THE EUROPA WORLD YEAR BOOK 2008

THE EUROPA WORLD YEAR BOOK 2008

VOLUME II

KAZAKHSTAN–ZIMBABWE

LONDON AND NEW YORK

First published 1926

© **Routledge 2008**
Albert House, 1–4 Singer Street, London, EC2A 4BQ, United Kingdom
(Routledge is an imprint of the Taylor & Francis Group, an Informa business)

All rights reserved. No part of this
publication may be photocopied, recorded,
or otherwise reproduced, stored in a retrieval
system or transmitted in any form or by any
electronic or mechanical means without the
prior permission of the copyright owner.

ISBN13: 978-1-85743-451-4 (The Set)
978-1-85743-453-8 (Vol. II)
ISBN10: 1-85743-451-X (The Set)
1-85743-453-6 (Vol. II)
ISSN 0071-2302
Library of Congress Catalog Card Number 59-2942

Senior Editor: Joanne Maher

Statistics Editor: Philip McIntyre

Regional Editors: Lynn Daniel, Katie Dawson, Lucy Dean, Iain Frame,
Imogen Gladman, Dominic Heaney, Juliet Love, Jillian O'Brien, Jacqueline West

International Organizations Editors: Catriona Appeatu Holman, Helen Canton

Associate Regional Editors: Meena Khan, Kirstie Macdonald,
Christopher Matthews, Anna Thomas

Assistant Editors: Kim Chamberlain, Laura Davis, David Gruar,
Catriona Marcham, Simon Molony, Adrian Reynolds,
Janine Tenzer, Gareth Vaughan, Elli Woollard

Associate Editor, Directory Research: James Middleton

Editorial Director: Paul Kelly

Typeset in New Century Schoolbook

Typeset by Data Standards Limited, Frome, Somerset

Printed and bound in Great Britain by Polestar Wheatons, Exeter

FOREWORD

THE EUROPA WORLD YEAR BOOK was first published in 1926. Since 1960 it has appeared in annual two-volume editions, and has become established as an authoritative reference work, providing a wealth of detailed information on the political, economic and commercial institutions of the world.

Volume I contains a comprehensive listing of some 1,900 international organizations and the first part of the alphabetical survey of countries of the world, from Afghanistan to Jordan. Volume II contains countries from Kazakhstan to Zimbabwe. An Index of Territories covered in both volumes is to be found at the end of Volume II.

The International Organizations section gives extensive coverage to the United Nations and its related agencies and bodies. There are also detailed articles concerning other major international and regional organizations; entries for many affiliated organizations appear within these articles. In addition, the section includes briefer details of some 1,500 other international organizations. A comprehensive Index of International Organizations is included at the end of Volume I.

Each country is covered by an individual chapter, containing: an introductory survey including recent history, economic affairs, government, defence, education, and public holidays; an economic and demographic survey using the latest available statistics on area and population, health and welfare, agriculture, forestry, fishing, industry, finance, trade, transport, tourism, the media, and education; and a directory section listing names, addresses and other useful facts about organizations in the fields of government, election commissions, political parties, diplomatic representation, judiciary, religions, the media, telecommunications, banking, insurance, trade and industry, development organizations, chambers of commerce, industrial and trade associations, utilities, trade unions, transport, and tourism.

The entire content of the print edition of THE EUROPA WORLD YEAR BOOK is available online at www.europaworld.com. This prestigious resource incorporates sophisticated search and browse functions as well as specially commissioned visual and statistical content. An ongoing programme of updates of key areas of information ensures currency of content, and enhances the richness of the coverage for which THE EUROPA WORLD YEAR BOOK is renowned.

Readers are referred to the nine titles in the Europa Regional Surveys of the World series: AFRICA SOUTH OF THE SAHARA, CENTRAL AND SOUTH-EASTERN EUROPE, EASTERN EUROPE, RUSSIA AND CENTRAL ASIA, THE FAR EAST AND AUSTRALASIA, THE MIDDLE EAST AND NORTH AFRICA, SOUTH AMERICA, CENTRAL AMERICA AND THE CARIBBEAN, SOUTH ASIA, THE USA AND CANADA, and WESTERN EUROPE, available both in print and online, offer comprehensive analysis at regional, sub-regional and country level. More detailed coverage of international organizations is to be found in THE EUROPA DIRECTORY OF INTERNATIONAL ORGANIZATIONS.

The content of THE EUROPA WORLD YEAR BOOK is extensively revised and updated by a variety of methods, including direct mailing to all the institutions listed. Many other sources are used, such as national statistical offices, government departments and diplomatic missions. The editors thank the innumerable individuals and organizations world-wide whose generous co-operation in providing current information for this edition is invaluable in presenting the most accurate and up-to-date material available.

May 2008

ACKNOWLEDGEMENTS

The editors gratefully acknowledge particular indebtedness for permission to reproduce material from the following sources: the United Nations' statistical databases and *Demographic Yearbook, Statistical Yearbook, Monthly Bulletin of Statistics, Industrial Commodity Statistics Yearbook* and *International Trade Statistics Yearbook*; the United Nations Educational, Scientific and Cultural Organization's *Statistical Yearbook* and Institute for Statistics database; the *Human Development Report* of the United Nations Development Programme; the Food and Agriculture Organization of the United Nations' statistical database; the statistical databases of the World Health Organization; the International Labour Office's statistical database and *Yearbook of Labour Statistics*; the World Bank's *World Bank Atlas, Global Development Finance, World Development Report* and *World Development Indicators*; the International Monetary Fund's statistical database, *International Financial Statistics* and *Government Finance Statistics Yearbook*; the US Geological Survey; the International Telecommunication Union; the World Tourism Organization's *Compendium* and *Yearbook of Tourism Statistics*; and *The Military Balance 2008*, a publication of the International Institute for Strategic Studies, Arundel House, 13–15 Arundel Street, London WC2R 3DX. Statistics Canada information is used with the permission of Statistics Canada. Users are forbidden to copy this material and/or redisseminate the data, in an original or modified form, for commercial purposes, without the expressed permission of Statistics Canada. Information on the availability of the wide range of data from Statistics Canada can be obtained from Statistics Canada's Regional Offices, its website at www.statcan.ca, and its toll-free access number 1-800-263-1136.

HEALTH AND WELFARE STATISTICS: SOURCES AND DEFINITIONS

Total fertility rate Source: WHO Statistical Information System. The number of children that would be born per woman, assuming no female mortality at child-bearing ages and the age-specific fertility rates of a specified country and reference period.

Under-5 mortality rate Source: WHO Statistical Information System. Defined by WHO as the probability of a child born in a specific year or period dying before the age of five, if subject to the age-specific mortality rates of that year or period.

HIV/AIDS Source: UNAIDS. Estimated percentage of adults aged 15 to 49 years living with HIV/AIDS. < indicates 'fewer than'.

Health expenditure Source: WHO Statistical Information System.
US $ per head (PPP)
International dollar estimates, derived by dividing local currency units by an estimate of their purchasing-power parity (PPP) compared with the US dollar. PPPs are the rates of currency conversion that equalize the purchasing power of different currencies by eliminating the differences in price levels between countries.
% of GDP
GDP levels for OECD countries follow the most recent UN System of National Accounts. For non-OECD countries a value was estimated by utilizing existing UN, IMF and World Bank data.
Public expenditure
Government health-related outlays plus expenditure by social schemes compulsorily affiliated with a sizeable share of the population, and extrabudgetary funds allocated to health services. Figures include grants or loans provided by international agencies, other national authorities, and sometimes commercial banks.

Access to water and sanitation Source: WHO/UNICEF Joint Monitoring Programme on Water Supply and Sanitation (JMP) (Mid-Term Assessment, 2004). Defined in terms of the percentage of the population using improved facilities in terms of the type of technology and levels of service afforded. For water, this includes house connections, public standpipes, boreholes with handpumps, protected dug wells, protected spring and rainwater collection; allowance is also made for other locally defined technologies. Sanitation is defined to include connection to a sewer or septic tank system, pour-flush latrine, simple pit or ventilated improved pit latrine, again with allowance for acceptable local technologies. Access to water and sanitation does not imply that the level of service or quality of water is 'adequate' or 'safe'.

Human Development Index (HDI) Source: UNDP, *Human Development Report* (2007/08). A summary of human development measured by three basic dimensions: prospects for a long and healthy life, measured by life expectancy at birth; knowledge, measured by adult literacy rate (two-thirds' weight) and the combined gross enrolment ratio in primary, secondary and tertiary education (one-third weight); and standard of living, measured by GDP per head (PPP US $). The index value obtained lies between zero and one. A value above 0.8 indicates high human development, between 0.5 and 0.8 medium human development, and below 0.5 low human development. A centralized data source for all three dimensions was not available for all countries. In some such cases other data sources were used to calculate a substitute value; however, this was excluded from the ranking. Other countries, including non-UNDP members, were excluded from the HDI altogether. In total, 177 countries were ranked for 2005.

CONTENTS

Abbreviations	Page ix
International Telephone Codes	xiii
Kazakhstan	2563
Kenya	2583
Kiribati	2605
The Democratic People's Republic of Korea (North Korea)	2613
The Republic of Korea (South Korea)	2643
Kosovo	2681
Kuwait	2687
Kyrgyzstan	2707
Laos	2725
Latvia	2741
Lebanon	2759
Lesotho	2789
Liberia	2802
Libya	2819
Liechtenstein	2839
Lithuania	2847
Luxembourg	2868
The former Yugoslav republic of Macedonia	2880
Madagascar	2899
Malawi	2917
Malaysia	2934
The Maldives	2973
Mali	2986
Malta	3003
The Marshall Islands	3014
Mauritania	3022
Mauritius	3038
Mexico	3054
The Federated States of Micronesia	3084
Moldova	3091
Monaco	3109
Mongolia	3116
Montenegro	3140
Morocco	3149
Mozambique	3174
Myanmar	3193
Namibia	3221
Nauru	3239
Nepal	3247
The Netherlands	3274
Netherlands Dependencies:	
Aruba	3301
The Netherlands Antilles	3308
New Zealand	3320
New Zealand's Dependent Territories:	
Ross Dependency	3344
Tokelau	3344
New Zealand's Associated States:	
The Cook Islands	3349
Niue	3356
Nicaragua	Page 3362
Niger	3382
Nigeria	3400
Norway	3426
Norwegian External Territories:	
Svalbard	3450
Jan Mayen	3452
Norwegian Dependencies	3452
Oman	3453
Pakistan	3467
Palau	3517
Palestinian Autonomous Areas	3524
Panama	3550
Papua New Guinea	3568
Paraguay	3591
Peru	3608
The Philippines	3632
Poland	3670
Portugal	3696
Qatar	3721
Romania	3734
The Russian Federation	3759
Rwanda	3800
Saint Christopher and Nevis	3817
Saint Lucia	3827
Saint Vincent and the Grenadines	3838
Samoa	3848
San Marino	3857
São Tomé and Príncipe	3864
Saudi Arabia	3874
Senegal	3897
Serbia	3921
Seychelles	3946
Sierra Leone	3954
Singapore	3971
Slovakia	3997
Slovenia	4017
Solomon Islands	4034
Somalia	4048
South Africa	4066
Spain	4101
Spanish External Territories:	
Ceuta	4145
Melilla	4150
Sri Lanka	4155
Sudan	4185
Suriname	4211
Swaziland	4224
Sweden	4238
Switzerland	4264
Syria	4289
Taiwan (see China, Vol. I)	
Tajikistan	4313

CONTENTS

Tanzania	Page 4332	Montserrat	Page 4724
Thailand	4353	The Pitcairn Islands	4731
Timor-Leste	4384	Saint Helena and Dependencies	4734
Togo	4402	South Georgia and the South Sandwich Islands	4738
Tonga	4420	The Turks and Caicos Islands	4739
Trinidad and Tobago	4430	The United States of America	4746
Tunisia	4448	United States Commonwealth Territories:	
Turkey	4467	The Northern Mariana Islands	4821
Turkmenistan	4503	Puerto Rico	4827
Tuvalu	4521	United States External Territories:	
Uganda	4528	American Samoa	4839
Ukraine	4547	Guam	4844
The United Arab Emirates	4577	The United States Virgin Islands	4851
The United Kingdom	4595	Other United States Territories	4857
United Kingdom Crown Dependencies:		Uruguay	4859
The Channel Islands	4668	Uzbekistan	4877
The Isle of Man	4675	Vanuatu	4896
United Kingdom Overseas Territories:		The Vatican City	4907
Anguilla	4680	Venezuela	4917
Bermuda	4687	Viet Nam	4944
The British Antarctic Territory	4694	Yemen	4972
The British Indian Ocean Territory	4695	Zambia	4993
The British Virgin Islands	4696	Zimbabwe	5010
The Cayman Islands	4703		
The Falkland Islands	4711	Index of Territories	5034
Gibraltar	4717		

ABBREVIATIONS

AB	Aktiebolag (Joint-Stock Company); Alberta
Abog.	Abogado (Lawyer)
Acad.	Academician; Academy
ACP	African, Caribbean and Pacific (countries)
ACT	Australian Capital Territory
AD	anno Domini
ADB	African Development Bank; Asian Development Bank
ADC	aide-de-camp
Adm.	Admiral
admin.	administration
AfDB	African Development Bank
AG	Aktiengesellschaft (Joint-Stock Company)
AH	anno Hegirae
a.i.	ad interim
AID	(US) Agency for International Development
AIDS	acquired immunodeficiency syndrome
AK	Alaska
Al.	Aleja (Alley, Avenue)
AL	Alabama
ALADI	Asociación Latinoamericana de Integración
Alt.	Alternate
AM	Amplitude Modulation
a.m.	ante meridiem (before noon)
amalg.	amalgamated
Apdo	Apartado (Post Box)
APEC	Asia-Pacific Economic Co-operation
approx.	approximately
Apt	Apartment
AR	Arkansas
ARV	advanced retroviral
AŞ	Anonim Şirketi (Joint-Stock Company)
A/S	Aktieselskab (Joint-Stock Company)
ASEAN	Association of South East Asian Nations
asscn	association
assoc.	associate
ASSR	Autonomous Soviet Socialist Republic
asst	assistant
AU	African Union
Aug.	August
auth.	authorized
av., Ave	Avenija, Avenue
Av., Avda	Avenida (Avenue)
Avv.	Avvocato (Lawyer)
AZ	Arizona
b.b.	bez broja (without number)
BC	British Columbia
BC	before Christ
Bd	Board
Bd, Bld, Blv., Blvd	Boulevard
b/d	barrels per day
BFPO	British Forces' Post Office
Bhd	Berhad (Public Limited Company)
Bldg	Building
blk	block
Blvr	Bulevar
BP	Boîte postale (Post Box)
br.(s)	branch(es)
Brig.	Brigadier
BSE	bovine spongiform encephalopathy
BSEC	(Organization of the) Black Sea Economic Co-operation
bte	boîte (box)
Bul.	Bulvar (boulevard)
bulv.	bulvarīs (boulevard)
C	Centigrade
c.	circa; cuadra(s) (block(s))
CA	California
CACM	Central American Common Market
Cad.	Caddesi (Street)
CAP	Common Agricultural Policy
cap.	capital
Capt.	Captain
CAR	Central African Republic
CARICOM	Caribbean Community and Common Market
CBSS	Council of Baltic Sea States
CCL	Caribbean Congress of Labour
Cdre	Commodore
CEMAC	Communauté économique et monétaire de l'Afrique centrale
Cen.	Central
CEO	Chief Executive Officer
CET	common external tariff
CFA	Communauté Financière Africaine; Coopération Financière en Afrique centrale
CFE	Treaty on Conventional Armed Forces in Europe
CFP	Common Fisheries Policy; Communauté française du Pacifique; Comptoirs français du Pacifique
Chair.	Chairman/person/woman
Chih.	Chihuahua
CI	Channel Islands
Cia	Companhia
Cía	Compañía
Cie	Compagnie
c.i.f.	cost, insurance and freight
C-in-C	Commander-in-Chief
circ.	circulation
CIS	Commonwealth of Independent States
CJD	Creutzfeldt-Jakob disease
cm	centimetre(s)
cnr	corner
CO	Colorado
Co	Company; County
c/o	care of
Coah.	Coahuila
Col	Colonel
Col.	Colima; Colonia
COMESA	Common Market for Eastern and Southern Africa
Comm.	Commission; Commendatore
Commdr	Commander
Commdt	Commandant
Commr	Commissioner
Cond.	Condiminio
Confed.	Confederation
Cont.	Contador (Accountant)
COO	Chief Operating Officer
Corp.	Corporate
Corpn	Corporation
CP	Case Postale, Caixa Postal, Casella Postale (Post Box); Communist Party
CPSU	Communist Party of the Soviet Union
Cres.	Crescent
CSCE	Conference on Security and Cooperation in Europe
CSTAL	Confederación Sindical de los Trabajadores de América Latina
CT	Connecticut
CTCA	Confederación de Trabajadores Centro-americanos
Cttee	Committee
cu	cubic
cwt	hundredweight
DC	District of Columbia; Distrito Capital; Distrito Central
d.d.	delniška družba, dioničko društvo (joint stock company)
DE	Delaware; Departamento Estatal
Dec.	December
Del.	Delegación
Dem.	Democrat; Democratic
Dep.	Deputy
dep.	deposits
Dept	Department
devt	development
DF	Distrito Federal
Dgo	Durango
Diag.	Diagonal
Dir	Director
Div.	Division(al)
DM	Deutsche Mark
DMZ	demilitarized zone
DNA	deoxyribonucleic acid
DN	Distrito Nacional
Doc.	Docent
Dott.	Dottore/essa
DPRK	Democratic People's Republic of Korea
Dr	Doctor
Dr.	Drive
Dra	Doctora
Dr Hab.	Doktor Habilitowany (Assistant Professor)
dr.(e)	drachma(e)
DR-CAFTA	Dominican Republic-Central American Free Trade Agreement
Drs	Doctorandus
DU	depleted uranium
dwt	dead weight tons
E	East; Eastern
EBRD	European Bank for Reconstruction and Development
EC	European Community
ECA	(United Nations) Economic Commission for Africa
ECE	(United Nations) Economic Commission for Europe
ECLAC	(United Nations) Economic Commission for Latin America and the Caribbean
ECO	Economic Co-operation Organization
Econ.	Economics; Economist
ECOSOC	(United Nations) Economic and Social Council
ECOWAS	Economic Community of West African States
ECU	European Currency Unit
Edif.	Edificio (Building)
edn	edition
EEA	European Economic Area
EFTA	European Free Trade Association
e.g.	exempli gratia (for example)
EIB	European Investment Bank
EMS	European Monetary System
EMU	Economic and Monetary Union
eMv	electron megavolt
Eng.	Engineer; Engineering

ABBREVIATIONS

EP	Empresa Pública	HSC	Harmonized System Classification	küç	küçasi (street)
ERM	Exchange Rate Mechanism			kv.	kvartal (apartment block); kvartira (apartment)
ESACA	Emisora de Capital Abierto Sociedad Anónima	HSH	His/Her Serene Highness	kW	kilowatt(s)
Esc.	Escuela; Escudos; Escritorio	Hwy	Highway	kWh	kilowatt hours
ESCAP	(United Nations) Economic and Social Commission for Asia and the Pacific	IA	Iowa	KY	Kentucky
		IBRD	International Bank for Reconstruction and Development	LA	Louisiana
ESCWA	(United Nations) Economic and Social Commission for Western Asia	ICC	International Chamber of Commerce; International Criminal Court	lauk	laukums (square)
				lb	pound(s)
esq.	esquina (corner)			LDCs	Least Developed Countries
est.	established; estimate; estimated	ICFTU	International Confederation of Free Trade Unions	Lic.	Licenciado
etc.	et cetera			Licda	Licenciada
EU	European Union	ICRC	International Committee of the Red Cross	LNG	liquefied natural gas
eV	eingetragener Verein			LPG	liquefied petroleum gas
excl.	excluding	ICT	information and communication technology	Lt, Lieut	Lieutenant
exec.	executive			Ltd	Limited
Ext.	Extension	ICTR	International Criminal Tribunal for Rwanda		
		ICTY	International Criminal Tribunal for the former Yugoslavia	m	metre(s)
F	Fahrenheit			m.	million
f.	founded	ID	Idaho	MA	Massachusetts
FAO	Food and Agriculture Organization	IDA	International Development Association	Maj.	Major
				Man.	Manager; managing
f.a.s.	free alongside ship	IDB	Inter-American Development Bank	MB	Manitoba
Feb.	February			mbH	mit beschränkter Haftung (with limited liability)
Fed.	Federal; Federation				
feds	federations	IDPs	internally displaced persons		
FL	Florida	i.e.	id est (that is to say)	MD	Maryland
FM	frequency modulation	IFC	International Finance Corporation	MDG	Millennium Development Goal
fmr(ly)	former(ly)			MDRI	multilateral debt relief initiative
f.o.b.	free on board	IGAD	Intergovernmental Authority on Development	ME	Maine
Fr	Father			Me	Maître
Fr.	Franc	IHL	International Humanitarian Law	mem.(s)	member(s)
Fri.	Friday	IL	Illinois	MEP	Member of the European Parliament
FRY	Federal Republic of Yugoslavia	ILO	International Labour Organization/Office		
ft	foot (feet)			Mercosul	Mercado Comum do Sul (Southern Common Market)
FTA	free trade agreement/area	IMF	International Monetary Fund		
FYRM	former Yugoslav republic of Macedonia	IML	International Migration Law	Mercosur	Mercado Común del Sur (Southern Common Market)
		in (ins)	inch (inches)		
		IN	Indiana	Méx.	México
		Inc, Incorp.		MFN	most favoured nation
g	gram(s)	Incd	Incorporated	mfrs	manufacturers
g.	gatve (street)	incl.	including	Mgr	Monseigneur; Monsignor
GA	Georgia	Ind.	Independent	MHz	megahertz
GATT	General Agreement on Tariffs and Trade	INF	Intermediate-Range Nuclear Forces	MI	Michigan
				MIA	missing in action
GCC	Gulf Co-operation Council	Ing.	Engineer	Mich.	Michoacán
Gdns	Gardens	Insp.	Inspector	MIGA	Multilateral Investment Guarantee Agency
GDP	gross domestic product	Int.	International		
Gen.	General	Inzå.	Engineer	Mil.	Military
GeV	giga electron volts	IP	intellectual property	Mlle	Mademoiselle
GM	genetically modified	IPU	Inter-Parliamentary Union	mm	millimetre(s)
GmbH	Gesellschaft mit beschränkter Haftung (Limited Liability Company)	Ir	Engineer	Mme	Madame
		IRF	International Road Federation	MN	Minnesota
		irreg.	irregular	mnt.	mante (road)
GMO(s)	genetically modified organism(s)	Is	Islands	MO	Missouri
GMT	Greenwich Mean Time	ISIC	International Standard Industrial Classification	Mon.	Monday
GNI	gross national income			Mor.	Morelos
GNP	gross national product	IT	information technology	MOU	memorandum of understanding
Gov.	Governor	ITU	International Telecommunication Union	MP	Member of Parliament
Govt	Government			MS	Mississippi
Gro	Guerrero	ITUC	International Trade Union Confederation	MSS	Manuscripts
grt	gross registered tons			MT	Montana
GSM	Global System for Mobile Communications	Iur.	Lawyer	MW	megawatt(s); medium wave
				MWh	megawatt hour(s)
Gto	Guanajuato				
GWh	gigawatt hours	Jal.	Jalisco		
		Jan.	January		
		Jnr	Junior	N	North; Northern
ha	hectares	Jr	Jonkheer (Esquire); Junior	n.a.	not available
HE	His/Her Eminence; His/Her Excellency	Jt	Joint	nab.	naberezhnaya (embankment, quai)
hf	hlutafelag (Limited Company)			NAFTA	North American Free Trade Agreement
HI	Hawaii	Kav.	Kaveling (Plot)		
HIPC	heavily indebted poor country	kg	kilogram(s)	nám.	náměstí (square)
HIV	human immunodeficiency virus	KG	Kommandit Gesellschaft (Limited Partnership)	Nat.	National
hl	hectolitre(s)			NATO	North Atlantic Treaty Organization
HM	His/Her Majesty	kHz	kilohertz		
Hon.	Honorary, Honourable	KK	Kaien Kaisha (Limited Company)	Nay.	Nayarit
hp	horsepower	km	kilometre(s)	NB	New Brunswick
HPAI	highly pathogenic avian influenza	kom.	komnata (room)	NC	North Carolina
		kor.	korpus (block)	NCD	National Capital District
HQ	Headquarters	k'och.	k'ochasi (street)	NCO	non-commissioned officer
HRH	His/Her Royal Highness	KS	Kansas		

ABBREVIATIONS

ND	North Dakota	Prof.	Professor	SITC	Standard International Trade Classification
NE	Nebraska; North-East	Propr	Proprietor		
NEPAD	New Partnership for Africa's Development	Prov.	Province; Provincial; Provinciale (Dutch)	SJ	Society of Jesus
				SK	Saskatchewan
NGO	non-governmental organization	prov.	provulok (lane)	Skt	Sankt (Saint)
NH	New Hampshire	pst.	puistotie (avenue)	SLP	San Luis Potosí
NJ	New Jersey	PT	Perseroan Terbatas (Limited Company)	SMEs	small and medium-sized enterprises
NL	Newfoundland and Labrador, Nuevo León	Pte	Private; Puente (Bridge)	s/n	sin número (without number)
NM	New Mexico	Pty	Proprietary	Soc.	Society
NMP	net material product	p.u.	paid up	Sok.	Sokak (Street)
no	numéro, número (number)	publ.	publication; published	Son.	Sonora
no.	number	Publr	Publisher	Şos.	Şosea (Road)
Nov.	November	Pue.	Puebla	SP	São Paulo
nr	near	Pvt.	Private	SpA	Società per Azioni (Joint-Stock Company)
nrt	net registered tons				
NS	Nova Scotia			Sq.	Square
NSW	New South Wales	QC	Québec	sq	square (in measurements)
NT	Northwest Territories	QIP	Quick Impact Project	Sr	Senior; Señor
NU	Nunavut Territory	Qld	Queensland	Sra	Señora
NV	Naamloze Vennootschap (Limited Company); Nevada	Qro	Querétaro	Srl	Società a Responsabilità Limitata (Limited Company)
		Q. Roo	Quintana Roo		
NW	North-West	q.v.	quod vide (to which refer)	SSR	Soviet Socialist Republic
NY	New York			St	Saint, Sint; Street
NZ	New Zealand			Sta	Santa
		Rag.	Ragioniere (Accountant)	Ste	Sainte
		Rd	Road	STI(s)	sexually transmitted infection(s)
OAPEC	Organization of Arab Petroleum Exporting Countries	R(s)	rand; rupee(s)	str.	strada, stradă (street)
		reg., regd	register; registered	str-la	stradelă (street)
OAS	Organization of American States	reorg.	reorganized	subs.	subscribed; subscriptions
OAU	Organization of African Unity	Rep.	Republic; Republican; Representative	Sun.	Sunday
Oax.	Oaxaca			Supt	Superintendent
Oct.	October	Repub.	Republic	SUV	sports utility vehicle
OECD	Organisation for Economic Cooperation and Development	res	reserve(s)	sv.	Saint
		retd	retired	SW	South-West
OECS	Organisation of Eastern Caribbean States	Rev.	Reverend		
		RI	Rhode Island		
Of.	Oficina (Office)	RJ	Rio de Janeiro	Tab.	Tabasco
OH	Ohio	Rm	Room	Tamps	Tamaulipas
OIC	Organization of the Islamic Conference	RN	Royal Navy	TAŞ	Turkiye Anonim Şirketi (Turkish Joint-Stock Company)
		ro-ro	roll-on roll-off		
OK	Oklahoma	RP	Recette principale	Tas	Tasmania
ON	Ontario	Rp.(s)	rupiah(s)	TD	Teachta Dàla (Member of Parliament)
OPEC	Organization of the Petroleum Exporting Countries	Rpto	Reparto (Estate)		
		RSFSR	Russian Soviet Federative Socialist Republic	tech., techn.	technical
opp.	opposite			tel.	telephone
OR	Oregon	Rt	Right	TEU	20-ft equivalent unit
Org.	Organization			Thur.	Thursday
ORIT	Organización Regional Interamericana de Trabajadores			TN	Tennessee
		S	South; Southern; San	tř	třída (avenue)
		SA	Société Anonyme, Sociedad Anónima (Limited Company); South Australia	Treas.	Treasurer
OSCE	Organization for Security and Cooperation in Europe			Tue.	Tuesday
				TV	television
		SAARC	South Asian Association for Regional Co-operation	TX	Texas
p.	page	SACN	South American Community of Nations		
p.a.	per annum			u.	utca (street)
PA	Palestinian Authority; Pennsylvania	SAECA	Sociedad Anónima Emisora de Capital Abierto	u/a	unit of account
				UAE	United Arab Emirates
Parl.	Parliament(ary)	SADC	Southern African Development Community	UEE	Unidade Económica Estatal
per.	pereulok (lane, alley)			UEMOA	Union économique et monetaire ouest-africaine
PE	Prince Edward Island	SAR	Special Administrative Region		
Perm. Rep.	Permanent Representative	SARL	Sociedade Anônima de Responsabilidade Limitada (Joint-Stock Company of Limited Liability)	UK	United Kingdom
PF	Postfach (Post Box)			ul.	ulica, ulitsa (street)
PICTs	Pacific Island countries and territories			UM	ouguiya
				UN	United Nations
PK	Posta Kutusu (Post Box)	SARS	Severe Acute Respiratory Syndrome	UNAIDS	United Nations Joint Programme on HIV/AIDS
Pl.	Plac, Plads (square)				
pl.	platz; place; ploshchad (square)	Sat.	Saturday	UNCTAD	United Nations Conference on Trade and Development
PLC	Public Limited Company	SC	South Carolina		
PLO	Palestine Liberation Organization	SD	South Dakota	UNDP	United Nations Development Programme
		Sdn Bhd	Sendirian Berhad (Private Limited Company)		
p.m.	post meridiem (after noon)			UNEP	United Nations Environment Programme
PMB	Private Mail Bag	SDR(s)	Special Drawing Right(s)		
PNA	Palestinian National Authority	SE	South-East	UNESCO	United Nations Educational, Scientific and Cultural Organization
POB	Post Office Box	Sec.	Secretary		
pp.	pages	Secr.	Secretariat		
PPP	purchasing-power parity	Sen.	Senior; Senator	UNHCHR	UN High Commissioner for Human Rights
PQ	Québec	Sept.	September		
PR	Puerto Rico	SER	Sua Eccellenza Reverendissima (His Eminence)	UNHCR	United Nations High Commissioner for Refugees
pr.	prospekt, prospekti (avenue)				
Pres.	President	SFRY	Socialist Federal Republic of Yugoslavia	UNICEF	United Nations Children's Fund
PRGF	Poverty Reduction and Growth Facility			Univ.	University
		SGP	Stability and Growth Pact	UNODC	United Nations Office on Drugs and Crime
Prin.	Principal	Sin.	Sinaloa		

ABBREVIATIONS

UNRWA	United Nations Relief and Works Agency for Palestine Refugees in the Near East	v-CJD	new variant Creutzfeldt-Jakob disease	WEU	Western European Union
				WFP	World Food Programme
UNWTO	World Tourism Organization	Ven.	Venerable	WFTU	World Federation of Trade Unions
Urb.	Urbanización (District)	Ver.	Veracruz		
US	United States	VHF	Very High Frequency	WHO	World Health Organization
USA	United States of America	VI	(US) Virgin Islands	WI	Wisconsin
USAID	United States Agency for International Development	Vic	Victoria	WSSD	World Summit on Sustainable Development
		Vn	Veien (Street)		
		vol.(s)	volume(s)	WTO	World Trade Organization
USSR	Union of Soviet Socialist Republics	VT	Vermont	WV	West Virginia
		vul.	vulitsa, vulytsa (street)	WY	Wyoming
UT	Utah				
		W	West; Western		
VA	Virginia	WA	Washington (State); Western Australia		
VAT	value-added tax			yr	year
VEB	Volkseigener Betrieb (Public Company)	WCL	World Confederation of Labour	YT	Yukon Territory
		Wed.	Wednesday	Yuc.	Yucatán

INTERNATIONAL TELEPHONE CODES

To make international calls to telephone and fax numbers listed in *The Europa World Year Book*, dial the international code of the country from which you are calling, followed by the appropriate country code for the organization you wish to call (listed below), followed by the area code (if applicable) and telephone or fax number listed in the entry.

	Country code	+ or − GMT*
Afghanistan	93	+4½
Albania	355	+1
Algeria	213	+1
Andorra	376	+1
Angola	244	+1
Antigua and Barbuda	1 268	−4
Argentina	54	−3
Armenia	374	+4
Australia	61	+8 to +10
Australian External Territories:		
Australian Antarctic Territory	672	+3 to +10
Christmas Island	61	+7
Cocos (Keeling) Islands	61	+6½
Norfolk Island	672	+11½
Austria	43	+1
Azerbaijan	994	+5
Bahamas	1 242	−5
Bahrain	973	+3
Bangladesh	880	+6
Barbados	1 246	−4
Belarus	375	+2
Belgium	32	+1
Belize	501	−6
Benin	229	+1
Bhutan	975	+6
Bolivia	591	−4
Bosnia and Herzegovina	387	+1
Botswana	267	+2
Brazil	55	−3 to −4
Brunei	673	+8
Bulgaria	359	+2
Burkina Faso	226	0
Burundi	257	+2
Cambodia	855	+7
Cameroon	237	+1
Canada	1	−3 to −8
Cape Verde	238	−1
Central African Republic	236	+1
Chad	235	+1
Chile	56	−4
China, People's Republic	86	+8
Special Administrative Regions:		
Hong Kong	852	+8
Macao	853	+8
China (Taiwan)	886	+8
Colombia	57	−5
Comoros	269	+3
Congo, Democratic Republic	243	+1
Congo, Republic	242	+1
Costa Rica	506	−6
Côte d'Ivoire	225	0
Croatia	385	+1
Cuba	53	−5
Cyprus	357	+2
'Turkish Republic of Northern Cyprus'	90 392	+2
Czech Republic	420	+1
Denmark	45	+1
Danish External Territories:		
Faroe Islands	298	0
Greenland	299	−1 to −4
Djibouti	253	+3
Dominica	1 767	−4
Dominican Republic	1 809	−4

	Country code	+ or − GMT*
Ecuador	593	−5
Egypt	20	+2
El Salvador	503	−6
Equatorial Guinea	240	+1
Eritrea	291	+3
Estonia	372	+2
Ethiopia	251	+3
Fiji	679	+12
Finland	358	+2
Finnish External Territory:		
Åland Islands	358	+2
France	33	+1
French Overseas Regions and Departments:		
French Guiana	594	−3
Guadeloupe	590	−4
Martinique	596	−4
Réunion	262	+4
French Overseas Collectivities:		
French Polynesia	689	−9 to −10
Mayotte	262	+3
Saint-Barthélemy	590	−4
Saint-Martin	590	−4
Saint Pierre and Miquelon	508	−3
Wallis and Futuna Islands	681	+12
Other French Overseas Territory:		
New Caledonia	687	+11
Gabon	241	+1
Gambia	220	0
Georgia	995	+4
Germany	49	+1
Ghana	233	0
Greece	30	+2
Grenada	1 473	−4
Guatemala	502	−6
Guinea	224	0
Guinea-Bissau	245	0
Guyana	592	−4
Haiti	509	−5
Honduras	504	−6
Hungary	36	+1
Iceland	354	0
India	91	+5½
Indonesia	62	+7 to +9
Iran	98	+3½
Iraq	964	+3
Ireland	353	0
Israel	972	+2
Italy	39	+1
Jamaica	1 876	−5
Japan	81	+9
Jordan	962	+2
Kazakhstan	7	+6
Kenya	254	+3
Kiribati	686	+12 to +13
Korea, Democratic People's Republic (North Korea)	850	+9
Korea, Republic (South Korea)	82	+9
Kosovo	381†	+3
Kuwait	965	+3
Kyrgyzstan	996	+5
Laos	856	+7
Latvia	371	+2

xiii

INTERNATIONAL TELEPHONE CODES

	Country code	+ or − GMT*
Lebanon	961	+2
Lesotho	266	+2
Liberia	231	0
Libya	218	+1
Liechtenstein	423	+1
Lithuania	370	+2
Luxembourg	352	+1
Macedonia, former Yugoslav republic	389	+1
Madagascar	261	+3
Malawi	265	+2
Malaysia	60	+8
Maldives	960	+5
Mali	223	0
Malta	356	+1
Marshall Islands	692	+12
Mauritania	222	0
Mauritius	230	+4
Mexico	52	−6 to −7
Micronesia, Federated States	691	+10 to +11
Moldova	373	+2
Monaco	377	+1
Mongolia	976	+7 to +9
Montenegro	382	+1
Morocco	212	0
Mozambique	258	+2
Myanmar	95	+6½
Namibia	264	+2
Nauru	674	+12
Nepal	977	+5¾
Netherlands	31	+1
Netherlands Dependencies:		
Aruba	297	−4
Netherlands Antilles	599	−4
New Zealand	64	+12
New Zealand's Dependent and Associated Territories:		
Tokelau	690	−10
Cook Islands	682	−10
Niue	683	−11
Nicaragua	505	−6
Niger	227	+1
Nigeria	234	+1
Norway	47	+1
Norwegian External Territory:		
Svalbard	47	+1
Oman	968	+4
Pakistan	92	+5
Palau	680	+9
Palestinian Autonomous Areas	970 or 972	+2
Panama	507	−5
Papua New Guinea	675	+10
Paraguay	595	−4
Peru	51	−5
Philippines	63	+8
Poland	48	+1
Portugal	351	0
Qatar	974	+3
Romania	40	+2
Russian Federation	7	+2 to +12
Rwanda	250	+2
Saint Christopher and Nevis	1 869	−4
Saint Lucia	1 758	−4
Saint Vincent and the Grenadines	1 784	−4
Samoa	685	−11
San Marino	378	+1
São Tomé and Príncipe	239	0
Saudi Arabia	966	+3
Senegal	221	0
Serbia	381	+1
Seychelles	248	+4
Sierra Leone	232	0

	Country code	+ or − GMT*
Singapore	65	+8
Slovakia	421	+1
Slovenia	386	+1
Solomon Islands	677	+11
Somalia	252	+3
South Africa	27	+2
Spain	34	+1
Sri Lanka	94	+5½
Sudan	249	+2
Suriname	597	−3
Swaziland	268	+2
Sweden	46	+1
Switzerland	41	+1
Syria	963	+2
Tajikistan	992	+5
Tanzania	255	+3
Thailand	66	+7
Timor-Leste	670	+9
Togo	228	0
Tonga	676	+13
Trinidad and Tobago	1 868	−4
Tunisia	216	+1
Turkey	90	+2
Turkmenistan	993	+5
Tuvalu	688	+12
Uganda	256	+3
Ukraine	380	+2
United Arab Emirates	971	+4
United Kingdom	44	0
United Kingdom Crown Dependencies	44	0
United Kingdom Overseas Territories:		
Anguilla	1 264	−4
Ascension Island	247	0
Bermuda	1 441	−4
British Virgin Islands	1 284	−4
Cayman Islands	1 345	−5
Diego Garcia (British Indian Ocean Territory)	246	+5
Falkland Islands	500	−4
Gibraltar	350	+1
Montserrat	1 664	−4
Pitcairn Islands	872	−8
Saint Helena	290	0
Tristan da Cunha	290	0
Turks and Caicos Islands	1 649	−5
United States of America	1	−5 to −10
United States Commonwealth Territories:		
Northern Mariana Islands	1 670	+10
Puerto Rico	1 787	−4
United States External Territories:		
American Samoa	1 684	−11
Guam	1 671	+10
United States Virgin Islands	1 340	−4
Uruguay	598	−3
Uzbekistan	998	+5
Vanuatu	678	+11
Vatican City	39	+1
Venezuela	58	−4½
Viet Nam	84	+7
Yemen	967	+3
Zambia	260	+2
Zimbabwe	263	+2

* The times listed compare the standard (winter) times in the various countries. Some countries adopt Summer (Daylight Saving) Time—i.e. +1 hour—for part of the year.

† Mobile telephone numbers for Kosovo use the country code for Monaco (377).

Free trial available!

Europa World *Plus*
Europa World and the Europa Regional Surveys of the World online
www.europaworld.com

Europa World *Plus* enables you to subscribe to Europa World together with as many of the nine Regional Surveys of the World online as you choose, in one simple annual subscription.

The Europa Regional Surveys of the World complement and expand upon the information in Europa World with in-depth, expert analysis at regional, sub-regional and country level.

Providing:

* An interactive online library for all the countries and territories of each of the world regions
* Impartial coverage of issues of regional importance from acknowledged experts
* A vast range of up-to-date economic, political and statistical data
* Book and periodical bibliographies - direct you to further research

* Extensive directory of research institutes specializing in the region
* Ability to search by content type across regions
* Thousands of click-through web links to external sites

The nine titles that make up the series are as follows: *Africa South of the Sahara; Central and South-Eastern Europe; Eastern Europe, Russia and Central Asia; The Far East and Australasia; The Middle East and North Africa; South America, Central America and the Caribbean; South Asia; The USA and Canada; Western Europe.*

For further information and to register for a free trial please contact us at:
Tel: + 44 (0) 20 7017 6062
Fax: + 44 (0) 20 7017 6720
E-mail: reference.online@tandf.co.uk

KAZAK...

Introducto...

Location, Climate, Language, Religion, Flag, Capital

The Republic of Kazakhstan extends 1,900 km (1,200 miles) from the Volga river in the west to the Altai mountains in the east, and about 1,300 km (800 miles) from the Siberian plain in the north to the Central Asian deserts in the south. To the south it borders Turkmenistan, Uzbekistan and Kyrgyzstan. To the east the border is with the People's Republic of China. There is a long border in the north with Russia and a coastline of 2,320 km (1,400 miles) on the Caspian Sea in the south-west. The climate is of a strongly continental type, but there are wide variations throughout the territory. Average temperatures in January range from −18°C (0°F) in the north to −3°C (27°F) in the south. In July average temperatures are 19°C (66°F) in the north and 28°C–30°C (82°F–86°F) in the south. Average annual rainfall in mountainous regions reaches 1,600 mm (63 ins), whereas in the central desert areas it is less than 100 mm (4 ins). The state language is Kazakh; however, Russian is employed officially in state and local government bodies. The predominant religion is Islam, most ethnic Kazakhs being Sunni Muslims of the Hanafi school. Other ethnic groups have their own religious communities, notably the (Christian) Eastern Orthodox Church, which is attended mainly by Slavs. The national flag (proportions 1 by 2) consists of a light blue field, at the centre of which is a yellow sun (a disc surrounded by 32 rays), framed by the wings of a flying eagle, also in yellow, with a vertical stripe of national ornamentation in yellow near the hoist. In November 1997 the capital was moved from Almaty to Akmola (formerly Tselinograd), now known as Astana.

Recent History

After the February Revolution and the Bolshevik coup in Russia in 1917, there was civil war throughout Kazakhstan, which had come under Russian control in the first half of the 18th century. Bolshevik forces finally overcame those of the White Army, foreign interventionists and local nationalists. In 1920 the Kyrgyz Autonomous Soviet Socialist Republic (ASSR) was created within the Russian Soviet Federative Socialist Republic (the Russian Federation): the Kazakhs were known to the Russians as Kyrgyz, to distinguish them from the unrelated Cossacks. In 1925 the Kyrgyz ASSR was renamed the Kazakh ASSR; the Karakalpak region (now part of Uzbekistan, as Qoraqalpog'iston) was detached in 1930, and became an autonomous republic within the Uzbek Soviet Socialist Republic (SSR) in 1936. In December 1936 the Kazakh ASSR became a full Union Republic of the USSR, as the Kazakh SSR.

Under Soviet rule parts of Kazakhstan were heavily industrialized. However, more than 1m. people were estimated to have died as a result of the starvation that accompanied the campaign in the early 1930s to collectivize agriculture and settle nomadic peoples. Many of those deported from parts of the USSR during the Second World War (including Germans, Crimean Tatars, Baltic and Caucasian peoples) were sent to the Republic. During Nikita Khrushchev's period in office as Soviet leader (1953–64) large areas of previously uncultivated land in Kazakhstan were transformed into arable land. This, along with intensive industrialization, and the development of nuclear-testing sites and the Baikonur space centre brought large numbers of ethnic Russians to Kazakhstan; the proportion of Russians increased from 19.7% of the population in 1926 to 42.7% in 1959.

In June 1989 Nursultan Nazarbayev, Chairman of the Republic's Council of Ministers since March 1984, was appointed First Secretary of the Communist Party of Kazakhstan (CPK). Political and administrative changes were instituted in September 1989: a permanent Supreme Kenges (Supreme Council or Supreme Soviet—legislature) was to be established, and elections were to be conducted on a multi-candidate basis. In addition, the state duties that had hitherto been the responsibility of the First Secretary of the CPK were transferred to the Chairman of the Supreme Kenges, to which post Nazarbayev was elected in February 1990. Many candidates stood unopposed at elections to the Supreme Kenges in March, and the system of reserved seats for CPK-affiliated organizations was retained, resulting in a substantial communist majority. In April the body elect... Kazakh... On 25 O... eignty, assert... the economy. Na... the respective all-... Kazakhstani Governme... new Union Treaty in ear... declared its sovereignty and sought economic sovereignty... resources and of enterprises were under all-Un... redefinition of

In the referendum on the future of... and the Soviet republics in March 1991, almo... ions on the voted in Kazakhstan, of whom 94% endo... ayev also preserve the USSR as a 'union of sovereign... ome 90% rights'. In June the Supreme Kenges voted, in pri... nine a draft union treaty. Kazakhstan was to sign th... rate August, but the event was forestalled by an attempt... to led by conservative communists, in Moscow, the Soviet Russian capital. As the coup attempt collapsed, Nazarbaye... resigned from the Politburo and Central Committee of the Communist Party of the Soviet Union (CPSU), in protest at the open support granted to the putschists by the CPSU leadership. The CPK was ordered to cease activities in state and government organs, and in September the party withdrew from the CPSU; elements from the party went to form the Socialist Party of Kazakhstan (SPK).

On 1 December 1991 Nazarbayev was elected unopposed as President of Kazakhstan in direct popular elections. On 8 December the leaders of Russia, Ukraine and Belarus signed an agreement establishing the Commonwealth of Independent States (CIS, see p. 215). On 16 December Kazakhstan became the last of the republics to declare independence from the USSR, as the Republic of Kazakhstan. The country was became a co-founder of the CIS on 21 December, when the leaders of 11 former Soviet countries met in Almaty.

The Constitution, adopted in January 1993, invoked legislation adopted in September 1989, denoting Kazakh as the state language and Russian as a language of inter-ethnic communication. The document required that the President be fluent in Kazakh. Meanwhile, increased emigration, particularly by ethnic Germans (more than 300,000 of whom left Kazakhstan in the early 1990s) and Russians, was accompanied, albeit on a much smaller scale, by the return of ethnic Kazakhs from Kyrgyzstan, Mongolia, Tajikistan and Turkmenistan.

In June 1991 some 5,000 people demonstrated in Almaty against continued communist predominance in the Government and Supreme Kenges, demanding the formation of a new, coalition administration. In October the three most prominent nationalist opposition parties (the Freedom—Azat movement, the Republican Party and the Jeltoqsan National Democratic Party) united to form the Republican Party—Freedom (RP—F). The Union of National Unity of Kazakhstan was established in February 1993, with the declared aim of promoting social harmony and countering radical nationalism. Nazarbayev (who had held no party affiliation since August 1991) became Chairman of the Union, which was reorganized as a political party, the People's Unity Party (PUP), later in 1993.

In December 1993 the Supreme Kenges voted to dissolve itself and to grant Nazarbayev the power to rule by decree pending elections to a new legislature, which was to be reduced in size from 360 to 177 seats. Kazakhstan's first multi-party elections were duly held on 7 March 1994, with the participation of 74% of the electorate; a number of irregularities were reported by international observers. The PUP obtained 33 seats, which, when combined with the 42 seats won by candidates from the so-called 'President's List' (candidates nominated by Nazarbayev) and those of pro-Nazarbayev independents, ensured that Nazarbayev's supporters emerged as the strongest force in the assembly. The Confederation of Kazakhstani Trade Unions (CKTU) won 11 seats, the People's Congress Party of Kazakhstan (PCPK) nine and the SPK eight. The CPK, which had continued to operate, was granted legal status in March, and in May claimed a membership of some 50,000. In that month the

bloc in the
s a guarantor
Supreme Kenges
n the Government's
in June Nazarbayev
anization. The Govern-
er since 1991) resigned in
re to reform the economy.
mist and First Deputy Prime
cil of Ministers, was appointed

Constitutional Court declared the
eral election to be invalid, owing to
es. In March the Government was forced
ation, on the grounds that it had been
constitutional parliament (although it was
nstated virtually unchanged). Nazarbayev was
vely empowered to rule by decree pending further
ections. At a national referendum on 29 April more
f voters endorsed the extension of Nazarbayev's five-
ndate until 1 December 2000.

May 1995 Nazarbayev ordered the establishment of a
al council to prepare (under his guidance) a new constitu-
on. The final draft, which was approved by 89.1% of the electorate in a referendum on 30 August, preserved the President's extensive executive powers. The Supreme Kenges was replaced by a bicameral Parliament, comprising a 47-member Senat (Senate—with 40 members elected by Kazakhstan's regional administrative bodies and seven appointed by the President) and a directly elected 67-member Majlis (Assembly). The Constitutional Court was replaced by a Constitutional Council, the rulings of which were to be subject to a presidential right of veto.

Indirect elections to the Senat took place on 5 December 1995. Direct elections were held to the Majlis on 9 December, with the participation of 80.7% of the electorate; further rounds of voting took place later in the month and in February 1996, in those constituencies where no candidate had obtained the requisite 50% of the votes. Foreign observers reported procedural violations.

Popular dissatisfaction with the Government's economic and social policies became more pronounced in 1996. In April a new opposition movement, Citizen (Azamat), was established. Prolonged delays in payments of wages, owing to the insolvency of numerous state-owned enterprises, were a principal cause of strikes and unauthorized demonstrations throughout 1997 and early 1998. The ongoing reform of pensions legislation also provoked protests.

Meanwhile, in late 1996 the relocation of civil servants from Almaty to the northern city of Akmola (formerly Tselinograd) marked the beginning of the transfer of the capital city (in July 1994 the Supreme Kenges had approved a proposal by Nazarbayev to transfer the capital to Akmola by 2000). In November 1997 the new capital was officially inaugurated by Nazarbayev, and a joint session of both chambers of Parliament was held for the first time in Akmola in the following month. A ceremony was held in June 1998 to mark the official opening of the capital under the new name of Astana.

In March 1997, while Kazhegeldin was out of the country, Nazarbayev undertook a major reorganization and rationalization of the state apparatus. The Ministry of Petroleum and Natural Gas was abolished and replaced by a new state company, KazakhOil. The Ministries of Defence and of Internal Affairs were among seven government institutions to become directly subordinate to the President, and the structure of regional government was reorganized. It was announced in October that Kazhegeldin had resigned, ostensibly for health reasons; in the previous month a Russian newspaper had published an admission by Kazhegeldin of his involvement, in the late 1980s, with the former Soviet state security service (KGB). Nazarbayev appointed Nurlan Balgymbayev, hitherto head of KazakhOil, as his replacement.

In January 1998 17 political parties and movements signed a 'memorandum on mutual understanding and co-operation', pledging their support for the President. In April an opposition leader was sentenced to one year's imprisonment, having been convicted of insulting the President during an unauthorized rally in November 1997. In September 1998 Nazarbayev outlined proposals for political reforms, including amendments to electoral procedures and enhanced legislative powers. In October, however, a joint session of Parliament rejected Nazarbayev's proposed constitutional reforms, amid concern that the President was attempting to mitigate his personal responsibility in the event of a future economic or political crisis. The session subsequently voted in favour of an amendment, proposed by Parliament, whereby a presidential election would take place before the expiry of Nazarbayev's extended mandate in 2000. Other amendments included a decrease in the percentage of votes required by parties in order to secure representation in the legislature, from 10% to 7%.

During November 1998 several opposition figures were deemed ineligible to contest the presidency by the Central Electoral Commission, in accordance with a presidential decree, enacted in May, which prevented those convicted of an administrative offence in the 12 months prior to an election from registering as a candidate. The most prominent disqualification was that of Kazhegeldin, who had been widely regarded as Nazarbayev's principal rival, after he attended a meeting of an unauthorized political organization. Kazhegeldin subsequently established a new political party, the Republican People's Party of Kazakhstan (RPPK). A number of other opposition parties were formed in late 1998 and early 1999, although many were prevented from registering. Among those to be accorded official status was the pro-presidential Fatherland party (Otan).

The Organization for Security and Co-operation in Europe (OSCE, see p. 354) was among international bodies to express serious concern at the conduct of the presidential election, contested by four candidates on 10 January 1999. Nazarbayev was elected to a further term, with 81.0% of the votes cast by 88.3% of the registered electorate. A new Government, headed by Balgymbayev, was appointed later in the month.

In August 1999 the President of KazakhOil, Nurlan Kaparov, was dismissed, having been accused by Nazarbayev of having exceeded his powers. Earlier that month the Minister of Defence, Gen. Mukhtar Altynbayev, and the Chairman of the National Security Committee (KNB), Nurtai Abykayev, had been dismissed, after admitting responsibility for the attempted illegal sale of military aircraft to the Democratic People's Republic of Korea. In September Kazhegeldin, who had been charged with tax evasion in April, was arrested at an airport in Moscow, but released following criticism of his detention by the OSCE. Owing to the outstanding charges against him, Kazhegeldin, together with two other leading members of the RPPK, was barred from registering as a candidate for the parliamentary elections in October. (Further charges were brought against him in February 2000.)

In late September 1999 the RPPK announced that it would boycott the forthcoming elections to the Majlis, in protest at the severe restrictions imposed on opposition parties by the President, although some of the party's members were to stand as independents. In early October Balgymbayev resigned the premiership and resumed his former position as President of KazakhOil. He was replaced as Prime Minister by Kasymzhomart Tokayev, a former Minister of Foreign Affairs. A government reorganization followed. Elections to the Majlis (as well as to municipal and local councils) were held on 10 October. Sixty-five candidates from nine political parties contested 10 seats allocated, for the first time, according to a party-list system, while almost 500 candidates contested the remaining 67 single-mandate constituency seats. All of the 10 party-list seats were filled at the first round (with Fatherland winning four seats and the CPK, the Agrarian Party of Kazakhstan (APK) and the Civic Party of Kazakhstan each taking two), but only 20 of the 67 directly elected seats were filled, and a second round of voting was held on 24 October. Final results indicated that Fatherland was to be the largest political grouping in the new Majlis, with 23 seats; the Civic Party held 13. Three other parties achieved representation, and 34 seats were taken by independent candidates. The rate of participation by voters was reported to be 62.6%. Observers from the OSCE cited numerous breaches of electoral law.

In June 2000 a law was approved awarding Nazarbayev certain lifetime guarantees and rights; the Constitutional Court upheld the legislation in the following month. In June 2001 a month-long amnesty was declared, to allow the return of capital that had been transferred abroad in violation of financial legislation; the Chairman of the National Bank of Kazakhstan (NBK) subsequently announced that US $480m. had been returned to domestic banks. However, the amnesty attracted criticism from Kazhegeldin, who claimed that the sale of petroleum had accounted for some $2,000m. in illegal transfers to

Caribbean banks in 2000. In September 2001 Kazhegeldin, who had been tried *in absentia* on charges of abuse of power, tax evasion and the illegal possession of weapons, was sentenced to 10 years' imprisonment.

In November 2001 Nazarbayev approved the resignation of Rakhat Aliyev as Deputy Chairman of the KNB, amid accusations of abuse of power. Persistent reports that Aliyev, the husband of Nazarbayev's daughter, Darigha Nazarbayeva, controlled the majority of Kazakhstan's media outlets and influenced their output, prompted the Akim (Governor) of Pavlodar Oblast, Galymzhan Zhakiyanov, and a number of other prominent political and business figures, including the Deputy Prime Minister, Uraz Jandosov, to form a new political movement, the Democratic Choice of Kazakhstan (DCK), in late November. The DCK, which aimed to revive democratic reform, decentralize political power and ensure the freedom of the mass media, criticized the concentration of power among members of Nazarbayev's family and a small group of leading entrepreneurs. Tokayev subsequently announced that two attempts to assassinate the President had been averted, and threatened to tender his resignation from the premiership unless the President dismissed ministers whom he denounced as disloyal, owing to their involvement in the formation of the DCK. Jandosov, Alikhan Baymenov (the Minister of Labour and Social Security) and two deputy ministers resigned shortly afterwards, announcing that they were unable to work with the Prime Minister; Nazarbayev dismissed Zhakiyanov on the same day. In early 2002 the United Democratic Party, which declared its main aim to be the creation of a parliamentary republic, was formed by the merger of the Citizen (Azamat) Democratic Party, the PCPK and the RPPK.

Meanwhile, in December 2001 Altynbayev was reappointed Minister of Defence. In January 2002 amendments to media legislation came into effect, which required 50% of all radio and television programmes to be broadcast in Kazakh, restricted the rebroadcast of foreign (mainly Russian) television programmes, and was intended to subject internet sites to the same controls as print media. In mid-January a further assassination attempt against the President was reported to have been thwarted. In late January Tokayev announced his resignation. On 31 January a new Government was sworn in, led by a former Deputy Prime Minister, Imangali Tasmagambetov; Tokayev was appointed State Secretary and Minister of Foreign Affairs. Meanwhile, divisions emerged within the DCK, prompting a number of its founding members, including Jandosov and Zhakiyanov, to form a new party, Bright Road (Ak Zhol).

Also in March 2002 a warrant was issued for the arrest of Zhakiyanov, on charges of abuse of power during his tenure as Akim of Pavlodar Oblast. He subsequently sought refuge in the French embassy until April, when agreement was reached between the Government and the ambassadors of France, Germany, the United Kingdom and the USA that Zhakiyanov would be permitted to go free until an investigation into the allegations had been carried out. However, less than one week later he was arrested and flown to the north-eastern city of Pavlodar, in contravention of the agreement. In mid-May it was reported that Zhakiyanov had been admitted to hospital following interrogation by security officials. Zhakiyanov's trial commenced in July, and he was sentenced to a seven-year term in August.

In July 2002 Nazarbayev signed into law new legislation on political parties, which required a party to demonstrate that it had at least 50,000 members (rather than the previous 3,000), representing every administrative region of the country, in order to qualify for registration. In the same month a former Minister of Energy, Industry and Trade and founding member of the DCK, Mukhtar Ablyazov, was sentenced to six years' imprisonment, having been found guilty of abuse of office. In late August Nazarbayev carried out a reorganization of the Government. On 8 October partial elections to fill 16 seats in the Senate were conducted; Fatherland remained the largest grouping in the chamber, accounting for 18 of the 47 senators.

In January 2003 it was reported that Jandosov had been appointed as an aide to President Nazarbayev, suggesting to many observers that Bright Road was in fact supportive of the incumbent leadership. In the same month the DCK's party registration was annulled by the Ministry of Justice, and in mid-January the establishment of a new opposition bloc, Democracy-Elections-Kazakhstan, was announced, with the aim of uniting those parties prevented from re-registering by the new legislation on political parties. By the end of the re-registration period in April, only seven parties had satisfied the criteria for registration.

In late January 2003 Sergei Duvanov, an independent journalist, was convicted of rape and sentenced to more than three years' imprisonment. He had been arrested in October 2002, shortly before he was due to travel to the USA to speak about press freedoms and human rights issues in Kazakhstan. Duvanov's conviction prompted the US embassy to express concern about judicial procedure during his trial. In mid-February 2003 the European Parliament adopted a resolution condemning the sentences awarded to Duvanov and the opposition politicians Ablyazov and Zhakiyanov, and demanding that an independent investigation into their trials be carried out. Ablyazov was pardoned in May, and subsequently announced his withdrawal from politics. (Duvanov was released in August 2004, and Zhakiyanov was released on parole in January 2006.) Meanwhile, in March 2003 Nazarbayev's links with US petroleum companies came under scrutiny when a US businessman was indicted in the USA for allegedly offering financial incentives to Kazakhstani officials, in an attempt to influence the award of important contracts (see below).

In May 2003 the Government defeated a parliamentary vote of no confidence, prompted by opposition to government plans to introduce legislation on land reform, which would permit the private ownership of land. However, on 9 June Tasmagambetov tendered his resignation, after it emerged that the results of the no confidence vote had been falsified by supporters of the Government. A new Government, led by Daniyal Akhmetov, a former Akim of Pavlodar Oblast, was appointed in June, which included more than two-thirds of the ministers of the outgoing administration. The land reform bill was approved by Parliament on 20 June.

In September 2003 Zautbek Turisbekov was appointed as Minister of Internal Affairs, replacing Col-Gen. Kairbek Suleimonov, after Nazarbayev reportedly decreed that the heads of the law-enforcement and security bodies should be civilian appointments. Elections to local councils took place on 20 September, with further rounds of voting in October–November. The OSCE was again critical of the conduct of the electoral process.

In October 2003 a new party, Mutual Help (Asar), led by Darigha Nazarbayeva, was officially registered. In March 2004 Nurtai Abykayev was appointed as Chairman of the Senat. In early May four political parties that had not been granted official registration were declared invalid by a court ruling: Kazakh Ely, the Republican People's Party of Kazakhstan, the Azamat Party and the People's Congress of Kazakhstan. However, in mid-June the Ministry of Justice officially registered the People's Communist Party of Kazakhstan and the Democratic Party of Kazakhstan (DPK).

On 19 September 2004 elections took place to the Majlis, with 'run-off' elections held on 3 October in 22 constituencies where no candidate had received an overall majority of the votes cast. Fatherland emerged as the largest grouping, with 42 seats, giving it an absolute majority in the chamber. An electoral coalition formed by the APK and the Civic Party of Kazakhstan won 11 seats, while Mutual Help obtained four seats. Bright Road and the DPK each obtained one seat, and 18 non-partisan candidates were elected. The rate of participation by the electorate was 56.7% in the first round of voting and 45.2% in the second round. Monitors from the OSCE criticized the conduct of the polls, and, in particular, the media. Alikhan Baymenov of Bright Road, who was effectively the only opposition representative elected to the new legislature, subsequently announced that he would not take up his seat in the Majlis, alleging that the results of the elections had been falsified. The Chairman of the outgoing legislature, Zharmakhan Tuyakbai, resigned from Fatherland in mid-October in order to protest against the conduct of the elections. At the inaugural session of the new Majlis, held on 3 November, Ural Mukhamejanov was elected Chairman.

In early December 2004, apparently inspired by mass protests in Ukraine against the falsification of presidential election results in that country (see the chapter on Ukraine), the DCK declared that it regarded the Kazakhstani Government to be illegitimate and urged non-violent civil disobedience. In January 2005 a court ordered that the DCK be dismantled, alleging that a recent statement by the party had breached national security laws. Later in the month at least 1,000 people took part in an unsanctioned rally organized by Bright Road, the DCK and the CPK to protest against the closure of the party; in October 2004 the three parties had established a Co-ordinating Council of

Opposition Democratic Forces of Kazakhstan, which aimed to draft a new constitution and create a more influential democratic movement in the country. In February 2005 the Co-ordinating Council of Opposition Democratic Forces of Kazakhstan announced that it was to establish a new national movement, to be known as For a Just Kazakhstan. In late March former members of the DCK announced the establishment of a new grouping, Forward (Alga), led by Asylbek Kozhakhmetov. (However, in February 2006 the party was refused registration.) In late April 2005 another new party, Real Bright Road (Naghyz Ak Zhol), held its founding congress, following divisions within Bright Road.

Meanwhile, in early December 2004 President Nazarbayev had issued a decree allowing village akims to be elected, and providing for 'experimental' elections of akims (who had hitherto been appointed) in several oblasts. Elections were duly held in villages and in four oblasts during 2005. Opposition representatives criticized the small number of administrative units covered, while the conduct of the elections to the oblast posts (in which all the incumbent candidates were returned to office, and in which all candidates had been nominated by the local authorities) was also criticised.

In April 2005 a law was introduced prohibiting demonstrations both during and after elections, and in June the Majlis approved legislation, which required all religious organizations and communities to register with the state authorities. Concern was expressed at an announcement in July that the security agencies were preparing to use force against any popular unrest that might arise around the time of the forthcoming presidential election: the Minister of Internal Affairs, Turisbekov, asserted that the country would not allow a repetition of the events that had taken place in 2003–05 in Georgia, Ukraine and Kyrgyzstan (where popular revolts, following disputed elections, had led to the collapse of the incumbent regimes). In early August 2005 the For a Just Kazakhstan coalition, led by Tuyakbai, and comprising the CPK, Forward, the Generation Pensioners' Movement and Real Bright Road, was officially registered with the Ministry of Justice.

On 19 August 2005 partial elections to the Senate, originally scheduled to be held in December, took place. Fatherland secured 10 of the 16 seats contested; three seats were won by other pro-Nazarbayev parties and three by independents. In September the Majlis confirmed that a presidential election would be held in December, one year earlier than had been anticipated. Later in September the For a Just Kazakhstan movement elected Tuyakbai to stand as its single opposition candidate in the election.

In the presidential ballot, conducted on 4 December 2005, Nazarbayev was re-elected as President, with 91.2% of the votes cast, according to official results; his candidacy was supported by an electoral bloc, the Popular Coalition, which included Fatherland, Mutual Help, the DPK, the APK and the Civic Party of Kazakhstan. Of the four other candidates, Nazarbayev's closest rival was Tuyakbai, who received 6.6% of the votes. The rate of participation was 76.8%. Monitors from the OSCE declared that the conduct of the election had not satisfied international standards of democracy. On 18 January both chambers of Parliament unanimously approved Nazarbayev's nomination of Akhmetov as Prime Minister. On the following day Nazarbayev approved a new Government, which retained most members of the previous administration. New appointments included those of Karim Masimov, a longstanding presidential aide and prominent economist, as Deputy Prime Minister and Natalya Korzhova as Minister of Finance.

In mid-February 2006 Altynbek Sarsenbayev, one of the leaders of Real Bright Road and a prominent supporter of Tuyakbai's presidential campaign, was shot and killed in Almaty. A special commission was established to investigate the killing, which opposition representatives claimed had been politically motivated. Those detained on suspicion of involvement in the case included five KNB officials and the head of the administration of the Senat, Erzhan Utembayev. The head of the KNB, Nartai Dutbayev, subsequently resigned as a result of the investigation. An unsanctioned protest rally was held in Almaty in late February, at which demonstrators urged the authorities to end the persecution of opposition representatives and to bring the perpetrators to trial; a number of organizers of the demonstration were later imprisoned. In March Real Bright Road was granted official registration.

In April 2006 Nazarbayev appointed Masimov to the additional post of Minister of the Economy and Budgetary Planning.

(He was replaced in this position by Aslan Musin in October.) In June the trial began of 10 suspects charged with involvement in the killing of Sarsenbayev. During the trial Utembayev pleaded not guilty to having ordered the murder, despite reportedly having earlier confessed to so doing. In June the Majlis adopted a number of controversial legislative amendments designed to enforce greater regulation over media outlets, which, despite strong criticism from the OSCE, were endorsed by the Senat on 29 June and signed into law by the President on 4 July. Also in July, at an extraordinary Fatherland party congress in Astana, the party merged with Nazarbayeva's Mutual Help party, thereby consolidating support for Nazarbayev in the Majlis prior to forthcoming legislative elections. In October President Nazarbayev appointed several new ministers in a governmental reorganization. In December the APK and Civic Party also merged with Fatherland; the new party, known as Light of the Fatherland (Nur Otan) controlled 57 seats in the Majlis.

On 8 January 2007 Akhmetov tendered his resignation as Prime Minister; it was reported that Nazarbayev had continually criticized him for poor organization and budget planning. On 10 January the Majlis voted to approve the President's nomination of Massimov as premier. Musin was appointed as Deputy Prime Minister (retaining the portfolio of the economy and budget planning), while Akhmetov became Minister of Defence. In May Parliament approved extensive constitutional amendments, proposed by President Nazarbayev, strengthening the powers of an expanded Majlis, which was henceforth to approve prime ministerial appointments. The presidential term of office was to be reduced from seven to five years with effect from 2012, while the restriction on the incumbent President to two terms in office was to be removed.

In June 2007 Rakhat Aliyev, now the Kazakhstani ambassador to Austria, was arrested in that country, after the Kazakhstani Government issued an arrest warrant against him in May for his alleged involvement in the kidnapping of two banking associates. The Austrian authorities began criminal proceedings against him on charges of financial malpractice, while Kazakhstan officially requested his extradition. (In March 2008 a military court sentenced Aliyev *in absentia* to 20 years' imprisonment.)

On 20 June 2007 President Nazarbayev dissolved the Majlis and announced that legislative elections were to be brought forward to 18 August (two years earlier than scheduled). At the elections the pro-presidential party, Light Of The Fatherland, won 88.4% of votes cast, securing all 98 contested seats in the enlarged 107-member Majlis. None of the other six parties participating in the poll achieved the 7% minimum of votes required to gain representation in the chamber; the newly established National Social-Democratic Party (NSDP) received 4.5% and Bright Road 3.1% of the votes cast. The leaders of the NSDP, Bright Road and the Communist People's Party refused to acknowledge the results and demanded that the poll be repeated. The OSCE announced that, despite some improvements, the poll had failed to meet international standards. In accordance with the amended Constitution, the Assembly of Nations of Kazakhstan (which represents the country's minority ethnic groups) elected the remaining nine deputies to the Majlis on 20 August. A reorganized Government was approved at the first session of the new Parliament on 2 September; most of the incumbent ministers retained their posts. Umirzak Shukeyev, hitherto Akim of Southern Kazakhstan Oblast, became the new Deputy Prime Minister, succeeding Musin, who was elected Chairman of the Majlis. In November the Minister of Emergency Situations (who was suspected of corruption) was replaced, and a new Minister of Finance was appointed.

The issue of the legal status of the Caspian Sea—and the division of the substantial mineral resources believed to be located in the seabed—has been a source of tension between the five littoral states: Azerbaijan, Iran, Kazakhstan, Russia and Turkmenistan. In July 1998 Nazarbayev and the Russian President, Boris Yeltsin, signed a bilateral agreement on the delineation of their countries' respective boundaries of the Caspian seabed, by which Russia for the first time formally recognized Kazakhstan's claim to, and right to exploit, its offshore petroleum resources, prompting particular criticism from Iran, which continued to assert that partitioning of the seabed required the consensus of all five littoral states. In October 2000 Nazarbayev and the recently elected President of Russia, Vladimir Putin, signed an additional agreement, on the definition of the legal status of the Caspian Sea, and the 1998 agreement was further augmented in May 2002, when an accord was signed on the equal division of three oilfields in the northern Caspian. Russia and Kazakhstan have also signed a Treaty of Eternal Friendship and Co-operation, which provides for mutual military assistance in the event of aggression by a third party. In November 2001 Kazakhstan concluded a bilateral agreement with Azerbaijan on the two countries' respective mineral rights in the Caspian Sea, prompting further protests from Iran. In May 2003 Azerbaijan, Kazakhstan and Russia signed a trilateral agreement. In November representatives of Azerbaijan, Iran, Kazakhstan, Russia and Turkmenistan, meeting in Tehran, Iran, signed a UN-sponsored framework Convention for the Protection of the Marine Environment of the Caspian Sea, which sought to alleviate environmental damage in the Caspian Sea region. In mid-January 2005 Nazarbayev and Putin signed a treaty in Moscow defining the 7,500-km land border between their two countries.

In the early 1990s the issue of the formerly Soviet, subsequently Russian-controlled, nuclear warheads deployed in Kazakhstan (effectively making the country the fourth largest nuclear power in the world) was the focus of international concern. In September 1992 the Kazakhstani legislature ratified the first Strategic Arms Reduction Treaty, signed by the USA and the USSR in July 1991. In December 1993 the Kazakhstani legislature ratified the Treaty on the Non-Proliferation of Nuclear Weapons. By April 1995 all nuclear warheads had been transferred to Russia, and in September 1996 Russia and Kazakhstan signed a final protocol governing the withdrawal of military units linked to the Russian nuclear weapons facilities in Kazakhstan. In November 2001 the Kazakhstani legislature ratified the Comprehensive Nuclear Test Ban Treaty.

In May 2001 the signatories of the CIS Collective Security Treaty (Armenia, Belarus, Kazakhstan, Kyrgyzstan, Russia and Tajikistan) agreed to form a Collective Rapid Reaction Force in Bishkek, Kyrgyzstan, to combat Islamist militancy in Central Asia; in January 2002 it was announced that the force was ready to undertake combat missions. An anti-terrorism centre became operational in Bishkek in August 2001. In late April 2003 a successor organization to the Collective Security Treaty was formed, when Armenia, Belarus, Kazakhstan, Kyrgyzstan, Russia and Tajikistan inaugurated the Collective Security Treaty Organization (CSTO).

In 1992 Kazakhstan joined the Economic Co-operation Organization (ECO, see p. 238), founded by Iran, Pakistan and Turkey. In 1994 Kazakhstan, Kyrgyzstan and Uzbekistan formed a trilateral economic area, and in February 1995 an Interstate Council was established to supervise its implementation. Several agreements to expand economic co-operation were signed by the three countries in 1996. In 1998 Tajikistan joined the alliance, which was renamed the Central Asian Co-operation Organization (CACO) in March 2002. Meanwhile, in January 1995 Kazakhstan established a customs union with Russia and Belarus, and in March 1996 the three members of the customs union were joined by Kyrgyzstan; Tajikistan joined the union in April 1998. In October 2000 a new economic body, the Eurasian Economic Community (EURASEC, see p. 412), was established to supersede the customs union, and this organization merged with CACO in January 2006. In October 2007 EURASEC leaders approved the legal basis for the establishment of a new customs union that was initially to comprise Belarus, Kazakhstan and Russia, with Kyrgyzstan, Tajikistan and Uzbekistan expected to join by 2011. In September 2002 President Nazarbayev and the President of Uzbekistan, Islam Karimov, signed a bilateral agreement on the delimitation of all disputed sectors of their countries' common border. A border agreement with Turkmenistan, which had been signed in July 2001, was ratified by the Senat in June 2003, and in July Nazarbayev signed a number of laws confirming the delimitation of Kazakhstan's borders with Kyrgyzstan, Turkmenistan and Uzbekistan.

In 1995 Nazarbayev made an official visit to the People's Republic of China, where an agreement was signed to improve long-term stability between the two countries, following concerns about Chinese underground nuclear tests near the border with eastern Kazakhstan. Bilateral relations were further strengthened by two accords concluded in 1997, whereby China was granted permission to exploit two of the largest oilfields in Kazakhstan. The agreements provided for the construction of a petroleum pipeline connecting the two countries, work on which commenced in September 2004. Construction, at an estimated cost of US $700m., was completed in late 2005. Meanwhile, in November 1998 Nazarbayev made a state visit to China, which resulted in the signature of a communiqué on the full settlement of outstanding border issues, and of an agreement outlining future bilateral relations. In July 2005 Nazarbayev and Chinese President Hu Jintao signed an agreement on the establishment of a strategic partnership between the two countries. China and Kazakhstan have attended annual summit meetings of the heads of state of the so-called Shanghai Five (also comprising Kyrgyzstan, Russia and Tajikistan), which aimed to promote economic co-operation and regional co-ordination on border and security issues. Members of the alliance, which became the Shanghai Co-operation Organization (SCO, see p. 425) upon the accession of Uzbekistan in 2001, signed the Shanghai Convention on Combating Terrorism, Separatism and Extremism in June 2001. In August 2003 Kazakhstan and China jointly hosted military manoeuvres involving the member states of the SCO. In July 2005, at a summit meeting in Astana, members of the SCO approved anti-terrorist measures, and signed a declaration advocating non-interference in the affairs of sovereign states. Several bilateral co-operation agreements were signed during a Chinese official visit in November 2007; a second stage in construction of the petroleum pipeline system linking Kazakhstan with China commenced in December.

Following the suicide attacks on the USA on 11 September 2001, President Nazarbayev expressed his support for US-led military action against the al-Qa'ida (Base) organization of the Saudi-born militant Islamist, Osama bin Laden, and the regime of its hosts, the Taliban, in Afghanistan (see the chapters on Afghanistan and the USA). The USA acknowledged Kazakhstan's strategic importance, and Kazakhstan offered the USA the use of airports, airspace and military bases. In February 2006 it was announced that US forces were to participate in Kazakhstani-British military exercises in Kazakhstan in September, and were to engage in the command component of the exercises for the first time. Meanwhile, Nazarbayev's links with US petroleum companies were subject to legal scrutiny from late March 2003, when James H. Giffen, a US businessman and former adviser to Nazarbayev, was indicted in the USA under the 1977 Foreign Corrupt Practices Act (which prohibits US companies or individuals from offering financial inducements to foreign officials in order to secure an agreement). He was accused of offering bribes to prominent Kazakhstani politicians, including Nazarbayev, in return for securing valuable contracts for US petroleum companies. In April 2004 a US federal court indicted Giffen and an executive of the petroleum company, ExxonMobil, on charges of corrupt business practices. In October 2005 a judge allowed Giffen to use classified information in his defence as evidence that the US Government had endorsed his actions. In September 2006 Nazarbayev met US President George W. Bush during an official visit to Washington, DC. The two Presidents subsequently issued a joint statement envisaging further bilateral co-operation in the energy sector. President Bush publicly thanked Nazarbayev for his assistance in the US-led military action and announced that the USA would support the efforts of Kazakhstan (which Bush referred to as a 'free nation') to join the World Trade Organisation (WTO, see p. 396). At an OSCE meeting in Madrid, Spain, at the end of November 2007, Kazakhstan secured approval to assume the rotating chairmanship of that body in 2010, despite criticism by OSCE monitors of the conduct of elections in August (see above) and continuing international concerns over the human rights situation in the country.

Government

Under the terms of the 1995 Constitution (to which a number of amendments were made in October 1998 and May 2007), the President of the Republic is Head of State and commander-in-chief of the armed forces, and holds broad executive powers. The President is directly elected by universal adult suffrage. (Under the constitutional amendments of May 2007, the presidential term was reduced from seven to five years, with effect from 2012.) The Government, headed by the Prime Minister, is responsible to the President. The supreme legislative organ is the bicameral Parliament, comprising the Senat (Senate, upper chamber) and the Majlis (Assembly, lower chamber). The Senat comprises 47 members, of whom 32 are elected by regional assemblies, while the remaining 15 deputies are appointed by the President. The Majlis comprises 107 deputies, of whom 98 are directly elected; the remaining nine deputies are elected by the Assembly of Nations of Kazakhstan (a 350-member body representing the country's minority ethnic groups). The Senat's term is six years, and that of the Majlis is five years. One-half of the elected deputies in the Senat are subject to election every three years.

KAZAKHSTAN

Introductory Survey

For administrative purposes, Kazakhstan is divided into 16 units (14 regions and the cities of Almaty and Astana). The city of Leninsk—now Turatam—serving the Baikonur space centre, and formerly one of Kazakhstan's administrative units, was transferred to Russian jurisdiction in August 1995. In January 2004 President Nazarbayev and the Russian President, Vladimir Putin, signed an agreement permitting Russia's continued use of the Baikonur space centre until 2050.

Defence

Following Kazakhstan's independence from the USSR in 1991, the armed forces were established by presidential decree in May 1992. The length of compulsory military service was reduced from two years to one year at the beginning of 2006. As assessed at November 2007, the estimated strength of the national armed forces was 49,000 (including an army of 30,000, air force of 12,000 and navy of 3,000). In addition, there were 31,500 paramilitary troops (including an estimated 20,000 troops attached to the Ministry of Internal Affairs, and an estimated 9,000 border guards). Kazakhstan participates, with Russia, Azerbaijan and Turkmenistan, in the operation of the Caspian Sea Flotilla, a former Soviet force based, under Russian command, at Astrakhan (Russia). In mid-1992 Kazakhstan signed a Collective Security Treaty with five other members of the Commonwealth of Independent States (CIS, see p. 215); in May 2001 it was announced that the signatory countries were to form a Collective Rapid Reaction Force to combat Islamist militancy in Central Asia. In April 2003 the Collective Security Treaty Organization (CSTO) was inaugurated as the successor to the CIS collective security system, with the participation of Armenia, Belarus, Kazakhstan, Kyrgyzstan, Russia and Tajikistan. A nuclear successor state to the USSR, Kazakhstan undertook to dismantle its nuclear capabilities, ratifying the first Strategic Arms Reduction Treaty in 1992 and the Treaty on the Non-Proliferation of Nuclear Weapons in 1993. All nuclear warheads had been transferred to Russia by mid-1995, and a final protocol for the withdrawal of the Russian strategic-missile troops was signed in September 1996. In May 1994 Kazakhstan joined the North Atlantic Treaty Organization's (NATO) 'Partnership for Peace' (see p. 342) programme of military co-operation. Kazakhstan became a full member of the UN Conference on Disarmament in August 1999. In early 2007 the Government announced a programme to reorganize the armed forces, in co-operation with Russia, by 2015. The budget for 2007 allocated 142,000m. tenge to defence.

Economic Affairs

In 2006, according to estimates by the World Bank, Kazakhstan's gross national income (GNI), measured at average 2004–06 prices, was US $57,982m., equivalent to $3,790 per head (or $7,780 per head on an international purchasing-power parity basis). During 1996–2006, it was estimated, the population decreased at an average annual rate of 0.2%, while gross domestic product (GDP) per head increased, in real terms, by an average of 7.6% per year. Overall GDP increased, in real terms, at an average annual rate of 10.3% in 1999–2006. Real GDP increased by 10.6% in 2006.

Agriculture (including forestry and fishing) contributed 5.3% of GDP in 2006 and provided 33.6% of total employment in 2004. There are large areas of land suitable for agriculture, and Kazakhstan is a major producer and exporter of agricultural products. The principal crops include fruit, sugar beet, vegetables, potatoes, cotton and, most importantly, cereals. Livestock-breeding is also important, and Kazakhstan is a significant producer of karakul and astrakhan wools. According to the World Bank, the GDP of the agricultural sector increased, in real terms, by an average of 2.4% per year in 1996–2006. Agricultural GDP increased by 7.3% in 2005, and by a further 1.0% in 2006.

Industry (including mining, manufacturing, construction, and power) contributed 39.3% of GDP in 2006, and 17.4% of total employment in 2004. The principal branches of industry include the fuel industry and metal-processing. According to World Bank figures, industrial GDP increased, in real terms, at an average annual rate of 9.1% in 1996–2006. The GDP of the sector increased by 10.3% in 2005 and by 10.0% in 2006.

Mining and quarrying provided 2.6% of employment in 2004. Kazakhstan possesses immense mineral wealth, and large-scale mining and processing industries have been developed. There are major coalfields (in the Karaganda, Turgai, Ekibastuz and Maikuben basins), as well as substantial deposits of iron ore, lead, zinc ore, titanium, magnesium, chromium, tungsten, molybdenum, gold, silver, copper and manganese. Petroleum is extracted, and Kazakhstan possesses substantial reserves of natural gas. The discovery of major petroleum reserves at the offshore Kashagan oilfield was announced in mid-2000 (see below). In January 2004 the state-owned hydrocarbons company KazMunaiGaz awarded the Russian energy company LUKoil a 50% stake in a 40-year production-sharing contract for the development of the Tyub-Karagan field in the Caspian Sea, which has petroleum reserves of an estimated 100m. metric tons. In January 2005 the Kazakhstani and Russian Presidents signed an agreement confirming the equal rights of both countries to the Imashevskoye natural gas field, the second largest natural gas field in Kazakhstan, which was to be developed jointly by KazMunaiGaz and the Russian energy company GazProm. Also in 2005 a subsidiary of KazMunaiGaz signed a production-sharing agreement with the Russian state-owned petroleum companies Zarubezhneft and Rosneft to develop the offshore Kurmanagazy oilfield, estimated to contain recoverable reserves of petroleum of between 900m. and 1,000m. metric tons. At the end of 2005 Kazakhstan's proven total reserves (on shore and off shore) of petroleum and natural gas were estimated at 39,800m. barrels and 3,000,000m. cu m, respectively.

Manufacturing provided 7.2% of employment in 2004, and, according to the World Bank, contributed 14.6% of GDP in 2005. The GDP of the manufacturing sector increased at an average annual rate of 6.5% in 1995–2005.

In 2004 coal-fired thermal power stations provided about 69.9% of annual domestic electricity production, while hydroelectric power stations accounted for 12.0% of production and natural gas for 10.6%. In 2006 mineral products accounted for 14.3% of total imports.

The services sector contributed some 55.4% of GDP in 2006 and provided 49.0% of employment in 2004. According to World Bank figures, the GDP of the services sector increased, in real terms, at an average annual rate of 7.0% during 1996–2006. Services GDP increased by 10.4% in 2005 and by 10.0% in 2006.

In 2006 Kazakhstan recorded a visible trade surplus of US $14,641.7m., and there was a deficit of $1,794.9m. on the current account of the balance of payments. In that year the principal source of imports was Russia, which accounted for 35.7% of total imports. Other major suppliers were the People's Republic of China (20.0%) and Germany. The principal market for exports in that year was Germany, which (accounting for 12.5% of total exports). Other important purchasers of exports were Russia, China, Italy and France The main exports were mineral products and base metals. The principal imports in that year were machinery and electrical equipment, mineral products, transportation equipment, base metals and chemical products.

In 2006 Kazakhstan recorded a preliminary budgetary surplus (excluding lending minus repayments) of some 81,600m. tenge (equivalent to around 0.8% of GDP). At the end of 2005 Kazakhstan's external debt amounted to US $43,354m. of which $2,184m. was long-term public debt. In that year the cost of debt-servicing was equivalent to 42.1% of the value of exports of goods and services. The annual rate of inflation averaged 8.9% during 1996–2005. Consumer prices increased by 6.9% in 2004 and by 7.5% in 2005. In 2006, according to provisional figures, 7.8% of the labour force were unemployed.

In addition to its membership of the economic bodies of the Commonwealth of Independent States (CIS, see p. 215), Kazakhstan has joined the ADB, is a 'Country of Operations' of the European Bank for Reconstruction and Development (EBRD, see p. 239) and is a member of the Economic Co-operation Organization (ECO, see p. 238).

After independence in 1991, contraction was recorded annually until 1995, when signs of an economic recovery emerged. In 1996 a large-scale privatization programme was extended to include the hydrocarbons and metallurgical sectors. In 1998 the economy was severely affected by the economic crises in Russia and Asia, and the subsequent decline in prices for Kazakhstan's principal exports. However, by mid-2000 Kazakhstan had repaid all debts owed to the IMF, seven years ahead of schedule. A National Oil Fund was created in 2001, to manage the country's wealth and guard against sudden declines in petroleum prices. By June 2005 the Fund's assets amounted to some US $5,200m. Meanwhile, commercial petroleum extraction from the Kashagan oilfield (which was discovered in July 2000) was not expected to ensue until 2011, six years later than initially scheduled. In January 2008 the Government successfully increased its ownership stake in the project to almost 17%;

KAZAKHSTAN

Statistical Survey

the oilfield was to be developed in partnership with a consortium of six international oil companies. Recoverable oil reserves at Kashagan were estimated at 18,000m. barrels and the authorities hoped to channel profits into fiscal expenditures and economic development projects. Petroleum exports increased significantly following the official opening, in November 2001, of a new, 1,500-km petroleum pipeline, connecting the onshore Tengiz field in western Kazakhstan with Novorossiisk, on the Russian Black Sea coast. In May 2005 a pipeline constructed to transport petroleum from Baku, Azerbaijan, via Tbilisi, Georgia, to Ceyhan, Turkey, and onto Western markets (known as the BTC pipeline) was officially inaugurated. In December 2007 a second stage in construction of a petroleum pipeline system linking Kazakhstan with the People's Republic of China commenced. In the same month Kazakhstan, Russia and Turkmenistan signed a formal agreement for the construction of a Caspian natural gas pipeline to transport Central Asian gas supplies to Russia. While economic growth remained strong at 8.7% in 2007, high levels of expenditure continued to increase inflation, which was estimated at 8.6%.

Education

General education (primary and secondary) is compulsory, and is fully funded by the state. Primary education begins at seven years of age and lasts for four years. Secondary education, beginning at 11 years of age, lasts for a further seven years, comprising a first cycle of five years and a second of two years. In 2004 total enrolment at primary schools included 93% of the relevant age-group, and the comparable ratio for secondary enrolment was 92%. After completing general education, pupils may continue their studies at specialized secondary schools. In 2004/05 there were a total of 181 higher schools (including universities), with a total enrolment of 747,100 students. Ethnic Kazakhs form a greater proportion (64% in 1995/96) of students in higher education than in general education, since many ethnic Russians choose to study at universities outside Kazakhstan. None the less, the majority of higher-education students (approximately 75% in 1997) are instructed in Russian. The number of private general schools in Kazakhstan increased from 18 in 1994/95 to 181 by 2005/06. In 2003/04 there were 179 private secondary vocational schools and 134 private higher schools (including universities). Government expenditure on education in 2001 was 105,024m. tenge (14.7% of total spending).

Public Holidays

2008: 1–2 January (New Year), 7 January (Orthodox Christmas), 8 March (International Women's Day), 22 March (Nauryz Meyramy, Spring Holiday), 1 May (Day of Unity of the Peoples of Kazakhstan), 9 May (Victory Day, Day of Remembrance), 30 August (Constitution Day), 25 October (Republic Day), 16 December (Independence Day), 8 December (Kurban Bayram—Feast of the Sacrifice).

2009: 1–2 January (New Year), 7 January (Orthodox Christmas), 8 March (International Women's Day), 22 March (Nauryz Meyramy, Spring Holiday), 1 May (Day of Unity of the Peoples of Kazakhstan), 9 May (Victory Day, Day of Remembrance), 30 August (Constitution Day), 25 October (Republic Day), 27 November (Kurban Bayram—Feast of the Sacrifice), 16 December (Independence Day).

Weights and Measures

The metric system is in force.

Statistical Survey

Source (unless otherwise stated): Statistical Agency of the Republic of Kazakhstan, 050009 Almaty, Abai 125; tel. (727) 261-13-23; fax (7272) 242-08-24; e-mail stat@mail.online.kz; internet www.stat.kz.

Area and Population

AREA, POPULATION AND DENSITY

Area (sq km)	2,724,900*
Population (census results)	
12 January 1989†	16,464,464
25 February–4 March 1999	
Males	7,201,785
Females	7,751,341
Total	14,953,126
Population (official estimates at 1 January)	
2006	15,219,291
2007	15,396,878
2008	15,565,647
Density (per sq km) at 1 January 2008	5.7

* 1,049,150 sq miles.

† Figure refers to the *de jure* population. The *de facto* total was 16,536,511.

PRINCIPAL ETHNIC GROUPS
(1 January 2004, official estimates)

	Number	%
Kazakh	8,550,986	57.19
Russian	4,072,337	27.24
Ukrainian	469,397	3.14
Uzbek	409,770	2.74
German	237,643	1.59
Tatar	232,735	1.56
Uigur	223,039	1.49
Others	755,293	5.05
Total	**14,951,200**	**100.00**

ADMINISTRATIVE DIVISIONS
(1 January 2008, official estimates)

	Area (sq km)	Population	Density (per sq km)	Capital city
Oblasts				
Akmola	146,200	747,208	5.11	Kokshetau
Aktobe	300,600	703,433	2.34	Aktobe
Almaty	224,000	1,642,324	7.33	Taldykorgan
Atyrau	118,600	490,218	4.13	Atyrau
Eastern Kazakhstan	283,200	1,416,393	5.00	Ust-Kamenogorsk
Jambul	144,300	1,018,305	7.06	Taraz
Karaganda	428,000	1,341,507	3.13	Karaganda
Kostanai	196,000	894,157	4.56	Kostanai
Kyzyl-Orda	226,000	631,816	2.80	Kyzyl-Orda
Mangystau	165,600	407,248	2.46	Aktau
Northern Kazakhstan	98,000	653,760	6.67	Petropavlovsk
Pavlodar	124,800	746,216	5.98	Pavlodar
Southern Kazakhstan	117,300	2,331,247	19.87	Chimkent
Western Kazakhstan	151,300	615,290	4.07	Oral
Cities				
Almaty	700	1,324,045	1,891.49	—
Astana (capital)	300	602,480	2,008.27	—
Total	**2,724,900**	**15,565,647**	**5.71**	—

KAZAKHSTAN

PRINCIPAL TOWNS
(population at 1999 census)

Almaty (Alma-Ata)	1,129,400	Petropavlovsk		203,500
Karaganda	436,900	Oral		195,500
Chimkent	360,100	Temirtau		170,500
Taraz*	330,100	Kyzyl-Orda		157,400
Astana† (capital)	313,000	Aktau‡		143,400
Ust-Kamenogorsk	311,000	Atyrau§		142,500
Pavlodar	300,500	Ekibastuz		127,200
Semipalatinsk	269,600	Kokchetau		123,400
Aktobe	253,100	Rudniy		109,500
Kostanai	221,400			

* Formerly Jambul.
† Formerly Akmola, and prior to that, Tselinograd.
‡ Formerly Shevchenko.
§ Formerly Guriyev.

Mid-2007 ('000, incl. suburbs, UN estimate): Almaty (Alma-Ata) 1,209 (Source: UN, *World Urbanization Prospects: The 2007 Revision*).

BIRTHS, MARRIAGES AND DEATHS

	Registered live births		Registered marriages		Registered deaths	
	Number	Rate (per 1,000)	Number	Rate (per 1,000)	Number	Rate (per 1,000)
1999	271,578	14.5	85,872	5.8	147,416	9.8
2000	222,054	14.9	90,873	6.1	149,778	10.0
2001	221,487	14.9	92,852	6.3	147,876	10.0
2002	227,171	15.3	98,986	6.7	149,381	10.1
2003	247,946	16.6	110,414	7.4	155,277	10.4
2004	273,028	18.2	114,685	7.6	152,250	10.1
2005	278,977	18.4	123,045	8.1	157,121	10.4
2006	301,756	19.7	137,204	9.0	157,210	10.3

Expectation of life (years at birth, WHO estimates): 63.5 (males 58.3; females 69.2) in 2005 (Source: WHO, *World Health Statistics*).

ECONOMICALLY ACTIVE POPULATION
(labour force survey, annual averages, '000 persons)

	2002	2003	2004
Agriculture, forestry and fishing	2,380.2	2,462.6	2,406.0
Mining and quarrying	167.3	181.7	186.0
Manufacturing	503.7	506.4	519.8
Electricity, gas and water supply	153.0	167.2	163.8
Construction	268.4	329.5	380.7
Wholesale and retail trade; repair of motor vehicles, motor cycles and personal and household goods	1,007.2	1,015.1	1,058.7
Hotels and restaurants	56.5	70.2	82.0
Transport, storage and communications	503.7	503.9	519.7
Financial intermediation	50.1	53.5	60.7
Real estate, renting and business activities	203.4	207.1	233.6
Public administration and defence; compulsory social security	280.4	318.2	334.7
Education	589.0	631.1	666.2
Health and social work	292.6	299.7	318.7
Community, social and personal services	186.3	196.3	201.3
Households with employed persons	66.8	42.5	49.4
Extra-territorial organizations and bodies	0.3	0.3	0.5
Total employed	6,708.9	6,985.2	7,181.8
Unemployed	690.7	672.1	658.8
Total labour force	7,399.6	7,657.3	7,840.6

Source: ILO.

Total employed (labour force survey, annual averages, '000 persons): 7,261.0 in 2005; 7,403.7 in 2006.

Health and Welfare

KEY INDICATORS

Total fertility rate (children per woman, 2005)	1.9
Under-5 mortality rate (per 1,000 live births, 2005)	31
HIV/AIDS (% of persons aged 15–49, 2005)	0.1
Physicians (per 1,000 head, 2003)	3.54
Hospital beds (per 1,000 head, 2005)	7.8
Health expenditure (2004): US $ per head (PPP)	263.8
Health expenditure (2004): % of GDP	3.8
Health expenditure (2004): public (% of total)	59.8
Access to water (% of persons, 2004)	86
Access to sanitation (% of persons, 2004)	72
Human Development Index (2005): ranking	73
Human Development Index (2005): value	0.794

For sources and definitions, see explanatory note on p. vi.

Agriculture

PRINCIPAL CROPS
('000 metric tons)

	2004	2005	2006
Wheat	9,936.9	11,066.0*	13,500.0
Rice (paddy)	275.8	310.0*	320.0*
Barley	1,387.9	1,545.0*	1,800.0*
Maize	457.8	510.0*	495.0*
Rye	20.3	23.0*	25.0*
Oats	130.3	145.0*	165.0*
Millet	50.7	56.0*	65.0*
Buckwheat	52.4	58.0*	66.0*
Potatoes	2,260.6	2,521.0	2,361.6
Sugar beet	397.9	310.8	339.0
Dry beans	5.0†	5.0*	6.5*
Dry peas	31.6	35.0*	37.0*
Soybeans	46.7	45.0†	48.0†
Sunflower seed	265.5	262.0	268.0
Safflower seed	76.1	75.0*	75.0*
Cottonseed†	257.0	256.0	250.0
Cabbages	321.5	338.0*	320.0*
Tomatoes	490.9	516.0*	485.0*
Cucumbers and gherkins	260.0	275.0*	258.0*
Aubergines (Eggplants)	48.3	50.0*	47.0*
Chillies and green peppers	73.5	77.0*	72.0*
Dry onions	327.3	345.0*	325.0*
Green broad beans	12.0†	13.0*	14.0*
Carrots	236.4	250.0*	235.0*
Watermelons	666.9	703.5*	660.0*
Apples	148.9	150.0*	150.0*
Pears	16.8	15.0*	15.0*
Cherries	14.6	12.0*	12.0*
Plums	7.8	8.0*	8.0*
Grapes	53.2	28.0*	28.0*
Tobacco (leaves)	14.3	14.0*	14.0*

* FAO estimate.
† Unofficial figure(s).

Aggregate production ('000 metric tons, may include official, semi-official or estimated data): Total cereals 12,333.8 in 2004, 13,736.6 in 2005, 16,461.6 in 2006; Total roots and tubers 2,260.6 in 2004, 2,521.0 in 2005, 2,361.6 in 2006; Total vegetables (incl. melons) 2,729.2 in 2004, 2,872.3 in 2005, 2,716.2 in 2006; Total fruits (excl. melons) 292.6 in 2004, 256.6 in 2005, 256.6 in 2006.

Source: FAO.

KAZAKHSTAN

LIVESTOCK
('000 head, year ending September)

	2004	2005	2006
Horses	1,064.3	1,120.4	1,163.5
Asses, mules or hinnies*	30.0	31.0	32.0
Cattle	4,871.0	5,204.0	5,457.0
Buffaloes*	9.0	9.0	10.0
Camels	114.9	125.7	130.5
Pigs	1,368.8	1,292.1	1,282.0
Sheep	10,420.1	11,397.0*	12,184.0*
Goats	1,827.0	2,012.1*	2,151.5*
Chickens	24,700†	25,500†	26,100*
Turkeys†	50	80	100
Rabbits*	60,000	62,000	64,000

* FAO estimate(s).
† Unofficial figures.

Source: FAO.

LIVESTOCK PRODUCTS
('000 metric tons)

	2004	2005	2006
Cattle meat	329.7	345.0*	365.5
Sheep meat	101.6	110.0*	105.6
Goat meat	7.7†	8.0*	10.0*
Horse meat*	57	55	56
Pig meat	198.6	200.0*	210.0*
Chicken meat	41.3	43.0*	50.0*
Cows' milk	4,504.0*	4,693.0	4,861.0*
Sheeps' milk	40.0*	42.0	47.0*
Goats' milk	13.0*	14.0	15.0*
Hen eggs†	128.5	139.4	138.3
Wool: greasy	28.5	30.4	32.4

* FAO estimate(s).
† Unofficial figure.

Source: FAO.

Forestry

ROUNDWOOD REMOVALS
(unofficial figures, cubic metres, excl. bark)

	2003	2004	2005
Sawlogs, veneer logs and logs for sleepers	103,920	216,800	513,600
Pulpwood	12,990	27,100	64,200
Other industrial roundwood	12,990	27,100	64,200
Fuel wood	170,900	202,000	210,000
Total	300,800	473,000	852,000

2006: Figures assumed to be unchanged from 2005 (FAO estimates).

Source: FAO.

SAWNWOOD PRODUCTION
(cubic metres, incl. railway sleepers)

	2003*	2004	2005*
Coniferous (softwood)	245,791	109,600	113,275
Broadleaved (hardwood)	19,293	24,600	25,425
Total	265,084	134,200	138,700

* Unofficial figures.

2006: Figures assumed to be unchanged from 2005 (FAO estimates).

Source: FAO.

Fishing
('000 metric tons, live weight)

	2003	2004	2005*
Capture	25.4	33.9	31.0
Freshwater bream	16.0	21.9	20.0
Common carp	0.9	0.6	0.7
Crucian carp	1.0	1.4	1.4
Roaches	1.7	1.6	1.5
Asp	0.7	0.9	0.8
Northern pike	0.9	0.8	0.8
Wels (Som) catfish	1.1	0.9	0.9
Pike-perch	1.4	2.7	2.1
Aquaculture	0.8	0.6	0.6
Total catch	26.2	34.5	31.6

* FAO estimates.

Source: FAO.

Mining
('000 metric tons, unless otherwise indicated)

	2004	2005	2006
Hard coal	86,875	86,617	96,231
Brown coal (incl. lignite)			
Crude petroleum*	50,672	50,870	54,339
Natural gas (million cu m)	22,102	24,973	26,382
Iron ore (gross weight)	20,303	19,471	22,263
Bauxite	4,706	4,815	4,884
Lead ore (metal content)	33	31	48
Zinc ore (metal content)	361	364	405
Manganese ore	2,318	2,233	2,531
Chromite	3,287	516	269
Silver ore (metal content, metric tons)	773,296	883,210	806,083
Gold (metal content, kg)	28,837	27,649	30,835
Asbestos	347	306	315

* Including gas condensate.

Industry

SELECTED PRODUCTS
('000 metric tons, unless otherwise indicated)

	2004	2005	2006
Wheat flour	2,126.6	2,756.0	2,849.9
Raw sugar	542.6	528.8	490.2
Wine ('000 hectolitres)	404	529	368
Beer ('000 hectolitres)	2,780	3,235	3,638
Cigarettes (million)	28,037.5	30,008.1	30,833.8
Woven cotton fabrics (metric tons)	20,301.9	35,530.2	56,459.6
Motor spirit (petrol)	1,927.5	2,359.2	2,345.3
Kerosene	294.3	248.7	313.6
Gas-diesel (distillate fuel) oils	2,887.6	3,704.7	3,887.5
Residual fuel oils (Mazout)	2,708.4	3,549.9	3,333.1
Cement	3,662.0	4,181.2	4,880.2
Crude steel	5,372	4,477	4,245
Copper (unrefined, metric tons)	445,268	418,356	427,723
Electric energy (million kWh)	66,942.4	67,919.7	71,668.5

KAZAKHSTAN

Finance

CURRENCY AND EXCHANGE RATES

Monetary Units
100 tein = 1 tenge.

Sterling, Dollar and Euro Equivalents (31 December 2007)
£1 sterling = 241.009 tenge;
US $1 = 120.300 tenge;
€1 = 177.094 tenge;
1,000 tenge = £4.15 = $8.31 = €5.65.

Average Exchange Rate (tenge per US $)
2005   132.88
2006   126.09
2007   122.55

Note: The tenge was introduced on 15 November 1993, replacing the old Russian (formerly Soviet) rouble at an exchange rate of 1 tenge = 500 roubles. On 18 November the rate was adjusted to 250 roubles per tenge. In April 1999 the tenge was allowed to 'float' on foreign exchange markets.

STATE BUDGET
(million tenge)

Revenue	2001	2002	2003
Tax revenue	635,792	752,785	947,251
Other current revenue	70,505	45,573	44,813
Capital revenue	25,363	9,494	12,502
Official transfers	233	—	—
Repayment of debt principal	12,719	13,308	17,690
Total	746,612	821,160	1,022,256

Expenditure	1999	2000	2001
General public services	28,856	35,114	47,771
Defence	17,198	20,379	32,347
Public order and security	32,507	47,738	63,681
Education	78,491	84,668	105,024
Health care	44,825	54,323	62,238
Social security and social assistance	159,064	171,065	186,641
Recreation and cultural activities	12,237	17,487	18,076
Housing and communal services	6,012	22,106	30,396
Economic affairs and services	48,794	87,761	132,188
Agriculture, forestry, water management, fishing and environmental protection	6,944	11,441	23,113
Mining and minerals (excl. fuel), manufacturing and construction	2,867	7,191	4,558
Transport and communications	12,865	37,804	41,651
Other purposes	19,442	35,541	37,764
Debt interest	19,442	35,541	37,764
Total	447,426	576,182	716,126

Revised expenditure totals (million tenge, rounded figures): Total expenditure (excluding lending minus repayments) 468,400 in 1999; 602,000 in 2000; 759,600 in 2001.

Expenditure in 2002 (million tenge, rounded figures): Total expenditure (excluding lending minus repayments) 834,200 (Defence 37,700; Social and cultural 416,500; Economic 123,800; Public administration 45,600).

Expenditure in 2003 (million tenge, rounded figures): Total expenditure (excluding lending minus repayments) 1,062,600 (Defence 47,500; Social and cultural 511,700; Economic 173,100; Public administration 63,900).

2004 (million tenge, rounded figures): Total revenue 1,286,700; Total expenditure (excluding lending minus repayments) 1,323,800 (Source: Asian Development Bank, *Key Indicators of Developing Asian and Pacific Countries*).

2005 (million tenge, rounded figures): Total revenue 2,098,500; Total expenditure (excluding lending minus repayments) 1,953,300 (Source: Asian Development Bank, *Key Indicators of Developing Asian and Pacific Countries*).

2006 (million tenge, rounded figures): Total revenue 2,338,100; Total expenditure (excluding lending minus repayments) 2,256,500 (Source: Asian Development Bank, *Key Indicators of Developing Asian and Pacific Countries*).

INTERNATIONAL RESERVES
(US $ million at 31 December)

	2004	2005	2006
Gold	803.6	985.5	1,376.2
IMF special drawing rights	1.2	1.2	1.3
Reserve position in IMF	0.0	0.0	0.0
Foreign exchange	8,471.9	6,083.0	17,749.5
Total	9,276.7	7,069.7	19,127.0

Source: IMF, *International Financial Statistics*.

MONEY SUPPLY
(million tenge at 31 December)

	2004	2005	2006
Currency outside banks	379,273	411,813	600,832
Demand deposits at commercial banks	295,523	381,360	663,600
Total money (incl. others)	677,468	799,440	1,281,549

Source: IMF, *International Financial Statistics*.

COST OF LIVING
(Consumer Price Index; base: 1995 = 100)

	2004	2005	2006
All items	243.6	262.0	283.9

Source: Asian Development Bank, *Key Indicators of Developing Asian and Pacific Countries*.

NATIONAL ACCOUNTS
('000 million tenge at current prices)

Expenditure on the Gross Domestic Product

	2004	2005	2006
Government final consumption expenditure	681.8	583.8	1,039.8
Private final consumption expenditure	3,142.5	3,784.4	4,635.5
Increase in stocks	72.1	228.1	378.1
Gross fixed capital formation	1,472.4	2,122.7	2,970.3
Total domestic expenditure	5,368.8	6,719.0	9,023.7
Exports of goods and services	3,081.8	4,064.2	5,223.0
Less Imports of goods and services	2,577.5	3,395.0	4,129.1
Sub-total	5,873.1	7,388.2	10,117.6
Statistical discrepancy*	–3.0	202.4	21.9
GDP in purchasers' values	5,870.1	7,590.6	10,139.5
GDP at constant 1994 prices	620.6	680.9	751.3

* Referring to the difference between the sum of the expenditure components and official estimates of GDP, compiled from the production approach.

Gross Domestic Product by Economic Activity

	2004	2005	2006
Agriculture, forestry and fishing	418.1	483.5	541.2
Industry*	1,719.4	2,261.2	2,998.3
Construction	355.8	595.0	985.7
Trade, restaurants and hotels	731.6	897.9	1,188.3
Transport, storage and communications	691.2	896.8	1,143.5
Other services			
Import duties	1,954.0	2,456.2	3,282.5
Less Imputed bank service charges			
GDP in purchasers' values	5,870.1	7,590.6	10,139.5

* Including mining and quarrying, manufacturing, and electricity, gas and water.

Source: Asian Development Bank, *Key Indicators of Developing Asian and Pacific Countries*.

KAZAKHSTAN

BALANCE OF PAYMENTS
(US $ million)

	2004	2005	2006
Exports of goods f.o.b.	20,603.1	28,300.6	38,762.1
Imports of goods f.o.b.	−13,817.7	−17,978.8	−24,120.4
Trade balance	6,785.4	10,321.8	14,641.7
Exports of services	2,009.2	2,228.4	2,807.6
Imports of services	−5,107.9	−7,495.7	−8,719.6
Balance on goods and services	3,686.7	5,054.5	8,729.7
Other income received	422.5	680.3	1,441.1
Other income paid	−3,285.6	−6,377.2	−10,758.3
Balance on goods, services and income	823.6	−642.4	−587.4
Current transfers received	352.9	810.0	904.2
Current transfers paid	−841.1	−1,223.5	−2,111.6
Current balance	335.4	−1,055.8	−1,794.9
Capital account (net)	−21.3	14.0	32.7
Direct investment abroad	1,278.9	145.9	404.2
Direct investment from abroad	4,157.2	1,971.2	6,221.7
Portfolio investment assets	−1,092.1	−5,157.1	−9,176.7
Portfolio investment liabilities	675.0	1,204.4	4,669.2
Financial derivatives assets	−44.6	−119.7	−91.6
Financial derivatives liabilities	−1.8	7.0	23.8
Other investment assets	−4,466.0	−4,310.4	−8,030.0
Other investment liabilities	4,194.2	7,156.7	22,070.6
Net errors and omissions	−1,015.9	−1,800.0	−3,254.5
Overall balance	3,999.0	−1,943.8	11,074.6

Source: IMF, *International Financial Statistics*.

External Trade

PRINCIPAL COMMODITIES
(US $ million)

Imports c.i.f.	2004	2005	2006
Prepared foodstuffs	611.1	741.1	1,082.6
Mineral products	1,873.5	2,322.8	3,375.3
Chemical products	1,128.3	1,337.0	1,638.6
Plastics and rubber	504.2	664.8	928.5
Base metals and articles thereof	1,666.1	2,546.3	3,149.7
Machinery, mechanical appliances and electrical equipment	3,421.9	4,902.3	6,479.1
Transportation equipment	1,777.2	2,341.7	3,717.3
Total (incl. others)	12,781.2	17,352.5	23,676.9

Exports f.o.b.	2004	2005	2006
Vegetable products	640.7	456.5	837.0
Mineral products	13,727.1	20,553.3	27,510.9
Chemical products	634.1	899.1	1,553.2
Pearls, precious and semi-precious stones, and metals	345.6	399.1	696.9
Base metals and articles thereof	3,897.2	4,419.1	6,159.4
Total (incl. others)	20,096.2	27,849.0	38,250.4

Source: Asian Development Bank, *Key Indicators of Developing Asian and Pacific Countries*.

PRINCIPAL TRADING PARTNERS
(US $ million)

Imports c.i.f.	2001	2002	2003
Belarus	46.3	54.8	94.9
China, People's Republic	172.0	313.0	523.7
Finland	71.4	73.4	97.2
France	141.6	110.2	196.9
Germany	490.2	586.2	734.2
Italy	268.9	219.1	250.2
Japan	142.0	164.6	212.0
Korea, Republic	110.6	110.2	114.6
Netherlands	85.4	87.5	127.6
Poland	61.3	74.7	117.2
Russia	2,891.9	2,548.8	3,282.1
Switzerland	67.6	60.2	61.7
Turkey	137.0	173.7	209.0
Ukraine	155.0	217.1	324.0
United Kingdom	249.4	259.7	248.6
USA	349.1	461.4	470.4
Uzbekistan	81.1	86.5	89.7
Total (incl. others)	6,446.0	6,584.0	8,408.7

Exports f.o.b.	2001	2002	2003
Bermuda	1,221.2	2,011.3	2,192.6
China, People's Republic	659.6	1,023.0	1,653.1
Finland	56.1	48.8	108.9
Germany	501.8	220.3	146.4
Italy	956.3	904.2	1,013.1
Korea, Republic	43.4	48.9	55.5
Kyrgyzstan	87.0	108.6	156.4
Netherlands	144.2	123.6	186.1
Poland	164.2	320.5	201.0
Russia	1,759.5	1,497.8	1,967.9
Switzerland	408.7	792.4	1,679.9
Tajikistan	61.2	45.7	75.7
Turkey	74.2	97.4	99.2
Ukraine	490.2	291.5	426.2
United Kingdom	294.3	131.8	143.2
USA	159.0	116.9	99.1
Uzbekistan	150.2	101.0	137.9
Total (incl. others)	8,639.1	9,670.3	12,926.7

2004 (US $ million): *Imports c.i.f.*: China, People's Republic 758.2; France 313.7; Germany 1,053.1; Italy 426.5; Japan 398.2; Russia 4,812.6; Turkey 342.4; Ukraine 722.6; United Kingdom 301.1; USA 563.2; Total (incl. others) 12,779.6. *Exports f.o.b.*: China, People's Republic 1,967.3; France 1,468.2; Germany 212.8; Iran 712.0; Italy 3,109.0; Romania 32.7; Russia 2,838.1; Switzerland 3,760.4; USA 273.9; Total (incl. others) 20,095.2 (Source: Asian Development Bank, *Key Indicators of Developing Asian and Pacific Countries*).

2005 (US $ million): *Imports c.i.f.*: China, People's Republic 4,288.8; France 638.6; Germany 1,424.5; Italy 555.9; Japan 195.3; Russia 7,181.7; Turkey 505.9; Ukraine 733.9; United Kingdom 308.1; USA 592.1; Total (incl. others) 20,138.6. *Exports f.o.b.*: China, People's Republic 2,638.4; France 2,033.2; Germany 2,825.2; Iran 906.6; Italy 2,105.2; Romania 1,196.3; Russia 2,918.3; Ukraine 144.0; USA 1,058.7; Total (incl. others) 23,610.3 (Source: Asian Development Bank, *Key Indicators of Developing Asian and Pacific Countries*).

2006 (US $ million): *Imports c.i.f.*: China, People's Republic 5,226.7; France 923.4; Germany 1,999.4; Italy 874.1; Japan 259.9; Russia 9,352.2; Turkey 764.5; Ukraine 861.0; United Kingdom 426.5; USA 710.6; Total (incl. others) 26,193.2. *Exports f.o.b.*: China, People's Republic 3,279.3; France 2,236.5; Germany 3,716.8; Iran 1,119.2; Italy 3,144.6; Romania 1,403.6; Russia 3,357.0; Switzerland 149.0; USA 907.5; Total (incl. others) 29,730.7 (Source: Asian Development Bank, *Key Indicators of Developing Asian and Pacific Countries*).

KAZAKHSTAN

Transport

RAILWAYS
(estimated traffic)

	2004	2005	2006
Passenger-km (million)	11,800	12,100	13,700
Freight net ton-km (million)	163,500	171,900	191,200

ROAD TRAFFIC
(motor vehicles in use at 31 December)

	2004	2005	2006
Passenger cars	1,204,100	1,405,300	1,745,000
Buses and coaches	62,894	65,698	75,042

SHIPPING
Merchant Fleet
(registered at 31 December)

	2004	2005	2006
Number of vessels	36	45	59
Total displacement (grt)	25,950	43,486	64,932

Source: Lloyd's Register-Fairplay, *World Fleet Statistics*.

CIVIL AVIATION
(traffic on scheduled services)

	2001	2002	2003
Passengers carried ('000)	884	1,036	1,275
Passenger-km (million)	1,901	2,179	2,654
Total ton-km (million)	44	53	94

Kilometres flown (million): 20 in 1996; 20 in 1997; 35 in 1998 (Source: UN, *Statistical Yearbook*).

Tourism

FOREIGN TOURIST ARRIVALS

Country of residence	2003	2004	2005
Armenia	9,730	4,684	5,765
Australia	1,465	1,614	2,040
Austria	1,477	1,433	1,964
Azerbaijan	24,690	37,179	67,030
Belarus	6,983	41,341	15,916
Canada	3,646	3,724	4,440
China, People's Republic	57,035	76,806	85,696
France	3,966	3,834	4,712
Georgia	2,656	5,375	5,278
Germany	56,384	72,529	84,534
Hungary	1,494	1,502	2,261
India	4,810	5,868	6,160
Iran	10,347	11,331	9,659
Israel	3,122	3,427	4,737
Italy	6,614	6,996	8,462
Japan	3,071	2,681	3,171
Korea, Republic	6,871	9,311	10,412
Kyrgyzstan	1,383,314	1,091,923	851,568

Country of residence—*continued*	2003	2004	2005
Lithuania	1,264	2,639	4,122
Mongolia	3,049	3,878	7,707
Netherlands	5,277	5,375	6,576
Pakistan	1,749	2,602	1,944
Poland	2,525	3,551	4,491
Romania	1,050	1,428	1,580
Russia	605,909	1,628,823	1,405,543
Switzerland	1,088	1,121	1,580
Tajikistan	202,744	260,487	286,042
Turkey	31,331	42,064	58,034
United Kingdom	16,956	16,530	19,659
USA	18,850	19,513	25,346
Uzbekistan	696,327	767,162	1,266,401
Total (incl. others)	3,249,344	4,291,040	4,364,949

Tourism receipts (US $ million, incl. passenger transport): 638 in 2003; 803 in 2004; 809 in 2005.

Source: World Tourism Organization.

Communications Media

	2004	2005	2006
Telephones ('000 main lines in use)	2,550.0	2,708.0	2,928.0
Mobile cellular telephones ('000 subscribers)	2,447.0	5,398.0	7,830.4
Internet users ('000)	400.0	609.2	1,247.0
Broadband subscribers ('000)	2.0	3.0	30.5

Book production (titles, incl. pamphlets): 1,223 in 1999.
Book production (copies, 1996): 21,014,000.
Daily newspapers (1996): Titles 3; Average circulation 500,000.
Radio receivers ('000 in use, 1997): 6,470.
Television receivers ('000 in use, 2001): 5,440.

Sources: UNESCO, *Statistical Yearbook*; UN, *Statistical Yearbook*; International Telecommunication Union.

Education

(state educational institutions, 2005/06, unless otherwise indicated)

	Institutions	Students ('000)
Pre-primary	1,179	185.4
Primary *and* Secondary: general	8,157	2,824.6
Secondary: vocational	415	397.6
Professional-technical schools	307	104.2
Higher	181	775.8

Note: In 2003/04 there were, additionally: 155 private primary and secondary-general schools, with 20,000 students; 179 private secondary-vocational schools, with 88,700 students; and 134 non-governmental higher education institutes, with 297,900 students.

Teachers: Pre-primary 15,412 in 2001/02; Primary 60,509 in 2002/03; Secondary—general 170,190 in 2002/03; Secondary—vocational 27,000 in 2005/06; Professional-technical schools 5,900 in 2005/06; Higher 43,400 in 2005/06.

Adult literacy rate (UNESCO estimates): 99.5% (males 99.8%; females 99.3%) in 1999 (Source: UNESCO Institute for Statistics).

Directory

The Constitution

The Constitution of the Republic of Kazakhstan was endorsed by 89% of the electorate voting in a national referendum on 30 August 1995, and was officially adopted on 6 September, replacing the Constitution of January 1993. A number of constitutional amendments were adopted on 8 October 1998 and on 18 May 2007. The following is a summary of the Constitution's main provisions:

GENERAL PROVISIONS

The Republic of Kazakhstan is a democratic, secular, law-based, unitary state with a presidential system of rule. The state ensures the integrity, inviolability and inalienability of its territory. State power belongs to the people, who exercise it directly through referendums and free elections, and also delegate the exercise of their power to state bodies. State power is separated into legislative, executive and judicial branches, with a system of checks and balances being applied.

Ideological and political diversity are recognized. State and private property are recognized. The state language is Kazakh. Russian is employed officially in state bodies and local government bodies on a par with Kazakh.

HUMAN AND CIVIL RIGHTS AND LIBERTIES

Citizenship of the Republic of Kazakhstan is acquired and terminated in accordance with the law. Citizenship of another state is not recognized for any citizen of Kazakhstan. The rights and liberties of the individual are recognized and guaranteed. No one may be subjected to discrimination on grounds of origin, sex, race, language, religious or other beliefs, or place of residence. No one may be subjected to torture, violence or other treatment or punishment that is cruel or degrading. Provision is made for the abolition of the death penalty. All are entitled to use their native language and culture. Freedom of speech and creativity are guaranteed. Censorship is prohibited. Citizens are entitled to assemble and to hold demonstrations peacefully and without weapons. Defence of the republic is the duty and obligation of every citizen. Human and civil rights and liberties may be restricted only by law and only to the extent that is necessary to defend the constitutional system and to safeguard public order. Any action capable of disrupting inter-ethnic accord is deemed unconstitutional.

THE PRESIDENT OF THE REPUBLIC

The President of the Republic is the Head of State, who determines the main directions of the state's domestic and foreign policy and represents Kazakhstan domestically and internationally. The President is elected for a seven-year term by secret ballot on the basis of general, equal and direct suffrage. (Under the constitutional amendments of May 2007, the presidential term was reduced to five years, with effect from 2012.) A citizen of the republic by birth, who is at least 40 years of age, has a fluent command of the state language, and has lived in Kazakhstan for no less than 15 years, may be elected President.

The President: addresses an annual message to the people; schedules regular and extraordinary elections to Parliament; signs and promulgates laws submitted by the Senat (Senate), or returns draft legislation for further discussion; appoints the Prime Minister and relieves him of office, subject to the approval of the Majlis (Assembly); with the consent of the Senat, appoints to and relieves of office the Chairman of the National Bank, the Prosecutor-General and the Chairman of the National Security Committee; appoints and recalls the heads of diplomatic missions of the republic; decides on the holding of referendums; negotiates and signs international treaties; is supreme Commander-in-Chief of the armed forces; bestows state awards and confers honours; resolves matters of citizenship and of granting political asylum; in the event of aggression against the republic, imposes martial law or announces a partial or general mobilization; forms the Security Council, the Supreme Judicial Council and other consultative and advisory bodies.

The President may be relieved of office only in the event of his having committed an act of treason or if he exhibits a consistent incapacity to carry out his duties owing to illness. A decision on the President's early dismissal is adopted at a joint sitting of the chambers of Parliament by a majority of no less than three-quarters of the total number of deputies of each chamber. The question of dismissal of the President may not be raised at the same time as he is considering early termination of the authority of Parliament.

PARLIAMENT

Parliament is the supreme representative body of the republic, exercising legislative functions. It consists of two chambers, the Senat and the Majlis. The Senat comprises 47 members, of whom 32 are elected at joint sittings of the deputies of all representative bodies of the regions and the capital city, while 15 deputies are appointed by the President. The Majlis comprises 107 deputies, of whom 98 are elected by general, equal and direct suffrage and on a basis of party-list proportional representation. The remaining nine deputies are elected by the Assembly of Nations of Kazakhstan (a 350-member body representing the country's minority ethnic groups). The Senat's term is six years, and that of the Majlis is five years. One-half of the elected deputies in the Senat are subject to election every three years.

THE GOVERNMENT

The Government exercises the executive power of the republic and is responsible to the President. The Government drafts the main areas of the state's socio-economic policy, defence capability, security and public order, and orders their implementation; presents to Parliament the republican budget and the report of its implementation, and ensures that the budget is implemented; submits draft legislation to the Majlis and provides for the implementation of laws; organizes the management of state property; formulates measures for the pursuit of Kazakhstan's foreign policy; directs the activity of Ministries, State Committees and other central and local executive bodies. The Prime Minister, who is a member of the parliamentary majority party, proposes members of the Government, subject to the approval of the Majlis, organizes and directs the activity of the Government and is personally responsible for its work. A motion of 'no confidence' in a new Government may be approved by a simple majority of votes in the Majlis.

LOCAL STATE ADMINISTRATION GOVERNMENT

Local state administration is exercised by local representative and executive bodies, which are responsible for the state of affairs on their own territory. The local representative councils (maslikhat) express the will of the population and, bearing in mind the overall state interest, define the measures necessary to realize this will and monitor their implementation. Councils are elected for a five-year term by a secret ballot on the basis of general, equal and direct suffrage. The local executive bodies (akimiyat) are part of the unified system of executive bodies of Kazakhstan, and ensure that the general state policy of the executive authority is implemented in co-ordination with the interests and development needs of the corresponding territory. Each local executive body is headed by the Akim (Governor) of the corresponding administrative-territorial unit, who is appointed by the President after the approval of the appropriate maslikhat.

The Government

HEAD OF STATE

President: NURSULTAN A. NAZARBAYEV (elected indirectly 24 April 1990; elected unopposed 1 December 1991; term extended by referendum 29 April 1995; re-elected 10 January 1999; re-elected 4 December 2005; inaugurated 11 January 2006).

GOVERNMENT
(April 2008)

Prime Minister: KARIM K. MASIMOV.

Deputy Prime Minister: UMIRZAK YE. SHUKEYEV.

Minister of Foreign Affairs: MARAT M. TAZHIN.

Minister of Defence: DANIAL K. AKHMETOV.

Minister of Internal Affairs: BAURZHAN A. MUKHAMEJANOV.

Minister of Health: ANATOLII G. DERNOVOI.

Minister of Industry and Trade: GALYM I. ORAZBAKOV.

Minister of Culture and Information: YERMUKHAMET K. YERTYSBAYEV.

Minister of Tourism and Sport: TEMIRKHAN M. DOSMUKHANBETOV.

Minister of Education and Science: ZHANSEIT K. TUIMEBAYEV.

Minister of Environmental Protection: NURLAN A. ISKAKOV.

Minister of Agriculture: AKHMETZHAN S. YESIMOV.

Minister of Transport and Communications: SERIK N. AKHMETOV.

Minister of Labour and Social Security: BERDIBEK M. SAPARBAYEV.

Minister of Finance: BOLAT B. ZHAMISHEV.

Minister of Emergency Situations: VLADIMIR K. BOZHKO.

Minister of the Economy and Budgetary Planning: BAKHYT T. SULTANOV.

KAZAKHSTAN   Directory

Minister of Energy and Mineral Resources: SAUAT A. MYNBAYEV.
Minister of Justice: ZAGIPA YA. BALIYEVA.

MINISTRIES

Office of the President: 010000 Astana, Beibitshilik 11; tel. (7172) 32-13-99; fax (7172) 32-61-72; internet www.akorda.kz.

Office of the Prime Minister: 010000 Astana, Beibitshilik 11; tel. (7172) 32-31-04; fax (7172) 32-40-89; internet www.government.kz.

Ministry of Agriculture: 010000 Astana, pr. Abaya 49; tel. (7172) 32-37-63; fax (7172) 32-62-99; e-mail mailbox@minagri.kz; internet www.minagri.kz.

Ministry of Culture and Information: 010000 Astana, pr. Respubliki 24; tel. and fax (7172) 33-32-82; e-mail prmin@mininfo.katelco.kz; internet www.sana.gov.kz.

Ministry of Defence: 010000 Astana, Beibitshilik 51A; tel. and fax (7172) 33-78-89; internet www.mod.kz.

Ministry of the Economy and Budgetary Planning: 010000 Astana, pr. Pobedy 11; tel. (7172) 71-77-70; fax (7172) 71-77-12; e-mail info@minplan.kz; internet www.minplan.kz.

Ministry of Education and Science: 010000 Astana, Beibitshilik 11; tel. (7172) 75-20-27; fax (7172) 75-28-71; e-mail pressa@edu.gov.kz; internet www.edu.gov.kz.

Ministry of Emergency Situations: 010000 Astana, Beibitshilik 22; e-mail chs@emer.kz; internet www.emer.kz.

Ministry of Energy and Mineral Resources: 010000 Astana, Beibitshilik 37; tel. (7172) 31-71-33; fax (7172) 31-71-64; e-mail ministr@minenergo.kegoc.kz; internet www.minenergo.kz.

Ministry of Environmental Protection: 010000 Astana, Sol zhagalau, ui. Ministrigi 35-8/14; tel. (7172) 59-19-44; fax (7172) 59-19-73; internet www.nature.kz.

Ministry of Finance: 010000 Astana, pl. Respubliki 60; tel. (7172) 28-00-65; fax (7172) 32-40-89; internet www.minfin.kz.

Ministry of Foreign Affairs: 010000 Astana, Beibitshilik 11; tel. (7172) 32-76-69; fax (7172) 32-76-67; e-mail midrk@mid.kz; internet www.mfa.kz.

Ministry of Health: 010000 Astana, Moskovskaya 86; tel. and fax (7172) 31-73-27; e-mail zdrav@mz.gov.kz; internet www.mz.gov.kz.

Ministry of Industry and Trade: 010000 Astana, pr. Kabanbai Batyr 49, 'Transport Tauer'; tel. (7172) 29-90-00; fax (7172) 24-12-13; internet www.mit.kz.

Ministry of Internal Affairs: 010000 Astana, Manasa 4; tel. (7172) 34-36-01; fax (7172) 34-17-38; e-mail press@mvd.kz; internet www.mvd.kz.

Ministry of Justice: 010000 Astana, pr. Pobedy 45; tel. (7172) 39-12-13; fax (7172) 32-15-54; internet www.minjust.kz.

Ministry of Labour and Social Security: 010000 Astana, Manasa 2; tel. (7172) 15-36-02; fax (7172) 15-36-54; e-mail inter@enbek.kz; internet www.enbek.kz.

Ministry of Tourism and Sport: 010000 Astana, pr. Abai 33; tel. (7172) 753010; fax (7172) 753430; internet www.mts.gov.kz.

Ministry of Transport and Communications: 010000 Astana, pr. Kabanbai batyra 47; tel. (7172) 24-17-70; fax (7172) 24-11-70; e-mail janibek@mtc.gov.kz; internet www.mtk.gov.kz.

President

Presidential Election, 4 December 2005

Candidates	Votes	%
Nursultan A. Nazarbayev	6,147,517	91.15
Zharmakhan A. Tuyakbai	445,934	6.61
Others	150,816	2.24
Total	6,744,267	100.00

Legislature

Parliament is a bicameral legislative body, comprising the Senat and the Majlis (Assembly).

Majlis

010000 Astana, Parliament House; tel. (7172) 15-30-19; fax (7172) 33-30-99; e-mail www@parlam.kz; internet www.parlam.kz.

Chairman: ASLAN MUSIN.

General Election, 18 August 2007

Parties	Votes	%	Seats
Light Of The Fatherland (Nur Otan)	5,247,720	88.41	98
National Social-Democratic Party	269,310	4.54	—
Bright Road—Democratic Party of Kazakhstan (Ak Zhol)	183,346	3.09	—
Village Kazakhstani Social-Democratic Party (Auyl)	89,855	1.51	—
Communist People's Party of Kazakhstan	76,799	1.29	—
Party of Patriots of Kazakhstan	46,436	0.78	—
Spirituality Party (Rukhaniyat)	22,159	0.37	—
Total (incl. others)	5,935,625	100.00	107*

*Including nine deputies elected by the Assembly of Nations of Kazakhstan (a body representing the country's minority ethnic groups) on 20 August 2007.

Senat

010000 Astana, pr. Abaya 33, Parliament House; tel. (7172) 15-33-76; fax (7172) 33-31-18; e-mail smimazh@parlam.kz; internet www.parlam.kz.

Chairman: KASYMZHOMART K. TOKAYEV.

The 47-member Senat is the upper chamber of Parliament. Elections are held every three years for one-half of the 32 seats elected by special colleges (comprising members of local councils) in Kazakhstan's 14 regions and two cities; the term of office for members of the Senat is six years. Partial elections to the Senat were held on 8 October 2002 and 19 August 2005. Under constitutional amendments adopted on 18 May 2007, the number of deputies appointed by the President increased from seven to 15; the additional eight members were officially appointed to the Senat by presidential decree in August.

Election Commission

Ortalyk Sailau Komissiyasy (Central Election Commission): 010000 Astana, Beibitshilik 4; tel. (7172) 152210; fax (7172) 333388; e-mail info@election.kz; internet www.election.kz; Chair. KUANDYK TURGANKULOV.

Political Organizations

A new law was introduced in July 2002, which required all parties to have a minimum of 50,000 members from among all the country's regions in order to qualify for official registration. In 2007 the following eight parties were registered.

Bright Road—Democratic Party of Kazakhstan (Ak Zhol) (Kazakstan Demokratiyalyk Partiyasy Ak Zhol): 010000 Astana, Imanov 18/7; tel. (7172) 22-10-66; fax (7172) 22-14-50; e-mail oral@kepter.kz; internet www.akzhol.kz; f. 2002 by former members of the Democratic Choice of Kazakhstan; merged with Justice Democratic Party (Adilet) in 2007; Chair. ALIKHAN M. BAYMENOV; 175,862 mems (2007).

Communist Party of Kazakhstan (CPK) (Kazakstan Kommunistik Partiyasy): 010000 Astana, Beibitshilik 27/49; tel. and fax (727) 221-32-97; e-mail pravdakz@list.ru; f. 1937; suspended Aug. 1991, re-registered Aug. 1998 and March 2003; contested 2004 legislative elections in alliance with Democratic Choice of Kazakhstan, as the People's Opposition Union of Communists and DVK bloc; mem. of For a Just Kazakhstan opposition bloc formed in 2005; Chair. SERIKBOLSYN A. ABDILDIN; 54,246 mems (2007).

Communist People's Party of Kazakhstan (Kazakstan Kommunistik Khalyk Partiyasy): 010000 Astana, Zheltoksan 36A/37; tel. (7172) 32-24-61; internet www.knpk.kz; f. 2004 by fmr mems of the Communist Party of Kazakhstan; Sec. of the Central Cttee VLADISLAV B. KOSAREV; 90,000 mems (2004).

Light Of The Fatherland People's Democratic Party (Nur Otan) ('Nur Otan' Khalyktyk Demokratiyalyk Partiyasy): 050000 Almaty, Abylai khana 79; tel. (727) 279-78-00; fax (727) 279-40-66; e-mail partyotan@nursat.kz; internet www.ndp-nurotan.kz; f. 2006 by merger of Fatherland, Civic Party of Kazakhstan and Agrarian Party of Kazakhstan; supports administration of President Nazarbayev; Chair. NURSULTAN A. NAZARBAYEV; First Deputy Chair. BAKYTZHAN T. ZHUMAGULOV; 607,557 mems (2007).

National Social-Democratic Party (Zhalpyulttyk Sotsial Demokratiyalyk Partiyasy—ZhSDP): 050000 Almaty, Kabanbai batyr 58; tel. (727) 663-64-06; fax (727) 266-36-43; e-mail ocdp@mail.ru; internet www.osdp.kz; f. 2006; merged with Real Bright Road—

KAZAKHSTAN

Democratic Party of Kazakhstan (Naghyz Ak Zhol) in 2007; Chair. ZHARMAKHAN A. TUYAKBAI; 140,000 mems (Jan. 2007).

Party of Patriots of Kazakhstan (PPK) (Kazakstan Patriottary Partiyasy): 050000 Almaty, Zhubek-zholy 76/318; tel. (7172) 22-98-34; fax (7172) 37-44-82; f. 2000; merged with the Union of Officers in 2004; Chair. GANI YE. KASYMOV; 172,000 mems (2007).

Spirituality Party (Rukhaniyat Partiyasy): 010000 Astana, Saryarka 5; tel. and fax (7172) 97-73-80; e-mail kazayelder@nursat.kz; internet www.rukhaniat.kz; f. 1995 as Renaissance Party of Kazakhstan; re-registered under new name 2003; supports Govt of President Nazarbayev; Chair. ALTYNSHASH K. JAGANOVA; 72,000 mems (2007).

Village Kazakhstani Social-Democratic Party (Auyl) ('Auyl' Kazakstandyk Sotsial-Demokratiyalyk Partiyasy): 010000 Astana, Beibitshilik 46/109; tel. and fax (7172) 31-71-57; internet auyl.by.ru; registered in 2002; seeks to strengthen government support for the agricultural sector; Chair. GANI A. KALIYEV; 61,043 mems (2006).

Diplomatic Representation

EMBASSIES IN KAZAKHSTAN

Afghanistan: 010000 Astana, Diplomatiyalyk kalashyk C-10; tel. and fax (727) 224-29-46; fax (727) 224-30-25; e-mail aziz59@mail.ru; Ambassador AZIZ ARYANFAR.

Armenia: 050025 Almaty, Seyfulin 57/9; tel. and fax (727) 291-71-26; e-mail armeniaemb_kz@hotmail.com; Ambassador LEVON KHACHATRIAN.

Austria: 010000 Astana, Saryarka 6/1310, Arman Business Centre; tel. (727) 299-01-44; fax (727) 299-02-27; e-mail astana-ob@bmeia.gv.at; Ambassador URSULA FARINGER.

Azerbaijan: 010000 Astana, Diplomatiyalyk kalashyk C-14; tel. (7172) 24-15-81; fax (7172) 24-15-32; e-mail astana@azembassy.kz; Ambassador LATIF GANDILOV.

Belarus: 010000 Astana, Kenesary 35; tel. (7172) 32-48-29; fax (7172) 32-06-65; e-mail kazakhstan@belembassy.org; internet kazakhstan.belembassy.org; Ambassador VASILII I. HAPEYEV.

Belgium: 010000 Astana, Kosmonavtov 62; tel. (7172) 97-78-48; fax (7172) 97-78-49; e-mail embassy.astana@diplobel.fed.be; Ambassador CHRISTIAN MEERSCHMAN.

Brazil: 010000 Astana, Kabanbai Batyr 6/1; tel. (7172) 92-51-12; fax (7172) 92-51-17; e-mail brasembastana@mre.gov.br; Ambassador ESTRADA MEYER.

Bulgaria: 050000 Almaty, Gornyi Gigant, 8-oi Gvardeiskoi Divizii; tel. (727) 264-67-10; fax (727) 262-99-56; e-mail bulgarianembassy@rambler.ru; internet www.mfa.bg/almaty; Ambassador NIKOLA F. BORISOV.

Canada: 050010 Almaty, Karasai Batyr 34; tel. (727) 250-11-51; fax (727) 258-24-93; e-mail almat@international.gc.ca; internet www.dfait-maeci.gc.ca/canadaeuropa/kazakhstan; Ambassador MARGARET SKOK.

China, People's Republic: 010000 Astana, Kabanbai batyr 37; tel. (7172) 79-35-70; fax (7172) 79-35-67; e-mail chinaemb_kz@mfa.gov.cn; internet kz.china-embassy.org; Ambassador ZHANG XIYUN.

Cuba: 010005 Astana, pr. Respublika 10/1; tel. and fax (7172) 22-14-19; e-mail embacuba@cubakaz.com; internet www.cubakaz.com; Ambassador TERESITA CAPOTE CAMACHO.

Czech Republic: 010000 Astana, Sary-Arka 6, Biznes-Tsentr Arman, 13th floor; tel. (7172) 99-01-43; fax (7172) 99-01-42; e-mail astana@embassy.mzv.cz; internet www.mzv.cz/astana; Ambassador (vacant).

Egypt: 050010 Almaty, Muhammed Haidar Dulati 80; tel. (727) 269-15-93; fax (727) 291-10-22; e-mail egyptianemb_kz@yahoo.com; Ambassador ABDEL MAWJOOD AHMED AL-HABASHI.

France: 010000 Astana, Kosmonavtov 62; tel. (7172) 79-51-00; fax (7172) 79-51-01; e-mail ambafrance@mail.ru; internet www.ambafrance-kz.kz; Ambassador ALAIN COUANON.

Georgia: 010000 Astana, Diplomatiyalyk kalashyk C-4; tel. and fax (7172) 24-32-58; fax (7172) 24-34-26; e-mail geoembassy@mail.online.kz; Ambassador ZURAB SHURGHAIA.

Germany: 010000 Astana, Kosmonavtov 62; tel. (7172) 79-12-00; fax (7172) 79-12-13; e-mail info@astana.diplo.de; internet www.astana.diplo.de; Ambassador RAINER EUGEN SCHLAGETER.

Greece: 050020 Almaty, Kyz Zhibek 80, mer Kok-Tobe; tel. (727) 250-39-61; fax (727) 250-39-38; e-mail hellenic.embassy@ducatmail.com; Chargé d'affaires GEORGIOS PARTHENIOU.

Holy See: 010000 Astana, Zelenaya Alleya 20; tel. (7172) 24-12-69; fax (7172) 24-16-04; e-mail nuntius_kazakhstan@lycos.com; Apostolic Nuncio (vacant).

Hungary: 050000 Almaty, ul. Musabayeva 4, POB 166; tel. (727) 255-12-06; fax (727) 258-18-37; e-mail mission.ala@kum.hu; Ambassador JÁNOS NÉMETH.

India: 010000 Astana, pr. Kabanbai Batyr 6/1, Kaskad Business Centre, 5th Floor; tel. (7172) 92-57-10; fax (7172) 92-57-16; e-mail admn.astana@mea.gov.in; internet www.indembassy.kz; Ambassador ASHOK SAJJANHAR.

Iran: 050000 Almaty, ul. Luganskogo 31–33; tel. (727) 254-19-74; fax (7272) 254-27-54; e-mail iranembassy@itte.kz; Ambassador RAMIN MEHMAN PARAST.

Israel: 010000 Astana, ul. Auezova 8; tel. (7172) 68-87-38; e-mail info@almaty.mfa.gov.il; internet www.almaty.mfa.gov.il; Ambassador RAN ICHAY.

Italy: 010000 Astana, Kosmonavtov 62; tel. (7172) 24-33-90; fax (7172) 24-38-68; e-mail ambasciata.astana@esteri.it; internet www.ambastana.esteri.it; Chargé d'affaires BRUNO ANTONIO PASQUINO.

Japan: 010000 Astana, Chubar sh-a, Kosmonavtov 62; tel. (7172) 97-78-43; fax (7172) 97-78-42; internet www.kz.emb-japan.go.jp/jp/index_r.htm; Ambassador TETSUO ITO.

Jordan: 010000 Astana; tel. (7172) 24-52-54; fax (7172) 24-52-53; Chargé d'affaires a.i. SULEIMAN ARABIAT.

Korea, Republic: 050000 Almaty, Jarkentskaya 2/77; tel. (727) 253-26-60; fax (727) 250-70-59; e-mail koreaemb-kz@mofat.go.kr; internet kaz.mofat.go.kr; Ambassador KIM IL-SOO.

Kyrgyzstan: 010000 Astana, Diplomatiyalyk kalashyk B-5; tel. (7172) 24-20-24; fax (7172) 24-24-12; e-mail kz@mail.online.kz; Ambassador JANUSH. RUSTENBEKOV.

Latvia: 010000 Astana, Kabanbai Batyr 6/1/122, Kaskad Business Centre; tel. (7172) 92-53-16; fax (7172) 92-53-19; Ambassador RETS PLĒSUMS.

Lebanon: 010000 Astana, Riksos Prezident Hotel, kom. 5013; tel. (7172) 24-50-50; Chargé d'affaires a.i. VAZKEN KAVLAKIAN.

Libya: 010000 Astana, Mikroraion Karaotkel–2 sh-a, kot. 110; tel. (7172) 24-18-79; fax (7172) 24-27-57; e-mail libya@nursat.kz; Chargé d'affaires a.i. AHMED ADDEB.

Lithuania: 050059 Almaty, Iskanderova 15, Gornyi Gigant; tel. (727) 293-46-06; fax (7172) 293-51-53; e-mail amb.kz@urm.lt; internet kz.mfa.lt; Ambassador ROMUALDAS KOZYROVIČIUS.

Malaysia: 050051 Almaty, Rubenshtein 9A; tel. (727) 333-44-83; fax (727) 387-28-25; e-mail mwalmaty@nursat.kz; Ambassador Dato THAN TAI HING.

Mongolia: 050000 Almaty, Musabayev 1; tel. (727) 269-35-70; fax (727) 258-17-27; e-mail monkazel@kazmail.asdc.kz; Ambassador RAVDANGIIN KHATANBAATAR.

Netherlands: 010000 Astana, Kosmonavtov 62/801; tel. (7172) 97-44-82; fax (7172) 97-44-80; e-mail ast@minbuza.nl; Ambassador PETER VAN LEEUWEN.

Oman: 010000 Astana, Chubar sh-a, Novostroitelnaya 3; tel. (7172) 24-18-61; fax (7172) 24-18-63; Ambassador AHMED BIN NASSER AL-MAHRIZI.

Pakistan: 050004 Almaty, Tulebayev 25; tel. (727) 273-15-02; fax (727) 273-13-00; e-mail parepalmaty@hotmail.com; Ambassador IRFAN-UR-REHMAN RAJA.

Poland: 050059 Almaty, Jarkent 9; tel. (727) 258-16-17; fax (727) 258-15-50; e-mail ambpol@mail.kz; internet www.almaty.polemb.net; Ambassador (vacant).

Qatar: 050000 Almaty.

Romania: 050010 Almaty, Pushkin 97; tel. (727) 261-57-72; fax (727) 258-83-17; e-mail amb@rom.ricc.kz; Ambassador EMIL RAPCEA.

Russia: 010000 Astana, Barayev 4; tel. (7172) 22-24-83; fax (7172) 22-38-49; e-mail rfe@nursat.kz; internet www.rfembassy.kz; Ambassador MIKHAIL N. BOCHARNIKOV.

Saudi Arabia: 010000 Astana; tel. (727) 250-28-71; fax (727) 250-28-11; e-mail kzemb@mofa.gov.sa; Ambassador HISHAM BIN ABDEL-WAHAB ZARAA.

Slovakia: 010000 Astana, Mikroraion Karaotkel–2, 5; tel. (7172) 24-11-91; fax (7172) 24-20-48; e-mail zuastana1@post.sk; internet www.mzv.sk/astana; Ambassador Dr DUŠAN PODHORSKÝ.

South Africa: 010000 Astana, Kabanbai batyr 6/1; tel. (7127) 259-82-60; fax (727) 259-82-59; e-mail almaty@foreign.gov.za; Ambassador BEKIZIZVE WISDOM GILA.

Spain: 010000 Astana, Kenesary 47/25; tel. (7172) 21-69-84; fax (7172) 20-03-17; e-mail emb.astana@maec.es; Ambassador SANTIAGO CHAMORRO Y GONZÁLEZ-TABLAS.

Tajikistan: 010000 Astana, Chubar sh-a, Marsovaya 15; tel. and fax (7172) 24-09-29; e-mail embassy_tajic@kepter.kz; Ambassador BAHROM M. KHOLNAZAROV.

Turkey: 050010 Almaty, Tole bi 29; tel. (727) 278-41-65; fax (727) 278-41-68; e-mail almatyturkbe@gmail.com; Ambassador TANER SEBEN.

KAZAKHSTAN

Turkmenistan: 010000 Astana, Otyrar 64; tel. and fax (7172) 28-08-82; e-mail tm_emb@at.kz; Ambassador KURBANMUKHAMMED G. KASYMOV.

Ukraine: 010000 Astana, Auezova 57; tel. (7172) 32-60-42; fax (7172) 32-68-11; e-mail emb_kz@mfa.gov.ua; internet ukrembassy.kepter.kz; Ambassador MYKOLA F. SELIVON.

United Arab Emirates: 010000 Astana, pos. Zarechnyi, 70 let Oktyabrya 71; tel. (7172) 24-36-75; fax (7172) 24-36-76; e-mail emaratembassy_kz@yahoo.com; Ambassador IBRAHIM HASSAN SAIF.

United Kingdom: 010000 Astana, Kosmonavtov 62, RENCO bldg; tel. (7172) 55-62-00; fax (7172) 55-62-11; e-mail britishembassy@mail.online.kz; internet www.britishembassy.kz; Ambassador PAUL BRUMMELL.

USA: 010010 Astana, Ak Bulak 4/23-22/3; tel. (7172) 70-21-00; fax (7172) 34-08-90; e-mail info@usembassy.kz; internet kazakhstan.usembassy.gov; Ambassador JOHN M. ORDWAY.

Uzbekistan: 050010 Almaty, Baribayeva 36; tel. (727) 291-02-35; fax (727) 291-10-55; Ambassador TURDIKUL S. BUTAYAROV.

Judicial System

Supreme Court of the Republic of Kazakhstan (Kazakhstan Respublikasynyn Zhogargy Soty): 010000 Astana, Levoberezhiye, Tayelsizdik 39; tel. (7172) 74-75-00; fax (7172) 74-78-13; e-mail ms@supcourt.kz; internet www.supcourt.kz; Chair. KAYRAT A. MAMI.

Constitutional Council of the Republic of Kazakhstan (Kazakhstan Respublikasy Konstitutsiyalyk Keneci): 010000 Astana, Levoberezhiye, Tayelsizdik 39, Zhogargy Soty, Blok A; tel. (7172) 74-76-31; fax (7172) 74-76-51; internet www.constcouncil.kz; f. 1995; seven mems; Chair. IGOR I. ROGOV.

Prosecutor-General: RASHID T. TUSIPBEKOV, 010000 Astana, Seifullin 37; e-mail gp-rk@mail.online.kz; internet www.procuror.kz.

Religion

The major religion of the Kazakhs is Islam. They are almost exclusively Sunni Muslims of the Hanafi school. The Russian Orthodox Church is the dominant Christian denomination; it is attended mainly by Slavs. There are also Protestant Churches (mainly Baptists), as well as a Roman Catholic (Latin Rite) presence and a Jewish community. In mid-2005 legislation was introduced, which required all religious organizations and communities to register with the state authorities.

ISLAM

The Kazakhs were converted to Islam only in the early 19th century, and for many years elements of animist practices remained. Over the period 1985–90 the number of mosques in Kazakhstan increased from 25 to 60. By 1991 there were an estimated 230 Muslim religious communities functioning in Kazakhstan and an Islamic institute had been opened in Almaty. The Islamic revival intensified following Kazakhstan's independence from the USSR, and during 1991–94 some 4,000 mosques were reported to have been opened.

Religious Administration of Muslims of Kazakhstan (Kazakstan musylmandary dini baskarmasy): 010000 Almaty; tel. (727) 230-63-65; fax (727) 297-94-23; e-mail susaev@bk.ru; internet www.muftyat.kz; Chair. Chief Mufti ABSATTAR B. Haji DERBISALI.

CHRISTIANITY

The Roman Catholic Church

The organization of the Roman Catholic Church in Kazakhstan comprises one archdiocese, two dioceses and one apostolic administration. There were an estimated 215,300 adherents at 31 December 2005.

Archbishop of the Archdiocese of the Most Holy Virgin Mary at Astana: Rt Rev. TOMASZ PETA, 010000 Astana, Tashenova 3, POB 622; tel. (7172) 37-29-35; fax (7172) 37-29-27; e-mail catholic_astana@mail.ru; internet www.catholic-kazakhstan.org.

The Russian Orthodox Church (Moscow Patriarchate)

Metropolitanate of Astana and Almaty: 050014 Almaty, mikroraion Dorozhnik 29; tel. (727) 298-94-15; e-mail office@orthodox.kz; internet www.orthodox.kz; f. 2003; three dioceses; Metropolitan MEFODII (NEMTSOV).

JUDAISM

Mitsva Association of Kazakhstan: Almaty; tel. (727) 273-5449; e-mail contact@mitsva.kz; internet www.mitsva.kz; f. 1992; unites Jewish communities from across Kazakhstan; Pres. ALEKSANDR BARON.

Rabbi of Almaty: Rabbi MENACHEM GERSHOVICH.

The Press

At July 2001 an estimated 950 newspaper and 342 periodical titles were published in Kazakhstan. In addition, 15 news agencies were operating in the country.

PRINCIPAL DAILY NEWSPAPERS

Almaty Asia Times: 050000 Almaty, Jandosova 60/412; tel. (727) 44-74-54; fax (727) 44-78-40.

Almaty Herald: 050000 Almaty, ul. Rozybakiyeva 37; tel. (727) 241-45-69; fax (727) 241-40-78; e-mail herald@nursat.kz; Editor-in-Chief OLESSYA IVANOVA.

Ekspress–K: 050044 Almaty, Abdullinykh 6; tel. (727) 259-60-00; fax (727) 259-60-39; e-mail daily@express-k.kz; internet www.express-k.kz; f. 1920; 5 a week; in Russian; Editor-in-Chief ADILKHAN NUSUPOV; circ. 19,500.

Kazakhstanskaya Pravda (Kazakhstani Truth): 050044 Almaty, Gogolya 39; tel. (727) 263-65-65; fax (727) 250-18-73; tel. (3172) 32-19-44; e-mail kpam@kaznet.kz; internet www.kazpravda.kz; f. 1920; 5 a week; publ. by the Govt; in Russian; Editor-in-Chief V. MIKHAILOV; circ. 34,115.

Khalyk Kenesi (Councils of the People): 010000 Astana; tel. (727) 233-10-85; f. 1990; 5 a week; publ. by Parliament; in Kazakh; Editor-in-Chief ZH. KENZHALIN.

Vechernii Almaty (Evening Almaty): 050016 Almaty, pr. Abylai khana 2; tel. and fax (727) 279-28-90; e-mail vecherni_almaty@mail.ru; internet www.vechorka.kz; f. 1968; in Russian; Editor-in-Chief ELMIRA R. PASHINA.

Yegemen Kazakhstan (Sovereign Kazakhstan): 050044 Almaty, Gogolya 39; Astana; tel. and fax (727) 263-25-46; tel. (7172) 34-16-41; e-mail astegemen@nursat.kz; f. 1919; 6 a week; organ of the Govt; in Kazakh; Editor-in-Chief M. SERKHANOV; circ. 31,840.

OTHER PUBLICATIONS

Aktsionery (Shareholders): 050004 Almaty, Chaikovskogo 11; tel. (727) 232-96-09; fax (727) 239-98-95; f. 1990; in Russian; two a week; business, investment; Editor-in-Chief VIKTOR SHATSKY.

Ana Tili (Native Language): 050044 Almaty, pr. Dostyk 7; tel. (727) 233-22-21; fax (727) 233-34-73; f. 1990; weekly; in Kazakh; Editor-in-Chief ZH. BEISENBAY-ULY; circ. 11,073.

Ara-Shmel (Bumble-bee): 050044 Almaty, Gogolya 39; tel. (727) 263-59-46; f. 1956; monthly; satirical; in Kazakh and Russian; Editor-in-Chief S. ZHUMABEKOV; circ. 53,799.

Arai (Dawn): 050000 Almaty, Furmanova 53; tel. (727) 232-29-45; f. 1987; every two months; socio-political; Editor-in-Chief S. KUTTYKADAMOV; circ. 7,500.

Atameken (Fatherland): 050010 Almaty, pr. Dostyk 85; tel. (727) 263-58-43; f. 1991; ecological; publ. by Ministry of Environmental Protection; circ. 25,063.

Aziya Kino (Asian Cinema): 050000 Almaty; tel. (727) 261-86-55; f. 1994; monthly; in Russian and Kazakh; Editor-in-Chief G. ABIKEYEVA.

Baldyrgan (Sprout): 050044 Almaty, pr. Zhibek-zholy 50; tel. (727) 233-16-73; f. 1958; monthly; illustrated; for pre-school and first grades of school; in Kazakh; Editor-in-Chief T. MOLDAGALIYEV; circ. 150,000.

Business World: 010000 Astana, Pushkina 166; tel. and fax (7172) 75-19-34; e-mail areket-kz@hotmail.com; f. 1999; weekly; circ. 10,000.

Continent: 050000 Almaty, POB 271; tel. (727) 250-10-39; fax (727) 250-10-41; e-mail bzchyt@kaznet.kz; f. 1999; policy and society journal; Editor-in-Chief ANDREI KUKUSHKIN; circ. 10,000.

Delovaya Nedelya (Business Week): 050044 Almaty, pr. Zhibek-zholy 64; tel. (727) 250-62-72; fax (727) 273-91-48; e-mail rikki@kazmail.asdc.kz; internet www.dn.kz; f. 1992; weekly; in Russian; Editor-in-Chief S. A. KORZHUMBAYEV; circ. 10,600.

Deutsche Allgemeine Zeitung: 050044 Almaty, pr. Zhibek-zholy 50/418; tel. (727) 273-42-69; fax (727) 273-92-91; e-mail daz@ok.kz; f. 1966; weekly; political, economic, cultural, social; in German; Editor-in-Chief IRINA ZIRENTSCHIKOWA; circ. 1,700.

Ekonomika i Zhizn (Economics and Life): 050000 Almaty; tel. (727) 263-96-86; f. 1926; monthly; publ. by the Govt; in Russian; Editor-in-Chief MURAT T. SARSENOV; circ. 4,800.

Ekspert Kazakhstan: 05000 Almaty, Furmanov 122; tel. (727) 295-28-32; fax (727) 295-28-33; e-mail expert@expertkazakhstan.kz;

internet www.expert.ru/printissues/kazakhstan/; f. 2003; weekly; business and economics; in Russian; Chief Editor ANDREI SKIRKA.

Globe: 050009 Almaty, pr. Abaya 155/13–14; tel. (727) 250-76-39; fax (727) 250-63-62; e-mail ipa@mailonline.kz; f. 1995; two a week; in English and Russian; Editor-in-Chief NURLAN ABLYAZOV; circ. 5,550.

Golos Kazakha/Kazakh Uni (Voice of a Kazakh): 050000 Almaty, Zenkov 75; tel. (727) 261-79-09; fax (727) 261-94-47; f. 1989; weekly; organ of the Federation of Trade Unions of Kazakhstan; in Russian and Kazakh.

Karavan (Caravan): 050000 Almaty, pl. Respubliki 13; tel. (727) 232-08-39; fax (727) 232-97-57; e-mail kaztag@caravan.kz; internet www.caravan.kz; f. 1991; weekly; in Russian; Editor-in-Chief ANDREI SHUKHOV; circ. 250,000.

Kazakh Adebiety (Kazakh Literature): 050000 Almaty, pr. Ablai-khana 105; tel. and fax (727) 269-54-62; f. 1934; weekly; organ of the Union of Writers of Kazakhstan; in Kazakh; Editor-in-Chief A. ZHAKSYBAYEV; circ. 7,874.

Kazakhstan: 050044 Almaty, pr. Zhibek-zholy 50; tel. (727) 233-13-56; f. 1992; weekly; economic reform; in English; Editor-in-Chief N. ORAZBEKOV.

Kazakhstan Aielderi (Women of Kazakhstan): 050044 Almaty, pr. Zhibek-zholy 50; tel. (727) 233-06-23; fax (727) 246-15-53; f. 1925; monthly; literary, artistic, social and political; in Kazakh; Editor-in-Chief ALTYNSHASH K. JAGANOVA; circ. 15,200.

Kazakhstan Business: 050044 Almaty, pr. Zhibek-zholy 50; tel. (727) 233-42-56; f. 1991; weekly; in Russian; Editor-in-Chief B. SUKHARBEKOV.

Kazakhstan Mektebi (Kazakh School): 050004 Almaty, pr. Ablai-khana 34; tel. (727) 239-76-65; f. 1925; monthly; in Kazakh; Editor-in-Chief S. ABISHEVA; circ. 10,000.

Kazakhstan Mugalimi (Kazakh Teacher): 050010 Almaty, Jambula 25; tel. (727) 261-60-58; f. 1935; weekly; in Kazakh; Editor-in-Chief ZH. TEMIRBEKOV; circ. 6,673.

Kazakstan Zaman (Kazakh Time): 050002 Almaty, pr. Dostyk 106G; tel. (727) 265-07-39; e-mail kazakstanzaman@mail.ru; f. 1992; in Kazakh and Turkish; weekly; circ. 15,000; Gen. Dir ERSIN DEMIRCI.

Korye Ilbo (Korean News): 050044 Almaty, pr. Zhibek-zholy 50; tel. (727) 233-90-10; fax (727) 263-25-46; f. 1923; weekly; in Korean and Russian; Editor-in-Chief YAN WON SIK.

Kredo (Credo): 100029 Karaganda, Oktyabrskaya 25; e-mail credogazeta@topmail.kz; internet www.catholic-kazakhstan.org/Credo/index.htm; f. 1995; monthly; Roman Catholic; in Russian; Chief Editor N. MAMAYEV.

Medicina (Medicine): 050004 Almaty, pr. Ablaikhana 63; tel. (727) 273-48-01; fax (727) 273-16-90; e-mail zdrav_kz@nursat.kz; f. 2000; monthly; in Kazakh; Editor-in-Chief A. SH. SEYSENBAYEV; circ. 5,000.

Novoye Pokoleniye (New Generation): 050091 Almaty, ul. Bogen-bai batyra 139/1–2; tel. (727) 261-31-06; fax (727) 250-95-46; e-mail np@host.kz; internet www.np.kz; f. 1998; weekly; in Russian; Editor-in-Chief SERGEI APARIN; circ. 95,000.

Oasis: 080000 Jambul obl., Taraz, ul. Lenina 31–34; tel. and fax (7262) 23-27-93; e-mail alex@zagribelny.jambyl.kz; organ of the Green Movement Socio-Ecological Centre; environmental matters; Editor-in-Chief ALEKSANDR ZAGRIBELNYI.

Panorama: 050013 Almaty, pl. Respubliki 15/647; tel. (727) 263-28-34; fax (727) 263-66-16; e-mail panorama@kazmail.asdc.kz; internet www.panorama.kz; f. 1992; weekly; in Russian; Editor-in-Chief LERA TSOY; circ. 18,500.

Parasat: 050000 Almaty, Aiteke bi 28; tel. (727) 293-94-71; fax (727) 293-94-74; f. 1958; monthly; socio-political, literary, illustrated; in Kazakh; Editor-in-Chief BAKKOZHA S. MUKAY; circ. 20,000.

Petroleum of Kazakhstan: 050091 Almaty, Nauryzbai batyr 58; tel. (727) 258-28-33; fax (727) 250-50-82; e-mail office@petroleumjournal.kz; internet www.petroleumjournal.kz; every two months; in Russian and English; Editor-in-Chief OLEG C. CHERVINSKY; circ. 2,000.

Prostor (Expanse): 050091 Almaty, pr. Ablai-khan 105; tel. (727) 272-61-87; e-mail info@prstr.samal.kz; internet prostor.samal.kz; f. 1933; monthly; literary and artistic; in Russian; Editor-in-Chief VALERII F. MIKHAILOV; circ. 1,800.

Respublika—Delovoye obozreniye (The Republic—Business Review): 050010 Almaty, Satpayeva 2/17; tel. and fax (727) 53-46-71; e-mail assandy@fromru.com; internet www.respublika.kz; weekly; in Russian; Editor-in-Chief IRINA PETRUSHOVA.

Russkii Yazyk i Literatura (Russian Language and Literature): 050091 Almaty, Ablylai-khan 34; tel. (727) 239-76-68; f. 1962; monthly; in Russian; Editor-in-Chief B. S. MUKANOV; circ. 17,465.

Sovety Kazakhstana (Councils of Kazakhstan): 050044 Almaty, pr. Zhibek-zholy 15; tel. (727) 234-92-19; f. 1990; weekly; publ. by Parliament; in Russian; Editor-in-Chief YU. GURSKII; circ. 30,000.

Turkistan: 050009 Almaty, ul. Abay 143; tel. (727) 243-32-42; fax (727) 243-58-11; e-mail turkestan_gazeta@mail.ru; internet www.turkystan.kz; f. 1994; weekly; political; in Kazakh; Editor SH. A. PATTEYEV; circ. 10,000.

Uigur Avazi (Uigur Voice): 050044 Almaty, pr. Zhibek-zholy 50; tel. (727) 233-84-59; f. 1957; 2 a week; publ. by the Govt; socio-political; in Uigur; Editor-in-Chief I. AZAMATOV; circ. 9,000.

Ulan (Hey You!): 050044 Almaty, pr. Zhibek-zholy 50; tel. (727) 233-80-03; f. 1930; weekly; in Kazakh; Editor-in-Chief S. KALIYEV; circ. 183,014.

Vremya (Time): 050000 Almaty, pr. Raiymbeka 115; tel. and fax (727) 258-10-06; internet www.time.kz; f. 1999; weekly; in Russian; Editor-in-Chief IGOR MELTSER; circ. 250,000 (2004).

Zerde (Intellect): 050044 Almaty, pr. Zhibek-zholy 50; tel. (727) 233-83-81; f. 1960; monthly; popular, scientific, technical; in Kazakh; Editor-in-Chief E. RAUSHAN-ULY; circ. 68,600.

Zhas Alash (Young Generation): 050044 Almaty, Makatayeva 22; tel. (727) 230-60-90; fax (727) 230-24-69; internet www.zhasalash.kz; f. 1921; publ. by the Kazakhstan Youth Union; in Kazakh; Editor-in-Chief ZHUSIPBEK KORGASBEK; circ. 133,000.

NEWS AGENCIES

Khabar News Agency: see Broadcasting and Communications.

National Information Agency 'Kazinform': 010000 Astana, Beibitshilik 10; tel. and fax (7172) 32-75-67; e-mail product@inform.kz; internet www.inform.kz; f. 1997; 100% state-owned open jt-stock co; provides information on govt activities in Kazakhstan and abroad; Pres. ZHANAI S. OMAROV.

Publishers

Gylym (Science): 050010 Almaty, Pushkin 111–113; tel. (727) 291-18-77; fax (727) 261-88-45; f. 1946; books on natural sciences, humanities and scientific research journals; Dir S. G. BAIMENOV.

Kainar (Spring): 050009 Almaty, pr. Abaya 143; tel. (727) 242-27-96; e-mail kainar_baspasy@mail.ru; f. 1962; agriculture, history, culture, religion; Dir ORAZBEK S. SARSENBAYEV.

Kazakhskaya Entsiklopediya (Kazakh Encyclopedia): 050000 Almaty; tel. (727) 262-55-66; f. 1968; Editor-in-Chief R. N. NURGALIYEV.

Kazakhstan Publishing House: 050000 Almaty, pr. Abaya 143; tel. and fax (727) 242-29-29; f. 1920; political science, economics, medicine, general and social sciences; Dir E. KH. SYZDYKOV; Editors-in-Chief M. D. SITKO, M. A. RASHEV.

Mektep: 050009 Almaty, pr. Abaya 143; tel. (727) 242-26-24; fax (727) 277-85-44; e-mail mektep@mail.ru; internet www.mektep.kz; f. 1947; mainly literature for educational institutions; dictionaries, phrase books, children's textbooks, teaching materials, reference books; publishes books in Kazakh, Russian, Uigur and Uzbek; Gen. Dir E. SATYBALDIYEV; Editor-in-Chief SH. GUSAKOVA.

Oner (Art): 050000 Almaty, pr. Abaya 143; tel. (727) 242-08-88; f. 1980; Dir S. S. ORAZALINOV; Editor-in-Chief A. A. ASKAROV.

Zhazushy (Writer): 050000 Almaty, pr. Abaya 143; tel. (727) 242-28-49; f. 1934; literature, literary criticism, essays and poetry; Dir D. I. ISABEKOV; Editor-in-Chief A. T. SARAYEV.

Broadcasting and Communications

GOVERNMENT AGENCY

Republican Agency for Information and Communications: 010000 Astana, Ministry Bldg, Left Bank, Ishim; tel. (7172) 74-01-35; fax (7172) 74-10-03; e-mail press@aic.gov.kz; internet www.aic.gov.kz; Chair. KUANYSHBEK B. YESEKEYEV.

TELECOMMUNICATIONS

Altel: 050000 Almaty, ul. Zhurgeneva 9; tel. (727) 230-16-30; fax (727) 230-01-43; e-mail info@altel.kz; internet www.altel.kz; f. 1994; provides mobile cellular communications in Kazakhstan (as Dalacom and PAThWORD).

GSM Kazakhstan: 050000 Almaty, Samal 2/100; tel. (727) 258-11-48; fax (727) 258-89-11; e-mail webmaster@kcell.kz; internet www.kcell.kz; f. 1998; 51% owned by Fintur Holdings (Finland/Turkey), 49% by Kazakhtelecom; provides mobile cellular telecommunications services (as K-Cell and Activ) in 180 settlements and along principal roads across Kazakhstan; 2m. subscribers (April 2005).

KAZAKHSTAN

KaR-tel (K-Mobile): 050000 Almaty, Tole bi 55; tel. (727) 250-60-60; fax (727) 295-23-97; e-mail csales@kartel.kz; internet www.k-mobile.kz; f. 1999; 100% subsidiary of VympelKom-Bilain (Russia); provides mobile cellular telecommunications services (as K-Mobile, Excess and Beeline) in more than 100 settlements and along principal roads across Kazakhstan; Gen. Dir DMITRII KROMSKII; 1.6m. subscribers (mid-2005).

Kazakhtelekom: 050000 Almaty, pr. Abylai-khan 86; tel. (727) 262-05-41; fax (727) 263-93-95; internet www.itte.kz; f. 1994; national telecommunications corpn; 60% state-owned, 40% owned by Daewoo Corpn (Republic of Korea); Pres. SERIK BURKITBAYEV.

KazTransCom: 050012 Almaty, Baitursynov 46A; tel. (727) 270-13-10; fax (727) 270-13-18; e-mail ktc@kaztranscom.kz; jt-stock co; provides telecommunications services to the petroleum and natural gas sectors; won licence in 2004 to provide long-distance and international telephone calls country-wide, becoming Kazakhstan's second long-distance provider.

BROADCASTING

Private radio and television stations began operating in Kazakhstan in the 1990s. In mid-2001 there were an estimated 124 radio and television stations.

Kazakh State Television and Radio Broadcasting Corpn: 050013 Almaty, Zheltoksan 175A; tel. (727) 263-37-16; f. 1920; Pres. YERMEK TURSUNOV.

Radio

Kazakh Radio: 050013 Almaty, Zheltoksan 175A; tel. (727) 263-19-68; fax (727) 265-03-87; e-mail kazradio@astel.kz; internet www.radio.kz; f. 1921; broadcasts in Kazakh, Russian, Uigur, German and other minority languages; Gen. Dir TOREKHAN DANIYAR.

Radio 31: 050060 Almaty, Tazhibayevoi 155; tel. (727) 315-29-31; e-mail radio@31.kz; internet www.31.kz; f. 1994; news and music; Dir SABIT SULEIMENOV.

Television

Khabar News Agency: 050013 Almaty, pl. Respubliki 13; tel. (727) 263-83-69; fax (727) 250-63-45; e-mail naz@khabar.almaty.kz; internet www.khabar.kz; f. 1959; international broadcasts in Kazakh, Uigur, Russian and German; two television channels; Chair. of the Bd of Dirs MAULEN ASHIMBAYEV; Dir GULNAR IKSANOVA.

KTK (Kazakh Commercial Television): 050013 Almaty, pl. Respubliki 13; tel. (727) 263-44-28; fax (727) 250-66-25; e-mail ktkao@kzaira.com; f. 1990; independent; Gen. Dir ANDREI SHUKHOV; Pres. SHOKAN LAUULIN.

NTK (Association of TV and Radio Broadcasters of Kazakhstan): 050013 Almaty, pl. Respubliki 13, 6th Floor; tel. (727) 270-01-83; fax (727) 270-01-85; e-mail kaztvradio@nursat.kz; f. 2000; privately owned; Pres. AIDAR ZHUMABAYEV.

Finance

(cap. = capital; res = reserves; dep. = deposits; m. = million; brs = branches; amounts in tenge, unless otherwise indicated)

BANKING

Central Bank

National Bank of Kazakhstan (NBK): 050040 Almaty, Koktem-3 21; tel. (727) 270-45-91; fax (727) 250-60-90; e-mail hq@nationalbank.kz; internet www.nationalbank.kz; f. 1990; cap. 20,000.0m., res 83,734.6m., dep. 2,325.4m. (Dec. 2006); Gov. ANVAR G. SAIDENOV; 19 brs.

Major Commercial Banks

Alliance Bank: 050000 Almaty, Furmanov 100A; tel. (727) 258-40-40; fax (727) 259-67-87; e-mail info@alb.kz; internet www.alb.kz; f. 1999; cap. 60,013m., res 3,557m., dep. 802,214m. (Dec. 2006); Chair. ZHOMART YERTAYEV.

ATF Bank: 050000 Almaty, Furmanova 100; tel. (727) 250-30-40; fax (727) 250-19-95; e-mail info@atfbank.kz; internet www.atfbank.kz; f. 1995; present name adopted 2002; cap. 45,600m., res 1,038.9m., dep. 951,461.3m. (Dec. 2006); Chair. TIMUR ISSATAYEV; 10 brs.

Bank Centercredit: 050000 Almaty, Panfilov 98; tel. (727) 259-85-98; fax (727) 258-45-10; e-mail info@centercredit.kz; internet www.centercredit.kz; f. 1988; present name adopted 1996; cap. 21,113.0m., res 91.0m., dep. 497,063.0m. (Dec. 2006); Chair. of Bd BAKHYTBEK R. BAYSEITOV; 19 brs.

Bank TuranAlem: 050051 Almaty, Samal 2, Zholdasbekov 97; tel. (727) 250-40-70; fax (727) 250-02-24; e-mail post@bta.kz; internet www.bta.kz; f. 1997; cap. 52,583.0m., res 61,318.0m., dep. 1,861,142.0m. (Dec. 2006); Chair. SADUAKAS MAMESHTEGI; 23 brs.

Caspian Bank (Bank Kaspiiskii): 050012 Almaty, Adi Sharipov 90; tel. (727) 279-57-92; fax (727) 250-95-96; e-mail office@bankcaspian.kz; internet www.bankcaspian.kz; 96% owned by Caspian Group (Netherlands); cap. 11,909.6m., res 2,212.3m., dep. 157,799.8m. (Dec. 2006); Chair. VYACHESLAV KIM; 17 brs.

Demır Kazakhstan Bank: 050012 Almaty, Tole bi 83; tel. (727) 244-92-44; fax (727) 244-92-35; e-mail demirbank@demirbank.kz; internet www.demirbank.kz; f. 1997; cap. 1,000m., res 39.5m., dep. 11,263.0m. (Dec. 2006); Gen. Man. YAVUZ AHMET EROL; 3 brs.

Development Bank of Kazakhstan: 010000 Astana, pr. Respublika 32; tel. (7172) 58-02-60; fax (7172) 58-02-76; e-mail info@kdb.kz; internet www.kdb.kz; wholly state-owned; cap. 70,572.9m., res 8,424.8m., dep. 95,413.4m. (Dec. 2005); Pres. KAMBAR SHALGIMBAYEV.

Eurasian Bank: 050002 Almaty, Kunayeva 56; tel. (727) 250-86-66; fax (727) 250-86-50; e-mail info@eurasian-bank.kz; internet www.eurasian-bank.kz; f. 1994; cap. 7,999.9m., res 1,136.9m., dep. 122,195.4m. (Dec. 2006); Chair. ALEKSANDR KONOPASSEVICH; 17 brs.

Eurasian Development Bank: 050000 Almaty, Panfilov 98; tel. (727) 244-40-44; fax (727) 244-65-70; e-mail info@eabr.org; f. 2006; cap. US $614.0m., res US $149.6m., dep. US $0.6m. (Dec. 2006); Chair. IGOR FINOGENOV.

Halyk Bank: 050046 Almaty, Rozybakiyeva 97; tel. (727) 259-07-77; fax (727) 259-02-71; e-mail halykbank@halykbank.kz; internet www.halykbank.kz; f. 1936 as br. of Savings Bank of USSR; fully privatized in Nov. 2001; cap. 60,684.1m., res 58,881.2m., dep. 851,066.3m. (Dec. 2006); Chair. GRIGORII MARCHENKO; 611 brs.

HSBC Bank Kazakhstan: 050010 Almaty, pr. Dostyk 43; tel. (727) 259-69-00; fax (727) 259-69-02; e-mail info@hsbc.kz; internet www.hsbc.kz; f. 1998; 100% owned by HSBC Bank PLC (United Kingdom); cap. 3,360.0m., res 422.7m., dep. 41,343.9m. (Dec. 2006); Chair of Bd of Dirs DEREK P. LUNT.

KazInvestBank: 050051 Almaty, pr. Dostyk 176; tel. (727) 261-90-60; fax (727) 259-86-58; e-mail info@kib.kz; internet www.kib.kz; f. 1993; open jt-stock co; cap. 4,501.0m., res 66.7m., dep. 19,265.0m. (Dec. 2006); Chief Exec. ADNAN ALLY AGHA; 3 brs.

Kazkommertsbank (KKB): 050060 Almaty, Gagarina 135; tel. (727) 258-53-01; fax (727) 258-51-61; e-mail mailbox@kkb.kz; internet www.kkb.kz; f. 1991; cap. 6,995.0m., res 241,659.0m. dep. 1,999,823.0m. (Dec. 2006); Chair. NURZHAN S. SUBKHANBERDIN; Man. Dir ANDREI I. TIMCHENKO; 23 brs.

Nurbank: 050010 Almaty, pr. Dostyk 38; tel. (727) 259-97-10; fax (727) 250-16-09; e-mail bank@nurbank.kz; internet www.nurbank.kz; f. 1992; cap. 14,994.0m., res 671.3m., dep. 176,780.9m. (Dec. 2006); Chair. ABILMAZHEN GILIMOV; 11 brs.

Temirbank: 050008 Almaty, pr. Abaya 68/74; tel. (727) 257-88-88; fax (727) 250-62-41; e-mail board@temirbank.kz; internet www.temirbank.kz; f. 1992; cap. 15,433.8m., res 23.5m., dep. 170,415.8m. (Dec. 2006); Chair. MURAT YULDASHEV; 15 brs.

Tsesnabank: 010000 Astana, Zhengis dangghyly 29; tel. (7172) 17-02-01; fax (7172) 17-01-95; e-mail tsb@tsb.kz; internet www.tsb.kz; f. 1992; cap. 7,500.9m., res 301.2m., dep. 71,827.0m. (Dec. 2006); Chair. KUAT KOZHAHMETOV; 9 brs.

Bankers' Organization

Bank Association of Kazakhstan: 010000 Almaty, Panfilova 98; tel. (727) 273-16-89; fax (727) 273-90-85; Pres. BAKHYTBEK BAISEITOV.

STOCK EXCHANGE

Kazakhstan Stock Exchange (KASE): 050000 Almaty, Aiteke bi 67; tel. (727) 272-98-98; fax (727) 272-09-25; e-mail info@kase.kz; internet www.kase.kz; f. 1993; Pres. and Chief Exec. AZAMAT M. JOLDASBEKOV.

INSURANCE

Almaty International Insurance Group: 050000 Almaty, Kabanbai batyr 112; tel. and fax (727) 250-12-31; internet www.aiig.escort.kz; f. 1994; Chair. SUREN AMBARTSUMIAN.

Centras Insurance: 050008 Almaty, Manas 32A; tel. (727) 259-77-55; fax (727) 259-77-66; e-mail insurance@centras.kz; internet www.centrasinsure.kz; f. 1997; life and non-life, insurance and reinsurance; Chair. TALGAT USENOV.

Dynasty Life Insurance Co: 050000 Almaty, Seifullina 410; tel. (727) 250-73-95; e-mail dynasty@bta.nursat.kz; Chair. SERIK TEMIRGALEYEV.

Industrial Insurance Group (IIG): 050046 Almaty, Nauryzbai Batyr 65–69; tel. (727) 250-96-95; fax (727) 250-96-98; e-mail iig@kaznet.kz; f. 1998; Pres. IVAN MIKHAILOV.

KazAgroPolits Insurance Co: 050000 Almaty, Nauryzbai Batyr 49–61; tel. (727) 232-13-24; fax (727) 232-13-26; e-mail kazagropolise@mail.banknet.kz; Chair. YERMEK USPANOV.

KAZAKHSTAN

Kazakhinstrakh (Kazakh International Insurance Co): 050044 Almaty, pr. Zhibek-zholy 69; tel. (727) 233-73-49; fax (727) 250-74-37; e-mail kiscentr@nursat.kz; Chair. NURLAN MOLDAKHMETOV.

Kazkommerts-Polits Insurance Co: 050013 Almaty, Satpayeva 24; tel. (727) 258-48-08; fax (727) 292-73-97; e-mail info@kkp.kz; internet www.kkp.kz; f. 1996; non-life; Chair. MEIRAM B. SERGAZIN; Dir TALGAT K. USSENOV.

MSCA (Medical Systems of Central Asia) Interteach: 050000 Almaty, Kabanbai batyr 122A; tel. and fax (727) 258-23-32; e-mail interteach@kaznet.kaz; f. 1989; medical and travel insurance, health care, accident and employee liability insurance; 290 employees; 48 brs; Gen. Dir ERNST M. KURLEUTOV.

Trade and Industry

GOVERNMENT AGENCY

Republican Agency for the Regulation of Natural Monopolies: 010000 Astana, Bukeikhan 14; tel. (7172) 59-16-77; fax (7172) 21-54-73; e-mail info@arem.kz; internet www.regulator.kz; Chair. NURLAN SH. ALDABERGENOV.

CHAMBERS OF COMMERCE

Union of Chambers of Commerce and Industry of Kazakhstan: 050000 Almaty, Masanchi 26; tel. (727) 292-00-52; fax (727) 250-70-29; e-mail tpprkaz@online.ru; internet www.ccikaz.kz; f. 1959; Chair. ABLAI MYRZAKHMETOV.

Aktobe Oblast Chamber of Commerce and Industry: 030000 Aktobe, Zhubanova 289/1; tel. (7132) 51-02-26; e-mail akbtpp@mail.ru; Chair. ELENA A. RUDENKO.

Almaty City Chamber of Commerce and Industry: 050000 Almaty, Tole bi 45; tel. (727) 262-03-01; e-mail alcci@nursat.kz; internet www.atpp.marketcenter.ru; Chair. ZULFIYA K. AKHMETZHANOVA.

Astana City Chamber of Commerce and Industry: 010000 Astana, Auezov 66, POB 1966; tel. (7172) 32-38-33; e-mail akmcci@dan.kz; internet www.chamber.kz; Chair. TATYANA I. KONONOVA.

Jambul Oblast Chamber of Commerce and Industry: 080012 Jambul obl., Taraz, Karakhana 2; tel. (7262) 43-05-98; Chair. ADILKHAN ZHAPARBEKOV.

Karaganda Oblast Chamber of Commerce and Industry: 100000 Karaganda, bulv. Mira 31; tel. (7212) 30-06-84; fax (7212) 30-05-05; e-mail karcci@mail.ru; f. 1994; Chair. NESIP SEITOVA.

Kostanai Oblast Chamber of Commerce and Industry: 110003 Kostanai, Taran 165; tel. (7142) 54-66-72; fax (7142) 54-44-03; e-mail ko_tpp@mail.kz; f. 1973; Chair. VALENTINA N. TRIBUSHNAYA.

Pavlodar Oblast Chamber of Commerce and Industry: 140002 Pavlodar, Toraigyrova 95/1; tel. (7182) 75-79-69; e-mail pav-cci@kaznet.kz; Chair. RAJHANGUL SATABAYEVA.

Southern Kazakhstan Oblast Chamber of Commerce and Industry: 160000 Southern Kazakhstan obl., Chimkent, Taukekhan 31; tel. (7252) 21-14-05; Chair. SYRLYBAJ ORDABEKOV.

EMPLOYERS' ORGANIZATIONS

Confederation of Employers of the Republic of Kazakhstan (KRRK): 050022 Almaty, Abai 42/44; tel. (727) 293-07-42; fax (727) 292-27-68; e-mail krrk@krrk.kz; internet www.krrk.kz; Pres. KADYR BAYIKENOV.

Kazakhstan Petroleum Association: 050010 Almaty, pr. Dostyk 43/517; tel. (727) 250-18-16; fax (727) 250-18-17; e-mail kpa@arna.kz; internet www.kpa.kz; f. 1998; Chair. NURZHAN KAMALOV; 61 mem. cos.

UTILITIES

Electricity

KEGOS—Kazakhstan Electricity Grid Operating Co (Elektr zhelilerin baskaru zhanindegi Kazakstan kompaniyasy): 050000 Almaty, ul. Kozybayeva 23; tel. (727) 271-93-59; internet www.kegoc.kz; f. 1997; technical electricity network operator; Pres. ALMASADAM M. SATKALIYEV.

Water

Almaty Vodocanal: 050057 Almaty, Zharokov 196; tel. (727) 274-00-17; fax (727) 274-98-41; e-mail info@almaty-vodokanal.kz; internet www.almaty-vodokanal.kz; f. 1936; state-owned; responsible for water supply and sewerage in Almaty and surrounding villages; Gen. Dir VADISLAV GALIYEV.

STATE HYDROCARBONS COMPANIES

KazMunaiGaz: 010000 Astana, Kabanbai Batyr 22; tel. (7172) 97-60-00; fax (7172) 97-60-01; e-mail info@kmg.kz; internet www.kmg.kz; f. 2002 by merger of KazakhOil and Transneftegas; national jt-stock co; subsidiaries include petroleum-transportation co KazTransOil, and gas-transportation co KazTransGas; Pres. UZAKBAI S. KARABALIN.

Munaigaz: 010000 Astana, Zheltoksan 7/1; tel. and fax (7172) 39-03-11; e-mail info@munaygas.com; internet www.munaygas.com; f. 1991; petroleum and gas prospecting and producing; Pres. T. A. KHAZANOV.

TRADE UNIONS

Confederation of Free Trade Unions of Kazakhstan: f. 1991; fmrly Independent Trade Union Centre of Kazakhstan; 9 regional brs with 2,200 mems; Chair. SERGEI BELKIN.

Confederation of Free Trade Unions of Coal and Mining Industries: 050000 Almaty; Chair. V. GAIPOV.

Federation of Trade Unions of Kazakhstan: 010000 Astana, Abai 94; tel. (7172) 216-68-14; fax (7172) 21-68-35; e-mail fprkastana@nursat.kz; internet www.fprk.kz; 30 affiliated unions with 2,300,000 mems (2001); Chair. SIYAZBEK MUKASHEV.

Transport

RAILWAYS

In 2003 the total length of rail track in use was 13,601 km (3,661 km of which were electrified). The rail network is most concentrated in the north of the country, where it joins the rail lines of Russia. In mid-2003 Kazakhstan and Kyrgyzstan announced that a 100-km railway link was to be built between Almaty and lake Issyk-Kul in Kyrgyzstan. Construction work was expected to be completed by 2008. A main line runs from Chimkent south to Uzbekistan, and another between Druzhba, on the eastern border of Kazakhstan, and Alataw Shankou, in the People's Republic of China.

In the early 2000s construction was under way of the first line of a new underground railway (metro) in Almaty.

In December 2004 a new rail line was opened, linking Altynsarino in Kostanai Oblast and Khromtau in Western Kazakhstan, greatly reducing travel time between the northern and central parts of the country and the petroleum-producing regions in the west.

Kazakstan Temir Zholy (Kazakhstan Railways): 010011 Astana, Zhengis dangghyly 98; tel. (7172) 93-44-00; fax (7172) 32-82-30; e-mail temirzhol@railways.kz; internet www.railways.kz; f. 1991; Pres. YERLAN D. ATAMKULOV.

ROADS

In 2004 Kazakhstan's total road network was 90,018 km, including 23,055 km of main roads.

INLAND WATERWAYS

Kazakhstan has an inland waterway network extending over some 4,000 km. The main navigable river is the Irtysh, accounting for approximately 80% of cargo transported by river. The Kazakhstan River Fleet Industrial Association, comprising 11 water companies, administers river traffic.

Department of Water Transport (Ministry of Transport and Communications): 010000 Astana, Abai 49; tel. (7172) 32-03-58; fax (7172) 32-10-58; Dir JENYS M. KASYMBEK.

SHIPPING

A ferry port was inaugurated at Aktau, on the eastern shore of the Caspian Sea, in September 2001 as part of the Transport Corridor Europa—Caucasus—Asia (TRACECA) programme, with services operating to Azerbaijan, Iran and Russia; the port was capable of processing some 10m. tons of petroleum and up to 30m. tons of dry goods per year. At 31 December 2006 Kazakhstan's merchant fleet comprised 59 vessels, with a combined total displacement of 64,932 grt.

Aktau International Commercial Sea Port: 130000 Mangystau obl., Aktauskii akimat, Umirzak; tel. (7292) 51-45-49; fax (7292) 44-51-01; e-mail aktauport@aktauport.kz; internet www.portaktau.kz; f. 1963; Dir TALGAT B. ABYLGAZIN; 429 employees.

CIVIL AVIATION

There are 18 domestic airports and four airports with international services (at Almaty, Aktau, Astana and Atyrau). A new passenger terminal opened at Astana International Airport in 2005.

KAZAKHSTAN

Department of Aviation (Ministry of Transport and Communications): 010000 Astana, Abai 49; tel. (7172) 32-63-16; fax (7172) 32-16-96; Dir S. BURANBAYEV.

Air Astana: 050000 Almaty, Biznes Tsentr Samal Tauers, ul. Zholdasbekova 97; tel. (7172) 58-41-35; fax (7172) 59-87-01; e-mail hr@air-astana.kz; internet www.air-astana.kz; f. 2001 jointly by the Government (51%) and BAE Systems (United Kingdom—49%); domestic and international flights; Pres. PETER FOSTER.

Tourism

Tourism is not widely developed in Kazakhstan. In 2005 there were 4.4m. tourist arrivals in Kazakhstan. In that year receipts from tourism (including passenger transport) amounted to US $809m.

Kazakhstan Tourist Association (KTA): 050022 Almaty, Abai 42/44/302; tel. (727) 292-53-31; fax (727) 292-48-53; e-mail kta@mail.kz; f. 1999.

KENYA

Introductory Survey

Location, Climate, Language, Religion, Flag, Capital

The Republic of Kenya lies astride the equator on the east coast of Africa, with Somalia to the north-east, Ethiopia and Sudan to the north, Uganda to the west and Tanzania to the south. The climate varies with altitude: the coastal region is hot and humid, with temperatures averaging between 20°C and 32°C (69°F–90°F), while inland, at more than 1,500 m (5,000 ft) above sea-level, temperatures average 7°C–27°C (45°F–80°F). The highlands and western areas receive ample rainfall (an annual average of 1,000 mm–1,250 mm) but most of northern Kenya is very dry (about 250 mm). Kiswahili is the official language, while English is widely spoken and 22% and 13% of the population, respectively, speak Kikuyu and Luo as their mother tongue. Most of the country's inhabitants follow traditional beliefs. There is a sizeable Christian community, while Muslims form a smaller proportion of the population. The national flag (proportions 2 by 3) has three broad horizontal stripes, of black, red and green, separated by two narrow white stripes. Superimposed in the centre is a red shield, with black and white markings, upon crossed white spears. The capital is Nairobi.

Recent History

Kenya was formerly a British colony (inland) and protectorate (along the coast). The first significant African nationalist organization was the Kenya African Union (KAU), founded in 1944, which was supported mainly by the Kikuyu, the largest ethnic group in Kenya. In 1947 Jomo Kenyatta, a Kikuyu, became President of the KAU. During 1952 a campaign of terrorism was launched by Mau Mau, a predominantly Kikuyu secret society that aimed to expel European (mainly British) settlers from Kenya. The British authorities declared a state of emergency in October 1952 and banned the KAU in 1953, when Kenyatta was imprisoned for alleged involvement with Mau Mau activities. The terrorist campaign ceased in 1956, and the state of emergency was revoked in January 1960.

Kenyatta was released from prison in 1961 and elected to the Legislative Council in 1962. Following general elections in May 1963, Kenya was granted internal self-government in June. The country became independent, within the Commonwealth, on 12 December 1963, and a republic exactly one year later. Kenyatta, then leader of the Kenya African National Union (KANU), was appointed Prime Minister in June 1963 and became the country's first President in December 1964. (He was subsequently re-elected to the presidency, unopposed, in 1969 and 1974.)

Kenyatta died in August 1978; the Vice-President, Daniel arap Moi, was proclaimed President in October, and was the sole candidate at a presidential election held (concurrently with a KANU-only general election) in November 1979. In June 1982 the National Assembly officially declared Kenya a one-party state. At a presidential election in September 1983 Moi was returned unopposed. In August 1986 KANU approved an open 'queue-voting' system to replace the secret ballot in the preliminary stage of a general election. In June 1987 it was announced that only members of the ruling party were to be entitled to vote during the preliminary stages of a general election.

In February 1988 Moi was nominated unopposed to serve a third term as President. In the same month preliminary elections under the 'queue-voting' system produced a KANU-approved list to contest 123 of the 188 elective seats in the National Assembly at a general election held in March (54 candidates received more than 70% of votes cast at the preliminary stage, and were thus deemed to have been elected, while 11 were elected unopposed). In an extensive cabinet reshuffle following the election, the Vice-President, Mwai Kibaki, was replaced by Josephat Karanja.

In April 1989 the National Assembly unanimously approved a motion of no confidence in Karanja, following allegations that he had abused his position as Vice-President to further his own personal and tribal interests. Karanja, while denying the charges against him, resigned shortly afterwards, and was replaced by the Minister of Finance, Prof. George Saitoti.

In December 1990 KANU abolished the system of 'queue-voting' and resolved to cease expelling party members, re-admitting 31 expelled members in the following month. In August six opposition leaders, including Oginga Odinga (Kenya's Vice-President in 1964–66), formed a new political movement, the Forum for the Restoration of Democracy (FORD); the Government outlawed the grouping, but it continued to operate.

In November 1991 several members of FORD were arrested prior to a planned pro-democracy rally in Nairobi, which was suppressed by the security forces. The Kenyan authorities were condemned internationally and bilateral and multilateral creditors suspended aid to Kenya indefinitely, pending the acceleration of both economic and political reforms. In December a special conference of KANU delegates acceded to the pressure for reform, resolving to introduce a multi-party political system. The National Assembly subsequently endorsed appropriate amendments to the Constitution. Former Vice-President Kibaki resigned as Minister of Health later in the month, in protest against alleged electoral malpractice by KANU and against the unsatisfactory outcome of the judicial inquiry into the death of Ouko, and founded the Democratic Party (DP).

During the first half of 1992 some 2,000 people were reportedly killed in tribal clashes in western Kenya. In March the Government banned all political rallies, and restrictions were placed on the activities of the press. Following a two-day general strike in April, organized by FORD, the Government ended the ban on political rallies. In August FORD split into two opposing factions, which were registered in October as separate political parties, FORD—Asili and FORD—Kenya, respectively led by Kenneth Matiba and Odinga.

At multi-party presidential and legislative elections held in December 1992 Moi was elected for a fourth term of office as President, winning 36.3% of the votes cast, ahead of Matiba (26.0%), Kibaki (19.5%) and Odinga (17.5%). Of the 188 elective seats in the National Assembly, KANU won 100 (including 16 uncontested); FORD—Asili and FORD—Kenya secured 31 seats each, and the DP took 23. Votes were cast predominantly in accordance with ethnic affiliations, with the two largest tribes, the Kikuyu and Luo, overwhelmingly rejecting KANU. An extensive reshuffle of cabinet posts was subsequently effected. In 1993 the international donor community agreed to resume the provision of aid to Kenya, in response to what it recognized as the Government's progress in implementing political and economic reforms.

In May 1995 leading opposition activists formed a new political organization, Safina. Dr Richard Leakey, a prominent white Kenyan and former Director of the Kenya Wildlife Service, was appointed as Safina's Secretary-General. The party aimed to combat corruption and human rights abuses by the Kenyan authorities and to campaign for the introduction of an electoral system of proportional representation.

During the mid-1990s Kenya's human rights record came under intense domestic and international scrutiny. In April 1995 the country's Roman Catholic bishops accused the Government of eroding judicial independence and of condoning police brutality and endemic corruption. In December the human rights organization Amnesty International alleged that the security forces were systematically torturing criminal suspects and opposition activists. In response to its critics, the Moi administration provisionally withdrew controversial draft legislation in January 1996 that would have severely restricted the freedom of the press and, in July, inaugurated a human rights committee to investigate alleged humanitarian abuses.

Divisions within opposition parties continued to undermine efforts to present a cohesive challenge to Moi and KANU prior to the 1997 elections. A renewed attempt to establish a coalition of opposition organizations, initiated in November 1995, was short-lived. Meanwhile, following an unsuccessful attempt to assume the leadership of FORD—Kenya, Raila Odinga (the son of Oginga Odinga, who died in January 1994, and a prominent opposition activist) left that party and subsequently became leader of the National Development Party (NDP). In October 1997 Matiba's faction of FORD—Asili registered as an independent party, the Forum for the Restoration of Democracy for the People (FORD—People). During the mid-1990s several opposition deputies, disaffected by these internal rivalries, defected to KANU. Within KANU itself rivalries also began to emerge, not least because the Constitution permitted Moi to stand for only one further term as President.

During the first half of 1997 Moi repeatedly refused to accede to opposition demands for a review of the Constitution prior to the forthcoming elections. Opposition organizations protested that constitutional reforms and a reorganization of the supervisory Electoral Commission were essential in order to eliminate an in-built electoral advantage for the Moi administration. In April the National Convention Executive Council (NCEC) was established as a forum embracing representatives of non-governmental organizations, religious groups and opposition parties (excluding, however, supporters of Matiba and Odinga). In mid-July Moi agreed to meet with opposition and religious leaders to discuss constitutional reform. It was subsequently announced that the opposition would henceforth be permitted to organize registered public meetings, and that a constitutional review commission would be established.

In August 1997 the IMF suspended assistance to Kenya, pending the implementation of decisive action to eliminate official corruption and to improve the system of revenue collection; the Government consequently announced the inauguration of an anti-corruption body. The NCEC organized a one-day general strike in early August, in support of its demands for constitutional reform. In late August serious unrest erupted in and around Mombasa. While the Government blamed the NCEC for orchestrating the attacks, the NCEC alleged that the Government was inciting inter-ethnic conflict with the aim of depriving opposition supporters from the predominantly Luo region of the opportunity to vote in the forthcoming elections by forcing them to flee their homes. In the following month the National Assembly approved legislation that amended the Constitution with the stated aim of ensuring free and fair democratic elections. All political parties were granted equal access to the media, and detention without trial was prohibited. In addition, the new legislation enabled the opposition to participate in selecting the 12 nominated members of the National Assembly and 10 of the 12 members of the supervisory Electoral Commission.

The presidential and legislative elections, which took place concurrently on 29 December 1997, were undermined by allegations of widespread fraud, as well as by logistical difficulties. Moi was re-elected President, winning 40.6% of the valid votes cast. Mwai Kibaki, the leader of the DP and former Vice-President, came second, with 31.5% of the votes cast. KANU secured 107 of the 210 elected seats in the enlarged National Assembly, while the remainder were divided between nine opposition parties, with the DP taking 39 seats, the NDP 21, FORD—Kenya 17 and the Social Democratic Party 15. Safina won five seats. Moi was inaugurated for a fifth (and final) term as President in January 1998. Shortly afterwards Moi appointed a new Cabinet. However, he postponed the designation of a new Vice-President, evidently in order not to give an indication of his preferred successor to the presidency.

In early 1998 inter-ethnic violence erupted once again in the volatile Rift Valley. The Moi administration blamed the conflict on bitterness in the Kikuyu and Luo communities at the outcome of the elections, while the latter alleged persecution both by the security forces and by smaller tribal groups that had voted predominantly for Moi and KANU. In July the authorities organized a judicial inquiry into the causes of the ethnic disturbances of both 1992 and 1998. Tension between the Kikuyu and Kalenjin communities in the Rift valley remained, however, especially over disputed land vacated by the Kikuyu during the clashes.

In early August 1998 a car-bomb exploded at the US embassy in central Nairobi, concurrently with a similar attack on the US mission in Dar es Salaam, Tanzania. Some 254 people were killed in Nairobi, and more than 5,000 suffered injuries. The attacks were believed to have been co-ordinated by international Islamist terrorists, and, in mid-August, the USA retaliated by launching air strikes against targets in Afghanistan and Sudan. Four men were convicted of involvement in the bombings by a court in New York, USA, in May 2001 and were later sentenced to life imprisonment. Other suspects, including Osama bin Laden, the fugitive Saudi-born Islamist activist whom the US authorities held ultimately responsible for the bombings, were still at large.

In April 1999 Saitoti was reappointed to the position of Vice-President (vacant since January 1998). In July Moi appointed Dr Leakey as head of the civil service and Secretary to the Cabinet, with responsibility for combating corruption in the public services. In September Moi effected a major reorganization of the Cabinet, merging several ministries and reducing the number of government ministers from 27 to 15.

In December 1999 the KANU-NDP majority in the National Assembly voted in favour of appointing a parliamentary select committee on constitutional review. However, a rival commission was established by an alliance of opposition and religious groups, known as Ufungamano, which intended to propose its own recommendations for constitutional change. Moi opposed the Ufungamano commission, although many Kenyans appeared to support it. In April 2000 the parliamentary committee, headed by Odinga, completed its review, proposing the establishment of a constitutional review commission, comprising 15 members, to be nominated by the National Assembly prior to their appointment by Moi. However, in November, following months of recriminations between the two rival commissions, Prof. Yash Pal Ghai, appointed by Moi to head the parliamentary commission, refused to be sworn into office. Ghai declared that he first wanted to negotiate with Ufungamano in an attempt to unite the two groups. The merger went ahead in May 2001; the new commission comprised 27 members, 12 of whom were drawn from Ufungamano.

In July 2000 the civil service commenced the reduction of its work-force as part of a programme of reforms to be effected over three years. Meanwhile, a parliamentary anti-graft committee sought the adoption by the National Assembly of a report in which the alleged perpetrators of corruption were named. (The Government later deleted the addendum containing the list of names, causing widespread outrage.) The committee also proposed legislation on economic crimes that would allow the anti-corruption authority (which had been established in 1997 at the insistence of the IMF) to prosecute alleged perpetrators of corruption without seeking permission from the Attorney-General. As a result of these measures, the IMF announced that it was to resume lending to Kenya. The Government agreed to a number of conditions, including the introduction of a law binding public officials to declare their wealth and liabilities and the enactment of the legislation on economic crimes. However, less than one month after the resumption of aid the High Court temporarily halted the retrenchment of civil servants, pending the final determination of a lawsuit on the issue, and ruled that all civil servants who had already been retrenched should be reinstated. In January 2001 the IMF and the World Bank expressed concern over the set-backs in the reforms, particularly the failure to approve legislation on public service ethics and economic crimes, and suspended aid to Kenya until the situation could be resolved. In August Kenyan deputies again refused to approve anti-corruption legislation, and the IMF suspended aid to Kenya indefinitely. Moi subsequently created a new police body to combat corruption. Meanwhile, in March Leakey resigned as head of the civil service and Secretary to the Cabinet (two months before the expiry of his contract) and was replaced by Dr Sally Kosgei, an ally of Moi. Leakey's departure, along with the dismissal of most of his colleagues, prompted a major reshuffle within the senior civil service. Many observers believed that Moi was now intent on gathering loyal followers around him in preparation for the 2002 elections.

In January 2001 Odinga, on behalf of the Luo-dominated NDP, signed a memorandum of understanding with KANU, which allowed Moi to appoint ministers from the NDP. In June Moi reorganized the Cabinet and appointed Odinga as Minister of Energy, thereby creating the first coalition Government in Kenya's history. Moi reshuffled the Cabinet again in November, introducing younger KANU ministers in an apparent attempt to provide suitable candidates for his succession; most notably Uhuru Kenyatta (son of the late President Jomo Kenyatta) and Cyrus Jirongo were appointed as Minister for Local Government and Minister for Rural Development, respectively.

The NDP was dissolved and absorbed into KANU in mid-March 2002, despite opposition from elements within both parties; Moi was elected as party Chairman, while Odinga became Secretary-General. In July some 12 opposition parties, including the DP, FORD—Kenya and the National Party of

Kenya, formed an electoral alliance, the National Alliance Party of Kenya (NAK).

In August 2002 Moi publicly announced that he favoured Uhuru Kenyatta as KANU's presidential candidate. However, several senior KANU members, including Vice-President Saitoti and Odinga, subsequently announced their intention to seek the party's presidential nomination and formed the Rainbow Alliance to campaign within KANU for a democratic vote to select its candidate. Moi responded by dismissing the Vice-President. In mid-October, in protest at Moi's attempts to impose his preferred successor, members of the Rainbow Alliance resigned from their posts in the Government and from KANU, together with some 30 KANU deputies. The Rainbow Alliance subsequently boycotted the KANU conference, at which Kenyatta's presidential candidacy was endorsed. Later in October the Rainbow Alliance established a new party, the Liberal Democratic Party (LDP), and joined with the NAK to form the National Rainbow Coalition (NARC), with Mwai Kibaki as its presidential candidate. The NARC proposed a vote of no confidence in Moi's Government, stating that the Government was illegally attempting to block the introduction of a new constitution. However, Moi forestalled the tabling of the motion by dissolving the National Assembly on 25 October, thereby ensuring that the elections would be held under the current Constitution.

At the presidential and legislative elections, held concurrently on 27 December 2002, the opposition secured an emphatic victory, with Kibaki winning 62.3% of the votes cast in the presidential election, and the NARC securing 125 of the 210 elected seats in the National Assembly, while Kenyatta received 31.2% of the votes cast for the presidency, and KANU won 64 seats in the legislature. The NARC were allocated a further seven appointed seats, increasing their representation to 132, and KANU a further four seats, bringing their total to 68. The electoral turn-out was 56.1%.

Following his inauguration as President on 30 December 2002, Kibaki promised reforms, including the adoption of a new constitution, under which certain powers would be transferred from the President to the legislature and the full independence of the judiciary guaranteed, the adoption of anti-corruption legislation, the privatization of state-owned companies and the dismissal of corrupt civil servants. In January 2003 Kibaki appointed a new Cabinet; however, divisions within the ruling coalition soon became apparent, as a group of 25 LDP deputies accused Kibaki of breaching a power-sharing agreement signed by the constituent parties of the NARC prior to the elections. In May the Anti-Corruption and Economic Crimes Act, which provided for the establishment of the Kenya Anti-Corruption Commission (KACC), and the Public Service (Code of Conduct and Ethics) Act, which required elected officials and senior civil servants to declare their wealth, came into effect.

In February 2003 Kibaki appointed a commission of inquiry into the Goldenberg financial scandal, in which public funds had been paid to the company Goldenberg International in 1990–93 as subsidies for non-existent exports of gold and diamonds. Evidence presented at the inquiry indicated that Goldenberg had initially received some Ks. 13,500m. (around US $180m.) under the Government's export compensation scheme. After thousands of transfers, including dubious foreign-exchange transactions, made with the alleged complicity of officials at the central bank, the payments to Goldenberg increased to Ks. 25,000m. ($600m.), equivalent to more than 10% of Kenya's annual GDP, although it was estimated that the total amount misappropriated could reach $4,000m. The scandal had also contributed to an IMF decision to suspend the disbursement to Kenya of loans worth some $500m. in 1997. Public hearings ended in November 2004, and the commission's findings were reported to Kibaki in February 2005. It had initially been expected that prosecutions would follow from the report; however, the Minister of Justice and Constitutional Affairs, Martha Karua, stated that further investigations were necessary before any charges could be brought.

Meanwhile, the constitutional review conference opened in April 2003, but divisions persisted over the proposed post of Prime Minister. The LDP advocated an executive Prime Minister with powers to appoint the Cabinet, while Kibaki and his supporters sought to maintain a strong presidency. The ensuing tensions between the NAK and LDP factions of the NARC threatened to split the ruling coalition. In August the death of Vice-President Wamalwa, who had been regarded as a moderating influence within the Government, led to an intensification of the power struggle. President Kibaki faced demands for a successor both from Wamalwa's Luhya ethnic group and from the Luo, who proposed the appointment of Odinga to the vice-presidency. In late September Kibaki named the Minister of Home Affairs, Arthur Moody Awori (a Luhya), as Vice-President and effected a minor government reshuffle. In March 2004 the constitutional review conference voted to reduce the powers vested in the presidency and to create the new post of executive Prime Minister following the next elections, which were scheduled to be held in December 2007. Under the recommendations adopted by the conference, greater power was to be accorded to the National Assembly. The Government withdrew from the conference in protest; however, the draft constitution was successfully presented to the Attorney-General, after which it was to be considered by the National Assembly. The High Court subsequently ruled that before the document could enter into force it required approval at a referendum. In December 2004 the National Assembly approved legislation to amend the draft constitution with the approval of a simple majority, rather than the two-thirds majority previously required. KANU and the LDP protested vehemently, as they believed that the President could use the legislation to reduce the proposed power of the Prime Minister.

The amended draft constitution, which was approved by the National Assembly in July 2005, confirmed the retention of the executive functions of the President, who would have the power to appoint and dismiss a non-executive Prime Minister. Devolution was to be on two levels (national and provincial), rather than the four levels originally envisaged, while the National Assembly was to remain unicameral.

There followed several months of campaigning punctuated by often violent demonstrations. Seven ministers announced their opposition to the proposed new constitution, including, most notably, Raila Odinga, whose LDP split from the NARC coalition and joined with KANU to form the Orange Democratic Movement (ODM). At the referendum, held on 21 November 2005, the draft constitution was rejected by 58.1% of voters. Some 53% of the electorate participated in the poll. Kibaki conceded defeat but ignored demands from Odinga and the ODM to hold legislative elections. Instead Kibaki moved swiftly to dismiss the entire Cabinet and in early December he unveiled a new administration, from which those ministers who had opposed the draft constitution were removed. Those NARC members who maintained their support for Kibaki subsequently formed a new coalition party, the National Rainbow Coalition—Kenya (NARC—Kenya), as a vehicle for contesting the 2007 elections. The fledgling party won three of the five available parliamentary seats at by-elections held in June 2006, justifying claims that the party was to be one of the main contenders in the forthcoming elections.

With a new constitution unlikely to be in place before the next general election a special review committee was established in September 2006. The committee submitted a report in November outlining proposals for a series of reforms targeting specific areas that were to be implemented prior to the elections, including reducing the number of members of the Electoral Commission from 22 to nine and the creation of 74 seats reserved for women. However, five parties, including the ODM, rejected these proposals and the process collapsed.

In 2004 it became increasingly apparent that corruption remained endemic in Kenya, despite the NARC Government's pledge to take measures to combat it. Four senior civil servants were suspended in May following their involvement in awarding contracts to supply passport printing equipment to a fictitious British company, Anglo Leasing Ltd. In July the British High Commissioner, Sir Edward Clay, claimed that corruption had cost Kenya some Ks. 15,000m. since Kibaki took office and warned that it could lead to a reduction in donor assistance—indeed, later that month the European Union (see p. 244) withheld substantial aid. Clay subsequently produced a dossier of some 20 allegedly dubious contracts involving corruption in four ministries, and in February 2005 reiterated his criticisms, urging Kibaki to remove corrupt ministers in order that investigations could proceed unhindered.

As public resentment increased, the issue of corruption became the subject of further attention in February 2005 when the Permanent Secretary for Governance and Ethics in the Office of the President, John Githongo, resigned citing his inability to continue working for the Government. Kibaki did not appoint a replacement for Githongo, and in November disbanded the Office of Governance and Ethics. Following Githongo's resignation, the USA and Germany announced that they would withhold anti-corruption aid, and the United Kingdom imposed travel restrictions on government ministers and others implicated in corruption. Awori admitted that there was massive corruption at senior levels, and there were demands from within the Government for the resignations of corrupt ministers. Kibaki subsequently reorganized the Cabinet, dismissing several high-ranking civil servants and effectively demoting a key presidential aide, the Minister of State for Provincial Administration and National Security in the Office of the President, Christopher Murungaru, to the Ministry of Transport. Kibaki also ordered the KACC to investigate procurement procedures in the National Security department.

Meanwhile, in February 2005 the Kenya Law Society announced that it was to prosecute senior figures on corruption charges, including Awori, the Attorney-General, Amos Wako, and the Minister of Finance, David Mwiraria. It was also revealed that the four senior civil servants suspended in May 2004 had agreed to act as prosecution witnesses and to testify that they had received instructions from government ministers to pursue the transactions for which they were being prosecuted. However, Wako invoked a provision in the Constitution granting him the power to take over private prosecutions initiated by individuals or institutions and entered a *nolle prosequi* to terminate the case.

In November 2005 Githongo presented Kibaki a dossier detailing his investigations into corruption in Kenya and death threats made against him, as well as accounts of his meetings with allegedly corrupt senior officials. Awori, Mwiraria, Murungaru and Kiraitu Murungi (the Minister of Energy) were implicated by Githongo in the Anglo Leasing scandal. Githongo claimed that, in total, the four intended to defraud the exchequer of US $700m. through false military and security contracts. He further alleged that two ministers had admitted that the money was to be used for party political campaigning. Awori, Mwiraria, Murungaru and Murungi were subsequently summoned to appear before the KACC; they all denied the allegations.

In January 2006 Githongo, who considered that Kibaki had failed to act upon the information supplied, released a copy of his dossier to the British media. (Githongo remained in exile in the United Kingdom.) He also released a recording of a meeting with Murungi in which the latter allegedly attempted to impede Githongo's investigation. Following Githongo's disclosure, a delegation of deputies representing the parliamentary Public Accounts Committee (PAC) travelled to the United Kingdom and interviewed Githongo at the Kenyan High Commission in London. In early February Mwiraria resigned from the Cabinet. Pressure increased on the Government and later that month Kibaki announced the resignations of Murungi and Saitoti, the Minister of Education. (Saitoti had also been implicated in the Goldenberg scandal—see above.) All three denied any wrongdoing. Kibaki reshuffled the Cabinet following the resignations, with Amos Kimunya assuming the finance portfolio, although Awori retained his position as Vice-President despite growing demands for his resignation. The PAC began questioning Awori, Mwiraria, Murungi and Saitoti in late February. In March Saitoti was also questioned by the police about his role in the Goldenberg affair, but the High Court of Kenya later rejected recommendations that he be charged. In a further cabinet reorganization in November, he was readmitted to the Government as Minister of Education, alongside Murungi, who resumed responsibility for the energy portfolio.

Division among the main parties intending to contest the forthcoming presidential and legislative elections emerged during 2007. In June NARC—Kenya indicated that Kibaki was to be named its presidential candidate, although this was not immediately confirmed. Dissension was also reported among ODM members and in May the party postponed for a fifth time the deadline for the submission of presidential nomination papers; however, Odinga began to emerge as the frontrunner for that party's presidential candidature. In October Minister of Health Charity Kaluki Ngilu was dismissed after she attended a rally at which Odinga launched his election campaign. Primary elections were held in November with Kibaki defecting from the ruling NARC—Kenya and choosing to contest the elections under his newly established Party of National Unity (PNU). Odinga was named the presidential candidate for the ODM. Shortly after the nominations were made an official report suggested that, despite Kibaki's renewed efforts in securing his re-election, the public was against him retaining office for a second term and Odinga held a significant lead in pre-election opinion polls.

At the legislative elections, held on 27 December 2007, the ODM secured 99 of the 210 seats in the National Assembly, the PNU won 43, the ODM—Kenya, which had broken away from the main party in August, 16 and KANU 14. Results in three constituencies were not released. The presidential election was held concurrently and the Electoral Commission of Kenya announced that, despite indications prior to the vote that Odinga had garnered greater popular support, Kibaki had narrowly been re-elected to the presidency with 4,584,721 votes; Odinga was reported to have secured 4,352,993 votes. Official figures detailing the total number of votes cast were not immediately made available. Odinga and other opposition candidates vehemently denounced the results, while independent international observers expressed scepticism regarding the credibility of the election, which had taken place amid allegations of widespread procedural violations. The results led to an upsurge in tribal conflict between Kibaki's Kikuyu supporters and Odinga's Luo followers. Nevertheless, on 30 December Kibaki was sworn in for a second term.

By mid-January 2008 some 600 people were reported to have been killed, and more than 250,000 displaced, as a result of the unrest. A mediation effort undertaken from 8 January by President John Kufuor of Ghana, in his capacity as Chairperson of the African Union (AU) Assembly, failed to bring about direct talks between Kibaki and Odinga. On that day Kibaki had announced the partial composition of his new Cabinet; despite the ODM having secured the largest number of seats in the legislature, no representatives from that party were included in the new Government. Further proposed AU-sponsored mediation was rejected by the Kenyan Government, and on 16 January the ODM, defying a ban on public demonstrations, commenced nation-wide protests scheduled to last for three days. These were violently dispersed by the security forces, resulting in additional fatalities.

On 29 January 2008 the former UN Secretary-General, Kofi Annan, formally launched a further round of negotiations, but observers believed that it would take time to resolve the deep-rooted ethnic problems that underpinned the political crisis, including the issue of land distribution. Ethnic fighting intensified and two senior ODM officials were killed. As a result Annan suspended discussions temporarily and the ODM appealed for calm. Talks resumed in early February and a proposal was made regarding the establishment of a power-sharing transitional government. Odinga had insisted that the elections be rerun, but signalled his willingness to consider this measure, which would allow for new elections to be conducted within a year. Negotiations continued haltingly throughout February with both parties reluctant to compromise. However, on 28 February Kibaki and Odinga signed an agreement on the division of power and the creation of the posts of Prime Minister and two Deputy Prime Ministers, pending a full constitutional review to be carried out within 12 months. Odinga conceded the presidency to Kibaki and accepted the role of Prime Minister. Despite the agreement, attacks were carried out in early March ahead of the opening of a new parliamentary session during which members were to debate the legislation required to legalize the power-sharing deal. The bills, which would allow a new coalition government to begin to implement a recovery programme and assist the numerous displaced persons across the country in returning to their homes, were ratified by the National Assembly later that month.

Following prolonged negotiations, in mid-April 2008 Kibaki named a new coalition Government, comprising members of the PNU, the ODM and ODM—Kenya, including Uhuru Kenyatta as Deputy Prime Minister and Minister of Trade and Wycliffe Musalia Mudavadi as Deputy Prime Minister and Minister of Local Government; Stephen Kalonzo Musyoka, who had been appointed as Vice-President and Minister of Home Affairs in January, and Moses Wetangula, who assumed responsibility for the foreign affairs portfolio at the same time, retained their positions in the new 40-member Cabinet.

Following the seizure of power by the National Resistance Army in Uganda in January 1986, Moi offered full co-operation to the new Ugandan President, Yoweri Museveni. After visits to Kenya by Museveni and President Ali Hassan Mwinyi of Tanzania in June, it was announced that joint commissions were to be formed to enhance co-operation between the three countries. In September, however, Ugandan authorities claimed that Kenya was harbouring anti-Museveni rebels, and stationed troops at the two countries' common border. These claims were denied, and in December, when Ugandan troops allegedly entered Kenya in pursuit of rebels, Ugandan and Kenyan armed forces exchanged fire across the border for several days; at least 15 people were reported to have been killed. Later in December Moi and Museveni agreed to withdraw troops from either side of the border. Moi visited Museveni in August 1990, indicating a renewed *détente* between Kenya and Uganda. In November 1994 Moi, Museveni and Mwinyi met in Arusha, Tanzania, and established a commission for co-operation; in March 1996 the Secretariat of the Permanent Tripartite Commission for East African Co-operation was formally inaugurated, with a view to reviving the East African Community (EAC), which had been dissolved in 1977. A treaty for the re-establishment of the EAC, providing for the promotion of free trade between the member states, the development of the region's infrastructure and economy and the creation of a regional legislative assembly and court, was ratified by the Kenyan, Tanzanian and Ugandan Heads of State in November 1999. The new EAC (see p. 412) was officially inaugurated in Arusha in January 2001. Talks on integrating the economies of the three EAC members followed, and in March 2004 Kibaki, Museveni and President Benjamin Mkapa of Tanzania signed a protocol on the creation of a customs union, eliminating most duties on goods traded within the Community, which took effect from January 2005. In May 2006 Kenya and Uganda agreed to share security information in an attempt to foster closer co-operation between the two countries.

Relations between Kenya and Sudan deteriorated in mid-1988, as the two countries made mutual accusations of aiding rebel factions. In early 1989 Sudan renewed a long-standing dispute with Kenya over the sovereignty of territory on the Kenyan side of the two countries' common border, known as the 'Elemi triangle'. During the late 1990s Kenya hosted a series of peace talks between the Sudanese Government and opposition leaders, under the auspices of the Intergovernmental Authority on Development (IGAD, see p. 311), in an attempt to resolve the conflict in southern Sudan. Further negotiations were held in Nairobi in September 2000 and June 2001, and in July 2002 the Sudanese Government and the opposition Sudan People's Liberation Movement (SPLM) signed an accord in Machakos, Kenya, which provided for the holding of a referendum on self-determination for southern Sudan after a transitional period of six years. In September 2003 Kenya and Sudan agreed to form a joint border committee. Talks aimed at achieving a final peace settlement between the Sudanese Government and the SPLM continued in Kenya throughout 2003 and 2004 (see the chapter on Sudan) and in January 2005 the Sudanese Government and southern rebels signed a peace accord in Nairobi, which officially ended the 21-year civil war.

Somalia has traditionally laid claim to part of north-eastern Kenya. During 1989 tension developed between the Kenyan authorities and ethnic Somalis from both sides of the Kenya–Somalia border, when Somalis were alleged to be largely responsible for wildlife-poaching and banditry in north-eastern Kenya. In September Moi protested strongly to the Somali Government, following an incursion into Kenya by Somali troops (reportedly pursuing Somali rebels), which resulted in the deaths of four Kenyans. In that month the Kenyan Minister of Foreign Affairs and International Co-operation stated that, while the Government supported the peace process in Somalia, it had not, as had been reported, officially declared recognition of the interim Somali President, Abdulkasim Hasan, or his Government. Moi later agreed to mediate between the interim Government and opposing rebel factions in Somalia. In July 2001 Kenya closed the border after numerous clashes were reported on the Somali side, which threatened to spill over into Kenya. However, Moi agreed to reopen the border in November. An IGAD-sponsored Somali reconciliation conference opened in the Kenyan town of Eldoret in October 2002 and was moved to Nairobi in February 2003; the talks continued throughout 2003 and early 2004, despite various disruptions, and in January 2004 representatives from more than 20 factions in attendance reached agreement on the establishment of a new Somali parliament, which was based in Nairobi until mid-2005 (see the chapter on Somalia).

Relations between the Kenyan and Ethiopian Governments became strained in 1997, owing to an increased incidence of cross-border cattle-rustling, including an attack in March during which 16 members of the Kenyan security forces were killed. A number of communiqués were subsequently signed by representatives of the two countries, agreeing to reinforce border security, to take measures to prevent the smuggling of arms and drugs, and to enhance trade. In November 1998 some 189 people (mainly Somalis) were found to have been massacred in north-eastern Kenya; Ethiopian guerrillas were widely believed to be responsible. In January 1999 the Kenyan Government protested to the Ethiopian authorities, following an incursion into Kenya by Ethiopian security forces, who were alleged to be in pursuit of Ethiopian rebels. Kenya deployed additional troops at the two countries' common frontier in May, following a series of land-mine explosions in the region, which had resulted in several fatalities. Bilateral relations deteriorated further during late 2000 after it was reported that some 50 Kenyans had been killed, allegedly by Ethiopian militia forces, in cross-border clashes. In January 2001 representatives from both countries met in Nairobi and agreed to initiate measures aimed at ending border disputes. In April 2006 Kenya closed part of its border with Ethiopia when militia forces allegedly entered Kenyan territory and fighting ensued. Seven people were reported to have been killed in further fighting that broke out in August.

In October 1995, despite strong condemnation from foreign Governments, the Kenyan authorities refused to permit the international tribunal that was investigating war crimes committed in Rwanda during 1994 access to alleged Rwandan perpetrators of genocide who had fled to Kenya. In June 1996 the Moi Government closed the Rwandan embassy in Nairobi in protest at the Rwandan Government's refusal to waive diplomatic immunity for an embassy official who was suspected of plotting a murder in Kenya; the diplomat was deported. In September, however, the first arrest in Kenya was made of a Rwandan Hutu suspected of involvement in genocide. Kenya strongly denied accusations, in November, of supplying arms to Rwandan Hutu rebels operating from within Zaire (now the Democratic Republic of the Congo). Following the *coup d'état* in Burundi in July 1996, Kenya, along with other countries of the region, imposed full economic sanctions on the administration of Maj. Pierre Buyoya; these sanctions were subsequently relaxed, and eventually withdrawn in January 1999. In November and December 1996 regional summit meetings were held in Nairobi to discuss the crisis in the Great Lakes region. Relations between the Kenyan and Rwandan Governments improved during 1997, when further Rwandan Hutus were arrested by the Kenyan security forces to stand trial on charges of genocide at the UN tribunal in Arusha, Tanzania. During a visit by Moi to Rwanda in May 2000 the two countries agreed to reopen the Kenyan embassy in Kigali and to establish a joint commission for bilateral relations.

In 1995 Kenya was reportedly sheltering about 200,000 refugees from the conflict in Somalia. The Moi Government, which claimed that the refugees placed an intolerable burden on the country's resources, repeatedly requested the UN to repatriate the total refugee population. By mid-1998 an estimated 155,000 Somalis had been repatriated from Kenya, with assistance from the office of the UN High Commissioner for Refugees. However, continuing instability in Somalia resulted in further influxes of refugees to Kenya. Kenya's total refugee population stood at 272,531 at the end of 2006, including 173,702 from Somalia and 73,004 from Sudan.

Government

Legislative power is vested in the unicameral National Assembly, with 224 members (210 elected by universal adult suffrage, the Attorney-General, the Speaker and 12 nominated members), who serve a term of five years, subject to dissolution. Executive power is held by the President, also directly elected for five years, who is assisted by an appointed Vice-President and Cabinet.

Defence

As assessed at November 2007, Kenya's active armed forces numbered 24,120, comprising an army of 20,000, an air force of 2,500 and a navy of 1,620; the paramilitary Police General Service Unit had a membership of 5,000. Military service is voluntary. Defence was allocated an estimated Ks. 25,600m. in the budget for 2006. Military assistance is received from the United Kingdom and from the USA, whose Rapid Deployment Force uses port and onshore facilities in Kenya.

Economic Affairs

In 2006, according to estimates by the World Bank, Kenya's gross national income (GNI), measured at average 2004–06 prices, was US $20,469m., equivalent to $580 per head (or $1,300 per head on an international purchasing-power parity basis). During 1996–2006, it was estimated, the population increased at an average annual rate of 2.3%, while gross domestic product (GDP) per head increased, in real terms, by an average of 0.7% per year. Overall GDP increased, in real terms, at an average annual rate of 3.0% in 1996–2006. Real GDP increased by 5.7% in 2006.

Agriculture (including forestry and fishing) contributed 27.9% of GDP in 2006 and accounted for 18.1% of workers engaged in paid employment in the formal sector in 2005. (According to FAO, agriculture employed 73.1% of the labour force in 2005.) The principal cash crops are tea (which contributed 17.2% of total export earnings in 2004) and coffee. Horticultural produce (Kenya is the world's fourth largest exporter of cut flowers), pyrethrum, sisal, sugar cane and cotton are also important. Maize is the principal subsistence crop. There is a significant dairy industry for domestic consumption and export. During 1996–2006, according to the World Bank, agricultural GDP increased at an average annual rate of 3.2%. Agricultural GDP increased by 3.0% in 2006.

Industry (including mining, manufacturing, construction and power) contributed 17.4% of GDP in 2006, and employed an estimated 19.5% of workers engaged in paid employment in the formal sector in 2005. During 1996–2006, according to the World Bank, industrial GDP increased at an average annual rate of 2.1%. Industrial GDP increased by 2.0% in 2006.

Mining contributed 0.6% of GDP in 2005 and employed 0.3% of those in paid formal sector employment in that year. Soda ash is the principal mineral export. Fluorspar, iron ore, salt, limestone, gold, gemstones (including rubies and sapphires), vermiculite and lead are also mined. Kenya has substantial reserves of titanium.

Manufacturing contributed an estimated 12.1% of GDP in 2006. The sector employed 13.7% of workers engaged in paid employment in the formal sector in 2005. During 1996–2006, according to the World Bank, manufacturing GDP increased at an average annual rate of 1.7%. Manufacturing GDP increased by 5.0% in 2006.

Hydroelectric power accounted for 51.5% of total electricity generated in 2004. It had accounted for an average of 81.9% during 1990–1998, whereafter recurrent droughts began to affect hydroelectric production. This shortfall was taken up by petroleum, which accounted for 24.1% in 2004 (as opposed to an average of 9.2% during 1990–1998). Kenya does not produce electricity from coal, natural gas or nuclear power. Energy for domestic use is derived principally from fuel wood and charcoal. The prolonged drought led to severe power shortages in 2000 and threatened to affect hydroelectric production in 2005–06. In February 2004 it was announced that the Kenyan and Tanzanian national grids were to be connected to that of Zambia under a cross-border energy project; the first phase of the project, which was to cost some US $300m., was to be commissioned in 2007, followed by a second phase in 2012. In 2004 imports of mineral fuels and lubricants (including crude petroleum intended for refining) comprised 24.3% of the value of total imports.

The services sector contributed an estimated 54.8% of GDP in 2006; it employed 62.4% of workers engaged in paid employment in the formal sector in 2005. Tourism makes an important contribution to Kenya's economy, and has been the country's principal source of foreign exchange since 1987. In 1998, however, a decline of 10.6% in tourist arrivals, to 894,300, was attributed partly to the effects of civil unrest in coastal areas during 1997. In 1999–2000 there was some recovery in tourism, with arrivals increasing to 1,036,628 in 2000. Following terrorist attacks in 2001, however, and subsequent warnings against travel to Kenya by the United Kingdom and the USA, the tourism industry again experienced difficulties. In 2005 tourist arrivals totalled 1,479,000, while receipts from tourism in 2004 amounted to US $808m. The GDP of the services sector increased at an average annual rate of 2.6% in 1996–2006, according to the World Bank. Services GDP increased by 3.7% in 2006.

In 2006 Kenya recorded a visible trade deficit of US $3,266.4m., and there was a deficit of $525.7m. on the current account of the balance of payments. In 2004 the principal source of imports was the United Arab Emirates (which supplied 14.4% of total imports in that year); other major suppliers were the USA, South Africa, Saudi Arabia, the United Kingdom, India and Japan. Uganda was the principal market for Kenya's exports (purchasing 17.4%) in that year; other important purchasers were the United Kingdom, Tanzania, the Netherlands and Pakistan. The principal exports in 2004 were refined petroleum products, tea, basic manufactures and vegetables and fruit. The principal imports in that year were petroleum and petroleum products, machinery and transport equipment, chemicals and related products, food and live animals and iron and steel.

In the financial year ending 30 June 2005 there was a budgetary deficit of Ks. 149,900m., equivalent to 10.6% of 2005 GDP. The country's external debt was US $6,826m. at the end of 2004, of which $5,978m. was long-term public debt. In that year the cost of debt-servicing was equivalent to 8.6% of the value of exports of goods and services. According to the IMF, the annual rate of inflation averaged 8.9% in 2000–06; consumer prices increased by 14.5% in 2006. Some 23% of the labour force were estimated to be unemployed in late 2000, and the rate of unemployment was reported to be approaching 30% by October 2001.

Kenya is a member of the Common Market for Eastern and Southern Africa (see p. 205) and, with Tanzania and Uganda, of the East African Community (see p. 412). The International Tea Promotion Association (see p. 409) is based in Kenya.

Kenya's economy is reasonably diversified, although most employment is dependent on agriculture. Agricultural development has been intermittently hindered by adverse weather conditions, resulting in sporadic food shortages, and also by rural ethnic unrest. Moreover, the country is highly vulnerable to fluctuations in international prices for its cash crops, most notably tea and coffee. Kenya's flower industry had been forecast to overtake tea and tourism as the country's leading source of foreign exchange, but by the mid-2000s this appeared unlikely. Drought, corruption and insecurity have all impacted negatively on the sector, and companies have been lured towards Ethiopia, further damaging the prospects of local growers. Poverty is widespread, with population growth considerably higher than growth in GNI per head, and the revelation in the mid-2000s that large scale corruption remained endemic in Kenya adversely affected business confidence and investment and led international donors to withhold aid. Nevertheless, in late 2006 President Kibaki stated intentions to transform the country into a middle income nation within 25 years, with a focus of the initiative being sustained annual economic growth of 10%. Outbreaks of violence that ensued following the disputed 2007 presidential election (see Recent History) precipitated temporary closures of key supply routes and forced many agricultural workers to abandon activities. Consequently, a severe downturn in maize production was reported in early 2008 and analysts warned of potential food shortages, particularly given that many farmers had been unable to plant crops for the next harvest. The crisis also disrupted the tourism sector, and it was estimated that more than 500,000 people required urgent humanitarian assistance. Meanwhile, the expiration of the Cotonou Agreement in December 2007 was expected to precipitate further difficulties in the agricultural sector. The accord (to which Kenya became a signatory in 2000) granted African, Caribbean and Pacific countries preferential access to the European Union (EU) market, a process which had strengthened Kenya's horticultural exports. The scheme was to be superseded by Economic Partnership Agreements requiring participating countries to reciprocate favourable terms of trade. There were concerns that an increase in imports of agricultural goods from the EU (where farmers benefited from large subsidies) would endanger Kenya's nascent horticultural industry. GDP grew by an estimated 6.4% in 2007, according to the IMF, and economic growth of 6.5% was projected for 2008.

Education

The Government provides, or assists in the provision of, schools. Primary education, which is compulsory, is provided free of charge. The education system involves eight years of primary education (beginning at six years of age), four years at secondary school and four years of university education. According to UNESCO estimates, in 2003/04 enrolment at primary schools included 76% of pupils in the relevant age group (males 76%; females 77%), while enrolment at secondary schools included 40% of children in the relevant age-group (males 40%; females 40%). Tertiary enrolment in 2001/02 included just 3% of those in the relevant age group (4% males; 2% females), according to UNESCO estimates. There are six state universities and seven private universities, with a total of 49,400 enrolled students in 1999/2000. The education sector was allocated Ks. 54,653m. in the budget for 2001/02 (equivalent to 25.6% of total budgetary expenditure by the central Government).

KENYA

Public Holidays

2008: 1 January (New Year's Day), 21–24 March (Easter), 1 May (Labour Day), 1 June (Madaraka Day, anniversary of self-government), 1 October* (Id al Fitr, end of Ramadan), 10 October (Moi Day), 20 October (Kenyatta Day), 12 December (Independence Day), 25–26 December (Christmas).

2009: 1 January (New Year's Day), 10–13 April (Easter), 1 May (Labour Day), 1 June (Madaraka Day, anniversary of self-government), 10 October (Moi Day), 20 September* (Id al Fitr, end of Ramadan), 20 October (Kenyatta Day), 12 December (Independence Day), 25–26 December (Christmas).

* These holidays are determined by the Islamic lunar calendar and may vary by one or two days from the dates given.

Weights and Measures

The metric system is in use.

Statistical Survey

Source (unless otherwise stated): Central Bureau of Statistics, Ministry of Finance and Planning, POB 30266, Nairobi; tel. (20) 333971; fax (20) 333030; internet www.cbs.go.ke.

Area and Population

AREA, POPULATION AND DENSITY

Area (sq km)	
Land area	571,416
Inland water	11,230
Total	582,646*
Population (census results)†	
24 August 1989	21,443,636
24 August 1999	
Males	14,205,589
Females	14,481,018
Total	28,686,607
Population (official projected estimates at mid-year)	
2005	33,368,802
2006	33,947,066
2007	34,528,249
Density (per sq km) at mid-2007	59.3

* 224,961 sq miles.
† Excluding adjustment for underenumeration.

PRINCIPAL ETHNIC GROUPS
(census of August 1989)

African	21,163,076		European	34,560
Arab	41,595		Other*	115,220
Asian	89,185		**Total**	21,443,636

* Includes persons who did not state 'tribe' or 'race'.

POPULATION BY PROVINCE
(2007, projected estimates)

Nairobi	2,940,911		Nyanza	5,039,776
Central	3,922,183		Rift Valley	8,586,066
Coast	3,031,879		Western	4,249,103
Eastern	5,389,546		**Total**	34,528,249
North-Eastern	1,368,785			

PRINCIPAL TOWNS
(estimated population at census of August 1999)

Nairobi (capital)	2,143,020		Meru	78,100
Mombasa	660,800		Kitale	63,245
Nakuru	219,366		Malindi*	53,805
Kisumu*	194,390		Nyeri*	46,969
Eldoret*	167,016		Kericho	30,023
Thika	82,665		Kisii	29,634

* Boundaries extended between 1979 and 1989.

Mid-2007 ('000, incl. suburbs, UN estimates): Nairobi 3,010; Mombasa 882 (Source: UN, *World Urbanization Prospects: The 2007 Revision*).

BIRTHS AND DEATHS
(annual averages, UN estimates)

	1990–95	1995–2000	2000–05
Birth rate (per 1,000)	38.6	38.0	39.1
Death rate (per 1,000)	9.4	11.4	13.2

Source: UN, *World Population Prospects: The 2006 Revision*.

Expectation of life (years at birth, WHO estimates): 51.3 (males 51.2; females 51.4) in 2005 (Source: WHO, *World Health Statistics*).

EMPLOYMENT
(labour force survey, selected urban and rural settlements, '000s)*

	2003	2004	2005†
Agriculture and forestry	316.1	320.6	327.5
Mining and quarrying	5.4	5.6	5.8
Manufacturing	239.7	242.0	247.5
Electricity and water	21.1	20.8	20.2
Construction	76.6	77.4	78.4
Wholesale and retail trade	162.8	168.0	175.8
Transport and communications	86.8	100.8	117.3
Finance, insurance, real estate and business services	83.8	83.6	85.7
Community, social and personal services	734.9	744.9	749.5
Total	1,727.3	1,763.7	1,807.7

* Data are for salaried employees in the formal sector only, and therefore exclude 66,800 self-employed and unpaid family workers and 6,407,200 workers in the informal sector. According to ILO, the 1999 census recorded an employed population of 14,474,200.
† Provisional figures.

Mid-2005 (estimates in '000): Agriculture, etc. 12,714; Total labour force 17,395 (Source: FAO).

Health and Welfare

KEY INDICATORS

Total fertility rate (children per woman, 2005)	5.0
Under-5 mortality rate (per 1,000 live births, 2005)	120
HIV/AIDS (% of persons aged 15–49, 2005)	6.1
Physicians (per 1,000 head, 2004)	0.14
Hospital beds (per 1,000 head, 2003)	1.97
Health expenditure (2004): US $ per head (PPP)	85.6
Health expenditure (2004): % of GDP	4.1
Health expenditure (2004): public (% of total)	42.7
Access to water (% of persons, 2004)	61
Access to sanitation (% of persons, 2004)	43
Human Development Index (2005): ranking	148
Human Development Index (2005): value	0.521

For sources and definitions, see explanatory note on p. vi.

KENYA   *Statistical Survey*

Agriculture

PRINCIPAL CROPS
('000 metric tons)

	2004	2005	2006
Wheat	379.4	368.9	358.1
Barley	39.2	41.2	81.1
Maize	2,607.1	2,905.6	3,247.2
Millet	50.5	53.1	68.7
Sorghum	69.5	149.7	131.2
Potatoes	1,084.4	980.2	783.8
Sweet potatoes	571.3	230.7	808.6
Cassava (Manioc)	642.9	347.8	841.2
Sugar cane	4,661.0	4,800.8	4,932.8
Dry beans	277.5	382.3	531.8
Dry cow peas	29.3	36.2	87.9
Pigeon peas	105.6	96.1	1,106.6
Cashew nuts*	10.0	11.2	11.2
Coconuts*	60.0	66.1	66.1
Seed cotton*	20.0	n.a.	20.0
Cottonseed*	13.0	13.0	13.0
Cabbages*	676.3	689.6	689.6
Tomatoes	330.0	330.0	330.0
Dry onions	68.0	68.0	68.0
Carrots*	44.8	42.9	42.9
Bananas	600.0	600.0	600.0*
Plantains	600.0	600.0	600.0*
Guavas, mangoes and mangosteens	118.0	149.3*	149.3*
Avocados*	70.0	72.0	72.0
Pineapples	600.0	600.0	600.0*
Papayas*	86.0	87.7	87.7
Coffee (green)	48.4	45.2	48.3
Tea (made)	324.6	328.5	310.6
Tobacco (leaves)*	20.0	n.a.	20.0
Sisal*	25.0	n.a.	25.0

* FAO estimate(s).

Aggregate production ('000 metric tons, may include official, semi-official or estimated data): Total cereals 3,199 in 2004, 3,585 in 2005, 3,955 in 2006; Total roots and tubers 2,328 in 2004, 1,582 in 2005, 2,464 in 2006; Total vegetables (incl. melons) 1,803 in 2004, 1,818 in 2005, 1,818 in 2006; Total fruits (excl. melons) 2,392 in 2004, 2,427 in 2005, 2,427 in 2006.

Source: FAO.

LIVESTOCK
('000 head, year ending September)

	2004	2005	2006
Cattle	13,022.4	13,019.0	12,430.3
Sheep	10,298.5	10,033.9	9,298.5
Goats	13,390.5	13,882.6	10,129.4
Pigs	379.8	320.0	321.1
Camels	1,193.6	931.3	1,057.9
Chickens	25,906	28,657	29,369

Source: FAO.

LIVESTOCK PRODUCTS
('000 metric tons)

	2004	2005	2006
Cattle meat	350.2	396.2	396.2*
Sheep meat	35.5	36.7	36.7*
Goats' meat	38.9	38.9	38.0
Pig meat	14.5	12.8	11.0
Chicken meat	19.2	18.2	18.2*
Game meat*	14.0	n.a.	14.0
Camel meat*	19.8	19.8	19.8
Cows' milk	2,829.9	2,650.0	3,500.0
Sheep's milk*	31.0	31.0	31.0
Goats' milk	118.5	129.0	129.0*
Camels' milk*	25.2	25.2	25.2
Hen eggs*	60.7	60.7	60.7
Honey	21.5	22.0	25.0

* FAO estimate(s).

Source: FAO.

Forestry

ROUNDWOOD REMOVALS
('000 cubic metres, excluding bark)

	2004	2005*	2006*
Sawlogs, veneer logs and logs for sleepers	241.0*	241.0	241.0
Pulpwood	391.0	391.0	391.0
Other industrial wood*	1,160.0	1,160.0	1,160.0
Fuel wood*	20,369.6	20,563.6	20,748.9
Total	22,161.6	22,355.6	22,540.9

* FAO estimate(s).

Source: FAO.

SAWNWOOD PRODUCTION
('000 cubic metres, including railway sleepers)

	2000*	2001	2002
Coniferous (softwood)	184	74	70
Broadleaved (hardwood)	1	10	8
Total	185	84	78

* FAO estimates.

2003–06: Production as in 2002.

Source: FAO.

Fishing

('000 metric tons, live weight)

	2003	2004	2005
Capture	124.1	130.9	152.1
Silver cyprinid	31.7	34.7	56.5
Nile tilapia	16.0	17.5	18.7
Other tilapias	4.5	3.9	4.0
Nile perch	55.2	57.2	53.1
Other freshwater fishes	5.9	5.7	8.7
Aquaculture	1.0	1.0	1.0
Total catch	125.1	131.9	153.2

Note: Figures exclude crocodiles, recorded by number rather than by weight. The number of Nile crocodiles caught was: 3,811 in 2003; 3,862 in 2004; 3,794 in 2005.

Source: FAO.

Mining

('000 metric tons, estimates)

	2003	2004	2005
Soda ash	352.6	353.8	360.2
Fluorspar	95.3	118.0	109.6
Salt	48.0	60.0	52.0
Limestone flux	33.0	34.0	35.0

Source: US Geological Survey.

Industry

SELECTED PRODUCTS
('000 metric tons, unless otherwise indicated)

	2003	2004	2005*
Wheat flour	248.6	262.3	271.6
Raw sugar	448.0	516.8	489.0
Beer ('000 hectolitres)	222.3	237.5	266.3
Cigarettes (million)	4,753.0	5,351.0	7,324.2
Cement	1,659.5	1,873.3	2,123.2
Electric energy (million kWh)	4,851.6	5,194.5	5,547.0

* Preliminary data.

2002: Kerosene and jet fuels 273; Motor spirit (petrol) 253; Gas-diesel (distillate fuel) oils 405; Residual fuel oils 533.

KENYA

Finance

CURRENCY AND EXCHANGE RATES

Monetary Units
100 cents = 1 Kenya shilling (Ks.).
Ks. 20 = 1 Kenya pound (K£).

Sterling, Dollar and Euro Equivalents (31 December 2007)
£1 sterling = Ks. 125.56;
US $1 = Ks. 62.68;
€1 = Ks. 92.26;
Ks. 1,000 = £7.96 sterling = $15.96 = €10.84.

Average Exchange Rate (Ks. per US $)
2005 75.554
2006 72.101
2007 67.318

Note: The foregoing information refers to the Central Bank's mid-point exchange rate. However, with the introduction of a foreign exchange bearer certificate (FEBC) scheme in October 1991, a dual exchange rate system is in effect. In May 1994 foreign exchange transactions were liberalized and the Kenya shilling became fully convertible against other currencies.

BUDGET
(Ks. million, year ending 30 June)

Revenue	1999/2000	2000/01	2001/02*
Tax revenue	151,359.5	160,771.6	160,394.2
Taxes on income and profits	53,317.0	53,428.9	55,861.9
Taxes on goods and services	69,437.3	78,538.9	82,948.6
Value-added tax	40,944.2	50,220.9	50,871.7
Excise duties	28,493.1	28,317.9	32,076.9
Taxes on international trade	28,605.2	28,803.7	21,583.7
Import duties	28,605.2	28,803.7	21,583.7
Non-tax revenue	27,585.1	26,306.1	25,399.4
Property income	6,482.4	4,786.1	4,105.5
Administrative fees and charges	21,538.1	21,538.1	21,293.9
Total (incl. others)	184,550.9	192,221.0	187,863.8

Expenditure	1999/2000	2000/01	2001/02*
General administration	44,080.7	62,943.3	57,584.5
Defence	10,427.2	14,202.8	16,268.2
Social services	59,670.4	67,611.1	71,953.1
Education	47,726.8	49,611.3	54,653.0
Health	9,188.6	15,629.3	14,336.5
Economic services	28,481.1	39,362.3	38,069.4
General administration	5,101.3	14,085.6	12,696.2
Agriculture, forestry and fishing	8,115.4	8,269.6	7,850.1
Roads	8,848.5	9,458.4	8,856.7
Interest on public debt	28,917.8	24,425.5	29,850.9
Total	171,577.2	208,545.7	213,726.2

* Forecasts.

2004/05 (year ending 30 June, Ks. '000 million, estimates): Revenue 342.3 (Direct taxes 140.5; Customs and excise 81.3; VAT and other indirect taxes 93.1); Expenditure 492.2 (General public services 70.8; Defence 27.0; Social services 158.0; Economic affairs 77.1; Other services 116.2).

INTERNATIONAL RESERVES
(excl. gold, US $ million at 31 December)

	2004	2005	2006
IMF special drawing rights	0.6	0.0	0.5
Reserve position in IMF	19.7	18.2	19.2
Foreign exchange	1,499.0	1,780.6	2,395.3
Total	1,519.3	1,798.8	2,415.0

Source: IMF, *International Financial Statistics*.

MONEY SUPPLY
(Ks. million at 31 December)

	2004	2005	2006
Currency outside banks	62,728	66,327	76,479
Demand deposits at commercial banks	136,729	157,460	206,583
Total money (incl. others)	209,368	230,845	291,741

Source: IMF, *International Financial Statistics*.

COST OF LIVING
(Consumer Price Index at December; base: October 1997 = 100)

	2000	2001	2002
Food and non-alcoholic beverages	136.3	134.8	142.5
Alcohol and tobacco	120.8	136.3	137.1
Clothing and footwear	109.9	109.8	110.7
Housing	121.6	129.3	133.9
Fuel and power	143.1	154.1	165.8
Household goods and services	117.6	119.0	120.8
Medical goods and services	134.1	152.6	158.8
Transport and communications	128.4	127.7	130.8
Recreation and education	120.2	129.6	132.8
Personal goods and services	118.2	120.5	122.8
All items (incl. others)	129.0	131.1	136.7

Source: IMF, *Kenya: Statistical Appendix* (July 2003).

All items (Consumer Price Index, annual averages; base 2000 = 100): 118.4 in 2003; 132.2 in 2004; 145.8 in 2005; 166.9 in 2006 (Source: IMF, *International Financial Statistics*).

NATIONAL ACCOUNTS

Expenditure on the Gross Domestic Product
(Ks. million at current prices)

	2003	2004	2005
Government final consumption expenditure	205,140	226,016	242,409
Private final consumption expenditure	875,154	965,528	1,077,071
Changes in inventories	7,288	10,546	−25,311
Gross fixed capital formation	179,282	206,634	263,063
Total domestic expenditure	1,266,865	1,408,724	1,557,231
Exports of goods and services	270,118	336,360	378,068
Less Imports of goods and services	338,394	434,234	529,749
Statistical discrepancy	−60,614	−28,345	9,605
GDP at market prices	1,137,975	1,282,504	1,415,155

Gross Domestic Product by Economic Activity
(Ks. million at current prices)

	2003	2004	2005
Agriculture, forestry and fishing	293,028	318,409	348,797
Mining and quarrying	6,217	6,491	7,173
Manufacturing	109,959	127,502	148,188
Electricity, gas and water	23,330	24,877	27,823
Construction	37,680	46,429	56,298
Wholesale and retail trade, repairs	104,074	126,986	153,528
Restaurants and hotels	10,713	16,214	19,533
Transport, storage and communication	104,411	127,271	154,412
Financial services	48,921	44,343	44,489
Real estate, renting and business services	67,316	72,702	79,015
Government services	167,040	186,346	204,614
Private households	4,561	5,224	5,787
Community, social and personal service activities	45,488	49,058	52,981
Sub-total	1,022,738	1,151,852	1,302,638
Less Imputed bank service charge	10,111	9,052	11,412
Indirect taxes, less subsidies	125,348	139,705	123,928
GDP in market prices	1,137,975	1,282,504	1,415,155

KENYA

BALANCE OF PAYMENTS
(US $ million)

	2004	2005	2006
Exports of goods f.o.b.	2,720.7	3,454.5	3,502.0
Imports of goods f.o.b.	−4,350.6	−5,601.7	−6,768.4
Trade balance	−1,629.9	−2,147.1	−3,266.4
Exports of services	1,556.5	1,880.0	2,461.1
Imports of services	−938.8	−1,137.6	−1,431.4
Balance on goods and services	−1,012.2	−1,404.8	−2,236.7
Other income received	45.0	73.3	99.4
Other income paid	−171.5	−181.7	−169.5
Balance on goods, services and income	−1,138.7	−1,513.3	−2,306.8
Current transfers received	1,044.7	1,319.2	1,829.0
Current transfers paid	−42.6	−66.6	−47.9
Current balance	−136.7	−260.6	−525.7
Capital account	145.2	103.3	168.4
Direct investment abroad	−4.4	−9.7	−24.0
Direct investment from abroad	46.1	21.2	50.7
Portfolio investment assets	−71.7	−45.9	−23.6
Portfolio investment liabilities	5.4	15.4	3.0
Other investment assets	−307.1	−200.6	−259.6
Other investment liabilities	372.0	730.8	927.1
Net errors and omissions	−61.9	−237.1	264.9
Overall balance	−13.1	117.0	581.3

Source: IMF, *International Financial Statistics*.

External Trade

PRINCIPAL COMMODITIES
(distribution by SITC, US $ million)

Imports c.i.f.	2002	2003	2004
Food and live animals	182.1	241.6	314.1
Cereals and cereal preparations	99.8	140.4	195.6
Crude materials (inedible) except fuels	75.7	80.2	116.4
Mineral fuels, lubricants, etc.	513.1	802.4	1,107.9
Petroleum, petroleum products, etc.	501.7	788.2	1,086.0
Crude petroleum oils	191.6	316.6	545.1
Refined petroleum products	305.2	465.4	531.6
Animal and vegetable oils, fats and waxes	163.5	164.7	112.4
Chemicals and related products	497.7	531.8	715.8
Medicinal and pharmaceutical products	104.2	117.4	135.6
Artificial resins, plastic materials, etc.	17.7	23.2	26.8
Basic manufactures	430.5	475.5	655.2
Iron and steel	142.7	168.6	277.6
Machinery and transport equipment	976.7	948.3	1,107.8
Power-generating machinery and equipment	62.1	36.7	71.0
Machinery specialized for particular industries	62.9	96.1	123.5
General industrial machinery, equipment and parts	87.0	103.9	115.7
Electrical machinery, apparatus, etc.	18.1	18.8	21.1
Road vehicles and parts*	235.3	263.7	337.2
Passenger motor cars (excl. buses)	84.3	105.3	125.2
Motor vehicles for goods transport and special purposes	62.7	71.3	95.3
Aircraft, associated equipment and parts*	255.9	216.8	107.4
Miscellaneous manufactured articles	205.8	213.8	389.9
Total (incl. others)	3,074.6	3,475.0	4,563.5

* Data on parts exclude tyres, engines and electrical parts.

Exports f.o.b.*	2002	2003	2004
Food and live animals	388.9	987.1	983.2
Vegetables and fruit	146.3	260.9	290.0
Fresh or simply preserved vegetables	74.9	153.3	160.9
Coffee, tea, cocoa and spices	178.1	583.7	570.8
Tea	140.9	481.2	462.1
Crude materials (inedible) except fuels	177.1	337.7	421.7
Cut flowers and foliage	101.4	179.4	234.8
Mineral fuels, lubricants, etc.	430.1	488.7	614.7
Petroleum, petroleum products, etc.	429.1	487.4	612.5
Refined petroleum products	427.8	483.9	609.1
Chemicals and related products	39.3	123.5	113.6
Basic manufactures	133.6	253.7	309.9
Iron and steel	31.2	61.8	96.7
Miscellaneous manufactured articles	90.5	173.8	113.9
Total (incl. others)	1,400.4	2,551.1	2,683.2

* Excluding re-exports.

PRINCIPAL TRADING PARTNERS
(Ks. million)

Imports c.i.f.	2003	2004	2005*
Belgium	6,757	9,689	8,000
China, People's Repub.	8,023	12,795	19,764
France	8,957	12,209	13,883
Germany	10,962	13,183	15,761
India	14,811	22,660	24,236
Indonesia	12,497	7,691	9,749
Italy	5,840	7,154	7,857
Japan	18,611	24,151	23,021
Korea, Repub.	2,966	3,289	3,386
Netherlands	6,256	7,310	9,629
Pakistan	4,456	3,247	2,532
Saudi Arabia	24,305	31,368	27,580
Singapore	2,352	4,452	7,574
South Africa	23,309	34,654	42,305
Spain	2,154	1,989	2,951
Sweden	1,615	2,007	2,404
United Arab Emirates	31,918	45,044	62,130
United Kingdom	19,621	27,124	26,134
USA	14,388	14,425	42,493
Total (incl. others)	281,844	364,557	430,740

Exports f.o.b.	2003	2004	2005*
Belgium	2,332	2,474	2,920
Egypt	5,453	6,918	8,839
France	3,100	3,592	5,086
Germany	5,330	4,574	5,221
India	2,498	4,147	4,000
Italy	1,671	1,764	2,170
Japan	1,215	1,593	1,855
Netherlands	14,139	17,094	18,316
Pakistan	9,153	11,359	14,072
Rwanda	6,012	6,190	7,273
Tanzania	14,588	17,921	19,887
Uganda	30,668	37,059	42,545
United Arab Emirates	2,108	2,396	3,923
United Kingdom	21,525	22,404	23,371
USA	2,796	4,502	4,518
Total (incl. others)	183,154	214,793	244,198

* Provisional.

KENYA   *Statistical Survey*

Transport

RAILWAYS
(traffic)

	2000	2001	2002*
Passenger-km (million)	302	216	288
Freight ton-km (million)	1,557	1,603	1,538

* Provisional figures.

ROAD TRAFFIC
(motor vehicles in use)

	2000	2001	2002*
Motor cars	244,836	255,379	269,925
Light vans	159,450	162,603	166,811
Lorries, trucks and heavy vans	57,796	58,501	59,835
Buses and mini-buses	38,930	42,629	46,606
Motorcycles and autocycles	44,894	46,004	47,451
Other motor vehicles	31,820	32,255	32,724

* Provisional figures.

2004: Motor cars 307,772; Buses 55,705; Lorries and vans 243,612; Motorcycles 53,508.

SHIPPING

Merchant Fleet
(registered at 31 December)

	2004	2005	2006
Number of vessels	41	41	38
Total displacement ('000 grt)	18.7	19.9	17.6

Source: Lloyd's Register-Fairplay, *World Fleet Statistics*.

International Sea-borne Freight Traffic
('000 metric tons)

	1999	2000	2001*
Goods loaded	1,845	1,722	1,998
Goods unloaded	6,200	7,209	8,299

* Provisional figures.

Freight handled ('000 metric tons at Kenyan ports): 11,931 in 2003; 12,920 in 2004; 13,282 in 2005.

CIVIL AVIATION
(traffic on scheduled services)

	2001	2002	2003
Kilometres flown (million)	32	36	41
Passengers carried ('000)	1,418	1,600	1,732
Passenger-km (million)	3,706	3,939	4,245
Total ton-km (million)	427	465	527

Source: UN, *Statistical Yearbook*.

Passengers carried ('000): 4,747 in 2003; 5,450 in 2004; 5,905 in 2005 (estimate).

Tourism

FOREIGN TOURIST ARRIVALS
(number of visitors by country of origin)

	2001	2002	2003
Austria	19,929	20,054	22,954
France	47,802	48,101	55,057
Germany	156,414	157,394	180,156
India	23,858	24,007	27,479
Italy	53,328	53,662	61,428
Sweden	34,376	34,591	39,593
Switzerland	39,081	39,326	45,013
Tanzania	111,735	112,435	128,695
Uganda	69,781	70,218	80,373
United Kingdom	153,968	154,933	177,339
USA	65,191	65,599	75,086
Total (incl. others)	993,600	1,001,297	1,146,099

Tourism receipts (US $ million, incl. passenger transport): 513 in 2002; 611 in 2003; 808 in 2004.

Source: World Tourism Organization.

Total arrivals ('000): 1,361 in 2004; 1,479 in 2005.

Communications Media

	2004	2005	2006
Telephones ('000 main lines in use)	299	282	293
Mobile cellular telephones ('000 subscribers)	2,546	4,612	6,485
Personal computers ('000 in use)	441	300	n.a.
Internet users ('000)	1,055	1,111	2,770

Source: International Telecommunication Union.

Television receivers ('000 in use, 2000): 768.

Radio receivers ('000 in use, 1999): 6,383.

Facsimile machines (number in use, year ending 30 June 1995): 3,800.

Daily newspapers (2000): 4 titles (average circulation 310,000 copies).

Book production (titles, 1994): 300 first editions (excl. pamphlets).

Sources: UNESCO, *Statistical Yearbook*; UN, *Statistical Yearbook*.

Education

(2003/04, unless otherwise indicated)

	Institutions	Teachers	Pupils
Pre-primary	23,977[1]	70,058	1,627,721
Primary	17,611[1]	149,893	5,926,078
Secondary:			
general secondary	3,057[1]	75,875	2,405,259
technical	36[2]	834[3]	14,597[3]
teacher training	26[4]	808[5]	18,992[6]
Higher	n.a.[7]	n.a.[7]	106,407

[1] 1998/99 figures.
[2] 1988 figure.
[3] UNESCO estimate.
[4] 1995 figure.
[5] 1985 figure.
[6] 1992 figure.
[7] In 1990 there were four universities, with 4,392 teachers.

Sources: Ministry of Education, Nairobi; UNESCO Institute for Statistics.

2005 ('000, estimates): Enrolment in primary schools 7,592; Enrolment in secondary schools 928; Enrolment in universities 90.

Adult literacy rate (UNESCO estimates): 73.6% (males 77.7%; females 70.2%) in 2000 (Source: UNESCO Institute for Statistics).

Directory

The Constitution

The Constitution was introduced at independence on 12 December 1963. Subsequent amendments, including the adoption of republican status on 12 December 1964, were consolidated in 1969. A further amendment in December 1991 permitted the establishment of a multi-party system. In September 1997 the National Assembly approved legislation which amended the Constitution with a view to ensuring free and fair democratic elections. All political parties were granted equal access to the media, and detention without trial was prohibited. In addition, the opposition was to participate in selecting the 12 nominated members of the National Assembly and 10 of the 12 members of the supervisory Electoral Commission. An amendment to the Constitution, approved by the National Assembly in November 1999, reduced the level of presidential control over the legislative process. The Constitution can be amended by the affirmative vote on Second and Third Reading of 65% of the membership of the National Assembly (excluding the Speaker and Attorney-General).

The central legislative authority is the unicameral National Assembly, in which there are 210 directly elected Representatives, 12 nominated members and two ex officio members, the Attorney-General and the Speaker. The maximum term of the National Assembly is five years from its first meeting (except in wartime). It can be dissolved by the President at any time, and the National Assembly may force its own dissolution by a vote of 'no confidence', whereupon presidential and Assembly elections have to be held within 90 days.

Executive power is vested in the President, Vice-President and Cabinet. Both the Vice-President and the Cabinet are appointed by the President, who must be a member of the Assembly and at least 35 years of age. Election of the President, for a five-year term, is by direct popular vote; the winning candidate at a presidential election must receive no less than 25% of the votes in at least five of Kenya's eight provinces. If a President dies, or a vacancy otherwise occurs during a President's period of office, the Vice-President becomes interim President for up to 90 days while a successor is elected.

The Government

HEAD OF STATE

President: MWAI KIBAKI (took office 30 December 2002; re-elected 27 December 2007).

CABINET
(April 2008)

A coalition of the Party of National Unity, the Orange Democratic Movement, and the Orange Democratic Movement—Kenya.

Prime Minister: RAILA AMOLLO ODINGA.
Vice-President and Minister of Home Affairs: STEPHEN KALONZO MUSYOKA.
Deputy Prime Minister and Minister of Trade: UHURU KENYATTA.
Deputy Prime Minister and Minister of Local Government: WYCLIFFE MUSALIA MUDAVADI.
Minister of the East African Community: AMASON KINGI JEFFAH.
Minister of Foreign Affairs: MOSES WETANGULA.
Minister of Finance: AMOS MUHINGA KIMUNYA.
Minister of Justice, National Cohesion and Constitutional Affairs: MARTHA KARUA.
Minister of Nairobi Metropolitan Development: MUTULA KILONZO.
Minister of Roads: KIPKAYLA KONES.
Minister of Public Works: CHRIS OBURE.
Minister of Transport: CHIRAU ALI MAKWERE.
Minister of Water and Irrigation: CHARITY KALUKI NGULI.
Minister of Regional Development Authorities: FREDRICK OMULO GUMO.
Minister of Information and Communications: SAMUEL LESRON POGHISIO.
Minister of Energy: KIRAITU MURUNGI.
Minister of Lands: AGGREY JAMES ORENGO.
Minister of the Environment and Mineral Resources: JOHN MICHUKI.
Minister of Forestry and Wildlife: NOAH WEKESA.
Minister of Tourism: MOHAMED NAJIB BALALA.
Minister of Agriculture: WILLIAM SAMOEI RUTO.
Minister of Livestock Development: MOHAMED ABDI KUTI.
Minister of Fisheries Development: PAUL NYONGESA OTUOMA.
Minister of the Development of Northern Kenya and Other Arid Lands: IBRAHIM ELMI MOHAMED.
Minister of Co-operatives Development: JOSEPH NYAGAH.
Minister of Industrialization: HENRY KIPRONO KOSGEY.
Minister of Housing: PETER SOITA SHITANDA.
Minister of Special Programmes: Dr NAOMI NAMSI SHABANI.
Minister of Gender and Children Affairs: ESTHER MURUGI MATHENGE.
Minister of Public Health and Sanitation: BETH WAMBUI MUGO.
Minister of Medical Services: Prof. PETER ANYANG' NYONG'O.
Minister of Labour: JOHN KIONGA MUNYES.
Minister of Youth and Sports: Dr HELEN JEPKEMOI SAMBILI.
Minister of Education: SAMSON KEGEO ONGERI.
Minister of Higher Education, Science and Technology: Dr SALLY JEPNGETICH KOSGEY.
Ministers of State in the Office of the President: Prof. GEORGE SAITOTI (Provincial Administration and Internal Security), YUSUF MOHAMED HAJI (Defence).
Ministers of State in the Office of the Vice-President: GERALD OTIENO KAJWANG' (Immigration and registration of Persons), WILLIAM OLE NTIMAMA (National Heritage and Culture).
Ministers of State in the Office of the Prime Minister: WYCLIFFE AMBETSA OPARANYA (Planning, National Development and Vision 2030), DALMAS ANYANGO OTIENO (Public Service).
Attorney-General: AMOS WAKO.

MINISTRIES

Office of the President: Harambee House, Harambee Ave, POB 30510, Nairobi; tel. (20) 227411; internet www.officeofthepresident.go.ke.

Office of the Vice-President and Ministry of Home Affairs: Jogoo House 'A', Taifa Rd, POB 30478, Nairobi; tel. (20) 228411; internet www.homeaffairs.go.ke.

Office of the Prime Minister: Nairobi.

Office of the Deputy Prime Minister and Ministry of Local Government: Jogoo House 'A', Taifa Rd, POB 30004, Nairobi; tel. (20) 217475; internet www.localgovernment.go.ke.

Office of the Deputy Prime Minister and Ministry of Trade: Teleposta Towers, Kenyatta Ave, POB 30430, Nairobi; tel. (20) 331030; fax (20) 248722; e-mail ps@tradeandindustry.go.ke; internet www.tradeandindustry.go.ke; Nairobi.

Ministry of Agriculture: Kilimo House, Cathedral Rd, POB 30028, Nairobi; tel. (20) 718870; fax (20) 720586; internet www.agriculture.go.ke.

Ministry of Co-operatives Development: Social Security House (NSSF) Bldg, Eastern Wing of Block 'A', POB 30547, 00100, Nairobi; tel. (20) 2731531; internet www.co-operative.go.ke.

Ministry of the Development of Northern Kenya and Other Arid Lands: Nairobi.

Ministry of the East African Community: Co-operative House, 16th Floor, Haile Sellasie Ave/Aga Khan Walk, POB 8846, 00200, Nairobi; tel. (20) 245741; fax (20) 253244.

Ministry of Education: Jogoo House 'B', Harambee Ave, POB 30040, Nairobi; tel. (20) 318581; e-mail info@education.go.ke; internet www.education.go.ke.

Ministry of Energy: Nyayo House, Kenyatta Ave, POB 30582, 00100 Nairobi; tel. (20) 310112; fax (20) 228314; internet www.energy.go.ke.

Ministry of the Environment and Natural Resources: NHIF Bldg, Ragati Rd, POB 30126, Nairobi; tel. (20) 2730808; fax (20) 2710015; e-mail mec@nbnet.co.ke; internet www.environment.go.ke.

KENYA

Ministry of Finance: Treasury Bldg, Harambee Ave, POB 30007, Nairobi; tel. (20) 252299; fax (20) 310833; internet www.treasury.go.ke.

Ministry of Fisheries Development: Nairobi.

Ministry of Foreign Affairs: Old Treasury Bldg, Harambee Ave, POB 30551, Nairobi; tel. (20) 318888; e-mail mfapress@nbnet.co.ke; internet www.mfa.go.ke.

Ministry of Forestry and Wildlife: Utalii House, off Uhuru Highway, POB 30027, Nairobi; tel. (20) 313010.

Ministry of Gender and Children Affairs: NSSF Bldg, Block 'A', Eastern Wing, POB 16936, 00100 Nairobi; tel. (20) 2727980; fax (20) 2734417; internet www.kenya.go.ke/gender.

Ministry of Higher Education, Science and Technology: Jogoo House 'B', Harambee Ave, POB 30040, Nairobi; tel. (20) 318581; e-mail info@education.go.ke; internet www.education.go.ke.

Ministry of Housing: Ardhi House, Ngong Rd, POB 30450, 00100 Nairobi; tel. (20) 2718050; fax (20) 2721248.

Ministry of Industrialization: Nairobi.

Ministry of Information and Communications: Teleposta Towers, Kenyatta Ave, POB 30025, Nairobi; tel. (20) 251152.

Ministry of Justice, National Cohesion and Constitutional Affairs: Cooperative Bank House, Haile Selassie Ave, POB 56057-00200, Nairobi; tel. (20) 224029; e-mail ps-justice@justice.go.ke; internet www.justice.go.ke.

Ministry of Labour: Social Security House, Block 'C', Bishop Rd, POB 40326, Nairobi; tel. (20) 2729800; fax (20) 2726497; internet www.labour.go.ke.

Ministry of Lands: Ardhi House, Ngong Rd, POB 30450, 00100 Nairobi; tel. (20) 2718050; fax (20) 2724470; e-mail pslands@wananchi.com; internet www.ardhi.go.ke.

Ministry of Livestock Development: Kilimo House, Cathedral Rd, POB 34188, 00100 Nairobi; tel. (20) 2718870; fax (20) 2711149; internet www.livestock.go.ke.

Ministry of Medical Services: Nairobi.

Ministry of Nairobi Metropolitan Development: Nairobi.

Ministry of Public Health and Sanitation: Medical HQ, Afya House, Cathedral Rd, POB 30016, Nairobi; tel. (20) 2717077; fax (20) 2725902; e-mail enquiries@health.go.ke; internet www.health.go.ke.

Ministry of Public Works: Ministry of Works Bldg, Ngong Rd, POB 30260, Nairobi; tel. (20) 2723101.

Ministry of Regional Development Authorities: NSSF Bldg, 21st Floor, Eastern Wing, POB 10280, 00100 Nairobi; tel. (20) 2724646; fax 2737693; internet www.regional-dev.go.ke.

Ministry of Roads: Ministry of Works Bldg, Ngong Rd, POB 30260, Nairobi; tel. (20) 2723101; fax (20) 720044; internet www.publicworks.go.ke.

Ministry of Special Programmes: Nairobi.

Ministry of Tourism: Utalii House, off Uhuru Highway, POB 30027, Nairobi; tel. (20) 313010; internet www.tourism.go.ke.

Ministry of Transport: Transcom House, Ngong Rd, POB 52692, Nairobi; tel. (20) 2729200; e-mail motc@insightkenya.com; internet www.transport.go.ke.

Ministry of Water: Maji House, Ngong Rd, POB 49720, Nairobi; tel. (20) 2716103; fax (20) 2727622.

Ministry of Youth and Sports: Nairobi.

President and Legislature

PRESIDENT

**Election, 27 December 2007*

Candidate	Votes
Mwai Kibaki (PNU)	4,584,721
Raila Odinga (ODM)	4,352,993
Stephen Kalonzo Musyoka (ODM—Kenya)	879,903
Others	59,411†

* Results released by the Office of the Government Spokesperson. The figure for the total number of votes cast at the election was not immediately made available.
† There were six other candidates.

NATIONAL ASSEMBLY

Speaker: KENNETH OTIATO MARENDE.

General Election, 27 December 2007

Party	Seats
ODM	99
PNU	43
ODM—Kenya	16
KANU	14
Safina	5
NARC—Kenya	4
FORD—People	3
NARC	3
New FORD—Kenya	2
CCU	2
PICK	2
DP	2
SKS	2
Others	10
Vacant	3*
Total	**210†**

* Results in three constituencies were not immediately made available.
† In addition to the 210 directly elected seats, 12 are held by nominees. The Attorney-General and the Speaker are, ex officio, members of the National Assembly.

Election Commission

Electoral Commission of Kenya: Anniversary Towers, University Way, POB 45371, Nairobi; tel. (20) 222072; e-mail eck@eck.or.ke; internet www.eck.or.ke; independent; Chair. SAMUEL KIVUITU.

Political Organizations

Chama Cha Uma (CCU): Nairobi; Leader DAVID NG'ETHE.

Dawa Ya Wakenya (Remedy for Kenya): f. 2007 by politicians from the North-Eastern region and the north of the Rift Valley to defend the rights of the inhabitants of those areas and to campaign for improved infrastructure, social services and security; Chair. HASSAN HAJI; Gen. Sec. MORU SHAMBARU.

Democratic Party of Kenya (DP): Gitanga Rd, POB 53695, 00200 Nairobi; tel. and fax (20) 3873595; e-mail info@democraticparty.co.ke; internet www.democraticparty.co.ke; f. 1991; Chair. MWAI KIBAKI; Sec. JOSEPH MUNYAO; rival faction led by NGENGI MUIGAI.

Forum for the Restoration of Democracy—Asili (FORD—Asili): Anyany Estate, POB 72595, Nairobi; f. 1992; Chair. GEORGE NTHENGE; Sec. MARTIN J. SHIKUKU.

Forum for the Restoration of Democracy—Kenya (FORD—Kenya): Odinga House, POB 57449, Nairobi; tel. (20) 570361; internet www.fordkenya.com; f. 1992; predominantly Luo support; Chair. MUSIKARI KOMBO.

Forum for the Restoration of Democracy for the People (FORD—People): Nairobi; f. 1997 by fmr mems of FORD—Asili; Leader SIMEON NYACHAE.

Growth and Development Party of Kenya (GDP): Nairobi; e-mail info@gdp.co.ke; internet www.gdp.co.ke; f. 2007; Chair. AURELIO REBELO.

Kenya African National Union (KANU): KICC POB 72394, Nairobi; tel. (20) 332383; internet www.kanuonline.com; f. 1960 as KANU; sole legal party 1982–91; absorbed the National Development Party (f. 1994) in 2002; Chair. UHURU KENYATTA.

Kenya National Congress (KNC): POB 9474, Nairobi; f. 1992; Chair. Prof. KATANA MKANGI; Sec.-Gen. ONESMUS MUSYOKA MBALI.

Kenya National Democratic Alliance (KENDA): Wetithe House, Nkrumah St, POB 1851, Thika; tel. (151) 562304; f. 1991; Chair. KAMLESH PATTNI (acting); Sec.-Gen. BERNARD KALOVE.

Kenya Social Congress (KSC): POB 55318, Nairobi; f. 1992; Chair. GEORGE MOSETI ANYONA; Sec.-Gen. KASHINI MALOBA FAFNA.

Labour Party Democracy: POB 7905, Nairobi; Chair. GEOFFREY MBURU; Sec. DAVID MBURI NGACHURA.

Liberal Democratic Party (LDP): Nairobi; f. 2002 by fmr mems of KANU; Chair. DAVID MUSHA; Sec.-Gen. J. J. KAMOTHO.

Liberal Party: Chair. WANGARI MAATHAI.

Mazingira Party of Kenya (MPK): f. 2007; campaigns for the equitable sharing of wealth, sustainable use of natural resources, women's rights and the defence of Kenyan cultural values; Leader WANGARI MAATHAI; Chair. MWANGI MAKANGA.

National Party of Kenya (NPK): Nairobi; internet nationalpartyofkenya.org; f. 1992; Chair. CHARITY KALUKI NGILU; Sec.-Gen. FIDELIS MWEKE.

National Rainbow Coalition (NARC): Mwenge House, Ole Odume Rd, off Gitanga Rd and near Methodist Guest House, Nairobi; tel. (20) 571506; f. 2002; Chair. CHARITY NGILU KALUKI.

National Rainbow Coalition—Kenya (NARC—Kenya): Woodland Rd, off Lenana Rd. Kilimani; POB 34200-00100, Nairobi; tel. (20) 2726783; fax (20) 2726786; e-mail info@narckenya.co.ke; internet www.narckenya.or.ke; f. 2005 by former mems of NARC; Chair. RAPHAEL TUJU; Sec.-Gen. Dr MUKHISA KITUYI.

New FORD—Kenya: Nairobi; f. 2007; Chair. SOITA SHITANDA.

New Kenya African National Union (New—KANU): Nairobi; f. 2006 by former members of KANU; Pres. NICHOLAS BIWOTT.

Orange Democratic Movement (ODM): POB 2478, 00202 Nairobi; tel. (720) 360934; e-mail info@odm07.com; internet www.odm07.com; f. 2005; split in August 2007; rival faction led by STEPHEN KALONZO MUSYOKA; Leader RAILA AMOLO ODINGA.

Orange Democratic Movement—Kenya (ODM—Kenya): Nairobi; e-mail odmk2007@yahoo.com; internet odmk.org; f. 2007 following split in the ODM; Leader STEPHEN KALONZO MUSYOKA.

Party of Independent Candidates of Kenya (PICK): Plot No 299/096 Kenyatta Ave, POB 21821, Nairobi; Chair. G. N. MUSYIMI; Sec. F. NGUGI.

Party of National Unity (PNU): Nairobi; internet www.pnuparty.com; f. 2007; coalition of 14 parties including: KANU, the SPK, the SKS, Safina, NARC—Kenya, the DP, New FORD—Kenya, FORD—People, FORD—Asili, FORD—Kenya and the MPK; Chair. MWAI KIBAKI.

Patriotic Pastoralist Alliance of Kenya: f. 1997; represents the interests of northern Kenyan pastoralist communities; Leaders KHALIF ABDULLAHI, IBRAHIM WOCHE, JACKSON LAISAGOR.

People's Alliance for Change in Kenya (PACK): Nairobi; f. 1999; aims to unite diverse ethnic groups; Sec.-Gen. OLANG SANA.

Safina ('Noah's Ark'): POB 135, Nairobi; f. 1995; aims to combat corruption and human rights abuses and to introduce proportional representation; Chair. CLEMENT MUTURI KIGANO; Sec.-Gen. MWANDAWIRO MGHANGA.

Shirikisho Party of Kenya (SPK): POB 70421, Nairobi; f. 1997; Sec.-Gen. YUSUF MAHMOUD ABOUBAKAR.

Sisi Kwa Sisi (SKS): Nairobi; f. 2001; Leader JOHN RUKENYA KABUGUA.

Social Democratic Party of Kenya (SDP): POB 55845, Nairobi; tel. (20) 260309; f. 1992; Chair. JUSTUS NYAGAYA; Sec.-Gen. Dr APOLLO LUGANO NJONJO.

United Agri Party of Kenya: f. 2001; Chair. GEORGE KINYUA; Sec.-Gen. SIMON MITOBIO.

United Democratic Movement: Nairobi; Chair. KIPRUTO RONO ARAP KIRWA; Sec.-Gen. STEPHEN TARUS.

United Patriotic Party of Kenya: POB 115, Athi River; Chair. JOSEPHAT GATHUA GATHIGA; Sec. MICHAEL NJUGUNA KIGANYA.

The following organizations are banned:

February Eighteen Resistance Army: believed to operate from Uganda; Leader Brig. JOHN ODONGO (also known as STEPHEN AMOKE).

Islamic Party of Kenya (IPK): Mombasa; f. 1992; Islamic fundamentalist; Chair. Sheikh KHALIFA MUHAMMAD (acting); Sec.-Gen. ABDULRAHMAN WANDATI.

Diplomatic Representation

EMBASSIES AND HIGH COMMISSIONS IN KENYA

Algeria: 37 Muthaiga Rd, POB 53902, Nairobi; tel. (20) 310440; fax (20) 310450; e-mail algerianembassy@mitsuminett.com; Ambassador MUHAMMAD-HACENE ECHARIF.

Argentina: Posta Sacco, 6th Floor, University Way, POB 30283, 00100 Nairobi; tel. (20) 339949; fax (20) 217693; e-mail argentina@form-net.com; Ambassador DANIEL CHUBURU.

Australia: ICIPE House, Riverside Dr., off Chiromo Rd, POB 39341, Nairobi; tel. (20) 445034; fax (20) 444718; internet www.kenya.embassy.gov.au; High Commissioner LISA FILIPETTO.

Austria: City House, 2nd Floor, Wabera St, POB 30560, 00100 Nairobi; tel. (20) 319076; fax (20) 342290; e-mail nairobi-ob@bmeia.gv.at; internet www.aussenministerium.at/nairobi; Ambassador ROLAND HAUSER.

Bangladesh: Lenana Rd, POB 41645, Nairobi; tel. (20) 562816; fax (20) 562817; High Commissioner YAKUB ALI.

Belgium: Muthaiga, Limuru Rd, POB 30461, Nairobi; tel. (20) 741564; fax (20) 442701; e-mail nairobi@diplobel.be; internet www.diplomatie.be/nairobi; Ambassador LEO WILLEMS.

Brazil: Tanar Center, UN Crescent Rd, UN Close, Gigiri, Nairobi; tel. (20) 7125765; fax (20) 7125767; Ambassador JOAQUIM AUGUSTO WHITAKER SALLES.

Burundi: Development House, 14th Floor, Moi Ave, POB 44439, Nairobi; tel. (20) 575113; fax (20) 219005; Ambassador JEREMIE NGENDAKUMANA.

Canada: Limuru Rd, POB 1013, 00621 Gigiri, Nairobi; tel. (20) 3663000; fax (20) 3663900; e-mail nrobi@international.gc.ca; High Commissioner ROSS HYNES.

Chile: Riverside Dr. 66, Riverside, POB 45554, 00100 Nairobi; tel. (20) 4452950; fax (20) 4443209; e-mail echile@echile.co.ke; Ambassador GAETE VIDAL PABLO RODRIGO.

China, People's Republic: Woodlands Rd, Kilimani District, POB 30508, Nairobi; tel. (20) 2722559; fax (20) 2726402; e-mail chinaemb_ke@mfa.gov.cn; internet ke.china-embassy.org; Ambassador ZHANG MING.

Colombia: International House, 6th Floor, Mam Ngina St, POB 48494, 00100 Nairobi; tel. (20) 246770; fax (20) 246771; e-mail enairobi@cancilleria.gov.co; Ambassador MARÍA VICTORIA DÍAZ DE SUÁREZ.

Congo, Democratic Republic: Electricity House, Harambee Ave, POB 48106, 00100 Nairobi; tel. (20) 2229772; fax (20) 3754253; e-mail ambardckenyal@yahoo.com; Ambassador TADUMI ON'OKOKO.

Cuba: International House, Mama Ngina St, 13th Floor, POB 41931, Nairobi; tel. (20) 241003; fax (20) 241023; e-mail embacuba@swiftkenya.com; Ambassador JULIO CÉSAR GONZÁLEZ MARCHANTE.

Cyprus: Eagle House, 5th Floor, Kimathi St, POB 30739, 00100 Nairobi; tel. (20) 220881; fax (20) 312202; e-mail cyphc@nbnet.co.ke; High Commissioner VASSOS CHAMBERLEN.

Czech Republic: Jumia Pl., Lenana Rd, POB 48785, 00100 Nairobi; tel. (20) 2731010; fax (20) 2731013; e-mail nairobi@embassy.mzv.cz; internet www.mzv.cz/nairobi; Ambassador PETER KOPŌIVA.

Denmark: Cassia House, Westlands Office Park, POB 40412, 00100 Nairobi; tel. (20) 4451460; fax (20) 4451474; e-mail nboamb@um.dk; internet www.ambnairobi.um.dk; Ambassador BO JENSEN.

Djibouti: Comcraft House, 2nd Floor, Haile Selassie Ave, POB 59528, Nairobi; tel. (20) 339640; Ambassador ADEN HOUSSEIN ABDILLAHI.

Egypt: Kingara Rd, Lavington, POB 30285, Nairobi; tel. (20) 570360; fax (20) 570383; Ambassador SAHER HASANEEN TAWFEEK HAMZA.

Eritrea: New Rehema House, 2nd Floor, Westlands, POB 38651, Nairobi; tel. (20) 443164; fax (20) 443165; e-mail eriembk@africaonline.co.ke; Ambassador SALIH OMAR ABDU.

Ethiopia: State House Ave, POB 45198, Nairobi; tel. and fax (20) 2732054; Ambassador DISSASA DIRBISSA WINSA.

Finland: International House, 2nd Floor, Mama Ngina St, POB 30379, 00100 Nairobi; tel. (20) 334777; fax (20) 335986; Ambassador HELI SIRVE.

France: Barclays Plaza, 9th Floor, Loita St, POB 41784, Nairobi; tel. (20) 2778000; fax (20) 2778180; e-mail ambafrance.nairobi@diplomatie.gouv.fr; internet www.ambafrance-ke.org; Ambassador ELIZABETH BARBIER.

Germany: Ludwig Krapf House, Riverside Dr. 113, POB 30180, Nairobi; tel. (20) 4262100; fax (20) 4262129; e-mail info@nairobi.diplo.de; internet www.nairobi.diplo.de; Ambassador WALTER JOHANNES LINDNER.

Greece: Nation Centre, 13th Floor, Kimathi St, POB 30543, Nairobi; tel. (20) 340722; fax (20) 216044; e-mail embgr@kenyaweb.com; Ambassador IOANNIS KORINTHIOS.

Holy See: Apostolic Nunciature, Manyani Rd West, Waiyaki Way, POB 14326, 00800 Nairobi; tel. (20) 4442975; fax (20) 4446789; e-mail nunciokenya@nunciokenya.org; Apostolic Nuncio Most Rev. ALAIN PAUL CHARLES LEBEAUPIN (Titular Archbishop of Vico Equense).

Hungary: Kabarsiran Ave, off James Gichuru Rd, Lavington, POB 61146, Nairobi; tel. (20) 560060; fax (20) 560114; e-mail huembnai@africaonline.co.ke; internet www.mfa.gov.hu/kulkepviselet/KE/en/; Ambassador GÁBOR SÁGI.

India: Jeevan Bharati Bldg, 2nd Floor, Harambee Ave, POB 30074, Nairobi; tel. (20) 225104; fax (20) 316242; e-mail hcindia@kenyaweb.com; internet www.hcinairobi.co.ke; High Commissioner PARAMPREET SINGH RANDHAWA.

Indonesia: Menengai Rd, Upper Hill, POB 48868, Nairobi; tel. (20) 2714196; fax (20) 2713475; e-mail indonbi@indonesia.or.ke; internet www.indonesia.or.ke; Ambassador DJISMUN KASRI.

Iran: Dennis Pritt Rd, POB 49170, Nairobi; tel. (20) 711257; fax (20) 339936; Ambassador MOHAMMAD RAESI.

KENYA

Directory

Israel: Bishop's Rd, POB 30354, Nairobi; tel. (20) 2722182; fax (20) 2715966; e-mail info@nairobi.mfa.gov.il; internet nairobi.mfa.gov.il; Ambassador EMMANUEL SERI.

Italy: International House, 9th Floor, Mama Ngina St, POB 30107, Nairobi; tel. (20) 247750; fax (20) 247086; e-mail ambasciata.nairobi@esteri.it; internet www.ambnairobi.esteri.it; Ambassador PIERANDREA MAGISTRATI.

Japan: Mara Rd, Upper Hill, POB 60202, Nairobi; tel. (20) 2898000; fax (20) 2898220; e-mail jinfocul@eojkenya.org; internet www.ke.emb-japan.go.jp; Ambassador SATORU MIYAMURA.

Korea, Republic: Anniversary Towers, 15th Floor, University Way, POB 30455, Nairobi; tel. (20) 333581; fax (20) 217772; e-mail emb-ke@mofat.go.kr; Ambassador YUM KI-SYUB.

Kuwait: Muthaiga Rd, POB 42353, Nairobi; tel. (20) 761614; fax (20) 762837; Chargé d'affaires a.i. JABER SALEM HUSSAIN EBRAHEEM.

Lesotho: Nairobi; tel. (20) 224876; fax (20) 337493; High Commissioner (vacant).

Mexico: Kibagare Way, off Loresho Ridge, POB 14145, Nairobi; tel. (20) 4182593; fax (20) 4181500; e-mail mexico@embamexken.com; Ambassador JUAN CARLOS CUE VEGA.

Morocco: Diamond Trust House, 3rd Floor, Moi Ave, POB 61098, Nairobi; tel. (20) 710647; fax (20) 222364; Ambassador ABDELILAH BENRYANE.

Mozambique: Bruce House, 3rd Floor, Standard St, POB 66923, Nairobi; tel. (20) 221979; fax (20) 222446; High Commissioner MARCOS NAMACHULUA; (temporarily closed in January 2008).

Netherlands: Riverside Lane, off Riverside Dr., POB 41537, Nairobi; tel. (20) 4288000; fax (20) 4447416; e-mail nlgovnai@africaonline.co.ke; internet www.netherlands-embassy.or.ke; Ambassador MARIA ALICE CRISPINA VAN DEN ASSUM.

Nigeria: Lenana Rd, Hurlingham, POB 30516, Nairobi; tel. (20) 564116; fax (20) 564117; High Commissioner N. TAPGUN.

Norway: Lion Pl., 1st Floor, Wayiaki Way, POB 46363, 00100 Nairobi; tel. (20) 4251000; fax (20) 4451517; e-mail emb.nairobi@mfa.no; internet www.norway.or.ke; Ambassador ELISABETH JACOBSEN.

Pakistan: St Michel Rd, Westlands Ave, POB 30045, 00100 Nairobi; tel. (20) 4443911; fax (20) 4446507; e-mail parepnairobi@iwayafrica.com; internet www.pakistanafrica.org; High Commissioner IFTIKHAR A. ARIAN.

Poland: Kabarnet Rd, off Ngong Rd, Woodley, POB 30086, 00100 Nairobi; tel. (20) 3872811; fax (20) 3872814; e-mail ambnairo@kenyaweb.com; internet www.nairobi.polemb.net; Ambassador WOJCIECH JASINSKI.

Portugal: Reinsurance Plaza, 10th Floor, Aga Khan Walk, POB 34020, 00100 Nairobi; tel. (20) 313203; fax (20) 214711; e-mail embassy.nairobi@portugal.co.ke; Ambassador LUIS LORUÁO.

Romania: Gardenia Rd, Gigiri, POB 63240, Nairobi; tel. (20) 7123109; fax (20) 7122061; e-mail secretariat@romanianembassy.co.ke; Ambassador MIHAIL CONSTANTIN COMAN.

Russia: Lenana Rd, POB 30049, Nairobi; tel. (20) 728700; fax (20) 721888; e-mail russemb@swiftkenya.com; Ambassador VALERY YEGOSHKIN.

Rwanda: International House, 12th Floor, Mama Ngina St, POB 48579, Nairobi; tel. (20) 560178; fax (20) 561932; Ambassador GEORGE WILLIAM KAYONGA.

Saudi Arabia: Muthaiga Rd, POB 58297, Nairobi; tel. (20) 762781; fax (20) 760939; Ambassador NBEEL KHALAF A. ASHOUR.

Slovakia: Milimani Rd, POB 30204, Nairobi; tel. (20) 721896; fax (20) 721898; Ambassador STEFAN MORAVEK.

Somalia: POB 30769, Nairobi; tel. (20) 580165; fax (20) 581683; Ambassador MOHAMMED ALI NUR.

South Africa: Roshanmaer Place, Lenana Rd, POB 42441, Nairobi; tel. (20) 2827100; fax (20) 2827219; e-mail sahc@africaonline.co.ke; High Commissioner TONY MSIMANGA.

Spain: International House, 3rd Floor, Mama Ngina St, POB 45503, 00100 Nairobi; tel. (20) 226568; fax (20) 332858; Ambassador NICOLÁS MARTÍN CINTO.

Sri Lanka: Lenana Rd, POB 48145 GPO, Nairobi; tel. (20) 572627; fax (20) 572141; e-mail slhckeny@africaonline.co.ke; internet www.lk/dipmissionf.html; High Commissioner HABEEB MOHAMMED FAROOK.

Sudan: Minet-ICDC Bldg, 7th Floor, Mamlaka Rd, POB 48784, Nairobi; tel. (20) 720853; fax (20) 721015; Ambassador OMER EL-SHEIKH.

Swaziland: Transnational Plaza, 3rd Floor, Mama Ngina St, POB 41887, Nairobi; tel. (20) 339231; fax (20) 330540; High Commissioner Prince SOLOMON MBILINI N. DLAMINI.

Sweden: Lion Pl., 3rd Floor, Waiyaki Way, Westlands, POB 30600, 00100 Nairobi; tel. (20) 4234000; fax (20) 4452008; e-mail ambassaden.nairobi@foreign.ministry.se; internet www.swedenabroad.com/nairobi; Ambassador ANNA BRANDT.

Switzerland: International House, 7th Floor, Mama Ngina St, POB 30752, Nairobi; tel. (20) 228735; fax (20) 217388; e-mail nai.vertretung@eda.admin.ch; Ambassador GEORGE MARTIN.

Tanzania: Continental House, Uhuru Highway, POB 47790, Nairobi; tel. (20) 331056; fax (20) 218269; e-mail tanzania@user.africaonline.co.ke; High Commissioner Maj.-Gen. MIRISHO SAM HAGGAI SARAKIKYA.

Thailand: Ambassador House, Rose Ave, POB 58349, Nairobi; tel. (20) 2715243; fax (20) 2715801; e-mail thainbi@thainbi.or.ke; internet www.thaiembassy.org/nairobi; Ambassador APICHIT ASATTHAWASI.

Turkey: Gigiri Rd, off Limuru Rd, POB 64748, 00620 Nairobi; tel. and fax (20) 7120404; fax (20) 7122778; e-mail tcbenair@accesskenya.com; internet www.turkishembassy.or.ke; Ambassador LEVENT ŞAHINKAYA.

Uganda: Uganda House, 5th Floor, Kenyatta Ave, POB 60853, Nairobi; tel. (20) 4449096; fax (20) 4443772; High Commissioner Brig. (retd) MATAYO KYALIGONZA.

United Kingdom: Upper Hill Rd, POB 30465, 00100 Nairobi; tel. (20) 2844000; fax (20) 2844033; e-mail bhcinfo@jambo.co.ke; internet www.britishhighcommission.gov.uk/kenya; High Commissioner ADAM WOOD.

USA: United Nations Ave, POB 606, Village Market, 00621 Nairobi; tel. (20) 3636000; fax (20) 537810; e-mail ircnairobi@state.gov; internet nairobi.usembassy.gov; Ambassador MICHAEL E. RANNEBERGER.

Venezuela: Ngong/Kabarnet Rd, POB 34477, Nairobi; tel. (20) 574646; fax (20) 337487; e-mail embavene@africaonline.co.ke; Ambassador MARÍA JACQUELINE MENDOZA.

Yemen: cnr Ngong and Kabarnet Rds, POB 44642, Nairobi; tel. (20) 564379; fax (20) 564394; Ambassador AHMAD MAYSARI.

Zambia: Nyerere Rd, POB 48741, Nairobi; tel. (20) 724850; fax (20) 718494; High Commissioner ENESS CHISHALA CHIYENGE.

Zimbabwe: Minet-ICDC Bldg, 6th Floor, Mamlaka Rd, POB 30806, Nairobi; tel. (20) 721071; fax (20) 726503; Ambassador KELEBERT NKOMANI.

Judicial System

The Kenya Court of Appeal

POB 30187, Nairobi.

The final court of appeal for Kenya in civil and criminal process; sits at Nairobi, Mombasa, Kisumu, Nakuru and Nyeri.

Chief Justice: JOHNSON EVANS GICHERU.

Justices of Appeal: MATHEW MULI, J. M. GACHUHI, J. R. O. MASIME, SAMUEL BOSIRE, R. O. KWACH, EFFIE OWUOR.

The High Court of Kenya: Between Taifa Rd and City Hall Way, POB 30041, Nairobi; tel. (20) 221221; e-mail hck-lib@nbnet.co.ke; has unlimited criminal and civil jurisdiction at first instance, and sits as a court of appeal from subordinate courts in both criminal and civil cases. The High Court is also a court of admiralty. There are three resident puisne judges at Mombasa and at Nakuru, two resident puisne judge at Eldoret, Kisumu and Meru and one resident puisne judge at Bungoma, Embu, Kakamega, Kissi, Kitale, Machakos, Malindi and Nyeri.

Resident Magistrates' Courts: have country-wide jurisdiction, with powers of punishment by imprisonment for up to five years or by fines of up to K£500. If presided over by a chief magistrate or senior resident magistrate the court is empowered to pass any sentence authorized by law. For certain offences, a resident magistrate may pass minimum sentences authorized by law.

District Magistrates' Courts: of first, second and third class; have jurisdiction within districts and powers of punishment by imprisonment for up to five years, or by fines of up to K£500.

Kadhi's Courts: have jurisdiction within districts, to determine questions of Islamic law.

Religion

According to official government figures, Protestants, the largest religious group, represent approximately 38% of the population. Approximately 25% of the population is Roman Catholic, 7% of the population practices Islam, 1% practices Hinduism and the remainder follows various traditional indigenous religions or offshoots of Christian religions. There are very few atheists. Muslim groups dispute government estimates; most often they claim to represent

KENYA

15% to 20% of the population, sometimes higher. Members of most religious groups are active throughout the country, although certain religions dominate particular regions. Muslims dominate North-Eastern Province, where the population is chiefly Somali. Muslims also dominate Coast Province, except for the western areas of the province, which are predominantly Christian. Eastern Province is approximately 50% Muslim (mostly in the north) and 50% Christian (mostly in the south). The rest of the country is largely Christian, with some persons following traditional indigenous religions. Many foreign missionary groups operate in the country, the largest of which are the African Inland Mission (Evangelical Protestant), the Southern Baptist Church, the Pentecostal Assembly of Kenya, and the Church Missionary Society of Britain (Anglican). The Government generally has permitted these missionary groups to assist the poor and to operate schools and hospitals. The missionaries openly promote their religious beliefs and have encountered little resistance.

CHRISTIANITY

National Council of Churches of Kenya: Church House, Moi Ave, POB 45009, Nairobi; tel. (20) 242278; fax (20) 224463; f. 1943 as Christian Council of Kenya; 35 full mems and eight assoc. mems; Chair. Rev. JOSEPH WAITHONGA; Sec.-Gen. Rev. MUTAVA MUSYIMI.

The Anglican Communion

Anglicans are adherents of the Church of the Province of Kenya, which was established in 1970. It comprises 28 dioceses, and has about 2.5m. members.

Archbishop of Kenya and Bishop of Nairobi: Most Rev. Dr DAVID M. GITARI, POB 40502, Nairobi; tel. (20) 2714755; fax (20) 2718442; e-mail davidgitari@insightkenya.com.

Greek Orthodox Church

Archbishop of East Africa: NICADEMUS OF IRINOUPOULIS, Nairobi; jurisdiction covers Kenya, Tanzania and Uganda.

The Roman Catholic Church

Kenya comprises four archdioceses, 20 dioceses and one Apostolic Vicariate. At 31 December 2005 an estimated 24.9% of the total population were adherents of the Roman Catholic Church.

Kenya Episcopal Conference

Kenya Catholic Secretariat, POB 13475, Nairobi; tel. (20) 443133; fax (20) 442910; e-mail csk@users.africaonline.co.ke; internet www.catholicchurch.or.ke.

f. 1976; Pres. Rt Rev. CORNELIUS K. ARAP KORIR (Bishop of Eldoret).

Archbishop of Kisumu: Most Rev. ZACCHAEUS OKOTH, POB 1728, Kisumu; tel. (57) 2020725; fax (57) 2022203; e-mail archdiocese-ksm@net2000ke.com.

Archbishop of Mombasa: Most Rev. JOHN NJENGA, Catholic Secretariat, Nyerere Ave, POB 84425, Mombasa; tel. (41) 2311801; fax (41) 2228217; e-mail demsa@africaonline.co.ke.

Archbishop of Nairobi: Cardinal JOHN NJUE, Archbishop's House, POB 14231, 00800 Nairobi; tel. (20) 241391; fax (20) 4447027; e-mail nairobiprocure@wananchi.com.

Archbishop of Nyeri: Most Rev. NICODEMUS KIRIMA, POB 288, 10100 Nyeri; tel. (61) 2030446; fax (61) 2030505; e-mail adn@wananchi.com.

Other Christian Churches

Africa Inland Church in Kenya: Bishop Rev. Dr TITUS M. KIVUNZI.

African Christian Church and Schools: POB 1365, Thika; e-mail accsheadoffice@yahoo.com; f. 1948; Moderator Rt Rev. JOHN NJUNGUNA; Gen. Sec. Rev. SAMUEL MWANGI; 50,000 mems.

African Church of the Holy Spirit: POB 183, Kakamega; f. 1927; 20,000 mems.

African Israel Nineveh Church: Nineveh HQ, POB 701, Kisumu; f. 1942; High Priest Rt Rev. JOHN KIVULI, II; Gen. Sec. Rev. JOHN ARAP TONUI; 350,000 mems.

Baptist Convention of Kenya: POB 14907, Nairobi; Pres. Rev. ELIUD MUNGAI.

Church of God in East Africa: Pres. Rev. Dr BYRUM MAKOKHA.

Evangelical Fellowship of Kenya: Co-ordinator Rt Rev. ARTHUR GITONGA; Sec.-Gen. Dr WASHINGTON NG'ENG'I.

Evangelical Lutheran Church in Kenya: POB 874, Kisii; tel. (40) 31231; fax (40) 30475; e-mail elok@africaonline.co.ke; Bishop Rev. FRANCIS NYAMWARO ONDERI; 65,000 mems.

Methodist Church in Kenya: POB 47633, 00100 Nairobi; tel. (20) 2724828; fax (20) 2729790; e-mail mckconf@wananchi.com; f. 1862; autonomous since 1967; Presiding Bishop Rev. Dr STEPHEN KANYARU M'IMPWII; 900,000 mems (2005).

Presbyterian Church of East Africa: POB 27573, 00506 Nairobi; tel. (20) 608848; fax (20) 609102; e-mail info@pcea.or.ke; internet www.pcea.or.ke; Moderator Rt Rev. Dr DAVID GITHI; Sec.-Gen. Rev. SAMUEL MURIGYH.

Other denominations active in Kenya include the Africa Gospel Church, the African Brotherhood Church, the African Independent Pentecostal Church, the African Interior Church, the Episcopal Church of Kenya, the Free Pentecostal Fellowship of Kenya, the Full Gospel Churches of Kenya, the Lutheran Church in Kenya, the National Independent Church of Africa, the Pentecostal Assemblies of God, the Pentecostal Evangelistic Fellowship of God and the Reformed Church of East Africa.

BAHÁ'Í FAITH

National Spiritual Assembly: POB 47562, Nairobi; tel. (20) 725447; mems resident in 9,654 localities.

ISLAM

Supreme Council of Kenyan Muslims (SUPKEM)
POB 45163, Nairobi; tel. and fax (20) 243109; Nat. Chair. Prof. ABD AL-GHAFUR AL-BUSAIDY; Sec.-Gen. MOHAMMED KHALIF.

Chief Kadhi: NASSOR NAHDI.

The Press

PRINCIPAL DAILIES

Daily Nation: POB 49010, Nairobi; tel. (20) 2221222; fax (20) 2337710; e-mail nation@africaonline.co.ke; internet www.nationaudio.com; f. 1960; English; owned by Nation Media Group; Editor-in-Chief WANGETHI MWANGI; Man. Editor JOSEPH ODINDO; circ. 195,000.

East African Standard: POB 30080, Nairobi; tel. (20) 2540280; fax (20) 2553939; e-mail online@eastandard.net; internet www.eastandard.net; f. 1902; Editor MUTUMA MATHIY; circ. 59,000.

Kenya Leo: POB 30958, Nairobi; tel. (20) 332390; f. 1983; Kiswahili; KANU party newspaper; Group Editor-in-Chief AMBOKA ANDERE; circ. 6,000.

Kenya Times: POB 30958, Nairobi; tel. (20) 2336611; fax (20) 2927348; internet www.timesnews.co.uk; f. 1983; evening; English; KANU party newspaper; Group Editor-in-Chief AMBOKA ANDERE; circ. 10,000.

The People: POB 10296, 00100 Nairobi; tel. (20) 249686; fax (20) 253344; e-mail info@people.co.ke; internet www.people.co.ke; f. 1993; Man. Editor MUGO THEURI; circ. 40,000.

Taifa Leo: POB 49010, Nairobi; tel. (20) 337691; Kiswahili; f. 1960; daily and weekly edns; owned by Nation Media Group; Editor ROBERT MWANGI; circ. 57,000.

Kenya has a thriving vernacular press, but titles are often short-lived. Newspapers in African languages include:

Kihooto (The Truth): Kikuyu; satirical.

Mwaria Ma (Honest Speaker): Nyeri; f. 1997; Publr Canon JAMLICK M. MIANO.

Mwihoko (Hope): POB 734, Muranga; f. 1997; Roman Catholic.

Nam Dar: Luo.

Otit Mach (Firefly): Luo.

SELECTED PERIODICALS

Weeklies and Fortnightlies

The Business Chronicle: POB 53328, Nairobi; tel. (20) 544283; fax (20) 532736; f. 1994; weekly; Man. Editor MUSYOKA KYENDO.

Coastweek: Oriental Bldg, 2nd Floor, Nkrumah Rd, POB 87270, Mombasa; tel. (41) 2230125; fax (41) 2225003; e-mail coastwk@africaonline.co.ke; internet www.coastweek.com; f. 1978; English, with German section; Friday; Editor ADRIAN GRIMWOOD; Man. Dir SHIRAZ D. ALIBHAI; circ. 54,000.

The East African: POB 49010, Nairobi; tel. (20) 221222; fax (20) 2213946; e-mail nation@africaonline.co.ke; internet www.nationaudio.com/news/eastafrican/current; f. 1994; weekly; English; owned by Nation Media Group; Editor-in-Chief JOE ODINDO; Man. Editor MBATAU WA NGAI.

The Herald: POB 30958, Nairobi; tel. (20) 332390; English; sponsored by KANU; Editor JOB MUTUNGI; circ. 8,000.

Kenrail: POB 30121, Nairobi; tel. (20) 2221211; fax (20) 2340049; quarterly; English and Kiswahili; publ. by Kenya Railways Corpn; Editor J. N. LUSENO; circ. 20,000.

Kenya Gazette: POB 30746, Nairobi; tel. (20) 334075; f. 1898; official notices; weekly; circ. 8,000.

KENYA

Post on Sunday: Nairobi; weekly; independent; Editor-in-Chief TONY GACHOKA.

Sunday Nation: POB 49010, Nairobi; f. 1960; English; owned by Nation Media Group; Man. Editor BERNARD NDERITU; circ. 170,000.

Sunday Standard: POB 30080, Nairobi; tel. (20) 552510; fax (20) 553939; English; Man. Editor DAVID MAKALI; circ. 90,000.

Sunday Times: POB 30958, Nairobi; tel. (20) 337798; Group Editor AMBOKA ANDERE.

Taifa Jumapili: POB 49010, Nairobi; f. 1987; Kiswahili; owned by Nation Media Group; Editor ROBERT K. MWANGI; circ. 56,000.

Taifa Weekly: POB 49010, Nairobi; tel. (20) 337691; f. 1960; Kiswahili; Editor ROBERT K. MWANGI; circ. 68,000.

Trans Nzoia Post: POB 34, Kitale; weekly.

The Weekly Review: Stellacom House, POB 42271, Nairobi; tel. (20) 2251473; fax (20) 2222555; f. 1975; English; Man. Dir JAINDI KISERO; circ. 16,000.

What's On: Rehema House, Nairobi; tel. (20) 27651; Editor NANCY KAIRO; circ. 10,000.

Monthlies

Africa Law Review: Tumaini House, 4th Floor, Nkrumah Ave, POB 53234, Nairobi; tel. (20) 330480; fax (20) 230173; e-mail alr@africalaw.org; f. 1987; English; Editor-in-Chief GITOBU IMANYARA.

East African Medical Journal: POB 41632, 00100 Nairobi; tel. (20) 2712010; fax (20) 2724617; e-mail eamj@ken.healthnet.org; English; f. 1923; Editor-in-Chief Prof. WILLIAM LORE; circ. 4,500.

East African Report on Trade and Industry: POB 30339, Nairobi; journal of Kenya Asscn of Mfrs; Editor GORDON BOY; circ. 3,000.

Executive: POB 47186, Nairobi; tel. (20) 530598; fax (20) 557815; e-mail spacesellers@wananchi.com; f. 1980; business; Publr SYLVIA KING; circ. 25,000.

Kenya Farmer (Journal of the Agricultural Society of Kenya): c/o English Press, POB 30127, Nairobi; tel. (20) 20377; f. 1954; English and Kiswahili; Editor ROBERT IRUNGU; circ. 20,000.

Kenya Yetu: POB 8053, Nairobi; tel. (20) 250083; fax (20) 340659; f. 1965; Kiswahili; publ. by Ministry of Information and Communications; Editor M. NDAVI; circ. 10,000.

Nairobi Handbook: POB 30127, Accra Rd, Nairobi; Editor R. OUMA; circ. 20,000.

News from Kenya: POB 8053, Nairobi; tel. (20) 253083; fax (20) 340659; publ. by Ministry of Information and Communications.

PC World (East Africa): Gilgil House, Monrovia St, Nairobi; tel. (20) 246808; fax (20) 215643; f. 1996; Editor ANDREW KARANJA.

Presence: POB 10988, 00400 Nairobi; tel. (20) 577708; fax (20) 4948840; f. 1984; economics, law, women's issues, fiction.

Sparkle: POB 47186, Nairobi; tel. (20) 530598; fax (20) 557815; e-mail spacesellers@wananchi.com; f. 1990; children's; Editor ANNA NDILA NDUTO.

Today in Africa: POB 60, Kijabe; tel. (25) 64210; English; Man. Editor MWAURA NJOROGE; circ. 13,000.

Other Periodicals

African Ecclesiastical Review: POB 4002, 30100 Eldoret; tel. (53) 2061218; fax (53) 2062570; e-mail gabapubs@africaonline.co.ke; internet www.gabapublications.org; f. 1969; scripture, religion and devt; 4 a year; Editor and Dir Sister JUSTIN C. NABUSHAWO; circ. 2,500.

Afya: POB 30125, Nairobi; tel. (20) 501301; fax (20) 506112; e-mail amrefkco@africaonline.co.ke; journal for medical and health workers; quarterly.

Azania: POB 30710, 00100 Nairobi; tel. (20) 4343190; fax (20) 4343365; f. 1966; annual (Dec.); English and French; history, archaeology, ethnography and linguistics of East African region; circ. 650.

Busara: Nairobi; literary; 2 a year; Editor KIMANI GECAU; circ. 3,000.

Defender: AMREF, POB 30125, Nairobi; tel. (20) 201301; f. 1968; quarterly; English; health and fitness; Editor WILLIAM OKEDI; circ. 100,000.

East African Agricultural and Forestry Journal: POB 30148, Nairobi; f. 1935; English; quarterly; Editor J. O. MUGAH; circ. 1,000.

Eastern African Economic Review: POB 30022, Nairobi; f. 1954; 2 a year; Editor J. K. MAITHA.

Economic Review of Agriculture: POB 30028, Nairobi; tel. (20) 728370; f. 1968; publ. by Ministry of Agriculture; quarterly; last issue 1999; Editor OKIYA OKOITI.

Education in Eastern Africa: Nairobi; f. 1970; 2 a year; Editor JOHN C. B. BIGALA; circ. 2,000.

Finance: Nairobi; monthly; Editor-in-Chief NJEHU GATABAKI.

Inside Kenya Today: POB 8053, Nairobi; tel. (20) 340010; fax (20) 340659; English; publ. by Ministry of Tourism; quarterly; Editor M. NDAVI; circ. 10,000.

Kenya Education Journal: Nairobi; f. 1958; English; 3 a year; Editor W. G. BOWMAN; circ. 5,500.

Kenya Statistical Digest: POB 30007, Nairobi; tel. (20) 338111; fax (20) 330426; publ. by Ministry of Finance; quarterly.

Safari: Norwich Bldg, 4th Floor, Mama Ngina St, POB 30339, Nairobi; tel. (20) 2246612; fax (20) 2215127; 6 a year; English.

Target: POB 72839, Nairobi; f. 1964; English; 6 a year; religious; Editor FRANCIS MWANIKI; circ. 17,000.

NEWS AGENCY

Kenya News Agency (KNA): Information House, POB 8053, Nairobi; tel. (20) 223201; internet www.kenyanewsagency.go.ke; f. 1963; Dir S. MUSANDU.

Publishers

Academy Science Publishers: POB 24916, Nairobi; tel. (20) 884401; fax (20) 884406; e-mail asp@africaonline.co.ke; f. 1989; part of the African Academy of Sciences; Editor-in-Chief Prof. KETO E. MSHIGENI.

Amecea Gaba Publications: Amecea Pastoral Institute, POB 4002, 30100 Eldoret; tel. (53) 2061218; fax (53) 2062570; e-mail gabapubs@africaonline.co.ke; internet www.gabapublications.org; f. 1989; anthropology, religious; Editor and Dir Sister JUSTIN C. NABUSHAWO.

Camerapix Publishers International: POB 45048, GPO 00100, Nairobi; tel. (20) 4448923; fax (20) 4448818; e-mail rukhsana@camerapix.co.ke; internet www.camerapix.com; f. 1960; travel, topography, natural history; Man. Dir RUKHSANA HAQ.

East African Educational Publishers: cnr Mpaka Rd and Woodvale Grove, Westlands, POB 45314, Nairobi; tel. (20) 222057; fax (20) 448753; e-mail eaep@africaonline.co.ke; internet www.eastafricanpublishers.com; f. 1965 as Heinemann Kenya Ltd; present name adopted 1992; academic, educational, creative writing; some books in Kenyan languages; Man. Dir and Chief Exec. HENRY CHAKAVA.

Evangel Publishing House: Lumumba Drive, off Kamiti Rd, Thika Rd, Private Bag 28963, 00200 Nairobi; tel. (20) 8560839; fax (20) 8562050; e-mail info@evangelpublishing.org; internet www.evangelpublishing.org; f. 1952; Christian literature; current backlist of about 300 titles; marriage and family, leadership, Theological Education by Extension (TEE); Gen. Man. BARINE A. KIRIMI.

Foundation Books: Nairobi; tel. (20) 765485; f. 1974; biography, poetry; Man. Dir F. O. OKWANYA.

Kenway Publications Ltd: POB 45314, Nairobi; tel. (20) 444700; fax (20) 4451532; e-mail sales@eastafricanpublishers.com; internet www.eastafricanpublishers.com/kenway/defult.htm; f. 1981; general, regional interests; Chair. HENRY CHAKAVA.

Kenya Literature Bureau: Bellevue Area, off Mombasa Rd, POB 30022, 00100 Nairobi; tel. (20) 600839; fax (20) 601474; e-mail customer@kenyaliteraturebureau.com; f. 1947; educational and general books; CEO M. A. KARAURI.

Jomo Kenyatta Foundation: Industrial Area, Enterprise Rd, POB 30533, 00100 Nairobi; tel. (20) 557222; fax (20) 531966; e-mail publish@jomokenyattaf.com; internet www.jkf.co.ke; f. 1966; primary, secondary, university textbooks; Man. Dir NANCY W. KARIMI.

Longman Kenya Ltd: Banda School, Magadi Rd, POB 24722, Nairobi; tel. (20) 891220; fax (20) 890004; f. 1966.

Macmillan Kenya Publishers Ltd: Judda Complex, Forest Rd, POB 30797, 00100 Nairobi; tel. (20) 6766962; fax (20) 6766963; e-mail info@macken.co.ke; f. 1970; atlases, children's educational, guide books, literature; Man. Dir DAVID MUITA.

Newspread International: POB 46854, Nairobi; tel. (20) 331402; fax (20) 607252; f. 1971; reference, economic devt; Exec. Editor KUL BHUSHAN.

Oxford University Press (Eastern Africa): Waiyaki Way, ABC Place, POB 72532, Nairobi; tel. (20) 440555; fax (20) 443972; f. 1954; children's, educational and general; Regional Man. ABDULLAH ISMAILY.

Paulines Publications Africa: POB 49026, 00100 Nairobi; tel. (20) 447202; fax (20) 442097; e-mail publications@paulinesafrica.org; internet www.paulinesafrica.org; f. 1985; African bible, theology, children's, educational; religious, psychology, audio cds, tapes, videos; Pres. Sister MARIA KIMANI; Dir Sister TERESA MARCAZZAN.

Transafrica Press: Kenwood House, Kimathi St, POB 48239, Nairobi; tel. (20) 331762; f. 1976; general, educational and children's; Man. Dir JOHN NOTTINGHAM.

KENYA

GOVERNMENT PUBLISHING HOUSE

Government Printing Press: POB 30128, Nairobi; tel. (20) 317840.

PUBLISHERS' ORGANIZATION

Kenya Publishers' Association: POB 42767, 00100 Nairobi; tel. (20) 3752344; fax (20) 3754076; internet www.kenyabooks.org; f. 1971; organizes Nairobi International Book Fair each Sept.; Chair. DAVID MUITA.

Broadcasting and Communications

TELECOMMUNICATIONS

Celtel: Parkside Towers, Mombasa Rd, Nairobi; tel. (20) 6910000; e-mail customercare@ke.celtel.com; internet www.ke.celtel.com; f. 2004; mobile cellular telephone network provider; subsidiary of Celtel International; CEO DAVID MURRAY.

KenCell Communications Ltd: Parkside Towers, City Sq., Mombasa Rd, POB 73146, 00200 Nairobi; e-mail info@kencell.co.ke; internet www.kencell.co.ke; f. 2000; operates a national mobile cellular telephone network; Man. Dir and CEO PHILLIPE VANDEBROUCK.

Telkom Kenya Ltd: Telposta Towers, Kenyatta Ave, POB 30301, Nairobi; tel. (20) 227401; fax (20) 251071; e-mail md@telkom.co.ke; f. 1999; 51% owned by France Telecom; operates a national fixed telephone network; Man. Dir SAMMY KIRUI.

Safaricom Ltd: Safaricom House, Waiyaki Way, Westlands, POB 46350, Nairobi; e-mail info@safaricom.co.ke; internet www.safaricom.co.ke; f. 1999; owned by Telkom Kenya Ltd and Vodafone Airtouch (UK); operates a national mobile cellular telephone network; Gen. Man. and CEO MICHAEL JOSEPH.

Regulatory Authority

Communications Commission of Kenya (CCK): Kijabe St, Longonot Place, POB 14448, Nairobi; tel. (20) 240165; fax (20) 252547; e-mail info@cck.go.ke; internet www.cck.go.ke; f. 1999; Dir-Gen. and Chief Exec. SAMUEL K. CHEPKONG'A.

BROADCASTING

Radio

Kenya Broadcasting Corpn (KBC): Broadcasting House, Harry Thuku Rd, POB 30456, Nairobi; tel. (20) 334567; fax (20) 220675; e-mail kbc@swiftkenya.com; internet www.kbc.co.ke; f. 1989; state corpn responsible for radio and television services; Chair. Dr JULIUS KIANO; Man. Dir JOE M. KHAMISI.

  Radio: National service (Kiswahili); General service (English); Vernacular services (Borana, Burji, Hindustani, Kalenjin, Kikamba, Kikuyu, Kimasai, Kimeru, Kisii, Kuria, Luo, Luhya, Rendile, Somali, Suba, Teso and Turkana).

Capital FM: Lonrho House, Standard St, POB 74933, Nairobi; tel. (20) 210020; fax (20) 332393; e-mail info@capitalfm.co.ke; internet www.capitalfm.co.ke; f. 1999; commercial station broadcasting to Nairobi and environs; Man. Dir LYNDA HOLT.

Citizen Radio: Ambank House, University Way, POB 45897, Nairobi; tel. (20) 249122; fax (20) 249126; commercial radio station broadcasting in Nairobi and its environs; Man. Dir S. K. MACHARIA.

IQRA Broadcasting Network: Bandari Plaza, 7th Floor, Woodvale Grove, Westlands, POB 45163 GPO, Nairobi; tel. (20) 4447624; fax (20) 4443978; e-mail iqrafm@swiftkenya.com; Islamic radio station broadcasting religious programmes in Nairobi; Man. Dir SHARIF HUSSEIN OMAR.

Kameme FM: Longonot Pl., Kijabe St, POB 49640, 00100 Nairobi; tel. (20) 217963; fax (20) 338129; commercial radio station broadcasting in Kikuyu in Nairobi and its environs; Man. Dir ROSE KIMOTHO.

Kitambo Communications Ltd: NSSF Bldg, POB 56155, Nairobi; tel. (20) 331770; fax (20) 212847; commercial radio and television station broadcasting Christian programmes in Mombasa and Nairobi; Man. Dir Dr R. AYAH.

Nation FM: Nation Centre, Kimathi St, POB 49010, Nairobi; tel. (20) 32088801; fax (20) 241892; e-mail philmatthews@nation.co.ke; internet www.nationmedia.com; f. 1999; commercial radio station broadcasting in English and Swahili; owned by Nation Media Group; Man. Dir IAN FERNANDES.

Radio Africa Ltd (KISS FM): Safina Towers, 16th Floor, University of Nairobi, POB 45897, Nairobi; tel. (20) 245368; fax (20) 245565; Man. Dir KIPRONO KITTONY.

Sauti ya Raheme RTV Network: POB 4139, Eldoret; Christian, broadcasts in Eldoret and its environs; Man. Dir Rev. ELI ROP.

Directory

Television

Kenya Broadcasting Corpn (KBC): see Radio
  Television: KBC-TV; services in Kiswahili and English; operates three channels—KBC1, KBC2 and Metro TV.

Citizen TV: POB 45897, Nairobi; tel. (20) 249122; fax (20) 249126; commercial station broadcasting in Nairobi and its environs.

Family TV: Dik Dik Gardens, off Gatundu Rd, Kileleshwa, POB 2330, Nairobi; tel. (20) 4200000; fax (20) 4200100; e-mail info@familykenya.com; internet www.familykenya.com.

Kenya Television Network (KTN-TV): Nyayo House, 22nd Floor, POB 56985, Nairobi; tel. (20) 227122; fax (20) 214467; e-mail news@ktnkenya.com; internet www.ktnkenya.tv; f. 1990; commercial station operating in Nairobi and Mombasa; Man. Dir D. J. DAVIES.

NTV: POB 49010, Nairobi; e-mail ntv@nation.co.ke; internet www.nationmedia.com/ntv; f. 1999 as Nation TV; commercial station; owned by Nation Media Group; Man. Dir IAN FERNANDES.

Stellagraphics TV (STV): NSSF Bldg, 22nd Floor, POB 42271, Nairobi; tel. (20) 218043; fax (20) 222555; f. 1998; commercial station broadcasting in Nairobi; Gen. Man. KANJA WARURU.

Finance

(cap. = capital; res = reserves; dep. = deposits; m. = million; brs = branches; amounts in Kenya shillings)

BANKING

Central Bank

Central Bank of Kenya (Banki Kuu Ya Kenya): Haile Selassie Ave, POB 60000, 00200 Nairobi; tel. (20) 226431; fax (20) 217940; e-mail info@centralbank.go.ke; internet www.centralbank.go.ke; f. 1966; bank of issue; cap. 1,500m., res 5,398m., dep. 79,897m. (March 2005); Gov. Prof. NJUGUNA S. NDUNG'U.

Commercial Banks

African Banking Corpn Ltd: ABC-Bank House, Mezzanine Floor, Koinange St, POB 46452, Nairobi; tel. (20) 223922; fax (20) 222437; e-mail ho@abcthebank.co.ke; internet www.abcthebank.com; f. 1984 as Consolidated Finance Co; converted to commercial bank and adopted present name 1995; cap. 350m., dep. 4,433m. (Dec. 2005); Man. Dir ASHRAF SAVANI; 7 brs.

Barclays Bank of Kenya Ltd: Barclays Plaza, Loita St, POB 30120, 00100 Nairobi; tel. (20) 332230; fax (20) 213915; e-mail barclays.kenya@barclays.com; f. 1978; cap. 2,037m., res 1,630m., dep. 77,417m. (Dec. 2003); Chair. SAMUEL O. J. AMBUNDO; Man. Dir ADAN MOHAMMED; 87 brs.

CFC Bank Ltd: CFC Centre, Chiromo Rd, POB 72833, 00200 Nairobi; tel. (20) 3752900; fax (20) 3752905; e-mail cfcbank@cfcgroup.co.ke; internet www.cfcbank.co.ke; f. 1955 as Credit Finance Corpn Ltd; became commercial bank and adopted present name 1995; cap. 720m., res 1,802m., dep. 14,137m. (Dec. 2004); Chair. P. K. JANI; Man. Dir R. J. BARRY.

Chase Bank (Kenya) Ltd: Prudential Assurance Bldg, Wabera St, POB 28987, Nairobi; tel. (20) 244035; fax (20) 246334; e-mail info@chasebank.co.ke; cap. 520m. (Dec. 2004); Chair. OSMAN MURGIAN; Man. Dir ZAFRULLAH KHAN.

Commercial Bank of Africa Ltd: Commercial Bank Bldg, cnr Wabera and Standard Sts, POB 30437, Nairobi; tel. (20) 228881; fax (20) 335827; e-mail cba@cba.co.ke; internet www.cba.co.ke; f. 1962; owned by Kenyan shareholders; cap. 1,000m., res 962m., dep. 167,788m. (Dec. 2004); Chair. M. H. DA GAMA-ROSE; Pres. and Man. Dir ISAAC O. AWUONDO; 9 brs.

Consolidated Bank of Kenya Ltd: Consolidated Bank House, Koinange St, POB 51133, Nairobi; tel. (20) 340551; fax (20) 340213; e-mail headoffice@consolidated-bank.com; internet www.consolidated-bank.com; f. 1989; state-owned; cap. 1,120m., res 102m., dep. 2,189m. (Dec. 2004); Chair. PHILIP J. NJUKI; Man. Dir DAVID K. WACHIRA.

Dubai Bank Kenya Ltd: ICEA Bldg, Kenyatta Ave, POB 11129, Nairobi; tel. (20) 330562; fax (20) 245242; e-mail info@dubaibank.co.ke; internet www.dubaibank.co.ke; 25% owned by World of Marble and Granite, Dubai (United Arab Emirates), 25% owned by Abdul Hassan Ahmed, 16% owned by Hassan Bin Hassan Trading Co LLC, Dubai (United Arab Emirates), 15% owned by Ahmed Mohamed Zubeidi; cap. 323m., res 39m., dep. 479m. (Dec. 2004); Chair. HASSAN AHMED ZUBEIDI; Man. Dir VIJU CHERIAN.

EABS Bank Ltd: Fedha Towers, 5th Floor, Muindi Mbingu St, POB 49584, 00100 Nairobi; tel. (20) 2883000; fax (20) 2883815; e-mail akiba.ho@akibabank.com; internet www.eabsbank.com; f. 1972 as Akiba Bank Ltd, present name adopted 2005; cap. 1,663m., res −376m., dep. 7,019m. (Dec. 2005); Chair. N. P. G. WARREN; CEO R. L. PANDIT; 3 brs.

KENYA

Equatorial Commercial Bank Ltd: Sasini House, Loita St, POB 52467, Nairobi; tel. (20) 2710455; fax (20) 2710700; e-mail Customerservice@ecb.co.ke; internet www.equatorialbank.co.ke; cap. 306m. (Dec. 2001); Chair. AHMED S. NDOPE; Man. Dir K. S. KRISHNAKUMAR.

Fidelity Commercial Bank Ltd: IPS Bldg, 7th Floor, Kimathi St, POB 34886, Nairobi; tel. (20) 242348; fax (20) 243389; e-mail customerservice@fidelitybankkenya.com; f. 1993 as Fidelity Finance; present name adopted 1996; CEO SULTAN KHIMJI.

Gulf African Bank (GAB): Nairobi; e-mail info@gulfafricanbank.com; internet www.gulfafricanbank.com; f. 2007; 20% owned by Bank Muscat International (BMI); 10% owned by the International Finance Corpn (IFC); Chair. SULEIMAN SHAHBAL; CEO YUSUF ABDULRAHMAN NZIBO.

Kenya Commercial Bank Ltd: Kencom House, Moi Ave, POB 48400, Nairobi; tel. (20) 223846; fax (20) 215565; e-mail kcbhq@kcb.co.ke; internet www.kcb.co.ke; f. 1970; 26.2% state-owned; cap. 1,996m., res 3,236m., dep. 64,639m. (Dec. 2005); CEO and Man. Dir MARTIN ODUOR-OTIENO; 105 brs and sub-brs.

Middle East Bank Kenya Ltd: Mebank Tower, Milimani Rd, POB 47387, 00100 Nairobi; tel. (20) 2723120; fax (20) 343776; e-mail ho@mebkenya.com; internet www.mebkenya.com; f. 1981; 25% owned by Banque Belgolaise SA (Belgium), 75% owned by Kenyan shareholders; cap. 506.8m., res 367.7m., dep. 1,880m. (Dec. 2007); Man. Dir PETER HARRIS; Exec. Dir. B. S. PAI; 2 brs.

National Bank of Kenya Ltd (Banki ya Taifa La Kenya Ltd): National Bank Bldg, Harambee Ave, POB 72866, Nairobi; tel. (20) 339690; fax (20) 330784; e-mail nbkops@nbnet.co.ke; internet www.nationalbank.co.ke; f. 1968; 64.5% state-owned; cap. 6,675m., res −4,050m., dep. 25,470m. (Dec. 2004); Exec. Chair. JOHN P. N. SIMBA; Gen. Man. A. H. AHMED; 25 brs.

Stanbic Bank Kenya Ltd: Stanbic Bank Bldg, Kenyatta Ave, POB 30550, Nairobi; tel. (20) 335888; fax (20) 330227; e-mail stanbickenya@stanbic.com; internet www.stanbic.co.ke; f. 1992; 89.5% owned by Stanbic Africa Holdings Ltd (London), 10.5% state-owned; cap. 1,260m., res 128m., dep. 5,526m. (Dec. 2001); Chair. J. B. WANJUI; Man. Dir M. L. DU TOIT; 3 brs.

Standard Chartered Bank Kenya Ltd: Stanbank House, Moi Ave, POB 30003, Nairobi; tel. (20) 330200; fax (20) 214086; e-mail mds.office@ke.standardchartered.com; internet www.standardchartered.com/ke; f. 1987; 74.5% owned by Standard Chartered Holdings (Africa) BV (Netherlands); cap. 1,236m., res 4,191m., dep. 54,358m. (Dec. 2003); Chair. HARRINGTON AWORI; CEO RICHARD ETEMESI; 43 brs.

Trans-National Bank Ltd: Transnational Plaza, 2nd Floor, Mama Ngina St, POB 34352, 00100 Nairobi; tel. (20) 252189; fax (20) 2222522; e-mail enquiries@tnbl.co.ke; internet www.tnbl.co.ke; f. 1985; cap. 584m., res 589m., dep. 1,196m. (Dec. 2004); Chair. MWAKAI SIO; CEO DHIRENDRA RANA; 5 brs.

Merchant Banks

Diamond Trust Bank of Kenya Ltd: Nation Centre, 8th Floor, Kimathi St, POB 61711, 00200 Nairobi; tel. (20) 210988; fax (20) 336836; e-mail user@dtbkenya.co.ke; f. 1945; cap. 398m., res 201m., dep. 9,304m. (Dec. 2004); Chair. ROBERT A. BIRD; Man. Dir NASIM DEVJI.

National Industrial Credit Bank Ltd (NIC): NIC House, Masaba Rd, POB 44599, Nairobi; tel. (20) 718200; fax (20) 718232; e-mail info@nic-bank.com; internet www.nic-bank.com; cap. 412m. (Dec. 2001); Chair. J. P. M. NDEGWA; Man. Dir JAMES MACHARIA.

Foreign Banks

Bank of Baroda (Kenya) Ltd (India): POB 30033, Baroda House, 29 Koinage St, 00100 Nairobi; tel. (20) 227869; fax (20) 316070; e-mail md.kenya@bankofbaroda.com; cap. 600m., res 126m., dep. 7,183m. (Dec. 2004); Chair. RAMA KRISHNAN; Man. Dir GIRIDHAR GOVINDRAO JOSHI; 6 brs.

Bank of India: Kenyatta Ave, POB 30246, 00100 Nairobi; tel. (20) 221414; fax (20) 229462; e-mail boinrb@futurenet.co.ke; internet www.bankofindiake.com; CEO A. K. JALOTA.

Citibank NA (USA): Citibank House, Upperhill Rd, POB 30711, 00100 Nairobi; tel. (20) 2711221; fax (20) 2714811; internet www.citibank.co.ke; f. 1974; Gen. Man. ADE AYAYEMI.

Habib Bank AG Zurich (Switzerland): Nagina House, Koinange St, POB 30584, 00100 Nairobi; tel. (20) 334984; fax (20) 218699; Country Man. IQBAL A. ALLAWALA.

Co-operative Bank

Co-operative Bank of Kenya Ltd: Co-operative Bank House, POB 48231, Nairobi; tel. (20) 32076000; fax (20) 249474; e-mail md@co-opbank.co.ke; internet www.co-opbank.co.ke; f. 1968; cap. 1,211m., res 589m., dep. 25,084m. (Dec. 2002); Chair. STANLEY C. MUCHIRI; Man. Dir GIDEON MURIUKI; 30 brs.

Development Banks

Development Bank of Kenya Ltd: Finance House, Loita St, POB 30483, 00100 Nairobi; tel. (20) 340401; fax (20) 338426; e-mail dbk@africaonline.co.ke; f. 1963 as Development Finance Co of Kenya; current name adopted 1996; owned by Industrial and Commercial Devt Corpn (30.5%), govt agencies of Germany and the Netherlands (28.8% and 22.8%, respectively), the Commonwealth Development Corpn (10.7%) and the International Finance Corpn (7.2%); cap. 348m., res 625m., dep. 586m. (Dec. 2004); Chair. Prof. HAROUN NGENY KIPKEMBOI MENGECH; Man. Dir SAJAL RAKHIT.

East African Development Bank: Rahimtulla Tower, 2nd Floor, Upper Hill Rd, Nairobi; tel. (20) 340642; fax (20) 2731590; internet www.eadb.org; Dirs J. KINYUA, F. KARUIRU.

Industrial Development Bank Ltd (IDB): National Bank Bldg, 18th Floor, Harambee Ave, POB 44036, Nairobi; tel. (20) 337079; fax (20) 334594; e-mail bizcare@idbkenya.com; f. 1973; 49% state-owned; cap. 272m., res 83m., dep. 190m. (Dec. 2002); Chair. DAVID LANGAT; Man. Dir L. A. MASAVIRU.

STOCK EXCHANGE

Nairobi Stock Exchange (NSE): Nation Centre, 1st Floor, Kimathi St, POB 43633, 00100 Nairobi; tel. (20) 230692; fax (20) 224200; e-mail info@nse.co.ke; internet www.nse.co.ke; f. 1954; Chair. JIMNAH MBARU; CEO CHRIS MWEBESA.

INSURANCE

American Life Insurance Co (Kenya) Ltd: POB 30364, 00100 Nairobi; tel. (20) 2711242; fax (20) 2711378; e-mail alicolife@alico-kenya.com; internet www.alico-kenya.com; f. 1964; life and general; Man. Dir ERWIN BREWSTER.

Apollo Insurance Co Ltd: POB 30389, Nairobi; tel. (20) 223562; fax (20) 339260; f. 1977; life and general; Chair. B. M. SHAH.

Blue Shield Insurance Co Ltd: POB 49610, Nairobi; tel. (20) 219592; fax (20) 337808; f. 1983; life and general.

Cannon Assurance (Kenya) Ltd: Haile Selassie Ave, POB 30216, Nairobi; tel. (20) 335478; fax (20) 331235; e-mail info@cannon.co.ke; internet www.cannon.co.ke; f. 1964; life and general; Man. Dir I. J. TALWAR.

Fidelity Shield Insurance Ltd: POB 47435, Nairobi; tel. (20) 430635; fax (20) 445699.

Heritage Insurance Co Ltd: CFC House, Mamlaka Rd, POB 30390, 00100 Nairobi; tel. (20) 2783000; fax (20) 2727800; e-mail info@heriaii.com; internet www.heritageinsurance.co.ke; f. 1976; general; Man. Dir JOHN H. D. MILNE.

Insurance Co of East Africa Ltd (ICEA): ICEA Bldg, Kenyatta Ave, POB 46143, Nairobi; tel. (20) 221652; fax (20) 338089; e-mail hof@icea.co.ke; internet www.icea.co.ke; life and general; Man. Dir J. K. NDUNGU.

Jubilee Insurance Co Ltd: POB 30376, Nairobi; tel. (20) 340343; fax (20) 216882; f. 1937; life and general; Chair. ABDUL JAFFER.

Kenindia Assurance Co Ltd: Kenindia House, Loita St, POB 44372, Nairobi; tel. (20) 333100; fax (20) 218380; e-mail kenindia@users.africaonline.co.ke; f. 1978; life and general; Exec. Dir R. S. BEDI.

Kenya Reinsurance Corpn Ltd (KenyaRe): Reinsurance Plaza, Taifa Rd, POB 30271, Nairobi; tel. (20) 240188; fax (20) 339161; e-mail kenyare@kenyare.co.ke; internet www.kenyare.co.ke; f. 1970; Man. Dir JOHNSON GITHAKA.

Lion of Kenya Insurance Co Ltd: POB 30190, Nairobi; tel. (20) 710400; fax (20) 711177; e-mail insurance@lionofkenya.com; f. 1978; general; CEO J. P. M. NDEGWA.

Mercantile Insurance Co Ltd: Nairobi; tel. (20) 218244; fax (20) 215528; e-mail mercantile@mercantile.co.ke; internet www.mercantile.co.ke; Man. Dir SUDHIR SATHE.

Monarch Insurance Co Ltd: Chester House, 2nd Floor, Koinange St, POB 44003, Nairobi; tel. (20) 330042; fax (20) 340691; e-mail monarch@form-net.com; f. 1975; general; Exec. Dir R. A. VADGAMA.

Pan Africa Insurance Co Ltd: POB 30065, Nairobi; tel. (20) 252168; fax (20) 217675; e-mail insure@pan-africa.com; f. 1946; life and general; Man. Dir WILLIAM OLOTCH.

Phoenix of East Africa Assurance Co Ltd: Ambank House, University Way, POB 30129, Nairobi; tel. (20) 338784; fax (20) 211848; general; Man. Dir D. K. SHARMA.

Prudential Assurance Co of Kenya Ltd: Yaya Centre, Argwings Kodhek Rd, POB 76190, Nairobi; tel. (20) 567374; fax (20) 567433; f. 1979; general; Man. Dir JOSEPH MURAGE.

PTA Reinsurance Co (ZEP-RE): Zep-Re Pl., Longonot Rd, Upper Hill, POB 42769, Nairobi; tel. (20) 212792; fax (20) 224102; e-mail

KENYA

Directory

mail@zep-re.com; internet www.zep-re.com; f. 1992; Man. Dir S. M. LUBASI.

Royal Insurance Co of East Africa Ltd: Mama Ngina St, POB 40001, Nairobi; tel. (20) 717888; fax (20) 712620; f. 1979; general; CEO S. K. KAMAU.

Standard Assurance (Kenya) Ltd: POB 42996, Nairobi; tel. (20) 224721; fax (20) 224862; Man. Dir WILSON K. KAPKOTI.

UAP Provincial Insurance Co of East Africa Ltd: Old Mutual Bldg, Kimathi St, POB 43013, Nairobi; tel. (20) 330173; fax (20) 340483; f. 1980; general; CEO E. C. BATES.

United Insurance Co Ltd: POB 30961, Nairobi; tel. (20) 227345; fax (20) 215609; Man. Dir G. KARRUIKI.

Trade and Industry

GOVERNMENT AGENCIES

Export Processing Zones Authority: Administration Bldg, Viwanda Rd, Athi River Export Processing Zone, off Nairobi-Namanga Highway, Athi River, POB 50563, Nairobi; tel. (45) 26421; fax (45) 26427; e-mail info@epzakenya.com; established by the Govt to promote investment in Export Processing Zones.

Export Promotion Council: Anniversary Towers, 1st and 16th Floors, University Way, POB 40247, Nairobi; tel. (20) 228534; fax (20) 218013; e-mail chiefexe@epc.or.ke; internet www.cbik.or.ke; f. 1992; promotes exports; CEO MATANDA WABUYELE.

Investment Promotion Centre: National Bank Bldg, 8th Floor, Harambee Ave, POB 55704, 00200 Nairobi; tel. (20) 221401; fax (20) 336663; e-mail info@investmentkenya.com; internet www.investmentkenya.com; f. 1986; promotes and facilitates local and foreign investment; CEO LUKA E. OBBANDA.

Kenya National Trading Corpn Ltd: Yarrow Rd, off Nanyuki Rd, POB 30587, Nairobi; tel. (20) 543121; fax (20) 532800; f. 1965; promotes national control of trade in both locally produced and imported items; exports coffee and sugar; CEO S. W. O. OGESSA.

Settlement Fund Trustees: POB 30449, Nairobi; administers a land purchase programme involving over 1.2m. ha for resettlement of African farmers.

DEVELOPMENT ORGANIZATIONS

Agricultural Development Corpn: POB 47101, Nairobi; tel. (20) 250695; fax (20) 243571; f. 1965 to promote agricultural devt and reconstruction; CEO WILLIAM K. KIRWA.

Agricultural Finance Corpn: POB 30367, Nairobi; tel. (20) 317199; fax (20) 219390; e-mail afc@wananchi.com; a statutory organization providing agricultural loans; Man. Dir OMUREMBE IYADI.

Horticultural Crops Development Authority: POB 42601, Nairobi; tel. (20) 8272601; fax (20) 827264; e-mail hcdamd@wananchi.com; internet www.hcda.or.ke; f. 1968; invests in production, dehydration, processing and freezing of fruit and vegetables; exports of fresh fruit and vegetables; Chair. Prof. ROSALIND W. MUTUA; Man. Dir S. P. GACHANJA.

Housing Finance Co of Kenya Ltd: Rehani House, cnr Kenyatta Ave and Koinange St, POB 30088, 00100 Nairobi; tel. (20) 317474; fax (20) 340299; e-mail housing@housing.co.ke; internet www.housing.co.ke; f. 1965; Chair. KUNG'U GATABAKI; Man. Dir FRANK M. IRERI.

Industrial and Commercial Development Corpn: Uchumi House, Aga Khan Walk, POB 45519, Nairobi; tel. (20) 229213; fax (20) 333880; e-mail icdcexe@africaonline.co.ke; f. 1954; govt-financed; assists industrial and commercial devt; Chair. JOHN NGUTHU MUTIO; Exec. Dir K. ETICH ARAP BETT.

Kenya Fishing Industries Ltd: Nairobi; Man. Dir ABDALLA MBWANA.

Kenya Industrial Estates Ltd: Nairobi Industrial Estate, Likoni Rd, POB 78029, Nairobi; tel. (20) 530551; fax (20) 534625; f. 1967 to finance and develop small-scale industries.

Kenya Industrial Research and Development Institute: POB 30650, Nairobi; tel. (20) 603842; fax (20) 607023; e-mail info@kirdi.go.ke; internet www.kirdi.go.ke; f. 1942; reorg. 1979; restructured 1995; research and devt in industrial and allied technologies including engineering, agro-industrial, mining and environmental technologies; Dir Dr TOM OGADA.

Kenya Tea Development Agency: POB 30213, Nairobi; tel. (20) 221441; fax (20) 211240; e-mail info@ktdateas.com; internet www.ktdateas.com; f. 1964 as Kenya Tea Development Authority; to develop tea growing, manufacturing and marketing among African smallholders; operates 51 factories; privatized in 2000; Chair. STEPHEN M. IMANYARA; Man. Dir ERIC KIMANI.

CHAMBER OF COMMERCE

Kenya National Chamber of Commerce and Industry: Ufanisi House, Haile Selassie Ave, POB 47024, Nairobi; tel. (20) 220867; fax (20) 334293; f. 1965; 69 brs; Nat. Chair. DAVID M. GITHERE; Chief Exec. TITUS G. RUHIU.

INDUSTRIAL AND TRADE ASSOCIATIONS

Central Province Marketing Board: POB 189, Nyeri.

Coffee Board of Kenya: Coffee Plaza, Exchange Lane, off Haile Selassie Ave, POB 30566, Nairobi; tel. and fax (20) 315754; e-mail info@coffeeboard.co.ke; internet www.coffeeboard.co.ke; f. 1947; Chair. JOHN NGARI ZACHARIAH; Gen. Man. AGGREY MURUNGA.

East African Tea Trade Association: Tea Trade Centre, Nyerere Ave, POB 85174, 80100 Mombasa; tel. (41) 2220093; fax (41) 2225823; e-mail info@eatta.co.ke; internet www.eatta.com; f. 1957; organizes Mombasa weekly tea auctions; Exec. Officer HADIJA SHAKOMBO; 264 mems in 11 countries.

Fresh Produce Exporters' Association of Kenya: Nairobi; Chair. JAMES MATHENGE.

Kenya Association of Manufacturers: Mwanzi Rd, off Peponi Rd, Westlands, POB 30225, Nairobi; tel. (20) 3746005; fax (20) 3746028; e-mail kam@users.africaonline.co.ke; internet www.kam.co.ke; Chair. MANU CHANDARIA; Exec. Sec. LUCY MICHENI; 200 mems.

Kenya Dairy Board: NSSF Bldg, 10th Floor, Bishops Rd, POB 30406, Nairobi; tel. (20) 310559; fax (20) 244064; e-mail info@kdb.co.ke; internet www.kdb.co.ke; f. 1958; Man. Dir MACHIRA GICHOHI.

Kenya Flower Council: Muthangari Gardens, off Gitanga Rd, POB 56325, 00200 Nairobi; tel. and fax (20) 3876597; e-mail kfc@wananchi.com; internet www.kenyaflowers.co.ke; regulates production of cut flowers; CEO JANE NGIGE.

Kenya Meat Corpn: POB 30414, Nairobi; tel. (20) 340750; f. 1953; purchasing, processing and marketing of beef livestock; Chair. H. P. BARCLAY.

Kenya Planters' Co-operative Union Ltd: Nairobi; e-mail gm@kpcu.co.ke; coffee processing and marketing; Chair. J. M. MACHARIA; Gen. Man. RUTH MWANIKI.

Kenya Sisal Board: Mutual Bldg, Kimathi St, POB 41179, Nairobi; tel. (20) 248919; f. 1946; CEO J. H. WAIRAGU; Man. Dir CHARLES K. KAGWIMI (acting).

Kenya Sugar Authority: Sukari Plaza, off Waiyaki Way, POB 51500, Nairobi; tel. (20) 631642; fax (20) 593273; e-mail ksa@africaonline.co.ke; Chair. LUKE R. OBOK; CEO F. M. CHAHONYO.

Mild Coffee Trade Association of Eastern Africa (MCTA): Nairobi; Chair. F. J. MWANGI.

National Cereals and Produce Board (NCPB): POB 30586, Nairobi; tel. (20) 536028; fax (20) 542024; e-mail cereals@africaonline.co.ke; f. 1995; grain marketing and handling, provides drying, weighing, storage and fumigation services to farmers and traders, stores and manages strategic national food reserves, distributes famine relief; Chair. JAMES MUTUA; Man. Dir NAFTALI MOGERE.

Pyrethrum Board of Kenya: POB 420, Nakuru; tel. (37) 211567; fax (37) 45274; e-mail pbk@pyrethrum.co.ke; internet www.kenya-pyrethrum.com; f. 1935; 14 mems; Chair. J. O. MARIARIA; CEO J. C. KIPTOON.

Tea Board of Kenya: Naivasha Rd, off Ngong Rd, POB 20064, 00200 Nairobi; tel. (20) 3874445; fax (20) 3862120; e-mail info@teaboard.or.ke; internet www.teaboard.or.ke; f. 1950; regulates tea industry on all matters of policy, licenses tea processing, carries out research on tea through **Tea Research Foundation of Kenya**, monitors tea planting and trade through registration, promotes Kenyan tea internationally; Chair. DUNSTAN M. NGUMO; Man. Dir SICILY K. KARIUKI.

EMPLOYERS' ORGANIZATIONS

Federation of Kenya Employers: Waajiri House, Argwings Kodhek Rd, POB 48311, Nairobi; tel. (20) 721929; fax (20) 721990; Chair. J. P. N. SIMBA; Exec. Dir TOM DIJU OWUOR.

Association of Local Government Employers: POB 52, Muranga; Chair. S. K. ITONGU.

Distributive and Allied Industries Employers' Association: POB 30587, Nairobi; Chair. P. J. MWAURA.

Engineering and Allied Industries Employers' Association: POB 48311, Nairobi; tel. (20) 721929; Chair. D. M. NJOROGE.

Kenya Association of Building and Civil Engineering Contractors: Nairobi; Chair. G. S. HIRANI.

Kenya Association of Hotelkeepers and Caterers: Heidelberg House, Mombasa Rd, POB 9977, 00100 Nairobi; tel. (20) 604419; fax (20) 602539; e-mail info@kahc.co.ke; internet www.kahc.co.ke; f. 1944; CEO KABANDO WA KABANDO.

KENYA

Kenya Bankers' Association: POB 73100, Nairobi; tel. (20) 221792; e-mail kba@kenyaweb.com; Chair. RICHARD ETEMESI.

Kenya Sugar Employers' Union: Kisumu; Chair. L. OKECH.

Kenya Tea Growers' Association: POB 320, Kericho; tel. (20) 21010; fax (20) 32172; Chair. M. K. A. SANG.

Kenya Vehicle Manufacturers' Association: POB 1436, Thika; Chair. C. PETERSON.

Motor Trade and Allied Industries Employers' Association: POB 48311, Nairobi; tel. (20) 721929; fax (20) 721990; Exec. Sec. G. N. KONDITI.

Sisal Growers' and Employers' Association: POB 47523, Nairobi; tel. (20) 720170; fax (20) 721990; Chair. A. G. COMBOS.

Timber Industries Employers' Association: POB 18070, Nairobi; Chair. H. S. BAMBRAH.

UTILITIES
Electricity

Energy Regulatory Commission: Integrity Centre, Milimani Rd, POB 42681, 00100 Nairobi; tel. (20) 2847000; fax (20) 2717603; e-mail info@erb.go.ke; internet www.erb.go.ke; f. 1997; govt-owned; regulates the generation, distribution, supply and use of electric power; Chair. HINDPAL SINGH JABBAL.

Kenya Electricity Generating Co Ltd (KenGen): Stima Plaza, Phase 3, Kolobot Rd, Parklands, POB 47936, Nairobi; tel. (20) 3666000; fax (20) 248848; e-mail comms@kengen.co.ke; internet www.kengen.co.ke; f. 1997 as Kenya Power Co; present name adopted 1998; generates 82% of Kenya's electricity requirements; partially privatized in 2006; CEO EDWARD NJOROGE.

Kenya Power and Lighting Co (KPLC): Stima Plaza, Kolobot Rd, POB 30099, Nairobi; tel. (20) 243366; fax (20) 337351; e-mail custcare@kplc.co.ke; internet www.kplc.co.ke; partially privatized in 2006; 4% owned by Transcentury Group; co-ordinates electricity transmission and distribution; Man. Dir SAMUEL GICHURU.

TRADE UNIONS

Central Organization of Trade Unions (Kenya) (COTU): Solidarity Bldg, Digo Rd, POB 13000, Nairobi; tel. (20) 761375; fax (20) 762695; f. 1965 as the sole trade union fed.; Chair. PETER G. MUTHEE; Sec.-Gen. JOSEPH J. MUGALLA.

Amalgamated Union of Kenya Metalworkers: POB 73651, Nairobi; tel. (20) 211060; Gen. Sec. F. E. OMIDO.

Bakers', Confectionary Manufacturing and Allied Workers' Union (Kenya): POB 57751, 00200 Nairobi; Lengo House, 3rd Floor, Room 20, Tom Mboya St, opposite Gill House, Nairobi; tel. (20) 330275; fax (20) 222735; e-mail bakers@form-net.com.

Communication Workers' Union of Kenya: POB 48155, Nairobi; tel. (20) 219345; e-mail cowuk@clubinternet.com.

Dockworkers' Union: POB 98207, Mombasa; tel. (11) 491427; f. 1954; Gen. Sec. J. KHAMIS.

Kenya Airline Pilots' Association: POB 57505, Nairobi; tel. (20) 716986.

Kenya Building, Construction, Timber, Furniture and Allied Industries Employees' Union: POB 49628, 00100 Nairobi; tel. (20) 223434; fax (20) 244779; e-mail kbctfaieu@yahoo.com; Gen. Sec. FRANCIS KARIMI MURAGE.

Kenya Chemical and Allied Workers' Union: POB 73820, Nairobi; tel. (20) 338815; Gen. Sec. WERE DIBI OGUTO.

Kenya Electrical Trades Allied Workers' Union: POB 47060, Nairobi; tel. (20) 334655.

Kenya Engineering Workers' Union: POB 73987, Nairobi; tel. (20) 333745; Gen. Sec. JUSTUS MULEI.

Kenya Game Hunting and Safari Workers' Union: Nairobi; tel. (20) 25049; Gen. Sec. J. M. NDOLO.

Kenya Jockey and Betting Workers' Union: POB 55094, Nairobi; tel. (20) 332120.

Kenya Local Government Workers' Union: POB 55827, Nairobi; tel. (20) 217213; Gen. Sec. WASIKE NDOMBI.

Kenya National Union of Fishermen: POB 83322, Nairobi; tel. (20) 227899.

Kenya Petroleum Oil Workers' Union: POB 48125, Nairobi; tel. (20) 338756; Gen. Sec. JACOB OCHINO.

Kenya Plantation and Agricultural Workers' Union: POB 1161, 20100 Nakuru; tel. and fax (51) 2212310; e-mail kpawu@africaonline.co.ke; Gen. Sec. FRANCIS ATWOLI.

Kenya Quarry and Mine Workers' Union: POB 332120, Nairobi; f. 1961; Gen. Sec. WAFULA WA MUSAMIA.

Kenya Railway Workers' Union: RAHU House, Mfangano St, POB 72029, Nairobi; tel. (20) 340302; f. 1952; Nat. Chair. FRANCIS O'LORE; Sec.-Gen. JOHN T. CHUMO.

Kenya Scientific Research, International Technical and Allied Institutions Workers' Union: Ngumba House, Tom Mboya St, POB 55094, Nairobi; tel. (20) 215713; Sec.-Gen. FRANCIS D. KIRUBI.

Kenya Shipping, Clearing and Warehouse Workers' Union: POB 84067, Mombasa; tel. (11) 312000.

Kenya Shoe and Leather Workers' Union: POB 49629, Nairobi; tel. (20) 533827; Gen. Sec. JAMES AWICH.

Kenya Union of Commercial, Food and Allied Workers: POB 2628, 00100 Nairobi; tel. (20) 245054; fax (20) 313118; e-mail kucfaw@yahoo.com.

Kenya Union of Domestic, Hotel, Educational Institutions, Hospitals and Allied Workers: POB 41763, 00100 Nairobi; tel. (20) 241509; fax (20) 243806; e-mail kudheihaworkers@hotmail.com; f. 1952; workers; Sec.-Gen. FESTUS MUTUNGA.

Kenyan Union of Entertainment and Music Industry Employees: Nairobi; tel. (20) 333745.

Kenya Union of Journalists: POB 47035, 00100 Nairobi; tel. (20) 250888; fax (20) 250880; e-mail info@kujkenya.org; f. 1962; Gen. Sec. and CEO EZEKIEL MUTUA; Chair. TERVIL OKOKO.

Kenya Union of Printing, Publishing, Paper Manufacturers and Allied Workers: POB 72358, Nairobi; tel. (20) 331387; Gen. Sec. JOHN BOSCO.

Kenya Union of Sugar Plantation Workers: POB 36, Kisumu; tel. (35) 22221; Gen. Sec. ONYANGO MIDIKA.

National Seamen's Union of Kenya: Mombasa; tel. (11) 312106; Gen. Sec. I. S. ABDALLAH MWARUA.

Tailors' and Textile Workers' Union: POB 72076, Nairobi; tel. (20) 338836.

Transport and Allied Workers' Union: POB 45171, Nairobi; tel. (20) 545317; Gen. Sec. JULIAS MALII.

Independent Unions

Academic Staff Association: Nairobi; e-mail dorata@uonbi.ac.ke; Interim Chair. Dr KORWA ADAR.

Kenya Medical Practitioners' and Dentists' Union: not officially registered. Nat. Chair. GIBBON ATEKA.

Kenya National Union of Teachers: POB 30407, Nairobi; f. 1957; Sec.-Gen. AMBROSE ADEYA ADONGO.

Transport

RAILWAYS

In 1999 there were some 2,700 km of track open for traffic.

Kenya Railways Corpn: POB 30121, Nairobi; tel. (20) 221211; fax (20) 224156; f. 1977; management of operations assumed by Rift Valley Railways consortium in Nov. 2006; Man. Dir A. HARIZ.

ROADS

At the end of 2004 there were an estimated 63,265 km of classified roads, of which 6,527 km were main roads and 18,885 km were secondary roads. Only an estimated 14.1% of road surfaces were paved. An all-weather road links Nairobi to Addis Ababa, in Ethiopia, and there is a 590-km road link between Kitale (Kenya) and Juba (Sudan). The rehabilitation of the important internal road link between Nairobi and Mombasa (funded by a US $165m. loan from the World Bank) was undertaken during the late 1990s.

Abamba Public Road Services: POB 40322, Nairobi; tel. (20) 556062; fax (20) 559884; operates bus services from Nairobi to all major towns in Kenya and to Kampala in Uganda.

East African Road Services Ltd: Nairobi; tel. (20) 764622; f. 1947; operates bus services from Nairobi to all major towns in Kenya; Chair. S. H. NATHOO.

Kenya Roads Board: Nairobi; tel. (20) 722865; f. 2000 to co-ordinate maintenance, rehabilitation and development of the road network; Chair. ALFRED JUMA.

Nyayo Bus Service Corpn: Nairobi; tel. (20) 803588; f. 1986; operates bus services within and between major towns in Kenya.

Speedways Trans-Africa Freighters: POB 75755, Nairobi; tel. (20) 544267; private road haulier; CEO HASSAN KANYARE.

SHIPPING

The major international seaport of Mombasa has 16 deep-water berths, with a total length of 3,044 m, and facilities for the off-loading of bulk carriers, tankers and container vessels. Mombasa port handled more than 8.5m. metric tons of cargo in 1998. An inland container depot with a potential full capacity of 120,000 20-ft (6-m) equivalent units was opened in Nairobi in 1984.

KENYA

Kenya Ports Authority: POB 95009, Mombasa; tel. (41) 312211; fax (41) 311867; internet www.kenya.ports.com; f. 1978; sole operator of coastal port facilities, and operates two inland container depots at Nairobi and Kisimu; Chair. Gen. (Retd) JOSEPH KIBWANA; Man. Dir ABDALLAH HEMED MWARURA.

Inchcape Shipping Services Kenya Ltd: Inchcape House, Archbishop Makarios Cl., off Moi Ave, POB 90194, 80100 Mombasa; tel. (41) 2314245; fax (41) 2314662; e-mail mail@iss-shipping.com; internet www.iss-shipping.com; covers all ports in Kenya and Tanzania; Man. Dir DAVID MACKAY.

Mackenzie Maritime Ltd: Maritime Centre, Archbishop Makarios Close, POB 90120, Mombasa; tel. (11) 221273; fax (11) 316260; e-mail mml@africaonline.co.ke; shipping agents; Man. Dir M. M. BROWN.

Marship Ltd: Mombasa; tel. (11) 314705; fax (11) 316654; f. 1986; shipbrokers, ship management and chartering agents; Man. Dir MICHELE ESPOSITO.

Mitchell Cotts Kenya Ltd: Cotts House, Wabera St, POB 30182, Nairobi; tel. (20) 221273; fax (20) 214228.

Motaku Shipping Agencies Ltd: Motaku House, Tangana Rd, POB 80419, 80100 Mombasa; tel. (41) 2229065; fax (41) 2220777; e-mail motaku@motakushipping.com; f. 1977; ship managers and shipping agents, freight broker and charter; Man. Dir KARIM KUDRATI.

PIL (Kenya) Ltd: 9th Floor, Canon Towers II, Moi Ave, POB 43050, Mombasa; tel. (11) 223700; fax (11) 225927.

Shipmarc Ltd: POB 99553, Mombasa; tel. (41) 229241; fax (41) 221390; e-mail info@shipmarckenya.com.

Southern Line Ltd: POB 90102, 80107 Mombasa; tel. (11) 229241; fax (11) 221390; e-mail shipmarc@africaonline.co.ke; operating dry cargo and tanker vessels between East African ports, Red Sea ports, the Persian (Arabian) Gulf and Indian Ocean islands.

Spanfreight Shipping Ltd: Cannon Towers, Moi Ave, POB 99760, Mombasa; tel. (11) 315623; fax (11) 312092; e-mail a23ke464@gncomtext.com; Exec. Dir DILIPKUMAR AMRITLAL SHAH.

Star East Africa Co: POB 86725, Mombasa; tel. (11) 314060; fax (11) 312818; shipping agents and brokers; Man. Dir YEUDA FISHER.

CIVIL AVIATION

Jomo Kenyatta International Airport (JKIA), in south-eastern Nairobi, and Moi International Airport, at Mombasa both service international flights. Wilson Airport, in south-western Nairobi, Eldoret Airport (which opened in 1997) and airports at Malindi and Kisumu handle internal flights. Kenya has about 150 smaller airfields. The rehabilitation and expansion of JKIA and Moi International Airport was undertaken during the late 1990s. A new cargo handling facility, The Nairobi Cargo Centre, opened at JKIA in June 1999, increasing the airport's capacity for storing horticultural exports.

Kenya Airports Authority: Jomo Kenyatta International Airport, POB 19001, Nairobi; tel. (20) 825400; fax (20) 822078; e-mail info@kenyaairports.co.ke; f. 1991; state-owned; responsible for the provision, management and operation of all airports and private airstrips; Man. Dir GEORGE MUHOHO.

African Airlines International: Airport North Rd, Jomo Kenyatta International Airport, POB 19202, Nairobi; tel. (20) 824333; fax (20) 823999; placed under receivership mid-1999; CEO Capt. MUSA BULHAN.

Airkenya Aviation: Wilson Airport, POB 30357, 00100 Nairobi; tel. (20) 605745; fax (20) 602951; e-mail info@airkenya.com; internet www.airkenya.com; f. 1985; operates internal scheduled and charter passenger services; CEO AMATZIA SNIR.

Blue Bird Aviation Ltd: Wilson Airport, Langata Rd, POB 52382, Nairobi; tel. (20) 602338; fax (20) 602337.

Eagle Aviation (African Eagle): POB 93926, Mombasa; tel. (11) 434502; fax (11) 434249; e-mail eaglemsa@africaonline.co.ke; f. 1986; scheduled regional and domestic passenger and cargo services; Chair. RAJA TANUJ; CEO Capt. KIRAN PATEL.

East African Safari Air: Mombasa; operates charter service.

Kenya Airways Ltd (KQ): Airport North Road, Jomo Kenyatta International Airport, POB 19142, Nairobi; tel. (20) 6422000; fax (20) 823488; e-mail contact@kenya-airways.com; internet www.kenya-airways.com; f. 1977; in private sector ownership since 1996; passenger services to Africa, Asia, Europe and Middle East; freight services to Europe; internal services from Nairobi to Kisumu, Mombasa and Malindi; also operates a freight subsidiary; Chair. EVANSON MWANIKI; Man. Dir and CEO TITUS NAIKUNI.

CIVIL AVIATION AUTHORITY

Kenya Civil Aviation Authority: Jomo Kenyatta International Airport, POB 30163, 00100 Nairobi; tel. (20) 827470; e-mail info@kcaa.or.ke; internet www.kcaa.or.ke; f. 2002; regulatory and advisory services for air navigation; Dir Gen. C. A. KUTO.

Tourism

Kenya's main attractions for visitors are its wildlife, with 25 National Parks and 23 game reserves, the Indian Ocean coast and an equable year-round climate. In 2005 there were 1,479,000 foreign visitors. Earnings from the sector totalled US $808m. in 2004.

Kenya Tourism Board: Kenya-Re Towers, Ragati Rd, POB 30630, 00100 Nairobi; tel. (20) 271126; fax (20) 2719925; e-mail info@kenyatourism.org; internet www.magicalkenya.com; f. 1997; promotes Kenya as a tourist destination, monitors the standard of tourist facilities.

Kenya Tourist Development Corpn: Utalii House, 11th Floor, Uhuru Highway, POB 42013, Nairobi; tel. (20) 2229751; fax (20) 2227817; e-mail info@ktdc.co.ke; internet www.ktdc.co.ke; f. 1965; Chair. CHARLES WACHIRA NGUNDO; Man. Dir OBONDO KAJUMBI.

KIRIBATI

Introductory Survey

Location, Climate, Language, Religion, Flag, Capital

The Republic of Kiribati (pronounced 'Kir-a-bas') comprises 33 atolls, in three principal groups, scattered within an area of about 5m. sq km (2m. sq miles) in the mid-Pacific Ocean. The country extends about 3,870 km (2,400 miles) from east to west and about 2,050 km (1,275 miles) from north to south. Its nearest neighbours are Nauru, to the west, and Tuvalu and Tokelau, to the south. The climate varies between maritime equatorial in the central islands and tropical in the north and south, with daytime temperatures varying between 26°C (79°F) and 32°C (90°F). There is a season of north-westerly trade winds from March to October and a season of rains and gales from October to March. Average annual rainfall, however, varies greatly, from 3,000 mm (118 ins) in the northern islands to 1,500 mm (59 ins) in Tarawa and 700 mm (28 ins) in the Line Islands. Droughts often occur in the central and southern islands. The principal languages are I-Kiribati (Gilbertese) and English, and the islands' inhabitants are mostly Christians. The national flag (proportions 1 by 2) depicts a golden frigate bird in flight, on a red background, above a rising sun and six alternating wavy horizontal lines of blue and white, representing the sea. The capital is the island of Bairiki, in Tarawa Atoll.

Recent History

In 1892 the United Kingdom established a protectorate over the 16 atolls of the Gilbert Islands and the nine Ellice Islands (now Tuvalu). The two groups were administered together by the Western Pacific High Commission (WPHC), which was based in Fiji until its removal to the British Solomon Islands (now Solomon Islands) in 1953. The phosphate-rich Ocean Island (now Banaba), west of the Gilberts, was annexed by the United Kingdom in 1900. The Gilbert and Ellice Islands were annexed in 1915, effective from January 1916, when the protectorate became a colony. The local representative of the WPHC was the Resident Commissioner, based on Tarawa Atoll in the Gilbert group. Later in 1916 the new Gilbert and Ellice Islands Colony (GEIC) was extended to include Ocean Island and two of the Line Islands, far to the east. Christmas Island (now Kiritimati), another of the Line Islands, was added in 1919, and the eight Phoenix Islands (then uninhabited) in 1937. The Line and Phoenix Islands, south of Hawaii, were also claimed by the USA. A joint British-US administration for two of the Phoenix group, Canton (now Kanton) and Enderbury, was agreed in April 1939. During the Second World War the GEIC was invaded by Japanese forces, who occupied the Gilbert Islands in 1942–43. Tarawa Atoll was the scene of some of the fiercest fighting in the Pacific between Japan and the USA.

As part of the British Government's programme to develop its own nuclear weapons, the first test of a British hydrogen bomb was conducted near Christmas Island in May 1957. Two further tests in the same vicinity followed later that year.

In 1963, to prepare the GEIC for self-government, the first of a series of legislative and executive bodies were established. In 1972 a Governor of the GEIC was appointed to assume almost all the functions previously exercised in the colony by the High Commissioner. The five uninhabited Central and Southern Line Islands, previously administered directly by the High Commissioner, became part of the GEIC at this time. In 1974 the Legislative Council was replaced by a House of Assembly, with 28 elected members and three official members. The House elected Naboua Ratieta as Chief Minister.

In October 1975 the Ellice Islands were allowed to secede from the GEIC to form a separate territory, Tuvalu (q.v.). The remainder of the GEIC was renamed the Gilbert Islands, and the House of Assembly's membership was reduced.

In 1975 the British Government refused to recognize as legitimate a demand for independence by the people of Ocean Island (Banaba), who had been in litigation with the British Government since 1971 over revenues derived from exports of phosphate. Open-cast mining had so adversely affected the island's environment that most Banabans had been resettled on Rabi Island, 2,600 km (1,600 miles) away in the Fiji group. The Banabans rejected the British Government's argument that phosphate revenues should be distributed over the whole territory of the Gilbert Islands. In 1976 the British High Court dismissed the Banabans' claim for unpaid royalties but upheld that for damages. An offer made by the British Government in 1977 of an *ex gratia* payment of $A10m., without admission of liability and on condition that no further judicial appeal would be made, was rejected.

The Gilbert Islands obtained internal self-government on 1 January 1977. Later in that year the number of elected members in the House of Assembly was increased to 36, and provision was subsequently made for a member appointed by the Rabi Council of Leaders. Following a general election in 1978, Ieremia Tabai, Leader of the Opposition in the previous House, was elected Chief Minister. On 12 July 1979 the Gilbert Islands became an independent republic within the Commonwealth, under the name of Kiribati. The House of Assembly was renamed the Maneaba ni Maungatabu, and Ieremia Tabai became the country's first President (Beretitenti). In September Kiribati signed a treaty of friendship with the USA, which relinquished its claim to the Line and Phoenix Islands, including Kanton and Enderbury. Kiribati did not become a member of the UN until September 1999, although it had previously joined some of the organization's agencies.

In 1981 the Banaban community on Rabi accepted the British Government's earlier *ex gratia* offer of compensation, but they continued to seek self-government. The 1979 Constitution provided for the establishment of an independent commission of inquiry to review the political status of the Banabans three years after Kiribati had achieved independence, but the inquiry was not commissioned until 1985.

The first general election since independence took place in March–April 1982. The members of the new Maneaba all sat as independents. In accordance with the 1979 Constitution, the legislature nominated from among its members candidates for the country's first presidential election, to be held on the basis of direct popular vote. President Tabai was confirmed in office at the election in May. The Government resigned in December, after the Maneaba had twice rejected proposals to increase salaries for civil servants. The legislature was dissolved, and a general election took place in January 1983. The formation of the new Maneaba necessitated a further presidential election in February, at which Tabai was re-elected for a third term of office. He was returned to office in May 1987 (following a general election in March). The May 1991 legislative election was followed by a presidential election in July, at which the former Vice-President, Teatao Teannaki, narrowly defeated Roniti Teiwaki to replace Tabai, who had served the maximum number of presidential terms permitted by the Constitution.

In 1992 the Maneaba approved an opposition motion urging the Government to seek compensation from Japan for damage caused during the Second World War. The intention to seek compensation was reiterated by President Teburoro Tito (see below) in late 1994.

In May 1994 the Government was defeated on a motion of confidence, following opposition allegations that government ministers had misused travel allowances. The Maneaba was dissolved, and at legislative elections in July five cabinet ministers lost their seats. Of the newly elected members, 13 were supporters of the Maneaban Te Mauri (Protect the Maneaba), while only eight were known to support the previously dominant National Progressive Party grouping. At the presidential election in September Teburoro Tito, of the Maneaban Te Mauri, was elected, receiving 51.1% of the total votes. The new President declared that reducing Kiribati's dependence on foreign aid would be a major objective for his Government. He also announced his intention to pursue civil and criminal action against members of the previous administration for alleged misuse of public funds while in office.

In 1995 a committee was created with the aim of assessing public opinion regarding possible amendments to the Constitution. In March 1998 more than 200 delegates attended a Constitutional Review Convention in Bairiki to consider the recommendations of a report presented to the Government in

1996, which included equalizing the status of men and women regarding the citizenship rights of foreigners marrying I-Kiribati and changes to the structure of the Council of State. Leaders of the Banaban community in Rabi, Fiji, were also consulted during 1998 as part of the review process.

A general election, held in September 1998 and contested by a record 191 candidates, failed to produce a conclusive result, necessitating a second round of voting one week later, at which the Government and opposition each lost seven seats. The new Maneaba convened in October, when it selected three presidential candidates. At a presidential election in November Tito was re-elected with 52.3% of total votes cast, defeating Dr Harry Tong, who obtained 45.8% of votes, and Ambreroti Nikora, with 1.8%.

In mid-1999 John Kum Kee, a member of the Maneaba, was sentenced to four years' imprisonment, having been convicted of bribing a customs official and evasion of customs duty. Controversy continued in 1999 regarding the renamed Millennium Island (previously Caroline Island). The island had been renamed in 1997 in an attempt to promote it as a tourist destination for the year 2000. In 1994 Kiribati had moved the international date-line to incorporate the Line and Phoenix Islands groups (including Millennium Island) in the same time zone as the Gilbert group, thus creating a large eastward anomaly in the date-line. Millennium Island's position as the first place to celebrate the New Year, however, was subsequently confirmed. In early 2000, however, opposition politicians severely criticized the Government for failing to attract the predicted numbers of tourists to the islands' millennium celebrations, despite expenditure of more than $A1m. Meanwhile, in April 1999 the Kiribati Government reiterated its desire to acquire Baker, Howland and Jarvis Islands (see US External Territories) from the USA, citing the potential economic value of their fishing resources.

In late 1999 concerns were expressed by a Pacific media organization after a New Zealand journalist working for Agence France-Presse was banned from entering Kiribati. The Kiribati Government claimed that a series of articles by the correspondent, unfavourable to Kiribati, which had been published in a regional magazine, were biased and sensationalist. In December former President Ieremia Tabai and a former member of the Maneaba, Atiera Tetoa, were fined, having been convicted of importing telecommunications equipment without a permit. They had launched Newair FM, an independent commercial radio station, 12 months previously; it had been immediately suspended and a criminal investigation was instigated by the police. Tabai subsequently established Kiribati's first private newspaper, the *Kiribati Newstar*, in an attempt to reduce the Government's control over the media in the islands.

In November 2000 the Vice-President and Minister for Home Affairs and Rural Development, Tewarika Tentoa, collapsed while addressing the Maneaba and died. The post of Vice-President was subsequently combined with the cabinet portfolio of finance and economic planning.

Campaigning for the general election during November 2002 was characterized by numerous allegations of improper conduct. Observers noted that officials from the Chinese embassy in Tarawa, accompanied by government candidates, had been donating gifts to the local community in the weeks preceding the election. (The Government had recently amended the Elections Act to allow gifts to be distributed to the public by candidates during their electoral campaigns, a practice that had been banned hitherto.) The opposition, which had stated its intention to close the Chinese satellite-tracking station (based on South Tarawa—see below) if elected, claimed that this action constituted a clear attempt to influence voters. Moreover, under a newly amended Newspaper Registration Act, Tito ordered police to seize opposition election pamphlets in November. Further allegations that the Government was attempting to stifle freedom of expression were made by former President Ieremia Tabai, whose private radio station was finally granted a licence to broadcast in December, following delays totalling almost four years in issuing the permit.

A total of 176 candidates contested the general election on 29 November 2002. The Government suffered significant losses with 14 of its supporters (including seven ministers) failing to retain their seats. The presidential election was postponed from its original date and finally took place on 25 February 2003. At the poll Tito received 14,160 votes, while the opposition candidate Taberannang Timeon secured 13,613. Tito was sworn in for his third term as President on 28 February and many of his former opponents in the legislature were expected to cross the floor to support him. However, in late March Tito was narrowly defeated on a motion of 'no confidence' and his Government was replaced by an interim administration, the Council of State (comprising the Speaker, the Chief Justice and the Public Service Commissioner). In accordance with the Constitution, another general election took place on 9 and 14 May, at which supporters of Tito secured a majority of seats. A presidential election took place in early July at which the opposition candidate, Anote Tong, narrowly defeated his brother, Harry Tong. Anote Tong's electoral campaign, which had focused on his pledge to review the lease of the Chinese satellite-tracking station on South Tarawa, had been characterized by a series of personal attacks on his brother.

A legislative election, contested by a total of 146 candidates, was held on 22 August 2007. Decisive majorities were achieved by candidates in only 18 constituencies, thus resulting in a second round of voting on 30 August. The ministers of the incumbent Government, with the exception of Martin Tofinga, were re-elected to the Maneaba ni Maungatabu, and the Boutokan Te Koaua (Pillars of Truth) grouping of Anote Tong secured 18 seats, defeating the Maneaban Te Mauri grouping, which won seven. Anote Tong defeated three other candidates to be re-elected to the post of President on 17 October, having received almost twice as many votes as his nearest rival, Nabuti Mwemwenikarawa. Prior to the presidential election, members of the opposition grouping protested against the omission of their candidates from the contest following their failure to gain sufficient parliamentary support. Anote Tong subsequently appointed a new Cabinet, retaining Teima Onorio in the position of Vice-President with additional responsibility for commerce, industry and co-operatives, and other erstwhile ministers including Natan Teewe, who became Minister for Finance and Economic Development.

In early November 2003 President Anote Tong announced the establishment of diplomatic relations with Taiwan. The Government's decision to transfer its recognition from the People's Republic of China to Taiwan caused considerable controversy within Kiribati and the region. Several hundred people staged a protest in Tarawa against the decision, claiming that it had been made in return for Taiwanese funding of Anote Tong's electoral campaign. The President strongly refuted this allegation, but did, however, state that Taiwan had offered extensive development funds to Kiribati for adopting its position. By late November it was reported that Chinese technicians were dismantling the satellite-tracking station, which had played an important role in China's recent first manned space flight. The Chinese embassy, however, remained open while China requested that Kiribati reconsider its decision. Despite its efforts, which many observers believed were motivated largely by the islands' strategic importance, in late November China suspended its diplomatic relations with Kiribati. In the same week the police in Kiribati announced that they were beginning an investigation into the death threats received by President Tong, believed to be from a Chinese source. A Taiwanese embassy was opened in Tarawa in January 2004. The continued presence of mainland Chinese officials in Kiribati (three diplomats remained as caretakers of the Chinese embassy building in Tarawa in mid-2004) caused the authorities some concern. In May 2005, as part of a diplomatic tour of Pacific nations, President Chen Shui-bian of Taiwan reportedly became the first foreign head of state to visit Kiribati in an official capacity. During a reciprocal visit by President Tong to Taiwan in May 2006, President Chen described Kiribati as a 'staunch ally' and drew attention to the bilateral projects instigated since the establishment of diplomatic relations.

As a result of discussions held at the Pacific Islands Forum (see p. 380) summit meeting in Kiribati in October 2000, Japan announced that it was willing to negotiate compensation claims with the islanders for damage caused during the Second World War. Furthermore, a six-day visit by President Tito to Japan in February 2001 resulted in a number of informal agreements aimed at enhancing relations between the two countries. These included a decision to try to resolve a dispute over tuna fishing, caused by Japan's refusal to sign a convention aimed at protecting tuna stocks in the central and western Pacific Ocean, and agreements to address their differences over whaling and nuclear-fuel shipments. Tito also appeared to modify his position on nuclear energy following the visit to Japan, stating that emissions of harmful 'greenhouse gases' could be reduced by replacing fossil with nuclear fuel.

KIRIBATI

In September 1995 Kiribati severed relations with France, in protest at the French Government's decision to renew nuclear-weapons testing at Mururoa Atoll in French Polynesia.

Reports that Palmyra Atoll (a privately owned uninhabited US territory some 200 km north of Kiribati's northern Line Islands) was to be sold and used by a US company for the storage of nuclear waste prompted a unanimous resolution of the Maneaba, in May 1996, urging the Government to convey to the US Government the islanders' concerns over the proposals. The islanders' anxieties centred largely on Palmyra's proximity to Kiribati, coupled with the belief that the atoll's fragility and porous structure make it an unstable environment for the storage of highly toxic materials. In November 2000, however, Palmyra was purchased by The Nature Conservancy, a conservation group that planned to preserve the natural state of the atoll.

Owing to the country's high rate of population growth (about 2% per year) and, in particular, the situation of over-population on South Tarawa and the associated social and economic problems, it was announced in 1988 that nearly 5,000 inhabitants were to be resettled on outlying atolls, mainly in the Line Islands. In November 2004 the Government announced a major new initiative, supported by the UN Development Programme and the Asian Development Bank, to establish up to four new urban areas in the outer islands as part of ongoing efforts to ease the overcrowding of South Tarawa.

A Chinese satellite-tracking station was opened on South Tarawa in late 1997 but was dismantled in late 2003 following the suspension of diplomatic relations between the two countries (see above). Sea Launch, an international consortium led by the US Boeing Commercial Space Company, also announced plans to undertake a rocket-launching project from a converted oil-rig near the islands. A prototype satellite was launched in March 1999, and commercial operations began in late 1999. Kiribati, which, together with the South Pacific Regional Environment Programme (SPREP, see p. 421), had expressed concerns regarding the potential negative environmental impact of the site, was not expected to benefit financially from the project, as the consortium had sought to carry out its activities in international waters near the outer limits of the islands' exclusive economic zone. The US authorities dismissed environmental concerns about the negative impact of the site (particularly the dumping of large quantities of waste fuel in the islands' waters), which were expressed by both the Government of Kiribati and SPREP in 1998. These fears were compounded in March 2000 after a rocket launched from the site crashed, and, furthermore, Sea Launch refused to disclose where it had landed. In November 1999 it was announced that the Government of Kiribati and the National Space Development Agency of Japan had reached agreement on the proposed establishment of a space-vehicle launching and landing facility on Kiritimati. In the following year the Japanese organization, which was subsequently renamed the Japan Aerospace Exploration Agency, was also given permission by the Kiribati Government to use land and runway facilities on the island, free of charge, until 2020.

In 1989 a UN report on the 'greenhouse effect' (the heating of the earth's atmosphere, and a resultant rise in sea-level, as a consequence of pollution) listed Kiribati as one of the countries that would completely disappear beneath the sea in the 21st century, unless drastic action were taken. None of the land on the islands is more than two metres above sea-level, making the country extremely vulnerable to the effects of climate change. It was feared that a rise in sea-level would not only cause flooding, but would also upset the balance between sea and fresh water (below the coral sands), rendering water supplies undrinkable. In late 1997 President Tito strongly criticized the Australian Government's refusal, at the Conference of the Parties to the Framework Convention on Climate Change (under the auspices of the UN Environment Programme, see p. 62) in Kyoto, Japan, to reduce its emission of gases known to contribute to the 'greenhouse effect'. In April 2001 the USA's decision to reject the Kyoto Protocol to the UN's Framework Convention on Climate Change was widely criticized. In March 2002 Kiribati, Tuvalu and the Maldives announced their decision to take legal action against the USA for its refusal to sign the Kyoto Protocol. In January 2006 the Australian Government reiterated its position, declaring that it believed there to be no evidence to suggest that the populations of the Pacific islands were in any imminent danger of being displaced by rising sea-levels. Vice-President Teima Onorio urged the UN to work towards a co-ordinated response to the challenge of global warming.

A report released by the World Bank in 2000 listed the flooding and loss of low-lying areas, more intense cyclones and droughts, the failure of subsistence crops and coastal fisheries, the death of coral reefs and the spread of mosquito-borne diseases such as malaria and dengue fever as consequences of the 'greenhouse effect' on Pacific island nations. Meanwhile, a state of emergency was declared in Kiribati in early 1999, owing to one of the worst droughts ever recorded in the islands. In mid-1999 it was announced that two of the country's uninhabited coral reefs had been submerged as a result of the 'greenhouse effect'. Concern among the islanders intensified in early 2001 when many of the causeways linking villages on Tarawa atoll were flooded by high tides, and by the early 21st century increasingly high 'king tides' were reported to be causing regular flooding.

In March 2006 President Anote Tong announced that one of the world's largest marine reserves was to be established in Kiribati. Commercial fishing was to be banned in the Phoenix Islands Protected Area (PIPA), which encompassed an area of 184,700 sq km and would afford protection to more than 120 species of coral and to 520 species of fish. A leading US aquarium and an international conservation group were to assist in the creation of the reserve. In January 2008 the projected area of PIPA was increased by 100%, thereby creating the largest protected marine area in the world.

In 2003 UNICEF established a field office in Kiribati as part of a wider strategy to increase the UN's presence in the region. In July 2007 the efforts of a team of Cuban doctors were reported to have resulted in an 80% decrease in infant mortality rates.

Government

Legislative power is vested in the unicameral Maneaba ni Maungatabu. It has 42 members elected by universal adult suffrage for four years (subject to dissolution), one nominated representative of the Banaban community and, if he is not an elected member, the Attorney-General as an ex-officio member. The Head of State is the Beretitenti (President), who is also Head of Government. The President is elected by direct popular vote. The President governs with the assistance of the Vice-President and Cabinet, whom he appoints from among members of the Maneaba. Executive authority is vested in the Cabinet, which is responsible to the Maneaba.

Defence

Kiribati has no defence forces: defence assistance is provided by Australia and New Zealand.

Economic Affairs

In 2006, according to estimates by the World Bank, Kiribati's gross national income (GNI), measured at average 2004–06 prices, was US $124.1m., equivalent to US $1,230 per head (or $9,970 on an international purchasing-power parity basis). During 1996–2006, it was estimated, the population increased at an average annual rate of 2.1% per year, while gross domestic product (GDP) per head increased, in real terms, by an estimated average of 1.5% per year. Overall GDP increased, in real terms, at an average annual rate of 3.7% in 1996–2006. According to estimates by the Asian Development Bank (ADB), GDP expanded by 1.1% in 2006 and by 0.5% in 2007.

Agriculture and fishing contributed an estimated 7.0% of GDP in 2006, according to figures from the ADB. In 2005, according to FAO estimates, agriculture engaged more than 25% of the economically active population. The principal cash crop is coconut, yielding copra as well as coconut oil. Export revenue from copra and copra cake reached almost $A1.8m. in 2004, accounting for 53.5% of the country's total revenue from exports and re-exports, while exports of crude coconut oil accounted for 26.2% of total receipts. Bananas, taro, screw-pine (*Pandanus*), breadfruit and papaya are cultivated as food crops. The cultivation of seaweed began in the mid-1980s. In 2004 seaweed provided 11.4% of total export earnings. Pigs and chickens are kept. The sale of fishing licences to foreign fleets (notably from South Korea, Japan, the People's Republic of China, Taiwan and the USA) has provided an important source of income: revenue from the sale of fishing licences reached a record $A52m. in 2001 but had declined to $A24.5m. by 2004. Nevertheless, in 2006 fees from fishing licences accounted for 43% of total government revenue. In September of that year a new six-year agreeement with the European Union (EU) entered into force: 16 Spanish vessels were permitted to fish for tuna in Kiribati waters, while the EU's annual financial contribution was to remain at US $0.6m. The GDP of the agricultural sector declined at an average annual rate of 8.7% in 1995–2006. According to the ADB, agricultural GDP contracted by 41.7% in 2005 but expanded by 6.0% in 2006.

Industry (including manufacturing, construction and utilities) contributed an estimated 6.5% of GDP in 2006. Industrial GDP increased by an average of 7.4% per year in 1995–2006. Compared with the previous year, industrial GDP was estimated by the ADB to have increased by 9.0% in 2005, but declined by 0.2% in 2006.

Mining of phosphate rock on the island of Banaba, which ceased in 1979, formerly provided some 80% of export earnings. Interest from a phosphate reserve fund (the Revenue Equalization Reserve Fund—RERF), established in 1956, continues to be an important source of income (see below). The production of solar-evaporated salt for export to other islands of the Pacific (for use on fishing vessels with brine refrigeration systems) began on Kiritimati in 1985.

Manufacturing, which was estimated to have contributed just 0.8% of GDP in 2006, is confined to the small-scale production of coconut-based products, soap, foods, handicrafts, furniture, leather goods and garments. Manufacturing GDP increased by an annual average of 1.2% in 1995–2006, according to ADB figures. Compared with the previous year, the GDP of the manufacturing sector decreased by 0.6% in 2005, but grew by 0.7% in 2006.

Production of electrical energy increased from 15.1m. kWh in 2001 to 21.0m. kWh in 2005. Mineral fuels accounted for an estimated 17% of total import costs in 2005. In 2001 the EU announced that it planned to fund the introduction of 1,500 new solar energy systems to Kiribati. Moreover, in May 2003 the Government announced the completion of a Japanese-funded programme to construct a new power station, to install two new generating units and to upgrade 16 km of power lines. The project was expected to ensure a power supply sufficient to meet Kiribati's increasing demand.

Services provided 86.5% of GDP in 2006. In that year the government sector accounted for an estimated 47% of GDP, compared with 30% in 2000. Although impeded by factors such as the high costs of transport, the tourism sector makes a significant contribution to the economy. The hotel and restaurant sector provided 6.6% of GDP in 2006, according to preliminary figures. Receipts from tourism totalled $3.0m. in 2001. An estimated 4,406 visitors arrived in Kiribati in 2006, rising to 4,709 in 2007. According to ADB figures, the GDP of the services sector increased at an annual average rate of 4.0% in 1995–2006. The services sector's GDP increased by 5.8% in 2005 and by 1.2% in 2006.

In 2006, according to the ADB, Kiribati recorded a trade deficit of an estimated US $103.3m., and a deficit of $42.6m. on the current account of the balance of payments. The ADB estimated that the deficit on the current account was equivalent to 76.3% of GDP in 2007, compared with a surplus equivalent to 10.1% of GDP in 2003. In 2005 the principal sources of imports were Australia (32.9%) and Fiji (27.0%). The principal recipients of exports in that year were the USA and Belgium. The major imports in 2005 were food and live animals, mineral fuels, manufactures, beverages and tobacco, and chemicals. The major domestic exports in 2004 included copra and copra cake, coconut oil and seaweed.

Current budgetary expenditure for 2004/05 reached $A78.6m. The projected budgetary deficit of $A23.8m. in 2005/06 required a drawdown of $A18.5m. from the RERF. It was anticipated that the budgetary deficit for 2006/07 would be financed wholly from this fund. In 2007, according to the ADB, the government deficit reached the equivalent of 2.5% of GDP. The country is reliant on foreign assistance for its development budget. Australia is a major provider of development assistance, with emphasis on the management of human resources, training, governance, health, education and improved customs procedures, within the framework of a new co-operation strategy. In 2007/08 aid from Australia was projected at $A15.0m. Aid from New Zealand was expected to total $NZ3.1m. in 2006/07. Through the ADB, Taiwan has provided aid to finance various development projects, as has Japan. Kiribati's total external debt was estimated by the ADB to have risen from US $47m. in 2006 to $52m. in 2007. The cost of debt-servicing was estimated to be the equivalent of 3.6% of the value of goods and services in 2006. The annual rate of inflation averaged 1.7% in 1996–2006. Consumer prices decreased by 1.5% in 2006, but rose by 3.5% in 2007. About 6.1% of the labour force were unemployed in 2005. Only around 8,600 people, equivalent to less than 20% of the working-age population, were formally employed in 2001, mainly in the public sector.

Kiribati is a member of the Pacific Community (see p. 377), the Pacific Islands Forum (see p. 380) and the Asian Development Bank (ADB, see p. 182); it is an associate member of the UN Economic and Social Commission for Asia and the Pacific (ESCAP, see p. 35), and is a signatory to the South Pacific Regional Trade and Economic Co-operation Agreement (SPARTECA, see p. 381) and to the Lomé Conventions and successor Cotonou Agreement (see p. 301) with the EU. The Council of Micronesian Government Executives, of which Kiribati was a founder member in 1996, aims to facilitate discussion of economic developments in the region and to examine possibilities for reducing the considerable cost of shipping essential goods between the islands.

Kiribati is one of the world's least developed nations. The country's export base is extremely limited, and the economy remains vulnerable to adverse weather conditions, as demonstrated by the severe drought of 2007/08, and to fluctuations in international copra prices. Kiribati depends on imports for almost all essential commodities, and import duties are a major source of government revenue. In most years the substantial trade deficit has been only partially offset by revenue from fishing licence fees, interest earned on the RERF and remittances from I-Kiribati working overseas. The majority of emigrant workers are seamen employed on foreign ships. The RERF usually provides the Government with investment income equivalent to around 33% of GDP per year. At October 2006 the value of the RERF was estimated at $A666m., compared with $A97m. in 1984. The Government also holds substantial offshore assets through the Kiribati Provident Fund. In addition to its efforts to assist Kiribati in the development of the outer islands, the ADB proposed to offer a loan of US $10m. to assist in the establishment of the Kiritimati Island Growth Center in 2007. In late 2007 it was reported that the accounts of the Government and government-owned companies had not been audited, thus raising concerns that donor countries might renege on their aid commitments. Furthermore, it was feared that the recent substantial increases in drawdowns from the RERF, which totalled $A45m. in 2007, might in the longer term jeopardize the Government's use of this important source of budgetary support. The 2008–11 National Sustainable Development Strategy was expected to focus on the strategic areas of economic growth, the reduction of poverty, health and education, the environment, improved governance and the upgrading of the country's infrastructure.

Education

Education is compulsory for nine years between the ages of six and 15 years, comprising six years of primary school and three years of junior secondary school, an initiative introduced in 1998. Students may then continue at secondary school for a further three years. Every atoll is provided with at least one primary and junior secondary school. In 2001/02 enrolment at primary schools reached 97.4% of pupils in the relevant age-group. In 2004/05 enrolment at secondary schools stood at 67.6% of students in the relevant age-group. In 2005 there were 91 primary schools and 35 secondary schools. In 2004/05 there were 16,133 pupils enrolled in primary school and 7,487 students enrolled in secondary school. The Government administers a technical college and training colleges for teachers, nurses and seamen (the last, the Marine Training Centre, trains about 200 seamen each year for employment by overseas shipping companies). An extra-mural centre of the University of the South Pacific (based in Fiji) is located on South Tarawa. In 2005 the Government allocated $A19.9m. (equivalent to 25.3% of total budgetary expenditure) to education.

Public Holidays

2008: 1 January (New Year), 21–24 March (Easter), 18 April (National Health Day), 11 July (National Church Day), 12–16 July (National Day Celebrations), 7 August (Youth Day), 11 December (Human Rights and Peace Day), 25–26 December (Christmas).

2009: 1 January (New Year), 10–13 April (Easter), 18 April (National Health Day), 11 July (National Church Day), 12–16 July (National Day Celebrations), 7 August (Youth Day), 11 December (Human Rights and Peace Day), 25–26 December (Christmas).

Weights and Measures

The metric system is in use.

KIRIBATI

Statistical Survey

Source (unless otherwise stated): Statistics Office, Ministry of Finance and Economic Planning, POB 67, Bairiki, Tarawa; tel. 21082; fax 21307; e-mail statistics@mfep.gov.ki; internet www.spc.int/prism/country/KI/Stats.

AREA AND POPULATION

Area: 810.5 sq km (312.9 sq miles). *Principal Atolls* (sq km): Banaba (island) 6.29; Tarawa 31.02 (North 15.26, South 15.76); Abemama 27.37; Tabiteuea 37.63 (North 25.78, South 11.85); Total Gilbert group (incl. others) 285.52; Kanton (Phoenix Is) 9.15; Tabuaeran (Fanning—Line Is) 33.73; Kiritimati (Christmas—Line Is) 388.39; Total Line and Phoenix group 525.0 (Line Is 496, Phoenix Is 29).

Population: 84,494 at census of 7 November 2000; 92,533 (males 45,612, females 46,921) at census of 7 November 2005 (provisional). *Principal Atolls* (2005, provisional): Banaba (island) 301; Abaiang 5,502; Tarawa 45,989 (North 5,678, South 40,311); Tabiteuea 4,898 (North 3,600, South 1,298); Total Gilbert group (incl. others) 83,683; Kanton (Phoenix Is) 41; Kiritimati 5,115; Total Line and Phoenix Group (incl. others) 8,850.

Density (2005 census): 114.2 per sq km.

Ethnic Groups (census of 2000): Micronesians 83,452; Polynesians 641; Europeans 154; Others 247; Total 84,494.

Principal Villages: (population at 2005 census): Betio 12,509; Bikenibeu 6,170; Teaoraereke 3,939; Bairiki (capital) 2,766; Eita 2,399; Bonriki 2,119; Temwaiku 2,011. Note: All of the listed villages are in South Tarawa atoll.

Births, Marriages and Deaths: Registered live births (1996) 2,299 (birth rate 29.5 per 1,000); Marriages (registrations, 1988) 352 (marriage rate 5.2 per 1,000); Death rate (estimate, 1995) 7 per 1,000. *2005:* Recorded births 2,419.

Expectation of Life (years at birth, WHO estimates): 65.0 (males 62.5; females 67.8) in 2005. Source: WHO, *World Health Statistics*.

Employment (paid employees, 2000 census): Agriculture, hunting, forestry and fishing 254; Manufacturing 150; Electricity, gas and water 187; Construction 346; Trade, restaurants and hotels 1,181; Transport, storage and communications 944; Financing, insurance, real estate and business services 317; Community, social and personal services 5,821; *Total employed* 9,200 (males 5,810, females 3,390). Note: Subsistence workers numbered 30,712 (males 14,502, females 16,210). *Mid-2005* (estimates in '000): Agriculture, etc. 12; Total labour force 47 (Source: FAO).

HEALTH AND WELFARE
Key Indicators

Total Fertility Rate (children per woman, 2005): 4.0.

Under-5 Mortality Rate (per 1,000 live births, 2005): 65.

Physicians (per 1,000 head, 1998): 0.30.

Hospital Beds (per 1,000 head, 2004): 1.5.

Health Expenditure (2004): US $ per head (PPP): 270.5.

Health Expenditure (2004): % of GDP: 13.7.

Health Expenditure (2004): public (% of total): 93.0.

Access to Water (% of persons, 2004): 65.

Access to Sanitation (% of persons, 2004): 40.

For sources and definitions, see explanatory note on p. vi.

AGRICULTURE, ETC.

Principal Crops ('000 metric tons, 2006, FAO estimates): Taro (Coco yam) 2.0; Other roots and tubers 7.8; Coconuts 109.8; Copra 8.5; Vegetables 5.9; Bananas 4.9; Other fruits 1.4.

Livestock ('000 head, year ending September 2006, FAO estimates): Pigs 12.4; Chickens 460.

Livestock Products (metric tons, 2006, FAO estimates): Pig meat 876; Poultry meat 428; Hen eggs 240.

Fishing (metric tons, live weight, 2005): Capture 34,000* (Emperors 2,950*; Mullets 2,200*; Snappers and jobfishes 3,750*; Jacks and crevalles 2,760*; Skipjack tuna 4,990; Yellowfin tuna 1,720; Other marine fishes 9,535*; Marine molluscs 5,525*); Aquaculture 12; Total catch 34,012*. Figures exclude aquatic plants (metric tons): 3,904* (all aquaculture).
* FAO estimate.
Source: FAO.

INDUSTRY

Copra Production (processed, metric tons): 10,501 in 2003; 12,334 in 2004; 6,194 in 2005.

Electric Energy (million kWh): 17.76 in 2003; 20.50 in 2004; 21.00 in 2005.

Source: Asian Development Bank, *Key Indicators of Developing Asian and Pacific Countries*.

FINANCE

Currency and Exchange Rates: Australian currency: 100 cents = 1 Australian dollar ($A). *Sterling, US Dollar and Euro Equivalents* (31 December 2007): £1 sterling = $A2.2725; US $1 = $A1.1343; €1 = $A1.6698; $A100 = £44.01 = US $88.16 = €59.89. *Average Exchange Rate* (Australian dollars per US $): 1.3095 in 2005; 1.3280 in 2006; 1.1951 in 2007.

Budget (central government operations, $A '000, year ending 30 June 2005): *Revenue:* Current 73,057 (Direct taxes 27,678, Property income 40,873, Fees, etc. 4,445, Other 61); Capital receipts 1; Total 73,058. *Current Expenditure:* General public services 7,691; Public order and safety 7,405; Education 19,880; Health 13,147; Welfare and environment 2,491; Community and culture 2,350; Agriculture, etc. 1,725; Construction affairs 2,296; Communications 2,910; Commerce 1,042; Labour affairs 2,009; Others 15,617; Total 78,563.

Cost of Living (Consumer Price Index; base: 2000 = 100): All items 110.3 in 2004; 110.0 in 2005; 108.3 in 2006. Source: ILO.

Gross Domestic Product ($A '000 at constant 1996 prices): 66,965 in 2004; 66,816 in 2005 (preliminary); 71,110 in 2006 (preliminary).

Expenditure on the Gross Domestic Product ($A million at current prices, 2006): Government final consumption expenditure 36; Private final consumption expenditure 61; Gross fixed capital formation 43; *Total domestic expenditure* 140; Exports of goods and services 30; *Less* Imports of goods and services 72; *GDP in purchasers' values* 99. Source: UN Statistics Division, National Accounts Main Aggregates Database.

Gross Domestic Product by Economic Activity ($A '000 at current prices, 2006): Agriculture and fishing 5,396; Manufacturing 646; Electricity, gas and water 370; Construction 3,980; Wholesale and retail trade 7,167; Transport and communications 8,782; Financial intermediation 10,096; Government administration 38,485; Other community, social and personal service activities 2,330; *Subtotal* 77,252; *Less* Imputed bank service charge 4,385; Indirect taxes, less subsidies 17,700; *GDP in purchasers' values* 90,567. Source: Asian Development Bank, *Key Indicators of Developing Asian and Pacific Countries*.

Balance of Payments (US $ '000, 2006): Exports of goods 1,986; Imports of goods −105,243; *Trade balance* −103,257; Exports of services and income 76,322; Imports of services and income −52,965; *Balance on goods, services and income* −79,900; Current transfers received 39,780; Current transfers paid −1,538; *Current balance* −42,581 (incl. adjustments); Capital account (net) 60,180; Portfolio investment (net) −11,433; Other investments (net) 11,743; Net errors and omissions 75,774; *Overall balance* 93,683. Source: Asian Development Bank, *Key Indicators of Developing Asian and Pacific Countries*.

EXTERNAL TRADE

Principal Commodities ($A '000): *Imports* (2005): Food and live animals 30,165; Beverages and tobacco 8,544; Crude materials (excl. fuels) 1,382; Mineral fuels, lubricants, etc. 16,473; Chemicals 4,237; Basic manufactures 11,622; Machinery and transport equipment 21,722; Miscellaneous manufactured articles 4,848; Total (incl. others) 100,081. *Exports (incl. re-exports)* (2004): Copra 1,579; Copra cake (meal) 218; Coconut oil (crude) 880; Seaweed 384; Total (incl. others) 3,358. *2005:* Total exports 4,656. *2006* (preliminary): Total imports 84,223; Total exports 8,374.

Principal Trading Partners (US $ million, 2005): *Imports*: Australia 25.6; Fiji 21.0; Japan 14.1; New Zealand 5.3; Total (incl. others) 77.7. *Exports* (incl. re-exports): USA 1.2; Belgium 1.1; Japan 0.7; Total (incl. others) 5.2.

Source: Asian Development Bank, *Key Indicators of Developing Asian and Pacific Countries*.

TRANSPORT

Road Traffic (motor vehicles registered on South Tarawa, 2000): Motor cycles 702; Passenger cars 477; Buses 10; Trucks 267; Minibuses 392; Others 13; Total 1,861.

Shipping: *Merchant Fleet* (registered, at 31 December 2006): 14 vessels; total displacement 27,704 grt. (Source: Lloyd's Register-Fairplay, *World Fleet Statistics*). *International Sea-borne Freight Traffic* ('000 metric tons, 1990): Goods loaded 15; Goods unloaded 26 (Source: UN, *Monthly Bulletin of Statistics*).

Civil Aviation (traffic on scheduled services, 1998): Passengers carried 28,000; Passenger-km 11 million; Total ton-km 2 million. Source: UN, *Statistical Yearbook*.

TOURISM

Foreign Tourist Arrivals (by air at Tarawa): 3,867 in 2003; 3,616 in 2004; 3,037 in 2005. *Arrivals at Kiritimati* (by air): 842 in 2003.

Tourist Arrivals by Country of Residence (by air at Tarawa, 2005): Australia 765; Fiji 438; Japan 229; Nauru 148; New Zealand 246; Solomon Islands 136; USA 300; Total (incl. others) 3,037.

Tourism Receipts ($A million): 2.1 in 1999; 2.2 in 2000; 3.0 in 2001.

COMMUNICATIONS MEDIA

Radio Receivers (1997): 17,000 in use.

Television Receivers (1997): 1,000 in use.

Telephones (main lines in use, 2005): 4,500.

Facsimile Machines (1996): 200 in use.

Mobile Cellular Telephones (subscribers, 2005): 600.

Personal Computers ('000 in use, 2005): 1.

Internet Users ('000, 2006): 2.

Non-daily Newspapers: 2 (estimated combined circulation 3,600) in 2002; 3 in 2004.

Sources: UNESCO, *Statistical Yearbook*; UN, *Statistical Yearbook*; International Telecommunication Union; Australian Press Council.

EDUCATION

Primary (2005): 91 schools; 16,133 students; 654 teachers.

Secondary (2005): 35 schools; 7,487 students; 665 teachers.

Teacher-training (2001): 198 students; 22 teachers.

Vocational (2001): 1,303 students; 17 teachers.

Adult Literacy Rate (UNESCO estimates): 92.5% (males 93%; females 92%) in 2001. Source: UNESCO, *Assessment of Resources, Best Practices and Gaps in Gender, Science and Technology in Kiribati*.

Directory

The Constitution

A new Constitution was promulgated at independence on 12 July 1979. The main provisions are as follows:

The Constitution states that Kiribati is a sovereign democratic Republic and that the Constitution is the supreme law. It guarantees protection of all fundamental rights and freedoms of the individual and provides for the determination of citizenship.

The President, known as the Beretitenti, is Head of State and Head of the Government and presides over the Cabinet which consists of the Beretitenti, the Kauoman-ni-Beretitenti (Vice-President), the Attorney-General and not more than eight other ministers appointed by the Beretitenti from an elected parliament known as the Maneaba ni Maungatabu. The Constitution stipulated that the pre-independence Chief Minister became the first Beretitenti, but that in future the Beretitenti would be elected. After each general election for the Maneaba, the chamber nominates, from among its members, three or four candidates from whom the Beretitenti is elected by universal adult suffrage. Executive authority is vested in the Cabinet, which is directly responsible to the Maneaba ni Maungatabu. The Constitution also provides for a Council of State consisting of the Chairman of the Public Services Commission, the Chief Justice and the Speaker of the Maneaba.

Legislative power resides with the single-chamber Maneaba ni Maungatabu, composed of 42 members elected by universal adult suffrage for four years (subject to dissolution), one nominated member (see below) and the Attorney-General as an ex-officio member if he is not elected. The Maneaba is presided over by the Speaker, who is elected by the Maneaba from among persons who are not members of the Maneaba.

One chapter makes special provision for Banaba and the Banabans, stating that one seat in the Maneaba is reserved for a nominated member of the Banaban community. The Banabans' inalienable right to enter and reside in Banaba is guaranteed and, where any right over or interest in land there has been acquired by the Republic of Kiribati or by the Crown before independence, the Republic is required to hand back the land on completion of phosphate extraction. A Banaba Island Council is provided for, as is an independent commission of inquiry to review the provisions relating to Banaba.

The Constitution also makes provision for finance, for a Public Service and for an independent judiciary (see Judicial System).

The Government

HEAD OF STATE

President (Beretitenti): ANOTE TONG (elected 4 July 2003; re-elected 17 October 2007).

Vice-President (Kauoman-ni-Beretitenti): TEIMA ONORIO.

THE CABINET
(April 2008)

President and Minister for Foreign Affairs and Immigration: ANOTE TONG.

Vice-President and Minister for Commerce, Industry and Co-operatives: TEIMA ONORIO.

Minister for Communications, Transport and Tourism Development: PATRICK TATIRETA.

Minister for Education: JAMES TAOM.

Minister for Environment, Lands and Agricultural Development: TETABO NAKARA.

Minister for Finance and Economic Development: NATAN TEEWE.

Minister for Fisheries and Marine Resource Development: TABERANNANG TIMEON.

Minister for Health and Medical Services: Dr KAUTU TENAUA.

Minister for Internal and Home Affairs: AMBEROTI NIKORA.

Minister for Labour and Human Resource Development: IOTEBA REDFERN.

Minister for the Line and Phoenix Islands Development: TAWITA TEMOKU.

Minister for Public Works and Utilities: KOURAITI BENIATO.

MINISTRIES

Office of the President (Beretitenti): POB 68, Bairiki, Tarawa; tel. 21183; fax 21145.

Ministry of Commerce, Industry and Co-operatives: POB 510, Betio, Tarawa; tel. 26158; fax 26233; e-mail commerce@tskl.net.ki.

Ministry of Communications, Transport and Tourism Development: POB 487, Betio, Tarawa; tel. 26003; fax 26193.

Ministry of Education, Youth and Sport Development: POB 263, Bikenibeu, Tarawa; tel. 28091; fax 28222.

Ministry of the Environment, Lands and Agricultural Development: POB 234, Bikenibeu, Tarawa; tel. 28507; fax 28334; internet www.melad.gov.ki.

Ministry of Finance and Economic Development: POB 67, Bairiki, Tarawa; tel. 21802; fax 21307; internet www.mfep.gov.ki.

Ministry of Foreign Affairs and Immigration: POB 68, Bairiki, Tarawa; tel. 21342; fax 21466; e-mail mfa@tskl.net.ki.

Ministry of Health and Medical Services: POB 268, Bikenibeu, Tarawa; tel. 28100; fax 28152.

Ministry of Human Resources and Development: POB 69, Bairiki, Tarawa; tel. 21068; fax 21452.

KIRIBATI

Ministry of Internal Affairs and Social Development: POB 75, Bairiki, Tarawa; tel. 21092; fax 21133; e-mail homeaffairs@tskl.net.ki.
Ministry of Line and Phoenix Islands: Kiritimati Island; tel. 21449; fax 81278.
Ministry of Natural Resources Development: POB 64, Bairiki, Tarawa; tel. 21099; fax 21120.
Ministry of Public Works and Utilities: POB 498, Betio, Tarawa; tel. 26192; fax 26172.

President and Legislature

PRESIDENT

Election, 17 October 2007

Candidate	Votes	% of votes
Anote Tong	15,676	64.3
Nabuti Mwemwenikarawa	8,151	33.4
Patrick Tatireta	356	1.5
Timon Aneri	198	0.8
Total	24,381	100.0

MANEABA NI MAUNGATABU
(House of Assembly)

This is a unicameral body comprising 42 elected members (most of whom formally present themselves for election as independent candidates), and one nominated representative of the Banaban community, along with the Attorney-General in an *ex-officio* capacity (if he or she is not elected). An election was held on 22 August 2007, with a second round of voting conducted on 30 August.
Speaker: TAOMATI IUTA.

Election Commission

Election Commission: Tarawa; Electoral Commissioner RINE UEARA.

Political Organizations

There are no organized political parties in Kiribati. However, loose groupings of individuals supporting similar policies do exist, the most prominent being the Maneaban Te Mauri (Protect the Maneaba) affiliated with Teburoro Tito and Harry Tong, the National Progressive Party, led by Teatao Teannaki, the Liberal Party, led by Tewareka Tentoa, the Boutokan Te Koaua (Pillars of Truth) group of Anote Tong, and the Maurin Kiribati Party.

Diplomatic Representation

EMBASSY AND HIGH COMMISSIONS IN KIRIBATI

Australia: POB 77, Bairiki, Tarawa; tel. 21184; fax 21904; internet www.kiribati.embassy.gov.au; High Commissioner ANNE QUINANE.
China (Taiwan): Bairiki, Tarawa; tel. 22557; fax 22535; e-mail Kir@mofa.gov.tw; Ambassador CHEN SHIH-LIANG.
New Zealand: POB 53, Bairiki, Tarawa; tel. 21400; fax 21402; e-mail nzhc@tskl.net.ki; High Commissioner CRAIG RICKIT.

Judicial System

There are 24 Magistrates' Courts (each consisting of one presiding magistrate and up to eight other magistrates) hearing civil, criminal and land cases. When hearing civil or criminal cases, the presiding magistrate sits with two other magistrates, and when hearing land cases with four other magistrates. A single magistrate has national jurisdiction in civil and criminal matters. Appeal from the Magistrates' Courts lies, in civil and criminal matters, to a single judge of the High Court, and, in matters concerning land, divorce and inheritance, to the High Court's Land Division, which consists of a judge and two Land Appeal Magistrates.

The High Court of Kiribati is a superior court of record and has unlimited jurisdiction. It consists of the Chief Justice and a Puisne Judge. Appeal from a single judge of the High Court, both as a Court of the First Instance and in its appellate capacity, lies to the Kiribati Court of Appeal, which is also a court of record and consists of a panel of three judges.

All judicial appointments are made by the Beretitenti (President).

High Court

POB 501, Betio, Tarawa; tel. 26007; fax 26149; e-mail robin.millhouse@gmail.com.
Chief Justice: ROBIN MILLHOUSE.
Judges of the Kiribati Court of Appeal: ROBIN MILLHOUSE (President), Sir MICHAEL HARDIE-BOYS, Sir DAVID TOMPKINS, ROBERT FISHER, BARRY PATTERSON.

Religion

CHRISTIANITY

Most of the population are Christians: 53.4% Roman Catholic and 39.2% members of the Kiribati Protestant Church, according to the 1990 census.

The Roman Catholic Church

Kiribati forms part of the diocese of Tarawa and Nauru, suffragan to the archdiocese of Suva (Fiji). At 31 December 2005 the diocese contained an estimated 60,636 adherents. The Bishop participates in the Catholic Bishops' Conference of the Pacific, based in Suva (Fiji).
Bishop of Tarawa and Nauru: Most Rev. PAUL EUSEBIUS MEA KAIUEA, Bishop's House, POB 79, Bairiki, Tarawa; tel. 21279; fax 21401; e-mail diocesetarawa@tskl.net.ki.

The Anglican Communion

Kiribati is within the diocese of Polynesia, part of the Anglican Church in Aotearoa, New Zealand and Polynesia. The Bishop in Polynesia is resident in Fiji.

Protestant Church

Kiribati Protestant Church: POB 80, Bairiki, Tarawa; tel. 21195; fax 21453; e-mail kpc@tskl.net.ki; f. 1988; Moderator Rev. BAITEKE NABETARI; Gen. Sec. Rev. TIAONTIN ARUE; 29,432 mems in 1998.

Other Churches

Seventh-day Adventist, Church of God and Assembly of God communities are also represented, as is the Church of Jesus Christ of Latter-day Saints (Mormon).

BAHÁ'Í FAITH

National Spiritual Assembly: POB 269, Bikenibeu, Tarawa; tel. and fax 28074; e-mail emi@tskl.net.ki; 2,400 mems resident in 100 localities in 1995.

The Press

Butim'aea Manin te Euangkerio: POB 80, Bairiki, Tarawa; tel. 21195; e-mail kpc@tskl.net.ki; f. 1913; Protestant Church newspaper; weekly; a monthly publication Te Kaotan te Ota is also produced; Editor Rev. TOOM TOAKAI.
Kiribati Business Link: Bairiki, Tarawa; English.
Kiribati Newstar: POB 10, Bairiki, Tarawa; tel. 21652; fax 21671; f. 2000; independent; weekly; English and I-Kiribati; Editor-in-Chief NGAUEA UATIOA.
Te Itoi ni Kiribati: POB 231, Bikenibeu, Tarawa; tel. 28138; fax 21341; f. 1914; Roman Catholic Church newsletter; monthly; circ. 2,300.
Te Mauri: Protestant Church newspaper; Editor BATIRI BATAUA.
Te Uekera: Broadcasting and Publications Authority, POB 78, Bairiki, Tarawa; tel. 21162; fax 21096; e-mail bpa_admin@tskl.net.ki; f. 1945; bi-weekly; English and I-Kiribati; Editor ROOTI TERUBEA; circ. 2,000.

Broadcasting and Communications

TELECOMMUNICATIONS

Telecom Kiribati Ltd: Bairiki, Tarawa; govt-owned; Gen. Man. ENOTA INGINTAU.
Telecom Services Kiribati Ltd: POB 72, Bairiki, Tarawa; tel. 20700; fax 21424; e-mail ceo@tskl.net.ki; internet www.tskl.net.ki; Chair. ELLIOT ALI; CEO BARANIKO TONGANIBEIA.

KIRIBATI

BROADCASTING

Regulatory Authority

Broadcasting and Publications Authority: POB 78, Bairiki, Tarawa; tel. 21187; fax 21096.

Radio

Radio Kiribati: Broadcasting and Publications Authority, POB 78, Bairiki, Tarawa; tel. 21187; fax 21096; f. 1954; statutory body; station Radio Kiribati broadcasting on SW and MW transmitters; programmes in I-Kiribati (90%) and English (10%); some advertising; Gen. Man. TANIERI TEIBUAKO.

Television

Television Kiribati Ltd: Betio, Tarawa; tel. 26036; fax 26045; internet www.tkl.com.ki.

Finance

(cap. = capital; dep. = deposits; res = reserves)

BANKING

The Bank of Kiribati Ltd: POB 66, Bairiki, Tarawa; tel. 21095; fax 21200; e-mail anzkiribati@anz.com; internet www.anz.com/kiribati; f. 1984; 75% owned by ANZ Bank, 25% by Govt of Kiribati; Chair. R. GOUDSWAARD; Pres. and Man. Dir NEVILLE OLDHAM; 3 brs.

Development Bank of Kiribati: POB 33, Bairiki, Tarawa; tel. 21345; fax 21297; e-mail dbk@tskl.net.ki; f. 1986; took over the assets of the National Loans Board; identifies, promotes and finances small-scale projects; auth. cap. $A2m.; Gen. Man. KIETAU TABWEBWEITI; 5 brs.

A network of lending entities known as 'village banks' operates throughout the islands, as do a number of credit unions under the management of the Credit Union League.

INSURANCE

Kiribati Insurance Corpn: POB 38, Bairiki, Tarawa; tel. 21260; fax 21426; e-mail kirins@tskl.net.ki; f. 1981; govt-owned; only insurance co; reinsures overseas; Gen. Man. TEAIRO TOOMA.

Trade and Industry

GOVERNMENT AGENCIES

Kiribati Housing Corporation: Bairiki, Tarawa; tel. 21092; operates the Housing Loan and Advice Centre; Chair. TOKOREAUA KAIRORO.

Kiribati Provident Fund: POB 76, Bairiki, Tarawa; tel. 21300; fax 21186; f. 1977; Gen. Man. TOKAATA NIATA.

CHAMBER OF COMMERCE

Kiribati Chamber of Commerce: POB 550, Betio, Tarawa; tel. 26351; fax 26332; Pres. WAYSANG KUM KEE; Sec.-Gen. TIARITE KWONG.

UTILITIES

Public Utilities Board: POB 443, Betio, Tarawa; tel. 26292; fax 26106; e-mail ceo.pub@tskl.net.ki; f. 1977; govt-owned; provides electricity, water and sewerage services in Tarawa; CEO TABOIA METUTERA.

Solar Energy Company (SEC): POB 493 Betio, Tarawa; tel. 26058; fax 26210; e-mail sec@tskl.net.ki; a co-operative administering and implementing solar-generated electricity projects in North Tarawa and the outer islands.

CO-OPERATIVE SOCIETIES

Co-operative societies dominate trading in Tarawa and enjoy a virtual monopoly outside the capital, except for Banaba and Kiritimati.

Bobotin Kiribati Ltd (BKL): POB 485, Betio, Tarawa; tel. 26092; fax 26224; e-mail bkl@tskl.net.ki; replaced Kiribati Co-operative Wholesale Society; govt-owned; Gen. Man. AKAU TIARE.

The Kiribati Copra Co-operative Society Ltd: POB 489, Betio, Tarawa; tel. 26534; fax 26391; e-mail kccs@tskl.net.ki; f. 1976; the sole exporter of copra; seven cttee mems; 29 mem. socs; Chair. RAIMON TAAKE; CEO RUTIANO BENETITO.

TRADE UNIONS

Kiribati Trades Union Congress (KTUC): POB 166, Bairiki, Tarawa; tel. 28157; fax 28712; e-mail ktc@tskl.net.ki; f. 1982; unions and asscns affiliated to the KTUC include the Fishermen's Union, the Co-operative Workers' Union, the Seamen's Union, the Teachers' Union, the Nurses' Asscn, the Public Employees' Asscn, the Bankers' Union, Butaritari Rural Workers' Union, Christmas Island Union of Federated Workers, the Pre-School Teachers' Asscn, Makim Island Rural Workers' Org., Nanolelei Retailers' Union, the Plantation Workers' Union of Fanning Island and the Overseas Fishermen's Union (formed in 1998); 2,500 mems; Pres. TATOA KAITEIE; Gen. Sec. TAMARETI TAAU.

Transport

ROADS

Wherever practicable, roads are built on all atolls, and connecting causeways between islets are also being built as funds and labour permit. A programme to construct causeways between North and South Tarawa was completed in the mid-1990s. Kiribati has about 670 km of roads that are suitable for motor vehicles; all-weather roads exist in Tarawa and Kiritimati.

SHIPPING

A major project to rehabilitate the port terminal and facilities at Betio, with finance totalling some US $22m. from Japan, was completed in 2000. There are other port facilities at Banaba, Kanton and English Harbour.

Inginimainiku Shipping Enterprises: Bikenibeu, Tarawa; fax 28539.

Kiribati Shipping Services Ltd: POB 495, Betio, Tarawa; tel. 26195; fax 26204; e-mail kssl@tskl.net.ki; operates three passenger/freight vessels on inter-island services and one landing craft; govt-owned; Gen. Man. Capt. ITIBWINNANG AIAIMOA.

Nikoraoi Shipping: Betio, Tarawa; tel. 26536; fax 26367.

CIVIL AVIATION

There are five international airports (Bonriki on South Tarawa, Cassidy on Kiritimati, Antekana on Butaritari, as well as others on Kanton and Tabuaeran) and several other airfields in Kiribati. Air Nauru (restyled as Our Airline in September 2006) and Air Marshall Islands also operate international services to Tarawa, and Aloha Airlines operates a charter flight service between Kiritimati Island and Honolulu, Hawaii.

Air Kiribati Ltd: POB 274, Bonriki, Tarawa; tel. 28088; fax 28216; e-mail airkiribati.admin@tsklnet.ki; f. 1977; fmrly Air Tungaru; national airline; operates scheduled services to 15 outer islands; Chair. TAKEI TAOABA; CEO BARANIKO BAARO.

Tourism

Kiribati's potential attractions include fishing and bird-watching opportunities, as well as the sites of Second World War battles. In 1997 Caroline Island, situated close to the recently realigned international date-line, was renamed Millennium Island in an attempt to maximize its potential for attracting visitors. However, attempts to establish tourism as a major source of revenue have been impeded by the remoteness of the islands. The number of visitor arrivals reached only 4,406 in 2006, rising to an estimated 4,709 in 2007. In 2001 the tourism industry earned some $3.0m.

Kiribati National Tourism Office: Ministry of Communications, Transport and Tourism Development, POB 487, Betio, Tarawa; tel. 26003; fax 26193; e-mail sto@mict.gov.ki; internet www.visit-kiribati.com; Sec. DAVID YEETING; Senior Tourist Officer TARATAAKE TEANNAKI.

THE DEMOCRATIC PEOPLE'S REPUBLIC OF KOREA

Introductory Survey

Location, Climate, Language, Religion, Flag, Capital

The Democratic People's Republic of Korea (North Korea) occupies the northern part of the Korean peninsula, bordered to the north by the People's Republic of China and, for a very short section to the north-east, by the Russian Federation, and to the south by the Republic of Korea. The climate is continental, with cold, dry winters and hot, humid summers; temperatures range from −6°C to 25°C (21°F to 77°F). The language is Korean. Buddhism, Christianity and Chundo Kyo are officially cited as the principal religions. The national flag (proportions 33 by 65) is red, with blue stripes on the upper and lower edges, each separated from the red by a narrow white stripe. Left of centre is a white disc containing a five-pointed red star. The capital is Pyongyang.

Recent History

Korea was formerly an independent monarchy. It was occupied by Japanese forces in 1905 and annexed by Japan in 1910, when the Emperor was deposed. Following Japan's surrender in August 1945, ending the Second World War, Korea was divided at latitude 38°N into military occupation zones, with Soviet forces in the North and US forces in the South. A Provisional People's Committee, led by Kim Il Sung of the Korean Communist Party (KCP), was established in the North in February 1946 and accorded government status by the Soviet occupation forces. In July the KCP merged with another group to form the North Korean Workers' Party. In 1947 a legislative body, the Choe Ko In Min Hoe Ui (Supreme People's Assembly—SPA), was established, and Kim Il Sung became Premier. A new Assembly was elected in August 1948, and the Democratic People's Republic of Korea (DPRK) was proclaimed on 9 September. In the same year the Republic of Korea (q.v.) was proclaimed in the South. Initially, the DPRK was recognized only by the USSR and other communist countries. Soviet forces withdrew from North Korea in December 1948. In the following year, as a result of a merger between communists in the North and South, the Korean Workers' Party (KWP) was formed, under the leadership of Kim Il Sung; it has held power in North Korea ever since.

The two republics each claimed to have legitimate jurisdiction over the whole Korean peninsula. North Korean forces crossed the 38th parallel in June 1950, precipitating a three-year war between North and South. The UN mounted a collective defence action in support of South Korea, and the invasion was repelled. North Korean forces were supported by the People's Republic of China from October 1950. Peace talks began in July 1951 and an armistice agreement was concluded in July 1953. The cease-fire line, which approximately follows the 38th parallel, remains the frontier between North and South Korea. A demilitarized zone (DMZ), supervised by UN forces, separates the two countries.

Through the 'personality cult' of Kim Il Sung (the 'Great Leader') and of his son Kim Jong Il (the 'Dear Leader'), and a policy of strict surveillance of the entire population, overt opposition to the KWP was effectively eliminated. The only organized opposition to the regime (albeit in exile) appeared to be the Salvation Front for the Democratic Unification of Chosun, established by former military and other officials of the DPRK in the early 1990s, with branches in Russia, Japan and China. International human rights organizations indicated that they believed there to be a number of concentration camps in North Korea, in which as many as 200,000 political prisoners were being held.

A new Constitution, adopted in December 1972, created the office of President, and Kim Il Sung was duly elected to the post. Kim Jong Il was appointed to several key positions within the KWP in 1980. In July 1984 Radio Pyongyang referred to Kim Jong Il, for the first time, as the 'sole successor' to his father, but there were reports of opposition to the President's heir, particularly among older members of the KWP.

Following elections to the eighth SPA, in November 1986 (when the 655 members were returned unopposed), Kim Il Sung was re-elected President, and a new Administration Council (cabinet) was formed. In March 1990 Kim Il Sung was returned to the post of President, and Kim Jong Il was appointed to his first state (as distinct from party) post, as First Vice-Chairman of the National Defence Commission. In February 1991 it was rumoured that there had been an unsuccessful military coup against Kim Jong Il. In December he was appointed Supreme Commander of the Korean People's Army (KPA), in place of his father, and in January 1992 he was reported to have been given control of foreign policy. In April Kim Jong Il was appointed to the rank of Marshal, while his father assumed the title of Grand Marshal.

In what was interpreted as a partial attempt to adapt to the change in international conditions following the collapse of communist regimes world-wide, the SPA (according to South Korean reports) made several amendments to the DPRK's Constitution in April 1992. Principal among these were the deletion of all references to Marxism-Leninism, and the promotion of 'economic openness' to allow limited foreign investment in the DPRK (although the KWP's guiding principle of *juche*, or self-reliance, was strongly emphasized). In September measures to address the deteriorating economic situation included a drastic devaluation of the national currency. At the fifth session of the ninth SPA in April 1993 Kim Jong Il was elected Chairman of the National Defence Commission. In July Kim Il Sung's younger brother, Kim Yong Ju, unexpectedly returned to political life after a 17-year absence, and was subsequently elevated to the position of Vice-President and to membership of the Central Committee of the KWP's Politburo.

Kim Il Sung died of heart failure on 8 July 1994. One hundred days of national mourning were observed, but, contrary to expectations, Kim Jong Il was not appointed to the leading post of President of the DPRK. Kim Jong Il did not appear in public during this period, reviving earlier speculation that he was either in poor health or that a struggle for power was taking place. It was thought that Kim Il Sung's widow, Kim Song Ae, who was the stepmother of Kim Jong Il, favoured her eldest son, Kim Pyong Il, for the presidency. In February 1995 the Minister of the People's Armed Forces, Marshal O Jin U, died; O had been a significant supporter within the military of Kim Jong Il's succession. Scheduled elections to the SPA did not take place in April 1995, and no session of the Assembly was convened in 1996. Meanwhile, from the mid-1990s, the influence of the KPA expanded significantly, as Kim Jong Il increasingly relied upon the military to maintain his power, and the policy of *Songun* ('military first') was emphasized as the regime's central doctrine. The 50th anniversary of the establishment of the KWP in October 1995 was dominated by the military rather than the party, and several generals were promoted. Kim Jong Il, however, failed to assume any new posts. In February 1996 Sung Hye Rim, a former consort of Kim Jong Il and mother of his eldest son, defected to a Western European country. In February 1997 Premier Kang Song San, who had made no public appearance since early 1996, was dismissed, and replaced on an acting basis by Hong Song Nam. Deepening social unrest was indicated by an increase in the rate of defections. In February 1997 Hwang Jang Yop, a close adviser to Kim Jong Il, sought political asylum in the South Korean embassy in China while returning from an official visit to Japan, and warned that the DPRK was preparing to launch a military assault on South Korea. Hwang's defection appeared to precipitate significant changes in the KWP and military high command, as did the deaths of the Minister of the People's Armed Forces, Marshal Choe Kwang, and of his deputy, Kim Kwang Jin. Many senior figures in the formal hierarchy were replaced, and some 123 generals, including many allies of Kim Jong Il, were promoted in rank in April. In August two senior North Korean diplomats, including the ambassador to Egypt, defected to the USA. There were also rumours of unrest and coup attempts, and several senior figures disappeared from public view without explanation. The official mourning period for

Kim Il Sung was formally declared to be at an end in July 1997, on the third anniversary of his death. It was announced that, henceforth, the country was to use the *Juche* calendar, with 1912, the year of Kim Il Sung's birth, designated the first year of the new calendar. On 8 October 1997, in accordance with the recommendations of recent municipal and provincial conferences of the KWP (including KPA delegates), Kim Jong Il was elected General Secretary of the KWP.

Elections to the SPA finally took place in July 1998, at which the single list of candidates received 100% of the votes cast. Some two-thirds of the 687 deputies were newcomers to the Assembly, while the military reportedly doubled its representation. The first session of the 10th SPA was convened in September. However, the anticipated appointment of Kim Jong Il as President of the DPRK did not occur, as the post was effectively abolished under major amendments to the Constitution that extensively revised the structure of government. The deceased Kim Il Sung was designated 'Eternal President', thus remaining *de jure* Head of State, while Kim Jong Il, who had been re-elected Chairman of the National Defence Commission (now apparently the highest office in the state hierarchy), assumed the role of *de facto* Head of State. Vice-Marshal Jo Myong Rok, the Director of the General Political Bureau of the KPA, was appointed First Vice-Chairman of the Commission, becoming the *de facto* second-ranking official in the DPRK. The Cabinet, as the Administration Council was redesignated, assumed many of the functions of the Central People's Committee, which was abolished. A new Presidium of the SPA was established, the President of which was to represent the State in diplomatic affairs; Kim Yong Nam, hitherto Minister of Foreign Affairs, was appointed to this position. Hong Song Nam was formally appointed Premier of the new Cabinet. Two 'technocrats', Jo Chang Dok and Kwak Pom Gi, were appointed Vice-Premiers.

Elections to the Local People's Assemblies were held in March 1999; it was reported that all candidates were fully endorsed. In October 2000 the Minister of Finance, Rim Kyong Suk, and the President of the central bank, Jong Song Thaek, were dismissed. They were replaced, respectively, by Mun Il Bong and Kim Wan Su. No reasons were given for their dismissal. The replacement of the Minister of Foreign Trade in December was also unexplained. The Minister of Agriculture was replaced in March 2001.

In January 2001 the Government urged a 'new way of thinking' to solve the country's economic and domestic problems and to complement the *Kangsong Taeguk* ('prosperous and powerful nation') philosophy adopted in the late 1990s. Meanwhile, the number of people defecting from the North to the South continued to increase, with nearly 650 such persons having settled in the latter since 1996. Several senior officials died or were replaced during 2001, including Ri Song Bok, the Secretary-General of the Party Central Committee and a senior aide to Kim Jong Il, who died in May.

In March 2002 the fifth session of the 10th SPA was held. A new land planning law was adopted with the aim of improving and intensifying land work. Premier Hong Song Nam also urged improved trade and economic co-operation, including joint ventures with other countries and international organizations. In April Kim Jong Il promoted some 55 military leaders, including Jang Song U, the elder brother of Kim's brother-in-law, Jang Song Thaek.

The question of the succession of the next generation of leadership became increasingly important during 2002–03, following Kim Jong Il's 60th birthday in February 2002. Kim was initially believed to have been preparing his eldest son, Kim Jong Nam, to succeed him. Kim Jong Nam had served in the Ministry of Public Security and as head of the country's information technology (IT) industry since the late 1990s; however, in May 2001 he was detained in Tokyo, on charges of entering Japan with a false passport, and subsequently deported to China. The incident discredited Kim Jong Nam, and thenceforth it was reported that Kim Jong Il was preparing for leadership Kim Jong Chol, the elder son of Ko Yong Hui, described as Kim Jong Il's unofficial wife. Kim Jong Nam spent much of 2002 in Russia, where his mother, Sung Hye Rim, died in July.

In September 2002 the Government designated the city of Sinuiju a 'Special Administrative Region' designed to attract foreign investment, and appointed Yang Bin, a Chinese-born Dutch citizen, as its first governor. However, within days of his appointment, Yang was arrested by the Chinese authorities on corruption charges, and he was unable to assume his post. None the less, the creation of the region was a significant development in the country's efforts to open up the economy. Under the 'Basic Law' establishing the region, Sinuiju would have its own government and legal system for a 50-year period, without interference from the DPRK. (In late 2004 there were indications that the Sinuiju project had been abandoned, although in July 2006 it was reported that DPRK loyalists and foreign-currency management groups were being moved into the area. In mid-2007 it was further reported that some 3,000 families were being relocated from Pyongyang to Sinuiju, which had apparently been declared a special economic zone earlier in that year.) In late 2002 the Government also established a special industrial zone in Kaesong, and a special tourist zone in the region of Mount Kumgang, although these did not have the same special status as Sinuiju. Despite these developments, a meeting of senior law enforcement officials was held in Pyongyang in December during which Premier Hong urged the elimination of 'non-socialist elements'. In early 2003 it was reported that travel restrictions within the country had been reintroduced, in order to improve security.

The sixth session of the 10th SPA was held in March 2003. Unlike previous sessions, Kim Jong Il did not attend the meeting. Having disappeared from public view for 50 days, according to South Korean observers, Kim reappeared in early April, and later in that month celebrations took place in Pyongyang to mark the 10th anniversary of Kim's election as Chairman of the National Defence Commission. Further celebrations took place in July to mark the 50th anniversary of the Korean War truce (celebrated as a triumph for the DPRK by the country's media). In August elections were held to form the 11th SPA. Voter turnout was reported to be have been 99.9%, and all 687 candidates were elected unopposed. At the first session of the 11th SPA in September, Kim Jong Il was re-elected as Chairman of the National Defence Commission. In October Kim Yong Sun, a member of the KWP Secretariat and Chairman of the Korea Asia-Pacific Peace Committee, died, reportedly as a result of a traffic accident. Kim Yong Sun had been an important figure in inter-Korean relations (see below).

In early 2004 reports from defectors, as well as some documentary evidence, indicated that mistreatment of political prisoners in the DPRK had included human experimentation for the purposes of chemical weapons development. On the occasion of Kim's 62nd birthday in February 2004, there was renewed speculation on the question of his successor. It was rumoured that Kim Jong Un, younger son of Ko Yong Hui, might have emerged as the most likely candidate, having been referred to by some sources as the 'Morning Star King'.

In April 2004 more than 150 people were killed and 1,300 injured by a massive explosion on a railway line at Ryongchon, a town near the border with China. Many children were among the victims of the accident, apparently caused when electric cables ignited chemical and other materials being transported by rail, only hours after a train carrying Kim Jong Il had travelled through the area. The North Korean authorities withheld information on the accident for two days, but subsequently accepted international humanitarian aid, including a donation (made through the Red Cross) from the USA. The railway accident drew attention to the shortcomings of the DPRK's health care system.

In July 2004 Ju Sang Song was appointed as Minister of People's Security, replacing Choe Ryong Su. Choe had been removed from his post only one year after being appointed, and the reason for his removal remained unclear. Also in July the 10th anniversary of the death of Kim Il Sung was commemorated. In August Ko Yong Hui, the mother of two of Kim Jong Il's sons (see above), was reported to have died. In November there was speculation that Kim's hold on power might be weakening, following reports that portraits of him had been removed from public locations. It was also noted that official news reports no longer referred to Kim by the honorific title of 'Dear Leader'. Some sources claimed that Kim himself was attempting to diminish the personality cult surrounding him. However, there were tentative suggestions throughout 2004 that a power struggle was taking place in Pyongyang. It was believed that in April Kim had removed his brother-in-law, Jang Song Thaek, from his position as vice-director of the KWP Central Committee and placed him under house arrest. Later in the year Jang's wife, Kim Jong Il's sister Kim Kyong Hui, was injured in a traffic incident, which was believed to have been a deliberate attack. The couple were described as the most powerful people in the DPRK after Kim Jong Il. Meanwhile, in April Kim's eldest son, Kim Jong Nam (see above), reportedly survived an assassination attempt in Austria, amid suggestions that the attempt on his life had been connected to the issue of leadership succession.

In May 2005 South Korean media reported that the North Korean Minister of Post and Telecommunications, Ri Kum Bom, had been dismissed, apparently as a result of his failure to control the revelation of information earlier in the year disclosing that the DPRK was in the process of combating outbreaks of avian influenza ('bird flu'). In July it was announced that his replacement was Ryu Yong Sop. In August an unspecified number of prisoners were granted an amnesty to mark the 60th anniversary of the liberation of the Korean peninsula from Japanese rule. In October the 60th anniversary of the KWP was celebrated. North Korean citizens were reportedly granted four public holidays in honour of the event. On 9 October, the day before the anniversary, the KWP held a national meeting in Pyongyang, at which the primacy of the *Songun* ('military first') policy was reaffirmed, as was the need for economic development in order to achieve the objective of *Kangsong Taeguk* ('prosperous and powerful nation'). The anniversary itself was commemorated with a large military parade in Pyongyang. In late October it was reported that Yon Hyong Muk, a Vice-Chairman of the National Defence Commission, who was regarded as a close adviser to Kim Jong Il, had died. North Korean media reports in November indicated that Ri Kwang Nam had been replaced as Minister of Extractive Industries by Kang Min Chol, while a report in December implied that Kim Jin Song had become Minister of Culture, replacing Choe Ik Kyu. In January 2006 Jang Song Thaek made his first public appearance since 2003, prompting speculation that he had been rehabilitated following his apparent removal from favour in 2004 (see above).

While thousands took to the streets in October 2006 for mass rallies to celebrate the nuclear test (see below), in November a rare protest against the authorities occurred in a town in North Hamkyong Province. Although the number of demonstrators was said to be little more than 100, the demonstration was highly significant, private mass activities being forbidden by North Korean law. According to a report on *Daily NK*, a website maintained by a group campaigning for democracy in the DPRK, residents of Hoiryeong were demonstrating against 'refurbishment fees' for a local market imposed on them by the town's officials. North Korean refugees living in China also reported growing discontent towards the regime, with 90% of the 1,300 refugees questioned by the bipartisan US Committee on Human Rights in North Korea agreeing that North Koreans were expressing their concerns about chronic food shortages.

In January 2007 the Minister of Foreign Affairs, Paek Nam Sun, was reported to have died of lung cancer. He was replaced by Pak Ui Chun, a former ambassador to Russia, in May. At the fifth session of the 11th SPA in mid-April, Premier Pak Pong Ju was replaced by Kim Yong Il, hitherto Minister of Land and Marine Transport. Although no official explanation was given, observers suggested that the new Premier's experience in infrastructure might indicate the future direction of government policy. At the same time Vice-Marshal Kim Yong Chun, hitherto Chief of General Staff of the KPA, was appointed as a Vice-Chairman of the National Defence Commission, filling the vacancy left by the death of Yon Hyong Muk in October 2005. Gen. Kim Kyok Sik became the new KPA Chief of General Staff. The permanent staff of the National Defence Commission was expanded as part of a further reorganization of senior military officials in May 2007, with the appointment of Gen. Ri Myong Su, the former operations director of the KPA, as a standing member. The changes at the National Defence Commission were generally interpreted as an attempt to enhance its role and powers. Rumours suggesting that Kim Jong Il's health was deteriorating prompted renewed speculation regarding his successor in mid-2007. This speculation intensified in August, following reports that Kim's eldest son, Kim Jong Nam, had returned from exile to work in the organization and guidance bureau of the KWP. However, Kim dismissed reports of his ill health during the inter-Korean summit meeting held in Pyongyang in early October (see below). Thae Jong Su was appointed as a Vice-Premier of the Cabinet later that month. In November it was reported that Jang Song Thaek had been promoted from the position of vice-director within the KWP to the directorship of the party's department responsible for state internal security, while Kim's second eldest son, Kim Jong Chol, had been appointed as a vice-director of another department of the KWP.

Meanwhile, the DPRK's economic difficulties and widespread food shortages were exacerbated by unusually serious flooding in 1995 and 1996, forcing the country to appeal to the UN and other international organizations for emergency food aid and flood relief. Assistance was provided by the USA, the Republic of Korea and Japan in 1995, but in early 1996 further shipments of cereals were halted, pending a positive response by the DPRK to US proposals for peace negotiations (see below). Renewed appeals for emergency aid were issued by the UN in mid-1996, to which the USA, South Korea and Japan responded on humanitarian grounds. In January 1997 it was reported that China had agreed to provide 500,000 metric tons of rice annually for five years. This was followed, in February, by an unprecedented admission from the DPRK that the country was experiencing 'temporary food problems' and that it had only one-half of the cereals necessary to feed its people.

In April and July 1997 the UN's World Food Programme (WFP) issued two further appeals for food and medical supplies. UN representatives sent to the DPRK to assess the extent of the crisis confirmed that chronic malnutrition was widespread, particularly among infants, and that the medical system was no longer able to provide even basic health care. The situation deteriorated in mid-1997, when severe drought devastated most of the North Korean maize crop; further damage was caused by a tidal wave on the western coast. In January 1998 WFP issued the largest appeal in the organization's history, requesting emergency aid valued at some US $380m. Agreement was reached with the DPRK whereby additional UN staff were to be permitted to enter the country in order to monitor the distribution of aid, following allegations that supplies had been diverted to the army. Despite the provision of aid, severe food shortages persisted during 1998 and malnutrition was widespread among children. In December the UN issued an appeal for humanitarian aid. In mid-1999 WFP announced that increased aid had prevented starvation in the country for the time being, although poor infrastructure continued to hamper food distribution, and entry to 49 of the country's 211 counties was still forbidden. In August serious flooding destroyed large areas of farm land.

Severe weather conditions during 2000 exacerbated food shortages in North Korea, leaving it in increased need of international aid. In November 2000 the UN estimated North Korea's food shortage for 2001 at some 1.2m. metric tons. In December 2000 the organization appealed to the international community for aid worth some US $390m., including 810,000 tons of food. In February 2001 WFP agreed to provide 810,000 tons of food and $93m. in aid. The UN subsequently urged members to provide $383m. in humanitarian aid in 2002. In April 2001 the head of WFP in the country stated that the most recent winter had been especially severe and could thus result in food shortages comparable to those of 1996–97. In May the South began deliveries of 200,000 tons of agricultural fertilizer, and in June WFP stated that the North had received 389,775 tons of food aid between January and May, but would require an additional 250,000 tons to prevent starvation later in the year. The official state media announced in June that the country had experienced 100 days of continuous drought since March; WFP subsequently estimated that the 2001 grain harvest would fall to 2.57m. tons, far less than the 4.8m. tons needed overall. In October WFP delivered emergency food supplies to flood-stricken Kangwon Province, and the Government began land rezoning programmes aimed at modernizing agricultural production in South Hwanghae Province. In November the head of the World Health Organization (WHO), Gro Harlem Brundtland, visited the DPRK and opened a permanent WHO office in Pyongyang. In December the Government launched an intensive campaign for potato and double-crop growing, in order to ease the famine.

In September–October 2002 representatives of FAO and WFP visited the DPRK and released a special report on the food situation. According to this report, in 2002 the harvest was believed to have improved somewhat. Overall food production was 49% higher than in 2001, but 6% below the levels of 1995/96. Total cereal production, including potato equivalents, for 2002/03 was expected to reach 3.8m. tons, whereas food requirements were forecast at 4.9m. tons, thus leaving a deficit of 1.1m. tons. Food consumption per caput per day was projected at 270g of cereal in cities, compared with 600g in rural areas. Thus, urban residents were forced to spend 75%–85% of income on food purchases. The introduction in July 2002 of a quasi-market pricing system caused a significant inflation of food prices, despite the concurrent increase in salaries.

In November 2003 the UN made a new appeal for humanitarian assistance to North Korea, stating that aid of more than US $200m. would be required in order to resolve the 'chronic emergency' in the DPRK. By February 2004 the aid crisis had deepened, with WFP stating that in early 2004 it would be able to give food rations to only 100,000 people, leaving the remainder of the 6.5m. people hitherto supported by WFP vulnerable to food shortages. A survey conducted by WFP in 2004 concluded that 37% of North Korean children aged six years and under were chronically malnourished. In November the UN stated that, despite relatively good harvests in 2004, 6.4m. people would remain in need of food aid in 2005, owing in part to a dramatic increase in food prices as a consequence of price reforms in 2002. In January 2005 it was reported that government food rations, upon which approximately two-thirds of the population were believed to depend, were to be reduced from 300g of grains per day to 250g. By May the head of the WFP's mission in the DPRK was warning that without increased contributions a number of people in the country could face 'famine-like conditions'. In the following month the USA pledged to supply 50,000 metric tons of food aid, its third successive annual donation, while simultaneously denying that this act was linked to the stalled negotiations on the DPRK's military nuclear programme (see below). In September, however, the North Korean Government announced that it had asked humanitarian aid agencies operating in the DPRK to terminate food aid programmes and withdraw the majority of their foreign staff by the end of the year. The Government asserted that, following a harvest that year reported to be the best in a decade, it was able to feed its people without assistance, and expressed a desire to progress from humanitarian to developmental aid. (Analysts speculated that the Government of the DPRK preferred to rely on food aid from China and the Republic of Korea, as the distribution of aid from these countries was monitored less closely and the political implications of allowing Westerners access to the country were thereby avoided.) Subsequently, WFP terminated its operations in North Korea in January 2006, although its activities were resumed after negotiations with the Government in May.

Severe flooding in July 2006, moreover, prompted the North Korean Government to seek further humanitarian aid. Reports from the South Korean Ministry of Unification in August suggested that, partly as a result of the flooding, the DPRK's food shortfall for 2006 might be as high as 1.6m. metric tons, and by October WFP was warning of renewed famine conditions. The shortage of food was exacerbated by the reluctance of donor nations to give aid to the DPRK following its missile tests in July and October (see below). South Korean reports in November suggested that, unofficially at least, the DPRK hoped for an early resumption of food aid. The South Korean Government, however, stated that more co-operation was needed from the DPRK over the issue of the country's nuclear programme before any further humanitarian assistance could be granted.

A report published by FAO in January 2007 estimated that the number of malnourished people in the DPRK had risen to 7.9m. in the period 2001–03, compared with 3.6m. in 1990–92. The UN Development Programme (UNDP) announced that it was suspending its non-humanitarian work in the country, pending an investigation into allegations by the USA that UN funding was being misappropriated by the North Korean Government. From March 2007 all UNDP's work in the DPRK was suspended after the North Korean authorities refused to comply with certain conditions for continued operations in the country. The preliminary findings of an investigation by the UN Board of Auditors into operations in the DPRK, which were presented at the end of May, indicated that there had been some breaches of regulations, but no systematic diversion of UN funds to the North Korean authorities. A second phase of the audit commenced later that year, while UNDP commissioned a separate external review into areas not covered by the Board of Auditors.

The DPRK suffered further severe flooding in August 2007, which led to some 600 deaths and left more than 100,000 people homeless, as well as causing widespread damage to roads, buildings and infrastructure. The North Korean authorities estimated that 11% of the country's cereal crops had been destroyed. In response, the UN and the Red Cross launched international appeals for US $14m. and $5.5m., respectively, while WFP announced plans to provide emergency food aid for 215,000 people over a three-month period. South Korea, which had resumed deliveries of fertilizer to the North in March and of food aid in June, pledged aid worth $47.5m. A typhoon in September led to further flooding of farm land and the destruction of buildings. FAO estimated that the import of more than 1m. metric tons of cereals would be required during 2007/08 in order to maintain annual cereal consumption at around 160 kg per caput. In April 2008 WFP warned of a humanitarian crisis, the food deficit for the coming year having been revised upwards to 1.66m. metric tons, more than double the shortfall of 2007.

In 1971 talks took place for the first time between the Red Cross Societies of North and South Korea. Negotiations were, however, suspended in 1973, and hopes for better relations were undermined by a series of clashes between North and South Korean vessels in disputed waters during 1974. Propaganda campaigns, suspended by agreement in 1972, were resumed by both sides. In October 1978 the UN Command (UNC—under which troops were stationed in South Korea) accused the DPRK of threatening the 1953 truce, after the discovery of an underground tunnel (the third since 1974) beneath the DMZ. During the 1980s the increasing prominence of Kim Jong Il, who advocated an uncompromising policy towards the South, appeared to aggravate the situation. In 1983 some 17 South Koreans, including four government ministers, were killed in a bomb explosion in Burma (now Myanmar), in what appeared to be an assassination attempt on the South Korean President, Chun Doo-Hwan. The DPRK was held responsible for the attack, and Burma severed relations with the country. In January 1984, none the less, the DPRK suggested tripartite talks on reunification, involving North and South Korea and the USA; however, the proposal was rejected by South Korea, which favoured bilateral talks. During 1984 the DPRK's propaganda campaign was moderated, and in September North Korea provided emergency relief to flood-stricken areas of the South. In November the first talks, on possible economic co-operation, were held, and negotiations continued in 1985. However, in February 1986, during the annual South Korean-US 'Team Spirit' military manoeuvres, North Korea suspended all negotiations with the South. The DPRK denied accusations by the South of North Korean involvement in the explosion of a South Korean airliner over Burma in November 1987, despite the subsequent confession of an alleged North Korean agent. In August 1988 three sessions of talks were held at the 'peace village' of Panmunjom (in the DMZ) between delegates of the legislatures of North and South Korea, although the discussions (the first formal contact between the two countries since 1986) produced no conclusive results. Further negotiations in 1989 were suspended by the DPRK.

Inter-Korean talks resumed in mid-1990, and in September the DPRK Premier visited the South Korean capital, Seoul, for discussions with his counterpart, the most senior-level bilateral contact since the end of the Korean War. Subsequent discussions culminated in the signing of an 'Agreement on Reconciliation, Non-aggression and Exchanges and Co-operation between the South and the North', in Seoul in December 1991. Both states pledged, *inter alia*, to desist from mutual slander, vilification and sabotage, to promote economic and other co-operation and the reunion of families separated by the war, and to work towards a full peace treaty to replace the 1953 armistice agreement. In November 1992, however, the DPRK threatened a complete suspension of contacts with the South, in protest at the latter's decision to resume the 'Team Spirit' military exercises in March 1993. (The 1992 exercises had been cancelled, owing to the improvement in relations between the two states.) Relations had also been seriously impaired by the South's announcement, in October 1992, that an extensive North Korean espionage network had been discovered in South Korea, and by the North's repeated refusals to agree to simultaneous nuclear inspections in both countries (see below).

The controversy surrounding the DPRK's suspected nuclear programme prevented any improvement in inter-Korean relations during 1993 and the first half of 1994, and contacts were also strained by the DPRK's withdrawal, in May 1994, of its mission to the Military Armistice Commission (the Panmunjom-based body overseeing the maintenance of the 1953 truce). Following talks between Kim Il Sung and former US President Jimmy Carter, who visited the DPRK (on a private initiative) in June 1994, it was announced that the first summit meeting at presidential level between the two Korean states would be held in Pyongyang in July. However, the death of Kim Il Sung led to the indefinite postponement of the summit meeting. The signature of the US-DPRK nuclear accord in October (see below) caused South Korea to make renewed efforts to resume the inter-Korean negotiations, and in February 1995 the South announced the cancellation of the annual 'Team Spirit' manoeuvres (for the second consecutive year), as a gesture of goodwill.

Tension increased markedly in April 1996, when the DPRK announced its decision to abandon the 1953 armistice. North

Korean troops subsequently made a number of incursions into the DMZ, thereby violating the provisions of the agreement. Later in the month, in an attempt to revitalize the peace process and replace the armistice agreement with a formal peace treaty, President Bill Clinton of the USA and President Kim Young-Sam of the Republic of Korea proposed four-way talks, involving the two Koreas, the USA and China. China responded positively, but the DPRK declared its willingness to hold discussions only with the USA. Relations between the two Koreas deteriorated considerably in September, when a submarine from North Korea was discovered abandoned in South Korean waters. One of the two surviving crew members claimed that this was the fourth such mission undertaken by armed North Koreans. South Korea suspended all contact with the DPRK, and the UN Security Council subsequently expressed 'serious concern' at the incident. Following protracted mediation by the USA, an unprecedented apology was broadcast in South Korea by the (North) Korean Central News Agency.

In March 1997 explanatory talks between delegates from the DPRK, the Republic of Korea and the USA were held in New York to discuss the proposed quadripartite negotiations. Following the talks, the DPRK announced that its participation in full quadripartite negotiations was conditional upon the receipt of substantial food aid. In May representatives of the Red Cross organizations of North and South Korea (in the first such meeting for five years) reached agreement on the provision of grain to the DPRK. Negotiations were concluded in October to allow foreign airlines, including those from South Korea, to use North Korean airspace.

Despite a military confrontation between North and South Korean troops in the DMZ in July 1997, full quadripartite negotiations, aimed at concluding a peace treaty between North and South Korea, finally opened in Geneva, Switzerland, in December. A second round of full discussions was held in March 1998, but proved unsuccessful, since the DPRK continued to insist on the inclusion on the agenda of the withdrawal of US troops from the Korean peninsula. In December 1997, meanwhile, negotiations in the Chinese capital of Beijing between the South and North Korean Red Cross organizations foundered, owing to North Korea's reluctance to allow South Korean officials access to the DPRK to monitor the distribution of food aid. At a subsequent meeting, in March 1998, the provision of additional food aid was agreed.

Following the inauguration of the new South Korean President, Kim Dae-Jung, in February 1998, the DPRK urged 'dialogue and negotiation' with the South Korean administration. Nevertheless, a ministerial-level meeting held in Beijing in April, to discuss the provision of fertilizer to North Korea (the first such direct contact for four years), broke down amid mutual accusations of inflexibility, when the South Koreans insisted that the DPRK enter into negotiations on the reunion of families. In that month, however, as part of Kim Dae-Jung's 'sunshine' policy of co-operation with the DPRK, the South Korean Government announced measures to encourage inter-Korean economic contacts, allowing the transfer of private funds to the North and relaxing legislation on investment. In June, in an historic development, Chung Ju-Yung, the founder of the South Korean conglomerate Hyundai, was permitted to cross the DMZ to deliver a gift of cattle to his home town; proposals for several other joint ventures were also discussed, including a plan to operate tour boats to Mount Kumgang, just north of the border. This improvement in relations seemed to be in jeopardy when, during the visit, a North Korean submarine was caught in the nets of a southern fishing boat; all nine crew members were found dead inside the vessel. The UNC condemned the incursion during a meeting with North Korean army officers in Panmunjom, the first such talks to be held in seven years. A further delivery of cattle was made by Chung Ju-Yung in October, when he also met with Kim Jong Il, and in November some 800 tourists from South Korea participated in the first visit to Mount Kumgang. In December, during Chung's third visit to North Korea, a proposal for the construction of an industrial complex at Haeju was approved. Following further visits in early 1999, it was announced that these would continue on a monthly basis. In December 1998, meanwhile, South Korean naval forces sank a suspected North Korean spy boat, after pursuing it into international waters.

In June 1999 a week-long confrontation between North and South Korean naval forces in the Yellow Sea resulted in a brief gun battle, during which one North Korean torpedo boat was sunk. Two rounds of bilateral talks in Beijing in June and July ended in failure. In September the DPRK declared invalid the Northern Limit Line (the maritime border that has separated the territorial waters of the two Koreas since 1953), in protest at the UNC's refusal to renegotiate its demarcation. Meanwhile, no discernible progress had been achieved at sessions of the quadripartite talks held in April and August 1999. None the less, Hyundai proceeded with its plans for a number of projects in North Korea: in October the company concluded an agreement with the DPRK on the construction of the proposed industrial complex, which, it was envisaged, would comprise some 850 businesses, employing some 220,000 people, and would be capable of producing export goods worth an estimated US $3,000m. annually. In February 2000 foreign residents in South Korea were permitted to visit Mount Kumgang for the first time. In December 1999 another major South Korean company, Samsung Electronics, announced that it had signed a contract with the DPRK for the joint development of computer software and the manufacture of electronic products. In February 2000 the construction of a motor vehicle assembly plant, in a joint venture with the Pyonghwa Motor Company of South Korea, began in Nampo, south-west of Pyongyang. According to South Korean estimates, inter-Korean trade increased by 50.2% in 1999. A number of joint North-South cultural and sporting events took place in 1999. In April 2000, following a series of senior-level bilateral contacts in Beijing, North and South Korea jointly announced that an historic summit meeting would take place between Kim Dae-Jung and Kim Jong Il in Pyongyang in June.

Following the presidential summit meeting in mid-June 2000, detailed agreements were signed pledging economic co-operation, the building of mutual trust and the resolution of reunification issues. In July ministerial-level delegations from both countries met in Seoul. This was the first visit to the South by North Korean officials since 1991. A joint communiqué was issued allowing for, *inter alia*, the reopening of liaison offices at Panmunjom, which had been closed in 1996, and the reconnection of the inter-Korean Kyongui railway line. The construction of a highway to run alongside the railway from North to South was subsequently agreed. In September 2000 Kim Dae-Jung formally inaugurated the project to remove thousands of landmines and rebuild the railway line and adjacent highway. Meanwhile, in August 100 North Korean families travelled to Seoul and 100 South Korean families visited Pyongyang simultaneously to meet with relatives from whom they had been separated by the Korean War. The second ministerial meeting between the two sides was held in Pyongyang later that month. It was agreed to hold two more cross-border family reunions by the end of 2000 and to commence talks on economic co-operation. In a symbolic display of unity, in September the two countries marched under the same flag in the opening ceremony of the Olympic Games in Sydney, Australia. In late September the DPRK's Minister of the People's Armed Forces, Vice-Marshal Kim Il Chol, visited the South and met his counterpart, Cho Seong-Tae, the first such ministerial meeting ever held. In October Kim Dae-Jung was awarded the Nobel Peace Prize in recognition of his reunification efforts. Further rounds of inter-ministerial, military and economic talks took place during 2000 and early 2001.

Despite the increased level of co-operation between the two countries, in December 2000 South Korea published its annual defence policy document, which described the North as its main enemy and alleged that it had expanded its military capacity along the DMZ. The DPRK was antagonized by its continued status as South Korea's most likely adversary. The North Korean Government was also displeased by the approval of a resolution by the South Korean legislature to demand the repatriation of prisoners of war who, it alleged, continued to be held by the North, despite the DPRK's denial of the existence of these prisoners.

In early 2001 the uncompromising attitude displayed by the new US Administration towards North Korea threatened to undermine the reconciliation process. In March the DPRK unilaterally postponed scheduled cabinet-level talks following a visit to the USA by Kim Dae-Jung, and in April North Korea denounced joint US-South Korean military exercises as a betrayal of the goodwill surrounding the June 2000 summit meeting. Ministerial discussions resumed in Seoul in September 2001, the sixth round of which was concluded in November without any agreement—the first such unsuccessful round since the presidential summit meeting.

US President George W. Bush's reference in January 2002 to North Korea as part of an 'axis of evil' threatened to damage inter-Korean relations. A stalemate in inter-Korean relations was broken in April, however, when the North received Kim Dae-Jung's special envoy, Lim Dong-Won. Following the visit, during which Lim met Kim Jong Il, the two sides agreed to further reunions for separated families (see below) and to continuing discussions on economic co-operation. The DPRK also agreed to Lim's request that it renew dialogue with the USA and Japan. In May Park Geun-Hye, a South Korean legislator and the daughter of former President Park Chung-Hee, visited the North and met Kim Jong Il. The visit was remarkable because North Korean agents had killed Park's mother in 1974 in a bid to assassinate her father. Despite the cordial visit, North Korea cancelled economic co-operation discussions with the South in May 2002.

In May 2002 the increasing number of defectors from the North received international attention as several groups sought asylum at Canadian, Japanese and South Korean diplomatic buildings in China. They were eventually allowed to travel to the South, albeit via the Philippines. The South Korean Ministry of Unification reported in January 2003 that during 2002 some 1,141 North Koreans had defected to the South, compared with 583 in 2001.

At the end of June 2002 a gun battle between North and South Korean vessels in the Yellow Sea resulted in the sinking of a Southern patrol boat and the deaths of six crew members. South Korean military sources estimated that 30 North Korean crewmen were also killed in the confrontation, which had started when two North Korean vessels accompanying a fishing boat reportedly crossed the Northern Limit Line. Following the incident, in July South Korea suspended rice shipments to the North and economic co-operation projects, reflecting widespread public anger. None the less, Kim Dae-Jung maintained his 'sunshine' policy towards the North.

In August 2002 North and South Korea held a seventh round of ministerial talks in Seoul, aimed at improving relations in the aftermath of the latest naval confrontation, and focusing on the issue of future family reunions, railway links (see below) and cultural exchanges. Regarding the latter, more than 300 North Korean athletes travelled to the South and participated in the Asian Games held in Busan during October. In September the first inter-Korean military 'hotline' was inaugurated to allow for improved communications during sensitive occasions.

The eighth round of ministerial talks was held in Pyongyang in October 2002 and mainly focused on economic co-operation issues, despite the fact that the USA had earlier revealed the existence of a secret nuclear weapons programme in the North (see below). At the end of that month a North Korean economic delegation began a nine-day tour of the South, including several major industrial facilities in the itinerary. Noteworthy was the fact that the delegation included Jang Song Thaek, Kim Jong Il's brother-in-law and reportedly one of his most trusted advisers, and also Kim Hi Thaek, the first deputy head of the KWP's Central Committee. At the end of December the South Korean Ministry of National Defence published a 'white paper' which, for the first time, excluded any reference to the North as its main enemy.

By late 2002 some of the goodwill generated by the historic inter-Korean summit meeting in June 2000 had been dissipated by the revelation that Kim Dae-Jung had arranged for the Korea Development Bank to give a Hyundai affiliate substantial funds to transfer to the North in order to finance the meeting. However, the election in December 2002 of Roh Moo-Hyun, the candidate of Kim's party, as President of the Republic of Korea heralded a continuation of Kim's 'sunshine' policy. In early January 2003 representatives of Roh secretly met North Korean officials in Beijing, and later in that month a ninth round of ministerial talks was held in Seoul.

North and South Korea continued their efforts to improve bilateral relations during 2003, despite a severe deterioration in relations between the North and the USA over the issue of the former's nuclear weapons programme (see below). The DPRK hosted the 10th round of ministerial talks at the end of April. In mid-May, however, Pyongyang announced that it no longer recognized a Joint Declaration of the Denuclearization of the Korean Pensinsula, signed with the South in 1992 (see below). Also in May 2003, at talks between the two Koreas on economic matters, North Korea warned that the South would risk 'unspeakable disaster' if it became too confrontational in co-operating with the USA on the nuclear issue (the threat followed a summit meeting between Roh and US President George W. Bush). Attempts to develop inter-Korean relations were also complicated by confirmation in June by South Korean investigators that former President Kim Dae-Jung had made a substanianl payment in order to arrange the historic inter-Korean summit meeting of 2000 (see above). In August 2003 the suicide of Hyundai official Chung Mong-Hun, who had been indicted in connection with the illegal payments to the North, further undermined the credibility of the 'sunshine' policy. Meanwhile, the 50th anniversary in July of the *de facto* end of the Korean War, celebrated as a triumph in North Korea, was commemorated in a sombre fashion in South Korea. Also in July, cross-border gunfire was exchanged between North and South Korean soldiers. In October North Korean official Kim Yong Sun, an important figure in inter-Korean affairs who had attended the presidential summit meeting in 2000, died, reportedly as a result of a traffic accident. In November 2003 two well-known North Korean defectors, Hwang Jang Yop (see above) and former North Korean official Kim Dok Hong, left their posts at the South Korean Institute of National Unification Policy. There was a suggestion that their resignations might have been due to fears that their criticism of the North Korean regime might be damaging to South Korean attempts to negotiate with North Korea. The resignation in January 2004 of the South Korean Minister of Foreign Affairs, Yoon Young-Kwan, was believed to have been related to tensions within the South Korean Government over the country's co-operation with the USA on the issue of North Korean weapons.

In April 2004, following a major railway accident in North Korea at Ryongchon (see above), the DPRK accepted emergency supplies and assistance from South Korea. At the end of the month a South Korean cargo plane arrived in Pyongyang carrying further emergency supplies, representing the first ever direct flight for humanitarian purposes. In May senior-level military discussions took place between the two sides, at which the establishment of a radio communication line between the North and South Korean navies was agreed. It was believed that the new communication line would reduce naval conflicts between the two sides; although later in the year there were none the less incidents of warning shots being fired by the South Korean navy at North Korean vessels considered to have intruded on the maritime border, amid accusations that in some instances South Korean navy officials had failed to report North Korean radio messages. In June, meanwhile, in a symbolic development, propaganda broadcasts across the DMZ were silenced for the first time in decades, with loudspeakers on both sides of the border being switched off. Also in June, a senior DPRK representative, Vice-Chairman of the Korea Asia-Pacific Peace Committee Ri Jong Hyok, made a visit to Seoul and met South Korean President Roh Moo-hyun to mark the fourth anniversary of the inter-Korean summit meeting of 2000 (see above). In July 2004 more than 450 North Korean defectors arrived in Seoul. The DPRK subsequently accused South Korean officials of kidnapping its citizens and suspended bilateral dialogue. Tensions were increased further in August following an admission by South Korea that it had in the past conducted secret nuclear experiments. It was believed that this disclosure would increase the DPRK's reluctance to dismantle its own nuclear programme. By the end of 2004 the number of North Koreans who had defected to South Korea had reportedly exceeded 6,000.

In February 2005 the South Korean Ministry of Defence urged the resumption of senior-level military talks, apparently to ease tension following North Korean accusations that Southern naval vessels had 'infiltrated' the waters of the DPRK. In April the most senior-level meeting between the two sides for five years took place when Kim Yong Nam, the President of the Presidium of the North Korean SPA, met South Korean Prime Minister Lee Hae-Chan during the course of an Asia-Africa summit meeting in Jakarta, Indonesia; the two reportedly agreed that bilateral dialogue, suspended since July of the previous year (see above), should continue. At vice-ministerial talks in May, South Korea pledged to provide 200,000 metric tons of fertilizer to ease the DPRK's food supply problems. Three North Korean freighters reportedly docked at Ulsan in South Korea to load the fertilizer later in the month, this being the first time since 1984 that North Korean ships had docked in a South Korean port. In June 2005 South Korean Minister of Unification Chung Dong-Young visited the DPRK to mark the fifth anniversary of the inter-Korean summit of 2000, and held an unscheduled meeting with Kim Jong Il; it was speculated that the DPRK's agreement to return to the six-party talks on its nuclear programme in the following month might have been influenced by incentives offered by Chung at this meeting, including the provision of electricity (see below). In July 2005 the 15th ministerial talks between North and South Korea, held in Seoul, concluded with a 12-point joint statement in which the two sides pledged, *inter alia*, to reopen military talks, resume reunions for separated families and hold North-South Red Cross talks to discuss the issue of 'the whereabouts of those reported missing during the Korean War' (see below). Further ministerial discussions were held in September and December. Meanwhile, a sizeable delegation from the DPRK, headed by Kim Ki Nam, a member of the KWP Politburo's Secretariat, travelled to Seoul in August to participate in celebrations commemorating the 60th anniversary of the liberation of the Korean peninsula from Japanese rule. In November it was announced that North and South Korea would present joint teams at the 2006 Asian Games in Doha, Qatar, and at the 2008 Olympic Games in Beijing, China. In March 2006 military negotiations were held between the two Koreas in the DMZ, following a break of some two years; these were reportedly the most senior-level military talks between the two sides since the 1953 armistice. In the same month, however, the Government of the DPRK postponed the scheduled 18th round of ministerial discussions between the two sides in protest at the South's conduct of joint military exercises with the USA; the annual exercises were thought to have incurred particular displeasure that year in consequence of the participation for the first time of a nuclear-powered aircraft carrier.

Relations between the two Koreas were strained further throughout 2006, mainly as a result of the DPRK's missile tests (see below). The testing of a *Taepo Dong 2* missile on 5 July prompted the Republic of Korea to announce an indefinite suspension of food aid; however, it insisted that business co-operation, notably at Kaesong and Mount Kumgang, would not be affected. Moreover, aid was resumed after North Korea suffered severe flooding later that month, with the South Korean Government granting US $10.5m. to the North via non-governmental organizations (NGOs) in August, followed by supplies of rice, cement, iron rods, excavators, vehicles, blankets and medical kits to the value of $200m. However, the testing of a nuclear device by the North on 9 October placed this emergency aid programme in jeopardy. While again pledging to continue its economic co-operation in Kaesong and Mount Kumgang (against express US pleas for these links to be severed), the South Korean Government announced an indefinite suspension of humanitarian aid. (NGOs, however, continued to provide relief shipments.) Although the South Korean Minister of Foreign Affairs, Ban Ki-Moon, reportedly stated that the DPRK deserved sanctions under the UN Security Council Resolution, he also urged a resumption of dialogue. Ironically, the nuclear test took place only a week after North and South Korea had conducted their first military talks since the missile tests in July. These discussions apparently ended inconclusively. However, in the weeks following the nuclear test the Republic of Korea appeared to relax its stance towards the DPRK. Significantly, the South Korean Government refused to join the US-led Proliferation Security Initiative (PSI), which provided for the stopping and searching of North Korean ships, and by early November South Korean President Roh was vowing to continue his policy of engagement with the North Korean Government. None the less, in a reversal of previous policy, in mid-November the Republic of Korea supported a UN resolution condemning the DPRK's human rights record (in previous votes it had been absent or abstained). Furthermore, a South Korean defence policy document published at the end of December described the DPRK as a 'serious threat' to the South—the most strongly worded assessment since the inception of the latter's policy of engagement in 2000. It was reported in February 2007 that the number of defectors from North to South Korea since 1953 had reached 10,000, with a record number of 1,578 arriving in 2006.

Following the progress made in mid-February 2007 at six-party talks on North Korea's nuclear programme (see below), North and South Korea held ministerial discussions later that month, and in late March South Korea shipped 12,500 metric tons of fertilizer to the North. Inter-Korean talks on economic co-operation were held in Pyongyang in April, shortly after North Korea had failed to meet a deadline agreed in February for the closure of its nuclear rector at Yongbyon. South Korea agreed to revive its food aid programme to the North, with the provision of 400,000 metric tons of rice, but only on condition that the DPRK demonstrate some progress in complying with its commitments under the February six-party accord. Senior-level military talks at Panmunjom in mid-May resulted in agreement on a trial run of trains along reinstated cross-border rail links (see below) and, in principle, on the creation of a joint fishing zone in the disputed Yellow Sea, where naval clashes had previously occurred. However, ministerial talks in Seoul in late May and early June ended without progress, as South Korea continued to refuse to dispatch any rice to the North while the latter's pledge to shut down the Yongbyon reactor remained unfulfilled. In late June, as IAEA inspectors were permitted to enter North Korea for the first time since December 2002, South Korea announced the resumption of food aid to the North with a first shipment of some 3,000 tons of rice; the remainder of the promised 400,000 tons was delivered over the following six-month period. In accordance with the February agreement, a first delivery of 13,700 tons (of a promised total of 50,000 tons) of heavy fuel oil followed in July 2007. None the less, difficulties remained in inter-Korean relations. Three days of senior-level military talks ended in stalemate in late July over the disputed maritime boundary, the Northern Limit Line, which the DPRK refused to recognize, and in early August North and South Korean soldiers exchanged gunfire across the DMZ.

In early October 2007 Kim Jong Il welcomed President Roh to Pyongyang for a three-day summit, which had been postponed from late August owing to severe flooding in the North. This was only the second meeting between the two countries' leaders since the Korean War. Following the meeting, Kim and Roh, who was approaching the end of his term of office, issued a declaration, in which they committed North and South Korea, *inter alia*, to working towards the replacement of the 1953 armistice agreement with a peace treaty; to making joint efforts for the smooth implementation of the six-party nuclear agreements; to creating a special 'peace zone' around Haeju; to establishing the planned joint fishing zone in the Yellow Sea; to expanding co-operation on economic and humanitarian projects; and to developing co-operation in a wide range of other areas (including education, technology, culture and sports). There was some scepticism in South Korea about Roh's motives for organizing the summit meeting, with the opposition Grand National Party (GNP) accusing the President of attempting to boost his own popularity and that of his party in advance of the forthcoming presidential and legislative elections. Several bilateral ministerial exchanges followed the meeting. A three-day visit to Seoul by Premier Kim Yong Il took place in mid-November 2007. During the first bilateral prime ministerial discussions since 1992 Kim and South Korean Prime Minister Han Duck-Soo agreed on a timetable for resuming cross-border freight rail services (see below) and on the establishment of a joint committee to advance the creation of the proposed 'peace zone' centred on Haeju, which was to involve the economic development of the city's port. Talks between the DPRK's Minister of the People's Armed Forces, Vice-Marshal Kim Il Chol, and his South Korean counterpart (the first since 2000 and only the second in more than 50 years) were held in Pyongyang later that month to discuss the security aspects of the agreements reached by the two countries' leaders, and in early December 2007 North Korean Vice-Premier Jon Sung Hun and the South Korean Deputy Prime Minister for Finance and the Economy, Kwon O-Kyu, held talks in Seoul on joint industrial projects. However, senior-level military talks in mid-December ended without agreement on the location of the proposed fishing zone in the Yellow Sea.

Lee Myung-Bak, of the conservative GNP, who was elected President of South Korea in December 2007, advocated the adoption of a more uncompromising approach towards North Korea than that pursued over the preceding 10 years by Presidents Kim Dae-Jung and Roh Moo-Hyun, demanding increased progress on denuclearization in return for the continuation of economic co-operation. In January 2008 Lee announced plans to review the agreements reached at the inter-Korean summit in the previous October and proposed merging the Ministry of Unification with the Ministry of Foreign Affairs. In the following month Lee yielded to demands by the United New Democratic Party (which held a narrow parliamentary majority pending elections in April) to retain the ministry, although it was to be scaled down. None the less, humanitarian projects, such as family reunions (see below) and food and fertilizer aid, were expected to continue, and Lee proposed the creation of a 37,500m. won investment fund for the DPRK if it abandoned its nuclear weapons programme, with the aim of raising the North's per caput income to US $3,000 within 10 years.

Meanwhile, the arrangements for further family reunions came under the auspices of the North and South Korean Red Cross organizations, which held several rounds of talks on the subject and co-ordinated the exchange of lists of potential candidates for reunion. Relations between the two sides deteriorated in late 2000, however, when North Korea accused the head of the South Korean Red Cross of defaming the former's political system. The official was replaced in January 2001. The DPRK continued to dictate terms for reunions, asking the Republic of Korea to limit the amount of money and gifts transferred during the events, which took place in November–December 2000 and in February 2001. It was subsequently reported that North Korean officials had confiscated money given to delegates for use as state funds. An historic accord between the two sides allowed 300 separated families from the North and South each to exchange letters in March. Further rounds of family reunions were held in April and September 2002 at Mount Kumgang, where officials from the two sides planned to build a centre for such meetings. In April 2004 a ninth round of reunions was delayed after a South Korean official made a joke concerning Kim Jong Il. Further rounds of reunions none the less took place during the year. As part of the reunion programme, in July 2005 the first private telephone line between North and South Korea since partition in 1945 was opened, in preparation for video conference family reunions, which took place in mid-August 2005 to coincide with the 60th anniversary of liberation from Japanese rule. Inter-Korean Red Cross talks held later that month at Mount Kumgang failed to resolve the question of South Korean soldiers and civilians 'abducted' to North Korea during and after the 1950–53 war: the South Korean Government estimated that more than 540 prisoners of war and some 485 abducted civilians were still alive and remained in detention in the DPRK. Further reunions were held, both in person and through video conference technology, in late 2005 and early 2006. At another Red Cross conference in February 2006, North Korea reportedly agreed to resolve the issue of South Korean prisoners of war and abductees held in the North, and a further family reunion took place in June. This reunion received particular international attention, as it involved the reuniting with his mother of a man who was said to have been abducted by North Korean security agents in 1978. However, the DPRK again suspended family reunions in July 2006, in response to the Republic's decision to suspend humanitarian aid following the North Korean missile tests. Following the test of a nuclear device in October, the prospect for further family reunions in the near future appeared uncertain. None the less, the family reunions arranged during 2006 helped to raise the total number of South Koreans visiting the North to more than 100,000 for the first time, a rise of 15.1% compared with the previous year. (Nearly 88,000 of the total of 101,708 were business people travelling to the Kaesong complex; the total figure excluded tourists visiting Mount Kumgang.) In January 2007 Choi Uk-Il, one of 33 South Korean fishermen abducted by a North Korean naval vessel in 1975, returned to the South after first fleeing to China. Inter-Korean ministerial talks held in Pyongyang in late February and early March 2007 resulted in an agreement on the resumption of family reunions, which took place by video conference in late March and in person at Mount Kumgang in mid-May. The 16th round of 'face-to-face' reunions was held in October.

As the DPRK's financial situation worsened, economic issues played an important part in inter-Korean relations from 2000. In January 2001 it was reported that the DPRK's energy shortages had reached crisis point, and that the country was desperately researching alternative power sources. A summit meeting took place between the two Koreas in February, at which the DPRK requested immediate and substantial electricity supplies to alleviate its needs. Frustration resulted from South Korean insistence on the necessity of on-site investigations prior to the commencement of deliveries. Meanwhile, in August 2000 Hyundai agreed to establish a technologically-advanced electronic industrial compound in Kaesong in the DPRK. Hyundai's financial problems, however, delayed the implementation of the project. In March 2001 the future of the Mount Kumgang tourist initiative was jeopardized by its lack of profitability, and Hyundai appealed to the South Korean Government for assistance; the Government subsequently pledged 90,000m. won to maintain the tourist cruises. Hyundai founder Chung Ju-Yung died in late March, and his funeral was attended by a delegation sent by Kim Jong Il. Progress on economic co-operation in Kaesong was made from 2002, with Kaesong being declared a special industrial zone in November of that year (see also Economic Affairs). In June 2003 the DPRK announced regulations for the development of the zone, as well as plans to develop an area of 3.3 sq km in a first phase of development extending to 2007. A South Korean company, Korea Land, was to invest around US $184m. in the project. These plans were finalized at a meeting of North and South Korean economic officials in November 2003. Although inter-Korean trade increased steadily, reportedly amounting to US $700m. in 2003, South Korea shared international concerns over North Korea's suspected illicit trade in weapons and narcotics. In June 2003 South Korean customs officials in the port of Busan seized 40 kg of methamphetamines believed to have originated in North Korea. There were also fears of very serious economic consequences for South Korea if reunification of the two Koreas were to become an imminent prospect. It was reported that in April 2004 some 1,600 South Korean companies had applied for a lease in the Kaesong special industrial zone, and in June Korea Land selected the first 15 companies that were to be permitted to conduct business in the zone. At the end of June a ceremony was held to signal the commencement of the first phase of development in Kaesong. In March 2005 the Korea Electric Power Corporation (KEPCO), of South Korea, began to supply electricity to Kaesong, representing the first cross-border flow of electricity since the peninsula's partition. In July the South Korean Minister of Unification reportedly proposed to Kim Jong Il that South Korea compensate the North with 2,000 MW of energy assistance if the latter were to abandon its nuclear weapons programme (see below). The DPRK, however, rejected the offer. In October the first joint governmental office operated by both North and South Korea, to handle cross-border economic projects, was opened in Kaesong, and in December the first commercial telephone link between Kaesong and Seoul commenced operation.

The construction of the major infrastructural facilities at Kaesong, which began in June 2003, was completed in October 2007, marking the end of the development phase. The complex was scheduled to be fully operational by the end of 2010, when it was anticipated that some 450 companies, employing a total of 100,000 North Koreans, would be conducting business there. By November 2007 the number of companies from the Republic of Korea operating in Kaesong had reached 52, according to the South Korean Ministry of Unification, with more than 20,000 North Koreans working at the complex. The construction of living quarters for 15,000 North Korean workers in Kaesong was scheduled to begin in the first half of 2008. Meanwhile, the expansion of the Kaesong complex contributed to a 33% rise in the value of inter-Korean trade in 2007, to US $1,798m., of which $1,431m. constituted 'commercial' trade (an increase of 54%) and $367m. 'non-commercial' trade (primarily general aid, as well as social and cultural exchanges and energy assistance).

Negotiations to re-establish the inter-Korean rail link continued during 2001. It was hoped that such a link would create a new Eurasian transport corridor that would reduce the cost and time involved in the transit of goods from North-East Asia to European markets from 25 days to about 15 days, bringing economic benefits to all participants. In February 2001 a meeting was held at the DMZ to arrange regulations for troops and workers employed to rebuild the line, and a parallel highway. However, the DPRK failed to attend a UN regional transport meeting held in Seoul in November, following the failure of the sixth round of ministerial talks. None the less, both Koreas agreed to accelerate the reconnection following bilateral talks in April 2002. Ground-breaking ceremonies for the reconnection of the railway and road links were held on both sides of the DMZ in September, and South Korea released a loan to the North to assist the funding of the work. In February 2003 the first road reconnecting the North with the South was completed, on the eastern coast of the Korean peninsula. In June rail links between the two Koreas were officially opened, although the connections remained largely symbolic, as construction on the North Korean side to link the new railways with wider networks was yet to be completed. In December 2004 it was reported that the road link along the eastern coast of the two Koreas had been opened to traffic. By late 2005 two major rail links between North and South Korea along the west and east coasts, with adjacent roads, were believed to be complete; however, the DPRK cancelled scheduled trial runs along the cross-border rail links in May 2006, citing military security issues. South Korea had also pledged to assist the DPRK in constructing several railway stations. Following senior-level military talks at Panmunjom, in May 2007 cross-border rail links were finally trialled when, for the first time in more than 50 years, passengers were conveyed on trains travelling in each direction. However, it remained uncertain when North Korea would permit the operation of regular services. At the inter-Korean summit held in October (see above), it was decided to resume a cross-border freight rail service. A daily freight service, connecting the South with Kaesong, was duly launched in December, although North Korea continued to oppose the introduction of regular passenger services. Inter-Korean talks on improving rail links, which were held in January 2008, resulted in agreement on a reduction in the number of carriages on the freight trains (owing to lack of use) and on the need to repair the North Korean section of the reconnected railway.

In the early 1990s there was growing international concern that the DPRK had intensified its clandestine nuclear programme at Yongbyon, north of Pyongyang, and would soon be capable of manufacturing a nuclear weapon. During 1991 pressure was increasingly applied, by the USA and Japan in particular, for the DPRK to sign the Nuclear Safeguards Agreement (NSA) with the International Atomic Energy Agency (IAEA, see p. 107). This was required by the DPRK's signature, in 1985, of the Treaty on the Non-Proliferation of Nuclear Weapons (the Non-Proliferation Treaty—NPT), in order that IAEA representatives might be permitted to inspect the country's nuclear facilities. However, the DPRK consistently refused to allow such inspections to take place unless there was to be a simultaneous inspection (or withdrawal) of US nuclear weapons sited in South Korea. Tension was eased considerably by the USA's decision, in October 1991, to remove all its tactical nuclear weapons from South Korea, and by South Korea's subsequent declaration that it would not manufacture, deploy or use nuclear, chemical or biological weapons. In December the South Korean Government stated that all US nuclear weapons had been withdrawn, and proposed that simultaneous inspections of military bases in the South and nuclear facilities in the North be conducted. Later in the month the two Korean states concluded an agreement 'to create a non-nuclear Korean peninsula', and in January 1992 the DPRK signed the NSA. In March delegates of North and South, meeting at Panmunjom, agreed to form a Joint Nuclear Control Commission (JNCC) to permit inter-Korean nuclear inspections to take place.

In May 1992 the DPRK submitted to the IAEA an unexpectedly detailed report on its nuclear facilities, describing, *inter alia*, the Yongbyon installation as a research laboratory. In the same month IAEA inspectors were permitted to visit North Korean nuclear facilities (the first in a series of official visits during that year). Despite the findings of the inspectors (who concluded that the Yongbyon plant was 'primitive' and far from completion, although potentially capable of producing plutonium), suspicions persisted regarding North Korean nuclear ambitions. Moreover, the DPRK repeatedly failed to agree to separate nuclear inspections by the JNCC, finally announcing in January 1993 its intention to boycott all future inter-Korean nuclear talks (in protest at the imminent resumption of the 'Team Spirit' manoeuvres). The situation became critical in February, when the DPRK refused to allow IAEA inspections of two 'undeclared' sites near Yongbyon, claiming that these were military installations unrelated to nuclear activities. In an unprecedented development, the DPRK announced in March that it was to withdraw from the NPT. In May the UN Security Council adopted a resolution urging the DPRK to reconsider its decision to withdraw from the NPT and calling on the country to allow an inspection by the IAEA of its nuclear facilities. Following negotiations with the USA, the DPRK agreed to suspend its withdrawal from the NPT; in return, the USA agreed to assist the DPRK in the development of its non-military nuclear programme. International concern regarding the North Korean weapons programme was, meanwhile, heightened by the successful testing of a medium-range missile, the *Rodong-1*, in May. In response to US pressure, the DPRK subsequently agreed to further negotiations with the IAEA. Talks at the organization's headquarters in Vienna, Austria, in September were, however, inconclusive, and further meetings were cancelled.

In February 1994, following further discussions between the DPRK and the USA, an agreement was reached whereby the IAEA would be allowed to visit all the country's declared nuclear facilities. In March, however, the inspectors were impeded in their efforts to remove samples from nuclear installations, and it was discovered that seals placed on nuclear materials by IAEA representatives during previous visits had been broken, leading the IAEA to conclude that the DPRK had, in all probability, produced more plutonium than had been admitted. In June the DPRK again threatened to withdraw from the NPT, and also to declare war against the Republic of Korea, if economic sanctions were imposed by the UN. In August the USA and the DPRK reached an agreement on the replacement of the latter's existing nuclear reactors by two light-water reactors, which were considered to be less easily adapted to the production of nuclear weaponry. The agreement also recommended the establishment of a restricted form of diplomatic representation between the two countries. Further negotiations in October led to the signing of an Agreed Framework whereby the USA undertook to establish an international consortium to finance and supply the light-water reactors, while the DPRK agreed to suspend operation of its existing reactors and halt construction at two further sites. To compensate for the DPRK's consequent shortfall in energy production until the new reactors were fully operational, the USA agreed to donate to the DPRK 500,000 metric tons annually of heavy fuel oil. IAEA inspectors subsequently travelled to Pyongyang to oversee the suspension of the country's nuclear programme.

In March 1995 several countries, led by the USA, the Republic of Korea and Japan, created the Korean Peninsula Energy Development Organization (KEDO), which insisted that the DPRK accept a South Korean-designed reactor. This demand was opposed by the DPRK. However, in August the North permitted a KEDO delegation to visit Sinpo, on the east coast of the DPRK, in order to assess its suitability as the site of the proposed nuclear power station. Finally, in December the DPRK and KEDO reached agreement on the details of implementing the October 1994 accord; this implied acceptance by the DPRK of South Korean light-water reactors. In January 1996 the DPRK announced its willingness to permit routine inspections of its nuclear installations by the IAEA. In March KEPCO was commissioned by KEDO as the principal contractor for the construction of the light-water reactors. Discussions between KEDO and the DPRK to negotiate the terms of repayment by the latter of the construction costs of the light-water reactors were successfully concluded in April 1997.

Meanwhile, US energy experts began the sealing of spent fuel rods at the DPRK's nuclear facilities. However, North Korea's continued refusal to grant IAEA inspectors access to several contentious laboratories again provoked concern that the DPRK was developing its nuclear programme. Preparation of the nuclear-reactor site at Sinpo formally began in August 1997. Negotiations held in early 1998 between the participants in KEDO (which the European Union—EU—had joined in mid-1997) concerning the financing of the light-water reactors (estimated at US $5,170m.) proved difficult, and were further complicated by South Korea's financial problems, raising fears that progress on the project would be hindered. In June 1998 the North Korean Government admitted to having sold nuclear missiles abroad, claiming that such exports were necessary, given ongoing US economic sanctions against the DPRK. Some progress was made at talks between the USA and the DPRK in New York, USA, in September, when the DPRK agreed to resume sealing of spent fuel rods (which had been suspended earlier that year), while the USA promised to deliver the delayed shipment of heavy fuel oil. The US Congress was, however, increasingly reluctant to approve financing for the purchase of fuel oil, obliging President Bill Clinton personally to authorize the disbursement of the necessary funds in October, in order to safeguard the 1994 nuclear accord.

Concerns regarding a suspected nuclear-related underground facility at Kumchang-ri, some 40 km north-west of Yongbyon, dominated a series of senior-level talks between the USA and the DPRK in late 1998 and early 1999. The North Korean authorities were angered by reports that KEDO had decided, in January 1999, to delay commencing the basic construction of the light-water reactors until mid-1999. In March, following protracted negotiations in New York, agreement was finally reached permitting US access to the suspected nuclear facility. The USA announced that it would donate substantial food aid to the DPRK, in addition to agricultural assistance, although it was emphasized that the aid was being granted on purely humanitarian grounds and did not constitute compensation. The US officials who inspected the Kumchang-ri site in May found it to be incomplete and largely empty.

In May 1999 William Perry, a former US Secretary of Defense who had been appointed to review policy towards the DPRK, visited Pyongyang, where he reportedly advised the North Korean Government to abandon its nuclear ambitions in exchange for substantial economic and political benefits. Talks held during mid-1999 between the USA and the DPRK culminated in September in a decision by the USA to ease several long-standing economic sanctions (principally on non-military trade, travel and banking) against the DPRK. In return, the country agreed to suspend missile test-firing for the duration of negotiations with the USA. Earlier in the month Perry had presented a report recommending a comprehensive, long-term approach to the establishment of normal relations with the DPRK to the US President and Congress. Discussions aimed at improving US-North Korean relations were held in Beijing in November 1999 and January 2000.

Meanwhile, in November 1999 it was reported that the IAEA was supervising the final stage of the sealing of spent fuel rods at Yongbyon. After several months of delays caused by disputes over the division of the costs of the project, in December KEDO and KEPCO finally signed the contract for the construction of the two light-water reactors; in February 2000 it was reported that construction of the reactors was unlikely to be completed before 2007, some four years later than scheduled. In November 2000 North Korea, frustrated by the delay, threatened to restart missile testing unless construction of the reactors was accelerated. The DPRK refuted the IAEA's claim that delays were due to the former's refusal to allow nuclear inspections.

In June 2000 the North Korean Government confirmed its moratorium on test flights of ballistic missiles. In July the USA rejected the DPRK's demand for annual payments from the USA of US $1,000m. in return for the curtailment of weapons exports. The fundamental issues of missile development and export remained unresolved. A planned visit to Pyongyang by the outgoing US President, Bill Clinton, was cancelled in December when the DPRK rejected a US proposal that the two sides prepare a draft missile accord to form a basis for talks. In early 2001 the new administration of George W. Bush adopted a less conciliatory stance towards the DPRK, officials reportedly referring to Kim Jong Il as a 'dictator', and refusing to grant economic aid unless transparency in North Korea's missile production and export was assured and verified. Since the late 1990s elements in Bush's Republican Party had been strongly arguing in favour of a planned 'national missile defence' (NMD) system to protect the USA from long-range missile attack, and had frequently cited North Korea as a developer and exporter of such missiles. US officials feared that the DPRK had developed an intercontinental ballistic missile, the *Taepo Dong 2*, capable of striking the west coast of the USA. Bush's commitment to develop NMD was denounced by the DPRK, which responded by threatening to abandon the 1994 framework, and to resume ballistic missile testing. In March 2001 US Secretary of State Colin Powell suggested that revisions to the 1994 framework might be required. In May 2001 an EU delegation travelled to North Korea, in an effort to renew diplomatic initiatives aimed at advancing the process of détente. Kim Jong Il reportedly agreed to maintain the moratorium on the testing of missiles until at least 2003. In June 2001 President Bush sought to broaden discussions with North Korea about its missile programme to include nuclear technology and a reduction of the country's conventional forces. The North responded that discussions on the latter would take place only following the withdrawal of the 37,000 US troops from the South, and that it was also seeking financial compensation for the delay in building KEDO's two light-water reactors, which were now not expected to be completed until 2008 at the earliest. In October 2001 the North rejected suggestions by the head of the IAEA and later by US officials that inspections of its nuclear facilities were necessary; however, in December it agreed to limited international access to certain laboratories. Meanwhile, in November, a team of North Korean nuclear engineers visited power plants in the South, indicating their commitment to acquire southern-style reactors. (See relations with the USA, below, for subsequent developments on the DPRK's nuclear weapons programme.)

The DPRK's relations with Japan have long been dominated by continuing hostility towards the latter as a result of the atrocities committed in Korea during the Japanese occupation (1910–45). The North Korean Government had demanded thousands of millions of dollars in compensation from Japan, before normal relations could be restored. In the 1980s, following the testimony of defectors, Japan began to suspect that North Korean agents had kidnapped a number of Japanese citizens during the late 1970s and early 1980s. Japan imposed sanctions on the DPRK after its agents were accused of attempting to assassinate the South Korean President in Burma in 1983. Following the destruction of a South Korean aircraft in 1987, allegedly by North Korean agents posing as Japanese citizens (see above), Japan reimposed sanctions during 1988; the DPRK then severed diplomatic contacts with Japan, although mutual trade continued. From late 1990 there was a significant rapprochement between the DPRK and Japan, and in January 1991 a Japanese government delegation visited Pyongyang for discussions concerning the possible normalization of diplomatic relations. The Japanese delegation offered apologies, on behalf of its Government, for Japanese colonial aggression on the Korean peninsula between 1910 and 1945. Moreover, the Japanese Government expressed its willingness to make reparations for Japanese abuses of human rights in Korea during this period. Subsequent negotiations in 1991 foundered, however, owing to the DPRK's demand for reparations for damage inflicted after 1945 (which the Japanese Government denied) and to Japan's insistence that North Korea's nuclear installations be opened to outside inspection; normalization talks collapsed in November 1992, as the North Korean delegation abandoned the proceedings. Relations with Japan were further strained after the DPRK's testing of the *Rodong-1* missile in the Sea of Japan in May 1993. The missile, according to US intelligence reports, would be capable of reaching most of Japan's major cities (and possibly of carrying either a conventional or a nuclear warhead). None the less, Japan, like the Republic of Korea, opposed the possible imposition of international economic sanctions on the DPRK in response to North Korea's refusal to allow inspections of its nuclear facilities. In March 1995 a Japanese parliamentary group visited the DPRK and reached an agreement for the resumption of normalization talks later that year. In May Japan agreed to North Korea's request for emergency rice aid, and later in the year Japan provided aid to help the DPRK overcome the effects of serious flooding (see above). In early 1996 Japan provided a shipment of fuel oil to alleviate the DPRK's energy shortfall.

Relations were complicated in 1997 by Japanese allegations that North Korea had abducted several Japanese citizens during the 1970s. However, in August 1997, for the first time since 1992, negotiations opened on the restoration of normal bilateral relations. An agreement was signed whereby some 1,800 Japanese women married to North Koreans, who had never been permitted to leave the DPRK, were to be allowed to visit their relatives in Japan for short periods; the first such visits took place in November 1997 and January 1998. Moreover, in October 1997 the Japanese Government resumed the provision of aid to North Korea, suspended since mid-1996, donating food and medical supplies in response to the renewed appeals issued by the UN. Relations deteriorated in mid-1998, however, when the North Korean Government cancelled a third visit of the Japanese women to their homeland, following Japan's rejection of a North Korean investigation into the alleged abduction of Japanese nationals. The testing by the DPRK of a suspected *Taepo Dong* missile over Japanese territory in August prompted Japan to break off normalization talks, suspend food aid and postpone its contribution to the KEDO project. The DPRK subsequently claimed that the object launched was in fact a satellite. Tension between the two countries increased in March 1999, when Japanese naval forces pursued and opened fire on suspected North Korean spy ships that had infiltrated Japanese waters. Relations improved, however, following the DPRK's agreement with the USA, in September, to suspend its reported plans to test a new long-range missile. In December, following a successful visit to the DPRK by a group of Japanese parliamentarians, Japan announced an end to its ban on food aid. Later in that month intergovernmental preparatory talks on re-establishing diplomatic relations were held in Beijing. Progress was achieved by the Japanese and North Korean Red Cross Societies at a meeting in March 2000. It was reported that the DPRK had agreed to co-operate in a further investigation into the fate of some 10 missing Japanese nationals, while Japan had agreed to a search for Korean citizens who had disappeared prior to 1945. In addition, visits to their homeland by Japanese women married to North Koreans were to resume, and Japan was to provide some 100,000 metric tons of rice to the DPRK through WFP. In late April 2000 Japanese charter flights to North Korea resumed. Following informal contacts between the North Korean and Japanese Governments, full normalization talks commenced in April; further rounds of discussions took place during the year, despite an announcement by Japan in September that relations between the two countries would not be normalized until the cases of Japanese citizens allegedly abducted by North Korean agents had been solved. In November the DPRK rejected an offer by Japan to extend economic aid rather than grant wartime compensation. Meanwhile, in September the long-delayed third visits home by the Japanese wives of North Korean men took place. In October Japan decided, on humanitarian grounds, to provide 500,000 metric tons of rice to North Korea.

In December 2000 the DPRK reiterated that normal relations with Japan could be restored only after the latter delivered an apology and compensation for its earlier colonial rule. In May 2001 Japan deported Kim Jong Nam, son of Kim Jong Il, for entering the country on a false passport (see above). In June the DPRK condemned Japan's refusal to issue visas to North Koreans planning to attend a conference on Japanese compensation for Korea, held in Japan. In August the DPRK demanded compensation for Korean victims of the atomic bombs dropped on Hiroshima and Nagasaki in 1945, and also for the collision of cargo ships from the two countries in July 2001.

The DPRK was one of several Asian countries that strongly condemned Japanese Prime Minister Junichiro Koizumi's visit to the Yasukuni Shrine in Tokyo, honouring Japan's war dead, in August 2001. In December the DPRK announced that it was abandoning efforts to locate missing Japanese nationals thought to have been abducted by North Korean agents. At the end of the month a suspected North Korean spy vessel was sunk by Japanese coastguard forces after it had been expelled from Japan's exclusive economic zone. The DPRK condemned the incident, but denied any involvement, accusing Japan of seeking to mislead world opinion. Japanese coastguard forces searched the sunken vessel in May 2002, and raised it in September of that year. In February the DPRK released a Japanese journalist who had been detained on spying charges since December 1999.

In an unexpected development, Junichiro Koizumi visited Pyongyang in September 2002, becoming the first incumbent Japanese Prime Minister to do so. His one-day visit, during which he held discussions with Kim Jong Il, was dominated by the latter's admission that North Korean agents had abducted 12 Japanese citizens in the 1970s and 1980s, of whom five were still alive. The remainder were said to have died of natural causes, although suspicions remained that they might have been executed, after the North Korean authorities failed to locate the graves. Kim apologized for the incidents, but attributed them to rogue elements within the security services. The admission led some sources to indicate that the total number of Japanese abductees might be as high as 100. The surviving captives were temporarily allowed to return to Japan in October 2002, although they had to leave behind any spouses or children. Among the abductees allowed to return was Hitomi Soga, the wife of Charles Jenkins, a US soldier who was believed to have defected to North Korea in 1965 and to have remained in the DPRK ever since. The couple's two daughters had never left the DPRK. The Japanese authorities refused to allow the abductees to return to the DPRK after the visit. Despite this, representatives from the two countries held the first round of resumed discussions on the restoration of normal diplomatic relations in Malaysia at the end of October 2002, but failed to make any progress.

In October 2002 the alleged admission by North Korean officials to their visiting US counterparts that the DPRK was pursuing a secret nuclear weapons programme alarmed Japan. Koizumi announced that Japan would halt further economic co-operation with the DPRK until the issues of the abducted Japanese citizens and the nuclear programme were resolved. The DPRK warned Japan that it would abandon its moratorium on missile testing if normalization talks failed to make any progress. In separate incidents in February and March 2003 the DPRK test-launched two short-range ground-to-ship missiles in the Sea of Japan, and in April tested a third missile in the Yellow Sea. However, it refrained from testing longer-range ballistic missiles, which Japan considered a threat to its security. In March the DPRK was angered by Japan's launching of two spy satellites, believed to be part of a programme of intelligence-gathering on the DPRK initiated following the suspected testing of the North Korean *Taepo Dong* missile over Japan in 1998 (see above).

In June 2003 the DPRK cancelled a voyage of the *Man Gyong Bong* passenger ferry, used by ethnic Korean residents in Japan to visit relatives in North Korea, apparently owing to more stringent inspections of North Korean ships by Japan; there was speculation that illegal goods were being transported by the ferry. In August a group of 10 North Korean refugees claimed asylum at the Japanese embassy in the Thai capital of Bangkok, in what was believed to be the first incident of this kind outside China. At the end of the month Japan was one of six nations taking part in talks on the North Korean nuclear weapons programme held in Beijing. At the talks, Japan reportedly attempted to raise the issue of Japanese citizens abducted by the DPRK (see above). In the same month, Japanese authorities seized premises owned by the General Association of Korean Residents in Japan (*Chongryon*), reportedly owing to tax evasion. Also in August, the *Man Gyong Bong* ferry arrived in the Japanese port of Niigata on its first trip to Japan in seven months. Departure of the ship from Niigata was subsequently delayed after the vessel failed safety inspections carried out by the Japanese authorities. Relatives of Japanese nationals abducted by North Korea, as well as Japanese right-wing groups, held anti-North Korean protests at the port. In October the DPRK announced that it did not wish Japan to participate in future negotiations on its nuclear weapons programme, claiming that Japan was 'an obstacle to the peaceful settlement' of the nuclear issue, and citing Japanese attempts to 'blockade' North Korea.

In January 2004 the Japanese House of Representatives approved legislation to permit the imposition of economic sanctions on the DPRK. In April legislation was approved requiring all ships entering Japanese ports from March 2005 to be insured against oil damage. This in practice amounted to a ban on entry by North Korean ships. Following a second visit by Japanese Prime Minister Koizumi to Pyongyang in May 2004, five children of the abductees who had returned to Japan in 2002 (see above) were permitted to fly to Tokyo. Their release had been secured in return for pledges of food aid and medical supplies. However, suspicions remained over the fate of other missing Japanese nationals. In July 2004 US soldier Charles Jenkins, husband of the Japanese abductee Hitomi Soga (see above), travelled to Indonesia with his two daughters and was reunited with his wife. (He subsequently received hospital treatment in Japan, and was then found guilty of desertion from the US army and sentenced to a short period of imprisonment.) In November the DPRK relinquished human remains which it claimed were those of Megumi Yokota, who had been kidnapped by North Korean agents in 1977. The DPRK claimed that she had committed suicide. However, subsequent DNA tests indicated that the remains were not those of Megumi Yokota. North Korea refused to accept the results of the tests. The Japanese Government subsequently suspended food aid to North Korea, and public pressure for the imposition of economic sanctions on the DPRK increased in Japan. In December 2004 the DPRK stated that it would regard the imposition of economic sanctions as tantamount to a declaration of war.

At the beginning of March 2005 legislation concerning insurance requirements for ships entering Japanese ports, which had been approved in early 2004 (see above), took effect, amounting to a ban on entry of all but 16 of an estimated 100 North Korean ships that were involved in trade with Japan. While most Japanese citizens were believed to favour the imposition of direct economic sanctions on the DPRK, the Japanese Government remained reluctant to do this, not wishing to jeopardize future negotiations concerning North Korea's nuclear weapons programme. The September 2005 six-party agreement (see below) contained a clause in which Japan and the DPRK undertook to 'take steps to normalize their relations'. Subsequently talks were held between the two countries in February 2006 to discuss issues including the alleged abductions of Japanese citizens, the development of ballistic missiles by the DPRK and the resumption of the nuclear negotiations. However, the talks ended inconclusively, and later that month Japan's Chief Cabinet Secretary, Shinzo Abe, announced that arrest warrants had been issued for two North Korean agents suspected of abducting four Japanese nationals in 1978.

In June 2006 the Japanese legislature enacted the North Korean Human Rights Act, which expressly linked the imposition of sanctions to issues of human rights in the DPRK. The Act stated that economic sanctions would be imposed unless the DPRK worked to resolve human rights issues; significantly, these included the abduction of Japanese nationals. When the DPRK conducted missile tests in July (see below) Japan was one of its most vehement critics, announcing unilateral sanctions against the DPRK in September. (The USA and Australia announced similar measures prior to the issuance of UN Security Council Resolution 1718 in October—see below.) The Japanese sanctions provided for the 'freezing' of transfers of funds to the DPRK by groups suspected of having links to the country's nuclear weapons or missiles programmes; this affected 15 groups and one individual. These followed more limited sanctions imposed in the immediate aftermath of the July missile tests, which included the banning of a North Korean trade ferry from

THE DEMOCRATIC PEOPLE'S REPUBLIC OF KOREA (NORTH KOREA)   *Introductory Survey*

Japanese ports and a moratorium on charter flights from Pyongyang.

The appointment of Shinzo Abe as Japanese Prime Minister in September 2006 signalled a firmer approach by Japan on the North Korean issue. Abe appointed a prime ministerial adviser on the issue of Japanese abductees, and also established a special government panel on the subject. Only three days after his appointment Prime Minister Abe met with families and supporters of abductees, a clear signal of the importance with which he regarded the issue.

Following the North Korean nuclear test on 9 October 2006, Japan was among the strongest supporters of tighter sanctions, and refused to accept the DPRK as a nuclear state. Not only did it support sanctions under the UN Security Council, but it also imposed firm measures of its own, banning all North Korean imports and prohibiting North Korean ships from entering Japanese waters. This stance provoked characteristic ire from the North Korean Government, which urged Japan not to attend the next round of six-party talks. In November the Japanese Government approved a ban on the export of luxury goods to the DPRK. (A similar ban was enacted by the USA in November.) However, the restoration of normal relations between the DPRK and Japan was one of the tenets of the agreement reached during six-party talks in February 2007 (see below), and a working group was established to conduct negotiations. The first bilateral discussions between the two countries for more than a year were held in Viet Nam in March, but they broke down over the issue of the Japanese abductees. In July the North Korean Ministry of Foreign Affairs issued a memorandum accusing Japan of attempting to obstruct the talks on the normalization of bilateral relations and to disrupt the six-party process with its refusal to provide energy aid and its insistence on the resolution of the abduction issue, which North Korea claimed had already been settled. The working group held its second round of bilateral discussions in Mongolia in September, reportedly in a more positive atmosphere than the March talks, although again no agreement was reached. In October Japan announced that it would not resume aid to North Korea and extended its ban on North Korean imports and the entry of North Korean ships into Japanese waters for a further six months, citing a continued lack of progress in the dispute over the abductees. Japan renewed its sanctions against the DPRK in April 2008.

The DPRK has considered the USA to be its main enemy since the time of the Korean War and repeatedly accused the Republic of Korea of being a US 'puppet' state. Relations deteriorated after the DPRK seized a US naval vessel, the *USS Pueblo*, in 1968 and detained its crew for several months. In 1969 the DPRK shot down a US reconnaissance aircraft which had apparently violated North Korean airspace, resulting in the deaths of 31 US servicemen. In 1987, in response to alleged North Korean involvement in the bombing of a South Korean airliner, the USA placed the DPRK on its list of countries supporting terrorism, and restricted contacts between US and North Korean diplomats. Relations with the USA in the 1990s were largely dominated by the DPRK's suspected nuclear ambitions (see above). In December 1994 it was announced that agreement had been reached to establish liaison offices in Washington, DC, and Pyongyang in 1995, in preparation for an eventual resumption of full diplomatic relations. The USA insisted, however, that normal relations would be restored only when the DPRK ceased to export ballistic missiles and withdrew its troops from the border with South Korea; the DPRK, in turn, stated that liaison offices could only be opened when light-water nuclear reactors, in accordance with the October 1994 agreement between the DPRK and the USA, had been supplied. Relations faltered following the shooting-down of a US army helicopter which had apparently entered North Korean airspace; the DPRK initially refused to negotiate, but, after direct bilateral talks in December, the pilot was repatriated. In January 1995 the DPRK opened its ports to US commercial shipping and removed restrictions on the import of goods from the USA. Following the severe flooding in the DPRK in 1995 and 1996, the USA provided food aid and other flood relief.

The issue of four-way talks (see above) dominated relations between the USA and the DPRK in 1996, but parallel negotiations were conducted concerning the estimated 8,100 US soldiers who were listed as 'missing in action' following the Korean War. The USA agreed to provide funds to assist in locating the bodies, and it was reported that the DPRK had requested additional food aid in return for its co-operation. In December, following the issuing of a (US-brokered) apology by the DPRK for the submarine incursion in September, it was reported that the USA was prepared partially to revoke its economic sanctions against North Korea, and to allow the gradual expansion of bilateral trade. In early 1997 the USA responded to a renewed appeal issued by the UN for food aid and humanitarian assistance for North Korea, as a result of which the DPRK announced its intention to take part in exploratory discussions about the proposed quadripartite talks. Bilateral discussions with the USA during 1997 focused on the establishment of liaison offices, missile non-proliferation and procedures for the exhumation of the US servicemen listed as 'missing in action'. In August, however, the defection to the USA of two North Korean diplomats (the most senior officials yet to seek asylum in North America) resulted in the suspension of the third round of missile non-proliferation talks. The DPRK was unsuccessful in attempting to make its participation in full quadripartite talks conditional upon the withdrawal of US forces from the Korean peninsula and upon the provision of food aid. None the less, the USA responded positively, on humanitarian grounds, to two further UN appeals for food aid during the year. Relations with the USA were dominated by nuclear issues and other concerns regarding the DPRK's missile development programme in 1998 and 1999 (see above). The exhumation of US soldiers listed as 'missing in action' proceeded, with 22 sets of remains returned to the USA in 1998. In October 1999 US officials visited Pyongyang to receive the remains of four soldiers, in the first such transfer to take place on North Korean territory without the involvement of the UNC. A further 15 sets of remains were returned in November 2000. Trade between the USA and the DPRK increased significantly following the partial revocation of economic sanctions against the latter in September 1999 (see above); US exports to the DPRK increased massively in 1999. Meanwhile, the USA continued to provide emergency food aid to the DPRK.

Relations between the DPRK and the USA were variable during 2000. In June the USA announced the partial easing of economic sanctions against the country. In September, however, officials from the DPRK declined to attend the UN Millennium summit meeting in New York, following a confrontation between the delegation and US security officials, who suspected the North Koreans of terrorism, at Frankfurt airport in Germany. The USA subsequently apologized, describing the incident as an 'innocent mistake' and refuting the DPRK's claim of a 'brazen plot'. In October Kim Jong Il's special envoy, Vice-Marshal Jo Myong Rok, paid a state visit to the USA, the most senior North Korean official ever to do so. Later that month the US Secretary of State, Madeleine Albright, reciprocated the visit and met Kim Jong Il, who agreed in principle to halt his country's long-range missile-testing programme. Shortly afterwards, however, tension arose when two US fighter aircraft participating in a US-South Korean joint manoeuvre briefly crossed the military demarcation line into North Korean airspace. The DPRK protested to the UN.

Relations between the DPRK and the USA deteriorated during 2001 following the inauguration of George W. Bush as US President. Bush adopted a tougher position towards the DPRK compared with his predecessor, and this also adversely affected inter-Korean relations (see above). The DPRK condemned the joint US-South Korean military exercises held in April. In May a non-governmental delegation from the USA visited the DPRK to examine evidence of atrocities committed by US troops during the Korean War. In June Bush stated that he was willing to resume negotiations with the DPRK, albeit linking these to a reduction in North Korea's missile programme and military deployments—terms rejected by the North.

Following the terrorist attacks on the USA in September 2001, the USA paid increasing attention to North Korea's biological, chemical and nuclear weapons programmes. Although the DPRK had condemned those attacks, it subsequently opposed the US bombing of Afghanistan. By late 2001 the DPRK was drawing increasing criticism from the USA, and in October the US State Department released its annual report on religious freedom, which included the DPRK on a list of countries suppressing such beliefs. Despite signing two UN treaties against terrorism in November, the DPRK remained on the USA's list of states sponsoring terrorism.

In January 2002 the DPRK's relations with the USA deteriorated further following President Bush's reference to North Korea as forming an 'axis of evil' with Iran and Iraq. Bush's comments were believed to reflect concern that the DPRK was exporting weapons technology to countries the USA considered to be 'rogue states'. (During the 1990s the DPRK had exported missiles and related technology to countries such as Egypt, Iran, Libya, Pakistan and Syria, allegedly earning up to US $1,000m. a year.) However, when Bush visited the DMZ on a visit to the South, he urged the North to open up to the outside world. Although the USA ruled out any military action against the DPRK, in March 2002 it was revealed that the DPRK was one of seven nations considered a potential target for a US nuclear first strike, in the event of emergency circumstances. The DPRK responded by threatening to withdraw from existing agreements with the USA (see above). However, in April the North accepted a South Korean request to reopen dialogue with the USA, and invited a US envoy, Jack Pritchard, to discuss outstanding issues. At the same time the USA announced that it would release US $95m. to the DPRK in order to accelerate the building of the replacement nuclear reactors—construction of which finally began in August 2002, with a view to completion in 2008. Pritchard himself attended the ground-breaking ceremony, but stated that the DPRK must accept international inspection of its nuclear facilities, a demand that the North Korean Government stated was not mandatory until 2005.

Meanwhile, in July 2002 the Minister of Foreign Affairs, Paek Nam Sun, held an informal meeting with the US Secretary of State, Colin Powell, on the sidelines of the ASEAN Regional Forum (ARF) in Brunei—the most senior-level contact between the DPRK and the Bush Administration. In August the DPRK rejected US demands for a significant reduction of its conventional military forces along its border with the South. The USA had long feared that these could be used to attack the 15,000 US troops deployed between Seoul and the DMZ in the event of hostilities.

Relations between the DPRK and the USA deteriorated significantly from October 2002 after the USA announced that senior North Korean officials had admitted to the visiting US Assistant Secretary of State for East Asian and Pacific Affairs, James Kelly, that the DPRK was pursuing a secret nuclear weapons programme in violation of the 1994 agreement. The clandestine programme was allegedly based on uranium extraction, whereas the suspended programme had been based on plutonium extraction. The admission reportedly came after Kelly presented his North Korean hosts with credible US intelligence reports about the programme, although officials of the DPRK later denied that they had made such an admission. Within days the USA declared the 1994 framework null and void and placed renewed pressure on the DPRK to halt its nuclear activities. The DPRK responded by stating that it would consider halting its nuclear programme if the USA would sign a non-aggression treaty guaranteeing it sovereignty, a demand rejected by the USA. The DPRK subsequently warned the USA of severe military measures if it continued to reject such a treaty. In mid-November 2002, however, the USA finally halted petroleum shipments to North Korea, citing the latter's violation of the 1994 framework. Further confusion over the nuclear programme emerged in November 2002 when North Korean radio reportedly admitted that the country already possessed nuclear weapons. However, the exact translation of the statement was in doubt, and most analysts concluded that the broadcast had stated that the DPRK was entitled to possess such weapons. At the same time it was widely reported that Pakistan had provided the technical expertise for North Korea's nuclear programme in exchange for ballistic missiles. Attention focused on the north-western city of Kusong, some 30 km northwest of Yongbyon, as the centre of the secret programme.

The diplomatic crisis between the DPRK and the USA worsened in December 2002 when the former announced that it would restart its nuclear reactor at Yongbyon, and the USA accused the DPRK of narcotics-trafficking. Later in that month the DPRK removed the IAEA's monitoring and surveillance equipment from the Yongbyon facility. The US Secretary of Defense, Donald Rumsfeld, warned the DPRK not to take advantage of the USA's planned attack on Iraq (see the chapter on Iraq) to raise regional tensions, stating that the USA could fight against both countries simultaneously. Security analysts, meanwhile, concluded that the DPRK already possessed between two and five nuclear devices. In late December the IAEA reported that North Korean technicians had transferred 1,000 fuel rods (out of 8,000 necessary to reactivate it) to the Yongbyon reactor, ostensibly for the production of electricity, but probably for the production of plutonium required to manufacture nuclear devices. The DPRK expelled the two remaining IAEA inspectors at the end of that year.

In January 2003 the DPRK announced its withdrawal from the NPT, and the IAEA responded by adopting a resolution condemning the country's recent behaviour. However, President Bush indicated that the USA would resume petroleum deliveries if the DPRK abandoned its nuclear weapons programme. In February the DPRK stated that the Yongbyon reactor was operating normally, and that any US military build-up in the region could lead the North to launch a pre-emptive strike on US forces anywhere in the world. The DPRK also threatened to withdraw from the 1953 armistice if the USA imposed a blockade on the country. Despite these threats, the USA deployed long-range bombers to its bases on the Pacific island of Guam as a precautionary measure, and warned that although it favoured a peaceful resolution of the crisis, it had not ruled out any options, including military action.

In early March 2003 the USA and South Korea began their annual joint military exercises amid condemnation by the North, which announced at the end of the month that it was severing military contacts with the USA at the liaison office in the DMZ. Also in early March four North Korean fighter aircraft intercepted a US reconnaissance aircraft in international airspace and closely pursued its flight, the first such incident in 32 years. Between late February and the beginning of April the DPRK also test-fired three short-range missiles, although it refrained from testing its longer-range ballistic missiles. The commencement of the US-led campaign in Iraq in late March alarmed the North Korean Government, which reportedly believed that the USA would target the DPRK at some future date. By early April the USA had imposed new sanctions on the DPRK's Government and its Changgwang Sinyong Corporation, for exporting ballistic missiles to Pakistan. However, the sanctions were largely symbolic, since the USA had minimal economic links with the DPRK. Later in the month, the seizure by Australian authorities of the *Pong Su*, a North Korean ship carrying 50 kg of heroin, confirmed US claims that the DPRK was involved in drugs-trafficking. Also in April, the UN Security Council held discussions on the North Korean crisis for the first time. The DPRK stated prior to the talks that the imposition of economic sanctions through the Security Council would amount to a declaration of war.

Tensions between the DPRK and the USA increased in late April 2003 after ambiguous statements by the North's official media in which it indicated it was preparing to reprocess, or was actually reprocessing, 8,000 spent fuel rods, a development that would enable it rapidly to produce nuclear weapons. Officials from North Korea, the USA and China held senior-level discussions in Beijing on the isse of the nuclear weapons programme. No agreements were reached, however, and US sources stated that the DPRK had, for the first time, admitted to possessing nuclear weapons and had threatened to carry out a nuclear test. In May the DPRK cited US behaviour against it as a reason for abandoning the Joint Declaration of the Denuclearization of the Korean Pensinsula, a 1992 commitment with the South on a nuclear-free peninsula.

In June 2003 the DPRK for the first time publicly defended its nuclear weapons strategy, declaring that the development of nuclear weapons was a 'deterrent', and that the programme 'was not aimed at threatening or blackmailing'. In July there were new indications from US and Asian intelligence sources that the DPRK was operating a second secret nuclear facility, in addition to the plant at Yongbyon. At the end of July it was announced that the DPRK had agreed to take part in multilateral talks on its nuclear weapons programme with the USA, the Republic of Korea, Japan, China and Russia. Prior to the talks, tensions were exacerbated by comments of US Under-Secretary of State John Bolton, who launched a virulent attack on Kim Jong Il in the course of a speech given in Seoul. The DPRK responded by describing Bolton as 'human scum' and refusing to negotiate with him at the talks. Furthermore, immediately in advance of the negotiations, Jack Pritchard resigned as US special envoy to North Korea. The six-party talks duly took place in Beijing in August, but little progress was achieved, the USA insisting that the DPRK unconditionally abandon its nuclear weapons programme, while the DPRK reiterated that it would continue to develop its nuclear capacity unless the USA provided a guarantee of non-aggression.

Following the six-party talks in Beijing, it was reported in September 2003 that President Bush had authorized his Assistant Secretary of State for East Asia and the Pacific, James Kelly, to abandon the USA's insistence on the full dismantling of the North Korean weapons programme before any concessions could be made. It was indicated that verifiable progress on dismantling might be sufficient. However, he said that a bilateral non-aggression treaty, as desired by the DPRK, was not a possibility, and that any guarantee would involve China, Russia, the Republic of Korea and Japan, as well as the USA. Also in October, the North Korean state news agency claimed that the DPRK had successfully completed the reprocessing of 8,000 spent fuel rods, thus generating sufficient plutonium to build a nuclear bomb. The USA, however, dismissed the claim. However, in November the Central Intelligence Agency (CIA) reported to the US Congress that it believed the DPRK had the technology to turn its nuclear fuel into functioning weapons. In early December KEDO (an international consortium established in 1995 following a 1994 agreement with the USA on assistance for energy development in the DPRK in return for nuclear non-proliferation, see above) announced that it would be suspending for one year its construction in the DPRK of two non-military nuclear reactors. Also in December 2003, the USA rejected an offer from the DPRK to 'freeze' its nuclear programme in return for concessions on security and energy aid.

In January 2004 a group of US nuclear scientists, including Siegfried Hecker, the former director of the Los Alamos nuclear research centre, was permitted to visit the Yongbyon plant in an unofficial capacity. Hecker subsequently stated that although he had seen no proof that the DPRK had produced a nuclear bomb, he had been shown radioactive plutonium metal. There was also speculation on the existence of a second nuclear programme for enriching uranium (in addition to the plutonium-reprocessing activities at Yongbyon). In February a fresh round of six-party talks took place in Beijing, but no significant resolutions were reached. In April a US expert on North Korea, Selig Harrison, visited Pyongyang and was reportedly assured by the President of the Presidium of the SPA, Kim Yong Nam, that the DPRK would not transfer nuclear technology to al-Qa'ida or other 'militant' groups. At a third round of six-party talks in June little progress was achieved, with the DPRK continuing to deny the existence of a uranium enrichment programme. In July US Secretary of State Colin Powell held discussions with the North Korean Minister of Foreign Affairs, Paek Nam Sun, in Jakarta, representing the most senior-level talks between the two countries since 2002. However, relations worsened after the Government of the DPRK, in response to criticism of Kim Jong Il by President Bush, issued a statement likening the US President to the Nazi leader, Adolf Hitler. Also in August 2004, it was reported that North Korea was developing a new sea-based long-range missile system, which would possibly be capable of targeting the USA. Disclosures in 2004 concerning the suspected inaccuracy of US intelligence on Iraq, which had been used to justify US military action against that country in 2003, increased uncertainty over the quality of US information on the DPRK's weapons capabilities. A fourth round of six-party talks scheduled for September 2004 was suspended when the DPRK refused to attend, citing US hostility. Tensions in relations with the USA increased further following the re-election of George W. Bush as US President in November. Later that month KEDO announced its intention to suspend plans for the construction in the DPRK of two non-military nuclear reactors.

In January 2005 the North Korean Government was angered by a description of the DPRK by Condoleezza Rice, the recently appointed US Secretary of State, as an 'outpost of tyranny'. Subsequently, in a state radio broadcast in February, the DPRK for the first time explicitly stated that it possessed nuclear weapons, and that it intended to postpone its participation in six-party negotiations for an indefinite period. Subsequent calls by the DPRK for bilateral talks with the USA were rejected by the latter. Early in 2005, meanwhile, Christopher Hill, hitherto the US ambassador in Seoul, replaced James Kelly as Assistant Secretary of State for East Asia and the Pacific and the USA's chief negotiator in the nuclear talks. In March Condoleezza Rice declared during a visit to Beijing that the USA would consider 'other options' if the DPRK persisted in refusing to participate in the six-party talks. In April, following a visit to the DPRK, Selig Harrison reported that the Yongbyon reactor was to be shut down in order to extract 8,000 spent fuel rods, to be reprocessed into plutonium for use in warheads. In May the DPRK announced that all 8,000 rods had been unloaded from the Yongbyon reactor 'in the shortest possible time', although there was speculation that this was unlikely to have been achieved so quickly and that the announcement might be a diplomatic ploy in advance of any resumption of talks. Also in May tension was increased when the DPRK test-fired a ballistic missile into the Sea of Japan, while Mohammad el-Baradei, Director-General of the IAEA, stated that he believed the DPRK possessed enough weapons-grade plutonium for five or six nuclear devices. However, an apparent improvement in relations in June included a US pledge of 50,000 metric tons of food aid, and the fourth round of six-party talks began in Beijing on 26 July. On the previous day bilateral discussions were held between the representatives of the DPRK and the USA in the hope of finding a compromise between their respective opening positions. The USA continued to insist that normalization of relations, lifting of sanctions and guarantees of security could only follow the 'complete, verifiable and irreversible dismantling' of the DPRK's nuclear weapons programme, while the latter reiterated that only after the normalization of relations, including the signing of a peace treaty ending the Korean War, and the removal of US nuclear weapons from South Korea (the presence of which the US side denied) would the North agree to abandon its military nuclear aspirations. (The USA had indicated that, for the purpose of these talks, it was prepared to disregard the issue of the possible existence of a uranium enrichment programme in the DPRK.) The talks went into recess in early August; their resumption was postponed until mid-September as a mark of protest by the DPRK at the annual joint military exercises performed by South Korea and the USA in late August and early September.

In mid-September 2005 a draft joint agreement was signed by all sides in the six-party negotiations, in which the DPRK committed itself to dismantle its nuclear weapons programme, return to the NPT and permit IAEA inspectors to visit its nuclear facilities. In return, the USA declared that it maintained no nuclear weapons on the Korean peninsula and had no intention of attacking the DPRK. The DPRK's right to peaceful nuclear energy was acknowledged, and it was envisioned that the provision of a civilian light-water nuclear reactor to North Korea would be discussed 'at an appropriate time'. The other five parties also pledged to provide the DPRK with energy assistance. Described in some quarters as a major breakthrough, the agreement was nevertheless vague and was compromised almost immediately when the North Korean Government insisted that it would take no steps towards dismantling its nuclear weapons programme until provided with a light-water reactor as specified in the agreement. The USA insisted that concessions such as the reactor could be expected to come into force only after the DPRK had fulfilled its dismantlement obligations. The fifth round of talks, which began in Beijing in November, was intended to discuss means of implementing the September agreement, but its opening was marred by North Korea's angry reaction to reported comments by President Bush during a visit to Brazil where he made reference to a 'tyrant in North Korea'. A five-point plan for dismantling its nuclear programme proposed at the talks by the DPRK was reportedly rejected by the USA; the discussions ended without agreement and without any setting of a date for the next round. Later in November KEDO announced that it was considering the termination of its light-water reactor construction project in the DPRK, which had been suspended since 2003. (All workers were withdrawn from KEDO's construction site in Kumho, DPRK, in January 2006, and in December KEDO's executive board signed an agreement to terminate the project. In January 2007 KEDO reportedly demanded nearly US $1,900m. in compensation.)

Meanwhile, the resumption of the six-party nuclear negotiations appeared to be jeopardized by a series of attacks by the USA on the alleged financial crimes of the DPRK. In September 2005 the US Administration had ordered that all transactions with Banco Delta Asia in Macao, China, be terminated, in relation to suspected money-laundering activities conducted with the bank by the North Korean Government, and had also 'frozen' the assets of eight North Korean companies, which it accused of proliferating weapons of mass destruction. In October the US Department of Justice accused the DPRK of having forged millions of US dollars' worth of counterfeit $100 bills since 1989, and in December 2005 Alexander Vershbow, US ambassador to the Republic of Korea, publicly described the DPRK as a 'criminal regime'. Although the US Administration insisted that the sanctions were purely a legal matter and had no political connection to the nuclear issue, the North Korean Government declared that no further six-party negotiations could be held until sanctions against it were removed. In April 2006 Christopher Hill rejected North Korean overtures for bilateral discussions in Tokyo, to coincide with a regional security forum at which all six participants in the nuclear talks were present, insisting that communication between the two sides was only possible within the context of the six-party talks.

By mid-2006 speculation was rife that the DPRK was soon to test-launch an intercontinental ballistic missile, thus breaking the moratorium on tests imposed in 1999. In the USA, officials reportedly telephoned North Korean diplomats in the UN to warn them of the consequences of proceeding with a test, while US Secretary of State Condoleezza Rice warned that a test would be regarded as a provocative act. Japan threatened stern action should a test missile be launched. However, North Korea continued to insist that it might be prepared to halt the planned test should the USA agree to direct bilateral talks, a request that the US Government once again rejected. Instead, the USA announced that it would deploy advanced *Patriot* missiles (capable of intercepting North Korean ballistic missiles, as well as cruise missiles and aircraft) on Japanese soil for the first time. The DPRK's decision to test seven missiles on 5 July 2006 was regarded as a deliberate attempt to provoke the USA, at a time when relations between the two countries were at a low point. Of the missiles tested, at least one was a *Taepo Dong 2* missile, thought to be capable of reaching Alaska, and although the US State Department claimed that the *Taepo Dong 2* failed in mid-air after about 42 seconds of flight, the North Korean Government hailed the tests as a success, announcing that more test launches were planned.

While the international community broadly condemned the tests, harsh criticism from the USA and Japan was tempered by the more cautious stance adopted by China, Russia and the Republic of Korea. The USA and Japan urged the UN Security Council to adopt sanctions against the DPRK, while Russia and China, which as permanent members of the Council held the power of veto, emphasized the importance of the resumption of dialogue. The UN Security Council adopted Resolution 1695 on 15 July 2006, requiring member states to bar the import and export of missile-related material to and from the DPRK, a motion that North Korean officials immediately rejected.

By August 2006 reports indicated that the North Korean missile programme was proceeding rapidly, with the construction of new underground missile bases and silos along the east coast. According to a South Korean security expert, around 200 *Rodong* missiles with ranges of up to 2,200 km and 50 SSN-6 missiles with ranges of 2,500–4,000 km were already deployed there. The South Korean report also suggested that the DPRK had built two underground missile bases deep within the mountains of the border region with China. The South Korean Minister of Foreign Affairs warned that a North Korean nuclear test would have serious consequences.

The USA attempted once more to revive the six-party talks in September 2006, with Assistant Secretary of State Christopher Hill travelling to Beijing, Tokyo and Seoul to hold talks with senior officials. However, he reiterated that the US position on the talks had not changed, and that no new incentives would be offered. (The DPRK accused the USA of threatening war by conducting a missile defence test from Alaska.) On 3 October 2006 the North Korean Ministry of Foreign Affairs officially announced that the DPRK would conduct a nuclear test in 'the near future'. The South Korean Government issued a 'grave warning' to the North, pointing out that such a test would violate the 1992 Joint Declaration of the Denuclearization of the Korean Peninsula.

In defiance of international opinion, however, the DPRK's nuclear test took place on 9 October 2006, reportedly from a test site near Kimchaek city in North Hampyong Province. The South Korean Minister for Unification, Lee Jong-Seok, denounced the test as a clear challenge to peace and stability around the world. Although the size of the nuclear device tested was thought to be very small, the detection of airborne radiation by US analysts confirmed that the device was nuclear in nature, and not, as earlier reports had suggested, a conventional weapon. The test immediately prompted an emergency meeting of the UN Security Council in New York, amid strong condemnation from the international community, notably the USA and Japan.

On 14 October 2006 the UN Security Council approved a unanimous resolution imposing sanctions on the DPRK, with Russia and China unexpectedly agreeing to a range of sanctions, albeit one that was purely economic and commercial, rather than military, in nature. Resolution 1718 called on the DPRK to suspend immediately its ballistic weapons programme and further nuclear tests and to return to the six-party talks without precondition. Sanctions included provision for the inspection of cargo entering and leaving North Korean ports, a ban on weapons-related imports, a travel ban on North Korean officials thought to be involved in the weapons programme and a 'freezing' of their assets, and a ban on the import of luxury goods.

At the end of October 2006 the DPRK indicated that it would return to the six-party talks, following discussions among Chinese, US and North Korean officials. While the DPRK set no conditions for its return to the talks, it expressed the hope that one of the topics would be the removal of financial sanctions and the release of North Korean assets. In mid-November, however, a draft UN resolution condemned the DPRK's human rights record (see above), and in the following week leaders from the Asia-Pacific Economic Co-operation (APEC, see p. 176) forum, meeting in the Vietnamese capital of Hanoi, issued a statement expressing their strong concern over the nuclear weapons test.

Talks held in Beijing in late November 2006 between the DPRK's senior nuclear negotiator Kim Kye Gwan and US Assistant Secretary of State Christopher Hill did little to solve the impasse. Not only did the two sides fail to confirm a date for the resumption of the six-party talks, but the DPRK remained adamant that while it was ready to implement its pledge made in September 2005 to relinquish nuclear weapons, it had no intention of doing so unilaterally. Intense diplomatic activity in the following weeks, however, resulted in the resumption of the six-nation talks on 18 December 2006. However, the DPRK stated that it would consider halting its nuclear programme only if the USA removed both its financial sanctions and the UN sanctions. The country also reiterated demands for a nuclear reactor to generate electricity. The US negotiators, meanwhile, were reported by South Korean sources to have offered a fresh programme of incentives, which would give the DPRK aid and security guarantees if it agreed to declare all its nuclear-related programmes and place them under permanent external inspection. However, the DPRK rejected the US overture, and the talks ended in deadlock. Meanwhile, a South Korean report by the National Assembly's Intelligence Committee suggested that the nuclear test had been conducted as part of a succession struggle within the DPRK; Kim Jong Il had allegedly agreed to the test to ensure that the military supported one of his sons.

Efforts to resume the six-party talks continued in January 2007 when, in an unprecedented development, US Assistant Secretary of State Christopher Hill held direct talks with North Korean nuclear negotiator Kim Kye Gwan in Berlin, Germany. While the DPRK stated that an agreement had been reached, Hill denied this, none the less describing the discussions as very useful. Discreet negotiations, meanwhile, continued to take place among the main parties concerned, and by the end of January the DPRK was reported by South Korean officials to be considering ending its nuclear programme in exchange for aid. On 30 January, as US treasury officials met their North Korean counterparts in Beijing to discuss financial sanctions, Chinese officials announced that the six-party talks were to resume.

The six-party talks held in February 2007 resulted in an apparently significant advance: among other points, the DPRK agreed to permit IAEA inspections and to shut down its nuclear reactor at Yongbyon within 60 days in exchange for the equivalent of 50,000 metric tons of heavy fuel oil and the assurance of negotiations on the restoration of normal relations with Japan and the USA, with the latter notably agreeing to begin the process of ending the designation of the DPRK as a state sponsoring terrorism. Five working groups were to be established to address North Korean relations with both Japan and the USA, economic and energy co-operation, denuclearization of the Korean peninsula, and the establishment of a North-East Asia peace and security mechanism. The DPRK was given an incentive of a further 950,000 tons of heavy fuel oil for immobilizing its nuclear facilities and providing a complete declaration of all its nuclear programmes as part of the next phase of the agreement. Although the formal accord did not directly mention the North Korean funds in the Banco Delta Asia in Macao that had been 'frozen' by the USA in 2005 (see above), this issue was covered by a reference to 'resolving pending bilateral issues', and the USA subsequently agreed to return the funds. Mohammad el-Baradei's visit to the DPRK in mid-March was an indication of further progress, with el-Baradei confirming the DPRK's evident commitment to the dismantling of its nuclear programme. A few days later, however, a further round of six-party talks faltered over delays to the release of the North Korean funds in Macao, and the DPRK missed the 14 April 2007 closure deadline for the Yongbyon reactor. Meanwhile, it was reported that the DPRK had offered to return the US naval vessel *USS Pueblo*, which had been seized in 1968 (see above), during the visit of a US delegation collecting the remains of six

US soldiers who had been killed in the Korean War. As progress on the implementation of the February 2007 agreement remained stalled, with commercial banks reportedly unwilling to transfer the Banco Delta Asia funds, North Korea test-fired three short-range missiles in late May and early June.

US Assistant Secretary of State Christopher Hill visited Pyongyang for the first time in late June 2007. Shortly afterwards North Korea confirmed that it had received the Banco Delta Asia funds, which amounted to US $25m. and had been transferred via a Russian bank, and on the following day IAEA inspectors arrived in North Korea for talks on the closure of the Yongbyon reactor. On their first visit to the DPRK since their expulsion in December 2002, the inspectors were given unlimited access to the nuclear site. In mid-July 2007 the DPRK announced that it had shut down Yongbyon, which was subsequently verified by the IAEA. Participants in the six-party talks met in Beijing a few days later, but failed to agree upon a timetable for the second phase of the February accord, i.e. the disclosure and disablement of all North Korea's nuclear facilities. Following the discussions, Kim Kye Gwan renewed demands that North Korea should be provided with a light-water reactor in exchange for immobilizing its Yongbyon nuclear reactor. Working groups established by the six nations involved in the talks on ending North Korea's nuclear weapons programme held meetings in Panmunjom in August to discuss the technical details of the next stage of the process. Following talks between the DPRK and the USA on improving their bilateral relations, which were held in Geneva in early September, Hill announced that North Korea had agreed to declare and disable all its nuclear facilities by the end of the year. The DPRK claimed that the US delegation had agreed to its removal from the US list of countries supporting terrorism and to lift economic sanctions, but Hill denied this, stating that such action would depend on progress towards ending North Korea's nuclear programme. A group of experts from the USA, China and Russia visited the DPRK in mid-September to examine ways of disabling its nuclear facilities.

A new round of six-party talks, which was held in Beijing in late September 2007, resulted in formal agreement on a deadline of 31 December for the completion of the second phase of the February accord, under which North Korea would receive a further 900,000 metric tons of heavy fuel oil (100,000 tons having already been supplied by South Korea and China). In mid-October a US team of government officials and nuclear experts spent a week in North Korea to discuss detailed plans for disablement. Work on immobilizing the Yongbyon reactor, which was to entail the removal of 8,000 fuel rods, commenced in early November under US supervision. Following a visit to North Korea in early December, Hill reported that disablement was progressing well. Meanwhile, in a personal letter to Kim Jong Il delivered by Hill, President Bush urged the DPRK to fulfil its pledge to provide a full and complete declaration of its nuclear programmes. However, North Korea failed to meet the deadline to disclose details of its nuclear activities. The disablement of the country's nuclear facilities had also not been completed by the end of 2007, although this was attributed to technical difficulties. Hill visited Japan, South Korea, China and Russia for consultations on the denuclearization process in mid-January 2008, suggesting in South Korea that the deadline could be extended until the end of February. In late January Kim Jong Il reportedly assured a visiting Chinese diplomat that the DPRK remained committed to implementing the agreements reached at six-party talks. Hill held talks with Kim Kye Gwan in Beijing in mid-February, later commenting that disagreement remained over the DPRK's continued denial of US claims of the existence of a covert North Korean nuclear programme for enriching uranium. Later that month an historic concert in Pyongyang by the New York Philharmonic orchestra, involving the largest US presence in North Korea since the Korean War, was hailed as a significant act of cultural diplomacy, although it was unlikely to influence political relations.

During the years of the so-called Sino-Soviet dispute the DPRK fluctuated in its allegiance to each of its powerful northern neighbours, the People's Republic of China and the USSR. Kim Il Sung made several official visits to China in the late 1980s, which were interpreted by some Western observers as an attempt to establish closer relations in view of the erosion of communist power in many Eastern European countries. However, the DPRK was aggrieved at China's establishment of full diplomatic relations with the Republic of Korea in August 1992. China appeared largely conciliatory with regard to North Korea's nuclear programme, and during 1993 and the first months of 1994 indicated that it would veto any attempt by the UN Security Council to impose economic sanctions on the DPRK. In 1997 China agreed to provide substantial food aid to the DPRK to alleviate the effects of flooding. Later in that year China accepted US and South Korean proposals for quadripartite negotiations with North Korea to conclude a new peace agreement with the South, and between December 1997 and August 1999 it participated in all six rounds of these negotiations. A senior North Korean delegation visited China in June 1999. During the visit China announced that it would provide the country with 150,000 metric tons of food aid and 400,000 tons of coke over the following months. In October 1999 the Chinese Minister of Foreign Affairs, Tang Jiaxuan, participated in celebrations held in Pyongyang to commemorate the 50th anniversary of the establishment of diplomatic relations between the two countries.

In late 1999 international attention was focused on the uncertain situation of the large number of North Koreans (estimated at some 30,000 by South Korean sources and at 200,000 by the voluntary organization Médecins Sans Frontières) who had crossed the border into China in recent years. In early 2000 it was reported that China had returned some 10,000 escapees to the DPRK during 1999. The number of migrants was thought to fluctuate, according to the season.

In February 2000 China permitted the DPRK to open a consulate-general in Hong Kong. In the following month Kim Jong Il attended a function at the Chinese embassy in Pyongyang. This was his first visit to the mission for 15 years. In May Kim Jong Il visited China, his first official trip abroad for 17 years. In January 2001 the North Korean leader paid a second visit to the People's Republic. During this visit, Kim held extensive talks with Chinese leaders in Beijing, and also toured the new business zones of Shanghai and Shenzhen, where he observed joint-venture projects with foreign multinational corporations, telecommunications projects and the Shanghai Stock Exchange.

In September 2001 Chinese President Jiang Zemin paid an official visit to North Korea, his first such visit since 1990. Jiang promised an additional 200,000 metric tons of food aid and 30,000 tons of diesel oil as a gesture of goodwill to alleviate North Korea's economic crisis. Jiang also reportedly urged North Korea to resume discussions with the South. By early 2002 it was thought that the DPRK was placing a renewed emphasis on relations with China in order to deflect criticism from the USA.

During 2002 the DPRK and China continued to seek the reconnection of the inter-Korean railway lines and their subsequent linking to China's own railway system. In May, however, China's forcible removal of North Korean refugees from South Korean embassy premises in the People's Republic again brought the issue of the refugees to international attention. Several groups of North Korean refugees had, in 2002, fled to Western, Japanese and South Korean diplomatic offices in China, embarrassing the latter, since the Chinese Government had signed a treaty with the DPRK providing for the repatriation of refugees. In June China allowed 24 North Korean refugees who had been concealed in the embassy of the Republic of Korea to leave for that country. After that incident, China began an operation against South Korean activists and missionaries who had been helping North Koreans to flee via China. It was estimated that as many as 300,000 North Korean refugees were already residing in China, with US sources stating that as many as 50,000 had fled to China in 2001 alone.

In February 2003 the President of the DPRK's SPA Presidium, Kim Yong Nam, visited Beijing and pledged to maintain strong bilateral relations. China was expected to use its influence with the DPRK to resolve the tension regarding North Korea's nuclear situation, albeit warning the UN Security Council not to involve itself in the matter. In March China cut its oil supply to the DPRK via a pipeline from Liaoning Province for three days, following North Korean missile tests in the Sea of Japan (see above).

In April 2003 China hosted and participated in senior-level meetings between the DPRK and the USA over Pyongyang's nuclear weapons programme (see above). Immediately prior to the talks, Vice-Marshal Jo Myong Rok, the DPRK's second highest ranking official, led a military delegation to China, and held meetings with President Hu Jintao and senior military leaders. Chinese diplomatic efforts played a major role in ensuring North Korean participation in the first round of six-party talks on the nuclear issue that were held in Beijing in August (as well as in subsequent rounds—see above). In April

THE DEMOCRATIC PEOPLE'S REPUBLIC OF KOREA (NORTH KOREA) *Introductory Survey*

2004 Kim Jong Il made a secretive visit to China, where he held talks with President Hu and other officials. Topics under discussion included the nuclear issue, with China reportedly urging the DPRK to modify its stance, and economic matters. During 2004 repeated instances of defectors from the DPRK seeking refuge in foreign embassies in Beijing posed a dilemma for China, which as an official ally of the DPRK continued to refuse to grant refugee status to such persons. Many defectors were none the less able to travel to Seoul via a third country. In November, however, China forcibly repatriated a group of 70 North Korean nationals. It was believed that they would be imprisoned and possibly executed upon their return to the DPRK. Meanwhile, following the DPRK's refusal to attend a fourth round of six-party talks on the nuclear issue in September, a member of the Standing Committee of the Politburo of the Chinese Communist Party, Li Changchun, headed a delegation to Pyongyang in an attempt to persuade the DPRK to resume negotiations. In March 2005 North Korean Premier Pak Pong Ju visited Beijing and Shanghai. Chinese diplomacy received considerable credit for the achievement of the joint draft agreement at the end of the fourth round of six-party talks in September (see above). In October President Hu made his first official visit to Pyongyang, in advance of the fifth round of nuclear talks in November. In January 2006 reports emerged that Kim Jong Il had travelled incognito to the People's Republic and was visiting the special economic zone of Shenzhen, to observe the methods and results of China's economic modernization. The visit was confirmed by North Korean media following Kim's return to the DPRK.

The DPRK's relations with China deteriorated in October 2006, however, following the North Korean nuclear weapon test (see above). The test embarrassed the Chinese Government, which had repeatedly urged the DPRK to forgo its plans. Somewhat unexpectedly, China agreed to UN sanctions against the country, while ensuring that they did not contain a threat of military action. Media reports following the test suggested that China was complying with UN Security Council Resolution 1718 by inspecting vehicles bound for the DPRK, and that Chinese soldiers were continuing to construct a barbed wire and concrete fence along part of the border. Moreover, the Chinese Government indicated that North Korean refugees being sheltered in a US consulate in north-eastern China would be allowed to travel to the Republic of Korea or the USA (a transfer that China had originally opposed), and stated that it would no longer object to Japan raising the issue of the abduction of Japanese citizens by North Korea at the six-party talks. At the same time, China Southern Airlines, the only Chinese airline offering regular flights to Pyongyang, indicated that it would suspend its operations to the North Korean capital. China reportedly threatened to cut off vital oil supplies to the DPRK should any further nuclear tests be conducted. This threat was supported by an official visit to Pyongyang by Chinese envoy Tang Jiaxuan, who returned to Beijing with assurances that no further tests were planned. China helped to broker another diplomatic advance at the end of October, when the DPRK indicated that it was willing to rejoin the six-way nuclear talks (see above). To give further encouragement to the North Korean Government, China was reported to have permitted the release of funds from the accounts of DPRK officials held in Banco Delta Asia the following month. In September 2007 China provided North Korea with 50,000 metric tons of fuel oil, in accordance with the agreement reached in February at the six-party talks (see above), which China continued to host. Following North Korea's failure to meet the deadline for the disablement of its nuclear facilities and disclosure of its nuclear activities, in late January 2008 the head of the Chinese Communist Party's international liaison department visited Pyongyang to urge Kim Jong Il to comply with his commitments under the six-party agreement. During a visit to Beijing in late February US Secretary of State Condoleezza Rice exerted pressure on the Chinese Government to use its influence to persuade the DPRK to implement the agreement fully.

In the mid-1980s the DPRK placed increased emphasis on its relations with the USSR. The DPRK's diplomatic isolation became more pronounced in the early 1990s, as former communist bloc countries attempted to foster relations with the Republic of Korea. Furthermore, the USSR announced that, from January 1991, its barter trading system with the DPRK would be abolished in favour of trade in convertible currencies at world market prices. However, an agreement was reported to have been signed in May 1993 by the DPRK and the Russian Federation (which, following the dissolution of the USSR, had assumed responsibility for many of the USSR's international undertakings) on technological and scientific co-operation. Discussions on the rescheduling of the terms of repayment of North Korea's debt to Russia took place in October 1997. In March 1999 a new bilateral treaty of friendship, good neighbourliness and co-operation was initialled in Pyongyang (to replace a 1961 bilateral treaty); a formal signing followed in February 2000, during a visit to Pyongyang by the Russian Minister of Foreign Affairs, Igor Ivanov. The treaty was ratified by the DPRK in April. In July President Vladimir Putin became the first Russian (or Soviet) leader to visit North Korea. Following Putin's visit, co-operation between Russia and the DPRK placed a strong emphasis on connecting the latter's rail system to the Trans-Siberian railway, with a view to creating a long-awaited Eurasian transport corridor, and in March 2001 the two countries signed a railway co-operation agreement.

In April 2001 the DPRK's Minister of the People's Armed Forces, Vice-Marshal Kim Il Chol, visited Moscow and reportedly negotiated the acquisition of defensive weapons such as SU-27 aircraft, anti-aircraft systems and intelligence-gathering equipment, in addition to signing a military co-operation protocol. In August Kim Jong Il paid a 24-day visit across Russia to Moscow, where he and President Putin signed a new declaration of co-operation in politics, the economy, military, science and technology, and culture. However, Russia also urged the DPRK to settle the latter's outstanding bilateral debt of as much as US $5,500m. The DPRK had repaid some of this amount by sending hundreds of forced-labour woodcutters to work in Khabarovsk Krai (territory)—although such labour camps were reportedly closed down by late 2002. Kim's visit suggested that the DPRK was seeking closer relations with Russia, in addition to China, to strengthen its international standing.

The DPRK continued to maintain strong relations with Russia in 2002. In April two separate Russian delegations, one led by the Mayor of St Petersburg, Vladimir Yakovlev, the other by the Russian Presidential Representative in the Far Eastern Federal Okrug (district), Konstantin Pulikovskii, visited Pyongyang to discuss co-operation in all fields, particularly business. In May the Minister of Foreign Affairs, Paek Nam Sun, visited Moscow, in the first such visit in 15 years. In July the Russian Minister of Foreign Affairs, Igor Ivanov, visited Pyongyang, and in August Kim Jong Il visited the Russian city of Vladivostok, where he held discussions with Putin, mainly focusing on the reconnection of railway links across the Korean peninsula. At the same time the DPRK and the Russian Oblast of Amur signed a co-operation agreement on agriculture and forestry. In October two North Korean military delegations visited Russia, and in December the Mayor of Moscow, Yurii Luzhkov, visited Pyongyang.

As the diplomatic crisis over the DPRK's nuclear weapons programme intensified in January 2003, Russia sought to defuse the situation by sending the Deputy Minister of Foreign Affairs, Aleksandr Losyukov, to Pyongyang, where he held discussions with Kim Jong Il. Losyukov, who had earlier visited China and subsequently the USA, urged a three-stage formula whereby the international community would accept a nuclear-free Korean peninsula, guarantees for the regime's security, and a resumption of aid. The DPRK reiterated that the crisis could be resolved only through discussions with the USA.

In March 2003 a hitherto unrealized Russian proposal to supply the DPRK with natural gas from the island of Sakhalin in return for the DPRK's abandonment of its nuclear programme was raised by the South Korean Government. In late 2003 Russia appeared to be expanding its economic links with the DPRK, with a team of Russian engineers inspecting a cargo port and petroleum refinery at Raijin, as well as assessing a stretch of railway linking the two countries across the Tumen river.

Russia supported the DPRK in early 2006; in March Glev Ivashentsov, the Russian ambassador to Seoul, was quoted by the South Korean media as stating that the use of international sanctions was not an effective measure. This stance was reiterated in July when, following the North's missile tests (see above), Russia and China ensured that attempts by the UN Security Council to impose sanctions on the DPRK were obstructed. However, Russia modified its strong anti-sanctions policy following the nuclear test of 9 October, like China using its power of veto and ensuring that UN Security Council Resolution 1718 did not include the threat of military action. The Russian authorities assisted in the process of transferring previously 'frozen' North Korean funds from the Banco Delta Asia in Macao to North Korea via a Russian bank in June 2007, thus removing the main obstacle to the implementation of the February agreement on the DPRK's nuclear programme (see above). In January 2008

THE DEMOCRATIC PEOPLE'S REPUBLIC OF KOREA (NORTH KOREA) *Introductory Survey*

Russia provided North Korea with 50,000 metric tons of fuel oil as part of its commitment under the six-party agreement on the dismantlement of North Korea's nuclear facilities (see above).

The DPRK's unilateral application for UN membership, first announced in May 1991, represented a radical departure from its earlier insistence that the two Koreas should occupy a single UN seat. This development was welcomed by the Republic of Korea, and both countries were admitted separately to the UN in September of that year. In September 1999, for the first time in seven years, the North Korean Minister of Foreign Affairs attended and addressed the annual session of the UN General Assembly, in what was perceived as an attempt to end the DPRK's diplomatic isolation. Furthermore, in January 2000 Italy became the first member of the Group of Seven (G-7) Western industrialized nations (and the sixth member of the EU) to establish diplomatic relations with the DPRK, and in May Australia restored diplomatic links with the DPRK. Diplomatic relations were established with the Philippines in July and with the United Kingdom in December. During 2001 the DPRK further expanded its range of diplomatic partners, opening relations with the Netherlands, Belgium, Canada, Spain, Germany, Luxembourg, Greece, Brazil, New Zealand, Kuwait, the EU, Bahrain, Turkey and Liechtenstein. Relations with Timor-Leste were established in late 2002. In May 2003 the DPRK opened an embassy in the United Kingdom, amid protests from human rights protesters. Relations with Ireland were established in December. In March 2004 the Australian ambassador to China, Alan Thomas, was instructed to present his credentials in Pyongyang.

In April 2000 the DPRK formally applied to join the Association of South East Asian Nations (ASEAN, see p. 185). Following the DPRK's admittance to the ASEAN Regional Forum (ARF), a meeting in Thailand in July was attended for the first time by the North Korean Minister of Foreign Affairs, Paek Nam Sun, who held unprecedented meetings with his South Korean, Japanese and US counterparts. In November the APEC forum supported the DPRK's guest status in that organization. Full membership was not expected to follow until 2010 at the earliest, following the announcement by the organization in September 2007, upon the expiry of a 10-year moratorium on new members, that it was to postpone any decision on enlargement for a further three years. Meanwhile, in July 2001 the President of the Presidium of the SPA, Kim Yong Nam, visited Viet Nam, Laos and Cambodia. In March 2002 Kim visited Thailand and Malaysia, where he discussed mainly trade issues. Prime Minister Mahathir bin Mohamad of Malaysia accepted an invitation to visit the DPRK, and Indonesian President Megawati Sukarnoputri visited the country at the end of March. Kim Yong Nam reciprocated Megawati's visit in July of that year. The President of Viet Nam, Tran Duc Luong, visited the DPRK in May and signed several economic and legal co-operation agreements. In 2003 there were reports that the DPRK was selling military equipment to Pakistan, and also that military relations with Myanmar were being developed; diplomatic relations with the latter were re-established in April 2007, and in September Myanmar's Deputy Minister of Foreign Affairs reportedly visited Pyongyang for official talks with the North Korean Government. In early 2004 Pakistani nuclear scientist Abdul Qadeer Khan confessed that he had sold nuclear secrets to the DPRK. In November 2005 it was reported that the Government of Thailand was investigating claims that a Thai woman missing since 1978 had been kidnapped by North Korean agents and was now living in the DPRK. North Korea denied that its agents had abducted the woman. However, in August 2007 the Thai Minister of Foreign Affairs announced that his North Korean counterpart had agreed to co-operate on investigations into the case. In late October and early November Premier Kim Yong Il led a senior-level trip by North Korean officials to South-East Asia, visiting Cambodia, Laos, Malaysia and Viet Nam.

The DPRK has maintained close links with a number of Middle Eastern countries, including Egypt, Libya, Syria and Iran. The President of the Presidium of the SPA, Kim Yong Nam, visited Libya and Syria in July 2002. The DPRK retained long-standing ties with many African nations, and reportedly had military advisers working in some 12 of that continent's countries in 2005. In January 2004 the Vice-President of the Presidium of the SPA, Yang Hyong Sop, visited Nigeria to discuss an agreement on military technology. In May it was reported that IAEA investigation of uranium delivered to the USA by Libya in late 2003 had revealed that the material had been supplied to Libya by the DPRK through an illicit nuclear technology procurement network operated by Pakistani nuclear scientist Abdul Qadeer Khan (see above). Further evidence concerning the transfer of nuclear material from the DPRK to Libya emerged in early 2005. In January 2007 North Korea was reported to have agreed to share its data from the October 2006 nuclear test with scientists from Iran. The alleged agreement reportedly followed a meeting between North Korean and Iranian nuclear scientists in the previous November. However, the DPRK strongly denied the allegations. In September 2007 the DPRK similarly rejected claims that it was assisting Syria to develop a nuclear weapons programme. In that month the United Arab Emirates announced that it had established diplomatic relations with North Korea at ambassadorial level.

Government

The highest organ of state power is the unicameral Supreme People's Assembly (SPA), with 687 members, elected (unopposed) for five years by universal adult suffrage. The SPA elects, for its duration, the Chairman of the National Defence Commission, who, since the effective abolition of the presidency in September 1998, holds the most senior accessible office of state (although this is not formally stated in the Constitution). The SPA elects the Premier and, on the latter's recommendation, appoints other Ministers to form the Cabinet. The President of the SPA Presidium, whose members are elected by the SPA, represents the State in its relations with foreign countries.

Political power is held by the communist Korean Workers' Party (KWP), which is the most influential party in the Democratic Front for the Reunification of the Fatherland (comprising the KWP and two minor parties). The Front presents an approved list of candidates for elections to representative bodies. The KWP's highest authority is the Party Congress, which elects a Central Committee to supervise party work. The Committee elects a Political Bureau (Politburo) to direct policy. The Presidium of the Politburo is the KWP's most powerful policy-making body.

The DPRK comprises nine provinces and two cities, each with an elected Local People's Assembly.

Defence

Military service is selective: army five to eight years, navy five to 10 years, and air force three to four years. The estimated total strength of the armed forces, as assessed at November 2007, was 1,106,000: army 950,000, air force 110,000, and navy 46,000. Security and border troops numbered 189,000, and there was a workers' and peasants' militia ('Red Guards') numbering about 3.5m. The ratio of North Korea's armed forces to total population is believed to be the highest in the world. Defence expenditure for 2006 was budgeted at an estimated 5,000m. won. South Korean intelligence sources estimated the real level of defence expenditure to be more than 30% of total spending in 2004.

Economic Affairs

The UN estimated that the DPRK's gross national income (GNI) per head increased from $472 in 2004 to $516 in 2005. According to estimates based on a different method of calculation, the Bank of Korea (South Korea) assessed North Korean GNI in 2006 at about US $25,600m., equivalent to some $1,108 per head, the latter figure being nearly 5% higher than that suggested in the previous year. During 1996–2006, according to estimates by the World Bank, the population increased by an annual average of 0.7%. It was estimated that in 1998 the North Korean economy declined for the ninth successive year, with gross domestic product (GDP) contracting by 1.1%, in real terms. In 1999–2005, however, GDP grew at an average annual rate of 2.9%, according to South Korean estimates. GDP was believed to have contracted by 1.1% in 2006. Some sources suggested a further contraction in 2007, while other observers believed that GDP remained at the same level as in the previous year.

Agriculture (including forestry and fishing) contributed an estimated 23.3% of GDP in 2006, according to South Korean sources. In mid-2005, according to FAO estimates, 26.6% of the economically active population were employed in agriculture. The principal crops are rice, maize, potatoes, sweet potatoes and soybeans. The DPRK is not self-sufficient in food, and imports substantial amounts of wheat, rice and maize annually. Intermittent food shortages became a serious problem from the mid-1990s (see Recent History). According to FAO estimates, grain production reached 5.1m. metric tons in 2005 and 5.0m. tons in 2006. Potato production exceeded 2.0m. tons in 2005, remaining at a similar level in 2006, according to estimates. The raising of livestock (principally cattle and pigs), forestry and fishing are important. During 1995–2004, according to South Korean estimates, agricultural GDP increased by an average of 2.7% per year. In 2004, again according to South Korean estimates, agricultural GDP rose by 4.1%, following increases of 1.7% in 2003 and 4.3% in 2002. Agricultural GDP was estimated to have expanded by 5.0% in 2005, before contracting by 2.6% in 2006. In early 2007 the DPRK suffered its first outbreak of foot-and-mouth disease since 1960, imported livestock being cited as the source of the infection. The adverse effects of the serious floods and resultant crop losses of August 2007 (see Recent History) were subsequently compounded by the exceptionally dry weather experienced during the winter of 2007/08.

In 2006, according to South Korean estimates, industry (including mining, manufacturing, construction and power) contributed 43.2% of GDP. In 1990 the industrial sector employed 31.6% of the labour force. During 1995–2004, according to South Korean sources, industrial GDP was estimated to have decreased by an average of 0.9% per year. Industrial GDP increased by 2.8% in 2003 and by 1.3% in 2004.

Mining contributed 10.2% of GDP in 2006, according to South Korean estimates. The DPRK possesses considerable mineral wealth, with large deposits of coal, iron, lead, copper, zinc, tin, silver and gold. Output of coal was estimated to have decreased from 23.5m. metric tons in 2005 to 22.5m. tons in 2006.There are unexploited offshore deposits of petroleum and natural gas. South Korean sources estimated that in 2004 output in the mining sector increased by 2.5%, compared with an increase of 3.2% in 2003 and a decline of 3.8% in 2002.

In 2006, according to South Korean estimates, the manufacturing sector contributed 19.5% of GDP. In the 1990s industrial development concentrated on heavy industry (metallurgy—notably steel production—machine-building, cement and chemicals). The textiles industry has provided significant exports. South Korean sources estimated that the GDP of the manufacturing sector increased by 0.3% in 2004, following an increase of 2.6% in 2003 and a decline of 1.9% in 2002.

In 2004 it was estimated that 56.9% of the DPRK's energy supply was derived from hydroelectricity, followed in importance by coal (38.6%) and petroleum (4.5%). A 30-MW nuclear reactor was believed to have been inaugurated in 1987. From the 1990s the DPRK experienced increasing power shortages, as generation declined and transmission infrastructure deteriorated. Futhermore, the production of hydroelectric power was adversely affected by intermittent drought. Electricity generation in 2004 was less than 75% of the amount generated in 1990. In 2006, according to South Korean sources, the DPRK's electricity production totalled 22,500m. kWh., compared with 21,974m. kWh in 2004. Petroleum imports in 2004 reached only 21% of the amount imported in 1990. The USA suspended fuel oil shipments to the DPRK in late 2002, following reports that the country was pursuing a secret nuclear programme. From the 1990s the DPRK sought greater foreign assistance in developing its offshore oilfields. A limited number of joint ventures have been established with foreign oil companies.

The services sector employed an estimated 30.4% of the labour force in 1990. South Korean sources estimated that in 2006 the DPRK's services sector accounted for 33.5% of GDP. In 2004 output in the sector was estimated to have increased by 1.4%, having risen by 0.6% in 2003 and decreased by 0.2% in 2002.

According to South Korean sources, in 2006 total exports, excluding trade with the Republic of Korea, reached $95m. and imports totalled $205m. The DPRK's principal source of imports in 2005 (again excluding the Republic of Korea) was the People's Republic of China, which accounted for 54% of total imports, followed by Russia (11%). China was the DPRK's principal market for exports in 2005, purchasing 50% of goods, followed by Japan (13%). China was a source of crude petroleum, food and vehicles, while Japan was a destination for industrial and agricultural goods. In 2006 the value of inter-Korean trade increased by nearly 27.8% to reach US $1,349.7m. The principal exports in 2002 were live animals (35.5% of the value of total exports, excluding trade with the Republic of Korea), textiles (16.7%) and machinery and electrical equipment (11.6%). Other export commodities in the late 1990s included tobacco and silk. The principal imports in 2002 were mineral products (15.5% of the value of total imports, excluding trade with the Republic of Korea), machinery and electrical equipment (15.4%), and textiles (10.4%). Other import items included road vehicles, chemicals and groceries.

The DPRK's total external debt was estimated to be US $12,460m. in 2000. Following the introduction of market-orientated reforms in 2002, the inflation rate was said to have reached 4,000% in that year. The 2006 budget reportedly envisaged expenditure of 388,950m. won. Budget expenditure was officially stated to have exceeded the Government's target in 2007. Compared with the previous year, budget revenue increased by 6.1% in 2007.

The lack of reliable statistical data impedes an accurate assessment of the North Korean economy. Critics of the regime allege that money-laundering and counterfeiting of US currency, together with suspected state-sponsored trade in weapons and narcotics, have played a crucial role. The country's situation deteriorated sharply from the early 1990s, following the abandonment of the DPRK's barter trading system with the USSR (then its major trading partner) and with China, in favour of trade conducted exclusively in convertible currencies. From the late 1990s the DPRK slowly began to modify its economy. A major reform initiated in 2002 was the establishment of a special industrial zone at Kaesong (see Recent History), on the border with South Korea, the first phase of which became operational in mid-2004. The development of the Kaesong zone contributed significantly to an increase in inter-Korean trade, and by early 2008 the cumulative value of production from the complex had exceeded US $300m. In March 2008 69 South Korean manufacturers, employing 23,953 North Korean workers, were reported to be operating in the complex. The five-year plan for 2008–12, announced in April 2008, accorded priority to improvements in the areas of science and technology. However, in comparison with the previous year the budgetary allocation to this sector was projected to rise by only 6.1% in 2008/09, following an increase of 60.3% in 2007/08. The 2008/09 budget was reported to have allocated 15.8% of total expenditure to defence. Meanwhile, the issue of food supplies remained a primary concern. The sharp rises in international grain prices in early 2008 were expected to exacerbate the problem of food shortages in the DPRK. In April the World Food Programme (WFP) declared that the country's situation was 'clearly bad and getting worse', urging increased action on the part of the international community. Food prices in Pyongyang were reported to have doubled within the previous year. Furthermore, prospects for economic development remained uncertain in the context of international tension over the DPRK's nuclear weapons programme.

Education

Universal compulsory primary and secondary education were introduced in 1956 and 1958, respectively, and are provided at state expense. Free and compulsory 11-year education in state schools was introduced in 1975. Children enter kindergarten at five years of age, and people's school at the age of six. After four years, they advance to senior middle school for six years. English is compulsory as a second language at the age of 14. A report submitted to UNESCO by the North Korean Government in 2000 stated that there were 27,017 nurseries for 1,575,000 pupils, 14,167 kindergartens for 748,416 pupils, 4,886 primary schools for 1,609,865 pupils, 4,772 senior middle schools for 2,181,524 pupils, and more that 300 universities and colleges with 1.89m. students and academics. The adult literacy rate was estimated by UNESCO in 2003 to be 98%.

Public Holidays

The *Juche* calendar was introduced in the DPRK in 1997; 1912, the year of the late Kim Il Sung's birth, was designated the first year of the new calendar.

2008: 1 January (New Year), 16–17 February (Kim Jong Il's Birthday), 8 March (International Women's Day), 15 April (Day of the Sun, Kim Il Sung's Birthday), 1 May (May Day), 15 August (Anniversary of Liberation), 9 September (Independence Day), 10 October (Anniversary of the foundation of the Korean Workers' Party), 27 December (Anniversary of the Constitution).

2009: 1 January (New Year), 16–17 February (Kim Jong Il's Birthday), 8 March (International Women's Day), 15 April (Day of the Sun, Kim Il Sung's Birthday), 1 May (May Day), 15 August (Anniversary of Liberation), 9 September (Independence Day), 10 October (Anniversary of the foundation of the Korean Workers' Party), 27 December (Anniversary of the Constitution).

Weights and Measures

The metric system is in force.

THE DEMOCRATIC PEOPLE'S REPUBLIC OF KOREA (NORTH KOREA)

Statistical Survey

Area and Population

AREA, POPULATION AND DENSITY*

Area (sq km)	122,762†
Population (census results) 31 December 1993	
Males	10,329,699
Females	10,883,679
Total	21,213,378
Population (UN estimates at mid-year)‡	
2005	23,616,000
2006	23,708,000
2007	23,790,000
Density (per sq km) at mid-2007	193.8

* Excluding the demilitarized zone between North and South Korea, with an area of 1,262 sq km (487 sq miles).
† 47,399 sq miles.
‡ Source: UN, *World Population Prospects: The 2006 Revision*.

PRINCIPAL TOWNS
(population at 1993 census)

Pyongyang (capital)	2,741,260	Wonsan	300,148
Nampo	731,448	Pyongsong	272,934
Hamhung	709,730	Sariwon	254,146
Chongjin	582,480	Haeju	229,172
Kaesong	334,433	Kanggye	223,410
Sinuiju	326,011	Hyesan	178,020

Source: UN, *Demographic Yearbook*.

Mid-2007 ('000, incl. suburbs, UN estimates): Pyongyang 3,300; Nampo 1,127; Hamhung 773 (Source: UN, *World Urbanization Prospects: The 2007 Revision*).

BIRTHS AND DEATHS
(annual averages, UN estimates)

	1990–95	1995–2000	2000–05
Birth rate (per 1,000)	21.1	19.0	15.1
Death rate (per 1,000)	6.0	7.9	9.3

Source: UN, *World Population Prospects: The 2006 Revision*.

Expectation of life (years at birth, WHO estimates): 66.4 (males 64.6; females 68.2) in 2005 (Source: WHO, *World Health Statistics*).

ECONOMICALLY ACTIVE POPULATION
('000 persons at mid-1990, ILO estimates)

	Males	Females	Total
Agriculture, etc.	2,027	1,877	3,904
Industry	2,206	1,043	3,249
Services	1,577	1,549	3,126
Total labour force	5,810	4,469	10,279

Source: ILO, *Economically Active Population: Estimates and Projections, 1950–2010*.

Mid-2005 (estimates in '000): Agriculture, etc. 3,097; Total labour force 11,661 (Source: FAO).

Health and Welfare

KEY INDICATORS

Total fertility rate (children per woman, 2005)	2.0
Under-5 mortality rate (per 1,000 live births, 2005)	55
HIV/AIDS (% of persons aged 15–49, 1994)	<0.01
Health expenditure (2004): US $ per head (PPP)	47.0
Health expenditure (2004): % of GDP	3.5
Health expenditure (2004): public (% of total)	85.6
Access to sanitation (% of persons, 2004)	59

For sources and definitions, see explanatory note on p. vi.

Agriculture

PRINCIPAL CROPS
('000 metric tons)

	2004	2005	2006
Wheat	175	267*	276†
Rice (paddy)	2,370	2,582†	2,478†
Barley	64	80†	90†
Maize	1,727	2,062†	1,964†
Rye	60†	50*	50†
Oats†	15	15	15
Millet	54†	30*	64*
Sorghum	20†	30*	32*
Potatoes	2,052	2,070*	2,000*
Sweet potatoes*	373	392	300
Dry beans*	310	310	280
Soybeans (Soya beans)†	350	340	345
Cottonseed†	25	25	25
Cabbages and other brassicas*	695	690	690
Tomatoes*	68	68	68
Pumpkins, squash and gourds*	89	90	90
Cucumbers and gherkins*	66	67	67
Aubergines (Eggplants)*	46	47	47
Chillies and green peppers*	59	60	60
Green onions and shallots*	96	97	97
Dry onions*	86	88	88
Garlic*	90	95	95
Apples*	665	668	668
Pears*	134	135	135
Peaches and nectarines*	122	124	124
Watermelons*	108	110	110
Cantaloupes and other melons	116	121*	121*
Tobacco (leaves)*	64	65	65
Cotton (lint)*	12	12	12

* FAO estimate(s).
† Unofficial figure(s).

Aggregate production ('000 metric tons, may include official, semi-official or estimated data): Total cereals 4,485 in 2004, 5,116 in 2005, 4,969 in 2006; Total roots and tubers 2,425 in 2004, 2,462 in 2005, 2,300 in 2006; Total vegetables (incl. melons) 3,950 in 2004, 3,968 in 2005, 3,968 in 2006; Total fruits (excl. melons) 1,406 in 2004, 1,417 in 2005, 1,417 in 2006.

Source: FAO.

THE DEMOCRATIC PEOPLE'S REPUBLIC OF KOREA (NORTH KOREA)

LIVESTOCK
('000 head)

	2003	2004	2005
Horses	48*	n.a.	n.a.
Cattle	576	566	570*
Pigs	3,178	3,194	3,200*
Sheep	171	171	172*
Goats	2,717	2,736	2,740*
Chickens	19,958	20,309	21,000*
Ducks	4,613	5,189	5,500*
Rabbits	19,576	19,677	n.a.

* FAO estimate.

2006: Figures assumed to be unchanged from 2005 (FAO estimates).

Source: FAO.

LIVESTOCK PRODUCTS
('000 metric tons, FAO estimates)

	2003	2004	2005
Cattle meat	21.8	21.0	21.1
Goat meat	11.1	11.2	11.3
Pig meat	162.5	165.0	167.5
Chicken meat	36.3	37.0	37.4
Cows' milk	94.0	94.0	94.0
Hen eggs	135.0	136.0	140.0

2006: Figures assumed to be unchanged from previous 2005 (FAO estimates).

Source: FAO.

Forestry

ROUNDWOOD REMOVALS
('000 cubic metres, excl. bark, FAO estimates)

	2004	2005	2006
Sawlogs, veneer logs and logs for sleepers	406	297	426
Other industrial wood	481	562	596
Fuel wood	2,463	2,465	2,469
Total	3,350	3,324	3,491

Sawnwood production ('000 cubic metres, incl. railway sleepers): 280 (coniferous 185, broadleaved 95) per year in 1970–2006 (FAO estimates).

Source: FAO.

Fishing

('000 metric tons, live weight, FAO estimates)

	2000	2001	2002
Capture	212.9	206.5	205.0
Freshwater fishes	8.0	4.9	5.0
Alaska pollock	60.0	60.0	60.0
Other marine fishes	112.2	109.0	107.6
Marine crustaceans	15.6	16.2	16.0
Squids	9.5	9.5	9.5
Aquaculture	66.7	63.7	63.7
Molluscs	63.0	60.0	60.0
Total catch	279.6	270.2	268.7

Note: Figures exclude aquatic plants (FAO estimates, '000 metric tons, aquaculture only): 401.0 in 2000; 391.0 in 2001; 444.3 in 2002.

2003–05: Figures assumed to be unchanged from 2002 (FAO estimates).

Source: FAO.

Mining

('000 metric tons, unless otherwise indicated, estimates)

	2004	2005	2006
Hard coal	22,800	23,500	22,500
Brown coal and lignite	6,500	7,000	6,500
Iron ore: gross weight	4,580	5,000	5,000
Iron ore: metal content	1,300	1,400	1,400
Copper ore*	12	12	12
Lead ore*	13	13	13
Zinc ore*	62	67	67
Tungsten concentrates (metric tons)*	600	600	600
Silver (metric tons)*	20	20	20
Gold (kg)*	2,000	2,000	2,000
Magnesite (crude)	1,200	1,000	1,000
Phosphate rock†	300	300	300
Fluorspar‡	12	13	13
Salt (unrefined)	500	500	500
Graphite (natural)	30	30	30
Talc, soapstone and pyrophyllite	50	50	50

* Figures refer to the metal content of ores and concentrates.
† Figures refer to gross weight.
‡ Metallurgical grade.

Note: No recent data are available for the production of molybdenum ore and asbestos.

Source: US Geological Survey.

Industry

SELECTED PRODUCTS
('000 metric tons, unless otherwise indicated)

	2002	2003	2004
Nitrogenous fertilizers*	17	n.a.	n.a.
Motor spirit (petrol)	189	185	188
Kerosene	38	37	37
Gas-diesel (distillate fuel) oils	207	201	203
Residual fuel oils	119	116	117
Coke-oven coke (excl. breeze)†	2,950	n.a.	n.a.
Cement†	5,320	5,540	5,500
Pig-iron‡	800	900	900
Crude steel‡	1,030	1,090	1,070
Refined copper (primary and secondary metal)‡	15	15	15
Refined lead (primary and secondary metal)‡	6	7	9
Zinc (primary and secondary metal)	65	65	67
Electric energy (million kWh)	19,777	21,035	21,974

* Output is measured in terms of nitrogen.
† Provisional or estimated figure(s).
‡ Estimated data from the US Geological Survey.

Source: mostly UN, *Industrial Commodity Statistics Yearbook*.

2005 ('000 metric tons, estimates): Cement 5,700; Pig-iron 900; Crude steel 1,070; Refined copper (primary and secondary metal) 15; Refined lead (primary and secondary metal) 9; Refined zinc (primary and secondary metal) 72 (Source: US Geological Survey).

2006 ('000 metric tons, estimates): Cement 5,700; Pig-iron 900; Crude steel 1,070; Refined copper (primary and secondary metal) 15; Refined lead (primary and secondary metal) 9; Refined zinc (primary and secondary metal) 72; Electric energy (million kWh) 22,500 (Sources: US Geological Survey; Bank of Korea, Republic of Korea).

THE DEMOCRATIC PEOPLE'S REPUBLIC OF KOREA (NORTH KOREA) *Statistical Survey*

Finance

CURRENCY AND EXCHANGE RATES

Monetary Units
100 chon (jun) = 1 won.

Sterling, Dollar and Euro Equivalents (30 November 2007)
£1 sterling = 287.230 won;
US $1 = 139.000 won;
€1 = 205.178 won;
1,000 won = £3.48 = $7.19 = €4.87.

Note: In August 2002 it was reported that a currency reform had been introduced, whereby the exchange rate was adjusted from US $1 = 2.15 won to $1 = 150 won: a devaluation of 98.6%.

BUDGET
(million won, projected)

	1992	1993	1994
Revenue	39,500.9	40,449.9	41,525.2
Expenditure	39,500.9	40,449.9	41,525.2
Economic development	26,675.1	27,423.8	28,164.0
Socio-cultural sector	7,730.6	7,751.5	8,218.3
Defence	4,582.1	4,692.2	4,816.9
Administration and management	513.1	582.4	326.0

1998 (million won, estimates): Total revenue 19,790.8; Total expenditure 20,015.2.

1999 (million won, estimates): Total revenue 19,801.0; Total expenditure 20,018.2.

2000 (million won, estimates): Total revenue 20,955.0; Total expenditure 20,903.0.

2001 (million won, projected): Total revenue 21,571.0; Total expenditure 21,571.0.

2002 (million won, projected): Total revenue 22,174.0; Total expenditure 22,174.0.

2003: Exact figures not made available following price reforms of August 2002.

2004 (million won, reported): Total revenue 337,546; Total expenditure 348,807.

2005 (million won, reported): Total expenditure 419,700.

2006 (million won, reported): Total expenditure 388,950.

NATIONAL ACCOUNTS

Gross Domestic Product by Economic Activity
('000 million won, unofficial estimates)*

	2002	2003	2004
Agriculture, forestry and fishing	6,429	5,961	6,341
Mining	1,652	1,820	2,065
Manufacturing	3,825	4,043	4,388
Electricity, gas and water	939	995	1,051
Construction	1,699	1,896	2,194
Government services	4,679	5,018	5,361
Other services	2,054	2,156	2,308
Total	21,277	21,887	23,707

* Totals may not be equal to sum of component parts, owing to rounding.

2005 (percentage distribution): Agriculture, forestry and fishing 25.0; Mining 9.9; Manufacturing 19.0; Electricity, gas and water 4.3; Construction 9.6; Government services 22.6; Other services 9.6.

2006 (percentage distribution): Agriculture, forestry and fishing 23.3; Mining 10.2; Manufacturing 19.5; Electricity, gas and water 4.5; Construction 9.0; Government services 23.7; Other services 9.8.

Source: Bank of Korea (Republic of Korea).

External Trade

PRINCIPAL COMMODITIES
(US $ million)*

Imports	2000	2001	2002
Live animals and animal products	20.3	73.9	103.4
Vegetable products	159.0	221.0	118.4
Animal or vegetable fats and oils; prepared edible fats; animal or vegetable waxes	89.1	89.9	72.3
Prepared foodstuffs; beverages, spirits and vinegar; tobacco and manufactured substitutes			
Mineral products	171.2	231.1	235.9
Products of chemical or allied industries	108.4	123.4	122.1
Plastics, rubber and articles thereof	67.5	66.0	66.0
Textiles and textile articles	171.9	203.9	158.5
Base metals and articles thereof	85.2	100.4	88.2
Machinery and mechanical appliances; electrical equipment; sound and television apparatus	205.1	243.8	234.7
Vehicles, aircraft, vessels and associated transport equipment	146.2	88.4	76.1
Total (incl. others)	1,406.5	1,620.3	1,525.4

Exports	2000	2001	2002
Live animals and animal products	97.9	158.4	261.1
Vegetable products	30.3	42.0	27.5
Mineral products	43.2	50.5	69.8
Products of chemical or allied industries	44.9	44.6	42.4
Plastics, rubber and articles thereof			
Wood, cork and articles thereof; wood charcoal; manufactures of straw, esparto, etc.	10.9	5.6	10.2
Textiles and textile articles	140.0	140.5	123.1
Natural or cultured pearls, precious or semi-precious stones, precious metals and articles thereof; imitation jewellery; coin	9.8	14.1	14.6
Base metals and articles thereof	43.9	60.2	57.4
Machinery and mechanical appliances; electrical equipment, sound and television apparatus	105.2	97.9	85.6
Total (incl. others)	565.8	650.2	735.0

* Excluding trade with the Republic of Korea (US $ million): *Imports:* 272.8 in 2000; 226.8 in 2001; 370.2 in 2002. *Exports:* 152.4 in 2000; 176.2 in 2001; 271.6 in 2002.

Source: Korea Trade-Investment Promotion Agency (KOTRA), Republic of Korea.

2005 (US $ million, unofficial estimates): *Excluding Republic of Korea:* Total imports 200; Total exports 100. *Republic of Korea only:* Total imports 715.5; Total exports 340.3 (Source: Bank of Korea, Republic of Korea).

2006 (US $ million, unofficial estimates): *Excluding Republic of Korea:* Total imports 205; Total exports 95. *Republic of Korea only:* Total imports 830.2; Total exports 519.5 (Source: Bank of Korea, Republic of Korea).

PRINCIPAL TRADING PARTNERS
(US $ million)*

Imports	2001	2002	2003
China, People's Republic	570.7	467.3	627.6
Germany	82.1	140.4	n.a.
Hong Kong	42.6	29.2	n.a.
India	154.8	186.6	157.9
Japan	249.1	135.1	91.5
Netherlands	9.1	27.6	n.a.
Russia	63.8	77.0	115.6
Singapore	112.3	83.0	n.a.
Spain	31.6	n.a.	n.a.
Thailand	106.0	172.0	203.6
United Kingdom	40.7	n.a.	n.a.
Total (incl. others)	1,620.3	1,525.4	1,614.4

Exports	2001	2002	2003
Bangladesh	38.0	32.3	n.a.
China, People's Republic	166.8	270.9	395.3
Germany	22.8	27.8	n.a.
Hong Kong	38.0	21.9	n.a.
India	3.1	4.8	1.6
Japan	225.6	234.4	173.8
Netherlands	10.4	6.4	n.a.
Russia	4.5	3.6	2.8
Spain	12.6	n.a.	n.a.
Thailand	24.9	44.6	50.7
Total (incl. others)	650.2	735.0	777.0

* Excluding trade with the Republic of Korea (US $ million): *Imports:* 226.8 in 2001; 370.2 in 2002; 435.0 in 2003. *Exports:* 176.2 in 2001; 271.6 in 2002; 289.3 in 2003.

Sources: Korea Trade-Investment Promotion Agency (KOTRA).

2004 (US $ million): *Imports:* China, People's Republic 800; Japan 89; Korea, Republic 439; Total (incl. others) 2,280. *Exports:* China, People's Republic 586; Japan 163; Korea, Republic 258; Total (incl. others) 1,280 (Source: Ministry of Unification, Republic of Korea).

Trade with Republic of Korea (US $ million, unofficial estimates): *Total imports:* 715.5 in 2005; 830.2 in 2006. *Total exports:* 340.3 in 2005; 519.5 in 2006 (Source: Bank of Korea, Republic of Korea).

Transport

SHIPPING
Merchant Fleet
(registered at 31 December)

	2004	2005	2006
Number of vessels	374	445	340
Total displacement ('000 grt)	1,122.8	1,257.8	1,052.6

Source: Lloyd's Register-Fairplay, *World Fleet Statistics*.

International Sea-borne Freight Traffic
(estimates, '000 metric tons)

	1988	1989	1990
Goods loaded	630	640	635
Goods unloaded	5,386	5,500	5,520

Source: UN, *Monthly Bulletin of Statistics*.

CIVIL AVIATION
(traffic on scheduled services)

	2001	2002	2003
Kilometres flown (million)	1	1	1
Passengers carried ('000)	79	84	75
Passenger-km (million)	33	35	32
Total ton-km (million)	5	5	5

Source: UN, *Statistical Yearbook*.

Tourism

	1996	1997	1998
Tourist arrivals ('000)	127	128	130

Source: World Tourism Organization.

Communications Media

	1994	1995	1996
Radio receivers ('000 in use)	2,950	3,000	3,300
Television receivers ('000 in use)	1,000	1,050	1,090
Telefax stations (number in use)	3,000*	n.a.	n.a.
Daily newspapers:			
number	11	11*	3
average circulation ('000 copies)*	5,000	5,000	4,500

* Estimate(s).

1997 ('000 in use): Radio receivers 3,360; Television receivers 1,200.

Telephones ('000 subscribers): 980 (estimate) in 2005.

Sources: UNESCO, *Statistical Yearbook*; UN, *Statistical Yearbook*.

Education
(2000)

	Institutions	Students
Kindergartens	14,167	748,416
Primary	4,886	1,609,865
Senior middle schools	4,772	2,181,524

Source: mainly Government of the Democratic People's Republic of Korea, *UNESCO Education for All Assessment Report 2000*.

Universities and Colleges: The *UNESCO Education for All Assessment Report 2000* identified more than 300 universities and colleges with 1.89m. students and academics.

Teachers (1987/88, UNESCO, *Statistical Yearbook*): Pre-primary 35,000, Primary 59,000, Secondary 111,000, Universities and colleges 23,000, Other tertiary 4,000.

Adult literacy rate (UNESCO estimate): 98.0% in 2003 (Source: UN Development Programme, *Human Development Report*).

Directory

The Constitution

A new Constitution was adopted on 27 December 1972. According to South Korean sources, several amendments were made in April 1992, including the deletion of references to Marxism-Leninism, the extension of the term of the Supreme People's Assembly from four to five years, and the promotion of limited 'economic openness'. Extensive amendments to the Constitution were approved on 5 September 1998. The main provisions of the revised Constitution are summarized below:

The Democratic People's Republic of Korea is an independent socialist state; the revolutionary traditions of the State are stressed (its ideological basis being the *juche* (self reliance) idea of the Korean Workers' Party), as is the desire to achieve national reunification by peaceful means on the basis of national independence. The Late President Kim Il Sung is the Eternal President of the Republic.

National sovereignty rests with the working people, who exercise power through the Supreme People's Assembly and Local People's Assemblies at lower levels, which are elected by universal, equal and direct suffrage by secret ballot.

THE DEMOCRATIC PEOPLE'S REPUBLIC OF KOREA (NORTH KOREA)

The foundation of an independent national economy, based on socialist and *juche* principles, is stressed. The means of production are owned solely by the State and socialist co-operative organizations.

Culture and education provide the working people with knowledge to advance a socialist way of life. Education is free, universal and compulsory for 11 years.

Defence is emphasized, as well as the rights of overseas nationals, the principles of friendly relations between nations based on equality, mutual respect and non-interference, proletarian internationalism, support for national liberation struggles and due observance of law.

The basic rights and duties of citizens are laid down and guaranteed. These include the right to vote and to be elected (for citizens who are more than 17 years of age), to work (the working day being eight hours), to free medical care and material assistance for the old, infirm or disabled, and to political asylum. National defence is the supreme duty of citizens.

THE STRUCTURE OF STATE

The Supreme People's Assembly

The Supreme People's Assembly is the highest organ of state power, exercises legislative power and is elected by direct, equal, universal and secret ballot for a term of five years. Its chief functions are: (i) to adopt, amend or supplement legal or constitutional enactments; (ii) to determine state policy; (iii) to elect the Chairman of the National Defence Commission; (iv) to elect the Vice-Chairmen and other members of the National Defence Commission (on the recommendation of the Chairman of the National Defence Commission); (v) to elect the President and other members of the Presidium of the Supreme People's Assembly, the Premier of the Cabinet, the President of the Central Court and other legal officials; (vi) to appoint the Vice-Premiers and other members of the Cabinet (on the recommendation of the Premier of the Cabinet); (vii) to approve the State Plan and Budget; (viii) to receive a report on the work of the Cabinet and adopt measures, if necessary; (ix) to decide on the ratification or abrogation of treaties. It holds regular and extraordinary sessions, the former being once or twice a year, the latter as necessary at the request of at least one-third of the deputies. Legislative enactments are adopted when approved by more than one-half of those deputies present. The Constitution is amended and supplemented when approved by more than two-thirds of the total number of deputies.

The National Defence Commission

The National Defence Commission, which consists of a Chairman, first Vice-Chairman, other Vice-Chairmen and members, is the highest military organ of state power, and is accountable to the Supreme People's Assembly. The National Defence Commission directs and commands the armed forces and guides defence affairs. The Chairman of the National Defence Commission serves a five-year term of office and has the most senior post in the state hierarchy.

The Presidium of the Supreme People's Assembly

The Presidium of the Supreme People's Assembly, which consists of a President, Vice-Presidents, secretaries and members, is the highest organ of power in the intervals between sessions of the Supreme People's Assembly, to which it is accountable. It exercises the following chief functions: (i) to convene sessions of the Supreme People's Assembly; (ii) to examine and approve new legislation, the State Plan and the State Budget, when the Supreme People's Assembly is in recess; (iii) to interpret the Constitution and legislative enactments; (iv) to supervise the observance of laws of State organs; (v) to organize elections to the Supreme People's Assembly and Local People's Assemblies; (vi) to form or abolish ministries or commissions of the Cabinet; (vii) to appoint or remove Vice-Premiers and other cabinet or ministry members, on the recommendation of the Premier, when the Supreme People's Assembly is not in session; (viii) to elect or transfer judges of the Central Court; (ix) to ratify or abrogate treaties concluded with other countries; (x) to appoint or recall diplomatic envoys; (xi) to confer decorations, medals, honorary titles and diplomatic ranks; (xii) to grant general amnesties or special pardon. The President of the Presidium represents the State and receives credentials and letters of recall of diplomatic representatives accredited by a foreign state.

The Cabinet

The Cabinet is the administrative and executive body of the Supreme People's Assembly and a general state management organ. It serves a five-year term and comprises the Premier, Vice-Premiers, Chairmen of Commissions and other necessary members. Its major functions are the following: (i) to adopt measures to execute state policy; (ii) to guide the work of ministries and other organs responsible to it; (iii) to establish and remove direct organs of the Cabinet and main administrative economic organizations; (iv) to draft the State Plan and adopt measures to make it effective; (v) to compile the State Budget and to implement its provisions; (vi) to organize and execute the work of all sectors of the economy, as well as education, science, culture, health and environmental protection; (vii) to adopt measures to strengthen the monetary and banking system; (viii) to adopt measures to maintain social order, protect State interests and guarantee citizens' rights; (ix) to conclude treaties; (x) to abolish decisions and directives of economic administrative organs which run counter to those of the Cabinet. The Cabinet is accountable to the Supreme People's Assembly.

Local People's Assemblies

The Local People's Assemblies and Committees of the province (or municipality directly under central authority), city (or district) and county are local organs of power. The Local People's Assemblies consist of deputies elected by direct, equal, universal and secret ballot. The Local People's Committees consist of a Chairman, Vice-Chairmen, secretaries and members. The Local People's Assemblies and Committees serve a four-year term and exercise local budgetary functions, elect local administrative and judicial personnel and carry out the decisions at local level of higher executive and administrative organs.

THE JUDICIARY

Justice is administered by the Central Court (the highest judicial organ of the State), local courts and the Special Court. Judges and other legal officials are elected by the Supreme People's Assembly. The Central Court protects state property and constitutional rights, guarantees that all state bodies and citizens observe state laws, and executes judgments. Justice is administered by the court comprising one judge and two people's assessors. The court is independent and judicially impartial. Judicial affairs are conducted by the Central Procurator's Office, which exposes and institutes criminal proceedings against accused persons. The Office of the Central Procurator is responsible to the Chairman of the National Defence Commission, the Supreme People's Assembly and the Central People's Committee.

The Government

HEAD OF STATE

President: President KIM IL SUNG died on 8 July 1994 and was declared 'Eternal President' in September 1998

Chairman of the National Defence Commission: Marshal KIM JONG IL.

Titular Head of State: KIM YONG NAM.

CABINET
(April 2008)

Premier: KIM YONG IL.

Vice-Premiers: RO TU CHOL, KWAK POM GI, JON SUNG HUN, THAE JONG SU.

Minister of Foreign Affairs: PAK UI CHUN.

Minister of People's Security: JU SANG SONG.

Minister of the People's Armed Forces: Vice-Marshal KIM IL CHOL.

Chairman of the State Planning Commission: KIM KWANG RIN.

Minister of Electric Power Industry: PAK NAM CHIL.

Minister of Coal Industries: KIM HYONG SIK.

Minister of Extractive Industries: KANG MIN CHOL.

Minister of the Metal Industry: KIM SUNG HYON.

Minister of Machine-Building Industries: JO PYONG JU.

Minister of Construction and Building Materials Industries: TONG JONG HO.

Minister of the Electronics Industry: O SU YONG.

Minister of Railways: KIM YONG SAM.

Minister of Land and Marine Transport: RA TONG HUI.

Minister of Agriculture: RI KYONG SIK.

Minister of Chemical Industry: RI MU YONG.

Minister of Light Industry: RI JU O.

Minister of Foreign Trade: RI RYONG NAM.

Minister of Forestry: SOK KUN SU.

Minister of Fisheries: SHIM KI YOP.

Minister of City Management: CHOE JONG GON.

Minister of Land and Environmental Protection: PAK SONG NAM.

Minister of State Construction Control: PAE TAL JUN.

THE DEMOCRATIC PEOPLE'S REPUBLIC OF KOREA (NORTH KOREA) — *Directory*

Minister of Commerce: Ri Yong Son.
Minister of Procurement and Food Administration: Choe Nam Gyun.
Minister of Education: Kim Yong Jin.
Minister of Post and Telecommunications: Ryu Yong Sop.
Minister of Culture: Kang Nung Su.
Minister of Finance: Mun Il Bong.
Minister of Labour: Jong Yong Su.
Minister of Public Health: Choe Chang Sik.
Minister of State Inspection: Kim Ui Sun.
Minister of the Crude Oil Industry: Ko Jong Sik.
Chairman of the Physical Culture and Sports Guidance Committee: Mun Jae Dok.
President of the National Academy of Sciences: Pyon Yong Rip.
President of the Central Bank: Kim Wan Su.
Director of the Central Statistics Bureau: Kim Chang Su.
Chief Secretary of the Cabinet: Jong Mun San.

MINISTRIES
All Ministries and Commissions are in Pyongyang.

Legislature

CHOE KO IN MIN HOE UI
(Supreme People's Assembly)

The 687 members of the 11th Supreme People's Assembly (SPA) were elected unopposed for a five-year term on 3 August 2003. The SPA's permanent body is the Presidium.

Chairman: Choe Tae Bok.
President of the Presidium: Kim Yong Nam.
Vice-Presidents of the Presidium: Yang Hyong Sop, Kim Yong Dae.

Political Organizations

Democratic Front for the Reunification of the Fatherland: Pyongyang; f. 1946; a vanguard organization comprising political parties and mass working people's organizations seeking the unification of North and South Korea; Mems of Presidium Pak Song Chol, Yang Hyong Sop, Ri Yong Su, Kim Pong Ju, Pyon Chang Bok, Ryu Mi Yong, Ryo Won Gu, Kang Ryon Hak.

The component parties are:

Chondoist Chongu Party: Pyongyang; tel. (2) 334241; f. 1946; follows the guiding principle of *Innaechon* (the realization of 'heaven on earth'); satellite party of the Korean Workers' Party; Chair. Ryu Mi Yong.

Korean Social Democratic Party (KSDP) (Joson Sahoeminju-dang): Pyongyang; tel. (2) 5211981; fax (2) 3814410; f. 1945; advocates national independence and a democratic socialist society; satellite party of the Korean Workers' Party; Chair. Kim Yong Dae; First Vice-Chair. Kang Pyong Hak.

Korean Workers' Party (KWP): Pyongyang; f. 1945; merged with the South Korean Workers' Party in 1949; the guiding principle is the *juche* idea, based on the concept that man is the master and arbiter of all things; most significant political entity in the DPRK; 3m. mems; Gen. Sec. Marshal Kim Jong Il.

SIXTH CENTRAL COMMITTEE OF THE KWP
General Secretary: Marshal Kim Jong Il.

POLITBURO OF THE KWP
Presidium: Marshal Kim Jong Il.
Full Members: Kim Yong Nam, Pak Song Chol, Kim Yong Ju, Jon Pyong Ho, Han Song Ryong.
Alternate Members: Yang Hyong Sop, Choe Tae Bok, Kim Chol Man, Choe Yong Rim, Ri Son Sil.
Secretariat: Marshal Kim Jong Il, Kye Ung Tae, Jon Pyong Ho, Han Song Ryong, Choe Tae Bok, Kim Ki Nam, Kim Kuk Tae, Kim Jung Rin, Jong Ha Chol.

The component mass working people's organizations (see under Trade Unions) are:

General Federation of Trade Unions of Korea (GFTUK).
Kim Il Sung Socialist Youth League.
Korean Democratic Women's Union (KDWU).
Union of Agricultural Working People of Korea.

Diplomatic Representation

EMBASSIES IN THE DEMOCRATIC PEOPLE'S REPUBLIC OF KOREA

Cambodia: Munsudong, Taedongkang District, Pyongyang; tel. (2) 3817283; fax (2) 3817625; e-mail recpyongyang@gmail.com; Ambassador Chhorn Hay.

China, People's Republic: Kinmauldong, Moranbong District, Pyongyang; tel. (2) 3823316; fax (2) 3813425; e-mail chinaemb_kp@mfa.gov.cn; internet kp.china-embassy.org; Ambassador Liu Xiaoming.

Cuba: Munsudong, Taedongkang District, Pyongyang; tel. (2) 3827380; fax (2) 3817703; e-mail embarpdc@di.chesin.com; Ambassador José Manuel Galego Montano.

Czech Republic: Taedongkang Guyok 38, Taehakgori, Puksudong, Pyongyang; tel. (2) 3817021; fax (2) 3817022; e-mail pyongyang@embassy.mzv.cz; internet www.mzc.cz/pyongyang; Ambassador Martin Tomčo.

Egypt: 39 Munsudong, Taedongkang District, Pyongyang; tel. (2) 3817414; fax (2) 3817611; Ambassador (vacant).

Ethiopia: POB 55, Munsudong, Taedongkang District, Pyongyang; tel. (2) 3827554; fax (2) 3827550; Chargé d'affaires Fekade S. G. Meskel.

Germany: Munsudong District, Pyongyang; tel. (2) 3817385; fax (2) 3817397; e-mail zreg@pjoe.auswaertiges-amt.de; Ambassador Thomas Schafer.

India: Block 53, Munsudong, Taehak St, Taedongkang District, Pyongyang; tel. (2) 3817274; fax (2) 3817619; e-mail indemhoc@di.chesin.com; Ambassador Zile Singh.

Indonesia: 5 Foreigners' Bldg, Munsudong, Taedongkang District, Pyongyang; tel. (2) 3827439; fax (2) 3817620; e-mail kompyg2@public2.bta.net.cn; Ambassador Daulat Hotma Audison Passaribu.

Iran: Munhungdong, Monsu St, Taedongkang District, Pyongyang; tel. (2) 3817492; fax (2) 3817612; Ambassador Morteza Moradian.

Laos: Munhungdong, Taedongkang District, Pyongyang; tel. (2) 3827363; fax (2) 3817722; Ambassador Chaleune Warinthrasak.

Libya: Munsudong, Taedongkang District, Pyongyang; tel. (2) 3827544; fax (2) 3817267; Secretary of People's Bureau Bashir Ramadan Khalifa Abu Janah.

Malaysia: Munhungdong Diplomatic Enclave, Pyongyang; tel. (2) 3817125; fax (2) 3817845; e-mail malpygyang@kln.gov.my; Chargé d'affaires a.i. Jamal Sharifuddin Bin Johan.

Mali: Pyongyang; Ambassador Nakounte Diakité.

Mongolia: Munsudong, Taedongkang District, Pyongyang; tel. (2) 3827322; fax (2) 3817323; Ambassador Sodovjamtsyn Khürelbaatar.

Nigeria: Munsudong, Taedongkang District, POB 535, Pyongyang; tel. (2) 3827558; fax (2) 3817293; Ambassador Sule Buba.

Pakistan: 23, Block 66, Munsudong, Taedongkang District, Pyongyang; tel. (2) 3827479; fax 3817622; e-mail parep.pyongyang@kcckp.net; Ambassador Noorullah Khan.

Poland: Munsudong, Taedongkang District, Pyongyang; tel. (2) 3817327; fax (2) 3817634; e-mail phenian@polemb.net; Ambassador Roman Iwaszkiewicz.

Romania: Munhungdong, Taedongkang District, Pyongyang; tel. (2) 3827336; fax (2) 3817336; e-mail ambrophe@kcckp.net; Chargé d'affaires a.i. Eugen Popa.

Russia: Sinyangdong, Central District, Pyongyang; tel. (2) 3823102; fax (2) 3813427; e-mail rusembdprk@yahoo.com; Ambassador Valery Sukhinin.

Sweden: Munsudung, Taedongkang District, Pyongyang; tel. (2) 3817485; fax (2) 3817663; e-mail ambassaden.pyongyang@foreign.ministry.se; Ambassador Mats Foyer.

Syria: Munsudong, Taedongkang District, Pyongyang; tel. (2) 3827473; fax (2) 3817635; Chargé d'affaires a.i. Muhammad Adib al-Hani.

Thailand: Pyongyang; Ambassador Nikhom Tantemsapya.

United Kingdom: Munsudong Diplomatic Compound, Pyongyang; tel. (2) 3817980; fax (2) 3817985; e-mail postmaster.PYONX@fco.gov.uk; Ambassador John Everard.

Viet Nam: Munsudong, Taedongkang District, Pyongyang; tel. (2) 3817353; fax (2) 3817632; Ambassador (vacant).

Judicial System

The judicial organs include the Central Court, the Court of the Province (or city under central authority) and the People's Court. Each court is composed of judges and people's assessors.

Procurators supervise the ordinances and regulations of all ministries and the decisions and directives of local organs of state power to ensure that they conform to the Constitution, laws and decrees, as well as to the decisions and other measures of the Cabinet. Procurators bring suits against criminals in the name of the State, and participate in civil cases to protect the interests of the State and citizens.

Central Court
Pyongyang.
The highest judicial organ; supervises the work of all courts.
President: KIM PYONG RYUL.
First Vice-President: YUN MYONG GUK.

Central Procurator's Office
Supervises work of procurator's offices in provinces, cities and counties.
Procurator-General: RI KIL SONG.

Religion

The religions that are officially reported to be practised in the DPRK are Buddhism, Christianity and Chundo Kyo, a religion peculiar to Korea combining elements of Buddhism and Christianity. Religious co-ordinating bodies are believed to be under strict state control. The exact number of religious believers is unknown.

Korean Religious Believers Council: Pyongyang; f. 1989; brings together members of religious organizations in North Korea; Chair. JANG JAE ON.

BUDDHISM
In 2002 it was reported that there were an estimated 300 Buddhist temples in the DPRK; the number of believers was estimated at about 10,000 in 2003.
Korean Buddhists Federation: POB 77, Pyongyang; tel. (2) 43698; fax (2) 3812100; f. 1945; Chair. Cen. Cttee PAK TAE HWA; Sec. SHIM SANG JIN.

CHRISTIANITY
In 2003 it was reported that there were approximately 13,000 Protestants and 3,000 Catholics in the country, many of whom worshipped in house churches (of which there were said to be about 500 in 2002). The construction of North Korea's first Russian Orthodox church was completed in August 2006.

Korean Christians Federation: Pyongyang; f. 1946; Chair. Cen. Cttee KANG YONG SOP; Sec. O KYONG U.

The Roman Catholic Church
For ecclesiastical purposes, North and South Korea are nominally under a unified jurisdiction. North Korea contains two dioceses (Hamhung and Pyongyang), both suffragan to the archdiocese of Seoul (in South Korea), and the territorial abbacy of Tokwon (Tokugen), directly responsible to the Holy See.
Diocese of Hamhung: Catholic Mission, Hamhung; 134-1 Waekwan-dong Kwan Eub, Chil kok kun, Gyeongbuk 718-800, Republic of Korea; tel. (545) 970-2000; Bishop (vacant); Apostolic Administrator of Hamhung and of the Abbacy of Tokwon Fr PLACIDUS DONG-HO RI.
Diocese of Pyongyang: Catholic Mission, Pyongyang; Bishop Rt Rev. FRANCIS HONG YONG HO (absent); Apostolic Administrator Most Rev. NICHOLAS CHEONG JIN-SUK (Archbishop of Seoul).
Korean Catholics Association: Changchung 1-dong, Songyo District, Pyongyang; tel. (2) 23492; f. 1988; Chair. Cen. Cttee JANG JAE ON; Vice-Chair. MUN CHANG HAK.

CHUNDO KYO
According to officials quoted in 2002, there were approximately 40,000 practitioners of Chundo Kyo in the DPRK.
Korean Chundoists Association: Pyongyang; tel. (2) 334241; f. 1946; Chair. of Central Guidance Cttee RYU MI YONG.

The Press

PRINCIPAL NEWSPAPERS
Choldo Sinmun: Pyongyang; f. 1947; every two days.
Joson Inmingun (Korean People's Army Daily): Pyongyang; f. 1948; daily; Editor-in-Chief RI TAE BONG.
Kyowon Sinmun: Pyongyang; f. 1948; publ. by the Education Commission; weekly.
Minju Choson (Democratic Korea): Pyongyang; f. 1946; govt organ; 6 a week; Editor-in-Chief KIM JONG SUK; circ. 200,000.
Nongup Kunroja: Pyongyang; publ. of Cen. Cttee of the Union of Agricultural Working People of Korea.
Pyongyang Sinmun: Pyongyang; f. 1957; general news; 6 a week; Editor-in-Chief SONG RAK GYUN.
Rodong Chongnyon (Working Youth): Pyongyang; f. 1946; organ of the Cen. Cttee of the Kim Il Sung Socialist Youth League; 6 a week; Editor-in-Chief RI JONG GI.
Rodong Sinmun (Labour Daily): Pyongyang; internet www.kcna.co.jp/today-rodong/rodong.htm; f. 1946; organ of the Cen. Cttee of the Korean Workers' Party; daily; Editor-in-Chief CHOE CHIL NAM; circ. 1.5m.
Rodongja Sinmun (Workers' Newspaper): Pyongyang; f. 1945; organ of the Gen. Fed. of Trade Unions of Korea; Editor-in-Chief RI SONG JU.
Saenal (New Day): Pyongyang; f. 1971; publ. by the Kim Il Sung Socialist Youth League; 2 a week; Deputy Editor CHOE SANG IN.
Sonyon Sinmun: Pyongyang; f. 1946; publ. by the Kim Il Sung Socialist Youth League; 2 a week; circ. 120,000.
Tongil Sinbo: Kangan 1-dong, Youth Ave, Songyo District, Pyongyang; f. 1972; non-affiliated; weekly; Chief Editor PAK JIN SIK; circ. 300,000.

PRINCIPAL PERIODICALS
Chollima: Pyongyang; popular magazine; monthly.
Choson (Korea): Pyongyang; social, economic, political and cultural; bi-monthly.
Choson Minju Juuiinmin Gonghwaguk Palmyonggongbo (Official Report of Inventions in the DPRK): Pyongyang; 6 a year.
Choson Munhak (Korean Literature): Pyongyang; organ of the Cen. Cttee of the Korean Writers' Union; monthly.
Choson Yesul (Korean Arts): Pyongyang; organ of the Cen. Cttee of the Gen. Fed. of Unions of Literature and Arts of Korea; monthly.
Economics: POB 73, Pyongyang; fax (2) 3814410; quarterly.
History: POB 73, Pyongyang; fax (2) 3814410; quarterly.
Hwahakgwa Hwahakgoneop: Pyongyang; organ of the Hamhung br. of the Korean Acad. of Sciences; chemistry and chemical engineering; 6 a year.
Jokook Tongil: Kangan 1-dong, Youth Ave, Songyo District, Pyongyang; organ of the Cttee for the Peaceful Unification of Korea; f. 1961; monthly; Chief Editor LI MYONG GYU; circ. 70,000.
Korean Medicine: POB 73, Pyongyang; fax (2) 3814410; quarterly.
Kunroja (Workers): 1 Munshindong, Tongdaewon, Pyongyang; f. 1946; organ of the Cen. Cttee of the Korean Workers' Party; monthly; Editor-in-Chief RYANG KYONG BOK; circ. 300,000.
Kwahakwon Tongbo (Bulletins of the Academy of Science): POB 73, Pyongyang; fax (2) 3814410; organ of the Standing Cttee of the Korean Acad. of Sciences; 6 a year.
Mulri (Physics): POB 73, Pyongyang; fax (2) 3814410; quarterly.
Munhwao Haksup (Study of Korean Language): POB 73, Pyongyang; fax (2) 3814410; publ. by the Publishing House of the Acad. of Social Sciences; quarterly.
Philosophy: POB 73, Pyongyang; fax (2) 3814410; quarterly.
Punsok Hwahak (Analysis): POB 73, Pyongyang; fax (2) 3814410; organ of the Cen. Analytical Inst. of the Korean Acad. of Sciences; quarterly.
Ryoksagwahak (Historical Science): Pyongyang; publ. by the Acad. of Social Sciences; quarterly.
Saengmulhak (Biology): Pyongyang; fax (2) 3814410; publ. by the Korea Science and Encyclopedia Publishing House; quarterly.
Sahoekwahak (Social Science): Pyongyang; publ. by the Acad. of Social Sciences; 6 a year.
Suhakkwa Mulli: Pyongyang; organ of the Physics and Mathematics Cttee of the Korean Acad. of Sciences; quarterly.

FOREIGN LANGUAGE PUBLICATIONS
The Democratic People's Republic of Korea: Korea Pictorial, Pyongyang; f. 1956; illustrated news; Korean, Russian, Chinese, English, French, Arabic and Spanish edns; monthly; Editor-in-Chief HAN POM CHIK.
Foreign Trade of the DPRK: Foreign Trade Publishing House, Potonggang District, Pyongyang; economic developments and export promotion; English, French, Japanese, Russian and Spanish edns; monthly.

Korea: Pyongyang; f. 1956; illustrated; Korean, Arabic, Chinese, English, French, Spanish and Russian edns; monthly.

Korea Today: Foreign Languages Publishing House, Pyongyang; current affairs; Chinese, English, French, Russian and Spanish edns; monthly; Vice-Dir and Editor-in-Chief HAN PONG CHAN.

Korean Women: Pyongyang; English and French edns; quarterly.

Korean Youth and Students: Pyongyang; English and French edns; monthly.

The Pyongyang Times: Sochondong, Sosong District, Pyongyang; tel. (2) 51951; English, Spanish and French edns; weekly.

NEWS AGENCY

Korean Central News Agency (KCNA): Potonggangdong 1, Potonggang District, Pyongyang; internet www.kcna.co.jp; f. 1946; sole distributing agency for news in the DPRK; publs daily bulletins in English, Russian, French and Spanish; Dir-Gen. KIM KI RYONG.

Press Association

Korean Journalists Union: Pyongyang; tel. (2) 36897; f. 1946; assists in the ideological work of the Korean Workers' Party; Chair. Cen. Cttee KIM SONG GUK.

Publishers

Academy of Sciences Publishing House: Nammundong, Central District, Pyongyang; tel. (2) 51956; f. 1953.

Academy of Social Sciences Publishing House: Pyongyang; Dir CHOE KWAN SHIK.

Agricultural Press: Pyongyang; labour, industrial relations; Pres. HO KYONG PIL.

Central Science and Technology Information Agency: Pyongyang; f. 1963; Dir JU SONG RYONG.

Education Publishing House: Pyongyang; f. 1945; Pres. KIM CHANG SON.

Foreign Language Press Group: Sochondong, Sosong District, Pyongyang; tel. (2) 841342; fax (2) 812100; f. 1949; Dir CHOE KYONG GUK.

Foreign Language Publishing House: Oesong District, Pyongyang; Dir KIM YONG MU.

Higher Educational Books Publishing House: Pyongyang; f. 1960; Pres. PAK KUN SONG.

Kim Il Sung University Publishing House: Pyongyang; f. 1965.

Korea Science and Encyclopedia Publishing House: POB 73, Pyongyang; tel. (2) 18111; fax (2) 3814410; publishes numerous periodicals and monographs; f. 1952; Dir Gen. KIM JUNG HYOP; Dir of International Co-operation JEAN BAHNG.

Korean People's Army Publishing House: Pyongyang; Pres. YUN MYONG DO.

Korean Social Democratic Party Publishing House: Pyongyang; tel. (2) 3818038; fax (2) 3814410; f. 1946; publishes quarterly journal Joson Sahoemingjudang (in Korean) and KSDP Says (in English); Dir KIM SOK JUN.

Korean Workers' Party Publishing House: Pyongyang; f. 1945; fiction, politics; Dir RYANG KYONG BOK.

Kumsong Youth Publishing House: Pyongyang; f. 1946; Dir HAN JONG SOP.

Literature and Art Publishing House: Pyongyang; f. by merger of Mass Culture Publishing House and Publishing House of the Gen. Fed. of Literary and Art Unions; Dir Gen. RI PHYO U.

Transportation Publishing House: Namgyodong, Hyongjaesan District, Pyongyang; f. 1952; travel; Editor PAEK JONG HAN.

Working People's Organizations Publishing House: Pyongyang; f. 1946; fiction, government, political science; Dir MIN SANG HYON.

WRITERS' UNION

Korean Writers' Union: Pyongyang; Chair. Cen. Cttee KIM PYONG HUN.

Broadcasting and Communications

North Korea established a satellite communications station in Pyongyang, through an agreement with France in 1986, which enabled North Korea to communicate by satellite with Western countries. In 1990 an agreement was reached on satellite communications for the operation of telephone, telex and telegram services between North Korea and Japan. In May the DPRK joined Intelsat (an international commercial satellite telecommunications organization). In October 2001 North Korea launched its first e-mail service provider in co-operation with China-based company Silibank.com, which was used for business and trade purposes. However, access to the internet remained severely limited, with information flow within North Korea still being conducted mainly via a closed intranet system (the Kwangmyong, meaning 'light', system). In 2002 a mobile telephone network was reportedly established in Pyongyang and surrounding areas, with mobile phone use being permitted to approximately 1,000 government officials. However, citizens have been banned from using mobile phones since mid-2004.

TELECOMMUNICATIONS

Korea Post and Telecommunications Co: Pyongyang; Dir KIM HYON JONG.

BROADCASTING

Regulatory Authorities

DPRK Radio and Television Broadcasting Committee: see Radio, below.

Pyongyang Municipal Broadcasting Committee: Pyongyang; Chair. KANG CHUN SHIK.

Radio

DPRK Radio and Television Broadcasting Committee: Jonsungdong, Moranbong District, Pyongyang; tel. (2) 3816035; fax (2) 3812100; programmes relayed nationally with local programmes supplied by local radio cttees; loudspeakers are installed in factories and in open spaces in all towns; home broadcasting 22 hours daily; foreign broadcasts in Russian, Chinese, English, French, German, Japanese, Spanish and Arabic; Chair. CHA SUNG SU.

Television

General Bureau of Television: Gen. Dir CHA SUNG SU.

DPRK Radio and Television Broadcasting Committee: see Radio.

Kaesong Television: Kaesong; broadcasts five hours on weekdays, 11 hours at weekends.

Korean Central Television Station: Ministry of Post and Telecommunications, Pyongyang; broadcasts five hours daily; satellite broadcasts commenced Oct. 1999.

Mansudae Television Station: Mansudae, Pyongyang; f. 1983; broadcasts nine hours of cultural programmes, music and dance, foreign films and news reports at weekends.

Finance

(cap. = capital; res = reserves; dep. = deposits; m. = million; brs = branches; amounts in won)

BANKING

During 1946–47 all banking institutions in North Korea, apart from the Central Bank and the Farmers Bank, were abolished. The Farmers Bank was merged with the Central Bank in 1959. The Foreign Trade Bank (f. 1959) conducts the international business of the Central Bank. Other banks, established in the late 1970s, are responsible for the foreign-exchange and external payment business of North Korean foreign trade enterprises.

The entry into force of the Joint-Venture Act in 1984 permitted the establishment of joint-venture banks, designed to attract investment into North Korea by Koreans resident overseas. The Foreign Investment Banking Act was approved in 1993.

Central Bank

Central Bank of the DPRK: Munsudong, Seungri St 58-1, Central District, Pyongyang; tel. (2) 3338196; fax (2) 3814624; e-mail kcb_idkb@co.chesin.com; f. 1946; bank of issue; supervisory and control bank; Pres. KIM WAN SU; 13 brs.

State Banks

Credit Bank of Korea: Chongryu 1-dong, Munsu St, Otandong, Central District, Pyongyang; tel. (2) 3818285; fax (2) 3817806; f. 1986; est. as International Credit Bank, name changed 1989; Pres. LI SUN BOK; Vice-Pres. SON YONG SUN.

Foreign Trade Bank of the DPRK: FTB Bldg, Jungsongdong, Seungri St, Central District, Pyongyang; tel. (2) 3815270; fax (2) 3814467; e-mail ftb@co.chesin.com; f. 1959; deals in international settlements and all banking business; Pres. and Chair. O KWANG CHOL; 12 brs.

THE DEMOCRATIC PEOPLE'S REPUBLIC OF KOREA (NORTH KOREA) *Directory*

International Industrial Development Bank: Jongpyong-dong, Pyongchon District, Pyongyang; tel. (2) 3818610; fax (2) 3814427; f. 2001; Pres. SHIN DOK SONG.

Korea Daesong Bank: Segoridong, Gyongheung St, Potonggang District, Pyongyang; tel. (2) 3818221; fax (2) 3814576; f. 1978; cap. 158,205.8m., res 25,917,6m., dep. 1,990,582.5m. (Dec. 2006); Pres. RI GYONG HA.

Koryo Bank: Ponghwadong, Potonggang District, Pyongyang; tel. (2) 3818168; fax (2) 3814033; e-mail krbankpy@co.chesin.com; f. 1989; est. as Koryo Finance Joint Venture Co, name changed 1994; co-operative, development, regional, savings and universal bank; Pres. PAK YONG CHIL; 10 brs.

Kumgang Bank: Jungsongdong, Central District, Pyongyang; tel. (2) 3818532; fax (2) 3814467; f. 1979; Chair. KIM JANG HO.

Private Banks

Bank of East Land: POB 32, BEL Bldg, Jonseung-dong, Moranbong District, Pyongyang; tel. (2) 3818923; fax (2) 3814410; f. 2001; commercial, investment, merchant, private and retail banking; Pres. PAK HYONG GIL.

Tanchon Commercial Bank: Saemaeul 1-dong, Pyongchon District, Pyongyang; tel. (2) 18111999; fax (2) 3814793; e-mail cbktm828@co.chesin.com; f. 1983; fmrly Changgwang Credit Bank, merged with Samchon-ri Bank and named as above Nov. 2003; cap. 50,043.9, res 93,817.9, dep. 875,021.9 (Dec. 2003); Chair. KIM CHOL HWAN; Pres. KYE CHANG HO.

Joint-Venture Banks

Korea Joint Bank (KJB): Ryugyongdong, Potonggang District, Pyongyang; tel. (2) 3818151; fax (2) 3814410; f. 1989; est. with co-operation of the Federation of Korean Traders and Industrialists in Japan; 50% Korea International General Joint Venture Co, 50% General Asscn of Koreans in Japan; Gen. Man. O HO RYOL; 6 domestic brs, 1 br in Tokyo.

Korea Joint Financial Co: f. 1988; joint venture with Koreans resident in the USA.

Korea Nagwon Joint Financial Co: f. 1987; est. by Nagwon Trade Co and a Japanese co.

Korea Rakwon Joint Banking Co: Pyongyang; Man. Dir HO POK DOK.

Korea United Development Bank: Central District, Pyongyang; tel. (2) 3814165; fax (2) 3814483; e-mail kudb888@yahoo.com; f. 1991; 51% owned by Zhongce Investment Corpn (Hong Kong), 49% owned by Osandok General Bureau; Pres. KIM SE HO.

Koryo Bank: Ponghwa-dong, Potonggang District, Pyongyang; tel. (2) 18333; fax (2) 3814410; e-mail krbankpy@co.chesin.com; Pres. YONG-CHIL PAK.

Koryo Commercial Bank: tel. (2) 3812060; fax (2) 3814441; f. 1988; jt venture with Koreans resident in the USA.

Foreign-Investment Banks

Daesong Credit Development Bank: Potonggang Hotel, 301 Ansan-dong, Pyongchon District, Pyongyang; tel. (2) 3814866; fax (2) 3814723; f. 1996; est. as Peregrine-Daesong Development Bank; fmrly jt venture between Oriental Commercial Holdings Ltd (Hong Kong) and Korea Daesong Bank; majority stake acquired by Global Group of Companies (UK) in May 2004; Man. NIGEL COWIE.

Golden Triangle Bank: Rajin-Sonbong Free Economic and Trade Zone; f. 1995.

INSURANCE

State Insurance Bureau: Central District, Pyongyang; tel. (2) 38196; handles all life, fire, accident, marine, hull insurance and reinsurance.

Korea Foreign Insurance Co (Chosunbohom): Central District, Pyongyang; tel. (2) 3818024; fax (2) 3814464; f. 1974; conducts marine, motor, aviation and fire insurance, reinsurance of all classes, and all foreign insurance; brs in Chongjin, Hungnam and Nampo, and agencies in foreign ports; overseas representative offices in Chile, France, Germany, Pakistan, Singapore; Pres. RI JANG SU.

Korea International Insurance Co: Pyongyang; Dir PAEK MYONG RON.

Korea Mannyon Insurance Co: Pyongyang; Pres. PAK IL HYONG.

Trade and Industry

GOVERNMENT AGENCIES

DPRK Committee for the Promotion of External Economic Co-operation: Jungsongdong, Central District, Pyongyang; tel. (2) 333974; fax (2) 3814498; Chair. PAEK HONG BONG.

DPRK Committee for the Promotion of International Trade: Central District, Pyongyang; Pres. RI SONG ROK; Chair. KIM YONG JAE.

Economic Co-operation Management Bureau: Ministry of Foreign Trade, Pyongyang; f. 1998; Dir KIM YONG SUL.

Korea International Joint Venture Promotion Committee: Pyongyang; Chair. CHAE HUI JONG.

Korean Association for the Promotion of Asian Trade: Pyongyang; Pres. RI SONG ROK.

Korean International General Joint Venture Co: Pyongyang; f. 1986; promotes joint economic ventures with foreign countries; Man. Dir RO TU CHOL.

CHAMBERS OF COMMERCE

DPRK Chamber of Commerce: POB 89, Jungsongdong, Central District, Pyongyang; tel. (2) 3815926; fax (2) 3815827; e-mail micom@co.chesin.com.

INDUSTRIAL AND TRADE ASSOCIATIONS

Korea Building Materials Trading Co: Tongdaewon District, Pyongyang; tel. (2) 18111–3818085; fax (2) 3814555; chemical building materials, woods, timbers, cement, sheet glass, etc.; Dir SHIN TONG BOM.

Korea Cereals Export and Import Corpn: Jungsongdong, Central District, Pyongyang; tel. (2) 18111-3818278; fax (2) 3813451; high-quality vegetable starches, etc.

Korea Chemicals Export and Import Corpn: Central District, Pyongyang; petroleum and petroleum products, raw materials for the chemical industry, rubber and rubber products, fertilizers, etc.

Korea Daesong General Trading Corpn: Pulgungori 1-dong, Potonggang District, Pyongyang; tel. (2) 18111; fax (2) 3814432; e-mail Daesong@silibank.com; Gen. Dir CHOE JONG SON.

Korea Daesong Jei Trading Corpn: Pulgungori 1-dong, Potonggang District, Pyongyang; tel. (2) 18111-3818213; fax (2) 3814431; machinery and equipment, chemical products, textiles, agricultural products, etc.

Korea Daesong Jesam Trading Corpn: Pulgungori 1-dong, Potonggang District, Pyongyang; tel. (2) 18111-3818562; fax (2) 3814431; remedies for diabetes, tonics, etc.

Korea Ferrous Metals Export and Import Corpn: Potonggang 2-dong, Potonggang District, Pyongyang; tel. (2) 18111-3818078; fax (2) 3814581; steel products.

Korea Film Export and Import Corpn: Daedongmundong, Central District, POB 113, Pyongyang; tel. (2) 180008034; fax (2) 3814410; f. 1956; feature films, cartoons, scientific and documentary films; Dir-Gen. CHOE HYOK U.

Korea First Equipment Export and Import Co: Central District, Pyongyang; tel. (2) 334825; f. 1960; export and import of ferrous and non-ferrous metallurgical plants, geological exploration and mining equipment, communication equipment, machine-building plant, etc.; construction of public facilities such as airports, hotels, tourist facilities, etc.; joint-venture business in similar projects; Pres. CHAE WON CHOL.

Korea Foodstuffs Export and Import Corpn: Kangan 2-dong, Songyo District, Pyongyang; tel. (2) 18111-3818289; fax (2) 3814417; cereals, wines, meat, canned foods, fruits, cigarettes, etc.

Korea Fruit and Vegetables Export Corpn: Central District, Pyongyang; tel. (2) 35117; vegetables, fruit and their products.

Korea General Corpn for External Construction (GENCO): Sungri St 25, Jungsongdong, Central District, Pyongyang; tel. (2) 18111-3818090; fax (2) 3814611; e-mail gen122@co.chesin.com; f. 1961; construction of dwelling houses, public establishments, factories, hydroelectric and thermal power stations, irrigation systems, ports, bridges, and transport services, technical services; Gen. Dir CHOE BONG SU.

Korea General Machine Co: Tongsin 3-dong, Tongdaewon, Pyongyang; tel. (2) 18555-3818102; fax (2) 3814495; Dir RA IN GYUN.

Korea Hyopdong Trading Corpn: Othan-dong, Kangan St, Central District, Pyongyang; tel. (2) 18111-3818011; fax (2) 3814454; fabrics, glass products, ceramics, chemical goods, building materials, foodstuffs, machinery, etc.

Korea Industrial Technology Co: Jungsongdong, Central District, Pyongyang; tel. (2) 18111-3818025; fax (2) 3814537; Pres. KWON YONG SON.

Korea International Chemical Joint Venture Co: Pyongyang; Chair. RYO SONG GUN.

Korea Jangsu Trading Co: Kyogudong, Central District, Pyongyang; tel. (2) 18111-3818834; fax (2) 3814410; medicinal products and clinical equipment.

Korea Jeil Equipment Export and Import Corpn: Jungsongdong, Central District, Pyongyang; tel. (2) 334825; f. 1960; ferrous and non-ferrous metallurgical plant, geological exploration and mining equipment, power plant, communications and broadcasting equipment, machine-building equipment, railway equipment, construction of public facilities; Pres. CHO JANG DOK.

Korea Koryo Trading Corpn: Jongpyongdong, Pyongchon District, Pyongyang; tel. (2) 18111-3818104; fax (2) 3814646; Dir KIM HUI DUK.

Korea Kwangmyong Trading Corpn: Jungsongdong, Central District, Pyongyang; tel. (2) 18111-3818111; fax (2) 3814410; dried herbs, dried and pickled vegetables; Dir CHOE JONG HUN.

Korea Light Industry Import-Export Co: Juchetab St, Tongdaewon District, Pyongyang; tel. (2) 37661; exports silk, cigarettes, canned goods, drinking glasses, ceramics, handbags, pens, plastic flowers, musical instruments, etc.; imports chemicals, dyestuffs, machinery, etc.; Dir CHOE PYONG HYON.

Korea Machine Tool Trading Corpn: Tongdaewon District, Pyongyang; tel. (2) 18555-381810; fax (2) 3814495; Dir KIM KWANG RYOP.

Korea Machinery and Equipment Export and Import Corpn: Potonggang District, Pyongyang; tel. (2) 333449; f. 1948; metallurgical machinery and equipment, electric machines, building machinery, farm machinery, diesel engines, etc.

Korea Mansu Trading Corpn: Chollima St, Central District, POB 250, Pyongyang; tel. (2) 43075; fax (2) 812100; f. 1974; antibiotics, pharmaceuticals, vitamin compounds, drugs, medicinal herbs; Dir KIM JANG HUN.

Korea Marine Products Export and Import Corpn: Central District, Pyongyang; canned, frozen, dried, salted and smoked fish, fishing equipment and supplies.

Korea Minerals Export and Import Corpn: Central District, Pyongyang; minerals, solid fuel, graphite, precious stones, etc.

Korea Namheung Trading Co: Sinri-dong, Tongdaewon District, Pyongyang; tel. (2) 18111-3818974; fax (2) 3814623; high-purity reagents, synthetic resins, vinyl films, essential oils, menthol and peppermint oil.

Korea Non-ferrous Metals Export and Import Corpn: Potonggang 2-dong, Potonggang District, Pyongyang; tel. (2) 18111-3818247; fax (2) 3814569.

Korea Okyru Trading Corpn: Kansongdong, Pyongchon District, Pyongyang; tel. (2) 18111-3818110; fax (2) 3814618; agricultural and marine products, household goods, clothing, chemical and light industrial products.

Korea Ponghwa Contractual Joint Venture Co: Pyongyang; Dir MUN YONG OK.

Korea Ponghwa General Trading Corpn: Jungsongdong, Central District, Pyongyang; tel. (2) 18111-3818023; fax (2) 3814444; machinery, metal products, minerals and chemicals.

Korea Publications Export and Import Corpn: Yokjondong, Yonggwang St, Central District, Pyongyang; tel. (2) 3818536; fax (2) 3814404; f. 1948; export of books, periodicals, postcards, paintings, cassettes, videos, CDs, CD-ROMs, postage stamps and records; import of books; Pres. RI YONG.

Korea Rungra Co: Sinwondong, Potonggang District, Pyongyang; tel. (2) 18111-3818112; fax (2) 3814608; Dir CHOE HENG UNG.

Korea Rungrado Trading Corpn: Segori-dong, Potonggang District, Pyongyang; tel. (2) 18111-3818022; fax (2) 3814507; food and animal products; Gen. Dir PAK KYU HONG.

Korea Ryongaksan General Trading Corpn: Pyongyang; Gen. Dir HAN YU RO.

Korea Samcholli General Corpn: Pyongyang; Dir JONG UN OP.

Korea Technology Corpn: Jungsongdong, Central District, Pyongyang; tel. (2) 18111-3818090; fax (2) 3814410; scientific and technical co-operation.

Korea Unha Trading Corpn: Rungra 1-dong, Taedonggang District, Pyongyang; tel. (2) 18111-3818236; fax (2) 3814506; clothing and fibres.

Korea Yonghung Trading Co: Tongan-dong, Central District, Pyongyang; tel. (2) 18111-3818223; fax (2) 3814527; e-mail greenlam@co.chesin.com; f. 1979; export of freight cars, vehicle parts, marine products, electronic goods, import of steel, chemical products; Pres. CHOE YONG DOK.

Pyongsu JV Co Ltd: Pyongyang; f. 2004; pharmaceutical mfr, medical products incl. analgesics; jt venture with Interpacific/Zuellig Pharma (Switzerland).

TRADE UNIONS

General Federation of Trade Unions of Korea (GFTUK): POB 333, Dongmun-dong, Daedonggang District, Pyongyang; fax (2) 3814427; f. 1945; 1.6m. mems (2003); seven affiliated unions (2003); Pres. RYOM SUN GIL.

Trade Union of Construction and Forestry Workers of Korea: Pyongyang; f. 1945; 160,000 mems (2003); Pres. WON HYONG GUK.

Trade Union of Educational and Cultural Workers: POB 333, Dongmun-dong, Daedonggang District, Pyongyang; fax (2) 3814427; f. 1946; 89,800 mems (2003); Pres. KIM YONG DO.

Trade Union of Light and Chemical Industries of Korea: Pyongyang; f. 1945; 372,500 mems (2003); Pres. RI JIN HAK.

Trade Union of Metal and Engineering Industries of Korea: Pyongyang; f. 1945; 332,800 mems (2003); Pres. CHOE GWANG HYON.

Trade Union of Mining and Power Industries of Korea: Pyongyang; f. 1945; 221,000 mems (2003); Pres. SON YONG JUN.

Trade Union of Public Employees and Service Workers of Korea: Pyongyang; f. 1945; 305,900 mems (2003); Pres. KIM GANG HO.

Trade Union of Transport and Fisheries Workers of Korea: Pyongyang; f. 1945; 119,800 mems (2003); Pres. CHOE RYONG SU.

General Federation of Agricultural and Forestry Technique of Korea: Chung Kuyuck Nammundong, Pyongyang; f. 1946; 523,000 mems.

General Federation of Unions of Literature and Arts of Korea: Pyongyang; f. 1946; seven br. unions; Chair. Cen. Cttee CHANG CHOL.

Kim Il Sung Socialist Youth League: Pyongyang; fmrly League of Socialist Working Youth of Korea; First Sec. KIM GYONG HO.

Korean Architects' Union: Pyongyang; f. 1954; 500 mems; Chair. Cen. Cttee PAE TAL JUN.

Korean Democratic Lawyers' Association: Ryonhwa 1, Central District, Pyongyang; fax (2) 3814644; f. 1954; Chair. HAM HAK SONG.

Korean Democratic Scientists' Association: Pyongyang; f. 1956.

Korean Democratic Women's Union: Jungsongdong, Central District, Pyongyang; fax (2) 3814416; f. 1945; Chief Officer RO SONG SIL.

Korean General Federation of Science and Technology: Jungsongdong, Seungri St, Central District, Pyongyang; tel. (2) 3224389; fax (2) 3814410; f. 1946; 550,000 mems; Chair. Cen. Cttee CHOE HUI JONG.

Korean Medical Association: Pyongyang; f. 1970; Chair. CHOE CHANG SHIK.

Union of Agricultural Working People of Korea: Pyongyang; f. 1965; to replace fmr Korean Peasants' Union; 2.4m. mems; Chair. Cen. Cttee KANG CHANG UK.

Transport

RAILWAYS

In 2005 the total length of track was estimated at 5,214 km, of which some 70% was electrified. There are international train services to Moscow (Russia) and Beijing (People's Republic of China). Construction work on the reconnection of the Kyongui (West Coast, Sinuiju–Seoul) and East Coast Line (Wonsan–Seoul) began in September 2002. The two lines were officially opened in June 2003, but were not yet open to traffic, as construction work on the Northern side remained to be completed. The lines were reportedly completed in 2005, and in May 2007 the first cross-border trial runs were conducted. Eventually the two were to be linked to the Trans-China and Trans-Siberian railways, respectively, greatly enhancing the region's transport links.

There is an underground railway system in Pyongyang, with two public lines serving 17 stations. Unspecified plans to expand the system were announced in February 2002.

ROADS

In 2000, according to South Korean estimates, the road network totalled 23,407 km (of which only about 8% was paved), including 682 km of multi-lane highways. Road links between the DPRK and the Republic of Korea were believed to have opened in late 2005.

INLAND WATERWAYS

In 2005 the total length of inland waterways was estimated at 2,253 km, most of which was navigable only by small craft. The Yalu (Amnok-gang) and Taedong, Tumen and Ryesong are the most important commercial rivers. Regular passenger and freight services: Nampo–Chosan–Supung; Chungsu–Sinuiju–Dasado; Nampo–Jeudo; Pyongyang–Nampo.

SHIPPING

The principal ports are Nampo, Wonsan, Chongjin, Rajin, Hungnam, Songnim and Haeju. At 31 December 2006 North Korea's merchant fleet comprised 340 vessels, with a combined displacement of 1,052,600 grt.

Bochon Shipping Co: Pyongchon District, Pyongyang.

Chon Song Shipping Co Ltd: Sochang-dong, Potonggang District, Pyongyang.

Korea Ansan Shipping Co: Nampo.

Korea Chartering Corpn: Central District, Pyongyang; arranges cargo transport and chartering.

Korea Daehung Shipping Co: Ansan 1–dong, Pyongchon District, Pyongyang; tel. (2) 18111, ext 8695; fax (2) 3814508; f. 1994; owns 6 reefers, 3 oil tankers, 1 cargo ship.

Korea East Sea Shipping Co: Pyongyang; Dir RI TUK HYON.

Korea Foreign Transportation Corpn: Central District, Pyongyang; arranges transport of cargoes for export and import (transit goods and charters).

Korea Myohyang Shipping Co: Ryonhwadong Changgoan St, Chung District, Pyongyang; tel. (3) 8160590; fax (3) 8146420.

Korea Myongsang Shipping Co: Chongpyong-dong, Pyongchon District, Pyongyang; tel. (2) 3815842; fax (2) 3815942.

Korea Tonghae Shipping Co: Changgwang St, Central District, POB 120, Pyongyang; tel. (2) 345805; fax (2) 3814583; arranges transport by Korean vessels.

Korea Undok Shipping Co Ltd: Nampo.

Korean-Polish Shipping Co Ltd: Moranbong District, Pyongyang; tel. (2) 3814384; fax (2) 3814607; f. 1967; maritime trade mainly with Polish, Far East and DPRK ports.

Ocean Maritime Management Co Ltd: Tonghungdong, Central District, Pyongyang.

Ocean Shipping Agency of the DPRK: Moranbong District, POB 21, Pyongyang; tel. (2) 3818100; fax (2) 3814531; Pres. O JONG HO.

CIVIL AVIATION

The international airport is at Sunan, 24 km from Pyongyang. In September 2003 the first tourist flight from Seoul to Pyongyang was completed by an Air Koryo aircraft, representing the first commercial flight between North and South Korea in more than 50 years. In January 2004 plans were announced for an aviation agreement between North and South Korea, which would allow regular inter-Korean flight routes to be opened.

Chosonminhang/General Civil Aviation Bureau of the DPRK: Sunan Airport, Sunan District, Pyongyang; tel. (2) 37917; fax (2) 3814625; f. 1954; internal services and external flights by Air Koryo to Beijing and Shenyang (People's Republic of China), Bangkok (Thailand), Macao, Nagoya (Japan), Moscow, Khabarovsk and Vladivostok (Russia), Sofia (Bulgaria) and Berlin (Germany); charter services are operated to Asia, Africa and Europe; Pres. KIM YO UNG.

Tourism

The DPRK was formally admitted to the World Tourism Organization in 1987. Tourism is permitted only in officially accompanied parties. In 1999 there were more than 60 international hotels (including nine in Pyongyang) with 7,500 beds. Tourist arrivals totalled 130,000 in 1998. A feasibility study was undertaken in 1992 regarding the development of Mount Kumgang as a tourist attraction. In November 1998 some 800 South Korean tourists visited Mount Kumgang, as part of a joint venture mounted by the North Korean authorities and Hyundai, the South Korean conglomerate. By November 2000 only 350,000 South Korean tourists had visited the attraction. In November 2002, in an effort to increase profitability, Mount Kumgang was designated a special tax-free economic zone. There were reports in 1998 that a heliport had been opened in the Zone, and in 1999 the resort was completed. Mount Chilbo, Mount Kuwol, Mount Jongbang and the Ryongmum Cave were transformed into new tourist destinations in that year. In August 2000 plans were announced for the development, jointly with the People's Republic of China, of the western part of Mount Paektu, Korea's highest mountain, as a tourist resort. In September 2003 South Korean tourists were able to visit Pyongyang for the first time. In 2003 it was estimated that around 1,500 Western tourists visited North Korea annually, while South Korean sources estimated that more than 80,000 South Koreans visited the North in 2005.

Korea International Tourist Bureau: Pyongyang; Pres. HAN PYONG UN.

Korean International Youth Tourist Co: Mankyongdae District, Pyongyang; tel. (2) 73406; f. 1985; Dir HWANG CHUN YONG.

Kumgangsan International Tourist Co: Central District, Pyongyang; tel. (2) 31562; fax (2) 3812100; f. 1988.

National Tourism Administration of the DPRK: Central District, Pyongyang; tel. (2) 3818901; fax (2) 3814547; e-mail nta@silibank.com; f. 1953; state-run tourism promotion organization; Dir RYO SUNG CHOL.

Ryohaengsa (Korea International Travel Company): Central District, Pyongyang; tel. (2) 3817201; fax (2) 3817607; f. 1953; has relations with more than 200 tourist companies throughout the world; Pres. CHO SONG HUN.

State General Bureau of Tourism: Pyongyang; Pres. RYO HAK SONG.

THE REPUBLIC OF KOREA

Introductory Survey

Location, Climate, Language, Religion, Flag, Capital

The Republic of Korea (South Korea) forms the southern part of the Korean peninsula, in eastern Asia. To the north, separated by a frontier which roughly follows the 38th parallel, is the country's only neighbour, the Democratic People's Republic of Korea (North Korea). To the west is the Yellow Sea, to the south is the East China Sea, and to the east is the Sea of Japan. The climate is marked by cold, dry winters, with an average temperature of −6°C (21°F), and hot, humid summers, with an average temperature of 25°C (77°F). The language is Korean. Confucianism, Mahayana Buddhism, and Chundo Kyo are the principal traditional religions. Chundo Kyo is peculiar to Korea, and combines elements of Shaman, Buddhist and Christian doctrines. There are some 17.5m. Christians, of whom about 83% are Protestants. The national flag (proportions 2 by 3) comprises, in the centre of a white field, a disc divided horizontally by an S-shaped line, red above and blue below, surrounded by four configurations of parallel, broken and unbroken black bars. The capital is Seoul.

Recent History

(For more details of the history of Korea up to 1953, including the Korean War, see the chapter on the Democratic People's Republic of Korea—DPRK.)

UN-supervised elections to a new legislature, the National Assembly (Kuk Hoe), took place in May 1948. The Assembly adopted a democratic Constitution, and South Korea became the independent Republic of Korea on 15 August 1948, with Dr Syngman Rhee, leader of the Liberal Party, as the country's first President. He remained in the post until his resignation in April 1960. Elections in July were won by the Democratic Party, led by Chang Myon, but his Government was deposed in May 1961 by a military coup, led by Gen. Park Chung-Hee. Power was assumed by the Supreme Council for National Reconstruction, which dissolved the National Assembly, suspended the Constitution and disbanded all existing political parties. In January 1963 the military leadership formed the Democratic Republican Party (DRP). Under a new Constitution, Gen. Park became President of the Third Republic in December.

Opposition to Park's regime led to the imposition of martial law in October 1972. A Constitution for the Fourth Republic, giving the President greatly increased powers, was approved by national referendum in November. A new body, the National Conference for Unification (NCU), was elected in December. The NCU re-elected President Park for a six-year term, and the DRP obtained a decisive majority in elections to the new National Assembly. In May 1975 opposition to the Government was effectively banned, and political trials followed. Elections to the NCU were held in May 1978, and the President was re-elected for a further six-year term in July. In October 1979 serious rioting erupted when Kim Young-Sam, the leader of the opposition New Democratic Party (NDP), was accused of subversive activities and expelled from the National Assembly. On 26 October Park was assassinated in an alleged coup attempt, led by the head of the Korean Central Intelligence Agency. Martial law was reintroduced (except on the island of Jeju), and in December the Prime Minister, Choi Kyu-Hah, was elected President by the NCU. Instability in the DRP and the army resulted in a military coup in December, led by the head of the Defence Security Command, Lt-Gen. Chun Doo-Hwan, who arrested the Army Chief of Staff and effectively took power. Nevertheless, President Choi was inaugurated on 21 December to complete his predecessor's term of office (to 1984).

Choi promised liberalizing reforms, but in May 1980 demonstrations by students and confrontation with the army led to the arrest of about 30 political leaders, including Kim Dae-Jung, former head of the NDP. Martial law was extended throughout the country, the National Assembly was suspended, and all political activity was banned. Almost 200 people were killed when troops stormed the southern city of Gwangju, which had been occupied by students and dissidents. In August Choi resigned, and Gen. Chun was elected President. Acting Prime Minister Nam Duck-Woo formed a new State Council (cabinet) in September. In the same month the sentencing to death of Kim Dae-Jung for plotting rebellion was condemned internationally. (This sentence was subsequently suspended.) In October a new Constitution was overwhelmingly approved by referendum.

Martial law was ended in January 1981, and new political parties were formed. In the following month President Chun was re-elected: the start of his new term, in March, inaugurated the Fifth Republic. Chun's Democratic Justice Party (DJP) became the majority party in the new National Assembly, which was elected shortly afterwards. Amid opposition demands for liberalization, Chun pledged that he would retire at the end of his term in 1988, thus becoming the country's first Head of State to transfer power constitutionally.

During 1984, following an escalation of student unrest, the Government adopted a more flexible attitude towards dissidents. Several thousand prisoners were released, and the political 'blacklist' was finally abolished in March 1985. In January 1985 the New Korea Democratic Party (NKDP) was established by supporters of Kim Young-Sam and Kim Dae-Jung. At the general election to the National Assembly held in February, the DJP retained its majority, but the NKDP emerged as the major opposition force, boosted by the return from exile of Kim Dae-Jung. The new party secured 67 of the Assembly's 276 seats, while the DJP won 148 seats. Chun appointed a new State Council, with Lho Shin-Yong as Prime Minister. Before the opening session of the new National Assembly many deputies defected to the NKDP, increasing the party's strength to 102 seats.

In April 1987 internal divisions within the NKDP led to the formation of a new opposition party, the Reunification Democratic Party (RDP); Kim Young-Sam was elected to its presidency in May. In April Chun unexpectedly announced the suspension of the process of reform until after the Olympic Games (due to be held in Seoul in September 1988). While confirming that he would leave office in February 1988, Chun indicated that his successor would be elected by the existing electoral college system, precipitating violent clashes between anti-Government demonstrators and riot police.

In June 1987 Roh Tae-Woo was nominated as the DJP's presidential candidate. However, Roh subsequently informed Chun that he would relinquish both the DJP chairmanship and his presidential candidature if the principal demands of the opposition for constitutional and electoral reform were not satisfied. Under international pressure, Chun acceded, and negotiations on constitutional amendments were announced. In August the DJP and the RDP announced that a bipartisan committee had agreed a draft Constitution. Among its provisions were the reintroduction of direct presidential elections by universal suffrage, and the restriction of the presidential mandate to a single five-year term; the President's emergency powers were also to be reduced, and serving military officers were to be prohibited from taking government office. Having been approved by the National Assembly, the amendments were endorsed in a national referendum in October, and the amended Constitution was promulgated shortly thereafter.

Kim Dae-Jung joined the RDP in August 1987; in November, however, he became President of a new Peace and Democracy Party (PDP), and declared himself a rival presidential candidate. At the election, in December, Roh Tae-Woo won some 36% of the votes, while Kim Dae-Jung and Kim Young-Sam each achieved about 27%. Roh Tae-Woo was inaugurated as President on 25 February 1988, whereupon the Sixth Republic was established. At the general election to the National Assembly, in April, the DJP failed to achieve an overall majority, securing 125 of the 299 seats. The PDP achieved 70 seats, thus becoming the main opposition party; the remainder went to the RDP and the New Democratic Republican Party (NDRP—the revived and renamed DRP), led by Kim Jong-Pil.

In February 1990 the DJP merged with the RDP and the NDRP to form the Democratic Liberal Party (DLP). Roh was subsequently elected President of the DLP, while Kim Young-Sam and Kim Jong-Pil were elected as two of the party's three Chairmen. The DLP thus controlled more than two-thirds of the seats in the National Assembly. The PDP, effectively isolated as the sole opposition party, condemned the merger and demanded new elections. In March a new opposition group, the Democratic Party (DP), was formed, largely comprising members of the RDP who had opposed the merger.

In July 1990 a large rally was held in Seoul to denounce the adoption by the National Assembly of several items of controversial legislation, including proposals to restructure the military leadership and to reorganize the broadcasting media. Shortly afterwards all the opposition members of the National Assembly tendered their resignation, in protest at the legislation. Although the Assembly's Speaker refused to accept the resignations, the PDP deputies returned to the National Assembly only in November, following an agreement with the DLP that local council elections would take place in the first half of 1991, to be followed by gubernatorial and mayoral elections in 1992. The DLP also agreed to abandon plans for the transfer, by constitutional amendment, of executive powers to the State Council. The local elections (the first to be held in the Republic of Korea for 30 years) took place in March and June 1991, and resulted in a decisive victory for the DLP.

Meanwhile, in April 1991 the PDP merged with the smaller opposition Party for New Democratic Alliance to form the New Democratic Party (NDP). In September the NDP and the DP agreed to merge (under the latter's name) to form a stronger opposition front. A further opposition group, the Unification National Party (UNP), was established in January 1992 by Chung Ju-Yung, the founder and honorary chairman of the powerful Hyundai industrial conglomerate.

At elections to the National Assembly in March 1992 the DLP unexpectedly failed to secure an absolute majority, obtaining a total of 149 of the 299 seats. The remainder of the seats were won by the DP (97), the UNP (31) and independent candidates (21). In May Kim Young-Sam was chosen as the DLP's candidate for the presidential election, scheduled for December, and in August he replaced Roh as the party's President. Roh's decision to resign from the DLP altogether, in order to create a neutral government in anticipation of the election, was welcomed by opposition deputies. Serious divisions within the DLP led to defections from the party by opponents of Kim Young-Sam.

The presidential election, on 18 December 1992, was won by Kim Young-Sam, with some 42% of the votes cast. Kim (who was inaugurated on 25 February 1993) was the first South Korean President since 1960 without military connections. The defeated Kim Dae-Jung subsequently announced his retirement from political life. In February 1993 Chung Ju-Yung resigned as President of the United People's Party (UPP—as the UNP had been renamed), following allegations that he had embezzled Hyundai finances to fund his election campaign. Kim Young-Sam appointed Hwang In-Sung as Prime Minister, and a new State Council was formed.

Kim Young-Sam acted swiftly to honour his campaign pledge to eliminate corruption in business and political life; in all, during 1993, Kim's anti-corruption measures were reported to have resulted in the dismissal of, or disciplinary action against, some 3,000 business, government and military officials. One of Roh Tae-Woo's former Ministers of National Defence, Lee Jong-Koo, was sentenced in November 1993 to three years' imprisonment, after having been convicted of accepting bribes from defence contractors. At the same time the announcement of measures to restrict the activities of the country's industrial conglomerates (*chaebol*) was accompanied by corruption proceedings against several prominent business executives. In November Chung Ju-Yung was sentenced to three years' imprisonment, although the sentence was suspended on account of his age (78) and past contribution to South Korean economic development.

Hwang In-Sung resigned as Prime Minister in December 1993 and was succeeded by Lee Hoi-Chang, hitherto Chairman of the Board of Audit and Inspection (BAI). However, he resigned in April 1994 and was replaced by Lee Yung-Duk, latterly the Deputy Prime Minister responsible for national unification.

In July 1994 the UPP and a smaller opposition party, the New Political Reform Party, merged to form the New People's Party (NPP). In October the Government announced that its inquiry into the role played by former Presidents Chun and Roh in the 1979 coup had found that both had participated in a 'premeditated military rebellion'. Prosecution proceedings were not initiated at this stage. In December 1994 Lee Hong-Koo (hitherto the Deputy Prime Minister responsible for national unification) was appointed Prime Minister, as part of a major restructuring of the State Council.

The DLP fared badly at elections for gubernatorial, mayoral and other municipal and provincial posts in May 1995 (the first full local elections to be held in the Republic of Korea for 34 years). A contributory factor to the DLP's poor performance was the success of a new party, the United Liberal Democrats (ULD), established in March by defectors from the DLP and led by Kim Jong-Pil (who had resigned as DLP Chairman earlier in the year). In September Kim Dae-Jung returned to political life, establishing his own party, the National Congress for New Politics (NCNP). The DP was severely undermined when many of its members left to join the NCNP.

A major scandal erupted in October 1995, when Roh Tae-Woo admitted in a televised address that he had amassed a large sum of money during his term of office. He was arrested in the following month; at his trial, which opened in December, Roh confessed to having received donations from South Korean businesses, but denied that these constituted bribes. Many senior politicians and business leaders were also detained and interrogated in connection with the affair. Kim Dae-Jung, meanwhile, unexpectedly admitted that his campaign for the 1992 presidential election had been supported by a donation of money from Roh's 'slush fund'. Kim Young-Sam denied opposition allegations that he too had benefited from a similar donation. In December 1995, in an effort to distance his party from the deepening scandal, Kim Young-Sam changed the DLP's name to the New Korea Party (NKP). A major reorganization of the State Council was effected, in which Lee Hong-Koo was replaced as Prime Minister by Lee Soo-Sung, the President of Seoul National University.

In late 1995 it was announced that Roh Tae-Woo and Chun Doo-Hwan were to be prosecuted for their involvement in the 1979 coup and the 1980 Gwangju massacre. Chun was arrested in December 1995, and in the following month he was additionally accused of accumulating a huge political 'slush fund'. At the opening of his trial for corruption in February 1996 Chun denied charges that the fund had been amassed as a result of bribe-taking. Legal proceedings in connection with the events of 1979 and 1980 opened in March 1996: Chun was charged with mutiny for his organization of the 1979 coup, and with sedition in connection with the Gwangju massacre, while Roh was charged with aiding Chun. Roh and Chun were convicted as charged in August 1996. For their role in the *coup d'état* and the Gwangju massacre, Chun was sentenced to death and Roh to $22\frac{1}{2}$ years' imprisonment; each was heavily fined in the corruption cases. Several others were also convicted for their part in the events of 1979 and 1980. Following an appeal, in which their contribution to the country's impressive economic growth and to the establishment of democratic government were cited as mitigating factors, Chun's sentence was commuted to one of life imprisonment, while Roh's term of imprisonment was reduced to 17 years.

Elections to the National Assembly took place in April 1996. Contrary to widespread predictions, the NKP only narrowly failed to retain its parliamentary majority, winning a total of 139 of the 299 seats. One factor contributing to the NKP's success was believed to have been the recent incursions into the demilitarized zone (DMZ, separating North and South Korea) by North Korean troops, which, although apparently intended to destabilize the electoral proceedings, in fact caused many voters to favour the ruling party out of concern for national security. The NCNP performed less well than had been expected, taking 79 seats; moreover, the party's leader, Kim Dae-Jung, failed to win a seat. By the time the National Assembly convened in June, the NKP had secured a working majority with the support of several opposition and independent members.

The revision of the Republic of Korea's labour laws, with the aim of introducing greater flexibility into the labour market (a condition of the country's impending membership of the Organisation for Economic Co-operation and Development, see p. 347—OECD), was initiated in May 1996. Reforms proposed by the Government in early December were severely criticized by trade unions and opposition parties. The country's principal workers' confederation, the Federation of Korean Trade Unions (FKTU), hitherto regarded as generally acquiescent to the Government, called a general strike in late December, after the Government convened a dawn session of the National Assembly, which approved the labour reform bill in the absence of opposition deputies. Many thousands of workers from key manufacturing industries, as well as public sector employees, participated in the strike, which lasted for three weeks. Anti-Government demonstrators in Seoul and other major cities frequently clashed with riot police, and warrants were issued for the arrest of several leaders of the Korean Confederation of Trade Unions (KCTU). Concern was expressed that President Kim might be resorting to a more authoritarian style of leadership, particularly when it was alleged that the DPRK was lending its support to the striking workers (a tactic used by the South Korean authorities in the past to justify the suppression of domestic dissent); furthermore, foreign labour officials were threatened with deportation for encouraging union action. By mid-January 1997 support for the strikes was abating; the KCTU proposed weekly one-day stoppages, in order to minimize financial losses, and suggested that it might accept a modification of the labour law, having previously insisted on its complete annulment. OECD issued a severe rebuke to the Government for failing to honour its pledges on the issue of labour reform, and, in a significant concession, Kim agreed to meet the leaders of the opposition parties to discuss amendments to the law; warrants for the arrest of union leaders were also suspended. In March the National Assembly approved a revised version of the legislation, whereby the implementation of certain proposals was delayed for two years, while the KCTU was granted immediate official recognition.

Meanwhile, political and economic scandals persisted throughout 1996, particularly concerning allegations of bribery, which resulted in several government resignations. The infiltration of a North Korean submarine into South Korean waters in September (see below) resulted in the dismissal of the Minister of Defence, Lee Yang-Ho. He was subsequently charged with divulging classified information and with receiving bribes in connection with the procurement of helicopters for the army, and in December was sentenced to four years' imprisonment.

In January 1997 a further major scandal erupted when Hanbo, one of the country's largest steel and construction conglomerates, was declared bankrupt. Allegations were made that Hanbo had bribed the Government to exert pressure on banks to provide substantial loans to the conglomerate. The chief executives of several large Korean banks were arrested on charges of receiving bribes, and in February the Minister of Home Affairs, Kim Woo-Suk, resigned following allegations that he too had accepted payments from the company. President Kim issued an official apology for the loan scandal, and in March Lee Soo-Sung resigned as Prime Minister in a gesture of contrition. He was replaced by Goh Kun, hitherto President of Myongju University. The repercussions of the Hanbo affair widened further, implicating, among others, Kim Soo-Han, the Speaker of the National Assembly, and President Kim himself, whose 1992 election campaign was alleged to have been funded partially by the conglomerate. In June 1997 the former Chairman of Hanbo and several senior banking officials and politicians, including Kim Woo-Suk, were convicted on charges relating to the scandal.

In July 1997 Lee Hoi-Chang, former Prime Minister and Chairman of the NKP, was nominated as the ruling party's candidate for the presidential election, scheduled for December. Lee's candidacy was severely affected by various scandals surrounding the NKP and his family. Moreover, Rhee In-Je, the defeated challenger in the contest for the NKP nomination, decided to contest the presidency, subsequently forming his own political organization, the New Party by the People. In September Lee was elected President of the NKP, replacing Kim Young-Sam, who subsequently resigned from the party in order to ensure his neutrality in the forthcoming election. In October the NCNP and the ULD established an alliance, uniting behind the NCNP presidential nominee, Kim Dae-Jung. In November the NKP announced its merger with the DP, to form the Grand National Party (GNP).

Internal party politics were, however, overshadowed by the crisis experienced by the Korean economy in the latter half of 1997. Many of the *chaebol* reported serious financial difficulties, having amassed huge debts which they were subsequently unable to service. Measures aimed at stabilizing the financial markets, announced in October, were unsuccessful. Moreover, in an unexpected reversal of its non-interventionist policy, the Government declared that part of the Kia Group, which was close to collapse, was to be nationalized, in an attempt to prevent further bankruptcies. Following the rejection by the legislature of the Government's financial liberalization measures, President Kim dismissed Kang Kyung-Shik, the Deputy Prime Minister and Minister of Finance and the Economy, in November, replacing him with Lim Chang-Yul, latterly Minister of Trade, Industry and Energy. An extensive economic stabilization programme, announced shortly afterwards, had little effect in curbing the depreciation of the national currency, the won, and the Government was forced to request the assistance of the IMF. This recourse to the IMF was condemned by opposition politicians and the media as a 'national shame'. The true extent of the country's economic crisis, described as the most serious in South Korean history, became apparent upon the conclusion of negotiations with the IMF in December. In the IMF's largest-ever rescue programme, worth US $57,000m., funds were to be allocated to prevent the Republic of Korea from defaulting on its repayments of external debt. Provision of the loans remained conditional upon the implementation of a programme of extensive financial and economic reforms.

The presidential election, held on 18 December 1997, was narrowly won by Kim Dae-Jung. Supporters of the ruling NKP were divided between Lee Hoi-Chang and Rhee In-Je, thus assuring victory for the NCNP-ULD alliance and the first peaceful transfer of power to an opposition politician in the Republic of Korea's history. Four other candidates contested the election. In a gesture to promote a sense of national unity, former Presidents Chun Doo-Hwan and Roh Tae-Woo were granted a presidential pardon and released from prison.

Legislation for financial reforms, to comply with the terms of the IMF agreement, was approved by the National Assembly in late December 1997. Discussions with South Korea's overseas creditors to renegotiate the terms of the country's debt repayments were successfully concluded at the end of January 1998. Compulsory reform of the *chaebol*, which had been widely criticized for contributing to the debt-repayment crisis through their extensive borrowing, and legislation to allow foreign investors to acquire majority shareholdings in South Korean companies, were among reform measures promulgated in early 1998.

Kim Dae-Jung was formally inaugurated as President in late February 1998. Despite resistance from the opposition, Kim Dae-Jung designated Kim Jong-Pil, the leader of the ULD, as acting Prime Minister, and a Cabinet was formed in early March, with the ministries divided equally between the NCNP and the ULD. Various administrative reforms were implemented, including the abolition of the two posts of Deputy Prime Minister, the merger of the Ministries for Home Affairs and Government Administration and a reduction in the powers of the Ministry of Finance and the Economy. The number of cabinet ministers was reduced to 17 (excluding the Prime Minister).

At the beginning of May 1998 a large rally organized by the KCTU in protest at job losses ended in violent clashes with riot police. Later that month a two-day strike was called to demand that the Government fully honour its pledge to improve unemployment benefits and to reform the *chaebol*; according to the KCTU, some 120,000 workers supported the first day of the strike. The NCNP and the ULD performed well in local elections in June, although the turn-out was low. As the economic recession deepened, with the unemployment rate rising above 7%, labour unrest increased. Tens of thousands participated in strikes in July to protest against unemployment, the Government's privatization proposals and plans from Hyundai Motor and Daewoo Motor for mass redundancies.

In August 1998 the National Assembly formally confirmed Kim Jong-Pil as Prime Minister, following months of legislative inactivity, during which the GNP had refused to support his nomination. The GNP, however, boycotted parliamentary sessions throughout September and into October, further delaying the consideration of urgent economic reforms, in protest at a government anti-corruption campaign, which it claimed was partisan and aimed at dividing the opposition. Several GNP members were placed under investigation on suspicion of illegally raising electoral campaign funds. In late October three former aides to Lee Hoi-Chang were charged in connection with an alleged attempt to bribe North Korean officials to organize a border incursion into the DMZ in December 1997, with the aim of aiding Lee's campaign for the presidency. The dispute escalated in December 1998, when a number of opposition deputies entered a room in the assembly buildings, which was being used by the intelligence agency, and removed confidential documents on 44 politicians. The GNP claimed that the agency had been carrying out surveillance of opposition deputies and subsequently boycotted legislative proceedings. In early January 1999, as the boycott continued, the ruling parties unilaterally passed 130 bills without debate, including legislation on banking reform and the endorsement of a controversial fishing agreement with Japan (see below). In mid-January, however, the ruling and opposition parties agreed that all issues relating to the affair be referred to the National Assembly's steering committee.

In May 1999 a major reorganization of the State Council was effected. In June, however, corruption scandals led to the replacement of the new Ministers of Justice and the Environment, and were believed to have contributed to the ruling coalition's failure to retain two parliamentary seats in by-elections held that month. In July Kim Dae-Jung and Kim Jong-Pil agreed not to seek a constitutional amendment on the adoption of a parliamentary, rather than presidential, system of government in 1999, despite protests from several senior ULD members.

Preparations for legislative elections (scheduled for April) dominated internal politics in early 2000. In January Kim Jong-Pil resigned as Prime Minister to chair the ULD, nominating Park Tae-Joon, the founder of Pohang Iron and Steel Company, as his successor. Kim Dae-Jung reshuffled the State Council, as a number of ministers resigned to concentrate on campaigning for parliamentary seats. Lee Hun-Jai, hitherto the Chairman of the Financial Supervisory Commission, was appointed as Minister of Finance and the Economy. There was speculation that with the appointments of Park and Lee, shortly before the elections, the ruling parties hoped to remind voters of the Government's relative success in overcoming the country's severe economic problems. Later in January 2000 Kim Dae-Jung established a new party, the Millennium Democratic Party (MDP), to succeed the ruling NCNP, having reportedly failed in attempts to effect a merger with the ULD. In February the National Assembly approved revisions to the election law, which reduced the number of legislative seats from 299 to 273 (227 directly elected and 46 allocated by proportional representation), and reversed a ban on campaigning by civic groups against candidates. A proposal by the MDP for the introduction of a two-ballot system was rejected by the National Assembly; the ULD was believed to have voted with the opposition GNP against its coalition partner. Lee Han-Dong, recently elected as President of the ULD, subsequently announced the party's withdrawal from the ruling coalition, claiming that the MDP had failed to fulfil its electoral pledges, although Prime Minister Park was to remain in the Government.

The elections to the National Assembly were held on 13 April 2000. The GNP, which won 133 of the 273 seats, retained its position as the largest party in the Assembly, but remained four seats short of a majority. The ruling MDP secured 115 seats, while the ULD suffered a serious reverse, taking only 17 seats (compared with 50 in the 1996 elections). Only two seats were won by the Democratic People's Party, which had been formed in February by defectors from the GNP who had failed to be nominated as parliamentary candidates by their former party. The New Korea Party of Hope won one seat, and independents five. In mid-May Park resigned as Prime Minister, amid increasing controversy over allegations of tax evasion. The designation of Lee Han-Dong as Park's successor indicated a restoration of MDP-ULD co-operation. Amid criticism that reform of the *chaebol* was proceeding too slowly, President Kim Dae-Jung effected a major government reorganization in August, which primarily concerned the economic portfolios.

President Kim enjoyed increasing respect within the international community, in October 2000 being awarded the Nobel Peace Prize for his contribution to democracy and human rights (and particularly for his successful attempts at reconciliation with the DPRK). However, his pursuit of reunification was criticized domestically by those who felt that the Republic of Korea, confronted by its own economic problems, could ill afford assistance to the DPRK, which was not perceived to be reciprocating in a magnanimous manner.

In November 2000 Kim Yong-Kap, a GNP member of the National Assembly, described the ruling MDP as a 'subsidiary of the North Korean KWP (Korean Workers' Party)'. The comments shocked and embarrassed both the MDP and the GNP, and the National Assembly was suspended. Shortly after the legislature reconvened the following evening, however, the GNP walked out in protest at an MDP motion to dismiss Kim Yong-Kap from his seat. A few days later there was renewed tension in the National Assembly as the GNP walked out again, this time prompted by the MDP's obstruction of a motion to impeach the Prosecutor-General, Park Soon-Yong, for alleged bias in the investigation of irregularities during the April elections. The GNP returned to the session one week later.

During 2000 and early 2001 dissatisfaction with the Government manifested itself on numerous occasions in the form of industrial and agricultural unrest. Strike action by doctors over legislation depriving physicians of their right to prescribe drugs took place in June 2000 and again in October. Mounting public anger obliged the abandonment of the renewed strike. In the following month farmers held a strike to demand that their debts be cancelled and that the Government intervene on their behalf at the World Trade Organization (WTO, see p. 396). Meanwhile, as the Daewoo Motor Company had been declared bankrupt, some 15,000 workers protested in November in Seoul against government-led corporate restructuring which would result, it was feared, in large-scale retrenchment.

In January 2001 a minor reorganization of the State Council was effected, when changes included Jin Nyum's elevation to the post of Deputy Prime Minister for Finance and the Economy. Simultaneously, a government organization law came into effect that conferred the status of Deputy Prime Minister on the portfolios of Finance and Economy and of Education and Human Resources. Han Wang-Sang assumed the latter position. A Ministry of Gender Equality was also created, for which Han Myeong-Sook was allocated responsibility. In March there was a major reorganization of the State Council, following the resignation of the Minister of Foreign Affairs and Trade, Lee Joung-Binn, who had caused controversy by signing a joint statement with Russia criticizing the USA's planned 'national missile defence' (NMD) system. Han Seung-Soo, a member of the Democratic People's Party, replaced him. The former Minister of Culture, Park Jie-Won, who had resigned in September 2000 following allegations of corruption, was appointed chief presidential policy adviser. Park had organized the historic inter-Korean summit in June 2000 (see below).

In early April 2001 the minor opposition Democratic People's Party joined the ruling MDP-led coalition, despite protests from within the MDP. Later that month the MDP suffered a defeat in local by-elections, and by May Kim Dae-Jung's popularity had fallen sharply, as voters grew disillusioned by his failure to implement political reforms. President Kim had also received criticism for his appointment of ministers and advisers from his home region of Jeolla, in the south-west, thereby antagonizing the south-eastern Gyeongsang region.

In August 2001 the Minister of Unification, Lim Dong-Won, came under heavy criticism from the opposition after delegates from several South Korean non-governmental organizations (NGOs) travelled to the North to mark the anniversary of Korean liberation from Japanese rule, on 15 August. In September Lim was forced to resign after the National Assembly approved a motion of no confidence in him, organized by the GNP and supported by the MDP's coalition partner, the ULD. The latter's actions effectively dissolved the ruling coalition, and President Kim appointed four new ministers. In addition, Hong Soon-Young, hitherto ambassador to China, was appointed Minister of Unification. Lim was immediately appointed presidential adviser on reunification, national security and foreign affairs, reaffirming Kim's confidence in him.

In October 2001 the GNP won three by-elections, increasing its seats in the National Assembly to 136—just one short of a majority. The opposition victory created new rifts within the ruling MDP between younger reformers and party veterans, and President Kim resigned from the party presidency in November, ostensibly in order to administer state affairs without being involved in party disputes. He was succeeded, on an interim basis, by Han Kwang-Ok. By early December some eight presidential candidates had emerged within the MDP.

In late January 2002 President Kim again reorganized the State Council, dismissing Minister of Unification Hong Soon-Young and reallocating seven other posts, as well as the positions of six of the eight senior presidential secretaries and his chief of staff. Park Jie-Won returned as Kim's special aide for policy, emphasizing his close relationship with the President. The changes were intended to strengthen Kim's authority during his final year in office. Within days, the Minister of Foreign Affairs and Trade, Han Seung-Soo, was also dismissed, owing to the country's strained relations with the USA.

The contest for the MDP's presidential nomination intensified during February 2002 as putative reformist candidates sought to present a joint candidate, and opponents of the leading contender, Rhee In-Je, moved against him. The opposition GNP also experienced a power struggle, resulting in the party Vice-President, Park Geun-Hye (daughter of former military ruler Park Chung-Hee), leaving the party later in the month, initially with the intention of standing for the presidency as an independent candidate. In May Park established a new party, the Korean Coalition for the Future (KCF), serving as its Chairwoman.

Meanwhile, in mid-2001 and early 2002 strike action was taken by employees of several sectors, notably airline pilots, nurses, railway staff and energy workers, who were protesting against various issues including the decline in real wage levels, privatization plans and shortened working hours. Intermittent strike action continued.

By late April 2002 Roh Moo-Hyun had secured the MDP presidential nomination, while the GNP remained mired in internal disputes; the party's eight vice-presidents all resigned on 24 March in order to 'renew the face of the party', and were succeeded by a collective leadership. Meanwhile, Lee Hoi-Chang had secured the GNP's nomination for the national presidency. Also in mid-April President Kim replaced the Deputy Prime Minister for Finance and the Economy, Jin Nyum, with Jeon Yun-Churl, hitherto the chief of staff to the President.

In early May 2002 President Kim and six of his ministers resigned from the MDP in order to focus on state affairs during the final months of Kim's presidency. By that time, Kim had become increasingly embarrassed by corruption scandals involving his second and third sons, Kim Hong-Up and Kim Hong-Gul respectively, and he publicly apologized for their behaviour. In early June Kim Hong-Gul was charged with bribery and tax evasion, and subsequently went on trial. Kim Hong-Up was arrested later that month, accused of receiving bribes from businessmen. Both were subsequently sentenced to prison terms, although the two-year sentence of the latter was suspended for three years. The scandals adversely affected the MDP's performance in local elections held in mid-June, in which the party secured only four posts, while the GNP won 11 posts and the ULD one post.

In early July 2002 President Kim reorganized the cabinet, nominating Chang Sang, hitherto President of Ewha Woman's University, as the country's first female Prime Minister. At the same time, six ministers were replaced. However, at the end of that month the National Assembly rejected Chang's appointment on the grounds of dubious property dealings and the fact that her son had adopted US citizenship. In her place, President Kim nominated Chang Dae-Whan, a former newspaper proprietor, but he too was rejected by the National Assembly in late August on the grounds of questionable financial practices. A third nominee, Kim Suk-Soo, a former Supreme Court judge and previously Head of the National Election Commission, was finally accepted by the National Assembly in October, thus ending months of political paralysis.

The MDP suffered further set-backs in by-elections held in August 2002 when the GNP won 11 out of 13 seats contested, giving it an overall majority in the National Assembly. In September Chung Mong-Joon (the sixth son of Hyundai founder Chung Ju-Yung), who was President of the Korean Football Association, announced that he was standing for the country's presidency. Chung's popularity had risen sharply following the Republic of Korea's successful co-hosting of the 2002 football World Cup. In November Chung formally established his 'National Unity 21' party, receiving support from a broad political spectrum. However, later in that month Chung and Roh agreed to present a joint candidate for the presidency, namely the latter, in order to prevent Lee Hoi-Chang's election as President in December. Under the terms of the Roh-Chung partnership, there was to be a constitutional amendment whereby the powers of the presidency would be reduced in favour of those of the Prime Minister. In the final months of 2002 the ruling MDP became mired in further scandals. In October it emerged that President Kim and Chung Mong-Joon had arranged for a Hyundai subsidiary to transfer a substantial sum of money to North Korea via the (Southern) state-owned Korea Development Bank prior to the historic inter-Korean summit of June 2000 (see below), effectively 'buying' the meeting. In November Park Geun-Hye, who had left the opposition GNP earlier in the year to form the new KCF (see above), agreed with Lee Hoi-Chang to merge her party with the GNP.

None the less, the presidential election, held on 19 December 2002, was narrowly won by Roh Moo-Hyun, who received 48.9% of the votes cast, against Lee Hoi-Chang's 46.6%. The level of participation was estimated at 70.8%. Roh's victory, despite the late withdrawal of Chung Mong-Joon's support, was generally attributed to his uncompromising stance in favour of a foreign policy more independent from the USA, whereas Lee was widely seen as having very close relations with the US Government. The MDP in early December accused the USA of supporting Lee in the election, citing a meeting between him and the US ambassador. Relations with the USA (see below) had become a major election issue.

In January 2003 President-elect Roh began making appointments to his new Government. Goh Kun, hitherto the president of Transparency International Korea, an anti-corruption agency, and himself a former Prime Minister, was reappointed to that post, while Moon Hee-Sang, an MDP legislator, was appointed chief of staff, and concurrently Chairman of the Civil Service Commission. Roh was inaugurated on 25 February 2003 and promptly appointed a new cabinet. President Roh also reorganized the military and intelligence services, appointing Gen. Kim Jong-Hwan as Chairman of the Joint Chiefs of Staff, and Ko Young-Koo, a human rights lawyer, as director of the National Intelligence Service (NIS). The latter appointment reflected Roh's determination to depoliticize the agency, which had been responsible for surveillance of political figures even after the transition to democracy.

President Roh faced immediate challenges on assuming office, most notably a diplomatic crisis between the DPRK and the USA. Other issues included the ongoing scandal surrounding Hyundai and the inter-Korean summit meeting of 2000. In March 2003 Roh appointed a special counsel to investigate the alleged transfer of funds by Hyundai to the DPRK in connection with the 2000 presidential summit meeting (see below). In the longer term Roh aimed to address regional imbalances and the disparity between rich and poor, to reduce corruption in business and the economy and to improve living standards and labour management.

In April 2003 the GNP won two out of three seats in by-elections to the National Assembly, raising its total representation to 153. However, the victory of a reformist ally of the MDP, Rhyu Si-Min, was welcomed by the Government as an indication of support for the reform process. Also in April, the National Assembly voted in favour of the dispatch of South Korean troops to support US military action in Iraq in a non-combat capacity. Despite his independent stance on relations with the USA (see above), President Roh justified the deployment in terms of strengthening Korean-US relations. There was widespread public opposition to the Iraq deployment. None the less, several hundred South Korean military medical and engineering personnel were sent to Iraq in May.

In June 2003 two aides of former President Kim Dae-Jung, former Minister of Unification Lim Dong-Won and former Minister of Culture and Tourism Park Jie-Won, were charged in connection with illegal payments made through the Hyundai group to the DPRK to arrange the 2000 presidential summit meeting (Lim received an 18-month prison sentence in September, and Park was sentenced to 12 years' imprisonment in December). Also implicated in the scandal was Hyundai heir Chung Mong-Hun, who committed suicide in August.

In September 2003 a faction of the MDP announced its intention to form a new party owing to internal divisions over corruption and other issues. President Roh subsequently relinquished his membership of the MDP, although he did not commit himself to joining the new organization, which was named the Uri (meaning 'our') Party in October. A large number of MDP legislators, including MDP Chairman Chyung Dai-Chul, joined the Uri Party, thus leaving the MDP with only 62 seats in the National Assembly. The Uri Party was officially inaugurated in November under a temporary leadership (Chung Dong-Young was elected Uri Party Chairman in early 2004). Another development in September, meanwhile, was the resignation of the Minister of Home Affairs, Kim Doo-Kwan, following an incident in which protesters had infiltrated a US base in Pocheon. The National Assembly had approved Kim Doo-Kwan's dismissal, despite President Roh's policy of increased independence in relations with the USA. In October there was renewed public protest over the country's involvement in Iraq, which intensified in late 2003 following the killing there of two South Korean engineers.

President Roh's declining popularity was further undermined in October 2003 by the investigation and subsequent arrest of his former aide Choi Do-Sul, who was accused of having received illegal funds from the SK Group following the 2002 presidential election. In an attempt to restore his popularity, Roh announced proposals for a referendum to be held on the issue of his presidency later in the year. However, the proposed referendum prompted further political instability, with Prime Minister Goh Kun and other government ministers offering their resignations

THE REPUBLIC OF KOREA (SOUTH KOREA)

Introductory Survey

(which were rejected by President Roh). Both the GNP and the MDP dismissed the referendum proposal as unconstitutional.

Official investigations into illegal campaign funding from leading *chaebol* during the 2002 presidential election, involving both the MDP and the GNP, were instigated in October 2003. Initially focusing on donations from the SK Group, the investigation widened in November, with forcible searches taking place at the offices of other *chaebol*, including Hyundai, LG Group and Samsung. At the end of November President Roh vetoed a bill, already approved by the National Assembly, which urged an independent investigation into the funding allegations. In December the National Assembly voted to rescind the veto, in the first reversal of a presidential decision since 1954. An independent investigator was subsequently appointed. In the same month President Roh announced that he would step down if the MDP were found by the investigation to have received one-10th of the illegal funding taken by the GNP. In a further development in December, the GNP's Lee Hoi-Chang, Roh's rival in the 2002 election, publicly admitted that his party had accepted US $42m. in illegal donations.

In January 2004 the Minister of Foreign Affairs and Trade, Yoon Young-Kwan, relinquished his post, reportedly following criticism of presidential policy by his advisers. The dispute was widely reported to have been related to President Roh's policy on independence from the USA over issues such as the North Korean nuclear weapons programme. However, there was also a suggestion that Yoon Young-Kwan's departure was due to internal divisions and was only incidentally connected to the Republic of Korea's relations with the USA. Yoon Young-Kwan was replaced by Ban Ki-Moon. There were further government changes in February, following the resignation of Kim Jin-Pyo, the Deputy Prime Minister for Finance and the Economy, in order to stand as a Uri Party candidate in the legislative elections scheduled for April. Kim was replaced as Deputy Prime Minister by Lee Hun-Jai, and three further new ministers were appointed in the same month. Also in February, the National Assembly approved the deployment of an additional 3,000 non-combat troops to Iraq (the deployment was later delayed owing to security concerns—see below).

Meanwhile, investigations into political corruption continued in early 2004, and both the former MDP Chairman, Chyung Dai-Chul (now of the Uri Party), and the former Secretary-General of the GNP, Kim Young-Iel, were arrested. In February there was also speculation that Park Geun-Hye, who had returned to the GNP in advance of the 2002 elections (see above), had received undeclared funds from the GNP for the purposes of a merger with her KCF. In March 2004 it was reported that President Roh's MDP election campaign had received 12,500m. won in illicit funds, amounting to one-seventh of the 84,000m. allegedly received by the GNP and thus to more than the proportion of one-10th that Roh had previously stated would prompt his resignation. At the end of March it was confirmed that Roh's former aide Choi Do-Sul (see above) had received US $530,000 in illegal funding.

As the legislative election of April 2004 approached, there were dramatic developments in mid-March with the impeachment of President Roh over the issue of his support for the pro-Government Uri Party, whereby he had allegedly violated electoral law. A total of 193 legislators, mostly from the GNP and Roh's former party, the MDP, voted in favour of the impeachment. There were vehement protests from supporters of President Roh in the National Assembly following the vote, as well as widespread public protests in support of the President, with opinion polls indicating that around 70% of the population did not support the impeachment. President Roh's position was to be reviewed by the Constitutional Court within six months, with Prime Minister Goh Kun becoming acting head of state for this period.

At the elections to the National Assembly on 15 April 2004, the Uri Party won a narrow majority in the legislature, securing 152 seats of the total of 299 in the newly expanded chamber (243 of which were determined by direct election and the remainder by proportional representation). The GNP, now under the leadership of Park Geun-Hye, secured 121 seats. Roh's former party, the MDP, won only nine seats. The success of the Uri Party was seen as a victory for Roh and an expression of public disapproval of his impeachment. It was believed that the Uri Party's majority might have been greater had it not been for comments made during the election campaign by the party's leader, Chung Dong-Young, who had offended older voters by suggesting that their participation in the election was unimportant. (Chung subsequently resigned as head of the Uri Party and was replaced by Shin Ki-Nam.) In May Roh was reinstated following the decision of the Constitutional Court to dismiss the case for impeachment. He became a formal member of the Uri Party in the same month.

Following the reinstatement of President Roh, Prime Minister Goh Kun resigned from his post; Lee Hae-Chan, a former education minister, was approved by the National Assembly as Prime Minister in June. Following his appointment, three new ministerial appointments were made, including that of Chung Dong-Young as Minister of Unification. Also in June, the Government announced that the deployment of 3,000 South Korean troops to Iraq, originally approved in February (see above), would take place in August. Public opposition to this decision increased dramatically a few days later when a South Korean translator, Kim Sun-Il, who had been taken hostage in Iraq, was beheaded by his captors. In July the Minister of National Defence, Cho Young-Kil, resigned, taking responsibility for an incident in which a South Korean ship had fired warning shots at a North Korean vessel believed to be intruding in South Korean waters, with naval staff reportedly having failed to report radio communication with the North Korean ship. Cho was replaced by Yoon Kwang-Woong. Meanwhile, during mid-2004 there were various instances of labour unrest, including strikes by subway workers and by employees of a major oil company. In August President Roh announced that investigations were to be held into the past conduct of politicians during the period of Japanese rule and of dictatorial governments extending into the 1980s. The first political leader to be adversely affected by these investigations was Uri Party leader Shin Ki-Nam, who was forced to resign after it was found that his father had committed human rights abuses as a policeman during the period of Japanese colonization. Shin was replaced by Lee Bu-Young. In September controversy arose over the anti-communist national security law, which dated back to the country's pre-democratic era. (The law had been invoked, for example, in the case of Korean-German scholar Song Doo-Yul, who had been charged under the law in 2003 in connection with his alleged links to North Korea.) Human rights groups, supported by President Roh, claimed that the law was outdated and subject to abuse. However, proposals to abolish the law were rejected by the Supreme Court. In October a number of reform bills submitted to the National Assembly by the Uri Party included a renewed attempt to abolish the national security law, amid strong opposition from the GNP. In November there were further instances of labour unrest in protest at government plans to reform labour legislation to prohibit strikes by public sector workers and to allow employers to hire staff on a temporary basis. In December the National Assembly approved a proposal for South Korean troops in Iraq to remain there until the end of 2005, despite continuing strong public opposition to the deployment.

A number of government changes took place in January 2005. In March the Deputy Prime Minister for Finance and the Economy, Lee Hun-Jai, resigned as a result of controversy over his wife's real-estate investments. He was replaced by Han Duck-Soo, hitherto the Minister of Government Policy Co-ordination. Further government changes took place in June, when Roh appointed Chun Jung-Bae as Minister of Justice and Lee Jae-Yong as Minister of the Environment.

In January 2005 Lee Bu-Young resigned from the leadership of the Uri Party, citing his party's failure to realize its reform aims such as the abolition of the anti-communist national security law. Moon Hee-Sang was elected party leader in April. The Uri Party had lost its majority in the National Assembly in the previous month when the Supreme Court upheld the convictions of two party legislators for malpractice in the election of April 2004, thereby depriving them of their seats and reducing the party's representation to 146. In all, six of the legislators elected in April 2004 had subsequently lost their seats as a result of malpractice convictions, temporarily reducing the National Assembly to 293 seats. At by-elections held in late April 2005 to fill these vacancies, the opposition GNP took five of the six contested seats, with the sixth being won by an independent candidate. In May it was announced that the MDP was changing its name to the Democratic Party (DP). From July President Roh repeatedly proposed that a coalition government be formed between the Uri Party and the GNP, offering in turn to relinquish some of the powers of his office. The proposal was comprehensively rejected by GNP Chairwoman Park Geun-Hye. Another round of by-elections was held in October to replace two legislators from the Uri Party and two from the GNP who had lost their seats, again owing to convictions for electoral malpractice.

The GNP won all four contested seats, thereby further reducing the Uri Party's parliamentary representation to 144 and prompting the resignation of the party's senior leadership, including Chairman Moon. Chung Sye-Kyun was appointed acting Chairman pending a leadership election in February 2006. Former party Chairman Chung Dong-Young resigned as Minister of Unification in December 2005 in order to stand in the leadership election, as did Kim Geun-Tae, the Minister of Health and Welfare.

Consequently, in January 2006 President Roh effected a government reorganization. Notably, Rhyu Si-Min was appointed Minister of Health and Welfare, while Lee Jong-Seok became Minister of Unification and acting Uri Party Chairman Chung Sye-Kyun was appointed Minister of Commerce, Industry and Energy (his replacement as acting Chairman was Yoo Jay-Kun). At the Uri Party's national convention in February Chung Dong-Young was elected to the post of Chairman for a second time. Another series of ministerial nominations was announced in March, to replace government members who subsequently resigned in order to stand at the forthcoming mayoral and gubernatorial elections scheduled for May. Also in March a scandal developed concerning the conduct of the Prime Minister, Lee Hae-Chan, with regard to a game of golf that he had played on 1 March, a public holiday that coincided with the first day of a national strike. Lee was criticized for choosing to play golf rather than oversee the Government's reaction to the strike. Objections were also raised to his choice of golfing partners, who reportedly included a businessman with a criminal record for the manipulation of share prices. Lee eventually resigned in mid-March in reaction to the scandal. Roh's nomination of Han Myeong-Sook as Lee's successor was approved by a vote in the National Assembly in mid-April, and she was thus appointed as the country's first female Prime Minister.

None the less, the appointment of a new Prime Minister failed to improve the fortunes of the Uri Party. (Conversely, the resignation of the Secretary-General of the GNP, Choi Yeon-Hee, following charges of sexual harassment, did little to boost the Uri Party's popularity.) Local elections held at the end of May 2006 resulted in victory for the GNP, which garnered 54.5% of the votes cast nation-wide, compared with just 21.2% received by the Uri Party. Significantly, of the 16 provincial governor and city mayoral positions, the Uri Party took only one, while the GNP secured 12, the DP two and an independent candidate the remaining one. In June, taking responsibility for the party's disastrous election performance, Chairman Chung Dong-Young resigned and was replaced by Kim Kun-Tae. By-elections held in July further emphasized the Uri Party's declining popularity; the GNP won three of the four seats contested, while the DP took the fourth.

Also in July 2006, President Roh effected a minor cabinet reorganization, appointing Kwon O-Kyu as Deputy Prime Minister for Finance and the Economy, Chang Byoung-Wan as Deputy Prime Minister for Planning and Budget and Kim Byong-Joon as Deputy Prime Minister for Education and Human Resources Development. (Kim, however, resigned just 13 days after his appointment, amid allegations of plagiarism in his university thesis; he was replaced by Kim Shin-Il.) All three of the new appointees were widely perceived as being close allies of Roh. In the following month Kim Sung-Ho, hitherto deputy head of the Commission Against Corruption, was named as Minister of Justice, replacing Chun Jung-Bae. This arrangement was regarded as a compromise; Roh had initially planned to appoint a former senior presidential secretary for civil affairs, but had withdrawn the nomination following accusations of cronyism.

The North Korean nuclear test on 9 October 2006 (see below) resulted in a further ministerial reorganization. Both the Minister of Unification, Lee Jong-Seok, and the Minister of National Defence, Yoon Kwang-Woong, resigned amid both domestic and international criticism of the South Korean Government's continuing policy of engagement with the North. The new Minister of Unification was Lee Jae-Joung, a former Uri Party legislator, while the Army Chief of Staff, Kim Jang-Soo, took the defence portfolio. Another new appointment was that of Song Min-Soon, who was nominated to the post of Minister of Foreign Affairs and Trade (a position vacated by Ban Ki-Moon, following his appointment as UN Secretary-General). Song was known for his belief that the South Korean Government needed to be more assertive and independent in its relations with the USA.

Parliamentary by-elections and local elections held in October 2006 resulted in defeat for the Uri Party's candidates, prompting debate on a possible political realignment within the party. While some members of the Uri Party remained staunch supporters of the embattled President, others began to indicate that they might establish a new party. Intra-party relations suffered a further set-back in November, when President Roh made a contentious nomination for the post of President of the Constitutional Court (the nomination was later withdrawn under pressure from the opposition and members of the ruling party). Both the nomination and a subsequent meeting with the opposition, convened without the knowledge of Uri Party leaders, revived speculation of a rift; the party's parliamentary leader, Kim Han-Gill, warned Roh to confine himself to economic and diplomatic issues rather than becoming involved in party politics.

In addition to the issue of engagement with North Korea, public dissatisfaction with President Roh's handling of the economy also increased; house prices had risen rapidly and the education system had undergone a controversial restructuring. Many South Koreans were also deeply suspicious of the Government's plans to sign a free trade agreement (FTA) with the USA, and in November thousands took to the streets to protest against the proposed deal, leading to violent clashes with the police (see below).

By late 2006 preparations for the next presidential election, due to be held in December 2007, were well under way, with three candidates having declared their intention to stand. First of these was Park Geun-Hye, the former GNP chairwoman and daughter of the late President Park Chung-Hee, said to be popular among conservative voters. Also entering the contest was her GNP colleague Lee Myung-Bak, the former mayor of Seoul and CEO of Hyundai Engineering and Construction Company. Former Prime Minister Goh Kun, meanwhile, expressed his intention to stand as an independent candidate, only to withdraw his candidacy in January 2007, owing to lack of popular support. Although the electoral rules barred President Roh from standing for re-election, in January 2007 he suggested that the law be amended to allow future Presidents to serve for a maximum of two four-year terms, as opposed to one five-year term under the present legislation. However, he later withdrew the proposal, which would have required the support of two-thirds of the members of the National Assembly, following opposition from the GNP. None the less, Roh secured the agreement of all the main parties to reconsider the issue following the next presidential and legislative elections.

In January 2007 the Uri Party announced formally that it would disband and form a new party. Initial reports suggested that the party would seek an alliance with the DP (defectors from which had originally formed the Uri Party in 2003), and that a number of Uri Party legislators had already switched their party allegiance to the DP. However, in February, before these plans could be implemented, 23 legislators announced their defection from the Uri Party, joining six others who had resigned in the previous fortnight. Following this mass defection, the GNP held 127 seats and the Uri Party 110 in the National Assembly. President Roh finally announced his departure from the Uri Party, in the hope of reversing its decline in popularity. This decision forced the President to engage more deeply with the GNP and other parties; without their support the Roh administration would be unable to secure the passage of important legislation.

In March 2007, after only 10 months in office, Prime Minister Han Myeong-Sook resigned, citing a desire to focus on her career as a lawmaker. However, speculation that she was seeking to contest the forthcoming presidential election was confirmed in June, when she formally declared her intention to stand, although she withdrew her candidacy in September. Meanwhile, she was succeeded as Prime Minister by Han Duck-Soo, who had been special adviser to the President on free trade affairs since being replaced as Deputy Prime Minister for Finance and the Economy in July 2006. Further government changes followed in mid-April 2007. New appointees included Kim Jong-Min as Minister of Culture and Tourism and Kang Moo-Hyun as Minister of Maritime Affairs and Fisheries.

The GNP suffered a reverse in by-elections held in late April 2007, securing only one of the three seats contested. It was defeated by the People First Party and the DP in the other two constituencies, where the Uri Party had opted not to field candidates, instead supporting the minor opposition parties, with which it hoped to form a 'grand alliance' in advance of the forthcoming presidential and legislative elections. The polls were marked by a particularly low turn-out of 27.7%. Moreover, the GNP lost five of six mayoral and gubernatorial posts being contested concurrently. The poor performance of the GNP, which some observers attributed to bribery allegations connected with the nomination of candidates, prompted the resignation of several senior officials from the party's leadership, although its Chairman, Kang Jae-Seop, remained in his post. The party was also damaged by the extreme antagonism between its two rival presidential contenders, Park Geun-Hye and Lee Myung-Bak, while the latter's reputation was also undermined by allegations that he had been involved in fraudulent business transactions. None the less, the GNP elected Lee as its presidential candidate by a narrow margin in mid-August.

Meanwhile, the disintegration of the Uri Party continued, with a series of further defections in June and July 2007, including that of former Chairman Chung Dong-Young, which left the party with only 58 seats in the National Assembly. In early August Chung and 79 other former legislators of the Uri Party joined with five defectors from the DP to form the United New Democratic Party (UNDP). Later that month the Uri Party finally disbanded and merged into the UNDP, thus making the new party the largest in the National Assembly, with 143 seats.

In early August 2007 Roh announced a minor government reorganization, in which Chung Soung-Jin, hitherto Chairman of the Commission Against Corruption, was allocated the justice portfolio, replacing Kim Sung-Ho, who had resigned following disagreements with the President. Also appointed to the State Council were Im Sang-Gyu as Minister of Agriculture and Forestry and Yoo Young-Hwan as Minister of Information and Communication.

Chung Dong-Young was elected as the UNDP's presidential candidate in October 2007. He subsequently made efforts to persuade minor parties such as the DP and the Democratic Labour Party to form an alliance with the UNDP ahead of the elections, but without success. In early November, in a move that threatened to split the conservative vote, former Prime Minister Lee Hoi-Chang unexpectedly announced that he was leaving the GNP to stand as an independent in a third bid to become the country's President, having been defeated in the 1997 and 2002 elections.

A major corruption scandal at Samsung arose in late October 2007, when the former head of its legal department, Kim Yong-Chul, claimed that senior executives at the *chaebol* had regularly bribed politicians, government officials and prosecutors using a 'slush fund' totalling 200,000m. won. In late November the National Assembly approved legislation authorizing an independent investigation into Kim's allegations, which Samsung vigorously denied. Also to be examined were claims that the conglomerate had made improper payments to candidates in the 2002 presidential election. (The investigation commenced in January 2008; in April, having been charged with tax evasion and breach of trust, the Chairman of Samsung, Lee Kun-Hee, resigned.) Meanwhile, the head of the National Tax Service and two of Roh's former presidential aides were also arrested on various corruption charges. These developments proved embarrassing for Roh, who had pledged to reduce corruption in business and politics when elected in 2002.

Corruption allegations against Lee Myung-Bak gained renewed momentum in mid-November 2007, when the extradition from the USA to the Republic of Korea of one of his former business partners, to answer charges of embezzlement and money-laundering, prompted speculation that Lee himself might be implicated in the case. In early December prosecutors concluded that there was no evidence to link Lee to the financial crimes with which his former associate had been charged, but later that month, only two days before the presidential election, the National Assembly voted to appoint an independent counsel to reinvestigate fraud claims against Lee, following the emergence of a video that purported to show the presidential candidate stating that he had established the investment company at the centre of the allegations. Lee denied any involvement in the scandal.

At the presidential election, which was held on 19 December 2007, the GNP's Lee Myung-Bak achieved a decisive victory, securing 48.7% of the votes cast, despite the allegations that had overshadowed the electoral campaign. Of the nine other candidates, his nearest rivals were Chung Dong-Young, with 26.1% of the votes, and Lee Hoi-Chang, with 15.1%. However, voter turnout, at 62.9%, was very low. Lee's win (by the largest margin since the reintroduction of direct elections in 1987) was attributed to a combination of the electorate's dissatisfaction with the achievements of the incumbent centre-left administration and its attraction to the new President-elect's focus on the economy.

During the election campaign he had pledged to improve the Republic of Korea's economic prospects with his so-called '7.4.7' vision: achieving annual growth of 7%, raising average annual income per caput to US $40,000 and making the country one of the world's seven largest economies by 2017. More controversially, Lee also proposed the construction of a 540-km inland canal, traversing the country from Seoul in the north-west to the port city of Busan in the south-east, at a cost of 14,000,000m. won, with the aim of easing road and rail congestion, creating employment and improving growth.

In mid-January 2008 President-elect Lee Myung-Bak proposed legislation to reduce the number of government ministries from 18 to 13 (through the closure or merger of the ministries responsible for unification, science and technology, information and communication, gender equality and maritime affairs and fisheries) and to consolidate other government agencies and offices. However, the UNDP, which remained the largest party in the National Assembly pending legislative elections scheduled for 9 April, expressed strong reservations about Lee's plans for government reorganization, particularly the proposed merger of the Ministry of Unification into the Ministry of Foreign Affairs, and a compromise was reached in February whereby the Ministries of Unification and of Gender Equality would be retained. Lee's transitional team also announced its intention to divide the country into regional economic zones, which would be encouraged to undertake independent industrial projects with the aim of decentralizing development policy.

Lee Myung-Bak was inaugurated as President of the Republic of Korea on 25 February 2008. Four days earlier he had been exonerated by the independent counsel re-examining the accusations of financial impropriety against him. The National Assembly subsequently approved Lee's appointment as Prime Minister of Han Seung-Soo, a veteran politician and diplomat, who had previously held various cabinet positions and was currently serving as a UN special envoy on climate change. The other members of the State Council were also designated in February, although three nominees withdrew following criticism of their property dealings. Meanwhile, there was some realignment of political parties in early 2008 in advance of the forthcoming legislative election. Lee Hoi-Chang created the Liberty Forward Party, which later absorbed the People First Party, and the UNDP and the DP merged to form the United Democratic Party, which held a total of 141 seats in the National Assembly, compared with the GNP's 130.

At the legislative election conducted on 9 April 2008 the GNP secured a narrow majority, winning 153 of the 299 seats in the National Assembly. The United Democratic Party garnered 81 seats, the Liberty Forward Party 18 seats and the pro-Park coalition 14 seats. A total of 245 candidates were directly elected, with the remaining seats being determined by proportional representation. The rate of participation by voters, at some 46%, was the lowest ever recorded at a general election. The success of the GNP was expected to facilitate the passage of legislation relating to the programme of economic reform proposed by newly appointed President Lee Myung-Bak.

During the 1980s relations with the DPRK were characterized by mutual suspicion, aggravated by various incidents; these included the discovery of several pro-North Korean spy rings and the death in October 1983 of four South Korean government ministers in a bomb explosion in Burma (now Myanmar), for which President Chun held the DPRK responsible. During 1985 representatives of the two states conferred on economic and humanitarian issues, but discussions were suspended in early 1986 when Kim Il Sung, the North Korean President, denounced the annual 'Team Spirit' military manoeuvres, held jointly with US troops in South Korea. Subsequent inter-Korean negotiations were likewise regularly suspended, owing to North Korean objections to the 'Team Spirit' exercises. In November 1987 the destruction of a South Korean airliner in flight over Burma, by a bomb that had allegedly been concealed aboard the aircraft by North Korean agents, caused a new outbreak of verbal hostility between the two countries.

However, with the appointment of Roh Tae-Woo as South Korean President in 1988, there appeared to be a greater willingness by the South to foster closer relations with the DPRK. Roh's announcement in early 1990 that the forthcoming 'Team Spirit' manoeuvres would be reduced in size and duration also contributed to an improvement in inter-Korean relations. In September of that year the North Korean Premier travelled to Seoul for discussions with his South Korean counterpart. The meeting represented the most senior-level contact between the two countries since the end of the Korean War in 1953. Further talks between the two premiers took place in late 1990. The DPRK's abandonment, announced in May 1991, of its long-standing position that the two Koreas should occupy a single seat at the UN was regarded as a significant concession. Accordingly, North and South Korea were admitted separately to the UN in September.

Prime-ministerial negotiations resumed in late 1991, and resulted in the signature of an 'Agreement on Reconciliation, Non-aggression and Exchanges and Co-operation between the South and the North'. At the end of December 1991 both states pledged to ban nuclear weapons from the Korean peninsula, and in early 1992 they agreed to form a joint commission to facilitate the simultaneous inspection of nuclear installations in the North and US military bases in the South. In recognition of the recent inter-Korean *rapprochement*, the Republic of Korea cancelled the 1992 'Team Spirit' exercises, and in the latter half of the year the DPRK permitted the inspection of its nuclear facilities by the International Atomic Energy Agency (IAEA, see p. 107). This apparent progress on military and nuclear issues was, however, reversed by the North's decision, in January 1993, to boycott all future inter-Korean nuclear talks, followed in March by its threatened withdrawal from the Treaty on the Non-Proliferation of Nuclear Weapons. Inter-Korean relations deteriorated further in early 1994, following the UN's announcement that it was considering the imposition of economic sanctions on North Korea: the DPRK, in turn, threatened to declare war on South Korea.

The DPRK's announcement, in April 1996, that it was abandoning the 1953 armistice agreement was followed by a series of incursions by North Korean troops into the DMZ. The USA and South Korea proposed the holding of quadripartite negotiations with the People's Republic of China and North Korea; China subsequently agreed to the proposal, but the North Korean administration refused to commit itself to discussions. In September 1996 tension increased when a North Korean submarine was found abandoned near the South Korean coast; armed crew members in South Korean military uniforms were found dead near the submarine, others were killed by South Korean troops, and one was captured and interrogated. The South Korean Government denounced the incident and, demanding an apology, suspended all contacts with the North, including the provision of emergency food aid. In an unprecedented development, in December the DPRK issued an apology for the incident and agreed to participate in preliminary talks about the proposed negotiations. These took place in the USA in March 1997. In May, in the first such meeting for five years, representatives of the Red Cross organizations of North and South Korea reached agreement on the provision of 50,000 metric tons of grain to the DPRK. In October negotiations to allow foreign airlines, including those from South Korea, to enter North Korean airspace reached a successful conclusion.

Despite a military confrontation between North and South Korean troops in the DMZ in July 1997, full quadripartite negotiations (with the USA and China), aimed at concluding a peace treaty between North and South Korea, opened in Geneva, Switzerland, in December. A second round of full discussions was held in March 1998. A meeting held in the Chinese capital of Beijing, in April, between North and South Korean government ministers, the first such direct contact for four years, broke down following mutual accusations of inflexibility.

A further improvement in relations between North and South Korea followed Kim Dae-Jung's inauguration in February 1998. Private and business-related inter-Korean contacts increased substantially during 1998, following the South Korean Government's introduction, in April, of measures designed to facilitate such activity, as part of Kim's new 'sunshine' policy of engagement with the North. Chung Ju-Yung, the founder of the Hyundai Group, initiated a number of historic joint ventures, including, in June and October, the delivery of cattle across the DMZ to his home town in North Korea and the organization, in November, of a visit of some 800 South Korean tourists to Mount Kumgang, just north of the border. Despite fears that this improvement in relations would be jeopardized by evidence of continued North Korean incursions, South Korea affirmed that it would continue to pursue a policy of conciliation.

In October 1999 Hyundai concluded an agreement with the DPRK on the construction of an industrial complex, and in December Samsung Electronics announced it had signed a contract with the DPRK for the joint development of computer software and the manufacture of electronic products. Inter-Korean trade increased by some 50.2% in 1999. In March 2000, during a visit to Germany, Kim Dae-Jung urged the DPRK to agree to government-level talks, and proposed the development of public sector economic co-operation in areas such as agriculture, communications and the construction of infrastructure in the North.

An historic summit meeting took place between Kim Dae-Jung and the North Korean leader, Kim Jong Il, in June 2000, during a three-day visit by the former to Pyongyang. Detailed agreements were then signed pledging economic co-operation, the development of mutual trust and the resolution of reunification issues. In July ministerial-level delegations from both countries met in Seoul. This was the first visit to the South Korean capital by officials of the DPRK since 1991. A joint communiqué was issued allowing for, *inter alia*, the reopening of liaison offices at Panmunjom, which had been closed in 1996, and the reconnection of the inter-Korean Kyongui railway line. The construction of a highway to run alongside the railway from North to South was subsequently agreed. In September 2000 Kim Dae-Jung formally inaugurated the project to remove thousands of landmines and rebuild the railway line and adjacent highway. Meanwhile, in August 100 South Korean families visited Pyongyang and 100 North Korean families travelled to Seoul simultaneously to meet with relatives from whom they had been separated by the Korean War. At a second bilateral ministerial meeting held later that month, it was agreed to hold more cross-border family reunions and to commence talks on economic co-operation. In September the South Korean Minister of National Defence, Cho Seong-Tae, received his North Korean counterpart for discussions held on Jeju Island, the first such ministerial meeting ever conducted. Further rounds of bilateral talks took place during 2000 and early 2001.

Despite this progress, in December 2000 the Republic of Korea published its annual defence policy document, which classified the DPRK as its main enemy, and alleged that it had expanded its military capacity along the DMZ, an accusation that angered the DPRK. Also in that month a resolution was passed by the South Korean legislature to demand the repatriation of prisoners of war who it alleged continued to be held by the North, despite the DPRK's denial of the existence of these prisoners. The two incidents seemed to demonstrate the growing reluctance of many South Koreans to continue with the process of reunification as it stood, which they regarded as having become increasingly unbalanced to the detriment of the South.

In early 2001 the uncompromising attitude adopted by the new US Administration towards the DPRK threatened to undermine the reconciliation process. In March the DPRK unilaterally postponed scheduled cabinet-level talks following Kim Dae-Jung's visit to the USA (see below), during which the latter had criticized the North Korean regime. In April the DPRK denounced joint US-South Korean military exercises as a betrayal of the goodwill surrounding the June 2000 summit meeting. Ministerial talks resumed in Seoul in September 2001, the sixth round of which was concluded in November without any agreement—the first unsuccessful such round since the presidential summit meeting.

US President George W. Bush's reference in January 2002 to North Korea as part of an 'axis of evil' further jeopardized inter-Korean relations. In March, however, the DPRK agreed to receive Kim Dae-Jung's special envoy, Lim Dong-Won. Following the visit in April, during which Lim met Kim Jong Il, the two sides agreed to further reunions for separated families (see below), and to continuing talks on economic co-operation. The DPRK also agreed to Lim's request that it renew dialogue with the USA and Japan. In May Park Geun-Hye visited the North and met Kim Jong Il. The visit was notable because North Korean agents had killed Park's mother in 1974 in a failed bid to assassinate her father.

In May 2002 the increasing number of defectors from the North to the South received international attention as several groups sought asylum at Canadian, Japanese and South Korean diplomatic buildings in China. They were eventually allowed to travel to the South, albeit via the Philippines. The South Korean Ministry of Unification reported in January 2003 that during 2002 some 1,141 North Koreans had defected to the South, compared with 583 in 2001.

At the end of June 2002 a gun battle between North and South Korean vessels in the Yellow Sea resulted in the sinking of a Southern patrol boat and the deaths of six crew members. South Korean military sources estimated that 30 North Korean crewmen had also been killed in the confrontation, which had started when two North Korean vessels accompanying a fishing boat reportedly crossed the Northern Limit Line (the maritime border separating the territorial waters of the two Koreas). Following the incident, South Korea suspended rice shipments to the North and economic co-operation projects, reflecting widespread public anger. None the less, Kim Dae-Jung maintained his 'sunshine' policy towards the North.

In August 2002 North and South Korea held a seventh round of ministerial talks in Seoul, aimed at improving relations in the aftermath of the latest naval confrontation and focusing on the issue of future family reunions, railway links (see below) and cultural exchanges. In September the first inter-Korean military 'hotline' was inaugurated to allow for improved communications during sensitive occasions.

The eighth round of ministerial talks was held in Pyongyang in October 2002 and focused mainly on economic co-operation issues, despite the fact that the USA had earlier revealed the existence of a secret nuclear weapons programme in the North (see the chapter on the Democratic People's Republic of Korea). At the end of that month a North Korean economic delegation began a nine-day tour of the South, including several major industrial facilities. At the end of December the South Korean Ministry of National Defence published a policy document that, for the first time, excluded any reference to the North as its main enemy.

By late 2002 some of the goodwill generated by the historic inter-Korean summit meeting in June 2000 had been undermined by the revelation that Kim Dae-Jung had arranged for the Korea Development Bank to give a Hyundai affiliate US $200m. to transfer to the North in order to arrange the summit. However, the election in December 2002 of Roh Moo-Hyun as President of the Republic of Korea heralded a continuation of Kim's 'sunshine' policy. In early January 2003 representatives of Roh secretly met North Korean officials in Beijing, and later in that month a ninth round of ministerial talks was held in Seoul.

North and South Korea continued their efforts to improve bilateral relations during 2003, despite a severe deterioration in relations between the North and the USA over the issue of the North Korean nuclear weapons programme (see the chapter on the Democratic People's Republic of Korea). In March Roh was exploring a long-standing idea of developing gas pipelines between Sakhalin, Russia, and the DPRK that would supply the latter with energy in return for an abandonment of its nuclear programme. In May, however, Pyongyang announced that it no longer recognized the Joint Declaration of the Denuclearization of the Korean Peninsula, signed with the South in 1992. Also in May 2003, at talks between the two Koreas on economic matters, North Korea warned that the South would risk 'unspeakable disaster' if it became too confrontational in co-operating with the USA on the nuclear issue (the threat followed a summit meeting between Roh and US President George W. Bush). Attempts to develop inter-Korean relations were also complicated by confirmation in June by South Korean investigators that former President Kim Dae-Jung had paid US $100m. to arrange the historic inter-Korean summit meeting of 2000 (see above). In August 2003 the suicide of Hyundai official Chung Mong-Hun, who had been indicted in connection with the illegal payments to the North, further undermined the credibility of the 'sunshine' policy. Meanwhile, the 50th anniversary in July of the *de facto* end of the Korean War, celebrated as a triumph in North Korea, was commemorated in a sombre fashion in South Korea. The resignation in January 2004 of the South Korean Minister of Foreign Affairs, Yoon Young-Kwan, was believed to have been related to tensions within the Government over South Korea's co-operation with the USA on the issue of North Korean weapons (see above).

In May 2004, following a 14th round of ministerial discussions early in the month, senior-level military discussions took place between the two sides, representing a departure from the DPRK's previous insistence that military matters be discussed only with the USA. At the talks the establishment of a radio communication line between the North and South Korean navies was agreed. It was believed that the new communication line would reduce naval conflicts between the two sides; although later in the year there were incidents of warning shots being fired by the South Korean navy at North Korean vessels considered to have intruded on the maritime border, amid accusations that in some instances South Korean navy officials had failed to report North Korean radio messages (one such incident in July led to the resignation of the South Korean Minister of National Defence, Cho Young-Kil—see above). In June, meanwhile, in a symbolic development, propaganda broadcasts across the DMZ were silenced for the first time in decades, with loudspeakers on both sides of the border being switched off. In July more than 450 defectors from the DPRK arrived in Seoul. North Korea subsequently accused the South of kidnapping its citizens, and refused to co-operate in preparations for ministerial and economic talks that had been scheduled for August (military discussions, however, resumed in October). Tensions were increased further in August following an admission by the Republic of Korea that it had in the past conducted secret nuclear experiments (see below). By the end of 2004 the number of North Korean refugees in South Korea had reportedly surpassed 6,000.

In February 2005 the South Korean Ministry of Defence urged that military talks be resumed at the highest level, apparently to ease tension after North Korea made accusations that South Korean naval vessels had 'infiltrated' the waters of the DPRK. In April the most senior-level bilateral meeting for five years occurred when the Prime Minister of South Korea, Lee Hae-Chan, met Kim Yong Nam, the President of the Presidium of the North Korean Supreme People's Assembly, on the periphery of an Asia-Africa summit meeting convened in the Indonesian capital of Jakarta; the two leaders were reported to have agreed that formal bilateral dialogue, suspended since mid-2004 (see above), should continue. At vice-ministerial talks held in May 2005, South Korea agreed to provide 200,000 metric tons of fertilizer, in an effort to ease the food supply problems that continued to prevail in the DPRK. Later in the month the docking of three North Korean freighters at the South Korean port of Ulsan prior to loading the fertilizer, was reported to be the first time that North Korean ships had docked in South Korea since 1984. In June 2005, to mark the fifth anniversary of the inter-Korean summit of 2000, the South Korean Minister of Unification, Chung Dong-Young, visited the DPRK, where he held an unscheduled meeting with Kim Jong Il. The 15th ministerial talks between North and South Korea, held in July 2005 in Seoul, concluded with a 12-point joint statement, which included pledges to reopen military talks, to resume reunions for separated families and, under the auspices of the Red Cross, to hold North-South discussions on the issue of 'the whereabouts of those reported missing during the Korean War' (see below). Meanwhile, celebrations held in Seoul in August to mark the 60th anniversary of the liberation of the Korean peninsula from Japanese rule were attended by a substantial delegation from the DPRK. In November, furthermore, it was announced that North and South Korea would field joint teams at the 2006 Asian Games to be held in Doha, Qatar, and also at the 2008 Olympic Games in Beijing. In March 2006 military talks were held between the two Koreas in the DMZ, following a break of some two years; these were reportedly the most senior-level military negotiations between the two sides since the 1953 armistice. Also in March 2006, however, the DPRK postponed the scheduled 18th round of ministerial talks in protest at the South's conduct of its annual joint military exercises with the USA, which were reported to have incurred particular objections on account of the participation for the first time of a nuclear-powered aircraft carrier.

Bilateral relations deteriorated sharply in 2006 when North Korea conducted two sets of missile tests: the first on 5 July and the second (of a nuclear device) on 9 October. The first test, involving at least one *Taepo Dong 2* intercontinental ballistic missile, thought to be capable of reaching Alaska, drew strong condemnation from the South Korean Government, which immediately announced a suspension of its aid programme to the North. None the less, in August the recent heavy flooding in the North prompted South Korea to announce a range of emergency aid measures, while emphasizing that this was entirely separate from its regular (suspended) food aid programme. Moreover, despite its condemnation of the missile tests, the South Korean Government insisted that its policy of *rapprochement* remained unchanged. However, the Republic of Korea refused a request by the DPRK to hold joint military talks (made just days before the missile test), describing the timing as 'inappropriate'. In September South Korean officials announced that the country had developed a cruise missile capable of striking most key targets in the North, and stated that the *Cheon Ryong* rocket would be deployed later in the year. North Korea's nuclear test in October placed the 'sunshine' policy of engagement towards the North (which was by now coming under heavy criticism from the South Korean public) in serious jeopardy. The test proceeded on 9 October, despite pleas from both the South Korean and Chinese Governments. The Republic of

THE REPUBLIC OF KOREA (SOUTH KOREA)

Korea was swift to condemn the test, which it denounced as a 'serious, provocative act'. Significantly, President Roh admitted that this development might require a review of the 'sunshine' policy. The Uri Party continued to emphasize the importance of dialogue, and in November the Government announced that it would not take part in the Proliferation Security Initiative (PSI), a US-led scheme to stop and search suspect North Korean ships. (The South Korean Government nevertheless agreed to comply with the sanctions imposed by the UN Security Council, and announced that North Koreans thought to be involved in the weapons programme would be banned from travelling to the South. It also suspended its programme of emergency flood aid to the North.) The GNP took the opposite stance, insisting (like the USA) that the Kaesong and Mount Kumgang projects (see below) be brought to an immediate halt. In November, in a reversal of previous policy, the Republic of Korea supported a UN resolution condemning the DPRK's human rights record; in previous votes on the issue, it had either been absent or abstained. Yet President Roh continued publicly to endorse a continuation of his Government's policy of engagement towards the North, warning that the two countries could not remain enemies forever.

In December 2006 the Republic of Korea prompted severe condemnation from the DPRK when prosecutors indicted five people, including one US citizen of Korean origin, on charges of spying for the North. According to prosecutors, the five men had passed on official secrets, including the movements of US troops in South Korea and the personal details of South Korean politicians, at the request of North Korean officials. The DPRK denounced the action as a 'calculated plot' against the North. Two of those arrested were members of the minor Democratic Labour Party. (In April 2007 the five defendants were convicted of espionage and sentenced to prison terms ranging from four to nine years.) Despite the continuing tensions, the new Minister of Unification, Lee Jae-Joung (who had been criticized by the GNP for his allegedly pro-DPRK views), described eventual unification with the North as a primary objective. None the less, the Republic of Korea remained concerned over the DPRK's military ambitions; a defence policy document published at the end of December 2006 described the DPRK as a 'serious threat' to the South—the most strongly worded assessment since the inception of the latter's policy of engagement in 2000.

Following the significant progress made at the six-party talks in mid-February 2007, when the DPRK pledged to shut down its nuclear reactor within 60 days in exchange for energy aid (for further details, see the chapter on the Democratic People's Republic of Korea), the South Korean Government finally agreed to resume shipments of relief supplies to the North, dispatching 12,500 metric tons of fertilizer in late March. At bilateral talks on economic co-operation in Pyongyang in April, South Korea made the revival of its food aid programme to the North conditional upon the DPRK demonstrating some progress in complying with its commitments under the February six-party accord, following its failure to meet the deadline for the closure of its reactor. In June, after IAEA inspectors were permitted to enter the DPRK for the first time since December 2002, South Korea dispatched a first shipment of some 3,000 tons of rice; a total of 400,000 tons was delivered over the following six-month period. In accordance with the February agreement, a first delivery of 13,700 tons (of a promised total of 50,000 tons) of heavy fuel oil followed in July 2007.

In October 2007 President Roh and Kim Jong Il held a three-day summit meeting in Pyongyang. Following the meeting, which was only the second between the two countries' leaders since the Korean War, Kim and Roh issued a declaration committing North and South Korea, *inter alia*, to working towards the replacement of the 1953 armistice agreement with a peace treaty; to making joint efforts for the smooth implementation of the six-party nuclear agreements; to creating a special 'peace zone' around Haeju; to establishing a planned joint fishing zone in the Yellow Sea; and to expanding co-operation in a wide range of other areas. There was some scepticism in South Korea about Roh's motives for organizing the summit meeting, with the GNP accusing the President of attempting to enhance his own political standing towards the end of his term of office, as well as that of the UNDP in advance of the forthcoming elections. The commitments made at the summit meeting were discussed further in November during a three-day visit to Seoul by North Korean Premier Kim Yong Il and in talks in Pyongyang between the two countries' ministers responsible for defence.

The GNP's Lee Myung-Bak, who was elected President of the Republic of Korea in December 2007, was expected to adopt a firmer stance towards the DPRK than his two immediate predecessors, linking the continuation of economic co-operation to greater progress on denuclearization. Lee announced plans to review the agreements reached at the inter-Korean summit in October and initially proposed merging the Ministry of Unification into the Ministry of Foreign Affairs, although he later reached a compromise with the UNDP to retain the ministry while reducing its role. None the less, Lee proposed the creation of a 37,500m. won investment fund for the DPRK if it abandoned its nuclear weapons programme, with the aim of raising the North's per caput income to US $3,000 within 10 years.

Meanwhile, the arrangements for further family reunions came under the auspices of the North and South Korean Red Cross organizations, which co-ordinated the exchange of lists of potential candidates for reunion. The DPRK continued to dictate terms for reunions, asking the Republic of Korea to limit the amount of money and gifts transferred during the events, which took place in November–December 2000 and in February 2001. There was a notable decline in the level of enthusiasm for the reunions, which were proceeding slowly and on a small scale, among the South Korean population (other than those who were directly involved). An historic accord between the two sides allowed 300 separated families from the North and South each to exchange letters in March. Further rounds of family reunions were held in April and September 2002 at Mount Kumgang, where officials from the two sides planned to build a centre for such meetings. In April 2004 a ninth round of reunions was delayed after a South Korean official made a joke concerning Kim Jong Il. As part of the reunion programme, in July 2005 the first private telephone line between North and South Korea since partition in 1945 was opened, in preparation for video conference family reunions. These were held in August 2005 to coincide with the 60th anniversary of liberation from Japanese rule. Inter-Korean Red Cross talks held later that month at Mount Kumgang failed to resolve the question of South Korean soldiers and civilians 'abducted' to North Korea during and after the 1950–53 war: the South Korean Government estimated that more than 540 prisoners of war and some 485 abducted civilians were still alive and detained in the DPRK. Further reunions were held, both in person and through video conference technology, in late 2005 and early 2006. At another conference held in February 2006 under the auspices of the Red Cross, North Korea reportedly agreed to resolve the issue of South Korean prisoners of war and abductees held in the North. One of the most noteworthy reunions of the year took place in June, when Kim Young-Nam, a South Korean citizen reported to have been abducted by North Korean agents in 1978, was allowed to meet his mother. Kim insisted, however, that he had not been abducted, maintaining that he had been rescued from a boat and thus confirming the official North Korean version of events. However, in July 2006, shortly after the DPRK had launched a series of missile tests (see above), South Korea's insistence that food aid would only be provided if the DPRK signalled its intention to return to the six-party talks on the nuclear issue prompted the North Korean branch of the Red Cross to suspend further reunions. In January 2007 Choi Uk-Il, one of 33 South Korean fishermen abducted by a North Korean naval vessel in 1975, returned home after having first fled to China. His wife accused the South Korean authorities of failing to facilitate his repatriation. Inter-Korean ministerial talks held in Pyongyang in late February and early March 2007 resulted in an agreement on the resumption of family reunions, which took place by video conference in late March and in person at Mount Kumgang in mid-May. The 16th round of 'face-to-face' reunions was held in October.

Of particular concern to those South Koreans who had begun to question the wisdom of extensive aid without firm preconditions was the fact that, as the DPRK's financial situation worsened, economic issues played an increasingly important part in inter-Korean relations from 2000. South Korea provided 52% of the total international aid to North Korea in 2000. A summit meeting took place between the two Koreas in February 2001, at which the DPRK requested immediate and substantial electricity supplies to alleviate its energy shortages. The Republic of Korea, however, insisted that on-site investigations be conducted prior to the commencement of deliveries. Meanwhile, in August 2000 Hyundai agreed to establish a technologically-advanced electronic industrial compound in Kaesong in the

DPRK. In March 2001 the future of the Mount Kumgang tourist initiative was jeopardized by its lack of profitability; the South Korean Government subsequently pledged 90,000m. won to maintain the tourist cruises. Progress on economic co-operation in Kaesong was made from 2002, with Kaesong being declared a special industrial zone in November of that year. In June 2003 the DPRK announced regulations for development of the zone, as well as plans to develop an area of 3.3 sq km in a first phase of development extending to 2007. A South Korean company, Korea Land, was to invest around US $184m. in the project. These plans were finalized at a meeting of South and North Korean economic officials in November 2003. It was reported that in April 2004 some 1,600 South Korean companies had applied for a lease in Kaesong, and in June Korea Land selected the first 15 companies that were to be permitted to conduct business in the zone. At the end of June a ceremony was held to signal the commencement of the first phase of development in Kaesong. In March 2005 the Korea Electric Power Corporation (KEPCO), of South Korea, began to supply electricity to Kaesong, representing the first cross-border flow of electricity since the peninsula's partition. In July the South Korean Minister of Unification, Chung Dong-Young, reportedly offered to provide North Korea with energy assistance totalling 2,000 MW if the country were to abandon its nuclear weapons programme. The DPRK, however, rejected the offer. In October the first joint governmental office operated by both North and South Korea, to handle cross-border economic projects, was opened in Kaesong, and in December the first commercial telephone link between Kaesong and Seoul entered into service.

Despite the tensions created by the North Korean missile tests in July 2006, bilateral economic co-operation was scarcely affected. In the previous month North and South Korea had held the 12th meeting of the Inter-Korean Economic Co-operation Promotion Committee on the South Korean island of Jeju, where the two sides concluded a nine-point accord. This included pledges by the Republic of Korea to help develop light industries in the DPRK and to assist in the joint development of the North's natural resources. However, the South Korean Government made it clear that the agreement would not be implemented until the DPRK agreed to the resumption of test runs on the inter-Korean rail link (see below), which the North had cancelled in May. Nevertheless, the Republic of Korea remained adamant that it was fully committed to both the Kaesong and Mount Kumgang projects. Even after the DPRK conducted its nuclear test in October and despite being urged by the USA to halt these schemes, Vice-Minister of Unification Shin Un-Sang continued to insist that economic co-operation was crucial to peace and stability on the Korean Peninsula.

The construction of the major infrastructural facilities at Kaesong, which began in June 2003, was completed in October 2007, marking the end of the development phase. The zone was scheduled to be fully operational by the end of 2010, when it was anticipated that some 450 companies, employing a total of 100,000 North Koreans, would be conducting business there. By November 2007 the number of companies from the Republic of Korea operating in Kaesong had reached 52, according to the South Korean Ministry of Unification, with more than 20,000 North Koreans working at the complex. Meanwhile, the expansion at Kaesong contributed to a 33% rise in the value of inter-Korean trade in 2007, to US $1,798m.

Negotiations to reconnect the inter-Korean rail link continued during 2001. It was hoped that such a link would create a new Eurasian transport corridor that would reduce the cost and time of the transit of goods from North-East Asia to European markets from 25 days to about 15 days, bringing economic benefits to all participants. In February a meeting was held at the DMZ to arrange regulations for troops and workers employed to rebuild the line, and a parallel highway. Ground-breaking ceremonies for the reconnection of the railway and road links were held on both sides of the DMZ in September 2002, and South Korea released a loan to the North to assist the funding of the work. In February 2003 the first road reconnecting the North with the South was completed, on the eastern coast of the Korean peninsula. In June rail links between the two Koreas were officially opened, though the connections remained largely symbolic, as construction on the North Korean side to link the new railways with wider networks was still to be completed. In December 2004 it was reported that the road link along the eastern coast of the two Koreas had been opened to traffic. By late 2005 two major rail links between North and South Korea along the west and east coasts, with adjacent roads, were believed to be complete; however, scheduled trial runs along the cross-border rail links were cancelled by the DPRK (which cited continuing military tensions) in May 2006. South Korea had also pledged to assist the DPRK in constructing several railway stations. In May 2007, in a historic development, trains carrying invited passengers crossed the border in each direction on the newly restored rail link. However, it remained uncertain when North Korea would permit the operation of regular passenger services. None the less, a daily freight service, connecting the South with Kaesong, commenced in December.

(For further details on North-South Korean relations, see the chapter on the Democratic People's Republic of Korea.)

Owing to its geographical position, Korea's foreign policy has long been dominated by its relations with the major powers of Russia, China, the USA and Japan. Following President Roh Tae-Woo's inauguration in 1988, relations with the communist bloc showed signs of improvement. Trade with the USSR and the People's Republic of China expanded, and in 1990 full diplomatic relations were established with the USSR. These developments were denounced by the DPRK, its diplomatic isolation being compounded by the Republic of Korea's establishment of full diplomatic relations with the People's Republic of China (hitherto the North's principal ally) in August 1992. Meanwhile, in 1991 the Republic of Korea had extended a substantial loan, of some US $1,470m., to the USSR; this debt was subsequently transferred to the Russian Federation (Russia) following the disintegration of the USSR later that year. In September 1993 it was announced that the Republic of Korea and Russia were to participate in joint naval exercises, and in 1994 it was reported that Russia was to supply 'defensive missiles' in order to repay a part of its debt to the Republic of Korea. Further arrangements were made concerning the settlement of Russia's debt, through the provision of commodities, in July 1997.

Relations were severely tested in mid-1998 by a diplomatic dispute, provoked by Russia's expulsion of a South Korean diplomat following allegations of espionage and bribery, which culminated in the resignation of the South Korean Minister of Foreign Affairs and Trade, Park Chung-Soo. During a state visit to Russia in May 1999, Kim Dae-Jung held a summit meeting with President Boris Yeltsin. Issues discussed included South Korea's engagement policy with North Korea, a proposed expansion of Russia's role in regional affairs and bilateral economic co-operation. The Russian Minister of Defence visited Seoul in September 1999, and the two countries conducted their first joint naval exercises in April 2000. President Vladimir Putin of Russia paid a three-day state visit to the Republic of Korea in February 2001, during which the two nations confirmed their commitment to improving bilateral relations, and Putin agreed to proceed with a tripartite framework of co-operation between Russia and both Koreas. Arrangements were made for Russia to supply weapons to the Republic of Korea, which were to be partially paid for by the cancellation of some Soviet-era debt. The Republic of Korea and Russia also issued a joint statement supporting the 1972 Anti-Ballistic Missile (ABM) treaty; however, US displeasure with this led to the resignation of the Minister of Foreign Affairs and Trade, Lee Joung-Binn. In December 2002 the Republic of Korea agreed to receive US $534m. worth of military equipment from Russia as part of a 1995 agreement aimed at repaying Moscow's $2,000m. debt to the Republic of Korea.

There were indications that Roh Moo-Hyun would seek to improve relations with Russia during his presidency, as part of a broader policy of reducing dependency on the USA. In March 2003 Roh revived the idea of building a 4,000-km pipeline that would provide the DPRK with Russian natural gas from Sakhalin in exchange for the abandonment of its nuclear weapons programme. At a summit meeting in Bangkok, Thailand, in October 2003 Roh and Putin agreed to co-operate on the North Korean nuclear issue. In late 2003 a team of Russian engineers was assessing a section of railway linking Russia with the Korean peninsula across the Tumen river, with a view to linking the South Korean rail network to the Trans-Siberian railway (discussions on the issue had taken place throughout 2001–02). In September 2003 President Roh visited Russia, and during the course of his visit a significant agreement between state-owned oil companies of the two countries (Korean National Oil Corporation—KNOC—and Russia's Rosneft) was signed. In April 2005 Minister of Defence Yoon Kwang-Woong visited Russia, where he met his Russian counterpart, Sergei Ivanov, to discuss the provision of Russian 'advanced weapons technology' by way of further servicing the Russian debt to the Republic of Korea.

Relations with China were strengthened in November 1998, when President Kim Dae-Jung paid an official visit to Beijing, meeting with Chinese President Jiang Zemin and Premier Zhu Rongji. Several accords were initialled during the visit. In August 1999 co-operative ties with China were further consolidated by the first visit of a South Korean defence minister to Beijing; a reciprocal visit to the Republic of Korea by the Chinese Minister of National Defence, Chi Haotian, took place in January 2000. The South Korean Government requested Chi's assistance in resolving the issue of seven North Korean defectors, who had recently been repatriated by China, despite South Korean protests. In October 2000 relations improved further when, during a visit to Seoul by Zhu Rongji, agreement was reached on the resumption of the quadripartite conference, incorporating the two Koreas, China and the USA, with the aim of establishing a peace mechanism for the Korean Peninsula. Later in the month, following strong opposition from China, the Republic of Korea refused to grant a visa to the Dalai Lama, Tibet's spiritual leader, on the grounds that it would be 'inappropriate'.

During 2001 China continued to seek stability on the Korean peninsula. A diplomatic dispute arose between the Republic of Korea and China in October, however, following the execution in China of a South Korean national and the alleged torture of another Korean prisoner, both convicted of drugs-trafficking. In November the ministers of economics, finance and foreign affairs from China, the Republic of Korea and Japan agreed to hold regular meetings to foster closer co-operation. In late 2001 there were concerns in South Korean business circles that China's admission to the WTO would divert investment and labour to the People's Republic and undercut the competitiveness of Korean goods. Nevertheless, the South Korean Minister of National Defence, Kim Dong-Shin, paid a week-long visit to China in December, where he sought closer military co-operation with his Chinese counterparts.

Tensions between South Korea and China temporarily increased in mid-2002 when the Chinese authorities sought to prevent North Korean refugees from seeking asylum in various diplomatic buildings in China, including the South Korean embassy in Beijing, where a group of 23 had hidden. In response, the Chinese authorities increased efforts to combat South Korean NGOs and religious groups that were seeking to increase the number of North Korean refugees in China. In September Lee Hoi-Chang visited China and met President Jiang Zemin. In October the Minister of Finance proposed a three-way alliance comprising the Republic of Korea, China and Japan to manage the region's development. Also in that month the Government decided to extend working visas for ethnic Koreans in China to two years, with unlimited extensions. The move was designed to reduce the illegal trafficking of ethnic Koreans from China and its associated problems.

The growing diplomatic crisis over North Korea's nuclear programme in late 2002 and early 2003 led South Korea to seek China's assistance in persuading the North to work towards a peaceful solution. Roh made a four-day state visit to Beijing in July. Chinese diplomatic efforts played a major role in ensuring North Korean participation in talks on the DPRK's nuclear weapons programme attended by six nations, including the Republic of Korea, in Beijing in August 2003, as well as in subsequent rounds of talks (see the chapter on the Democratic People's Republic of Korea). In August 2004 relations between China and the Republic of Korea were damaged by controversy over the issue of the historical kingdom of Koguryo, which had covered the area of modern North Korea and part of South Korea, as well as areas of northern China. Following the deletion of references to Koguryo from the Chinese Ministry of Foreign Affairs website, the South Korean Government feared that China was planning to claim Koguryo as part of Chinese, rather than Korean, history, and to use this historical 'distortion' as a basis for present-day expansionism. In September, however, the Chinese Ministry of Foreign Affairs issued a statement declaring that its reference to Koguryo as an ancient Chinese province had been a mistake. The issue of Koguryo dominated discussions between President Roh and Chinese Prime Minister Wen Jiabao held in September 2006, not least because China was in the process of applying to the UN to register Mount Paekdu (half of which belonged to North Korea, half to China, and regarded by Korean nationalists as a sacred symbol) as a historic site. Meanwhile, in August South Korean officials stated that they would seek an FTA with China, following the conclusion of negotiations on a similar agreement with the USA (see below). Several rounds of preliminary discussions aimed at examining the potential benefits and costs of a bilateral FTA were held during 2007.

Relations between the Republic of Korea and the USA were frequently strained in the late 1970s, in particular by the proposal to withdraw US ground troops from South Korea (which was abandoned in 1979) and by the trial of Kim Dae-Jung (see above). Disputes between the Republic of Korea and the USA in the late 1980s over trade issues had subsided by mid-1991. President George Bush of the USA visited the country in January 1992, and the two leaders agreed to cancel that year's 'Team Spirit' exercises. In December 1991 it had been announced that all US nuclear weapons had been withdrawn from South Korean territory. The 'Team Spirit' exercises were resumed in 1993. In July, during a visit to Seoul, US President Bill Clinton affirmed his country's continuing commitment to the defence of the Republic of Korea; he subsequently stated that an attack by the DPRK on the Republic of Korea would be tantamount to an act of aggression against the USA. In January 1994 it was announced that the USA was to deploy air-defence missiles on South Korean territory. In April 1996, during a visit to Seoul, President Clinton issued a joint US-South Korean proposal for quadripartite negotiations with the DPRK and the People's Republic of China (see above). In October 1997 the US Government asked the South Korean administration to reconsider its decision to order an air-defence missile system from France. The Republic of Korea, however, was seeking to reduce its dependence on the USA for military technology. Later in that year the USA pledged financial support for the Republic of Korea, following the conclusion of an agreement with the IMF.

President Kim Dae-Jung was warmly received on a state visit to the USA in June 1998, during which he outlined his 'sunshine' policy of engagement towards North Korea. A reciprocal visit was made by President Clinton to Seoul in November. In March 1999 the South Korean Government welcomed a breakthrough in negotiations between the DPRK and the USA on US access to a suspected nuclear site in North Korea (for further details, see the chapter on the Democratic People's Republic of Korea). During a second visit by Kim Dae-Jung to the USA in July, the US Administration reaffirmed its support for the 'sunshine' policy. US-South Korean talks were held in late 1999 and early 2000 regarding the Republic of Korea's proposed extension of its missile range, from 180 km to 300 km for military purposes, and to 500 km for research and development. (In January 2001 a revised missile accord was signed between the Republic of Korea and the USA, permitting the former to develop missiles with greatly increased ranges and payloads.) In October 1999 the US and South Korean Governments began investigations into the alleged massacre of as many as 300 Korean refugees by US troops near Nogun-ri, in the South Korean province of North Chungcheong, shortly after the beginning of the Korean War. Revelations surrounding the use of defoliants in the DMZ in the late 1960s created further controversy in November 1999. The herbicides, which had apparently been provided by the USA but applied by South Korean troops, included Agent Orange, which had later been found to be highly toxic. The South Korean Government announced that it was prepared to compensate both soldiers and civilians adversely affected by the defoliants, but the USA reportedly refused to accept any liability. In December a lawsuit was filed against seven US chemical companies by a group of Koreans demanding compensation for damage they claimed to have suffered as a consequence of the herbicides.

In May 2000 there was further tension between the two countries when a US aircraft accidentally released several bombs close to a village south-west of Seoul, causing minor injuries and damage to property. Violent protests were held outside the US embassy in Seoul, and the USA subsequently agreed to cease using the Koon-ni range for such training missions. (Operations subsequently resumed, the USA citing a lack of suitable alternative facilities.) Following the incident, opposition politicians demanded a review of the Status of Forces Agreement (SOFA), which governed the 37,000 US troops stationed in South Korea. In August negotiations were held on the issue, and resulted in partial agreement. Further talks held in December successfully revised the agreement, which was signed in January 2001. South Korean civic groups, however, protested that the partnership between the two countries remained biased in favour of the USA. In January 2001 outgoing US President Bill Clinton made an unprecedented statement of regret for the massacre near Nogun-ri. Many South Koreans, however, were angry that no apology was forthcoming. Later, in January 2002, a British Broadcasting Corporation (BBC) investigation

THE REPUBLIC OF KOREA (SOUTH KOREA)

Introductory Survey

revealed that US commanders had repeatedly ordered troops to fire on refugees at Nogun-ri and elsewhere during the opening months of the Korean War. Some South Korean historians were, in late 2001, also investigating the USA's possible role in the massacre by South Korean troops of 30,000 people on Jeju Island in a suppression of communist elements in late 1948 and early 1949. Meanwhile, the USA welcomed the improvement in inter-Korean relations during 2000. US Secretary of State Madeleine Albright visited Seoul in June and in October of that year to discuss developments. In March 2001 Kim Dae-Jung paid a visit to the new Bush Administration in Washington, DC, hoping to secure support for his 'sunshine' policy. US President George W. Bush, however, took a firmer stance than his predecessor and declared that North Korea must prove its abandonment of its missile testing and development programme prior to any improvement in relations or release of aid.

The Republic of Korea immediately pledged support to the USA following terrorist attacks on the latter in September 2001, and in December the National Assembly endorsed the deployment of non-combat troops to assist the US-led campaign in Afghanistan, mainly in a logistical capacity. Meanwhile, in November the USA and the Republic of Korea agreed to a major 'land-swap' whereby existing US bases would relocate to other areas within the country, allowing a consolidation of bases and training facilities over the next 10 years.

In January 2002 the Republic of Korea reacted with concern to President Bush's reference to North Korea as being part of an 'axis of evil', a remark that further undermined Kim Dae-Jung's 'sunshine' policy. None the less, the South Korean military planned to purchase US $800m. worth of surface-to-surface missiles, capable of attacking most of North Korea, from US manufacturers. At the same time GNP leader Lee Hoi-Chang visited the USA and met senior US officials, his attitude to the DPRK generally being closer to that of Bush than of Kim. Lee favoured a policy of 'strategic engagement' based on reciprocity and transparency. Bush himself visited South Korea in February and urged the North to change its ways, while ruling out any US invasion.

In March 2002 the USA announced plans to deploy a new mobile military force unit to South Korea by 2007. Later in the month the USA agreed to sell a combat-radar system to the Republic of Korea, and the two countries held their biggest-ever joint military exercises, which antagonized the North. Also in that month the Republic of Korea reacted angrily to Bush's imposition of new tariffs on imported steel, since the country was a major steel exporter. At the end of the month the Ministry of National Defence announced that the Boeing Company of the USA had secured a US $4,500m. contract to supply the Republic of Korea with 40 F-15K fighter planes. The Republic of Korea hoped to develop an indigenous fighter aircraft by 2015.

Relations between the Republic of Korea and the USA deteriorated noticeably after an accident in June 2002 in which a US army vehicle killed two teenaged Korean girls. The US military charged two US soldiers with negligent homicide, and the South Korean authorities subsequently requested their submission for trial at a local court, but this was rejected by the US army. In November the two soldiers were acquitted by a US military court, leading to a significant increase in anti-US sentiment among the public. Although President Bush apologized for the incident, in mid-December hundreds of thousands of people attended anti-US rallies in Seoul and across the country, and there were several incidents of assaults on and hostility towards US troops and businesses. Although precipitated by the issue of the acquittals, the rallies became a forum of protest against the country's dependency on the USA and that country's policy towards North Korea. Meanwhile, in October a new joint base pact came into force whereby the US military would reduce the number of its bases from 41 to 23 and return 50% of the land it used to South Korea. However, there had yet to be changes to the SOFA that governed the conduct of US troops in Korea—amendments to which had long been demanded by South Koreans. Public anger towards the USA was further raised by the crash of a U2 reconnaissance plane in January, causing destruction of property.

The election of Roh Moo-Hyun as President raised fears that the Republic of Korea's relations with the USA would be further undermined, since Roh had once called for the removal of US troops from South Korea (although he had subsequently rescinded such demands) and had campaigned for a foreign policy more independent from the USA. However, in January 2003 he indicated a more conciliatory stance, but nevertheless warned the USA against attacking North Korea, instead urging the USA to resume dialogue with the DPRK. He also instructed the military to prepare contingency plans for the possible withdrawal of US troops, and the US Secretary of Defense, Donald Rumsfeld, in March stated that the troops could be reduced or withdrawn completely. The USA announced that it planned to remove its 15,000 troops stationed between Seoul and the DMZ and deploy them in the south of the country. Kim Dae-Jung had previously criticized the USA's policy of 'tailored containment' to isolate the DPRK, warning that it would be ineffective.

In February 2003 the commander of the United States Forces Korea, Gen. Leon LaPorte, stated that the USA and South Korea would review their 1953 Mutual Defense Treaty, with the possibility of ending provisions under the 'Combined Forces Command' for the transfer of control over South Korea's military to the USA in wartime. However, it was noted that South Korea still remained dependent on the USA for military intelligence. Despite disagreements, South Korea and the USA held their annual joint military exercises during March. In April the US military announced that it would move its main base away from Seoul as part of a global redeployment of forces, and the two countries began major discussions on the long-term future of their alliance. The USA envisaged eventually consolidating its forces in two major hubs: the Osan-Pyeongtaek and Daegu-Busan regions. Meanwhile, Roh arranged to send 700 non-combatant troops to Iraq in support of the USA, despite domestic protests. Roh visited President Bush in Washington, DC, in mid-May, and the two leaders agreed to work towards a peaceful solution to the crisis over North Korea's nuclear programme, although differences remained between US and South Korean policies towards the DPRK. In July South Korea rejected US calls for UN intervention in the North Korean nuclear crisis.

In March 2003, meanwhile, Donald Rumsfeld stated that the USA was considering withdrawing troops from the North–South Korean border, and in June plans were confirmed to withdraw US troops to locations 120 km south of the DMZ, as part of a wider reorganization of US forces in South Korea. There was some concern in South Korea that these developments were in preparation for an attack by the USA on North Korean nuclear facilities. Also in June, some 20,000 people protested at the US embassy in Seoul to mark the anniversary of the killing of two Korean girls by a US army vehicle (see above). In November Rumsfeld visited the Republic of Korea to discuss the US military presence as well as the deployment of South Korean troops to Iraq.

In January 2004 the two countries agreed to relocate US troops out of Seoul. In May the USA announced its intention to transfer 3,600 US troops currently stationed in South Korea to Iraq. In June, furthermore, the USA outlined plans to reduce the number of troops in South Korea by about one-third by the end of 2005. Meanwhile, the deployment of 3,000 South Korean troops to Iraq, which had been approved by the National Assembly in February (see above), remained suspended, despite US requests for the troops to be sent. In August, during talks between South Korean and US officials, South Korea expressed its desire that the proposed withdrawal of one-third of US troops be delayed until 2006. In the same month, an admission by the South Korean Government that it had conducted secret experiments for uranium enrichment and plutonium extraction in 2000 and the early 1980s represented a serious potential threat to the country's relations with the USA (as well as to its relations with the IAEA), although the amounts of nuclear material involved were reported to have been small. Also in August, despite public outrage at the beheading of a South Korean hostage in June (see above), the Government refused to abandon its plans for the scheduled deployment of 3,000 South Korean troops to Iraq. In September it was announced that US troops would withdraw from the DMZ by the end of October (South Korean forces duly assumed responsibility for patrolling the border zone from the beginning of November). In October an agreement for the planned withdrawal of one-third of all US troops in South Korea was reached. The withdrawal was now due to take place in three phases extending to 2008.

In December 2004, following a vote in the National Assembly, it was announced that South Korean troops in Iraq (now numbering around 3,600) would remain there throughout 2005. Joint US-South Korean military exercises were held in mid-2005 and early 2006, eliciting protest on both occasions from the DPRK (see above, and the chapter on the Democratic People's Republic of Korea). In December 2005 the National Assembly voted to reduce the number of South Korean troops in Iraq to

2,300 and to extend their deployment until the end of 2006. In January 2006, meanwhile, a court in Seoul ordered two US pharmaceutical companies responsible for producing the toxic herbicide Agent Orange to pay compensation to some 6,800 South Koreans, who had been affected by the chemical while serving alongside the US military during the Viet Nam war.

In February 2006 it was announced that negotiations had commenced with regard to an important FTA between the Republic of Korea and the USA. As negotiations proceeded, however, in July an estimated 30,000 demonstrators took to the streets of Seoul to protest against what they described as 'economic subjugation'. South Korean farmers, in particular, were concerned that the proposed FTA might prove detrimental to their livelihoods. Furthermore, the Government was insistent that the South Korean rice market should be exempt from the zero tariffs proposed by the USA. Major corporations expressed reservations with regard to US demands that trade-related legislation, including fair trade laws, be applied to the South Korean *chaebol*. A further obstacle was the pharmaceutical sector, owing to the USA's strong objections to a new South Korean drug pricing system intended to ensure that medicines were available at reasonable cost to those on low incomes. Another fundamental issue was the South Korean policy of engagement towards the DPRK. The USA insisted that goods produced in the North Korean industrial complex of Kaesong should be exempt from the trade pact, while the South Korean Government regarded Kaesong as a symbol of reconciliation, serving to promote peace and stability on the Korean Peninsula. As public opposition to the proposed FTA increased, in November at least 65,000 protesters took to the streets across South Korea, as part of a general strike organized by the KCTU, to demonstrate their disapproval. Further demonstrations later in the month were severely curtailed by a heavy police presence. None the less, an estimated 5,000 farmers and their supporters defied a police ban to hold a protest in early December, to coincide with the start of the fifth round of FTA negotiations, which were again dominated by the issues of pharmaceuticals and rice. The sixth round of talks, which took place in early 2007, drew further protests, with up to 8,000 farmers and workers taking to the streets of Seoul.

In April 2007 the Republic of Korea and the USA finally reached a compromise on the terms of the FTA. The principal elements of the agreement included wider access to the US market for South Korean carmakers, a reduction of taxes payable by television and mobile phone manufacturers and the cessation of duties levied on beef imports. Critics claimed that these measures would have a drastic impact on South Korean farmers, although the agreement did not encompass rice imports, as the Republic of Korea objected to the liberalization of that particular market. The conclusion of the FTA led to renewed protests by various sections of South Korean society. Many argued that increased US imports would render local businesses uncompetitive, thus threatening numerous livelihoods. Several senior opposition politicians joined the protests when they began a hunger strike. However, the Government took a more positive view of the agreement, regarding it as the most important bilateral development since the two nations signed the military alliance in 1953. None the less, the FTA remained subject to ratification by both countries' legislatures. Several amendments to the FTA, incorporating stricter labour and environmental provisions, were agreed before it was formally signed at the end of June 2007, mainly in order to facilitate the ratification process in the US Congress. Tens of thousands of workers participated in several days of strike action organized by the Korean Metal Workers' Union that month in protest against the agreement. The South Korean Government hoped to complete ratification of the FTA by the end of May 2008, when the current legislature was scheduled to be dissolved following elections in April. The situation in the USA was more uncertain, with a presidential election due to take place in November, and was further complicated by US demands that the Republic of Korea remove restrictions on the import of US beef that had been imposed in late 2003 in response to the detection of bovine spongiform encephalopathy (BSE) at a US cattle farm. In April 2008, however, prior to a visit to the USA by the newly elected President Lee Myung-Bak, the South Korean Government agreed to relax the restrictions on imports of US beef.

Meanwhile, also under discussion in 2006–07 was the continuing issue of the US military presence in the Republic of Korea. By August 2006 joint studies had been conducted on the terms of a new military alliance. In February 2007, at a meeting in Washington, DC, the South Korean Minister of National Defence, Kim Jang-Soo, and the US Secretary of Defense, Robert Gates, agreed to transfer operational control of South Korean military forces from the USA to South Korea in the event of war and to disband the Combined Forces Command on 17 April 2012 (three years later than the USA had proposed). A new 'supporting-supported command relationship' was to be established, under which the United States Forces Korea would continue to support the South Korean military. Kim and Gates also reaffirmed earlier agreements on the relocation of US forces from Seoul to the Osan-Pyeongtaek and Daegu-Busan regions and on a reduction in the number of US troops stationed in the Republic of Korea from around 30,000 to 25,000 by 2008. The election of Lee Myung-Bak as South Korean President in mid-December 2007 prompted speculation that the new administration might attempt to renegotiate the arrangement on the transfer of wartime military control. The GNP remained staunchly opposed to the agreement concluded under Roh. Lee pledged to forge closer relations with the USA, asserting that the Republic of Korea continued to require US protection. Later that month the National Assembly voted to extend the deployment of South Korean troops in Iraq until the end of 2008, but to reduce their number from around 1,250 to 650. The South Korean Government had come under pressure from the Bush Administration to maintain its military presence in Iraq, despite continued domestic public opposition to the deployment.

Relations between the Republic of Korea and Japan, which had long been strained, were eased by President Chun's official visit to Japan in September 1984 (the first such visit undertaken by a South Korean Head of State), during which Emperor Hirohito and Prime Minister Nakasone formally expressed their regret for Japanese aggression in Korea in the past. In May 1990, during President Roh's visit to Japan, Emperor Akihito offered official apologies for the cruelties of Japanese colonial rule in Korea. In January 1992 the Japanese Prime Minister, Kiichi Miyazawa, visited the Republic of Korea, where he publicly expressed regret at the enslavement during the Second World War of an estimated 100,000 Korean women, who were used by the Japanese military for sexual purposes ('comfort women'). In late 1994 the Japanese Government announced that it would not make compensation payments directly to individuals, but would finance a programme to construct vocational training centres for the women concerned. In August 1995, on the 50th anniversary of the end of the Second World War, the Japanese Prime Minister, Tomiichi Murayama, issued a statement expressing 'deep reflection and sincere apologies' for Japanese colonial aggression. At the end of a summit meeting with President Kim in June 1996, the Japanese Prime Minister, Ryutaro Hashimoto, issued a public apology to the 'comfort women'. However, the South Korean Government regarded Japanese proposals to provide compensation through private sources of funding, rather than government money, as amounting to a denial of moral responsibility. The conclusion of new defence co-operation guidelines between Japan and the USA in September 1997 was of concern for the Republic of Korea, which feared an expansion in Japanese military capability. Negotiations for a new fisheries agreement, under way since mid-1996, were unilaterally terminated by Japan in January 1998, following the continuing disagreement regarding sovereignty of a group of islets in the Sea of Japan, to which both countries laid claim. In April 1998 the South Korean Government announced its intention to make payments itself to surviving 'comfort women', apparently abandoning its attempts to gain compensation for the women from the Japanese Government. Later that month, however, a Japanese district court ordered the Government to pay compensation to three former 'comfort women' from the Republic of Korea. Another group of South Korean 'comfort women' was refused the right to recompense by the Japanese High Court in November 2000, and in March 2001 the 1998 compensation ruling was overturned by a regional High Court.

Relations with Japan improved considerably in October 1998, meanwhile, during a four-day state visit to Tokyo by President Kim Dae-Jung. A joint declaration was signed, in which Japan apologized for the suffering inflicted on the Korean people during Japanese colonial rule. In addition, the Republic of Korea agreed to revoke a ban on the import of various Japanese goods, while Japan promised financial aid to the Republic of Korea in support of its efforts to stimulate economic recovery. In November the two countries concluded negotiations on the renewal of their bilateral fisheries agreement, which came into effect in January 1999, despite the objections of the main South Korean opposition party, which protested that it failed positively to affirm the Republic of Korea's claim to sovereignty over the disputed islets. Differences over the accord and its implementation continued to create tension in early 1999, particularly in the Republic of Korea, where protests from fishermen, who were apparently suffering heavy losses because of the revised agreement, forced the resignation of the Minister for Maritime Affairs and Fisheries. In March increasing co-operation between the two countries was highlighted during a visit to the Republic of Korea by the Japanese Prime Minister, Keizo Obuchi, despite protests against Japan's military ties with the USA and failure fully to compensate the 'comfort women'. Both countries agreed to strengthen bilateral economic relations, and Japan pledged a further US $1,000m. in aid to the Republic of Korea. The Japanese Prime Minister, Yoshiro Mori, visited Seoul in May 2000 and met with Kim Dae-Jung.

During 2001 relations with Japan deteriorated owing to the publication in February of new Japanese history textbooks which sought to justify Japan's aggression towards its Asian neighbours during the Second World War, and neglected to mention the forced prostitution of Asian (mainly Korean) 'comfort women' by the Japanese army and the forcible transfer and use of Koreans as slave labour in Japan. Large-scale protests were held in Seoul, and the Japanese ambassador was summoned to the Ministry of Foreign Affairs and Trade. In April the Republic of Korea temporarily withdrew its ambassador from Japan. President Kim Dae-Jung urged Japan to adopt 'a correct understanding of history', and the South Korean National Assembly pressed the Government to reconsider any further opening of its markets to Japanese cultural products unless the books were abandoned. The South Korean Ministry of Foreign Affairs and Trade demanded 35 major revisions to the books, but in July Japan's Ministry of Education ruled out any further significant changes, prompting Kim Dae-Jung to refuse to receive a visiting Japanese delegation and the suspension of bilateral military co-operation. Protests also took place outside the Japanese embassy in Seoul. In August the Republic of Korea was further outraged by the visit of the Japanese Prime Minister, Junichiro Koizumi, to the controversial Yasukuni Shrine in Tokyo honouring Japan's war dead. Koizumi's visit was seen as a sign of resurgent Japanese nationalism and was denounced by the Republic of Korea, as well as by Japan's other Asian neighbours. Koizumi visited Seoul in October and delivered an apology for the suffering of Koreans under Japanese rule, but his visit was greeted by protests and he was forced to cancel a visit to the National Assembly owing to the hostile sentiment of some legislators. However, both sides recognized the need to improve relations prior to co-hosting the football World Cup in 2002.

Along with China and North Korea, South Korea condemned Koizumi's visits to the Yasukuni Shrine in April 2002 and January 2003. However, in March 2002 Koizumi and Kim Dae-Jung agreed to begin discussions on a possible bilateral FTA, and in May Koizumi attended the opening ceremony of the 2002 football World Cup in Seoul. Also in attendance was Prince Takamado and his wife, who were making the first official visit to the Republic of Korea by a member of the Imperial family. The football tournament, a major source of prestige for both countries, passed off without incident. Any remaining mutual hostility between the two countries was overshadowed in 2002 by the need for co-operation in engaging with the North, and in December Koizumi and South Korean President-elect Roh Moo-Hyun agreed to forge a united front in this regard. Koizumi subsequently attended Roh's inauguration in February 2003. In June Roh made his first state visit to Japan and had discussions with Koizumi on the issue of North Korea's nuclear weapons programme. Although both leaders opposed any development of nuclear weapons in North Korea, Roh urged dialogue with the DPRK, whereas Koizumi favoured stricter measures towards the DPRK. Japan and the Republic of Korea continued efforts towards reaching an FTA from 2003, but negotiations faltered in November 2004, reportedly over disagreement regarding the liberalization of trade in agricultural and fisheries products.

In February 2005 tensions arose over a statement by the Japanese ambassador to Seoul, Toshiyuki Takano, implying that the uninhabited Dokdo islands (or 'Takeshima' in Japanese, located in the East Sea—also known as the Sea of Japan—between South Korea and Japan) belonged to Japan. The issue of the Dokdo islands aroused anger once more in March when the local legislature of Japan's Shimane Prefecture, which claimed the islands as part of its territory, voted to establish a 'Takeshima Day'. In response, the South Korean Minister of Foreign Affairs and Trade, Ban Ki-Moon, cancelled a scheduled visit to Japan, while protests were staged outside the Japanese embassy in Seoul. Further public demonstrations took place in April in reaction to the approval for use in Japanese schools of history textbooks, including one first published in 2001 (see above), which were regarded by Koreans (and Chinese) as failing to address the true nature of Japanese wartime conduct. Another visit to the Yasukuni Shrine by Prime Minister Koizumi in October provoked condemnation from the Republic of Korea, and prompted President Roh to cancel a scheduled visit to Japan in December. Throughout 2006 the Republic of Korea's continued requests for the shrine visits to end were disregarded by the Japanese Government. On 15 August (Liberation Day in Korea) Koizumi made another visit to the shrine, and the South Korean Ministry of Foreign Affairs and Trade issued a statement declaring that the visit would strain bilateral relations and obstruct regional co-operation and friendship. This shrine visit took place just days after the Minister of Foreign Affairs and Trade, Ban Ki-Moon, embarked upon his first trip to Japan for 10 months, not only to attend the memorial service for former Japanese Prime Minister Ryutaro Hashimoto, but also to protest against Koizumi's shrine visits and to discuss the North Korean missile crisis. In the following month officials from the two countries held discussions in Seoul aimed at improving bilateral relations, particularly with regard to the disputed Dokdo or Takeshima islands, but no progress was forthcoming. The Republic of Korea had antagonized the Japanese authorities in July when it had conducted a survey of the waters around the islands, against the express wishes of Japan (which, in turn, had announced plans to conduct a similar survey in April, prompting the South Korean Government to announce a five-year plan to develop facilities on the island and to explore the area's marine and mineral resources).

Relations deteriorated further in early 2007 after remarks made by the new Japanese Prime Minister, Shinzo Abe, regarding the treatment of 'comfort women' by Japanese soldiers during the Second World War caused public outrage in the Republic of Korea. Abe inferred that there was no direct evidence to prove that South Korean women had been coerced into sexual servitude. President Roh later expressed his disappointment at what he perceived as a succession of errors on the part of the Japanese Government in relation to the fractious history of the two countries, claiming that it had repeatedly failed to apologize for any ill-treatment suffered by South Koreans during the war. In March, furthermore, the Japanese Prime Minister refused to apologize for his previous comments. He partially eased tensions in April, however, by deciding not to emulate his predecessor with regard to visits to the Yasukuni Shrine (despite a clandestine visit in the previous year). Instead, Abe sent a sacred plant to the shrine, thereby appeasing both South Koreans and opponents within his own Government while ensuring that he did not offend his conservative supporters or Japanese war veterans. In early May the Republic of Korea declared its intention to seize assets secured by nine alleged collaborators during Japanese colonial rule. Land, worth some US $3.9m. and belonging to the descendants of the collaborators, would be seized in an effort to 'restore South Korean people's dignity'. The proceeds were to be used to assist former combatants, while other land was allocated for the purposes of commemorating the Korean independence movement.

Yasuo Fukuda, who succeeded Abe as Japanese Prime Minister in September 2007, identified strengthening relations with the Republic of Korea as a priority, notably pledging not to visit the controversial Yasukuni Shrine. The election of Lee Myung-Bak as South Korean President in December was also regarded as a positive development for the bilateral relationship. Fukuda attended Lee's inauguration in late February 2008, following which the two leaders held a meeting and agreed to undertake regular reciprocal visits and to promote the resumption of negotiations on the establishment of an FTA (stalled since late 2004). Meanwhile, in January, in a gesture of reconciliation, the relatives of 101 South Koreans who had been forced to fight for the Japanese army during the Second World War were invited to a memorial service in Tokyo to mark the return of their remains. Japan had relinquished more than 1,000 sets of remains to South Korean diplomats since 2004, but this was the first time that the families of the dead had participated in events.

In November 2000, after eight years' suspension, the 25th Joint Conference of Korea-Taiwan Business Councils took place in Seoul. It was agreed that henceforth conferences would be held annually alternately in Seoul and Taipei. In the same month a

Korean passenger aircraft flew from Seoul to Taipei for the first time since 1992, when diplomatic relations had been severed. The Republic of Korea also maintained close relations with South-East Asian countries, and Minister of Defence Kim Dong-Shin and Prime Minister Lee Han-Dong visited Viet Nam in December 2001 and April 2002 respectively. Security, economic and trade issues were the main topics of discussions. Viet Nam had already become the principal recipient of South Korean aid. In early 2003 a South Korean newspaper funded the opening of a peace park in southern Viet Nam, as a gesture of atonement for atrocities committed by South Korean soldiers, some 300,000 of whom had fought on behalf of South Viet Nam during the Viet Nam war.

An agreement on free trade in merchandise goods was reached between the Republic of Korea and nine of the 10 members of the Association of South East Asian Nations (ASEAN, see p. 185) in August 2006. Under the agreement, which was ratified by the South Korean National Assembly in May 2007 and took effect on 1 June, 97% of South Korean products exported to the nine ASEAN countries were exempt from tariffs or would carry tariffs of less than 5% by 2010. The South Korean Government thus envisaged a substantial increase in its trade surplus with the nine South-East Asian signatories. Although more commonly known as the South Korea-ASEAN FTA, the arrangement did not include Thailand, which refused to participate in protest against the Republic of Korea's insistence on the exclusion of rice from the agreement. However, several rounds of free trade negotiations were held between the two countries during 2007, and in January 2008 it was reported that an agreement had been reached whereby Thailand would be allowed more flexibility in reducing or waiving its tariffs compared with the other ASEAN nations. Meanwhile, in November 2007 the Republic of Korea and all 10 members of ASEAN signed an agreement on free trade in services; a futher accord, covering investment, was also envisaged. An FTA between South Korea and Iceland, Liechtenstein and Switzerland took effect in September 2006. In May 2007 South Korea and the European Union (EU) commenced negotiations on the establishment of an FTA; in February 2008, following a sixth round of talks, the EU's chief negotiator reported that 70% of issues had been resolved. As with the South Korean FTA with the USA (see above), farmers were resolutely opposed to such an agreement. Meanwhile, negotiations aimed at concluding an FTA between South Korea and Canada, which commenced in July 2005, were also ongoing.

Taliban militants seized a group of 23 South Korean Christians in Afghanistan in mid-July 2007. Following the killing of two of the hostages later that month, direct talks between South Korean officials and the Taliban were held in August. By the end of August the Taliban had released the remaining 21 hostages, who claimed to have been undertaking aid work rather than missionary activities. The South Korean authorities refused to confirm or deny speculation that a ransom had been paid to the Taliban, but stated that it had agreed to withdraw its troops from Afghanistan by the end of the year, as scheduled, and to prevent missionary groups from travelling to the country. The withdrawal of South Korea's 210-strong contingent in the International Security Assistance Force in Afghanistan (comprising military medical and engineering personnel) was indeed completed by mid-December.

Government

Under the Constitution of the Sixth Republic (adopted in October 1987), executive power is held by the President, who is directly elected for one term of five years by universal suffrage. The President appoints and governs with the assistance of the State Council (Cabinet), led by the Prime Minister. Legislative power is vested in the unicameral National Assembly (Kuk Hoe), popularly elected for a four-year term. The Assembly has 299 members.

Defence

Protection of the frontier separating North and South Korea is the responsibility of the UN. Military service lasts for 26 months in the South Korean army, and for 30 months in the navy and in the air force. As assessed at November 2007, the strength of the active armed forces was 687,000 (including an estimated 159,000 conscripts): army 560,000, navy 63,000, air force 64,000. Paramilitary forces included a 3.5m.-strong civilian defence corps. In November 2007 US forces stationed in South Korea comprised 18,366 army personnel, 244 navy, 8,369 air force and 135 marines. Expenditure on defence was budgeted at 24,700,000m. won for 2007. In November 2004 a plan was announced to reform the armed services and to increase the defence budget between 2005 and 2008. This was in order to compensate for the withdrawal of US troops from South Korea (see Recent History). The total expenditure on military reform was to amount to around 99,000,000m. won.

Economic Affairs

In 2006, according to estimates by the World Bank, the Republic of Korea's gross national income (GNI), measured at average 2004–06 prices, was US $856,565m., equivalent to $17,690 per head (or $23,800 per head on an international purchasing-power parity basis). During 1996–2006, it was estimated, the population increased at an average annual rate of 0.6%, while gross domestic product (GDP) per head increased, in real terms, by an average of 3.6% per year. Overall GDP increased, in real terms, at an average annual rate of 4.3% in 1996–2006. According to the Asian Development Bank (ADB), GDP rose by 5.1% in 2006 and by 5.0% in 2007.

Agriculture (including forestry and fishing) contributed an estimated 3.0% of GDP and engaged 7.4% of the employed labour force in 2007. The principal crop is rice, but maize, barley, potatoes, sweet potatoes and fruit are also important, as is the raising of livestock (principally pigs and cattle). Fishing provides food for domestic consumption, as well as a substantial surplus for export. In the early 2000s South Korea remained one of the world's leading ocean-fishing nations. During 1995–2006, according to figures from the ADB, the GDP of the agricultural sector increased by an average of 0.6% per year. According to data issued by the central bank, agricultural GDP decreased by 2.6% in 2006 before growing by an estimated 0.6% in 2007.

Industry (including mining and quarrying, manufacturing, utilities and construction) contributed an estimated 39.4% of GDP in 2007, and engaged 26.3% of the employed labour force in 2006. Industry is dominated by large conglomerate companies (*chaebol*), with greatly diversified interests, especially in construction and manufacturing. According to figures from the ADB, during 1995–2006 industrial GDP increased at an average annual rate of 5.7%. The sector's GDP increased by 6.6% in 2006 and by 5.5% in 2007.

South Korea is not richly endowed with natural resources. Mining and quarrying contributed less than 0.4% of GDP in 2007, employing a negligible percentage of the labour force. There are deposits of coal (mainly anthracite). Other minerals include iron ore, lead, zinc, silver, gold and limestone. Substantial offshore reserves of natural gas have been discovered.

Manufacturing contributed an estimated 27.9% of GDP and engaged 17.6% of the employed labour force in 2007. The most important branches of manufacturing include electrical machinery, transport equipment (mainly road motor vehicles and shipbuilding) non-electrical machinery, chemicals, food products, iron and steel, and textiles. During 1995–2006 manufacturing GDP increased by an average of 7.4% per year, according to figures from the ADB. According to central bank estimates, the manufacturing sector's GDP expanded by 6.4% in 2007.

Energy is derived principally from nuclear power, coal and petroleum. In 2004 38.2% of total electricity output was generated by nuclear power, while thermal and hydroelectric power provided 58.8% and 1.7%, respectively. In 2000 it was announced that another eight nuclear plants were to be constructed by 2015, in addition to the four already under construction at that time. At the end of 2004 there were 20 nuclear units in operation in the country. The Republic of Korea also produces liquefied natural gas for domestic and industrial consumption. Imports of petroleum and its products comprised an estimated 20.8% of the value of merchandise imports in 2007.

The services sector contributed 57.6% of GDP in 2007, and engaged 66.0% of the employed labour force in 2006. Receipts from tourism are significant (totalling an estimated US $8,148m. in 2005). During 1995–2006, according to figures from the ADB, the GDP of the services sector increased at an average annual rate of 4.1%. The GDP of the sector increased by 4.2% in 2006 and by 4.8% in 2007.

In 2006 the Republic of Korea recorded a visible trade surplus of US $29,214m., and there was a surplus of $6,092m. on the current account of the balance of payments. The People's Republic of China and Japan were the principal sources of imports in 2007 (accounting for, respectively, 17.6% and 15.8% of total imports in that year); other important suppliers were the USA and Saudi Arabia. The People's Republic of China was the principal market for exports in 2006 (purchasing 22.1%), followed by the USA (12.3%). Other important markets included Japan and Hong Kong. The main exports in 2006 were electrical machinery, basic manufactures, road vehicles, and chemical products. The principal imports in that year were machinery and transport equipment (especially electrical machinery), petroleum and petroleum products, basic manufactures and chemical products.

The budget for 2009 projected expenditure of 256,789,100m. won (including capital expenditure), an increase of 7.4% compared with the previous year. A budget surplus equivalent to 1.0% of GDP was envisaged. At the end of 2007, according to the ADB, the Republic of Korea's total external debt reached US $380,665m. In that year the cost of debt-servicing was equivalent to 5.3% of the value of exports of goods and services. The average annual rate of inflation was 3.4% in 1995–2007. Consumer prices increased by an average of 2.5% in 2007. The average rate of unemployment was 3.2% in 2007.

The Republic of Korea is a member of the UN Economic and Social Commission for Asia and the Pacific (ESCAP, see p. 35), the Asian Development Bank (ADB, see p. 182), Asia-Pacific Economic Co-operation (APEC, see p. 176), the Colombo Plan (see p. 411) and the Organisation for Economic Co-operation and Development (OECD, see p. 347).

Following the Republic of Korea's strong recovery from the regional financial crisis of 1997–98, the economy briefly re-entered recession in the first half of 2003, prior to resuming its robust growth. Although foreign direct investment declined for the third consecutive year in 2007 (when according to the ADB it reached only US $1,579m., compared with $3,586m. in 2006), domestic demand remained strong and private investment, notably in the manufacturing sector, continued to expand. In 2007 the value of the South Korean won reached its highest level against the US dollar since the financial crisis of 1997–98, prompting renewed concern that this might have an adverse effect on the competitiveness of the South Korean export sector; however, the won weakened against the Japanese yen in the latter part of the year. The deceleration of the economy of the USA, an important export market, was also expected to have an adverse effect on South Korean trade in 2008, but this was likely to be partially offset by increasing demand from China and elsewhere. In 2003, meanwhile, the Republic of Korea signed its first free trade agreement (FTA), with Chile. Negotiations with various countries on similar FTAs followed (see Recent History). An agreement with the Association of South East Asian Nations (ASEAN, see p. 185) was reached in 2006. The conclusion in April 2007 of an FTA with the USA was expected to be of major benefit to the South Korean economy; however, ratification of this accord continued to await approval by the US Congress in early 2008.

The completion of negotiations regarding an FTA with Japan was delayed by disagreement over the liberalization of trade in agricultural products, as well as by political tensions, but discussions were expected to resume in 2008. Among the principal challenges confronting the newly elected President Lee Myung-Bak, who took office in February 2008, were a recent increase in unemployment and a growing disparity in income levels. The incoming President pledged to create 3m. jobs within five years. Prior to his assumption of office, President Lee had projected a GDP growth rate of about 7% for 2008, but this was subsequently revised downwards to 6%.

Education

Education, available free of charge, is compulsory between the ages of six and 15. Primary education begins at six years of age and lasts for six years. In 2005 enrolment at primary schools included 99.4% of children in the appropriate age-group. Secondary education begins at 12 years of age and lasts for up to six years, comprising two cycles of three years each, the first of which is compulsory. Enrolment at secondary schools in 2005 included 90.4% of children in the appropriate age-group (males 90%; females 91%). In 2005 there were 173 university-level institutions, with a student enrolment of 1,859,639. In that year there were 1,051 graduate schools, with a student enrolment of 282,225. Expenditure on education by the central Government was projected at 26,384,100m. won for 2004.

Public Holidays

2008: 1 January (New Year's Day), 6–8 February (Lunar New Year), 1 March (Sam Il Jol, Independence Movement Day), 5 April (Arbor Day), 5 May (Children's Day), 12 May (Buddha's Birthday), 6 June (Memorial Day), 17 July (Constitution Day), 15 August (Liberation Day), 13–15 September (Juseok, Korean Thanksgiving Day), 3 October (National Foundation Day), 25 December (Christmas Day).

2009: 1 January (New Year's Day), 25–27 January (Lunar New Year), 1 March (Sam Il Jol, Independence Movement Day), 5 April (Arbor Day), 2 May (Buddha's Birthday), 5 May (Children's Day), 6 June (Memorial Day), 17 July (Constitution Day), 15 August (Liberation Day), 2–4 October (Juseok, Korean Thanksgiving Day), 3 October (National Foundation Day), 25 December (Christmas Day).

Weights and Measures

The metric system is in force, although a number of traditional measures are also used.

Statistical Survey

Source (unless otherwise stated): National Statistical Office, Bldg III, Government Complex-Daejeon 920, Dunsan-dong, Seo-gu, Daejeon 302-701; tel. (42) 481-2001; fax (42) 481-2460; internet www.nso.go.kr.

Area and Population

AREA, POPULATION AND DENSITY*

Area (sq km)	99,646†
Population (census results)‡	
1 November 2000	46,136,101
1 November 2005	
Males	23,620,000
Females	23,634,000
Total	47,254,000
Population (mid-year estimates)	
2006	48,297,184
2007	48,456,369
Density (per sq km) at mid-2007	486.3

* Excluding the demilitarized zone between North and South Korea, with an area of 1,262 sq km (487 sq miles).

† 38,474 sq miles. The figure indicates territory under the jurisdiction of the Republic of Korea, surveyed on the basis of land register in 2005.

‡ Excluding adjustment for underenumeration.

ADMINISTRATIVE DIVISIONS
(population at 31 December 2005, according to resident registration programme)

Province	Area (sq km)	Population	Density (per sq km)
Seoul	605.4	10,297,004	17,008.6
Busan	764.4	3,657,840	4,785.1
Daegu	884.5	2,525,836	2,855.8
Incheon	994.1	2,632,178	2,647.7
Gwangju	501.4	1,408,106	2,808.3
Daejeon	539.8	1,462,535	2,709.5
Ulsan	1,057.1	1,095,105	1,035.9
Gyeonggi-do	10,130.9	10,853,157	1,071.3
Gangwon-do	16,613.5	1,521,099	91.6
Chungcheongbuk-do	7,431.4	1,501,674	202.1
Chungcheongnam-do	8,600.5	1,982,495	230.5
Jeollabuk-do	8,054.6	1,895,500	235.3
Jeollanam-do	12,073.5	1,976,465	163.7
Gyeongsangbuk-do	19,026.0	2,711,900	142.5
Gyeongsangnam-do	10,520.8	3,187,110	302.9
Jeju-do	1,848.3	559,747	302.8
Total	**99,646.2**	**49,267,751**	**494.4**

THE REPUBLIC OF KOREA (SOUTH KOREA)

PRINCIPAL TOWNS
(population at 1995 census)

Seoul (capital)	10,231,217	Jeonju (Chonju)	563,153
Busan (Pusan)	3,814,325	Jeongju (Chongju)	531,376
Daegu (Taegu)	2,449,420	Masan	441,242
Incheon (Inchon)	2,308,188	Jinju (Chinju)	329,886
Daejeon (Taejon)	1,272,121	Kunsan	266,559
Gwangju (Kwangju)	1,257,636	Jeju (Cheju)	258,511
Ulsan	967,429	Mokpo	247,452
Seongnam (Songnam)	869,094	Chuncheon (Chunchon)	234,528
Suwon	755,550		

2000 census: Seoul 9,853,972; Busan 3,655,437; Daegu 2,473,990; Incheon 2,466,338; Daejeon 1,365,961; Gwangju 1,350,948; Ulsan 1,012,110.

Mid-2007 ('000, incl. suburbs, UN estimates): Seoul 9,796; Busan 3,480; Incheon 2,550; Daegu 2,460; Daejeon 1,486; Gwangju 1,440; Suwon 1,078; Ulsan 1,061; Seongnam 942; Goyang 903 (Source: UN, *World Urbanization Prospects: The 2007 Revision*).

BIRTHS, MARRIAGES AND DEATHS*

	Registered live births		Registered marriages		Registered deaths	
	Number	Rate (per 1,000)	Number	Rate (per 1,000)	Number	Rate (per 1,000)
2000	636,780	13.4	334,030	7.0	247,346	5.2
2001	557,228	11.6	320,063	6.7	242,730	5.1
2002	494,625	10.3	306,573	6.4	246,515	5.1
2003	493,471	10.2	304,932	6.3	245,817	5.1
2004	476,052	9.8	310,944	6.4	245,771	5.1
2005	438,062	9.0	316,375	6.5	245,511	5.0
2006	451,514	9.2	332,752	6.8	243,934	5.0
2007†	497,000	10.1	345,592	7.0	n.a.	n.a.

* Owing to late registration, figures are subject to continuous revision.
† Preliminary.

Expectation of life (years at birth, WHO estimates): 78.5 (males 75.1; females 81.8) in 2005 (Source: WHO, *World Health Statistics*).

ECONOMICALLY ACTIVE POPULATION*
(labour force survey, '000 persons aged 15 years and over)

	2004	2005	2006
Agriculture, forestry and fishing	1,825	1,815	1,785
Mining and quarrying	16	17	18
Manufacturing	4,290	4,234	4,167
Electricity, gas and water	72	71	76
Construction	1,820	1,814	1,835
Wholesale and retail trade, repair of motor vehicles and personal and household goods	3,805	3,748	3,713
Restaurants and hotels	2,057	2,058	2,049
Transport, storage and communications	1,376	1,429	1,470
Financial intermediation	738	746	786
Real estate, renting and business activities	1,914	2,037	2,168
Public administration and defence; compulsory social security	768	791	801
Education	1,506	1,568	1,658
Health and social work	594	646	686
Other community, social and personal service activities	1,627	1,727	1,781
Households with employed persons	125	130	138
Extra-territorial organizations and bodies	24	24	20
Total employed	22,557	22,856	23,151
Unemployed	860	887	827
Total labour force	23,417	23,743	23,978
Males	13,727	13,883	13,977
Females	9,690	9,860	10,000

* Excluding armed forces.
Source: ILO.

2007 (labour force survey, '000 persons aged 15 years and over): Agriculture, forestry and fishing 1,726; Mining and quarrying 18; Manufacturing 4,119; Electricity, gas and water, construction and services 7,495; *Total employed* 23,433; Unemployed 783; *Total labour force* 24,216 (males 14,124, females 10,092).

Health and Welfare

KEY INDICATORS

Total fertility rate (children per woman, 2005)	1.2
Under-5 mortality rate (per 1,000 live births, 2005)	6
HIV/AIDS (% of persons aged 15–49, 2005)	<0.1
Physicians (per 1,000 head, 2003)	1.6
Hospital beds (per 1,000 head, 2004)	8.9
Health expenditure (2004): US $ per head (PPP)	1,134.6
Health expenditure (2004): % of GDP	5.5
Health expenditure (2004): public (% of total)	52.6
Access to water (% of persons, 2004)	92
Access to sanitation (% of persons, 2000)	63
Human Development Index (2005): ranking	26
Human Development Index (2005): value	0.921

For sources and definitions, see explanatory note on p. vi.

Agriculture

PRINCIPAL CROPS
('000 metric tons)

	2004	2005	2006
Rice (paddy)	6,736.9	6,435.0	6,305.5
Barley	277.7	286.9	260.0
Maize	77.6	73.5	64.6
Potatoes	642.6	894.2	631.1
Sweet potatoes	345.2	282.5	285.8
Dry beans	9.3	7.1	6.4
Chestnuts	71.8	76.4	76.4*
Soybeans (Soya beans)	138.6	183.3	156.4
Sesame seed	20.9	23.5	15.6
Cabbages	3,139.4	2,602.6	3,068.1
Lettuce	204.8	167.0	160.3
Spinach	118.7	109.0	103.7
Tomatoes	394.6	439.0	433.2
Pumpkins, squash and gourds	304.3	339.1	322.0
Cucumbers and gherkins	407.5	403.3	389.6
Chillies and green peppers	410.3	395.3	395.3*
Green onions and shallots	700.2	513.2	543.0
Dry onions	947.8	1,023.3	889.6
Garlic	357.8	375.0	331.4
Carrots	80.0	117.7	130.4
Mushrooms	27.8	28.4	29.0
Watermelons	823.7	905.9	778.4
Cantaloupes and other melons	243.1	199.8	219.7
Tangerines, mandarins, clementines and satsumas	584.4	638.0	620.3
Apples	357.2	367.5	407.6
Pears	451.9	443.3	431.5
Peaches and nectarines	200.5	223.7	193.8
Plums	72.0	76.0	64.4
Strawberries	202.5	202.0	205.3
Grapes	367.9	381.4	330.0
Persimmons	299.0	363.8	352.8
Tobacco (leaves)	36.4†	n.a.	35.0*

* FAO estimate.
† Unofficial figure.

Aggregate production ('000 metric tons, may include official, semi-official or estimated data): Total cereals 7,115 in 2004, 6,816 in 2005, 6,653 in 2006; Total vegetables (incl. melons) 11,846 in 2004, 10,965 in 2005, 11,138 in 2006; Total fruits (excl. melons) 2,631 in 2004, 2,812 in 2005, 2,727 in 2006.

Source: FAO.

LIVESTOCK
('000 head)

	2004	2005	2006
Cattle	2,163	2,298	2,484
Pigs	8,908	8,962	9,382
Goats	527	523	523*
Chickens	106,736	109,628	119,181

* FAO estimate.
Source: FAO.

THE REPUBLIC OF KOREA (SOUTH KOREA)

LIVESTOCK PRODUCTS
('000 metric tons)

	2004	2005	2006
Cattle meat	207.0	217.7	224.0*
Pig meat	959.7	899.4	860.0†
Chicken meat†	386.0	536.0	496.0
Duck meat†	46.0	64.0	67.0
Cows' milk	2,255.0	2,228.8	2,184.0†
Goats' milk*	5.2	n.a.	5.2
Hen eggs	508.0	514.9	514.9*
Other poultry eggs*	26.0	28.0	28.0
Honey	15.7	23.8	23.8*

* FAO estimate(s).
† Unofficial figure(s).
Source: FAO.

Forestry

ROUNDWOOD REMOVALS
('000 cubic metres, excl. bark)

	2004	2005	2006
Sawlogs, veneer logs and logs for sleepers	406	297	426
Pulpwood	1,354	1,491	1,422
Other industrial wood	481*	562	596
Fuel wood*	2,463	2,465	2,469
Total	4,704	4,815	4,913

* FAO estimate(s).
Source: FAO.

SAWNWOOD PRODUCTION
('000 cubic metres, incl. sleepers)

	2002	2003	2004
Coniferous (softwood)	4,209	4,200	4,200*
Broadleaved (hardwood)	201	180	166†
Total	4,410	4,380	4,366*

* FAO estimate.
† Unofficial figure.
2005–06: Figures assumed to be unchanged from 2004 (FAO estimates).
Source: FAO.

Fishing

('000 metric tons, live weight)

	2003	2004	2005
Capture	1,642.9	1,575.3	1,639.1
Croakers and drums	29.5	27.3	43.5
Japanese anchovy	250.1	196.6	249.5
Skipjack tuna	153.3	162.2	171.6
Chub mackerel	122.1	185.6	135.7
Largehead hairtail	62.9	66.3	60.1
Argentine shortfin squid	91.4	20.4	42.9
Japanese flying squid	233.3	212.8	189.1
Aquaculture	387.8	405.7	436.2
Pacific cupped oyster	238.3	239.3	251.7
Total catch	2,030.7	1,981.1	2,075.3

Note: Figures exclude aquatic plants ('000 metric tons): 457.2 (capture 5.2, aquaculture 452.1) in 2003 (FAO estimates); 556.2 (capture 9.1, aquaculture 547.1) in 2004; 528.0 (capture 15.2, aquaculture 512.8) in 2005. Also excluded are aquatic mammals, recorded by number rather than by weight; the number of dolphins and whales caught was: 237 in 2003; 480 in 2004; 386 in 2005.
Source: FAO.

Mining

('000 metric tons, unless otherwise indicated)

	2004	2005	2006
Hard coal (Anthracite)	3,191	2,832	2,824
Iron ore: gross weight	233	266	227
Iron ore: metal content	127	119	155
Lead ore (metric tons)*	40	50	17
Zinc ore (metric tons)*	14	77	16
Kaolin	2,780	2,767	2,399
Feldspar	541.8	508.6	427.4
Salt (unrefined)	340.8	378.9	285.6
Mica (metric tons)	59,238	36,623	30,356
Talc (metric tons)	79,313	83,471	64,118
Pyrophyllite	827.9	885.6	677.5

* Figures refer to the metal content of ores.
Source: US Geological Survey.

Industry

SELECTED PRODUCTS
('000 metric tons, unless otherwise indicated)

	2002	2003	2004
Wheat flour	1,814	1,792	1,891
Refined sugar	1,273	n.a.	n.a.
Beer (million litres)	18,224	17,863	18,033
Cigarettes (million)	94,433	123,166	133,206
Cotton yarn—pure and mixed	301.3	n.a.	n.a.
Plywood ('000 cu m)	797	827	704
Newsprint	1,597	1,538	1,679
Rubber tyres ('000)*	71,103	n.a.	n.a.
Caustic soda (metric tons)	1,340	1,365	1,508
Liquefied petroleum gas	3,477	3,273	3,312
Naphtha	18,754	17,039	19,204
Kerosene	7,934	8,152	6,364
Gas-diesel (distillate fuel oil)	28,732	28,033	29,383
Residual fuel oil	28,569	30,816	30,509
Cement	56,823	60,725	56,955
Pig-iron	26,879	27,314†	27,556†
Crude steel	45,482	46,310†	47,521†
Television receivers ('000)	9,157	n.a.	n.a.
Passenger cars—produced ('000 units)	2,653	n.a.	n.a.
Lorries and trucks—produced (number)	288,992	n.a.	n.a.
Electric energy (million kWh)	336,237	352,352	371,011
Carbon black†	460.0	464.9	473.8
Products of petroleum refineries ('000 barrels)†	940,000‡	796,000‡	886,415

* Tyres for passenger cars and commercial vehicles.
† Source: US Geological Survey.
‡ Estimate.

Shipbuilding (merchant ships launched, '000 grt): 8,977 in 1999; 11,211 in 2000; 8,385 in 2001.

Source: mostly UN, *Industrial Commodity Statistics Yearbook*.

2005 ('000 metric tons, unless otherwise indicated): Cement 51,391; Crude steel 47,820; Pig-iron 27,309; Carbon black 471.7; Products of petroleum refineries ('000 barrels) 919,627 (Source: US Geological Survey).

2006 ('000 metric tons, unless otherwise indicated): Cement 53,971; Crude steel 48,437; Pig-iron 27,548; Carbon black 484.3; Products of petroleum refineries ('000 barrels) 947,433 (Source: US Geological Survey).

THE REPUBLIC OF KOREA (SOUTH KOREA) *Statistical Survey*

Finance

CURRENCY AND EXCHANGE RATES

Monetary Units
100 chun (jeon) = 10 hwan = 1 won.

Sterling, Dollar and Euro Equivalents (31 December 2007)
£1 sterling = 1,879.59 won;
US $1 = 938.20 won;
€1 = 1,381.12 won;
10,000 won = £5.32 = $10.66 = €7.24.

Average Exchange Rate (won per US $)
2005   1,024.12
2006   954.79
2007   929.21

BUDGET
('000 million won)

Revenue	2004	2005	2006*
Current revenue	177,432	190,165	208,092
Tax revenue	140,643	152,371	165,359
Non-tax revenue	36,788	37,794	42,733
Capital revenue	1,329	1,281	1,482
Total	178,760	191,447	209,574

Expenditure	2004	2005	2006*
Current expenditure	145,148	160,274	173,688
General public services	11,909	14,743	17,208
Defence	19,995	21,976	23,428
Education	22,113	27,467	28,457
Social security and welfare	15,125	16,716	18,536
Economic services	30,753	28,250	30,115
Transport and communications	14,458	14,041	13,903
Capital expenditure	26,992	24,648	26,493
Net lending	1,398	3,024	5,746
Total	173,538	187,946	205,928

* Preliminary figures.

INTERNATIONAL RESERVES
(US $ million at 31 December)

	2004	2005	2006
Gold (national valuation)	72.3	73.6	74.2
IMF special drawing rights	32.8	43.7	54.1
Reserve position in IMF	788.4	305.8	440.4
Foreign exchange	198,175.3	209,967.7	238,387.9
Total	199,068.9	210,390.8	238,956.6

Source: IMF, *International Financial Statistics*.

MONEY SUPPLY
('000 million won at 31 December)

	2004	2005	2006
Currency outside banks	20,772	21,959	23,224
Demand deposits at deposit money banks	47,424	55,045	62,395
Total money (incl. others)	68,423	77,274	85,831

Source: IMF, *International Financial Statistics*.

COST OF LIVING
(Consumer Price Index; base: 2005 = 100)

	2004	2006	2007
Food and non-alcoholic beverages	97.0	102.0	104.8
Alcoholic beverages and cigarettes	87.1	99.8	100.2
Housing, water and fuels	98.2	102.9	105.2
Furnishings and household goods	97.9	101.8	105.9
Clothing and footwear	99.0	102.7	105.4
Health	97.8	102.0	103.8
Education	95.9	104.9	111.2
Communication	101.8	98.7	96.7
Transport	95.2	104.6	108.4
All items (incl. others)	97.3	102.0	104.8

NATIONAL ACCOUNTS
('000 million won at current prices)

National Income and Product

	2005	2006	2007*
Compensation of employees	365,160.8	385,003.6	410,749.3
Operating surplus	237,710.9	241,763.8	255,167.8
Domestic factor incomes	602,871.7	626,767.4	665,917.1
Consumption of fixed capital	111,106.3	117,313.1	122,314.7
Gross domestic product (GDP) at factor cost	713,978.0	744,080.5	788,231.8
Indirect taxes, *less* subsidies	96,537.9	103,964.1	112,956.8
GDP in purchasers' values	810,515.9	848,044.6	901,188.6
Net factor income from abroad	–1,216.1	1,116.5	1,352.7
Gross national income	809,299.8	849,161.2	902,541.3
Less Consumption of fixed capital	111,106.3	117,313.1	122,314.7
National income in market prices	698,193.5	731,848.0	780,226.7

* Preliminary.

Expenditure on the Gross Domestic Product

	2005	2006	2007*
Final consumption expenditure	541,528.8	580,598.5	623,582.7
Households	417,425.1	444,859.7	476,528.6
Non-profit institutions serving households	9,265.5	10,096.0	10,878.5
General government	114,838.2	125,642.8	136,175.6
Gross capital formation	243,659.5	253,118.5	264,665.9
Gross fixed capital formation	237,239.5	246,298.0	259,353.4
Changes in inventories	6,420.0	6,820.5	5,312.5
Total domestic expenditure	785,188.3	833,717.0	888,248.6
Exports of goods and services	342,588.0	364,718.4	410,940.3
Less Imports of goods and services	323,466.8	356,929.9	403,418.2
Statistical discrepancy	6,206.3	6,539.1	5,417.9
GDP in market prices	810,515.9	848,044.6	901,188.6
GDP at constant 2000 prices	723,126.8	760,251.2	798,057.0

* Preliminary.

THE REPUBLIC OF KOREA (SOUTH KOREA)

Gross Domestic Product by Economic Activity

	2005	2006	2007*
Agriculture, forestry and fishing	24,631.4	24,635.1	23,982.2
Mining and quarrying	2,626.2	2,612.4	2,839.4
Manufacturing	204,701.0	210,948.4	223,324.2
Electricity, gas and water	16,838.7	17,526.7	18,050.7
Construction	66,375.0	67,731.0	71,118.0
Wholesale and retail trade, restaurants and hotels	67,862.2	71,014.2	74,351.1
Transport, storage and communications	52,429.5	53,814.3	57,451.1
Financial intermediation	60,483.5	63,965.4	70,904.9
Real estate, renting and business activities	90,482.4	95,836.2	102,172.0
Public administration and defence, compulsory social security	45,429.4	48,794.8	51,421.8
Education	41,569.8	44,635.2	47,442.3
Health and social work	22,069.3	25,639.2	28,574.7
Other service activities	24,975.6	26,851.1	28,671.6
Gross value added at basic prices	721,474.2	754,004.1	800,304.1
Taxes, less subsidies, on products	89,041.7	94,040.6	100,884.5
Total	810,515.9	848,044.6	901,188.6

* Preliminary.
Source: Bank of Korea.

BALANCE OF PAYMENTS
(US $ million)

	2004	2005	2006
Exports of goods f.o.b.	257,710	288,971	331,845
Imports of goods f.o.b.	−220,141	−256,288	−302,631
Trade balance	37,569	32,683	29,214
Exports of services	41,882	45,129	51,873
Imports of services	−49,928	−58,788	−70,637
Balance on goods and services	29,523	19,025	10,451
Other income received	9,410	10,432	13,596
Other income paid	−8,328	−11,994	−14,134
Balance on goods, services and income	30,606	17,462	9,912
Current transfers received	9,151	10,004	9,337
Current transfers paid	−11,583	−12,486	−13,157
Current balance	28,174	14,981	6,092
Capital account (net)	−1,753	−2,340	−3,033
Direct investment abroad	−4,650	−4,291	−7,126
Direct investment from abroad	9,246	6,309	3,645
Portfolio investment assets	−9,918	−14,136	−26,908
Portfolio investment liabilities	18,375	14,114	8,435
Financial derivatives assets	2,523	3,461	4,331
Financial derivatives liabilities	−2,360	−5,167	−8,402
Other investment assets	−8,138	−2,658	−8,759
Other investment liabilities	4,282	9,473	56,438
Net errors and omissions	2,895	119	−2,624
Overall balance	38,675	19,864	22,089

Source: IMF, *International Financial Statistics*.

External Trade

PRINCIPAL COMMODITIES
(distribution by SITC, US $ million)*

Imports c.i.f.	2005	2006	2007
Food and live animals	9,956.0	11,357.9	13,630.4
Crude materials (inedible) except fuels	15,353.8	19,664.5	24,071.8
Mineral fuels, lubricants, etc.	67,500.9	86,706.7	96,503.6
Petroleum, petroleum products, etc.	51,303.8	66,689.2	74,059.9
Crude petroleum oils, etc.	42,605.8	n.a.	n.a.
Gas (natural and manufactured)	10,754.2	14,699.9	15,998.6
Chemicals and related products	24,502.4	27,573.0	32,432.5
Organic chemicals	8,321.5	8,662.6	9,778.6
Basic manufactures	35,849.4	42,313.9	51,932.9
Iron and steel	15,032.8	15,890.4	21,446.4
Machinery and transport equipment	82,533.4	92,717.6	107,499.3
Machinery specialized for particular industries	7,219.2	8,423.4	13,506.7
General industrial machinery, equipment and parts	8,714.4	9,728.1	11,916.6
Office machines and automatic data-processing machines	7,047.1	8,028.2	7,920.0
Telecommunications and sound equipment	6,694.8	7,537.6	9,204.0
Other electrical machinery, apparatus, etc.	39,106.9	41,776.9	46,088.1
Thermionic valves and tubes, microprocessors, transistors, etc.	23,870.9	24,712.8	28,420.3
Digital monolithic integrated units	17,800.5	18,026.1	n.a.
Miscellaneous manufactured articles	23,434.3	26,684.0	27,572.4
Total (incl. others)	261,238.3	309,382.6	356,845.7

Exports f.o.b.	2005	2006	2007
Mineral fuels, lubricants, etc.	15,709.4	20,920.4	24,630.9
Petroleum, petroleum products, etc.	15,622.7	20,788.7	24,516.1
Chemicals and related products	27,745.2	31,806.1	37,544.7
Organic chemicals	10,388.1	12,549.4	14,968.0
Plastics in primary forms	10,673.6	11,610.9	13,541.2
Basic manufactures	41,023.2	46,559.2	52,041.3
Textile yarn, fabrics, etc.	10,390.8	10,109.5	10,373.4
Iron and steel	14,345.9	15,823.6	18,802.4
Machinery and transport equipment	173,491.6	192,359.8	216,730.2
Office machines and automatic data-processing machines	17,756.9	17,884.2	13,331.2
Automatic data-processing machines and units, etc.	9,240.5	8,511.4	3,107.4
Parts and accessories for office machines and automatic data-processing equipment	8,141.8	9,011.1	8,622.7
Telecommunications and sound equipment	37,746.0	37,300.4	46,612.9

THE REPUBLIC OF KOREA (SOUTH KOREA)

Exports f.o.b.—continued	2005	2006	2007
Transmission apparatus for radio or television	19,476.1	17,321.6	44.4
Other electrical machinery, apparatus, etc.	42,942.9	48,545.9	50,962.8
Thermionic valves and tubes, microprocessors, transistors, etc.	27,488.3	28,486.4	32,737.5
Digital monolithic integrated units	18,159.8	18,159.8	21,998.3
Road vehicles	37,310.9	42,418.4	48,958.5
Motor cars and other motor vehicles	27,256.1	30,597.2	34,482.8
Other transport equipment	17,616.5	22,290.7	27,533.6
Ships, boats and floating structures	17,231.5	21,492.9	26,632.0
Miscellaneous manufactured articles	20,292.0	26,630.2	32,239.1
Total (incl. others)	284,418.7	325,464.8	371,489.1

* Excluding trade with the Democratic People's Republic of Korea.

Source: Korea International Trade Association.

PRINCIPAL TRADING PARTNERS
(US $ million)*

Imports c.i.f.	2005	2006	2007
Australia	9,859.1	11,309.4	13,232.5
Brazil	2,500.8	2,706.9	2,793.7
Canada	2,603.7	3,091.3	3,254.5
China, People's Republic	38,648.2	48,556.7	63,027.8
France	2,759.0	3,219.4	4,043.2
Germany	9,774.2	11,364.6	13,534.3
Hong Kong	2,043.1	2,101.3	2,142.3
Indonesia	8,184.4	8,848.6	9,113.8
Iran	3,534.9	5,049.2	6,481.8
Italy	2,777.7	2,915.6	3,582.8
Japan	48,403.2	51,926.3	56,250.1
Kuwait	5,977.0	8,133.5	8,746.8
Malaysia	6,011.6	7,242.5	8,442.2
Oman	3,705.1	5,128.7	3,813.9
Philippines	2,316.0	2,186.6	2,438.3
Qatar	5,599.3	6,985.2	8,454.0
Russia	3,936.6	4,573.0	6,977.5
Saudi Arabia	16,105.8	20,552.1	21,163.5
Singapore	5,317.7	5,886.7	6,859.7
Taiwan	8,049.6	9,287.5	9,966.5
Thailand	2,688.8	3,328.4	3,769.2
United Arab Emirates	10,018.3	12,930.9	12,656.2
United Kingdom	3,149.1	2,976.5	3,580.8
USA	30,585.9	33,654.2	33,654.2
Total (incl. others)	261,238.3	309,382.6	356,845.7

Exports f.o.b.	2005	2006	2007
Australia	3,812.1	4,692.1	4,691.2
Brazil	2,410.7	3,063.4	3,487.5
Canada	3,446.2	3,620.4	3,506.4
China, People's Republic	61,915.0	69,459.2	81,985.2
France	3,172.3	3,415.5	3,478.2
Germany	10,304.0	10,056.2	11,542.5
Hong Kong	15,531.1	18,978.9	18,654.5
India	4,597.8	5,532.8	6,600.0
Indonesia	5,045.6	4,873.5	5,770.6
Iran	2,141.2	2,559.3	3,265.6
Italy	4,296.9	4,286.3	4,151.4
Japan	24,027.4	26,534.0	26,370.2
Malaysia	4,608.2	5,227.2	5,704.2
Mexico	3,789.1	6,284.6	7,482.0
Netherlands	3,646.7	3,609.4	4,488.7
Philippines	3,219.7	3,930.5	4,420.3
Russia	3,864.2	5,179.2	8,087.7

Exports f.o.b.—continued	2005	2006	2007
Singapore	7,406.6	9,489.3	11,949.5
Spain	2,867.1	3,479.2	3,924.8
Taiwan	10,862.9	12,995.7	13,027.1
Thailand	3,380.8	4,246.1	4,488.4
Turkey	2,782.0	3,035.8	4,087.4
United Arab Emirates	2,732.7	2,896.0	3,704.7
United Kingdom	5,338.8	5,635.1	6,870.0
USA	41,342.6	43,183.5	45,766.1
Viet Nam	3,431.7	3,927.5	5,760.1
Total (incl. others)	284,418.7	325,464.8	371,489.1

* Excluding trade with the Democratic People's Republic of Korea.

Source: Korea International Trade Association.

Trade with the Democratic People's Republic of Korea (US $ million, unofficial estimates): *Total imports:* 340.3 in 2005; 519.5 in 2006. *Total exports:* 715.5 in 2005; 830.2 in 2006 (Source: Bank of Korea, Republic of Korea).

Transport

RAILWAYS
(traffic)

	2003	2004	2005
Passengers carried ('000)	894,620	921,223	950,995
Passenger-km (million)	27,228	28,459	31,004
Freight ('000 metric tons)	47,110	44,512	41,669
Freight ton-km (million)	11,057	10,641	10,108

ROAD TRAFFIC
(motor vehicles in use at 31 December)

	2002	2003	2004
Passenger cars	9,737,428	10,278,923	10,464,827
Goods vehicles	2,894,412	3,016,407	3,942,573
Buses and coaches	1,275,319	1,246,629	98,954
Motorcycles and mopeds	1,708,457	1,730,193	1,728,463

SHIPPING

Merchant Fleet
(registered at 31 December)

	2004	2005	2006
Number of vessels	2,700	2,778	2,820
Total displacement ('000 grt)	7,826.1	9,251.1	10,477.1

Source: Lloyd's Register-Fairplay, *World Fleet Statistics*.

Sea-borne Freight Traffic
('000 metric tons)*

	2002	2003	2004
Goods loaded	319,570	340,527	317,799
Goods unloaded	615,555	616,326	593,361

* Including coastwise traffic loaded and unloaded.

THE REPUBLIC OF KOREA (SOUTH KOREA)

CIVIL AVIATION*

	2003	2004	2005
Passengers ('000)	42,839	45,824	46,841
Passenger-km (million)	82,231	96,583	101,664
Freight ('000 metric tons)	2,632	2,978	2,989
Freight ton-km (million)	11,696	13,810	13,597

* Domestic and international flights.

Tourism

FOREIGN VISITOR ARRIVALS*

Country of nationality	2003	2004	2005
China, People's Republic	513,236	627,264	709,836
Hong Kong	156,373	155,058	166,204
Japan	1,802,171	2,443,070	2,439,806
Philippines	216,647	213,434	222,622
Russia	168,051	156,890	143,850
Taiwan	194,681	304,908	351,421
USA	421,709	511,170	530,629
Total (incl. others)	4,753,604	5,818,138	6,022,752

* Including same-day visitors (excursionists) and crew members from ships; also including Korean nationals resident abroad.

Receipts from tourism (US $ million, incl. passenger transport): 7,005 in 2003; 8,226 in 2004; 8,148 in 2005.

Source: World Tourism Organization.

Communications Media

	2004	2005	2006
Telephones ('000 main lines in use)	26,058.1	23,745.2	26,865.9
Mobile cellular telephones ('000 subscribers)	36,586.1	38,342.3	40,971.1
Personal computers ('000 in use)	26,201	n.a.	n.a.
Internet users ('000)	31,580	33,010	34,120
Broadband subscribers ('000)	11,921.4	12,190.7	14,042.7
Book production:			
titles	27,527	n.a.	n.a.
copies ('000)	82,097	n.a.	n.a.
Registered daily newspapers (titles)	168	187	203

1996: Facsimile machines (estimate, '000 in use): 400.

1997: Radio receivers ('000 in use) 47,500.

2000: Television receivers ('000 in use) 17,229.

Sources: mainly UNESCO, *Statistical Yearbook*; UN, *Statistical Yearbook*; International Telecommunication Union; Korean Association of Newspapers.

Education

(2005)

	Institutions	Teachers	Pupils
Kindergarten	8,275	31,033	541,603
Primary schools	5,646	160,143	4,022,801
Middle schools	2,935	103,835	2,010,704
General high schools	1,382	79,158	1,259,792
Vocational high schools	713	37,253	503,104
Junior colleges	158	12,027	853,089
Teachers' colleges	11	798	25,141
Universities and colleges	173	49,200	1,859,639
Graduate schools	1,051	1,673	282,225

Adult literacy rate (UNESCO estimates): 97.9% (males 99.2%; females 96.6%) in 2001 (Source: UN Development Programme, *Human Development Report*).

Directory

Note: from 2001 the romanization of place-names in South Korea was in the process of change. Transliteration of names of people and corporations was to remain unchanged for the time being.

The Constitution

The Constitution of the Sixth Republic (Ninth Amendment) was approved by national referendum on 29 October 1987. It came into effect on 25 February 1988. The main provisions are summarized below:

THE EXECUTIVE

The President

The President shall be elected by universal, equal, direct and secret ballot of the people for one term of five years. Re-election of the President is prohibited. In times of national emergency and under certain conditions the President may issue emergency orders and take emergency action with regard to budgetary and economic matters. The President shall notify the National Assembly of these measures and obtain its concurrence, or they shall lose effect. He may, in times of war, armed conflict or similar national emergency, declare martial law in accordance with the provisions of law. He shall lift the emergency measures and martial law when the National Assembly so requests with the concurrence of a majority of the members. The President may not dissolve the National Assembly. He is authorized to take directly to the people important issues through national referendums. The President shall appoint the Prime Minister (with the consent of the National Assembly) and other public officials.

The State Council

The State Council shall be composed of the President, the Prime Minister and no more than 30 and no fewer than 15 others appointed by the President (on the recommendation of the Prime Minister), and shall deliberate on policies that fall within the power of the executive. No member of the armed forces shall be a member of the Council, unless retired from active duty.

The Board of Audit and Inspection

The Board of Audit and Inspection shall be established under the President to inspect the closing of accounts of revenue and expenditures, the accounts of the State and other organizations as prescribed by law, and to inspect the administrative functions of the executive agencies and public officials. It shall be composed of no fewer than five and no more than 11 members, including the Chairman. The Chairman shall be appointed by the President with the consent of the National Assembly, and the members by the President on the recommendation of the Chairman. Appointments shall be for four years and members may be reappointed only once.

THE NATIONAL ASSEMBLY

Legislative power shall be vested in the National Assembly. The Assembly shall be composed of not fewer than 200 members, a number determined by law, elected for four years by universal, equal, direct and secret ballot. The constituencies of members of the Assembly, proportional representation and other matters pertaining

THE REPUBLIC OF KOREA (SOUTH KOREA)

to the Assembly elections shall be determined by law. A regular session shall be held once a year and extraordinary sessions shall be convened upon requests of the President or one-quarter of the Assembly's members. The period of regular sessions shall not exceed 100 days and of extraordinary sessions 30 days. The Assembly has the power to recommend to the President the removal of the Prime Minister or any other Minister. The Assembly shall have the authority to pass a motion for the impeachment of the President or any other public official, and may inspect or investigate state affairs, under procedures to be established by law.

THE CONSTITUTIONAL COURT

The Constitutional Court shall be composed of nine members appointed by the President, three of whom shall be appointed from persons selected by the National Assembly and three from persons nominated by the Chief Justice. The term of office shall be six years. It shall pass judgment upon the constitutionality of laws upon the request of the courts, matters of impeachment and the dissolution of political parties. In these judgments the concurrence of six members or more shall be required.

THE JUDICIARY

The courts shall be composed of the Supreme Court, which is the highest court of the State, and other courts at specified levels (for further details, see section on Judicial System). The Chief Justice and justices of the Supreme Court are appointed by the President, subject to the consent of the National Assembly. When the constitutionality of a law is a prerequisite to a trial, the Court shall request a decision of the Constitutional Court. The Supreme Court shall have the power to pass judgment upon the constitutionality or legality of administrative decrees, and shall have final appellate jurisdiction over military tribunals. No judge shall be removed from office except following impeachment or a sentence of imprisonment.

ELECTION MANAGEMENT

Election Commissions shall be established for the purpose of fair management of elections and national referendums. The National Election Commission shall be composed of three members appointed by the President, three appointed by the National Assembly and three appointed by the Chief Justice of the Supreme Court. Their term of office is six years, and they may not be expelled from office except following impeachment or a sentence of imprisonment.

POLITICAL PARTIES

The establishment of political parties shall be free and the plural party system guaranteed. However, a political party whose aims or activities are contrary to the basic democratic order may be dissolved by the Constitutional Court.

AMENDMENTS

A motion to amend the Constitution shall be proposed by the President or by a majority of the total number of members of the National Assembly. Amendments extending the President's term of office or permitting the re-election of the President shall not be effective for the President in office at the time of the proposal. Proposed amendments to the Constitution shall be put before the public by the President for 20 days or more. Within 60 days of the public announcement, the National Assembly shall decide upon the proposed amendments, which require a two-thirds' majority of the National Assembly. They shall then be submitted to a national referendum not later than 30 days after passage by the National Assembly and shall be determined by more than one-half of votes cast by more than one-half of voters eligible to vote in elections for members of the National Assembly. If these conditions are fulfilled, the proposed amendments shall be finalized and the President shall promulgate them without delay.

FUNDAMENTAL RIGHTS

Under the Constitution all citizens are equal before the law. The right of habeas corpus is guaranteed. Freedom of speech, press, assembly and association are guaranteed, as are freedom of choice of residence and occupation. No state religion is to be recognized and freedom of conscience and religion is guaranteed. Citizens are protected against retrospective legislation, and may not be punished without due process of law.

Rights and freedoms may be restricted by law when this is deemed necessary for the maintenance of national security, order or public welfare. When such restrictions are imposed, no essential aspect of the right or freedom in question may be violated.

GENERAL PROVISIONS

Peaceful unification of the Korean peninsula, on the principles of liberal democracy, is the prime national aspiration. The Constitution mandates the State to establish and implement a policy of unification. The Constitution expressly stipulates that the armed forces must maintain political neutrality at all times.

The Government

HEAD OF STATE

President: LEE MYUNG-BAK (took office 25 February 2008).

STATE COUNCIL
(April 2008)

Prime Minister: HAN SEUNG-SOO.
Minister for Strategy and Finance: KANG MAN-SOO.
Minister of Unification: KIM HA-JOONG.
Minister of Foreign Affairs and Trade: YU MYUNG-HWAN.
Minister of Justice: KIM KYUNG-HAN.
Minister of National Defence: LEE SANG-HEE.
Minister of Public Administration and Security: WON SEI-HOON.
Minister of Education, Science and Technology: KIM DOH-YEON.
Minister of Culture, Sports and Tourism: YU IN-CHON.
Minister of Food, Agriculture, Forestry and Fisheries: CHUNG WOON-CHUN.
Minister of Knowledge Economy: LEE YOUN-HO.
Minister of Health, Welfare and Family Affairs: KIM SOUNG-YEE.
Minister of the Environment: LEE MAN-EUI.
Minister of Labour: LEE YOUNG-HEE.
Minister of Gender Equality: BYUN DO-YOON.
Minister of Land, Transport and Maritime Affairs: CHUNG JONG-HWAN.

MINISTRIES

Office of the President: Chong Wa Dae (The Blue House), 1, Sejong-no, Jongno-gu, Seoul; tel. (2) 770-0055; fax (2) 770-0344; e-mail president@cwd.go.kr; internet www.bluehouse.go.kr.

Office of the Prime Minister: 77, Sejong-no, Jongno-gu, Seoul; tel. (2) 737-0094; fax (2) 739-5830; e-mail m-opm@opm.go.kr; internet www.opm.go.kr.

Ministry of Culture, Sports and Tourism: 82-1, Sejong-no, Jongno-gu, Seoul 110-703; tel. (2) 3704-9114; fax (2) 3704-9119; e-mail webadmin@www.mct.go.kr; internet www.mcst.go.kr.

Ministry of Education, Science and Technology: 77-6, Sejong-no, Jongno-gu, Seoul 110-760; tel. (2) 2100-6570; fax (2) 2100-6579; internet www.mest.go.kr.

Ministry of Environment: 1, Jungang-dong, Gwacheon City, Gyeonggi Prov. 427-729; tel. (2) 2110-6546; fax (2) 504-9277; e-mail chanchan@me.go.kr; internet www.me.go.kr.

Ministry for Food, Agriculture, Forestry and Fisheries: 3-108 Gwacheon Government Office Bldg, 1, Jungang-dong, Gwacheon City, Gyeonggi Prov.; tel. (2) 2110-4000; fax (2) 503-7238; e-mail wmaster@maf.go.kr; internet www.mifaff.go.kr.

Ministry of Foreign Affairs and Trade: 95-1, Doryeom-dong, Jongno-gu, Seoul 110-787; tel. (2) 3703-2114; fax (2) 2100-7999; e-mail web@mofat.go.kr; internet www.mofat.go.kr.

Ministry of Gender Equality: 55, Sejong-no, 1-ga, Jongno-gu, Seoul 110-760; tel. (2) 2100-6600; fax (2) 2106-5145; e-mail webadmin@mogef.go.kr; internet www.moge.go.kr.

Ministry for Health, Welfare and Family Affairs: 1, Jungang-dong, Gwacheon City, Gyeonggi Prov. 427-721; tel. (2) 502-8272; fax (2) 2110-6453; e-mail webmaster@mohw.go.kr; internet www.mohw.go.kr.

Ministry of Justice: 1, Jungang-dong, Gwacheon City, Gyeonggi Prov.; tel. (2) 503-7023; fax (2) 504-3337; e-mail webmaster@moj.go.kr; internet www.moj.go.kr.

Ministry of Knowledge Economy: 3, Jungang-dong, Gwacheon City, Gyeonggi Prov. 427-721; tel. (2) 2110-5291; fax (2) 503-3142; internet www.mke.go.kr.

Ministry of Labour: 1, Jungang-dong, Gwacheon City, Gyeonggi Prov. 427-716; tel. (2) 503-9713; fax (2) 503-8862; e-mail m_molab@molab.go.kr; internet www.molab.go.kr.

Ministry of Land, Transport and Maritime Affairs: 1, Jungang-dong, Gwacheon City, Gyeonggi Prov. 427-712; tel. (2) 504-9114; fax (2) 503-7400; e-mail webmaster@moct.go.kr; internet www.mltm.go.kr.

THE REPUBLIC OF KOREA (SOUTH KOREA)

Ministry of National Defence: 1, 3-ga, Yeongsan-dong, Yeongsan-gu, Seoul 140-701; tel. (2) 795-0071; fax (2) 703-3109; e-mail cyber@mnd.go.kr; internet www.mnd.go.kr.

Ministry of Public Administration and Security: Central Government Complex, 77-6, Sejong-no, 1-ga, Jongno-gu, Seoul 110-760; tel. (2) 2100-6767; fax (2) 3703-5502; e-mail hdchoi@mogaha.go.kr; internet www.mopas.go.kr.

Ministry of Strategy and Finance: Government Complex II, 88 Gwanmunro, Gwacheon City, Gyeonggi Prov. 427-725; tel. (2) 2110-2348; fax (2) 504-1335; e-mail fppr@mofe.go.kr; internet www.mofe.go.kr.

Ministry of Unification: 77-6, Sejong-no, Jongno-gu, Seoul 110-760; tel. (2) 720-2424; fax (2) 720-2149; e-mail ispark@unikorea.go.kr; internet www.unikorea.go.kr.

President and Legislature

PRESIDENT

Election, 19 December 2007

Candidate	Votes	% of total
Lee Myung-Bak (Grand National Party)	11,492,389	48.7
Chung Dong-Young (United New Democratic Party)*	6,174,681	26.1
Lee Hoi-Chang (Independent)	3,559,963	15.1
Moon Kuk-Hyun (Creative Korea Party)	1,375,498	5.8
Kwon Young-Gil (Democratic Labour Party)	712,121	3.0
Lee In-Je (Democratic Party)	160,708	0.7
Huh Kyung-Young (Economic Republican Party)	96,756	0.4
Geum Min (Korea Socialist Party)	18,223	0.1
Chung Kun-Mo (True Owner Coalition)	15,380	0.1
Chun Kwan (Chamsaram Society Full True Act)	7,161	0.0
Total (incl. others)	23,732,854	100.0

* The United New Democratic Party changed its name to the United Democratic Party in February 2008.

LEGISLATURE

Kuk Hoe
(National Assembly)

1 Yeouido-dong, Yeongdeungpo-gu, Seoul 150-701; tel. (2) 788-2001; fax (2) 788-3375; e-mail webmaster@assembly.go.kr; internet www.assembly.go.kr.

Speaker: LIM CHAE-JUNG.

General Election, 9 April 2008

Party	Elected	Proportional	Total
Grand National Party	131	22	153
United Democratic Party	66	15	81
Liberty Forward Party	14	4	18
Pro-Park Coalition*	6	8	14
Democratic Labour Party	2	3	5
Creative Korea Party	1	2	3
Independents	25	—	25
Total	245	54	299

* Comprising supporters of Park Geun-Hye, former Chairwoman of the GNP.

Election Commission

National Election Commission: 2-3 Junggang-dong, Gwacheon-si, Gyeonggi-do 427-727; tel. (2) 504-2761; e-mail e_nec@nec.go.kr; internet www.nec.go.kr; Chair. KOH HYUN-CHUL.

Political Organizations

Centrist Reformists Democratic Party: 25-4, Yeouido-dong, Yeongdeungpo-gu, Seoul; tel. (2) 784-7007; fax (2) 780-4074; internet minjoo.org.kr; f. 2005; fmrly Millennium Democratic Party; Pres. LEE IN-JE.

Creative Korea Party (CKP): 28-130, Yeongdeungpo 2-dong, Yeongdeungpo-gu, Seoul; tel. (2) 784-4701; fax (2) 784-4705; internet www.ckp.kr; f. 2007; Pres. MOON KOOK-HYUN.

Democratic Labour Party (DLP): 25-1, Jongdo Bldg, Moonrae-dong, Yeongdeungpo-gu, Seoul; tel. (2) 2139-7777; fax (2) 2139-7890; e-mail kdlpinter@hotmail.com; internet www.kdlp.org; f. 2000; Pres. KIM HYE-KYUNG.

Grand National Party (GNP) (Hannara Party): 247-17, Yeomchang-dong, Gangseo-gu, Seoul 157-863; tel. (2) 3786-3000; fax (2) 3786-3610; internet www.hannara.or.kr; f. 1997; est. by merger of Democratic Party and New Korea Party; Chair. KANG JAE-SEOP.

Korea Socialist Party: BS Tower, 106-7 Nogosan-dong, Mapo-gu, Seoul; tel. (2) 711-4592; fax (2) 706-4118; internet sp.or.kr; f. 1998; Pres. GEUM MIN.

Liberty Forward Party (LFP): c/o National Assembly, 1 Yeouido-dong, Yeongdeungpo-gu, Seoul 150-701 1 Seoul; tel. (2) 780-3988; e-mail master@new-party.org; internet www.jayou.or.kr; Leader LEE HOI-CHANG.

United Democratic Party (UDP): 15–16 Yeouido-dong, Yeongdeungpo-gu, Seoul 150-701; e-mail help@undp.kr; internet minjoo.kr; f. 2007; Pres. SOH HAK-KYU; est. as United New Democratic Party in 2007 by defectors and mems of the Uri Party and the Democratic Party; name changed to above following merger with Democratic Party in 2008.

Other parties that presented candidates for the 2007 presidential election were the Economic Republican Party, the True Owner Coalition and the Chamsaram Society Full True Act.

Civic groups play an increasingly significant role in South Korean politics. These include: the People's Solidarity for Participatory Democracy (Dir JANG HASUNG); the Citizens' Coalition for Economic Justice (Sec.-Gen. PARK BYEONG-OK); and the Citizens' Alliance for Political Reform (Leader KIM SOK-SU).

Diplomatic Representation

EMBASSIES IN THE REPUBLIC OF KOREA

Afghanistan: 27-2, Hannam-dong, Yeongsan-gu, Seoul 140-210; tel. (2) 793-3535; fax (2) 795-2662; e-mail info@afghanistanembassy.or.kr; internet www.afghanistanembassy.or.kr; Ambassador MOHAMMAD KARIM RAHIMI.

Algeria: 2-6, Itaewon 2-dong, Yeongsan-gu, Seoul 140-857; tel. (2) 794-5034; fax (2) 794-5040; e-mail sifdja01@kornet.net; internet www.algerianemb.or.kr; Ambassador RABAH HADID.

Argentina: Chun Woo Bldg, 5th Floor, 534 Itaewon-dong, Yeongsan-gu, Seoul 140-861; tel. (2) 793-4062; fax (2) 792-5820; e-mail info@argentina.or.kr; internet www.argentina.or.kr; Ambassador ALFREDO A. ALCORTA.

Australia: Kyobo Bldg, 11th Floor, 1, 1-ga, Jongno-gu, Seoul 110-714; tel. (2) 2003-0100; fax (2) 722-9264; e-mail seoul-inform@dfat.gov.au; internet www.southkorea.embassy.gov.au; Ambassador PETER ROWE.

Austria: Kyobo Bldg, Rm 1913, 1-1, 1-ga, Jongno, Jongno-gu, Seoul 110-714; tel. (2) 732-9071; fax (2) 732-9486; e-mail seoul-ob@bmeia.gv.at; internet www.bmeia.gv.at/seoul; Ambassador WILHELM DONKO.

Azerbaijan: 3/F, Annex Bldg, Hannam Tower, 730 Hannam-dong, Yeongsan-gu, Seoul 140-893; tel. (2) 797-1765; fax (2) 792-1767; e-mail seoul@mission.mfa.gov.az; internet www.azembassy.co.kr; Ambassador ROVSHAN JAMSHIDOV.

Bangladesh: 7-18, Woo Sung Bldg, Dongbinggo-dong, Yeongsan-gu, Seoul; tel. (2) 796-4056; fax (2) 790-5313; Ambassador MOHAMMAD SHAHIDUL ISLAM.

Belarus: 432-1636 Sindang 2-dong, Jung-gu, Seoul; tel. (2) 2237-8171; fax (2) 2237-8174; e-mail korea@belembassy.org; internet korea.belembassy.org; Ambassador ALEKSANDR GURYANOV.

Belgium: 737-10, Hannam-dong, Yeongsan-gu, Seoul 140-895; tel. (2) 749-0381; fax (2) 797-1688; e-mail seoul@diplobel.org; internet www.belgium.or.kr; Ambassador VICTOR WEI.

Brazil: Ihn Gallery Bldg, 4th and 5th Floors, 141 Palpan-dong, Jongno-gu, Seoul; tel. (2) 738-4970; fax (2) 738-4974; e-mail braseul@kornet.net; internet www.brasemb.or.kr; Ambassador CELINA ASSUMPÇÃO DO VALLE PEREIRA.

Brunei: 737-11, Hannam-dong, Yeongsan-gu, Seoul 140-210; tel. (2) 790-1078; fax (2) 790-1084; e-mail kbnbd_seoul@yahoo.com; Ambassador Dato' PADUKA HAJI HARUN BIN HJ ISMAIL.

Bulgaria: 723-42, Hannam 2-dong, Yeongsan-gu, Seoul 140-894; tel. (2) 794-8626; fax (2) 794-8627; e-mail ebdy1990@unitel.co.kr; Ambassador ALEXANDER SAVOV.

THE REPUBLIC OF KOREA (SOUTH KOREA)

Cambodia: 657-162, Hannam-dong, Yeongsan-gu, Seoul 140-910; tel. (2) 3785-1041; fax (2) 3785-1040; e-mail camboemb@korea.com; Ambassador LIM SAMKOL.

Canada: POB 6299, 9/F Kolon Bldg, 45, Mugyo-dong, Jung-gu, Seoul; tel. (2) 3455-6000; fax (2) 3455-6123; e-mail canada@cec.or.kr; internet www.korea.gc.ca; Ambassador TED LIPMAN.

Chile: 1801 Coryo Daeyungak Tower, 25-5 Chungmoro 1-ga, Jung-gu, Seoul 100-706; tel. (2) 779-2610; fax (2) 779-2615; e-mail echilekr@yahoo.co.kr; internet www.echilecor.or.kr; Ambassador ADOLFO CARAFÍ MELERO.

China, People's Republic: 54, Hyoja-dong, Jongno-gu, Seoul; tel. (2) 738-1038; fax (2) 738-1059; e-mail chinaemb_kr@mfa.gov.cn; internet www.chinaemb.or.kr; Ambassador NING FUKUI.

Colombia: Kyobo Bldg, 13th Floor, 1-ga, Jongno, Jongno-gu, Seoul; tel. (2) 720-1369; fax (2) 725-6959; e-mail eseul@cancilleria.gov.co; Ambassador ALEJANDRO BORDA ROJAS.

Congo, Democratic Republic: 702, Daewoo Complex Bldg, 167 Naesu-dong, Jongno-gu, Seoul; tel. (2) 722-7958; fax (2) 722-7998; e-mail congokoreambassy@yahoo.com; Ambassador N. CHRISTOPHE NGWEY.

Costa Rica: Iljin Bldg, 7, 50-1, Dohwa-dong, Mapo-gu, Seoul 121-040; tel. (2) 707-9248; fax (2) 707-9255; e-mail embajadacr@ecostarica.or.kr; internet www.ecostarica.or.kr; Ambassador FERNANDO BORBÓN ARIAS.

Côte d'Ivoire: Chungam Bldg, 2nd Floor, 794-4, Hannam-dong, Yeongsan-gu, Seoul; tel. (2) 3785-0561; fax (2) 3785-0564; e-mail abenikof@hotmail.com; Ambassador HONORAT ABENI KOFFI.

Czech Republic: 1-121, 2-ga, Shinmun-ro, Jongno-gu, Seoul 110-062; tel. (2) 725-6765; fax (2) 734-6452; e-mail seoul@embassy.mzv.cz; internet www.mzv.cz/seoul; Ambassador TOMÁŠ SMETÁNKA.

Denmark: Namsong Bldg, 5th Floor, 260-199, Itaewon-dong, Yeongsan-gu, Seoul 140-200; tel. (2) 795-4187; fax (2) 796-0986; e-mail selamb@um.dk; internet www.ambseoul.um.dk; Ambassador POUL O. G. HOINESS.

Dominican Republic: Taepyeong-no Bldg, 19th Floor, 2-ga, 310 Taepyeong-no, Jung-gu, Seoul; tel. (2) 756-3513; fax (2) 756-3514; e-mail embadom@kornet.net; Ambassador HÉCTOR GALUÁN.

Ecuador: Korea First Bldg, 19th Floor, 100, Gongpyeong-dong, Jongno-gu, Seoul; tel. (2) 739-2401; fax (2) 739-2355; e-mail mecuadorcor1@kornet.net; Ambassador JOSÉ ENRIQUE NÚÑEZ TAMAYO.

Egypt: POB 3734, 46-1, Hannam-dong, Yeongsan-gu, Seoul 140-210; tel. (2) 749-0787; fax (2) 795-2588; e-mail embassyegyptkorea@yahoo.com; Ambassador MOHAMED REDA KAMEL EL-TAIFY.

El Salvador: Samsung Life Insurance Bldg, 20th Floor, Taepyeong-no 2-ga, Jung-gu, Seoul 100-716; tel. (2) 753-3432; fax (2) 753-3456; e-mail koembsal@hananet.net; Ambassador ZOILA DEL CARMEN AGUIRRE DE MAY.

Finland: POB 1602, Kyobo Bldg 15/F, Suite 1602, 1-1, 1-ga, Jongno, Jongno-gu, Seoul 110-714; tel. (2) 732-6737; fax (2) 723-4969; e-mail sanomat.seo@formin.fi; internet www.finland.or.kr; Ambassador KIM LUOTONEN.

France: 30, Hap-dong, Seodaemun-gu, Seoul 120-030; tel. (2) 3149-4300; fax (2) 3149-4328; e-mail ambafrance@korea.com; internet www.ambafrance-kr.org; Ambassador PHILIPPE THIÉBAUD.

Gabon: Yoosung Bldg, 4th Floor, 738-20, Hannam-dong, Yeongsan-gu, Seoul; tel. (2) 793-9575; fax (2) 793-9574; e-mail amgabsel@unitel.co.kr; Ambassador JEAN-PIERRE SOLE-EMANE.

Germany: 308-5, Dongbinggo-dong, Yeongsan-gu, Seoul 140-816; tel. (2) 748-4114; fax (2) 748-4161; e-mail info@seoul.diplo.de; internet www.seoul.diplo.de; Ambassador NORBERT BAAS.

Ghana: 5-4, Hannam-dong, Yeongsan-gu, Seoul (CPOB 3887); tel. (2) 3785-1427; fax (2) 3785-1428; e-mail ghana3@kornet.net; internet www.ghanaembassy.or.kr; Ambassador (vacant).

Greece: Hanwha Bldg, 27th Floor, 1, Janggyo-dong, Jung-gu, Seoul 100-797; tel. (2) 729-1401; fax (2) 729-1402; e-mail greekemb@kornet.net; Ambassador KONSTANTINOS DRAKAKIS.

Guatemala: 614, Lotte Hotel, 1, Sogong-dong, Jung-gu, Seoul 100-635; tel. (2) 771-7582; fax (2) 771-7584; e-mail embcorea@minex.gob.gt; Ambassador RAFAEL A. SALAZAR.

Holy See: POB 393, Kwang Hwa Mun, Seoul 110-603 (Apostolic Nunciature); tel. (2) 736-5725; fax (2) 739-5738; e-mail nunseoul@kornet.net; Apostolic Nuncio Most Rev. EMIL PAUL TSCHERRIG (Titular Archbishop of Voli).

Honduras: Jongno Tower Bldg, 2nd Floor, 6, Jongno 2-ga, Jongno-gu, Seoul 110-160; tel. (2) 738-8402; fax (2) 738-8403; e-mail hondseul@kornet.net; Ambassador RENE FRANCISCO UMANA CHINCHILLA.

Hungary: 1-103, Dongbinggo-dong, Yeongsan-gu, Seoul 140-230; tel. (2) 792-2105; fax (2) 792-2109; e-mail mission.sel@kum.hu; internet www.mfa.gov.hu/emb/seoul; Ambassador MIKLÓS LENGYEL.

India: 37-3, Hannam-dong, Yeongsan-gu, CPOB 3466, Seoul 140-210; tel. (2) 798-4257; fax (2) 796-9534; e-mail eoiseoul@sinbiro.com; internet www.indembassy.or.kr; Ambassador N. PARTHASARATHI.

Indonesia: 55, Yeouido-dong, Yeongdeungpo-gu, Seoul 150-010; tel. (2) 783-5675; fax (2) 780-4280; e-mail komsel@soback.kornet.nm.kr; internet www.indonesiaseoul.org; Ambassador JAKOB TOBING.

Iran: 726-126, Hannam-dong, Yeongsan-gu, Seoul; tel. (2) 793-7751; fax (2) 792-7052; e-mail iranemb@hotmail.com; Ambassador MOHAMMAD REZA BAKHTIARI.

Iraq: 310-49, Dongbinggo-dong, Yeongsan-gu, Seoul; tel. (2) 792-6671; fax (2) 792-6674.

Ireland: Daehan Fire and Marine Insurance Bldg, 15th Floor, 51-1, Namchang-dong, Jung-gu, Seoul; tel. (2) 774-6455; fax (2) 774-6458; e-mail irelandkor@kornet.net; internet www.irelandhouse-korea.com/embassy.html; Ambassador CONOR MURPHY.

Israel: 18th Fl., Kabool Bldg, 149 Seorin-dong, Jongno-gu, Seoul 110-726; tel. (2) 739-8666; fax (2) 739-8667; e-mail seoul@israel.org; internet seoul.mfa.gov.il; Ambassador YIGAL B. CASPI.

Italy: 1-398, Hannam-dong, Yeongsan-gu, Seoul 140-210; tel. (2) 796-0491; fax (2) 797-5560; e-mail embassy.seoul@esteri.it; internet www.ambseoul.esteri.it; Ambassador MASSIMO ANDREA LEGGERI.

Japan: 18-11, Junghak-dong, Jongno-gu, Seoul; tel. (2) 2170-5200; fax (2) 734-4528; e-mail info@japanem.or.kr; internet www.kr.emb-japan.go.jp; Ambassador TOSHINORI SHIGEIE.

Kazakhstan: 484-24, Bukak Village 11, Pyeongchang-dong, Jongno-gu, Seoul; tel. (2) 379-9714; fax (2) 395-9719; e-mail kazkor@chollian.net; internet www.kazembassy.org; Ambassador DULAT BAKISHEV.

Kuwait: 309-15, Dongbinggo-dong, Yeongsan-gu, Seoul; tel. (2) 749-3688; fax (2) 749-3687; Ambassador MOHAMMED ABDULRASUL AL-AWADI.

Laos: 657-93, Hannam-dong, Yeongsan-gu, Seoul; tel. (2) 796-1713; fax (2) 796-1771; e-mail laoseoul@korea.com; Ambassador SOUKTHAVONE KEOLA.

Lebanon: 310-49, Dongbinggo-dong, Yeongsan-gu, Seoul 140-230; tel. (2) 794-6482; fax (2) 794-6485; e-mail emleb@lebanonembassy.net; internet www.lebanonembassy.net; Ambassador ISSAM MUSTAPHA.

Malaysia: 4-1, Hannam-dong, Yeongsan-gu, Seoul 140-884; tel. (2) 795-9203; fax (2) 794-5480; e-mail mwseoul@kornet.net; internet www.malaysia.or.kr; Ambassador Dato' M. SANTHANANABAN.

Mexico: 33-6, Hannam 1-dong, Yeongsan-gu, Seoul 140-885; tel. (2) 798-1694; fax (2) 790-0939; e-mail srecor@uriel.net; internet portal.sre.gob.mx/corea; Ambassador LEANDRO ARELLANO.

Mongolia: 33-5, Hannam-dong, Yeongsan-gu, Seoul 140–885; tel. (2) 794-1350; fax (2) 794-7605; e-mail mongol5@kornet.net; internet www.mongolembassy.com; Ambassador DORJPALAMYN GEREL.

Morocco: S-15, UN Village, 270-3, Hannam-dong, Yeongsan-gu, Seoul; tel. (2) 793-6249; fax (2) 792-8178; e-mail sifamase@kornet.net; internet www.moroccoemb.or.kr; Ambassador AHMED BOURZAIM.

Myanmar: 724-1, Hannam-dong, Yeongsan-gu, Seoul 140-210; tel. (2) 792-3341; fax (2) 796-5570; e-mail myanmare@ppp.kornet.net; Ambassador U NYO WIN.

Nepal: 244-143, Huam-dong, Yeongsan-gu, Seoul; tel. (2) 3789-9770; fax (2) 736-8848; e-mail info@nepembseoul.gov.np; internet www.nepembseoul.gov.np; Ambassador KAMAL KOIRALA.

Netherlands: Kyobo Bldg, 14th Floor, 1-ga, Jongno, Jongno-gu, Seoul 110-714; tel. (2) 737-9514; fax (2) 735-1321; e-mail seo@minbuza.nl; internet www.nlembassy.or.kr; Ambassador HANS HEINSBROEK.

New Zealand: Kyobo Bldg, 15th Floor, 1, 1-ga, Jongno, Jongno-gu, KPO Box 2258, Seoul 110-110; tel. (2) 3701-7700; fax (2) 3701-7701; e-mail nzembsel@kornet.net; internet www.nzembassy.com/korea; Ambassador JANE COOMBS.

Nigeria: 310-19, Dongbinggo-dong, Yeongsan-gu, Seoul; tel. (2) 797-2370; fax (2) 796-1848; e-mail chancery@nigerianembassy.or.kr; internet www.nigerianembassy.or.kr; Ambassador ABBA A. TIJJANI.

Norway: 258-8, Itaewon-dong, Yeongsan-gu, Seoul 140-200; tel. (2) 795-6850; fax (2) 798-6072; e-mail emb.seoul@mfa.no; internet www.norway.or.kr; Ambassador DIDRIK TØNSETH.

Oman: 309-3, Dongbinggo-dong, Yeongsan-gu, Seoul; tel. (2) 790-2431; fax (2) 790-2430; e-mail omanembs@ppp.kornet.nm.kr; Ambassador MOUSSA HAMDAN AT-TAE.

Pakistan: 124-13, Itaewon-dong, Yeongsan-gu, Seoul 140-200; tel. (2) 796-8252; fax (2) 796-0313; Ambassador MURAD ALI.

Panama: Northgate Bldg, 6th Floor, 66, Jeokseon-dong, Jongno-gu, Seoul; tel. (2) 734-8610; fax (2) 734-8613; e-mail panaemba@kornet.net; Ambassador JUAN JOSÉ AMADO, III.

THE REPUBLIC OF KOREA (SOUTH KOREA)

Papua New Guinea: 36-1, Hannam 1-dong, Yeongsan-gu, Seoul; tel. (2) 798-9854; fax (2) 798-9856; e-mail pngembsl@ppp.kornet.nm.kr; Ambassador KUMA AUA.

Paraguay: Hannam Tower Annex Bldg, 3rd Floor, 730 Hannam-dong, Yeongsan-gu, Seoul; tel. (2) 792-8335; fax (2) 792-8334; e-mail pyemc2@kornet.net; internet www.embaparcorea.org; Ambassador CEFERINO ADRIAN VALDEZ PERALTA.

Peru: Daeyungak Bldg, Suite 2002, 25-5, 1-ga, Jungmu-no, Jung-gu, Seoul 100-706; tel. (2) 757-1735; fax (2) 757-1738; e-mail lpruseul@uriel.net; Ambassador DORALIZA LÓPEZ BRAVO VDA DE RUÍZ.

Philippines: 34-44, Itaewon 1-dong, Yeongsan-gu, Seoul; tel. (2) 796-7387; fax (2) 796-0827; e-mail seoulpe@gmail.com; Ambassador LUIS TEODORO CRUZ.

Poland: 70, Sagan-dong, Jongno-gu, Seoul; tel. (2) 723-9681; fax (2) 723-9680; e-mail embassy@polandseoul.org; internet www.polandseoul.org; Ambassador MAREK CAŁKA.

Portugal: Wonseo Bldg, 2nd Floor, 171, Wonseo-dong, Jongno-gu, Seoul; tel. (2) 3675-2251; fax (2) 3675-2250; e-mail ambport@chollian.net; Ambassador HENRIQUE SILVEIRA BORGES.

Qatar: 309-5, Dongbinggo-dong, Yeongsan-gu, Seoul 140-817; tel. (2) 798-2444; fax (2) 790-1027; e-mail qatarseoul@hotmail.com; Ambassador AHMAD S. AL-MIDHADI.

Romania: 1-42, UN Village, Hannam-dong, Yeongsan-gu, Seoul 140-210; tel. (2) 797-4924; fax (2) 794-3114; e-mail romemb@uriel.net; Chargé d'affaires a.i. CONSTANTIN SOARE.

Russia: 34-16, Jeong-dong, Jung-gu, Seoul 100-120; tel. (2) 318-2116; fax (2) 754-0417; e-mail rusemb@uriel.net; internet www.russian-embassy.org; Ambassador GLEB A. IVASHENTSOV.

Saudi Arabia: 1-112, 2-ga, Sinmun-no, Jongno-gu, Seoul; tel. (2) 739-0631; fax (2) 732-3110; Ambassador ABDULLAH A AL-A'IFAN.

Serbia, Republic: 730 Hannam-dong, Yeongsan-gu, Seoul; tel. (2) 797-5109; fax (2) 790-6109; e-mail emserbseul@yahoo.com; internet www.embserb.or.kr; Ambassador ZORAN VELJIĆ.

Singapore: Seoul Finance Bldg, 28th Floor, 84, 1-ga, Taepyeong-no, Jung-gu, Seoul 100-102; tel. (2) 774-2464; fax (2) 773-2465; e-mail singemb@unitel.co.kr; internet www.mfa.gov.sg/seoul; Ambassador CHUA THAI KEONG.

Slovakia: 389-1, Hannam-dong, Yeongsan-gu, Seoul 140-210; tel. (2) 794-3981; fax (2) 794-3982; e-mail slovakemb@yahoo.com; Ambassador PAVEL HRMO.

South Africa: 1-37, Hannam-dong, Yeongsan-gu, Seoul 140-210; tel. (2) 792-4855; fax (2) 792-4856; e-mail general@southafrica-embassy.or.kr; internet www.southafrica-embassy.or.kr; Ambassador STEFANUS JOHANNES SCHOEMAN.

Spain: 726-52, Hannam-dong, Yeongsan-gu, Seoul; tel. (2) 794-3581; fax (2) 796-8207; e-mail emb.seul@mae.es; internet www.mae.es/embajadas/seul/es/home; Ambassador DELFÍN COLOMÉ PUJOL.

Sri Lanka: Kyobo Bldg, Rm 2002, 1-1, 1-ga, Jongno, Jongno-gu, Seoul 110-714; tel. (2) 735-2966; fax (2) 737-9577; e-mail lankaemb@chollian.net; Ambassador JOHN ASITHA IVON PERERA.

Sudan: 653-24, Hannam-dong, Yeongsan-gu, Seoul; tel. (2) 793-8692; fax (2) 793-8693; e-mail sudansol@yahoo.com; Ambassador MOHAMMED SALAH ELDIN ABBAS.

Sweden: Seoul Central Bldg, 12th Floor, 136, Seorin-dong, Jongno-gu, KPO Box 1154, Seoul 110-611; tel. (2) 3703-3700; fax (2) 3703-3701; e-mail embassy@swedemb.or.kr; internet www.swedenabroad.com/seoul; Ambassador LARS VARGÖ.

Switzerland: 32-10, Songwol-dong, Jongno-gu, POB 2900, Seoul 110-101; tel. (2) 739-9511; fax (2) 737-9392; e-mail swissemb@elim.net; internet www.eda.admin.ch/seoul; Ambassador CHRISTIAN HAUSWIRTH.

Thailand: 653-7, Hannam-dong, Yeongsan-gu, Seoul 140-210; tel. (2) 795-3098; fax (2) 798-3448; e-mail rteseoul@kornet.net; internet www.thaiembassy.or.kr; Ambassador VASIN TEERAVECHYAN.

Tunisia: 1-17, Dongbinggo-dong, Yeongsan-gu, Seoul 140-809; tel. (2) 790-4334; fax (2) 790-4333; e-mail ambtnkor@kornet.net; Ambassador MUSTAPHA KHAMMARI.

Turkey: Vivien Corpn Bldg, 4th Floor, 4-52, Seobinggo-dong, Yeongsan-gu, Seoul; tel. (2) 794-0255; fax (2) 797-8546; e-mail tcseulbe@kornet.net; Ambassador DENIZ OZMEN.

Ukraine: 1-97, Dongbinggo-dong, Yeongsan-gu, Seoul; tel. (2) 790-5696; fax (2) 790-5697; e-mail secretary@ukrembrk.com; internet www.ukrembrk.com; Ambassador YURII MUSHKA.

United Arab Emirates: 5-5, Hannam-dong, Yeongsan-gu, Seoul; tel. (2) 790-3235; fax (2) 790-3238; Ambassador ABDULLAH MUHAMMADD AL-MAAINAH.

United Kingdom: Taepyeongno 40, 4, Jeong-dong, Jung-gu, Seoul 100-120; tel. (2) 3210-5500; fax (2) 725-1738; e-mail bembassy@uk.or.kr; internet www.britishembassy.or.kr; Ambassador MARTIN UDEN.

USA: 32, Sejong-no, Jongno-gu, Seoul 110-710; tel. (2) 397-4114; fax (2) 735-3903; e-mail EmbassySeoulPA@state.gov; internet seoul.usembassy.gov; Ambassador ALEXANDER R. VERSHBOW.

Uruguay: 14F LIG Kangnam Bldg, 708-6 Yeoksam-dong, Gangnam-gu, Seoul; tel. (2) 6245-3179; fax (2) 6245-3181; e-mail uruseul@embrou.or.kr; Ambassador NELSON YEMIL CHABEN.

Uzbekistan: Diplomatic Center, Rm. 701, 1376-1, Seocho 2-dong, Seocho-gu, Seoul; tel. (2) 574-6554; fax (2) 578-0576; Ambassador VITALI V. FEN.

Venezuela: 16th Floor, SC First Bank Bldg, 100 Gongpyeong-dong, Jongno-gu, 110-702 Seoul; tel. (2) 732-1546; fax (2) 732-1548; e-mail emvesel@soback.kornet.net; internet www.venezuelaemb.or.kr; Chargé d'affaires a.i. WOLFGANG GONZÁLEZ.

Viet Nam: 28-58, Samcheong-dong, Jongno-gu, Seoul 140-210; tel. (2) 738-2318; fax (2) 739-2064; e-mail vndsq@yahoo.com; Ambassador PHAM TIEN VAN.

Yemen: 11-444, Hannam-dong, Yeongsan-gu, Seoul 140-210; tel. (2) 792-9883; fax (2) 792-9885; internet www.gpc.org.ye; Ambassador YAHYA AHMAD AL-WAZIR.

Judicial System

SUPREME COURT

The Supreme Court is the highest court, consisting of 14 Justices, including the Chief Justice. The Chief Justice is appointed by the President, with the consent of the National Assembly, for a term of six years. Other Justices of the Supreme Court are appointed for six years by the President on the recommendation of the Chief Justice. The appointment of the Justices of the Supreme Court, however, requires the consent of the National Assembly. The Chief Justice may not be reappointed. The court is empowered to receive and decide on appeals against decisions of the High Courts, the Patent Court, and the appellate panels of the District Courts or the Family Court in civil, criminal, administrative, patent and domestic relations cases. It is also authorized to act as the final tribunal to review decisions of courts-martial and to consider cases arising from presidential and parliamentary elections.

Chief Justice: LEE YONG-HOON, 967, Seocho-dong, Seocho-gu, Seoul; tel. (2) 3480-1002; fax (2) 533-1911; internet www.scourt.go.kr.

Justices: KOH HYUN-CHUL, KIM YONG-DAM, KIM YOUNG-RAN, YANG SEUNG-TAE, KIM HWANG-SIK, PARK SI-HWAN, KIM JI-HYUNG, LEE HONG-HOON, PARK ILL-HOAN, KIM NUNG-HWAN, JEON SOO-AHN, AHN DAI-HEE.

CONSTITUTIONAL COURT

The Constitutional Court is composed of nine adjudicators appointed by the President, of whom three are chosen from among persons selected by the National Assembly and three from persons nominated by the Chief Justice. The Court adjudicates the following matters: constitutionality of a law (when requested by the other courts); impeachment; dissolution of a political party; disputes between state agencies, or between state agencies and local governments; and petitions relating to the Constitution.

President: LEE KANG-KUK, 83 Jae-dong, Jongno-gu, Seoul 110-250; tel. (2) 708-3456; fax (2) 708-3566; internet www.ccourt.go.kr.

HIGH COURTS

There are five courts, situated in Seoul, Daegu, Busan, Gwangju and Daejeon, with five chief, 78 presiding and 145 other judges. The courts have appellate jurisdiction in civil and criminal cases and can also pass judgment on administrative litigation against government decisions.

PATENT COURT

The Patent Court opened in Daejeon in March 1998, to deal with cases in which the decisions of the Intellectual Property Tribunal are challenged. The examination of the case is conducted by a judge, with the assistance of technical examiners.

DISTRICT COURTS

District Courts are established in 13 major cities; there are 13 chief, 241 presiding and 966 other judges. They exercise jurisdiction over all civil and criminal cases in the first instance.

MUNICIPAL COURTS

There are 103 Municipal Courts within the District Court system, dealing with small claims, minor criminal offences, and settlement cases.

THE REPUBLIC OF KOREA (SOUTH KOREA) *Directory*

FAMILY COURT
There is one Family Court, in Seoul, with a chief judge, four presiding judges and 16 other judges. The court has jurisdiction in domestic matters and cases of juvenile delinquency.

ADMINISTRATIVE COURT
An Administrative Court opened in Seoul in March 1998, to deal with cases that are specified in the Administrative Litigation Act. The Court has jurisdiction over cities and counties adjacent to Seoul, and deals with administrative matters, including taxes, expropriations of land, labour and other general administrative matters. District Courts will deal with administrative matters within their districts until the establishment of regional administrative courts is complete.

COURTS-MARTIAL
These exercise jurisdiction over all offences committed by armed forces personnel and civilian employees. They are also authorized to try civilians accused of military espionage or interference with the execution of military duties.

Religion
BUDDHISM
Korean Mahayana Buddhism has about 80 denominations. The Chogye-jong is the largest Buddhist order in Korea, having been introduced from China in AD 372. The Chogye Order accounts for almost two-thirds of all Korean Buddhists. Won Buddhism combines elements of Buddhism and Confucianism.

Korean United Buddhist Association (KUBA): 46-19, Soosong-dong, Jongno-gu, Seoul 110-140; tel. (2) 732-4885; 28 mem. Buddhist orders; Pres. Song Wol-Joo.

CHRISTIANITY
National Council of Churches in Korea: Christian Bldg, Rm 706, 136-46, Yeonchi-dong, Jongno-gu, Seoul 110-736; tel. (2) 763-8427; fax (2) 744-6189; e-mail kncc@kncc.or.kr; internet www.kncc.or.kr; f. 1924; est. as National Christian Council; present name adopted 1946; eight mem. churches; Gen. Sec. Rev. Paik Do-Woong.

The Anglican Communion
South Korea has three Anglican dioceses, collectively forming the Anglican Church of Korea (founded as a separate province in April 1993), under its own Primate, the Bishop of Seoul.

Bishop of Pusan (Busan): Rt Rev. Joseph Dae-Yong Lee, 455-2, Oncheon-1-dong, Dongnae-gu, Busan 607-061; tel. (51) 554-5742; fax (51) 553-9643; e-mail bpjoseph@hanmail.net.

Bishop of Seoul: Most Rev. Matthew Chung Chul-Bum, 3, Jeong-dong, Jung-gu, Seoul 100-120; tel. (2) 738-6597; fax (2) 723-2640; e-mail bishop100@hosanna.net.

Bishop of Taejon (Daejeon): Rt Rev. Paul Yoon Hwan, 88-1, Sonhwa 2-dong, POB 22, Daejeon 300-600; tel. (42) 256-9987; fax (42) 255-8918.

The Roman Catholic Church
For ecclesiastical purposes, North and South Korea are nominally under a unified jurisdiction. South Korea comprises three archdioceses, 12 dioceses, one military ordinate and one territorial abbacy. At 31 December 2005 some 4,278,168 people were adherents of the Roman Catholic Church.

Bishops' Conference
Catholic Bishops' Conference of Korea, 643-1, Junggok-dong, Gwangjin-gu, Seoul 143-912; tel. (2) 460-7500; fax (2) 460-7505; e-mail cbck@cbck.or.kr; internet www.cbck.or.kr.
f. 1857; Pres. Most Rev. Andreas Choi Chang-Mou (Archbishop of Gwangju).

Archbishop of Kwangju (Gwangju): Most Rev. Andreas Choi Chang-Mou, Archdiocesan Office, 5-32, Im-dong, Buk-gu, Gwangju 500-868; tel. (62) 510-2838; fax (62) 525-6873; e-mail biseo@kjcatholic.or.kr.

Archbishop of Seoul: Cardinal Nicholas Cheong Jin-Suk, Archdiocesan Office, 1, 2-ga, Myeong-dong, Jung-gu, Seoul 100-022; tel. (2) 727-2114; fax (2) 773-1947; e-mail ao@seoul.catholic.or.kr.

Archbishop of Taegu (Daegu): Most Rev. Paul Ri Moon-Hi, Archdiocesan Office, 225-1, Namsan 3-dong, Jung-gu, Daegu 700-804; tel. (53) 253-7011; fax (53) 253-9441; e-mail taegu@tgcatholic.or.kr.

Protestant Churches
Korean Methodist Church: 64-8, 1-ga, Taepyeong-no, Jung-gu, Seoul 100-101; KPO Box 285, Seoul 110-602; tel. (2) 399-4300; fax (2) 399-4307; e-mail bishop@kmcweb.or.kr; internet www.kmcweb.or.kr; f. 1885; 1,417,213 mems (2003); Bishop Kim Jin Ho.

Presbyterian Church in the Republic of Korea (PROK): Academy House, San 76, Suyu 6-dong, Kangbuk-ku, Seoul 142-070; tel. (2) 3499-7600; fax (2) 3499-7630; e-mail prok3000@chollian.net; internet www.prok.org; f. 1953; 337,188 mems (2005); Gen. Sec. Rev. Yoon Kil-Soo.

Presbyterian Church of Korea (PCK): The Korean Church Centennial Memorial Bldg, 135, Yunji-dong, Jongno-gu, Seoul 110-470; tel. (2) 745-4640; fax (2) 743-7982; e-mail thepck@pck.or.kr; internet www.pck.or.kr; 2,395,323 mems (Dec. 2003); Moderator Rev. Young Tae Kim; Gen. Sec. Rev. Seongi Cho.

There are some 160 other Protestant denominations in the country, including the Korea Baptist Convention and the Korea Evangelical Church.

OTHER RELIGIONS
Chundo Kyo, a religion indigenous and unique to Korea, combines elements of Shaman, Buddhist, and Christian doctrines. Confucianism also has a significant number of followers. Taejong Gyo is Korea's oldest religion, dating back 4,000 years, and comprising beliefs in the national foundation myth, and the triune god, Hanul. By the 15th century the religion had largely disappeared, but a revival began in the late 19th century.

The Press
NATIONAL DAILIES
(In Korean, unless otherwise indicated)

Chosun Ilbo: 61, 1-ga, Taepyeong-no, Jung-gu, Seoul 100-756; tel. (2) 724-5114; fax (2) 724-5059; e-mail webmaster@chosun.com; internet www.chosun.com; f. 1920; morning, weekly and children's edns; independent; Korean, English, Chinese and Japanese; Executive Editor Byun Yong-Shik; circ. 2,470,000.

Daily Sports Seoul: 25, 1-ga, Taepyeong-no, Jung-gu, Seoul; tel. (2) 721-5114; fax (2) 721-5396; internet www.seoul.co.kr; f. 1985; morning; sports and leisure; Pres. Lee Han-Soo; Man. Editor Son Chu-Whan.

Dong-A Ilbo: 139-1, 3-ga, Sejong-no, Jongno-gu, Seoul 100-715; tel. (2) 2020-0114; fax (2) 2020-1239; e-mail newsroom@donga.com; internet www.donga.com; f. 1920; morning; independent; Pres. Kim Hak-Joon; Editor-in-Chief Lee Hyun-Nak; circ. 2,150,000.

Han-Joong Daily News: 91-1, 2-ga, Myeong-dong, Jung-gu, Seoul; tel. (2) 776-2801; fax (2) 778-2803; Chinese.

Hankook Ilbo: 14, Junghak-dong, Jongno-gu, Seoul; tel. (2) 724-2114; fax (2) 724-2244; internet www.hankooki.com; f. 1954; morning; independent; Pres. Chang Chae-Keun; Editor-in-Chief Yoon Kook-Byung; circ. 2,000,000.

Hankuk Kyungje Shinmun (Korea Economic Daily): 441, Junglim-dong, Jung-gu, Seoul 100-791; tel. (2) 360-4114; fax (2) 779-4447; internet www.hankyung.com; f. 1964; morning; Pres. and CEO Shin Sang-Min; Man. Dir and Editor-in-Chief Choi Yu-Young.

Hankyoreh Shinmun (One Nation): 116-25, Gongdeok-dong, Mapo-gu, Seoul 121-020; tel. (2) 710-0114; fax (2) 710-0210; internet www.hani.co.kr; f. 1988; centre-left; Korean, English; CEO and Publr Chung Tae-Ki; Editor-in-Chief Sung Han-Pyo; circ. 500,000.

Ilgan Sports (The Daily Sports): 14, Junghak-dong, Jongno-gu, Seoul 110-792; tel. (2) 724-2114; fax (2) 724-2299; internet www.dailysports.co.kr; morning; f. 1969; Pres. Chang Chae-Keun; Editor Kim Jin-Dong; circ. 600,000.

Jeil Economic Daily: 146 Ssangrin-dong, Jung-gu, Seoul; tel. (2) 6325-3114; e-mail ysk@jed.co.kr; internet www.jed.co.kr; f. 1988; morning; Pres. Park Jung-Gu; Editor-in-Chief Jang Chang-Yong.

JoongAng Ilbo (JoongAng Daily News): 7, Soonhwa-dong, Jung-gu, 100-759 Seoul; tel. (2) 751-9215; fax (2) 751-9219; e-mail iht@joongang.co.kr; internet www.joins.com; f. 1965; morning; Korean and English; Publr Kil Jeong-Woo; Exec. Dir Chang Sung-Hyo; circ. 2,300,000.

Kookmin Ilbo: 12, Yeouido-dong, Yeongdeungpo-gu, Seoul; tel. (2) 781-9114; fax (2) 781-9781; internet www.kukminilbo.co.kr; Pres. Ro Seung-Sook.

Korea Daily News: 25, 1-ga, Taepyeong-no, Jung-gu, Seoul; tel. (2) 2000-9000; fax (2) 2000-9659; e-mail webmaster@seoul.co.kr; internet www.kdaily.com; f. 1945; morning; independent; Publr and Pres. Son Chu-Hwan; Man. Editor Lee Dong-Hwa; circ. 700,000.

The Korea Herald: 1-17, Jeong-dong, Jung-gu, Seoul; tel. (2) 727-0114; fax (2) 727-0670; internet www.koreaherald.co.kr; f. 1953; morning; English; independent; Pres. Wook Hong-Jung; Man. Editor Yu Kun-Ha; circ. 150,000.

THE REPUBLIC OF KOREA (SOUTH KOREA)

The Korea Times: 14, Junghak-dong, Jongno-gu, Seoul 110-792; tel. (2) 724-2114; fax (2) 732-4125; e-mail kt@koreatimes.co.kr; internet www.koreatimes.co.kr; f. 1950; morning; English; independent; Pres. YOON KOOK-BYUNG; Man. Ed. LEE SANG-SEOK; circ. 100,000.

Kyung-hyang Shinmun: 22, Jeong-dong, Jung-gu, Seoul; tel. (2) 3701-1114; fax (2) 737-6362; internet www.khan.co.kr; f. 1946; evening; independent; Pres. HONG SUNG-MAN; Executive Editor KIM JI-YOUNG; circ. 733,000.

Maeil Business Newspaper: 51-9, 1-ga, Bil-dong, Jung-gu, Seoul 100-728; tel. (2) 2000-2114; fax (2) 2269-6200; internet www.mk.co.kr; f. 1966; evening; economics and business; Korean, English; Pres. CHANG DAE-WHAN; Editor JANG BYUNG-CHANG; circ. 235,000.

Munhwa Ilbo: 68, 1-ga, Chungjeong-no, Jung-gu, Seoul 110-170; tel. (2) 3701-5114; fax (2) 722-8328; internet www.munhwa.co.kr; f. 1991; evening; Pres. and Publr LEE BYUN-KYU; Editor-in-Chief KANG SIN-KU.

Naeway Economic Daily: 1-12, 3-ga, Hoehyon-dong, Jung-gu, Seoul 100; tel. (2) 727-0114; fax (2) 727-0661; internet www.naeway.co.kr; f. 1973; morning; Pres. KIM CHIN-OUK; Man. Editor HAN DONG-HEE; circ. 300,000.

Segye Times: 63-1, 3-ga, Hangang-no, Yeongsan-gu, Seoul; tel. (2) 799-4114; fax (2) 799-4520; internet www.segyetimes.co.kr; f. 1989; morning; Pres. SA KWANG-KEE; Editor MOK JUNG-GYUM.

Seoul Kyungje Shinmun (Seoul Economic Daily): 19, Junghak-dong, Jongno-gu, Seoul 100; tel. (2) 724-2114; fax (2) 732-2140; e-mail webmaster@hanooki.com; internet www.sed.co.kr; f. 1960; morning; Pres. LIM KONG-JON; Man. Editor LEE JONG-WHAN; circ. 500,000.

Sports Chosun: 61, 1-ga, Taepyeong-no, Jung-gu, Seoul; tel. (2) 724-6114; fax (2) 724-6979; internet www.sportschosun.com; f. 1964; Publr BANG SANG-HOON; circ. 400,000.

LOCAL DAILIES

Chungchong Daily News: 304, Sachang-dong, Hungduk-gu, Cheongju, N. Chungcheong Prov.; tel. (43) 279-5114; fax (43) 262-2000; e-mail webmaster@ccilbo.com; internet www.ccilbo.com; f. 1946; morning; Pres. SEO JEONG-OK; Editor IM BAIK-SOO.

Daegu Ilbo: 81-2, Sincheon 3-dong, Dong-gu, Daegu; tel. (53) 757-4500; fax (53) 751-8086; internet www.tgnews.co.kr; f. 1953; morning; Pres. LEE TAE-YEUL; Editor KIM KYUNG-PAL.

Daejon Ilbo: 1-135, Munhwa 1-dong, Jung-gu, Daejeon; tel. (42) 251-3311; fax (42) 253-3320; f. 1950; evening; Pres. CHO JOON-HO; Editor KWAK DAE-YEON.

Halla Ilbo: 568-1, Samdo 1-dong, Jeju; tel. (64) 750-2114; fax (64) 750-2520; internet www.hallailbo.com; f. 1989; evening; Chair. KANG YONG-SOK; Man. Editor HONG SONG-MOK.

Incheon Ilbo: 18-1, 4-ga, Hang-dong, Jung-gu, Incheon; tel. (32) 763-8811; fax (32) 763-7711; internet www.itimes.co.kr; f. 1988; evening; Chair. MUN PYONG-HA; Man. Editor LEE JAE-HO.

Jeju Daily News: 2324-6, Yeon-dong, Jeju; tel. (64) 740-6114; fax (64) 740-6500; e-mail webmaster@jejunews.com; internet www.jejunews.com; f. 1945; evening; Pres. KIM DAE-SUNG; Man. Editor KANG BYUNG-HEE.

Jeonbuk Domin Ilbo: 207-10, 2-ga, Deokjin-dong, Deokjin-gu, Jeonju, N. Jeolla Prov.; tel. (63) 251-7114; fax (63) 251-7127; internet www.domin.co.kr; f. 1988; morning; Pres. LIM BYOUNG-CHAN; Man. Editor YANG CHAE-SUK.

Jeonbuk Ilbo: 710-5, Kumam-dong, Deokjin-gu, Jeonju, N. Jeolla Prov.; tel. (63) 250-5500; fax (63) 250-5550; f. 1950; evening; Chair. SUH CHANG-HOON; Man. Editor LEE KON-WOONG.

Jeonju Ilbo: 568-132, Sonosong-dong, Deokjin-gu, Jeonju, N. Jeolla Prov.; tel. (63) 285-0114; fax (63) 285-2060; f. 1991; morning; Chair. KANG DAE-SOON; Man. Editor SO CHAE-CHOL.

Jeonnam Ilbo: 700-5, Jungheung-dong, Buk-gu, Gwangju 500-758; tel. (62) 527-0015; fax (62) 510-0436; f. 1989; morning; Pres. PARK KEE-JUNG; Editor-in-Chief KIM YONG-OK.

Joongdo Ilbo: 274-7, Galma-dong, Seo-gu, Daejeon; tel. (42) 530-4114; fax (42) 535-5334; f. 1951; morning; CEO KIM WOK-SIK; Man. Editor SONG HYOUNG-SOP.

Kangwon Ilbo: 53, 1-ga, Jungang-no, Chuncheon, Gangwon Prov.; tel. (33) 252-7228; fax (33) 252-5884; internet www.kwnews.co.kr; f. 1945; evening; Pres. CHOI SEUNG-IK; Editor-in-Chief KIM SUNG-KEE.

Kookje Daily News: 76-2, Goje-dong, Yeonje-gu, Busan 611-702; tel. (51) 500-5114; fax (51) 500-4274; e-mail jahwang@ms.kookje.co.kr; internet www.kookje.co.kr; f. 1947; morning; Pres. ROH KI-TAE; Editor-in-Chief JEONG WON-YOUNG.

Kwangju Ilbo: 1, 1-ga, Geumnam-no, Dong-gu, Gwangju; tel. (62) 222-8111; fax (62) 227-9500; e-mail webmaster@kwangju.co.kr; internet www.kwangju.co.kr; f. 1952; evening; Chair. KIM CHONG-TAE; Man. Editor CHO DONG-SU.

Kyeonggi Ilbo: 452-1, Songjuk-dong, Changan-gu, Suwon, Gyeonggi Prov.; tel. (31) 247-3333; fax (31) 247-3349; e-mail webmaster@kgib.co.kr; internet www.kgib.co.kr; f. 1988; evening; Pres. SHIN CHANG-GI; Man. Editor LEE CHIN-YONG.

Kyeongin Ilbo: 1121-11, Ingye-dong, Paldal-gu, Suwon, Gyeonggi Prov.; tel. (31) 231-5114; fax (31) 232-1231; e-mail webmaster@kyeongin.com; internet www.kyeongin.com; f. 1960; evening; Pres. WOO JE-CHAN; Man. Editor KIM HWA-YANG.

Kyungnam Shinmun: 100-5, Sinwol-dong, Changwon, S. Gyeongsang Prov.; tel. (55) 283-2211; fax (55) 283-2227; internet www.knnews.co.kr; f. 1946; evening; Pres. KIM DONG-KYU; Editor PARK SUNG-KWAN.

Maeil Shinmun: 71, 2-ga, Gyesan-dong, Jung-gu, Daegu; tel. (53) 255-5001; fax (53) 255-8902; internet www.m2000.co.kr; f. 1946; evening; Pres. CHO HWAN-KIL; Editor LEE YONG-KEUN; circ. 300,000.

Pusan Daily News: 1-10, Sujeong-dong, Dong-gu, Busan 601-738; tel. (51) 461-4114; fax (51) 463-8880; internet www.pusanilbo.co.kr; f. 1946; Pres. JEONG HAN-SANG; Man. Editor AHN KI-HO; circ. 427,000.

Yeongnam Ilbo: 111, Sincheon-dong, Dong-gu, Daegu; tel. (53) 757-5114; fax (53) 756-9009; internet www.yeongnam.co.kr; f. 1945; morning; Chair. PARK CHANG-HO; Man. Editor KIM SANG-TAE.

SELECTED PERIODICALS

Academy News: 50, Unjung-dong, Bundang-gu, Seongnam, Gyeonggi Prov. 463-791; tel. (31) 709-8111; fax (31) 709-9945; organ of the Acad. of Korean Studies; Pres. HAN SANG-JIN.

Eumak Dong-A: 139, Sejong-no, Jongno-gu, Seoul 110-715; tel. (2) 781-0640; fax (2) 705-4547; f. 1984; monthly; music; Publr KIM BYUNG-KWAN; Editor KWON O-KIE; circ. 85,000.

Han Kuk No Chong (FKTU News): Federation of Korean Trade Unions, FKTU Bldg, 168-24 Chungam-dong, Yongsan-gu, Seoul 140-050; tel. (2) 715-3954; fax (2) 715-7790; e-mail fktuintl@fktu.co.kr; internet www.fktu.or.kr; f. 1961; labour news; circ. 20,000.

Hyundae Munhak: Seoul; tel. (2) 516-3770; fax (2) 516-5433; e-mail webmaster@hdmh.co.kr; internet www.hdmh.co.kr; f. 1955; literature; Publr KIM SUNG-SIK; circ. 200,000.

Korea Business World: Yeouido, POB 720, Seoul 150-607; tel. (2) 532-1364; fax (2) 594-7663; f. 1985; monthly; English; Publr and Pres. LEE KIE-HONG; circ. 40,200.

Korea Buyers Guide: Rm 2301, Korea World Trade Center, 159, Samseong-dong, Gangnam-gu, Seoul; tel. (2) 551-2376; fax (2) 551-2377; e-mail info@buyersguide.co.kr; internet www.buykorea21.com; f. 1973; monthly; consumer goods; quarterly, hardware; Pres. YOU YOUNG-PYO; circ. 30,000.

Korea Journal: Korean National Commission for UNESCO, CPOB 64, Seoul 100-600; tel. (2) 755-6225; fax (2) 755-7478; e-mail kj@unesco.or.kr; internet www.ekoreajournal.net; organ of the UNESCO Korean Commission; Publr SAMUEL LEE; Editor-in-Chief LIM SEUNG-HO.

Korea Newsreview: 1-12, 3-ga, Hoehyeon-dong, Jung-gu, Seoul 100-771; tel. (2) 756-7711; weekly; English; Publr and Editor PARK CHUNG-WOONG.

Korea and World Affairs: Rm 1723, Daewoo Center Bldg, 5-541, Namdaemun-no, Jung-gu, Seoul 100-714; tel. (2) 777-2628; fax (2) 319-9591; organ of the Research Center for Peace and Unification of Korea; Pres. CHANG DONG-HOON.

Korean Business Review: FKI Bldg, 28-1, Yeouido-dong, Yeongdeungpo-gu, Seoul 150-756; tel. (2) 3771-0114; fax (2) 3771-0138; monthly; publ. by Fed. of Korean Industries; Publr KIM KAK-CHOONG; Editor SOHN BYUNG-DOO.

Literature and Thought: Seoul; tel. (2) 738-0542; fax (2) 738-2997; f. 1972; monthly; Pres. LIM HONG-BIN; circ. 10,000.

Monthly Travel: Cross Bldg, 2nd Floor, 46-6, 2-ga, Namsan-dong, Jung-gu, Seoul 100-042; tel. (2) 757-6161; fax (2) 757-6089; e-mail kotfa@unitel.co.kr; Pres. SHIN JOONG-MOK; circ. 50,000.

News Maker: 22, Jung-dong, Jung-gu, Seoul 110-702; tel. (2) 3701-1114; fax (2) 739-6190; e-mail hudy@kyunghyang.com; internet www.kyunghyang.com/newsmaker; f. 1992; Pres. JANG JUN-BONG; Editor PARK MYUNG-HUN.

Reader's Digest: 295-15, Deoksan 1-dong, Geumcheon-gu, Seoul 153-011; tel. (2) 3398-2654; fax (2) 3398-2669; internet www.readersdigest.co.kr; f. 1978; monthly; general; Pres. YANG SUNG-MO; Editor PARK SOON-HWANG; circ. 115,000.

Shin Dong-A (New East Asia): 139, Chungjeong-no, Seodaemun-gu, Seoul 120-715; tel. (2) 361-0974; fax (2) 361-0988; e-mail hans@donga.com; internet shindonga.donga.com; f. 1931; monthly; general; Publr KIM HAK-JUN; Editor LEE HYUNG-SAM; circ. 150,000.

Taekwondo: Sinmun-no Bldg, 5th Floor, 238, Sinmun-no, 1-ga, Jongno-gu, Seoul 110-061; tel. (2) 566-2505; fax (2) 553-4728; e-mail

THE REPUBLIC OF KOREA (SOUTH KOREA)

wtf@unitel.co.kr; internet www.wtf.org; f. 1973; organ of the World Taekwondo Fed; Pres. Dr KIM UN-YONG.

Vantage Point: 85-1, Susong-dong, Jongno-gu, Seoul, 110-140; tel. (2) 398-3519; fax (2) 398-3539; e-mail kseungji@yna.co.kr; internet www.yna.co.kr; f. 1978; monthly; developments in North Korea; Editor KWAK SEUNG-JI.

Weekly Chosun: 61, Taepyeong-no 1, Jung-gu, Seoul; tel. (2) 724-5114; fax (2) 724-6199; weekly; Publr BANG SANG-HOON; Editor CHOI JOON-MYONG; circ. 350,000.

The Weekly Hankook: 14, Junghak-dong, Jongno-gu, Seoul; tel. (2) 732-4151; fax (2) 724-2444; f. 1964; Publr CHANG CHAE-KUK; circ. 400,000.

Wolgan Mot: 139, Sejong-no, Jongno-gu, Seoul 110-715; tel. (2) 733-5221; f. 1984; monthly; fashion; Publr KIM SEUNG-YUL; Editor KWON O-KIE; circ. 120,000.

Women's Weekly: 14, Junghak-dong, Jongno-gu, Seoul; tel. (2) 735-9216; fax (2) 732-4125.

Yosong Dong-A (Women's Far East): 139, Sejong-no, Jongno-gu, Seoul 110-715; tel. (2) 721-7621; fax (2) 721-7676; f. 1933; monthly; women's magazine; Publr KIM BYUNG-KWAN; Editor KWON O-KIE; circ. 237,000.

NEWS AGENCY

Yonhap News Agency: 85-1, Susong-dong, Jongno-gu, Seoul; tel. (2) 398-3114; fax (2) 398-3257; internet www.yonhapnews.co.kr; f. 1980; Pres. KIM KUN.

PRESS ASSOCIATIONS

Journalists Association of Korea (JAK): Korea Press Centre Bldg, 25 1-ga, Taepyeong-no, Jung-gu, Seoul; tel. (2) 737-2483; fax (2) 738-1003; internet www.journalist.or.kr; Pres. CHUNG IL-YONG.

Korean Association of Newspapers: Korea Press Center, 13th Floor, 25, Taepyeong-no, Jung-gu, Seoul 100-745; tel. (2) 733-2251; fax (2) 720-3291; e-mail iwelcome@presskorea.or.kr; internet www.presskorea.or.kr; f. 1962; 48 mems; Pres. CHANG DAE-WHAN; Sec.-Gen. PARK SU-MAN.

Korean Newspaper Editors' Association: Korea Press Center, 13th Floor, 25, 1-ga, Taepyeong-no, Jung-gu, Seoul; tel. (2) 732-1726; fax (2) 739-1985; f. 1957; 416 mems; Pres. SEONG BYONG-WUK.

Seoul Foreign Correspondents' Club: Korea Press Center, 18th Floor, 25, 1-ga, Taepyeong-no, Jung-gu, Seoul; tel. (2) 734-3272; fax (2) 734-7712; f. 1956; Pres. PARK HAN-CHUN.

Publishers

Ahn Graphics Ltd: 532-1, Paju Book City, Munbal-ri, Gyoha-eup, Paju-si, Gyeonggi-do; tel. (31) 955-7766; fax (2) 955-7744; e-mail lbr@ag.co.kr; internet www.ag.co.kr; f. 1985; computer graphics; Pres. KIM OK-CHUL.

Bak-Young Publishing Co: 13-31, Pyeong-dong, Jongno-gu, Seoul; tel. (2) 733-6771; fax (2) 736-4818; f. 1952; sociology, philosophy, literature, linguistics, social science; Pres. AHN JONG-MAN.

BIR Publishing Co Ltd: 4/F, Gangnam Publishing Culture Center, 506 Sinsa-dong, Gangnam-Gu, Seoul 135-887; tel. (2) 3443-4318; fax (2) 3442-4661; e-mail bir@bir.co.kr; internet www.bir.co.kr; children's books.

Bobmun Sa Publishing Co: Hanchung Bldg, 4th Floor, 161-7, Yomni-dong, Mapo-gu, Seoul 121-090; tel. (2) 703-6541; fax (2) 703-6594; internet www.bobmunsa.co.kr; f. 1954; law, politics, philosophy, history; Pres. BAE HYO-SEON.

Bookhouse Publishing Co Ltd: 6/F, Dongsomun Bldg, Seoul 136-034; tel. (2) 924-4736; fax (2) 924-4738; e-mail editor@bookhouse.co.kr; internet www.bookhouse.co.kr; business, foreign novels, health.

Bumwoo Publishing Co: 525-2, Paju Book City, Munbal-ri, Gyoha-eup, Paju-si, Gyeonggi-do; tel. (31) 955-6900; fax (31) 955-6905; e-mail help@bumwoosa.co.kr; internet www.bumwoosa.co.kr; f. 1966; philosophy, religion, social science, technology, art, literature, history; Pres. YOON HYUNG-DOO.

Chaeksesang Publishing Co (Book World): tel. (2) 704-1251; fax (2) 719-1258; e-mail webmaster@bkworld.co.kr; internet www.bkworld.co.kr; f. 1975.

Chajaknamu: 21-1, Sangsoo-dong, Seoul 121-160; tel. (2) 3142-9150; fax (2) 3142-9160; humanities.

Changhae Publishing: 336-10, Ahyun 2-dong, Seoul 121-012; tel. (2) 313-3200; fax (2) 313-3204; e-mail nanal21@changhae.com; internet www.changhae.

Cheong Moon Gak Publishing Co Ltd: 486-9, Kirum 3-dong, Seongbuk-gu, Seoul 136-800; tel. (2) 985-1451; fax (2) 988-1456; e-mail cmgbook@cmgbook.co.kr; internet www.cmgbook.co.kr;

f. 1974; science, technology, business; subsidiaries HanSeung Publishers, Lux Media; Pres. KIM HONG-SEOK; Man. Dir HANS KIM.

Crayon House Co Ltd: 5/F, Crayon House Bldg, Seoul; tel. (2) 3436-1711; fax (2) 3436-1410; e-mail crayon@korea.com; internet www.crayonhouse.co.kr; f. 1996; children's books.

Dai Won Publishing Co: 40-456, Hangangno 3-ga, Yeongsan-gu, Seoul 140-880; tel. (2) 2071-2000; fax (2) 793-8994; e-mail int@daiwon.co.kr; internet www.daiwon.co.kr; f. 1990; comics.

Design House Publishing Co: Paradise Bldg, 186-210, Jangchung-dong, 2-ga, Jung-gu, Seoul 100-392; tel. (2) 2275-6151; fax (2) 2275-7884; internet www.design.co.kr; f. 1987; social science, art, literature, languages, children's periodicals; Pres. LEE YOUNG-HEE.

Dong-A Publishing Co Ltd: 295-15, Toksan-dong, Seoul 140-100; tel. (2) 866-8800; fax (2) 862-0410; f. 1945; children's books, arts, humanities.

Dong-Hwa Publishing Co: 130-4, 1-ga, Wonhyoro, Yeongsan-gu, Seoul 140-111; tel. (2) 713-5411; fax (2) 701-7041; f. 1968; language, literature, fine arts, history, religion, philosophy; Pres. LIM IN-KYU.

Dongmoonsun Publishing Co: 4, Kwanhum-dong, Jongno-gu, Seoul 110-300; tel. (2) 733-4901; fax (2) 723-4518; e-mail dmoonsun@netsgo.com; humanities.

Doosan Corporation Publishing BG: 14-34, Yeouido-dong, Yeongdeungpo-gu, Seoul; tel. (2) 2167-0601; fax (2) 2167-0668; e-mail dudvkf@doosan.com; internet www.bookdonga.com; f. 1951; general works, school reference, social science, periodicals; Pres. CHOI TAE-KYUNG.

E*Public Co: 923-11, Mok 1-dong, Yangcheon-gu, Seoul 158-051; tel. (2) 653-5131; fax (2) 653-2454; e-mail skliu@panmun.co.kr; internet www.panmun.co.kr; f. 1955; social science, pure science, technology, medicine, linguistics; Pres. and CEO LIU SUNG-KWON.

Ehak Publishing Co Ltd: 17-1, Anhuk-dong, Jongno-gu, Seoul 110-240; tel. (2) 720-4572; fax (2) 720-4573; e-mail legosum@dreamwiz.com.

Eulyoo Publishing Co Ltd: 46-1, Susong-dong, Jongno-gu, Seoul 110-603; tel. (2) 733-8151; fax (2) 732-9154; e-mail eulyoo@chollian.net; f. 1945; linguistics, literature, social science, history, philosophy; Pres. CHUNG CHIN-SOOK.

Gilbut Publishing Co Ltd: 380-15, Seogyo-dong, Mapo-gu, Seoul; tel. (2) 332-0931; fax (2) 323-0586; e-mail gilbut@gilbut.co.kr; internet www.gilbut.co.kr; f. 1991.

Gimm-Young Publishers Inc: 17, Kahoe-dong, Jongno-gu, Seoul 110-260; tel. (2) 3668-3202; fax (2) 745-4827; e-mail marketing@gimmyoung.com; f. 1979; current affairs, humanities, history, religion, children's books.

Hainaim Publishing Co Ltd: 5/F, Hainaim Bldg, 368-4, Seogyo-dong, Mapo-gu, Seoul; tel. (2) 326-1600; fax (2) 326-1624; e-mail hainaim@chollian.net; internet www.hainaim.com; f. 1983; philosophy, literature, children's; Pres. SONG YOUNG-SUK.

Haksan Publishing Co: tel. (2) 828-8988; fax (2) 828-8890; internet www.haksanpub.co.kr; f. 1995; children's books, comics, magazines.

Hakwon Publishing Co Ltd: Seocho Plaza, 4th Floor, 1573-1, Seocho-dong, Seocho-gu, Seoul; tel. (2) 587-2396; fax (2) 584-9306; f. 1945; general, languages, literature, periodicals; Pres. KIM YOUNG-SU.

Hangilsa Corpn: 520-11, Paju Book City, Munbal-ri, Gyoha-eup, Paju-si, Gyeonggi-do; tel. (31) 955-2000; fax (31) 955-2005; e-mail hangilsa@hangilsa.co.kr; internet www.hangilsa.co.kr; f. 1976; social science, history, literature; Pres. KIM EOUN-HO.

Hanul Publishing Company: 3/F Seoul Bldg, 105-90 Gongdeok-dong, Mapo-gu, Seoul 121-801; tel. (2) 336-6183; fax (2) 333-7543; internet www.hanulbooks.co.kr; f. 1980; general, philosophy, university books, periodicals; Pres. KIM CHONG-SU.

Hollym Corporation: 13-13, Gwancheol-dong, Jongno-gu, Seoul 110-111; tel. (2) 735-7551; fax (2) 730-5149; e-mail hollym@chollian.net; internet www.hollym.co.kr; f. 1963; academic and general books on Korea in English; Pres. HAM KI-MAN.

Hyang Mun Sa Publishing Co: 645-20, Yeoksam-dong, Gangnam-gu, Seoul 135-081; tel. (2) 538-5672; fax (2) 538-5673; f. 1950; science, agriculture, history, engineering, home economics; Pres. NAH JOONG-RYOL.

Hyonam Publishing Co Ltd: 627-5, Ahyun 3-dong, Mapo-gu, Seoul 121-013; tel. (2) 365-5056; fax (2) 365-5251; e-mail lawhyun@chollian.net; f. 1951; general, children's, literature, periodicals; Pres. CHO KEUN-TAE.

Hyungseul Publishing Co: 33, Tongeui-dong, Jongno-gu, Seoul; tel. (2) 738-6052; fax (2) 736-7134; e-mail hs@hyungseul.co.kr; internet www.hyungseul.co.kr.

Il Jin Sa Publishing Co: 5-104, Hyochang-dong, Yeongsan-gu, Seoul; tel. (2) 704-1616; fax (2) 715-3536; e-mail webmaster@iljinsa.com; internet www.iljinsa.com; f. 1956; literature, social sciences,

THE REPUBLIC OF KOREA (SOUTH KOREA)

juvenile, fine arts, philosophy, linguistics, history; Pres. KIM SUNG-JAE.

Ilchokak Publishing Co Ltd: 1-335, Sinmunno 2-ga, Jongno-gu, Seoul 110-062; tel. (2) 733-5430; fax (2) 738-5857; e-mail ilchokak@hanmail.net; internet www.ilchokak.co.kr; f. 1953; history, literature, sociology, linguistics, medicine, law, engineering; Pres. HAN MAN-NYUN.

Jigyungsa Publishers Ltd: 790-14, Yeoksam-dong, Gangnam-gu, Seoul 135-080; tel. (2) 557-6351; fax (2) 557-6352; e-mail jigyung@uriel.net; internet www.jigyung.co.kr; f. 1979; children's, periodicals; Pres. KIM BYUNG-JOON.

Jihak Publishing Co Ltd: 180-20, Dongkyo-dong, Mapo-gu, Seoul 121-200; tel. (2) 330-5220; fax (2) 325-5835; e-mail webmaster@jihak.co.kr; internet www.jihak.co.kr; f. 1965; philosophy, language, literature; Pres. KWON BYONG-IL.

Jipmoondang: 95, Waryon-dong, Jongno-gu, Seoul 110-360; tel. (2) 743-3098; fax (2) 743-3192; internet www.jimoon.co.kr; philosophy, social science, Korean studies, history, Korean folklore; Pres. LIM KYOUNG-HWAN.

Jisik Sanup Publications Co Ltd: 35-18, Dongui-dong, Jongno-gu, Seoul 110-040; tel. (2) 734-1978; fax (2) 720-7900; e-mail jsp@jisik.co.kr; internet www.jisik.co.kr; f. 1969; religion, social science, art, literature, history, children's; Pres. KIM KYUNG-HEE.

Joongang Publishing Co Ltd: 172-11, Yomni-dong, Mapo-gu, Seoul 121-090; tel. (2) 717-2111; fax (2) 716-1369; f. 1972; study books, children's; Pres. KIM DUCK-KI.

Kemongsa Publishing Co Ltd: 772, Yeoksam-dong, Gangnam-gu, Seoul 135-080; tel. (2) 531-5335; fax (2) 531-5520; internet www.kemongsa.co.kr; f. 1946; picture books, juvenile, encyclopaedias, history, fiction; Pres. RHU SEUNG-HEE.

Kookminbooks Co Ltd: 514-4, Paju Book City, Munbal-ri, Gyoha-eup, Paju-si, Gyeonggi-do; tel. (31) 955-7861; fax (31) 955-7855; internet www.kmbooks.com; f. 1961; children's books.

Korea Britannica Corpn: 117, 1-ga, Jungchung-dong, Seoul 100-391; tel. (2) 272-2151; fax (2) 278-9983; f. 1968; encyclopaedias, dictionaries; Pres. JANG HO-SANG, SUJAN ELEN TAPANI.

Korea University Press: 5-1, Anam-dong, 5-ga, Seongbuk-gu, Seoul 136-701; tel. (2) 3290-4231; fax (2) 923-6311; e-mail kupress@korea.ac.uk; internet www.kupress.com; f. 1956; philosophy, history, language, literature, Korean studies, education, psychology, social science, natural science, engineering, agriculture, medicine; Pres. EUH YOON-DAE.

Kum Sung Publishing Co: 242-63, Gongdeok-dong, Mapo-gu, Seoul 121-022; tel. (2) 713-9651; fax (2) 718-4362; e-mail webmaster@kumsungpub.co.kr; internet www.kumsung.co.kr; f. 1965; literature, juvenile, social sciences, history, fine arts; Pres. KIM NAK-JOON.

Kyohak-sa Publishing Co Ltd: 105-67, Gongdeok-dong, Mapo-gu, Seoul 121-020; tel. (2) 707-5110; fax (2) 707-5160; internet www.kyohak.co.kr; f. 1952; dictionaries, educational, children's; Pres. YANG CHEOL-WOO.

Kyung Hee University Press: 1, Hoeki-dong, Dongdaemun-gu, Seoul 130-701; tel. (2) 961-0106; fax (2) 962-8840; f. 1960; general, social science, technology, language, literature; Pres. CHOE YOUNG-SEEK.

Kyungnam University Press: 28-42, Samchung-dong, Jongno-gu, Seoul 110-230; tel. (2) 370-0700; fax (2) 735-4359; Pres. PARK JAE-KYU.

Minumsa Publishing Co Ltd: 5/F Kangnam Publishing Culture Centre, 506, Sinsa-dong, Gangnam-gu, Seoul 135-120; tel. (2) 515-2000; fax (2) 515-2007; e-mail michellenam@minumsa.com; internet www.minumsa.com; f. 1966; literature, philosophy, linguistics, pure science; Pres. PARK MAENG-HO.

Munhakdongne Publishing Co Ltd: 513-8, Paju Book City, Munbal-ri, Gyoha-eup, Paju-si, Gyeonggi-do 413-832; tel. (31) 955-8888; fax (2) 955-8855; e-mail editor@munhak.com; internet www.munhak.com; f. 1993; art, literature, science, philosophy, non-fiction, children's, periodicals; Pres. KANG BYUNG-SUN.

Sakyejul Publishing Ltd: 1513-3, Paju Book City, Munbal-ri, Gyoha-eup, Paju-si, Gyeonggi-do; tel. (31) 955-8558; fax (31) 955-8596; e-mail kec@sakyejul.co.kr; internet www.sakyejul.co.kr; f. 1982; social sciences, art, literature, history, children's; Pres. KANG MAR-XILL.

Sam Joong Dang Publishing Co: 261-23, Soke-dong, Yeongsan-gu, Seoul 140-140; tel. (2) 704-6816; fax (2) 704-6819; f. 1931; literature, history, philosophy, social sciences, dictionaries; Pres. LEE MIN-CHUL.

Sam Seong Dang Publishing Co: 101-14, Non Hyun-dong, Gangnam-gu, Seoul 135-010; tel. (2) 3442-6767; fax (2) 3442-6768; e-mail kyk@ssdp.co.kr; f. 1968; literature, fine arts, history, philosophy; Pres. KANG MYUNG-CHAE.

Sam Seong Publishing Co Ltd: 1516-2, Seocho-dong, Seocho-gu, Seoul 137-070; tel. (2) 3470-6900; fax (2) 597-1507; f. 1951; literature, history, juvenile, philosophy, arts, religion, science, encyclopaedias; Pres. KIM JIN-YONG.

Samsung Publishing Co Ltd: Samsung Publishing Bldg, 1516-2, Seocho 3-dong, Seocho-gul 137-871; tel. (2) 3470-6900; fax (2) 521-8534; e-mail lisababy@ssbooks.com; internet www.ssbooks.com; www.samsungbooks.com; children's books, comics, cooking, parenting, health, travel; f. 1951; Chief Editor BOSUNG KONG.

Segyesa Publishing Co Ltd: 217-1 Poi-dong, Gangnam-gu, Seoul 135-260; tel. (2) 577-2341; fax (2) 576-9853; f. 1988; general, philosophy, literature, periodicals; Pres. CHOI SUN-HO.

Se-Kwang Music Publishing Co: 232-32, Seogye-dong, Yeongsan-gu, Seoul 140-140; tel. (2) 719-2652; fax (2) 719-2656; f. 1953; music, art; Pres. PARK SEI-WON; Chair. PARK SHIN-JOON.

Seong An Dang Publishing Co: 4579, Singil-6-dong, Yeongdeungpo-gu, Seoul 150-056; tel. (2) 3142-4151; fax (2) 323-5324; f. 1972; technology, text books, university books, periodicals; Pres. LEE JONG-CHOON.

Seoul National University Press: San 56-1, Sillim-dong, Gwanak-gu, Seoul; tel. (2) 880-0434; fax (2) 888-4148; e-mail snubook@snu.ac.kr; internet www.snupress.com; f. 1961; philosophy, engineering, social science, art, literature; Pres. LEE KI-JUN.

Si-sa-young-o-sa, Inc: 55-1, 2-ga, Jongno, Jongno-gu, Seoul 110-122; tel. (2) 274-0509; fax (2) 271-3980; internet www.ybmsisa.co.kr; f. 1959; language, literature; Pres. CHUNG YOUNG-SAM.

Sogang University Press: 1, Sinsu-dong, Mapo-gu, Seoul 121-742; tel. (2) 705-8212; fax (2) 705-8612; f. 1978; philosophy, religion, science, art, history; Pres. LEE HAN-TAEK.

Sookmyung Women's University Press: 53-12, 2-ga, Jongpa-dong, Yeongsan-gu, Seoul 140-742; tel. (2) 710-9162; fax (2) 710-9090; f. 1968; general; Pres. LEE KYUNG-SOOK.

Sungkyunkwan University Press: 53, Myeongnyun-dong 3-ga, Jongno-gu, Seoul; tel. (2) 760-1252; fax (2) 762-7452; internet www7.skku.ac.kr/skkupress.

Sungshin Women's University Press: 249-1, Dongsun-dong 3-ga, Seongbuk-gu, Seoul; tel. (2) 920-7327; fax (2) 920-7326; internet www.sungshin.ac.kr/press.

Tam Gu Dang Publishing Co: 158, 1-ga, Hanggangno, Yeongsan-gu, Seoul 140-011; tel. (2) 3785-2271; fax (2) 3785-2272; f. 1950; linguistics, literature, social sciences, history, fine arts; Pres. HONG SUK-WOO.

Woongjin Think Big Co. Ltd: Woongjin Bldg, 112-2, Inui-dong, Jongno-gu, Seoul; tel. (2) 3670-1832; fax (2) 766-2722; e-mail lois.kim@email.woongjin.com; internet www.woongjin.com; children's; Pres. YOON SUCK-KEUM.

Yearimdang Publishing Co Ltd: Yearim Bldg, 153-3, Samseong-dong, Gangnam-gu, Seoul 135-090; tel. (2) 566-1004; fax (2) 567-9610; e-mail yearim@yearim.co.kr; internet www.yearim.co.kr; f. 1973; children's; Pres. NA CHOON-HO.

Yonsei University Press: 134, Sincheon-dong, Seodaemun-gu, Seoul 120-749; tel. (2) 361-3380; fax (2) 393-1421; e-mail ysup@yonsei.ac.kr; f. 1955; philosophy, religion, literature, history, art, social science, pure science; Pres. KIM BYUNG-SOO.

Youl Hwa Dang: Paju Book City, 520-10, Munbal-li, Gyoha-eup, Paju-si, Gyeonggi-do 413-832; tel. (31) 955-7000; fax (31) 955-7010; e-mail yhdp@youlhwadang.co.kr; internet www.youlhwadang.co.kr; f. 1971; art; Pres. YI KI-UNG.

Younglim Cardinal Inc: Hyecheon Bldg, 831, Yeoksam-dong, Gangnam-gu, Seoul 135-792; tel. (2) 553-8516; fax (2) 552-0436; e-mail edit@ylc21.co.kr; internet www.ylc21.co.kr; f. 1987.

PUBLISHERS' ASSOCIATION

Korean Publishers' Association: 105-2, Sagan-dong, Jongno-gu, Seoul 110-190; tel. (2) 735-2702; fax (2) 738-5414; e-mail kpa@kpa21.or.kr; internet www.kpa21.or.kr; f. 1947; Pres. PARK MAENG-HO; Sec.-Gen. KO HUNG-SIK.

Broadcasting and Communications

TELECOMMUNICATIONS

Hanaro Telecom Inc: Kukje Electronics Center Bldg, 24th Floor, 1445-3, Seocho-dong, Seocho-gu, Seoul 137-728; tel. (2) 6266-4114; fax (2) 6266-4379; internet www.hanaro.com; local telecommunications and broadband internet services; Pres. and CEO YOON CHANG-BUN.

Korea Telecom: 206 Jungja-dong, Bundang-gu, Seongnam-si, Gyeonggi Prov. 463-711; tel. (2) 727-0114; fax (2) 750-3994; internet www.kt.co.kr; domestic and international telecommunica-

THE REPUBLIC OF KOREA (SOUTH KOREA)   *Directory*

tions services and broadband internet services; privatized in June 2002; CEO JOONG SOO-NAM.

Korea Telecom (KT) Freetel: Seoul; internet www.ktf.co.kr; subsidiary of Korea Telecom; 10m. subscribers (2002); CEO JOONG SOO-NAM.

LG Dacom Corpn: Dacom Bldg, 706-1, Yeoksam-dong, Gangnam-gu, Seoul 135-610; tel. (2) 6220-0220; fax (2) 6220-0702; internet www.lgdacom.net; f. 1982; domestic and international long-distance telecommunications services and broadband internet services; CEO PARK JONG-WOOK.

LG Telecom: LG Gangnam Tower, 19th Floor, 679 Yeoksam-dong, Gangnam-gu, Seoul 135-985; tel. (2) 2005-7114; fax (2) 2005-7505; e-mail englishweb@lgtel.co.kr; internet www.lgtelecom.com; subsidiary of LG Corpn; mobile telecommunications and wireless internet services; commenced commercial CDMA2000 1x service in May 2001; 4m. subscribers (2002); CEO JUNG IL-JAE.

Onse Telecom: 192-2, Gumi-dong, Bundang-gu, Seongnam-si, Gyeonggi Prov. 463-500; tel. and fax (31) 738-6000; internet www.onse.net; domestic and international telecommunications services; Pres. and CEO HWANG KYU-BYUNG.

SK Telecom Co Ltd: 11, Euljiro, 2-ga, Jung-gu, Seoul 100-999; tel. (2) 6100-2114; fax (2) 2121-3999; e-mail webmaster@sktelecom.com; internet www.sktelecom.com; cellular mobile telecommunications and wireless internet services; merged with Shinsegi Telecom in Jan. 2002; 16m. subscribers (2002); Pres. and CEO SHIN BAE-KIM.

BROADCASTING

Regulatory Authority

Broadcasting and Communications Commission: KBS Bldg, 923-5, Mok-dong, Yangcheon-gu, Seoul 158-715; tel. (2) 3219-5117; fax (2) 3219-5371; e-mail admin@kbc.go.kr; internet www.kbc.go.kr; Chair. CHOI SI-JUNG.

Radio

Korean Broadcasting System (KBS): 18, Yeouido-dong, Yeongdeungpo-gu, Seoul 150-010; tel. (2) 781-1000; fax (2) 781-4179; internet www.kbs.co.kr; f. 1926; publicly owned corpn with 26 local broadcasting and 855 relay stations; overseas service in Korean, English, German, Indonesian, Chinese, Japanese, French, Spanish, Russian and Arabic; Pres. JUNG YUN-JOO.

Buddhist Broadcasting System (BBS): 140, Mapo-dong, Mapo-gu, Seoul 121-050; tel. (2) 705-5114; fax (2) 705-5229; e-mail webmaster@bbsfm.co.kr; internet www.bbsfm.co.kr; f. 1990; Pres. CHO HAE-HYONG.

Christian Broadcasting System (CBS): 917-1, Mok-dong, Yangcheon-gu, Seoul 158-701; tel. (2) 650-7000; fax (2) 654-2456; e-mail changsoo@cbs.co.kr; internet www.cbs.co.kr; f. 1954; independent religious network with 14 network stations, incl. Seoul, Daegu, Busan and Gwangju; also satellite, cable and digital media broadcasting; programmes in Korean; Pres. LEE JEONG-SIK.

Educational Broadcasting System (EBS): 92-6, Umyeon-dong, Seocho-gu, Seoul 137-791; tel. (2) 526-2000; fax (2) 526-2179; internet www.ebs.co.kr; f. 1990; Pres. Dr PARK HEUNG-SOO.

Far East Broadcasting Co (FEBC): 89, Sangsu-dong, Mapo-gu, Seoul 121-707; tel. (2) 320-0114; fax (2) 320-0129; e-mail febcadm@febc.net; internet www.febc.net; Christian programmes; nine local stations; Pres. Dr BILLY KIM.

Radio Station HLAZ: MPO Box 88, Seoul 121-707; tel. (2) 320-0114; fax (2) 320-0129; e-mail febcadm@febc.net; internet www.febc.net; f. 1973; religious, educational service operated by Far East Broadcasting Co; programmes in Korean, Chinese, Russian and Japanese; Pres. Dr BILLY KIM.

Radio Station HLKX: MPO Box 88, Seoul 121-707; tel. (2) 320-0114; fax (2) 320-0129; e-mail febcadm@febc.net; internet www.febc.net; f. 1956; religious, educational service operated by Far East Broadcasting Co; programmes in Korean, Chinese and English; Pres. Dr BILLY KIM.

Munhwa Broadcasting Corpn (MBC): 31, Yeouido-dong, Yeongdeungpo-gu, Seoul 150-728; tel. (2) 784-2000; fax (2) 784-0880; e-mail mbcir@imbc.com; internet www.imbc.com; f. 1961; public; Pres. KIM JOONG-BAE.

Pyong Hwa Broadcasting Corpn (PBC): 2-3, 1-ga, Jeo-dong, Jung-gu, Seoul 100-031; tel. (2) 270-2114; fax (2) 270-2210; internet www.pbc.co.kr; f. 1990; religious and educational programmes; Pres. Rev. PARK SHIN-EON.

Seoul Broadcasting System (SBS): 10-2, Yeouido-dong, Yeongdeungpo-gu, Seoul 150-010; tel. (2) 786-0792; fax (2) 780-2530; internet www.sbs.co.kr; f. 1991; Pres. HA KUM-LOUL.

US Forces Network Korea (AFN Korea): Seoul; tel. (2) 7914-6495; fax (2) 7914-5870; e-mail info@afnkorea.net; internet afnkorea.com; f. 1950; six originating stations and 19 relay stations; 24 hours a day.

Television

Educational Broadcasting System (EBS): see Radio.

Jeonju Television Corpn (JTV): 656-3, Sonosong-dong, Deokjin-gu, Jeonju, N. Jeolla Prov.; tel. (63) 250-5231; fax (63) 250-5249; e-mail jtv@jtv.co.kr; f. 1997.

Korean Broadcasting System (KBS): 18, Yeouido-dong, Yeongdeungpo-gu, Seoul 150-790; tel. (2) 781-1000; fax (2) 781-4179; internet www.kbs.co.kr; f. 1961; publicly owned corpn with 25 local broadcasting and 770 relay stations; Pres. JUNG YUN-JOO.

Munhwa Broadcasting Corpn (MBC-R/TV): 31, Yeouido-dong, Yeongdeungpo-gu, Seoul 150-728; tel. (2) 789-2851; fax (2) 782-3094; e-mail song@mbc.co.kr; internet www.imbc.com; f. 1961; public; owned by the Foundation for Broadcast Culture (70%) and the Chung-Soo Scholarship Foundation (30%); includes terrestrial, cable and satellite TV stations, regional stations and radio stations; Pres. and CEO CHOI MOON-SOON.

Seoul Broadcasting System (SBS): see Radio.

US Forces Network Korea (AFN Korea): Seoul; tel. (2) 7914-2711; fax (2) 7914-5870; f. 1950; main transmitting station in Seoul; 19 rebroadcast transmitters and translators; 168 hours weekly.

Finance

(cap. = capital; res = reserves; dep. = deposits; m. = million; brs = branches; amounts in won, unless otherwise indicated)

REGULATORY AUTHORITIES

Financial Services Commission: 27, Yeouido-dong, Yeongdeungpo-gu, Seoul 150-743; tel. (2) 3771-5083; internet www.fsc.go.kr; f. 1998; deliberates on and resolves financial supervision issues; supervises the Financial Supervisory Service; Chair. JUN KWANG-WOO.

Financial Supervisory Service: 27, Yeouido-dong, Yeongdeungpo-gu, Seoul 150-743; tel. (2) 3771-5000; fax (2) 785-3475; internet www.fss.or.kr; f. 1999; examines and supervises financial institutions; Gov. KIM JONG-CHANG.

BANKING

In 2003 there were 59 commercial banks in South Korea, comprising eight nation-wide banks, six regional commercial banks, five specialized banks and 40 branches of foreign banks. In mid-2006 there were 32 foreign banks operating in South Korea. The Financial Supervisory Service oversees the operations of commercial banks and the financial services sector.

Central Bank

Bank of Korea: 110, 3-ga, Namdaemun-no, Jung-gu, Seoul 100-794; tel. (2) 759-4114; fax (2) 759-4139; e-mail bokdplp@bok.or.kr; internet www.bok.or.kr; f. 1950; bank of issue; res 3,774,800m., dep. 267,811,200m. (Dec. 2006); Gov. PARK SEUNG; Dep. Gov. LEE SEONG-TAE; 16 domestic brs, 6 overseas offices.

Commercial Banks

Citibank Korea Inc: 39, Da-dong, Jung-gu, Seoul 100-180; tel. (2) 3455-2114; fax (2) 3455-2966; e-mail shk@goodbank.com; internet www.goodbank.com; f. 1983; fmrly KorAm Bank, name changed as above 2004; acquired by Citigroup in 2004; cap. 1,309,515m., res 751,858m., dep. 32,810,010m. (Dec. 2005); CEO and Chair. HA YUNG-KU; 222 brs.

Hana Bank: 101-1, 1-ga, Ulchi-no, Jung-gu, Seoul 100-191; tel. (2) 2002-1111; fax (2) 775-7472; e-mail webmaster@hanabank.co.kr; internet www.hanabank.co.kr; f. 1991; merged with Boram Bank in Jan. 1999; merged with Seoulbank in Dec. 2002; cap. 987,161m., res 1,918,840m., dep. 88,193,052m. (Dec. 2006); Chair. and CEO KIM JONG-YEOL; 574 brs.

Kookmin Bank: 9-1, 2-ga, Namdaemun-no, Jung-gu, CPOB 815, Seoul 100-703; tel. (2) 2073-7114; fax (2) 2073-3296; e-mail corres@kookminbank.com; internet www.kookminbank.com; f. 1963; est. as Citizen's National Bank, renamed 1995; re-est. Jan. 1999, following merger with Korea Long Term Credit Bank; merged with H & CB in Nov. 2001; cap. 1,681,896m., res 7,157,839m., dep. 155,002,422m. (Dec. 2006); Chair. CHUNG DONG-SOO; Pres. and CEO KANG CHUNG-WON; 1,122 domestic brs, 6 overseas brs.

Korea Exchange Bank: 181, 2-ga, Ulchi-no, Jung-gu, Seoul 100-793; tel. (2) 729-0114; fax (2) 775-2565; internet www.keb.co.kr; f. 1967; merged with Korea International Merchant Bank in Jan. 1999; cap. 3,224,534m., res 1,190,241m., dep. 44,795,258m. (Dec.

THE REPUBLIC OF KOREA (SOUTH KOREA) Directory

2006); Chair. ROBERT E. FALLON; Pres. and CEO RICHARD F. WACKER; 269 domestic brs, 19 overseas brs.

Shinhan Bank: 120, 2-ga, Taepyeong-no, Jung-gu, Seoul 100-102; tel. (2) 756-0505; fax (2) 774-7013; e-mail corres@shinhan.com; internet www.shinhan.com; f. 1982; merged with Chohung Bank in April 2006; cap. 1,224,034m., res 1,103,678m., dep. 56,324,841m. (Dec. 2005, pre-merger figures); Pres. and CEO SHIN SANG-HOON; 957 domestic brs, 12 overseas brs.

Standard Chartered First Bank Korea Limited: 100, Gong-pyeong-dong, Jongno-gu, Seoul 110702; tel. (2) 3702-3114; fax (2) 3702-4934; e-mail master@kfb.co.kr; internet www.kfb.co.kr; f. 1929; acquired by Standard Chartered Bank in Jan. 2005, name changed from Korea First Bank to above in Sept. 2005; cap. 1,115,963m., res 279,862m., dep. 48,692,373m. (Dec. 2005); Chair. ROBERT T. BARNUM; Pres. and CEO ROBERT COHEN; 410 domestic brs, 2 overseas brs.

Woori Bank: 203, 1-ga, Hoehyeon-dong, Jung-gu, Seoul; tel. (2) 2002-3000; fax (2) 2002-5687; internet www.wooribank.com; f. 2002; est. by merger of Hanvit Bank and Peace Bank of Korea; 78% government-owned; privatization expected by 2008; cap. 3,179,783m., res 6,473,596m., dep. 126,852,686m. (Dec. 2006); Chair. HWANG YOUNG KEY; 712 domestic brs.

Development Banks

Export-Import Bank of Korea: 16-1, Yeouido-dong, Yeong-deungpo-gu, Seoul 150-873; tel. (2) 3779-6114; fax (2) 7841-1030; e-mail kexim@koreaexim.go.kr; internet www.koreaexim.go.kr; f. 1976; cap. 3,305,755m., res 612,607m. (Dec. 2006); Chair. and Pres. SHIN DONG-KYU; 11 brs.

Korea Development Bank: 16-3, Yeouido-dong, Yeongdeungpo-gu, Seoul 150-973; tel. (2) 787-4000; fax (2) 787-6191; internet www.kdb.co.kr; f. 1954; cap. 8,241,861m., res 2,475,452m., dep. 56,740,805m. (Dec. 2005); Gov. KIM CHANG-LOK; 40 domestic brs, 6 overseas brs.

Specialized Banks

Industrial Bank of Korea: 50, 2-ga, Ulchi-no, Jung-gu, Seoul 100-758; tel. (2) 729-6114; fax (2) 729-6402; e-mail ifd@ibk.co.kr; internet www.ibk.co.kr; f. 1961; est. as the Small and Medium Industry Bank; 85.5% govt-owned; cap. 2,291,385m., res 1,645,176m., dep. 50,054,053m. (Dec. 2004); Chair. and CEO KANG KWON-SEOK; 387 domestic brs, 5 overseas brs.

Meritz Investment Bank: 5/F Seoul Financial Center, 84 Tae-pyeongno 1-ga, Jung-gu, Seoul 100-768; tel. (2) 777-7711; fax (2) 318-7060; internet www.imeritzbank.com; f. 1977; fmrly known as Korean-French Banking Corpn (SogeKo).

National Agricultural Co-operative Federation (NACF): 75, 1-ga, Chungjeong-no, Jung-gu, Seoul 100-707; tel. (2) 397-5114; fax (2) 397-5140; e-mail nacfico@nuri.net; internet www.nonghyup.com; f. 1961; merged with National Livestock Co-operatives Federation in July 2000; cap. 2,564,400m., res 1,395,800m., dep. 64,063,500m. (2002); Chair. and Pres. CHUNG DAE-KUN; 2,025 brs and member co-operatives.

National Federation of Fisheries Co-operatives: 11-6, Sincheon-dong, Songpa-gu, Seoul 138-730; tel. (2) 2240-2114; fax (2) 2240-3049; internet www.suhyup.co.kr; f. 1962; cap. 1,158,100m., res 301,900m., dep. 4,371,000m. (2002); Chair. and Pres. CHANG BYUNG-KOO; 120 brs.

Provincial Banks

Daegu Bank Ltd: 118, 2-ga, Susong-dong, Susong-gu, Daegu 706-712; tel. (53) 740-2543; fax (53) 756-2095; internet www.daegubank.co.kr; f. 1967; cap. 660,625m., res 17,041m., dep. 14,766,294m. (Dec. 2005); Chair. and Pres. KIM KUK-NYON; 247 brs.

Jeju Bank: 1349, Ido-1-dong, Jeju 690-021, Jeju Prov.; tel. (64) 734-1711; fax (64) 720-0183; internet www.chejubank.co.kr; f. 1969; cap. 55,500m., res. 30,700m., dep. 1,044,100m. (2002); merged with Central Banking Co in 2000, joined the Shinhan Financial Group in 2002; Chair. and Pres. KANG JOON-HONG; 29 brs.

Jeonbuk Bank Ltd: 669-2, Geumam-dong, Deokjin-gu, Jeonju 561-711, N. Jeolla Prov.; tel. (63) 250-7114; fax (63) 250-7078; internet www.jbbank.co.kr; f. 1969; cap. 170,591m., res 625m., dep. 3,898,228m. (2005); Chair. and Pres. HONG SUNG-JOO; 74 brs.

Kwangju Bank Ltd: 7-12, Daein-dong, Dong-gu, Gwangju 501-719; tel. (62) 239-5000; fax (62) 239-5199; e-mail kbjint1@nuri.net; internet www.kjbank.com; f. 1968; cap. 220,403m., res 24,426m., dep. 8,986,515m. (Dec. 2005); Chair. and Pres. UM JONG-DAE; 135 brs.

Kyongnam Bank: 246-1, Sokjeon-dong, Hoewon-gu, Masan 630-010, Gyeongsang Prov.; tel. (551) 290-8000; fax (551) 294-9426; internet www.knbank.co.kr; f. 1970; est. as Gyeongnam Bank Ltd, name changed 1987; cap. 259,000m., res 24,699m., dep. 10,426,712m. (Dec. 2005); Chair. and Pres. JUNG KYONG-DUCK; 110 brs.

Banking Association

Korea Federation of Banks: 4-1, 1-ga, Myeong-dong, Jung-gu, Seoul 100-021; tel. (2) 3705-5000; fax (2) 3705-5337; internet www.kfb.or.kr; f. 1928; Chair. SHIN DONG-HYUCK; Vice-Chair. KIM KONG-JIN.

STOCK EXCHANGE

Korea Exchange (KRX): 5-50 Jungang-dong, Jung-gu, Busan 600-015; tel. (51) 662-2000; internet www.krx.co.kr; f. 2005; formed by merger of Korea Stock Exchange, Korea Futures Exchange, Kosdaq Stock Market, Korea Securities Dealers Association; Chair. and CEO YOUNG-TAK LEE.

INSURANCE

Principal Life Companies

Allianz Life Insurance Co Ltd: Allianz Tower, 45-21 Yeouido-dong, Yeongdeungpo-gu, Seoul 150-978; tel. (2) 3787-7000; e-mail webadmin@allianzlife.co.kr; internet www.allianzlife.co.kr; fmrly Allianz Jeil Life Insurance; formed in 2000 following acquisition of Jeil (First Life) by Allianz Group; renamed as above in 2002; Pres. and CEO MANUEL BAUER.

American International Assurance Korea: 9/F, Hanil Bldg, Chungmu-ro 2ga, Chung-gu, Seoul 100-012; tel. (2) 3707-4800; fax (2) 776-7109; internet www.aiglife.co.kr; f. 1977; CEO SANG LEE.

Dongbu Life Insurance Co Ltd: Dongbu Bldg, 7th Floor, 891-10, Daechi-dong, Gangnam-gu, Seoul 135-820; tel. (2) 1588-3131; fax (2) 3011-4100; internet www.dongbulife.co.kr; f. 1989; cap. 85,200m. (2003); CEO CHO JAE-HONG.

Green Cross Life Insurance Co Ltd: 395-68, Shindaebang-dong, Dongjak-gu, Seoul; tel. (2) 3284-7000; fax (2) 3284-7455; internet www.healthcare.co.kr; CEO LEE JUNG-SANG.

Hana HSBC Life Insurance Ltd: 17/F, Hana Bank HQ Bldg, 101-1 Ulchiro-1ga, Jung-gu, Seoul 100-191; tel. (2) 3709-7300; fax (2) 755-0668; jt venture between HSBC Insurance (Asia-Pacific) Holdings Ltd and Hana Financial Group; CEO DAVID YOON.

Hungkuk Life Insurance Co Ltd: 226, Sinmun-no 1-ga, Jongno-gu, Seoul 100-061; tel. (2) 2002-7000; fax (2) 2002-7804; e-mail webmaster@hungkuk.co.kr; internet www.hungkuk.co.kr; f. 1958; Pres. and CEO RYU SEOK-KEE.

ING Life Insurance Co Korea Ltd: Sean Bldg, 116, Sinmun-no, Jongno-gu, Seoul 110-700; tel. (2) 3703-9500; fax (2) 734-3309; internet www.inglife.co.kr; f. 1991; cap. 64,820m. (2002); Pres. and CEO RON VAN OIJEN.

KB Life Insurance Co Ltd: 6/F, Daewoo Bldg, 167, Naesu-dong, Jongno-gu, Seoul; tel. (2) 398-6800; fax (2) 398-6843; e-mail webmaster@kbli.co.kr; internet www.kbli.co.kr.

Korea Life Insurance Co Ltd: 60, Yeouido-dong, Yeongdeungpo-gu, Seoul 150-603; tel. (2) 789-5114; fax (2) 789-8173; internet www.korealife.com; f. 1946; cap. 3,550,000m. (2002); CEO EUN CHUL-SHIN.

Korean Reinsurance Company: 80, Susong-dong, Jongno-gu, Seoul 110-733; tel. (2) 3702-6000; fax (2) 739-3754; internet www.koreanre.co.kr; f. 1963; Pres. PARK JONG-WON.

Kumho Life Insurance Co Ltd: 57, 1-ga, Sinmun-no, Jongno-gu, Seoul 110-061; tel. (2) 6303-5000; fax (2) 771-7561; internet www.kumholife.co.kr; f. 1988; acquired Dong-Ah Life Insurance in 2000; cap. 211,249m. (2002); Pres. CHOI BYEONG-GIL.

Kyobo Life Insurance Co Ltd: 1, 1-ga, Jongno, Jongno-gu, Seoul 110-714; tel. (2) 721-2121; fax (2) 737-9970; internet www.kyobo.co.kr; f. 1958; cap. 92,500m.; Chair. and CEO SHIN CHANG-JAE; 84 main brs.

Life Insurance Association of North America: 14/F, Seoul City Tower, 581, Namdaemunro-5-ga, Jung-gu, Seoul; tel. (2) 3781-1000; fax (2) 792-6063; internet www.lina.co.kr; f. 1987; CEO YOUNG HO LEE.

LIG Life Insurance Co Ltd: 3, Sujung-dong, Dong-gu, Busan 601-716; tel. (51) 461-7700; fax (51) 465-0581; internet www.liglife.com; f. 1988; fmrly Lucky Life Insurance Co Ltd; cap. 139,054m. (2002); Pres. LEE YOUNG-MOON.

MetLife Insurance Co of Korea Ltd: Sungwon Bldg, 8th Floor, 141, Samseong-dong, Gangnam-gu, Seoul 135-716; tel. (2) 3469-9600; fax (2) 3469-9700; internet www.metlifekorea.co.kr; f. 1989; cap. 97,700m. (2002); Pres. STUART B. SOLOMON.

Mirae Asset Life Insurance: 168, Kongduk-2-dong, Mapo-gu, Seoul 121-705; tel. (2) 3271-4114; fax (2) 3271-4400; internet www.miraeassetlife.com; f. 2005; CEO PARK HYEON-JOO.

New York Life Insurance Ltd: 10/F, Shinyoung Bldg, 68-5, Chung Dam-dong, Gangnam-gu, Seoul; tel. (2) 2107-4600; fax (2) 2107-4700; internet www.nyli.co.kr; f. 1990.

THE REPUBLIC OF KOREA (SOUTH KOREA) *Directory*

PCA Life Insurance Co Ltd: 18/F, Seoul City Tower, 581 Namdaemunro-5ga, Jung-gu, Seoul 135-749; tel. (2) 2129-1700; fax (2) 2129-1640; internet www.pcakorea.co.kr; f. 1990; cap. 52,100m. (2002); Pres. MIKE BISHOP.

Prudential Life Insurance Co of Korea Ltd: Prudential Bldg, Yeoksam-dong, Gangnam-gu, Seoul; tel. (2) 2144-2000; fax (2) 2144-2100; internet www.prudential.co.kr; f. 1989; cap. 26,400m.; Pres. JAMES C. SPACKMAN.

Samsung Life Insurance Co Ltd: 150, 2-ga, Taepyeong-no, Jung-gu, Seoul 100-716; tel. (2) 751-8000; fax (2) 751-8100; internet www.samsunglife.com; f. 1957; cap. 100,000m. (2002); Pres. BAE JUNG-CHOONG; 1,300 brs.

Shinhan Life Insurance Co Ltd: 120, 2-ga, Taepyeong-no, Jung-gu, Seoul 100-102; tel. (2) 3455-4000; fax (2) 753-9351; internet www.shinhanlife.co.kr; f. 1990; Pres. HAN DONG-WOO.

Tong Yang Life Insurance Co Ltd: 185, Ulchi-no 2-ga, Jung-gu, Seoul 100-192; tel. (2) 728-9114; fax (2) 771-1347; internet www.myangel.co.kr; f. 1989; cap. 340,325m. (2002); Pres. KU JA-HONG.

Non-Life Companies

AIG General Insurance: 18/F, Seoul Central Bldg, 136 Seorin-dong, Jongno-gu, Seoul; tel. (2) 2260-6800; fax (2) 2260-6707; internet www.aiggeneral.co.kr; f. 1947; Pres. GARY MUNSTERMAN.

Daehan Fire and Marine Insurance Co Ltd: 51-1, Namchang-dong, Jung-gu, Seoul 100-778; tel. (2) 3455-3114; fax (2) 756-9194; e-mail dhplane@daeins.co.kr; internet www.daeins.co.kr; f. 1946; cap. 19,500m.; Pres. and CEO LEE JUN-HO.

Dongbu Insurance Co Ltd: Dongbu Financial Center, 891-10, Daechi-dong, Gangnam-gu, Seoul 135-840; tel. (2) 2262-3450; fax (2) 2273-6785; e-mail dongbu@dongbuinsurance.co.kr; internet www.idongbu.com; f. 1962; cap. 30,000m.; Pres. KIM SOON-HWAN.

First Fire and Marine Insurance Co Ltd: 12-1, Seosomun-dong, Jung-gu, Seoul 100-110; CPOB 530, Seoul 100-110; tel. (2) 316-8114; fax (2) 771-7319; internet www.insumall.co.kr; f. 1949; cap. 17,200m.; Pres. KIM WOO-HOANG.

GreenFire Marine Insurance Co Ltd: Seoul City Tower, 581, 5-ga, Namdaemun-no, Jung-gu, Seoul 100-803; tel. (2) 1588-5959; fax (2) 773-1214; internet www.greenfire.co.kr; Pres. LEE YOUNG-DOO.

Hyundai Marine and Fire Insurance Co Ltd: 178, Sejongno, Jongno-gu, Seoul 110-731; tel. (2) 3701-8000; fax (2) 732-5687; e-mail webpd@hdinsurance.co.kr; internet www.hi.co.kr; f. 1955; cap. 30,000m.; Pres. and CEO HA JONG-SUN.

Korean Reinsurance Co: 80, Susong-dong, Jongno-gu, Seoul 100-733; tel. (2) 3702-6000; fax (2) 739-3754; e-mail service@koreanre.co.kr; internet www.koreanre.co.kr; f. 1963; cap. 34,030m.; Pres. PARK JONG-WON.

Kyobo Auto Insurance Co Ltd: 76-4, Jamwon-dong, Seocho-gu, Seoul 137-909; tel. (2) 3479-4900; fax (2) 3479-4800; internet www.kyobodirect.com; Pres. SHIN YONG-KIL.

LIG Insurance Co Ltd: LG Da-dong Bldg, 85, Da-dong, Jung-gu, Seoul 100-180; tel. (2) 310-2391; fax (2) 753-1002; e-mail webmaster@lginsure.com; internet www.lginsure.com; f. 1959; fmrly LG Insurance Co; Pres. KOO CHA-HOON.

Meritz Fire & Marine Insurance Co Ltd: 25-1, Yeouido-dong, Yeongdeungpo-gu, Seoul 150-878; tel. (2) 3786-2114; fax (2) 3786-2115; internet www.meritzfire.com; f. 1922; Pres. and CEO WOHN MYUNG-SOO.

Samsung Fire and Marine Insurance Co Ltd: Samsung Insurance Bldg, 87, 1-ga, Ulchi-no, Jung-gu, Seoul 100-191; tel. (2) 758-7948; fax (2) 758-7831; internet www.samsungfire.com; f. 1952; cap. 6,566m.; Pres. LEE SOO-CHANG.

Seoul Guarantee Insurance Co: 136-74, Yeonchi-dong, Jongno-gu, Seoul 110-470; tel. (2) 3671-7459; fax (2) 3671-7480; internet www.sgic.co.kr; Pres. JUNG KI-HONG.

Shindongah Fire and Marine Insurance Co Ltd: 43, 2-ga, Taepyeong-no, Jung-gu, Seoul; tel. (2) 6366-7000; fax (2) 755-8006; internet www.sdafire.com; f. 1946; cap. 60,220m.; CEO KWON CHU-SIN.

Ssangyong Fire and Marine Insurance Co Ltd: 60, Doryeom-dong, Jongno-gu, Seoul 110-716; tel. (2) 724-9000; fax (2) 730-1628; e-mail sfmi@ssy.insurance.co.kr; internet www.insurance.co.kr; f. 1948; cap. 27,400m.; Pres. YANG IN-JIP.

Insurance Associations

General Insurance Association of Korea: KRIC Bldg, 6th Floor, 80, Susong-dong, Jongno-gu, Seoul; tel. (2) 3702-8539; fax (2) 3702-8549; internet www.knia.or.kr; f. 1946; 16 corporate mems; fmrly Korea Non-Life Insurance Asscn; Chair. AHN KONG-HYUK.

Korea Life Insurance Association: Kukdong Bldg, 16th Floor, 60-1, 3-ga, Jungmu-no, Jung-gu, Seoul 100-705; tel. (2) 2262-6600; fax (2) 2262-6580; internet www.klia.or.kr; f. 1950; Chair. HOON NAM-KOONG.

Trade and Industry

GOVERNMENT AGENCIES

Fair Trade Commission: 1, Jungang-dong, Gwacheon-si, Gyeonggi Prov. 427-760; internet www.ftc.go.kr; Chair. KWON OH-SEUNG; Sec.-Gen. LEE DONG-KYU.

Federation of Korean Industries: FKI Bldg, 2nd Floor, 28-1, Yeouido-dong, Yeongdeungpo-gu, Seoul 150-756; tel. (2) 3771-0114; fax (2) 3771-0110; e-mail webmaster@fki.or.kr; internet www.fki.or.kr; f. 1961; conducts research and survey work on domestic and overseas economic conditions and trends; advises the Govt and other interested parties on economic matters; exchanges economic and trade missions with other countries; sponsors business conferences; 366 corporate mems and 63 business asscns; Chair. CHO SUK-RAI.

Korea Appraisal Board: 171-2, Samseong-dong, Gangnam-gu, Seoul; tel. (2) 2189-8000; internet www.kab.co.kr; Chair. KANG KIL-BOO.

Korea Asset Management Corpn (KAMCO): 814, Yeoksam-dong, Gangnam-gu, Seoul; tel. (2) 2103-6134; fax (2) 2103-7423; e-mail irkamco@kamco.or.kr; internet www.kamco.or.kr; f. 1963; collection and foreclosure agency; appointed following Asian financial crisis as sole institution to manage and dispose of non-performing loans for financial institutions; Chair. and CEO LEE CHOL-HWI.

Korea Export Industrial Corpn: 33, Seorin-dong, Jongno-gu, Seoul; tel. (2) 853-5573; f. 1964; encourages industrial exports, provides assistance and operating capital, conducts market surveys; Pres. KIM KI-BAE.

Korea Export Insurance Corpn: 136, Seorin-dong, Jongno-gu, Seoul 110-729; tel. (2) 399-6800; fax (2) 399-6679; internet www.keic.or.kr; f. 1992; official export credit agency of Korea; Chair. and Pres. CHO HWAN-EIK.

Korea Industrial Research Institutes: FKI Bldg, 28-1, Yeouido-dong, Yeongdeungpo-gu, Seoul; tel. (2) 780-7601; fax (2) 785-5771; f. 1979; analyses industrial and technological information from abroad; Pres. KIM CHAE-KYUM.

Korea Institute for Industrial Economics and Trade (KIET): 206-9, Cheongnyangni-dong, Dongdaemun-gu, Seoul; tel. (2) 3299-3114; fax (2) 963-8540; internet www.kiet.re.kr; f. 1976; economic and industrial research; Pres. OH SANG-BONG.

Korea Resources Corpn (KORES): Seoul; tel. (2) 840-5682; e-mail sbchoi@kores.or.kr; internet www.kores.or.kr; f. 1967; provides technical and financial support for the national mining industry; Pres. LEE HAN-HO.

Korea Trade-Investment Promotion Agency (KOTRA): 300-9, Yeomgok-dong, Seocho-gu, Seoul; tel. (2) 3460-7114; fax (2) 3460-7777; e-mail digitalkotra@kotra.or.kr; internet www.kotra.or.kr; f. 1962; various trade promotion activities, market research, cross-border investment promotion, etc.; 102 overseas brs; Pres. HONG KI-WHA.

Korean Intellectual Property Office: Government Complex-Daejeon, Dunsan-dong, Seo-gu, Daejeon; tel. (42) 481-5027; fax (42) 481-3455; internet www.kipo.go.kr; Commissioner JUN SANG-WOO.

CHAMBER OF COMMERCE

Korea Chamber of Commerce and Industry: 45, 4-ga, Namdaemun-no, Jung-gu, Seoul 100-743; tel. (2) 316-3114; fax (2) 757-9475; internet www.korcham.net; f. 1884; over 47,000 mems; 70 local chambers; promotes development of the economy and of international economic co-operation; Chair. SOHN KYUNG-SHIK; Pres. and CEO KIM SANG-YEOL.

INDUSTRIAL AND TRADE ASSOCIATIONS

Construction Association of Korea: Construction Bldg, 8th Floor, 71-2, Nonhyon-dong, Gangnam-gu, Seoul 135-701; tel. (2) 547-6101; fax (2) 542-6264; internet www.cak.or.kr; f. 1947; national licensed contractors' asscn; 6,823 mem. firms (2006); Pres. KWON HONG-SA.

Korea Agro-Fisheries Trade Corpn (aT): AGRO-TRADE & Exhibition Center, 232 Yangjae-dong, Seocho-gu, Seoul; tel. (2) 6300-1114; fax (2) 6300-1600; internet www.at.co.kr; f. 1967; fmrly Agricultural and Fishery Marketing Corpn; integrated devt for secondary processing and marketing distribution for agricultural products and fisheries products; Pres. AHN KYO-DUCK; Exec. Vice-Pres. KIM JIN-KYU.

THE REPUBLIC OF KOREA (SOUTH KOREA) *Directory*

Korea Automobile Manufacturers Association: 1461-15, Seocho 3-dong, Seocho-gu, Seoul 137-720; tel. (2) 3660-1800; fax (2) 3660-1900; e-mail cwkim@kama.or.kr; internet www.kama.or.kr; f. 1988; Chair. CHO NAM-HONG.

Korea Coal Association: 80-6, Susong-dong, Jongno-gu, Seoul; tel. (2) 734-8891; fax (2) 734-7959; f. 1949; 49 corporate mems; Chair. AHN JONG-BEOM.

Korea Consumer Goods Exporters Association: KWTC Bldg, Rm 1802, 159, Samseong-dong, Gangnam-gu, Seoul; tel. (2) 551-1865; fax (2) 551-1870; f. 1986; 230 corporate mems; Pres. YONG WOONG-SHIN.

Korea Electronics Association: 648, Yeoksam-dong, Gangnam-gu, CPOB 5650, Seoul 135-080; tel. (2) 553-0941; fax (2) 555-6195; e-mail webmaster@gokorea.org; internet www.gokea.org; f. 1976; 328 mems; Chair. YUN JONG-YONG.

Korea Federation of Textile Industries: Textile Center, 16/F, 944-31, Daechi-3dong, Gangnam-gu, Seoul 135-713; tel. (2) 528-4005; fax (2) 528-4069; e-mail kofoti@kofoti.or.kr; internet www.kofoti.or.kr; f. 1980; 50 corporate mems; Chair. CHAN RO-HEE.

Korea Foods Industry Association: 1002-6, Bangbae-dong, Seocho-gu, Seoul; tel. (2) 585-5052; fax (2) 586-4906; internet www.kfia.or.kr; f. 1969; 104 corporate mems; Pres. CHUN MYUNG-KE.

Korea Importers Association (KOIMA): 218, Hangang-no, 2-ga, Yeongsan-gu, Seoul 140-875; tel. (2) 792-1581; fax (2) 785-4373; e-mail info@aftak.com; internet www.koima.or.kr; f. 1970; 6,804 mems; Chair. KWON SOON-HAN.

Korea International Trade Association: 159-1, Samseong-dong, Gangnam-gu, Seoul; tel. (2) 6000-5114; fax (2) 6000-5115; internet www.kita.org; f. 1946; private, non-profitmaking business org. representing all licensed traders in South Korea; provides foreign businesses with information, contacts and advice; 80,000 corporate mems; Chair. and CEO LEE HEE-BEOM.

Korea Iron and Steel Association: 19/F, Posteel Tower, 735-3, Yeoksam-dong, Gangnam-gu, Seoul; tel. (2) 559-3508; internet www.kosa.or.kr; f. 1975; 39 corporate mems; Chair. YOO SANG-BOO.

Korea Oil Association: 28-1, Yeouido-dong, Yeongdeungpo-gu, Seoul; tel. (2) 555-8322; fax (2) 555-7825; internet www.koreaoil.or.kr; f. 1980; Pres. CHOI DOO-HWAN.

Korea Productivity Center: 122-1, Jeokseon-dong, Jongno-gu, Seoul 110-052; tel. (2) 724-1114; fax (2) 736-0322; internet www.kpc.or.kr; f. 1957; services to increase productivity of the industries, consulting services, education and training of specialized personnel; Chair. and CEO KIM JAE-HYUN.

Korea Sericultural Association: 17-9, Yeouido-dong, Yeongdeungpo-gu, Seoul; tel. (2) 783-6072; fax (2) 780-0706; e-mail silk@chollian.net; internet www.silktopia.or.kr; f. 1946; improvement and promotion of silk production; 50,227 corporate mems; Pres. CHOI YON-HONG.

Korea Shipbuilders' Association: 18/F, Landmark Tower, 837-36, Yeoksam-dong, Gangnam-gu, Seoul 135–937; tel. (2) 2112-8181; fax (2) 2112-8182; internet www.koshipa.or.kr; f. 1977; 9 mems; Chair. PARK KYU-WON.

Korea Textiles Trade Association: Textile Center, 16/F, 944-31, Daechi-3dong, Gangnam-gu, Seoul 135-713; tel. (2) 528-5158; fax (2) 528-5188; e-mail webmaster@textra.or.kr; internet www.textra.or.kr; f. 1981; 947 corporate mems; Pres. KANG TAE-SEUNG.

Korean Apparel Industry Association: Textile Centre, 16/F, 944-31 Daechi-3dong, Gangnam-gu, Seoul 135-713; tel. (2) 528-0114; fax (2) 528-0120; internet www.kaia.or.kr; f. 1993; 741 corporate mems; Pres. PARK PUNGEON.

Mining Association of Korea: 35-24, Dongui-dong, Jongno-gu, Seoul 110; tel. (2) 737-7748; fax (2) 720-5592; f. 1918; 128 corporate mems; Pres. KIM SANG-BONG.

Spinners and Weavers Association of Korea: 43-8, Gwancheol-dong, Jongno-gu, Seoul 110; tel. (2) 735-5741; fax (2) 735-5749; internet www.swak.org; f. 1947; 20 corporate mems; Chair. KIM HYONG-SANG.

EMPLOYERS' ORGANIZATION

Korea Employers' Federation: KEF Bldg, 276-1 Daeheung-dong, Mapo-gu, Seoul 121-726; tel. (2) 3270-7310; fax (2) 706-1059; e-mail delee@kef.or.kr; internet www.kef.or.kr; f. 1970; advocates employers' interests with regard to labour and social affairs; 13 regional employers' asscns, 20 economic and trade asscns, and 4,000 major enterprises; Chair. LEE SOO-YOUNG.

UTILITIES

Electricity

Korea Electric Power Corpn (KEPCO): 167, Samseong-dong, Gangnam-gu, Seoul; tel. (2) 3456-3630; fax (2) 3456-3699; internet www.kepco.co.kr; f. 1961; transmission and distribution of electric power, and development of electric power sources; six power generation subsidiaries formed in 2001; Pres. and CEO LEE WON-GUL.

Oil and Gas

Daegu City Gas Co Ltd: 2268-1, Namsan 4-dong, Jung-gu, Daegu; tel. (53) 606-1000; fax (53) 606-1004; internet www.taegugas.co.kr; f. 1983; Pres. and CEO JUNG CHOONG-YUNG.

Daehan City Gas: 27-1, Daechi-dong, Kangnam-gu, Seoul; tel. (2) 3410-8000; internet www.daehancitygas.com; f. 1978; supplies liquefied natural gas (LNG) to customers in Seoul and Gyeonggi Province; Co-CEO NAH SEONG-HWA; Co-CEO KIM BOK-HWAN.

GS Caltex: 135-985, 679 Yeoksam-dong, Gangnam-gu, Seoul; tel. (2) 2005-1114; internet www.gscaltex.com; subsidiary of GS Holdings Corpn; fmrly LG Caltex Oil, renamed as above March 2005; Chair. and CEO HUR DONG-SOO.

Hanjin City Gas: 711, Sanggye 6-dong, Nowon-gu, Seoul; tel. (2) 950-5000; fax (2) 950-5001; e-mail webmaster@hjcgas.com; internet www.hjcgas.com; f. 1985; supplies natural gas to Seoul and Gyeonggi; CEO PARK JIN-DO.

Incheon City Gas Corpn: 178-24, Gajoa-dong, Seo-gu, Incheon; tel. (32) 576-4121; fax (32) 576-2710; internet www.icgas.co.kr; f. 1983; CEO KIM JUNG-CHI.

Jungbu City Gas Co Ltd: ; fax (41) 533-6748; e-mail websmaster@jbcitygas.com; internet www.cbcitygas.co.kr; f. 1992.

Korea Gas Corpn: 215, Jeongja-dong, Bundang-gu, Seongnam, Gyeonggi Prov.; tel. (31) 710-0114; fax (31) 710-0117; e-mail kogasmaster@kogas.or.kr; internet www.kogas.or.kr; f. 1983; state-owned; privatization pending; Chair., Pres. and CEO LEE SOO-HO.

Korea National Oil Corpn (KNOC): ; tel. 380-2114; fax 387-9321; e-mail webmaster@knoc.co.kr; internet www.knoc.co.kr; Pres. HWANG DOO-YUL.

KyungDong City Gas Co: 939, Jinjang-dong, Book-gu, Ulsan; tel. (52) 219-5300; internet www.kdgas.co.kr; distributes liquefied natural gas (LNG) to residential, commercial and industrial customers in Ulsan and Yangsan; CEO SONG JAE-HO.

Kyungnam Energy Co Ltd: 55-5 Ungnam-dong, Changwon, Gyeongsangnam 641-290; tel. (55) 260-4432; fax (55) 260-4435; internet www.knenergy.co.kr; f. 1972; supplies natural gas to Changwon and the surrounding area; Pres. and CEO CHUNG YEUN-WOOK.

Samchully Co Ltd: 35-6, Yeouido-dong, Yeongdeungpo-gu, Seoul; tel. (2) 368-3300; fax (2) 783-1206; e-mail webmaster@samchully.co.kr; internet www.samchully.co.kr; f. 1966; gas supply co for Seoul metropolitan area and Gyeonggi Prov; Chair. LEE YOUNG-BOK.

Seoul City Gas Co: 281, Yeomchang-dong, Gangseo-gu, Seoul 157-864; tel. (2) 810-8000; fax (2) 828-6740; internet www.seoulgas.co.kr; f. 1983; distributes gas in Seoul and Gyeonggi Province; Chair. and CEO KIM YOUNG-MIN.

SK E & S: 99 Seorin-dong, Jongno-gu, Seoul; tel. (2) 2121-3114; fax (2) 2121-3198; internet www.sk-enron.com; f. 1999; jt venture between SK Corpn and Enron Corpn (USA); supplies natural gas through nine city gas cos: Chongju City Gas, Chonnam City Gas, Chungnam City Gas, Iksan City Gas, Iksan Energy, Kangwon City Gas, Kumi City Gas and Pusan City Gas; Pres. and CEO KIM JOONG-HO.

Yesco Co Ltd: 249-8, Yongdap-dong, Sungdong-gu, Seoul; tel. (2) 1644-0303; fax (2) 3390-3117; e-mail webmaster@lsyesco.com; internet www.gaspia.com; f. 1981; fmrly Kukdong City Gas Co; part of the LS Group; supplies liquefied natural gas (LNG) to the Seoul metropolitan area; CEO and Pres. CHOI KYUNG-HOON.

Water

Korea Water Resources Corpn: 6-2, Yeonchuk-dong, Daedeok-gu, Daejeon; tel. (42) 629-3114; fax (42) 623-0963; internet www.kowaco.or.kr.

Office of Waterworks, Seoul Metropolitan Govt: 27-1 Hap-dong, Seodaemun-gu, Seoul; tel. (2) 390-7332; fax (2) 362-3653; f. 1908; responsible for water supply in Seoul; Head SON JANG-HO.

Ulsan City Water and Sewerage Board: 646-4, Sin-Jung 1-dong, Nam-gu, Ulsan; tel. (52) 743-020; fax (52) 746-928; f. 1979; responsible for water supply and sewerage in Ulsan; Dir HO KUN-SONG.

CO-OPERATIVES

Korea Auto Industries Co-operative Association: 1638–3, Seocho-dong, Seocho-gu, Seoul 137-070; tel. (2) 587-0014; fax (2) 583-7340; e-mail kaica@kaica.or.kr; internet www.kaica.or.kr; f. 1962; Chair. SHIN DAL-CHUK.

Korea Computers Co-operative: 14-8, Yeouido-dong, Yeongdeungpo-gu, Seoul; tel. (2) 780-0511; fax (2) 780-7509; f. 1981; Pres. MIN KYUNG-HYUN.

THE REPUBLIC OF KOREA (SOUTH KOREA)

Korea Federation of Knitting Industry Co-operatives: 586-1, Sinsa-dong, Gangnam-gu, Seoul; tel. (2) 548-2131; fax (2) 3444-9929; internet www.knit.or.kr; f. 1962; Chair. JOUNG MAN-SUB.

Korea Federation of Non-ferrous Metal Industry Co-operatives: Backsang Bldg, Rm 715, 35-2, Yeouido-dong, Yeongdeungpo-gu, Seoul; tel. (2) 780-8551; fax (2) 784-9473; f. 1962; Chair. PARK WON-SIK.

Korea Federation of Plastic Industry Co-operatives: tel. (2) 2280-8200; fax (2) 2277-3915; internet www.koreaplastic.or.kr; f. 1973.

Korea Federation of Small and Medium Business (Kbiz): 16-2, Yeouido-dong, Yeongdeungpo-gu, Seoul 150-010; tel. (2) 2124-3114; fax (2) 782-0247; e-mail webmaster@kbiz.or.kr; internet www.kbiz.or.kr; f. 1962; Chair. KIM KI-MUN.

Korea Federation of Weaving Industry Co-operatives: tel. (2) 752-8097; fax (2) 755-6994; e-mail weaving3@hanmail.net; internet www.weaving.or.kr; f. 1964.

Korea Information and Communication Industry Co-operative: tel. (2) 711-2266; fax (2) 7111-2272; e-mail webmaster@kicic.or.kr; internet www.kicic.or.kr; f. 1962; CEO JOO DAE-CHULL.

Korea Metal Industry Co-operative: tel. (2) 780-4411; fax (2) 785-5067; e-mail master@koreametal.or.kr; internet www.koreametal.or.kr; f. 1962.

Korea Mining Industry Co-operative: 35-24, Dongui-dong, Jongno-gu, Seoul; tel. (2) 735-3490; fax (2) 735-4658; f. 1966; Chair. JEON HYANG-SIK.

Korea Steel Industry Co-operative: 915-14, Bangbae-dong, Seocho-gu, Seoul; tel. (2) 587-3121; fax (2) 588-3671; internet www.kosic.or.kr; f. 1962; Pres. KIM DUK-NAM.

National Agricultural Co-operative Federation (NACF): 75, 1-ga, Chungjeong-no, Jung-gu, Seoul; tel. (2) 397-5114; fax (2) 397-5380; internet www.nonghyup.com; f. 1961; international banking, marketing, co-operative trade, utilization and processing, supply, co-operative insurance, banking and credit services, education and research; Chair. CHOI WUN-BYUNG.

National Federation of Fisheries Co-operatives: 11-6, Sincheon-dong, Songpa-gu, Seoul; tel. (2) 2240-3114; fax (2) 2240-3024; internet www.suhyup.co.kr; f. 1962; Pres. HONG JONG-MOON.

TRADE UNIONS

Federation of Korean Trade Unions (FKTU): 35 Yeouido-dong, Yeongdeungpo-gu, Seoul; tel. (2) 6277-0072; fax (2) 6277-0077; e-mail fktuintl@fktu.or.kr; internet www.efktu.or.kr/~fktueng; f. 1941; Pres. LEE YONG-DEUK; affiliated to ITUC; 24 union federations are affiliated, including:

Federation of Korean Chemical Workers' Unions: FKTU Bldg 802, Yeouido-dong 35, Yeongdeungpo-gu, Seoul 150-980; tel. (2) 6299-1234; fax (2) 6299-1235; e-mail fkcu@chollian.net; internet www.fkcu.or.kr; f. 1961; Pres. PARK HUN-SOO; 116,286 mems.

Federation of Korean Metal Workers Trade Unions: 150-980, 9/F, 35 Yeouido-dong, Yeongdeungpo-gu, Seoul; tel. (2) 6277-2015; fax (2) 6277-2017; e-mail dykim@metall.or.kr; internet www.metall.or.kr; f. 1961; Pres. JANG SOEK-CHUN; 130,000 mems.

Federation of Korean Public Service Unions: Sukchun Bldg, 3rd Floor, 32-100, 4-ga, Dangsan-dong, Yeongdeungpo-gu, Seoul; tel. (2) 769-1330; fax (2) 769-1332; internet www.fkpu.or.kr; f. 1997; Pres. LEE KWAN-BOO; 15,641 mems.

Federation of Korean Seafarers' Unions: 544, Donhwa-dong, Mapo-gu, Seoul; tel. (2) 716-2764; fax (2) 702-2271; e-mail fksu@chollian.net; internet www.fksu.or.kr; f. 1961; Pres. PARK HEE-SUNG; 60,037 mems.

Federation of Korean State-invested Corporation Unions: Sunwoo Bldg, 501, 350-8, Yangjae-dong, Seocho-gu, Seoul; tel. (2) 529-2268; fax (2) 529-2270; internet www.publicunion.or.kr; f. 1998; Pres. JANG DAE-IK; 19,375 mems.

Federation of Korean Taxi & Transport Workers' Unions: 415-7, Janan 1-dong, Dongdaemun-gu, Seoul; tel. (2) 2210-8500; fax (2) 2247-7890; internet www.ktaxi.or.kr; f. 1988; Pres. KWAN OH-MAN; 105,118 mems.

Federation of Korean United Workers' Unions: Sukchun Bldg, 32-100, 4-ga, Dangsan-dong, Yeongdeungpo-gu, Seoul; internet www.fkuwu.or.kr; f. 1961; 51,802 mems.

Korea Automobile & Transport Workers' Federation: 678-27, Yeoksam-dong, Gangnam-gu, Seoul; tel. (2) 554-0890; fax (2) 554-1558; f. 1963; Pres. KANG SUNG-CHUN; 84,343 mems.

Korea Federation of Bank & Financial Workers' Unions: 88, Da-dong, Jung-gu, Seoul; tel. (2) 756-2389; fax (2) 754-4893; internet www.kfiu.or.kr; f. 1961; 113,994 mems.

Korea Federation of Communication Trade Unions: 10th Floor, 106-6, Guro 5-dong, Guro-gu, Seoul; tel. (2) 864-5099; fax (2) 864-5519; internet www.ictu.co.kr; f. 1961; Pres. OH DONG-IN; 18,810 mems.

Korea Federation of Food Industry Workers' Unions: 106-2, 1-ga, Yanpyeong-dong, Yeongdeungpo-gu, Seoul; tel. (2) 679-6441; fax (2) 679-6444; e-mail hpunion@hanmir.com; internet food.inochong.org; f. 2000; Pres. BAEK YOUNG-GIL; 19,146 mems.

Korea Federation of Port & Transport Workers' Unions: 19th Floor, Pyouk-San Bldg, 12-5 Dongja-dong, Yeongsan-gu, Seoul; tel. (2) 727-4741; fax (2) 727-4749; e-mail kfptwu@chollian.net; f. 1980; Pres. CHOI BONG-HONG; 33,347 mems.

Korea National Electrical Workers' Union: 167, Samseong-dong, Gangnam-gu, Seoul; tel. (2) 3456-6017; fax (2) 3456-6004; internet www.knewu.or.kr; f. 1961; Pres. KIM JU-YOUNG; 16,741 mems.

Korea Tobacco & Ginseng Workers' Unions: 100, Pyeongchon-dong, Daedeok-gu, Daejeon; tel. (42) 932-7118; fax (42) 931-1812; e-mail ktgson35@ktng.com; internet www.ktgwu.or.kr; f. 1960; Pres. KANG TAE-HEUNG; 6,008 mems.

Korea Union of Teaching and Educational Workers: ; tel. (2) 2691-5335; fax (2) 2691-8558; e-mail leemo@korea.com; internet www.kute.or.kr; f. 1999; 18,337 mems.

Korean Postal Workers' Union: 154-1, Seorin-dong, Jongno-gu, Seoul 110-110; tel. (2) 2195-1773; fax (2) 2195-1761; e-mail cheshin@chol.com; internet www.kpwu.or.kr; f. 1958; Pres. JUNG HYUN-YOUNG; 23,500 mems.

Korean Railway Workers' Union: 40, 3-ga, Hangang-no, Yeongsan-gu, Seoul; tel. (2) 3780-5980; fax (2) 3780-5971; internet www.krwu.or.kr; f. 1947; Pres. KIM JONG-WOOK; 31,041 mems.

Korean Tourist Industry Workers' Federation: 749, 5-ga, Namdaemun-no, Jung-gu, Seoul 100-095; tel. (2) 779-1297; fax (2) 779-1298; f. 1970; Pres. JEONG YOUNG-KI; 27,273 mems.

Korean Confederation of Trade Unions: 5th Daeyoung Bldg, 139, 2-ga, Yeouido-dong, Yeongdeungpo-gu, Seoul 150-032; tel. (2) 2636-0165; fax (2) 2635-1134; internet www.kctu.org; f. 1995; legalized 1999; Chair. CHO JUN-HO; 600,000 mems.

Transport

RAILWAYS

At the end of 2001 there were 3,392 km of railways in operation. The first phase of construction of a new high-speed rail system connecting Seoul to Busan (412 km) via Cheonan, Daejeon, Daegu, and Gyungju, was completed in early 2004, with services commencing operation from April. The second phase, Daejeon–Busan, was scheduled for completion in 2010. Construction work on the reconnection of the Kyongui (West Coast, Sinuiju–Seoul) and East Coast Line (Wonsan–Seoul) began in September 2002. The two lines were reportedly completed in 2005. Scheduled cross-border trial runs took place in May 2007. Eventually the two were to be linked to the Trans-China and Trans-Siberian railways respectively.

Korean National Railroad: 139 Seonsa-ro, Seo-gu, Daejon 302-701; tel. (42) 472-3001; fax (42) 472-3020; internet www.korail.com; f. 1963; operates all railways under the supervision of the Ministry of Land, Transport and Maritime Affairs; total track length of 6,819 km (2001); Pres. PARK KWANG-SEOK (acting).

City Underground Railways

Busan Subway: Busan Urban Transit Authority, 861-1, Bumchun-dong, Busan 614-021; tel. (51) 633-8783; e-mail ipsubway@buta.or.kr; internet subway.busan.kr; f. 1988; length of 71.6 km (2 lines, with a further 3rd line under construction); Pres. LEE HYANG-YEUL.

Daegu Metropolitan Subway Corpn: 1500 Sangin 1-dong, Dalseo-gu, Daegu; tel. (53) 640-2114; fax (53) 640-2229; e-mail webmaster@daegusubway.co.kr; internet www.daegusubway.co.kr; length of 28.3 km (one line, with a further five routes totalling 125.4 km planned or under construction); Pres. YOON JIN-TAE.

Daejeon Metropolitan Express Transit Corpn: tel. (42) 539-3114; fax (42) 539-3119; e-mail qnsdlqkr@hanmail.net; internet www.djet.co.kr; f. 2006; operates one line, with a further four lines planned.

Gwangju Metropolitan Rapid Transit Corpn: 529 Sangmu-no, Seo-gu, Gwangju; tel. (62) 604-8000; internet www.subway.gwangju.kr; f. 2004; one line, with a further line planned; Pres. OH HAENG-WON.

Incheon Rapid Transit Corpn: 67-2, Gansok-dong, Namdong-gu, Incheon 405-233; tel. (32) 451-2114; fax (32) 451-2160; internet www.irtc.co.kr; length of 24.6 km (22 stations, 1 line), with two further lines planned; Pres. CHOUNG IN-SOUNG.

THE REPUBLIC OF KOREA (SOUTH KOREA)

Seoul Metropolitan Rapid Transit Corporation: 133-170 Seongdong-gu, Yongdap-dong 223-3, Seoul; tel. (2) 6211-2000; e-mail webadmin@smrt.co.kr; internet www.smrt.co.kr; operates lines 5–8.

Seoul Metropolitan Subway Corpn: 447-7, Bangbae-dong, Seocho-gu, Seoul; tel. (2) 520-5020; fax (2) 520-5039; internet www.seoulsubway.co.kr; f. 1981; length of 134.9 km (115 stations, lines 1-4); Pres. KIM JUNG-GOOK.

ROADS

At the end of 2005 there were 102,293 km of roads, of which 76.8% were paved. A network of motorways (2,637 km) links all the principal towns, the most important being the 428-km Seoul–Busan motorway. Improvements in relations with North Korea resulted in the commencement of work on a four-lane highway to link Seoul and the North Korean capital, Pyongyang, in September 2000. In February 2003 a road link between the two countries was reportedly opened.

Korea Highway Corpn: 293-1, Kumto-dong, Sujong-gu, Seongnam, Gyeonggi Prov.; tel. (822) 2230-4114; fax (822) 2230-4308; internet www.freeway.co.kr; f. 1969; responsible for construction, maintenance and management of toll roads; Pres. OH JUM-LOCK.

SHIPPING

In December 2006 South Korea's merchant fleet (2,820 vessels) had a total displacement of 10,477,100 grt. Major ports include Busan, Incheon, Donghae, Masan, Yeosu, Gunsan, Mokpo, Pohang, Ulsan, Jeju and Gwangyang.

Busan Port Authority: c79-9, Jungangdong 4-ga, Junggu, Busan 600-817; tel. (2) 999-3000; fax (2) 988-8878; e-mail bpmaster@busanpa.com; internet www.busanpa.com; f. 2004.

Korea Shipowners' Association: Sejong Bldg, 10th Floor, 100, Dangju-dong, Jongno-gu, Seoul 110-071; tel. (2) 739-1551; fax (2) 739-1564; e-mail korea@shipowners.or.kr; internet www.shipowners.co.kr; f. 1960; 145 shipping co mems (March 2008); Chair. LEE JIN-BANG.

Korea Shipping Association: 66010, Dungchon 3-dong, Gangseo-gu, Seoul 157-033; tel. (2) 6096-2024; fax (2) 6096-2029; e-mail kimny@haewoon.co.kr; internet www.haewoon.co.kr; f. 1962; management consulting and investigation, mutual insurance; 1,189 mems; Chair. PARK HONG-JIN.

Principal Companies

DooYang Line Co Ltd: 166-4, Samseong-dong, Gangnam-gu, Seoul 135-091; tel. (2) 550-1700; fax (2) 550-1777; internet www.dooyang.co.kr; f. 1984; world-wide tramping and conventional liner trade; Pres. CHO DONG-HYUN.

Hanjin Shipping Ltd: 25-11, Yeouido-dong, Yeongdeungpo-gu, Seoul; tel. (2) 3770-6114; fax (2) 3770-6740; internet www.hanjin.com; f. 1977; marine transport, harbour service, warehousing, shipping and repair, vessel sales, harbour department and cargo service; Pres. CHOI WON-PYO.

Hyundai Merchant Marine Co Ltd: 66, Jeokseon-dong, Jongno-gu, Seoul 110-052; tel. (2) 3706-5114; fax (2) 723-2193; internet www.hmm.co.kr; f. 1976; Chair. HYUN YUNG-WON.

Korea Line Corpn: Dae Il Bldg, 43, Insa-dong, Jongno-gu, Seoul 110-290; tel. (2) 3701-0114; fax (2) 733-1610; f. 1968; world-wide transport service and shipping agency service in Korea; Pres. JANG HAK-SE.

Pan Ocean Shipping Co Ltd: 51-1, Namchang-dong, Jung-gu, CPOB 3051, Seoul 100-060; tel. (2) 316-5114; fax (2) 316-5296; f. 1966; transport of passenger cars and trucks, chemical and petroleum products, dry bulk cargo; Pres. CHIANG JIN-WON.

CIVIL AVIATION

There are international airports at Incheon (Seoul), Gimpo (Seoul), Busan, Cheongju, Daegu, Gwangju, Jeju and Yangyang. The main gateway into Seoul is Incheon International Airport, which opened for service in 2001. The second phase began construction in 2002, with completion due by 2008. When complete, the airport will handle 44m. passengers and 4.5m. tons of cargo annually. The airport is located 52 km from Seoul. A new airport, Yangyang International Airport, in Gangwon Province, opened in 2002.

Asiana Airlines Inc: 47, Osae-dong, Gangseo-gu, Seoul; tel. (2) 758-8114; fax (2) 758-8008; e-mail asianacr@asiana.co.kr; internet www.asiana.co.kr; f. 1988; serves 14 domestic cities and 36 destinations in 16 countries; fmrly Seoul Air International; CEO PARK SAM-KOO.

Hansung Airlines: Cheongju; tel. 1599-1090; fax (43) 210-0520; internet www.gohansung.com; f. 2004; operates low-cost flights between Cheongju and Jeju City; CEO HAN WOO-BONG.

Jeju Air: tel. (64) 746-7003; fax (64) 746-7011; internet www.jejuair.net; f. 2005; 25% owned by Jeju provincial govt, 75% by the Aekyung Group; operates low-cost flights between Jeju and the mainland; CEO JOO SANG-KIL.

Korean Air: 1370, Gonghang-dong, Gangseo-gu, Seoul; tel. (2) 656-7092; fax (2) 656-7289; internet www.koreanair.com; f. 1962; est. by the Govt, privately owned since 1969; fmrly Korean Air Lines (KAL); operates domestic and regional services and routes to the Americas, Europe, the Far East and the Middle East, serving 73 cities in 26 countries; Chair. and CEO CHO YANG-HO.

Tourism

South Korea's mountain scenery and historic sites are the principal attractions for tourists. Jeju Island, located some 100 km off the southern coast, is a popular resort. In 2005 there were 6.0m. visitors to South Korea, of whom some 41% came from Japan. Receipts from tourism in 2005 amounted to US $8,148m.

Korea National Tourism Organization: KNTO Bldg, 10, Da-dong, Jung-gu, CPOB 903, Seoul 100; tel. (2) 729-9600; fax (2) 757-5997; e-mail webmaster@mail.knto.or.kr; internet english.tour2korea.com; f. 1962; as Korea Tourist Service; Pres. (vacant).

Korea Tourism Association: Saman Bldg, 11th Floor, 945, Daechi-dong, Gangnam-gu, Seoul; tel. (2) 556-2356; fax (2) 556-3818; f. 1963; Pres. CHO HANG-KYU, KIM JAE-GI.

KOSOVO

Introductory Survey

On 17 February 2008 the Serbian province of Kosovo made a declaration of independence, which was strongly opposed by Serbia. By early May 39 countries had formally recognized the Republic of Kosovo. However, several countries, including the People's Republic of China and Russia, continued to withhold recognition.

Location, Climate, Language, Religion, Flag, Capital

The Republic of Kosovo (Kosova), formerly the province officially named Kosovo and Metohija within the Republic of Serbia, is situated in the central Balkan peninsula in south-eastern Europe. There are borders with Serbia in the north-west and north-east, the former Yugoslav republic of Macedonia in the south, Albania in the south-west, and Montenegro to the west. The climate is continental. Under a new Constitution, approved in April 2008, the official languages of Kosovo are Albanian and Serbian, while the Turkish, Bosnian and Roma languages are also accorded official status at municipal level. The principal religion in Kosovo is Islam. Serbs are principally adherents of Orthodox Christianity, as represented by the Serbian Orthodox Church. The state flag adopted at independence (proportions 2 by 3) is blue, with an arc of six white stars above a golden map of Kosovo. The capital is Prishtina (Prishtinë—Priština).

Recent History

Kosovo was part of the Serbian state established by the Nemanja dynasty in 1166. The Serbian Orthodox Patriarchate was established in Kosovo in the 13th century, and the territory was the location of the defeat of the Serbs by the Turkish Ottoman Empire at Fushë Kosovë (Kosovo Polje—'the Field of Blackbirds') in 1389. After continued Albanian resistance to Ottoman rule, the League of Prizren was established in 1878. Kosovo remained under Ottoman rule until its annexation by Serbia during the First Balkan War in 1912. During the Second World War Kosovo was annexed by Albania (in personal union with the Italian Crown). Following the establishment of the Federative People's Republic of Yugoslavia, Kosovo (together with Vojvodina) became an autonomous region of Serbia under the Constitution of 1946. Following Albanian campaigning for greater autonomy, Kosovo received the status of an Autonomous Province in the Constitution of 1974.

From the mid-1980s increasing Serb nationalism, with the rise to power of Slobodan Milošević, exacerbated tensions in the province. A new Serbian Constitution of 1990 revoked the autonomy of Kosovo and Vojvodina. The abolition of the autonomous status of the two provinces was confirmed in April 1992 under a new federal Constitution, which created the Federal Republic of Yugoslavia. A republic-wide referendum on the new Serbian Constitution, largely boycotted by the ethnic Albanians, was conducted on 2 July, and a majority of Serbs approved the new Constitution. It was formally promulgated on 28 September, whereupon Kosovo was officially renamed Kosovo and Metohija. Meanwhile, following the constitutional referendum, 114 of 180 deputies in the Kosovo Assembly (Kuvendi i Kosovës/Skupština Kosova) met and declared Kosovo independent of Serbia. On 5 July the Serbian authorities dissolved the provincial Assembly and Government. The Kosovo presidency resigned in protest, and Serbia introduced a special administration. On 7 September members of the old representative body declared the Kosovo Assembly to have been reconvened and subsequently proclaimed a basic law of the 'Republic of Kosovo'. Meanwhile, elections, which were declared illegal by the Serbian authorities, were held in the province on 24 May. The Democratic Alliance of Kosovo (DAK) secured the most seats in the 130-member Assembly, and the DAK leader, Ibrahim Rugova, was elected President of the self-proclaimed 'Republic of Kosovo'.

Throughout the mid-1990s there were reports of harassment of Kosovo Albanians by Serbian police. The situation deteriorated further in 1996 with the emergence, in February, of an ethnic Albanian terrorist organization, the Kosovo Liberation Army (KLA), which announced its intention to achieve independence for Kosovo through armed resistance against the Serbian authorities, and began attacks against security forces. Special Serbian security forces, which were dispatched to the region, undertook reprisals against the Albanian population.

Negotiations regarding the implementation of a cease-fire in Kosovo and the withdrawal of Serbian forces continued throughout 1998 and in October, following a North Atlantic Treaty Organization (NATO, see p. 340) ultimatum, federal President Milošević agreed to the presence in Kosovo of an Organization for Security and Co-operation in Europe (OSCE, see p. 354) mission, which began deployment in early November. Nevertheless, armed clashes between Serbian forces and the KLA increased. In January 1999 the bodies of 45 Albanians were discovered in the village of Reçak (Račak), increasing international concerns of a humanitarian crisis. In February–March Serbian and ethnic Albanian delegations, including KLA representatives, attended a peace conference in Rambouillet, France. Despite the reluctance of the KLA to accept conditions for disarmament, the Albanian delegation signed the peace agreement on 18 March. However, the Serbian delegation continued to present objections to the peace plan; on 23 March the Serbian legislature adopted a resolution condemning aggression against its country and opposing the deployment of NATO forces in Kosovo. On 24 March a NATO-led aerial bombardment of military and civilian installations in Serbia, and also some targets in Montenegro, commenced. Serbian security forces in Kosovo subsequently intensified the mass expulsions and large-scale massacres of the Albanian civilian population, resulting in the continued exodus of refugees from the province. According to the UN High Commissioner for Refugees (UNHCR), a total of 848,100 Albanians fled or were expelled from Kosovo. On 3 June 1999 a peace agreement providing for the withdrawal of Serbian forces from Kosovo and the deployment of a joint NATO-Russian peace-keeping force was approved by the Serbian legislature. On 10 June, following a Military Technical Agreement between NATO and the Federal Government, the withdrawal of Serbian forces from Kosovo commenced, and NATO officially suspended its air operations. On the same day a UN Security Council resolution was passed, authorizing the deployment of international civil and security presences in Kosovo, and providing for the establishment of the UN Interim Administration Mission in Kosovo (UNMIK) as the supreme legal and executive authority in the region. On 12 June Russian and NATO troops entered Kosovo. By 20 June the Serb withdrawal had been completed and the multinational NATO-led Kosovo Force (KFOR), which had an authorized strength of up to 50,000 personnel, was established in the province. Some three weeks after the end of the conflict, an estimated 600,000 Albanians had returned to Kosovo. Over the same period some 180,000 Serbs and Roma fled the province, fearing retaliatory attacks.

In February 2000 Rugova announced the dissolution of the 'Republic of Kosovo' and of the DAK. Following the completion of a voter registration process, local government elections took place in Kosovo on 28 October. Rugova's Democratic League of Kosovo (DLK—which had been formed as a successor organization to the DAK) secured 58% of the votes cast to 30 municipal councils, while the Democratic Party of Kosovo (DPK), led by a former KLA Commander, Hashim Thaçi, won 27% of the votes. Elections to 100 seats of the 120-member Kosovo Assembly were conducted on 17 November 2001, under a UNMIK programme for establishing partial provisional self-government in the province. (The remaining 20 seats were allocated proportionally to Serbs and other ethnic groups.) Rugova's DLK secured 47 seats, while the DPK won 26 seats and a coalition of Serbian parties, Povratak (Return), 22 seats. However, repeated attempts to elect Rugova as President of Kosovo proved unsuccessful, owing to a boycott of the vote by the other parties represented in the legislature. On 4 March 2002, following protracted inter-party discussions, Rugova was elected President of Kosovo. Under the coalition agreement, a member of the DPK, Bajram Rexhepi, became Prime Minister, and a 10-member Government (in which the DLK held four portfolios and the DPK a further two) was subsequently established. In April the Povratak coalition finally agreed to join the administration.

In March 2004 the deaths of three Albanian boys, who had allegedly been pursued by a group of Serbs into the Ibar River, precipitated rioting in Kosovska Mitrovica (Mitrovicë), which escalated into several days of clashes between the Serbian and Albanian communities throughout the province. NATO deployed some 2,000 KFOR reinforcements in the province to quell the violence. At the end of the month it was reported that 19 civilians had been killed (11 Albanians and eight Serbs), while some 4,000 Serbs and Roma had been forced to flee from their residences, after being attacked by Albanian rioters. At elections to the Kosovo Assembly on 23 October, Rugova's DLK secured 45.4% of the votes cast, thereby retaining 47 seats in the 120-member legislature, while the DPK won 28.9% of the votes, increasing its representation to 30 seats, and the Alliance for the Future of Kosovo 8.4%, with nine seats. Having again failed to obtain an outright majority, the DLK negotiated a coalition agreement, whereby the leader of the AFK, Ramush Haradinaj, became the new Prime Minister on 3 December. The election of Haradinaj, a former senior KLA leader who had been under investigation by the International Criminal Tribunal for the former Yugoslavia (ICTY, see p. 18) for alleged war crimes in Kosovo, was strongly criticized by Serbian parties. While the overall rate of participation by voters in the province was recorded at some 53.6% of the registered electorate, only about 0.3% of the Serb community were reported to have participated in the poll, following a boycott urged by Serbian political leaders. (Serbs retained an allocation of 10 seats in the Assembly, but continued to boycott the provisional institutions.) On 8 March 2005 Haradinaj, having received an indictment from the ICTY on a total of 37 charges, resigned from the office of Prime Minister and surrendered to the Tribunal. His indictment prompted widespread protests in the province (causing the dispatch of British military reinforcements). On 23 March a new Kosovo Government, led by Bajram Kosumi, also of the AFK, was established. (In April 2008 the ICTY acquitted Haradinaj of all charges.)

Following a favourable report of the European Commission on Serbia and Montenegro in early April 2005, the resolution of Kosovo's future status became an increasingly pressing issue. The European Commission pledged to continue support for the eventual integration of Kosovo into European institutions, provided that the Kosovo Government demonstrated commitment to reforms and democratic principles. In September delegations from the Governments of Serbia and Kosovo met in Vienna, Austria, for preliminary discussions. On 4 October a UN Special Envoy officially submitted a review on Kosovo to the Secretary-General, stating that the Government had made significant progress in establishing executive, legislative and judicial institutions. On 24 October the UN Security Council endorsed the initiation of final status negotiations on Kosovo. In November the Serbian Government adopted a unanimous resolution rejecting independence in Kosovo, while the Kosovo Assembly approved a motion stating that it would only accept independence as final status. Later that month a former Finnish President, Martti Ahtisaari, who had been appointed by UN Secretary-General Kofi Annan as the UN Special Envoy for the Future Status Process for Kosovo, commenced separate discussions with Serbian and Kosovo leaders. On 21 January 2006 Rugova died after an illness. Later that month the DLK nominated Fatmir Sejdiu to succeed Rugova; on 10 February he was elected unopposed as the new President by the Kosovo Assembly. The first round of final status negotiations on Kosovo subsequently began in Vienna on 20–21 February. Direct high-level discussions, the first to involve the Presidents and Prime Ministers of Serbia and Kosovo since 1999, were conducted in Vienna in July; the Kosovo delegation reiterated demands for full independence for the province by the end of that year, while the Serbian Prime Minister, Dr Vojislav Koštunica, maintained that Serbia would not accept a loss of territory. The Kosovo delegation remained opposed to increased decentralization (including a Serbian proposal that a number of new Serb municipalities with autonomous powers be created), owing to concern that an effectively autonomous Serb polity would be established within the province. By the end of 2006 the two delegations had failed to reach any agreement.

On 2 February 2007 Ahtisaari presented his recommendations for the future status of Kosovo to the Serbian and Kosovo authorities and invited the delegations to engage in consultations on the draft in Vienna. The discussions, which commenced later that month, ended in mid-March, with a meeting of the Serbian and Kosovo government leaders; Ahtisaari concluded that, in view of the failure of the delegations to compromise on previously stated positions, there was no further prospect of achieving a negotiated agreement. On 26 March Ahtisaari submitted to the UN Security Council the finalized Comprehensive Proposal for the Kosovo Status Settlement, which recommended independence for the province, to be supervised for an initial period by an international military and civilian presence. Kosovo was to adopt a constitution, flag and anthem, and be granted rights to membership in international organizations; the rights of all minority groups living in the province, particularly the Kosovo Serbs, were to be protected. Under the Proposal, an International Civilian Representative, operating under a UN and European Union (EU, see p. 244) mandate, would be appointed to supervise the implementation of the Settlement, and would be empowered to veto legislation and dismiss local officials. KFOR would continue to provide security in the province, while the EU would deploy a police mission to assist in the development of law-enforcement institutions. On 3 April, at the beginning of a debate in the UN Security Council, Prime Minister Koštunica declared that Serbia rejected the Proposal (following a vote in the Serbian legislature in February). On 5 April Ahtisaari's Proposal was approved by 100 of the 101 votes cast in the Kosovo Assembly. During a visit to Belgrade later that month, the Russian Minister of Foreign Affairs reiterated previous statements that Russia (as a permanent member of the Security Council) would not support an imposed resolution on the status of Kosovo that was not acceptable to the Serbian Government. The Prime Minister of Kosovo, Agim Çeku, insisted that Kosovo was prepared to declare unilateral independence in the event of a protracted delay, while UNMIK officials warned of increasing tension amongst Albanians in the province. From the end of April intensive discussions on Ahtisaari's Proposal were conducted in the UN Security Council; however, on 20 July it was announced that it had proved impossible to secure a resolution, after Russia continued to oppose several drafts. In August a further series of negotiations began between Serbian and Kosovo delegations, with mediation by the USA, the EU and Russia, but again failed to resolve the impasse, with Serbia remaining categorically opposed to full independence for Kosovo. On 10 December the UN Secretary-General was informed that agreement could not be reached between the two sides.

Meanwhile, amid increasing expectations of a unilateral declaration of independence, in view of the lack of progress in negotiations, legislative elections were conducted in Kosovo on 17 November 2007. According to official results, Thaçi's DPK secured the highest number of votes cast, with 34.3%, taking 37 seats in the Assembly, while the DLK received some 22.6% of the votes and 25 seats. With a further boycott of the elections by Serb parties, a rate of participation of about 43% of the electorate was recorded. After lengthy negotiations, it was announced that the DPK and the DLK had reached a coalition agreement, according to which Thaçi was designated as Prime Minister. On 9 January 2008 an 18-member, coalition Government, headed by Thaçi, was approved by the Assembly; the new administration comprised a further eight members of the DPK and six members of the DLK, while two ministerial posts were allocated to representatives of the Serb ethnic community and one to a representative of the Turkish ethnic community. With both main parties in favour of independence, Thaçi confirmed to the Assembly that a declaration of independence was imminent, and would be achieved with the approval of the USA and most EU member states. On the same day Sejdiu was re-elected as President in a third round of voting in the Assembly for a term that was, in an amendment to the existing Constitutional Framework for Provisional Government, extended to five years. Jakup Krasniqi (a member of the DPK) was elected President of the Assembly.

On 17 February 2008 the Assembly of Kosovo endorsed a declaration establishing the province as the Republic of Kosovo (Kosova), a sovereign state independent from Serbia, the resolution adopted being based on Ahtisaari's Comprehensive Proposal for the Kosovo Status Settlement and in accordance with UN Security Council Resolution 1244 (of 1999). Serbia immediately protested that the declaration of independence contravened international law and demanded that it be annulled. An emergency meeting of the UN Security Council failed to agree on a new resolution, with Russia, in continued strong support of Serbia, opposing Kosovo's sovereignty and the People's Republic of China also withholding recognition. Several countries, including Albania, France, the USA and the United Kingdom, extended recognition to Kosovo on 18 February 2008; by early May 39 UN member nations, including 19 EU member nations, had formally

KOSOVO

recognized Kosovo, while a number of diplomatic missions in Prishtina had become embassies. An International Steering Group appointed Dutch diplomat Pieter Feith, already the EU Special Representative, as an International Civilian Representative, who was to supervise the implementation of the Settlement. An EU Rule of Law Mission (EULEX Kosovo), comprising some 1,900 foreign personnel, was to be deployed in Kosovo to support the authorities in maintaining public order. In March one member of UNMIK was killed in severe clashes between Serb protesters (who had seized control of a courthouse) and UNMIK and KFOR troops in Mitrovica. Serbia insisted that it intended to organize polls for its legislative and local elections (scheduled for 11 May) in the Serb-dominated municipalities in Kosovo. (In addition, a Kosovo Serb leader, Marko Jakšić, announced that Serbs planned to form their own legislature in Kosovo after the Serbian elections.) A new Constitution, which had been drafted by a Constitutional Commission in accordance with the principles of the Settlement, was adopted by the Assembly on 9 April, after being approved by Feith. Following a transitional period, the Constitution was expected to enter into effect on 15 June, when UNMIK had originally been scheduled to transfer authority to government institutions. However, it was reported that Kosovo Serb reluctance to accept the EULEX mission presented an impediment to UNMIK's withdrawal. A report by the UN Secretary-General on developments in Kosovo, published at the beginning of April, stated that UNMIK's mandate would remain in force under Resolution 1244 (with a possible adjustment in its competencies), pending a further decision by the UN Security Council.

Government

In June 1999 the UN Interim Administration Mission in Kosovo (UNMIK) was established as the supreme executive and legal authority in the province of Kosovo. Under the Constitutional Framework for Provisional Government, enacted in May 2001, the Kosovo Assembly (Kuvendi i Kosovës/Skupština Kosova) comprises 120 deputies, of whom 100 are directly elected (the remaining 20 seats are reserved for the elected representatives of specified minority ethnic communities, including eight allocated to Serbs). The Assembly has a nine-member Presidency. The President of Kosovo is elected by the Assembly for a five-year term (renewable only once), and nominates a Prime Minister, who proposes a Government, for approval by the Assembly. Kosovo comprises seven regions, which are divided into 30 municipalities.

The Assembly adopted a declaration of independence on 17 February 2008, with a resolution based on the Comprehensive Proposal for the Kosovo Status Settlement drawn up by the UN Special Envoy of the Secretary-General for the Future Status Process for Kosovo, Martti Ahtisaari, and in accordance with UN Security Council Resolution 1244 (of 1999). An International Civilian Representative, who was also European Union (EU, see p. 244) Special Representative, was appointed by an International Steering Group to supervise the implementation of the Settlement. An EU Rule of Law Mission (EULEX Kosovo) of some 1,900 foreign personnel was to be deployed in Kosovo to maintain public order and security, and to assist in the development of law institutions, while UNMIK was to continue to exercise its executive authority for a transitional period. A new Constitution was adopted by the Assembly on 9 April; it was expected to enter into effect on 15 June, when UNMIK was originally scheduled to transfer its authority to government institutions. (In April it was stated that UNMIK's mandate would remain provisionally in force under Resolution 1244, with a possible adjustment in its competencies.) The International Steering Group was to conduct its first review of the implementation of the Status Settlement after a period of two years.

Defence

Under an agreement between the North Atlantic Treaty Organization (NATO, see p. 340) and the Federal Government, reached in June 1999 (see Recent History), and a subsequent UN resolution, the NATO-led Kosovo Force (KFOR—with a maximum authorized strength of 50,000 personnel) was deployed in the province of Kosovo, and the UN Interim Administration Mission in Kosovo (UNMIK) was installed. In September, following the disarmament of the paramilitary organization, the Kosovo Liberation Army, the movement became reconstituted as a 5,000-member civil emergency security force, the Kosovo Protection Corps. After Kosovo's declaration of independence in February 2008, an EU Rule of Law Mission (EULEX Kosovo), comprising some 1,900 foreign personnel and 1,100 local staff, was to be deployed in Kosovo, with an initial mandate of two years. At the end of February UNMIK comprised 1,996 police officers and 40 military observers. Some 16,000 KFOR troops were to maintain security, in support of Kosovo's institutions. The Kosovo Protection Corps was to be dissolved within one year and a new, multi-ethnic, 2,500-member Kosovo Security Force established.

Economic Affairs

The figures given in the Economic Affairs section of the chapter on Serbia include data pertaining to Kosovo.

Education

Responsibility for education was transferred to the Ministry of Education, Science and Technology in 2002. The system of compulsory education was extended from eight to nine years in 2003/04, henceforth comprising a five-year period of primary education, beginning at seven years, and two cycles of secondary education, lasting four years and three years, respectively. The higher education system operates through two state universities, the University of Prishtina, with a total of 28,832 students in 2004/05, and the University of Mitrovica.

Public Holidays

2008: 1 January (New Year's Day), 7 January (Orthodox Christmas), 17 February (Independence Day), 21–24 March (Roman Catholic Easter), 1 May (International Labour Day), 2 September (Beginning of Ramadan), 1 October* (Small Bayram, end of Ramadan), 28 November (Independence and Liberation Day), 8 December* (Great Bayram, Feast of the Sacrifice), 25 December (Christmas Day).

2009: 1 January (New Year's Day), 7 January (Orthodox Christmas), 17 February (Independence Day), 10–13 April (Roman Catholic Easter), 1 May (International Labour Day), 22 August (Beginning of Ramadan), 20 September* (Small Bayram, end of Ramadan), 27 November* (Great Bayram, Feast of the Sacrifice), 28 November (Independence and Liberation Day), 25 December (Christmas Day).

*These holidays are dependent on the Islamic lunar calendar and may vary by one or two days from the dates given.

Directory

The Constitution

In June 1999 the UN Interim Administration Mission in Kosovo (UNMIK) was established as the supreme executive and legal authority in the province of Kosovo, with Kosovo remaining part of the territory of Serbia. Under the Constitutional Framework for Provisional Government, enacted in May 2001, the Kosovo Assembly (Kuvendi i Kosovës/Skupština Kosova) is the highest representative and legislative institution of Kosovo. The Assembly comprises 120 deputies, of whom 100 are directly elected (the remaining 20 seats are reserved for the elected representatives of specified minority ethnic communities, including eight allocated to Serbs). The Assembly has a nine-member presidency. Under a 2007 amendment to the existing Constitutional Framework, the President of Kosovo is elected by the Assembly for a five-year term (renewable only once). The President nominates a Prime Minister, who proposes a Government, for approval by the Assembly.

Following Kosovo's unilateral declaration of independence on 17 February 2008, the President appointed a Constitutional Commission on 19 February. The Commission subsequently promulgated a draft Constitution, based on the principles of the Comprehensive Proposal for the Kosovo Status Settlement of UN Special Envoy Martti Ahtisaari, which guaranteed the rights of minority ethnic communities. After being approved by a newly appointed International Civilian Representative, the new Constitution was adopted by the Assembly on 9 April; it was expected to enter into effect on 15 June.

The Government

INTERNATIONAL REPRESENTATIVES

Special Representative of the Secretary-General of the UN, Head of the UN Interim Administration Mission in Kosovo (UNMIK): Joachim Rücker.

European Union Special Representative in Kosovo and International Civilian Representative in Kosovo: Pieter Feith.

PRESIDENT

President of Kosovo: Fatmir Sejdiu.

GOVERNMENT
(April 2008)

An administration comprising representatives of the Democratic Party of Kosovo (DPK), the Democratic League of Kosovo (DLK), the Independent Liberal Party (SLS) and the Turkish Democratic Party of Kosovo (KDTP).

Prime Minister: Hashim Thaçi (DPK).
Deputy Prime Ministers: Hajredin Kuçi (DPK), Rame Manaj (DLK).
Minister of Finance and the Economy: Ahmet Shala (DPK).
Minister of Public Services: Arsim Bajrami (DPK).
Minister of Education, Science and Technology: Enver Hoxhaj (DPK).
Minister of Culture, Youth and Sports: Skënder Hyseni (DLK).
Minister of Transport and Telecommunications: Fatmir Limaj (DPK).
Minister of the Interior: Blerim Kuçi (DLK).
Minister of Justice: Nekibe Kelmendi (DLK).
Minister of Local Government Administration: Sadri Ferati (DLK).
Minister of the Environment and Spatial Planning: Mahir Yağcilar (KDTP).
Minister of Labour and Social Welfare: Nenad Rašić (SLS).
Minister of Trade and Industry: Lutfi Zharku (DLK).
Minister of Energy and Mining: Justina Pula-Shiroka (DPK).
Minister of Health: Alush Gashi (DLK).
Minister of Returnees and Communities: Boban Stanković (SLS).
Minister of Agriculture, Forestry and Rural Development: Ideriz Vehapi (DPK).

MINISTRIES

Office of the President: 10000 Prishtina, Rruga Nënë Terezë; tel. (38) 213222; e-mail beqiri@president-ksgov.net; internet www.president-ksgov.net.

Office of the Government: 10000 Prishtina, Rruga Nënë Terezë; internet www.ks-gov.net.

Ministry of Agriculture, Forestry and Rural Development: 10000 Prishtina; tel. (38) 20038473; e-mail tome.hajdaraj@ks-gov.net; internet www.mbpzhr-ks.org.

Ministry of Culture, Youth and Sports: 10000 Prishtina; internet www.mkrs-ks.org.

Ministry of Education, Science and Technology: 10000 Prishtina, Rruga Musine Kokollari 18, Lagjja Dadania Blloku-III; tel. (38) 540973; e-mail masht@ks-gov.net; internet www.ks-gov.net/masht.

Ministry of Energy and Mining: 10000 Prishtina, Rruga Qyteza Pejton dne Sejdi Kryeziu 5; tel. (38) 20021301; fax (38) 20021302; e-mail metush.zenuni@ks-gov.net; internet www.ks-gov.net/mem.

Ministry of the Environment and Spatial Planning: 10000 Prishtina, Rruga Nazim Gafurri 31; tel. (38) 517800; fax (38) 517845; e-mail webmaster.mmph@ks-gov.net; internet www.ks-gov.net/mmph.

Ministry of Finance and the Economy: 10000 Prishtina, Rruga Bill Klinton dhe Nënë Terezë; tel. (38) 213115; fax (38) 213113; e-mail info@mfe-ks.org; internet www.mfe-ks.org.

Ministry of Health: 10000 Prishtina, Rruga Zagrebi; tel. (38) 211191; fax (38) 211371; e-mail skender.berisha@ks-gov.net; internet www.mshgov-ks.org.

Ministry of Internal Affairs: 10000 Prishtina, Rruga Nënë Terezë, Ndërtesa e Qeverisë; tel. (38) 20019024; e-mail blerim.kuci@ks-gov.net; internet www.mpb-ks.org.

Ministry of Justice: 10000 Priština; internet www.md-ks.org.

Ministry of Labour and Social Welfare: 10000 Prishtina, Ndërtesa e re e Fakultetit Ekonomik; tel. (38) 244228; fax (38) 244229; e-mail agron.bacaj@ks-gov.net; internet www.mpms-ks.org.

Ministry of Local Government Administration: 10000 Prishtina; tel. (38) 542574; e-mail aziz.lila@ks-gov.net; internet www.mapl-ks.net.

Ministry of Public Services: 10000 Prishtina, Rruga Nëna Tereze, Zona C-213, Ndërtesa e Gërmisë; tel. (38) 20030956; e-mail info-mshp@ks-gov.net; internet www.ks-gov.net/mshp.

Ministry of Returnees and Community: 10000 Prishtina.

Ministry of Trade and Industry: 10000 Prishtina, Rruga Agim Ramadani, Ndërtesa e re e Fakultetit Ekonomik; tel. (38) 20036010; fax (38) 200211985; internet www.mti-ks.org.

Ministry of Transport and Telecommunications: 10000 Prishtina; internet www.mtpt.org.

Legislature

Kosovo Assembly
(Kuvendi i Kosovës/Skupština Kosova)
10000 Prishtina, Rruga Nënë Terezë; tel. (38) 211186; fax (38) 211188; internet www.assembly-kosova.org.

President: Jakup Krasniqi.

Election, 17 November 2007

Parties	Votes	% of votes	Seats
Democratic Party of Kosovo	196,207	34.32	37
Democratic League of Kosovo	129,410	22.63	25
New Kosovo Alliance	70,165	12.27	13
Democratic League of Dardania–Albanian Christian Democratic Party of Kosovo	57,002	9.97	11
Alliance for the Future of Kosovo	54,611	9.55	10
ORA Reformist Party	23,722	4.14	—
Justice Party	9,789	1.73	—
Others	30,760	5.38	4*
Reserved seats for representatives of designated minority ethnic groups†	—	—	20
Total	**571,767**	**100.00**	**120**

* The other parties to obtain representation (one seat apiece) on the basis of national proportional representation were: the Turkish Democratic Party of Kosovo; the Vakat Coalition; the Democratic Ashkali Party of Kosovo; and the Party of Democratic Action (all four of these parties additionally obtained representation among those seats reserved for representatives of minority ethnic groups, q.v.).

† The 20 seats reserved for representatives of designated minority ethnic groups (10 seats are elected by Serbs, four by a constituency comprising Roma, Ashkali and 'Egyptians'—a subset of Roma, three by Bosniaks, two by Turks and one by Gorani) were allocated as follows, following voting within each constituent group: the Civic Initiative of Gora (1 seat); the Democratic Ashkali Party of Kosovo (2 seats); the Independent Liberal Party (3 seats); New Democracy (1 seat); the New Democratic Initiative of Kosovo (1 seat); the Party of Democratic Action (1 seat); the Serb Democratic Party of Kosovo and Metohija (3 seats); the Serb Kosovo and Metohija Party (1 seat); the Serb People's Party (1 seat); the Turkish Democratic Party of Kosovo (2 seats); Union of Independent Social Democrats of Kosovo and Metohija (1 seat); the United Roma Party of Kosovo (1 seat); and the Vakat Coalition (2 seats).

Election Commission

Kosovo Central Election Commission: 10000 Prishtina, Rruga Qyteza Pejton Mujo Ulqinaku 7; tel. (38) 246599; fax (38) 246602; e-mail kqz.sekretariati@cec-ko.org; internet www.cec-ko.org; f. 2004; Chair. Tim Guldimann.

Political Organizations

Albanian Christian Democratic Party of Kosovo (PShDK) (Partia Shqiptare Demokristane e Kosovës): 10000 Prishtina, B. Pejani 3; tel. (38) 221536; f. 2000; Chair. Mark Krasniqi.

Alliance for the Future of Kosovo (AFK) (Aleanca për Ardhmërinë e Kosovës): 10000 Prishtina, Kodra e Trimave; tel. (44) 219080; f. 2002; coalition; Leader Ramush Haradinaj.

Democratic League of Dardania (Lidhja Demokratike e Dardanisë): 10000 Prishtina, Rruga Robert Gajdiku, Lagja Velania; tel. and fax (38) 248586; e-mail info@ldd-kosova.org; internet www

KOSOVO

.ldd-kosova.org; f. Jan. 2007 by fmr mems of Democratic League of Kosovo; Leader NEXHAT DACI.

Democratic League of Kosovo (DLK) (Lidhja Demokratike e Kosovës): 10000 Prishtina, Kompleksi Qafa; tel. (38) 242242; fax (38) 245305; e-mail ldk@ldk-kosova.org; internet www.ldk-kosova.org; f. 2000 as successor to the Democratic Alliance of Kosovo; Chair. FATMIR SEJDIU.

Democratic Party of Kosovo (DPK) (Partia Demokratike e Kosovës): 10000 Prishtina, Rruga Nënë Terezë 20; tel. (44) 156774; e-mail pdk@pdk-ks.org; internet www.pdk-ks.org; fmrly Party for the Democratic Party of Kosovo; Chair. HASHIM THAÇI.

Independent Liberal Party (SLS) (Samostalna liberalna stranka): 10000 Prishtina; internet www.sls-ks.org; f. 2006; represents Serb interests; Chair. SLOBODAN PETROVIĆ.

Justice Party (Partia e Drejtësisë): 10000 Prishtina, Rexhep Luci 9; tel. (44) 155688; f. 2000; Chair. SYLEJMAN ÇERKEZI.

Liberal Party of Kosovo (Partia Liberale e Kosovës—PLK): 10000 Prishtina, Rruga Nënë Terezë dne Goleshi 10/2; tel. and fax (38) 244780; e-mail info@plk-kosova.org; internet n.1asphost.com/mend/base; Chair. Prof. GJERGJ DEDAJ.

New Democracy (Nova Demokratija): 10000 Prishtina; f. 2007; represents Serb interests; Leader BRANISLAV GRBIĆ.

New Kosovo Alliance (AKR) (Aleanca Kosova e Re): 10000 Prishtina, Rruga UÇK 55; tel. (38)247988; fax (38) 247988; e-mail info@akr-ks.com; internet www.akr-ks.info; f. 2006; Leader BEHGJET PACOLLI.

ORA Reformist Party (Partia Reformiste ORA): 10000 Prishtina; tel. (38) 246600; e-mail info@ora-kosova.org; internet www.ora-kosova.org; Chair. VETON SORRAI.

People's Movement of Kosovo (Lëvizja Popullore e Kosovës): 10000 Prishtina, Rruga Thimi Mitko 6; tel. (44) 131832; e-mail info@lpk-kosova.com; internet www.lpk-kosova.com; f. 1982; Chair. EMRUSH XHEMAJLI.

Serb List for Kosovo and Metohija (Srpska Lista za Kosovo i Metohiju): Kosovska Mitrovica; coalition of representatives of the Serbian Renewal Movement (q.v.), the Democratic Party (q.v.) and the Social Democratic Party (q.v.) in Kosovo.

Turkish Democratic Party of Kosovo (KDTP) (Kosova Demokratik Türk Partisi): 10000 Prizren, Rruga Adem Jashari 122; e-mail kosova_dtp@hotmail.com; internet www.kdtp.org; Chair. MAHIR YAĞCILAR.

Vakat Coalition (Koalicija Vakat): Dragaš; coalition of representatives of the Bosniak Democratic Party, the Fatherland (Vatan) Democratic Party and the Bosniak Party of Kosovo.

Other political parties represented in the Kosovo Assembly (Kuvendi i Kosovës/Skupština Kosova), following elections on 17 November 2007, were: the Democratic Ashkali Party of Kosovo (Partia Demokratike e Ashkanlive të Kosovës); the Serb Democratic Party of Kosovo and Metohija (Srpska Demokratska Stranka Kosova i Metohije), led by SLAVIŠA PETKOVIĆ; the Party of Democratic Action (Stranka Demokratske Akcije); the Serb People's Party (Srpska Narodna Stranka), led by MIHAJL ŚĆEPANOVIĆ; the Civic Initiative of Gora (Građanska Inicijativa Gore); the Serb Kosovo and Metohija Party (Srpska Kosovsko-Metohijka Stranka), led by DRAGIŠA MIRIĆ; the New Democratic Initiative of Kosovo (Iniciativa e re Demokrarike e Kosovës), representing the 'Egyptian' (a subset of Roma) minority ethnic group; the Union of Independent Social Democrats of Kosovo and Metohija (Savez Nezavisnih Socijaldemokrata Kosova i Metohije), led by NEBOJŠA ŽIVIĆ; and the United Roma Party of Kosovo (Partia Rome e Bashkuar e Kosovës).

Diplomatic Representation

EMBASSIES IN KOSOVO

Albania: Prishtina, Qyteza Pejton, Rruga Mujo Ulqinaku 18; tel. (38) 248208; fax (38) 248209; e-mail mission.kosova@mfa.gov.al; Ambassador ISLAM LAUKA.

Austria: 38000 Prishtina, Fan Noli 22, Dragodan I; tel. (38) 249284; fax (38) 249285; e-mail pristina-as@bmeia.gv.at.

Germany: 10000 Prishtina, Arbëri, Rruga Azem Jashanica 17; tel. (38) 254500; fax (38) 254536; e-mail info@pris.auswaertiges-amt.de; internet www.pristina.diplo.de; Ambassador HANS-DIETER STEINBACH.

Switzerland: 10060 Prishtina, Adrian Krasniqi 11; tel. (38) 248088; fax (38) 248078; e-mail pri.vertretung@eda.admin.ch; internet www.eda.admin.ch/pristina; Ambassador LUKAS BEGLINGER.

United Kingdom: 10000 Prishtina, Arbëri, Rruga Ismail Qemali 6; tel. (38) 254700; fax (38) 249799; e-mail britishoffice.pristina@fco.gov.uk; Ambassador ANDREW SPARKES.

USA: 1000 Prishtina, Arbëri, Nazim Hikmet 30; tel. (38) 593000; fax (38) 549890; e-mail papristina@state.gov; internet www.pristina.usembassy.gov; Chargé d'affaires TINA S. KAIDANOW.

Judicial System

The court system comprises a Supreme Court, district courts, municipal courts and minor offences courts.

Supreme Court of Kosovo: 10000 Prishtina; Pres. REXHEP HAXHIMUSA.

Religion

Most of the inhabitants of Kosovo are adherents of Islam, although most Serbs are Orthodox Christians, and several sites of historic importance to Serbian Orthodoxy are located within Kosovo. A significant minority of the Kosovo Albanian population are Roman Catholics.

ISLAM

Islamic Community: 10000 Prishtina; Pres. of the Mesihat Dr REDZEP BOJE.

CHRISTIANITY

The Eastern Orthodox Church

The Patriarchate of the Serbian Orthodox Church is located at Pej (Peć), in central Kosovo.

The Roman Catholic Church

At 31 December 2005 there were an estimated 65,000 Roman Catholics within the Apostolic Administration of Prizren.

Apostolic Administrator of Prizren: GJERGJU DODË, 20000 Prizren, Rruga I. L. Ribar 7; tel. (29) 41933; fax (29) 41232; e-mail ipeshkvia_pz@yahoo.com.

The Press

PRINCIPAL DAILIES

Bota Sot (The World Today): 10000 Prishtina, Rruga Jakove Xoxa; tel. (38) 249846; fax (38) 249845; e-mail bota-sot@ipko.net; in Albanian; Editor BAJRUSH MORINA.

Gazeta Express: 10000 Prishtina, Dardania 1/1; tel. (38) 542270; e-mail info@gazetaexpress.com; internet www.gazetaexpress.com; f. 2005; in Albanian; seven a week; Chief Exec. BATON HAXHIU.

Infopress: 10000 Prishtina; popular; supportive of Democratic Party of Kosovo; Editor AVNI AZEMI.

Koha Ditore: 10000 Prishtina, POB 202; tel. (38) 249104; e-mail koha@magnet.ch; internet www.koha.net; in Albanian; Editor AGRON BAJRAMI.

Kosova Sot (Kosovo Today): 10000 Prishtina, Pallati i Shtypit; tel. (38) 525049; fax (38) 545070; e-mail kosovasot2001@yahoo.com; f. 1998; in Albanian; Dir MARGARITA KADRIU.

Lajm (The News): 10000 Prishtina; tel. (38) 243009; e-mail info@gazetalajm.info; internet www.gazetalajm.info; f. 2004; in Albanian; supportive of the New Kosovo Alliance; Chief Exec. BEHGJET PACOLLI.

PERIODICALS

Fokus Kosova/Fokus Kosovo/Focus Kosovo: 10000 Prishtina, UNMIK Administrative Headquarters; e-mail focuskosovo@un.org; internet www.unmikonline.org/pio/fokus_kosovo_eng.htm; f. 2001; publ. by UNMIK; Albanian, Serbian and English edns; seven a year; Publisher ALEXANDER IVANKO; Editor MYRIAM DESSABLES (Albanian and Serbian edns), RICARDO Z. DUNN.

Official Gazette of the Republic of Kosovo (Gazeta Zyrtare e Republikës së Kosovës/Sluzbeni list Republike Kosova/Kosova Cumhuriyeti Resmi Gazetesi/Sluzbeni Novine Republike Kosova): 10000 Prishtina, Ndërtesa e re e Qeverisë; tel. (38) 20114039; e-mail gazetazyrtare@ks-gov.net; internet www.ks-gov.net/GazetaZyrtare; f. 2005; monthly; publishes official text of laws adopted by the Kosovo Assembly (Kuvendi i Kosovës/Skupština Kosova) as promulgated by the Special Representative of the Secretary-General, resolutions adopted by the Kosovo Assembly, secondary and other legislation issued by the Government and ministries of Kosovo, agreements of international character, etc.; edns in Albanian, Serbian, English, Turkish and Bosnian; administered by the Office of the Prime Minister; Editor ARBEN VESELAJ.

Zeri: 10000 Prishtina; in Albanian; Editor-in-Chief BARDH HAMZAJ.

Publishers

Panorama: 10000 Prishtina; f. 1994; publishes newspapers and journals in Serbian, Albanian and Turkish; Dir JORDAN RISTIĆ.

Rilindja Publishing House: 10000 Prishtina, Dom štampe pa nr; tel. (38) 23868; popular science, literature, children's fiction, travel books, textbooks in Albanian; Dir NAZMI RRAHMANI.

Broadcasting and Communications

TELECOMMUNICATIONS

Regulatory Authority

Telecommunications Regulatory Authority (Kosovo) (ART) (Autoriteti Rregullativ i Telekomunikacionit): 10000 Prishtina; tel. (38) 212345; e-mail info@art-ks.org; internet www.art-ks.org; Chair. ANTON BERISHA.

Service Provider

PTK (Posts and Telecommunications of Kosovo): 10100 Prishtina, Dardania pa nr,. Kati VIII, zyra 808; tel. (38) 524583; e-mail postaekosoves@ptkonline.com; internet www.ptkonline.com; f. 1959; became jt-stock co in 2005; provides postal and telecommunications services in Kosovo, including mobile cellular telephone services operated under the brand name Vala; Chair. of Bd of Dirs ILIR SALIHU.

BROADCASTING

Radio Televizioni i Kosovës (RTK) (Radio-Television Kosovo): 10000 Prishtina, Rruga Xhemail Prishtina 12; tel. (38) 230102; fax (38) 235336; e-mail post@rtklive.com; internet www.rtklive.com; subsidiaries include Radio Kosova and Radio Blue Sky; Chair. Dr VJOSA DOBRUNA; Dir-Gen. AGIM ZATRIQI.

RadioTelevizioni21 (RTV21): 10000 Prishtina, Pallati i Mediave, Aneks II; tel. and fax (38) 550088; e-mail lajmet@rtv21.tv; internet www.rtv21.tv; radio and television broadcaster.

Finance

(cap. = capital; res = reserves; dep. = deposits; m. = million; br. = branch)

BANKING

Regulatory Authority

Central Banking Authority of Kosovo (Autoriteti Qendror Bankar I Kosovës): 10000 Prishtina, Rruga Garibaldi 33; tel. (38) 222055; fax (38) 243763; e-mail publicrelations@cbak-kos.org; internet www.cbak-kos.org; f. 2006 on the basis of the UNMIK Banking and Payments Authority of Kosovo; supervises and regulates banking, insurance, pensions and micro-finance sectors in Kosovo, and fulfils other roles typically carried out by a Central Bank; Man. Dir MICHEL SVETCHINE.

Selected Banks

NLB Banka e Re e Kosovës: 10000 Prishtina, Rruga Nënë Terezë; tel. (38) 223976; fax (38) 225152; e-mail info@brk-bank.com; internet www.brk-bank.com; f. 2001; 87.3% owned by Nova Ljubljanska Banka (Slovenia); cap. €7.8m., res −€1.3m., dep. €48.2m. (Dec. 2006); Chair. of Bd of Dirs REMZI EJUPI.

ProCredit Bank Kosova: 10000 Prishtina, Skënderbeu, Kosovo; tel. (39) 240248; fax (38) 248777; e-mail info@procreditbank-kos.com; internet www.procreditbank-kos.com; f. 2000 as Micro Enterprise Bank; present name adopted 2003; cap. €10.1m., res €0.5m., dep. €343.7m. (Dec. 2005); Gen. Man. FRIEDER WÖHRMANN.

INSURANCE

At the end of 2005 there were nine registered insurance companies operating in Kosovo.

Kompania e Sigurimeve Dukagjini (Dukagjini Insurance Co): 10000 Prishtina, Bulevardi i Dëshmorëve 145; tel. (38) 543575; fax (38) 543576; e-mail info@insurancedukagjini.co; internet www.insurancedukagjini.com; f. 2002; Dir EKREM LLUKA.

Trade and Industry

GOVERNMENT AGENCIES

Investment Promotion Agency of Kosovo (IPAK): 10000 Prishtina, Qyteza Pejton, Perandori Justinian 3–5; tel. and fax (38) 20036041; e-mail info@invest-ks.org; internet www.invest-ks.org.

Kosovo Trust Agency: 10000 Prishtina, Rruga Vellusha II, Green Bldg; tel. (38) 500400; fax (38) 248076; e-mail soetenders@eumik.org; internet www.kta-kosovo.org; Kosovo's privatization agency, supervised by UNMIK.

CHAMBER OF COMMERCE

Kosovo Chamber of Commerce (Oda Ekonomike e Kosovës): 10000 Prishtina, Rruga Nënë Terezë 20; tel. (38) 224741; fax (38) 224299; e-mail info@oek-kcc.org; internet www.kosovo-eicc.org; Chair. Dr BESIM BEQAJ.

UTILITIES

Korporata Energetike e Kosovës/Energetska Korporacija Kosova (KEK) (Kosovo Energy Corpn): 10000 Prishtina; tel. (38) 240245; e-mail nezir.sinani@kek-energy.com; internet www.kek-energy.com; generation and distribution of electricity.

TRADE UNIONS

Union of Independent Trade Unions of Kosovo (BSPK) (Bashkimi i Sindikatave të Pavarura të Kosovës): 38000 Prishtina, Rruga Nëna Terezë 35; tel. (38) 221782; fax (38) 223175; e-mail bspk@etuc.org; internet www.bskp.org; 120,000 mems in 18 federations (2006); Chair. HAXHI ARIFI.

Transport

RAILWAYS

In 2005 there were 436 km of railways and 33 railway stations in operation in Kosovo.

Hekurudhat e Kosovës/Kosovske Železnice (Kosovo Railways): Fushë Kosovë, Sheshi i lirisë pn; tel. (38) 536355; fax (38) 536307; e-mail info@kosovorailway.com; internet www.kosovorailway.com; f. 2005 to replace UNMIK Railway; jt-stock co; operates railway services within Kosovo and international services to Skopje, former Yugoslav republic of Macedonia; Man. Dir XHEVAT RAMOSAJ.

CIVIL AVIATION

There is an international airport at Prishtina.

KUWAIT

Introductory Survey

Location, Climate, Language, Religion, Flag, Capital

The State of Kuwait lies at the north-west extreme of the Persian (Arabian) Gulf, bordered to the north-west by Iraq and to the south by Saudi Arabia. The State comprises a mainland region and nine small islands, of which the largest is Bubiyan and the most populous is Failaka. Immediately to the south of Kuwait, along the Gulf, lies a Neutral (Partitioned) Zone of 5,700 sq km, which is shared between Kuwait and Saudi Arabia. Much of Kuwait is arid desert, and the climate is generally hot and humid. Temperatures in July and August often exceed 45°C (113°F), and in the winter months are frequently above 20°C (68°F)—although there is often frost at night. Average annual rainfall is only 111 mm. The official language is Arabic, which is spoken by the majority of Kuwaiti nationals (estimated, by official definition, to have comprised 39.8% of Kuwait's population at the census of April 2005, according to preliminary results) and by many of the country's non-Kuwaiti residents. Apart from other Arabs, the non-Kuwaitis are mainly Iranians, Indians and Pakistanis. At the 1975 census 95.0% of the population were Muslims (of whom about 70% are now thought to belong to the Sunni sect), while 4.5% were Christians, Hindus or adherents of other faiths. The national flag (proportions 1 by 2) has three equal horizontal stripes, of green, white and red, with a superimposed black trapezoid at the hoist. The capital is Kuwait City.

Recent History

Kuwait became part of Turkey's Ottoman Empire in the 16th century. During the later years of Ottoman rule Kuwait became a semi-autonomous Arab monarchy, with local administration controlled by a Sheikh of the Sabah family, which is still the ruling dynasty. In 1899, fearing an extension of Turkish control, the ruler of Kuwait made a treaty with the United Kingdom, accepting British protection while surrendering control over external relations. Nominal Turkish suzerainty over Kuwait ended in 1918, with the dissolution of the Ottoman Empire.

Petroleum was first discovered in Kuwait in 1938, but exploration was interrupted by the Second World War. After 1945 drilling resumed on a large scale, and extensive deposits of petroleum were found. Sheikh Ahmad (ruler since 1921) was succeeded in 1950 by his cousin, Sheikh Abdullah as-Salim as-Sabah, who inaugurated a programme of public works and educational development, funded by petroleum revenues, which transformed Kuwait's infrastructure and introduced a comprehensive system of welfare services.

Kuwait became fully independent on 19 June 1961, when the United Kingdom and Kuwait agreed to terminate the 1899 treaty. The ruler took the title of Amir and assumed full executive power. Kuwait was admitted to the League of Arab States (the Arab League, see p. 332) despite opposition from Iraq, which claimed that Kuwait was historically part of Iraqi territory. Kuwait's first election took place in December 1961, when voters chose 20 members of a Constituent Assembly (the other members being cabinet ministers appointed by the Amir). The Assembly drafted a new Constitution, which was adopted in December 1962. A 50-member Majlis al-Umma (National Assembly) was elected, under a limited franchise (see Government, below), in January 1963. In the absence of formal political parties (which remain illegal), candidates contested the poll as independents, although some known opponents of the Government were elected. In the same month the Amir appointed his brother, Sheikh Sabah as-Salim as-Sabah (the heir apparent), to be Prime Minister. Iraq renounced its claim to Kuwait in October, and diplomatic relations were established.

In January 1965, following conflict between the paternalistic ruling family and the democratically inclined Majlis, the powers of the Council of Ministers were strengthened. The Amir died in November 1965, and Sheikh Sabah succeeded to the throne. He was replaced as Prime Minister by his cousin, Sheikh Jaber al-Ahmad as-Sabah, who was named heir apparent in May 1966. The Neutral (Partitioned) Zone between Kuwait and Saudi Arabia was formally divided between the two countries in 1969: revenues from oil production in the area are shared equally.

As Kuwait's petroleum sector expanded during the 1960s, the country became increasingly wealthy. The Government effected an extensive redistribution of income, through public expenditure and a land compensation scheme, but there was some popular discontent concerning corruption and official manipulation of the media and the Majlis. A more representative legislature was elected in January 1971 (again under a limited franchise). A further general election took place in January 1975, but in August 1976 the Amir dissolved the Majlis, on the grounds that it was acting against the best interests of the state. Sheikh Sabah died in December 1977 and was succeeded by Crown Prince Jaber. In January 1978 the new Amir appointed Sheikh Saad al-Abdullah as-Salim as-Sabah to be his heir apparent. The new Crown Prince, hitherto Minister of Defence and the Interior, became Prime Minister in the following month. In accordance with an Amiri decree of August 1980, a new Majlis was elected in February 1981, although only one-half of the eligible 6% of the population registered to vote.

The collapse of Kuwait's unofficial stock exchange, the Souk al-Manakh, in September 1982 caused a prolonged financial crisis, and eventually led to the resignations of the Ministers of Finance (in 1983) and of Justice (in 1985). The Majlis subsequently opposed several government measures, including proposed price increases for public services, educational reforms and legislation to restrict the press, and questioned the competence of certain ministers. In July 1986 the Council of Ministers submitted its resignation to the Amir, who then dissolved the Majlis and suspended some articles of the Constitution, declaring his intention to rule by decree. The Crown Prince was immediately reappointed Prime Minister. An Amiri decree accorded the Council of Ministers greater powers of censorship, including the right to suspend publication of newspapers for up to two years.

In late 1989 the Amir refused to accept a petition, signed by more than 20,000 Kuwaiti citizens, seeking the restoration of the Majlis. In January 1990 police dispersed two pro-democracy demonstrations, although later in the month the Government agreed to relax press censorship. In June 62% of eligible voters participated in a general election for 50 members of a 'provisional' National Council; a further 25 members were appointed by the Amir. The election was boycotted by pro-democracy activists, who continued to demand the full restoration of the Majlis.

Of all the Gulf states, Kuwait has been most vulnerable to regional disruption. Immediately after independence British troops (soon replaced by an Arab League force) were dispatched to support the country against the territorial claim by Iraq. The force remained until 1963, and relations between Kuwait and Iraq were stable until 1973, when Iraqi troops occupied a Kuwaiti outpost on their joint border. Kuwait none the less supplied aid to Iraq from the outbreak of the Iran–Iraq War in 1980. As a result, Kuwaiti petroleum installations and shipping in the Persian (Arabian) Gulf were targeted intermittently by Iranian forces, and by pro-Iranian groups within Kuwait, for much of the 1980s. A large number of Iranians were among 27,000 expatriates deported in 1985–86, and in 1987 the Government initiated a five-year plan to reduce the number of expatriates in the Kuwaiti work-force. Kuwait resumed diplomatic relations with Iran following the 1988 cease-fire between Iran and Iraq.

In July 1990 the Iraqi Government implicitly criticized Kuwait (among other states) for disregarding the petroleum production quotas stipulated by the Organization of the Petroleum Exporting Countries (OPEC, see p. 373). It also declared that Kuwait should cancel Iraq's war debt and compensate it for losses of revenue incurred during the war with Iran, and as a result of Kuwait's overproduction of petroleum—to which Iraq attributed a decline in international oil prices. In addition, Iraq alleged that Kuwait had established military posts and drilled oil wells on Iraqi territory. Despite regional mediation efforts, Iraq subsequently began to deploy armed forces on the Kuwait–Iraq border.

Direct negotiations in Jeddah, Saudi Arabia, at the end of the month between Kuwaiti and Iraqi officials collapsed, and on 2 August some 100,000 Iraqi troops invaded Kuwait (whose total military strength was about 20,000): Iraq stated that it had entered at the invitation of insurgents who had overthrown the Kuwaiti Government. The Amir and other government members fled to Saudi Arabia, where they established a 'Government-in-exile', while Iraq declared that a provisional Government had been formed in Kuwait comprising Iraqi-sponsored Kuwaiti dissidents. The UN Security Council immediately adopted a series of resolutions, of which the first (Resolution 660) condemned the invasion, demanded the immediate and unconditional withdrawal of Iraqi forces from Kuwait, and appealed for a negotiated settlement of the conflict. A trade embargo was then imposed on Iraq and Kuwait. Meanwhile, the USA and member states of the European Community (now European Union—EU, see p. 244) froze all Kuwait's overseas assets to prevent their repatriation. Five days after the invasion US troops and aircraft were deployed in Saudi Arabia, with the stated aim of securing that country's borders with Kuwait in the event of further Iraqi territorial expansion. A number of European governments, together with some Arab League states, agreed to provide military support for the US forces. The Iraqi Government subsequently announced the formal annexation of Kuwait, and ordered the closure of foreign diplomatic missions there. At the end of August most of Kuwait was officially declared to be the 19th Governorate of Iraq, while a northern strip was incorporated into the Basra Governorate.

In the months following the invasion apparent attempts at demographic manipulation—by settling Iraqis and Palestinians in Kuwait and by forcing Kuwaitis to assume Iraqi citizenship—were documented. The population was estimated to have decreased from approximately 2m. prior to the invasion to some 700,000, of whom Kuwaitis constituted about 300,000, Palestinians 200,000, and the remainder comprised other Arab and Asian expatriates. Many Kuwaitis, and Arab and Asian expatriates, had fled Iraq and Kuwait into Jordan, while most European and US expatriates were detained as hostages; by the end of 1990 it was claimed that all hostages had been released.

UN Security Council Resolution 678, adopted in November 1990, authorized the multinational force by now stationed in Saudi Arabia and the Gulf region to use 'all necessary means' to liberate Kuwait. It was implied that should Iraq not begin, by 15 January 1991, to implement the terms of 10 resolutions hitherto adopted regarding the invasion, military action would ensue. Renewed international diplomatic attempts failed to avert a military confrontation. On the night of 16–17 January the US-led multinational force launched an intensive aerial bombardment of Iraq. Ground forces entered Kuwait during the night of 23–24 February, encountering relatively little effective Iraqi opposition. Within three days the Iraqi Government had agreed to comply with the terms of all Security Council resolutions concerning Kuwait, and on 28 February the USA announced a suspension of military operations. Resolutions 686 and 687, adopted by the UN Security Council in March and April respectively, dictated the terms to Iraq for a permanent cease-fire: Iraq was required to release all allied prisoners of war and Kuwaitis detained as hostages, repeal all laws and decrees concerning the annexation of Kuwait, and recognize the inviolability of the Iraq–Kuwait border. Iraq promptly announced its compliance with both resolutions. Resolution 689, adopted in April, provided for the establishment of a demilitarized zone, to be supervised by a UN Iraq-Kuwait Observation Mission (UNIKOM).

Meanwhile, in October 1990, at a conference in Jeddah of some 1,000 prominent Kuwaitis, the exiled Crown Prince Saad agreed to establish government advisory committees on political, social and financial matters, and pledged to restore the country's Constitution and legislature and to organize free elections after Kuwait's eventual liberation. In February 1991, however, the Government-in-exile excluded the possibility of early elections, maintaining that the need to rebuild and repopulate the country took precedence over that for political reform. Immediately following liberation an Amiri decree imposed martial law in Kuwait, and in March the formation of a state security committee was announced: its objectives included the investigation of individuals suspected of collaboration with the Iraqi authorities in Kuwait, the prevention of unofficial acts of reprisal and the identification of those civilians relocated to Kuwait by Iraq. Palestinians in Kuwait were a particular target of reprisals, and it was alleged by several human rights organizations that they were subject to torture by Kuwaiti security forces. Kuwait's Palestinian population, which had totalled around 400,000 prior to the Iraqi invasion, was estimated to have declined to less than 50,000 by early 1992.

The Amir, the Prime Minister and other members of the exiled regime returned to Kuwait in March 1991. The Council of Ministers resigned later that month, apparently in response to public discontent at the Government's failure to restore essential services. Although several specialists were appointed to strategic posts within the new Government named by Sheikh Saad in April (most notably to the finance, planning and oil portfolios), other important positions (including the foreign affairs, interior and defence ministries) were allocated to members of the as-Sabah family.

In May 1991 it was revealed that some 900 people were under investigation in Kuwait in connection with crimes committed during the Iraqi occupation; about 200 of these were accused of collaboration. The Government undertook to investigate alleged abuses documented by the human rights organization Amnesty International, which claimed that trials were being conducted without the provision of adequate defence counsel and that in some cases torture had been used to extract confessions. Martial law was ended in June, and 29 death sentences hitherto imposed on convicted collaborators were commuted to custodial terms. Outstanding trials relating to the occupation were to be referred to civilian courts, and in August a tribunal, said to guarantee defendants the right to greater legal protection as well as a right of appeal, was established to replace the martial law courts. Amid continuing international criticism of Kuwait's record on human rights, measures were subsequently taken to prevent clandestine deportations of alleged collaborators and to permit international supervision of the expulsion of foreign nationals. However, it was widely believed that Kuwait had been motivated to curb human rights abuses primarily in an attempt to procure international support for its efforts to secure the release of Kuwaiti nationals detained in Iraq.

It was announced in May 1991 that a US military presence would remain in Kuwait until September, by which time, it was envisaged, a regional defence force would be established. However, little progress was achieved in negotiations for such a force, and in August the USA announced that it would maintain 1,500 troops in Kuwait for several more months. In September the US and Kuwaiti Governments signed a 10-year military co-operation agreement, permitting the storage of US supplies and equipment in Kuwait, and providing for joint military training and exercises. (The agreement was renewed for a further 10 years in February 2001.) Defence accords were signed with both the United Kingdom and France in 1992.

In June 1993 the State Security Court was reported to have issued death sentences against 17 people who had been found guilty of collaborating with Iraq in 1990–91; Alaa Hussein Ali, the leader of the provisional Government installed by Iraq in August 1990, was convicted *in absentia*. In February 1994 Amnesty International asserted that at least 120 alleged collaborators had been convicted by trials that failed to satisfy international minimum standards. Human rights organizations therefore welcomed the endorsement by the Majlis, in August 1995, of government proposals to abolish the State Security Court. In January 1997 the Government announced the creation of a new human rights committee within the Ministry of the Interior.

Press censorship was partially relaxed in January 1992. Elections to the new Majlis, on 5 October, were contested by some 280 candidates, many of whom (although nominally independent) were affiliated to one of several quasi-political organizations. The franchise was again restricted, with only about 81,400 men eligible to vote. Anti-Government candidates, notably those representing Islamist groups, were unexpectedly successful, securing 31 of the Assembly's 50 seats. The Prime Minister subsequently formed a new Government, including six members of the Majlis, who were allocated, *inter alia*, the oil and justice portfolios; members of the ruling family retained control of foreign affairs, the interior and defence.

The Majlis voted in December 1992 to establish a commission of inquiry into the circumstances surrounding the 1990 invasion. The commission's report, published in May 1995, revealed profound negligence on the part of government and military officials, who had apparently ignored warnings of an imminent invasion. The report also claimed that the immediate flight of members of the royal family and the Council of Ministers had deprived the country of political leadership and military organization.

Meanwhile, in January 1993 legislation was enacted whereby the Majlis would have automatic access to the financial accounts of all state-owned companies and investment organizations, and stricter penalties would be imposed in cases of abuse of public funds. Demands for greater parliamentary scrutiny of the state's investments were largely prompted by revelations of the misappropriation of funds by the London-based Kuwait Investment Office (KIO), responsible for much of Kuwait's overseas investment portfolio (22 former KIO executives, including Sheikh Fahd Muhammad as-Sabah—its Chairman at the time of the Iraqi invasion—were reportedly implicated in the allegations), and also by emerging evidence of financial misconduct at the state-owned Kuwait Oil Tanker Co. In July 1996 three former executives received prison sentences of between 15 and 40 years, having been convicted of corruption by the criminal court; they were ordered to repay embezzled funds, together with fines totalling more than US $100m. In June 1999 the High Court in London ruled that Sheikh Fahd and two other former KIO senior executives were guilty, *in absentia*, of conspiracy and fraud involving some $460m. against the KIO's Spanish subsidiary during 1988–92.

The ruling family again retained control of the key portfolios following a reorganization of the Council of Ministers in April 1994. In June the Majlis approved legislation extending the franchise to sons of naturalized Kuwaitis. In July 1995 the Assembly approved a bill reducing from 30 years to 20 the minimum period after which naturalized Kuwaitis would become eligible to vote. In July 1996 the Ministry of the Interior announced that an electorate of just over 107,000 men was entitled to vote in the forthcoming elections to the Majlis, scheduled for 7 October. Pro-Government candidates were the most successful, securing the majority of the 50 seats. Sheikh Saad was reappointed Prime Minister, and his new Council of Ministers included four newly elected deputies.

In March 1998 Sheikh Saad submitted his Government's resignation, after members of the Majlis proposed a motion of no confidence in the Minister of Information, Sheikh Sa'ud Nasir as-Sa'ud as-Sabah, who had allowed what were deemed 'un-Islamic' publications to be exhibited at a book fair in Kuwait. The Amir immediately reappointed the Crown Prince as Prime Minister, and a new Government was named at the end of the month. The promotion of Sheikh Sa'ud to the post of Minister of Oil was controversial not only because of the recent action taken against him, but also because the oil portfolio was not customarily allocated to a member of the ruling family. An institutional crisis appeared imminent in June, when the Majlis sought to cross-examine the Minister of the Interior, Sheikh Muhammad Khalid al-Hamad as-Sabah, on issues including corruption, illicit drugs and human rights. However, the ministry in question was deemed by the Government to be 'sovereign' and therefore exempt from parliamentary examination. Tensions between the Government and the Majlis were swiftly revived in July, when the Government introduced amendments to legislation enacted in 1993 (which had already been amended in 1995) regarding repayment of debts arising from the collapse of the Souk al-Manakh in 1982. Many deputies regarded new arrangements for the discharge of liabilities to be unduly favourable to debtors, many of whom were members of the ruling family, and boycotted an initial vote before reluctantly approving the amendments in August 1998.

Confrontation persisted between the Government and the Majlis, which in February 1999 refused to refer to its finance committee government proposals for economic reform. In May the Amir dissolved the legislature and called fresh elections, after deputies had in the previous month questioned the Minister of Justice and of Awqaf (Religious Endowments) and Islamic Affairs over errors that had appeared in copies of the Koran printed and distributed by his ministry. Some 80% of an eligible electorate of 113,000 Kuwaiti men voted in the election, which took place on 3 July. Pro-Government candidates recorded the greatest losses, taking only 12 seats; Islamist candidates won 20 seats and liberals 14, with the remaining four seats won by independents. A new Council of Ministers led by the Prime Minister, Sheikh Saad, was inaugurated in mid-July. The ruling family retained control of the strategic foreign affairs, oil, interior and defence portfolios, although a number of liberal deputies joined the Government.

During the period between the dissolution of the Majlis and the election, the Government had promulgated some 60 decrees (subject to legislative approval), most notably one proposing that women should be allowed to contest and to vote in elections from 2003. However, the law on female suffrage was defeated by a considerable majority in the new Majlis in November 1999, as liberal deputies, who supported women's enfranchisement, registered their protest at what they considered to be the unconstitutionality of legislation by decree by joining Islamist and conservative deputies in voting against the measure. Liberal deputies immediately submitted identical legislation regarding women's suffrage, but this was narrowly defeated in a vote at the end of the month. Kuwaiti women suffered a further reverse in their attempts to secure greater rights in January 2001, when the Constitutional Court rejected a lawsuit brought by a male citizen against the state's election department for having failed to register the names of five women on electoral lists in his constituency. In March the Majlis rejected, on procedural grounds, draft legislation that would increase women's political rights.

In January 2000 Alaa Hussein Ali, leader of the provisional Government installed by Iraq in August 1990, who had been in self-imposed exile since Kuwait's liberation, returned to Kuwait in order to appeal against the death sentence pronounced in June 1993 (see above). In May 2000 it was announced that Hussein had lost his appeal at the Court of First Instance, and that he planned a further challenge to his sentence. The Court of Appeal upheld the previous ruling in July, but in March 2001 commuted Hussein's death sentence to one of life imprisonment.

In July 2000 unrest was reported in the Al-Jahra region, where a community of *bidoun* ('stateless' Arabs) form the majority of the population. (About 100,000 *bidoun* reside in Kuwait, but the authorities refuse to recognize their claims to Kuwaiti nationality.) The unrest followed the approval, in May, of a draft amendment to the Citizenship Law that would grant only a small number of *bidoun* the right to Kuwaiti citizenship. Some 1,000 *bidoun* obtained Kuwaiti citizenship in early 2001, leading to protests by those whose applications had been refused.

Sheikh Saad tendered his Government's resignation in January 2001. The Crown Prince denied that this constituted an attempt to prevent parliamentary scrutiny of the Minister of Justice and of Awqaf and Islamic Affairs, Saad Jasem Yousuf al-Hashil, relating to allegations of inefficiency and corruption in his ministry. The Amir immediately reappointed Sheikh Saad as Prime Minister, and a new 15-member Government was named in February. The new administration included five younger members of the ruling family, as well as four members of the Majlis. The outgoing Deputy Prime Minister and Minister of Defence, Sheikh Salim Sabah as-Salim as-Sabah, left the Government, although the defence, foreign affairs and interior portfolios remained in the hands of the as-Sabah family. Some controversy was caused by the allocation of the oil portfolio to Dr Adil Khalid as-Sabih, the minister previously responsible for the electricity, water and housing portfolios who had recently survived a parliamentary vote of no confidence in respect of his business interests.

Meanwhile, during November 2000, as the crisis in Israeli–Palestinian relations deepened, 16 suspected Islamist militants (Kuwaitis and other Arab nationals) were arrested in Kuwait, accused of involvement in plotting bomb attacks on US military installations in the Gulf region in retaliation for perceived US support for Israel. The arrests of the alleged saboteurs followed reports that a Moroccan aide to the Saudi-born leader of the militant Islamist al-Qa'ida (Base) organization, Osama bin Laden, had entered Kuwait from Afghanistan; however, the aide subsequently fled to Iran. In June 2001 a senior Kuwaiti military official was convicted of concealing weapons to be used for terrorist purposes; he received a 10-year prison sentence, but in December this was reduced to seven years. (Eight of the suspected militants were given suspended sentences and ordered to pay fines; the remainder were acquitted.)

In January 2002 four people died following a major explosion at Raudhatain, Kuwait's second largest oilfield, to the north of Kuwait City. Adil Khalid as-Sabih immediately submitted his resignation as Minister of Oil, stating that he accepted responsibility for the incident; he also ordered an investigation into the cause of the explosion. The Minister of Information, Sheikh Ahmad al-Fahd al-Ahmad as-Sabah, was subsequently named as acting Minister of Oil. However, a political crisis ensued after it proved impossible to find a permanent replacement for Dr as-Sabih, and Sheikh Ahmad was asked to remain in charge of the oil portfolio until the general election (scheduled for mid-2003). Meanwhile, several members of the increasingly assertive Majlis demanded the resignation of the entire Government, alleging that the explosion at Raudhatain was the result of state corruption and mismanagement. In January 2003 the Amir accepted the resignation of the Minister of Finance, of Planning and Minister of State for Administrative Development Affairs, Dr Yousuf Hamad al-Ibrahim, who had been the object of severe parliamentary criticism. Dr al-Ibrahim, a leading reformist, had in July 2002 survived a vote of no confidence instigated by Islamist Majlis deputies who accused him of poor management of the Government's fiscal affairs.

After a campaign that was overshadowed by the US-led military intervention in Iraq (which was largely conducted from Kuwaiti territory), parliamentary elections were held, as scheduled, on 5 July 2003. Islamist candidates secured 21 of the 50 seats in the Majlis, while pro-Government candidates won 14 seats, independents (regarded as being aligned with the Government) 12 and liberals three. The rate of voter participation was reported to be only 45% of the 6% of the total population who formed the electorate. The results were viewed as a major setback for those seeking political reform, and were widely interpreted as signalling popular dissatisfaction with the entire political process. In 2004 the Majlis debated proposals to reduce the number of constituencies, thereby requiring successful candidates to gain a wider appeal among voters.

Meanwhile, following the elections, in July 2003 the ailing Crown Prince relinquished the position of Prime Minister. The appointment of Sheikh Sabah as his replacement represented an unprecedented separation between the post of Prime Minister and the position of Crown Prince, and provided some encouragement to reformists after their heavy electoral losses. A new Council of Ministers, including six new appointments, was also announced in mid-July. The most significant change was the merger of the oil portfolio with the Ministry of Electricity and Water to form the Ministry of Energy, to be headed by Sheikh Ahmad al-Fahd al-Ahmad as-Sabah.

In October 2003 and May 2004 the Council of Ministers approved legislation that would permit women to vote in and contest municipal and parliamentary elections, respectively. The Majlis gave provisional approval for the former piece of legislation in April 2005, but subsequently failed to ratify the legislation at a second vote in May. Both new laws were approved later in the month; however, this was too late to allow women to participate in the June municipal elections. By early 2006 it was reported that there were already considerably more women than men registered as voters. Kuwaiti women received their first opportunity to vote and to stand in elections at a municipal by-election on 4 April 2006, where two of the eight candidates were female. Some 28 women registered to contest legislative elections in June of the same year (see below).

In March 2004 the Minister of Finance, Mahmud Abd al-Khaliq an-Nuri, narrowly survived a vote of no confidence, having been heavily criticized by the Majlis for mismanagement during the sale of state property. Citing health reasons, an-Nuri resigned shortly after the vote; however, he continued in the role of Minister of Finance until Bader Mishari al-Humaidhi, formerly Director-General of the Kuwait Fund for Arab Economic Development, was appointed as his replacement on 4 April 2005. Meanwhile, in the previous month Dr Anas Muhammad Ahmad ar-Rashaid was finally appointed as Minister of Information; he replaced Muhammad Abu al-Hassan, who had resigned in January, shortly before he was to be questioned in the Majlis by Islamist members over allowing 'immoral' Western-style concerts in Kuwait. The day after the appointment of al-Humaidhi, the Minister of Health, Muhammad Ahmad al-Jarallah, resigned in advance of a parliamentary vote on a motion of no confidence, which had been lodged on 4 April, accusing him of mismanagement. Al-Jarallah thus became the third member of the Council of Ministers to resign in connection with hostile parliamentary questioning since the elections to the Majlis in July 2003. The Prime Minister subsequently warned the Majlis that a vote of no confidence in al-Jarallah, should it be carried, could 'negatively impact on our national unity', which in some quarters was interpreted as a sign that the increasingly assertive nature of the Majlis had begun to concern the ruling as-Sabah family. Al-Jarallah's resignation was accepted by the Prime Minister on 10 April 2005, and the Minister of Energy, Sheikh Ahmad al-Fahd as-Sabah, assumed the health portfolio in an acting capacity. In June the Prime Minister appointed Dr Massouma Saleh al-Mubarak as Minister of Planning and Minister of State for Administrative Development Affairs. Dr al-Mubarak, a human rights activist, thus became Kuwait's first female member of the Council of Ministers.

Meanwhile, in February 2005 the Majlis approved legislation giving security agencies flexible new powers to search for and seize illegal firearms, following several recent battles between government forces and armed militants. Some of the recent violence was linked to reports of hostility towards Westerners, particularly US citizens, and al-Qa'ida was believed by some to be implicated in the violence. Additionally, in January the army announced that a number of soldiers had been detained under suspicion of plotting to attack US troops. The new legislation was to be renewed on an annual basis.

On 15 January 2006 the death was announced of the Amir, Sheikh Jaber. He was automatically succeeded by the Crown Prince, Sheikh Saad, who had, however, for some time been beset by rumours that he was too ill to accede to the role. In an unprecedented development, on 24 January Sheikh Saad, who had yet to take the oath of office, was indeed removed from the position of Amir on health grounds, following a formal request from the Council of Ministers that the Majlis debate the issue. Under the Constitution, the law of succession required a two-thirds' majority of Majlis deputies in order to dismiss an Amir; but in the event, the vote in favour of replacing Sheikh Saad was unanimous. It was reported that Sheikh Saad and his close supporters had, after nine days of intense negotiation, reluctantly agreed to his removal from office prior to the Majlis debate; however, his abdication letter did not bear an official stamp and was disregarded by parliamentarians. In the absence of a nominated Crown Prince, the Prime Minister, Sheikh Sabah, who was in any case regarded as the de facto ruler of the emirate, assumed the powers of the Amir until the nomination of a permanent head of state by the Council of Ministers. Sheikh Sabah was duly sworn in as Amir on 29 January, after his widely predicted nomination had been unanimously approved by the Majlis. The sole controversy attached to Sheikh Sabah's accession was that, like the late Sheikh Jaber, he belonged to the al-Jaber branch of the ruling as-Sabah family that, by tradition, alternated the position of Amir with the as-Salim branch of the family, of which Sheikh Saad was a member.

The new Amir accepted the resignation of the Council of Ministers on 30 January 2006. In early February Sheikh Sabah appointed Sheikh Nasser al-Muhammad al-Ahmad as-Sabah, a former diplomat and the Amir's nephew, as the new Prime Minister and the erstwhile Deputy Prime Minister and Minister of the Interior, Sheikh Nawwaf al-Ahmad al-Jaber as-Sabah, the Amir's brother, as Crown Prince. The appointments, which maintained the post-2003 separation between the roles of premier and Crown Prince, emphasized the channelling of power towards the al-Jaber branch of the ruling family, although both men were respected for their extensive political experience. On the following day the Amir approved Sheikh Nasser's first Council of Ministers. Although strategic portfolios (including those of foreign affairs, finance and energy) remained unaltered, a notable change was the addition of the interior portfolio to the responsibilities of the Minister of Defence, Sheikh Jaber Mubarak al-Hamad as-Sabah, who also became First Deputy Prime Minister.

In March 2006 the Majlis approved new legislation repealing an official ban, imposed in 1976, on the establishment of daily newspapers. The new press law, *inter alia*, prohibited the publication of material that attacked religious groups or incited hatred, violence or public dissension, and banned the imprisonment of journalists for offences other than blasphemy, apostasy and proselytizing, the maximum imprisonment terms for which were reduced.

A long-running campaign for electoral reform, which sought to reduce the number of electoral constituencies in Kuwait in order to diminish the opportunities for vote-buying, began to attract extensive popular support from May 2006. A proposal by the Government to reduce the number of constituencies from 25 to 10 was rejected by the opposition, which advocated a more comprehensive reduction, to just five constituencies. Following efforts by the Majlis to cross-examine the Prime Minister on the matter, the Amir dissolved parliament and called for elections to be held on 29 June, just over one year earlier than scheduled. A loose alliance of 29 pro-reform members of the outgoing legislature was formed to contest the elections, comprising candidates from across the political spectrum. Reformists made significant gains at the polls, winning 34 of the 50 seats contested. The remaining 16 seats were won by independents and pro-Government candidates; no female candidates were elected. Voter participation

KUWAIT

Introductory Survey

was reported to be 65% of those registered to vote; despite constituting 65% of the electorate, women accounted for only 35% of the total number of votes cast. A reform bill drafted by the new Majlis proposing the introduction of a five-constituency electoral system was passed into law in July. Meanwhile, in early July a new Council of Ministers was named under Prime Minister Sheikh Nasser. Although the key portfolios remained unchanged, the Minister of Energy, Sheikh Ahmad al-Fahd as-Sabah, failed to be reappointed, after he was accused by members of the opposition and pro-reformists of having interfered in the electoral process and of seeking to block reforms. Dr Massouma al-Mubarak assumed the communications portfolio.

In December 2006 the Minister of Information, Muhammad Nasser as-Sanousi, resigned following a move by the increasingly confrontational Majlis to question him over allegations that he had curbed media freedom during the recent election campaign. In the following month deputies made a similar request to question the Minister of Health, Sheikh Ahmad Abdullah al-Ahmad as-Sabah, on four charges related to the mismanagement of, and deterioration in, the medical sector. Following the cross-examination of Sheikh Ahmad in February 2007, a motion of no confidence was filed against the minister; however, in early March, one day before the Majlis was due to debate the motion, the entire Council of Ministers resigned. A new cabinet, approved by the Amir in late March, excluded Sheikh Ahmad but retained most of the key ministers in the same posts. Dr al-Mubarak was awarded the health portfolio, while Nouriya Subeeh Barrak as-Subeeh was appointed Minister of Education, increasing to two the number of female cabinet ministers. The reorganization also included the division of the recently created Ministry of Energy into the Ministry of Oil and the Ministry of Electricity and Water; the latter was to be headed by Muhammad Abdullah Hadi al-Olaim, spokesman of the Islamic Constitutional Movement. At the end of June the Minister of Oil, Sheikh Ali al-Jarrah as-Sabah, resigned; the Majlis had been scheduled to debate a motion of no confidence in the minister after having questioned him over allegations of corruption (reportedly involving the embezzlement of state funds by a relative of his in the 1990s). Al-Olaim replaced Ali as-Sabah in an acting capacity. In late August Minister of Health al-Mubarak also announced her resignation, after a fire at a hospital in Kuwait City had resulted in the deaths of two patients. Towards the end of October the Prime Minister, Sheikh Nasser, instigated an extensive reorganzation of the Council of Ministers, which was approved by the Amir; the cabinet changes were apparently intended to prevent an escalation of the ongoing difficulties between the Government and the Majlis. New appointments included Sheikh Jaber Khalid al-Jaber as-Sabah as Minister of the Interior, Bader Mishari al-Humaidhi as Minister of Oil and Mustafa Jassem ash-Shimali as Minister of Finance. However, in early November al-Humaidhi resigned amid continuing controversy relating to his previous role as Minister of Finance (see above).

In late January 2008 the liberal Minister of Education, Nouriya as-Subeeh, survived a no-confidence vote in the Majlis, having undergone a lengthy interrogation by Islamist and tribal deputies with regard to alleged mismanagement of the education sector, legal irregularities and a reported failure to guarantee the complete segregation of male and female students at Kuwait's universities. The fact that political infighting was increasingly damaging Kuwait's prospects for economic and social development was said to be causing growing frustration among the population. On 17 March the entire Council of Ministers tendered its resignation, stating that relations with the Majlis had become untenable, and that parliament was continuing to obstruct ministers' attempts to carry out their duties effectively. Parliamentary deputies countered this argument by claiming that the blame for the political crisis lay with the executive, in which the as-Sabah family continued to exert considerable power. The immediate cause of the latest crisis involved a dispute concerning salary increases for state employees, with deputies asserting that the Government's proposed pay rise was too low. Having cut short a visit to Morocco, on 19 March Sheikh Sabah ordered the dissolution of the Majlis in order for fresh elections to take place on 17 May. In his speech the Amir referred to the need to 'safeguard the unity of the nation', adding that he had taken the decision to suspend parliament owing to 'irresponsible behaviour'. The May elections would be the first to use the five-constituency system adopted into law in July 2006. In early April 2008 the Minister of Commerce and Industy, Dr Falah Fahd al-Hajeri, and the Minister of State for Housing Affairs and for National Assembly Affairs, Abd al-Wahid Mahmoud al-Awadhi, tendered their resignations in order to stand as candidates in the forthcoming polls. Minister of Finance Mustafa Jassem ash-Shimali and Minister of Health Abdullah Abd ar-Rahman at-Taweel assumed responsibility for their respective portfolios pending the elections.

Meanwhile, in February 2008 tensions increased between Sunni and Shi'a Muslims in the emirate after several hundred people from the minority Shi'a community had held a rally to commemorate the death of a senior commander of the militant Shi'a organization Hezbollah in Lebanon. Imad Mughniyeh, who was killed in a bomb attack in the Syrian capital, Damascus, in that month, was described by the Kuwaiti Government as a 'terrorist', who, they claimed, had been responsible for the hijacking of a Kuwait Airways plane in 1988, in which two Kuwaiti passengers were murdered. A number of prominent Shi'a politicians and clerics were questioned by the authorities over their involvement in the rally, and many arrests were reported; Kuwaiti officials claimed that all of those under investigation were members of an illegal opposition group, Hezbollah Kuwait.

Friction between Kuwait and Iraq in the aftermath of the Gulf War was exacerbated by the issue of the demarcation of their joint border. The UN commission with responsibility for delineating the frontier formalized the land border as it had been defined by British administrators in 1932 (and officially agreed by Kuwait and Iraq in 1963). The boundary, the validity of which was now rejected by Iraq, was established some 570 m north of its pre-war position, dividing the Iraqi port of Umm Qasr, with the effect that Iraq retained the town and much of the harbour while Kuwait was awarded hinterland which included an abandoned Iraqi naval base; the border also situated several Iraqi oil wells on Kuwaiti territory. In January 1993 the USA led air attacks on Iraq, and more than 1,000 US troops were dispatched to Kuwait, in response to a series of incursions by Iraqi forces into Kuwaiti territory in the days immediately preceding the designated entry into force of the new border; its formal delineation was completed in March, when the UN commission defined the maritime border along the median line of the Khawr Abd Allah waterway. Allegations made by Kuwait of Iraqi violations of the border, and of attempts to impede construction of a trench along the land border, intensified during the second half of 1993, and there were sporadic reports of exchanges of fire in the border region. In November a 775-strong armed UNIKOM reinforcement was deployed in northern Kuwait, with authorization (under specific circumstances) to use its weapons to assist the unarmed force already in the demilitarized zone.

In October 1994 Iraq deployed some 70,000 troops and 700 tanks near the border with Kuwait, in an apparent attempt to force an easing of UN economic sanctions. Kuwait immediately mobilized its army reserves, and dispatched some 20,000 troops to the border region. The USA committed almost 40,000 land, naval and air forces to the region; France and the United Kingdom deployed naval vessels, and the United Kingdom dispatched about 1,200 troops. Following Russian mediation, Iraq announced its willingness to recognize Kuwait's sovereignty and borders, on condition that the UN ease sanctions against Iraq after six months. However, the UN Security Council adopted a resolution (No. 949) requiring Iraq's unconditional recognition of Kuwait's sovereignty and borders and restricting the movement of Iraqi troops in the border area. In November Iraq officially recognized Kuwait's sovereignty, territorial integrity and political independence, as well as its UN-defined borders. Most of the US and British reinforcements deployed in the region in October had been withdrawn by the end of the year. Kuwait's relations with Iraq deteriorated sharply in September 1996, after the Kuwaiti Government agreed to the deployment in Kuwait of US military aircraft and troops in support of a US operation to force the withdrawal of Iraqi armed forces from the Kurdish 'safe haven' in northern Iraq. In December the USA announced that some 4,200 US troops deployed in Kuwait during 1996 would be withdrawn by the end of the year, although the deployment of US F-117 *Stealth* fighter aircraft was to be extended.

Kuwait and Iraq made mutual accusations of territorial violations and attacks on shipping during 1997. Meanwhile, Kuwait continued to support the maintenance of international sanctions against Iraq, and to demand adherence by Iraq to all relevant UN resolutions adopted since the Gulf crisis. Furthermore, statements by the Iraqi Government that it was holding no Kuwaiti prisoners of war were refuted by Kuwait: the Kuwaiti authorities, asserting that some 600 Kuwaitis remained captive in Iraq, claimed in late 1997 to be in possession of documentation, passed by Iraq to the International Committee of the Red Cross (ICRC), relating to 126 Kuwaiti prisoners of war. As the crisis involving weapons inspections in Iraq by the UN Special Commission (see the Recent History of Iraq) deepened in February 1998, fears were expressed for Kuwait's security—in particular that an attack on Iraq might result in the use of chemical or other weapons of mass destruction against Kuwait. Although Kuwait was the only country in the region to announce its approval of the use of force against Iraq should diplomatic efforts fail, it emphasized that any military action would exacerbate hardship suffered by the Iraqi people and increase regional instability. The USA, supported by the United Kingdom, undertook a military deployment in the Gulf region at this time: by the end of the month, when the UN Secretary-General and the Iraqi Government reached a compromise agreement regarding weapons inspections, some 6,000 US ground troops had been dispatched to Kuwait. Following a series of air-strikes against targets in Iraq by US and British forces from December 1998, Iraq accused Kuwait of collaborating in the air attacks, and frequently reiterated claims to Kuwaiti territory. In September 1999 Kuwait lodged an official protest over changes made to the final draft of an Arab League report to which, Kuwait asserted, references to the formation of a 'mechanism' to resolve the issue of Kuwaiti and other prisoners of war in Iraq had been added; Kuwait maintained that the ICRC was the only body empowered to deal with the issue. In November the Majlis established a committee to examine future relations with Iraq, and in December the Kuwaiti Government welcomed UN Security Council Resolution 1284 (establishing a new weapons inspectorate for Iraq, q.v.), which incorporated demands for: the repatriation of Kuwaiti and other prisoners from Iraq; Iraq's co-operation with the ICRC; and the return of Kuwaiti property seized during the occupation.

In September 2000 ministers responsible for foreign affairs of the Co-operation Council for the Arab States of the Gulf (Gulf Co-operation Council—GCC, see p. 219) expressed concerns after the Iraqi leadership had repeatedly denounced both Kuwait and Saudi Arabia for allowing US and British military aircraft to use their airspace in order to conduct military attacks on Iraq, and had vowed to launch a new invasion of Kuwait. Iraq also renewed its long-standing accusation that Kuwait was drilling oil wells on Iraqi territory, and accused Kuwait and Saudi Arabia of inflicting suffering on the Iraqi population through the maintenance of UN sanctions. In late 2000 Kuwait reinforced security along its border with Iraq, partly to prevent a possible influx of *bidoun*, who had reportedly entered the demilitarized zone from Iraq and who were demanding the right of return to Kuwait (from where they had been excluded since the Gulf crisis).

In March 2001 a summit meeting of Arab League heads of state, held in Amman, Jordan, was considered to have made the most comprehensive effort hitherto in addressing divisions arising from the Gulf conflict. None the less, a draft resolution presented by the Iraqi delegation urging an end to UN sanctions and a resumption of civilian flights failed to secure adoption, owing to Iraq's unwillingness—on the grounds that it had already done sufficient to make clear its recognition of Kuwait's territorial integrity—to accede to a requirement of a specific guarantee that Iraq would not repeat the invasion of 1990. In November 2001 Kuwait issued a formal complaint to the UN following an alleged violation of its territory by Iraq. The incident occurred shortly after a senior Iraqi official had reiterated claims of sovereignty over Kuwait. In January 2002 the Kuwaiti leadership was reported to have rejected attempts by the Arab League to persuade it to accept Iraqi proposals apparently aimed at improving bilateral relations: as part of Iraq's diplomatic offensive to secure the support of the Arab world in view of the threat of US-led military action against Saddam Hussain's regime, the Iraqi leader had conveyed an appeal to Arab states to set aside their differences, referring specifically to the need to improve relations with Kuwait and Saudi Arabia. Later in the month it was reported that Iraq had announced its preparedness to allow a delegation from Kuwait to visit Iraq to verify that no Kuwaiti prisoners of war were being held. (Kuwait continued to assert that Iraq was detaining at least 90 Kuwaiti nationals.) At the Arab League summit held in Beirut, Lebanon, in March 2002, however, it was announced that Kuwait and Iraq had reached agreement on the resolution of outstanding differences. The summit's final communiqué welcomed Iraq's assurances that it would respect the 'independence, sovereignty and security' of Kuwait, and safeguard its 'territorial integrity'; Iraq was urged to co-operate in seeking a 'definitive solution' to issues of Kuwaiti prisoners and detainees, and of the return of property, while Kuwait was called upon to 'co-operate with what Iraq offers with respect to its nationals' reported as missing through the ICRC.

Relations with Iraq were profoundly affected by the political repercussions of the suicide attacks against New York and Washington, DC, USA, in September 2001. Kuwait, which strongly condemned the attacks, thereafter assumed an important role in persuading other Gulf states to join the US-led 'coalition against terror'. US bases in Kuwait were subsequently used to provide logistical support to the US-led campaign against al-Qa'ida (held by the USA to be principally responsible for the suicide attacks) and its Taliban hosts in Afghanistan during late 2001. Meanwhile, in October the Kuwaiti authorities revoked the citizenship of the official spokesman of al-Qa'ida, Sulayman Abu Ghaith, after remarks he had made via the Qatar-based Al-Jazeera television station. In late 2001 the Central Bank of Kuwait implemented measures designed to prevent Islamic charitable organizations from using Kuwaiti financial institutions to channel funds to al-Qa'ida.

During the course of 2002 increased speculation that the US Administration of George W. Bush intended to extend the 'war on terror' to target the regime of Saddam Hussain in Iraq threatened to fuel opposition to a continued US presence in the region and exacerbate an increasingly tense political situation in Kuwait. At the end of December some 12,000 US troops were stationed in Kuwait, and in early 2003 Kuwait's Ministry of Defence declared that the entire northern half of Kuwait would be designated a closed military zone from mid-February. Several US soldiers and civilians were killed in late 2002 and early 2003 in attacks by Kuwaitis, some of whom, it was alleged, had links to al-Qa'ida. In March an emergency meeting of the Arab League, hosted by Qatar, to discuss the deepening crisis descended into a bitter exchange of insults between, primarily, a senior Iraqi official and the Kuwaiti Minister of Information. Kuwait subsequently supported a proposal made by the President of the United Arab Emirates (UAE) for Saddam Hussain to go into exile in order to prevent a US-led war to remove his regime. At the outset of military action, which commenced in late March, US-led troops in Kuwait, the base for the main ground assault on Iraq, numbered some 140,000. Iraqi armed forces launched several missiles at Kuwaiti territory, although little damage was caused in the emirate during the course of the conflict. In the aftermath of the most intense period of fighting, which President Bush declared to have ended by early May, Kuwait renewed its financial demands against Iraq, while a number of Kuwaiti firms entered into agreements with the US-led occupying powers. In October the demilitarized zone between Iraq and Kuwait was ended and, having fulfilled its mandate, UNIKOM's operations were terminated. The resumption of diplomatic relations between Iraq and Kuwait was announced in mid-2004. In 2005 Kuwait began the construction of a 200-km steel barrier along the border with Iraq, parts of which were destroyed by Iraqi militants who claimed that it was encroaching upon their land; however, in November 2006 Iraq agreed to allow the fence to be completed. In April 2007 the Kuwaiti Government expressed its hope that the two countries would open diplomatic missions in their respective capitals in the near future.

Meanwhile, in May 1994 the governing body of the UN Compensation Commission (UNCC), responsible for considering claims for compensation arising from the 1990–91 Gulf crisis, approved the first disbursements (to 670 families or individuals in 16 countries), totalling US $2.7m. By late 1996 payments amounting to $3,000m. (to be financed partly by Iraqi petroleum revenues) had been endorsed by the UN, which had yet to consider claims for a further $190,000m. In December international arbitrators recommended that a payment of $610m. should be made to the Kuwait Oil Company (KOC), in compensation for the cost of extinguishing oil wells set alight by retreating Iraqi troops in early 1991. In March 1997 the Kuwaiti general committee responsible for evaluating war damages stated that it was to begin compensation payments, initially to some 4,500 citizens who had incurred losses valued at less than $100,000. The disbursement of a further $84m. to some 33,800 individuals was authorized by the UN in February 1999. In September 2000 the UN Security Council approved the payment to the Kuwait Petroleum Corporation (which controls the KOC) of $15,900m. in compensation for lost petroleum revenues arising from the Iraqi occupation; this was the largest claim to have been considered by the UNCC hitherto. However, the Security Council decided at the same time to reduce the share of Iraqi petroleum revenues to

KUWAIT   Introductory Survey

be paid into the compensation fund from 30% to 25%. France and Russia, which increasingly opposed the maintenance of sanctions against Iraq, had delayed a decision by the UNCC on the payment, and Russia had warned of its inclination to oppose Kuwaiti claims to reparations unless the levy on Iraqi petroleum revenues was reduced. By mid-2003 the majority of individual claimants (Kuwaitis and expatriates in Kuwait and Iraq during the Gulf war) had received compensation, with total disbursements being valued at some $17,600m. Meanwhile, the UNCC was considering a claim of $86,000m. by the Kuwait Investment Agency, principally in recompense for lost earnings during the conflict. However, in a deposition issued in June 2003, the UNCC rejected all but $1,500m. of the claim. In May 2003 UN Security Council Resolution 1483 had reduced the share of Iraqi petroleum revenue to be used for compensation payments from 25% to 5%, which was expected to result in outstanding compensation payments believed to total more than $30,000m. remaining unpaid for several decades. In January 2004, after a meeting with US envoy James Baker and following similar announcements by the Governments of the UAE and Qatar, Sheikh Sabah stated that Kuwait was prepared to waive a 'significant proportion' of the estimated $16,000m. owed by Iraq. This did not, however, include any war reparations still claimed by the Government. In March 2005 the UN panel overseeing payments to victims of the Gulf crisis approved a further disbursement of $265m. to families of those who had died in Iraqi detention. At a final session of the UNCC governing body, held in June, a further $367m. in compensation was awarded to successful claimants. In April 2008 payments worth $972.4m. were made by the UNCC, principally to Kuwaiti state-owned and private companies for losses incurred as a result of the Iraqi invasion and occupation (including losses caused by environmental damage).

Relations with Jordan, which had deteriorated following that country's failure openly to denounce the Iraqi invasion, gradually eased in the mid-1990s. Flights between Kuwait and Jordan by both countries' national airlines, which had been suspended in 1990, resumed in July 1997, and the normalization of relations generally continued thereafter. In March 1999 the Jordanian embassy in Kuwait, which had been closed in 1990, was re-opened. In September of that year new King Abdullah of Jordan made his first visit to Kuwait (his father, King Hussein, had not visited after 1990), where he held talks with the Amir. Jordan and Kuwait signed a bilateral free trade agreement in December.

In July 2000 Kuwait and Saudi Arabia signed an agreement finalizing the delineation of their maritime borders. Kuwait subsequently commenced negotiations with Iran on the demarcation of respective rights to the continental shelf, following complaints by the Kuwaiti and Saudi authorities over Iran's decision to begin drilling for gas in a disputed offshore area. Iraq asserted that, as a concerned party, it should be included in the Kuwaiti-Iranian discussions. Iran suspended drilling pending the conclusion of the talks. In December a defence agreement was signed by the six member states of the GCC. Kuwait opposes any military action being taken by the USA against Iran, and supports the Iranian Government's right to develop a peaceful nuclear energy programme (see the chapter on Iran). In July 2007 the US Administration unveiled a US $20,000m. package of military assistance and weapons sales to Kuwait and the other GCC member states, in an attempt to bolster security in the Gulf region and to encourage the GCC to side with the USA in its dispute with the Iranian regime regarding the latter's nuclear programme.

Government
Under the 1962 Constitution, executive power is vested in the Amir, the Head of State (who is chosen by and from members of the ruling family), and is exercised through the Council of Ministers. The Amir appoints the Prime Minister and, on the latter's recommendation, other ministers. Legislative power is vested in the unicameral Majlis al-Umma (National Assembly), with 50 elected members who serve for four years (subject to dissolution), along with some 15 government ministers who sit as ex officio members. In May 2005 legislation was approved allowing women to vote in legislative and municipal elections for the first time. The country is divided administratively into six governorates.

Defence
As assessed at November 2007, Kuwait's active armed forces numbered 15,500—a land army of 11,000 (including up to 3,700 foreign personnel), an air force of an estimated 2,500 and a navy of around 2,000—and there were reserve forces of 23,700. Paramilitary forces comprised an estimated 6,600-strong national guard and a 500-strong coastguard. Military service is voluntary. The defence budget for 2007 was estimated at KD 1,100m. A US force has been deployed in Kuwait as part of 'Operation Iraqi Freedom' launched in 2003 (see the chapter on Iraq), and there are also small contingents of troops from the United Kingdom, Japan and the Republic of Korea (South Korea).

Economic Affairs
In 2005, according to estimates by the World Bank, Kuwait's gross national income (GNI), measured at average 2003–05 prices, was US $77,660m., equivalent to $30,630 per head (or $29,200 on an international purchasing-power parity basis). During 1996–2006, it was estimated, the population increased at an average annual rate of 3.2%, while gross domestic product (GDP) per head increased, in real terms, by an average of 1.4% per year in 1996–2005. Overall GDP was estimated to have increased, in real terms, at an average annual rate of 8.0% in 2000–06. Real GDP increased by 6.6% in 2006.

Agriculture (including hunting, forestry and fishing) contributed 0.2% of GDP in 2006. The sector engaged 2.1% of the labour force in the previous year. The principal crops are potatoes, tomatoes, cucumbers, aubergines and dates. Owing to scarcity of water, little grain is produced, and the bulk of food requirements is imported. (Imports of food and live animals accounted for 12.3% of merchandise imports in 2004.) Livestock, poultry and fishing are also important. Agricultural GDP increased, in real terms, by an average annual rate of 7.5% in 2000–06. The agricultural sector grew by 3.9% in 2006.

Industry (including mining, manufacturing, construction and power) provided 62.0% of GDP in 2006, and employed 15.4% of the labour force in 2005. During 2000–06 industrial GDP increased, in real terms, at an average annual rate of 6.3%. The sector expanded by 5.0% in 2006.

Mining and quarrying contributed 52.9% of GDP in 2006, although the sector engaged only 0.5% of the labour force in 2005. The production of petroleum and its derivatives is the most important industry in Kuwait, providing an estimated 95.2% of export revenue in 2007. At the end of 2006 the country's proven recoverable reserves of petroleum were 101,500m. barrels, representing about 8.4% of world reserves. According to oil industry figures, Kuwait's petroleum production averaged 2.70m. barrels per day (b/d) in 2006; the Government aimed to increase its production capacity to 4.0m. b/d by 2020. As a member of the Organization of the Petroleum Exporting Countries (OPEC, see p. 373), Kuwait is subject to production quotas agreed by the Organization's Conference. There are significant reserves of natural gas (1,780,000m. cu m at the end of 2006) associated with the petroleum deposits. Moreover, in March 2006 a major discovery of non-associated gas in the north of the country was announced. During 2000–06 the GDP of the mining sector increased, in real terms, at an average rate of 4.8% per year. The sector's GDP increased by 2.8% in 2006.

Manufacturing provided 6.4% of GDP in 2006, and employed 6.3% of the labour force in the previous year. Petroleum refineries accounted for 60.5% of manufacturing activity, measured by gross value of output, in 2004. Of the other branches of manufacturing, the most important are the production of building materials (and related activities such as aluminium extrusion), fertilizer production, food processing and the extraction of salt and chlorine. During 2000–06 manufacturing GDP increased, in real terms, at an average annual rate of 9.7%. Growth in the manufacturing sector was 5.8% in 2006.

Electrical energy is derived from Kuwait's own resources of petroleum (providing 79.5% of total electricity production in 2004) and both local and imported natural gas (20.5%). The value of fuel imports in 2003 was equivalent to 0.5% of the value of total merchandise imports. Total installed electricity-generating capacity increased from 6,898 MW in 1996 to 9,298 MW in 2000, following the completion of a 2,400-MW plant at Subahiya; capacity had risen to some 9,800 MW by early 2007. In 2005 the construction of a 1,000-MW gas turbine power plant at az-Zour was completed. Two further power projects were also planned: the 2,400-MW az-Zour North plant and the 1,000-MW az-Zour South II facility (although progress had been slow by 2007). Negotiations for the supply of 8,000m. cu m–15,000m. cu m per year of natural gas to Kuwait's energy industry via an offshore pipeline from Qatar were in progress in 2006.

Services contributed 37.8% of GDP in 2006, and employed 82.4% of the labour force in 2005. Kuwait's second most important source of revenue is investment abroad, both in petroleum-related ventures and in other industries, chiefly in the USA, Western Europe and Japan; many such investments are held by the Reserve Fund for Future Generations (RFFG—to which 10% of petroleum revenues must by law be contributed each year, and which is intended to provide an income after hydrocarbon resources have been exhausted) and managed by the Kuwait Investment Authority. Prior to the Iraqi invasion the value of the RFFG was believed to have been some US $100,000m. As part of its efforts to diversify the economy, the Government planned to develop the islands of Bubiyan and Failaka into major tourist resorts. In January 2004 a US company was selected as project manager for the Bubiyan island project, the first phase of which—the construction of a new port—was expected to cost about $800m. It was reported in June 2007 that a Chinese firm was the principal contractor of this phase, which also included construction of a bridge linking Bubiyan island with the mainland. The combined GDP of the service sectors increased, in real terms, at an average rate of 10.0% per year during 2000–06. The services sector grew by 8.4% in 2006.

In 2006 Kuwait recorded a visible trade surplus of US $44,288m., and there was a surplus of $50,996m. on the current account of the balance of payments. In 2004 the principal sources of imports were Germany and the USA, which provided, respectively, 11.5% and 10.8% of total imports; other important suppliers in that year were Saudi Arabia, the People's Republic of China, Japan and Italy. Details concerning the destination of Kuwait's petroleum exports are not available for recent years; however, the major markets for non-petroleum exports in 2004 included Saudi Arabia (10.8%), the UAE (10.0%), Indonesia, Pakistan, the USA and India. The principal exports are petroleum and petroleum products. The principal imports are machinery and transport equipment, which accounted for 40.3% of total imports in 2004, basic manufactures and other manufactured goods, food and live animals, and chemicals and related products.

A budget surplus of KD 5,202.9m. was recorded for the financial year ending 30 June 2007. A deficit of KD 2,979.7m. was forecast for 2007/08, although actual revenue from Kuwait's petroleum interests would undoubtedly be far greater than the projected figure. Kuwait's total external debt in 2004 was estimated at US $13,237m. The average annual rate of inflation in 2000–06 was 1.9%; consumer prices increased by an average of 3.0% in 2006. National unemployment among Kuwaitis was estimated at only 1.5% in mid-2003; however, underemployment was unofficially reported to be up to 50%. There were 24,921 unemployed people in Kuwait in 2006.

Kuwait is a member of the Co-operation Council for the Arab States of the Gulf (Gulf Co-operation Council—GCC, see p. 219); the six GCC states established a unified regional customs tariff in January 2003, and it has been agreed to create a single market and currency no later than January 2010. (On 1 January 2003 Kuwait pegged the dinar to the US dollar, as part of the GCC plan; however, this peg was replaced by a basket of currencies in May 2007, amid concerns about the declining value of the dollar.) The economic convergence criteria for the monetary union were agreed at a GCC summit in Abu Dhabi, the UAE, in December 2005, and in January 2008 the GCC launched its common market. Kuwait also belongs to the Organization of Arab Petroleum Exporting Countries (OAPEC, see p. 366) and to OPEC. Kuwait is a major aid donor, disbursing loans to developing countries through the Kuwait Fund for Arab Economic Development (KFAED) and the Arab Fund for Economic and Social Development (AFESD, see p. 174).

Despite its significant, oil-based wealth, Kuwait has a number of fundamental weaknesses in its economic structure: instability in its relations with Iraq have necessitated a high level of defence expenditure; reliance on petroleum revenues has impeded diversification into other industries; and its constitutional commitment to provide employment for all Kuwaitis has resulted in a heavy burden on government spending. During the early years of this century plans by the Kuwait Petroleum Corpn to allow foreign participation in a development project (known as 'Project Kuwait'), valued at US $8,500m., for the northern oilfields made extremely slow progress; the project aimed to increase production from 2.5m. b/d to 4m. b/d by 2020. However, approval by the Majlis was still required, and, despite assurances that all reserves would remain Kuwaiti-owned, many Kuwaitis remained opposed to any foreign involvement in the petroleum sector. Nevertheless, in 2003 the Majlis passed legislation that would increase foreign investment in the economy, including the limited participation of international oil companies in the petroleum sector and measures that would permit foreign banks to operate in Kuwait. The recovery in world petroleum prices from late 1999 was the principal factor contributing to budget surpluses during 1999/2000–2006/07. (As in previous years, a projected deficit in 2007/08 was expected to be more than covered by higher than predicted petroleum prices.) The main disadvantage of the huge petroleum windfalls accrued in recent years is that incentives for the Government to introduce much-needed reforms, particularly in the non-oil sector, have been further reduced. Ostensibly, the Government remained committed to its four-year action programme, which was launched in 2004 to stimulate the private sector's role in the economy and improve the fiscal position through tax and labour market reforms and privatization; however, legislative delays hindered implementation of the proposed changes and there remained high levels of opposition to any reduction in public sector employment and salaries. None the less, huge infrastructure and tourism projects provided some grounds for optimism by 2006 that the economy could be successfully diversified. In addition, after the US-led military campaign in 2003, the removal of the threat to Kuwait from Saddam Hussain's Baathist regime in Iraq provided a special impetus to the non-hydrocarbons sector. Meanwhile, the lack of success by Kuwait and other Gulf petroleum producers in expanding oil export capacity has led to a sharp increase in international oil prices. In the case of Kuwait, this problem will require attention if recently discovered new oil and gas deposits are to be exploited. In May 2007 the Government decided to revalue the currency and to remove its peg to the US dollar, replacing this with a basket of currencies. The decision, precipitated by the weakening US currency, was viewed as a threat to the proposed introduction of a single GCC currency by 2010. In January 2008 the Council of Ministers approved the budget for the 2008/09 fiscal year: this proposed a record deficit of KD 5,100m., mainly owing to increased government spending. Planned revenues were also projected to increase by 52.8%, to reach KD 12,680m., of which oil revenues were estimated to reach KD 7,450m. Meanwhile, it was reported in February 2008 that the Government planned to spend some $51,000m. on the development of the petroleum sector during 2008–13.

Education

Education is compulsory for eight years between the ages of six and 14. Although private schools exist, state education is free, and is graded into pre-primary (for children between four and six years of age), primary (for children aged six to 10), intermediate (10 to 14) and secondary (14 to 18). In 2004/05 enrolment at primary schools included 86.5% of children in the relevant age-group, while in 2001/02 secondary enrolment included 77.6% of children in the relevant age-group. There is a teacher-training college, a technical college, and a university (where some 20,000 students were enrolled in 2006). A KD 1,000m. project to build a new university campus and to gather the institution's dispersed facilities onto one site was in progress in early 2006. More than 4,500 Kuwaiti students receive education abroad. Expenditure on education by the central Government in 2005/06 was budgeted at KD 573.9m. (7.9% of total expenditure).

Public Holidays

2008: 1 January (New Year's Day), 10 January*† (Islamic New Year), 25 February (Kuwaiti National Day), 26 February (Liberation Day), 20 March* (Birth of the Prophet), 30 July* (Leilat al-Meiraj, Ascension of the Prophet), 1 October* (Id al-Fitr, end of Ramadan), 9 December* (Id al-Adha, Feast of the Sacrifice), 29 December*† (Islamic New Year).

2009: 1 January (New Year's Day), 25 February (Kuwaiti National Day), 26 February (Liberation Day), 9 March* (Birth of the Prophet), 19 July* (Leilat al-Meiraj, Ascension of the Prophet), 20 September* (Id al-Fitr, end of Ramadan), 27 November* (Id al-Adha, Feast of the Sacrifice).

* These holidays are dependent on the Islamic lunar calendar and may vary by one or two days from the dates given.

† This festival occurs twice (marking the start of the Islamic years AH 1429 and 1430) within the same Gregorian year.

Weights and Measures

The metric system is in force.

KUWAIT   Statistical Survey

Statistical Survey

Sources (unless otherwise stated): Economic Research Department, Central Bank of Kuwait, POB 15, 13001 Safat, Kuwait City; tel. 2403257; fax 2440887; e-mail cbk@cbk.gov.kw; internet www.cbk.gov.kw; Central Statistical Office, Ministry of Planning, POB 26188, 13122 Safat, Kuwait City; tel. 2454968; fax 2430464; e-mail salah@mop.gov.kw; internet cso.gov.kw.

Note: Unless otherwise indicated, data refer to the State of Kuwait as constituted at 1 August 1990, prior to the Iraqi invasion and annexation of the territory and its subsequent liberation. Furthermore, no account has been taken of the increase in the area of Kuwait as a result of the adjustment to the border with Iraq that came into force on 15 January 1993.

Area and Population

AREA, POPULATION AND DENSITY

Area (sq km)	17,818*
Population (census results)†‡	
20 April 1995	1,575,570
20 April 2005 (preliminary results)	
Males	1,310,067
Females	903,336
Total	2,213,403
Density (per sq km) at 2005 census	124.2§

* 6,880 sq miles.
† Figures include Kuwaiti nationals abroad. The total population at the 2005 census comprised 880,774 Kuwaiti nationals (433,977 males, 446,797 females) and 1,332,629 non-Kuwaitis (876,090 males, 456,539 females).
‡ Excluding adjustment for underenumeration.
§ Preliminary.

GOVERNORATES
(population at 2005 census, preliminary)

Governorate	Area (sq km)*	Population	Density (per sq km)
Capital	199.8	261,013	1,306.4
Hawalli	} 368.4	487,514	} 3,491.2
Mubarak al-Kabir		176,519	
Farwaniya		622,123	
Al-Jahra	11,230.2	272,373	24.3
Al-Ahmadi	5,119.6	393,861	76.9
Total	16,918.0	2,213,403	130.8

* Excluding the islands of Bubiyan and Warba (combined area 900 sq km).

PRINCIPAL TOWNS
(population at 1995 census)

Kuwait City (capital)	28,747	Subbah as-Salem	54,608
Salmiya	129,775	Sulaibiah	53,639
Jaleeb ash-Shuyukh	102,169	Farwaniya	52,928
Hawalli	82,154	Al-Kreen	50,689
South Kheetan	62,241	Subahiya	50,644

Mid-2007 ('000, incl. suburbs, UN estimate): Kuwait City 2,063 (Source: UN, *World Urbanization Prospects: The 2007 Revision*).

BIRTHS, MARRIAGES AND DEATHS

	Registered live births		Registered marriages		Registered deaths	
	Number	Rate (per 1,000)	Number	Rate (per 1,000)	Number	Rate (per 1,000)
1993	37,379	25.6	10,077	6.9	3,441	2.4
1994	38,868	24.0	9,550	5.9	3,464	2.1
1995	41,169	22.8	9,515	5.3	3,781	2.1
1996	44,620	23.6	9,022	4.8	3,812	2.0
1997	42,817	21.6	9,610	4.9	4,017	2.0
1998	41,424	20.4	10,335	5.1	4,216	2.1
1999	41,135	19.5	10,847	5.1	4,187	2.0
2000	41,843	19.1	10,785	4.9	4,227	1.9

2004: Total births 29,665; Total deahs 4,793; Total marriages 12,359.

Expectation of life (years at birth, WHO estimates): 77.9 (males 77.0; females 79.0) in 2005 (Source: WHO, *World Health Statistics*).

ECONOMICALLY ACTIVE POPULATION
('000 persons aged 15 years and over, mid-2005)

	Kuwaitis	Non-Kuwaitis	Total
Agriculture, hunting and fishing	0.1	32.1	32.2
Mining and quarrying	4.7	2.3	7.0
Manufacturing	8.5	86.7	95.2
Electricity, gas and water	8.1	2.5	10.6
Construction	2.5	118.3	120.8
Wholesale and retail trade	6.3	237.3	243.5
Transport, storage and communications	7.6	43.2	50.9
Finance, insurance, real estate and business services	10.7	63.6	74.3
Public administration	244.7	634.0	878.7
Activities not adequately defined	19.3	194.1	213.4
Total labour force	312.6	1,414.0	1,726.6
Males	185.4	1,119.9	1,305.3
Females	127.2	294.1	421.3

Source: IMF, *Kuwait: Statistical Appendix* (April 2006).

Health and Welfare

KEY INDICATORS

Total fertility rate (children per woman, 2005)	2.3
Under-5 mortality rate (per 1,000 live births, 2005)	12
HIV/AIDS (% of persons aged 15–49, 1994)	<0.2
Physicians (per 1,000 head, 2004)	1.53
Hospital beds (per 1,000 head, 2005)	1.9
Health expenditure (2004): US $ per head (PPP)	537.5
Health expenditure (2004): % of GDP	2.8
Health expenditure (2004): public (% of total)	77.6
Human Development Index (2005): ranking	33
Human Development Index (2005): value	0.891

For sources and definitions, see explanatory note on p. vi.

Agriculture

PRINCIPAL CROPS
('000 metric tons)

	2003	2004	2005
Potatoes	20.8	20.7	20.7
Cabbages and other brassicas	7.7	9.3	9.5*
Lettuce	6.3	7.2*	7.8*
Tomatoes	63.8	55.1*	55.8*
Cauliflowers and broccoli	6.3	7.6*	8.3*
Pumpkins, squash and gourds	5.1	5.5*	6.0*
Cucumbers and gherkins	34.1	35.7*	37.3*
Aubergines (Eggplants)	14.7	17.1*	18.3*
Chillies and green peppers	7.5	7.7*	8.2*
Dry onions	7.6	8.0*	8.0*
Dates	15.8	16.0	16.4*

* FAO estimate.

Aggregate production ('000 metric tons, may include official, semi-official or estimated data): Total cereals 3.3 in 2003, 3.3 in 2004, 3.8 in 2005; Total roots and tubers 20.8 in 2003, 20.7 in 2004, 20.7 in 2005; Total vegetables (incl. melons) 208.2 in 2003, 208.3 in 2004, 214.4 in 2005; Total fruits (excl. melons) 16.7 in 2003, 16.9 in 2004, 17.3 in 2005.

2006: Figures assumed to be unchanged from 2005 (FAO estimates).

Source: FAO.

KUWAIT

LIVESTOCK
('000 head, year ending September)

	2003	2004*	2005*
Cattle	27.4	28.0	28.0
Camels	4.9*	5.0	5.0
Sheep	850*	900	900
Goats	152.4	150.0	150.0
Chickens	31,312	32,000	32,500

* FAO estimate(s).

2006: Figures assumed to be unchanged from 2005 (FAO estimates).

Source: FAO.

LIVESTOCK PRODUCTS
('000 metric tons)

	2003	2004*	2005*
Cattle meat	1.8*	1.8	1.8
Sheep meat	30.6*	29.8	29.8
Chicken meat	37.4	43.3	46.5
Cows' milk	40.1	40.0	40.0
Goats' milk	2.8	4.0	4.5
Hen eggs	20.4	22.0	22.0

* FAO estimate(s).

2006: Figures assumed to be unchanged from 2005 (FAO estimates).

Source: FAO.

Fishing

(metric tons, live weight, FAO estimates)

	2003	2004	2005
Capture	4,059	4,833	4,895
Hilsa shad	205	135	154
Mullets	103	298	220
Groupers	202	171	152
Grunts and sweetlips	30	109	60
Croakers and drums	625	865	674
Yellowfin seabream	164	269	280
Indo-Pacific king mackerel	101	125	97
Carangids	93	121	100
Natantian decapods	1,376	1,666	1,890
Aquaculture	366	375	327
Total catch	4,425	5,208	5,222

Source: FAO.

Mining*

	2004	2005	2006
Crude petroleum (million barrels)	838	939	980
Natural gas (million cu metres)†	9,800	11,000	11,500

* Estimates, including an equal share of production with Saudi Arabia from the Neutral/Partitioned Zone.
† On a dry basis.

Source: US Geological Survey.

Industry

SELECTED PRODUCTS
('000 metric tons, unless otherwise stated)

	2000	2001	2002
Bran and flour*	210.0	211.2	225.1†
Sulphur (by-product)‡	512	524	634§
Chlorine*	14.8	17.7	19.0†
Caustic soda (Sodium hydroxide)*	18.5	20.0	56.6†
Salt*	36.8	37.5	42.5†
Nitrogenous fertilizers‡||	288	290	320§
Motor spirit (petrol) (million barrels)‡¶	12	10	15§
Kerosene (million barrels)‡¶	45	30	45§
Gas-diesel (Distillate fuel) oils (million barrels)‡¶	84	70	85§
Residual fuel oils (million barrels)‡¶	57	60	75§
Petroleum bitumen (asphalt)§¶	331	252	297
Liquefied petroleum gas ('000 barrels)*¶	35	35	33
Quicklime‡	40	40	40§
Cement‡	1,187	921	1,584§
Electric energy (million kWh)*¶	32,300	34,500	36,400†

2003‡§ ('000 metric tons, unless otherwise stated): Sulphur (by-product) 714; Motor spirit (petrol) (million barrels) 15¶; Kerosene (million barrels) 45¶; Gas-diesel (Distillate fuel) oils (million barrels) 85¶; Residual fuel oils (million barrels) 70¶; Quicklime 40; Cement 1,600.

2004‡ ('000 metric tons, unless otherwise stated): Sulphur (by-product) 730; Motor spirit (petrol) (million barrels) 15¶; Kerosene (million barrels) 45¶; Gas-diesel (Distillate fuel) oils (million barrels) 85¶; Residual fuel oils (million barrels) 75¶; Quicklime 40; Cement 1,600.

* Source: IMF, *Kuwait: Statistical Appendix* (July 2004).
† Figure for January–October.
‡ Source: US Geological Survey.
§ Provisional or estimated figure(s).
\|\| Production in terms of nitrogen.
¶ Including an equal share of production with Saudi Arabia from the Neutral/Partitioned Zone.

Finance

CURRENCY AND EXCHANGE RATES

Monetary Units
  1,000 fils = 10 dirhams = 1 Kuwaiti dinar (KD).

Sterling, Dollar and Euro Equivalents (31 December 2007)
  £1 sterling = 546.93 fils;
  US $1 = 273.00 fils;
  €1 = 401.88 fils;
  10 Kuwaiti dinars = £18.28 = $36.63 = €24.88.

Average Exchange Rate (fils per US $)
  2005   292.0
  2006   290.2
  2007   284.2

From 1 January 2003 the official exchange rate was fixed within the range of US $1 = 289 fils to $1 = 310 fils (KD 1 = $3.4602 to KD 1 = $3.2258), but this 'peg' to the US dollar was abandoned in May 2007 in favour of a basket of currencies including the pound sterling, the euro and the yen.

GENERAL BUDGET
(KD million, year ending 30 June)

Revenue	2005/06	2006/07	2007/08*
Tax revenue	247.1	287.6	279.7
International trade and transactions	176.0	190.4	177.7
Non-tax revenue	13,481.0	15,221.7	8,040.6
Oil revenue	12,955.5	14,511.5	7,449.9
Total operating revenue of government enterprises	411.3	449.0	516.4
Total	13,728.1	15,509.3	8,320.3

KUWAIT

Statistical Survey

Expenditure	2005/06	2006/07	2007/08*
Current expenditure	4,767.5	5,902.0	7,218.0
Land acquisitions	181.9	361.2	267.9
Capital expenditure	58.6	77.1	216.0
Construction expenditure	568.6	628.3	1,790.1
Other expenditure	1,285.3	3,337.9	1,808.0
Total	6,862.0	10,306.4	11,300.0

* Projections.

INTERNATIONAL RESERVES
(US $ million at 31 December)

	2004	2005	2006
Gold (national valuation)	107.7	108.7	109.8
IMF special drawing rights	181.8	183.9	207.3
Reserve position in IMF	712.7	298.5	181.1
Foreign exchange	7,347.4	8,380.4	12,177.6
Total	8,349.6	8,971.5	12,675.8

Source: IMF, *International Financial Statistics*.

MONEY SUPPLY
(KD million at 31 December)

	2004	2005	2006
Currency outside banks	531.0	578.7	656.3
Demand deposits at deposit money banks	2,643.3	3,148.7	2,893.9
Total money	3,174.2	3,727.4	3,550.2

Source: IMF, *International Financial Statistics*.

COST OF LIVING
(Consumer Price Index; base: 2000 = 100)

	2004	2005	2006
Food	110.0	119.4	124.0
Beverages and tobacco	111.2	112.2	114.3
Clothing and footwear	111.0	118.1	122.8
Housing services	104.6	105.3	108.0
All items (incl. others)	104.5	108.8	112.1

NATIONAL ACCOUNTS
(KD million at current prices)

Expenditure on the Gross Domestic Product

	2004	2005	2006
Government final consumption expenditure	3,478	3,707	4,029
Private final consumption expenditure	6,555	7,386	8,086
Increase in stocks	3,186	4,961	5,543
Gross fixed capital formation			
Total domestic expenditure	13,219	16,054	17,658
Exports of goods and services	9,970	15,094	19,038
Less Imports of goods and services	5,672	6,670	7,123
GDP in purchasers' values	17,517	24,478	29,573

Gross Domestic Product by Economic Activity

	2004	2005	2006
Agriculture, hunting, forestry and fishing	70.9	71.1	74.4
Mining and quarrying	7,844.5	12,865.2	16,256.2
Manufacturing	1,455.9	1,712.9	1,973.4
Electricity, gas and water	306.9	319.1	336.6
Construction	401.9	437.1	479.3
Trade	950.2	1,017.8	1,088.8
Restaurants and hotels	170.5	168.0	171.2
Transport, storage and communications	1,048.0	1,230.7	1,397.4
Finance, insurance, real estate and business services	2,880.6	4,306.1	5,460.3
Community, social and personal services	2,950.0	3,228.3	3,478.7
Sub-total	18,079.4	25,356.3	30,716.3
Import duties	161.5	173.6	174.6
Less Imputed bank service charges	−724.2	−1,052.1	−1,318.1
GDP in purchasers' values	17,516.7	24,477.8	29,572.8

BALANCE OF PAYMENTS
(US $ million)

	2004	2005	2006
Exports of goods f.o.b.	30,089	46,971	58,638
Imports of goods f.o.b.	−11,663	−14,238	−14,350
Trade balance	18,426	32,733	44,288
Exports of services	3,743	4,723	6,972
Imports of services	−7,586	−8,604	−10,192
Balance on goods and services	14,583	28,852	41,068
Other income received	6,584	9,413	14,659
Other income paid	−456	−556	−1,274
Balance on goods, services and income	20,712	37,709	54,453
Current transfers received	88	86	113
Current transfers paid	−2,638	−3,487	−3,571
Current balance	18,162	34,308	50,996
Capital account (net)	433	797	882
Direct investment abroad	−2,526	−5,142	−7,892
Direct investment from abroad	24	250	110
Portfolio investment assets	−14,216	−10,006	−25,532
Portfolio investment liabilities	288	−542	101
Other investment assets	−292	−19,965	−23,683
Other investment liabilities	−107	4,260	8,896
Net errors and omissions	−1,136	−3,341	−293
Overall balance	629	619	3,584

Source: IMF, *International Financial Statistics*.

External Trade

PRINCIPAL COMMODITIES
(distribution by SITC, KD million)

Imports c.i.f.	2002	2003	2004
Food and live animals	382.9	432.3	462.2
Chemicals and related products	238.6	270.6	325.2
Basic manufactures	510.5	593.3	763.8
Machinery and transport equipment	1,089.5	1,368.3	1,511.1
Miscellaneous manufactured articles	378.1	443.8	487.3
Total (incl. others)	2,735.8	3,274.1	3,749.5

KUWAIT

Statistical Survey

Exports f.o.b.	2002	2003	2004
Mineral fuels, lubricants, etc.	4,276	n.a.	n.a.
Petroleum, petroleum products, etc.*	4,273	5,832	5,430
Chemicals and related products	248	n.a.	321
Total (incl. others)*	4,666	6,495	8,867

* Estimates by the Central Bank of Kuwait.

2005 (KD million): Total imports 4,613.9; Total exports 13,101.6 (Petroleum, petroleum products, etc. 12,392.6).

2006 (KD million): Total imports 4,629.2; Total exports 16,166.7 (Petroleum, petroleum products, etc. 15,430.7).

2007 (KD million): Total imports 5,510.0; Total exports 17,688.7 (Petroleum, petroleum products, etc. 16,845.7).

PRINCIPAL TRADING PARTNERS
(KD million)*

Imports c.i.f.	2002	2003	2004
Australia	103.3	108.6	94.4
Brazil	25.0	35.1	40.6
Canada	41.3	48.9	48.6
China, People's Repub.	142.4	187.1	252.3
France (incl. Monaco)	88.0	95.2	113.7
Germany	255.1	336.4	426.4
India	106.4	122.7	157.8
Iran	43.8	56.5	62.5
Italy	153.0	168.0	202.3
Japan	292.4	322.9	238.4
Korea, Repub.	70.0	81.4	103.9
Malaysia	36.8	40.4	47.1
Netherlands	44.1	44.9	55.9
Saudi Arabia	176.5	222.1	294.9
Spain	43.3	48.3	48.8
Switzerland-Liechtenstein	39.5	41.7	49.8
Syria	27.4	17.4	21.6
Taiwan	31.2	34.9	42.7
Thailand	33.6	35.4	42.3
Turkey	56.3	66.6	95.6
United Arab Emirates	96.5	121.7	167.1
United Kingdom	122.0	146.1	151.2
USA	299.7	380.5	400.2
Total (incl. others)	2,735.8	3,274.1	3,722.2

Exports f.o.b.†	2002	2003	2004
Bahrain	7.7	12.5	10.5
Belgium-Luxembourg	5.7	3.1	2.0
China, People's Repub.	23.9	25.0	22.5
Egypt	10.6	12.0	13.1
India	25.1	29.4	31.5
Indonesia	39.5	37.3	51.2
Iran	7.8	6.8	6.4
Japan	5.8	2.4	1.0
Jordan	9.1	11.5	13.7
Korea, Repub.	0.7	1.0	1.8
Lebanon	5.5	4.7	8.3
Malaysia	7.0	5.7	1.3
Oman	6.5	5.5	6.2
Pakistan	17.6	24.0	39.0
Philippines	8.7	7.0	4.4
Qatar	11.1	9.6	10.0
Saudi Arabia	52.4	68.3	61.1
Spain	15.7	7.7	8.2
Syria	8.3	11.1	13.9
Taiwan	4.0	3.5	4.6
Turkey	8.0	4.6	2.9
United Arab Emirates	41.9	49.7	56.5
USA	2.9	27.7	32.0
Total (incl. others)	393.4	498.5	567.0

* Imports by country of production; exports by country of last consignment.
† Excluding petroleum exports.

Transport

ROAD TRAFFIC
(motor vehicles in use at 31 December)

	1995	1996	1997
Passenger cars	662,946	701,172	747,042
Buses and coaches	11,937	12,322	13,094
Goods vehicles	116,813	121,753	127,386

1999: Buses and coaches 12,775; Goods vehicles 97,706.

2000: Buses and coaches 10,974; Goods vehicles 80,378.

2001: Passenger cars 715,000; Commercial vehicles 226,000.

2004: Passenger cars, 858,055; Buses and coaches, 37,789; Commercial vehicles, 143,151.

SHIPPING
Merchant Fleet
(registered at 31 December)

	2004	2005	2006
Number of vessels	213	222	220
Displacement ('000 grt)	2,377.6	2,315.7	2,156.8

Source: Lloyd's Register-Fairplay, *World Fleet Statistics*.

International Sea-borne Freight Traffic
('000 metric tons)*

	1988	1989	1990
Goods loaded	61,778	69,097	51,400
Goods unloaded	7,123	7,015	4,522

* Including Kuwait's share of traffic in the Neutral/Partitioned Zone.

Source: UN, *Monthly Bulletin of Statistics*.

Goods loaded ('000 metric tons): 89,945 in 1997.

Goods unloaded ('000 metric tons): 746 in 1991 (July–December only); 2,537 in 1992; 4,228 in 1993; 5,120 in 1994; 5,854 in 1995; 6,497 in 1996; 6,049 in 1997.

CIVIL AVIATION
(traffic on scheduled services)

	2001	2002	2003
Kilometres flown (million)	37	41	39
Passengers carried ('000)	2,085	2,299	2,186
Passenger-km (million)	6,010	6,706	6,311
Total ton-km (million)	777	867	795

Source: UN, *Statistical Yearbook*.

Tourism

VISITOR ARRIVALS BY COUNTRY OF ORIGIN
(incl. excursionists)

	2002	2003	2004
Bahrain	74,979	77,512	84,934
Bangladesh	75,423	90,327	111,060
Egypt	256,867	289,401	327,460
India	314,054	363,724	413,109
Iran	99,066	100,474	121,642
Lebanon	61,687	63,735	74,629
Pakistan	84,224	111,055	123,128
Philippines	56,335	60,264	73,656
Saudi Arabia	725,025	777,831	896,102
Sri Lanka	62,586	63,269	62,676
Syria	176,375	185,946	234,726
Total (incl. others)	2,315,568	2,602,300	3,056,093

Tourism receipts (US $ million, incl. passenger transport): 330 in 2003; 413 in 2004; 408 in 2005.

Source: World Tourism Organization.

Communications Media

	2003	2004	2005
Telephones ('000 main lines in use)	486.9	497.0	510.3
Mobile cellular telephones ('000 subscribers)	1,420.0	2,000.0	2,379.8
Personal computers ('000 in use)	400	450	600
Internet users ('000)	567	600	700

1996: Daily newspapers 8 (average circulation 635,000 copies); Non-daily newspapers 78.

1999: Radio receivers 1,200,000 in use; Television receivers 910,000 in use; Facsimile machines 60,000 in use; Book titles published 219.

2000: Television receivers 930,000 in use.

2004: Daily newspapers 8; Non-daily newspapers 91.

Internet users ('000): 816.7 in 2006.

Broadband subscribers ('000): 25.0 in 2005.

Sources: UNESCO, *Statistical Yearbook*; UN, *Statistical Yearbook*; International Telecommunication Union.

Education

(state-controlled schools, 2000/01)

	Schools	Teachers	Males	Females	Total
Kindergarten	153	3,379	22,142	22,128	44,270
Primary	184	8,151	48,796	49,322	98,118
Intermediate	165	9,073	47,955	47,509	95,464
Secondary	117	9,234	34,868	41,353	76,221
Religious institutes	7	351	n.a.	n.a.	2,454
Special training institutes	33	756	n.a.	n.a.	543

Private education (1996/97): 63 kindergarten schools (598 teachers, 12,172 students); 80 primary schools (2,341 teachers, 47,111 students); 82 intermediate schools (1,860 teachers, 36,254 students); 66 secondary schools (1,576 teachers, 20,932 students).

2000/01 (private education): 112 schools; 7,324 teachers; 128,204 students.

2004/05: *Teaching staff:* kindergarten 4,958; primary 16,815; intermediate 12,300; secondary 11,762; *Student enrolment:* kindergarten 50,911; primary 202,826; intermediate 142,146; secondary 106,749; tertiary 38,630 (Source: UNESCO Institute for Statistics).

Adult literacy rate (UNESCO estimates): 93.3% (males 94.4%; females 91.0%) in 2005 (Source: UNESCO Institute for Statistics).

Directory

The Constitution

The principal provisions of the Constitution, promulgated on 16 November 1962, are set out below. On 29 August 1976 the Amir suspended four articles of the Constitution dealing with the National Assembly, the Majlis al-Umma. On 24 August 1980 the Amir issued a decree ordering the establishment of an elected legislature before the end of February 1981. The new Majlis was elected on 23 February, and fresh legislative elections followed on 20 February 1985. The Majlis was dissolved by Amiri decree in July 1986, and some sections of the Constitution, including the stipulation that new elections should be held within two months of dissolving the legislature (see below), were suspended. A new Majlis was elected on 5 October 1992 and convened on 20 October. In 2005 the Majlis approved legislation allowing women to vote in and stand as candidates for parliamentary and local elections.

SOVEREIGNTY

Kuwait is an independent sovereign Arab State; its sovereignty may not be surrendered, and no part of its territory may be relinquished. Offensive war is prohibited by the Constitution.

Succession as Amir is restricted to heirs of the late Mubarak as-Sabah, and an Heir Apparent must be appointed within one year of the accession of a new Amir.

EXECUTIVE AUTHORITY

Executive power is vested in the Amir, who exercises it through the Council of Ministers. The Amir will appoint the Prime Minister 'after the traditional consultations', and will appoint and dismiss ministers on the recommendation of the Prime Minister. Ministers need not be members of the Majlis al-Umma, although all ministers who are not members of parliament assume membership ex officio in the legislature for the duration of office. The Amir also formulates laws, which shall not be effective unless published in the *Official Gazette*. The Amir establishes public institutions. All decrees issued in these respects shall be conveyed to the Majlis. No law is issued unless it is approved by the Majlis.

LEGISLATURE

A National Assembly, the Majlis al-Umma, of 50 members is elected for a four-year term by all natural-born Kuwaitis over the age of 21 years, except servicemen and police, who may not vote. (Unelected cabinet ministers also sit in the Majlis, bringing the total membership to around 65.) Candidates for election must possess the franchise, be over 30 years of age and literate. The Majlis will convene for at least eight months in any year, and new elections shall be held within two months of the last dissolution of the outgoing legislature.

Restrictions on the commercial activities of ministers include an injunction forbidding them to sell property to the Government.

The Amir may ask for reconsideration of a bill that has been approved by the Majlis and sent to him for ratification, but the bill would automatically become law if it were subsequently adopted by a two-thirds' majority at the next sitting, or by a simple majority at a subsequent sitting. The Amir may declare martial law, but only with the approval of the legislature.

The Majlis may adopt a vote of no confidence in a minister, in which case the minister must resign. Such a vote is not permissible in the case of the Prime Minister, but the legislature may approach the Amir on the matter, and the Amir shall then either dismiss the Prime Minister or dissolve the Majlis.

CIVIL SERVICE

Entry to the civil service is confined to Kuwaiti citizens.

PUBLIC LIBERTIES

Kuwaitis are equal before the law in prestige, rights and duties. Individual freedom is guaranteed. No one shall be seized, arrested or exiled except within the rules of law.

No punishment shall be administered except for an act or abstaining from an act considered a crime in accordance with a law applicable at the time of committing it, and no penalty shall be imposed more severe than that which could have been imposed at the time of committing the crime.

Freedom of opinion is guaranteed to everyone, and each has the right to express himself through speech, writing or other means within the limits of the law.

The press is free within the limits of the law, and it should not be suppressed except in accordance with the dictates of law.

Freedom of performing religious rites is protected by the State according to prevailing customs, provided it does not violate the public order and morality.

Trade unions will be permitted and property must be respected. An owner is not banned from managing his property except within the boundaries of law. No property should be taken from anyone, except within the prerogatives of law, unless a just compensation be given.

Houses may not be entered, except in cases provided by law. Every Kuwaiti has freedom of movement and choice of place of residence within the State. This right shall not be controlled except in cases stipulated by law.

Every person has the right to education and freedom to choose his type of work. Freedom to form peaceful societies is guaranteed within the limits of law.

The Government

HEAD OF STATE

Amir of Kuwait: His Highness Sheikh SABAH AL-AHMAD AL-JABER AS-SABAH (acceded 29 January 2006).

COUNCIL OF MINISTERS
(April 2008)

Following the resignation of the entire Council of Ministers on 17 March 2008, Sheikh Sabah dissolved the Majlis al-Umma (National Assembly) on 19 March and called for fresh elections to be held on 17 May. The ministers listed below remained in their posts in an interim capacity.

Prime Minister: Sheikh NASSER AL-MUHAMMAD AL-AHMAD AS-SABAH.
First Deputy Prime Minister and Minister of Defence: Sheikh JABER MUBARAK AL-HAMAD AS-SABAH.
Deputy Prime Minister and Minister of Foreign Affairs: Sheikh Dr MUHAMMAD SABAH AS-SALIM AS-SABAH.
Deputy Prime Minister and Minister of State for Cabinet Affairs: FAISAL MUHAMMAD AL-HAJJI BUKHADHOUR.
Minister of the Interior: Sheikh JABER KHALID AL-JABER AS-SABAH.
Minister of Finance and Acting Minister of Commerce and Industry: MUSTAFA JASSEM ASH-SHIMALI.
Minister of Electricity and Water and Acting Minister of Oil: MUHAMMAD ABDULLAH HADI AL-OLAIM.
Minister of Public Works and Minister of State for Municipal Affairs: MOUSSA HUSSEIN ABDULLAH AS-SARRAF.
Minister of Education and Higher Education: NOURIYA SUBEEH BARRAK AS-SUBEEH.
Minister of Justice and of Social Affairs and Labour: JAMAL AHMAD ASH-SHIHAB.
Minister of Awqaf (Religious Endowments) and Islamic Affairs and of Communications: ABDULLAH SAUD AL-MUHAILBI.
Minister of Information: Sheikh SABAH KHALID AL-HAMAD AS-SABAH.
Minister of Health and Acting Minister of State for Housing Affairs and for National Assembly Affairs: ABDULLAH ABD AR-RAHMAN AT-TAWEEL.

PROVINCIAL GOVERNORS

Al-Ahmadi: Sheikh Dr IBRAHIM AD-DUAIJ AL-IBRAHIM AS-SABAH.
Farwaniya: ABD AL-HAMID HAJJI ABD AR-RAHIM.
Mubarak al-Kabir: Sheikh ALI ABDULLAH AS-SALIM AS-SABAH.
Hawalli: ABDULLAH ABD AR-RAHMAN AL-FARIS.
Al-Jahra: Sheikh MUBARAK AL-HUMOUD AS-SABAH.
Kuwait (Capital): Sheikh ALI JABER AL-AHMAD AS-SABAH.

MINISTRIES

Ministry of Awqaf (Religious Endowments) and Islamic Affairs: POB 13, 13001 Safat, Kuwait City; tel. 2487225; internet www.islam.gov.kw.
Ministry of Commerce and Industry: POB 2944, 13030 Safat, Kuwait City; tel. 248000; fax 2424411; internet www.moci.gov.kw.
Ministry of Communications: POB 15, 13001 Safat, Kuwait City; tel. 4819033; internet www.mockw.net.
Ministry of Defence: POB 1170, 13012 Safat, Kuwait City; tel. 4848300; fax 4846059; internet www.mod.gov.kw.
Ministry of Education: POB 7, 13001 Safat, Hilali St, Kuwait City; tel. 4836800; fax 2423676; e-mail webmaster@moe.edu.kw; internet www.moe.edu.kw.
Ministry of Electricity and Water: POB 12, 13001 Safat, Kuwait City; tel. 5371000; internet www.energy.gov.kw.
Ministry of Finance: POB 9, 13001 Safat, al-Morkab St, Ministries Complex, Kuwait City; tel. 2480000; fax 2404025; e-mail webmaster@mof.gov.kw; internet www.mof.gov.kw.
Ministry of Foreign Affairs: POB 3, 13001 Safat, Gulf St, Kuwait City; tel. 2425141; fax 2412169; e-mail emad@mofa.org; internet www.mofa.gov.kw.
Ministry of Health: POB 5, 13001 Safat, Arabian Gulf St, Kuwait City; tel. 4863840; fax 4863485; e-mail health@moh.gov.kw; internet www.moh.gov.kw.
Ministry of Higher Education: tel. 2401300; e-mail info_minister@mohe.edu.kw; internet www.mohe.edu.kw.
Ministry of Information: POB 193, 13002 Safat, as-Sour St, Kuwait City; tel. 2415301; fax 2419642; e-mail info@media.gov.kw; internet www.media.gov.kw.
Ministry of the Interior: POB 11, 13001 Safat, Kuwait City; tel. 2430500; fax 2561268; e-mail contact@moi.gov.kw; internet www.moi.gov.kw.
Ministry of Justice: POB 6, 13001 Safat, al-Morkab St, Ministries Complex, Kuwait City; tel. 2486012; fax 2442257; e-mail info@moj.gov.kw; internet www.moj.gov.kw.
Ministry of Oil: POB 5077, 13051 Safat, Kuwait City; tel. 2406990; e-mail alnaft@moo.gov.kw; internet www.moo.gov.kw.
Ministry of Planning: POB 15, 13001 Safat, Kuwait City; tel. 2428200; fax 2430403; e-mail info@mop.gov.kw; internet www.mop.gov.kw.
Ministry of Public Works: POB 8, 13001 Safat, Kuwait City; tel. 5385520; fax 5380829; e-mail undersecretary@mpw.gov.kw; internet www.mpw.gov.kw.
Ministry of Social Affairs and Labour: POB 563, 13006 Safat, Kuwait City; tel. 2480000; fax 2419877; internet www.mosal.gov.kw.

Legislature

MAJLIS AL-UMMA
(National Assembly)

Speaker: JASEM AL-KHARAFI.

Elections to the 50-seat Majlis took place one year early on 29 June 2006, following the dissolution of parliament by Sheikh Sabah on 21 May (precipitated by a dispute between the Government and opposition over proposed electoral reform). A loose coalition of Islamist, liberal and nationalist candidates secured 34 seats; the remaining seats were won by pro-Government candidates and independents. Sheikh Sabah again dissolved parliament on 19 March 2008 (see Recent History), and fresh elections to the Majlis were called for 17 May.

Political Organizations

Political parties are not permitted in Kuwait. However, several quasi-political organizations are in existence. Among those that have been represented in the Majlis since 1992 are:

Constitutional Group: supported by merchants.
Islamic Constitutional Movement: Sunni Muslim; political arm of the Muslim Brotherhood; Spokesman MUHAMMAD ABDULLAH HADI AL-OLAIM.
Kuwait Democratic Forum: f. 1991; loose asscn of secular, liberal and Arab nationalist groups; campaigned for the extension of voting rights to women.
National Action Bloc: Liberal.
National Democratic Rally (NDR): f. 1997; secular, liberal; Sec.-Gen. Dr AHMAD BISHARA.
National Islamic Movement: Shi'a Muslim.
Salafeen (Islamic Popular Movement): Sunni Muslim.

Diplomatic Representation

EMBASSIES IN KUWAIT

Afghanistan: POB 33186, 73452 Rawdah, Block 6, Surra St, Across Surra Co-op Society House 16, Kuwait City; tel. 5329461; fax 5326274; e-mail afg_emb_kuw@hotmail.com; Ambassador MUHAMMAD YOUSUF SAMAD.
Algeria: POB 578, 13006 Safat, Istiqlal St, Kuwait City; tel. 2519220; fax 2519497; e-mail ambalgkt@qualitynet.net; Ambassador MUHAMMAD BURUBA.
Argentina: POB 3788, 40188 Mishref, Kuwait City; tel. 5379211; fax 5379212; e-mail ekuwa@mrecic.gov.ar; Ambassador RICARDO E. INSUA.
Australia: Dar al-Awadi Complex (Level 12), Ahmad al-Jaber St, Sharq, Kuwait City; tel. 2322422; fax 2322430; e-mail austemb.kuwait@dfat.go.au; internet www.kuwait.embassy.gov.au; Ambassador GLENN MILES.
Austria: POB 15013, Daiyah, Area 3, Shawki St, House 10, 35451 Kuwait City; tel. 2552532; fax 2563052; e-mail kuwait-ob@bmaa.gv.at; Ambassador GEORG STILLFRIED.
Azerbaijan: Al-Yarmouk, Block No. 2, St 1, Bldg 15, Kuwait City; tel. 5355247; fax 535546; e-mail embazerbaijan@yahoo.com; internet www.azerembassy-kuwait.org; Ambassador SHAHIN ABDULLAYEV.

KUWAIT

Bahrain: POB 196, 13002 Safat, Area 6, Surra Rd, Villa 35, Kuwait City; tel. 5318530; fax 5330882; e-mail b111b@kems.net; Ambassador Sheikh KHALIFA BIN HAMAD AL-KHALIFA.

Bangladesh: POB 22344, 13084 Safat, Khaldya, Block 6, Ali bin Abi Taleb St, House 361, Kuwait City; tel. 5316042; fax 5316041; e-mail bdoot@ncc.moc.kw; Ambassador NAZRUL ISLAM KHAN.

Belgium: POB 3280, 13033 Safat, Baghdad St, Block 8, House 15, Kuwait City; tel. 5722014; fax 5748389; e-mail kuwait@diplobel.org; internet www.diplomatie.be/kuwait; Ambassador GILES HEYVAERT.

Bhutan: POB 1510, 13016 Safat, Adailiya-Block 3, Issa Abd ar-Rahman al-Assoussi St, Jadda 32, Villa 7, Kuwait City; tel. 2516640; fax 2516550; e-mail bhutankuwait@hotmail.com; Ambassador TSHERING WANGDI.

Bosnia and Herzegovina: POB 6131, 32036 Hawalli, Bayan, Block 6, St 4, House 25, Kuwait City; tel. 5392637; fax 5392106; Ambassador ŠERIF MUJKANOVIĆ.

Brazil: POB 39761, 73058 Nuzha, Block 2, St 1, Jadah 1, Villa 8, Kuwait City; tel. 5328610; fax 5328613; e-mail brasemkw@qualitynet.net; internet www.brazilianembassykw.com; Ambassador MARIO DA GRAÇA ROITER.

Bulgaria: POB 12090, 71651 Shamiya, Jabriya, Block 11, St 107 and St 1, Villa 272, Kuwait City; tel. 5314458; fax 5321453; e-mail bgembkw@qualitynet.net; Ambassador ANGEL N. MANTCHEV.

Canada: POB 25281, 13113 Safat, Daiyah, Area 4, 24 al-Mutawakkel St, Kuwait City; tel. 2563025; fax 2560173; e-mail kwait@international.gc.ca; internet www.dfait-maeci.gc.ca/kuwait; Ambassador DENIS THIBAULT.

China, People's Republic: POB 2346, 13024 Safat, Yarmouk, Sheikh Ahmad al-Jaber Bldgs 4 & 5, St 1, Villa 82, Kuwait City; tel. 5333340; fax 5333341; e-mail chinaemb_kw@mfa.gov.cn; Ambassador WU JIUHONG.

Czech Republic: al-Nuzha, Block 3, St 34, Bldg 13, Kuwait City; tel. 2529018; fax 2529021; e-mail kuwait@embassy.mzv.cz; internet www.mzv.cz/kuwait; Ambassador ANTONÍN BLAŽEK.

Egypt: POB 11252, 35153 Dasmah, Istiqlal St, Kuwait City; tel. 2519955; fax 2563877; Ambassador ABD ELRAHIM ISMAIL SHALABY.

Eritrea: POB 53016, 73015 Nuzha, Jabriya, Block 9, St 21, House 9, Kuwait City; tel. 5317427; fax 6631304; Ambassador MAHMOUD OMAR CHIROUM.

Ethiopia: POB 939, 45710 Safat, Jabriya, Block 10, St 107, Villa 30, Kuwait City; tel. 5330128; fax 5331179; e-mail ethiokuwait@yahoo.com; Ambassador KADAFOU MUHAMMAD HANFARY.

France: POB 1037, 13011 Safat, Mansouriah, Block 1, St 13, Villa 24, Kuwait City; tel. 2582020; fax 2571058; e-mail cad.koweit-amba@diplomatie.gouv.fr; internet www.ambafrance-kwt.org; Ambassador CORINNE BREUZÉ.

Georgia: Qurtoba, Block 2, Area 1, Ave 3, Villa 6, Kuwait City; tel. 5352909; fax 5354707; e-mail kuwait.emb@mfa.gov.ge; Ambassador GOCHA JAPARIDZE.

Germany: POB 805, 13009 Safat, Dahiya Abdullah as-Salem, Area 1, Ave 14, Villa 13, Kuwait City; tel. 2520857; fax 2520763; e-mail info@kuwait.diplo.de; internet www.kuwait.diplo.de; Ambassador Dr MICHAEL WORBS.

Greece: POB 23812, 13099 Safat, Khaldiya, Block 4, St 44, House 4, Kuwait City; tel. 4817100; fax 4817103; e-mail grembkw@hotmail.com; Ambassador STAVROS LYKIDIS.

Hungary: POB 23955, 13100 Safat, Bayan, Block 13, St 13, Villa 381, Kuwait City; tel. 5379351; fax 5379350; e-mail huembkwi@quality.net; internet www.mfa.gov.hu/kulkepviselet/Kuwait/en; Ambassador JÁNOS GYURIS.

India: POB 1450, 13015 Safat, Diplomatic Enclave, Arabian Gulf St, Kuwait City; tel. 2530600; fax 2525811; e-mail contact@indembkwt.org; internet www.indembkwt.org; Ambassador M. GANAPATHI.

Indonesia: POB 21500, 13076 Safat, Kaifan, Block 6, Al-Andalus St, House 29, Kuwait City; tel. 4839927; fax 4819250; e-mail unitkom@kbrikuwait.org; internet www.kbrikuwait.org; Ambassador SUDIRMAN FAISAL ISMAIL.

Iran: POB 4686, 13047 Safat, Daiyah, Embassies Area, Block B, Kuwait City; tel. 2560694; fax 2529868; e-mail iranebassy@hotmail.com; Ambassador ALI JANNATI.

Italy: POB 4453, 13045 Safat, Kuwait City; tel. 5356010; fax 5356030; e-mail ambasciata.alkuwait@esteri.it; internet www.ambalkuwait.esteri.it; Ambassador GIORGIO DI PIETROGIACOMO.

Japan: POB 2304, 13024 Safat, Kuwait City, Area 9, Plot 496, St 101, Kuwait City; tel. 5312870; fax 5326168; e-mail info@embjp-kw.org; internet www.kw.emb-japan.go.jp; Ambassador MASATOSHI MUTO.

Jordan: POB 39891, 73059 Kuwait City; tel. 2533261; fax 2533270; e-mail kujor@qualitynet.net; Ambassador MUHAMMAD AL-QURAAN.

Korea, Republic: POB 20771, 13068 Safat, Rawda, Block 1, St 10, House 17, Kuwait City; tel. 2554206; fax 2526874; Ambassador SONG KEUN HO.

Lebanon: POB 253, 13003 Safat, Da'Yiah Diplomatic Area Plot 6, Kuwait City; tel. 2562103; fax 2571682; Ambassador BASSAM NA'AMANI.

Libya: POB 21460, 13075 Safat, 27 Istiqlal St, Kuwait City; tel. 2575183; fax 2575182; Chargé d'affaires ALI JAFFERE.

Malaysia: POB 4105, 13042 Safat, Daiya, Diplomatic Enclave, Area 5, Istiqlal St, Plot 5, Kuwait City; tel. 2550394; fax 2550384; e-mail malkuwait@kln.gov.my; internet www.kln.gov.my/perwakilan/kuwait; Ambassador Dato' ASHAARY BIN SANI.

Morocco: Yarmouk, Block 2, St 2, Villa 14, Kuwait City; tel. 5312980; fax 5317423; e-mail ambkow@yahoo.fr; Ambassador MUHAMMAD BELAICH.

Netherlands: POB 21822, 13079 Safat, Jabriya, Area 9, St 1, Plot 40A, Kuwait City; tel. 5312650; fax 5326334; e-mail kwe@minbuza.nl; internet www.netherlandsembassy.gov.kw; Ambassador Dr CORNELIS G. J. VAN HONK.

Niger: POB 44451, 32059 Hawalli, Salwa Block 12, St 6, Villa 183, Kuwait City; tel. 5652943; fax 5640478; Ambassador ASSOUMANE GUIAOURI.

Nigeria: POB 6432, 32039 Hawalli, Surra, Area 1, St 14, House 24, Kuwait City; tel. 5320794; fax 5320834; Ambassador MUHAMMAD ADAMU JUMBA.

Oman: POB 21975, 13080 Safat, al-Odeilia Block 3, St 3, Villa 25, Kuwait City; tel. 2561956; fax 2561963; Ambassador SAEED IBN ALI AL-KALBANI.

Pakistan: POB 988, 13010 Safat, Jabriya, Police Station Rd, St 101, Plot 5, Block 11, Villa 7, Kuwait City; tel. 5327649; fax 5328013; e-mail pavepkw@pakembkw.org; internet www.pakembkw.org; Ambassador MOHAMMAD ASLAM.

Philippines: POB 26288, 13123 Safat, Area 7, No. 103, Villa 503 Jabriya, Kuwait City; tel. 5349099; fax 5329319; e-mail kuwaitpe@dfa.gov.ph; internet www.philembassykuwait.gov.kw; Ambassador RICARDO M. ENDAYA.

Poland: POB 5066, 13051 Safat, Jabriya, Plot 7, St 3, House 20, Kuwait City; tel. 5311571; fax 5311576; e-mail embassy@kuwejt.polemb.net; internet www.kuwejt.polemb.net; Ambassador JANUSZ SZWEDO.

Qatar: POB 1825, 13019 Safat, Diiyah, Istiqlal St, Kuwait City; tel. 2523107; fax 2513604; e-mail kuwait@mofa.gov.qa; Ambassador ABD AL-AZIZ BIN SAAD AL-FEHAID.

Romania: POB 11149, 35152 Dasmah, Keifan, Area 4, Moona St, House 34, Kuwait City; tel. 4845079; fax 4848929; e-mail ambsa@qualitynet.net; Ambassador CONSTANTIN VOLODEA NISTOR.

Russia: POB 1765 Safat, Daya Diplomatic Area, Block 17, Kuwait City; tel. 2560427; fax 2524969; e-mail rospos@kuwait.net; Ambassador AZAMAT R. KULMUKHAMETOV.

Saudi Arabia: POB 20498, 13065 Safat, Istiqlal St, Kuwait City; tel. 2550021; fax 2420654; Ambassador ABD AL-AZIZ AL-FAYEZ.

Senegal: POB 23892, 13099 Safat, Rawdah, Block 3, St 35, House 9, Kuwait City; tel. 2573477; fax 2542044; e-mail senegal_embassy@yahoo.com; internet www.diplomatie.gouv.sn/maeuase/ambassene_koweit.htm; Ambassador ABDOU LAHAD MBACKE.

Serbia: POB 20511, 13066 Safat, Jabriya, Block 7, St 12, Villa 3, Kuwait City; tel. 5327548; fax 5327568; e-mail embrskw@qualitynet.net; Chargé d'affaires a.i. ZLATAN MALTARIĆ.

Somalia: POB 22766, 13088 Safat, Bayan, St 1, Block 7, Villa 25, Kuwait City; tel. 5394795; fax 5394829; e-mail soamin1@hotmail.com; Ambassador ABDUL KHADIR AMIN SHEIKH ABUBAKER.

South Africa: POB 2262, 40173 Mishref, Salwa Block 10, St 1, Villa 91, Unit 3, Kuwait City; tel. 5617988; fax 5617917; e-mail saemb@southafricaq8.com; internet www.southafricaq8.com; Ambassador ASHRAF SULIMAN.

Spain: POB 22207, 13083 Safat, Surra, Block 3, St 14, Villa 19, Kuwait City; tel. 5325827; fax 5325826; e-mail embespkw@mail.mae.es; Ambassador JESÚS CARLOS RIOSALIDO GAMBOTTI.

Sri Lanka: Jabriya, Block 10, St 107, Villa 1, Kuwait City; tel. 5339140; fax 5339154; e-mail lankaemb@qualitynet.net; internet www.slembkwt.org; Ambassador S. A. C. M. ZUHYLE.

Switzerland: POB 23954, 13100 Safat, Qortuba, Block 2, St 1, Villa 122, Kuwait City; tel. 5340172; fax 5340176; e-mail vertretung@kow.rep.admin.ch; internet www.eda.admin.ch/kuwait; Ambassador MICHEL GOTTRET.

Syria: POB 25600, 13116 Safat, Kuwait City; tel. 5396560; fax 5396509; Ambassador ALI ABD AL-KARIM.

Thailand: POB 66647, 43757 Bayan, Block 6, St 8, Villa 1, Jabriya, Kuwait City; tel. 5317530; fax 5317532; e-mail thaiemkw@kems.net; Ambassador DUSIT CHANTASEN.

Tunisia: POB 5976, 13060 Safat, Nuzha, Plot 2, Nuzha St, Villa 45, Kuwait City; tel. 2542144; fax 2528995; e-mail tunemrku@ncc.moc.kw; Ambassador HICHEM BAYOUDH.

KUWAIT

Turkey: POB 20627, 13067 Safat, Block 16, Plot 10, Istiqlal St, Kuwait City; tel. 2531785; fax 2560653; e-mail turkishembassykuwait@hotmail.com; internet www.turkish-embassy.org.kw; Ambassador ŞAKIR FAKILI.

Ukraine: POB 7588, 32096 Hawalli, Jabriya, Block 10, St 6, House 5, Kuwait City; tel. 5318507; fax 5318508; e-mail emb_kw@mfa.gov.ua; internet www.mfa.gov.ua/kuwait; Ambassador SERHIY A. PUSHARSKY.

United Arab Emirates: POB 1828, 13019 Safat, Plot 70, Istiqlal St, Kuwait City; tel. 2528544; fax 2526382; Ambassador YOUSUF A. AL-ANSARI.

United Kingdom: POB 2, 13001 Safat, Arabian Gulf St, Kuwait City; tel. 2594320; fax 2594339; e-mail kuwait.generalenquiries@fco.gov.uk; internet www.britishembassy-kuwait.org; Ambassador STUART LAING.

USA: POB 77, 13001 Safat, Bayan, Al-Masjed al-Aqsa St, Plot 14, Block 14, Kuwait City; tel. 2591001; fax 5380282; e-mail paskuwaitm@state.gov; internet kuwait.usembassy.gov; Ambassador DEBORAH K. JONES.

Uzbekistan: Kuwait City; Ambassador ABDURAFIK A. HOSHIMOV.

Venezuela: POB 24440, 13105 Safat, Block 5, St 7, Area 356, Surra, Kuwait City; tel. 5324367; fax 5324368; e-mail embavene@qualitynet.net; Ambassador ELOY FERNÁNDEZ AZUAJE.

Yemen: POB 7182, Al-Jabriya St, Kuwait City; tel. 5349416; fax 5349415; Ambassador Dr ALI AL-AHMADI.

Zimbabwe: POB 36484, 24755 Salmiya, Kuwait City; tel. 5621517; fax 5621491; e-mail zimkuwait@hotmail.com; Ambassador MARK GREY MARONGWE.

Judicial System

SPECIAL JUDICIARY

Constitutional Court: Comprises five judges. Interprets the provisions of the Constitution; considers disputes regarding the constitutionality of legislation, decrees and rules; has jurisdiction in challenges relating to the election of members, or eligibility for election, to the Majlis al-Umma.

ORDINARY JUDICIARY

Court of Cassation: Comprises five judges. Is competent to consider the legality of verdicts of the Court of Appeal and State Security Court; Chief Justice MUHAMMAD YOUSUF AR-RIFA'I.

Court of Appeal: Comprises three judges. Considers verdicts of the Court of First Instance; Chief Justice RASHED AL-HAMMAD.

Court of First Instance: Comprises the following divisions: Civil and Commercial (one judge), Personal Status Affairs (one judge), Lease (three judges), Labour (one judge), Crime (three judges), Administrative Disputes (three judges), Appeal (three judges), Challenged Misdemeanours (three judges); Chief Justice MUHAMMAD AS-SAKHOBY.

Summary Courts: Each governorate has a Summary Court, comprising one or more divisions. The courts have jurisdiction in the following areas: Civil and Commercial, Urgent Cases, Lease, Misdemeanours. The verdict in each case is delivered by one judge.

There is also a **Traffic Court**, with one presiding judge.

Prosecutor-General: HAMED AL-OTHMAN.

Religion

ISLAM

The majority of Kuwaitis are Muslims of the Sunni or Shi'a sects. The Shi'ite community comprises about 30% of the total.

CHRISTIANITY

The Roman Catholic Church

Latin Rite

For ecclesiastical purposes, Kuwait forms an Apostolic Vicariate. At 31 December 2005 there were an estimated 250,000 adherents in the country.

Vicar Apostolic: CAMILLO BALLIN (Titular Bishop of Arna), Bishop's House, POB 266, 13003 Safat, Kuwait City; tel. 2434637; fax 2409981; e-mail vicariate_clergy@hotmail.com; internet www.catholic-church.org/kuwait.

Melkite Rite

The Greek-Melkite Patriarch of Antioch is resident in Damascus, Syria. The Patriarchal Exarchate of Kuwait had an estimated 800 adherents at 31 December 2005.

Exarch Patriarchal: Rev. BOUTROS GHARIB, Vicariat Patriarcal Greek-Melkite, POB 1205, Salwa Block 12, St No. 6, House 58, 22013 Salmiya, Kuwait City; tel. and fax 6016691; e-mail greekcatholickuwait@yahoo.com.

Syrian Rite

The Syrian Catholic Patriarch of Antioch is resident in Beirut, Lebanon. The Patriarchal Exarchate of Basra and Kuwait, with an estimated 820 adherents at 31 December 2005, is based in Basra, Iraq.

The Anglican Communion

Within the Episcopal Church in Jerusalem and the Middle East, Kuwait forms part of the diocese of Cyprus and the Gulf. The Anglican congregation in Kuwait is entirely expatriate. The Bishop in Cyprus and the Gulf is resident in Cyprus, while the Archdeacon in the Gulf is resident in Bahrain.

Other Christian Churches

National Evangelical Church in Kuwait: POB 80, 13001 Safat, Kuwait City; tel. 2407195; fax 2431087; e-mail elc@ncc.moc.kw; Rev. NABIL ATTALLAH (pastor of the Arabic-language congregation), Rev. JERRY A. ZANDSTRA (senior pastor of the English-speaking congregation); an independent Protestant Church founded by the Reformed Church in America; services in Arabic, English, Korean, Malayalam and other Indian languages; combined weekly congregation of some 20,000.

The Armenian, Greek, Coptic and Syrian Orthodox Churches are also represented in Kuwait.

The Press

Freedom of the press and publishing is guaranteed in the Constitution, although press censorship was in force between mid-1986 and early 1992 (when journalists adopted a voluntary code of practice). In February 1995 a ruling by the Constitutional Court effectively endorsed the Government's right to suspend publication of newspapers; however, legislation passed in 2006 rendered this illegal without a court order. The Government provides financial support to newspapers and magazines.

DAILIES

Al-Anbaa (The News): POB 23915, 13100 Safat, Kuwait City; tel. 4831168; fax 4837914; internet www.alanba.com.kw; f. 1976; Arabic; general; Editor-in-Chief BIBI KHALID AL-MARZOOQ; circ. 85,000.

Arab Times: POB 2270, Airport Road, Shuwaikh, 13023 Safat, Kuwait City; tel. 4849144; fax 4818267; e-mail arabtimes@arabtimesonline.com; internet www.arabtimesonline.com; f. 1977; English; political and financial; no Fri. edn; Editor-in-Chief AHMAD ABD AL-AZIZ AL-JARALLAH; Man. Editor MISHAL AL-JARALLAH; circ. 41,922.

Kuwait Times: POB 1301, 13014 Safat, Kuwait City; tel. 4833199; fax 4835621; e-mail info@kuwaittimes.net; internet www.kuwaittimes.net; f. 1961; English, Malayalam and Urdu; political; Dep. Editor-in-Chief ABD AR-RAHMAN ALYAN; circ. 32,000.

Al-Qabas (Firebrand): POB 21800, 13078 Safat, Kuwait City; tel. 4812822; fax 4834355; e-mail info@alqabas.com.kw; internet www.alqabas.com.kw; f. 1972; Arabic; independent; Gen. Man. FOUZAN AL-FARES; Editor-in-Chief WALEED ABD AL-LATIF AN-NISF; circ. 60,000.

Ar-Ra'i al-'Aam (Public Opinion): POB 761, 13008 Safat, Kuwait City; tel. 4817777; fax 4838352; internet www.alraialaam.com; f. 1961; Arabic; political, social and cultural; Editor-in-Chief YOUSUF AL-JALAHMA; circ. 101,500.

As-Seyassah (Policy): POB 2270, Shuwaikh, Kuwait City; tel. 4813566; fax 4846905; e-mail alseyassah@alseyassah.com; internet www.alseyassah.com; f. 1965; Arabic; political and financial; Editor-in-Chief AHMAD ABD AL-AZIZ AL-JARALLAH; circ. 70,000.

Al-Watan (The Homeland): POB 1142, 13012 Safat, Kuwait City; tel. 4840950; fax 4818481; e-mail alwatan@alwatan.com.kw; internet www.alwatan.com.kw; f. 1962; Arabic; political; Editor-in-Chief MUHAMMAD ABD AL-QADER AL-JASEM; Gen. Man. YOUSUF BIN JASEM; circ. 91,726.

WEEKLIES AND PERIODICALS

Al-Balagh (Communiqué): POB 4558, 13046 Safat, Kuwait City; tel. 4818606; fax 4819008; f. 1969; weekly; Arabic; general, political and

Islamic affairs; Editor-in-Chief ABD AR-RAHMAN RASHID AL-WALAYATI; circ. 29,000.

Byzance: Kuwait City; f. 2007; bi-monthly; Arabic and French; lifestyle magazine, incl. features on fashion, jewellery, furniture and art; Man. Editor JEAN-PIERRE GUEIRARD; Exec. Editor-in-Chief ANTOINE DAHER.

Ad-Dakhiliya (The Interior): POB 71655, 12500 Shamiah, Kuwait City; tel. 2410091; fax 2410609; e-mail moipr@qualitynet.net; monthly; Arabic; official reports, transactions and proceedings; publ. by Public Relations Dept, Ministry of the Interior; Editor-in-Chief Lt-Col AHMAD A. ASH-SHARQAWI.

Dalal Magazine: POB 6000, 13060 Safat, Kuwait City; tel. 4832098; fax 4832039; e-mail alyaqza@alyaqza.com; internet www.alyaqza.com; f. 1997; monthly; Arabic; family affairs, beauty, fashion; Editor-in-Chief AHMAD YOUSUF BEHBEHANI.

Friday Times: POB 1301, 13014 Safat, Kuwait City; tel. 4833199; fax 4835621; e-mail info@kuwaittimes.net; internet www.kuwaittimes.net; f. 2005; weekend edn of *Kuwait Times*.

Al-Hadaf (The Objective): POB 2270, 13023 Safat, Kuwait City; tel. 4813566; fax 4816042; e-mail alhadaf@alseyassah.com; internet www.alseyassah.com/alhadaf; f. 1964; weekly; Arabic; social and cultural; Editor-in-Chief AHMAD ABD AL-AZIZ AL-JARALLAH; circ. 268,904.

Hayatuna (Our Life): POB 26733, 13128 Safat, Kuwait City; tel. 2530120; fax 2530736; f. 1968; fortnightly; Arabic; medicine and hygiene; publ. by Al-Awadi Press Corpn; Editor-in-Chief ABD AR-RAHMAN AL-AWADI; circ. 6,000.

Al-Iqtisadi al-Kuwaiti (Kuwaiti Economist): POB 775, 13008 Safat, Kuwait City; tel. 805580; fax 2412927; e-mail kcci@kcci.org.kw; internet www.kcci.org.kw; f. 1960; monthly; Arabic; commerce, trade and economics; publ. by Kuwait Chamber of Commerce and Industry; Editor MAJED B. JAMALUDDIN; circ. 6,000.

Journal of the Gulf and Arabian Peninsula Studies: POB 17073, 72451 Khaldiya, Kuwait University, Kuwait City; tel. 4833215; fax 4833705; e-mail jotgaaps@kuc01.kuniv.edu.kw; internet pubcouncil.kuniv.edu.kw/jgaps; f. 1975; quarterly; Arabic and English; publ. by Academic Publication Council of Kuwait Univ.; Editor-in-Chief Dr FATIMA HUSSAIN AL-ABDULRAZZAQ.

Al-Khaleej Business Magazine: POB 25725, 13118 Safat, Kuwait City; tel. 2433765; e-mail aljabriya@gulfweb.com; Editor-in-Chief AHMAD ISMAIL BEHBEHANI.

Kuwait Medical Journal (KMJ): POB 1202, 13013 Safat, Kuwait City; tel. 5316023; fax 5312630; e-mail kmj@kma.org.kw; internet www.kma.org.kw/KMJ; f. 1967; quarterly; English; publ. by the Kuwait Medical Asscn; original articles, review articles, case reports, short communications, letters to the editor and book reviews; Editor-in-Chief Prof. FOUAD ABDULLAH M. HASSAN; circ. 10,000.

Kuwait al-Youm (Kuwait Today): POB 193, 13002 Safat, Kuwait City; tel. 4842167; fax 4831044; f. 1954; weekly; Arabic; statistics, Amiri decrees, laws, govt announcements, decisions, invitations for tenders, etc.; publ. by the Ministry of Information; circ. 5,000.

Al-Kuwaiti (The Kuwaiti): Information Dept, POB 9758, 61008 Ahmadi, Kuwait City; tel. 3989111; fax 3983661; e-mail kocinfo@kockw.com; f. 1961; monthly journal of the Kuwait Oil Co; Arabic; Editor-in-Chief ALI H. MURAD; circ. 6,500.

The Kuwaiti Digest: Information Dept, POB 9758, 61008 Ahmadi, Kuwait City; tel. 3980651; fax 3983661; e-mail kocinfo@kockw.com; f. 1972; quarterly journal of Kuwait Oil Co; English; Editor-in-Chief RA'AD SALEM AL-JANDAL; circ. 7,000.

Al-Majaless (Meetings): POB 5605, 13057 Safat, Kuwait City; tel. 4841178; fax 4847126; e-mail qasem@almajaless.com; internet www.almajaless.com; weekly; Arabic; current affairs; Editor-in-Chief QASIM ABD AL-QADIR; circ. 60,206.

Mejallat al-Kuwait (Kuwait Magazine): POB 193, 13002 Safat, Kuwait City; tel. 2415300; fax 2419642; f. 1961; monthly; Arabic; illustrated magazine; science, arts and literature; publ. by the Ministry of Information.

Mirat al-Umma (Mirror of the Nation): POB 1142, 13012 Safat, Kuwait City; tel. 4837212; fax 4838671; weekly; Arabic; Editor-in-Chief MUHAMMAD AL-JASSEM; circ. 79,500.

An-Nahdha (The Renaissance): POB 695, 13007 Safat, Kuwait City; tel. 4813133; fax 4849298; f. 1967; weekly; Arabic; social and political; Editor-in-Chief THAMER AS-SALAH; circ. 170,000.

Osrati (My Family): POB 2995, 13030 Safat, Kuwait City; tel. 4813233; fax 4838933; e-mail info@osratimag.com; f. 1978; weekly; Arabic; women's magazine; publ. by Fahad al-Marzouk Establishment; Editor GHANIMA F. AL-MARZOUK; circ. 10,500.

Sawt al-Khaleej (Voice of the Gulf): POB 659, Safat, Kuwait City; tel. 4815590; fax 4839261; f. 1962; politics and literature; Arabic; Editor-in-Chief CHRISTINE KHRAIBET; Owner BAKER ALI KHRAIBET; circ. 20,000.

At-Talia (The Ascendant): POB 1082, 13011 Safat, Kuwait City; tel. 4831200; fax 4840471; f. 1962; weekly; Arabic; politics and literature; Editor AHMAD YOUSUF AN-NAFISI; circ. 10,000.

Al-Yaqza (The Awakening): POB 6000, 13060 Safat, Kuwait City; tel. 4831318; fax 4832039; f. 1966; weekly; Arabic; political, economic, social and general; Editor-in-Chief AHMAD YOUSUF BEHBEHANI; circ. 91,340.

NEWS AGENCY

Kuwait News Agency (KUNA): POB 24063, 13101 Safat, Kuwait City; tel. 4834546; fax 4813424; e-mail kuna@kuna.net.kw; internet www.kuna.net.kw; f. 1979; public corporate body; independent; also publishes research digests on topics of common and special interest; Chair. and Man. Dir Sheikh MUBARAK AD-DUAIJ AS-SABAH.

PRESS ASSOCIATION

Kuwait Journalists Association: POB 5454, 13055 Safat, Kuwait City; tel. 4843351; fax 4842874; e-mail kja@kja-kw.com; internet www.kja-kw.com; Chair. AHMAD YOUSUF BEHBEHANI.

Publishers

Al-Abraj Translation and Publishing Co WLL: POB 26177, 13122 Safat, Kuwait City; tel. 2442310; fax 2407024; Man. Dir Dr TARIQ ABDULLAH.

Dar as-Seyassah Publishing, Printing and Distribution Co: POB 2270, 13023 Safat, Kuwait City; tel. 4813566; fax 4833628; publ. *Arab Times*, *As-Seyassah* and *Al-Hadaf*.

Gulf Centre Publishing and Publicity: POB 2722, 13028 Safat, Kuwait City; tel. 2402760; fax 2458833; Propr HAMZA ISMAIL ESSLAH.

Kuwait National Advertising and Publishing Co (KNAPCO): POB 2268, Safat 13023; tel. 5745776; fax 5745779; e-mail support@knapco.com; internet www.knapco.com; f. 1995; publ. annual commercial business directory, *Teledymag*.

Kuwait Publishing House Co: POB 1446, 13015 Safat, Kuwait City; tel. 2449686; fax 2436956; e-mail info@kuwaitpocketguide.com; Dir ESAM AS'AD ABU AL-FARAJ.

Kuwait United Co for Advertising, Publishing and Distribution WLL: POB 29359, 13153 Safat, Kuwait City; tel. 4817111; fax 4817797.

At-Talia Printing and Publishing Co: POB 1082, Airport Rd, Shuwaikh, 13011 Safat, Kuwait City; tel. 4840470; fax 4815611; Man. AHMAD YOUSUF AN-NAFISI.

GOVERNMENT PUBLISHING HOUSE

Ministry of Information: see Ministries.

Broadcasting and Communications

TELECOMMUNICATIONS

The privatization of the state telecommunications sector, and the reorganization of the Ministry of Communications as a company, designated the Kuwaiti Communications Corporation, were completed in 2000. The Government announced at the end of 2006 that it was to issue a third mobile telecommunications licence, and in November 2007 the Saudi Telecommunications Company won the public auction for a 26% stake in the third mobile operator. It was anticipated that this new operator would launch mobile services during the latter part of 2008.

National Mobile Telecommunications Co KSC (Wataniya Telecom): POB 613, 13007 Safat, Kuwait City; tel. 2435500; fax 2436600; e-mail info@wataniya.com; internet www.wataniya.com; f. 1999; Chair. and Man. Dir Sheikh ABDULLAH BIN MUHAMMAD BIN SAUD ATH-THANI; CEO and Gen. Man. SCOTT GEGENHEIMER.

Zain Kuwait: POB 22244, 1308 Safat, Kuwait City; tel. 4644444; fax 4837755; e-mail cust_care@kw.zain.com; internet www.kw.zain.com; f. 1983 as Mobile Telecommunications Co; in Sept. 2007 began operating under new global brand, Zain; Chair. ASAAD AL-BANWAN; Dep. Chair. and Man. Dir Dr SAAD AL-BARRAK.

BROADCASTING

Radio

Radio of the State of Kuwait: POB 397, 13004 Safat, Kuwait City; tel. 2423774; fax 2456660; e-mail info@media.gov.kw; internet www.media.gov.kw; f. 1951; broadcasts daily in Arabic, Farsi, English and Urdu, some in stereo; Dir of Radio Dr ABD AL-AZIZ ALI MANSOUR; Dir of Radio Programmes ABD AR-RAHMAN HADI.

KUWAIT

Television

Kuwait Television: POB 193, 13002 Safat, Kuwait City; tel. 2413501; fax 2438403; e-mail info@media.gov.kw; internet www.media.gov.kw; f. 1961; transmission began privately in Kuwait in 1957; transmits in Arabic; colour television service began in 1973; has a total of five channels; Head of News Broadcasting MUHAMMAD AL-KAHTANI.

Ar-Rai: Kuwait City; internet www.alrai.tv; f. 2004; first private satellite television station in Kuwait; admin. offices in Kuwait and transmission facilities in Dubai (United Arab Emirates); owned by the Ar-Rai Media Group.

Finance

(cap. = capital; res = reserves; dep. = deposits; m. = million; brs = branches; amounts in Kuwaiti dinars unless otherwise stated)

BANKING

Central Bank

Central Bank of Kuwait: POB 526, 13006 Safat, Abdullah as-Salem St, Kuwait City; tel. 2449200; fax 2464887; e-mail cbk@cbk.gov.kw; internet www.cbk.gov.kw; f. 1969; cap. 5.0m., res 394.0m., dep. 1,700.8m. (March 2006); Governor Sheikh SALEM ABD AL-AZIZ SA'UD AS-SABAH.

National Banks

Al-Ahli Bank of Kuwait KSC: POB 1387, 13014 Safat, Ahmad al-Jaber St, Kuwait City; tel. 2400900; fax 2424557; e-mail marketing@abkuwait.com; internet www.eahli.com/abk; f. 1967; wholly owned by private Kuwaiti interests; cap. 95.9m., res 167.2m., dep. 2,033.5m. (Dec. 2006); Chair. AHMAD YOUSUF BEHBEHANI; Dep. Chair. and Man. Dir ALI HILAL AL-MUTAIRI; 19 brs.

Bank of Kuwait and the Middle East KSC (BKME): POB 71, 13001 Safat, Joint Banking Centre, East Tower, Darwazat Abd ar-Razzak, Kuwait City; tel. 2459771; fax 2461430; e-mail hayakom@bkme.com.kw; internet www.bkme.com; f. 1971; 75% owned by Ahli United Bank (Bahrain); cap. 84.5m., res 150.6m., dep. 1,629.6m. (Dec. 2006); Chair. and Man. Dir HAMAD ABD AL-MOHSEN AL-MARZOUQ; 22 brs.

BBK: POB 24396, 13104 Safat, Ahmad al-Jaber St, Kuwait City; tel. 2417140; fax 2440937; e-mail bbkp@batelco.com.bh; internet www.bbkonline.com; f. 1971 as Bank of Bahrain and Kuwait BSC; name changed as above in 2005; cap. BD 64.0m., res BD 80.2m., dep. BD 1,493.3m. (Dec. 2006); Chair. MURAD ALI MURAD.

Boubyan Bank KSC: POB 25507, 13116 Safat, Kuwait City; tel. 2325000; fax 2454263; e-mail info@bankboubyan.com; internet www.bankboubyan.com; f. 2004; cap. 99.9m., res 4.6m., dep. 375.8m. (Dec. 2006); Chair. and Man. Dir YACOB YOUSUF AL-MUZAINI.

Burgan Bank SAK: POB 5389, 12170 Safat, Abd al-Haih al-Ahmad St, Kuwait City; tel. 2439000; fax 2461148; e-mail info@burgan.com; internet www.burgan.com; f. 1975; 33.9% Kuwait Projects Co (Holding), Safat; cap. 86.1m., res 124.4m., dep. 1,826.9m. (Dec. 2006); Chair. TARIQ MUHAMMAD ABD AS-SALAM; CEO JONATHAN DAVID LYON; 18 brs.

Commercial Bank of Kuwait SAK: POB 2861, 13029 Safat, Mubarak al-Kabir St, Kuwait City; tel. 2411001; fax 2450150; e-mail cbkinq@cbk.com; internet www.cbk.com; f. 1960 by Amiri decree; cap. 115.4m., res 333.2m., dep. 2,319.2m. (Dec. 2006); Chair. ABD AL-MAJID ASH-SHATTI; CEO and Gen. Man. JAMAL ABD AL-HAMID AL-MUTAWA; 45 brs.

Gulf Bank KSC: POB 3200, 13032 Safat, Mubarak al-Kabir St, Kuwait City; tel. 2449501; fax 2445212; e-mail customerservice@gulfbank.com.kw; internet www.e-gulfbank.com; f. 1960; cap. 94.8m., res 209.1m., dep. 3,498.2m. (Dec. 2006); Chair. and Man. Dir BASSAM YOUSUF AL-GHANIM; CEO and Chief Gen. Man. LOUIS MYERS; 40 brs.

Industrial Bank of Kuwait KSC (IBK): POB 3146, 13032 Safat, Joint Banking Centre, Darwazzat Abd ar-Razaq, Commercial Area 9, Kuwait City; tel. 2457661; fax 2462057; e-mail ibk@ibkuwt.com; internet www.ibkuwt.com; 31.4% state-owned; f. 1973; cap. 20.0m., res 167.2m., dep. 83.7m. (Dec. 2006); Chair. and Man. Dir ABD AL-MOHSEN YOUSUF AL-HANIF; Gen. Man. ALI ABD AN-NABI KHAJA.

Kuwait Finance House KSC (KFH): POB 24989, 13110 Safat, Abdullah al-Mubarak St, Kuwait City; tel. 2445050; fax 2455135; e-mail kfh@kfh.com; internet www.kfh.com; f. 1977; Islamic banking and investment co; 45% state-owned; cap. 122.5m., res 580.0m., dep. 4,809.9m. (Dec. 2006); Chair. and Man. Dir BADER ABD AL-MOHSEN AL-MUKHAISEEM; Gen. Man. MUHAMMAD SULAYMAN AL-OMAR; 27 brs.

Kuwait International Bank KSC: POB 22822, 13089 Safat, West Tower, Joint Banking Centre, Mubarak al-Kabir St, Kuwait City; tel. 2458177; fax 2462516; e-mail contact@kreb.com.kw; internet www.kreb.com.kw; f. 1973 as Kuwait Real Estate Bank KSC; name changed as above in 2007; wholly owned by private Kuwaiti interests; cap. 85.7m., res 47.3m., dep. 600.5m. (Dec. 2006); Chair. and Man. Dir ABD AL-WAHAB MUHAMMAD AL-WAZZAN; Gen. Man. ADIL AHMAD; 6 brs.

National Bank of Kuwait SAK (NBK): POB 95, 13001 Safat, Abdullah al-Ahmad St, Kuwait City; tel. 2422011; fax 2431888; e-mail webmaster@nbk.com; internet www.nbk.com; f. 1952; cap. 195.0m., res 557.2m., dep. 6,680.4m. (Dec. 2006); Chair. MUHAMMAD ABD AR-RAHMAN AL-BAHAR; CEO IBRAHIM S. DABDOUB; 41 brs in Kuwait, 16 brs abroad.

INSURANCE

Al-Ahleia Insurance Co SAK: POB 1602, Ahmad al-Jaber St, 13017 Safat, Kuwait City; tel. 2240033; fax 2430308; e-mail aic@alahleia.com; internet www.alahleia.com; f. 1962; all forms of insurance; cap. 11.7m. (July 2004); Chair. and Man. Dir SULAYMAN HAMAD MUHAMMAD AD-DALALI.

Arab Commercial Enterprises WLL (Kuwait): POB 2474, 13025 Safat, Kuwait City; tel. 2413854; fax 2409450; e-mail acekwt@ace-ins.com; f. 1952; Man. SALIM ABOU HAIDER.

Gulf Insurance Co KSC: POB 1040, 13011 Safat, Ahmad al-Jaber St, Kuwait City; tel. 802080; fax 2422320; e-mail contacts@gulfins.com.kw; internet info@gic.com; f. 1962; cap. 11.3m. (2002); all forms of insurance; Chair. FARKAD ABDULLAH AS-SANEA; Man. Dir and CEO KHALED SAOUD AL-HASSAN.

Al-Ittihad al-Watani Insurance Co for the Near East SAL: POB 781, 13008 Safat, Kuwait City; tel. 4842988; fax 2432424; Man. JOSEPH ZACCOUR.

Kuwait Insurance Co SAK (KIC): POB 769, 13008 Safat, Abdullah as-Salem St, Kuwait City; tel. 884433; fax 2428530; e-mail info@kic-kw.com; internet www.kic-kw.com; f. 1960; cap. US $64.6m.; all life and non-life insurance; Chair. MUHAMMAD SALEH BEHBEHANI; Gen. Man. Dr ALI HAMAD AL-BAHAR.

Kuwait Reinsurance Co KSCC: POB 21929, 13080 Safat, Kuwait City; tel. 2432011; fax 2427823; e-mail kuwaitre@kuwaitre.com; internet www.kuwaitre.com; f. 1972; cap. 10.0m., total assets 59.3m. (2006); Chair. FAHED AL-IBRAHIM; Gen. Man. AMIR AL-MUHANNA.

Kuwait Technical Insurance Office: POB 25349, 13114 Safat, Kuwait City; tel. 2409600; fax 2413986.

Mohd Saleh Behbehani & Co: POB 341, 13004 Safat, Kuwait City; tel. 4721670; fax 4760070; e-mail msrybco@qualitynet.net; f. 1963; Pres. MUHAMMAD SALEH YOUSUF BEHBEHANI.

New India Assurance Co: POB 370, 13004 Safat, Kuwait City; tel. 2412085; fax 2412089.

The Northern Insurance Co Ltd: POB 579, 13006 Safat, Kuwait City; tel. 2427930; fax 2462739.

The Oriental Insurance Co Ltd: POB 22431, 13085 Safat, Kuwait City; tel. 2424016; fax 2424017; Man. JUGAL KISHORE MADAAN.

Sumitomo Marine & Fire Insurance Co (Kuwait Agency): POB 3458, 13035 Safat, Kuwait City; tel. 2433087; fax 2430853; Contact ABDULLAH BOUDROS.

Warba Insurance Co SAK: POB 24282, 13103 Safat, Kuwait City; tel. 2445140; fax 2466131; e-mail warba@warbaonline.com; internet www.warbaonline.com; f. 1976; cap. 7.7m. (2002), total assets 80.1m. (Dec. 2005); all forms of insurance; Chair. Dr HAIDER HASSAN ABD AR-RASOL AL-JUMAA; 3 brs.

STOCK EXCHANGE

Kuwait Stock Exchange: POB 22235, 13083 Safat, Mubarak al-Kabir St, Kuwait City; tel. 2992000; fax 2420779; e-mail borse@kse.gov.kw; internet www.kse.com.kw; f. 1983; 197 cos and one mutual fund listed in early 2008; Dir-Gen. SALEH MUBARAK AL-FALAH.

Markets Association

Kuwait Financial Markets Association (KFMA): POB 25228, 13113 Safat, Block 12, St 101, Complex 182, Villa 4, Kuwait City; tel. 5339776; fax 5339778; e-mail kfma@kfma.org.kw; internet www.kfma.org.kw; f. 1977; represents treasury, financial and capital markets and their mems; Pres. AQEEL NASSER HABEEB; Sec.-Gen. TAREQ M. AL-BASSAM.

Trade and Industry

GOVERNMENT AGENCY

Kuwait Investment Authority (KIA): POB 64, 13001 Safat, Kuwait City; tel. 2485600; fax 2454059; e-mail information@kia.gov.kw; internet www.kia.gov.kw; oversees the Kuwait Investment Office (London); responsible for the Kuwaiti General Reserve; Chair.

MUSTAFA JASSEM ASH-SHIMALI (Minister of Finance); Exec. Dir AHMAD M. A. BASTAKI.

DEVELOPMENT ORGANIZATIONS

Arab Planning Institute (API): POB 5834, 13059 Safat, Kuwait City; tel. 4843130; fax 4842935; e-mail api@api.org.kw; internet www.arab-api.org; f. 1966; 15 Arab mem. states; publishes *Journal of Development and Economic Policies* (twice-yearly) and proceedings of seminars and discussion group meetings, offers research, training programmes and advisory services; Dir-Gen. ESSA AL-GHAZALI.

Industrial and Financial Investments Co (IFIC): POB 26019, 13121 Safat, Joint Banking Complex, 8th Floor, Industrial Bank Bldg, Derwaza Abdulrazak, Kuwait City; tel. 2429073; fax 2448850; e-mail ific@ific.net; internet www.ific.net; f. 1983; invests directly in industry; privatized in 1996; Chair. and Man. Dir Dr TALEB AHMAD ALI.

Kuwait Fund for Arab Economic Development (KFAED): POB 2921, 13030 Safat, cnr Mubarak al-Kabir St and al-Hilali St, Kuwait City; tel. 2999000; fax 2999090; e-mail info@kuwait-fund.org; internet www.kuwait-fund.org; f. 1961; cap. KD 2,000m.; state-owned; provides and administers financial and technical assistance to developing countries; Chair. Sheikh Dr MUHAMMAD SABAH AS-SALIM AS-SABAH (Minister of Foreign Affairs); Dir-Gen. ABDULWAHAB A. AL-BADER.

Kuwait International Investment Co SAK (KIIC): POB 22792, 13088 Safat, as-Salhiya Commercial Complex, Kuwait City; tel. 2438273; fax 2454931; 30% state-owned; domestic real estate and share markets; Chair. and Man. Dir JASEM MUHAMMAD AL-BAHAR.

Kuwait Investment Co SAK (KIC): POB 1005, 13011 Safat, 5th Floor, al-Manakh Bldg, Mubarak al-Kabir St, Kuwait City; tel. 2438111; fax 2444896; e-mail info@kic.com.kw; internet www.kic.com.kw; f. 1981; 88% state-owned, 12% owned by private Kuwaiti interests; cap. KD 50.0m. (2002); international banking and investment; Chair. and Man. Dir BADER NASSER AS-SUBAIEE.

Kuwait Planning Board: c/o Ministry of Planning, POB 15, 13001 Safat, Kuwait City; tel. 2428200; fax 2414734; f. 1962; supervises long-term devt plans; through its Central Statistical Office publishes information on Kuwait's economic activity; Dir-Gen. AHMAD ALI AD-DUAIJ.

Mega Projects Agency (MPA): c/o Ministry of Public Works, POB 8, 13001 Safat, Kuwait City; f. 2005; supervises the progress of Failaka and Bubiyan island devts; Man. Dir WALID ATH-THAQEB.

National Industries Group (Holding) SAK (NIG): POB 417, 13005 Safat, Kuwait City; tel. 4815466; fax 4839582; e-mail nigroup@nig.com.kw; internet www.nigroup.net; f. 1960; cap. KD 55.8m. (2002); has controlling interest in various construction enterprises; privatized in 1995; Chair. and Man. Dir SAAD MUHAMMAD AS-SAAD.

Public Authority for Industry (PAI): POB 4690, 13047 Safat, Kuwait City; POB 10033, Shuaiba; tel. 3260903; f. 1997; successor to Shuaiba Area Authority (f. 1964); develops, promotes and supervises industry in Kuwait; CEO Dr FALAH FAHD AL-HAJERI (Minister of Commerce and Industry); Dir-Gen. ALI FAHAD AL-MUDHAF.

CHAMBER OF COMMERCE

Kuwait Chamber of Commerce and Industry: POB 775, 13008 Safat, Chamber's Bldg, Abdulaziz Hamad ash-Sager St, Kuwait City; tel. 805580; fax 2460693; e-mail kcci@kcci.org.kw; internet www.kcci.org.kw; f. 1959; 50,000 mems; Chair. ALI MUHAMMAD THUNAYAN AL-GHANIM; Dir-Gen. AHMAD RASHED AL-HAROUN.

STATE HYDROCARBONS COMPANIES

Kuwait Petroleum Corpn (KPC): POB 26565, 13126 Safat, as-Salhiya Commercial Complex, Fahed as-Salem St, Kuwait City; tel. 2455455; fax 2467159; e-mail info@kpc.com.kw; internet www.kpc.com.kw; f. 1980; co-ordinating org. to manage the petroleum industry; controls Kuwait Aviation Fuelling Co (KAFCO), Kuwait Foreign Petroleum Exploration Co (KUFPEC), Kuwait Gulf Oil Co (KGOC), Kuwait National Petroleum Co (KNPC), Kuwait Oil Co (KOC), Kuwait Oil Tanker Co (KOTC), Kuwait Petroleum International (Q8), Petrochemical Industries Co (PIC); Chair. MUHAMMAD ABDULLAH HADI AL-OLAIM; CEO SAAD ASH-SHUWAYIB.

    Kuwait Aviation Fuelling Co KSC (KAFCO): POB 1654, 13017 Safat, Kuwait City; tel. 4330507; fax 4330475; e-mail airfuel@kafco.com; internet www.kafco.com; f. 1963; Dep. Chair. and Gen. Man. NASSER BADER AL-MUDHAF; 70 employees.

    Kuwait Foreign Petroleum Exploration Co KSC (KUFPEC): POB 5291, 13053 Safat, Kuwait City; tel. 836000; fax 4920018; internet www.kufpec.com; f. 1981; state-owned; overseas oil and gas exploration and devt; Chair. and Man. Dir FAHED AL-AJMI; 169 employees.

    Kuwait Gulf Oil Co KSC (KGOC): POB 9919, Ahmadi 61010; tel. 3980883; e-mail info@kgoc.com; internet www.kgoc.com; f. 2002 to take over Kuwait's interest in the Partitioned Zone's offshore operator, Khafji Joint Operations, and all of Kuwait's other offshore exploration and production activities; Chair. and Man. Dir ABD AL-HADI MARZOUK AL-AWAD.

    Kuwait National Petroleum Co KSC (KNPC): POB 70, 13001 Safat, Ali as-Salem St, Kuwait City; tel. 2420121; fax 2433839; internet www.knpc.com.kw; f. 1960; oil refining, production of liquefied petroleum gas, and domestic marketing and distribution of petroleum by-products; Chair. and Man. Dir FAROUK AZ-ZANKI; 5,611 employees.

    Kuwait Oil Co KSC (KOC): POB 9758, 61008 Ahmadi; tel. 3989111; fax 3984971; e-mail kocinfo@kockw.com; internet www.kockw.com; f. 1934; state-owned; Chair. and Man. Dir SAMI FAHED AR-RUSHAID; 4,815 employees.

    Kuwait Petroleum International (Q8): POB 26565, 13126 Safat, Kuwait City; tel. 2455455; fax 2407523; e-mail info-kuwait@q8.com; internet www.q8.com; marketing division of KPC; controls 6,500 petrol retail stations in Europe, and European refineries with capacity of 235,000 b/d; Man. Dir HUSSEIN AL-ISMAIL.

UTILITIES

The Government planned to create regulatory bodies for each of Kuwait's utilities, with a view to facilitating their privatization.

Ministry of Electricity and Water: see Ministries; provides subsidized services throughout Kuwait.

TRADE UNIONS

Federation of Petroleum and Petrochemical Workers: Kuwait City; f. 1965; Chair. JASEM ABD AL-WAHAB AT-TOURA.

KOC Workers Union: Kuwait City; f. 1964; Chair. HAMAD SAWYAN.

Kuwait Trade Union Federation (KTUF): POB 5185, 13052 Safat, Kuwait City; tel. 5636389; fax 5627159; e-mail ktuf@hotmail.com; internet www.ktuf.org; f. 1967; central authority to which all trade unions are affiliated; KHALED ALAZEMI.

Transport

RAILWAYS

There are currently no railways in Kuwait. However, it was announced in early 2008 that a national rail network and a metro system were both at the planning stages; the projects were expected to be completed by 2016.

ROADS

Roads in the towns are metalled, and the most important are motorways or dual carriageways. There are metalled roads linking Kuwait City to Ahmadi, Mina al-Ahmadi and other centres of population in Kuwait, and to the Iraqi and Saudi Arabian borders. In 2004 the total road network was estimated at 5,749 km (613 km of motorways, 5,136 km of secondary roads), of which 85% was paved. A causeway linking Kuwait City with Subahiya was under consideration in the mid-2000s; the design-and-build contract was projected to be worth some US $1,500m.

Kuwait Public Transport Co SAK (KPTC): POB 375, 13004 Safat, Murghab, Safat Sq., Kuwait City; tel. 2469420; fax 2401265; e-mail info@kptc.com.kw; internet www.kptc.com.kw; f. 1962; state-owned; provides internal bus service; regular service to Mecca, Saudi Arabia; Chair. and Man. Dir MAHMOUD A. AN-NOURI.

SHIPPING

Kuwait has three commercial seaports. The largest, Shuwaikh, situated about 3 km from Kuwait City, was built in 1960. By 1987 it comprised 21 deep-water berths, with a total length of 4 km, three shallow-water berths and three basins for small craft, each with a depth of 3.35 m. In 1988 3.6m. metric tons of cargo were imported and 133,185 tons were exported through the port. A total of 1,189 vessels passed through Shuwaikh in 1988.

Shuaiba Commercial Port, 56 km south of Kuwait City, was built in 1967 to facilitate the import of primary materials and heavy equipment, necessary for the construction of the Shuaiba Industrial Area. By 1987 the port comprised a total of 20 berths, plus two docks for small wooden boats. Four of the berths constitute a station for unloading containers. Shuaiba handled a total of 3,457,871 metric tons of dry cargo, barge cargo and containers in 1988.

Doha, the smallest port, was equipped in 1981 to receive small coastal ships carrying light goods between the Gulf states. It has 20 small berths, each 100 m long. Doha handled a total of 20,283 metric tons of dry cargo, barge cargo and containers in 1988.

The oil port at Mina al-Ahmadi, 40 km south of Kuwait City, is capable of handling the largest oil tankers afloat, and the loading of over 2m. barrels of oil per day. By 1987 the port comprised 12 tanker

KUWAIT

berths, one bitumen-carrier berth, two LPG export berths and bunkering facilities.

Plans for the privatization of Kuwait's ports were under development in the mid-2000s. A new US $1,500m. facility at Bubiyan was scheduled for completion in 2010.

At 31 December 2006 Kuwait's merchant fleet numbered 220 vessels, with a total displacement of 2,156,836 grt.

Kuwait Ports Authority: POB 3874, 13039 Safat, Kuwait City; tel. 4812622; fax 4819714; e-mail info@kpa.com.kw; internet www.kpa.com.kw; f. 1977; Dir-Gen. Dr SABER JABER AL-ALI AS-SABAH.

Principal Shipping Companies

Arab Maritime Petroleum Transport Co (AMPTC): POB 22525, 13086 Safat, Kuwait City; tel. 4844500; fax 4842996; e-mail amptc.kuwait@amptc.net; internet www.amptc.net; f. 1973; four crude petroleum tankers, two LPG carriers and one product carrier; owned by Algeria, Bahrain, Egypt, Iraq, Kuwait, Libya, Qatar, Saudi Arabia and the UAE; Gen. Man. SULAYMAN I. AL-BASSAM.

Heavy Engineering Industries and Shipbuilding Co (Heisco): POB 21998, 13080 Safat, Kuwait City; tel. 4835488; fax 4830291; e-mail marine@heisco.com; internet www.heisco.com; f. 1974 as Kuwait Shipbuilding and Repairyard Co; name changed as above in 2003; ship repairs and engineering services, underwater services, maintenance of refineries, power stations and storage tanks; maintains floating dock for vessels up to 35,000 dwt; synchrolift for vessels up to 5,000 dwt with transfer yard; seven repair jetties up to 550 m in length and floating workshop for vessels lying at anchor; Chair. JUHAIL MUHAMMAD AL-JUHAIL.

KGL Ports Int. Co (KGL PI): POB 24565, 13106 Safat, Kuwait City; tel. 4827804; fax 4827806; internet www.kglq8.com; f. 2005; subsidiary of Kuwait and Gulf Link Transport Co; port management and stevedoring; operates Shuaiba Commercial Port Container Terminal; also operations and management contracts with ports in United Arab Emirates and Saudi Arabia; Gen. Man. and Man. Dir SAID ISMAIL DASHTI.

Kuwait Maritime Transport Co KSC (KMTC): POB 22595, 13086 Safat, Nafisi and Khatrash Bldg, Jaber al-Mubarak St, Kuwait City; tel. 2449974; fax 2420513; f. 1981; Chair. YOUSUF AL-MAJID.

Kuwait Oil Tanker Co SAK (KOTC): POB 810, 13009 Safat, as-Salhiya Commercial Complex, Blocks 3, 5, 7 and 9, Kuwait City; tel. 2455455; fax 2445907; e-mail ysm@kotc.com.kw; internet www.kotc.com.kw; f. 1957; state-owned; operates eight crude oil tankers, 11 product tankers and five LPG vessels; sole tanker agents for Mina al-Ahmadi, Shuaiba and Mina al-Abdullah and agents for other ports; LPG filling and distribution; Chair. and Man. Dir ABDULLAH HAMAD AR-ROUMI.

United Arab Shipping Co SAG (UASC): POB 3636, 13037 Safat, Shuwaikh, Airport Rd, Kuwait City; tel. 839999; fax 4845388; e-mail info@uasc.com.kw; internet www.uasc.net; f. 1976; national shipping co of six Arabian Gulf countries; services between Europe, Far East, Mediterranean ports, Japan and east coast of USA and South America, and ports of participant states on Persian (Arabian) Gulf and Red Sea; operates 33 vessels; subsidiary cos include: United Arab Shipping Agencies Co (Kuwait), Arab Transport Co (Aratrans), United Arab Chartering Ltd (United Kingdom), Middle East Container Repair Co (UAE), Arabian Chemicals Carriers (Saudi Arabia), United Arab Agencies Inc. (USA) and United Arab Shipping Agencies Co (Saudi Arabia); Pres. and CEO KEN SOERENSEN.

CIVIL AVIATION

Kuwait International Airport opened in 1980, and by 2007 handled 6.9m. passengers, compared with 3.8m. in 2001. The airport is undergoing a major programme of expansion: the first phase of the project was to expand the airport's annual capacity to 20m. passengers and to modernize facilities, with a further final phase of development intended to achieve passenger capacity of 55m.

Directorate-General of Civil Aviation (DGCA): POB 17, 13001 Safat, Kuwait City; tel. 4335599; fax 4713504; Pres. Sheikh JABER AL-MUBARAK AS-SABAH; Dir-Gen. YACOUB Y. AS-SAQER.

Jazeera Airways: POB 29288, 13153 Safat, Kuwait City; e-mail helpdesk@jazeeraairways.com; internet www.jazeeraairways.com; f. 2005; low-cost airline owned by Boodai Group; serves 26 destinations in the Middle East, North Africa, Europe and Asia; Chair. and CEO MARWAN BOODAI.

Kuwait Airways Corpn (KAC): POB 394, Kuwait International Airport, 13004 Safat, Kuwait City; tel. 4345555; fax 4314118; e-mail info@kuwait-airways.com; internet www.kuwait-airways.com; f. 1954; scheduled and charter passenger and cargo services to the Arabian peninsula, Asia, Africa, the USA and Europe; scheduled for privatization; Chair. and Man. Dir HAMAD A. LATIF AL-FALAH.

Kuwait National Airways: Kuwait City; f. 2006; CEO GEORGE COOPER.

Tourism

Attractions for visitors include the Kuwait Towers leisure and reservoir complex, the Entertainment City theme park, the Kuwait Zoological Garden in Omariya and the Khiran Resort tourist village near the border with Saudi Arabia, as well as extensive facilities for sailing and other water sports. In early 2005 there were some 4,000 rooms available for visitors; it was intended to increase this figure to around 6,000 by 2008. Foreign tourist arrivals totalled some 3.1m. in 2004, while tourism receipts of US $408m. were recorded in 2005.

Department of Tourism: Ministry of Information, Tourism Affairs, POB 193, 18th Floor, Fahad as-Salem Tower, Fahad as-Salem St, 13002 Safat, Kuwait City; tel. 2457591; fax 2401540; e-mail tourism_kw@media.gov.kw.

Touristic Enterprises Co (TEC): POB 23310, 13094 Safat, Kuwait City; tel. 5650111; fax 5650514; e-mail info@tec.com.kw; internet www.kuwaittourism.com; f. 1974; 92% state-owned; manages 23 tourist facilities; Chair. BADER AL-BAHAR; Vice-Chair. SHAKER AL-OTHMAN.

KYRGYZSTAN

Introductory Survey

Location, Climate, Language, Religion, Flag, Capital

The Kyrgyz Republic (formerly the Kyrgyz Soviet Socialist Republic and, between December 1990 and May 1993, the Republic of Kyrgyzstan) is a small, land-locked state situated in eastern Central Asia. It borders Kazakhstan to the north, Uzbekistan to the west, Tajikistan to the south and west, and the People's Republic of China to the east. There are distinct variations in climate between low-lying and high-altitude areas. In the valleys the mean July temperature is 28°C (82°F), whereas in January it falls to an average of −18°C (−0.5°F). Annual rainfall ranges from 180 mm (7 ins) in the eastern Tien Shan mountains to 750 mm–1,000 mm (30 ins–39 ins) in the Farg'ona (Fergana) mountain range. In the settled valleys the annual average varies between 100 mm and 500 mm (4 ins–20 ins). The state language is Kyrgyz; Russian additionally has the status of an official language. The major religion is Islam, with the majority of ethnic Kyrgyz being Sunni Muslims of the Hanafi school. The national flag (proportions 3 by 5) consists of a red field, at the centre of which is a yellow sun, with 40 counter-clockwise rays surrounding a red-bordered yellow disc, on which are superimposed two intersecting sets of three red, curved, narrow bands. The capital is Bishkek.

Recent History

Following the October Revolution of 1917 in Russia, Kyrgyzstan (which had been formally incorporated into the Russian Empire in 1876) experienced a period of civil war, with anti-Bolshevik forces, including the Russian White Army and local armed groups (*basmachi*), fighting against the Bolshevik Red Army. Soviet power was established in the region by 1919. In 1918 the Turkestan Autonomous Soviet Socialist Republic (ASSR) was established within the Russian Soviet Federative Socialist Republic (the Russian Federation). In 1924 the Kara-Kyrgyz Autonomous Oblast (Region) was created. (At this time the Russians used the term Kara-Kyrgyz to distinguish the Kyrgyz from the Kazakhs, then known as Kyrgyz by the Russians.) In 1925 the region was renamed the Kyrgyz Autonomous Oblast, and it became the Kyrgyz ASSR in February 1926. On 5 December 1936 the Kyrgyz Soviet Socialist Republic (SSR) was established as a full union republic of the USSR.

During the 1920s considerable economic and social developments were made in Kyrgyzstan, when land reforms resulted in the settlement of many of the nomadic Kyrgyz. The agricultural collectivization programme of the early 1930s was strongly opposed in the republic. Despite the suppression of nationalism under Stalin (Iosif V. Dzhugashvili—Soviet leader in 1924–53), many aspects of Kyrgyz national culture were retained, although many so-called 'national communists' were expelled from the Kyrgyz Communist Party (KCP) and often imprisoned or exiled, particularly during the late 1930s. Tensions with the all-Union (Soviet) authorities continued following the death of Stalin in 1953.

The election of Mikhail Gorbachev as Soviet leader in 1985, and his introduction of the policies of perestroika (restructuring) and glasnost (openness), led to the resignation of Turdakan Usubaliyev as First Secretary of the KCP and the dismissal from office of his allies by Absamat Masaliyev, his successor. The republic's Supreme Soviet (Zhogorku Kenesh or Supreme Council—legislature) adopted Kyrgyz as the official language, although Russian was retained as a language of inter-ethnic communication. However, the conservative republican leadership opposed the development of unofficial quasi-political groups, although one such group, Ashar, was partially tolerated by the authorities and soon developed a wider political role. A notable group at this time was Osh Aymaghi, based in Osh Oblast (Region) of the Farg'ona (Fergana) valley (which is shared between Kyrgyzstan, Tajikistan and Uzbekistan). Osh Aymaghi attempted to obtain land and housing provision for ethnic Kyrgyz in the ethnic Uzbek-dominated region (Osh had been incorporated into Kyrgyzstan in 1924 but ethnic Uzbeks had recently begun to demand the establishment of an Uzbek autonomous region) and in 1990 disputes over land and homes developed into violent confrontation between ethnic Kyrgyz and Uzbeks. According to official reports, more than 300 people died, and a state of emergency and a curfew were introduced in the region, the former remaining in force until 1995; the Uzbekistani–Kyrgyzstani border was also closed.

Elections to the 350-member Kyrgyzstani Supreme Soviet in February 1990 were conducted along Soviet lines, with KCP candidates winning most seats unopposed, and in April Masaliyev was elected to the new office of Chairman of the Supreme Soviet. In October an extraordinary session of the Supreme Soviet was convened to elect the President, but Masaliyev had been discredited by the conflict in Osh. Furthermore, the opposition, which had united as the Democratic Movement of Kyrgyzstan (DMK), had become a significant political force and in the first round of voting Masaliyev failed to achieve the requisite proportion of votes to be elected; in a further round a compromise candidate, Askar Akayev, the President of the Kyrgyz Academy of Sciences, was elected to the executive presidency. Akayev rapidly allied himself with reformist politicians and economists, including leaders of the DMK. In December Masaliyev resigned as Chairman of the Supreme Soviet, and was replaced by Medetkan Sherimkulov. (Masaliyev resigned as First Secretary of the KCP in April 1991). Also in December 1990, the Supreme Soviet voted to change the name of the republic from the Kyrgyz SSR to the Republic of Kyrgyzstan. In January 1991 Akayev replaced the Council of Ministers with a smaller cabinet, comprising mainly reformist politicians. In February the capital, Frunze (named after a Red Army commander), reverted to its pre-1926 name of Bishkek. However, in a referendum held in nine Soviet Union Republics in March, 87.7% of eligible voters in Kyrgyzstan approved the proposal to retain the USSR as a 'renewed federation'.

In August 1991, when the conservative communist State Committee for the State of Emergency (SCSE) announced that it had assumed power in the Russian and Soviet capital, Moscow, there was an attempt to depose Akayev in Kyrgyzstan. Akayev dismissed the Chairman of the republican Committee of State Security (KGB) and ordered interior ministry troops to guard strategic buildings in Bishkek. He publicly denounced the coup (which the KCP had supported) and issued a decree prohibiting activity by any political party in government or state bodies. After the coup had collapsed in Moscow, Akayev and republican Vice-President German Kuznetsov renounced their membership of the Communist Party of the Soviet Union, and the entire politburo and secretariat of the KCP resigned. On 31 August the Kyrgyzstani Supreme Soviet voted to declare independence from the USSR. Akayev (the sole candidate) was re-elected President of Kyrgyzstan by direct popular vote on 12 October, receiving 95% of the votes cast.

In October 1991 Akayev signed, with representatives of seven other republics, a treaty to establish a new economic community. On 21 December Kyrgyzstan was among the 11 signatories to the Almaty (Alma-Ata) Declaration, which formally established the Commonwealth of Independent States (CIS, see p. 215).

Discussions were held throughout 1992 to draft a new constitution. The Constitution, which was finally promulgated on 5 May 1993, provided for a parliamentary system of government, with the Prime Minister as head of the executive. Legislative power was to be vested in a smaller (105-member) Zhogorku Kenesh, following a general election, which was due to be held by 1995; in the mean time, the existing assembly continued to act as the republic's parliament. Russian was accorded the constitutional status of a language of inter-ethnic communication. The country's official name was changed from the Republic of Kyrgyzstan to the less ethnically neutral Kyrgyz Republic. In July Akayev's attempts to encourage non-Kyrgyz to remain in the republic suffered a serious reverse when Kuznetsov, by this time the First Deputy Prime Minister announced his decision to return to Russia. By mid-1993 it was estimated that some 145,000 Russians had left the republic since 1989.

Akayev's presidency was destabilized during 1993 by a series of corruption scandals. Two commissions of inquiry were established to investigate the business dealings of the Vice-President, Feliks Kulov, and to examine allegations that senior politicians—including the Prime Minister since February 1992, Tursunbek Chyngyshev—had been involved in unauthorized gold exports. In December 1993 Kulov resigned and the legislature subsequently held a vote of confidence in Chyngyshev's Government: the motion failed to secure the required two-thirds' majority and Akayev dismissed the entire cabinet. A new Government, headed by Apas Jumagulov (Chairman of the Council of Ministers in 1986–91), was approved later in the month. A referendum of confidence in the presidency was held (on Akayev's initiative) in January 1994, at which 96.2% of voters endorsed Akayev's leadership.

In June 1994, in an attempt to curb the rate of emigration, Akayev issued a decree promoting the use of Russian, simplifying the procedure of application for dual citizenship, and guaranteeing the equitable representation of ethnic Russians in the state administration. The Zhogorku Kenesh adopted a resolution based on the decree in March 1996.

In September 1994 more than 180 deputies demanded the dissolution of the Kenesh and the holding of fresh elections, in protest at the continuing obstruction of the economic reform process. The Government tendered its resignation, and Akayev announced that fresh parliamentary elections would be held. The Government was promptly reinstated by Akayev, who announced the holding of a referendum in October on constitutional amendments, at which the majority of the electorate endorsed proposals for a restructured Zhogorku Kenesh, comprising a 70-member El Okuldor Palatasy (People's Assembly—upper chamber) to represent regional interests at twice-yearly sessions and a permanent, 35-member Myizam Chygaru Palatasy (Legislative Assembly—lower chamber) to represent the population as a whole. Elections to the two chambers of the new Zhogorku Kenesh were held in two rounds in February 1995. The two chambers of the Zhogorku Kenesh held their inaugural sessions on 28 March. A new Government, again led by Jumagulov, was appointed in April.

In September 1995 the Myizam Chygaru Palatasy vetoed a proposal to hold a referendum on extending the President's term of office until 2000. A direct presidential election was held on 24 December 1995, at which Akayev emerged as the victor, receiving a reported 71.6% of the votes cast; Masaliyev (who had recently been reinstated as the leader of the revived KCP) won 24.4% of the votes. The rate of participation by the electorate was some 82%. Akayev was inaugurated on 30 December. Following a decree issued by Akayev, a referendum was held on 10 February 1996, at which the majority of the electorate endorsed amendments to the Constitution increasing presidential powers and decreasing those of the legislature. The Government resigned later that month; Jumagulov was reinstated as Prime Minister in March and Akayev approved a new Government shortly afterwards.

In January 1998 a new criminal code was promulgated, which effectively abolished the death penalty by imposing a moratorium on its implementation. In March Jumagulov announced his retirement and the Zhogorku Kenesh endorsed the appointment of Kuvachbek Jumaliyev as the new Prime Minister. A cabinet reorganization was also effected. A further cabinet reshuffle was undertaken in early April. In July the Constitutional Court ruled that Akayev was permitted to seek a third term in the presidential election due to be held in 2000. A referendum on several constitutional amendments took place on 17 October, with the participation of about 96% of the electorate, and some 90% of voters approved the following amendments: the number of deputies in the Myizam Chygaru Palatasy was to increase to 60, and representation in the El Okuldor Palatasy was to be reduced to 45; the electoral system was to be reformed; restrictions on parliamentary immunity were to be introduced; private land ownership was to be legalized; the presentation of unbalanced or unattainable budgets was to be banned; and the adoption of any legislation restricting freedom of speech or of the press was to be prohibited. The Zhogorku Kenesh and the majority of political parties declared their opposition to the constitutional changes and, in particular, to the introduction of private land ownership, which they feared would result in the transfer of land to foreign ownership.

By mid-December 1998 some 383 government officials had been dismissed on grounds of corruption, and in late December the President dissolved the Government for its failure to address the country's economic problems. Jumabek Ibraimov was appointed Prime Minister and a new Government was formed, in which 10 ministers from the previous administration retained their portfolios. Akayev also issued a decree extending the Prime Minister's mandate, giving him the right to appoint and dismiss ministers and heads of departments (which had previously been the exclusive right of the President). Ibraimov died in April 1999, and Amangeldy Muraliyev was appointed in his stead.

A new electoral law was introduced at the end of May 1999 whereby, henceforth, 15 seats in the Myizam Chygaru Palatasy were to be allocated on a proportional basis for those parties that secured a minimum of 5% of the votes; the legislation also banned the use of foreign and private funds in electoral campaigns. In June legislation came into effect, banning political organizations considered a threat to Kyrgyzstan's stability and ethnic harmony. In July two new opposition parties were established: the Dignity (Ar-Namys) Party, led by Kulov (by this time Mayor of Bishkek), and the Justice (Adilettuuluk) Party.

At the elections to both chambers of the Zhogorku Kenesh, held on 20 February 2000, a total of six parties passed the 5% threshold required to secure party-list seats in the Myizam Chygaru Palatasy. A number of electoral violations were reported by the Organization for Security and Co-operation in Europe (OSCE, see p. 354). In a second round of voting on 12 March, the KCP secured 27.7% of the votes cast, ahead of the Union of Democratic Forces, with 18.6%, and the Democratic Women's Party of Kyrgyzstan, with 12.7%. The Union of Democratic Forces achieved the greatest representation of any party or bloc in the combined Zhogorku Kenesh, securing a total of 12 seats, compared with the KCP's six. Nominally independent candidates took 73 of the 105 seats in the two chambers. Kulov, who stood as an independent after Dignity was prohibited from participating, failed to win a seat, prompting opposition protests and allegations of official corruption. Later in March Kulov was arrested on charges of abuse of office during his tenure as Minister of National Security in 1997–98. Although Kulov was acquitted in August 2000, a retrial was ordered, and he was sentenced to seven years' imprisonment in January 2001. An appeal was rejected in March, and in May 2002 Kulov was also found guilty of embezzlement.

Meanwhile, at the presidential election, held on 29 October 2000, Akayev secured 74.5% of the votes cast. The leader of the Fatherland Socialist Party (Ata-Meken), Omurbek Tekebayev, won 13.9% and the leader of the Social Democratic Party of Kyrgyzstan, Almazbek Atambayev, obtained 6.0% of the ballot. According to the Central Commission for Elections and Referendums, 74% of the electorate participated. However, on the day of the election a criminal case opened in Bishkek following the discovery, by international observers, of several hundred ballot papers, marked in favour of Akayev, before polling had begun officially. Moreover, opposition parties claimed that they had been prevented from participating in media broadcasts. The Chairman of the Central Commission for Elections and Referendums was forced to concede that electoral violations had taken place, leading to international condemnation. Despite mass protests and demands for the election to be repeated, on 10 November the Constitutional Court formally endorsed the results.

Akayev was inaugurated for a third term on 9 December 2000 and on 21 December Kurmanbek Bakiyev, hitherto the Governor of Chui Oblast, was appointed Prime Minister; a new Government was announced at the beginning of January 2001. In April the leaders of nine opposition parties formally announced the establishment of an alliance known as the People's Patriotic Movement, the stated objectives of which were the safeguarding of democracy and of human and constitutional rights. The movement organized demonstrations against the erosion of the independent media and against the imprisonment of Kulov. In November opposition parties including Dignity, the Fatherland Socialist Party (Ata-Meken) and the Liberty (Erkindik) party announced the formation of a new People's Congress, and elected the imprisoned Kulov its Chairman. In the following month the President signed into law a constitutional amendment granting Russian the status of official language, in what was considered a further attempt to halt the emigration of ethnic Russians from Kyrgyzstan.

In January 2002 the arrest of Azimbek Beknazarov, an opposition deputy, was denounced as politically motivated (Beknazarov had publicly criticized President Akayev's signature of a Sino-Kyrgyzstani border treaty in 1999). In March 2002 six people were reported to have been killed during clashes between protesters and security forces in the southern city of Jalal-Abad, where Beknazarov's trial was being held; it was subsequently suspended. In May the Myizam Chygaru Palatasy ratified the controversial Sino-Kyrgyzstani treaty, prompting two weeks of anti-Government demonstrations, hunger strikes and acts of civil disobedience. Protesters demanded that the Government accept responsibility for the violence of March, rescind the ratification of the border treaty (which they claimed had been signed illegally by President Akayev, since he had agreed to cede land to the People's Republic of China without the consent of the legislature), and close the criminal case against Beknazarov. Nevertheless, the El Okuldor Palatasy ratified the treaty later in May, and it was duly signed into law by the President.

In May 2002 Prime Minister Bakiyev tendered his resignation. The First Deputy Prime Minister, Nikolai Tanayev, was appointed Prime Minister and a new Government was announced in June. Meanwhile, in May Beknazarov received a one-year, suspended prison sentence. Following an appeal and further large-scale demonstrations, Beknazorov's sentence was annulled (although the initial guilty verdict was upheld), enabling him to retain his parliamentary seat. In June the Myizam Chygaru Palatasy approved an amnesty, proposed by Tanayev for both protesters and law enforcement officials involved in the disturbances of March.

In January 2003 President Akayev announced that a referendum on several constitutional amendments was to be held on 2 February. The amendments, which provided for the introduction of a unicameral legislature in 2005, in which all deputies were to be elected in single-member constituencies, were duly approved by 76.6% of the electorate, while 78.7% of voters supported Akayev's remaining in office until 2005; the reported rate of participation was 86.7%. The hasty scheduling of the referendum attracted criticism from international human rights organizations, and there were also allegations of procedural violations.

A major government reorganization took place in February 2004. In April the President introduced a new law designating Kyrgyz the state language, and stipulating measures for its promotion, apparently in order to encourage bilingualism in Kyrgyz and Russian, which was to remain an official language. In May, in advance of legislative elections, opposition parties, including Dignity, the Fatherland Socialist Party (Ata-Meken) and the Social Democratic Party of Kyrgyzstan, announced the formation of an electoral bloc, the Civic Union For Fair Elections. The formation of a larger electoral bloc, known as the People's Movement of Kyrgyzstan, was announced in September, under Bakiyev's leadership.

In January 2005 Roza Otunbayeva, a former ambassador to the United Kingdom, and the leader of the recently formed opposition Fatherland Party (Ata-Jurt), was refused permission to register as a candidate in the parliamentary elections, on the grounds that she had not been resident in the country for the previous five years; several other former diplomatic representatives were also prohibited from contesting the elections. Campaigning for the elections officially began on 2 February. Protests against the exclusion of candidates and opposition rallies demanding free and fair parliamentary elections, or the impeachment of Akayev, continued throughout February. In the first round of legislative voting on 27 February, the rate of participation by the electorate was reported to be 60%. Some 31 candidates (each of whom had received an absolute majority of votes cast in their respective electoral districts) were elected to the restructured, single-chamber, 75-member Zhogorku Kenesh. The majority of those elected were nominally independent candidates, including supporters of Akayev. Forward, Kyrgyzstan (Alga, Kyrgyzstan), established in 2003 and regarded as generally sympathetic to Akayev's administration, became the largest party faction to achieve representation, with 10 members reportedly elected. OSCE monitors concluded that the elections had not fully complied with democratic standards, while opposition and independent observers asserted that large-scale electoral fraud had taken place. Protests to dispute local polling results took place in various regions in advance of the second round of elections, held on 13 March, and the suppression of media outlets supportive of the opposition or critical of the authorities was reported. Following the second round of voting, a further 37 candidates were reported to have been elected (with a participation rate of 55%); only six opposition candidates obtained representation in the new legislature.

Dissatisfaction at the conduct of the elections, and at the failure of the opposition to obtain significant representation in the legislature, resulted in large-scale protests in a number of cities, initially in the south of Kyrgyzstan. From mid-March 2005 demonstrators occupied the regional governor's office in Jalal-Abad for several weeks and later in the month, demonstrators took control of a government building in Osh. On 22 March the Central Commission for Elections and Referendums declared that the results of voting for 69 of the 75 seats were valid; investigations into the conduct of voting in the remaining six districts were to continue. The Supreme Court, however, while emphasizing that the ruling did not constitute an annulment of the poll results, revoked the mandate of the newly elected Zhogorku Kenesh, asserting that the previous bicameral legislature continued to hold authority. On 23 March Akayev dismissed the Prosecutor-General, Myktybek Abdyldayev, and the Minister of Internal Affairs, Bakirdin Subanbekov, who had declared that he would not use force to end the protests.

By 24 March 2005 demonstrations had spread to Bishkek, and protesters stormed the presidential palace and government buildings. Akayev fled the country (maintaining that he remained Kyrgyzstan's Head of State) and Tanayev resigned as Prime Minister, while protesters freed Kulov from gaol. On the same day, at an emergency session, the lower chamber of the legislature elected in 2000 named Bakiyev acting Prime Minister (he automatically became acting President in Akayev's absence). On 25 March Bakiyev announced the appointment of several senior officials in the interim Government, including Otunbayeva as Minister of Foreign Affairs, Abdyldayev as Minister of Internal Affairs, Gen. Ismail Isakov as Minister of Defence, and Beknazarov as acting Prosecutor-General. Kulov was given responsibility for overseeing the country's law enforcement agencies and armed forces. After the Central Commission for Elections and Referendums announced that the powers of the bicameral legislature elected in 2000 were terminated, the lower and upper chambers dissolved themselves on 28 and 29 March, respectively, thereby effectively confirming the legitimacy of the recently elected legislature, and apparently overturning the ruling of the Supreme Court. Meanwhile, on 28 March the new Zhogorku Kenesh voted to confirm Bakiyev as interim Prime Minister, and to elect Tekebayev as legislative Chairman. (In late April Tekebayev was also appointed as Chairman of the Constitutional Court.) On 30 March Kulov resigned his post, reportedly owing to disagreement with Bakiyev.

On 4 April 2005 Akayev, speaking at the Kyrgyzstani embassy in Moscow, announced his resignation as President (the decision was approved by the Zhogorku Kenesh on 11 April). On 8 April Parliament voted to deprive Akayev of certain privileges associated with his status as a former president, and to remove immunity from prosecution from members of his family, allowing them to be investigated on corruption charges. The Zhogorku Kenesh subsequently scheduled a presidential election for 10 July. From mid-April protests were staged outside the Supreme Court against aspects of the legislative elections, demanding, inter alia, the resignation of the Chairman of the Court, Kurmanbek Osmonov, who was regarded as an ally of Akayev. However, although Osmonov submitted his resignation in late April, it was rejected by Bakiyev. In mid-May Bakiyev reached an agreement with Kulov, whose convictions had been overturned by the Supreme Court in April and who was considered his strongest rival in the presidential contest, according to which Kulov agreed to withdraw his candidacy in return for a guarantee that Bakiyev would appoint him Prime Minister should he secure the presidency. Also in mid-May, Bakiyev dismissed acting Minister of Internal Affairs Abdyldayev and replaced him with Murat Sutalinov. Violent unrest in Bishkek was reported in June.

On 10 July 2005 Bakiyev won 88.7% of the votes cast in the presidential election, which was contested by six candidates. The OSCE reported some irregularities in the counting of votes. Bakiyev was inaugurated as President on 14 August, and on 1 September the Zhogorku Kenesh confirmed Kulov's appointment as Prime Minister. In mid-September Bakiyev removed Beknazarov from his position as Prosecutor-General, together with his deputy, accusing them of negligence. Busurmankul Tabaldiyev was appointed to succeed Beknazarov on an acting basis; however, he resigned in October, and was replaced by Kambaraly Kongantiyev. Meanwhile, in late September the Zhogorku Kenesh approved 10 of the 16 ministers proposed by Bakiyev. Many ministers in the outgoing interim administration retained their portfolios, notably Isakov as Minister of Defence and Akylbek Zhaparov as Minister of the Economy and Finance. Following the rejection of Otunbayeva's nomination as Minister of Foreign Affairs, Alikbek Jekshenkulov was appointed to the post. (Otunbayeva and Beknazarov subsequently became co-chairmen of the Banner—Asaba—Party of National Revival.)

Adakhan Madumarov was appointed Deputy Prime Minister and Marat Kaipov became Minister of Justice. In October the Office of the Prosecutor-General charged former Prime Minister Tanayev, who was under house arrest in Bishkek, with abuse of power and corruption. (In May 2006 it was reported that the criminal case against Tanayev had been closed.) Also in October 2005 Bakiyev appointed Daniyar Usenov, an opponent of Kulov, to the post of acting First Deputy Prime Minister, although his nomination was rejected in November, and in the following month the Zhogorku Kenesh approved the appointment of Medetbek Kerimkulov. The Government was sworn in on 20 December.

Meanwhile, in September 2005 Bayaman Erkinbayev, a parliamentary deputy and businessman who had actively participated in Akayev's removal from power (and who was alleged to have links to criminal groups), was murdered in Bishkek; another parliamentary deputy had been assassinated in July. In October a further parliamentary deputy, Tynychbek Akmatbayev, was killed by inmates during an official visit to a gaol. Large rallies, led by Akmatbayev's brother, Ryspek, a prominent and controversial figure alleged to be involved in organized crime (see below), subsequently took place to demand the dismissal of Kulov, whom the protesters accused of having collaborated with prisoners to organize the killing of Akmatbayev.

In January 2006 President Bakiyev decreed that measures be taken to organize a referendum on the division of power between the President and Parliament; Bakiyev had pledged to award the legislature increased powers following his election. Also in early January, representatives of 17 political movements and organizations agreed to establish an opposition bloc, the People's Coalition of Democratic Forces, which united those dissatisfied with the new regime. In late January Kulov demanded reform of the judicial system and the entire law enforcement system, and criticized the Chairman of the National Security Service (SNB), Tashtemir Aitbayev, for allowing criminal elements to infiltrate the organization. Although Bakiyev rejected demands by parliamentary deputies for Aitbayev's dismissal, in early February he removed the deputy head of the SNB, and accepted the resignation of the Deputy Secretary of the Security Council. Also in early February further tensions between the Zhogorku Kenesh and the President arose when Bakiyev accused the legislature of fomenting political instability and exceeding its mandate, causing Tekebayev to tender his resignation from the parliamentary chairmanship. Although the Zhogorku Kenesh initially rejected Tekebayev's resignation, leading to further strains between the legislature and the President, it was accepted in late February. Marat Sultanov was elected as the new Chairman of the Zhogorku Kenesh in early March, and pledged to attempt to resolve disagreements with the executive without recourse to confrontation. In March President Bakiyev signed a decree officially suspending the Chairman of the National Bank, Ulan Sarbanov, from office, during his trial on charges of having illegally transferred some US $420,000 to former President Akayev in 1999. Meanwhile, in early March Bakiyev had signed a decree designating 24 March, the anniversary of Akayev's effective removal from power as a result of the so-called 'tulip revolution', a national holiday, to be known as the Day of the People's Revolution.

Parliamentary by-elections, scheduled to take place in three districts in April 2006, generated considerable controversy owing to the candidacy of Rysbek Akmatbayev. Akmatbayev, convicted twice during the 1990s for, *inter alia*, assault and robbery, had been tried, but acquitted, in early 2006 for the murder of a policeman; however, his acquittal was in the process of being appealed at the time of the polls, thus rendering his candidacy illegitimate according to the terms of the Constitution; a court also ruled that Akhmatbayev was ineligible to contest the election on the grounds that he had not fulfilled the residency criteria, although this decision was subsequently overturned. In protest at Akmatbayev's participation, thousands of demonstrators amassed in the streets of the capital on the eve of the by-elections, urging the Government to adopt a tougher stance against organized crime. The by-elections proceeded as planned on 9 April, and Akmatbayev secured a comfortable victory in the constituency that he contested. Another large-scale demonstration took place in the capital in late April when several thousand people gathered to protest against widespread corruption among state officials, demanding that Bakiyev implement the reforms that he had pledged during his election campaign. In May Akmatbayev was shot dead by unknown assailants in Bishkek.

Further evidence of a rift between the executive and the legislature materialized in late April 2006, when the Zhogorku Kenesh voted to evaluate the performance of individual members of the Government: only Prime Minister Kulov, two ministers and the head of a state committee were given positive appraisals, and in early May 14 ministers resigned. Although President Bakiyev rejected their resignations and the ministers subsequently agreed to remain in their posts, Bakiyev effected a cabinet reorganization in mid-May, which included the appointment of Usenov as First Deputy Prime Minister. The nomination of Ishengul Boljurova as a Deputy Prime Minister was rejected by the Zhogorku Kenesh in the following month. Also in mid-May Bakiyev dismissed Kombaraaly Kongantiyev as Prosecutor-General and Usen Sydykov as Chief of the Presidential Administration, and replaced Tashtemir Aitbayev as Chairman of the SNB with former Prosecutor-General Busurmankul Tabaldiyev.

In November 2006 thousands of opposition supporters attended a rally in Bishkek demanding constitutional reform and the resignation of President Bakiyev. Following a week of mass protests, the Zhogorku Kenesh approved a new Constitution on 8 November, which was to diminish the power afforded to the President and to augment that of the legislature, the capacity of which was to be enlarged to 90 members; the membership of governments was henceforth to be determined by the Zhogorku Kenesh, rather than the President. President Bakiyev signed the new Constitution into effect on 9 November. In mid-December Prime Minister Kulov tendered his resignation (together with that of his Government), with the stated aim of forcing early parliamentary elections and thereby addressing the ongoing political crisis.

At the end of December 2006 the legislature voted to adopt a number of amendments to the new Constitution, including the retraction of the legislature's power to appoint the Government, which was henceforth to be appointed by the President at the suggestion of the Prime Minister, without the need for legislative approval. These amendments were signed into law on 17 January 2007. In late January the Zhogorku Kenesh formally approved President Bakiyev's nomination of Azim Isabekov, hitherto acting Minister of Agriculture, Water Resources and Processing Industry, as Prime Minister, having twice rejected the President's nomination of Kulov. In early February Isabekov formed a new Government, in which the majority of key posts were allocated to close associates of President Bakiyev, including Daniyar Usenov, who retained the position of First Deputy Prime Minister, Ednan Karabayev, who was appointed Minister of Foreign Affairs, and Igor Chudinov, who was awarded the newly-created industry, energy and fuel resources portfolio. In the same month Kulov added his voice to opposition calls for the President's resignation, strongly suggesting that the appointment of a new Prime Minister and Government would do little to restore political stability to Kyrgyzstan. On 29 March Isabekov resigned as premier, after Bakiyev reversed his decision to remove five government ministers that had been taken in response to continuing mass protests in Bishkek. The appointment of Atambayev as Prime Minister, which was regarded as an attempt to satisfy opposition demands, was approved by the Zhogorku Kenesh on the following day. A subsequent government reorganization included the dismissal of Usenov as First Deputy Prime Minister. Later in April large-scale protests in Bishkek, organized by the recently established opposition grouping led by Kulov, the United Front For A Worthy Future For Kyrgyzstan, were dispersed by the security forces, and an encampment of tents established by protesters in the city centre was removed; some 100 demonstrators were arrested and two prominent opposition leaders were detained on charges of inciting unrest.

In September 2007 the Constitutional Court ruled that the adoption of the Constitutions of both November 2006 and January 2007 had been illegal, since the drafts had not been submitted to a national referendum; consequently the Constitution in place prior to November 2006 again entered into force. Bakiyev subsequently announced that a further new constitutional text was to be proposed at a referendum on 21 October. In early October Bakiyev dismissed the Minister of Economic Development and Trade for failing to address rising food prices in the country. Later that month Bakiyev established a political party, Bright Road (Ak Zhol). An estimated 77% of the electorate (with a voter turnout of 81.6%) endorsed the Constitution proposed at the national referendum on 21 October; henceforth, in legislative elections single-member constituencies were to be replaced by a proportional party list system, while the number of parliamentary deputies was to increase from 75 to 90. On the following day Bakiyev dissolved the Zhorgorku Kenesh and announced that early legislative elections were to take place later in the year; these were subsequently scheduled for 16 December. The Government submitted its resignation on 24 October, but remained in office in an interim capacity.

On 29 November 2007 Bakiyev removed Atambayev from the premiership; on the same day he appointed Iskenderbek Aydaraliyev, hitherto Governor of Jalal-Abad Oblast, as First Deputy Prime Minister and also assigned him the role of acting Prime Minister. At the elections on 16 December Bright Road won about 47.0% of votes cast, securing 71 seats in the 90-member Zhorgorku Kenesh, ahead of the Social Democratic Party of Kyrgyzstan, with 5.1% of the votes cast and 11 seats, and the Communist Party of Kyrgyzstan, with 5.1% of the votes cast and eight seats. The Fatherland Socialist Party (Ata-Meken), despite gaining 8.3% of votes overall, narrowly failed to qualify for representation, owing to the new electoral requirement that each party obtain at least 0.5% of the votes cast in each of the country's seven oblasts and two largest cities. Although the stipulation was particularly criticized by OSCE observers, who stated that the conduct of the elections failed to meet democratic standards, and was also contested by Fatherland Socialist Party (Ata-Meken), the electoral commission upheld the results. On 25 December Chudinov was appointed Prime Minister. A new Government, which retained the principal ministers of the former administration, was approved in the Zhorgorku Kenesh on 27 December.

In January 1994 Kyrgyzstan joined the economic zone newly established by Kazakhstan and Uzbekistan, and in February 1995 an Interstate Council was formed to co-ordinate economic activity in the zone. Following the admission of Tajikistan in March 1998, in May the four countries were formally constituted as the Central Asian Economic Union (known as the Central Asian Co-operation Organization—CACO—from March 2002). Meanwhile, in March 1996 Kyrgyzstan signed a treaty with Russia, Belarus and Kazakhstan to create a 'community of integrated states', in an attempt to achieve closer economic, cultural and social integration, and joined a customs union established by the three other countries. In April 1998 Tajikistan joined the union, and in October 2000 it was superseded by a new economic body, the Eurasian Economic Community (EURASEC, see p. 412), which merged with CACO in January 2006. Kyrgyzstan was not to participate in the first stage of a customs union to be established by some of the member states of EURASEC, but it was anticipated that it would join the union by 2011.

In May 2001 the signatories of the CIS Collective Security Treaty—Armenia, Belarus, Kazakhstan, Kyrgyzstan, Russia and Tajikistan—agreed to form a Collective Rapid Reaction Force in Bishkek to combat Islamist militancy in Central Asia; in January 2002 it was announced that the force was ready to undertake combat missions. In April 2003 a successor organization to the Collective Security Treaty was formed, with the inauguration of the Collective Security Treaty Organization (CSTO). In 2003 the Islamic Party of Turkestan and the clandestine, transnational, Islamist Hizb-ut-Tahrir al-Islami (Party of Islamic Liberation) continued to be considered threats to stability in Kyrgyzstan. The latter, which aimed to unite Muslim countries and establish Islamic law, apparently solely through peaceful means, had become the most widespread illegal movement in Kyrgyzstan, particularly in southern regions, despite government attempts to suppress it.

Kyrgyzstan's campaign against Islamist extremism intensified in mid-1999, when Islamist groups believed to be based in Uzbekistan and Tajikistan took hostages in separate instances near Osh. In August Kyrgyzstani and Uzbekistani forces launched airstrikes against Tajikistani militants in the Osh region, in an attempt to prevent further acts of insurgency. However, later that month a senior Kyrgyzstani military commander was among more than 25 people kidnapped by a group of rebels, which captured three villages near the Tajikistani border. The rebels were believed to be members of the Islamic Movement of Uzbekistan (IMU), which demanded the release of Islamists imprisoned in that country. The hostage crisis intensified, with Kyrgyzstani government troops engaging in a large-scale military operation in order to defeat the rebels and free the captives. It was announced in October that all of the hostages had been released. (However, it was reported in November that the body of a police officer, taken hostage in August, had been discovered.) From August 2000 Islamist militants made a further series of incursions into Kyrgyzstan from Tajikistan, leading to armed conflict with government forces. The number of insurgents amassing on the Kyrgyzstani–Tajikistani border increased, despite intensive shelling and aerial bombardment by Kyrgyzstani troops. By the end of October, however, the Government claimed that all the rebels had left Kyrgyzstan and that it had regained full control of the border regions.

In April 2001 a local government official accused the Uzbekistani authorities of laying land-mines along the border with Kyrgyzstan, and demanded the removal of Uzbekistani troops, deployed in an effort to combat the incursions of Islamist militants and drugs-traffickers, from Kyrgyzstani border territories. Meanwhile, reports in May indicated that Islamist rebels were increasingly recruiting from southern Kyrgyzstan. In July 2003 it was reported that Kyrgyzstan was to commence the unilateral removal of land-mines along the border with Uzbekistan.

Relations with Uzbekistan were further strained in mid-2005, when the Kyrgyzstani Government refused to return a large number of refugees who had fled Uzbekistan after violence broke out in the city of Andijon in May (see the chapter on Uzbekistan). Although some refugees were repatriated, most were either given refuge in Kyrgyzstan or allowed to travel on to other countries. Apparently in response to Kyrgyzstan's refusal to co-operate with its demands, in August the Government of Uzbekistan annulled a bilateral agreement to supply natural gas to Kyrgyzstan. In September Uzbekistan issued a report accusing Kyrgyzstan of having permitted religious extremists to use bases in the south of the country to prepare to foment unrest in Andijon. In August 2006 the Kyrgyzstani authorities attracted international censure for the decision to repatriate to Uzbekistani a number of refugees from Andijon. In the same month Rafiq Qori Kamoluddin, a prominent imam in Kyrgyzstan and an ethnic Uzbek, was shot dead in an operation to crackdown on alleged Islamist extremists conducted by the Kyrgyzstani and Uzbekistani national security services.

Kyrgyzstan endeavoured to maintain good relations with the largest and most influential CIS member, Russia. In June 1992 Akayev and the Russian President, Boris Yeltsin, signed a treaty of friendship, co-operation and mutual assistance. A further declaration on friendship, alliance and partnership was signed in July 2000. Military agreements, including a treaty of non-aggression, have also been concluded. An agreement concerning the expansion of Russian-Kyrgyzstani military co-operation was concluded in October 1997, whereby Russia was to lease four military installations in Kyrgyzstan in return for training Kyrgyzstani army recruits. In October 2003 a Russian airbase became operational at Kant, some 30 km from an airbase at Manas, occupied by the US-led anti-terrorism coalition (see below); the new base was the first Russian military installation to be established outside Russia since the collapse of the USSR. In March 2005 Putin offered Akayev the opportunity to take up residence in Russia, after he fled to that country during what became known as the 'tulip revolution' (see above). In September the Russian Minister of Defence, Sergei Ivanov, declared that Russia was to provide Kyrgyzstan with several million US dollars in military aid, to be used primarily to combat terrorism.

Kyrgyzstan reached a series of bilateral co-operation agreements with the People's Republic of China during 1996, the terms of which provided for the partial demarcation of their shared border, which was undertaken from mid-2001. A border treaty signed in August 1999 ceded almost 95,000 ha of disputed territory to China. Akayev signed the agreement without the consent of the legislature, prompting widespread protests upon its ratification in 2002 (see above). Meanwhile, an agreement signed in April 1997 with China, Russia, Kazakhstan and Tajikistan (which, together with Kyrgyzstan, constituted the so-called Shanghai Five, later known as the Shanghai Forum) aimed to improve joint border security. The alliance, renamed the Shanghai Co-operation Organization (SCO) upon the accession of Uzbekistan, signed the Shanghai Convention on Combating Terrorism, Separatism and Extremism in mid-2001. In August an associated anti-terrorism centre became operational in Bishkek. The Presidents of Kazakhstan and Kyrgyzstan signed a border agreement in December. In March 2002 China agreed to provide Kyrgyzstan with military assistance worth some US $1.2m. In August 2003 Kyrgyzstani forces participated in major anti-terrorist manoeuvres, hosted by China and Kazakhstan. In September 2004 Tanayev and the Chinese Prime Minister, Wen Jiabao, signed a 10-year co-operation agreement on combating terrorism, separatism and religious extremism, and a protocol on the demarcation of the border between the two countries. In addition, China announced that it would provide Kyrgyzstan with a $6m. grant as part of an agreement on technical and economic co-operation. In April 2006 Minister of Defence Isakov met his Chinese counterpart, Gen. Cao Gangchuan, for sideline discussions during a meeting of the SCO in the Chinese capital, Beijing. The two ministers pledged further to consolidate bilateral relations and also to improve military co-operation in order to safeguard regional security and stability.

Following the suicide attacks on the US cities of New York and Washington, DC, on 11 September 2001, President Akayev announced that he was prepared to give US military aircraft access to Kyrgyzstani airspace for the aerial bombardment of militants of the al-Qa'ida (Base) organization (held responsible by the USA for having co-ordinated the attacks) and its Taliban hosts in Afghanistan. In late November the Government agreed to give the US-led anti-terrorism coalition access to its military bases and, later, the airbase at Manas airport. Kyrgyzstan undertook joint exercises with US troops in February 2002, which aimed to facilitate attempts to counter insurgency in the country's mountainous regions. In September Akayev met the US President, George W. Bush, and the US Secretary of State, Colin Powell, in Washington, DC, where they discussed Kyrgyzstan's human rights record, the USA's declared 'war against terrorism' and economic issues. Although Kyrgyzstan stated that it would permit the USA to use the Manas airbase until the situation in Afghanistan stabilized, in early 2006 Kyrgyzstan presented the USA with new conditions for the use of the facility, apparently proposing to increase the rent payable by the USA from US $2m. to $200m.; President Bakiyev maintained that the proposed charge was in accordance with international norms. In July the Kyrgyzstani authorities expelled two US diplomats from Bishkek, owing to 'inappropriate' contact with local non-governmental organizations; it was also alleged that the diplomats were working for the US Central Intelligence Agency (CIA), allegations that the USA adamantly denied. Notwithstanding this dispute, Kyrgyzstan and the USA signed an agreement later that month allowing the latter to continue using the airbase at Manas airport in exchange for 'assistance and co-operation' of some $150m. Nevertheless, in early 2008 President Bakiyev announced that the Kyrgyzstani Government planned eventually to request the closure of the airbase.

Government

Supreme legislative power in the Kyrgyz Republic is vested in the unicameral, 90-member Zhogorku Kenesh (Supreme Council). The Zhogorku Kenesh is elected by universal suffrage for a term of five years. The President of the Republic, who is directly elected for a five-year term, is Head of State and Commander-in-Chief of the Armed Forces, and also holds extensive executive powers. The Prime Minister is appointed by the President, subject to the approval of the Zhogorku Kenesh; the remaining members of the Government are appointed by the President. The Prime Minister is empowered to appoint and dismiss ministers and heads of departments. For administrative purposes, Kyrgyzstan is divided into seven oblasts (regions) and the municipality of Bishkek (the capital).

Defence

Kyrgyzstan began to raise a national army in 1992. As assessed at November 2007, Kyrgyzstan's total armed forces numbered 10,900 (army 8,500, air force 2,400). There were also an estimated 9,500 paramilitary forces (including 5,000 border guards, 3,500 troops attached to the Ministry of Internal Affairs). Military service is compulsory and lasts for 18 months. Kyrgyzstan joined the defence structures of the Commonwealth of Independent States (CIS, see p. 215) by signing, with five other member states, a collective security agreement in May 1992; in May 2001 it was announced that the signatory countries were to form a Collective Rapid Reaction Force to combat Islamist militancy in Central Asia. In April 2003 the Collective Security Treaty Organization (CSTO) was inaugurated as the successor to the CIS collective security system, with the participation of Armenia, Belarus, Kazakhstan, Kyrgyzstan, Russia and Tajikistan. In June 1994 Kyrgyzstan joined the North Atlantic Treaty Organization's (NATO) 'Partnership for Peace' (see p. 342) programme of military co-operation. In early 2008 the US Administration stationed some 1,000 forces at its base at Manas airport, while about 400 Russian troops were deployed at the Kant airbase (established by Russia in October 2003). In 2007 state expenditure on defence totalled some 1,460m. soms.

Economic Affairs

In 2006, according to estimates by the World Bank, Kyrgyzstan's gross national product (GNI), measured at average 2004–06 prices, was US $2,554m., equivalent to $490 per head (or $1,990 per head on an international purchasing-power parity basis). During 1996–2006, it was estimated, the population increased by an annual average of 1.1%, while gross domestic product (GDP) per head increased, in real terms, at an average annual rate of 3.1%. Overall GDP increased, in real terms, at an estimated average annual rate of 3.9% in 1999–2006. Real GDP decreased by 0.2% in 2005, but grew by 2.7% in 2006.

Agriculture (including forestry and fishing) contributed an estimated 33.6% of GDP in 2007, according to preliminary official figures. In 2005 38.5% of the employed labour force were engaged in the sector. By tradition, the Kyrgyz are a pastoral nomadic people, and the majority of the population (some 64.2% in 2005, according to UN estimates) reside in rural areas. Livestock-rearing, once the mainstay of agricultural activity, is declining in importance. Only about 7% of the country's land area is arable; of this, some 70% depends on irrigation. The principal crops are grain, potatoes, vegetables and sugar beet. By 2002, according to government figures, collective farms accounted for only around 6% of agricultural production, while state farms accounted for just under 2%. The GDP of the agricultural sector increased, in real terms, by an average of 5.1% per year in 1995–2006; according to the Asian Development Bank (ADB, see p. 182), agricultural GDP declined by 4.5% in 2005, but increased by 1.8% in 2006.

Industry (comprising manufacturing, mining, utilities and construction) contributed 18.9% of GDP in 2007, according to preliminary official data. The industrial sector provided 17.6% of employment in 2005. Real industrial GDP increased at an average annual rate of 2.1% in 1995–2006; according to the ADB, the GDP of the sector declined by 9.5% in 2005, and by 5.3% in 2006.

In 2007 the mining and quarrying sector provided 0.5% of GDP, according to preliminary figures. The sector engaged 0.6% of the employed work-force in 2005. Kyrgyzstan has considerable mineral deposits, including coal, gold, tin, mercury, antimony, zinc, tungsten and uranium. In May 2001 the Government announced the discovery of new deposits of petroleum, estimated to total 70m. barrels, in an oilfield in the west. Production of gold from the Kumtor mine, which is believed to contain the eighth largest deposit of gold in the world (over 200 metric tons), began in January 1997. As a result, by 2001 Kyrgyzstan had become the 10th largest extractor and seller of gold world-wide. The Kumtor mine reportedly produced almost 4.4m. ounces of gold between 1997 and the end of 2003. Production of gold from the Jeruy deposit, which was not expected to produce significant quantities until 2006–07, commenced in 2002. In April 2006 an agreement was signed with a Kazakhstani company on the development of the Taldy Bulak Levoberezhny gold deposit. Gold production totalled 10.5 tons in 2006.

Manufacturing contributed 11.3% of GDP in 2007, according to preliminary figures. The manufacturing sector employed 7.9% of the work-force in 2005. In 2005 the principal branches of manufacturing, measured by gross value of output, were metallurgy (50.6% of the total) and food products, beverages and tobacco (18.2%). Real manufacturing GDP declined by an average of 3.7% per year in 1996–2006, according to the World Bank; the GDP of the sector decreased by 16.8% in 2005, and by 12.8% in 2006.

Kyrgyzstan's principal source of domestic energy production (and a major export) is hydroelectricity (generated by the country's mountain rivers), which provided 93.1% of the country's total energy requirements in 2004. Kyrgyzstan has insufficient petroleum and natural gas to meet its needs, and substantial imports of hydrocarbons are thus required; Kyrgyzstan exports electricity to Kazakhstan and Uzbekistan in return for coal and natural gas, respectively. Imports of mineral products comprised 30.7% of the value of total recorded imports in 2006. Exports of electricity contributed some 15.8% of the value of total exports in 2000.

In 2007, according to preliminary official figures, the services sector contributed an estimated 47.5% of GDP, and the sector provided 43.9% of employment in 2005. In 1995–2006 the GDP of the sector increased, in real terms, by an average of 4.3% per year; according to the ADB, services GDP increased by 13.8% in 2005 and by 8.4% in 2006.

In 2006 Kyrgyzstan recorded a visible trade deficit of US $981.5m., and there was a deficit of $403.0m. on the current account of the balance of payments. In 2006 the principal source of imports (accounting for 38.0% of the total) was Russia; other major suppliers were the People's Republic of China (14.4%), Kazakhstan (11.6%) and the USA (5.7%). The main market for exports in that year was Switzerland (which accounted for 26.2% of all exports); other principal markets were Kazakhstan (20.5%), Russia (19.4%) and Afghanistan (9.4%). The main exports in 2006 were precious and semi-precious stones and metals, mineral products and textiles. The principal imports in that year were mineral products (mostly petroleum and natural gas), machinery, and electrical equipment and chemicals.

In 2007 Kyrgyzstan recorded an overall budgetary surplus of 130.0m. soms, equivalent to less than 0.1% of GDP. Kyrgyzstan's total external debt was US $2,032m. at the end of 2005, of which $1,670m. was long-term public debt. In that year the cost of debt-servicing was equivalent to 10.0% of the value of exports of goods and services. The annual rate of inflation averaged 0.9% in 2000–06. Consumer prices increased by 0.2% in 2005 and by 1.2% in 2006. The average rate of unemployment was 9.0% in 2005.

Kyrgyzstan participates in the economic bodies of the Commonwealth of Independent States (CIS, see p. 215), and has also joined the European Bank for Reconstruction and Development (EBRD, see p. 239), as a 'Country of Operations', the Economic Co-operation Organization (ECO, see p. 238) and the ADB. In 1998 Kyrgyzstan became the first CIS country to join the World Trade Organization (WTO, see p. 396).

Following independence in 1991, the Government embarked on an ambitious programme of economic reforms. Significant growth was recorded from 1996, although it slowed in 1998–99, apparently owing to the financial crisis in Russia. In 2001 an annual rate of inflation of less than 10% was recorded for the first time since independence. In 2002 GDP declined for the first time since 1995, largely owing to reduced industrial output after a landslide at the Kumtor gold mine. However, growth was recorded in 2003 and 2004, partly owing to increased foreign trade and changes to fiscal regulations concerning small businesses, which had served to reduce tax evasion. In February 2005 the IMF approved a new Poverty Reduction and Growth Facility arrangement for 2005–07. In early 2007 the IMF reviewed the country's progress under the initiative and, although generally positive about its findings, it underscored the importance of the rapid implementation of measures to tackle the high levels of corruption. In March 2005 the 'Paris Club' of official creditors announced that it was cancelling US $124m. of Kyrgyzstan's sovereign debt and rescheduling a further $431m. Meanwhile, a decline in gold production and the political instability resulting from the removal of President Askar Akayev and the subsequent change of government in 2005 slowed economic development, and GDP contracted in that year. The new Government declared that poverty reduction and combating corruption were among its principal aims, although by early 2007 little discernible progress to this end had been made. Political instability intensified in 2006–07, and inflation was reported to have reached 19.5% for the 11 months between January–November 2007, although the 2008 budget forecast an annual rate of inflation of 12% The IMF estimated growth of 7.0% for 2008, compared with the 7.5% growth recorded for 2007, although preliminary official figures reported growth of 18.4% in that year. In the medium term, the economy's reliance on the output of the Kumtor mine (accounting for some 38.5% of industrial production in 2005) was likely to have a detrimental effect on growth, the closure of which was anticipated in 2010. In addition, the need to reduce foreign debt remained an important factor limiting growth. Ultimately, sustained economic growth would be dependent on the greater diversification of both exports and industry, and on a restoration of political stability.

Education

Education is officially compulsory for nine years, comprising four years of primary school (between the ages of seven and 10), followed by five years of lower secondary school (ages 11 to 15). Pupils may then continue their studies in upper secondary schools (two years' duration), specialized secondary schools (two to four years) or technical and vocational schools (from 15 years of age). In 2004 total enrolment at primary schools included 90.1% of the relevant age-group; enrolment at secondary-school level in that year was equivalent to 88.0% of the relevant age group. A decree signed in December 2001 abolished free schooling. In 2004/05 there were 49 institutes of higher education, providing courses lasting between four and six years, and attended by 218,273 students. In 2007 budgetary expenditure on education amounted to 9,178.0m. soms (25.6% of total spending).

Public Holidays

2008: 1 January (New Year's Day), 7 January (Christmas), 8 March (International Women's Day), 21 March (Nooruz, Spring Holiday), 24 March (Day of the People's Revolution), 1 May (International Labour Day), 5 May (Constitution Day), 9 May (Victory Day), 31 August (Independence Day), 1 October* (Orozo Ait, Id al-Fitr or end of Ramadan), 31 December* (Kurban Ait, Id al-Adha or Feast of the Sacrifice).

2009: 1 January (New Year's Day), 7 January (Christmas), 8 March (International Women's Day), 21 March (Nooruz, Spring Holiday), 24 March (Day of the People's Revolution), 1 May (International Labour Day), 5 May (Constitution Day), 9 May (Victory Day), 31 August (Independence Day), 20 September* (Orozo Ait, Id al-Fitr or end of Ramadan), 27 November* (Kurban Ait, Id al-Adha or Feast of the Sacrifice).

* These holidays are dependent on the Islamic lunar calendar and may vary by one or two days from the dates given.

Weights and Measures

The metric system is in force.

Statistical Survey

Source (unless otherwise stated): National Statistical Committee, 720033 Bishkek, Frunze 374; tel. (312) 22-63-63; fax (312) 22-07-59; e-mail zkudabaev@nsc.bishkek.su; internet www.stat.kg.

Area and Population

AREA, POPULATION AND DENSITY

Area (sq km)	199,900*
Population (census results)†	
12 January 1989	4,257,755
24 March 1999	
Males	2,380,465
Females	2,442,473
Total	4,822,938
Population (official estimates at 31 December)	
2005	5,138,700
2006	5,189,800
2007	5,224,300
Density (per sq km) at 31 December 2007	26.1

* 77,182 sq miles.
† The figures refer to *de jure* population. The *de facto* total was 4,290,442 at the 1989 census and 4,850,700 at the 1999 census.

PRINCIPAL ETHNIC GROUPS
(permanent inhabitants, 1999 census)

	Number	%
Kyrgyz	3,128,147	64.86
Uzbek	664,950	13.79
Russian	603,201	12.51
Dungan	51,766	1.07
Ukrainian	50,442	1.05
Others	324,432	6.73
Total	**4,822,938**	**100.00**

ADMINISTRATIVE DIVISIONS
(1999 census)

	Area (sq km)	Population	Density (per sq km)	Principal city
Oblasts (Regions)				
Batken	17,000	382,426	22.5	Batken
Chui	20,200	770,811	38.2	Tokmok
Issyk-Kul	43,100	413,149	9.6	Karakol
Jalal-Abad	33,700	869,259	25.8	Jalal-Abad
Naryn	45,200	249,115	5.5	Naryn
Osh	29,200	1,175,998	40.3	Osh
Talas	11,400	199,872	17.5	Talas
City				
Bishkek	100	762,308	7,623.1	—
Total	**199,900**	**4,822,938**	**24.1**	

PRINCIPAL TOWNS
(population at census of March 1999)

Bishkek (capital)*	750,327	Karakol†	64,322
Osh	208,520	Tokmok	59,409
Jalal-Abad	70,401	Kara-Balta	53,887

* Known as Frunze between 1926 and 1991.
† Formerly Przhevalsk.

Mid-2007 (incl. suburbs, UN estimate): Bishkek 837,000 (Source: UN, *World Urbanization Prospects: The 2007 Revision*).

BIRTHS, MARRIAGES AND DEATHS

	Registered live births		Registered marriages		Registered deaths	
	Number	Rate (per 1,000)	Number	Rate (per 1,000)	Number	Rate (per 1,000)
1997	102,050	21.6	26,588	5.6	34,540	7.3
1998	104,183	21.7	25,726	5.4	34,596	7.2
1999	104,068	21.4	26,033	5.4	32,850	6.8
2000	96,770	19.7	24,294	4.9	34,111	6.9
2001	98,138	19.8	27,455	5.5	32,677	6.6
2002	101,012	20.2	31,240	6.3	35,235	7.1
2003	105,490	20.9	34,266	6.8	35,941	7.1
2004	109,939	21.6	34,542	6.8	35,061	6.9

2005: Birth rate 21.4 per 1,000 persons; Death rate 7.2 per 1,000 persons.
2006: Birth rate 23.3 per 1,000 persons; Death rate 7.4 per 1,000 persons.
Expectation of life (years at birth, official estimates): 67.7 (males 63.5; females 71.9) in 2006.

ECONOMICALLY ACTIVE POPULATION
(annual averages, '000 persons)

	2003	2004	2005
Agriculture, hunting and forestry	834.2	773.9	799.0
Fishing	0.5	0.7	0.6
Mining and quarrying	12.5	13.5	12.4
Manufacturing	140.2	153.4	163.9
Electricity, gas and water supply	35.0	39.1	35.2
Construction	102.2	144.0	153.7
Wholesale and retail trade; repair of motor vehicles, motor cycles and personal and household goods	257.8	281.6	301.5
Hotels and restaurants	34.1	44.5	49.0
Transport, storage and communications	97.6	112.9	115.7
Financial intermediation	10.0	8.5	8.2
Real estate, renting and business activities	28.4	38.4	34.1
Public administration and defence; compulsory social security	91.1	91.8	102.3
Education	156.4	161.8	161.8
Health and social work	80.9	73.9	85.4
Other services	49.5	53.2	54.2
Total employed	**1,930.5**	**1,991.2**	**2,077.1**
Unemployed	212.3	185.7	183.5
Total labour force	**2,142.8**	**2,176.9**	**2,260.6**
Males	1,296.1	1,239.5	1,291.6
Females	945.9	937.4	969.0

Source: ILO.

Health and Welfare

KEY INDICATORS

Total fertility rate (children per woman, 2005)	2.6
Under-5 mortality rate (per 1,000 live births, 2005)	67
HIV/AIDS (% of persons aged 15–49, 2005)	0.1
Physicians (per 1,000 head, 2003)	2.51
Hospital beds (per 1,000 head, 2005)	5.1
Health expenditure (2004): US $ per head (PPP)	101.6
Health expenditure (2004): % of GDP	5.6
Health expenditure (2004): public (% of total)	40.9
Access to water (% of persons, 2004)	77
Access to sanitation (% of persons, 2004)	59
Human Development Index (2005): ranking	116
Human Development Index (2005): value	0.696

For sources and definitions, see explanatory note on p. vi.

Agriculture

PRINCIPAL CROPS
('000 metric tons)

	2004	2005	2006
Wheat	998.2	950.1	928.0
Rice (paddy)	18.3	17.1	18.7
Barley	233.4	213.5	214.4
Maize	452.9	437.3	438.0
Potatoes	1,362.5	1,141.5	1,254.9
Sugar beet	642.4	288.8	226.0
Sunflower seed	67.2	69.2	77.0*
Cabbages and other brassicas	113.2	94.7	98.0†
Tomatoes	168.1	171.2	177.0†
Cucumbers and gherkins	55.7	62.4	64.5†
Dry onions	117.1	110.0	113.5†
Garlic	25.0	24.2	25.0†
Carrots and turnips	127.1	144.9	150.0†
Apples	124.5*	102.4*	130.0†
Apricots	15.4*	13.0*	16.5†
Peaches and nectarines*	3.5	3.0	3.8†
Grapes	14.6	11.4	14.7
Watermelons	88.1	85.8	97.7
Cotton (lint)†	40.0	39.0	39.0
Cottonseed†	72.0	70.0	69.0
Tobacco (leaves)	13.0	13.4	13.7

* Unofficial figure.
† FAO estimate(s).

Aggregate production ('000 metric tons, may include official, semi-official or estimated data): Total cereals 1,708.9 in 2004, 1,621.6 in 2005, 1,605.9 in 2006; Total roots and tubers 1,362.5 in 2004, 1,141.5 in 2005, 1,254.9 in 2006; Total vegetables (incl. melons) 830.3 in 2004, 825.1 in 2005, 859.0 in 2006; Total fruits (excl. melons) 190.6 in 2004, 158.6 in 2005, 201.4 in 2006.

Source: FAO.

LIVESTOCK
('000 head at 1 January)

	2004	2005	2006
Horses	341	347	350*
Asses, mules or hinnies	49	44	42*
Cattle	1,004	1,035	1,074
Pigs	83	83	78
Sheep	2,884	2,965	3,062†
Goats	770	808	814†
Chickens	3,949	4,121	4,300*
Turkeys	149	154	160

* FAO estimate.
† Unofficial figure.

Source: FAO.

LIVESTOCK PRODUCTS
('000 metric tons)

	2004	2005	2006
Cattle meat	94.6	90.9	91.2*
Sheep meat	37.7	39.2	39.4*
Goat meat	7.1	7.2	7.2*
Pig meat	25.2	18.7	18.8*
Horse meat	18.1	20.3	20.4*
Chicken meat	4.9	5.4	5.4*
Cows' milk	1,132.5	1,151.4	1,157.0*
Hen eggs	16.6	17.7	18.3*
Honey	1.3	1.3	1.4*
Wool: greasy	10.2	10.0	10.6

* FAO estimate.

Source: FAO.

Forestry

ROUNDWOOD REMOVALS
('000 cubic metres, excl. bark, unofficial figures)

	2002	2003	2004
Sawlogs, veneer logs and logs for sleepers	6	6	5
Other industrial wood	6	6	5
Fuel wood	25	25	18
Total	37	37	28

2005–06: Figures assumed to be unchanged from 2004 (FAO estimates).

Source: FAO.

SAWNWOOD PRODUCTION
('000 cubic metres, incl. railway sleepers)

	2002*	2003	2004
Coniferous (softwood)	2.0	8.0	6.3
Broadleaved (hardwood)	4.0	7.2	15.7
Total	6.0	15.2	22.0

* FAO estimates.

2005–06: Figures assumed to be unchanged from 2004 (FAO estimates).

Source: FAO.

Fishing

(metric tons, live weight)

	2003	2004	2005*
Capture	14	7	7
Freshwater bream	1	2	2
Common carp	1	—	—
Silver carp	2	—	—
Other cyprinids	5	1	1
Pike-perch	1	2	2
Whitefishes	3	1	1
Aquaculture	12	20	20
Common carp	7	8	8
Grass carp	1	2	2
Silver carp	4	10	10
Total catch	26	27	27

* FAO estimates.

Source: FAO.

Mining

('000 metric tons, unless otherwise indicated)

	2003	2004	2005
Coal	415.3	456.3	331.6
Crude petroleum	69.5	73.8	74.4
Natural gas (million cu metres)	27.1	28.6	24.7

Gold (metric tons): 22.1 in 2004; 16.7 in 2005; 10.5 in 2006 (Source: Gold Fields Mineral Services, *Gold Survey 2007*).

Industry

SELECTED PRODUCTS
('000 metric tons, unless otherwise indicated)

	2003	2004	2005
Vegetable oil	10.7	12.3	15.2
Refined sugar	75.5	88.1	44.5
Vodka ('000 hectolitres)	24.3	21.8	16.5
Beer ('000 hectolitres)	7.7	11.6	12.3
Cigarettes (million)	3,102.4	3,169.5	3,164.7
Textile fabrics ('000 sq metres)	1,814.2	1,264.8	1,921.2
Footwear ('000 pairs)	237.8	245.7	220.5
Motor spirit (petrol)	25.0	19.7	14.0
Gas-diesel (distillate fuel) oil	21.9	26.3	31.4
Cement	757.3	870.1	975.1
Electric energy (million kWh)	14,021.1	15,091.2	14,838.7

Finance

CURRENCY AND EXCHANGE RATES

Monetary Units
100 tyiyns = 1 som.

Sterling, Dollar and Euro Equivalents (31 December 2007)
£1 sterling = 71.118 soms;
US $1 = 35.499 soms;
€1 = 52.258 soms;
1,000 soms = £14.06 = $28.17 = €19.14.

Average Exchange Rate (soms per US $)
2005   41.012
2006   40.153
2007   37.316

Note: In May 1993 Kyrgyzstan introduced its own currency, the som, replacing the Russian (former Soviet) rouble at an exchange rate of 1 som = 200 roubles.

BUDGET
(million soms)*

Revenue†	2005	2006	2007
Taxation	16,361.4	19,981.2	26,544.8
Corporate income taxes	1,744.2	1,820.3	2,322.9
Personal income taxes	1,283.2	1,191.6	1,736.1
Value-added tax	7,088.6	9,150.6	10,701.6
Excise taxes	1,149.7	1,205.4	1,448.2
Taxes on international trade and transactions	1,664.0	2,803.3	3,789.5
Other current revenue	3,567.9	4,696.0	7,195.3
Capital revenue	46.1	138.0	465.3
Total	19,975.4	24,815.2	34,205.4

Expenditure‡	2005	2006	2007
General public services	3,039.6	3,358.4	5,154.8
Education	4,917.7	6,314.2	9,178.0
Health care	2,283.3	3,059.1	4,028.8
Social insurance and security	2,858.1	3,610.6	3,816.9
Housing and public utilities	1,040.6	1,415.5	2,657.3
Cultural and religious activity	606.9	813.0	1,239.9
Total (incl. others)	20,143.7	25,297.8	35,864.9

* Figures represent a consolidation of the budgetary transactions of the central Government and local governments. The operations of extra-budgetary accounts, including the Social Fund (formed in 1994 by an amalgamation of the Pension Fund, the Unemployment Fund and the Social Insurance Fund), are excluded.
† Excluding grants received (million soms): 392.6 in 2005; 266.1 in 2006; 1,789.5 in 2007.
‡ Including lending minus repayments.

Source: National Bank of the Kyrgyz Republic.

INTERNATIONAL RESERVES
(US $ million at 31 December)

	2004	2005	2006
Gold	36.4	42.6	52.8
IMF special drawing rights	19.9	5.3	33.3
Foreign exchange	508.3	564.5	731.1
Total	564.6	612.4	817.2

Source: IMF, *International Financial Statistics*.

MONEY SUPPLY
(million soms at 31 December)

	2004	2005	2006
Currency outside banks	11,109	13,065	19,410
Demand deposits at banking institutions	1,935	2,123	3,655
Total money	13,045	15,188	23,065

Source: IMF, *International Financial Statistics*.

COST OF LIVING
(Retail Price Index; base: previous year = 100)

	2005	2006	2007
Food and nonalcoholic drinks	107.0	109.5	114.7
Fuel and light	108.5	107.3	113.2
Clothing and footwear	101.1	101.1	102.9
All items (incl. others)	104.3	105.6	110.2

NATIONAL ACCOUNTS
(million soms at current prices)

Expenditure on the Gross Domestic Product

	2004	2005	2006
Final consumption expenditure	88,893.1	102,972.4	128,722.7
Households	69,983.4	83,471.4	105,799.4
Non-profit institutions serving households	1,763.6	1,833.8	2,453.7
General government	17,146.0	17,667.3	20,469.6
Gross capital formation	13,669.9	16,565.8	27,534.8
Gross fixed capital formation	13,739.1	16,150.0	26,211.6
Changes in stocks	−255.5	208.5	867.9
Acquisitions, less disposals, of valuables	186.3	207.3	455.3
Total domestic expenditure	102,563.0	119,538.2	156,257.5
Exports of goods and services (net)	−8,212.3	−18,639.0	−42,457.4
GDP in purchasers' values	94,350.7	100,899.2	113,800.1

Source: National Bank of the Kyrgyz Republic.

Gross Domestic Product by Economic Activity

	2005	2006	2007*
Agriculture, forestry and fishing	28,739.4	32,638.2	40,552.9
Mining	556.4	488.7	548.7
Manufacturing	12,968.0	12,509.0	13,687.8
Electricity, gas and water supply	3,896.7	3,937.4	3,922.8
Construction	2,725.9	3,041.9	4,711.0
Trade, repair of motor vehicles, household appliances and articles of personal use	18,001.6	20,883.9	25,484.4
Hotels and restaurants	1,350.6	1,549.0	1,870.6
Transport and communications	6,617.7	6,887.2	10,181.7
Housing, social and personal services	1,197.9	1,531.4	1,860.4
Health care and social services	2,064.9	2,588.5	2,711.7

KYRGYZSTAN

—continued	2005	2006	2007*
Education	3,854.4	4,561.6	5,409.8
Financial activities	2,250.8	2,986.4	605.7
Real estate, rent and rendering services	2,814.1	3,321.7	3,777.9
Government administration	4,659.8	5,053.9	5,474.7
Sub-total	91,698.2	101,978.8	120,800.1
Less Imputed bank service charge	1,735.2	2,380.7	—
GDP at basic prices	89,963.0	99,598.1	120,800.1
Taxes on products } *Less* Subsidies on products	10,936.2	14,202.0	18,949.3
GDP in purchasers' values	100,899.2	113,800.1	139,749.4

* Preliminary figures.

BALANCE OF PAYMENTS
(US $ million)

	2004	2005	2006
Exports of goods f.o.b.	733.2	686.8	810.8
Imports of goods f.o.b.	−903.8	−1,105.5	−1,792.3
Trade balance	−170.6	−418.7	−981.5
Exports of services	209.8	255.5	374.5
Imports of services	−223.5	−291.3	−460.9
Balance on goods and services	−184.3	−454.4	−1,068.0
Other income received	7.8	16.5	35.7
Other income paid	−109.4	−91.7	−69.8
Balance on goods, services and income	−285.9	−529.5	−1,102.1
Current transfers received	306.9	513.6	749.0
Current transfers paid	−17.6	−37.9	−50.0
Current balance	3.4	−53.9	−403.0
Capital account (net)	−19.9	−20.5	−43.9
Direct investment abroad	−43.9	—	—
Direct investment from abroad	175.5	42.6	182.0
Portfolio investment assets	−9.5	−2.3	−3.0
Portfolio investment liabilities	—	—	—
Financial derivatives assets	−20.5	—	—
Other investment assets	−35.8	−51.8	−19.8
Other investment liabilities	114.3	92.3	174.9
Net errors and omissions	−19.0	57.5	289.6
Statistical discrepancy	—	4.5	—
Overall balance	144.5	68.4	176.7

Source: IMF, *International Financial Statistics*.

External Trade

PRINCIPAL COMMODITIES
(US $ million)

Imports c.i.f.	2004	2005	2006
Vegetable products	23.0	40.6	62.6
Prepared foodstuffs, beverages and tobacco	83.0	101.3	141.6
Mineral products	273.3	334.0	527.4
Products of chemical or allied industries	112.9	130.8	145.5
Plastics, rubber and articles thereof	56.0	60.1	85.2
Textiles and fabrics	42.6	36.6	51.0
Metals and articles thereof	65.0	66.5	104.9
Machinery, electrical equipment and parts	107.3	156.1	271.9
Vehicles and transport equipment	70.3	41.4	136.6
Total (incl. others)	941.0	1,101.3	1,718.2

Exports f.o.b.	2004	2005	2006
Vegetable products	26.2	19.9	35.6
Prepared foodstuffs, beverages and tobacco	42.9	37.2	28.9
Mineral products	94.1	96.8	177.8
Products of chemical or allied industries	21.7	13.5	14.4
Raw hides and skins, leather, fur, travel articles and bags	9.3	12.2	14.3
Textiles and fabrics	79.5	77.4	96.7
Natural and cultured pearls, precious and semi-precious stones, precious metals and products, and coins	291.2	236.2	212.6
Metals and articles thereof	31.7	23.2	27.0
Machinery, electrical equipment and parts	35.5	32.1	51.1
Vehicles and transport equipment	14.8	18.5	23.8
Total (incl. others)	718.8	672.0	794.2

PRINCIPAL TRADING PARTNERS
(US $ million)

Imports c.i.f.	2004	2005	2006
Belarus	4.2	7.1	18.7
Belgium	2.3	4.5	16.8
Canada	12.6	15.0	32.2
China, People's Republic	80.1	102.9	246.7
Germany	52.6	37.6	39.9
Japan	11.6	11.7	13.3
Kazakhstan	202.9	174.4	199.8
Korea, Republic	25.1	27.8	29.1
Netherlands	15.7	18.9	27.7
Poland	10.3	11.6	12.5
Russia	293.7	378.9	652.2
Turkey	33.2	33.4	39.5
Ukraine	23.3	40.1	41.9
USA	44.6	67.2	97.5
Uzbekistan	51.9	60.1	65.0
Total (incl. others)	941.0	1,101.3	1,718.2

Exports f.o.b.	2004	2005	2006
Afghanistan	8.0	12.4	74.8
Canada	42.7	22.5	0.2
China, People's Republic	39.3	26.6	38.1
Iran	3.5	3.9	7.3
Kazakhstan	87.3	116.1	162.6
Russia	137.7	134.4	153.8
Switzerland	101.8	65.3	207.7
Tajikistan	22.1	22.9	23.9
Turkey	17.0	18.2	27.2
United Arab Emirates	189.3	173.1	8.9
Uzbekistan	14.7	17.1	27.9
Total (incl. others)	718.8	672.0	794.1

Transport

RAILWAYS
(traffic)

	2002	2003	2004
Passenger-km (million)	43	50	45
Freight net ton-km (million)	395	562	715

ROAD TRAFFIC
(vehicles in use at 31 December)

	2001	2002	2003
Passenger cars	189,796	188,711	188,900
Motorcycles and mopeds	14,319	12,288	11,221

KYRGYZSTAN

CIVIL AVIATION
(traffic on scheduled services)

	2002	2003	2004
Kilometres flown (million)	6	7	7
Passengers carried ('000)	185	218	258
Passenger-km (million)	342	411	459
Total ton-km (million)	39	43	46

Tourism

FOREIGN TOURIST ARRIVALS

Country of residence	2003	2004	2005
China, People's Republic	8,268	11,822	15,747
Germany	8,553	9,724	9,128
Kazakhstan	160,335	236,712	150,904
Korea, Republic	2,700	3,127	3,850
Russia	36,071	36,540	32,001
Tajikistan	6,289	8,190	4,565
Turkey	6,398	9,032	9,362
USA	11,667	11,111	11,727
Uzbekistan	36,153	40,655	49,376
Total (incl. others)	341,990	398,078	315,290

Tourism receipts (US $ million, incl. passenger transport): 65 in 2003; 97 in 2004; 94 in 2005.

Source: World Tourism Organization.

Communications Media

	2002	2003	2004
Television receivers ('000 in use)	7	7	7
Telephones ('000 main lines in use)	394.8	396.2	416.4
Mobile cellular telephones ('000 subscribers)	53.1	138.3	263.4
Internet users ('000)	152	200	263
Personal computers ('000 in use)	65	75	87
Daily newspapers:			
number	1	2	2
average circulation	35,900	65,000	21,000
Non-daily newspapers:			
number	62	77	83
average circulation	319,100	376,600	427,800
Book production:			
titles	672	642	703
copies ('000)	1,056.6	1,885.0	1,600.3

Radio receivers ('000 in use): 520 in 1997 (Source: UNESCO, *Statistical Yearbook*).

Telephones ('000 main lines in use): 438.2 in 2005.

Mobile cellular telephones ('000 subscribers): 541.7 in 2005.

Personal computers ('000 in use): 100 in 2005.

Internet users ('000): 280.0 in 2005; 298.1 in 2006.

Broadband subscribers ('000): 2.5 in 2005.

Source: International Telecommunication Union.

Education

(2004/05)

	Institutions	Teachers	Students
Pre-primary	440	2,333	50,935
Primary	2,104	17,729	436,159
Secondary: general	n.a.	50,526	692,724
Secondary: vocational	187	6,212	59,659
Higher (all institutions)	49	13,337	218,273

Adult literacy rate (official estimate): 98.7% in 2006.

Directory

The Constitution

In September 2007 the Constitutional Court ruled that the adoption of two successive Constitutions in November 2006 and January 2007 had been illegal. It restored the Constitution that had been proclaimed on 5 May 1993, and that was subsequently revised on numerous occasions. President Kurmanbek Bakiyev subsequently scheduled a referendum on the adoption of a new Constitution for 21 October 2007. The new Constitution, which was approved by 76.1% of votes cast at the national referendum, entered into effect on 23 October. The following is a summary of its main provisions.

GENERAL PROVISIONS

The Kyrgyz Republic is a sovereign, unitary, democratic republic founded on the principle of the rule of law. All state power originates from the people of Kyrgyzstan, who exercise this power through elections and referendums, and through the state bodies and bodies of local self-government, on the basis of the Constitution and laws. Matters of legislation and other issues pertaining to the state may be decided by the people by referendum. The President of the Republic, the deputies of the Zhogorku Kenesh (Supreme Council) and representatives of local administrative bodies are all elected directly by the people. Elections are held on the basis of universal, equal and direct suffrage by secret ballot. All citizens of 18 years and over are eligible to vote.

The territory of the Kyrgyz Republic is integral and inviolable. The state language is Kyrgyz, and Russian is used as an official language. The equality and free use of other languages by representatives of the national and ethnic groups that constitute the people of Kyrgyzstan are guaranteed. The rights and freedoms of citizens may not be restricted on account of ignorance of the state language. The adoption of a state religion is prohibited. Political parties may not be formed on a religious basis, and certain provisions provide for a separation of the activities of political parties from those of the organs of the State.

HUMAN RIGHTS AND CIVIL LIBERTIES

Human rights and freedoms are absolute and inalienable. All people are equal before the laws and courts of the Kyrgyz Republic.

The freedoms of movement, association, peaceful assembly, of place of residence within the territories of the Kyrgyz Republic, and of property ownership are guaranteed. The privacy of written and telephonic conversation is respected. The freedoms of religion and thought, speech and expression are guaranteed. Citizens of the Kyrgyz Republic are permitted to obtain citizenship of another state, subject to international agreements entered into by the Kyrgyz Republic.

THE PRESIDENT

The President of the Kyrgyz Republic is Head of State. The President is a symbol of the unity of the people and state power, a guarantor of the Constitution, human rights and civil liberties. The term of office is five years, and no more than two consecutive terms may be served. The President is directly elected by the people. Any citizen of the republic between the ages of 35 and 65, who has a command of the state language, and who has resided in the Republic for at least 15 years, is permitted to contest the presidency. Presidential candidates must be nominated by no less than 50,000 electors.

The President: appoints the Prime Minister and members of the Government; dismisses members of the Government either of his own accord or at the behest of the Prime Minister; appoints heads of local state administration in consultation with the Prime Minister and orders their dismissal; appoints other leading state posts; and appoints one-half of the members of the Central Commission for Elections and Referendums. With the agreement of the Zhogorku Kenesh, he appoints the Prosecutor-General, other senior judicial posts, the Chairman of the National Bank and the Chairman of the Central Commission for Elections and Referendums. The President: presents draft legislation to the Zhogorku Kenesh; signs legislation approved by the Zhogorku Kenesh or returns it for further scrutiny; signs international agreements; may call referendums on issues of state on his own initiative or in response to proposals presented by at least 300,000 electors and a majority of deputies in the Zhogorku Kenesh; and calls elections to the Zhogorku Kenesh and to local assemblies. The President declares a state of war.

The President may be removed from office only on the basis of a charge of high treason or relating to other grave crimes made by the Zhogorku Kenesh, as confirmed by the Prosecutor-General. Any ensuing demands for a vote of impeachment must be supported by no less than two-thirds of the total membership of the Zhogorku Kenesh. For the vote of impeachment to be approved it must be supported by no less than three-quarters of the total membership of the Zhogorku Kenesh; this vote must be held no more than three months after the vote to commence impeachment proceedings was taken. In the event of impeachment being approved, the executive duties of the President are assumed on an acting basis by the Chairman of the Zhogorku Kenesh; in the event that the Chairman of the Zhogorku Kenesh is unable to assume executive powers, they are transferred to the Prime Minister. Elections for a new President must be held no later than three months after the removal from office of the outgoing President.

ZHOGORKU KENESH

Supreme legislative power is vested in the Zhogorku Kenesh, which comprises one 90-member chamber. Deputies are elected for a term of five years on the basis of party lists. Any citizen of the Kyrgyz Republic aged 25 years or older, and enjoying full civil rights, may be elected to the Zhogorku Kenesh.

The Zhogorku Kenesh: adopts the Constitution; approves amendments and additions to the Constitution; enacts legislation; confirms the republican budget and supervises its execution; determines questions pertaining to the administrative and territorial structure of the republic; designates presidential elections; approves the governmental structure proposed by the Prime Minister; may approve a vote of 'no confidence' in the Government or in individual members thereof; consents to the appointment of the Procurator-General, as nominated by the President; elects judges of the Constitutional court, judges of the Supreme Court and the Chairman of the National Bank, at the proposal of the President; and ratifies or abrogates international agreements. The Zhogorku Kenesh may be dissolved by resolution of no less than two-thirds of its deputies.

THE GOVERNMENT

The Government of the Kyrgyz Republic is the highest organ of executive power in Kyrgyzstan. A political party that receives more than 50% of the mandates in the Zhogorku Kenesh presents its candidate for the Prime Minister for presidential approval, no later than five days from the convening of a new Zhogorku Kenesh. In the event that the nominated candidate fails to obtain the approval of the Zhogorku Kenesh, the President may request a second political party to nominate a candidate as Prime Minister, and similarly from a third political party in the event that the second candidate is not approved. In the event that the third candidate for the premiership is rejected, the President shall form an interim Government pending fresh legislative elections. A vote of 'no confidence' in the Government may be held if demanded by at least one-third of the membership of the Zhogorku Kenesh, except in the six-month period before a presidential election, when such a vote may not be held. The President is not obliged to dismiss the Government following a vote of 'no confidence', unless two such votes take place within a period of three months, in which case the President may either dismiss the Government and appoint a new administration or call fresh legislative elections. The President is obliged to dismiss an individual member of the Government subject to two votes of 'no confidence' in a six-month period.

The Government: determines all questions of state administration, other than those ascribed by the Constitution to the competence of the President and the Zhogorku Kenesh; drafts the republican budget and submits it to the Zhogorku Kenesh for approval; co-ordinates budgetary, financial, fiscal and monetary policy; administers state property; takes measures to defend the country and state security; executes foreign policy; and strives to guarantee the rights and freedoms of the citizens and to protect property and social order.

The authorities, duties, organization and form of local territorial-administrative bodies are determined by law.

THE CENTRAL ORGANS OF STATE POWER

The central organs of state power of the Kyrgyz Republic comprise: the Office of the Prosecutor-General; the National Bank; the Central Commission for Elections and Referendums; the Audit Chamber; and the Akyikatchi (Ombudsman), which protects the observation of human rights and civil freedoms in the Republic.

JUDICIAL SYSTEM

The judicial system comprises the Constitutional Court, the Supreme Court and regional courts. Courts are independent and governed only by the Constitution and by law. Judges of all courts remain in office for as long as their behaviour is deemed to be irreproachable. Judges of the Constitutional Court and the Supreme Court are elected by the Zhogorku Kenesh, on the recommendation of the President. Judges of local courts are appointed by the President of the Republic at the proposal of the National Council for the Judiciary, for terms of five years. The Constitutional Court comprises seven judges. The Supreme Court is the highest organ of judicial power in the sphere of civil, criminal and administrative justice.

ON REFORM

The proposed introduction of amendments or additions to the existing Constitution, or the proposed adoption of a new Constitution, may be examined by the Zhogorku Kenesh in response to a request of the President or of a majority of deputies of the Zhogorku Kenesh, or in response to an initiative supported by no less than 300,000 electors. A law amending and supplementing the existing Constitution may be adopted by a majority of no less than two-thirds of the total membership of the Zhogorku Kenesh after the holding of no fewer than two readings with an interval of three months between readings. At the demand of the majority of the total membership of the Zhogorku Kenesh a law amending and supplementing the present Constitution may be submitted to referendum.

The Government

HEAD OF STATE

President: KURMANBEK S. BAKIYEV (elected 10 July 2005; inaugurated 14 August 2005).

GOVERNMENT
(April 2008)

Prime Minister: IGOR V. CHUDINOV.

First Deputy Prime Minister: ISKENDERBEK R. AYDARALIYEV.

Deputy Prime Minister: DOSBOL NUR UULU.

Head of the Government Staff, Minister: MURAT A. ISMAILOV.

Minister of Foreign Affairs: EDNAN O. KARABAYEV.

Minister of Defence: Gen. ISMAIL I. ISAKOV.

Minister of Internal Affairs: MOLDOMUSA T. KONGANTIYEV.

Minister of Justice: MARAT T. KAIYYPOV.

Minister of Finance: TAZHIKAN B. KALIMBETOVA.

Minister of Economic Development and Trade: AKYLBEK U. ZHAPAROV.

Minister of Agriculture, Water Resources and Processing Industry: ARSTANBEK I. NOGOYEV.

Minister of Transport and Communications: NURLAN CH. SULAIMANOV.

Minister of Emergency Situations: KAMCHIBEK K. TASHIYEV.

Minister of Education and Science: ISHENKUL S. BOLJUROVA.

Minister of Health: MARAT A. MAMBETOV.

Minister of Culture and Information: SULTAN A. RAYEV.

Minister of Labour and Social Welfare: UKTOMKHAN A. ABDULLAYEVA.

Minister of Industry, Energy and Fuel Resources: SAPAR E. BALKIBEKOV.

Note: The Chairmen of the State Committees for National Security, Migration and Labour, for the Management of State Property, for Taxes and Collections, and for Customs are also members of the Government.

MINISTRIES

Office of the President: 720003 Bishkek, Dom Pravitelstva; tel. (312) 21-24-66; fax (312) 21-86-27; e-mail office@mail.gov.kg; internet www.president.kg.

Office of the Prime Minister: 720003 Bishkek, Dom Pravitelstva; tel. (312) 66-12-20; fax (312) 66-66-58; e-mail pmoffice@mail.gov.kg; internet www.government.gov.kg.

Ministry of Agriculture, Water Resources and Processing Industry: 720040 Bishkek, Kiyevskaya 96A; tel. (312) 62-14-27; fax (312) 62-36-32; e-mail mawr@elcat.kg.

KYRGYZSTAN

Ministry of Culture and Information: 720040 Bishkek, Pushkina 78; tel. (312) 62-12-00; internet www.minculture.gov.kg.

Ministry of Defence: 720001 Bishkek, Logvinenko 26; tel. (312) 66-38-28; fax (312) 66-16-02; e-mail ud@bishkek.gov.kg; internet www.mil.kg.

Ministry of Economic Development and Trade: 720002 Bishkek, pr. Chui 106; tel. (312) 66-38-00; fax (312) 66-34-98; e-mail postmaster@mvtp.bishkek.gov.kg.

Ministry of Education and Science: 720040 Bishkek, Tynystanova 257; tel. (312) 62-36-33; fax (312) 62-36-22; e-mail monk@monk.bishkek.gov.kg.

Ministry of Emergency Situations: 720055 Bishkek, Toktonaliyeva 2/1; tel. (312) 54-79-86; fax (312) 54-11-79; e-mail mecd@bishkek.gov.kg; internet www.mecd.gov.kg.

Ministry of Finance: 720040 Bishkek, pr. Erkindik 58; tel. (312) 66-13-50; fax (312) 66-16-45; e-mail it@minfin.kg; internet www.minfin.kg.

Ministry of Foreign Affairs: 720040 Bishkek, bul. Erkindik 57; tel. (312) 62-05-45; fax (312) 66-05-01; e-mail gendep@mfa.gov.kg; internet www.mfa.kg.

Ministry of Health: 720040 Bishkek, Moskovskaya 148; tel. (312) 62-26-80; fax (312) 66-07-17; e-mail e_bayalinova@foms.med.kg; internet www.med.kg.

Ministry of Industry, Energy and Fuel Resources: 720002 Bishkek, pr. Chui 106; tel. (312) 66-19-45; fax (312) 66-18-37; e-mail postmaster@mvtp.bishkek.gov.kg.

Ministry of Internal Affairs: 720040 Bishkek, Frunze 469; tel. (312) 66-24-50; fax (312) 68-20-44; e-mail mail@mvd.bishkek.gov.kg; internet www.mvd.kg.

Ministry of Justice: 720040 Bishkek, M. Gandi 32; tel. (312) 65-64-90; fax (312) 65-65-02; e-mail admin@minjust.gov.kg; internet www.minjust.gov.kg.

Ministry of Labour and Social Welfare: 720041 Bishkek, Tynystanova 215; tel. (312) 66-34-00; fax (312) 66-57-24; e-mail mlsp@mlsp.kg; internet www.mlsp.kg.

Ministry of Transport and Communications: 720017 Bishkek, Isanova 42; tel. (312) 61-04-72; fax (312) 66-47-81; e-mail mtk@mtk.gov.kg; internet www.mtk.gov.kg.

President

Presidential Election, 10 July 2005*

Candidates	Votes	%
Kurmanbek S. Bakiyev	1,776,156	88.72
Tursunbai Bakir-uulu	78,701	3.93
Akbaraly Y. Aitikeyev	72,604	3.63
Others	38,864	1.94
Total†	**2,001,974**	**100.00**

* Preliminary official results.
† Including 18,197 votes (0.91% of the total) 'against all candidates' and 17,452 invalid votes (0.87% of the total).

Legislature

**Zhogorku Kenesh
(Supreme Council)**

720053 Bishkek, ul. Abdymomunov 207; tel. (312) 61-16-04; fax (312) 62-50-12; e-mail zs@kenesh.gov.kg; internet www.kenesh.kg.

Chairman: ADAKHAN MADUMAROV.

General Election, 16 December 2007*

Parties	% of votes†	Seats
Bright Road (Ak Zhol)	46.90	71
Social Democratic Party of Kyrgyzstan	5.12	11
Communist Party of Kyrgyzstan	5.05	8
Fatherland Socialist Party (Ata-Meken)	8.29	—
Others	34.64	—
Total	**100.00**	**90**

* Provisional final results.
† Parties were required to obtain at least 0.5% of votes cast in each of the country's six regions and two largest cities in order to be eligible for legislative representation.

Election Commission

Kyrgyz Respublikasynyn Shailoo Zhana Referendum Otkoruu Boyuncha Borborduk Komissiyasy (Central Commission for Elections and Referendums of the Kyrgyz Republic): 720003 Bishkek, Dom Pravitelstva; tel. (312) 62-62-87; e-mail muhina@shailoo.gov.kg; independent govt organ; one-half of the mems are appointed by the President of the Republic, and one-half by the Zhogorku Kenesh; Chair. KLARA KABILOVA.

Political Organizations

At December 2005 some 67 political organizations were registered with the Ministry of Justice. The following were among the most important operating in early 2008.

Agrarian Party of Kyrgyzstan: 720000 Bishkek, Kiyevskaya 96; tel. (312) 22-68-52; f. 1993; re-registered 2001; campaigns for agrarian reform, and for the protection of the rights and interests of people working in agriculture; Chair. MEDETBEK SHAMSHIBEKOV; c. 8,000 mems (1999).

Banner (Asaba) Party of National Revival: 720000 Bishkek, pr. Chui 26; tel. (312) 43-04-45; fax (312) 28-53-64; f. 1990; re-registered 2001; nationalist, pro-democracy; mem. of the People's Movement of Kyrgyzstan electoral alliance; critical of the progress made by the administration of Kurmanbek Bakiyev in tackling issues such as crime and corruption; Co-Chair. AZIMBEK BEKNAZAROV, ROZA OTUNBAYEVA.

Bright Road People's Party (Ak Zhol) (Ak Zhol Eldik Partiyasy): 720000 Bishkek, Toktogul 175/15; tel. (312) 62-82-45; internet www.akjolnarod.kg; f. Oct. 2007; supports administration of Pres. Bakiyev; Chair. ELMIRA S. IBRAIMOVA (acting).

Democratic Movement of Kyrgyzstan: 720000 Bishkek, Abdymomunova 205; tel. (312) 27-14-95; f. 1990; registered as a political party in 1993, re-registered in 2000; campaigns for civil liberties, for democratic social and legal development; participated in 2005 legislative elections as mem. of People's Movement of Kyrgyzstan electoral bloc; Leader JYPAR JEKSHEYEV; Chair. of the Exec. Cttee EDILBEK SARYBAYEV; Chair. of the Political Council VIKTOR CHERNOMORETS.

Dignity (Ar-Namys): 720040 Bishkek, Orozbekova 87; tel. and fax (312) 62-78-89; e-mail ar-namys@mail.kg; internet www.ar-namys.org; f. 1999; pro-democracy; mem. of political bloc For a Worthy Future of Kyrgyzstan United Front, formed Feb. 2007; Chair. FELIKS KULOV; c. 11,000 mems.

Fatherland (Ata Meken) Socialist Party (Ata Meken Sotsialisttik Partiyasy): 720040 Bishkek, Orozbekova 110A/2; tel. (312) 66-34-92; fax (312) 66-46-38; e-mail atameken@elcat.kg; internet www.atameken.kg; f. 1992; nationalist; supports state control of the economy; participated in 2005 legislative elections as mem. of For Fair Elections electoral bloc; mem. of political bloc People's Coalition of Democratic Forces, formed Jan. 2006 with declared aim of introducing parliamentary system of govt; Leader OMURBEK CH. TEKEBAYEV; more than 2,000 mems.

Forward, Kyrgyzstan (Alga, Kyrgyzstan): 720000 Bishkek, Moskovskaya 217; tel. (312) 65-13-57; f. 2003 by merger of the Manas El Party of Spiritual Revival, New Time, New Movement and the Party of Co-operators; merged with Birimdik in 2003, and with the Unity Party of Kyrgyzstan in 2004; fmrly supportive of regime of President Akayev; Chair. BOLOT BEGALIYEV; c. 7,000 mems (2004).

Free Kyrgyzstan Progressive-Democratic Party (ERK) (Erkin Kyrgyzstan): 720000 Bishkek, Abdymomunova 207; tel. (312) 22-49-57; fax (312) 22-60-35; f. 1991; social-democratic; participated in 2005 legislative elections as mem. of People's Movement of Kyrgyzstan electoral alliance; Chair. BEKTUR ASANOV.

Justice (Adilet): 720000 Bishkek, Bokonbayev 109; tel. (312) 66-48-17; fax (312) 66-50-84; f. 1999; re-registered 2003; campaigns for economic reform, modernization and investment; Hon. Chair. CHINGIZ T. AITMATOV; Co-Chair. TOICHUBEK KASYMOV, KUBANYCHBEK JUMALIYEV, ALTAI BORUBAYEV; c. 15,000 mems (2003).

Liberty (Erkindik): 720000 Bishkek; f. 2000; participated in 2005 legislative elections as mem. of People's Movement of Kyrgyzstan electoral bloc; Chair. TOPCHUBEK TURGUNALIYEV; c. 3,700 mems (June 2004).

New Kyrgyzstan (Jany Kyrgyzstan): 720000 Bishkek, Kiyevskaya 120; tel. (312) 21-19-61; fax (312) 21-65-04; f. 1994 as Agrarian Labour Party of Kyrgyzstan; re-registered 2001; participated in 2005 legislative elections as mem. of People's Movement of Kyrgyzstan electoral bloc; Chair. DOSBOL NUR UULU.

Party of Communists of Kyrgyzstan (KCP): 720001 Bishkek, pr. Chui 104/206; tel. (312) 62-49-99; fax (312) 67-02-55; e-mail anashparties@mail.ru; disbanded 1991, re-established 1992, re-registered 2007; successor to the Communist Party of Kyrgyz SSR;

participated in 2005 legislative elections as mem. of People's Movement of Kyrgyzstan election bloc; Chair. ISKHAK MASALIYEV; 25,000 mems.

Republican Party of Kyrgyzstan (RPK): 720000 Bishkek, Isanova 8; tel. (312) 21-14-16; registered in 1999; advocates absolute freedom of speech, full equality of all citizens before the law and environmental protection; participated in 2005 legislative elections as mem. of People's Movement of Kyrgyzstan electoral alliance; Chair. GIYAZ TOKOMBAYEV.

Social Democratic Party of Kyrgyzstan: 720000 Bishkek, Alma-Atinskaya 4B/203; tel. (312) 43-15-07; f. 1993; mem. of political bloc People's Coalition of Democratic Forces, formed Jan. 2006 with declared aim of reforming Kyrgyzstan's constitution and introducing parliamentary system of govt; Chair. ALMAZBEK ATAMBAYEV.

Union of Democratic Forces: 720040 Bishkek, Abdumomunova 207; tel. (312) 66-19-10; fax (312) 62-50-27; e-mail smanbaeva@kenesh.kg; f. 2005; registered Dec. 2005; seeks constitutional, judicial and economic reform in order to combat corruption, stimulate the economy and establish a strong state; advocates creation of parliamentary republic and introduction of parliamentary elections by party lists; mem. of political bloc People's Coalition of Democratic Forces (led by party's leader), formed Jan. 2006 with declared aim of reforming Kyrgyzstan's constitution and introducing parliamentary system of govt; Leader KUBATBEK BAIBOLOV.

The following Islamist groups were banned by the Supreme Court in November 2003: **Hizb-ut-Tahrir al-Islami** (Party of Islamic Liberation), the **Islamic Party of Turkestan**, the **East Turkestan Islamic Party** (Sharq Turkestan Islam Partiyasy) and the **East Turkestan Liberation Organization** (Sharq azzat Turkestan).

Diplomatic Representation

EMBASSIES IN KYRGYZSTAN

Afghanistan: 720040 Bishkek, Gorkogo 210; tel. (312) 69-01-76; fax (312) 69-03-30; e-mail afghanemb_bishkek@yahoo.com; Ambassador SHAHJAHAN AHMADI.

Azerbaijan: 720040 Bishkek; ARIF AGHAYEV.

Belarus: 720040 Bishkek, Moskovskaya 210; tel. (312) 65-13-65; fax (312) 65-11-77; e-mail kyrgyzstan@belembassy.org; Ambassador VALERY A. BRYLYOV.

China, People's Republic: 720001 Bishkek, Toktogula 196; tel. (312) 61-08-58; fax (312) 66-30-14; e-mail chinaemb_kg@mfa.gov.cn; Ambassador ZHANG YANNIAN.

Germany: 720040 Bishkek, Razzakova 28; tel. (312) 90-50-00; fax (312) 66-66-30; e-mail info@bischkek.diplo.de; internet www.bischkek.diplo.de; Ambassador Prof. Dr KLAUS WERNER GREWLICH.

India: 720044 Bishkek, ul. Aeroportinskaya 15A; tel. (312) 54-92-14; fax (312) 54-32-45; e-mail indembas@infotel.kg; Ambassador JYOTI SWARUP PANDE.

Iran: 720026 Bishkek, Razzakova 36; tel. (312) 62-49-17; fax (312) 22-74-98; e-mail sefabish@amil.elcat.gg; Ambassador MUHAMMAD REZA SABOURI.

Japan: 720033 Bishkek, Frunze 503; tel. (312) 61-18-75; fax (312) 61-18-82; Ambassador TETSUO ITO.

Kazakhstan: 720040 Bishkek, pr. Mira 95 A; tel. (312) 66-21-01; fax (312) 69-20-94; e-mail kaz_emb@kazemb.elcat.kg; Ambassador UMIRZAK U. UZBEKOV.

Pakistan: 720040 Bishkek, Serova Bayalinova 37; tel. (312) 62-17-11; fax (312) 66-15-50; e-mail parepbishkek@elcat.kg; Ambassador ALAM BROHI.

Russia: 720040 Bishkek, Razzakova 17; tel. (312) 62-47-38; fax (312) 62-18-23; e-mail rusemb@elcat.kg; internet www.kyrgyz.mid.ru; Ambassador VALENTIN S. VLASOV.

Syria: 720000 Bishkek; Ambassador WAHIB FADEL.

Tajikistan: 720031 Bishkek, ul. Kara-Darinskaya 36; tel. (312) 51-23-43; fax (312) 51-14-64; e-mail tojsaforat@exnet.kg; Ambassador MAKHMUD N. SOBIROV.

Turkey: 720040 Bishkek, Moskovskaya 89; tel. (312) 62-23-54; fax (312) 66-05-19; e-mail biskbe@infotel.kg; Ambassador FATMA SERPIL ALPMAN.

Ukraine: 720040 Bishkek, bulv. Panfilova 150; tel. (312) 66-55-90; fax (312) 66-20-12; e-mail emb_kg@mfa.gov.ua; internet www.mfa.gov.ua/kirgizia; Ambassador VOLODYMYR M. TYAHLO.

USA: 720016 Bishkek, pr. Mira 171; tel. (312) 55-12-41; fax (312) 55-12-64; internet bishkek.usembassy.gov; Ambassador MARIE L. YOVANOVITCH.

Uzbekistan: 720040 Bishkek, Tynystanova 213; tel. (312) 66-20-65; fax (312) 66-44-03; e-mail uzbembish@infotel.kg; Ambassador ZIYADULLA S. PULATKHOJAYEV.

Judicial System

Supreme Court: 720000 Bishkek, Orozbekova 37; tel. (312) 66-33-18; fax (312) 66-29-46; e-mail scourt@bishkek.gov.kg; Chair. JANYL ALIYEVA.

Constitutional Court: 720040 Bishkek, pr. Erkindik 39; tel. (312) 62-04-95; fax (312) 66-28-19; e-mail konsud@bishkek.gov.kg; Chair. SVETLANA SYDYKOVA.

Office of the Prosecutor-General: 720040 Bishkek; Prosecutor-General ELMURZA R. SATYBALDIYEV.

Religion

ISLAM

The majority of Kyrgyz are Sunni Muslims (Hanafi school), as are some other groups living in the republic, such as Uzbeks and Tajiks.

Chief Mufti of the Muslims of Kyrgyzstan: Haji MURATALY AJY JUMANOV, 720000 Bishkek.

International Islamic Centre of Kyrgyzstan: 714018 Osh; Pres. Haji SADYKZHAN KAMALUDDIN.

CHRISTIANITY

Roman Catholic Church

The Church is represented in Kyrgyzstan by an Apostolic Administration, established in March 2006. There were an estimated 500 adherents in the country at 31 December 2005.

Apostolic Administrator: Most Rev. NIKOLAUS MESSMER (Titular Bishop of Carmeiano), 720072 Bishkek, Vasilyeva 203; tel. and fax (312) 21-78-32; e-mail nikmessmer@hotmail.com; internet www.catholic-kyrgyzstan.org.

Russian Orthodox Church (Moscow Patriarchate)

The Russian Orthodox Church (Moscow Patriarchate) in Kyrgyzstan comes under the jurisdiction of the Eparchy of Tashkent and Central Asia, headed by the Metropolitan of Tashkent and Central Asia, VLADIMIR (IKIM), resident in Uzbekistan.

JUDAISM

At the 1989 census, around 6,000 Jews were enumerated as living within the Kyrgyz SSR, mostly in Bishkek. By 1993 around 3,000 Jews had emigrated from Kyrgyzstan, mostly to Israel, and outmigration continued subsequently.

Chief Rabbi: Rabbi ARIYE RAICHMAN, 720000 Bishkek, Sutombayev 193, Khabad Lyubavich Synagogue; tel. and fax (312) 68-19-66; e-mail arier@mail.ru.

The Press

In 2004 there were 83 non-daily newspapers, with an average circulation of 427,800 copies. Two daily newspapers were published in that year, with an average circulation of 21,000 copies.

PRINCIPAL NEWSPAPERS

Asaba (The Standard): 720000 Bishkek; tel. (312) 26-47-39; weekly; in Kyrgyz; supplement in Russian *Asaba-Bishkek*; Editors JUMABEK MEDERALIYEV (*Asaba*), BERMET BUKASHEVA (*Asaba-Bishkek*).

Belyi Parokhod (White Steamship): 720040 Bishkek, Ibraimova 24; tel. (312) 42-24-80; e-mail parohod@list.ru; internet www.parohod.kg; f. 1997; in Russian; independent.

Bishkek Observer: 720021 Bishkek, Frunze 429; tel. (312) 28-95-96; fax (312) 68-22-61; e-mail observer@elcat.kg; f. 2000; weekly; independent; in English; Editor AVTAR SINGH.

Bishkek Taims (Bishkek Times): 720040 Bishkek, Pushkina 70; tel. (312) 62-15-68; e-mail b-times@yandex.ru; internet www.presskg.com/bt; Editor-in-Chief NURALY KAPAROV.

Chui Baayni/Chuiskiye Izvestiya (Chui News): 720300 Bishkek, Ibraimova 24; tel. (312) 42-83-31; weekly; organ of Chui Oblast administration; Kyrgyz and Russian edns; Editor (Kyrgyz edn) KURMANBEK RAMATOV; Editor (Russian edn) A. BLINDINA.

Delo N^o... (Case Number...): 720000 Bishkek; tel. (312) 62-19-80; fax (312) 66-38-66; e-mail cactus@elcat.kg; internet delo.to.kg; f. 1991; weekly; in Russian; independent; politics, crime; Editor VIKTOR ZAPOLSKII; circ. 30,000.

Erkin Too (Free Mountain): 720040 Bishkek, Ibraimova 24; tel. (312) 42-03-15; fax (312) 42-22-42; f. 1991; 2 a week; organ of the Government; publishes laws, presidential, parliamentary and govt decrees, and other legal documents; Kyrgyz; Editor-in-Chief NURLAN SHAKIYEV; circ. 10,000.

KYRGYZSTAN

Gazeta.kg: 720000 Bishkek; internet gazeta.kg; online only, in Russian and English; independent; politics and analysis of current affairs; culture; regional news; f. 2003.

Kyrgyz Madaniyaty (Kyrgyz Culture): 720301 Bishkek, Bokonbayeva 99; tel. (312) 26-14-58; f. 1967; weekly; organ of the Union of Writers; Editor NURALY KAPAROV; circ. 15,940.

Kyrgyz Rukhu: 720040 Bishkek, Abdymomunova 193; tel. and fax (312) 66-45-43; f. 1991; weekly; Kyrgyz; Editor-in-Chief BAKBYRBEK ALENOV; circ. c. 5,000.

Kyrgyz Tuusu (Flag of Kyrgyzstan): 720040 Bishkek, Abdymomunova 193; tel. (312) 62-20-18; fax (312) 62-20-25; e-mail tuusu@infotel.kg; internet www.tuusu.kg; f. 1924; fmrly *Sovettik Kyrgyzstan*; daily; organ of the Government; Kyrgyz; Editor-in-Chief ZHEDIGER I. SAALAYEV; circ. 17,000–20,000.

Limon (Lemon): 720040 Bishkek, Moskovskaya 189; tel. (312) 65-03-03; fax (312) 65-02-04; e-mail limon@akipress.org; internet www.limon.kg; f. 1994; in Russian; youth newspaper; independent; Editor-in-Chief VENERA JAMONA KULOVA.

MSN—Moya Stolitsa—Novosti (My Capital City—News): 720001 Bishkek, Turusbekova 47; tel. (312) 21-29-79; fax (312) 21-58-94; e-mail city@infotel.kg; internet www.msn.kg; f. 2001; independent; 3 a week; in Russian; Editor-in-Chief ALEXANDER KIM; circ. 5,000 (Tues. and Thurs.), 50,000 (Fri.).

Slovo Kyrgyzstana (Word of Kyrgyzstan): 720004 Bishkek, Abdymomunova 193; tel. (312) 66-60-88; fax (312) 66-59-28; e-mail slovo@infotel.kg; internet www.sk.kg; f. 1925; daily; organ of the Government; in Russian; Editor ALEKSANDR I. MALEVANY.

The Times of Central Asia: 720000 Bishkek, Abdrakhmanova 175A/303–304; tel. (312) 66-17-37; fax (312) 66-42-95; e-mail edittimes@infotel.kg; internet www.timesca-europe.com; f. 1995; weekly; in English; also distributed in Kazakhstan, Turkmenistan and Uzbekistan, and internationally; Editor-in-Chief LYDIA SAVINA.

Vechernii Bishkek (Bishkek Evening News): 720021 Bishkek, Usenbayeva 2; tel. (312) 68-21-21; fax (312) 68-02-68; e-mail webmaster@vb.kg; internet www.vb.kg; f. 1974; daily; independent; in Russian; Editor-in-Chief GENNADII A. KUZMIN; circ. (Mon.–Thur.) 20,000, (Fri.) 50,000.

Zaman Kyrgyzstan (Herald of Kyrgyzstan): 720040 Bishkek, Ibraimova 24; tel. (312) 42-62-35; e-mail zamantur@elcat.kg; f. 1992; weekly; independent; in Kyrgyz, Turkish and English; Editor-in-Chief A. KUSH; circ. 15,000.

PRINCIPAL PERIODICALS

Monthly, unless otherwise indicated.

Aalam (Universe): 720000 Bishkek, Baitik Baatyra 73; tel. (312) 54-42-07; fax (312) 54-42-09; e-mail aalamga@hotmail.kg; f. 1991; independent; Kyrgyz; weekly; Editor-in-Chief ELNURA SHABDANBEKOVA; circ. 18,000.

Agym (Current): 720040 Bishkek, pr. Manasa 40; tel. (312) 66-56-70; fax (312) 66-55-48; e-mail agym@users.kyrnet.kg; internet presskg.com/agym; f. 1992; 2 a week; in Kyrgyz; political; Editor-in-Chief MELIS ESHIMKANOV.

AKIpress: 720010 Bishkek, Moskovskaya 189; tel. and fax (312) 61-18-23; fax (312) 65-02-02; e-mail admin@akipress.org; internet www.akipress.org; f. 1993; in Russian; monthly; independent; analysis of political and economic affairs; Editor-in-Chief SAMAGAN AITYMBETOV; circ. 1,000.

Kut Bilim (Good Knowledge): 720001 Bishkek, Tynystanova 257; tel. (312) 62-04-86; e-mail kutbilim@elcat.kg; internet kb.host.net.kg; f. 1953 as *Mugalimder Gazetasy*; current name adopted 1993; organ of the Ministry of Education, Science and Youth Affairs; weekly; in Kyrgyz; Editor-in-Chief KUBATBEK CHEKIROV; circ. 6,000.

Literaturnyi Kyrgyzstan (Literary Kyrgyzstan): 720301 Bishkek, Pushkina 70; tel. (312) 626-16-01; e-mail literary_kyrgyzstan@rambler.ru; internet www.lk.to.kg; f. 1955; journal of the Union of Writers; fiction, literary criticism, journalism; in Russian; Editor-in-Chief A. I. IVANOV; circ. 3,000.

Zdravookhraneniye Kyrgyzstana (Healthcare of Kyrgyzstan): 720005 Bishkek, Moskovskaya 148; tel. (312) 62-26-80; fax (312) 66-07-17; e-mail mz@med.kg; f. 1938; 4 a year; publ. by the Ministry of Health; health research; in Russian; Editor-in-Chief T. ABDRAIMOV; circ. 3,000 (2007).

NEWS AGENCY

Kabar Kyrgyz News Agency: 720011 Bishkek, Sovetskaya 175; tel. (312) 62-05-74; fax (312) 66-11-68; e-mail s1@kabar.gov.kg; internet www.kabar.kg; Dir OLEG RYABOV.

Publishers

Ilim (Science): 720071 Bishkek, pr. Chui 265A; tel. (312) 65-56-88; e-mail ilimph@mail.ru; f. 1954; state-owned; scientific and science fiction; Dir L. V. TARASOVA.

Kyrgyz-Russian Slavic University Publishing House (Izdatelstvo Kyrgyzsko-Rossiiskogo slavyanskogo universiteta): 720000 Bishkek, Kiyevskaya 44; tel. (312) 25-53-60; internet www.krsu.edu.kg/Rus/EduIzd.htm; f. 1995; academic works of university staff; textbooks; Dir. LARISA V. TARASOVA.

Kyrgyzstan: 720000 Bishkek, Abdrakhmanova 170; tel. (312) 62-19-47; politics, science, economics, literature; Dir BERIK N. CHALAGYZOV.

Tsentr Gosudarstvennogo Yazyka i Kyrgyzskoi Entsiklopedii (Centre for the State Language and the Kyrgyz Encyclopedia): 720040 Bishkek, bul. Erkindik 56; tel. (312) 62-50-72; fax (312) 62-50-03; e-mail gocst.ensk@mail.ru; dictionaries and encyclopedias; Dir BAKTYGUL KALDYBAYEVA; Editor-in-Chief USEN A. ASANOV.

Broadcasting and Communications

National Communications Agency of the Kyrgyz Republic: 720005 Bishkek, Baytik Baatyra 7B; tel. (312) 54-41-03; fax (312) 54-41-05; internet www.nas.kg; f. 1997; Dir KUBAT S. KYDYRALIYEV.

TELECOMMUNICATIONS

BiMoKom: tel. (555) 50-00-00; fax (312) 90-52-40; internet www.megacom.kg; f. 2006; provides mobile cellular telecommunications services in Bishkek, Manas Airport, the shores of Lake Issyk-Kul and in Chui, Issyk-Kul, Osh, Dzalal-Abad, Naryn, Talas and Batken Oblasts under the Megacom brand name; Dir ANDREI G. SILICH; c. 600,000 subscribers (Jan. 2008).

Kyrgyztelekom: 720000 Bishkek, pr. Chui 96; tel. (312) 68-16-16; fax (312) 66-24-24; e-mail info@kt.kg; internet www.kt.kg; f. 1993, transformed into joint stock co in 1997; state telecommunications co; 77.84% state-owned; 51% scheduled for privatization; Chair. of the Bd of Dirs SALAIDIN A. AVAZOV; Mems of the Bd of Dirs MYKTARBEK JUMABAYEV, BURKAN JUMABAYEV, DUISHENBEK R. ABDYLDAYEV, MYRBEK T. BATAKANOV.

Sky Mobile: 720011 Bishkek, pr. Chui 121; tel. (312) 58-79-15; fax (312) 90-09-16; e-mail office@bitel.kg; internet www.bitel.kg; f. 1997; provides mobile cellular telecommunications services under the Bitel and Mobi brand names; Dir-Gen. D. V. SHERSHNEV; over 1m. subscribers (Jan. 2008).

BROADCASTING

Radio and Television

State National Television and Radio Broadcasting Corpn: 720010 Bishkek, Molodoi Gvardii 59; tel. (312) 65-56-77; internet www.ktr.kg; Pres. MELIS ESHIMKANOV.

Kyrgyz Public Educational Radio and Television (Kyrgyzskoye Obshchestvennoye Obrazovatelnoye Radio i Televideniye—KOORT): 720031 Bishkek, Ibraimova 24; tel. (312) 54-77-27; fax (312) 54-77-15; e-mail office@koort.kg; f. 1997; broadcasts in Kyrgyz and Russian; educational programmes and entertainment; Gen. Dir AZIMA ABDIMAMINOVA; 103 employees.

Radio

Radio Azattyk: 720000 Bishkek; tel. (312) 66-88-17; fax (312) 66-68-14; internet www.azattyk.org; Kyrgyz language news broadcasts by Radio Free Europe/Radio Liberty (USA—based in the Czech Republic); Dir TYNTCHTYKBEK TCHOROEV; Bureau Chief KUBAT OTORBAEV.

Kyrgyz Radio: 720010 Bishkek, Molodoi Gvardii 59; tel. (312) 25-79-36; fax (312) 65-10-64; internet www.ktr.kg; f. 1931; broadcasts in Kyrgyz, Russian, English, German, Ukrainian, Uzbek, Dungan and Uigur; subsidiary of State National Television and Radio Broadcasting Corpn; Dir BAIMA SUTENOVA.

Radio Television Pyramid: 720300 Bishkek, Jantosheva 70; tel. and fax (312) 51-00-15; e-mail pyramid@tom.kg; f. 1992; privately owned; broadcasts to Bishkek and neighbouring regions; Pres. MIRBEK OROZOV.

There are several other private radio stations operating in Kyrgyzstan.

Television

Kyrgyz Television: 720300 Bishkek, Molodoi Gvardii 63; tel. (312) 25-79-36; fax (312) 25-79-30; internet www.ktr.kg; subsidiary of State National Television and Radio Broadcasting Corpn; Pres. KYYAS MOLDOKASYMOV.

KYRGYZSTAN

TV Pyramid: 720005 Bishkek; tel. and fax (312) 41-01-31; e-mail pyramid@ss5-22.kyrnet.kg; f. 1991; privately owned; broadcasts to Bishkek and neighbouring regions; Pres. ADYLBEK T. BIINAZAROV.

Finance

(cap. = capital; res = reserves; m. = million; brs = branches; amounts in soms, unless otherwise indicated)

BANKING

Central Bank

National Bank of the Kyrgyz Republic (Kyrgyz Respublikasynyn Uluttuk Banky): 720040 Bishkek, Umetaliyeva 101; tel. (312) 66-90-08; fax (312) 61-04-56; e-mail pr@nbkr.kg; internet www.nbkr.kg; f. 1991, name changed in 1992, and as above in 1993; cap. 50m., res 921.9m., dep. 9,840.0m. (Dec. 2005); Chair. MARAT O. ALAPAYEV.

Other Banks

Amanbank: 720400 Bishkek, Tynystanova 249; tel. and fax (312) 62-20-77; fax (312) 90-04-97; e-mail bank@amanbank.kg; internet www.amanbank.kg; f. 1995; cap. 65m., res 8.6m., dep. 116.0m. (Aug. 2006); Chair. JOHN I. JAPARKULOV; 6 brs.

AsiaUniversalBank: 720001 Bishkek, Toktogula 187; tel. (312) 62-02-52; fax (312) 62-02-50; e-mail reception@aub.kg; internet www.aub.kg; f. 1997; present name adopted 2000; cap. 300.0m., res 296.4m., dep. 4,772.6m. (Dec. 2006); Chair. MIKHAIL NADEL; Chief Exec. NURDIN ABDRAZAKOV; 2 brs.

ATFBank-Kyrgyzstan: 720070 Bishkek, Jibek Jolu 493; tel. and fax (312) 67-04-71; e-mail bank@atfbank.kg; internet www.atfbank.kg; f. 1992; fmrly Energobank, present name adopted 2006; cap. 500.0m., res 1.5m., dep. 1,876.0m. (Dec. 2006); Pres. BAKIRDIN E. SARTKAZIYEV; 7 brs.

Bank Bakai: 720001 Bishkek, Isanov 77; tel. (312) 66-06-10; fax (312) 66-06-12; e-mail bank@bakai.kg; internet www.bakai.kg; f. 1998; cap. 100.0m., res 544.2m. (Aug. 2007); Chair. BAKYTA MUNDUZBAYEVA; Pres. MUHAMMAD IBRAGIMOV; 5 brs.

Demir Kyrgyz International Bank (DKIB): 720001 Bishkek, pr. Chui 245; tel. (312) 61-06-10; fax (312) 66-64-44; e-mail dkib@demirbank.kg; internet www.demirbank.kg; f. 1997; cap. 132.5m., res 0.0, dep. 124.3m. (Dec. 2006); Chair. ISMAIL HASAN AKCAKAYALIOGLU; Gen. Man. AHMET KAMIL PARMAKSIZ; 3 brs.

Ecobank: 720031 Bishkek, Geologicheskii per. 17; tel. (312) 54-35-82; fax (312) 54-35-80; e-mail office@ecobank.kg; internet www.ecobank.kg; f. 1996 as Bank Rossiiskii Kredit; name changed 1998; joint-stock commercial bank; cap. 78.0m., dep. 181.5m. (Oct. 2003); Chair. NURLANBEK A. SAGYNDYKOV; Deputy Chair. GALINA V. HOHLOVA, LARISA G. CHENGIZ; 5 brs.

Investment Export-Import Bank—Ineximbank: 720001 Bishkek, Kalyk Akiyeva 57; tel. (312) 65-06-10; fax (312) 62-06-54; e-mail info@ineximbank.com; internet www.ineximbank.com; f. 1996; present name adopted 2001; cap. 480.0m., res 3.4m., dep. 2,894.2m. (Dec. 2006); Chair.of Bd MURAT KUNAKUNOV; 4 brs.

Kyrgyz Investment and Credit Bank: 720001 Bishkek, Ibraimova 115A, Dordoi Plaza Business Centre; tel. (312) 69-05-55; fax (312) 69-05-60; e-mail kicb@kicb.net; internet www.kicb.net; f. 2001; cap. US $10m., res $23.3m., dep. $23.3m. (Dec. 2005); Chief Exec. KUANG YOUNG CHOI.

Kyrgyzstan Bank: 720001 Bishkek, Togolok Moldo 54A; tel. (312) 61-16-66; fax (312) 61-02-20; e-mail akb@bankkg.kg; internet www.bankkg.kg; f. 1991; cap. 120.9m., res 6.3m., dep. 1,035.5m. (Dec. 2004); Chair. ABIROV NURBEK; 29 brs.

Tolubay Bank: 720010 Bishkek, Toktogula 247; tel. (312) 24-02-46; fax (312) 25-63-14; e-mail tolubay@infotel.kg; internet www.tolubaybank.kg; f. 1996; cap. 48m., res 1.6m., dep. 195.4m. (Dec. 2005); Chair. JENISHBEK S. BAIGUTTIYEV; 1 br.

COMMODITY EXCHANGE

Kyrgyzstan Commodity and Raw Materials Exchange: 720001 Bishkek, Belinskaya 40; tel. (312) 22-13-75; fax (312) 22-27-44; f. 1990; Gen. Dir TEMIR SARIYEV.

STOCK EXCHANGE

Kyrgyz Stock Exchange (Kyrgyz Fonduk Birzhasy/Kyrgyzskaya Fondovaya Birzha): 720010 Bishkek, Moskovskaya 172; tel. (312) 66-50-59; fax (312) 66-15-95; e-mail kse@kse.kg; internet www.kse.kg; Pres. ANDREI V. ZALEPO.

INSURANCE

At 1 July 2005 there were 12 private insurance companies operating in Kyrgyzstan, including two that were partly Russian-owned and three that were entirely British-owned. In late 2007 there were 15 insurance companies operating in the country.

Anglo-Kyrgyz Insurance Co: 720000 Bishkek, ul. Akhunbaeva 100; tel. (312) 54-90-23; fax (312) 54-90-49; e-mail anglokgz@elcat.kg.

ATN Polis: 720000 Bishkek, ul. Isanova 42/1; tel. (312) 93-79-37; fax (312) 90-32-52; e-mail info@atnpolis.kg; internet www.atnpolis.kg; f. 2001; life and non-life.

Insurance Group of Central Asia: 720000 Bishkek, Baitik Baatyra 191, Hyatt Hotel, room 103; tel. (312) 68-12-21.

Kyrgyzinstrakh: 720001 Bishkek, pr. Chui 219; tel. (312) 21-95-54; fax (312) 21-99-44; e-mail kinstrakh@infotel.kg; internet kyrgyzinstrakh.com.kg; f. 1996 by the Russian joint-stock insurance company Investstrakh, Kyrgyz insurance companies and the Kyrgyz Government to insure foreign investors; brs in Karakol and Osh; insurance and reinsurance; Chair. of Bd E. M. SEIDAKHMETOVA.

Kyrgyzstan Insurance Co: 720000 Bishkek, ul. Moskovskaya 76B; tel. (312) 28-28-15; e-mail office@insurance.kg; internet www.insurance.kg; f. 1991; Dir MARIYA ADENOVA.

Trade and Industry

GOVERNMENT AGENCIES

National Institute of Standards and Metrology: 720040 Bishkek, Panfilova 197; tel. (312) 62-68-70; fax (312) 66-13-67; e-mail nism@nism.gov.kg; internet www.nism.gov.kg; f. 1927 as the Division of the Chamber of Measures and Weights; present name adopted 2005; certification, control and testing of products and services; standardization, metrology, accreditation; Dir PATIDIN ATAKHANOV.

State Agency for Geology and Mineral Resources: 720739 Bishkek, pr. Erkindik 2; tel. (312) 66-49-01; fax (312) 66-03-91; e-mail mail@geoagency.bishkek.gov.kg; internet www.kgs.bishkek.gov.kg; Chair. SHEISHENALY MURZAGAZIYEV.

State Committee for Management of State Property: 720017 Bishkek, Moskovskaya 151; tel. (312) 62-68-52; fax (312) 66-02-36; e-mail mail@spf.bishkek.gov.kg; internet www.spf.gov.kg; f. 1991; responsible for the privatization of state-owned enterprises and deals with bankruptcies; Chair. TURSUN O. TURDUMAMBETOV.

CHAMBER OF COMMERCE

Chamber of Commerce and Industry of the Kyrgyz Republic: 720001 Bishkek, Kiyevskaya 107; tel. (312) 21-05-65; fax (312) 21-05-75; e-mail cci-kr@totel.kg; internet www.ihk-kg.de; f. 1959; supports foreign economic relations and the development of small and medium-sized enterprises; Pres. BORIS V. PERFILIYEV.

TRADE ASSOCIATION

Kyrgyzvneshtorg: 720033 Bishkek, Abdymomunova 276; tel. (312) 21-39-78; fax (312) 66-08-36; e-mail kvt@infotel.kg; f. 1992; export-import org.; Gen. Dir KADYRBEK K. KALIYEV.

UTILITIES

Electricity

NES Kyrgyzstana (National Electric Grid of Kyrgyzstan) (NESK): 720070 Bishkek, pr. Jibek Zholu 326; tel. (312) 66-10-00; fax (312) 66-06-56; e-mail nesk@elcat.kg; internet www.energo.kz; f. 2001; comprises seven companies, including four regional distribution companies, Severeletro, Oshelektro, Zhalabadelektro, Vostoelektro; one heating company, Bishkekteploset; 80.5% state-owned, 13.2% by the Social Fund of the Kyrgyz Republic; reorganization and privatization pending in 2008; cap. 1,597.4m. som (June 2006); Gen. Dir AVTANDIL CH. SYDYKOV.

Gas

KyrKazGaz: 720000 Bishkek, Baytik Baatyr 3/10; tel. (312) 56-40-51; fax (312) 59-57-05; e-mail office@kyrkazgaz.elcat.kg; internet www.kyrkazgaz.kg; f. 2004 by union of Kyrgyzgaz (which distributes gas within Kyrgyzstan) and KazTransGaz (which operates gas pipelines in Kazakhstan, Kyrgyzstan and Uzbekistan); Dir-Gen (KyrKazGaz) KYBANYCHBEK K. JUSUPOV; Dir-Gen.(Kyrgyzgaz) SADAMAT K. AYTIKEYEV.

TRADE UNIONS

Kyrgyzstan Federation of Trade Unions: 720032 Bishkek, Chui 207; tel. (312) 21-49-30; fax (312) 21-76-87; affiliated with the General Confed. of Trade Unions; Chair. SAGYN BOZGUNBAYEV.

Transport

RAILWAYS

Kyrgyzstan's railway network consists of only one main line (340 km) in northern Kyrgyzstan, which connects the country, via Kazakhstan, with the railway system of Russia. Osh, Jalal-Abad and other towns in regions of Kyrgyzstan bordering Uzbekistan are linked to that country by short lengths of railway track. In 2001 the Governments of Kyrgyzstan and the People's Republic of China signed a memorandum on the construction of a rail link from Kashgar (China) to Bishkek. In 2003 Kyrgyzstan and Kazakhstan announced that a 100-km railway link was to be built between Issyk-Kul and Almaty, Kazakhstan, although by mid-2007 work had yet to commence.

Kyrgyz Railway Administration (Kyrgyz Temir Jolu): 720009 Bishkek, L. Tolstogo 83; tel. (312) 62-48-65; fax (312) 65-06-90; e-mail asoup@imfiko.bishkek.su; internet railway.aknet.kg; f. 1992; Pres. I. S. OMURKULOV.

ROADS

In 1999 Kyrgyzstan's road network totalled an estimated 18,500 km, including 140 km of motorway; in 1996 there were 3,200 km of main roads and 6,380 km of secondary roads. About 91% of roads were paved. Work on the third and final phase of a project to reconstruct the main Bishkek—Osh highway was completed in 2004.

CIVIL AVIATION

There are three international airports at Bishkek (Manas), Osh and Tamchy (in the Issyk-Kul region).

Air Kyrgyzstan (AK): 720040 Bishkek, pr. Manasa 12A; tel. (312) 61-02-47; fax (312) 61-02-35; e-mail company@air.kg; internet www.air.kg; f. 2006 by merger of Altyn Air and Kyrgyzstan Airlines; state-owned; charter passenger services.

Tourism

There was little tourism in Kyrgyzstan during the Soviet period. However, the Government hoped that the country's spectacular and largely unspoilt mountain scenery, as well as the great crater lake of Issyk-Kul, might attract foreign tourists and investment. In 2005 there were 315,290 tourist arrivals, compared with 398,078 in 2004. Tourism receipts (including passenger transport) amounted to US $94m. in 2005.

State Committee for Tourism, Sport and Youth Policy: 720033 Bishkek, Togolok Moldo 17; tel. (312) 62-24-99; fax (312) 21-28-45; e-mail gktsm@gks.gov.kg; Chair. TURUSBEK CH. MAMASHEV.

LAOS

Introductory Survey

Location, Climate, Language, Religion, Flag, Capital

The Lao People's Democratic Republic is a land-locked country in South-East Asia, bordered by the People's Republic of China to the north, by Viet Nam to the east, by Cambodia to the south, by Thailand to the west and by Myanmar (formerly Burma) to the north-west. The climate is tropical, with a rainy monsoon season lasting from May to September. The temperature in the capital ranges between 23°C and 38°C in the hottest month, April, and between 14°C and 28°C in the coolest month, January. Laos comprises 47 ethnic groups. The official language, Lao or Laotian, is spoken by about two-thirds of the population. French is also spoken, and there are numerous tribal languages, including Meo. The principal religion is Buddhism. There are also some Christians and followers of animist beliefs. The national flag (proportions 2 by 3) has three horizontal stripes, of red, blue (half the total depth) and red, with a white disc in the centre. The capital is Vientiane (Viangchan).

Recent History

Laos was formerly a part of French Indo-China and comprised the three principalities of Luang Prabang, Vientiane and Champasak. These were merged in 1946, when France recognized Sisavang Vong, ruler of Luang Prabang since 1904, as King of Laos. In May 1947 the King promulgated a democratic constitution (although women were not allowed to vote until 1957). The Kingdom of Laos became independent, within the French Union, in July 1949, and full sovereignty was recognized by France in October 1953. The leading royalist politician was Prince Souvanna Phouma, who was Prime Minister in 1951–54, 1956–58, 1960 and in 1962–75. King Sisavang Vong died in October 1959, and was succeeded by his son, Savang Vatthana.

From 1950 the Royal Government was opposed by the Neo Lao Haksat (Lao Patriotic Front—LPF), an insurgent movement formed by a group of former anti-French activists. The LPF's Chairman was Prince Souphanouvong, a half-brother of Prince Souvanna Phouma, but its dominant element was the communist People's Party of Laos (PPL), led by Kaysone Phomvihane. During the 1950s the LPF's armed forces, the Pathet Lao, gradually secured control of the north-east of the country with the assistance of the Vietnamese communists, the Viet Minh, who were engaged in war with the French (until 1954). Several agreements between the Royal Government and the LPF, attempting to end the guerrilla war and reunite the country, failed during the 1950s and early 1960s. By 1965 the *de facto* partition of Laos was established, with the LPF refusing to participate in national elections and consolidating its power over the north-eastern provinces.

During the 1960s, as the 'Ho Chi Minh Trail' (the communist supply route to South Viet Nam) ran through Pathet Lao-controlled areas, Laos remained closely involved with the war between communist forces and anti-communist troops (supported by the USA) in Viet Nam. In 1973 the Viet Nam peace negotiations included provisions for a cease-fire in Laos. A new Government was formed in April 1974 under Prince Souvanna Phouma, with royalist, neutralist and LPF participation; Prince Souphanouvong was appointed Chairman of the Joint National Political Council. However, the LPF increased its power and eventually gained effective control of the country. This was confirmed by election victories in October and November 1975. In November King Savang Vatthana abdicated, and Prince Souvanna Phouma resigned.

In December 1975 the National Congress of People's Representatives (264 delegates elected by local authorities) abolished the monarchy and elected a 45-member legislative body, the Supreme People's Council. Souphanouvong was appointed President of the renamed Lao People's Democratic Republic and President of the Supreme People's Council. Kaysone Phomvihane, who had become Secretary-General of the Phak Pasason Pativat Lao (Lao People's Revolutionary Party—LPRP, a successor to the PPL), was appointed Prime Minister. The former King, Savang Vatthana, was designated Supreme Counsellor to the President, but he refused to co-operate with the new regime and was arrested in March 1977. (He was subsequently stated to have died in a 're-education camp'.) The LPF was replaced in February 1979 by the Lao Front for National Construction (LFNC), under the leadership of the LPRP.

In October 1986 the ailing Souphanouvong announced his resignation from his duties as President of the Republic (while retaining the title) and of the Supreme People's Assembly (as the Supreme People's Council had been renamed). Phoumi Vongvichit, formerly a Vice-Chairman in the Council of Ministers, became acting President of the Republic, while Sisomphon Lovansai, a Vice-President of the Supreme People's Assembly and a member of the LPRP Political Bureau (Politburo), became acting President of the Assembly. In November Kaysone Phomvihane was re-elected Secretary-General of the LPRP. In September 1987 it was announced that Phoumi Vongvichit had also replaced Souphanouvong as Chairman of the LFNC.

In June 1988 elections (the first since the formation of the Lao People's Democratic Republic) took place to determine the members of 113 district-level People's Councils. The LFNC approved 4,462 candidates to contest 2,410 seats. Provincial prefectural elections took place in November, when 898 candidates contested 651 seats. At the legislative election of March 1989, 121 candidates contested 79 seats in the enlarged Supreme People's Assembly. At its inaugural session in May, Nouhak Phoumsavanh (a Vice-Chairman of the Council of Ministers) was elected President of the Assembly.

Armed opposition to the Government persisted during the 1980s, particularly among hill tribes. In October 1982 Gen. Phoumi Nosavan, a 'conservative' who had been living in exile since 1965, formed the anti-communist Royal Lao Democratic Government, led by former Laotian military officers. However, many prominent exiles and resistance fighters in the United Front for the National Liberation of the Lao People (UFNLLP—formed in September 1980, and reportedly led by Gen. Phoumi since mid-1981) dissociated themselves from the Royal Government, which had established itself in southern Laos. In October 1988 the Government announced the capture of the Chief of Staff of the UFNLLP.

In December 1989 the right-wing United Lao National Liberation Front (ULNLF) proclaimed the 'Revolutionary Provisional Government' of Laos. The self-styled Government, which was headed by Outhong Souvannavong (the former President of the Royal Council of King Savang Vatthana), claimed to have used military force to 'liberate' one-third of Laotian territory. Although there were reports of attacks by insurgent guerrillas in northern Laos at this time, it was widely assumed that the ULNLF's claims were exaggerated and that its proclamation was an attempt to elicit popular support. Responsibility for defence was reportedly allocated to Gen. Vang Pao, a leader of the Hmong tribe who in the 1970s had been a commander of the Royalist army (and who had lived in exile in the USA since 1975); Somphorn Wang (also formerly a prominent Royalist) was described as secretary of state in the 'Revolutionary Provisional Government'. In late 1992 Gen. Vang Pao reportedly travelled to Singapore to direct an unsuccessful military operation from Thailand. In October Gen. Vang Pao's brother, Vang Fung, and another Hmong rebel, Moua Yee Julan (who were allegedly preparing an incursion into Laos under Gen. Vang Pao's command), were arrested in Thailand. In September 1993 Thai troops launched an offensive against Gen. Vang Pao's forces, expelling 320 rebels from Thai territory.

In June 1990 a draft Constitution, enshrining free-market principles, was published in the LPRP newspaper, *Pasason*. Later in the same month the Supreme People's Assembly approved legislation that included provision for the ownership of property, for inheritance rights and contractual obligations. In October three former government officials were arrested in connection with what were termed 'activities aimed at overthrowing the regime'. It was reported in Thailand that they had formed part of a 'Social Democrat Group', which was actively seeking the introduction of multi-party democracy. In November 1992 all three were sentenced to 14 years' imprisonment.

In March 1991, at the Fifth Congress of the LPRP, Souphanouvong retired from all his party posts. Phoumi Vongvichit and

Sisomphon Lovansai also retired, and the three were appointed to a newly created advisory board to the LPRP Central Committee. Kaysone Phomvihane's title was altered from General Secretary to President of the LPRP, and his power was slightly enhanced following the abolition of the party Secretariat. A new Political Bureau and (younger) Party Central Committee were elected. Gen. Sisavat Keobounphan, the military Chief of the General Staff, was not re-elected to the Political Bureau. The leadership pledged a continuance of free-market economic reforms, but denied the need for political pluralism. However, the national motto ('peace, independence, unity, socialism') was changed to 'peace, independence, democracy, unity, prosperity'.

On 14 August 1991 the Supreme People's Assembly adopted a new Constitution, which provided for a National Assembly, confirmed the leading role of the LPRP, enshrined the right to private ownership, and endowed the presidency with executive powers; new electoral legislation was also promulgated. Kaysone Phomvihane was appointed President of Laos. Gen. Khamtay Siphandone, a Vice-Chairman of the Council of Ministers, Minister of National Defence and Supreme Commander of the Lao People's Army, replaced Kaysone Phomvihane as Chairman of the Council of Ministers, restyled Prime Minister.

Kaysone Phomvihane died in November 1992. He was replaced as President of the LPRP by Gen. Khamtay Siphandone, and on 25 November a specially convened meeting of the Supreme People's Assembly elected Nouhak Phoumsavanh as President of State. Elections to the new National Assembly took place on 20 December; 99.33% of eligible voters participated in the election, in which 154 LFNC-approved candidates contested 85 seats. On 22 February 1993 the new National Assembly re-elected Nouhak Phoumsavanh as President, confirmed Khamtay Siphandone as Prime Minister, and implemented the most extensive reorganization of the Council of Ministers since the LPRP's accession to power in 1975. Phoumi Vongvichit died in January 1994, and Souphanouvong in January 1995.

Although the 20th anniversary of the beginning of communist rule was celebrated in 1995, the Laotian Government was gradually attempting to replace communist ideology with Lao nationalism, as Laos developed as a market economy with increasing foreign participation. In July senior Buddhist monks were assembled in Vientiane (as Buddhism was deemed central to Laotian cultural identity) and were encouraged by the Government to lead a 'cultural renaissance'. Meanwhile, the Government urged the security forces to suppress social problems, particularly corruption and prostitution, perceived as arising from increasing external influences.

The outcome of the LPRP congress at the end of March 1996 consolidated the country's apparent progress towards a form of military-dominated authoritarian government. The armed forces gained a majority of seats on the new nine-member Political Bureau; Khamtay Siphandone was elected as its President (replacing Nouhak Phoumsavanh, who retired from this post), and the Minister of National Defence and Commander-in-Chief of the armed forces, Lt-Gen. Choummali Saignason, was promoted to third position, after the Chairman of the National Assembly, Lt-Gen. Saman Vignaket. The most significant development was the failure of Khamphoui Keoboualapha, a Deputy Prime Minister responsible for many of Laos's reforms, to be re-elected either to the Political Bureau or to the Central Committee. Lts-Gen. Choummali Saignason and Saman Vignaket were widely reported to be opposed to rapid economic and political reform.

At the opening session of the National Assembly in April 1996 Nouhak Phoumsavanh was, despite his retirement from the Political Bureau, confirmed as Head of State until the end of his term of office in February 1998. Sisavat Keobounphan (who had been restored to the Political Bureau at the previous month's elections) was elected to the new office of Vice-President, in order to relieve Nouhak Phoumsavanh of a number of presidential duties. Boungnang Volachit was approved by the National Assembly as a Deputy Prime Minister, although, contrary to expectation, Khamphoui Keoboualapha also retained his posts as Deputy Prime Minister and Chairman of the State Committee for Planning and Co-operation. However, it was expected that the latter's influence would be diminished by his exclusion from the Political Bureau and also by the establishment of a new State Planning Committee, which was to assume some of the responsibilities hitherto exercised by Khamphoui's Committee.

Elections to the National Assembly took place on 21 December 1997, at which 159 LFNC-approved candidates, including 41 members of the outgoing legislature, contested 99 seats. The three members of the LPRP Political Bureau and 10 Central Committee members who stood for election were all successful; one of the four 'independent' candidates without affiliation to the LPRP was elected. The level of participation by voters was officially registered to have been 99.37%. The first session of the new National Assembly was held on 23–26 February 1998, during which the Assembly elected Gen. Khamtay to succeed Phoumsavanh as President of State. The Assembly also endorsed the appointment of Sisavat Keobounphan as Prime Minister and of Oudom Khattigna in his place as Vice-President, re-elected Saman Vignaket as President of the National Assembly, and approved a redistribution of ministerial posts.

In March 2001 the Seventh Congress of the LPRP confirmed the military's control of the Political Bureau. In the same month, as part of another reorganization of the Council of Ministers, Oudom was replaced as the country's Vice-President by Lt-Gen. Choummali Saignason, who had relinquished his bid for the premiership owing to ill health. Prime Minister Sisavat Keobounphan was forced to resign, in order to take responsibility for the mismanagement of the economy following the Asian financial crisis of 1997/98. His successor, the former Deputy Prime Minister and Minister of Finance, Boungnang Volachit, provided a civilian balance to the entirely military executive branch. The appointment of Thongloun Sisolit to the post of Deputy Prime Minister further enhanced the greater civilian representation on the Council of Ministers.

From the mid-1990s uprisings against the Government became more frequent. In July 1995 an army unit based near Luang Prabang mutinied after its commander, a Hmong general, was passed over for promotion. Five members of the armed forces died in the rebellion, which was believed to be symptomatic of the resentment felt by hill tribes over the political and military dominance of the lowland Lao. About 2,000 troops were dispatched to Luang Prabang to restore order. In November several people were killed in an armed assault on a bus near Luang Prabang, which was attributed to disaffected Hmong tribesmen. In October a shipment of explosives, allegedly destined for Hmong insurgents, had been intercepted on the Mekong River. Several incidents in the Luang Prabang region during 1996 were ascribed to Hmong rebels. Meanwhile, fund-raising by the Hmong community in the USA was reportedly a cause for concern within the Laotian Government.

In October 1999 an anti-Government demonstration by students and teachers was held in Vientiane. The protest, which constituted an extremely rare overt demonstration of public dissatisfaction, was reportedly swiftly dispersed by police. The Government subsequently repudiated claims that about 50 people who were involved or suspected to have been involved in the protest had been arrested, and, furthermore, denied that the demonstration had taken place; in March 2000, however, it was reported that the whereabouts of one professor and at least five students arrested during the protest remained unknown.

Civil unrest intensified throughout 2000, with a spate of bomb attacks. The first occurred in a restaurant in March, immediately drawing international attention to the event, as several tourists were injured in the blast. Two further attacks took place in Vientiane in May, coinciding with the respective visits of the Thai Prime Minister, Chuan Leekpai, and his Minister of Foreign Affairs, Surin Pitsuwan. Two more strikes followed within a week of each other, bringing the total to five explosions within three months, more than 20 people having been injured and at least two killed. Under pressure, the Government, blaming the campaign on Hmong insurgents, claimed to have arrested two men (one Lao and one Hmong) carrying explosive devices in mid-June. Despite the arrests, the bombing operation continued unabated. A bomb was defused near the Vietnamese embassy in Vientiane at the end of July, lending credence to the suspicion that the action was part of an internal power struggle between pro-Chinese and pro-Vietnamese governmental factions. In total, at least nine bombs exploded between March 2000 and January 2001, with the penultimate detonation occurring on the eve of the meeting of the European Union and the Association of South East Asian Nations (see p. 185) (EU-ASEAN summit) in December 2000.

Although no group admitted responsibility for the bombings, a pre-dawn raid in July 2000 on immigration and customs offices in Vang Tao, opposite the Chong Mek border checkpoint, indicated the involvement of royalist rebels. The Government claimed that the attack was merely a robbery, but during the incursion the former royal flag was raised over the immigration office. (In October 2004, following their extradition from Thailand, 16 Lao nationals were convicted of robbery in connection with the raid and sentenced to prison terms of between two and 12 years.) In mid-November 2000 about 200 workers and students were reported to have staged a demonstration in the southern province of Champasak, calling for democracy. The protest was swiftly quelled, with 15 people being arrested. The timing of the demonstration, however, exacerbated the increasing sense of instability, as less than two weeks previously, Helen Clark, the Prime Minister of New Zealand, had confirmed that her Government had granted political asylum to Khamsay Souphanouvong, a minister attached to the Prime Minister's office and son of the first President of the Lao People's Democratic Republic.

In October 2001 five European activists, including Olivier Dupuis, a Belgian member of the European Parliament, were arrested for handing out pro-democracy leaflets at a peaceful protest in Vientiane. The protest was held to commemorate the second anniversary of the disappearance of five students who had participated in the demonstration of October 1999. In November 2001, following expressions of concern at the conditions the detainees were being forced to endure, Romani Prodi, President of the European Commission, warned the Laotian authorities that the continued detention of the activists would threaten diplomatic relations with the EU. In the same month, following a swift trial, the prisoners were convicted of attempting to spread unrest and ordered to be deported. They were also fined and given two-year suspended prison terms.

On 24 February 2002 elections took place from among 166 LFNC-approved candidates for the 109 seats available in the National Assembly. Only one of the elected members was not affiliated to the LPRP, ensuring that the ruling party secured a comprehensive victory. In April, at the opening session of the National Assembly, the existing Cabinet was almost wholly re-elected. The former Minister of the Interior, Maj.-Gen. Asang Laoli, became Deputy Prime Minister and Maj.-Gen. Soudchai Thammasith subsequently assumed the interior portfolio. In January 2003 a cabinet reorganization was announced in an apparent attempt to strengthen the national economy. The former Governor of the Central Bank, Chansy Phosikham, was appointed Minister of Finance, Onneua Phommachanh became Minister of Industry and Handicrafts and Soulivong Daravong was placed in charge of the Ministry of Commerce and Tourism.

In September 2002 a bomb exploded at the Si Muang temple in Vientiane, injuring two children; it was unclear whether the attack was linked to the bombings that had occurred in 2000. In January 2003, for the first time, national celebrations were held to commemorate the anniversary of the birth of King Fa Ngoum, accredited with founding the Kingdom of Lane Xang in 1353; a statue was erected and a public holiday declared. In the following month a group of armed men ambushed a bus near the town of Vang Vieng; the attack resulted in the deaths of 13 people, including three foreign nationals, two of whom were tourists. It was feared that the incident might discourage tourists from visiting the country. Such fears were intensified in April by a further attack on a bus travelling between Luang Prabang and Vientiane; at least 12 people died as a result of the incident, which was thought to have been perpetrated by Hmong rebels. In August an attack on a bus in the north of the country killed five people. In October three bombs exploded in Vientiane. A previously unknown group, the Free Democratic People's Government of Laos (FDPGL), claimed responsibility for the bombings, as well as for the spate of bomb attacks that had occurred in the capital since 2000. It was believed that the group consisted of disaffected former members of the armed forces. However, a German-based organization, the Committee for Independence and Democracy in Laos, later claimed responsibility for all the bombings, including two further attacks that occurred in early 2004, one in Savannakhet and one in Vientiane.

In June 2003 it was reported that two European journalists, together with their Lao-US interpreter, had been arrested owing to their suspected involvement in the murder of a Lao national and for reporting from the country in contravention of the terms of their tourist visas. The journalists had allegedly been researching the Hmong insurgency in the country, which they had found to be almost exhausted and desperate for assistance. Following a summary trial, the three were sentenced to 15-year prison terms. Three Hmong defendants were given 20-year prison sentences. However, following intense diplomatic pressure from their respective Governments, the three foreign nationals were released in the following month. In October Political Bureau member Bouasone Bouphavanh was appointed fourth Deputy Prime Minister, with responsibility for home affairs. His appointment was believed to be, in part, a governmental response to the deteriorating security situation in the country.

In March 2004 an official from the Ministry of National Defence claimed that some 700 Hmong, including five senior commanders, had recently surrendered to the authorities, having been offered amnesty. Five bomb attacks reportedly occurred in April and May, the most serious of which killed one person and injured six others in southern Laos. In September the human rights organization Amnesty International alleged that up to 40 government troops had assaulted and murdered five Hmong children in the Xaysomboun special zone in northern Laos in May; the Government denied the accusations. Security was heightened in Vientiane in November, following two minor bomb explosions near the Thai border (for which the FDPGL claimed responsibility) and warnings of further possible attacks in advance of the ASEAN summit meeting, which was held in the capital at the end of the month. Two small bombs exploded in a village outside the capital a few days before the opening of the meeting, but no injuries were reported.

In February 2006 it was announced that a legislative election would be held at the end of April, almost a year ahead of schedule. President Khamtay Siphandone stated that the decision to hold elections before the expiry of the mandate of the current Assembly had been made in order to enable the new Council of Ministers and the incoming legislature to commence their respective terms of office within close proximity of one another, in order to facilitate the forging of a strong working relationship. In March the LPRP held its Eighth Party Congress, during which Gen. Khamtay tendered his resignation as party leader; he was replaced by Vice-President Lt-Gen. Choummali Saignason. Khamtay also resigned from the Political Bureau, to which two new members were elected: Deputy Prime Minister and Minister of Foreign Affairs Somsavat Lengsavat; and Phani Yathothu, the only female member of the Bureau. During the Party Congress elections for a new Central Committee were also held, at which 55 members were selected. On 30 April the legislative election was duly held; an estimated 2.7m. voters cast their ballot. The counting of votes was delayed by torrential rain across parts of the country, which hindered attempts to collect ballot boxes from the affected regions. The results of polling, announced in mid-May, showed that two nominally independent candidates (of the three who had contested the election) had been elected, alongside 113 members of the LPRP. However, some 71 of the incoming deputies had not previously been members of the National Assembly, and therefore were described by some commentators as constituting a new generation of legislators. The new National Assembly convened at the beginning of June, electing Thongsing Thammavong, Politburo member and Governor of Vientiane, as its President. As widely anticipated, Lt-Gen. Choummali Saignason was chosen to succeed Gen. Khamtay as President of Laos. Boungnang Volachit became Vice-President, while Bouasone Bouphavanh was appointed to replace him as Prime Minister. Among the new members of the Council of Ministers were two women; other notable changes included the transfer of the foreign affairs portfolio from Somsavat Lengsavat to Thongloun Sisolit, both of whom remained as Deputy Prime Ministers, along with Maj.-Gen. Asong Laoli. Maj.-Gen. Douangchai Phichit retained the defence portfolio and was promoted to the position of Deputy Prime Minister. Chansy Phosikham remained Minister of Finance. In a structural reorganization, the Ministries of Commerce and of Industry were combined to form one entity, and a new Ministry of Energy and Mining was established.

In June 2007 10 Hmong resident in the USA and a former officer of the California National Guard were arrested in the USA and charged in connection with an alleged plot to overthrow the Laos Government that had been uncovered by US federal agents. Most of the 11 defendants, including Gen. Vang Pao, who was accused of being the leader of the group, were released on bail in July.

The National Assembly approved several ministerial changes proposed by Prime Minister Bouasone Bouphavanh in early July 2007. Chansy Phosikham was replaced as Minister of Finance by his deputy, Somdy Douangdy, and three new Ministers to the Office of the Prime Minister were appointed. Chansy succeeded Somphet Phetmala as Governor of Vientiane, with the latter becoming Deputy Minister of National Defence. At the same time the Assembly adopted new legislation on public security and state auditing and inspection. Addressing the National Assembly in the previous month, Bouasone had emphasized the need to combat rising corruption among government officials.

From 1975 Laos was dependent on Vietnamese economic and military assistance, permitting the stationing of Vietnamese troops (estimated in 1987 to number between 30,000 and 50,000) on its territory. In 1977 a 25-year treaty of friendship between the two countries was signed, and Laos supported the Vietnamese-led overthrow of the Khmer Rouge regime in Kampuchea (Cambodia) in January 1979. Following the outbreak of hostilities between Viet Nam and the People's Republic of China in that year, Laos allied itself with the former. Viet Nam withdrew its military presence from Laos during 1988. The two countries signed a protocol governing military co-operation in March 1994. In July 2001 Prime Minister Bougnang Volachit visited Viet Nam on his first overseas trip since assuming office in March. In May 2002 President Khamtay Siphandone paid an official friendship visit to Viet Nam, which was reciprocated in October by the Chairman of the Vietnamese National Assembly, Nguyen Van An. The visits affirmed the strength of ties between the two countries. In February 2006 a major border crossing was opened between Sekong province in Laos and Quang Nam province in Viet Nam. It was hoped that this would facilitate economic co-operation between the two countries and would also help to control smuggling along the common border. Discussions held during an official visit to Laos by the Vietnamese President, Nguyen Minh Triet, in February 2007 also focused on the expansion of economic co-operation. Various joint activities were organized later that year to celebrate the 45th anniversary of the establishment of diplomatic relations between Laos and Viet Nam and the 30th anniversary of the signing of the treaty of friendship. In February 2008 it was reported that Viet Nam had become the second largest foreign investor in Laos, investing some US $600m. in economic development projects since 1989, including $270m. in the energy sector.

In February 1993 Laos, Thailand, Viet Nam and Cambodia signed a joint communiqué providing for the resumption of co-operation in the development of the Mekong River. In April 1995 in Chiang Rai, Thailand, representatives of the four countries signed an agreement on the joint exploitation and development of the lower Mekong. The accord provided for the establishment of the Mekong River Commission (see p. 413) as a successor to the Committee for Co-ordination of Investigations of the Lower Mekong Basin. In February 2008 Laos, Cambodia and Viet Nam concluded a draft agreement on defining the intersection point of their borders.

In July 1992 Laos strengthened ties with members of ASEAN by signing the ASEAN Treaty of Amity and Co-operation, which provided for wider regional co-operation and was regarded as a preliminary step to full membership of the Association. Laos attended ASEAN meetings with observer status from this time, and applied for membership of the organization in March 1996. The country was formally admitted as a full member at the organization's meeting of ministers responsible for foreign affairs in July 1997. As Chair of ASEAN for 2004/05, Laos hosted the 10th summit meeting of the Association in November 2004 and the 38th Ministerial Meeting in July 2005. Despite bomb threats made to staff at the US embassy in Vientiane, apparently by groups opposed to the Laotian Government, in the period prior to the summit meeting in November 2004, both the summit meeting itself and the ministerial conference proceeded without incident and did much to raise the international profile of Laos. In February 2008 Laos ratified the new ASEAN Charter, which codified the principles and purposes of the Association and had been signed in November 2007 at the 13th summit meeting in Singapore.

Relations with the People's Republic of China improved in December 1986, when a Chinese delegation, led by the Deputy Minister of Foreign Affairs, made the first official Chinese visit to Laos since 1978. In December 1987, after an assurance from the People's Republic of China that support would be withdrawn from Laotian resistance groups operating from within China, the two countries agreed to restore full diplomatic relations and to encourage bilateral trade. Relations between the LPRP and the Chinese Communist Party were fully restored in August 1989. In October 1991 the Laotian and Chinese Prime Ministers signed a border treaty, which established a framework for meetings of a Laotian-Chinese joint border committee. In January 1992 the committee adopted a resolution providing for the demarcation of the common border, and in June an agreement on the delineation of boundaries was signed. In November 1994 Laos and China signed a reciprocal agreement on the transport of passengers and goods on each other's sections of the Mekong River. In February 1996 Laos and China opened a section of their border to highway traffic. In October 1997 Chinese Vice-Premier Wu Bangguo made a three-day visit to Laos, and in early 1999 Prime Minister Sisavat Keobounphan made an eight-day official visit to China. The first visit ever made by a Chinese head of state to Laos was by President Jiang Zemin in November 2000. As the volume of bilateral trade continued to increase, wider co-operation with China was expected to follow a state visit by President Hu Jintao to Laos in November 2006. Relations were further strengthened in August 2007 by a seven-day official visit to China by Prime Minister Bouasone Bouphavanh, during which six agreements on co-operation in a range of areas were signed.

Relations with Thailand from 1975 were characterized by mutual suspicion. Thailand intermittently closed its border to Laotian imports and exports, causing considerable hardship. Disputed sovereignty claims in border areas were a cause of friction, and led to clashes between Laotian and Thai troops in 1984. Further hostilities began in December 1987, resulting in hundreds of casualties. In February 1988 the two sides agreed to declare a cease-fire, to withdraw their troops from the combat area, and to attempt to negotiate a peaceful solution. In March 1991 (following the recent military coup in Thailand) representatives of the two countries signed an agreement providing for the immediate withdrawal of troops from disputed areas. The Thai Government also undertook to suppress the activities of Laotian insurgents operating from Thai territory. In December Thailand and Laos signed a border co-operation agreement.

In June 1992 the Thai Crown Prince, Maha Vajiralongkorn, visited Vientiane for the first time. On the following day, however, about 300 guerrillas from a Thai-based rebel group, the Free Democratic Lao National Salvation Force, attacked three Laotian government posts, killing two people and causing significant damage. In the same month Laos refuted allegations made by a senior Thai military officer that a Laotian government unit was receiving training in chemical warfare from Cuban and Vietnamese experts, and also dismissed previous accusations by Laotian resistance fighters and Western aid agencies of its use of chemical warfare to suppress the activities of rebel groups. Bilateral relations improved in July, when the Thai authorities announced the arrest of 11 Laotian citizens accused of planning subversive activities against the Government in Vientiane. The first bridge (over the Mekong River) linking Laos and Thailand was opened in April 1994. In September 1996 the countries' Joint Co-operation Commission agreed to establish a boundary commission, in an effort to resolve demarcation problems. Despite various diplomatic efforts to stimulate further co-operation between the two countries, such as the signing of an extradition treaty in January 2001, the relationship was strained by the July 2000 incursion launched from Thai territory by suspected royalist rebels. (In July 2004, following a lengthy legal dispute, Thailand handed over to the Laotian authorities 16 Lao nationals who were allegedly involved in the incursion, despite an earlier ruling by a Thai court rejecting their extradition.) Meanwhile, the situation deteriorated further in August 2000 after Laotian troops occupied two islands in the Mekong River, evicting 65 Thai farming families. Laos claimed that under a 1926 treaty it had sovereignty over all the islands in the Mekong, while Thailand merely requested the withdrawal of the troops. Nevertheless, in April 2001 the Thai Minister of Foreign Affairs, Surakiart Sathirathai, visited Laos, affirming the beginning of a new era of friendly Lao-Thai relations based on shared cultural values. In June Thai Prime Minister Thaksin Shinawatra arrived in Vientiane on a two-day official visit intended further to consolidate co-operative ties between the two countries. In late 2003, following a meeting of the Joint Co-operation Commission, the two countries pledged to resolve all outstanding border demarcation issues, as well as agreeing to work together on a variety of social development initiatives. In March 2004, for the first time, the Thai and Laotian Governments held a joint cabinet meeting to discuss bilateral co-operation. The meeting ended with Prime Ministers Thaksin Shinawatra and Bougnang Volachit presiding over a ceremony to lay the foundation stone for a second Mekong Friendship Bridge, which was officially opened in December 2006. In June 2007 the People's Republic of China, Laos and Thailand signed an agreement on the construction of a further bridge across the Mekong River, which would provide a direct road link from the Chinese province of Yunnan, through Laos, to the Thai capital, Bangkok. Scheduled for completion in 2011, the bridge was to be financed jointly by China and Thailand. In February 2008 Laos and Thailand agreed to complete the demarcation of their land border that year, as the area remaining under dispute covered only 12 km, followed by that of the maritime border in 2010. At the end of February the new Thai Prime Minister, Samak Sundaravej, visited Laos on his first foreign trip since taking office earlier that month.

During the 1970s and 1980s thousands of Laotian refugees fled to Thailand to escape from civil war and food shortages. In January 1989 an estimated 90,000 Laotian refugees remained in border camps in Thailand. The office of the UN High Commissioner for Refugees (UNHCR) began a programme of voluntary repatriation in 1980. By late 1990 fewer than 6,000 refugees had been repatriated under UNHCR supervision, while some 15,000 had returned independently, and others had been resettled abroad. In June 1991 UNHCR, Laos and Thailand signed an agreement guaranteeing the repatriation or resettlement in a third country of the remaining 60,000 Laotian refugees in Thailand by the end of 1994; however, this deadline was subsequently revised on several occasions. In December 1996, according to UNHCR, 3,293 Laotian refugees remained in Thailand. In December 1997 UNHCR announced that a final review of the status of the last remaining refugees at Ban Napho camp in Thailand would be completed by January 1998, whereupon they would be repatriated or resettled in a third country. Among the camp's 1,344 refugees were reportedly 964 Hmong, most of whom were unwilling to return to Laos. In December 2003 the USA agreed to accept around 15,000 Laotian Hmong refugees living in refugee camps in Thailand. The first group of refugees was resettled in the USA in June 2004, under the aegis of the International Organization for Migration.

In early 2006 tension arose between Laos and Thailand concerning 27 Hmong refugees (all but one of whom were children), who had been reported missing from a refugee camp in Phetchabun province, north-eastern Thailand, in December 2005. The group was subsequently discovered in Laos, allegedly having been forcibly repatriated by the Thai authorities. Laos and Thailand entered into negotiations regarding the possibility of reuniting the children with their parents at the Phetchabun refugee camp, although it was later reported that the children had disappeared. In June Thai police arrested some 270 Hmong migrants who had allegedly entered Thailand illegally from Laos; however, officials of the latter country denied that the migrants were necessarily Laotian citizens. In August officials from the respective Ministries of Foreign Affairs of Laos and Thailand declared that their countries were ready to co-operate in addressing the Hmong refugee issue, for which neither side took responsibility. The Laotian Deputy Prime Minister, Somsavat Lengsavat, suggested in November that Laos might allow repatriation of Hmong refugees if they were proven to be of Laotian nationality, but reiterated that the Government had not persecuted the Hmong. In the following month UNHCR urged the Thai Government to abandon its plan for the forcible repatriation of more than 150 Hmong migrants to Laos, arguing that they would be at risk if they returned. The Thai Ministry of Foreign Affairs responded that Thai and Laotian immigration officials were determining the nationality of the migrants, who, it was stated, would not be repatriated against their will. In January 2007 the Thai Government agreed to halt the deportation process after the USA, Canada, Australia and the Netherlands agreed to provide asylum to the migrants, some of whom had protested against repatriation by locking themselves inside their detention centre. In January 2008, however, the group of Hmong, now numbering 149, including 90 children, and all recognized as refugees, remained in an immigration detention centre in Thailand, according to UNHCR, which urged the Thai authorities to release them so that they could take up the previous offers of asylum in other countries.

Meanwhile, in mid-December 2006 a meeting between the Laotian Prime Minister and his Thai counterpart reportedly resulted in an agreement to repatriate the more than 7,000 Hmong living in refugee camps in Thailand's Phetchabun province, who were alleged to be economic migrants (and to whom UNHCR did not have access), following verification of their origin. In January 2007 UNHCR expressed concern about reports that Thailand had returned 16 Hmong to Laos who had apparently not been screened to ascertain if they required international protection, urging the suspension of deportations pending the introduction of procedures to allow a proper assessment of the needs and claims of the Hmong. Thai and Laotian officials held further discussions on the repatriation of the Hmong in Phetchabun province in September, later confirming that around 200 Hmong had already been resettled in Laos in that year and that the process of verifying the identity of those remaining in Phetchabun was ongoing. A site in Kaxi district, some 150 km from Vientiane, had been prepared for those who could not return to their homes in Laos. In February 2008, following a visit to Laos, the Thai Minister of Foreign Affairs announced that the Thai authorities were nearing the completion of the screening process. Later that month Thai defence officials announced that 10 Hmong were being repatriated from Phetchabun in advance of an official visit by the Thai Prime Minister to Laos; UNHCR sought reassurance that their return was voluntary, as claimed by the officials.

From the 1990s Laos forged closer links with Myanmar and with Cambodia. In February 1992 Khamtay Siphandone was the first foreign head of government to visit Myanmar since the military coup in that country in 1988, and in June 1994 Senior Gen. Than Shwe visited Laos, his first foreign visit as Myanmar's Head of State. Bilateral contacts continued on a frequent basis. Laos signed a treaty of friendship and assistance with Cambodia in December 1995, further to which Joint Co-operation Committees were established. In November 2001 Prince Norodom Ranariddh headed a Cambodian delegation on an official goodwill visit to Laos.

From 1989 the Laotian Government sought to improve relations with non-communist countries, in order to reduce its (especially economic) dependence on the USSR and Viet Nam. Following a visit to Japan in that year by Kaysone Phomvihane (his first official visit to a non-communist country), the Japanese Government agreed to increase grant aid to Laos. In December 1995 Japan announced that it would resume the provision of official loans to Laos in 1996. In January 2000 the Japanese Prime Minister, Keizo Obuchi, made an official visit to Laos, and in August 2000 a bridge over the Mekong, built with a 5,460m.-yen grant from the Japanese Government, was officially opened in Paksé. In mid-2001 Prince Akishino of Japan made a 10-day unofficial visit to Laos and, in September, Japan agreed a further loan to fund the construction of the second Mekong Friendship Bridge. Bilateral relations were further strengthened in May 2007, during a four-day visit to Japan by Laotian Prime Minister Bouasone Bouphavanh. Bouasone held a meeting with his Japanese counterpart, Shinzo Abe, who pledged to provide continued economic assistance to Laos, including approximately US $1m. for the clearance of unexploded ordnance remaining from the Viet Nam war (see below), which was impeding development. Furthermore, it was hoped that a bilateral agreement on the liberalization, promotion and protection of investment, which was signed in January 2008, would encourage the participation of Japanese businesses in the Laotian economy.

In November 2002 the Prime Minister of India, Atal Bihari Vajpayee, paid the first visit to Laos by an Indian head of government in more than 45 years. During his stay the two countries signed agreements on co-operation in defence issues and control of drugs-trafficking. The Indian Government also agreed to provide US $10m. of credit to Laos at low interest rates.

During the Viet Nam war US aircraft completed almost 600,000 bombing missions over Laos, leaving large amounts of undetonated explosives, which were estimated to cause 50–100 fatalities per year in the 1990s. The National Unexploded Ordnance Awareness and Clearance Programme was established in Laos in May 1995, with support from the UN.

In 1985 Laos agreed to co-operate with the USA in recovering the remains of US soldiers 'missing in action' in Laos since the war in Viet Nam. In August 1987 a US delegation visited Vientiane to discuss 'humanitarian co-operation' by Laos in tracing missing US soldiers, and agreed to provide Laos with aid. The first remains of US soldiers were passed to the US Government in February 1988; further operations to locate the remains of US soldiers took place in the 1990s and 2000s. In November 1991, in response to continued Laotian co-operation and the implementation of limited political and economic reforms, the US Government announced that diplomatic relations with Laos were to be upgraded to ambassadorial level. In January 1993, following 17 months of hearings, a special US Senate panel concluded that (despite considerable public speculation to the contrary) there was 'no compelling evidence' of the survival of US servicemen in the region. In May 1995 the USA announced the ending of a 20-year embargo on aid to Laos. In November 1997 the US Deputy Secretary of State, Strobe Talbott, led the most senior-level US delegation to Laos since the mid-1970s. During the visit further US support was pledged for a programme to clear unexploded ordnance from the Viet

Nam war, which had been supported by the USA since 1996. In mid-1998 US officials agreed to extend financial and logistical support for the programme until September 1999. In December 2004, following its adoption by Congress, President George W. Bush of the USA signed legislation according normal trade relations (NTR) status to Laos, which had been suspended in 1975. The US Senate had separately approved a resolution condemning Laos's human rights record, concerns over which had delayed the approval of NTR status. A bilateral trade agreement signed by the USA and Laos in September 2003 consequently entered into force in February 2005.

Government

Under the terms of the 1991 Constitution, executive power is vested in the President of State, while legislative power resides with the National Assembly. The President is elected for five years by the National Assembly. Members of the National Assembly are elected for a period of five years by universal adult suffrage. The Lao People's Revolutionary Party remains the sole legal political party. With the approval of the National Assembly, the President appoints the Prime Minister and members of the Council of Ministers, who conduct the government of the country. The President also appoints provincial governors and mayors of municipalities, who are responsible for local administration.

Defence

As assessed at November 2007, according to Western estimates, the strength of the armed forces was 29,100 (Lao People's Army 25,600—including an army marine section of 600—and air force 3,500). Military service is compulsory for a minimum of 18 months. There is a paramilitary self-defence force numbering more than 100,000. In 2006 defence expenditure was budgeted at an estimated 135,000m. kips.

Economic Affairs

In 2006, according to estimates by the World Bank, Laos's gross national income (GNI), measured at average 2004–06 prices, was US $2,879m., equivalent to $500 per head (or $2,050 per head on an international purchasing-power parity basis). During 1996–2006, it was estimated, the population increased by an annual average of 1.8%, while gross domestic product (GDP) per head increased, in real terms, by an average of 4.4% per year. Overall GDP increased, in real terms, at an average annual rate of 6.4% in 1999–2006, expanding by 7.6% in 2006. The Asian Development Bank (ADB) estimated that GDP grew by 8.0% in 2007.

Agriculture (including forestry and fishing) contributed an estimated 42.6% of GDP in 2006. According to FAO, an estimated 75.6% of the working population were employed in the sector in mid-2005. Rice is the staple crop. Other crops include sweet potatoes, maize, cassava, sugar cane and sesame seed. Coffee, production of which reached an estimated 25,000 metric tons in 2005, is grown for export. In 2000 forest covered about 55.4% of the country's total land area. Timber remained a significant export commodity in 2006, accounting for an estimated 15.9% of total export revenue in that year. The illicit cultivation of narcotic drugs has been widespread. Although the UN Office on Drugs and Crime (UNODC—formerly the UN Office of Drug Control and Crime Prevention) estimated that the area under opium poppy cultivation in Laos had decreased from 26,800 ha in 1998 to 1,800 ha in 2005, in 2006 the cultivated area was estimated to have expanded to 2,500 ha, with the country's potential opium production increasing by almost 40% to reach 20 metric tons. During 1995–2006 agricultural GDP, measured at constant 1990 prices, increased by an estimated average of 4.1% per year. The sector's rate of growth was estimated by the ADB at 2.7% in 2007.

Industry (including mining, manufacturing, construction and utilities) contributed an estimated 31.8% of GDP in 2006. According to the ADB, the sector employed 9.3% of the working population in 2003. During 1995–2006 industrial GDP, measured at constant 1990 prices, increased at an average annual rate of 11.6%. Growth in the industrial sector was estimated by the ADB at 14.0% in 2007.

Mining contributed only an estimated 5.4% of GDP in 2006, although this represented a significant increase from 1.5% in 2004. Laos has considerable mineral resources: iron ore, copper, coal, tin, gold, gemstones and gypsum are among the minerals that are exploited. Other mineral deposits include zinc, nickel, potash, lead, limestone and silver. Copper production in 2005 reached an estimated 30,480 metric tons, and this rose to some 60,803 tons in 2006. Exports of copper were valued at an estimated at US $409.3m. in 2006, compared with $112.1m. in the previous year. Gold exports (including re-exports) totalled $116.1m. in 2006. During 1995–2006 the GDP of the mining sector increased by an average of 43.0% per year. Expansion in this sector was largely concentrated in 2003 (during which year mining GDP increased by 267.5%, according to figures from the ADB) owing to the start of gold production in Laos. The sector contracted by 5.1% in 2004 before recovering in 2005, when mining GDP increased by 121.3%. According to official estimates, the sector expanded by a further 86.9% in 2006, a result attributed to increased copper production (see above) and an associated rise in mineral exports.

Manufacturing contributed an estimated 20.6% of GDP in 2006, although the sector employed less than 1% of the working population in the mid-1980s. It is mainly confined to the processing of raw materials (chiefly sawmilling) and agricultural produce, the production of textiles and garments (a principal export commodity), and the manufacture of handicrafts and basic consumer goods for the domestic market. Manufacturing GDP increased at an estimated average annual rate of 10.2% in 1995–2006. Manufacturing GDP increased by an estimated 8.1% in 2006.

Electrical energy is principally derived from hydroelectric power. Electricity is exported to Thailand and Viet Nam, and is one of Laos's principal sources of foreign exchange. Laos's total hydroelectric power potential was estimated at 25,000 MW in 2000. In 2006 the country's total hydroelectricity generation reached an estimated 3,606m. kWh. In 2002 the Government granted a concession to the Nam Theun 2 Power Company (NTPC), enabling it to assume control of the construction of a major new hydroelectric dam, which was originally scheduled for completion in 2009. Under an agreement reached with Thailand in 2006, annual exports of electricity from Laos were to increase to as much as 5,000 MW. Laos is dependent on imports, mainly from Thailand, for supplies of mineral fuels.

The services sector contributed an estimated 25.6% of GDP in 2006, and engaged 8.6% of the total labour force in 2003. Receipts from tourism increased from US $119m. in 2004 to $146m. in 2005. Tourist arrivals increased from 894,806 in 2004 to 1,095,315 in 2005. The GDP of the services sector, measured at constant 1990 prices, increased at an estimated average annual rate of 6.7% in 1995–2006. The sector grew by 7.2% in 2007, according to the ADB.

In 2006 Laos recorded a visible trade deficit of US $178.2m., and there was a surplus of $41.3m. on the current account of the balance of payments. Remittances from relatives residing overseas are a significant source of income for many Lao. In 2006 Thailand was the principal source of imports, supplying an estimated 69.1% (including any goods in transit) of the total. The People's Republic of China was also an important source of imports (11.4%) in that year, along with Viet Nam, Singapore, Japan and Australia. The principal destination of exports from Laos in 2006 was Thailand, which purchased 43.1% (including any goods in transit) of the total. Other significant purchasers in that year were Viet Nam (9.6%), China (4.3%) and Germany (3.3%). The main exports in 2006 were copper, timber, garments, gold and electricity. The principal imports were capital goods, petroleum and material for the garment industry.

In the financial year ending 30 September 2007 an overall budget deficit of 1,392,000m. new kips, equivalent to 3.7% of GDP, was envisaged. At the end of 2007 the country's external debt totalled US $2,625m.; in that year the cost of debt-servicing was equivalent to 6.1% of revenue from exports of goods and services. Consumer prices increased by an annual average of 29.8% in 1996–2005. According to the ADB, the annual rate of inflation averaged 6.9% in 2006 and 4.5% in 2007. The unemployment rate was estimated at 5.1% of the labour force in 2003.

Laos is a member of the UN Economic and Social Commission for Asia and the Pacific (ESCAP, see p. 35), of the Asian Development Bank (ADB, see p. 182), of the Association of South East Asian Nations (ASEAN, see p. 185), of the Colombo Plan (see p. 411), which promotes economic and social development in Asia and the Pacific, and of the Mekong River Commission (see p. 413).

Despite the introduction in 1986 of a programme of reform, Laos has remained underdeveloped. In 2005 a study published by the World Bank reported that approximately 37% of educated Laotians were working abroad—a serious impediment to the country's prospects. The investment approval process was simplified in 2003. Inflows of foreign direct investment were estimated to have risen from US $650m. in 2006 to $770m. in 2007, largely as a result of substantial investments in the mining sector and in hydroelectricity projects. The Sixth National Socio-economic Development Plan, for the period 2006–10, envisaged average annual growth of between 7.5% and 8.0%. The industrial sector was targeted for particularly rapid expansion. Other areas to be accorded priority were the development of agriculture, infrastructure, health and education. The improvement of governance and of the management of natural resources, as well as the encouragement of the private sector, were also envisaged. The Government hoped to create 652,000 new jobs during the plan period and to reduce the incidence of poverty (estimated at more than 30% in 2003) among households in Laos to less than 15%. The limitations of the Laotian infrastructure had previously impeded the timely transport of exports; however, improvements to the road network facilitated an expansion in external trade in 2007. In that year China continued to increase its volume of trade with Laos, which thus reduced the latter's dependency on neighbouring Thailand somewhat. It was also expected that increasing demand from China would stimulate development in Laos's agricultural and industrial sectors, particularly with regard to the cultivation of rubber and the manufacture of garments. The Government continued its attempts to address weaknesses in the system of revenue collection, and it was hoped that the introduction of value-added tax (VAT) in 2008 would raise the funds required to promote wider social and economic development. In the hope of joining the World Trade Organization (WTO, see p. 396) by 2010, the Government aimed to improve conditions for trade and investment in the country. The ADB envisaged GDP growth of 7.7% in 2008.

Education

Education was greatly disrupted by the civil war, causing a high illiteracy rate, but educational facilities subsequently improved significantly. Lao is the medium of instruction. A comprehensive education system is in force. In 1990 the Government issued a decree permitting the establishment of private schools, in an effort to accommodate the increasing number of students.

Primary education begins at six years of age and lasts for five years. In 2004/05 enrolment in pre-primary education included 10% of pupils in the relevant age-group (males 10%; females 10%). In the same year enrolment in primary education included 83% of children in the relevant age-group (males 85%; females 80%). Secondary education, beginning at the age of 11, lasts for six years, comprising two three-year cycles. In 2004/05 enrolment in secondary education included 36% of pupils in the relevant age-group (males 38%; females 33%). In 2006/07 there were 1,087 pre-primary institutions, 8,654 primary schools, 717 secondary schools (including 47 vocational schools, at which 26,300 pupils were enrolled) and 41 tertiary institutions (including 3 universities, at which 30,600 students were enrolled). Government expenditure on education for 1997/98 was forecast at 37,400m. kips, representing 6.9% of total projected expenditure.

Public Holidays

2008: 1 January (New Year's Day), 6 January (Pathet Lao Day), 20 January (Army Day), 7 February (Chinese New Year), 8 March (Women's Day), 22 March (People's Party Day), 13–15 April (Lao New Year), 1 May (Labour Day), 2 June (Children's Day), 13 August (Free Laos Day), 23 August (Liberation Day), 12 October (Liberation from the French Day, Vientiane only), 2 December (Independence Day).

2009: 1 January (New Year's Day), 6 January (Pathet Lao Day), 20 January (Army Day), 26 January (Chinese New Year), 8 March (Women's Day), 22 March (People's Party Day), 13–15 April (Lao New Year), 1 May (Labour Day), 1 June (Children's Day), 13 August (Free Laos Day), 23 August (Liberation Day), 12 October (Liberation from the French Day, Vientiane only), 2 December (Independence Day).

Weights and Measures

The metric system is in force.

Statistical Survey

Source (unless otherwise stated): National Statistics Centre, rue Luang Prabang, Vientiane; tel. (21) 214740; fax (21) 219129; e-mail nscp@laotel.com; internet www.nsc.gov.la.

Area and Population

AREA, POPULATION AND DENSITY

Area (sq km)	236,800*
Population (census results)	
1 March 1995	4,581,258
1 March 2005	
Males	2,800,551
Females	2,821,431
Total	5,621,982
Population (official estimate at mid-year)	
2006	5,747,000
Density (per sq km) at mid-2006	24.3

* 91,400 sq miles.

PROVINCES
(population at mid-2005, official estimates)

	Area (sq km)	Population ('000)	Density (per sq km)
Vientiane (municipality)	3,920	698	178.1
Phongsali	16,270	166	10.2
Luang Namtha	9,325	145	15.5
Oudomxay	15,370	265	17.2
Bokeo	6,196	145	23.4
Luang Prabang	16,875	407	24.1
Houaphanh	16,500	281	17.0
Sayabouri	16,389	339	20.7
Xiangkhouang	15,880	230	14.5
Vientiane	18,526	389	21.0
Bolikhamsai	14,863	225	15.1
Khammouane	16,315	337	20.7
Savannakhet	21,774	826	37.9
Saravan	10,691	324	30.3
Sekong	7,665	85	11.1
Champasak	15,415	607	39.4
Attopu	10,320	112	10.9
Xaysomboun SR	4,506	39	8.7
Total	**236,800**	**5,622**	**23.7**

Note: In January 2006 the Xaysomboun SR special region was dissolved, and its administrative responsibilities were transferred to Vientiane and Xiangkhouang provinces.

LAOS

PRINCIPAL TOWNS
(population at 1995 census)

Viangchan (Vientiane—capital)	160,000	Xam Nua (Sam Neua)	33,500
Savannakhet (Khanthaboury)	58,500	Luang Prabang	25,500
Pakxe (Paksé)	47,000	Thakek (Khammouan)	22,500

Source: Stefan Helders, *World Gazetteer* (internet www.world-gazetteer.com).

Mid-2007 (incl. suburbs, UN estimate): Vientiane 745,000 (Source: UN, *World Urbanization Prospects: The 2007 Revision*).

BIRTHS AND DEATHS
(annual averages, UN estimates)

	1990–95	1995–2000	2000–05
Birth rate (per 1,000)	41.4	34.5	28.4
Death rate (per 1,000)	11.9	9.5	8.0

Source: UN, *World Population Prospects: The 2006 Revision*.

Expectation of life (years at birth, WHO estimates): 59.8 (males 58.8; females 60.9) in 2005 (Source: WHO, *World Health Statistics*).

ECONOMICALLY ACTIVE POPULATION
('000 persons in 2003)

	Total
Agriculture, etc.	2,085
Industry	235
Services	217
Total labour force	**2,537**

Source: Asian Development Bank, *Key Indicators of Developing Asian and Pacific Countries*.

Mid-2005 (estimates in '000): Agriculture, etc. 2,278; Total labour force 3,013 (Source: FAO).

Health and Welfare

KEY INDICATORS

Total fertility rate (children per woman, 2005)	4.6
Under-5 mortality rate (per 1,000 live births, 2005)	79
HIV/AIDS (% of persons aged 15–49, 2005)	0.1
Physicians (per 1,000 head, 1996)	0.59
Hospital beds (per 1,000 head, 2003)	1.10
Health expenditure (2004): US $ per head (PPP)	73.7
Health expenditure (2004): % of GDP	3.9
Health expenditure (2004): public (% of total)	20.5
Access to adequate water (% of persons, 2004)	51
Access to adequate sanitation (% of persons, 2004)	30
Human Development Index (2005): ranking	130
Human Development Index (2005): value	0.601

For sources and definitions, see explanatory note on p. vi.

Agriculture

PRINCIPAL CROPS
('000 metric tons)

	2003	2004	2005
Rice (paddy)	2,375	2,529	2,568
Maize	143	204	373
Potatoes	36*	35†	35†
Sweet potatoes	140	120	130
Cassava (Manioc)	4	56	51
Sugar cane	308	223	196
Watermelons	84	60	65†
Cantaloupes and other melons†	36	35	35
Bananas†	55	46	48
Oranges†	28	30	31
Tangerines, mandarins, clementines and satsumas†	23	23	25
Pineapples†	36	36	37
Coffee (green)	28	23	25
Tobacco (leaves)	26	33	28

* Unofficial figure.
† FAO estimate(s).

2006 ('000 metric tons): Rice (paddy) 2,660; Sugar cane 240 (FAO estimate).

Aggregate production ('000 metric tons, may include official, semi-official or estimated data): Total cereals 2,733 in 2004, 2,941 in 2005, 3,033 in 2006; Total vegetables (incl. melons) 759 in 2004, 775 in 2005, 773 in 2006; Total fruits (excl. melons) 204 in 2004, 211 in 2005, 211 in 2006.

Source: FAO.

LIVESTOCK
('000 head, year ending September)

	2003	2004	2005
Horses*	31	31	31
Cattle	1,244	1,249	1,272
Buffaloes	1,111	1,112	1,097
Pigs	1,655	1,728	1,827
Goats	137	141	143*
Chickens	19,474	19,481	19,802
Ducks*	2,600	3,000	3,200

* FAO estimate(s).
Source: FAO.

LIVESTOCK PRODUCTS
('000 metric tons)

	2003	2004*	2005*
Cattle meat	21.5	22.0	22.5
Buffalo meat	18.3	18.5	18.6
Pig meat	35.5	35.5	36.4
Chicken meat	14.4	15.2	16.0
Cows' milk*	6.0	6.0	6.0
Hen eggs	12.8	12.0	12.5

* FAO estimates.
Source: FAO.

Forestry

ROUNDWOOD REMOVALS
('000 cubic metres, excl. bark, FAO estimates)

	2004	2005	2006
Sawlogs, veneer logs and logs for sleepers	148	62	62
Other industrial wood	132	132	132
Fuel wood	5,928	5,944	5,944
Total	**6,209**	**6,137**	**6,137**

Source: FAO.

LAOS

SAWNWOOD PRODUCTION
('000 cubic metres, incl. railway sleepers)

	2004	2005	2006
Total (all broadleaved) . . .	125	130	130

Source: FAO.

Fishing

('000 metric tons, live weight)

	2003*	2004*	2005
Capture*	29.8	29.8	29.8
Cyprinids*	4.5	4.5	4.5
Other freshwater fishes* . .	25.3	25.3	25.3
Aquaculture	64.9	64.9	78.0
Common carp	16.2	16.2	5.8
Roho labeo	2.7	2.7	5.3
Mrigal carp	2.7	2.7	4.7
Bighead carp	3.8	3.8	6.5
Silver carp	3.8	3.8	8.0
Nile tilapia	29.2	29.2	19.6
Total catch	94.7	94.7	107.8

* FAO estimates.
Source: FAO.

Mining

('000 metric tons, unless otherwise indicated)

	2004	2005	2006*
Coal (all grades)	298.8	300.0	233.0
Gemstones, sapphire ('000 carats)	712.3	710.0	750.0
Gypsum	201.1	131.5	150.0
Salt	15.0	34.1	35.0
Copper (metric tons)†	—	30,480*	60,803
Tin (metric tons)†	400	100	70

* Estimate(s).
† Figures refer to metal content.
Source: US Geological Survey.

Industry

SELECTED PRODUCTS

	2004	2005	2006
Beer ('000 hectolitres) . . .	827	927	1,059
Soft drinks ('000 hectolitres) . .	187	194	n.a.
Cigarettes (million packs) . . .	84	105	n.a.
Garments (million pieces) . . .	37	39	68
Plastic products (metric tons) . .	5,500	6,000	n.a.
Detergent (metric tons) . . .	860	880	1,082
Agricultural tools ('000) . . .	4	4	n.a.
Nails (metric tons)	900	980	2,099
Bricks (million)	120	135	n.a.
Hydroelectric energy (million kWh)	3,348	3,492	3,606
Tobacco (metric tons)	1,897	3,080	3,836
Plywood (million sheets) . . .	1,300	1,320	n.a.

Source: Ministry of Industry and Handicrafts, Vientiane.

Finance

CURRENCY AND EXCHANGE RATES

Monetary Units
100 at (cents) = 1 new kip.

Sterling, Dollar and Euro Equivalents (31 October 2007)
£1 sterling = 19,611.3 new kips;
US $1 = 9,457.6 new kips;
€1 = 13,663.4 new kips;
100,000 new kips = £5.10 = $10.57 = €7.32.

Average Exchange Rate (new kips per US $)
2004   10,585.5
2005   10,655.2
2006   10,159.9

Note: In September 1995 a policy of 'floating' exchange rates was adopted, with commercial banks permitted to set their rates.

GENERAL BUDGET
('000 million new kips, year ending 30 September)*

Revenue†	2004/05	2005/06	2006/07‡
Tax revenue	2,803	3,641	4,086
Profits tax	307	459	733
Income tax	215	234	241
Turnover tax	673	887	872
Excise tax	523	800	870
Import duties	429	515	518
Timber royalties	189	172	150
Other tax revenue . . .	467	574	703
Non-tax revenue	584	625	602
Payment for depreciation or dividend transfers . .	178	175	180
Overflight	222	229	227
Other revenue	185	222	195
Total	3,387	4,266	4,689

Expenditure	2004/05	2005/06	2006/07‡
Current expenditure . . .	2,517	3,124	3,603
Wages and salaries . . .	1,058	1,263	1,540
Compensation and allowances	317	674	874
Subsidies and transfers . .	196		
Interest	318	277	394
Other recurrent expenditure .	626	911	795
Capital expenditure and net lending	2,261	2,529	2,788
Domestically-financed . .	468	403	517
Foreign-financed	1,531	1,956	2,416
Onlending (net)	261	171	−145
Debt repayment	347	348	370
Total	5,124	6,002	6,761

* Since 1992 there has been a unified budget covering the operations of the central Government, provincial administrations and state enterprises.
† Excluding grants received ('000 million new kips): 499 in 2004/05; 696 in 2005/06; 681 in 2006/07 (budget).
‡ Budget.

Source: IMF, *Lao People's Democratic Republic: Selected Issues and Statistical Appendix* (November 2007).

INTERNATIONAL RESERVES
(US $ million at 31 December)

	2004	2005	2006
Gold (national valuation) . .	4.10	5.10	7.35
IMF special drawing rights . .	15.37	14.09	14.71
Foreign exchange	207.87	220.21	312.16
Total	227.35	239.40	334.22

Source: IMF, *International Financial Statistics*.

LAOS

MONEY SUPPLY
(million new kips at 31 December*)

	2004	2005	2006
Currency outside banks	666,420	948,550	1,230,590
Demand deposits at commercial banks	537,540	610,260	767,660
Total (incl. others)	1,207,290	1,558,910	1,998,320

* Figures rounded to the nearest ten million.

Source: IMF, *International Financial Statistics*.

COST OF LIVING
(Consumer Price Index for Vientiane; base: 2000 = 100)

	2004	2005	2006
All items	152.2	163.1	174.2

Source: IMF, *International Financial Statistics*.

NATIONAL ACCOUNTS
Gross Domestic Product by Economic Activity
(million new kips at current prices)

	2004	2005	2006*
Agriculture, hunting, forestry and fishing	12,377,759	13,593,364	14,940,091
Mining and quarrying	396,740	941,003	1,878,248
Manufacturing	5,372,876	6,274,388	7,242,166
Electricity, gas and water	720,339	821,750	906,384
Construction	700,037	895,608	1,143,571
Wholesale and retail trade	2,763,900	3,178,374	3,680,580
Hotels and restaurants	528,336	690,773	848,901
Transport, storage and communications	1,703,280	1,912,611	2,195,012
Finance and insurance	83,972	109,925	137,406
Ownership of dwellings	682,470	749,674	820,656
Public administration	957,228	1,082,575	1,224,336
Other services	65,913	74,801	84,409
GDP at factor cost	26,352,850	30,324,846	35,101,760
Import duties, etc.	237,281	269,239	305,502
GDP in purchasers' values	26,590,131	30,594,085	35,407,262

* Estimates.

BALANCE OF PAYMENTS
(US $ million)

	2004	2005	2006
Exports of goods f.o.b.	363.3	553.1	882.0
Imports of goods c.i.f.	−712.7	−882.0	−1,060.2
Trade balance	−349.4	−328.9	−178.2
Services and other income (net)	81.5	69.2	92.9
Balance on goods, services and income	−267.9	−259.7	−85.3
Current transfers received	119.2	124.2	151.5
Current transfers paid	−40.6	−57.0	−24.9
Current balance	−189.3	−192.5	41.3
Direct investment (net)	16.9	27.7	187.3
Other investments (net)	77.2	126.7	42.6
Net errors and omissions	107.2	48.8	−173.9
Overall balance	12.0	10.8	97.3

Source: Asian Development Bank, *Key Indicators of Developing Asian and Pacific Countries*.

External Trade

PRINCIPAL COMMODITIES
(US $ million)

Imports c.i.f.	2004	2005	2006*
Petroleum	107.6	159.5	201.3
Capital goods	467.6	615.0	728.0
Materials for garments industry	115.5	103.0	98.6
Electricity	18.2	23.1	25.1
Total (incl. others)	977.2	1,205.6	1,384.1

* Estimates.

Exports f.o.b.	2004	2005	2006*
Timber	144.9	136.8	158.1
Coffee	14.4	21.9	29.9
Garments	154.7	138.0	132.0
Electricity	91.1	107.0	107.1
Copper	—	112.1	409.3
Gold (incl. re-exports)	57.8	90.7	116.1
Total (incl. others)	499.6	646.3	996.0

* Estimates.

Source: IMF, *Lao People's Democratic Republic: Selected Issues and Statistical Appendix* (November 2007).

PRINCIPAL TRADING PARTNERS
(US $ million)

Imports	2004	2005	2006
Australia	18.3	21.0	20.5
China, People's Republic	108.8	115.9	185.6
France	10.5	13.5	11.3
Germany	28.0	11.3	12.0
Hong Kong	8.0	8.3	15.5
Japan	15.4	21.3	22.7
Korea, Republic	9.9	11.8	18.0
Singapore	42.3	44.1	45.2
Thailand*	639.5	846.2	1,127.6
Viet Nam	74.8	89.3	86.2
Total (incl. others)	1,056.7	1,267.3	1,632.7

Exports	2004	2005	2006
Belgium	13.4	15.6	16.5
China, People's Republic	11.4	23.2	45.1
France	43.4	41.9	27.9
Germany	28.7	31.6	34.6
Italy	11.8	8.9	6.6
Netherlands	10.9	13.4	12.8
Thailand*	104.3	204.4	454.7
United Kingdom	26.8	8.3	1.4
Viet Nam	72.5	86.6	101.8
Total (incl. others)	540.5	694.6	1,055.0

* Trade with Thailand may be overestimated, as it may include goods in transit to and from other countries.

Source: Asian Development Bank, *Key Indicators of Developing Asian and Pacific Countries*.

Transport

ROAD TRAFFIC
(motor vehicles in use at 31 December, estimates)

	1994	1995	1996
Passenger cars	18,240	17,280	16,320
Buses and coaches	440	n.a.	n.a.
Lorries and vans	7,920	6,020	4,200
Motorcycles and mopeds	169,000	200,000	231,000

Source: International Road Federation, *World Road Statistics*.

SHIPPING

Inland Waterways
(traffic)

	2002	2003	2004
Freight ('000 metric tons)	770.0	893.0	939.9
Freight ton-kilometres (million)	69.9	55.5	49.6
Passengers ('000)	2,025.0	2,203.0	2,183.5
Passenger-kilometres (million)	76.9	45.3	22.4

Source: Ministry of Communications, Transport, Post and Construction.

Merchant Fleet
(registered at 31 December)

	2004	2005	2006
Number of vessels	1	2	2
Displacement ('000 grt)	2.4	2.9	2.9

Source: Lloyd's Register-Fairplay, *World Fleet Statistics*.

CIVIL AVIATION
(traffic on scheduled services)

	2001	2002	2003
Kilometres flown (million)	2	2	3
Passengers carried ('000)	211	220	219
Passenger-kilometres (million)	86	91	90
Total ton-kilometres (million)	9	9	9

Source: UN, *Statistical Yearbook*.

Tourism

FOREIGN VISITOR ARRIVALS
(incl. excursionists)

Country of nationality	2003	2004	2005
China, People's Republic	21,232	33,019	39,210
France	23,958	27,806	35,371
Japan	17,766	20,319	20,319
Thailand	377,748	489,677	603,189
United Kingdom	22,541	27,402	29,977
USA	30,133	37,181	47,427
Viet Nam	41,594	130,816	165,151
Total (incl. others)	636,361	894,806	1,095,315

Tourism receipts (US $ million, excl. passenger transport): 87 in 2003; 119 in 2004; 146 in 2005.

Source: World Tourism Organization.

Communications Media

	2003	2004	2005
Telephones ('000 main lines in use)	69.8	75.0	75.3
Mobile cellular telephones ('000 subscribers)	112.3	204.2	638.2
Personal computers ('000 in use)	20	22	100
Internet users ('000)	19.0	20.9	25.0
Broadband subscribers ('000)	n.a.	n.a.	0.1

Radio receivers ('000 in use): 730 in 1997.

Television receivers ('000 in use): 280 in 2001.

Facsimile machines (estimated number in use): 500 in 1994 (Source: UN, *Statistical Yearbook*).

Book production (1995): Titles 88; copies ('000) 995.

Daily newspapers (2004): 6 (average circulation 14,558).

Non-daily newspapers (1988, estimates): 18 (average circulation 34,550).

Sources (unless otherwise specified): International Telecommunication Union; UNESCO, *Statistical Yearbook*.

Education

(2006/07)

	Institutions	Teachers	Students
Pre-primary	1,087	3,000	49,000
Primary	8,654	28,000	892,000
Secondary:			
lower	642	10,000	243,000
upper	28	500	148,000
vocational	47	1,500	26,300
University level	3	1,300	30,600
Other higher	38	1,100	30,100

Note: Figures for teachers and students are rounded to the nearest 100 persons.

Source: Ministry of Education, Vientiane.

Adult literacy rate (UNESCO estimates): 68.7% (males 77.0%; females 60.9%) in 2001 (Source: UNESCO Institute for Statistics).

Directory

The Constitution

The new Constitution was unanimously endorsed by the Supreme People's Assembly on 14 August 1991. Its main provisions are summarized below:

POLITICAL SYSTEM

The Lao People's Democratic Republic (Lao PDR) is an independent, sovereign and united country and is indivisible.

The Lao PDR is a people's democratic state. The people's rights are exercised and ensured through the functioning of the political system, with the Lao People's Revolutionary Party as its leading organ. The people exercise power through the National Assembly, which functions in accordance with the principle of democratic centralism.

The State respects and protects all lawful activities of Buddhism and the followers of other religious faiths.

The Lao PDR pursues a foreign policy of peace, independence, friendship and co-operation. It adheres to the principles of peaceful co-existence with other countries, based on mutual respect for independence, sovereignty and territorial integrity.

SOCIO-ECONOMIC SYSTEM

The economy is market-orientated, with intervention by the State. The State encourages all economic sectors to compete and co-operate in the expansion of production and trade.

Private ownership of property and rights of inheritance are protected by the State.

The State authorizes the operation of private schools and medical services, while promoting the expansion of public education and health services.

FUNDAMENTAL RIGHTS AND OBLIGATIONS OF CITIZENS

Lao citizens, irrespective of their sex, social status, education, faith and ethnic group, are equal before the law.

Lao citizens aged 18 years and above have the right to vote, and those over 21 years to be candidates, in elections.

Lao citizens have freedom of religion, speech, press and assembly, and freedom to establish associations and to participate in demonstrations which do not contradict the law.

THE NATIONAL ASSEMBLY

The National Assembly is the legislative organ, which also oversees the activities of the administration and the judiciary. Members of the National Assembly are elected for a period of five years by universal adult suffrage. The National Assembly elects its own Standing Committee, which consists of the Chairman and Vice-Chairman of the National Assembly (and thus also of the National Assembly Standing Committee) and a number of other members. The National Assembly convenes its ordinary session twice annually. The National Assembly Standing Committee may convene an extraordinary session of the National Assembly if it deems this necessary. The National Assembly is empowered to amend the Constitution; to endorse, amend or abrogate laws; to elect or remove the President of State and Vice-Presidents of State, as proposed by the Standing Committee of the National Assembly; to adopt motions expressing no confidence in the Government; to elect or remove the President of the People's Supreme Court, on the recommendation of the National Assembly Standing Committee.

THE PRESIDENT OF STATE

The President of State, who is also Head of the Armed Forces, is elected by the National Assembly for a five-year tenure. Laws adopted by the National Assembly must be promulgated by the President of State not later than 30 days after their enactment. The President is empowered to appoint or dismiss the Prime Minister and members of the Government, with the approval of the National Assembly; to appoint government officials at provincial and municipal levels; and to promote military personnel, on the recommendation of the Prime Minister.

THE GOVERNMENT

The Government is the administrative organ of the State. It is composed of the Prime Minister, Deputy Prime Ministers and Ministers or Chairmen of Committees (which are equivalent to Ministries), who are appointed by the President, with the approval of the National Assembly, for a term of five years. The Government implements the Constitution, laws and resolutions adopted by the National Assembly and state decrees and acts of the President of State. The Prime Minister is empowered to appoint Deputy Ministers and Vice-Chairmen of Committees, and junior-level government officials.

LOCAL ADMINISTRATION

The Lao PDR is divided into provinces, municipalities, districts and villages. Provincial governors and mayors of municipalities are appointed by the President of State. Deputy provincial governors, deputy mayors and district chiefs are appointed by the Prime Minister. Administration at village level is conducted by village heads.

THE JUDICIARY

The people's courts comprise the People's Supreme Court, the people's provincial and municipal courts, the people's district courts and military courts. The President of the People's Supreme Court and the Public Prosecutor-General are elected by the National Assembly, on the recommendation of the National Assembly Standing Committee. The Vice-President of the People's Supreme Court and the judges of the people's courts at all levels are appointed by the National Assembly Standing Committee.

The Government

HEAD OF STATE

President of State: Lt-Gen. CHOUMMALI SAIGNASON (elected 8 June 2006).
Vice-President: BOUNGNANG VOLACHIT.

COUNCIL OF MINISTERS
(April 2008)

Prime Minister: BOUASONE BOUPHAVANH.
Deputy Prime Minister and Minister of Foreign Affairs: THONGLOUN SISOLIT.
Deputy Prime Minister and Minister of National Defence: Maj.-Gen. DOUANGCHAI PHICHIT.
Deputy Prime Ministers: Maj.-Gen. ASANG LAOLI, SOMSAVAT LENGSAVAT.
Minister of Finance: SOMDY DOUANGDY.
Minister of Security: THONGBANH SENGAPHONE.
Minister of Justice: CHALEUN YIAPAOHEU.
Minister of Agriculture and Forestry: SITAHENG LATSAPHONE.
Minister of Communications, Transport, Post and Construction: SOMMATH PHOLSENA.
Minister of Industry and Commerce: Dr NAM VIYAKET.
Minister of Information and Culture: MOUNKEO OLABUN.
Minister of Labour and Social Welfare: ONECHANH THAMMAVONG.
Minister of Education: Prof. SOMKOT MANGNOMEK.
Minister of Public Health: Dr PONEMEKH DARALOY.
Minister of Energy and Mining: Dr BOSAIKHAM VONGDARA.
Minister to the Office of the President: SOUBANH SRITHIRATH.
Ministers to the Office of the Prime Minister: BOUNTIEM PHITSAMAY, ONNEUA PHOMMACHANH, KHAM-OUANE BOUPPHA, SAISENGLI TENGIACHU, KHAMLOUAT SITLAKON, CHEUANG SOMBOUNKHAN, BUNPHENG MUNGPHOSAI, SOMPHONG MONGKONVILAI, KHEMPHENG PHOLSENA, PHOUTHONG SAENGAKHOM, DOUANGSAVAT SOUPHANAOUVONG.
President of the State Planning Committee: SOULIVONG DARAVONG.
Governor of the Central Bank: PHOUPHET KHAMPHOUNVONG.

MINISTRIES

Office of the President: rue Lane Xang, Vientiane; tel. (21) 214200; fax (21) 214208.
Office of the Prime Minister: Ban Sisavat, Vientiane; tel. (21) 213653; fax (21) 213560.
Ministry of Agriculture and Forestry: Ban Phonxay, Vientiane; tel. (21) 412359; fax (21) 412344; internet www.maf.gov.la.
Ministry of Commerce: 104/4-5 rue Khounboulom, BP 4107, Vientiane; tel. (21) 216207; fax (21) 213623; e-mail citd@moc.gov.la; internet www.moc.gov.la.
Ministry of Communications, Transport, Post and Construction: ave Lane Xang, Vientiane; tel. (21) 412251; fax (21) 414123.
Ministry of Education: 1 rue Lane Xang, BP 67, Vientiane; tel. (21) 216013; fax (21) 216006; e-mail esitc@moe.gov.la; internet www.moe.gov.la.
Ministry of Energy and Mining: Vientiane.
Ministry of Finance: rue That Luang, Ban Phonxay, Vientiane; tel. (21) 412401; fax (21) 412415.
Ministry of Foreign Affairs: rue That Luang 01004, Ban Phonxay, Vientiane; tel. (21) 413148; fax (21) 414009; e-mail cabinet@mofa.gov.la; internet www.mofa.gov.la.
Ministry of Information and Culture: rue Setthathirath, Ban Xiengnheun, Vientiane; tel. (21) 212897; fax (21) 212408; e-mail email@mic.gov.la.
Ministry of Justice: Ban Phonxay, Vientiane; tel. (21) 414105.
Ministry of Labour and Social Welfare: rue Pangkham, Ban Sisaket, Vientiane; tel. (21) 213003.
Ministry of National Defence: rue Phone Kheng, Ban Phone Kheng, Vientiane; tel. (21) 412803.
Ministry of Public Health: Ban Simeuang, Vientiane; tel. (21) 214002; fax (21) 214001; e-mail cabinet.fr@moh.gov.la.
Ministry of Security: rue Nongbone, Ban Hatsady, Vientiane; tel. (21) 212500.

Legislature

At the election held on 30 April 2006 113 candidates of the Lao People's Revolutionary Party (LPRP) and two independents were elected to the National Assembly. (All but three candidates contesting the elections were members of the LPRP.)

President of the National Assembly: THONGSING THAMMAVONG.
Vice-Presidents: PANY YATHOTU, Dr XAYSOMPHONE PHOMVIHANE.

Political Organizations

COMMUNIST PARTY

Phak Pasason Pativat Lao (Lao People's Revolutionary Party—LPRP): Vientiane; f. 1955 as the People's Party of Laos; reorg. under present name in 1972; Cen. Cttee of 55 full mems elected at Eighth Party Congress in March 2006; Gen. Sec. Lt-Gen. CHOUMMALI SAIGNASON.

Political Bureau (Politburo)

Full members: Lt-Gen. CHOUMMALI SAIGNASON, Lt-Gen. SAMAN VIGNAKET, THONGSIN THAMMAVONG, BOUNGNANG VOLACHIT, Gen. SISAVAT KEOBOUNPHAN, Maj.-Gen. ASANG LAOLI, THOUNGLONG SISO-

LIT, Maj.-Gen. DOUANGCHAI PHICHIT, BOUASONE BOUPHAVANH, SOMSAVAT LENGSAVAT, PHANI YATHOTHU.

OTHER POLITICAL ORGANIZATIONS

Lao Front for National Construction (LFNC): Thanon Khouvieng, Ban Sisakhet, Muang Chanthaboury, Vientiane; tel. (21) 213752; fax (21) 213752; f. 1979 to replace the Lao Liberal Front and the Lao Patriotic Front; comprises representatives of various political and social groups, of which the LPRP (see above) is the dominant force; fosters national solidarity; Chair. Gen. SISAVAT KEOBOUNPHANH; Vice-Chair. SIHO BANNAVONG, KHAMPHOUI CHANTHASOUK, TONG YEUTHOR.

Numerous factions are in armed opposition to the Government. The principal groups are:

Democratic Chao Fa Party of Laos: led by Pa Kao Her until his death in Oct. 2002; Pres. SOUA HER; Vice-Pres. TENG TANG.

Free Democratic Lao National Salvation Force: based in Thailand.

United Front for the Liberation of Laos: Leader PHOUNGPHET PHANARETH.

United Front for the National Liberation of the Lao People: f. 1980; led by Gen. PHOUMI NOSAVAN until his death in 1985.

United Lao National Liberation Front: Sayabouri Province; comprises an estimated 8,000 members, mostly Hmong (Meo) tribesmen; Sec.-Gen. VANG SHUR.

Diplomatic Representation

EMBASSIES IN LAOS

Australia: rue Pandit J. Nehru, quartier Phonxay, BP 292, Vientiane; tel. (21) 413600; fax (21) 413601; e-mail austemb.laos@dfat.gov.au; internet www.laos.embassy.gov.au; Ambassador MICHELE FORSTER.

Brunei: Unit 12, Ban Thoungkang, Lao-Thai Friendship Rd, Sisathanak, Vientiane; tel. (21) 352294; fax (21) 352291; e-mail embdlaos@laotel.com; Ambassador Hajik SIDEK ALI.

Cambodia: rue Thadeua, Km 3, BP 34, Vientiane; tel. (21) 314952; fax (21) 314951; e-mail recamlao@laotel.com; Ambassador DAN YI.

China, People's Republic: rue Wat Nak, Muang Sisattanak, BP 898, Vientiane; tel. (21) 315100; fax (21) 315104; e-mail embassyprc@laonet.net; Ambassador PAN GUANGXUE.

Cuba: Ban Saphanthong Neua 128, BP 1017, Vientiane; tel. (21) 314902; fax (21) 314901; e-mail embacuba@laonet.net; Ambassador EDUARDO VALIDO GARCÍA.

France: rue Setthathirath, BP 06, Vientiane; tel. (21) 215253; fax (21) 215250; e-mail contact@ambafrance-laos.org; internet www.ambafrance-laos.org; Ambassador FRANÇOIS SÉNÉMAUD.

Germany: rue Sok Paluang 26, Muang Sisattanak, BP 314, Vientiane; tel. (21) 312110; fax (21) 351152; e-mail info@vien.diplo.de; Ambassador PETER WIENAND.

India: 2 Ban Wat Nak, rue Thadeua, Km 3, Sisattanak District, Vientiane; tel. (21) 352301; fax (21) 352300; e-mail indiaemb@laotel.com; internet indemblao.nic.in; Ambassador Shri SURESH K. GOEL.

Indonesia: ave Phone Keng, BP 277, Vientiane; tel. (21) 413909; fax (21) 214828; e-mail kbrivte@laotel.com; Ambassador SUTJIPTORAHHARDJO DONOKUSUMO.

Japan: rue Sisangvone, Vientiane; tel. (21) 414401; fax (21) 414406; internet www.la.emb-japan.go.jp; Ambassador MASAAKI MIYASHITA.

Korea, Democratic People's Republic: quartier Wat Nak, Vientiane; tel. (21) 315261; fax (21) 315260; Ambassador PAK MYONG GU.

Korea, Republic: rue Lao-Thai Friendship, Ban Wat Nak, Sisattanak District, BP 7567, Vientiane; tel. (21) 415833; fax (21) 415831; e-mail koramb@laotel.com; internet lao.mofat.go.kr; Ambassador PARK JAE-HYUN.

Malaysia: 23 rue Singha, quartier Phonxay, BP 789, Vientiane; tel. (21) 414205; fax (21) 414201; e-mail mwvntian@laopdr.com; internet www.kln.gov.my/perwakilan/vientiane; Ambassador ZAINAL ABIDIN AHMAD.

Mongolia: rue Wat Nak, Km 3, BP 370, Vientiane; tel. (21) 315220; fax (21) 315221; e-mail embmong@laotel.com; Ambassador TOGTOKHYN BATBAATAR.

Myanmar: Ban Thong Kang, rue Sok Paluang, BP 11, Vientiane; tel. (21) 314910; fax (21) 314913; e-mail mev@loxinfo.co.th; Ambassador U TIN OO.

Philippines: Ban Saphanthong Kang, Sisattanak, BP 2415, Vientiane; tel. (21) 452490; fax (21) 452493; e-mail pelaopdr@laotel.com; Ambassador ELIZABETH P. BUENSUCESO.

Poland: 263 Ban Thadeua, Km 3, quartier Wat Nak, BP 1106, Vientiane; tel. (21) 312940; fax (21) 312085; e-mail polembv@yahoo.com; internet www.vientiane.polemb.net; Chargé d'affaires Dr TOMASZ GERLACH.

Russia: Ban Thadeua, quartier Thaphalanxay, BP 490, Vientiane; tel. (21) 312222; fax (21) 312210; e-mail rusemb@laotel.com; Ambassador VLADIMIR PLOTNIKOV.

Singapore: Unit 12, Ban Naxay, rue Nong Bong, Muang Sat Settha, Vientiane; tel. (21) 416860; fax (21) 416854; e-mail singemb_vte@sgmfa.gov.sg; internet www.mfa.gov.sg/vientiane; Ambassador BENJAMIN WILLIAM.

Thailand: ave Kaysone Phomvihane, Xaysettha, Vientiane; tel. (21) 214581; fax (21) 214580; e-mail thaivtn@mfa.go.th; internet www.thaiembassy.org/vientiane; Ambassador WIBOON KHUSAKUL.

USA: 19 rue Bartholonie, BP 114, That Dam, Vientiane; tel. (21) 267000; fax (21) 267190; e-mail khammanhpx@state.gov; internet vientiane.usembassy.gov; Ambassador RAVIC ROLF HUSO.

Viet Nam: 85 23 rue Singha, Phonxay, Xaysettha, Vientiane; tel. (21) 413409; fax (21) 413379; e-mail dsqvn@laotel.com; internet www.mofa.gov.vn/vnemb.la; Ambassador NGUYEN HUY QUANG.

Judicial System

President of the People's Supreme Court: KHAMMY SAYAVONG.

Vice-President: DAVON VANGVICHIT.

People's Supreme Court Judges: NOUANTHONG VONGSA, NHOTSENG LITTHIDETH, PHOUKHONG CHANTHALATH, SENGSOUVANH CHANTHALOUNNAVONG, KESON PHANLACK, KONGCHI YANGCHY, KHAMPON PHASAIGNAVONG.

Public Prosecutor-General: SOMPHANE PHENGKHAMMY.

Religion

The 1991 Constitution guarantees freedom of religious belief. The principal religion of Laos is Buddhism.

BUDDHISM

Lao Unified Buddhists' Association: Maha Kudy, Wat That Luang, Vientiane; f. 1964; Pres. (vacant); Sec.-Gen. Rev. SIHO SIHAVONG.

CHRISTIANITY

The Roman Catholic Church

For ecclesiastical purposes, Laos comprises four Apostolic Vicariates. At 31 December 2005 an estimated 0.6% of the population were adherents.

Episcopal Conference of Laos and Cambodia

c/o Mgr Pierre Bach, Paris Foreign Missions, 254 Silom Rd, Bangkok 10500, Thailand.

f. 1971; Pres. Most Rev. DESTOMBES EMILE (Titular Bishop of Altava).

Vicar Apostolic of Luang Prabang: (vacant), Evêché, BP 113, Luang Prabang.

Vicar Apostolic of Paksé: Mgr LOUIS-MARIE LING MANGKHANEKHOUN (Titular Bishop of Proconsulari), Centre Catholique, BP 77, Paksé, Champasak; tel. (31) 212879; fax (31) 251439.

Vicar Apostolic of Savannakhet: Mgr JEAN SOMMENG VORACHAK (Titular Bishop of Muzuca in Proconsulari), Centre Catholique, BP 12, Thakek, Khammouane; tel. (51) 212184; fax (51) 213070.

Vicar Apostolic of Vientiane: Mgr JEAN KHAMSÉ VITHAVONG (Titular Bishop of Moglaena), Centre Catholique, BP 113, Vientiane; tel. (21) 216593; fax (21) 215085.

The Anglican Communion

Laos is within the jurisdiction of the Anglican Bishop of Singapore.

The Protestant Church

Lao Evangelical Church: BP 4200, Vientiane; tel. (21) 169136; Exec. Pres. Rev. KHAMPHONE KOUTHAPANYA.

BAHÁ'Í FAITH

National Spiritual Assembly: BP 189, Vientiane; tel. and fax (21) 216996; e-mail usme@laotel.com; f. 1956; Sec. SUSADA SENCHANTHISAY.

The Press

Aloun Mai (New Dawn): rue That Luang, Ban Nongbone, Xaysettha, Vientiane; tel. (21) 413029; fax (21) 413037; f. 1985; quarterly; theoretical and political organ of the LPRP; Editor-in-Chief SISOUK PHILAVONG.

Finance: rue That Luang, Ban Phonxay, Vientiane; tel. (21) 412401; fax (21) 412415; organ of Ministry of Finance.

Heng Ngan: 87 ave Lane Xang, BP 780, Vientiane; tel. (21) 212756; fax (21) 219750; fortnightly; organ of the Federation of Lao Trade Unions; Editor CHANSING KOKKEOBOUNMA.

Khao Tourakit (Business News): rue Sihom, Ban Sihom, Chanthaboury, Vientiane; tel. (21) 219244; fax (21) 219223; e-mail bsnews@laotel.com; f. 1999; fortnightly; organ of the Lao National Chamber of Commerce and Industry; Editor-in-Chief SOMCHIT THIPTHIENGTHAM.

Khaokila (Sports Daily News): Ban Mixay, Chanthaboury, Vientiane; tel. (21) 252908; fax (21) 252909; e-mail khaokila@hotmail.com; f. 1999; Editor-in-Chief SUKSAKHONE SIPRASEUTH.

Lao Dong (Labour): 87 ave Lane Xang, Vientiane; f. 1986; fortnightly; organ of the Federation of Lao Trade Unions; circ. 46,000.

Laos: 80 rue Setthathirath, BP 3770, Vientiane; tel. (21) 21447; fax (21) 21445; quarterly; published in Lao and English; illustrated; Editor V. PHOMCHANHEUANG; English Editor O. PHRAKHAMSAY.

Meying Lao: rue Manthatoarath, BP 59, Vientiane; e-mail chansoda@hotmail.com; f. 1980; monthly; women's magazine; organ of the Lao Women's Union; Editor-in-Chief VATSADY KHUTNGOTHA; Editor CHANSODA PHONETHIP; circ. 7,000.

Noum Lao (Lao Youth): rue Phonthan, Ban Phonthan Neua, Xaysettha, Vientiane; tel. (21) 951067; fax (21) 416727; f. 1979; fortnightly; organ of the Lao People's Revolutionary Youth Union; Editor KHANKAB BUDARAT; circ. 1,500.

Pasason Van Athit: rue Pangkham, Ban Xiengyeun Thong, Chanthaboury, Vientiane; tel. (21) 212471; fax (21) 212470; weekly; Editor THONGLITH LIEMXAYYACHAK; circ. 2,000.

Pasaxon (The People): 80 rue Setthathirath, BP 110, Vientiane; tel. (21) 212466; fax (21) 212470; e-mail infonews@pasaxon.org.la; internet www.pasaxon.org.la; f. 1940; daily; Lao; organ of the Cen. Cttee of the LPRP; Editor BOUABAN VOLAKHOUN; circ. 28,000.

Pathet Lao: 80 rue Setthathirath, Vientiane; tel. (21) 212447; f. 2001; daily; Lao and English; organ of the Lao News Agency, Khao San Pathet Lao (KPL); Editor KHEMTHONG SANOUBAN.

Sciences and Technics: Science, Technology and the Environment Agency (STEA), BP 2279, Vientiane; f. 1991; est. as Technical Science Magazine; quarterly; organ of the Dept of Science and Technology; scientific research and development.

Siang Khong Gnaovason Song Thanva (Voice of the 2nd December Youths): Vientiane; monthly; youth journal.

Sieng Khene Lao: Vientiane; monthly; organ of the Lao Writers' Association.

Suksa Mai: Vientiane; monthly; organ of the Ministry of Education.

Valasan Khosana (Propaganda Journal): Vientiane; f. 1987; organ of the Cen. Cttee of the LPRP.

Vannasinh: Vientiane; monthly; literature magazine.

Vientiane Mai (New Vientiane): 36 rue Setthathirath, BP 989, Vientiane; tel. (21) 212623; fax (21) 215989; e-mail admin@vientianemai.net; internet www.vientianemai.net; f. 1975; morning daily; organ of the LPRP Cttee of Vientiane province and city; Editor SOMPHET INTHISARATH; circ. 2,500.

Vientiane Times: rue Pangkham, BP 5723, Vientiane; tel. (21) 216364; fax (21) 216365; e-mail info@vientianetimes.gov.la; internet www.vientianetimes.org.la; f. 1994; daily; English; Editor-in-Chief SAVANKHONE RAZMOUNTRY; circ. 3,000.

Vientiane Tourakit Sangkhom (Vientiane Business-Social): 36 rue Setthathirath, Vientiane; tel. (21) 2623; fax (21) 6365; weekly; publ. in conjunction with Vientiane Mai; Editor SOMPHET INTHISARATH; circ. 2,000.

There is also a newspaper published by the Lao People's Army, and several provinces have their own newsletters.

NEWS AGENCY

Khao San Pathet Lao (Lao News Agency—KPL): 80 rue Setthathirath, BP 3770, Vientiane; tel. (21) 215090; fax (210 212446; e-mail kplnews@yahoo.com; internet www.kplnet.net; f. 1968; dept of the Ministry of Information and Culture; news service for press, radio and television broadcasting; daily bulletins in Lao, English and French; Gen. Dir KHAMSENE PHONGSA; English Editor BOUNLERT LOUANEDOUANGCHANH.

PRESS ASSOCIATION

The Journalists' Association of the Lao PDR: BP 122, Vientiane; tel. (21) 212420; fax (21) 212408; Pres. BOUABANE VORAKHOUNE; Sec.-Gen. KHAM KHONG KONGVONGSA.

Publishers

Khoualuang Kanphim: 2–6 Khoualuang Market, Vientiane.

Lao-phanit: Ministry of Education, Bureau des Manuels Scolaires, rue Lane Xang, Ban Sisavat, Vientiane; educational, cookery, art, music, fiction.

Pakpassak Kanphin: 9–11 quai Fa-Hguun, Vientiane.

State Printing Enterprise: 314/C rue Samsemthai, BP 2160, Vientiane; tel. (21) 213273; fax (21) 215901; Dir NOUPHAY KOUNLAVONG.

Broadcasting and Communications

TELECOMMUNICATIONS

Entreprises des Postes et Télécommunications de Laos: ave Lane Xang, 01000 Vientiane; tel. (21) 215767; fax (21) 212779; e-mail laoposts@laotel.com; state enterprise, responsible for the postal service and telecommunications; Dir-Gen. KIENG KHAMKETH.

Lao Télécommunications Co Ltd: ave Lane Xang, BP 5607, 0100 Vientiane; tel. (21) 216465; fax (21) 219690; e-mail marketin@laotel.com; internet www.laotel.com; f. 1996; a jt venture between a subsidiary of the Shinawatra Group of Thailand and Entreprises des Postes et Télécommunications de Laos; awarded a 25-year contract by the Government in 1996 to undertake all telecommunications projects in the country; Dir-Gen. HOUMPHANH INTHARATH.

BROADCASTING

Radio

In addition to the national radio service, there are several local stations.

Lao National Radio: rue Phangkham, Km 6, BP 310, Vientiane; tel. (21) 212468; fax (21) 212430; e-mail laonradio@lnr.org.la; internet www.lnr.org.la; f. 1960; state-owned; programmes in Lao, French, English, Thai, Khmer and Vietnamese; domestic and international services; Dir-Gen. BOUNTHANH INTHAXAY.

In 1990 resistance forces in Laos established an illegal radio station, broadcasting anti-Government propaganda: Satthani Vithayou Kachai Siang Latthaban Potpoi Sat Lao (Radio Station of the Government for the Liberation of the Lao Nation): programmes in Lao and Hmong languages; broadcasts four hours daily.

Television

A domestic television service began in December 1983. In May 1988 a second national television station commenced transmissions from Savannakhet. In December 1993 the Ministry of Information and Culture signed a 15-year joint-venture contract with a Thai firm on the development of broadcasting services in Laos. Under the resultant International Broadcasting Corporation Lao Co Ltd, IBC Channel 3 was inaugurated in 1994 (see below).

Lao National Television (TVNL): rue Chommany Neua, Km 6, BP 5635, Vientiane; tel. (21) 710617; fax (21) 710182; e-mail lntv2007@yahoo.co.th; f. 1983; colour television service; Dir-Gen. BOUMCHOM VONGPHET.

Laos Television 3: BP 860, Vientiane; tel. (21) 315449; fax (21) 215628; operated by the International Broadcasting Corpn Lao Co Ltd; f. 1994 as IBC Channel 3; 30% govt-owned, 70% owned by the International Broadcasting Corpn Co Ltd of Thailand; programmes in Lao.

Finance

(cap. = capital; dep. = deposits; br.(s) = branch(es); m. = million)

BANKING

The banking system was reorganized in 1988–89, ending the state monopoly of banking. Some commercial banking functions were transferred from the central bank and the state commercial bank to a new network of autonomous banks. The establishment of joint ventures with foreign financial institutions was permitted. Foreign banks have been permitted to open branches in Laos since 1992. In 1998 there were nine private commercial banks in Laos, most of them Thai. In March 1999 the Government consolidated six state-owned banks into two new institutions—Lane Xang Bank Ltd and Lao May Bank Ltd; these in turn merged in 2001.

Central Bank

Banque de la RDP Lao: rue Yonnet, BP 19, Vientiane; tel. (21) 213109; fax (21) 213108; e-mail bol@pan-laos.net.la; internet www.bol.gov.la; f. 1959 as the bank of issue; became Banque Pathetlao 1968; took over the operations of Banque Nationale du Laos 1975; known as Banque d'Etat de la RDP Lao from 1982 until adoption of present name; dep. 394,017m. kips, total assets US $361m. (Dec. 2002); Gov. PHOUPHET KHAMPHOUNVONG.

Commercial Banks

Agriculture Promotion Bank: 58 rue Hengboun, Ban Haysok, BP 5456, Vientiane; tel. (21) 212024; fax (21) 213957; e-mail apblaopdr@laonet.net; Man. Dir BOUNSONG SOMMALAVONG.

Banque pour le Commerce Extérieur Lao (BCEL): 1 rue Pangkham, BP 2925, Vientiane; tel. (21) 213200; fax (21) 213202; e-mail bcelhovt@etllao.com; internet www.bcellaos.com; f. 1975; 100% state-owned; Chair. AKSONE BOUPHAKONEKHAM; Man. Dir SONEXAY SITPHAXAY.

Joint Development Bank: 82 ave Lane Xang, BP 3187, Vientiane; tel. (21) 213531; fax (21) 213530; e-mail jdb@jdbbank.com; internet www.jdbbank.com; f. 1989; the first joint-venture bank between Laos and a foreign partner; 30% owned by Banque de la RDP Lao, 70% owned by Thai company, Phrom Suwan Silo and Drying Co Ltd; cap. US $4m.

Lao May Bank Ltd: 39 rue Pangkham, BP 2700, Vientiane; tel. (21) 213300; fax (21) 213340; f. 1999 as a result of the consolidation by the Government of ParkTai Bank, Lao May Bank and Nakornluang Bank; merged with Lane Xang Bank Ltd in 2001.

Lao-Viet Bank (LVB): 5 ave Lane Xang, Ban Hatsady, Chanthaboury, Vientiane; tel. (21) 216316; fax (21) 212197; e-mail lvbho@laotel.com; f. 1999; joint venture between BCEL and the Bank for Investment and Development of Vietnam.

Phongsavanh Bank: 77 Unit 09, Samsenthai Rd, Ban Anou, Chanthaboury, Vientiane; tel. (21) 212666; e-mail info@phongsavanhbank.com; internet www.phongsavanhbank.com; f. 2007; cap. US $10m. (2007).

Vientiane Commercial Bank Ltd: 33 ave Lane Xang, Ban Hatsady, Chanthaboury, Vientiane; tel. (21) 222700; fax (21) 213513; e-mail vccbank@laotel.com; f. 1993; privately-owned joint venture by Laotian, Thai, Taiwanese and Australian investors; Man. Dir SOP SISOMPHOU.

INSURANCE

Assurances Générales du Laos (AGL): Vientiane Commercial Bank Bldg, ave Lane Xang, BP 4223, Vientiane; tel. (21) 215903; fax (21) 215904; e-mail agl@agl-allianz.com; internet www.agl-allianz.com; f. 1990; jt venture between Lao Govt (49%) and Assurances Générales de France (51%); sole licensed insurance co in Laos; Group Chair. Dr MICHAEL DIEKMANN; Man. Dir PHILIPPE ROBINEAU.

Trade and Industry

GOVERNMENT AGENCY

National Economic Research Institute (NERI): rue Luang Prabang, Sithanneua, Vientiane; tel. (21) 351369; fax (21) 216660; e-mail neri@pan-laos.net; govt policy development unit; Dir SOUPHAN KEOMISAY.

DEVELOPMENT ORGANIZATIONS

Department of Domestic and Foreign Investment (DDFI): rue Luang Prabang, 01001 Vientiane; tel. (21) 222690; fax (21) 215491; e-mail fimc@laotel.com; internet invest.laopdr.org; fmrly Foreign Investment Management Committee (FIMC); provides information and assistance to existing and potential investors.

Department of Livestock and Fisheries: Ministry of Agriculture and Forestry, Ban Phonxay, BP 811, Vientiane; tel. (21) 416932; fax (21) 415674; e-mail eulaodlf@laotel.com; public enterprise; imports and markets agricultural commodities; produces and distributes feed and animals; Dir-Gen. SINGKHAM PHONVISAY.

National Agriculture and Forestry Research Institute (NAFRI): Nongviengkham, BP 7170, Vientiane; tel. (21) 770084; fax (21) 770047; e-mail info@nafri.org.la; internet www.nafri.org.la; f. 1999; br. of the Ministry of Agriculture and Forestry; supports sectoral devt and the strategic formulation of policies and programmes in accordance with govt policy; Dir-Gen. Dr BOUNTHONG BOUAHOM.

State Committee for State Planning: Office of the Prime Minister, Ban Sisavat, Vientiane; tel. (21) 213653; fax (21) 213560; Pres. SOULIVONG DARAVONG.

CHAMBER OF COMMERCE

Lao National Chamber of Commerce and Industry (LNCCI): ave Kaysone Phomvihane, Sat Settha District, BP 4596, Vientiane; tel. (21) 452579; fax (21) 452580; e-mail lncci@laopdr.com; internet www.lncci.laotel.com; f. 1989; 800 mems; Pres. KISSANA VONGSAY; Sec.-Gen. KHAMPANH SENGTHONGKHAM.

TRADE ASSOCIATION

Société Lao Import-Export (SOLIMPEX): 43–47 ave Lane Xang, BP 2789, Vientiane; tel. (21) 213818; fax (21) 217054; Dir KANHKEO SAYCOCIE; Dep. Dir PHONGSAMOUTH VONGKOT.

UTILITIES

Electricity

Electricité du Laos: rue Nongbone, BP 309, Vientiane; tel. (21) 451519; fax (21) 416381; e-mail edlgmo@laotel.com; internet www.edl-laos.com; responsible for production and distribution of electricity; Man. Dir KHAMMANY INTHIRATH (acting).

Lao National Grid Co: Vientiane; responsible for Mekong hydro-electricity exports.

Water

In 1998 the Government adopted a policy of decentralization with regard to water supply and sanitation in Laos. As a result, the national water supply authority, Nam Papa Lao, was divided into Nam Papa Vientiane, with jurisdiction over the capital, and a number of provincial authorities. Activities within the sector were subsequently co-ordinated by a newly established body, the Water Supply Authority.

Nam Papa Vientiane (Vientiane Water Supply Authority): rue Phone Kheng, Thatluang Neue Village, Sat Settha District, Vientiane; tel. (21) 412880; fax (21) 414378; e-mail daophet@laotel.com; f. 1962; fmrly Nam Papa Lao; authority responsible for the water supply of Vientiane; Gen. Man. DAOPHET BOUAPHA.

Water Supply Authority (WASA): Dept of Housing and Urban Planning, Ministry of Communications, Transport, Post and Construction, ave Lane Xang, Vientiane; tel. and fax (21) 451826; e-mail mctpcwwa@laotel.com; internet www.wasa.gov.la; f. 1998; Dir NOUPHEUAK VIRABOUTH.

STATE ENTERPRISES

Agricultural Forestry Development Import-Export and General Service Co: trading co of the armed forces.

Bolisat Phatthana Khet Phoudoi Import-Export Co: rue Khoun Boulom, Vientiane; tel. (21) 216234; fax (21) 215046; f. 1984; trading co of the armed forces.

Dao-Heuang Import-Export Co: Ban Thaluang, Paksé, Champasak Province; tel. (31) 213805; fax (31) 212438; e-mail info@dao-heuang.com; internet www.daoheuangcoffee.com; f. 1990; imports and distributes whisky, beer, mineral water, coffee and foodstuffs.

Lao Commodities Export Co Ltd (Lacomex): Ban Wattuang, Paksé, Champasak Province; tel. (31) 212552; fax (31) 212553; e-mail sisanouk@laotel.com; f. 1994; exports coffee under the Paksong Cafe Lao brand; Man. Dir SISANOUK SISOMBAT.

Lao Houng Heuang Export-Import Co: rue Nongbone, Vientiane; tel. (21) 217344; fax (21) 212107.

Lao State Material Import-Export Co (Lasmac): 59 Ban Hatsady Tai, Chanthaboury, Vientiane; tel. (21) 216578; fax (21) 217149; e-mail lasmac@laotel.com; internet www.lasmac.laotel.com; f. 1983; mfr of wood products and woven plastic; exports agricultural and wood products; imports construction materials.

Luen Fat Hong Lao Plywood Industry Co: BP 83, Vientiane; tel. (21) 314990; fax (21) 314992; e-mail lfhsdsj@laotel.com; internet www.luenfathongyada.laopdr.com; development and management of forests, logging and timber production.

CO-OPERATIVES

Central Leading Committee to Guide Agricultural Co-operatives: Vientiane; f. 1978; to help organize and plan regulations and policies for co-operatives; by the end of 1986 there were some 4,000 co-operatives, employing about 74% of the agricultural labour force; Chair. (vacant).

TRADE UNION ORGANIZATION

Federation of Lao Trade Unions: 87 ave Lane Xang, BP 780, Vientiane; tel. (21) 212754; e-mail kammabanlao@pan-laos.net.la;

f. 1956; 21-mem. Cen. Cttee and five-mem. Control Cttee; Pres. BOSAIKHAM VONGDALA (acting); 70,000 mems.

Transport

RAILWAYS

The construction of a 30-km rail link between Vientiane and the Thai border town of Nong Khai began in January 1996 but was indefinitely postponed in February 1998 as an indirect consequence of a severe downturn in the Thai economy. In 1997 the Government announced plans to develop a comprehensive railway network, and awarded a contract to a Thai company, although no timetable for the implementation of the scheme was announced. In 2003 the Thai Government agreed to finance a 3.5-km rail link from Tha Naleng (near Vientiane) to Nong Khai, North-East Thailand; construction was completed in April 2008. Draft proposals to extend the track, to link Tha Naleng with Vientiane and to extend southwards and eastwards to Vinh in Viet Nam via Thakek in central Laos, were subsequently announced.

ROADS

The Asian Development Bank is supporting an extensive development programme for the road network in Laos, in order to promote integration in the Mekong region. The road network provides the country's main method of transport, accounting for about 90% of freight traffic and 95% of passenger traffic in 1993. In 1999 there were an estimated 21,716 km of roads, of which 9,664 km were paved. The main routes link Vientiane and Luang Prabang with Ho Chi Minh City in southern Viet Nam and with northern Viet Nam and the Cambodian border, Vientiane with Savannakhet, Phongsali to the Chinese border, Vientiane with Luang Prabang and the port of Ha Tinh (northern Viet Nam), and Savannakhet with the port of Da Nang (Viet Nam). In 2002 Laos, Thailand and China agreed to a US $45m. road project intended to link the three countries; most of the construction on the Kunming–Bangkok Highway would be carried out in Laos. The project was initially expected to be completed in 2007, but in early 2008 the sections in Laos and Thailand had yet to be finished. In February 2004 construction of a 245-km national road (Route 9) was completed, linking Laos with Thailand and Viet Nam.

The Friendship Bridge across the Mekong River, linking Laos and Thailand between Tha Naleng and Nong Khai, was opened in April 1994. In early 1998 construction work began in Paksé on another bridge across the Mekong River. The project was granted substantial funding from the Japanese Government, and was completed in August 2000. Construction commenced in December 2003 on a second Friendship Bridge, also funded by the Japanese Government, linking Savannakhet and Mukdahan. Part of the bridge collapsed into the Mekong River during construction work in mid-2005; nevertheless, the bridge was opened on schedule in December 2006. In 2008 plans were announced to construct a new bridge linking Thailand's northern province of Chiang Rai with Huayxai in Laos. The bridge was scheduled to open in 2011.

INLAND WATERWAYS

The Mekong River, which forms the western frontier of Laos for much of its length, is the country's greatest transport artery. However, the size of river vessels is limited by rapids, and traffic is seasonal. In April 1995 Laos, Cambodia, Thailand and Viet Nam signed an agreement regarding the joint development of the lower Mekong, and established a Mekong River Commission. There are about 4,600 km of navigable waterways.

CIVIL AVIATION

Wattay airport, Vientiane, is the principal airport. Following the signing of an agreement in 1995, the airport was to be upgraded by Japan; renovation work commenced in 1997, and a new passenger terminal was opened in 1998. The development of Luang Prabang airport by Thailand, at a cost of 50m. baht, began in May 1994 and the first phase of the development programme was completed in 1996; the second phase was completed in 1998. In April 1998 Luang Prabang airport gained formal approval for international flights. The airports at Paksé and Savannakhet were also scheduled to be upgraded to enable them to accommodate wide-bodied civilian aircraft; renovation work on the airport at Savannakhet was completed in April 2000. Construction of a new airport in Oudomxay Province was completed in the late 1990s.

In mid-2004 the Laotian Government announced that a memorandum of understanding was to be signed with Thailand by the end of 2005 providing for the development of Savannakhet Airport into an international landing strip, to be used jointly by Japan, which would partially fund the development. The plan constituted part of the east–west economic corridor project, a proposed transport network linking Laos with Myanmar, Thailand and Viet Nam.

Lao Civil Aviation Department: BP 119, Vientiane; tel. and fax (21) 512163; fax (21) 520237; e-mail laodca@laotel.com; Dir-Gen. YAKUA LOPANGKAO.

Lao Airlines: National Air Transport Co, 2 rue Pangkham, BP 6441, Vientiane; tel. (21) 212057; fax (21) 212065; e-mail laoairlines@laoairlines.com; internet www.laoairlines.com; f. 1975; state airline, fmrly Lao Aviation; operates internal and international passenger and cargo transport services within South-East Asia; CEO SOMPHONE DOUANGDARA.

Tourism

Laos boasts spectacular scenery and ancient pagodas. Luang Prabang was approved by UNESCO as a World Heritage site in 1998. Total arrivals increased from 894,806 in 2004 to 1,095,315 in 2005, in which year receipts reached $146m.

National Tourism Administration of Lao PDR: ave Lane Xang, BP 3556, Hadsady, Chanthaboury, Vientiane; tel. (21) 212251; fax (21) 212769; e-mail tmpd_lnta@yahoo.com; internet www.tourismlaos.gov.la; 17 provincial offices; Chair. SOMPHONG MONGKHONVILAY.

LATVIA

Introductory Survey

Location, Climate, Language, Religion, Flag, Capital

The Republic of Latvia is situated in north-eastern Europe, on the east coast of the Baltic Sea. The country is bounded by Estonia to the north and by Lithuania to the south and south-west. To the east it borders Russia, and to the south-east Belarus. Owing to the influence of maritime factors, the climate is relatively temperate, but changeable. Average temperatures in January range from −2.8°C (26.6°F) in the western coastal town of Liepāja to −6.6°C (20.1°F) in the inland town of Daugavpils. Mean temperatures for July range from 16.7°C (62.1°F) in Liepāja to 17.6°C (63.7°F) in Daugavpils. Average annual rainfall in Rīga is 617 mm (24 ins). The official language is Latvian. The major religion is Christianity: most ethnic Latvians are traditionally Lutherans or Roman Catholics, whereas ethnic Russians are mainly adherents of the Russian Orthodox Church. The national flag (proportions 1 by 2) has a maroon background, with a narrow white horizontal stripe superimposed across the central part. The capital is Rīga (Riga).

Recent History

In November 1917 representatives of Latvian nationalist groups elected a provisional national council, which informed the Russian Government of its intention to establish a sovereign, independent Latvian state. On 18 November 1918 the Latvian National Council, which had been constituted on the previous day, proclaimed the independent Republic of Latvia, with Jānis Čakste as President. Independence, under the nationalist Government of Kārlis Ulmanis, was fully achieved after the expulsion of the Bolsheviks from Rīga in May 1919, with the aid of German troops, and from the eastern province of Latgale, with Polish and Estonian assistance, in January 1920. A Latvian-Soviet peace treaty was finally signed in August. Latvia's first Constitution was adopted in 1922. An electoral system based on proportional representation permitted a large number of small parties to be represented in the Saeima (Parliament). As a result, there was little administrative stability, with 18 changes of government in 1922–34. None the less, under the dominant party, the Latvian Farmers' Union (LZS, led by Ulmanis), agrarian reforms were successfully introduced and agricultural exports flourished. The world-wide economic decline of the early 1930s, together with domestic political fragmentation, prompted a (bloodless) *coup d'état* in May 1934, led by Ulmanis. Martial law was introduced, the Saeima was dissolved and all political parties, including the LZS, were banned. A Government of National Unity, with Ulmanis as Prime Minister, assumed the legislative functions of the Saeima. Ulmanis became President in 1936.

Under the Treaty of Non-Aggression (the 'Molotov-Ribbentrop Pact'), signed by Germany and the USSR in August 1939, the incorporation of Latvia into the USSR was agreed by the two powers. A Treaty of Mutual Aid between the USSR and Latvia allowed the establishment of Soviet military bases in Latvia, and in June 1940 it was occupied by Soviet forces. A 'puppet' administration, under Augusts Kirhenšteins, was installed, and the election to the Saeima of Soviet-approved candidates took place in July. In that month the legislature proclaimed the Latvian Soviet Socialist Republic, which was formally incorporated into the USSR as a constituent union republic in August.

In the first year of Soviet rule almost 33,000 Latvians were deported to Russia and Kazakhstan, and a further 1,350 were killed. Latvian language, traditions and culture were also suppressed. In July 1941 Soviet rule in Latvia was interrupted by German occupation. Most German troops had withdrawn by 1944, although the Kurzeme region, in south-western Latvia, was retained by Germany until the end of the Second World War. Soviet Latvia was re-established in 1944–45 and the process of 'sovietization' was resumed. There were further mass deportations of Latvians to Russia and Central Asia. Independent political activities were prohibited and exclusive political power was exercised by the Communist Party of Latvia (CPL). A process of industrialization encouraged significant and sustained Russian and other Soviet immigration into the republic. Under CPL First Secretary Arvīds Pelše (appointed in 1959) and his successor, Augusts Voss (First Secretary, 1966–84), limited autonomy gained in the 1950s was reversed.

There was a revival in traditional Latvian culture from the late 1970s. Political groups began to be established, including the Environmental Protection Club and Helsinki-86, established to monitor Soviet observance of the Helsinki Final Act adopted in 1975 by the Conference on (now Organization for) Security and Co-operation in Europe (CSCE—now OSCE, see p. 354). In June and August 1986 anti-Soviet demonstrations, organized by Helsinki-86, were suppressed by the police. In 1987 there were further demonstrations on the anniversaries of significant events in Latvian history. Such movements, fostered by the greater freedom of expression permitted under the new Soviet policy of *glasnost* (openness), were strongly opposed by the CPL. In 1988 opposition movements in Latvia began to unite, and in October representatives of the leading movements organized the inaugural congress of the Latvian Popular Front (LTF), at which delegates resolved to seek sovereignty for Latvia within a renewed Soviet federation. The LTF, chaired by Dainis Ivāns, rapidly became the largest and most influential political force in Latvia, with an estimated membership of 250,000 by the end of 1988.

In September 1988 Boris Pugo was replaced as First Secretary of the CPL by Jānis Vagris. The new CPL leadership came increasingly under the influence of members of the LTF. At the end of September Latvian was designated the state language. In March 1989 candidates supported by the LTF won 26 of the 34 contested seats in elections to the USSR's Congress of People's Deputies. On 28 July, following similar measures in Lithuania and Estonia, the Latvian Supreme Soviet (Supreme Council—legislature) adopted a declaration of sovereignty and economic independence. However, there was growing support within the republic for full independence, as advocated by the Latvian National Independence Movement (LNNK), formed in 1988, particularly among ethnic Latvians (who, however, were outnumbered by ethnic Slavs in Rīga and the other large cities in the republic as a result of the Soviet policy of large-scale immigration). In December 1989 candidates supported by the LTF won some 75% of seats contested in local elections.

In January 1990 the Latvian Supreme Soviet voted to abolish the constitutional provisions that guaranteed the CPL's political predominance. In the following month the Supreme Soviet adopted a declaration condemning the Latvian legislature's decision to request admission to the USSR in 1940, and the flag, state emblems and anthem of pre-1940 Latvia were restored to official use. At elections to the Supreme Soviet in March and April 1990, pro-independence candidates endorsed by the LTF won 131 of the 201 seats; the CPL and the anti-independence Interfront (International Front—dominated by members of the Russian-speaking population) together won 59 seats. The CPL subsequently split into two parties: the majority of delegates at an extraordinary congress rejected a motion to leave the Communist Party of the Soviet Union (CPSU), and elected Alfrēds Rubiks, an opponent of independence, as First Secretary.

The new Supreme Council was convened in early May 1990, and elected Anatolijs Gorbunovs of the CPL as its Chairman (*de facto* President of the Republic). On 4 May the Supreme Council adopted a resolution that declared the incorporation of Latvia into the USSR in 1940 as unlawful, and announced the beginning of a transitional period that was to lead to full political and economic independence. Four articles of the 1922 Constitution, defining Latvia as an independent democratic state and asserting the sovereignty of the Latvian people, were restored, and were to form the basis of the newly declared Republic of Latvia's legitimacy. Ivars Godmanis, the Deputy Chairman of the LTF, was elected Prime Minister in a new, LTF-dominated Government. Meanwhile, a rival body to the Supreme Soviet had been convened at the end of April 1990. This Congress of Latvia had been elected in an unofficial poll, in which some 700,000 people were reported to have participated: only citizens of the pre-1940 republic and their descendants had been entitled to vote. The Congress, in which members of the LNNK predominated,

LATVIA

Introductory Survey

declared Latvia to be an occupied country and adopted resolutions on independence and the withdrawal of Soviet troops.

The Supreme Council's resolutions, although more cautious than independence declarations adopted in Lithuania and Estonia, severely strained relations with the Soviet authorities. On 14 May 1990 the Soviet President, Mikhail Gorbachev, issued a decree that annulled the Latvian declaration of independence, condemning it as a violation of the USSR Constitution. The declaration was also opposed within the republic by some ethnic Slavs, who organized protest strikes and demonstrations. In subsequent months local anti-Government movements (allied with Soviet troops stationed in Latvia) conducted a campaign of propaganda and harassment. In December the Latvian Government claimed that special units (OMON) of the Soviet Ministry of Internal Affairs had been responsible for a series of explosions in Rīga, and in January 1991 OMON troops seized the Rīga Press House, previously the property of the CPL. Later in January a 'Committee of Public Salvation', headed by Alfrēds Rubiks, declared itself as a rival Government to the Godmanis administration; on the same day five people died when OMON troops attacked the Ministry of the Interior in Rīga. (In November 1999 10 former Soviet officers were convicted of attempting to overthrow the Latvian Government in 1991; seven received suspended prison sentences of up to four years' duration.)

The attempted seizure of power by Rubiks' Committee reinforced opposition in Latvia to inclusion in the new union treaty being prepared by nine Soviet republics. Latvia refused to conduct the all-Union referendum on the future of the USSR, which was scheduled for 17 March 1991 (although some 680,000 people, mostly Russians and Ukrainians, did participate, on an unofficial basis). Instead, a referendum on Latvian independence took place on 3 March. Of those eligible to vote, 87.6% participated, of whom, according to official results, 73.7% endorsed proposals for a democratic, independent Latvian republic.

At the time of the attempted overthrow of the Gorbachev administration in the Russian and Soviet capital, Moscow, in August 1991, immediate Soviet military intervention in Latvia was widely anticipated. However, an emergency session of the Supreme Council was convened and the full independence of Latvia was proclaimed. As the coup collapsed, the Godmanis Government took prompt action to assert control in Latvia, banning the CPL and detaining Rubiks. (In July 1995 Rubiks was found guilty of involvement in the coup attempt. He was released in November 1997.) On 6 September 1991 the USSR State Council formally recognized the independent Republic of Latvia, and the country was admitted to the UN later that month. In late 1991 the Supreme Council adopted legislation guaranteeing the right of citizenship to all citizens of the pre-1940 republic (including non-ethnic Latvians) and their descendants. Remaining residents of Latvia (mainly Russians and other Slavs) were to be required to apply for naturalization after final legislation governing citizenship was determined by a restored Saeima.

The first legislative elections since the restoration of independence took place in June 1993, with the participation of about 90% of the electorate. Only citizens of pre-1940 Latvia and their descendants were entitled to vote; consequently, some 27% of the adult population (mainly ethnic Russians) were excluded from the election. A total of 23 parties, movements and alliances contested the poll, of which eight secured representation in the 100-seat Saeima. Latvian Way (LC), a broadly-based movement established earlier in the year, emerged as the strongest party, with more than 32% of the votes and 36 seats in the assembly. The results of the elections demonstrated strong popular support for the more moderate nationalist parties, and socialist-orientated parties (including the successor of the CPL, the Latvian Socialist Party—LSP) failed to win representation. The LTF also failed to secure any seats. Only 11 of the elected deputies were non-ethnic Latvians (six of whom were ethnic Russians).

The new Saeima voted to restore the Constitution of 1922, and undertook to elect the President of the Republic from among three prominent deputies. At a third round of voting on 7 July 1993 Guntis Ulmanis (great-nephew of Kārlis Ulmanis) of the revived LZS succeeded in winning a majority, with 53 votes. He was inaugurated as President the following day, whereupon he appointed Valdis Birkavs (formerly a Deputy Chairman of the Supreme Council and a leading member of LC) as Prime Minister. Birkavs' Cabinet of Ministers represented a coalition agreement between LC (the majority partner) and the LZS.

The requirements for naturalization proposed by the Government's draft citizenship law included a minimum of 10 years' permanent residence, a knowledge of Latvian to conversational level and an oath of loyalty to the republic. In March 1994 the Saeima approved the establishment of the new post of State Minister for Human Rights, in an attempt to counter accusations of violations of minority rights. Following international criticism, the Saeima adopted an amended citizenship law in July. Latvia was admitted to the Council of Europe (see p. 225) in February 1995.

Meanwhile, in July 1994 the LZS announced its withdrawal from the governing coalition, following disagreements with LC over economic and agricultural policy. A new Cabinet was appointed in September. It, too, was dominated by LC members, including the Prime Minister, Māris Gailis; Birkavs became Deputy Prime Minister and Minister of Foreign Affairs.

A general election was held on 30 September–1 October 1995. Nine parties and coalitions succeeded in obtaining the 5% of the votes required for representation in the Saeima; as a result, the assembly was highly fragmented. LC's share of the 100 seats was reduced by more than one-half, to 17, while the largest number of seats (18) was won by the newly established, leftist Democratic Party Saimnieks (The Master—DPS). The People's Movement for Latvia (Zigerists' Party—PML), an extreme nationalist party led by a German-Latvian, Joahims Zigerists, won 16 seats. (Zigerists was linked to an extremist right-wing organization in Germany, and in 1994 had been convicted in that country for inciting racial hatred.) In December 1995 the Saeima finally endorsed a Cabinet of Ministers led by Andris Šķēle (an entrepreneur with no party affiliation). The new Government was a broad coalition of the DPS, LC, the For Fatherland and Freedom Union (TB), the Latvian National Conservative Party (LNCP), as the LNNK had been renamed, the LZS and the Latvian Unity Party (LVP). The PML was, notably, excluded from the coalition. Former Prime Ministers Gailis and Birkavs were appointed to the new Cabinet, the former as a Deputy Prime Minister, and the latter as Minister of Foreign Affairs. In May 1996 the Deputy Prime Minister and Minister of Agriculture, Alberīs Kauls, was dismissed, after criticizing the Prime Minister's agricultural policies. The LVP (of which Kauls was the leader) temporarily withdrew its support from the coalition, but shortly afterwards rejoined the Government, having secured approval for a new candidate as Minister of Agriculture.

On 18 June 1996 the Saeima re-elected Guntis Ulmanis as President for a second three-year term. In July it was announced that the LVP was to merge with the DPS, reinforcing the DPS's position as the dominant party in the coalition. None the less, instability in both the Government and the legislature continued. In January 1997 Šķēle resigned as Prime Minister, but was swiftly reappointed by Ulmanis, who indicated his support for Šķēle's economic and structural reforms, and a new, largely unaltered Cabinet was appointed in February. Local elections conducted in March demonstrated a considerable increase in support for the LZS.

By July 1997 the governing coalition had begun to disintegrate, not least because a series of corruption scandals had, since May, prompted the resignation of several ministers, and at the end of the month Šķēle announced the resignation of the Government. Ulmanis invited Guntars Krasts, the outgoing Minister of the Economy, to form a new administration. In early August the Saeima approved Krasts' proposals for a new, five-party coalition, comprising his own party, formed in the previous month by the merger of the TB and the LNNK (to which designation the LNCP had reverted), known as the TB/LNNK, the DPS, LC, the LZS and the Christian Democratic Union of Latvia. In early 1998 Krasts was accused of negligence with regard to a privatization proposal for the state power utility, Latvenergo, during his tenure as Minister of the Economy. In March Krasts formally requested that the Saeima conduct a vote of confidence in his personal integrity, in order to confirm his mandate. The refusal of any parliamentary faction to organize such a vote was interpreted by the Prime Minister as an endorsement of his leadership. In that month Šķēle announced the formation of a new political party, later named the People's Party (TP), to contest the forthcoming elections.

In April 1998 the Minister of the Economy, Atis Sausnītis, was dismissed. Anticipating the collapse of Krasts' Government, the DPS announced its withdrawal from the coalition. At the end of the month, however, Krasts survived a parliamentary vote of no confidence proposed by the LZS and LC. At the same session the Saeima approved appointments to a new coalition Government, with members of the Cabinet of Ministers drawn from the LZS, LC, and an alliance of the Latvian National Reform Party and the Latvian Green Party.

In April 1998 draft amendments to the strict legislation regulating rights to citizenship were adopted, in response to recommendations made by the OSCE. The amendments, which removed the age-related system of naturalization that allocated dates for application by age-group, granted citizenship to stateless children (permanently resident in Latvia) born after the 1991 declaration of independence and relaxed the citizenship requirements for Russian-speakers, were approved by the Saeima in June 1998. Although widely welcomed elsewhere in Europe, the amendments were deemed inadequate by Russia, and nationalist groups within the Latvian legislature secured sufficient support inside and outside the Saeima to force a delay to the enactment of the new legislation and the organization of a referendum on the subject. The referendum was duly conducted concurrently with the 3 October general election; 52.5% of the votes were cast in favour of the amendments, which were promulgated later in the month.

At the general election, Škēle's TP was the most successful single party, taking 21.2% of the votes (and 24 of the 100 legislative seats), ahead of LC with 18.1% (21 seats) and TB/LNNK with 14.7% (17 seats). Only six of the 21 participating political parties secured the minimum 5% of the votes necessary for representation in the Saeima. It was not until the end of November 1998 that the Saeima approved a new, three-party, minority coalition Government, headed by Vilis Krištopans of LC. The coalition, comprising LC, TB/LNNK and the New Party (which held eight legislative seats), also drew support from the Latvian Social Democratic Alliance, which controlled 14 seats in the Saeima. In early February 1999 the Social Democrats formally joined the coalition with the appointment of one of their members to the agriculture portfolio in the Cabinet of Ministers.

On 17 June 1999 Vaira Viķe-Freiberga was elected President at a seventh round of voting in the Saeima, with the support of 53 deputies (compared with 20 for Valdis Birkavs of LC and nine for Ingrīda Ūdre of the New Party). Born in Latvia, but resident in Canada from the end of the Second World War until 1998, Viķe-Freiberga, a non-partisan figure who had trained as a psychologist, thus became the first female President in central or eastern Europe. At her inauguration on 8 July 1999 Viķe-Freiberga identified as priorities for her presidency Latvia's entry into the European Union (EU, see p. 244) and the North Atlantic Treaty Organization (NATO, see p. 340). Three days before her inauguration, Krištopans announced his Government's resignation, apparently in response to the recent signing by TB/LNNK of a co-operation accord with the opposition TP. President Viķe-Freiberga subsequently asked Škēle to form a new government. Škēle thus became Prime Minister for the third time, leading a coalition of his TP, the TB/LNNK and LC.

In early July 1999 the Saeima adopted controversial new language legislation, which, notably, required that all business and all state- and municipally-organized gatherings be conducted in Latvian. Russia immediately denounced the legislation as discriminatory, and it was also condemned by the OSCE, the Council of Europe, the European Commission and, within Latvia, by groups representing ethnic Slavs. Revised legislation, approved in early December, incorporated amendments urged by the OSCE, and was said by its proponents to allow the preservation and strengthening of the Latvian language, while ensuring compliance with international standards: Latvian was to be used for all business in the state sector, and for certain private-sector activities. The revised language law came into effect at the beginning of September 2000.

Škēle resigned the premiership in April 2000, after LC withdrew from the governing coalition, owing to a dispute over the running of the Latvian Privatization Agency. President Viķe-Freiberga asked Andris Bērziņš, hitherto the Mayor of Rīga, to form a new government; his cabinet (a coalition principally comprising the TP, LC and TB/LNNK) was approved by the Saeima in early May.

In November 2001 Einārs Repše resigned as Governor of the Bank of Latvia, in order to found a new political party, New Era (JL). The rightist party attracted immediate popular support, and Repše was elected Chairman at its founding congress in February 2002. In May a new Christian democratic party, the Latvian First Party (LPP), was formed.

In legislative elections, held on 5 October 2002, JL won 23.9% of the votes cast (26 seats); the leftist, pro-Russian electoral bloc For Human Rights in a United Latvia (PCTVL), which included the People's Harmony Party (TSP) and the LSP, obtained 18.9% of the votes (25 seats); and the TP received 16.7% (20 seats). Other groups to achieve representation in the Saeima were the Greens' and Farmers' Union (ZZS—an alliance of the Centre Party, the LZS and the Latvian Green Party—LZP), with 12 seats, the LPP (10 seats) and TB/LNNK (seven); LC failed to obtain a seat in the Saeima. The rate of participation by the electorate was some 72.5%. Repše formed a coalition government comprising members of JL, the LPP, the ZZS and TB/LNNK, which was approved by the Saeima on 7 November. The Minister of Defence, Ģirts Kristovskis, was the only member of the Cabinet of Ministers to have retained his previous portfolio; a new post of Deputy Prime Minister was established, to which Ainārs Šlesers of the LPP was appointed. In late November Atis Slakteris replaced Škēle as Chairman of the TP.

In February 2003 the TSP withdrew from the PCTVL alliance, apparently in a desire to pursue more moderate policies. In June the LSP also announced its withdrawal; the remainder of the PCTVL coalition was officially reconstituted as a united organization later that year. In mid-June Prime Minister Repše survived a vote of no confidence in the Saeima, proposed by the TP. On 20 June Viķe-Freiberga was re-elected unopposed (with 88 votes) to serve a second term of office as President; she was inaugurated on 8 July. In late September tensions emerged within the Government, when its constituent parties (with the exception of JL) issued a statement expressing a lack of confidence in the Prime Minister, accusing him of authoritarianism. A compromise agreement was reached, following inter-party discussions, and in mid-November the Chairmen of the four ruling parties signed a memorandum of understanding. In late January 2004 Repše dismissed Šlesers as Deputy Prime Minister; Šlesers alleged that his dismissal had been prompted by a proposal to establish a special investigative committee to examine the premier's property dealings. Two days later the LPP withdrew from the Government, and on 5 February Repše announced the resignation of his administration.

Following the collapse of the Government, President Viķe-Freiberga emphasized the need to maintain a stable political course in preparation for Latvia's impending accession to full membership of NATO and the EU, and on 20 February 2004 nominated the Co-Chairman of the LZP, Indulis Emsis, as premier. In early March Emsis secured the support of the ZZS alliance, the LPP and the TP, and a new, right-of-centre, coalition Government was approved by the Saeima on 9 March, with the parliamentary support of the TSP. Šlesers was re-appointed Deputy Prime Minister.

Following Latvia's official accession to the EU on 1 May 2004 (see below), elections to the European Parliament were conducted on 13 June; the opposition TB/LNNK won four of the nine seats available, while its ally JL won two, and PCTVL, the LPP and LC each won one seat. Neither of the two major parties of the ruling coalition obtained representation. The Minister of Foreign Affairs, Rihards Piks, resigned from the Cabinet in order to take up his seat in the European Parliament; he was replaced by Artis Pabriks.

The Government survived motions of confidence in the Saeima in June and September 2004. However, on 28 October the draft budget was defeated in a parliamentary vote, precipitating the collapse of the ruling coalition. President Viķe-Freiberga nominated Aigars Kalvītis of the TP (which had led opposition to the proposed budget) to form a new government, and on 2 December, following prolonged negotiations, the Saeima approved the formation of a Government comprising members of the TP, JL, the ZZS alliance and the LPP. Several members of the outgoing administration were retained in the same posts, including Pabriks and Oskars Spurdziņš (both of the TP), as Minister of Foreign Affairs and Minister of Finance, respectively. Viķe-Freiberga reportedly opposed the proposed nomination of Škēle as Minister of Health, and consequently Gundars Bērziņš, of the TP, was appointed to that position. The new Government was able to command a majority of votes in the legislature, which approved the draft budget on 20 December.

Local elections, held on 12 March 2005, were marred by allegations of electoral malpractice in Jūrmala and Rēzekne. In early July Jānis Jurkāns resigned as leader of the TSP, in protest at the party's decision, following electoral defeats at both European and local level, to form an alliance with the New Centre, led by Sergejs Dolgopolovs, who had been expelled from the TSP in 2003. The new union, which became known as the Harmony Centre (SC) alliance, was joined by the LSP in December 2005. Jānis Urbanovičs was elected to succeed Jurkāns as leader of the TSP in November. LC and the LPP also formed a political alliance in October, in preparation for legislative elections due to take place in October 2006.

In mid-October 2005 the Minister of the Interior, Ēriks Jēkabsons, tendered his resignation, after attracting criticism for his performance in office, and for his contacts with the controversial, self-exiled Russian businessman Boris Berezovskii (which aggravated tensions with Russia, where he was charged with fraud). In early November Jēkabsons was replaced by Dzintars Jaundzeikars of the LPP. In late December Einārs Repše resigned as Minister of Defence, following the announcement of a criminal investigation into his property investments; although Repše denied any impropriety, he resigned his parliamentary seat and temporarily withdrew from the leadership of JL. Linda Mūrniece succeeded Repše as Minister of Defence. In mid-March 2006 Kalvītis dismissed Slesers as Minister of Transport, after evidence emerged that implicated him in electoral malpractice in the 2005 municipal elections. In April 2006 the Ministry of the Interior launched an inquiry into allegations of financial misconduct against the JL Minister of the Economy, Krišjānis Kariņš. JL accused the LPP, which held the interior portfolio, of misusing its control of the ministry and subsequently withdrew its seven representatives from the Government, after Kalvītis (of the TP) rejected its demand that the LPP be removed from the governing coalition. On 8 April a three-party minority Government (which excluded JL) was approved by the Saeima.

At elections to the Saeima on 7 October 2006 the TP won some 19.6% of the votes cast and 23 seats, the ZZS alliance 16.7% of the votes (18 seats), JL 16.4% of the votes (18 seats), the SC alliance 14.4% of the votes (17 seats), the LPP, allied with LC, 8.6% of the votes (10 seats), TB/LNNK 6.9% (eight seats) and PCTVL 6.0% (six seats). The governing coalition of the TP, the ZZS alliance and the LPP consequently secured a narrow parliamentary majority. Around 62.3% of the electorate participated in the elections, significantly less than had done so in 2002. Kalvītis invited TB/LNNK to join the governing coalition in order to strengthen its parliamentary majority and subsequently formed a new administration, comprising representatives of those four parties, which was approved by 58 deputies in the Saeima on 7 November 2006. In early December the Supreme Court ruled that regulations on campaign financing had been contravened, notably by the TP and the LPP, on the grounds that two independent organizations had supported their party advertising prior to the October elections. In the same month a congress of the TSP approved the consolidation of the SC alliance as a merged association (although the LSP retained its separate status as an affiliated party).

In March 2007 President Viķe-Freiberga refused to endorse new legislation, which had been approved by the Saeima, providing for an increase in the powers vested in the Prime Minister with regard to national security, and declared that a national referendum would be conducted on the issue; following the collection of the signatures of more than 10% of the electorate, the referendum was scheduled for 7 July. On 31 May Valdis Zatlers, the presidential candidate proposed by the ruling coalition, was elected by the Saiema as the new President, to succeed Viķe-Freiberga. Zatlers (a medical doctor without political experience) was inaugurated on 8 July. Meanwhile, the referendum on new national security legislation, conducted as scheduled, was declared by the Central Election Commission to be invalid, owing to an inadequate rate of participation, estimated at only about 37%; some 95% of those participating had voted in favour of abandoning the legislation. Kalvītis subsequently announced that national security legislation would be drafted in consultation with the Saeima. In August the LPP officially merged with LC; the reconstituted LPP/LC was jointly chaired by Ainārs Slesers and former Prime Minister Godmanis (previously the Chairman of LC).

In September 2007 the Minister of the Economy, a member of the TB/LNNK, tendered his resignation. In October Kalvītis dismissed the Minister of Regional Development and Local Government, who had voted against a government motion to remove the director of the anti-corruption bureau, Aleksejs Loskutovs; Loskutovs had been suspended from his post on the grounds that irregularities in the accounts of the bureau had been discovered. The Minister of Foreign Affairs resigned in protest at the decision to replace Loskutovs, which opponents of Kalvītis claimed was motivated by the bureaus's investigations into corruption allegations involving the ruling coalition. The crisis precipitated a mass anti-Government demonstration in Rīga; however, the administration won a motion of no confidence in the Saeima. At the end of October the Minister of Welfare, Dagnija Stake of the ZZS, resigned, following opposition to her plans to reform the state pension system. In early December, in response to increasing pressure, Kalvītis finally tendered the resignation of his Government. Zatlers, after rejecting an attempt by the TP to propose a further candidate, nominated Godmanis (who had hitherto held the interior portfolio) to the premiership. On 20 December a new coalition Government, comprising representatives of the TP, the LPP/LC, the ZZS and the TB/LNNK, was approved by the Saeima.

Latvia's post-independence relations with Russia were troubled by two issues. The first concerned the citizenship and linguistic rights of Latvia's large Russian-speaking community (see above). Of comparable importance was the issue of the 100,000 former Soviet troops still stationed in Latvia (jurisdiction over whom had been transferred, following the dissolution of the USSR, to Russia). Following negotiations, withdrawal of the troops began in early 1992. The process was hampered by a series of disagreements, in particular over the issue of a Russian military radar station at Skrunda, in western Latvia, that the Russians wished to retain. However, in April 1994 agreements were concluded on the complete withdrawal of the remaining 10,000 Russian troops by the end of August, as well as on social guarantees for the estimated 22,000 Russian military pensioners residing in Latvia. Installations at the Skrunda base were subsequently dismantled.

Negotiations regarding the demarcation of the Latvian–Russian border, and Latvia's claim to some 1,640 sq km of land transferred from Latvia to Russia during the Soviet era, commenced in April 1996. Latvia initially insisted (as Estonia had done) that any future border agreement should include a reference to the 1920 treaty in which Russia recognized Latvia's independence. However, in February 1997 the Latvian administration abandoned this demand, and agreed that claims to property in the disputed territory should be discussed separately from the main border agreement. In March a draft treaty on the demarcation of the border was agreed by the two countries, and full agreement on a border treaty was reached in October (although it remained unratified). In January 2007 the Latvian Government agreed to remove a declaration from the draft treaty, which had been interpreted by Russia as a territorial claim on the land formerly part of Latvia, thereby providing for the official endorsement of the treaty. In early February the Saeima approved legislation authorizing the Government to sign the border treaty with Russia. On 27 March Kalvītis and his Russian counterpart, Mikhail Fradkov, officially signed the treaty in Moscow. The treaty was endorsed by Viķe-Freiberga in May and by Russian President Vladimir Putin in October; a legal challenge against it, proposed by JL, was rejected by the Constitutional Court in November.

Relations became strained in March 1998, following the organization, in Rīga, of a rally of Latvian veterans of Nazi German *Waffen SS* units, who had fought Soviet forces during the Second World War; the participation of senior Latvian politicians and military personnel attracted particular criticism from the Russian authorities. When the rally was repeated in March 2000 government officials and serving military officers were not permitted to take part. Meanwhile, tensions arising from repeated Russian threats to impose economic sanctions against Latvia, if the Government did not promptly address perceived infringements of minority rights, were exacerbated by Latvia's new state language law (see above) in 1999. The revised language law, as approved by the Saeima in December, was again denounced by Russia. Economic issues threatened to raise further tensions between the two countries in early 2003, following Russia's decision to cease using the port of Ventspils for its petroleum exports, primarily owing to the opening of a new Russian petroleum terminal on the Baltic coast at Primorsk, Leningrad Oblast. Russia also condemned amendments to legislation on education, which took effect from September 2004, and in accordance with which 60% of lessons in minority schools were to be taught in the Latvian language; in February thousands of ethnic Russians had protested in Rīga against the reforms.

On 9 May 2005 President Viķe-Freiberga travelled to Moscow to attend celebrations to commemorate the 60th anniversary of the end of the Second World War in Europe. (Notably, the Heads of State of Estonia and Lithuania declined to attend.) Three days later the Saeima adopted a declaration denouncing the Soviet occupation of Latvia and urging Russia to accept moral, legal and financial responsibility for the losses incurred by the Latvian people under Soviet rule. In late May the Saeima ratified the Council of Europe's Framework Convention for the Protection of National Minorities; however, a declaration was appended, stipulating that only Latvian citizens would be regarded as members of a national minority, thus excluding large numbers of ethnic Russians who had failed to obtain citizenship. In August a commission was established to calculate the economic damage and human loss sustained by Latvia under Soviet governance; it was estimated that the commission might take up to five years to complete its research. Latvia (together with Estonia and Lithuania) was unhappy with the signature in September of an agreement between Russia and Germany on the construction of a North European Gas Pipeline, which was to carry natural gas from Russia to Germany under the Baltic Sea, bypassing the Baltic countries. In August 2006 the Latvian authorities introduced a new citizenship law provision, stipulating that applicants who failed a Latvian language test three times would be disqualified permanently from obtaining citizenship.

Latvia enjoys close relations with Estonia and Lithuania, and the three countries have established institutions to promote co-operation, including the interparliamentary Baltic Assembly and the Baltic Council of Ministers (which meets twice yearly). In 1992 Latvia became a founder member, with Estonia, Lithuania and other countries of the region, of the Council of Baltic Sea States, a principal aim of which was to assist the political and economic development of its former communist member states (which included Russia). Differences arose in the mid-1990s between Latvia and its two closest Baltic neighbours, in particular concerning the demarcation of maritime borders. However, agreement on the delimitation of the sea border with Estonia was reached in May 1996, and the document was ratified by both countries' legislatures in August. A further agreement on fishing rights was concluded in early 1997. The demarcation of the land border between the two countries was completed in December. Negotiations between Latvia and Lithuania on their maritime border were complicated in October 1996 by the Saeima's ratification of an agreement with two foreign petroleum companies to explore and develop offshore oilfields in disputed areas of the Baltic Sea. Although the two countries signed an agreement on the delimitation of their territorial waters in July 1999, protests from the Latvian fishing industry prevented the agreement from being ratified by the Saeima. In December 2000 a protocol was signed on the re-demarcation of the land border between the two countries. In early 2006 the leaders of all three Baltic states reached agreement on the construction of a new nuclear power plant to replace that at Ignalina, Lithuania, and various other co-operative measures aimed at reducing Russian dominance in the supply of regional energy.

A priority of Latvian foreign policy was attaining full membership of the EU. Latvia applied for membership in October 1995, and formal negotiations on accession commenced in February 2000. In December 2002 Latvia, together with nine other countries, was formally invited to become a full member of the EU in 2004. A referendum on EU membership was held in Latvia on 20 September 2003. Of the 72.5% of the electorate who participated in the plebiscite, 66.8% voted in support of Latvia's accession to the EU, although in certain areas of the country, particularly in the predominately Russian-speaking, south-eastern regions around the second city of Daugavpils, a majority of votes were cast against EU membership. The country became a full member on 1 May 2004. In December 2007 Latvia, together with eight other nations, implemented the EU's Schengen Agreement, enabling its citizens to travel to and from other member states, without border controls.

In February 2002 the Secretary-General of NATO warned the Latvian Government that its existing language requirements, which demanded that candidates standing in regional and national elections be fluent in Latvian, threatened to affect adversely the likelihood of the country being admitted to the Alliance; amendments to the electoral law were duly passed in May. At a summit meeting held in Prague, Czech Republic, in November, Latvia was one of seven countries invited to join NATO in 2004. Latvia became a full member of the Alliance on 29 March 2004.

Government

Under the terms of the 1922 Constitution, which was restored in July 1993 (and amended in December 1997), Latvia is an independent democratic parliamentary republic. The supreme legislative body is the Saeima (Parliament), the 100 members of which are elected by universal adult suffrage for a four-year term. The President of the Republic, who is Head of State, is elected by a secret ballot of the Saeima, also for a period of four years. The President, who is also Head of the Armed Forces, may not serve for more than two consecutive terms. Executive power is held by the Cabinet of Ministers, which is headed by the Prime Minister. The Prime Minister is appointed by the President; the remaining members of the Cabinet are nominated by the Prime Minister. For administrative purposes, Latvia is divided into 26 districts and seven towns (including the capital, Rīga).

Defence

Until independence in August 1991, Latvia had no armed forces separate from those of the USSR. A Ministry of Defence was established in November of that year. As assessed at November 2007, Latvia's total armed forces numbered 5,696, including an army of 1,526, a navy of 603 and an air force of 480. The remainder comprised administration and command staff, central support staff and other forces. Reserve forces in the national guard numbered 11,204. Military service is compulsory from 19 years of age and lasts for 12 months. In August 1994 the withdrawal from Latvia of all former Soviet forces was completed. Latvia joined the North Atlantic Treaty Organization's (NATO) 'Partnership for Peace' (see p. 342) programme in February 1994, and became a full member of the Alliance on 29 March 2004. The budget for 2007 allocated US $471m. to defence.

Economic Affairs

In 2006, according to estimates by the World Bank, Latvia's gross national income (GNI), measured at average 2004–06 prices, was US $18,525m., equivalent to $8,100 per head (or $15,350 per head on an international purchasing-power parity basis). During 1996–2006, it was estimated, the population decreased by an annual average of 0.9%, while gross domestic product (GDP) per head increased at an average annual rate of 8.7%, in real terms. Overall GDP increased, in real terms, by an annual average of 7.7% in 1996–2006; according to official figures, real GDP increased by 10.2% in 2007.

Agriculture (including hunting, forestry and fishing) contributed 3.4% of GDP in 2007, and provided 11.0% of employment in 2006. The principal sectors are dairy farming and pig-breeding. Cereals, sugar beet, potatoes and fodder crops are the main crops grown. As part of the process of land reform and privatization, the dissolution of collective and state farms was undertaken in the early 1990s. In 2003 Latvia approved a seven-year ban on the sale of rural land to foreign purchasers. Fishing makes an important contribution to the economy (an estimated 70% of the total annual catch is exported). There was considerable growth potential in the forestry industry (43.9% of Latvia's land area is classified as forest), and output increased from 1996. Agricultural GDP increased, in real terms, by an average of 3.1% per year in 1996–2006; the real GDP of the sector increased by 7.8% in 2007.

Industry (comprising mining and quarrying, manufacturing, construction and utilities) contributed 21.6% of GDP in 2007, and provided 27.6% of employment in 2006. Industrial GDP increased, in real terms, at an average annual rate of 7.1% in 1996–2006. The GDP of the industrial sector increased, in real terms, by 5.2% in 2007.

Mining and quarrying contributed just 0.4% of GDP in 2007, and employed 0.4% of workers in 2006. Latvia has limited mineral resources, the most important being peat, dolomite, limestone, gypsum, amber, gravel and sand. Offshore and onshore petroleum reserves have been located. The GDP of the mining sector increased at an annual average rate of 20.1% in 1997–2007. According to official figures, the GDP of the mining sector increased by 14.9% in 2007.

The manufacturing sector contributed 10.9% of GDP in 2007, and provided 15.6% of employment in 2006. Real manufacturing GDP increased by an average of 6.4% per year in 1996–2006. The GDP of the sector increased, in real terms, by 6.2% in 2006, but declined by 3.3% in 2007.

Latvia is highly dependent on imported fuels to provide energy. In 2006 mineral products represented 13.4% of the total value of Latvia's imports. Electric energy is supplied primarily by Estonia and Lithuania, and petroleum products are supplied by Russia and Lithuania. In 2004 hydroelectric plants provided some 66.4% of annual domestic electricity production in Latvia; a further 30.6% was derived from natural gas.

The services sector has increased in importance; the sector contributed 75.0% of GDP in 2007, and accounted for 61.4% of employment in 2006. The GDP of the sector increased, in real terms, by an annual average of 8.2% in 1996–2006; real services

GDP increased by 10.9% in 2007. The tourism sector expanded markedly in the mid-2000s, following a significant expansion in air services between Rīga and cities in central and western Europe. Total visitor arrivals numbered 816,297 in 2006, compared with 545,366 in 2004.

In 2006 Latvia recorded a visible trade deficit of US $4,941m., and there was a deficit of $4,280m. on the current account of the balance of payments. The principal source of imports in 2006 was Germany, which accounted for 15.5% of total imports; other major sources were Lithuania, Russia, Estonia, Poland, Finland and Sweden. The main market for exports in that year was Lithuania, which accounted for 14.7% of the total; other significant purchasers were Estonia, Germany, the United Kingdom, Russia, Sweden and Denmark. The principal exports in 2006 were wood and wood articles, followed by base metals and manufactures, machinery and electrical equipment, textiles, foodstuffs, beverages and tobacco, chemicals and mineral products. The principal imports in that year were machinery and electrical equipment, vehicles and transport equipment, mineral products, base metals, chemicals, foodstuffs and beverages, and plastics and rubber.

In 2006 the consolidated state budget recorded a deficit of 215.6m. lats (equivalent to 1.9% of GDP). At the end of 2005 Latvia's external debt totalled US $14,283m., of which $1,318m. was long-term public debt. In that year the cost of debt-servicing was equivalent to 37.4% of the value of exports of goods and services. Annual consumer-price inflation averaged 4.4% in 1996–2007. However, consumer prices increased by 10.1% in 2007. According to official statistics, some 5.4% of the population were registered as unemployed at the end of 2007.

Latvia became a member of the World Trade Organization (WTO, see p. 396) in February 1999. In May 2004 Latvia acceded to the European Union (EU, see p. 244).

Latvia's external trade underwent a significant reorientation in the 1990s, away from Russia and the successor states of the USSR, and towards the markets of central and western Europe. Conversely, in the early 2000s Latvia was able to reorientate its trade eastwards, to capitalize on rapid growth in the Russian economy and the concurrent slow rates of growth in several of the principal EU economies. Although growth slowed in the immediate aftermath of the Russian economic crisis of 1998, the Latvian economy demonstrated a recovery thereafter. Although in terms of GDP per head Latvia was the poorest country to accede to full membership of the EU in May 2004, its economy had enjoyed one of the highest rates of growth in the region. Strong growth had improved employment levels significantly, but it also led to price and wage inflation (which increased markedly in the mid-2000s) and a large deficit on the current account of the balance of payments; expanding international energy prices increased the severity of the situation, while labour shortages in many sectors also became apparent. Latvia was admitted to the EU's exchange rate mechanism (ERM 2) in May 2005, in advance of its eventual adoption of the common European currency, the euro. The annual rate of consumer-price inflation reached 10.1% in 2007, compared with 6.6% in 2006. The Government predicted that inflation would increase at an average annual rate of between 9% and 11% in 2008, although banking analysts anticipated that rising fuel costs could cause that figure to increase to as much as 20%. Growth was expected to slow to some 6% in 2008, owing to reduced economic activity in property, construction and banking. The appointment in December 2007 of an experienced politician and former Prime Minister, Ivars Godmanis, to the premiership, following a succession of corruption allegations against the previous Government, was made in the hope that he could succeed in restoring public confidence and stabilizing the economic situation.

Education

Primary education begins at seven years of age and lasts for four years. Secondary education, beginning at the age of 11, comprises a first cycle of five years and a second of three years. Only the first nine years of education are officially compulsory. In 2004 primary enrolment was equivalent to 93% of children in the relevant age-group (males 94%; females 91%), while the comparable ratio for secondary education was 97% (males 97%; females 96%). In the 2004/05 academic year some 65% of school-age pupils were taught in Latvian-language schools and some 25% were taught in Russian-language schools; 10% were taught in schools offering instruction in both Latvian and Russian. In 2005 higher education was offered at 57 institutions. Enrolment totalled 129,503 students in 2006/07. According to official figures, in 2006 consolidated central government expenditure on education amounted to 626.3m. lats (representing 15.5% of expenditure).

Public Holidays

2008: 1 January (New Year's Day), 21–24 March (Easter), 1 May (Labour Day), 4 May (Declaration of Independence Day), 23–24 June (Midsummer Festival), 18 November (National Day, proclamation of the Republic), 25–26 December (Christmas), 31 December (New Year's Eve).

2009: 1 January (New Year's Day), 10–13 April (Easter), 1 May (Labour Day), 4 May (Declaration of Independence Day), 23–24 June (Midsummer Festival), 18 November (National Day, proclamation of the Republic), 25–26 December (Christmas), 31 December (New Year's Eve).

Weights and Measures

The metric system is in force.

Statistical Survey

Source (unless otherwise stated): Central Statistical Bureau of Latvia, Lāčpleša iela 1, Rīga 1301; tel. 6736-6850; fax 6783-0137; e-mail csb@csb.lv; internet www.csb.lv.

Area and Population

AREA, POPULATION AND DENSITY

Area (sq km)	64,589*
Population (census results)†	
12 January 1989	2,666,567
31 March 2000	
Males	1,094,964
Females	1,282,419
Total	2,377,383
Population (official estimates at 1 January)‡	
2006	2,294,600
2007	2,281,300
2008	2,269,600
Density (per sq km) at 1 January 2008	35.1

* 24,938 sq miles.
† Figures refer to the resident population.
‡ Figures are rounded to the nearest 100 persons.

POPULATION BY ETHNIC GROUP
(official estimates, 1 January 2007)

	Number	%
Latvian	1,346,686	59.0
Russian	645,435	28.3
Belarusian	85,274	3.7
Ukrainian	57,642	2.5
Polish	54,744	2.4
Lithuanian	30,975	1.4
Others	60,549	2.7
Total	**2,281,305**	**100.0**

LATVIA

PRINCIPAL TOWNS
(population at 1 January 2007, official estimates)

Rīga (Riga, capital)	722,485	Jūrmala		55,408
Daugavpils	108,091	Ventspils		43,544
Liepāja	85,477	Rēzekne		36,345
Jelgava	66,051			

BIRTHS, MARRIAGES AND DEATHS

	Registered live births Number	Rate (per 1,000)	Registered marriages Number	Rate (per 1,000)	Registered deaths Number	Rate (per 1,000)
2000	20,248	8.5	9,211	3.9	32,205	13.6
2001	19,664	8.3	9,258	3.9	32,991	14.0
2002	20,044	8.6	9,738	4.2	32,498	13.9
2003	21,006	9.0	9,989	4.3	32,437	13.9
2004	20,334	8.8	10,370	4.5	32,024	13.8
2005	21,497	9.3	12,554	5.5	32,777	14.2
2006	22,264	9.7	14,616	6.4	33,087	14.4
2007	23,070	10.1	15,451	6.8	32,940	14.4

Expectation of life (years at birth, WHO estimates): 71.0 (males 65.4; females 76.5) in 2005 (Source: WHO, *World Health Statistics*).

IMMIGRATION AND EMIGRATION

	2005	2006	2007
Immigrants	1,886	2,801	3,252
Emigrants	2,450	5,252	5,085

ECONOMICALLY ACTIVE POPULATION
(annual averages, '000 persons aged 15–74 years)

	2004	2005	2006
Agriculture, hunting and forestry	132	122	118
Fishing	2	3	2
Mining and quarrying	2	2	4
Manufacturing	163	154	170
Electricity, gas and water	25	23	22
Construction	87	91	104
Wholesale and retail trade; repair of motor vehicles, motorcycles and personal and household goods	151	158	170
Hotels and restaurants	26	28	29
Transport, storage and communications	96	95	101
Financial intermediation	18	20	25
Real estate, renting and business activities	40	49	61
Public administration and defence, compulsory social security	73	82	88
Education	83	91	88
Health and social work	54	58	51
Other community, social and personal service activities	60	58	49
Total employed (incl. others)	1,018	1,036	1,088
Males	522	534	559
Females	496	502	528
Unemployed	119	95	76
Total labour force	1,136	1,131	1,164

Health and Welfare

KEY INDICATORS

Total fertility rate (children per woman, 2005)	1.3
Under-5 mortality rate (per 1,000 live births, 2005)	10
HIV/AIDS (% of persons aged 15–49, 2005)	0.8
Physicians (per 1,000 head, 2003)	3.01
Hospital beds (per 1,000 head, 2005)	7.70
Health expenditure (2004): US $ per head (PPP)	851.6
Health expenditure (2004): % of GDP	7.1
Health expenditure (2004): public (% of total)	56.6
Human Development Index (2005): ranking	45
Human Development Index (2005): value	0.855

For sources and definitions, see explanatory note on p. vi.

Agriculture

PRINCIPAL CROPS
('000 metric tons)

	2004	2005	2006
Wheat	499.9	676.5	598.3
Barley	274.8	365.8	307.0
Rye	96.8	87.2	116.8
Oats	107.4	122.0	91.6
Triticale (wheat-rye hybrid)	42.1	31.8	22.2
Potatoes	628.4	658.2	550.9
Sugar beet	505.6	519.9	473.9
Dry peas	2.7	2.5	0.8
Rapeseed	103.6	145.7	120.6
Cabbages	73.9	64.4	63.3
Cucumbers and gherkins	12.1	12.3	6.4
Dry onions	19.8	15.9	13.6
Carrots	33.3	34.7	31.6
Apples	6.9	37.5	37.5
Currants	3.9	5.2	5.2
Cranberries*	3.4	n.a.	n.a.

* Unofficial figures.

Aggregate production ('000 metric tons, may include official, semi-official or estimated data): Total cereals 1,059.5 in 2004, 1,323.2 in 2005, 1,167.6 in 2006; Total roots and tubers 628.4 in 2004, 658.2 in 2005, 550.9 in 2006; Total vegetables (incl. melons) 181.4 in 2004, 172.7 in 2005, 197.6 in 2006; Total fruits (excl. melons) 17.8 in 2004, 55.0 in 2005, 55.0 in 2006.

Source: FAO.

LIVESTOCK
('000 head at 1 January)

	2004	2005	2006
Cattle	379	371	385
Pigs	444	436	428
Sheep	39	39	42
Goats	15	15	15
Horses	15	16	14
Chickens*	3,403	3,450	3,480

* Unofficial figures.

Source: FAO.

LIVESTOCK PRODUCTS
('000 metric tons, unless otherwise indicated)

	2004	2005	2006
Cattle meat	21.6	20.4	20.7
Pig meat	36.8	38.5	37.8
Chicken meat	14.3	17.2	20.6
Cows' milk	784.0	806.8	812.1
Hen eggs	31.6	32.3	33.1

Source: FAO.

Forestry

ROUNDWOOD REMOVALS
('000 cubic metres, excl. bark)

	2004	2005	2006
Sawlogs, veneer logs and logs for sleepers	7,892	7,951	8,372
Pulpwood	3,292	3,318	2,659
Other industrial wood	600	624	835
Fuel wood	970	950	979
Total	12,754	12,843	12,845

Source: FAO.

SAWNWOOD PRODUCTION
('000 cubic metres, incl. railway sleepers)

	2004	2005	2006
Coniferous (softwood)	2,880	3,225	3,296
Broadleaved (hardwood)	1,108	1,002	1,024
Total	3,988	4,227	4,320

Source: FAO.

Fishing

('000 metric tons, live weight)

	2003	2004	2005
Capture	114.5	125.4	150.6
Atlantic cod	4.6	5.0	4.0
Jack and horse mackerels	8.7	13.8	25.7
Atlantic herring	24.2	23.6	22.2
Sardinellas	8.7	7.0	9.7
European sprat	41.7	52.4	64.6
Chub mackerel	10.5	9.0	4.6
Northern prawn	3.7	3.2	2.4
Aquaculture	0.6	0.5	0.5
Total catch	115.2	125.9	151.1

Source: FAO.

Mining

('000 metric tons)

	2004	2005	2006
Peat	595.1	791.0	1,000.0
Gypsum	266.2	273.9	235.7
Limestone	344.0	377.3	468.1

Industry

SELECTED PRODUCTS
('000 metric tons, unless otherwise indicated)

	2002	2003	2004
Sausages	30	33	38
Preserved fish	88	70	62
Whole milk (million litres)	22.3	15.9	26.4
Yoghurt	51	54	58
Ice-cream (million litres)	12.4	14.8	13.1
Mayonnaise	7.3	7.4	8.2
Beer ('000 hectolitres)	1,199	1,364	1,315
Woven fabrics (million sq metres)	38	44	47
Leather footwear ('000 pairs)	99	169	90
Plywood ('000 cu metres)	236	237	268
Paper	21	n.a.	n.a.
Crude steel	520	n.a.	n.a.
Electric energy (million kWh)	3,975	3,975	4,689

Source: partly UN, *Industrial Commodity Statistics Yearbook*.

Finance

CURRENCY AND EXCHANGE RATES

Monetary Units
100 santimi = 1 lats.

Sterling, Dollar and Euro Equivalents (31 December 2007)
£1 sterling = 96.96 santimi;
US $1 = 48.40 santimi;
€1 = 71.25 santimi;
10 lats = £10.31 = $20.66 = €14.04.

Average Exchange Rate (lats per US $)
2005   0.565
2006   0.560
2007   0.514

Note: Between March and June 1993 Latvia reintroduced its national currency, the lats, replacing the Latvian rouble (Latvijas rublis), at a conversion rate of 1 lats = 200 Latvian roubles. The Latvian rouble had been introduced in May 1992, replacing (and initially at par with) the Russian (formerly Soviet) rouble.

GOVERNMENT FINANCE
(general government operations, million lats)

Summary of Balances

	2004	2005	2006
Revenue	2,522.2	3,200.0	4,002.3
Less Expense	2,461.9	3,109.6	3,786.7
Net operating balance	60.3	90.4	215.6
Less Net acquisition of non-financial assets	137.6	188.0	245.9
Net lending/borrowing	−77.3	−97.6	−30.3

Revenue

	2004	2005	2006
Tax revenue	1,385.3	1,802.5	2,340.5
Taxes on income, profits and capital gains	563.3	689.8	911.0
Taxes on goods and services	739.8	1,021.6	1,331.4
Taxes on property	56.8	61.6	66.4
Social contributions	641.2	751.1	958.5
Grants	154.4	255.0	267.9
Other revenue	341.3	391.4	435.4
Total	2,522.2	3,200.0	4,002.3

LATVIA

Expense/Outlays

Expense by economic type	2004	2005	2006
Compensation of employees	654.4	778.7	970.4
Use of goods and services	433.3	539.0	664.0
Interest	54.6	52.6	57.6
Subsidies	38.5	44.0	72.2
Social benefits	681.6	778.7	927.7
Other expense	599.5	916.6	1,094.8
Total	2,461.9	3,109.6	3,786.7

Outlays by function of government	2004	2005	2006
General public services	406.6	506.9	599.2
Defence	90.1	107.7	168.4
Public order and safety	163.7	192.4	247.7
Education	429.9	510.1	626.3
Health care	245.7	306.7	421.0
Social security and social welfare	730.4	841.9	1,010.6
Housing and community amenities	135.0	191.5	205.2
Recreation, sport, cultural and religious affairs	95.1	108.7	149.5
Economic affairs	303.0	531.7	604.7
Total	2,599.5	3,297.6	4,032.6

Source: IMF, *Government Finance Statistics Yearbook*.

INTERNATIONAL RESERVES
(US $ million at 31 December)

	2004	2005	2006
Gold (national valuation)	110.27	128.45	156.10
IMF special drawing rights	0.15	0.14	0.16
Reserve position in IMF	0.09	0.08	0.08
Foreign exchange	1,911.74	2,231.91	4,353.26
Total	2,022.25	2,360.58	4,509.60

Source: IMF, *International Financial Statistics*.

MONEY SUPPLY
(million lats at 31 December)

	2004	2005	2006
Currency outside banks	645.41	786.39	969.31
Demand deposits	860.97	1,264.02	1,916.53
Total money (incl. others)	1,507.68	2,052.42	2,892.15

Source: IMF, *International Financial Statistics*.

COST OF LIVING
(Consumer Price Index; base: 2000 = 100)

	2005	2006	2007
Food and non-alcoholic beverages	130.5	141.1	160.1
Fuel and light	121.0	139.6	158.4
Clothing (incl. footwear)	106.2	106.2	108.7
Rent	126.5	141.0	167.3
All items (incl. others)	121.9	129.9	143.0

NATIONAL ACCOUNTS
(million lats at current prices)*

Expenditure on the Gross Domestic Product

	2005	2006	2007
Government final consumption expenditure	1,580.7	1,904.4	2,493.2
Private final consumption expenditure	5,666.1	7,347.8	9,303.1
Gross fixed capital formation	2,773.8	3,871.3	5,109.4
Changes in inventories	341.5	414.2	—
Total domestic expenditure	10,362.1	13,537.7	16,905.7
Exports of goods and services	4,334.7	4,981.0	6,112.0
Less Imports of goods and services	5,637.8	7,253.9	8,970.2
GDP in market prices	9,059.1	11,264.7	14,047.5
GDP at constant 2000 prices	7,041.5	7,881.2	8,688.5

Gross Domestic Product by Economic Activity

	2005	2006	2007
Agriculture, hunting and forestry	308.9	354.9	414.6
Fishing	9.5	10.1	11.0
Mining and quarrying	27.3	34.1	45.3
Manufacturing	1,009.7	1,176.3	1,350.3
Electricity, gas and water supply	204.5	244.3	309.6
Construction	490.9	678.8	968.0
Wholesale and retail trade; repair of motor vehicles, motorcycles and personal and household goods	1,616.7	2,075.9	2,496.2
Hotels and restaurants	137.6	175.4	216.4
Transport, storage and communications	1,118.1	1,290.3	1,524.9
Financial intermediation	478.4	615.1	865.4
Real estate, renting and business activities	1,137.9	1,466.8	1,943.2
Public administration and defence; compulsory social security	556.2	660.2	790.2
Education	386.4	437.6	529.8
Health and social work	237.7	310.7	369.4
Other community, social and personal service activities	309.6	400.6	544.6
GDP at basic prices	8,029.4	9,931.2	12,378.9
Taxes *less* subsidies on products	1,029.7	1,333.5	1,668.6
GDP in purchasers' values	9,059.1	11,264.7	14,047.5

* Figures revised in accordance with standard EU classification.

BALANCE OF PAYMENTS
(US $ million)

	2004	2005	2006
Exports of goods f.o.b.	4,221	5,361	6,051
Imports of goods f.o.b.	−7,002	−8,379	−10,992
Trade balance	−2,781	−3,018	−4,941
Exports of services	1,780	2,165	2,670
Imports of services	−1,178	−1,557	−1,984
Balance on goods and services	−2,179	−2,410	−4,255
Other income received	500	768	1,074
Other income paid	−788	−957	−1,579
Balance on goods, services and income	−2,467	−2,598	−4,760
Current transfers received	1,289	1,373	1,787
Current transfers paid	−595	−776	−1,307
Current balance	−1,774	−2,002	−4,280
Capital account (net)	144	212	237
Direct investment abroad	−103	−127	−148
Direct investment from abroad	638	730	1,635
Portfolio investment assets	−21	−268	−242
Portfolio investment liabilities	260	150	248
Financial derivatives assets	−35	58	134
Financial derivatives liabilities	−13	−134	−71
Other investment assets	−1,779	−400	−1,895
Other investment liabilities	3,015	2,620	6,439
Net errors and omissions	71	−317	−79
Overall balance	403	524	1,979

Source: IMF, *International Financial Statistics*.

LATVIA

External Trade

PRINCIPAL COMMODITIES
(million lats)

Imports c.i.f.	2004	2005	2006
Prepared foodstuffs; beverages spirits and vinegar; tobacco and manufactured substitutes	229.0	293.7	379.2
Mineral products	481.6	752.8	854.8
Products of chemical or allied industries	350.1	409.2	530.4
Plastics, rubber and articles thereof	190.2	250.3	322.6
Paper-making material; paper and paperboard and articles thereof	126.3	143.7	135.5
Textiles and textile articles	216.6	236.6	297.0
Base metals and articles thereof	388.4	447.6	606.7
Machinery and mechanical appliances; electrical equipment; sound and television apparatus	755.7	967.7	1,257.0
Vehicles, aircraft, vessels and associated transport equipment	413.7	523.1	868.3
Total (incl. others)	3,805.3	4,866.9	6,378.5

Exports f.o.b.	2004	2005	2006
Prepared foodstuffs; beverages spirits and vinegar; tobacco and manufactured substitutes	132.4	200.1	245.2
Mineral products	114.1	265.2	182.2
Products of chemical or allied industries	123.5	160.3	222.6
Wood, cork and articles thereof; wood charcoal; manufactures of straw, esparto, etc.	655.3	717.6	739.5
Textiles and textile articles	230.0	249.0	269.3
Base metals and artices thereof	303.3	379.3	488.1
Machinery and mechanical appliances; electrical equipment; sound and television apparatus	169.2	269.4	324.0
Miscellaneous manufactured articles	114.3	128.1	149.3
Total (incl. others)	2,150.0	2,888.2	3,293.2

PRINCIPAL TRADING PARTNERS
(million lats)*

Imports c.i.f.	2004	2005	2006
Austria	56.6	78.8	98.4
Belarus	181.5	281.5	297.7
Belgium	60.7	79.4	108.7
China, People's Rep.	47.9	73.4	106.3
Czech Republic	58.5	68.4	112.1
Denmark	116.0	141.3	173.3
Estonia	272.3	383.3	494.1
Finland	247.1	284.9	363.0
France	91.6	100.2	156.4
Germany	556.9	679.0	988.5
Hungary	34.8	56.2	63.8
Italy	131.0	163.5	216.8
Lithuania	476.6	665.5	827.7
Netherlands	131.3	171.2	206.1
Norway	38.0	57.7	128.5
Poland	213.7	309.9	459.4
Russia	332.0	413.8	499.1
Spain	36.3	59.6	59.9
Sweden	239.7	248.5	321.0
Switzerland	57.9	50.9	69.5
Ukraine	99.7	92.9	67.1
United Kingdom	80.0	88.6	124.6
USA	50.0	51.7	58.6
Total (incl. others)	3,805.3	4,866.9	6,378.5

Exports f.o.b.	2004	2005	2006
Belarus	45.1	57.6	75.9
Belgium	19.2	20.4	46.4
Denmark	123.0	153.5	164.8
Estonia	180.2	312.3	419.1
Finland	54.7	101.7	96.2
France	40.8	51.8	57.3
Germany	267.5	295.9	332.3
Ireland	31.3	43.8	48.1
Italy	38.2	47.0	67.7
Lithuania	203.5	317.8	483.0
Netherlands	56.9	61.3	77.4
Norway	40.7	57.1	78.0
Poland	79.6	150.7	79.7
Russia	137.5	228.3	291.9
Spain	11.8	37.2	38.1
Sweden	222.2	225.0	212.9
Switzerland	31.8	46.7	40.2
Ukraine	34.2	39.8	57.7
United Kingdom	278.5	291.7	257.2
USA	63.1	78.6	61.8
Total (incl. others)	2,150.0	2,888.2	3,293.2

* Imports by country of origin; exports by country of destination.

Transport

RAILWAYS
(traffic)*

	2004	2005	2006
Passenger journeys (million)	23.9	25.9	27.4
Passenger-kilometres (million)	811	892	n.a.
Freight transported (million metric tons)	55.9	60.1	48.7
Freight ton-kilometres (million)	18,618	19,779	n.a.

* Data relating to passengers include railway personnel, and data on freight include passengers' baggage, parcel post and mail.

ROAD TRAFFIC
(motor vehicles in use at 31 December)

	2004	2005	2006
Passenger cars	686,128	742,447	822,011
Buses and coaches	10,740	10,644	10,628
Lorries and vans	107,553	113,113	121,120

SHIPPING

Merchant Fleet
(registered at 31 December)

	2004	2005	2006
Number of vessels	162	164	153
Total displacement ('000 grt)	294.3	304.8	333.3

Source: Lloyd's Register-Fairplay, *World Fleet Statistics*.

International Sea-borne Freight Traffic
('000 metric tons)

	2004	2005	2006
Goods loaded	54,101	55,890	53,069
Goods unloaded	3,299	4,152	6,428

LATVIA

CIVIL AVIATION
(traffic)

	2003	2004	2005
Passengers carried ('000)	408.3	674.2	1,150.7
Passenger-kilometres (million)	424.0	825.1	1,478.1
Cargo ton-kilometres (million)	21.1	40.1	9.9

Source: Ministry of Transport, Rīga.

Tourism

FOREIGN TOURIST ARRIVALS*

Country of residence	2004	2005	2006
Denmark	14,326	15,325	14,739
Estonia	50,883	64,103	82,074
Finland	65,321	90,845	88,533
Germany	87,757	123,981	108,716
Italy	17,472	25,394	25,551
Lithuania	45,193	62,279	72,790
Norway	15,573	20,894	43,687
Poland	17,514	23,732	23,030
Russia	43,545	40,488	50,040
Sweden	26,116	45,021	52,115
United Kingdom	29,090	56,370	73,760
USA	18,245	17,377	n.a.
Total (incl. others)	545,366	730,146	816,297

* Figures refer to arrivals at accommodation establishments.

Tourism receipts (US $ million): 271 in 2003; 343 in 2004; 446 in 2005 (Source: World Tourism Organization).

Communications Media

	2004	2005	2006
Telephones ('000 main lines in use)*	631	731	657
Mobile cellular telephones ('000 subscribers)	1,526.7	1,871.6	2,183.7
Personal computers ('000 in use)	501	501	n.a.
Internet users ('000)	810	1,030	1,071
Broadband subscribers ('000)	49	61	110
Book production: titles	2,591	2,371	2,427
Book production: copies ('000)	4,882	4,822	4,700
Newspapers: number	252	261	248
Newspapers: average annual circulation (million copies)	201	206	224
Other periodicals: number	353	366	387
Other periodicals: average annual circulation (million copies)	32.1	45.0	45.4

* At 31 December.

Radio receivers ('000 in use): 1,760 in 1997.

Television receivers ('000 in use): 1,220 in 1997.

Facsimile machines (number in use): 900 in 1996.

Sources: partly UNESCO, *Statistical Yearbook*; UN, *Statistical Yearbook*; and International Telecommunication Union.

Education

(2006/07 unless otherwise indicated)

	Institutions*	Students
Pre-primary	551	77,278
Schools†	1,017	279,872
Primary (Grades 1–4)	58	n.a.
Basic (Grades 1–9)	483	n.a.
Secondary (Grades 10–12)	378	n.a.
Special	64	9,793
Vocational schools	96‡	40,439
Higher education institutions	57‡	129,503

* 2005/2006 figures unless otherwise indicated.
† Figures are for full-time general schools.
‡ Figure at 1 January 2005.

Teachers (2002): Pre-primary 7,996 (2004); Primary (including basic schools) 9,252; Secondary 16,495; Special schools 1,837; Vocational 5,639; Higher 4,535 (2004).

Adult literacy rate (UNESCO estimates): 99.7% (males 99.6%; females 99.6%) in 2000 (Source: UNESCO Institute for Statistics).

Directory

The Constitution

The Constitution of the Republic of Latvia, which had been adopted on 15 February 1922, was annulled at the time of the Soviet annexation in 1940. Latvia became a Union Republic of the USSR and a new Soviet-style Constitution became the legal basis for the governmental system of the republic. The constitutional authority for Latvian membership of the USSR, the Resolution on Latvian Entry into the USSR of 21 July 1940, was declared null and void on 4 May 1990. In the same declaration the Latvian Supreme Council announced the restoration of Articles 1, 2 and 3 of the 1922 Constitution, which describe Latvia as an independent and sovereign state, and Article 6, which states that the legislature (the Saeima) is elected by universal, equal, direct and secret vote, on the basis of proportional representation. On 6 July 1993 the 1922 Constitution was fully restored by the Saeima, following its election on 5 and 6 June. A summary of the Constitution's main provisions (including amendments adopted since its restoration) is given below.

BASIC PROVISIONS

Latvia is an independent, democratic republic, in which the sovereign power of the State belongs to the people. The territory of the Republic of Latvia comprises the provinces of Vidzeme, Latgale, Kurzeme and Zemgale, within the boundaries stipulated by international treaties.

THE SAEIMA

The Saeima (Parliament) comprises 100 representatives of the people and, according to a constitutional amendment adopted in December 1997, is elected by universal, equal, direct and secret vote, on the basis of proportional representation, for a period of four years. All Latvian citizens who have attained 18 years of age are entitled to vote and are eligible for election to the Saeima.

The Saeima elects a Board, which consists of the Chairperson, two Deputies, and Secretaries. The Board convenes the sessions of the Saeima and decrees regular and extraordinary sittings. The sessions of the Saeima are public (sittings in camera are held only by special request).

The right of legislation belongs to both the Saeima and the people. Draft laws may be presented to the Saeima by the President of the Republic, the Cabinet of Ministers, the Committees of the Saeima, no fewer than five members of the Saeima, or, in special cases, by one-tenth of the electorate. Before the commencement of each financial year, the Saeima approves the state budget, the draft of which is submitted by the Cabinet of Ministers. The Saeima decides on the

LATVIA

strength of the armed forces during peacetime. The ratification of the Saeima is indispensable to all international agreements dealing with issues resolved by legislation.

THE PRESIDENT OF THE REPUBLIC

According to a constitutional amendment adopted by the Saeima in December 1997, the President of the Republic is elected by a secret ballot of the Saeima for a period of four years. At least 51 deputies must vote for the winning candidate. No person of less than 40 years of age may be elected President of the Republic. The office of President is not compatible with any other office, and the President may serve for no longer than two consecutive terms.

The President represents the State in an international capacity; he or she appoints Latvian representatives abroad, and receives representatives of foreign states accredited to Latvia; implements the decisions of the Saeima concerning the ratification of international treaties; is Head of the Armed Forces; appoints a Commander-in-Chief in time of war; and has the power to declare war on the basis of a decision of the Saeima.

The President has the right to pardon criminals serving penal sentences; to convene extraordinary meetings of the Cabinet of Ministers for the discussion of an agenda prepared by him or her, and to preside over such meetings; and to propose the dissolution of the Saeima. The President may be held criminally accountable if the Saeima sanctions thus with a majority vote of no fewer than two-thirds of its members.

THE CABINET OF MINISTERS

The Cabinet comprises the Prime Minister and the ministers nominated by him/her. This task is entrusted to the Prime Minister by the President of the Republic. All state administrative institutions are subordinate to the Cabinet, which, in turn, is accountable to the Saeima. If the Saeima adopts a vote expressing 'no confidence' in the Prime Minister, the entire Cabinet must resign. The Cabinet discusses all draft laws presented by the ministries as well as issues concerning the activities of the ministries. If the State is threatened by foreign invasion or if events endangering the existing order of the State arise, the Cabinet has the right to proclaim a state of emergency.

THE JUDICIARY

All citizens are equal before the law and the courts. Judges are independent and bound only by law. The appointment of judges is confirmed by the Saeima. Judges may be dismissed from office against their will only by a decision of the Supreme Court. The retiring age for judges is stipulated by law. Judgment may be passed solely by institutions that have been so empowered by law and in such a manner as specified by law. A Constitutional Court was established in 1996 to examine the legality of legislation.

The Government

HEAD OF STATE

President: VALDIS ZATLERS (inaugurated 8 July 2007).

CABINET OF MINISTERS
(May 2008)

A coalition of the People's Party (TP), the Latvian First Party/Latvian Way (LPP/LC), the Greens' and Farmers' Union (ZZS) and the For Fatherland and Freedom Union/Latvian National Independence Movement (TB/LNNK).

Prime Minister: IVARS GODMANIS (LPP/LC).
Minister of Defence: VINETS VELDRE (TP).
Minister of Foreign Affairs: MĀRIS RIEKSTIŅŠ (TP).
Minister of Finance: ATIS SLAKTERIS (TP).
Minister of the Economy: KASPARS GERHARDS (TB/LNNK).
Minister of the Interior: MAREKS SEGLIŅŠ (TP).
Minister of Education and Science: TATJANA KOĶE (ZZS).
Minister of Agriculture: MĀRTIŅŠ ROZE (ZZS).
Minister of Culture: HELĒNA DEMAKOVA (TP).
Minister of Welfare: IVETA PURNE (ZZS).
Minister of Transport: AINĀRS ŠLESERS (LPP/LC).
Minister of Justice: GAIDIS BĒRZIŅŠ (TB/LNNK).
Minister of the Environment, and of Special Assignment on Electronic Government Affairs: RAIMONDS VĒJONIS (ZZS).
Minister of Health: IVARS EGLĪTIS (TP).
Minister of Regional Development and Local Government: EDGARS ZALĀNS (TP).
Minister of Children and Family Affairs: AINARS BAŠTIKS (LPP/LC).
Minister of Special Assignment on Social Integration Affairs: OSKARS KASTĒNS (LPP/LC).
Minister of Special Assignment on the Administration of European Union Funds: NORMUNDS BROKS (TB/LNNK).

MINISTRIES

Chancery of the President: Pils lauk. 3, Rīga 1050; tel. 6737-7548; fax 6709-2106; internet www.president.lv.
Office of the Cabinet of Ministers: Brīvības bulv. 36, Rīga 1520; tel. 6708-2800; fax 6728-0469; e-mail vk@mk.gov.lv; internet www.mk.gov.lv.
Ministry of Agriculture: Republikas lauk. 2, Rīga 1981; tel. 6702-7107; fax 6702-7250; internet www.zm.gov.lv.
Ministry of Children and Family Affairs: Basteja bulv. 14, Rīga 1050; tel. 6735-6497; fax 6735-6464; e-mail pasts@bm.gov.lv; internet www.bm.gov.lv.
Ministry of Culture: K. Valdemāra iela 11A, Rīga 1364; tel. 6707-8110; fax 6707-8107; e-mail info@km.gov.lv; internet www.km.gov.lv.
Ministry of Defence: K. Valdemāra iela 10–12, Rīga 1473; tel. 6721-0124; fax 6721-2307; e-mail kanceleja@mod.gov.lv; internet www.mod.gov.lv.
Ministry of the Economy: Brīvības iela 55, Rīga 1519; tel. 6701-3101; fax 6728-0882; e-mail em@em.gov.lv; internet www.em.gov.lv.
Ministry of Education and Science: Vaļņu iela 2, Rīga 1050; tel. 6722-2415; fax 6721-3992; internet www.izm.gov.lv.
Ministry of the Environment: Peldu iela 25, Rīga 1494; tel. 6702-6400; fax 6782-0442; e-mail pasts@vidm.gov.lv; internet www.vidm.gov.lv.
Ministry of Finance: Smilšu iela 1, Rīga 1050; tel. 6609-5405; fax 6609-5503; e-mail info@fm.gov.lv; internet www.fm.gov.lv.
Ministry of Foreign Affairs: Brīvības bulv. 36, Rīga 1395; tel. 6701-6201; fax 6782-8121; e-mail mfa.cha@mfa.gov.lv; internet www.mfa.gov.lv.
Ministry of Health: Brīvības iela 72, Rīga 1011; tel. 6787-6000; fax 6787-6002; internet www.vm.gov.lv.
Ministry of the Interior: Raiņa bulv. 6, Rīga 1050; tel. 6721-9210; fax 6722-8283; e-mail pc@iem.gov.lv; internet www.iem.gov.lv.
Ministry of Justice: Brīvības bulv. 36, Rīga 1536; tel. 6708-8220; fax 6728-5575; e-mail info@tm.gov.lv; internet www.tm.gov.lv.
Ministry of Regional Development and Local Government: Lāčplēša iela 27, Rīga 1011; tel. 6777-0401; fax 6777-0479; e-mail pasts@raplm.gov.lv; internet www.raplm.gov.lv.
Ministry of Transport: Gogoļa iela 3, Rīga 1743; tel. 6722-6922; fax 6721-7180; e-mail satmin@sam.gov.lv; internet www.sam.gov.lv.
Ministry of Welfare: Skolas iela 28, Rīga 1331; tel. 6702-1600; fax 6727-6445; e-mail lm@lm.gov.lv; internet www.lm.gov.lv.

Legislature

Saeima
(Parliament)

Jekaba iela 11, Rīga 1811; tel. 6708-7111; fax 6708-7100; e-mail web@saeima.lv; internet www.saeima.lv.

Chairman: GUNDARS DAUDZE.

General Election, 7 October 2006

Parties and coalitions	Votes	%	Seats
People's Party	177,481	19.55	23
Greens' and Farmers' Union*	151,595	16.70	18
New Era	148,602	16.37	18
Harmony Centre†	130,887	14.42	17
Latvian First Party and Latvian Way	77,869	8.58	10
For Fatherland and Freedom Union/Latvian National Independence Movement	62,989	6.94	8
For Human Rights in a United Latvia	54,684	6.02	6
Others	97,558	10.75	—
Total‡	907,640	100.00	100

* Comprising the Latvian Green Party and the Centre Party Latvian Farmers' Union.
† Coalition comprising the People's Harmony Party and the New Centre.
‡ Including 5,975 invalid votes (0.66% of the total).

LATVIA   *Directory*

Election Commission

Central Election Commission (Centrālā vēlēšanu komisija—CVK): Smilšu iela 4, Rīga 1050; tel. 6732-2688; fax 6732-5251; e-mail cvk@cvk.lv; internet web.cvk.lv; Chair. ARNIS CIMDARS.

Political Organizations

There were some 69 political organizations registered in Latvia in January 2005. The following were among the most influential in 2008:

All for Latvia (Visu Latvijai): Ģertrūdes iela 2–46, Rīga 1011; tel. 6738-3171; e-mail imants@agni.lv; internet www.visulatvijai.lv; f. 2006 as a political party; nationalist; Chair. IMANTS PARĀDNIEKS.

Centre Party Latvian Farmers' Union (CP LZS) (Centriskā partija Latvijas Zemnieku savienība): Republikas lauk. 2, Rīga 1010; tel. 6702-7163; fax 6702-7467; e-mail lzs@latnet.lv; internet www.lzs .lv; f. 1990; rural, centrist; contested 2002 and 2006 legislative elections as mem. of Greens' and Farmers' Union; Chair. AUGUSTS BRIGMANIS.

For Fatherland and Freedom Union/Latvian National Independence Movement (TB/LNNK) (Apvienība 'Tēvzemei un Brīvībai'/Latvijas Nacionālās Neatkarības Kustība): Jēkaba iela 20/22–9, Rīga 1050; tel. and fax 6721-6762; e-mail tb@tb.lv; internet www.tb.lv; f. 1997 by merger; Chair. ROBERTS ZĪLE.

For Human Rights in a United Latvia (PCTVL) (Par cilvēka tiesībām vienotā Latvijā/Za prava cheloveka v yedinoi Latvii): Rūpniecības iela 9, Rīga 1010; tel. and fax 6732-0290; e-mail info@zapchel.lv; internet www.pctvl.lv; f. 1998 as electoral alliance; became united party Nov. 2003; represents interests of Russian-speaking communities in Latvia; opposed to Latvian membership of NATO; Leaders TATJANA ŽDANOKA, JAKOVS PLINERS, JURIS SOKOLOVSKIS.

Harmony Centre (SC) (Saskaņas Centrs/ Tsentr soglasiya): Rīga; tel. 6921-8855; internet www.saskanascentrs.lv; f. 2005 as electoral alliance of the National Harmony Party, Latvian Socialist Party (LSP), New Centre and Daugavpils City Party; officially merged Dec. 2006 (excl. LSP, which remained affil.); Chair. NILS UŠAKOVS.

Latvian First Party/Latvian Way (LPP/LC) (Latvijas Pirmā Partija/Latvijas ceļš): Kungu iela 8, Rīga 1050; tel. 6722-6070; fax 6722-6831; e-mail lpp@lpp.lv; internet www.lpplc.lv; f. Aug. 2007 by merger of Latvian First Party (f. 2002) and Latvian Way (f. 1993); contested Oct. 2006 elections as a political union; Christian democratic; Chair. AINĀRS ŠLESERS, IVARS GODMANIS.

Latvian Green Party (LZP) (Latvijas Zaļā partija): Kalnciema iela 30, Rīga 1046; tel. and fax 6761-4272; internet www.zp.lv; f. 1990; forms part of the Greens' and Farmers' Union; Co-Chair. INDULIS EMSIS, VIESTURS SILENIEKS, RAIMONDS VĒJONIS.

Latvian Social Democratic Workers' Party (LSDSP) (Latvijas Sociāl-demokrātiskā strādnieku partija): Aldaru iela 8, Rīga 1050; tel. 6735-6585; fax 6735-6588; e-mail lsdsp@lis.lv; internet www .lsdsp.lv; f. 1904; Chair. JĀNIS DINEVIČS.

Latvian Socialist Party (LSP) (Latvijas Sociālistiskā partija/Sotsialisticheskaya partiya Latvii): Burtnieku iela 23, Rīga; tel. and fax 6755-5535; internet www.latsocpartija.lv; f. 1994; mem. of the For Human Rights in a United Latvia bloc in 1998–2003; joined the Harmony Centre alliance in Dec. 2005, remained affil. to Harmony Centre; Chair. ALFRĒDS RUBIKS.

New Era (JL) (Jaunais laiks): Jēkaba Kazarmās, Torņa iela 4/3B, Rīga 1050; tel. 6720-5472; fax 6720-5473; e-mail birojs@jaunaislaiks .lv; internet www.jaunaislaiks.lv; f. 2002; right-wing; Leaders SOLVITA ĀBOLTIŅA, ARTIS KAMPARS; Sec.-Gen. ĒRIKS ŠKAPARS.

People's Party (TP) (Tautas partija): Dzirnavu iela 68, Rīga; tel. 6728-6441; fax 6728-6405; e-mail info@tautaspartija.lv; internet www.tautaspartija.lv; f. 1998; Chair. ATIS SLAKTERIS.

Diplomatic Representation

EMBASSIES IN LATVIA

Austria: Elizabetes iela 21A/11, Rīga 1010; tel. 6721-6125; fax 6721-4401; e-mail riga-ob@bmaa.gv.at; Ambassador HERMINE POPPELLER.

Azerbaijan: Raiņa bulv. 3/1, Rīga 1050; tel. 6714-2889; fax 6714-2896; e-mail office@azembassy.lv; f. 2005; Ambassador TOFIQ ZULFUGAROV.

Belarus: Jēzusbaznīcas iela 12, Rīga 1050; tel. 6722-2560; fax 6732-2891; e-mail latvia@belembassy.org; internet belembassy.org/latvia; Ambassador ALYAKSANDR GERASIMENKA.

Belgium: Alberta iela 13, Rīga 1010; tel. 6711-4852; fax 6711-4855; e-mail riga@diplobel.be; internet www.diplomatie.be/riga; f. 2004; Ambassador CHRISTIAN VERDONCK.

Canada: Baznicas iela 20–22, Rīga 1010; tel. 6781-3945; fax 6781-3960; e-mail riga@international.gc.ca; internet www.dfait-maeci.gc .ca/dfait/missions/baltiks; Ambassador CLAIRE A. POULIN.

China, People's Republic: Ganību dambis 5, Rīga 1045; tel. 6735-7023; fax 6735-7025; e-mail chinaemb_lv@mfa.gov.cn; Ambassador ZHANG LIMIN.

Czech Republic: Elizabetes iela 29A, Rīga 1010; tel. 6721-7814; fax 6721-7821; e-mail riga@embassy.mzv.cz; internet www.mfa.cz/riga; Ambassador TOMÁŠ PŠTROSS.

Denmark: Pils iela 11, Rīga 1863; tel. 6722-6210; fax 6722-9218; e-mail rixamb@um.dk; internet www.ambriga.um.dk; Ambassador ARNOLD CHRISTIAN DE FINE SKIBSTED.

Estonia: Skolas iela 13, Rīga 1010; tel. 6781-2020; fax 6781-2029; e-mail embassy.riga@mfa.ee; internet www.estemb.lv; Ambassador JAAK JÕERÜÜT.

Finland: Kalpaka bulv. 1, Rīga 1605; tel. 6707-8800; fax 6707-8814; e-mail sanomat.rii@formin.fi; internet www.finland.lv; Ambassador PEKKA WUORISTO.

France: Raiņa bulv. 9, Rīga 1050; tel. 6703-6600; fax 6703-6615; e-mail webmastre.ambafrance-lv@diplomatie.gouv.fr; internet www .ambafrance-lv.org; Ambassador ANDRÉ-JEAN LIBOUREL.

Georgia: Raiņa bulv. 3–19, Rīga 1050; tel. and fax 6722-5812; e-mail riga.emb@mfa.gov.ge; Ambassador KONSTANTIN KORKELIA.

Germany: Raiņa bulv. 13, Rīga 1050; tel. 6708-5100; fax 6708-5149; e-mail mailbox@deutschebotschaft-riga.lv; internet www .deutschebotschaft-riga.lv; Ambassador EBERHARD SCHUPPIUS.

Greece: Elizabetes iela 11–5, 1010 Rīga; tel. 6735-6345; fax 6735-6351; e-mail greekemb-riga@mfa.gr; internet www.greekembassy .se; Ambassador CHRYSSANTHIE PANAYOTOPOULOU.

Hungary: Alberta iela 4, Rīga 1010; tel. 6721-7500; fax 6721-7878; e-mail mission.rix@kum.hu; internet www.mfa.gov.hu/emb/riga; Ambassador Dr ISTVÁN MOHÁCSI.

Ireland: Valdemara Centrs 632, Kr. Valdemara iela 21, Rīga 1010; tel. 6703-5286; fax 6703-5323; e-mail irijas.vestnieciba@gmail.com; Ambassador TIM MAWE.

Israel: Elizabetes iela 2, Rīga 1010; tel. 6732-0739; fax 6783-0170; e-mail press@rig.mfa.gov.il; internet riga.mfa.gov.il; Ambassador CHEN IVRI.

Italy: Teātra iela 9, Rīga 1050; tel. 6721-6069; fax 6721-6084; e-mail ambitalia.riga@apollo.lv; internet www.ambriga.esteri.it; Ambassador FRANCESCO PUCCIO.

Japan: Kr. Valdemāra iela 21, Rīga 1010; tel. 6781-2001; fax 6781-2004; e-mail eoj.001@latnet.lv; Ambassador AKIRA NAKAJIMA.

Lithuania: Rūpniecibas iela 24, Rīga 1010; tel. 6732-1519; fax 6732-1589; e-mail lt@apollo.lv; internet lv.urm.lt; Ambassador ANTANAS VINKUS.

Moldova: Basteja bulv. 14, 1050 Rīga; tel. 6735-9160; fax 6735-9165; e-mail riga@moldovaembassy.lv; Ambassador EDUARD MELNIC.

Netherlands: Torņu iela 4, Jēkaba Kazarmas 1A, Rīga 1050; tel. 6732-6147; fax 6732-6151; e-mail info@netherlandsembassy.lv; internet www.netherlandsembassy.lv; Ambassador ROBERT SCHUDDEBOOM.

Norway: Zirgu iela 14, POB 1173, Rīga 1050; tel. 6781-4100; fax 6781-4108; e-mail emb.riga@mfa.no; internet www.norvegija.lv; Ambassador NILS OLAV STAVA.

Poland: Mednieku iela 6B, Rīga 1010; tel. 6703-1500; fax 6703-1549; e-mail ambpol@apollo.lv; internet www.ambpolriga.lv; Ambassador MACIEJ KLIMCZAK.

Portugal: Balasta Dambis 60, Oģļu iela, Ķipsala, 1048 Rīga; tel. 6782-1926; fax 6733-4233; e-mail embporturiga@gmail.com; Ambassador JOÃO LUIS NIZA PINHEIRO.

Russia: Antonijas iela 2, Rīga 1010; tel. 6733-2151; fax 6783-0209; e-mail rusembas@delfi.lv; internet www.latvia.mid.ru; Ambassador ALEKSANDR VESHNYAKOV.

Slovakia: Smilšu iela 8, Rīga 1050; tel. 6781-4280; fax 6781-4290; e-mail embassy@slovakia.lv; Ambassador IVAN ŠPILDA.

Spain: Elizabetes iela 11, 3rd Floor, 1010 Rīga; tel. 6732-0281; fax 6732-5005; Ambassador PAULINO GONZÁLEZ FERNÁNDEZ-CORUGEDO.

Sweden: A. Pumpura iela 8, Rīga 1010; tel. 6768-6600; fax 6768-6601; e-mail ambassaden.riga@foreign.ministry.se; internet www .swedenemb.lv; Ambassador GÖRAN HÅKANSSON.

Switzerland: Elizabetes iela 2, Rīga 1340; tel. 6733-8351; fax 6733-8354; e-mail vertretung@rig.rep.admin.ch; internet www.eda.admin .ch/riga; Ambassador ANNE BAUTY.

Turkey: A. Pumpura iela 2, 1010 Rīga; tel. 6782-1600; fax 6732-0334; e-mail turkishembassy.riga@gmail.com; Ambassador DURAY POLAT.

LATVIA

Ukraine: Kalpaka bulv. 3, Rīga 1010; tel. 6724-3082; fax 6732-5583; e-mail embassy@ml.lv; Ambassador RAUL CHILACHAVA.
United Kingdom: J. Alunāna iela 5, Rīga 1010; tel. 6777-4700; fax 6777-4707; e-mail british.embassy@apollo.lv; internet www.britain.lv; Ambassador RICHARD MOON.
USA: Raiņa bulv. 7, Rīga 1510; tel. 6703-6206; fax 6722-2132; internet www.usembassy.lv; Ambassador CHARLES W. LARSON, JR.
Uzbekistan: Elizabetes iela 11–11, Rīga 1010; tel. 6732-2424; fax 6732-2306; e-mail posoluz@apollo.lv; internet www.latvia.mfa.uz; Ambassador KOBILJON S. NAZAROV.

Judicial System

Constitutional Court of the Republic of Latvia (Satversmes tiesa): J. Alunāna iela 1, Rīga 1010; tel. 6722-1412; fax 6722-0572; e-mail aivars.e@satv.tiesa.gov.lv; internet www.satv.tiesa.gov.lv; f. 1996; comprises seven judges, appointed by the Saeima for a term of 10 years; Chair. AIVARS ENDZIŅŠ.

Supreme Court (Latvijas Republikas Augstākā tiesa): Brīvības bulv. 36, Rīga 1050; tel. 6702-0350; fax 6702-0351; e-mail at@at.gov.lv; internet www.at.gov.lv; Chair. ANDRIS GUĻĀNS.

Office of the Prosecutor-General: Kalpaka bulv. 6, Rīga 1801; tel. 6704-4400; fax 6704-4449; e-mail una.brenca@lrp.gov.lv; internet www.lrp.gov.lv; Prosecutor-General JĀNIS MAIZĪTIS.

Religion

From the 16th century the traditional religion of the Latvians was Lutheran Christian, although there remained a substantial Roman Catholic population. Russian Orthodoxy is the religion of much of the Slavic population of Latvia. During the period of Soviet rule many places of religious worship were closed. Following the restoration of independence in 1991, religious organizations regained their legal rights and property. In 2004 the statutes of 1,122 religious congregations were registered, of which 304 were Lutheran, 251 Roman Catholic, 118 Orthodox, 93 Baptist, 48 Pentecostal, 67 Old Believer, 50 Adventist, 34 evangelical Christian, 12 Methodist, 13 Jewish and 13 Muslim.

Board of Religious Affairs: Pils lauk. 4, Rīga 1050; tel. 6722-0585; e-mail zlp@zlp.gov.lv; f. 2000; govt agency, attached to the Ministry of Justice; Principal IRETA ROMANOVSKA.

CHRISTIANITY

Protestant Churches

Evangelical Lutheran Church of Latvia: M. Pils iela 4, Rīga 1050; tel. 6722-6057; fax 6782-0041; e-mail konsistorija@lutheran.lv; internet www.lutheran.lv; f. 1922; Archbishop JĀNIS VANAGS.

Latvian Conference of Seventh-day Adventists in Latvia: Baznīcas iela 12A, Rīga 1010; tel. and fax 6724-0013; e-mail viesturs@baznica.lv; internet www.adventistu.baznica.lv; f. 1920; Pres. of Council VIESTURS REĶIS.

Latvian Pentecostal Union: J. Asara iela 8, Jelgava 3001; tel. 6308-1401; fax 6308-1407; e-mail lvdaddf@hotmail.com; f. 1989; Bishop JĀNIS OZOLINKEVIČS.

Union of Baptist Churches in Latvia: Lāčplēša iela 37, Rīga 1011; tel. and fax 6722-3379; internet www.lbds.lv; f. 1860; Bishop Dr PĒTERIS SPROĢIS.

United Methodist Church in Latvia: Klaipēdas iela 56, Liepāja 3401; tel. 6343-2161; fax 6346-9848; re-est. 1991; Supt ĀRIJS VĪKSNA.

The Roman Catholic Church

Latvia comprises one archdiocese and three dioceses. At 31 December 2005 there were an estimated 429,053 adherents in the country (equivalent to 18.6% of the population).

Bishops' Conference

M. Pils iela 2A, Rīga 1050; tel. 6722-7266; fax 6722-0775; Pres. Cardinal JĀNIS PUJATS.

Archbishop of Rīga: Cardinal JĀNIS PUJATS, M. Pils iela 2A, Rīga 1050; tel. 6722-7266; fax 6722-0775; e-mail curia@e-apollo.lv; internet www.catholic.lv.

The Orthodox Church

Although the Latvian Orthodox Church has close ties with the Moscow Patriarchate, it has administrative independence.

Latvian Orthodox Church (Moscow Patriarchate): Pils iela 14, Rīga 1050; tel. 6722-5855; fax 6722-4345; e-mail sinode@orthodoxy.lv; internet www.pareizticiba.lv; f. 1850; Metropolitan of Rīga and all Latvia ALEKSANDR (KUDRJASHOV).

Latvian Old Believer (Old Ritualist) Pomor Church: Krasta iela 73, Rīga 1003; tel. 6711-3083; fax 6714-4513; e-mail oldbel@junik.lv; f. 1760 in split from Moscow Patriarchate; Head of Central Council IVANS MIZOĻUBOVS (Fr Ioann).

JUDAISM

Jewish Religious Community of Rīga: Peitavas iela 6/8, Rīga 1050; tel. 6722-4549; f. 1764; Rabbi NATAN BARKAN.

The Press

The joint-stock company Preses nams (Press House—q.v.) is the leading publisher of newspapers and magazines in Latvia. In 2002 there were eight daily newspapers, with an average circulation of 183,000. In 2006 a total of 248 daily and non-daily newspapers and 387 other periodicals were published. The publications listed below are in Latvian, unless otherwise indicated.

DAILIES

Bizness & Baltiya (Business and the Baltics): Kr. Valdemāra iela 149, Rīga 1013; tel. 6703-3011; fax 6703-3010; e-mail media@bb.lv; internet www.bb.lv; f. 1991; 5 a week; in Russian; Editor-in-Chief YURII ALEKSEYEV; circ. 12,000 (2007).

Chas (Hour): Peldu iela 15, Rīga 1050; tel. 6708-8712; fax 6721-1067; internet www.chas-daily.com; f. 1997; in Russian; Editor-in-Chief XENIA ZAGOROVSKAYA; circ. 16,050 (weekdays), 22,000 (Saturdays).

Diena (Day): Mūkusalas iela 15, Rīga 1004; tel. 6706-3100; fax 6706-3169; e-mail diena@diena.lv; internet www.diena.lv; f. 1990; social and political issues; associated with free newspaper *5min*, launched in Sept. 2005; Editor-in-Chief SARMĪTE ĒLERTE; circ. 62,000.

Jaunā Avīze: Brīvības iela 75, Rīga 1001; tel. 6724-2437; e-mail ja@parks.lv.

Neatkarīgā Rīta Avīze (Independent Morning Paper): Balasta dambis 3, Rīga 1081; tel. 6706-2462; fax 6706-2465; e-mail redakcija@nra.lv; internet www.nra.lv; f. 1990; Editor-in-Chief ALDIS BĒRZIŅŠ; circ. 40,000.

Rīgas Balss (RB) (Voice of Rīga): Balasta dambis 3, Rīga 1081; tel. 6706-2420; fax 6706-2400; e-mail balss@rb.lv; internet www.rigasbalss.lv; f. 1957; city evening newspaper; Editor-in-Chief IVETA MEDINA; circ. 18,100 (Mon.–Thur.), 42,700 (Fri.).

Vakara Ziņas (The Evening News): Bezdelīgas iela 12, Rīga 1007; tel. 6761-7595; fax 6761-2383; e-mail vakara.zinas@vz.lv; internet www.vz.lv; f. 1993; popular; Editor-in-Chief AINĀRS VLADIMIROVS; circ. 53,000.

Vesti Segodnya (News Today): Mūkusalas iela 41, Rīga 1004; tel. 6706-3230; fax 6706-3232; e-mail sm@fenster.lv; in Russian; Editor-in-Chief ALEKSANDRS BĻINOVS; circ. 24,000.

OTHER NEWSPAPERS

The Baltic Times: Rupniciebas iela 1–5, Rīga 1010; tel. 6722-9978; fax 6722-6041; e-mail office@baltictimes.com; internet www.baltictimes.com; f. 1996; news from Estonia, Latvia and Lithuania; in English; Man. Dir VERA ĻIOLE; Editor-in-Chief STEVE ROMAN; circ. 12,000 (2007).

Dienas Bizness (Daily Business): Balasta dambis 3, POB 2, Rīga 1081; tel. 6706-2622; fax 6706-2309; e-mail nberch@db.lv; internet www.db.lv; f. 1992; Editor-in-Chief JURIS PAIDERS; circ. 17,000.

Ieva (Eve): Stabu iela 34, Rīga 1011; tel. 6700-6102; fax 6700-6111; e-mail ieva@santa.lv; f. 1997; weekly; illustrated journal for women; Editor-in-Chief INGA GORBUNOVA; circ. 73,650.

Izglītība un Kultūra (Education and Culture): Palasta iela 10, Rīga 1502; tel. 6735-7585; fax 6735-7584; e-mail info@izglitiba-kultura.lv; internet www.izglitiba-kultura.lv; f. 1948; Editor ANITA KALMANE.

Latvijas Avīze (Latvian Newspaper): Dzirnavu iela 21, Rīga 1010; tel. 6709-6600; fax 6709-6645; e-mail mlredaktors@la.lv; internet www.la.lv; f. 1988; fmrly *Lauku Avīze* (Country Newspaper); present name adopted 2004; 3 a week; popular; agriculture, politics and sport; Editor-in-Chief LINDA RASA; circ. 59,500.

Latvijas Vēstnesis (Latvian Herald): Bruņinieku iela 36/2, Rīga 1001; tel. 6729-8833; fax 6729-9410; e-mail redakcija@lv.lv; internet www.lv.lv; f. 1993; official newspaper; 4 a week; Editor-in-Chief OSKARS GERTS; circ. 3,500.

Privātā Dzīve (Private Life): Stabu iela 34, Rīga 1011; tel. 6700-6104; fax 6700-6111; e-mail pdz@santa.lv; weekly; Editor-in-Chief SANDIJA ŠĶĒLE; circ. 76,000.

Rīgas Viļņi (Riga Waves): Bruņinieku iela 49, korp. 3, Rīga 1011; tel. 6784-2577; fax 6784-2578; e-mail info@rigasvilni.lv; internet www.rigasvilni.lv; weekly.

LATVIA

PRINCIPAL PERIODICALS

Baltiskii Kurs/The Baltic Course: Vesetas 9/205, Rīga 1013; tel. 6738-9694; fax 6738-9696; e-mail baltkurs@baltkurs.com; internet www.baltkurs.com; f. 1996; quarterly; business; in Russian and English; Int. Editor EUGENE ETERIS; Editor-in-Chief OLGA PAVUK.

Daugava: Balasta dambis 3, Rīga 1081; tel. 6728-0290; e-mail ravdin@mailbox.riga.lv; f. 1977; 6 a year; literary journal; Editor-in-Chief ZHANNA EZIT; circ. 500.

Karogs (Banner): Kuršu iela 24, Rīga 1006; tel. 6755-4145; fax 6755-4146; e-mail karogs@apollo.lv; f. 1940; literary monthly; Editor-in-Chief IEVA KOLMANE; circ. 1,500.

Klubs (Club): Balasta dambis 3, Rīga 1081; tel. 6746-4420; fax 6746-1438; e-mail klubs@santa.lv; f. 1994; monthly; politics, business, fashion; Editor-in-Chief JURIS ŠLEIERS; circ. 18,000.

Latvijas Ekonomists: Ieriķu ielā 67A, Rīga 1084; tel. 6703-1090; e-mail birojs@ekonomists.lv; internet www.ekonomists.lv; f. 1992; monthly; in Latvian and Russian; Dir INESE LAPIŅA.

Māksla Plus (M+): Akadēmijas laukums 1, a.k. 41, Rīga 1027; tel. 6722-0722; fax 6782-0608; e-mail makslaplus@inbox.com; internet www.makslaplus.lv; cultural magazine (cinema, music, theatre, photography); Editor-in-Chief SANITA BUČINIECE.

Mans Mazais: Balasta dambis 3, Rīga 1081; tel. 6762-8274; fax 6246-5450; e-mail mansmazais@santa.lv; f. 1994; monthly; illustrated journal for young parents; Editor-in-Chief VITA BEĻAUNIECE; circ. 20,000.

Mūsmājas (Our Home): Pērnavas iela 43, Rīga 1009; tel. 6727-3311; fax 6729-2701; e-mail pasts@mgtops.lv; internet www.musmajas.lv; f. 1993; monthly; home and family magazine; Editor-in-Chief ILZE STRAUTIŅA; circ. 50,000.

Mūzikas Saule (Musical Sun): Arhitektu 1–305, Rīga 1050; tel. 6722-0161; fax 6957-7765; internet www.m-saule.lv; music; Editor-in-Chief IEVA ROZENTĀLE.

Rīgas Laiks (Rīga Times): Lāčplēša iela 25, Rīga 1011; tel. 6728-7922; fax 6783-0542; e-mail pasts@rigaslaiks.lv; internet www.rigaslaiks.lv; f. 1993; monthly; Editor-in-Chief INESE ZANDERE; circ. 10,000.

Santa: Balasta dambis 3, POB 32, Rīga 1081; tel. 6762-8274; fax 6246-5450; e-mail santa@santa.lv; f. 1991; monthly; illustrated journal for women; Editor-in-Chief SANTA ANCHA; circ. 42,000.

Zinātnes Vēstnesis (Scientific Herald): Akadēmijas lauk. 1, Rīga 1524; tel. 6721-2706; fax 6782-1109; e-mail lzs@ac.lza.lv; internet www.lza.lv/zv00.htm; f. 1989; published by the Latvian Scientific Council, the Latvian Academy of Science and the Latvian Society of Scientists; two a month; Editor-in-Chief ZAIGA KIPERE.

NEWS AGENCIES

Baltic News Service: Baznīcas iela 8, Rīga 1010; tel. 6708-8600; fax 6708-8601; internet bnsnews.bns.lv; f. 1990; news from Latvia, Lithuania, Estonia and the CIS; in English, Russian and the Baltic languages; Dir LIGA MENGELSONA.

LETA Latvian News Agency: Palasta iela 10, Rīga 1502; tel. 6722-2509; fax 6722-3850; e-mail leta.marketing@leta.lv; internet www.leta.lv; independent; Chair. MĀRTIŅŠ BARKĀNS.

PRESS ASSOCIATION

Latvian Journalists' Union (Latvijas Žurnālistu savienība): Marstaļu iela 2, Rīga 1050; tel. 6721-1433; fax 6782-0233; e-mail reiterns@zn.apollo.lv; f. 1992; 700 mems; Pres. LIGITA AZOVSKA.

Publishers

Izdevniecība AGB (AGB Publishing House): K. Barona iela 31, Rīga 1011; tel. 6728-0464; fax 6728-0356; e-mail info@izdevnieciba.com; internet www.izdevnieciba.com.

Avots (Spring): Puskina iela 1A, Rīga 1050; tel. 6721-1394; fax 6722-5824; e-mail avots@apollo.lv; f. 1980; non-fiction, dictionaries, crafts, hobbies, etc.; Pres. JĀNIS LEJA.

Elpa (Breath): Doma lauk. 1, Rīga 1050; tel. 6721-1776; fax 6722-6497; e-mail elpa@apollo.lv; f. 1990; books and newspapers; Pres. MAIRITA SOLIMA.

Jāņa sēta: Elizabetes iela 83–85, Rīga 1050; tel. 6709-2290; fax 6709-2292; e-mail janaseta@janaseta.lv; internet www.janaseta.lv; f. 1991; travel and culinary books; Dir AIVARS ZVIRBULIS.

Jumava: Dzirnavu iela 73, Rīga 1011; tel. and fax 6728-0314; e-mail jumava@parks.lv; internet www.jumava.lv; f. 1994; translations, dictionaries, fiction, etc.; Pres. JURIS VISOCKIS.

Kontinents: Elijas iela 17, Rīga 1050; tel. 6720-4130; fax 6720-4129; e-mail kontinent@ml.lv; internet www.kontinents.lv; f. 1991; translated fiction, non-fiction and colour children's books; Chair. of Bd OLEG MIHALEVICH.

Nordik: Daugavgrīvas 36–9, Rīga 1048; tel. 6760-2672; fax 6760-2818; e-mail nordik@nordik.lv; internet www.nordik.lv; f. 1992; sister co, Tapals, at same address; Dir JĀNIS JUŠKA; Editor-in-Chief IEVA JANAITE.

Preses nams (Press House): Balasta dambis 3, Rīga 1081; tel. 6246-5732; internet www.presesnams.lv; f. 1990; newspapers, magazines, encyclopedias and scientific literature; controlling interest owned by Ventspils Nafta; Dir EGONS LAPIŅŠ.

Smaile (Peak): Brīvības iela 104, Rīga 1001; tel. 6731-5137; f. 1999; fiction, poetry, fine arts; Dir ANDREJS BRIMERBERGS.

Zinātne Publishers Ltd (Science): Akadēmijas lauk. 1, Rīga 1050; tel. 6721-2797; fax 6722-7825; e-mail zinatne@navigator.lv; f. 1951; non-fiction, text books, dictionaries, reference books; Dir INGRĪDA SEGLINA.

Zvaigzne ABC: K. Valdemāra iela 6, Rīga 1010; tel. 6750-8799; fax 6750-8798; e-mail info@zvaigzne.lv; internet www.zvaigzne.lv; f. 1966; privately owned; educational literature, textbooks, dictionaries, non-fiction for children and adults, fiction; Head of Bd VIJA KILBLOKA.

PUBLISHERS' ASSOCIATION

Latvian Publishers' Assen (Latvijas Grāmatizdevēju asociācija): K. Barona iela 36/4, Rīga 1011; tel. 6728-2392; fax 6728-0549; e-mail lga@gramatizdeveji.lv; internet www.gramatizdeveji.lv; f. 1993; 40 mems; Pres. INGRIDA VAVERNIECE.

Broadcasting and Communications

TELECOMMUNICATIONS

In 2006 there were 657,000 main telephone lines in use; 69% of lines were digital in 2001. In 2005 there were four providers of mobile telecommunications services.

Regulatory Organizations

Dept of Communications (Ministry of Transport): Gogoļa iela 3, Rīga 1190; tel. 6724-2321; fax 6782-0636; e-mail diana.ainep@sam.gov.lv; f. 1991; Dir INĀRA RUDAKA.

Public Utilities Regulatory Commission (Sabiedrisko Pakalpojumu Regulēšanas Komisija): see Trade and Industry (Utilities) section.

Major Service Providers

Lattelecom SIA: Dzirnavu iela 105, Rīga 1011; tel. 6705-5222; fax 6705-5001; e-mail nils.melngailis@lattelecom.lv; internet www.lattelecom.lv; f. 1992; 49% owned by TeliaSonera AB (Sweden); CEO NILS MELNGAILIS; 3,000 employees.

Latvian Mobile Telephone Co (Latvijas Mobilais Telefons SIA—LMT): Ropazu iela 6, Rīga 1039; tel. 6777-3200; fax 6753-5353; e-mail info@lmt.lv; internet www.lmt.lv; f. 1992; 24.5% owned by Sonera Holding BV (Finland), 24.5% owned by TeliaSonera AB (Sweden), 23.0% owned by SIA Lattelekom, 23.0% owned by Digitālais Latvijas radio un televīzijas centrs, a/s; Gen. Man. JURIS BINDE; 150 employees.

SIA Radiokoms: Elizabetes iela 45–47, Rīga 1010; tel. 6733-3355; e-mail radiokoms@radiokoms.lv; internet www.radiokoms.lv; Dir JANA BALODE.

Tele2: Kurzemes pr. 3, Rīga 1067; tel. 6706-0069; fax 6706-0176; internet www.tele2.lv; f. 1991; owned by Tele2 AB (Sweden); fmrly Baltkom GSM; Pres. BILL BUTLER; 110 employees.

BROADCASTING

Regulatory Organization

National Broadcasting Council of Latvia (Nacionālā Radio un Televizijas padome): Smilšu iela 1/3, Rīga 1939; tel. 6722-1848; fax 6722-0448; e-mail Zita.Janitena@nrtp.lv; internet www.nrtp.lv; f. 1995; Chair. AIVARS BERKIS.

Radio

Latvijas Radio (Latvian Radio): Doma lauk. 8, Rīga 1505; tel. 6720-6722; fax 6720-6709; e-mail radio@radio.org.lv; internet www.radio.org.lv; f. 1925; state-operated service; broadcasts in Latvian, Russian and English; supports four programme services: Latvijas Radio 1, Latvijas Radio 2, Latvijas Radio 3—Klasika and Latvijas Radio 4—Doma Square; Dir-Gen. AIGĀRS SEMEVICS.

Alise Plus: Raiņa iela 28, Daugavpils 5403; e-mail alise_plus@daugavpils.apollo.lv; 24-hour transmissions in Russian and Latvian.

LATVIA

European Hit Radio: Elijas iela 17, Rīga 1050; tel. 6957-5757; fax 6720-4407; e-mail radio@superfm.lv; internet www.europeanhitradio.com; f. 1994; 24-hour transmissions in Latvian, Russian, Estonian, Lithuanian and English; Pres. Ugis Polis; Dir Richard Zakss.

Latvijas Kristīgais Radio (Latvian Christian Radio): Lāčplēša iela 37, Rīga 1011; tel. 6721-3704; fax 6782-0633; e-mail lkr@lkr.lv; internet www.lkr.lv; f. 1993; 24-hour transmissions in Latvian and Russian.

Radio Ef-Ei: Atbrvōsanas aleja 98, Rēzekne 4600; e-mail efei@mailbox.riga.lv; 24-hour transmissions in Russian and Latvian.

Radio Imanta: Tērbatas iela 1, Valmiera 4201; tel. 6420-7349; fax 6420-7350; e-mail radio.imanta@tl.lv; internet www.radioimanta.lv; 24-hour transmissions in Russian and Latvian; Chief Editor Nils Interbergs.

Radio Mix FM: L. Nometņu iela 62, Rīga 1002; 24-hour transmissions in Russian.

Radio Sigulda: L. Paegles iela 3, Sigulda 2150; tel. 6797-2678; fax 6797-3786; e-mail mail@radiosigulda.lv; internet www.radiosigulda.lv; f. 1991; 24-hour transmissions in Latvian; music radio; Dir Aivars Plucis.

Radio SWH: Skanstes iela 13, Rīga 1013; tel. 6737-0067; fax 6782-8283; e-mail radio@radioswh.lv; internet www.radioswh.lv; Pres. Zitmars Liepinsch.

Radio Trīs: Vaļņu iela 5, Cēsis 4101; tel. 6412-4566; fax 6412-7041; e-mail radio@radio3.lv; internet www.radio3.lv; f. 1994; 24-hour transmissions in Latvian; Dir Egils Viskrints.

Radio Zemgale: Grāfa lauk. 6, Lecava 3913; e-mail rz@apollo.lv; internet www.radiozemgalei.lv; f. 2000; 24-hour transmissions in Latvian; Dir Dace Dubkeviča.

Television

Latvijas Televīzija (Latvian Television): Zaķusalas krastmala 3, Rīga 1509; tel. 6720-0315; fax 6720-0025; internet www.ltv.lv; f. 1954; state-operated service; two channels in Latvian (Channel II also includes programmes in Russian, Polish, Ukrainian, German, English and French); Dir Edgars Kots.

Latvijas Neatkariga Televizija (Latvian Independent Television—LNT): Elijas iela 17, Rīga 1050; tel. 6707-0200; fax 6782-1128; e-mail lnt@lnt.lv; internet www.lnt.lv; f. 1996; entertainment, news reports; Dir-Gen. Andrejs Ēķis.

TV3 Latvia: Mūkusalas iela 72b, Rīga 1004; tel. 6762-9366; fax 6760-0599; e-mail tv3@tv3.lv; internet www.tv3.lv; owned by Modern Times Group—MTG (Sweden); affiliated with channel 3+, targeted at a Russian-speaking audience; Dir Kaspars Ozolins.

Finance

(cap. = capital; res = reserves; dep. = deposits; m. = million; brs = branches; amounts in lats)

BANKING

A crisis in the banking sector in 1995 was contained by early 1996. Reorganization of the sector subsequently took place. At the end of 2004 there were 23 banks in operation.

Central Bank

Bank of Latvia (Latvijas Banka): K. Valdemāra iela 2a, Rīga 1050; tel. 6702-2300; fax 6702-2420; e-mail info@bank.lv; internet www.bank.lv; f. 1990; cap. 25.0m., res 71.9m., dep. 1,305.0m. (Dec. 2006); Gov. and Chair. of Council Ilmārs Rimšēvičs.

Commercial Banks

Aizkraukles Banka: Elizabetes iela 23, Rīga 1010; tel. 6777-5222; fax 6777-5200; e-mail bank@ab.lv; internet www.ab.lv; f. 1993; cap. 15.0m., res 28.0m., dep. 719.4m. (Dec. 2006); Chair. of Bd Ernests Bernis.

Baltic Trust Bank—BTB: 13 Janvāra iela 3, Rīga 1050; tel. 6702-4747; fax 6721-1985; e-mail btb@btb.lv; internet www.btb.lv; f. 1992; present name adopted 2004; cap. 15.6m., res 16.1m., dep. 191.7m. (Dec. 2006); Chair. of Bd Ieva Racenaja; 30 brs.

DnB Nord Banka Latvija: Smilšu iela 6, Rīga 1803; tel. 6701-5204; fax 6732-3449; e-mail office@dnbnord.lv; internet www.dnbnord.lv; f. 1989; fmrly Rīgas Komercbanka PLC and AS NORD/LB Latvija; 99.76% owned by Bank DnB NORD (Denmark); cap. 57.0m., res 14.4m., dep. 1,190.0m. (Dec. 2006); Pres. and Chair. of Bd Andris Ozolins; 10 brs.

Hansabanka: Balasta dambis 1a, Rīga 1048; tel. 6702-4555; fax 6702-4400; e-mail info@hansabanka.lv; internet www.hansabanka.lv; f. 1992; present name adopted 1999; 100% owned by AS Hansapank (Estonia); cap. 186.0m., res 0.1m., dep. 3,398.6m. (Dec. 2006); Chair. of Bd Maris Avotiņš; 76 brs.

Latvijas Biznesa Banka (Latvian Business Bank): 3 Antonijas iela, Rīga 1010; tel. 6777-5888; fax 6777-5849; e-mail info@lbb.lv; internet www.lbb.lv; f. 1992; present name adopted 2004; 99.87% owned by Bank of Moscow (Russian Federation); cap. 10.8m., res 0.6m., dep. 36.8m. (Dec. 2006); Chair. and Pres. Artis Birkmanis.

Latvijas Hipotēku un Zemes Banka (Mortgage and Land Bank of Latvia): Doma lauk. 4, Rīga 1977; tel. 6800-0100; fax 6777-4152; e-mail banka@hipo.lv; internet www.hipo.lv; f. 1993; present name adopted in 2000; state-owned; cap. 48.5m., res 1.4m., dep. 605.9m. (Dec. 2006); Pres. and Chair. of Bd Inesis Feiferis; 32 brs.

Latvijas Tirdzniecības banka (Latvian Trade Bank): Grēcinieku iela 22, Rīga 1050; tel. 6704-3500; fax 6704-3511; e-mail ltb@ltblv.com; internet www.ltblv.com; f. 1991; owned by MDM Bank (Russian Federation); cap. 8.2m., res 4.5m., dep. 250.5m. (Dec. 2006); Chair. Armands Steinbergs.

Multibanka: Elizabetes iela 57, Rīga 1772; tel. 6701-9100; fax 6782-8232; e-mail info@multibanka.com; internet www.multibanka.com; f. 1994; cap. 7.0m., res 0.3m., dep. 27.8m. (Dec. 2006); Pres. Svetlana Dzene.

Norvik Banka: E. Birznieka-Upiša iela 21, Rīga 1011; tel. 6704-1100; fax 6704-1111; e-mail welcome@norvik.lv; internet www.norvik.lv; f. 1992; fmrly Lateko Bank; present name adopted 2006; cap. 30.5m., res 13.9m., dep. 218.2m. (June 2007); Chair. of Bd Andrejs Svirčenkovs; 13 brs.

Parex Banka: Smilšu iela 3, Rīga 1522; tel. 6701-0000; fax 6701-0001; e-mail info@parex.lv; internet www.parex.lv; f. 1992; cap. 65.0m., res 10.7m., dep. 2,132.4m. (Dec. 2006); Pres. and Chair. of Bd Valery Kargin; Chair. of Council Victor Krasovitsky; 71 brs.

Paritate Banka: Terbatas iela 4, Rīga 1134; tel. 6704-1300; fax 6728-2981; e-mail info@paritate.lv; internet www.paritate.com; f. 1992; cap. 3.6m., res 2.2m., dep. 95.4m. (Dec. 2006); Chair. of Bd Oleksandr Trubakov.

Regional Investment Bank (Regionala investīciju banka): J. Alunāna iela 2, Rīga 1010; tel. 6750-8989; fax 6750-8988; e-mail banka@rib.lv; internet www.rib.lv; f. 2001; cap. 5.5m., res 1.7m., dep. 56.2m. (Dec. 2006); Chair. of Bd Haralds Āboliņš.

Rietumu Banka: tel. 6702-5555; fax 6702-5588; e-mail info@rietumu.lv; internet www.rietumu.lv; f. 1992; cap. 22.5m., res 39.1m., dep. 827.0m. (Dec. 2006); Pres. and Chair. of Exec. Bd Alexander Kalinovski.

Sampo Banka: Cesu iela 31, Rīga 1012; tel. 6777-2676; fax 6728-2788; e-mail info@sampobanka.lv; internet www.sampo.lv; f. 1997 as Māras banka; present name adopted 2005; 100% owned by Sampo Bank (Finland); mortgage banking; cap. 8.5m., res 2.2m., dep. 126.1m. (Dec. 2006); Chair. of Council Georg Schubiger; Pres. Ingus Grasis.

SEB Latvijas Unibanka: Unicentrs, Kekavas pagasts, Rīga 1076; tel. 6721-5535; fax 6721-5335; e-mail sekretars@seb.lv; internet www.seb.lv; f. 1993; present name adopted 2005; wholly owned by Skandinaviska Enskilda Banken AB (Sweden); cap. 37.1m., res 1.5m., dep. 2,284.1m. (Dec. 2006); Pres. and Chair. Viesturs Neimanis; 68 brs.

Trasta komercbanka—TKB (Trust Commercial Bank): Miesnieku iela 9, Rīga 1050; tel. 6702-7777; fax 6702-7700; e-mail info@tkb.lv; internet www.tkb.lv; f. 1989; present name adopted 1996; cap. 5.5m., res 4.0m., dep. 230.3m. (Dec. 2006); Pres. and Chair. Gundars Grieze.

UniCredit Bank: Elizabetes iela 63, Rīga 1050; tel. 6708-5500; fax 6708-5507; e-mail info@unicreditbank.lv; internet www.unicreditbank.lv; f. 1997; fmrly Vereinsbank Rīga; present name adopted 2005; 100% owned by Bayerische Hypo-und Vereinsbank AG (Germany); cap. 41.7m., res 1.9m., dep. 311.3m. (Dec. 2006); Chair. of Bd Juris Jakobsons.

Savings Bank

Latvijas Krājbanka (Latvian Savings Bank): Dalina iela 15, Rīga 1013; tel. 6709-2001; fax 6721-2000; e-mail info@lkb.lv; internet www.krajbanka.lv; f. 1924; present name adopted 1998; 83.0% owned by Snoras Bankas (Lithuania); cap. 9.1m., res 8.4m., dep. 373.2m. (Dec. 2006); Pres. Martins Bondars; 10 brs.

Regulatory Authority

Financial and Capital Markets Commission (Finanšu un kapitāla tirgus komisija—FKTK): Kungu iela 1, Rīga 1050; tel. 6777-4800; fax 6722-5755; e-mail fktk@fktk.lv; internet www.fktk.lv; f. 2001; Chair. Uldis Cērps.

Banking Association

Association of Latvian Commercial Banks (Latvijas Komercbanku asociācija): Pērses iela 9–11, Rīga 1011; tel. 6728-4528; fax

LATVIA

6782-8170; e-mail office@bankasoc.lv; internet www.bankasoc.lv; f. 1992; 23 mems; Pres. TEODORS TVERIJONS.

INSURANCE

At September 2004 there were 18 insurance companies in Latvia, of which six were involved in life insurance and 12 in non-life insurance operations (including one mutual non-life insurance co-operative society).

Balta Insurance Co: Raunas iela 10/12, Rīga 1039; tel. 6708-2233; fax 6708-2345; internet www.balta.lv; f. 1992; automobile, property, freight, travel, agricultural insurance; Pres. JANIS ABASINS.

Balva: K. Valdemāra iela 36, Rīga 1010; tel. 6750-6955; fax 6750-6956; e-mail balva@balva.lv; internet www.balva.lv; f. 1992; partly owned by Ingosstrakh (Russia); non-life insurance; Chair. of Bd ANDREW SHAKHMATOV; 31 brs.

BTA Apdrošināšana: K. Valdemāra iela 63, Rīga 1142; tel. 6702-5100; fax 6702-5190; e-mail bta@bta.lv; internet www.bta.lv; f. 1993.

Colemont FKB Latvia: Dārzaugļu iela 1–50, Rīga 1012; tel. 6724-0066; fax 6720-1737; e-mail info@colemont.lv; internet www.colemont.lv; f. 2000; 60% owned by Colemont Insurance Brokers (USA); fmrly Finansu Konsultanti Un Brokeri (FKB); name changed in 2006; Chair. of Bd BEERH SURINDER KUMAR.

ERGO Latvija: Ūnijas iela 45, Rīga 1039; tel. 6708-1700; fax 6784-0102; e-mail info@ergo.lv; internet www.ergo.lv; owned by Alte Leipziger (Germany); life and non-life; Pres. of Bd ILMARS VEIDE.

Estora Reinsurance Co: Elizabetes iela 14, Rīga 1010; tel. 6733-3335; fax 6733-3898; e-mail estora@estora.com; internet www.estora.com; f. 1992; reinsurance; Dir-Gen. JERGENIJS TOLOČKOVS.

SEB Dzīvības Apdrošināšana (SEB Life Insurance): Antonijas iela 9, Rīga 1010; tel. 6707-9800; fax 6707-9808; e-mail dziviba@seb.lv; internet www.seb.lv; f. 1940; present name adopted 2005; Chair. of Bd UĢIS VORONS.

Seesam Latvia: Vienības gatve 87H, Rīga 1004; tel. 6706-1000; fax 6706-1022; e-mail seesam@seesam.lv; internet www.seesam.lv; f. 1993; owned by Pohjola Group Plc (Finland).

COMMODITY AND STOCK EXCHANGES

Rīga Stock Exchange (Rīgas Fondu birža): Vaļņu iela 1, Rīga 1050; tel. 721-2431; fax 722-9411; e-mail riga@omxgroup.com; internet www.omxgroup.com/riga; f. 1993; owned by HEX Helsinki Stock Exchange (Finland)—OMX ABforms Group; Pres. DAIGA AUZINA-MELALKSNE.

Trade and Industry

GOVERNMENT AGENCY

Latvian Privatization Agency (Latvijas Privatizācijas agentūra): K. Valdemāra iela 31, Rīga 1887; tel. 6702-1358; fax 6783-0363; e-mail lpa@mail.bkc.lv; internet www.lpa.bkc.lv; f. 1994; became state joint-stock co in 2004; Dir-Gen. ARTURS GRANTS.

DEVELOPMENT ORGANIZATIONS

Latvian Investment and Development Agency (Latvijas Investīciju un Attīstibas Aģentūra—LIAA): Pērses iela 2, Rīga 1442; tel. 6703-9400; fax 6703-9401; e-mail invest@liaa.gov.lv; internet www.liaa.gov.lv; f. 1993; promotion of business development in Latvia and foreign markets; Dir ANDRIS OZOLS.

CHAMBER OF COMMERCE

Latvian Chamber of Commerce and Industry (Latvijas Tirdzniecības un rūpniecības kamera): K. Valdemāra iela 35, Rīga; tel. 6722-5595; fax 6782-0092; e-mail info@chamber.lv; internet www.chamber.lv; f. 1934; re-est. 1990; Pres. ANDRIS BĒRZIŅŠ; Dir-Gen. ANDRIS GŪTMANIS.

INDUSTRIAL AND TRADE ASSOCIATIONS

Latvian Employers' Confederation: Vilandes iela 12–1, Rīga 1010; tel. 6722-5162; fax 6722-4469; e-mail lddk@lddk.lv; internet www.lddk.lv; f. 1993 by merger of Latvian Employers' Central Assocn and Latvian Private Entrepreneurs' (Employers') Union; Pres. VITĀLIJS GAVRILOVS.

Latvian Construction Contractors' Association (LCCA) (Latvijas būvnieku asociācija—LBA): Grēcinieku ielā 22/24, kab. 201, Rīga 1050; tel. 6722-8584; fax 6721-0023; e-mail lba@latnet.lv; internet www.building.lv/lba; f. 1996; Pres. VIKTORS PURIŅŠ; 6 brs.

Latvian Electrical Engineering and Electronics Industry Association (LETERA): Dzirnavu iela 93, Rīga 1011; tel. and fax 6728-8360; e-mail letera@latnet.lv; internet www.letera.lv; f. 1995; 50 mems (enterprises and education institutions); Pres. NORMUNDS BERGS.

Latvian Fuel Traders' Association (Latvijas Degvielas Tirgotāju Asociācija): Citadeles iela 7/43, Rīga 1010; tel. 6732-0229; fax 6732-0228; e-mail birojs@ldta.lv; internet www.ldta.lv; Chair. of Bd O. KARČEVSKIS; Exec. Dir U. SAKNE.

Latvian Information Technology and Telecommunications Association (LITTA): Stabu iela 47–1, Rīga 1011; tel. 6731-1821; fax 6731-5567; e-mail litta@dtmedia.lv; internet www.litta.lv; f. 1998; Pres. IMANTS FREIBERGS.

Latvian Timber Exporters' Association (LTEA) (Latvijas Kokmateriālu Eksportētāju Asociācija): Skaistkalnes iela 1, Rīga 1004; tel. 6706-7369; fax 6786-0268; e-mail ltea@latvianwood.lv; internet www.latviantimber.lv; f. 1998; Pres. JANIS APSITIS.

UTILITIES

Regulatory Authority

Public Utilities Commission of Latvia (PUC) (Sabiedrisko Pakalpojumu Regulēšanas Komisija): Brīvības iela 55, Rīga 1010; tel. 6709-7200; fax 6709-7277; e-mail sprk@sprk.gov.lv; internet www.sprk.lv; f. 2001; to replace the Energy Regulation Council; multi-sector regulator overseeing electricity, gas, telecommunications, post and railway sectors; Chair. VALENTĪNA ANDRĒJEVA.

Electricity

Latvenergo: Pulkveža Brieža iela 12, Rīga 1230; tel. 6772-8309; fax 6772-8811; e-mail latvenergo@latvenergo.lv; internet www.latvenergo.lv; state-owned joint-stock co; transmits and distributes electricity and heat; seven regional subsidiary cos; Chair. of Bd KĀRLIS MIĶELSONS.

Gas

Latvian Gas (Latvijas gāze): A. Briana iela 6, Rīga 1001; tel. 6736-9132; fax 6782-1406; e-mail latvijas_gaze@lg.lv; internet www.lg.lv; partially privatized in 2000–01; 8% state-owned; Chair. MĀRIS GAILIS; 2,817 employees.

Water

Major suppliers include:

Aizkraukle Water Co (Aizkraukles ūdens): Torņu iela 1, Aizkraukle 5101; fax 6512-2150; e-mail udensall@inbox.lv.

Bauska Water Co (Bauskas ūdens): Birzu iela 8A, Bauska 3901; tel. 6396-0565; fax 6396-0566; e-mail baude@apollo.lv.

Daugavpils Water Co (Daugavpils ūdens): Ūdensvada iela 3, Daugavpils 5403; tel. 6544-4565; fax 6542-5547; e-mail kontakti@daugavpils.udens.lv; internet www.daugavpils.udens.lv; f. 1889.

Liepāja Water Co (Liepājas ūdens): K. Valdemāra iela 12, Liepāja 3401; tel. 6541-1416; fax 6541-0769; e-mail dmeu@dpu.lv.

Rīga Water Co (Rīgas ūdens): Basteja bulv. l/5, Rīga 1495; tel. 6708-8555; fax 6722-2660; e-mail office@ru.lv; internet www.rw.lv; water supply and sewage treatment.

TRADE UNIONS

Free Trade Union Confederation of Latvia (Latvijas Brīvo Arodbiedrību Savienība—LBAS): Bruņinieku iela 29–31, Rīga 1001; tel. 6727-0351; fax 6727-6649; e-mail lbas@lbas.lv; internet www.lbas.lv; f. 1990; Pres. PETERIS KRIGERS.

Transport

RAILWAYS

In 2005 there were 2,270 km of railways on the territory of Latvia, of which 257 km were electrified. In 2006 Latvian railways carried 27.4m. passengers and 48.7m. metric tons of freight.

Latvian Railways (Latvijas Dzelzceļš): Gogoļa iela 3, Rīga 1547; tel. 6723-4940; fax 6782-0231; e-mail biruta.sakse@ldz.lv; internet www.ldz.lv; f. 1993; state joint-stock co; Chair. of Bd UGIS MAGONIS.

ROADS

In 2004 Latvia's total road network was 69,532 km, of which 6,963 km were main roads.

Latvian State Roads (Latvijas Valsts Ceļi): Gogoļa iela 3, Rīga 1050; tel. 6702-8169; fax 6702-8171; e-mail lad@lvceli.lv; internet www.lvceli.lv; f. 2004 to replace Latvian Road Administration; state joint-stock co; manages state road network, administers State Road Fund; Chair. TĀLIS STRAUME.

SHIPPING

At 31 December 2006 the Latvian-registered merchant fleet numbered 153 vessels, with a combined total displacement of 333,275 grt. In 2006 some 53.1m. metric tons of sea-borne freight were transported through the country's three main (Ventspils, Rīga and Liepāja) and seven smaller ports. Ventspils is particularly important for the shipping of petroleum and fuel exports and is included in a special economic zone; Rīga and Ventspils operate in a free port regime.

Maritime Department (Ministry of Transport): Gogoļa iela 3, Rīga 1743; tel. 6702-8198; fax 6733-1406; e-mail aigars.krastins@sam.gov.lv; internet www.sam.gov.lv; Dir AIGARS KRASTIŅŠ.

Port Authorities

Liepāja Port Authority: Liepāja Special Economic Zone, Feniksa iela 4, Liepāja 3401; tel. 6342-7605; fax 6348-0252; e-mail authority@lsez.lv; internet www.lsez.lv; Man. Dir AIVARS BOJA.

Rīga Commercial Free Port SSC: Katrinas iela 5A, Rīga 1227; tel. 6732-9224; fax 6783-0215; e-mail rto@mail.bkc.lv; internet www.rto.lv; f. 1996.

Rīga Free Port Authority (Rīgas Brīvostas Pārvalde): Kalpaka bulv. 12, Rīga 1050; tel. 6703-0800; fax 6703-0835; e-mail rop@mail.rop.lv; internet www.rop.lv; f. 1994; Chief Exec. LEONIDS LOGINOVS; Chair. of Bd ANDRIS ARGALIS.

Ventspils Free Port Authority (Ventspils brīvostas pārvalde): Jāņa iela 19, Ventspils 3601; tel. 6362-2586; fax 6362-1297; e-mail info@vbp.lv; internet portofventspils.lv; f. 1991; Chief Exec. IMANTS SARMULIS.

Ventspils Commercial Port Authority (Ventspils Tirdzniecības Ostā): Dzintaru iela 22, Ventspils 3602; tel. 6366-8706; fax 6366-8860; e-mail vcp@vto.lv; internet www.vcp.lv; Pres. OLEGS STEPANOVS.

Shipping Company

Latvijas kuģniecība (LASCO) (Latvian Shipping Co): Elizabetes iela 2, Rīga 1807; tel. 6702-0111; fax 6782-8106; e-mail lsc@lsc.riga.lv; internet www.lk.lv; f. 1991; tanker, reefer, liquid petroleum gas and dry-cargo transportation; 49.94% owned by Ventspils Nafta; Pres. IMANTS VIKMANIS.

CIVIL AVIATION

There is an international airport at Rīga.

Civil Aviation Agency of Latvia (Latvijas Civilās Aviācijas Administrācija): Rīga Airport 1011, Rīga 1053; tel. 6783-0936; fax 6783-0967; internet www.caa.lv; Dir MĀRIS GORODCOVS.

Department of Aviation (Ministry of Transport): Gogoļa iela 3, Rīga 1743; tel. 6702-8209; fax 6721-7180; Dir ARNIS MUIŽNIEKS.

airBaltic Corpn: Rīga Airport, Rīga 1053; tel. 6720-7069; fax 6720-7369; e-mail info@airbaltic.lv; internet www.airbaltic.com; f. 1995; 52.6% govt-owned, 47.2% owned by Scandinavian Airlines System—SAS (Sweden/Denmark); fleet of 24 aircraft; operates services between Rīga and 44 European destinations, and domestic services between Rīga and Liepāja; also operates services between Vilnius (Lithuania) and 18 international destinations; operates direct flights between Kaliningrad (Russia) and Copenhagen (Denmark), Liepāja and Hamburg (Germany), and Liepāja and Copenhagen; Pres. and Chief Exec. BERTOLT FLICK.

RAF-AVIA Airlines: J. Alunana iela 2A, Rīga 1010; tel. 6732-4661; fax 6732-4671; e-mail rafavia@mail.interfeis.lv; f. 1991; scheduled and charter flights; Pres. JURIJS HMELEVSKII.

Tourism

Among Latvia's principal tourist attractions are the historic centre of Rīga, with its medieval and art nouveau buildings, the extensive beaches of the Baltic coastline, and Gauja National Park, which stretches east of the historic town of Sigulda for nearly 100 km along the Gauja river. Sigulda also offers winter sports facilities, while Rīga also has an extensive cultural life. Revenue from tourism in 2005 was some €446m., compared with €271m. in 2003. Foreign tourist arrivals at accommodation establishments in 2006 numbered 816,297, of whom 13.3% were from Germany.

Latvian Tourism Development Agency: Pils lauk. 4, Rīga 1050; tel. and fax 6722-9945; fax 6735-8128; e-mail tda@latviatourism.lv; internet www.latviatourism.lv; f. 1993; Dir ULDIS VITOLINS.

LEBANON

Introductory Survey

Location, Climate, Language, Religion, Flag, Capital

The Republic of Lebanon lies in western Asia, bordered by Syria to the north and east, and by Israel and the Palestinian Autonomous Areas to the south. The country has a coastline of about 220 km (135 miles) on the eastern shore of the Mediterranean Sea. The climate varies widely with altitude. The coastal lowlands are hot and humid in summer, becoming mild (cool and damp) in winter. In the mountains, which occupy much of Lebanon, the weather is cool in summer, with heavy snowfalls in winter. Rainfall is generally abundant. The official language is Arabic, which is spoken by almost all of the inhabitants. French is widely used as a second language, while Kurdish and Armenian are spoken by small ethnic minorities. According to the UN Relief and Works Agency for Palestine Refugees in the Near East (UNRWA), at December 2007 there were 413,962 Palestinian refugees registered in Lebanon. The major religions are Islam and Christianity, and there is a very small Jewish community. In the early 1980s it was estimated that 57% of Lebanon's inhabitants were Muslims, with about 43% Christians; these figures were believed to have changed to 63% and 37%, respectively, by 1994. The principal Muslim sects are Shi'a and Sunni, while there is also a significant Druze community. By the 1980s it was generally considered that Shi'a Muslims, totalling an estimated 1.2m., constituted Lebanon's largest single community. Most Christians adhere to the Roman Catholic Church, principally the Maronite rite. In 1994 it was estimated that 29%–32% of the population of Lebanon were Shi'a Muslims, 25%–28% Maronites, 16%–20% Sunni Muslims and 3.5% Druzes. There are also Armenian, Greek and Syrian sects (both Catholic and Eastern Orthodox) and small groups of Protestants. The national flag (proportions 2 by 3) has three horizontal stripes, of red, white (half the depth) and red, with a representation of a cedar tree (in green and brown) in the centre of the white stripe. The capital is Beirut.

Recent History

Lebanon, the homeland of the ancient Phoenicians, became part of the Turkish Ottoman Empire in the 16th century, and following the dissolution of the Ottoman Empire after the First World War (1914–18), a Greater Lebanese state was created by the Allied powers. The new state was formed in order to meet the nationalist aspirations of the area's predominantly Christian population, but it also included largely Muslim-populated territories traditionally considered to be part of Syria. Lebanon was administered by France, under a League of Nations mandate, from 1920 until independence was declared on 26 November 1941. A republic was established in 1943, and full autonomy was granted in January 1944.

Religious and cultural diversity is Lebanon's defining feature. At the time of independence Christians formed a slight majority of the population, the largest single community (nearly 30% of the total) being the Maronite Christians, who mostly inhabited the north of the country and the capital, Beirut. Other Christian groups included Greek Orthodox communities, Greek Catholics and Armenians. The Muslim groups were the Sunnis, living mainly in the coastal towns of Sur (Tyre), Saida (Sidon) and Beirut, the Shi'ites, a predominantly rural community in southern Lebanon and the northern Beka'a valley, and, in much smaller numbers, the Druzes, an ancient community in central Lebanon. The relative size of the various communities provided the basis for the unwritten 'national pact' of 1943, whereby executive and legislative posts were to be shared in the ratio of six Christians to five Muslims, and seats in the Chamber of Deputies (renamed the National Assembly in March 1979) were distributed on a religious, rather than a politico-ideological, basis. The convention according to this 'confessional' arrangement was that the President was a Maronite Christian, the Prime Minister a Sunni Muslim, and the President of the National Assembly a Shi'a Muslim.

Lebanon's first President, from 1943 until 1952, was Sheikh Bishara el-Khoury. His successor was Camille Chamoun, whose reforms included the enfranchisement of women. Following elections to the Chamber of Deputies in 1957 there was considerable unrest, mainly among Muslims who mistrusted Chamoun's pro-Western foreign policy and advocated Lebanon's closer alignment with Syria and Egypt. In July 1958 Chamoun appealed to the USA for military assistance; US forces remained in Beirut until October, by which time peace had been restored. Meanwhile, Chamoun was persuaded not to seek a further presidential term, and the Chamber elected Gen. Fouad Chehab as his successor. Chehab, who took office in September 1958, adopted a foreign policy of non-alignment, and introduced state provision of health, education and other services. In 1964 he was succeeded by Charles Hélou, who continued many of Chehab's policies but was faced by increasing controversy over the status of Palestinians in Lebanon.

After the establishment of Israel in 1948, and during the subsequent Arab–Israeli wars, thousands of Palestinians fled to Lebanon, where most were housed in refugee camps in the south of the country. Following the creation of the Palestine Liberation Organization (PLO) in 1964, military training centres for Palestinian guerrilla fighters were established in the camps. From 1968 these self-styled *fedayeen* ('martyrs') began making raids into Israel, provoking retaliatory attacks by Israeli forces. In 1969 there were clashes between Lebanese security forces and the *fedayeen*. Many Christians, particularly the Maronites, advocated strict government control over the Palestinians' activities, but the majority of Muslims strongly supported Palestinian operations against Israel.

Hélou's successor, Sulayman Franjiya, took office in 1970. During his presidency the Palestinian issue was exacerbated by an influx of Palestinian fighters expelled from Jordan in July 1971. Conflict between Israeli forces and Palestinians based in Lebanon intensified, while Christian groups began their own armed campaign against the *fedayeen*. In July 1974 Palestinian forces clashed with militia of the Phalangist Party (the Phalanges libanaises, or al-Kataeb, a militant right-wing Maronite Christian group). From April 1975 the conflict between the Palestinians and Phalangists quickly descended into full-scale civil war between the Lebanese National Movement (LNM) of left-wing Muslims (including Palestinians), led by Kamal Joumblatt of the Parti socialiste progressiste (PSP, a mainly Druze-supported group), and conservative Christian groups, mainly the Phalangist militia. Constitutional matters overtook the status of Palestinians as the main divisive issue, with the LNM advocating an end to the 'confessional' system, claiming that this unduly favoured Christians (who by now were generally accepted as no longer forming a majority of the population). Despite diplomatic efforts by Arab and Western countries, no durable cease-fire was achieved until October 1976, largely as a result of intervention in the conflict (in order to prevent an outright LNM victory) by Syrian forces in mid-1976. Under the terms of the cease-fire a 30,000-strong Arab Deterrent Force (ADF), composed mainly of Syrian troops, entered Lebanon.

President Franjiya was succeeded by Elias Sarkis in September 1976, and Prime Minister Rashid Karami by Selim al-Hoss in December. Legislative elections, due in April 1976, were postponed for an initial period of 26 months—the term of the Chamber of Deputies was subsequently extended further. Although the constitutional status quo remained intact, more than 30,000 people had died in the civil war and the militias of the various warring factions controlled most of the country. East Beirut and much of northern Lebanon was controlled by the Lebanese Forces (LF), a coalition of Maronite militias formed in September 1976; west Beirut was controlled by Muslim groups; and Palestinians dominated much of south-west Lebanon.

In March 1978 Israeli forces advanced into southern Lebanon in a counter-attack against forces of Fatah (the Palestine National Liberation Movement), the main guerrilla group within the PLO. UN Security Council Resolution 425, adopted on 17 March, demanded an Israeli withdrawal from Lebanon (thereby respecting its territorial integrity, sovereignty and independence) and also established a UN Interim Force in Lebanon (UNIFIL, see p. 80), initially of 4,000 troops. Israeli forces withdrew in June, but transferred control of a border strip to the pro-Israeli Christian militias of Maj. Saad Haddad. In

October, following several months of renewed fighting in Beirut between Syrian troops of the ADF and right-wing Christian militias, the ADF states agreed on a peace plan (the Beiteddin Declaration), which aimed to restore the authority of the Lebanese Government and army. Attempts to implement the plan were unsuccessful, however, and Lebanon's fragmentation deepened.

Al-Hoss resigned the premiership in June 1980 and was replaced in October by Chafic al-Wazzan. In August 1982, in an election boycotted by most Muslim deputies, the renamed National Assembly designated Bachir Gemayel (the younger son of the founder of the Phalangist Party and commander of the LF) to succeed President Sarkis. The President-elect was assassinated in September, and his brother, Amin, was elected in his place. Following the assassination, Phalangist forces (with the apparent complicity of occupying Israeli forces) entered the Palestinian refugee camps of Sabra and Chatila, in west Beirut, killing some 2,000 refugees. Israeli forces had re-entered Lebanon in June 1982, with the declared aim of finally eliminating the PLO's military threat to Israel's northern border; they quickly defeated Palestinian forces in south-west Lebanon and surrounded the western sector of Beirut, trapping more than 6,000 Palestinian fighters. A US-led diplomatic initiative resulted in an agreement enabling the PLO fighters to disperse among several Arab states, and a multinational peace-keeping force was deployed in Beirut. (In September 1983 intense fighting between rival factions of Fatah resulted in a truce agreement, brokered by Saudi Arabia and Syria, which led to a second evacuation of some 4,000 Palestinian fighters, most notably of the PLO Chairman, Yasser Arafat, who was exiled to Tunisia.) Negotiations between Lebanon and Israel began in December 1982, culminating in May 1983 in an agreement to end all hostilities (including the theoretical state of war that had existed between the two countries since 1948) and to withdraw all foreign troops from Lebanon. However, Syria did not recognize the accord, leaving 40,000 of its own troops and 7,000 PLO fighters in the Beka'a valley and northern Lebanon. Israel, meanwhile, redeployed a reduced force of 10,000 troops along the Awali river, south of Beirut. Maj. Haddad's South Lebanon Army (SLA) was to police southern areas as Israel's role lessened. Meanwhile, the multinational force in Beirut (comprising some 5,800 mainly French, Italian and US personnel) was drawn increasingly into the fighting, coming under frequent attack from Muslim militias who opposed its tantamount support for the Christian-led Government. In October 241 US and 58 French marines were killed in suicide bombings by Muslim groups.

The failure to conclude a peaceful settlement, and in particular the resumption of heavy fighting in February 1984 (which the reconstituted, US-trained Lebanese army was unable to suppress), led to the resignation of Prime Minister al-Wazzan, followed shortly afterwards by the withdrawal of the USA, Italy and the United Kingdom from the peace-keeping force. French troops were withdrawn in March. By this time successive defeats had left Gemayel's forces with effective control only in the mainly Christian-populated east Beirut. In March President Gemayel abrogated the May 1983 agreement with Israel, and in April 1984, with Syrian support, he formed a Government of national unity under former premier Rashid Karami. The Lebanese army failed to gain control of Beirut, and Gemayel's efforts to obtain approval for constitutional reform, already constrained by his fear of alienating his Christian supporters, were further undermined by divisions within the Cabinet.

The Israeli Government formed by Shimon Peres in September 1984 pledged to withdraw Israeli forces from Lebanon. However, while the Lebanese authorities demanded that UNIFIL police the Israeli–Lebanese border, by the time the Israeli withdrawal was completed, in June 1985, Israel had ensured that a narrow buffer zone, policed by the SLA (now commanded by Gen. Antoine Lahad), was in place along the border. With the Israeli presence in Lebanon reduced to a token force, Syria withdrew about one-third of its troops from the Beka'a valley in July, leaving some 25,000 in position.

In December 1985 the leaders of the three main Lebanese militias (the Druze forces, Amal and the LF) signed an accord in the Syrian capital, Damascus, providing for an immediate cease-fire and for the cessation of the civil war within one year. The militias were to be disarmed and disbanded, and a new constitutional regime was to be introduced within three years. However, the militias of the Sunni Murabitoun and the Iranian-backed Shi'ite Hezbollah were not parties to the agreement, which was also opposed by influential Christian elements. Furthermore, there were clashes later in December between supporters of the agreement within the LF and those who resented the concessions made by their leader, Elie Hobeika. In January 1986 Hobeika was forced into exile and replaced as LF leader by Samir Geagea, who urged renegotiation of the Damascus accord.

During 1986 Palestinian guerrillas resumed rocket attacks on settlements in northern Israel, provoking retaliatory air attacks by Israel on targets in the Beka'a valley and southern Lebanon. Meanwhile, Hezbollah escalated its attacks on SLA positions within the Israeli buffer zone, and also clashed with UNIFIL. Fighting between Palestinian guerrillas and Shi'ite Amal militiamen for control of the refugee camps in south Beirut escalated in May, before a cease-fire was imposed around the camps in June, as part of a Syrian-sponsored peace plan for Muslim west Beirut. The activities of the Amal, Druze and Sunni militias in west Beirut were temporarily curtailed by the deployment of Lebanese and Syrian troops, but fighting across the so-called 'Green Line', which had effectively divided the area from Christian east Beirut since early 1984, continued. By the time Amal and the PLO agreed in September 1987 to end hostilities, more than 2,500 people had died in the 'war of the camps'. Despite renewed fighting near Sidon in October, the Amal leader, Nabih Berri, in January 1988 announced an end to the siege of the Palestinian refugee camps in Beirut and southern Lebanon, avowedly as a gesture of support for the *intifada* (uprising) by Palestinians in the Israeli-occupied territories.

After Prime Minister Karami was killed in a bomb explosion in June 1987, Selim al-Hoss (Prime Minister in 1976–80) was appointed acting premier. In 1988 a political crisis developed as it proved impossible to find a successor to President Gemayal that was acceptable to all the warring factions. The three leading contenders for the presidency were Gen. Michel Awn (Commander-in-Chief of the Lebanese army), Raymond Eddé (leader of the Maronite Bloc National) and Sulayman Franjiya (President in 1970–76). Franjiya was Syria's preferred candidate but was notably opposed by Geagea, who apparently ensured that the National Assembly was inquorate when it convened for the presidential election in August 1988. In September the USA and Syria agreed to support another candidate, Mikhail ad-Daher, but Christian army and LF leaders remained opposed to the imposition of any candidate by foreign powers. Gemayel's term of office expired later in the month, when a further attempt by the National Assembly to hold an election was inquorate. The outgoing President appointed an interim military administration, comprising three Christians and three Muslims, with Awn as Prime Minister. However, the three nominated Muslim officers immediately refused to serve in the new administration, while two Christian members of the al-Hoss Government resigned, signalling their recognition of the interim military administration. The constitutional crisis, with two Governments claiming legitimacy, was further complicated in November, when the Minister of Defence in the al-Hoss Government dismissed Awn as Commander-in-Chief of the Lebanese army; however, Awn retained the loyalty of large sections of the military and thus remained its de facto leader.

In September 1989, following six months of fighting in Beirut between Awn's Lebanese army and Syrian forces, a Tripartite Arab Committee—formed in May by an emergency session of Arab leaders, and comprising King Hassan of Morocco, King Fahd of Saudi Arabia and President Chadli of Algeria—announced a peace plan whereby, most notably, the Lebanese National Assembly would meet to discuss a draft charter of national reconciliation. The Committee's charter was approved by the Syrian Government and the leaders of Lebanon's Muslim militias. Awn initially rejected its terms, on the grounds that it did not provide for the withdrawal of Syrian forces, but he was forced to relent, in view of support for the charter by almost every Arab country, as well as the USA, the USSR, the United Kingdom and France; a cease-fire accordingly took effect. The National Assembly subsequently met in Ta'if, Saudi Arabia, to discuss the charter, which was finally approved (with some amendments) in October by 58 of the 62 attending deputies (of the 99 deputies elected in May 1972, only 73 survived); it became known as the 'Ta'if agreement'. The charter provided for the transfer of executive power from the presidency to a cabinet, with portfolios divided equally between Christian and Muslim ministers. The number of seats in the National Assembly was to be increased to 108, comprising equal numbers of Christian and Muslim deputies. Following the election of a President and the formation of a new government, all militias involved in the Lebanese conflict were to be disbanded within six months, while the internal security forces would be strengthened; the Syrian armed forces would assist the new Government in implementing the security plan for a maximum of two years.

The National Assembly elected René Mouawad, a Maronite Christian deputy and a former Minister of Education and Arts, as President in early November 1989. The Assembly also unanimously endorsed the Ta'if agreement. However, Awn, who denounced the agreement as a betrayal of Lebanese sovereignty, declared the presidential election unconstitutional and its result null and void, proclaiming himself President. Mouawad was assassinated only 17 days after his election. The National Assembly again convened and elected Elias Hrawi as the new President; the legislature also voted to extend its own term until 1994. A new Cabinet was formed by Selim al-Hoss in late November 1989.

The Christian communities were divided over the Ta'if agreement, and Geagea's refusal to reject the agreement precipitated violent clashes between his LF and Awn's forces in January 1990: by March more than 800 people had been killed in inter-Christian fighting. (Geagea eventually announced the LF's recognition of the al-Hoss Government, and hence the Ta'if agreement, in April.) In August the National Assembly duly approved amendments to the Constitution, increasing the number of seats in the National Assembly to 108, to be divided equally between Muslims and Christians. On 21 September the Second Lebanese Republic was officially inaugurated when President Hrawi formally endorsed the amendments. In October Awn and his forces (who continued to reject the Ta'if agreement) were expelled from east Beirut by Syrian forces and units of the Lebanese army loyal to Hrawi. The Lebanese army began to deploy in Beirut in December, by which time all militia forces had withdrawn from the city. In the same month al-Hoss submitted his Government's resignation, and Hrawi invited Omar Karami (Minister of Education and Arts in the outgoing administration) to form a government of national unity, as stipulated by the Ta'if agreement. By early 1991 the Lebanese army was established in most major southern Lebanese towns; by September the militias had been largely disbanded (although Hezbollah maintained armaments in southern Lebanon and the Beka'a valley). In May the National Assembly approved amendments to the electoral law, and in June the Cabinet appointed 40 deputies to fill the seats that had become vacant since the 1972 election as well as the nine new seats created under the Ta'if agreement. In August 1991 the National Assembly approved a general amnesty for crimes perpetrated during the civil war, although its terms excluded several specified crimes committed during 1975–90. Under a presidential pardon, Awn was allowed to leave the French embassy compound (where he had been sheltering since his defeat in 1990) and to depart for exile in France.

In May 1991 Lebanon and Syria signed a bilateral treaty establishing formal relations in political, military and economic affairs, and confirming the role of the Syrian army as guarantor of the security plans enshrined in the Ta'if agreement. Israel immediately condemned the treaty as a further step towards the formal transformation of Lebanon into a Syrian protectorate, while its opponents within Lebanon denounced it as a threat to the country's independence. In September Lebanon and Syria concluded a mutual security agreement. Syrian forces began to withdraw from Beirut in March 1992, in preparation for their scheduled withdrawal to eastern Lebanon by September. Israel, meanwhile, reasserted its intention of maintaining a military presence in the buffer zone, and its support for the SLA, by launching severe attacks on Palestinian bases in southern Lebanon in June 1991. Lebanese forces began to take up positions in Sidon in July. Initial resistance from Palestinians loyal to Arafat was swiftly overcome, and an agreement was concluded with the PLO to allow the Lebanese army to assume control of the area. The conflict escalated further in February 1992, following the assassination by the Israeli air force of the Secretary-General of Hezbollah, Sheikh Abbas Moussawi.

The deteriorating economic situation in early 1992, combined with allegations of government corruption and incompetence, and a series of general strikes, provoked the resignation of Karami and his Cabinet in May. Subsequent talks in Damascus between President Hrawi and the Syrian leadership led to the reappointment of Rashid Solh as Prime Minister (a position that he had previously held in 1974–75). In July 1992 the National Assembly approved a new electoral law whereby the number of seats in the Assembly was raised from 108 to 128, to be divided equally between Christian and Muslim deputies. The Government's intention to conduct legislative elections in mid-1992 had prompted Christian groups to threaten a boycott of the polls, since it was not certain that Syrian forces would have withdrawn to the eastern area of the Beka'a valley by that time, in accordance with the Ta'if agreement. The Government, for its part, stated that the Lebanese army was not yet able to guarantee the country's security in the absence of Syrian troops.

Lebanon's first legislative elections for 20 years were held in three rounds, on 23 August (in the governorates of the North and the Beka'a valley), 30 August (Beirut and Mount Lebanon) and 6 September 1992 (South and An-Nabatiyah). Electoral turn-out was low (averaging 32%), especially in Maronite districts where leaders had urged a boycott. Hezbollah, contesting the elections for the first time as a political party, enjoyed considerable success in southern constituencies. The Amal leader, Nabih Berri, was appointed President of the new National Assembly in October, and Hrawi invited Rafik Hariri, a Lebanese-born Saudi Arabian business executive, to form a new government, amid hopes that he would restore some confidence in the Lebanese economy and oversee the country's reconstruction. Hariri's Cabinet was dominated by technocrats, and the system of distributing portfolios on an entirely 'confessional' basis was somewhat diluted. It emerged after the elections that Syria would only withdraw its armed forces from Lebanon once a comprehensive peace treaty had been concluded between Syria and Israel.

In December 1992 the Lebanese army took up positions in southern suburbs of Beirut for the first time in eight years, apparently meeting no resistance from Hezbollah, which had hitherto effectively controlled the areas. In mid-1993 the Lebanese Government was said to be attempting to curtail the activities of the Damascus-based Popular Front for the Liberation of Palestine—General Command (PFLP—GC), which had begun to mount guerrilla attacks on Israeli military positions from southern Lebanon. In July Israeli armed forces launched their heaviest artillery and air attacks on targets in southern Lebanon since 1982. The declared aim of 'Operation Accountability' was to eradicate the threat posed by Hezbollah and Palestinian guerrillas, and to create a flow of refugees so as to compel the Lebanese and Syrian authorities to take action against these groups. According to Lebanese sources, the week-long offensive displaced some 300,000 civilians towards the north and resulted in 128 (mainly civilian) deaths. Although a US-brokered cease-fire 'understanding' entered effect at the end of July 1993, hostilities continued in subsequent months.

In June 1994 Hezbollah reported that 26 of its fighters had been killed in an Israeli air-strike on one of its training camps in the Beka'a valley; Hezbollah responded with rocket attacks into the security zone and northern Israel. In October an Israeli attack on the town of An-Nabatiyah at-Tahta (Nabatiyah), in which seven civilians died, was apparently provoked by the deaths of 22 people in a bomb attack, attributed to Palestinian militants of the Islamic Resistance Movement (Hamas), in the Israeli city of Tel-Aviv: hitherto, Israeli operations in Lebanon had tended to be in reprisal for terrorist activity in the security zone. Clashes in southern Lebanon in December reportedly resulted in the killing by Hezbollah of several members of the Israeli military and SLA. Israeli attacks south of Beirut in January 1995 targeted alleged PFLP—GC bases.

In March 1994, meanwhile, the National Assembly approved legislation instituting the death penalty for 'politically motivated' murders. Shortly afterwards the Maronite LF was proscribed (on the grounds that it had sought the country's partition) and its leader, Samir Geagea, was arrested and charged, along with several of his associates, in connection with the murder, in October 1990, of Dany Chamoun, son of former President Camille Chamoun and the leader of the right-wing Maronite Parti national libéral (PNL), and with the bombing of a Maronite church outside Beirut in January 1994. In September Geagea was reportedly relieved of the organization's leadership and his recognition of the Ta'if agreement revoked; the LF command had also reportedly countermanded Geagea's formal dissolution, under the Ta'if agreement, of the organization's militia status. (A successor political organization, the Lebanese Forces Party, had been created in September 1990.) In June 1995 Geagea and a co-defendant were convicted of instigating the murder of Chamoun, and were (together with seven others convicted *in absentia*) sentenced to death; the sentences were immediately commuted to life imprisonment with hard labour. In July 1996 Geagea was acquitted of involvement in the Maronite church bombing. However, by mid-1997 Geagea had received another two death sentences (one for ordering the assassination of another Maronite rival in 1990, and the other for attempting to assassinate the Minister of Defence, Michel Murr, in 1991—both of which were later commuted to life imprisonment); another sentence of life imprisonment for orchestrating the death of Prime Minister Rashid Karami in 1987; and a 10-year gaol term for attempting to recruit and arm militiamen after 1991 (when all militias had been banned).

In October 1995 the National Assembly voted to amend the Constitution to extend President Hrawi's mandate for a further three years. Prime Minister Hariri had sought an extension of the presidential term in the stated interest of promoting stability in the economic reconstruction process, and the amendment had been facilitated following intervention by Syria to resolve a procedural dispute between Hariri and the President of the National Assembly, Nabih Berri.

Elections to the National Assembly took place, in five rounds, in August–September 1996. Pro-Hariri candidates enjoyed considerable success in the first three rounds of voting (in Mount Lebanon, North Lebanon and Beirut governorates), with the Prime Minister himself winning the largest number of votes at the third round; there were, however, allegations of vote-buying involving Hariri's supporters in Beirut. In the fourth and fifth rounds (in the South and An-Nabatiyah, and in the Beka'a valley) an electoral alliance led by Amal and Hezbollah was reported to have won all but one of the 46 seats. Prior to the fifth round Syria had redeployed some 12,000 of its estimated 30,000 troops in Lebanon to the eastern part of the Beka'a valley. (Under the terms of the Ta'if agreement, the redeployment should have been completed in 1992.) The overall rate of participation averaged about 45%, suggesting that many voters had disregarded demands particularly by Awn, Gemayel and other exiled figures for a boycott of the polls. Berri was re-elected President of the National Assembly when the new legislature convened in October 1996, and in the following month a new Government was formed under Hariri.

In April 1996 Israel commenced a sustained military offensive (code-named 'Operation Grapes of Wrath') in southern Lebanon and suburbs to the south of Beirut, aimed at preventing rocket attacks by Hezbollah on settlements in northern Israel. Some 400,000 Lebanese were displaced northwards, and the shelling by Israeli forces of a UNIFIL base at Qana, which resulted in the deaths of more than 100 Lebanese civilians who had been sheltering there, and of four UNIFIL soldiers, provoked international condemnation. After more than two weeks of hostilities a cease-fire 'understanding' took effect in late April. As in 1993, this was effectively a compromise confining the conflict to the area of the security zone, recognizing both Hezbollah's right to resist Israeli occupation and Israel's right to self-defence; the 'understanding' also envisaged the establishment of an Israel-Lebanon Monitoring Group (ILMG), comprising representatives of Israel, Lebanon, Syria, France and the USA, to supervise the cease-fire. According to the Israeli authorities, Operation Grapes of Wrath resulted in no Israeli deaths, while 170–200 Lebanese civilians, in addition to some 50 fighters, were killed. Hezbollah claimed to have sustained minimal casualties, and its military capacity appeared largely undiminished.

A subsequent UN report on the killing of Lebanese civilians at Qana concluded that it was 'unlikely' that the shelling of the UNIFIL base had, as claimed by the Israelis, been the result of 'gross technical and/or procedural errors'. Prior to the first meeting of the ILMG, in July 1996, Israel and Hezbollah reportedly exchanged prisoners and bodies of members of their armed forces for the first time since 1991. However, despite the April 1996 cease-fire 'understanding', sporadic clashes continued during 1997–98. The extent of Israeli casualties as a result of the occupation of southern Lebanon prompted a vocal campaign within Israel for a unilateral withdrawal from the security zone. In April 1998 Israel's 'inner' Security Cabinet voted to adopt UN Security Council Resolution 425, but with the stipulation that Lebanon provide guarantees of the security of Israel's northern border. Lebanon, however, emphasized that Resolution 425 demanded an unconditional withdrawal, and stated that neither would it be able to guarantee Israel's immunity from attack, nor would it be prepared to deploy the Lebanese army in southern Lebanon for this purpose; furthermore, Lebanon could not support the continued presence there of the SLA. Concern was also expressed that a unilateral withdrawal from Lebanon in the absence of a comprehensive Middle East peace settlement might foment regional instability.

Meanwhile, in late 1996 the Government had ordered the closure of about 150 radio and 50 television stations; licences to broadcast political items had been granted to only a limited number of stations, most of which were owned by prominent political figures. In September 1997 the authorities began to close down unlicensed broadcasters, and in December the Minister of the Interior, deputy premier Michel Murr, prohibited a televised satellite broadcast, from France, by Gen. Michel Awn, on the grounds that such transmissions were undermining national security. The ban provoked a violent demonstration in Beirut, which resulted in a number of protesters being arrested and tried on charges of defying restrictions on public demonstrations imposed in 1993. (Awn's interview was eventually broadcast in January 1998 by a private terrestrial channel.)

Voting in Lebanon's first municipal elections since 1963 took place, in four rounds, in May–June 1998. At the first round (in Mount Lebanon governorate), Hezbollah won convincing victories in Beirut's southern suburbs, while right-wing organizations opposed to the Government also took control of several councils. At the second round (in North Lebanon), efforts failed to achieve an inter-community balance in Tripoli, where a council comprising 23 Muslims and only one Christian was elected; elsewhere in the governorate there was notable success for candidates loyal to Samir Geagea. However, a joint list of candidates supported by Hariri and Berri won control of the Beirut council at the third round, while Berri's Amal gained overall control in Tyre. At the final round of voting (in the Beka'a valley), Hezbollah candidates were largely defeated by their pro-Syrian secular rivals and by members of the governorate's leading families. Other than in Beirut, the rate of voter participation was high (about 70%). (Municipal elections did not take place in southern Lebanon until September 2001, following the withdrawal of Israeli troops in 2000.)

As President Hrawi's mandate neared completion in 1998, the Commander-in-Chief of the Army, Gen. Emile Lahoud, emerged as a suitable successor: his strong leadership, firm stance on corruption and success in having reconstructed the army following the civil war, were thought likely to assist the process of political reform and economic regeneration. Moreover, Syria, which remained a major influence on Lebanese politics, endorsed Lahoud's candidacy, despite his strong nationalist tendency. To enable Lahoud's appointment, the National Assembly overwhelmingly adopted an exceptional amendment to Article 49 of the Constitution—which requires that senior civil servants resign their post two years prior to seeking political office—and Lahoud was duly elected President on 15 October, with the approval of all 118 National Assembly deputies present (the vote was boycotted by the Druze leader, Walid Joumblatt, and his supporters). Lahoud took office on 24 November; law enforcement and the elimination of official corruption were identified as priorities for his administration. Hariri unexpectedly declined an invitation from Lahoud to form a new government, and at the beginning of December Selim al-Hoss (who had headed four administrations during the civil war) was designated Prime Minister. His new Cabinet, which was almost halved in size (to 16 members), included only two ministers from the previous administration—Michel Murr notably retained the post of deputy premier as well as the interior portfolio. Several reformists were appointed to the Cabinet, which excluded representatives of the various 'confessional' blocs and former militia leaders whose rivalries had frequently undermined previous governments. Hezbollah declined to participate in the new Government. At the Cabinet's first session, held later in December, Gen. Michel Sulayman was appointed to succeed Lahoud as head of the armed forces. The al-Hoss Government's programme emphasized anti-corruption measures, economic liberalization and reduction of the public debt, as well as accelerated electoral reform. To that effect the judiciary was granted powers to investigate a number of political scandals and bring former high-ranking officials to trial. The incoming Government also revoked the five-year ban on the holding of public demonstrations.

Clashes persisted in southern Lebanon following Israel's 'adoption' of Resolution 425, amid continuing protests of violations of the April 1996 cease-fire 'understanding'. In May 1998 at least 10 people were killed in an Israeli air raid on a Fatah training camp in the central Beka'a valley; in two separate incidents in November, seven Israeli soldiers were killed as a result of attacks by Hezbollah on Israeli patrols in the occupied zone. Following further serious exchanges in December, in January 1999 Israel's Security Cabinet voted to respond to future Hezbollah offensives by targeting infrastructure in central and northern Lebanon (thereby extending the conflict beyond suspected guerrilla bases in the south). Hostilities escalated in February, when Israeli forces annexed the village of Arnoun, just outside the occupied zone; Israel also launched intensive air attacks on Hezbollah targets, following an ambush in the security zone that had killed Brig.-Gen. Erez Gerstein, the commander of the Israeli army's liaison unit with the SLA.

In 1999 the Palestinian militant organizations in Lebanon were riven by factional infighting, and both the Lebanese and Syrian Governments undertook measures to seek to bring the groups to order. In May a senior official of the Fatah faction of the PLO and his wife were killed in Sidon by unidentified gunmen, believed to be PLO activists opposed to Fatah's willingness to negotiate with Israel, while a car bomb in southern Lebanon shortly afterwards seriously wounded another Fatah official, leading to fears of a renewed cycle of violence between the rival Palestinian factions. In October a senior Fatah commander, Sultan Abu al-Aynayn (a close ally of Yasser Arafat), was sentenced to death *in absentia* by a military court in Beirut, having been found guilty of leading a militia and of encouraging anti-Government rebellion. (In December 2000, again *in absentia*, al-Aynayn was convicted of weapons-trafficking and of plotting terrorist actions in southern Lebanon; he was sentenced to 15 years' imprisonment.) Several other Fatah officials were detained by the Lebanese authorities in subsequent months. In January 2000 the Government ordered a judicial inquiry into the recent upsurge in sectarian violence.

In July 1999 the Lebanese Government was angered by an announcement made by the new Israeli Prime Minister, Ehud Barak, elected in May, that Palestinian refugees residing in Lebanon would under no circumstances be permitted to return to Israel. President Lahoud responded by demanding that any permanent peace agreement should guarantee the right of Palestinians to return home; he subsequently initiated legislation to prevent Palestinian refugees in Lebanon from being granted Lebanese citizenship.

During his election campaign Barak had pledged to withdraw Israeli forces from southern Lebanon by July 2000. In June 1999 the SLA completed a unilateral withdrawal from the enclave of Jezzine, in the north-east of the occupied zone. Following further Hezbollah attacks on northern Israel, in late June the outgoing administration of Binyamin Netanyahu ordered a series of airstrikes against infrastructure targets in central and southern Lebanon—the heaviest aerial bombardment since Operation Grapes of Wrath in 1996. In December 1999 an 'understanding in principle' was reportedly reached between Israel and Syria in order to curb the fighting in southern Lebanon, although the informal cease-fire ended in late January 2000 when a senior SLA commander was killed; the deaths of three Israeli soldiers at the end of the month led Israel to declare that peace talks with Syria (again postponed indefinitely) could resume only if Syria took action to restrain Hezbollah. In February, after suffering further military casualties in the security zone, Israel announced that its Prime Minister would henceforth be empowered to order immediate retaliatory raids against Hezbollah without discussion with the Security Cabinet. In March the Israeli Cabinet voted unanimously to withdraw its forces from southern Lebanon by July, even if no agreement had been reached on the Israeli-Syrian track of the Middle East peace process. In April, having released 13 Lebanese prisoners held without trial for more than a decade as 'bargaining counters' for Israeli soldiers missing in Lebanon, Israel gave the UN official notification that it intended to withdraw its forces from southern Lebanon 'in one phase' by 7 July. The Lebanese Government made the unprecedented admission that it would accept a UN peace-keeping force in southern Lebanon after the Israeli withdrawal.

On 23 May 2000 Israel's Security Cabinet voted to accelerate the withdrawal of its remaining troops from Lebanon, after Hezbollah had taken control of about one-third of southern Lebanon following the evacuation by the SLA of outposts transferred to its control by the Israeli army. Both the Israeli Government and the UN had expected the withdrawal to take place on 1 June; however, the rapid and chaotic withdrawal of Israeli forces from southern Lebanon was completed on 24 May, almost six weeks ahead of Barak's original deadline. In June the UN Security Council officially declared that the Israeli withdrawal had been completed. However, both the Lebanese Government and Hezbollah maintained that Israel was still required to depart from territory known as Shebaa Farms and to release all Lebanese prisoners. (The UN maintains that Shebaa Farms is part of territory captured by Israel from Syria, and as such must be considered under the Israeli-Syrian track of the peace process.) In July a limited contingent of UNIFIL troops began to redeploy close to the Lebanese border with Israel, to fill the vacuum created by the departure of Israeli forces. At the same time the UN Security Council voted to extend UNIFIL's mandate for a further six months. In August a Joint Security Force of some 1,000 Lebanese troops and Internal Security Forces reportedly deployed in southern Lebanon (other than in the border area), charged with the provision of general security in the territory. Responsibility for the border with Israel remained with UNIFIL (whose troops in Lebanon now numbered some 5,600). By January 2001 an estimated 2,041 SLA militiamen were reported to have been convicted of having collaborated with Israel during its occupation of southern Lebanon.

Elections to the National Assembly took place on 27 August (Mount Lebanon and North Lebanon) and 3 September 2000 (Beirut, the Beka'a valley, An-Nabatiyah and the South). For the first time since 1972 Lebanese citizens in the former Israeli-occupied zone of southern Lebanon participated in the elections. Voting patterns in the first round swiftly indicated a rejection of al-Hoss's premiership, as the Druze leader, Walid Joumblatt (one of former premier Rafik Hariri's staunchest allies), secured an overwhelming victory in Mount Lebanon governorate. Moreover, the election of Pierre Gemayel, son of Amin Gemayel, in the Maronite Northern Metn district (north-east of Beirut) was regarded as a considerable reverse for President Lahoud. Voter participation was an estimated 51%, apparently indicating that the electorate had largely ignored appeals by some Christian parties for a boycott of the poll. At the second round of voting, Hariri's Al-Karamah (Dignity) list secured 18 of the 19 assembly seats in Beirut; al-Hoss lost his own seat in the legislature. In the south an alliance of Hezbollah and Amal candidates took all the governorate's 23 seats, while Hezbollah enjoyed similar successes in the Beka'a valley. Independent monitors reported numerous instances of electoral malpractice. Overall, Hariri was reported to have the support of between 92–106 of the 128 seats in the new legislature. In October President Lahoud formally appointed Rafik Hariri to the premiership. The composition of his radically altered Cabinet (newly expanded to 30 members) was announced a few days later, with Issam Fares named as Deputy Prime Minister and Elias Murr, the son-in-law of President Lahoud and a non-parliamentarian, replacing his father, Michel Murr, as Minister of the Interior and of Municipal and Rural Affairs. (Resistance and Development, the party list including Hezbollah, had declined to join the Government.) Hariri and President Lahoud were reported to have reached an informal power-sharing agreement, according to which Hariri would be responsible for economic policy and the President would take charge of defence and foreign affairs.

Divisions between pro- and anti-Syrian elements within Lebanon had become increasingly vocal in the aftermath of the Israeli withdrawal from southern Lebanon in May 2000 and the death of Syria's President Hafiz al-Assad in the following month. An unofficial visit to Beirut by his successor, Bashar al-Assad, for meetings with key Lebanese politicians shortly before the legislative elections appeared to indicate that he intended to continue his late father's role as power-broker in Lebanon. However, the decisive rejection of the Syrian-backed Government of Selim al-Hoss, combined with Joumblatt's electoral successes, suggested a redefinition of Syria's role in Lebanon. In September Maronite bishops issued a statement urging the departure of the Syrian military from Lebanon. While the Maronite community and other Christian groups maintained that the departure of Syrian forces was necessary in order for full Lebanese sovereignty to be attained, both President Lahoud and Prime Minister Hariri continued to defend Syria's military presence. In December Syria—which had never previously confirmed that it was holding Lebanese prisoners—freed 46 Lebanese political prisoners (including many Christians who had been detained by Syrian troops during 1975–90), apparently as a gesture of 'goodwill'. In January 2001 the Lebanese Government established a commission to examine the issue of Lebanese prisoners held in Syria. In the same month a Jordanian newspaper reported that the former Christian militia leader, Gen. Michel Awn, had declared himself ready to return to Lebanon from exile in France in order to appear before the Lebanese judiciary. In April, following student protests demanding the withdrawal of Syrian troops, the Government banned all unlicensed demonstrations against Syria.

The outbreak of the so-called 'al-Aqsa *intifada*' in the Palestinian territories in September 2000 resulted in a renewed crisis in the Middle East, prompting uncertainty in Lebanon about the permanence of the Israeli withdrawal, particularly as Hezbollah had renewed its campaign against the Israeli military. In October Hezbollah fighters captured three Israeli soldiers in Shebaa Farms, with the demand that Israel release 19 Lebanese and dozens of Palestinians from Israeli detention. The UN Secretary-General, Kofi Annan, visited Beirut for talks regarding the soldiers' release; however, in the following week a senior Israeli army reservist and businessman, Elhanan Tannenbaum, was kidnapped in Switzerland, apparently by Hezbollah (which claimed that the officer was working for Israeli intelligence). The killing of an Israeli soldier in Shebaa Farms at the end of November prompted Israel to launch air-strikes against suspected Hezbollah targets in southern Lebanon. In mid-November the UN Security Council had urged the Lebanese Government to comply with international law by deploying its armed forces on the Israeli border with southern Lebanon (where Hezbollah still controlled the line of withdrawal, or 'Blue Line'), but Lebanon rejected such a deployment until Israel had signed a comprehensive peace treaty with both Lebanon and Syria. In January 2001 the UN Security Council voted to extend UNIFIL's mandate in Lebanon until July, when its operational strength was to be reduced to about 4,500—the number of troops deployed prior to the Israeli withdrawal.

The Lebanese leadership was generally pessimistic as to the prospects for peace in the Middle East following the election, in February 2001, of Likud leader Ariel Sharon as Israeli Prime Minister. (Most Lebanese hold Sharon responsible for the deaths of 2,000 Palestinian refugees in the Sabra and Chatila camps in September 1982, at which time he was Israel's Minister of Defence.) In February 2001 Israel launched mortar attacks close to Shebaa Farms, in reprisal for the death of an Israeli soldier in a bomb attack there. In April Israel responded to the killing by Hezbollah of another of its soldiers in Shebaa Farms with the first military action against Syrian troops since 1996, launching air raids on a Syrian radar base to the east of Beirut. According to Syrian sources, at least one Syrian soldier died in the attack, which Israel claimed had been provoked by Syria's sponsorship of Hezbollah.

In June 2001 Syria withdrew an estimated 6,000–10,000 troops from the largely Christian eastern and southern suburbs of Beirut and from Mount Lebanon, and redeployed the majority to the Beka'a valley. However, Syria's withdrawal from the Lebanese capital was widely regarded as merely symbolic, since Syria retained 15 military bases in strategic parts of Beirut. In early August the Maronite patriarch, Cardinal Sfeir, and the Druze leader, Walid Joumblatt, held discussions, apparently to indicate a new era of 'reconciliation' between the two communities. Within days, however, the mainly pro-Syrian army intelligence service began mass arrests of Maronite Christians (mostly members of the banned LF or supporters of Awn) who were again demanding a complete Syrian withdrawal from Lebanon. Many Christian and Muslim deputies condemned the detentions as 'unconstitutional', while protesters demonstrating against the growing influence of the military clashed with police. Hariri's political standing appeared to have been weakened by the security forces' actions, which had been undertaken when he was out of the country, as in mid-August the National Assembly approved legislation granting increased powers to President Lahoud.

Israel launched a further air attack on a Syrian radar station in eastern Lebanon at the beginning of July 2001, again apparently in response to an assault by Hezbollah against the Israeli military in Shebaa Farms. At the end of July the UN Security Council voted for an extension of UNIFIL's mandate for a further six months; the peace-keeping force was to be reduced in size from 4,500 to 3,600 troops, with the possibility that its status would be downgraded to that of an observer mission (this was implemented before the expiry of the six-month mandate). In October Hezbollah guerrillas broke what had effectively been a three-month cease-fire by launching an attack against two Israeli military positions in Shebaa Farms, to which Israeli forces responded by shelling a Hezbollah patrol in the area. Israel alleged, furthermore, that Hezbollah was directly involved in the Palestinian intifada, and was supplying weapons to Palestinians in the West Bank and Gaza. (In March 2002 Hezbollah Secretary-General Sheikh Hasan Nasrallah admitted that two Lebanese militants detained in Jordan had been attempting to smuggle weapons into the West Bank, and in April 2006 he acknowledged for the first time that Hezbollah funded Palestinian militant groups.) In January 2002 the UN Security Council expressed concern regarding recent Israeli violations of Lebanese airspace, and criticized Hezbollah for its frequent interference with the freedom of movement of UNIFIL. The UN again urged the Lebanese Government to deploy its army along the Blue Line. The observer mission's mandate was extended for further six-month periods in January and July; by the end of 2002 the strength of the force had been reduced to some 2,000 troops.

Lebanon's political and religious leadership were unequivocal in their condemnation of the September 2001 suicide attacks on New York and Washington, DC. Lebanese Shi'ites feared, however, that Hezbollah might be targeted in any retaliatory campaign against militant Islamist groups deemed to be involved in terrorism. In mid-October Muslim clerics in Lebanon issued a ruling in support of the Afghan people following the commencement of US-led military action in Afghanistan against the Taliban regime and alleged bases of the al-Qa'ida (Base) organization, the militant Islamist network held by the USA to be principally responsible for September's atrocities. Three Lebanese men, believed to be members of Hezbollah involved in the 1985 hijacking of a US commercial flight, had been included on a list of 22 'most wanted' terrorist suspects, published in early October 2001 by the US Federal Bureau of Investigation. Lebanese security forces detained two men in Tripoli in mid-October, on charges of plotting terrorist actions against US targets in the Middle East. (In March 2002 a military court sentenced one of the defendants to a three-year prison term, and the other to 18 months' imprisonment, both with hard labour.)

In January 2002 Elie Hobeika, the former leader of the Christian LF militia, was killed (along with three aides and two bystanders) in a car bombing in Beirut. A previously unknown anti-Syrian group, the 'Lebanese for a Free and Independent Lebanon', claimed responsibility for the attack, alleging that Hobeika was a 'Syrian agent'. Israel denied in the strongest terms assertions made by some Lebanese sources that Israeli interests had instigated the killing, since Hobeika had declared his willingness to give evidence to an investigation being carried out by a Belgian court into alleged 'crimes against humanity' by Ariel Sharon, owing to his implication in the massacre of Palestinians in the Sabra and Chatila refugee camps in 1982 (see above). Hobeika was the first prominent Lebanese politician to be assassinated since the civil war ended in 1990. (A Belgian appeals court judged the case against Sharon to be inadmissible in June 2002.)

It was feared in early 2002 that rising tensions between Israel and Lebanon might escalate into a 'second front' of Arab–Israeli conflict; in February Iran denied allegations made by Israeli officials that it was supplying Hezbollah with vast consignments of *Katyusha* rockets and had sent a number of its Revolutionary Guards to Lebanon. In March Hezbollah initiated cross-border mortar, missile and machine-gun attacks against Israeli military targets in Shebaa Farms, asserting that these were in retaliation for Israeli violations of Lebanese airspace. Israel responded by shelling suspected militant bases in southern Lebanon. In April the UN condemned Hezbollah for increasing the instability along the Blue Line, and also for an incident in which five UNIFIL personnel allegedly came under attack by Hezbollah guerrillas near Shebaa Farms. In response to Hezbollah attacks on Shebaa Farms in August, the Israeli Government targeted suspected Hezbollah bases in southern Lebanon, and issued a firm warning to Lebanon and Syria that they must take immediate action to end such attacks.

President Bashar al-Assad of Syria undertook an historic visit to Beirut in March 2002 for discussions with President Lahoud. This first official visit by a Syrian leader to Beirut since 1947 was welcomed by many Lebanese as a formal recognition by Syria of Lebanese sovereignty. The talks resulted in several agreements regarding closer economic co-operation, including a pledge by Syria to reduce the cost of imported natural gas. It was reported in April 2002 that Syrian troops were soon to redeploy from central Lebanon to the Beka'a valley, thus fulfilling one of the requirements of the 1989 Ta'if agreement. However, hundreds of Syrian intelligence officers were likely to remain in central Lebanon.

In March 2002 Beirut hosted the annual summit meeting of the Council of the Arab League, at which the principal issue under discussion was a peace initiative for the Middle East proposed by Crown Prince Abdullah of Saudi Arabia. However, only 10 out of 22 Arab heads of state attended the summit, while President Mubarak of Egypt and King Abdullah of Jordan reportedly declined to participate in the discussions as a demonstration of solidarity with the President of the Palestinian (National) Authority (PA), Yasser Arafat, who was effectively blockaded by Israeli forces in the West Bank. At the conclusion of the summit Arab leaders unanimously endorsed the Saudi peace initiative. Incorporated in the Beirut Declaration, this required from Israel a complete withdrawal from all Arab territories occupied in June 1967, and what were termed 'territories still occupied in southern Lebanon', a 'just solution' to the issue of Palestinian refugees, and acceptance of the establishment of a sovereign Palestinian state in the West Bank and Gaza Strip with East Jerusalem as its capital; in return, the Arab states undertook to consider the Arab–Israeli conflict at an end, to sign a peace agreement with Israel, and to establish normal relations with Israel within this comprehensive peace framework. The initiative was, however, rejected by Israel, which maintained that it would lead to the destruction of the State of Israel. During a visit to Lebanon by the US Secretary of State, Colin Powell, in April 2002, the Lebanese leadership maintained its stance that its obligation to respect the Blue Line did not exclude resistance (by Hezbollah) to 'liberate' Shebaa Farms, while President Assad gave no indication that he would exert his influence to halt Hezbollah offensives from southern Lebanon against Israel.

Jihad Jibril, the head of the PFLP—GC's military operations and son of the group's leader, was killed by a car bomb in west Beirut in May 2002. The Lebanese security forces blamed intra-Palestinian rivalries for the assassination, although many PFLP—GC officials held the Israeli intelligence services responsible. In August two people were killed in the worst factional fighting at the Ain al-Hilweh Palestinian refugee camp for several years. Tensions had escalated following the arrest of an Islamist militant in the previous month by the Lebanese army, aided by Fatah. (The Israeli daily *Ha'aretz* subsequently alleged that the violence at Ain al-Hilweh was linked to the presence there of up to 200 al-Qa'ida militants who had returned from the war in Afghanistan.) In September clashes between the Lebanese army and Palestinian militants at the al-Jalil refugee camp, near Ba'albak (Ba'albek), left one soldier and three Palestinians dead.

The Lebanese Government closed down a Christian opposition-controlled television station, Murr Television, and its sister radio station, Radio Mount Lebanon, in September 2002, claiming that they had undermined relations with Syria and violated electoral legislation banning party political broadcasts during a recent by-election in the Metn district, where one of the stations' owners, the nephew of Minister of the Interior Elias Murr, had won the seat. The ruling against Murr Television was upheld in December and a final appeal was rejected in April 2003, resulting in the station's permanent closure.

In November 2002 international donors attending a conference in Paris, France, agreed to provide Lebanon with an aid package worth some US $4,300m. to assist the country with its heavy burden of debt and to finance development projects. In April 2003, following weeks of reported disagreements between members of the Cabinet over economic and other domestic policies, the Prime Minister, Rafik Hariri, tendered his resignation and that of his Government. However, after his premiership was endorsed by the Lebanese parliament, Hariri was asked by President Lahoud to form a new 30-member cabinet. The new Government, announced two days after Hariri's resignation, brought in 11 new ministers, including Jean Obeid, who replaced Mahmoud Hammoud as Minister of Foreign Affairs and Emigrants; Hammoud was named as the new Minister of National Defence. The new Cabinet was widely considered to be the most pro-Syrian for more than a decade; it contained no members of the Christian opposition, nor of Hezbollah. Syria was still believed to be exerting considerable influence over Lebanese domestic affairs, despite the decreasing Syrian military presence in the country: in February 2003 Syria had commenced the redeployment of more than 4,000 troops stationed in northern Lebanon, under the terms of the Ta'if agreement; the withdrawal was reportedly carried out over several months.

It was reported in May 2003 that Lebanese security forces had arrested at least nine suspected al-Qa'ida operatives in Sidon. The suspects were accused of plotting to attack the US embassy in Beirut and to kidnap members of the Lebanese Cabinet. Moreover, they were believed to be linked to the al-Qa'ida militants thought to be in hiding in the Ain al-Hilweh refugee camp. In December 27 Lebanese were found guilty, and given varying prison sentences, on charges of carrying out bomb attacks against mostly US and British businesses in Lebanon between the end of 2002 and April 2003. However, a military court in Beirut acquitted three defendants of plotting to assassinate the US ambassador to Lebanon.

The Israeli Cabinet agreed in November 2003 to release more than 400 Palestinian, Lebanese (mostly Hezbollah) and other Arab prisoners in exchange for the remains of three soldiers kidnapped by Hezbollah in Shebaa Farms in 2000, as well as the return of the abducted Israeli businessman, Elhanan Tannenbaum. Israel also hoped to receive information on the fate of a missing Israeli airman, Ron Arad, who had been shot down over Lebanon in 1986, and was still believed to be held in Lebanese detention. Germany, which had mediated the negotiations between Israel and Hezbollah, oversaw the exchange, and in January 2004 the first 30 Lebanese and other Arab prisoners to be released by Israel were flown to the airport at Cologne, Germany, where they were exchanged for Tannenbaum and the remains of the Israeli soldiers. The remaining Palestinian prisoners, and the remains of 59 Lebanese militants held by Israel, were later released at Israeli border posts.

Allegations of repeated violations of Lebanese airspace by Israel led Hezbollah in November 2004 to send a drone over Israeli territory, and to declare that it possessed drone aircraft capable of launching attacks on targets inside Israel. In January 2005 at least one Israeli officer and two UN observers were killed when Israeli soldiers retaliated against Hezbollah guerrilla attacks on an Israeli military vehicle patrolling Shebaa Farms. UN Secretary-General Kofi Annan criticized Israel's persistent violations of Lebanese airspace and Hezbollah's launching of a drone over Israel, both of which he considered to be provocative acts; he also urged Lebanon to respect the Blue Line. On 28 January the mandate of the UNIFIL observer mission (see above), already extended four times since July 2002, was extended until 31 July 2005; the UN Security Council expressed grave concern at the persistent violence along the Blue Line. The mission's mandate was extended again in July 2005 and February 2006. Meanwhile, in November 2005 Hezbollah launched what was apparently its heaviest attack on Israeli troops in the Shebaa Farms area since October 2000. Four Hezbollah militants were killed and 11 Israeli soldiers injured in the ensuing violence, in which the two sides exchanged heavy artillery fire across the border.

Meanwhile, four rounds of voting took place in municipal elections held in May 2004. At the first round (in Mount Lebanon governorate), Hezbollah and other pro-Syrian groups, such as the PSP and independent Christian candidates, defeated the primarily Christian opposition, which was reportedly suffering from internal divisions. At the second round, a list of candidates supported by Hariri won in Beirut (where turn-out was reportedly only 23%) against lists connected to the Parti communiste libanais (PCL) and the opposition Christian Free Patriotic Movement; in the Beka'a valley Hezbollah took the majority of municipalities that it contested, again securing victory over its opposition, Amal. At the third round, Hezbollah achieved further success, particularly in the mostly Shi'a villages on the Israeli border, where elections took place for the first time since the withdrawal of Israeli troops. The list supported by Hariri suffered an overwhelming defeat in the region's capital and the Prime Minister's home town, Sidon, while Amal secured an unexpected victory over Hezbollah in some mainly Shi'a villages. At the final round of elections in north Lebanon, a candidate considered to be a potential rival to Hariri as Prime Minister, Najib Mikati (also the Minister of Public Works and Transport and a close friend of Syrian President Assad), achieved success.

In August 2004, in advance of the expiry of President Lahoud's six-year term of office in November, the Cabinet voted to amend the Constitution, which prevented Lahoud from seeking a second term, to extend Lahoud's mandate by three years. Both Muslim and Christian politicians and Hariri protested against the decision, but Hariri eventually offered his support for the amendment after a meeting with Syrian politicians, including President Assad. The USA and France expressed their opposition to the move, and presented a resolution to the UN in early September in an attempt to forestall it. The UN subsequently adopted Resolution 1559, demanding that: Lebanon's sovereignty be respected; a 'free and fair' presidential election be held; the Government assert its power throughout the whole country; all foreign forces leave Lebanon; and all militias in the country, both Lebanese and non-Lebanese, disband and disarm. The resolution did not explicitly refer to Syria or its forces and agents, however. The Security Council gave Lebanon 30 days to comply with the resolution's demands, threatening to take measures against that country if it failed to meet them. Nevertheless, the National Assembly approved the constitutional amendment by 96 votes to 29, prompting the resignation of four cabinet ministers in protest.

The Syrian army responded to Resolution 1559 by redeploying about 3,000 special forces from positions to the south of Beirut, although some 14,000 Syrian troops remained in Lebanon. (Further redeployments of Syrian troops took place in December 2004, from the northern town of Batrun and from Beirut's southern suburbs and the airport to the Beka'a valley.) In October 2004, after UN Secretary-General Kofi Annan had reported Lebanon's non-compliance with the resolution, the Security Council ordered Annan to provide a report every six months detailing steps towards its fulfilment. Hariri dissolved his Cabinet a day after the release of the statement, declaring that he would not attempt to head the next government. The following day he was replaced by Omar Karami, who revealed the composition of his Cabinet five days later (which for the first time included two women). The former Minister of Public Health, Sulayman Franjiya, assumed the post of Minister of the Interior and Municipalities, while Mahmoud Hammoud became Minister of Foreign Affairs and Emigrants; Hammoud's former national defence portfolio was allocated to Abd ar-Rahim Mrad, previously a Minister of State without portfolio. The new Government, which received legislative approval in November, was considered to be still more favourable than its predecessor to continued Syrian influence in Lebanese affairs. The new Prime Minister criticized the recent UN Security Council resolution, asserting that: the fulfilment of its demands would lead to crises of security and stability in Lebanon; the resolution constituted external pressure on Syria and Lebanon; and the presence of Syrian troops in Lebanon was a matter only for the two countries involved. The USA exerted further pressure on Lebanon in January 2005, when it vowed to include Lebanon among its list of states deemed to sponsor terrorism if the country did not end its support for Hezbollah.

On 22 November 2004 (Independence Day) some 3,000 students from several universities and right-wing Christian activists demonstrated in Beirut against what they perceived to be Syria's dominance in Lebanon, in defiance of a government ban. At the end of the month the Government supported a march by over 100,000 demonstrators in Beirut in praise of Syria's influence in the country and rejecting the terms of UN Resolution 1559. In December parties opposed to the Lebanese Government's support of Syrian involvement in Lebanese affairs, including the main Christian opposition group, the Qornet Shehwan Gathering, Kamal Joumblatt's mainly Druze-supported PSP and the proscribed Lebanese Forces Party, issued a joint statement demanding a cessation of foreign interference in Lebanon and calling for the release of Lebanese Forces Party leader Samir Geagea, who had been imprisoned on murder charges in 1994. They also demanded an electoral law that would allow people of all political sensibilities to participate in governing the country.

On 14 February 2005 a car bombing in Beirut killed Rafik Hariri, the former Prime Minister and business executive, and 22 other people; at least 100 were injured in the blast. The attack provoked condemnation from Syrian President Assad. However, the USA, emphasizing the problems caused by the Syrian military presence in Lebanon and the inability of the Syrian-dominated intelligence services to forestall the attack, removed its ambassador to Syria for consultations, and later demanded that all Syrian troops withdraw from Lebanon. Later in the month Syria announced that it would redeploy its troops in Lebanon to the Beka'a valley. On 28 February, following a general strike and mass protests in Beirut advocated by opposition parties, at which demonstrators demanded the complete withdrawal of Syrian troops from Lebanon and an end to Syrian influence in Lebanese politics, Karami dissolved his Cabinet and resigned as premier. Nevertheless, Lahoud requested that Karami and his ministers remain in office in an interim capacity pending the appointment of a new government.

Lebanese opposition groups demanded in March 2005 that President Assad and the public prosecutor and senior security officials in Lebanon resign their posts in order to ensure that the investigation into Hariri's death be conducted legitimately and with integrity. They also announced their refusal to participate in any discussions on the formation of a new government until their demands were met. Also in March US Secretary of State Condoleezza Rice reiterated demands by President George W. Bush, the Lebanese opposition and several other countries that Syria withdraw its troops and security forces from Lebanon. Assad and Lahoud agreed at a summit meeting to the withdrawal of Syrian troops to the Beka'a valley by the end of the month; Syria later pledged to withdraw all troops prior to Lebanon's general election, scheduled to begin in May, and to provide the UN with a timetable for the withdrawal. Although Rice praised the decision, she urged the two countries to complete the process more quickly. Meanwhile, protests took place in Beirut in support of the Syrian influence and military presence in Lebanon. Syria reportedly withdrew 4,000–6,000 of its soldiers and intelligence agents from Lebanon to Syria in mid-March; 8,000–10,000 troops remained in the Beka'a valley. A UN report released later that month accused Syria of allowing political tension in Lebanon to be heightened before the murder of Hariri, and criticized Lebanon's initial attempts to investigate the incident. In April the UN Security Council approved Resolution 1595, establishing an International Independent Investigation Commission (UNIIIC) to investigate Hariri's murder. The German prosecutor appointed to head the commission, Detlev Mehlis, arrived in Lebanon in May. In April Syria had declared that it had fulfilled its promise to withdraw all troops, military assets and intelligence apparatus, and in May a UN team dispatched to Lebanon to confirm the withdrawal announced that thus far it had not found a single Syrian soldier in areas that it had inspected. However, it reported that an armed guard had blocked the road and fired shots in the air when members of the team had attempted to approach a base in Qussaya, a border village in which the PFLP—GC (which attributed the incident to a misunderstanding) had positions.

President Lahoud reappointed Karami to the post of Prime Minister on 10 March 2005. In the following month Karami, having failed to form a new administration, tendered his resignation for a second time, and Najib Mikati was appointed to the post of caretaker Prime Minister. Mikati named a new Cabinet (approved by the National Assembly on 27 April), which was to be responsible for the implementation of legislation facilitating a general election. Elias Murr was appointed Deputy Prime Minister and Minister of National Defence, while Mahmoud Hammoud retained responsibility for foreign affairs and emigrants. In late April three senior Lebanese security officials with close ties to Syria announced their resignations, and by mid-May a number of other pro-Syrian security officials, whose replacement had been demanded by the opposition, had been dismissed from their posts.

Elections to the National Assembly were held in four rounds between 29 May and 19 June 2005. The first round of voting took place in the Beirut region, where turn-out was a reported 28%. The anti-Syrian Rafik Hariri Martyr List, headed by the Future Movement (Tayar al-Mustaqbal) of Rafik Hariri's son, Saad ed-Din Hariri, and including the PSP, the Lebanese Forces Party and the Qornet Shehwan Gathering, won all 19 seats. Four days later the prominent anti-Syrian journalist Dr Samir Kassir was killed in a car bombing in a Christian district of Beirut. The anti-Syrian opposition accused remaining Syrian intelligence agents of involvement in the murder, and again called on President Lahoud to resign. An estimated 45% of registered voters participated in the second round of elections conducted on 5 June in southern Lebanon; as in the first round, turn-out was reportedly lower in Christian than in Muslim districts. The Resistance and Development Bloc, consisting of the pro-Syrian Shi'a organizations Amal and Hezbollah and their allies, secured all 23 seats. The third round was held on 12 June in Mount Lebanon, where candidates contested 35 seats and turn-out was unofficially estimated at 54%, and the Beka'a Valley, where an estimated 49% of registered voters elected deputies to 23 seats. Immediately prior to the poll, Gen. Michel Awn allied himself with pro-Syrian factions as the Free Patriotic Movement (Tayar al-Watani al-Horr), declaring that he was no longer hostile to Syria now that it had withdrawn its troops from Lebanon. Awn's alliance took 21 seats, while Hariri's list secured 25. However, in the final round in north Lebanon on 19 June, at which turn-out was officially estimated at 49%, Hariri's list won all 28 seats. Consequently, according to final results, the Rafik Hariri Martyr List secured 72 of the National Assembly's 128 seats, allowing the officially prohibited Lebanese Forces Party to achieve parliamentary representation for the first time; the Resistance and Development Bloc won 35 seats; and the Free Patriotic Movement took 21. Following their victory, the various anti-Syrian factions continued to demand that President Lahoud resign.

In June 2005 George Hawi, the former Secretary-General of the PCL and an outspoken critic of Syrian interference in

Lebanese politics, was killed by a car bomb in Beirut. The anti-Syrian opposition attributed the attack to Syrian agents and their allies in the Lebanese security services. Further bomb explosions took place in the capital throughout 2005, causing a number of fatalities. In July two people were killed in an explosion that injured pro-Syrian Deputy Prime Minister Murr, and in December the anti-Syrian publisher of the daily newspaper *An-Nahar* (The Day), Gebran Tueni, and three others were killed in a car bombing.

Meanwhile, pro-Syrian Nabih Berri was re-elected President of the National Assembly in June 2005. Two days later President Lahoud appointed Fouad Siniora of the Future Movement, a close ally of Rafik Hariri, as Prime Minister, and asked him to form a new government. In July Siniora announced the composition of a new Cabinet: Elias Murr remained Deputy Prime Minister and Minister of National Defence, while Fawzi Salloukh was appointed Minister of Foreign Affairs and Emigrants; Muhammad Fneish became the first representative of Hezbollah to hold cabinet office, assuming responsibility for energy and water. In the same month the National Assembly passed a law pardoning Lebanese Forces Party leader Samir Geagea, as demanded by some of the opposition (see above). Almost 40 Islamist militants, some of whom were allegedly linked to al-Qa'ida, were also released by parliamentary approval. Prime Minister Siniora met Syrian President Assad and Prime Minister Otari in Syria in August. The two states reportedly agreed to improve relations based on mutual respect, and Siniora emphasized Lebanon's support of Syria and its commitment to bilateral agreements.

Following reports that Syrian intelligence agents might not have completely withdrawn from Lebanon, the UN announced in June 2005 that it was considering sending a commission to the country to investigate the claims; Syria continued to insist that it had removed all its security personnel. UNIIIC began its inquiry into Rafik Hariri's assassination in mid-June, with a three-month mandate. In August UNIIIC arrested the three former security officials who had tendered their resignations in April (see above) for questioning regarding the assassination. A fourth security chief, who had retained his post after Hariri's murder, was also sought, and subsequently handed himself in to the organization; a former pro-Syrian parliamentary deputy was also detained. In October, shortly before UNIIIC issued its first report on the investigation, the Syrian Minister of the Interior, Maj.-Gen. Ghazi Kanaan, was found shot dead in his office. The official Syrian Arab News Agency announced that he had committed suicide. A former head of Syrian military intelligence in Lebanon, Kanaan had become Chief of Political Intelligence in Syria in 2002, and had been appointed Minister of the Interior in October 2004 (see the chapter on Syria). Shortly before his apparent suicide, Kanaan had told a Lebanese radio station that he had been questioned by UNIIIC, but had not given any evidence against Syria. According to its report, issued in October 2005, UNIIIC had found evidence that Lebanese and Syrian intelligence and security services were directly involved in Hariri's assassination. Moreover, the report reasoned, the act was too complex and too well planned to have taken place without the approval of senior Syrian security officials and their Lebanese counterparts. UNIIIC expressed its extreme concern at the lack of co-operation by the Syrian authorities. Lebanon and Syria, which denounced the investigation's findings as politically motivated, rejected the report, and Syria announced that it had established a special judicial commission to deal with all matters relating to UNIIIC's mission. The commission was granted an extension to its mandate until December.

The UN Security Council responded to the first UNIIIC report by adopting in October 2005 a resolution, sponsored by the USA, France and the United Kingdom, establishing measures against suspects in the assassination, including prohibitions on travel and the freezing of assets. The Security Council urged Syria to co-operate fully with the investigation commission and detain suspects identified by the inquiry, threatening unspecified 'further action' should Syria fail to comply with the resolution's demands by the stipulated deadline of 15 December. Syria reported in November that it had arrested six government officials for questioning. Meanwhile, in October the UN Special Envoy, Terje Roed-Larsen, issued his report on the implementation of UN Security Council Resolution 1559, in which he praised the withdrawal of Syrian troops from Lebanon, but noted that Lebanon had still not complied with the demands that Lebanese and non-Lebanese militias disarm and disband, and that government authority be extended throughout the country. Lebanon rejected the report, asserting that the Government would deal with armed groups through national dialogue.

In December 2005 UNIIIC began questioning five Syrian officials suspected of involvement in Hariri's assassination in Vienna, Austria. Detlev Mehlis presented his second report on the investigating body's work to the UN Security Council later in the month. While noting that Syria had presented five officials suspected of involvement in the murder to the commission for interrogation, the report again accused Syria of reluctance to co-operate with the investigating body and of hindering the investigation. It stated that UNIIIC had found further evidence that the Lebanese and Syrian intelligence and security services had been involved in the assassination, and revealed that Mehlis had identified 19 suspects, six of whom were Syrian (of which five were those being questioned in Vienna). Mehlis resigned as the head of UNIIIC shortly after he presented the body's findings, citing personal and professional reasons; he was replaced by Serge Brammertz. UNIIIC's mandate was extended to 15 June 2006.

In January 2006 UNIIIC investigators declared that they wished to question Syrian President Assad and Minister of Foreign Affairs Farouk ash-Shara' in relation to Hariri's murder. (A few days earlier the Vice-President of Syria, Abd al-Halim Khaddam, who had been living in exile in Paris, having resigned his post in June 2005, had accused Assad of personally threatening Hariri. He subsequently declared that, in his view, Assad had ordered Hariri's assassination, although he awaited the final decision of the investigating commission.) However, the following day the Syrian Minister of Information announced that Syria would not permit UNIIIC to interview Assad. Ash-Shara' announced in March 2006 that he had reached an agreement with UNIIIC that provided for full Syrian co-operation with the investigation, while preserving the country's 'sovereignty and dignity'.

Ministers from Hezbollah and Amal announced in February 2006 that they were ending a boycott of cabinet meetings begun in December in protest against the Government's decision to allow an international investigation into Hariri's assassination. The ministers had also demanded that the Government describe Hezbollah as a 'resistance movement' rather than a militia. The announcement came shortly after Prime Minister Fouad Siniora declared to the National Assembly that the Government had always considered Hezbollah to be a movement of national resistance. Meanwhile, protests were taking place in Beirut and throughout the world against caricatures of the Prophet Muhammad (portrayal of whom is considered blasphemous in Islam), originally published in a Danish newspaper in September 2005, but subsequently reprinted in newspapers in various countries. In Beirut the protests, which had apparently been infiltrated by Islamist extremists, culminated in February 2006 in riots during which the Danish embassy was attacked and around 200 people were arrested. Apparently in response to this outbreak of disorder, the Minister of the Interior and Municipalities, Hassan as-Sabaa, resigned. The Minister of Youth and Sports, Ahmad Fatfat, assumed his responsibilities in an acting capacity.

Lebanese army sources claimed in May 2006 that four Israeli aircraft had violated southern Lebanese airspace. In the following month UNIIIC published its latest findings in its investigation into the assassination of Rafik Hariri. While maintaining that progress had been made in terms of the investigators' understanding of the links between those who had orchestrated and those who had executed the attack, the report acknowledged that it was not immediately feasible to reach any conclusions concerning possible connections between Hariri's murder and the killing of several other anti-Syrian personalities since October 2004. UNIIIC's mandate was duly extended until 15 June 2007.

On 12 July 2006 Hezbollah soldiers conducted a cross-border raid in which three Israeli troops were killed and two were captured; five more Israeli soldiers were killed during an attempt to rescue the kidnapped men. Their abduction prompted the Israeli Government to call an emergency cabinet meeting, following which it accused the Lebanese Government of having organized the incident and maintained that Israel reserved the right to defend its interests. Prime Minister Siniora denied the Israeli claims of his Government's culpability and insisted that he did not condone the raid. Later that same day Israel launched a series of air raids on a number of suspected Hezbollah positions across southern Lebanon. Further strikes during the night caused extensive damage to civilian infrastructure in the area.

Hezbollah declared 'open war' on 14 July, firing barrages of rockets into northern Israel in response to Israeli air-strikes. On the same day the UN Security Council held an emergency meeting, which was reported to have been called by Lebanon and at which Lebanon accused Israel of instigating the violence.

Numerous strikes were exchanged between the two warring factions on a daily basis and, despite claims to the contrary from both sides, who insisted that they were targeting political and military targets exclusively, many civilians were killed or injured in the conflict and thousands of homes were destroyed. Israel systematically targeted Lebanese infrastructure—roads and bridges were destroyed, seaports were blockaded and Beirut International Airport was bombed, forcing all international flights to be diverted to Cyprus. An estimated 70% of civilians living in southern Lebanon fled to the north of the country to escape the worst of the violence. In late July 2006 at least 28 civilians, including 19 children, were reported to have been killed when a residential building in the Lebanese village of Qana was struck by missiles during an Israeli air raid. At an emergency session of the UN Security Council, convened on the following day, members issued a statement expressing 'extreme shock and distress' at the attack; UN Secretary-General Kofi Annan, while apportioning blame for the initial outbreak of the conflict to Hezbollah, denounced the Israeli response as excessive and as being responsible for 'death and suffering on a wholly unacceptable scale'. Nevertheless, in early August the Israeli Cabinet approved a plan to send a large number of ground troops further into Lebanon, as far as the Litani river (approximately 30 km—18 miles—north of the Israeli–Lebanese border).

The USA and France agreed at the beginning of August 2006 upon the content of a draft resolution to be submitted to the UN Security Council, which duly convened to discuss the proposed terms. (The USA had come under criticism for apparently blocking earlier attempts to impose a cease-fire, which had led to allegations that the Bush Administration was implicitly encouraging Israel to wreak damage upon Hezbollah.) On 11 August the Security Council adopted Resolution 1701, which had been unanimously approved and which called for: an immediate and full cessation of hostilities; the extension of the Lebanese Government's authority over the whole country; and the delineation of Lebanese international boundaries, with particular regard to disputed sectors such as Shebaa Farms. The resolution was endorsed by the Lebanese Government on 12 August, and Sheikh Nasrallah announced that Hezbollah would honour the call for a cease-fire; however, 24 Israeli soldiers were killed on that same day—the greatest loss of life on any single day since the conflict began. Similarly, despite Israel's Cabinet approving the resolution on 13 August, on the following day Israeli troops launched an attack on a refugee camp in Sidon, killing an UNRWA staff member approximately one hour before the cease-fire was scheduled to take effect.

In late August 2006 Sheikh Nasrallah acknowledged that Hezbollah's kidnapping of the two Israeli soldiers that had triggered the conflict had, with hindsight, been deeply regrettable and that talks concerning their possible return, in exchange for Lebanese nationals detained by Israel, were ongoing. However, he remained defiant, claiming during a rally staged in Beirut in September that Hezbollah was stronger than it had been prior to the conflict and that the organization possessed in excess of 20,000 rockets in its arsenal. Earlier that month Israel had lifted its naval blockade of Lebanon and rescinded its restrictions on air travel to and from Lebanon, thereby formalizing the end of the conflict. However, much of southern Lebanon remained uninhabitable owing to the presence of unexploded cluster bombs, and at the end of 2006 an estimated 200,000 Lebanese had yet to return to their homes (although many of these were able to do so during 2007). According to figures released by Lebanon's Higher Relief Council, an estimated 1,191 Lebanese civilians were killed during the conflict, and a further 4,410 were thought to have been injured. According to the Israeli Ministry of Foreign Affairs, 119 Israeli troops and 43 Israeli civilians had died in the fighting, and more than 530 Hezbollah members had also been killed. In November the findings of an official UN investigation into the conflict determined that Israel had fired artillery shells containing white phosphorus, an incendiary substance the use of which against civilians, or against legitimate military targets within residential areas, is banned under the terms of the Geneva Convention. However, the Israeli Government refuted the claim, insisting that the shells had been aimed solely at military targets in open ground. Meanwhile, in September 2006 the human rights group Amnesty International accused Hezbollah of having committed war crimes by deliberately targeting Israeli civilians in its air-strikes during the recent conflict.

In October 2006 Sheikh Nasrallah demanded that Hezbollah be allocated one-third of the seats in an expanded national unity government, prompting accusations that he was attempting to attain the right of veto in order to protect the Syrian Government from prosecution in the ongoing investigation into the assassination of Rafik Hariri. Nasrallah's demands were ignored, however, and in the following month five ministers—two members of Hezbollah and three from its ally, Amal—resigned from the Cabinet, thereby removing any Shi'a presence from the Government. A sixth resignation, that of a Christian pro-Syrian minister, followed soon afterwards. The assassination later in November of Pierre Gemayel, the Minister of Industry since 2005, rendered the political situation even more unstable. Gemayel was shot dead in his car in a suburb of Beirut, and many Lebanese leaders were quick to blame Syria for his murder. Since the Lebanese Constitution decrees that any government in which one-third of the ministers have vacated their posts must automatically be dissolved and a new government appointed, Gemayel's assassination meant that, should just one further minister leave the Cabinet for any reason, it would force the collapse of the Government.

In December 2006 thousands of demonstrators gathered in Beirut and erected tents in the capital's main square, besieging government buildings and proclaiming that the Cabinet was now constitutionally invalid. When the protests, aimed at pressurizing the Government into resigning, had failed to achieve any tangible results by late January 2007, the opposition intensified its efforts and called for a general strike, which brought commercial districts of the capital to a virtual standstill; at least three people were killed during clashes between protesters and the authorities. The security forces appeared to do little to remove the road blockades that were in place, leading to allegations that the police and the army were colluding with the opposition to bring about the Government's collapse. Nevertheless, the strike had a minimal effect on the resolve of the Government, which, at early May 2008, remained in place, despite the continuing efforts of those participating in the sit-in protest and the rapid intensification of sectarian violence (see below). Yet, despite the Government's refusal to submit to the wishes of the opposition, the presence of two separate Lebanese delegations at the annual summit meeting of the Arab League, held in Saudi Arabia in March 2007, aptly symbolized the endemic divisions threatening the country's future stability.

Meanwhile, a disagreement between pro-Government Sunni and anti-Government Shi'a students at Beirut Arab University in January 2007 escalated into violent clashes that spilled out onto the streets; up to four people were killed and more than 150 were injured. The incident further fuelled concerns that Lebanon was about to spiral into full-scale sectarian conflict again, fears that appeared to be shared by the Government, which responded to the latest violence by imposing an overnight curfew in Beirut—the first of its kind in a decade. In February two bombs were detonated on commuter buses travelling through Ein Alaq, a village to the north-east of Beirut, killing three people. The attacks, which took place on the eve of the second anniversary of Hariri's assassination, were widely considered to have been timed so as to deter people from travelling to Beirut to attend a rally to mark the occasion; however, amid tight security, tens of thousands of people congregated on the following day to honour their former leader. In March Hassan as-Sabaa, who had retracted his resignation as Minister of the Interior and Municipalities in November 2006, announced that four Syrian members of Fatah al-Islam—a militant Islamist Palestinian group, inspired by al-Qa'ida and alleged by the Lebanese authorities to be supported by Syria—had been arrested on suspicion of involvement in the bus explosions in Ein Alaq.

In March 2007 UNIIIC released its latest report into the assassination of Rafik Hariri, in which again it claimed to have made considerable progress in acquiring further evidence, but declined to give specific details. Brammertz did, however, state that UNIIIC had identified 250 individuals whom it wanted to question; 50 of these were to be interviewed within the next three months. UNIIIC's mandate was extended to 15 June 2008. Also in March 2007 recently appointed UN Secretary-General Ban Ki-Moon issued his report on the implementation of UN Security Council Resolution 1701, in which he rebuked both Israel and Lebanon for failing to adhere to all of its terms. However, he praised both sides' overall commitment to maintaining the cease-fire, and proposed the establishment of an independent assessment mission to assist with the monitoring of the Israeli–Lebanese border and thereby to facilitate the full implementation of the resolution.

A copy of the interim report of Israel's Winograd Commission, a government-appointed commission of inquiry into Israel's military campaign in Lebanon, was made public at the end of April 2007. This preliminary report, which focused specifically on the period between Israel's withdrawal from southern Lebanon in 2000 to mid-July 2006, contained severe criticism of prominent Israeli government officials, notably Prime Minister Olmert, Minister of Defence Amir Peretz and the Chief of Staff of the Armed Forces during the conflict, Lt-Gen. Dan Halutz (who had resigned in January 2007). Olmert was accused of having initiated the military action against Hezbollah 'hastily' and without due consideration for the likely outcome and repercussions of such action, while Halutz was deemed to have provided inadequate information to the Prime Minister and Minister of Defence regarding the shortcomings of the Israeli armed forces. Sheikh Nasrallah welcomed the findings of the Commission (for further details, see the chapter on Israel) and acknowledged the level of self-criticism that Israel had demonstrated, conceding that this was worthy of 'respect'.

At the end of May 2007 the UN Security Council adopted Resolution 1757, authorizing the formation of an international tribunal to try suspects in Hariri's assassination. The Special Tribunal for Lebanon was to comprise 11 independent judges (or 14, should a second trial chamber be created), of whom seven were to be international judges and four were to be Lebanese; should a second trial chamber be created, there were to be nine international and five Lebanese judges. For security reasons, the tribunal would not be based in Lebanon itself, and in August it was reported that the Netherlands was close to reaching an agreement with the UN to allow the tribunal to be hosted by The Hague. While the creation of the tribunal was welcomed by the Siniora Government, the Hezbollah-led opposition was quick to challenge its validity. Sheikh Nasrallah insisted that any such tribunal not approved by the Lebanese legislature was illegitimate, suggesting that the new body would be unable to rely on the co-operation of Hezbollah should no agreement concerning its establishment be reached between the opposition and the Government.

In mid-June 2007 Walid Eido, a revered anti-Syrian legislator and member of Saad ed-Din Hariri's Future Movement, was killed along with nine other people, including Eido's son, in a car bombing in Beirut. Once again, suspicions were immediately raised regarding Syria's involvement; however, Syrian officials vehemently denied the allegations. A few days later, following a request by Prime Minister Siniora, the UN Security Council announced that UNIIIC was to assist with the investigation into Eido's assassination. By-elections to select replacements for Eido, in Beirut's second district, and for Pierre Gemayel, in the Metn district, were held in August. The former seat was won comfortably by the pro-Government Muhammad Amin Itani, of the Future Movement, while the latter was secured by pro-Syrian Camille Khoury, of the Free Patriotic Movement, in a very tight contest against his closest rival, former President Amin Gemayel. Khoury's victory was a considerable reverse for the Lebanese leadership, which had hoped to fill both seats with supporters of Siniora; since the assassination of Eido had reduced the number of pro-Government legislators to 68, the loss of just three more seats, for whatever reason, would result in the loss of the Siniora administration's majority quorum.

Meanwhile, the latest UNIIIC report (the sixth compiled during the tenure of Serge Brammertz) was released in mid-July 2007. The report asserted that a 'number of persons' had now been identified who might have been involved in Hariri's assassination, and stated that Syria and other states had continued to provide a 'mostly positive response' to UNIIIC's requests for co-operation and information. Also in July Lebanese investigators concluded that Fatah al-Islam had been responsible for the killing of Pierre Gemayel. In the previous month two UN armoured vehicles travelling between the villages of Marjayoun and Khaim, close to the Israeli border, were hit by a roadside bomb; three Spanish and three Colombian UN personnel were killed in the incident. In August the UN Security Council voted to extend the mandate of UNIFIL by another year; at the end of November UNIFIL had a strength of 13,264 military personnel, as well as 887 international and local civilian staff. The 10th UNIIIC report, and the first to be published since the appointment in early 2008 of Daniel Bellemare in place of Brammertz, was issued in March 2008. In the report, the UN body revealed that the evidence it had examined thus far indicated that a network of people was behind Hariri's murder, without mentioning specific individuals. In early April Bellemare asked the UN Security Council for a further six months to investigate the crime.

At the beginning of September 2007 a 105-day siege of the Nahr al-Bared refugee camp in Tripoli was finally concluded when the Lebanese army seized control from Islamist militants. The siege had begun in late May, after members of Fatah al-Islam had fled to the camp having conducted a bank robbery in the town of Amioun, south of Tripoli. In the ensuing weeks more than 300 people were believed to have been killed in fierce clashes between the army and militants within the camp, which forced an estimated 40,000 Palestinian refugees to flee in order escape the violence. Fatah al-Islam's leader—Shaker al-Abassi, who had been sentenced to death *in absentia* in April 2004 for the murder in 2002 of a US diplomat, Laurence Foley (see the chapter on Jordan)—was reported to have been killed in the closing stages of the fighting; however, subsequent DNA tests carried out on the body thought to have been that of al-Abassi proved negative, suggesting that the militant leader might have fled the camp before the siege was concluded. The Syrian Government commended the efforts of the Lebanese army in ending the siege, and continued to deny ongoing claims that it in any way supported or condoned the activities of Fatah al-Islam. In mid-March 2008 al-Abassi was charged with incitement to murder, in connection with the bus explosions at Ein Alaq in February 2007.

With the scheduled expiry, in November 2007, of Lahoud's presidential term, the attention of the Government and the opposition in the preceding months came increasingly to focus on the election of his successor. The first session of the National Assembly to elect a new president was duly arranged for 25 September 2007—the first time that the legislature was to have met since October 2006. In a conciliatory overture, the President of the Assembly, Nabih Berri, proposed an initiative whereby the opposition would relinquish its long-standing demand for a national unity government if the rival factions could agree on a presidential candidate, although the response from Siniora and his supporters to the proposal was muted. The ambiguity of the Lebanese Constitution meant that, in the event of political divisions between the two camps preventing agreement on a common candidate, the likely eventuality remained deeply uncertain. According to the Constitution, if a new president was not elected by 23 November 2007, then Siniora and his Cabinet would automatically assume executive control. However, the Constitution also authorizes the President to decree the resignation of the Cabinet, allowing Lahoud, should he choose, to appoint a new, opposition cabinet, which would almost certainly elect a pro-Syrian, anti-Government president. Lebanon experienced a further political assassination in late September, just six days before the scheduled presidential election, when Antoine Ghanem, a Christian Phalangist legislator, was killed in a car bombing in a predominantly Christian district of Beirut. Five others died in the explosion, for which Syrian officials were again obliged to deny claims of involvement by certain Lebanese leaders. Since the Government and opposition demonstrated an unwillingness to co-operate in order to elect a new president, the National Assembly failed to achieve the requisite two-thirds' quorum of members on 25 September owing to an opposition boycott; a second vote was thus scheduled for 23 October. Speculation increased at this time about the possibility of a return to a dual-government system, effectively formalizing the intense divisions in Lebanon.

Following mediation by German diplomats and representatives of the International Committee of the Red Cross, Hezbollah and Israel carried out a limited exchange of prisoners and bodies in mid-October 2007—the first such exchange between the two sides since their conflict of the previous year. However, the two Israeli soldiers whose abduction by Hezbollah militants in July 2006 had apparently provoked the conflict were not included in the arrangement. In late January 2008 Sheikh Nasrallah alleged that Hezbollah was holding the remains of a number of Israeli troops killed during the 2006 conflict.

The second postponement of the scheduled ballot to elect a successor to President Lahoud was announced by Berri on 22 October 2007, the day before the vote was to take place; a new date of 12 November was declared. In early October US President Bush had warned the Syrian Government not to interfere in Lebanon's internal affairs, since it was a boycott of the National Assembly by pro-Syrian opposition members that had rendered the parliament inquorate. Thus began a seven-month period during which no fewer than 17 further postponements of the presidential election were ordered, owing to a failure by the opposing factions to agree first on a mutually acceptable candidate, and then on the exact nature of administration to be formed after a new president had been elected. When the parliamentary session scheduled for 23 November—at the end of which Lahoud's term of office expired—was postponed until 30 November, it meant that Lahoud was obliged to leave office without a successor having been appointed. Under the terms of the Constitution, therefore, presidential duties were assumed by the Siniora Government in an acting capacity, although, shortly before the expiry of his mandate, Lahoud had issued a statement asserting that, owing to conditions being present for a 'state of emergency', he would hand over responsibility for the country's security to the armed forces. (He and other representatives of the pro-Syrian opposition refused to recognize the legitimacy of the Government following the ministerial resignations of November 2006.) Yet Lahoud's stance was firmly rejected by the Prime Minister, who insisted that no Head of State could call a state of emergency without the approval of the Cabinet. This represented the first time that Lebanon had been without a president since the civil war ended in 1990.

Although the Commander-in-Chief of the Army, Gen. Michel Sulayman (a Maronite Christian), was chosen as a 'compromise candidate' acceptable to both pro-Government and pro-opposition politicians towards the end of November 2007, disagreements remained as to how to amend the Constitution in order to permit Sulayman, as a serving senior state official, to assume the office of Head of State. Amid a flurry of international and regional diplomatic meetings, the ministers responsible for the foreign affairs of Arab League member states, meeting in Cairo, Egypt, in early January 2008, approved details of a plan intended to bring to an end Lebanon's presidential vacuum. The three-phase proposals included the election of Sulayman as president, establishment of a Lebanese government of national unity (where Sulayman would have the deciding vote in any dispute) and approval of new electoral legislation. It was reported that the Arab League plan had received the support of both the Lebanese and Syrian administrations, but that Hezbollah and its principal allies continued to demand that they receive at least one-third of government portfolios in any new cabinet, thus granting them the right to veto important decisions. Following a 19th postponement of the National Assembly session to elect a president on 13 May, a new date of 10 June was set. In early April, meanwhile, Sulayman had announced his intention to retire from his military post in August, three months in advance of the scheduled date.

In mid-December 2007 Brig.-Gen. François al-Hajj, the army's head of operations, was killed, along with three other people, in a car bomb attack in east Beirut. Observers noted the significance of the fact that al-Hajj had been widely expected to be promoted to Commander-in-Chief of the Army should Sulayman be elected as Lahoud's successor. It was, however, unclear as to which group had carried out the assassination, with Syria, Israel and the militant group Fatah al-Islam all being accused by various parties of responsibility for the blast. An explosion apparently aimed at US embassy officials in mid-January 2008 resulted in the deaths of four Lebanese bystanders. There was a further wave of unrest in the principally Shi'ite suburbs of southern Beirut in late January, which had been precipitated by popular frustration over power shortages; seven protesters were reported to have died in the ensuing clashes with security forces. A group of army officers was detained and charged by the authorities in February, amid criticism of the military's handling of the protests. Towards the end of January, meanwhile, Capt. Wissam Eid, a senior member of the police team charged with investigating the recent bombings and assassinations, was himself killed in another car bomb attack in a suburb of the capital; Eid's driver and up to 10 others also died in the explosion. In mid-February Imad Mughniyeh, one of Hezbollah's most senior militants, was killed in a car bombing in the Syrian capital. Hezbollah representatives immediately blamed Israel for Mughniyeh's death; however, Israeli officials rejected such claims. Mughniyeh had been implicated in a number of high-profile kidnappings of Western journalists, military personnel and religious envoys in Lebanon during the 1980s, and his funeral in Beirut attracted significant levels of support from Hezbollah members.

Lebanon's political situation deteriorated rapidly in early May 2008, when a decision taken by the Government to shut down a private telecommunications network controlled by Hezbollah and to close Beirut International Airport (where Hezbollah was accused of using surveillance equipment to spy on pro-Government politicians) prompted fierce clashes between members of the Shi'a opposition group and government loyalists. Moreover, a general strike called by the opposition in protest against price increases and to demand higher salaries descended into violence. As Sheikh Nasrallah called the Government's actions against his organization a 'declaration of war', gunmen from Hezbollah and its allies besieged the Beirut offices of the media controlled by the Future Movement's Saad ed-Din Hariri, while major roads were blocked. Observers noted that west Beirut was now effectively controlled by militants of the Hezbollah-led opposition. After several days of violent clashes, which spread to other cities such as Tripoli, more than 65 people had been killed, and some 200 wounded, in Lebanon's worst period of unrest since the civil war. However, by mid-May the Government and army claimed to have regained control, and, following mediation by the Arab League, the Cabinet voted to revoke the measures that had provoked the recent violence—an outcome widely viewed as a demonstration of Hezbollah's growing military strength and influence.

Government

Under the 1926 Constitution (as subsequently amended), legislative power is held by the National Assembly (called the Chamber of Deputies until 1979), with 128 members elected by universal adult suffrage for four years (subject to dissolution), on the basis of proportional representation. Seats are allocated on a religious or 'confessional' basis (divided equally between Christians and Muslims). The President of the Republic (who must be a Maronite Christian) is elected for six years by the National Assembly. The President, in consultation with deputies and the President of the National Assembly, appoints the Prime Minister (a Sunni Muslim) and other ministers to form the Cabinet, in which executive power is vested. The Ta'if agreement of October 1989, which was incorporated into the Constitution in August 1990, stated that cabinet portfolios must be distributed equally between Christian and Muslim ministers.

Defence

As assessed at November 2007, the Lebanese armed forces numbered 56,000 (army 53,900, air force 1,000, navy 1,100). Paramilitary forces included an estimated 20,000 members of the Internal Security Force, which was attached to the Ministry of the Interior and Municipalities. Compulsory military service was formally abolished in February 2007. Hezbollah's active members numbered some 2,000 in August 2005. In August 2004 there were an estimated 16,000 Syrian troops in Lebanon; however, following several redeployments, it was reported in April 2005 that Syria had withdrawn all of its forces from the country (see Recent History). Israeli armed forces and the Israeli-backed South Lebanon Army (SLA) withdrew from Lebanon in May 2000. Government expenditure on defence was budgeted at £L953,000m. in 2007.

The UN Interim Force in Lebanon (UNIFIL, see p. 80) observer mission numbered 1,980 troops in January 2006, assisted by about 50 military observers of the UN Truce Supervision Organization (UNTSO). At November 2007, following the adoption in August 2006 of UN Resolution 1701, which authorized an expansion of UNIFIL's capacity up to a maximum of 15,000 personnel, UNIFIL military personnel numbered 13,264, and were supported by 887 international and local civilian personnel.

Economic Affairs

In 2006, according to estimates by the World Bank, Lebanon's gross national income (GNI), measured at average 2004–06 prices, was US $22,253m., equivalent to $5,490 per head (or $5,460 per head on an international purchasing-power parity basis). During 1996–2006, it was estimated, the population increased at an average annual rate of 1.3%, while gross domestic product (GDP) per head increased, in real terms, by an average of 1.4% per year. Overall GDP increased, in real terms, at an average annual rate of 2.7% in 1996–2006; GDP growth of some 1.0% was recorded in 2005, and zero growth was recorded in 2006.

Agriculture (including hunting, forestry and fishing) contributed an estimated 6.5% of GDP in 2005. According to FAO data, some 2.6% of the labour force were employed in the sector in that year. The principal crops are potatoes, tomatoes, cucumbers citrus fruits and grapes. Viticulture is also significant. Hashish is a notable, albeit illegal, export crop, although the Government is attempting to persuade growers to switch to other crops. The GDP of the agricultural sector was estimated to have increased by an average of 2.0% annually in 1996–2005; agricultural GDP grew by some 1.0% in 2005.

The industrial sector (including manufacturing, construction and power) contributed an estimated 22.3% of GDP in 2005. Some 25.9% of the labour force were employed in industry in 1997. Lebanon's only mineral resources consist of small reserves of lignite and iron ore, and their contribution to GDP is insignificant. The GDP of the industrial sector increased by an estimated average of 0.7% per year in 1996–2005; industrial GDP expanded by about 1.0% in 2005.

Manufacturing contributed an estimated 13.6% of GDP in 2005. The sector employed about 10% of the labour force in 1985. The most important branches have traditionally been food-processing, petroleum refining, textiles and furniture and wood-working. Manufacturing GDP was estimated to have increased at an average annual rate of 1.9% in 1996–2005; however, the GDP of the sector decreased by some 4.1% in 2005.

Energy is derived principally from thermal power stations, using imported petroleum (which accounted for 89.0% of total electricity production in 2004). Plans for the construction of an offshore pipeline—capable of importing 6m. cu m–9m. cu m of natural gas per day from Syria—in order to meet Lebanon's growing energy requirements, comply with UN regulations on climate change, and reduce state and consumer expenditure on energy, were postponed indefinitely in July 2004. A second pipeline, costing an estimated US $100m., was also planned that would enable Lebanon to import an estimated 9m. cu m of natural gas per day from Egypt. The second phase of the gas pipeline project, which would also provide Syria, Jordan and Turkey with natural gas from Egypt, was initiated in January 2004. It was also expected that Lebanon would eventually be able to convert power plants in Zahrani, Hreiche, Zouk and Jieh from petroleum to natural gas, to be connected by an offshore pipeline. The Government estimated the damage inflicted on the country's electrical infrastructure during Israeli air-strikes in mid-2006 to be worth some $208m.

The services sector contributed an estimated 71.2% of GDP in 2005. In 1997 some 65.1% of the working population were employed in the sector, which has traditionally been dominated by trade and finance (accounting for an estimated 39.8% and 6.6% of GDP, respectively, in 2004). Financial services, in particular, withstood many of the disruptions inflicted on the economy by the civil conflict during 1975–90, although the Beirut Stock Exchange did not recommence trading until 1996. Lebanon is also becoming increasingly important as a centre for telecommunications. Recent efforts to revive the tourism industry have been a major source of growth in the construction industry. Tourist arrivals increased by 25.9% in 2004, with the number of tourists from Gulf and other Arab states reported to have grown significantly in recent years. However, the number of tourists declined by 10.9% in 2005 and the situation worsened in mid-2006 as a result of the conflict between Israel and Hezbollah (see Recent History). The GDP of the services sector increased at an average annual rate of some 3.5% in 1996–2005; the sector's GDP was estimated to have risen by 3.7% in 2005.

In 2006 Lebanon recorded a trade deficit of US $5,755m., and there was a deficit of $1,484m. on the current account of the balance of payments. The principal market for exports in 2006 was Switzerland (which took 24.3% of Lebanese exports); other significant purchasers included the United Arab Emirates and Syria (both 9.5%), Saudi Arabia, Iraq and Turkey. The principal supplier of imports in the same year was the USA (10.8%); France, the People's Republic of China, Italy and Germany were also important suppliers. The principal exports in 2006 were jewellery, machinery and electrical equipment, base metals, food, beverages and tobacco, and chemical products. The principal imports in that year were mineral products, machinery and electrical equipment, chemical products, vehicles, base metals, and food, beverages and tobacco.

In 2007 Lebanon recorded an overall budget deficit of £L3,891,000m., equivalent to 33.6% of recorded expenditure. At the end of 2005 Lebanon's total external debt was US $22,373m., of which $17,912m. was long-term public debt. The cost of debt-servicing in that year was equivalent to 17.7% of the value of exports of goods and services. According to the Ministry of Finance, Lebanon's total domestic and external debt totalled L£53,520,000m. at the end of March 2005. The annual rate of inflation averaged 2.2% in 1997–2007; consumer prices increased by 9.3% in 2007. In 1997, according to official figures, 8.5% of the labour force were unemployed (representing a significant decline from a level of 35% in 1990), although youth unemployment was reported to be much higher. The unemployment rate was estimated to be close to 20% in late 2006.

Lebanon is a member of the Arab Fund for Economic and Social Development (see p. 174), the Arab Monetary Fund (see p. 175) and the Islamic Development Bank (see p. 329). A customs union with Syria entered into effect in January 1999, and in the early 2000s the creation of a free trade zone was under discussion. Lebanon is also involved in efforts to finalize the establishment of a Greater Arab Free Trade Area. A Euro-Mediterranean Association Agreement was signed with the European Union (EU, see p. 244) in June 2002. Lebanon has observer status with the World Trade Organization (see p. 396), but by early 2008 had yet to satisfy all the requirements for full membership of the organization.

The reconstruction process following Lebanon's civil war (1975–90) was undertaken with the support of the international donor community, which in late 1996 pledged grants and concessionary loans totalling some US $3,200m. However, GDP growth since 1996 has been considerably lower than the targeted annual average of 8% under the Horizon 2000 investment programme for 1995–2007, principally owing to the failure to control both the budget deficit and the accumulated public debt (equivalent to an estimated 185% of GDP by 2007). In 1999 the World Bank agreed to disburse some $600m. in concessionary loans over a three-year period, and in 2000 the EU granted aid worth around $47.9m. In 2001–02 international donors agreed to provide the Lebanese authorities with close to $5,000m., in order to provide further assistance with debt restructuring and to finance development projects. However, the inability to reach a consensus on proposed measures to stimulate growth prevented the administration under Rafik Hariri in the early 2000s from implementing fully its comprehensive economic reform programme. By October 2004, when Hariri was replaced as Prime Minister by Omar Karami, the Lebanese economy was beset by many traditional problems, manifested in growing levels of debt and a large budget deficit. Furthermore, the privatization of vital state assets saw little progress under Hariri's administrations, partly as a result of ongoing political disagreements.

The Lebanese authorities were generally considered to have handled the upheaval surrounding Rafik Hariri's assassination in February 2005 successfully, preventing devastating effects on the economy. Nevertheless, the economy showed only 1% growth in 2005, although some optimism was afforded by the appointment of Fouad Siniora to the premiership in June of that year; as a long-serving Minister of Finance, he pledged to revitalize Hariri's failed economic reform programme. According to the Ministry of Finance, the new Prime Minister's fiscal programme would allow Lebanon to reduce its debt to around 110% of GDP within five years, providing that annual economic growth averaged 3%. Even with financial support from the international community and domestic creditors, however, such growth remained dependent on political stability, institutional reforms and the implementation of a successful privatization plan. The war between Israel and Hezbollah in July–August 2006, and the political turmoil that followed, adversely affected Lebanon's economic growth, causing a steep decline towards the end of the year and rising inflation. Israel's military campaign against Lebanese targets in mid-2006 had caused extensive damage to infrastructure, destroying bridges and damaging major roads, ports, schools, hospitals, and broadcasting and telecommunications sites. According to estimates by Lebanon's Council for Development and Reconstruction, the Israeli bombardments caused $3,600m. of damage, resulted in a sharp increase in unemployment and had a particularly disastrous effect on the agricultural, industrial and tourism sectors. Furthermore, amid widening divisions between the Government and opposition, it looked increasingly unlikely that Lebanon's various economic targets, which relied upon political consensus and reform, would be met. Amid fears that Lebanon's high level of public debt would rise further, countries at the 'Paris III' conference of international donors in January 2007 pledged a further $7,600m. to the Siniora Government. This followed an initial $940m. in the form of an early recovery plan, secured at a donor conference in Stockholm, Sweden, in August 2006. In December 2007 the EU agreed to assist Lebanon with $117m. to restore public finances and support the economy. In early 2008 preparations were being made for the privatization of the country's mobile phone network, which was anticipated to take place in 2009. The tourism sector has suffered a detrimental impact from the political instability of the region in recent years, with several Arab nations recently forbidding their citizens from visiting Lebanon. Despite the obvious damage to related sectors, the Minister of Finance insisted that GDP growth had been more than 3% in 2007. The IMF projected growth of some 3.5% in 2008, with inflation anticipated to decline towards 2.5%.

Education

There are state-controlled primary and secondary schools, but private institutions provide the main facilities for secondary and higher education. Education is not compulsory, but state education is provided free of charge. Primary education begins at six years of age and lasts for five years. Secondary education, beginning at the age of 11, lasts for a further seven years, comprising a first cycle of four years and a second of three years. In 2004/05 enrolment at primary schools included 92.4% of the relevant age-group; in the same year enrolment at secondary schools was equivalent to 89.1% of the relevant age-group. Some 165,730 Lebanese students were enrolled in higher education in the 2004/05 academic year. In 1998 Lebanon secured a loan of US $60m. from the World Bank, in order to restructure the country's system of technical and vocational education. Expenditure on education by the central Government in 2003 was some £L810,000m. (9.4% of total budgetary expenditure).

Public Holidays

2008: 1 January (New Year's Day), 10 January*† (Muharram, Islamic New Year), 19 January* (Ashoura), 9 February (Feast of St Maron), 20 March* (Mouloud/Yum an-Nabi, birth of Muhammad), 22 March (Arab League Anniversary), 24 March (Easter, Western Church), 25–28 April (Greek Orthodox Easter), 1 May (Ascension Day, Western Church), 30 July* (Leilat al-Meiraj, ascension of Muhammad), 15 August (Assumption), 1 October* (Id al-Fitr, end of Ramadan), 1 November (All Saints' Day), 22 November (Independence Day), 9 December* (Id al-Adha, Feast of the Sacrifice), 25 December (Christmas Day), 29 December*† (Muharram, Islamic New Year).

2009: 1 January (New Year's Day), 7 January*‡ (Ashoura), 9 February (Feast of St Maron), 9 March* (Mouloud/Yum an-Nabi, birth of Muhammad), 22 March (Arab League Anniversary), 13 April (Easter, Western Church), 17–20 April (Greek Orthodox Easter), 21 May (Ascension Day, Western Church), 19 July* (Leilat al-Meiraj, ascension of Muhammad), 15 August (Assumption), 20 September* (Id al-Fitr, end of Ramadan), 1 November (All Saints' Day), 22 November (Independence Day), 27 November* (Id al-Adha, Feast of the Sacrifice), 18 December* (Muharram, Islamic New Year), 25 December (Christmas Day), 27 December*‡ (Ashoura).

* These holidays are determined by the Islamic lunar calendar and may vary by one or two days from the dates given.
† This festival occurs twice (marking the start of the Islamic years AH 1429 and 1430) within the same Gregorian year.
‡ This festival occurs twice (in the Islamic years AH 1430 and 1431) within the same Gregorian year.

Weights and Measures

The metric system is in force.

Statistical Survey

Sources (unless otherwise stated): Central Administration for Statistics, Beirut; internet www.cas.gov.lb; Direction Générale des Douanes, Beirut.

Area and Population

AREA, POPULATION AND DENSITY

Area (sq km)	10,452*
Population (official estimate)	
15 November 1970†	
Males	1,080,015
Females	1,046,310
Total	2,126,325
Population (UN estimates at mid-year)‡	
2005	4,011,000
2006	4,055,000
2007	4,099,000
Density (per sq km) at mid-2007	392.2

* 4,036 sq miles.
† Figures are based on the results of a sample survey, excluding Palestinian refugees in camps. The total number of registered Palestinian refugees in Lebanon was 413,962 at 31 December 2007.
‡ Source: UN, *World Population Prospects: The 2006 Revision*.

PRINCIPAL TOWNS
(population in 2003)*

Beirut (capital)	1,171,000	Jounieh	79,800
Tarabulus (Tripoli)	212,900	Zahle	76,600
Saida (Sidon)	149,000	Baabda	58,500
Sur (Tyre)	117,100	Ba'albak (Ba'albek)	29,800
An-Nabatiyah at-Tahta (Nabatiyah)	89,400	Alayh	26,700

* Figures are rounded.

Source: Stefan Helders, *World Gazetteer* (internet www.world-gazetteer.com).

Mid-2007: Beirut 1,846,000 (Source: UN, *World Urbanization Prospects: The 2007 Revision*).

BIRTHS, MARRIAGES AND DEATHS
(annual averages, UN estimates)

	1990–95	1995–2000	2000–05
Birth rate (per 1,000)	24.9	22.6	19.3
Death rate (per 1,000)	7.1	7.1	7.0

Source: UN, *World Population Prospects: The 2006 Revision*.

2004 (numbers registered, official estimates): Live births 73,900; Marriages 30,014; Deaths 17,774.

2005 (numbers registered, official estimates): Live births 73,770; Marriages 29,705; Deaths 18,012.

2006 (numbers registered, official estimates): Live births 72,790; Marriages 29,078; Deaths 18,787.

Expectation of life (years at birth, WHO estimates): 70.2 (males 67.9; females 72.5) in 2005 (Source: WHO, *World Health Statistics*).

EMPLOYMENT
(ISIC major divisions)

	1975	1985*
Agriculture, hunting, forestry and fishing	147,724	103,400
Manufacturing	139,471	45,000
Electricity, gas and water	6,381	10,000
Construction	47,356	25,000
Trade, restaurants and hotels	129,716	78,000
Transport, storage and communications	45,529	20,500
Other services	227,921	171,000
Total	**744,098**	**452,900**

* Estimates.

1997 (provisional estimates at mid-year): Total employed 1,246,000; Unemployed 116,000; Total labour force 1,362,000.

Source: National Employment Office.

Mid-2005 (estimates in '000): Agriculture, etc. 35; Total labour force 1,337.

Source: FAO.

LEBANON

Health and Welfare

KEY INDICATORS

Total fertility rate (children per woman, 2005)	2.2
Under-5 mortality rate (per 1,000 live births, 2005)	30
HIV/AIDS (% of persons aged 15–49, 2005)	0.1
Physicians (per 1,000 head, 2003)	3.18
Hospital beds (per 1,000 head, 2005)	3.6
Health expenditure (2004): US $ per head (PPP)	816.5
Health expenditure (2004): % of GDP	11.6
Health expenditure (2004): public (% of total)	36.0
Access to sanitation (% of persons, 2004)	98
Human Development Index (2005): ranking	88
Human Development Index (2005): value	0.772

For sources and definitions, see explanatory note on p. vi.

Agriculture

PRINCIPAL CROPS
('000 metric tons)

	2004	2005	2006*
Wheat	137	144	144
Barley	24	29	29
Potatoes	499	511	511
Almonds	28*	28	28
Olives	83	90	90
Cabbages	91	80	80
Lettuce	32	29	29
Tomatoes	225	277	277
Cauliflower	37	31	31
Pumpkins, squash and gourds	24	24	24
Cucumbers and gherkins	159	131	131
Aubergines (Eggplants)	23	20	20
Dry onions	52	51	51
Garlic	4	3	3
Green beans	18	13	13
Carrots	9	11	11
Watermelons	86	74	74
Cantaloupes and other melons	9	6	6
Bananas	86	81	81
Oranges	234	236	236
Tangerines, mandarins, clementines and satsumas	40	32	32
Lemons and limes	107	113	113
Grapefruit and pomelos	15	12	12
Apples	113	115	115
Pears	37	37	37
Apricots	29	32	32
Sweet cherries	31	30	30
Peaches and nectarines	35	34	34
Plums	26	26	26
Strawberries	3	3	3
Grapes	123	111	111
Figs	10	7	7

* FAO estimate(s).

Aggregate production ('000 metric tons, may include official, semi-official or estimated data): Total cereals 165 in 2004, 177 in 2005, 177 in 2006; Total roots and tubers 500 in 2004, 512 in 2005, 512 in 2006; Total vegetables (incl. melons) 831 in 2004, 811 in 2005, 811 in 2006; Total fruits (excl. melons) 966 in 2004, 946 in 2005, 946 in 2006.

Source: FAO.

LIVESTOCK
('000 head, year ending September)

	2003	2004	2005
Horses*	6	6	6
Asses, mules or hinnies*	31	31	31
Cattle	86	80	77
Pigs	14	15*	15*
Sheep	303	305	337
Goats	428	432	495
Chickens*	34,000	35,000	35,000

* FAO estimate(s).

2006: Figures assumed to be unchanged from 2005 (FAO estimates).

Source: FAO.

LIVESTOCK PRODUCTS
('000 metric tons)

	2003	2004	2005
Cattle meat*	52.5	52.5	52.5
Sheep meat*	14.3	14.7	14.7
Goat meat*	2.6	2.7	2.7
Pig meat*	1.3	1.3	1.3
Chicken meat	127.2	131.3*	136.1*
Cows' milk	194.6	186.3	189.8
Sheep's milk	23.4	21.6	22.8
Goats' milk	36.5	36.1	39.3
Hen eggs	46.5	46.8*	47.1*
Wool: greasy*	1.8	1.9	2.0

* FAO estimate(s).

2006: Figures assumed to be unchanged from 2005 (FAO estimates).

Source: FAO.

Forestry

ROUNDWOOD REMOVALS
('000 cubic metres, excluding bark, FAO estimates)

	2004	2005	2006
Sawlogs, veneer logs and logs for sleepers*	7.2	7.2	7.2
Fuel wood	81.6	81.4	80.6
Total	88.7	88.5	87.8

* Assumed to be unchanged since 1992.

Source: FAO.

SAWNWOOD PRODUCTION
('000 cubic metres, including railway sleepers)

	1991	1992	1993
Total (all broadleaved)	10.9	9.1	9.1*

* FAO estimate.

1994–2006: Figures assumed to be unchanged from 1993 (FAO estimates).

Source: FAO.

LEBANON

Fishing

(metric tons, live weight)

	2003	2004	2005
Capture	3,898	3,866	3,798
Groupers and seabasses	265	245	250
Porgies and seabreams	370	365	370
Surmullets (Red mullets)	200	200	190
Barracudas	250	250	240
Mullets	365	360	365
Scorpionfishes	125	125	110
Carangids	400	400	380
Clupeoids	600	600	580
Tuna-like fishes	400	400	385
Mackerel-like fishes	300	300	320
Marine crustaceans	60	60	55
Aquaculture	790	790	803
Rainbow trout	700	700	708
Total catch	**4,688**	**4,656**	**4,601**

Source: FAO.

Mining

('000 metric tons)

	2004	2005*	2006*
Salt (unrefined)*	5	5	5
Phosphoric acid	175	180	180

* Estimated production.

Source: US Geological Survey.

Industry

SELECTED PRODUCTS
('000 metric tons, unless otherwise indicated)

	2003	2004	2005
Olive oil, virgin*†	6.5	7.5	7.0
Sunflower seed oil*†	3.7	5.2	2.3
Wine*‡	15.0	15.0	15.0
Beer of barley*‡	15.4	24.1	24.1
Plywood ('000 cubic metres)*‡	34	34	34
Paper*‡	100	103	103
Cement§‖	3,500	4,000	4,500
Sulphuric acid (gross weight)§	485	495	500

* Source: FAO.
† Unofficial figures.
‡ FAO estimates.
§ Source: US Geological Survey.
‖ Estimates.

2006 ('000 metric tons, estimates): Cement 5,000; Sulphuric acid (gross weight) 500 (Source: US Geological Survey).

Electric energy (million kWh): 10,547 in 2003; 10,192 in 2004 (Source: UN, *Industrial Commodity Statistics Yearbook*).

Finance

CURRENCY AND EXCHANGE RATES

Monetary Units
100 piastres = 1 Lebanese pound (£L).

Sterling, Dollar and Euro Equivalents (30 November 2007)
£1 sterling = £L3,115.1;
US $1 = £L1,507.5;
€1 = £L2,225.2;
£L10,000 = £3.21 sterling = $6.63 = €4.49.

Exchange Rate: The official exchange rate has been maintained at US $1 = £L1,507.5 since September 1999.

BUDGET
(£L '000 million)*

Revenue	2005	2006	2007†
Tax revenue	4,867	4,922	5,347
Taxes on income, profits and capital gains	1,047	1,166	1,200
Taxes on property	414	579	441
Domestic taxes on goods and services	1,896	2,457	2,942
Taxes on international trade and transactions	1,268	461	493
Other taxes	241	259	271
Other current revenue	2,117	1,945	2,328
Income from public enterprises	1,663	1,428	1,843
Administrative fees and charges	365	426	393
Fines and confiscations	4	4	4
Other	85	87	88
Total	**6,984**	**6,867**	**7,675**

Expenditure	2005	2006	2007†
Personnel costs	3,193	3,307	3,803
Salaries and wages	2,129	2,188	2,588
Interest payments and financial charges	3,534	4,557	4,900
Materials and supplies	213	140	315
External services	82	87	120
Subsidies and transfers	827	756	1,664
Reserves	75	80	162
Acquisitions of land, buildings, for the construction of roads, ports, airports and water networks	15	12	9
Equipment	25	25	45
Construction in progress	413	435	412
Maintenance	46	48	92
Other expenditures related to fixed capital assets	35	32	44
Total	**8,459**	**9,478**	**11,566**
Current	7,925	8,927	10,964
Capital	534	551	601

* Figures, which are rounded, represent the consolidated operations of the central Government's General Budget and the Council for Development and Reconstruction. The accounts of other central government units with individual budgets (including the general social security scheme) are excluded.
† Budget proposals.

Source: Ministry of Finance.

INTERNATIONAL RESERVES
(US $ million at 31 December)

	2004	2005	2006
Gold (national valuation)	4,006.0	4,736.4	5,807.3
IMF special drawing rights	32.9	31.4	34.9
Reserve position in IMF	29.2	26.9	28.3
Foreign exchange	11,672.4	11,828.7	13,313.3
Total	**15,740.5**	**16,623.4**	**19,183.8**

Source: IMF, *International Financial Statistics*.

LEBANON

MONEY SUPPLY
(£L '000 million at 31 December)

	2004	2005	2006
Currency outside banks	1,586.5	1,534.7	1,809.2
Demand deposits at commercial banks	1,389.3	1,358.5	1,450.0
Total money (incl. others)	3,030.6	2,893.2	3,321.7

Sources: IMF, *International Financial Statistics*.

COST OF LIVING
(Consumer Price Index for Beirut; base: December 1998 = 100)

	2005	2006	2007
Food and beverages	97.8	109.5	125.7
Water, electricity and gas	124.7	121.6	147.0
Clothing and footwear	124.9	126.5	127.6
Transport and communications	140.4	148.7	153.8
All items (incl. others)	107.5	113.5	124.1

NATIONAL ACCOUNTS
(US $ million at current prices, UN estimates)

Expenditure on the Gross Domestic Product

	2002	2003	2004
Government final consumption expenditure	3,187.4	3,348.6	3,600.6
Private final consumption expenditure	15,621.2	16,411.9	17,646.4
Increase in stocks / Gross fixed capital formation	3,395.0	3,566.8	3,834.8
Total domestic expenditure	22,203.6	23,327.3	25,081.8
Exports of goods and services	2,927.3	3,075.3	3,306.8
Less Imports of goods and services	6,668.6	7,006.3	7,533.0
GDP in purchasers' values	18,462.3	19,396.3	20,855.7
GDP at constant 1995 prices	17,050.4	17,561.7	18,439.7

Gross Domestic Product by Economic Activity

	2002	2003	2004
Agriculture, hunting, forestry and fishing	1,075.9	1,130.3	1,215.2
Manufacturing	2,154.5	2,263.3	2,433.8
Electricity, gas and water	179.7	188.4	202.9
Construction	1,422.2	1,493.8	1,605.9
Trade, restaurants and hotels	7,349.9	7,722.0	8,302.5
Transport, storage and communications	1,197.3	1,257.7	1,352.5
Finance and insurance	1,218.5	1,280.2	1,376.4
Real estate and business services	1,535.6	1,613.2	1,734.6
Government services	2,328.3	2,447.1	2,631.5
Statistical discrepancy	0.4	0.3	0.4
GDP in purchasers' values	18,462.3	19,396.3	20,855.7

Source: UN Economic and Social Commission for Western Asia, *National Accounts Studies of the ESCWA Region*.

BALANCE OF PAYMENTS
(US $ million)

	2004	2005	2006
Exports of goods f.o.b.	2,050	2,278	2,792
Imports of goods f.o.b.	−8,502	−8,397	−8,547
Trade balance	−6,452	−6,118	−5,755
Exports of services	9,704	10,858	11,611
Imports of services	−8,230	−7,895	−8,708
Balance on goods and services	−4,978	−3,155	−2,852
Other income received	1,060	1,733	2,060
Other income paid	−1,877	−1,910	−1,849
Balance on goods, services and income	−5,795	−3,332	−2,641
Current transfers received	5,325	4,399	5,033
Current transfers paid	−3,609	−3,337	−3,876

—*continued*	2004	2005	2006
Current balance	−4,079	−2,270	−1,484
Capital account (net)	50	27	1,925
Direct investment abroad	−213	−122	−71
Direct investment from abroad	1,993	2,751	2,794
Portfolio investment assets	−614	−111	−188
Portfolio investment liabilities	−93	648	1,308
Other investment assets	3,864	3,658	−1,492
Other investment liabilities	1,214	48	821
Net errors and omissions	−2,902	−4,173	−3,466
Overall balance	−780	458	146

Source: IMF, *International Financial Statistics*.

External Trade

PRINCIPAL COMMODITIES
(US $ million)*

Imports c.i.f.	2004	2005	2006
Live animals and animal products	452.6	427.6	443.7
Vegetable products	440.9	383.8	365.8
Prepared foodstuffs; beverages, spirits and vinegar; tobacco and manufactured substitutes	527.0	530.2	534.2
Mineral products	2,068.1	2,226.1	2,412.6
Products of chemical or allied industries	828.5	819.7	886.8
Plastics, rubber and articles thereof	349.3	356.6	360.6
Textiles and textile articles	507.9	486.1	464.3
Natural or cultured pearls, precious or semi-precious stones, precious metals and articles thereof; imitation jewellery; coin	526.8	491.5	290.9
Base metals and articles thereof	596.1	650.7	682.2
Machinery and mechanical appliances; electrical equipment; sound and television apparatus	1,109.1	1,060.5	1,123.3
Vehicles, aircraft, vessels and associated transport equipment	843.4	809.3	764.3
Total (incl. others)	9,397.0	9,339.9	9,397.6

Exports f.o.b.	2004	2005	2006
Vegetable products	82.5	76.5	80.3
Prepared foodstuffs; beverages, spirits and vinegar; tobacco and manufactured substitutes	148.1	191.1	187.1
Products of chemical or allied industries	149.2	162.7	162.4
Textiles and textile articles	78.0	81.5	87.3
Natural or cultured pearls, precious or semi-precious stones, precious metals and articles thereof; imitation jewellery; coin	287.1	223.6	554.6
Base metals and articles thereof	227.9	275.8	320.8
Machinery and mechanical appliances; electrical equipment; sound and television apparatus	274.0	314.3	333.6
Total (incl. others)	1,747.0	1,879.8	2,282.5

* Figures are calculated on the basis of the official dollar rate, which is the previous month's average exchange rate of Lebanese pounds per US dollar.

Source: Ministry of Economy and Trade.

LEBANON

PRINCIPAL TRADING PARTNERS
(US $ million)*

Imports c.i.f.	2002	2003	2004
Belgium	207.0	156.3	170.0
China, People's Republic	435.0	530.7	717.8
Egypt	134.4	174.4	294.9
France	779.5	582.9	730.7
Germany	878.4	579.0	729.3
Greece	109.3	83.1	68.6
India	107.0	84.4	114.1
Indonesia	n.a.	40.3	52.3
Italy	1,045.2	674.3	930.5
Japan	327.8	269.1	349.2
Korea, Republic	76.9	79.0	103.0
Malaysia	n.a.	54.4	67.6
Netherlands	222.1	229.8	171.5
Russia	370.8	321.2	542.5
Saudi Arabia	138.9	219.6	413.5
Spain	263.3	198.3	189.7
Switzerland	402.8	216.2	395.8
Syria	312.5	207.2	240.0
Taiwan	63.2	54.5	75.9
Thailand	63.0	65.7	92.4
Turkey	258.7	234.1	258.2
Ukraine	102.2	166.6	145.9
United Kingdom	252.6	315.5	385.6
USA	464.5	431.5	553.2
Total (incl. others)	6,444.8	7,168.2	9,397.0

Exports f.o.b.	2002	2003	2004
Belgium	33.7	10.4	16.5
Canada	n.a.	7.4	7.3
Cyprus	n.a.	12.9	14.2
Egypt	27.6	28.0	39.8
France	29.7	24.0	35.0
Germany	14.1	20.2	22.8
Greece	10.9	5.4	8.4
India	14.3	13.8	27.3
Iraq	71.1	121.8	255.5
Italy	22.7	28.5	18.7
Jordan	35.3	48.4	62.8
Kuwait	32.4	50.8	67.4
Malta	18.0	14.0	7.9
Netherlands	15.6	13.4	11.1
Saudi Arabia	96.0	104.3	112.8
Spain	16.7	16.4	11.1
Switzerland	132.1	379.1	187.3
Syria	75.6	99.5	145.2
Turkey	32.1	63.3	127.3
United Arab Emirates	94.7	104.4	135.2
United Kingdom	20.7	16.1	21.3
USA	53.5	66.2	48.5
Total (incl. others)	1,045.5	1,523.9	1,747.0

* Imports by country of production; exports by country of last consignment.

Source: Ministry of Economy and Trade.

2005 (US $ million): *Imports c.i.f.:* Belgium 175.1; Brazil 159.9; China, People's Republic 734.4; Egypt 303.4; France 788.1; Germany 657.3; India 139.4; Italy 975.7; Japan 307.0; Netherlands 152.1; Russia 509.1; Saudi Arabia 329.0; Spain 167.7; Switzerland 422.3; Syria 196.1; Turkey 199.6; United Arab Emirates 136.8; United Kingdom 323.2; USA 547.7; Total (incl. others) 9,339.9. *Exports c.i.f.:* Bahrain 21.5; Belgium 23.0; China, People's Republic 26.0; Egypt 54.6; France 32.1; Germany 18.3; India 20.4; Iran 25.8; Iraq 178.4; Jordan 75.2; Kuwait 81.2; Nigeria 27.0; Qatar 36.2; Saudi Arabia 139.8; Switzerland 125.1; Syria 187.4; Turkey 121.6; United Arab Emirates 155.0; United Kingdom 28.8; USA 57.6; Total (incl. others) 1,879.8

2006 (US $ million): *Imports c.i.f.:* Belgium 153.6; Brazil 227.1; China, People's Republic 751.6; Egypt 379.1; France 761.1; Germany 659.9; India 117.8; Italy 710.0; Japan 285.0; Netherlands 150.0; Russia 260.7; Saudi Arabia 296.4; Spain 148.9; Switzerland 212.0; Syria 178.0; Turkey 257.8; United Arab Emirates 132.1; United Kingdom 406.7; USA 1,016.0; Total (incl. others) 9,397.6. *Exports c.i.f.:* Bahrain 20.1; Belgium 46.8; China, People's Republic 45.6; Egypt 47.9; France 39.1; Germany 22.2; India 12.0; Iran 36.1; Iraq 136.3; Jordan 84.2; Kuwait 82.5; Nigeria 33.8; Qatar 63.8; Saudi Arabia 146.2; Switzerland 451.0; Syria 175.7; Turkey 102.3; United Arab Emirates 176.2; United Kingdom 31.5; USA 52.6; Total (incl. others) 1,856.0.

Transport

ROAD TRAFFIC
(motor vehicles in use)

	1995	1996*	1997*
Passenger cars (incl. taxis)	1,197,521	1,217,000	1,299,398
Buses and coaches	5,514	5,640	6,833
Lorries and vans	79,222	81,000	85,242
Motorcycles and mopeds	53,317	54,450	61,471

* Estimates.

Source: International Road Federation, *World Road Statistics*.

Passenger cars ('000, incl. taxis): 1,370.6 in 1999; 1,370.8 in 2000; 1,370.9 in 2001 (Source: UN, *Statistical Yearbook*).

SHIPPING

Merchant Fleet
(registered at 31 December)

	2004	2005	2006
Number of vessels	79	76	65
Total displacement ('000 grt)	184.1	399.5	157.0

Source: Lloyd's Register-Fairplay, *World Fleet Statistics*.

International Sea-borne Freight Traffic
('000 metric tons)

	1988	1989	1990
Goods loaded	148	150	152
Goods unloaded	1,120	1,140	1,150

Source: UN, *Monthly Bulletin of Statistics*.

2002 ('000 metric tons, Beirut port only): Goods loaded 393; Goods unloaded 4,827.

2003 ('000 metric tons, Beirut port only): Goods loaded 499; Goods unloaded 4,306.

2004 ('000 metric tons, Beirut port only): Goods loaded 727; Goods unloaded 4,334.

CIVIL AVIATION
(traffic on scheduled services)

	2001	2002	2003
Kilometres flown (million)	20	20	20
Passengers carried ('000)	816	874	935
Passenger-km (million)	1,658	1,749	1,905
Total ton-km (million)	229	244	253

Source: UN, *Statistical Yearbook*.

Tourism

FOREIGN TOURIST ARRIVALS
('000)*

Country of nationality	2003	2004	2005
Australia	31.9	45.9	38.6
Canada	43.1	52.4	48.5
Egypt	39.0	46.1	34.3
France	76.4	94.3	80.5
Germany	37.9	48.4	51.9
Iran	70.4	89.8	92.9
Italy	13.1	15.6	14.1
Jordan	87.8	92.8	135.2
Kuwait	56.0	79.8	64.2
Saudi Arabia	162.2	200.9	124.7
Sri Lanka	17.1	22.1	20.4
United Kingdom	28.0	34.5	35.5
USA	60.1	78.8	68.4
Total (incl. others)	1,015.8	1,278.5	1,139.5

* Figures exclude arrivals of Syrian nationals, Palestinians and students.

Tourism receipts (US $ million, incl. passenger transport): 6,782 in 2003; 5,931 in 2004; 5,869 in 2005.

Source: World Tourism Organization.

Communications Media

	2004	2005	2006
Telephones ('000 main lines in use)	630.0	634.7	681.4
Mobile cellular telephones ('000 subscribers)	888.0	993.6	1,103.4
Personal computers ('000 in use)	400	409	n.a.
Internet users ('000)	600	700	950
Broadband subscribers ('000)	80	130	170

Radio receivers ('000 in use): 2,850 in 1997.

Facsimile machines (number in use): 3,000 in 1992.

Television receivers ('000 in use): 1,170 in 2000.

Daily newspapers (number of titles): 13 in 2000.

Daily newspapers (total average circulation, estimates, '000 copies): 220 in 2000.

Non-daily newspapers (number of titles): 7 in 2000.

Book production (number of titles): 289 in 1998.

Sources: UNESCO Institute for Statistics; UNESCO, *Statistical Yearbook*; UN, *Statistical Yearbook*; and International Telecommunication Union.

Education

(2004/05, unless otherwise indicated)

	Institutions	Teachers	Students
Pre-primary	1,938*	9,435	145,453
Primary	2,160*	31,752	452,607
Secondary:			
general	n.a.	30,062	313,729
vocational	275†	11,210	48,637
Higher	n.a.	20,764	165,730

* 1996/97 figure.
† 1994 figure.

Sources: UNESCO Institute for Statistics; Banque du Liban, *Annual Report*.

Adult literacy rate (UNESCO estimates): 86.5% (males 92.4%; females 81.0%) in 2001 (Source: UN Development Programme, *Human Development Report*).

Directory

The Constitution

The Constitution was promulgated on 23 May 1926 and amended by the Constitutional Laws of 1927, 1929, 1943, 1947 and 1990.

According to the Constitution, the Republic of Lebanon is an independent and sovereign state, and no part of the territory may be alienated or ceded. Lebanon has no state religion. Arabic is the official language. Beirut is the capital.

All Lebanese are equal in the eyes of the law. Personal freedom and freedom of the press are guaranteed and protected. The religious communities are entitled to maintain their own schools, on condition that they conform to the general requirements relating to public instruction, as defined by the state. Dwellings are inviolable; rights of ownership are protected by law. Every Lebanese citizen over 21 is an elector and qualifies for the franchise.

LEGISLATIVE POWER

Legislative power is exercised by one house, the National Assembly, with 108 seats (raised, without amendment of the Constitution, to 128 in 1992), which are divided equally between Christians and Muslims. Members of the National Assembly must be over 25 years of age, in possession of their full political and civil rights, and literate. They are considered representative of the whole nation, and are not bound to follow directives from their constituencies. They can be suspended only by a two-thirds' majority of their fellow members. Secret ballot was introduced in a new election law of April 1960.

The National Assembly holds two sessions yearly, from the first Tuesday after 15 March to the end of May, and from the first Tuesday after 15 October to the end of the year. The normal term of the National Assembly is four years; general elections take place within 60 days before the end of this period. If the Assembly is dissolved before the end of its term, elections are held within three months of dissolution.

Voting in the Assembly is public—by acclamation, or by standing and sitting. A quorum of two-thirds and a majority vote is required for constitutional issues. The only exceptions to this occur when the Assembly becomes an electoral college, and chooses the President of the Republic or Secretaries to the National Assembly, or when the President is accused of treason or of violating the Constitution. In such cases voting is secret, and a two-thirds' majority is needed for a proposal to be adopted.

EXECUTIVE POWER

With the incorporation of the Ta'if agreement into the Lebanese Constitution in August 1990, executive power was effectively transferred from the presidency to the Cabinet. The President is elected for a term of six years and is not immediately re-eligible. He is responsible for the promulgation and execution of laws enacted by the National Assembly, but all presidential decisions (with the exception of those to appoint a Prime Minister or to accept the resignation of a government) require the co-signature of the Prime Minister, who is head of the Government, implementing its policies and speaking in its name. The President must receive the approval of the Cabinet before dismissing a minister or ratifying an international treaty. The ministers and the Prime Minister are chosen by the President of the Republic in consultation with the members and President of the National Assembly. They are not necessarily members of the National Assembly, although they are responsible to it and have access to its debates. The President of the Republic must be a Maronite Christian, and the Prime Minister a Sunni Muslim; the choice of the other ministers must reflect the level of representation of the communities in the Assembly.

Note: In October 1998 the National Assembly endorsed an exceptional amendment to Article 49 of the Constitution to enable the election of Gen. Emile Lahoud, then Commander-in-Chief of the Army, as President of the Republic: the Constitution requires that senior state officials relinquish their responsibilities two years prior to seeking public office. In September 2004 the National Assembly voted in favour of a constitutional amendment extending President Lahoud's term of office for a further three years.

The Government

HEAD OF STATE

President: (vacant).

Note: Gen. Emile Lahoud's extended term of office expired at the end of 23 November 2007. Since the National Assembly had failed to elect a successor by this date, presidential duties were assumed by the Cabinet of Prime Minister Fouad Siniora in an acting capacity.

CABINET
(April 2008)

Prime Minister: Fouad Siniora.

Deputy Prime Minister and Minister of National Defence: Elias Murr.

Minister of the Interior and Municipalities: Hassan as-Sabaa.

Minister of Justice: Charles Rizq.

Minister of Industry: (vacant).

Minister of Energy and Water: (vacant).

Minister of Public Works and Transport: Muhammad as-Safadi.

Minister of Finance: Jihad Azour.

Minister of Economy and Trade: Sami Haddad.

Minister of Education and Higher Education: Khalid Qabbani.

Minister of Culture and Acting Minister of Foreign Affairs and Emigrants: Tariq Mitri.

Minister of Information: Ghazi al-Aridi.

Minister of Tourism: Joseph Sarkis.

Minister of Telecommunications: Marwan Hamadeh.

Minister of Labour: (vacant).

LEBANON

Minister of Agriculture: (vacant).
Minister of the Environment: (vacant).
Minister of Public Health: (vacant).
Minister of Social Affairs: NAYLA MOUAWAD.
Minister of the Displaced: NEHME TOHME.
Minister of Youth and Sports: AHMAD FATFAT.
Minister of State for Administrative Reform: JEAN OGHASABIAN.
Minister of State for Parliamentary Affairs: MICHEL FAROUN.

MINISTRIES

Presidency of the Lebanese Republic: POB 40001, Presidential Palace, Baabda, Beirut; tel. (5) 920900; fax (5) 922400; e-mail president_office@presidency.gov.lb; internet www.presidency.gov.lb.

Office of the President of the Council of Ministers: Grand Sérail, place Riad es-Solh, Beirut; tel. (1) 746800; fax (1) 865630; internet www.pcm.gov.lb.

Ministry of Agriculture: Embassies St, Bir Hassan, Beirut; tel. (1) 849600; fax (1) 849620; e-mail ministry@agriculture.gov.lb; internet www.agriculture.gov.lb.

Ministry of Culture: Immeuble Hatab, rue Madame Curie, Verdun, Beirut; tel. (1) 744250; fax (1) 756303; e-mail omarhala_48@hotmail.com; internet www.culture.gov.lb.

Ministry of the Displaced: Minet el-Hosn, Starco Centre, Beirut; tel. (1) 366373; fax (1) 503040; e-mail mod@dm.net.lb.

Ministry of Economy and Trade: rue Artois, Hamra, Beirut; tel. (1) 982292; fax (1) 982293; e-mail sdabaghy@economy.gov.lb; internet www.economy.gov.lb.

Ministry of Education and Higher Education: Unesco Quarter, Habib Abi Chahla, Beirut; tel. (1) 789611; fax (1) 789606; e-mail info@higher-edu.gov.lb; internet www.higher-edu.gov.lb.

Ministry of Energy and Water: Beirut River Highway, Beirut; tel. (1) 565100; e-mail mew@terra.net.lb; internet www.energyandwater.gov.lb.

Ministry of the Environment: POB 11-2727, 7th and 8th Floors, Lazarieh Centre, Beirut; tel. (1) 976555; fax (1) 976530; e-mail webmaster@moe.gov.lb; internet www.moe.gov.lb.

Ministry of Finance: 4e étage, Immeuble MOF, place Riad es-Solh, Beirut; tel. (1) 981001; fax (1) 981059; e-mail infocenter@finance.gov.lb; internet www.finance.gov.lb.

Ministry of Foreign Affairs and Emigrants: rue Sursock, Achrafieh, Beirut; tel. (1) 333100; e-mail info@emigrants.gov.lb; internet www.emigrants.gov.lb.

General Directorate of Emigrants: Immeuble as-Sultan, Jnah, Beirut; tel. (1) 840921; fax (1) 840924; e-mail director@emigrants.gov.lb; internet www.emigrants.gov.lb.

Ministry of Industry: Ministry of Industry and Oil Bldg, ave Sami Solh, Beirut; tel. (1) 423338; fax (1) 427112; e-mail ministry@industry.gov.lb; internet www.industry.gov.lb.

Ministry of Information: rue Hamra, Beirut; tel. (1) 754400.

Ministry of the Interior and Municipalities: Grand Sérail, place Riad es-Solh, Beirut; tel. (1) 751613; e-mail ministry@interior.gov.lb; internet www.moim.gov.lb.

Ministry of Justice: rue Sami Solh, Beirut; tel. (1) 422944; e-mail info@justice.gov.lb; internet www.justice.gov.lb.

Ministry of Labour: Shiah, Beirut; tel. (1) 274140.

Ministry of National Defence: Yarze, Beirut; tel. (5) 420000; fax (5) 951035; e-mail ministry@lebarmy.gov.lb; internet www.lebarmy.gov.lb.

Ministry of Public Health: Hussein Mansour Bldg, Museum St, Beirut; tel. (1) 615775; fax (1) 615771; e-mail ministry@public-health.gov.lb; internet www.public-health.gov.lb.

Ministry of Public Works and Transport: Shiah, Beirut; tel. (1) 428980.

Ministry of State for Administrative Reform: Immeuble Starco, rue Omar Daouk, Beirut; tel. (1) 371510; fax (1) 371599; e-mail webmaster@omsar.gov.lb; internet www.omsar.gov.lb.

Ministry of Telecommunications: 1st Floor, Ministry of Telecom Bldg, place Riad es-Solh, Beirut; tel. (1) 979161; fax (1) 979164; e-mail webmaster@mpt.gov.lb; internet www.mpt.gov.lb.

Ministry of Tourism: POB 11-5344, rue Banque du Liban 550, Beirut; tel. (1) 340940; fax (1) 340945; internet www.destinationlebanon.gov.lb.

Ministry of Youth and Sports: rue Sami Solh, Beirut; tel. (1) 425770; fax (1) 424387; e-mail minijes@cyberia.net.lb.

Legislature

MAJLIS AN-NUAB
(National Assembly)

The equal distribution of seats among Christians and Muslims is determined by law, and the Cabinet must reflect the level of representation achieved by the various religious denominations within that principal division. Deputies of the same religious denomination do not necessarily share the same political or party allegiances. The distribution of seats is as follows: Maronite Catholics 34; Sunni Muslims 27; Shi'a Muslims 27; Greek Orthodox 14; Druzes 8; Greek-Melkite Catholics 8; Armenian Orthodox 5; Alawites 2; Armenian Catholics 1; Protestants 1; Others 1.

President: NABIH BERRI.
Vice-President: ELIE FERZLI.
General election, 29 May–19 June 2005

Party list	Seats
Rafik Hariri Martyr List*	72
Resistance and Development Bloc†	35
Free Patriotic Movement‡	21
Total	128

* Electoral list comprising the Future Movement (which won 36 seats), Parti socialiste progressiste (16), Lebanese Forces Party (6), Qornet Shehwan Gathering (6), Tripoli Bloc (3), Democratic Renewal (1), Democratic Left (1) and independents (3).
† Election list comprising Amal (which won 15 seats), Hezbollah (14), the Syrian Social Nationalist Party (2) and others (4).
‡ Election list comprising the Free Patriotic Movement itself (which won 14 seats), the Skaff bloc (5) and the Murr bloc (2).

Political Organizations

Amal (Hope—Afwaj al-Muqawamah al-Lubnaniyyah—Lebanese Resistance Detachments): e-mail post@amal-movement.com; internet www.amal-movement.com; f. 1975 as a politico-military organization; Shi'ite political party; contested 2005 legislative elections with Hezbollah as Resistance and Development Bloc; Leader NABIH BERRI.

Armenian Revolutionary Federation (ARF) (Tashnag): rue Spears, Beirut; f. 1890; principal Armenian party; historically the dominant nationalist party in the independent Armenian Republic of Yerevan of 1917–21, prior to its becoming part of the USSR; socialist ideology; collective leadership.

Al-Baath (Baath Arab Socialist Party): Beirut; f. 1948; local branch of secular pro-Syrian party with policy of Arab union; Leader ASSEM QANSO.

Al-Baath (Baath Arab Socialist Party): f. 1966, following split in Syrian branch of Al-Baath; part of pro-Iraqi faction of Al-Baath; Sec.-Gen. ABD AL-MAJID RAFEI.

Bloc national libanais (National Bloc): rue Pasteur, Gemmayze, Beirut; tel. (1) 584585; fax (1) 584591; f. 1943; right-wing Lebanese party with policy of power-sharing between Christians and Muslims and the exclusion of the military from politics; Pres. CARLOS EDEH.

Free Patriotic Movement (Tayar al-Watani al-Horr): Beirut; tel. (3) 122858; e-mail info@tayyar.org; internet www.tayyar.org/tayyar/index.php; aims to recover sovereignty and complete independence for Lebanon; majority of leaders and supporters are from the Christian community; contested 2005 legislative elections in alliance with the Skaff and Murr blocs; Leader Gen. MICHEL AWN.

Future Movement (Tayar al-Mustaqbal): Beirut; opposed to Syrian influence in Lebanese affairs; contested 2005 legislative elections on the Rafik Hariri Martyr List with the Qornet Shehwan Gathering, Lebanese Forces Party and Parti socialiste progressiste; Leader SAAD ED-DIN HARIRI.

Hezbollah (Party of God): Beirut; e-mail info@moqawama.net; internet www.moqawama.org; f. 1982 by Iranian Revolutionary Guards who were sent to Lebanon; militant Shi'ite faction, which has become the leading organization of Lebanon's Shi'a community and a recognized political party; demands the withdrawal of Israeli forces from the occupied Shebaa Farms area of what it considers to be southern Lebanon (but which is designated by the UN as being part of Syria) and the release of all Lebanese prisoners from Israeli detention; contested 2005 legislative elections with Amal as Resistance and Development Bloc, and achieved parliamentary and govt representation; Chair. MUHAMMAD RA'D; Leader and Sec.-Gen. Sheikh HASAN NASRALLAH; Spiritual Leader Ayatollah MUHAMMAD HUSSAIN FADLALLAH.

Al-Kataeb (Phalanges libanaises—Phalangist Party): POB 992, place Charles Hélou, Beirut; tel. (1) 584107; e-mail admin@kataeb

.com; internet www.lebanese-kataeb.com; f. 1936 by the late Pierre Gemayel; nationalist, reformist, democratic social party; largest Maronite party; mem. of the Qornet Shehwan Gathering; 100,000 mems; Supreme Pres. AMIN GEMAYEL; Pres. KARIM PAKRADOUNI.

National Lebanese Front: Beirut; f. 1999; Pres. ERNEST KARAM.

Parti communiste libanais (Lebanese Communist Party—PCL): rue Al-Bahatri, Al-Watuat, Beirut; tel. and fax (1) 739615; e-mail lcparty@lcparty.org; internet www.lcparty.org; f. 1924; officially dissolved 1948–71; Marxist, with much support among intellectuals; Pres. MAURICE NOHRA; Sec.-Gen. KHALID HADDADEH.

Parti socialiste progressiste (At-Takadumi al-Ishteraki—PSP): POB 11-2893, Beirut 1107 2120; tel. (1) 303455; fax (1) 301231; e-mail secretary@psp.org.lb; internet www.psp.org.lb; f. 1949; progressive party, advocates constitutional road to socialism and democracy; over 25,000 mems; mainly Druze support; contested 2005 legislative elections as part of the Rafik Hariri Martyr List; Pres. WALID JOUMBLATT; Sec.-Gen. SHARIF FAYAD.

Qornet Shehwan Gathering: f. 2001; Christian coalition of parties of diverse political persuasions and incorporating Maronite (incl. Al-Kataeb), Orthodox and Greek Catholic mems; advocates full national sovereignty for Lebanon; supports the establishment of a Palestinian state; rejects violence as a means of solving disputes; contested 2005 legislative elections as part of the Rafik Hariri Martyr List; Maronite Christian Patriarch Cardinal NASRALLAH BOUTROS (PIERRE) SFEIR is the group's unofficial patron.

Resistance and Development Bloc: electoral bloc consisting principally of Amal and Hezbollah; the two parties contested the 2000 and, with the Syrian Social Nationalist Party, 2005 legislative elections as this alliance; Leader NABIH BERRI.

Syrian Social Nationalist Party (al-Hizb as-Suri al-Qawmi al-Ijtima'i): e-mail administrator@ssnp.com; internet www.ssnp.com; f. 1932 in Beirut; banned 1962–69; seeks creation of a 'Greater Syrian' state, incl. Lebanon, Syria, Iraq, Jordan, the Palestinian territories, Kuwait, Cyprus and parts of Egypt, Iran and Turkey; advocates separation of church and state, the redistribution of wealth and a strong military; supports Syrian involvement in Lebanese affairs; contested 2005 legislative elections as mem. of the Resistance and Development Bloc (consisting principally of Amal and Hezbollah); Leader JIBRAN ARAIJI.

Al-Wa'ad (National Secular Democratic Party—Pledge): Beirut; f. 1986 by the late Elie Hobeika; pro-Syrian splinter group of Lebanese Forces (see below).

Other parties include the **Independent Nasserite Movement** (Murabitoun; Sunni Muslim Militia; Leader IBRAHIM QULAYAT) and the **Lebanese Popular Congress** (Pres. KAMAL SHATILA). The **Nasserite Popular Organization** and the **Arab Socialist Union** merged in January 1987, retaining the name of the former. The **Islamic Amal** is a breakaway group from Amal, based in Ba'albak (Ba'albek) (Leader HUSSEIN MOUSSAVI). **Islamic Jihad** (Islamic Holy War) is a pro-Iranian fundamentalist guerrilla group (Leader IMAAD MOUGNIEH). The **Popular Liberation Army** (f. 1985 by the late MUSTAFA SAAD) is a Sunni Muslim faction, active in the south of Lebanon. **Tawhid Islami** (the Islamic Unification Movement; f. 1982; Sunni Muslim) and the **Arab Democratic Party** (or the Red Knights; Alawites; pro-Syrian; Leader ALI EID) are based in Tripoli.

The **Lebanese Forces Party** (f. 1990; www.lebanese-forces.org), the political successor to the **Lebanese Forces (LF)** (f. 1976; coalition of Maronite militias), is still active in Lebanon, despite proscription by the Government in 1994. Its leader, SAMIR GEAGEA, was imprisoned in 1995 on murder charges, but was pardoned and released in 2005.

Diplomatic Representation

EMBASSIES IN LEBANON

Algeria: POB 4794, face Hôtel Summerland, rue Jnah, Beirut; tel. (1) 826712; fax (1) 826711; Ambassador AHMAD BOUTEHRI.

Argentina: 2nd Floor, Residence des Jardins, Immeuble Moutran, 161 rue Sursock, Achrafieh, Beirut; tel. (1) 210800; fax (1) 210802; e-mail elbno@mrecic.gov.ar; Chargé d'affaires a.i. GUILLERMO LUIS NICOLÁS.

Armenia: POB 70607, rue Jasmin, Rabieh, Mtaileb, Beirut; tel. (4) 402952; fax (4) 418860; e-mail armenia@dm.net.lb; Ambassador VAHAN TER-GHEVONDYAN.

Australia: Embassy Complex, Semail Hill, Beirut; tel. (1) 974030; fax (1) 974029; e-mail austemle@dfat.gov.au; internet www.lebanon.embassy.gov.au; Ambassador LYNDALL SACHS.

Austria: POB 11-3942, 8th Floor, Immeuble Tabaris, 812 ave Charles Malek, Achrafieh, Beirut; tel. (1) 217360; fax (1) 217772; e-mail beirut-ob@bmeia.gv.at; Chargé d'affaires a.i. GERHARD LUTZ.

Bahrain: Sheikh Ahmed ath-Thani Bldg, Raoucheh, Beirut; tel. (1) 805495; Ambassador MUHAMMAD BAHLOUL.

Belgium: POB 11-1600, Riad es-Solh, Beirut; tel. (1) 976001; fax (1) 976007; e-mail beirut@diplobel.org; internet www.diplomatie.be/beirut; Ambassador STÉPHANE DE LOECKER.

Brazil: POB 40242, Baabda, Beirut; tel. (5) 921255; fax (5) 923001; e-mail braemlib@dm.net.lb; Ambassador EDUARDO AUGUSTO IBIAPINA DE SEIXAS.

Bulgaria: POB 11-6544, Immeuble Hibri, rue de l'Australie 55, Raouche, Beirut; tel. (1) 452883; fax (1) 452892; Ambassador VANELIN DIMITROV LAZAROV.

Canada: POB 60163, 1e étage, Immeuble Coolrite, Autostrade Jal ed-Dib 43, Beirut; tel. (4) 713900; fax (4) 710595; e-mail berut.webmaster@dfait-maeci.gc.ca; internet www.dfait-maeci.gc.ca/beirut; Ambassador LOUIS DE LORIMIER.

Chile: Nouvelle Naccache, 21 Bifurcation après La Belle Antique avant Carpacio, Beirut; tel. (4) 418670; fax (4) 418672; e-mail echilelb@dm.net.lb; Ambassador FELIPE DU MONCEAU DE BERGENDAL.

China, People's Republic: POB 11-8227, 72 rue Nicolas Ibrahim Sursock, Ramletbaida, Beirut 1107 2260; tel. (1) 850314; fax (1) 822492; e-mail chinaemb_lb@mfa.gov.cn; internet lb.china-embassy.org; Ambassador LIU ZHIMING.

Colombia: 5th Floor, Mazda Centre, Jal ed-Dib, Beirut; tel. (4) 712646; fax (4) 712656; e-mail ebeirut@minrelext.gov.co; Ambassador GEORGINE MALLAT.

Cuba: Center Farrania, Saïd Freiha St, Mar-Takla, Hazmieh, Beirut 2901 6727; tel. (1) 459925; fax (1) 950070; e-mail libancub@cyberia.net.lb; internet www.embacubalebanon.com; Ambassador DARÍO DE URRA TORRIENTE.

Czech Republic: POB 40195, Baabda, Beirut; tel. (5) 929010; fax (5) 922120; e-mail beirut@embassy.mzv.cz; internet www.mzv.cz/beirut; Ambassador JAN ČÍŽEK.

Denmark: POB 11-5190, Immeuble 812 Tabaris, 4e étage, ave Charles Malek, Achrafieh, Beirut; tel. (1) 335828; fax (1) 335851; e-mail dk-emb@dm.net.lb; internet www.ambbeirut.um.dk; Ambassador JAN TOP CHRISTENSEN.

Egypt: POB 5037, rue Thomas Eddison, ar-Ramla el-Baida, Beirut; tel. (1) 862917; fax (1) 863751; Ambassador AHMAD AL-BIDYAWI.

France: rue de Damas, Beirut; tel. (1) 420000; fax (1) 420013; e-mail ambafr@ciberia.net.lb; internet www.ambafrance-lb.org; Chargé d'affaires a.i ANDRÉ PARANT.

Gabon: POB 11-1252, Riad es-Solh, Hadath, Beirut 1107 2080; tel. (5) 924649; fax (5) 924643; Ambassador SIMON NTOUTOUME EMANE.

Germany: POB 11-2820, Riad es-Solh, Beirut 1102 2110; tel. (4) 929600; fax (4) 929616; e-mail info@beirut.diplo.de; internet www.beirut.diplo.de; Ambassador HANSJOERG HABER.

Greece: POB 11-0309, Immeuble Boukhater, rue des Ambassades, Nouvelle Naccache, Beirut; tel. (4) 418772; fax (4) 418774; e-mail hellas.emb@inco.com.lb; Ambassador NIKOLAOS VAMVOUNAKIS.

Holy See: POB 1061, Jounieh (Apostolic Nunciature); tel. (9) 263102; fax (9) 264488; e-mail naliban@terra.net.lb; Apostolic Nuncio Most Rev. LUIGI GATTI (Titular Archbishop of Santa Giusta).

Hungary: POB 90618, Centre Massoud, 2e étage, Fanar, Beirut; tel. (1) 898840; fax (1) 873391; e-mail mission.bej@kum.hu; internet www.mfa.gov.hu/kulkepviselet/LB/en; Ambassador LAJOS TAMÁS.

India: POB 113-5240, Immeuble Sahmarani, rue Kantari 31, Hamra, Beirut; tel. (1) 353892; fax (1) 869806; e-mail indembei@dm.net.lb; Ambassador NANTU SARKAR.

Indonesia: POB 40007, ave Palais Presidential, rue 68, Secteur 3, Baabda, Beirut; tel. (5) 924682; fax (5) 924678; e-mail indobey@cyberia.net.lb; internet www.welcome.to/indobey; Ambassador SYAM SOEMANAGARA.

Iran: POB 5030, Bir Hassan, Beirut; tel. (1) 821224; fax (1) 821230; Ambassador MUHAMMAD-REZA RAOUF SHEIBANI.

Iraq: Beirut; tel. (1) 453209; fax (1) 459850; e-mail brtemb@iraqmofamail.net; Ambassador JAWAD AL-HA'IRI.

Italy: rue du Palais Présidentiel, Baabda, Beirut; tel. (5) 954955; fax (5) 959616; e-mail amba.beirut@esteri.it; internet www.ambbeirut.esteri.it; Ambassador GABRIELE CHECCHIA.

Japan: POB 11-3360, Army St, Zkak al-Blat, Serail Hill, Beirut; tel. (1) 985751; fax (1) 989754; e-mail japanemb@japanemb.org.lb; internet www.lb.emb-japan.go.jp; Ambassador YOSHIHISA KURODA.

Jordan: POB 109, Beirut 5113; tel. (5) 922500; fax (5) 922502; e-mail joremb@dm.net.lb; Ambassador ZIYAD MAJALI.

Korea, Republic: POB 40-290, Baabda, Beirut; tel. (5) 953167; fax (5) 953170; e-mail koreamdm@dm.net.lb; Ambassador YOUNG-SUN KIM.

Kuwait: POB 4530, Rond-point du Stade, Bir Hassan, Beirut; tel. (1) 756100; fax (1) 756103; e-mail info@kuwaitinfo.net; internet www.kuwaitinfo.net; Ambassador ALI SULEIMAN AS-SAID.

LEBANON

Mexico: POB 70-1150, Antélias; tel. (4) 418871; fax (4) 418873; e-mail mail@embassyofmexicoinlebanon.org; internet www.embassyofmexicoinlebanon.org; Ambassador JORGE ÁLVAREZ FUENTES.

Morocco: Bir Hassan, Beirut; tel. (1) 859829; fax (1) 859839; e-mail sifmar@cyberia.net.lb; Ambassador ALI OUMLIL.

Netherlands: POB 167190, Netherlands Tower, ave Charles Malek, Achrafieh, Beirut; tel. (1) 204663; fax (1) 204664; e-mail nlgovbei@sodetel.net.lb; internet www.netherlandsembassy.org.lb; Ambassador ROBERT ZELDENRUST.

Norway: POB 113-7001, Immeuble Dimashki, rue Bliss, Ras Beirut, Hamra, Beirut 1103 2150; tel. (1) 372977; fax (1) 372979; e-mail norleb@cyberia.net.lb; internet www.norway-lebanon.org; Chargé d'affaires a.i. AUD LISE NORHEIM.

Pakistan: POB 135506, Immeuble Shell, 11e étage, Raoucheh, Beirut; tel. (1) 863041; fax (1) 864583; e-mail pakemblb@cyberia.net.lb; Ambassador ASMA ANEESA.

Philippines: POB 136631, 1er et 2e étages, Immeuble Design, rue Abdullah Machnouk, Beirut; tel. (1) 791092; fax (1) 791095; e-mail beirutpe@cyberia.net.lb; Ambassador RAMONITO S. MARINO.

Poland: POB 40-215, Immeuble Khalifa, ave Président Sulayman Franjiya 52, Baabda, Beirut; tel. (5) 924881; fax (5) 924882; e-mail polamb@cyberia.net.lb; Ambassador WALDEMAR MARKIEWICZ.

Qatar: POB 11-6717, 1er étage, Immeuble Deebs, Shouran, Beirut; tel. (1) 865271; fax (1) 810460; e-mail beirut@mofa.gov.qa; Ambassador JABOR BIN ABDULLAH AS-SWAIDI.

Romania: Route du Palais Presidentiel, Baabda, Beirut; tel. (5) 924848; fax (5) 924747; e-mail romembey@inco.com.lb; Ambassador AUREL CALIN.

Russia: POB 5220, rue Mar Elias et-Tineh, Wata Mseitbeh, Beirut; tel. (1) 300041; fax (1) 303837; e-mail rusembei@cyberia.net.lb; internet www.lebanon.mid.ru; Ambassador SERGEI NIKOLAYEVICH BUKIN.

Saudi Arabia: POB 136144, Kuraitem, Beirut; tel. (1) 860351; fax (1) 861524; e-mail lbemb@mofa.gov.sa; Ambassador ABD AL-AZIZ MAHI ED-DIN AL-KHOJA.

Spain: POB 11-3039, Palais Chehab, Hadath Antounie, Beirut; tel. (5) 464120; fax (5) 464030; e-mail embesplb@mail.mae.es; Ambassador MIGUEL BENZO PEREA.

Sri Lanka: POB 175, Hazmieh, Mar-Takla, Beirut; tel. (5) 924765; fax (5) 924768; e-mail slemblbn@cyberia.net.lb; Ambassador MOHAMED MOHIDEEN AMANUL FAROUQUE.

Sudan: POB 2504, Hamra, Beirut; tel. (1) 350057; fax (1) 353271; Ambassador SAYED AHMAD AL-BAKHIT.

Switzerland: Immeuble Bourj al-Ghazal, ave Fouad Chehab, Achrafieh, Beirut; tel. (1) 324129; fax (1) 324167; e-mail bey.vertretung@eda.admin.ch; Ambassador FRANÇOIS BARRAS.

Tunisia: Hazmieh, Mar-Takla, Beirut; tel. (5) 457431; fax (5) 950434; Ambassador NAZIHA ZARROUK.

Turkey: POB 70-666, zone II, rue 1, Rabieh, Beirut; tel. (4) 520929; fax (4) 407557; e-mail trbebeyr@intracom.net.lb; Ambassador SAKIR TORUNLAR.

Ukraine: POB 431, Jardin al-Bacha, Jisr al-Bacha, Sin el-Fil, Beirut; tel. (1) 510527; fax (1) 510531; e-mail ukrembassy@inco.com.lb; Ambassador BORIS ZHARSHOK.

United Arab Emirates: Immeuble Wafic Tanbara, Jnah, Beirut; tel. (1) 857000; fax (1) 857009; e-mail eembassy@uae.org.lb; Ambassador MUHAMMAD SULTAN AS-SOWAIDI.

United Kingdom: POB 11-471, Serail Hill, Beirut Central District, Beirut; tel. (1) 990400; fax (1) 990420; e-mail chancery@cyberia.net.lb; internet www.britishembassy.gov.uk/lebanon; Ambassador FRANCES GUY.

USA: POB 70-840, Antélias; tel. (4) 542600; fax (4) 544136; e-mail pasbeirut@state.gov; internet lebanon.usembassy.gov; Chargé d'affaires a.i. MICHELE J. SISON.

Uruguay: POB 2051, Centre Stella Marris, 7e étage, rue Banque du Liban, Jouniêh; tel. (9) 636529; fax (9) 636531; e-mail uruliban@dm.net.lb; internet www.embauruguaybeirut.org; Ambassador JORGE LUIS JURE.

Venezuela: POB 603, Immeuble Baezevale House, 5e étage, Zalka, Beirut; tel. (1) 888701; fax (1) 900757; e-mail embavene@dm.net.lb; Ambassador JOEL RAMÓN PÉREZ.

Yemen: Bir Hassan, Beirut; tel. (1) 852688; fax (1) 821610; Ambassador AHMAD ABDULLAH AL-BASHA.

Note: Lebanon and Syria have very close relations but do not exchange formal ambassadors. Libya closed its embassy in Beirut in September 2003, but still maintains diplomatic relations with Lebanon.

Judicial System

Law and justice in Lebanon are administered in accordance with the following codes, which are based upon modern theories of civil and criminal legislation:

Code de la Propriété (1930).

Code des Obligations et des Contrats (1932).

Code de Procédure Civile (1933).

Code Maritime (1947).

Code de Procédure Pénale (Code Ottoman Modifié).

Code Pénal (1943).

Code Pénal Militaire (1946).

Code d'Instruction Criminelle.

The following courts are now established:

(*a*) Fifty-six **'Single-Judge Courts'**, each consisting of a single judge, and dealing in the first instance with both civil and criminal cases; there are 17 such courts in Beirut and seven in Tripoli.

(*b*) Eleven **Courts of Appeal**, each consisting of three judges, including a President and a Public Prosecutor, and dealing with civil and criminal cases; there are five such courts in Beirut.

First President of the Courts of Appeal of Beirut: TANIOS EL-KHOURY.

(*c*) Four **Courts of Cassation**, three dealing with civil and commercial cases and the fourth with criminal cases. A Court of Cassation, to be properly constituted, must have at least three judges, one being the President and the other two Councillors. If the Court of Cassation reverses the judgment of a lower court, it does not refer the case back but retries it itself.

General Prosecutor of Cassation: SAID MIRZA.

(*d*) **State Consultative Council**, which deals with administrative cases.

President of the State Consultative Council: GHALEB GHANEM.

(*e*) **The Court of Justice**, which is a special court consisting of a President and four judges, deals with matters affecting the security of the State; there is no appeal against its verdicts.

In addition to the above, the Constitutional Council considers matters pertaining to the constitutionality of legislation. Military courts are competent to try crimes and misdemeanours involving the armed and security forces. Islamic (*Shari'a*), Christian and Jewish religious courts deal with affairs of personal status (marriage, death, inheritance, etc.).

President of the Constitutional Council: AMIN FARIS NASSER.
Chief of the Military Court: Brig.-Gen. MAHER SAFI ED-DIN.

Religion

Of all the regions of the Middle East, Lebanon probably presents the closest juxtaposition of sects and peoples within a small territory. Estimates for 1983 assessed the sizes of communities as: Shi'a Muslims 1.2m., Maronites 900,000, Sunni Muslims 750,000, Greek Orthodox 250,000, Druzes 250,000, Armenians 175,000. There is also a small Jewish community. In 1994 it was estimated that 29%–32% of the population of Lebanon were Shi'a Muslims, 25%–28% Maronites, 16%–20% Sunni Muslims and 3.5% Druzes. The Maronites, a uniate sect of the Roman Catholic Church, inhabited the old territory of Mount Lebanon, i.e. immediately east of Beirut. In the south, towards the Israeli frontier, Shi'a villages are most common, while between the Shi'a and the Maronites live the Druzes (divided between the Yazbakis and the Joumblatis). The Beka'a valley has many Greek Christians (both Roman Catholic and Orthodox), while the Tripoli area is mainly Sunni Muslim.

CHRISTIANITY

The Roman Catholic Church

Armenian Rite

Patriarchate of Cilicia: Patriarcat Arménien Catholique, rue de l'Hôpital orthodoxe, Jeitawi, Beirut 2078 5605; tel. (1) 570555; fax (1) 570563; e-mail nerbed19@magnarama.com; f. 1742; established in Beirut since 1932; includes patriarchal diocese of Beirut, with an estimated 12,000 adherents (31 December 2005); Patriarch Most Rev. NERSES BEDROS XIX TARMOUNI; Protosyncellus Rt Rev. VARTAN ACHKARIAN (Titular Bishop of Tokat—Armenian Rite).

Chaldean Rite

Diocese of Beirut: Evêché Chaldéen de Beyrouth, POB 373, Hazmieh, Beirut; tel. (5) 457732; fax (5) 457731; e-mail

LEBANON

chaldepiscopus@hotmail.com; an estimated 10,000 adherents (31 December 2005); Bishop of Beirut MICHEL KASSARJI.

Latin Rite

Apostolic Vicariate of Beirut: Vicariat Apostolique, POB 11-4224, Riad es-Solh, Beirut 1107 2160; tel. (9) 236101; fax (9) 236102; e-mail vicariatlat@hotmail.com; an estimated 15,000 adherents (31 December 2005); Vicar Apostolic PAUL DAHDAH (Titular Archbishop of Arae in Numidia).

Maronite Rite

Patriarchate of Antioch and all the East: Patriarcat Maronite, Bkerké; tel. (9) 915441; fax (9) 938844; e-mail jtawk@bkerke.org.lb; includes patriarchal dioceses of Jounieh, Sarba and Jobbé; the Maronite Church in Lebanon comprises four archdioceses and six dioceses, with an estimated 1,411,645 adherents (31 December 2005); Patriarch Cardinal NASRALLAH BOUTROS (PIERRE) SFEIR.

Archbishop of Antélias: Most Rev. JOSEPH MOHSEN BÉCHARA, Archevêché Maronite, POB 70400, Antélias; tel. (4) 410020; fax (4) 415872.

Archbishop of Beirut: Most Rev. PAUL YOUSSEF MATAR, Archevêché Maronite, 10 rue Collège de la Sagesse, Achrafieh, Beirut; tel. (1) 561980; fax (1) 561930; e-mail maronitebeyrouth@yahoo.fr; also representative of the Holy See for Roman Catholics of the Coptic Rite in Lebanon.

Archbishop of Tripoli: Most Rev. GEORGES BOU-JAOUDÉ, Archevêché Maronite, POB 104, rue al-Moutran, Karm Sada, Tripoli; tel. (6) 624324; fax (6) 629393; e-mail rahmat@inco.com.lb.

Archbishop of Tyre: Most Rev. CHUCRALLAH-NABIL HAGE, Archevêché Maronite, Tyre; tel. (7) 740059; fax (7) 344891.

Melkite Rite

Patriarch of Antioch: Patriarcat Grec-Melkite Catholique, POB 22249, 12 ave az-Zeitoon, Bab Charki, Damascus, Syria; tel. (1) 5441030; fax (1) 5418966; e-mail gcp@pcg-lb.org; the Melkite Church in Lebanon comprises seven archdioceses, with an estimated 387,300 adherents (31 December 2005); The Patriarch of Antioch and all the East, of Alexandria and of Jerusalem Most Rev. GRÉGOIRE III LAHAM.

Archbishop of Ba'albek: Most Rev. ELIAS RAHAL, Archevêché Grec-Catholique, Ba'albek; tel. (8) 370200; fax (8) 373986.

Archbishop of Baniyas: Most Rev. GEORGES NICOLAS HADDAD, Archevêché de Panéas, Jdeidet Marjeyoun; tel. (3) 830007; fax (7) 200270.

Archbishop of Beirut and Gibail: JOSEPH KALLAS, Archevêché Grec-Melkite-Catholique, POB 11-901, 655 rue de Damas, Beirut; tel. (1) 616104; fax (1) 616109; e-mail agmcb@terra.net.lb.

Archbishop of Saida (Sidon): Most Rev. GEORGES KWAÏTER, Archevêché Grec-Melkite-Catholique, POB 247, rue el-Moutran, Sidon; tel. (7) 720100; fax (7) 722055; e-mail mkwaiter@inco.com.lb.

Archbishop of Tripoli: Most Rev. GEORGE RIASHI, Archevêché Grec-Catholique, rue al-Kanaess, Tripoli; tel. (6) 431602; fax (6) 441716.

Archbishop of Tyre: Most Rev. GEORGES BAKOUNY, Archevêché Grec-Melkite-Catholique, POB 257, Tyre; tel. (7) 740015; fax (7) 349180; e-mail eegc@inco.com.lb.

Archbishop of Zahleh and Furzol: Most Rev. ANDRÉ HADDAD, Archevêché Grec-Melkite-Catholique, Saidat en-Najat, Zahleh; tel. (8) 800333; fax (8) 822406; e-mail arch_zahle@hotmail.com.

Syrian Rite

Patriarchate of Antioch: Patriarcat Syrien Catholique d'Antioche, rue de Damas, POB 116/5087, Beirut 1106 2010; tel. (1) 615892; fax (1) 616573; e-mail psc_lb@yahoo.com; jurisdiction over about 150,000 Syrian Catholics in the Middle East, incl. (at 31 December 2005) 14,700 in the diocese of Beirut; Patriarch Most Rev. IGNACE PIERRE VIII ABDEL AHAD; Protosyncellus Mgr GEORGES MASRI.

The Anglican Communion

Within the Episcopal Church in Jerusalem and the Middle East, Lebanon forms part of the diocese of Jerusalem (see the chapter on Israel).

Other Christian Groups

Armenian Apostolic Orthodox Church: Armenian Catholicosate of Cilicia, POB 70317, Antélias; tel. (4) 410001; fax (4) 419724; e-mail info@armenianorthodoxchurch.org; internet www.armenianorthodoxchurch.org; f. 301 in Armenia, re-established in 1293 in Cilicia (now in Turkey), transferred to Antélias, Lebanon, 1930; Leader His Holiness ARAM KESHISHIAN I (Catholicos of Cilicia); jurisdiction over an estimated 3.5m. adherents in Lebanon, Syria, Cyprus, Kuwait, Greece, Iran, Qatar, the United Arab Emirates, South America, the USA and Canada.

National Evangelical Synod of Syria and Lebanon: POB 70890, Antélias; tel. (4) 525030; fax (4) 411184; e-mail nessl@synod-sl.org; internet www.nes-sl.org; f. 1959; 20,000 adherents (2006); Gen. Sec. Rev. JOSEPH KASSAB.

Patriarchate of Antioch and all the East (Greek Orthodox): Patriarcat Grec-Orthodoxe, POB 9, Damascus, Syria; tel. (11) 5424400; fax (11) 5424404; e-mail info@antiochpat.org; internet www.antiochpat.org; Patriarch His Beatitude IGNATIUS (HAZIM) IV.

Patriarchate of Antioch and all the East (Syrian Orthodox): Patriarcat Syrien Orthodoxe, Bab Toma, POB 22260, Damascus, Syria; tel. 5432401; fax 5432400; Patriarch IGNATIUS ZAKKA I IWAS.

Supreme Council of the Evangelical Community in Syria and Lebanon: POB 70/1065, rue Rabieh 34, Antélias; tel. (4) 525036; fax (4) 405490; e-mail suprcoun@minero.net; Pres. Rev. Dr SALIM SAHIOUNY.

Union of the Armenian Evangelical Churches in the Near East: POB 11-377, Beirut; tel. (1) 565628; fax (1) 565629; e-mail uaecne@cyberia.net.lb; f. 1846 in Turkey; comprises about 30 Armenian Evangelical Churches in Syria, Lebanon, Egypt, Cyprus, Greece, Iran, Turkey and Australia; 7,500 mems (1990); Pres. Rev. MEGRDICH KARAGOEZIAN; Gen. Sec. SEBOUH TERZIAN.

ISLAM

Shi'a Muslims: Leader Imam Sheikh SAYED MOUSSA AS-SADR (went missing during visit to Libya in August 1978); President of the Supreme Islamic Council of the Shi'a Community of Lebanon ABD AL-AMIR QABALAN; Beirut.

Sunni Muslims: Grand Mufti of Lebanon, Dar el-Fatwa, rue Ilewi Rushed, Beirut; tel. (1) 422340; Leader Sheikh Dr MUHAMMAD RASHID QABBANI.

Druzes: Supreme Spiritual Leader of the Druze Community, Beirut; tel. (1) 341116; Supreme Spiritual Leader Sheikh AL-AQL BAHJAT GHAITH; Political Leader WALID JOUMBLATT.

Alawites: a schism of Shi'ite Islam; there are an estimated 50,000 Alawites in northern Lebanon, in and around Tripoli.

JUDAISM

Jews: Leader CHAHOUD CHREIM (Beirut).

The Press

DAILIES

Al-Amal (Hope): POB 992, place Charles Hélou, Beirut; tel. (1) 382992; f. 1939; Arabic; organ of Al-Kataeb (Phalangist Party); Chief Editor ELIAS RABABI; circ. 35,000.

Al-Anwar (Lights): c/o Dar Assayad, POB 11-1038, Hazmieh, Beirut; tel. (5) 456374; fax (5) 452700; e-mail info@alanwar.com; internet www.alanwar.com; f. 1959; Arabic; independent; supplement, Sunday; cultural and social; publ. by Dar Assayad SAL; Editors-in-Chief MICHEL RAAD, RAFIK KHOURY; circ. 14,419.

Aztag: POB 80-860, Shaghzoyan Cultural Centre, Bourj Hammoud; tel. (1) 258526; fax (1) 258529; e-mail aztag@inco.com.lb; internet www.aztagdaily.com; f. 1927; Armenian; Editor-in-Chief SHAHAN KANDAHARIAN; circ. 6,500.

Al-Bairaq (The Standard): Immeuble Dimitri Trad, rue Issa Maalouf, Achrafieh, Beirut; tel. (1) 216393; fax (1) 338928; e-mail dalwl@dm.net.lb; f. 1913; Arabic; publ. by Dar Alf Leila wa Leila Publishing House; politics and society; circ. 10,000.

Bairut: Beirut; f. 1952; Arabic.

Ach-Chaab (The People): POB 5140, Beirut; f. 1961; Arabic; Nationalist; Propr and Editor MUHAMMAD AMIN DUGHAN; circ. 7,000.

Ach-Chams (The Sun): Beirut; f. 1925; Arabic.

Ach-Charq (The East): POB 11-0838, rue Verdun, Riad es-Solh, Beirut; tel. (1) 810820; fax (1) 866105; e-mail info@elshark.com; f. 1926; Arabic; Gen. Dir and Editor-in-Chief AOUNI AL-KAAKI.

Daily Star: 6th Floor, Marine Tower, rue de la Sainte Famille, Achrafieh, Beirut; tel. (1) 587277; fax (1) 561333; e-mail editorial@dailystar.com.lb; internet www.dailystar.com.lb; f. 1952; English; Publr and Editor-in-Chief JAMIL K. MROUE; circ. 10,550.

Ad-Diyar (The Homeland): an-Nahda Bldg, Yarze, Beirut; tel. (5) 923830; fax (5) 923773; e-mail aldiyar2002@yahoo.com; f. 1987; Arabic; Propr and Editor-in-Chief CHARLES AYYUB.

Ad-Dunya (The World): Beirut; f. 1943; Arabic; political; Chief Editor SULIMAN ABOU ZAID; circ. 25,000.

Al-Hakika (The Truth): Beirut; Arabic; publ. by Amal.

LEBANON

Al-Hayat (Life): POB 11-1242, rue Maarad, place Riad es-Solh, Beirut; tel. (1) 987990; fax (1) 983395; e-mail information@alhayat.com; internet www.alhayat.com; f. 1946; Arabic; independent; circ. 196,800.

Al-Jarida (The (News) Paper): POB 220, place Tabaris, Beirut; f. 1953; Arabic; independent; Editor ABDULLAH SKAFF; circ. 22,600.

Al-Jumhuriya (The Republic): Beirut; f. 1924; Arabic.

Journal al-Haddis: POB 300, Jounieh; f. 1927; Arabic; political; Owner GEORGES ARÈGE-SAADÉ.

Al-Khatib (The Speaker): rue Georges Picot, Beirut; Arabic.

Al-Kifah al-Arabi (The Arab Struggle): POB 5158-14, Immeuble Rouche-Shams, Beirut; tel. (1) 809300; fax (1) 808281; e-mail editor@kifaharabi.com; internet www.kifaharabi.com; f. 1974; Arabic; political, socialist, pan-Arab; Publr and Chief Editor WALID HUSSEINI.

Lisan ul-Hal (The Organ): rue Châteaubriand, Beirut; e-mail lebanon@lissan-ul-hal.com; internet www.lissan-ul-hal.com; f. 1877; Arabic; Editor GEBRAN HAYEK; circ. 33,000.

Al-Liwa' (The Standard): POB 11-2402, Beirut; tel. (1) 735745; fax (1) 735749; e-mail events@aliwaa.com.lb; internet www.aliwaa.com; f. 1963; Arabic; Propr ABD AL-GHANI SALAM; Editor SALAH SALAM; circ. 26,000.

Al-Mustaqbal: POB 14-5426, Beirut; tel. (1) 797770; fax (1) 869264; e-mail rnakib@almustaqbal.com.lb; internet www.almustaqbal.com.lb; f. 1999; Dir TOUFIK KHATTAB; Editor HANI HAMMOUD; circ. 20,000.

An-Nahar (The Day): Immeuble An-Nahar, place des Martyrs, Marfa', Beirut 2014 5401; tel. (1) 994888; fax (1) 996777; e-mail webmaster@annahar.com.lb; internet www.annahar.com; f. 1933; Arabic; independent; Exec. Editor-in-Chief EDMOND SAAB; circ. 50,000.

An-Nida (The Appeal): Beirut; f. 1959; Arabic; publ. by the Lebanese Communist Party; Editor KARIM MROUÉ; circ. 10,000.

An-Nidal (The Struggle): Beirut; f. 1939; Arabic.

L'Orient-Le Jour: POB 11-2488, Kantari, Immeuble Kantari Corner, Beirut; tel. (1) 365365; fax (1) 375888; e-mail administration@lorientlejour.com; internet www.lorientlejour.com; f. 1942; French; independent; Pres. Dir MICHEL EDDÉ; Editor-in-Chief NAJUIB AOUN; circ. 23,000.

Rayah (Banner): POB 4101, Beirut; Arabic.

Le Réveil: Beirut; tel. (1) 890700; f. 1977; French; Editor-in-Chief JEAN SHAMI; Dir RAYMOND DAOU; circ. 10,000.

Sada Lubnan (Echo of Lebanon): Beirut; f. 1951; Arabic; pan-Arab; Editor MUHAMMAD BAALBAKI; circ. 25,000.

As-Safir: POB 113/5015, Immeuble as-Safir, rue Monimina, Hamra, Beirut 1103-2010; tel. (1) 350001; fax (1) 743602; e-mail mail@assafir.com; internet www.assafir.com; f. 1974; Arabic; political; Publr and Editor-in-Chief TALAL SALMAN; circ. 45,000.

Sawt al-Uruba (The Voice of Europe): POB 3537, Beirut; f. 1959; Arabic; organ of the An-Najadeh Party; Editor ADNANE AL-HAKIM.

Le Soir: POB 1470, rue de Syrie, Beirut; f. 1947; French; independent; Dir DIKRAN TOSBATH; Editor ANDRÉ KECATI; circ. 16,500.

Telegraf—Bairut: rue Béchara el-Khoury, Beirut; f. 1930; Arabic; political, economic and social; Editor TOUFIC ASSAD MATNI; circ. 15,500 (5,000 outside Lebanon).

Al-Yaum (Today): Beirut; f. 1937; Arabic; Editor WAFIC MUHAMMAD CHAKER AT-TIBY.

Az-Zamane: Beirut; f. 1947; Arabic.

Zartonk: POB 11-617, rue Nahr Ibrahim, Beirut; tel. and fax (1) 566709; e-mail zartonk@dm.net.lb; f. 1937; Armenian; official organ of Armenian Liberal Democratic Party; Man. Editor BAROUYR H. AGHBASHIAN.

WEEKLIES

Achabaka (The Net): c/o Dar Assayad SAL, POB 11-1038, Hazmieh, Beirut; tel. (5) 456373; fax (5) 452700; e-mail achabaka@achabaka.com; internet www.achabaka.com; f. 1956; Arabic; society and features; Founder SAID FREIHA; Editor ELHAM FREIHA; circ. 139,775.

Al-Ahad (Sunday): Beirut; Arabic; political; organ of Hezbollah; Editor RIAD TAHA; circ. 32,000.

Al-Akhbar (The News): Beirut; f. 1954; Arabic; publ. by the Parti communiste libanais; circ. 21,000.

Al-Alam al-Lubnani (The Lebanese World): POB 462, Beirut; f. 1964; Arabic, English, Spanish, French; politics, literature and social economy; Editor-in-Chief FAYEK KHOURY; Gen. Editor CHEIKH FADI GEMAYEL; circ. 45,000.

Al-Anwar Supplement: c/o Dar Assayad, POB 11-1038, Hazmieh, Beirut; tel. (5) 450406; fax (5) 452700; e-mail info@alanwar.com; internet www.alanwar.com; cultural and social; every Sun.; supplement to daily Al-Anwar; Editor ISSAM FREIHA; circ. 90,000.

Assayad (The Hunter): c/o Dar Assayad, POB 11-1038, Hazmieh, Beirut; tel. (5) 450933; fax (5) 452700; e-mail assayad@inco.com.lb; internet www.darassayad.net; f. 1943; Arabic; political and social; Editor-in-Chief MOUNIR NAJJAR; circ. 76,192.

Dabbour: place du Musée, Beirut; tel. and fax (1) 616770; e-mail addabbour@yahoo.com; internet www.addabbour.com; f. 1922; Arabic; CEO JOSEPH RICHARD MOUKARZEL; circ. 12,000.

Ad-Dyar: Immeuble Bellevue, rue Verdun, Beirut; f. 1941; Arabic; political; circ. 46,000.

Al-Hadaf (The Target): Beirut; tel. (1) 420554; f. 1969; organ of Popular Front for the Liberation of Palestine; Arabic; Editor-in-Chief SABER MOHI ED-DIN; circ. 40,000.

Al-Hawadeth (Events): POB 1281, rue Clémenceau, Beirut; tel. (1) 216393; fax (1) 200961; e-mail info@al-hawadeth.com; internet www.al-hawadeth.com; publ. from London, United Kingdom (183–185 Askew Rd, W12 9AX; tel. (20) 8740-4500; fax. (20) 8749-9781); f. 1911; Arabic; news; Editor-in-Chief MELHIM KARAM; circ. 120,000.

Al-Hiwar (Dialogue): Beirut; f. 2000; Arabic; Chair. FOUAD MAKHZOUMI; Editor-in-Chief SAM MOUNASSA.

Al-Hurriya (Freedom): Beirut; f. 1960; Arabic; organ of the Democratic Front for the Liberation of Palestine; Editor DAOUD TALHAME; circ. 30,000.

Al-Iza'a (Broadcasting): POB 462, rue Selim Jazaerly, Beirut; f. 1938; Arabic; politics, art, literature and broadcasting; Editor FAYEK KHOURY; circ. 11,000.

Al-Jumhur (The Public): POB 1834, Moussaitbé, Beirut; f. 1936; Arabic; illustrated weekly news magazine; Editor FARID ABU SHAHLA; circ. 45,000, of which over 20,000 outside Lebanon.

Kul Shay' (Everything): POB 3250, rue Béchara el-Khoury, Beirut; Arabic.

Magazine: POB 11-1404, Immeuble Sayegh, rue Sursock, Beirut; tel. (1) 202070; fax (1) 202663; e-mail info@ediori.com.lb; internet www.magazine.com.lb; f. 1956; French; political, economic and social; published by Editions Orientales SAL; Pres. CHARLES ABOU ADAL; Editor-in-Chief PAUL KHALIFEH; circ. 18,000.

Massis: Immeuble Eglise Ste Croix des Arméniens Catholiques, rue Zoghbi, Zalka, Beirut; tel. (4) 715263; e-mail hebdomassis@sodetel.net.lb; internet www.armeniancatholic.org; f. 1947; Armenian; Catholic; Editor-in-Chief Fr ANTRANIK GRANIAN; Dir SARKIS NADJARIAN; circ. 2,500.

Al-Moharrir (The Liberator): Beirut; f. 1962; Arabic; circ. 87,000; Gen. Man. WALID ABOU ZAHR.

Monday Morning: POB 165612, Immeuble Dimitri Trad, rue Issa Maalouf, Achrafieh, Beirut; tel. (1) 200961; fax (1) 335079; e-mail info@mmorning.com; internet www.mmorning.com; f. 1971; political and social affairs; publ. by Dar Alf Leila wa Leila Publishing House; circ. 15,000; Editor-in-Chief MELHEM KARAM.

An-Nass (The People): POB 4886, ave Fouad Chehab, Beirut; tel. (3) 376185; fax (8) 376610; f. 1959; Arabic; weekly news magazine; Editor-in-Chief HASSAN YAGHI; circ. 22,000.

Al-Ousbou' al-Arabi (Arab Week): POB 11-1404, Immeuble Sayegh, rue Sursock, Beirut; tel. (1) 202070; fax (1) 202663; e-mail info@arabweek.com.lb; internet www.arabweek.com.lb; f. 1959; Arabic; political and social; publ. by Editions Orientales SAL; Chair. and Editor-in-Chief CHARLES ABOU ADAL; circ. 88,407 (circulates throughout the Arab world).

Phoenix: POB 113222, Beirut; tel. (1) 363133; fax (1) 371186; e-mail dolfins@cyberia.net.lb; for women; publ. by Al-Khal.

Ar-Rassed: Beirut; Arabic; Editor GEORGE RAJJI.

La Revue du Liban (Lebanon Review): POB 165612, Immeuble Dimitri Trad, rue Issa Maalouf, Achrafieh, Beirut; tel. (1) 200961; fax (1) 338929; e-mail rdl@rdl.com.lb; internet www.rdl.com.lb; f. 1928; French; political, social, cultural; publ. by Dar Alf Leila wa Leila Publishing House; Publr MELHEM KARAM; Gen. Man. MICHEL MISK; circ. 22,000.

Sabah al-Khair (Good Morning): Beirut; Arabic; publ. by the Syrian Nationalist Party.

Samar: c/o Dar Assayad, POB 11-1038, Hazmieh, Beirut; tel. (5) 452700; fax (5) 452957; Arabic; for teenagers; publ. by Dar Assayad SAL.

Ash-Shira' (The Sail): POB 13-5250, Beirut; tel. (1) 703000; fax (1) 866050; internet www.alshiraa.com; Arabic; Editor HASSAN SABRA; circ. 40,000.

OTHER SELECTED PERIODICALS

Alam at-Tijarat (Business World): Immeuble Strand, rue Hamra, Beirut; f. 1965; monthly; commercial; Editor NADIM MAKDISI; international circ. 17,500.

Al Computer, Communications and Electronics (ACCE): c/o Dar Assayad, POB 1038, Hazmieh, Beirut; tel. (5) 450935; fax (5) 452700; e-mail assayad@inco.com.lb; internet www.darassayad.net;

LEBANON

f. 1984; monthly; computer technology; publ. by Dar Assayad International; Chief Editor ANTOINE BOUTROS; circ. 31,912 (Jan.–June 2006).

Arab Construction World: POB 13-5121, Chouran, Beirut 1102 2802; tel. (1) 352413; fax (1) 352419; e-mail info@acwmag.com; internet www.acwmag.com; f. 1985; monthly; English and Arabic; publ. by Chatila Publishing House; Pres. and Publr FATHI CHATILA; Editor-in-Chief MUHAMMAD RABIH CHATILA; circ. 10,100.

Arab Defense Journal: c/o Dar Assayad, POB 11-1038, Hazmieh, Beirut; tel. (5) 456374; fax (5) 450609; e-mail adj2004a@yahoo.com; internet www.darassayad.net; f. 1976; monthly; military; publ. by Dar Assayad International; Chief Editor FAWZI ABOU FARHAT; circ. 24,831 (July–Dec. 2005).

Arab Economist: POB 11-6068, Beirut; monthly; publ. by Centre for Economic, Financial and Social Research and Documentation SAL; Chair. HEKMAT KASSIR.

Arab Health World: POB 13-5121, Chouran, Beirut 1102 2802; tel. (1) 748333; fax (1) 352419; e-mail editorial@ahwmag.net; internet www.ahwmag.net; f. 1986 as Arab Health magazine, but publ. suspended in 1993; relaunched as above 2006; bi-monthly; English and Arabic; publ. by Chatila Publishing House; Pres. and Publr FATHI CHATILA; Editor-in-Chief Dr RAJAA CHATILA ALAYLI.

Arab Water World: POB 13-5121, Chouran, Beirut 1102-2802; tel. (1) 748333; fax (1) 352419; e-mail editorial@awwmag.com; internet www.awwmag.com; f. 1977; monthly; English and Arabic; publ. by Chatila Publishing House; Pres., Publr and Editor-in-Chief FATHI CHATILA; circ. 8,400.

The Arab World: POB 567, Jounieh; tel. and fax (9) 935096; e-mail naaman@lynx.net.lb; internet www.naamanculture.com; f. 1985; 24 a yr; publ. by Dar Naamān lith-Thaqāfa; Editor NAJI NAAMAN.

Argus: POB 16-5403, 6 rue Arguse Sodeco, Beirut; tel. (1) 219113; fax (1) 219955; e-mail argus@cyberia.net.lb; monthly; Arabic, French and English; economics and law; circ. 1,000.

Le Commerce du Levant: Kantari, Immeuble Kantari Corner, 11e étage, Beirut 2021 2502; tel. (1) 362361; fax (1) 360379; e-mail lecommerce@inco.com.lb; internet www.lecommercedulevant.com; f. 1929; monthly; French; commercial and financial; publ. by Société de la Presse Economique; Chief Editor SIBYLLE RIZK; circ. 15,000.

Déco: POB 11-1404, Immeuble Sayegh, rue Sursock, Beirut; tel. (1) 202070; fax (1) 202663; e-mail info@decomag.com.lb; internet www.decomag.com.lb; f. 2000; quarterly; French; architecture and interior design; publ. by Editions Orientales SAL; Pres. CHARLES ABOU ADAL; circ. 14,000.

Fairuz International: Dar Assayad, POB 11-1038, Hazmieh, Beirut; tel. (5) 456373; fax (5) 450609; e-mail assayad@inco.com.lb; internet www.darassayad.net; f. 1982; monthly; Arabic; for women; publ. by Dar Assayad International; Chief Editor ELHAM FREIHA; circ. 93,892 (July–Dec. 2005).

Fann at-Tasswir: POB 16-5947, Beirut; tel. (1) 498950; monthly; Arabic; photography.

Al Fares: c/o Dar Assayad, POB 11-1038, Hazmieh, Beirut; tel. (5) 450406; fax (5) 450609; e-mail assayad@inco.com.lb; internet www.darassayad.net; f. 1991; monthly; Arabic; men's interest; publ. by Dar Assayad International; Chief Editor ELHAM FREIHA; circ. 79,237 (July–Dec. 2005).

Al-Idari (The Manager): c/o Dar Assayad, POB 11-1038, Hamzieh, Beirut; tel. (5) 450406; fax (5) 450609; e-mail assayad@inco.com.lb; internet www.darassayad.net; f. 1975; monthly; Arabic; business management, economics, finance and investment; publ. by Dar Assayad International; Pres. BASSAM FREIHA; Gen. Man. ELHAM FREIHA; circ. 31,867.

Al-Intilak (Outbreak): Al-Intilak Printing and Publishing House, POB 4958, Beirut; tel. (1) 302018; e-mail tonehnme@cyberia.net.lb; f. 1960; monthly; Arabic; literary; Chief Editor MICHEL NEHME.

Al-Jeel (The Generation): Beirut; monthly; Arabic; literary.

Al-Khalij Business Magazine: POB 11-8440, Beirut; tel. (1) 345568; fax (1) 602089; e-mail massaref@dm.net.lb; f. 1981; fmrly based in Kuwait; 6 a year; Arabic; Editor-in-Chief ZULFICAR KOBEISSI; circ. 16,325.

Lebanese and Arab Economy: POB 11-1801, Sanayeh, Beirut; tel. (1) 744160; fax (1) 353395; e-mail info@.ccib.org.lb; internet www.ccib.org.lb; f. 1951; monthly; Arabic, English and French; publ. by Chamber of Commerce, Industry and Agriculture of Beirut and Mount Lebanon.

Majallat al-Iza'at al-Lubnaniat (Lebanese Broadcasting Magazine): c/o Radio Lebanon, rue des Arts et Métiers, Beirut; tel. (1) 863016; f. 1959; monthly; Arabic; broadcasting affairs.

Al-Mar'a: POB 11-1404, Immeuble Sayegh, rue Sursock, Beirut; tel. (1) 202070; fax (1) 202663; e-mail info@almara.com.lb; internet www.almara.com.lb; f. 2000; monthly; Arabic; for women; publ. by Editions Orientales SAL; Pres. CHARLES ABOU ADAL; circ. 20,000.

Middle East Food: POB 13-5121, Chouran, Beirut 1102 2802; tel. (1) 352413; fax (1) 352419; e-mail info@mefmag.com; internet www.mefmag.com; f. 1985; 9 a yr; publ. by Chatila Publishing House; Editor-in-Chief ROULA HAMDAN; circ. 8,650.

Al-Mouktataf (The Selection): Beirut; monthly; Arabic; general.

Al-Mukhtar (Reader's Digest): Beirut; monthly; general interest.

Qitāboul A'lamil A'rabi (The Arab World Book): POB 567, Jounieh; tel. and fax (9) 935096; e-mail naaman@lynx.net.lb; internet www.naamanculture.com; f. 1991; 6 a yr; Arabic; publ. by Dar Naamān lith-Thaqāfa; Editor NAJI NAAMAN.

Rijal al-Amal (Businessmen): Beirut; f. 1966; monthly; Arabic; business; Publr and Editor-in-Chief MAHIBA AL-MALKI; circ. 16,250.

Scoop: POB 165612, rue Issa Maalouf, Sioufi, Beirut; tel. (1) 482185; fax (1) 490307; weekly; general interest; publ. by La Régie Libanaise de Publicité; circ. 100,000.

As-Sihāfa wal I'lām (Press and Information): POB 567, Jounieh; tel. and fax (9) 935096; e-mail naamanculture@lynx.net.lb; internet www.naamanculture.com; f. 1987; 12 a yr; Arabic; publ. by Dar Naaman lith-Thaqāfa; Owner NAJI NAAMAN.

Siyassa was Strategia (Politics and Strategy): POB 567, Jounieh; tel. and fax (9) 935096; e-mail naamanculture@lynx.net.lb; internet www.naamanculture.com; f. 1981; 36 a year; Arabic; publ. by Dar Naaman lith-Thaqāfa; Editor NAJI NAAMAN.

Tabibok (Your Doctor): POB 90434, Beirut; tel. (3) 604159; fax in Syria (963-11) 3738901; e-mail tabibokmag@mail.sy; internet www.tabibokmag.com; f. 1956; monthly; Arabic; medical, social, scientific; Editor Dr SAMI KABBANI; circ. 90,000.

Takarir Wa Khalfiyat (Background Reports): c/o Dar Assayad, POB 11-1038, Hazmieh, Beirut; tel. (5) 456374; fax (5) 452700; internet www.darassayad.net; f. 1976; monthly; Arabic; political and economic bulletin; publ. by Dar Assayad SAL; Editor-in-Chief HASSAN EL-KHOURY.

At-Tarik (The Road): Beirut; monthly; Arabic; cultural and theoretical; publ. by the Parti communiste libanais; circ. 5,000.

Travaux et Jours (Works and Days): Rectorat de l'Université Saint-Joseph, rue de Damas, Beirut; tel. (1) 421170; fax (1) 421005; e-mail travauxetjours@usj.edu.lb; internet www.usj.edu.lb; f. 1961; publ. twice a year; French; political, social and cultural; Editor MOUNIR CHAMOUN.

Welcome to Lebanon and the Middle East: Beirut; f. 1959; monthly; English; entertainment, touring and travel; Editor SOUHAIL TOUFIK ABOU JAMRA; circ. 6,000.

NEWS AGENCY

National News Agency (NNA): Hamra, Beirut; tel. (1) 754400; fax (1) 745776; e-mail nna-leb@nna-leb.gov.lb; internet www.nna-leb.gov.lb; state-owned; Dir ANDRE KASSAS.

PRESS ASSOCIATION

Lebanese Press Order: POB 3084, ave Saeb Salam, Beirut; tel. (1) 865519; fax (1) 865516; e-mail mail@pressorder.org; internet www.pressorder.org; f. 1911; 18 mems; Pres. MUHAMMAD AL-BAALBAKI; Vice-Pres. GEORGES SKAFF; Sec. ABD AL-KARIM EL-KHALIL.

Publishers

Dar al-Adab: POB 11-4123, Beirut; tel. (1) 1795135; fax (1) 861633; e-mail d_aladab@cyberia.net.lb; internet www.adabmag.com; f. 1953; dictionaries, literary and general; Man. RANA IDRISS; Editor-in-Chief SAMAH IDRISS.

Arab Institute for Research and Publishing (Al-Mouasasah al-Arabiyah Lildirasat Walnashr): POB 11-5760, Beirut; tel. and fax (1) 751438; e-mail mkayyali@nets.com.jo; f. 1969; Dir MAHER KAYYALI; works in Arabic and English.

Arab Scientific Publishers BP: POB 13-5574, Immeuble Ein at-Tenah Reem, rue Sakiet al-Janzir, Beirut; tel. (1) 786233; fax (1) 786230; e-mail asp@asp.com.lb; internet www.asp.com.lb; computer science, biological sciences, cookery, travel, politics, fiction, children's; Pres. BASSAM CHEBARO.

Dar Assayad Group (SAL and International): POB 11-1038, Hazmieh, Beirut; tel. (5) 450406; fax (5) 452700; e-mail assayad@inco.com.lb; internet www.darassayad.net; Dar Assayad SAL founded in 1943; Dar Assayad International founded in 1983 and provides publishing, advertising and distribution services; publishes in Arabic Al-Anwar (daily), Assayad (weekly), Achabaka (weekly), Background Reports, Arab Defense Journal (monthly), Fairuz (international monthly edition), Al-Idari (monthly), Al Computer, Communications and Electronics (monthly), Al-Fares (monthly); also publishes monthly background reports; has offices and correspondents in Arab countries and most parts of the world; CEO BASSAM FREIHA; Gen. Man. ELHAM FREIHA.

LEBANON

Chatila Publishing House: POB 13-5121, Chouran, Beirut 1102 2802; tel. (1) 352413; fax (1) 352419; e-mail info@cph.com.lb; internet www.chatilapublishing.com; f. 1977; publishes Arab Construction World (monthly), Arab Health World (monthly), Arab Water World (nine per year), Middle East Food (every two months), Middle East and World Construction Directory (bi-annual), Middle East and World Food Directory (bi-annual), Middle East and World Health Directory (bi-annual), Middle East and World Water Directory (bi-annual); Pres. and Publr FATHI CHATILA; Gen. Man. MUHAMMAD RABIH CHATILA.

Edition Française pour le Monde Arabe (EDIFRAMO): POB 113-6140, Immeuble Elissar, rue Bliss, Beirut; tel. (1) 862437; Man. TAHSEEN S. KHAYAT.

Editions Orientales SAL: POB 11-1404, Immeuble Sayegh, rue Sursock, Beirut; tel. (1) 202070; fax (1) 202663; e-mail info@ediori.com.lb; internet www.ediori.com.lb; political and social newspapers and magazines; Pres. and Editor-in-Chief CHARLES ABOU ADAL.

GeoProjects SARL: POB 113-5294, Immeuble Barakat, 13 rue Jeanne d'Arc, Beirut; tel. (1) 344236; fax (1) 342005; e-mail geproj@cyberia.net.lb; internet www.geoprojects.net; f. 1978; cartographers, researchers, school textbook publrs; Dir-Gen. RIDA ISMAIL.

Dar el-Ilm Lilmalayin: POB 1085, Centre Metco, rue Mar Elias, Beirut 2045 8402; tel. (1) 306666; fax (1) 701657; e-mail info@malayin.com; internet www.malayin.com; f. 1945; dictionaries, encyclopaedias, reference books, textbooks, Islamic cultural books; CEO TAREF OSMAN.

Institute for Palestine Studies, Publishing and Research Organization (IPS): POB 11-7164, rue Anis Nsouli, off Verdun, Beirut 1107 2230; tel. (1) 868387; fax (1) 814193; e-mail ipsbrt@palestine-studies.org; internet palestine-studies.org; f. 1963; independent non-profit Arab research org., which promotes better understanding of the Palestine problem and the Arab–Israeli conflict; publishes books, reprints, research papers, etc.; Chair. Dr HISHAM NASHABE; Dir MAHMOUD SOUEID.

The International Documentary Center of Arab Manuscripts: POB 2668, Immeuble Hanna, Ras Beirut, Beirut; e-mail alafaq@cyberia.net.lb; f. 1965; publishes and reproduces ancient and rare Arabic texts; Propr ZOUHAIR BAALBAKI.

Dar al-Kashaf: POB 112091, rue Assad Malhamee, Beirut; tel. (1) 296805; f. 1930; publrs of Al-Kashaf (Arab Youth Magazine), maps, atlases and business books; printers and distributors; Propr M. A. FATHALLAH.

Khayat Book and Publishing Co SARL: 90–94 rue Bliss, Beirut; Middle East, Islam, history, medicine, social sciences, education, fiction; Man. Dir PAUL KHAYAT.

Dar al-Kitab al-Lubnani: Beirut; tel. (1) 861563; fax (1) 351433; f. 1929; Man. Dir HASSAN EZ-ZEIN.

Librairie du Liban Publishers: POB 11-9232, Beirut; tel. (9) 217735; fax (9) 217734; e-mail info@ldlp.com; internet www.ldlp.com; f. 1944; publr of children's books, dictionaries and reference books; distributor of books in English and French; Man. Dirs HABIB SAYEGH, PIERRE SAYEGH.

Dar al-Maaref Liban SARL: Beirut; tel. (1) 931243; f. 1959; children's books and textbooks in Arabic; Man. Dir Dr FOUAD IBRAHIM; Gen. Man. JOSEPH NACHOU.

Dar al-Machreq SARL: POB 11-946, Beirut 1107 2060; tel. (1) 202423; e-mail machreq@cyberia.net.lb; internet www.darelmachreq.com; f. 1848; religion, art, Arabic and Islamic literature, history, languages, science, philosophy, school books, dictionaries and periodicals; Man. Dir CAMILLE HÉCHAIMÉ.

Dar Naamān lith-Thaqāfa (Maison Naaman pour la Culture): POB 567, Jounieh; tel. and fax (9) 935096; e-mail naamanculture@lynx.net.lb; internet www.naamanculture.com; f. 1979; publishes Mawsou'atul 'Alamil 'Arabiyyil Mu'asser (Encyclopaedia of the Contemporary Arab World), Mawsou'atul Waqa'e'il 'Arabiyya (Encyclopaedia of Arab Events), Qitāboul A'lamil A'rabi, Siyassa was Strategia, As-Sahafa wal I'lam in Arabic, and The Arab World in English; Propr NAJI NAAMAN; Exec. Man. MARCELLE AL-ASHKAR.

Editions Dar an-Nahar SAL: BP 11-226, 36 rue Andraos, Immeuble Media Centre, Beirut; tel. (1) 561687; fax (1) 561693; e-mail darannahar@darannahar.com; internet www.darannahar.com; f. 1967; a pan-Arab publishing house; Pres. GHASSAN TUÉNI; Gen. Man. SAMIA SHAMI.

Naufal Group SARL: POB 11-2161, Immeuble Naufal, rue Sourati, Beirut; tel. (1) 354898; fax (1) 354394; e-mail naufalgroup@terra.net.lb; f. 1970; subsidiary cos Macdonald Middle East Sarl, Les Editions Arabes; encyclopaedias, fiction, children's books, history, law and literature; Man. Dir TONY NAUFAL.

Publitec Publications: POB 16-6142, Beirut; tel. (1) 495401; fax (1) 493330; e-mail info@whoswhointhearabworld.info; internet www.whoswhointhearabworld.info; f. 1965; publishes Who's Who in Lebanon and Who's Who in the Arab World (both bi-annual); Pres. CHARLES GEDEON; Man. KRIKOR AYVAZIAN.

Dar ar-Raed al-Lubnani: POB 93, Immeuble Kamal al-Assad, Hazmieh, Sammouri, Beirut; tel. (5) 450757; f. 1971; CEO RAYED SAMMOURI.

Rihani Printing and Publishing House: Beirut; f. 1963; Propr ALBERT RIHANI; Man. DAOUD STEPHAN.

World Book Publishing: POB 11-3176, 282 rue Emile Eddé, Sanayeh, Beirut; tel. (1) 349370; fax (1) 351226; e-mail info@wbpbooks.com; internet www.wbpbooks.com; f. 1926; literature, education, philosophy, current affairs, self-help, children's books; Chair. M. SAID EZ-ZEIN; Man. Dir RAFIK EZ-ZEIN.

Broadcasting and Communications

TELECOMMUNICATIONS

Regulatory Authority

Direction Générale des Télécommunications pour l'Exploitation et la Maintenance: Ministry of Telecommunications (see above); Dir-Gen. ABDUL M. YOUSSEF.

Service Providers

OGERO (Organisme de Gestion et d'Exploitation de l'ex Radio Orient): POB 11-12226, Bir Hassan, Beirut 1107 2070; tel. (1) 840000; fax (1) 826823; internet www.ogero.gov.lb; f. 1972; 100% state-owned; plans for the incorporation of OGERO and two depts of the Ministry of Telecommunications into a single operator, Liban Télécom, were announced in 2005; preparations were stalled as a result of the conflict between Hezbollah and Israel in mid-2006, but have subsequently resumed; fixed-line operator.

In March 2004 Mobile Telecommunications Co (MTC) of Kuwait (now Zain) and Detecon (Germany) were awarded the contracts to replace Cellis and LibanCell SAL as the principal operators of mobile services in Lebanon.

Detecon: subsidiary of Deutsch Telecom (Germany); mobile services.

MTC Touch: POB 17-5051, Immeuble MTC Touch, ave Charles Helou, Beirut; tel. (1) 566111; fax (1) 564185; e-mail info@mtc.com.lb; internet www.mtctouch.com.lb; owned by Zain Group (fmrly Mobile Telecommunications Co—Kuwait); mobile services; Gen. Man. CLAUDE BASSIL.

BROADCASTING

Radio

Radio Liban: rue Arts et Métiers, Beirut; tel. (1) 343217; fax (1) 347489; internet www.96-2.com; run by the Ministry of Information in conjunction with Radio France International; f. 1937; scheduled for privatization; Dir-Gen. FOUAD KABALAN HAMDAN.

The Home Service broadcasts in Arabic on short wave, and the Foreign Service broadcasts in Portuguese, Armenian, Arabic, Spanish, French and English.

Television

Lebanese Broadcasting Corpn (LBC) Sat Ltd: POB 111, Zouk, Beirut 165853; tel. (9) 850850; fax (9) 850916; e-mail lbcsat@lbcsat.com.lb; internet www.lbcgroup.tv; f. 1985 as Lebanese Broadcasting Corpn International SAL; name changed 1996; operates satellite channel on Arabsat 2C, Arabsat 3A and Nilesat 102; programmes in Arabic, French and English; broadcasts to Lebanon, the Middle East, Europe, the USA and Australia; Chair. Sheikh PIERRE ED-DAHER.

Télé-Liban (TL) SAL: POB 11-5055, Hazmieh, 4848 Beirut; tel. (1) 793000; fax (1) 950286; e-mail tl@tele-liban.com.lb; f. 1959; commercial service; programmes in Arabic, French and English on three channels; privatization pending; Chair. and Dir-Gen. IBRAHIM EL-KHOURY; Dep. Dir-Gen. MUHAMMAD S. KARIMEH.

Future Television (Al-Mustaqbal): POB 13-6052, White House, rue Spears, Sanayeh, Beirut; tel. (1) 355355; fax (1) 753434; e-mail future@future.com.lb; internet www.future.com.lb; commercial; privately owned; Gen. Man. NADIM AL-MONLA.

Al-Manar (Lighthouse): Bir Hassan, Beirut; tel. (1) 540440; fax (1) 553138; e-mail pr@manartv.com; internet www.manartv.com.lb; f. 1991; television station owned by Lebanese Communication Group; broadcasts to Arab and Muslim audiences worldwide; operates satellite channel since May 2000; partially controlled by Hezbollah; Chair. of Bd ABDALLAH KASSIR.

During 1996–98 the Government took measures to close down unlicensed private broadcasters, and to restrict the activities of those licensed to operate. In particular, the broadcasting of news and political programmes by private satellite television channels was banned.

LEBANON *Directory*

Finance

(cap. = capital; dep. = deposits; res = reserves; m. = million; brs = branches)

BANKING

Beirut was, for many years, the leading financial and commercial centre in the Middle East, but this role was destroyed by the civil conflict during 1975–90. To restore the city as a regional focus for investment banking has been a key element of the Government's reconstruction plans.

Central Bank

Banque du Liban: POB 11-5544, rue Masraf Loubnane, Beirut; tel. (1) 750000; fax (1) 747600; e-mail bdlfx@bdl.gov.lb; internet www.bdl.gov.lb; f. 1964 as successor in Lebanon to the Banque de Syrie et du Liban; cap. and res £L1,974,363m., dep. £L33,888,223m. (Dec. 2006); Gov. RIAD T. SALAMEH; 9 brs.

Principal Commercial Banks

Al-Ahli International Bank SAL: POB 11-5556, Immeuble International, Bab Idris, rue Omar Daouk, Beirut; tel. (1) 970921; fax (1) 970939; e-mail aibmgt@dm.net.lb; f. 1964 as Bank of Lebanon and Kuwait SAL; merged with Lebanon brs of Jordan National (now Ahli) Bank and name changed as above 2001; subsidiary of Jordan Ahli Bank (97.9%); Pres. and Chair. Dr RAJAJ AL-MOUASHER; 8 brs.

Arab Finance House SAL (Islamic Bank) (AFH): POB 11-273, Riad es-Solh, Beirut 1107 2020; tel. (1) 329595; fax (1) 329797; e-mail info@arabfinancehouse.com; internet www.arabfinancehouse.com; f. 2003 as Arab Finance House SAL; merged into Arab Finance Investment House SAL in 2005, when name changed as above; commercial and investment banking; commercial and investment banking; cap. £L30.0m., res £L59.3m., dep. £L37.0m. (Dec. 2006); Chair. and Gen. Man. MUHAMMAD ABD AL-LATIF AL-MANAA.

Audi Saradar Private Bank SAL: Immeuble Clover, ave Charles Malek, Achrafieh, Beirut 1107 2805; tel. (1) 205400; fax (1) 205480; e-mail contactus@audisaradarpb.com; internet www.saradar.com; f. 1948 as Banque Marius Saradar; succeeded by Banque Saradar SAL 1956; became part of Audi Saradar Group in 2004; name changed as above 2005; cap. £L40,000m., res £L72,202m., dep. £L1,627,588m. (Dec. 2005); Chair. and Gen. Man. MARIO JOSEPH SARADAR; 7 brs.

Bank Audi SAL—Audi Saradar Group: POB 11-2560, Riad es-Solh, Beirut 1107 2808; tel. (1) 994000; fax (1) 990555; e-mail bkaudi@audi.com.lb; internet www.audi.com.lb; f. 1962 as Bank Audi; acquired Orient Credit Bank 1997 and Banque Nasr 1998; absorbed into Audi Saradar Group in 2004; cap. £L577,317m., res £L1,717,377m., dep. £L18,325,710m. (Dec. 2006); Chair. and Gen. Man. RAYMOND W. AUDI; 78 brs in Lebanon, 7 brs in Jordan.

Bank of Beirut SAL: POB 11-7354, Bank of Beirut SAL Bldg, Foch St, Beirut Central District, Beirut; tel. and fax (1) 983999; e-mail contactus@bankofbeirut.com; internet www.bankofbeirut.com.lb; f. 1973; acquired Transorient Bank 1999, Beirut Riyad Bank 2002; cap. £L158,648m., res £L223,245m., dep. £L5,209,233m. (Dec. 2006); Chair. and Gen. Man. SALIM G. SFEIR; 43 brs in Lebanon, 7 offices abroad.

Bank of Kuwait and the Arab World SAL: POB 113-6248, Bellevue Bldg, Ain at-Tineh, Verdun, Beirut 1103 2110; tel. (1) 866306; fax (1) 865299; e-mail info@bkawbank.com; internet www.bkawbank.com; f. 1959; 74% owned by Achour Group, 15% by Maacaron Group, 10% by Merhi Group and 1% by Dr Cheaib; cap. £L50,000m., res £L8,638m., dep. £L671,548m. (Dec. 2006); Chair. and Gen. Man. ABD AR-RAZZAK ACHOUR; 14 brs in Lebanon.

BankMed SAL: POB 11-0348, Centre Groupe Méditerranée, 482 rue Clémenceau, Beirut 2022 9302; tel. (1) 373937; fax (1) 362706; internet www.bankmed.com.lb; f. 1944 as Banque Naaman et Soussou; name changed to Eastern Commercial Bank 1955, Banque de la Méditerranée SAL 1970 and as above 2006; acquired Allied Bank SAL in 2006; cap. £L530,000m., res £L321,512m., dep. £L8,693,4726m. (Dec. 2006); Chair. and Gen. Man. MUHAMMAD HARIRI; Exec. Gen. Man. NEMEH SABBAGH; 46 brs.

Banque Bemo SAL: POB 16-6353, Immeuble Bemo, place Sassine, ave Elias Sarkis, Achrafieh, Beirut 1100 2120; tel. (1) 200505; fax (1) 992821; e-mail bemosal@dm.net.lb; internet www.bemobank.com; f. 1964 as Future Bank SAL; name changed to BEMO (Banque Européenne pour le Moyen-Orient) SAL 1994 and as above 2006; cap. £L16,200m. (Dec. 2006), res £L20,798m., dep. £L843,624m. (Dec. 2005); Chair. HENRY YORDAN OBEGI; Gen. Man. SAMIH H. SAADEH; 8 brs in Lebanon, 1 br. in Cyprus.

Banque de Crédit National SAL: POB 110-204, Immeuble Marfaa, 157 rue Saad Zaghloul, Beirut; tel. (1) 990808; fax (1) 975140; e-mail bncrena@dm.net.lb; f. 1920; cap. £L118,092m., res £L2,024m., dep. £L27,440m. (Dec. 2006); Pres. and Chair. ABDULLAH TAMARI; Vice-Chair. and Gen. Man. ANDRE BOULOS.

Banque de l'Industrie et du Travail SAL (BIT Bank): POB 11-3948, Immeuble BIT, 89 Riad es-Solh, Beirut 1107 2150; tel. (1) 985680; fax (1) 985681; e-mail info@bitbank.com.lb; internet www.bitbank.com.lb; f. 1960; cap. £L25,444m., res £L26,217m., dep. £L538,599m. (Dec. 2005); Chair. and Gen. Man. Sheikh FOUAD JAMIL EL-KHAZEN; Exec. Dir and Gen. Man. NABIL N. KHAIRALLAH; 12 brs.

Banque Libano-Française SAL: POB 11-0808, Tour Liberty, rue de Rome, Beirut 1107 2804; tel. and fax (1) 791332; e-mail info@eblf.com; internet www.eblf.com; f. 1967; cap. £L200,000m., res £L361,063m., dep. £L6,716,815m. (Dec. 2006); Pres., Chair. and Gen. Man. FARID RAPHAËL; 32 brs.

Banque Misr-Liban SAL: rue Riad es-Solh, Beirut 2011 9301; tel. (1) 986666; fax (1) 964296; e-mail mail@bml.com.lb; internet www.bml.com.lb; f. 1929 as Banque Misr Syrie Liban; name changed as above 1958; cap. £L27,000m., res £L24,226m., dep. £L570,055m. (Dec. 2005); Chair. MUHAMMAD KAMAL ED-DIN BARAKAT; Gen. Man. HADI NAFFI; 14 brs.

Al-Baraka Bank Lebanon SAL: POB 113-5683, 2nd Floor, Verdun 2000 Centre, Rashid Karameh St, Beirut; tel. (1) 808008; fax (1) 806499; e-mail info@al-baraka.com; internet www.al-baraka.com; f. 1992; Islamic banking; Chair. ADNAN AHMAD YOUSSEF; Gen. Man. MUTASIM MAHMASSANI; 6 brs.

BBAC (Bank of Beirut and the Arab Countries) SAL: POB 11-1536, Immeuble de la Banque, 250 rue Clémenceau, Riad es-Solh, Beirut 1107 2080; tel. (1) 366630; fax (1) 365200; e-mail marketing@bbac.com.lb; internet www.bbacbank.com; f. 1956; cap. £L114,120m., res £L60,810m., dep. £L3,496,404m. (Dec. 2005); Chair. and Gen. Man. GHASSAN T. ASSAF; 34 brs.

BLC Bank SAL: POB 11-1126, BLC Bldg, Adlieh Sq., Beirut 2064 5809; tel. and fax (1) 429000; e-mail info@blcbank.com; internet www.blcbank.com; f. 1950; owned by Supreme Council for Economic Affairs and Investment (Qatar) 96.2%; cap. £L40,320m., res –£L31,103m., dep. £L2,756,634m. (Dec. 2005); Chair. and Gen. Man. SHADI A. KARAM; 35 brs.

BLOM Bank SAL: POB 11-1912, Immeuble BLOM Bank, rue Rachid Karameh, Verdun, Beirut 1107 2807; tel. (1) 743300; fax (1) 738946; e-mail blommail@blom.com.lb; internet www.blom.com.lb; f. 1951 as Banque du Liban et d'Outre-Mer; name changed as above 2000; cap. £L240,000m., res £L1,339,613m., dep. £L18,999,225m. (Dec. 2006); Pres., Chair. and Gen. Man. Dr NAAMAN AZHARI; Vice-Chair. SAAD AZHARI; 47 brs in Lebanon, 28 brs abroad.

Byblos Bank SAL: POB 11-5605, ave Elias Sarkis, Achrafieh, Beirut 1107 2811; tel. (1) 335200; fax (1) 339436; e-mail byblosbk@byblosbank.com.lb; internet www.byblosbank.com; f. 1959; merged with Banque Beyrouth pour le Commerce SAL 1997; acquired Byblos Bank Europe SA 1998, Wedge Bank Middle East SAL 2001 and ABN AMRO Bank Lebanon 2002; cap. £L494,456m., res £L415,286m., dep. £L10,691,471m. (Dec. 2006); Pres., Chair. and Gen. Man. Dr FRANÇOIS SEMAAN BASSIL; 73 brs in Lebanon, 7 brs abroad.

Creditbank SAL: POB 16-5795, Immeuble Crédit Bancaire SAL, 680 blvd Bachir Gemayel, Achrafieh, Beirut 1100 2802; tel. (1) 485148; fax (1) 485245; e-mail info@creditbank.com.lb; internet www.creditbank.com.lb; f. 1981 as Crédit Bancaire SAL; name changed as above following merger with Crédit Lyonnais Liban SAL 2002; cap. £L23,445m., res £L27,016m., dep. £L766,321m. (Dec. 2005); Chair. and Gen. Man. TAREK JOSEPH KHALIFÉ; Vice-Chair. SALAH FOUAD ZOGHBY; 15 brs.

Crédit Libanais SAL: POB 16-6729, Centre Sofil, 5e étage, ave Charles Malek, Beirut 1100 2811; tel. (1) 200028; fax (1) 325713; e-mail info@creditlibanais.com.lb; internet www.creditlibanais.com.lb; f. 1961; cap. £L250,000m., res £L290,845m., dep. £L4,509,643m. (Dec. 2006); Pres., Chair. and Gen. Man. Dr JOSEPH M. TORBEY; 57 brs in Lebanon, 2 brs abroad.

Federal Bank of Lebanon SAL: POB 11-2209, Immeuble Renno, ave Charles Malek, St Nicolas, Beirut; tel. (1) 212300; fax (1) 215847; e-mail federal@cyberia.net.lb; f. 1952; cap. £L13,019m., res £L7,672m., dep. £L357,779m. (Dec. 2005); Chair. and Gen. Man. AYOUB FARID MICHEL SAAB; Vice-Chair. and Dep. Gen. Man. FADI MICHEL SAAB; 8 brs.

First National Bank SAL: POB 11-0435, Immeuble 147, rue Allenby, Riad es-Solh, Beirut 2012 6004; tel. (1) 963000; fax (1) 973090; e-mail info@fnb.com.lb; internet www.fnb.com.lb; f. 1996; acquired Société Bancaire du Liban SAL 2002; cap. £L57,964m., res £L9,972m., dep. £L1,661,453m. (Dec. 2005); Chair. and Gen. Man. RAMI REFAAT EN-NIMER; 16 brs.

Fransabank SAL: POB 11-0393, Riad es-Solh, Beirut 1107 2803; tel. (1) 340180; fax (1) 354572; e-mail fsb@fransabank.com; internet www.fransabank.com; f. 1978 as a result of merger between Banque Sabbag SAL and Banque Française por le Moyen Orient SAL; acquired Banque Tohmé SAL 1993, Universal Bank SAL 1999, United Bank of Saudi and Lebanon SAL 2001 and Banque de la Beka'a SAL 2003; Banque de la Beka'a was subsequently sold to Bank of Sharjah Ltd (United Arab Emirates) in July 2007; cap. £L315,000m., res £L246,261m., dep. £L6,654,311m. (Dec. 2006);

Chair. and Gen. Man. ADNAN KASSAR; Vice-Chair. and Vice-Gen. Man. ADEL KASSAR; 63 brs.

Intercontinental Bank of Lebanon SAL: POB 11-5292, Immeuble Ittihadiah, ave Charles Malek, Beirut 1107 2190; tel. (1) 200350; fax (1) 204505; e-mail ibl@ibl.com.lb; internet www.ibl.com.lb; f. 1961; cap. £L30,000m., res £L15,935m., dep. £L2,195,311m. (Dec. 2005); Chair. and Gen. Man. SALIM Y. HABIB; 13 brs in Lebanon, 2 abroad.

Jammal Trust Bank SAL: POB 11-5640, Immeuble Jammal, rue Verdun, Beirut; tel. (1) 805702; fax (1) 864170; e-mail services@jammalbank.com.lb; internet www.jammalbank.co.lb/home.html; f. 1963 as Investment Bank SAL; cap. £L58,000m., res £L8,165m., dep. £L442,289m. (Dec. 2006); Chair. and Gen. Man. ALI AL-JAMMAL; 21 brs in Lebanon, 4 brs in Egypt.

Lebanese Canadian Bank: POB 11-2520, Immeuble Ghantous, blvd Dora, Riad es-Solh, Beirut 1107 2110; tel. and fax (1) 379922; e-mail lebcan@lebcanbank.com; internet www.lebcanbank.com; f. 1960 as Banque des Activités Economiques; name changed to The Royal Bank of Canada (Middle East) SAL 1970 and as above 1988; cap. £L110,700.0m., res £L42,386.1m., dep. £L3,824,537.0m. (Dec. 2006); Chair. and Gen. Man. GEORGES ZARD ABOU JAOUDÉ; 32 brs in Lebanon, 1 rep. office in Canada.

Lebanese Swiss Bank SAL: POB 11-9552, Immeuble Hoss, 6e étage, rue Emile Eddé, place Hamra, Ras Beirut, Beirut; tel. (1) 354501; fax (1) 346242; e-mail lbs@t-net.com.lb; f. 1962; cap. £L40,000m., res £L20,882m., dep. £L552,866m. (Dec. 2006); Pres., Chair. and Gen. Man. Dr TANAL SABBAH; 10 brs.

Lebanon and Gulf Bank SAL: POB 11-3360, 124 Allenby St, Beirut Central District, Beirut; tel. (1) 965000; fax (1) 965999; e-mail info@lgb.com.lb; internet www.lgb.com.lb; f. 1963 as Banque de Crédit Agricole; name changed as above 1980; cap. £L50,000m., res £L11,218m., dep. £L1,351,804m. (Dec. 2006); Pres., Chair. and Gen. Man. ABD AL-HAFIZ MAHMOUD ITANI; 11 brs.

MEAB SAL: POB 14-5958, Beirut 1105 2080; tel. (1) 826740; fax (1) 841190; e-mail meab@meabank.com; internet www.meabank.com; f. 1991 as Middle East and Africa Bank SAL; name changed as above 2003; cap. £L24,000m., res £L8,739m., dep. £L556,717m. (Dec. 2006); Chair. HASSAN M. HEJEIJ; Man. Dir KASSEM HEJEIJ; Gen. Man. MOUNIR KARAM; 5 brs.

National Bank of Kuwait (Lebanon) SAL: POB 11-5727, BAC Bldg, Sanayeh Sq., Justinien St, Riad es-Solh, Beirut 1107 2200; tel. (1) 741111; fax (1) 747866; e-mail info@nbk.com.lb; internet www.nbk.com.lb; f. 1963 as Rifbank; name changed as above 1996; cap. £L40,020m., res £L6,425m., dep. £L320,859m. (Dec. 2006); Chair. IBRAHIM DABDOUB; Gen. Man. HANY SHERIF; 10 brs.

Near East Commercial Bank SAL: POB 16-5766, SNA Bldg, Said Akl St, Achrafieh, Beirut 1100 2070; tel. and fax (1) 200770; fax 339000; e-mail necb@necbbank.com; internet www.necbbank.com; f. 1978; cap. £L26,575m., res £L670m., dep. £L182,270m. (Aug. 2007); Chair. DOMINIQUE LANG; 5 brs.

North Africa Commercial Bank SAL: POB 11-9575, Centre Aresco, rue Justinian, Beirut; tel. (1) 759000; fax (1) 346322; e-mail info@nacb.com.lb; internet www.nacb.com.lb; f. 1973; cap. £L45,687m., res L£14m., dep. £L817,545m. (Dec. 2006); Pres. and Chair. ABOUBAKER ALI ASH-SHARIF; Gen. Man. NAJIB ABD AL-HAMID LATRASH; 2 brs.

Société Générale de Banque au Liban (SGBL): POB 11-2955, rond-point Salomé, Sin el-Fil, Beirut; tel. (1) 499813; fax (1) 502820; e-mail sgbl@sgbl.com.lb; internet www.sgbl.com.lb; f. 1953 as Banque Belgo-Libanaise; name changed to Société Générale Libano Européenne de Banque SAL in 1969; present name adopted in 2001; cap. £L10,600m., res £L12,600m. (Dec. 2006); CEO ANTOUN SEHNAOUI; 41 brs in Lebanon, 23 abroad.

Société Nouvelle de la Banque de Syrie et du Liban SAL (SNBSL): POB 11-957, rue Riad es-Solh, Beirut; tel. (1) 980080; fax (1) 980091; e-mail snbsl@snbsl.com.lb; f. 1963; cap. £L36,225m., res £L14,400m., dep. £L756,510m. (Dec. 2006); Chair. RAMSAY A. EL-KHOURY; Gen. Man. SÉLIM STÉPHAN; 17 brs.

Standard Chartered Bank SAL: POB 70216, Antélias; tel. and fax (4) 542474; e-mail aamir.hussain@standardchartered.com; internet www.standardchartered.com/lb; f. 1979 as Metropolitan Bank SAL; acquired by Standard Chartered Bank 2000; cap. £L12,000m., res £L603m., dep. £L150,902m. (Dec. 2005); Chair. MARTIN FISH; CEO AAMIR HUSSEIN; 5 brs.

Syrian Lebanese Commercial Bank SAL: POB 113-5127, Immeuble Cinéma Hamra, rue Hamra, Hamra, Beirut; tel. (1) 738274; fax (1) 738228; e-mail hamra@slcbk.com; internet www.slcb.com.lb; f. 1974; cap. £L90,000m., res £L14,860m., dep. £L330,854m. (Dec. 2006); Chair. and Gen. Man. Dr DOURAID AHMAD DERGHAM; Vice-Chair. MARCEL EL-KHOURY; 3 brs in Lebanon, 2 offices in Syria.

Development Bank

Audi Saradar Investment Bank SAL: POB 16-5110, Bank Audi Plaza, Omar ad-Daouk St, Beirut; tel. (1) 994000; fax (1) 999406; e-mail contactus@asib.com; internet www.asib.com; f. 1974 as Investment and Finance Bank; name changed to Audi Investment Bank SAL 1996 and as above 2004; medium- and long-term loans, 100% from Lebanese sources; owned by Bank Audi SAL—Audi Saradar Group; cap. £L25,075m., res £L100,099m., dep. £L1,193,352m. (Dec. 2005); Chair. and Gen. Man. Dr MARWAN M. GHANDOUR.

Banking Association

Association of Banks in Lebanon: POB 976, Association of Banks in Lebanon Bldg, Gouraud St, Saifi, Beirut; tel. (1) 970500; fax (1) 970501; e-mail abl@abl.org.lb; internet www.abl.org.lb; f. 1959; serves and promotes the interests of the banking community in Lebanon; mems: 63 banks and 8 banking rep. offices; Pres. and Chair. Dr FRANÇOIS BASSIL; Sec.-Gen. Dr MAKRAM SADER.

STOCK EXCHANGE

Beirut Stock Exchange (BSE): POB 11-3552, 4e étage, Bloc A3, Immeuble Azareih, Beirut; tel. (1) 993555; fax (1) 993444; e-mail bse@bse.com.lb; internet www.bse.com.lb; f. 1920; recommenced trading in Jan. 1996; 10 cttee mems; Cttee Pres. Dr FADI KHALAF.

INSURANCE

About 80 insurance companies were registered in Lebanon in the late 1990s, although fewer than one-half of these were operational. An insurance law enacted in 1999 increased the required capital base for insurance firms and provided tax incentives for mergers within the sector.

Arabia Insurance Co SAL: POB 11-2172, Arabia House, rue de Phénicie, Beirut; tel. (1) 363610; fax (1) 365139; e-mail arabia@arabia-ins.com.lb; internet www.arabiainsurance.com; f. 1944; cap. £L51,000m.; Chair. WAHBÉ A. TAMARI; CEO FADY SHAMMAS.

Bankers Assurance SAL: POB 11-4293, Immeuble Capitole, rue Riad es-Solh, Beirut; tel. (1) 988777; fax (1) 984004; e-mail mail@bankers-assurance.com; internet www.bankers-assurance.com; f. 1972; Chair. SABA NADER; Gen. Man. EUGÈNE NADER.

Commercial Insurance Co (Lebanon) SAL: POB 11-4351, Centre Starco, North Block, 9th Floor, Beirut; tel. (1) 373070; fax (1) 373071; e-mail comins@commercialinsurance.com.lb; internet www.commercialinsurance.com.lb; f. 1962; cap. £L6,000m. (March 2006); Chair. MAX R. ZACCAR; 2 brs.

Compagnie Libanaise d'Assurances SAL: POB 3685, rue Riad es-Solh, Beirut; tel. (1) 868988; f. 1951; Chair. JEAN F. S. ABOUJAOUDÉ; Gen. Man. JIHAD SHAKER.

Al-Ittihad al-Watani: POB 11-1270, Jisr al-Wati, Immeuble Al-Ittihad al-Watani, Beirut; tel. (1) 426480; fax (1) 426486; e-mail webmaster@alittihadalwatani.com.lb; internet www.alittihadalwatani.com.lb; f. 1947; cap. £L20.6m. (2005); Chair. and Gen. Man. TANNOUS FEGHALI.

Libano-Suisse Insurance Co SAL: POB 11-3821, Commerce and Finance Bldg, Beirut 1107 2150; tel. (1) 364461; fax (1) 368724; e-mail libasuis@dm.net.lb; internet www.libano-suisse.com; f. 1959; cap. £L4,050m. (2000); Chair. MICHEL PIERRE PHARAON; Gen. Man. LUCIEN LETAYEF, Jr.

Al-Mashrek Insurance and Reinsurance SAL: POB 16-6154, Al-Mashrek Bldg, 65 Aabrine St, Achrafieh, Beirut 1100 2100; tel. (1) 204666; fax (1) 337625; e-mail almashrek@almashrek.com.lb; internet www.almashrek.com.lb; f. 1962; Chair. and CEO ABRAHAM MATOSSIAN.

'La Phénicienne' SAL: POB 11-5652, Immeuble Hanna Haddad, rue Amine Gemayel, Sioufi, Beirut; tel. (1) 425484; fax (1) 424532; f. 1964; Chair. and Gen. Man. TANNOUS C. FEGHALI.

Société Nationale d'Assurances SAL: POB 16-6528, Immeuble SNA, Hazmieh, Beirut 1100 2130; tel. (1) 956600; fax (1) 956624; e-mail sna@sna.com.lb; internet www.sna.com.lb; f. 1963; cap. £L13,264m. (2006); Chair., CEO and Gen. Man. ANTOINE WAKIM.

Trade and Industry

DEVELOPMENT ORGANIZATIONS

Council for Development and Reconstruction (CDR): POB 116-5351, Tallet es-Serail, Beirut; tel. (1) 643982; fax (1) 647947; e-mail general@cdr.gov.lb; internet www.cdr.gov.lb; f. 1977; an autonomous public institution reporting to the Cabinet, the CDR is charged with the co-ordination, planning and execution of Lebanon's public reconstruction programme; it plays a major role in attracting foreign funds; Pres. NABIL JISR.

LEBANON   *Directory*

Investment Development Authority of Lebanon (IDAL): POB 113-7251, Azarieh Tower, 4th Floor, Emir Bechir St, Riad es-Solh, Beirut; tel. (1) 983306; fax (1) 983302; e-mail invest@idal.com.lb; internet www.idal.com.lb; f. 1994; state-owned; Chair. and Gen. Man. NABIL ITANI.

Société Libanaise pour le Développement et la Reconstruction de Beyrouth (SOLIDERE): POB 11-9493, 149 rue Saad Zaghoul, Beirut 2012 7305; tel. (1) 980650; fax (1) 980662; e-mail solidere@solidere.com.lb; internet www.solidere.com.lb; f. 1994; real estate co responsible for reconstruction of Beirut Central District after the civil war; Chair. NASSER CHAMMAA; Gen. Man. MOUNIR DOUAIDY.

CHAMBERS OF COMMERCE AND INDUSTRY

Federation of the Chambers of Commerce, Industry and Agriculture in Lebanon: POB 11-1801, Immeuble CCIAB, rue Justinian, Sanayeh, Beirut; tel. (1) 744702; fax (1) 349614; e-mail fccial@cci-fed.org.lb; internet www.cci-fed.org.lb; f. 1996; Pres. GHAZI KRAYTEM.

Chamber of Commerce, Industry and Agriculture of Beirut and Mount Lebanon: POB 11-1801, rue Justinian, Sanayeh, Beirut; tel. (1) 744160; fax (1) 353395; e-mail information@ccib.org.lb; internet www.ccib.org.lb; f. 1898; 32,000 mems; Pres. GHAZI KRAYTEM.

Chamber of Commerce, Industry and Agriculture of Tripoli and North Lebanon: POB 47, rue Bechara Khoury, Tripoli; tel. (6) 627162; fax (6) 442042; e-mail abdallahg@cciat.org.lb; internet www.cciat.org.lb; Chair. ABDALLAH GHANDOUR.

Chamber of Commerce, Industry and Agriculture in Sidon and South Lebanon: POB 41, rue Maarouf Saad, Sidon; tel. (7) 720123; fax (7) 722986; e-mail chamber@ccias.org.lb; internet www.ccias.org.lb; f. 1933; Pres. MUHAMMAD ZAATARI.

Chamber of Commerce, Industry and Agriculture of Zahleh and Beka'a: POB 100, Zahleh; tel. (8) 802602; fax (8) 800050; e-mail info@cciaz.org.lb; internet www.cciaz.org.lb; f. 1939; 2,500 mems; Pres. EDMOND JREISSATI.

EMPLOYERS' ASSOCIATION

Association of Lebanese Industrialists: Chamber of Commerce and Industry Bldg, 5e étage, rue Justinien, Sanayeh, Beirut; tel. (1) 350280; fax (1) 351167; e-mail ali@ali.org.lb; internet www.ali.org.lb; Pres. FADY ABBOUD; Gen. Man. SAAD S. OUEINI.

UTILITIES

Electricity

Electricité du Liban (EdL): POB 131, Immeuble de l'Electricité du Liban, 22 rue du Fleuve, Beirut; tel. (1) 442720; fax (1) 583084; e-mail info@edl.gov.lb; internet www.edl.gov.lb; f. 1954; state-owned; scheduled for privatization from 2003; Chair. and Dir-Gen. KAMAL F. HAYEK.

Water

From the late 1990s the Government began a process of establishing five new regional water authorities (in the governorates of the North, South, Beka'a, Beirut and Mount Lebanon), to replace the existing water authorities and committees. Under the reorganization the new authorities were to operate under the supervision of the Ministry of Energy and Water.

Beirut Water Supply Office: Beirut; Pres. LUCIEN MOBAYAD.

North Lebanon Water Authority: Chair. and Gen. Man. JAMAL ABD AL-LATIF KARIM.

South Lebanon Water Authority: Chair. and Gen. Man. AHMAD HASSAN NIZAM.

TRADE UNION FEDERATION

Confédération Générale des Travailleurs du Liban (CGTL): POB 4381, Beirut; f. 1958; 300,000 mems; only national labour centre in Lebanon and sole rep. of working classes; comprises 18 affiliated feds incl. all 150 unions in Lebanon; Pres. GHASSAN GHOSN.

Transport

RAILWAYS

Office des Chemins de Fer de l'Etat Libanais et du Transport en Commun: POB 11-109, Gare St Michel, Nahr, Beirut; tel. (1) 587211; fax (1) 447007; since 1961 all railways in Lebanon have been state-owned. The original network of some 412 km is no longer functioning. However, in 2004 work began on a project to reconstruct a section of the railway network between Tripoli and the Syrian border; Dir-Gen. and Pres. RADWAN BOU NASSER ED-DIN.

ROADS

At 31 December 1996 Lebanon had an estimated 6,350 km of roads, of which 2,170 km were highways, main or national roads and 1,370 km were secondary or regional roads. The total road network in 1999 was estimated at 7,300 km, of which 84.9% was paved. The two international motorways are the north–south coastal road and the road connecting Beirut with Damascus in Syria. Among the major roads are those crossing the Beka'a and continuing south to Bent-Jbail and the Shtaura–Ba'albek road. Hard-surfaced roads connect Jezzine with Moukhtara, Bzebdine with Metn, Meyroub with Afka and Tannourine. A road construction project, costing some US $100m., was planned for Beirut in the late 1990s. A new, 8-km highway, linking around 26 villages in southern Lebanon, was inaugurated in August 2000. It was reported in late July 2006 that up to 80% of Lebanon's major roads, and almost all of its bridges, had been destroyed as a result of the Israeli military offensive against infrastructural targets alleged to be in use by Hezbollah militants during Israel's conflict with the organization, which began in early July.

SHIPPING

In the 1990s a two-phase programme to rehabilitate and expand the port of Beirut commenced, involving the construction of an industrial free zone, a fifth basin and a major container terminal, at an estimated cost of US $1,000m.; the container terminal became operational in February 2005. Tripoli, the northern Mediterranean terminus of the oil pipeline from Iraq (the other is Haifa, Israel—not in use since 1948), is also a busy port, with good equipment and facilities. Jounieh, north of Beirut, is Lebanon's third most important port. A new deep-water sea port is to be constructed south of Sidon. The reconstructed port of an-Naqoura, in what was then the 'security zone' along the border with Israel, was inaugurated in June 1987. Several ports were bombed by Israeli forces during the conflict of July–August 2006 and a complete sea blockade of Lebanon was imposed by Israel at this time.

Port Authorities

Gestion et Exploitation du Port de Beyrouth: POB 1490, Beirut; tel. (1) 580211; fax (1) 585835; e-mail info@portdebeyrouth.com; internet www.portdebeyrouth.com; Pres., Dir-Gen. and Man. Dir HASSAN KAMEL KRAYTEM; Harbour Master MAROUN KHOURY.

Service d'Exploitation du Port de Tripoli: El Mina, Tripoli; tel. (6) 601225; fax (6) 220180; e-mail tport@terra.net.lb; f. 1959; Harbour Master MARWAN BAROUDI.

Principal Shipping Companies

Youssef A Abourahal and Hanna N Tabet: POB 11-5890, Immeuble Ghantous, autostrade Dora, Beirut; tel. (1) 263872.

Ets Paul Adem: Centre Moucarri, 6e étage, autostrade Dora, Bourj Hammoud, Beirut; tel. (1) 244610; fax (1) 244612; e-mail padco@inco.com.lb; f. 1971; ship owners, operators, maritime agents, brokers, consultants; Gen. Man. PAUL ADEM.

Ademar Shipping Lines: POB 175-231, rue Shafaka, Al-Medawar, Beirut; tel. and fax (1) 445093; e-mail ademar@sodetel.net.lb.

Agence Générale Maritime (AGEMAR) SARL: POB 9255, Centre Burotec, 7e étage, rue Pasteur, Beirut; tel. (1) 583885; fax (1) 583884; Dirs S. MEDLEJ, N. MEDLEJ.

Amin Kawar & Sons (Jordan): POB 4230, Beirut; tel. (1) 352525; fax (1) 353802; e-mail amkawar@inco.com.lb; internet www.kawar.com; f. 1963; Chair. TAWFIQ AMIN KAWAR; CEO RUDAIN KAWAR.

Arab Shipping and Chartering Co: POB 1084, Immeuble Ghandour, ave des Français, Beirut; tel. (1) 371044; fax (1) 373370; e-mail arabship@dm.net.lb; agents for China Ocean Shipping Co.

Associated Levant Lines SAL: POB 110371, Immeuble Mercedes, autostrade Dora, Beirut; tel. (1) 255366; fax (1) 255362; e-mail tgf-all@dm.net.lb; Dirs T. GARGOUR, N. GARGOUR, H. GARGOUR.

Wafic Begdache: Immeuble Wazi, 4e étage, rue Moussaitbé, Beirut; tel. (1) 319920; fax (1) 815002; e-mail mody@lebaneseshipping.com.

Consolidated Bulk Inc: POB 70-152, Centre St Elie, Bloc A, 6e étage, Antélias, Beirut; tel. (4) 410724; fax (4) 402842; e-mail info@bulkgroup.net.

Continental Ship Management SARL: POB 90-1413, Centre Dora Moucarri, 8e étage, appt 804, Beirut; tel. (1) 583654; fax (1) 584440.

O. D. Debbas & Sons: POB 16-6678, Immeuble Debbas, 530 blvd Corniche du Fleuve, Beirut; tel. (1) 585253; fax (1) 587135; e-mail oddebbas@oddebbas.com; internet www.oddebbas.com; f. 1892; Man. Dir OIDIH ELIE DEBBAS.

Dery Shipping Lines Ltd: POB 5720-113, Beirut; tel. (1) 862442; fax (1) 344146.

Diana K Shipping Co: POB 113-5125, Immeuble Ajouz, rue Kenedi, Ein Mreisseh, Beirut; tel. (1) 363314; fax (1) 369712;

e-mail dianak@cyberia.net.lb; Marine Dept Man. Capt. AMIN HABBAL.

Fauzi Jemil Ghandour: POB 1084, Beirut 1107 2070; tel. (1) 373376; fax (1) 360048; e-mail ali@seahorsenet.com; agents for Ecuadorian Line.

Gezairi Chartering and Shipping Co (GEZACHART): POB 11-1402, Immeuble Gezairi, place Gezairi, Ras Beirut 2034 0716; tel. (1) 783783; fax (1) 784784; e-mail gezairi@gezairi.com; internet www.gezairi.com; ship management, chartering, brokerage.

Gulf Agency Co (Lebanon) Ltd: POB 11 4392, Riad es-Solh, Beirut 1107 2160; tel. (1) 446189; fax (1) 446097; e-mail lebanon@gacworld.com; f. 1969; Gen. Man. SIMON G. BEJJANI.

Lebanese Navigators Co SARL: POB 11-0239, Immeuble Aleddine, blvd Ghobeiry, Beirut; tel. (1) 822664; fax (1) 603334.

Medawar Shipping Co SARL: POB 8962/11, Immeuble Kanafani, rue al-Arz, Saifi, Beirut; tel. (1) 447277; fax (1) 447662.

Mediterranean Feedering Co SARL: POB 70-1187, Immeuble Akak, autostrade Dbayeh, Beirut; tel. (1) 403056; fax (1) 406444; e-mail mfcbeirut@attmail.com; Man. Dir EMILE AKEF EL-KHOURY.

Orient Shipping and Trading Co SARL: POB 11-2561, Immeuble Moumneh, no 72, rue Ain al-Mraisseh 54, Beirut; tel. (1) 644252; fax (1) 602221; Dirs ELIE ZAROUBY, EMILE ZAROUBY.

Rassem Shipping Agency: POB 11-8460, Immeuble Agha, Raoucheh, Beirut; tel. (1) 866372; fax (1) 805593.

Riga Brothers: POB 17-5134, Immeuble Mitri Haddad, rue du Port, Beirut; tel. (1) 406882.

G. Sahyouni & Co SARL: POB 17-5452, Mar Mikhael, Beirut 1104 2040; tel. (1) 257046; fax (1) 241317; e-mail lloydsbey@inco.com.lb; f. 1989; agents for Baltic Control Lebanon Ltd, SARL, and Lloyds; Man. Dir GEORGE SHYOUNI; Financial Man. HENRY CHIDIAC.

Sinno Trading and Navigation Agency: POB 113-6977, 4e étage, Immeuble Rebeiz, Beirut; tel. and fax (1) 446707; Chair. MUHIEDDINE F. SINNO; Man. Dir AHMED JABBOURY.

A. Sleiman Co & Sons: Immeuble Saroulla, 3e étage, rue Hamra, Beirut; tel. (1) 354240; fax (1) 340262.

Union Shipping and Chartering Agency SAL: POB 2856, Immeuble Ghandour, ave des Français, Beirut 1107 2120; tel. (1) 373376; fax (1) 360048; e-mail ucsa@seahorsenet.com; agents for Jadroslobodna, Jugo Oceania, Atlanska Plovidba, Jadroplov and Maruba.

CIVIL AVIATION

Services from the country's principal airport, in Beirut, were subject to frequent disruptions after 1975; its location in predominantly Muslim west Beirut made it virtually inaccessible to non-Muslims. In 1986 a new airport, based on an existing military airfield, was opened at Halat, north of Beirut, by Christian concerns, but commercial operations from the airport were not authorized by the Government. Services to and from Beirut by Middle East Airlines (MEA) were suspended, and the airport closed, in January 1987, after the Maronite Lebanese Forces (LF) militia shelled the airport and threatened to attack MEA aircraft if services from their own airport, at Halat, did not receive official authorization. Beirut airport was reopened in May, after the LF accepted government assurances that Halat would receive the necessary authorization for civil use. However, the commission concluded that Halat did not possess the facilities to cater for international air traffic. Some 3.3m. passengers used Beirut International Airport in 2004. In late 2001 a major expansion project at the airport was completed, at an estimated cost of US $600m.; facilities included a new terminal building and two new runways, increasing handling capacity to 6m. passengers a year. In May 2005 the airport was renamed Beirut Rafik Hariri International Airport in honour of the former Prime Minister who had been killed in February. However, the airport was targeted by Israeli armed forces in July 2006, and was closed to commercial flights during the conflict between Israel and Hezbollah. Following extensive repairs to damaged runways and other infrastructure, the airport reopened to commercial operations in August.

MEA (Middle East Airlines, Air Liban SAL): POB 11-206, blvd de l'Aéroport, Beirut 1107 2801; tel. (1) 628888; fax (1) 629260; e-mail mikaouir@mea.com.lb; internet www.mea.com.lb; f. 1945; acquired Lebanese International Airways in 1969; privatization pending; regular services throughout Europe, the Middle East, North and West Africa, and the Far East; Chair. and Dir-Gen. MUHAMMAD A. EL-HOUT; Commercial Man. NIZAR KHOURY.

Trans-Mediterranean Airways SAL (TMA): POB 30-1001, Beirut International Airport, Beirut; tel. (1) 629210; fax (1) 629219; e-mail cargo@tmacargo.com; internet www.tma.com.lb; f. 1953; scheduled services, charter activities and aircraft lease operations covering Europe, the Middle East, Africa and the Far East; also provides handling, storage and maintenance services; Chair. and Pres. FADI N. SAAB.

Tourism

Before the civil war, Lebanon was a major tourist centre, and its scenic beauty, sunny climate and historic sites attracted some 2m. visitors annually. In 1974 tourism contributed about 20% of the country's income. Since the end of the civil conflict, tourist facilities (in particular hotels) have begun to be reconstructed, and the Government has chosen to concentrate its efforts on the promotion of cultural as well as conference and exhibition-based tourism. In 1999 UNESCO declared Beirut as the Cultural Capital of the Arab World. Lebanon is also being promoted as an 'eco-tourism' destination. Excluding Syrian visitors, the annual total of tourist arrivals increased from 177,503 in 1992 to some 1.28m. in 2004; arrivals declined to 1.14m. in 2005. Tourism receipts fell from US $1,221m. in 1998 to $742m. in 2000, before rising again, to reach $5,931m. in 2004; there was a slight decrease, to $5,869m., in 2005. The Lebanese tourism industry experienced a significant downturn in the aftermath of the conflict between Israel and Hezbollah in mid-2006. By early 2008 the prospects for an imminent recovery in the sector were particularly gloomy, owing to the ongoing political crisis (see Recent History) and following a series of politically motivated bombings and assassinations; it was reported that several Gulf states had advised their citizens against travelling to Lebanon.

Ministry of Tourism: see section on The Government (Ministries).

LESOTHO

Introductory Survey

Location, Climate, Language, Religion, Flag, Capital

The Kingdom of Lesotho is a land-locked country, entirely surrounded by South Africa. The climate is generally mild, although cooler in the highlands: lowland temperatures range from a maximum of 32°C (90°F) in summer (October to April) to a minimum of −7°C (20°F) in winter. Rainfall averages about 725 mm (29 ins) per year, mostly falling in summer. The official languages are English and Sesotho; other languages spoken include Zulu and Xhosa. About 90% of the population are Christians. The largest denominations are the Roman Catholic, Lesotho Evangelical and Anglican Churches. The national flag (official proportions 2 by 3) has three horizontal stripes from top to bottom of blue, white and green, with a black traditional Basotho hat in the centre of the white stripe. The capital is Maseru.

Recent History

Lesotho was formerly Basutoland, a dependency of the United Kingdom. In 1868, at the request of the Basotho people's chief, the territory became a British protectorate. Basutoland was annexed to Cape Colony (now part of South Africa) in 1871, but detached in 1884. It became a separate British colony and was administered as one of the High Commission Territories in southern Africa (the others being the protectorates of Bechuanaland, now Botswana, and Swaziland). The British Act of Parliament that established the Union of South Africa in 1910 also provided for the possible inclusion in South Africa of the three High Commission Territories, subject to local consent: the native chiefs opposed requests by successive South African Governments for the transfer of the three territories.

Within Basutoland a revised Constitution, which established the colony's first Legislative Council, was introduced in 1956. A new document, granting limited powers of self-government, was adopted in September 1959. Basutoland's first general election, on the basis of universal adult suffrage, took place on 29 April 1965, and full internal self-government was achieved the following day. Moshoeshoe II, Paramount Chief since 1960, was recognized as King. The Basutoland National Party (BNP), a conservative group supporting limited co-operation with South Africa, narrowly won a majority of the seats in the new Legislative Assembly. The BNP's leader, Chief Leabua Jonathan, was appointed Prime Minister in July 1965. Basutoland became independent, as Lesotho, on 4 October 1966. The new Constitution provided for a bicameral legislature, comprising the 60-seat National Assembly and the 33-member Senate; executive power was vested in the Cabinet, which was presided over by the Prime Minister. The King was designated Head of State.

The BNP, restyled the Basotho National Party, remained in power at independence. A general election was held in January 1970, at which the opposition Basotho Congress Party (BCP), a pan-Africanist group led by Dr Ntsu Mokhehle, appeared to have won a majority of seats in the National Assembly. Chief Jonathan declared a state of emergency, suspended the Constitution and arrested several BCP organizers. The election was annulled, and the legislature prorogued. King Moshoeshoe II was placed under house arrest and subsequently exiled, although he returned in December after accepting a government order banning him from participating in politics. The country was thus effectively under the Prime Minister's personal control. An interim National Assembly, comprising the former Senate (mainly chiefs) and 60 members nominated by the Cabinet, was inaugurated in April 1973. The state of emergency was revoked in July. However, following a failed coup attempt in January 1974 by alleged supporters of the BCP, Chief Jonathan introduced stringent security laws. Mokhehle and other prominent members of the BCP went into exile abroad, and the party split into two factions, internal and external. The latter, led by Mokhehle, was supported by the Lesotho Liberation Army (LLA), which was responsible for terrorist attacks in Lesotho during the late 1970s and the 1980s.

Although Lesotho was economically dependent on South Africa, and the Government's official policy during the 1970s was one of 'dialogue' with its neighbour, Chief Jonathan repeatedly criticized the apartheid regime, and supported the then banned African National Congress of South Africa (ANC). In December 1982 South African forces launched a major assault on the homes of ANC members in Maseru, killing more than 40 people. Lesotho's persistent refusal to sign a joint non-aggression pact led South Africa to impound consignments of armaments destined for Lesotho, and again, in August 1984, to threaten economic sanctions.

In December 1985 South African commando troops were held responsible by the Lesotho Government for a raid in Maseru in which nine people (including several ANC members) were killed. South Africa imposed a blockade on the border with Lesotho from the beginning of 1986. Five of Lesotho's opposition leaders were arrested on their return from talks in South Africa, and there were reports of fighting between factions of the armed forces. On 20 January Chief Jonathan's Government was overthrown in a coup led by Maj.-Gen. Justin Lekhanya, the head of the armed forces. A Military Council, chaired by Lekhanya, was established and executive and legislative powers were to be vested in King Moshoeshoe, assisted by the Military Council and a (mainly civilian) Council of Ministers. About 60 ANC members were subsequently deported from Lesotho, and the South African blockade was ended. In March 1986 the Military Council suspended all formal political activity. In September the Council of Ministers was restructured, giving increased responsibility to Lekhanya, and the Military Council held discussions with the leaders of the five main opposition parties.

Although the South African Government denied having any part in the coup, the Lekhanya regime proved to be more amenable to South Africa's regional security policy. In March 1986 it was announced that the two countries had reached an informal agreement whereby neither would allow its territory to be used for attacks against the other. Moreover, the Lesotho Government did not join other African states in pressing for international economic sanctions against South Africa. In March 1988 Lesotho and South Africa reached final agreement on the Lesotho Highlands Water Project (LHWP), a major scheme to supply water to South Africa.

In May 1988 Mokhehle was allowed to return to Lesotho after 14 years of exile. In 1989 the LLA was said to have disbanded, and by 1990 the two factions of the BCP had apparently reunited under Mokhehle's leadership.

In February 1990 Lekhanya dismissed three members of the Military Council and one member of the Council of Ministers, accusing them of 'insubordination'. When Moshoeshoe refused to approve new appointments to the Military Council, Lekhanya suspended the monarch's executive and legislative powers, which were assumed by the Military Council in March. Moshoeshoe (who remained Head of State) was exiled in the United Kingdom. Lekhanya announced that a general election would take place during 1992; however, party political activity remained outlawed. In June 1990 a National Constituent Assembly (including Lekhanya, members of the Council of Ministers, representatives of banned political parties, traditional chiefs and business leaders) was inaugurated to draft a new constitution. In October Lekhanya invited the King to return from exile. Moshoeshoe responded that his return would be conditional upon the ending of military rule and the establishment of an interim government, pending the readoption of the 1966 Constitution. On 6 November 1990 Lekhanya promulgated an order dethroning the King with immediate effect. Lesotho's 22 principal chiefs elected Moshoeshoe's elder son, Prince David Mohato Bereng Seeiso, as the new King; on 12 November he acceded to the throne, as King Letsie III, having undertaken to remain detached from politics.

On 30 April 1991 Lekhanya was deposed in a coup organized by disaffected army officers. Col (later Maj.-Gen.) Elias Phitsoane Ramaema succeeded Lekhanya as Chairman of the Military Council. Ramaema repealed the ban on party political activity, and by July the National Constituent Assembly had completed the draft Constitution. In May 1992 Lesotho and South Africa agreed to establish diplomatic relations at ambassadorial level. Following talks in the United Kingdom with Ramaema, former King Moshoeshoe returned from exile in July.

The general election was eventually held in March 1993. The BCP secured all 65 seats in the new National Assembly, winning 54% of the votes cast. In April Mokhehle was inaugurated as Prime Minister, and King Letsie swore allegiance to the new Constitution, under the terms of which he remained Head of State with no executive or legislative powers; executive authority was vested in the Cabinet.

A mutiny in November 1993 by the Royal Lesotho Defence Force (RLDF), was apparently precipitated by a proposal to place the military under the command of a senior member of the LLA. Four senior army officers were subsequently reported to have resigned their posts. Skirmishes near Maseru in January 1994 escalated into more serious fighting between some 600 rebel troops and a 150-strong contingent of forces loyal to the Government, reportedly resulting in the deaths of at least five soldiers and three civilians. Following mediation efforts involving representatives of Botswana, South Africa, Zimbabwe, the Commonwealth (see p. 206), the Organization of African Unity (OAU, now the African Union, see p. 164—AU) and the UN, a truce entered force, and at the beginning of February the rival factions surrendered their weapons and returned to barracks. In April, however, the Deputy Prime Minister, Selometsi Baholo (who also held the finance portfolio), was killed during an abduction attempt by disaffected troops.

A commission to investigate the armed forces unrest of January and April 1994 began work in July. In that month Mokhehle appointed a commission of inquiry into the dethronement of King Moshoeshoe II. On 17 August Letsie announced that he had dissolved the National Assembly, dismissed the Government and suspended sections of the Constitution, citing 'popular dissatisfaction' with the BCP administration. Although several thousand people gathered outside the royal palace in Maseru in support of the deposed Government, army and police support for Letsie's 'royal coup' was evident, and subsequent clashes between demonstrators and the security forces reportedly resulted in five deaths. A well-known human rights lawyer, Hae Phoofolo, was appointed Chairman of a transitional Council of Ministers, and the Secretary-General of the BNP, Evaristus Retselisitsoe Sekhonyana, was appointed Minister of Foreign Affairs. Phoofolo identified as a priority for his administration the amendment of the Constitution to facilitate the restoration of Moshoeshoe; in the mean time, King Letsie was to act as executive and legislative Head of State.

The suspension of constitutional government was widely condemned outside Lesotho. The Presidents of Botswana, South Africa and Zimbabwe led diplomatic efforts to restore the elected Government, supported by the OAU and the Commonwealth. The USA withdrew financial assistance, and several other countries threatened sanctions. Following negotiations in South Africa, in September 1994 King Letsie and Mokhehle signed an agreement, guaranteed by Botswana, South Africa and Zimbabwe, providing for the restoration of Moshoeshoe II as reigning monarch and for the restitution of the elected organs of government; the commission of inquiry into Moshoeshoe's dethronement was to be abandoned; all those involved in the 'royal coup' were to be immune from prosecution; the political neutrality of the armed forces and public service was to be guaranteed, and consultations were to be undertaken with the aim of broadening the democratic process. Moshoeshoe was restored to the throne on 25 January 1995, undertaking not to interfere in politics. Letsie took the title of Crown Prince.

King Moshoeshoe was killed in a motor accident on 15 January 1996. The College of Chiefs subsequently elected Crown Prince David to succeed his father, and the prince was restored to the throne, resuming the title King Letsie III, on 7 February. Letsie undertook not to involve the monarchy in any aspect of political life.

In April 1997 the National Assembly approved legislation for a reduction in the age of eligibility to vote (from 21 to 18 years), and for the establishment of a three-member Independent Electoral Commission (IEC). In June, following a protracted struggle between rival factions for control of the party, Mokhehle resigned from the BCP and formed the Lesotho Congress for Democracy (LCD), to which he transferred executive power. Mokhehle's opponents denounced the move as a 'political coup', declaring that he should have resigned from the premiership and sought a dissolution of the National Assembly and new elections. However, some 38 members of the National Assembly joined the LCD. In July Molapo Qhobela was elected leader of the BCP.

There was further controversy in August, when the Speaker of the National Assembly designated the BCP as the official opposition party. In October members of the Senate (most of whom apparently refused to recognize the legitimacy of Mokhehle's Government) voted to suspend discussion of proposed legislation, pending the King's response to appeals for the dissolution of the National Assembly. At the first annual conference of the LCD, held in January 1998, Mokhehle resigned as leader, and was made Honorary Life President of the party. In February Deputy Prime Minister Bethuel Pakalitha Mosisili was elected to succeed him as party leader. (Mokhehle died in January 1999.)

Elections to an expanded National Assembly took place on 23 May 1998. An application by the three main opposition parties—the BCP, the BNP and the Marematlou Freedom Party (MFP)—for a postponement of the poll, on the grounds that the IEC had not allowed sufficient time for parties to examine the electoral register, had been rejected by the High Court. The LCD secured an overwhelming victory, winning 78 of the Assembly's 80 seats; the BNP was the only other party to win representation. Voting for one seat was postponed, owing to the death of a candidate. The IEC and observers representing the Southern African Development Community (SADC, see p. 386) and the Commonwealth concluded that the polls had been generally free and fair. Mosisili was elected Prime Minister by the National Assembly in late May, and a new Government was appointed in June. At the end of June the BCP, the BNP and the MFP appealed to the High Court to annul the election results; in the following month the Court ordered the IEC to permit the opposition parties to inspect election documents.

In August 1998 opposition activists began a mass vigil outside the royal palace; within one week some 2,000 people were reported to have joined the protest against the outcome of the poll. Tensions escalated as LCD militants blocked access roads to the capital, in a stated attempt to prevent supplies of weapons to the protesters. Following consultations involving the Lesotho Government and the main opposition parties, with mediation by the Government of South Africa, Mosisili announced the establishment of an independent commission, comprising representatives of the SADC 'troika' of Botswana, South Africa and Zimbabwe, to investigate the conduct and results of the May election. The commission was to be chaired by Pius Langa, the Deputy President of South Africa's Constitutional Court.

Meanwhile, revelations that state funds had been used to purchase farmland for the Commander of the Lesotho Defence Force (LDF, as the RLDF had been redesignated), Lt-Gen. Makhula Mosakeng, fuelled opposition allegations of the Commander's complicity in corruption and vote-rigging. (Mosakeng stated that the land had been acquired for army, rather than personal, use.) However, Mosakeng later announced his resignation and stated that 26 members of the military command had been dismissed.

The Langa Commission's report, which was finally released on 17 September 1998, expressed serious concerns at apparent irregularities and discrepancies in the conduct of the May general election, but the Commission was 'unable to state that the invalidity of the elections had been conclusively established'. There was considerable confusion in the days following the publication of the report. Rumours that the Mosisili Government had been overthrown were denied; however, it was confirmed that Lesotho had appealed to SADC for assistance, in view of a breakdown in security. On 22 September an SADC peace-keeping force, initially comprising 600 South African troops and 200 from Botswana, entered Lesotho. In response to criticism that he had not consulted King Letsie prior to requesting external military assistance, Mosisili stated that the monarch had, by harbouring opposition protesters in the palace grounds, contributed to the instability that had necessitated SADC intervention. (It was subsequently reported that the King had been prevented from making a broadcast to the nation.) Within Lesotho, there was widespread outrage at what was perceived as an effective 'invasion' by South Africa, and the SADC force encountered unexpectedly strong resistance. There was sustained fighting between the intervention force and rebel units of the LDF before strategic points, including military bases and the Katse Dam (part of the LHWP essential to the supply of water to South Africa), were secured, while rioting in Maseru and other towns targeted in particular South African interests and caused widespread destruction. Mosakeng and his officers, who had fled to South Africa earlier in the month, returned to resume the army command on 24 September: Mosakeng stated that his

LESOTHO

Introductory Survey

resignation had been exacted under duress and, since it had not been approved by the King, was invalid.

Following meetings with representatives of the SADC 'troika', in early October 1998 it was reported that the LCD and the main opposition parties had agreed in principle that fresh elections should be held within 15–18 months. In the mean time, the IEC was to be restructured, and the electoral system was to be reviewed, with the aim of ensuring wider inclusion in political affairs (many parties felt that the simple majority voting system was incompatible with the nature of Lesotho's political evolution). In mid-October agreement was reached on a transitional structure, designated the Interim Political Authority (IPA), to comprise representatives of 12 political parties, as well as government and parliamentary delegates, to oversee preparations for fresh elections to the National Assembly.

Shortly after the conclusion of this interim settlement it was announced that some 30 members of the LDF had been arrested on suspicion of involvement in the army rebellion of September 1998. Multi-party talks took place in Pretoria, South Africa, during November, but progress towards the establishment of the IPA was impeded after warrants were issued for the arrest, on murder charges, of several opposition activists, including two leading members of the BCP and BNP youth wings. The opposition parties stated that they would not co-operate in arrangements for the IPA until outstanding security matters, including the release of all rebel soldiers, had been expedited. A court martial in October 1999 ruled against the discharge of a total of 38 members of the LDF accused of mutiny.

The withdrawal of the SADC intervention force was completed in May 1999. This force was immediately succeeded by a new SADC mission, comprising some 300 military personnel from South Africa, Botswana and (subsequently) Zimbabwe, which remained until May 2000, assisting in the retraining and restructuring of the LDF.

Meanwhile, the 24-member IPA was inaugurated on 9 December 1998. After protracted consultations, the IPA announced in September 1999 that the number of seats in the National Assembly was to be increased by 50, to 130, effective from the elections scheduled for April 2000, with seats to be allocated according to a combination of proportional representation and simple majority voting. However, arbitration was required to resolve divisions within the IPA as to the number of seats to be decided by each method, and it was not until December 1999 that a Commonwealth-brokered agreement was signed, providing for 80 seats to be allocated on the basis of simple majority in single-member constituencies, and 50 by proportional representation. The mandate of the IPA was to be extended until elections took place. In the mean time, the Presidents of South Africa, Botswana, Mozambique and Zimbabwe, together with the UN, OAU and Commonwealth Secretaries-General, were to act as guarantors to ensure the implementation of the accord.

In February 2000 the IPA accused the Government of reneging on the December 1999 accord, after the LCD-dominated National Assembly voted to submit the proposed electoral changes to a referendum. Further arbitration concluded in May 2000 that the elections should proceed within 10–12 months. In July the IEC identified 26 May 2001 as the provisional date for the elections; however, delays in enacting legislation concerning voter registration and the electoral model caused the abandonment of this date.

In April 2000 the establishment of a commission of inquiry to investigate political events during July–November 1998 was announced. The commission, comprising three senior judges and chaired by Nigel Leon, met for the first time in June 2000 and heard evidence from several public figures. However, a number of opposition politicians criticized the commission, expressing doubts as to its impartiality. In August three LDF members were convicted by a court martial of participation in the mutiny of September 1998 and sentenced to a combined 29 years' imprisonment; a further 33 LDF members were convicted in November. The Leon commission of inquiry, which submitted its report to Prime Minister Mosisili in October 2001, rejected demands for a general amnesty to be granted to perpetrators of violence during the period under review, recommending the indictment of a number of opposition politicians and members of the armed forces. The commission also proposed measures aimed at ensuring the political neutrality of the armed forces and the police, and the establishment of an informal body, comprising the King, traditional chiefs and representatives of the armed forces, the police, churches, political organizations, and the industrial and agricultural sectors, to discuss issues affecting Basotho.

In January 2001 a congress of the LCD re-elected Mosisili as leader of the party, for a five-year term. Shakhane Mokhehle, the incumbent and brother of the party's founder, was defeated in the election to the post of Secretary-General of the LCD by the Minister in the Prime Minister's Office, Sephiri Motanyane. In a minor cabinet reshuffle in July Mokhehle, who had disputed the results of the LCD elections, was dismissed as Minister of Justice, Human Rights and Rehabilitation, Law and Constitutional Affairs. Deputy Prime Minister Kelebone Maope resigned from the Government in September and broke away from the LCD, together with Mokhehle, to form a new opposition party, the Lesotho People's Congress (LPC), to prepare for forthcoming elections. By mid-October a total of 27 deputies had defected from the LCD to join the LPC, which was declared the main opposition party. Mosisili made new cabinet appointments in October, in an effort to consolidate his position ahead of the elections.

In mid-January 2002 a protracted dispute over the leadership of the BCP, which had been ongoing since the late 1990s, also appeared to be resolved, when the High Court ruled in favour of Tseliso Makhakhe's leadership of the party. Qhobela subsequently formed a new party, known as the Basutoland African Congress (BAC), which had been the name of the BCP in 1952–59.

Meanwhile, divisions over the electoral model, notably regarding the number of seats to be allocated by proportional representation, had continued to impede progress towards the elections. In January 2002 Parliament finally approved amendments to the electoral legislation, providing for the expansion of the National Assembly to 120 members, with 80 to be elected on a constituency basis and 40 selected by proportional representation.

The LCD won a resounding victory at the general election, which took place on 25 May 2002, retaining 77 of the 78 contested constituency seats, with 54.9% of the valid votes cast. The BNP became the second largest legislative party, securing 21 of the 40 seats allocated by proportional representation (known as compensatory seats), with 22.4% of the votes cast; the LPC won one constituency seat and four compensatory seats. Voting in two constituencies was postponed, owing to the deaths of candidates. Of the remaining 15 compensatory seats, the National Independent Party secured five, the BAC and the BCP both won three, while four smaller parties each took one seat. Mosisili was re-elected Prime Minister by the National Assembly in early June and a new Cabinet was subsequently appointed.

In mid-October 2004 a 30-member committee was established to direct a parliamentary reform programme; the committee was chaired by the leader of the Popular Front for Democracy, Lekhetho Rakuoane, and comprised government ministers and members of the National Assembly and the Senate. In mid-November the Cabinet was reorganized: Monyane Moleleki was appointed Minister of Foreign Affairs and was replaced as Minister of Natural Resources by Dr 'Mamphono Khaketla, while the Deputy Prime Minister, Lesao Lehohola, also assumed the home affairs portfolio; the former Minister of Home Affairs, Thomas Thabane, became Minister of Communications, Science and Technology. Other notable changes included the appointment of Mothejoa Metsing as the Minister of Justice, Human Rights and Rehabilitation, Law and Constitutional Affairs, and the appointment of Mpeo Mahase-Moiloa as Minister of Employment and Labour.

In mid-February 2005, following an amendment to the Local Government Act in September 2004, the IEC announced that elections to local councils were to be held, for the first time, on 30 April 2005; the elections had initially been scheduled for 1998. Voting took place in 1,272 electoral divisions, of which some 390 were reserved for women candidates, in accordance with SADC guidelines. Over 1,000 new councillors were elected to 129 councils replacing previous councils comprising traditional leaders and government officials. The ruling LCD won over three-quarters of the seats; the rate of voter participation, recorded by the IEC at less than 30%, was officially attributed to the fact that it was the first such election to be held.

In late January 2006 Khauhelo Raditapole and Kelebone Maope, the leaders of the BAC and the LPC, respectively, announced that their parties would form an alliance, following appeals by the BCP for reconciliation between political parties. Legislative elections took place on 17 February 2007, at which the LCD retained its parliamentary majority, although the party's total number of seats in the National Assembly was reduced from 77 to 61. The National Independent Party took 21 of the 40 compensatory seats, thus becoming the second largest legislative party, while the All Basotho Convention secured 17 constituency seats and the Lesotho Workers' Party 10 compensatory seats. Voting in one constituency was postponed, owing to the death of a candidate. The Alliance of Congress Parties won one constituency seat and one compensatory seat, while five other parties each secured one compensatory seat. Observers from SADC and the AU declared the elections to have been free and fair. Mosisili was reappointed Prime Minister later that month and in early March a new Cabinet was sworn in. Most notably, Mohlabi Tsekoa, hitherto Minister of Education and Training, was appointed Minister of Foreign Affairs; Mahase-Moiloa became Minister of Law and Constitutional Affairs.

As exemplified by South Africa's prominent role in the resolution of the 1994 constitutional crisis and by its intervention in the political crisis of September 1998, Lesotho's internal affairs continue to be strongly influenced by South Africa. Long-standing problems of border security and, in particular, the issue of disputed land in South Africa's Free State (formerly Orange Free State) have periodically caused friction between the two countries. During a two-day state visit to Lesotho in July 1995, President Nelson Mandela of South Africa advocated the pursuit of mutually beneficial policies of regional integration, and he and Prime Minister Mokhehle agreed that the issue of sovereignty in Free State should be discussed by 'appropriate' authorities. Relations between the two countries were strained in August 2000 when Lesotho withdrew its support shortly before the scheduled signing of an agreement with Botswana, Namibia and South Africa on the management of water resources from the Orange river. In September an official at the South African High Commission was killed in Maseru. Representatives of both countries met in Pretoria in November and recommended increased co-operation in areas including education and criminal justice. During a visit to Lesotho by President Thabo Mbeki of South Africa in April 2001, it was agreed to replace an intergovernmental liaison committee that had been established following SADC intervention in 1998 (see above) with a joint binational commission at ministerial level, with the aim of enhancing bilateral relations. Relations between Lesotho and South Africa were further enhanced in May 2002, when their ministers of foreign affairs signed the Joint Bilateral Commission of Co-operation programme, which aimed to raise Lesotho from its current status as a 'least developed country'.

Government

Lesotho is an hereditary monarchy. Under the terms of the Constitution, which came into effect following the March 1993 election, the King, who is Head of State, has no executive or legislative powers. The College of Chiefs is theoretically empowered, under traditional law, to elect and depose the King by a majority vote. Executive power is vested in the Cabinet, which is headed by the Prime Minister. Legislative power is exercised by the National Assembly, which is elected, at intervals of no more than five years, by universal adult suffrage in the context of a multi-party political system. A system of mixed member proportional representation was introduced at the general election of May 2002, when the National Assembly was expanded to 120 members (80 elected by simple majority in single-member constituencies and 40 selected from party lists). The upper house, the Senate, comprises traditional chiefs and 11 nominated members. Lesotho comprises 10 administrative districts, each with an appointed district co-ordinator.

Defence

Military service is voluntary. As assessed at November 2007, the Lesotho Defence Force (LDF, formerly the Royal Lesotho Defence Force) comprised 2,000 men, including an air wing of 110 men. The creation of a new commando force unit, the first professional unit in the LDF, was announced in October 2001, as part of ongoing efforts to restructure the armed forces. Projected budgetary expenditure on defence for 2007 was M230m.

Economic Affairs

In 2006, according to estimates by the World Bank, Lesotho's gross national income (GNI), measured at average 2004–06 prices, was US $1,839m., equivalent to $1,030 per head (or $4,340 per head on an international purchasing-power parity basis). During 1996–2006, it was estimated, the population increased at an average annual rate of 0.4%, while gross domestic product (GDP) per head increased, in real terms, by an average of 1.9% per year. Overall GDP increased, in real terms, at an average annual rate of 2.3% in 1996–2006; growth in 2006 was 2.8%.

Agriculture, forestry and fishing contributed an estimated 15.5% of GDP in 2006 and employed some 94.3% of the labour force at mid-2005, according to FAO estimates. The principal agricultural exports are cereals and live animals. The main subsistence crops are potatoes, maize, sorghum and wheat. Lesotho remains a net importer of staple foodstuffs, largely owing to its vulnerability to adverse climatic conditions, especially drought. According to the World Food Programme, less than 10% of land is arable and there is no irrigation. During 1996–2006 agricultural GDP increased at an average annual rate of 0.2%. Agricultural GDP increased by 1.8% in 2006.

Industry (including mining, manufacturing, construction and power) provided an estimated 41.6% of GDP in 2006, and engaged 9.3% of the labour force in 1999. During 1996–2006 industrial GDP increased by an average of 3.9% per year. Industrial GDP increased by 4.4% in 2006.

Mining contributed an estimated 6.6% of GDP in 2006. Lesotho has reserves of diamonds, which during the late 1970s provided more than 50% of visible export earnings, but large-scale exploitation of these ceased in 1982. The Lets'eng-la-Terae diamond mine reopened in April 2004 and by the time of its official inauguration in November gems with an estimated value of US $28m. had been recovered. Industrial mining at other sites was also envisaged, including a second diamond mine at Liqhobong. Lesotho also possesses deposits of uranium, lead and iron ore, and is believed to have petroleum deposits. The GDP of the mining sector increased by an average of 66.1% per year in 1997–2006; growth in 2005 was 239.2% and growth in 2006 was estimated at 40%.

Manufacturing contributed an estimated 14.6% of GDP in 2006. During 1996–2006 manufacturing GDP increased by an average of 2.3% per year; manufacturing GDP contracted by 8.0% in 2005 but increased by 4.1% in 2006.

The Lesotho Highlands Water Project (LHWP) provides hydroelectricity sufficient for all Lesotho's needs and for export to South Africa; phases 1A and 1B were inaugurated in 1998 and 2004, respectively. In late September 2005 an agreement was signed for a feasibility study concerning the location of the second phase of the project. The scheme was expected to be completed by about 2030. The R200m. (US $30m.) that Lesotho receives annually in royalties from South Africa for the LHWP represents the country's largest single source of foreign exchange. Prior to the LHWP more than 90% of Lesotho's energy requirements were imported from South Africa. Imports of mineral fuels and lubricants comprised 6.2% of the total value of imports in 2001. Legislation providing for the privatization of the Lesotho Electricity Corporation was presented to the National Assembly in January 2005.

The services sector contributed 42.9% of GDP in 2006. During 1996–2006 the GDP of the services sector increased at an average annual rate of 2.7%. Services GDP increased by 2.7% in 2006.

In 2006 Lesotho recorded a visible trade deficit of US $667.2m., but there was a surplus of $66.6m. on the current account of the balance of payments. In 2005 the principal source of imports (83.9%) was the Southern African Customs Union (SACU—i.e. chiefly South Africa—see below), which was also the second largest market for exports (17.2%), behind the USA (61.4%); the European Union was also a significant market for exports (17.1%). The principal exports in that year were basic manufactures, clothing, foodstuffs and telecommunication equipment. The principal imports in 2001 were manufactured goods, food and live animals, and machinery and transport equipment.

In the financial year ending 31 March 2006 there was an overall budgetary surplus of M266.7m. The 2006/07 budget projected a surplus of M1,637.5m. Lesotho's external debt totalled US $689.7m. at the end of 2005, of which $646.7m. was long-term public debt. In that year the cost of debt-servicing was equivalent to 5.0% of revenue from exports of goods and services. The annual rate of inflation averaged 6.6% in 2001–06; consumer prices increased by 6.0% in 2006. In 1999 231,742 people were registered as unemployed, equivalent to 27.3% of the labour force. In 2006 51,595 Basotho were employed as miners in South Africa compared with 129,000 in 1989. The number was expected to continue to decrease in the coming years. According to the Central Bank of Lesotho, in 2004 Basotho miners' remittances amounted to M1,795.0m. and accounted for more than 70% of total earnings during the period 1997–2004. South African officials estimated that around 300,000 Basotho were employed in South Africa at any given time.

LESOTHO

Lesotho is a member of the Common Monetary Area (with Namibia, South Africa and Swaziland), and a member of SACU (with Botswana, Namibia, South Africa and Swaziland). Lesotho also belongs to the Southern African Development Community (SADC, see p. 386).

Impediments to economic development in Lesotho include vulnerability to drought and serious land shortages, combined with the country's dependence on South Africa (the Lesotho currency, the loti, is fixed at par with the South African rand, exposing Lesotho to fluctuations within the South African economy). By the late 1990s the strong growth that had prevailed for most of the decade was being eroded, while retrenchment in the South African gold-mining sector resulted in a marked decline in remittances from Basotho working abroad. The textile industry benefited considerably from the USA's African Growth and Opportunities Act (AGOA), for which Lesotho was first declared eligible in April 2001; under its terms, textiles and clothing made in Lesotho had unlimited access to the US market, and by early 2002 exports of these products to the USA had increased by nearly 40%. Lesotho's qualification for the benefits of the AGOA attracted interest from foreign investors in Lesotho, notably Taiwanese textile manufacturers. However, faced with increasing competition from producers in Asia, between mid-2004 and January 2005 eight textile factories closed with the loss of more than 23,000 jobs. The textile and garment sector improved markedly in 2007, owing to a depreciation of the rand and the reduction in 2006 of rates of company tax and taxes paid by manufacturers, resulting in estimated GDP growth of 4.9% in 2007. These had been lowered as an incentive to attract investors and the decision to exempt exporters from company tax entirely was seen as a measure favouring textile producers in particular. In 2006 the Government had also stated that it would seek to diversify Lesotho's economy, promoting agriculture and 'agroprocessing', diamond and sandstone mining and tourism as possible alternatives. Nevertheless, the country faced ongoing difficulties as a result of the high level of HIV/AIDS infection among the population. In 2005 Lesotho had the third highest prevalence of HIV/AIDS in the world, affecting some 23% of adults in the country, and almost 100,000 children had been orphaned as a result of the pandemic.

Education

As part of an initiative begun in 2000, all primary education is available free of charge, provided mainly by the three main Christian missions (Lesotho Evangelical, Roman Catholic and Anglican), under the direction of the Ministry of Education. Officially, primary education is compulsory for seven years between six and 13 years of age. Secondary education, beginning at the age of 13, lasts for up to five years, comprising a first cycle of three years and a second of two years. According to UNESCO estimates, of children in the relevant age-groups in 2003/04, 86% (males 83%; females 88%) were enrolled at primary schools, while only 23% (males 18%; females 28%) were enrolled at secondary schools. Some 3,266 students were enrolled at the National University of Lesotho, at Roma, in 2002. Proposed expenditure on education under the 2006/07 budget was M927.4m. (representing more than 20% of total government expenditure). In January 2006 17 new schools constructed with the assistance of the Government of Japan were opened; they were expected to accommodate some 14,000 pupils.

Public Holidays

2008: 1 January (New Year's Day), 11 March (Moshoeshoe Day), 21–24 March (Easter), 1 May (Workers' Day and Ascension Day), 25 May (Africa Day and Heroes' Day), 17 July (King's Birthday), 4 October (National Independence Day), 25 December (Christmas Day), 26 December (Boxing Day).

2009: 1 January (New Year's Day), 11 March (Moshoeshoe Day), 10–13 April (Easter), 1 May (Workers' Day), 21 May (Ascension Day), 25 May (Africa Day and Heroes' Day), 17 July (King's Birthday), 4 October (National Independence Day), 25 December (Christmas Day), 26 December (Boxing Day).

Weights and Measures

The metric system of weights and measures is in force.

Statistical Survey

Sources (unless otherwise stated): Bureau of Statistics, POB 455, Maseru 100; tel. 22323852; fax 22310177; internet www.bos.gov.ls; Central Bank of Lesotho, POB 1184, Maseru 100; tel. 22314281; fax 22310051; e-mail cbl@centralbank.org.ls; internet www.centralbank.org.ls.

Area and Population

AREA, POPULATION AND DENSITY

Area (sq km)	30,355*
Population (*de jure* census results)	
14 April 1996	1,841,967
9 April 2006	
Males	911,848
Females	960,873
Total	1,872,721
Density (per sq km) at April 2006	61.7

* 11,720 sq miles.

DISTRICTS
(*de jure* population at 2006 census, preliminary figures)

District	Population
Berea	248,225
Butha-Buthe	109,139
Leribe	296,673
Mafeteng	192,795
Maseru	436,399
Mohale's Hoek	173,706
Mokhotlong	95,332
Qacha's Nek	71,756
Quthing	119,811
Thaba-Tseka	128,885
Total	**1,872,721**

PRINCIPAL TOWNS
(population at 1986 census)

Maseru (capital)	109,400		Hlotse	9,600
Maputsoa	20,000		Mohale's Hoek	8,500
Teyateyaneng	14,300		Quthing	6,000
Mafeteng	12,700			

Source: Stefan Helders, *World Gazetteer* (www.world-gazetteer.com).

Mid-2007 (including suburbs, UN estimate): Maseru 210,000 (Source: UN, *World Urbanization Prospects: The 2007 Revision*).

BIRTHS AND DEATHS
(annual averages, UN estimates)

	1990–95	1995–2000	2000–05
Birth rate (per 1,000)	35.0	34.0	31.3
Death rate (per 1,000)	10.3	11.9	17.7

Source: UN, *World Population Prospects: The 2006 Revision*.

Expectation of life (years at birth, WHO estimates): 41.5 (males 41.7; females 41.4) in 2005 (Source: WHO, *World Health Statistics*).

LESOTHO

ECONOMICALLY ACTIVE POPULATION
(household survey, persons aged 10 years and over, 1999)

	Males	Females	Total
Agriculture	270,919	175,760	446,679
Fishing	125	—	125
Mining and quarrying	2,392	611	3,003
Manufacturing	7,957	13,839	21,795
Electricity, gas and water supply	1,722	1,541	3,263
Construction	18,947	10,548	29,495
Wholesale and retail trade; repair of motor vehicles, motorcycles and household goods	11,099	17,915	29,014
Hotels and restaurants	918	3,529	4,447
Transport, storage and communications	9,307	1,363	10,670
Financial intermediation	1,041	810	1,851
Real estate, renting and business activities	3,405	2,032	5,437
Public administration and defence; compulsory social security	5,181	2,395	7,576
Education	5,125	8,099	13,224
Health and social work	2,070	2,895	4,965
Other community, social and personal service activities	1,765	7,686	9,451
Households with employed persons	4,474	21,970	26,444
Extra-territorial organizations and bodies	126	—	126
Total employed	346,573	270,993	617,566
Unemployed	90,964	140,778	231,742
Total labour force	437,537	411,771	849,308

Source: ILO.

Mid-2005 (estimates in '000): Agriculture, etc. 684; Total 725 (Source: FAO).

Health and Welfare

KEY INDICATORS

Total fertility rate (children per woman, 2005)	3.4
Under-5 mortality rate (per 1,000 live births, 2005)	132
HIV/AIDS (% of persons aged 15–49, 2005)	23.2
Physicians (per 1,000 head, 2003)	0.05
Health expenditure (2004): US $ per head (PPP)	138.5
Health expenditure (2004): % of GDP	6.5
Health expenditure (2004): public (% of total)	84.2
Access to water (% of persons, 2004)	79
Access to sanitation (% of persons, 2004)	37
Human Development Index (2005): ranking	138
Human Development Index (205): value	0.549

For sources and definitions, see explanatory note on p. vi.

Agriculture

PRINCIPAL CROPS
('000 metric tons)

	2004	2005	2006
Wheat	11.6	2.1	n.a.
Maize	81.0	76.1	102.0
Sorghum	10.3	15.8	n.a.
Potatoes*	90	90	n.a.
Dry beans	4.8	1.0	0.5
Dry peas	1.5	0.9	2.0
Vegetables*	18	18	18
Fruit*	13	13	13

*FAO estimates.
Source: FAO.

LIVESTOCK
('000 head, year ending September)

	2003	2004*	2005*
Cattle	644.6	650	650
Sheep	1,030.8	1,000	1,000
Goats	789.6	790	790
Pigs	79.0	65	65
Horses	37.7	100	100
Asses, mules or hinnies	76.3	155.2	155.2
Poultry	1,800*	1,800	1,800

*FAO estimate(s).
2006: No data were available.
Source: FAO.

LIVESTOCK PRODUCTS
('000 metric tons, FAO estimates)

	2003	2004	2005
Cows' milk	23.8	23.8	23.8
Pig meat	2.8	2.8	2.9
Chicken meat	1.8	1.8	2.0
Game meat	3.9	3.9	n.a.
Other meat	15.9	16.0	19.9
Hen eggs	15.1	15.1	15.0
Wool (greasy)	2.6	n.a.	n.a.

2006 ('000 metric tons, FAO estimate): Hen eggs 15.0.
Source: FAO.

Forestry

ROUNDWOOD REMOVALS
('000 cubic metres, excluding bark, FAO estimates)

	2004	2005	2006
Total (all fuel wood)	2,046.6	2,052.8	2,060.5

Source: FAO.

Fishing

(metric tons, live weight)

	2003	2004	2005
Capture	42	45	45
Common carp	12	15	15
North African catfish	5	5	5
Other freshwater fishes	25	25	25
Aquaculture	4	2	2
Common carp	4	2	1
Total catch	46	47	46

Source: FAO.

Mining

(cubic metres, unless otherwise indicated)

	2003	2004	2005*
Fire clay	14,470	15,000*	15,000
Diamond (carats)	2,099	14,000	37,000
Gravel and crushed rock	389,695	300,000*	300,000

*Estimate(s).
Source: US Geological Survey.

LESOTHO

Statistical Survey

Finance

CURRENCY AND EXCHANGE RATES

Monetary Units
100 lisente (singular: sente) = 1 loti (plural: maloti).

Sterling, Dollar and Euro Equivalents (31 December 2007)
£1 sterling = 13.643 maloti;
US $1 = 6.810 maloti;
€1 = 10.025 maloti;
100 maloti = £7.33 = $14.68 = €9.98.

Average Exchange Rate (maloti per US $)
2005   6.3593
2006   6.7716
2007   7.0454

Note: The loti is fixed at par with the South African rand.

BUDGET
(million maloti, year ending 31 March)

Revenue*	2004/05	2005/06	2006/07†
Tax revenue	3,678.3	4,003.1	6,008.0
Taxes on net income and profits	901.9	924.6	994.5
Company tax	219.2	194.9	203.7
Individual income tax	567.4	612.0	654.7
Other income and profit taxes	115.3	117.8	136.1
Taxes on goods and services	749.8	723.0	734.7
Customs duties	2,012.4	2,306.0	4,208.3
Other taxes	14.2	49.4	70.4
Non-tax revenue	452.1	473.3	510.0
Water royalties	194.7	235.9	268.4
Total	**4,130.4**	**4,476.3**	**6,517.9**

Expenditure and net lending	2004/05	2005/06	2006/07†
Wages and salaries	1,174.3	1,263.7	1,391.6
Goods and services	828.2	1,114.8	1,285.8
Subsidies and transfers	765.0	988.5	1,360.5
Interest payments	152.2	223.9	124.5
Capital expenditure (incl. lending minus repayments)	693.8	702.3	793.6
Total	**3,613.5**	**4,293.2**	**4,955.9**

* Excluding grants received (million maloti): 231.4 in 2004/05; 83.6 in 2005/06; 75.5 in 2006/07.
† Projections.

INTERNATIONAL RESERVES
(US $ million at 31 December)

	2004	2005	2006
IMF special drawing rights	0.62	0.44	0.22
Reserve position in IMF	5.53	5.15	5.45
Foreign exchange	495.35	513.42	652.74
Total	**501.50**	**519.01**	**658.41**

Source: IMF, *International Financial Statistics*.

MONEY SUPPLY
(million maloti at 31 December)

	2004	2005	2006
Currency outside banks	204.54	212.78	309.42
Demand deposits at commercial banks	1,197.50	1,427.86	2,187.20
Total money (incl. others)	**1,589.42**	**1,829.48**	**2,688.81**

Source: IMF, *International Financial Statistics*.

COST OF LIVING
(Consumer Price Index; base: April 1997 = 100)

	2004	2005	2006
Food (incl. non-alcoholic beverages)	181.2	186.0	202.8
Alcoholic beverages and tobacco	189.3	200.4	212.8
Housing, water, electricity, and other fuels	164.5	175.8	191.8
Clothing (incl. footwear)	149.0	153.1	157.4
All items (incl. others)	**169.4**	**175.3**	**185.9**

NATIONAL ACCOUNTS
(million maloti at current prices)

Expenditure on the Gross Domestic Product

	2004	2005	2006*
Government final consumption expenditure	9,577.9	9,400.3	10,951.6
Private final consumption expenditure			
Increase in stocks	8.7	15.0	—
Gross fixed capital formation	3,045.1	3,239.1	3,886.9
Statistical discrepancy	180.6	157.9	—
Total domestic expenditure	**12,631.7**	**12,812.3**	**14,838.5**
Exports of goods and services	4,928.1	4,540.4	5,481.4
Less Imports of goods and services	9,222.7	8,089.1	9,946.4
GDP in purchasers' values	**8,517.7**	**9,263.6**	**10,373.2**
GDP at constant 1995 prices	**4,399.6**	**4,529.3**	**4,809.1**

* Preliminary.

Gross Domestic Product by Economic Activity

	2004	2005	2006*
Agriculture	1,275.9	1,354.9	1,481.1
Mining and quarrying	174.7	425.9	632.0
Manufacturing	1,380.5	1,307.9	1,403.0
Electricity and water	370.2	555.8	659.8
Construction	1,100.6	1,185.0	1,291.3
Wholesale and retail trade	814.3	808.9	866.0
Restaurants and hotels	160.4	177.6	201.7
Transport and communication	353.4	406.2	470.1
Financial intermediation and insurance	397.5	439.8	527.7
Real estate and business services	136.5	152.0	164.3
Ownership of dwellings	267.3	272.7	294.8
Public administration	561.6	636.9	692.7
Education	568.8	606.2	658.6
Health and social work	123.4	133.2	145.1
Other services	84.9	88.3	94.9
Sub-total	**7,770.0**	**8,551.3**	**9,583.1**
Less Imputed bank service charge	293.4	325.5	365.0
GDP at factor cost	**7,476.6**	**8,225.8**	**9,218.1**
Indirect taxes, less subsidies	1,041.1	1,037.8	1,155.1
GDP at market prices	**8,517.7**	**9,263.6**	**10,373.2**

* Preliminary.

LESOTHO

BALANCE OF PAYMENTS
(US $ million)

	2004	2005	2006
Exports of goods f.o.b.	707.3	650.0	693.6
Imports of goods f.o.b.	−1,302.0	−1,306.1	−1,360.8
Trade balance	−594.8	−656.2	−667.2
Exports of services	63.9	56.4	59.9
Imports of services	−96.1	−103.3	−95.2
Balance on goods and services	−626.9	−703.1	−702.5
Other income received	379.1	369.9	412.1
Other income paid	−76.3	−65.3	−32.6
Balance on goods, services and income	−324.1	−398.5	−323.0
Current transfers received	250.7	303.8	392.1
Current transfers paid	−2.5	−3.2	−2.6
Current balance	−75.9	−97.9	66.6
Capital account (net)	33.4	21.3	11.0
Direct investment abroad	−0.1	—	—
Direct investment from abroad	123.5	92.6	77.8
Other investment assets	−48.9	−0.1	−87.8
Other investment liabilities	−11.2	−53.7	−19.2
Net errors and omissions	−17.0	81.5	142.3
Overall balance	3.8	43.7	190.8

Source: IMF, *International Financial Statistics*.

External Trade

PRINCIPAL COMMODITIES
(distribution by SITC, million maloti)

Imports c.i.f.*	1999	2000	2001
Food and live animals	787.8	928.7	768.7
Beverages and tobacco	33.7	115.6	386.6
Crude materials, inedible except fuels	177.7	228.6	167.7
Mineral fuels and lubricants	323.7	840.8	317.0
Animal and vegetable oils, fats and waxes	54.2	104.2	67.0
Chemicals and related products	309.4	254.6	525.1
Manufactured goods	715.6	558.7	1,026.5
Machinery and transport equipment	674.6	426.4	620.0
Miscellaneous manufactured articles	458.5	486.7	797.3
Total (incl. others)	3,888.5	4,236.2	5,119.1

*Unrevised figures.

Exports	2002	2003	2004
Foodstuffs, etc.	197.6	194.0	180.8
Cereals	75.7	71.2	55.2
Beverages and tobacco	94.9	96.5	98.5
Live animals	20.4	20.4	16.8
Livestock materials	64.6	90.3	3.3
Wool	56.1	80.6	1.8
Manufactures	3,439.8	3,238.1	4,433.3
Chemicals and petroleum	45.5	49.3	21.0
Telecommunication equipment	291.7	289.7	153.6
Machinery	50.0	53.9	55.1
Furniture and parts	37.4	33.1	2.9
Clothing, etc.	2,745.2	2,555.6	3,462.0
Footwear	135.1	130.5	128.7
Other manufactures	39.8	35.2	566.8
Total (incl. others)	3,739.9	3,557.4	4,652.2

Source: IMF, *Kingdom of Lesotho: Selected Issues and Statistical Appendix* (December 2005).

Exports (million maloti, 2005): Foodstuffs 227.3 (Cereals 65.0; Beverages and tobacco 134.6); Diamonds 637.7; Manufactures 3,214.1 (Telecommunication equipment 143.6; Machinery 158.9; Clothing, etc. 2,704.8; Footwear 95.8); Total 4,134.6. Source: IMF, *Kingdom of Lesotho: Selected Issues and Statistical Appendix* (November 2006).

PRINCIPAL TRADING PARTNERS
(million maloti)

Imports c.i.f.*	2003	2004	2005
Africa	7,242.7	6,628.7	6,641.8
SACU†	7,234.1	6,584.0	6,603.3
Asia	1,141.7	2,183.5	1,133.1
China, People's Repub.	241.8	457.4	205.8
Hong Kong	401.3	623.9	332.8
Taiwan	367.6	670.4	386.3
European Union	8.9	70.3	53.0
North America	15.1	97.5	32.8
USA	14.5	97.5	27.4
Total (incl. others)	8,411.6	9,036.5	7,870.1

Exports f.o.b.	2003	2004	2005
Africa	695.6	657.5	812.6
SACU†	689.7	622.2	713.6
European Union	3.7	692.0	710.4
North America	2,849.1	3,168.6	2,597.8
Canada	19.7	48.3	56.1
USA	2,829.4	3,120.3	2,541.7
Total (incl. others)	3,557.4	4,533.3	4,134.6

*Valuation exclusive of import duties. Figures also exclude donated food.
†Southern African Customs Union, of which Lesotho is a member; also including Botswana, Namibia, South Africa and Swaziland.

Source: IMF, *Kingdom of Lesotho: Selected Issues and Statistical Appendix* (November 2006).

Transport

ROAD TRAFFIC
(motor vehicles in use at 31 December, estimates)

	1994	1995	1996
Passenger cars	9,900	11,160	12,610
Lorries and vans	20,790	22,310	25,000

Source: International Road Federation, *World Road Statistics*.

CIVIL AVIATION
(traffic on scheduled services)

	1997	1998	1999
Kilometres flown (million)	0	1	0
Passengers carried ('000)	10	28	1
Passenger-km (million)	3	9	0
Total ton-km (million)	0	1	0

Source: UN, *Statistical Yearbook*.

Tourism

FOREIGN TOURIST ARRIVALS BY COUNTRY OF RESIDENCE

	2003	2004	2005
Botswana	3,970	1,973	2,129
Germany	2,878	1,687	1,775
South Africa	286,349	282,070	280,399
Swaziland	2,380	1,408	1,481
United Kingdom	2,005	1,970	1,950
USA	2,196	955	1,054
Zimbabwe	3,590	1,963	2,088
Total (incl. others)	329,301	303,530	303,578

Tourism receipts (US $ million, excl. passenger transport): 28 in 2003; 34 in 2004; n.a. in 2005.

Source: World Tourism Organization.

LESOTHO

Communications Media

	2003	2004	2005
Telephones ('000 main lines in use)	35.1	37.2	48.0
Mobile cellular telephones ('000 subscribers)	101.5	159.0	249.8
Internet users ('000)	30	43	52

2006: 37,200 main telephone lines in use.

Facsimile machines (number in use, year ending 31 March 1996): 569.

Radio receivers ('000 in use): 104 in 1997.

Television receivers ('000 in use): 70 in 2001.

Daily newspapers (1998): 2 (estimated average circulation 15,750 copies).

Non-daily newspapers (1996): 7 (average circulation 74,000 copies).

Sources: UNESCO Institute for Statistics; International Telecommunication Union.

Education

(2003)

	Institutions	Teachers	Students Males	Females	Total
Primary	1,355	9,294	214,746	214,974	429,720
Secondary: general	228	3,470	36,621	46,483	83,104
technical and vocational	8	166	n.a.	n.a.	1,837
teacher training	1	n.a.	n.a.	n.a.	1,855
University	1	n.a.	n.a.	n.a.	4,195

Adult literacy rate (UNESCO estimates): 82.2% (males 73.7%; females 90.3%) in 2001 (Source: UNESCO Institute for Statistics).

Directory

The Constitution

The Constitution of the Kingdom of Lesotho, which took effect at independence in October 1966, was suspended in January 1970. A new Constitution was promulgated following the March 1993 general election. Its main provisions, with subsequent amendments, are summarized below:

Lesotho is an hereditary monarchy. The King, who is Head of State, has no executive or legislative powers. Executive authority is vested in the Cabinet, which is headed by the Prime Minister, while legislative power is exercised by the 120-member National Assembly, which comprises 80 members elected on a single-member constituency basis and 40 selected by a system of proportional representation. The National Assembly is elected, at intervals of no more than five years, by universal adult suffrage in the context of a multi-party political system. There is also a Senate, comprising 22 traditional chiefs and 11 nominated members. The Prime Minister is the official head of the armed forces.

The Government

HEAD OF STATE

King: HM King LETSIE III (acceded to the throne 7 February 1996).

CABINET
(February 2008)

Prime Minister and Minister of Defence and National Security: BETHUEL PAKALITHA MOSISILI.

Deputy Prime Minister and Minister of Home Affairs and Public Safety and Parliamentary Affairs: ARCHIBALD LESAO LEHOHLA.

Minister of Natural Resources (Water, Lesotho Water Highlands Project, Energy, Mining and Technology): MONYANE MOLELEKI.

Minister of Gender, Youth, Sports and Recreation: 'MATHABISO LEPONO.

Minister of Foreign Affairs and International Relations: MOHLABI TSEKOA.

Minister of Local Government and Chieftainship: Dr PONTŠO SUZAN 'MATUMELO SEKATLE.

Minister in the Prime Minister's Office: Dr MOTLOHELOA PHOKO.

Minister of Employment and Labour: REFILOE MASAMENE.

Minister of Finance and Development Planning: Dr TIMOTHY THAHANE.

Minister of Tourism, Environment and Culture: LEBOHANG NTŚINYI.

Minister of Education and Training: Dr 'MAMPHONO KHAKETLA.

Minister of Forestry and Land Reclamation: LINCOLN RALECHATE 'MOKOSE.

Minister of Trade, Industry, Co-operatives and Marketing: POPANE LEBESA.

Minister of Justice, Human Rights and Correctional Services, Law and Constitutional Affairs: MPEO MAHASE-MOILOA.

Minister of Communications, Science and Technology: MOTHEJOA METSING.

Minister of Public Service: SEMANO SEKATLE.

Minister of Agriculture and Food Security: Dr LESOLE MOKOMA.

Minister of Health and Social Welfare: Dr MPHU RAMATLAPENG.

Minister of Public Works and Transport: TS'ELE CHAKELA.

There were also five assistant ministers.

MINISTRIES

Office of the Prime Minister: POB 527, Maseru 100; tel. 22311000; fax 22310578; internet www.lesotho.gov.ls.

Ministry of Agriculture and Food Security: POB 24, Maseru 100; tel. 22316407; fax 22310906; e-mail tvmofilikoane@yahoo.com.

Ministry of Communications, Science and Technology: POB 36, Maseru 100; tel. 22323561; fax 22310264; e-mail n.sello@mcst.gov.ls.

Ministry of Defence and National Security: POB 527, Maseru 100; tel. 22316570; fax 22310518; e-mail nmokatsa@yahoo.co.uk.

Ministry of Education and Training: POB 47, Maseru 100; tel. 22313045; fax 22310562; e-mail semakaleM@education.gov.ls; internet www.education.gov.ls.

Ministry of Employment and Labour: Private Bag A116, Maseru 100; tel. 22322602; fax 22310374.

Ministry of Finance and Development Planning: POB 395, Maseru 100; tel. 22311101; fax 22310964; e-mail ps@finance.gov.ls; internet www.finance.gov.ls.

Ministry of Foreign Affairs and International Relations: POB 1387, Maseru 100; tel. 22311150; fax 22310178; e-mail moear@foreign.gov.ls.

Ministry of Forestry and Land Reclamation: POB 24, Maseru 100; tel. 22316407; fax 22310146.

Ministry of Gender, Youth, Sports and Recreation: POB 729, Maseru 100; tel. 22314763; fax 22310506.

Ministry of Health and Social Welfare: POB 514, Maseru 100; tel. 22317707; fax 22321014; e-mail lesenyehom@health,gov.ls; internet www.health.gov.ls.

Ministry of Home Affairs and Public Safety and Parliamentary Affairs: POB 174, Maseru 100; tel. 22323771; fax 22310319; e-mail hkoali@homeaffairs.gov.ls.

Ministry of Justice, Human Rights and Correctional Services, Law and Constitutional Affairs: POB 402, Maseru 100; tel. 22322683; fax 22311092; e-mail dps@justice.gov.ls; internet www.justice.gov.ls.

Ministry of Local Government and Chieftainship: POB 174, Maseru 100; tel. 22323771; fax 22310587; e-mail lesedi_ntho@hotmail.com.

Ministry of Natural Resources: POB 772, Maseru 100; tel. 22323163; fax 22310520.

LESOTHO

Ministry of Public Service: POB 527, Maseru 100; tel. 22311000; e-mail m.leteketa@mps.gov.ls; internet www.publicservice.gov.ls.

Ministry of Public Works and Transport: POB 20, Maseru 100; tel. 22311362; fax 22310125; e-mail cio@mopwt.gov.ls.

Ministry of Tourism, Environment and Culture: POB 52, Maseru 100; tel. 22313034; fax 22310194; e-mail pmasita.mohale@mtec.gov.ls; internet www.mtec.gov.ls.

Ministry of Trade, Industry, Co-operatives and Marketing: POB 747, Maseru 100; tel. 22312938; fax 22310644; e-mail nkaotal@mticm.gov.ls.

Legislature

PARLIAMENT

National Assembly

POB 190, Maseru; tel. 22323035; fax 22310023; internet www.parliament.ls/TheNationalAssembly/About.aspx.

Speaker: NTLHOI MOTSAMAI.

General Election, 17 February 2007

Party	Constituency seats	Compensatory seats*	Total seats
Lesotho Congress for Democracy	61	—	61
National Independent Party	—	21	21
All Basotho Convention	17	—	17
Lesotho Workers' Party	—	10	10
Basotho National Party	—	3	3
Alliance of Congress Parties	1	1	2
Basotho Batho Democratic Party	—	1	1
Basotho Congress Party	—	1	1
Basotho Democratic National Party	—	1	1
Marematlou Freedom Party	—	1	1
Popular Front for Democracy	—	1	1
Total	79†	40	119†

* Allocated by proportional representation.

† Voting in Makhaleng constituency was postponed, owing to the death of a candidate. The Lesotho Congress for Democracy secured the seat at a by-election held on 30 June 2007.

Senate

POB 553, Maseru 100; tel. 22315338; fax 22310023; internet www.parliament.ls/Senate/AboutSenate.aspx.

Speaker: Chief SEMPE LEJAHA.

The Senate is an advisory chamber, comprising 22 traditional chiefs and 11 members appointed by the monarch.

Election Commission

Independent Electoral Commission (IEC): POB 12698, Kingsway 100, Maseru; tel. 314991; fax 310398; internet www.iec.org.ls; f. 1997 as successor to the Constituency Delimitation Commission; Chair. LESHELE THOAHLANE.

Political Organizations

All Basotho Convention (ABC): Maseru; f. 2006 by fmr mems of the Lesotho Congress for Democracy; Pres. MOTSOAHAE TOM THABANE.

Basotho Batho Democratic Party: f. 2006.

Basotho Congress Party (BCP): POB 111, Maseru 100; tel. 8737076; f. 1952; Leader NTSUKUNYANE MPHANYA.

Basotho Democratic Alliance (BDA): Maseru; f. 1984; Pres. S. C. NKOJANE.

Basotho Democratic National Party: internet bdnp.blogspot.com; f. 2006; Leader THABANG NYEOE.

Basotho National Party (BNP): POB 124, Maseru 100; f. 1958; Leader Maj.-Gen. JUSTIN METSING LEKHANYA; Sec.-Gen. RANTHOMENG MATETE; 280,000 mems.

Basutoland African Congress (BAC): Maseru; f. 2002 following split in the BCP; Leader Dr KHAUHELO RADITAPOLE; Sec.-Gen. MAHOLELA MANDORO.

Khokanyana-Phiri Democratic Alliance: Maseru; f. 1999; alliance of opposition parties comprising:

Christian Democratic Party: Maseru.

Communist Party of Lesotho (CPL): Maseru; f. 1962; banned 1970–91; supported mainly by migrant workers employed in South Africa; Sec.-Gen. MOKHAFISI KENA.

Kopanang Basotho Party (KBP): Maseru; f. 1992; campaigns for women's rights; Leader LIMAKATSO NTAKATSANE.

National Independent Party (NIP): Maseru; f. 1984; Pres. ANTHONY CLOVIS MANYELI.

National Progressive Party (NPP): Maseru; f. 1995 following split in the BNP; Leader Chief PEETE NKOEBE PEETE.

Popular Front for Democracy (PFD): Maseru; f. 1991; leftwing; Leader LEKHETHO RAKUOANE.

Social Democratic Party: Maseru; Leader MASITISE SELESO.

Lesotho Congress for Democracy (LCD): POB 7, Mohole's Hoek; tel. 785207; f. 1997 as a result of divisions within the BCP; Leader BETHUEL PAKALITHA MOSISILI; Chair. MOEKETSI MOLETSANE; Sec.-Gen. MPHO MALIE; 200,000 mems.

Lesotho Labour Party (LLP): Maseru; f. 1991; Leader MUTHUTHULEZI TYHALI.

Lesotho People's Congress (LPC): f. 2001 following split in the LCD; Leader KELEBONE ALBERT MAOPE; Sec.-Gen. SHAKHANE MOKHEHLE.

Lesotho Workers' Party (LWP): Maseru; f. 2001; Leader MACAEFA BILLY.

Marematlou Freedom Party (MFP): POB 0443, Maseru 105; tel. 315804; f. 1962 following merger between the Marema Tlou Party and Basutoland Freedom Party; Leader (vacant); Dep. Leader THABO LEANYA; 300,000 mems.

Sefate Democratic Union (SDU): Maseru; Leader BOFIHLA NKUEBE.

United Democratic Party (UDP): POB 776, Maseru 100; f. 1967; Chair. BEN L. SHEA; Leader CHARLES DABENDE MOFELI; Sec.-Gen. MOLOMO NKUEBE; 26,000 mems.

United Party (UP): Maseru; Pres. MAKARA SEKAUTU.

Diplomatic Representation

EMBASSIES AND HIGH COMMISSIONS IN LESOTHO

China, People's Republic: POB 380, Maseru 100; tel. 22316521; fax 22310489; e-mail chinaemb_ls@mfa.gov.cn; internet ls.china-embassy.org; Ambassador QIU BOHUA.

Korea, Republic: Maseru; Ambassador KIM EUN SOO.

South Africa: Lesotho Bank Tower, 10th Floor, Kingsway, Private Bag A266, Maseru 100; tel. 22325758; fax 22310128; e-mail sahcmas@leo.co.ls; High Commissioner WILLIAM LESLIE.

USA: 254 Kingsway, POB 333, Maseru 100; tel. 22312666; fax 22310116; e-mail infomaseru@state.gov; internet maseru.usembassy.gov; Ambassador ROBERT NOLAN.

Judicial System

HIGH COURT

The High Court is a superior court of record, and in addition to any other jurisdiction conferred by statute it is vested with unlimited original jurisdiction to determine any civil or criminal matter. It also has appellate jurisdiction to hear appeals and reviews from the subordinate courts. Appeals may be made to the Court of Appeal.

POB 90, Maseru; tel. 22312188; internet www.justice.gov.ls/judiciary/high_court.html.

Chief Justice: MAHAPELA LEHOHLA.

Judges: T. NOMNGCONGO, W. C. M. MAQUTU, B. K. MOLAI, T. E. MONAPATHI, K. MAFOSO-GUNI, G. MOFOLO, S. PEETE, M. HLAJOANE, N. MAJARA.

COURT OF APPEAL

POB 90, Maseru; tel. 22312188; internet www.justice.gov.ls/judiciary/appeal.html.

President: J. H. STEYN.

Judges: M. M. RAMODIBEDI, M. E. KUMBLEBEN, H. GROSSKOPF, C. PLEWMAN, J. J. GAUNTLETT, L. S. MELUNSKY (acting).

SUBORDINATE COURTS

Each of the 10 districts possesses subordinate courts, presided over by magistrates.

Chief Magistrate: MOLEFI MAKARA.

LESOTHO

JUDICIAL COMMISSIONERS' COURTS

These courts hear civil and criminal appeals from central and local courts. Further appeal may be made to the High Court and finally to the Court of Appeal.

CENTRAL AND LOCAL COURTS

There are 71 such courts, of which 58 are local courts and 13 are central courts which also serve as courts of appeal from the local courts. They have limited civil and criminal jurisdiction.

Religion

About 90% of the population profess Christianity.

CHRISTIANITY

African Federal Church Council (AFCC): POB 70, Peka 340; f. 1927; co-ordinating org. for 48 African independent churches.
Christian Council of Lesotho (CCL): POB 547, Maseru 100; tel. 22313639; fax 22310310; f. 1833; 112 congregations; 261,350 mems (2003); Chair. Rev. M. MOKHOSI; Sec. CATHERINE RAMOKHELE.

The Anglican Communion

Anglicans in Lesotho are adherents of the Anglican Church of Southern Africa (formerly the Church of the Province of Southern Africa). The Metropolitan of the Province is the Archbishop of Cape Town, South Africa. Lesotho forms a single diocese, with an estimated 200,000 members.
Bishop of Lesotho: Rt Rev. PHILIP STANLEY MOKUKU, Bishop's House, POB 87, Maseru 100; tel. 22311974; fax 22310161; e-mail diocese@ilesotho.com.

The Roman Catholic Church

Lesotho comprises one archdiocese and three dioceses. At 31 December 2005 there were some 1,100,667 adherents of the Roman Catholic Church, equivalent to an estimated 48.8% of the total population.
Lesotho Catholic Bishops' Conference
Catholic Secretariat, POB 200, Maseru 100; tel. 22312525; fax 22310294.
f. 1972; Pres. Rt Rev. EVARISTUS THATHO BITSOANE (Bishop of Qacha's Nek).
Archbishop of Maseru: Most Rev. BERNARD MOHLALISI, Archbishop's House, 19 Orpen Rd, POB 267, Maseru 100; tel. 22312565; fax 22310425; e-mail archmase@lesoff.co.za.

Other Christian Churches

At mid-2000 there were an estimated 279,000 Protestants and 257,000 adherents professing other forms of Christianity.
African Methodist Episcopal Church: POB 223, Maseru 100; tel. 22311801; fax 22310548; e-mail bishopsarah@leo.co.ls; f. 1903; Presiding Prelate Rt Rev. SARAH F. DAVIS; 15,000 mems.
Lesotho Evangelical Church: POB 260, Maseru 100; tel. 22323942; f. 1833; independent since 1964; Pres. Rev. JOHN RAPELANG MOKHAHLANE; Exec. Sec. Rev. A. M. THEBE; 230,000 mems (2003).
Other denominations active in Lesotho include the Apostolic Faith Mission, the Assemblies of God, the Dutch Reformed Church in Africa, the Full Gospel Church of God, Methodist Church of Southern Africa and the Seventh-day Adventists. There are also numerous African independent churches.

BAHÁ'Í FAITH

National Spiritual Assembly: POB 508, Maseru 100; tel. 22312346; fax 22310092; mems resident in 444 localities.

The Press

Lesotho does not have a daily newspaper.
Leseli ka Sepolesa (The Police Witness): Press Dept, Police Headquarters, Maseru CBD, POB 13, Maseru 100; tel. 22317262; fax 22310045; fortnightly; Sesotho; publ. by the Lesotho Mounted Police Services.
Leselinyana la Lesotho (Light of Lesotho): Morija Printing Works, POB 7, Morija 190; tel. 22360205; fax 22360005; f. 1863; fortnightly; Sesotho, with occasional articles in English; publ. by the Lesotho Evangelical Church; Editor SELBORNE MOTLATSI MOHLALISI; circ. 10,000.
Lesotho Today/Lentsoe la Basotho (Voice of the Lesotho Nation): Lesotho News Agency Complex, Lerotholi St, opp. Royal Palace, POB 36, Maseru 100; tel. 22323561; fax 22322764; f. 1974; weekly; Sesotho; publ. by Ministry of Communications, Science and Technology; Editor KAHLISO LESENYANE; circ. 14,000.
Makatolle: POB 111, Maseru 100; tel. 22850990; f. 1963; weekly; Sesotho; Editor M. RAMANGOEI; circ. 2,000.
The Mirror/Setsomi sa Litaba: Mothamo House, 1st Floor, POB 903, Maseru 100; tel. 22323208; fax 22320941; f. 1986; weekly; English and Sesotho; Owner TEBELLO PITSO-HLOHLONGOANE; Editor NAT MOLOMO; circ. 4,000.
MoAfrika: MoAfrika Broadcasting and Publishing Services, Carlton Centre Bldg, 1st Floor, POB 7234, Maseru 100; tel. 22321854; fax 22321956; f. 1990 as *The African*; weekly; Sesotho and English; Editor-in-Chief Prof. SEBONONOLA R. K. RAMAINOANE; circ. 5,000.
Moeletsi oa Basotho: Mazenod Institute, POB 18, Mazenod 160; tel. 22350465; fax 22350010; e-mail mzpwrks@lesoff.co.za; f. 1933; weekly; Sesotho; publ. by the Roman Catholic Church; Editor FRANCIS KHOARIPE; circ. 20,000.
Mohahlaula: Allied Bldg, 1st Floor, Manonyane Centre, POB 14430, Maseru 100; tel. 22312777; fax 22320941; weekly; Sesotho; publ. by Makaung Printers and Publrs; Editor WILLY MOLLUNGOA.
Mololi: Cooperatives Bldg, Main North 1 Rd, POB 9933, Maseru 100; tel. 22312287; fax 22327912; 1997; publ. suspended in 2000; Sesotho; organ of the Lesotho Congress for Democracy; Editor MONYANE MOLELEKI.
Mopheme (The Survivor): Allied Bldg, 1st Floor, Manonyane Centre, POB 14184, Maseru; tel. and fax 22311670; e-mail mopheme@lesoff.co.za; weekly; English and Sesotho; publ. by Newsshare Foundation; Owner and Editor LAWRENCE KEKETSO; circ. 2,500.
Public Eye/Mosotho: House No. 14A3, Princess Margaret Rd, POB 14129, Old Europa, Maseru 100; tel. 22321414; fax 22310614; e-mail editor@publiceye.co.ls; internet www.publiceye.co.ls; f. 1997; weekly; 80% English, 20% Sesotho; publ. by Voice Multimedia; also publ. *Eye on Tourism* and *Family Mirror* magazines; Editor-in-Chief BETHUEL THAI; circ. 20,000 (Lesotho and South Africa).
Southern Star: POB 7590, Maseru; tel. 22312269; fax 22310167; e-mail ba-holdings@ilesotho.com; weekly; English; Editor FRANK BOFFOE; circ. 1,500.

PERIODICALS

Justice and Peace: Catholic Bishops' Conference, Our Lady of Victories Cathedral Catholic Centre, POB 200, Maseru 100; tel. 22312750; fax 22312751; quarterly; publ. by the Roman Catholic Church.
Moqolotsi (The Journalist): House No. 1B, Happy Villa, POB 14139, Maseru 100; tel. and fax 22320941; e-mail medinles@lesoff.co.za; monthly newsletter; English; publ. by the Media Institute of Lesotho (MILES).
NGO Web: 544 Hoohlo Extension, Florida, Maseru 100; tel. 22325798; fax 22317205; e-mail lecongo@lecongo.org.ls; quarterly; English and Sesotho; publ. of the Lesotho Council of NGOs; circ. 2,000.
Review of Southern African Studies: Institute of Southern African Studies, National University of Lesotho, PO Roma 180; tel. 22340247; fax 22340601; 2 a year; arts, social and behavioural sciences; Editor TANKIE KHALANYANE.
Shoeshoe: POB 36, Maseru 100; tel. 22323561; fax 22310003; quarterly; women's interest; publ. by Ministry of Communications, Science and Technology.
Other publications include *Mara LDF Airwing/Airsquadron* and *The Sun/Thebe*.

NEWS AGENCY

Lesotho News Agency (LENA): Lesotho News Agency Complex, Lerotholi St, opp. Royal Palace, POB 36, Maseru 100; tel. 22325317; fax 22324608; e-mail l_lenanews@hotmail.com; internet www.lena.gov.ls; f. 1985; Dir NKOE THAKALI; Editor VIOLET MARAISANE.

Publishers

Longman Lesotho (Pty) Ltd: 104 Christie House, 1st Floor, Orpen Rd, Old Europa, POB 1174, Maseru 100; tel. 22314254; fax 22310118; Man. Dir SEYMOUR R. KIKINE.
Macmillan Boleswa Publishers Lesotho (Pty) Ltd: 523 Sun Cabanas Hotel, POB 7545, Maseru 100; tel. 22317340; fax 22310047; e-mail macmillan@lesoff.co.ls; Man. Dir PAUL MOROLONG.
Mazenod Institute: POB 39, Mazenod 160; tel. 22350224; f. 1933; Roman Catholic; Man. Fr B. MOHLALISI.
Morija Sesuto Book Depot: POB 4, Morija 190; tel. and fax 22360204; f. 1862; owned by the Lesotho Evangelical Church; religious, educational and Sesotho language and literature.

St Michael's Mission: The Social Centre, POB 25, Roma; tel. 22316234; f. 1968; religious and educational; Man. Dir Fr M. FERRANGE.

GOVERNMENT PUBLISHING HOUSE

Government Printer: POB 268, Maseru; tel. 22313023.

Broadcasting and Communications

TELECOMMUNICATIONS

Lesotho Telecommunications Authority (LTA): Moposo House, 6th Floor, Kingsway Rd, POB 15896, Maseru 100; tel. 22224300; fax 22310984; e-mail lta@lta.org.ls; internet www.lta.org.ls; f. 2000; regulates telecommunications and broadcasting; Chief Exec. MONEHELA POSHOLI.

Telecom Lesotho: POB 1037, Maseru 100; tel. 22211100; fax 22310183; internet www.telecom.co.ls; 70% holding acquired by the Mountain Kingdom Communications consortium in 2000; 30% state-owned; Chair. JOHN BAYLEY; CEO ADRI VAN DER VEER.

Vodacom Lesotho (Pty) Ltd: Block B, Development House, Kingsway Rd, POB 7387, Maseru 100; tel. 52212201; fax 22311079; internet www.vodacom.co.ls; f. 1996; jt venture between Telecom Lesotho and Vodacom (Pty) Ltd; fmrly VCL Communications; mobile cellular telecommunications provider; Man. Dir MERVYN VISAGIE.

BROADCASTING

RADIO

The first licences for private radio stations were issued in 1998. Licences are issued by the Lesotho Telecommunications Authority. Radio Lesotho is the only station to broadcast nationwide; all the other stations are restricted to urban areas and their peripheries.

Catholic Radio FM: Our Lady of Victories Cathedral, Catholic Centre POB 200, Maseru 100; tel. 22323247; fax 22310294; f. 1999.

Joy FM: Lesotho Sun Hotel, Suites 2204–2206, Private Bag A457, Maseru 100; tel. 22310920; fax 22310104; internet www.joyfm.co.ls; f. 2001; Sesotho and English; relays Voice of America broadcasts.

Khotso FM: Institute of Extramural Studies, National University of Lesotho POB 180, Roma; Private Bag A47, Maseru 100; tel. 22322038; fax 22340000; community radio station; sister station of DOPE FM (f. 2004).

MoAfrika FM: Carlton Centre, 2nd Floor, Kingsway, POB 7234, Maseru 100; tel. and fax 22321956; e-mail info@moafrika.co.ls; internet www.moafrika.co.ls; affiliated to the *MoAfrika* newspaper; Sesotho, Xhosa and Mandarin; news and entertainment; Man. and Editor-in-Chief Prof. SEBONONOLA R. K. RAMAINOANE.

People's Choice Radio (PCFM): LNDC Centre, Development House, Level 9, Block D, POB 8800, Maseru 100; tel. 22322122; fax 22310888; internet www.pcfm.co.ls; f. 1998; news and entertainment; Man. Dir MOTLATSI MAJARA.

Radio Lesotho: Lesotho News Agency Complex, Lerotholi St, opp. Royal Palace, POB 552, Maseru 100; tel. and fax 22323371; e-mail enquiries@africanextension.com; internet www.radiolesotho.co.ls; f. 1964; state-owned; part of Lesotho Nat. Broadcasting Services; Sesotho and English; Dir of Broadcasting LEBOHANG DADA MOQASA.

TELEVISION

Lesotho Television (LTV): Lesotho News Agency Complex, Lerotholi St, opp. Royal Palace, POB 36, Maseru 100; tel. 22324735; fax 22310149; e-mail mfalatsa@yahoo.com; f. 1988 in association with M-Net, South Africa; state-owned; part of Lesotho Nat. Broadcasting Services; Sesotho and English.

Finance

(cap. = capital; res = reserves; dep. = deposits; m. = million; brs = branches; amounts in maloti)

BANKING

Central Bank

Central Bank of Lesotho: cnr Airport and Moshoeshoe Rds, POB 1184, Maseru 100; tel. 22314281; fax 22310051; e-mail cbl@centralbank.org.ls; internet www.centralbank.org.ls; f. 1978 as the Lesotho Monetary Authority; present name adopted in 1982; bank of issue; cap. 25.0m., res 1,676.2m., dep. 1,544.7m. (Dec. 2002); Gov. and Chair. ESSELEN MOTLATSI MATEKANE.

Commercial Banks

Nedbank Lesotho: Nedbank Building, 361 Kingsway, POB 1001, Maseru 100; tel. 22312696; fax 22310025; f. 1997; fmrly Standard Chartered Bank Lesotho Ltd; 100% owned by Nedcor Group (South Africa); cap. 20m., res 21.5m., dep. 704.2m. (Dec. 2002); Chair. WILLEM P. FROST; Man. Dir PHILIP D. OPPERMAN; 3 brs and 7 agencies.

Standard Lesotho Bank: Banking Bldg, 1st Floor, Kingsway Rd, Kingsway Town Centre, POB 115, Maseru 100; tel. 22312423; fax 22310235; internet www.standardbank.co.ls; f. 2006 following merger between Lesotho Bank (1999) Ltd (f. 1972) and Standard Bank Lesotho Ltd (fmrly Stanbic Bank Lesotho Ltd); Chair. THABO MAKEBA; Man. Dir COLIN ADDIS; 6 brs.

INSURANCE

Alliance Insurance Co Ltd: Alliance House, 4 Bowker Rd, POB 01118, Maseru West 105; tel. 22312357; fax 22310313; e-mail alliance@alliance.co.ls; internet www.alliance.co.ls; f. 1993; life and short-term insurance; Man. Dir JOHANN PIENAAR; Gen. Mans MOK'HAPHEK'HA LAZARO, THABISO MADIBA.

Customer Protection Insurance Co Ltd: POB 201, Maseru 100; tel. 22312643; e-mail craigb@relyant.co.za; wholly owned subsidiary of Ellerine Holdings Ltd, South Africa; general short-term insurance; Chair. DENZIL MCGLASHAN.

Lesotho National Insurance Group (LNIG): Lesotho Insurance House, Kingsway, Private Bag A65, Maseru 100; tel. 22313031; fax 22310008; f. 1977; 50% state-owned; part-privatized in 1995; incorporating subsidiaries specializing in life and short-term insurance; Chair. Dr M. SENAOANA; CEO M. MOLELEKOA.

Metropolitan Lesotho Ltd: POB 645, Maseru; tel. 22323970; fax 22317126; f. 2003; subsidiary of Metropolitan Holdings Ltd, South Africa; Man. Dir TSOANE MPHAHLELE.

Trade and Industry

GOVERNMENT AGENCIES

Privatisation Unit: Privatisation Project, Lesotho Utilities Sector Reform Project, Ministry of Finance and Development Planning, Lesotho Bank Mortgage Division Bldg, 2nd Floor, Kingsway St, Private Bag A249, Maseru 100; tel. 22317902; fax 22317551; internet www.privatisation.gov.ls; CEO MOSITO KHETHISA.

Trade Promotion Unit: c/o Ministry of Trade, Industry, Cooperatives and Marketing, POB 747, Maseru 100; tel. 322138; fax 310121.

DEVELOPMENT ORGANIZATIONS

Basotho Enterprises Development Corpn (BEDCO): POB 1216, Maseru 100; tel. 22312094; fax 22310455; e-mail admin@bedco.org.ls; f. 1980; promotes and assists in the establishment and devt of Basotho-owned enterprises, with emphasis on small- and medium-scale; CEO VICTOR R. LECHESA.

Lesotho Council of Non-Governmental Organizations: House 544, Hoohlo Extension, Private Bag A445, Maseru 100; tel. 22317205; fax 22310412; e-mail seabatam@lecongo.org.ls; internet www.lecongo.org.ls; f. 1990; promotes sustainable management of natural resources, socio-economic devt and social justice; Exec. Dir SEABATA MOTSAMAI.

Lesotho Highlands Development Authority (LHDA): Bank Tower, 3rd Floor, Kingsway, POB 7332, Maseru 100; tel. 22311280; fax 22310060; internet www.lhda.org.ls; f. 1986 to supervise the Lesotho Highlands Water Project, being undertaken jtly with South Africa; Chair. JOHN J. EAGER (acting); CEO MASILO PHAKOE (acting).

Lesotho National Development Corpn (LNDC): Development House, Block A, Kingsway, Private Bag A96, Maseru 100; tel. 22312012; fax 22310038; e-mail info@lndc.org.ls; internet www.lndc.org.ls; f. 1967; state-owned; total assets M477.5m. (March 2006); interests in manufacturing, mining, food-processing and leisure; Chair. MOHLOMI RANTEKOA; CEO PEETE MOLAPO.

Lesotho Co-operative Handicrafts: Basotho Hat Bldg, Kingsway, PO Box 148, Maseru; tel. 22322523; e-mail ich@ilesotho.com; f. 1978; marketing and distribution of handicrafts; Gen. Man. KHOTSO MATLA.

CHAMBER OF COMMERCE

Lesotho Chamber of Commerce and Industry: Kingsway Ave, POB 79, Maseru 100; tel. 22316937; fax 22322794; Pres. SIMON PHAFANE.

INDUSTRIAL AND TRADE ASSOCIATIONS

Livestock Marketing Corpn: POB 800, Maseru 100; tel. 22322444; f. 1973; sole org. for marketing livestock and livestock products; liaises with marketing boards in South Africa; projects incl. an abattoir, tannery, poultry and wool and mohair scouring plants; Gen. Man. S. R. MATLANYANE.

EMPLOYERS' ORGANIZATION

Association of Lesotho Employers: 8 Bowker Rd, POB 1509, Maseru 100; tel. 22315736; fax 22325384; f. 1961; represents mems in industrial relations and on govt bodies, and advises the Govt on employers' concerns; Treas. R. LEBOELA; Exec. Dir THABO MAKEKA.

UTILITIES

Lesotho Electricity Corpn (LEC): POB 423, Maseru 100; tel. 22312236; fax 22310093; internet www.lec.co.ls; f. 1969; bids for transfer to the private sector were under consideration in mid-2004; Man. Dir S. L. MHAVILLE.

Lesotho Water and Sewerage Authority (WASA): POB 426, Maseru 100; tel. 22312449; fax 22312006; Chair. REFILOE TLALI.

TRADE UNIONS

Congress of Lesotho Trade Unions (COLETU): POB 13282, Maseru 100; tel. 22320958; fax 22310081; f. 1998; Sec.-Gen. JUSTICE TSIUKULU; 15,587 mems.

Construction and Allied Workers' Union of Lesotho (CAWULE): Manonyana Centre, 2nd Floor, Room 24, POB 132282, Maseru 100; tel. 63023484; fax 22321951; f. 1967; affiliated to the Building and Wood Workers International; Pres. L. PUTSOANE; Sec. T. TLALE.

Factory Workers' Union (FAWU): Maseru; f. 2003 following split from the Lesotho Clothing and Allied Workers' Union; Pres. KHABILE TSILO; Sec.-Gen. MACAEFA BILLY.

Lesotho Association of Teachers (LAT): POB 12528, Maseru 100; tel. and fax 22317463; affiliated to the Education International; Exec. Sec. PAUL P. SEMATLANE.

Lesotho Clothing and Allied Workers' Union (LECAWU): LNDC Centre, 2nd Floor, Rm 12–14, Kingsway Rd, POB 11767, Maseru 100; tel. 22324296; fax 22320958; e-mail lecawu@lesoff.co.ls; affiliated to the Int. Textile, Garment and Leather Workers' Fed.; Sec.-Gen. DANIEL MARAISANE; 6,000 mems.

Lesotho General Workers' Union: POB 322, Maseru 100; f. 1954; Chair. J. M. RAMAROTHOLE; Sec. T. MOTLOHI.

Lesotho Congress of Democratic Unions (LECODU): POB 15851, Maseru 100; tel. and fax 22323559; f. 2004; Sec.-Gen. E. T. RAMOCHELA; 15,279 mems (2005).

Lesotho Teachers' Trade Union (LTTU): POB 0509, Maseru West 105; tel. 22322774; fax 22321951; e-mail lecawu@lesoff.co.ls; affiliated to the Education International; Pres. CHEFANE JOSEPH CHEFANE; Gen. Sec. MALIMABE JOAKIM MOTOPELA.

Lesotho Transport and Allied Workers' Union: Maseru 100; f. 1959; Pres. M. BERENG; Gen. Sec. TSEKO KAPA.

Lesotho University Teachers' and Researchers' Union (LUTARU): Maseru; Pres. Dr FRANCIS MAKOA.

Transport

RAILWAYS

Lesotho is linked with the South African railway system by a short line (2.6 km in length) from Maseru to Marseilles, on the Bloemfontein–Natal main line.

ROADS

In 1999 Lesotho's road network totalled 5,940 km, of which 1,084 km were main roads and 1,950 km were secondary roads. About 18.3% of roads were paved. In 1996 the International Development Association granted US $40m. towards the Government's rolling five-year road programme. From 1996/97 an extra-budgetary Road Fund was to finance road maintenance. In March 2000 a major road network was opened, linking Maseru with the Mohale Dam.

CIVIL AVIATION

King Moshoeshoe I International Airport is at Thota-Moli, some 20 km from Maseru; in January 2002 the Government announced plans for its expansion. International services between Maseru and Johannesburg are operated by South African Airlink. The national airline company, Lesotho Airways, was sold to a South African company in 1997 as part of the Government's ongoing privatization programme; however, after two years of losses the company was liquidated in 1999.

Tourism

Spectacular mountain scenery is the principal tourist attraction, and a new ski resort was opened in 2003. Tourist arrivals totalled 303,578 in 2005. In 2004 receipts from tourism amounted to an estimated US $34m.

Lesotho Tourism Development Corpn (LTDC): cnr Linare and Parliament Rds, POB 1378, Maseru 100; tel. 22312238; fax 22310189; e-mail ltdc@ltdc.org.ls; internet www.ltdc.org.ls; f. 2000; successor to the Lesotho Tourist Board; CEO MTHWALO MTHWALO.

LIBERIA

Introductory Survey

Location, Climate, Language, Religion, Flag, Capital

The Republic of Liberia lies on the west coast of Africa, with Sierra Leone and Guinea to the north, and Côte d'Ivoire to the east. The climate is tropical, with temperatures ranging from 18°C (65°F) to 49°C (120°F). English is the official language but the 16 major ethnic groups speak their own languages and dialects. Liberia is officially a Christian state, although some Liberians hold traditional beliefs. There are about 670,000 Muslims. The national flag (proportions 10 by 19) has 11 horizontal stripes, alternately of red and white, with a dark blue square canton, containing a five-pointed white star, in the upper hoist. The capital is Monrovia.

Recent History

Founded by liberated black slaves from the southern USA, Liberia became an independent republic in 1847. The leader of the True Whig Party (TWP), William Tubman, who had been President of Liberia since 1944, died in July 1971 and was succeeded by his Vice-President, William R. Tolbert, who was re-elected in October 1975.

In April 1980 Tolbert was assassinated in a military coup, led by Master Sgt (later Commander-in-Chief) Samuel Doe, who assumed power as Chairman of the newly established People's Redemption Council (PRC), suspending the Constitution and proscribing all political parties. The new regime attracted international criticism for its summary execution of 13 former senior government officials who had been accused of corruption and mismanagement. In July 1981 all civilian ministers received commissions, thus installing total military rule.

A draft Constitution was approved by 78.3% of registered voters in a national referendum in July 1984. In the same month Doe dissolved the PRC and appointed a 58-member Interim National Assembly. The ban on political organizations was repealed in the same month, to enable parties to secure registration prior to presidential and legislative elections, which were due to take place in October 1985. In August 1984 Doe established the National Democratic Party of Liberia (NDPL) and formally announced his candidature for the presidency. By early 1985 a total of 11 political associations had been formed; however, two influential parties, the Liberian People's Party (LPP) and the United People's Party (UPP), were proscribed, and apart from the NDPL only three parties—the Liberian Action Party (LAP), the Liberia Unification Party (LUP) and the Unity Party (UP)—were eventually permitted to participate in the elections. Doe won the presidential election, receiving 50.9% of the votes. At the concurrent elections to the bicameral National Assembly, the NDPL won 22 of the 26 seats in the Senate and 51 of the 64 seats in the House of Representatives.

On 6 January 1986 Doe was inaugurated as President. He appointed a new Cabinet (which largely comprised members of the previous administration). Six members of the opposition parties continued to boycott the National Assembly, and their seats were taken by NDPL representatives at a by-election in December. In March 1988 Gabriel Kpolleh, the leader of the LUP, was among several people arrested on charges of planning to overthrow the Government. In October he and nine others were sentenced to 10 years' imprisonment for treason.

In December 1989 an armed insurrection by rebel forces began in the north-eastern border region of Nimba County. In early 1990 several hundred deaths ensued in fighting between the Liberian army (the Armed Forces of Liberia—AFL) and the rebels, who claimed to be members of a hitherto unknown opposition group, the National Patriotic Front of Liberia (NPFL), led by a former government official, Charles Taylor. The fighting swiftly degenerated into a war between Doe's ethnic group, the Krahn, and the local Gio and Mano tribes, and many thousands of people took refuge in neighbouring Guinea and Côte d'Ivoire. Following the advance of rebels on the capital, Monrovia, in May, most foreign residents were evacuated. NPFL forces entered Monrovia in July; Taylor's authority as self-proclaimed President of his own interim administration, known as the National Patriotic Reconstruction Assembly, was, however, challenged by a faction of the NPFL, led by Prince Yormie Johnson, which rapidly secured control of parts of Monrovia. In the subsequent conflict both government and rebel forces were responsible for numerous atrocities against civilians. The Economic Community of West African States (ECOWAS, see p. 232) repeatedly failed to negotiate a cease-fire, and in late August it dispatched a military force to restore peace in the region. Doe and Johnson accepted this Monitoring Group (ECOMOG, see p. 235), but its initial occupation of the port area of Monrovia encountered armed opposition by Taylor's forces.

On 30 August 1990 exiled representatives of Liberia's principal political parties and other influential groups met at a conference convened by ECOWAS in the Gambian capital, Banjul, where they elected Dr Amos Sawyer, the leader of the LPP, as President of an Interim Government of National Unity (IGNU). Doe was taken prisoner by Johnson's rebel Independent National Patriotic Front of Liberia (INPFL) on 9 September, and was killed on the following day. In early October, following Taylor's rejection of a proposed peace settlement, ECOMOG began an offensive aimed at establishing a neutral zone in Monrovia separating the three warring factions. By mid-October ECOMOG had gained control of central Monrovia. On 22 November Sawyer was inaugurated as Interim President, under the auspices of ECOWAS, in Monrovia. Later that month, following ECOWAS-sponsored negotiations in the Malian capital, Bamako, the AFL, the NPFL and the INPFL signed a cease-fire agreement. By January 1991 all rebel forces had withdrawn from Monrovia, and in that month Sawyer nominated ministers to the IGNU. Legislative power was vested in a 28-member Interim National Assembly, which represented the principal political factions, including the INPFL; however, the NPFL refused to participate. On 19 April a national conference re-elected Sawyer as Interim President and appointed a member of the INPFL, Peter Naigow (a former minister in Doe's administration), as Vice-President. In June Sawyer nominated a new Council of Ministers, which was subsequently approved by the Interim National Assembly. In August, however, the INPFL representatives, including Naigow, resigned from the IGNU, after Sawyer denounced the execution, apparently at Johnson's instigation, of four members of the INPFL who had reportedly complied with arrangements to relinquish weapons to ECOMOG.

In April 1991, after members of the NPFL perpetrated several incursions into Sierra Leone, Sierra Leonean forces entered Liberian territory and launched retaliatory attacks, while the NPFL reportedly advanced within Sierra Leone. It was claimed that NPFL forces were supporting a Sierra Leonean resistance movement, the Revolutionary United Front (RUF), in hostilities against government forces of that country (see the chapter on Sierra Leone). In September members of a newly emerged rebel movement, comprising former supporters of Doe, the United Liberation Movement of Liberia for Democracy (ULIMO), began attacks from Sierra Leone against NPFL forces in north-western Liberia.

At the end of October 1991 a summit meeting between Sawyer and Taylor, which took place in Yamoussoukro, Côte d'Ivoire, under the aegis of an ECOWAS five-nation committee, resulted in a peace agreement whereby the troops of all warring factions were to be disarmed and restricted to camps, while the NPFL was to relinquish the territory under its control to ECOMOG. It was also agreed that all Liberian forces would be withdrawn from Sierra Leone, and that a demilitarized zone, under the control of ECOMOG, would be created along Liberia's border with Sierra Leone. In January 1992 the Interim Election Commission and Supreme Court were established, in accordance with the peace accord. At the end of April, in response to pressure from within the NPFL, Taylor agreed to withdraw NPFL troops from the border with Sierra Leone. In May ECOMOG began to disarm the rebel factions and to deploy troops in NPFL-controlled territory, and, despite continued fighting between ULIMO and NPFL forces, established a demilitarized zone along the border with Sierra Leone.

In August 1992 ULIMO launched a renewed offensive in western Liberia, gaining control of Bomi and Grand Cape Mount

Counties. In October the NPFL claimed that Nigerian aircraft under ECOMOG command had bombed its bases at Kakata and Harbel (the site of the Robertsfield International Airport and the country's principal rubber plantation), and at Buchanan, following an NPFL attack on ECOMOG forces stationed near Monrovia. The NPFL subsequently seized a number of strategic areas on the outskirts of Monrovia. ECOMOG forces (who were supported by members of the AFL and militia loyal to the IGNU) began retaliatory attacks against NPFL positions around the capital. In late October ECOMOG units succeeded in capturing the INPFL base at Caldwell, near Monrovia, and forcing Johnson to surrender. (The INPFL was subsequently disbanded.) In November the UN Security Council adopted a resolution imposing a mandatory embargo on the supply of armaments to Liberia, and authorized the UN Secretary-General to send a special representative to the country. In December ECOMOG announced that it had regained control of the area surrounding Monrovia, and in early 1993 began to advance in south-eastern Liberia, recapturing Harbel, while ULIMO was reported to have gained control of Lofa County in the west. In March ULIMO accepted an invitation from Sawyer to join the IGNU; ULIMO forces in Monrovia were subsequently disarmed. Following a major offensive, ECOMOG announced in April that it had gained control of Buchanan (which was reopened to shipping later that year).

In July 1993 a conference, attended by the factions involved in the hostilities, was convened (under the auspices of the UN and ECOWAS) in Geneva, Switzerland. Following several days of negotiations, the IGNU, the NPFL and ULIMO agreed to a cease-fire (to be monitored by a joint committee of the three factions, pending the deployment of UN observers and a reconstituted peace-keeping force), and to the establishment of a transitional administration. The peace accord was formally signed in Cotonou on 25 July. Under its terms, the IGNU was to be replaced by the Liberian National Transitional Government (LNTG), with a five-member transitional Council of State and a 35-member Transitional Legislative Assembly (comprising 13 representatives of the IGNU, 13 of the NPFL and nine of ULIMO), pending elections. In response to demands by Taylor, the dominance in ECOMOG of the Nigerian contingent was to be reduced.

The cease-fire came into effect at the end of July 1993; however, ECOMOG subsequently accused the NPFL of violating the Cotonou accord by repeatedly entering territory under its control. In August the IGNU, the NPFL and ULIMO each appointed a representative to the Council of State, while a list of nine candidates, nominated by the three factions, elected the two remaining members (who were representatives of the IGNU and ULIMO respectively) from among their number. Dr Bismark Kuyon, a member of the IGNU, was subsequently elected Chairman of the Council of State. Shortly afterwards, however, Kuyon announced that the inauguration of the Council of State (originally scheduled to take place on 24 August) was to be postponed, pending the clear implementation of the process of disarmament.

In September 1993 the UN Security Council approved the establishment of a 300-member UN Observer Mission in Liberia (UNOMIL), which was to co-operate with ECOMOG and the Organization of African Unity (now the African Union, see p. 164) in monitoring the transitional process. In October the Transitional Legislative Assembly was established, in accordance with the peace agreement. Sawyer dismissed Kuyon (who had reportedly dissociated himself from the IGNU's refusal to relinquish power prior to disarmament) and appointed Philip Banks, hitherto Minister of Justice, in his place.

Meanwhile, it was feared that renewed hostilities in several areas of the country would jeopardize the peace accord. An armed faction styling itself the Liberia Peace Council (LPC), which reportedly comprised members of the Krahn ethnic group from Grand Gedeh County, joined by a number of disaffected AFL troops, emerged in September 1993 and subsequently entered into conflict with the NPFL in south-eastern Liberia. In December fighting between ULIMO and a newly formed movement, the Lofa Defence Force (LDF), was also reported in Lofa County. The NPFL denied involvement with the LDF, which occupied territory previously controlled by ULIMO in the north-west.

In February 1994 the Council of State elected David Kpomakpor, a representative of the IGNU, as its Chairman. In early March units belonging to UNOMIL and the new ECOMOG force (which had been reinforced by contingents from Tanzania and Uganda) were deployed, and the disarmament of all factions commenced. On 7 March the Council of State was inaugurated; it was envisaged that the presidential and legislative elections (originally scheduled for February) would take place in September. However, the disarmament process was subsequently impeded by an increase in rebel activity: in addition to continuing clashes involving the LDF and the LPC, more than 200 people were killed in fighting within ULIMO between members of the Krahn and Mandingo ethnic groups, particularly in the region of Tubmanburg (in Bomi County, where the movement was officially based). The hostilities were prompted by resentment among the Krahn at the predominance of the Mandingo in ULIMO's representation in the transitional institutions.

UNOMIL's mandate was renewed in April 1994. In May, following prolonged controversy over the allocation of principal portfolios, a 19-member Cabinet was installed, comprising seven representatives of the NPFL, seven of ULIMO and five of the former IGNU. In July, however, a faction known as ULIMO—K (led by Alhaji G. V. Kromah) launched an offensive to recapture Tubmanburg, which was under the control of Maj.-Gen. Roosevelt Johnson's forces (ULIMO—J). In early September (when the original mandate of the LNTG was due to expire) a meeting of the NPFL, the AFL and ULIMO—K took place in Akosombo, Ghana. On 12 September Taylor, Kromah and the Chief of Staff of the AFL, Lt-Gen. Hezekiah Bowen, signed a peace accord providing for the immediate cessation of hostilities and for the establishment later that month of a reconstituted Council of State, in which four of the five members were to be nominated, respectively, by the three factions and a civilian Liberian National Conference (LNC—which had been convened in Monrovia at the end of August). Meanwhile, following clashes between dissident members of the NPFL and troops loyal to Taylor, the dissidents' Central Revolutionary Council (CRC) announced that Taylor had been deposed and replaced by the Minister of Labour in the LNTG, Thomas Woewiyu, who indicated that he was not prepared to accept the Akosombo agreement. In mid-September disaffected members of the AFL, led by a former officer who had served in the Doe administration, Gen. Charles Julu, seized the presidential mansion, but were subsequently overpowered by ECOMOG forces. (Almost 80 members of the AFL, including Julu, were later arrested, and a further 2,000 troops were disarmed by ECOMOG.) Later that month the CRC, apparently in alliance with elements of the AFL, ULIMO, the LPC and the LDF, took control of Taylor's base at Gbarnga (in central Bong County); Taylor was reported to have fled to Côte d'Ivoire.

In October 1994 both the ECOMOG and UNOMIL contingents were reduced in size, in view of the lack of progress achieved in the peace process. In November a conference, attended by Bowen, Taylor, Woewiyu, the leader of the LPC, Dr George Boley, and the leader of the LDF, François Massaquoi, together with representatives of the LNC and the LNTG, was convened in Accra, Ghana, to discuss preparations for the installation of a reconstituted Council of State. Meanwhile, the NPFL had regained control of much of the territory, including Gbarnga, that the CRC had captured in September. On 22 December the participants of the peace conference reached agreement for a cease-fire to enter into force later that month and reaffirmed the terms of the Akosombo agreement, including provisions for the establishment of demilitarized zones throughout Liberia and for the installation of a reconstituted Council of State, to comprise a single representative of each of the NPFL, ULIMO, the 'Coalition Forces' (a loose alliance comprising the CRC, the LPC, the LDF and elements of the AFL), and the LNC, with a fifth member elected jointly by the NPFL and ULIMO from traditional rulers. Later in December 1994 the UN Security Council extended the mandate of UNOMIL (now comprising some 90 observers) until April 1995, while the Nigerian Government reduced its ECOMOG contingent to 6,000 (from about 10,000). The cease-fire entered into force on 28 December 1994; however, factional fighting, particularly between the NPFL and LPC, continued in early 1995. The UN and ECOWAS expressed further dissatisfaction with the suspension of the peace process, and at the end of April Tanzania withdrew its 800-member ECOMOG contingent, owing to lack of funding.

Negotiations regarding the composition of the Council of State were impeded by Taylor's persistent demand to be granted its chairmanship. On 19 August 1995, following a further ECOWAS summit meeting in Abuja, the armed factions (the NPFL, ULIMO—K, the LPC, the CRC, the LDF, ULIMO—J and the AFL) finally signed a compromise agreement providing for the installation of a reconstituted Council of State, which was to remain in power, pending elections, for one year. An academic with no factional affiliations, Prof. Wilton Sankawulo, was to assume the office of Chairman, while the other seats were to be allocated to Taylor, Kromah, Boley, the LNC representative, Oscar Quiah, and a traditional ruler who had been nominated by ULIMO and the NPFL, Chief Tamba Taylor. Later that month a cease-fire entered into force, in compliance with the terms of the peace accord. The Council of State was formally installed on 1 September, and was to remain in place pending elections, scheduled for 20 August 1996. The Council of State subsequently appointed a transitional Council of Ministers, comprising members of the seven factions that had signed the Abuja agreement. Later in September the UN Security Council extended UNOMIL's mandate until the end of January 1996.

In November 1995 a demilitarized zone was established between NPFL and ULIMO—K forces in the region of St Paul River (between Bong and Lofa Counties). Deployment of ECOMOG forces commenced, in accordance with the Abuja peace terms, in December. Following continued clashes between the ULIMO factions, however, ULIMO—J attacked ECOMOG troops near Tubmanburg. ECOMOG suspended deployment of its forces, and launched a counter-offensive in an attempt to restore order. Hostilities continued in early 1996, with large numbers of civilians killed or displaced.

In February 1996 ULIMO—J officials stated that Johnson had been replaced as leader of the movement in the interests of the peace process. In March the Council of State announced his removal from the Council of Ministers. In subsequent clashes between the two factions of ULIMO—J, forces loyal to Johnson allegedly killed a supporter of the new leadership, prompting the Council of State to order that he be arrested on charges of murder. Johnson, however, refused to surrender to the authorities, and became effectively besieged in his private residence in Monrovia. In April government forces, led by Charles Taylor, engaged in hostilities with Johnson's supporters, in an effort to force him to surrender. The principal factions represented in the transitional authorities thus became involved in the conflict: elements of the LPC and AFL (which were predominantly Krahn) supported Johnson's forces, while the NPFL and ULIMO—K opposed them. Fighting rapidly intensified in central Monrovia and ECOMOG (which had refrained from military intervention) deployed its forces in the region, with the aim of negotiating between the warring factions. Following a lull in the fighting, however, some of Johnson's supporters launched attacks in the residential area of Mamba Point (where embassies and offices of humanitarian organizations were situated) and seized a number of civilians as hostages. Later in April a further cease-fire agreement was negotiated under the aegis of the US Government, the UN and ECOWAS, allowing the deployment of ECOMOG troops throughout Monrovia, while most of the remaining hostages were released by Johnson's supporters.

In May 1996, during the absence of Johnson (who had left the country under US protection, to attend a planned ECOWAS summit meeting), the NPFL launched a further attack against the Barclay Training Centre, prompting large numbers of civilians to flee to Monrovia Freeport. At the end of May the UN Security Council renewed the mandate of UNOMIL for a further three months, but warned the armed factions that international support would be withdrawn if fighting continued; UNOMIL was henceforth to comprise only the remaining five military and 20 civilian personnel, following the evacuation of the main mission of about 90 observers in April. In June Johnson's supporters agreed to disarm, while an ECOWAS arbitration mission commenced discussions with the faction leaders in an effort to restore the peace process.

In August 1996, at an ECOWAS conference in Abuja, the principal faction leaders (apart from Johnson, who remained abroad) signed a further peace agreement, whereby a reconstituted Council of State was to be installed by the end of that month, with a former senator, Ruth Perry, replacing Sankawulo as Chairman; Taylor and Boley were to remain members of the new administration. Under a revised schedule, elections were to take place at the end of May 1997, and power was to be transferred to an elected government by mid-June, following the dissolution of the armed factions by the end of January of that year. In order to implement the new timetable, ECOMOG (which then numbered 8,500) was to be reinforced by personnel from several West African states. At the end of August 1996 the mandate of UNOMIL was again extended.

Perry was inaugurated as Chairman of the Council of State in early September 1996; Johnson was again allocated a ministerial portfolio in a subsequent reorganization of the Cabinet. Following the expiry of the deadline for the completion of the disarmament process, which had been extended to early February 1997,

ECOMOG announced that about 91% of the rebel forces (who numbered 30,000–35,000, according to revised estimates) had relinquished their armaments.

In January 1997 Taylor announced that the NPFL had been officially dissolved, in accordance with the peace agreement; the movement was subsequently reconstituted as a political organization, the National Patriotic Party (NPP). In the same month Kromah declared that ULIMO—K had also ceased to exist as a military organization, and was to be reconstituted as the All Liberian Coalition Party (ALCOP). Meanwhile, political parties that had become inactive during the civil conflict were revived, and new groupings applied for official registration. In March Taylor, Kromah and Boley resigned from the Council of State, in compliance with the peace agreement, to allow their candidacy in the forthcoming elections. From March a number of West African countries began to dispatch additional contingents to reinforce ECOMOG (which was expected to be increased in size to about 16,000 personnel prior to the elections), with the USA providing logistical and financial assistance. In May, however, following a request by several political parties, the elections were postponed until 19 July to allow all the newly registered organizations sufficient time for preparation.

A 10-day voter registration process commenced at the end of June 1997. A total of 13 presidential candidates had emerged by this time, among them Ellen Johnson-Sirleaf (a former minister in the Tolbert administration and subsequently a World Bank official, who was to contest the election on behalf of the UP). Despite demands for a further postponement, the elections proceeded on 19 July. The elections commission announced on 23 July that Taylor had been elected President, with 75.3% of votes cast; Johnson-Sirleaf (who had been widely expected to be Taylor's strongest opponent) received only 9.6% of the votes. In the concurrent elections to the bicameral legislature (at which seats were allocated on a proportionate basis), the NPP secured 49 seats in the 64-member House of Representatives and 21 seats in the 26-member Senate, the UP won seven seats in the House of Representatives and three in the Senate, while ALCOP obtained three seats in the House of Representatives and two in the Senate. Kromah (who had won only 4.0% of the votes) subsequently declared that serious irregularities had occurred, but international observers declared the conduct of the elections to have been 'free and fair'. Taylor's overwhelming victory was generally ascribed to the widely held perception that he was the candidate most likely to achieve long-term stability in the country.

Taylor was inaugurated as President on 2 August 1997, and subsequently nominated a 19-member Cabinet, which was approved by the Senate. The new Government retained several members of the previous transitional administration, including Johnson and Woewiyu. A nine-member National Security Council, comprising several government ministers, the Chief of Staff of the Armed Forces and the Commander of ECOMOG, was established with the aim of ensuring the maintenance of civil order.

At an ECOWAS summit meeting, convened in Abuja, at the end of August 1997, it was agreed that ECOMOG was to be reconstituted and would henceforth assist in the process of national reconstruction, including the restructuring of the armed and security forces, and the maintenance of security; it was further envisaged that the contingent's mandate (officially due to expire on 2 February 1998) would be extended in agreement with the Liberian Government. Following the military coup in Sierra Leone in May 1997, ECOMOG was authorized to enforce international sanctions against the new junta led by Maj. Johnny Paul Koroma (see the chapter on Sierra Leone). In October, however, Taylor announced that he opposed the use of military force to oust the Koroma regime, and that ECOMOG would no longer be permitted to launch offensives against Sierra Leone from Liberian territory. Taylor ordered the closure of Liberia's border with Sierra Leone in response to civil disorder within that country. At the end of October Taylor established a National Human Rights Commission, which was empowered to investigate complaints of human rights violations.

In November 1997, following several months of rumours of the increasing strength in Guinea of Liberian rebel militia (principally members of the former ULIMO), constituting a threat to security in both countries, it was reported that some 30 members of ULIMO had been arrested in southern Guinea. The alleged presence of former Liberian factions in Guinea was discussed at a meeting between Taylor and the Guinean President, Gen. Lansana Conté, in December. Taylor subsequently appointed

Kromah (who had taken up residence in Guinea following his electoral defeat in July) to the post of Chairman of a National Commission on Reconciliation.

By early 1998 the ECOMOG contingent had been reduced to about 5,000 and the Government had notified ECOWAS of its desire for ECOMOG to withdraw formally by 2 February, but had also requested that Nigeria, Ghana, Burkina Faso and Niger continue to provide military assistance. Following the seizure of the Sierra Leonean capital, Freetown, by ECOMOG troops, Taylor protested that the arrest by ECOMOG of about 25 senior members of Sierra Leone's ousted junta at James Spriggs Payne Airport was an infringement of Liberian territory. The Liberian Government recalled its ambassador in Nigeria for consultations, and subsequently submitted a formal complaint to ECOWAS.

In March 1998 violent clashes erupted in Monrovia between the security forces and Johnson's supporters; Johnson subsequently claimed that members of Taylor's special security forces had attacked his private residence. ECOMOG troops were deployed to prevent further violence, and, in an attempt to ease tension in the capital, Johnson was removed from the Cabinet and appointed ambassador to India. In the same month Kromah, who had expressed concern regarding his own safety, was removed from his position as Chairman of the National Commission on Reconciliation. Later that month, following increasing tension between ECOMOG troops and Liberian security forces, the Government and ECOWAS signed an agreement revising ECOMOG's mandate in the country; the contingent was henceforth banned from intervening in civil disputes.

In September 1998 security forces attempted to arrest Johnson (who had not yet assumed his ambassadorial post), pursuing him to the US embassy compound, where he and a number of his supporters had taken refuge; some 50 people were killed in ensuing clashes between members of the security forces and Johnson's followers. The Government subsequently announced that Johnson, Kromah and 21 of his associates had been charged with treason, following an abortive coup attempt, and demanded that US embassy officials relinquish Johnson to Liberian authority. After discussions with the Liberian authorities, however, US officials transported Johnson to Sierra Leone. In response to an incursion by Liberian security forces into the US embassy compound during the fighting, the US Government temporarily closed the embassy and deployed a naval vessel near the Liberian coast to facilitate the evacuation of US nationals in the event of an escalation of violence in Monrovia. The Liberian Government subsequently issued a formal apology to the USA and announced that an investigation would be conducted into the incident, in co-operation with the US authorities. In October 32 people (several, including Johnson, *in absentia*) were formally charged with treason; their trial commenced in November. In the same month Taylor reorganized the Cabinet.

By November 1998 most of the ECOMOG forces in Liberia had been redeployed in Sierra Leone, owing to increased rebel activity in that country, and to continued tension between the Liberian Government and ECOMOG officials. In late December the Government closed Liberia's border with Sierra Leone, in response to the escalation in civil conflict in the neighbouring country, and pledged support for the administration of President Ahmed Kabbah. In January 1999 it was announced that further ECOMOG troops in Liberia were to be relocated to Sierra Leone, following a major offensive by RUF forces against Freetown. A small number of ECOMOG forces remained in Liberia to provide military assistance to the armed forces. In April 13 of the defendants on trial for treason were convicted and sentenced to 10 years' imprisonment.

In August 1999 members of a rebel movement reported to comprise former members of ULIMO—K, known as the Joint Forces for the Liberation of Liberia (JFLL), attacked principal towns in Lofa County from Guinea. Some 80 aid workers, including six foreign nationals, were taken hostage by the JFLL, but were released a few days later, following negotiations by humanitarian relief officials. Taylor ordered the closure of the border with Guinea and declared a temporary state of emergency in Lofa County. At an ECOWAS meeting on relations between Liberia and Guinea, which took place in Abuja in September, it was agreed that a commission would be established to address the issue of security at the border between Liberia, Guinea and Sierra Leone. The border was reopened in February 2000.

Reports of increased activity by Liberian dissidents, both in Sierra Leone, where rebels had allied with Kamajor militia, and in Guinea, resulted in a further deterioration in relations between the Liberian authorities and the Governments of those countries. In July 2000 rebel forces again launched an offensive from Guinean territory against Voinjama. Another hitherto unknown movement, Liberians United for Reconciliation and Democracy (LURD), believed to be a grouping of former members of the armed factions (particularly ULIMO–K), claimed responsibility for the attacks. Taylor and Conté subsequently conducted further discussions, with mediation from the Malian President, Alpha Oumar Konaré. In August Johnson-Sirleaf and a further 14 prominent opposition leaders (many of whom were abroad) were charged with alleged involvement with the LURD dissidents.

In September 2000 Conté claimed that Liberian and Sierra Leonean refugees in Guinea were supporting the activity of rebels attempting to overthrow his Government (see the chapter on Guinea), and ordered them to leave the country. Following a further rebel attack on the Guinean border town of Macenta, staged from Liberian territory, government forces bombarded the Liberian town of Zorzor, 220 km north-east of Monrovia, where dissident Liberian forces were based. In January 2001 the Liberian Government withdrew its ambassador in Guinea, following further Guinean bombardment of towns in the Foya district of northern Liberia. In the same month a committee of the UN Security Council reported that the Liberian Government actively supported the RUF and proposed the imposition of UN sanctions against Liberia. In early February the authorities announced that the Commander of the RUF, Sam Bockarie, had left the country, and that the rebels' liaison office had been closed. In early March the UN Security Council renewed the embargo on the supply of armaments to Liberia and voted in favour of a 12-month ban on diamond exports from Liberia and restrictions on the foreign travel of senior government and military officials; these latter measures were, however, deferred for a period of two months to allow the Government time to comply with demands that it expel RUF members from Liberia and end financial and military aid to the rebels. (In October 2000 the US Government had announced the imposition of diplomatic sanctions against Taylor, his relatives and close associates, prohibiting them from entering the USA until Liberia withdrew support for the RUF.) In late March 2001 Taylor expelled the ambassadors of Guinea and Sierra Leone from Liberia, claiming that they had been engaged in activity incompatible with their office, and announced the closure of the border with Sierra Leone. The Sierra Leonean authorities subsequently retaliated by ordering the Liberian chargé d'affaires to leave the country.

In April 2001 François Massaquoi, the former leader of the LDF, and Minister of Youth and Sport since 1997, was killed, after LURD forces fired on the helicopter transporting him to Voinjama. The Government subsequently intensified operations to suppress the continuing insurgency in northern Lofa County, near the border with Guinea. By May, however, the LURD claimed to have gained control of that region, and to have advanced to the neighbouring newly created Gbarpolu County, prompting the displacement of several thousand civilians. Early that month, in response to Taylor's perceived failure to comply with UN demands, the embargo on exports of diamonds from Liberia, together with the travel restrictions on senior government and military officials, entered into effect. Taylor condemned the imposition of UN sanctions, claiming that he had ended all connections with the RUF, while a large demonstration was staged in Monrovia in protest at the measures.

In July 2001 Taylor offered a general amnesty to active rebel supporters and to opposition members in exile who had been charged with treason or associated crimes. In August the Government announced that its order of expulsion against the ambassadors of Guinea and Sierra Leone accredited to Liberia had been formally withdrawn, following a request by ECOWAS. In September Johnson-Sirleaf (who had been charged with supporting anti-Government activities) returned to Monrovia under the terms of the general amnesty. In October a five-member UN commission issued a report recommending the extension of the existing sanctions against Liberia. The UN report also stated that the Liberian Government continued to use revenue generated by the timber industry and maritime activities to finance illicit trade in armaments with the RUF, and proposed the imposition of additional sanctions on timber exports.

By early 2002 LURD forces had gained considerable territory from government troops, and continued to advance southwards towards Monrovia. In response, Taylor declared a national state of emergency on 8 February (which was subsequently ratified by the legislature, and was to be revised after three months). Later that month the Government announced that it was to establish a permanent security presence at the country's northern border with Sierra Leone and Guinea. At the beginning of March the leader of LURD, Sekou Damate Conneh, announced that his forces aimed to depose Taylor and install a transitional administration in Monrovia. The rebels declared a few days later that they were prepared to enter into dialogue with government officials, but demanded that Taylor be excluded from discussions, on the grounds that he was not the legitimate Head of State of Liberia. The Government insisted that it would not contemplate the negotiation of a power-sharing agreement with the movement. Later that month a meeting of representatives of the Liberian authorities and opposition was convened at Abuja, under the aegis of ECOWAS; however, representatives of LURD failed to attend the negotiations, purportedly owing to the logistical difficulties in travelling to Abuja. At the conclusion of the discussions delegates representing 29 political and civil society associations, including major opposition leaders, urged the Government and LURD forces to declare a cease-fire. Nevertheless, fighting continued, particularly at Liberia's northern border with Guinea. At the end of March ECOWAS imposed travel restrictions on the LURD leadership, on the grounds that the movement had renewed hostilities against the Government.

On 6 May 2002 the UN Security Council adopted a resolution extending the armaments and diamond embargoes, and the travel ban, for a further 12 months. Also in May the Liberian legislature extended for a further six months the national state of emergency, after LURD forces gained further territory, seizing control of Gbarnga, in Bong County. In September 12 registered political parties attended a National Peace and Reconciliation Conference to discuss preparations for forthcoming elections. In the same month Taylor ended the national state of emergency and the ban on political demonstrations, announcing that government forces had regained control of much of the territory captured by the LURD, including the significant town of Bopolu, 100 km north-west of Monrovia.

During early 2003 hostilities frequently crossed into the territory of Côte d'Ivoire, and reports emerged that Ivorian rebel groups, notably the Mouvement pour la justice et la paix (MJP) and the Mouvement populaire ivoirien du grand ouest (MPIGO), had become allied with LURD. LURD forces regained control of Bopolu in February and briefly captured Robertsport and Bo Waterside, in Grand Cape Mount County. In March LURD occupied Klay, followed by the Ricks Institute Camp for internally displaced civilians, only 20 km from Monrovia, causing large numbers of civilians to take refuge in the capital. Simultaneous heavy fighting for control of Gbarnga was reported; LURD forces had recaptured the town by April. Meanwhile, a new rebel faction, the Movement for Democracy in Liberia (MODEL), attacked and secured Zwedru in Grand Geddeh County. MODEL was believed to comprise former members of the AFL and Doe loyalists, who were mainly based in Côte d'Ivoire (and reportedly supported by the Ivorian Government). Following fierce fighting in Sinoe County in April, MODEL captured the logging port of Greenville and continued to advance towards Buchanan. By this time members of the Ivorian MJP and MPIGO had clashed with the Liberian rebel and RUF members formerly allied with them. At the end of April Taylor and President Laurent Gbagbo of Côte d'Ivoire agreed to deploy joint border patrols. On 6 May the UN Security Council renewed the existing embargoes in force against Liberia for a further year, and imposed an additional ban on timber exports (which entered into effect in early July). Also in early May the Liberian authorities announced that Bockarie (who had been indicted by the Special Court established in Sierra Leone to try suspects of war crimes committed during the 10-year conflict in the country) had been killed in Liberia during an attempt to arrest him. (It was reported that he had been leading former RUF elements involved in the conflict in Liberia.) Subsequently, however, officials at the Special Court claimed that Bockarie and his immediate family had been captured and murdered by Liberian security forces to prevent him from testifying against prominent regional leaders.

The international community repeatedly urged unconditional negotiations within the framework of a mediation process led by ECOWAS, and in March 2003 LURD finally agreed, in principle, to enter into dialogue with Taylor. LURD and MODEL halted their advances on Monrovia and Buchanan at the end of May and pledged to observe a cease-fire, provided that the Government also suspended attacks. Peace discussions, attended by Taylor and LURD, commenced in Accra on 4 June, but were disrupted by the announcement of Taylor's indictment for war crimes by the Special Court, in connection with his alleged longstanding involvement with the RUF. On the following day Taylor returned to Monrovia, where he immediately announced that the authorities had suppressed an attempted coup. On the same day LURD forces launched a major attack on Monrovia from the movement's base in Tubmanburg, and rapidly reached the capital's western outskirts, causing an exodus from refugee camps towards the city centre. On 7 June a government counter-offensive forced the rebels to withdraw back over a strategic bridge, which separated the western suburbs from the city centre. LURD's political leadership issued an ultimatum demanding Taylor's resignation, and French military forces commenced the evacuation of foreign nationals in response to the increasingly critical situation. Following the arrival of a MODEL delegation, the peace discussions in Ghana resumed on 9 June. Repeated demands by LURD for Taylor's resignation as a precondition to the suspension of hostilities, and Taylor's insistence that his indictment by the Sierra Leone Special Court be withdrawn, impeded progress. On 17 June, however, a cease-fire agreement was signed by the LURD and MODEL leaders, and by the Minister of Defence, Daniel Chea, on behalf of the Liberian Government. Immediately beforehand, government troops recaptured Greenville, forcing LURD to withdraw to positions some 35 km from Monrovia. The cease-fire agreement required the deployment of a multinational stabilization force and a 30-day period of discussions to resolve outstanding issues, prior to the adoption of a comprehensive peace accord.

Shortly after the cease-fire agreement was signed in Accra, however, Taylor declared that he would remain in office at least until the end of his presidential term in January 2004, and rejected the Special Court indictment against him. Serious breaches of the cease-fire were reported, and on 26 June 2003, after the resumption of heavy fighting between government and rebel forces in and around Monrovia, in which about 300 civilians were killed, US President George W. Bush urged Taylor to resign. On the following day the rebel leadership declared a unilateral cease-fire (which was, however, rapidly abandoned). At the end of June the UN Secretary-General recommended to the Security Council that a multinational peace-keeping force be deployed in Liberia in response to the critical humanitarian situation, and urged US military intervention. On 6 July Taylor announced that he had accepted, in principle, an offer of asylum from the Nigerian Head of State, Olusegun Obasanjo, but stipulated that he would not leave the country until a peace-keeping operation was installed. Following continued appeals from Liberian civilians for foreign intervention to prevent the humanitarian disaster, a US mission of military observers was dispatched to Liberia. However, Bush indicated that he would only deploy peace-keeping troops in Liberia after Taylor had left the country and a West African mission had restored order. Later in July, after the rebel offensive to oust Taylor had reached the centre of the capital, the US embassy compound (in which some 10,000 Liberian civilians had taken refuge) was repeatedly bombarded. Some 100 US marines were flown in to defend the building, while US naval vessels were stationed off the Liberian coast. Meanwhile, following the resumption of discussions between the government, LURD and MODEL delegations in Accra, it was announced that a peace accord, based on the terms of the failed cease-fire agreement, had been drafted.

On 22 July 2003 a summit meeting of ECOWAS Heads of State was convened in the Senegalese capital, Dakar. Following pressure from the UN Secretary-General, the West African delegates agreed to dispatch an initial 1,300 Nigerian peace-keeping troops (including a battalion redeployed from neighbouring Sierra Leone) to Liberia. On 1 August the UN Security Council officially authorized the establishment of a multinational force with a maximum strength of 3,250 troops, to be known as the ECOWAS Mission in Liberia (ECOMIL), which was to restore security to allow the distribution of emergency humanitarian assistance, and prepare for the deployment of a longer-term UN stabilization force (envisaged for October). On 11 August, following continued pressure from West African Governments and the international community, Taylor relinquished power to the Vice-President, Moses Zeh Blah, before leaving Liberia for exile in the town of Calabar, in south-eastern Nigeria. Blah was inaugurated as interim Head of State, pending the installation of a government of national unity, which was the subject of continuing negotiations between the government and rebel delegations in Accra. Taylor's departure fulfilled the main demand of the rebel leadership, and was celebrated in Monrovia. Rebels ceded control of Monrovia Freeport to ECOMIL, and a further 200 US military personnel arrived in Liberia to support the peace operation. On 18 August delegates of the incumbent Government, rebel factions, political opposition and civil organizations, under the aegis of the UN, reached a comprehensive peace agreement, which provided for the establishment of a transitional power-sharing government and legislature, to comprise representatives of the participating groupings. Under the accord, Blah was to transfer power to the new administration on 14 October, all armed militia were to be disbanded, and democratic elections were to be conducted by October 2005. On 21 August 2003 the delegations elected Gyude Bryant, a prominent church figure and leader of the LAP, as Chairman of the transitional administration. Perceived as being most neutral, Bryant defeated a further two candidates for the office, Johnson-Sirleaf and Rudolph Sherman of the TWP. By the end of August a UN Joint Monitoring Committee had been dispatched to Monrovia, and ECOMIL troops (then numbering 1,500) were slowly taking control of rebel-held territory.

On 19 September 2003 the UN Security Council formally established the UN Mission in Liberia (UNMIL, see p. 83), which was mandated to support the transitional authorities and the implementation of the August peace agreement; the first contingent, of about 4,000, commenced deployment in the country (replacing ECOMIL) on 1 October. On 14 October, under the terms of the peace agreement, Bryant was officially inaugurated as Chairman of the two-year power-sharing administration, the National Transitional Government, while the leader of the UPP, Wesley Johnson, became Vice-Chairman. At the same time a 76-member unicameral legislature, the National Transitional Legislative Assembly (NTLA), comprising representatives of the groupings signatory to the August agreement and 15 deputies nominated by the counties, was installed. A prominent member of LURD, George Dweh, was subsequently elected Speaker of the new Assembly. Shortly before his inauguration, Bryant had signed an agreement for the resumption of diplomatic relations with the People's Republic of China (thereby ending links with Taiwan); the Chinese Government was expected to finance substantially reconstruction projects in the country. Later in October LURD and MODEL (which were each allocated five ministries in the National Transitional Government) submitted ministerial nominees for approval by the legislature (although MODEL remained undecided on the selection of two representatives). Of the former Taylor loyalists, Chea retained the post of Minister of Defence, while LURD representatives were awarded the portfolios of justice and finance, and the leader of MODEL, Thomas Nimely Yaya, became Minister of Foreign Affairs. (However, the political opposition and civil society groups failed to agree on representatives for the remaining six portfolios divided between them.) In early December the International Criminal Police Organization (INTERPOL) issued an arrest notice against Taylor (who remained in Nigeria) for suspected war crimes.

On 22 December 2003 the UN Security Council adopted a resolution maintaining the embargoes on imports of armaments and on exports of timber and diamonds for a minimum of one year, but envisaged that these would be ended in response to progress in the peace process and in efforts by the National Transitional Government to prevent the illicit exploitation of resources. In January 2004 it was reported that Conneh's wife, Aisha, had ousted him from the leadership of LURD, with the support of other military commanders, resulting in the division of the movement. LURD and MODEL continued to demand Bryant's resignation from the chairmanship of the interim administration as a precondition to disarmament. On 23 March, after the remaining ministerial portfolios were finally designated, Bryant finally inaugurated the National Transitional Government. In mid-April UNMIL resumed the disarmament programme.

In May 2004 the Civil Society Organizations of Liberia, a grouping of pro-democracy and human rights organizations, presented a petition to the NTLA in support of the extradition of Taylor by the Nigerian Government. (Legal representatives of Taylor continued to plead at the Special Court in Sierra Leone that, as serving President at the time of his indictment, he was immune from prosecution.) In June, in a further struggle for leadership within LURD, the national executive council announced the removal of Sekou Conneh and his replacement by Chayee Doe (a brother of the former President). Conneh refused to acknowledge the statement, and continued to reject demands by his opponents within the movement for the replacement of the LURD Minister of Finance, Lusine Kamara. In September the International Criminal Court (ICC, see p. 314) announced that Liberia had ratified the signatory treaty, thereby allowing the Court jurisdiction to prosecute crimes committed during the civil conflict. On 17 September the UN Security Council adopted a resolution extending the mandate of UNMIL for a further year (while welcoming the progress made in the peace process).

The disarmament process, under which a total of some 96,000 former combatants had relinquished armaments, officially ended on 31 October 2004, with a ceremony at which the three former armed factions were also officially dissolved (although operations continued after that date). In December the UN Security Council conducted a review of the sanctions in force on Liberia and concluded that, following the report of an assessment mission to the country, the National Transitional Government had not met the requisite conditions. The sanctions on armaments, timber and travel were consequently renewed for a further year, while, in view of preparations by the authorities to introduce a certification system, the embargo on the export of diamonds was extended for six months (and again extended in mid-2005).

Electoral reform legislation, which had been submitted to the NTLA at the end of August 2004, became an issue of contention, following attempts by the NTLA to add an amendment requiring a prior population census to be conducted, which would effectively prevent the elections from taking place in October 2005 (as specified in the comprehensive peace agreement). Ensuing disputes over the legislation between the NTLA and the Government were resolved only by sustained pressure from Bryant and the US Ambassador, thereby delaying the adoption of the legislation until December 2004. Nevertheless, in February 2005 the National Elections Commission (NEC) announced that the presidential and legislative elections would be conducted on 11 October. Some 40 prospective presidential candidates had emerged, notably including George Manneh Weah, a Liberian national who had gained international renown as an association footballer. In mid-March NTLA Speaker Dweh, together with the Deputy Speaker and two parliamentary deputies, were suspended from office on suspicion of corruption, following a report by a parliamentary committee that they had spent government funds without authorization. Dweh denied the charges against him, insisting that his suspension was not legitimate, and the UNMIL presence in Monrovia was reinforced, amid concerns of renewed unrest.

At the first round of presidential voting on 11 October 2005, which was contested by a total of 22 candidates, Weah secured 28.3% of votes cast, while Johnson-Sirleaf won 19.8% of votes and Charles Brumskine of the Liberty Party (LP) 13.9% of votes. At the elections to the 64-member lower House of Representatives Weah's party, the Congress of Democratic Change (CDC), won 15 seats, the LP nine seats, an alliance known as the Coalition for the Transformation of Liberia (COTOL) eight seats and the UP eight seats. At the elections to the 30-member Senate the COTOL secured seven seats, while the CDC, the UP and the LP each received three seats. Some 74.9% of the registered electorate voted in the presidential ballot and 76.5% in the legislative elections. Since no presidential candidate had secured an absolute majority, a second round was conducted on 8 November: Johnson-Sirleaf defeated Weah by securing 59.4% of votes cast (with 61.0% of the electorate participating). Weah immediately protested that electoral malpractice had been perpetrated and accused the NEC of bias towards Johnson-Sirleaf; a demonstration in his support was staged in Monrovia. On 23 November the NEC officially declared that Johnson-Sirleaf had won the presidential election. Nevertheless, Weah continued to claim that the election results were fraudulent, and threatened to prevent Johnson-Sirleaf's inauguration. Violent demonstrations by his supporters in Monrovia resulted in clashes with security forces and the arrest of some 40 protesters. In mid-December, following international pressure, however, Weah agreed to suspend his legal challenge to Johnson-Sirleaf's election at the Supreme Court, and subsequently announced that he would abandon his claim to the presidency in the interests of national reconciliation. Later that month the UN Security Council again extended the sanctions on armaments and travel for a further year and those on diamonds and timber for six months, and urged the establishment of a panel of experts to assess the authorities' compliance with requirements.

Johnson-Sirleaf was inaugurated as President on 16 January 2006, thereby becoming the first woman to be elected Head of State in Africa. The two legislative chambers were officially installed on the same day. The election of a close former associate of Taylor, Edwin Snowe, as Speaker of the House of Representatives attracted controversy. Johnson-Sirleaf subsequently began to nominate ministers, who, in accordance with the Constitution, were to be approved by the Senate. Opposition leaders criticized a number of presidential appointments, including that of a US officer as Johnson-Sirleaf's military adviser. In February Johnson-Sirleaf established a seven-member Truth and Reconciliation Commission, which was to investigate human rights abuses perpetrated during the civil conflict. Johnson-Sirleaf (despite having previously indicated that national reconstruction was the greatest priority for the new Government) pledged commitment to bringing Taylor to trial. In the same month the Nigerian Government announced that it had received an official request from Liberia for Taylor's extradition. (In early November 2005 the UN Security Council had extended the mandate of UNMIL to authorize Taylor's arrest and dispatch to the Special Court in Sierra Leone, in the event that he return to Liberia.) In response to Johnson-Sirleaf's request, President Obasanjo declared that he would engage in consultations with other regional leaders. Later in March 2006 Taylor fled from his residence in Calabar, but was apprehended two days later in Borno State, near the border with Cameroon, and dispatched to Liberia, from where he was immediately extradited by UNMIL peace-keepers to the Special Court. In early April Taylor pleaded 'not guilty' to all charges at the Special Court. Tribunal officials subsequently requested that his trial be transferred to the ICC at The Hague, Netherlands, (while remaining under the jurisdiction of the Special Court), in the interests of regional stability. The Dutch authorities acceded to that request on the condition that any sentence handed down to Taylor was served in another country. The United Kingdom subsequently agreed to host Taylor should he be imprisoned and, following the unanimous approval of the UN Security Council, on 20 June Taylor was transferred to The Hague where his trial commenced on 4 June 2007. Proceedings were subsequently postponed until January 2008 to allow his legal representatives additional time to prepare his case.

Meanwhile, in May 2006 ethnic tensions re-emerged as Liberians returned to Nimba County from refugee camps across West Africa to find their homes occupied by the local Gio and Mano tribes who had driven them out of the region during the 1990s (see above). UN peace-keeping forces were mobilized when rumours of an imminent attack by Liberian refugees from Guinea brought people of the Gio and Mano tribes into the streets armed with machetes. Negotiations mediated by local government officials failed to secure the return of land and property, and they called for the central Government to intervene before the situation degenerated into violent conflict.

In November 2006 the Minister of Information, Culture and Tourism, Johnny McClain, resigned from office citing insufficient funding and a lack of support from the Government. He was replaced by Rev. Dr Lawrence Bropleh. In February 2007 Willis D. F. Knuckles, the Minister of State for Presidential Affairs, resigned after allegations were published in the press of inappropriate behaviour and the sexual exploitation of young women. Johnson-Sirleaf announced in March that Dr Edward McClain would assume Knuckles' vacated portfolio on a temporary basis, pending the appointment of a new minister. In August Johnson-Sirleaf implemented a major reorganization of the Government in which Bankie King Akerele replaced George W. Wallace as Minister of Foreign Affairs. Philip Banks became Minister of Justice, replacing Frances Johnson-Morris, who assumed the commerce and industry portfolio.

In July 2007 former armed forces leader Julu was arrested, along with a number of other senior military officials, and charged with an attempted coup; they remained in custody pending trial. In December, during the trial, Julu insisted that he had no involvement in a plot to depose Johnson-Sirleaf. Meanwhile, Former President Bryant, who had been arrested and charged with embezzlement in February, was ordered to organize a new defence team, having earlier dismissed two of his lawyers. Bryant continued to plead his innocence. In January 2008 Taylor's trial resumed in The Hague as scheduled.

Government

Under the Constitution of January 1986, legislative power is vested in the bicameral National Assembly, comprising the 64-member House of Representatives and the 30-member Senate. Members of the House of Representatives are elected by legislative constituency for a term of six years, while each county elects two members of the Senate (one for a term of nine years and one for six years). Executive power is vested in the President, who is elected to office for a six-year term (renewable only once), and who appoints the Government (subject to the approval of the Senate). Following a peace agreement in August 2003, a democratically elected administration was installed in January 2006 (replacing the power-sharing National Transitional Government). The country comprises 15 counties, which are divided into 64 districts.

Defence

Following a major rebel offensive against the capital in June 2003, the UN Security Council on 1 August authorized the establishment of an Economic Community of West African States (ECOWAS) peace-keeping contingent, the ECOWAS Mission in Liberia (ECOMIL), which was to restore security and prepare for the deployment of a longer-term UN stabilization force. The UN Mission in Liberia (UNMIL, see p. 83), which was officially established on 19 September and replaced ECOMIL on 1 October, was mandated to support the implementation of a comprehensive peace agreement, and a two-year transitional administration. With a total authorized strength of up to 15,000, at the end of November 2007 UNMIL numbered 13,335 troops, 199 military observers and 1,183 civilian police, supported by 502 international civilian personnel, 945 local staff and 245 UN volunteers. Following the completion of the disarmament programme, in January 2005 a US military commission arrived in Liberia to assist in the restructuring of the armed forces, which was ongoing in 2008. In June 2006 the armed forces began recruiting women as part of the reform process. A 3,500-member police force trained by UNMIL was also to be established. As assessed at November 2007, the total strength of the Liberian armed forces was 2,400. In 2007 defence expenditure was estimated at US $58m. (equivalent to 6.0% of GDP).

Economic Affairs

In 2006, according to the World Bank, Liberia's gross domestic product (GDP) was US $469m., equivalent to $140 per head. During 1996–2006, it was estimated, the population increased at an average annual rate of 4.0%, while GDP per head rose by 9.2%. Overall GDP increased, in real terms, at an average annual rate of 13.4% in 1996–2006; real GDP increased by 7.8% in 2006.

Agriculture and forestry, measured at constant 1992 prices, contributed an estimated 61.5% of GDP in 2006. An estimated 9.2% of the formal labour force were employed in the sector in that year, although FAO estimated that in mid-2005 65.0% of the total labour force were employed in the sector. The principal cash crops are rubber (which accounted for an estimated 95.3% of export earnings in 2006) and iron ore. The principal food crops are cassava, bananas, rice, plantains, yams and sweet potatoes. Timber production has traditionally represented an important source of export revenue, providing an estimated 50.1% of export earnings in 2003 (when, however, sanctions on timber exports were imposed). According to African Development Bank (ADB) figures, agricultural GDP declined at an average annual rate of 5.5% in 2000–06; however, the GDP of the agricultural sector increased by 3.3% in 2005, and by 7.0% in 2006.

Industry (including mining, manufacturing, construction and power), measured at constant 1992 prices, contributed an estimated 16.3% of GDP in 2006, and employed an estimated 1.9% of the formal labour force in the same year. Industrial GDP, according to ADB figures, increased at an average annual rate of 4.7% in 2000–06; the GDP of the industrial sector increased by 7.8% in 2006.

The mining sector, measured at constant 1992 prices, contributed an estimated 0.2% of GDP in 2006, and engaged 0.8% of the formal labour force in the same year. Gold and diamonds are mined, and Liberia possesses significant amounts of barytes and kyanite. The production and export of mineral products were severely disrupted from 1990, as a result of the civil conflict. In 1997 total mineral reserves were estimated to include more than 10m. carats of diamonds and 3m. troy oz of gold. In January 2005 the Government prohibited diamond mining in order to support the enforcement of UN sanctions on the export of diamonds (imposed in 2001—see below). The GDP of the mining sector, according to the IMF, declined at an average annual rate of 40.1% in 1988–2002; mining GDP increased by 49.8% in 2000, but declined by 74.9% in 2001 and by an estimated 69.9% in 2002.

Manufacturing, measured at constant 1992 prices, provided an estimated 12.8% of GDP in 2006, and engaged an estimated

0.8% of the formal labour force in the same year. Manufacturing GDP, according to ADB figures, increased at an average annual rate of 4.6% in 2000–06; the GDP of the manufacturing sector increased by 7.8% in 2006.

Energy is derived from the consumption of fossil fuels (62.2%) and from hydroelectric power (37.8%). In 2003 the authorities announced plans to restore power throughout the country by a programme to rehabilitate a major hydroelectric power installation, which had been damaged in the civil conflict. Liberia is dependent on imports of petroleum, which comprised an estimated 27.5% of the value of total imports in 2006.

The services sector, measured at constant 1992 prices, contributed an estimated 22.2% of GDP in 2006, and employed 88.9% of the formal labour force in that year. The GDP of the services sector, according to ADB figures, increased at an average annual rate of 2.3% in 2000–06; the GDP of the sector increased by 10.1% in 2006.

Liberia's large open-registry ('flag of convenience') merchant shipping fleet has become an increasingly significant source of foreign exchange. In 2006 revenue from Liberia's maritime programme accounted for an estimated 8.0% of total revenue.

In 2007 Liberia recorded an estimated visible trade deficit of US $260m., and there was a deficit of $255m. on the current account of the balance of payments. In 2004 the principal source of imports (37.8%) was the Republic of Korea. The principal market for exports in 2006 was the USA (73.7%); the other major purchaser was Belgium. The principal export in 2006 was rubber. The principal imports in that year were petroleum, food (particularly rice) and live animals, machinery and transport equipment, basic manufactures and chemicals and related products.

Liberia's overall budgetary surplus was US $25.3m. in 2006/07, according to IMF figures. The country's external debt totalled $2,581m. at the end of 2005, of which $1,115m. was long-term public debt. The annual rate of inflation averaged 10.9% in 2000–2006; consumer prices increased by 8.0% in 2006. In 2006 unemployment was estimated at about 85.0% of the labour force.

Liberia is a member of the Economic Community of West African States (ECOWAS, see p. 232) and the Mano River Union (see p. 413), both of which aim to promote closer economic co-operation in the region.

The 1989–96 civil conflict severely disrupted Liberia's economy, and from 2000 a progressive deterioration in the country's relations with donors and external creditors resulted in a suspension in the disbursement of post-conflict financial assistance. In May 2001 a UN embargo on exports of diamonds from Liberia was imposed (see Recent History), and in 2003 an additional ban on the export of timber entered into effect. Following the removal from power of President Charles Taylor a comprehensive agreement between the Government and rebels was signed, providing for the creation of a power-sharing administration, the National Transitional Government, which was installed in October (see Recent History). In early February 2004 a UN-sponsored conference of international donors pledged some US $520m. (exceeding expectations) to support reconstruction and humanitarian efforts, and projects for infrastructural rehabilitation and employment generation. The transitional period ended when presidential and legislative elections were conducted successfully in October and November 2005; Ellen Johnson-Sirleaf, a former World Bank economist, was inaugurated as President in January 2006. She immediately appealed for international support for reconstruction, and announced measures to end endemic corruption, including the organization of a comprehensive financial audit of government institutions, and the introduction of restrictions on the conduct of public officials. UN sanctions on the export of timber were lifted in September and those on diamond exports in April 2007; the following month Liberia became a participant in the Kimberley Process. A Canadian renewable energy company, meanwhile, was looking to rebuild the Liberian rubber sector by providing investment of $15m. and equipment worth some $10m. for biomass fuel production. In late 2007 the country became eligible for two debt reduction programmes, the first of which provided funding from the UN for post-conflict countries to rebuild vital infrastructure; the second provided $1,463m. in debt relief from the World Bank, the IMF and the ADB under the initiative for heavily indebted poor countries, which it was hoped would accelerate national development. By early 2008 the ADB had cancelled $225m. of Liberia's debt. In February 2007 the Government announced an agenda for national development, which placed emphasis on providing the necessary conditions for job creation. The consolidation of national peace and the reconstruction of basic infrastructure and public services were also identified as vital to sustained economic recovery. The 2007/08 budget allocated an additional 44% to education funding and a 28% increase in expenditure on health services. The IMF estimated GDP growth of 9.4% in 2007 and forecasted growth of 10.4% for 2008.

Education

Education is provided by a mixture of government, private, church and mosque schools. The civil conflicts of 1989–96 and 1999–2003 devastated the education system as buildings and equipment were damaged and looted, and teachers, parents and children became refugees or internally displaced. By September 2005 3,817 of the country's 4,500 schools were reported to be functioning again. Education in Liberia is officially compulsory for 10 years, between six and 16 years of age. Primary education begins theoretically at six years of age and lasts for six years (grades 1–6). Secondary education, beginning theoretically at 12 years of age, lasts for a further six years, and is divided into two three-year cycles, known in Liberia as 'junior high school' (grades 7–9) and 'senior high school' (grades 10–12). Pre-primary education is undertaken from the age of five or younger and is important for those students whose mother language is not English, since English is the language of instruction throughout the school system. School attendance is not enforced and in 2000 an estimated 34% of primary school age children did not attend school (26% of boys and 42% of girls). Although the 1984 Liberian Constitution includes the aspiration to provide universal free education, school attendance is discouraged by the poor quality of education offered and by official and unofficial school fees, charges and the cost of uniforms and travel. In 2004 UNESCO estimated the adult literacy rate at 52% (58% male and 46% female). The higher education sector consists of the University of Liberia in Monrovia, Cuttington University College in Bong County, the Booker Washington Institute in Kakata, Margibi County, and the William V. S. Tubman College in Maryland County. According to UNESCO, a total of 44,107 students were enrolled in tertiary education in 2000.

Public Holidays

2008: 1 January (New Year's Day), 11 February (Armed Forces Day), 12 March (Decoration Day), 15 March (J. J. Robert's Birthday), 21 March (Good Friday), 11 April (Fast and Prayer Day), 14 May (National Unification Day), 25 May (Africa Day), 26 July (Independence Day), 24 August (Flag Day), 1 November (All Saints' Day), 12 November (National Memorial Day), 29 November (President Tubman's Birthday), 25 December (Christmas Day).

2009: 1 January (New Year's Day), 11 February (Armed Forces Day), 11 March (Decoration Day), 15 March (J. J. Robert's Birthday), 10 April (Good Friday), 14 April (Fast and Prayer Day), 14 May (National Unification Day), 25 May (Africa Day), 26 July (Independence Day), 24 August (Flag Day), 1 November (All Saints' Day), 12 November (National Memorial Day), 29 November (President Tubman's Birthday), 25 December (Christmas Day).

Weights and Measures

Imperial weights and measures, modified by US usage, are in force.

Statistical Survey

Sources (unless otherwise stated): the former Ministry of Planning and Economic Affairs, POB 9016, Broad St, Monrovia; the Central Bank of Liberia, POB 2048, Corner of Warren and Carey St, Monrovia; tel. 22-669-91; fax 22-61-14; internet www.cbl.org.lr/index.php.

Area and Population

AREA, POPULATION AND DENSITY

Area (sq km)	97,754*
Population (census results)	
1 February 1974	1,503,368
1 February 1984 (provisional)	
Males	1,063,127
Females	1,038,501
Total	2,101,628
Population (UN estimates at mid-year)†	
2005	3,442,000
2006	3,579,000
2007	3,750,000
Density (per sq km) at mid-2007	38.4

* 37,743 sq miles.
† Source: UN, *World Population Prospects: The 2006 Revision*.

ADMINISTRATIVE DIVISIONS
(population at 1984 census)

Counties:				
Bomi	66,420		Nimba	313,050
Bong	255,813		Rivercess	37,849
Grand Bassa	159,648		Sinoe	64,147
Grand Cape Mount	79,322		*Territories:*	
Grand Gedeh	102,810		Gibi	66,802
Lofa	247,641		Kru Coast	35,267
Maryland	85,267		Marshall	31,190
Montserrado	544,878		Sasstown	11,524
			Total	**2,101,628**

Note: The counties of Grand Kru and Margibi were subsequently established. Two further counties, River Gee and Gbarpolu, were created in 1998 and 2001, respectively.

PRINCIPAL TOWNS
(2003)

Monrovia (capital)	550,200		Harbel	17,700
Zwedru	35,300		Tubmanburg	16,700
Buchanan	27,300		Gbarnga	14,200
Yekepa	22,900		Greenville	13,500
Harper	20,000		Ganta	11,200
Bensonville	19,600			

Source: Stefan Helders, *World Gazetteer* (internet www.world-gazetteer.com).

BIRTHS AND DEATHS
(annual averages, UN estimates)

	1990–95	1995–2000	2000–05
Birth rate (per 1,000)	50.0	49.7	49.9
Death rate (per 1,000)	23.0	21.2	19.8

Source: UN, *World Population Prospects: The 2006 Revision*.

Expectation of life (years at birth, WHO estimates): 42.8 (males 41.5; females 44.2) in 2005 (Source: WHO, *World Health Statistics*).

ECONOMICALLY ACTIVE POPULATION
(formal sector)

	2004	2005	2006*
Agriculture and forestry	11,100	11,200	12,200
Mining	850	918	1,009
Manufacturing	882	950	1,045
Construction	450	486	535
Wholesale and retail trade	42,500	42,700	43,500
Transport	1,300	1,400	1,540
Business services	2,250	2,430	2,475
Social and community services	10,500	11,340	12,470
Government	60,000	64,000	58,500
Total	**129,832**	**135,424**	**133,274**

* Estimates.

Total employed in informal sector: 420,000 in 2004; 430,000 in 2005; 470,000 in 2006 (estimate).

Mid-2005 (estimates in '000): Agriculture, etc. 796; Total labour force 1,225 (Source: FAO).

Health and Welfare

KEY INDICATORS

Total fertility rate (children per woman, 2005)	6.8
Under-5 mortality rate (per 1,000 live births, 2005)	235
HIV/AIDS (% of persons aged 15–49, 2003)	5.9
Physicians (per 1,000 head, 2004)	0.03
Health expenditure (2004): US $ per head (PPP)	22.2
Health expenditure (2004): % of GDP	5.6
Health expenditure (2004): public (% of total)	63.9
Access to water (% of persons, 2004)	61
Access to sanitation (% of persons, 2004)	27

For sources and definitions, see explanatory note on p. vi.

Agriculture

PRINCIPAL CROPS
('000 metric tons)

	2004	2005	2006
Rice (paddy)	110*	96*	66†
Sweet potatoes†	19	19	20
Cassava (Manioc)†	480	483	635
Taro (Coco yam)†	26	26	26
Yams†	21	22	20
Sugar cane†	255	255	255
Oil palm fruit†	174	183	183
Bananas†	116	120	116
Plantains†	44	47	42
Natural rubber (dry weight)*	115	112	115

* Unofficial figure(s).
† FAO estimate(s).

Aggregate production ('000 metric tons, may include official, semi-official or estimated data): Total cereals 110 in 2004, 96 in 2005, 66 in 2006; Total roots and tubers 545 in 2004, 550 in 2005, 700 in 2006; Total vegetables (incl. melons) 76 in 2004, 76 in 2005, 84 in 2006; Total fruits (excl. melons) 177 in 2004, 183 in 2005, 176 in 2006.

Source: FAO.

LIBERIA

LIVESTOCK
('000 head, year ending September, FAO estimates)

	2003	2004	2005
Cattle	36	36	36
Pigs	130	130	130
Sheep	210	210	210
Goats	220	220	220
Chickens	4,800	5,000	5,300
Ducks	200	200	200

2006: Figures assumed to be unchanged from 2005 (FAO estimates).
Source: FAO.

LIVESTOCK PRODUCTS
(metric tons, FAO estimates)

	2004	2005	2006
Pig meat	4,404	4,417	5,100
Chicken meat	8,000	8,480	8,960
Game meat	6,500	6,500	6,500
Cows' milk	715	715	735
Hen eggs	4,320	4,320	4,500

Source: FAO.

Forestry

ROUNDWOOD REMOVALS
('000 cubic metres, excluding bark)

	2004	2005	2006
Sawlogs, veneer logs and logs for sleepers	100	100	120
Other industrial wood*	180	180	180
Fuel wood*	5,576	5,811	6,033
Total	5,856	6,091	6,333

*FAO estimates.
Source: FAO.

SAWNWOOD PRODUCTION
('000 cubic metres, including railway sleepers)

	2004	2005	2006
Total (all broadleaved)	50	50	60

Source: FAO.

Fishing

(metric tons, live weight, capture)

	2003*	2004	2005*
Freshwater fishes	4,000	4,000	4,000
Dentex	250	4	4
Sardinellas	1,000	643	620
Sharks, rays, skates, etc.	440	60	40
Total catch (incl. others)	10,700	10,359	10,000

*FAO estimates.
Source: FAO.

Mining

	2003	2004	2005
Diamonds ('000 carats)*	25	40	40
Gold (kilograms)*	40	10	10

*Estimates.

Note: In addition to the commodities listed, Liberia produced significant quantities of a variety of industrial minerals and construction materials (clays, gypsum, sand and gravel, and stone), but insufficient information is available to make reliable estimates of output levels.

Source: US Geological Survey.

Industry

SELECTED PRODUCTS
(litres, unless otherwise indicated)

	2004	2005	2006*
Beverages	15,463,113	15,393,455	17,413,502
Cement (metric tons)	121,059	143,847	132,226
Paint (gallons)	31,540	168,750	72,174
Nails (kilograms)	78,450	50,938	n.a.
Candles (kilograms)	557,814	390,653	539,911
Bleach	380,202	362,505	654,075
Rubbing alcohol	201,137	277,323	268,184
Mattresses (number)	48,178	68,834	100,402
Water			
Deep well (gallons)	60,415,605	63,918,844	54,720,361
Treatment plant (gallons)	432,521,479	462,168,224	643,436,265

*Estimates.

Electrical energy (million kWh): 320 in 2002; 320 in 2003; 330 in 2004 (Source: UN, *Industrial Commodity Statistics Yearbook*).

Finance

CURRENCY AND EXCHANGE RATES

Monetary Units
100 cents = 1 Liberian dollar (L $).

Sterling, Dollar and Euro Equivalents (31 May 2007)
£1 sterling = L $123.581;
US $1 = L $62.500;
€1 = L $84.081;
L $1,000 = £8.09 = US $16.00 = €11.89.

Average Exchange Rate (L $ per US $)
2004   54.9058
2005   57.0958
2006   57.0133

Note: The aforementioned data are based on market-determined rates of exchange. Prior to January 1998 the exchange rate was a fixed parity with the US dollar (L $1 = US $1).

BUDGET
(US $ million)

Revenue*	2005/06	2006/07	2007/08†
Tax revenue	81.0	140.0	149.5
Taxes on income and profits	25.1	42.5	48.6
Taxes on goods and services	20.3	26.1	26.9
Maritime revenue	12.1	11.8	13.0
Taxes on international trade and transactions	35.3	69.9	70.1
Other taxes	0.3	1.4	3.8
Non-tax revenue	3.6	6.9	36.2
Stumpage fees and land rental	0.0	0.1	2.2
Total	84.6	146.8	185.7

LIBERIA

Expenditure‡	2005/06	2006/07	2007/08†
Current expenditure	67.2	106.4	167.6
Wages and salaries	32.5	40.6	67.5
Other goods and services	22.0	46.1	59.8
Subsidies, transfers and net lending	11.2	19.1	32.7
Interest on debt	1.4	0.5	7.6
Capital expenditure	6.3	16.6	21.1
Total	73.5	123.0	188.7

* Excluding grants received (US $ million): 1.0 in 2005/06; 1.5 in 2006/07; 0.0 in 2007/08 (budget projection).
† Budget projection.
‡ Includes net lending.

Source: IMF, *Liberia: Fourth Review of Performance Under the Staff-Monitored Program and Request for Three-Year Arrangement Under the Poverty Reduction and Growth Facility and the Extended Fund Facility—Staff Report; Press Release on the Executive Board Discussion* (March 2008).

INTERNATIONAL RESERVES
(US $ million at 31 December)

	2004	2005	2006
Reserve position in IMF	0.05	0.04	0.05
Foreign exchange	18.69	25.35	71.94
Total	18.74	25.40	71.99

Source: IMF, *International Financial Statistics*.

MONEY SUPPLY
(L $ million at 31 December)

	2004	2005	2006
Currency outside banks*	1,754.9	2,168.9	2,647.6
Demand deposits at commercial banks	1,971.9	2,701.9	3,973.2
Total money (incl. others)	3,727.5	4,871.6	6,663.5

* Figures refer only to amounts of Liberian coin in circulation. US notes and coin also circulate, but the amount of these in private holdings is unknown. The amount of Liberian coin in circulation is small in comparison to US currency.

Source: IMF, *International Financial Statistics*.

COST OF LIVING
(Consumer Price Index; base: May 1998 = 100)

	2003	2004	2005
Food	140.9	153.8	167.0
Fuel and light	154.4	217.6	342.1
Clothing	121.2	128.7	137.3
Rent	131.8	156.1	180.9
All items (incl. others)	157.0	169.3	187.6

Source: IMF, *Liberia: Selected Issues and Statistical Appendix* (May 2006).

All items (Consumer Price Index; base 2000 = 100): 160.8 in 2004; 171.9 in 2005; 185.7 in 2006 (Source: African Development Bank).

NATIONAL ACCOUNTS
Expenditure on the Gross Domestic Product
(US $ million at current prices)

	2004	2005	2006
Government final consumption expenditure	48	59	65
Private final consumption expenditure	452	476	625
Gross fixed capital formation	61	87	85
Total domestic expenditure	561	622	775
Exports of goods and services	171	201	233
Less Imports of goods and services	235	275	320
GDP in purchasers' values	497	548	687
GDP at constant 1990 prices	361	380	407

Source: UN Statistics Division, National Accounts Main Aggregates Database.

Statistical Survey

Gross Domestic Product by Economic Activity
(US $ million, at constant 1992 prices)

	2004	2005	2006*
Agriculture	176.0	184.8	192.3
Forestry	69.2	71.3	74.1
Mining and quarrying	0.8	0.7	0.7
Manufacturing	47.8	51.7	55.5
Electricity and water	2.6	2.8	3.0
Construction	7.6	8.0	11.3
Trade, restaurants and hotels	18.3	20.1	29.2
Transport and communications	27.0	28.6	30.9
Financial institutions	9.8	10.3	10.8
Government services	9.3	9.9	10.4
Other services	13.1	13.6	14.9
GDP in purchasers' values	381.5	401.8	433.2

* Estimates.

BALANCE OF PAYMENTS
(US $ million)

	2006*	2007*	2008†
Exports of goods f.o.b.	158	227	333
Imports of goods c.i.f.	–401	–487	–844
Trade balance	–243	–260	–511
Services (net)	–91	–111	–152
Balance on goods and services	–334	–371	–663
Income (net)	–168	–175	–165
Balance on goods, services and income	–502	–546	–828
Current transfers (net)	274	291	298
Current balance	–228	–255	–529
Capital and financial account (incl. net errors and omissions)	96	117	442
Overall balance	–133	–138	–87

* Estimates.
† Projections.

Source: IMF, *Liberia: Fourth Review of Performance Under the Staff-Monitored Program and Request for Three-Year Arrangement Under the Poverty Reduction and Growth Facility and the Extended Fund Facility—Staff Report; Press Release on the Executive Board Discussion* (March 2008).

External Trade

PRINCIPAL COMMODITIES
(US $ million, estimates)

Imports c.i.f.	2004	2005	2006*
Food and live animals	77.4	68.2	121.4
Rice	n.a.	17.2	70.4
Beverages and tobacco	11.5	8.4	19.4
Mineral fuels and lubricants	5.4	28.9	15.8
Petroleum	84.5	91.1	121.9
Chemicals and related products	8.9	9.2	22.2
Basic manufactures	31.7	27.3	43.8
Machinery and transport equipment	63.3	32.6	65.7
Miscellaneous manufactured articles	47.8	30.3	9.1
Total (incl. others)	336.8	309.9	443.8

Exports f.o.b.	2004	2005	2006*
Rubber	93.4	126.7	172.3
Cocoa beans and coffee	3.4	0.3	0.2
Iron ore	—	—	1.0
Total (incl. others)	103.8	131.3	180.8

* Estimates.

LIBERIA

PRINCIPAL TRADING PARTNERS
(US $ million)

Imports c.i.f.	1986	1987	1988
Belgium-Luxembourg	8.5	11.2	15.0
China, People's Repub.	7.1	14.7	4.8
Denmark	10.6	7.6	5.9
France (incl. Monaco)	6.5	6.4	4.7
Germany, Fed. Repub.	32.7	52.3	39.5
Italy	2.5	2.2	7.3
Japan	20.1	15.0	12.0
Netherlands	20.6	26.8	14.4
Spain	2.5	6.6	3.1
Sweden	2.4	0.6	4.6
United Kingdom	24.2	18.4	12.7
USA	42.5	58.0	57.7
Total (incl. others)	259.0	307.6	272.3

Source: UN, *International Trade Statistics Yearbook*.

Exports f.o.b.	2004	2005	2006*
Belgium	30.6	28.5	39.2
China, People's Repub.	5.5	1.2	n.a.
France	1.7	n.a.	n.a.
USA	63.7	96.8	133.3
Total (incl. others)	103.8	131.8	180.8

*Estimates.

Transport

RAILWAYS
(estimated traffic)

	1991	1992	1993
Passenger-km (million)	406	417	421
Freight ton-km (million)	200	200	200

Source: UN Economic Commission for Africa, *African Statistical Yearbook*.

ROAD TRAFFIC
(estimates, '000 vehicles in use at 31 December)

	1999	2000	2001
Passenger cars	15.3	17.1	17.1
Commercial vehicles	11.9	12.8	12.8

2002: Figures assumed to be unchanged from 2001.

Source: UN, *Statistical Yearbook*.

SHIPPING
Merchant Fleet
(registered at 31 December)

	2004	2005	2006
Number of vessels	1,538	1,653	1,907
Displacement ('000 gross registered tons)	53,898.8	59,600.2	68,405.1

Source: Lloyd's Register-Fairplay, *World Fleet Statistics*.

International Sea-borne Freight Traffic
(estimates, '000 metric tons)

	1991	1992	1993
Goods loaded	16,706	17,338	21,653
Goods unloaded	1,570	1,597	1,608

Source: UN Economic Commission for Africa, *African Statistical Yearbook*.

CIVIL AVIATION
(traffic on scheduled services)

	1990	1991	1992
Passengers carried ('000)	32	32	32
Passenger-km (million)	7	7	7
Total ton-km (million)	1	1	1

Source: UN, *Statistical Yearbook*.

Communications Media

	1995	1996	1997
Radio receivers ('000 in use)	675	715	790
Television receivers ('000 in use)	56	60	70
Telephones ('000 main lines in use)	5	5	6
Daily newspapers:			
number	8	6	6
average circulation ('000 copies, estimates)	35	35	36

Sources: UNESCO Institute for Statistics; UN, *Statistical Yearbook*.

Telephones ('000 main lines in use): 6.7 in 2000; 6.8 in 2001; 6.9 in 2002 (Source: International Telecommunication Union).

Mobile cellular telephones ('000 subscribers): 47.2 in 2003; 94.4 in 2004; 160.0 in 2005 (Source: International Telecommunication Union).

Internet users ('000): 0.3 in 1999; 0.5 in 2000; 1.0 in 2001 (Source: UN, *Statistical Yearbook*).

Daily newspapers: 6 in 1998 (estimated average circulation 36,600); 3 in 2004 (Source: UNESCO Institute for Statistics).

Education
(1999/2000)

	Teachers	Males	Females	Total
Pre-primary	4,322	82,215	72,908	155,123
Primary	12,966	288,227	208,026	496,253
Secondary:				
general	4,529	52,072	38,370	90,442
technical and vocational	603	26,988	18,079	45,067
Post-secondary technical and vocational	430	8,842	6,789	15,631
University	723	25,236	18,871	44,107

Source: UNESCO Institute for Statistics.

Adult literacy rate (UNESCO estimates): 51.9% (males 58.3%; females 45.7%) in 2004 (Source: UNESCO Institute for Statistics).

Directory

The Constitution

The Constitution of the Republic of Liberia entered into effect on 6 January 1986, following its approval by national referendum in July 1984. Its main provisions are summarized below:

PREAMBLE

The Republic of Liberia is a unitary sovereign state, which is divided into counties for administrative purposes. There are three separate branches of government: the legislative, the executive and the judiciary. No person is permitted to hold office or executive power in more than one branch of government. The fundamental human rights of the individual are guaranteed.

LEGISLATURE

Legislative power is vested in the bicameral National Assembly, comprising a Senate and a House of Representatives. Deputies of both chambers are elected by universal adult suffrage. Each county elects two members of the Senate (one for a term of nine years and one for six years), while members of the House of Representatives are elected by legislative constituency for a term of six years. Legislation requires the approval of two-thirds of the members of both chambers, and is subsequently submitted to the President for endorsement. The Constitution may be amended by two-thirds of the members of both chambers.

EXECUTIVE

Executive power is vested in the President, who is Head of State and Commander-in-Chief of the armed forces. The President is elected by universal adult suffrage for a term of six years, and is restricted to a maximum of two terms in office. A Vice-President is elected at the same time as the President. The President appoints a Cabinet, and members of the judiciary and armed forces, with the approval of the Senate. The President is empowered to declare a state of emergency.

JUDICIARY

Judicial power is vested in the Supreme Court and any subordinate courts, which apply both statutory and customary laws in accordance with standards enacted by the legislature. The judgments of the Supreme Court are final and not subject to appeal or review by any other branch of government. The Supreme Court comprises one Chief Justice and five Associate Justices. Justices are appointed by the President, with the approval of the Senate.

POLITICAL PARTIES AND ELECTIONS

Political associations are obliged to comply with the minimum registration requirements imposed by the Elections Commission. Organizations that endanger free democratic society, or that organize, train or equip groups of supporters, are to be denied registration. Prior to elections, each political party and independent candidate is required to submit statements of assets and liabilities to the Elections Commission. All elections of public officials are determined by an absolute majority of the votes cast. If no candidate obtains an absolute majority in the first ballot, a second ballot is conducted between the two candidates with the highest number of votes. Complaints by parties or candidates must be submitted to the Elections Commission within seven days of the announcement of election results. The Supreme Court has final jurisdiction over challenges to election results.

The Government

HEAD OF STATE

President: ELLEN JOHNSON-SIRLEAF (inaugurated 16 January 2006).

THE CABINET
(February 2008)

Vice-President: JOSEPH NYUMAH BOAKAI.
Minister of Agriculture: J. CHRISTOPHER TOE.
Minister of Commerce and Industry: FRANCES JOHNSON-MORRIS.
Minister of Defence: BROWNIE SAMUKAI.
Minister of Education: JOSEPH KORTO.
Minister of Finance: ANTOINETTE SAYEH.
Minister of Foreign Affairs: BANKIE KING AKERELE.
Minister of Gender and Development: VARBAH GAYFLOR.
Minister of Health and Social Welfare: WALTER GWENIGALE.
Minister of Information, Culture and Tourism: Rev. Dr LAWRENCE K. BROPLEH.
Minister of Internal Affairs: AMBULLAI JOHNSON.
Minister of Justice: PHILLIP BANKS.
Minister of Labour: SAMUEL KOFI WOODS.
Minister of Lands, Mines and Energy: EUGENE SHANNON.
Minister of Planning and Economic Affairs: TOGA G. McINTOSH.
Minister of Posts and Telecommunications: JEREMIAH SULUNTEH.
Minister of Public Works: LUSENI DONZO.
Minister of National Security: ANTHONY B. KROMAH (acting).
Minister of Transport: JACKSON E. DOE.
Minister of Youth and Sport: ETMONIA TARPEH.
Minister of State for Presidential Affairs: Dr EDWARD McCLAIN.
Minister of State for Finance, Economic and Legal Affairs: MORRIS SAYTUMAH.

MINISTRIES

Office of the President: Executive Mansion, POB 10-9001, Capitol Hill, 1000 Monrovia 10; e-mail rpailey@emansion.gov.lr; internet www.emansion.gov.lr.

Ministry of Agriculture: Tubman Blvd, POB 10-9010, 1000 Monrovia 10; tel. 226399; internet www.moa.gov.lr.

Ministry of Commerce and Industry: Ashmun St, POB 10-9014, 1000 Monrovia 10; tel. 226283; internet www.moci.gov.lr.

Ministry of Defence: Benson St, POB 10-9007, 1000 Monrovia 10; tel. 226077; internet www.mod.gov.lr.

Ministry of Education: E. G. N. King Plaza, Broad St, POB 10-1545, 1000 Monrovia 10; tel. and fax 226216; internet www.moe.gov.lr.

Ministry of Finance: Broad St, POB 10-9013, 1000 Monrovia 10; tel. (4) 7510680; internet www.mof.gov.lr.

Ministry of Foreign Affairs: Mamba Point, POB 10-9002, 1000 Monrovia 10; tel. 226763; internet www.mofa.gov.lr.

Ministry of Gender and Development: Monrovia; internet www.mogd.gov.lr.

Ministry of Health and Social Welfare: Sinkor, POB 10-9004, 1000 Monrovia 10; tel. 226317; internet www.moh.gov.lr.

Ministry of Information, Culture and Tourism: Capitol Hill, POB 10-9021, 1000 Monrovia 10; tel. and fax 226269; internet www.micat.gov.lr.

Ministry of Internal Affairs: cnr Warren and Benson Sts, POB 10-9008, 1000 Monrovia 10; tel. 226346; internet www.moia.gov.lr.

Ministry of Justice: Ashmun St, POB 10-9006, 1000 Monrovia 10; tel. 227872; internet www.moia.gov.lr.

Ministry of Labour: Mechlin St, POB 10-9040, 1000 Monrovia 10; tel. 226291; internet www.mol.gov.lr.

Ministry of Lands, Mines and Energy: Capitol Hill, POB 10-9024, 1000 Monrovia 10; tel. 226281; internet www.molme.gov.lr.

Ministry of Planning and Economic Affairs: Broad St, POB 10-9016, 1000 Monrovia 10; tel. 226962; internet www.mopea.gov.lr.

Ministry of Posts and Telecommunications: Carey St, 1000 Monrovia 10; tel. (6) 433715; e-mail ministryofposttelecommunication@yahoo.com.

Ministry of Presidential Affairs: Executive Mansion, Capitol Hill, 1000 Monrovia 10; tel. 228026; internet www.emansion.gov.lr.

Ministry of Public Works: Lynch St, POB 10-9011, 1000 Monrovia 10; tel. 227972; internet www.mopw.gov.lr.

Ministry of Transport: 1000 Monrovia 10; internet www.mopt.gov.lr.

Ministry of Youth and Sports: Monrovia; internet www.lys.gov.lr.

President and Legislature

PRESIDENT

Presidential Election, First Round, 11 October 2005

Candidate	Votes	% of votes
George Manneh Weah (Congress for Democratic Change)	275,265	28.26
Ellen Johnson-Sirleaf (Unity Party)	192,326	19.75
Charles Walker Brumskine (Liberty Party)	135,093	13.87
Winston A. Tubman (National Democratic Party of Liberia)	89,623	9.20
Harry Varney Gboto-Nambi Sherman (Coalition for the Transformation of Liberia)	76,403	7.85
Roland Chris Yarkpah Massaquoi (National Patriotic Party)	40,361	4.14
Joseph D. Z. Korto (Liberia Equal Rights Party)	31,814	3.27
Alhaji G. V. Kromah (All Liberian Coalition Party)	27,141	2.79
Togba-Nah Tipoteh (Alliance for Peace and Democracy)	22,766	2.34
Others	82,998	8.52
Total	**973,790**	**100.00**

Presidential Election, Second Round, 8 November 2005

Candidate	Votes	% of votes
Ellen Johnson-Sirleaf (Unity Party)	478,526	59.40
George Manneh Weah (Congress for Democratic Change)	327,046	40.60
Total	**805,572**	**100.00**

LEGISLATURE

House of Representatives

Speaker: ALEX JANEKAI TYLER.

General Election, 11 October 2005

Party	% of votes	Seats
Congress for Democratic Change	23.4	15
Liberty Party	14.1	9
Unity Party	12.5	8
Coalition for the Transformation of Liberia	12.5	8
Independents	10.9	7
Alliance for Peace and Democracy	7.8	5
National Patriotic Party	6.3	4
New Deal Movement	4.7	3
All Liberian Coalition Party	3.1	2
National Democratic Party of Liberia	1.6	1
United Democratic Alliance	1.6	1
National Reformation Party	1.6	1
Total	**100.0**	**64**

Senate

President: ISAAC NYENABO.

General Election, 11 October 2005

Party	% of votes	Seats
Coalition for the Transformation of Liberia	23.3	7
Congress for Democratic Change	10.0	3
Unity Party	10.0	3
Liberty Party	10.0	3
Alliance for Peace and Democracy	10.0	3
National Patriotic Party	10.0	3
Independents	10.0	3
National Democratic Party of Liberia	6.7	2
National Reformation Party	3.3	1
All Liberian Coalition Party	3.3	1
United Democratic Alliance	3.3	1
Total	**100.0**	**30**

Election Commission

National Elections Commission: Tubman Blvd, 16th St, Sinkor, Monrovia; internet www.necliberia.org; independent; Chair. JAMES FLOMOYAN.

Political Organizations

At the end of January 1997 the armed factions in Liberia officially ceased to exist as military organizations; a number of them were reconstituted as political parties, while long-standing political organizations re-emerged. In August 2003 the two main rebel movements in conflict with government forces, Liberians United for Reconciliation and Democracy and the Movement for Democracy in Liberia, signed a peace agreement, which provided for their inclusion in a power-sharing administration. Following the completion of the disarmament process in November 2004, these were officially dissolved. A total of 30 political parties had been granted registration prior to presidential and legislative elections in October and November 2005.

Alliance for Peace and Democracy (APD): Benson St, Monrovia; tel. (6) 547710; internet www.members.tripod.com/tipoteh12/index.html; f. 2005; Leader TOGBA-NAH TIPOTEH; Chair. DUSTY WOLOKOLIE.

    Liberian People's Party (LPP): Monrovia; f. 1984 by fmr mems of the Movement for Justice in Africa; Leader DUSTY WOLOKOLIE.

    United People's Party (UPP): Monrovia; f. 1984 by fmr mems of the Progressive People's Party, which led opposition prior to April 1980 coup; Leader WESLEY JOHNSON.

All Liberian Coalition Party (ALCOP): Broad St, Monrovia; tel. (6) 524735; f. 1997 from elements of fmr armed faction the United Liberation Movement of Liberia for Democracy; Leader Alhaji G. V. KROMAH; Chair. JOHNSTON P. FANNEBRDE.

Coalition for the Transformation of Liberia (COTOL): Monrovia; f. 2005; Leader HARRY VARNEY GBOTO-NAMBI SHERMAN.

    Liberian Action Party (LAP): Monrovia; f. 1984; Leader GYUDE BRYANT.

    Liberian Unification Party (LUP): Monrovia; f. 1984; Leader LAVELI SUPUWOOD.

    People's Democratic Party of Liberia (PDPL): Monrovia; Leader FIYAH GBOLIE.

    True Whig Party (TWP): Monrovia; Leader RUDOLPH SHERMAN.

Congress for Democratic Change: Bernard Beach Compound, Monrovia; tel. (6) 513469; f. 2004; Leader GEORGE MANNEH WEAH; Chair. J. BANGULA COLE.

Free Democratic Party (FDP): Center St, Monrovia; tel. (6) 582291; Leader DAVID M. FARHAT; Chair. S. CIAPHA GBOLLIE.

Liberia Equal Rights Party (LERP): Duala Gas Station, Bushrod Island, Opposite Duala Market, Monrovia; f. 2005; Leader JOSEPH D. Z. KORTO; Chair. SOLOMON KING.

Liberia Destiny Party (LDP): Congo Town Back Rd, Monrovia; tel. (6) 511531; f. 2005; Leader MILTON NATHANIEL BARNES; Sec.-Gen. BORBOR B. KROMAH.

Liberty Party (LP): Old Rd, Sinkor Opposite Haywood Mission, POB 1340, Monrovia; tel. (6) 547921; f. 2005; Leader CHARLES WALKER BRUMSKINE; Chair. LARRY P. YOUQUOI.

National Democratic Party of Liberia (NDPL): Capital Bye Pass, Monrovia; f. 1997 from the fmr armed faction the Liberia Peace Council; Leader WINSTON A. TUBMAN; Chair. NYANDEH SIEH.

National Patriotic Party (NPP): Sinkor, Tubman Bldg, Monrovia; tel. (6) 515312; f. 1997 from the fmr armed faction the National Patriotic Front of Liberia; won the majority of seats in legislative elections in July 1997; Leader ROLAND CHRIS YARKPAH MASSAQUOI; Chair. LAWRENCE A. GEORGE.

National Reformation Party (NRP): Duala Market, Monrovia; tel. (6) 511531; Leader Bishop ALFRED GARPEE REEVES; Chair. Rev. SAMUEL TORMETIEE.

New Deal Movement (NDM): Randall St, Monrovia; tel. (6) 567470; f. 2003; Leader Prof. GEORGE KLAY KIEH, Jr; Chair. T. WILSON GAYE.

Progressive Democratic Party (PRODEM): McDonald St, Monrovia; tel. (6) 521091; f. early 2005 by mems of fmr rebel movement, Liberians United for Reconciliation and Democracy (emerged 1999); Leader SEKOU DAMATE CONNEH.

Reformed United Liberia Party (RULP): 70 Ashmun St, POB 1000, Monrovia; tel. (6) 571212; f. 2005; Leader WILLIAM VACANARAT SHADRACH TUBMAN.

United Democratic Alliance (UDA): Monrovia; f. 2005 by the **Liberia National Union (LINU)**; led by HENRY MONIBA; the **Liberia Education and Development Party (LEAD)**; and the

LIBERIA

Reformation Alliance Party (RAP), led by HENRY BOIMAH FAHN-BULLEH; Leader JOHN SEMBE MORLU.

Unity Party (UP): 86 Broad St, Monrovia; tel. (6) 512528; e-mail info@theunityparty.org; internet www.theunityparty.org; f. 1984; Leader ELLEN JOHNSON-SIRLEAF; Chair. Dr CHARLES CLARKE.

Diplomatic Representation

EMBASSIES IN LIBERIA

Algeria: Capitol By-Pass, POB 2032, Monrovia; tel. 224311; Chargé d'affaires a.i. MUHAMMAD AZZEDINE AZZOUZ.

Cameroon: 18th St and Payne Ave, Sinkor, POB 414, Monrovia; tel. 261374; Ambassador VICTOR E. NDIBA.

China, People's Republic: Tubman Blvd, Congotown, POB 5970, Monrovia; tel. 228024; fax 226740; e-mail Chinaemb_lr@mfa.gov.cn; internet lr.china-embassy.org; Ambassador ZHOU YUXIAO.

Congo, Democratic Republic: Spriggs Payne Airport, Sinkor, POB 1038, Monrovia; tel. 261326; Ambassador (vacant).

Côte d'Ivoire: Tubman Blvd, Sinkor, POB 126, Monrovia; tel. 261123; Ambassador CLÉMENT KAUL MELEDJE.

Cuba: 17 Kennedy Ave, Congotown, POB 3579, Monrovia; tel. 262600; Ambassador Dr MIGUEL GUSTAVO PÉREZ CRUZ.

Egypt: Coconut Plantation, Randal St, Mamba Point, POB 462, Monrovia; tel. 226226; fax 226122; Ambassador OMAR ABD EL AZIZ EL SHEEMY.

Ghana: cnr 11th St and Gardiner Ave, Sinkor, POB 471, Monrovia; tel. 261477; Ambassador Maj.-Gen. FRANCIS ADU-AMANFOH.

Guinea: Monrovia; Ambassador ABDOULAYE DORÉ.

Lebanon: 12th St, Monrovia; tel. 262537; Ambassador MANSOUR ABDALLAH.

Libya: Monrovia; Ambassador MUHAMMAD UMARAT-TABI.

Morocco: Tubman Blvd, Congotown, Monrovia; tel. 262767; Ambassador MOHAMED LASFAR.

Nigeria: Congotown, POB 366, Monrovia; tel. 227345; fax 226135; Ambassador EINEJE ONOBU.

Russia: Payne Ave, Sinkor, POB 2010, Monrovia; tel. 261304; Ambassador ANDREY V. POKROVSKII.

Senegal: Monrovia; Ambassador MOCTAR TRAORÉ.

Sierra Leone: Tubman Blvd, POB 575, Monrovia; tel. 261301; Ambassador PATRICK J. FOYAH.

USA: 111 United Nations Dr., Mamba Point, POB 10-0098, Monrovia; tel. (7) 7054826; fax (7) 710370; e-mail ConsularMonrovia@state.gov; internet monrovia.usembassy.gov; Ambassador DONALD E. BOOTH.

Judicial System

In February 1982 the People's Supreme Tribunal (which had been established following the April 1980 coup) was renamed the People's Supreme Court, and its Chairman and members became the Chief Justice and Associate Justices of the People's Supreme Court. The judicial system also comprised People's Circuit and Magistrate Courts. The five-member Supreme Court was established in January 1992 to adjudicate in electoral disputes.

Chief Justice of the Supreme Court of Liberia: JOHNNIE LEWIS.

Justices: KABINEH JA'NEH, FRANCIS KORPKPOR, GLADYS JOHNSON.

Religion

Liberia is officially a Christian state, although complete religious freedom is guaranteed. Christianity and Islam are the two main religions. There are numerous religious sects, and many Liberians hold traditional beliefs.

CHRISTIANITY

Liberian Council of Churches: 15 St, Sinkor, POB 10-2191, 1000 Monrovia; tel. (6) 517879; e-mail bendlartey46@yahoo.com; f. 1982; 11 mems, two assoc. mems, one fraternal mem.; Pres. Rt Rev. SUMOWARD E. HARRIS.

The Anglican Communion

The diocese of Liberia forms part of the Church of the Province of West Africa, incorporating the local Episcopal Church. Anglicanism was established in Liberia in 1836, and the diocese of Liberia was admitted into full membership of the Province in 1982. In 1985 the Church had 125 congregations, 39 clergy, 26 schools and about 20,000 adherents in the country. The Metropolitan of the Province is the Bishop of Koforidua, Ghana.

Bishop of Liberia: Rt Rev. EDWARD NEUFVILLE, POB 10-0277, 1000 Monrovia 10; tel. 224760; fax 227519.

The Roman Catholic Church

Liberia comprises the archdiocese of Monrovia and the dioceses of Cape Palmas and Gbarnga. At 31 December 2005 there were an estimated 174,050 adherents in the country, equivalent to 5.2% of the total population.

Catholic Bishops' Conference of Liberia POB 10-2078, 1000 Monrovia 10; tel. 227245; fax 226175. f. 1998; Pres. Rt Rev. LEWIS ZEIGLER (Bishop of Gbarnga).

Archbishop of Monrovia: Most Rev. MICHAEL KPAKALA FRANCIS, Archbishop's Office, POB 10-2078, 1000 Monrovia 10; tel. (6) 519766; fax (7) 7003719; e-mail apostolic_adm@yahoo.com.

Other Christian Churches

Assemblies of God in Liberia: POB 1297, Monrovia; f. 1908; 14,578 adherents, 287 churches; Gen. Supt JIMMIE K. DUGBE, Sr.

Lutheran Church in Liberia (LCL): POB 10-1046, 13th St, Payne Ave, Sinkor, 1000 Monrovia 10; tel. 226262; e-mail lutheranchurchinliberia@yahoo.com; f. 1947 as Evangelical Lutheran Church, reorg. in 1965 under indigenous leadership as LCL; 71,000 adherents; Pres. Bishop SUMOWARD E. HARRIS.

Providence Baptist Church: cnr Broad and Center Sts, Monrovia; f. 1821; 2,500 adherents, 300 congregations, 6 ministers, 8 schools; Pastor Rev. A. MOMOLUE DIGGS.

Liberia Baptist Missionary and Educational Convention, Inc: POB 390, Monrovia; tel. 222661; f. 1880; 72,000 adherents, 270 churches (2007); Pres. Rev. J. K. LEVEE MOULTON; Nat. Vice-Pres. Rev. J. GBANA HALL; Gen. Sec. CHARLES W. BLAKE.

United Methodist Church in Liberia: cnr 12th St and Tubman Blvd, POB 1010, 1000 Monrovia 10; tel. 223343; f. 1833; c. 68,300 adherents, 600 congregations, 700 ministers, 394 lay pastors, 121 schools, one university; Resident Bishop Rev. Dr JOHN G. INNIS; Sec. Rev. Dr SAMUEL J. QUIRE, Jr.

Other active denominations include the National Baptist Mission, the Pentecostal Church, the Presbyterian Church in Liberia, the Prayer Band and the Church of the Lord Aladura.

ISLAM

The total community numbers about 670,000.

National Muslim Council of Liberia: Monrovia; Leader Shaykh KAFUMBA KONNAH.

The Press

NEWSPAPERS

The Inquirer: POB 3600, Monrovia; tel. (6) 538573; fax 227036; e-mail theinquirernews@yahoo.com; internet www.theinquirer.com.lr; New Era Publications, Ltd; daily; Man. Editor PHILIP WESSEH.

Monrovia Guardian: 58 Broad Street, POB 2131, Monrovia; weekly; independent; Editor B. IGNATIUS GEORGE.

News: ACDB Bldg, POB 10-3137, Carey Warren St, Monrovia; tel. 227820; independent; weekly; Chair. WILSON TARPEH; Editor-in-Chief JEROME DALIEH.

PERIODICALS

The Kpelle Messenger: Kpelle Literacy Center, Lutheran Church, POB 1046, Monrovia; Kpelle-English; monthly; Editor Rev. JOHN J. MANAWU.

Liberia Orbit: Voinjama; e-mail orbit@tekmail.com; internet www.liberiaorbit.org; national current affairs; Editor LLOYD SCOTT.

Liberian Post: e-mail info@liberian.org; internet www.liberian.org; f. 1998; independent internet magazine; tourist information; Publr WILLEM TIJSSEN.

New Democrat: Monrovia; e-mail newdemnews@yahoo.com; internet www.newdemocrat.org; national news and current affairs.

Patriot: Congotown 1000, Monrovia; internet www.allaboutliberia.com/patriot.htm.

The People Magazine: Bank of Liberia Bldg, Suite 214, Carey and Warren Sts, POB 3501, Monrovia; tel. 222743; f. 1985; monthly; Editor and Publr CHARLES A. SNETTER.

PRESS ORGANIZATIONS

Liberia Institute of Journalism: Kashour Bldg, 2nd Floor, cnr Broad and Johnson Sts, POB 2314, Monrovia; tel. 227327; Dir VINICIUS HODGES.

Press Union of Liberia: Benson St, POB 20-4209, Monrovia; tel. and fax 227105; f. 1985; Pres. ELIZABETH HOFF.

NEWS AGENCIES

Liberian News Agency (LINA): POB 9021, Capitol Hill, Monrovia; tel. 222229; Dir-Gen. ERNEST KIAZOLY (acting).

Broadcasting and Communications

TELECOMMUNICATIONS

LiberCell: Monrovia; e-mail info@awli.net; internet www.libercell .info; f. 2004; mobile cellular telephone provider; CEO AZZAM SBAITY; Gen. Man. MOHAMMED ALAWIE.

Liberia Telecommunications Corpn: Monrovia; tel. 227523; Man. Dir JOE GBALAH.

Mobile cellular services are also provided by Cellcom, Comium and Lone Star.

BROADCASTING

Radio

Liberia Communications Network: Congotown 1000, Monrovia; govt-operated; broadcasts information, education and entertainment 24 hours daily in English, French and several African languages; short-wave service.

Liberia Rural Communications Network: POB 10-02176, 1000 Monrovia 10; tel. 271368; f. 1981; govt-operated; rural devt and entertainment programmes; Dir J. RUFUS KAINE (acting).

Radio Veritas: POB 3569, Monrovia; tel. (4) 712834; e-mail radioveritas@hotmail.com; internet radioveritas.org; f. 1981; Catholic; independent; nation-wide shortwave broadcasts.

Star Radio: Sekou Toure Ave, Mamba Point, Monrovia; tel. 226820; fax 227360; e-mail star@liberia.net; independent news and information station; f. July 1997 by Fondation Hirondelle, Switzerland, with funds from the US Agency for International Development; broadcasts in English, French and 14 African languages; operations suspended by the Govt in March 2000; ban on transmissions ended Nov. 2003; Dir GEORGE BENNETT.

Television

Liberia Broadcasting System: POB 594, Monrovia; tel. 224984; govt-owned; Dir-Gen. CHARLES SNETTER.

Finance

(cap. = capital; res = reserves; dep. = deposits; m. = million; br. = branch; amounts in Liberian dollars, unless otherwise indicated)

BANKING

Following intensive fighting between government and rebel forces in the capital in mid-2003, it was reported that commercial banks had resumed operations at the end of August. At that time, however, only four (of a total of 18 deposit banks established since 1954) were active, the remainder having been closed as a result of poor bank management or the 1989–96 civil conflict. The Liberian Bank for Development and Investment is the only locally owned bank.

Central Bank

Central Bank of Liberia: cnr Warren and Carey Sts, POB 2048, Monrovia; tel. 226144; fax 227685; e-mail webmaster@cbl.org.lr; internet www.cbl.org.lr; f. 1974 as National Bank of Liberia; name changed March 1999; bank of issue; cap. 7,240.8m., res 2,995.4m., dep. 1,093.6m. (Dec. 2004); Gov. JOSEPH MILLS JONES.

Other Banks

Ecobank Liberia Ltd: Ashmun and Randall Sts, POB 4825, Monrovia; tel. 226428; fax (7) 7012290; e-mail ecobanklr@ecobank .com; internet www.ecobank.com; commenced operations Aug. 1999; cap. and res US $2.1m., total assets US $10.2m. (Dec. 2001); Chair. EUGENE H. COOPER; Man. Dir ESIJOLONE OKORODUDU.

First International Bank (Liberia) Ltd: Luke Bldg, Broad St, Monrovia; tel. 77026241; e-mail info@fib-lib.com; internet www .fib-lib.com; f. April 2005; Chair. FRANCIS L. M. HORTON; Exec. Dir ARISA AWA.

Global Bank Liberia Ltd (GBLL): Ashmun and Mechlin Sts, POB 2053, Monrovia; tel. (6) 425760; e-mail mail@globalbankliberia.com; internet www.globalbankliberia.com; f. 2005; Italian-owned; Pres. RICCARDO SEMBIANTE.

International Bank (Liberia) Ltd: 64 Broad St, POB 292, Monrovia; tel. 226092; fax 226505; e-mail tjeffrey@ibliberia.com; internet www.ibliberia.com; f. 1948 as International Trust Co of Liberia; name changed April 2000; cap. 2m. (1989), dep. 96.4m. (Dec. 1996); Pres. F. A. GUIDA; Gen. Man. THOMAS S. JEFFREY; 1 br.

Liberian Bank for Development and Investment (LBDI): Ashmun and Randall Sts, POB 547, Monrovia; tel. 226366; fax 226359; e-mail lbdi@lbdi.net; internet www.lbdi.net; f. 1961; 18.7% govt-owned; cap. and res US $12.5m., total assets US $26.8m. (Dec. 2001); Chair. NATHANIEL BARNES; Pres. FRANCIS A. DENNIS.

Banking Association

Liberia Bankers' Association: POB 292, Monrovia; mems include commercial and devt banks; Pres. LEN MAESTRE.

INSURANCE

American National Underwriters, Inc: Carter Bldg, 39 Broad St, POB 180, Monrovia; tel. 114921; general; Gen. Man. S. B. MENSAH.

American Life Insurance Co: Carter Bldg, 39 Broad St, POB 60, Monrovia; f. 1969; life and general; Vice-Pres. ALLEN BROWN.

Insurance Co of Africa: 64 Broad St, POB 292, Monrovia; f. 1969; life and general; Pres. SAMUEL OWAREE MINTAH.

National Insurance Corpn of Liberia (NICOL): LBDI Bldg Complex, POB 1528, Sinkor, Monrovia; tel. 262429; f. 1983; state-owned; sole insurer for Govt and parastatal bodies; also provides insurance for the Liberian-registered merchant shipping fleet; Man. Dir MIATTA EDITH SHERMAN.

Royal Exchange Assurance: Ashmun and Randall Sts, POB 666, Monrovia; all types of insurance; Man. RONALD WOODS.

United Security Insurance Agencies Inc: Randall St, POB 2071, Monrovia; life, personal accident and medical; Dir EPHRAIM O. OKORO.

Trade and Industry

GOVERNMENT AGENCIES

Budget Bureau: Capitol Hill, POB 1518, Monrovia; tel. 226340; Dir-Gen. AUGUSTINE K. NGAFUAN.

General Services Agency (GSA): Sinkor, Monrovia; tel. 226745; Dir-Gen. WILLIARD RUSSELL.

DEVELOPMENT ORGANIZATIONS

Forestry Development Authority: POB 3010, 1000 Monrovia; tel. 224940; fax 226000; f. 1976; responsible for forest management and conservation; Chair. EDWIN ZELEE; Man. Dir JOHN T. WOODS.

Liberia Industrial Free Zone Authority (LIFZA): One Free Zone, Monrovia; tel. 533671; e-mail mskromah@lifza.com; internet www.lifza.com; f. 1975; 98 mems; Man. Dir MOHAMMED S. KROMAH.

National Investment Commission (NIC): Fmr Executive Mansion Bldg, POB 9043, Monrovia; tel. 226685; internet www.nic.gov.lr; f. 1979; autonomous body negotiating investment incentives agreements on behalf of Govt; promotes agro-based and industrial devt; Chair. RICHARD TOLBERT.

CHAMBER OF COMMERCE

Liberia Chamber of Commerce: Warren St, POB 92, Monrovia; tel. 223738; e-mail liberiachamber2006@yahoo.com; f. 1951; Pres. HENRY REED COOPER; Sec.-Gen. EMMETT C. A. GOODING.

INDUSTRIAL AND TRADE ASSOCIATIONS

Liberian Produce Marketing Corpn: POB 662, Monrovia; tel. 222447; f. 1961; govt-owned; exports Liberian produce, provides industrial facilities for processing of agricultural products and participates in agricultural devt programmes; Man. Dir NYAH MARTEIN.

Liberian Resources Corpn (LIBRESCO): controls Liberia's mineral resources; 60% govt-owned; 40% owned by South African co, Amalia Gold.

EMPLOYERS' ASSOCIATION

National Enterprises Corpn: POB 518, Monrovia; tel. 261370; importer, wholesaler and distributor of foodstuffs, and wire and metal products for local industries; Pres. EMMANUEL SHAW, Sr.

UTILITIES

Electricity

Liberia Electricity Corpn (LEC): Waterside, POB 165, Monrovia; tel. 226133; Chair. DUNSTAN MACAULEY; Man. Dir HARRY YUAN.

National Oil Co of Liberia (NOCL): Episcopal Church Plaza, Ashmun and Randall Sts, Monrovia; Chair. CLEMENCEAU B. UREY.

TRADE UNIONS

Congress of Industrial Organizations: 29 Ashmun St, POB 415, Monrovia; f. 1960; Pres. Gen. J. T. PRATT; Sec.-Gen. AMOS N. GRAY; 5 affiliated unions.

Labor Congress of Liberia: 71 Gurley St, Monrovia; Sec.-Gen. P. C. T. SONPON; 8 affiliated unions.

Liberian Federation of Labor Unions: J. B. McGill Labor Center, Gardnersville Freeway, POB 415, Monrovia; f. 1980; Sec.-Gen. AMOS GRAY; 10,000 mems (1983).

Transport

RAILWAYS

Railway operations were suspended in 1990, owing to the civil conflict. Large sections of the 480-km rail network were subsequently dismantled.

Bong Mining Co Ltd: POB 538, Monrovia; tel. 225222; fax 225770; f. 1965; Gen. Man. HANS-GEORG SCHNEIDER.

Liberian Mining Co: Monrovia; tel. 221190; govt-owned; assumed control of LAMCO JV Operating Co in 1989.

National Iron Ore Co Ltd: POB 548, Monrovia; f. 1951; Gen. Man. S. K. DATTA RAY.

ROADS

In 1999 the road network in Liberia totalled an estimated 10,600 km, of which about 657 km were paved. The main trunk road is the Monrovia–Sanniquellie motor road, extending north-east from the capital to the border with Guinea, near Ganta, and eastward through the hinterland to the border with Côte d'Ivoire. Trunk roads run through Tapita, in Nimba County, to Grand Gedeh County and from Monrovia to Buchanan. A bridge over the Mano river connects with the Sierra Leone road network, while a main road links Monrovia and Freetown (Sierra Leone). Although principal roads were officially reopened to commercial traffic in early 1997, following the 1989–96 armed conflict, much of the infrastructure remained severely damaged. In late 2003 the Liberian authorities announced plans for the extensive rehabilitation of the road network, including a highway linking Monrovia with Harper, which was to be funded by the People's Republic of China.

SHIPPING

In December 2005 Liberia's open-registry fleet (1,907 vessels), the second largest in the world (after Panama) in terms of gross tonnage, had a total displacement of 68.4m. grt. Commercial port activity in Liberia was frequently suspended from 1990, as a result of hostilities. At September 2004 only Monrovia Freeport had fully resumed operations and (compared with the corresponding period in 2003) experienced a rise in vessel traffic of 95.2%, owing to increasing commercial and humanitarian activities.

Bureau of Maritime Affairs: Tubman Blvd, POB 10-9042, 1000 Monrovia 10; tel. and fax 226069; e-mail maritime@liberia.net; internet www.maritime.gov.lr; Commissioner (vacant).

Liberia National Shipping Line (LNSL): Monrovia; f. 1987; jt venture by the Liberian Govt and private German interests; routes to Europe, incl. the United Kingdom and Scandinavia.

National Port Authority: POB 1849, Monrovia; tel. 226646; fax 226180; e-mail natport@liberia.net; f. 1967; administers Monrovia Freeport and the ports of Buchanan, Greenville and Harper; Chair. Dr WILLIAM ALLEN; Man. Dir GEORGE TUBMAN.

CIVIL AVIATION

Liberia's principal airports are Robertsfield International Airport, at Harbel, 56 km east of Monrovia, and James Spriggs Payne Airport, at Monrovia.

ADC Liberia Inc: Monrovia; f. 1993; services to the United Kingdom, the USA and destinations in West Africa.

Air Liberia: POB 2076, Monrovia; f. 1974; state-owned; scheduled passenger and cargo services; Man. Dir JAMES K. KOFA.

LIBYA

Introductory Survey

Location, Climate, Language, Religion, Flag, Capital

The Great Socialist People's Libyan Arab Jamahiriya extends along the Mediterranean coast of North Africa. Its neighbours are Tunisia and Algeria to the west, Niger and Chad to the south, Egypt to the east, and Sudan to the south-east. The climate is very hot and dry. Most of the country is part of the Sahara, an arid desert, but the coastal regions are cooler. Average temperatures range from 13°C (55°F) to 38°C (100°F), but a maximum of 57.3°C (135°F) has been recorded in the interior. Arabic is the official language, although English and Italian are also used in trade. Almost all of the population are Sunni Muslims. The national flag (proportions 2 by 3) is plain green. The administrative capital was formerly Tripoli (Tarabulus), but under a decentralization programme announced in September 1988 most government departments and the legislature were relocated to Sirte (Surt), while some departments were transferred to other principal towns.

Recent History

Libya, formerly an Italian colony and occupied by British and French troops in 1942, attained independence as the United Kingdom of Libya on 24 December 1951. Muhammad Idris as-Sanusi, Amir of Cyrenaica, became King Idris of Libya. British and US forces maintained bases in Libya in return for economic assistance; however, the discovery of petroleum reserves in 1959 greatly increased the country's potential for financial autonomy.

King Idris was deposed in September 1969, in a bloodless revolution led by a group of young nationalist army officers. A Revolution Command Council (RCC) was established, with Col Muammar al-Qaddafi as Chairman, and a Libyan Arab Republic was proclaimed. British and US military personnel withdrew from Libya in 1970, and in 1972 British oil interests in Libya were nationalized.

The Arab Socialist Union (ASU) was established in June 1971 as the country's sole political party. People's Congresses and Popular Committees were formed, and an undertaking was made to administer the country in accordance with Islamic principles. The General National Congress of the ASU (which comprised members of the RCC, leaders of the People's Congresses and Popular Committees and of trade unions and professional organizations) held its first session in January 1976; it was subsequently restyled the General People's Congress (GPC).

In March 1977 the GPC endorsed constitutional changes, recommended by Qaddafi, whereby the official name of the country was changed to the Socialist People's Libyan Arab Jamahiriya. Power was vested in the people through the GPC and its constituent parts. The RCC was dissolved, and a General Secretariat of the GPC (with Qaddafi as Secretary-General) was established. The GPC elected Qaddafi as Revolutionary Leader of the new state. The Council of Ministers was replaced by a General People's Committee, initially with 26 members—each a secretary of a department.

In March 1979 Qaddafi resigned from the post of Secretary-General of the General Secretariat of the GPC to devote more time to 'preserving the revolution'. The creation in early 1984 of the post of Secretary for External Security and of an office, attached to the Secretariat for Foreign Liaison, to 'combat international terrorism', combined with repressive measures to curb the activity of dissidents, apparently reflected Qaddafi's increasing sensitivity to the growth of opposition groups—principally the National Front for the Salvation of Libya (NFSL), which he accused foreign governments of fostering. In 1986 the country's official name was changed to the Great Socialist People's Libyan Arab Jamahiriya.

From 1988, in an apparent attempt to allay domestic dissatisfaction and international criticism, Qaddafi initiated a series of liberalizing economic and political reforms. In foreign policy he adopted a more pragmatic approach to his ambition of achieving Maghreb union (see below), and to his relations with other Arab and African countries. Within Libya he accused the 'revolutionary committees' (young, pro-Qaddafi activists) of murdering political opponents of his regime. Qaddafi encouraged the reopening of private businesses, in recognition of the inadequacy of state-sponsored supermarkets, and declared an amnesty for all prisoners, other than those convicted of violent crimes or of conspiring with foreign powers. Libyan citizens were guaranteed freedom to travel abroad, and the powers of the revolutionary committees were curbed. The GPC created a People's Court and People's Prosecution Bureau to replace the revolutionary courts, and approved a charter of human rights. In August Qaddafi announced that the army was to be replaced by a force of 'Jamahiri Guards', which would be supervised by 'people's defence committees'. In September it was decided to relocate all but two of the secretariats of the GPC, mostly to the town of Sirte (Surt), 400 km east of Tripoli, and in January 1989 Qaddafi announced that all state institutions, including the state intelligence service and the official Libyan news agency, were to be abolished.

In October 1990 the GPC implemented extensive changes to the General People's Committee, creating three new secretariats and electing a new Secretary-General, Abu Sa'id Omar Durdah, as well as 11 new secretaries. Three of the five-member General Secretariat of the GPC were replaced, and Abd ar-Raziq as-Sawsa was appointed Secretary-General of the GPC; in November 1992 as-Sawsa was replaced by Muhammad az-Zanati. In the same month there was a further reorganization of the General People's Committee; the former Secretary for Economic Planning, Omar al-Muntasir, was named Secretary for Foreign Liaison and International Co-operation. Regarded as a moderate, al-Muntasir's appointment was viewed by some observers as a sign of Libya's willingness to resume dialogue with the West over the Lockerbie issue (see below).

Western media reported in October 1993 that elements loyal to Qaddafi had suppressed an attempted military *coup d'état*, and that Libya's second-in-command, Maj. Abd as-Salam Jalloud, was among many placed under house arrest. Qaddafi denied that a coup had been attempted, but the appointment of known loyalists to senior positions in the General People's Committee was announced in January 1994. Most notably, Abd al-Majid al-Aoud, a member of Qaddafi's closest personal entourage, replaced Durdah, a close associate of Jalloud, as Secretary-General.

At its annual convention in March 1997 the GPC made changes to the composition and structure of the General People's Committee. Muhammad Ahmad al-Manqush was appointed Secretary-General of the Committee in December, as part of a further reorganization. The Secretariat for Arab Unity was abolished in a restructuring of the General People's Committee in December 1998, in accordance with Qaddafi's recently stated intention to forge closer relations with African rather than Arab countries.

In January 2000 Qaddafi unexpectedly attended the opening session of the GPC, at the end of which he demanded that the budget for 2000 be redrafted, with a view to channelling petroleum revenues into education, health and public services. Furthermore, he urged that the current administrative system, based on General People's Committees, be abandoned in favour of an alternative form of government. Accordingly, a radical decentralization of the Government was announced in March, whereby almost all of the People's Committees were dissolved and their responsibilities devolved mainly to local level: only those areas described as 'sovereign' were to remain under the control of the General People's Committee, now led by Mubarak Abdallah ash-Shamikh. Most notably, Ali Abd as-Salam at-Turayki was allocated the new post of Secretary for African Unity, being replaced as Secretary for Foreign Liaison and International Co-operation by Abd ar-Rahman Muhammad Shalgam. Al-Ujayli Abd as-Salam Burayni replaced Muhammad Abdullah Bait al-Mal as Secretary for Finance in October, when a further restructuring of the General People's Committees was announced; it had been reported in July that Bait al-Mal, along with the President of the Central Bank of Libya and a further 22 senior Libyan bankers, had been implicated in allegations of financial impropriety.

In September 2000 clashes occurred throughout the country between Libyans and nationals of several other African countries. The confrontations were believed to reflect resentment within Libya at the increasing numbers of black African migrants entering the country. A large number of Chadians and Sudanese were reportedly killed in incidents in the town of Az-Zawiyah, some 30 km west of Tripoli, and thousands more were interned in military camps. The Nigerian embassy in Tripoli was ransacked, and Libyan youths were also held responsible for an attack on a camp which was razed to the ground. The GPC announced its intention formally to investigate the incidents, and in October the evacuation and deportation of migrant workers from Nigeria, Chad, Niger, Sudan and Ghana commenced. It was estimated that as a result of the clashes more than 100 Africans had been killed and as many as 30,000 migrants had left Libya. Qaddafi subsequently apportioned blame for the incidents on 'foreign hostile hands' opposed to his plans to create an African Union. In May 2001 two Libyans, four Nigerians and one Ghanaian were sentenced to death for their roles in the violence. A further 12 defendants were sentenced to life imprisonment.

A minor reorganization of the General People's Committee was announced in September 2001, including the creation of a new Secretariat for Infrastructure, Urban Planning and Environment. In November it was announced that more than 40 government and bank officials had been sentenced to varying terms of imprisonment for corruption and embezzlement; reportedly among those convicted was Secretary for Finance Burayni, who received a one-year prison sentence for negligence.

In January 2003 Libya was elected to chair the session of the UN Human Rights Commission scheduled to be held in March. It was the first time since the formation of the Commission in 1947 that the decision had been voted upon, with Libya securing 33 of the 53 votes, and 17 countries, including the United Kingdom, abstaining; the USA, Canada and Guatemala opposed the proposal. Libya's election was widely criticized by a number of international human rights organizations.

In June 2003 Qaddafi dismissed ash-Shamikh from the post of Secretary of the General People's Committee, replacing him with Shukri Muhammad Ghanem, who was succeeded as Secretary for the Economy and Trade by Abd al-Qadir Balkheir. It was also announced that the Secretariat for African Unity had been merged with the Secretariat for Foreign Liaison and International Co-operation; Shalgam assumed responsibility for both portfolios. In March 2004 Qaddafi announced a further reorganization of the General People's Committee, which included the creation of four new secretariats (for national security, youth and sport, training and labour, and culture) and the restoration of the Secretariat for Energy, which had been abolished in 2000.

It was announced in October 2005 that 84 members of banned opposition group the Muslim Brotherhood, originally convicted and imprisoned in 2002, were to be retried, following the abolition in January 2005 of the unpopular People's Court, which had passed the original verdicts; the prisoners were subsequently released in March 2006. An extensive reorganization of the General People's Committee was announced that same month, including the creation of seven new secretariats. Ghanem was replaced as Secretary of the General People's Committee by the former Deputy Secretary for Production, Dr al-Baghdadi Ali al-Mahmoudi, and was handed the role of Chairman of the National Oil Corporation, while Muhammad Ali al-Houeiz, hitherto Secretary for Finance, was promoted to Deputy Secretary. The Secretariat for Energy, only reinstated in March 2004, was restructured and renamed the Secretariat for Industry, Electricity and Mines.

In May 2006 the US-based organization Human Rights Watch (HRW) called for the immediate release of Fathi al-Jahmi, a political dissident detained since March 2004 for criticizing Qaddafi. The Libyan Government avowed that the trial of al-Jahmi, who faced the death sentence if convicted, had commenced in 2005; however, no details of the specific charges were made available. HRW urged the Libyan Government to build upon its recent renunciation of terrorism by allowing peaceful opponents freely to express their opinions. In June 2006 HRW also pressed the Libyan Government to allow a full, independent investigation into the deaths of hundreds of inmates at Abu Salim prison in Tripoli in 1996; the alleged massacre was reported to have been caused by security officers opening fire on prisoners protesting against poor living conditions. In September 2006 HRW released a report in which it claimed that the Libyan Government routinely subjected refugees and asylum-seekers to violence, arrest without due cause and forcible deportation; the report urged members of the European Union (EU, see p. 244) to apply pressure on Libya to protect the rights of the hundreds of thousands of foreigners residing therein. The report also alleged endemic failings within the Libyan criminal justice system, which, it claimed, had expended insufficient effort both to prevent foreigners from being tortured while detained in police custody and to ensure the legitimacy of their trials.

In October 2006 Abu Salim prison was again the scene of controversy when one inmate was killed and a further 17 people were injured in clashes between prisoners and guards. The disturbance, reported predominantly to have involved detainees who were members of the Libyan Islamic Fighting Group (LIFG), followed the decision by a Tripoli court earlier that same day to uphold the convictions, on charges of having links with the LIFG, of 190 inmates housed at the prison. The Libyan People's Prosecution Bureau, however, indicated that the violence had erupted when guards moved to end a sit-in protest against delays in legal proceedings. Amnesty International appealed for a thorough independent investigation into the incident.

Meanwhile, in July 2006 Qaddafi claimed that Libya had come close to building a nuclear bomb before abandoning in December 2003 its programmes to produce weapons of mass destruction (see below). In November 2006 an official source in Tripoli announced that Qaddafi's second son, Seif al-Islam, a popular figure among Libyans on account of his ongoing efforts to effect political and economic change, was to leave the country to take up employment with an international economic institution. His departure from Libya, which many feared would severely lessen hopes of genuine, lasting reform, was widely perceived to have been orchestrated by the Government in reaction to his outspoken criticism of the regime during a speech at a youth activist rally in Sirte in August; Seif al-Islam had articulated grave concerns about the undemocratic nature of the national political system, the dishevelled state of the health and education sectors, the lack of a free press and corruption within state institutions.

A reorganization of the General People's Committee was announced in January 2007, comprising nine changes, of which five were new appointments. Notable changes included the appointment of Dr Abd al-Hafid Mahmud Zalitni as Deputy Secretary and the modification of the recently restructured Secretariat for Industry, Electricity and Mines, its responsibilities henceforth to be shared between the newly created Secretariats for Industry and Mineral Resources and for Electricity, Water and Gas.

In a speech broadcast live on state television in August 2007, Seif al-Islam Qaddafi urged the drafting of a new constitution or 'social contract' that would establish, *inter alia*, an independent central bank and a free media and judiciary. He also criticized the Libyan political system for its lack of a freely elected legislature, its refusal to allow the creation of political parties and its ongoing intolerance of political dissent, and called for political power to be more widely distributed, beyond the GPC and the General People's Committee. While few observers questioned Seif al-Islam's commitment to these proposals, it was widely believed that his father would never allow such radical reforms to be implemented.

In November 2007 an audio tape purporting to be from Dr Ayman az-Zawahiri, the deputy leader of the militant Islamist organization al-Qa'ida (Base), was released, and included a message from Abu Laith al-Libi, the leader of al-Qa'ida in Afghanistan, who identified himself on the tape as also being a member of the LIFG. Al-Libi declared that the LIFG had pledged allegiance to al-Qa'ida, a development that some feared might signal the beginning of an intensification of militant Islamist activity within Libya. The recruitment of the LIFG to the al-Qa'ida network was symptomatic of a wider drive on the part of the latter organization to turn local militant Islamist groups within North Africa into branches of its global movement. Az-Zawahiri's own message, meanwhile, called for the overthrow of the Libyan, Algerian, Moroccan and Tunisian Governments, and criticized Qaddafi for surrendering Libya's nuclear weapons materials to 'crusader masters'. In early April 2008 it was reported that around 90 members of the LIFG had been released from a prison in Tripoli, after they were said to have renounced violence.

Qaddafi effected a reorganization of the General Secretariat of the GPC and of the General People's Committee in early March 2008. Changes to the former included the replacement of az-Zanati as Secretary by Muftah Muhammad Kaiba and the appointment of Huda Fathi ben Amer to the position of Secretary for Women's Affairs; changes to the latter included the appointment of former General People's Committee Secretary Mubarak Abdallah ash-Shamikh to the position of Deputy Secretary and that of Gen. Abd al-Fattah Yunis al-Abaidi as the new Secretary for National Security. At the same time Qaddafi announced that he intended to abolish the majority of secretariats within the General People's Committee by the end of that year, owing to his frustration with the 'labyrinthine bureaucracy' of the Committee, 'in which corruption and maladministration reign'. The secretariats' powers were instead to be handed over to the people to enable them to manage their own affairs, requiring privatization of many sectors of Libyan society; only the secretariats for defence, internal security and foreign affairs would be retained, along with those responsible for strategic infrastructural projects, such as the Great Man-made River Project (see Economic Affairs). At mid-2008 it remained unclear, however, as to whether these proposed structural reforms would actually be implemented.

Various plans for pan-Arab unity led to the formation, in January 1972, of the Federation of Arab Republics, comprising Libya, Egypt and Syria. In 1972 Libya concluded an agreement with Egypt to merge the two countries in 1973. Neither union was effective, and proposals for union with Tunisia in 1974, Syria in 1980, Chad in 1981, Morocco in 1984, Algeria in 1987 and Sudan in 1990 also proved abortive.

Relations with Egypt, already tense following the failure of the Libya-Egypt union, deteriorated further when President Anwar Sadat launched the October 1973 war against Israel without consulting Qaddafi. In common with the other members of the League of Arab States (the Arab League, see p. 332), Libya strongly objected to Sadat's peace initiative with Israel, which culminated in the signing of the Camp David accords in 1978, and Libya also condemned the proposals for Middle East peace that were agreed by other Arab states in Fez, Morocco, in 1982. From the late 1980s, none the less, Egypt and Libya forged a close relationship, with Egypt acting as an intermediary between Libya and Western nations (particularly in negotiations resulting from the Lockerbie bombing—see below). Following the suspension of UN sanctions against Libya in April 1999 (see below), EgyptAir resumed regular flights to Tripoli in July 2000, and Libyan flights to Egypt recommenced later that month.

In 1973 Libyan forces occupied the 'Aozou strip', a reputedly mineral-rich region of 114,000 sq km in the extreme north of Chad, to which it laid claim on the basis of an unratified border treaty concluded by Italy and France in 1935. Thereafter, Libya became embroiled in the lengthy struggle for political control between rival forces in Chad (q.v.). During 1987 intense fighting took place for control of north-western Chad, and in August President Hissène Habré's forces advanced into the 'Aozou strip', occupying the town of Aozou. Libya responded by bombing towns in northern Chad, and recaptured Aozou. In September Chadian forces destroyed an airbase 100 km inside Libya (allegedly a base for Libyan raids on Chad). Later in September, however, the two countries agreed to observe a cease-fire sponsored by the Organization of African Unity (OAU, now African Union—AU, see p. 164), and in October 1988 Libya and Chad restored diplomatic relations. In August 1989, with Algerian mediation, Chad and Libya concluded an agreement to attempt to resolve the dispute over sovereignty of the 'Aozou strip' through a political settlement. Accordingly, the issue was submitted to the International Court of Justice in The Hague, Netherlands, which in February 1994 ruled against Libya's claim. All Libyan troops remaining in the 'Aozou strip' were withdrawn in May. In June Libya and Chad concluded a treaty of friendship, neighbourly terms and co-operation. In May 1998 Qaddafi made his first visit to Chad for 17 years, and in November the two countries officially opened two of their common border posts. Chad's President Idriss Deby (who had overthrown Habré in 1990) and members of his administration made several visits to Libya after 1997 and in January 2002 Libyan mediation resulted in the brokering of a peace agreement between the Chadian Government and the rebel Mouvement pour la démocratie et la justice au Tchad, which had been in conflict since late 1998. In February 2005 Libya hosted talks between Chad and Sudan, attended by Deby and President Omar Hassan Ahmad al-Bashir of Sudan, which aimed to reduce tensions between the two countries.

Libya's outspoken criticism of other Arab regimes, and perceived interference in the internal affairs of other countries, led to years of relative political isolation. However, in 1987 Qaddafi sought to realign Libyan policy with that of the majority of Arab states. Qaddafi was reconciled in March with Yasser Arafat's Fatah wing of the Palestine Liberation Organization (PLO—against which he had previously advocated revolt, owing to its more moderate policies) and attempted to reunite the opposing factions of the Palestinian movement. In September Libya re-established 'fraternal' links with Iraq, modifying its support for Iran in the Iran-Iraq War.

A summit meeting of North African heads of state, held in Morocco in February 1989, concluded a treaty proclaiming the Union du Maghreb arabe (UMA—Union of the Arab Maghreb, see p. 414), comprising Algeria, Libya, Mauritania, Morocco and Tunisia. The treaty envisaged: the establishment of a council of heads of state; regular meetings of ministers of foreign affairs; and the eventual free movement of goods, people, services and capital throughout the countries of the region. During 1989–92 the member states formulated 15 regional co-operation conventions. In February 1993, however, it was announced that, in view of the differing economic orientations of each signatory, no convention had actually been implemented, and the UMA's activities were to be limited. UMA leaders met in April 1994 (and subsequently on an annual basis). In 1994 Libya threatened to leave the UMA unless member states ceased to comply with UN sanctions imposed on Libya (see below), and in 1995 it refused to assume the chairmanship of the organization, owing to their continuing compliance.

In February 1997, at a meeting hosted by Libya and attended by the Presidents of Sudan, Chad, Mali and Niger, and government ministers from Egypt, Burkina Faso and Tunisia, a treaty establishing the Community of Sahel-Saharan States (COMESSA, now CEN-SAD, see p. 411) was signed. CEN-SAD's general secretariat was temporarily located in Tripoli, and provisions were made for the establishment of a development bank, a council of heads of state and an executive council.

Libya's relations with the USA, which had been strained for many years, deteriorated significantly under the presidency of Ronald Reagan (1981–89), who accused the Libyan Government of sponsoring international terrorism. In January 1986 Reagan severed all economic and commercial relations with Libya, and in March Libyan forces fired missiles at US fighter aircraft, which were challenging Libya's attempts to enforce recognition of the whole of the Gulf of Sirte as its territorial waters. In retaliatory attacks in April US military aircraft bombed military installations, airports and official buildings, as well as alleged terrorist training camps and communication centres, in Tripoli and Benghazi. A total of 101 people, including many civilians, were reported to have died in the raids. The US Administration claimed in justification to have irrefutable proof of Libyan involvement in terrorist attacks and plots against US targets in Europe and the Middle East (including the recent bombing of a discothèque in Berlin, Germany—see below).

In November 1991 the US and British Governments announced that they would seek to extradite two Libyan citizens, Abd al-Baset Ali Muhammad al-Megrahi (a former head of security at Libyan Arab Airlines) and Al-Amin Khalifa Fhimah (an employee of the airline), alleged to have been responsible for an explosion that destroyed a Pan American World Airways (Pan Am) passenger aircraft over Lockerbie, Scotland, in December 1988, resulting in the deaths of 270 people. The Libyan Government denied any involvement in the bombing, and recommended that the allegations be investigated by a neutral body. In January 1992 the UN Security Council adopted a resolution (No. 731) demanding Libya's compliance with requests for the extradition of its two nationals and its co-operation with a French inquiry into the bombing over Niger, in September 1989, of a UTA passenger airline, in which all 171 passengers and crew had been killed. Libya's offer to try on its own territory the two men accused of the Lockerbie bombing was rejected by the USA, the United Kingdom and France, which urged the UN to impose sanctions on Libya. On 31 March 1992 the UN Security Council adopted a resolution (No. 748) providing for the imposition of economic sanctions against Libya if it refused to comply with Resolution 731, and to commit itself to a renunciation of international terrorism, by 15 April. Sanctions, including the severance of international air links, the prohibition of trade in arms and the reduction of Libya's diplomatic representation abroad, were duly imposed on the specified date. In May, at Qaddafi's instigation, 1,500 People's Congresses were convened in Libya and abroad, to enable the country's citizens to decide the fate of the two Lockerbie suspects and their response to the UN sanctions. The GPC announced in the following month its decision to allow the two Lockerbie suspects to be tried abroad, provided that the proceedings were 'fair and just'.

In August 1993 the USA, the United Kingdom and France announced that they would request the UN Security Council to strengthen the sanctions in force against Libya if, by 1 October, Libya had still not complied with Resolutions 731 and 748. The Libyan Government rejected this ultimatum, but stated its willingness to commence discussions with those three countries on an appropriate venue for the trial of the two Lockerbie suspects. In October the UN Secretary-General, Dr Boutros Boutros-Ghali, met the Libyan Secretary for Foreign Liaison and International Co-operation, but failed to secure agreement on a timetable for the surrender of the two suspects to either the USA or the United Kingdom. (US and British officials remained convinced that there was sufficient evidence of Libyan involvement to continue to seek the suspects' extradition, despite various reports issued in the early 1990s which alleged that Iranian, Syrian and Palestinian agents—sometimes separately, sometimes in collaboration—had been responsible for the bombing.) In November the Security Council adopted a resolution (No. 883) providing for the strengthening of the economic sanctions in force against Libya in the event of the country's failure fully to comply with Resolutions 731 and 748 by 1 December. The sanctions, which were duly applied, included: the closure of all Libyan Arab Airlines' offices abroad; a ban on the sale of equipment and services for the civil aviation sector; the sequestration of all Libyan financial resources overseas; and a ban on the sale to Libya of specified items for use in the petroleum and gas industries.

In January 1994 the Scottish lawyer representing the two Lockerbie suspects stated that they might be willing to stand trial in The Hague; this was subsequently endorsed as an appropriate venue by Qaddafi. In February, however, US President Bill Clinton recommended that an embargo be imposed on Libya's sales of petroleum (which accounted for some 98% of its export earnings) if the country continued to defy the international community. In mid-1996, following its repeated failure to persuade the UN to agree yet more stringent sanctions against Libya, the US Congress approved unilateral 'secondary' sanctions against Libya (and Iran). The Iran-Libya Sanctions Act (ILSA) sought to penalize companies operating in US markets that were investing more than US $40m. (later amended to $20m.) in Libya's oil and gas industries.

In July 1997 the Arab League, which had been criticized by Qaddafi for its lack of support, formally proposed that the two Libyan suspects in the Lockerbie case be tried by Scottish judges under Scottish law in a neutral country. In September the members of the League urged a relaxation of the air embargo on Libya and voted to defy UN sanctions by permitting aircraft carrying Qaddafi, and other flights for religious or humanitarian purposes, to land on their territory.

In August 1998 the United Kingdom and the USA proposed that the trial of the two Lockerbie suspects be held in the Netherlands under Scottish law and presided over by Scottish judges. (In April the official spokesman for the families of the British victims of the bombing, together with an expert in Scottish law, had held talks with Qaddafi in Libya, during which Qaddafi had agreed to the Netherlands as a suitable neutral country.) The UN Security Council adopted a resolution (No. 1192) welcoming the initiative and providing for the suspension of sanctions upon the arrival in the Netherlands of the two suspects; additional sanctions were threatened if the Libyan authorities did not comply with the resolution.

In December 1998 the UN Secretary-General, Kofi Annan, held a meeting with Qaddafi in Libya in an attempt to expedite a trial of the Lockerbie suspects. Shortly afterwards the GPC endorsed the principle of a trial, but requested that the USA and the United Kingdom remove 'all remaining obstacles'. In a bid to break the impasse arising from Qaddafi's demand that the trial include a panel of international judges, envoys from Saudi Arabia and South Africa were dispatched to Libya in January 1999 to negotiate with Qaddafi. In February it was reported that the envoys had reached an understanding with the Libyan leader whereby UN observers would be allowed to monitor the two Libyan suspects during the trial, to ensure that they were not questioned by US and British agents, and afterwards, if they were convicted and imprisoned in Scotland. The diplomatic initiative culminated in March with a visit by President Nelson Mandela of South Africa to Libya, during which Qaddafi undertook to surrender the suspects by 6 April. The two Libyans duly arrived for trial in the Netherlands on 5 April and were transferred to Camp Zeist, a former US airbase near Utrecht, designated Scottish territory for the purposes of the trial, where they were formally arrested and charged with murder, conspiracy to murder and contravention of the 1982 Aviation Security Act. The UN Security Council immediately voted to suspend sanctions against Libya indefinitely, although they were not to be permanently revoked until Libya had complied with other conditions stipulated in Resolution 1192 (including the payment of compensation to the families of victims of the Lockerbie bombing). The USA refused to remove the 'secondary' sanctions against Libya, but subsequently announced that it would permit the sale of food and medical items to Libya on a 'case-by-case' basis. In June 1999 the US and Libyan ambassadors to the UN took part in what represented the first official contact between the two countries in 18 years. During the talks the USA informed Libya that it could not support a permanent end to UN sanctions until Libya had fully complied with Resolution 1192.

The two Libyan suspects appeared before the Scottish court in the Netherlands for the first time in December 1999, at a pre-trial hearing to decide on the court's jurisdiction. The presiding Scottish judge ruled that the two suspects could be tried on all three charges, and that they could be described as members of the Libyan intelligence services. (Defence lawyers had argued that to describe the Libyans as such was irrelevant and prejudicial.) The trial of al-Megrahi and Fhimah eventually commenced on 3 May 2000; both pleaded not guilty to the charges brought against them, and defence lawyers accused a number of organizations, including militant Palestinian resistance groups, of perpetrating the bombing.

In January 2001 prosecution lawyers unexpectedly announced that they would no longer pursue charges of conspiracy to murder and contravention of the 1982 Aviation Security Act. Accordingly, the trial proceeded on the sole charge of murder. On 31 January 2001 the judges announced that they had unanimously found al-Megrahi guilty of the murder of 270 people and sentenced him to life imprisonment, with the recommendation that he serve a minimum of 20 years. The judges accepted that al-Megrahi was a member of the Libyan intelligence services, and although they acknowledged their awareness of what they termed 'uncertainties and qualifications' in the case, they concluded that the evidence against him combined to form 'a real and convincing pattern' which left them with no reasonable doubt as to his guilt. Fhimah, however, was unanimously acquitted, owing to lack of proof, and freed to return to Libya. Despite mounting pressure from Arab League states, the British Government asserted that sanctions against Libya would not be permanently revoked until Libya accepted responsibility for the bombing and paid 'substantial' compensation. The newly inaugurated US President, George W. Bush, also indicated his support for this stance, and in July 2001 ILSA was extended for a further five-year term.

Meanwhile, demands for further investigation into the bombing, and Qaddafi's role in it, were rejected by senior Scottish legal officials, who stated that there was insufficient evidence to justify any further proceedings against those alleged to have abetted al-Megrahi, despite the fact that he had apparently not acted alone. Lawyers for al-Megrahi subsequently lodged an appeal against his conviction; the hearing, before five Scottish judges, began at Camp Zeist in January 2002. Al-Megrahi's lawyers based their case on what they termed new 'strong circumstantial evidence', which raised the possibility that the bomb had been placed on the aircraft at London, United Kingdom, and not in Malta, as the trial judges had concluded. In February Seif al-Islam Qaddafi indicated that Libya would pay compensation to the families of those killed in the Lockerbie bombing, regardless of the outcome of the appeal. In March the appeal was unanimously rejected, and al-Megrahi was transferred to a prison in Scotland to begin his sentence.

In July 1999 Libya and the United Kingdom reached agreement on the full restoration of diplomatic relations after Qaddafi issued a statement in which he accepted Libya's 'general responsibility' for the death of Yvonne Fletcher, a British policewoman who was shot outside the Libyan People's Bureau in London in 1984, and agreed to co-operate with the investigation into the killing. The payment by Libya, in November 1999, of compensation to the victim's family facilitated the reopening of the British embassy in Tripoli the following month. In January 2000, however, the British Government confirmed that its customs officials had, in late 1999, seized a consignment of *Scud* missile parts that had arrived in the United Kingdom from Taiwan and was bound for Libya via Malta. (It subsequently transpired that the parts had been impounded in mid-1999, prior to the full restoration of diplomatic relations between the United Kingdom and Libya.) Despite this incident and the delivery of the Lockerbie trial verdict, the normalization of relations between the United Kingdom and Libya progressed and in March 2001 Libya appointed an ambassador to the United Kingdom for the first time in 17 years. In August 2002 a minister of the British Foreign and Commonwealth Office visited Libya for talks with Qaddafi.

In April 2003 it was confirmed that, following negotiations in London between senior British, US and Libyan representatives, Libya had agreed to accept civil responsibility for the actions of its officials in the Lockerbie case and would pay US $10m. in compensation to the families of the victims. Payment of the compensation was to be a three-stage process: $4m. would be paid to each family on the permanent lifting of UN sanctions; a further $4m. would follow upon the removal of unilateral US sanctions; and a final payment of $2m. would be made when Libya was removed from the list of countries that the USA deemed to support international terrorism. However, Libya would pay only an additional $1m. to each family if the USA did not complete the second and third stages.

After further negotiations, on 16 August 2003 Libya delivered a letter to the President of the UN Security Council stating that it: accepted 'responsibility for the actions of its officials' in the Lockerbie bombing; agreed to pay compensation to the families of the victims; pledged co-operation in any further Lockerbie inquiry; agreed to continue its co-operation in the 'war on terror'; and to take practical measures to ensure that such co-operation was effective. Following the transfer of US $2,700m. in compensation to the International Bank of Settlements, the United Kingdom submitted a draft resolution to the Security Council requesting the formal lifting of UN sanctions against Libya. It was feared, however, that France, which had demanded a similar amount of compensation for families of victims of the UTA bombing in 1989 (see above), would veto the resolution unless Libyan officials agreed to an additional payment. The United Kingdom, France and the USA eventually agreed to postpone the vote on the draft resolution to allow more time for such an agreement to be reached. On 12 September 2003 13 of the 15 members of the UN Security Council approved the lifting of the sanctions imposed against Libya; France and the USA abstained from the vote. Later that month Libya announced its intention to commence dialogue with the USA aimed at normalizing bilateral relations. Nevertheless, the US Administration continued to insist that unilateral sanctions would remain in place until the Libyan Government addressed ongoing US concerns such as the infringement of human rights in the country and the pursuit of weapons of mass destruction.

In September 2003, following an intervention by the French President, Jacques Chirac, the Libyan Government and the families of the UTA bombing had reached partial agreement on the payment of additional compensation to the victims' relatives. Talks between Libya and France in October aimed at reaching a final settlement regarding the issue of compensation for the UTA bombing were suspended following a number of disagreements between the two sides. However, in January 2004 Libya agreed to pay an additional US $170m. to the relatives of the victims; the payment was to be made in four equal instalments, resulting in the families of each victim receiving an additional $1m.

Meanwhile, in October 2003 an official of the US Department of State accused Libya of having increased its efforts to purchase components for biological and chemical weapons since the lifting of UN sanctions the previous month, and warned that Libya would be added to the group of countries described by President Bush as forming an 'axis of evil'—comprising Iran, Iraq and the Democratic People's Republic of Korea (North Korea). In mid-December, however, in an unexpected development, the British Prime Minister, Tony Blair, announced that Libya had agreed to disclose and dismantle its programme to develop weapons of mass destruction and long-range ballistic missiles. The statement was the culmination of nine months of clandestine negotiations between Qaddafi and British and US diplomats, during which the Libyan authorities had reportedly shown evidence of a 'well advanced' nuclear weapons programme, as well as the existence of large quantities of chemical weapons and bombs designed to carry poisonous gas. Libya also agreed to adhere to the Chemical Weapons Convention and to sign an additional protocol allowing the International Atomic Energy Agency (IAEA) to carry out random inspections of its facilities. Upon visiting a number of sites in Tripoli in late December, in order to commence the process of dismantling Libya's weapons development projects, the Director-General of the IAEA, Dr Muhammad el-Baradei, insisted that these projects had been in the initial stages of development, contradicting the assessment given by the United Kingdom and the USA. In January 2004 the US Department of State confirmed that British and US intelligence agents had, in October 2003, intercepted a shipment of centrifuges capable of developing weapons-grade uranium destined for Tripoli. Also in January 2004 it was announced that Libya had ratified the IAEA's Comprehensive Nuclear Test Ban Treaty.

Further disagreements in January 2004 between the USA, the United Kingdom and the IAEA concerning their respective roles in the process of dismantling Libya's weapons facilities were finally resolved late that month: it was agreed that US and British officials would be responsible for destroying and removing the nuclear material and that the IAEA would verify that the dismantling process was complete. In February Libyan officials held talks with the US Assistant Secretary of State in London and it was also confirmed that an American diplomat had been stationed in the US interests section of the Belgian embassy in Tripoli, providing the USA with its first permanent diplomatic presence in Libya for 25 years. Also in February the Libyan Secretary for Foreign Liaison and International Co-operation, Abd ar-Rahman Muhammad Shalgam, visited London for talks with his British counterpart and Prime Minister Blair; this represented the first meeting between cabinet-level ministers of the two countries in more than 20 years.

The Secretary of the General People's Committee, Shukri Muhammad Ghanem, caused controversy in late February 2004 when he claimed that compensation was being paid to the families of the Lockerbie victims in order to 'buy peace' and avoid sanctions, and that the country did not accept responsibility for the Lockerbie bombing; he also denied any Libyan involvement in the murder of Yvonne Fletcher. The following day, however, Shalgam issued a statement in which he announced his regret at Ghanem's comments and reiterated that Libya stood by its acceptance of responsibility for the Lockerbie bombing. The USA subsequently lifted the restrictions on its citizens travelling to Libya. In March Libya signed an additional IAEA protocol allowing the agency to carry out random inspections of its nuclear facilities; moreover, Libya commenced the destruction of its supplies of chemical weapons and transported all of its remaining nuclear weapons-related equipment to the USA. Later that month the Organisation for the Prohibition of Chemical Weapons verified that Libya's declaration of its chemical weapons inventory (submitted to the UN in early March) had been accurate, after a series of inspections carried out by the agency's officials. In May it was announced that Libya would no longer conduct military trade with those countries that it believed to be involved in the proliferation of weapons of mass destruction.

Meanwhile, in late March 2004 William Burns, the US Assistant Secretary of the Bureau of Near Eastern Affairs, became the highest-ranking US official to visit Libya in more than 30 years; the principal issues under discussion were further moves towards the lifting of US sanctions on Libya and the restoration of normal bilateral relations. In April the USA announced that it would remove the restrictions that prevented US petroleum companies and banks from conducting commercial activities in Libya and that Libyan students would be allowed to study in the USA; however, it also declared that all Libyan assets held in the USA would remain frozen. In June it was revealed that Libya had resumed exports of petroleum to the USA. At the end of the month formal diplomatic relations were re-established between the two countries when a US liaison office was opened in Tripoli, and it was reported that Libya was preparing to establish diplomatic representation in Washington, DC. In September President Bush lifted all travel restrictions for charter and commercial flights between Libya and the USA. He also announced that the US $1,300m. of Libyan assets held in the USA or in US banks abroad would be unfrozen. In February 2005 the US authorities lifted all restrictions on Libyan diplomats travelling within the USA.

Relations between Libya and the United Kingdom continued to improve in 2004. In March Blair visited Tripoli and held talks with Qaddafi, after which the British Prime Minister stated that there was genuine hope for a 'new relationship', while Qaddafi insisted that he was willing to join the international 'war on terror'. It was also announced that British police officers would travel to Libya in April to continue investigations into the murder of Fletcher. In October 2005 Libya signed a memorandum of understanding with the British Government, which allowed for the deportation from the United Kingdom of Libyans suspected of involvement in terrorist activities. (The United Kingdom is legally prevented from deporting foreign nationals to countries that it suspects of using inhumane or degrading treatment.) Blair visited Libya again in May 2007, as part of a wider tour of Africa during his final weeks in office. At the same time, the British oil company BP (formerly British Petroleum) announced that it was to return to Libya, more than three decades after its expulsion from the country when Qaddafi had nationalized the oil industry in 1974; BP was granted onshore and offshore exploratory rights in a deal worth an estimated US $900m., a development welcomed by Blair as evidence of a 'transformed' bilateral relationship.

Meanwhile, in December 2004, with the unilateral sanctions imposed upon Libya by the USA having been lifted, Libya paid the second instalment of its compensation to the families of those killed in the Lockerbie explosion. In August 2005 the head of the Senate Foreign Relations Committee, Senator Richard Lugar, visited Libya to hold talks with Qaddafi; two months previously officials from the US State Department had praised Libya for its co-operation in the fight against international terrorism. In May 2006 the US Secretary of State, Condoleezza Rice, announced the US Administration's intention to restore full diplomatic relations between the two countries in recognition of Libya's 'continued commitment to its renunciation of terrorism', a development regarded by observers as the natural culmination of a process initiated in 2003 by Qaddafi's decision to abandon Libya's nuclear weapons programme; the US liaison office in Tripoli was formally upgraded to an embassy at the end of that month. In June 2006 Libya was removed from the US Department of State's list of countries deemed to support international terrorism. The renewal of full ties was expected significantly to boost both political and economic co-operation between the two nations, and was extended by the Bush Administration as an implicit incentive to the Iranian and North Korean Governments to dismantle their respective nuclear programmes.

In June 2006 tensions arose when Libyan lawyers in the USA insisted that, as a result of the expiration in December 2004 of an agreement concerning the transfer of the final portion of compensation for families of the victims of the Lockerbie bombing, the Libyan Government was no longer obligated to pay the final US $2m. promised to each family. Nevertheless, in July the USA lifted all air transport sanctions against Libya. In March 2007 the Libyan Government announced that it had reached an agreement with the USA that would aid the development of Libya's programme of nuclear energy generation; US officials contested that negotiations had been restricted to the possible establishment of a nuclear medicine centre in Libya. In further evidence of the improving relationship between the two countries, Shalgam made an official visit to Washington, DC, in January 2008, and held discussions with Condoleezza Rice—the first State Department visit by a Libyan foreign secretary in almost four decades. Rice called on Libya to improve its human rights record and to resolve the problem of outstanding compensation payments still owed to families of victims of the Lockerbie bombing; the US Secretary of State also pledged to visit Tripoli at an 'appropriate' time.

In January 2000 (shortly after the revelation of the seizure of missile parts by the United Kingdom) the EU withdrew an invitation to Qaddafi, issued by the Commission President, Romano Prodi, to visit the European Commission headquarters in Brussels, Belgium, on the grounds that Libya had not accepted EU conditions regarding commitment to human rights, democracy, free trade and support for the Middle East peace process. Apparently in reprisal, Libya immediately announced major commercial contracts with Russia and the People's Republic of China. Qaddafi none the less attended the EU-Africa summit meeting in Cairo, Egypt, in April, at which talks with Prodi and other European officials were described as 'positive'. Relations with the EU, and particularly with France, generally improved following talks in early 1996 between Libyan and EU representatives in Belgium. In July Qaddafi granted the French authorities investigating the 1989 bombing of the UTA passenger aircraft unprecedented access to Libyan evidence. This resulted in February 1998 in a judge's decision to try *in absentia* six Libyans suspected of involvement in the attack, and in March 1999 a French court sentenced the six suspects to life imprisonment. The French authorities issued international arrest warrants for the Libyans, and threatened to intensify sanctions against Libya if it did not impose the verdicts on the accused. In July Libya began payment of some US $31m. in compensation to the families of those killed in the bomb attack. France stated that this represented an acknowledgement by Libya of the responsibility of its citizens for the bombing, although attempts by French lawyers on behalf of the victims' families to prosecute Qaddafi for complicity in the bombing of the aircraft were unsuccessful. Nevertheless, it was announced in January 2004 that Libya had agreed to pay an additional $170m. to the relatives of the victims (see above). During an official visit to Libya in November, French President Jacques Chirac affirmed his commitment to rebuilding diplomatic ties with Libya. In December 2005 the Libyan Government was ordered by a French court to pay an additional $4m. in compensation to families of victims of the 1989 bombing not included in the previous agreement. Despite the ongoing process of reparation, relations between the French and Libyan Governments improved in 2005 after France expressed its interest in assisting the development of civil nuclear technology in Libya. In March 2006 a deal on co-operation regarding the development of nuclear energy in Libya was signed by representatives of the two countries during a visit to Tripoli by the Director of France's Commissariat à l'Energie Atomique; it was the first such agreement since Libya had relinquished its nuclear weapons programme in 2003. In October 2006 it was reported that Libya and France were conducting negotiations about further possible military accords. Meanwhile, in April 2004 Qaddafi, who was visiting Europe for the first time in 15 years, met with several senior EU politicians in Brussels and addressed the European Commission. The lifting of economic sanctions and an arms embargo imposed on Libya by the EU in 1986 was ratified by EU ministers in October 2004.

In October 1996, meanwhile, the German authorities announced that evidence existed to prove the Libyan Government's direct involvement in a bomb attack on a discothèque in Berlin in 1986. Arrest warrants were subsequently issued for the four Libyans suspected of carrying out the bombing, but in March 1997 a German parliamentary delegation recommended that regular contact between the German Parliament and the GPC should continue. In April 1998 Libya resolved to allow the German authorities to question the Libyan suspects. In May the two countries signed an agreement on economic co-operation. Following a lengthy trial, in November 2001 a court in Berlin sentenced four people, including a Libyan national, to between 12 and 14 years' imprisonment for their involvement in the bomb attack. Although Qaddafi's personal complicity in the incident could not be proven, the presiding judge stated that there was sufficient evidence to ascertain that the bombing had been carried out by members of the Libyan secret service and employees of the Libyan People's Bureau in the former East Germany.

In August 2003 the Qaddafi International Foundation for Charitable Associations (now the Qaddafi Development Foundation), a charity run by Seif al-Islam Qaddafi, offered to compensate the relatives of the three victims of the Berlin bomb attack. While negotiations between the USA and Libya regarding this compensation continued, a new round of talks between Germany and Libya began in July 2004 to decide upon compensation payments for the non-US citizens injured in the attack. The talks were finalized in the following month, and the Libyan authorities signed a deal in September agreeing to pay US $35m. to compensate some 160 non-US victims. The agreement signalled the start of improved relations between Germany and Libya, and in October Chancellor Gerhard Schröder paid an official visit to Libya. In talks with Schröder, Qaddafi requested compensation for the millions of landmines left behind by the Nazi German forces during the Second World War. While no compensation was offered, the German Chancellor agreed to provide assistance with mine detection and medical aid for victims. In March 2006 the trial commenced in Mannheim, Germany, of a German engineer arrested in 2004 on charges of aiding Libya's nuclear weapons programme; the arrest followed the interception in 2003 of centrifuge parts on board a German vessel destined for Libya. In July 2006 the case was dismissed owing to an apparent withholding of evidence by the prosecution, and it remained unclear as to whether a retrial was to be conducted. In November the German Minister of Foreign Affairs, Frank-Walter Steinmeier, visited Tripoli during a tour of North Africa, which was intended to consolidate bilateral relations. Steinmeier praised the progress made by the Libyan Government in renouncing terrorism and its nuclear weapons programme, and urged Libya to continue its gradual return to the international fold.

In February 1998 a Spanish minister visited Tripoli, following an announcement of Spain's intention to renew political and economic ties with Libya. However, the decision by France, Spain, Italy and Portugal to create a rapid reaction force in the Mediterranean was strongly condemned by Qaddafi. In July Italy formally apologized for its colonial rule of Libya, and commitments were made to improve bilateral relations. The Italian Minister of Foreign Affairs, Lamberto Dini, visited Libya in April 1999, immediately after the suspension of international sanctions. Italy's Prime Minister, Massimo D'Alema, travelled to Libya in December, thus becoming the first EU premier to visit the country since 1992. In December 2000 officials from the two countries signed accords regarding political consultation, visas and the removal of landmines during talks in Rome. In September 2003, just days after the lifting of UN sanctions against Libya, the Spanish Prime Minister, José María Aznar López, visited Tripoli for talks with Qaddafi. In February 2004 the Italian Prime Minister, Silvio Berlusconi, became the first Western leader to meet with Qaddafi following the Libyan renouncement of its nuclear weapons programme. In August Berlusconi exerted pressure on Qaddafi to place stricter border controls on the country's northern coastline following an influx of illegal immigrants into the Italian island of Lampedusa from Libya. In October, as a result of a sudden increase in the number of illegal immigrants arriving from North Africa (up to 1,700 a week), the Italian Government began a mass expulsion of illegal immigrants to Libya. Having agreed to assist with the immigration problem, Libya returned some 1,000 of these people to Egypt. Also in October Qaddafi agreed to lift a ban that prohibited some 20,000 Italian settlers who had been expelled from Libya in 1970 (following Qaddafi's rise to power) from visiting the country.

Diplomatic relations between Libya and Italy soured, however, in early 2006. In February the Italian consulate in Benghazi and the residence of the consul were attacked and set alight by protesters, following the publication in numerous countries, including Italy, of cartoons originally printed in a Danish newspaper depicting the Prophet Muhammad, which were deemed to be offensive towards Islam. A day prior to the protests, the Italian Minister without Portfolio for Institutional Reforms and Devolution, Roberto Calderoli, had appeared on Italian television wearing an item of clothing bearing one of the cartoons; it was claimed that Calderoli's television appearance had provoked the disturbances in Benghazi, during which 11 people were killed. Libyan Secretary for National Security Nasser al-Mabrouk was suspended and referred for investigation over the conduct of security forces during the protests; Calderoli later resigned from the Italian Council of Ministers. In the immediate aftermath of the protests, Berlusconi and Qaddafi gave assurances that bilateral relations would not be harmed. However, in March a statement by Qaddafi appeared to contradict his previous stance. The Libyan leader was quoted by Italian newspapers as warning of further attacks against Italian interests should the issue of compensation for Italian colonial rule of Libya not be resolved.

Meanwhile, Libya came under heavy criticism from EU officials in May 2004 after five Bulgarian nurses and a Palestinian doctor were sentenced to death for deliberately infecting more than 400 children at a Benghazi hospital in 1999 with blood containing the HIV virus. The trials were also criticized by international human rights associations as being unfair, and the nurses stated that their confessions had been extracted through torture. In December 2004 it was announced that Libya would review the sentences and later in the month Seif al-Islam Qaddafi reportedly stated that the medics would not be executed. By March 2005, however, the sentences remained in place and the medics launched an official appeal. The judgment regarding the medics' appeal, which was expected in May, was delayed until November. Meanwhile, Libya continued to reject calls from Bulgaria, the USA and the EU to release the medics, and demanded compensation from Bulgaria for the families affected by the case. The Bulgarian Government refused, stating that any payment would constitute an admission of the medics' guilt. In November the Supreme Court rescheduled the ruling for January 2006. However, in December 2005 the previous sentences were overturned by the Supreme Court and a retrial was ordered.

The retrial began in May 2006 but, following a brief initial hearing, was adjourned for procedural reasons until 13 June. Despite calls from the presiding judge to accelerate the pace of legal proceedings, which were now into their seventh year, the trial was beset by numerous subsequent delays and adjournments. Eventually, however, in December 2006, notwithstanding data arising from genetic analysis that strongly suggested that the children had been infected with HIV prior to the defendants' arrival in Libya in 1998, the original verdict was upheld and the six death sentences were reinstated. The EU Commissioner for Justice, Franco Frattini, called for the ruling to be reviewed, branding it an 'obstacle' to comfortable EU-Libyan relations, while the office of the UN High Commissioner for Human Rights urged the Libyan Government to intervene, citing 'serious and credible concerns' about the legitimacy of the trial. A few days after the ruling, the Government declared that it would not succumb to international pressure to invalidate the verdict, insisting that the Supreme Court had sole jurisdiction in the matter.

In January 2007 Qaddafi denounced 'Western intervention and pressure', reiterating the Government's argument that the outcome of the trial was a strictly juridical matter. However, it was reported later that month that the Libyan Government had extended an offer to free the six medical staff in exchange for the release of al-Megrahi, convicted for his part in the Lockerbie bombing (see above). Qaddafi, who claimed that the infections had arisen as a result of illicit experiments conducted on the children at the hospital by either the US or Israeli state intelligence agencies, linked the HIV case with the Lockerbie attack on numerous occasions, and demanded compensation of US $2,700m. to be paid to the affected families—the same amount tendered by the Libyan Government to the families of Lockerbie victims. In early 2007 the six defendants were also charged with slandering the Libyan police service, owing to their allegations of having been tortured during official interrogations; a verdict in the ensuing trial was expected to be delivered on 27 May. Meanwhile, in February the defence filed an appeal against the verdict reached in December 2006, but this was rejected in mid-July 2007 and the death sentences were upheld. A few days later, however, the High Judicial Court commuted the sentences to terms of life imprisonment, following the successful brokerage of a compensation deal, according to which the victims' families would receive a reported US $1m. for each child infected. The Bulgarian Government urged Libya to allow the medics to complete their sentences in Bulgaria, and Benita Ferrero-Waldner, the EU Commissioner responsible for External Relations and European Neighbourhood Policy, and Cécilia Sarkozy, then the wife of the French President Nicolas Sarkozy, both travelled to Tripoli to lobby the Libyan Government to this end. Libya finally acquiesced to the Bulgarian request, and the medics were duly released from Libyan detention on 24 July. Upon their return to Bulgaria, they were immediately pardoned by the President of that country, Georgi Parvanov, a decision that incensed Qaddafi, who threatened to sever diplomatic ties with Bulgaria and urged other member states of the Arab League to do likewise. In the following month Seif al-Islam Qaddafi stated publicly that the medics had been tortured during their detention, although the Libyan Government continued to refute such a claim.

During the late 1990s and 2000s Qaddafi oscillated between identifying Libya as an African nation on the one hand, and emphasizing Libya's links with the Arab world on the other, often to suit his own political aims. In mid-1998 Qaddafi announced his intention to ally Libya more closely with African rather than Arab countries; later in the year numerous African heads of state visited Tripoli, all of whom defied UN sanctions by travelling to Libya by air. In October, as further evidence of his dissatisfaction with Arab states, Qaddafi changed the name of Libya's mission to the Arab League from 'permanent' to 'resident'. In September 1999, on the 30th anniversary of his seizure of power, Qaddafi hosted an extraordinary OAU summit in Sirte, at which he presented his vision of a United States of Africa and demanded that Africa be given veto power on the UN Security Council. The 'Sirte Declaration', a final document adopted by the 43 attending heads of state and government, called for the strengthening of the OAU, the establishment of a pan-African parliament, African monetary union and an African court of justice. At a further extraordinary summit of the OAU in Sirte in March 2001 it was announced that the organization's member states had overwhelmingly endorsed the proposals to declare the formation of the AU. In July 2002 Qaddafi travelled to Durban, South Africa, for the 38th and final summit of the OAU, which saw the formal creation of the new AU, chaired by South African

President Thabo Mbeki. During the summit Mbeki and numerous other African heads of state attempted to persuade Qaddafi to abandon his hostility towards the New Partnership for Africa's Development, a contract between Africa and the international community under which, in exchange for aid and investment, the African states agreed to strive towards democracy and good governance. In October Libya notified the Arab League of its intention to withdraw from the organization. Although no official reason for the withdrawal was given, reports indicated that senior Libyan officials had cited the Arab League's 'inefficiency' in dealing with the crises in Iraq and the Palestinian territories as its motives. In March 2003 Libyan officials confirmed that the threat of withdrawal was 'serious and official'.

Meanwhile, Qaddafi's growing influence in Africa was somewhat checked in January 2003 following the removal of some 300 Libyan troops from the Central African Republic, to whose Government they had been providing protection. In the previous month an agreement between Libya and Zimbabwe that would have resulted in the exchange of Libyan fuel for Zimbabwean beef, sugar and tobacco was abandoned. Attempts to revive the trade pact in mid-2003, which would have resulted in Zimbabwe mortgaging its petroleum assets to Libya, proved unsuccessful, and the abolition of the Secretariat for African Unity was widely interpreted as evidence of the failure of Qaddafi's African policy. In June 2004 it was reported that in mid-2003 Qaddafi had ordered the assassination of Crown Prince Abdullah of Saudi Arabia, the kingdom's de facto leader, following a dispute between the two leaders at the Arab League summit held in March. (Libya also reportedly accused Saudi Arabia of financing Libyan opposition groups that had attempted to assassinate Qaddafi.) Libyan officials strongly refuted these allegations; however, in December 2004 Saudi Arabia recalled its ambassador from Tripoli and dismissed the Libyan ambassador in the Saudi capital, Riyadh. In the same month Libya announced that it had decided to relinquish its chairmanship of the UMA, assumed in December 2003, citing the failure of the organization to achieve regional co-operation.

In May 2006 Sudanese President Omar Hassan Ahmad al-Bashir expressed gratitude to Qaddafi for the latter's role in finding a resolution to the crisis in Darfur and proposed the establishment of a tripartite committee, comprising representatives of the Libyan and Sudanese Governments and the Sudan Liberation Movement, to oversee the implementation of the peace agreement signed between the two latter parties on 5 May (see the chapter on Sudan). In October Qaddafi and Egyptian President Muhammad Hosni Mubarak met in Tripoli to discuss the situation in Darfur, whereupon they concurred on the importance of the AU in resolving the crisis, and urged a rejection of foreign intervention, articulating their mutual opposition to a planned deployment of UN peace-keeping forces therein. In November Qaddafi accused the USA and other Western countries of involving themselves in the Darfur crisis not because of genuine compassion but in order to secure oil, and, by means of the deployment of UN troops, to effect the return of colonialism to Africa. In July 2007 Libya hosted an international conference on Darfur, which was co-chaired by the AU and the UN.

In June 2006 ministers responsible for foreign affairs from Algeria, Libya, Mauritania, Morocco and Tunisia convened in Tripoli to discuss a potential revivification of the five-nation UMA, which had remained dormant for more than a decade predominately owing to Algerian–Moroccan disagreements concerning Western Sahara (see the chapters on Algeria and Morocco). If revived, the Union was expected markedly to improve political and economic co-operation among the countries of North Africa. In January 2007 Qaddafi met with the Presidents of Algeria and Egypt in Sirte to discuss the respective situations in Iraq, Lebanon and Sudan. In the same month a three-day period of mourning was declared in Libya, following the execution of deposed Iraqi President Saddam Hussain in December 2006. In March 2007 Qaddafi announced his decision to boycott the Arab League summit meeting in Riyadh, insisting that Libya was an African nation and had 'turned its back to Arabs'. Later that year Qaddafi embarked upon a tour of western Africa, including visits to Côte d'Ivoire, Guinea, Mali and Sierra Leone, and culminating with his attendance in July at an AU summit meeting, held in the Ghanaian capital, Accra, which focused predominantly on proposals to establish a pan-African government. However, Qaddafi was reported to have left the session abruptly when the majority of those present rejected his call for the immediate creation of a United States of Africa, and in February 2008 he threatened to sever Libyan ties with Africa, pledging to transfer Libya's African investments to alternative destinations in Arab and European countries if his vision for African unity continued to be ignored.

Meanwhile, in January 2004 it was reported that a senior Israeli diplomat had held talks in Paris, France, in December 2003 with Libyan representatives, with the aim of establishing diplomatic relations between the two countries. While an Israeli official confirmed that a meeting had taken place, the Libyan Government denied that any contact had been made. Paris was the scene of another controversial meeting in December 2007, when Qaddafi made an official visit to the French capital at the invitation of President Nicolas Sarkozy—the first such invitation from a Western nation since Libya had abandoned its nuclear weapons programme in 2003 and interpreted by some as a reward for the Libyan leader's decision to release the Bulgarian medics earlier in 2007 (see above). The visit provoked strong censure from both French and Libyan opposition politicians, as well as international human rights groups, owing to Libya's questionable human rights record. In an attempt to appease his critics, Sarkozy insisted that he had broached the issue of human rights with the Libyan leader, but Qaddafi was reported as saying that human rights had not in fact been discussed. During Qaddafi's visit deals worth an estimated €10,000m. were signed between the two countries, including plans for a joint-venture nuclear-powered water desalination plant and the sale of French Airbus aeroplanes; Libya also expressed a keen interest in the future purchase of military equipment, including 14 fighter jets, 35 helicopters and an air defence radar system.

Government

Power is vested in the people through People's Congresses, Popular Committees, Trade Unions, Vocational Syndicates, and with the General People's Congress (GPC) and its General Secretariat. The Head of State is the Revolutionary Leader, elected by the GPC; however, Col Muammar al-Qaddafi himself rejects this nomenclature and all other titles. Executive power is exercised by the General People's Committee. The country is divided into three provinces, 10 governorates and 1,500 administrative communes.

Defence

As assessed at November 2007, Libya's active armed forces totalled 76,000 (including an estimated 25,000 conscripts): army an estimated 50,000; air force 18,000; navy 8,000. Military service is by selective conscription, lasting up to two years. There was additionally a People's Militia of some 40,000 reserves. Libya's defence budget for 2007 was LD 807m.

Economic Affairs

In 2006, according to estimates by the World Bank, Libya's gross national income (GNI), measured at average 2004–06 prices, was US $44,011m., equivalent to $7,380 per head. During 1996–2006, it was estimated, the population increased at an average annual rate of 2.0%, while gross domestic product (GDP) per head increased, in real terms, by an average of 1.7% per year. According to the African Development Bank (ADB), overall GDP increased, in real terms, at an average annual rate of 3.5% in 1996–2006. Real GDP increased by 5.0% in 2006.

Agriculture (including forestry and fishing) contributed 2.8% of GDP in 2005, according to preliminary figures, and engaged 6.3% of the employed labour force. The principal subsistence crops are wheat and barley; other crops include potatoes, olives, tomatoes, onions, watermelons, dates and citrus fruits. Output is limited by climatic conditions and irrigation problems, although cultivable land was being significantly increased by the Great Man-made River Project, whereby water was to be carried from the south of the country to the north and thence to the east and west. In July 2005 contracts for engineering, construction and supply during the third phase of the project were awarded to a Turkish company, Tekfen, and SNC Lavalin of Canada; however, the project was not expected to be completed for more than 20 years. Agriculture is based mainly on animal husbandry; sheep are the principal livestock, but goats, cattle, camels, horses and chickens are also kept. During 1996–2006, according to the ADB, agricultural GDP increased at an average annual rate of 2.1%; the sector's GDP increased by 2.0% in 2006.

Industry (including mining, manufacturing, construction and power) contributed 77.3% of GDP in 2005, according to preliminary figures, and engaged 20.6% of the employed labour force. Virtually all of the industrial sector is state-controlled. During 1996–2006, according to ADB figures, the GDP of the industrial sector increased at an average annual rate of 2.5%; industrial GDP increased by 3.7% in 2006.

Mining contributed 72.2% of GDP in 2005, according to preliminary figures, but engaged only 4.7% of the employed labour force in 2004. The petroleum and natural gas sector contributed an estimated 71.3% of GDP in 2005, and engaged 2.7% of the employed labour force in 2004. Libya's economy depends almost entirely on its petroleum and natural gas resources. The National Oil Corporation of Libya controls about three-quarters of the petroleum produced in Libya, largely through production-sharing agreements. At the end of 2006 proven recoverable reserves of petroleum were estimated at 41,500m. barrels, the largest proven reserves in Africa and sufficient to enable production to be maintained—at that year's levels, averaging 1.84m. barrels per day (b/d)—for some 62 years. As a member of the Organization of the Petroleum Exporting Countries (OPEC, see p. 373), Libya is subject to production quotas agreed by the Organization's Conference. Libya's natural gas reserves are extensive (estimated at 1,320,000m. cu m at the end of 2006). Libya also has reserves of iron ore, salt, limestone, clay, sulphur and gypsum. The GDP of the mining sector increased, in real terms, by an annual average of 3.8% in 2000–05; mining GDP increased by an estimated 5.1% in 2005.

Manufacturing contributed 1.4% of GDP in 2005, according to preliminary figures, and engaged 13.8% of the employed labour force. The principal manufacturing activity is petroleum refining. There are five refineries, including facilities at Brega, Ras Lanouf and Az-Zawiyah. A petrochemicals site is located at Brega, and in the mid-2000s plans were under way to construct a new refinery complex at Sebha, 700 km south of Tripoli. Other important manufacturing activities were the production of iron, steel and cement, and the processing of agricultural products. According to the ADB, the GDP of the manufacturing sector declined at an average annual rate of 0.7% during 1996–2006; the sector's GDP increased by 2.0% in 2006.

Energy is derived principally from petroleum (which contributed 80.7% of total electricity output in 2004), but another source is natural gas (19.3%). Libya is a net exporter of fuels (less than 10% of petroleum production is used for domestic energy requirements), with imports of mineral fuels and related products comprising only an estimated 0.4% of the value of merchandise imports in 2005.

Services contributed an estimated 19.9% of GDP in 2005, according to preliminary figures, and engaged 73.1% of the employed labour force. In an attempt to stimulate growth in the tourism sector, the Government has invested heavily in recent years to expand and rehabilitate the country's tourism infrastructure. Visitor arrivals had declined from some 1.8m. in 1995 to 857,952 in 2002, but increased to 999,343 in 2004. Receipts from tourism amounted to some US $301m. in 2005. During 1996–2006, according to ADB figures, the GDP of the services sector increased at an annual average rate of 5.2%; services GDP increased by 7.2% in 2006.

In 2006 Libya recorded a visible trade surplus of US $35,742m., and there was a surplus of $34,290m. on the current account of the balance of payments. In 2004 the principal sources of imports were Italy (which provided 18.3% of total imports), Germany (12.0%), Japan and the Republic of Korea. The principal market for exports in 2000 was Italy (42.6%); Germany, Spain, Turkey and France were also important purchasers. The petroleum sector is overwhelmingly Libya's principal generator of exports revenue: exports of mineral fuels and lubricants accounted for 92.6% of Libya's export earnings in 1998. The principal imports in 2005 were plant and equipment, basic manufactures, and food and live animals.

A budgetary surplus of some LD 25,131m. was recorded in 2006, compared with a surplus of LD 15,933m. in the previous year. Libya's total external debt was about US $3,800m. at the end of 1999, according to estimates quoted by the *Middle East Economic Digest*. According to the Central Bank of Libya, the annual rate of inflation averaged 3.1% during 2000–06; consumer prices increased by 3.5% in 2006. The rate of unemployment was unofficially estimated to be about 30% in 2004.

Libya is a member of the Arab Monetary Fund (see p. 175), the Council of Arab Economic Unity (see p. 222), the Islamic Development Bank (see p. 329), the Organization of Arab Petroleum Exporting Countries (OAPEC, see p. 366), OPEC (see p. 373) and the Union du Maghreb arabe (UMA—Union of the Arab Maghreb, see p. 414) In July 2004 Libya was permitted to begin accession negotiations with the World Trade Organization (WTO, see p. 396), having first applied to join the WTO in 2001.

Prospects for the improvement and modernization of the Libyan economy were bolstered during 2003–04 by a number of extremely important political decisions, including the appointment in mid-2003 of Shukri Muhammad Ghanem, a former Libyan representative to OPEC, as Secretary of the General People's Committee. Ghanem announced plans to divest more than 360 state-owned entities, although he emphasized that the privatization scheme would not involve companies in the hydrocarbons or chemical sectors. The replacement of Ghanem as Secretary by Deputy Secretary for Production Dr al-Baghdadi Ali al-Mahmoudi in March 2006 was widely interpreted as a reverse as far as prospects for further economic reforms were concerned. In February 2007, amid considerable frustration that Libya had not taken sufficient advantage of significant potential benefits such as high petroleum revenues and the lifting of sanctions (see below), the Libyan Economic Development Board was launched, with the principal aim of encouraging a more competitive economy with a high level of entrepreneurial activity. (The new body formed part of the National Economic Strategy—an ambitious plan for reforming and modernizing the economy initiated in 2005 with a group of US advisers.) A Libyan Stock Exchange Market was established in March 2007. Meanwhile, the decision by the Libyan Government in September 2003 to accept civil responsibility for the Lockerbie bombing (see Recent History) facilitated the formal removal of UN sanctions, which had been imposed in 1992 and suspended in 1999, and in April 2004 the USA lifted the unilateral 'secondary' sanctions, which had outlawed commercial activities and financial transactions between Libyan and US companies since 1996. In June 2006 the USA removed Libya from its list of state sponsors of terrorism, thus facilitating the Government's aim of attracting more foreign direct investment, particularly in the hydrocarbons sector. In late 2007 41 oil exploration licences were being tendered in the latest international round, with much competition reported. However, in early 2008 Libya placed conditions on a US $900m. exploration project agreed with British company BP, namely the repatriation of convicted Lockerbie bomber al-Megrahi. The Libyan Government has pledged to increase petroleum production capacity to more than 3m. b/d by 2015. It was announced in late 2006 that an oil refinery costing around $3,000m. would be constructed in western Libya in order to supply other Arab, African and US markets. In early 2006 the IMF praised the authorities for achieving success in their attempts at economic diversification; however, by mid-2006 only some 66 out of the planned 216 small enterprises had been privatized, and it was announced that the programme would be broadened to include sectors such as insurance, health and transport. Attempts are under way to develop the country's largely untapped tourism potential after the enactment of a five-year investment plan, at a cost of some $7,000m., and in February 2004 the lifting of sanctions on US citizens travelling to Libya significantly opened up the tourism market. However, in November 2007 Libya introduced the requirement that Western passports be translated into Arabic in order to gain entry to the country. In September of that year Seif al-Islam Qaddafi unveiled the Green Mountain eco-tourism project, based in the ancient city of Cyrene; it was hoped that the project would further bolster the tourism sector and help preserve the city's previously vulnerable antiquities.

Education

Education is compulsory for children between six and 15 years of age. Primary education begins at the age of six and lasts for six years. Secondary education, from the age of 12, is divided into two three-year periods: an intermediate and vocational stage, and a further secondary and advanced vocational stage. In 2004/05 enrolment at the secondary level was equivalent to 98.4% of the relevant age-group. Libya also has institutes for agricultural, technical and vocational training, of which there were 84 in 2004. In 1995 the number of public universities had reached 13, but subsequent policy changes resulted in a reduction of this number, to nine, by the mid-2000s. In 1992 enrolment at the tertiary level was equivalent to 18.4% of the relevant age-group; in 2004 there were an estimated 196,500 students enrolled in tertiary education.

LIBYA

Public Holidays

2008: 10 January*† (Muharram, Islamic New Year), 19 January* (Ashoura), 20 March* (Mouloud, Birth of Muhammad), 28 March (Evacuation Day), 11 June (Evacuation Day), 30 July* (Leilat al-Meiraj, Ascension of Muhammad), 1 September (Revolution Day), 1 October* (Id al-Fitr, end of Ramadan), 7 October (Evacuation Day), 9 December* (Id al-Adha, Feast of the Sacrifice), 29 December*† (Muharram, Islamic New Year).

2009: 7 January*‡ (Ashoura), 9 March* (Mouloud, Birth of Muhammad), 28 March (Evacuation Day), 11 June (Evacuation Day), 19 July* (Leilat al-Meiraj, Ascension of Muhammad), 1 September (Revolution Day), 20 September* (Id al-Fitr, end of Ramadan), 7 October (Evacuation Day), 27 November* (Id al-Adha, Feast of the Sacrifice), 18 December* (Muharram, Islamic New Year), 27 December*‡ (Ashoura).

* These holidays are dependent on the Islamic lunar calendar and may vary by one or two days from the dates given.

† This festival occurs twice (marking the start of the Islamic years AH 1429 and 1430) within the same Gregorian year.

‡ This festival occurs twice (in the Islamic years AH 1430 and 1431) within the same Gregorian year.

Weights and Measures

The metric system is in force.

Statistical Survey

Sources (unless otherwise stated): National Corporation for Information and Documentation; Census and Statistical Dept, Secretariat of Planning, Sharia Damascus 40, 2nd Floor, Tripoli; tel. (21) 3331731; Central Bank of Libya, POB 1103, Sharia al-Malik Seoud, Tripoli; tel. (21) 3333591; fax (21) 4441488; e-mail info@cbl.gov.ly; internet www.cbl.gov.ly.

Area and Population

AREA, POPULATION AND DENSITY

Area (sq km)	1,775,500*
Population (census results)	
August 1995 (provisional)	
Males	2,236,943
Females	2,168,043
Total	4,404,986†
2003 (provisional)	5,678,484
Population (UN estimates at mid-year)	
2005	5,918,000
2006	6,039,000
2007	6,160,000
Density (per sq km) at mid-2007	3.5

* 685,524 sq miles.
† Excluding 406,916 non-Libyans.

Sources: UN, *World Population Prospects: The 2006 Revision*; National Authority for Information and Authentication.

POPULATION BY REGION
(1995 census, provisional figures)

Al-Batnan	151,240	Misratah (Misurata)	488,573
Jebel Akhdar	381,165	Najghaza	244,553
Banghazi (Benghazi)	665,615	Tarabulus (Tripoli)	1,313,996
Al-Wosta	240,574	Az-Zawiyah (Zawia)	517,395
Al-Wahat	62,056	Jebel Gharbi	316,970
Al-Jufra	39,335	Fazzan (Fezzan)	314,029
Sofuljin	76,401	**Total**	**4,811,902**

PRINCIPAL TOWNS
(population at census of 2003)

Tarabulus (Tripoli, the capital)	1,149,957	Az-Zawiyah (Zawia)	197,177
Banghazi (Benghazi)	636,992	Al-Jabal al-Akhader	194,185
Misratah (Misurata)	360,521	Ajdabiya (Ejdabia)	165,839
Almirqeb	328,292	Garyan (Ghryan)	161,408
Turhona and Misllatah	296,092	Sirte (Surt)	156,839
Al-Jfara	289,340	Surman and Subratha	152,521
An-Niikat al-Ghames	208,954		

Source: National Authority for Information and Authentication.

BIRTHS, MARRIAGES AND DEATHS

	Registered live births		Registered marriages*		Registered deaths*	
	Number	Rate (per 1,000)	Number	Rate (per 1,000)	Number	Rate (per 1,000)
1994	98,423	20.1	19,190	3.9	14,036	2.9
1995	88,779	17.9	21,358	4.3	13,538	4.6
1996	90,428	17.8	18,743	3.7	12,281	2.4

* Registration is incomplete.

Source: UN, *Demographic Yearbook*.

2002*: Registered live births 111,053 (rate per 1,000 20.2); Registered marriages 33,323; Registered deaths 19,362 (Source: mostly UN, *Population and Vital Statistics Report*).

Expectation of life (years at birth, WHO estimates): 72.0 (males 69.7; females 74.9) in 2005 (Source: WHO, *World Health Statistics*).

EMPLOYMENT
('000 persons)

	2000	2001	2004*
Agriculture, forestry and fishing	239.1	103.4	113.4
Oil and gas extraction	39.9	40.0	43.9
Mining and quarrying	12.5	28.9	31.7
Manufacturing	169.6	172.1	188.8
Electricity, gas and water	41.0	50.9	55.8
Construction	222.0	45.2	49.6
Trade, restaurants and hotels	69.5	161.2	176.8
Transport and communications	143.4	55.5	60.9
Financing, insurance and real estate	33.0	38.1	41.8
Public administration	118.9	219.2	240.5
Education	198.2	365.5	401.0
Health services	86.1	158.3	173.7
Other services	71.8	20.1	22.1
Total	**1,445.0**	**1,458.4**	**1,600.0**
Libyans	1,257.1	1,335.4	1,543.1
Non-Libyans	187.9	123.0	56.9

* Figures for 2002–03 were not available.

Source: IMF, *Socialist People's Libyan Arab Jamahiriya: Statistical Appendix* (May 2007).

2005 ('000 persons): Agriculture 63.5; Manufacturing industries 140.1; Electricity, gas and water 40.2; Building and constructions 29.1; Trade, restaurants and hotels 123.9; Transport and communications 37.8; Public services 515.2; Other services 65.8; Total 1,015.6 (Libyans 863.8, Expatriates 151.8).

LIBYA
Statistical Survey

Health and Welfare

KEY INDICATORS

Total fertility rate (children per woman, 2005)	2.9
Under-5 mortality rate (per 1,000 live births, 2005)	19
HIV/AIDS (% of persons aged 15–49, 2003)	0.30
Physicians (per 1,000 head, 1997)	1.29
Hospital beds (per 1,000 head, 2004)	3.4
Health expenditure (2004): US $ per head (PPP)	328.1
Health expenditure (2004): % of GDP	3.8
Health expenditure (2004): public (% of total)	74.9
Access to water (% of persons, 2002)	72
Access to sanitation (% of persons, 2004)	97
Human Development Index (2005): ranking	56
Human Development Index (2005): value	0.818

For sources and definitions, see explanatory note on p. vi.

Agriculture

PRINCIPAL CROPS
('000 metric tons)

	2004	2005	2006
Wheat*	125	125	100
Barley*	85	100	100
Potatoes	195*	195*	200†
Dry broad beans†	14	14	14
Almonds	25	24†	24†
Groundnuts (in shell)	23	24†	24†
Olives†	190	211	211
Tomatoes†	204	213	213
Pumpkins, squash and gourds†	28	28	28
Cucumbers and gherkins†	13	13	13
Chillies and green peppers†	14	13	13
Green onions and shallots†	53	53	53
Dry onions	182	182†	182†
Green peas	6	7†	7†
Carrots and turnips	25	24†	24†
Watermelons	240	263†	263†
Cantaloupes and other melons	26	27†	27
Oranges	44	33†	33†
Tangerines, mandarins, etc.†	11	12	12
Lemons and limes	17	18†	18†
Apples	20	24†	24†
Apricots	18	17†	17†
Peaches and nectarines	10	9†	9†
Plums and sloes	32	35†	35†
Grapes	30*	33†	33†
Figs	10*	6†	6†
Dates	150	181†	181†

* Unofficial figure(s).
† FAO estimate(s).

Aggregate production ('000 metric tons, may include official, semi-official or estimated data): Total cereals 218 in 2004, 234 in 2005, 209 in 2006; Total roots and tubers 195 in 2004, 195 in 2005, 200 in 2006; Total vegetables (incl. melons) 883 in 2004, 917 in 2005, 917 in 2006; Total fruits (excl. melons) 347 in 2004, 372 in 2005, 372 in 2006.

Source: FAO.

LIVESTOCK
('000 head, year ending September, FAO estimates)

	2002	2003	2004
Horses	45	45	45
Asses, mules or hinnies	30	30	30
Cattle	130	130	130
Camels	46	47	47
Sheep	4,500	4,500	4,500
Goats	1,265	1,265	1,265
Poultry	25	25	25

2005–06: Figures assumed to be unchanged from 2004 (FAO estimates).
Source: FAO.

LIVESTOCK PRODUCTS
('000 metric tons)

	2003	2004	2005
Cattle meat*	6	6	6
Sheep meat	27*	27*	27
Goat meat	6*	6*	6
Chicken meat*	99	108	113
Cows' milk*	130	130	130
Sheep's milk*	56	56	56
Goats' milk	15	15*	15
Hen eggs*	60	60	60
Wool: greasy	9*	9	10*

* FAO estimate(s).
2006: Figures assumed to be unchanged from 2005 (FAO estimates).
Source: FAO.

Forestry

ROUNDWOOD REMOVALS
('000 cubic metres, excl. bark, FAO estimates)

	2004	2005	2006
Sawlogs, veneer logs and logs for sleepers*	63	63	63
Other industrial wood	53	53	53
Fuel wood	536	536	901
Total	652	652	1,017

* Annual output assumed to be unchanged since 1978.
Source: FAO.

SAWNWOOD PRODUCTION
('000 cubic metres, incl. railway sleepers, FAO estimates)

	1976	1977	1978
Total (all broadleaved)*	9	21	31

* Annual output assumed to be unchanged since 1978 (FAO estimates).
Source: FAO.

Fishing
(metric tons, live weight, FAO estimates)

	2003	2004	2005
Capture	46,671	46,077	46,076
Groupers	3,000	3,000	3,000
Bogue	3,100	3,100	3,100
Porgies and seabreams	4,800	4,800	4,800
Surmullet	4,500	4,500	4,500
Jack and horse mackerels	5,200	5,200	5,200
Sardinellas	9,500	9,500	9,500
'Scomber' mackerels	4,200	4,200	4,200
Aquaculture	58	266	266
Total catch (incl. others)	46,729	46,343	46,342

Source: FAO.

Mining

('000 metric tons, unless otherwise indicated, estimates)

	2004	2005	2006
Crude petroleum ('000 barrels)	587,000	630,000	660,000
Natural gas (million cu m)*	14,900	15,000	17,000
Salt	40	40	40
Gypsum (crude)	175	175	175

* Figures refer to gross volume. The dry equivalent (estimates, million cubic metres) was: 10,700 in 2004; 11,700 in 2005; 14,800 in 2006.

Source: US Geological Survey.

Industry

SELECTED PRODUCTS
('000 metric tons, unless otherwise indicated)

	2002	2003	2004
Olive oil (crude)	8	7	9
Paper and paperboard	6	n.a.	n.a.
Jet fuels	1,525	1,491	1,504
Motor spirit (petrol)	2,020	1,972	1,991
Naphthas	1,375	1,345	1,358
Kerosene	326	319	322
Gas-diesel (distillate fuel) oil	4,843	4,737	4,782
Residual fuel oils	4,659	4,556	4,597
Liquefied petroleum gas: from petroleum refineries	315	310	310
Petroleum bitumen (asphalt)	140	147	154
Cement*	3,300	n.a.	n.a.
Electric energy (million kWh)	17,351	18,943	20,202

* Provisional or estimated figure.

Source: UN, *Industrial Commodity Statistics Yearbook*.

Finance

CURRENCY AND EXCHANGE RATES

Monetary Units
1,000 dirhams = 1 Libyan dinar (LD).

Sterling, Dollar and Euro Equivalents (30 November 2007)
£1 sterling = 2.5111 dinars;
US $1 = 1.2152 dinars;
€1 = 1.7937 dinars;
100 Libyan dinars = £39.82 = $82.29 = €55.75.

Average Exchange Rate (Libyan dinar per US $)
2004 1.3050
2005 1.3084
2006 1.3136

Note: In March 1986 the value of the Libyan dinar was linked to the IMF's special drawing right (SDR). Between November 1994 and November 1998 the official mid-point exchange rate was SDR 1 = 525 dirhams (LD 1 = SDR 1.90476). In February 1999 a rate of LD 1 = SDR 1.577 (SDR 1 = 634.1 dirhams) was introduced, but from September 1999 to September 2000 the value of the dinar fluctuated. In September 2000 a new rate of LD 1 = SDR 1.4204 (SDR 1 = 704.03 dirhams) was established, but in June 2001 the Libyan dinar was devalued to SDR 1.224 (SDR 1 = 816.99 dirhams). The latter rate remained in effect until the end of December 2001. In January 2002 the value of the Libyan dinar was adjusted to SDR 0.608 (SDR 1 = LD 1.64474): a devaluation of 50.3%.

BUDGET
(LD million)

Revenue	2004	2005	2006
Hydrocarbon budget allocation	20,141	34,764	43,566
Non-hydrocarbon	3,131	2,650	3,523
Non-hydrocarbon tax revenue	1,617	1,526	1,768
Taxes on income and profits	309	397	691
Taxes on international trade	602	517	527
Other tax revenue	705	611	569
Non-hydrocarbon non-tax revenue	1,515	1,124	1,736
Total	**23,272**	**37,413**	**47,088**

Expenditure	2004	2005	2006
Current	10,195	8,245	9,693
Administrative budget	5,611	7,166	8,219
Expenditure on goods and services	4,647	5,669	6,655
Wages and salaries	3,445	4,007	4,575
Subsidies and other current transfers	964	1,497	1,564
Extrabudgetary current expenditure	3,690	99	705
Oil reserve fund	3,690	99	705
Capital	6,933	8,395	11,105
Development budget	6,135	7,570	10,079
Extrabudgetary capital expenditure	798	825	1,026
Total*	**17,230**	**19,060**	**21,377**

* Including net lending (LD million): 102 in 2004; 2,420 in 2005; 580 in 2006.

Source: IMF, *The Socialist People's Libyan Arab Jamahiriya: Statistical Appendix* (May 2007).

INTERNATIONAL RESERVES
(US $ million at 31 December)

	2004	2005	2006
Gold (national valuation)	194	194	194
IMF special drawing rights	738	707	787
Reserve position in IMF	614	565	595
Foreign exchange	24,336	38,235	57,907
Total	**25,882**	**39,701**	**59,483**

Source: IMF, *International Financial Statistics*.

MONEY SUPPLY
(LD million at 31 December)

	2004	2005	2006
Currency outside banks	2,612.7	3,310.6	3,932.9
Private-sector deposits at Central Bank	246.3	529.8	537.5
Demand deposits at commercial banks	6,801.6	8,666.2	10,506.9
Total money (incl. others)	**10,154.0**	**13,383.9**	**15,455.3**

Source: IMF, *International Financial Statistics*.

COST OF LIVING
(Consumer Price Index; base: 1999 = 100)

	2004	2005	2006
Personal services and others	78.7	77.5	80.2
Medical care	103.5	107.6	115.7
Recreation and education	82.3	82.4	81.0
Transport and communication	95.9	98.3	100.1
Clothing and shoes	60.8	61.3	61.6
Furniture	70.9	71.2	71.1
Housing	83.2	86.9	99.1
Food, beverages and tobacco	74.8	77.4	78.8
All items	**76.4**	**77.9**	**80.6**

LIBYA   Statistical Survey

NATIONAL ACCOUNTS
(LD million at current prices)
National Income and Product

	1983	1984	1985
Compensation of employees	2,763.1	2,865.8	2,996.2
Operating surplus	5,282.7	4,357.8	4,572.4
Domestic factor incomes	8,045.8	7,223.6	7,568.6
Consumption of fixed capital	436.1	457.5	481.6
Gross domestic product (GDP) at factor cost	8,481.9	7,681.1	8,050.2
Indirect taxes	470.0	462.2	389.0
Less Subsidies	146.7	130.0	162.2
GDP in purchasers' values	8,805.2	8,013.3	8,277.0
Factor income from abroad	200.2	142.8	122.5
Less Factor income paid abroad	989.0	727.7	397.9
Gross national product	8,016.4	7,428.4	8,001.6
Less Consumption of fixed capital	436.1	457.5	481.6
National income in market prices	7,580.3	6,970.9	7,520.0
Other current transfers from abroad	8.6	2.3	2.6
Less Other current transfers paid abroad	25.2	27.9	16.0
National disposable income	7,563.7	6,945.3	7,506.6

Source: UN, *National Accounts Statistics*.

Expenditure on the Gross Domestic Product

	2003	2004	2005*
Government final consumption expenditure	4,643.3	5,132.4	6,712.5
Private final consumption expenditure	14,061.8	15,669.3	18,148.6
Gross fixed capital formation	3,330.7	3,987.5	4,807.0
Changes in inventories	138.0	167.0	202.1
Total domestic expenditure	22,173.8	24,956.2	29,870.2
Exports of goods and services	18,770.0	27,928.0	40,613.0
Less Imports of goods and services	9,212.0	11,398.0	14,458.0
GDP in purchasers' values	31,731.8	41,486.2	56,025.2
GDP at constant 1997 prices	16,160.6	17,025.7	17,971.2

Gross Domestic Product by Economic Activity

	2003	2004	2005*
Agriculture, forestry and fishing	1,375.8	1,439.3	1,554.5
Oil and natural gas production	18,940.5	27,228.0	39,937.5
Other mining	360.2	411.0	495.5
Manufacturing	764.7	761.1	799.0
Electricity, gas and water	303.1	334.4	379.0
Construction	1,249.0	1,424.9	1,718.0
Trade, restaurants and hotels	2,193.9	2,392.1	2,797.9
Transport, storage and communications	1,515.0	1,663.6	1,947.5
Finance, insurance and real estate	439.9	478.9	560.1
Ownership of houses	534.1	591.6	614.1
Education, health and other public services	3,606.5	4,286.0	4,682.4
Other services	448.9	475.5	539.3
Total	31,731.8	41,486.2	56,025.2

* Preliminary figures.

BALANCE OF PAYMENTS
(LD million)

	2004	2005	2006
Exports of goods f.o.b.	22,619	37,792	51,453
Imports of goods f.o.b.	−11,398	−14,638	−15,711
Trade balance	11,221	23,154	35,742
Exports of services	568	700	1,273
Imports of services	−2,487	−3,077	−3,638
Balance on goods and services	9,302	20,777	33,377
Other income (net)	−65	−369	1,079
Balance on goods, services and income	9,237	20,408	34,456
Current transfers (net)	−3,261	−831	−166
Current balance	5,976	19,577	34,290
Direct investment (net)	92	1,192	1,942
Portfolio investment (net)	−243	−515	−2,573
Other investment (net)	−252	−162	−5,976
Net errors and omissions	479	1,308	−3,953
Statistical discrepancy	—	—	−353
Overall balance	6,052	21,400	23,377

External Trade

PRINCIPAL COMMODITIES

Imports c.i.f. (LD million)	2004	2005
Food and live animals	1,159.8	1,177.4
Beverages and tobacco	15.1	30.2
Animal and vegetable oils and fats	156.5	111.6
Crude materials (inedible) except fuels	118.1	145.8
Mineral fuels and related materials	56.4	30.0
Chemical materials	334.4	458.1
Basic manufactures	1,646.7	1,650.0
Plant and equipment	3,960.3	3,787.0
Miscellaneous products	807.9	563.1
Total	8,255.2	7,953.5

Exports f.o.b. (US $ million)*	1997	1998
Mineral fuels, lubricants, etc.	8,557.4	5,678.4
Petroleum, petroleum products, etc.	8,386.7	5,587.5
Crude petroleum oils, etc.	6,897.5	4,524.8
Refined petroleum products	1,489.2	1,062.7
Gasoline and other light oils	282.3	226.6
Residual fuel oils	1,206.9	836.1
Chemicals and related products	294.2	258.4
Total (incl. others)	9,028.7	6,131.4

* Excluding military goods.

2006 (LD million): Total imports c.i.f. 7,934.7.

Source: partly UN, *International Trade Statistics Yearbook*.

PRINCIPAL TRADING PARTNERS
(US $ million)*

Imports c.i.f.	2003	2004
Argentina	25.7	99.6
Belgium	101.3	118.3
Brazil	50.7	81.2
Canada	37.2	114.4
China, People's Republic	85.1	207.3
Egypt	129.7	131.6
France (incl. Monaco)	274.3	255.4
Germany	486.2	760.8
Greece	47.7	40.9
India	12.8	162.6
Italy	925.9	1,156.7
Japan	321.9	525.4
Korea, Republic	96.5	471.2
Malta	160.6	78.0

LIBYA

Imports c.i.f.—continued	2003	2004
Netherlands	69.9	72.0
Spain	64.4	92.7
Sweden	22.6	68.3
Switzerland-Liechtenstein	93.9	41.9
Tunisia	135.8	145.6
Turkey	92.1	111.3
United Arab Emirates	99.1	23.8
United Kingdom	300.8	260.2
USA	20.3	157.0
Total (incl. others)	4,322.5	6,317.6

Exports f.o.b.	1998	1999	2000
Austria	125.2	87.0	18.9
Egypt	97.6	94.1	57.1
France (incl. Monaco)	236.8	509.8	574.4
Germany	1,002.9	1,507.1	1,556.2
Greece	161.6	186.1	270.7
Italy	2,449.9	2,987.0	4,343.8
Netherlands	141.0	81.8	70.0
Portugal	29.6	20.6	49.9
Spain	685.9	1,084.5	1,555.0
Switzerland-Liechtenstein	0.9	105.2	18.4
Tunisia	303.6	320.6	423.2
Turkey	394.4	5.7	769.3
United Kingdom	158.0	104.4	233.6
Total (incl. others)	6,131.4	7,905.1	10,194.9

*Imports by country of origin; exports by country of destination. Figures exclude trade in gold.

Source: UN, *International Trade Statistics Yearbook*.

Transport

ROAD TRAFFIC
(motor vehicles in use at 31 December)

	2000	2001
Passenger cars	549,600	552,700
Commercial vehicles	177,400	195,500

Buses and coaches: 1,424 in 1995; 1,490 in 1996.
Motorcycles and mopeds: 1,078 in 1995; 1,112 in 1996.
Sources: IRF, *World Road Statistics*; UN, *Statistical Yearbook*.

SHIPPING
Merchant Fleet
(registered at 31 December)

	2004	2005	2006
Number of vessels	136	140	139
Total displacement ('000 grt)	130.1	117.3	105.4

Source: Lloyd's Register-Fairplay, *World Fleet Statistics*.

International Sea-borne Freight Traffic
(estimates, '000 metric tons)

	1991	1992	1993
Goods loaded	57,243	59,894	62,491
Goods unloaded	7,630	7,710	7,808

Source: UN Economic Commission for Africa, *African Statistical Yearbook*.

CIVIL AVIATION
(traffic on scheduled services)

	2001	2002	2003
Kilometres flown (million)	4	4	8
Passengers carried ('000)	583	559	742
Passenger-km (million)	409	409	825
Total ton-km (million)	33	33	69

Source: UN, *Statistical Yearbook*.

Tourism

VISITOR ARRIVALS*

Country of origin	2002	2003	2004
Algeria	70,416	71,657	73,459
Egypt	354,189	429,220	441,230
Morocco	19,076	19,120	20,803
Tunisia	329,145	346,331	366,871
Total (incl. others)	857,952	957,896	999,343

*Including same-day visitors (excursionists).

Tourism receipts (US $ million, incl. passenger transport): 243 in 2003; 261 in 2004; 301 in 2005.

Source: World Tourism Organization.

Communications Media

	2003	2004	2005
Telephones ('000 main lines in use)	750	750	750
Mobile cellular telephones ('000 subscribers)	127	235	235
Personal computers ('000 in use)	130	130	n.a.
Internet users ('000)	160	205	205

1994: Book production (titles) 26.
1997: Radio receivers ('000 in use) 1,350; Television receivers ('000 in use) 730.
1998: Daily newspapers 4 (estimated average circulation 71,100).
2006: Telephones ('000 main lines in use) 483.0; Mobile cellular telephones ('000 subscribers) 3,927.6.

Sources: UNESCO, *Statistical Yearbook*; International Telecommunication Union.

Education

(1995/96, unless otherwise indicated)

	Institutions	Teachers	Students
Primary and preparatory: general	2,733*	122,020	1,333,679
Primary and preparatory: vocational	168	n.a.	22,490
Secondary: general	n.a.	17,668	170,573
Secondary: teacher training	n.a.	2,760†	23,919
Secondary: vocational	312	n.a.	109,074
Universities	13	n.a.	126,348

* 1993/94.
† 1992/93.

Source: partly UNESCO, *Statistical Yearbook*.

1998: 1,160,315 primary school students (Source: World Bank).
Students (UNESCO estimates, 2005/05 unless otherwise indicated): Pre-primary 15,912; Primary 713,902; Secondary 701,536; Tertiary 375,028 (2002/03) (Source: UNESCO Institute for Statistics).
Teachers (UNESCO estimates, 2005/06 unless otherwise indicated): Pre-primary 2,211; Primary 148,476; Secondary 152,338; Tertiary 15,711 (2002/03) (Source: UNESCO Institute for Statistics).
Adult literacy rate (UNESCO estimates): 84.2% (males 92.8%; females 74.8%) in 2004 (Source: UNESCO Institute for Statistics).

Directory

The Constitution

The Libyan Arab People, meeting in the General People's Congress in Sebha from 2–28 March 1977, proclaimed its adherence to freedom and its readiness to defend it on its own land and anywhere else in the world. It also announced: its adherence to socialism and its commitment to achieving total Arab Unity; its adherence to the moral human values; and confirmation of the march of the revolution led by Col Muammar al-Qaddafi, the Revolutionary Leader, towards complete People's Authority.

The Libyan Arab People announced the following:

(i) The official name of Libya is henceforth the Socialist People's Libyan Arab Jamahiriya.

(ii) The Holy Koran is the social code in the Socialist People's Libyan Arab Jamahiriya.

(iii) The Direct People's Authority is the basis for the political order in the Socialist People's Libyan Arab Jamahiriya. The People shall practise its authority through People's Congresses, Popular Committees, Trade Unions, Vocational Syndicates and the General People's Congress, in the presence of the law.

(iv) The defence of our homeland is the responsibility of every citizen. The whole people shall be trained militarily and armed by general military training, the preparation of which shall be specified by the law.

The General People's Congress in its extraordinary session held in Sebha issued four decrees:

The first decree announced the establishment of the People's Authority in compliance with the resolutions and recommendations of the People's Congresses and Trade Unions.

The second decree stipulated the choice of Col Muammar al-Qaddafi, the Revolutionary Leader, as Secretary-General of the General People's Congress.

The third decree stipulated the formation of the General Secretariat of the General People's Congress (see The Government, below).

The fourth decree stipulated the formation of the General People's Committee to carry out the tasks of the various former ministries (see The Government, below).

In 1986 it was announced that the country's official name was to be the Great Socialist People's Libyan Arab Jamahiriya.

The Government

HEAD OF STATE*

Revolutionary Leader: Col MUAMMAR AL-QADDAFI (took office as Chairman of the Revolution Command Council 8 September 1969).

GENERAL SECRETARIAT OF THE GENERAL PEOPLE'S CONGRESS
(April 2008)

Secretary: MUFTAH MUHAMMAD KAIBA.
Assistant Secretary for Popular Congresses: (vacant).
Secretary for Culture and Mass Mobilization: ABD AL-HAMID AS-SID ZINTANI.
Secretary for Trade Unions, Leagues and Professional Unions: ABDALLAH IDRIS IBRAHIM.
Secretary for Social Affairs: SALIMA SHAIBAN ABD AL-JABAR.
Secretary for Infrastructure, Urban Planning and Environment: Dr SALIM AHMAD FUNAYT.
Secretary for Human Resources: Dr AL-BAGHDADI ALI AL-MAHMOUDI.
Secretary for Foreign Affairs: SULEIMAN SASI ASH-SHAHOUMI.
Secretary for Economy: ABD AS-SALAM AHMAD NUWEIR.
Secretary for Legal Affairs and Human Rights: HUSSEIN AL-WAHISHI AS-SADIQ.
Secretary for Security Affairs: MUFTAH ABD AS-SALAM BUKAR.
Secretary for Women's Affairs: HUDA FATHI BEN AMER.
Secretary for Union Syndicates and Vocational Association Affairs: Dr MUHAMMAD BIN HUSSEIN JABRAIL.

*Qaddafi himself rejects this nomenclature and all other titles.

GENERAL PEOPLE'S COMMITTEE
(April 2008)

Secretary: Dr AL-BAGHDADI ALI AL-MAHMOUDI.
Deputy Secretary: MUBARAK ABDALLAH ASH-SHAMIKH.
Secretary for Justice: MOUSTAFA MUHAMMAD ABU AL-JELIL.
Secretary for Finance: MUHAMMAD ALI AL-HOUEIZ.
Secretary for Foreign Liaison and International Co-operation: ABD AR-RAHMAN MUHAMMAD SHALGAM.
Secretary for Tourism: AMMAR AT-TAEF.
Secretary for the Economy, Trade and Investment: Dr ALI ABDALLAH AL-ESSAWI.
Secretary for Health and Environment: Dr MUHAMMAD ABU UJAYLAH RASHID.
Secretary for Industry and Mineral Resources: ALI YOUSUF ZIKRI.
Secretary for Electricity, Water and Gas: OMRAN IBRAHIM ABU KRAA.
Secretary for Youth and Sport: MOUSTAFA MIFTAH BEL'ID AD-DERSI.
Secretary for Culture and Information: NURI DHAW AL-HUMEIDI.
Secretary for Manpower, Training and Employment: MAATUK MUHAMMAD MAATUK.
Secretary for Planning: Dr ABD AL-HAFID MAHMUD ZALITNI.
Secretary for Agriculture and Animals: ABU BAKR MABROUK AL-MANSURI.
Secretary for National Security: Gen. ABD AL-FATTAH YUNIS AL-ABAIDI.
Secretary for Social Affairs: Dr IBRAHIM AZ-ZARRUQ ASH-SHARIF.
Secretary for Transport and Communications: Dr MUHAMMAD ABU JALLAH AL-MABROUK.
Secretary for General Education: Dr ABD AL-QADIR MUHAMMAD AL-BAGHDADI.
Secretary for Higher Education: Dr AGAIL HUSSEIN AGAIL.

Legislature

GENERAL PEOPLE'S CONGRESS

The Senate and House of Representatives were dissolved after the *coup d'état* of September 1969, and the provisional Constitution issued in December 1969 made no mention of elections or a return to parliamentary procedure. However, in January 1971 Col Qaddafi announced that a new legislature would be appointed, not elected; no date was mentioned. All political parties other than the Arab Socialist Union were banned. In November 1975 provision was made for the creation of the 1,112-member General National Congress of the Arab Socialist Union, which met officially in January 1976. This later became the General People's Congress, which met for the first time in November 1976 and in March 1977 began introducing the wide-ranging changes outlined in the Constitution (above).

Secretary-General: MUFTAH MUHAMMAD KAIBA.

Political Organizations

In June 1971 the Arab Socialist Union (ASU) was established as the country's sole authorized political party. The General National Congress of the ASU held its first session in January 1976 and later became the General People's Congress (see Legislature).

The following groups are in opposition to the Government:

Ansarollah (Followers of God): f. 1996.
Islamic Martyrs' Movement (IMM): seeks to establish an Islamic republic; Leader ABU SHALTILAH; Spokesman ABDALLAH AHMAD.
Libyan Baathist Party.
Libyan Change and Reform Movement: breakaway group from NFSL.
Libyan Conservatives' Party: f. 1996.
Libyan Constitutional Grouping.
Libyan Democratic Authority: f. 1993.
Libyan Democratic Conference: f. 1992.
Libyan Democratic Movement: f. 1977; external group.

Libyan Islamic Fighting Group (LIFG): f. 1995; seeks to establish an Islamic regime; claimed responsibility for subversive activities in early 1996, and engaged in armed clashes with security forces in mid- to late 1990s; Leader ANAS SEBAI.

Libyan Movement for Change and Reform: POB 3423, London, NW6 7TZ, United Kingdom; f. 1994.

Libyan National Alliance: f. 1980 in Cairo, Egypt.

Libyan National Democratic Grouping: Leader MAHMOUD SULAYMAN AL-MAGHRABI.

Movement of Patriotic Libyans: f. 1997; aims to establish a 'free Libyan state' based on a market economy.

National Front for the Salvation of Libya (NFSL): e-mail info@libya-nfsl.org; internet www.libya-nfsl.org; f. 1981 in Khartoum, Sudan; aims to replace the existing regime by a democratically elected govt; Leader MUHAMMAD MEGARIEF.

Diplomatic Representation

EMBASSIES IN LIBYA

Afghanistan: POB 4245, Sharia Mozhar al-Aftes, Tripoli; tel. (21) 4775192; fax (21) 609876; Chargé d'affaires MUHAMMAD AMER ALZAIDY.

Algeria: Sharia Kairouan 12, Tripoli; tel. (21) 4440025; fax (21) 3334631; Ambassador MUHAMMAD SEGHIR KARA.

Argentina: POB 932, Gargaresh, Madina Syahia, Tripoli; tel. (21) 4834956; fax (21) 4840928; e-mail embartrip@hotmail.com; Ambassador JUAN CARLOS VALLE RALEIGH.

Austria: POB 3207, Sharia Khalid ibn al-Walid, Garden City, Tripoli; tel. (21) 4443379; fax (21) 4440838; e-mail tripolis-ob@bmaa.gv.at; Ambassador Dr THOMAS WUNDERBALDINGER.

Bangladesh: POB 5086, Hi Damasq, Tripoli; tel. (21) 4911198; fax (21) 4906616; e-mail bdtripoli@bsisp.net; Ambassador JAMILUDDIN AHSAN.

Belarus: POB 1530, Tripoli; tel. (21) 4444708; fax (21) 3332994; e-mail libya@belembassy.org; Ambassador DEREVYASHKO ALEKSANDR NIKOLAEVICH.

Belgium: POB 91650, Jasmin St, Hay Andalus, Tripoli; tel. (21) 4782044; fax (21) 4782046; e-mail tripoli@diplobel.be; internet www.diplomatie.be/tripoli; Ambassador ALPHONSE CREUSEN.

Benin: POB 6676, Sharia Ghout ash-Shaal, Tripoli; tel. (21) 4837663; fax (21) 834569; Ambassador LAFIA CHABI.

Bosnia and Herzegovina: POB 6946, Sharia Abd al-Melik bin Kutn, Tripoli; tel. and fax (21) 4776442; Ambassador SETA FERHAT.

Brazil: POB 2270, Sharia ben Ashour, Tripoli; tel. (21) 3614894; fax (21) 3614895; e-mail brcastripoli@lttnet.net; Ambassador JOAQUIM PALMEIRO.

Bulgaria: POB 2945, Sharia Selma ben Al-Ukua, Ben Ashour Area No. 58-6, Tripoli; tel. (21) 3609988; fax (21) 3609990; e-mail tripoli@embassy.transat.bg; Ambassador Dr ZDRAVKO VELEV.

Burkina Faso: POB 81902, Route de Gargeresh, Tripoli; tel. (21) 4771221; fax (21) 4778037; Ambassador YOUSSOUF SANGARE.

Burundi: POB 2817, Sharia Ras Hassan, Tripoli; tel. (21) 608848; Ambassador RAPHAËL BITARIHO.

Canada: POB 93392, Al-Fateh Tower Post Office, Tripoli; tel. (21) 3351633; fax (21) 3351630; e-mail trpli@dfait-maeci.gc.ca; internet www.dfait-maeci.gc.ca/libya; Ambassador HAIG SARAFIAN.

Chad: POB 1078, Sharia Muhammad Mussadeq 25, Tripoli; tel. (21) 4443955; Ambassador IBRAHIM MAHAMAT TIDEI.

China, People's Republic: POB 5329, Sharia Menstir, Andalus, Gargaresh, Tripoli; tel. (21) 4832914; fax (21) 4831877; e-mail chinaemb_ly@mfa.gov.cn; Ambassador HUANG JIEMEN.

Croatia: Great al-Fatah Towers, Floor 12, Room 125, Tripoli; tel. (21) 3351381; fax (21) 3351486; e-mail croemb.tripoli@mvpei.hr; Ambassador JOVAN VEJNOVIĆ.

Cuba: POB 83738, Sharia ibn al-Youmin, Ahmed al-Mahzumi, Tripoli; tel. (21) 4775216; fax (21) 4776294; e-mail embacuba.libia@lttnet.net; Ambassador PABLO ANGEL REYES DOMÍNGUEZ.

Cyprus: POB 3284, Sharia adh-Dhul 60, Ben Ashour, Tripoli; tel. (21) 3601274; fax (21) 3613516; e-mail cyprusembassy@mail.lttnet.net; Ambassador YANNIS IACOVOU.

Czech Republic: POB 1097, Sharia Ahmad Lutfi Sayed, Sharia ben Ashour, Tripoli; tel. (21) 3615436; fax (21) 3615437; e-mail tripoli@embassy.mzv.cz; internet www.mzv.cz/tripoli; Ambassador DUŠAN ŠTRAUCH.

Egypt: POB 1105, The Grand Hotel, Tripoli; tel. (21) 4448909; fax (21) 4449262; e-mail egyemblib@hotmail.com; Ambassador MUHAMMAD FATIHY REFA'A ET-TAHTAWI.

Equatorial Guinea: Tripoli.

Eritrea: POB 91279, Tripoli; tel. (21) 4773568; fax (21) 4780152; Ambassador ABDALLAH MUSSA.

France: POB 312, Sharia Beni al-Amar, Hay Andalus, Tripoli; tel. (21) 4774891; fax (21) 4778266; e-mail info@ambafrance-ly.org; internet www.ambafrance-ly.org; Ambassador JEAN-LUC SIBIUDE.

Germany: POB 302, Sharia Hassan al-Mashai, Tripoli; tel. (21) 3330554; fax (21) 4448968; e-mail info@tripolis.diplo.de; internet www.tripolis.diplo.de; Ambassador BERND WESTPHAL.

Ghana: POB 4169, Andalus 21/A, nr Funduk Shati Gargaresh, Tripoli; tel. (21) 4772534; fax (21) 4773557; e-mail ghaemb@all-computers.com; Ambassador GEORGE KUMI.

Greece: POB 5147, Sharia Jalal Bayar 18, Tripoli; tel. (21) 3338563; fax (21) 4441907; e-mail grembtri@hotmail.com; Ambassador CHRYSANTHI PANAGIOTOPOULOU.

Guinea: POB 10657, Hay Andalus, Tripoli; tel. (21) 4772793; fax (21) 4773441; e-mail magatte@lttnet.net; Ambassador ABDUL AZIZ SOUMAH.

Holy See: Tripoli; Apostolic Nuncio Most Rev. FÉLIX DEL BLANCO PRIETO (Titular Archbishop of Vannida, resident in Malta).

Hungary: POB 4010, Sharia Talha ben Abdullah, Tripoli; tel. (21) 3618218; fax (21) 3618220; e-mail hutpi9@hotmail.com; Ambassador Dr ISTVAN CSEJTEI.

India: POB 3150, 16 Sharia Mahmud Shaltut, Tripoli; tel. (21) 4441835; fax (21) 3337560; e-mail indembtrip@hotmail.com; Ambassador D. P. SRIVASTAVA.

Indonesia: POB 5921, Tripoli; tel. (21) 4842067; fax (21) 4842069; e-mail indonesia@bsisp.net; Ambassador ACHMAD NAWAWI HASBI.

Iran: POB 6185, Tripoli; tel. (21) 3609552; fax (21) 3611674; e-mail iran_em_tripoli@hotmail.com; Ambassador MUHAMMAD MENHAJ.

Italy: POB 912, Sharia Vahran 1, Tripoli; tel. (21) 3334133; fax (21) 3331673; e-mail ambasciata.tripoli@esteri.it; internet www.ambtripoli.esteri.it; Ambassador FRANCESCO TRUPIANO.

Japan: POB 3265, Sharia Jamal ad-Din al-Waeli, Hay Andalus, Tripoli; tel. (21) 4781041; fax (21) 4781044; Ambassador AKIRA WATANABE.

Korea, Democratic People's Republic: Tripoli; Ambassador KIM TONG JE.

Korea, Republic: POB 4781, Gargaresh, Tripoli; tel. (21) 4831322; fax (21) 4831324; Ambassador KIM JOONG-JAE.

Kuwait: POB 2225, Beit al-Mal Beach, Tripoli; tel. (21) 4440281; fax (21) 607053; Chargé d'affaires (vacant).

Lebanon: POB 927, Auss bin al-Arkam, Ben Achour 10, Tripoli; tel. (21) 3615744; fax (21) 3611740; e-mail emblebanon_ly@hotmail.com; Chargé d'affaires a.i. NAZIH ACHOUR.

Lesotho: Ambassador PAUL KHOASHANE MOTHOLO.

Madagascar: POB 652, Maidane az-Zajeir, Tripoli; tel. (21) 3408257; fax (21) 3408256; e-mail ambamtri@yahoo.fr; Ambassador DIEUDONNÉ MARIE MICHEL RAZAFINDRANDRIATSIMANIRY.

Malaysia: POB 6309, Hay Andalus, Tripoli; tel. (21) 4830854; fax (21) 4831496; e-mail mwtripoli@lttnet.net; Ambassador Dato' ZULKIFLI YAACOB.

Mali: POB 2008, Sharia Jaraba Saniet Zarrouk, Tripoli; tel. (21) 4444924; Ambassador OUSMANE TANDIA.

Malta: POB 2534, Sharia Ubei ben Ka'ab, Tripoli; tel. (21) 3611181; fax (21) 3611180; e-mail maltaembassy.tripoli@gov.mt; Ambassador Dr JOSEPH CASSAR.

Mauritania: Sharia Aïssa el-Wakwak, Tripoli; tel. (21) 4443223; Ambassador YAHIA MUHAMMAD EL-HADI.

Morocco: POB 908, Ave 7 Avril, Tripoli; tel. (21) 3617809; fax (21) 3614762; e-mail sifmatripo@hotmail.com; Ambassador DRISS ALAOUI.

Netherlands: POB 3801, Sharia Jalal Bayar 20, Tripoli; tel. (21) 4441549; fax (21) 4440386; e-mail tri@minbuza.nl; internet www.mfa.nl/tri-uk; Ambassador BART VON BARTHELD.

Niger: POB 2251, Fachloun Area, Tripoli; tel. (21) 4443104; Ambassador AMADOU TIDJANI ALI.

Nigeria: POB 4417, Sharia Bashir al-Ibrahim, Tripoli; tel. (21) 4443038; Ambassador Prof. DANDATTI ABD AL-KADIR.

Pakistan: POB 2169, Sharia Huzayfa bin al-Yaman, Manshiya bin Ashour, Tripoli; tel. (21) 3610937; fax (21) 3600412; e-mail pareptripoli@hotmail.com; Ambassador MUHAMMAD FAROOQ QARI.

Philippines: POB 12508, Km 7 Abu Nawas, Hay Andalus, Gargaresh, Tripoli; tel. (21) 4833966; fax (21) 4836158; e-mail tripoli_pe76@lttnet.net; Ambassador BAYANI V. MANGIBIN.

Poland: POB 519, Sharia ben Ashour 61, Tripoli; tel. (21) 3608569; fax (21) 3615199; e-mail poland@trypolis.polemb.net; internet www.trypolis.polemb.net; Ambassador JÓSEF OSAS.

Qatar: POB 3506, Sharia ben Ashour, Tripoli; tel. (21) 4446660; Ambassador SAAD BEN ALI AL-MAHANDY.

LIBYA

Romania: POB 5085, Sharia Ali bin Talib, Ben Ashour, Tripoli; tel. (21) 3615295; fax (21) 3607597; e-mail ambaromatrip@hotmail.com; Ambassador STAN NICULAE.

Russia: POB 4792, Sharia Mustapha Kamel, Tripoli; tel. (21) 3330545; fax (21) 4446673; Ambassador VALERYIAN V. SHUVAYEV.

Rwanda: POB 6677, Villa Ibrahim Musbah Missalati, Andalus, Tripoli; tel. (21) 72864; fax (21) 70317; Chargé d'affaires CHRISTOPHE HABIMANA.

Saudi Arabia: Sharia Kairouan 2, Tripoli; tel. (21) 30485; Chargé d'affaires MUHAMMAD HASSAN BANDAH.

Senegal: POB 6392, El-Arabia Gotchalle 246/5, Gargaresh, Tripoli; tel. (21) 4836090; fax (21) 4838955; e-mail ambassene.tripoli@stcc.presidence.sn; Chargé d'affaires a.i. MAMADOU DIOP.

Serbia: POB 1087, 14–16 Sharia Turkia, Tripoli; tel. (21) 3330819; fax (21) 3334114; e-mail serbianembassy_tripoli@yahoo.com; Ambassador Dr DUSAN SIMEONOVIC.

Sierra Leone: Tripoli; Ambassador el Hadj MOHAMMED SAMURA.

Slovakia: POB 5721, Gargaresh 3 Km, Hay Andalus, Tripoli; tel. (21) 4781388; fax (21) 4781387; e-mail slovembtrp@slovembtrp.com; Ambassador JÁN BÓRY.

Spain: POB 2302, Sharia el-Amir Abd al-Kader al-Jazairi 36, Tripoli; tel. (21) 3336797; fax (21) 4443743; e-mail emb.tripoli@mae.es; Ambassador JOAQUÍN ANTONIO PÉREZ VILLANUEVA Y TOVAR.

Sudan: POB 1076, Sharia Gargaresh, Tripoli; tel. (21) 4775387; fax (21) 4774781; e-mail sudtripoli@hotmail.com; internet www.sudtripoli.net; Ambassador OSMAN M. O. DIRAR.

Switzerland: POB 439, Sharia al-Moussawer ben Maghzamah, off Sharia ben Ashour, Tripoli; tel. (21) 3614118; fax (21) 3614238; e-mail tri.vertretung@eda.admin.ch; internet www.eda.admin.ch/tripoli; Ambassador MARTIN AESCHBACHER.

Syria: POB 4219, Sharia Muhammad Rashid Reda 4, Tripoli (Relations Office); tel. (21) 3331783; Head MUNIR BORKHAN.

Togo: POB 3420, Sharia Khaled ibn al-Walid, Tripoli; tel. (21) 4447551; fax (21) 3332423; Ambassador TCHAO SOTOU BERE.

Tunisia: POB 613, Sharia Bashir al-Ibrahim, Tripoli; tel. (21) 3331051; fax (21) 4447600; High Representative MUHAMMAD B'RAHEM.

Turkey: POB 947, Sharia Zaviya Dahmani, Tripoli; tel. (21) 3401140; fax (21) 3401146; e-mail trablusbe@yahoo.com; Ambassador RIZA ERKMENOĞLU.

Uganda: POB 80215, Sharia Jaraba, Tripoli; tel. and fax (21) 3603083; fax (21) 3634471; e-mail ugembatp60@hotmail.com; internet www.ugandaembassy.org.ly; Ambassador MOSES SEBUNYA.

Ukraine: POB 4544, Sharia Dhil, Tripoli; tel. (21) 3608665; fax (21) 3608666; e-mail emb_ly@mfa.gov.ua; Ambassador OLEKSIY RYBAK.

United Kingdom: POB 4206, Tripoli; tel. (21) 3403644; fax (21) 3403648; e-mail tripoli.press@fco.gov.uk; internet www.britishembassy.gov.uk/libya; Ambassador Sir VINCENT FEAN.

USA: Corinthia Bab Africa Hotel, Souq at-Tlat al-Qadim, Tripoli; tel. (21) 3351831; e-mail paotripoli@state.gov; internet libya.usembassy.gov; Chargé d'affaires a.i. JOHN CHRISTOPHER STEVENS.

Venezuela: POB 2584, Sharia ben Ashour, Jamaa as-Sagaa Bridge, Tripoli; tel. (21) 3600408; fax (21) 3600407; Ambassador DAVID PARAVISINI.

Viet Nam: POB 587, Sharia Gargaresh, Tripoli; tel. (21) 4835587; fax (21) 4836962; e-mail dsqvnlib@yahoo.com; Ambassador DO BA KHOA.

Yemen: POB 4839, Sharia Ubei ben Ka'ab 36, Tripoli; tel. (21) 607472; Ambassador HUSSEIN ALI HASSAN SABAH.

Judicial System

The judicial system is composed, in order of seniority, of the Supreme Court, Courts of Appeal, and Courts of First Instance and Summary Courts.

All courts convene in open session, unless public morals or public order require a closed session; all judgments, however, are delivered in open session. Cases are heard in Arabic, with interpreters provided for aliens.

The courts apply the Libyan codes, which include all the traditional branches of law, such as civil, commercial and penal codes, etc. Committees were formed in 1971 to examine Libyan law and ensure that it coincides with the rules of Islamic *Shari'a*. The proclamation of People's Authority in the Jamahiriya provides that the Holy Koran is the law of society.

Attorney-General: SALIM MUHAMMAD SALIM.

SUPREME COURT

The judgments of the Supreme Court are final. It is composed of the President and several Justices. Its judgments are issued by circuits of at least three Justices (the quorum is three). The Court hears appeals from the Courts of Appeal in civil, penal, administrative and civil status matters.

President: ABD AR-RAHMAN MUHAMMAD ABU TOTAH.

COURTS OF APPEAL

These courts settle appeals from Courts of First Instance; the quorum is three Justices. Each court of appeal has a court of assize.

COURTS OF FIRST INSTANCE AND SUMMARY COURTS

These courts are first-stage courts in the Jamahiriya, and the cases heard in them are heard by one judge. Appeals against summary judgments are heard by the appellate court attached to the court of first instance, whose quorum is three judges.

PEOPLE'S PROSECUTION BUREAU

Established by order of the General People's Congress in March 1988.
Secretary: MUHAMMAD ALI AL-MISURATI.

Religion

ISLAM

The vast majority of Libyan Arabs follow Sunni Muslim rites, although Col Qaddafi has rejected the Sunnah (i.e. the practice, course, way, manner or conduct of the Prophet Muhammad, as followed by Sunnis) as a basis for legislation.

Chief Mufti of Libya: Sheikh TAHIR AHMAD AZ-ZAWI.

CHRISTIANITY

The Roman Catholic Church

Libya comprises three Apostolic Vicariates and one Apostolic Prefecture. At 31 December 2005 there were an estimated 104,000 adherents in the country.

Apostolic Vicariate of Benghazi: POB 248, Benghazi; tel. and fax (91) 9081599; e-mail apostvicar@yahoo.com; Vicar Apostolic Mgr SYLVESTER CARMEL MAGRO (Titular Bishop of Saldae).

Apostolic Vicariate of Derna: c/o POB 248, Benghazi; Vicar Apostolic (vacant).

Apostolic Vicariate of Tripoli: POB 365, Dahra, Tripoli; tel. (21) 3331863; fax (21) 3334696; e-mail bishoptripolibya@hotmail.com; Vicar Apostolic Mgr GIOVANNI INNOCENZO MARTINELLI (Titular Bishop of Tabuda).

The Anglican Communion

Within the Episcopal Church in Jerusalem and the Middle East, Libya forms part of the diocese of Egypt (q.v.).

Other Christian Churches

The Coptic Orthodox Church is represented in Libya.

The Press

Most newspapers and periodicals are published either by the Jamahiriya News Agency (JANA), by government secretariats, by the Press Service or by trade unions.

DAILIES

Al-Fajr al-Jadid (The New Dawn): POB 91291, Press Bldg, Sharia al-Jamahiriya, Tripoli; tel. (21) 3606393; fax (21) 3605728; internet www.alfajraljadeed.com; f. 1969; publ. by JANA; also publishes bi-monthly English version.

Ash-Shams: POB 82331, As-Sahafa Bldg, Sharia al-Jamhouria, Tripoli; tel. (21) 4442524; fax (21) 609315; internet www.alshames.com.

Az-Zahf al-Akhdar (The Green March): POB 14273, As-Sahafa Bldg, Sharia al-Jamhouria, Tripoli; tel. (21) 4776890; fax (21) 4772502; e-mail info@azzahfalakhder.com; internet www.azzahfalakhder.com; ideological journal of the revolutionary cttees.

PERIODICALS

Al-Amal (Hope): POB 4845, Tripoli; e-mail info@alamalmag.com; internet www.alamalmag.com; monthly; social, for children; publ. by the Press Service.

Ad-Daawa al-Islamia (Islamic Call): POB 2682, Sharia Sawani, km 5, Tripoli; tel. (21) 4800294; fax (21) 4800293; f. 1980; weekly (Wed.); Arabic, English, French; cultural; publ. by the World Islamic Call Society; Eds MUHAMMAD IMHEMED AL-BALOUSHI, ABDULAHI MUHAMMAD ABD AL-JALEEL.

LIBYA

Economic Bulletin: POB 2303, Tripoli; tel. (21) 3337106; monthly; publ. by JANA.

Al-Jamahiriya: POB 4814, Tripoli; tel. (21) 4449294; e-mail info@aljamahiria.com; internet www.aljamahiria.com; f. 1980; weekly; Arabic; political; publ. by the revolutionary cttees.

Al-Jarida ar-Rasmiya (The Official Newspaper): Tripoli; irregular; official state gazette.

Libyan Arab Republic Gazette: Secretariat of Justice, NA, Tripoli; weekly; English; publ. by the Secretariat of Justice.

Risalat al-Jihad (Holy War Letter): POB 2682, Tripoli; tel. (21) 3331021; f. 1983; monthly; Arabic, English, French; publ. by the World Islamic Call Society.

Scientific Bulletin: POB 2303, Tripoli; tel. (21) 3337106; monthly; publ. by JANA.

Ath-Thaqafa al-Arabiya (Arab Culture): POB 4587, Tripoli; f. 1973; weekly; cultural; circ. 25,000.

The Tripoli Post: POB 1159, Al-Fateh Tower, 1st Floor, Office No. 74, Tripoli; tel. (21) 3337422; fax (21) 3351740; e-mail editor@tripolipost.com; internet www.tripolipost.com; f. 1999; weekly; English; privately owned; Editor-in-Chief Dr SAID LASWAD.

Al-Usbu ath-Thaqafi (The Cultural Week): POB 4845, Tripoli; weekly.

Al-Watan al-Arabi al-Kabir (The Greater Arab Homeland): Tripoli; f. 1987.

NEWS AGENCY

Jamahiriya News Agency (JANA): POB 2303, Sharia al-Fatah, Tripoli; tel. (21) 3402606; fax (21) 3402421; e-mail janadmin@jananews.com; internet www.jananews.com; f. 1964; brs and correspondents throughout Libya and abroad; provides Arabic, English and French news services.

Publishers

Ad-Dar al-Arabia Lilkitab (Maison Arabe du Livre): POB 3185, Tripoli; tel. (21) 4447287; f. 1973 by Libya and Tunisia.

Ad-Dar al-Hikma Publishing House: Tripoli; tel. (21) 3606571; fax (21) 3606610; e-mail info@elgabooks.com.

Al-Fatah University, General Administration of Libraries, Printing and Publications: POB 13543, Tripoli; tel. (21) 4628034; fax (21) 4625045; e-mail m.alfituri@hotmail.com; f. 1955; academic books.

General Co for Publishing, Advertising and Distribution: POB 921, Sirte (Surt); tel. (54) 63170; fax (54) 62100; general, educational and academic books in Arabic and other languages; makes and distributes advertisements throughout Libya.

Ghouma Publishing: POB 80092, Tripoli; tel. (21) 3630864; e-mail ghoumapub@hotmail.com; f. 1993; book publishing, distribution and art production; Gen. Man. MUSTAFA FETOURI.

Broadcasting and Communications

TELECOMMUNICATIONS

Communications General Authority: Tripoli; f. 2007; supervisory body reporting directly to the General People's Committee.

General Directorate of Posts and Telecommunications: POB 81686, Tripoli; tel. (21) 3604101; fax (21) 3604102; Dir-Gen. ABU ZAID JUMA AL-MANSURI.

General Post and Telecommunications Co: POB 886, Sharia Zawia, Tripoli; tel. (21) 3600777; fax (21) 3609515; f. 1985; Chair. FARAJ AMARI.

BROADCASTING

Radio

Great Socialist People's Libyan Arab Jamahiriya Broadcasting Corporation: POB 80237, Tripoli; tel. (21) 3402107; fax (21) 3403468; e-mail info@en.ljbc.net; internet www.ljbc.net; f. 1968; broadcasts in Arabic; additional satellite channel broadcast for 18 hours a day from 1982; Sec.-Gen. ABDULLAH MANSOUR.

Voice of Africa: POB 4677, Sharia al-Fateh, Tripoli; tel. (21) 4449209; fax (21) 4449875; f. 1973 as Voice of the Greater Arab Homeland; adopted current name in 1998; broadcasts in Arabic, French, English, Swahili and Hausa; Dir-Gen. ABDALLAH AL-MEGRI.

Television

People's Revolution Broadcasting TV: POB 80237, Tripoli; tel. (21) 3402107; fax (21) 3403468; e-mail info@en.ljbc.net; internet www.ljbc.net; f. 1957; broadcasts in Arabic; additional satellite channels broadcast for limited hours in English; Dir ABDULLAH MANSOUR.

Finance

(cap. = capital; res = reserves; dep. = deposits; m. = million; brs = branches; amounts in Libyan dinars)

BANKING

Central Bank

Central Bank of Libya: POB 1103, Sharia al-Malik Seoud, Tripoli; tel. (21) 3333591; fax (21) 4441488; e-mail info@cbl.gov.ly; internet www.cbl.gov.ly; f. 1955 as National Bank of Libya; name changed to Bank of Libya 1963, to Central Bank of Libya 1977; state-owned; bank of issue and central bank carrying govt accounts and operating exchange control; commercial operations transferred to National Commercial Bank 1970; cap. 500.0m., res 250.0m., dep. 65,484.9m. (Dec. 2006); Gov. and Chair. FARHAT OMAR BENGDARA.

Other Banks

Alwafa Bank: POB 84212, Sharia Alfallah, Tripoli; tel. (21) 4815123; fax (21) 4801247; e-mail alwafa-bank@hotmail.com; f. 2003; private bank; Chair. and Gen. Man. HADI M. GITELI.

Gumhouria Bank: POB 65004, Gharyan; tel. (21) 4440848; fax (21) 3333793; e-mail edari@gumhouriabank.com; internet www.gumhouria-bank.com; f. 1969 as successor to Barclays Bank International in Libya; known as Masraf al-Jumhuriya until March 1977, and as Jamahiriya Bank until Dec. 2000; plans for a merger with Umma Bank SAL announced mid-2007; expected to be completed mid-2008; wholly owned subsidiary of the Central Bank; cap. 100.0m., res 63.0m., dep. 3,901.2m. (Dec. 2005); Chair. HAMED ARABI AL-HOUDERI; Gen. Man. MELLAD MUHAMMAD ELGHOOL; 82 brs.

Libyan Foreign Bank: POB 2542, Tower 2, Dat al-Imad Complex, Tripoli; tel. (21) 3350155; fax (21) 3350164; e-mail it@lafbank.com; internet www.lafbank.com; f. 1972 under the name Libyan Arab Foreign Bank; present name adopted 2005; offshore bank wholly owned by Central Bank of Libya; cap. 757.8m., res 249.7m., dep. 9,292.6m. (Dec. 2005); Chair. Dr MUHAMMAD A. BEIT EL-MAL.

National Commercial Bank SAL: POB 543, Aruba Ave, al-Baida; tel. (21) 3610306; fax (21) 3612267; e-mail ncbly@lttnet.net; internet www.ncb.ly; f. 1970 to take over commercial banking division of Central Bank (then Bank of Libya) and brs of Aruba Bank and Istiklal Bank; wholly owned by Central Bank of Libya; cap. 35m., res 83.8m., dep. 2,637.0m. (Dec. 2005); Chair. BADER A. ABU AZIZA; Gen. Man. AHMAD F. BELKHEIR; 51 brs.

Sahara Bank SPI: POB 70, Sharia 1 September 10, Tripoli; tel. (21) 3330724; fax (21) 3337922; e-mail sahbankgm1@lttnet.net; f. 1964 to take over br. of Banco di Sicilia; the Govt announced in early 2007 the proposed sale of a 19% stake to an international financial institution; cap. and res 208.2m., total assets 1,951.8m. (March 2003); Chair. and Gen. Man. Dr SALEM MUFTAH EL-GHAMATI; 20 brs.

Umma Bank SAL: POB 685, 1 Giaddat Omar al-Mokhtar, Tripoli; tel. (21) 3334031; fax (21) 3332505; e-mail info@umma-bank.com; internet www.umma-bank.com; f. 1969 to take over brs of Banco di Roma; wholly owned by Central Bank of Libya; plans for a merger with Gumhouria Bank announced mid-2007; expected to be completed mid-2008; cap. 23m. (Dec. 2004), res 30.0m., dep. 1,793.5m. (Dec. 2005); Chair. OMAR M. SAGHIAR; Gen. Man. ABD AL-FATAH S. GHAFFAR; 38 brs.

Wahda Bank: POB 452, Fadiel Abu Omar Sq., El-Berkha, Benghazi; tel. (61) 2224256; fax (21) 2224122; e-mail wahda@wahdabank.com; internet www.wahdabank.com; f. 1970 to take over Bank of North Africa, Commercial Bank SAL, Nahda Arabia Bank, Société Africaine de Banque SAL, Kafila al-Ahly Bank; 87%-owned by Central Bank of Libya; cap. 108m., res 94.1m., dep. 2,396.5m. (Dec. 2006); Chair. Dr FAROUK EL-KHAROUF; Gen. Man. SAID A. RASHWAN; 72 brs.

STOCK EXCHANGE

Libyan Stock Exchange Market: Sharia Omar Maukhtar, Tripoli; tel. (21) 3365026; e-mail info@lsm.gov.ly; internet www.lsm.gov.ly; f. 2007; Gen. Dir SULIMAN SALEM ASH-SHOHOMIY.

INSURANCE

Libya Insurance Co: POB 80087, Aman Bldg, Sharia At-Taha, Tripoli; tel. (21) 4444174; fax (21) 4444176; e-mail infolt@libtamin.com; internet www.libtamin.com; f. 1964; merged with Al-Mukhtar Insurance Co in 1981; all classes of insurance; Man. ALI AMAR AR-RAGAYEE.

Trade and Industry

There are state trade and industrial organizations responsible for the running of industries at all levels, which supervise production, distribution and sales. There are also central bodies responsible for the power generation industry, agriculture, land reclamation and transport.

GOVERNMENT AGENCIES

Council for Oil and Gas Affairs: Tripoli; f. 2006; reports to the General People's Committee; holds ultimate responsibility for all matters involving oil, gas and their by-products; Chair. Dr AL-BAGHDADI ALI AL-MAHMOUDI.

Great Man-made River Water Utilization Authority (GMRA): POB 7217, Benghazi; tel. (61) 2230392; fax (61) 2230393; e-mail info@gmrwua.com; internet www.gmrwua.com; supervises construction of pipeline carrying water to the Libyan coast from beneath the Sahara desert, to provide irrigation for agricultural projects; Sec. for the Great Man-made River project ABD AL-MAJID AL-AOUD.

Libyan Economic Development Board (LEDB): Tripoli; f. 2007; charged with the drafting and execution of reform campaigns, and the facilitation of decision-making and action on critical economic issues; Chair. OMRAN BUKHRES.

DEVELOPMENT ORGANIZATIONS

Arab Organization for Agricultural Development: POB 12898, Zohra, Tripoli; tel. and fax (21) 3619275; e-mail arabagri@lycos.com; internet www.aoad.org; responsible for agricultural devt projects.

General National Organization for Industrialization: Sharia San'a, Tripoli; tel. (21) 3334995; f. 1970; public org. responsible for the devt of industry.

Kufra and Sarir Authority: Council of Agricultural Development, Benghazi; f. 1972 to develop the Kufra oasis and Sarir area in southeast Libya.

CHAMBERS OF COMMERCE

Benghazi Chamber of Commerce, Trade, Industry and Agriculture: POB 208 and 1286, Benghazi; tel. (61) 3372319; fax (61) 3380761; f. 1956; Pres. Dr BADIA; Gen. Man. Dr TAREK TARBAGHIA; 150,000 mems.

Tripoli Chamber of Commerce and Industry: POB 2321, Sharia Najed 6–8, Tripoli; tel. (21) 3336855; fax (21) 3332655; f. 1952; Chair. MUHAMMAD KANOON; Dir-Gen. ABDULMONEM H. BURAWI; 30,000 mems.

UTILITIES

Electricity

General Electricity Company of Libya (GECOL): POB 668, Tripoli; tel. (21) 4445068; fax (21) 4447023; e-mail gecol@gecol.ly; internet www.gecol.ly; Sec. of People's Cttee Eng. OMRAN IBRAHIM ABU KRAA.

STATE HYDROCARBONS COMPANIES

Until 1986 petroleum affairs in Libya were dealt with primarily by the Secretariat of the General People's Committee for Petroleum. This body was abolished in March 1986, and sole responsibility for the administration of the petroleum industry passed to the national companies that were already in existence. The Secretariat of the General People's Committee for Petroleum was re-established in March 1989 and incorporated into the new Secretariat for the General People's Committee for Energy in October 1992. This was dissolved in March 2000, and responsibility for local oil policy was transferred to the National Oil Corporation, under the supervision of the General People's Committee. Since 1973 the Libyan Government has entered into participation agreements with some of the foreign oil companies (concession holders), and nationalized others. It has concluded 85%:15% production-sharing agreements with various oil companies.

National Oil Corporation (NOC): POB 2655, Tripoli; tel. (21) 4446180; fax (21) 3331390; e-mail info@noclibya.com; internet en .noclibya.com.ly; f. 1970 to: undertake jt ventures with foreign cos; build and operate refineries, storage tanks, petrochemical facilities, pipelines and tankers; take part in arranging specifications for local and imported petroleum products; participate in general planning of oil installations in Libya; market crude and refined petroleum and petrochemical products; and establish and operate oil terminals; from 2000 responsible for deciding local oil policy, under supervision of General People's Committee; Chair. Dr SHUKRI MUHAMMAD GHANEM.

Oilinvest International: Tripoli; wholly owned subsidiary of the NOC; Chair. and Gen. Man. AHMAD ABD AL-KARIM AHMAD.

Agip North Africa and Middle East Ltd—Libyan Branch: POB 346, Tripoli; tel. and fax (21) 3335135; Sec. of People's Cttee OMAR AS-SWEIFI.

Arabian Gulf Oil Co (AGOCO): POB 263, Benghazi; tel. (61) 28931; fax (21) 49031; Chair. TAWSIG MESMARI.

Az-Zawiyah Oil Refining Co: POB 15715, Zawia; tel. (23) 620125; fax (23) 605948; e-mail arcp@lttnet.net; f. 1976; Gen. Man. AL-MOAMARE A. SWEDAN.

Brega Oil Marketing Co: POB 402, Sharia Bashir as-Saidawi, Tripoli; tel. (21) 4440830; f. 1971; Chair. Dr DOKALI B. AL-MEGHARIEF.

International Oil Investments Co: Tripoli; f. 1988, with initial capital of US $500m. to acquire 'downstream' facilities abroad; Chair. MUHAMMAD AL-JAWAD.

National Drilling and Workover Co: POB 1454, 208 Sharia Omar Mukhtar, Tripoli; tel. (21) 3332411; f. 1986; Chair. IBRAHIM BAHI.

Ras Lanouf Oil and Gas Processing Co (RASCO): POB 1971, Ras Lanouf, Benghazi; tel. (21) 3605177; fax (21) 607924; f. 1978; Chair. ABULKASIM M. A. ZWARY.

Sirte Oil Co: POB 385, Marsa el-Brega, Tripoli; tel. (21) 607261; fax (21) 601487; f. 1955 as Esso Standard Libya, taken over by Sirte Oil Co 1982; absorbed the National Petrochemicals Co in October 1990; exploration, production of crude oil, gas and petrochemicals, liquefaction of natural gas; Chair. M. M. BENNIRAN.

Umm al-Jawaby Petroleum Co: POB 693, Tripoli; Chair. and Gen. Man. MUHAMMAD TENTTOUSH.

Waha Oil Co: POB 395, Tripoli; tel. (21) 3337161; fax (21) 3337169; Chair. SALEH M. KAABAR.

Zueitina Oil Co: POB 2134, Tripoli; tel. (21) 3338011; fax (21) 3339109; f. 1986; Chair. of Management Cttee BASHIR BAZAZI.

TRADE UNIONS

General Federation of Producers' Trade Unions: POB 734, Sharia Istanbul 2, Tripoli; tel. (21) 4446011; f. 1952; affiliated to ITUC; Sec.-Gen. BASHIR IHWIJ; 17 trade unions with 700,000 mems.

General Union for Oil and Petrochemicals: Tripoli; Chair. MUHAMMAD MITHNANI.

Pan-African Federation of Petroleum Energy and Allied Workers: Tripoli; affiliated to the Organisation of African Trade Union Unity.

Transport

Department of Road Transport and Railways: POB 14527, Sharia az-Zawiyah, Secretariat of Communications and Transport Bldg, Tripoli; tel. (21) 609011; fax (21) 605605; Dir-Gen. (Projects and Research) MUHAMMAD ABU ZIAN.

RAILWAYS

There are, at present, no railways in Libya. In mid-1998, however, the Government invited bids for the construction of a 3,170 km-railway, comprising one branch, 2,178 km in length, running from north to south, and another, 992 km in length, running from east to west along the north coast. The railway may eventually be linked to other North African rail networks.

Railway Executive Board: Tripoli; tel. (21) 3609486; fax (21) 626734; e-mail info@libyanrailways.com; oversees the planning and construction of railways.

ROADS

The most important road is the 1,822-km national coast road from the Tunisian to the Egyptian border, passing through Tripoli and Benghazi. It has a second link between Barce and Lamluda, 141 km long. Another national road runs from a point on the coastal road 120 km south of Misurata through Sebha to Ghat near the Algerian border (total length 1,250 km). There is a branch 247 km long running from Vaddan to Sirte (Surt). A 690-km road, connecting Tripoli and Sebha, and another 626 km long, from Ajdabiya in the north to Kufra in the south-east, were opened in 1983. The Tripoli–Ghat section (941 km) of the third, 1,352-km national road was opened in September 1984. There is a road crossing the desert from Sebha to the frontiers of Chad and Niger.

In addition to the national highways, the west of Libya has about 1,200 km of paved and macadamized roads and the east about 500 km. All the towns and villages of Libya, including the desert oases, are accessible by motor vehicle. In 1999 Libya had an estimated total road network of 83,200 km, of which 47,590 km was paved.

SHIPPING

The principal ports are Tripoli, Benghazi, Mersa Brega, Misurata and as-Sider. Zueitina, Ras Lanouf, Mersa Hariga, Mersa Brega and as-Sider are mainly oil ports. A pipeline connects the Zelten oilfields with Mersa Brega. Another pipeline joins the Sarir oilfield with Mersa Hariga, the port of Tobruk, and a pipeline from the Sarir field to Zueitina was opened in 1968. A port is being developed at Darnah. Libya also has the use of Tunisian port facilities at Sand Gabès, to alleviate congestion at Tripoli. At 31 December 2006 Libya's merchant fleet consisted of 139 vessels, with a combined displacement of 105,368 grt.

General National Maritime Transport Co: POB 80173, esh-Shaab Terminal, Tripoli; tel. (21) 3339631; fax (21) 4441710; e-mail info@gnmtc.com; internet www.gnmtc.com; f. 1971 to handle all projects dealing with maritime trade; state-owned; Chair. Capt. ALI BELHAG AHMED.

Libya Shipping Agency: POB 4288, Tripoli; tel. (21) 3402528; fax (21) 3403496; e-mail info@libyashipping.com; internet www.libyashipping.com; provides chartering, land transportation and customs clearance services; Gen. Man. IMAD FELLAH.

CIVIL AVIATION

There are four international airports: Tripoli International Airport, situated at ben Gashir, 34 km (21 miles) from Tripoli; Benina Airport 19 km (12 miles) from Benghazi; Sebha Airport; and Misurata Airport. There are a further 10 regional airports. A US $800m. programme to improve the airport infrastructure and air traffic control network was approved in mid-2001. In the mid-2000s plans were announced for the upgrade and expansion of Tripoli International Airport, which were to include the construction of two new terminals, following which the airport's annual passenger capacity was expected to increase to some 20m., compared with 3m. in 2007. Work on the project was scheduled to commence in August 2008. Meanwhile, in August 2007 a Canadian company was awarded a $541m. contract for the construction of a new international airport at Benghazi.

Afriqiyah Airways: 1st Floor, Waha Bldg, Sharia Omar al-Mokhtar, Tripoli; tel. (21) 4449734; fax (21) 3341181; e-mail customerservice@afriqiyah.aero; internet www.afriqiyah.aero; f. 2001; state-owned; flights to 23 destinations in Africa, Europe and Saudi Arabia; Chair. Capt. SABRI S. ABDALLA.

Buraq Air: Tripoli International Airport, Tripoli; e-mail lias@buraqair.com; internet www.buraqair.com; f. 2000; first privately owned Libyan airline; scheduled international passenger and cargo flights to Morocco, Syria and Turkey; domestic flights from Tripoli, Benghazi and Misurata; Chair. and Man. Dir Capt. MUHAMMAD A. BUBEIDA.

Libyan Arab Airlines: POB 2555, ben Fernas Bldg, Sharia Haiti, Tripoli; tel. (21) 3614102; fax (21) 3614815; internet www.ln.aero; f. 1989 by merger of Jamahiriya Air Transport (which in 1983 took over operations of United African Airlines) and Libyan Arab Airlines (f. 1964 as Kingdom of Libya Airlines and renamed 1969); passenger and cargo services from Tripoli, Benghazi and Sebha to destinations in Europe, North Africa, the Middle East and Asia; domestic services throughout Libya; Chair. and CEO Eng. TARIK AREBI.

Tourism

The principal attractions for visitors to Libya are Tripoli, with its beaches and annual International Fair, the ancient Roman towns of Sabratha, Leptis Magna and Cyrene, and historic oases. There were 999,343 visitor arrivals in 2004; in 2005 receipts totalled some US $301m.

Tripoli International Fair Department: POB 891, Sharia Omar Mukhtar, Tripoli; tel. (21) 3332255; fax (21) 4448385; Head of Fairs KHALIL S. AS-SENUSSI.

General Board of Tourism and Traditional Industries: POB 82063, Tripoli; tel. (21) 3334673; fax (21) 4445336; e-mail info@libyan-tourism.net; internet www.libyan-tourism.org; Chair. MUHAMMAD SEALNA.

LIECHTENSTEIN

Introductory Survey

Location, Climate, Language, Religion, Flag, Capital

The Principality of Liechtenstein is in central Europe. The country lies on the east bank of the Upper Rhine river, bordered by Switzerland to the west and south, and by Austria to the north and east. Liechtenstein has an Alpine climate, with mild winters. The average annual temperature is about 10°C, while average annual rainfall is about 1,000 mm. The official language is German, of which a dialect—Alemannish—is spoken. Almost all of the inhabitants profess Christianity, and about 79% are adherents of the Roman Catholic Church. The national flag (proportions 3 by 5) consists of two equal horizontal stripes, of royal blue and red, with a golden princely crown, outlined in black, in the upper hoist. The capital is Vaduz.

Recent History

Liechtenstein has been an independent state since 1719, except while under French domination briefly in the early 19th century. In 1919 Switzerland assumed responsibility for Liechtenstein's diplomatic representation, replacing Austria. In 1920 a postal union with Switzerland was agreed, and in 1924 a treaty was concluded with Switzerland whereby Liechtenstein was incorporated in a joint customs union. Franz Josef II succeeded as Reigning Prince in 1938. In 1950 Liechtenstein became a party to the Statute of the International Court of Justice (ICJ, see p. 20), in 1973 it joined the Organization for Security and Co-operation in Europe (see p. 354) and in 1978 it was admitted to the Council of Europe (see p. 225). Liechtenstein became a member of the UN in September 1990 (hitherto the country had been a member of some UN specialized agencies). In the following year Liechtenstein became a full member of the European Free Trade Association (EFTA, see p. 412).

After 42 years as the dominant party in government, the Fortschrittliche Bürgerpartei (FBP—Progressive Citizens' Party) was defeated by the Vaterländische Union (VU—Patriotic Union) at a general election to the Landtag (parliament) in February 1970. Four years later the FBP regained its majority. At the general election to the Landtag in February 1978, the VU, led by Hans Brunhart, won eight of the 15 seats, although with a minority of the votes cast, while the remaining seats were taken by the FBP, led by Dr Walter Kieber, the Head of Government since March 1974. After protracted negotiations, Brunhart replaced Kieber in April 1978. At the general election in February 1982, the distribution of seats remained unchanged, although the VU gained a majority of votes. Following a referendum in July 1984, women were granted the right to vote on a national basis. However, women were still not permitted to vote on communal affairs in three of Liechtenstein's 11 communes until April 1986, when they were finally accorded full voting rights. (An amendment to the Constitution, declaring equality between men and women, took effect in 1992.) In August 1984 Prince Franz Josef transferred executive power to his son, Prince Hans-Adam, although he remained titular Head of State until his death in November 1989, when he was succeeded by Hans-Adam (Hans-Adam II).

The composition of the Landtag remained unchanged following a general election in February 1986, when women voted for the first time in a national poll. In January 1989 the Landtag was dissolved by Prince Hans-Adam, following a dispute between the VU and the FBP regarding the construction of a new museum to accommodate the royal art collection. At the subsequent general election, which took place in March, the number of seats in the Landtag was increased from 15 to 25; the VU retained its majority, securing 13 seats, while the FBP took the remaining 12 seats.

At the next general election, which took place in February 1993, the VU lost its majority, taking only 11 of the Landtag's 25 seats. The FBP retained 12 seats, and two seats were won by an environmentalist party, the Freie Liste (FL—Free List). Lengthy negotiations resulted in the formation of a new coalition between the FBP and the VU, in which the FBP was the dominant party, and Markus Büchel of the FBP became Head of Government. In September, however, following a unanimous vote in the Landtag expressing 'no confidence' in his leadership, Büchel was dismissed from his post, and Prince Hans-Adam dissolved the legislature. At a further general election, which was held in October, the VU regained its majority, winning 13 seats, while the FBP took 11 seats and the FL one. The VU became the dominant party in a new coalition with the FBP, with Mario Frick of the VU as Head of Government.

In October 1992 almost 2,000 people demonstrated in Vaduz to protest against a threat by Prince Hans-Adam that he would dissolve the Landtag if deputies did not submit to his wish to hold a proposed referendum to endorse Liechtenstein's entry to the nascent European Economic Area (EEA) shortly in advance of a similar vote in Switzerland. The Prince believed that the outcome of the Swiss poll might be prejudicial to that of the Liechtenstein vote, and that, in the event of voters' rejecting EEA membership at an early referendum, Liechtenstein might still be able to join other EFTA members in applying for admission to the European Community (EC, now European Union—EU, see p. 244). A compromise was reached, whereby the referendum was scheduled to take place shortly after the Swiss vote, while the Government agreed actively to promote a vote in favour of the EEA and to explore the possibility of applying to the EC should EEA membership be rejected. (The authorities subsequently decided that admission to the EU would not be beneficial to the Principality.) At the referendum in December, although Switzerland's voters had rejected accession to the EEA, Liechtenstein's membership was approved by 55.8% of those who voted (about 87% of the Principality's electorate); consequently, the two countries' joint customs union was renegotiated. In April 1995 a further national referendum was held, at which 55.9% of those who voted (around 82% of the electorate) approved the revised customs arrangements. Liechtenstein joined the EEA in May.

In March 1996 the Landtag adopted a unanimous motion of loyalty to the hereditary monarchy, after Prince Hans-Adam offered to resign (following tension between the Prince and the legislature—see above). At the next general election, which took place in February 1997, the VU retained its majority with 13 seats, while the FBP secured 10 seats and the FL two. Frick remained Head of Government. In April the FBP withdrew from the ruling coalition, leaving a single party (the VU) to govern alone for the first time since 1938. The constitutional role of the Reigning Prince came under renewed scrutiny in 1997, when, against the wishes of the Landtag, Prince Hans-Adam refused to reappoint Dr Herbert Wille, a senior judge who had advocated that constitutional issues should be decided by the Supreme Court rather than the Monarch. Dr Wille subsequently presented a formal complaint to the European Court of Human Rights, which ruled, in November 1999, that Prince Hans-Adam had restricted Wille's right to free speech; the Prince was required to pay 100,000 Swiss francs in costs.

In December 1999 Prince Hans-Adam requested an Austrian prosecutor, Kurt Spitzer, to investigate allegations in the German press based on an unpublished report of April 1999 by the German secret service that international criminals were using financial institutions in Liechtenstein to launder the proceeds of organized crime. As a result, five people were placed under investigative arrest in May 2000, including the brothers of both the Deputy Head of Government and of one of the Principality's most senior judges; all five were later released without charge. In his final report, which was released at the end of August, Spitzer concluded that Liechtenstein was no more culpable of money-laundering than other countries in Europe. He blamed the current problems on the Principality's over-bureaucratic and inefficient banking system and the poor application of existing legislation designed to combat economic crimes; criminal proceedings were initiated against two judges for abusing their authority. Spitzer also revealed that a money-laundering investigation was under way against Herbert Batliner, a lawyer who had been implicated in the party-funding scandal involving the former Federal Chancellor of Germany, Helmut Kohl, and his party, the Christlich-Demokratische Union Deutschlands (CDU—Christian Democratic Union), and in another case involving proceeds from drugs-trafficking in Colombia. In June the

Financial Action Task Force on Money Laundering (FATF), a commission of the Organisation for Economic Co-operation and Development (OECD, see p. 347), included Liechtenstein on a list of countries considered unco-operative in international attempts to combat money-laundering. In an effort to improve the country's international reputation, the Liechtenstein Bankers' Association announced in July that anonymous accounts would be abolished. In the same month the Government approved the establishment of a new financial investigative unit within the police force and measures to accelerate legal assistance to foreign countries in money-laundering investigations. Legislation was promulgated in December requiring financial institutions to maintain tighter controls over accounts and transactions, including the abolition of anonymous accounts. Liechtenstein was removed from the FATF's list of unco-operative countries in 2001, and, in October of that year, the Government appointed the former head of the Swiss anti-money-laundering authority, Daniel Thelesklaf, to administer a new financial surveillance unit, which was to enforce new regulations requiring banks and lawyers to be able to verify the identity of their clients. However, Liechtenstein was among seven jurisdictions identified by OECD as 'unco-operative tax havens' lacking financial transparency in April 2002, under its initiative to abolish 'harmful tax practices'. Although four jurisdictions were subsequently removed from the list, in early 2008 Liechtenstein remained one of three countries so designated.

In the general election that took place in February 2001 the VU lost its parliamentary majority, securing only 11 of the 25 seats in the Landtag, while the FBP won 13 seats and the FL obtained one. The VU administration's popularity had been adversely affected by an unresolved dispute with Prince Hans-Adam over his demands for constitutional changes, notably with regard to appointments in the judiciary (the Prince advocated that judges be nominated by the reigning Monarch rather than by parliamentary deputies); the Prince claimed that these amendments would benefit the people, whilst the VU regarded them as an attempt to extend the royal prerogative. A new Government comprising solely the FBP, under the leadership of Otmar Hasler, took office in April. The Prince had previously announced that if he failed to secure the support of the new Government for his proposed constitutional reforms, he would seek a national referendum; in December he also threatened to leave the Principality and take up residence in Austria.

The issue of constitutional reform was finally resolved by a national referendum, held on 14 and 16 March 2003, in which 64.3% of the votes cast were in favour of granting the Prince new powers; the voter participation rate was 87.7%. As a result of the referendum, the Prince gained the right to dismiss a government even if it retained parliamentary confidence, to appoint an interim administration pending elections, to preside over a panel to select judges, to veto laws by not signing them within a six-month period and to adopt emergency legislation. Conversely, citizens could now force a referendum on any subject (including the future of the monarchy) by collecting a minimum of 1,500 signatures. A compromise proposal put forward by a cross-party group that included former premier Frick (the Volksinitiative für Verfassungsfrieden—People's Initiative for Constitutional Peace), which suggested that a princely veto could be overruled by a referendum and sought to limit the Prince's use of emergency legislation to times of war, received the support of only 16.5% of the voters. The overwhelming support for the Prince's proposed changes was partially attributed to widespread fear that, if fulfilled, his threat of self-imposed exile as a symbolic monarch would cause economic decline and social upheaval. Prince Hans-Adam dismissed the findings of a commission established by the Council of Europe, which stated that the constitutional amendments would constitute a retrograde step for democracy and could lead to the isolation of Liechtenstein in Europe. On 15 August 2004 Prince Hans-Adam transferred his sovereign powers to his son, Prince Alois, in accordance with an announcement that he had made in August 2003. Prince Hans-Adam, however, remained Head of State.

At the general election held on 11 and 13 March 2005 the FBP failed to retain an absolute majority, winning 12 of the 25 seats, with 48.7% of the votes cast; voter participation was 86.5%. The VU won 10 seats (38.2% of the votes), while the FL increased its representation from one seat to three (with 13.0% of the votes). In April the FBP and the VU formed a coalition Government, which comprised three representatives of the FBP, including Hasler, who remained as Prime Minister, and two of the VU, with Dr Klaus Tschütscher becoming Deputy Prime Minister.

In August 2005 a conservative group known as the Volksinitiative für das Leben (People's Initiative For Life) submitted 1,889 signatures to the Government in support of its demands for a national referendum to be held on constitutional revisions. The group hoped to amend Article 14 of the Constitution so that the highest responsibility of the state would be 'to protect human life from conception until natural death' and also aimed to insert a reference to the state's responsibility to protect human dignity. The initiative was intended to address the potential legalization of abortion (which was the subject of much public debate) and, indirectly, the issues of euthanasia, genetic technology and stem-cell research. Having failed to secure sufficient support in the Landtag, the proposals were to be subject to a national referendum. Considering the initiative to be too restrictive, the FBP and VU jointly drafted a counterproposal to make the protection of life and human dignity a right for Liechtenstein citizens rather than a duty of the state. A further amendment was added explicitly prohibiting the death penalty (which had already been abolished by a revision of the criminal code in 1985). Following its approval by the Landtag in September, the counterproposal was presented to the referendum concurrently with the People's Initiative For Life. At the referendum, held on 25 and 27 November, the initiative, which opponents claimed would prevent abortion, birth control and assisted suicide, was rejected by 80.9% of the votes cast, while the counterproposal was adopted, with the support of 79.4% of voters.

In February 2008, following a meeting of EU ministers responsible for justice and home affairs in Brussels, Belgium, Liechtenstein became an associate member of the EU's Schengen Agreement (which binds signatories to the abolition of border controls) and the Dublin Convention on Asylum (relating to common formal arrangements on asylum). Liechtenstein was expected to implement the Schengen Agreement, concurrently with Switzerland, in November.

In the latter half of the 20th century Liechtenstein's relations with the Czech Republic and Slovakia were strained. This stemmed from the expulsion of ethnic Germans from Czechoslovakia and the confiscation of their land (without compensation) following the Second World War, under the controversial Beneš Decrees. The Liechtenstein royal family lost a large part of its estates during this time—including the castles of Feldsberg and Eisgrub, now estimated to be worth some €100m. Liechtenstein, which was a sovereign, neutral state throughout both the First and Second World Wars, claimed that it was unfairly grouped together with Germany under the terms of the Decrees. Czechoslovakia, however, considered the Liechtenstein royal family to have been collaborators with the Nazi regime in Germany during the Second World War, and that its action was thus legitimate. Liechtenstein also sought damages from Germany for assets that it claimed Germany had improperly awarded to Czechoslovakia after the Second World War as reparations. The German position was that the assets were seized by Czechoslovakia and that Germany was not responsible. In February 2005, however, the ICJ ruled that it was not competent to make a decision on the claim as it predated the 1980 agreement between the two countries that disputes between them should be settled by the ICJ.

At the beginning of the 21st century the Czech Republic and Slovakia still refused to recognize Liechtenstein as a sovereign state. In October 2003 Prince Hans-Adam blocked the entry of the Czech Republic and Slovakia (along with that of the eight other EU accession states) into the EEA; the 10 countries were due to become members of the EU on 1 May 2004 and would, under normal circumstances, have automatically joined the EEA. Their accession to the EEA was delayed until November 2003, when Liechtenstein agreed to sign the enlargement treaty on the EEA; Slovakia subsequently agreed immediately to establish diplomatic relations with Liechtenstein. Liechtenstein reiterated its demand that the Czech Republic and Slovakia acknowledge that the Principality was a sovereign, neutral state through both World Wars. To do so, however, would expose these two countries to the possibility of legal action being brought against them by Liechtenstein for the illegal seizure of land.

Following a four-year investigation, in April 2005 an Independent Commission of Historians charged with examining Liechtenstein's role in the Second World War reported that no Jewish assets were confiscated and no forced labour was used during the War, and that while 165 refugees from Nazi-controlled Austria were turned away by Liechtenstein between 1933 and 1945, 400 others were taken in and thousands more allowed safe passage to Switzerland. The Commission was appointed by the Government in 2001 after the World Jewish Congress accused the Principality's financial institutions of having hidden plundered Jewish assets for the Nazis during the War.

Relations with Germany were strained in early 2008, following the revelation that the German Federal Intelligence Service had paid some €4m. to a former employee of Liechtenstein's LGT Bank for access to records detailing accounts held by German nationals. In the aftermath of the revelations, senior members of the German Government, including the Federal Chancellor, Angela Merkel, criticized Liechtenstein's banking system and called for greater financial transparency in that country, as well as greater co-operation regarding tax evasion. Merkel's comments were strongly rejected by Prince Alois, who accused Germany of attempting to undermine Liechtenstein's sovereignty. In late February the Prime Minister, Hasler, travelled to the German capital, Berlin, for talks with Merkel, during which the Federal Chancellor urged Hasler to begin co-operation with other countries regarding fiscal data.

Government

The Constitution of the hereditary Principality provides for a unicameral Landtag (parliament), comprising 25 members, who are elected by universal adult suffrage for a term of four years (subject to dissolution), on the basis of proportional representation. The country is divided into the two election districts of Oberland (Upper Country) and Unterland (Lower Country), in which the seats are allocated separately. The Oberland district has 15 seats, the smaller Unterland district has 10 seats. A five-member Government is nominated by the Reigning Prince, on the recommendation of the Landtag, for four years. In March 2003 constitutional changes that extended the powers of the monarch were approved by a referendum; he was empowered to dismiss governments (even if they retained parliamentary confidence), appoint an interim administration pending an election, approve judicial nominees, veto laws and invoke emergency legislation. Citizens could force a referendum on any subject, including the future of the monarchy, by collecting 1,500 signatures. On 15 August 2004 the sovereign rights pertaining to the Reigning Prince were transferred to the Hereditary (Crown) Prince, who was to exercise them as the representative of the Reigning Prince, who remained Head of State.

Defence

Although Liechtensteiners under the age of 60 years are liable to military service in an emergency, there has been no standing army since 1868 and there is only a small police force, with 63 members.

Economic Affairs

In 2005, according to official estimates, Liechtenstein's gross national income (GNI) was 3,892m. Swiss francs, equivalent to 111,990 Swiss francs per head (establishing Liechtenstein among the world's most affluent nations in per-capita terms). During 1996–2006 the population increased at an average annual rate of 1.2%. According to UN estimates, during 1996–2006, gross domestic product (GDP) grew, in real terms, at an average annual rate of 3.2%; the UN estimated that GDP increased by 2.7% in 2006.

Following the Second World War, the importance of agriculture declined in favour of industry. According to official provisional estimates, in 2005 the agricultural sector (together with household producers) accounted for 7% of GDP. Within the agricultural sector the emphasis is on cattle-breeding, dairy-farming and market gardening. The principal crops are maize and potatoes. In addition, wine is produced, and forestry is a significant activity. In 2006 1.3% of those employed in Liechtenstein worked in agriculture (including forestry).

In 2005, according to official provisional estimates, industry (including production of goods) contributed some 39% of GDP, while 43.7% of those employed in Liechtenstein worked in industrial activity (including mining and quarrying, processing industries, energy and water supply and construction) in 2006. The metal, machinery and precision instruments industry is by far the most prominent sector. Other important areas are the pharmaceutical, textiles and ceramics industries.

In 2006 more than 90% of energy requirements were imported from other countries. In that year natural gas supplied 28.8% of energy requirements, electricity 26.3%, fuel oil 20.5%, motor fuel (petrol) 14.3% and diesel 7.9%.

According to official provisional estimates, in 2005 54% of GDP was generated by the services sector, while in 2006 the sector engaged 55.1% of those employed in Liechtenstein. Financial services are of great importance. Numerous foreign corporations, holding companies and foundations (estimated to number about 75,000) have nominal offices in Liechtenstein, benefiting from the Principality's stable political situation, tradition of bank secrecy (although stricter banking legislation was introduced in 1997 and in 2000–02, partly to increase the transparency of the sector) and low fiscal charges. Such enterprises pay no tax on profit or income, contributing instead an annual levy on capital or net worth. These levies account for about 20% of the Principality's annual direct revenue. In 1980 Liechtenstein adopted legislation to increase controls on foreign firms, many of which were thereafter subject to audit and entered in the public register. Following the Principality's accession to the European Economic Area (EEA) in 1995, the registration of foreign banks was permitted. New legislation governing insurance companies was approved in 1996, and during the late 1990s the insurance sector expanded rapidly. In December 2004 the Government and the European Union (EU, see p. 244) signed an accord on savings tax, which entered into force on 1 July 2005. Under the agreement, savings income, in the form of interest payments made in Liechtenstein to residents of the EU, became subject to a withholding tax. The building and hotel trades and other service industries are also highly developed. The Government initiated a publicity campaign in 2004 to promote Liechtenstein, with the launch of a national logo (a 'democratic crown' on an aubergine background). The objective was to increase tourism and investment and further to develop the Principality as a business centre.

With a very limited domestic market, Liechtenstein's industry is export-orientated. In 2007, according to preliminary figures, total exports amounted to 4,182.0m. Swiss francs (with imports totalling 2,416.4m. Swiss francs). Switzerland is the principal trading partner. In 2005 Switzerland purchased 11.7% of total exports of members of the Liechtenstein Chamber of Commerce and Industry and the EEA accounted for 44.1%. Specialized machinery, dental technology, vehicle components and frozen food are important exports.

In 2006 there was a fiscal surplus of 353.0m. Swiss francs. The annual average rate of inflation decreased gradually from 5.4% in 1990 to 0.6% in 2003. Consumer prices increased by an average of 1.2% in 2005, 1.1% in 2006 and 0.7% in 2007. Traditionally the unemployment rate has been negligible; in 2006 the rate of unemployment (as a percentage of those employed) was 2.2%. More than one-third of Liechtenstein's population are resident foreigners, many of whom provide the labour for industry, while in December 2006 14,604 workers crossed the borders from Austria and Switzerland each day to work in the Principality.

Liechtenstein has important economic links with neighbouring Switzerland. It is incorporated in a customs union with that country, and uses the Swiss franc as its currency. Liechtenstein became a member of the European Free Trade Association (EFTA, see p. 412) in May 1991 and the EEA in May 1995. The Principality is also a member of the European Bank for Reconstruction and Development (EBRD, see p. 239).

Education

Compulsory education begins at seven years of age. Basic instruction is given for five years at a primary school (Primarschule), after which a pupil may transfer to a lower secondary school (Oberschule) or secondary school (Realschule) for four years, with the option of an additional year, or to the Liechtensteinisches Gymnasium (grammar school) for eight years. There is no university. Many Liechtensteiners continue their studies at universities in Austria and Switzerland. Liechtenstein has a further education college for the study of philosophy, a technical college (Fachhochschule), a music school, an art school, an adult education centre and a school for mentally disabled children. Government expenditure on education totalled 136.2m. Swiss francs in 2006 (18.7% of total expenditure).

Public Holidays

2008: 1 January (New Year's Day), 2 January (St Berchtold's Day), 6 January (Epiphany), 2 February (Candlemas), 5 February (Shrove Tuesday), 19 March (St Joseph's Day), 21 March (Good Friday), 24 March (Easter Monday), 1 May (Labour Day and Ascension Day), 12 May (Whit Monday), 22 May (Corpus Christi), 15 August (National Holiday and Assumption), 8 September (Nativity of the Virgin Mary), 1 November (All Saints' Day), 8 December (Immaculate Conception), 25 December (Christmas), 26 December (St Stephen's Day).

LIECHTENSTEIN

2009: 1 January (New Year's Day), 2 January (St Berchtold's Day), 6 January (Epiphany), 2 February (Candlemas), 24 February (Shrove Tuesday), 19 March (St Joseph's Day), 10 April (Good Friday), 13 April (Easter Monday), 1 May (Labour Day), 21 May (Ascension Day), 1 June (Whit Monday), 11 June (Corpus Christi), 15 August (National Holiday and Assumption), 8 September (Nativity of the Virgin Mary), 1 November (All Saints' Day), 8 December (Immaculate Conception), 25 December (Christmas), 26 December (St Stephen's Day).

Weights and Measures
The metric system is in force.

Statistical Survey

Source: Amt für Volkswirtschaft, Gerberweg 5, 9490 Vaduz; tel. 2366111; fax 2366895; e-mail info.statistik@avw.llv.li; internet www.avw.llv.li.

AREA AND POPULATION

Area: 160.0 sq km (61.8 sq miles).

Population: 35,322, incl. 11,927 resident aliens at mid-2007.

Density (mid-2007): 220.8 per sq km.

Municipalities (population at mid-2007): Schaan 5,764; Vaduz (capital) 5,091; Triesen 4,701; Balzers 4,475; Eschen 4,112; Mauren 3,794; Triesenberg 2,550; Ruggell 1,917; Gamprin 1,491; Schellenberg 1,028; Planken 399; Total 35,322.

Births, Marriages and Deaths (2005, provisional): Live births 381 (10.9 per 1,000); Marriages 188 (5.4 per 1,000); Deaths 215 (6.2 per 1,000). *2006:* Marriages 290; Deaths 220.

Economically Active Population (2006): Agriculture and forestry 398; Industry and skilled trades 13,569 (Mining and quarrying 45, Processing industries 10,813, Energy and water supply 207, Construction 2,504); Services 17,107 (Retail, repairs, etc. 2,393, Hotels and restaurants 823, Transport and communications 1,123, Banking and insurance 2,339, Real estate, business services, etc. 2,838, Legal consultancy and trust management 2,390, Public administration 1,479, Education 925, Health and social services 1,617, Other services 1,180); *Total employed* 31,074; Unemployed 689; *Total labour force* 31,763.

HEALTH AND WELFARE
Key Indicators

Under-5 Mortality Rate (per 1,000 live births, 2004): 5.

Physicians (per 1,000 head, 1997): 1.31 (Source: Statistik des Fürstentums Liechtenstein, *Statistisches Jahrbuch (1998)*).

For sources (unless specified) and definitions, see explanatory note on p. vi.

AGRICULTURE, ETC.

Note: Figures are for farms with a minimum of either 1 ha of arable land, 30 acres of specialized cultivation, 10 acres of protected cultivation, 8 sows, 80 porkers (or capacity for 80 porkers) or 300 head of poultry, and where livestock owners are covered by the Tierseuchenfond (insurance against epidemics).

Principal Crops (metric tons, 1987): Wheat 460; Oats 4; Barley 416; Silo-maize 27,880; Potatoes 1,040. *2006:* Grapes 157 metric tons (FAO estimate) (Source: partly FAO).

Livestock (2006): Cattle 5,826; Pigs 1,723; Horses 426; Sheep 3,661; Goats 358; Hens 11,712.

Dairy Produce (2006, metric tons): Milk delivered to dairies 13,225; Milk for consumption and pasteurization 905; Milk for processing 5,270; Cream 1,759; Yoghurt 198.

Forestry ('000 cubic metres, 2006, FAO estimates): Roundwood removals (excl. bark) 22 (Sawlogs, veneer logs and logs for sleepers 18, Fuel wood 4). Source: FAO.

FINANCE

Currency and Exchange Rates: Swiss currency: 100 Rappen (centimes) = 1 Franken (Swiss franc). *Sterling, Dollar and Euro Equivalents* (31 December 2007): £1 sterling = 2.2548 Franken; US $1 = 1.1255 Franken; €1 = 1.6568 Franken; 10 Franken = £4.43 = $8.88 = €6.04. For average exchange rate, see chapter on Switzerland.

Budget (million Swiss francs, 2006): *Revenue:* Current 1,206.8 (Taxes and duties 687.1; Revenues from assets 463.0); Capital 15.8; Total 1,222.6. *Expenditure:* Current 772.4 (Personnel 147.1; Regular contributions 348.4; Financial allocations 155.8); Capital 97.2; Total 869.6.

National Income and Product (million Swiss francs at current prices, 2005, provisional): Compensation of employees 2,510.2; Gross operating surplus 1,418.1; Gross mixed income 390.9; *GDP at factor cost* 4,319.2; Taxes on production and imports 331.6; Subsidies –95.5; *GDP in market prices* 4,555.3.

Production Account for GDP (million Swiss francs at current prices, 2005, provisional): Total output 11,671.1; Financial intermediation services indirectly measured –341.8; *Gross value added in basic prices* 11,329.3; Taxes, less subsidies, on products 188.7; Intermediate consumption at purchasers' prices –6,962.7; *GDP in market prices* 4,555.3.

Gross Value Added by Economic Activity (percentage, 2005, provisional): Agriculture and households 7; Industry and production of goods 39; Financial services 29; General services 25.

EXTERNAL TRADE

Note: Imports and exports to and from Liechtenstein presented at Swiss customs, not including trade with Switzerland and goods traffic via Switzerland.

Principal Commodities ('000 Swiss francs, 2006, provisional): *Imports:* Food, animals and other products of agriculture 82,455; Raw materials, metals, construction and chemical products 321,983; Vehicles and transport equipment 81,956; Machinery and electrical products 687,448; Metal manufactures and other finished and semi-finished goods 792,864; Glass, ceramic and textile manufactures 197,303; Total 2,164,009. *Exports:* Food, animals and other products of agriculture 275,243; Raw materials, metals, construction and chemical products 374,861; Vehicles and transport equipment 323,599; Machinery and electrical products 1,150,541; Metal manufactures and other finished and semi-finished goods 1,192,803; Glass, ceramic and textile manufactures 286,636; Total (incl. others) 3,603,683.

Principal Trading Partners ('000 Swiss francs, 2007, provisional): *Imports:* Austria 892,644; China, People's Republic 35,664; France 43,469; Germany 972,257; Italy 125,189; Netherlands 28,582; Poland 37,141; United Kingdom 34,326; USA 44,329; Total (incl. others) 2,416,359. *Exports:* Austria 479,404; China, People's Republic 85,179; France 413,314; Germany 834,810; Hong Kong 39,695; Italy 264,427; Japan 75,586; Mexico 41,441; Poland 54,104; Russia 78,842; Singapore 53,284; Spain 162,778; Sweden 69,902; United Arab Emirates 55,736; United Kingdom 160,021; USA 596,549; Total (incl. others) 4,182,040.

TRANSPORT

Road Traffic (registered motor vehicles, 1 July 2007): Passenger cars 24,368; Commercial vehicles 2,566; Motorcycles 3,256; Total (incl. others) 31,900.

TOURISM

Arrivals by Country of Residence (2007): Austria 3,047; France 1,316; Germany 18,819; Italy 2,143; Netherlands 1,326; Switzerland 15,947; United Kingdom 2,644; USA 2,363; Total (incl. others) 59,603.

COMMUNICATIONS MEDIA

Daily Newspapers (2004): 2 (total circulation 18,387 copies). Source: UNESCO Institute for Statistics.

Radio Receivers (1998): 12,451 in use.

Television Receivers (1998): 12,089 in use.

Telephones (2006): 20,100 main lines in use. Source: International Telecommunication Union.

Mobile Cellular Telephones (2006): 28,800 subscribers. Source: International Telecommunication Union.

Internet Users (2006): 22,000. Source: International Telecommunication Union.

Broadband Subscribers (2006): 10,000. Source: International Telecommunication Union.

LIECHTENSTEIN

EDUCATION

(2006/07, unless otherwise indicated*)

Kindergarten: 51 classrooms; 80 teachers; 758 pupils.
Primary†: 119 classrooms; 270 teachers; 2,149 pupils.
High School: 33 classrooms; 111 teachers; 406 pupils.
Secondary: 40 classrooms; 120 teachers; 712 pupils.
Optional 10th School Year: 20 teachers; 84 pupils.
Vocational Training: 16 teachers; 120 pupils.
Grammar Schools (2004/05, unless otherwise indicated): 38 classrooms (2001/02); 103 teachers; 744 pupils.
Music (2004/05): 91 teachers; 2,519 pupils.
Higher Education (2004/05)‡: 527 students.

* Excluding private institutions.
† Including pre-school and reception classes.
‡ Those studying in Liechtenstein only (931 students attended institutions abroad).

Directory

The Constitution

Under the Constitution of 5 October 1921 (as amended in 1969, 1984, 2003 and 2005), the monarchy is hereditary in the male line. The Reigning Prince, who is constitutionally responsible for foreign affairs, exercises legislative power jointly with the Landtag (parliament). The Landtag comprises 25 members, who are elected for a term of four years (subject to dissolution) by universal adult suffrage, on a basis of proportional representation. Of those 25 members, 15 are elected by voters in the Oberland (Upper Country) and 10 by voters in the Unterland (Lower Country). Under the Constitution, all citizens of over 18 years of age are eligible to vote. The voters participate directly in legislation through referendums.

The Government is a collegial body consisting of five Ministers, including the Prime Minister. Each Minister has an Alternate who takes part in the meetings of the collegial Government if the Minister is unavailable. The Prime Minister, the other Ministers and their Alternates are appointed by the Reigning Prince on the recommendation of the Landtag. On the recommendation of the Landtag, the Reigning Prince appoints one of the Ministers as Deputy Prime Minister. Only native Liechtenstein citizens who meet the requirements for election to the Landtag are eligible for appointment to the Government. Each of the two regions of Liechtenstein, the Upper Country and the Lower Country, is entitled to at least two Ministers. Their respective Alternates must come from the same region. The term of office is four years (subject to dissolution).

In a referendum on 14 and 16 March 2003 the electorate approved constitutional amendments extending the powers of the monarch. He was awarded the right to dismiss governments (even if they retained parliamentary confidence), to appoint an interim administration pending fresh elections, to veto laws by not signing them within a six-month period, to dismiss individual Ministers, subject to approval by the Landtag, to preside over a panel to select judges (with a casting vote) and to invoke emergency legislation. Citizens were accorded the right to force a referendum on any subject, including the future of the monarchy, by collecting 1,500 signatures.

In a referendum on 25 and 27 November 2005 the electorate approved constitutional amendments on the protection of human dignity and the right to life. The death penalty (abolished by a revision of the criminal code in 1985) was explicitly prohibited, as was the inhumane or degrading treatment of individuals.

In accordance with a treaty concluded with Switzerland in 1924, Liechtenstein is incorporated in Swiss customs territory, and uses Swiss currency, customs and postal administration.

The Government

HEAD OF STATE

Reigning Prince: HSH Prince HANS-ADAM II (Prince of Liechtenstein, Duke of Troppau and Jägerndorf, Count of Rietberg—succeeded 13 November 1989).

On 15 August 2004 Prince Hans-Adam II transferred the execution of his sovereign powers to his son, Hereditary Prince Alois.

GOVERNMENT
(April 2008)

A coalition of the Fortschrittliche Bürgerpartei (FBP) and the Vaterländische Union (VU).

Prime Minister and Minister of General Government Affairs, of Finance and of Construction and Public Works: OTMAR HASLER (FBP).
Deputy Prime Minister and Minister of Economic Affairs, of Justice and of Sports: Dr KLAUS TSCHÜTSCHER (VU).
Minister of Foreign Affairs, of Culture and of Family and Equal Opportunity: RITA KIEBER-BECK (FBP).
Minister of the Interior, of Public Health and of Transport and Telecommunications: Dr MARTIN MEYER (FBP).
Minister of Education, of Social Affairs and of Environmental Affairs, Land Use Planning, Agriculture and Forestry: HUGO QUADERER (VU).
Alternate Ministers: URSULA BATLINER-ELKUCH (FBP), MAURO PEDRAZZINI (FBP), PATRICK SCHÜRMANN (FBP), HEIKE LINS-SELE (VU), RENATE MÜSSNER (VU).

GOVERNMENT OFFICES

Regierungsgebäude: Postfach 684, 9490 Vaduz; tel. 2366111; fax 2366022; e-mail office@liechtenstein.li; internet www.liechtenstein.li.

Legislature

LANDTAG

Landtagssekretariat des Fürstentums Liechtenstein: Städtle 47, 9490 Vaduz; tel. 2366576; fax 2366580; e-mail info@landtag.li; internet www.landtag.li.

President: KLAUS WANGER (FBP).
Vice-President: IVO KLEIN (VU).

General Election, 11 and 13 March 2005

Party	Votes	% of votes	Seats
FBP	94,547	48.74	12
VU	74,162	38.23	10
FL	25,286	13.03	3
Total	193,995	100.00	25

Election Commissions

Hauptwahl- oder Hauptabstimmungskommission Oberland: c/o Heiligkreuz 18, Postfach 684, 9490 Vaduz; tel. 2322202; fax 2361961; e-mail nv@viv.li; independent; Chair. NORBERT VOGT (Vaduz).

Hauptwahl- oder Hauptabstimmungskommission Unterland: c/o Postfach 684, 9490 Vaduz; independent; Chair. ALOIS ALLGÄUER (Eschen).

Political Organizations

Fortschrittliche Bürgerpartei (FBP) (Progressive Citizens' Party): Aeulestr. 56, Postfach 1213, 9490 Vaduz; tel. 2377940; fax 2377949; e-mail marcus.vogt@fbp.li; internet www.fbp.li; f. 1918; Pres. MARCUS VOGT.

Freie Liste (FL) (Free List): Postfach 254, 9494 Schaan; tel. 3732042; e-mail info@freieliste.li; internet www.freieliste.li; f. 1985; progressive social democratic and ecological party; Pres CLAUDIA HEEB-FLECK, EGON MATT.

Vaterländische Union (VU) (Patriotic Union): Bartlegroschstr. 19, 9490 Vaduz; tel. 2398282; fax 2398289; e-mail vu@vu-online.li; internet www.vu-online.li; f. 1936 by merger of the People's Party (f. 1918) and the Heimatdienst movement; Pres. ADOLF HEEB; Sec.-Gen. HANSJÖRG GOOP.

LIECHTENSTEIN
Directory

Diplomatic Representation

According to an arrangement concluded in 1919, Switzerland has agreed to represent Liechtenstein's interests in countries where it has diplomatic missions and where Liechtenstein is not represented in its own right. In so doing, Switzerland always acts only on the basis of mandates of a general or specific nature, which it may either refuse or accept, while Liechtenstein is free to enter into direct relations with foreign states or to establish its own additional missions. Liechtenstein has nine diplomatic missions abroad, comprising embassies in Berlin (Germany), Bern (Switzerland), Brussels (Belgium, including a permanent mission to the European Union), Washington, DC (USA), Vienna (Austria, including permanent missions to the Organization for Security and Co-operation in Europe and the UN), as well as a permanent representative to the Council of Europe in Strasbourg (France), a permanent mission to the UN in New York (USA) and a permanent mission in Geneva (Switzerland). Liechtenstein also has a non-resident ambassador to the Holy See. There are 38 consular representatives accredited to Liechtenstein, of which 22 have offices in the Principality (representing Austria, the Central African Republic, Chad, Cyprus, Denmark, France, Germany, Hungary, Iceland, the Republic of Korea, Luxembourg, the former Yugoslav republic of Macedonia, Malta, Monaco, the Netherlands, Poland, Romania, Russia, Saint Vincent and the Grenadines, Spain, Sweden and Ukraine).

Judicial System

CIVIL AND CRIMINAL COURTS

Landgericht (County Court): Äulestr. 70, 9490 Vaduz; tel. 2366111; fax 2366539; Court of First Instance; one presiding judge, and 13 other judges; Presiding Judge Dr BENEDIKT MARXER.

Kriminalgericht (Criminal Court): bench of five judges; Presiding Judge Lic. Iur. UWE ÖHRI.

Schöffengericht (Court of Assizes): 9490 Vaduz; for minor misdemeanours; bench of three judges; Presiding Judge Dr BENEDIKT MARXER.

Jugendgericht (Juvenile Court): 9490 Vaduz; bench of three judges; Presiding Judge Lic. Iur. UWE ÖHRI.

Obergericht (Superior Court): 9490 Vaduz; Court of Second Instance; divided into three senates, each with bench of five judges; Presiding Judge and Chair. of First Senate Lic. Iur. MAX BIZOZZERO; Chair. of Second Senate Lic. Iur. RUDOLF FEHR; Chair. of Third Senate Dr GERHARD MISLIK.

Oberster Gerichtshof (Supreme Court): 9490 Vaduz; Court of Third Instance; bench of five judges; Presiding Judge Dr HANSJÖRG RÜCK.

ADMINISTRATIVE COURTS

Verwaltungsgerichtshof (Administrative Court of Appeal): Städtle 49, Postfach 804, 9490 Vaduz; tel. 2366111; appeal against decrees and decisions of the Government may be made to this court; five members; Presiding Judge Lic. Iur. ANDREAS BATLINER.

Staatsgerichtshof (State Court): Geschäftsstelle, Städtle 36, Postfach 729, 9490 Vaduz; tel. 2391010; fax 2391039; e-mail kontakt@stgh.li; internet www.stgh.li; five members; exists for the protection of Public Law; Presiding Judge Lic. Iur. MARZELL BECK.

Religion

CHRISTIANITY

The Principality comprises a single archdiocese, Vaduz, created in 1997, which is directly responsible to the Holy See. At 31 December 2005 there were an estimated 26,800 adherents (some 78.8% of the population). The few Protestants (7.3%) belong to the parish of Vaduz.

Archdiocese of Vaduz: Erzbischöfliche Kanzlei, Fürst-Franz-Josef-Str. 112, Postfach 103, 9490 Vaduz; tel. 2332311; fax 2332324; e-mail erzbistum@powersurf.li; internet www.erzbistum-vaduz.li; Archbishop Most Rev. WOLFGANG HAAS.

The Press

Exclusiv: Aubündt 28, 9490 Vaduz; tel. 2328080; fax 2328081; e-mail info@exclusiv.li; internet www.exclusiv.li; f. 1996; monthly; Publr ALBERT MENNEL.

Liechtensteiner Vaterland: Fürst-Franz-Josef-Str. 13, 9490 Vaduz; tel. 2361616; fax 2361617; e-mail redaktion@vaterland.li; internet www.vaterland.li; f. 1913; publ. by Vaduzer Medienhaus AG; daily (Monday to Saturday); organ of the VU; Editor-in-Chief GÜNTHER FRITZ; circ. 10,295.

Liechtensteiner Volksblatt: Zollstr. 13, 9494 Schaan; tel. 2375161; fax 2375155; e-mail redaktion@volksblatt.li; internet www.volksblatt.li; f. 1878; daily (Monday to Saturday); organ of the FBP; Editor-in-Chief TINO QUADERER; circ. 7,503.

Liewo Sonntagszeitung: Fürst-Franz-Josef-Str. 13, 9490 Vaduz; tel. 2361616; fax 2361617; e-mail redaktion@liewo.li; internet www.liewo.li; f. 1993 as Liechtensteiner Wochenzeitung; publ. by Vaduzer Medienhaus AG; weekly (Sunday); Editor-in-Chief CORINNA BECK; circ. 32,000.

Wirtschaft Regional: Fürst-Franz-Josef-Str. 13, 9490 Vaduz; tel. 2361616; fax 2361617; e-mail info@wirtschaftregional.li; internet www.wirtschaftregional.li; f. 2001; publ. by Vaduzer Medienhaus AG; weekly; Editor-in-Chief MATTHIAS HASSLER.

PRESS AGENCY

Presse- und Informationsamt (PIA) (Press and Information Office): St Florinsgasse 3, 9490 Vaduz; tel. 2366721; fax 2366460; e-mail info@pia.llv.li; internet www.pia.llv.li; f. 1962; Dir DANIELA CLAVADETSCHER.

Publishers

Alpenland Verlag AG: Feldkircher Str. 13, 9494 Schaan; tel. 2395030; fax 2395031; e-mail office@buchzentrum.li; internet www.buchzentrum.li.

BONAFIDES Verlags-Anstalt: Pflugstr. 20, Postfach 82, 9490 Vaduz; tel. 2654680; fax 3900594; e-mail bva-fl@adon.li.

BVD Druck+Verlag AG: Landstr. 153, 9494 Schaan; tel. 2361836; fax 2361840; e-mail bvd@bvd.li; internet www.bvd.li; Pres. KURT GÖPPEL.

van Eck Publishers: Haldenweg 8, 9495 Triesen; tel. 3923000; fax 3922277; e-mail info@vaneckverlag.li; internet www.vaneckverlag.li; f. 1982; art, local interest, juvenile, golf, crime fiction; Man. Dirs FRANK P. VAN ECK, PETER GÖPPEL.

Ex Jure Verlagsanstalt: Aeulestr. 74, Postfach 86, 9490 Vaduz; tel. 2360404; fax 2360481; e-mail service@exjure.li; internet www.exjure.net; f. 1968; legal.

A. R. Gantner Verlag KG: Industriestr. 105A, Postfach 131, 9491 Ruggell; tel. 3771808; fax 3771802; e-mail bgc@adon.li; internet www.gantner-verlag.com; botany; Dir BRUNI GANTNER-CAPLAN.

GMG Verlag AG: Landstr. 30, 9494 Schaan; tel. 2381166; fax 2381160; e-mail verlag@gmg.biz; internet www.gmg.biz/verlag; f. 1990.

Lehrmittelverlag: Pflugstr. 30, 9490 Vaduz; tel. 2366390.

Liechtenstein-Verlag AG: Landstr. 30, 9494 Schaan; tel. 2396010; fax 2396019; e-mail flbooks@lol.li; internet www.liechtensteinverlag.com; f. 1947; belles-lettres and legal and scientific books; agents for international literature; Man. ARTHUR GASSNER.

Litag Anstalt—Literarische, Medien und Künstler Agentur: Industriestr. 105A, Postfach 131, 9491 Ruggell; tel. 3771808; fax 3771802; e-mail bgc@adon.li; f. 1956; Dir BRUNI GANTNER-CAPLAN.

MM-Verlag Buchhandlung Irmgard Meier: Pradafant 20, 9490 Vaduz; tel. 2329448; fax 2329449; e-mail mm.verlag@buchhandlung.li.

Neue Verlagsanstalt: In der Fina 18, Postfach 29, 9494 Schaan; tel. 2334381; fax 2334382; e-mail info@neue-verlagsanstalt.li; internet www.neue-verlagsanstalt.li; magazine publisher; Dir JANINE HILLERT.

Sändig Reprint Verlag Wohlwend: Am Schrägen Weg 12, 9490 Vaduz; tel. 2323627; fax 2323649; e-mail saendig@adon.li; internet www.saendig.com; f. 1981; natural sciences, linguistics, freemasonry, fiction, folklore, music, history; Dir CHRISTIAN WOHLWEND.

Topos Verlag AG: Industriestr. 26A, Postfach 551, 9491 Ruggell; tel. 3771111; fax 3771119; e-mail topos@supra.net; internet www.topos.li; f. 1977; law, politics, literature, social science, periodicals; Dir GRAHAM A. P. SMITH.

Verlag der Liechtensteinischen Akademischen Gesellschaft (LAG): Bildgass 52, Postfach 829, 9494 Schaan; tel. 2323028; fax 2331449; e-mail info@verlag-lag.li; internet www.verlag-lag.li; f. 1972; Dir NORBERT JANSEN.

LIECHTENSTEIN   *Directory*

Broadcasting and Communications

TELECOMMUNICATIONS

Amt für Kommunikation: Kirchstr. 10, 9490 Vaduz; tel. 2366488; fax 2366489; e-mail info@ak.llv.li; internet www.ak.llv.li; national regulatory authority; Dir KURT BÜHLER.

Telecom Liechtenstein AG: Schaanerstr. 1, 9490 Vaduz; tel. 2377400; fax 2377499; e-mail telecom@telecom.li; internet www.telecom.li; f. 1999; fixed-line and mobile cellular telecommunications, broadband internet access, digital television; Pres. OLIVER GERSTGRASSER.

BROADCASTING

Radio Liechtenstein: Dorfstr. 24, 9495 Triesen; tel. 3991313; fax 3991366; e-mail redaktion@radio.li; internet www.radio.li; f. 1995; Pres. CLEMENS LATERNSER; Editor-in-Chief MARTIN FROMMELT.

Finance

(cap. = capital; res = reserves; dep. = deposits; m. = million; brs = branches; amounts in Swiss francs)

REGULATORY AUTHORITY

Finanzmarktaufsicht Liechtenstein (FMA) (Financial Market Authority of Liechtenstein): Heiligkreuz 8, Postfach 684, 9490 Vaduz; tel. 2367373; fax 2367374; e-mail info@fma-li.li; internet www.fma-li.li; f. 2005; independent authority under the auspices of the Landtag; regulates banks and credit institutions, insurance cos and Liechtensteinische Post AG (Liechtenstein Postal Service); Chair. RENÉ H. MELLIGER; Pres., Management Bd MARIO GASSNER (acting).

BANKING

In early 2008 there were 15 banks in Liechtenstein.

Alpe-Adria-Privatbank: Landstr. 126A, Postfach 324, 9494 Schaan; tel. 2350111; fax 2350102; e-mail info@hypo-alpe-adria.li; internet www.hypo-alpe-adria.li; f. 1999 as Hypo-Alpe-Adria-Bank (Liechtenstein) AG; present name adopted 2007; 51% owned by BayernLB (Germany), 49% by Hypo Group Alpe-Adria (Austria); cap. 50m., res 10m., dep. 527m. (Dec. 2006); Pres. DIETMAR FALSCHLEHNER; Chair., Management Bd MARKUS MÜLLER.

Bank Alpinum AG: Städtle 17, 9490 Vaduz; tel. 2396211; fax 2396221; e-mail info@bankalpinum.com; internet www.bankalpinum.com; fmrly NewCenturyBank, renamed as above April 2006; Chair. WOLFGANG SEEGER; CEO URBAN B. EBERLE.

Bank von Ernst (Liechtenstein) AG: Egertastr. 10, Postfach 112, 9490 Vaduz; tel. 2655353; fax 2655363; e-mail info@bve.li; internet www.bve.li; wholly owned by EFG Bank (Switzerland); cap. 25m., res 4m., dep. 280m. (Dec. 2005); Chair. JEAN-PIERRE CUONI; Gen. Mans MAX CADERAS, ERNST WEDER.

Bank Frick & Co. AG: Landstr. 14, Postfach 43, 9496 Balzers; tel. 3882121; fax 3882122; e-mail bank@bfc.li; internet www.bfc.li; Chair. KUNO FRICK, Sr; CEO JÜRGEN FRICK.

Bank Vontobel (Liechtenstein) AG: Pflugstr. 20, Postfach 786, 9490 Vaduz; tel. 2364141; fax 2364142; e-mail postmaster@vontobel.li; internet www.vontobel.li; f. 2000; Pres. WALTER THOMA.

Banque Pasche (Liechtenstein) SA: Austr. 61, Postfach 832, 9490 Vaduz; tel. 2393333; fax 2393300; e-mail pasche.liechtenstein@pasche.li; internet www.pasche.li; fmrly Swissfirst Bank (Liechtenstein) AG; 52.5% owned by Banque Pasche CM-CIC Private Banking (Switzerland); Chair. JEAN-FRANÇOIS KURZ; CEO WALTER RUPF.

Centrum Bank AG: Kirchstr. 3, Postfach 1168, 9490 Vaduz; tel. 2383838; fax 2383839; e-mail info@centrumbank.com; internet www.centrumbank.com; f. 1993; cap. 20m., res 131m., dep. 838m. (Dec. 2006); Chair. Dr PETER MARXER; CEO Dr STEFAN LATERNSER.

Hypo Investment Bank (Liechtenstein) AG: Austr. 59, Postfach 23, 9490 Vaduz; tel. 2655656; fax 2655699; e-mail info@hypo.li; internet www.hypo.li; f. 1998; CEO, Management Bd Dr ANDREAS INSAM.

Kaiser Ritter Partner Privatbank AG: Pflugstr. 16, Postfach 725, 9490 Vaduz; tel. 2378000; fax 2378001; e-mail bank@serica.com; internet www.kaiserritterpartner.com; f. 1999; cap. 10m., res 22m., dep. 423m. (Dec. 2006); Pres. Dr PETER RITTER; Man. Dir K. HEINZ BECK.

LGT Bank in Liechtenstein Ltd (LGT): Herrengasse 12, Postfach 85, 9490 Vaduz; tel. 2351122; fax 2351522; e-mail info@lgt.com; internet www.lgt.com; f. 1920; present name adopted 1996; cap. 291m., res 1,042m., dep. 13,269m. (Dec. 2006); Group CEO Prince MAXIMILIAN.

Liechtensteinische Landesbank AG (State Bank): Städtle 44, Postfach 384, 9490 Vaduz; tel. 2368811; fax 2368822; e-mail llb@llb.li; internet www.llb.li; f. 1861; present name adopted 1955; cap. 164m., res −345m., dep. 13,184m. (Dec. 2006); Chair., Bd of Dirs Dr HANS-WERNER GASSNER; Chair., Management Bd Dr JOSEF FEHR; 4 brs.

Neue Bank AG: Marktgass 20, Postfach 1533, 9490 Vaduz; tel. 2360808; fax 2329260; e-mail info@neuebankag.li; internet www.neuebankag.li; f. 1992; cap. 40m., res 42m., total assets 1,257m. (Dec. 2007); Chair. GEORG VOGT.

Raiffeisen Bank (Liechtenstein) AG: Austr. 51, Postfach 1621, 9490 Vaduz; tel. 2370707; fax 2370777; e-mail info@raiffeisen.li; internet www.raiffeisen.li; f. 1998; total assets 252m. (Dec. 2006); Chair. WILLI FRITZ.

Verwaltungs- und Privat-Bank AG (VP Bank): Aeulestr. 6, 9490 Vaduz; tel. 2356655; fax 2356500; e-mail info@vpbank.com; internet www.vpbank.com; f. 1956; cap. 59m., res 445m., dep. 6,385m. (Dec. 2006); Chair. HANS BRUNHART; Gen. Man. ADOLF E. REAL; 4 brs.

Volksbank AG: Feldkircher Str. 2, 9494 Schaan; tel. 2390404; fax 2390405; e-mail info@volksbank.li; internet www.volksbank.li; f. 1997; Man. Dir GERHARD HAMEL.

Bankers' Association

Liechtensteinischer Bankverband: Pflugstr. 20, Postfach 254, 9490 Vaduz; tel. 2301323; fax 2301324; e-mail info@bankenverband.li; internet www.bankenverband.li; f. 1969; Pres. ADOLF E. REAL; Dir MICHAEL LAUBER; 15 mems.

INSURANCE

In early 2008 there were 37 insurance companies in Liechtenstein.

Fortuna Lebens-Versicherungs-AG: Städtle 35, 9490 Vaduz; tel. 2361545; fax 2361546; e-mail fl.service@fortuna.li; internet www.fortuna.li; f. 1996; Man. Dir HEINER KEIL.

Liechtensteinische AHV-IV-FAK: Gerberweg 2, Postfach 84, 9490 Vaduz; tel. 2381616; fax 2381600; e-mail ahv@ahv.li; internet www.ahv.li; state-owned; Dir WALTER KAUFMANN.

Swisscom Re AG: Kirchstr. 12, 9490 Vaduz; tel. 2301665; fax 2301666; Man. Dirs BERNHARD LAMPERT, URS LUGINBÜHL, MARCEL VON VIVIS, THOMAS WITTBJER.

Swiss Life (Liechtenstein) AG: In der Specki 3, 9494 Schaan; tel. 3777000; fax 3777099; e-mail office@swisslife.li; internet www.swisslife.li; absorbed CapitalLeben Versicherung AG in 2007; life insurance.

Transmarine Insurance Co Ltd: Aeulestr. 38, 9490 Vaduz; tel. 2334488; fax 2334489; f. 1996.

Valorlife Lebensversicherungs-AG: Heiligkreuz 43, 9490 Vaduz; tel. 3992950; fax 3992959; e-mail info@valorlife.com; internet www.valorlife.com; f. 1998; subsidiary of Vaudoise Versicherungsgruppe (Switzerland); Pres. ROLF MEHR; Dir SERGE HEDIGER.

Insurance Association

Liechtensteinischer Versicherungsverband eV (LVV): c/o Fortuna Lebens-Versicherungs AG, Städtle 35, 9490 Vaduz; tel. 2361549; fax 2361548; e-mail office@versicherungsverband.li; internet www.versicherungsverband.li; f. 1998; Pres. HEINER KEIL; 25 mems.

Trade and Industry

CHAMBER OF COMMERCE

Liechtensteinische Industrie- und Handelskammer (Liechtenstein Chamber of Commerce and Industry): Altenbach 8, 9490 Vaduz; tel. 2375511; fax 2375512; e-mail info@lihk.li; internet www.lihk.li; f. 1947; Pres. KLAUS RISCH; Gen. Man. JOSEF BECK; 40 mems.

INDUSTRIAL ASSOCIATION

Vereinigung Bäuerlicher Organisationen im Fürstentum Liechtenstein (VBO) (Agricultural Union): Duxweg 14, 9494 Mauren; tel. 3759050; fax 3759051; e-mail vbo@kba.li; Pres. THOMAS BÜCHEL.

UTILITIES

Electricity

Liechtenstein imported some 93% of its electricity in 2006, mainly from Switzerland.

Liechtensteinische Kraftwerke (LKW): Im alten Riet 17, 9494 Schaan; tel. 2360111; fax 2360112; e-mail lkw@lkw.li; internet www.lkw.li; Pres. Dr ALEXANDER OSPELT; Dir-Gen. GERALD MARXER.

LIECHTENSTEIN

Gas

Liechtensteinische Gasversorgung (LGV): Im Rietacker 4, 9494 Schaan; tel. 2361555; fax 2361566; e-mail lgv@lgv.li; internet www.lgv.li; f. 1985; Dir ROLAND RISCH.

Water

Wasserversorgung Liechtensteiner Unterland (WLU): Industriestr. 36, 9487 Gamprin-Bendern; tel. 3732555; fax 3735136; e-mail info@wlu.li; supplies water to Eschen, Gamprin, Mauren, Ruggell, and Schellenberg.

Gruppenwasserversorgung Liechtensteiner Oberland (GWO): supplies water to Balzers, Planken, Schaan, Triesen, Triesenberg and Vaduz.

TRADE UNIONS

Liechtensteiner ArbeitnehmerInnenverband (LANV) (Employees' Asscn): Dorfstr. 24, 9495 Triesen; tel. 3993838; fax 3993839; e-mail info@lanv.li; internet www.lanv.li; Pres. SIGI LANGENBAHN; Sec. JÜRGEN SCHÄDLER; 1,200 mems.

Wirtschaftskammer Liechtenstein: Zollstr. 23, 9494 Schaan; tel. 2377788; fax 2377789; e-mail info@wirtschaftskammer.li; internet www.wirtschaftskammer.li; f. 1936; aims to protect the interests of Liechtenstein artisans and tradespeople; Pres. ARNOLD MATT; Gen. Man. JÜRGEN NIGG; 3,000 mems.

Transport

RAILWAYS

Liechtenstein is traversed by some 18.5 km of railway track, which is administered by Austrian Federal Railways. There is a station at Nendeln, as well as two halts at Schaan and Schaanwald. A local service connects Feldkirch in Austria and Buchs in Switzerland via Liechtenstein, and the Arlberg express (Paris, France, to Vienna, Austria) passes through the Principality.

ROADS

Modern roads connect the capital, Vaduz, with all the towns and villages in the Principality. There are approximately 250 km of roads, all of which are paved. The Rhine and Samina valleys are connected by a tunnel 740 m long. Public transport is provided by a well-developed network of postal buses.

Liechtenstein Bus Anstalt (LBA): Städtle 38, 9490 Vaduz; tel. 2366310; fax 2366311; e-mail info.lba@tba.llv.li; internet www.lba.li; operates 42 buses on 13 routes over 105 km; Man. Dir ULRICH FEISST.

INLAND WATERWAYS

A canal of 26 km, irrigating the Rhine valley, was opened in 1943.

Tourism

Liechtenstein has an Alpine setting in the Upper Rhine area. The principal tourist attractions include a renowned postal museum, a National Museum and the Liechtenstein State Art Collection at Vaduz, as well as the Prince's castle (although this is closed to the public) and two ruined medieval fortresses at Schellenberg. Annually about two-fifths of foreign tourists visit the winter sports resort at Malbun, in the south-east of the Principality. For summer visitors there are some 400 km of hiking trails and an extensive network of cycling paths. In 2007 Liechtenstein received 59,603 foreign visitors.

Liechtenstein Tourismus: Postfach 139, Städtle 37, 9490 Vaduz; tel. 2396300; fax 2396301; e-mail info@tourismus.li; internet www.tourismus.li; Dir ROLAND BÜCHEL.

LITHUANIA

Introductory Survey

Location, Climate, Language, Religion, Flag, Capital

The Republic of Lithuania (formerly the Lithuanian Soviet Socialist Republic) is situated on the eastern coast of the Baltic Sea, in north-eastern Europe. It is bounded by Latvia to the north, by Belarus to the south-east, by Poland to the south-west and by the Russian exclave, Kaliningrad Oblast, to the west. Lithuania's maritime position moderates an otherwise continental-type climate. Temperatures range from an average of −4.9°C (23.2°F) in January to a July mean of 17.0°C (62.6°F). Rainfall levels vary considerably from region to region: in the far west the annual average is 700 mm–850 mm (28 ins–33 ins), but in the central plain it is about 600 mm (24 ins). The official language is Lithuanian. The predominant religion is Christianity. Most ethnic Lithuanians are Roman Catholics by belief or tradition, but there are small communities of Lutherans and Calvinists, as well as a growing number of modern Protestant denominations. Adherents of Russian Orthodoxy are almost exclusively ethnic Slavs, while most Tatars have retained an adherence to Islam. The national flag (proportions 3 by 5) consists of three equal horizontal stripes of yellow (top), green and red (bottom). The capital is Vilnius.

Recent History

Prior to annexation by the Russian Empire in 1795, Lithuania was united in a Commonwealth with Poland. In 1915, after the outbreak of the First World War, it was occupied by German troops. A 'Lithuanian Conference' was convened in September 1917, which demanded the re-establishment of an independent Lithuanian state and elected a 'Lithuanian Council', headed by Antanas Smetona; it proceeded to declare independence on 16 February 1918. The new state survived both a Soviet attempt to create a Lithuanian-Belarusian Soviet republic and a Polish campaign aimed at reincorporating Lithuania. In October 1920 Poland annexed the region of Vilnius, but was forced to recognize the rest of Lithuania as an independent state (with its provisional capital at Kaunas). Soviet Russia had recognized Lithuanian independence in the Treaty of Moscow, signed in July. Lithuania's first Constitution, which declared Lithuania a parliamentary democracy, was adopted in August 1922. In December 1926 Smetona seized power in a military *coup d'état* and established an authoritarian regime, which endured until 1940.

According to the 'Secret Protocols' to the Treaty of Non-Aggression (the Molotov-Ribbentrop Pact), signed on 23 August 1939 by the USSR and Germany, Lithuania was to be part of the German sphere of influence. However, the Nazi-Soviet Treaty on Friendship and Existing Borders, agreed in September (following the outbreak of the Second World War), permitted the USSR to take control of Lithuania. In October Lithuania was compelled to agree to the stationing of 20,000 Soviet troops on its territory. In return, the USSR granted the city and region of Vilnius (which had been seized by Soviet troops in September) to Lithuania. In June 1940 the USSR dispatched a further 100,000 troops to Lithuania and forced the Lithuanian Government to resign. A Soviet-approved People's Government was formed. Elections to a People's Seim (parliament), which only pro-Soviet candidates were permitted to contest, took place in July. The Seim proclaimed the Lithuanian Soviet Socialist Republic on 21 July, and on 3 August Lithuania formally became a Union Republic of the USSR. The establishment of Soviet rule was followed by the arrest and imprisonment of many Lithuanian politicians and government officials.

Some 210,000 people, mainly Jews, were killed during the Nazi occupation of Lithuania (1941–44). The return of the Soviet Army, in 1944, was not welcomed by most Lithuanians, and anti-Soviet partisan warfare continued until 1952. Lithuanian agriculture was forcibly collectivized and rapid industrialization was implemented. Meanwhile, some 150,000 people were deported, many to Kazakhstan or to Russian Siberia and the Far East, and leaders and members of the Roman Catholic Church were persecuted and imprisoned. Lithuanian political parties were disbanded, and political power became the exclusive preserve of the Communist Party of Lithuania (CPL), the local branch of the Communist Party of the Soviet Union (CPSU). The leader (First Secretary) of the CPL in 1940–74 was Antanas Sniečkus.

A significant dissident movement was established during the 1960s and 1970s. With the introduction of the policy of *glasnost* (openness) by the Soviet leader, Mikhail Gorbachev, in the mid-1980s, a limited discussion of previously censored aspects of Lithuanian history appeared in the press. Dissident groups took advantage of a more tolerant attitude to political protests, organizing a demonstration in August 1987 to denounce the Nazi-Soviet Pact. However, in February 1988 security forces were deployed to prevent the public celebration of the 70th anniversary of Lithuanian independence. This, together with frustration among the intelligentsia at the slow pace of reform in the republic, led to the establishment in June of the Lithuanian Movement for Reconstruction (Sąjūdis). Sąjūdis organized mass demonstrations to protest against environmental pollution, the suppression of national culture and 'russification', and to condemn the signing of the Molotov-Ribbentrop Pact. The movement appealed to the CPL to support a declaration of independence and the recognition of Lithuanian as the state language. The latter demand was adopted by the Lithuanian Supreme Soviet (Supreme Council—legislature) in November, and traditional Lithuanian state symbols were restored. Other concessions made by the CPL during 1988 included the restoration of Independence Day as a public holiday and the return of buildings to the Roman Catholic Church.

Sąjūdis won 36 of the 42 popularly elected Lithuanian seats at elections to the all-Union Congress of People's Deputies in March 1989. Thereafter, the CPL began to adopt a more radical position, in an attempt to retain some measure of popular support. On 18 May the CPL-dominated Supreme Soviet approved a declaration of Lithuanian sovereignty, which asserted the supremacy of Lithuania's laws over all-Union legislation. Public debate concerning the legitimacy of Soviet rule in Lithuania intensified: a commission of the Lithuanian Supreme Soviet declared the establishment of Soviet power in 1940 to have been unconstitutional and, in August, on the 50th anniversary of the signing of the Pact with Nazi Germany, more than 1m. people participated in a 'human chain' extending from Tallinn in Estonia, through Latvia, to Vilnius.

Despite denunciations of Baltic nationalism by the all-Union authorities, the Lithuanian Supreme Soviet continued to adopt reformist legislation, including the establishment of freedom of religion and the legalization of a multi-party system. In December 1989 the CPL declared itself an independent party, no longer subordinate to the CPSU, adopting a new programme and declaring support for multi-party democracy and independent statehood. Shortly afterwards a group of former CPL members who were opposed to independence formed a separate movement, the Lithuanian Communist Party on the CPSU Platform (LCP). Meanwhile, Algirdas Brazauskas, First Secretary of the CPL since October 1988, was elected Chairman of the Presidium of the Lithuanian Supreme Soviet, defeating three other candidates, including Romualdas Ozolas, a leading member of Sąjūdis. None the less, Sąjūdis remained the dominant political force in the republic, and its supporters won an overall majority in the elections to the Lithuanian Supreme Soviet in February–March 1990. This new, pro-independence parliament elected Vytautas Landsbergis, the Chairman of Sąjūdis, to replace Brazauskas as its Chairman (*de facto* President of Lithuania), and on 11 March declared the restoration of Lithuanian independence: Lithuania thus became the first of the Soviet republics to make such a declaration. The Supreme Council also restored the pre-1940 name of the country (the Republic of Lithuania) and suspended the USSR Constitution on Lithuanian territory. Kazimiera Danutė Prunskienė, a member of the CPL and hitherto a Deputy Chairman of the Council of Ministers, was appointed to be the first Prime Minister of the restored republic.

The Lithuanian declarations were condemned by a special session of the all-Union Congress of People's Deputies as unconstitutional, and Soviet forces occupied CPL buildings in Vilnius and took control of newspaper presses. An economic embargo was imposed on Lithuania in April 1990, and vital fuel supplies were suspended; the embargo remained in force for more than two months, until Lithuania agreed to a six-month moratorium on the independence declaration, pending formal negotiations. However, talks, which began in August, were soon terminated by the Soviet Government, and in January 1991 Landsbergis revoked the suspension of the declaration of independence, since negotiations on Lithuania's status had not resumed. Tension increased in the republic when the Soviet authorities dispatched to Vilnius troops (led by the special OMON units of the Soviet Ministry of Internal Affairs), who occupied former CPSU properties that had been nationalized by the Lithuanian Government. Landsbergis mobilized popular support to help to defend the parliament building, which he believed to be under threat. In mid-January 13 people were killed and about 500 injured, when Soviet troops seized the broadcasting centre in Vilnius. (In August 1999 six former officers of the LCP were convicted of complicity in attempts to overthrow the Lithuanian Government in January 1991, and sentenced to between three and 12 years' imprisonment.)

Meanwhile, policy differences had arisen within the Lithuanian leadership, and earlier in January 1991 Prunskienė and her Council of Ministers had resigned after the Supreme Council refused to sanction proposed price increases. Gediminas Vagnorius, a member of the Supreme Council, was appointed Prime Minister. The military intervention strengthened popular support for independence. A referendum on this issue took place on 9 February, at which 90.5% of voters expressed support for the re-establishment of an independent Lithuania and for the withdrawal of the Soviet army from the republic. In common with five other Soviet republics, Lithuania refused to conduct the all-Union referendum on the future of the USSR, which was held in March. (Voting did take place unofficially in predominantly Russian- and Polish-populated areas of Lithuania, where the majority endorsed the preservation of the USSR.)

A series of attacks by OMON forces on members of the nascent Lithuanian defence force and on the customs posts on the border with Belarus, combined with the seizure of power in Moscow by the conservative communist 'State Committee for the State of Emergency' (SCSE) in August 1991, led to fears in Lithuania that there would be a renewed attempt to overthrow the Landsbergis administration and reimpose Soviet rule. Soviet military vehicles entered Vilnius, but did not prevent the convening of an emergency session of the Supreme Council, which condemned the SCSE and issued a statement supporting Boris Yeltsin, President of the Russian Federation. As the coup collapsed, the Lithuanian Government ordered the withdrawal of Soviet forces from the republic and banned the LCP. (The successor party to the CPL, the Lithuanian Democratic Labour Party—LDLP, was not banned.) The Government also began to assume effective control of the country's borders. The failed coup prompted the recognition of Lithuanian independence by other states, and on 6 September the USSR State Council recognized the independence of Lithuania and the other Baltic republics (Estonia and Latvia), all three of which were admitted to the UN and the Conference on (now Organization for) Security and Co-operation in Europe (OSCE, see p. 354) later in the month.

During the first half of 1992 there was an increasing polarity within the Supreme Council between Sąjūdis deputies and those of the mainly left-wing opposition parties, most prominently the LDLP, led by Brazauskas. In April 10 members of the Council of Ministers criticized Vagnorius's 'dictatorial' methods, and two ministers subsequently resigned. Vagnorius tendered his resignation as Prime Minister in May, but remained in the post until July, when the legislature approved a motion of no confidence in his leadership. The Seimas (Parliament—as the Supreme Council had been renamed) appointed Aleksandras Abišala, a close associate of Landsbergis, as Prime Minister; a new Council of Ministers was named shortly afterwards. Meanwhile, the growing division within the legislature had led to a boycott by pro-Sąjūdis deputies, rendering it frequently inquorate. In July, however, the Seimas approved a new electoral law, whereby Lithuania's first post-Soviet legislative elections, scheduled for late 1992, would be held under a mixed system of majority voting (for 71 seats) and proportional representation on the basis of party lists (70 seats).

The LDLP emerged as the leading party in the elections to the Seimas, which took place on 25 October and 15 November 1992, winning a total of 73 of the 141 seats. The defeat of Sąjūdis (which, in alliance with the Citizens' Charter of Lithuania, secured 30 seats) was largely attributed to popular disenchantment with its management of economic reform. The Christian Democratic Party of Lithuania (CDPL), which was closely aligned with Sąjūdis, won 16 seats. Also on 25 October a referendum approved a new Constitution, which was adopted by the Seimas on 6 November. Pending an election to the new post of President of the Republic, Brazauskas was elected by the Seimas to be its Chairman and acting Head of State. In December Brazauskas appointed Bronislovas Lubys (hitherto a Deputy Prime Minister) as Prime Minister. Lubys formed a new coalition Council of Ministers, retaining six members of the previous Government and including only three representatives of the LDLP.

The presidential election on 14 February 1993 was won by Brazauskas, with some 60% of the votes cast. His only rival was Stasys Lozoraitis, Lithuania's ambassador to the USA. Brazauskas subsequently announced his resignation from the LDLP. In March Adolfas Šleževičius replaced Lubys as Prime Minister and in April Šleževičius was appointed Chairman of the LDLP. In May a new political organization, the Conservative Party of Lithuania (CP), also known as the Homeland Union (Lithuanian Conservatives), was formed. Mainly comprising former members of Sąjūdis, and chaired by Landsbergis, the CP rapidly established itself as the principal opposition party.

The Minister of the Economy resigned in October 1995, following the collapse of several small commercial banks and in view of the slow progress achieved in the privatization programme. In November the Government survived its second vote of no confidence, initiated by the conservative opposition, which accused the LDLP of economic mismanagement. The banking crisis culminated in December with the suspension of the operations of the country's two largest commercial banks, owing to insolvency; senior officials of both institutions were arrested on charges of fraud. In January 1996 it was revealed that Šleževičius had withdrawn funds from the Lithuanian Joint Stock Innovation Bank (LJIB) only two days before the bank's suspension. Later in January Romasis Vaitekūnas resigned as Minister of the Interior, following intense public criticism of his handling of the crisis; it was revealed that Vaitekūnas had also withdrawn funds from the LJIB before its closure. Kazys Ratkevičius, the Chairman of the Bank of Lithuania (the central bank), also resigned. Šleževičius initially disregarded a presidential decree that he should leave office, which was upheld by the Seimas in February. He was replaced as Prime Minister by Laurynas Mindaugas Stankevičius, hitherto Minister of Government Reforms and Local Governments. Šleževičius also resigned as Chairman of the LDLP, and was succeeded by Česlovas Juršėnas, the Chairman of the Seimas. In October Šleževičius was charged with abuse of office.

A general election took place in two rounds on 20 October and 10 November 1996. The results confirmed the substantial loss of popular support for the LDLP, which retained only 12 seats in the Seimas. The CP obtained 70 seats, and the CDPL 16. The right-wing Lithuanian Centre Union won 13 seats and the Lithuanian Social Democratic Party (LSDP) 12. Some 53% of eligible voters participated in the first round, and about 40% took part in the second. Following the election, a coalition agreement was signed by the leaders of the CP and the CDPL. Landsbergis was elected Chairman of the Seimas at the assembly's first sitting in late November, and shortly afterwards the Seimas approved the appointment of Vagnorius as Prime Minister. His Government was dominated by members of the CP, with three representatives of the CDPL and two of the Centre Union. In January 1997 the Minister of Finance, Rolandas Matiliauskas, resigned, amid allegations of financial impropriety. The Prosecutor-General, Valdas Nikitinas, also resigned, following criticism of his handling of investigations into the financial crises of 1995.

Brazauskas did not contest a further term of office in the presidential election held on 21 December 1997, and in the first round of voting none of the seven candidates won the overall majority of votes required to secure the presidency. In a second round of voting on 4 January 1998 the second-placed candidate after the first round, Valdas Adamkus (a former environmental-protection executive, who had been naturalized in the USA), narrowly defeated Artūras Paulauskas (a prominent lawyer and deputy Prosecutor-General, supported by the Lithuanian Liberal Union), with 50.4% of the votes. The new President immediately endorsed the mandate of the incumbent Government, and in March Vagnorius was confirmed as Prime Minister by the Seimas. In April Paulauskas announced the formation of a new, centre-left political party, the New Union (Social Liberals—NU), which hoped to attract the support of young voters.

LITHUANIA

A serious conflict of interests between Adamkus and Vagnorius intensified in April 1999, following the President's public criticism of what he regarded as the Government's inadequate attempts to eradicate corruption in the public sector. Although Vagnorius secured the confidence of the Seimas in a non-binding vote, at the end of the month he announced his intention to resign. In mid-May Adamkus invited the Mayor of Vilnius, Rolandas Paksas (a member of the CP), to form a new government. His Council of Ministers, announced at the beginning of June, was again formed from a coalition led by the CP and the CDPL. In October Paksas indicated that he would not endorse an agreement to sell a one-third stake in the state-owned Mažeikiai Nafta petroleum refinery to a US oil company, Williams International, under the terms of which Lithuania would be required to provide long-term financing equivalent to more than twice the price paid by the US company, in order to offset the refinery's debts. None the less, the Council of Ministers endorsed the sale, which was strongly supported by Adamkus and the majority of the CP, prompting the resignations of the Ministers of National Economy and of Finance, and, in late October, of Paksas.

At the end of October 1999 Adamkus nominated Andrius Kubilius, the First Deputy Chairman of the Seimas, as Prime Minister. Kubilius' Council of Ministers, approved by the legislature in mid-November, retained largely the same membership as the previous administration. Following the appointment of the new Government, the Lithuanian Centre Union announced that it was to become an opposition party; the party's leader, Romualdas Ozolas, had resigned as a Deputy Chairman of the Seimas after criticizing Landsbergis (who chaired both the CP and the legislature). In mid-November Paksas announced his resignation from the CP; in early December he was elected Chairman of the Lithuanian Liberal Union. Local elections in March 2000 resulted in considerable successes for parties of the left, most notably the NU, which had campaigned against the sale of principal state properties to foreign interests. A lack of support for the CP apparently precipitated a split in the party, as several deputies established a 'moderate' faction in the Seimas, thus depriving the CP-CDPL coalition of an automatic majority in the legislature. In May, in advance of scheduled legislative elections the country's two largest left-wing parties, the LSDP and the LDLP, agreed to contest the election in alliance. The New Democracy Party and the Lithuanian Russians' Union subsequently joined the alliance, which was known as the A. Brazauskas Social Democratic Coalition, after the former President, who had been elected Honorary Chairman.

Some 56.2% of eligible voters participated in legislative elections held on 8 October 2000, which were contested by 28 political parties and alliances. The CP won only nine seats (compared with 70 in 1996). The A. Brazauskas Social Democratic Coalition obtained the largest representation, with 51 seats. However, the Lithuanian Liberal Union (with 34 seats) and the NU (with 29), which had formed an informal alliance prior to the elections, subsequently signed a coalition agreement and were able to form a parliamentary majority with partners that included the Lithuanian Centre Union and the Modern Christian-Democratic Union. On 26 October the legislature approved the appointment of Paksas as Prime Minister; Paulauskas was elected Chairman of the Seimas. The new Council of Ministers, in which notable appointments included that of Antanas Valionis of the NU as Minister of Foreign Affairs, was approved at the end of the month. However, in subsequent months a number of ministers resigned from the cabinet, including the Minister of the Economy, Eugenijus Maldeikis, who was replaced by Eugenijus Gentvilas. Formalizing their electoral alliance, the LDLP merged with the LSDP at a joint congress held in January 2001; the LSDP thereby became the single party with the greatest number of seats in the Seimas, and Brazauskas was elected its Chairman. Further political consolidation took place in May, when the CDPL merged with the Christian Democratic Union to form the Lithuanian Christian Democrats.

In mid-June 2001 the six NU members of the Council of Ministers resigned their portfolios, following disagreements with the Lithuanian Liberal Union over privatization of the energy sector and economic reform, and criticism of the Prime Minister's style of leadership. Paksas was subsequently unable to form an alternative coalition government and, despite surviving a vote of no confidence, resigned on 20 June. Hopes that the previous coalition could be resurrected were short-lived, and the NU sought a new alliance with the LSDP. At the end of the month President Adamkus offered the post of Prime Minister to Brazauskas, who was confirmed on 3 July. The LSDP did not, however, offer the NU a formal coalition agreement, but instead agreed to an informal accord, which granted the NU the same six ministerial positions from which it had withdrawn in June (including the foreign affairs portfolio). In September Paksas resigned as Chairman of the Lithuanian Liberal Union, in compliance with intra-party demands; Gentvilas was appointed acting Chairman, and was confirmed in the post in October. In December Paksas and 10 other deputies left the parliamentary faction of the Lithuanian Liberal Union, owing, in part, to its failure to nominate Paksas as First Deputy Chairman of the Seimas. Paksas and the former Lithuanian Liberal Union deputies were formally expelled from the party in January 2002, and in March they founded the rightist Lithuanian Liberal Democratic Party (LLDP), with Paksas as its Chairman.

The results of the first round of voting in the presidential election, held on 22 December 2002, were inconclusive. A second round took place on 5 January 2003, in which Paksas obtained 54.7% of the votes cast, defeating Adamkus, with 45.3%, despite the fact that most major political parties had expressed support for the latter candidate. (However, observers noted that Adamkus appeared to have lost popularity through his implementation of market economic reforms.) Paksas was inaugurated as President on 26 February. On 4 March Brazauskas was reappointed as Prime Minister; he nominated a Council of Ministers that was substantially unchanged from the outgoing administration. Following the presidential election, Paksas resigned as Chairman of the LLDP; Valentinas Mazuronis was elected as his successor. In May Kubilius was elected as Chairman of the CP, in succession to Landsbergis. In the same month the Lithuanian Centre Union, the Lithuanian Liberal Union and the Modern Christian-Democratic Union merged to form the Lithuanian Liberal and Centre Union, with Artūras Zuokas as Chairman. In June a faction of the Lithuanian Centre Union that did not support the merger founded the National Centre Party, and elected Romualdas Ozolas as its Chairman. In February 2004 the CP merged with the Lithuanian Union of Political Prisoners and Deportees to form the Homeland Union—Conservatives, Political Prisoners and Deportees, Christian Democrats (HU).

Meanwhile, following the nomination by President Paksas of a new Director-General of the State Security Department, in October 2003 a classified departmental report was disclosed, which claimed to provide evidence of links between the presidential adviser on national security, Remigijus Acas, and Yurii Borisov, an ethnic Russian with purported connections with organized crime groups, who had contributed significant funds to Paksas' presidential election campaign. It was revealed that in April Paksas had signed a presidential decree permitting Borisov to hold dual citizenship, despite warnings from the State Security Department that he was suspected of involvement in the illegal trading of weapons. In November an emergency session of the Seimas established a special parliamentary commission to investigate Paksas' alleged links with Russian organized crime and the associated threat to national security, and the Prosecutor-General launched a criminal investigation into Borisov. Paksas subsequently dismissed a number of his senior advisers, but refused to appear before the commission. In December the Seimas approved the commission's conclusion that the President's conduct had jeopardized national security, and the following day both Brazauskas and Paulauskas appealed for the President's resignation. On 18 December the Seimas approved a draft resolution to initiate impeachment proceedings against Paksas, and an investigative commission was subsequently established to consider the charges.

On 18 February 2004 the investigative commission endorsed six charges, which were to form the basis for the impeachment of the President: that Paksas represented a threat to national security; that he had failed to protect classified information; that he had attempted illegally to influence the operations of private companies; that he was unable to reconcile his public and private interests; that he had hindered the operations of state institutions; and that he had failed to prevent his advisers from abusing their positions. On the following day the Seimas voted to initiate formal impeachment proceedings and, in the mean time, agreed to seek a ruling from the Constitutional Court as to whether the charges technically constituted a breach of the Constitution. Paksas continued to deny the charges against him, and in late February he demanded that the Seimas initiate impeachment proceedings against the parliamentary Chairman, Paulauskas, whom he accused of the unauthorized disclosure of the confidential report that had been made public in October 2003 (the request was rejected, on the grounds that the Constitution provided only for the impeachment of deputies, and not of the parliamentary Chairman). On 24 March 2004 Paksas unexpectedly announced the nomination of Borisov as a presidential adviser, but he subsequently retracted the nomination, alleging that it had been prompted by a blackmail attempt. In response to this development, on the following day the Seimas adopted a resolution urging Paksas to resign; Borisov was placed under house arrest for having violated a pledge to avoid contact with the President. On 31 March the Constitutional Court ruled that the President had severely violated the Constitution by: granting Borisov dual citizenship in exchange for financial support; failing to protect state secrets; and using his presidential office illegally to influence the actions of a company's shareholders. The ruling was followed by a parliamentary vote on Paksas' impeachment, which took place on 6 April. Paksas was removed from office, after the necessary three-fifths' majority in the Seimas supported impeachment on the three charges confirmed by the Constitutional Court. Paulauskas immediately assumed the presidency, in an acting capacity, pending a presidential election, and subsequently suspended his membership of the NU, in compliance with the Constitution. In May the Constitutional Court ruled that legislation recently passed by the Seimas, preventing an impeached head of state from seeking presidential office again, was in accordance with the Constitution, and Paksas was obliged to withdraw his candidacy from the forthcoming presidential election.

The first round of the presidential election, held on 13 June 2004 and contested by five candidates, proved inconclusive. In the second round, held on 27 June, Adamkus was narrowly elected, receiving 52.6% of the votes cast, and defeating Prunskienė. Meanwhile, Lithuania's first elections to the European Parliament, following the accession of the country to full membership of the European Union (EU, see p. 244) on 1 May (see below), were held concurrently with the first round of presidential voting, with the participation of 46% of the electorate. The recently founded Lithuanian Labour Party (LLP), headed by a controversial, ethnically Russian business executive, Viktor Uspaskikh, won five of the 13 mandates allocated to Lithuania; the governing LSDP, the Lithuanian Liberal and Centre Union and the HU each obtained two seats, while the LLDP and the Peasants' and New Democracy Union (PNDU—led by Prunskienė) each won one seat. Adamkus was inaugurated on 12 July, and on the following day the Seimas approved his nomination of Brazauskas as Prime Minister.

Elections to the Seimas, held in two rounds on 10 and 24 October 2004, demonstrated that the LLP had further consolidated its support. It became the largest single party in the Seimas, receiving 28.4% of the votes cast on the basis of party lists, and obtaining 39 of the 141 mandates available. A coalition of the LSDP and the NU, known as Working for Lithuania, received 20.7% of the votes cast on the basis of party lists, and 31 seats. The HU obtained 25 seats, and the Liberal and Centre Union 18. The Order and Justice coalition, comprising the Liberal Democratic Party and the Lithuanian People's Union for a Free Lithuania, received 11 seats, while the PNDU obtained 10.

In October 2004 the Vilnius District Court effectively cleared Paksas of disclosing state secrets by ruling that there was no indisputable evidence that Borisov had learnt from Paksas that his telephones were being monitored by the State Security Department. (However, this decision was overturned by the Court of Appeal in March 2005, when Paksas was ordered to pay a fine of 9,735 litai.) In December 2004 a congress of the LLDP re-elected Paksas as the party's Chairman.

Meanwhile, following prolonged negotiations, a coalition government of the LLP, the LSDP, the NU and the PNDU was presented for presidential approval in November 2004. Brazauskas was to remain as Prime Minister, while several prominent members of the LSDP and the NU were to retain the posts they had held in the outgoing administration. Uspaskikh was nominated as Minister of the Economy and Prunskienė as Minister of Agriculture. The Seimas approved the new Government in the following month.

It emerged in January 2005 that the Minister of Foreign Affairs, Antanas Valionis, a member of the NU, had previously served as a reservist in the Committee for State Security (KGB), the Soviet security service. However, although this revelation proved controversial, reservists were exempt from a law stating that all former KGB agents must formally declare their association with the organization. Later that month a Deputy Chairman of the Seimas and Chairman of the parliamentary Committee on European Affairs, Alfredas Pekeliunas, also came under investigation for membership of the KGB, a charge he denied; Pekeliunas resisted demands for his resignation. In April Algirdas Butkevičius submitted his resignation as Minister of Finance, after the governing coalition rejected a proposed tax-reform programme. He was replaced by Zigmantas Balčytis, hitherto the Minister of Transport, in May. In mid-June Uspaskikh resigned from both the Government and the Seimas after an ad hoc parliamentary ethics commission concluded that he had violated the principle of the separation of public and private interests; Kęstutis Daukšys replaced him as Minister of the Economy. Meanwhile, in early June the Mayor of Vilnius, Artūras Zuokas, temporarily resigned as Chairman of the Liberal and Centre Union, pending an investigation into corruption allegations; Zuokas had been involved in a public dispute with Uspaskikh, with each accusing the other of corruption, which had led President Adamkus to appeal for their resignations. In December a parliamentary commission concluded that it was likely that Zuokas had received unauthorized financial inducements in his role as Mayor; nevertheless, in February 2006 he survived a vote of no confidence.

Meanwhile, in December 2005 the Supreme Court ruled that Paksas was not guilty of divulging confidential state information, and Yurii Borisov was granted permission to remain resident in the country. In January 2006 an investigation into Brazauskas' business affairs was closed, after no evidence was found to substantiate allegations of financial impropriety relating to the privatization of a Soviet-era hotel owned by his wife.

In mid-April 2006 Artūras Paulauskas, the Chairman of the NU, was removed from his position as parliamentary speaker, following a secret ballot in the Seimas, amid accusations that he had been aware of a scandal involving the unauthorized use of official vehicles by government employees. The NU immediately announced its intention to withdraw from the governing coalition. The remaining members of the coalition, the LSDP, the LLP and the PNDU, signed a new agreement on the following day, and Viktoras Muntianas of the LLP was subsequently elected as the new Chairman of the Seimas. At the end of April Paulauskas was re-elected as Chairman of the NU, which in early May declared itself to be in opposition to the Government. Later that month President Adamkus expressed a lack of confidence in the Minister of Culture, Vladimiras Prudnikovas, and the Minister of Health Care, Žilvinas Padaiga, amid allegations that both LLP ministers had been involved in severe financial impropriety.

In early May 2006 seven LLP deputies renounced their party membership and defected to the newly reconstituted Civil Democracy Party (formerly the Citizens' Union), citing dissatisfaction with the LLP leadership, in particular Chairman Viktor Uspaskikh, as the primary reason for their departure. The ruling coalition's number of seats in the 141-member Seimas was thereby reduced to just 62. Uspaskikh, the subject of ongoing corruption allegations, tendered his resignation as party Chairman later that month. At the end of May the LLP withdrew from the ruling coalition, effectively forcing the resignation of Prime Minister Brazauskas and of the Council of Ministers. Minister of Finance Balčytis was appointed Prime Minister in an acting capacity, but the Seimas opted to approve in July the nomination of Gediminas Kirkilas, Vice-Chairman of the LSDP, as premier. The new Council of Ministers, approved in the same month, comprised six members of the LSDP, three members of the Lithuanian Peasant Nationalists' Union, and two members each of the Civil Democracy Party and of the Liberal and Centre Union. Balčytis retained the finance portfolio, while Petras Vaitiekūnas of the LPNU was appointed Minister of Foreign Affairs.

Kęstutis Dauksys was elected Chairman of the LLP in August 2006. Uspaskikh, meanwhile, had fled to Russia, but was detained there in September, following the issuing of a European warrant for his arrest by the Lithuanian Office of the Prosecutor-General; he was subsequently released without charge. In January 2007 it was reported that Uspaskikh had registered as an LLP candidate to contest the municipal elections scheduled to take place in February (see below). Meanwhile, in September 2006 the Order and Justice—Liberal Democrats party initiated a motion of no confidence against Muntianas, claiming that comments made by him concerning a recent court decision not to deport Jurijus Borisovas (a close associate of Paksas) had breached the terms of the Constitution. Muntianas comfortably survived the ensuing vote, which was supported by only 36 deputies.

From August 2006 pressure mounted on Balčytis to resign from the Council of Ministers, amid claims that his son had abused office while an employee of the Lithuanian Business Support Agency, which was responsible for the distribution of EU funding. Balčytis refused to relinquish his post until legal proceedings against his son had been concluded. In the event, however, Balčytis announced his resignation the day after his son was cleared of the charges against him.

The rate of participation at the municipal elections held on 25 February 2007 failed for the first time in the country's history to exceed 40% of the electorate. The HU was placed first, with 17.1% of the votes cast, while the LSDP came a close second, with 16.3%; the LLP ranked sixth, with 6.4% of the ballot. Uspaskikh and Paksas won seats in Kedainiai and Vilnius, respectively. The results in two municipalities were invalidated by the Central Electoral Committee, and polls repeated there, owing to alleged violations of electoral law, including vote-buying and the misuse of administrative resources to influence voters. In September Uspaskikh returned to Lithuania from Russia, despite the outstanding charges against him; he was subsequently placed under house arrest.

In December 2007 the Minister of the Interior and the head of the police service resigned from their posts, after a police official under the influence of alcohol fatally injured three children in an automobile accident. In January 2008 an agreement was signed on the expansion of the ruling coalition to include the NU, thereby giving it a majority in the Seimas, with 73 seats. Later that month NU Chairman Paulauskas joined the Government as Minister of the Environment; representatives of the NU were also offered posts at the head of parliamentary commissions. In April the Speaker of the Seimas was replaced, following media allegations of corruption. In early April the Minister of Education and Science, Roma Žakaitienė, tendered her resignation, although she agreed to remain in the post pending a new appointment to the position.

Whereas Lithuania's Baltic neighbours, Estonia and Latvia, have large national minorities, ethnic Lithuanians constitute much of the republic's population: in the 2001 census ethnic Lithuanians represented some 84% of the total, while the two largest minority groups, Poles and Russians, represented 7% and 6%, respectively, of the total population. As a result, the requirements for naturalization of non-ethnic Lithuanians were less stringent than in the neighbouring Baltic republics, where national identity was perceived in some quarters as being under threat. Under citizenship laws adopted in late 1989, all residents, regardless of ethnic origin, were eligible to apply for naturalization; by early 1993 more than 90% of the country's non-ethnic Lithuanian residents had been granted citizenship. None the less, the population of Lithuania declined by some 191,000 between 1989 and 2001. In an attempt to counter emigration (in particular to the USA), in September 2002 the Seimas approved legislation permitting Lithuanian citizens to hold dual citizenship, thereby facilitating the eventual return of Lithuanian nationals to the country.

Mainly because of its citizenship laws, Lithuania's relations with Russia have generally been less strained than have those of Estonia and Latvia. During 1992 negotiations took place between Lithuania and Russia for the withdrawal of the estimated 38,000 former Soviet troops remaining in Lithuania. Agreement was reached in September, and the final troops left, as scheduled, on 31 August 1993, whereupon full state sovereignty was perceived as having been restored in Lithuania.

In November 1993 Lithuania and Russia signed several agreements, including an accord on most-favoured nation status in bilateral trade, and another concerning the transportation, via Lithuania, of Russian military equipment and troops from the Russian exclave of Kaliningrad Oblast, on the Baltic coast. However, there was disagreement between the two countries during 1994, following Lithuania's decision to introduce new regulations governing military transits. A compromise appeared to have been reached in January 1995, when the Lithuanian Government extended until December the existing procedure for military transits; Russia duly indicated that the agreement on bilateral trade would enter into force immediately. In October 1997 President Brazauskas undertook the first official visit to Russia by a Baltic head of state since the disintegration of the former USSR. During the visit a state border delimitation treaty was signed by both sides, and bilateral co-operation agreements on joint economic zones, and on the Baltic continental shelf, were also concluded. The border treaty was ratified by the Seimas in October 1999, but was not ratified by the Russian side until May 2003. Lithuania expressed support for an agreement between the EU and Russia in late 2002, which proposed simplified visa arrangements for Russian citizens traversing Lithuania to reach the exclave of Kaliningrad. New transit arrangements were implemented in Lithuania at the beginning of February 2003, in advance of Lithuania's accession to the EU in the following year. Tensions were reported in the first half of 2005, following the refusal of President Adamkus to attend a commemoration held in Moscow in May to mark the 60th anniversary of the end of the Second World War in Europe. All three Baltic Governments were concerned at an agreement signed between Russia and Germany, in September 2005, on the construction of a North European Gas Pipeline, which was to carry natural gas from Russia to Germany under the Baltic Sea, bypassing the Baltic countries, which would allow Russia to interrupt the supply of gas to the Baltic states without having to compromise supplies to Western Europe. In June 2006 Russian petroleum supplies to the Mažeikiai Nafta petroleum refinery were indefinitely suspended, on the grounds that its pipeline link had been damaged; Russia subsequently refused assistance to repair the pipeline, prompting speculation that the halt in pipeline exports was in reprisal for the majority acquisition in that year of the refinery by Polish enterprise PKN Orlen, rather than by a Russian company.

Lithuania's relations with neighbouring Poland were largely concerned with the status of the Polish minority in Lithuania. Following the failed coup attempt of August 1991 in Moscow, leaders of councils in Polish-populated regions of Lithuania were dismissed, in response to their alleged support for the coup, and direct rule was introduced. However, in January 1992 Lithuania and Poland signed a 'Declaration on Friendly Relations and Neighbourly Co-operation', which guaranteed the rights of the respective ethnic minorities and also recognized the existing border between the two countries. A full treaty of friendship and co-operation was signed by the respective Heads of State in April 1994. The treaty, notably, did not include a condemnatory reference to Poland's occupation of the region of Vilnius in 1920–39 (a provision that had originally been demanded by Lithuania). An agreement on free trade was signed by the two countries in June 1996, and during 1997 the Lithuanian and Polish Governments established regular forums for inter-presidential and inter-parliamentary discussion. In May 2005 the Chairmen of the national legislatures of Lithuania, Poland and Ukraine, meeting in Lutsk, Ukraine, signed a declaration establishing a new Inter-Parliamentary Assembly, which aimed to help fulfil Ukraine's objective of attaining membership of the EU and the North Atlantic Treaty Organization (NATO, see p. 340), by sharing the successful reform measures undertaken in Lithuania and Poland. In September 2006 President Adamkus made an official visit to the Polish capital, Warsaw.

Lithuania enjoys close relations with Estonia and Latvia. Relations between the three states are co-ordinated through the consultative inter-parliamentary Baltic Assembly, the Council of Baltic Sea States (see p. 224) and the Baltic Council (see p. 423). However, in the mid-1990s Lithuania's relations with Latvia came under strain, as a result of disagreement over the demarcation of the countries' maritime border. In October 1995 the Lithuanian Government protested at Latvia's signature of a preliminary agreement with two foreign petroleum companies to explore oilfields in the disputed waters. Tension increased following the ratification of the agreement by the Latvian parliament in October 1996, although in July 1999 the two countries signed an agreement on the Delimitation of the Territorial Sea, Exclusive Economic Zone and Continental Shelf in the Baltic Sea. However, protests from the Latvian fishing industry prevented the agreement from being ratified by the Latvian parliament. In December 2000 a protocol was signed for the re-demarcation of the land border between the two countries. In early 2008 Prime Minister Kirkilas welcomed a decision by the Latvian Government that ratification of the maritime border treaty would proceed separately to the signing of an economic co-operation agreement between the two countries. Meanwhile, in early 2006 the leaders of all three Baltic states had reached agreement on the construction of a new nuclear power plant to replace that at Ignalina (see below) and various other co-operative measures aimed at reducing Russian dominance in the supply of regional energy.

Lithuania pursued close co-operation with, and eventual integration into, the political, economic and defence systems of western Europe, notably NATO and the EU. In December 1999 a summit meeting of EU Heads of State and Government in Helsinki, Finland, endorsed proposals to begin accession talks

LITHUANIA
Introductory Survey

with a number of countries, including Lithuania; formal negotiations commenced in February 2000. As a concession to achieve EU membership, the Government approved a draft national energy strategy in September 1999, which provided for the decommissioning of the first unit of the Ignalina nuclear power plant by 2005. In June 2002 Lithuania agreed to decommission the plant's remaining unit in 2009, in return for a significant contribution from the EU towards the cost of the endeavour. In December 2002 Lithuania, and nine other countries, were formally invited to join the EU on 1 May 2004; at a national referendum, held on 10–11 May 2003, 90.0% of participants voted in favour of membership, and Lithuania duly acceded to the EU as scheduled. In December 2007 Lithuania, together with eight other nations, implemented the EU's Schengen Agreement, enabling its citizens to travel to and from other member states without border controls. Meanwhile, in November 2002 Lithuania was one of seven countries invited to join NATO in 2004. Lithuania became a full member of the Alliance on 29 March 2004.

Government
Under the terms of the Constitution that was approved in a national referendum on 25 October 1992, supreme legislative authority resides with the Seimas (Parliament), which has 141 members, elected by universal adult suffrage for a four-year term (71 deputies are directly elected by majority vote, with 70 being elected from party lists on the basis of proportional representation). The President of the Republic (who is Head of State) is elected by direct popular vote for a period of five years (and a maximum of two consecutive terms). Executive power is vested in the Council of Ministers. This is headed by the Prime Minister, who is appointed by the President with the approval of the Seimas. For administrative purposes, Lithuania is divided into 10 counties.

Defence
Until independence Lithuania had no armed forces separate from those of the USSR. The Department of State Defence (established in April 1990) was reorganized as the Ministry of Defence in October 1991. As assessed at November 2007, Lithuania's active armed forces totalled an estimated 13,850: army 12,500 (including 1,900 conscripts), navy 450 (including 300 conscripts) and air force 900 (including 100 conscripts). There was also a paramilitary force of 14,600 (including a border guard of 5,000) and a total of 6,700 reserves. Military service is compulsory and lasts for 12 months. The budget for 2007 allocated 1,140m. litai to defence. Lithuania became a full member of the North Atlantic Treaty Organization (NATO, see p. 340) on 29 March 2004.

Economic Affairs
In 2006, according to estimates by the World Bank, Lithuania's gross national income (GNI), measured at average 2004–06 prices, was US $26,734m., equivalent to $7,870 per head (or $14,930 per head on an international purchasing-power parity basis). During 1996–2006 the population decreased by an annual average of 0.6%, while gross domestic product (GDP) per head increased, in real terms, by an average of 6.9% per year. Overall GDP increased, in real terms, by an average of 6.2% annually during 1996–2006. Real GDP increased by 8.8% in 2007.

Agriculture (including hunting, forestry and fishing) contributed 5.5% of GDP in 2007, and engaged an estimated 12.4% of the employed population in 2006. The principal crops are cereals, sugar beet, potatoes and vegetables. Legislation approved in January 2003 authorized the sale of agricultural land to foreign owners, although its implementation was to be subject to a seven-year transition period. Agricultural GDP increased, in real terms, by an annual average of 0.9% during 1996–2006. The GDP of the sector declined by 10.5% in 2006, but recovered in 2007, increasing by 13.2%.

Industry (including mining, manufacturing, construction and power) contributed 33.7% of GDP in 2007, and engaged an estimated 29.7% of the employed population in 2006. Industrial GDP increased by an annual average of 6.9% during 1996–2006; the GDP of the sector increased by 7.9% in 2007.

Mining and quarrying contributed 0.5% of GDP in 2006, and provided only an estimated 0.3% of employment in that year. Lithuania has significant reserves of peat and materials used in construction (limestone, clay, dolomite, chalk, and sand and gravel), as well as small deposits of petroleum and natural gas. In terms of gross value added, the sector registered growth of 3.0% in 2004, according to official data.

The manufacturing sector provided 20.5% of GDP in 2006, and engaged 17.7% of the employed labour force in the same year. Based on the value of sales (excluding refined petroleum products), in 2005 the principal branches of manufacturing were food products (particularly dairy products), wood products (particularly furniture), chemicals (including fertilizers) and clothing. Manufacturing GDP increased, in real terms, by an annual average of 9.0% during 1996–2006. Sectoral GDP increased by 7.0% in 2006.

In 2004 nuclear power accounted for 80.5% of gross electricity production, and natural gas accounted for 14.4%. Lithuania has substantial petroleum-refining and electricity-generating capacities, which enable it to export refined petroleum products and electricity. Lithuania has been a net exporter of electricity, although the Ignalina power plant is due to be decommissioned (see below). In 2007 imports of mineral fuels accounted for 16.3% of the total value of merchandise imports.

The services sector contributed 60.8% of GDP in 2007, and provided 57.9% of total employment in 2006. The Baltic port of Klaipėda (Memel) is a significant entrepôt for regional trade. The GDP of the services sector increased, in real terms, by an annual average of 6.2% in 1996–2006. Real services GDP increased by 8.8% in 2007.

In 2006 Lithuania recorded a visible trade deficit of US $4,209.3m., and there was a deficit of $3,218.1m. on the current account of the balance of payments. In 2007 the principal source of imports was Russia (accounting for 18.2% of the total); other major sources were Germany, Poland and Latvia. Russia was also the main market for exports in that year (accounting for 15.0% of the total); other principal markets were Latvia, Germany, Poland and Estonia. In 2007 the principal exports were mineral products, machinery and electrical equipment, vehicles and transportation equipment, chemical products, plastics and rubber, textiles, and miscellaneous manufactured articles. The principal imports were mineral products, machinery and electrical equipment, vehicles and transportation equipment, nuclear reactors and boilers, chemical products, base metals, electrical machinery, and plastics and rubber.

In 2007 there was a budgetary deficit of 477.8m. litai (equivalent to 0.5% of GDP). Lithuania's total external debt was US $11,201m. at the end of 2005, of which $1,511m. was long-term public debt. In that year the cost of debt-servicing was equivalent to 16.5% of the value of exports of goods and services. Annual inflation averaged 2.3% in 1996–2006. The rate of inflation was 3.7% in 2006. The average rate of unemployment was 4.3% in 2007, compared with 11.4% in 2004.

In December 2000 Lithuania became a member of the World Trade Organization (WTO, see p. 396). Lithuania acceded to full membership of the European Union (EU, see p. 244) on 1 May 2004.

In an effort to facilitate increased integration with EU economies and further reorientate foreign trade, from February 2002 the national currency's fixed rate of exchange was linked to the common European currency, the euro, instead of the US dollar. In June formal agreement was reached with the EU on the closure of the Ignalina nuclear power plant. The first of the plant's reactors was decommissioned in late 2004 and the second was due to be decommissioned in 2009, in return for substantial financial compensation from the EU. In February 2006 the Prime Ministers of the Baltic states of Estonia, Latvia and Lithuania reached agreement on the construction of a new nuclear plant to replace the existing Ignalina plant by 2015, with equal investment from each country. Meanwhile, Lithuania was one of three new member states of the EU (along with Estonia and Slovenia) to be admitted to the EU's exchange rate mechanism (ERM 2) in June 2004, ahead of the country's planned adoption of the euro. In March 2006 Lithuania formally applied to become a member of the euro zone from 1 January 2007. However, increases in global energy prices and rapid economic growth had stimulated consumer-price inflation in 2005, and in May 2006 the European Commission and the European Central Bank concluded that Lithuania would not be ready to adopt the euro in 2007; in October 2006 the Government announced a new target date of 2010. With rising wages, increasing utility costs and high global fuel prices, annual inflation reached an estimated 5.2% in 2007. Despite government plans to reduce inflation in order to enter the euro zone, inflation was forecast to increase to as much as 8.5% in 2008, and the IMF urged the Government to attempt to constrain the rate of growth. Meanwhile, it was reported in early 2008 that amendments to the gas supply contract between Lithuania and the Russian gas monopoly Gazprom had resulted

LITHUANIA

in an increase of almost 50% in the price of gas. Russia also retained the option to price gas supplies in Russian roubles rather than US dollars, a measure that would further inflate the price for Lithuanian importers.

Education

Education, beginning at six years of age, is free and compulsory until the age of 18. Pre-school education is available for children aged between one and six years. Children spend four years at primary school (Grades 1–4), followed by six years at lower secondary school (basic education, Grades 5–10) and two years at upper secondary school or gymnasium (Grades 10–12). Vocational training is available. From 2003 a uniform tuition fee was introduced for students in higher education, although there were exemptions for the highest achievers. In 2005/06 94.9% of the relevant age-group was enrolled in primary education, while the comparable rate of enrolment in secondary education was 95.2%. In the 2006/07 academic year 560,000 students were enrolled in 1,582 general and vocational schools. In that year there were 29 schools of higher education and 22 universities; total enrolment in institutions of higher education was 199,520. In 1991 the first private schools were opened; by 2006 there were 27 private schools, 13 private colleges and seven private universities. Lithuanian is the main language of instruction, although in 1999/2000 7.7% of students at comprehensive schools were taught in Russian and 3.8% were taught in Polish. The state budget for 2001 allocated 925.5m. litai (7.3% of total expenditure) to education. The 2003 budget allocated 5.9% of GDP to education.

Public Holidays

2008: 1 January (New Year's Day), 16 February (Day of the Restoration of the Lithuanian State), 11 March (Day of the Re-establishment of Independence), 24 March (Easter Monday), 1 May (Mothers' Day), 6 July (Anniversary of the Coronation of Grand Duke Mindaugas of Lithuania), 15 August (Assumption), 1 November (All Saints' Day), 25–26 December (Christmas).

2009: 1 January (New Year's Day), 16 February (Day of the Restoration of the Lithuanian State), 11 March (Day of the Re-establishment of Independence), 13 April (Easter Monday), 1 May (Mothers' Day), 6 July (Anniversary of the Coronation of Grand Duke Mindaugas of Lithuania), 15 August (Assumption), 1 November (All Saints' Day), 25–26 December (Christmas).

Weights and Measures

The metric system is in force.

Statistical Survey

Source (unless otherwise indicated): Department of Statistics to the Government of Lithuania (Statistics Lithuania), Gedimino pr. 29, Vilnius 01500; tel. (52) 236-4800; fax (5) 236-4845; e-mail statistika@stat.gov.lt; internet www.stat.gov.lt.

Area and Population

AREA, POPULATION AND DENSITY

Area (sq km)	65,300*
Population (census results)	
12 January 1989†	3,674,802
6 April 2001	
Males	1,629,148
Females	1,854,824
Total	3,483,972
Population (official estimates at 1 January)	
2005	3,425,324
2006	3,403,284
2007	3,384,879
Density (per sq km) at 1 January 2007	51.8

* 25,212 sq miles.
† Figure refers to the *de jure* population. The *de facto* total was 3,689,779.

POPULATION BY ETHNIC GROUP
(permanent inhabitants at 2001 census)

	Number	%
Lithuanian	2,907,293	84.5
Polish	234,989	6.8
Russian	219,789	6.4
Belarusian	42,866	1.2
Others	34,035	1.0
Total	**3,483,972**	**100.0**

ADMINISTRATIVE DIVISIONS
(at 1 January 2007)

County	Area (sq km)	Population	Density (per sq km)
Alytus	5,425	178,955	33.0
Kaunas	8,089	677,284	83.7
Klaipėda	5,209	379,472	72.8
Marijampolė	4,463	182,587	40.9
Panevėžys	7,881	287,119	36.4
Šiauliai	8,540	353,713	41.4
Tauragė	4,411	128,679	29.2
Telšiai	4,350	174,573	40.1
Utena	7,201	174,743	24.3
Vilnius	9,731	847,754	87.1
Total	**65,300**	**3,384,879**	**51.8**

PRINCIPAL TOWNS
(population at 2001 census)

Vilnius (capital)	542,287	Šiauliai	133,883
Kaunas	378,943	Panevėžys	119,749
Klaipėda	192,954	Alytus	71,491

2005 (official estimate at 1 January): Vilnius 541,278.

LITHUANIA

BIRTHS, MARRIAGES AND DEATHS

	Registered live births Number	Rate (per 1,000)	Registered marriages Number	Rate (per 1,000)	Registered deaths Number	Rate (per 1,000)
1999	36,415	10.3	17,868	5.1	40,003	11.3
2000	34,149	9.8	16,906	4.8	38,919	11.1
2001	31,546	9.1	15,764	4.5	40,399	11.6
2002	30,014	8.6	16,151	4.7	41,072	11.8
2003	30,598	8.9	16,975	4.9	40,990	11.9
2004	30,419	8.8	19,130	5.6	41,340	12.0
2005	30,541	8.9	19,938	5.8	43,799	12.8
2006	31,265	9.2	21,246	6.3	44,813	13.2

2007: Marriages 23,605.

Expectation of life (years at birth, WHO estimates): 71.3 (males 65.3; females 77.4) in 2005 (Source: WHO, *World Health Statistics*).

IMMIGRATION AND EMIGRATION

	2004	2005	2006
Immigrants	5,553	6,789	7,745
Emigrants	15,165	15,571	12,602

ECONOMICALLY ACTIVE POPULATION
(annual averages, '000 persons)*

	2004	2005	2006
Agriculture, hunting and forestry	225.6	204.2	183.9
Fishing	1.9	2.8	2.7
Mining and quarrying	4.3	3.3	4.3
Manufacturing	254.9	266.5	264.6
Electricity, gas and water	29.5	26.5	27.1
Construction	116.2	132.5	148.7
Wholesale and retail trade; repair of motor vehicles, motorcycles and personal and household goods	228.0	233.3	254.6
Hotels and restaurants	32.7	33.1	39.0
Transport, storage and communications	93.9	93.9	98.9
Financial intermediation	15.0	16.3	16.6
Real estate, renting and business activities	77.9	81.7	75.7
Public administration and defence; compulsory social security	55.8	62.3	78.3
Education	141.0	148.0	131.5
Health and social work	98.4	98.6	105.7
Other community, social and personal service activities	55.8	63.7	63.7
Private households with employed persons	5.0	7.1	3.6
Extra-territorial organizations and bodies	0.2	0.2	0.1
Total	1,436.3	1,473.9	1,499.0
Unemployed	184.4	132.9	89.3
Total labour force	1,620.6	1,606.8	1,588.3
Males	824.4	818.0	802.5
Females	796.3	788.8	785.8

* Official estimates based on results of 2001 census.

2007: Total employed 1,534.2; Unemployed 69.0; Total labour force 1,603.2 (males 812.3; females 790.8).

Health and Welfare

KEY INDICATORS

Total fertility rate (children per woman, 2005)	1.3
Under-5 mortality rate (per 1,000 live births, 2005)	9
HIV/AIDS (% of persons aged 15–49, 2005)	0.2
Physicians (per 1,000 head, 2003)	3.97
Hospital beds (per 1,000 head, 2005)	8.1
Health expenditure (2004): US $ per head (PPP)	843.1
Health expenditure (2004): % of GDP	6.5
Health expenditure (2004): public (% of total)	75.0
Human Development Index (2005): ranking	43
Human Development Index (2005): value	0.862

For sources and definitions, see explanatory note on p. vi.

Agriculture

PRINCIPAL CROPS
('000 metric tons)

	2004	2005	2006
Wheat	1,430.2	1,379.4	809.8
Barley	859.8	948.3	743.8
Rye	140.6	108.3	90.0
Oats	117.7	114.1	62.8
Triticale (wheat-rye hybrid)	263.4	201.1	110.4
Potatoes	1,021.4	894.7	457.1
Sugar beet	904.9	798.5	717.1
Dry peas	22.0	21.1	15.8
Rapeseed	204.7	201.2	169.6
Cabbages and other brassicas	134.1	141.4	72.7
Dry onions	33.4	22.3	11.5
Carrots and turnips	77.5	82.6	41.2
Apples	34.0	96.5	99.5

Aggregate production ('000 metric tons, may include official, semi-official or estimated data): Total cereals 2,859.4 in 2004, 2,811.1 in 2005, 1,857.8 in 2006; Total roots and tubers 1,021.4 in 2004, 894.7 in 2005, 457.1 in 2006; Total vegetables (incl. melons) 347.3 in 2004, 338.0 in 2005, 184.0 in 2006; Total fruits (excl. melons) 50.4 in 2004, 124.0 in 2005, 126.5 in 2006.

Source: FAO.

LIVESTOCK
('000 head at 1 January)

	2004	2005	2006
Horses	64	64	63
Cattle	812	792	800
Pigs	1,057	1,073	1,115
Sheep	17	22	29
Goats	27	27	22
Chickens	7,870	8,227	9,201
Turkeys	98	93	103
Rabbits and hares	98	96	99

Source: FAO.

LIVESTOCK PRODUCTS
('000 metric tons)

	2004	2005	2006
Cattle meat	47.6	52.9	47.3
Pig meat	97.1	105.6	106.2
Chicken meat	49.1	56.5	56.5*
Cows' milk	1,841.6	1,853.6	1,884.6
Hen eggs	50.8	50.9	53.4
Honey	1.1	1.3	1.4

* FAO estimate.

Source: FAO.

LITHUANIA Statistical Survey

Forestry

ROUNDWOOD REMOVALS
('000 cubic metres, excl. bark)

	2004	2005	2006
Sawlogs, veneer logs and logs for sleepers	3,420	3,520	3,285
Pulpwood	1,430	1,390	1,355
Other industrial wood	10	5	—
Fuel wood	1,260	1,130	1,230
Total	6,120	6,045	5,870

Source: FAO.

SAWNWOOD PRODUCTION
('000 cubic metres, incl. railway sleepers)

	2004	2005	2006
Coniferous (softwood)	980	1,025	996
Broadleaved (hardwood)	470	420	470
Total	1,450	1,445	1,466

Source: FAO.

Fishing

(metric tons, live weight)

	2003	2004	2005
Capture	157,205	161,988	139,785
Largehead hairtail	4,590	601	556
Atlantic redfishes	21,631	7,136	2,359
Jack and horse mackerels	32,439	49,312	55,831
Sardinellas	29,517	35,372	19,328
European sprat	3,032	6,185	8,635
European anchovy	22,000	27,584	20,500
Chub mackerel	21,264	15,868	14,962
Northern prawn	5,539	7,057	5,860
Aquaculture	2,356	2,697	2,013
Total catch	159,561	164,685	141,798

Source: FAO.

Mining

('000 metric tons, unless otherwise indicated)

	2004	2005	2006
Crude petroleum	382	302	216
Dolomite ('000 cubic metres)	796	1,016	1,300
Limestone	960	1,178	1,279
Clay ('000 cubic metres)	200	261	281
Peat	345	361	495

Industry

SELECTED PRODUCTS
('000 metric tons, unless otherwise indicated)

	2004	2005	2006
Sausages and smoked meat products	73.5	76.3	76.7
Flour	239.1	223.6	214.4
Refined sugar	132.9	124.7	96.6
Beer ('000 hectolitres)	269.0	289.5	293.4
Wine ('000 hectolitres)	516	785	797
Cotton fabrics (million sq m)	21.9	22.0	20.4
Woollen fabrics (million sq m)	21.5	20.2	22.5
Fabrics of man-made fibres	21.2	19.9	19.4
Footwear—excl. rubber and plastic ('000 pairs)*	1,200	1,100	1,000
Plywood ('000 cubic metres)	49.9	46.6	47.1
Particle board ('000 cubic metres)	422.5	440.1	433.4
Paper and paperboard	98.2	112.6	119.2
Sulphuric acid	1,019	1,091	1,117
Nitrogenous fertilizers	612	n.a.	n.a.
Cement*	800	800	1,100
Cast iron	14.7	11.3	10.0
Television sets ('000)	1,201.7	1,152.4	711.3
Refrigerators and freezers ('000)	456.8	443.8	434.9
Bicycles ('000)	348	418	330
Electric energy (million kWh)*	19,100	14,900	11,900

* Figures are rounded.

Finance

CURRENCY AND EXCHANGE RATES

Monetary Units
100 centas = 1 litas (plural: litai).

Sterling, Dollar and Euro Equivalents (31 December 2007)
£1 sterling = 4.7224 litai;
US $1 = 2.3572 litai;
€1 = 3.4528 litai;
100 litai = £21.18 = $42.42 = €28.96.

Average Exchange Rate (litai per US $)
2005 2.7740
2006 2.7522
2007 2.5237

Note: In June 1993 Lithuania reintroduced its national currency, the litas, replacing a temporary coupon currency, the talonas, at a conversion rate of 1 litas = 100 talonai. The talonas had been introduced in May 1992, initially circulating alongside (and at par with) the Russian (formerly Soviet) rouble. An official mid-point exchange rate of US $1 = 4.00 litai was in operation from 1 April 1994 until 1 February 2002. From 2 February 2002 the litas was linked to the euro, with the exchange rate set at €1 = 3.4528 litai.

GOVERNMENT FINANCE
(general government transactions, non-cash basis, million litai)

Summary of Balances

	2004	2005	2006
Revenue	19,939.4	23,770.4	27,644.6
Less Expense	19,555.9	22,588.8	25,499.7
Net operating balance	383.5	1,181.6	2,144.9
Less Net acquisition of non-financial assets	1,348.3	1,547.4	2,333.9
Net lending/borrowing	−964.8	−365.8	−189.0

LITHUANIA

Revenue

	2004	2005	2006
Taxes	12,379.0	14,439.1	17,143.9
Taxes on income and profits	5,428.9	6,461.1	7,918.7
Taxes on goods and services	6,598.8	7,703.5	8,919.5
Other taxes	351.3	274.5	305.7
Social security contributions	5,746.4	6,449.8	7,584.1
Grants	560.0	704.7	1,094.9
Other revenue	1,254.0	2,176.8	1,821.7
Property income	451.1	494.1	422.6
Sales of goods and services	703.0	1,172.7	1,021.1
Other revenue	99.0	510.0	387.0
Total revenue	19,939.4	23,770.4	27,644.6

Expense*

	2004	2005	2006
Compensation of employees	5,542.7	7,157.5	8,307.4
Use of goods and services	2,956.7	3,932.3	4,721.3
Consumption of fixed capital	682.1	888.8	1,018.1
Interest	626.0	600.8	375.3
Subsidies	438.2	590.0	584.6
Grants	332.2	547.1	627.2
Social benefits	7,795.0	7,490.8	8,898.0
Other expense	1,183.0	1,381.5	967.8
Total expense	19,555.9	22,588.8	25,499.7

* Excluding net acquisition of non-financial assets.

Source: Ministry of Finance, Vilnius.

INTERNATIONAL RESERVES
(US $ million at 31 December)

	2004	2005	2006
Gold (national valuation)	81.40	95.34	118.14
IMF special drawing rights	0.09	0.08	0.10
Reserve position in IMF	0.02	0.02	0.05
Foreign exchange	3,512.47	3,720.14	5,654.26
Total	3,593.98	3,815.58	5,772.55

* National valuation.

Source: IMF, *International Financial Statistics*.

MONEY SUPPLY
(million litai at 31 December)

	2004	2005	2006
Currency outside banks	5,122	6,118	7,245
Demand deposits at banking institutions	9,988	14,770	17,578
Total money (incl. others)	15,126	20,901	24,835

Source: IMF, *International Financial Statistics*.

COST OF LIVING
(Consumer Price Index; base: 2000 = 100)

	2004	2005	2006
Food (incl. beverages)	101.2	105.3	111.7
Fuel and light	104.9	109.7	106.5
Clothing	89.1	87.5	79.6
Rent	108.6	115.0	123.1
All items (incl. others)	101.6	104.3	108.2

Source: ILO.

NATIONAL ACCOUNTS
(million litai at current prices)

National Income and Profit

	2005	2006	2007
Compensation of employees	29,415.1	34,966.8	41,784.9
Operating surplus and mixed income	26,745.8	29,370.3	34,080.6
Domestic primary incomes	56,160.9	64,337.1	75,865.5
Consumption of fixed capital	8,341.5	9,492.4	10,823.5
Gross domestic product (GDP) at factor cost	64,502.4	73,829.5	86,689.0
Taxes on production and imports	8,221.9	9,477.6	11,653.8
Less Subsidies	1,334.9	1,401.9	1,570.1
Statistical discrepancy	–9.0	—	—
GDP in market prices	71,380.4	81,905.2	96,772.5
Primary incomes received from abroad	2,112.8	2,429.6	2,954.6
Less Primary incomes paid abroad	3,251.4	4,193.6	6,656.2
Gross national income (GNI)	70,241.8	80,141.3	93,071.0
Less Consumption of fixed capital	8,341.5	9,492.4	10,823.5
Net national income	61,900.3	70,648.9	82,247.6
Current transfers from abroad	1,786.0	3,327.1	4,290.4
Less Current transfers paid abroad	536.2	1,642.7	1,936.2
Net national disposable income	63,150.2	72,333.3	84,601.7

Expenditure on the Gross Domestic Product

	2005	2006	2007
Final consumption expenditure	58,683.9	68,272.9	79,826.9
Households	46,308.8	53,309.8	63,170.1
Non-profit institutions serving households	144.5	183.5	244.4
General government	12,230.6	14,779.5	16,412.3
Gross capital formation	17,923.8	22,137.6	28,246.4
Gross fixed capital formation	16,302.2	20,290.8	25,648.1
Changes in inventories	1,590.8	1,794.2	2,522.5
Acquisitions, less disposals, of valuables	30.8	52.7	75.8
Total domestic expenditure	76,607.7	90,410.5	108,073.3
Exports of goods and services	41,440.1	48,892.6	53,581.4
Less Imports of goods and services	46,667.4	57,397.9	64,882.2
GDP in market prices	71,380.4	81,905.2	96,772.5
GDP at chain-linked 2000 prices	66,549.5	71,649.1	77,935.2

Gross Domestic Product by Economic Activity

	2004	2005	2006
Agriculture, hunting and forestry	3,262.5	3,601.1	3,753.3
Fishing	45.6	51.6	53.7
Mining and quarrying	301.9	344.6	393.4
Manufacturing	11,838.4	13,475.0	15,165.7
Electricity, gas and water supply	2,497.9	2,584.1	2,791.5
Construction	4,102.1	4,916.6	6,515.7
Wholesale and retail trade; repair of motor vehicles, motorcycles and personal and household goods	9,940.7	11,321.1	12,568.5
Hotels and restaurants	835.6	906.2	1,008.0
Transport, storage and communication	7,181.5	8,281.9	9,409.7
Financial intermediation	1,202.8	1,308.0	1,821.0
Real estate, renting and business activities	3,062.8	3,309.6	3,846.4

LITHUANIA

—continued

	2004	2005	2006
Public administration and defence; compulsory social security	5,897.3	7,425.4	8,716.3
Education	3,050.2	3,164.9	3,495.5
Health and social work	1,667.2	1,948.5	2,306.3
Other community, social and personal service activities	1,610.5	1,729.2	1,885.1
Private households with employed persons	74.4	106.7	85.5
Statistical discrepancy	—	9.1	—
Gross value added at basic prices	56,571.5	64,483.6	73,815.6
Taxes on products	6,671.1	7,832.9	9,037.6
Less Subsidies on products	655.9	936.1	948.0
GDP in market prices	62,586.7	71,380.4	81,905.2

2007 (million litai at current prices): Agriculture, hunting, forestry and fishing 4,727.2; Industry 29,229.3 (Construction 8,628.7); Services 52,742.2 (Public administration, social services and community activities 27,278.4, Trade, hotels and restaurants, and transport, storage and communication 12,442.7, Financial intermediation, real estate, and renting and business activities 13,021.1); *Gross value added at basic prices* 86,698.7; Taxes on products 11,128.1; *Less* Subsidies on products –1,054.3; *GDP in market prices* 96,772.5.

BALANCE OF PAYMENTS
(US $ million)

	2004	2005	2006
Exports of goods f.o.b.	9,306.3	11,774.4	14,150.6
Imports of goods f.o.b.	–11,688.9	–14,690.4	–18,359.8
Trade balance	–2,382.6	–2,916.0	–4,209.3
Exports of services	2,444.4	3,104.3	3,623.2
Imports of services	–1,632.1	–2,054.6	–2,540.0
Balance on goods and services	–1,570.2	–1,866.3	–3,126.0
Other income received	354.9	448.3	589.9
Other income paid	–967.3	–1,075.4	–1,406.9
Balance on goods, services and income	–2,182.5	–2,493.4	–3,943.0
Current transfers received	612.1	951.3	1,425.1
Current transfers paid	–154.2	–289.1	–700.2
Current balance	–1,724.6	–1,831.2	–3,218.1
Capital account (net)	287.2	331.1	351.4
Direct investment abroad	–262.6	–343.0	–289.5
Direct investment from abroad	773.2	1,031.8	1,840.2
Portfolio investment assets	–219.9	–778.5	–1,105.8
Portfolio investment liabilities	431.1	541.6	852.1
Financial derivatives assets	60.0	27.4	9.5
Financial derivatives liabilities	–57.4	–14.5	–20.5
Other investment assets	–683.8	–785.6	–475.7
Other investment liabilities	1,100.7	2,582.6	3,852.4
Net errors and omissions	191.8	–49.4	–289.1
Overall balance	–104.4	712.3	1,506.7

Source: IMF, *International Financial Statistics*.

External Trade

PRINCIPAL COMMODITIES
(million litai)

Imports c.i.f.	2005	2006	2007
Prepared foodstuffs; beverages, spirits and vinegar; tobacco and manufactured substitutes	1,597.4	2,140.4	2,543.1
Mineral products	10,996.5	12,481.0	10,549.1
Mineral fuels	10,572.3	11,980.1	9,965.0
Products of the chemical or allied industries	3,360.5	4,497.5	5,920.5
Plastics, rubber and articles thereof	2,419.3	2,745.0	3,144.3
Textiles and textile articles	2,418.6	2,679.9	2,954.7
Base metals and articles thereof	2,990.8	3,756.1	4,781.4
Machinery and mechanical appliances; electrical equipment; sound and television apparatus	7,737.1	9,402.8	10,695.6
Nuclear reactors, boilers, etc.	4,584.7	5,491.8	5,996.1
Electrical machinery, sound and television recorders and parts thereof	3,152.4	3,910.9	4,699.4
Vehicles, aircraft, vessels and associated transport equipment	5,068.8	7,383.5	9,981.4
Total (incl. others)	43,151.9	53,274.6	60,987.4

Exports f.o.b.	2005	2006	2007
Live animals and animal products	1,468.9	1,769.6	2,374.9
Vegetable products	978.9	1,314.3	2,193.8
Prepared foodstuffs; beverages, spirits and vinegar; tobacco and manufactured substitutes	1,691.5	2,234.4	2,653.6
Mineral products	8,939.8	9,292.4	5,976.6
Mineral fuels	8,859.7	9,192.6	5,865.4
Products of the chemical or allied industries	2,389.7	2,514.7	3,480.0
Fertilizers	1,453.0	1,433.5	2,134.9
Plastics, rubber and articles thereof	1,186.5	1,999.6	3,431.2
Wood, cork and articles thereof; wood charcoal; manufactures of straw, esparto, etc.	1,494.9	1,584.2	1,993.1
Textiles and textile articles	3,043.0	3,228.3	3,261.4
Articles of apparel and clothing accessories, not knitted	1,236.5	1,252.2	1,148.0
Base metals and articles thereof	1,434.2	1,779.7	2,259.4
Machinery and mechanical appliances; electrical equipment; sound and television apparatus	4,079.0	4,885.8	5,561.5
Vehicles, aircraft, vessels and associated transport equipment	2,707.4	3,948.4	4,540.3
Miscellaneous manufactured articles	1,950.5	2,425.2	2,955.8
Total (incl. others)	32,767.3	38,888.3	43,234.2

PRINCIPAL TRADING PARTNERS
(million litai)

Imports c.i.f.	2005	2006	2007
Austria	441.0	586.0	699.1
Belarus	753.6	944.7	1,218.1
Belgium	962.6	1,321.3	1,766.8
China, People's Republic	1,005.5	1,275.8	1,719.3
Czech Republic	643.0	760.4	957.2
Denmark	1,300.3	1,533.9	1,675.2
Estonia	1,222.8	1,639.3	2,189.3
Finland	1,325.1	1,547.8	1,693.9
France	1,209.7	1,679.3	2,123.7
Germany	6,538.4	7,916.2	9,108.4
Italy	1,277.2	1,798.8	2,407.8

LITHUANIA

Imports c.i.f.—continued	2005	2006	2007
Latvia	1,707.9	2,541.8	3,326.1
Netherlands	1,601.5	1,988.0	2,586.8
Poland	3,585.0	5,070.1	6,479.3
Russia	12,006.3	12,975.4	11,070.6
Spain	438.8	625.3	968.0
Sweden	1,481.8	1,777.1	2,296.5
Ukraine	511.1	721.6	847.4
United Kingdom	955.1	1,417.8	1,712.2
USA	843.0	859.3	1,356.1
Total (incl. others)	43,151.9	53,274.6	60,987.4

Exports f.o.b.	2005	2006	2007
Belarus	1,063.0	1,472.8	1,733.4
Belgium	617.5	482.4	729.4
Canada	939.5	765.7	192.0
Denmark	1,420.1	1,634.4	1,752.4
Estonia	1,937.0	2,515.4	2,509.9
France	2,301.8	1,626.8	1,575.8
Germany	3,075.5	3,344.9	4,531.8
Italy	631.5	822.8	980.2
Latvia	3,362.7	4,303.9	5,551.3
Netherlands	1,005.7	1,885.4	1,287.9
Norway	524.8	724.0	993.4
Poland	1,812.3	2,361.4	2,711.3
Russia	3,422.1	4,956.1	6,472.9
Singapore	918.2	901.5	197.5
Spain	833.1	740.6	607.2
Sweden	1,633.1	1,749.0	1,627.3
Ukraine	743.5	1,005.6	1,176.3
United Kingdom	1,542.1	1,714.0	1,970.5
USA	1,543.4	1,681.9	1,109.2
Total (incl. others)	32,767.3	38,888.3	43,234.2

Transport

RAILWAYS
(traffic)

	2004	2005	2006
Passenger journeys ('000)	6,983.2	6,719.9	6,193.8
Passenger-km (million)	443	428	431
Freight transported ('000 metric tons)	45,554.8	49,287.3	50,224.8
Freight ton-km (million)	11,637	12,457	12,896

ROAD TRAFFIC
(public transport and freight)

	2004	2005	2006
Passenger journeys ('000)	430,073.9	443,418.7	445,484.9
Passenger-km (million)	3,548	3,691	3,695
Freight transported ('000 metric tons)	51,456.1	55,333.5	56,026.0
Freight ton-km (million)	12,279	15,908	18,134

ROAD TRAFFIC
(motor vehicles in use at 31 December)

	2004	2005	2006
Passenger cars	1,315,914	1,455,276	1,592,238
Buses and coaches	14,377	14,839	15,134
Lorries and vans	101,284	106,247	117,427
Motorcycles and mopeds	22,861	24,027	25,478

Statistical Survey

INLAND WATERWAYS

	2004	2005	2006
Passenger journeys ('000)	1,973.9	2,122.8	2,248.1
Passenger-km (million)	2	3	3
Freight transported ('000 metric tons)	621.0	745.4	879.5
Freight ton-km (million)	1	1	2

SHIPPING
Merchant Fleet
(registered at 31 December)

	2004	2005	2006
Number of vessels	162	164	132
Total displacement ('000 grt)	453.4	476.7	448.6

Source: Lloyd's Register-Fairplay, *World Fleet Statistics*.

International Sea-borne Freight Traffic
('000 metric tons)

	1999	2000	2001
Goods loaded	12,864	18,552	18,144
Goods unloaded	2,796	4,296	4,224

Source: UN, *Monthly Bulletin of Statistics*.

CIVIL AVIATION
(traffic on scheduled services)

	2004	2005	2006
Passengers carried ('000)	591.5	674.6	729.7
Passenger-km (million)	896	1,099	1,200
Freight transported (million metric tons)	6.6	7.6	5.6
Freight ton-km (million)	9	10	5

Tourism

FOREIGN VISITORS BY COUNTRY OF ORIGIN
(arrivals at accommodation establishments)

	2003	2004	2005
Belarus	21,810	22,039	29,977
Denmark	10,855	16,438	15,337
Estonia	19,067	23,456	27,834
Finland	21,300	27,303	32,996
Germany	79,182	113,974	137,317
Italy	11,548	23,475	26,518
Latvia	28,114	35,769	43,660
Norway	8,884	11,492	14,385
Poland	59,564	85,457	94,881
Russia	50,290	49,240	50,829
Sweden	14,618	17,687	20,133
United Kingdom	19,770	22,751	32,941
USA	14,267	19,419	19,980
Total (incl. others)	438,299	590,043	681,487

Receipts from tourism (US $ million, incl. passenger transport): 700 in 2003; 834 in 2004; 975 in 2005.

Source: World Tourism Organization.

Communications Media

	2004	2005	2006
Telephones ('000 main lines in use)	820.0	801.1	792.4
Mobile cellular telephones ('000 subscribers)	3,051.2	4,353.4	4,718.2
Internet users ('000)	767.0	882.9	1,083.0
Broadband subscribers ('000)	129.1	234.1	368.7
Personal computers ('000 in use)	533	n.a.	n.a.
Book titles (incl. brochures)	4,270	4,223	4,548
Newspapers: number	340	325	334
Newspapers: average circulation (million copies)	215.9	218.2	258.3
Other periodicals	536	543	566

1997: Radio receivers ('000 in use) 1,900; Facsimile machines (number in use) 6,200.

Sources: International Telecommunication Union; UNESCO, *Statistical Yearbook*; UN, *Statistical Yearbook* and Ministry of Education and Science, Vilnius.

Education

(2006/07)

	Institutions	Teachers	Students
General schools	1,502	43,885	514,600
Vocational schools	80	4,692	45,400
Professional college	1	n.a.	20
Colleges	28	3,605	56,300
Universities	22	9,640	143,200

Adult literacy rate (UNESCO estimates): 99.6% (males 99.6%; females 99.6%) in 2001 (Source: UNESCO Institute for Statistics).

Directory

The Constitution

The Constitution was approved in a national referendum on 25 October 1992 and adopted by the Seimas on 6 November. The following is a summary of its main provisions:

THE STATE

The Republic of Lithuania is an independent and democratic republic; its sovereignty is vested in the people, who exercise their supreme power either directly or through their democratically elected representatives. The powers of the State are exercised by the Seimas (Parliament), the President of the Republic, the Government and the Judiciary. The most significant issues concerning the State and the people are decided by referendum.

The territory of the republic is integral. Citizenship is acquired by birth or on other grounds determined by law. With certain exceptions established by law, no person may be a citizen of Lithuania and of another state at the same time. Lithuanian is the state language.

THE INDIVIDUAL AND THE STATE

The rights and freedoms of individuals are inviolable. Property is inviolable, and the rights of ownership are protected by law. Freedom of thought, conscience and religion are guaranteed. All persons are equal before the law. No one may be discriminated against on the basis of sex, race, nationality, language, origin, social status, religion or opinion. Citizens may choose their place of residence in Lithuania freely, and may leave the country at their own will. Citizens are guaranteed the right to form societies, political parties and associations. Citizens who belong to ethnic communities have the right to foster their language, culture and customs.

SOCIETY AND THE STATE

The family is the basis of society and the State. Education is compulsory until the age of 16. Education at state and local government institutions is free of charge at all levels. State and local government establishments of education are secular, although, at the request of parents, they may offer classes in religious instruction. The State recognizes traditional Lithuanian and other churches and religious organizations, but there is no state religion. Censorship of mass media is prohibited. Ethnic communities may independently administer the affairs of their ethnic culture, education, organizations, etc. The State supports ethnic communities.

NATIONAL ECONOMY AND LABOUR

Lithuania's economy is based on the right to private ownership and freedom of individual economic activity. Every person may freely choose an occupation, and has the right to adequate, safe and healthy working conditions, adequate compensation for work, and social security in the event of unemployment. Trade unions may be freely established and may function independently. Employees have the right to strike in order to protect their economic and social interests. The state guarantees the right of citizens to old-age and disability pensions, as well as to social assistance in the event of unemployment, sickness, widowhood, etc.

THE SEIMAS

Legislative power rests with the Seimas. It comprises 141 members, elected for a four-year term on the basis of universal, equal and direct suffrage by secret ballot. Any citizen who has attained 25 years of age may be a candidate for the Seimas. Members of the Seimas may not be found criminally responsible, may not be arrested, and may not be subjected to any other restrictions of personal freedom, without the consent of the Seimas. The Seimas convenes for two regular four-month sessions every year.

The Seimas considers and enacts amendments to the Constitution; enacts laws; adopts resolutions for the organization of referendums; announces presidential elections; approves or rejects the candidature of the Prime Minister, as proposed by the President of the Republic; establishes or abolishes government ministries, upon the recommendation of the Government; supervises the activities of the Government, with the power to express a vote of 'no confidence' in the Prime Minister or individual ministers; appoints judges to the Constitutional Court and the Supreme Court; approves the state budget and supervises the implementation thereof; establishes state taxes and other obligatory payments; ratifies or denounces international treaties whereto the republic is a party, and considers other issues of foreign policy; establishes administrative divisions of the republic; issues acts of amnesty; imposes direct administration and martial law, declares states of emergency, announces mobilization, and adopts decisions to use the armed forces.

THE PRESIDENT OF THE REPUBLIC

The President of the Republic is the Head of State. Any Lithuanian citizen by birth, who has lived in Lithuania for at least the three preceding years, who has reached 40 years of age and who is eligible for election to the Seimas, may be elected President of the Republic. The President is elected by the citizens of the republic, on the basis of universal, equal and direct suffrage by secret ballot, for a term of five years. No person may be elected to the office for more than two consecutive terms.

The President resolves basic issues of foreign policy and, in conjunction with the Government, implements foreign policy; signs international treaties and submits them to the Seimas for ratification; appoints or recalls, upon the recommendation of the Government, diplomatic representatives of Lithuania in foreign states and international organizations; appoints, upon the approval of the Seimas, the Prime Minister, and charges him or her with forming the Government, and approves its composition; removes, upon the approval of the Seimas, the Prime Minister from office; appoints or dismisses individual ministers, upon the recommendation of the Prime Minister; appoints or dismisses, upon the approval of the Seimas, the Commander-in-Chief of the armed forces and the head of the Security Service.

THE GOVERNMENT

Executive power is held by the Government of the Republic (Council of Ministers), which consists of the Prime Minister and other ministers. The Prime Minister is appointed and dismissed by the President of the Republic, with the approval of the Seimas. Ministers

LITHUANIA

are appointed by the President, on the nomination of the Prime Minister.

The Government administers the affairs of the country, protects the inviolability of the territory of Lithuania, and ensures state security and public order; implements laws and resolutions of the Seimas as well as presidential decrees; co-ordinates the activities of the ministries and other governmental institutions; prepares the draft state budget and submits it to the Seimas; executes the state budget and reports to the Seimas on its fulfilment; drafts legislative proposals and submits them to the Seimas for consideration; establishes and maintains diplomatic representation with foreign countries and international organizations.

JUDICIAL SYSTEM

The judicial system is independent of the authority of the legislative and executive branches of government. It consists of a Constitutional Court, a Supreme Court, a Court of Appeal, and district and local courts (for details, see section on Judicial System below).

The Government

HEAD OF STATE

President: VALDAS ADAMKUS (inaugurated 12 July 2004).

COUNCIL OF MINISTERS
(April 2008)

A coalition of the Civil Democracy Party (CDP), the Liberal and Centre Union (LCU), Lithuanian Social Democratic Party (LSDP), the Lithuanian Peasant Nationalists' Union (LPNU) and the New Union (Social Liberals—NU).

Prime Minister: GEDIMINAS KIRKILAS (LSDP).
Minister of the Economy: VYTAS NAVICKAS (LPNU).
Minister of Finance: RIMANTAS ŠADŽIUS (LSDP).
Minister of National Defence: JUOZAS OLEKAS (LSDP).
Minister of Culture: JONAS JUČAS (LCU).
Minister of Social Security and Labour: VILIJA BLINKEVIČIŪTĖ (LSDP).
Minister of Justice: PETRAS BAGUŠKA (CDP).
Minister of Transport and Communications: ALGIRDAS BUTKEVIČIUS (LSDP).
Minister of Health Care: RIMVYDAS TURČINSKAS (CDP).
Minister of Foreign Affairs: PETRAS VAITIEKŪNAS (LPNU).
Minister of the Interior: REGIMANTAS ČIUPAILA (LCU).
Minister of Agriculture: KAZIMIERA DANUTĖ PRUNSKIENĖ (LPNU).
Minister of Education and Science: ROMA ŽAKAITIENĖ (LSDP) (acting).
Minister of the Environment: ARTŪRAS PAULAUSKAS (NU).

MINISTRIES

Office of the President: S. Daukanto 3/8, Vilnius 01021; tel. (5) 266-4154; fax (5) 266-4145; e-mail info@president.lt; internet www.president.lt.
Office of the Prime Minister: Gedimino pr. 11, Vilnius 01103; tel. (5) 266-3874; fax (5) 216-3877; internet www.ministraspirmininkas.lt.
Ministry of Agriculture: Gedimino pr. 19, Vilnius 01103; tel. (5) 239-1032; fax (5) 239-1212; e-mail zum@zum.lt; internet www.zum.lt.
Ministry of Culture: J. Basanavičiaus 5, Vilnius 01118; tel. (5) 261-9486; fax (5) 262-3120; e-mail culture@muza.lt; internet www.muza.lt.
Ministry of the Economy: Gedimino pr. 38/2, Vilnius 01104; tel. (5) 262-3863; fax (5) 262-3974; e-mail kanc@ukmin.lt; internet www.ukmin.lt.
Ministry of Education and Science: A. Volano 2/7, Vilnius 01516; tel. (5) 274-3126; fax (5) 261-2077; e-mail smmin@smm.lt; internet www.smm.lt.
Ministry of the Environment: A. Jakšto 4/9, Vilnius 01105; tel. (5) 266-3661; fax (5) 266-3663; e-mail kanceliarija@am.lt; internet www.am.lt.
Ministry of Finance: J. Tumo-Vaižganto 8 A/2, Vilnius 01512; tel. (5) 239-0005; fax (5) 212-6387; e-mail finmin@finmin.lt; internet www.finmin.lt.
Ministry of Foreign Affairs: J. Tumo-Vaižganto g. 2, Vilnius 01511; tel. (5) 236-2444; fax (5) 231-3090; e-mail urm@urm.lt; internet www.urm.lt.

Ministry of Health Care: Vilniaus g. 33, Vilnius 01119; tel. (5) 268-5110; fax (5) 266-1402; e-mail ministerija@sam.lt; internet www.sam.lt.
Ministry of the Interior: Šventaragio 2, Vilnius 01510; tel. (5) 271-7130; fax (5) 271-8551; e-mail korespondencija@vrm.lt; internet www.vrm.lt.
Ministry of Justice: Gedimino pr. 30/1, Vilnius 01104; tel. (5) 262-4670; fax (5) 262-5940; e-mail tminfo@tic.lt; internet www.tm.lt.
Ministry of National Defence: Totorių 25/3, Vilnius 01121; tel. (5) 262-4821; fax (5) 212-6082; e-mail vis@kam.lt; internet www.kam.lt.
Ministry of Social Security and Labour: A. Vivulskio 11, Vilnius 03610; tel. (5) 266-4201; fax (5) 266-4209; internet www.socmin.lt.
Ministry of Transport and Communications: Gedimino pr. 17, Vilnius 01505; tel. (5) 261-2363; fax (5) 212-4335; e-mail transp@transp.lt; internet www.transp.lt.

President

Presidential Election, First Ballot, 13 June 2004

Candidates	Valid votes cast	% of valid votes cast
Valdas Adamkus	387,837	31.14
Kazimiera Danutė Prunskienė	264,681	21.25
Petras Auskevičius	240,413	19.30
Vilija Blinkevičiūtė	204,819	16.45
Česlovas Juršėnas	147,610	11.85
Total	**1,245,360**	**100.00**

Second Ballot, 27 June 2004

Candidates	Valid votes cast	% of valid votes cast
Valdas Adamkus	723,891	52.65
Kazimiera Danutė Prunskienė	651,024	47.35
Total	**1,374,915**	**100.00**

Legislature

Seimas
(Parliament)

Gedimino pr. 53, Vilnius 01109; tel. (5) 239-6212; fax (5) 239-6330; e-mail priim@lrs.lt; internet www.lrs.lt.

Chairman: ČESLOVAS JURŠĖNAS.

General Election, 10 and 24 October 2004

Parties and blocs	% of votes	Seats (Party lists)	Single-member constituency seats	Total seats
Lithuanian Labour Party	28.44	22	17	39
Working for Lithuania coalition*	20.65	16	15	31
Homeland Union (Conservatives, Political Prisoners and Deportees, Christian Democrats)	14.75	11	14	25
Order and Justice coalition†	11.36	9	2	11
Liberal and Centre Union	9.19	7	11	18
Peasants' and New Democracy Union	6.60	5	5	10
Lithuanian Poles' Electoral Action	3.79	—	2	2
Others	5.22	—	—	—
Independents	—	—	5	5
Total	**100.00**	**70**	**71**	**141**

* A coalition of the Lithuanian Social Democratic Party and the New Union (Social Liberals).
† A coalition of the Liberal Democratic Party and the Lithuanian People's Union for A Free Lithuania.

LITHUANIA
Directory

Election Commission

Lietuvos Republikos Vyriausioji rinkimų komisija (Central Electoral Committee of the Republic of Lithuania): Gedimino pr. 53, Vilnius 8860715; tel. (5) 239-6969; fax (5) 239-6960; e-mail rinkim@lrs.lt; internet www.vrk.lt; Chair. ZENONAS VAIGAUSKAS.

Political Organizations

In early 2008 38 political parties were officially registered. The following were among the most significant:

Civil Democracy Party: Vilnius; f. 2006; fmrly Civic Union; joined by fmr members of the Lithuanian Labour Party and the Liberal Democratic Party in 2006; Chair. VIKTORAS MUNTIANAS.

Christian-Conservative Social Union (Krikščionių Konservatorių Socialinė Sąjunga): Odminių 5, Vilnius 01122; tel. and fax (5) 212-6874; e-mail sekretoriatas@nks.lt; internet www.nks.lt; f. 2000; centre-right; Chair. GEDIMINAS VAGNORIUS.

Homeland Union—Conservatives, Political Prisoners and Deportees, Christian Democrats (HU) (Tėvynės Sąjunga—TS): L. Stuokos-Gucevičiaus g. 11, Vilnius 01122; tel. (5) 212-1657; fax (5) 278-4722; e-mail sekretoriatas@tsajunga.lt; internet www.tsajunga.lt; f. 1993 as the Conservative Party of Lithuania (Homeland Union); absorbed the Lithuanian Rightist Union in Nov. 2003; merged with the Lithuanian Union of Political Prisoners and Deportees in Feb. 2004, and name changed as above; Chair. ANDRIUS KUBILIUS; 16,000 mems.

Labour Party (LP) (Darbo Partija): Ankštoji 3, Vilnius 01109; tel. (5) 210-7152; fax (5) 210-7153; e-mail info@darbopartija.lt; internet www.darbopartija.lt; f. 2003; Chair. KĘSTUTIS DAUKSYS.

Liberal and Centre Union (Liberalų Centro Sąjunga): Vilniaus g. 22/1, Vilnius 01119; tel. (5) 231-3264; fax (5) 261-9363; e-mail info@lics.lt; internet www.lics.lt; f. 2003 by a merger of the Lithuanian Centre Union, the Lithuanian Liberal Union and the Modern Christian-Democratic Union; Chair. ARTŪRAS ZUOKAS; over 5,000 mems.

Liberal Movement of the Republic of Lithuania (Lietuvos Respublikos liberalų sąjūdis): J. Jasinskio g. 10, Vilnius 01013; tel. and fax (5) 249-6959; e-mail info@liberalusajudis.lt; internet www.liberalusajudis.lt; f. 2006; formed by a splinter group of the Liberal and Centre Union; Leader ELIGIJUS MASIULIS.

Lithuanian Christian Democrats (Lietuvos Krikščionys Demokratai): Pylimo g. 36/2, Vilnius 01135; tel. (5) 262-6126; fax (5) 212-7387; e-mail lkdp@takas.lt; internet www.lkdp.lt; f. 2001 by merger of the Christian Democratic Party of Lithuania and the Christian Democratic Union; Chair. VALENTINAS STUNDYS; 12,000 mems.

Lithuanian Peasant Nationalists' Union (LPNU) (Lietuvos Valstiečių Liaudininkų Sąjunga—LVLS): Pamėnkalnio g. 26, Vilnius 01114; tel. and fax (5) 239-4195; e-mail lvls@zebra.lt; internet www.lvls.lt; f. 2001 by the merger of the New Democracy Party and the Lithuanian Peasants' (Farmers') Party; fmrly Peasants' (Farmers) and New Democratic Party Union (VNDS); present name adopted Feb. 2006; Chair. KAZIMIERA DANUTĖ PRUNSKIENĖ; 1,500 mems.

Lithuanian Polish Electoral Action (Lietuvos lenkų rinkimų akcija—LLRA): Pilies g. 16, Vilnius 01123; tel. (5) 279-1887; e-mail info@awpl.lt; internet www.awpl.lt; f. 1994; Chair. WALDEMAR TOMASZEWSKI.

Lithuanian Polish People's Party (Lietuvos Lenkų Liaudies Partija/Polska Partia Ludowa): Kauno g. 1A, Vilnius 03212; tel. and fax (5) 216-2874; e-mail lllp@mail.lt; internet www.lllp.lt; f. 2002; Chair. ANTONINA POŁTAWIEC.

Lithuanian Russians' Union (Lietuvos rusų sąjunga/Soyuz Russkikh Litvy): Pamėnkalnio g. 3–27, Vilnius 01116; tel. (5) 262-4248; e-mail srl@pochta.ru; internet sojuzru.tts.lt; f. 1995; Chair. SERGEI DMITRIYEV.

Lithuanian Social Democratic Party (LSDP) (Lietuvos Socialdemokratų Partija): Barboros Radvilaites g. 1, Vilnius 01124; tel. (5) 261-3907; fax (5) 261-5420; e-mail info@lsdp.lt; internet www.lsdp.lt; absorbed the Lithuanian Democratic Labour Party in 2001; Chair. ALGIRDAS BRAZAUSKAS; 11,000 mems.

New Union (Social Liberals) (NU) (Naujoji sąjunga—Socialliberalai): Gedimino pr. 10/1, Vilnius 01103; tel. (5) 210-7600; fax (5) 210-7602; e-mail centras@nsajunga.lt; internet www.nsajunga.lt; f. 1998; centre-left; Chair. ARTŪRAS PAULAUSKAS.

Order and Justice—Liberal Democrats (Tvarka ir teisingumas—Liberalai demokratai): Gedimino pr. 10/1, Vilnius 01103; tel. and fax (5) 269-1618; e-mail tt@tvarka.lt; internet www.ldp.lt; f. 2002; fmrly Liberal Democratic Party (LDP), renamed as above May 2006; right-wing; Chair. ROLANDAS PAKSAS; 6,500 mems (2007).

Diplomatic Representation

EMBASSIES IN LITHUANIA

Austria: Gaono g. 6, Vilnius 01131; tel. (5) 266-0580; fax (5) 279-1363; e-mail wilna-ob@bmaa.gv.at; Ambassador ANDREA WICKE.

Azerbaijan: Olimpiečių g. 5-7, Vilnius; tel. (5) 219-0042; fax (5) 279-1504; Ambassador NAIRA SHAKHTAKHTINSKAYA.

Belarus: Mindaugo g. 13, Vilnius 03225; tel. (5) 266-2200; fax (5) 266-2212; e-mail lithuania@belembassy.org; internet www.belarus.lt; Ambassador ULADZIMIR DRAZHIN.

Belgium: Kalinausko g. 2B, Vilnius 03107; tel. (5) 266-0820; fax (5) 212-6444; e-mail vilnius@diplobel.org; internet www.diplomatie.be/vilnius; Ambassador FILNIUS CUMPS.

Bulgaria: Pylimo 8, Palangos 2, 01118 Vilnius; tel. (5) 249-9274; fax (5) 261-9174; e-mail vilnius@bgembassy.lt; Ambassador IVAN PENTCHEV DANTCHEV.

China, People's Republic: Algirdo g. 36, Vilnius 03218; tel. (5) 216-2861; fax (5) 216-2682; e-mail chinaemb_lithuania@mfa.gov.cn; internet www.chinaembassy.lt; Ambassador YANG XIUPING.

Czech Republic: Birutės g. 16, Vilnius 08117; tel. (5) 266-1040; fax (5) 266-1066; e-mail vilnius@embassy.mzv.cz; internet www.mzv.cz/vilnius; Ambassador ALOIS BUCHTA.

Denmark: T. Kosciuškos g. 36, Vilnius 01100; tel. (5) 264-8760; fax (5) 231-2300; e-mail vnoamb@um.dk; internet www.ambvilnius.um.dk; Ambassador LAURIDS MIKAELSEN.

Estonia: Mickevičiaus g. 4A, Vilnius 08119; tel. (5) 278-0200; fax (5) 278-0201; e-mail sekretar@estemb.lt; internet www.estemb.lt; Ambassador ANDRES TROPP.

Finland: Klaipėdos g. 6, Vilnius 01117; tel. (5) 212-1621; fax (5) 212-2463; e-mail sanomat.vil@formin.fi; internet www.finland.lt; Ambassador TIMO LAHELMA.

France: Švarco g. 1, Vilnius 01131; tel. (5) 212-2979; fax (5) 212-4211; e-mail ambafrance.vilnius@diplomatie.gouv.fr; internet www.ambafrance-lt.org; Ambassador GUY YELDA.

Georgia: Poškos g. 13, Vilnius 08123; tel. (5) 273-6959; fax (5) 272-3623; e-mail vilnius.emb@mfa.gov.ge; Ambassador DAVIT APSIAURI.

Germany: Z. Sierakausko g. 24/8, Vilnius 03105; tel. (5) 210-6400; fax (5) 210-6446; e-mail info@wilna.diplo.de; internet www.deutschebotschaft-wilna.lt; Ambassador VOLKER HEINSBERG.

Greece: Didžioji 33/Rūdininkų 2; tel. (5) 261-0526; fax (5) 261-0536; e-mail embassy@grembvil.w3.lt; Ambassador GEORGE CHRISTOFIS.

Holy See: Kosciuškos g. 28, Vilnius 01100; tel. (5) 212-3696; fax (5) 212-4228; e-mail nuntiusbalt@aiva.lt; Apostolic Nuncio Most Rev. PETER STEPHAN ZURBRIGGEN (Titular Archbishop of Glastonia).

Hungary: Jojailos g. 4, Vilnius 01116; tel. (5) 269-0038; fax (5) 269-0041; e-mail vilnius@kum.hu; Ambassador PÉTER NOSZKÓ-HORVATH.

Ireland: Gedimino pr.1, Vilnius 01103; tel. (5) 262-9460; fax (5) 262-9462; e-mail vilniusembassy@dfa.ie; f. 2005; Ambassador DÓNAL DENHAM.

Italy: Vytauto g. 1, Vilnius 08118; tel. (5) 212-0620; fax (5) 212-0405; e-mail ambasciata.vilnius@esteri.it; internet www.ambvilnius.esteri.it; Ambassador Dr GIULIO PRIGIONI.

Japan: M. K. Čiurlionio g. 82B, Vilnius 03100; tel. (5) 231-0462; fax (5) 231-0461; Ambassador MASAKI OKADA.

Kazakhstan: Birutės g. 20A/35, Vilnius 08117; tel. (5) 212-2123; fax (5) 231-3580; e-mail kazemb@iti.lt; internet kazakhstan.embassy.lt; Ambassador TLEUKHAN KABDRAKHMANOV.

Latvia: M. K. Čiurlionio g. 76, Vilnius 03100; tel. (5) 213-1260; fax (5) 213-1130; e-mail embassy.lithuania@mfa.gov.lv; internet www.am.gov.lv/vilnius; Ambassador HARDIJS BAUMANIS.

Moldova: Miglos g. 61A, Vilnius; tel. (5) 260-7914; fax (5) 260-7915; e-mail ambasada.vilnius@gmail.com; Ambassador ION CIORNII.

Netherlands: Business Centre 2000, 4th Floor, Jogailos g. 4, Vilnius 01116; tel. (5) 269-0072; fax (5) 269-0073; e-mail vil@minbuza.nk; internet www.netherlandsembassy.lt; Ambassador JOHANNA GERARDA MARIA RUIGROK.

Norway: Mėsinių g. 5/2, Vilnius 01133; tel. (5) 261-0000; fax (5) 261-0100; e-mail emb.vilnius@mfa.no; internet www.norvegija.lt; Ambassador STEINAR GIL.

Poland: Smėlio g. 20A, Vilnius 10323; tel. (5) 270-9001; fax (5) 270-9007; e-mail ampol@tdd.lt; internet www.polandembassy.lt; Ambassador JANUSZ SKOLIMOWSKI.

Portugal: Gedimino pr. 5, Vilnius 01103; tel. (5) 262-0511; fax (5) 262-0509; e-mail vilnius@embportugal.lt; Ambassador ANTÓNIO MANUEL MOREIRA TANGER CORREA.

Romania: Vivulskio g. 19, Vilnius 03115; tel. (5) 231-0527; fax (5) 231-0652; e-mail ambromania@romania.lt; internet www.romania.lt; Ambassador GHEORGHE TOKAY.

LITHUANIA

Russia: Latvių g. 53/54, Vilnius 08113; tel. (5) 272-1763; fax (5) 272-3877; e-mail post@rusemb.lt; internet www.rusemb.lt; Ambassador BORIS A. TSEPOV.

Spain: Algirdo g. 4, Vilnius 03220; tel. (5) 231-3961; fax (5) 231-3962; e-mail vilnius@mcx.es; f. 2004; Ambassador JOSÉ LUÍS SOLANO GADEA.

Sweden: Didžioji g. 16, Vilnius 01128; tel. (5) 268-5010; fax (5) 268-5030; e-mail ambassaden.vilnius@foreign.ministry.se; internet www.swedishembassy.lt; Ambassador MALIN KÄRRE.

Turkey: Didžioji g. 37, Vilnius 01128; tel. (5) 264-9570; fax (5) 212-3277; e-mail turemvil@eunet.lt; Ambassador OGUZ ÖZGE.

Ukraine: Teatro g. 4, Vilnius 03107; tel. (5) 212-1536; fax (5) 212-0475; e-mail ukrembassy@post.5ci.lt; internet www.mfa.gov.ua/lithuania; Chargé d'affaires a.i. (vacant).

United Kingdom: Antakalnio g. 2, Vilnius 10308; tel. (5) 246-2900; fax (5) 246-2901; e-mail be-vilnius@britain.lt; internet www.britain.lt; Ambassador COLIN ROBERTS.

USA: Akmenų g. 6, Vilnius 03106; tel. (5) 266-5300; fax (5) 266-5310; e-mail webemailvilnius@state.gov; internet vilnius.usembassy.gov; Ambassador JOHN A. CLOUD.

Judicial System

The organs of justice are the Supreme Court, the Court of Appeal, district courts, local courts of administrative areas and a special court—the Commercial Court. The Seimas (Parliament) appoints and dismisses from office the judges of the Supreme Court in response to representations made by the President of the Republic (based upon the recommendation of the chairman of the Supreme Court). Judges of the Court of Appeal are appointed by the President with the approval of the Seimas (on the recommendation of the Minister of Justice), while judges of district and local courts are appointed and dismissed by the President. The Council of Judges submits recommendations to the President of the Republic concerning the appointment of judges, as well as their promotion, transfer or dismissal from office.

The Constitutional Court decides on the constitutionality of acts of the Seimas, as well as of the President and the Government. It consists of nine judges, who are appointed by the Seimas for a single term of nine years; one-third of the Court's members are replaced every three years.

The Office of the Prosecutor-General is an autonomous institution of the judiciary, comprising the Prosecutor-General and local and district prosecutors' offices which are subordinate to him. The Prosecutor-General and his deputies are appointed for terms of seven years by the President, subject to approval by the Seimas, while the prosecutors are appointed by the Prosecutor-General. The Office of the Prosecutor-General incorporates the Department for Crime Investigation. The State Arbitration decides cases of business litigation. A six-volume Civil Code, in accordance with European Union and international law, came into effect in 2001, replacing the Soviet civil legal system, which had, hitherto, remained in operation.

Constitutional Court of the Republic of Lithuania (Lietuvos Respublikos Konstitucinis Teismas): Gedimino pr. 36, Vilnius 01104; tel. (5) 261-1466; fax (5) 212-7975; e-mail mailbox@lrkt.lt; internet www.lrkt.lt; f. 1993; Chair. KĘSTUTIS LAPINSKAS.

Court of Appeal: Gedimino pr. 40/1, Vilnius 01503; tel. (5) 266-3433; fax (5) 266-3060; Chair. VYTAS MILIUS.

Supreme Court of Lithuania (Leituvos Aukščiausiasis Teismas): Gynėjų g. 6, Vilnius 01109; tel. (5) 261-0560; fax (5) 262-7950; e-mail lat@lat.lt; internet www.lat.lt; Chair. VYTAUTAS GREIČIUS.

Office of the Prosecutor-General: A. Smetonos 4, Vilnius 01515; tel. (5) 266-2305; fax (5) 266-2317; e-mail info@prokuraturos.lt; internet www.prokuraturos.lt; Prosecutor-General ALGIMANTAS VALANTINAS.

Religion

Lithuania adopted Christianity at the end of the 14th century. However, the country's geographical position and history have long predetermined a diversity of religious communities. The restoration of independence, in 1991, stimulated the revival of religious practice, which was widely suppressed during the Soviet period. Religious communities that existed prior to Soviet rule were re-established and new ones came into existence. In 2001 there were 923 traditional and 176 non-traditional religious organizations registered in the country.

CHRISTIANITY
The Roman Catholic Church

Roman Catholicism has been the principal religious affiliation in Lithuania since its adoption by the Lithuanian State in 1387. The Roman Catholic Church in Lithuania comprises two archdioceses and five dioceses. There are three seminaries at Vilnius, Kaunas and Telšiai. At 31 December 2005 the Roman Catholic Church estimated there to be 2.8m. adherents in Lithuania (equivalent to some 78.8% of the population).

Lithuanian Bishops' Conference

Skapo 4, Vilnius 01122; tel. (5) 212-5455; fax (5) 212-0972; e-mail lvk@lcnl.lt; internet lvk.lcn.lt.

f. 2002; Pres. Most Rev. SIGITUS TAMKEVIČIUS (Archbishop of Kaunas).

Archbishop of Kaunas: Most Rev. SIGITUS TAMKEVIČIUS, Rotušės 14A, Kaunas 44279; tel. (37) 409026; fax (37) 320090; e-mail kurija@kn.lcn.lt; internet www.kaunas.lcn.lt.

Archbishop of Vilnius: Cardinal AUDRYS JUOZAS BAČKIS, Šventaragio 4, Vilnius 01122; tel. (5) 262-7098; fax (5) 212-2807; e-mail curia@vilnensis.lt; internet vilnius.lcn.lt.

Orthodox Churches
Russian Orthodox Church (Moscow Patriarchate)

The first communities appeared during the 12th century and the first monastery was established in Vilnius in 1597. While Lithuania formed part of the Russian Empire (1795–1915), Orthodoxy was considered the state religion. At 1 January 1996 there were 41 communities. There were an estimated 180,000 adherents in 2001.

Lithuanian Orthodox Church (Moscow Patriarchate): Aušros Vartų 10/3, Vilnius 01129; tel. (5) 212-7765; internet www.orthodoxy.lt; Metropolitan of Vilnius and Lithuania CHRYZOSTOM (MARTISHKIN).

Lithuanian Old Believers Pomor Church

The first communities settled in Lithuania in 1679 and the Church was established in 1709. At 1 January 1996 there were approximately 34,000 adherents (mainly ethnic Russians) in 58 communities, with 23 clergymen and 50 churches.

Supreme Council of the Old Believers Pomor Church in Lithuania: Naujininkų g. 20, Vilnius 02109; tel. (5) 269-5271; f. 1925; Chair. MARK SEMIONOV (acting).

Protestant Churches
Lithuanian Evangelical Lutheran Church

The first parishes were established in 1539–69. In 1563 the Evangelical Church divided into Lutheran and Reformed Churches. Church attendance revived after 1990. The Lithuanian Evangelical Lutheran Church comprises one diocese. At 1 January 1998 there were approximately 30,000 adherents in 54 parishes (with 18 priests and 41 churches).

Consistory of the Lithuanian Evangelical Lutheran Church (Lietuvos Evangeliku-Liuteronu Bažnycia): Tumo-Vaižganto 50, Tauragė 72263; tel. and fax (446) 61145; e-mail redakcija@liuteronai.lt; internet www.liuteronai.lt; Bishop MINDAUGAS SABUTIS.

Lithuanian Evangelical Reformed Church

The first parishes were established after 1563. At 1 January 1996 there were approximately 12,000 adherents in 11 parishes (with two pastors and nine churches).

Lithuanian Evangelical Reformed Church: POB 661, Vilnius 04008; tel. and fax (5) 245-0656; Pres. of Synodie Collegium POVILAS A. JAŠINSKAS.

Lithuanian Baptist Union and Other Churches

Parliament awarded the Baptist Union 'recognized' status in July 2001, the first religious community to be awarded this status. There has been a Baptist presence in Lithuania since the 18th century. The United Methodist Church, the New Apostolic Church, the Pentecostal Union and the Adventist Church ETH are all similarly seeking such status, beyond their status as 'registered'.

ISLAM

Sunni Islam is the religion of the ethnic Tatars of Lithuania. The first Tatar communities settled there in the 14th century. The first mosque in Vilnius was erected in 1558. At 1 January 1996 there were five Tatar religious communities (with 10 clergymen, four mosques and one prayer house). In 2001 there were an estimated 5,000 adherents in Lithuania.

LITHUANIA *Directory*

Sunni Muslim Religious Centre—Muftiate in Lithuania: A. Vivulskio g. 3, Vilnius 03220; tel. (5) 242-5124; fax (5) 260-3451; e-mail ramazanas@is.lt; f. 1998; Mufti ROMUALDAS KRINICKIS.

JUDAISM

The first Jewish communities appeared in Lithuania in the 15th century. In the 15th–17th centuries Lithuania, and particularly Vilnius, was an important centre of Jewish culture and religion. Before the Second World War approximately 200,000 Jews lived in Lithuania; an estimated 90% were murdered during the German occupation (1941–44). At 1 January 1996 there were five religious communities, with two synagogues (in Vilnius and Kaunas). There were an estimated 5,000 adherents in Lithuania in 2001. There are small number of Karaites (Karaim), who originate from Crimea (now in Ukraine), and who speak a Turkic language and follow a form of Judaism resident in Lithuania, principally in Trakai, near Vilnius.

Jewish Community of Lithuania: Pylimo g. 4, Vilnius 01117; tel. (5) 261-3003; fax (5) 212-7915; e-mail jewishcom@post.5ci.lt; internet www.litjews.org; f. 1992 to replace and expand the role of the Jewish Cultural Society; Chair. SIMONAS ALPERAVIČIUS; Chief Rabbi CHAIM BURSHTEIN.

The Press

In 2006 there were 334 newspapers and 566 periodicals published in Lithuania.

The publications listed below are in Lithuanian, except where otherwise indicated.

PRINCIPAL NEWSPAPERS

Kauno diena (Kaunas Daily): Kęstučio g. 86, 44296 Kaunas; tel. (37) 302250; fax (37) 423404; e-mail redakcija@kaunodiena.lt; internet www.kaunodiena.lt; f. 1945; 6 a week; Editor-in-Chief OVIDIJUS LUKOŠIUS; circ. 50,000.

Klaipėda: Šaulių g. 21, Klaipėda 92233; tel. (46) 397750; fax (46) 397700; e-mail office@klaipeda.daily.lt; internet www.klaipeda .daily.lt; Editor VALDEMARAS PUODŽIŪNAS.

Kurier Wileński (Vilnius Courier): Birbynių g. 4A, Vilnius 02121; tel. and fax (5) 260-8444; e-mail info@kurierwilenski.lt; internet www.kurierwilenski.lt; f. 1953; 5 a week; in Polish; Editor-in-Chief ROBERT MICKIEWICZ; circ. 8,000.

Lietuvos aidas (Lithuanian Echo): Gedimino pr. 2, 2000 Vilnius; tel. (52) 261-0544; fax (5) 212-4876; e-mail centr@aidas.lt; internet www.aidas.lt; f. 1917; re-est. 1990; 5 a week; Editor-in-Chief ALGIRDAS PILVELIS; circ. 20,000.

Lietuvos rytas (Lithuanian Morning): Gedimino pr. 12A, Vilnius 01103; tel. (5) 274-3600; fax (5) 274-3700; e-mail news@lrytas.lt; internet www.lrytas.lt; f. 1990; 6 a week, with 3 supplements per week; Editor-in-Chief RIMVYDAS VALATKA; circ. 65,000 (Mon.–Fri.), 200,000 (Sat.).

Lietuvos žinios (Lithuanian News): Kęstučio g. 4/14, Vilnius 08117; tel. (5) 249-2152; fax (5) 275-3131; e-mail red@lzinios.lt; internet www.lzinios.lt; 6 a week; Gen. Dir and Editor-in-Chief VASILIAUSKAS VASILIAUSKAS.

Respublika (Republic): A. Smetonos g. 2, Vilnius 01115; tel. (5) 212-3112; fax (5) 212-3538; e-mail press@respublika.lt; f. 1989; 6 a week in Lithuanian, with 5 Russian editions per week; Editor-in-Chief VITAS TOMKUS; circ. 55,000.

Šiaulių kraštas: P. Višinskio g. 26, Šiauliai 77155; tel. (41) 591555; fax (41) 524581; e-mail redakcija@skrastas.lt; internet www .skrastas.lt.

Vakaro žinios (Evening News): Jogailos g. 11/2-11, Vilnius 01116; tel. and fax (5) 261-6875; e-mail vakarozinios@takas.lt; daily; circ. 70,000.

Vakarų ekspresas (Western Express): M. Mažvydo 3, Klaipėda 92131; tel. (46) 411308; fax (46) 310102; e-mail sekretore@ve.lt; internet www.ve.lt; f. 1990; 6 a week; Editor-in-Chief GINTARAS TOMKUS; circ. 16,000–22,000.

Verslo žinios (Business News): J. Jasinskio 16A, Vilnius 01112; tel. (5) 252-6300; fax (5) 252-6313; e-mail info@vz.lt; internet vz.lt; f. 1994; 5 a week; circ. 9,000; Editor LINAS KMIELIAUSKAS.

PRINCIPAL PERIODICALS

Artuma (Presence): Rotušės a. 23, Kaunas 44279; tel. and fax (37) 209683; e-mail redakcija@artuma.lt; internet www.artuma.lt; f. 1989 as *Caritas*; name changed as above in 1997; monthly; Catholic family magazine; Editor-in-Chief DARIUS CHMIELIAUSKAS; circ. 12,500.

Dienovidis (Midday): Pilies g. 23A, Vilnius 01123; tel. (5) 212-1911; fax (5) 212-3101; e-mail dienovidis@takas.lt; f. 1990; weekly; Editor-in-Chief ALDONA ŽEMAITYTĖ; circ. 4,500.

Kultūros barai (Domains of Culture): Latako g. 3, Vilnius 01125; tel. (5) 261-6696; fax (5) 261-0538; e-mail kulturosbarai@takas.lt; internet www.eurozine.com; f. 1965; monthly; independent cultural magazine; Editor-in-Chief BRONYS SAVUKYNAS; circ. 3,000.

Laima: K. Donelaičio g. 70–10, Kaunas 44248; tel. (5) 272-8083; fax (5) 272-1614; e-mail laima@redakcija.lt; f. 1993; monthly; lifestyle and feature magazine for women; Editor-in-Chief GITANA BUKAUSKIENĖ; circ. 30,000.

Liaudies kultūra (Ethnic Culture): Barboros Radvilaitės 8, Vilnius 01124; tel. (5) 261-3412; fax (5) 212-4033; e-mail lkredaktore@llkc.lt; internet www.llkc.lt; f. 1988; 6 a year; Gen. Editor DALIA ANTANINA RASTENIENĖ; circ. 800.

Lietuvos sportas (Lithuanian Sports): Odminių g. 9, Vilnius 01122; tel. and fax (5) 261-6757; f. 1922; re-est. 1992; 3 a week; Editor-in-Chief BRONIUS ČEKANAUSKAS; circ. 18,000.

Lietuvos ūkis (Lithuanian Economy): Vilnius; tel. (5) 213-6718; f. 1921; monthly; Editor-in-Chief ALGIRDAS JASIONIS.

Literatūra ir menas (Literature and Art): Mesiniu 4, Vilnius 01133; tel. (5) 269-1977; fax (5) 212-6556; e-mail lmenas@takas.lt; internet www.culture.lt/lmenas; f. 1946; weekly; publ. by the Lithuanian Writers' Union; Editor-in-Chief KORNELIJUS PLATELIS; circ. 2,000.

Lithuania in the World: J. Basanavičiaus g. 7, Vilnius 01118; tel. (5) 261-4432; fax (5) 212-5560; e-mail info@liw.lt; internet www.liw .lt; f. 1993; 6 a year; in English and Lithuanian; Exec. Editor JOLANTA LAUMENSKAITĖ; circ. 10,000.

Magazyn Wileński (Vilnius Journal): Laisvės pr. 60, Vilnius 05120; tel. (5) 242-7718; fax (5) 242-9065; e-mail magazyn@magwil.lt; internet www.magwil.lt; f. 1990; monthly; political, cultural; in Polish; Editor-in-Chief MICHAŁ MACKIEWICZ; circ. 5,000.

Metai (Year): K. Sirvydo g. 6, Vilnius 01101; tel. (5) 261-7344; e-mail metai@takas.lt; f. 1991; monthly; journal of the Lithuanian Writers' Union; Editor-in-Chief DANIELIUS MUŠINSKAS; circ. 2,000.

Mokslas ir gyvenimas (Science and Life): Antakalnio g. 36, Vilnius 10305; tel. and fax (5) 234-1572; e-mail mgredacija@takas.lt; internet ausis.gf.vu.lt/mg/; f. 1957; monthly; popular and historical science; Editor-in-Chief JUOZAS BALDAUSKAS; circ. 3,500.

Moteris (Woman): P. Smuglevičiaus g. 21, Vilnius 08311; tel. and fax (5) 247-7711; e-mail info@moteris.lt; internet www.moteris.lt; f. 1952; monthly; popular, for women; Editor-in-Chief EGLE STRIAUKIENE; circ. 20,000.

Naujasis Židinys-Aidai (New Hearth–Echoes): Tilto g. 8/3–11, Vilnius 01001; tel. (5) 212-0311; fax (5) 212-2363; e-mail aidai@ aidai.lt; internet www.aidai.lt/zidinys; f. 1991; monthly; religion, culture and social affairs; Editor-in-Chief SAULIUS DRAZDAUSKAS; circ. 1,000.

Nemunas: Gedimino g. 45, Kaunas 44239; tel. and fax (37) 322244; e-mail nemunas.redakcija@centras.lt; f. 1967; weekly; journal of the Lithuanian Writers' Union; Editor-in-Chief VIKTORAS RUDZIANSKAS; circ. 1,500.

Panelė (Young Miss): P. Smuglevičiaus g. 23, Vilnius 08311; tel. (5) 247-7716; fax (5) 247-7715; e-mail magazine@panele.lt; internet www.panele.lt; f. 1994; monthly; popular, for ages 12–25; Editor-in-Chief JURGA BALTRUKONYTĖ; circ. 66,000.

Septynios meno dienos (7 meno dienos) (Seven Days of Art): Bernardinų g. 10, Vilnius 01124; tel. (5) 261-3039; fax (5) 261-1926; e-mail 7md@takas.lt; internet www.culture.lt/7menodienos; f. 1992; weekly; Editor-in-Chief LINAS VILDŽIŪNAS; circ. 1,500.

Švyturys (Beacon): Maironio g. 1, Vilnius 01124; tel. (5) 261-0791; fax (5) 261-4690; f. 1949; monthly; politics, economics, history, culture, fiction; Editor-in-Chief JUOZAS BAUŠYS; circ. 10,000.

Tremtinys (Deportee): Laisvės al. 39, Kaunas 44282; tel. (37) 323204; e-mail tremtinys@erdvas.lt; internet www.lpkts.lt/ tremtinys.htm; f. 1988; weekly; publ. of fmr Lithuanian Union of Political Prisoners and Deportees (now part of Homeland Union); Editor-in-Chief AUDRONĖ KAMINSKIENĖ; circ. 4,500.

Valstiečių laikraštis (Farmer's Newspaper): Laisvės pr. 60, Vilnius 05120; tel. and fax (5) 242-1281; e-mail redakcija@valstietis.lt; internet www.valstietis.lt; f. 1940; 2 a week; Editor-in-Chief JONAS ŠVOBA; circ. 68,000.

Vasario 16 (16 February): J. Gruodžio g. 9/404, Kaunas 44293; tel. (37) 225219; f. 1988; fortnightly; journal of Order and Justice—Liberal Democrats; Sec. PRIMAS NOREIKA; circ. 1,600.

NEWS AGENCIES

Baltic News Service (BNS): Jogailos g. 9/1, Vilnius 01116; tel. (5) 231-2410; fax (5) 268-1515; e-mail bns@bns.lt; f. 1991; Dir JURGITA LITVINIENĖ (acting).

ELTA Lithuanian News Agency (ELTA Lietuvos Naujienų Agentūra): Gedimino pr. 21/2, Vilnius 01103; tel. (5) 262-8864; fax (5) 261-9507; e-mail zinios@elta.lt; internet www.elta.lt; f. 1920; 18.4%

owned by Ziniu Partneriai; 39.5% owned by Respublikos Investicija (both cos controlled by Respublika Gp); Dir GRAZINA RAMANAUSKAITĖ-TIUMENEVIENĖ.

Publishers

Alma littera: A. Juozapavičiaus 6/2, Vilnius 09310; tel. (5) 263-8877; fax (5) 272-8026; e-mail post@almali.lt; internet www.almali.lt; f. 1990; fiction, children's books, textbooks; Dir-Gen. ARVYDAS ANDRIJAUSKAS.

Baltos lankos leidykla (White Meadows Publishing House): Aušros Vartų g. 29/1, Vilnius 01129; tel. (5) 240-8673; fax (5) 240-7446; e-mail leidykla@baltoslankos.lt; internet www.baltoslankos.lt; f. 1992; literature, humanities, social sciences, fiction and textbooks; Dir SAULIUS ŽUKAS.

Eugrimas: Kalvariju 98/36, Vilnius 08211; tel. and fax (5) 273-3955; e-mail info@eugrimas.lt; internet www.eugrimas.lt; f. 1995; academic and professional literature, incl. economics, business, law and politics; Dir EUGENIJA PETRULIENĖ.

Katalikų pasaulio leidiniai (Editions of the Catholic World): Pylimo 27/14, Vilnius 01141; tel. (5) 212-2422; fax (5) 212-0375; internet www.katalikuleidiniai.lt; f. 1990; Dir BIRUTĖ BARTASŪNAITE.

Lietuvos rašytojų sąjungos leidykla (Lithuanian Writers' Union Publishers): K. Sirvydo 6, Vilnius 01101; tel. and fax (5) 262-8945; e-mail info@rsleidykla.lt; internet www.rsleidykla.lt; f. 1990; fiction, essays, literary heritage, children's books; Dir GIEDRE SORIENE.

Mintis leidykla (Mintis Publishing House): Z. Sierakausko g. 15, Vilnius 03105; tel. (5) 233-2943; fax (5) 216-3157; e-mail redakcija@mintis.org; internet www.mintis.org; f. 1949; philosophy, politics, history, law, mythology, textbooks, encyclopedias, biographies, fiction; also book distributor, bookshop; Dir LEONARDAS ARMONAS.

Mokslo ir enciklopedijų leidybos institutas (Science and Encyclopedia Publishing Institute): L. Asanavičiūtės 23, Vilnius 04315; tel. (5) 245-8526; fax (5) 245-8537; e-mail meli@meli.lt; internet www.meli.lt; f. 1992; encyclopedias, science and reference books, dictionaries, higher education textbooks, books for the general reader; Dir RIMANTAS KARECKAS.

Presvika: Kauno g. 28, Vilnius 03202; tel. (5) 262-3182; fax (5) 262-3110; e-mail presvika@vilnius.balt.net; internet www.presvika.lt; f. 1996; psychological and educational literature, textbooks and fiction; Dir VIOLETA BILAIŠYTĖ.

Šviesa (Light): E. Ožeškienės g. 10, Kaunas 44252; tel. (37) 409126; fax (37) 342032; e-mail mail@sviesa.lt; internet www.sviesa.lt; f. 1945; textbooks and pedagogical literature; Dir ARŪNAS BUTKUS.

Tyto alba: J. Jasinskio g. 10, Vilnius 01112; tel. (5) 249-7453; fax (5) 298-8602; internet www.tytoalba.lt; f. 1993; contemporary Lithuanian literary fiction and non-fiction, fiction in translation; Dir LOLITA VARANAVIČIENĖ.

UAB Leidykla Vaga (Furrow Publishing House Ltd): Gedimino pr. 50, Vilnius 01110; tel. (5) 249-8121; fax (5) 249-8122; e-mail info@vaga.lt; internet www.vaga.lt; f. 1945 as Lithuanian State Publishing House of Fiction; privatized and restructured in 1994; fiction, non-fiction, art, children's books; Dir VYTAS V. PETROŠIUS.

UAB Versus Aureus leidykla: Rūdninkų g. 10, Vilnius 01135; tel. and fax (5) 265-2730; e-mail versus@versus.lt; internet www.versus.lt; f. 2003; fiction, non-fiction and educational literature.

PUBLISHERS' ASSOCIATION

Lietuvos Leidėjų Asociacija (Lithuanian Publishers' Association): A. Jakšto 22–13, Vilnius 01105; tel. and fax (5) 261-7740; e-mail lla@centras.lt; internet www.lla.lt; f. 1989; Pres. EUGENIJUS KAZILIŪNAS.

Broadcasting and Communications

TELECOMMUNICATIONS

Regulatory Authority

Communications Regulatory Authority (Ryšių reguliavimo tarnyba): Algirdo 27, Vilnius 03219; tel. (5) 210-5633; fax (5) 216-1564; e-mail rrt@rrt.lt; internet www.rrt.lt; f. 2001; Dir TOMAS BARAKAUSKAS.

Service Providers

UAB BITĖ Lietuva: Žemaitės 15, Vilnius 03118; tel. (6) 560-0656; fax (6) 990-0111; e-mail info@bite.lt; internet www.bite.lt; mobile telecommunications service provider; 1.8m. subscribers (Dec. 2006); CEO MARTIN AMTOFT-CHRISTENSEN.

UAB Eurocom: Ozo g. 25, Vilnius 07150; tel. (5) 274-4699; fax (5) 274-4612; e-mail eurocom@eurocom.lt; internet www.eurocom.lt; f. 2001; fixed line and mobile telecommunications service provider; a subsidiary of VP Market; Dir SEDIMINAS JOVAIŠA.

Omnitel UAB: T. Ševčenkos 25, Vilnius 03503; tel. (698) 63333; fax (5) 274-5574; e-mail info@omnitel.net; internet www.omnitel.lt; f. 1991 as Litcom; owned by Telia Sonera (Sweden); largest mobile GSM communications provider in Lithuania; Pres. ANTANAS JUOZAS ZABULIS.

UAB Tele2: POB 147, Vilnius 01003; tel. (684) 00212; fax (5) 236-6301; e-mail tele2@tele2.lt; internet www.tele2.lt; f. 1999; owned by Tele2 AB (Sweden); provider of GSM, internet and fixed-line telecommunications services; Chief Exec. PETRAS MASIULIS.

Teo LT AB: Savanorių pr. 28, Vilnius 03116; tel. (5) 262-1511; fax (5) 212-6655; internet www.teo.lt; f. 1992 under the name Lietuvos Telekomas AB; present name adopted 2006; privatized 1998; operates public telecommunications network, repairs telecommunications equipment; monopoly withdrawn in 2003; Chair. ERIK HALLBERG; Gen. Man. ARŪNAS ŠIKŠTA; 3,200 employees.

BROADCASTING

Regulatory Authority

Lietuvos radijo ir televizijos komisija (Radio and Television Commission of Lithuania): Vytenio 6, Vilnius 03113; tel. (5) 233-0660; fax (5) 264-7125; e-mail lrtk@rtk.lt; internet www.rtk.lt; f. 1996; licensing and licence compliance; Chair. JONAS LINIAUSKAS.

Radio

Lietuvos radijas ir televizija (LRT) (Lithuanian Radio and Television): S. Konarskio 49, Vilnius 03123; tel. (5) 236-3209; fax (5) 236-3208; e-mail lrt@lrt.lt; internet www.lrt.lt; f. 1926; govt-owned; non-profit public broadcasting co; operates two national radio channels and two national television channels; Chair. of Council ROMAS PAKALNIS; Dir-Gen. AUDRIUS SIAURUSEVIČIUS; 650 employees.

Lietuvos radijas (Lithuanian Radio): S. Konarskio 49, Vilnius 03123; tel. (5) 236-3000; fax (5) 213-5333; e-mail rimgel@lrt.lt; internet www.lrt.lt; f. 1926; broadcasts in Lithuanian, Russian, Polish, Yiddish, Belarusian and Ukrainian; Dir RIMGAUDAS GELEŽEVIČIUS.

A2 Radijo Stotis: Laisvės pr. 3, Vilnius 04215; tel. (5) 245-4922; e-mail a2@a2.lt; internet www.a2.lt; private, commercial; Dir VYDAS IVANAUSKAS.

UAB Aukštaitijos radijas (AR): Laisvės a. 1, Panevėžys 35175; tel. and fax (45) 596969; e-mail ar@laineta.lt; private, commercial; Dir ALGIRDAS ŠATAS.

FM 99: Rotušės a. 2, POB 119, Alytus 62141; tel. (315) 76120; fax (315) 74646; e-mail fm99@fm99.lt; internet www.fm99.lt; private, commercial; broadcast by UAB Alytaus radijas; Dir LIUDAS RAMANAUSKAS.

Kauno fonas 105.4: Savanorių pr. 192–802, Kaunas 44151; tel. (37) 327427; fax (37) 327447; internet www.kf.lt; private, commercial; Dir ŪDRYS STASELKA.

UAB Laisvoji banga: Lvovo g. 25, Vilnius 09320; tel. (5) 216-3591; fax (5) 215-1458; e-mail info@laisvojibanga.lt; internet www.europeanhitradio.lt; private, commercial; broadcasts European Hit Radio; Dir JŪRATĖ OVERLINGIENĖ.

Laluna: Taikos pr. 81, Klaipėda 94114; tel. (46) 390808; fax (46) 390805; e-mail laluna@laluna.lt; internet www.laluna.lt; private, commercial; Dir TADAS ŽEMAITIS.

M-1: Laisvės pr. 60, Vilnius 05120; tel. (5) 236-0360; fax (5) 236-0366; e-mail m-1@m-1.fm; internet www.m-1.fm; f. 1989; private, commercial; Gen. Man. RŪTA GRUŠNIENĖ.

Mažeikių aidas (MA): POB 17, Ventos g. 49, Mažeikiai 89103; tel. (443) 65055; fax (443) 65600; e-mail info@mazeikiuaidas.lt; internet www.mazeikiuaidas.lt; f. 1996; private, commercial; Dir TOMAS RUGINIS.

Pūkas, UAB: Ringuvos g. 61, Kaunas 45242; tel. (37) 342424; fax (37) 342434; e-mail pukas@pukas.lt; internet www.pukas.lt; f. 1991; private, commercial; operates two radio stations and a television station; Dir KĘSTUTIS PŪKAS.

Radiocentras, UAB: Laisvės pr. 60, Vilnius 05120; tel. (5) 212-8706; fax (5) 242-9073; e-mail biuras@rc.lt; internet www.rc.lt; f. 1991; private, commercial; Gen. Man. ARTŪRAS MIRONCIKAS.

Saulės radijas, UAB: Aušros al. 64, Šiauliai 76235; tel. (41) 525141; fax (41) 424404; e-mail info@saulesradijas.lt; internet www.saulesradijas.lt; private, commercial; Dir RASA AKUČKIENĖ.

Tau: Draugystės g. 19–357, Kaunas 51230; tel. (37) 352790; fax (37) 352128; e-mail info@tau.lt; internet www.tau.lt; private, commercial; Dir GIEDRIUS GIPAS.

LITHUANIA

Vš Į Kauno radijas ir televizija: S. Daukanto 28A, Kaunas 44246; tel. (37) 321010; fax (37) 322570; e-mail kaunas@lrtv.lt; Dir P. GARNYS.

Znad Wilii, UAB: Laisvės pr. 60, Vilnius 05120; tel. (5) 249-0870; fax (5) 278-4446; e-mail radio@znadwilii.lt; internet www.znadwilii.lt; f. 1992; private, commercial; Dir-Gen. MIROSLAVAS JUCHNEVIČIUS.

Television

Lietuvos televizija (LTV): S. Konarskio g. 49, Vilnius 03123; tel. (5) 236-3100; fax (5) 216-3282; e-mail lrt@lrt.lt; internet www.lrt.lt; f. 1957; subsidiary of LRT (see Radio); programmes in Lithuanian, Russian, Polish, Ukrainian and Belarusian; Dir ŠARŪNAS KALINAUSKAS.

Aidas, UAB (Echo): Birutės skg. 42, Trakai 21114; tel. (528) 52480; fax (528) 55656; e-mail tvaidas@uab.lt; mainly relays German programmes; private, commercial; Dir ČESLOVAS RULEVIČIUS.

Baltijos televizija (BTV): Laisvės pr. 60, Vilnius 05120; tel. (5) 278-0805; fax (5) 278-0804; internet www.btv.lt; f. 1993; broadcasts own programmes and relays German, Polish and US broadcasts; private, commercial; Dir-Gen. GINTARAS SONGAILA.

KTV plius: Nemuno g. 79, Panevėžys 37355; tel. (45) 514103; fax (45) 443561; e-mail pictura@kateka.lt; internet www.ktvplius.lt; private, commercial; Pres. ROLANDAS MEILIŪNAS.

LNK TV (UAB Laisvas ir nepriklausomas kanalas): Šeškinės g. 20, Vilnius 07156; tel. (5) 212-4061; fax (5) 278-4530; e-mail info@lnk.lt; internet www.lnk.lt; private, commercial; broadcasts TV1; Dir PAULIUS KOVAS.

PAN-TV: Respublikos g. 19–8, Panevėžys 35185; tel. (45) 464267; e-mail pantv@takas.lt; private, commercial; Dir SAULIUS BUKELIS.

Raseiniu TV: Vytauto Vilniaus 1A, Raseiniai 60187; tel. (428) 54433; fax (428) 70422; e-mail office@mirkliai.lt; broadcast by VšĮ Raseinių televizijos ir radijo centras; Dir KĘSTUTIS SKAMARAKAS.

Šiaulių TV: Liejyklos g. 10, Šiauliai 78147; tel. and fax (41) 523809; internet www.stv.lt; private; Dir ANDRIUS SEDŽIUS.

TV3: Nemenčinės pl. 4, Vilnius 10102; tel. (5) 276-4264; fax (5) 276-4253; e-mail postmaster@tv3.lt; internet www.tv3.lt; broadcasts own programmes (20% of schedule) in Lithuanian and English, and relays international satellite channels; private, commercial; Dir RAMŪNAS ŠAUČIKOVAS.

Vilniaus TV: Vivulskio 23, Vilnius 2600; tel. (5) 213-5560; fax (5) 233-7904; e-mail vtv@iti.lt; f. 1994; private, commercial; Dir LINAS RYŠKUS.

Finance

(cap. = capital; res = reserves; dep. = deposits; m. = million; brs = branches; amounts in litai)

BANKING

Central Bank

Bank of Lithuania (Lietuvos bankas): Gedimino pr. 6, Vilnius 01103; tel. (5) 268-0029; fax (5) 262-8124; e-mail info@lb.lt; internet www.lb.lt; f. 1922; re-est. 1990; central bank, responsible for bank supervision; cap. 133.0m., res 564.7m., dep. 3,651.0m. (Dec. 2005); Chair. of Bd REINOLDIJUS ŠARKINAS; 2 brs.

Commercial Banks

Bankas Hansabankas: Savanorių pr. 19, Vilnius 03502; tel. (5) 268-4444; fax (52) 268-4700; e-mail info@hansa.lt; internet www.hansa.lt; f. 1919; as Lietuvos Taupomasis Bankas; present name adopted 2003; 99.5% owned by AS Hansapank (Estonia); cap. 569.7m., res 150.3m., dep. 12,394.9m. (Dec. 2006); Chair. of Bd GIEDRIUS DUSEVIČIUS.

Bankas Snoras: A. Vivulskio g. 7, Vilnius 03221; tel. (5) 239-2239; fax (5) 232-7300; e-mail info@snoras.com; internet www.snoras.com; f. 1992; 68.7% owned by Chairman of the Supervisory Bd, 25.1% by Chairman of Management Bd; cap. 504.5m., dep. 3,627m., total assets 5,754m. (Dec. 2007); Chair. of Supervisory Bd VLADIMIR ANTONOV; Chair. of Management Bd RAIMONDAS BARANAUSKAS.

DnB NORD Bankas: J. Basanavičiaus g. 26, Vilnius 03601; tel. (5) 239-3444; fax (5) 213-9056; e-mail info@dnbnord.lt; internet www.dnbnord.lt; f. 1924; registered as AB Lietuvos Žemės Ūkio Bankas in 1993; privatized in March 2002; present name adopted 2006; 93.1% obtained by Bank DnB Nord A/S (Denmark) in Dec. 2005; cap. 404.5m., res 4.4m., dep. 6,769.5m. (Dec. 2006); Chair. of Management Bd, Pres. and CEO WERNER SCHILLI; 77 brs.

Medicinos Bankas (Medical Bank): Pamėnkalnio g. 40, Vilnius 01114; tel. (5) 264-4800; fax (5) 264-4801; e-mail info@medbank.lt; internet www.medbank.lt; f. 1992; cap. 34.3m., res 9.3m., dep. 337.8m. (Dec. 2006); Chair. of Bd KĘSTUTIS OLSAUSKAS; 7 brs.

Directory

Parex Bankas: K. Kalinausko g. 13, Vilnius 03107; tel. (5) 266-4600; fax (5) 266-4601; e-mail info@parex.lt; internet www.parex.lt; f. 1996; owned by Parex Group (Latvia); cap. 115.0m., res 0.5m., dep. 445.9m. (June 2007); Chair. and Chief Exec. ALMA VAITKUNSKIENE; 6 brs.

Sampo Bankas: Geležinio Vilko g. 18, Vilnius 08500; tel. (5) 210-9400; fax (5) 210-9409; e-mail bankas@sampo.lt; internet www.sampo.lt; f. 1994; fmrly Lithuanian Development Bank; present name adopted 2004; 100% owned by Danske Bank A/S (Denmark); cap. 234.9m., res 3.7m., dep. 3,781.9m. (Dec. 2006); Chair. of Bd GINTAUTAS GALVANAUSKAS.

SEB Vilniaus Bankas (Bank of Vilnius): Gedimino pr. 12, Vilnius 01103; tel. (5) 268-2512; fax (5) 268-2333; e-mail info@seb.lt; internet www.seb.lt; f. 1990 as Spaudos Bankas; present name adopted 2005; 98.9% owned by Skandinaviska Enskilda Banken AB (Sweden); cap. 1,034.6m., res 24.0m., dep. 16,950.1m. (Dec. 2006); Pres. and Chief Exec. AUDRIUS ŽIUGŽDA; 17 brs.

Šiaulių Bankas: Tilžės g. 149, Šiauliai 76348; tel. (41) 595607; fax (41) 430774; internet www.sb.lt; f. 1992; cap. 121.0m., res 17.1m., dep. 1,068.9m. (July 2007); Chair. of Bd ALGIRDAS BUTKUS; 49 brs and client service centres (2007).

Ūkio Bankas: Maironio g. 25, Kaunas 44250; tel. (37) 301301; fax (37) 323188; e-mail ub@ub.lt; internet www.ub.lt; f. 1989; cap. 176.7m., res 180.0m., dep. 2,695.6m. (Dec. 2006); Chair. of Bd EDITA KARPAVIČIENE; Chief Exec. GINTARAS UGIANSKIS; 12 brs.

Property Bank

Turto Bankas AB: Kęstučio g. 45, Vilnius 08124; tel. (5) 278-0900; fax (5) 275-1155; e-mail info@turtas.lt; internet www.turtas.lt; f. 1996; cap. and res 9.7m., total assets 69.5m. (Dec. 2003); recovery of non-performing loans, administration of loans of the Ministry of Finance; Chair. of Bd JONAS BUDREVIČIUS; 6 brs.

Banking Association

Association of Lithuanian Banks (Lietuvos Bankų Asociacija): Ankštoji g. 5/3, Vilnius 01109; tel. (5) 249-6669; fax (5) 249-6139; e-mail info@lba.lt; internet www.lba.lt; f. 1991; Pres. RIMANTAS BUSILA; 9 mems.

STOCK EXCHANGE

Vilnius Stock Exchange (VSE) (Vilniaus vertybinių popierių birža): Konstitucijos pr. 7, Vilnius 08501; tel. (5) 272-3871; fax (5) 272-4894; e-mail vilnius@omxgroup.com; internet www.lt.omxgroup.com; f. 1993; 93.1% owned by HEX Helsinki Stock Exchange Ltd (Finland)—OMX ABforms Group; Chair. of Bd ARMINTA SALADŽIENĖ.

INSURANCE

Principal Insurance Companies

Commercial Union Lietuva Gyvybės draudimas: Jogailos g. 4, Vilnius 01116; tel. (5) 269-0169; fax (5) 269-0269; internet www.commercialunion.lt; f. 2001; owned by Commercial Union Polska—Towarzystwo Ubezpieczeń na Zycie SA (Poland), part of the Aviva Group (United Kingdom); Dir A. UNGULAITIENĖ.

Ergo Lietuva: Geležinio vilko g. 6A, Vilnius 03507; tel. (5) 268-3000; fax (5) 268-3005; e-mail info@ergo.lt; internet www.ergo.lt; f. 1991; owned by Ergo International AG (Germany); formerly Drauda UAB; name changed as above in 2000; in 2002 merged with Preventa; Dir S. JOKUBAITIS.

Hansa Gyvybės draudimas UAB: J. Basanavičiaus g. 8/ Vingrių g. 1, Vilnius 01118; tel. (5) 266-5966; fax (5) 268-5866; e-mail info@hansa.lt; internet www.hansadraudimas.lt; f. 1995; owned by Hansabankas AB (Estonia); formerly Lietuvos Draudimo Gyvybės draudimas; Lithuania's leading life insurer; Dir D. VALENTUKEVIČIUS.

Lietuvos draudimas AB (Lithuanian Insurance): J. Basanavičiaus g. 12, Vilnius 03600; tel. (5) 268-6300; fax (5) 231-4138; e-mail info@ldr.lt; internet www.lietuvosdraudimas.lt; f. 1921; privatized in 1999; owned by Codan AS (Denmark); principal non-life insurance co in Lithuania; Dir K. ŠERPYTIS.

PZU Lietuva UAB: Konstitucijos pr. 7, Vilnius 09308; tel. (5) 279-0007; fax (5) 279-0019; e-mail info@pzu.lt; internet www.pzu.lt; f. 1993; owned by Powszechny Zaklad Ubezpieczen (PZU) SA (Poland); Dir G. MAŽEIKA.

SEB VB Gyvybės Draudimas UAB: Gedimino pr. 12, Vilnius 01103; tel. (5) 268-1555; fax (5) 268-1556; e-mail draudimas@seb.lt; internet www.vbgd.lt; f. 1999; owned by SEB Vilniaus bankas AB; Dir B. KAMUNTAVIČIENĖ.

Insurance Association

Association of Lithuanian Insurers: Vytenio g. 50, Vilnius 03229; tel. (5) 231-0381; e-mail asociacija@draudikai.lt; internet www.draudikai.lt; f. 1992; Dir ANDRIUS ROMANOVSKIS.

Supervisory Body

Insurance Supervisory Commission: Ukmergės g. 222, Vilnius 07157; tel. (5) 243-1370; fax (5) 272-3689; e-mail dpk@dpk.lt; internet www.dpk.lt; Chair. MINDAUGAS ŠALČIUS.

Trade and Industry

GOVERNMENT AGENCIES

Lithuanian Development Agency for Small and Medium-sized Enterprises (Lietuvos smulkaus ir vidutinio verslo plėtros agentūra—SMEDA/LSVVPA): Žalgirio g. 92, Vilnius 09303; tel. (5) 205-1235; fax (5) 205-1246; e-mail info@svv.lt; internet www.smeda.lt; f. 1996; under the Ministry of the Economy; Dir ARVYDAS DARULIS.

State Property Fund (Valstybės Turto Fondas—VTS): Vilniaus g. 16, Vilnius 01507; tel. (5) 268-4999; fax (5) 268-4997; e-mail info@vtf.lt; internet www.vtf.lt; f. 1995; privatization and management of state-owned and municipal property; Chair. GEDIMINAS RAINYS; Dir-Gen. AUDRIUS RUDYS.

DEVELOPMENT AGENCY

National Regional Development Agency (Nacionalinė Regionų Plėtros Agentūra): Lukiskių g. 5/502, Vilnius 01108; tel. and fax (5) 233-4151; e-mail nrda@nrda.lt; internet www.nrda.lt; f. 1999 by the Asscn of Lithuanian Chambers of Commerce, Industry and Crafts; Dir VAIDAS KAZAKEVIČIUS.

CHAMBERS OF COMMERCE

Association of Lithuanian Chambers of Commerce, Industry and Crafts (Lietuvos prekybos, pramonės ir amatų rūmų asociacija): J. Tumo-Vaižganto g. 9/1–63A, Vilnius 01108; tel. (5) 261-2102; fax (5) 261-2112; e-mail info@chambers.lt; internet www.chambers.lt; f. 1992; mem. of International Chamber of Commerce and of Asscn of European Chambers of Commerce and Industry; Pres. DARIUS MOCKUS.

Kaunas Chamber of Commerce, Industry and Crafts: K. Donelaičio g. 8, POB 2111, Kaunas 44213; tel. (37) 229212; fax (37) 208330; e-mail chamber@chamber.lt; internet www.chamber.lt; f. 1925; re-est. 1991; br. at Marijampolė; Pres. Prof. M. RONDOMANSKAS.

Klaipėda Chamber of Commerce, Industry and Crafts: Danės g. 17, POB 148, Klaipėda 92117; tel. (46) 390861; fax (46) 410626; internet www.kcci.lt; Pres. SIGITAS PAULAUSKAS; Dir VIKTORAS KROLIS; 250 mems.

Panevėžys Chamber of Commerce, Industry and Crafts: Respublikos g. 34, Panevėžys 35173; tel. (45) 463687; fax (45) 462227; e-mail panevezys@chambers.lt; internet www.ccic.lt; f. 1991; Pres. VYTAUTAS ŠIDLAUSKAS; Gen. Dir VYTAUTAS KAZAKEVIČIUS.

Šiauliai Chamber of Commerce, Industry and Crafts: Vilniaus g. 88, Šiauliai 76285; tel. (41) 523224; fax (41) 523903; e-mail siauliai@chambers.lt; internet www.rumai.lt; f. 1993; Dir-Gen. RIMUNDAS DOMARKAS.

Vilnius Chamber of Commerce, Industry and Crafts: Algirdo g. 31, Vilnius 03219; tel. (5) 213-5550; fax (5) 213-5542; e-mail vilnius@chambers.lt; internet www.cci.lt; f. 1991; Dir-Gen. BORISAS ZAUBIDOVAS; 480 mems.

INDUSTRIAL ASSOCIATION

Lithuanian Confederation of Industrialists (Lietuvos pramonininkų konfederacija—LPK): A. Vienuolio g. 8, Vilnius 01104; tel. (5) 212-5217; fax (5) 212-5209; e-mail sekretoriatas@lpk.lt; internet www.lpk.lt; f. 1989; Pres. BRONISLOVAS LUBYS.

EMPLOYERS' ORGANIZATION

Lithuanian Business Employers' Confederation (Lietuvos verslo darbdavių konfederacija—LVDK): Algirdo g. 31, Vilnius 03219; tel. (5) 249-8345; fax (5) 249-6448; e-mail info@lvdk.w3.lt; internet www.ldkonfederacija.lt; f. 1999; Gen. Dir DANAS ARLAUSKAS.

UTILITIES

Energy Agency (Energetikos Agentura): Gedimino pr. 38/2, Vilnius 01104; tel. (5) 262-9731; fax (5) 262-6845; e-mail eainfo@ukmin.lt; internet www.ena.lt; f. 1993; state enterprise; attached to the Ministry of the Economy; Dir MARIJUS FRANCKEVIČIUS.

Electricity

Ignalina Nuclear Power Plant (Ignalinos Atominė Elektrinė): Karklų k., Visaginas 31500; tel. (386) 28350; fax (386) 29350; e-mail info@mail.iae.lt; internet www.iae.lt; f. 1985; Dir VIKTOR ŠEVALDIN.

Lietuvos energija AB (Lithuanian Power): Žvejų g. 14, Vilnius 09310; tel. (5) 262-6822; fax (5) 212-6736; e-mail info@lietuvosenergija.lt; internet www.lpc.lt; f. 1995; restructured in 2000; Man. Dir RYMANTAS JUOZAITIS.

Rytų Skirstomieji Tinklai AB (RST) (Eastern Distribution Networks): P. Lukšio g. 5B, Vilnius 08221; tel. (5) 277-7524; fax (5) 277-7514; e-mail info@rst.lt; internet www.rst.lt; f. 2001 following the reorganization of Lietuvos Energija AB; distribution network operator and public supplier of four regions; scheduled for privatization; 156,000 customers (Dec. 2002); Dir RIMANTAS MILIŠAUSKAS.

Vakarų skirstomieji tinklai AB (VST): Jasinskio g. 16C, Vilnius 01112; tel. (5) 2781259; fax (5) 2781269; e-mail vst@vst.lt; internet www.vest.lt; f. 2001; distribution in central and western Lithuania; 96.5% of shares divested to NDX Energija in 2003–04; Chief Exec. DARIUS NEDZINSKAS; 2,000 employees.

Gas

Lietuvos Dujos AB (Lithuanian Gas): Aguonų g. 24, Vilnius 03212; tel. (5) 236-0210; fax (5) 236-0200; e-mail ld@lietuvosdujos.lt; internet www.dujos.lt; f. 1995; natural gas import, sale and transportation; 17.7% state-owned; 38.9% owned by E.ON Ruhrgas International AG (Germany); 37.1% owned by OAO Gazprom (Russia); Chair. ALEXANDER RYAZANOV; Gen. Man. VIKTORAS VALENTUKEVIČIUS; 1,900 employees.

TRADE UNIONS

Lithuanian Labour Federation (Lietuvos Darbo Federacija): Vytauto g. 14, Vilnius 03106; tel. and fax (5) 231-2029; e-mail ldforg@ldf.lt; internet www.ldf.lt; f. 1919 as a Christian trade-union org.; re-est. 1991; 20,000 mems; Chair. VYDAS PUSKEPALIS; Sec.-Gen. JANINA ŠVEDIENĖ.

Lithuanian Trade Union Confederation (LPSK): J. Jasinskio g. 9–213, Vilnius 01111; tel. (5) 249-6921; fax (5) 249-8078; e-mail lpsk@lpsk.lt; internet www.lpsk.lt; f. 2002 by merger of Lithuanian Union of Trade Unions (LPSS) and Lithuanian Trade Union Centre (LPSC); 25 branch trade unions with 120,000 mems; Pres. ARTŪRAS ČERNIAUSKAS.

Lithuanian Trade Union: Solidarumas (Lietuvos profesinė sąjunga 'Solidarumas'): V. Mykolaičio-Putino g. 5, Vilnius 03106; tel. (5) 262-1743; fax (5) 213-3295; e-mail info@solidarumasmokymai.lt; internet www.lps.lt; f. 2002; fmrly the Lithuanian Workers' Union: Labora (f. 1989); Pres. ALDONA BALSIENĖ; 52,000 mems.

Transport

RAILWAYS

In 2006 there were 1,771 km of railway track in use in Lithuania; in 2003 some 122 km of track were electrified. Main lines link Vilnius with Minsk (Belarus), Kaliningrad (Russia) and Warsaw (Poland), in the latter case by way of the Belarusian town of Grodno (Horadnia).

Lithuanian Railways (Lietuvos geležinkeliai): Mindaugo g. 12–14, Vilnius 03603; tel. (5) 269-2038; fax (5) 269-2028; e-mail lgkanc@litrail.lt; internet www.litrail.lt; f. 1991; Dir-Gen. STASYS DAILYDKA; 10,392 employees.

ROADS

In 2006 the total length of the road network was estimated at 79,984 km; the motorway network totalled 309 km. In 2005 some 89% of roads were paved.

Lithuanian Road Administration (Lietuvos automobilių kelių direkcija—LAKD): J. Basanavičiaus g. 36/2, Vilnius 03109; tel. (5) 232-9600; fax (5) 232-9609; e-mail lra@lra.lt; internet www.lra.lt; Gen. Dir VIRGAUDAS PUODŽIUKAS.

SHIPPING

The main port is at Klaipėda. In 2006 there were 441 km of inland navigable waterways.

Port Authority

Klaipėda State Seaport Authority: J. Janonio g. 24, Klaipėda 92251; tel. (46) 499799; fax (46) 499777; e-mail info@port.lt; internet www.port.lt; multi-purpose, deep-water universal port; connects sea, land and rail routes from east and west; Gen. Dir SIGITAS DOBILINSKAS.

Shipowning Company

Lithuanian Shipping Company (AB Lietuvos Jūrų Laivininkystė): Malunininku g. 3, Klaipėda 92264; tel. (46) 393105; fax (46) 393119; e-mail gp@ljl.lt; internet www.ljl.lt; f. 1969 as LISCO; partially privatized and renamed as above in June 2001; 73.24% state-owned; transportation of cargo; owns 18 vessels; Gen. Dir VYTAUTAS VISMANTAS.

LITHUANIA

CIVIL AVIATION

There are international airports at Vilnius, Kaunas, Palanga and Šiauliai.

Directorate of Civil Aviation (Oro Navigacija): Rodūnios kelias 2, Vilnius 02188; tel. (5) 273-9102; fax (5) 273-9161; e-mail info@ans.lt; internet www.ans.lt; Gen. Dir ALGIMANTAS RAŠČIUS.

flyLAL—Lithuanian Airlines: A. Gustaičio g. 4, Vilnius 02512; tel. (5) 252-5555; fax (5) 216-6828; e-mail info@flylal.lt; internet www.flylal.lt; f. 1991; owned by the LAL Group; operates passenger and cargo flights to regional and European destinations; Chief Exec. SAULIUS STASIŪNAS.

Tourism

Tourist attractions in Lithuania include the historic cities of Vilnius, Kaunas, Kėdainiai, Trakai and Klaipėda, coastal resorts, such as Palanga and Kuršių Nerija, and picturesque countryside. Some 681,487 tourists visited the country in 2005; tourist receipts totalled US $975m. (including passenger transport).

Lithuanian State Department of Tourism: A. Juozapavičiaus g. 13, Vilnius 09311; tel. (5) 210-8796; fax (5) 210-8753; e-mail vtd@tourism.lt; internet www.tourism.lt; Dir ALVITIS LUKOŠEVIČIUS.

LUXEMBOURG

Introductory Survey

Location, Climate, Language, Religion, Flag, Capital

The Grand Duchy of Luxembourg is a land-locked country in western Europe. It is bordered by Belgium to the west and north, by France to the south, and by Germany to the east. The climate is temperate, with cool summers and mild winters. In Luxembourg-Ville the average temperature ranges from 1°C (33°F) in January to 18°C (64°F) in July, while annual rainfall averages 782 mm. Lëtzebuergesch (Luxembourgish), a German-Moselle-Frankish dialect, is the spoken language and became the official language in 1984. French is generally used for administrative purposes, while German is the principal written language of commerce and the press. Almost all of the inhabitants profess Christianity: about 87% are Roman Catholics and a small minority are Protestants. The national flag (proportions 3 by 5) consists of three equal horizontal stripes, of red, white and blue. The capital is Luxembourg-Ville (Lützelburg).

Recent History

As a founder member of the European Community (EC, now European Union—EU, see p. 244), of which Luxembourg-Ville is one of the main bases, Luxembourg has played a significant role in progress towards European integration since the Second World War. Luxembourg's commitment to such integration was exemplified by its status as one of the original signatories to the Schengen Agreement (named after the town in Luxembourg where the accord was signed by a number of EC member countries in June 1990), which binds signatories to the abolition of internal border controls.

The Belgo-Luxembourg Economic Union (BLEU) has existed since 1921, except for the period from 1940–44, when the Grand Duchy was subject to wartime occupation by Germany. In 1948 the Benelux Economic Union (see p. 411) was inaugurated between Belgium, Luxembourg and the Netherlands, becoming effective in 1960, and establishing the three countries as a single customs area in 1970.

In November 1964 Grand Duchess Charlotte abdicated, after a reign of 45 years, and was succeeded by her son, Prince Jean.

Pierre Werner, leader of the Chrëschtlech Sozial Vollekspartei (CSV—Christian Social Party), became Prime Minister in February 1959 and, during 1959–74, led successive coalition governments in which the CSV was the dominant partner, along with either the Demokratesch Partei (DP—Democratic Party) or the Lëtzebuerger Sozialistesch Arbechterpartei (LSAP—Socialist Workers' Party of Luxembourg). However, at a general election in May 1974 the CSV suffered a decrease in popularity, and, for the first time since 1919, entered into opposition. In the following month a centre-left coalition between the LSAP and the DP was formed under the premiership of the leader of the DP, Gaston Thorn, who had been Minister of Foreign Affairs in the previous administration. At the next general election, which took place in June 1979, the CSV increased its representation in the 59-member Chambre des Députés from 18 to 24 seats. In July Werner again formed a coalition Government, comprising the CSV and the DP, which held 15 seats.

At a general election in June 1984 the CSV again secured the largest number of seats (25) in the enlarged 64-member legislature. However, the success of the LSAP, which took 21 seats (compared with 14 in the previous election), was widely attributed to general dissatisfaction with an economic austerity programme, which had been introduced during the early 1980s, and with the rising level of unemployment. A centre-left coalition was formed in July 1984 between the CSV and the LSAP, with Jacques Santer of the CSV (hitherto Minister of Finance, Labour and Social Security) as Prime Minister. Elections to the Chambre des Députés (whose membership had been reduced to 60 in January 1989) took place in June 1989. The CSV, the LSAP and the DP each lost three seats (returning 22, 18 and 11 deputies, respectively). In the following month Santer renewed the outgoing coalition. At the next general election, in June 1994, the CSV and the LSAP each lost one representative in the Chambre des Députés, winning 21 and 17 seats, respectively; the DP secured 12 seats. The CSV-LSAP coalition was again renewed, under Santer as Prime Minister. In January 1995 Santer took office as President of the Commission of the EU. He was succeeded as Prime Minister by Jean-Claude Juncker of the CSV, hitherto Minister of the Budget, of Finance and of Labour. In January 1998 the Minister of the Environment and of Health, Johny Lahure, resigned from the Government, following the disclosure of a financial scandal within the Ministry of Health.

The two coalition partners both recorded losses at the general election held concurrently with elections to the European Parliament on 13 June 1999, the CSV winning 19 seats and the LSAP 13. The DP increased its representation from 12 to 15 seats, while the conservative Aktiounskomitee fir Demokratie a Rentegerechtegkeet (ADR—Action Committee for Democracy and Pensions Justice) took seven seats (an increase of two). The environmentalist party, Déi Gréng (The Greens), retained its five seats in the legislature. Juncker, who remained as Prime Minister, subsequently formed a new centre-right coalition of the CSV and the DP, which took office in early August.

In March 1998 Grand Duke Jean conferred broad constitutional powers upon his eldest son and heir, Prince Henri, permitting him to deputize for the Grand Duke in all official capacities. On 7 October 2000 Prince Henri succeeded his father as Head of State.

Luxembourg's banking secrecy laws have for many years been a cause of concern. In April 1993 legislation was introduced which permitted the confiscation of deposits in Luxembourg banks accruing from suspected illegal drugs-related activities. Further legislation was introduced in 1997 that extended the state's powers of confiscation to include funds believed to be derived from other illegal sources, including arms-smuggling. During 1997 the country's financial sector came under renewed scrutiny when the Belgian authorities conducted an investigation into alleged widespread tax evasion by Belgian citizens and companies based in Luxembourg. The German authorities also launched a similar investigation. Luxembourg was further criticized for refusing, as did Switzerland, to endorse the code of conduct with respect to tax havens drafted by the Organisation for Economic Co-operation and Development (OECD, see p. 347) in April 1998. During 1998 Luxembourg also opposed European Commission proposals for European taxation harmonization, which would oblige Luxembourg to impose tax on non-residents' interest and dividend income for the first time, thereby reducing the attraction of Luxembourg as a financial centre. In May 2000, however, Luxembourg for the first time endorsed OECD proposals aimed at limiting the use of bank secrecy laws for the purpose of tax evasion. In October the Chambre des Députés approved a relaxation of bank secrecy laws to facilitate co-operation with the US Internal Revenue Service in its attempts to halt tax evasion. Luxembourg was exempted for at least six years from a requirement for EU member states to exchange banking information from 2005 under new EU taxation rules concerning overseas investments agreed in early 2003 (see Economic Affairs).

In December 2000 the Government was prominent during negotiations regarding the Treaty of Nice, which aimed to reform the institutions of the EU in light of its forthcoming enlargements. The terms of the Treaty substantially safeguarded Luxembourg's privileged position in the EU: Luxembourg was to continue to have a European Commissioner, to maintain its six seats in the European Parliament and to continue to enjoy a voting weight in the Council of the European Union out of proportion to its size. In July 2001 the Chambre des Députés ratified the Treaty by a large majority. At the same time, Luxembourg continued, much to the frustration of most of its EU partners, to oppose the removal from Luxembourg-Ville of the Secretariat of the European Parliament, together with its 1,500 staff, whose continued presence was considered by the Luxembourg Government to be vital to the local economy.

At the general election held on 13 June 2004 the CSV increased its representation in the legislature from 19 to 24 seats. The LSAP secured 14 seats, while the DP took 10, five fewer than in 1999. Déi Gréng won seven seats and the ADR secured five. On 20 July Lydie Polfer of the DP tendered her resignation as

Deputy Prime Minister and Minister of Foreign Affairs and External Trade, and of the Civil Service and Administrative Reform. A new coalition Government comprising members of the CSV and the LSAP was sworn in on 31 July, again under the leadership of Juncker. The CSV assumed nine of the 15 ministerial posts, retaining the finance and justice portfolios and gaining the Ministry of the Interior and Spatial Planning, which was now headed by Jean-Marie Halsdorf. Jean Asselborn of the LSAP was appointed as Deputy Prime Minister and Minister of Foreign Affairs and Immigration.

A minor reorganization of the CSV government portfolios, which took effect in February 2006, was designed to enable the ministers concerned to focus on the areas of employment and the budget. Jean-Louis Schiltz, hitherto Minister of Co-operation and Humanitarian Action and Minister-delegate of Communications, assumed full ministerial responsibility for communications from Juncker and was also allocated the defence portfolio, becoming Minister of Co-operation and Humanitarian Action, of Communications and of Defence. The former Minister of Defence, Luc Frieden, retained his responsibilities as Minister of Justice and of the Treasury and Budget. Furthermore, François Biltgen, the Minister of Culture, Further Education and Research, of Labour and Employment and of Religious Affairs, ceded greater control over culture, further education and research to Octavie Modert, the Secretary of State in charge of that portfolio.

In April 2006 the ADR adopted a new name, Alternativ Demokratesch Reformpartei (Alternative Democratic Reform Party), in an attempt to broaden its appeal. However, the concurrent redesign of the party's logo to incorporate the colours of the national flag provoked criticism that it was adopting a more right-wing, nationalist stance. Several members of the ADR subsequently resigned from the party, including one of its five deputies, who remained in the legislature as an independent; the ADR consequently lost its status as an official parliamentary group.

Meanwhile, in January 2006 Luxembourg's largest private sector employer, the steel company Arcelor, was the subject of a hostile takeover bid by a major competitor, Netherlands-based Mittal Steel. Widespread concerns regarding potential job losses at steel plants in Luxembourg led the Government (which held a 5.6% stake in Arcelor) strongly to oppose the bid. However, some observers feared that the Government's opposition to the takeover would damage Luxembourg's reputation as an economy open to foreign investment. Following protracted negotiations, in June the two companies announced an agreement to merge to create a new company, Arcelor Mittal, which would retain Arcelor's headquarters in Luxembourg-Ville.

In late February 2008 Luxembourg became the third EU member state (along with Belgium and the Netherlands) to approve legislation decriminalizing euthanasia and assisted suicide, despite opposition from the governing CSV. The legislation was due to enter into effect by mid-2008.

Popular opposition in Luxembourg to a potential US-led military campaign in Iraq to remove the regime of Saddam Hussain culminated in nation-wide demonstrations on 15 February 2003. The Government's opposition to the military intervention (which was undertaken the following month without the support of a UN resolution), although muted, adversely affected relations with the USA. Following the swift removal of the Iraqi regime, however, the Luxembourg Government announced the allocation of €3.5m. for the financing of a humanitarian aid programme for Iraq. In March Parliament approved the secondment of 10 officers and men to the International Security Assistance Force in Afghanistan (ISAF), and, as part of the EU's first ever military operation, that of one officer to the Union's peace-keeping mission to the former Yugoslav republic of Macedonia. Four EU countries—Luxembourg, Belgium, France and Germany—all of which had opposed the US-led military campaign in Iraq, held a special summit in April to discuss defence matters, at which it was agreed to establish an autonomous European military command headquarters near Brussels, Belgium. The plan, which provoked protests from the USA and the United Kingdom, was superseded in December by a compromise agreement between France, Germany and the United Kingdom to create an EU 'planning cell' within existing defence structures.

On 1 January 2005 Juncker commenced a two-year appointment as Chairman of the Eurogroup (comprising the EU member states that belong to the euro zone). In this capacity Juncker would represent the members of the euro zone at global financial summits and would be instrumental in shaping European economic policy. Also in January Luxembourg assumed the rotating six-month presidency of the Council of the European Union. During the Luxembourg presidency the reform of the Stability and Growth Pact was successfully negotiated, the Lisbon Agenda, which aimed to create sustainable economic prosperity and full employment, was relaunched, and a new framework for relations with Russia was adopted. On 10 July Luxembourg held a national referendum (the first since 1936) on the EU constitutional treaty, which had finally been approved by the EU in mid-2004. Although there were concerns that the proposed constitution was not wholly advantageous for the smaller member states of the EU, the vast majority of political parties in Luxembourg supported the document and Juncker threatened to resign if the electorate rejected the treaty. Opposition to the treaty increased when the French and Dutch, at respective referendums in May and June, voted against its ratification. None the less, the draft treaty was approved by some 56.5% of the Luxembourg electorate. In late June 2007, at a summit meeting of EU heads of state and of government in Brussels, a preliminary agreement was reached over a reform treaty to replace the constitutional treaty rejected by French and Dutch voters in 2005. On 13 December 2007 the reform treaty was signed by EU leaders, including Juncker, following a summit meeting in Lisbon, Portugal. The so-called Treaty of Lisbon was expected to be ratified by parliamentary vote by the end of 2008.

Government

Luxembourg is an hereditary and constitutional monarchy. Legislative power is exercised by the unicameral Chamber of Deputies (Chambre des Députés), with 60 members elected by universal adult suffrage for five years (subject to dissolution) on the basis of proportional representation. Some legislative functions are also entrusted to the advisory State Council (Conseil d'Etat), with 21 members appointed for life by the Grand Duke, but decisions made by this body can be overruled by the legislature.

Executive power is vested in the Grand Duke, but is normally exercised by the Council of Ministers, led by the President of the Government (Prime Minister). The Grand Duke appoints ministers, but they are responsible to the legislature. Luxembourg is divided into three districts (Luxembourg, Diekirch, Grevenmacher), 12 cantons and 118 municipalities.

Defence

Luxembourg was a founder member of the North Atlantic Treaty Organization (NATO, see p. 340) in 1949. Compulsory military service was abolished in 1967, but Luxembourg maintains an army of volunteers, totalling 900, and a gendarmerie numbering 612 (in November 2006). Expenditure of some €263m. was allocated to defence in the budget for 2007. In March 1987 the country became a signatory of the Benelux military convention, together with Belgium and the Netherlands, which was intended to standardize training methods and military equipment in the three countries. In November 2004 the European Union (EU, see p. 244) ministers responsible for defence agreed to create 13 'battlegroups' (each numbering about 1,500 men), which could be deployed at short notice to crisis areas around the world. The EU battlegroups, two of which were to be ready for deployment at any one time, following a rotational schedule, reached full operational capacity from 1 January 2007. Luxembourg participated in a battlegroup with France, Germany and Belgium.

Economic Affairs

In 2006, according to estimates by the World Bank, Luxembourg's gross national income (GNI), measured at average 2004–06 prices, was US $35,133m., equivalent to $76,040 per head (or $59,560 per head on an international purchasing-power parity basis). During 1996–2006, it was estimated, the population increased at an average rate of 1.1% per year, while gross domestic product (GDP) per head grew, in real terms, by an average of 4.1% per year during the same period. Overall GDP increased, in real terms, at an average annual rate of 5.2% in 1996–2006; growth was 6.1% in 2006.

Agriculture (including forestry and fishing) contributed 0.4% of GDP in 2006. In 2005 1.3% of the employed labour force were engaged in the agricultural sector. The principal crops are cereals, potatoes and wine grapes. Livestock-rearing is also of some importance. Agricultural GDP decreased at an average annual rate of 4.0% in 1996–2006. Real agricultural GDP declined by 5.3% in 2006.

Industry (including mining, manufacturing, construction and power) provided 14.6% of GDP in 2006, and engaged 21.2% of the employed labour force in 2005. Industrial GDP increased, in real terms, at an average annual rate of 3.4% in 1996–2006, and rose by 3.7% in 2006.

Manufacturing activities constitute the most important industrial sector, contributing 7.9% of GDP in 2006 and engaging 10.6% of the employed work-force in 2005. Although the country's deposits of iron ore are no longer exploited, the iron and steel industry remains one of the most important sectors of the Luxembourg economy; metal manufactures accounted for an estimated 33.4% of total exports in 2007. The Luxembourg steel industry is dominated by Arcelor, which was formed in June 2001 by the merger of the Luxembourg-based Aciéries Réunies de Burbach-Eich-Dudelange SA—ARBED—and the steel companies Usinor, of France, and Aceralia, of Spain, to form the world's largest steel group. In January 2003 Arcelor announced that no further investment would be made in the two smelting furnaces in the Val du Fensch and that hot-phase production would gradually cease. The steelworks, which employed around 1,500 workers and contributed 85% of the Val du Fensch's annual revenue, would eventually close in 2010. In January 2006 Arcelor rejected a takeover bid by Mittal Steel, which had overtaken Arcelor as the world's largest steel group in the previous year following a number of acquisitions. However, in June the two companies agreed to merge to form Arcelor Mittal. Machinery and other equipment provided 18.7% of total exports in 2007. Other important branches of manufacturing are basic manufactures and chemicals and related products. Real manufacturing GDP increased by an average of 3.3% per year in 1996–2006; it grew by 3.3% in 2006.

In 2005 66.1% of net electricity production was thermal, while 20.9% was from hydroelectric installations. Imports of mineral fuels and lubricants comprised 12.8% of the value of total imports in 2007.

The services sector contributed 85.1% of GDP in 2006, and engaged 77.7% of the employed labour force in 2005. Favourable laws governing banking secrecy and taxation encouraged the development of Luxembourg as a major international financial centre. Financial services contributed 29.2% of GDP in 2006. In 2007 there were 156 banks in Luxembourg. In 2005 there were 12,600 holding companies registered in Luxembourg. In accordance with the demands of the European Commission, however, Luxembourg abolished its preferential tax regime for holding companies from 1 January 2007, although existing companies were permitted to retain their tax benefits until 2010. The replacement regime, the Family Private Assets Management Company, which was aimed at the wealth management sector, was introduced in 2007. Stock exchange activities (notably the 'Eurobond' market and investment portfolio management) are also prominent. From the mid-1990s Luxembourg has had the largest investment fund sector in Europe: in 2005 investment funds accounted for 8% of GDP. In 2006 there were 95 approved insurance companies in Luxembourg, as well as 262 reinsurance companies. The GDP of the services sector increased, in real terms, at an average annual rate of 5.7% in 1996–2006; it rose by 8.4% in 2006.

In 2006, according to IMF figures, Luxembourg recorded a visible trade deficit of US $4,427m., but there was a surplus of $4,370m. on the current account of the balance of payments. Other members of the European Union (EU, see p. 244) account for much of Luxembourg's foreign trade. In 2007 the principal source of imports (33.8%) was Belgium; other major providers were Germany (29.3%), France (11.6%) and the Netherlands (6.2%). The principal market for exports in that year was Germany (26.4%); other major purchasers were France (16.6%), Belgium (12.5%) and Italy (5.4%). The principal exports in 2007 were manufactured goods, particularly metal manufactures, and machinery. The principal imports were machinery, transport equipment, manufactured articles, notably metal manufactures, and mineral fuels and lubricants.

In 2006 a budgetary surplus of €233,500, equivalent to 0.7% of GDP, was recorded. Government debt was equivalent to 7.3% of GDP in 2006. The annual rate of inflation averaged 2.2% in 1996–2006; consumer prices rose by 2.7% in 2006 and by 2.3% in 2007. The rate of unemployment averaged 4.2% in 2006. In the same year cross-border commuters from neighbouring states totalled 143,858, constituting more than one-third of the total employed in Luxembourg.

Luxembourg was a founder member of the EU, and participated in the introduction of the European single currency, the euro, on 1 January 1999. It also belongs to the Benelux Economic Union (see p. 411).

Luxembourg's economy expanded at an average annual rate of more than 5% during 1985–2000, recording increases in GDP even in the early 1990s when neighbouring countries were in recession. The country's economic success was based on its development as an international financial centre, following the decline in the importance of the country's previously dominant iron and steel industry. Rapid economic expansion in Luxembourg attracted an increasing number of cross-border workers from neighbouring countries. These workers, who account for more than one-third of the work-force, pay social security contributions in Luxembourg, but retire to their native countries to spend their pensions, which are financed by Luxembourg. The solution advanced by the Government was to eschew further job creation in favour of the development of high-technology industries (with a substantial value added), which do not require a larger work-force. This plan was also expected to help to diversify the economy away from too great a dependence on the financial sector, the future profitability of which was likely to be eroded by the effects of EU integration, including the harmonization of taxation and regulatory structures. New EU taxation rules concerning overseas investments agreed in early 2003 required most EU countries to begin exchanging account details from 2005 in an attempt to eliminate tax fraud. However, they allowed Luxembourg (as well as Austria and Belgium) to retain banking secrecy for at least the next six years. In these countries a withholding tax was to be levied on non-residents' savings instead. The tax was to rise incrementally from 15% in 2005 to 35% in 2011. Crucially, Switzerland would have to apply the same rate of tax, thus avoiding 'capital flight' from Luxembourg. Moreover, Luxembourg secured an agreement that it would not be forced to exchange banking information in the future without parallel action from Switzerland (which was extremely unlikely). Luxembourg also hoped to diversify into the potentially lucrative cross-border pensions fund market, and installed a flexible regulatory regime in order to take full advantage of an EU directive (incorporated into Luxembourg's national legislation in July 2005, ahead of a September deadline) allowing pension-fund providers to offer services and products to customers across the EU. The rapid economic expansion of the late 1990s declined significantly in 2000–03, when GDP growth averaged only 2.9% per year. A recovery followed, with GDP growth rising to 4.9% in 2004, 5.0% in 2005 and 6.1% in 2006. This strong growth was largely attributed to innovation within the banking and insurance sectors, and to the expansion of international financial markets, which stimulated Luxembourg's financial intermediation and business services. However, the growth rate in the financial sector was expected to slow as the sector matured. GDP growth of 4%–5% was forecast for 2007–08. Meanwhile, a deteriorating fiscal position prompted the IMF and the Organisation for Economic Co-operation and Development (OECD) to recommend that the Government restrain expenditure, particularly on public sector salaries and social benefits. The increasing unemployment rate and high level of cross-border workers were also a cause for concern.

Education

Education in Luxembourg is compulsory from the age of four to 15 years. Primary education begins at six years of age and lasts for six years. German is the initial language of instruction at primary level. French is added to the programme in the second year, and replaces German as the language of instruction at higher secondary level. In 2005 enrolment in primary education included 97% of children in the relevant age-group (males 96%; females 97%).

At the age of 12, pupils can choose between secondary school (lycée) and technical education (lycée technique). The first year of secondary school is a general orientation course on comprehensive lines, which is then followed by a choice between two sections: the Classical Section, with an emphasis on Latin, and the Modern Section, which stresses English and other modern languages. The completed secondary course lasts seven years, and leads to the Certificat de Fin d'Etudes Secondaires, which qualifies for university entrance. The technical education course (six to eight years) leads either to a vocational diploma, a technician's diploma (diplôme de technicien) or a technical baccalaureate diploma (bac technique) and is devised in three parts: an orientation and observation course, an intermediate course and an upper course. In 2005 enrolment in secondary education included 83% of children in the relevant age-group (males 81%; females 86%).

LUXEMBOURG

The Centre Universitaire was established in 1969, offering one-year or two-year courses in the humanities, sciences and law and economics, as well as training courses for lawyers and teachers, following which the students generally attended other European universities. The Institut Supérieur de Technologies (IST) is an institute for higher education at university level in civil engineering, electrical engineering, applied computer sciences and mechanical engineering. In August 2003 the Government founded the University of Luxembourg, operating from three campuses, Kirchberg, Limpertsberg and Walferdange, and offering a full range of degrees and post-graduate qualifications taught in French, German and English. In December 2005 the Government announced that a single site was to be developed at Belval-Ouest, near Esch-sur-Alzette, to accommodate all university faculties and services.

Consolidated government expenditure on education in 2006 was €1,556.6m. (equivalent to 11.8% of total expenditure).

Public Holidays

2008: 1 January (New Year's Day), 4 February (Carnival), 24 March (Easter Monday), 1 May (Labour Day and Ascension Day), 12 May (Whit Monday), 23 August (National Day), 15 August (Assumption), 1 September (Luxembourg City Fête, Luxembourg City only), 1 November (All Saints' Day), 25 December (Christmas), 26 December (St Stephen's Day).

2009: 1 January (New Year's Day), 23 February (Carnival), 13 April (Easter Monday), 1 May (Labour Day), 21 May (Ascension Day), 1 June (Whit Monday), 23 August (National Day), 15 August (Assumption), 1 September (Luxembourg City Fête, Luxembourg City only), 1 November (All Saints' Day), 25 December (Christmas), 26 December (St Stephen's Day).

Weights and Measures

The metric system is in force.

Statistical Survey

Source (unless otherwise stated): Service Central de la Statistique et des Etudes Economiques (STATEC), Centre Administratif Pierre Werner, 13 rue Erasme, 1468 Luxembourg; tel. 478-42-52; fax 46-42-89; e-mail statec.post@statec.etat.lu; internet www.statec.lu.

AREA AND POPULATION

Area: 2,586 sq km (999 sq miles).

Population: 384,634 at census of 1 March 1991; 439,539 (males 216,540, females 222,999) at census of 15 February 2001; 476,200 (males 235,800, females 240,400) official estimate at 1 January 2007.

Density (January 2007): 184.1 per sq km.

Principal Towns ('000, 2007): Luxembourg-Ville (capital) 83.8; Esch-sur-Alzette 29.1; Differdange 20.1; Dudelange 18.0; Pétange 15.0; Sanem 14.1; Hesperange 12.1.

Births, Marriages and Deaths (2006): Live births 5,514 (birth rate 12.0 per 1,000); Marriages 1,948 (marriage rate 4.2 per 1,000); Deaths 3,766 (death rate 8.2 per 1,000).

Expectation of Life (years at birth, WHO estimates): 79.1 (males 75.8; females 82.1) in 2005. Source: WHO, *World Health Report*.

Immigration and Emigration (2005): Arrivals 13,512; Departures 10,841.

Employment ('000 persons, incl. armed forces, 2005): Agriculture, hunting, forestry and fishing 3.9; Mining and quarrying 0.3; Manufacturing 32.6; Electricity, gas and water supply 1.8; Construction 30.3; Wholesale and retail trade, repair of motor vehicles, motorcycles and personal and household goods 42.8; Hotels and restaurants 14.2; Transport, storage and communications 22.9; Financial intermediation 34.1; Real estate, renting and business activities 52.0; Public administration and defence and compulsory social security 16.7; Education 14.4; Health and social work 22.8; Other community, social and personal service activities 10.6; Private households with employed persons 8.2; *Total employed* 307.3.

HEALTH AND WELFARE

Key Indicators

Total Fertility Rate (children per woman, 2005): 1.7.

Under-5 Mortality Rate (per 1,000 live births, 2005): 5.

HIV/AIDS (% of persons aged 15–49, 2005): 0.2.

Physicians (per 1,000 head, 2003): 2.66.

Hospital Beds (per 1,000 head, 2004): 6.3.

Health Expenditure (2004): US $ per head (PPP): 5,177.6.

Health Expenditure (2004): % of GDP: 8.0.

Health Expenditure (2004): public (% of total): 90.4.

Human Development Index (2005): ranking: 18.

Human Development Index (2005): value: 0.944.

For sources and definitions, see explanatory note on p. vi.

AGRICULTURE, ETC.

Principal Crops ('000 metric tons unless otherwise indicated, 2006, FAO estimates): Wheat 75.6; Rye 6.2; Barley 50.1; Oats 6.7; Triticale (wheat-rye hybrid) 19.7; Potatoes 16.4; Rapeseed 16.3; Mushrooms 5.0 (metric tons); Apples 3.8; Grapes 16.9.

Livestock ('000 head, year ending September 2006): Cattle 183.6; Horses 4.3; Pigs 84.2; Sheep 9.6; Poultry 81.3.

Livestock Products (metric tons, 2006, FAO estimates): Cattle meat 16,833; Pig meat 12,757; Chicken meat 122; Milk 267,073.

Forestry ('000 cubic metres, 2006, FAO estimates): *Roundwood Removals:* 268 (Sawlogs, veneer logs and logs for sleepers 154, Fuel wood 13, Pulpwood 93, Other 9); *Sawnwood Production* (incl. railway sleepers) 133 (Coniferous 113, Broadleaved 20).

Source: FAO.

INDUSTRY

Selected Products ('000 metric tons, 2006, unless otherwise indicated): Crude steel 2,802; Rolled steel products 3,648; Wine ('000 hl) 123.7 (2006/07); Beer ('000 hl) 373.7 (2005); Electric energy (million kWh) 4,334.

FINANCE

Currency and Exchange Rates: 100 cent = 1 euro (€). Sterling and Dollar Equivalents (31 December 2007): £1 sterling = 1.3609 euros; US $1 = 0.6793 euros; €10 = £7.35 = $13.72. *Average Exchange Rate* (euros per US dollar): 0.8041 in 2005; 0.7971 in 2006; 0.7306 in 2007. Note: The national currency was formerly the Luxembourg franc. From the introduction of the euro, with Luxembourg's participation, on 1 January 1999, a fixed exchange rate of €1 = 40.3399 Luxembourg francs was in operation. Euro notes and coins were introduced on 1 January 2002. The euro and local currency circulated alongside each other until 28 February, after which the euro became the sole legal tender.

Consolidated Budget (€ million, 2006): *Revenue:* Total 13,434.6. *Expenditure:* General services 1,380.4; Defence 78.0; Public order and security 330.0; Economic affairs and services 1,560.2; Environmental protection 354.0; Housing and community regeneration 233.2; Health 1,589.9; Leisure, recreation and culture 588.7; Education 1,556.6; Social protection 5,529.9; Total 13,201.1.

International Reserves (US $ million at 31 December 2006): Gold 47.04; IMF special drawing rights 18.40; Reserve position in IMF 43.65; Foreign exchange 156.03; Total 265.12. Source: IMF, *International Financial Statistics*.

Money Supply (€ million at 31 December 2006): Currency issued 1,412*; Demand deposits at banking institutions 75,771. Source: IMF, *International Financial Statistics*.

* Currency put into circulation by the Banque Centrale du Luxembourg was €41,224m.

Cost of Living (Consumer Price Index; base: 2000 = 100): All items 109.3 in 2004; 112.0 in 2005; 115.0 in 2006. Source: IMF, *International Financial Statistics*.

Gross Domestic Product (€ million at constant 2000 prices): 25,141.5 in 2004; 26,404.2 in 2005; 28,019.7 in 2006.

National Income and Product (€ million at current prices, 2006): Compensation of employees 15,290.4; Operating surplus and mixed income (incl. consumption of fixed capital) 14,877.8; *Gross domestic product (GDP) at factor cost* 30,168.2; Taxes, *less* subsidies on production and imports 3,684.2; *GDP in market prices* 33,852.4; Primary incomes received from abroad 94,448.0; *Less* Primary incomes paid abroad 100,596.9; *Gross national income* 27,703.4; *Less* Consumption of fixed capital 3,597.5; *Net national income* 24,106.0.

Expenditure on the Gross Domestic Product (€ million at current prices, 2006): Final consumption expenditure 17,369.3 (Households 11,603.8, Non-profit institutions serving households 573.2, General government 5,192.4); Gross capital formation 6,443.9 (Gross fixed capital formation 6,220.9, Changes in inventories 162.1, Acquisitions, less disposals, of valuables 61.0); *Total domestic expenditure* 23,813.2; Exports of goods and services 56,225.6; *Less* Imports of goods and services 46,186.4; *GDP in market prices* 33,852.4.

Gross Domestic Product by Economic Activity (€ million at current prices, 2006): Agriculture, hunting, forestry and fishing 109.7; Mining and quarrying 29.4; Manufacturing 2,419.1; Electricity, gas and water supply 398.5; Construction 1,615.6; Wholesale and retail trade, repair of motor vehicles, motorcycles and personal and household goods 2,835.6; Hotels and restaurants 543.8; Transport and communications 3,035.8; Financial services 8,951.4; Real estate, renting and business activities 5,884.0; Other community, social and personal service activities 4,787.7; *Gross value added in basic prices* 30,610.8; Taxes, less subsidies, on products 3,241.6; *GDP in market prices* 33,852.4.

Balance of Payments (US $ million, 2006): Exports of goods f.o.b. 16,371; Imports of goods f.o.b. −20,798; *Trade balance* −4,427; Exports of services 51,007; Imports of services −30,207; *Balance on goods and services* 16,373; Other income received 99,947; Other income paid −110,322; *Balance on goods, services and income* 5,998; Current transfers received 5,295; Current transfers paid −6,922; *Current balance* 4,370; Capital account (net) −243; Direct investment abroad −109,614; Direct investment from abroad 126,459; Portfolio investment assets −177,656; Portfolio investment liabilities 248,961; Financial derivatives liabilities 10,366; Other investment assets −265,130; Other investment liabilities 163,232; Net errors and omissions −774; *Overall balance* −28. Source: IMF, *International Financial Statistics*.

EXTERNAL TRADE

Principal Commodities (€ million, 2007): *Imports:* Food and live animals 1,117.7; Beverages and tobacco 423.7; Crude materials (inedible) except fuels 1,292.8; Mineral fuels, lubricants, etc. 2,075.4; Chemicals and related products 1,566.3; Metal manufactures 1,785.5; Other basic manufactures 1,252.9; Machinery and other equipment 2,577.9; Transport equipment 2,569.1; Miscellaneous manufactured articles 1,572.4; Total (incl. others) 16,233.8. *Exports:* Food and live animals 535.2; Chemicals and related products 785.8; Metal manufactures 3,928.5; Other basic manufactures 1,832.6; Machinery and other equipment 2,202.2; Transport equipment 862.8; Miscellaneous manufactured articles 1,107.8; Total (incl. others) 11,766.5.

Principal Trading Partners (€ million, 2007): *Imports:* Belgium 5,487.2; France 1,878.3; Germany 4,757.1; Italy 375.5; Netherlands 1,000.9; Switzerland 168.3; United Kingdom 283.6; USA 632.2; Total (incl. others) 16,233.8. *Exports:* Austria 255.8; Belgium 1,473.4; France 1,957.3; Germany 3,104.0; Italy 636.1; Netherlands 641.8; Spain 431.5; Sweden 169.3; Switzerland 142.2; United Kingdom 549.3; USA 298.6; Total (incl. others) 11,766.5.

TRANSPORT

Railways (traffic, million, 2006): Passenger-kilometres 298; Freight ton-kilometres 466.

Road Traffic (motor vehicles in use at 1 January 2007): Cars 314,718; Motorcycles 14,609; Buses and coaches 1,380; Goods vehicles 25,755; Tractors 29,169; Total 385,631.

Shipping: River Traffic (Port of Mertert, '000 metric tons, 2006): Goods loaded 232, Goods unloaded 1,057. *Merchant Fleet* (vessels registered at 31 December 2006): Number of vessels 62; Total displacement 779,871 grt (Source: Lloyd's Register-Fairplay, *World Fleet Statistics*).

Civil Aviation (traffic on scheduled services, 2006): Passengers carried 1,613,475; Freight (metric tons) 752,635.

TOURISM

Tourist Arrivals (at accommodation establishments): 912,798 in 2005; 908,171 in 2006; 917,334 in 2007.

Arrivals by Country (2007): Belgium 190,819; France 107,157; Germany 134,655; Italy 23,490; Netherlands 202,639; Spain 16,245; United Kingdom 61,894; USA 22,522; Total (incl. others) 917,334.

Tourism Receipts (US $ million): 2,577 in 2002; 3,134 in 2003; 3,889 in 2004.

COMMUNICATIONS MEDIA

Facsimile Machines: 20,000 in use (1998).

Mobile Cellular Telephones: 713,800 in 2006.

Telephones: 246,700 main lines in use in 2006.

Personal Computers ('000 in use): 290 in 2005.

Internet Users ('000): 339 in 2006.

Broadband Subscribers ('000): 93.2 in 2006.

Daily Newspapers: 6 (2005).

Book Production: 513 titles (1997).

Radio Receivers: 285,000 in use (1997).

Television Receivers: 260,000 in use (2000).

Sources: partly UNESCO, *Statistical Yearbook*; International Telecommunication Union.

EDUCATION

(2005/06, unless otherwise indicated)

Nursery: 1,233 teachers; 10,411 pupils.

Primary: 3,191 teachers; 33,138 pupils.

Secondary and Technical Secondary: 3,667 teachers (state sector only); 11,114 pupils (secondary), 22,759 pupils (technical secondary).

University-level: 9,227 students, incl. 6,063 studying abroad.

Schools (2004/05): 375 offering a combination of nursery and primary education; 32 secondary (5 private).

Directory

The Constitution

The Constitution now in force dates back to 17 October 1868, but in 1919 a constituent assembly introduced some important changes, declaring that the sovereign power resided in the nation, that all secret treaties were denounced and that deputies were to be elected by a list system by means of proportional representation, on the basis of universal adult suffrage. Electors must be citizens of Luxembourg and must have attained 18 years of age. Candidates for election must have attained 18 years of age (reduced from 21 years of age by the electoral law of 18 February 2003). The Grand Duke, who is Sovereign, chooses government ministers, may intervene in legislative questions and has certain judicial powers. There is a single-chamber legislature, the Chamber of Deputies (Chambre des Députés), with 60 members elected for five years. There are four electoral districts: the North, the Centre, the South and the East. By the law of 9 October 1956 the Constitution was further revised to the effect that: 'The exercise of prerogatives granted by the Constitution to the legislative, executive and judiciary powers, can, by treaty, be temporarily vested in institutions of international law.'

The Constitution was further amended on 12 December 1994, 12 July 1996 (introducing a Constitutional Court) and 12 January 1998. In addition to the Council of Ministers, which consists of the President of the Government (Prime Minister) and at least three other ministers, the State Council (Conseil d'Etat—which is the supreme administrative tribunal and which also fulfils certain legislative functions) comprises 21 members nominated by the Sovereign who serve for 15 years (not necessarily continuous) or until the age of 72.

The Government

HEAD OF STATE

Grand Duke: HRH Henri Albert Félix Marie Guillaume (succeeded to the throne 7 October 2000).

Marshal of the Court: Jean-Jacques Kasel.

LUXEMBOURG

COUNCIL OF MINISTERS
(April 2008)

A coalition of the Chrëschtlech Sozial Volkspartei (CSV) and the Lëtzebuerger Sozialistesch Arbechterpartei (LSAP).

Prime Minister and Minister of State and of Finance: JEAN-CLAUDE JUNCKER (CSV).

Deputy Prime Minister and Minister of Foreign Affairs and Immigration: JEAN ASSELBORN (LSAP).

Minister of Agriculture, Viticulture and Rural Development and of Small Business, Tourism and Housing: FERNAND BODEN (CSV).

Minister of Family Affairs and Integration and of Equal Opportunities: MARIE-JOSÉE JACOBS (CSV).

Minister of National Education and Vocational Training: MADY DELVAUX-STEHRES (LSAP).

Minister of Justice and of the Treasury and Budget: LUC FRIEDEN (CSV).

Minister of Labour and Employment, of Culture, Higher Education and Research and of Religious Affairs: FRANÇOIS BILTGEN (CSV).

Minister of the Economy and External Trade and of Sport: JEANNOT KRECKÉ (LSAP).

Minister of Health and of Social Security: MARS DI BARTOLOMEO (LSAP).

Minister of the Environment and of Transport: LUCIEN LUX (LSAP).

Minister of the Interior and Land Management: JEAN-MARIE HALSDORF (CSV).

Minister of the Civil Service and Administrative Reform and of Public Works: CLAUDE WISELER (CSV).

Minister of Co-operation and Humanitarian Action, of Communications and of Defence: JEAN-LOUIS SCHILTZ (CSV).

Minister-delegate of Foreign Affairs and Immigration: NICOLAS SCHMIT (LSAP).

Secretary of State for Parliamentary Relations, for Agriculture, Viticulture and Rural Development and for Culture, Higher Education and Research: OCTAVIE MODERT (CSV).

MINISTRIES

Office of the Prime Minister: Hôtel de Bourgogne, 4 rue de la Congrégation, 1352 Luxembourg; tel. 478-21-00; fax 46-17-20.

Ministry of Agriculture, Viticulture and Rural Development: 1 rue de la Congrégation, 1352 Luxembourg; tel. 478-24-78; fax 46-40-27; e-mail info@ma.public.lu; internet www.ma.public.lu.

Ministry of the Civil Service and Administrative Reform: 63 ave de la Liberté, BP 1807, 1931 Luxembourg; tel. 478-31-00; fax 26-48-36-21; e-mail info@mfpra.public.lu; internet www.mfpra.public.lu.

Ministry of Culture, Higher Education and Research: 20 montée de la Pétrusse, 2273 Luxembourg; tel. 478-1; fax 29-21-86; e-mail info@mcesr.public.lu; internet www.mcesr.public.lu.

Ministry of the Economy and External Trade: 19–21 blvd Royal, 2449 Luxembourg; tel. 478-1; fax 46-04-48; e-mail info@eco.public.lu; internet www.eco.public.lu.

Ministry of the Environment: 18 montée de la Pétrusse, 2327 Luxembourg; tel. 478-68-24; fax 40-04-10; e-mail info@environnement.public.lu; internet www.environnement.public.lu.

Ministry of Equal Opportunities: 12–14 ave Emile Reuter, 2921 Luxembourg; tel. 478-58-14; fax 24-18-86; e-mail info@mega.public.lu; internet www.mega.public.lu.

Ministry of Family Affairs and Integration: 12–14 ave Emile Reuter, 2919 Luxembourg; tel. 478-65-00; fax 478-65-71; internet www.fm.etat.lu.

Ministry of Finance: 3 rue de la Congrégation, 1352 Luxembourg; tel. 478-1; fax 47-52-41; internet www.mf.public.lu.

Ministry of Foreign Affairs and Immigration: Hôtel St Maximin, 5 rue Notre-Dame, 2240 Luxembourg; tel. 478-1; fax 22-31-44; e-mail officielle.boite@mae.etat.lu; internet www.mae.lu.

Ministry of Health: Villa Louvigny, allée Marconi, 2120 Luxembourg; tel. 478-24-78; fax 46-79-62; e-mail ministere-sante@ms.etat.lu; internet www.ms.etat.lu.

Ministry of the Interior and Land Management: 19 rue Beaumont, 1219 Luxembourg; tel. 478-46-00; fax 22-11-25; e-mail info@miat.public.lu; internet www.miat.public.lu.

Ministry of Justice: Centre Administratif Pierre Werner, 13 rue Erasme, 2934 Luxembourg; tel. 478-1; fax 26-68-48-61; e-mail info@mj.public.lu; internet www.mj.public.lu.

Ministry of Labour and Employment: 26 rue Zithe, 2763 Luxembourg; tel. 478-61-18; fax 48-63-25; e-mail joseph.faber@mt.etat.lu; internet www.mt.etat.lu.

Ministry of National Education and Vocational Training: 29 rue Aldringen, 2926 Luxembourg; tel. 478-51-00; fax 478-51-13; e-mail info@men.public.lu; internet www.men.public.lu.

Ministry of Public Works: 4 blvd F. D. Roosevelt, 2450 Luxembourg; tel. 478-33-00; fax 46-27-09; e-mail contact@tp.etat.lu; internet www.mtp.etat.lu.

Ministry of Religious Affairs: 4 rue de la Congrégation, 2910 Luxembourg; tel. 478-21-00; fax 46-17-20.

Ministry of Small Business, Tourism and Housing: 6 ave Emile Reuter, 2937 Luxembourg; tel. 478-47-15; fax 478-47-40; internet www.mcm.public.lu (small business), www.mdt.public.lu (tourism), www.logement.lu (housing).

Ministry of Social Security: 26 rue Sainte Zithe, 2936 Luxembourg; tel. 478-63-11; fax 478-63-28; e-mail info@mss.public.lu; internet www.mss.public.lu.

Ministry of State: 4 rue de la Congrégation, 1352 Luxembourg; tel. 478-21-00; fax 46-17-20; e-mail ministere.etat@me.etat.lu; internet www.etat.lu.

Ministry of Transport: 19–21 blvd Royal, 2449 Luxembourg; tel. 478-44-00; fax 22-85-68; e-mail info@mt.public.lu; internet www.mt.public.lu.

Legislature

CHAMBER OF DEPUTIES

Chambre des Députés: Hôtel de la Chambre des Députés, 19 rue du Marché-aux-Herbes, 1728 Luxembourg; tel. 966-1; fax 22-02-30; e-mail info@chd.lu; internet www.chd.lu.
President: LUCIEN WEILER (Chrëschtlech Sozial Volkspartei).

General Election, 13 June 2004

Party	% of votes	Seats
Chrëschtlech Sozial Volkspartei	36.11	24
Lëtzebuerger Sozialistesch Arbechterpartei	23.37	14
Demokratesch Partei	16.09	10
Déi Gréng	11.58	7
Aktiounskomitee fir Demokratie a Rentegerechtegkeet*	9.95	5
Déi Lénk	1.90	—
Kommunistesch Partei Lëtzebuerg	0.92	—
Frai Partei Lëtzebuerg	0.12	—
Total	100.00	60

*Changed its name to Alternativ Demokratesch Reformpartei in April 2006, prompting one of its deputies to leave the party to sit as an independent.

Advisory Councils

Conseil Economique et Social: Centre Administratif Pierre Werner, 13 rue Erasme, BP 1306, 1468 Luxembourg; tel. 43-58-51; fax 42-27-29; e-mail ces@ces.etat.lu; internet www.ces.etat.lu; f. 1966; consultative body on economics and social affairs; 39 mems; Pres. ROMAIN SCHMIT; Sec.-Gen. MARIANNE NATI-STOFFEL.

Conseil d'Etat: 5 rue Sigefroi, 2536 Luxembourg; tel. 47-30-71; fax 46-43-22; e-mail info@conseil-etat.public.lu; internet www.conseil-etat.public.lu; 21 mems nominated by the Sovereign; Pres. ALAIN MAYER; Sec.-Gen. MARC BESCH.

Political Organizations

Alternativ Demokratesch Reformpartei (ADR) (Alternative Democratic Reform Party): 9 rue de la Loge, 1945 Luxembourg; tel. 46-37-42; fax 46-37-45; e-mail adr@chd.lu; internet www.adr.lu; f. 1987 as Aktiounskomitee 5/6 Pensioun fir jiddfereen (Action Committee 5/6 Pensions for Everyone); name changed to Aktiounskomitee fir Demokratie a Rentegerechtegkeet (Action Committee for Democracy and Pensions Justice) in 1994; present name adopted 2006; conservative; established to campaign for improved pension rights for private sector employees, but subsequently sought to broaden its concerns; Pres. ROBERT (ROBY) MEHLEN.

Chrëschtlech Sozial Volkspartei (CSV) (Christian Social Party): 4 rue de l'Eau, BP 826, 2018 Luxembourg; tel. 22-57-31-1; fax 47-27-16; e-mail csv@csv.lu; internet www.csv.lu; f. 1914;

LUXEMBOURG

Directory

advocates political stability, sustained economic expansion, ecological and social progress; 9,500 mems; Pres. FRANÇOIS BILTGEN; Sec.-Gen. MARCO SCHANK.

Déi Gréng (The Greens): 1 rue de Fort Elisabeth, 1463 Luxembourg; tel. 27-48-27-1; fax 27-48-27-22; e-mail greng@greng.lu; internet www.greng.lu; f. 1983; fmrly Déi Gréng Alternativ (Green Alternative Party); merged with the Gréng Lëscht Ekologesch Initiativ (Green List Ecological Initiative) in 1995; advocates 'grass-roots' democracy, environmental protection, social concern and increased aid to developing countries; Spokespersons TILLY METZ, CARLO DI TOFFOLI.

Déi Lénk (The Left): BP 817, 2018 Luxembourg; tel. 26-20-20-72; fax 26-20-20-73; e-mail sekretariat@dei-lenk.lu; internet www.dei-lenk.lu; f. 1999; individual membership; no formal leadership.

Demokratesch Partei (DP) (Democratic Party): 9 rue du St Esprit, BP 510, 2015 Luxembourg; tel. 22-10-21; fax 22-10-13; e-mail secretariat@dp.lu; internet www.dp.lu; liberal; Leader CLAUDE MEISCH; Gen. Sec. GEORGES GUDENBURG.

Kommunistesch Partei Lëtzebuerg (KPL) (Communist Party of Luxembourg): 2 rue Astrid, 1143 Luxembourg; tel. 44-60-66-21; fax 44-60-66-66; e-mail kpl@zlv.lu; internet www.kp-l.org; f. 1921; Pres. ALI RUCKERT.

Lëtzebuerger Sozialistesch Arbechterpartei (LSAP d'Sozialisten) (Socialist Workers' Party of Luxembourg): 68 rue de Gasperich, 1617 Luxembourg; tel. 45-65-73-1; fax 45-65-75; e-mail info@lsap.lu; internet www.lsap.lu; f. 1902; social democrat; 6,000 mems; Pres. ALEX BODRY; Secs ROMAIN SCHNEIDER, CHANTAL BOLY.

Diplomatic Representation

EMBASSIES IN LUXEMBOURG

Austria: 3 rue des Bains, 1212 Luxembourg; tel. 47-11-88; fax 46-39-74; e-mail luxemburg-ob@bmeia.gv.at; internet www.bmeia.gv.at/luxemburg; Ambassador Dr CHRISTINE STIX-HACKL.

Belgium: 4 rue des Girondins, 1626 Luxembourg; tel. 44-27-46-1; fax 45-42-82; e-mail luxembourg@diplobel.org; internet www.diplomatie.be/luxemburg; Ambassador ALAIN KUNDYCKI.

Cape Verde: 46 rue Goethe, 1637 Luxembourg; tel. 26-48-09-48; fax 26-48-09-49; e-mail ambcvlux@pt.lu; Chargé d'affaires FERNANDA TAVARES FERNANDES.

China, People's Republic: 2 rue Van der Meulen, Dommeldange, 2152 Luxembourg; tel. 43-69-91-1; fax 42-24-23; e-mail ambchine@pt.lu; internet lu.china-embassy.org; Ambassador MA ZHIXUE.

Czech Republic: 2 rond-point Robert Schuman, 2525 Luxembourg; tel. 26-47-78-11; fax 26-47-78-20; e-mail luxembourg@embassy.mzv.cz; internet www.mzv.cz/luxembourg; Ambassador KATEŘINA LUKEŠOVÁ.

Denmark: 4 rue des Girondins, 1626 Luxembourg; tel. 22-21-22-1; fax 22-21-24; e-mail luxamb@um.dk; internet www.ambluxembourg.um.dk; Ambassador OLE LISBORG.

Finland: 2 rue Heine, 1720 Luxembourg; tel. 49-55-51; fax 49-46-40; e-mail sanomat.lux@formin.fi; internet www.finlande.lu; Ambassador TARJA LAITIAINEN.

France: 8B blvd Joseph II, BP 359, 2013 Luxembourg; tel. 45-72-71; fax 45-72-71-227; e-mail ambassade@ambafrance-lu.org; internet www.ambafrance-lu.org; Ambassador CHARLES DE BANCALIS.

Germany: 20–22 ave Emile Reuter, BP 95, 2010 Luxembourg; tel. 45-34-45-1; fax 45-56-04; internet www.luxembourg.diplo.de; Ambassador Dr HUBERTUS VON MORR.

Greece: 27 rue Marie-Adélaïde, 2128 Luxembourg; tel. 44-51-93; fax 45-01-64; e-mail ambgrec@pt.lu; Ambassador DIONYSIOS KODELAS.

Hungary: 36 rue Marie-Adélaïde, 2128 Luxembourg; tel. 45-91-77; fax 45-82-89; e-mail ambhongr@pt.lu; internet www.mfa.gov.hu/kulkepviselet/lu; Ambassador TIBOR KECSKÉS.

Ireland: 28 route d'Arlon, 1140 Luxembourg; tel. 45-06-10-1; fax 45-88-20; e-mail luxembourg@dfa.ie; Ambassador MARTIN BURKE.

Italy: 5–7 rue Marie-Adélaïde, 2128 Luxembourg; tel. 44-36-44-1; fax 45-55-23; e-mail ambasciata.lussemburgo@esteri.it; internet www.amblussemburgo.esteri.it; Ambassador ROBERTO BETTARINI.

Japan: 62 ave de la Faïencerie, BP 92, 2010 Luxembourg; tel. 46-41-51-1; fax 46-41-76; e-mail embjapan@pt.lu; internet www.lu.emb-japan.go.jp; Ambassador KAZUHITO TATEBE.

Netherlands: 6 rue Ste Zithe, 2763 Luxembourg; tel. 22-75-70; fax 40-30-16; e-mail lux@minbuza.nl; internet www.paysbas.lu; Ambassador GERTJAN STORM.

Poland: 2 rue de Pulvermühl, 2356 Luxembourg; tel. 26-00-32; fax 26-68-75-54; e-mail ambapol@pt.lu; internet www.luksemburg.polemb.net; Ambassador BARBARA LABUDA.

Portugal: 24 rue Guillaume Schneider, 2522 Luxembourg; tel. 46-61-90-1; fax 46-51-69; e-mail embport@pt.lu; Ambassador RUI ALFREDO DE VASCONCELOS FÉLIX ALVES.

Romania: 41 blvd de la Pétrusse, 2320 Luxembourg; tel. 45-51-59; fax 45-51-63; e-mail ambroum@pt.lu; internet luxemburg.mae.ro; Ambassador VLAD TUDOR ALEXANDRESCU.

Russia: Château de Beggen, 1719 Luxembourg; tel. 42-23-33; fax 42-23-34; e-mail ambruslu@pt.lu; internet www.ruslux.mid.ru; Ambassador EDUARD R. MALAYAN.

Spain: 4–6 blvd Emmanuel Servais, BP 290, 2012 Luxembourg; tel. 46-02-55; fax 46-12-88; e-mail emb.luxemburgo@mae.es; internet www.mae.es/embajadas/luxemburgo; Ambassador MARÍA ASUNCIÓN ANSORENA CONTO.

Sweden: 2 rue Heinrich Heine, 1720 Luxembourg; tel. 26-64-61; fax 29-69-09; e-mail ambassaden.luxemburg@foreign.ministry.se; internet www.swedenabroad.com/luxembourg; Ambassador AGNETA SÖDERMAN.

Switzerland: Immeuble Forum Royal, 25A blvd Royal, 3e étage, 2449 Luxembourg; tel. 22-74-74-1; fax 22-74-74-20; e-mail lux.vertretung@eda.admin.ch; internet www.eda.admin.ch/luxembourg; Ambassador PHILIPPE GUEX.

Turkey: 49 rue Siggy vu Lëtzebuerg, 1933 Luxembourg; tel. 44-32-81; fax 44-32-81-34; e-mail ambtrlux@pt.lu; Chargé d'affaires a.i. IHSAN SAKARYA.

United Kingdom: 5 blvd Joseph II, 1840 Luxembourg; tel. 22-98-64; fax 22-98-67; e-mail britemb@internet.lu; internet www.britain.lu; Ambassador PETER BATEMAN.

USA: 22 blvd Emmanuel Servais, 2535 Luxembourg; tel. 46-01-23; fax 46-14-01; internet luxembourg.usembassy.gov; Ambassador ANN LOUISE WAGNER.

Judicial System

The lowest courts in Luxembourg are those of the Justices of the Peace, of which there are three, at Luxembourg-Ville, Esch-sur-Alzette and Diekirch. These are competent to deal with civil, commercial and criminal cases of minor importance. Above these are the two District Courts, Luxembourg being divided into the judicial districts of Luxembourg and Diekirch. These are competent to deal with civil, commercial and criminal cases. The Superior Court of Justice includes both a court of appeal, hearing decisions made by District Courts, and the Cour de Cassation. As the judicial system of the Grand Duchy does not employ the jury system, a defendant is acquitted if a minority of the presiding judges find him or her guilty. The highest administrative court is the Comité du Contentieux du Conseil d'Etat. Special tribunals exist to adjudicate upon various matters of social administration such as social insurance. The department of the Procureur Général (Attorney-General) is responsible for the administration of the judiciary and the supervision of judicial police investigations. In July 1996 an amendment to the Constitution introduced a Constitutional Court.

Judges are appointed for life by the Grand Duke, and are not removable except by judicial sentence.

President of the Superior Court of Justice: MARC SCHLUNGS.

Attorney-General: ROBERT BIEVER.

Religion

CHRISTIANITY

The Roman Catholic Church

For ecclesiastical purposes, Luxembourg comprises a single archdiocese, directly responsible to the Holy See. At 31 December 2005 adherents numbered 393,800 (around 86.5% of the total population).

Archbishop of Luxembourg: Most Rev. FERNAND FRANCK, Archevêché, 4 rue Génistre, BP 419, 2014 Luxembourg; tel. 46-20-23; fax 47-53-81; e-mail archeveche@cathol.lu; internet www.cathol.lu.

The Anglican Communion

Within the Church of England, Luxembourg forms part of the diocese of Gibraltar in Europe.

Chaplain: Rev. CHRISTOPHER LYON, 89 rue de Muhlenbach, 2168 Luxembourg; tel. and fax 43-95-93; e-mail chris.lyon@anglican.lu; internet www.anglican.lu; English-speaking church (Anglican Chaplaincy).

Protestant Church

Protestant Church of Luxembourg: 5 rue de la Congrégation, 1352 Luxembourg; tel. 22-96-70; fax 46-71-88; e-mail mail@protestant.lu; internet www.protestant.lu; f. 1818 as Protestant

Garnison Church, 1868 as multiconfessional community for the Grand Duchy; there are about 1,500 Evangelicals; Pres. Pasteur MICHEL FAULLIMMEL.

ISLAM

Centre Culturel Islamique de Luxembourg: 2 route d'Arlon, 8210 Mamer, Luxembourg; tel. 31-00-60; fax 31-04-26; internet www.islam.lu; Imam HALIL AHMETSPAHIC.

JUDAISM

Chief Rabbi: JOSEPH SAYAGH, 34 rue Alphouse Munchen, 2172 Luxembourg; tel. 45-23-66; fax 25-04-30.

Consistoire Israélite de Luxembourg (Jewish Community of Luxembourg): 45 ave Monterey, 2018 Luxembourg; tel. 45-29-14; fax 47-37-72; e-mail cil@pt.lu; Pres. GUY AACH.

The Press

DAILIES

Lëtzebuerger Journal: Résidence de Beauvoir, 51 rue de Strasbourg, BP 2101, 1021 Luxembourg; tel. 49-30-33-1; fax 49-20-65; e-mail journal@journal.lu; internet www.journal.lu; f. 1948; organ of the Democratic Party; Editor-in-Chief CLAUDE KARGER.

Luxemburger Wort: 2 rue Christophe Plantin, 2988 Luxembourg; tel. 49-93-1; fax 49-93-384; e-mail wort@wort.lu; internet www.wort.lu; f. 1848; German; Catholic; Christian Democrat; Chief Editor LÉON ZECHES; circ. 87,126 (2000).

Tageblatt/Zeitung fir Lëtzebuerg: 44 rue du Canal, 4050 Esch-sur-Alzette; tel. 54-71-31-1; fax 54-71-30; e-mail tageblatt@tageblatt.lu; internet www.tageblatt.lu; f. 1913; French and German; Editor-in-Chief DANIÈLE FONCK.

La Voix du Luxembourg: 2 rue Christophe Plantin, 2988 Luxembourg; tel. 49-93-94-00; fax 49-93-773; e-mail voix@voix.lu; internet www.voix.lu; Editor LAURENT MOYSE.

Zeitung vum Lëtzebuerger Vollek: BP 3008, 1030 Luxembourg; tel. 44-60-66-1; fax 44-60-66-66; internet www.zlv.lu; f. 1946; organ of the Communist Party; Editor ALI RUCKERT.

PERIODICALS

Carrière: BP 2535, 1025 Luxembourg; tel. and fax 85-89-19; e-mail carrieremag@logic.lu; internet www.logic.lu/carriere; f. 1988; women's interest; French and German; Editor MONIQUE MATHIEU; circ. 8,000.

Contacto: 2 rue Christophe Plantin, 2988 Luxembourg; tel. 49-93-470; fax 49-93-448; e-mail contacto@saint-paul.lu; internet www.jornal-contacto.lu; Portuguese; weekly; Editors ARMAND THILL, MARC WILLIÈRE; circ. 22,800.

Correio: 459 route de Longwy, 1941 Bertrange; tel. 44-34-92; fax 44-34-93; e-mail correio@correio.lu; Portuguese; Editor JOSÉ DIAS; circ. 10,000.

Echo de l'Industrie: 7 rue Alcide de Gasperi, BP 1304, 1013 Luxembourg; tel. 43-53-66-1; fax 43-23-28; e-mail echo@fedil.lu; internet www.fedil.lu/Echo; f. 1920; 6 a year; industry, commerce; publ. by Fédération des Industriels Luxembourgeois; Dir NICOLAS SOISSON.

D'Handwierk: 2 circuit de la Foire Internationale, BP 1604, 1016 Luxembourg; tel. 42-45-11-1; fax 42-45-25; e-mail info@fda.lu; internet www.fda.lu; monthly; organ of the Fédération des Artisans and the Chambre des Métiers; Editor CHRISTIAN REUTER.

Horesca: 7 rue Alcide de Gasperi, BP 2524, 1025 Luxembourg; tel. 42-13-55-1; fax 42-13-55-299; e-mail info@horesca.lu; internet www.horesca.lu; monthly; hotel trade, tourism, gastronomy; Editor DAVE GIANNANDREA; circ. 6,000.

Le Jeudi: 44 rue du Canal, 4050 Esch-sur-Alzette; tel. 22-05-50; fax 22-05-44; e-mail redaction@le-jeudi.lu; internet www.lejeudi.lu; f. 1997; weekly; French; Dir DANIÈLE FONCK; circ. 11,602 (2006).

De Konsument: 55 rue des Bruyères, 1274 Howald; tel. 49-60-22-1; fax 49-49-57; e-mail ulc@pt.lu; internet www.ulc.lu; 12 a year; consumer affairs; Man. GUY GOEDERT.

De Lëtzeburger Bauer: 16 blvd d'Avranches, 2980 Luxembourg; tel. 48-81-61-1; fax 40-03-75; e-mail letzeburger.bauer@netline.lu; f. 1944; weekly; journal of Luxembourg farming; circ. 7,500.

D'Lëtzeburger Land: 59 rue Glesener, BP 2083, 1020 Luxembourg; tel. 48-57-57; fax 49-63-09; e-mail land@land.lu; internet www.land.lu; f. 1954; weekly, Fri.; political, economic, cultural affairs; Managing Editor ROMAIN HILGERT; circ. 7,500.

Lux-Post: Editions Saphir, 23 rue des Gênets, 1621 Luxembourg; tel. 49-53-63; fax 48-53-70; local news; four regional edns; French and German.

Muselzeidung: 30 rue de Trèves, POB 36, 6701 Grevenmacher; tel. 75-87-47; fax 75-84-32; e-mail burton@pt.lu; internet www.muselzeidung.lu; f. 1981; regional magazine; monthly; German; Editor TANIA USELDINGER.

OGB-L Aktuell: 60 blvd Kennedy, BP 149, 4002 Esch-sur-Alzette; tel. 54-05-45-1; fax 54-16-20; e-mail ogb-l@ogb-l.lu; internet www.ogb-l.lu; f. 1919; articles in both French and German; monthly; journal of the Luxembourg General Confederation of Labour; Editor-in-Chief DANIÈLE NIELES; circ. 43,000.

Revue/D'Lëtzebuerger Illustréiert: 2 rue Dicks, BP 2755, 1027 Luxembourg; tel. 49-81-81-1; fax 48-77-22; e-mail revue@revue.lu; internet www.revue.lu; f. 1945; weekly; illustrated; Man. Dir GUY LUDIG; Editor-in-Chief CLAUDE WOLF; circ. 31,000.

Revue Technique Luxembourgeoise: 4 blvd Grande-Duchesse Charlotte, 1330 Luxembourg; tel. 45-13-54; fax 45-09-32; e-mail aliasbl@pt.lu; internet www.aliai.lu; f. 1908; quarterly; technology.

Sauerzeidung: 30 rue de Trèves, BP 36, 6701 Grevenmacher; tel. 75-87-47; fax 75-84-32; e-mail burton@pt.lu; internet www.muselzeidung.lu; f. 1988; regional newspaper; monthly; German; Publr EUGENE BURTON; circ. 10,000.

Soziale Fortschrett/Progrès Social: 11 rue du Commerce, BP 1208, Luxembourg; tel. 49-94-24-1; fax 49-94-24-49; e-mail info@lcgb.lu; internet www.lcgb.lu; f. 1921; monthly; journal of the Confederation of Christian Trade Unions of Luxembourg; Pres. ROBERT WEBER; circ. 36,000.

Télécran: 2 rue Christophe Plantin, BP 1008, 1010 Luxembourg; tel. 49-93-50-0; fax 49-93-59-0; e-mail telecran@telecran.lu; internet www.telecran.lu; f. 1978; TV and family weekly; illustrated; Editor-in-Chief ROLAND ARENS; circ. 41,877 (2006).

Transport: 13 rue du Commerce, BP 2615, 1026 Luxembourg; tel. 22-67-86-1; fax 22-67-09; e-mail syprolux@pt.lu; internet www.fcpt-syprolux.lu; fortnightly; circ. 3,800.

Woxx: 51 ave de la Liberté, 2e étage, BP 684, 2016 Luxembourg; tel. 29-79-99-0; fax 29-79-79; e-mail woxx@woxx.lu; internet www.woxx.lu; f. 1988 as GréngeSpoun; weekly; social, ecological, environmental and general issues; circ. 3,000.

NEWS AGENCY

Agence Europe SA: BP 428, 2014 Luxembourg; tel. 22-00-32; fax 46-22-77; e-mail info@agenceurope.com; internet www.agenceurope.eu; f. 1953.

PRESS ASSOCIATIONS

Association Luxembourgeoise des Editeurs de Journaux: 44 rue du Canal, Luxembourg; tel. 54-71-31; fax 53-05-87; e-mail asold@tageblatt.lu; Pres. ALVIN SOLD.

Association Luxembourgeoise des Journalistes: BP 1732, 1017 Luxembourg; tel. 44-00-44; fax 85-88-40; Pres. LUCIEN MONTEBRUSCO.

Publishers

Editions Guy Binsfeld: 14 place du Parc, 2313 Luxembourg; tel. 49-68-68; fax 40-76-09; e-mail editions@binsfeld.lu; internet www.editionsguybinsfeld.lu; f. 1979; Man. Dir GUY BINSFELD; Chief Editor ROB KIEFFER.

Editions Phi: BP 321, 4004 Esch-sur-Alzette; tel. 54-13-82-820; fax 54-13-87; e-mail editions.phi@editpress.lu; internet www.phi.lu; f. 1980; fmrly Editions Francis van Maele; literature, art; Dirs A. THOME, A. FIXMER.

Editions Schortgen: 108 rue d'Alzette, BP 367, 4004 Esch-sur-Alzette; tel. 54-64-87; fax 53-05-34; e-mail editions@schortgen.lu; internet www.schortgen.lu; art, literature, factual, cuisine, comics; Dir JEAN-PAUL SCHORTGEN.

Editpress Luxembourg SA: 44 rue du Canal, BP 147, 4050 Esch-sur-Alzette; tel. 54-71-31-1; fax 54-71-30; e-mail tageblatt@tageblatt.lu; internet www.tageblatt.lu; Dir ALVIN SOLD.

Edouard Kutter: BP 319, 2013 Luxembourg; tel. 22-35-71; fax 47-18-84; e-mail kuttered@pt.lu; internet www.kutter.lu; art, photography, facsimile edns on Luxembourg.

Imprimerie Beffort SA: 7A rue de Bitbourg, 1273 Luxembourg; tel. 25-44-55-1; fax 25-44-19; e-mail jmkerschen@beffort.lu; f. 1869; scientific, economic reviews; Dir JEAN-MARIE KERSCHEN.

Saint-Paul Luxembourg SA: 2 rue Christophe Plantin, 2988 Luxembourg; tel. 49-93-1; fax 49-93-386; e-mail direction@saint-paul.lu; internet www.saint-paul.lu; f. 1887; Man. Dir LÉON ZECHES.

LUXEMBOURG   *Directory*

PUBLISHERS' ASSOCIATION

Fédération Luxembourgeoise des Editeurs de Livres: 31 blvd Konrad Adenauer, BP 482, 2014 Luxembourg; tel. 43-94-44; fax 43-94-50; e-mail info@clc.lu; internet www.clc.lu; Dir ALBERT DAMING; Pres. ROMAIN JEBLICK.

Broadcasting and Communications

TELECOMMUNICATIONS

Regulatory Authority

Institut Luxembourgeois de Régulation (ILR): 45 allée Scheffer, 2922 Luxembourg; tel. 45-88-45-1; fax 45-88-45-88; e-mail info@ilr.lu; internet www.ilr.lu; Dir ODETTE WAGENER.

Major Service Providers

Cegecom SA: 3 rue Jean Piret, BP 2708, 1027 Luxembourg; tel. 26-49-91; fax 26-49-96-99; e-mail info@cegecom.net; internet www.cegecom.lu; Man. Dirs MICHAEL LEIDINGER, GEORGES MULLER, BERTHOLD WEGMANN.

Coditel SA: 283 route d'Arlon, 8011 Strassen; tel. 34-93-93-1; fax 34-93-98; e-mail info@coditel.lu; internet www.coditel.lu; offers digital television, fixed-line telecommunications and broadband internet access; Dir CHRISTIAN DURLET.

Entreprise des Postes et Télécommunications (P&TLuxembourg): 8A ave Monterey, 2020 Luxembourg; tel. 47-65-1; fax 47-51-10; e-mail contact@pt.lu; internet www.pt.lu; f. 1992; post, telecommunications and internet service provider; Pres. GASTON REINESCH; CEO MARCEL GROSS.

LUXGSM SA: 90A rue de Strasbourg, 1171 Luxembourg; tel. 24-62-1; fax 24-62-60-00; e-mail communication@luxgsm.lu; internet www.luxgsm.lu; f. 1993; mobile cellular telephone operator; subsidiary of Entreprise des Postes et Télécommunications; Man. Dir MARC ROSENFELD.

Tele2Tango: 75 route de Longwy, 8080 Bertrange; tel. 27-77-71-01; fax 27-77-78-88; e-mail info@tele2tango.lu; internet www.tele2tango.lu; fmrly Millicom Luxembourg; fixed and mobile telephony, as well as data network and internet services; owned by Tele2 AB (Sweden); CEO RAFAEL ROS MONTERO.

BROADCASTING

Regulatory Authority

Commission Indépendante de la Radiodiffusion: 5 rue Large, 1917 Luxembourg; tel. 47-82-07-5; e-mail isabelle.marinov@smc.etat.lu; Pres. GEORGES SANTER.

Radio

Eldoradio: 47 Mühlenweg, BP 1344, 1013 Luxembourg; tel. 40-95-09-1; fax 40-95-09-509; e-mail eldoradio@eldoradio.lu; internet www.eldoradio.lu; music station.

Radio 100,7: 45A ave Monterey, BP 1833, 2163 Luxembourg; tel. 44-00-44-1; fax 44-00-44-940; e-mail dweyler@100komma7.lu; internet www.100komma7.lu; f. 1993; non-commercial cultural broadcaster; Dir FERNAND WEIDES.

Radio Ara: 2 rue de la Boucherie, BP 266, 1247 Luxembourg; tel. 22-22-89; fax 22-22-66; e-mail radioara@pt.lu; internet www.ara.lu; music broadcaster.

Radio DNR: 12 rue Christophe Plantin, 2988 Luxembourg; tel. 40-70-60; fax 40-79-98; e-mail dnr@dnr.lu; internet www.dnr.lu; e-mail dnr@dnr.lu; music broadcaster; Dir JEAN-MARC STURM.

Radio Latina: 3 rue du Fort Bourbon, 1249 Luxembourg; tel. 29-95-96-201; fax 40-24-76; internet www.radiolatina.lu; programmes for foreign communities in Luxembourg; Dir LUIS BARREIRA.

Radio LRB: BP 8, 3201 Bettembourg; tel. and fax 52-44-88; e-mail info@lrb.lu; internet www.lrb.lu; Man. CHRISTIAN FEDERSPIL.

Radio WAKY Power FM 107: 300D route de Thionville, BP 70, 5801 Hespérange; tel. 48-20-85; fax 48-21-13; e-mail waky@waky.lu; internet www.waky.lu; English and Lëtzebuergesch.

RTL Group: 45 blvd Pierre Frieden, 1543 Luxembourg; tel. 24-86-1; fax 24-86-27-60; e-mail oliver.herrgesell@rtlgroup.com; internet www.rtlgroup.com; f. 2000 by merger of CLT-UFA and Pearson TV; 90.3% owned by Bertelsmann AG (Germany); 9.7% private shareholders; 32 radio stations and 42 television channels in 10 countries; CEO GERHARD ZEILER.

RTL Radio Lëtzebuerg: tel. 42-14-2; fax 42-14-22-737; e-mail news@rtl.lu; internet www.rtl.lu; broadcasts in Lëtzebuergesch; Station Man. FERNAND MATHES; Chief Editor MARC LINSTER.

SES Astra: Château de Betzdorf, 6815 Betzdorf; tel. 710-725-1; fax 710-725-227; e-mail yves.feltes@ses.com; internet www.ses.com; f. 2001; owned by SES; operates 13 satellites (broadcasting 1,800 digital and analogue television and radio channels); Chair. ROMAIN BAUSCH; CEO FERDINAND KAYSER.

Television

RTL Télé Lëtzebuerg: 45 blvd Pierre Frieden, 1543 Luxembourg; tel. 42-14-28-10; fax 42-14-27-438; e-mail online@rtl.lu; internet www.rtl.lu; subsidiary of RTL Group; CEO ALAIN BERWICK.

Finance

(cap. = capital; res = reserves; dep. = deposits; m. = million; brs = branches; amounts in euros unless otherwise indicated)

BANKING

In 2007 there were 156 banks in Luxembourg, most of which were subsidiaries or branches of foreign banks; a selection of the principal banks operating internationally is given below.

Central Bank

Banque centrale du Luxembourg: 2 blvd Royal, 2983 Luxembourg; tel. 47-74-1; fax 47-74-49-10; e-mail info@bcl.lu; internet www.bcl.lu; f. 1998; represents Luxembourg within the European System of Central Banks (ESCB); cap. 25.0m., res 135.6m., dep. 10,284.8m. (Dec. 2006); Pres. YVES MERSCH; Exec. Dirs ANDRÉE BILLON, SERGE KOLB.

Principal Banks

ABN AMRO Bank (Luxembourg) SA: 46 ave J. F. Kennedy, 185 Luxembourg; tel. 26-07-1; fax 26-07-29-99; internet www.abnamroprivatebanking.com/luxembourg; f. 1991 by merger; cap. 372.0m., res 15.9m., dep. 6,040.5m. (Dec. 2005); Chair. JAN KOOPMAN; Man. Dir TONIKA HERDMAN.

Banque et Caisse d'Epargne de l'Etat, Luxembourg: 1 pl. de Metz, 1930 Luxembourg; tel. 40-15-1; fax 40-15-20-99; internet www.bcee.lu; f. 1856 as Caisse de l'Epargne de l'Etat du Grand-Duché de Luxembourg; present name adopted 1989; govt-owned; cap. 173.5m., res 979.9m., dep. 37,587.6m. (Dec. 2006); Chair. VICTOR ROD; Pres. and CEO JEAN-CLAUDE FINCK; 80 brs.

Banque Degroof Luxembourg SA: 12 rue Eugène Ruppert, 2453 Luxembourg; tel. 45-35-45-1; fax 25-07-21; e-mail investors.relation@degroof.lu; internet www.degroof.be; f. 1987; cap. 37.0m., res 75.7m., dep. 1,536.3m. (Sept. 2006); Chair. ALAIN PHILIPPSON; Man. Dirs GEERT DE BRUYNE, PATRICK KEUSTERS.

Banque BI&A SA (BI&A): 287 route d'Arlon, 1150 Luxembourg; tel. 44-50-80; fax 26-29-26-26; e-mail customer@bia.lu; internet www.bia.lu; f. 1989 as Banque Ippa et Associés; merged with Bank Anhyp Luxembourg SA in 2000; present name adopted 2006; cap. 11.0m., res 5.5m., dep. 162.8m. (Dec. 2005); Chair. PHILIPPE HAVAUX; Man. Dir YVES LAHAYE.

Banque LBLux SA: 3 rue Jean Monnet, BP 602, 2180 Luxembourg; tel. 42-43-41; fax 42-43-45-09-9; e-mail bank@lblux.lu; internet www.lblux.lu; f. 1973; present name adopted 2002; 75% owned by BayernLB, 25% by Helaba (both Germany); cap. 300.0m., res 120.6m., dep. 12,869.0m. (Dec. 2006); Chair. RUDOLF HANISCH; Man. Dir HENRI STOFFEL.

Banque de Luxembourg SA: 14 blvd Royal, BP 2221, 1022 Luxembourg; tel. 26-20-26-60; fax 499-24-55-99; e-mail banque.de.luxembourg@bdl.lu; internet www.banquedeluxembourg.com; f. 1920; 71% owned by Crédit Industriel d'Alsace et de Lorraine (France); cap. 100.0m., res 285.1m., dep. 11,700.7m. (Dec. 2006); Chair. PIERRE AHLBORN; Pres. ROBERT RECKINGER; 4 brs.

Banque Raiffeisen SC: 46 rue Charles Martel, 2134 Luxembourg; tel. 24-50-1; fax 22-50-22-52; internet www.raiffeisen.lu; f. 1926 as Caisse Centrale Raiffeisen SC; present name adopted 2001; res 137.0m., dep. 3,398.0m. (Dec. 2006); Chair. PAUL LAUTERBOUR; CEO and Gen. Man. ERNEST CRAVATTE.

Banque Safra Luxembourg SA: 10A blvd Joseph II, BP 887, 2018 Luxembourg; tel. 45-47-73-1; fax 45-47-86; internet www.safra.lu; cap. Swiss francs 24.2m., res Swiss francs 236.7m., dep. Swiss francs 1,957.5m. (Dec. 2005); Man. Dir JORGE ALBERTO KININSBERG.

BHF-BANK International: 283 route d'Arlon, BP 258, 2012 Luxembourg; tel. 45-76-76-1; fax 45-83-20; f. 1972; present name adopted 2005; 100% owned by BHF-Bank AG (Germany); cap. 26.0m., res 54.0m., dep. 4,807.2m. (Dec. 2006); Chair. LOUIS GRAF VON ZECH; Man. Dir Dr HARTMUT ROTHACKER.

BNP Paribas Luxembourg: 10A blvd Royal, 2093 Luxembourg; tel. 46-46-1; fax 46-46-90-00; internet www.bnpparibas.lu; absorbed Banca Nazionale del Lavoro International in 2007; cap. 105.0m., res 833.4m., dep. 17,642.0m. (Dec. 2006); Chair. ALAIN PAPIASSE; Man. Dir ERIC MARTIN.

LUXEMBOURG

Capitalia Luxembourg SA: 26 blvd Royal, BP 692, 2449 Luxembourg; tel. 47-79-06-1; fax 47-28-07; e-mail info@capitalia.lu; internet www.capitalia.lu; f. 1992 by merger of Banco di Roma International and Banco di Santo Spirito (Luxembourg); present name adopted 2006; owned by Capitalia SpA (Italy); cap. 120.0m., res 50.1m., dep. 994.9m. (Dec. 2005); Chair. GIANFRANCO IMPERATORI; Gen. Man. ANGELO BRIZI.

Clearstream Banking SA: 42 ave J. F. Kennedy, 1855 Luxembourg; tel. 243-0; fax 24-33-80-00; e-mail inquiries@clearstream.com; internet www.clearstream.com; f. 1970 as Cedelbank; present name adopted 2000; subsidiary of Deutsche Börse AG; private bank; acts as the central bank's securities depository; total assets 10,600,000m. (Dec. 2007); Chair. ANDRÉ ROELANTS; CEO JEFFREY TESSLER.

Commerzbank International SA (CISAL): 25 rue Edward Steichen, 2540 Luxembourg; tel. 47-79-11-1; fax 47-79-11-270; e-mail cisal@commerzbank.com; internet www.commerzbank.lu; f. 1969; cap. 579.8m., res 155.4m., dep. 9,409.0m. (Dec. 2006); Pres. and Chair. KLAUS-PETER MÜLLER; Man. Dirs BERND HOLZENTHAL, CORNELIUS OBERT.

Crédit Agricole Luxembourg Bank: 287–289 route d'Arlon, 1150 Luxembourg; tel. 45-78-80-1; fax 45-23-96; internet www.ca-luxembourgbank.com; f. 1988; fmrly Bank Sarasin Europe, acquired by Crédit Agricole (France) in 2007; merger with Crédit Agricole Luxembourg Private Bank expected mid-2008; cap. 16.3m., res 21.9m., dep. 642.2m. (Dec. 2005); Man. Dir THOMAS WITTLIN.

Crédit Agricole Luxembourg Private Bank: 39 allée Scheffer, BP 1104, 1011 Luxembourg; tel. 47-67-1; fax 46-24-42; e-mail marketing@ca-luxembourg.com; internet www.e-private.com; f. 2005 by merger of Crédit Lyonnais Luxembourg and Crédit Agricole Indosuez Luxembourg; cap. 84.2m., res 52.4m., dep. 3,597.1m. (Dec. 2006); Chair. JACQUES HAFFNER; Gen. Man. CHARLES HAMER.

Crédit Suisse (Luxembourg) SA: 56 Grand-Rue, BP 40, 2010 Luxembourg; tel. 46-00-11-1; fax 46-32-70; internet www.credit-suisse.com; f. 1974; cap. Swiss francs 43.0m., res Swiss francs 27.3m., dep. Swiss francs 5,103.7m. (Dec. 2006); Man. Dir HANS-ULRICH HÜGLI.

Danske Bank International SA: 2 rue du Fossé, 2011 Luxembourg; tel. 46-12-75-1; fax 47-30-78; e-mail information@danskebank.lu; internet www.danskebank.lu; f. 1976; cap. 90.6m., res 34.5m., dep. 4,841.5m. (Dec. 2006); Chair. PER DAMBORG SKOVHUS; Man. Dir KLAUS MØNSTED PEDERSEN.

DekaBank Deutsche Girozentrale Luxembourg SA: 38 ave J. F. Kennedy, 1855 Luxembourg; tel. 34-09-35; fax 34-09-37; e-mail info@dekabank.lu; internet www.dekabank.lu; f. 1971 as Deutsche Girozentrale International SA; present name adopted 2002, after merger with DekaBank Luxembourg SA; cap. 50.0m., res 106.1m., dep. 8,705.2m. (Dec. 2006); Chair. HANS-JÜRGEN GUTENBERGER; Man. Dir RAINER MACH.

Deutsche Bank Luxembourg SA: 2 blvd Konrad Adenauer, 1115 Luxembourg; tel. 42-12-21; fax 42-12-24-49; internet www.db.com/luxembourg; f. 1970 as Deutsche Bank Compagnie Financière Luxembourg; present name adopted 1987; cap. 215.0m., res 1,117.1m., dep. 60,520.8m. (Dec. 2006); Chair. Dr HUGO BÄNZIGER; CEO ERNST WILHELM CONTZEN.

Deutsche Postbank International SA: PB Finance Centre, 18–20 Parc d'Activités Sydrall, 5365 Munsbach; tel. 34-95-31-1; fax 34-62-06; e-mail deutsche.postbank@postbank.lu; internet www.postbank.de; f. 1993; cap. 600.0m., res 9.9m., dep. 16,440.5m. (Dec. 2006); Chair. LOUKAS RIZOS; Gen. Mans CHRISTOPH SCHMITZ, JOCHEN BEGAS.

Dexia Banque Internationale à Luxembourg SA (Dexia BIL): 69 route d'Esch, 2953 Luxembourg; tel. 45-90-1; fax 45-90-20-10; e-mail contact@dexia-bil.lu; internet www.dexia-bil.lu; f. 1856 as Banque Internationale à Luxembourg; present name adopted 2000; 99.9% owned by Dexia (Belgium); cap. 141.2m., res 1,103.9m., dep. 51,100.3m. (Dec. 2006); Chair. PIERRE RICHARD; 40 brs.

Dresdner Bank Luxembourg SA: 26 rue de Marché-aux-Herbes, 2097 Luxembourg; tel. 47-60-1; fax 47-60-33-1; e-mail info@dresdner-bank.lu; internet www.dresdner-bank.lu; f. 1967 as Cie Luxembourgeoise de Banque SA; present name adopted 1989; cap. 125.0m., res 286.6m., dep. 9,500.9m. (Dec. 2006); Chair. Dr ANDREAS GEORGI; CEO BENEDIKT BUHL; 1 br.

DZ Bank International SA: 4 rue Thomas Edison, 1445 Strassen; tel. 44-90-31; fax 44-90-32-00-1; e-mail info@dzi.lu; internet www.dzi.lu; f. 1978 as DG Bank Luxembourg SA; present name adopted 2001, after merger with GZ Bank International SA; 89.7% owned by DZ Bank AG Deutsche Zentral-Genossenschaftsbank; cap. 80.7m., res 229.7m., dep. 14,240.6m. (Dec. 2006); Chair. of Bd of Dirs HEINZ HILGERT.

EFG Private Bank (Luxembourg) SA: 5 rue Jean Monnet, BP 897, 2018 Luxembourg; tel. 42-07-24-1; fax 42-07-24-650; e-mail info@efgbank.lu; internet www.efgbank.lu; f. 1986; owned by EFG Eurobank Ergasias (Greece); cap. 70.0m., res 30.2m., dep. 907.3m. (Dec. 2006); Chair. FRANÇOIS REIS; Man. Dir LENA LASCARI.

Fortis Banque Luxembourg SA: 50 ave J. F. Kennedy, 2951 Luxembourg; tel. 42-42-1; fax 42-42-25-79; e-mail info@fortisbanque.lu; internet www.fortisbanque.lu; f. 1919 as Banque Générale du Luxembourg SA; merged with Fortis Bank Luxembourg SA 2001; present name adopted 2005; cap. 350.0m., res 2,695.3m., dep. 45,626.3m. (Dec. 2006); Chair. JEAN MEYER; CEO CARLO THILL; 37 brs.

HSBC Private Bank (Luxembourg) SA: 32 blvd Royal, BP 733, 2017 Luxembourg; tel. 47-93-31-1; fax 47-93-31-33-7; e-mail hrlu@hsbcpb.com; internet www.hsbcpb.com; f. 1985; cap. 53.0m., res 56.8m., dep. 1,840.0m. (Dec. 2006); Chair. MICHEL S. ELIA; Man. Dir and CEO PETER YEATES.

HSBC Trinkaus & Burkhardt (International) SA: 1–7 rue Nina et Julien Lefèvre, BP 579, 2015 Luxembourg; tel. 47-18-47-1; fax 47-18-47-61-3; e-mail contact@hsbctrinkhaus.lu; f. 1977 as Trinkhaus & Burhardt (International) SA; present name adopted 1999; cap. 15.5m., res 63.4m., dep. 2,036.6m. (Dec. 2006); Pres. Dr OLAF HUTH; Man. Dirs HANS-JOACHIM ROSTECK, JÖRG MEIER.

HSH Nordbank Private Banking SA: 2 rue Jean Monnet, BP 612, 2016 Luxembourg; tel. 42-41-21-1; fax 42-41-21-50-9; e-mail info@hsh-nordbank-pb.com; internet www.hsh-nordbank-pb.com; f. 1983; cap. 12.9m., res 4.1m., dep. 886.6m. (Dec. 2006); Chair. BERNHARD VISKER; Man. Dirs ERNST-WILHELM MÜNSTER, MICHAEL RIVERA, CARSTEN BÄCKER.

HVB Banque Luxembourg SA (HVB Luxembourg): 4 rue Alphonse Weicker, 2721 Luxembourg; tel. 42-72-1; fax 42-72-45-00; e-mail contact@hvb.lu; internet www.hvb.lu; f. 1998 by merger of Hypobank International SA and Vereinsbank International SA Luxembourg; present name adopted 2001; owned by HVB Group (Germany); cap. 238.0m., res 708.0m., dep. 28,896.9m. (Dec. 2006); Pres. and Chair. Dr WOLFGANG SPRISSLER; Man. Dirs ERNST-DIETER WIESNER, MARCELLO MANCINI.

IKB International SA: 12 rue Erasme, BP 771, 2017 Luxembourg; tel. 42-37-77-0; fax 42-06-03; e-mail ikb.luxemburg@ikb.de; internet www.ikb.de; f. 1979; cap. 272.5m., res 164.0m., dep. 8,055.5m. (March 2007); Chair. STEFAN ORTSEIFEN; Dirs WOLFGANG GÜTH, ROBERT SPLIID.

ING Luxembourg SA: 52 route d'Esch, 1470 Luxembourg; tel. 44-99-11; fax 44-99-12-31; internet www.ing.lu; f. 1960 as Crédit Européen SA; present name adopted 2003; owned by ING Belgium SA/NV; cap. 83.4m., res 1,185.7m., dep. 10,497.5m. (Dec. 2006); Chair. JAN OP DE BEECK; 15 brs.

Kredietbank SA Luxembourgeoise: 43 blvd Royal, 2955 Luxembourg; tel. 47-97-1; fax 47-97-73-90-0; internet www.kbl.lu; f. 1949; 99% owned by KBC Bank NV (Belgium); cap. 189.0m., res 1,134.0m., dep. 20,309.0m. (Dec. 2006); Pres. and Gen. Man. ETIENNE VERWILGHEN; 3 brs.

Landesbank Berlin International SA: 30 blvd Royal, 2449 Luxembourg; tel. 47-78-1; fax 47-78-20-09; e-mail contact@lbb.lu; internet www.lbb.lu; f. 1995 by merger; present name adopted 2006; cap. 57.0m., res 128.6m., dep. 4,175.5m. (Dec. 2005); Chair. SERGE DEMOLIÈRE; Man. Dirs RALPH BIEDINGER, UWE JUNGERWIRTH.

LRI Landesbank Rheinland-Pfalz International SA: 10–12 blvd F.D. Roosevelt, BP 84, 2010 Luxembourg; tel. 47-59-21-1; fax 47-59-21-31-4; e-mail info@lri.lu; internet www.lri.lu; f. 1978; present name adopted 2003; cap. 315.0m., res 285.2m., dep. 13,124.1m. (Dec. 2006); Chair. PAUL K. SCHMINKE; Man. Dirs ALAIN BAUSTERT, ROBY HAAS.

Norddeutsche Landesbank Luxembourg SA: 26 route d'Arlon, BP 121, 2011 Luxembourg; tel. 45-22-11-1; fax 45-22-11-31-9; e-mail info@nordlb.lu; internet www.nordlb.lu; f. 1972; cap. 205.0m., res 376.4m., dep. 21,307.7m. (Dec. 2006); Man. Dir and CEO HANS HARTMANN.

Nordea Bank SA: 672 rue de Neudorf-Findel, BP 562, 2015 Luxembourg; tel. 43-88-71; fax 43-93-52; e-mail nordea@nordea.lu; internet www.nordea.lu; f. 1976 as Privatbanken International (Denmark) SA, Luxembourg; changed name to Unibank SA in 1990, present name adopted 2001; cap. 25.0m., res 166.2m., dep. 3,271.7m. (Dec. 2006); Chair. GUNN WAERSTED; Man. Dir JHON MORTENSEN.

Sanpaolo Bank SA: 12 ave de la Liberté, BP 2062, 1020 Luxembourg; tel. 40-37-60-1; fax 40-37-60-35-0; e-mail sanpaolo@sanpaolo.lu; f. 1981 as Sanpaolo-Lariano Bank SA; present name adopted 1995; cap. 140.0m., res 131.1m., dep. 3,530.3m. (Dec. 2005); Man. Dir GIUSEPPE LA SORDA.

Skandinaviska Enskilda Banken SA: 6A circuit de la Foire Internationale, BP 487, 2014 Luxembourg; tel. 26-23-1; fax 26-23-20-01; e-mail marketing@sebprivatebank.com; internet www.sebprivatebank.com; f. 1977; present name adopted 1999; cap. 118.0m., res 20.9m., dep. 1,488.7m. (Dec. 205); Chair. ULF PETERSON; Man. Dir LARS FRIBERG.

LUXEMBOURG   *Directory*

Société Européenne de Banque SA: 19–21 blvd du Prince Henri, BP 21, 2010 Luxembourg; tel. 46-14-11; fax 22-37-55; e-mail contact@seb.lu; internet www.seb.lu; f. 1976; cap. 45.0m., res 42.4m., dep. 3,897.9m. (Dec. 2006); subsidiary of Intesa Sanpaolo (Italy); Chair. Prof. ANGELO CALOIA; Man. Dir and CEO MARCO BUS.

Société Générale Bank & Trust: 11 ave Emile Reuter, BP 1271, 2420 Luxembourg; tel. 47-93-111; fax 22-88-59; e-mail sgbt.lu@socgen.com; internet www.sgbt.lu; f. 1956 as International and General Finance Trust; present name adopted 1995; cap. 1,179.0m., res 501.9m., dep. 33,539.4m. (Dec. 2006); Chair. PHILIPPE COLLAS; Man. Dir VINCENT DECALF.

UBS (Luxembourg) SA: 33A ave J. F. Kennedy, 1855 Luxembourg; tel. 45-12-11; fax 45-12-12-70-0; internet www.ubs.com; f. 1998 by merger of Swiss Bank Corporation (Luxembourg) SA and Union de Banques Suisses (Luxembourg) SA; cap. Swiss francs 150m., res Swiss francs 310.4m., dep. Swiss francs 19,350.4m. (Dec. 2006); Chair. ARTHUR DECURTINS; Man. Dir and CEO ROGER H. HARTMANN.

WestLB International SA: 32–34 blvd Grande-Duchesse Charlotte, BP 420, 2014 Luxembourg; tel. 44-74-11; fax 44-74-12-10; e-mail info@westlb.lu; internet www.westlb.lu; f. 1972; owned by WestLB AG (Germany); cap. 65.0m., res 185.9m., dep. 19,151.0m. (Dec. 2006); Pres. ROBERT M. STEIN; Man. Dirs Dr JOHANNES SCHEEL, NORBERT LERSCH.

Banking Association

Association des Banques et Banquiers Luxembourg (ABBL): 59 blvd Royal, BP 13, 2010 Luxembourg; tel. 46-36-60-1; fax 46-09-21; e-mail mail@abbl.lu; internet www.abbl.lu; f. 1939; Pres. JEAN MEYER.

STOCK EXCHANGE

Société de la Bourse de Luxembourg SA: 11 ave de la Porte-Neuve, BP 165, 2011 Luxembourg; tel. 47-79-36-1; fax 47-32-98; e-mail info@bourse.lu; internet www.bourse.lu; f. 1928; Chair. RAYMOND KIRSCH; CEO MICHEL MAQUIL.

INSURANCE

In 2006 there were 95 approved insurance companies and, in addition, 262 reinsurance companies. A selection of insurance companies is given below:

Aon Insurance Managers (Luxembourg) SA: 19 rue de Bitbourg, BP 593, 2015 Luxembourg; tel. 22-34-22-1; fax 31-71-74; e-mail lambert_schroeder@aon.com; internet www.aon.com; f. 1994; Man. Dir. LAMBERT SCHROEDER.

Assurances Mutuelles d'Europe: 7 blvd Joseph II, BP 787, 1840 Luxembourg; tel. 47-46-93; fax 47-46-90; e-mail ame@ame.lu; internet www.ame.lu; f. 1989.

AXA Luxembourg: 7 rue de la Chapelle, 1325 Luxembourg; tel. 44-24-24-1; fax 44-24-24-45-90; e-mail info@axa.lu; internet www.axa.lu; f. 1977; all branches and life; Dir-Gen. PAUL DE COOMAN.

Fortis Assurances Luxembourg: 16 blvd Royal, 2449 Luxembourg; tel. 24-18-58-1; fax 24-18-58-90-00; e-mail info@fortisinsurance.lu; internet www.fortisinsurance.lu; f. 1996 by merger of AG Luxembourg and CGA Luxembourg; life and non-life insurance; CEO DIRK BILLEMON.

Groupe Foyer: 12 rue Léon Laval, 2986 Luxembourg; tel. 43-74-37; fax 43-74-32-49-9; e-mail contact@foyer.lu; internet www.foyer.lu; f. 1922; all branches and life.

La Luxembourgeoise SA d'Assurances: 10 rue Aldringen, 1118 Luxembourg; tel. 47-61-1; fax 47-61-30-0; e-mail groupell@lalux.lu; internet www.lalux.lu; f. 1989; all branches of non-life; Chair. GABRIEL DEIBENER; Dir-Gen. PIT HENTGEN.

West of England Shipowners' Mutual Insurance Asscn (Luxembourg): 33 blvd du Prince Henri, BP 841, 1724 Luxembourg; tel. 47-00-67-1; fax 22-52-53; e-mail philip.aspden@westpandi.com; internet www.westpandi.com; f. 1970; marine mutual insurance; Gen. Man. PHILIP ASPDEN.

Insurance Association

Association des Compagnies d'Assurances (ACA): 75 rue de Mamer, BP 29, 8005 Bertrange; tel. 44-21-44-1; fax 44-02-89; e-mail aca@aca.lu; internet www.aca.lu; f. 1956; Pres. PIT HENTGEN; 71 mems.

Trade and Industry

GOVERNMENT AGENCY

Société Nationale de Crédit et d'Investissement (SNCI): 7 rue du Saint Esprit, BP 1207, 1475 Luxembourg; tel. 46-19-71-1; fax 46-19-79; e-mail snci@snci.lu; internet www.snci.lu; f. 1978; cap. €164m., res €120m., dep. €583m., assets €728m. (Dec. 2006); SNCI finances participations in certain cos, provides loans for investment and research and devt projects, provides export credit; Pres. GASTON REINESCH; Sec.-Gen. EVA KREMER.

CHAMBER OF COMMERCE

Chambre de Commerce du Grand-Duché de Luxembourg: 7 rue Alcide de Gasperi, 2981 Luxembourg-Kirchberg; tel. 42-39-39-1; fax 43-83-26; e-mail chamcom@cc.lu; internet www.cc.lu; f. 1841; Pres. MICHEL WURTH; 35,000 mems.

INDUSTRIAL AND TRADE ASSOCIATIONS

Centrale Paysanne Luxembourgeoise: 16 blvd d'Avranches, 2980 Luxembourg; tel. 48-81-61; fax 40-03-75; f. 1945; Pres. MARC FISCH; Sec. LUCIEN HALLER; groups all agricultural organizations.

Chambre d'Agriculture (Landwirtschaftskammer): 261 route d'Arlon, BP 81, 8001 Strassen; tel. 31-38-76; fax 31-38-75; e-mail info@lwk.lu; internet www.lwk.lu; Pres. MARCO GAASCH; Sec.-Gen. ROBERT LEY.

Confédération Luxembourgeoise du Commerce (CLC): Bâtiment C, 2e étage, 7 rue Alcide de Gasperi, BP 482, 2014 Luxembourg; tel. 43-94-44; fax 43-94-50; e-mail info@clc.lu; internet www.clc.lu; f. 1909; Pres. ERNY LAMBORELLE; Dir THIERRY NOTHUM; 50,000 individual mems and 10,000 mem. cos.

Fédération des Artisans du Grand-Duché de Luxembourg: 2 circuit de la Foire Internationale, BP 1604, 1016 Luxembourg; tel. 42-45-11-1; fax 42-45-25; e-mail info@fda.lu; internet www.federation-des-artisans.lu; f. 1905; Chair. NORBERT GEISEN; Dir ROMAIN SCHMIT; 51 mem. feds.

FEDIL—Business Federation Luxembourg: 7 rue Alcide de Gasperi, BP 1304, 1013 Luxembourg; tel. 43-53-66-1; fax 43-23-28; e-mail fedil@fedil.lu; internet www.fedil.lu; f. 1918; Pres. ROBERT DENNEWALD; Dir NICOLAS SOISSON; c. 450 mems.

UTILITIES

Regulatory Authority

Service de l'Energie de l'Etat (SEE): 34 ave de la Porte-Neuve, BP 10, 2010 Luxembourg; tel. 46-97-46-1; fax 22-25-24; e-mail see.direction@eg.etat.lu; internet www.see.lu; f. 1967; civil service dept with responsiblity for testing, standardization and certification; Dir JEAN-MARIE REIFF.

Electricity

Cegedel (Compagnie Grand-Ducale d'Electricité de Luxembourg): 2 rue Thomas Edison, 1445 Strassen; tel. 26-24-1; fax 26-24-61-00; e-mail mail@cegedel.lu; internet www.cegedel.lu; f. 1928; produces and distributes electricity; 33% state-owned; Chair. ROLAND MICHEL; Dir-Gen. ROMAIN BECKER.

Cegedel Net SA: 2 rue Thomas Edison, 1445 Strassen; tel. 26-24-1; fax 26-24-61-00; e-mail mail@cegedel.lu; internet www.cegedelnet.lu; f. 2004; operates the Cegedel distribution grid; Chair. ETIENNE SCHNEIDER; Dir-Gen. CARLO BARTOCCI.

Société Electrique de l'Our (SEO): 2 rue Pierre d'Aspelt, BP 37, 2010 Luxembourg; tel. 44-90-21; fax 45-13-68; e-mail seo@seo.lu; internet www.seo.lu; f. 1951; electricity production and supply; Pres. ETIENNE SCHNEIDER.

SOTEL Réseau & Cie: 4 rue de Soleuvre, 4321 Esch-sur-Alzette; tel. 55-19-21; fax 57-22-13; f. 2001; distributor of electricity; Man. Dir NICO WIETOR.

Gas

SOTEG SA: 19–21 bd Royal, 2449 Luxembourg; tel. 57-44-11-1; fax 26-55-20-05; internet www.soteg.lu; f. 1974 as Société de Transport de Gaz SA; 21% state-owned; gas transportation and supply; Pres. MARCO HOFFMANN; Dir-Gen. JEAN LUCIUS.

SUDGAZ SA: 150 rue Jean-Pierre Michels, BP 383, 4004 Esch-sur-Alzette; tel. 55-66-551; fax 57-20-44; e-mail contact@sudgaz.lu; internet www.sudgaz.lu; f. 1899; gas distribution co; Pres. WILL HOFFMANN; Dir JO SIMON.

TRADE UNIONS

FNCTTFEL—Landesverband der Eisenbahner, Transportarbeiter, Funktionäre und Beamten, Luxemburg (National Union of Luxembourg Railway and Transport Workers and Employees): 63 rue de Bonnevoie, 1260 Luxembourg; tel. 48-70-44-1; fax 48-85-25; e-mail info@landesverband.lu; internet www.landesverband.lu; f. 1909; affiliated to CGT and International Transport Workers' Federation; Pres. NICO WENNMACHER; Gen. Sec. GUY GREIVELDING; 8,000 mems.

Lëtzebuerger Chrëschtleche Gewerkschaftsbond (LCGB) (Confederation of Luxembourg Christian Trade Unions): 11 rue du

LUXEMBOURG

Commerce, BP 1208, 1012 Luxembourg; tel. 49-94-24-1; fax 49-94-24-49; e-mail info@lcgb.lu; internet www.lcgb.lu; f. 1921; affiliated to European Trade Union Confederation and World Confederation of Labour; Pres. ROBERT WEBER; Gen. Sec. MARC SPAUTZ; 40,000 mems.

Onofhängege Gewerkschaftsbond-Lëtzebuerg/Confédération Syndicale Indépendente du Luxembourg (OGB-L) (Luxembourg Independent Confederation of Labour): 60 blvd J. F. Kennedy, BP 149, 4002 Esch-sur-Alzette; tel. 54-05-45-1; fax 54-16-20; e-mail ogbl@ogbl.lu; internet www.ogb-l.lu; f. 1921; comprises 15 mem. unions; Pres. JEAN-CLAUDE REDING; c. 58,000 mems.

Transport

RAILWAYS

At 31 December 2006 there were 275 km of railway track, of which 262 km were electrified. A high-speed link from Luxembourg-Ville to Paris, France, opened in June 2007.

Société Nationale des Chemins de Fer Luxembourgeois: 9 place de la Gare, BP 1803, 1018 Luxembourg; tel. 49-90-0; fax 49-90-44-70; e-mail info@cfl.lu; internet www.cfl.lu; f. 1946; Pres. JEANNOT WARINGO; Dir-Gen. and CEO ALEX KREMER.

ROADS

At 1 January 2006 there were 2,894 km of roads, of which motorways comprised 147 km.

Ministry of Public Works: (see Ministries).

INLAND WATERWAYS AND SHIPPING

Rhine shipping has direct access to the Luxembourg inland port of Mertert as a result of the canalization of the Moselle river. An 'offshore' shipping register was established in 1991.

CIVIL AVIATION

There is an international airport situated at Findel, north-west of Luxembourg-Ville.

Luxair SA (Société Luxembourgeoise de Navigation Aérienne): Aéroport de Luxembourg, 2987 Luxembourg; tel. 456-42-55; fax 456-46-05; e-mail information@luxair.lu; internet www.luxair.lu; f. 1962; regular services to destinations in Europe and North Africa; Pres. and CEO ADRIEN NEY.

Cargolux Airlines International SA: Aéroport de Luxembourg, 2990 Luxembourg; tel. 42-11-1; fax 43-54-46; e-mail info@cargolux.com; internet www.cargolux.com; f. 1970; regular international all-freighter services; technological devt; owned by Luxair, a consortium of Luxembourg banks and SAir Logistics (Switzerland); Pres. and CEO ULRICH OGIERMANN.

Tourism

Many tourist resorts have developed around the ruins of medieval castles such as Clerf, Esch/Sauer, Vianden and Wiltz. The Benedictine Abbey at Echternach is also much visited. There is a thermal centre at Mondorf-les-Bains, supplied by three mineralized springs. In addition, there are numerous footpaths and hiking trails. Luxembourg-Ville, with its many cultural events and historical monuments, is an important centre for congresses. In 2007 there were 917,334 tourist arrivals at hotels and other accommodation establishments, of which there were 409. Receipts from tourism totalled US $3,889m. in 2004. In 2007 Luxembourg and Greater Region, which includes the German states of Saarland and Rhineland-Palatinate, the French region of Lorraine and the Belgian region of Wallonia, was a European Capital of Culture.

Office National du Tourisme (ONT): 68–70 blvd de la Pétrusse, BP 1001, 1010 Luxembourg; tel. 42-82-82-1; fax 42-82-82-38; e-mail info@ont.lu; internet www.ont.lu; f. 1931; 192 mems; Chair. M. SCHANK; Dir ROBERT L. PHILIPPART.

THE FORMER YUGOSLAV REPUBLIC OF MACEDONIA

Introductory Survey

Location, Climate, Language, Religion, Flag, Capital

The former Yugoslav republic of Macedonia (FYRM) is situated in south-eastern Europe. The FYRM is a land-locked state and is bounded by Serbia to the north, Kosovo (a former Serbian province, which made a declaration of independence in February 2008) to the north-west, Albania to the west, Greece to the south and Bulgaria to the east. The republic is predominantly mountainous with a continental climate, although the Vardar (Axiós) river valley, which bisects the country from north-west to south-east, across the centre of the republic and into Greece, has a mild Mediterranean climate with an average summertime temperature of 27°C (80°F). The official language of the republic, under the Constitution of November 1991, was originally stipulated as Macedonian, and is most frequently written in the Cyrillic script. Constitutional amendments adopted in November 2001 accorded any minority language, such as Albanian (written in the Latin script), the status of official language in communities where its speakers constitute 20% of the population. Most of the population is nominally Christian and of the Eastern Orthodox faith. The ethnic Macedonians (who accounted for 64.2% of the total population at the 2002 census) are traditionally adherents of the Macedonian Orthodox Church, which claims autocephaly, although this is not recognized by other Orthodox churches. Most of the ethnic Albanians (officially recorded as 25.2% of the population) are Muslims, as are the majority of the remaining minority groups. The national flag (proportions 1 by 2) comprises, in the centre of a red field, a yellow disc, with eight yellow rays extending to the edges of the flag. The capital is Skopje.

Recent History

After the First World War, during which Macedonia was occupied by the Bulgarians and the Central Powers of Austria-Hungary and Germany, Vardar Macedonia, the area now known as the former Yugoslav republic of Macedonia (FYRM), became part of the new Kingdom of Serbs, Croats and Slovenes (formally named Yugoslavia in 1929), being widely referred to as 'South Serbia'. In the Second World War, however, the Bulgarian occupation of 1941–44 disillusioned many Yugoslav Macedonians. From 1943 the Partisans of Josip Broz (Tito), the General-Secretary of the banned Communist Party of Yugoslavia, began to increase their support in the region, and after the war the new Federal People's Republic of Yugoslavia and its communist rulers resolved to include a Macedonian nation as a federal partner (having rejected the idea of a united Macedonia under Bulgaria). A distinct Macedonian identity was promoted, and a linguistic policy that encouraged the establishment of a Macedonian literary language distinct from Bulgarian and Serbian, together with the consolidation of an historical and cultural tradition, increased Macedonian self-awareness. In 1967 the Orthodox Church in Macedonia declared itself autocephalous, a move strongly contested by the Serbian Orthodox Church and not recognized by other Orthodox jurisdictions.

The presence of a large ethnic Albanian minority in western Macedonia added to Macedonian insecurities. The proximity of the neighbouring Serbian province of Kosovo (officially Kosovo and Metohija from 1990), which had a majority ethnic Albanian population, and demands, from the late 1960s, for the creation of a Albanian republic within Yugoslavia alarmed the Macedonian authorities, which became particularly active against Albanian nationalism from 1981. In 1989 the communists amended the republican Constitution to allow for the introduction of a multi-party system; however, Macedonia was declared to be a 'nation-state' of the ethnic Macedonians, and mention of the 'Albanian and Turkish minorities' was excluded. Tension continued into the early 1990s (see below).

In November and December 1990 the first multi-party elections to a unicameral republican Sobranie (Assembly) were held in Macedonia. The Front for Macedonian National Unity, which principally comprised a nationalist party, the Internal Macedonian Revolutionary Organization—Democratic Party for Macedonian National Unity (IMRO—DPMNU), led by Ljubčo Georgievski, and which had previously declared its support for the return of territories within Serbia, alleged irregularities after failing to win any seats at the first round. Following two further rounds of voting, however, the IMRO—DPMNU unexpectedly emerged as the single party with the most seats (a total of 37) in the 120-member Sobranie. The League of Communists of Macedonia—Party for Democratic Reform (LCM—PDR, as the League of Communists of Macedonia had renamed itself), led by Petar Gosev, won 31 seats and the two predominantly Albanian parties (the Party for Democratic Prosperity—PDP—and the People's Democratic Party) a total of 25. The republican branch of the federal Alliance of Reform Forces (ARF, subsequently the Liberal Party of Macedonia—LPM) won 19 seats. Following lengthy negotiations to establish a parliamentary coalition, in January 1991 Kiro Gligorov of the LCM—PDR was elected President of the Republic, with Georgievski as Vice-President, and Stojan Andov of the ARF was elected President of the Sobranie. The three parties agreed to support a government largely comprising members without political affiliation. In March the Sobranie approved a new administration, headed by Nikola Kljušev. The LCM—PDR was renamed the Social Democratic Alliance of Macedonia (SDAM) in April.

On 25 January 1991 the Sobranie unanimously adopted a motion declaring the republic a sovereign territory. After June declarations of Croatian and Slovenian 'dissociation', Macedonia, wary of Serbian domination of the remaining federal institutions, declared its neutrality and emphasized its sovereign status. On 8 September a referendum (boycotted by the ethnic Albanian population) approved the sovereignty of Macedonia.

Georgievski resigned the vice-presidency in October 1991, and the IMRO—DPMNU announced that it had joined the opposition, stating that the party had been excluded from the decision-making process. The preparation of the new Constitution was delayed by the IMRO—DPMNU's proposal for an introductory nationalist statement, which was strongly opposed by the predominantly ethnic Albanian parties and was finally abandoned. On 17 November the Constitution, which declared the sovereignty of the 'Republic of Macedonia', was endorsed by 96 of the 120 Assembly members, with opposition from the majority of ethnic Albanian deputies. In January 1992 an unofficial referendum conducted among the ethnic Albanian population (declared illegal by the Macedonian authorities) reportedly resulted in 99.9% of votes being cast in favour of territorial and political autonomy for the ethnic Albanian population.

The complete withdrawal of federal troops from Macedonia in March 1992, in conjunction with the adoption in April of a new Constitution in the Federal Republic of Yugoslavia (FRY), referring only to Serbia and Montenegro, effectively signalled Yugoslav acceptance of Macedonian secession from the federation. Macedonia established diplomatic relations with Slovenia in March, and with Croatia in April.

Macedonian affairs were subsequently dominated by the question of wider international recognition. The republic, although no longer part of Yugoslavia, was unable to act as an independent nation in the international community. Bulgaria recognized the state of Macedonia (although not the existence of a distinct Macedonian nationality or language) in January 1992, closely followed by Turkey in February, provoking mass protests in Thessaloníki, the capital of the Greek region of Macedonia. The Greek authorities insisted that 'Macedonia' was a geographical term delineating an area that included a large part of northern Greece, and expressed fears that the republic's independence under the name 'Macedonia' might foster a false claim to future territorial expansion. Greece was instrumental in the formulation of a European Community (EC, now European Union, EU, see p. 244) policy, adopted in early 1992, that the republic should be awarded no formal recognition of independence until stringent constitutional requirements had been fulfilled. In May Gligorov rejected a statement by the EC that it was 'willing to recognize Macedonia as a sovereign and independent state within its existing borders under a name that can be accepted by all concerned'. Negotiations with Greece ended in failure in June. In July, after a motion expressing no confidence in the Government received strong support in the Sobranie (and following large demonstrations at its failure to gain international recognition for an independent Macedonia), the Government resigned. The IMRO—DPMNU failed to form a new alliance and, eventually, in September Branko Crvenkovski, the Chairman of the SDAM, was installed as Prime Minister of a coalition Government.

The adoption of a new flag in August 1992 attracted particular opposition from Greece, which objected to the depiction outside Greece of the 'Vergina Star' (regarded as an ancient Greek symbol of Philip of Macedon and Alexander the Great). As a result of a blockade of petroleum deliveries imposed on Macedonia by Greece, reserves at the Skopje petroleum refinery were exhausted by September. In February 1993 Greece agreed to international arbitration over the issue of Macedonia's name, undertaking to abide by its final outcome. On 8 April the republic was admitted to the UN under the temporary name of 'the former Yugoslav republic of Macedonia', pending settlement of the issue of a permanent name by international mediators. However, Greece continued to assert, and the FYRM to deny, that the use of the 'Vergina Star' emblem and the name 'Macedonia' implied territorial claims on Greek territory, and in October Greece announced its withdrawal from UN-sponsored negotiations on the issue of a permanent name. In January 1994 Greece requested that the other nations of the EU prevail upon the FYRM (which was by this time recognized by all the other EU member states) to make concessions concerning its name, flag and Constitution, and threatened to ban trade with the FYRM. From February (shortly after Russia and the USA had formally recognized the FYRM) Greece blocked all non-humanitarian shipments to the FYRM from the port of Thessaloníki, and also road and rail transport links with the FYRM. In April the European Commission, which contested that the Greek embargo was in violation of EU trade legislation, initiated legal proceedings against Greece at the Court of Justice of the European Communities. In April 1995, however, the Court issued a preliminary opinion that the embargo was not in breach of Greece's obligations under the Treaty of Rome. Meanwhile, Greece agreed to resume negotiations in April with the FYRM, under the auspices of the UN; in May the Organization for Security and Co-operation in Europe (OSCE, see p. 354) announced that it was to join the mediation efforts. In September an interim accord was signed at the UN headquarters in New York, USA, by the FYRM Minister of Foreign Affairs and his Greek counterpart. The agreement provided for the mutual recognition of existing frontiers and respect for the sovereignty and political independence of each state, and for the free movement of goods and people between the two countries. Greece was to end its trade embargo and veto on the FYRM's entry into international organizations, while the FYRM undertook to abandon its use of the Vergina emblem in any form, and to amend parts of its Constitution that had been regarded by Greece as 'irredentist'. (The issue of a permanent name for the FYRM was to be the subject of further negotiations.) In early October the Sobranie approved a new state flag, depicting an eight-rayed sun in place of the Vergina emblem. The interim accord was ratified by the Sobranie on 9 October, and was formally signed in Skopje by representatives of the FYRM and Greece on 13 October. The border between the two countries was subsequently reopened.

The Albanian Government formally recognized the FYRM in April 1993. However, relations between the FYRM authorities and the country's ethnic Albanian minority continued to deteriorate. In November several ethnic Albanians were arrested in the western towns of Gostivar and Tetovo (both of which had predominantly Albanian populations) and in Skopje. The Government announced that a conspiracy to form paramilitary groups, with the eventual aim of establishing an Albanian republic in the west of the country, had been discovered. Further arrests followed, and in June 1994 Mithat Emini, the former General Secretary of the PDP, was sentenced to eight years' imprisonment, after being convicted of conspiring to engage in hostile activity; nine others received custodial sentences of between five and eight years. (In February 1995 all the sentences were reduced by two years.)

In February 1994, after months of disunity, the PDP split when a faction led by Xheladin Murati (the Deputy President of the Sobranie) and including the PDP's representatives in the Government and in the legislature, withdrew from the party's congress. The remaining grouping, led by Arben Xhaferi, made more radical demands regarding the status of ethnic Albanians in the FYRM. Organizations representing ethnic Albanians protested that inadequate preparations for a national census, conducted in mid-1994, effectively prevented the full enumeration of the ethnic Albanian community. It was reported that many ethnic Albanians boycotted the census, despite appeals by their political leaders for full participation. Following the publication of the census results, ethnic Albanian groups continued to assert that their community was considerably larger than officially indicated. The sentencing of Emini and his co-defendants prompted ethnic Albanian deputies to boycott the Sobranie in July (although they resumed their seats to defeat a motion, proposed by the IMRO—DPMNU, expressing no confidence in the Government). Murati resigned from the leadership of his PDP faction (and from his role at the Sobranie) later in July, reportedly in protest at the sentences; he was succeeded as party leader by Abdurahman Aliti.

Gligorov, representing the Alliance for Macedonia (an electoral coalition of the SDAM, the LPM and the Socialist Party of Macedonia—SPM) was re-elected to the presidency on 16 October 1994, winning 78.4% of the valid votes cast; his only challenger was Georgievski of the IMRO—DPMNU. A first round of voting to the new Sobranie took place on the same day. The IMRO—DPMNU, which failed to secure any seats, alleged widespread electoral fraud in both elections, and boycotted the second round of legislative voting, which took place on 30 October (a third round was necessary in 10 constituencies on 13 November, owing to irregularities in earlier rounds). The final results confirmed that the Alliance for Macedonia had won the majority of seats in the Sobranie (with the SDAM taking 58 seats, the LPM 29 and the SPM eight). Aliti's 'moderate' PDP, which had been legally recognized as the successor to the original party, secured 10 seats; members of the 'radical' PDP had been obliged to stand as independent candidates (Xhaferi was among the independent candidates to be elected). Gligorov subsequently requested that Crvenkovski form a new government, and the SDAM-led administration, which also included members of the LPM, Aliti's PDP and the SPM, was approved by the Sobranie in December.

Tensions were exacerbated by efforts by the ethnic Albanian community to establish an Albanian-language university in Tetovo, following continued claims by ethnic Albanian groups that the education system of the FYRM disadvantaged ethnic minorities. Despite government objections that to establish such an institution would be unconstitutional, the university was formally established in December 1994. In February 1995 the opening of the university provoked considerable unrest; an ethnic Albanian was killed in clashes with security forces, and several people were arrested, including the university's rector. In July 1996 five of the university's founders, including its rector, received custodial sentences for inciting the riots, prompting protests by ethnic Albanians in Tetovo and other parts of the country. (In May 2000 the Sobranie approved legislation granting the university at Tetovo legal status as a private foundation, and in January 2004 further legislation was passed, transforming it into a state university.)

In October 1995 Gligorov was injured in a car-bomb attack in Skopje; he resumed full presidential duties in January 1996. Meanwhile, divisions had emerged within the governing Alliance for Macedonia, which collapsed in February, prompting the LPM to be excluded from the Government. Andov resigned as President of the Sobranie in early March, stating that Crvenkovski had acted unconstitutionally in expelling the LPM from the Government. A new penal code, under which the death penalty was abolished, entered into force in November.

In September 1996, prior to local elections scheduled for 17 November, the Sobranie approved legislation reorganizing the territorial division of the FYRM into 123 municipalities. In October three opposition parties, the IMRO—DPMNU, the PDP and the newly established Movement for All-Macedonian Action—Conservative Party, formed a coalition to contest the elections. Xhaferi's faction, which had been reconstituted as the Party of Democratic Prosperity of Albanians in Macedonia (PDPAM), and the (also ethnic Albanian) National Democratic Party (NDP) agreed to present joint candidates in some constituencies. The SDAM received the greatest number of votes, followed by the coalition led by the IMRO—DPMNU, and the

PDP. Observers from the Council of Europe (see p. 225) declared that, overall, the elections had been conducted fairly.

In January 1997, following a campaign by ethnic Albanian students, legislation was adopted to permit Albanian to become the language of instruction at the teacher-training faculty of the university at Skopje. This provoked outrage among ethnic Macedonian students at the faculty, and a series of protests by university and secondary-school students ensued. Ethnic tensions were further compounded by the civil conflict in Albania in early 1997. A financial scandal emerged in the FYRM in March, involving the embezzlement of funds invested in 'pyramid' savings schemes. Crvenkovski pledged an investigation to identify those responsible for the losses sustained by large numbers of investors, and several senior officials were subsequently arrested on suspicion of involvement. Although the Government won a vote of confidence in its management of the affair, the LPM deputies withdrew from the parliamentary chamber to register their disapproval of the measures undertaken. In April the Government announced plans to reimburse losses incurred by investors, following the failure of a major savings institution in the south-western town of Bitola; in May the Sobranie approved the replacement of the Governor of the central bank, who was believed to have been involved in the failure of the investment scheme. Following an IMRO—DPMNU demonstration in Skopje to demand the resignation of the Government, a reorganized administration was approved by the Sobranie at the end of May.

In May 1997 ethnic Albanians in Gostivar took part in protests against a ruling by the Constitutional Court that prohibited the use of the Albanian flag in the FYRM. In June the President of the Constitutional Court issued a statement demanding that the Government enforce the ruling. In early July the Sobranie adopted legislation stipulating that the use of the Albanian flag, and flags of other ethnic minorities, would only be permitted on national holidays, with the Macedonian flag being displayed at the same time. None the less, the mayors of Gostivar and Tetovo continued to refuse to comply with the order of the Constitutional Court, and government officials forcibly removed Albanian flags that had been displayed at municipal buildings. Ensuing protests in Gostivar resulted in violent clashes between security forces and demonstrators, as a result of which three ethnic Albanians were killed; some 500 protesters were arrested. In September the mayor of Gostivar, Rufi Osmani, received a custodial sentence of some 13 years (reduced to seven years in February 1998), after being convicted on charges of inciting ethnic tension and rebellion, while the Chairman of the municipal council was sentenced to three years' imprisonment for failing to adopt the ruling of the Constitutional Court. In April 1998 the Democratic Party of Albanians (DPA—which had been formed in July 1997 by the amalgamation of the PDPAM and the NDP) announced that it was to withdraw its representatives from all government bodies, in protest at Osmani's imprisonment.

In August 1998 the PDP and the DPA established an alliance to contest forthcoming legislative elections. In early September the IMRO—DPMNU and the newly formed Democratic Alternative (DA) formed an electoral coalition, For Changes. The legislative elections were conducted in two rounds on 18 October and 1 November 1998; the For Changes coalition secured an absolute majority in the Sobranie, with 58 seats, while the SDAM obtained 29 seats, and the alliance of the PDP and the DPA 24. Owing to irregularities, a further round of voting took place in two electoral districts, at which one seat was won by the For Changes alliance, and the other by the PDP–DPA alliance. Later in November Georgievski was nominated as Prime Minister. The DPA was subsequently invited to join the governing coalition of the IMRO—DPMNU and the DA. In early December a new Government, comprising 14 representatives of the IMRO—DPMNU, eight of the DA and five of the DPA, was formed. At the end of December the Sobranie approved legislation (supported by the new Government) providing for the release of some 8,000 prisoners, among them Osmani. Although Gligorov refused to approve the amnesty in January 1999, in the following month the amnesty legislation was resubmitted to the Sobranie (in accordance with the Constitution) and subsequently adopted.

The first round of the presidential election on 31 October 1999 was contested by six candidates: Tito Petkovski, representing the SDAM, secured 33.2% of the votes cast, and Boris Trajkovski, the IMRO—DPMNU candidate, won 20.6%; Vasil Tupurkovski, the DA leader, took 16.0%, and Muharem Nexipi, the DPA candidate, 14.8%. Since no candidate had secured an outright majority of the votes, Petkovski and Trajkovski progressed to a second round, held on 14 November; Trajkovski was elected to the presidency with 52.8% of the votes cast (after DPA and DA voters transferred support to his candidacy). In late November the Supreme Court upheld a legal appeal by the SDAM against the results, and ruled that a further ballot take place in some western regions. A partial round, affecting about 10% of the total electorate, consequently took place on 5 December. However, the overall results were almost unchanged, with Trajkovski receiving 52.9% of the votes cast. Although the SDAM again claimed that irregularities had taken place, Petkovski finally accepted Trajkovski's election to the presidency. Trajkovski was formally inaugurated as President on 15 December. Following negotiations between the two leaders of the For Changes coalition, Georgievski and Tupurkovski, the IMRO—DPMNU, DA and DPA reached agreement on the formation of a new Government. The coalition administration, which contained seven new ministers (including Tupurkovski, as a Deputy Prime Minister), was formally approved by the Sobranie on 27 December.

In January 2000 the Government announced that amendments to the Constitution, which would allow higher education to be conducted in the language of ethnic minorities, would be submitted for approval by the Sobranie. In April legislation was adopted, obliging the authorities to return property expropriated under the communist regime. In the same month disaffected members of the IMRO—DPMNU, headed by a former Minister of Finance, Boris Zmejkovski, established a breakaway faction, which became known as the IMRO—True Macedonian Reform Option (IMRO—TMRO). In May the SDAM, the Liberal-Democratic Party (LDP) and the Democratic League—Liberal Party established an electoral alliance. In July Georgievski reorganized the Government, reducing the number of ministries from 21 to 14. Local government elections took place in two rounds on 10 and 24 September, amid reports of numerous violent incidents. After a further round of voting took place, owing to electoral irregularities, it was announced at the end of the month that the parties of the governing coalition had secured 75 of the 123 municipalities. Following prolonged dissent between Georgievski and Tupurkovski, the DA withdrew from the coalition Government and from the Sobranie at the end of November. Georgievski subsequently formed a new administration, which, for the first time, included members of the LDP.

In early 2001 ethnic Albanian militants, members of the self-styled National Liberation Army (NLA—which had emerged as the successor movement to the KLA), began to infiltrate northern parts of the FYRM from Kosovo, clashing with FYRM security forces. In early March NLA forces seized the border village of Tanusevci, north of Skopje, prompting counter-attacks from government troops. The border with Kosovo was officially closed, after senior government officials visiting the border region were attacked and temporarily besieged by the NLA. Although the authorities succeeded in regaining control of Tanusevci, in mid-March some 200 NLA forces attempted to occupy Tetovo, precipitating the imposition of curfew regulations in the city. Following an appeal by the Government to the international community for military assistance, the North Atlantic Treaty Organization (NATO, see p. 340) reinforced its military presence at the border with Kosovo to prevent the NLA from receiving supplies from the province. On 21 March the UN Security Council adopted Resolution 1345, condemning the violence by ethnic Albanian nationalists in the FYRM as constituting a threat to the stability of the region. Despite reports that the ethnic Albanian rebels aimed to establish a 'greater Albania' (to include some northern and western regions of the FYRM), the NLA insisted that the conflict had been initiated to pressurize the FYRM Government to institute constitutional changes guaranteeing equal rights for ethnic Albanians. The prolonged bombardment of rebel positions by government forces resulted in a withdrawal by the NLA from the Tetovo region, and hostilities temporarily subsided in early April. However, at the end of the month eight members of the state security forces were killed in an NLA attack near the border with Kosovo. Their funeral precipitated rioting and attacks by Macedonians on Albanian-owned property in the southern town of Bitola. Government troops subsequently launched an offensive against rebel ethnic Albanian positions near Kumanovo, after two further members of the armed forces were killed.

Meanwhile, in early April 2001, following the temporary suppression of the insurgency, inter-party discussions regarding the ethnic Albanian demands commenced. After signing a Stabilization and Association Agreement with the EU, the Government pledged to initiate political, social and economic reforms by mid-2001. Ethnic Albanian proposals included: the postponement of the national census, due to take place in May, until October, to allow the return of refugees who had fled the conflict; state funding for the university at Tetovo; and the conversion of the state television's third service into an Albanian-language channel. However, the Government continued to oppose principal demands that the Constitution be amended to grant the ethnic Albanian population (hitherto officially categorized as a minority) equal rights with the Macedonian population, and Albanian the status of a second official language.

In early May 2001, following the resumption of intensive hostilities in the north of the country, the Government announced that the declaration of a state of war (which would allow the authorities to adopt emergency powers and Trajkovski to rule by decree) was under debate; the declaration, which required the approval of a two-thirds' majority in the Sobranie, was strongly opposed by ethnic Albanian deputies. Intensive discussions ensued between the principal political parties, with EU and NATO mediation, and it was agreed that the SDAM, the DPA and the PDP would join a government of national unity, and the parliamentary debate on the declaration of a state of war was suspended. The PDP subsequently demanded that the Government declare a cease-fire in the conflict in the north, as a precondition to the ethnic Albanian party's participation in the new administration. After the government offensive against the rebels was temporarily suspended, the Government of national unity (which was again headed by Georgievski) was approved by the Sobranie on 13 May. NLA leaders stated that the rebel movement (which still held several villages) would continue hostilities until the Government agreed to enter into negotiations.

On 8 June 2001 Trajkovski announced proposals for a comprehensive peace plan, which provided for the proportional representation of ethnic Albanians at all levels of government, the increased official use of the Albanian language, and a partial amnesty for NLA combatants. Despite EU support for the plan, the NLA demanded that the Government end hostilities and enter into negotiations on constitutional reforms, and rebel forces seized the town of Aracinovo, some 6 km east of Skopje. Later in June the Government announced the suspension of its offensive against the NLA, following pressure from international envoys. However, violent protests were staged by Macedonian nationalists at the parliament building in Skopje, in response to the NATO-mediated cease-fire arrangement at Aracinovo, which was perceived to be lenient towards the ethnic Albanian rebels. On 29 June NATO formally approved an operation to deploy a 3,500-member multinational force in the FYRM to assist in the disarmament of the NLA, which was, however, conditional on the imposition of a lasting cease-fire. On 5 July the Government announced that an official cease-fire agreement had been signed by both sides, and negotiations resumed between leaders of the principal Macedonian and ethnic Albanian parties regarding a permanent peace settlement. However, Georgievski and his nationalist cabinet supporters strongly opposed proposals, detailed by the EU and US special envoys, for the extension of the use of the Albanian language, and accused them of bias towards the rebels. The cease-fire collapsed after 17 days, when the NLA launched further attacks on government forces deployed near Tetovo. (By that time some 60,000 ethnic Albanians had fled to Kosovo, while a further 30,000 had become internally displaced.) International diplomatic efforts subsequently intensified, following renewed fears of widespread civil conflict. On 26 July it was announced that an accord had been reached to restore the cease-fire between government forces and the ethnic Albanian rebels, who had agreed to withdraw from newly captured territory near Tetovo. At the end of July further negotiations on the peace proposals, between government and ethnic Albanian representatives, commenced at the western town of Ohrid. Progress in the discussions was reported, following the resolution of the two main issues of contention (the extension of the official use of the Albanian language and the right to proportional representation of the ethnic Albanian community in the security forces). In response to increasing pressure from the EU and the USA, the Government announced a unilateral cease-fire, and on 13 August the Government and ethnic Albanian leaders at Ohrid signed a framework peace agreement, providing for the amendment of the Constitution to grant greater rights to the ethnic Albanian community. On the following day the NLA leader, Ali Ahmeti, agreed that the NLA, numbering an estimated 2,500–3,000, would relinquish its armaments to NATO troops. Following an assessment of the security situation, NATO announced that the cease-fire was generally being observed, and on 22 August the activation order for a NATO mission, Operation Essential Harvest, was released. The force, which finally comprised 4,500 troops (of which the United Kingdom contributed about 1,900), had a mandate to disarm the ethnic Albanian combatants and destroy their weapons within 30 days of its deployment. The Ministry of Internal Affairs claimed the NLA to be in possession of some 85,000 armaments; however, NATO estimated the number of weapons to be collected at 3,000–4,000.

In early September 2001 parliamentary debate on constitutional reform was delayed by mass nationalist protests against the peace plan. Macedonian nationalist parties in the legislature continued to dispute the details of a number of the proposed amendments, while ethnic Albanian representatives insisted that attempts to limit the reforms would provoke renewed conflict. Meanwhile, investigators from the International Criminal Tribunal for the former Yugoslavia (ICTY, see p. 18) at the Hague, Netherlands, had been dispatched to the FYRM to conduct preliminary inquiries into the killing of six ethnic Albanian civilians in the village of Ljuboten in early August; the nationalist Minister of Internal Affairs, Ljube Boskovski, was suspected of responsibility for the operation. On 26 September NATO's 30-day disarmament programme was declared to have been successful, with the collection of some 3,875 armaments. On the same day the establishment of a further, reduced NATO mission, Operation Amber Fox, was authorized. (In response to international pressure, the Government had invited NATO to retain a military presence in the country, despite domestic opposition.) The new mission, comprising 700 troops, together with 300 forces already stationed in the FYRM, was deployed under German leadership, with a three-month renewable mandate to protect EU and OSCE monitors supervising the implementation of the peace agreement. On 27 September Ahmeti announced that the NLA had been formally dissolved, following the completion of the disarmament process. In early October the EU criticized delays in implementing constitutional reforms, after Macedonian parties announced that the legislative process would be suspended pending the release of 14 Macedonian civilians allegedly seized by the NLA earlier that year. Following pressure from Trajkovski, and the international community, which urged acceptance of the plan, discussion on the measures resumed in the Sobranie. Later that month Trajkovski approved plans for the deployment of ethnically-mixed security units in regions formerly held by the NLA.

On 16 November 2001 the Sobranie finally adopted 15 main amendments to the existing Constitution (although the extent of some provisions had been reduced at the insistence of the Macedonian parties). The principal reforms were: the revision of the Constitution's preamble to include a reference to members of non-ethnic Macedonian communities as citizens of the country; the introduction in the Sobranie of a 'double majority' system, whereby certain legislation would require the approval of a minority group; the establishment of Albanian as the second official language in communities where ethnic Albanians comprised more than 20% of the population; and the right to proportional representation for ethnic Albanians in the Constitutional Court, all areas of government administration and the security forces. The adoption of the reforms was received with approval by the international community. Later in November the SDAM and the LDP withdrew from the coalition Government (which was subsequently reorganized), on the grounds that their participation was no longer necessary.

In early December 2001 NATO extended the mandate of Operation Amber Fox until 26 March 2002, and it was subsequently extended until 26 June. An EU-sponsored international donor conference on economic assistance for the FYRM, originally scheduled to take place in October 2001, was further postponed in December, pending the implementation of additional reforms. In January 2002 new legislation providing for the devolution of greater authority to local government (thereby granting a measure of self-rule to predominantly ethnic Albanian regions) was approved by the Sobranie, and the donor conference duly took place in March. Also in January a Deputy Prime Minister, Dosta Dimovska (who was considered to be a moderate), resigned from the Government, following disagreement with Georgievski over issues relating to the deployment of security units in previously NLA-controlled villages. In February the three principal ethnic Albanian political parties (the DPA, the PDP and the NDP) and the former NLA leadership officially established a co-ordinating council. In March the

Sobranie adopted legislation granting immunity from prosecution to several thousand former NLA insurgents (excluding those indictable by the ICTY), in accordance with the peace settlement. In May the mandate of Operation Amber Fox was further extended, to 26 October. In accordance with the peace agreement, the Sobranie was dissolved on 18 July, prior to legislative elections, which were scheduled for 15 September and were to be monitored by the OSCE.

In May 2002 Ahmeti established a new political party, the Democratic Union for Integration (DUI), which was believed to comprise mainly former NLA combatants. Later that month two ministers belonging to the IMRO—TMRO resigned from the Government, on the grounds that former NLA members had become dominant within the principal ethnic Albanian parties. In the same month the Sobranie approved legislation whereby Albanian became an official language, in accordance with the Ohrid peace accord. At the end of August ethnic Albanians took hostage five Macedonian civilians at Gostivar; security forces surrounded an ethnic Albanian base and killed two of the kidnappers. None the less, the elections to the legislature took place peacefully on 15 September, attracting commendation from the international community, after OSCE observers declared them to have been conducted democratically. Georgievski's Government was removed from power by a 10-party alliance (led by the SDAM and the LDP), known as Together for Macedonia, which secured 60 of the 120 seats in the Sobranie. The IMRO—DPMNU won 33 seats and the DUI 16 seats. The Together for Macedonia alliance and the DUI subsequently signed an agreement for the establishment of a coalition Government (which was, however, to exclude former NLA combatants). The new administration, comprising members of the SDAM, the LDP and the DUI, and headed by Crvenkovski, was officially approved by the Sobranie on 1 November.

In October 2002 NATO agreed to extend the mandate of Operation Amber Fox until December. On 14 December Operation Amber Fox was succeeded by a 450-member mission, Allied Harmony, with a mandate to protect international monitors and advise FYRM security forces. On 31 March 2003 this contingent was, in turn, replaced by an EU-led mission, known as Operation Concordia, comprising 350 military personnel; 13 EU member states and 14 non-EU nations were to participate in the force. The purpose of the operation, which was deployed at the official request of Trajkovski, was to maintain security in order to facilitate the implementation of the Ohrid peace agreement. Meanwhile, in early 2003 a newly emerged ethnic Albanian extremist group, the Albanian National Army (ANA), threatened to launch a military offensive against the Government. In September, after ethnic Albanian militants clashed with a security patrol at the border with Kosovo, the authorities dispatched security forces to the region in an operation to suppress dissident activity (a measure that was criticized by the DUI).

In May 2003 Nikola Gruevski became the new leader of the IMRO—DPMNU. In November Ljupco Jordanovski of the SDAM was elected as the new President of the Sobranie, replacing Nikola Popovski, who had been appointed as Deputy Prime Minister and Minister of Finance. In December Operation Concordia was replaced by a 200-member EU mission, Operation Proxima, which, in addition to maintaining security and combating organized crime in the country, was to advise the FYRM police forces (the mandate of Operation Proxima expired in December 2005). In early 2004 the Government announced plans to redemarcate municipal boundaries, as part of a process of administrative decentralization included in the provisions of the Ohrid agreement, although there was widespread popular opposition to the proposals.

On 26 February 2004 President Trajkovski, together with eight government officials, was killed, when an aircraft transporting him to a international investment conference in Bosnia and Herzegovina crashed in a southern, mountainous region of that country. Jordanovski, as speaker of the Sobranie, assumed the presidency in an acting capacity, pending an election, which, under the terms of the Constitution, was to take place within 40 days. At the presidential election, held on 14 April, Crvenkovski, representing the SDAM, won 42.5% of the votes cast; since he failed to secure the 50% of the votes necessary to be elected outright, he progressed to a second round with Sasko Kedev, hitherto a parliamentary deputy and a member of the IMRO—DPMNU (who had won 34.1% of the votes). Two former NLA commanders, the DUI Secretary-General, Gzim Ostreni, and Zudi Xhelili of the DPA, also contested the election, obtaining 14.8% and 8.7% of the votes cast, respectively. On 28 April Crvenkovski was elected to the presidency with 62.7% of the votes. Kedev immediately claimed that widespread malpractice had been perpetrated and appealed against the election results, which were, however, described as legitimate by OSCE monitors. Crvenkovski was inaugurated on 12 May.

On 2 June 2004 the Sobranie approved the formation of a coalition administration, with Hari Kostov of the SDAM as Prime Minister, and comprising members of that party, the DUI and the LDP. The only new ministerial appointment was that of Siljan Avramovski as Minister of Internal Affairs, replacing Kostov. In July, after lengthy negotiations and under pressure from the international community, the parties of the governing coalition reached an agreement on the planned redemarcation of the country's municipal boundaries. The total number of administrative districts was to be reduced from 123 to 85, with the ethnic balance of 26 districts becoming predominantly Albanian, and the adoption of Albanian as a second official language in a number of these, including Skopje and Struga. The agreement prompted immediate strong public criticism. Protests in Struga escalated into violence; it was reported that 15 protesters and 24 members of the security forces had been injured. On 26 July a large demonstration was staged in Skopje, in protest at the draft agreement on decentralization, which had been submitted for approval to the Sobranie.

On 7 November 2004, following a petition presented by Macedonian nationalist parties, a referendum on the proposed redemarcation of administrative districts was conducted. However, the governing coalition, together with representatives of the international community, urged a boycott and voter participation in the referendum was estimated at only 26%, thereby invalidating the results and allowing the local government reforms to proceed. In mid-November Kostov tendered his resignation as Prime Minister, claiming that the DUI had obstructed the parliamentary approval of reforms essential to attract foreign investment and that the DUI Minister of Transport and Communications, in particular, had been involved in corrupt practices. Later that month Crvenkovski nominated Vlado Buckovski, hitherto the Minister of Defence, as Prime Minister, shortly after his election as Chairman of the SDAM. On 17 December the Sobranie approved a new Government, formed by Buckovski, who pledged his commitment to the implementation of economic reforms, and again comprising members of the SDAM, the LDP and the DUI. In mid-March 2005 the ICTY issued indictments against Boskovski and a former head of security, John Tarculovski, in connection with the August 2001 killings in Ljuboten. At the beginning of April Boskovski pleaded 'not guilty' to all charges before the Tribunal.

The first round of local government elections, which were to effect the significant devolution of powers to 85 municipal authorities (including the City of Skopje), took place, with some reported irregularities, on 13 March 2005. A second round of voting for 47 of the 85 municipalities was conducted on 27 March. After upholding claims of irregularities in the first round, the Supreme Court had ordered polls to be repeated in several constituencies, and an OSCE observer mission announced that the second round of the elections again failed to meet OSCE and Council of Europe standards in some municipalities. (Buckovski insisted, however, that irregularities had been recorded in only a small proportion of constituencies.) The DPA and the PDP, which had urged a boycott of the vote, refused to recognize the results. Supporters of the IMRO—DPMNU staged protests in Ohrid to demand that the second round be repeated in that municipality on grounds of malpractice. On 10 April further ballots were conducted in 19 municipalities and the City of Skopje, where electoral irregularities had occurred. According to official results, 36 of the mayoral contests were won by the Together for Macedonia governing coalition, and 15 by the DUI, with the IMRO—DPMNU securing 21 mayoralties. In mid-July, in accordance with the Ohrid Agreement, the Sobranie adopted legislation enabling any ethnic minority community to display its flag, together with the Macedonian flag, in regions where it constituted at least 50% of the population (in effect, in 19 municipalities, of which 16 were predominantly ethnic Albanian, two ethnic Turkish and one Roma).

In September 2005 the Government survived a motion of no confidence in the Sobranie, which had been proposed by opposition parties alleging economic mismanagement and demanding early elections. In December the Sobranie approved a series of constitutional amendments providing for extensive reform of the judicial system; the process of ensuring the complete independence of the judiciary, regarded as important to the country's application for EU membership (see below), was to be implemented over several years. In March 2006 the Sobranie adopted a series of amendments to electoral regulations, in preparation for legislative elections. In May the Sobranie abolished custodial sentences for those convicted on press offences.

In the legislative elections, held on 5 July 2006, the IMRO—DPMNU secured 32.5% of the votes cast, defeating Prime Minister Buckovski's SDAM, which obtained only 23.3% of the votes. A coalition of the DUI and the PDP secured the majority of ethnic Albanian votes, attracting 12.2% of the total ballot, while Xhaferi's DPA received 7.2% of the votes. Reported electoral irregularities caused the Supreme Court to demand that elections be repeated in eight constituencies, following which the IMRO—DPMNU's number of seats in the Sobranie was increased from 44 to 45. In August Gruevski, the Chairman of the IMRO—DPMNU, was formally appointed as Prime Minister and his Government was approved by the Sobranie a few days later. The new coalition administration comprised 10 members of the IMRO—DPMNU (including Trajko Slaveski as Minister of Finance and Antonio Milososki as Minister of Foreign Affairs), four of the DPA, three of the NSDP and one each of the LPM and of the SPM. Ljubiša Georgievski was appointed as President of the Sobranie. In his first address to the Sobranie as Prime Minister, Gruevski identified his Government's main priorities as intensifying efforts to combat corruption and improving living standards, the rate of employment and inter-ethnic relations.

In November 2006 the Sobranie adopted amendments to the FYRM's anti-corruption legislation, which included a widening of the range of activities that the Government was prohibited from engaging in during election campaigns. In early March 2007 a number of police officers and customs officials were arrested on suspicion of accepting bribes in a security operation, which met with extensive popular support. Later that month the Government announced the creation of a special agency that was to be charged with the management of confiscated illegal property in the hope of limiting the opportunities for corruption.

Meanwhile, in January 2007 the DUI and the PDP announced a boycott of parliamentary proceedings, in protest at their continued exclusion from Gruevski's Government. In February Ahmeti announced two preconditions to the resumption of political dialogue: a reconsideration by the Government of the composition of the Committee for Cross-Community Relations and a constitutional amendment to ensure fairer representation for ethnic minorities within future governments. In mid-March representatives of the ruling coalition and of the DUI convened to discuss the political impasse; however, the DUI insisted that it would not commit to a return to the Sobranie until concessions had been made.

In February 2007 the Sobranie approved a government reorganization, which included the appointment of Imer Aliu (hitherto Minister of the Environment and Physical Planning) to the position of Deputy Prime Minister, responsible for the implementation of the Ohrid Framework Agreement. In April Boskovski and Tarculovski became the first of those accused of war crimes during the 2001 insurgency to stand trial at the ICTY; the trial concluded in May 2008, and the court was expected to reach a verdict within three months.

At the end of May 2007 the PDP announced that its representatives were to resume participation in the Sobranie, after reaching an agreement with the IMRO—DPMNU permitting it to join the Government; members of the PDP received several state posts. The DUI also ended its boycott of the Sobranie, but criticized the PDP's admission to the Government. The return of the PDP and the DUI enabled the Sobranie to adopt, on 5 June, legislation providing for full co-operation with the ICTY by the Government. Two days later the Government survived a motion of no confidence proposed by the SDAM. In July DUI deputies withdrew from a parliamentary session, owing to their dissatisfaction that the regulation of use of minority languages was not under debate. In September the DUI again suspended participation in the Sobranie, following a violent disagreement between PDP and DUI deputies, prompted by criticism of the DUI by the PDP Chairman, Abduladi Vejseli. In December legislation amending the judicial system was approved, as part of the requirements for NATO accession.

In December 2007 Abduraman Memeti of the PDP announced his resignation as Minister of Local Self-Government. In January 2008 the Minister of the Economy, Vera Rafajlovska, also tendered her resignation, citing personal reasons, although the DPA had proposed a motion of no confidence over the controversial privatization of a power installation. (However, neither minister was replaced, pending a reorganization.) In March the DPA announced its withdrawal from the Government, in protest at the failure of the IMRO—DPMNU to recognize the independence of Kosovo (see below), and to provide increased rights for the use of the Albanian language and flag. Later that month, however, it was reported that the DPA had retracted its decision (with only Aliu expected to resign from his post), after reaching an agreement with the IMRO—DPMNU on inter-party co-operation to adopt legislation on the use of language, in accordance with the Constitution and the Ohrid Framework Agreement. Following the failure of negotiations with Greece on the issue of the country's official name, and Greece's consequent decision to veto NATO membership for the FYRM at a summit meeting of the Alliance held on 2 April (see below), the DUI proposed a motion for the dissolution of the Sobranie. The motion received the support of the IMRO—DPMNU, on the grounds that the existing legislature had obstructed reforms and, despite opposition from Crvenkovski, was approved on 12 April by 70 deputies in the Sobranie (with SDAM representatives boycotting the vote). Early legislative elections were scheduled for 1 June.

Both the September 1995 interim agreement with Greece and the November Dayton peace accord (for further details, see the chapter on Bosnia and Herzegovina) were of great significance for the FYRM, despite the unresolved issue of a permanent name for the country. The FYRM was admitted to the Council of Europe in late September, and to the OSCE in mid-October; in the following month the FYRM joined NATO's 'Partnership for Peace' programme (see p. 342). The agreement with Greece facilitated the establishment of full diplomatic relations with the EU from January 1996, and negotiations subsequently began for a co-operation accord; a declaration on co-operation was, furthermore, signed with the European Free Trade Association (see p. 412) in early April. By the end of 1996 more than 75 countries had recognized the FYRM, with about two-thirds using the country's constitutional name, the Republic of Macedonia. The FYRM Government signed a Stabilization and Association Agreement with the EU in April 2001, which came into effect on 1 April 2004. A formal application for membership of the EU was submitted on 22 March 2004 (having been postponed from February, following the death of President Trajkovski—see above). In November 2005 the European Commission recommended that the FYRM be granted the status of candidate country. The FYRM was officially declared to have candidate status at an EU summit meeting in Brussels, Belgium, in mid-December, prompting public celebrations in Skopje. However, this provided no guarantee of formal accession, although the holding of legislative elections in accordance with international standards in July 2006 did much to bolster Macedonian hopes of membership. The breakdown in political dialogue in early 2007 (see above) provoked considerable censure from, *inter alia*, the EU, NATO and the USA, which urged the FYRM Government more fully to implement reform measures announced in 2006. Prime Minister Gruevski assured the international community that his Government would accelerate the pace of reform. In October 2007 NATO member states adopted a resolution supporting the accession application of the FYRM (together with Albania and Croatia). The Government expressed confidence that an official invitation would be extended at a NATO summit meeting in Bucharest, Romania, on 2 April 2008; however, the unresolved dispute with Greece over the issue of the country's permanent name presented an obstacle, and despite intensified diplomatic efforts by the UN special envoy (see below), as a result of the continued impasse Greece vetoed the FYRM's application. NATO confirmed that the country had fulfilled other membership pre-requisites, and that an invitation would be extended upon the settlement of the issue.

In July 1995 the FYRM and Turkey signed a 20-year co-operation agreement and a mutual security accord. Turkey, together with Albania, Bulgaria and Italy, was involved (between February 1994 and October 1995) in providing trading routes to permit the FYRM to bypass the Greek blockade. None the less, the issue of ethnic Albanian rights in the FYRM was a frequent source of tension with Albania, and relations with Bulgaria continued to be impeded, specifically by the question of its recognition of a distinct Macedonian language and nationality.

Regular trade with Greece and the FRY resumed in late 1995, and discussions continued between FYRM, Greek and UN officials regarding the issue of a permanent name for the FYRM. By 1999 the FYRM's relations with Greece had improved significantly, and the principal border crossing between the

FYRM and Greece was reopened at the end of 2000. Meanwhile, work on the construction of a 214-km pipeline to transport petroleum from the FYRM's capital, Skopje, to Thessaloníki was officially completed in July 2002. Greece strongly opposed a decision by the USA, announced in November 2004, that it would henceforth recognize the FYRM by its constitutional name of 'Republic of Macedonia'; UN-mediated negotiations on the issue continued in 2005. In April the UN proposed the adoption of the name 'Republic of Macedonia-Skopje'; however, the compromise arrangement was rejected by both countries, although Greece indicated that it might provide a basis for further dialogue. The announcement in December 2006 that the international airport near Skopje was to be renamed after Alexander 'the Great' provoked renewed tension with Greece, which considers the historical figure part of its own cultural heritage; the Greek Minister of Foreign Affairs, Dora Bakoyannis, strongly criticized the decision. Discussions continued in Ohrid in January 2007, but again resulted in little progress; it was reported that the FYRM authorities were only prepared to accept a 'double formula', whereby 'Republic of Macedonia' would be used for international instances and a separate name adopted for bilateral communications with Greece. In January 2008 negotiations resumed between Greek and FYRM officials on a further proposal by the UN special envoy on the issue. In March the UN special envoy increased pressure on both Governments to reach a compromise resolution prior to a NATO conference in early April. Demonstrations against changing the country's constitutional name were staged in Skopje, and at the end of March the Greek ambassador formally protested to the Macedonian Government at the public display of posters depicting the Greek flag overprinted with a Nazi swastika. Following the FYRM's failure to receive an invitation to join NATO, owing to the continued impasse, the Government pledged to intensify efforts to resolve the dispute, and early legislative elections were subsequently scheduled for June (see above), in the hope that the efficacy of governance would be improved.

Although the FYRM formally supported the UN embargo on the FRY, there was frequent evidence that the FYRM Government permitted violations of the blockade. An agreement signed by the FYRM and the FRY in early April 1996, regulating bilateral relations and promoting mutual co-operation, was regarded as particularly significant in formalizing the FRY's recognition of the FYRM as a sovereign state, although it was criticized by most opposition groups within the FYRM. Meanwhile, the FYRM, Bosnia and Herzegovina, Croatia and Slovenia co-operated in efforts to secure international recognition for all the former republics as successor states to the SFRY, and thereby win access to a share of the assets of the former Yugoslavia. In September the FRY Prime Minister, Radoje Kontić, on his first official visit to the FYRM, signed several bilateral agreements. The Governments of the FYRM and Serbia and Montenegro (as the FRY was renamed in February 2003) increased bilateral co-operation in a number of areas, particularly measures to combat organized crime and promote regional stability.

In late 1992 the UN Security Council approved the deployment of members of the UN Protection Force (UNPROFOR) along the FYRM's border with the FRY and Albania, in an effort to protect the FYRM from any external threat to its security; in March 1995 the operation in the FYRM was renamed the UN Preventive Deployment Force (UNPREDEP). Following a reduction in UNPREDEP's authorized strength by the Security Council, the US contingent of military personnel was placed under direct US administration. In April 1997 the mandate of UNPREDEP was extended to the end of May, in view of the civil disorder in Albania (q.v.); it was further extended in June and December. Following the civil unrest in Albania, a number of border incursions by armed groups of Albanian rebels were reported. In October the Ministers of Defence of the FYRM and Albania signed an agreement providing for increased security along the joint border between the two countries.

In early 1998 increasing clashes were reported in Kosovo between members of the Serbian security forces and the ethnic Albanian KLA. In late July the UN Security Council extended the mandate of UNPREDEP until 28 February 1999 and agreed to increase the size of the contingent from 750 to about 1,100, with the aim of reinforcing border control. In early December 1998, following discussions between President Gligorov and NATO officials, it was announced that a NATO 'extraction force' was to be deployed in the FYRM to effect the evacuation of OSCE monitors in Kosovo in the event of large-scale conflict. In late February 1999 the People's Republic of China vetoed a UN Security Council resolution to extend the mandate of UNPREDEP for a further six months, following a decision by the FYRM Government to extend diplomatic recognition to Taiwan, which also prompted the People's Republic of China to suspend diplomatic relations with the FYRM. Following the commencement by NATO forces of an intensive aerial bombardment of strategic targets in the FRY in late March (see the chapter on Serbia), by early April some 140,000 refugees had fled to the FYRM. By mid-April about 14,000 NATO troops were deployed near the FYRM border with Kosovo, and were involved in assisting the refugees. Owing to concern over internal destabilization, the FYRM authorities repeatedly closed the border with Kosovo to prevent the continued arrival of large numbers of ethnic Albanians, and demanded that the international community fulfil pledges to accept a proportion of the refugees. By late May some 60,000 refugees had been transported from the FYRM for provisional resettlement abroad, while an estimated 250,000 remained in the country. In early June the strength of NATO forces stationed in the FYRM was increased to 16,000. Shortly afterwards the Yugoslav Government accepted a peace plan, which provided for the withdrawal of Serbian forces from Kosovo, the return of ethnic Albanian refugees and the deployment of a NATO-led Kosovo Force (KFOR). NATO troops, which were to be deployed under the KFOR mandate, entered Kosovo from the FYRM. On 20 June NATO announced that the air campaign had officially ended, and large numbers of ethnic Albanian refugees subsequently began to return to the province from the FYRM.

In June 2001 the FYRM and the People's Republic of China agreed to restore diplomatic relations, thereby ensuring Chinese support in the UN Security Council for the deployment of a NATO peace-keeping operation from August (following an ethnic Albanian insurgency—see above); Taiwan subsequently severed relations with the FYRM. In March 2004 the FYRM Minister of Foreign Affairs met the Head of the UN Interim Administration Mission in Kosovo (UNMIK) and NATO and US envoys for emergency discussions on Kosovo, following an outbreak of ethnic Albanian violence in the province, amid concern that the clashes would result in further destabilization in the FYRM. In March 2005 Prime Minister Buckovski urged a resolution on demarcation of the border between the FYRM and Kosovo (contested since a 2001 agreement between the Governments of the FYRM and Serbia and Montenegro, owing to the continued unresolved status of Kosovo). Prolonged negotiations between Kosovan Albanian and Serbian delegations on the final status of Kosovo, which commenced in early 2006, and subsequent deliberations in the UN Security Council failed to result in a resolution. Kosovo's declaration of independence, with the support of many EU member states and the USA, on 17 February 2008 (see the chapter on Kosovo) was celebrated by ethnic Albanians in Skopje. The FYRM Government reacted with caution to the declaration (while indicating that it would extend diplomatic recognition in the future) and requested that the new Kosovo authorities rapidly proceed with demarcation of the border between the two countries in order to avert regional instability. Although it was reported that some members of the Kosovo Government had insisted that recognition precede the beginning of work to resolve the issue, a joint border demarcation commission began operations in Skopje in March.

Government

According to the 1991 Constitution, which was amended in November 2001, legislative power is vested in the Sobranie (Assembly), with 120 members, elected for a four-year term by universal adult suffrage (85 in single-seat constituencies and 35 members by proportional representation). The President is directly elected for a five-year term, and appoints a Prime Minister to head the Government. The Ministers are elected by the Sobranie. For the purposes of local government, the FYRM is divided into 85 municipalities (including the City of Skopje).

Defence

As assessed at November 2007, the armed forces of the FYRM totalled 10,890 in active service: army 9,760 and air force 1,130. Paramilitary forces comprised a police force of 7,600. There was also a reserve force of 21,000. Conscription was officially abolished by the legislature in May 2006 (with effect from the beginning of 2007). On 31 March 2003 the North Atlantic Treaty Organization (NATO, see p. 340) contingent in the FYRM was replaced by a European Union (EU, see p. 244) mission, Operation Concordia, which was, in turn, replaced on 15 December by a 200-member EU police mission, Operation Proxima. The mandate of Operation Proxima, which had been renewed for one year, expired at the end of 2005. The EU subsequently provided support and assistance for the FYRM police force. The budget for 2007 allocated 7,020m. new denars to defence.

Economic Affairs

In 2006, according to World Bank estimates, the FYRM's gross national income (GNI), measured at average 2004–06 prices, was US $6,237m., equivalent to $3,060 per head (or $7,610 per head on an international purchasing-power parity basis). During 1996–2006, it was estimated, the population increased by an average of 0.3% per year, while gross domestic product (GDP) per head increased, in real terms, at an average annual rate of 2.0%. Overall GDP increased, in real terms, at an average annual rate of 2.3% in 1996–2006; real GDP increased by 3.7% in 2006.

Agriculture (including hunting, forestry and fishing) contributed 12.5% of GDP in 2006, and engaged 20.1% of the employed labour force. Dairy farming is significant, and the principal agricultural exports are tobacco, vegetables and fruit. The wine industry is of considerable importance, and the FYRM is also a producer of wheat, maize and barley. During 1996–2006, according to the World Bank, the GDP of the agricultural sector increased at an average annual rate of 0.6%; real agricultural GDP increased by 0.6% in 2006.

Industry contributed 29.2% of GDP in 2006, when it engaged 32.6% of the employed labour force. During 1996–2006, according to the World Bank, the GDP of the industrial sector increased, in real terms, at an average annual rate of 3.4%; real industrial GDP increased by 2.8% in 2006.

Mining contributed 0.6% of GDP and engaged 0.7% of the employed labour force in 2006. The only major mining activity is the production of lignite (brown coal), although there are also deposits of iron, zinc, lead, copper, chromium, manganese, antimony, silver, gold and nickel. Production in the mining and quarrying sector increased at an average annual rate of 5.9% in 1996–2000.

The manufacturing sector contributed an estimated 18.4% of GDP and engaged 21.5% of the employed labour force in 2006. The GDP of the manufacturing sector increased, in real terms, at an average annual rate of 1.1% in 1996–2006; real manufacturing GDP increased by 2.1% in 2006.

Energy is derived principally from coal and lignite, which provided 77.6% of the electricity generated in 2004. Hydroelectric sources accounted for another 22.2% of production. The first stage of a pipeline from the Bulgarian border to carry natural gas to the FYRM from Russia became operational in 1995. A 214-km pipeline to transport petroleum from the Greek port of Thessaloníki to Skopje was inaugurated in July 2002. Mineral fuels accounted for 18.7% of the value of total imports in 2007, according to preliminary data.

Services accounted for 58.3% of GDP in 2006, when the sector engaged 47.3% of the employed labour force. Regional instability, notably ethnic hostilities in the north of the FYRM in 2001, had an adverse impact on tourist activity, although tourist receipts increased thereafter. During 1996–2006, according to the World Bank, the GDP of the services sector increased, in real terms, at an average annual rate of 1.9%; services GDP increased by 3.7% in 2006.

In 2006 the FYRM recorded a visible trade deficit of US $1,263.1m., and there was a deficit of $23.7m. on the current account of the balance of payments. In 2007 the principal source of imports was Russia (accounting for an estimated 12.3% of total imports); other major sources were Germany, the former Serbia and Montenegro, Greece, Italy and Bulgaria. The principal markets for exports in that year were Montenegro and Serbia (taking a combined total of 19.1% of all exports, according to provisional data); other important purchasers were Germany, Greece, Italy, Bulgaria and Spain. The principal exports in 2007 were basic manufactures, miscellaneous manufactured articles, food and live animals, beverages and tobacco, and inedible crude materials. The main imports in that year were basic manufactures, machinery and transport equipment, mineral fuels and lubricants (notably petroleum and petroleum products), chemical products, food and live animals, miscellaneous manufactured articles, and inedible crude materials.

The FYRM recorded an overall budgetary deficit of 3,497m. new denars in 2007. At the end of 2005 the FYRM's external debt totalled US $2,243m., of which $1,613m. was long-term public debt. In that year the cost of debt-servicing was equivalent to 8.6% of the value of exports of goods and services. The annual rate of inflation averaged 1.9% in 1996–2006. Consumer prices increased by 3.2% in 2006. The rate of unemployment was 36.0% in 2006.

The FYRM is a member of the European Bank for Reconstruction and Development (EBRD, see p. 239). It became a member of the World Trade Organization (WTO, see p. 396) in 2003. The FYRM joined the Central European Free Trade Association (CEFTA) in February 2006.

The FYRM's economic prospects were significantly improved by the removal, in late 1995, of a Greek embargo on trade with the FYRM (see Recent History) and UN sanctions against the FRY, which had severely disrupted the FYRM's trading links. A subsequent improvement in relations between Greece and the FYRM allowed substantial Greek investment. A Stabilization and Association Agreement was signed with the European Union (EU, see p. 244) in April 2001. However, ethnic hostilities in the north of the country in early 2001 caused a substantial deterioration of the fiscal position. A peace agreement was negotiated in August, and in March 2002 a donor aid conference, sponsored by the EU and the World Bank, resulted in considerable pledges to support reconstruction. In September the Government, which had been widely regarded as responsible for mismanagement and corruption, was replaced. A new stand-by credit agreement with the IMF was signed in early 2003. In March 2004 the FYRM submitted a formal application for membership of the EU. A new Government, established in December, appeared to make some progress in attracting major investment projects (regarded as essential in addressing the critically high rate of unemployment). In August 2005 the IMF approved a further three-year stand-by arrangement to finance the Government's economic programme. In December the EU formally granted the FYRM candidate status. Legislative elections were conducted in accordance with international standards in July 2006. In early 2008 the IMF commended the strong economic growth (particularly in the industrial sector) and increased levels of investment achieved during 2007. With the aim of improving further the FYRM's investment grade, the 2008 budget reduced the corporate tax rate from 15% to 10%. The Government also removed the minimum capital requirement previously applied to new enterprises. A budgetary deficit of 1.5% and real GDP growth of 6.0% were targeted for 2008. Improved fiscal discipline enabled the Government to increase pensions by an average of 15% in early 2008. Despite government measures to contain inflation, further sharp price rises in April prompted concern. As a result of the unresolved dispute with Greece over the country's permanent name, the FYRM failed to receive an invitation to join NATO in early April (see Recent History) and, despite progress made in reforms, the issue was expected to obstruct the country's EU accession aspirations until its settlement. Early legislative elections were subsequently scheduled for the beginning of June (with a likely negative impact on the economy), in an attempt to improve the efficacy of governance.

Education

Elementary education is provided free of charge, and is officially compulsory for all children between the ages of seven and 15 years. Various types of secondary education, beginning at 15 years of age and lasting for four years, are available to those who qualify. In 2003/04 enrolment in primary education included 92.8% of children in the relevant age-group, while the comparable ratio for secondary education was 80.7%. The Constitution guarantees nationals the right to elementary and secondary education in their mother tongue. In 2001/02 Albanian was the language of education in 275 primary schools and 24 secondary schools, Turkish in 55 primary schools and five secondary schools, and Serbian in 13 primary schools. In 2003/04 some 46,637 students were enrolled at the universities at Skopje and at Bitola. In July 2000 new legislation permitted the use of Albanian and other languages in private tertiary institutions, and an Albanian-language university (the South-East Europe University) at Tetovo opened as a private institution, with funding from the international community, in November 2001. In 2004, under further amendments to legislation on higher education, the Albanian-language Tetovo University (previously declared illegal) became the third state-funded university. Expenditure on education by the central Government in 2002 was budgeted at 7,591m. denars (11.4% of total expenditure).

Public Holidays

2008: 1 January (New Year), 6–7 January (Orthodox Christmas), 14–15 January (Orthodox New Year), 8 March (International Women's Day), 27–28 April (Orthodox Easter), 1 May

THE FORMER YUGOSLAV REPUBLIC OF MACEDONIA

(Labour Day), 24 May (Day of the Apostles SS Methodius), 2 August (National Day), 8 September (Independence Day), 1 October* (Small Bayram, end of Ramadan), 11 October (Anti-Fascism Day), 8 December* (Great Bayram, Feast of the Sacrifice).

2009: 1 January (New Year), 6–7 January (Orthodox Christmas), 14–15 January (Orthodox New Year), 8 March (International Women's Day), 19–20 April (Orthodox Easter), 1 May (Labour Day), 24 May (Day of the Apostles SS Cyril and Methodius), 2 August (National Day), 8 September (Independence Day), 20 September* (Small Bayram, end of Ramadan), 11 October (Anti-Fascism Day), 27 November* (Great Bayram, Feast of the Sacrifice).

* These holidays are dependent on the Islamic lunar calendar and may vary by one or two days from the dates given.

Weights and Measures
The metric system is in force.

Statistical Survey

Source (unless otherwise indicated): State Statistical Office of the Republic of Macedonia, 91000 Skopje, Dame Gruev 4, POB 506; tel. (2) 114904; fax (2) 111336; e-mail info@stat.gov.mk; internet www.stat.gov.mk.

Area and Population

AREA, POPULATION AND DENSITY

Area (sq km)	25,713*
Population (census results)†	
20 June 1994	1,945,932
31 October 2002	
Males	1,015,377
Females	1,007,170
Total	2,022,547
Population (official estimates at mid-year)	
2004	2,032,000
2005	2,037,000
2006	2,041,000
Density (per sq km) at mid-2006	79.4

* 9,928 sq miles.
† Comprising persons with an official place of residence in the country (including those temporarily abroad for less than a year), persons from other countries who have been granted a residence permit in the FYRM and have been present there for at least a year and foreigners with refugee status; excluding foreign diplomatic and military personnel.

PRINCIPAL ETHNIC GROUPS
(census of 31 October 2002)

	Number	%
Macedonian	1,297,981	64.2
Albanian	509,083	25.2
Turkish	77,959	3.9
Roma (Gypsy)	53,879	2.7
Serb	35,939	1.8
Muslim	17,018	0.8
Vlach	9,695	0.5
Others	21,193	1.0
Total	**2,022,547**	**100.0**

PRINCIPAL TOWNS
(official estimates, 2004)*

Skopje (capital)	515,419	Prilep	76,768
Kumanovo	105,484	Struga	63,376
Bitola	95,385	Ohrid	55,749
Tetovo	86,580	Velec	55,108
Gostivar	81,042	Strumica	54,676

* Population by municipality, except for Skopje, which comprises 10 municipalities.

Source: Ministry of Local Self-Government, Skopje.

BIRTHS, MARRIAGES AND DEATHS

	Registered live births		Registered marriages		Registered deaths	
	Number	Rate (per 1,000)	Number	Rate (per 1,000)	Number	Rate (per 1,000)
1999	27,309	13.5	14,172	7.0	16,789	8.3
2000	29,308	14.5	14,255	7.0	17,253	8.5
2001	27,010	13.3	13,267	6.5	16,919	8.3
2002	27,761	13.7	14,522	7.2	17,962	8.9
2003	27,011	13.3	14,402	7.1	18,006	8.9
2004	26,883	13.2	14,073	6.9	18,265	9.0
2005	22,697	11.1	14,500	7.1	18,406	9.0
2006	22,786	11.2	14,908	7.3	18,630	9.1

Expectation of life (years at birth, WHO estimates): 73.4 (males 70.8; females 76.1) in 2005 (Source: WHO, *World Health Statistics*).

ECONOMICALLY ACTIVE POPULATION
(sample surveys, '000 persons aged 15 years and over)

	2004	2005	2006
Agriculture, hunting and forestry	87.6	106.2	114.5
Fishing	0.4	0.4	0.3
Mining and quarrying	2.8	3.6	3.9
Manufacturing	116.3	120.0	123.1
Electricity, gas and water	15.8	17.0	16.0
Construction	36.5	35.2	43.2
Wholesale and retail trade, repair of motor vehicles, motorcycles and articles for personal use and for households	74.2	74.7	73.0
Hotels and restaurants	12.7	13.6	19.0
Transport, storage and communications	30.8	32.7	30.0
Financial intermediation	7.7	6.3	7.1
Real estate, renting and business activities	13.5	14.8	15.4
Public administration and defence, compulsory social security	39.7	38.3	39.3
Education	33.6	31.7	33.4
Health and social work	29.9	31.3	32.6
Other community, social and personal services	19.7	18.2	18.3
Private households with employed persons	0.2	0.4	0.5
Extra-territorial organizations and bodies	1.6	0.9	1.0
Total employed	**523.0**	**545.3**	**570.4**
Unemployed	309.3	323.9	321.3
Total labour force	**832.3**	**869.2**	**891.7**
Males	506.9	523.3	543.8
Females	325.4	345.9	347.8

Source: ILO.

THE FORMER YUGOSLAV REPUBLIC OF MACEDONIA

Health and Welfare

KEY INDICATORS

Total fertility rate (children per woman, 2005)	1.5
Under-5 mortality rate (per 1,000 live births, 2005)	17
HIV/AIDS (% of persons aged 15–49, 2005)	<0.1
Physicians (per 1,000 head, 2001)	2.19
Hospital beds (per 1,000 head, 2005)	4.7
Health expenditure (2004): US $ per head (PPP)	471.2
Health expenditure (2004): % of GDP	8.0
Health expenditure (2004): public (% of total)	71.0
Human Development Index (2005): ranking	69
Human Development Index (2005): value	0.801

For sources and definitions, see explanatory note on p. vi.

Agriculture

PRINCIPAL CROPS
('000 metric tons)

	2004	2005	2006
Wheat	356.8	333.9	287.5
Rice (paddy)	14.7	12.6	12.4*
Barley	150.0	136.9	135.2
Maize	146.1	148.2	147.3
Rye	10.3	9.5	8.8
Potatoes	199.0	186.7	186.7*
Sugar beet	52.2	57.8	63.0*
Dry beans	14.6	6.3	7.5*
Olives*	12.5	10.9	10.9
Cabbages	68.3	66.5	66.5*
Tomatoes	116.8	116.6	116.6*
Cucumbers and gherkins	35.7	36.2	36.2*
Chillies and green peppers*	116.1	119.1	119.1
Dry onions	34.2	38.5	38.5*
Green beans*	13.8	13.8	13.8
Watermelons	125.4	132.9	132.9*
Apples	82.4	86.2	86.2*
Peaches and nectarines	11.6	11.0	11.0*
Plums	26.0	25.3	25.3*
Grapes	247.7	265.7	265.7*
Tobacco (leaves)	21.1	27.7	27.7*

* FAO estimate(s).

Aggregate production ('000 metric tons, may include official, semi-official or estimated data): Total cereals 682.0 in 2004, 644.6 in 2005, 595.1 in 2006; Total roots and tubers 199.0 in 2004, 186.7 in 2005, 186.7 in 2006; Total vegetables (incl. melons) 528.3 in 2004, 542.0 in 2005, 541.9 in 2006; Total fruits (excl. melons) 395.4 in 2004, 415.4 in 2005, 415.4 in 2006.

Source: FAO.

LIVESTOCK
('000 head, year ending September)

	2003	2004	2005
Horses*	57	57	57
Cattle	260	255	248
Pigs	179	158	156
Sheep	1,239	1,432	1,244
Chickens	2,417	2,725	2,617

* FAO estimates.

2006: Figures assumed unchanged from 2005 (FAO estimates).
Source: FAO.

Statistical Survey

LIVESTOCK PRODUCTS
('000 metric tons)

	2003	2004	2005
Cattle meat	8.7	8.8	7.6
Sheep meat	5.9	7.0	6.9
Pig meat	9.6	9.4	8.9
Chicken meat	4.1	3.2	3.8
Cows' milk	191.5	212.9	197.5
Sheep's milk	52.5	47.9	48.7
Hen eggs	15.5	18.7	19.0*
Honey	1.0	0.9	1.0*
Wool: greasy	2.0	3.2	1.8

* FAO estimate.

2006: Figures assumed to be unchanged from 2005 (FAO estimates).
Source: FAO.

Forestry

ROUNDWOOD REMOVALS
('000 cubic metres, excl. bark)

	2004	2005	2006
Sawlogs, veneer logs and logs for sleepers	126	144	140
Other industrial wood	10	14	22
Fuel wood	705	664	740
Total	841	822	902

Source: FAO.

SAWNWOOD PRODUCTION
('000 cubic metres, incl. railway sleepers)

	2004	2005	2006
Coniferous (softwood)	8	5	4
Broadleaved (hardwood)	20	13	13
Total	28	18	17

Source: FAO.

Fishing

(metric tons, live weight)

	2003	2004	2005
Capture	162	213	246
Trouts	130	125	142
Aquaculture	910	959	868
Common carp	174	248	187
Other freshwater fishes	18	n.a.	214
Trouts	672	711	442
Huchen	46	n.a.	n.a.
Total catch	1,072	1,172	1,114

Source: FAO.

THE FORMER YUGOSLAV REPUBLIC OF MACEDONIA

Mining

('000 metric tons, unless otherwise indicated)

	2003	2004	2005
Lignite	8,360	8,500	8,200
Copper concentrates*	3	n.a.	5
Gold (kilograms)	400	n.a.	700
Gyps	20	20	20

* Figures refer to the metal content of concentrates.
Silver: 10,000 kg in 2003.
Source: US Geological Survey.

Industry

SELECTED PRODUCTS
('000 metric tons, unless otherwise indicated)

	2002	2003	2004
Flour	114	98	95
Refined sugar	37	33	n.a.
Wine ('000 hectolitres)	254	873	n.a.
Beer ('000 hectolitres)	657	680	716
Soft drinks ('000 hectolitres)	1,021	1,149	1,094
Cigars (million)	6,567	5,162	n.a.
Footwear, excl. rubber ('000 pairs)	1,654	1,586	n.a.
Sulphuric acid	95	45	n.a.
Motor spirit (petrol)	78	126	146
Naphthas	97	160	183
Gas-diesel (distillate fuel) oil	172	322	359
Residual fuel oils	254	343	282
Cement	777	832	812
Ferro-alloys*	77	65	70
Crude steel*	244.6	291.4	315.0
Lead: refined*	19.8	8.0	n.a.
Zinc: refined*	38.0	15.1	n.a.
Electric energy (million kWh)	6,090	6,737	6,665

* Data from US Geological Survey.

Source (unless otherwise indicated): UN, *Industrial Commodity Statistics Yearbook*.

Finance

CURRENCY AND EXCHANGE RATES

Monetary Units
100 deni = 1 new Macedonian denar.

Sterling, Dollar and Euro Equivalents (31 December 2007)
£1 sterling = 83.455 new denars;
US $1 = 41.656 new denars;
€1 = 61.322 new denars;
1,000 new denars = £11.98 = $24.01 = €16.31.

Average Exchange Rate (new denars per US $)
2005   49.284
2006   48.802
2007   44.730

Note: The Macedonian denar was introduced in April 1992, replacing (initially at par) the Yugoslav dinar. In May 1993 a new Macedonian denar, equivalent to 100 of the former units, was established as the sole legal tender.

BUDGET
(million new denars)*

Revenue	2005	2006	2007
Tax revenue	54,018	58,688	66,734
Personal income tax	8,231	8,256	8,320
Profit tax	2,571	4,423	5,721
Value-added tax	26,325	27,374	31,841
Excises	11,457	11,652	13,200
Import duties	4,867	5,483	5,652
Special revenue accounts tax	256	240	211
Social contributions	29,573	30,579	31,325
Pension insurance	18,996	19,933	20,878
Unemployment contributions	1,320	1,370	1,390
Health insurance	9,257	9,276	9,057
Non-tax revenue	16,555	15,994	15,445
Capital revenue	630	700	564
Foreign donations	4,236	2,430	1,819
Repayment of loans	1	400	20
Total	105,269	109,031	116,118

Expenditure	2005	2006	2007
Current expenditure	92,742	99,555	105,307
Wage, salaries and allowances	23,177	23,860	24,335
Other purchases of goods and services	14,253	14,392	17,166
Transfers	52,553	57,541	61,053
Pensions	25,296	26,884	28,532
Unemployment benefits	3,048	2,152	1,748
Social benefits	4,141	4,280	4,152
Health care	15,142	16,087	16,032
Interest payments	2,659	3,362	2,753
Guarantees	—	400	—
Capital expenditure	14,757	11,914	14,306
Total	107,499	111,469	119,615

* Figures refer to the consolidated accounts of the general Government, comprising the transactions of the central Government and the operations of extrabudgetary funds.

Source: Ministry of Finance, Skopje.

INTERNATIONAL RESERVES
(US $ million at 31 December)

	2004	2005	2006
Gold (national valuation)	86.5	112.0	138.8
IMF special drawing rights	0.8	0.8	3.0
Foreign exchange	904.2	1,227.7	1,747.6
Total	991.5	1,340.5	1,889.4

Source: IMF, *International Financial Statistics*.

MONEY SUPPLY
(million new denars at 31 December)

	2004	2005	2006
Currency outside banks	14,162	14,439	16,206
Demand deposits at deposit money banks	13,154	15,206	18,504
Total (incl. others)	28,884	31,219	36,591

Source: IMF, *International Financial Statistics*.

COST OF LIVING
(Consumer Price Index; base: 2000 = 100)

	2004	2005	2006
Food	104.0	102.7	105.0
Fuel and light	112.8	114.0	118.2
Clothing (incl. footwear)	111.6	114.0	114.2
Housing	120.0	120.4	119.5
All items (incl. others)	108.2	108.8	112.3

Source: ILO.

THE FORMER YUGOSLAV REPUBLIC OF MACEDONIA

Statistical Survey

NATIONAL ACCOUNTS
(million new denars at current prices)

National Income and Product

Expenditure on the Gross Domestic Product

	2004	2005	2006
Government final consumption expenditure	53,133	53,990	57,559
Private final consumption expenditure	209,075	222,726	242,005
Changes in inventories	9,430	10,481	10,763
Gross fixed capital formation	47,286	48,868	56,485
Total domestic expenditure	318,924	336,065	366,812
Exports of goods and services	106,758	128,137	149,669
Less Imports of goods and services	160,425	177,582	207,709
GDP in purchasers' values	265,257	286,619	308,772
GDP at constant 1995 prices	202,192	210,486	218,375

Gross Domestic Product by Economic Activity

	2004	2005	2006
Agriculture, hunting and forestry	30,073	31,018	33,939
Fishing	21	28	47
Mining and quarrying	1,042	1,415	1,593
Manufacturing	39,663	44,517	50,065
Electricity, gas and water supply	11,080	10,164	10,323
Construction	14,736	15,954	17,506
Wholesale and retail trade	36,000	39,022	40,631
Hotels and restaurants	4,172	4,280	4,429
Transport and communications	20,642	23,763	26,494
Financial services	7,510	8,299	10,940
Real estate and business services*	24,515	23,618	25,339
Public administration and defence	17,874	20,760	21,141
Education	9,913	10,253	10,820
Health care and social work	9,650	9,675	11,516
Other community, social and personal services	5,984	6,186	7,059
Sub-total	232,876	248,952	271,842
Less Imputed bank service charge	4,720	5,933	6,805
Gross value added at basic prices	228,156	243,019	265,037
Value-added tax	31,290	38,688	39,318
Import duties	5,815	5,398	5,423
Less Subsidies on products	4	486	1,006
GDP in purchasers' values	265,257	286,619	308,772

*Including imputed rents of owner-occupied dwellings.

BALANCE OF PAYMENTS
(US $ million)

	2004	2005	2006
Exports of goods f.o.b.	1,672.4	2,039.6	2,396.3
Imports of goods f.o.b.	−2,784.5	−3,097.1	−3,681.5
Trade balance	−1,112.1	−1,057.5	−1,285.2
Exports of services	407.9	471.6	601.3
Imports of services	−462.3	−505.3	−576.1
Balance on goods and services	−1,166.4	−1,091.2	−1,260.0
Other income received	84.6	97.6	134.9
Other income paid	−123.8	−152.7	−138.0
Balance on goods, services and income	−1,205.7	−1,146.2	−1,263.1
Current transfers received	836.9	1,109.5	1,282.8
Current transfers paid	−46.0	−44.7	−43.4
Current balance	−414.8	−81.4	−23.7
Capital account (net)	−4.6	−2.0	−1.1
Direct investment abroad	−1.2	−2.8	−0.2
Direct investment from abroad	157.0	99.8	350.5
Portfolio investment assets	−0.9	0.8	−0.5
Portfolio investment liabilities	14.7	235.0	83.3
Other investment assets	6.8	−89.2	−150.5
Other investment liabilities	263.4	263.1	117.8
Net errors and omissions	7.7	−12.9	9.7
Overall balance	28.0	410.6	385.3

Source: IMF, *International Financial Statistics*.

External Trade

PRINCIPAL COMMODITIES
(distribution by SITC, US $ million)

Imports c.i.f.	2002	2003	2004
Food and live animals	246.5	270.6	337.1
Meat and meat preparations	70.9	70.2	86.5
Mineral fuels, lubricants, etc.	263.2	322.0	377.3
Petroleum, petroleum products, etc.	205.7	257.9	295.9
Crude petroleum and bituminous oils	96.2	192.0	220.3
Refined petroleum products	100.5	55.1	59.6
Chemicals and related products	211.7	254.7	303.7
Basic manufactures	264.8	332.8	696.1
Iron and steel	44.6	75.8	298.6
Machinery and transport equipment	408.0	433.4	545.7
Telecommunications, sound recording and reproducing equipment	50.6	89.4	73.7
Electrical machinery, apparatus, etc. (excl. telecommunications and sound equipment)	70.9	75.9	81.6
Road vehicles and parts*	130.9	101.9	184.1
Passenger motor vehicles (excl. buses)	91.3	59.2	129.8
Miscellaneous manufactured articles	113.3	128.5	171.3
Total (incl. others)	1,995.1	2,299.9	2,903.4

*Data on parts exclude tyres, engines and electrical parts.

Source: UN, *International Trade Statistics Yearbook*.

2005 (US $ million): Food and live animals 343.1; Crude materials (inedible) except fuels 106.7; Mineral fuels, lubricants, etc. 618.4; Chemicals and related products 333.9; Basic manufactures 947.6; Machinery and transport equipment 563.0; Miscellaneous manufactured articles 252.0; Total (incl. others) 3,228.0.

2006 (US $ million, preliminary): Food and live animals 369.0; Crude materials (inedible) except fuels 133.6; Mineral fuels, lubricants, etc. 760.1; Chemicals and related products 365.3; Basic manufactures 1,118.8; Machinery and transport equipment 688.6; Miscellaneous manufactured articles 260.9; Total (incl. others) 3,762.7.

2007 (US $ million, preliminary): Food and live animals 513.9; Crude materials (inedible) except fuels 293.5; Mineral fuels, lubricants, etc. 979.5; Chemicals and related products 482.8; Basic manufactures 1,483.1; Machinery and transport equipment 1,030.8; Miscellaneous manufactured articles 354.5; Total (incl. others) 5,227.6.

Exports f.o.b.	2002	2003	2004
Food and live animals	74.7	91.1	125.6
Vegetables and fruit	36.0	42.4	63.4
Beverages and tobacco	124.9	136.7	127.8
Beverages	48.7	55.4	54.9
Tobacco and tobacco manufactures	76.2	81.3	72.8
Crude materials (inedible) except fuels	35.4	39.9	47.7
Mineral fuels, lubricants, etc.	25.1	73.8	78.3
Refined petroleum products	22.5	68.6	70.4
Chemicals and related products	69.3	70.2	79.6
Basic manufactures	316.2	397.2	542.7
Textile yarn, fabrics, etc.	35.8	42.4	52.6
Iron and steel	156.1	250.5	401.8
Ferro-alloys	32.6	74.9	116.3
Sheets and plates	72.3	113.1	169.1
Non-ferrous metals	62.0	40.7	7.2
Zinc	40.1	20.4	0.7

THE FORMER YUGOSLAV REPUBLIC OF MACEDONIA

Statistical Survey

Exports f.o.b.—*continued*	2002	2003	2004
Machinery and transport equipment	74.5	80.6	98.8
Electrical machinery, apparatus, etc. (excl. telecommunications and sound equipment)	42.0	44.4	49.4
Miscellaneous manufactured articles	388.9	470.3	568.7
Clothing and accessories (excl. footwear)	334.1	409.3	488.3
Total (incl. others)	1,115.5	1,363.2	1,673.5

Source: UN, *International Trade Statistics Yearbook*.

2005 (US $ million): Food and live animals 167.2; Beverages and tobacco 163.1; Crude materials (inedible) except fuels 67.8; Mineral fuels, lubricants, etc. 163.6; Chemicals and related products 90.7; Basic manufactures 682.5; Machinery and transport equipment 109.9; Miscellaneous manufactured articles 589.9; Total (incl. others) 2,041.3.

2006 (US $ million, preliminary): Food and live animals 191.1; Beverages and tobacco 192.0; Crude materials (inedible) except fuels 111.8; Mineral fuels, lubricants, etc. 225.1; Chemicals and related products 100.5; Basic manufactures 852.6; Machinery and transport equipment 117.9; Miscellaneous manufactured articles 604.1; Total (incl. others) 2,400.7.

2007 (US $ million, preliminary): Food and live animals 248.1; Beverages and tobacco 207.3; Crude materials (inedible) except fuels 170.1; Mineral fuels, lubricants, etc. 165.1; Chemicals and related products 132.2; Basic manufactures 1,502.7; Machinery and transport equipment 149.8; Miscellaneous manufactured articles 776.5; Total (incl. others) 3,356.2.

PRINCIPAL TRADING PARTNERS
(US $ million)

Imports c.i.f.	2005	2006	2007*
Austria	69.2	80.6	101.4
Bulgaria	234.3	250.2	267.1
China, People's Republic	115.0	139.4	242.7
Croatia	75.2	79.0	109.7
France	61.0	66.3	n.a.
Germany	334.9	369.3	525.3
Greece	296.8	319.9	413.3
Italy	193.7	226.9	303.5
Netherlands	53.2	59.8	73.9
Poland	94.6	117.7	162.4
Romania	64.9	91.9	n.a.
Russia	424.5	569.6	643.3
Serbia and Montenegro	264.2	282.9	448.4
Slovenia	128.0	129.4	154.5
Spain	32.3	51.7	50.8
Switzerland-Liechtenstein	63.7	59.3	49.9
Turkey	113.6	123.9	194.8
Ukraine	72.0	105.6	n.a.
United Kingdom	44.0	37.2	49.9
USA	45.2	41.0	77.9
Total (incl. others)	3,228.0	3,762.7	5,227.6

Exports f.o.b.	2005	2006	2007*
Bosnia and Herzegovina	50.5	64.7	88.0
British Virgin Islands	83.6	n.a.	n.a.
Bulgaria	76.1	130.1	242.5
Croatia	81.1	124.2	163.9
France	19.9	10.3	n.a.
Germany	364.0	375.5	484.0
Greece	312.9	361.2	420.4
Italy	169.6	236.8	346.8
Netherlands	44.6	55.4	71.8
Russia	21.4	25.5	23.6
Serbia and Montenegro	459.5	55.8	639.4
Slovenia	31.8	41.2	68.7
Spain	50.4	50.4	173.0
Turkey	46.3	55.2	53.2
United Kingdom	42.9	36.5	75.1
USA	44.3	22.4	51.6
Total (incl. others)	2,041.3	2,400.7	3,356.2

* Preliminary.

Transport

RAILWAYS
(traffic)

	2005	2006	2007
Passenger journeys ('000)	903	962	1,102
Passenger-km (million)	94	101	109
Freight carried ('000 metric tons)	3,129	3,797	4,686
Freight ton-km (million)	531	614	778

ROAD TRAFFIC
(motor vehicles in use at 31 December)

	2000	2001	2002
Motorcycles	3,729	4,483	2,918
Passenger cars	299,588	309,562	307,581
Buses	2,498	2,620	2,497
Commercial vehicles	20,763	21,727	20,213
Special vehicles	8,552	9,554	10,292
Tractors and working vehicles	1,417	1,560	918

INLAND WATERS
(lake transport)

	2000	2001	2002
Passengers carried ('000)	10	3	6
Passenger-km ('000)	321	117	389

CIVIL AVIATION
(traffic on scheduled services)

	2001	2002	2003
Kilometres flown (million)	5	3	3
Passengers carried ('000)	315	166	201
Passenger-kilometres (million)	377	236	280
Total ton-kilometres (million)	36	21	25

Source: UN, *Statistical Yearbook*.

Tourism

TOURISTS BY COUNTRY OF ORIGIN*

	2003	2004	2005
Albania	11,338	12,470	15,392
Austria	2,511	2,433	2,604
Bosnia and Herzegovina	2,450	3,118	3,546
Bulgaria	12,375	11,110	15,894
Croatia	4,754	5,767	6,770
France	3,429	2,785	2,881
Germany	6,159	6,337	6,762
Greece	26,514	28,661	31,504
Hungary	2,171	1,270	1,554
Italy	3,558	3,537	4,160
Netherlands	2,380	2,524	3,995
Serbia and Montenegro	24,190	27,141	33,212
Slovenia	4,094	4,848	6,754
Turkey	5,498	6,010	6,795
United Kingdom	4,462	3,988	4,976
USA	7,286	7,531	7,353
Total (incl. others)	148,508	153,644	181,484

* Figures refer to arrivals from abroad at all accommodation establishments.

Tourism receipts (US $ million, incl. passenger transport): 65 in 2003; 77 in 2004; 92 in 2005.

Source: World Tourism Organization.

THE FORMER YUGOSLAV REPUBLIC OF MACEDONIA

Communications Media

	2000	2001	2002
Television receivers ('000 in use)	570	n.a.	n.a.
Telephones ('000 main lines in use)	507.3	538.5	578.3
Mobile cellular telephones ('000 subscribers)	99.9	221.3	365.3
Internet users ('000)	50	70	100
Book production: titles*	727	737	1,102
Book production: copies ('000)*	968	1,061	1,899
Daily newspapers: titles	6	8	9
Daily newspapers: average circulation ('000 copies)	32,640	43,689	45,536
Non-daily newspapers: titles	33	29	30
Non-daily newspapers: average circulation ('000 copies)	2,619	2,961	2,618

* Including pamphlets.

Radio receivers ('000 in use): 410 in 1997.

Facsimile machines (number in use): 3,000 in 1997.

Telephones ('000 main lines in use): 537.0 in 2004; 533.2 in 2005; 490.9 in 2006.

Mobile cellular telephones ('000 subscribers): 985.6 in 2004; 1,261.3 in 2005; 1,417.0 in 2006.

Personal computers ('000 in use): 118 in 2003; 140 in 2004; 451 in 2005.

Internet users ('000): 159.0 in 2004; 159.9 in 2005; 268.0 in 2006.

Broadband subscribers ('000): 12.4 in 2005; 36.5 in 2006.

Sources: mainly International Telecommunication Union; UNESCO, *Statistical Yearbook*; and UN, *Statistical Yearbook*.

Education

(2005/06, unless otherwise indicated)

	Institutions	Teachers	Students
Primary and lower secondary	1,005	14,917	235,185
Upper secondary	100	6,136	93,908
University level*	29	1,487	44,731
Other higher*	1	32	893

* 2002/03 figures.

Adult literacy rate (UNESCO estimates): 96.1% (males 98.2%; females 94.1%) in 2002 (Source: UNESCO Institute for Statistics).

Directory

The Constitution

The Constitution of the former Yugoslav republic of Macedonia was promulgated on 17 November 1991. The September 1995 interim agreement with Greece required guarantees that the Macedonian Constitution enshrined or implied no claim to territory beyond the country's existing borders. Some amendment of the 1991 document was thus necessitated. Following the framework agreement between the principal Macedonian and ethnic Albanian parties, reached in August 2001 (see Recent History), the Constitution was revised on 16 November to include 15 principal amendments. The following is a summary of the main provisions of the Constitution, which describes the country as the Republic of Macedonia:

GENERAL PROVISIONS

The Republic of Macedonia is a sovereign, independent, democratic state, where sovereignty derives from democratically elected citizens, referendums and other forms of expression. The citizens of the Republic of Macedonia are defined as the Macedonian people, as well as citizens living within its borders who are, *inter alia*, ethnic Albanians, ethnic Turks, ethnic Serbs and Vlach. The fundamental values defined by the Constitution are: basic human rights, free expression of nationality, the rule of law, a policy of pluralism and the free market, local self-government, entrepreneurship, social justice and solidarity, and respect for international law. State power is divided into legislative, executive and judicial power.

BASIC RIGHTS

The following rights and freedoms are guaranteed and protected in the Republic: the right to life, the inviolability of each person's physical and moral integrity, the right to freedom of speech, public appearance, public information, belief, conscience and religion, and the freedom to organize and belong to a trade union or a political party. All forms of communication and personal data are secret, and the home is inviolable.

The Macedonian language is the official language in use throughout the Republic of Macedonia. Any other language spoken by at least 20% of the population is also an official language. The official personal documentation of citizens speaking an official language other than Macedonian will also be issued in that language.

Military and semi-military associations, which do not belong to the Armed Forces of the Republic, are prohibited.

Any citizen who has reached the age of 18 years has the right to vote and to be elected to organs of government. The right to vote is equal, general and direct, and is realized in free elections by secret ballot. The proportional representation of each community must be assured in the public services and in all areas of public life. Citizens enjoy equal freedoms and rights without distinction as to sex, race, colour, national and social origin, political and religious conviction, material and social position. All religious creeds are separate from the State and are equal under the law. They are identified, *inter alia*, as the Macedonian Orthodox Church, the Islamic Community of Macedonia, the Roman Catholic Church, the Evangelical Methodist Church and the Jewish Community. The members of all such communities are free to establish schools and other charitable institutions in the fields of culture, art and education.

GOVERNMENT

Legislature

Legislative power resides with the Sobranie (Assembly), which consists of between 120 and 140 deputies elected for four years. The Sobranie adopts and amends the Constitution, enacts laws and gives interpretations thereof, adopts the budget of the Republic, decides on war and peace, chooses the Government, elects judges and releases them from duty. The Sobranie may decide, by a majority vote, to call a referendum on issues within its competence. A decision is adopted at a referendum if the majority of voters taking part in the ballot votes in favour of it and if more than one-half of the electorate participates in the vote. The Sobranie forms a Council for Inter-Ethnic Relations, comprising seven representatives from each of the ethnic Macedonian and Albanian communities, and five representatives of other nationalities living in the state. Parliamentary legislation on issues of culture and identity, particularly in the areas of language and education, can only be adopted if a majority of the deputies representing these communities votes in favour, in addition to the overall majority. Three of the nine judges of the Constitutional Court and three of the seven members of the Republican Judicial Council must also be elected by a double majority vote.

President

The President of the Republic represents the country and is responsible for ensuring respect for the Constitution and laws. He is Commander of the Armed Forces and appoints the Prime Minister. He appoints three members of the Security Council of the Republic (of which he is President) and ensures that the Council reflects the composition of the country's population.

Ministers

Executive power in the Republic resides with the Prime Minister and Ministers, who are not permitted concurrently to be deputies in the Sobranie. The Ministers are elected by the majority vote of all the deputies in the Sobranie. The Ministers implement laws and the state budget, and are responsible for foreign and diplomatic relations.

Judiciary

Judicial power is vested in the courts, and is autonomous and independent. The Supreme Court is the highest court. The election and dismissal of judges is proposed by the Republican Judicial Council.

Local Government

Legislation at local and municipal level is adopted by a two-thirds' majority vote of the total number of representatives. Legislation regulating such areas as local finance, elections and municipal boundaries must be adopted by a majority of the representatives representing the minority communities, as well as by an overall majority. In units of local self-government, citizens participate in decision-making on issues of local relevance directly, and through representatives.

OTHER PROVISIONS

The Sobranie elects an Ombudsman to ensure that constitutional rights are upheld, particularly the principles of non-discrimination and fair representation of the respective communities in public life. Revision of the Constitution must be approved by a two-thirds' majority in the Sobranie. Certain articles, such as the Preamble and those relating to local councils and minority rights, also require a majority of the vote by deputies from the minority communities.

The Government

HEAD OF STATE

President of the Republic: BRANKO CRVENKOVSKI (elected 28 April 2004; inaugurated 12 May 2004).

GOVERNMENT
(April 2008)

A coalition of the Internal Macedonian Revolutionary Organization—Democratic Party for Macedonian National Unity (IMRO—DPMNU), the Democratic Party of Albanians (DPA), the New Social Democratic Party (NSDP), the Liberal Party of Macedonia (LPM), the Socialist Party of Macedonia (SPM), the Party for the Movement of Turks in Macedonia and the Party for Democratic Prosperity (PDP).

Prime Minister: NIKOLA GRUEVSKI (IMRO—DPMNU).
Deputy Prime Minister, in charge of Economic Affairs: ZORAN STAVREVSKI (IMRO—DPMNU).
Deputy Prime Minister, responsible for the implementation of the Ohrid Framework Agreement: IMER ALIU (DPA).
Deputy Prime Minister, in charge of Eurointegration: GABRIELA KONEVSKA-TRAJKOVSKA (IMRO—DPMNU).
Deputy Prime Minister, in charge of Agriculture and Education: ZIVKO JANKULOVSKI (NSDP).
Minister of Finance: TRAJKO SLAVESKI (IMRO—DPMNU).
Minister of Foreign Affairs: ANTONIO MILOŠOSKI (IMRO—DPMNU).
Minister of Internal Affairs: GORDANA JANKULOVSKA (IMRO—DPMNU).
Minister of Defence: LAZAR ELENOVSKI (NSDP).
Minister of Labour and Social Welfare: LJUPCO MESKOV (LPM).
Minister of Justice: MIHAJLO MANEVSKI (IMRO—DPMNU).
Minister of the Economy: VERA RAFAJLOVSKA (NSDP).
Minister of Health: IMER SELMANI (DPA).
Minister of Transport and Communications: MILE JANAKIESKI (IMRO—DPMNU).
Minister of Agriculture, Forestry and Water Resources: ACO SPASENOVSKI (SPM).
Minister of Education and Science: SULEJMAN RUSHITI (DPA).
Minister of Culture: ARIFHIKMET XHEMAILI (DPA).
Minister of Local Self-Government: ABDURAMAN MEMETI (PDP).

Minister of the Environment and Physical Planning: XHELIL BAJRAMI (DPA).
Ministers without Portfolio: GLIGOR TASKOVIĆ (IMRO—DPMNU), VELE SAMAK (IMRO—DPMNU), ADNAN CAHIL (Party for the Movement of Turks in Macedonia).
Minister without Portfolio, in charge of Information: IVO IVANOVSKI (IMRO—DPMNU).

MINISTRIES

Office of the President: 1000 Skopje, 11 Oktomvri bb; tel. (2) 3113318; fax (2) 3112147; internet www.president.gov.mk.
Office of the Prime Minister: 1000 Skopje, Ilindenska bb; tel. (2) 3115455; fax (2) 3112561; internet www.vlada.mk.
Ministry of Agriculture, Forestry and Water Resources: 1000 Skopje, Leninova 2; tel. (2) 3134477; fax (2) 3239429; e-mail irena.ristoska@mzsv.gov.mk; internet www.mzsv.gov.mk.
Ministry of Culture: 1000 Skopje, ul. Gjuro Gjakovik 61; tel. (2) 3240600; fax (2) 3240561; e-mail info@kultura.gov.mk; internet www.kultura.gov.mk.
Ministry of Defence: 1000 Skopje, Orce Nikolov bb; tel. and fax (2) 3282042; e-mail info@morm.gov.mk; internet www.morm.gov.mk.
Ministry of the Economy: 1000 Skopje, Jurij Gagarin 15; tel. (2) 3084470; fax (2) 3084472; e-mail ms@mt.net.mk; internet www.economy.gov.mk.
Ministry of Education and Science: 1000 Skopje, Dimitrija Čupovski 9; tel. (2) 3117277; fax (2) 3118414; e-mail contact@mofk.gov.mk; internet www.mon.gov.mk.
Ministry of the Environment and Physical Planning: 1000 Skopje, ul. Drezdenska 52; tel. (2) 3066930; fax (2) 3066931; e-mail info@moepp.gov.mk; internet www.moepp.gov.mk.
Ministry of Finance: 1000 Skopje, Dame Gruev 14; tel. (2) 3117288; fax (2) 3117280; internet www.finance.gov.mk.
Ministry of Foreign Affairs: 1000 Skopje, Dame Gruev 6; tel. (2) 3110333; fax (2) 3115790; e-mail mailmnr@mfa.gov.mk; internet www.mfa.gov.mk.
Ministry of Health: 1000 Skopje, Vodnjanska bb; tel. (2) 3112500; fax (2) 3113014; internet www.zdravstvo.gov.mk.
Ministry of Internal Affairs: 1000 Skopje, Dimitar Mirchev bb; tel. (2) 3117222; fax (2) 3112468; internet www.mvr.gov.mk.
Ministry of Justice: 1000 Skopje, Dimitrija Čupovski 9; tel. (2) 3117277; fax (2) 3226975; e-mail webmaster@zic.gov.mk; internet www.covekovi-prava.gov.mk.
Ministry of Labour and Social Welfare: 1000 Skopje, Dame Gruev 14; tel. (2) 3106410; fax (2) 3110251; e-mail mtsp@mtsp.gov.mk; internet www.mtsp.gov.mk.
Ministry of Local Self-Government: 1000 Skopje, Dame Gruev 14; tel. (2) 3106302; fax (2) 3106303; internet www.mls.gov.mk.
Ministry of Transport and Communications: 1000 Skopje, pl. Crvena skopska opstina 4; tel. (2) 3126228; fax (2) 3123292; internet www.mtc.gov.mk.

President

Presidential Election, First Ballot, 14 April 2004

Candidate	Votes	% of votes
Branko Crvenkovski (SDAM)	385,347	42.47
Sasko Kedev (IMRO—DPMNU)	309,132	34.07
Gzim Ostreni (DUI)	134,208	14.79
Zudi Xhelili (DPA)	78,714	8.67
Total	907,401	100.00

Second Ballot, 28 April 2004

Candidate	Votes	% of votes
Branko Crvenkovski (SDAM)	553,522	62.70
Sasko Kedev (IMRO—DPMNU)	329,271	37.30
Total	882,793	100.00

Legislature

Sobranie
(Assembly)

1000 Skopje, 11 Oktomvri bb; tel. (2) 3112255; fax (2) 3237947; e-mail sobranie@sobranie.mk; internet www.sobranie.mk.

THE FORMER YUGOSLAV REPUBLIC OF MACEDONIA

President: LJUBIŠA GEORGIEVSKI.

General Election, 5 July 2006*

Party	% of votes	Seats
Internal Macedonian Revolutionary Organization—Democratic Party for Macedonian National Unity coalition	32.51	45
Together for Macedonia†	23.31	32
Democratic Union for Integration-Party for Democratic Prosperity	12.15	17
Democratic Party of Albanians	7.21	11
Internal Macedonian Revolutionary Organization—People's Party	5.85	6
New Social Democratic Party	5.81	7
Democratic Renewal of Macedonia	1.78	1
Party of European Integration	1.30	1
Others	10.08	—
Total	**100.00**	**120**

* Provisional results. Elections were repeated in eight constituencies on 19 July. Members of the Sobranie are elected according to a regional proportional system without a minimum requirement.
† Electoral coalition, led by the Social Democratic Alliance of Macedonia and the Liberal-Democratic Party.

Election Commission

State Election Commission: 1000 Skopje, 11 Oktomvri bb; tel. (2) 3244744; fax (2) 3244745; e-mail izbori@sec.mk; internet www.sec.mk; Chair. STEVO PENDAROVSKI.

Political Organizations

Democratic Alternative (DA) (Demokratska Alternativa): 1000 Skopje, ul. Dame Gruev 1; tel. (2) 3212361; fax (2) 3227810; f. 1998; Chair. VASIL TUPURKOVSKI.

Democratic Party of Albanians (DPA) (Partia Demokratike Shqiptare) (PDSh): Tetovo, Maršal Tito 2; tel. and fax (44) 7332572; e-mail webmaster@pdsh.org; internet www.pdsh.org; f. 1997 by a merger of the Party of Democratic Prosperity of Albanians in Macedonia (f. 1994) and the National Democratic Party (f. 1990); officially registered in July 2002; absorbed the National Democratic Party (f. 2001) and the Republican Party of Albanians (f. 2002) in June 2003; Chair. MENDUH THAÇI.

Democratic Party of Serbs in Macedonia (DPSM): Skopje, 27 Mart 11; tel. (2) 3254274; f. 1996; Pres. IVAN STOILKOVIĆ.

Democratic Party of Turks in Macedonia (DPTM) (Demokratska Partija na Turcite na Makedonija): 1000 Skopje, bul. Koco Racin br. 26; tel. (2) 3114696; fax (2) 3214053; e-mail info@tdp.org.mk; internet www.tdp.org.mk; Leader Dr KENAN HASIP.

Democratic Renewal of Macedonia (Demokraticka Obnova na Makedonija): 1000 Skopje; tel. (2) 3214107; fax (2) 3121987; internet www.dom.org.mk; f. Jan. 2006; Leader LILJANA POPOVSKA.

Democratic Union for Integration (DUI) (Bashkimi Demokratik për Integrim/Demokratska Unija za Integracija) (BDI): 1200 Tetovo, Rruga 170 Nr 2, Reçicë e Vogël; tel. (4) 4334398; fax (4) 4334397; e-mail bdi@bdi.org.mk; internet www.bdi.org.mk; f. 2002; ethnic Albanian, dominated by former mems of rebel National Liberation Army; Chair. ALI AHMETI; Sec.-Gen. GËZIM OSTRENI.

Internal Macedonian Revolutionary Organization—Democratic Party for Macedonian National Unity (IMRO—DPMNU) (Vnatrešno-Makedonska Revolucionerna Organizacija—Demokratska Partija za Makedonsko Nacionalno Edinstvo—VMRO—DPMNE): 1000 Skopje, Petar Drapshin br. 36; tel. (2) 3111441; fax (2) 3211586; e-mail info@vmro-dpmne.org.mk; internet www.vmro-dpmne.org.mk; nationalist; Pres. NIKOLA GRUEVSKI; Sec. DEN DONCEV.

Internal Macedonian Revolutionary Organization—People's Party (IMRO—People's Party) (Vnatrešno Makedonska Revolucionerna Organizacija—Narodna Partija—VMRO—NP): 1000 Skopje, ul. Nikola Vapcarov br. 2; tel. and fax (2) 3223555; e-mail contact@vmro-np.org.mk; internet www.vmro-np.org.mk; f. July 2004 by fmr Prime Minister Ljubčo Georgievski as breakaway party of IMRO—DPMNU; Chair. VESNA JANEVSKA.

Liberal-Democratic Party (LDP) (Liberalno-Demokratska Partija): 1000 Skopje, Partizanski odredi 89; tel. (2) 3298261; fax (2) 3298268; e-mail contact@ldp.org.mk; internet www.ldp.org.mk; f. 1996 by a merger of the Liberal Party and the Democratic Party; Chair. RISTO PENOV; Sec.-Gen. ROZA TOPUZOVA-KAREVSKA.

Liberal Party of Macedonia (LPM) (Liberalna Partija na Makedonija): 1000 Skopje, ul. Vasko Karangeleski 66; tel. (2) 2464955; fax (2) 2464956; e-mail info@lp.org.mk; internet www.lp.org.mk; Chair. STOJAN ANDOV; Sec.-Gen. IVON VELICKOVSKI.

New Social Democratic Party (NSDP) (Nova Socijaldemokratska Partija): 1000 Skopje, Dame Gruev 5; tel. and fax (2) 3238775; fax (2) 3290465; e-mail nsdp@nsdp.org.mk; internet www.nsdp.org.mk; f. 2005; Leader TITO PETKOVSKI.

Party for Democratic Prosperity (PDP) (Partija za Demokratski Prosperitet): Tetovo, Rruga Ilindenska; tel. (44) 336950; fax (44) 336948; e-mail kontakt@ppd.org.mk; internet www.ppd.org.mk; f. 1990; split 1994; predominantly ethnic Albanian and Muslim party; Chair. ABDULADI VEJSELI; Sec.-Gen. ZEMRI ELEZI.

Party of European Integraton (Partija za Evropska Idnina): Skopje; internet www.pei.org.mk; Leader FIJAT CANOSKI.

Party of Free Democrats (PSD): Skopje; f. 2007; Leader LJUPCO JORDANOVSKI.

Social Democratic Alliance of Macedonia (SDAM) (Socijaldemokratski Sojuz na Makedonija—SDSM): 1000 Skopje, Bihačka 8; tel. (2) 3293101; fax (2) 3293111; e-mail contact@sdsm.org.mk; internet www.sdsm.org.mk; f. 1943; name changed from League of Communists of Macedonia—Party of Democratic Reform in 1991; led alliance, Together for Macedonia, which held govt in Sept. 2002–July 2006; Chair. RADMILA SEKERINSKA.

Socialist Party of Macedonia (SPM) (Socijalistiska Partija na Makedonija): 1000 Skopje, 11 Oktomvri 17; tel. (2) 3228015; fax (2) 3220025; e-mail spm@mol.com.mk; f. 1990; left-wing; Chair. LJUBISAV IVANOV.

Diplomatic Representation

EMBASSIES IN THE FORMER YUGOSLAV REPUBLIC OF MACEDONIA

Albania: 1000 Skopje, Majka Tereza 22; tel. (2) 3246726; fax (2) 3246727; e-mail ambshquip@mt.net.mk; Ambassador VLADIMIR PRELJA.

Austria: 1000 Skopje, Mile Popjordanov 8; tel. (2) 3083400; fax (2) 3083150; e-mail skopje-ob@bmeia.gv.at; Ambassador Dr ALOIS KRAUT.

Bosnia and Herzegovina: 1000 Skopje, Mile Popjordanov 56; tel. (2) 3086216; fax (2) 3086221; Ambassador MILAN BALABAN.

Bulgaria: 1000 Skopje, Ivo Ribar Lola 40; tel. (2) 3229444; fax (2) 3246491; e-mail bgemb@unet.com.mk; Ambassador MIHO MIHOV.

China, People's Republic: 1000 Skopje, 474 No 20; tel. (2) 3213163; fax (2) 3212500; Ambassador DONG CHUNFENG.

Croatia: 1000 Skopje, Mitropolit Teodosij Gologanov 44; tel. (2) 3246012; fax (2) 3246004; e-mail croemb.skopje@mvpei.hr; Ambassador IVAN KUJUNDŽIĆ.

Czech Republic: 1000 Skopje, Salvador Aljende 35; tel. (2) 3109805; fax (2) 3178380; e-mail skopje@embassy.mzv.cz; internet www.mzv.cz/belgrade; Ambassador JOZEF BRAUN.

France: 1000 Skopje, Salvador Aljende 73; tel. (2) 3244300; fax (2) 3117760; e-mail franamba@mt.net.mk; internet www.ambafrance-mk.org; Ambassador BERNARD VALERO.

Germany: 1000 Skopje, Leninska 59; tel. (2) 3093900; fax (2) 3093899; e-mail dtboskop@unet.com.mk; internet www.deutschebotschaft-skopje.com.mk/mk/; Ambassador RALF ANDREAS BRETH.

Hungary: 1000 Skopje, Mirka Ginova 27; tel. (2) 3063423; fax (2) 3063070; e-mail hungemb@mt.net.mk; Ambassador Dr FERENC KÉKESI.

Italy: 1000 Skopje, VIII Udarna brig. 22; tel. (2) 3236500; fax (2) 3117087; Ambassador DONATINO MARCON.

Montenegro: 1000 Skopje, Vasil Stefanovski 7; tel. (2) 3227277; fax (2) 3227254; Ambassador DUŠKO LALIĆEVIĆ.

Netherlands: 1000 Skopje, Leninova 69–71; tel. (2) 3129319; fax (2) 3129309; e-mail sko@minbuza.nl; internet www.nlembassy.org.mk; Ambassador SIMONE FILIPPINI.

Norway: 1000 Skopje, 8 Udarna brig. 2; tel. (2) 3129165; fax (2) 3111138; e-mail emb.skp@mfa.no; internet www.norway.org.mk; Ambassador CARL SCHIØTZ WIBYE.

Poland: 1000 Skopje, Djuro Djakovic 50; tel. and fax (2) 3112647; fax (2) 3119744; e-mail ambasada@skopje.polemb.net; internet www.skopje.polemb.net; Ambassador DARIUSZ KAROL BACHURA.

THE FORMER YUGOSLAV REPUBLIC OF MACEDONIA

Romania: 1000 Skopje, Rajko Zinzifov 42; tel. (2) 3228055; fax (2) 3228036; e-mail romanamb@on.net.mk; Ambassador ADRIAN STEFAN CONSTANTINESCU.
Russia: 1000 Skopje, Pirinska 44; tel. (2) 3117160; fax (2) 3117808; e-mail embassy@russia.org.mk; internet www.russia.org.mk; Ambassador VLADIMIR SOLOTSINSKII.
Serbia: 1000 Skopje, Pitu Guli 8; tel. (2) 3129298; fax (2) 3129427; e-mail yuamb@unet.com.mk; Ambassador ZORAN POPOVIĆ.
Slovenia: 1000 Skopje, Vodnjanska 42; tel. (2) 3178730; fax (2) 3176631; e-mail vsk@gov.si; Ambassador ALAIN BRIAN BERGANT.
Spain: 1000 Skopje, 27 Mart 7; tel. (2) 3231002; fax (2) 3220612; e-mail ambspanija@mt.net.mk; Ambassador JOSÉ MANUEL PAZ Y AGÜERAS.
Sweden: 1000 Skopje, 8 Udarna Brigada 2; tel. (2) 3297880; fax (2) 3112065; e-mail swedembsk@mt.net.mk; Ambassador ULRIKA CRONENBERG-MOSSBERG.
Switzerland: 1000 Skopje, Maksim Gorki 19; tel. (2) 3103320; fax (2) 3103301; e-mail sko.vertretung@eda.admin.ch; internet www.eda.admin.ch/skopje; Ambassador NICOLE WYRSCH.
Turkey: 1000 Skopje, Slavej Planina bb; tel. (2) 3113270; fax (2) 3117024; e-mail turkish@mol.com.mk; Ambassador TANER KARAKAŞ.
Ukraine: 1000 Skopje, Pitu Guli 3; tel. and fax (2) 3178120; e-mail ukrambas@mt.net.mk; Ambassador VITALIY MOSKALENKO.
United Kingdom: 1000 Skopje, Salvador Aljende 73; tel. (2) 3299299; fax (2) 3179726; e-mail britishembassyskopje@fco.gov.uk; internet www.britishembassy.gov.uk/macedonia; Ambassador ANDREW KEY.
USA: 1000 Skopje, Ilindenska bb; tel. (2) 3116180; fax (2) 3117103; internet skopje.usembassy.gov; Ambassador GILLIAN ARLETTE MILOVANOVIĆ.

Judicial System

The FYRM has 27 Courts of First Instance and three Courts of Appeal. The Republican Judicial Council, which comprises seven members elected by the Sobranie for a term of six years, proposes the election or dismissal of judges to the Sobranie. The Constitutional Court, comprising nine judges elected by the Sobranie with a mandate of nine years, is responsible for the protection of constitutional and legal rights, and ensures that there is no conflict in the exercise of legislative, executive and judicial powers. The Supreme Court is the highest court in the country, and guarantees the equal administration of legislation by all courts. In December 2005 the Sobranie approved a series of constitutional amendments providing for extensive reform of the judicial system; as part of the reform, the Sobranie was no longer responsible for the appointment of judges.

Constitutional Court of the Republic of Macedonia (Ustaven Sud na Republika Makedonija): 1000 Skopje, 12 Udarna brig. 2; tel. and fax (2) 3119355; e-mail usud@usud.gov.mk; internet www.usud.gov.mk; Pres. TRENDAFIL IVANOVSKI.
Supreme Court: 1000 Skopje, Krste Misirkova bb; tel. (2) 3234064; fax (2) 3237538; Pres. SIMEON GELEVSKI.
Republican Judicial Council: 1000 Skopje, Veljko Vlahovik bb; tel. (2) 3218130; fax (2) 3218131; Pres. LENČE SOFRONIEVSKA.
Office of the Public Prosecutor: 1000 Skopje, Krste Misirkova bb; tel. (2) 3229314; Public Prosecutor ALEKSANDR PRCEVSKI.

Religion

Most ethnic Macedonians are adherents of the Eastern Orthodox Church, and since 1967 there has been an autocephalous Macedonian Orthodox Church. However, the Serbian Orthodox Church (of which the Macedonian Church formed a part) does not recognize the autocephalous church, and nor do the Ecumenical Patriarchate (based in Istanbul, Turkey) and other Orthodox Churches. There are some adherents of other Orthodox jurisdictions in the country. Those Macedonian (and Bulgarian) Slavs who converted to Islam during the Ottoman era are known as Pomaks or as ethnic Muslims. The substantial Albanian population is mostly Muslim (mainly Sunni, but some adherents of a Dervish sect); there are a few Roman Catholic Christians and a small Jewish community.

CHRISTIANITY

Macedonian Orthodox Church: Skopje, Partizanski Odredi 12, POB 69; tel. (2) 3230697; fax (2) 3230685; internet www.mpc.org.mk; Metropolitan See of Ohrid revived in 1958; autocephaly declared 1967; 1.5m. mems; comprises seven bishoprics in Macedonia and three abroad; Head of Church and Archbishop of Ohrid and Macedonia Metropolitan Archbishop STEFAN VELJANOVSKI (of Skopje).

Evangelical Methodist Church of Macedonia: Strumica; 14 congregations; mem. of the Methodist Conference of Central and Southern Europe, based in Geneva (Switzerland); Superintendent WILHELM NAUSNER (based in Linz, Austria); Pastor MIHAIL CEKOV.

The Roman Catholic Church

The diocese of Skopje, suffragan to the archdiocese of Vrhbosna (based in Sarajevo, Bosnia and Herzegovina), covers most of the FYRM. The Bishop is also Apostolic Exarch for Catholics of the Byzantine Rite in the FYRM. At 31 December 2005 there were an estimated 3,730 adherents of the Latin Rite in the diocese, and the country had an estimated 11,491 adherents of the Byzantine Rite.

Bishop of Skopje: Rt Rev. KIRO STOJANOV, 1000 Skopje, Risto Siškov 31; tel. and fax (2) 3164123; e-mail katbiskupija@mt.net.mk.

ISLAM

Islamic Community of Macedonia (Bashkësia Fetare Islame e Republikës së Maqedonisë): Skopje, Çairska 52; tel. (2) 3117410; fax (2) 3117883; e-mail bim@bim.org.mk; internet www.bim.org.mk; fmrly headquarters of the Skopje Region, one of the four administrative divisions of the Yugoslav Muslims; Leader Haji ARIF EMINI.

JUDAISM

Jewish Community: 1000 Skopje, Borka Taleski 24.

The Press

In 2002 a total of 39 newspapers and 178 magazines were published in the FYRM.

PRINCIPAL DAILY NEWSPAPERS

Denes (Today): 1000 Skopje, M. H. Jasmin 50; tel. (2) 3110239; fax (2) 3110150; e-mail denes@unet.com.mk; Editor NIK DENES.
Dnevnik (Daily): 1000 Skopje, Teodosij Gologanov 28; tel. (2) 3297555; fax (2) 3297554; e-mail dnevnik@dnevnik.com.mk; internet www.dnevnik.com.mk; independent; Editor-in-Chief BRANKO GEROSKI.
Flaka e vëllazërimit (Flame of Brotherhood): 1000 Skopje, Mito Hadživasilev bb; tel. (2) 3112025; fax (2) 3224829; f. 1945; relaunched 1994; in Albanian; Editor-in-Chief ABDULHADI ZULFIQARI; circ. 4,000.
Nova Makedonija (New Macedonia): 1000 Skopje, Mito Hadživasilev Jasmin bb; tel. and fax (2) 3233500; e-mail contact@novamakedonija.com.mk; internet www.novamakedonija.com.mk; f. 1944; morning; in Macedonian; Editor-in-Chief MIRCHE ADAMCHEVSKI; circ. 25,000.
Utrinski Vesnik (Morning Herald): 1000 Skopje, Dame Gruev 5; tel. (2) 3236900; fax (2) 3236901; e-mail contact@utrinskivesnik.com.mk; internet www.utrinskivesnik.com.mk; Dir EROL RIZAOV; Editor-in-Chief BRANKO TRICKOVSKI.
Večer (The Evening): 1000 Skopje, Mito Hadživasilev bb; tel. (2) 3111537; fax (2) 3238327; f. 1963; evening; Editor-in-Chief STOJAN NASEV; circ. 29,200.
Vest (News): Skopje; internet www.vest.com.mk; popular.

PERIODICALS

Delo: Skopje, Petar Drapshin 26; tel. (2) 3231949; fax (2) 3115748; f. 1993; weekly; nationalist; Editor-in-Chief BRATISLAV TASKOVSKI.
Fokus: Skopje, Zheležnička 53; tel. (2) 3111327; fax (2) 3111685; weekly; independent; Editor-in-Chief NIKOLA MLADENOV.
Makedonsko Vreme/Macedonian Times: 1000 Skopje, Vasil Gorgov 39; tel. and fax (2) 3121182; e-mail mian@mian.com.mk; internet www.unet.com.mk/mian; f. 1994; monthly; politics and current affairs; in Macedonian and English; Editor-in-Chief JOVAN PAVLOSKI.
Puls (Pulse): 1000 Skopje, Mito Hadživasilev bb; tel. (2) 3117124; fax (2) 3118024; internet www.puls.com.mk; weekly; business and technology; Editor-in-Chief MIRCE TOMOVSKI.
Roma Times: Skopje; e-mail mail@dostae.net.mk; internet www.dostae.net.mk/mk/press_mk_roma.htm; f. 2001; 3 a week; circ. 3,000.
Sport Magazine: 1000 Skopje, Mito Hadživasilev Jasmin bb; tel. and fax (2) 3116254; e-mail lav@unet.com.mk; f. 1991; weekly; circ. 6,000.
Trudbenik (Worker): 1000 Skopje, Udarna brigada 12; weekly; organ of Macedonian Trade Unions; Editor SIMO IVANOVSKI.

NEWS AGENCIES

Agency for Information (Agencija za Informacii): 1000 Skopje, Veljko Vlahonik 11; tel. (2) 3127453; fax (2) 3114695; e-mail sinf@sinf

MADAGASCAR

Introductory Survey

Location, Climate, Language, Religion, Flag, Capital

The Republic of Madagascar comprises the island of Madagascar, the fourth largest in the world, and several much smaller offshore islands, in the western Indian Ocean, about 500 km (300 miles) east of Mozambique, in southern Africa. The inland climate is temperate; in Antananarivo temperatures are generally between 8°C (48°F) and 27°C (81°F), with cooler, dryer weather between May and October. The coastal region is tropical, with an average daily maximum temperature of 32°C (90°F). The rainy season extends from November to April in the highlands (average annual rainfall is 1,000 mm–1,500 mm) but is more prolonged on the coast, where average annual rainfall can reach 3,500 mm. The official languages are Malagasy and French. Following a referendum held in April 2007, English was adopted as the third official language. Hova and other dialects are also widely spoken. More than 50% of the population follow animist beliefs, while about 41% are Christians and the remainder are Muslims. The national flag (proportions 2 by 3) has a vertical white stripe (one-third of the length) at the hoist and two equal horizontal stripes, of red and green, in the fly. The capital is Antananarivo.

Recent History

A French possession since 1896, Madagascar became an autonomous state within the French Community in October 1958, as the Malagasy Republic. In May 1959 Philibert Tsiranana, leader of the Parti social démocrate (PSD), was elected President. The country achieved full independence on 26 June 1960. Prior to independence France supported the PSD, which was identified with the majority coastal tribes (*côtiers*), as an alternative to the more nationalistic highland people, the Merina, who were the traditional ruling group in the island.

After 1967 the economy deteriorated, and there was growing opposition to the Government's alleged authoritarianism and subservience to French interests. In May 1972, following civil unrest, President Tsiranana transferred full powers to the Army Chief of Staff, Gen. Gabriel Ramanantsoa. In October 1973 pro-Government parties secured a decisive victory in legislative elections. A prolonged crisis followed an attempted military coup in December 1974, and in early February 1975 Ramanantsoa transferred power to Col Richard Ratsimandrava, hitherto Minister of the Interior; however, Ratsimandrava was assassinated shortly afterwards. On 12 February Brig.-Gen. Gilles Andriamahazo assumed power and imposed martial law. All political parties were suspended. In June Andriamahazo was succeeded as Head of State by Lt-Commdr (later Adm.) Didier Ratsiraka, a *côtier* and a former Minister of Foreign Affairs, who became Chairman of the Supreme Revolutionary Council (SRC).

In a referendum in December 1975 more than 94% of voters approved a new Constitution, which provided for radical administrative and agrarian reforms, and the appointment of Ratsiraka as President of the Republic for a term of seven years. The country's name was changed to the Democratic Republic of Madagascar, and a 'Second Republic' was proclaimed. In March the Avant-garde de la révolution malgache (AREMA—Antoky Ny Revolosiona Malagasy) was founded as the nucleus of the Front national pour la défense de la révolution socialiste malgache (FNDR), the only political organization permitted by the Constitution.

At local government elections in March–June 1977 AREMA secured the majority of votes, resulting in division within the FNDR. The left-wing Mouvement national pour l'indépendance de Madagascar (Monima Ka Miviombio, known as Monima), led by Monja Jaona, withdrew from the FNDR and was subsequently proscribed. At legislative elections in June AREMA secured 112 of the 137 seats in the National People's Assembly. A new Council of Ministers was formed in August, and the membership of the SRC was extended to include leaders of the former political parties and additional *côtiers*, in an effort to restore political equilibrium.

In November 1982 Ratsiraka was re-elected President, receiving 80.2% of the votes cast. At elections to the National People's Assembly in August 1983 AREMA won 117 of the 137 seats. Open dissatisfaction with the Government's policies persisted, however.

In February 1988 the Prime Minister, Col Désiré Rakotoarijaona, resigned, owing to poor health, and was replaced by Lt-Col Victor Ramahatra, formerly Minister of Public Works. Ratsiraka was re-elected to the presidency in March 1989 for a further seven-year term, with 62.7% of the total votes cast. At legislative elections in May AREMA won 120 seats. The Mouvement pour le pouvoir prolétarien (Mpitolona ho amin'ny Fonjakan'ny Madinika—MFM), which obtained only seven seats, rejected the official results, alleging electoral misconduct. The Élan populaire pour l'unité nationale (Vonjy Iray Tsy Mivaky, known as Vonjy) secured four seats, AKFM/Fanavaozana (a newly formed group, comprising former members of the Parti du congrès de l'indépendance de Madagascar—AKFM), won three seats, the original AKFM two seats, and Monima only one seat.

In August 1989 Ratsiraka assented to opposition demands for discussions about the future role and structure of the FNDR. In December the National People's Assembly adopted a constitutional amendment abolishing the requirement for political parties to be members of the FNDR (thereby effectively dissolving the FNDR), despite opposition from MFM deputies.

In March 1990 the Government formally permitted the resumption of multi-party politics. Numerous new organizations emerged, while other parties that had hitherto operated within the FNDR became official opposition movements. Several pro-Government political associations joined AREMA to form a new coalition, the Mouvement militant pour le socialisme malagasy (MMSM). The principal opposition movements included the Union nationale pour le développement et la démocratie (UNDD) and the MFM (restyled the Mouvement pour le progrès de Madagascar, or Mpitolona ho amin'ny Fandrosoan'ny Madagasikara). An informal alliance, the Comité des forces vives—subsequently known as Forces vives (FV, Hery Velona)—was formed by 16 opposition factions, and trade unions and other groups.

In May 1991 legislation providing for extensive constitutional amendments was submitted to the National People's Assembly. Opposition parties criticized the proposals, on the grounds that the revised Constitution would retain references to socialism. In June opposition leaders applied to the Constitutional High Court to effect Ratsiraka's removal from office, while the FV organized demonstrations in support of its demands for the resignation of the President and the convening of a national conference to draft a new constitution. Later in June the FV formed a 'parallel' administration, which it termed the 'Provisional Government'.

In July 1991 the FV organized a general strike, warning that it would continue until the Government acceded to its demands for constitutional reform. The FV appointed Jean Rakotoharison, a retired army general, as President of the 'Provisional Government', and Albert Zafy, the leader of the UNDD, as its Prime Minister. However, Rakotonirina Manandafy, the leader of the MFM, rejected the formation of the 'Provisional Government', favouring further negotiations, and withdrew his party from the FV. Members of the 'Provisional Government' subsequently occupied the premises of six official government ministries. Later in July Ratsiraka ordered the detention of several members of the 'Provisional Government' and imposed a state of emergency in Antananarivo. The FV withdrew from negotiations with the MMSM, in protest against the arrests, while the French Government appealed to Ratsiraka to release the opposition leaders. In response to increasing public pressure, Ratsiraka dissolved the Council of Ministers and pledged to organize a constitutional referendum before the end of 1991. Members of the 'Provisional Government' were released from custody, and Ratsiraka repealed legislation that authorized the detention of opponents of the Government.

In August 1991 Ratsiraka appointed Guy Razanamasy, the mayor of Antananarivo, as Prime Minister. Later that month Ratsiraka declared Madagascar to be a federation of six states, with himself as President, and claimed to command the support of five provinces where AREMA continued to hold the majority of seats in regional councils. At the end of August Razanamasy formed an interim Government, which did not include any members of the FV or the MFM.

On 31 October 1991 representatives of the Government, the FV, the MFM, church leaders and the armed forces signed an agreement providing for the suspension of the Constitution and the creation of a transitional Government, which was to remain in office for a maximum period of 18 months, pending presidential and legislative elections. The SRC and the National People's Assembly were to be replaced by interim bodies, respectively the High State Authority for Transition to the Third Republic and the National Committee for Economic and Social Regeneration. On an interim basis, Ratsiraka was to remain as President of the Republic and Razanamasy as Prime Minister. Zafy was designated President of the High State Authority, which was to comprise 18 representatives of the FV, seven of the MFM and six of the MMSM. Manandafy and Pastor Richard Andriamanjato, the leader of AKFM/Fanavaozana, were appointed as joint Presidents of the 131-member National Committee for Economic and Social Regeneration. The power to appoint or to dismiss government ministers, hitherto vested in the President, was granted to Razanamasy. A new constitution was to be submitted to a national referendum by the end of 1991. Zafy subsequently rejected the agreement, on the grounds that Ratsiraka was to retain the nominal post of Commander-in-Chief of the Armed Forces. In November Razanamasy formed a new interim Government, which included three representatives of the MFM and one MMSM member. Francisque Ravony, of the MFM, was appointed to the new post of Deputy Prime Minister. Owing to Zafy's refusal to participate in the Government, 10 portfolios that had been allocated to the FV remained vacant. Later in November, however, Zafy agreed to accept the presidency of the High State Authority.

In December 1991 Razanamasy announced that the formation of the coalition Government had proved unsuccessful, and 11 ministers, including Ravony, resigned. Razanamasy appointed a larger Government of national consensus, in which 14 (of 36) portfolios were allocated to the FV. In January 1992 it was announced that all political factions had now accepted the terms of the October 1991 agreement. The institutions that had been established by the accord were to prepare for the constitutional referendum, now scheduled for June 1992, and for local, presidential and legislative elections, which were to take place by the end of the year. In February the High State Authority for Transition to the Third Republic announced the dissolution of the SRC and the National People's Assembly, in accordance with the October 1991 agreement, and indicated that a new body was to be created to supervise local elections, replacing the existing system of government, based on village assemblies (*fokontany*). However, the MMSM claimed that the High State Authority was not empowered to dissolve the local government structure. The Government subsequently announced that control of local government was to be transferred from elected councils to special delegations, and that security commissions were to be established to organize the *fokontany*.

The draft Constitution of the Third Republic, as submitted to the Government in April 1992, envisaged a unitary state and provided for a bicameral legislature, comprising a Senate and a National Assembly. Two-thirds of the members of the Senate were to be selected by an electoral college, with the remaining one-third to be appointed by the President, while the 184-member National Assembly was to be elected by universal suffrage, under a system of proportional representation, for a four-year term. The authority of the President was reduced, and executive power was vested in the Prime Minister, who was to be appointed by the National Assembly. Ratsiraka reiterated his intention to contest the presidential election and demanded that a draft providing for a federal system of government also be submitted to the forthcoming referendum.

The new Constitution was approved by 72.2% of votes cast in a national referendum on 19 August 1992. Federalists forcibly prevented the electorate from voting in a number of regions, and several people were killed in clashes between supporters of the MMSM and members of the FV at Toamasina.

In September 1992 several prominent political figures, including Zafy and Manandafy, announced that they were to contest the forthcoming presidential election. Later in September a committee of government officials and church leaders proposed that a stipulation restricting the President to two terms of office be incorporated in the electoral code. Shortly afterwards MMSM supporters unilaterally declared Antsiranana, Toliary, Toamasina and Fianarantsoa to be federal states, and suspended infrastructural links between these provinces and Antananarivo. In October federalists in Antsiranana, apparently supported by members of the presidential guard, took hostage members of the FV and seized control of the radio and television stations. Razanamasy declared the unilateral proclamation of independence of the four provinces to be illegal, but initiated negotiations with the federalists, in an effort to prevent disruption of the presidential election. Later that month there were further clashes in Toliary between supporters of the FV and federalists, led by Monja Jaona, who had declared himself to be Governor of the province. At the end of October, however, the federalists agreed to participate in the presidential election, although the MMSM continued officially to reject the new Constitution.

The presidential election took place on 25 November 1992, contested by eight candidates. Zafy secured 45.1% of votes cast, and Ratsiraka 29.2%. Prior to a second round of voting, on 10 February 1993, the remaining six candidates withdrew in favour of Zafy, who thus secured 66.7% of the votes cast. Zafy's inauguration, on 27 March, was accompanied by violent clashes between security forces and federalists in the north. In accordance with the Constitution, Zafy resigned as President of the UNDD at a party congress in May; Emmanuel Rakotovahiny, the Minister of State for Agriculture and Rural Development, was elected as his successor.

Several constituent parties of the FV that had not supported Zafy in the first round of the presidential election subsequently presented independent lists of candidates for the forthcoming legislative elections; the remaining parties in the alliance became known as Forces vives Rasalama (Hery Velona Rasalama—HVR). The elections, to a reduced 138-member National Assembly, took place on 16 June 1993, and were contested by 121 political associations. The HVR secured 46 seats, the MFM 15, and a new alliance of pro-Ratsiraka parties 11 seats. The official results indicated that parties supporting Zafy had won 75 seats in the National Assembly. In August Francisque Ravony was elected Prime Minister and formed a new Council of Ministers. Richard Andriamanjato was elected President of the National Assembly.

In October 1994 controversy over a local subsidiary enterprise, Flamco Madagascar, which had failed to reimburse funds advanced by the Government, prompted increased division between Ravony and Andriamanjato regarding economic policy. Meanwhile, opposition leaders demanded the removal of Zafy, Ravony and Andriamanjato, amid general resentment towards the Government, which had been precipitated by an increase in the rate of inflation resulting from the flotation of the Malagasy franc. At a regional congress of AREMA, which took place at the end of October, Ratsiraka urged the resignation of Ravony and the dissolution of the Government. In January 1995 Ravony dismissed the Governor of the central bank, who had approved the financial transaction with Flamco Madagascar, at the insistence of the IMF and World Bank, and (apparently as a concession to Andriamanjato) also dismissed Raserijaona, assuming the finance and budget portfolio himself.

In July 1995, apparently at Zafy's instigation, deputies belonging to the HVR, the UNDD and AKFM/Fanavaozana proposed a motion of censure against Ravony in the National Assembly (which was, however, rejected by a large majority). Zafy subsequently announced that he was unable to co-operate with Ravony and decreed that a constitutional amendment empowering the President, rather than the National Assembly, to select the Prime Minister, be submitted for approval in a national referendum. Ravony indicated that he would resign after the referendum, regardless of the outcome. In August Ravony formed a new Council of Ministers, comprising representatives of the parliamentary majority that had supported him in the previous month. The referendum proceeded in September, at which the constitutional amendment was approved by 63.6% of votes cast. Ravony duly resigned in October, and Zafy appointed Rakotovahiny as Prime Minister.

Dissension emerged between the parties that supported Zafy over the composition of the new Council of Ministers, and in December 1995 associates of Andriamanjato demanded that an alternative cabinet be appointed. In May 1996 a motion of censure against Rakotovahiny's Government was approved by a large majority in the National Assembly. Rakotovahiny submitted his administration's resignation, and Zafy appointed Norbert Ratsirahonana, hitherto President of the Constitutional High Court, as Prime Minister.

Zafy refused to approve the new Government initially proposed by Ratsirahonana, insisting on the inclusion of five UNDD members who had served in the previous Council of Ministers. Ratsirahonana, however, won a vote of confidence in the legislature in July, by associating the vote with legislation providing for the implementation of economic reforms stipulated by the IMF and the World Bank. On 26 July a motion in the National Assembly to remove Zafy from office for numerous contraventions of the Constitution was supported by 99 of 131 votes cast. (Meanwhile, local elections, which had been scheduled for August, and were to replace the existing six provinces with 28 regions, were postponed as a result of the presidential crisis.) The Constitutional High Court endorsed the President's impeachment in September, upholding the majority of the charges against him; Zafy maintained that his impeachment was illegal, but resigned the same day. Ratsirahonana was appointed interim President by the Constitutional High Court, pending an election; he formed a new interim Government that represented the majority in the National Assembly and excluded members of the UNDD. Zafy announced his intention to contest the forthcoming election, as did Ratsiraka and Ratsirahonana.

In all, 15 candidates stood in the first round of the presidential election, which proceeded peacefully on 3 November 1996; Ratsiraka (with 36.6% of the votes cast) and Zafy (with 23.4%) qualified to contest the second round. The head of Libéralisme économique et action démocratique pour la reconstruction nationale (LEADER/Fanilo), Herizo Razafimahaleo, obtained 15.1%, and Ratsirahonana 10.1%, of the votes. Razafimahaleo urged his supporters to vote for Ratsiraka. None of the unsuccessful candidates chose to support Zafy, who declared his intention, if elected, to retain Ratsirahonana (who had successfully concluded an agreement with the IMF in August) as Prime Minister; Ratsirahonana, however, refused to endorse either candidate. At the second round, which took place on 29 December, Ratsiraka narrowly won, with 50.7% of the valid votes cast, although more than 50% of the registered electorate abstained from voting. Ratsiraka was inaugurated as President on 9 February. He appointed Pascal Rakotomavo (a former Minister of Finance) as Prime Minister. Rakotomavo's Government included Razafimahaleo as Deputy Prime Minister, responsible for Foreign Affairs.

In May 1997 legislative elections, which had been scheduled for August, were postponed, officially to allow time for identity cards to be issued to voters. In August a commission that had been appointed by the Prime Minister to draft constitutional amendments presented its proposals. However, apparently following intervention from Andriamanjato, who was said to have insisted that the National Assembly alone was responsible for constitutional revision, regional forums, attended by local officials and representatives of non-governmental organizations, were held in September to put forward proposals for one constitutional project. (Ratsiraka had originally favoured submitting two alternatives to a referendum, one for a federal state, the other for a decentralized but unitary state.) A new constitution was then to be drafted by a 15-member National Consultative Commission, nominated by Ratsiraka, Rakotomavo and Andriamanjato.

In early 1998 Ratsiraka announced that a constitutional referendum would take place on 15 March 1998, to be followed by legislative elections. The draft amendments to the Constitution envisaged a 'federal-style' state, composed of six autonomous provinces, and also provided for increased presidential powers.

In February 1998 a motion of impeachment against Ratsiraka failed to gain the requisite two-thirds' majority in the National Assembly. Later that month the principal opposition parties urged voters to boycott the forthcoming referendum, claiming that the Government had ignored the views presented at the regional forums and the proposals of the National Consultative Commission, and had deliberately delayed discussion on legislation proposed by Manandafy (who had chaired the Commission) whereby any draft constitution would require the approval of more than 50% of all registered voters in order to become law. The referendum proceeded on 15 March 1998, when extensive revisions to the Constitution were narrowly endorsed by 50.96% of votes cast. Manandafy's proposed legislation was approved by the National Assembly later that month. However, Ratsiraka referred the legislation back to the National Assembly, and in April it was rejected after further deliberation.

Elections to an expanded National Assembly followed on 17 May 1998, under a new electoral law. Of the 150 seats, 82 were to be filled from single-member constituencies, with the remaining deputies to be elected by a system of proportional representation in 34 two-member constituencies. Ratsiraka's party, AREMA, performed well in the elections, winning 63 seats, while the pro-presidential LEADER/Fanilo and the Rassemblement pour le socialisme et la démocratie (RPSD) secured 16 and 11 seats, respectively. Ratsirahonana's party, Ny asa vita no ifampitsara (AVI), emerged as the strongest opposition party, with 14 seats, while Zafy's new party—Asa, Faharaminana, Fampandrasoana, Arinda (AFFA)—won six seats; independent candidates took 32 seats. The AVI and 24 independent deputies were subsequently reported to have joined the AREMA majority, leaving the AFFA and the remaining independents as the only significant parliamentary opposition. In July Tantely Andrianarivo, hitherto Deputy Prime Minister, was appointed as Prime Minister, retaining responsibility for finance and the economy. The 31-member Council of Ministers was dominated by AREMA, with the key portfolios largely unchanged; 12 new ministers were appointed.

The first local government elections—communal voting for 20,000 councillors and 1,392 mayors—since the reintroduction of the three-tier system of local government (provinces, regions and communes), under the amended Constitution of 1998, took place on 14 November 1999. The greatest successes were recorded by nominally independent candidates. Most notably, Marc Ravalomanana, the head of the country's largest agro-industrial processor, Tiko, was elected mayor of Antananarivo; Ravalomanana had been a principal donor of electoral funds to the AVI, but had stood as an independent. Roland Ratsiraka, a nephew of the President, was elected independent mayor of Toamasina. Provincial elections took place on 3 December 2000 to elect 336 councillors, as a preliminary step to the decentralization of certain powers to six autonomous provinces (legislation on the organization of which had been approved by the National Assembly in August). It was reported that AREMA had secured control of most of the major towns, although the AVI won a majority of seats in Antananarivo.

On 18 March 2001 a 1,727-member electoral college, which included mayors and local councillors, elected 60 members of the new Senate. AREMA won 49 of the 60 seats, while LEADER/Fanilo secured five seats and opposition parties a total of six, including two for the AVI. President Ratsiraka subsequently named the remaining 30 senators who would constitute the 90-seat upper house.

A presidential election took place on 16 December 2001, contested by six candidates, including Ratsiraka, Zafy, Razafimahaleo and Ravalomanana. According to the official results, Ravalomanana, whose candidacy was supported by a number of opposition parties, most notably the AVI, the RPSD and the MFM, secured 46.2% of the votes cast and Didier Ratsiraka 40.9%, thereby necessitating a second round of voting. However, Ravalomanana's own electoral observers disputed this result, claiming that he had won an outright victory, with 52.2% of the votes, and demanded a public comparison of voting records. The opposition was supported in these demands by international electoral observers. A re-count was subsequently conducted, and on 25 January 2002 the Constitutional High Court endorsed the official results and ruled that a second round of voting should take place within 30 days. Ravalomanana rejected this verdict and called for a national strike in protest. Some 500,000 people responded by gathering in Antananarivo; government offices, public utilities and banks ceased operations, and air traffic was suspended. Ravalomanana's supporters also closed the central bank in order to prevent Ratsiraka from withdrawing special funds from the treasury. Strike action continued, in varying forms, for eight weeks. Following a meeting between Ravalomanana and Ratsiraka in mid-February, negotiations were conducted between their representatives, with mediation by the Organization of African Unity (OAU); Ratsiraka's delegates rejected Ravalomanana's proposals for the formation of an interim government and new appointments to the Constitutional High Court and electoral committee. Meanwhile, the Minister of the Armed Forces, Gen. Marcel Ranjeva, declared that the army would remain neutral in the electoral dispute.

On 22 February 2002 Ravalomanana accelerated events by unilaterally declaring himself President at a ceremony in Antananarivo attended by 100,000 supporters. The President of the Senate immediately declared Ravalomanana's proclamation to be illegal, and it was widely condemned by the international community. In response, President Ratsiraka declared a three-month 'state of national necessity', according himself broad powers, including the right to pass laws by decree. On 26 February Ravalomanana named Jacques Sylla, a former Minister of Foreign Affairs under Zafy's presidency, as his Prime Minister. On the following day Ratsiraka's Minister of Foreign Affairs and

Minister of Post and Telecommunications both resigned. Meanwhile, after weeks of largely peaceful protests, violent clashes erupted between supporters of Ratsiraka and Ravalomanana in Antananarivo, prompting Ratsiraka to decree martial law and appoint a military governor, Gen. Léon-Claude Raveloarison, in the capital. None the less, Ravalomanana proceeded with the formation of his rival Government in early March, while opposition supporters erected barricades against the army and set fire to the military headquarters; 17 of those appointed to Ravalomanana's administration were successfully installed in government offices, accompanied by large crowds of supporters and unopposed by the military. On the same day the governors of the five remaining provinces of the country declared their allegiance to Ratsiraka, recognizing his hometown, Toamasina (where Ratsiraka and his ministers had relocated) as a temporary 'alternative capital'. A few days later Gen. Ranjeva resigned as Minister of the Armed Forces, shortly after Ravalomanana's rival Government had taken control of his offices in Antananarivo. Gen. Raveloarison resigned as military governor of Antananarivo some three weeks after his appointment, having failed to apply martial law and order troops to end protests, on the grounds that this would have incurred deaths. Later in March 58 of Madagascar's 150 deputies attended a parliamentary session called by Ravalomanana and elected an interim President of the National Assembly.

An OAU mission held talks with Ravalomanana and Ratsiraka in March 2002, in an attempt to resolve the ongoing political crisis, but its proposal for a 'government of national reconciliation' was rejected by both sides. At the beginning of April supporters of Ratsiraka, who had erected roadblocks to isolate Antananarivo in February, destroyed two of the bridges located on its supply routes to the rest of the island, in an effort to intensify the effective siege of the capital, which was already suffering from severe fuel shortages. The situation fostered fears of ethnic conflict, with Ravalomanana supported by the predominantly Merina population of Antananarivo and the central highlands, and Ratsiraka by the *côtiers*. This concern was exacerbated by Ravalomanana's appeal for his supporters to overthrow the roadblocks around the capital, declaring the country to be in a state of war and listing the names of those considered to be enemies. The OAU condemned Ravalomanana's statements as incitement to violence.

On 10 April 2002 the Supreme Court ruled that there had been irregularities in the appointment, shortly before the presidential election, of six of the nine judges of the Constitutional High Court, which had endorsed the official results; one week later the Supreme Court annulled the disputed results and ordered a re-count of the votes. On the following day Ratsiraka and Ravalomanana signed a peace accord in Dakar, Senegal, where they had been holding talks under the auspices of the OAU and the UN, and with mediation by the Presidents of Senegal, Benin, Côte d'Ivoire and Mozambique. Following the completion of the re-count, in late April, the Constitutional High Court ruled that Ravalomanana had secured the presidency, with 51.5% of the votes cast, while Ratsiraka had won 35.9%. Ratsiraka, who had failed to remove the blockade of Antananarivo (in contravention of the Dakar accord), refused to accept the Court's decision. Nevertheless, Ravalomanana was inaugurated as President on 6 May, largely without international recognition, and appointed a new Council of Ministers later that month. Four of the country's six provincial governors, who were loyal to Ratsiraka, subsequently threatened to secede. Ravalomanana and Ratsiraka failed to reach agreement at further talks in Dakar in early June. Heavy fighting ensued, as troops loyal to Ravalomanana conducted a military offensive against areas controlled by Ratsiraka, securing two provincial capitals, Mahajanga and Toliary, in mid-June.

In mid-June 2002 Ravalomanana dissolved the Government that he had formed in May, immediately reappointing Sylla as Prime Minister; however, despite nominating six new members of the Council of Ministers, he failed to appoint a government of national unity. At the end of June the USA recognized Ravalomanana as the legitimate leader of Madagascar; endorsement soon followed from France and, in contravention of the policy of the OAU, Senegal. Meanwhile, the OAU suspended Madagascar from its meetings, pending the staging of free and fair elections leading to the establishment of a legitimate government; this decision was upheld by the African Union (AU, see p. 164), which replaced the OAU in July. In early July Ravalomanana's government troops took control of Antsiranana and Toamasina, and Ratsiraka sought exile in France; this apparent admission of defeat allowed for an international conference to take place in Paris, France, on the donation of aid for the reconstruction of Madagascar. The new Government was in full control of the island by the middle of the month. Ravalomanana replaced the 30 presidentially appointed members of the Senate, with the approval of the Constitutional High Court, despite the fact that those appointed by Ratsiraka had been appointed for a tenure of six years. In August six of the nine members of the Constitutional High Court were also replaced. In early October Ravalomanana dismissed Narisoa Rajaonarivony as Deputy Prime Minister and Minister of Finance and Development and altered the portfolio of Benjamin Andriamparany Radavidson from Minister of the Economy and Planning to that of Minister of the Economy, Finance and the Budget.

In mid-October 2002 the National Assembly was dissolved in preparation for legislative elections, brought forward from May 2003, in response to pressure from aid donors, in order to finalize the legitimacy of Ravalomanana's mandate. At the elections, which took place on 15 December 2002, Ravalomanana's party, Tiako i Madagasikara (TIM—I Love Madagascar), won 104 of the 160 seats and the pro-Ravalomanana Firaisankinam-Pirenena, an alliance of the AVI and elements of the RPSD, secured a further 22 seats; notably, 23 independent deputies were elected, and the formerly incumbent AREMA party won only three seats. (Foreign observers were permitted to be present at the elections for the first time in Malagasy electoral history.) In mid-January 2003 a new Government was appointed, which included 10 new ministers and was reduced in overall size from 30 to 20 ministers; the former Minister of Public Works, Jean Lahiniriako, was elected President of the National Assembly. Madagascar's suspension from meetings of the AU—hitherto the only remaining significant authority not to have recognized the new Government—was formally revoked at the organization's General Assembly in July of that year; the legitimacy of the Ravalomanana administration was thus considered finally to have been established. In August former President Ratsiraka was sentenced, *in absentia*, to 10 years' hard labour for the embezzlement of public funds and declared unfit for public office.

In January 2004 Ravalomanana restructured and reshuffled the Council of Ministers, reducing its membership to 17 ministers and two secretaries of state. Several former supporters of Ratsiraka were appointed in order to diversify the ethnic composition of the Government, which had hitherto been dominated by the Merina. In March the President granted pardons to those sentenced to less than three years' imprisonment for involvement with the pro-Ratsiraka resistance; those with more serious sentences would have the right to apply individually for an amnesty.

Civil unrest was evident from January 2004, initially among army reservists protesting at the non-payment of their demobilization bonuses. More generalized public demonstrations subsequently took place, in response to economic hardship, caused by high global petroleum prices and the suspension of import taxes and tariffs on a range of goods from August 2003 which had led to a large increase in imports, thus undermining the national currency and inflating consumer prices. This atmosphere culminated in a series of grenade attacks on associates of President Ravalomanana in June, July and November.

In December 2004 the TIM held its first national congress, at which Sylla resigned as Secretary-General; a reshuffle of the Council of Ministers was effected early in the same month. President Ravalomanana increased the accountability of the Government with ministerial performances being graded, financial bonuses awarded for the attainment of performance targets and the introduction of possible dismissal from office as the result of failure to reach such targets.

In March 2005 Zaza Ramandimbiarisona resigned as Deputy Prime Minister in charge of Economic Programmes and the post was subsequently abolished, although a successor was appointed to his secondary role as Minister of Transport and Public Works. As part of that reorganization the office of Secretary of State for Decentralization and National and Regional Development was redesignated as a ministerial portfolio. In October a further minor reorganization was effected, with the appointment of Roger-Marie Rafanomezantsoa as Minister of Industry, Trade and the Development of the Private Sector and of Tombo Ramandimbisoa to the Ministry of Youth and Sports. Furthermore, the Minister of the Interior and Administrative Reform, Gen. Soja, was unexpectedly dismissed in November, following an alleged attempt on the President's life; he was replaced by Lt-Gen. Charles Rabemananjara. Meanwhile, in October the Government forcibly closed the Fiangonana Protestanta Vaovao eto Madagasikara (FPVM) protestant church, for illegally occupying churches of the Fiangonan' i Jesoa Kristy eto Madagasikara (FJKM), of which President Ravalomanana was a senior official, and posing a threat to public order. Some observers feared a threat to the secular status of the country, with the President declaring that he hoped for a Christian nation. The FPVM challenged the closure, but it was ruled by a civil court that only the President could overturn the decision.

In mid-November 2006 Gen. Randrianafidiosa, a senior member of the armed forces whose candidacy for the presidential election scheduled for the following month had been rejected by the Constitutional Court, attempted a military coup to overthrow what he termed an 'illegitimate' Government. An aircraft aboard which President Ravalomanana was returning from Europe was diverted as gunfire broke out near the airport at Antananarivo, and it was reported that a member of the security forces had been shot dead outside a military base. Randrianafidiosa initially evaded capture, but was arrested by the authorities in mid-December.

The presidential election was held on 3 December 2006. According to results released by the Constitutional Court on 23 December, Ravalomanana secured 54.79% of votes cast in the first-round ballot, thus obviating the requirement for a second round of voting. His closest rival was Jean Lahiniriko, who took 11.65% of the votes. The poll was generally accepted by independent observers as free and fair. President Ravalomanana was formally sworn in for a second term in office on 19 January 2007 and the following day he appointed Gen. Charles Rabemananjara, hitherto Minister of the Interior and Administrative Reform, as Prime Minister. The majority of those appointed to the new Government announced later that month were members of the FJKM church, including, most notably, Harison Edmond Randriarimanana, who was appointed to head the newly created Ministry of the Economy, Planning, the Private Sector and Commerce.

At a national referendum conducted on 4 April 2007 75.3% of participants voted in favour of amendments to the Constitution, which included the abolition of autonomous powers for the six provinces. Voter turn-out was reported at just 44%. The new Constitution also adopted English as the country's third official language alongside Malagasy and French and granted extended powers to the President, including the right to legislate by decree in the event of the declaration of a state of emergency.

President Ravalomanana dissolved the National Assembly on 24 July 2007, claiming that its composition was no longer representative of the recently restructured regional and national administrative order. Elections to the 127 seats (reduced from 160) were held on 23 September, in which the TIM secured 105 seats while independent candidates won 11. However, results in two constituencies were annulled owing to alleged voting irregularities. In October the President of the TIM, Razoharimihaja Solofonantenaina, resigned citing ill health; Yvan Randriasandratriniony, the Minister of Decentralization and Territorial Development, was selected as his successor. Later that month, in a governmental reorganization, Cécile Manorohanta was appointed Minister of National Defence, while Bakolalao Ramanandraibe Ranaivoharivony was named as Minister of Justice and Keeper of the Seals; Haja Nirina Razafinjatovo became Minister of Finance and the Budget.

Madagascar's foreign policy is officially non-aligned: while it formerly maintained close links with communist countries (particularly the People's Republic of China, the Democratic People's Republic of Korea and the former USSR), the Zafy Government established relations with Israel, South Africa and the Republic of Korea. Relations with France have been affected by disputes over compensation for nationalized French assets and over the continuing French claim to the Iles Glorieuses, north of Madagascar, and three other islets in the Mozambique Channel. In 1980 the UN voted in favour of restoring all the disputed islets to Madagascar. In early 1986 the Government announced the extension of Madagascar's exclusive economic zone to include the Iles Glorieuses and the three islets. In 1997 government announcements regarding future privatization plans in Madagascar prompted renewed appeals from France for compensation for nationalized French assets. In response, the Government allocated some 50,000m. francs MG as initial compensation in the budget for 1998. In February 2000 it was agreed that the Iles Glorieuses would be co-administered by France, Madagascar and Mauritius, without prejudice to the question of sovereignty. In April 2004, during a state visit to Madagascar by Prime Minister Paul Bérenger of Mauritius, political and economic co-operation agreements between the two countries were signed.

Relations with China were strengthened in January 1999, during a visit by Vice-President Hu Jintao; agreements were signed on the expansion of bilateral economic relations and China's provision of preferential loans to Madagascar. In September 2000 the representative office for Taiwan in Madagascar was closed down, following an official visit by the Malagasy Minister of Foreign Affairs to China. (It was claimed that this was carried out by the Government in support of the 'one China' policy; however, the Taiwanese claimed that the office had never functioned effectively.) In 2005 Prime Minister Sylla denounced the Taiwanese authorities' decision to terminate the National Unification Council, which had been established in 1990 to oversee the island's eventual unification with China.

Government

The Constitution of the Third Republic was endorsed by national referendum on 19 August 1992, but was extensively revised by amendments that were endorsed by national referendum on 15 March 1998. The amended Constitution enshrined a 'federal-style' state, composed of six autonomous provinces (faritany), each with a provincial council (holding legislative power) elected by universal suffrage for a term of five years. Each provincial council elected a governor; however, these officials were replaced on an interim basis by presidentially appointed representatives following the governmental crisis in 2002 (see above). Legislation was passed subsequently whereby local administration was restructured into 22 regions and in September 2004 each region was nominated a regional chief responsible for decentralizing operations. A national referendum held on 4 April 2007 approved a number of further amendments to the Constitution, including the abolition of autonomy for the six provinces. The first local elections (for communal councillors and mayors) under the restored three-tier system of provinces, regions and communes, as envisaged in the Constitution, took place in November 1999. Provincial elections were held in December 2000 and in November 2003. The Constitution provides for a bicameral legislature, comprising a Senate (established in March 2001) and a National Assembly. Two-thirds of the members of the Senate are elected by the autonomous provinces, and the remaining one-third of the members are appointed by the President, while the National Assembly is elected by universal suffrage for a five-year term of office. The constitutional Head of State is the President, who is elected for a term of five years, and can be re-elected for two further terms. The President appoints the Prime Minister and, on the latter's recommendation, the other members of the Council of Ministers.

Defence

As assessed at November 2007, total armed forces numbered about 13,500 men: army 12,500, navy 500 and air force 500. There is a paramilitary gendarmerie of 8,100. The defence budget for 2007 was estimated at 700,000m. ariary.

Economic Affairs

In 2006, according to estimates by the World Bank, Madagascar's gross national income (GNI), measured at average 2004–06 prices, was US $5,343m., equivalent to about $280 per head (or $960 per head on an international purchasing-power parity basis). During 1996–2006, it was estimated, the population increased at an average annual rate of 2.9%, while gross domestic product (GDP) per head increased, in real terms, by an average of 0.4% per year. Overall GDP increased, in real terms, at an average annual rate of 3.3% in 1996–2006; GDP increased by 4.9% in 2006.

In 2007 the agricultural sector (including forestry and fishing) accounted for an estimated 27.0% of GDP and employed an estimated 82.0% of the economically active population in 2005. Rice, the staple food crop, is produced on some 50% of cultivated land. Since 1972, however, imports of rice have been necessary to supplement domestic production. The most important cash crops are vanilla (which accounted for an estimated 27.8% of total export revenue in 2004), cloves and coffee. Following a long drought in 2003, vanilla production was estimated to have halved in that year, leading to a dramatic escalation in world prices and the development of the crop in other countries, as well as an increase in synthetic alternatives; however, prices had declined significantly at the beginning of 2005, having a negative impact on producers. Sugar, coconuts, tropical fruits, cotton and sisal are also cultivated. Cattle-farming is important. Sea fishing by coastal fishermen (particularly for crustaceans) is being expanded, while vessels from the European Union fish for tuna and prawns in Madagascar's exclusive maritime zone, within 200 nautical miles (370 km) of the coast, in return for compensation. According to World Bank figures, agricultural GDP increased by an average of 2.1% per year in 1996–2006; the sector's GDP increased by 2.2% in 2006.

Industry (including mining, manufacturing, construction and power) contributed an estimated 15.3% of Madagascar's GDP in 2007, and employed 3.4% of the employed labour force in 2005. According to the World Bank, industrial GDP increased at an average annual rate of 3.0% in 1996–2006; the sector's GDP increased by 2.7% in 2006.

The mining sector contributed only 0.3% of GDP in 1991 and engaged 0.2% of the employed labour force in 2005. However, Madagascar has sizeable deposits of a wide range of minerals, principally chromite (chromium ore), which, with graphite and mica, is exported, together with small quantities of semi-precious stones. A major project to resume the mining of ilmenite (titanium ore) in south-eastern Madagascar, which would generate US $550m. over a 30-year period but which had prompted considerable controversy on environmental grounds, received approval from the Government in 2001, on the basis that QIT Madagascar Minerals would pursue simultaneously a strong environmental conservation programme. Construction of the mining facilities and rehabilitation of a deep-sea multi-purpose port at Ehoala, near Fort Dauphin (Tolagnaro) commenced in 2006, with an estimated budget of $585m. The operation was expected to commence production in late 2008, with an initial capacity of 750,000 metric tons. Other potential mineral projects included the exploitation of an estimated 100m. tons of bauxite in the south-east of the country, and of nickel and cobalt deposits in Ambatovy, central Madagascar. The presence of significant grades of the platinum group of metals were confirmed, as well as copper and nickel, in 2004. Renewed interest was also shown in that year in reviving the country's long-inactive uranium mines. An agreement with the People's Republic of China in 2005 for the export of chrome ore held significant potential for the development of that sector. Following exploratory drilling for petroleum at three offshore areas in the early 1990s, it was announced that only non-commercial deposits of petroleum and gas had been discovered, although contracts for further exploration were granted in 1997 and 1999. In late 2007 it was announced that a large nickel mining project was due to begin production by 2010, with annual output expected to reach 60,000 tons of nickel and 5,600 tons of cobalt. The project was expected to provide employment for some 5,000 workers.

According to the World Bank, manufacturing contributed 13.4% of GDP in 2006 and engaged some 2.8% of the employed labour force in 2005. The petroleum refinery at Toamasina, using imported petroleum, provides a significant share of export revenue. Other important branches of manufacturing are textiles and clothing, food products, beverages and chemical products. The introduction of a new investment code in 1990 and the creation of a number of export-processing zones achieved some success in attracting foreign private investment, particularly in the manufacturing branches of textiles, cement, fertilizers and pharmaceuticals. According to the World Bank, manufacturing GDP increased at an average annual rate of 2.9% in 1996–2006; the GDP of the sector increased by 2.7% in 2006.

Energy generation depends on imports of petroleum (which accounted for an estimated 22.9% of the value of total imports in 2004) to fuel thermal installations, although hydroelectric resources have also been developed, and accounted for an estimated 67.6% of electricity production in 2001.

The services sector accounted for an estimated 57.8% of GDP in 2007, and engaged some 14.6% of the employed labour force in 2005. An information communication technologies business park was under development in Antananarivo as part of an effort to diversify Madagascar's economic growth. According to the World Bank, the GDP of the services sector increased by an average of 3.7% per year in 1996–2006; services GDP increased by 7.0% in 2006.

In 2005 Madagascar recorded a visible trade deficit of US $592m., and there was a deficit of $626m. on the current account of the balance of payments. The principal source of imports in 2004 was France (15.3%); other major suppliers were the People's Republic of China, Bahrain and South Africa. France was also the principal market for exports (accounting for 35.8% of exports in that year); the USA, Mauritius and Singapore were also important purchasers. The principal exports in 2004 were vanilla, crustaceans and cloves; food and live animals constituted 60.5% of the value of total exports. The principal imports in that year were basic manufactures, machinery and transport equipment, food and live animals and mineral fuels.

Madagascar's overall budget deficit for 2007 (excluding grants) was estimated at 1,265,800m. ariary. Madagascar's external debt totalled US $3,465m. at the end of 2005, of which $3,178m. was long-term public debt. The cost of debt-servicing that year was estimated to be equivalent to 17.0% of the value of exports of goods and services. The annual rate of inflation averaged 10.7% in 2000–06; consumer prices increased by 20.4% in 2006. About 2.8% of the labour force was unemployed in 2005.

Madagascar is a member of the Indian Ocean Commission (see p. 412) and of the Common Market for Eastern and Southern Africa (COMESA, see p. 205). In August 2005 Madagascar joined the Southern African Development Community (SADC, see p. 386).

Economic activity in Madagascar was paralysed from the beginning of 2002—amid political uncertainty caused by the disputed presidential election (see Recent History)—by the strikes called by Marc Ravalomanana and the blockades ordered by Didier Ratsiraka. The closure of the central bank from the end of January resulted in the freezing of the nation's assets, rendering Madagascar unable to service its debts and at risk of default; real GDP for the year declined by 11.9%. Companies in the export-processing zone (EPZ) and in the agricultural sector were severely affected by the political crisis, being highly dependent on foreign purchasers and the transportation network, while tourism also was drastically curtailed. In July international donors pledged some US $2,300m. (one-half of which was to be supplied by the Bretton Woods institutions) over a period of four years towards the reconstruction and development of the country; this subsequently enabled the authorities to repay the arrears on all external payments. In October the IMF fully disbursed a structural adjustment credit of $100m., and in November it approved an Emergency Economic Recovery Credit and other loans aimed at public sector management and private sector development. The economy recovered significantly in 2003, and in November 2004, following Madagascar's completion of its obligations under the IMF's initiative for heavily indebted poor countries, the 'Paris Club' of international creditors restructured the country's debt; many participants, including France and, subsequently, Japan and the USA, cancelled the entire amount owed to them, reaching a total reduction of some $836m. Madagascar was also one of the first countries to negotiate a compact with the USA under its Millennium Challenge Account foreign-aid programme; this constituted some $110m. to be disbursed over four years as part of a poverty-reduction project which was to: expand property rights for citizens, strengthen the financial sector and promote investment in agriculture. In July 2005 the World Bank announced $129.8m. of funding under an 'integrated growth poles' project, aimed at broadening the base of the country's growth and employment beyond the narrow sector of textiles in the EPZ. The authorities subsequently announced a major road improvement project for 2006, which was intended to provide employment in the medium term and improve trade in the long term. (Road restoration remains a challenge, with useable roads in that year measuring just 15,000 km compared with 35,000 km in 1960). In early 2008, following the second and third reviews under a three-year Poverty Reduction and Growth Facility, a further $25m. was released by the IMF, bringing the total financial disbursement under the programme to $49.9m. The World Bank, meanwhile, approved a loan of $40m. for poverty reduction as part of the Madagascar Action Plan, which aimed to reduce the poverty rate in the country to below 50% of the population and sustain economic growth of between 8%–10% from 2012. GDP growth for 2007 was estimated by the IMF at 6.5%, with growth of 7.3% projected for 2008.

Education

Six years' education, to be undertaken usually between six and 13 years of age, is officially compulsory. Madagascar has both public and private schools, although legislation that was enacted in 1978 envisaged the progressive elimination of private education. In 2002 primary school fees were abolished. Primary education generally begins at the age of six and lasts for five years. Secondary education, beginning at 11 years of age, lasts for a further seven years, comprising a first cycle of four years and a second of three years. According to UNESCO estimates, in 2003/04 primary enrolment included 89% of children in the relevant age-group (males 89%; females 89%), while in 1998/

MADAGASCAR

99 secondary enrolment included 11% of children in the relevant age-group (males 11%; females 11%). In 1998/99 31,013 students attended institutions providing tertiary education; there are six universities in Madagascar. In 1999 the OPEC Fund granted a loan worth US $10m. to support a government programme to improve literacy standards and to increase access to education. In 2001 the Arab Bank for Economic Development in Africa granted a loan of $8m. to finance a project in support of general education. The budget for 2004 allocated 205,400m. ariary (22.9% of budgetary expenditure) to education.

Public Holidays

2008: 1 January (New Year), 29 March (Martyr's Day, Commemoration of 1947 Rebellion), 24 March (Easter Monday), 1 May (Labour Day and Ascension Day), 11 May (Whitsun), 25 May (Organization of African Unity Day), 26 June (Independence Day), 15 August (Assumption), 1 November (All Saints' Day), 25 December (Christmas).

2009: 1 January (New Year), 29 March (Martyr's Day, Commemoration of 1947 Rebellion), 13 April (Easter Monday), 1 May (Labour Day), 21 May (Ascension Day), 25 May (Organization of African Unity Day), 31 May (Whitsun), 26 June (Independence Day), 15 August (Assumption), 1 November (All Saints' Day), 25 December (Christmas).

Weights and Measures

The metric system is in force.

Statistical Survey

Source (unless otherwise stated): Institut National de la Statistique Malagache, BP 485, Anosy Tana, 101 Antananarivo; tel. (20) 2227418; e-mail dridnstat@wanadoo.mg; internet www.instat.mg; Ministry of Economy, Finance and Budget, BP 61, 101 Antananarivo; internet www.mefb.gov.mg.

Area and Population

AREA, POPULATION AND DENSITY

Area (sq km)	587,041*
Population (census results)	
1974–75†	7,603,790
1–19 August 1993	
Males	5,991,171
Females	6,100,986
Total	12,092,157
Population (UN estimates at mid-year)‡	
2005	18,643,000
2006	19,159,000
2007	19,683,000
Density (per sq km) at mid-2007	33.5

* 226,658 sq miles.
† The census took place in three stages: in provincial capitals on 1 December 1974; in Antananarivo and remaining urban areas on 17 February 1975; and in rural areas on 1 June 1975.
‡ Source: UN, *World Population Prospects: The 2006 Revision*.

PRINCIPAL ETHNIC GROUPS
(estimated population, 1974)

Merina (Hova)	1,993,000	Sakalava	470,156*
Betsimisaraka	1,134,000	Antandroy	412,500
Betsileo	920,600	Antaisaka	406,468*
Tsimihety	558,100		

* 1972 figure.

PRINCIPAL TOWNS
(population at 1993 census)

Antananarivo (capital)	1,103,304	Mahajanga (Majunga)	106,780
Toamasina (Tamatave)	137,782	Toliary (Tuléar)	80,826
Antsirabé	126,062	Antsiranana (Diégo-Suarez)	59,040
Fianarantsoa	109,248		

2001 (estimated population, incl. Renivohitra and Avaradrano): Antananarivo 1,111,392.

Mid-2007 ('000, incl. suburbs, UN estimate): Antananarivo 1,697 (Source: UN, *World Urbanization prospects: The 2007 Revision*).

BIRTHS AND DEATHS

	2004	2005	2006
Birth rate (per 1,000)	38.6	38.0	37.4
Death rate (per 1,000)	11.7	11.5	11.4

Source: African Development Bank.

Expectation of life (years at birth, WHO estimates): 58.2 (males 56.4; females 60.2) in 2005 (Source: WHO, *World Health Statistics*).

ECONOMICALLY ACTIVE POPULATION
(labour force survey, '000 persons)

	2005
Agriculture, hunting and forestry	7,745.3
Fishing	99.0
Mining and quarrying	18.8
Manufacturing	267.5
Electricity, gas and water	27.5
Construction	13.0
Wholesale and retail trade; repair of motor vehicles, motor cycles and personal and household goods	470.5
Hotels and restaurants	63.9
Transport, storage and communications	86.3
Financial intermediation	4.1
Public administration and defence; compulsory social security	202.4
Education	44.5
Health and social work	9.9
Other community, social and personal service activities	517.7
Total employed	9,570.4
Unemployed	274.3
Total labour force	9,844.7
Males	4,942.2
Females	4,902.4

Source: ILO.

Health and Welfare

KEY INDICATORS

Total fertility rate (children per woman, 2005)	5.1
Under-5 mortality rate (per 1,000 live births, 2005)	119
HIV/AIDS (% of persons aged 15–49, 2005)	0.5
Physicians (per 1,000 head, 2004)	0.29
Hospital beds (per 1,000 head, 2002)	0.42
Health expenditure (2004): US $ per head (PPP)	28.9
Health expenditure (2004): % of GDP	3.0
Health expenditure (2004): public (% of total)	59.1
Access to water (% of persons, 2004)	50
Access to sanitation (% of persons, 2004)	34
Human Development Index (2005): ranking	143
Human Development Index (2005): value	0.533

For sources and definitions, see explanatory note on p. vi.

MADAGASCAR

Agriculture

PRINCIPAL CROPS
('000 metric tons)

	2004	2005	2006
Rice (paddy)	3,030	3,400	3,485
Maize	350	293	293*
Potatoes	281	281	220*
Sweet potatoes	542	526	526*
Cassava (Manioc)	1,949	2,144	2,359
Taro (Coco yam)*	200	n.a.	200
Sugar cane	2,224	2,446	2,691
Dry beans	70	62*	70*
Groundnuts (in shell)	35	38	42
Coconuts*	85	85	85
Oil palm fruit*	21	21	21
Cottonseed†	9	6	9
Tomatoes*	22	23	23
Bananas*	290	303	303
Oranges*	83	83	83
Guavas, mangoes and mongosteens*	210	211	211
Avocados*	23	24	24
Pineapples*	51	51	51
Cashewapple*	68	n.a.	68
Coffee (green)	68	61*	82
Vanilla	1	1	1*
Cinnamon (Canella)*	2	1	1
Cloves*	18	20	22
Cotton (lint)	7*	n.a.	4*
Sisal	17	n.a.	17*
Tobacco (leaves)	2	2	2*

* FAO estimate(s).
† Unofficial figures.

Aggregate production ('000 metric tons, may include official, semi-official or estimated data): Total cereals 3,391 in 2004, 3,705 in 2005, 3,790 in 2006; Total roots and tubers 2,972 in 2004, 3,152 in 2005, 3,305 in 2006; Total vegetables (incl. melons) 344 in 2004, 346 in 2005, 346 in 2006; Total fruits (excl. melons) 891 in 2004, 906 in 2005, 906 in 2006.

Source: FAO.

LIVESTOCK
('000 head, year ending September)

	2003	2004	2005
Cattle	8,020	8,105	9,687
Pigs*	1,600	1,600	1,600
Sheep	843	650*	703
Goats	1,252	1,249	1,200*
Chickens*	24,000	24,000	24,000
Ducks*	3,800	3,800	3,800
Geese and guinea fowls*	3,000	3,000	3,000
Turkeys*	2,000	2,000	2,000

* FAO estimate(s).

2006: Figures assumed to be unchanged from 2005 (FAO estimates).
Source: FAO.

LIVESTOCK PRODUCTS
('000 metric tons, FAO estimates)

	2002	2003	2004
Cattle meat	111.6	114.8	146.6
Sheep meat	2.5	3.2	2.5
Goat meat	6.1	6.1	6.1
Pig meat	70	73	74
Chicken meat	35.5	35.5	35.5
Duck meat	10.6	10.6	10.6
Goose meat	12.6	12.6	12.6
Turkey meat	8.4	8.4	8.4
Cows' milk	535	535	535
Hen eggs	14.9	14.9	14.9
Other eggs	4.5	4.5	4.5
Honey	4.0	4.0	4.0

2005–06: Production assumed to be unchanged from 2004 (FAO estimates).
Source: FAO.

Forestry

ROUNDWOOD REMOVALS
('000 cubic metres, excl. bark)

	2004	2005	2006
Sawlogs, veneer logs and logs for sleepers	160	160	160
Pulpwood*	23	23	23
Fuel wood†	10,770	11,055	11,339
Total	10,953	11,238	11,522

* Production assumed to be unchanged from 2000 (FAO estimates).
† FAO estimates.
Source: FAO.

SAWNWOOD PRODUCTION
('000 cubic metres, incl. railway sleepers)

	2002	2003	2004
Coniferous (softwood)	4*	8	8
Broadleaved (hardwood)	91	485	886
Total	95	493	894

* FAO estimate.

2005–06: Production assumed to be unchanged from 2004 (FAO estimates).
Source: FAO.

Fishing

('000 metric tons, live weight)

	2003	2004	2005
Capture	140.8	146.8	136.4
Cichlids	21.5	21.5	21.5
Other freshwater fishes	4.5	4.5	4.5
Narrow-barred Spanish mackerel	12.0	12.0	12.0
Other marine fishes	82.1	89.9	80.0
Shrimps and prawns	13.3	11.3	10.9
Aquaculture	9.5	8.7	8.5*
Giant tiger prawn	7.0	6.2	6.0*
Total catch	150.3	155.5	144.9*

* FAO estimate.

Note: Figures exclude aquatic plants ('000 metric tons, capture only): 1.7 in 2003; n.a. in 2004; n.a. in 2005. Also excluded are crocodiles, recorded by number rather than weight, and shells. The number of Nile crocodiles caught was: 7,300 in 2003; 4,760 in 2004; 4,850 in 2005. The catch of marine shells (in metric tons) was: 194 in 2003; n.a. in 2004; n.a. in 2005.

Source: FAO.

Mining

(metric tons, estimates)

	2003	2004	2005
Chromite*	45,040	77,386	140,000
Salt	26,000	26,000	26,000
Graphite (natural)	15,000	15,000	15,000
Mica	90	90	90

* Figures refer to gross weight. The estimated chromium content is 27%.
Source: US Geological Survey.

Industry

SELECTED PRODUCTS
(metric tons, unless otherwise indicated)

	1999	2000	2001
Raw sugar	61,370	62,487	67,917
Beer ('000 hectolitres)	610.1	645.5	691.7
Cigarettes	3,839	4,139	4,441
Woven cotton fabrics (million sq metres)	20.4	23.3	29.6
Leather footwear ('000 pairs)	460	570	568
Plastic footwear ('000 pairs)	375	303	291
Paints	1,918	1,487	1,554
Soap	15,884	15,385	15,915
Motor spirit—petrol ('000 cu metres)	98.0	122.6	128.3
Kerosene ('000 cu metres)	65.0	65.2	75.1
Gas-diesel (distillate fuel) oil ('000 cu metres)	119.0	150.4	150.2
Residual fuel oils ('000 cu metres)	198.8	225.7	247.2
Cement	45,701	50,938	51,882
Electric energy (million kWh)*	721.3	779.8	833.9

* Production by the state-owned utility only, excluding electricity generated by industries for their own use.

2002: Raw sugar 35,000 metric tons; Beer 439,000 hectolitres; Woven cotton fabrics 20m. sq metres; Soap 14,100 metric tons; Motor spirit—petrol 112,000 metric tons (estimate); Kerosene 66,000 metric tons (estimate); Gas-diesel (distillate fuel) oil 57,000 metric tons (estimate); Residual fuel oils 77,000 metric tons (estimate); Electric energy 790m. kWh (Source: mostly UN, *Industrial Commodity Statistics Yearbook*).

2003: Motor spirit—petrol 113,000 metric tons (estimate); Kerosene 67,000 metric tons (estimate); Gas-diesel (distillate fuel) oil 57,000 metric tons (estimate); Residual fuel oils 77,000 metric tons (estimate); Electric energy 900m. kWh (Source: mostly UN, *Industrial Commodity Statistics Yearbook*).

2004: Electric energy 990m. kWh (Source: mostly UN, *Industrial Commodity Statistics Yearbook*).

Cement ('000 metric tons, estimates): 80 in 2003; 130 in 2004; 180 in 2005 (Source: US Geological Survey).

Finance

CURRENCY AND EXCHANGE RATES

Monetary Units
5 iraimbilanja = 1 ariary.

Sterling, Dollar and Euro Equivalents (31 December 2007)
£1 sterling = 3,579.46 ariary;
US $1 = 1,786.69 ariary;
€1 = 2,630.19 ariary;
100,000 ariary = £2.79 = $5.60 = €3.80.

Average Exchange Rate (ariary per US $)
2005   2,003.0
2006   2,142.3
2007   1,873.9

Note: A new currency, the ariary, was introduced on 31 July 2003 to replace the franc malgache (franc MG). The old currency was to remain legal tender until 30 November. Some figures in this survey are still given in terms of francs MG.

BUDGET
('000 million ariary, central government operations)

Revenue and grants	2005	2006*	2007†
Tax revenue	1,020.0	1,259.2	1,523.8
Non-tax revenue	82.8	80.8	28.3
Grants	579.5	5,580.0	699.3
Total	1,682.3	6,920.0	2,251.4

Expenditure	2005	2006*	2007†
Current expenditure	1,107.2	1,240.6	1,411.1
Budgetary expenditure	1,021.5	1,226.2	1,397.5
Wages and salaries	456.4	596.9	721.0
Other non-interest expenditure	298.5	375.9	455.3
Interest payments	266.6	253.4	221.1
Treasury operations (net)	84.2	12.5	13.7
Counterpart funds-financed operations	1.5	1.9	—
Capital expenditure	1,038.3	1,290.3	1,406.8
Total	2,145.5	2,530.9	2,817.9

* Provisional.
† Forecasts.

INTERNATIONAL RESERVES
(US $ million at 31 December)

	2004	2005	2006
IMF special drawing rights	0.2	0.0	0.0
Foreign exchange	503.3	481.2	583.1
Total	503.5	481.2	583.1

Source: IMF, *International Financial Statistics*.

MONEY SUPPLY
('000 million ariary at 31 December)

	2004	2005	2006
Currency outside banks	591.38	599.12	715.05
Demand deposits at deposit money banks	808.05	815.57	1,035.75
Total money	1,399.43	1,414.69	1,750.81

Source: IMF, *International Financial Statistics*.

COST OF LIVING
(Consumer Price Index for Madagascans in Antananarivo; base: 2000 = 100)

	2004	2005	2006
Food	135.1	170.1	177.6
Clothing*	119.3	122.0	136.2
Rent	150.8	174.8	215.1
All items (incl. others)	140.0	152.6	183.7

* Including household linen.
Source: ILO.

NATIONAL ACCOUNTS

Expenditure on the Gross Domestic Product
('000 million ariary at current prices)

	2004	2005	2006*
Government final consumption expenditure	778.0	849.1	993.4
Private final consumption expenditure	6,725.1	8,349.2	9,739.2
Increase in stocks / Gross fixed capital formation	1,980.8	2,276.3	2,563.5
Total domestic expenditure	9,483.9	11,474.6	13,296.1
Exports of goods and services	2,650.7	2,674.8	3,230.6
Less Imports of goods and services	3,979.0	4,052.0	4,766.0
Statistical discrepancy†	—	461.7	33.0
GDP in purchasers' values	8,155.7	10,559.1	11,793.7
GDP at constant 1984 prices	498.8	521.7	546.4

* Provisional.
† Representing the difference between the expenditure and production approaches.

MADAGASCAR

Gross Domestic Product by Economic Activity
('000 million francs MG at current prices)

	2002	2003	2004
Agriculture, hunting, forestry and fishing	8,963	9,073	9,857
Mining and quarrying } Manufacturing } Electricity, gas and water }	4,078	4,777	5,456
Construction	552	652	794
Trade, restaurants and hotels	3,555	3,909	4,316
Transport, storage and communications	4,817	5,154	5,796
Financial intermediation	246	293	324
Administration	1,641	2,140	2,281
Other services	4,610	5,289	5,644
Sub-total	28,462	31,287	34,468
Less imputed bank charges	196	226	251
GDP at factor cost	28,265	31,061	34,217
Indirect taxes, less subsidies	1,777	2,803	3,435
GDP in purchasers' values	30,042	33,863	37,651

Source: Ministry of the Economy, Finance and Budget.

2004 ('000 million ariary at current prices): Agriculture, hunting, forestry and fishing 2,135.2; Industry 1,182.6; Services 4,148.8; *Sub-total* 7,466.6; Imputed bank charges –52.4; *GDP at factor cost* 7,414.2; Indirect taxes, less subsidies 741.5; *GDP in purchasers' values* 8,155.7.

2005 ('000 million ariary at current prices): Agriculture, hunting, forestry and fishing 2,668.8; Industry 1,476.6; Services 5,519.2; *Sub-total* 9,664.6; Imputed bank charges –70.2; *GDP at factor cost* 9,574.4; Indirect taxes, less subsidies 981.6; *GDP in purchasers' values* 10,559.1.

2006 ('000 million ariary at current prices, provisional): Agriculture, hunting, forestry and fishing 2,967.5; Industry 1,656.7; Services 6,143.1; *Sub-total* 10,767.3; Imputed bank charges –79.6; *GDP at factor cost* 10,688.0; Indirect taxes, less subsidies 1,105.6; *GDP in purchasers' values* 11,793.7.

2007 ('000 million ariary at current prices, estimates): Agriculture, hunting, forestry and fishing 3,363.6; Industry 1,906.1; Services 7,204.8; *Sub-total* 12,474.5; Imputed bank charges –94.7; *GDP at factor cost* 12,378.1; Indirect taxes, less subsidies 1,313.5; *GDP in purchasers' values* 13,691.6.

BALANCE OF PAYMENTS
(US $ million)

	2003	2004	2005
Exports of goods f.o.b.	854	990	834
Imports of goods f.o.b.	–1,111	–1,427	–1,427
Trade balance	–258	–437	–592
Exports of services	322	425	498
Imports of services	–619	–637	–615
Balance on goods and services	–555	–649	–710
Other income received	16	15	24
Other income paid	–94	–89	–104
Balance on goods, services and income	–632	–723	–790
Current transfers received	357	245	208
Current transfers paid	–183	–62	–45
Current balance	–458	–541	–626
Capital account (net)	143	182	192
Direct investment from abroad	13	53	85
Other investment assets	–29	295	11
Other investment liabilities	–110	–97	–102
Net errors and omissions	67	–35	91
Overall balance	–374	–143	–349

Source: IMF, *International Financial Statistics*.

External Trade

PRINCIPAL COMMODITIES
(US $ million)

Imports c.i.f.	2002	2003	2004
Food and live animals	60.3	123.7	117.8
Cereals and cereal preparations	23.7	79.0	67.4
Rice	10.3	50.2	34.4
Mineral fuels, lubricants and related materials	219.2	233.4	280.3
Petroleum, petroleum products and related materials	216.9	231.6	275.5
Crude petroleum and oils obtained from bituminous materials	77.8	84.1	0.0
Residual petroleum products	2.5	3.8	7.8
Gas oils	136.6	143.7	267.7
Chemicals and related products	61.9	107.0	103.2
Medicinal and pharmaceutical products	27.0	35.8	36.6
Basic manufactures	71.9	162.3	196.5
Textile yarn and related products	11.5	31.0	45.1
Woven cotton fabrics	2.7	4.8	6.0
Machinery and transport equipment	92.9	218.8	369.3
Electric machinery, apparatus and appliances	16.8	36.8	42.2
Road vehicles	28.8	69.3	121.3
Miscellaneous manufactures	34.6	86.9	78.3
Total (incl. others)	566.1	992.9	1,204.2

Exports f.o.b.	2002	2003	2004
Food and live animals	390.2	366.2	258.2
Fish, crustaceans and molluscs and preparations thereof	162.3	69.1	61.7
Crustaceans and molluscs	130.5	66.5	59.3
Vegetables and fruit	22.5	16.8	26.5
Coffee, tea, cocoa, spices	203.6	275.9	158.4
Spices	191.1	263.1	147.7
Vanilla	165.5	231.5	118.6
Cloves	23.2	29.4	26.9
Crude materials, inedible, except fuels	35.4	38.4	47.1
Basic manufactures	33.5	28.6	31.8
Miscellaneous manufactures	145.9	10.4	53.4
Articles of apparel and clothing accessories	113.2	1.7	1.6
Men's and boys' outerwear	32.0	0.2	0.1
Women's, girls' and infants' outerwear	17.4	0.5	0.6
Knitted or crocheted outerwear	46.2	0.0	0.0
Total (incl. others)	639.7	494.5	426.6

Source: UN, *International Trade Statistics Yearbook*.

PRINCIPAL TRADING PARTNERS
(US $ million)

Imports	2002	2003	2004
Bahrain	57.2	19.0	107.7
Belgium	8.8	20.0	38.7
China, People's Repub.	33.2	96.9	123.6
France	85.6	162.5	184.5
Germany	14.9	36.8	50.1
Hong Kong	1.3	1.1	2.6
India	21.0	48.7	52.2
Indonesia	12.3	23.7	20.3
Italy	8.8	17.8	22.3
Japan	10.3	26.8	51.1
Korea, Republic	6.4	13.3	15.5

MADAGASCAR

Imports—continued	2002	2003	2004
Malaysia	8.4	16.9	21.2
Mauritius	18.0	26.0	19.0
Pakistan	3.5	23.9	15.4
Qatar	17.6	0.5	0.5
South Africa	29.7	85.6	87.6
Thailand	2.9	13.6	30.6
United Arab Emirates	79.1	27.4	17.7
United Kingdom	4.2	11.4	19.3
USA	14.3	28.6	38.6
Total (incl. others)	566.1	992.9	1,204.2

Exports	2002	2003	2004
Belgium	8.6	5.2	4.0
Canada	13.8	9.4	8.8
France	267.4	152.2	152.6
Germany	31.0	20.6	13.2
Hong Kong	7.4	7.7	7.6
Italy	19.4	8.0	12.7
Japan	23.9	13.5	10.2
Mauritius	19.9	43.3	24.5
Netherlands	8.4	3.8	5.0
Singapore	20.9	25.2	23.9
South Africa	1.2	4.2	1.6
Spain	13.7	5.1	9.6
Thailand	6.8	7.9	3.2
United Kingdom	21.7	7.6	3.1
USA	128.9	129.5	87.9
Total (incl. others)	639.7	494.5	426.6

Source: UN, *International Trade Statistics Yearbook*.

Transport

RAILWAYS
(traffic)

	1997	1998	1999
Passengers carried ('000)	359	293	273
Passenger-km (million)	37	35	31
Freight carried ('000 metric tons)	227	213	141
Ton-km (million)	81	71	46

Source: Réseau National des Chemins de Fer Malagasy.

2000: Passenger-km (million) 19; Ton-km (million) 26 (Source: UN, *Statistical Yearbook*).

ROAD TRAFFIC
(vehicles in use)

	1994	1995	1996*
Passenger cars	54,821	58,097	60,480
Buses and coaches	3,797	4,332	4,850
Lorries and vans	35,931	37,232	37,972
Road tractors	488	560	619

* Estimates.

Source: IRF, *World Road Statistics*.

1998 ('000): Passenger cars 64.0; Commercial vehicles 9.1 (Source: UN, *Statistical Yearbook*).

SHIPPING

Merchant Fleet
(registered at 31 December)

	2004	2005	2006
Number of vessels	103	103	103
Displacement ('000 gross registered tons)	32.9	33.2	33.6

Source: Lloyd's Register-Fairplay, *World Fleet Statistics*.

International Sea-borne Freight Traffic
('000 metric tons)

	1987	1988	1989
Goods loaded:			
Mahajanga	17	18	29
Toamasina	252	350	361
other ports	79	100	137
Total	348	468	527
Goods unloaded:			
Mahajanga	37	32	31
Toamasina	748	778	709
other ports	48	53	52
Total	833	863	792

1990 ('000 metric tons): Goods loaded 540; Goods unloaded 984 (Source: UN, *Monthly Bulletin of Statistics*).

CIVIL AVIATION
(traffic on scheduled services)

	2001	2002	2003
Kilometres flown (million)	7	2	4
Passengers carried ('000)	146	241	140
Passenger-km (million)	654	266	562
Total ton-km (million)	86	42	60

Source: UN, *Statistical Yearbook*.

Tourism

TOURIST ARRIVALS BY NATIONALITY

	2004	2005
Canada and USA	9,151	13,808
France	129,263	145,192
Germany	9,609	12,025
Italy	17,159	22,657
Japan	3,432	5,952
Mauritius	9,609	9,825
Réunion	22,878	31,861
Switzerland	4,576	4,987
United Kingdom	6,864	6,732
Total (incl. others)	228,785	277,422

2003: No data available for individual countries; Total arrivals 139,000.

Tourism receipts (US $ million, incl. passenger transport): 69 in 2003; 84 in 2004; 98 in 2005.

Source: World Tourism Organization.

Communications Media

	2004	2005	2006
Telephones ('000 main lines in use)	58.7	66.9	129.8
Mobile cellular telephones ('000 subscribers)	333.9	510.3	1,045.9
Personal computers ('000 in use)	91	91	n.a.
Internet users ('000)	90	100	110

Source: International Telecommunication Union.

1995: Radio receivers ('000 in use) 2,850; Book production (incl. pamphlets): titles 131, copies ('000) 292; Daily newspapers: number 6, circulation ('000 copies) 59 (Source: UNESCO, *Statistical Yearbook*).

1996: Radio receivers ('000 in use) 2,950; Book production (incl. pamphlets): titles 119, copies ('000) 296; Daily newspapers: number 5, circulation ('000 copies) 66 (Source: UNESCO, *Statistical Yearbook*).

1997: Radio receivers ('000 in use) 3,050 (Source: UNESCO, *Statistical Yearbook*).

2000: Television receivers ('000 in use) 375.

2004: Daily newspapers (number) 9 (Source: UNESCO Institute for Statistics).

Education

(2004/05, unless otherwise indicated, UNESCO estimates, public and private schools)

	Teachers	Males	Females	Total
Pre-primary (all programmes)*	3,520	n.a.	n.a.	169.2
Primary (all programmes)	67,137	1,838.3	1,759.5	3,597.7
Secondary:				
Lower secondary (general programmes)†	19,500	244.6	241.6	486.2
Upper secondary (general programmes)	6,586	53.9	52.7	106.6
Total secondary (general programmes)	26,086	298.4	294.4	592.8
Tertiary	1,763	23.8	21.1	44.9

* 2003/04.
† Lower secondary, all programmes: 498.2 (males 252.0, females 246.2).
Source: UNESCO Institute for Statistics.

2003/04: Primary schools 19,961 (3,556,042 pupils) (Source: IMF, *Republic of Madagascar: Poverty Reduction Strategy Paper Progress Report*, December 2004).

2005/06: 6 universities; 14 private institutes of higher education.

Adult literacy rate (UNESCO estimates): 70.7% (males 76.5%; females 65.3%) in 2000 (Source: UNESCO Institute for Statistics).

Directory

The Constitution

The Constitution of the Third Republic of Madagascar was endorsed by national referendum on 19 August 1992, but was substantially altered by amendments that were endorsed in a national referendum on 15 March 1998. The amended Constitution enshrines a 'federal-style' state, composed of six autonomous provinces—each with a governor and up to 12 general commissioners (holding executive power) and a provincial council (holding legislative power). It provides for a government delegate to each province, who is charged with supervising the division of functions between the state and the province. The bicameral legislature consists of the National Assembly (the lower house), which is elected by universal adult suffrage in single-seat constituencies for a five-year term of office. The Constitution also provides for a Senate (the upper house), of which one-third of the members are presidential nominees and two-thirds are elected in equal numbers by the provincial councillors and mayors of each of the six autonomous provinces, for a term of six years. The constitutional Head of State is the President. If no candidate obtains an overall majority in the presidential election, a second round of voting is to take place a maximum of 30 days after the publication of the results of the first ballot. Any one candidate can be elected for a maximum of three five-year terms. The powers of the President were greatly increased by constitutional amendments of March 1998: he has the power to determine general state policy in the Council of Ministers, to call referendums on all matters of national importance, and to dissolve the National Assembly not less than one year after a general election. Executive power is vested in a Prime Minister, who is appointed by the President. The President appoints the Council of Ministers, on the recommendation of the Prime Minister. In a national referendum held on 4 April 2007 a number of constitutional reforms were endorsed, including the abolition of autonomous powers for the six provinces. The amended Constitution conferred on the President new powers, including the right to legislate by decree in the event of a state of emergency. English was also adopted as the country's third official language.

The Government

HEAD OF STATE

President: MARC RAVALOMANANA (inaugurated 6 May 2002, re-elected 3 December 2006).

COUNCIL OF MINISTERS
(March 2008)

Prime Minister and Minister of the Interior: CHARLES RABEMANANJARA.

Minister at the Presidency, responsible for Decentralization and Territorial Development: YVAN RANDRIASANDRATRINIONY.

Minister of Foreign Affairs: Gen. MARCEL RANJEVA.

Minister of National Defence: CÉCILE MANOROHANTA.

Minister of Justice and Keeper of the Seals: BAKOLALAO RAMANANDRAIBE RANAIVOHARIVONY.

Minister of Agriculture, Livestock and Fisheries: MARIUS RATOLONJANAHARY.

Minister of National Education and Scientific Research: ANDRIAMPARANY BENJAMIN RADAVIDSON.

Minister of Public Works and Meteorology: ROLAND RANDRIAMAMPIONONA.

Minister of Health and Family Planning: ROBINSON JEAN LOUIS.

Minister of the Economy, Commerce and Industry: IVOHASINA RAZAFIMAHEFA.

Minister of Finance and the Budget: HAJA NIRINA RAZAFINJATOVO.

Minister of the Environment, Water, Forests and Tourism: HARISON EDMOND RANDRIARIMANANA.

Minister of Energy and Mines: ELISÉ RAZAKA.

Minister of the Civil Service, Labour and Social Legislation: JACKY MAHAFALY TSIANDOPY.

Minister of Telecommunications, Post and Communications: BRUNO RAMAROSON ANDRIANTAVISON.

Minister of Transport: JULIEN RAVELONARIVO LAPORTE.

Minister of Sports, Culture and Leisure: PATRICK RAMIARAMANANA.

Deputy Minister of Health and Family Planning: MARIE PERLINE RAHANTANIRINA.

Secretary of State for Public Security at the Ministry of the Interior and Administrative Reform: DÉSIRÉ RASOLOFOMANANA.

MINISTRIES

Office of the President: Antananarivo; e-mail communication@presidency.gov.mg; internet www.madagascar-presidency.gov.mg.

MADAGASCAR

Office of the Prime Minister: BP 248, Palais d'Etat Mahazoarivo, 101 Antananarivo; tel. (20) 2264498; fax (20) 2233116; e-mail dircom@primature.gov.mg; internet www.primature.gov.mg.

Ministry of Agriculture, Livestock and Fisheries: BP 301, Anosy, 101 Antananarivo; tel. (20) 2261002; fax (20) 2264308; e-mail info@maep.gov.mg; internet www.maep.gov.mg.

Ministry of the Civil Service, Labour and Social Legislation: BP 207, Cité des 67 Hectares, 101 Antananarivo; tel. (20) 2224209; fax (20) 2233856; e-mail ministre@mfptls.gov.mg; internet www.mfptls.gov.mg.

Ministry of Decentralization and Territorial Development: BP 24 bis, 101 Antananarivo; tel. (20) 2235881; fax (20) 2237516; internet www.mprdat.gov.mg.

Ministry of National Defence: BP 08, Ampahibe, 101 Antananarivo; tel. (20) 2222211; fax (20) 2235420; e-mail mdn@wanadoo.fr; internet 196.192.32.105/MDN.

Ministry of the Economy, Commerce and Industry: Bâtiment Commerce, Ambohidahy, 101 Antananarivo; tel. (20) 2264681; fax (20) 2234530; e-mail sg@mepspc.gov.mg; internet www.mepspc.gov.mg.

Ministry of Energy and Mines: BP 527, Immeuble de l'Industrie, Antaninarenina, 101 Antananarivo; tel. (20) 2228928; fax (20) 2232554; internet www.mem.gov.mg.

Ministry of the Environment, Water, Forests and Tourism: rue Farafaty, BP 571 Ampandrianomby, 101 Antananarivo; tel. (20) 2261359; fax (20) 2241919; e-mail minenv@wanadoo.mg; internet www.minenvef.gov.mg.

Ministry of Finance and the Budget: BP 61, Antaninarenina, Antananarivo; tel. (20) 2230173; fax (20) 2264680; internet www.mefb.gov.mg.

Ministry of Foreign Affairs: BP 836, Anosy, 101 Antananarivo; tel. (20) 2221198; fax (20) 2234484; e-mail contact@madagascar-diplomatie.net; internet www.madagascar-diplomatie.net.

Ministry of Health and Family Planning: BP 88, Ambohidahy, 101 Antananarivo; tel. (20) 2263121; fax (20) 2264228; e-mail cabminsan@wanadoo.mg; internet www.sante.gov.mg.

Ministry of the Interior: BP 833, Anosy, 101 Antananarivo; tel. (20) 2223084; fax (20) 2235579; internet www.mira.gov.mg.

Ministry of Justice: rue Joel Rakotomalala, BP 231, Faravohitra, 101 Antananarivo; tel. (20) 2237684; fax (20) 2264458; e-mail presse.justice@justice.gov.mg; internet www.justice.gov.mg.

Ministry of National Defence: BP 08, Ampahibe, 101 Antananarivo; tel. (20) 2222211; fax (20) 2235420; e-mail mdn@wanadoo.fr; internet 196.192.32.105/MDN.

Ministry of National Education and Scientific Research: BP 247, Anosy, 101 Antananarivo; tel. (20) 2224308; fax (20) 2223897; e-mail mlraharimalala@yahoo.fr; internet 196.192.32.105/menrs/.

Ministry of Public Works and Meteorology: BP 295, 101 Antananarivo; tel. (20) 2228715; fax (20) 2220890; e-mail secreab@mtpm.gov.mg.

Ministry of Telecommunications, Post and Communications: pl. de l'Indépendance, Antaninarenina, 101 Antananarivo; tel. (20) 2222902; fax (20) 2234115; internet www.mtpc.gov.mg.

Ministry of Transport: BP 610, rue Fernand Kasanga Tsimbazaza, 101 Antananarivo; tel. (20) 2262816; fax (20) 2235410.

Ministry of Sports, Culture and Leisure: Ambohijatovo, pl. Goulette, BP 681, 101 Antananarivo; tel. (20) 2227780; fax (20) 2234275; e-mail mjs_101@yahoo.fr; internet www.mjs.gov.mg.

State Secretariat for Public Security: BP 23 bis, 101 Antananarivo; tel. (20) 2221029; fax (20) 2231861.

President and Legislature

PRESIDENT

Presidential Election, 3 December 2006

Candidate	Votes	% of votes
Marc Ravalomanana	2,435,199	54.79
Jean Lahiniriko	517,994	11.65
Iarovana Roland Ratsiraka	450,717	10.14
Herizo J. Razafimahaleo	401,473	9.03
Norbert Lala Ratsirahonana	187,552	4.22
Ny Hasina Andriamanjato	185,624	4.18
Others	266,191	5.99
Total	**4,444,750***	**100.00**

* Excluding 87,196 invalid votes.

LEGISLATURE

Senate

President: GUY RAJEMISON RAKOTOMAHARO.

Senatorial Election, 18 March 2001

Party	Seats
AREMA	49
LEADER/Fanilo	5
Independents	3
AVI	2
AFFA	1
Total	**60***

* Elected by a 1,727-member electoral college of provincial councillors and mayors. An additional 30 seats were appointed by the President.

National Assembly

President: JACQUES HUGUES SYLLA.

General Election, 23 September 2007, provisional results

Party	Seats
TIM	105
Independents	11
Others	9
Total	**125***

* The total number of seats is 127; however, results in two constituencies were annulled, owing to alleged voting irregularities.

Election Commission

Conseil national électoral (CNE): Immeuble Microréalisation, 4 étage, 67 ha, 101 Antananarivo; tel. (20) 2225179; fax (20) 2225881; e-mail cne@wanadoo.mg; internet www.cne.mg; Pres. THÉODORE RANDREZASON.

Political Organizations

Following the restoration of multi-party politics in March 1990, more than 120 political associations emerged, of which six secured representation in the National Assembly in 2002. The following were among the more influential political organizations in 2007:

Association pour la renaissance de Madagascar (Andry sy riana enti-manavotra an'i Madigasikara) (AREMA): f. 1975 as Avant-garde de la révolution malgache; adopted present name 1997; party of fmr Pres. Adm. (retd) Ratsiraka (now in exile); control disputed between two factions, headed by Gen. Sec. PIERROT RAJAO-NARIVELO (in exile), and Asst. Gen. Sec. PIERRE RAHARIJAONA.

Comité pour la Réconciliation Nationale (CRN): Villa la Franchise, Lot II-I 160 A, Alarobia, Antananarivo; tel. (20) 2242022; f. 2002 by fmr President Zafy; radical opposition; does not recognize the presidency of Marc Ravalomanana; formed part of the 3FN (Trois Forces Nationales) group of opposition parties, established in Sept. 2005; Leader ALBERT ZAFY.

Herim-Bahoaka Mitambatra (HBM) (Union of Popular Forces): formed part of the coalition supporting Pres. Ravalomanana prior to the presidential election; Leader TOVONANAHARY RABETSITONTA.

Libéralisme économique et action démocratique pour la reconstruction nationale (LEADER/Fanilo) (Torch): f. 1993 by Herizo Razafimahaleo; Leader Prof. MANASSE ESOAVELOMANDROSO.

Mouvement pour le progrès de Madagascar (Mpitolona ho amin'ny Fandrosoan'ny Madagasikara) (MFM): 42 & 44 Cité Ampefiloha Bldg, 101 Antananarivo; tel. (20) 2437560; e-mail servasia@wanadoo.mg; internet www.votemfm.com; f. 1972 as Mouvement pour le pouvoir prolétarien (MFM); adopted present name in 1990; advocates liberal and market-orientated policies; Leader RAKOTONIRINA MANANDAFY; Sec.-Gen. OLIVIER RAKOTOVAZAHA.

Ny asa vita no ifampitsara (AVI) (People are judged by the work they do): f. 1997 to promote human rights, hard work and development; Leader NORBERT RATSIRAHONANA.

Parti socialiste et démocratique pour l'union de Madagascar (PSDUM): f. 2006; Pres. JEAN LAHINIRIKO.

Rassemblement des forces nationales (RFN): f. 2005; a coalition of parties comprising the AKFM, LEADER/Fanilo and Fihavanantsika (led by Pasteur Daniel Rajakoba); formed part of the 3FN (Trois

MADAGASCAR

Forces Nationales) group of opposition parties, established in Sept. 2005; Leader Pasteur EDMOND RAZAFIMAHEFA.

Rassemblement pour le socialisme et la démocratie (RPSD): f. 1993 by fmr mems of PSD; also known as Renaissance du parti social-démocratique; Jean-Eugène Voninahitsy formed a breakaway party known as the RPSD Nouveau in 2003; Leader EVARISTE MARSON.

Tiako i Madagasikara (TIM) (I Love Madagascar): internet www.tim-madagascar.org; f. 2002; supports Pres. Ravalomanana; Pres. YVAN RANDRIASANDRATRINIONY.

Diplomatic Representation

EMBASSIES IN MADAGASCAR

China, People's Republic: Ancien Hôtel Panorama, BP 1658, 101 Antananarivo; tel. (20) 2240129; fax (20) 2240215; e-mail chinaemb_mg@mfa.gov.cn; internet mg.china-embassy.org; Ambassador LI SHULI.

Comoros: Antananarivo; tel. (20) 2265819; Ambassador Col HALIDI CHARIF.

Egypt: Lot MD 378 Ambalatokana Mandrosoa Ivato, BP 4082, 101 Antananarivo; tel. (20) 2245497; fax (20) 2245379; Ambassador MAGID FOAD SALEH FOAD.

France: 3 rue Jean Jaurès, BP 204, 101 Antananarivo; tel. (20) 2239898; fax (20) 2239927; e-mail ambatana@wanadoo.mg; internet www.ambafrance-mada.org; Ambassador GILDAS LE LIDEC.

Germany: 101 rue du Pasteur Rabeony Hans, BP 516, Ambodirotra, 101 Antananarivo; tel. (20) 2223802; fax (20) 2226627; e-mail amballem@wanadoo.mg; internet www.antananarivo.diplo.de; Ambassador Dr WOLFGANG MOSER.

Holy See: Amboniloha Ivandry, BP 650, 101 Antananarivo; tel. (20) 2242376; fax (20) 2242384; e-mail nuntiusantana@wanadoo.mg; Apostolic Nuncio Most Rev. AUGUSTINE KASUJJA (Titular Archbishop of Caesarea de Numidia).

India: 4 Làlana Emile Rajaonson, Tsaralalana, BP 1787, 101 Antananarivo; tel. (20) 2223334; fax (20) 2233790; e-mail indembmd@wanadoo.mg; Ambassador DILJIT SINGH PANNUN.

Indonesia: 26–28 rue Patrice Lumumba, BP 3969, 101 Antananarivo; tel. (20) 2224915; fax (20) 2232857; Chargé d'affaires a.i. SLAMET SUYATA SASTRAMIHARDZA.

Iran: route Circulaire, Lot II L43 ter, Ankadivato, 101 Antananarivo; tel. (20) 2228639; fax (20) 2222298; Ambassador ABDOL RAHIM HOMATASH.

Japan: 8 rue du Dr Villette, BP 3863, Isoraka, 101 Antananarivo; tel. (20) 2226102; fax (20) 2221769; Ambassador TETSURO KAWAGUCHI.

Korea, Democratic People's Republic: 101 Antananarivo; tel. (20) 2244442; Ambassador RI YONG HAK.

Libya: Lot IIB, 37A route Circulaire Ampandrana-Ouest, 101 Antananarivo; tel. (20) 2221892; Chargé d'affaires a.i. Dr MOHAMED ALI SHARFEDIN AL-FITURI.

Mauritius: Anjaharay, route Circulaire, BP 6040, Ambanidia, 101 Antananarivo; tel. (20) 2221864; fax (20) 2221939; Ambassador ERNEST GÉRARD LEMAIRE.

Morocco: Bâtiment D1, Rez-de-chaussée, Ankorondrano, BP 12, 104 Antananarivo; tel. (20) 2221347; fax (20) 2221124; e-mail amar_med@hotmail.com; Ambassador MUHAMMAD AMAR.

Norway: Explorer Business Park, Bâtiment 2D, Antananarivo; tel. (20) 2230507; fax (20) 2237799; e-mail emb.antananarivo@mfa.no; internet www.amb-norvege.mg; Ambassador HANS FREDERIK LEHNE.

Russia: BP 4006, Ivandry-Ambohijatovo, 101 Antananarivo; tel. (20) 2242827; fax (20) 2242642; e-mail ambrusmad@wanadoo.mg; Ambassador VLADIMIR B. GONCHARENKO.

Senegal: Lot II R, 179B Ambohirakely, Betongolo, Antananarivo; tel. (20) 2252186; fax (20) 2252186; Ambassador CÉSAR COLY.

South Africa: Villa Chandella, Lot Bonnet 38, Ivandry, BP 12101-05, 101 Antananarivo; tel. (20) 2243350; fax (20) 2243386; e-mail antanarivo@foreign.gov.za; Ambassador MOKGETHI SAMUEL MONAISA.

Switzerland: Immeuble ARO, Solombavambahoaka, Frantsay 77, BP 118, 101 Antananarivo; tel. (20) 2262997; fax (20) 2228940; e-mail ant.vertretung@eda.admin.ch; internet www.eda.admin.ch/antananarivo; Chargé d'affaires a.i. BENOÎT GIRARDIN.

USA: 14–16 rue Rainitovo, Antsahavola, BP 620, 101 Antananarivo; tel. (20) 2221257; fax (20) 2234539; internet www.usmission.mg; Ambassador R. NIELS MARQUARDT.

Judicial System

HIGH CONSTITUTIONAL COURT

Haute Cour Constitutionnelle: POB 835, Ambohidahy, 101 Antananarivo; tel. (20) 2266061; e-mail hcc@simicro.mg; internet www.simicro.mg/hcc; interprets the Constitution and rules on constitutional issues; nine mems; Pres. JEAN-MICHEL RAJAONARIVONY.

HIGH COURT OF JUSTICE

Haute Cour de Justice: 101 Antananarivo; nine mems.

SUPREME COURT

Cour Suprême: Palais de Justice, Anosy, 101 Antananarivo; Pres. ALICE RAJAONAH (acting); Attorney-General COLOMBE RAMANANTSOA (acting); Chamber Pres YOLANDE RAMANGASOAVINA, FRANÇOIS RAMANANDRAIBE.

COURT OF APPEAL

Cour d'Appel: Palais de Justice, Anosy, 101 Antananarivo; Pres. AIMÉE RAKOTONIRINA; Pres of Chamber CHARLES RABETOKOTANY, PÉTRONILLE ANDRIAMIHAJA, BAKOLALAO RANAIVOHARIVONY, BERTHOLIER RAVELONTSALAMA, LUCIEN RABARIJHON, NELLY RAKOTOBE, ARLETTE RAMAROSON, CLÉMENTINE RAVANDISON, GISÈLE RABOTOVAO, JEAN-JACQUES RAJAONA.

OTHER COURTS

Tribunaux de Première Instance: at Antananarivo, Toamasina, Antsiranana, Mahajanga, Fianarantsoa, Toliary, Antsirabé, Ambatondrazaka, Antalaha, Farafangana and Maintirano; for civil, commercial and social matters, and for registration.

Cours Criminelles Ordinaires: tries crimes of common law; attached to the Cour d'Appel in Antananarivo but may sit in any other large town. There are also 31 Cours Criminelles Spéciales dealing with cases concerning cattle.

Tribunaux Spéciaux Economiques: at Antananarivo, Toamasina, Mahajanga, Fianarantsoa, Antsiranana and Toliary; tries crimes specifically relating to economic matters.

Tribunaux Criminels Spéciaux: judges cases of banditry and looting; 31 courts.

Religion

It is estimated that more than 50% of the population follow traditional animist beliefs, some 41% are Christians (about one-half of whom are Roman Catholics) and some 7% are Muslims.

CHRISTIANITY

Fiombonan'ny Fiangonana Kristiana eto Madagasikara (FFKM)/Conseil Chrétien des Eglises de Madagascar (Christian Council of Churches in Madagascar): Vohipiraisama, Ambohijatovo-Atsimo, BP 798, 101 Antananarivo; tel. (20) 2229052; f. 1980; four mems and one assoc. mem.; Pres. Pastor EDMOND RAZAFIMAHALEO; Gen. Sec. Rev. RÉMY RALIBERA.

Fiombonan'ny Fiangonana Protestanta eto Madagasikara (FFPM)/Fédération des Eglises Protestantes à Madagascar (Federation of the Protestant Churches in Madagascar): VK 3 Vohipiraisana, Ambohijatovo-Atsimo, BP 4226, 101 Antananarivo; tel. (20) 2415888; f. 1958; two mem. churches; Pres Rev. Dr ENDOR MODESTE RAKOTO; Gen. Sec. Rev. Dr EDMOND RAZAFIMANANTSOA.

The Anglican Communion

Anglicans are adherents of the Church of the Province of the Indian Ocean, comprising six dioceses (four in Madagascar, one in Mauritius and one in Seychelles). The Archbishop of the Province is the Bishop of Antananarivo. The Church has about 160,000 adherents in Madagascar, including the membership of the Eklesia Episkopaly Malagasy (Malagasy Episcopal Church), founded in 1874.

Bishop of Antananarivo (also Archbishop of the Province of the Indian Ocean): Most Rev. RÉMI JOSEPH RABENIRINA, Evêché anglican, Lot VK57 ter, Ambohimanoro, 101 Antananarivo; tel. (20) 2220827; fax (20) 2261331; e-mail eemdanta@wanadoo.mg.

Bishop of Antsiranana: Rt Rev. ROGER CHUNG PO CHEN, Evêché anglican, 4 rue Grandidier, BP 278, 201 Antsiranana; tel. (20) 8222650; e-mail eemdants@wanadoo.mg.

Bishop of Fianarantsoa: Rt Rev. GILBERT RATELOSON RAKOTONDRAVELO, Evêché anglican, BP 1418, 531 Fianarantsoa.

Bishop of Mahajanga: Rt Rev. JEAN-CLAUDE ANDRIANJAFIMANANA, Evêché anglican, BP 169, 401 Mahajanga; e-mail eemdmaha@wanadoo.mg.

MADAGASCAR

Bishop of Toamasina: Rt Rev. JEAN PAUL SOLO, Evêché anglican, rue James Seth, BP 531, 501 Toamasina; tel. (20) 5332163; fax (20) 5331689.

The Roman Catholic Church

Madagascar comprises four archdioceses and 17 dioceses. At 31 December 2005 the number of adherents in the country represented about 27.0% of the total population.

Bishops' Conference

Conférence episcopale de Madagascar, 102 bis, rue Cardinal Jerôme Rakotomalala, BP 667, 101 Antananarivo; tel. (20) 2220478; fax (20) 2224854; e-mail ecar@vitelcom.mg.

f. 1969; Pres. Most Rev. FULGENCE RABEONY (Archbishop of Toliara).

Archbishop of Antananarivo: ODON ARSÈNE RAZANAKOLONA, Archevêché, Andohalo, BP 3030, 101 Antananarivo; tel. (20) 2220726; fax (20) 2264181; e-mail didih@simicro.org.

Archbishop of Antsiranana: Most Rev. MICHEL MALO, Archevêché, 5 blvd le Myre de Villers, BP 415, 201 Antsiranana; tel. (82) 21605; e-mail archevediego@blueline.mg.

Archbishop of Fianarantsoa: Most Rev. FULGENCE RABEMAHAFALY, Archevêché, pl. Mgr Givelet, BP 1440, Ecar Ambozontany, 301 Fianarantsoa; tel. (20) 7550027; fax (20) 7551436; e-mail ecarfianar@mel.wanadoo.mg.

Archbishop of Toliara: Most Rev. FULGENCE RABEONY, Archevêché, Maison Saint Jean, BP 30, 601 Toliary; tel. (20) 9442416; e-mail diocese_tulcar@wanadoo.mg.

Other Christian Churches

Fiangonan'i Jesoa Kristy eto Madagasikara/Eglise de Jésus-Christ à Madagascar (FJKM): Lot 11 B18, Tohatohabato Ranavalona 1, Trano 'Ifanomezantsoa', BP 623, 101 Antananarivo; tel. (20) 2226845; fax (20) 2226372; f. 1968; Pres. LALA HAJA RASENDRAHASINA; Gen. Sec. Rev. RÉMY RALIBERA; 2m. mems.

Fiangonana Loterana Malagasy (Malagasy Lutheran Church): BP 1741, 101 Antananarivo; tel. (20) 2422703; fax (20) 2423856; e-mail flm@wanadoo.mg; f. 1867; Pres. Rev. Dr ENDOR MODESTE RAKOTO; 600,000 mems.

The Press

In December 1990 the National People's Assembly adopted legislation guaranteeing the freedom of the press and the right of newspapers to be established without prior authorization.

PRINCIPAL DAILIES

Bulletin de l'Agence Nationale d'Information 'TARATRA' (ANTA): 8/10 Làlana Rainizanabololona, Antanimena, BP 194, 101 Antananarivo; tel. (20) 2234308; e-mail taratramada@blueline.mg; internet www.taratramada.com; f. 1977; Malagasy; Editor-in-Chief HANITRA RABETOKOTANY.

L'Express de Madagascar: BP 3893, 101 Antananarivo; tel. (20) 2221934; fax (20) 2262894; e-mail lexpress@malagasy.com; internet www.lexpressmada.com; f. 1995; French and Malagasy; Editor (vacant); circ. 10,000.

Gazetiko: rue Ravoninahitriniarivo, BP 1414 Ankorondrano, 101 Antananarivo; tel. (20) 2269779; fax (20) 2227351; e-mail gazetiko@midi-madagasikara.mg; internet www.gazetiko.com; Malagasy; circ. 50,000.

La Gazette de la Grande Ile: Lot II, W 23 L Ankorahotra, route de l'Université, Antananarivo; tel. (20) 2261377; fax (20) 2265188; internet www.lagazette-dgi.com; French; 24 pages; Pres. LOLA RASOAMAHARO; circ. 15,000–30,000.

Imongo Vaovao: 11K 4 bis Andravoahangy, BP 7014, 101 Antananarivo; tel. (20) 2221053; f. 1955; Malagasy; Dir CLÉMENT RAMAMONJISOA; circ. 10,000.

Madagascar Tribune: Immeuble SME, rue Ravoninahitriniarivo, BP 659, Ankorondrano, 101 Antananarivo; tel. (20) 2222635; fax (20) 2222254; e-mail tribune@wanadoo.mg; internet www.madagascar-tribune.com; f. 1988; independent; French and Malagasy; Editor RAHAGA RAMAHOLIMIHASO; circ. 12,000.

Maresaka: Cité Logt. 288, Analamahitsy, 101 Antananarivo; tel. (20) 2231665; f. 1953; independent; Malagasy; Editor R. RABEFANANINA; circ. 5,000.

Midi Madagasikara: Làlana Ravoninahitriniarivo, BP 1414, Ankorondrano, 101 Antananarivo; tel. (20) 2269779; fax (20) 2227351; e-mail infos@midi-madagasikara.mg; internet www.midi-madagasikara.mg; f. 1983; French and Malagasy; Dir MAMY RAKOTOARIVELO; circ. 21,000 (Mon.–Fri.), 35,000 (Sat.).

Les Nouvelles: BP 194, 101 Antananarivo; tel. (20) 2235433; fax (20) 2229993; e-mail administration@les-nouvelles.com; internet www.les-nouvelles.com; in French and Taratra; f. 2003; Editors-in-Chief RENAUD RAHARIJAONA, ANDRY TSILEFERINTSOA.

Ny Vaovaontsika: BP 11137, MBS Anosipatrana; tel. (20) 2227717; e-mail nyvaovaontsika@mbs.mg; f. 2004; re-estd as a daily; Malagasy; Malagasy Broadcasting System; Editor-in-Chief ROLAND ANDRIAMAHENINA; circ. 10,000.

Le Quotidien: BP 11 097, 101 Antananarivo; tel. (20) 2227717; fax (20) 2265447; e-mail lequotidien@mbs.mg; internet www.lequotidien.mg; f. 2003; owned by the Tiko Group plc; French.

PRINCIPAL PERIODICALS

Basy Vava: Lot III E 96, Mahamasina Atsimo, 101 Antananarivo; tel. (20) 2220448; f. 1959; daily; Malagasy; Dir GABRIEL RAMANANJATO; circ. 3,000.

Bulletin de la Société du Corps Médical Malgache: Imprimerie Volamahitsy, 101 Antananarivo; Malagasy; monthly; Dir Dr RAKOTOMALALA.

Dans les Médias Demain (DMD): Immeuble Jeune Afrique, 58 rue Tsiombikibo, BP 1734, Ambatovinaky, 101 Antananarivo; tel. (20) 2230755; fax (20) 2230754; e-mail dmd@wanadoo.mg; internet www.dmd.mg; f. 1986; independent; economic information and analysis; weekly; Editorial Dir JEAN ERIC RAKOTOARISOA; circ. 4,000.

Feon'ny Mpiasa: Lot M8, Isotry, 101 Antananarivo; trade union affairs; Malagasy; monthly; Dir M. RAZAKANAIVO; circ. 2,000.

Fiaraha-Miasa: BP 1216, 101 Antananarivo; Malagasy; weekly; Dir SOLO NORBERT ANDRIAMORASATA; circ. 5,000.

Gazetinao: Lot IPA 37, BP 1758, Anosimasina, 101 Antananarivo; tel. (33) 1198161; e-mail jamesdigne@caramail.com; f. 1976; French and Malagasy; monthly; Editors-in-Chief ANDRIANIAINA RAKOTOMAHANINA, JAMES FRANKLIN; circ. 3,000.

L'Hebdo: BP 3893, 101 Antananarivo; tel. (20) 2221934; f. 2005; French and Malagasy; weekly; Editor-in-Chief NASOLO VALIAVO ANDRIAMIHAJA.

Isika Mianakavy: Ambatomena, 301 Fianarantsoa; f. 1958; Roman Catholic; Malagasy; monthly; Dir J. RANAIVOMANANA; circ. 21,000.

Journal Officiel de la République de Madagascar/Gazetim-Panjakan' Ny Repoblika Malagasy: BP 248, 101 Antananarivo; tel. (20) 2265010; fax (20) 2225319; f. 1883; official announcements; Malagasy and French; weekly; Dir HONORÉE ELIANNE RALALAHARISON; circ. 1,545.

Journal Scientifique de Madagascar: BP 3855, Antananarivo; f. 1985; Dir Prof. MANAMBELONA; circ. 3,000.

Jureco: BP 6318, Lot IVD 48 bis, rue Razanamaniraka, Behoririka, 101 Antananarivo; tel. (20) 2255271; e-mail jureco@malagasy.com; internet www.jureco.com; law and economics; monthly; French; Dir MBOARA ANDRIANARIMANANA.

Lakroan'i Madagasikara/La Croix de Madagascar: BP 7524, CNPC Antsimena, 101 Antananarivo; tel. (20) 2266128; fax (20) 2224020; e-mail info@lakroa.org; internet www.geocities.com/lakroam; f. 1927; Roman Catholic; French and Malagasy; weekly; Dir Fr VINCENT RABEMAHAFALY; circ. 25,000.

La Lettre de Madagascar (LLM): Antananarivo; f. 2003; 2 a month; in French and English; economic; Editor-in-Chief DANIEL LAMY.

Mada—Economie: 15 rue Ratsimilaho, BP 3464, 101 Antananarivo; tel. (20) 2225634; f. 1977; reports events in south-east Africa; monthly; Editor RICHARD-CLAUDE RATOVONARIVO; circ. 5,000.

Mpanolotsaina: BP 623, 101 Antananarivo; tel. (20) 2226845; fax (20) 2226372; e-mail fjkm@wanadoo.mg; religious, educational; Malagasy; quarterly; Dir RAYMOND RAJOELISOL.

New Magazine: BP 7581, Newprint, Route des Hydrocarbures, 101 Antananarivo; tel. (20) 2233335; fax (20) 2236471; e-mail newmag@wanadoo.mg; internet www.newmagazine.mg; monthly; in French; Dir CLARA RAVOUAVAHY.

Ny Mpamangy-FLM: 9 rue Grandidier Isoraka, BP 538, Antsahamanitra, 101 Antananarivo; tel. (20) 2232446; f. 1882; monthly; Dir Pastor JEAN RABENANDRASANA; circ. 3,000.

Ny Sakaizan'ny Tanora: BP 538, Antsahaminitra, 101 Antananarivo; tel. (20) 2232446; f. 1878; monthly; Editor-in-Chief DANIEL PROSPER ANDRIAMANJAKA; circ. 5,000.

PME Madagascar: rue Hugues Rabesahala, BP 953, Antsakaviro, 101 Antananarivo; tel. (20) 2222536; fax (20) 2234534; f. 1989; French; monthly; economic review; Dir ROMAIN ANDRIANARISOA; circ. 3,500.

Recherche et Culture: BP 907, 101 Antananarivo; tel. (20) 2226600; f. 1985; publ. by French dept of the University of Antananarivo; 2 a year; Dir GINETTE RAMAROSON; circ. 1,000.

Revue Ita: BP 681, 101 Antananarivo; tel. (20) 2230507; f. 1985; controlled by the Ministry of Population, Social Protection and Leisure; monthly; Dir FILS RAMALANJAONA; circ. 1,000.

MADAGASCAR

Revue de l'Océan Indien: Communication et Médias Océan Indien, rue H. Rabesahala, BP 46, Antsakaviro, 101 Antananarivo; tel. (20) 2222536; fax (20) 2234534; e-mail roi@dts.mg; internet www.madatours.com/roi; f. 1980; monthly; French; Man. Dir GEORGES RANAIVOSOA; Sec.-Gen. HERY M. A. RANAIVOSOA; circ. 5,000.

Sahy: Lot VD 42, Ambanidia, 101 Antananarivo; tel. (20) 2222715; f. 1957; political; Malagasy; weekly; Editor ALINE RAKOTO; circ. 9,000.

Sosialisma Mpiasa: BP 1128, 101 Antananarivo; tel. (20) 2221989; f. 1979; trade union affairs; Malagasy; monthly; Dir PAUL RABEMANANJARA; circ. 5,000.

Vaovao: BP 271, 101 Antananarivo; tel. (20) 2221193; f. 1985; French and Malagasy; weekly; Dir MARC RAKOTONOELY; circ. 5,000.

NEWS AGENCIES

Agence Nationale d'Information 'TARATRA' (ANTA): 7 rue Jean Ralaimongo, Ambohiday, BP 386, 101 Antananarivo; tel. and fax (20) 2236047; e-mail taratra.mtpc@mtpc.gov.mg; f. 1977; Man. Dir JOÉ ANACLET RAKOTOARISON.

Mada: Villa Joëlle, Lot II J 161 R, Ivandry, 101 Antananarivo; tel. (20) 2242428; e-mail communication@mada.mg; internet www.mada.mg; f. 2003; independent information agency; Dir RICHARD CLAUDE RATOVONARIVO.

Publishers

Edisiona Salohy: BP 4226, 101 Antananarivo; Dir MIRANA VOLOLOARISOA RANDRIANARISON.

Editions Ambozontany Analamalintsy: BP 7553, 101 Antananarivo; tel. and fax (20) 2243111; e-mail editionsj@wanadoo.mg; f. 1962; religious, educational, historical, cultural and technical textbooks; Dir Fr GUILLAUME DE SAINT PIERRE RAKOTONANDRATONIARIVO.

Foibe Filankevitry Ny Mpampianatra (FOFIPA): BP 202, 101 Antananarivo; tel. (20) 2227500; f. 1971; textbooks; Dir Frère RAZAFINDRAKOTO.

Imprimerie Nouvelle: PK 2, Andranomahery, route de Majunga, BP 4330, 101 Antananarivo; tel. (20) 2221036; fax (20) 2269225; e-mail nouvelle@wanadoo.mg; Dir EUGÈNE RAHARIFIDY.

Imprimerie Takariva: 4 rue Radley, BP 1029, Antanimena, 101 Antananarivo; tel. (20) 2222128; f. 1933; fiction, languages, school textbooks; Man. Dir PAUL RAPATSALAHY.

Madagascar Print and Press Co (MADPRINT): rue Rabesahala, Antsakaviro, BP 953, 101 Antananarivo; tel. (20) 2222536; fax (20) 2234534; f. 1969; literary, technical and historical; Dir GEORGES RANAIVOSOA.

Maison d'Edition Protestante Antso: 19 rue Venance Manifatra, Imarivolanitra, BP 660, 101 Antananarivo; tel. (20) 2220886; fax (20) 2226372; e-mail fjkm@dts.mg; f. 1972; religious, school, social, political and general; Dir HANS ANDRIAMAMPIANINA.

Nouvelle Société de Presse et d'Edition (NSPE): Immeuble Jeune Afrique, 58 rue Tsiombikibo, BP 1734, Ambatorinaky, 101 Antananarivo; tel. (20) 2227788; fax (20) 2230629.

Office du Livre Malgache: Lot 111 H29, Andrefan' Ambohijanahary, BP 617, 101 Antananarivo; tel. (20) 2224449; f. 1970; children's and general; Sec.-Gen. JULIETTE RATSIMANDRAVA.

Société Malgache d'Edition (SME): BP 659, Ankorondrano, 101 Antananarivo; tel. (20) 2222635; fax (20) 2222254; e-mail tribune@wanadoo.mg; f. 1943; general fiction, university and secondary textbooks; Man. Dir RAHAGA RAMAHOLIMIHASO.

Société Nouvelle de l'Imprimerie Centrale (SNIC): Làlana Ravoninahitriniarivo, BP 1414, 101 Antananarivo; tel. (20) 2221118; e-mail mrakotoa@wanadoo.mg; f. 1959; science, school textbooks; Man. Dir MAMY RAKOTOARIVELO.

Société de Presse et d'Edition de Madagascar: Antananarivo; non-fiction, reference, science, university textbooks; Man. Dir RAJAOFERA ANDRIAMBELO.

Trano Printy Fiangonana Loterana Malagasy (TPFLM): BP 538, 9 ave Général Gabriel Ramanantsoa, 101 Antananarivo; tel. (20) 2223340; fax (20) 2262643; e-mail impluth@wanadoo.mg; f. 1877; religious, educational and fiction; Man. RAYMOND RANDRIANATOANDRO.

GOVERNMENT PUBLISHING HOUSE

Imprimerie Nationale: BP 38, 101 Antananarivo; tel. (20) 2223675; e-mail dinm@wanadoo.mg; all official pubs; Dir JEAN DENIS RANDRIANIRINA.

Broadcasting and Communications

TELECOMMUNICATIONS

Office Malagasy d'Etudes et de Régulation des Télécommunications (OMERT): BP 99991, Route des Hydrocarbures-Alarobia, 101 Antananarivo; tel. (20) 2242119; fax (20) 2321516; e-mail omert@moov.mg; internet www.omert.mg; f. 1997; Gen. Man. GILBERT ANDRIANIRINA RAJAONASY.

Celtel Madagscar: Explorer Business Park, Ankorondrano, Antananarivo 101; tel. (33) 1100100; e-mail service_clientele@mg.celtel.com; internet www.mg.celtel.com; f. 2006; Dir-Gen. EMILLIENNE MACAULEY.

Madacom SA: BP 763, Bâtiments B1-B2, Explorer Business Park, Ankorondrano, 101 Antananarivo; tel. (22) 66055; fax (20) 66056; e-mail madacom@madacom.mg; internet www.madacom.com; f. 1997; mobile telecommunications GSM network provider; partly owned by Celtel International B. V. (Netherlands); Dir EMILIENNE MACAULEY.

Orange Madagascar: Antananarivo; internet www.orange.mg; f. 1998; fmrly Antaris, la Société Malgache de Mobiles; name changed as above 2003; mobile telecommunication GSM network provider; market leader; Dir-Gen. PATRICE PEZAT.

Télécom Malagasy SA (TELMA): BP 763, 101 Antananarivo; tel. (20) 2242705; fax (20) 2242654; e-mail telmacorporate@telma.mg; internet www.telma.mg; 68% owned by Distacom (Hong Kong); owns DTS Wanadoo internet service provider; Chair. DAVID WHITE; Dir-Gen. RON ALLARD.

BROADCASTING

Radio

In 2001 there were an estimated 127 radio stations.

Radio MBS (Malagasy Broadcasting System): BP 11137, Anosipatrana, Antananarivo; tel. (20) 2266702; fax (20) 2268941; e-mail marketing@mbs.mg; internet www.mbs.mg; broadcasts by satellite; Man. SARAH RAVALOMANANA.

Radio Nationale Malagasy: BP 442, Anosy, 101 Antananarivo; tel. (20) 2221745; fax (20) 2232715; e-mail radmad@wanadoo.mg; internet www.takelaka.dts/radmad; state-controlled; part of the Office de Radiodiffusion et de Télévision de Madagascar (ORTM); broadcasts in French and Malagasy; Dir ALAIN RAJAONA.

Le Messager Radio Evangélique: BP 1374, 101 Antananarivo; tel. (20) 2234495; broadcasts in French, English and Malagasy; Dir JOCELYN RANJARISON.

Radio Antsiva: BP 632, Enceinte STEDIC, Village des Jeux, Zone Industrielle Nord, Route des Hydrocarbures, 101 Antananarivo; tel. (20) 2254849; e-mail antsiva@freenet.mg; internet www.antsiva.mg; f. 1994; broadcasts in French and Malagasy; Dir LALATIONE RAKOTONDRAZAFY.

Radio Don Bosco: BP 60, 105 Ivato; tel. (20) 2244387; fax (20) 2244511; e-mail rdb@wanadoo.mg; internet www.radiodonbosco.mg; f. 1996; Catholic, educational and cultural; Chair. Fr GIUSEPPE MIELE.

Radio Feon'ny Vahoaka (RFV): 103 Immeuble Ramaroson, 8e étage, 101 Antananarivo; tel. (20) 2233820; broadcasts in French and Malagasy; Dir ALAIN RAMAROSON.

Radio Lazan'iarivo (RLI): Lot V A49, Andafiavaratra, 101 Antananarivo; tel. (20) 2229016; fax (20) 2267559; e-mail rli@simicro.mg; broadcasts in French, English and Malagasy; privately owned; specializes in jazz music; Dir IHOBY RABARIJOHN.

Radio Tsioka Vao (RTV): Ambohitsimbina, Antananarivo 101; tel. (20) 2221749; f. 1992; broadcasts in French, English and Malagasy; Dir DETKOU DEDONNAIS.

Television

MA TV: BP 1414 Ankorondrano, 101 Antananarivo; tel. (20) 2220897; fax (20) 2234421.

MBS Television (Malagasy Broadcasting System): BP 11137, Anosipatrana, Antananarivo; tel. (20) 2266702; fax (20) 2268941; e-mail journaltv@mbs.mg; internet www.mbs.mg; broadcasts in French and Malagasy.

Radio Télévision Analamanga (RTA): Immeuble Fiaro, 101 Antananarivo; e-mail rta@rta.mg; internet www.rta.mg; including four provincial radio stations; Gen. Man. PATRICK COTTRELLE.

Télévision Nasionaly Malagasy: BP 1202, Anosy, 101 Antananarivo; tel. (20) 2222381; state-controlled; part of the Office de Radiodiffusion et de Télévision de Madagascar (ORTM); broadcasts in French and Malagasy; Dir-Gen. RAZAFIMAHEFA HERINIRINA LALA.

MADAGASCAR

Finance

(cap. = capital; res = reserves; dep. = deposits; m. = million; brs = branches; amounts in Malagasy francs)

BANKING

Central Bank

Banque Centrale de Madagascar: rue de la Révolution Socialiste Malgache, BP 550, 101 Antananarivo; tel. (20) 2221751; fax (20) 2234532; e-mail banque-centrale@banque-centrale.mg; internet www.banque-centrale.mg; f. 1973; bank of issue; cap. 1,000m., res −87,555.6m., dep. 3,842,281.0m. (Dec. 2004); Gov. FRÉDÉRIC RASAMOELY.

Other Banks

Bank of Africa (BOA)—Madagascar: 2 pl. de l'Indépendance, BP 183, 101 Antananarivo; tel. (20) 2239100; fax (20) 2266125; e-mail boa@boa.mg; internet www.boa.mg; f. 1976 as Bankin'ny Tantsaha Mpamokatra; name changed as above 1999; 35.1% owned by African Financial Holding, 15% state-owned; commercial bank, specializes in micro-finance; cap. 40.0m., res 17.4m., dep. 2,075.7m. (Dec. 2004); Pres. PAUL DERREUMAUX; Gen. Man. ALAIN LEPATRE LAMONTAGNE; 51 brs.

Banque Industrielle et Commerciale de Madagascar (BICM): 2 rue du Dr Raseta Andraharo, BP 889, 101 Antananarivo; tel. (20) 2356568; fax (20) 2356656; e-mail bicm@bicm.mg; internet www.bicm.mg; f. 2002; successor of the Banque Internationale Chine Madagascar, fmrly Compagnie Malgache de Banque; cap. 21,167.0m., res −5,377.9m., dep. 51,656.3m. (Dec. 2004); Dir Gen. DELMOTTE NICOLAS.

Banque Malgache de l'Océan Indien (BMOI) (Indian Ocean Malagasy Bank): pl. de l'Indépendance, BP 25 bis, Antaninarenina, 101 Antananarivo; tel. (20) 2234609; fax (20) 2234610; e-mail karine.rabefaritra@africa.bnpparibas.com; internet www.bmoi.mg; f. 1990; 75% owned by BNP Paribas SA (France); cap. 30,000m., res 121,700m., dep. 1,942,000m. (Dec. 2004); Pres. GASTON RAMENASON; Dir-Gen. JEAN-CLAUDE HERIDE; 8 brs.

Banque SBM Madagascar (SBM): rue Andrianary Ratianarivo Antsahavola 1, 101 Antananarivo; tel. (20) 2266607; fax (20) 2266608; e-mail sbmm@wanadoo.mg; f. 1998; 79.99% owned by SBM Global Investments Ltd (Mauritius), 20.01% owned by Nedbank Africa Investments Ltd (South Africa); cap. and res 20,873.4m., dep. 186,682.8m. (Dec. 2002); Chair. CHAITLALL GUNNESS; Gen. Man. KRISHNADUTT RAMBOJUN.

BFV—Société Générale: 14 Làlana Jeneraly Rabehevitra, BP 196, Antananarivo 101; tel. (20) 2220691; fax (20) 2237140; internet www.bfvsg.mg; f. 1977 as Banky Fampandrosoana ny Varotra; changed name in 1998; 70% owned by Société Générale (France) and 28.5% state-owned; cap. 70,000m., res 24,300.3m., dep. 1,114,111.4m. (Dec. 2004); Chief Exec. MARCEL LENGUIN; 30 brs.

BNI—Crédit Lyonnais Madagascar: 74 rue du 26 Juin 1960, BP 174, 101 Antananarivo; tel. (20) 2223951; fax (20) 2233749; e-mail info@bni.mg; internet www.bni.mg; f. 1976 as Bankin 'ny Indostria; 51% owned by Crédit Lyonnais Global Banking (France), 32.58% state-owned; cap. and res 232,489.0m., dep. 2,374,632.0m. (Dec. 2004); Pres. and Chair. EVARISTO MARSON; Dir-Gen. PASCAL FALL; 22 brs.

Union Commercial Bank SA (UCB): 77 rue Solombavambahoaka Frantsay, Antsahavola, BP 197, 101 Antananarivo; tel. (20) 2227262; fax (20) 2228740; e-mail ucb.int@wanadoo.mg; f. 1992; 70% owned by Mauritius Commercial Bank Ltd; cap. 6,000m., res 60,087.6m., dep. 327,141.9m. (Dec. 2002); Pres. RAYMOND HEIN; Gen. Man. MARC MARIE JOSEPH DE BOLLIVIER; 3 brs.

INSURANCE

ARO (Assurances Réassurances Omnibranches): Antsahavola, BP 42, 101 Antananarivo; tel. (20) 2220154; fax (20) 2234464; state-owned; Pres. GUY ROLLAND RASOANAIVO; Dir-Gen. (vacant).

Compagnie Malgache d'Assurances et de Réassurances 'Ny Havana': Immeuble 'Ny Havana', Zone des 67 Ha, BP 3881, 101 Antananarivo; tel. (20) 2226760; fax (20) 2224303; e-mail nyhavana@wanadoo.mg; f. 1968; state-owned; cap. 5,435.6m. (2006); Dir-Gen. BERA RAZANAKOLONA.

Mutuelle d'Assurances Malagasy (MAMA): Lot 1F, 12 bis, rue Rainibetsimisaraka, Ambalavao-Isotry, BP 185, 101 Antananarivo; tel. (20) 2261882; fax (20) 2261883; f. 1965; Pres. FRÉDÉRIC RABARISON.

Société Malgache d'Assurances (SMA—ASCOMA): 13 rue Patrice Lumumba, BP 673, 101 Antananarivo; tel. (20) 2223162; fax (20) 2222785; e-mail ascoma@simicro.mg; f. 1952; Dir VIVIANE RAMANITRA.

Directory

Trade and Industry

DEVELOPMENT ORGANIZATIONS

Bureau d'Information pour les Entreprises (BIPE): Nouvel Immeuble ARO, Ampefiloha, 101 Antananarivo; tel. (20) 2230512; internet www.bipe.mg; part of the Ministry of Industry, Trade and the Development of the Private Sector.

Economic Development Board of Madagascar (EDBM): Nouvel Immeuble Aro Ampefiloha, Antananarivo; tel. (20) 2268121; fax (20) 2266105; e-mail edbm@edbm.mg; internet www.edbm.gov.mg; f. 2006; service for the facilitation and promotion of investment in Madagascar; advisory service for starting a business, obtaining visas and land acquisition; CEO PREGA RAMSAMY.

La maison de l'entreprise: rue Samuel Ramahefy Ambatonakanga, BP 74, 101 Antananarivo; tel. (20) 2225386; fax (20) 2233669; e-mail cite@cite.mg; internet www.cite.mg; f. 1967; supports and promotes Malagasy businesses; Dir-Gen. ISABELLE GACHIE.

Office des Mines Nationales et des Industries Stratégiques (OMNIS): 21 Làlana Razanakombana, BP 1 bis, 101 Antananarivo; tel. (20) 2224439; fax (20) 2222985; e-mail omnis@simicro.mg; f. 1976; promotes the exploration and exploitation of mining resources, in particular oil resources; Dir-Gen. ELISE ALITERA RAZAKA.

Société d'Etude et de Réalisation pour le Développement Industriel (SERDI): BP 3180, 101 Antananarivo; tel. (20) 2225204; fax (20) 2229669; f. 1966; Dir-Gen. RAOILISON RAJAONARY.

CHAMBER OF COMMERCE

Fédération des Chambres de Commerce, d'Industrie et d'Agriculture de Madagascar: BP 166, 20 rue Henri Razantseheno, Antaninarenina, Antananarivo 101; tel. (20) 2220211; fax (20) 2220213; e-mail cciaa@tana-cciaa.org; internet www.tana-cciaa.org; 12 mem. chambers; Pres. SIMON RAKOTONDRAHOVA; Chair. HENRI RAZANATSEHENO; Sec.-Gen. HUBERT RATSIANDAVANA.

Chambre de Commerce, d'Industrie, d'Artisanat et d'Agriculture—Antananarivo (CCIAA): BP 166, 20 rue Henri Razanatseheno, Antaninarenina, 101 Antananarivo; tel. (20) 2220211; fax (20) 2220213; e-mail cciaa@tana-cciaa.org; internet www.tana-cciaa.org; f. 1993.

TRADE ASSOCIATION

Société d'Intérêt National des Produits Agricoles (SINPA): BP 754, rue Fernand-Kasanga, Tsimbazaza, Antananarivo; tel. (20) 2220558; fax (20) 2220665; f. 1973; monopoly purchaser and distributor of agricultural produce; Chair. GUALBERT RAZANAJATOVO; Gen. Man. JEAN CLOVIS RALIJESY.

EMPLOYERS' ORGANIZATIONS

Groupement des Entreprises de Madagascar (GEM): Kianja MDRM sy Tia Tanindrazana, Ambohijatovo, BP 1338, 101 Antananarivo; tel. (20) 2223841; fax (20) 2221965; e-mail gem@simicro.mg; internet www.gem-madagascar.com; f. 1976; 10 nat. syndicates and five regional syndicates comprising 700 cos and 47 directly affiliated cos; Pres. NAINA ANDRIANTSITOHAINA; Sec.-Gen. ZINAH RASAMUEL RAVALOSON.

Groupement National des Exportateurs de Vanille de Madagascar (GNEV): BP 21, Antalaha; tel. (13) 20714532; fax (13) 20816017; e-mail rama.anta@sat.blueline.mg; 18 mems; Pres. JEAN GEORGES RANDRIAMIHARISOA.

Malagasy Entrepreneurs' Association (FIV.MPA.MA): Lot II, 2e étage, Immeuble Santa Antaninarenina; tel. (20) 2229292; fax (20) 2229290; e-mail fivmpama@simicro.mg; comprises 10 trade assocs, representing 200 mems, and 250 direct business mems; Chair. HERINTSALAMA RAJAONARIVELO.

Syndicat Professionel des Producteurs d'eExtraits Aromatiques, Alimentaires et Medicinaux de Madagascar (SYPEAM): Lot II M 80 bis, Antsakaviro, BP 8530, 101 Antananarivo; tel. (20) 2226934; fax (20) 2261317.

Syndicat des Industries de Madagascar (SIM): Immeuble Holcim, Lot 1 bis, Tsaralalàna; BP 1695, 101 Antananarivo; tel. (20) 2224007; fax (20) 2222518; e-mail syndusmad@wanadoo.mg; internet www.syndusmad.com; f. 1958; Chair. SAMUEL RAVELOSON; 82 mems (2006).

Syndicat des Planteurs de Café: 37 Làlana Razafimahandry, BP 173, 101 Antananarivo.

Syndicat Professionnel des Agents Généraux d'Assurances: Antananarivo; f. 1949; Pres. SOLO RATSIMBAZAFY; Sec. IHANTA RANDRIAMANDRANTO.

MADAGASCAR   Directory

UTILITIES

Electricity and Water

Office de Regulation de l'Électricité (ORE): Antananarivo; f. 2004; Dir Mamy Rakotomizao.

Jiro sy Rano Malagasy (JIRAMA): BP 200, 149 rue Rainandriamampandry, Faravohitra, 101 Antananarivo; tel. (20) 2220031; fax (20) 2233806; e-mail dgjirama@wanadoo.mg; f. 1975; controls production and distribution of electricity and water; managed by Lahmeyer International (Germany) from April 2005; Chair. Patrick Ramiaramanana; Dir-Gen. Bernard Romahn.

TRADE UNIONS

Cartel National des Organisations Syndicales de Madagascar (CARNOSYMA): BP 1035, 101 Antananarivo.

Confédération des Travailleurs Malagasy Révolutionnaires (FISEMARE): Lot IV N 76-A, Ankadifotsy, BP 1128, Befelatanana-Antananarivo 101; tel. (20) 2221989; fax (20) 2267712; f. 1985; Pres. Paul Rabemananjara.

Confédération des Travailleurs Malgaches (Fivomdronamben'ny Mpiasa Malagasy—FMM): Lot IVM 133 A Antetezanafovoany I, BP 846, 101 Antananarivo; tel. (20) 2224565; e-mail rjeannot2002@yahoo.fr; f. 1957; Sec.-Gen. Jeannot Ramanarivo; 30,000 mems.

Fédération des Syndicats des Travailleurs de Madagascar (Firaisan'ny Sendika eran'i Madagaskara—FISEMA): Lot III, rue Pasteur Isotry, BP 172, 101 Antananarivo; f. 1956; Pres. Désiré Ralambotahina; Sec.-Gen. M. Razakanaivo; 8 affiliated unions representing 60,000 mems.

Sendika Kristianina Malagasy (SEKRIMA) (Christian Confederation of Malagasy Trade Unions): Soarano, route de Mahajanga, BP 1035, 101 Antananarivo; tel. (20) 2223174; f. 1937; Pres. Marie Rakotoanosy; Gen. Sec. Raymond Rakotoarisaona; 158 affiliated unions representing 40,000 mems.

Union des Syndicats Autonomes de Madagascar (USAM): Lot III M 33 BC, Andrefan'Ambohijanahary, BP 1038, 101 Antananarivo; tel. and fax (20) 2227485; e-mail usam@moov.mg; f. 1954; Pres. Jean Henri Randriambaoarisoa; Sec.-Gen. Samuel Rabemanantsoa; 46 affiliated unions representing 30,000 mems.

Transport

RAILWAYS

In 2001 there were 893 km of railway, including four railway lines, all 1-m gauge track. The northern system, which comprised 720 km of track, links the east coast with Antsirabé, in the interior, via Moramanga and Antananarivo, with a branch line from Moramanga to Lake Alaotra and was privatized in 2001. The southern system, which comprised 163 km of track, links Manakara, on the east coast, with Fianarantsoa.

Réseau National des Chemins de Fer Malagasy (RNCFM): 1 ave de l'Indépendance, BP 259, Soarano, 101 Antananarivo; tel. (20) 2220521; fax (20) 2222288; f. 1909; in the process of transfer to private sector; Administrator Daniel Razafindrabe.

Fianarantsoa-Côte Est (FCE): FCE Gare, Fianarantsoa; tel. (20) 7551354; e-mail fce@blueline.mg; internet www.fce-madagascar .com; f. 1936; southern network, 163 km.

Madarail: Gare de Soarano, 1 ave de l'Indépendance, BP 1175, 101 Antananarivo; tel. (20) 2234599; fax (20) 2221883; e-mail madarail@wanadoo.mg; internet www.comazar.com/madarail.htm; f. 2001; jt venture, operated by Comazar, South Africa; 45% of Comazar is owned by Sheltam Locomotive and Rail Services, South Africa; 31.6% is owned by Spoornet, South Africa; operates the northern network of the Madagascan railway (650 km); Chair. Eric Peiffer; Gen. Dir Patrick Claes; 878 employees.

ROADS

In 2001 there were an estimated 49,837 km of classified roads; about 11.6% of the road network was paved. In 1987 there were 39,500 km of unclassified roads, used only in favourable weather. A road and motorway redevelopment programme, funded by the World Bank (€300m.) and the European Union (EU—€61m.), began in June 2000. In August 2002 the EU undertook to disburse US $10m. for the reconstruction of 11 bridges destroyed during the political crisis in that year. In 2003 Japan pledged $28m. to build several bridges and a 15-km bypass. The Government planned to have restored and upgraded 14,000 km of highways and 8,000 km of rural roads to an operational status by 2015. In 2005, according to the IMF, 8,982 km of roads had been maintained or rehabilitated.

INLAND WATERWAYS

The Pangalanes canal runs for 600 km near the east coast from Toamasina to Farafangana. In 1990 432 km of the canal between Toamasina and Mananjary were navigable.

SHIPPING

There are 18 ports, the largest being at Toamasina, which handles about 70% of total traffic, and Mahajanga; several of the smaller ports are prone to silting problems. A new deep-sea port was to be constructed at Ehoala, near Fort Dauphin, in order to accommodate the activity of an ilmenite mining development by 2008.

CMA—CGM Madagascar: BP 12042, Village des jeux, Bat. C1 Ankorondrano, 101 Antananarivo; tel. (20) 2235949; fax (20) 2266120; e-mail tnr@cma-cgm.mg; internet www.cma-cgm.com; maritime transport; Gen. Man. Philippe Murcia.

Compagnie Générale Maritime Sud (CGM): BP 1185, Lot II U 31 bis, Ampahibe, 101 Antananarivo; tel. (20) 2220113; fax (20) 2226530.

Compagnie Malgache de Navigation (CMN): rue Rabearivelo, BP 1621, 101 Antananarivo; tel. (20) 2225516; fax (20) 2230358; f. 1960; coasters; 13,784 grt; 97.5% state-owned; privatization pending; Pres. Elinah Bakoly Rajaonson; Dir-Gen. Aristide Emmanuel.

SCAC-SDV Shipping Madagascar: rue Rabearivelo Antsahavola, BP 514, 102 Antananarivo; tel. (20) 2220631; fax (20) 2247862; operates the harbour in Antananarivo Port.

Société Malgache des Transports Maritimes (SMTM): 6 rue Indira Gandhi, BP 4077, 101 Antananarivo; tel. (20) 2227342; fax (20) 2233327; f. 1963; 59% state-owned; privatization pending; services to Europe; Chair. Alexis Razafindratsira; Dir-Gen. Jean Ranjeva.

CIVIL AVIATION

The Ivato international airport is at Antananarivo, while the airports at Mahajanga, Toamasina and Nossi-Bé can also accommodate large jet aircraft. There are 211 airfields, two-thirds of which are privately owned. In 1996 the Government authorized private French airlines to operate scheduled and charter flights between Madagascar and Western Europe.

Air Madagascar (Société Nationale Malgache des Transports Aériens): 31 ave de l'Indépendance, Analakely, BP 437, 101 Antananarivo; tel. (20) 2222222; fax (20) 2233760; e-mail commercial@airmadagascar.com; internet www.airmadagascar.com; f. 1962; 90.60% state-owned; 3.17% owned by Air France (France); transfer to the private sector pending; restructured and managed by Lufthansa Consulting since 2002; extensive internal routes connecting all the principal towns; external services to France, Italy, the Comoros, Kenya, Mauritius, Réunion, South Africa and Thailand; Chair. Heriniaina Razafimahefa; Chief Exec. Ulrich Lang.

Air Transport et Transit Régional (ATTR): tel. (32) 0518811; fax (32) 3205218; e-mail attr.reservation@blueline.mg; internet www .attrmada.com; f. 2006; private; regular local and regional services; Dir Gen. Frédéric Rabesahala.

Aviation Civile de Madagascar (ACM): BP 4414, 101 Tsimbazaza-Antananarivo; tel. (20) 2222438; fax (20) 2224726; e-mail acm@acm.mg; f. 2000; Chair. Maxime Ravelojaoma; Dir-Gen. François Xavier Randriamahandry.

Transports et Travaux Aériens de Madagascar (TAM): 17 ave de l'Indépendance, Analakely, Antananarivo; tel. (20) 2222222; fax (20) 2224340; e-mail tamdg@wanadoo.mg; f. 1951; provides airline services; Administrators Lala Razafindrakoto, François Dane.

Tourism

Madagascar's attractions include unspoiled scenery, many unusual varieties of flora and fauna, and the rich cultural diversity of Malagasy life. In 2005 some 277,422 tourists visited Madagascar, the majority were from France (52.3%). Revenue from tourism in that year was estimated at US $98m.

Direction d'Appui aux Investissements Publiques: Ministry of Culture and Tourism, BP 610, rue Fernand Kasanga Tsimbazaza, 101 Antananarivo; tel. (20) 2262816; fax (20) 2235410; e-mail mintourdati@wandaoo.mg; internet www.tourisme.gov.mg.

La Maison du Tourisme de Madagascar: pl. de l'Indépendance, BP 3224, 101 Antananarivo; tel. (20) 2235178; fax (20) 2269522; e-mail mtm@simicro.mg; internet www.tourisme.madagascar.com; Exec. Dir André Andriamboavonjy.

MALAWI

Introductory Survey

Location, Climate, Language, Religion, Flag, Capital

The Republic of Malawi is a land-locked country in southern central Africa, with Zambia to the west, Mozambique to the south and east, and Tanzania to the north. Lake Malawi forms most of the eastern boundary. The climate is tropical, but much of the country is sufficiently high above sea-level to modify the heat. Temperatures range from 14°C (57°F) to 18°C (64°F) in mountain areas, but can reach 38°C (100°F) in low-lying regions. There is a rainy season between November and April. The official language is English, although Chichewa is being promoted as the basis for a 'Malawi Language'. Chitumbuka, a national language, and Yao are also widely spoken. More than 70% of the population profess Christianity, while a further 20%, largely Asians, are Muslims. Most of the remaining Malawians follow traditional beliefs, although there is also a Hindu minority. The national flag (proportions 2 by 3) has three equal horizontal stripes, of black, red and green, with a rising sun, in red, in the centre of the black stripe. The capital is Lilongwe.

Recent History

Malawi was formerly the British protectorate of Nyasaland. In 1953 it was linked with two other British dependencies, Northern and Southern Rhodesia (now Zambia and Zimbabwe), to form the Federation of Rhodesia and Nyasaland. Elections in August 1961 gave the Malawi Congress Party (MCP), led by Dr Hastings Kamuzu Banda, a majority of seats in the Legislative Council. Dr Banda became Prime Minister in February 1963, and the Federation was dissolved in December. Nyasaland gained independence, as Malawi, on 6 July 1964. The country became a republic and a one-party state, with Banda as its first President, on 6 July 1966. Malawi created a major controversy among African states in 1967 by officially recognizing the Republic of South Africa. In 1971 Banda, named Life President in that year, became the first African head of state to visit South Africa. In 1976, however, Malawi recognized the communist-backed Government in Angola in preference to the South African-supported forces. Malawi did not recognize the 'independence' granted by South Africa to four of its African 'homelands'.

Until 1993 all Malawian citizens were obliged to be members of the MCP; no political opposition was tolerated, and only candidates who had been approved by Banda were allowed to contest elections to the National Assembly. Frequent reorganizations of the Cabinet effectively prevented the emergence of any political rival to Banda. However, it was reported in 1983 that a conflict had developed between Dick Matenje, the Minister without Portfolio in the Cabinet and Secretary-General of the MCP, and John Tembo, the Governor of the Reserve Bank of Malawi, concerning the eventual succession to Banda. In May the authorities reported that Matenje and three other senior politicians had died in a road accident; Malawian exiles claimed that the four men had been shot while attempting to flee the country.

Opposition to the Government intensified during 1992: in March Malawi's Roman Catholic bishops criticized the Government's alleged abuses of human rights. In April Chakufwa Chihana, a prominent trade union leader who had demanded multi-party elections, was arrested. In July Chihana was charged with sedition, and in August the police detained 11 church leaders and prohibited a planned rally by pro-democracy supporters. In September opposition activists formed the Alliance for Democracy (AFORD), a pressure group operating within Malawi, under the chairmanship of Chihana, which aimed to campaign for democratic political reform. Another opposition grouping, the United Democratic Front (UDF), was formed in October. In that month Banda conceded that a referendum on the introduction of a multi-party system would take place. However, in November the Government banned AFORD. In the following month Chihana was found guilty of sedition and sentenced to two years' hard labour (reduced to nine months' in March 1993).

At the referendum on the introduction of a multi-party system, held on 14 June 1993, 63.2% of those who participated (some 63.5% of the electorate) voted for an end to single-party rule. Banda rejected opposition demands for the immediate installation of an interim government of national unity. He agreed, however, to the establishment of a National Executive Council to oversee the transition to a multi-party system and the holding of free elections, and of a National Consultative Council to implement the necessary amendments to the Constitution. Both councils were to include members of the Government and the opposition. Banda announced an amnesty for thousands of political exiles, and stated that a general election would be held, on a multi-party basis, within a year. In late June the Constitution was amended to allow the registration of political parties other than the MCP: by mid-August five organizations, including AFORD and the UDF, had been accorded official status.

In September 1993 Banda carried out an extensive cabinet reshuffle, relinquishing the post of Minister of External Affairs, which he had held since 1964. In October 1993 Banda underwent neurological surgery in South Africa. Interim executive power was assumed by a three-member Presidential Council, chaired by the new Secretary-General of the MCP, Gwandaguluwe Chakuamba. The two other members, Tembo and the Minister of Transport and Communications, Robson Chirwa, were also senior MCP officials. In November a further cabinet reshuffle relieved Banda of all ministerial responsibilities. Later in November the National Assembly approved a Constitutional Amendment Bill, which, *inter alia*, abolished the institution of life presidency, ended the requirement that election candidates be members of the MCP, repealed the right of the President to nominate members of the legislature exclusively from the MCP, and lowered the minimum voting age from 21 to 18 years.

Having made a rapid and unexpected recovery, Banda resumed full presidential powers in December 1993. Shortly afterwards, in response to increasing pressure from the opposition, the Government amended the Constitution to provide for the appointment of an acting President in the event of the incumbent being incapacitated. In February 1994 the MCP announced that Banda was to be the party's presidential candidate in the forthcoming general election (scheduled for May); Chakuamba was named as the MCP's candidate for the vice-presidency. Also in February the National Assembly approved an increase in the number of elective seats in the legislature from 141 to 177.

On 16 May 1994 the National Assembly adopted a provisional Constitution, which provided for the appointment of a Constitutional Committee and of a human rights commission, and abolished the system of 'traditional' courts. Malawi's first multi-party parliamentary and presidential elections took place on 17 May. In the presidential election the Secretary-General of the UDF, (Elson) Bakili Muluzi (a former government minister and MCP Secretary-General), took 47.3% of the votes cast, defeating Banda (who won 33.6% of the votes). Eight parties contested the legislative elections: of these, the UDF won 85 seats in the National Assembly, the MCP 56 and AFORD 36. The Constitution was introduced for a one-year period on 18 May; it was to be subject to further review prior to official ratification one year later.

President Muluzi and his Vice-President, Justin Malewezi, were inaugurated on 21 May 1994. The new UDF-dominated Government proclaimed an amnesty for the country's remaining political prisoners, and commuted all death sentences to terms of life imprisonment. In August it was announced that Banda, while remaining honorary Life President of the MCP, was to retire from active involvement in politics. Chakuamba, as Vice-President of the party, effectively became the leader of the MCP.

In September 1994 a number of AFORD members were appointed to the Government, including Chihana as Second Vice-President and Minister of Irrigation and Water Development. Meanwhile, the creation of the post of Second Vice-President had necessitated a constitutional amendment, and provoked severe criticism from the MCP. Moreover, the National Constitutional Conference recommended that the post be abolished. In March, however, the National Assembly (in the absence of MCP deputies, who boycotted the vote) approved the retention of the second vice-presidency; the Assembly also endorsed recommendations for the establishment—although not before May 1999—of a second chamber of parliament. The Constitution took effect on 18 May 1995.

In June 1994 Muluzi established an independent commission of inquiry to investigate the deaths of Matenje and his associates in May 1983. In January 1995, in accordance with the findings of the commission, Banda was placed under house arrest and Tembo and two former police-officers were detained; the four were charged with murder and conspiracy to murder. A former inspector-general of police was charged later in the month. In April Cecilia Kadzamira, Tembo's niece and the former President's 'Official Hostess', was charged with conspiracy to murder and was subsequently released on bail. The trial opened later that month, but was immediately adjourned, owing to Banda's failure to appear in court (his defence counsel asserted that he was too ill to stand trial) and to the failure of the state prosecution to submit certain evidence to the defence. Hearings resumed, in Banda's absence, in July. In September Tembo and the two former police-officers were granted bail, and most restrictions on Banda's movements were ended. The case against Kadzamira was abandoned in December, owing to lack of evidence, and later that month Banda, Tembo and the other defendants were found not guilty of conspiracy to murder and conspiracy to defeat justice. In January 1996 an MCP-owned newspaper printed a statement by Banda in which he admitted that he might unknowingly have been responsible for brutalities perpetrated under his regime and apologized to Malawians for 'pain and suffering' inflicted during his presidency.

Meanwhile, there were further allegations that the Muluzi administration had been involved in dubious financial transactions. It emerged, in mid-1995, that the President had authorized the payment of some 6.2m. kwacha from the state poverty alleviation account to UDF deputies (to enable the payment of loans to their constituents); there was also evidence of the involvement of government ministers in the smuggling of maize to neighbouring countries. In February 1996 Muluzi announced that an independent Anti-Corruption Bureau (ACB) was to be established to investigate allegations of corruption.

In July 1995 the UDF and AFORD signed a formal co-operation agreement. In December, however, Chihana warned that AFORD might withdraw from the coalition Government, alleging that the UDF was using public funds to secure political influence, and complaining of a lack of openness in the Muluzi administration. Chihana resigned from the Government in May 1996, expressing his intention to devote himself more fully to the work of his party. The post of Second Vice-President remained vacant following a subsequent reorganization of the Cabinet. In June AFORD withdrew from its coalition with the UDF, declared that remaining AFORD ministers should resign, and appointed a 'shadow cabinet'. Five members were dismissed from AFORD's National Executive, and another was suspended, having refused to relinquish their ministerial posts. AFORD and the MCP insisted that AFORD ministers should be regarded as members of the UDF. The rejection of this demand resulted in a parliamentary boycott by both opposition parties. At the beginning of December the AFORD ministers remaining in the Cabinet asserted that they were independent and had not joined the UDF. In March 1997 AFORD stated that the party would continue its boycott until the ministers resigned both their government posts and parliamentary seats. In April the MCP and AFORD ended their parliamentary boycott, following a meeting with Muluzi at which he had allegedly promised to amend the Constitution to prevent parliamentary delegates from changing their political affiliation without standing for re-election.

In November 1997 Banda died in South Africa, where he had been undergoing emergency medical treatment. He was accorded a state funeral, with full military honours.

In June 1998 the National Assembly approved legislation providing for the introduction of a single-ballot electoral system to replace the existing multiple-ballot system and for a strengthening of the authority and independence of the Malawi Electoral Commission (MEC). In November legislation was adopted to allow presidential and parliamentary elections to run concurrently (as Muluzi's term was due to end several weeks earlier than that of the National Assembly), and the elections were subsequently scheduled for 18 May 1999. An electoral alliance between the MCP and AFORD, which was officially announced in February 1999, created serious divisions within the MCP, when the party's leader and presidential candidate, Chakuamba, chose Chihana, the leader of AFORD, as the candidate for the vice-presidency, in preference to Tembo. Thousands of Tembo's supporters were reported to have mounted protests to demand Chakuamba's resignation. The Chakuamba-Chihana partnership also provoked a wider dispute with the UDF and the MEC, which claimed that the arrangement was unconstitutional. In February the National Assembly adopted a controversial report by the MEC that recommended the creation of a further 72 parliamentary seats, including an additional 42 in the Southern Region, a UDF stronghold. In response to widespread opposition to the proposals, however, only 16 of the 72 seats were approved.

Having been postponed twice, the presidential and legislative elections were held on 15 June 1999. Muluzi was re-elected to the presidency, securing 51.4% of the votes cast, while Chakuamba obtained 43.3%. Turn-out was high, with some 93.8% of registered voters reported to have participated. At the elections to the expanded National Assembly the ruling UDF won 94 seats, while the MCP secured 66 seats, AFORD 29 and independent candidates four. Despite declarations from international observers that the elections were largely free and fair, the MCP-AFORD alliance filed two petitions with the High Court, challenging Muluzi's victory and the results in 16 districts. The opposition alleged irregularities in the voter registration process and claimed that Muluzi's victory was unconstitutional, as he had failed to gain the support of 50% of all registered voters. None the less, Muluzi was inaugurated later in June, and a new Cabinet was appointed. In mid-August the UDF regained a parliamentary majority when the four independent deputies decided to ally themselves with the UDF, of which they had previously been members.

Chakuamba, who had maintained a boycott of the new parliament pending the result of his party's challenge to the outcome of the elections, was suspended from the chamber in June 2000. Tembo assumed the leadership of the opposition and appointed his supporters to prominent posts within the MCP. Chakuamba was reinstated in September, and a dispute between the two factions ensued. In October the opposition's petitions against the election results were dismissed by the High Court.

The country's first multi-party local elections were held in November 2000. The MCP was disqualified from contesting a number of wards where both factions of the party had submitted nominations. Amid allegations of electoral malpractice, the UDF secured victory in 610 of the 860 contested wards, AFORD winning 120 seats and the MCP 84.

In January 2001 deputies from the Tembo faction of the MCP ensured the approval by the National Assembly of a UDF proposal to abandon plans (ostensibly for financial reasons) for the creation of a second legislative chamber, the Senate, which would have had powers to impeach the President; AFORD boycotted the vote. In March six people were arrested and charged with treason for allegedly planning a coup against Muluzi; the leader of the plot was said to be Sudi Sulaimana, a political activist who had previously been arrested in 1993 for attempting to overthrow Banda. However, Chakuamba claimed that the Government had fabricated the plot in order to curb the activities of its political opponents. In October the leader of the opposition National Democratic Alliance (NDA), Brown Mpinganjira, was arrested and charged with treason for alleged involvement in the March coup attempt, but was released after a court ruled that his detention was unconstitutional. In November seven deputies who had joined the NDA were excluded from the National Assembly for abandoning the political parties for which they had been elected, an action proscribed by law since May, when the UDF acted to prevent defections to the NDA; Sam Mpasu, the Speaker, defied an order of the High Court restraining him from expelling the deputies.

In January 2002 Muluzi effected a minor cabinet reshuffle. In the meantime, negotiations between Chihana and Muluzi on the possible formation of a government of national unity had created divisions within AFORD. The minister responsible for poverty alleviation, Leonard Mangulama, was dismissed in August after a report was published implicating him in the sale of emergency maize reserves to Kenya when Minister of Agriculture and Irrigation Development. A minor reorganization of ministerial portfolios took place in September. In the same month it was reported that Mpinganjira had fled the country following the murder of a supporter of the UDF in late August.

Proposed legislation to change the Constitution to allow Muluzi to seek a third presidential term failed to gain the requisite support of two-thirds of the members of the National Assembly in July 2002. A further attempt to introduce a constitutional amendment also failed in January 2003, when the bill was withdrawn. The UDF declared that it would hold a referendum on the issue later in the year. However, in late March Muluzi declared that he would not seek a third presidential term, and proposed Dr Bingu wa Mutharika, recently appointed Minister of Economic Planning and Development, as his successor, to contest the presidential election scheduled for May 2004. (Mutharika had represented the United Party at the 1999 presidential election, but subsequently defected to the UDF.) In early April 2003 Muluzi dismissed his entire Cabinet, apparently without explanation. However, several ministers reported that Muluzi had imposed the appointment of Mutharika on the party without sufficient consultation, and suggested that they had been dismissed for expressing opposition to the President's decision; Muluzi appointed a new administration later that month.

In May 2003, at a party convention in Blantyre that was disrupted by violent incidents, Tembo and Chakuamba were elected, respectively, as President and Vice-President of the MCP. Tembo was subsequently named as the MCP's candidate to contest the 2004 presidential election. Chakuamba resigned from the MCP and formed the Republican Party (RP). On 1 January 2004 Justin Malewezi, Malawi's First Vice-President and Minister responsible for Privatization, announced his resignation from the UDF for 'personal reasons'. He did not, however, relinquish his position in the Government, stating that he would remain in office, but on leave, until after the presidential election had taken place. One week after leaving the UDF Malewezi joined the People's Progressive Movement (PPM), an opposition party founded in April 2003. Later in January 2004 Aleke Banda, who had resigned from the UDF in May 2003, was elected as President of the PPM, while Malewezi was chosen as its Vice-President.

In February 2004 the Government initiated legal proceedings aimed at having Malewezi's position within the Cabinet declared vacant on the grounds that he had resigned as Vice-President 'by implication or by his own conduct'. Meanwhile, in late January several opposition parties, including the PPM and the RP, announced their formation of the Mgwirizano Coalition to contest the forthcoming presidential election; Chakuamba was elected as the coalition's presidential candidate in February. Malewezi subsequently announced that he would contest the election as an independent. A minor cabinet reshuffle was effected in late February, and Muluzi appointed Hetherwick Ntaba, the leader of the New Congress for Democracy (NCD), as Minister of Energy and Mining at the end of March, following the NCD's decision to join the UDF-AFORD electoral alliance. Presidential and legislative elections were to take place on 18 May, but were subsequently postponed, in compliance with a judicial ruling, until 20 May, after the opposition lodged complaints of irregularities in the voters' register.

At the presidential election held on 20 May 2004 Mutharika, representing the ruling UDF, secured 35.89% of the valid votes cast, according to official results. Tembo, of the MCP, and Chakuamba, representing the Mgwirizano Coalition, took 27.13% and 25.72% of the vote, respectively. Cassim Chilumpha, of the UDF, was elected as Vice-President. At concurrent elections to the National Assembly, however, the MCP emerged as the largest party, winning 56 of the 193 seats in the legislature, while the UDF secured 49 seats and the Mgwirizano Coalition 25; 39 of the remaining seats were taken by independent candidates, while voting in six constituencies was not conducted owing to irregularities. International observers criticized the conduct of the polls and opposition parties disputed the results. Mutharika was sworn in as President on 24 May amid rioting by opposition supporters. The new Cabinet, appointed in mid-June 2004, comprised 21 ministers, compared with 32 under the previous administration. Mutharika, in defiance of critics who believed he would merely serve to act as Muluzi's 'puppet', pledged to take measures to combat corruption and to effect wide-ranging economic reforms. In late October the former Minister of Finance, Friday Jumbe, was arrested in connection with illegal sales of maize during 2001–02 (see above) when he held the position of General Manager of the Agriculture Development and Marketing Corporation; he was subsequently charged with four counts of corruption. The Director of Public Prosecutions, Ishmael Wadi, also announced in October 2004 that at least 10 former senior ministers were under investigation by the ACB following the disappearance of more than 10,000m. kwacha during the Muluzi presidency.

In early January 2005 three members of the UDF were arrested for attempting to enter the presidential palace carrying handguns, prior to a scheduled meeting with Mutharika. The three were suspected of being part of an assassination plot and were charged with treason; however, the men were later pardoned by Mutharika and released. (Ministers were legally permitted to carry weapons for protection.) Mutharika subsequently ordered the dissolution of the National Intelligence Bureau (NIB), according to official explanations, for restructuring. It was believed that the NIB remained sympathetic to Muluzi and thus undermined the new President.

In early February 2005 Mutharika resigned from the leadership of the UDF—of which Muluzi was Chairman—claiming that the party was opposing his campaign against corruption. Prior to the announcement, Mutharika dismissed three members of the Government loyal to Muluzi, including the Minister of Labour, Lilian Patel, and Chihana, who was replaced as Minister of Agriculture, Irrigation and Food Security by Chakuamba. Later that month Mutharika announced his intention to form a new political party, the Democratic Progressive Party (DPP), which was formally registered in mid-March. In late May the Minister of Education and Human Resources, Yusuf Mwawa, was arrested on charges of corruption, fraud and misuse of public funds. He was replaced by the former Secretary-General of the MCP, Kate Kainja Kaluluma. (In February 2006 Mwawa was sentenced to five years' imprisonment.) Meanwhile, in late June 2005 the UDF introduced before the National Assembly a motion of impeachment against Mutharika, alleging statutory violations of the Constitution and misuse of public funds. The session was suspended following the collapse of the Speaker, Rodwell Munyenyembe, who died several days later. Louis Chimango of the MCP was elected as Speaker in early July and the impeachment debate resumed later that month.

In late July 2005 Mutharika faced criticism for increasing the size of the Cabinet from 27 members to 33. A new Ministry of Irrigation and Water Development was created, headed by Chakuamba, while the agriculture and food security portfolio was awarded to Uladi Mussa, who was replaced as Minister of Home Affairs and Internal Security by Anna Kachikho. In early September Sidik Mia replaced Chakuamba at the Ministry of Irrigation and Water Development. Chakuamba was dismissed in advance of an investigation by the ACB over misuse of World Bank funds; he was arrested later that month for allegedly slandering the President at a rally for the RP.

In October 2005 Muluzi was summoned to appear before the ACB, which was investigating the misappropriation of 1,400m. kwacha in foreign aid during his presidency. It was alleged that much of this money had been diverted to personal bank accounts and had also been used to finance the 2004 presidential campaign. Muluzi was able to obtain an injunction from the High Court, which allowed him to refuse to answer the ACB's questions. However, later that month police and ACB officers raided three properties belonging to Muluzi, confiscating computer equipment and banking documents. In November Vice-President Chilumpha was arrested in connection with the alleged embezzlement of 187m. kwacha during his tenure as Minister of Education. However, Chilumpha obtained an injunction against criminal proceedings being initiated against him on the grounds that as the incumbent Vice-President he was immune from prosecution.

Following an agreement between the UDF and Tembo, in mid-October 2005 the National Assembly voted in favour of beginning proceedings to impeach Mutharika. Envoys from several donor countries (including the United Kingdom, the USA and South Africa) were signatories to a letter to the opposition requesting them to reconsider their decision in the interests of the country at large. Despite their appeal Mutharika was summoned to face indictment before the National Assembly later that month. However, the impeachment process was halted by the High Court after concern was expressed over the constitutionality of the process. At by-elections in December (following the deaths of five UDF members of the National Assembly and the conviction of a sixth) the DPP won all six seats, suggesting that there was general support for Mutharika among the populace. Later that month, in South Africa, former regional heads of state—Nelson Mandela of South Africa, Joachim Chissano of Mozambique and Sir Ketumile Masire of Botswana—brokered talks between Mutharika, Muluzi and Tembo in an attempt to halt the impeachment proceedings; however, they ended without success.

The impeachment motion was eventually withdrawn in late January 2006, prompting the resignation of seven UDF members, five of whom subsequently joined the DPP. The next session of Parliament, scheduled for February, was postponed owing to the continuing food crisis (see below) as it was believed that the allocated budget would be more beneficial to ongoing relief efforts. (Expenditure on the previous four-week session had amounted to 56m. kwacha and had been largely occupied with the failed impeachment proceedings.) In early February it was announced that Mutharika had accepted Chilumpha's 'constructive resignation'. In a letter to Chilumpha the President asserted that Chilumpha had abandoned his duties as Vice-President, leading the Cabinet to conclude that he had resigned. Chilumpha refuted the allegations made against him—*inter alia*, that he had only attended 16 out of 48 cabinet meetings and had left the country without informing Mutharika—and brought the matter before the High Court on the grounds that his dismissal was unconstitutional: as an elected minister he could only be dismissed by Parliament, not by the President. In March the High Court apparently ordered Chilumpha's full restitution; however, the Supreme Court ruled later that month that although Chilumpha was confirmed in his position as Vice-President the Government was permitted to strip him of all benefits and entitlements. In late April Chilumpha was arrested and charged with treason and conspiring to murder the President. In May he was granted bail but confined to house arrest; the restrictions on his movement were relaxed in November. Meanwhile in mid-May the Attorney-General, Ralph Kasambara, was dismissed, following allegations that he was implicated in events that led to Chilumpha's resignation; in July Jane Ansah was appointed to replace Kasambara.

In October 2006 Mutharika dismissed Mussa and the Minister of Economic Planning and Development, David Faiti. The President assumed responsibility for their respective portfolios. In February 2007 Mussa was questioned over his alleged involvement in the attempted assassination of the President the previous year, although this was not given as the reason for his dismissal from the Cabinet. Days later the President also accused Mussa of the misappropriation of fertilizer subsidies, which some small-scale farmers claimed not to have received. Mussa denied both allegations.

In November 2006 a High Court ruling stated that the section of the Constitution which stipulated that the Speaker must declare vacant the parliamentary seat of any member of the legislature wishing to move to a different political party did not breach any other principle of the Constitution. The decision was passed after it was noted that many deputies had realigned themselves with the ruling DPP without first consulting their constituency. It was alleged that only five of some 90 DPP parliamentarians had been elected while serving that party. The DPP challenged the decision; however, in June 2007 the Supreme Court of Appeal ruled that the Speaker had the authority to expel from the National Assembly any member of that body who switched party allegiances. Opposition deputies insisted upon the expulsions and in July members of the MCP and the UDF refused to participate in discussions regarding the budget for the 2007/08 financial year. The following month an injunction was granted allowing the opposition to continue their delay of the debate on the budget, although that order was overturned after an appeal by the Attorney-General. In mid-August the debate began without the participation of opposition deputies, and in mid-September the budget was finally approved.

In early February 2008 President Mutharika carried out a reorganization of the Cabinet, in which the Minister of Defence and the Minister of Health were replaced.

Despite being the only African country to have maintained full diplomatic relations with South Africa during the apartheid era, Malawi joined the Southern African Development Co-ordination Conference (subsequently the Southern African Development Community, see p. 386—SADC), which originally aimed to reduce the dependence of southern African countries on South Africa.

Relations with Mozambique were frequently strained during the early and mid-1980s by the widely held belief that the Banda regime was supporting the Resistência Nacional Moçambicana (Renamo—see the chapter on Mozambique). Following the death of President Machel of Mozambique in an air crash in South Africa in October 1986, the South African Government claimed that documents discovered in the wreckage revealed a plot by Mozambique and Zimbabwe to overthrow the Banda Government. Angry protests from Malawi were answered by denials of the accusations from the Mozambican and Zimbabwean Governments. In December, however, Malawi and Mozambique signed an agreement on defence and security matters, which was believed to include co-operation in eliminating Renamo operations. In July 1988, during an official visit to Malawi, President Chissano of Mozambique stated that he did not believe Malawi to be supporting Renamo. In December of that year Malawi, Mozambique and the office of the UN High Commissioner for Refugees (UNHCR) signed an agreement to promote the voluntary repatriation of an estimated 650,000 Mozambican refugees who had fled into Malawi during the previous two years. However, by mid-1992 the number of Mozambican refugees in Malawi had reportedly reached 1m. Large numbers of refugees returned to Mozambique in 1993–94, but in May 1995 Malawi demanded the repatriation of the remainder—estimated to total some 39,000—stating that food aid and other assistance to those who failed to leave would be reduced. The programme of the Malawi-Mozambique-UNHCR commission officially ended in November: it was estimated that a total of 1m. refugees had been repatriated.

Until early 2008 Malawi was one of a small number of nations which accorded Taiwan recognition as an independent country. In January of that year, however, it was announced that Malawi had withdrawn its support for Taiwan and established diplomatic relations with the People's Republic of China.

Government

The Head of State is the President, who is elected by universal adult suffrage, in the context of a multi-party political system, for a term of five years. Executive power is vested in the President, and legislative power in the National Assembly, which has 193 elective seats. Members of the Assembly are elected for five years, by universal adult suffrage, in the context of a multi-party system. Cabinet ministers are appointed by the President. The country is divided into three administrative regions (Northern, Central and Southern), sub-divided into 24 districts.

Defence

Malawi's active defence forces, as assessed at November 2007, comprised a land army of 5,300, a marine force of 220 and an air force of 200; all form part of the army. There was also a paramilitary police force of 1,500. Projected budgetary expenditure on defence was 3,000m. kwacha in 2007.

Economic Affairs

In 2006, according to estimates by the World Bank, Malawi's gross national income (GNI), measured at average 2004–06 prices, was US $2,263m., equivalent to $170 per head (or $720 per head on an international purchasing-power parity basis). During 1996–2006, it was estimated, the population increased at an average annual rate of 2.5%, while gross domestic product (GDP) per head increased, in real terms, by an average of 0.9% per year. Overall GDP increased, in real terms, at an average annual rate of 3.4% in 1996–2006; real GDP increased by 6.5% in 2006.

Agriculture (including forestry and fishing) contributed an estimated 30.6% of GDP in 2006, and engaged an estimated 80.8% of the labour force in 2005. The principal cash crops are tobacco (which accounted for 45.8% of total export earnings in 2004), sugar cane and tea. The principal food crops are cassava, potatoes, maize, pulses, bananas and groundnuts. Periods of severe drought and flooding have necessitated imports of basic foods in recent years (see below). During 1996–2006, according to the World Bank, agricultural GDP increased at an average annual rate of 3.1%; agricultural GDP declined by 9.1% in 2005; however, it increased by 10.1% in 2006.

Industry (including manufacturing, mining, construction and power) contributed an estimated 23.4% of GDP in 2006, and engaged 4.5% of the employed labour force in 1998. During 1996–2006, according to the World Bank, industrial GDP increased by an average of 3.1% per year. Industrial GDP increased by 10.1% in 2006.

Mining and quarrying contributed an estimated 0.8% of GDP in 2006, and engaged less than 0.1% of the employed labour force in 1998. Limestone, coal and gemstones are mined, and there are plans to develop deposits of bauxite, high-calcium marble and graphite. There are also reserves of phosphates, uranium, glass sands, asbestos and vermiculite. Environmental and financial concerns have delayed plans to exploit an estimated 30m. metric tons of bauxite deposits at Mount Mulanje. The GDP of the mining sector increased at an average annual rate of 15.1% in 1994–2003, according to official figures; mining GDP increased by 18.6% in 2003, but decreased by 12.1% in 2004.

Manufacturing contributed an estimated 19.7% of GDP in 2006, and engaged 2.7% of the employed labour force in 1998. During 1996–2006, according to the World Bank, manufacturing GDP increased by an average of 1.7% per year. Manufacturing GDP increased by 11.1% in 2006.

Production of electrical energy is by hydroelectric (principally) and thermal installations. Some 90% of energy for domestic use is derived from fuel wood. In October 1997 an agreement was signed to link Malawi's electricity system to the Cahora Bassa hydroelectric dam in Mozambique. In October 2000 a hydroelectric power plant, with a generation capacity of 64 MW, was opened at Kapichira. In 2003 full capacity of Malawi's hydroelectric power plants was 240 MW. However, as a result of flooding at the Nkula plant in March overall capacity was reduced to 140 MW and power was rationed until June. In January 2001 the Government introduced a campaign to widen access to electricity, especially in rural areas; in 2005 it was reported that only 4% of Malawians had access to electricity. By October 2004 five coalfields had been identified in Malawi with estimated reserves of 20m. metric tons and probable reserves of up to 750m. tons; at that time there was only one coal producer in Malawi, which mainly supplied domestic manufacturers. Imports of fuel comprised an 10.5% of the value of total imports in 2005.

The services sector contributed an estimated 46.0% of GDP in 2006, and engaged 11.0% of the employed labour force in 1998. The GDP of the services sector increased by an average of 2.6% per year in 1996–2006, according to the World Bank. Services GDP increased by 5.6% in 2006.

Malawi recorded a visible trade deficit of 69,615.6m. kwacha in 2006, while there was a deficit of 97,779.9m. kwacha on the current account of the balance of payments. In 2004 the principal source of imports was South Africa (31.7%); Mozambique and the United Kingdom were also notable suppliers. South Africa was also the principal market for exports (14.6%) in that year; other important markets were the USA, the United Kingdom, Germany and Mozambique. The principal imports in 2004 were machinery and transport equipment (particularly road vehicles), basic manufactures, chemicals and related products, and food and live animals. The principal exports in that year were tobacco and food and live animals.

In the financial year ending 30 June 2006 Malawi's overall budget deficit was an estimated 20,213.2m. kwacha. The country's external debt totalled US $3,155m. at the end of 2005, of which $3,040m. was long-term public debt. In 2003 the cost of debt-servicing was equivalent to 9.0% of the value of exports of goods and services. The annual rate of inflation averaged 14.6% in 2000–05; consumer prices increased by an average of 13.9% in 2006. Some 1.1% of the labour force were unemployed in 1998.

Malawi is a member of the Southern African Development Community (see p. 386) and the Common Market for Eastern and Southern Africa (COMESA, see p. 205). Nine members of COMESA, including Malawi, became inaugural members of the COMESA Free Trade Area in October 2000. The country belongs to the International Tea Promotion Association (see p. 409) and to the International Tobacco Growers' Association (see p. 409). Malawi was also a signatory to the Cotonou Agreement with the European Union (EU), which expired on 31 December 2007 and was to be superseded by an Economic Partnership Agreement (EPA). The terms of trade embodied in the new arrangement had not been finalised in early 2008.

Malawi's natural impediments to growth (including its landlocked position, the vulnerability of the dominant agricultural sector to drought, and a high rate of population growth), were compounded by the severe mismanagement of economic affairs and in late 2001 and early 2002 the EU, the USA and other donors suspended aid to Malawi, in response to concerns regarding corruption. In April 2002 Malawi was suspended from the World Bank's initiative for heavily indebted poor countries (HIPC) and the dispersal of funds under the IMF's Poverty Reduction and Growth Facility (PRGF) was delayed until December 2003. (It was not until August 2005 that approval was finally given for a three-year PRGF programme worth US $55m.) The report on the first review of the PRGF programme, published in March 2006, commended the Government for its ongoing efforts to reduce public expenditure and observe budget limits, while acknowledging that spending on food security remained a priority. In February the EU provided assistance in launching a $27m. income-generating public works programme, as an extension of a four-year programme which had ended the previous year. In the short term the programme would provide rural employment in road construction and rehabilitation, forestry, irrigation and aquaculture, with the long-term aim of improving food security. A severe scarcity of food was experienced in 2005/06, with the 2005 harvest declared the worst in a decade by the UN World Food Programme; however, an improved harvest was recorded in 2006. Furthermore, the 2006/07 budget allocated considerable additional resources to the Ministry of Agriculture and Food Security, in order that future potential humanitarian crises be avoided. Improvements in this sector resulted in a 22% increase in maize production during 2007, thereby allowing Malawi to donate a portion of its surplus crop to less affluent countries in Southern Africa. Rising agricultural output also facilitated a decline in inflation, which the IMF recorded at 7.0% in 2007. In 2006 the Government had unveiled the Malawi Growth and Development Strategy, covering the period from 2006/07–2010/11, which sought to create wealth through sustainable economic growth and infrastructure development as a means of achieving poverty reduction. This programme was expected to transform the country from a predominantly importing and consuming economy to a manufacturing and exporting economy. Real GDP increased by an estimated 5.5% in 2007 and the IMF forecast further growth of 5.2% for 2008. However, the political impasse which delayed the approval of the 2007/08 budget (see Recent History) also threatened the effective delivery of public services and the supply of donor assistance.

Education

Primary education is officially compulsory, beginning at six years of age and lasting for eight years. Secondary education, which begins at 14 years of age, lasts for four years, comprising two cycles of two years. According to UNESCO estimates, in 2003/04 primary enrolment included 95% of children in the relevant age-group (males 93%; females 98%), while in 2003/04 secondary enrolment included 25% of children in the relevant age-group (males 27%; females 23%). A programme to expand education at all levels has been undertaken; however, the introduction of free primary education in September 1994 led to the influx of more than 1m. additional pupils, resulting in severe overcrowding in schools. There were 4,757 students attending the country's two universities in 2003. Some students attend institutions in the United Kingdom and the USA. Expenditure on education in 2003/04 was estimated at 8,714m. kwacha (equivalent to 19.6% of total expenditure).

Public Holidays

2008: 1 January (New Year's Day), 15 January (John Chilembwe Day), 3 March (Martyrs' Day), 21–24 March (Easter), 1 May (Labour Day), 14 June (Freedom Day), 6 July (Republic Day), 13 October (Mothers' Day), 25–26 December (Christmas).

2009: 1 January (New Year's Day), 15 January (John Chilembwe Day), 3 March (Martyrs' Day), 10–13 April (Easter), 1 May (Labour Day), 14 June (Freedom Day), 6 July (Republic Day), 13 October (Mothers' Day), 25–26 December (Christmas).

Weights and Measures

The metric system is in use.

MALAWI

Statistical Survey

Sources (unless otherwise indicated): National Statistical Office of Malawi, POB 333, Zomba; tel. 1524377; fax 1525130; e-mail enquiries@statistics.gov.mw; internet www.nso.malawi.net; Reserve Bank of Malawi, POB 30063, Capital City, Lilongwe 3; tel. 1770600; fax 1772752; e-mail webmaster@rbm.mw; internet www.rbm.mw.

Area and Population

AREA, POPULATION AND DENSITY

Area (sq km)	118,484*
Population (census results)	
1–21 September 1987	7,988,507
1–21 September 1998	
Males	4,867,563
Females	5,066,305
Total	9,933,868
Population (official projected estimates)	
2005	12,341,170
2006	12,757,883
2007	13,187,632
Density (per sq km) at mid-2007	111.3

* 45,747 sq miles. The area includes 24,208 sq km (9,347 sq miles) of inland water.

REGIONS
(official projected estimates, 2007)

Region	Area (sq km)*	Population	Density (per sq km)	Regional capital
Southern	31,753	6,068,428	191.1	Blantyre
Central	35,592	5,568,238	156.4	Lilongwe
Northern	26,931	1,550,966	57.6	Mzuzu
Total	94,276	13,187,632	139.9	

* Excluding inland waters, totalling 24,208 sq km.

PRINCIPAL TOWNS
(population at census of September 1998)

Blantyre	502,053	Karonga	27,811
Lilongwe (capital)	440,471	Kasungu	27,754
Mzuzu	86,890	Mangochi	26,570
Zomba	65,915	Salima	20,355

2007 (population, official projected estimates): Blantyre 778,827; Lilongwe 744,436; Mzuz 150,065; Zomba 113,106.

BIRTHS AND DEATHS
(annual averages, UN estimates)

	1990–95	1995–2000	2000–05
Birth rate (per 1,000)	49.1	47.0	43.8
Death rate (per 1,000)	17.1	17.2	17.5

Source: UN, *World Population Prospects: The 2006 Revision*.

Expectation of Life (years at birth, WHO estimates): 46.6 (males 46.9; females 46.2) in 2005 (Source: WHO, *World Health Statistics*).

ECONOMICALLY ACTIVE POPULATION*
(persons aged 10 years and over, 1998 census)

	Males	Females	Total
Agriculture, hunting, forestry and fishing	1,683,006	2,082,821	3,765,827
Mining and quarrying	2,206	293	2,499
Manufacturing	94,545	23,938	118,483
Electricity, gas and water	6,656	663	7,319
Construction	70,196	3,206	73,402
Trade, restaurants and hotels	176,466	80,923	257,389
Transport, storage and communications	29,438	3,185	32,623
Financing, insurance, real estate and business services	10,473	3,484	13,957
Public administration	82,973	18,460	101,433
Community, social and personal services	52,980	33,016	85,996
Total employed	2,208,940	2,249,989	4,458,929
Unemployed	34,697	15,664	50,361
Total labour force	2,243,637	2,265,653	4,509,290

* Excluding armed forces.

Mid-2005 (estimates in '000): Agriculture, etc. 4,903; Total labour force 6,068 (Source: FAO).

Health and Welfare

KEY INDICATORS

Total fertility rate (children per woman, 2005)	5.9
Under-5 mortality rate (per 1,000 live births, 2005)	125
HIV/AIDS (% of persons aged 15–49, 2005)	14.1
Physicians (per 1,000 head, 2004)	0.02
Hospital beds (per 1,000 head, 1998)	1.34
Health expenditure (2004): US $ per head (PPP)	57.8
Health expenditure (2004): % of GDP	12.9
Health expenditure (2004): public (% of total)	74.7
Access to water (% of persons, 2004)	73
Access to sanitation (% of persons, 2004)	61
Human Development Index (2005): ranking	164
Human Development Index (2005): value	0.437

For sources and definitions, see explanatory note on p. vi.

Agriculture

PRINCIPAL CROPS
('000 metric tons)

	2004	2005	2006
Rice (paddy)	49.7	50.0*	50.0*
Maize	1,733.1	1,253.0†	1,600.0*
Millet	17.3	17.5*	17.5*
Sorghum	40.9	41.0*	41.0*
Potatoes	1,784.7	1,800.0*	1,800.0*
Cassava (Manioc)	2,559.3	2,075.0†	2,075.0*
Dry beans	79.4	80.0*	80.0*
Chick-peas*	34.4	34.1	34.1
Cow peas (dry)*	54.0	n.a.	54.0
Pigeon peas*	79.0	n.a.	79.0
Groundnuts (in shell)	161.2	92.0†	145.0†
Cottonseed	34.8	24.0†	24.0*
Cabbages and other brassicas	50.0	37.5*	37.5*

MALAWI

—continued	2004	2005	2006
Tomatoes*	35.0	34.9	35.0
Onions (dry)	50.0	50.0*	50.0*
Guavas, mangoes and mangosteens*	33.0	44.5	44.5
Bananas	360.0	54.2*	54.2*
Plantains	300.0	247.6*	247.6*
Sugar cane	2,100	n.a.	2,400*
Coffee (green)	1.6	1.5†	1.5†
Tea	50.1	38.0	38.4
Tobacco (leaves)*	69.5	n.a.	69.5
Cotton (lint)	18.8	19.0*	19.0*

* FAO estimate(s).
† Unofficial figure.

Aggregate production ('000 metric tons, may include official, semi-official or estimated data): Total cereals 1,843 in 2004, 1,363 in 2005, 1,710 in 2006; Total roots and tubers 4,344 in 2004, 3,875 in 2005, 3,875 in 2006; Total vegetables (incl. melons) 310 in 2004, 298 in 2005, 297 in 2006; Total fruits (excl. melons) 878 in 2004, 532 in 2005, 532 in 2006.

Source: FAO.

LIVESTOCK
('000 head, year ending September)

	2004	2005	2006*
Cattle	765	750*	750
Pigs*	456.3	n.a.	456.3
Sheep*	115	n.a.	115
Goats	1,900	1,900*	1,900
Chickens*	15,200	15,200	15,200

* FAO estimate(s).
Source: FAO.

LIVESTOCK PRODUCTS
('000 metric tons, FAO estimates)

	2004	2005	2006
Cattle meat	15.7	16.0	16.0
Goat meat	6.6	6.6	6.6
Pig meat	23.1	24.5	24.5
Chicken meat	16.0	16.4	16.4
Cows' milk	35.0	n.a.	35.0
Hen eggs	19.5	n.a.	19.5

Source: FAO.

Forestry

ROUNDWOOD REMOVALS
('000 cubic metres, excluding bark, FAO estimates)

	2004	2005	2006
Sawlogs, veneer logs and logs for sleepers	130	130	130
Other industrial wood	390	390	390
Fuel wood	5,101.7	5,140.7	5,189.3
Total	5,621.7	5,660.7	5,709.3

Source: FAO.

SAWNWOOD PRODUCTION
('000 cubic metres, including railway sleepers)

	1991*	1992†	1993
Coniferous (softwood)	28	28	30
Broadleaved (hardwood)	15	15	15†
Total	43	43	45

* Unofficial figures.
† FAO estimate(s).

1994–2006: Annual production as in 1993 (FAO estimates).

Source: FAO.

Statistical Survey

Fishing
('000 metric tons, live weight)

	2003	2004	2005
Capture	53.8	56.5	59.4
Cyprinids	6.7	7.1	7.2
Tilapias	5.7	6.0	6.0
Cichlids	29.8	31.4	33.6
Torpedo-shaped catfishes	8.2	8.7	8.7
Other freshwater fishes	3.1	3.3	3.3
Aquaculture	0.7	0.7	0.8
Total catch	54.5	57.2	60.2

Note: Figures exclude aquatic mammals, recorded by number rather than weight. The number of Nile crocodiles caught was: 301 in 2003; 20 in 2004; 637 in 2005.

Source: FAO.

Mining
('000 metric tons, unless otherwise indicated)

	2004	2005	2006
Bituminous coal	40.9	44.9	48.0
Lime	23.1	22.0	21.1
Gemstones (kilograms)	1,820	1,620	2,171
Aggregate	168.6	170.0*	170.0*
Limestone	21.2	28.0*	34.2

* Estimates.
Source: US Geological Survey.

Industry

SELECTED PRODUCTS
('000 metric tons, unless otherwise indicated)

	2000	2001	2002
Raw sugar	96	107	260*
Beer ('000 hectolitres)	739	1,033	n.a.
Blankets ('000)	574	281	n.a.
Cement	198	111	174

* Natural sodium carbonate (Na_2Co_3).

2003 ('000 metric tons): Raw sugar (Na_2Co_3) 257; Cement 190 (Source: US Geological Survey).

Electric energy (million kWh): 1,129 in 2002; 1,177 in 2003; 1,270 in 2004.

Source (unless otherwise indicated): UN, *Industrial Commodity Statistics Yearbook*.

Cement ('000 metric tons, hydraulic): 119.5 in 2004; 160.0 in 2005 (estimate); 200.0 in 2006 (Source: US Geological Survey).

Finance

CURRENCY AND EXCHANGE RATES
Monetary Units
  100 tambala = 1 Malawi kwacha (K).

Sterling, Dollar and Euro Equivalents (31 July 2007)
  £1 sterling = 284.000 kwacha;
  US $1 = 139.812 kwacha;
  €1 = 191.640 kwacha;
  1,000 Malawi kwacha = £3.52 = $7.15 = €5.22.

Average Exchange Rate (kwacha per US $)
  2004 108.898
  2005 118.420
  2006 136.014

MALAWI

BUDGET
(K million, year ending 30 June)

Revenue	2003/04	2004/05	2005/06*
Tax revenue	27,793.2	43,635.0	55,797.8
Taxes on income and profits	12,706.6	19,854.0	23,973.0
Companies	4,796.6	5,386.0	6,710.3
Individuals	7,910.0	14,468.0	17,263.5
Taxes on goods and services	12,160.4	18,830.0	25,909.8
Surtax	8,630.0	13,739.0	17,796.6
Excise duties	3,530.4	5,091.0	8,113.2
Taxes on international trade	3,766.1	5,952.0	7,374.4
Less Tax refunds	840.0	1,001.0	1,460.2
Non-tax revenue	4,874.0	4,461.0	8,127.0
Departmental receipts	1,173.2	2,447.0	4,595.3
Total	**32,667.2**	**48,096.0**	**63,924.8**

Expenditure	2003/04	2004/05	2005/06*
General public services	21,889.6	22,719.7	35,519.5
General administration	19,445.9	17,581.0	26,997.5
Defence	1,139.1	2,552.6	4,157.3
Public order and safety	1,304.6	2,586.1	4,364.7
Social and community services	12,606.7	17,509.0	24,363.2
Education	6,310.1	8,631.9	9,500.8
Health	3,692.4	5,247.6	11,057.9
Social security and welfare	2,105.7	2,706.4	2,221.3
Housing and community amenities	356.7	395.8	1,325.6
Recreational, cultural and other social services	75.4	76.8	106.2
Broadcasting and publishing	66.4	450.5	151.3
Economic affairs and services	4,799.0	8,721.1	6,927.3
Energy and mining	108.9	105.2	115.4
Agriculture and natural resources	2,482.4	4,345.5	2,837.2
Tourism	150.0	—	—
Physical planning and development	101.6	1,144.3	527.9
Transport and communications	1,496.3	2,048.5	2,299.1
Industry and commerce	210.7	390.0	599.6
Labour relations and employment	231.2	346.5	404.2
Environmental protection and conservation	—	—	—
Scientific and technological services	—	314.4	144.0
Other economic services	17.9	26.7	—
Unallocable expenditure	1,505.2	677.3	—
Total recurrent expenditure	**40,800.5**	**49,627.0**	**66,810.0**
Debt amortization	18,736.5	18,752.0	17,328.0
Total	**59,537.0**	**68,379.0**	**84,138.0**

* Estimates.

INTERNATIONAL RESERVES
(US $ million at 31 December)

	2004	2005	2006
Gold (national valuation)	0.54	0.54	0.54
IMF special drawing rights	1.20	1.05	0.68
Reserve position in IMF	3.56	3.27	3.48
Foreign exchange	123.30	154.59	129.61
Total	**128.60**	**159.45**	**134.31**

Source: IMF, *International Financial Statistics*.

MONEY SUPPLY
(K million at 31 December)

	2004	2005	2006
Currency outside banks	10,992.8	11,947.0	15,470.9
Demand deposits at commercial banks	14,730.2	19,356.1	20,217.8
Total money (incl. others)	**25,723.0**	**31,303.1**	**35,688.7**

Source: IMF, *International Financial Statistics*.

COST OF LIVING
(Consumer Price Index; base: 2000 = 100)

	2004	2005	2006
Food (incl. beverages)	154.4	181.0	209.1
Clothing (incl. footwear)	179.5	192.8	208.8
Rent	211.7	236.9	266.9
All items (incl. others)	**172.0**	**198.5**	**226.1**

Source: ILO.

NATIONAL ACCOUNTS
Expenditure on the Gross Domestic Product
(K million at current prices)

	2004	2005	2006*
Government final consumption expenditure	34,990.1	41,344.5	49,124.8
Private final consumption expenditure	324,697.4	395,671.5	435,651.9
Gross capital formation	25,091.9	29,106.9	32,783.5
Total domestic expenditure	**384,779.4**	**466,122.9**	**517,560.2**
Exports of goods and services	58,914.3	61,785.8	84,188.8
Less Imports of goods and services	135,181.6	164,387.6	166,523.9
GDP in purchasers' values	**308,512.1**	**363,521.1**	**435,225.0**
GDP at 2002 factor cost	271,050.6	276,801.2	300,123.6

Gross Domestic Product by Economic Activity
(K million at current prices)

	2004	2005	2006*
Agriculture, forestry and fishing	88,955.7	81,395.9	91,814.5
Mining and quarrying	1,450.5	2,177.2	2,386.2
Manufacturing	52,040.1	55,786.9	59,022.6
Electricity and water	3,434.4	3,740.0	4,016.8
Building and construction	3,904.4	4,189.5	4,759.2
Wholesale and retail trade services	53,418.1	58,118.9	62,826.6
Hotels and restaurants	10,804.3	11,470.0	12,341.3
Transport and communication	14,584.4	15,926.2	16,802.1
Financial intermediation and insurance	8,405.0	9,069.0	9,540.6
Business activities and real estate	9,815.1	10,050.6	10,362.2
Ownership of dwellings	2,407.2	2,457.8	2,583.1
Private social services	7,984.7	8,240.2	8,808.8
Government services	13,846.7	14,179.0	14,859.6
Sub-total	**271,050.6**	**276,801.2**	**300,123.6**
Net indirect taxes	25,706.2	31,813.3	40,000.0
Adjustment to current prices	11,755.2	54,906.6	95,101.4
GDP in market prices	**308,512.0**	**363,521.1**	**435,225.0**

* Projected figures.

BALANCE OF PAYMENTS
(K million)

	2004	2005	2006
Exports of goods f.o.b.	54,419.6	60,251.3	73,790.2
Imports of goods f.o.b.	−88,308.4	−119,101.8	−143,405.8
Trade balance	**−33,888.9**	**−58,850.5**	**−69,615.6**
Net services	−18,238.5	−24,560.2	−28,974.6
Balance on goods and services	**−52,127.4**	**−83,410.7**	**−98,590.2**
Net other income	−4,992.8	−5,008.6	−4,847.3
Balance on goods, services and income	**−57,120.2**	**−88,419.3**	**−103,437.5**
Net transfers	1,888.0	4,924.7	5,657.5
Current balance	**−55,232.1**	**−83,494.6**	**−97,779.9**
Government transfers (net)	24,186.2	23,361.7	20,634.5
Government drawings on loans	3,625.7	10,499.4	6,112.3
Public enterprises (net)	1,173.1	1,319.4	1,632.0
Private sector (net)	391.9	425.7	489.1
Short-term capital (net)	65.0	70.6	81.1
Errors and omissions	19,016.2	35,334.7	51,730.8
Overall balance*	**−6,774.0**	**−12,483.0**	**−17,100.1**

* Excluding debt relief (K million): 5,125.2 in 2003; 7,079.1 in 2004; 14,925.4 in 2006.

MALAWI

External Trade

PRINCIPAL COMMODITIES
(distribution by SITC, US $ million)

Imports c.i.f.	2002	2003	2004
Food and live animals	128.3	56.9	40.2
Cereals and cereal preparations	104.6	30.9	15.5
Beverages and tobacco	16.9	46.0	11.9
Tobacco and tobacco products	14.3	43.8	10.1
Mineral fuels, lubricants, etc.	77.1	86.3	13.0
Petroleum, petroleum products, etc.	73.8	85.2	11.7
Refined petroleum products	71.1	82.0	9.1
Chemicals and related products	120.1	121.5	80.7
Medicinal and pharmaceutical products	23.1	26.2	22.6
Manufactured fertilizers	49.2	43.3	13.8
Basic manufactures	106.6	130.9	106.1
Paper, paperboard, etc.	16.1	22.6	15.8
Textile yarn, fabrics, etc.	29.3	33.7	31.7
Iron and steel	19.5	21.9	16.5
Machinery and transport equipment	163.6	188.5	152.5
Machinery specialized for particular industries	21.1	32.6	26.4
General industrial machinery, equipment and parts	17.0	23.8	19.3
Office machinery and automatic data processing equipment	13.9	12.2	15.3
Electrical machinery, apparatus, etc.	17.0	26.3	21.1
Road vehicles	73.8	76.2	49.1
Goods vehicles (lorries and trucks)	29.9	32.4	14.6
Miscellaneous manufactured articles	52.4	58.6	55.2
Total (incl. others)	695.0	723.5	477.6

Exports f.o.b.	2002	2003	2004
Food and live animals	87.1	162.6	145.7
Sugar and honey	34.8	105.4	75.6
Raw beet and cane sugars	27.5	92.5	72.4
Coffee, tea, cocoa and spices	42.2	36.3	50.9
Tea	36.7	32.8	47.2
Beverages and tobacco	232.1	225.0	221.4
Tobacco and tobacco products	232.0	224.9	221.4
Unstripped tobacco	143.9	123.7	130.3
Stripped or partly stripped tobacco	88.1	101.3	91.1
Crude materials (inedible) except fuels	12.1	15.3	35.5
Textile fibres	7.4	5.8	21.0
Basic manufactures	34.7	40.8	57.9
Clothing and accessories	32.0	34.2	44.3
Total (incl. others)	377.4	457.0	483.3

Source: UN, *International Trade Statistics Yearbook*.

PRINCIPAL TRADING PARTNERS
(K million)

Imports	2002	2003	2004
France	1,379	530	2,680
Germany	504	1,099	1,116
Japan	1,597	3,202	3,924
Mozambique	1,576	4,061	13,705
Netherlands	431	429	579
South Africa	22,272	30,621	32,221
United Kingdom	2,806	4,079	5,193
USA	2,264	2,874	2,795
Zambia	968	2,172	3,915
Zimbabwe	3,118	4,996	4,800
Total (incl. others)	53,657	76,650	101,554

Exports	2002	2003	2004
France	451	1,726	385
Germany	3,321	3,655	3,974
Japan	1,238	2,681	1,052
Mozambique	548	1,873	3,050
Netherlands	863	3,174	2,319
South Africa	4,246	7,865	7,706
United Kingdom	2,905	3,822	5,197
USA	4,659	6,394	5,934
Zambia	255	884	1,114
Zimbabwe	485	851	1,002
Total (incl. others)	31,416	51,672	52,627

Transport

RAILWAYS
(traffic)

	2002	2003	2004
Passengers carried ('000)	402	488	394
Passenger-kilometres ('000)	23,845	30,311	29,523
Net freight ton-kilometres ('000)	86,018	26,009	26,055

ROAD TRAFFIC
(estimates, motor vehicles in use at 31 December)

	1994	1995	1996
Passenger cars	23,520	25,480	27,000
Lorries and vans	26,000	29,000	29,700

Source: International Road Federation, *World Road Statistics*.

SHIPPING

Inland Waterways
(lake transport)

	2002	2003	2004
Passengers carried ('000)	78	68	55
Passenger-km ('000)	6,955	5,659	4,299
Net freight-ton km	392	1,438	316

MALAWI

CIVIL AVIATION
(traffic on scheduled services)

	2001	2002	2003
Kilometres flown (million)	3	3	4
Passengers carried ('000)	113	105	109
Passenger-km (million)	221	140	147
Total ton-km (million)	23	14	16

Source: UN, *Statistical Yearbook*.

Freight carried (metric tons): 3,468 in 2002; 2,768 in 2003; 4,011 in 2004.

Passengers carried ('000): 335 in 2004.

Tourism

FOREIGN TOURIST ARRIVALS BY COUNTRY OF RESIDENCE

	2003	2004	2005
Mozambique	92,200	104,698	95,019
North America	17,210	19,431	17,278
Southern Africa*	49,200	54,230	48,155
United Kingdom and Ireland	31,220	17,030	28,157
Zambia	50,540	45,817	43,855
Zimbabwe	63,910	57,518	60,807
Total (incl. others)	424,000	427,360	437,718

* Comprising South Africa, Botswana, Lesotho and Swaziland.

Tourism receipts (US $ million, excl. passenger transport): 33 in 2003; 24 in 2004; n.a. in 2005.

Source: World Tourism Organization.

Communications Media

	2003	2004	2005
Telephones ('000 main lines in use)	85.0	93.0	102.7
Mobile cellular telephones ('000 subscribers)	135.1	222.1	429.3
Personal computers ('000 in use)	16	20	25
Internet users ('000)	36.0	46.1	51.5
Broadband subscribers ('000)	—	0.1	0.4

2006: Internet users ('000) 59.7.

Radio receivers ('000 in use): 4,929 in 1998.

Television receivers ('000 in use): 40 in 2001.

Facsimile machines (number in use): 1,250 in 1997.

Book production (first editions only): 120 titles in 1996.

Daily newspapers: 5 in 1998 (estimated average circulation 26,000 copies).

Non-daily newspapers: 4 in 1996 (estimated average circulation 120,000 copies).

Sources: UNESCO Institute for Statistics; UN, *Statistical Yearbook*; International Telecommunication Union.

Education

(2003)

	Institutions	Teachers	Students
Primary	3,160*	45,100	3,112,513
Secondary	n.a.	7,076	131,100
Universities	6	654	4,757

* 1997 figure. Source: UNESCO Institute for Statistics.

Primary education (2004): Schools 5,103; Students 3,166,786; Teachers 43,952 (Source: partly Ministry of Education, Science and Technology).

Adult literacy rate (UNESCO estimates): 64.1% (males 74.9%; females 54.0%) in 1998 (Source: UNESCO Institute for Statistics).

Directory

The Constitution

A new Constitution, replacing the (amended) 1966 Constitution, was approved by the National Assembly on 16 May 1994, and took provisional effect for one year from 18 May. During this time the Constitution was to be subject to review, and the final document was promulgated on 18 May 1995. The main provisions (with subsequent amendments) are summarized below:

THE PRESIDENT

The President is both Head of State and Head of Government. The President is elected for five years, by universal adult suffrage, in the context of a multi-party political system. The Constitution provides for up to two Vice-Presidents.

PARLIAMENT

Parliament comprises the President, the Vice-President(s) and the National Assembly. The National Assembly has 193 elective seats, elections being by universal adult suffrage, in the context of a multi-party system. Cabinet ministers who are not elected members of parliament also sit in the National Assembly. The Speaker is appointed from among the ordinary members of the Assembly. The parliamentary term is normally five years. The President has power to prorogue or dissolve Parliament.

In 1995 the National Assembly approved proposals for the establishment of a second chamber, the Senate, to be implemented in 1999. The chamber was not established by that date, however, and in January 2001 the National Assembly approved a proposal to abandon plans for its creation.

EXECUTIVE POWER

Executive power is exercised by the President, who appoints members of the Cabinet.

The Government

HEAD OF STATE

President: Dr BINGU WA MUTHARIKA (took office 24 May 2004).
Vice-President: Dr CASSIM CHILUMPHA.

CABINET
(March 2008)

President and Commander-in-Chief of the Malawi Defence Force and Police Service, Minister of Agriculture and Food Security and Minister of Education, Science and Technology: Dr BINGU WA MUTHARIKA.

Minister for Presidential and Parliamentary Affairs: DAVIES KATSONGA.

Minister of Finance: Dr GOODALL E. GONDWE.

Minister of Foreign Affairs: JOYCE BANDA.

Minister of Industry and Trade: HENRY MUSSA.

Minister of Energy and Mines: TED KALEBE.

Minister of Local Government and Rural Development: Dr GEORGE CHAPONDA.

Minister of Transport, Public Works and Housing: HENRY CHIMUNTHU BANDA.

Minister of Economic Planning and Development: KEN LIPENGA.

MALAWI
Directory

Minister of Irrigation and Water Development: MOHAMMED SIDIK MIA.
Minister of National Defence: AARON SANGALA.
Minister of Information and Civic Education: PATRICIA KALIATI.
Minister of Lands and Natural Resources: JOHN B. KHUMBO CHIRWA.
Minister of Home Affairs and Internal Security: ERNEST MALENGA.
Minister of Justice: HENRY DAMA PHOYA.
Attorney-General: JANE ANSAH.
Minister of Labour: DAVIS KATSONGA.
Minister of Health: KUMBO KACHALI.
Minister of Women and Child Development: ANNA KACHIKO.
Minister of Youth Development and Sports: SYMON VUWA KAUNDA.
Minister of Persons with Disabilities and the Elderly: CLEMENT KHEMBO.
Minister of Tourism and Wildlife: CALLISTA CHAPOLA CHIMOMBO.
There were also 21 Deputy Ministers.

MINISTRIES

Office of the President and Cabinet: Private Bag 301, Capital City, Lilongwe 3; tel. 1789311; fax 1788456; internet www.malawi.gov.mw/opc/opc.htm.

Office of the Vice President: POB 30399, Capital City, Lilongwe; tel. 1788444; fax 1788218; e-mail vicepres@malawi.gov.mw.

Ministry of Agriculture and Food Security: POB 30134, Capital City, Lilongwe 3; tel. 1789033; fax 1789218; e-mail agriculture@agriculture.gov.mw; internet www.malawi.gov.mw/Agriculture/Home%20%20Agriculture.htm.

Ministry of Economic Planning and Development: POB 30136, Capital City, Lilongwe 3; tel. 1788390; fax 1788131; e-mail epd@malawi.net; internet www.malawi.gov.mw/Economic%20Planning/Home%20Economic%20Planning.htm.

Ministry of Education Science and Technology: Private Bag 328, Lilongwe 3; tel. 1789422; fax 1788064; e-mail education@malawi.gov.mw; internet www.malawi.gov.mw/Education/Home%20%20Education.htm.

Ministry of Energy and Mines: Private Bag 350, Lilongwe 3; tel. 1789488; fax 1773379; internet www.malawi.gov.mw/natres/natres.htm.

Ministry of Finance: Capital Hill, POB 30049, Lilongwe 3; tel. 1789355; fax 1789173; internet www.malawi.gov.mw/Finance/Home%20Finance.htm.

Ministry of Foreign Affairs: POB 30315, Lilongwe 3; tel. 1789323; fax 1788482; e-mail foreign@malawi.net; internet www.malawi.gov.mw/Foreign%20Affairs/Home%20ForeignAffairs.htm.

Ministry of Health: POB 30377, Capital City, Lilongwe 3; tel. 1789400; fax 1789431; e-mail doccentre@malawi.net; internet www.malawi.gov.mw/Health/Home%20Health.htm.

Ministry of Home Affairs and Internal Security: Private Bag 331, Lilongwe 3; tel. 1789177; fax 1789509; internet www.malawi.gov.mw/Home%20Affairs/Home%20HomeAffairs.htm; comprises the Immigration Dept, Prison and Police Services.

Ministry of Industry and Trade: POB 30366, Capital City, Lilongwe 3; tel. 1770244; fax 1770680; e-mail minci@malawi.net; internet www.malawi.gov.mw/Trade/Home%20%20Trade.htm.

Ministry of Information and Civic Education: Private Bag 326, Capital City, Lilongwe 3; tel. 1775499; fax 1770650; e-mail psinfo@sdnp.org.mw; internet www.malawi.gov.mw/Information/Home%20Information.htm.

Ministry of Irrigation and Water Development: Tikwere House, Private Bag 390, Capital City, Lilongwe 3; tel. 1770238; fax 1773737; internet www.malawi.gov.mw/water/Home%20%20Water.htm.

Ministry of Justice: Private Bag 333, Capital City, Lilongwe 3; tel. 1788411; fax 1788332; e-mail justice@malawi.gov.mw; internet www.malawi.gov.mw/Justice/Home%20%20Justice.htm; also comprises the Attorney-General's Chambers and the Directorate of Public Prosecutions.

Ministry of Labour: Private Bag 344, Capital City, Lilongwe 3; tel. 1773277; fax 1773803; e-mail labour@malawi.net; internet www.malawi.gov.mw/Labour/Home%20%20Labour.htm.

Ministry of Lands and Natural Resources: POB 30548, Lilongwe 3; tel. 1774766; fax 1773990.

Ministry of Local Government and Rural Development: POB 30312, Lilongwe 3; tel. 1789388; fax 1788083; internet www.malawi.gov.mw/LocalGovt/Home%20%20LocalGovt.htm.

Ministry of National Defence: Private Bag 339, Lilongwe 3; tel. 1789600; fax 1789176; internet www.malawi.gov.mw/Defence/Home%20Defence.htm.

Ministry of Persons with Disabilities and the Elderly: Lilongwe 3.

Ministry of Tourism and Wildlife: Lilongwe 3.

Ministry of Transport, Public Works and Housing: Private Bag 322, Capital City, Lilongwe 3; tel. 1789377; fax 1789328; internet www.malawi.gov.mw/Transport/Home%20Transport.htm.

Ministry of Women and Child Development: Private Bag 330, Capital City, Lilongwe 3; tel. 1770411; fax 1770826.

Ministry of Youth Development and Sports: Lingadzi House, Private Bag 384, Lilongwe 3; tel. 1774999; fax 1771018; e-mail sports@malawi.gov.mw; internet www.malawi.gov.mw/Youth/Home%20%20Youth.htm.

President and Legislature

PRESIDENT

Presidential Election, 20 May 2004

Candidate	Votes	% of votes
Bingu wa Mutharika (UDF)	1,119,738	35.89
John Tembo (MCP)	846,457	27.13
Gwandaguluwe Chakuamba (Mgwirizano Coalition*)	802,386	25.72
Brown Mpinganjira (NDA)	272,172	8.72
Justin Malewezi (Independent)	78,892	2.53
Total	3,119,645	100.00

* Comprising the Malawi Democratic Party, the Malawi Forum for Unity and Development, the Movement for Genuine Democratic Change (MGODE), the National Unity Party, the People's Progressive Movement, the People's Transformation Party and Chakuamba's Republican Party (RP); in early June 2004 MGODE and the RP signed a memorandum of understanding on co-operation with the UDF.

NATIONAL ASSEMBLY

National Assembly: Parliament Bldg, Private Bag B362, Lilongwe 3; tel. 1773566; fax 1774196; internet www.malawi.gov.mw/parliament/parliament.htm.

Speaker: LOUIS JOSEPH CHIMANGO.

General Election, 20 May 2004*

Party	Seats
Malawi Congress Party (MCP)	56
United Democratic Front (UDF)	49
Republican Party (RP)†	15
National Democratic Alliance (NDA)	8
Alliance for Democracy (AFORD)	6
People's Progressive Movement (PPM)†	6
Movement for Genuine Democratic Change (MGODE)†	3
Congress for National Unity (CONU)	1
People's Transformation Party (PETRA)†	1
Independents	39
Total	193‡

* Provisional results.
† Contested the election as part of the Mgwirizano Coalition, which also comprised the Malawi Democratic Party, the Malawi Forum for Unity and Development and the National Unity Party; in early June 2004 MGODE and the RP signed a memorandum of understanding on co-operation with the UDF.
‡ Disputed results in three constituencies remained under investigation in early June 2004, while voting in a further six constituencies was not conducted owing to irregularities.

Election Commission

Malawi Electoral Commission (MEC): Development House, Private Bag 113, Blantyre; tel. 1822033; fax 1823960; internet www.sdnp.org.mw/~solomon/mec/index.htm; f. 1998; Chair. JAMES KALAILE; Chief Elections Officer DAVID KAMBAUWA (acting).

Political Organizations

Alliance for Democracy (AFORD): Private Bag 28, Lilongwe; f. 1992; in March 1993 absorbed membership of fmr Malawi Freedom Movement; Pres. CHAKUFWA CHIHANA; First Vice-Pres. KALUNDI CHIRWA; Sec.-Gen. WALLACE CHIUME.

Congress for National Unity (CONU): Lilongwe; f. 1999; Pres. Bishop DANIEL KAMFOSI NKHUMBWA.

Democratic Progressive Party (DPP): Lilongwe 3; internet dppmw.org; f. 2005 following Bingu wa Mutharika's resignation from the UDF; Leader Dr BINGU WA MUTHARIKA; Sec.-Gen. HEATHERWICK NTABA.

Malawi Congress Party (MCP): Private Bag 388, Lilongwe 3; tel. 1730388; f. 1959; sole legal party 1966–93; Pres. JOHN TEMBO.

Malawi Democratic Party (MDP): Lilongwe; Pres. KAMLEPO KALUA.

Malawi Forum for Unity and Development (MAFUNDE): f. 2002; aims to combat corruption and food shortages; Pres. GEORGE MNESA.

Movement for Genuine Democratic Change (MGODE): Lilongwe; f. 2003 by fmr mems of AFORD; Pres. EGBERT CHIBAMBO (acting); Nat. Chair. GREENE LULILO MWAMONDWE; Sec.-Gen. ROGERS NKHWAZI.

National Democratic Alliance (NDA): POB 994, Blantyre; tel. 1842593; f. 2001 by fmr mems of the UDF; officially merged with the UDF in June 2004 but maintained independent structure; Pres. BROWN JAMES MPINGANJIRA; Nat. Chair. JAMES MAKHUMULA NKHOMA.

National Solidarity Movement: Leader NGWAZI KAZUNI KUMWENDA.

National Unity Party (NUP): Blantyre; Pres. HARRY CHIUME; Sec.-Gen. HARRY MUYENZA.

New Dawn for Africa (NDA): Lilongwe; f. 2003; associated with the UDF; Pres. THOM CHIUMIA; Sec.-Gen. CHIKUMBUTSO MTUMODZI.

People's Progressive Movement (PPM): f. 2003 by fmr mems of the UDF; Pres. ALEKE KADONAPHANI BANDA; Sec.-Gen. KNOX VARELA.

People's Transformation Party (PETRA): POB 31964, Chichiri, Blantyre 3; tel. 1871577; fax 1871573; e-mail umunthu@sdnp.org.mw; internet www.petra.mw; f. 2002; Pres. KAMUZU CHIBAMBO; Sec.-Gen. DEREK LAKUDZALA.

Republican Party (RP): f. 2004; Leader (vacant).

Social Democratic Party (SDP): Pres. ISON KAKOME.

United Democratic Front (UDF): POB 5446, Limbe; internet www.udf.malawi.net; f. 1992; officially merged with the NDA in June 2004 but maintained independent structure; Nat. Chair. Dr BAKILI MULUZI; Sec.-Gen. KENNEDY MAKWANGWALA.

United Front for Multi-party Democracy (UFMD): f. 1992 by three exiled political groups: the Socialist League of Malawi, the Malawi Freedom Party and the Malawi Dem. Union; Pres. EDMOND JIKA.

The Movement for the Restoration of Democracy in Malawi (f. 1996) is based in Mozambique and consists of fmr Malawi Young Pioneers; it conducts occasional acts of insurgency.

Diplomatic Representation

EMBASSIES AND HIGH COMMISSIONS IN MALAWI

China, People's Republic: Lilongwe; FAN GUIJIN (designate).

Egypt: 10/247 Tsoka Rd, POB 30451, Lilongwe 3; tel. 1780668; fax 1780691; Ambassador ADEL EL-HAMID AHMED MARZOUK.

Germany: Convention Dr., POB 30046, Lilongwe 3; tel. 1772555; fax 1770250; e-mail info@lilongwe.diplo.de; internet www.lilongwe.diplo.de; Ambassador ALBERT JOSEF GISY.

Ireland: Lilongwe; tel. 1706640; e-mail lilongweemdiplomats@dfa.ie; Ambassador LIAM MACGABHANN.

Mozambique: POB 30579, Lilongwe 3; tel. 1774100; fax 1771342; High Commissioner JORGE DE SOUSA MATEUS.

Norway: Plot 13–14, Arwa House, City Centre, Private Bag B323, Lilongwe 3; tel. 1774211; fax 1772845; e-mail emb.lilongwe@mfa.no; Ambassador GUNNAR FØRELAND.

South Africa: Kang'ombe House, 3rd Floor, City Centre, POB 30043, Lilongwe 3; tel. 1773722; fax 1772571; e-mail sahc@malawi.net; High Commissioner N. M. TSHEOLE.

Tanzania: POB 922, Capital City, Lilongwe 3; tel. 1770150; fax 1770148; e-mail tanzanianhighcomm@tz.lilongwe.mw; High Commissioner Maj.-Gen. (retd) MAKAME RASHID.

United Kingdom: British High Commission Bldg, Capital Hill, POB 30042, Lilongwe 3; tel. 1772400; fax 1772657; e-mail bhclilongwe@fco.gov.uk; internet www.britishhighcommission.gov.uk/malawi; High Commissioner RICHARD WILDASH.

USA: Area 40, Plot No. 18, 16 Jomo Kenyatta Rd, POB 30016, Lilongwe 3; tel. 1773166; fax 1770471; e-mail ConsularLilongwe@state.gov; internet lilongwe.usembassy.gov; Ambassador ALAN W. EASTHAM.

Zambia: Area 40/2, City Centre, POB 30138, Lilongwe 3; tel. 1772100; fax 1774349; High Commissioner (vacant).

Zimbabwe: POB 30187, Lilongwe 3; tel. 1774988; fax 1772382; e-mail zimhighcomllw@malawi.net; High Commissioner THANDIWE S. DUMBUTSHENA.

Judicial System

The courts administering justice are the Supreme Court of Appeal, High Court and Magistrates' Courts.

The High Court, which has unlimited jurisdiction in civil and criminal matters, consists of the Chief Justice and five puisne judges. Traditional Courts were abolished under the 1994 Constitution. Appeals from the High Court are heard by the Supreme Court of Appeal in Blantyre.

High Court of Malawi

POB 30244, Chichiri, Blantyre 3; tel. 1670255; fax 1670213; e-mail highcourt@sdnp.org.mw; internet www.judiciary.mw; Registrar SYLVESTER KALEMBERA.

Chief Justice: JAMES KALAILE (acting).

Justices of Appeal: J. B. KALAILE, D. G. TAMBALA, H. M. MTEGHA, A. S. E. MSOSA, I. J. MTAMBO, A. K. TEMBO.

High Court Judges: D. F. MWAUNGULU, A. K. C. NYIRENDA, G. M. CHIMASULA PHIRI, B. S. CHIUDZA BANDA, E. B. TWEA, R. R. MZIKAMANDA, Dr J. M. ANSAH, R. R. CHINANGWA, A. C. CHIPETA, F. E. KAPANDA, L. P. CHIKOPA, H. S. B. POTANI, E. CHOMBO, J. N. KATSALA, J. S. MANYUNGWA, M. L. KAMWAMBE, M. C. C. MKANDAWIRE, I. C. KAMANGA.

Religion

More than 70% of the population profess Christianity. Islam, the fastest growing religion, is practised by about 20% of the population. Traditional beliefs are followed by about 10% of the population. The Asian community includes Hindus.

CHRISTIANITY

Malawi Council of Churches (MCC): POB 30068, Capital City, Lilongwe 3; tel. 1783499; fax 1783106; f. 1939; Chair. Rev. HOWARD MATIYA NKHOMA; Gen. Sec. Rev. Dr A. C. MUSOPOLE; 22 mem. churches.

The Anglican Communion

Anglicans are adherents of the Church of the Province of Central Africa, covering Botswana, Malawi, Zambia and Zimbabwe. The Church comprises 15 dioceses, including four in Malawi. There were about 230,000 adherents in Malawi at mid-2000.

Archbishop of the Province of Central Africa and Bishop of Upper Shire: Most Rev. BERNARD AMOSI MALANGO, Private Bag 1, Chilema, Zomba; tel. and fax 1539203; e-mail esjopembamoyo@malawi.net.

Bishop of Lake Malawi: (vacant), POB 30349, Capital City, Lilongwe 3; tel. 1797858; fax 1797548; e-mail anglama@eomw.net.

Bishop of Northern Malawi: Rt Rev. CHRISTOPHER JOHN BOYLE, POB 120, Mzuzu; tel. 1331486; fax 1333805; e-mail angdioofnm@sdnp.org.mw.

Bishop of Southern Malawi: Rt Rev. JAMES TENGATENGA, POB 30220, Chichiri, Blantyre 3; tel. 1641218; fax 1641235; e-mail angsoma@sdnp.org.mw.

Protestant Churches

At mid-2001 there were an estimated 2.1m. Protestants in Malawi.

Assemblies of God in Malawi: POB 1220, Lilongwe; tel. 1761057; fax 1762056; 639,088 mems in 3,114 churches (2005).

Baptist Convention of Malawi (BACOMA): Lali Lubani Rd, POB 30212, Chichiri, Blantyre 3; tel. 1671170; e-mail bacoma@sdnp.org.mw; 175,000 adherents, 1,375 churches (2007); Gen. Sec. Rev. FLETCHER KAIYA.

Church of Central Africa (Presbyterian) (CCAP): Blantyre Synod, POB 413, Blantyre; tel. and fax 1633942; comprises three synods in Malawi (Blantyre, Livingstonia and Nkhoma); Co-ordinator Rev. J. J. MPHATSE; Gen. Sec. DANIEL GUNYA; Exec. Dir ROBSON CHITENGO; more than 1m. adherents in Malawi.

MALAWI

Directory

Evangelical Association of Malawi: POB 2120, Blantyre; tel. and fax 9936681; Chair. Rev. Dr LAZARUS CHAKWERA; Gen. Sec. FRANCIS MKANDAWIRE.

Lutheran Church of Central Africa—Malawi Conference: POB 748, Blantyre; tel. and fax 1630821; e-mail pwegner@africa-online.net; f. 1963; Pres. FRACKSON B. CHINYAMA; Co-ordinator PAUL WENGER; 30,000 mems.

Seventh-day Adventist Church: Robins Rd, Kabula Hill, POB 951, Blantyre; tel. 1620264; fax 1620528; e-mail musda@malawi.net; Pres. SAUSTIN K. MFUNE; Exec. Sec. BAXTER D. CHILUNGA; 200,000 mems.

The African Methodist Episcopal Church, the Churches of Christ, the Free Methodist Church, the New Apostolic Church and the United Evangelical Church in Malawi are also active. At mid-2000 there were an estimated 2m. adherents professing other forms of Christianity.

The Roman Catholic Church

Malawi comprises one archdiocese and six dioceses. At 31 December 2005 there were some 3.5m. adherents of the Roman Catholic Church (equivalent to approximately 21.7% of the total population).

Episcopal Conference of Malawi

Catholic Secretariat of Malawi, Chimutu Rd, POB 30384, Capital City, Lilongwe 3; tel. 1782066; fax 1782019; e-mail ecm@malawi.net. f. 1969; Pres. Most Rev. TARCISIUS GERVAZIO ZIYAYE (Archbishop of Blantyre).

Archbishop of Blantyre: Most Rev. TARCISIUS GERVAZIO ZIYAYE, Archbishop House, POB 385, Blantyre; tel. and fax 1637905; e-mail archdblantyre@africa-online.net.

ISLAM

Muslim Association of Malawi (MAM): POB 497, Blantyre; tel. 1622060; fax 1623581; f. 1946 as the Nyasaland Muslim Asscn; umbrella body for Muslim orgs; provides secular and Islamic education; Sec.-Gen. MOHAMMED IMRAN SHAREEF.

BAHÁ'Í FAITH

National Spiritual Assembly: POB 30922, Lilongwe 3; tel. 1771177; fax 1771713; e-mail bahaimalawi@africa-online.net; f. 1970; mems resident in over 1,200 localities.

The Press

The Chronicle: Private Bag 77, Lilongwe; tel. 1756530; e-mail thechronicle@africa-online.net; f. 1993; publ. by Jamieson Publications; Mon. and Thurs.; English; ceased publ. in Dec. 2006; Owner and Editor-in-Chief ROBERT JAMIESON; circ. c. 5,000 (2006).

The Daily Times: Private Bag 39, Blantyre; tel. 1670115; fax 1671114; e-mail bnl@sdnp.org.mw; f. 1895; fmrly the *Nyasaland Times*; Mon.–Fri., Sun.; English; publ. by Blantyre Newspapers Ltd (Chayamba Trust); affiliated to the MCP; Editor-in-Chief JIKA NKOLOKOSA; circ. Mon.–Fri. c. 20,000, Sun. c. 40,000 (2006).

The Democratus: Aquarius House, Convention Dr., City Centre, Box 1100, Lilongwe 3; tel. 1770033; internet democratusmalawi.blogspot.com; f. 2004; publ. by Democratus Ltd; Wed. and Sun.; Chair. ZIKHALE NG'OMA.

The Dispatch: The Dispatch Publications Ltd, POB 30353, Capital City, Lilongwe 3; tel. 1751639; fax 9510120; e-mail thedispatchmw@sdnp.org.mw; Thurs. and Sun.; Publr and Man. Editor MARTINES NAMINGAH; circ. Thurs. 5,000, Sun. 7,000.

The Enquirer: POB 1745, Blantyre; tel. 1670022; e-mail pillycolette@yahoo.co.uk; English and Nyanja; affiliated to the UDF; Owner LUCIOUS CHIKUNI.

The Guardian: Area 47, Lilongwe; Man. Dir DUWA MUTHARIKA-KAFOTEKA; circ. c. 5,000 (2006).

The Lamp: Montfort Media, POB 280, Balaka, Zomba; tel. 1545267; e-mail montfortmedia@malawi.net; f. 1995; fortnightly; Roman Catholic and ecumenical; Editor Fr GAMBA PIERGIORGIO; circ. 5,500.

Malawi Government Gazette: Government Printer, POB 37, Zomba; tel. 1523155; fax 1522301; f. 1894; weekly.

Malawi News: Private Bag 39, Blantyre; tel. 1671679; fax 1671233; f. 1959; weekly; English and Chichewa; publ. by Blantyre Newspapers Ltd (Chayamba Trust); Gen. Man. JIKA NKOLOKOSA; Man. Editor EDWARD CHISAMBO; Editor FREDERICK NDALA, Jr; circ. c. 40,000 (2006).

The Malawi Standard: POB 31781, Blantyre 3; tel. 1674013; e-mail bligomeka@yahoo.co.uk; fortnightly; Editor BRIAN LIGOMEKA.

The Mirror: POB 30721, Blantyre; tel. 1675043; f. 1994; weekly; English and Nyanja; affiliated to the UDF; Owner and Publr BROWN MPINGANJIRA; circ. 10,000.

The Nation: POB 30408, Chichiri, Blantyre 3; tel. 1673611; fax 1674343; e-mail nation@nationmalawi.com; internet www.nationmalawi.com; f. 1993; daily; publ. by Nation Publs Ltd; weekly edn of *The Weekend Nation* (circ. 30,000); English and Nyanja; Owner ALEKE BANDA; Editor-in-Chief ALFRED NTONGA; circ. 15,000.

Odini: POB 133, Lilongwe; tel. 1721135; fax 1721141; f. 1949; fortnightly; Chichewa and English; Roman Catholic; Dir P. I. AKOMENJI; circ. 12,000.

UDF News: POB 3052, Blantyre; tel. 1645314; fax 1645725; e-mail echapusa@yahoo.co.uk; organ of the UDF; fortnightly; English and Nyanja.

The Weekly News: Dept of Information, POB 494, Blantyre; tel. 1642600; fax 1642364; f. 1996; English and Nyanja; publ. by the Ministry of Information; Editor-in-Chief GEORGE TUKHUWA.

Weekly Courier: Lilongwe 3; affiliated to the Democratic Progressive Party; Man. Editor DENIS MZEMBE; circ. c. 3,000 (2006).

PERIODICALS

Boma Lathu: POB 494, Blantyre; tel. 1620266; fax 1620039; internet www.maform.com/bomalathu.htm; f. 1973; quarterly; Chichewa; publ. by the Ministry of Information; circ. 100,000.

Business Monthly: POB 906646, Blantyre 9; tel. 16301114; fax 1620039; f. 1995; English; economic, financial and business news; Editor ANTHONY LIVUZA; circ. 10,000.

Fairlane Magazine: POB 1745, Blantyre; tel. 1880205; e-mail fairlane@sndp.org.mw; internet www.fairlane.emalawi.com; f. 2006; 6 a year; lifestyle magazine; English and Chichewa; Man. Dir MARIE FRANCE CHIKUNI; Editor AGNES DUMISANI MIZERE.

Journal of Humanities: Faculty of Humanities, Univ. of Malawi, Chancellor College, POB 280, Zomba; tel. (1) 522622; fax (1) 524046; e-mail publications@chanco.unima.mw; annually; focus on east, central and southern Africa; Chief Editor DAVESON NYABANI; circ. 250.

Kuunika (The Light): POB 17, Nkhoma, Lilongwe; tel. 1722807; e-mail nkhomasynod@globemw.net; f. 1909; monthly; Chichewa; publ. by the Church of Central Africa (Presbyterian) Nkhoma Synod; Presbyterian; Editor Rev. M. C. NKHALAMBAYAUSI; circ. 6,000.

Malawi Journal of Science and Technology: The Research Co-ordinator, University Office, POB 278, Zomba; tel. (1) 522622; fax (1) 522760; e-mail publications@chanco.unima.mw; annually; applied and natural sciences; Editor Dr M. W. MFITILODZE.

Malawi Medical Journal: College of Medicine and Medical Asscn of Malawi, Private Bag 360, Blantyre 3; tel. 1676444; fax 1675774; e-mail mchilongo@mlw.medcol.mw; f. 1980; replaced *Medical Quarterly*; quarterly; Chair. Prof. ERIC BORGSTEIN; Editor-in-Chief Prof. MALCOLM E. MOLYNEUX.

Moni Magazine: POB 5592, Limbe; tel. 1651833; fax 1651171; f. 1964; monthly; Chichewa and English; Editor PRINCE SHONGA; circ. 40,000.

Moyo Magazine: Health Education Unit, POB 30377, Lilongwe 3; 6 a year; English; publ. by the Ministry of Health; Editor-in-Chief JONATHAN NKHOMA.

Pride: POB 51668, Limbe; tel. 1640569; f. 1999; quarterly; Publr JOHN SAINI.

This is Malawi: POB 494, Blantyre; tel. 1620266; fax 1620807; f. 1964; monthly; English and Chichewa edns; publ. by the Dept of Information; Editor ANTHONY LIVUZA; circ. 12,000.

Together: Montfort Media, POB 280, Balaka, Zomba; tel. 1545267; e-mail together@sdnp.org.mw; f. 1995; quarterly; Roman Catholic and ecumenical, youth; Editor LUIGI GRITTI; circ. 6,000.

Other publications include *Dzukani*, *Inspiration* and *Msilikali*.

NEWS AGENCIES

Malawi News Agency (MANA): POB 28, Blantyre; tel. 1622122; fax 1634867; f. 1966.

Publishers

Christian Literature Association in Malawi (CLAIM): POB 503, Blantyre; tel. 1620839; f. 1968; Chichewa and English; general and religious; Gen. Man. J. T. MATENJE.

Likuni Press and Publishing House: POB 133, Lilongwe; tel. 1721388; fax 1721141; f. 1949; English and Chichewa; general and religious.

MALAWI
Directory

Macmillan Malawi Ltd: Private Bag 140, Kenyatta Dr., Chitawira, Blantyre; tel. 1676499; fax 1675751; e-mail macmillan@macmillanmw.net; Gen. Man. HASTINGS MATEWERE.

Montfort Press and Popular Publications: POB 5592, Limbe; tel. 1651833; fax 1641126; f. 1961; general and religious; Gen. Man. VALES MACHILA.

GOVERNMENT PUBLISHING HOUSE

Government Press: Government Printer, POB 37, Zomba; tel. 1525515; fax 1525175.

Broadcasting and Communications

TELECOMMUNICATIONS

Celtel Malawi: Mwai House, City Centre, POB 57, Lilongwe; tel. 1774800; fax 1774802; e-mail helpdesk@mw.celtel.com; internet www.mw.celtel.com; f. 1999; 80% owned by Mobile Systems Int. Cellular Investments Holding B.V., 10% owned each by Malawi Devt Corpn and Investment and Devt Bank of Malawi Ltd; Man. Dir CHARLES ZOUZOUA.

Malawi Telecommunications Ltd (MTL): Lamya House, Masauko Chipembere Highway, POB 537, Blantyre; tel. 1620977; fax 1624445; e-mail mtlceo@malawi.net; f. 2000 following division of Malawi Posts and Telecommunications Corpn into two separate entities; privatized in 2006; 80% owned by Telecom Holdings Ltd, 20% state-owned; CEO EMMANUEL MAHUKA.

Telekom Networks Malawi (TNM): POB 3039, Munif House, Livingstone Ave, Limbe, Blantyre; tel. 1644398; fax 1642805; e-mail nasirbah@malawi.net; internet www.telekom.co.mw; f. 1995; 60% owned by Telekom Malaysia Berhad; operates mobile cellular telephone network; CEO ROSLI MUSTAFFA.

BROADCASTING

Radio

Malawi Broadcasting Corpn: POB 30133, Chichiri, Blantyre 3; tel. 1671222; fax 1671257; e-mail dgmbc@malawi.net; internet www.mbcradios.com; f. 1964; statutory body; semi-commercial, partly state-financed; two channels: MBC 1 and Radio 2 (MBC 2); programmes in English, Chichewa, Chitonga, Chitumbuka, Kyangonde, Lomwe, Sena and Yao; Chair. LEONARD NAMWERA; Dir-Gen. OWEN MAUNDE.

Private commercial and religious radio stations include:

African Bible College Radio (Radio ABC): POB 1028, Lilongwe; tel. 1761965; e-mail radioabc@malawi.net; f. 1995; regional Christian religious programming; Asst Station Man. MCLEOD MUNTHALI.

Calvary Family Radio: POB 30239, Blantyre 3; tel. 1671627; fax 1671642; e-mail calvaryministries@hotmail.com; operated by the Calvary Family Church; religious community radio station.

Capital Radio 102.5 FM: Plot 475, cnr Victoria Ave and Juachim Chissano Rd, Sunnyside; Private Bag 437, Chichiri, Blantyre 3; tel. 1620858; fax 1623282; e-mail stationmanager@capitalradiomalawi.com; internet www.capitalradiomalawi.com; f. 1999; commercial radio station; music and entertainment; Man. Dir and Editor-in-Chief ALAUDIN OSMAN.

Channel for All Nations (CAN): POB 1220, Lilongwe; tel. 1761763; fax 1762056; e-mail kawembale@yahoo.com; f. 2004; operated by the Assemblies of God church; regional Christian religious programming.

Dzimwe Community Radio (DCR): POB 425, Chichiri, Blantyre; tel. 1672288; fax 1624330; e-mail mamwa@yahoo.com; f. 1997; operated by the Malawi Media Women's Ascn; focus on rural women's issues; Station Man. JANET KARIM.

Joy FM: Private Bag 17, Limbe, Blantyre; tel. 1638330; fax 1638329; e-mail joyradio@globemalawi.net; commercial radio station; Owner BAKILI MULUZI.

MIJ FM: POB 30165, Chichiri, Blantyre 3; tel. 1675087; fax 1675649; e-mail mij@clcom.net; f. 1996; operated by students of the Malawi Institute of Journalism; community radio station; closed by the Govt during May 2004.

Nkhota Kota Community Radio: Nkhota Kota; f. 2003 with assistance from UNESCO; focus on social and devt issues.

Power 101 FM: POB 761, Blantyre; tel. 1844101; fax 1841387; e-mail fm101@malawi.net; f. 1998; commercial radio station; music and entertainment; Dir and Station Man. OSCAR THOMSON.

Radio Alinafe: Maula Cathedral, POB 631, Lilongwe; tel. 1759971; fax 1752767; e-mail radioalinafe@sdnp.org.mw; f. 2002; Chichewa and English; operated by the Archdiocese of Lilongwe; regional Roman Catholic religious programming; Dir GABRIEL JANA; Editor MOSES KAUFA.

Radio Islam: PO Box 5400, Limbe; tel. 1641408; e-mail zakaat@globemw.net; f. 2001; operated by the Islamic Zakaat Fund; religious programming; Dir MAHMUD SARDAR ISSA.

Radio Maria Malawi: POB 408, Mangochi; tel. 1599626; fax 1599691; e-mail radiomaria@malawi.net; internet www.radiomaria.mw; f. 2003; operated by Ascn of Radio Maria Malawi as part of the World Family of Radio Maria, Italy; Roman Catholic religious programming; Chichewa, Chiyao and English; Gen. Man. JOSEPH KIMU; Dir of Programmes HENRY SAINDI.

Radio Tigawane: Bishop's House, POB 252, Mzuzu; tel. 1332271; e-mail tigawane@sndp.org.mw; f. 2005; operated by the Diocese of Mzuzu; regional Roman Catholic religious programming; Tumbuka, Chichewa and English; Project Co-ordinator EUGENE NGOMA.

Star FM: Everest House, Lower Sclatter Rd, Blantyre; f. 2006; commercial radio station; Station Man. PATRICK KAMKWATIRA.

Trans World Radio Malawi (TWR): POB 52, Lilongwe; tel. and fax 1751763; e-mail twr@malawi.net; f. 2000; part of Trans World Radio-Africa, South Africa; Christian religious programming; Dir PATRICK SEMPHERE.

Zodiak Broadcasting Station (ZBS): Private Bag 312, Lilongwe 3; f. 2005; operated by Zodiak Broadcasting Services; programmes in Chichewa and English; Man. Dir GOSPEL KAZAKO.

Television

Television Malawi (TVM): Private Bag 268, Blantyre; tel. 1675033; fax 1762627; e-mail tvmalawi@sdnp.org.mw; f. 1999; broadcasts 55 hours per week, of which 10 hours are produced locally; relays programmes from France, Germany, South Africa and the United Kingdom; Chair. MOHAMMED KULESI; Dir-Gen. KENSON M'BWANA.

Finance

(cap. = capital; res = reserves; dep. = deposits; m. = million; br(s). = branch(es); amounts in kwacha)

BANKING

Central Bank

Reserve Bank of Malawi: Convention Dr., POB 30063, Capital City, Lilongwe 3; tel. 1770600; fax 1772752; internet www.rbm.malawi.net; f. 1965; bank of issue; cap. 306m., res –1,361m., dep. 17,388m. (Dec. 2004); Gov. and Chair. VICTOR MBEWE; br. in Blantyre.

Commercial Banks

Finance Bank Malawi Ltd: Finance House, Victoria Ave, POB 421, Blantyre; tel. 1624232; fax 1622957; f. 1995; 93.6% owned by Finance Holdings Corpn Ltd (International), 6.4% owned by Finance Bank Zambia Ltd; cap. and res 439.2m., total assets 4,152m. (Dec. 2003); Chair. Dr RAJAN L. MAHTANI; CEO A. S. PILLAI; 5 brs, 1 agency.

INDEBank Ltd: INDEBank House, Kaohsiung Rd, Top Mandala, POB 358, Blantyre; tel. 1820055; fax 1823353; internet www.indebank.com; f. 1972 as Investment and Devt Bank of Malawi Ltd; total assets 2,162.6m. (Dec. 2003); 41.38% owned by TransAfrica Holdings Ltd, 30% owned by Press Trust, 25.67% owned by ADMARC Investments Holding, 2.95% owned by Employee Ownership Scheme; commercial and devt banking; provides loans to statutory corpns and to private enterprises in the agricultural, industrial, tourism, transport and commercial sectors; Chair. FRANKLIN KENNEDY; Man. Dir and CE) GEORGE NAMANDWA (acting).

Loita Investment Bank Ltd: Loita House, cnr Victoria Ave and Henderson St, Private Bag 389, Chichiri, Blantyre 3; tel. 1620099; fax 1622683; internet www.loita.com; total assets 3,100.3m. (Dec. 2003); 100% owned by Loita Capital Partners Int.; Chair. N. JUSTIN CHIMYANTA; CEO AUBERY CHALERA (acting); 2 brs.

National Bank of Malawi: Victoria Ave, POB 945, Blantyre; tel. 1620622; fax 1620321; e-mail natbank@malawi.net; internet www.natbank.mw.com; f. 1971; 51.8% owned by Press Corpn Ltd, 20.7% owned by ADMARC (Investments Holding Co), 11.2% owned by Old Mutual Life Assurance; cap. 456m., res 895m., dep. 24,254m. (Dec. 2005); Chair. Dr M. A. P. CHIKAONDA; CEO ISAAC K. NSAMALA; 13 brs; 10 agencies.

NBS Bank Ltd: Ginnery Cnr, Chipembere Highway, off Masajico, POB 32251 Chichiri, Blantyre; tel. 1876222; fax 1875041; e-mail nbs@nbsmw.com; internet www.nbsmw.com; f. 2003; 74% owned by NICO, 16% owned by the Govt, 10% owned by the Nat. Investment Trust 10%; fmrly New Building Society; 10,978m. (Mar. 2007); Chair. FELIX L. MLUSU; Gen. Man. JOHN S. BIZIWICK.

Nedbank (Malawi) Ltd: Development House, cnr Henderson St and Victoria Ave, POB 750, Blantyre; tel. 1620477; fax 1620102; e-mail office@mw.nedcor.com; f. 1999; fmrly Fincom Bank of Malawi

MALAWI

Ltd; 68.8% owned by Nedbank Africa Investments Ltd, 28.4% owned by SBM Nedcor Holdings Ltd; total assets 1,426.9m. (Dec. 2003); Chair. C. DREW; Man. Dir PAUL TUBB.

Stanbic Bank Ltd: Kaomba Centre, cnr Sir Glyn Jones Rd and Victoria Ave, POB 1111, Blantyre; tel. 1620144; fax 1620360; e-mail malawi@stanbic.com; internet www.stanbicbank.co.mw; f. 1970 as Commercial Bank of Malawi; present name adopted June 2003; 60% owned by Stanbic Africa Holdings Ltd, 20% owned by Nat. Insurance Co; cap. 200m., res 1,818m., dep. 13,774m. (Dec. 2005); Chair. ALEX CHITSIME; Man. Dir PHILIP ODERA; 8 brs.

Development Bank

Opportunity International Bank of Malawi Ltd (OIBM): Kamuzu Procession Rd, Plot No. 4/044, Private Bag A71, Lilongwe; tel. 1758403; fax 1758400; e-mail oibm@oibm.mw; internet www.oibm.mw; f. 2003; 63.7% owned by Opportunity Transformation Investments, USA, 25.3% owned by Opportunity Micro Investments (UK) Ltd, United Kingdom, 11% owned by Trust for Transformation; total assets 967.4m. (Dec. 2005); Chair. FRANCIS PELEKAMOYO; CEO RODGER VOORHIES.

Discount Houses

Continental Discount House: Unit House, 5th Floor, Victoria Ave, POB 1444, Blantyre; tel. 1821300; fax 1822826; e-mail discount@cdh-malawi.com; internet www.cdh-malawi.com; f. 1998; 84% owned by Trans-Africa Holdings; total assets 6,728.8m. (Dec. 2005); Chair. ROBERT SEKOH ABBEY; CEO JOSEPH MWANAMVEKHA.

First Discount House Ltd: Umoyo House, Upper Ground Floor, 8 Victoria Ave North, POB 512, Blantyre; tel. 1820219; fax 1523044; e-mail fdh@fdh.co.mw; internet www.fdh.co.mw; f. 2000; 40.16% owned by Kingdom Financial Holdings Ltd, 39.84% owned by Thomson F. Mpinganjira Trust, 20% owned by Old Mutual Life Assurance Co (Malawi) Ltd; total assets 5,960.7m. (Dec. 2004); CEO THOMSON FRANK MPINGANJIRA; Chair. NIGEL CHAKANIRA.

Merchant Banks

First Merchant Bank Ltd: Livingstone Towers, Glyn Jones Rd, Private Bag 122, Blantyre; tel. 1821955; fax 1821978; e-mail fmb.headoffice@fmbmalawi.com; internet www.fmbmalawi.com; f. 1994; cap. 100.0m., res 411.8m., dep. 6,015.4m. (Dec. 2005); 44.9% owned by Zambezi Investments Ltd, 22.5% owned by Simsbury Holdings Ltd, 11.2% owned each by Prime Capital and Credit Ltd, Kenya, and Prime Bank Ltd, Kenya; Chair. RASIKBHAI C. KANTARIA; Man. Dir KASHINATH N. CHATURVEDI; 7 brs.

Leasing and Finance Co of Malawi Ltd: Livingstone Towers, Glyn Jones Rd, POB 1963, Blantyre; tel. 1820233; fax 1820275; f. 1986; subsidiary of First Merchant Bank Ltd since June 2002; total assets 2,087.4m. (Dec. 2006); Chair. HITESH ANADKAT; Gen. Man. MBACHAZWA LUNGU.

Savings Bank

Malawi Savings Bank: Umoyo House, Victoria Ave, POB 521, Blantyre; tel. 1625111; fax 1621929; 99.9% state-owned; total assets 1,191.7m. (Dec. 2003); Sec.-Treas. P. E. CHILAMBE; Gen. Man. IAN C. BONONGWE.

STOCK EXCHANGE

Malawi Stock Exchange: Old Reserve Bank Bldg, 17 Victoria Ave, Private Bag 270, Blantyre; tel. 1824233; fax 1823636; e-mail mse@mse-mw.com; internet www.mse.co.mw; f. 1996; Chair. KRISHNA SAVJANI; CEO SYMON W. MSEFULA; 11 cos listed in 2007.

INSURANCE

In 2005 the insurance sector comprised 10 local companies and one foreign company; there was also one reinsurance company. Of these, eight companies dealt in non-life insurance.

NICO Holdings Ltd: NICO House, 3 Stewart St, POB 501, Blantyre; tel. 1822699; fax 1822364; e-mail info@nicomw.com; internet www.nicomw.com; f. 1970; fmrly National Insurance Co Ltd; transferred to private sector in 1996; incorporates NICO Gen. Insurance Co Ltd, NICO Life Insurance Co Ltd and NICO Technologies Ltd; cap. and res 104.7m. (Sept. 1997); offices at Blantyre, Lilongwe, Mzuzu and Zomba; agencies country-wide; CEO and Man. Dir FELIX L. MLUSU.

Old Mutual Malawi: Trust Finance Ltd, Michiru House, Ground Floor, Victoria Ave, POB 1396, Blantyre; tel. 0623856; f. 1845; subsidiary of Old Mutual PLC, United Kingdom; Chair. MIKE LEVETT; Man. Dir JEAN DU PLESSIS.

Royal Insurance Co of Malawi Ltd: Hannover House, Independence Dr., POB 442, Blantyre; tel. 1824044; fax 1823862; e-mail royalbt@royal.mw; internet www.royalinsure.com/malawi.htm; associate of Royal and SunAlliance PLC, United Kingdom; Man. Dir ROBERT G. NDUNGU; Gen. Man. DAMIANO K. PHIRI.

United General Insurance Co Ltd (UGI): Michiru House, Victoria Ave, POB 383, Blantyre; tel. 1621770; fax 1621980; e-mail ugi@malawi.net; internet www.ugimalawi.com; f. 1986 as Pearl Assurance Co Ltd; latterly Property and Gen. Insurance Co Ltd; present name adopted following merger with Fide Insurance Co Ltd in July 1998; subsidiary of ZimRE Holdings, Zimbabwe; Chair. ALBERT NDUNA; Man. Dir IAN K. KUMWENDA.

Vanguard Life Assurance Co (Pvt) Ltd: MDC House, 2nd Floor, Sir Glyn Jones Rd, POB 1625, Blantyre; tel. 1623356; fax 1623506; f. 1999; 90% owned by Fidelity Life Assurance Ltd, Zimbabwe; Man. Dir THEMBA MPALA.

Trade and Industry
GOVERNMENT AGENCIES

Agricultural Development and Marketing Corpn (ADMARC): POB 5052, Limbe; tel. 1640500; fax 1640486; f. 1971; involved in cultivation, processing, marketing and export of grain and other crops; Chair. Prof. KANYAMA PHIRI; CEO Dr CHARLES J. MATABWA.

Malawi Export Promotion Council (MEPC): Kanabar House, 2nd Floor, Victoria Ave, POB 1299, Blantyre; tel. 1820499; fax 1820995; e-mail mepco@malawi.net; internet www.malawiepc.com; f. 1971; promotes and facilitates export and investment, and provides technical assistance and training to exporters; Gen. Man. LAWRENCE M. CHALULUKA.

Malawi Investment Promotion Agency (MIPA): Aquarius House, Private Bag 302, Lilongwe 3; tel. 1770800; fax 1771781; e-mail mipa@mipamw.org; internet www.malawi-invest.net; f. 1993; promotes and facilitates local and foreign investment; CEO JAMES R. KAPHWELEZA BANDA.

Petroleum Control Commission: POB 2827, Blantyre; e-mail sichioko@pccmalawi.com; state-owned; held monopoly on fuel imports until 2000; also serves regulatory role; Chair. Rev Dr LAZARUS CHAKWERA; Gen. Man. ISHMAEL CHIOKO.

Privatisation Commission of Malawi: Livingstone Towers, 2nd Floor, Glyn Jones Rd, POB 937, Blantyre; tel. 1823655; fax 1821248; e-mail info@pcmalawi.org; internet www.pcmalawi.org; f. 1996; has sole authority to oversee divestiture of govt interests in public enterprises; Chair. EDWARD SAWERENGERA; Exec. Dir JIMMY LIPUNGA (acting); 66 privatizations completed by January 2006.

Tobacco Control Commission: POB 40045, Kanengo, Lilongwe 4, Malawi; tel. 1712777; fax 1712632; regulates tobacco production and marketing; Chair Dr ANDREW MZUMACHARO IV; Gen. Man. Dr GODFREY M. CHAPOLA; brs in Mzuzu and Limbe.

DEVELOPMENT ORGANIZATIONS

Council for Non-Governmental Organizations in Malawi (CONGOMA): Chitawira, Waya Bldg, POB 480, Blantyre; tel. 1676459; fax 1677908; internet www.congoma.org; f. 1992; promotes social and economic devt; Chair. TADEYO SHABA; Exec. Dir EMMANUEL TED NANDOLO; 86 mem. orgs (2004).

Human Rights Consultative Committee (HRCC): c/o Centre for Human Rights and Rehabilitation, POB 2340 Lilongwe; tel. 1761700; fax 1761122; e-mail chrr@sdnp.org.mw; f. 1995; umbrella body comprising 40 mem orgs; promotes human rights and the rule of law; Chair. ROGERS NEWA.

Small Enterprise Development Organization of Malawi (SEDOM): POB 525, Blantyre; tel. 1622555; fax 1622781; e-mail sedom@sdnp.org.mw; f. 1982; financial services and accommodation for indigenous small- and medium-scale businesses; Chair. STELLA NDAU.

CHAMBER OF COMMERCE

Malawi Confederation of Chambers of Commerce and Industry (MCCCI): Masauko Chipembere Highway, Chichiri Trade Fair Grounds, POB 258, Blantyre; tel. 1671988; fax 1671147; e-mail ckaferapanjira@mccci.org; internet www.mccci.org; f. 1892; promotes trade and encourages competition in the economy; Pres. MARTIN KANSICHI; CEO CHANCELLOR L. KAFERAPANJIRA; 400 mems.

INDUSTRIAL AND TRADE ASSOCIATIONS

Dwangwa Cane Growers Trust (DCGT): POB 156, Dwangwa; tel. 1295111; fax 1295164; e-mail dcgt@malawi.net; f. 1999; fmrly Smallholder Sugar Authority; Chair (vacant).

National Hawkers and Informal Business Association (NAHIBA): Chichiri Trade Fair, POB 60544, Ndirande, Blantyre; tel. 1945315; fax 1624558; e-mail nazulug@yahoo.com; f. 1995; Exec. Dir EVA JOACHIM.

MALAWI

Directory

Smallholder Coffee Farmers Trust: POB 20133, Luwinga, Mzuzu 2; tel. 1332899; fax 1333902; e-mail mzuzucoffee@malawi.net; f. 1971; successor to the Small Holder Coffee Authority, disbanded in 1999; producers and exporters of arabica coffee; Gen. Man. HARRISON KARUA; 4,000 mems.

Smallholder Tea Co (STECO): POB 135, Mulanje; f. 2002 by the merger of the Smallholder Tea Authority and Malawi Tea Factory Co Ltd.

Tea Association of Malawi Ltd (TAML): Kidney Crescent Rd, POB 930, Blantyre; tel. 1671182; fax 1671427; e-mail taml@malawi.net; f. 1936; CEO CLEMENT C. THINDWA; 20 mems.

Tobacco Association of Malawi (TAMA): 13/69 Independence Dr., TAMA House, POB 31360, Lilongwe 3; tel. 1773099; fax 1773493; e-mail tama@eomw.net; f. 1929; Pres. CHARLES A. KAMULAGA; Chief Exec. FELIX MKUMBA; brs in Mzuzu, Limbe and Chinkhoma; 60,000 mems.

Tobacco Exporters' Association of Malawi Ltd (TEAM): Private Bag 403, Kanengo, Lilongwe 4; tel. 1775839; fax 1774069; f. 1930; Chair. CHARLES A. M. GRAHAM; Gen. Man. H. M. MBALE; 9 mems.

EMPLOYERS' ORGANIZATIONS

Employers' Consultative Association of Malawi (ECAM): POB 2134, Blantyre; tel. and fax 1830151; e-mail ecam@malawi.net; f. 1963; Pres. DICKENS CHAULA; Exec. Dir Dr VINCENT SINJANI; 250 mem. asscns and six affiliates representing 80,000 employees.

Master Printers' Association of Malawi: POB 2460, Blantyre; tel. 1632948; fax 1632220; f. 1963; Chair. PAUL FREDERICK; 21 mems.

Motor Traders' Association: POB 311, Blantyre; tel. and fax 1624754; f. 1954; Chair. A. R. OSMAN; 24 mems (2003).

UTILITY

Electricity

Electricity Supply Commission of Malawi (ESCOM): ESCOM House, Haile Selassie Rd, POB 2047, Blantyre; tel. and fax 1622008; f. 1966; controls electricity distribution; Chair. ABDUL WAHAB MIA; CEO Dr ALLEXON CHIWAYA.

TRADE UNIONS

According to the Malawi Congress of Trade Unions, in 2005 some 18% of the workforce was unionized.

Congress of Malawi Trade Unions (COMATU): POB 1443 Lilongwe; tel. 1757255; fax 1770885; Pres. THOMAS L. BANDA; Gen. Sec. PHILLMON E. CHIMBALU.

Malawi Congress of Trade Unions (MCTU): POB 1271, Lilongwe; tel. 1754581; fax 1755614; e-mail mctu@malawi.net; f. 1994 as successor to the Trade Union Congress of Malawi (f. 1964); affiliated to the Int. Trade Union Confed.; Pres. LUTHER MAMBALA (acting); Gen. Sec. AUSTIN KALIMANJIRA; 93,973 paid-up mems (2006).

Affiliated unions incl.:

Building Construction, Civil Engineering and Allied Workers' Union (BCCEAWU): c/o MCTU, POB 5094, Limbe; tel. 1620381; fax 1622304; e-mail johnmwafulirwa@yahoo.com; f. 1961; Pres. LAWRENCE KAFERE; Gen. Sec. JOHN O. MWAFULIRWA; 6,401 mems (2006).

Commercial Industrial and Allied Workers' Union (CIAWU): c/o MCTU, POB 5094, Limbe; tel. 1820716; fax 1622303; e-mail mareydzinyemba@yahoo.com; affiliated to the Int. Textile, Garment and Leather Workers' Fed. and Union Network Int.; Pres. TRYSON KALANDA; Gen. Sec. MARY DZINYEMBA; 3,075 mems (2006).

Communications Workers' Union of Malawi: Armarsi Odvarji Plaza, 1st Floor, Chipembere Highway, Private Bag 186, Blantyre; tel. 1820716; fax 1830830; e-mail cowuma@yahoo.co.uk; f. 1997; Pres. BATWELL KULEMERO; Gen. Sec. ROBERT JAMES DANIEL MKWEZALAMBA; 2,854 mems (2006).

Electronic Media Workers' Union: POB 30133, Chichiri, Blantyre 3; tel. 1871343; e-mail mmsowoya@hotmail.com; Pres. LASTEN KUNKEYANI; Gen. Sec. MALANI MSOWOYA; 243 mems (2006).

ESCOM Staff Union: POB 2047, Blantyre; tel. 1773447; Pres. OSCAR CHIMWEZI; affiliated to the Int. Fed. of Chemical, Energy, Mine and General Workers' Unions; Gen. Sec. RACHEL CHASWEKA; 1,899 mems (2006).

Hotels, Food and Catering Service Union: c/o MCTU 5094, Limbe; tel. 1820314; e-mail hfpcwu@sdnp.org.mw; affiliated to the Int. Union of Food, Agricultural, Hotel, Restaurant, Catering, Tobacco and Allied Workers' Asscns; Pres. AUSTIN KALIMANJIRA; Gen. Sec. DOROTHEA MAKHASU; 3,565 mems (2006).

Malawi Housing Co-operation Workers' Union: c/o MHC, POB 84, Mzuzu; tel. 1332655; Pres. GREY SADIKI; Gen. Sec. ROOSEVELT MSISKA; 236 mems (2006).

Plantation and Agriculture Workers' Union: POB 181, Lucheza; Pres. PATRICK KADYANJI; Gen. Sec. DENNIS BANDA; 2,086 mems (2006).

Private Schools Employees' Union of Malawi (PSEUM): c/o MCTU, Kepell Compton Cres., Area 3/089, POB 1271, Lilongwe; tel. 1755614; fax 1752162; e-mail hendrixbanda@yahoo.com; Pres. SAMUEL NJIWA; Gen. Sec. HENDRIX S. BANDA; 1,713 mems (2006).

Railway Workers' Union of Malawi (Central East African Railway Workers' Union—CEARWU): POB 5393, Limbe; tel. 1640844; e-mail cear@cearcdn.mw; f. 1954; affiliated to the Int. Transport Workers' Fed.; Pres. DINA M'MERA; Gen. Sec. LUTHER MAMBALA; 485 mems (2006).

Sugar Plantation and Allied Workers' Union (SPAWUM): c/o Illovo Sugar (Malawi) Ltd, Private Bag 50, Blantyre; tel. 1425200; e-mail spawum@illovo.co.za; Pres. KEEPER GUMBO; Gen. Sec. STEPHEN MKWAPATIRA; 8,598 mems (2006).

Teachers' Union of Malawi: Aphunzitsi Centre, Private Bag 11, Lilongwe; tel. 1724224; fax 1755614; e-mail tum@sdnp.org.mw; Pres. BERNARD MANDA; Gen. Sec. LUCIEN CHIKADZA; 46,207 mems (2006).

Textile, Garment, Leather and Security Services Workers' Union: POB 5094, Limbe; tel. 8345576; e-mail textilegarmentunion@yahoo.com; f. 1995; affiliated to the Int. Textile, Garment and Leather Workers' Fed.; Gen. Sec. GRACE NYIRENDA; 5,514 mems (2006).

Tobacco Tenants Workers' Union: POB 477, Nkhotakota; tel. 1292288; e-mail totawum@malawi.net; affiliated to the Int. Union of Food, Agricultural, Hotel, Restaurant, Catering, Tobacco and Allied Workers' Asscns; Pres. LUTHER MAMBALA; Gen. Sec. RAPHAEL SANDRAM; 5,579 mems (2006).

Transport and General Workers' Union: POB 2778, Blantyre; tel. 8877795; fax 1830219; e-mail ronaldmbewe2002@yahoo.com; f. 1945; affiliated to the Int. Transport Workers' Fed.; Pres. FRANCIS ANTONIO; Gen. Sec. RONALD MBEWE; 3,257 mems (2006).

Water Employees' Trade Union of Malawi (WETUM): c/o Lilongwe Water Board, Madzi House, off Likuni Rd, POB 96, Lilongwe; tel. 1750366; fax 1752294; affiliated to the Public Services Int.; Pres. ANTHONY A. CHIMPHEPO; Gen. Sec. OLIVIA KUNJE; 1,195 mems (2006).

Transport

RAILWAYS

The Central East African Railways Co (fmrly Malawi Railways) operates between Nsanje (near the southern border with Mozambique) and Mchinji (near the border with Zambia) via Blantyre, Salima and Lilongwe, and between Nkaya and Nayuchi on the eastern border with Mozambique, covering a total of 797 km. The Central East African Railways Co and Mozambique State Railways connect Malawi with the Mozambican ports of Beira and Nacala. These links, which traditionally form Malawi's principal trade routes, were effectively closed during 1983–85, owing to insurgent activity in Mozambique. The rail link to Nacala was reopened in October 1989; however, continued unrest and flooding in Mozambique prevented full use of the route until the completion of a programme of improvements in September 2000; the service was temporarily suspended in 2002 while safety was improved. There is a rail/lake interchange station at Chipoka on Lake Malawi, from where vessels operate services to other lake ports in Malawi.

Central East African Railways Co Ltd (CEAR): Station Rd, POB 5144, Limbe; tel. 1640844; fax 1643496; f. 1994 as Malawi Railways Ltd; sold to a consortium owned by Mozambique's Empresa Nacional dos Portos e Caminhos de Ferro de Moçambique and the USA's Railroad Corpn in mid-1999 and subsequently renamed as above; ceased passenger services in Oct. 2005; Dir RUSSELL NEELY.

ROADS

In 2004 Malawi had a total road network of some 15,500 km, of which 3,600 km was paved. In addition, unclassified community roads total an estimated 10,000 km. All main roads, and most secondary roads, are all-weather roads. Major routes link Lilongwe and Blantyre with Harare (Zimbabwe), Lusaka (Zambia) and Mbeya and Dar es Salaam (Tanzania). A 480-km highway along the western shore of Lake Malawi links the remote Northern Region with the Central and Southern Regions. A project to create a new trade route, or 'Northern Corridor', through Tanzania, involving road construction and improvements in Malawi, was completed in 1992.

Department of Road Traffic: c/o Ministry of Transport and Public Works, Private Bag 257, Capital City, Lilongwe 3; tel. 1756138; fax 1752592; comprises the Nat. Road Authority.

Road Transport Operators' Association: Chitawira Light Industrial Site, POB 30740, Chichiri, Blantyre 3; tel. 1870422; fax 1871423; e-mail rtoa@sdnp.org.mw; f. 1956; Chair. P. CHAKHUMBIRA; Exec. Dir SHADRECK MATSIMBE; 200 mems (2004).

Shire Bus Lines Ltd: POB 176, Blantyre; tel. 1671388; fax 1670038; 100% state-owned; operates local and long-distance bus services between Mzuzu, Lilongwe, and Blantyre; services to Harare (Zimbabwe) and Johannesburg (South Africa); Chair. Al-haj Sheik ALIDI LIKONDE.

SHIPPING

There are 23 ports and landing points on Lake Malawi. The four main ports are at Chilumba, Nkhata Bay, Chipoka and Monkey Bay. Ferry services carry around 60,000 passengers annually; the principal cargoes transported are sugar, fertilizer, dried fish and maize. The amount of cargo transported was expected to rise from August 2005 with the inclusion of a new landing point at Ngala, near Dwangwa, to carry sugar to Chipoka. Smaller vessels are registered for other activities including fishing and tourism. Lake Malawi is at the centre of the Mtwara Development Corridor transport initiative agreed between Zambia, Malawi, Tanzania and Mozambique in mid-December 2004.

Department of Marine Services: c/o Department of Transport and Public Works, Private Bag A-81; tel. 1751531; fax 1756290; e-mail marinedepartment@malawi.net; responsible for vessel safety and control, ports services, and maritime pollution control.

Malawi Lake Services (MLS): POB 15, Monkey Bay; tel. and fax 1587221; e-mail ilala@malawi.net; f. 1994; privatized in 2001; 20-year operating concession granted to Glens Waterways Ltd; operates passenger and freight services to Mozambique, and freight services to Tanzania; Gen. Man. ANTON BOTES; 9 vessels, incl. 3 passenger and 4 cargo vessels; carried 14,000 metric tons of cargo in 2005/06.

CIVIL AVIATION

Kamuzu (formerly Lilongwe) International Airport was opened in 1982. There are also international airports at Chileka, and at Mzuzu and Karonga in the Northern region. There is one domestic airport, Club Makokola, at Mangochi.

Department of Civil Aviation: c/o Ministry of Transport and Public Works, Private Bag B311, Lilongwe 3; tel. 1770577; fax 1774986; e-mail aviationhq@malawi.net; Dir L. Z. PHESELE.

Air Malawi Ltd: 4 Robins Rd, POB 84, Blantyre; tel. 1820811; fax 1820042; e-mail cd@airmalawi.net; internet www.airmalawi.net; f. 1967; privatization, begun in 1999, was postponed in 2003; scheduled domestic and regional services; Chair. JIMMY KOREIA-MPATSA; CEO Capt. A. B. W. MCHUNGULA.

Tourism

Fine scenery, beaches on Lake Malawi, big game and an excellent climate form the basis of the country's tourist potential. According to official figures, the number of foreign visitor arrivals was 437,718 in 2005. Receipts from tourism totalled US $24m. in that year.

Department of Tourism: POB 402, Blantyre; tel. 1620300; fax 1620947; f. 1969; responsible for tourism policy; inspects and licenses tourist facilities, sponsors training of hotel staff and publishes tourist literature; Dir of Tourism Services ISAAC K. MSISKA.

Malawi Tourism Association (MTA): POB 1044, Lilongwe; tel. 1770010; fax 1770131; e-mail mta@malawi.net; internet www.malawi-tourism-association.org.mw; f. 1998; Exec. Dir SAM BOTOMANI.

MALAYSIA

Introductory Survey

Location, Climate, Language, Religion, Flag, Capital

The Federation of Malaysia, situated in South-East Asia, consists of 13 states. Eleven of these are in Peninsular Malaysia, in the southern part of the Kra peninsula (with Thailand to the north and the island of Singapore to the south), and two, Sabah and Sarawak, are on the north coast of the island of Borneo, two-thirds of which comprises the Indonesian territory of Kalimantan. Sarawak also borders Brunei, a coastal enclave in the north-east of the state. The climate is tropical, there is rain in all seasons and temperatures are generally between 22°C (72°F) and 33°C (92°F), with little variation throughout the year. The official language is Bahasa Malaysia, based on Malay, but English is also widely used. Chinese, Tamil and Iban are spoken by minorities. Islam is the established religion, practised by about 53% of the population (including virtually all Malays), while about 19%, including most of the Chinese community, follow Buddhism. The Indians are predominantly Hindus. There is a minority of Christians among all races, and traditional beliefs are practised, particularly in Sabah and Sarawak. Malaysia's national flag (proportions 1 by 2) has 14 horizontal stripes, alternating red and white, with a blue rectangular canton, containing a yellow crescent and a 14-pointed yellow star, in the upper hoist. The capital is Kuala Lumpur. A new administrative capital, Putrajaya, has been developed south of Kuala Lumpur.

Recent History

The 11 states of Malaya, under British protection, were united as the Malayan Union in April 1946 and became the Federation of Malaya in February 1948. An armed communist offensive began in 1948, and was not effectively suppressed until the mid-1950s. After 1960 the remainder of the banned Communist Party of Malaya (CPM) took refuge in southern Thailand. Meanwhile, Malaya was granted independence, within the Commonwealth, on 31 August 1957.

Malaysia was established on 16 September 1963, through the union of the independent Federation of Malaya (renamed the States of Malaya), the internally self-governing state of Singapore, and the former British colonies of Sarawak and Sabah (North Borneo). Singapore left the federation in August 1965, reducing the number of Malaysia's component states from 14 to 13. The States of Malaya were designated West Malaysia in 1966 and later styled Peninsular Malaysia.

In 1970 serious inter-communal rioting, engendered by Malay resentment of the Chinese community's economic dominance and of certain pro-Chinese electoral results, precipitated the resignation of Tunku Abdul Rahman, who had been Prime Minister of Malaya (and subsequently of Malaysia) since independence. The new Prime Minister, Tun Abdul Razak, widened the government coalition, dominated by the United Malays National Organization (UMNO), to create a national front, Barisan Nasional (BN). The BN originally comprised 10 parties, absorbing most of the former opposition parties. In January 1976 the Prime Minister died and was succeeded by the Deputy Prime Minister, Dato' Hussein bin Onn.

Political stability was subsequently threatened by the resurgence of the communist guerrilla movement, which conducted a series of terrorist attacks in Peninsular Malaysia during 1976–78. However, CPM activity subsequently declined, owing to co-operation between Malaysia and Thailand in military operations along their common border. In 1987, in a Thai-sponsored amnesty, about 700 Malaysian communists surrendered to the Thai authorities. In December 1989, following a year of negotiations with the Thai Government, the remaining 1,188 rebels (including recruits from Thailand and Singapore) agreed to terminate all armed activities. The peace agreements, signed by the leader of the CPM and representatives of the Malaysian and Thai Governments, made provision for the resettlement of the insurgents in either Malaysia or Thailand and their eventual participation in legitimate political activity in Malaysia.

In October 1977 the expulsion of the Chief Minister (Menteri Besar) of Kelantan from the dominant Parti Islam se Malaysia (PAS—Islamic Party of Malaysia) resulted in violent political disturbances in Kelantan and the declaration of a state of emergency by the federal Government. Direct rule was imposed in Kelantan, and the PAS was expelled from the BN coalition in December. In the federal and state elections of July 1978 Hussein consolidated the position of the BN, while the PAS, in opposition, suffered a serious reversal. In 1978, following the federal Government's rejection of proposals for a Chinese university, racial and religious tensions re-emerged.

In July 1981 Hussein was succeeded as Prime Minister by Dato' Seri Dr Mahathir Mohamad, Deputy Prime Minister since 1976. Mahathir called a general election in April 1982; the BN coalition won convincingly in all states and increased its overall strength in the House of Representatives.

A new political party, the Parti Bersatu Sabah (PBS—Sabah United Party), won control of the Sabah State Legislative Assembly at an election in April 1985. The legality of the new PBS Government was challenged by Muslim opponents, and in February 1986 the Chief Minister (Ketua Menteri) called a further election. In the May election the PBS won an increased majority of seats in the Assembly, and in June the BN agreed to admit the PBS into its ruling coalition, together with the United Sabah National Organization (USNO), which had been expelled in 1984.

In February 1986 Mahathir's leadership of the federal Government and of UMNO was challenged when Datuk Musa Hitam, the Deputy Prime Minister, resigned from the Government, owing to 'irreconcilable differences' with Mahathir. However, Musa retained his position as Deputy President of UMNO. During the following months Musa's supporters became increasingly critical of Mahathir. At an early general election in August, the BN coalition took 148 of the 177 seats in an enlarged House of Representatives: UMNO secured 83 seats, while the Malaysian Chinese Association (MCA) won 17. Of the opposition parties, the Democratic Action Party (DAP) won 24 seats, having gained support from ethnic Chinese voters who were disillusioned with the MCA. In state elections held simultaneously, the BN retained control of all the State Legislative Assemblies in Peninsular Malaysia. Several ministers who had supported Musa were subsequently demoted or removed from the Government.

In early 1987 there was a serious challenge for the presidency of UMNO from Tengku Razaleigh Hamzah, the Minister of Trade and Industry. At the UMNO General Assembly in April, none the less, Mahathir was elected UMNO President for the third time (and thus retained the position of Prime Minister at the head of the BN coalition), albeit with a greatly reduced majority. The General Assembly also narrowly elected Abdul Ghafar Baba (who had replaced Musa as Deputy Prime Minister in February 1986) as UMNO Deputy President. Mahathir subsequently announced the resignation of Razaleigh.

Criticism of Mahathir's leadership persisted during 1987, both from within UMNO and from other political parties. At the same time, racial tensions intensified in various parts of the country over Chinese-language education, religion and other issues. In October–November, allegedly to prevent violent racially-motivated riots between Chinese and Malays over politically sensitive issues, 106 people were detained under the provisions of the Internal Security Act (ISA), which allows detention without trial on grounds of national security. Those detained included politicians from all parties (most notably the leader of the DAP, Lim Kit Siang), lawyers, journalists and leaders of pressure groups. Three newspapers were closed by the Government, and political rallies were prohibited. In November the Government introduced legislation to impose stringent penalties on editors and publishers disseminating what the Government regarded as 'false' news. From December the Minister of Information was empowered to monitor all radio and television broadcasts, and to revoke the licence of any private broadcasting company not conforming with 'Malaysian values'. By April 1989 all the detainees under the ISA had been released (although often under restrictive conditions).

In February 1988 the High Court gave a ruling on a suit filed by dissatisfied members of UMNO, who claimed that, since some of the delegations taking part in the UMNO elections of April 1987 had not been legally registered, the elections should be declared null and void. On account of the irregularities, the Court ruled that UMNO was an 'unlawful society' and that there had been 'no election at all'. Mahathir maintained that the ruling did not affect the legal status of the Government, and the Head of State, Tunku Mahmood Iskandar, expressed support for Mahathir. Later in February 1988 Mahathir announced that UMNO Baru (New UMNO) had been formed and that members of the original party would have to re-register in order to join. In March it was stated that Razaleigh and his supporters were to be excluded from the new party. The assets of UMNO Baru (hereafter referred to as UMNO) were 'frozen' and placed under judicial control until the party's legal status had been resolved; they were finally returned in September 1994.

Tension between the executive and the judiciary was intensified by Parliament's approval in March 1988 of constitutional amendments limiting the power of the judiciary to interpret laws. The Lord President of the Supreme Court, Tun Mohammed Salleh bin Abas, wrote to the Head of State to complain about government attempts to reduce the independence of the judiciary, and was subsequently dismissed from office. In June 1989 the Government introduced a security law removing the right of persons being detained under provisions of the ISA to have recourse to the courts.

In September 1988 Razaleigh and 12 others followed two earlier dissidents and left the BN to join the opposition in the House of Representatives as independents. They were joined in October by Musa. In December Musa and his supporters drafted a six-point resolution (the Johore Declaration), specifying the terms under which they would consent to join UMNO. These terms were accepted by UMNO in January 1989 but were binding only in the state of Johor. Following the defeat at a by-election in that month of an opposition representative by an MCA candidate with UMNO support, Musa announced his membership of UMNO, prompting a further eight dissident representatives in Johor to join the party.

In March 1989 Razaleigh's movement established an alliance with the fundamentalist PAS. In May Razaleigh's party registered as Semangat '46 (Spirit of 1946, a reference to the year of foundation of the original UMNO). The DAP, whose followers were largely urban Chinese, agreed to co-operate with Semangat '46 and the PAS, but refused to join a formal alliance, owing to their opposition to the PAS's proclaimed policy of forming an Islamic state in Malaysia. In June a former breakaway faction from the PAS, Barisan Jama'ah Islamiah Sa-Malaysia, left the BN coalition to join Semangat '46, the PAS and the Parti Hisbul Muslimin Malaysia in an opposition coalition, Angkatan Perpaduan Ummah (APU—Muslim Unity Movement). APU subsequently won a by-election in Trengganu. In December Mahathir held a cordial but unproductive meeting with Razaleigh, in an attempt to heal the rift in the ethnic Malay community.

A general election took place in October 1990. The opposition parties formed an informal electoral alliance, Gagasan Rakyat (People's Might). (Gagasan Rakyat was formally registered in April 1992, and Razaleigh was elected as Chairman in July.) Prior to the election the PBS withdrew from the BN and aligned itself with the opposition. None the less, the BN controlled 127 of the 180 seats in the enlarged House of Representatives, thus retaining the two-thirds' majority necessary to amend the Constitution. Elections to 11 of the 13 State Legislative Assemblies (excluding Sabah and Sarawak) took place simultaneously. The BN obtained a majority of seats in every state except Kelantan, where APU won every seat in both the federal and state elections.

In November 1990, at a meeting of the UMNO General Assembly, Mahathir and Abdul Ghafar Baba were unanimously re-elected as President and Deputy President of the party. Two incumbent Vice-Presidents of UMNO, Dato' Anwar Ibrahim, the Minister of Education, and Dato' Abdullah Ahmad Badawi, a former Minister of Defence (who had been dismissed in 1987 for supporting Razaleigh's leadership challenge), were re-elected; Datuk Seri Sanusi Junid, the Minister of Agriculture, was also elected a Vice-President. In February 1991 Mahathir announced cabinet changes, appointing Anwar as Minister of Finance and Abdullah Badawi as Minister of Foreign Affairs.

In January 1991 the Chief Minister of Sabah and President of the PBS, Datuk Seri Joseph Pairin Kitingan, was arrested and charged with corruption. It was widely conjectured that his arrest and his press adviser's detention, under the ISA, were politically motivated. In May UMNO secured its first seat in Sabah, in a by-election necessitated by the defection to UMNO of USNO's founder and President, Tun Mustapha Harun. Shortly afterwards Jeffrey Kitingan (the brother of the Chief Minister) was detained under the ISA, accused of plotting Sabah's secession from Malaysia.

At the UMNO General Assembly in November 1991, Mahathir made reference to the nine hereditary rulers' supposed abuse of privilege for personal gain. In February 1992 a delegation of senior UMNO representatives (excluding Mahathir) presented the Sultans with a memorandum that alleged interference by the rulers in both political and commercial spheres. UMNO criticism of the Sultans was widely suspected to be due, in part, to the Sultan of Kelantan's open support for Razaleigh (a prince of Kelantan) in the 1990 general election. In July 1992 four of the nine Sultans approved a Proclamation of Constitutional Principles, drafted in consultation with UMNO, establishing a code of conduct for the Sultans. Mahathir, who in 1983 had successfully forced the Sultans to surrender their right to refuse assent to laws passed by Parliament, proposed to remove the rulers' constitutional immunity from prosecution. In January 1993 Parliament approved amendments ending the Sultans' legal immunity, curtailing their power to pardon the offences of family members, and allowing parliamentary criticism of their misdeeds. However, under the terms of the Constitution, the Sultans' privileges could not be restricted without the consent of the Conference of Rulers, comprising the nine Sultans. The Sultans indicated initially that they would approve the amendments, but, two hours before Parliament met, the rulers rejected the changes entirely. Mahathir responded by withdrawing from the Sultans various customary royal privileges (many of them financial) not stipulated in the Constitution. A constitutional crisis was averted when, in February, the Conference of Rulers agreed to the amendments with the inclusion of slight modifications; they were thus finally adopted with royal consent in March.

In August 1993 Anwar announced his decision to contest the post of UMNO Deputy President in the party's divisional elections, which Mahathir had postponed until November. The post was particularly significant as the Deputy President of UMNO was traditionally also accorded the position of Deputy Prime Minister. In October Mahathir was returned unopposed as President of UMNO. Ghafar submitted his resignation as Deputy Prime Minister, seemingly in protest against Mahathir's failure actively to support his candidacy for the party post. By November Anwar, representing the *Malayu baru* (new Malays—younger, urban, mainly professional Malays who had prospered as a result of economic expansion), had secured overwhelming support for his candidacy, prompting the more traditional Ghafar to withdraw from the contest and also resign from UMNO. Anwar was duly elected Deputy President of UMNO, and all three vice-presidential posts were won by his self-styled 'Vision Team', which comprised Tan Sri Haji Muhyiddin Yassim (the Chief Minister of Johor), Datuk Seri Najib Razak (the Minister of Defence) and Tan Sri Dato' Mohammad Haji Mohammad Taib (the Chief Minister of Selangor). Anwar was appointed Deputy Prime Minister in December.

In April 1993 USNO, now led by Tun Mustapha Amirkahar (the son of Tun Mustapha Harun), left the opposition in the Sabah State Legislative Assembly to form a coalition with the ruling PBS. Prior to the announcement six of the 11 elected representatives of USNO joined UMNO. USNO's defection prompted the federal Government successfully to seek the party's deregistration in August, on the grounds that it had breached its own statutes. In the same month Tun Mustapha Harun was appointed to the federal post of Minister of Sabah Affairs.

In January 1994 Pairin Kitingan dissolved the Sabah State Legislative Assembly in preparation for early elections. Shortly afterwards Pairin Kitingan was convicted on charges of corruption by the High Court. However, he was fined less than the minimum RM 2,000 that was required to disqualify him from office. Although Pairin Kitingan gained popular sympathy owing both to his perceived victimization in the corruption case and to his resistance to federal encroachment on Sabahan authority, a faction emerged in the PBS that favoured more harmonious relations with the federal Government. Former members of the deregistered USNO joined the PBS for the election, and the party also gained the support of Tun Mustapha Harun, who had resigned as Minister of Sabah Affairs and as a member of UMNO in January. (Tun Mustapha Harun died in January 1995.) At the election, which took place in February 1994, the PBS won a narrow majority, securing 25 of the 48 elective seats.

Pairin Kitingan was sworn in as Chief Minister. In March, however, several PBS members defected to the opposition; among these was Jeffrey Kitingan, who had been released from detention under the ISA in December 1993. Although he was initially confined to Seremban town in Negeri Sembilan for two years, all restrictions on him were swiftly revoked, encouraging suspicions of an agreement with the federal authorities. In March 1994 Pairin Kitingan resigned as Chief Minister, and on the following day Tan Sri Sakaran Dandai, a leader of the Sabah wing of UMNO, was sworn in at the head of a new administration.

In June 1994 the BN coalition agreed to admit two breakaway parties from the PBS, the Parti Demokratik Sabah (Sabah Democratic Party), led by Datuk Bernard Dompok, and the Parti Bersatu Rakyat Sabah (PBRS—United Sabah People's Party), led by Joseph Kurup. In August Dompok was appointed as Minister in the Prime Minister's Department and Jeffrey Kitingan became Deputy Minister for Housing and Local Government. Also in June Jeffrey Kitingan was cleared of corruption in the High Court.

In May 1994 the House of Representatives approved the 1994 Constitution (Amendment) Act, which further restricted the powers of the monarchy and provided for the restructuring of the judiciary. Hitherto the Yang di-Pertuan Agong (Head of State) had been competent to withhold assent from and return legislation, within 30 days, to Parliament for further consideration. The amendment required the Yang di-Pertuan Agong to give his assent to a bill within 30 days; if he failed to do so, the bill would, none the less, become law. The changes to the judiciary in the amendment included the creation of a Court of Appeal, the restyling of the Supreme Court as the Federal Court and of the Lord President as the Chief Justice.

From June 1994 the Government took action to suppress the activities of Al-Arqam, an Islamic sect that had been founded by Ashaari Muhammad in 1968. Al-Arqam was believed to have about 10,000 members in Malaysia, many of whom were public servants, and was alleged to control considerable assets. Although Al-Arqam had traditionally eschewed politics, the Government asserted that the group was a threat to national security and denounced its Islamic teachings as 'deviationist'; moreover, the Malaysian authorities accused it of training a military force in Thailand, although this was denied by both Al-Arqam and the Thai Government. In July UMNO threatened to expel party members who refused to leave Al-Arqam, and in August the National Fatwa (Islamic Advisory) Council banned the sect on the grounds that its doctrine contravened Islamic principles.

A general election took place in April 1995. Following an often acrimonious campaign, the BN won an overwhelming majority, taking 162 of the 192 seats in the House of Representatives (with some 64% of the total votes cast). The PBS won eight of Sabah's federal seats, including those held by Jeffrey Kitingan and Dompok. Although this constituted a loss of six seats, it was an indication that, despite the BN's assumption of power at state level through the defection of former PBS members of the legislature, the PBS remained a significant political force in Sabah. The BN also retained control of 10 of the 11 State Legislative Assemblies for which voting took place, in most cases securing a two-thirds' majority. In Kelantan, which remained the only state under opposition control, a coalition of the PAS and Semangat '46 took 35 of the 43 state seats.

Despite his overwhelming election victory, Mahathir's position appeared vulnerable during the divisional elections of UMNO in 1995. The defeat of several Mahathir supporters was widely attributed to the influence of Anwar's associates, and prompted speculation that Anwar might challenge Mahathir for the leadership. In November, however, UMNO's General Assembly adopted an unprecedented resolution to avoid any contest for the two senior party positions in 1996; Anwar finally declared that he would not challenge Mahathir, and Mahathir for the first time said that he would retire in the near future and again named Anwar as his successor.

Semangat '46 was formally dissolved in October 1996, and its members were admitted to UMNO. At that month's UMNO General Assembly Mahathir and Anwar were, as anticipated, returned unopposed to their posts. In contrast to the 1993 party elections, in which Anwar's supporters had been particularly successful, a large proportion of Mahathir loyalists were now elected. Notably, in the elections for the vice-presidencies, Muhyiddin Yassim, the only member of Anwar's 'Vision Team' who had remained loyal to the Deputy President, was defeated by Abdullah Badawi (the Minister of Foreign Affairs, who had been a vice-president prior to 1993); Najib Razak and Mohammad Taib were re-elected. However, the Minister of International Trade and Industry, Dato' Seri Paduka Rafidah Aziz, a Mahathir loyalist, who had been investigated in 1994 by the Anti-Corruption Agency for corrupt share-dealing, was defeated as head of the women's wing by a candidate favoured by Anwar, while Tan Sri Datuk Rahim Thamby Chik was ousted from the youth-wing leadership by another supporter of Anwar. No former member of Semangat '46, including Razaleigh, secured a position on the UMNO Supreme Council.

In October 1996 the PAS announced that it was to abandon its attempt (of some six years' standing) to replace secular criminal laws with *hudud*, the Islamic criminal code, in Kelantan, unless this was approved by the federal Government: Mahathir was known to be strongly opposed to such a policy. The PAS won a by-election for the State Legislative Assembly in Kelantan in January 1997. Although the PAS took the seat by only a narrow margin (the seat had been won convincingly at the previous election by a Semangat '46 candidate), the results were nevertheless indicative of Razaleigh's weakened position in the state.

In May 1997 Mahathir appointed Anwar as Acting Prime Minister while he took two months' leave of absence from the post. On his return, Mahathir's response to the currency crisis affecting the region, following Thailand's effective devaluation of the baht in early July, was widely perceived to have exacerbated Malaysia's economic position. His criticism of international investors resulted in further losses to the value of both the currency and shares on the stock exchange. Meanwhile, Anwar benefited politically from the situation, appearing to act responsibly in reassuring investors and rescinding the newly imposed financial restrictions. However, political opponents attempted to undermine Anwar through the circulation of a series of letters accusing him of sexual indiscretions. International criticism of Mahathir's outspokenness prompted popular demonstrations of support for the premier within Malaysia and near unanimous support for a vote of confidence in his leadership, which was held in the House of Representatives during November. In the same month Mahathir announced the formation of an executive authority to address the economic crisis, the National Economic Action Council. The composition of the Council, including the appointment of the former Minister of Finance, Dato' Paduka Daim Zainuddin, as Executive Director of the Council, was approved by the Cabinet in January 1998. At the UMNO annual convention in September 1997 Mahathir criticized the increasing tendency of Malaysian Muslims to attach excessive importance to external symbols of Islam (such as beards and headscarves) and warned of the dangers of extremism. Mahathir's speech, which was resented by many Muslims, followed the widely publicized arrest, in June, of three Muslim women for taking part in a beauty contest in Selangor. The arrests prompted debate concerning the position of women in Malaysian society and resulted in demands for the reform of the Islamic Syariah (Shariah) courts; a *fatwa* (religious edict) had the force of law in the state in which it was issued, which arguably violated the liberties of Malaysians as guaranteed under the federal Constitution. In November 10 men were detained under the ISA for disseminating Shia Muslim teachings (Malaysian Muslims belong predominantly to the Sunni sect) that were perceived as militant and a threat to national security. Many non-governmental organizations and political parties urged that the detainees be released or allowed to stand trial under the Sedition Act.

At internal elections for divisional committee members in UMNO, which took place in March 1998, most of Mahathir's supporters retained their positions. However, evidence of a growing division between Mahathir and Anwar became apparent at the UMNO annual party congress held in June, where Ahmad Zahid Hamidi, the head of the youth wing of UMNO and one of Anwar's supporters, made a speech criticizing what he termed the debilitating impact of corruption in the party. Zahid's speech, which was reminiscent of Anwar's recent condemnation of corruption and political restrictions, was perceived as an attack on the party's leadership; Mahathir responded by publishing a list of hundreds of people and companies who had received privatization contracts in recent years, which included close associates of Anwar and members of his family. During the following weeks Mahathir acted to counter the influence of Anwar. He promoted Daim Zainuddin (a close personal ally) to the position of Minister of Special Functions in charge of economic development, thus undermining Anwar's position as

Minister of Finance. Mahathir also dismissed newspaper editors close to Anwar and ordered the arrest of an associate of Anwar on firearms charges, which carried the death penalty under Malaysian law. The resignation in August of the Governor (a close ally of Anwar) and Deputy Governor of the central bank, reportedly owing to a disagreement over policy with Mahathir, served as an indication of the intensification of the rift within the Government. Supporters loyal to the Prime Minister responded to the perceived threat to Mahathir's leadership by circulating a brochure entitled *Fifty Reasons Why Anwar Cannot Become Prime Minister*, in which Anwar was accused of sexual offences and corruption.

Allegations of Anwar's supposed sexual misconduct increased throughout the months following the UMNO congress, and, following Anwar's refusal to resign, culminated in Mahathir's dismissal of Anwar as Deputy Prime Minister and Minister of Finance on 2 September 1998, on the grounds that he was morally unfit to hold office. On the following day Anwar was expelled from UMNO, and affidavits accusing him of sexual impropriety were filed with the High Court. The allegations were denied by Anwar, who asserted that they constituted part of a political conspiracy, at senior level, to discredit him. Anwar began a tour of the country, drawing extensive support for his calls for the wide-ranging reform of the political system from the many thousands who attended his public appearances. His supporters adopted the slogan *'reformasi'* (reform), which had united the popular forces that ousted President Suharto in Indonesia. In mid-September Anwar's adoptive brother, Sukma Darmawan Samitaat Madja, and a former speech-writer for Anwar, Munawar Ahmad Anees, were each sentenced to six months' imprisonment after they confessed to illegal homosexual activity with Anwar. The following day, at a meeting attended by at least 40,000 people in Kuala Lumpur, Anwar called directly for Mahathir's resignation; he was arrested shortly afterwards and detained under the ISA. A further 17 people, including a number of close associates of Anwar, were also detained under the same act. Anwar's arrest provoked demonstrations of protest, which erupted into violence when demonstrations involving up to 60,000 people were violently dispersed by the security forces; 132 people were arrested.

Following Anwar's arrest, his wife, Wan Azizah Wan Ismail, emerged as the *de facto* leader of the opposition movement. Despite a restriction order issued against Wan Azizah, barring her from holding rallies at her residence, demonstrations in protest at Anwar's detention were held throughout September 1998 and became the forum for demands for widespread political reform and the removal of the restrictions on freedom of speech and assembly imposed under the ISA. Anwar finally appeared in court in Petaling Jaya at the end of September, where he pleaded not guilty to five charges of corruption and five charges of sexual impropriety. Allegations made by Anwar, who appeared in court with visible bruising to his face, that he had been severely beaten while in police custody and had subsequently been denied medical attention for a number of days, provoked expressions of extreme concern from foreign Governments—in particular from the Presidents of the Philippines and Indonesia—and prompted the UN Secretary-General, Kofi Annan, to urge the Malaysian Government to ensure humane treatment for Anwar. The Malaysian Government initially dismissed Anwar's claims of assault; however, it was subsequently announced that a special investigation would be established. In December the Inspector-General of the Malaysian police force, Tan Sri Abdul Rahim Noor, resigned after an initial inquiry blamed the police for the injuries Anwar had received. Malaysia's Attorney-General publicly admitted in January 1999 that Anwar had been assaulted by the police while in custody, and a Royal Commission of Inquiry into Anwar's injuries, which was completed in March, found Rahim Noor to be personally responsible for the beating. In accordance with the recommendations of the inquiry, in April Rahim Noor was charged with assaulting Anwar. In March 2000 Rahim Noor was sentenced to two months' imprisonment and fined RM 2,000 after pleading guilty to a lesser charge of assault against Anwar.

Anwar's trial on four charges of corruption (which related to efforts allegedly made by him in 1997 to obtain through the police written denials that he was guilty of sexual misconduct and sodomy) began in November 1998. The presiding judge ruled that official foreign observers were not to be allowed at the trial. The credibility of the prosecution was undermined by the professed willingness of a principal witness to lie under oath, the withdrawal by a witness for the prosecution of his claims to have engaged in illegal homosexual activity with Anwar and the retraction by Anwar's adoptive brother and his speech-writer of their confessions, which they claimed had been obtained through police coercion. The defence suffered a number of reverses during the trial: in November the judge sentenced one of Anwar's lawyers to three months' imprisonment for contempt of court, because of a motion he had filed on behalf of Anwar to have two of the prosecutors dismissed from the case; the charges against Anwar were unexpectedly amended in January 1999, with the emphasis being shifted from sexual misconduct to abuse of power (the amendment meant that the prosecution would no longer have to prove that Anwar had committed sexual offences, but only that he had attempted to use his position to influence the police to quash the investigation into the allegations, effectively making it far easier for the prosecution to obtain a conviction). In addition, the judge ruled that all evidence given by several witnesses was inadmissible, despite requests from Anwar's lawyers that some parts of the testimony be retained as evidence for the defence. Following a disagreement between the defence and the presiding judge over the judge's refusal to hear a motion tabled by the defence that he be dismissed, the defence team refused to sum up its case, and the trial was ended abruptly in late March. In mid-April Anwar was found guilty on each of the four charges of corruption and a sentence of six years' imprisonment was imposed (under Malaysian law, this would be followed by a five-year period of disqualification from political office). Following the delivery of the verdict, supporters of the former Deputy Prime Minister clashed with security forces outside the court. Violent protests continued for the next three days, resulting in the arrest of 18 demonstrators. Following the trial, the three prosecution witnesses who had withdrawn their testimony against Anwar were charged with perjury. In late April Anwar was further charged with one count of illegal homosexual activity, to which he pleaded not guilty; it was announced that four other similar charges and one additional corruption charge against him had been suspended.

On the first day of Anwar's second trial in early June 1999 the prosecution amended the wording of its charge, changing the month and year (for the second time) in which the alleged crimes were supposedly committed. The trial was adjourned in September and Anwar was sent for medical examination following claims by the defence that Anwar had proven high levels of arsenic in his blood and was quite possibly the victim of deliberate poisoning. In the same month some 10,000 Anwar supporters gathered to demonstrate against the Government's treatment of the former Deputy Prime Minister and Minister of Finance; following the protests, several prominent allies of Anwar were reported to have been arrested. Anwar's trial resumed in late September, however, after medical tests found that he showed no clinical signs of arsenic poisoning, although concerns over his health continued to be expressed in October. In his testimony in court in October and November, Anwar made potentially damaging allegations of corruption against members of the Government (including the Minister of Finance, Daim, and the Minister of Domestic Trade and Consumer Affairs, Dato' Seri Megat Junid bin Megat Ayob) who, he alleged, had conspired to remove him from office. In mid-November the trial of Anwar was adjourned indefinitely without explanation; supporters of Anwar claimed that the adjournment was a government attempt to silence him in the approach to the general election, which was to be held in late November. The trial resumed on 25 January 2000, but was adjourned again in late February at the request of the defence. Meanwhile, in April 2000 the Court of Appeal upheld Anwar's conviction on four charges of corruption.

Anwar suffered a further set-back in early June 2000, after the Court of Appeal rejected his plea for a stay of proceedings, ordering the trial on charges of sodomy to continue. In July the presiding judge ordered Anwar's defence lawyers to conclude their case, although they protested that they had intended to call further witnesses. Despite an indefinite postponement of the verdict, initially scheduled for early August, by the judge, and several police warnings, some 200 protesters gathered outside the High Court in a pro-Anwar rally. The High Court found Anwar guilty of sodomy, sentencing him to a further nine years' imprisonment, thus bringing his term to a total of 15 years. His adoptive brother, Sukma Darmawan, was sentenced to six years' imprisonment and four strokes of the cane for the same offence. Although the verdict of guilty had been widely expected, observers were surprised by the severity of the sentence and by the judge's ruling that the punishments should be served consecutively rather than concurrently.

Although Anwar had been effectively removed from public office for 15 years, the affair continued to receive prominence in the media. Anwar was hospitalized in November, suffering from an acute back problem that required critical surgery. The Government refused a request for Anwar to travel abroad for surgery and, after becoming exasperated at Anwar's indecision, in April 2001 issued an ultimatum to Anwar either to accept treatment in a state hospital or return to his cell. He returned to his cell in May. In the same month public prosecutors announced that the remaining charges of corruption and sodomy against him were to be abandoned and, in July, Anwar lodged an appeal against his sodomy conviction. Meanwhile, in June 2001 the contempt verdict passed against one of Anwar's lawyers was overruled when the High Court concluded that the lawyer had been acting only in the interests of his client. In July 2002 Anwar lost his final appeal against his corruption conviction. In October of the same year Mahathir launched bankruptcy proceedings against Anwar, following his refusal to pay the costs of a defamation lawsuit he had brought against the Prime Minister in 1999. In April 2003 Anwar's appeal against his final conviction for sodomy was rejected by the Court of Appeal. A few days previously he had completed his sentence for corruption, the last two years of his six-year sentence having been remitted for good behaviour. Despite speculation that the accession of Abdullah Badawi to the premiership in October 2003 (see below) would bring about a change in the Government's stance towards Anwar, in January 2004 a court denied his application for bail pending the result of a further appeal against his sodomy conviction.

In early September 2004 Anwar was released from prison after his appeal against his conviction for sodomy was upheld by the Federal Court, which found the evidence against Anwar unreliable. Shortly afterwards Anwar travelled to Germany for surgery on the back condition that he claimed had resulted from the severe beatings he had received in police custody in 1998, returning to Malaysia at the end of October 2004. Although he remained disqualified from holding political office until April 2008 owing to his corruption conviction, against which the Federal Court refused to allow a new appeal, Anwar announced his intention to resume his campaign for political reform.

In January 1999, meanwhile, prior to the closure of the first trial of Anwar, Mahathir effected a major cabinet reorganization, in which Abdullah Badawi was appointed as Deputy Prime Minister and Minister for Home Affairs (a post relinquished by Mahathir) and Daim Zainuddin was allocated the finance portfolio, which had been assumed by Mahathir following the dismissal of Anwar in September 1998. Also in January 1999 the UMNO Supreme Council announced its decision to postpone for 18 months elections for senior posts within the party, previously scheduled to be held in June, effectively preventing any potential challenge to Mahathir's leadership from within the party. The BN won a significant victory in the elections to the State Legislative Assembly in Sabah on 12–13 March, securing 31 of the 48 seats; however, Mahathir indicated that the result would not induce him to call an early general election. In early April a new opposition party, the Parti Keadilan Nasional (PKN—National Justice Party), was launched by Wan Azizah in anticipation of the general election; the new party reportedly aimed to establish itself as a multi-ethnic and multi-religious party and declared that its first act, should it come to power, would be to seek a royal pardon for Anwar. However, Anwar himself did not join the new party. Despite its stated aspirations to multi-ethnicity, the initial membership of the party appeared to be predominantly Muslim.

In November 1999 the Government unexpectedly announced that a general election was to be held later in the same month. The opposition expressed dissatisfaction at the limited period of time allowed for campaigning. At the election, which was held on 29 November, a decisive victory was won by the governing BN coalition, which gained 148 of a total of 193 seats in the House of Representatives, thereby retaining the two-thirds' majority required to allow the Government to amend the Constitution. The opposition coalition, the Barisan Alternatif (Alternative Front—which had been formed by the PAS, the PKN, the DAP and the Parti Rakyat Malaysia (PRM—Malaysian People's Party) in June 1999 and which subsequently selected Anwar as its prime ministerial candidate) won a total of 42 seats, while the opposition PBS (which remained outside the Barisan Alternatif) secured three seats. Despite the BN's victory, UMNO experienced a significant decline in support amongst Malay voters (mainly to the PAS, which secured 27 seats) and lost 23 seats, including those of four cabinet ministers. The party also performed poorly in the assembly elections held simultaneously in 11 Malaysian states: the PAS secured control of the state legislature in Trengganu, retained power in Kelantan and made significant gains in Mahathir's home state of Kedah. This erosion of confidence in UMNO was widely believed to be a result of the Government's treatment of Anwar and the concomitant decline of public confidence in the country's institutions, including the police and the judicial system. While there were a number of new appointments to the Cabinet, which was announced in early December, many of the key portfolios remained unchanged. However, in an unexpected development, Mahathir promoted the unelected academic, Musa Mohamad, neither an existing government minister nor a member of UMNO, to the influential post of Minister of Education; Musa replaced Dato' Seri Najib Abdul Razak, a former potential successor to Mahathir, who was transferred to the less powerful Ministry of Defence in what was perceived by many as an effective demotion. Also in December Mahathir announced that he intended this (his fifth) term of office to be his last, and for the first time formally identified the Deputy Prime Minister, Abdullah Badawi, as his preferred successor. In the same month the Barisan Alternatif nominated Fadzil Nor, President of the PAS, as the new parliamentary leader of the opposition. He replaced Lim Kit Siang, who had lost his seat in the general election and who in early December resigned as the Secretary-General of the DAP.

In May 2000, at the UMNO party elections, Mahathir and Abdullah Badawi were formally elected President and Deputy President of the party, respectively. Recognizing the need for change in order to improve the increasingly unfavourable public image of the Government, in November the Prime Minister appointed Mohamed Dzaiddin Abdullah as the new Chief Justice, in a bid to enhance the credibility of the judiciary, tarnished by the Anwar trials. Later that month UMNO held a special general assembly, at which measures were approved to revitalize the image of the party and to attract more young professionals, including women. These developments failed to prevent the opposition PKN from taking a seat from the BN coalition at a by-election in the Lunas constituency of Kedah.

In April 2001 the Minister of Finance, Daim Zainuddin, took a two-month leave of absence. The leave was seen as having been enforced by Mahathir, who wanted to distance himself from criticism arising from two controversial nationalization agreements involving the heavily indebted Malaysia Airlines and Time dotCom (the telecommunications unit of the Renong Group) in late 2000, both companies being connected to protégés of Daim. In June 2001 Daim formally resigned from his post, following widespread allegations that he had taken advantage of public funds to help business associates. Mahathir assumed the finance portfolio on an interim basis.

Possibly fearing a split in the Malay vote over the Anwar affair, Mahathir attempted to strengthen support by using the race issue in August 2000, when he criticized Suqiu, the Malaysian Chinese Organizations' Election Appeals Committee, describing some of its members as extremists and likening them to communists for urging the abolition of the New Vision Policy. The policy had for 30 years ensured favouritism for the Malay majority in education and commerce, in an attempt to reduce the inequality of wealth between Malays and Chinese. The effect of the criticism may have been merely to alienate Chinese supporters, integral to the BN's 1999 victory, although Suqiu did withdraw its demands after a series of meetings with UMNO in January 2001. In March Mahathir confirmed that the New Vision Policy, due to end in 2001, was to be extended for a further 10 years.

In January 2000, meanwhile, government suppression of dissent increased significantly. Three prominent members of the opposition were arrested; the deputy leader of the DAP and Anwar's legal representative, Karpal Singh, and the Vice-President of the PKN, Marina Yusoff, were charged under the Sedition Act. Mohamad Ezam Mohamad Noor was charged under the Official Secrets Act and subsequently placed on trial. In the same month the editor and the printer of the popular PAS newspaper, *Harakah*, were also charged with sedition in connection with an article concerning the trial of Anwar that reportedly included a quote accusing the authorities of conspiring against him. The arrests were perceived by observers to constitute an attempt by the Government to curb the influence of the PAS following the party's strong performance in the general election. In early March 2000 the Government ordered that *Harakah* be published just twice a month instead of twice weekly and restricted sales of the publication to members of the PAS only. In an apparent further attempt by the Government to stifle dissent, the group editor of the *New Straits Times*, Kadir Jasin, was forced to resign in January following the publication of an editorial that questioned the decision by the UMNO Supreme Council to reject demands that the party's two most senior positions be contested from within the party in the forthcoming UMNO internal elections (the Supreme Council proposed instead that Mahathir and Abdullah Badawi be renominated for the party presidency and vice-presidency unopposed). In January 2002 public prosecutors abandoned the sedition charges against Karpal Singh. No explanation was given for the decision.

The Anwar issue continued to incite public unrest, and in April 2000 a protest to mark the anniversary of Anwar's conviction for corruption was broken up by riot police, 48 PKN activists being arrested. Public criticism of the Government, and subsequent detentions, became more frequent after Anwar's second conviction, as confidence in Mahathir's leadership continued to decline. Mohamad Ezam Mohamad Noor was arrested in March 2001 as a result of allegedly seditious comments, despite already being on trial for releasing a secret report on corruption. A month later he was detained again, along with six other opposition leaders, including the PKN Vice-President, Tian Chua, and the PKN youth Vice-Chairman, N. Gobala Krishnan, under the ISA (which allows for detention without trial for up to two years). The aim of these arrests seemed to be to dissuade protesters from gathering for the second anniversary of Anwar's conviction. The effect was significant as only 2,000 demonstrators defied the authorities' ban to attend the peaceful 'Black 14' rally, named after and coinciding with the date of Anwar's first conviction, 14 April. However, the seven detainees were not immediately released after the rally, and three more arrests were made under the ISA. During late April the PKN youth leaders, Dr Badrul Amin Baharom and Lokman Noor Adam, were arrested, as was the human rights activist, Badarudiin Ismail, thus bringing the total of recent detainees under the provisions of the ISA to 10. In August 2002 Mohamad Ezam Mohamad Noor was sentenced to a two-year prison term, having been convicted of 'leaking' state secrets. In June 2003 he was freed on bail, pending an appeal; his conviction was overruled by the High Court in April 2004.

In early August 2001 an extraordinary session of the Court of Final Appeal heard arguments against the detention of five people under the ISA. Significantly, the judges ruled that the onus was on the State to produce evidence that those arrested posed a real threat to national security. Meanwhile, Nik Adli Nik Abdul Aziz, son of PAS spiritual leader Datuk Haji Nik Abdul Aziz Nik Mat, was one of 10 men detained under the Act on suspicion of membership of the Kumpulan Mujahidin Malaysia (KMM), an Islamist fundamentalist group believed to be engaged in a long-term plot to overthrow the Government. Seven of those taken into custody were also members of the PAS. Soon afterwards 25 supporters of Anwar Ibrahim were freed from prison and promptly rearrested on new charges, before being granted bail. In September the Government announced that Nik Adli Nik Abdul Aziz was to be detained for two years without trial under the provisions of the ISA. Eight of the nine men arrested with him were also imprisoned. Human rights activists accused the Government of exploiting the aftermath of the terrorist attacks on the USA in the same month (see the chapter on the USA) to suppress national opposition groups. Further arrests continued to be made under the ISA, as the Government tightened its control of national security.

In September 2001 the opposition was destabilized by the withdrawal of the DAP from the Barisan Alternatif. The party accused the PAS of alienating Chinese voters through its support for an Islamic state. In the same month an election in Malaysia's largest state, Sarawak, confirmed the strength of the ruling coalition. The BN won 60 out of 62 available seats in the state legislature. The DAP secured one seat; an independent candidate the other. In November the PBS decided to rejoin the Government following more than a decade of absence from power; the party was formally readmitted to the BN in January 2002. Also in January, at a by-election in the Perlis district of Indera Kayangan, the PKN was heavily defeated by the BN. The PAS accused the Government of using devious methods to exploit popular fear of Islamist militancy in the aftermath of the September terrorist attacks.

On 21 November 2001 the Head of State, Sultan Salahuddin Abdul Aziz Shah Al-Haj ibni Al-Marhum Sultan Hisamuddin Alam Shah Al-Haj, died at the age of 75. On 13 December the Raja of Perlis, Tuanku Syed Sirajuddin Syed Putra Jamalullail, was sworn in as the new monarch, following his election by secret ballot from amongst the remaining eight Malay rulers. The Sultan of Terengganu continued as his deputy.

In December 2001 a court convicted 19 members of the Islamist cult al-Ma'unah of treason for plotting to overthrow the Government. The men had been arrested following the murder of two hostages during a confrontation with security forces after a weapons robbery in July 2000. Ten other cult members had pleaded guilty to lesser charges and received 10-year prison terms. Three of the sect's ringleaders were sentenced to death for their part in the armed rebellion. The remaining men were given life terms. (In November 2003 15 members of the cult, who had played only minor roles in the robbery and who later expressed remorse for their actions, were released, having been held under the ISA.) Also in December 2001 *The Sun* published a story claiming the existence of a plot to assassinate Prime Minister Mahathir. The story was later proved to be false and more than one-half of the editorial staff were dismissed, leading to allegations that the authorities had plotted to discredit the newspaper and thus more easily subject it to Malaysia's rigorous censorship laws. In January 2002 the Government announced further measures intended to stifle potential sources of dissent, stating that, with effect from May, students and staff at public universities would be required to sign a pledge declaring allegiance to their king, country and government. Students had played a leading role in the protests that had followed the dismissal of Anwar Ibrahim in 1998.

In June 2002, during a speech to the annual congress of UMNO, Prime Minister Mahathir made the dramatic announcement that he intended to resign from the Government, with immediate effect. However, he was persuaded to withdraw his resignation shortly afterwards and, following some discussion, it was decided that he would remain in power until October 2003, when he would be succeeded by the Deputy Prime Minister, Abdullah Badawi. During the transition period Abdullah Badawi would assume increased responsibility for the running of the Government. Fadzil Nor, President of the PAS, died following complications arising from heart surgery in June 2002; Abdul Hadi Awang assumed the party leadership on an interim basis.

In July 2002 Abdul Hadi Awang announced the imposition of Islamic law in Terengganu state, of which he was the Chief Minister. However, the Government continued to oppose efforts to enforce the new law code. In the same month, at a by-election to the Kedah seat of Pendang, which had become vacant upon the death of Fadzil Nor, the BN secured a narrow victory.

In October 2002 police arrested five men, believed to be members of the regional Islamist organization Jemaah Islamiah (JI), under the ISA. The arrests brought the total number of ISA detainees to approximately 70. Members of JI were believed to be responsible for the recent terrorist attack on the Indonesian island of Bali (see the chapter on Indonesia), which had resulted in the deaths of 202 people, including many tourists. In November the ISA attracted renewed criticism when a court ordered the release of Nasharuddin Nasir, who had been detained under its provisions since April of that year, on the grounds that no evidence had been provided to substantiate claims that he had engaged in terrorist activities. The Government, in contravention of the judicial order, rearrested him almost immediately after his release. It was announced subsequently that the ISA was to be strengthened in order to prevent further challenges by the courts. Meanwhile, Prime Minister Mahathir announced the appointment of Datuk Dr Jamaluddin Jarjis as Minister of Finance II; Mahathir himself continued to hold the other finance portfolio.

In May 2003 Minister of Transport Ling Liong Sik announced his resignation. In the following month it was announced that three members of the PKN who had been imprisoned under the ISA for more than two years were to be released. In August the PKN merged with the smaller PRM, forming the Parti Keadilan Rakyat (PKR—People's Justice Party), in advance of the general election scheduled to be held in 2004. It was hoped that the merger would strengthen opposition to the BN and promote Anwar's cause. The President of the PKN, Wan Azizah, continued as President of the new party. In September it was announced that nine suspected members of the KMM who had been detained under the ISA in August 2001, including Nik Adli Nik Abdul Aziz, would be imprisoned for a further two years.

On 31 October 2003 Prime Minister Mahathir Mohamad retired, having spent 22 years in power. His designated successor, Deputy Prime Minister Abdullah Badawi, was then sworn in as Prime Minister, retaining the home affairs portfolio and, in addition, assuming Mahathir's role as Minister of Finance. In November Abdullah Badawi was also endorsed as the new Chairman of the BN. Meanwhile, the PAS announced plans to transform Malaysia fully into an Islamic state should it come to power, attracting criticism not only from non-Muslim members of the BN but also from political allies of the PAS, including the PKR. In January 2004 the new Prime Minister effected his first cabinet reorganization, nominating Minister of Defence Najib Razak as Deputy Prime Minister. Amongst other changes, the economist Nor Mohamed Yakcop became Minister of Finance II, replacing Jamaluddin Jarjis, who was allocated the domestic trade and consumer affairs portfolio.

In February 2004, as a result of an ongoing anti-corruption campaign initiated by the new Prime Minister, both the Minister of Land and Co-operative Development, Tan Sri Datuk Kasitah bin Gaddam, and the former head of the national steel company Perwaja Steel Bhd, Eric Chia Eng Hock, were arrested and charged with corruption. Kasitah announced his resignation shortly afterwards. (The charges against Chia were dismissed in June 2007; the judge in his trial criticized the prosecutors involved in the case, notably over their failure to call important witnesses. Kasitah's trial continued in early 2008.) Also in February 2004 a national service programme was introduced with the intention of promoting national unity; conscripts were to perform military service for three months. A Royal Commission into the police force was also appointed in February. The Commission's preliminary report, presented in August, included numerous allegations of corruption and evidence that excessive force had been used against detainees. The Commission's final report, published in May 2005, urged the swift establishment of an Independent Police Complaints and Misconduct Commission, in order to render the police more accountable to the public; the report noted that the incidence of corruption within the police force was higher than in other government agencies. Meanwhile, in early March 2004 it was announced that Parliament was to be dissolved and a general election held later in that month, several months before the constitutional deadline of November. Later in March it was reported that six suspected Indonesian members of JI had been captured in Malaysia and were being held under the ISA, bringing the total number of suspected militants detained under the ISA to 96.

On 21 March 2004, following a brief campaign period, elections took place to an enlarged 219-member House of Representatives and to 12 of the 13 State Legislative Assemblies (Sarawak was exempted, having held elections to its legislature in September 2001). The BN secured a commanding victory, winning 198 of the 219 seats in the House of Representatives and taking control of 11 of the 12 State Legislative Assemblies, including that of Terengganu, which had previously been governed by the PAS. The PAS retained control of Kelantan by a narrow margin. The DAP secured 12 seats in the House of Representatives, followed by the PAS, which won seven (compared with 27 at the election of 1999) and the PKR, which retained only one seat, that held by Wan Azizah. Having been sworn in again as head of government, Abdullah Badawi announced a major reorganization of his Cabinet, which was enlarged through the creation of two new ministries—the Ministry of Federal Territories and the Ministry of Natural Resources and the Environment—and the division of three existing ministries, those of Home Affairs, Education and Culture, Arts and Tourism. Abdullah Badawi retained the finance portfolio and that of internal security, created following the division of the Ministry of Home Affairs. Najib Razak continued as Deputy Prime Minister and Minister of Defence.

The Prime Minister launched a National Integrity Plan in April 2004, aimed at reducing corruption and abuse of power. In late May the Government allowed journalists to visit a detention centre for those held under the ISA, in an attempt to dispel recent allegations, made by the US-based organization Human Rights Watch, that detainees had been tortured. In August the BN succeeded in retaining its seat at a state assembly by-election in Kuala Berang in Terengganu, increasing its majority in the constituency.

Abdullah Badawi's control over UMNO was questioned in September 2004, when three members of his Cabinet failed to secure re-election to the party's Supreme Council at its General Assembly; some observers attributed their defeat to a reaction by party members against the Prime Minister's anti-corruption campaign. In addition, only one of those elected to the three posts of Vice-President was regarded as being a close ally of the Prime Minister: incumbent Tan Sri Dato' Muhyiddin bin Mohd Yassin, the Minister of Agriculture and Agro-based Industry. Tan Sri Mohamed Isa Abdul Samad, the Minister of Federal Territories, and Datuk Wira Mohamed Ali Rustam, the Chief Minister (Ketua Menteri) of Melaka (Malacca), were also elected as Vice-Presidents. Allegations of vote-buying emerged after the announcement of the results. None the less, Abdullah Badawi and Najib Razak were formally endorsed as the party's President and Deputy President. UMNO leaders ruled out a return to the party for Anwar Ibrahim, who had been freed from prison earlier in September (see above). Anwar's release was widely regarded as evidence that the Prime Minister was fulfilling a pledge to respect the independence of the judiciary. In December Anwar launched a nation-wide campaign against the ISA.

In January 2005 police responsible for religious matters conducted a raid on a night-club in Kuala Lumpur, arresting about 100 Muslims, including many women, on charges of public indecency and other 'anti-Islamic' crimes. Amid the ensuing public outcry, the legitimacy of these arrests was questioned, as the application of Islamic law in federal territories was restricted to marriage and related matters. In the following month the Government instructed the Federal Territories Islamic Department to abandon the charges. In July 21 members of the religious group Sky Kingdom, one of 22 organizations deemed by the Government earlier that month to be 'deviant sects of Islam', were arrested at the group's compound in Terengganu and charged with propagating teachings that 'humiliated' Islam. One of those arrested pleaded guilty and was sentenced to a one-year period of religious 'rehabilitation' under the supervision of local Islamic officials. Two of the detainees, who claimed to have previously renounced Islam, applied for a hearing at the Federal Court on the question of whether the right to profess a religion under Article 11 of the Constitution (which prescribes religious freedom for all) included the right of a Muslim to renounce Islam. In December the federal High Court in Kuala Lumpur rejected their application, ruling that the jurisdiction to decide whether or not a person had renounced Islam rested with the Syariah courts. (One of the two was sentenced to two years' imprisonment in March 2008 by the Syariah High Court, having been convicted of apostasy.) Meanwhile, the remaining 18 detainees pleaded not guilty and opted for trial before an Islamic Court. The forthcoming verdicts, regarded as being of considerable significance in the continuing debate about the issue of religious tolerance within Malaysia, were awaited with great interest by the international community. In August 2005 Anwar Ibrahim was awarded RM 4.5m. in damages by the High Court for the false allegations contained within the pamphlet *Fifty Reasons Why Anwar Ibrahim Cannot Become Prime Minister*, published in 1998.

In October 2005 Tan Sri Mohamed Isa Abdul Samad resigned from the position of Minister of Federal Territories, having been found guilty by the ruling party of vote-buying and political corruption pertaining to the UMNO party elections of September 2004. The UMNO Supreme Council subsequently rejected Isa's appeal against his three-year suspension from the party. In November 2005 a new Malaysian coastguard agency was launched, with operations initially focused on the Strait of Melaka, where piracy remained a serious problem. The Government was to disburse an estimated RM 578m. by the end of 2007 to finance the agency's operations, which were to be expanded gradually to cover Malaysia's other territorial waters. Malaysia, Indonesia and Singapore agreed to improve co-operation in their efforts to protect vessels traversing the busy maritime trade route. In the same month Azahari Husin, a notorious Malaysian bomb-maker thought to be responsible for many of JI's operations, was killed in Indonesia during a police raid on a property in Batu, near Malang, East Java. In January 2006 another prominent Malaysian Islamist militant, Noordin Mohammad Top, released a message in which he claimed responsibility for the bombings on the Indonesian island of Bali in 2005 (see the chapter on Indonesia) and declared himself to be the head of a new South-East Asian Islamist militant organization, namely Tanzam Qaedat al Jihad (Organization of the Basis of Jihad). The statement served to remind Malaysia of the threat posed by its own nationals to regional security. Later that month Anwar Ibrahim filed a lawsuit against former Prime Minister Mahathir Mohamad for falsely having depicted him as a homosexual and causing 'irreparable damage' to his reputation. (In September 2005 Mahathir had controversially admitted to reporters that he had dismissed Anwar in order to avert the prospect of the appointment of a homosexual prime minister.) However, in July 2007 the High Court dismissed the lawsuit, which Mahathir had claimed was a ploy by Anwar to 'rehabilitate himself for high office'.

In February 2006 the Prime Minister effected a reorganization of the Cabinet. Datuk Paduka Abdul Kadir Sheikh Fadzir had previously announced his resignation from the position of Minister of Information and was replaced by Datuk Zainuddin Maidin. Other notable changes included the appointment of Datuk Seri Radzi Sheikh as Minister of Home Affairs, in place of Datuk Azmi Khalid, and the appointment of Dato' Haji Zulhasnan Rafique as Minister of Federal Territories. In the same month the Malaysian Government suspended indefinitely the licence of the *Sarawak Tribune*, in response to the newspaper's decision to reprint controversial cartoons depicting the Prophet Muhammad, which had first been published in a Danish newspaper and had provoked outrage from the international Muslim community. This was the first time in almost two decades that a Malaysian publication had had its licence revoked, and the episode renewed concerns about the status of religious freedom and freedom of expression. Shortly afterwards the licences of *Guang Ming Daily* and *Berita Petang Sarawak* were also revoked, for a two-week period, after they too reprinted the cartoons. Also in February, the Government announced plans to slaughter all poultry in four villages, following official confirmation of the first outbreak of avian influenza ('bird flu') in the country for more than a year: 40 chickens on a farm near Kuala Lumpur had been diagnosed with the deadly H5N1 strain of the virus earlier that month, prompting the Singapore Government to ban all imports from the affected region. Further cases followed.

The Sarawak State Legislative Assembly was dissolved in April 2006 and an election held in May. The BN won 62 of the 71 seats in the expanded state legislature, while the DAP took six seats and the remaining three were divided among the PKR, the Sarawak National Party and an independent candidate.

In April 2006 relations with Singapore became a source of internal disharmony when the Malaysian Prime Minister suspended the construction of a bridge designed to replace the Johor Strait causeway to Singapore. It was hoped that the new bridge would reduce congestion on the route and allow the passage of ships through the waterway. Singapore had expressed uncertainty about the plan on financial and environmental grounds but, in the absence of a bilateral consensus, construction work on the Malaysian half of the bridge had nevertheless begun in January. Abdullah Badawi remarked that other related negotiations would also be suspended, in a statement that cast doubt over Singapore's request for the provision of Malaysian materials for the purposes of land reclamation work, as well as access to Malaysian airspace for military training. The incident provoked a harsh reaction from former Prime Minister Mahathir, who was outspoken in his criticism of what he regarded as a 'surrender (of) sovereignty' to Singapore. In June the rupture in relations deepened when the former leader, who remained powerful in many quarters, appeared to question his own choice of successor, and expressed disapproval at the Prime Minister's reluctance to complete certain projects started in the Mahathir era. The UMNO Supreme Council responded by voicing its support for Abdullah Badawi, both as Prime Minister and UMNO President. For some observers the episode signified the beginning of a power struggle that would reach its culmination at the forthcoming UMNO party election in 2008 (it was later announced that the party election would not take place until after the next legislative election). Mahathir continued his apparent campaign against Abdullah Badawi and his administration in the months that followed, warning in August 2006 that he had evidence to substantiate his accusations of government corruption. In September Mahathir was unable to secure election as a delegate to the annual UMNO assembly scheduled for November, amid speculation that he had intended to use the meeting to renew his offensive against the Government of Abdullah Badawi.

In October 2006 Nik Adli Nik Abdul Aziz was released from prison, having been incarcerated for more than five years without charge (see above). Sultan Tuanku Mizan Zainal Abidin ibni al-Marhum Sultan Mahmud, the Sultan of Terengganu, was sworn in as the country's Yang di-Pertuan Agong on 13 December and enthroned on 26 April 2007. Severe flooding in December 2006 and January 2007, particularly in the southern state of Johor, displaced more than 100,000 people.

Several corruption scandals, involving senior officials, emerged in early 2007. In March it was revealed that the Anti-Corruption Agency was investigating allegations that the Deputy Minister of Internal Security, Datuk Mohd Johari Baharum, had accepted more than RM 5m. in bribes in return for the release of three men suspected of being involved in organized crime. Meanwhile, the Director-General of the Anti-Corruption Agency, Datuk Seri Zulkipli Mat Noor, had himself been accused by a former colleague of illicit self-enrichment. The Prime Minister's Office announced at the end of March that Zulkipli's contract, which had just expired, would not be renewed. Moreover, the position of the Deputy Prime Minister and Minister of Defence, Najib Razak, was undermined by opposition attempts to link him to a murder that his political adviser, Abdul Razak Baginda, was charged with abetting. In late April Najib denied having any connection to the killing or the victim. The trial of Abdul Razak Baginda and the two members of a special police unit who were accused of perpetrating the murder commenced in June and continued in early 2008. In July 2007 the Attorney-General halted investigations into the activities of Johari and Zulkipli owing to lack of evidence.

A state assembly by-election held in Ijok, in Selangor, in late April 2007 marked the return to active politics of Anwar Ibrahim, who campaigned vigorously on behalf of the PKR candidate. None the less, the ruling BN retained the seat with an increased majority. Anwar declared his intention to contest the presidency of the PKR at its annual conference in late May, despite being barred from holding public office until April 2008, but at a very late stage withdrew his candidacy, amid some internal dissent over his decision to stand; Wan Azizah was consequently re-elected unopposed. Anwar's renewed prominence was not welcomed by all members of the PKR and prompted the resignation from the party of a number of senior members. Meanwhile, Abdullah Badawi's announcement that civil servants would receive pay rises of up to 35% (the first increase in 15 years) prompted speculation that the Prime Minister intended to call an early general election.

In late May 2007 the Federal Court rejected an appeal by a convert from Islam to Christianity to have the word 'Islam' removed from the religion section of her identity card, ruling that Syariah courts held jurisdiction in this area. Observers noted that the judgment effectively made it impossible to renounce Islam legally, given that apostasy was a criminal offence under Islamic law, and raised renewed questions about the right to religious freedom prescribed by Article 11 of the Constitution. This was perhaps the most high-profile of a number of similar cases that were provoking religious tension in Malaysia. In late August the Government suspended publication of the Tamil-language newspaper *Makkal Osai* for one month, after the newspaper published an image of Jesus Christ apparently smoking a cigarette and drinking alcohol. In December controversy arose over the use of the word 'Allah' by non-Muslims, when a Roman Catholic weekly newspaper, *The Herald*, encountered difficulties in renewing its publishing permit because its Malay-language section employed 'Allah' when referring to the Christian God. Dato' Abdullah bin Mohamad Zin, the Minister in the Prime Minister's Department responsible for Islamic affairs, reportedly stated that the Government had decided that the use of 'Allah' by non-Muslims might create confusion among Muslims.

In mid-November 2007 police used tear gas and water cannons to disperse up to 30,000 protesters who were marching in Kuala Lumpur to campaign for electoral reform. The demonstration, which had been declared illegal, was organized by the Gabungan Pilihanraya Bersih dan Adil (Bersih—the Coalition for Clean and Fair Elections), comprising a number of opposition parties, including the DAP, the PAS and the PKR, and civil society organizations. Bersih's main demands were equal access to the state-controlled media for all parties, a complete revision of the electoral register, the use of indelible ink to prevent multiple voting, and the abolition of postal voting except for diplomats and overseas voters. A second banned demonstration, involving at least 8,000 ethnic Indians, took place outside the British High Commission in Kuala Lumpur later that month, ending in violence, as police clashed with the protesters. The rally was organized by the Hindu Rights Action Force (Hindraf, a coalition of some 30 Hindu non-governmental organizations) to highlight perceived discrimination against Indians in Malaysia (who accounted for some 7% of the population) and, more specifically, in support of a lawsuit, filed in the British courts in August, demanding that the British Government pay reparations to the descendants of Indians transported to Malaysia as indentured labourers during the 19th century. In December five Hindraf members were detained under the ISA on the grounds that their actions had threatened national security.

The Minister of Health, Datuk Seri Chua Soi Lek, resigned in early January 2008 after admitting his involvement in a sexual scandal; he was replaced by Dato' Seri Ong Ka Ting. In mid-February Abdullah Badawi announced the dissolution of Parliament, and a general election was called for 8 March, more than one year earlier than the constitutional deadline. The Prime Minister gave no explanation for his decision, which observers attributed to a desire to secure a renewed mandate in advance of a widely anticipated deterioration in economic conditions. The timing of the election also ensured the exclusion of Anwar Ibrahim, whose disqualification from seeking public office was not due to expire until a month later. Also in mid-February, several hundred ethnic Indians participated in another banned demonstration organized by Hindraf in Kuala Lumpur to protest against the alleged marginalization of the Indian minority.

On 8 March 2008 the BN sustained heavy losses in elections to an enlarged House of Representatives and to 12 of the 13 State Legislative Assemblies (Sarawak having conducted elections to its legislature in May 2006). The ruling coalition failed to retain its two-thirds' majority in the House of Representatives, taking only 140 of the 222 seats, and lost control of the Legislative Assemblies of Kedah, Penang, Perak and Selangor. Of the opposition parties, which had pledged not to present candidates against each other, the PKR made the most significant gains in the House of Representatives, winning a total of 31 seats (compared with only one in 2004), while the DAP and the PAS both increased their representation by 16 seats, to 28 seats and 23 seats, respectively. The PAS also strengthened its majority in the Kelantan state legislature. The BN's poor performance was attributed to public discontent with renewed ethnic tensions and rising inflation, as well as concern about crime levels and corruption. Having dismissed demands for his resignation, including from within UMNO, Abdullah Badawi reorganized his Cabinet 10 days after the election. Although Najib Razak remained Deputy Prime Minister and Minister of Defence, most other portfolios were affected by the reallocation. The most notable departure from the Government was perhaps that of Dato' Seri Paduka Rafidah binti Aziz, who had served as Minister of International Trade and Industry since 1987, but had been criticized in 2006 over procedures for the import of foreign vehicles; she was replaced by Tan Sri Dato' Haji Muhyiddin bin Mohd Yassin, hitherto Minister of Agriculture and Agro-Based Industry. New appointees included Datuk Mohd Zaid bin Ibrahim, a former lawyer and member of UMNO, who had previously been critical of the Government, as a Minister in the Prime Minister's Department. Zaid was charged with reforming the judiciary, which had been damaged in the second half of 2007 by allegations of corruption in the appointment process for judges.

Malaysia's foreign policy was dominated by its membership of the regional grouping, the Association of South East Asian Nations (ASEAN, see p. 185), founded in 1967. In February 2008 Malaysia ratified the new ASEAN Charter, which codified the principles and purposes of the Association and had been signed in November 2007 at the 13th summit meeting in Singapore.

Mahathir was instrumental in bringing Myanmar into ASEAN in 1997 under the Policy of Constructive Engagement. Malaysia also played an integral role in bringing together the military junta and opposition leader Aung San Suu Kyi for negotiations in late 2000, although it was thought that financial considerations might have been significant, with a promise of direct investment in Myanmar by Malaysia's national petroleum corporation, PETRONAS, in return for a semblance of progress on the part of the junta. Mahathir's visit to Myanmar in January 2001 confirmed Malaysia's interest in Myanmar, a possible alternative source of natural gas. In September 2001 the Myanma leader, Gen. Than Shwe, paid an official visit to Malaysia during which a number of bilateral agreements were signed. In August 2002 Mahathir visited Myanmar again; during his visit he met with Aung San Suu Kyi and, it was thought, attempted to encourage the junta to engage in further dialogue with the opposition. In March 2006 the Malaysian Minister of Foreign Affairs, Syed Hamid Albar, was denied access to Aung San Suu Kyi on a visit to Myanmar as an ASEAN envoy to assess the country's progress towards political reform. Albar, who had held a meeting with Lt-Gen. Soe Win, the Myanma Prime Minister, was initially positive about the visit. However, ASEAN's forbearance with regard to the military regime of Myanmar seemed to be decreasing in July when Albar implied that the Association's development was being impeded by Myanmar, claiming that ASEAN could no longer defend the country as Myanmar was 'not making an attempt to co-operate or help itself'.

Relations with Singapore had always been characterized by mistrust, after the city-state left the Federation of Malaya in 1965. Resentment increased as Singapore advanced more swiftly than Malaysia economically, creating a certain acrimonious competition between the two countries. However, as Malaysia also developed, bilateral relations became more cordial, and co-operation increased. The visit in August 2000 by Singapore's Senior Minister and figurehead, Lee Kuan Yew, to Mahathir in Kuala Lumpur demonstrated the growing convergence of the two countries' viewpoints. In September 2001 Lee Kuan Yew travelled to Kuala Lumpur again, on a visit intended to further enhance ties between the two countries. Relations were threatened from early 2002, however, as tensions arose over the renegotiation of a 1961 agreement by which Malaysia supplied Singapore with water. Negotiations took place in July and October 2002 in an attempt to resolve the problems arising from the water dispute, but without success. In February 2003 Prime Minister Mahathir stated that, while Malaysia would cease to supply Singapore with untreated water in 2011, it would continue to supply filtered water, at a reasonable price, for as long as necessary. Following the retirement of Mahathir in October 2003, bilateral relations showed signs of improvement under new Prime Minister Abdullah Badawi. In January 2004 the Malaysian Prime Minister and his Singaporean counterpart, Goh Chok Tong, exchanged visits and discussed the tensions in the relationship. In October, on his first official visit to Malaysia, the new Prime Minister of Singapore, Lee Hsien Loong, announced that his predecessor, Goh, now Senior Minister in the Prime Minister's Office, would lead his country's efforts to resolve outstanding bilateral issues. Abdullah Badawi and Goh held talks in Kuala Lumpur in December. Issues discussed included the dispute over the sale of water to Singapore; the use of Malaysian airspace by Singapore's air force; the joint development of unused railway land in Singapore; the release of pension funds owed to Malaysians who had worked in Singapore; and the proposed construction of a bridge between the two countries. In January 2005 Malaysia and Singapore appeared to have resolved a dispute over the latter's land reclamation project in the Straits of Johor, which separate the two countries. Malaysia accepted that the reclamation work could proceed, while Singapore agreed to co-operate with Malaysia to ensure navigational safety and environmental protection of the waterway. In 2006, however, relations became strained over the Johor Strait bridge dispute (see above), and deteriorated further in September, when Singapore's Minister Mentor and former Prime Minister, Lee Kuan Yew, remarked that Malaysia's Chinese minority was being systematically marginalized because of its success. Lee later apologized to Abdullah Badawi for causing him 'discomfort' and stated that he did not want to interfere in Malaysian politics. Prime Minister Lee Hsien Loong visited Malaysia in May 2007 for two days of informal talks with Abdullah Badawi. The main outcome of the discussions was a decision to form a joint ministerial committee to oversee collaboration on Malaysia's plan to establish a 2,217-sq-km economic development zone in southern Johor, to be known as the Iskandar Development Region, with both leaders agreeing that outstanding issues of dispute, such as water sales to Singapore and the suspended construction of the Johor Strait bridge, should not be allowed to impede bilateral co-operation in other areas.

In January 1993 Gen. Fidel Ramos visited Malaysia, the first Philippine President to do so since 1968, owing to strained relations over the Philippines' claim to Sabah. Mahathir and Ramos agreed to establish a joint commission to address bilateral problems. In February 1994 Mahathir made the first official visit by a Malaysian head of government to the Philippines. Relations with the Philippines were strained in April 2000, however, when Muslim separatists from the southern Philippines abducted a group of tourists from the Malaysian resort of Sipadan, off the coast of Sabah. Following a similar kidnapping incident in September, the Malaysian Government dispatched an additional 600 troops to the region.

Relations with Indonesia generally improved from the mid-1990s. In June 1996 the two countries agreed on joint measures to limit the flow of illegal workers into Malaysia. Wide-ranging amendments to the Immigration Act in Malaysia in October 1996 failed to halt the flow of illegal immigrants, which was blamed for rising social tensions. The regional economic crisis, which began in mid-1997, led to an increase in illegal immigrants arriving in Malaysia and prompted Malaysia to begin a repatriation programme to Indonesia and elsewhere. Violent protests against deportation took place in detention centres in March 1998. In addition, groups of illegal Indonesian immigrants entered the compounds of several foreign embassies and the office of the UN High Commissioner for Refugees in March and April and requested political asylum to prevent their repatriation to the Indonesian province of Aceh, where they claimed that, as members of secessionist groups, they would be subject to persecution. Some of the immigrants were subsequently granted asylum by Denmark and Norway. In November 2000 Malaysia and Indonesia agreed to intensify border patrols, after four Malaysians were detained by Indonesian police in June of that year for allegedly stealing logs.

Relations with both Indonesia and the Philippines, meanwhile, were strained in 1998 following the arrest in September of the former Malaysian Deputy Prime Minister and Minister of Finance, Anwar Ibrahim: both the President of Indonesia and the President of the Philippines made explicit criticisms of the Malaysian Government regarding its treatment of Anwar. Although the controversy surrounding Anwar's treatment receded as an international issue in 1999, bilateral relations with the Philippines were adversely affected by President Estrada's granting of an audience to Anwar's wife, Wan Azizah Wan Ismail, when she visited the Philippines in April. The new President of Indonesia, Abdurrahman Wahid, demonstrated the close relations between Indonesia and Malaysia by visiting Kuala Lumpur immediately after his election in October 1999.

In August 2001 President Wahid's successor, Megawati Sukarnoputri, visited Malaysia on the final stage of her tour of ASEAN nations. In the same month the new President of the Philippines, Gloria Macapagal Arroyo, also paid her first official visit to the country. However, relations with Indonesia soon threatened to deteriorate again. In 2001 the Government announced that it would deport 10,000 Indonesian illegal immigrants each month in an attempt to tighten controls on foreign labour in the country at a time of economic slowdown. In December 2001 and January 2002 a series of riots by Indonesian labourers led Prime Minister Mahathir to comment that Malaysia might give workers of different nationalities preference in the labour market owing to the problems caused by the illegal immigrants. In late January a temporary ban was imposed on new workers arriving from Indonesia. Soon afterwards the Indonesian Government issued a formal apology for the behaviour of its workers and stated that it hoped that the trouble caused would not affect an otherwise harmonious relationship. Relations with the Philippines were also threatened in November 2001 when the authorities arrested the fugitive Philippine rebel leader, Nur Misuari, on charges of attempting to enter Malaysia illegally. After much indecision, he was finally deported in January 2002 to face trial in Manila (see the chapter on the Philippines). In May Malaysia, Indonesia and the Philippines signed an anti-terrorism pact enabling them to exchange intelligence and to launch joint police operations, in an effort to combat regional terrorist organizations; Thailand and Cambodia also acceded to the pact later in the year. In August the implementation of new legislation requiring that all illegal immigrants leave the country, or face penalties including fines, imprisonment and caning, strained relations with both the Philippines and Indonesia, as the majority of the workers affected were citizens of those countries. In September the Malaysian Government announced that, owing to diplomatic pressure, exacerbated by public protests being held in Indonesia and the Philippines over the apparently inhumane nature of the expulsions, deportations were being temporarily halted. In early 2004 relations with Indonesia were threatened again when the Indonesian Government urged a global boycott of Malaysian timber, following the release of a report alleging that protected trees from Indonesia were being smuggled across the joint border, 'laundered' and re-exported. The Government denied the claims. At the end of October a 17-day amnesty began for illegal migrant workers to leave Malaysia voluntarily without penalty. Thousands of Indonesians had fled to Malaysia since the Indonesian authorities had commenced military operations against separatists in the province of Aceh in May 2003. In November 2004 Malaysia agreed to extend the amnesty until the end of the year in response to disquiet expressed by the Indonesian Government. The amnesty was subsequently further extended following a written request from President Susilo Bambang Yudhoyono of Indonesia, who was concerned at the prospect of an influx of migrants, at a time when the country was still struggling to recover from the devastation caused by a series of tsunamis in late December (which had killed at least 111,000 people in Indonesia and some 68 in Malaysia). None the less, it was reported that around 380,000 of an estimated 1.2m. illegal foreign workers had left Malaysia by the end of January 2005. In mid-February, following talks with President Yudhoyono in Kuala Lumpur, the Malaysian Prime Minister announced that the amnesty would expire at the end of the month, and in March the forced repatriation of illegal immigrants recommenced. Human rights organizations, including Amnesty International, expressed serious misgivings about the standard of training and supervision given to officers of the Malaysian Immigration Department, amid allegations of widespread physical abuse of immigrants. In July 2006 it was estimated by the Minister of Home Affairs, Radzi Sheikh, that approximately 500,000 illegal immigrants were still living in Malaysia. According to the Minister, another major deportation campaign was to be undertaken by the Government. In October 2007 a temporary ban was imposed on Malaysian employers recruiting new workers from Bangladesh, following a series of cases of ill-treatment of migrants, including the abandonment of several thousand at Kuala Lumpur airport. In January 2008 it was reported that the Malaysian Government aimed to reduce the number of foreign workers in the country from some 2.3m. to 1.8m. in 2009, and to 1.5m. by 2015, by introducing stricter regulations on their employment.

In August 2005 the Malaysian Government expressed frustration at the Indonesian authorities' apparent failure adequately to address the recurrent issue of the heavy smoke emanating from forest fires lit by farmers to clear land for crop plantations on the Indonesian island of Sumatra. Owing to the dangerously high levels of air pollution, the Government declared a state of emergency in western and central regions of the country, including Kuala Lumpur.

In 1994 Malaysian and Indonesian officials commenced discussions to resolve their conflicting claims to the sovereignty of Sipadan and Ligitan, two small islands off the coast of Borneo. In October 1996 an agreement was reached by both countries to refer the issue to the International Court of Justice (ICJ, see p. 20). In December 2002 the ICJ ruled that Malaysia would be awarded sovereignty of the islands, thus bringing an end to the dispute. Another territorial claim being pursued through negotiations was the dispute with Singapore over the island of Batu Putih (Pedra Branca). In February 2003 the two countries finally signed a formal agreement referring the dispute to the ICJ. The Court began deliberating its judgment in November 2007, following the conclusion of public hearings on the case. Malaysia is also involved with Brunei, Viet Nam, the People's Republic of China, the Philippines and Taiwan in disputed sovereignty claims over the Spratly Islands in the South China Sea. In November 2002 the ASEAN member states approved a Code of Conduct for the islands; the agreement was also sanctioned by China.

Relations with Thailand were strained at the end of 1995 following the killing by the Malaysian navy of two Thai citizens fishing illegally in Malaysian waters. In December the two countries agreed to establish a committee to resolve a long-standing dispute over fishing rights. In February 1996 relations deteriorated, owing to Thailand's opposition to Malaysia's construction of a 27-km wall (completed in 1997) along its border with Thailand, intended to deter illegal immigration from that country. However, in January 1997 the two countries agreed to co-operate in preventing Bangladeshi migrant workers from entering Malaysia and in expediting the return of illegal Thai workers from Malaysia. The arrest in January 1998 of three Thai Muslim separatists by the Malaysian authorities and their deportation to Thailand demonstrated continued co-operation between the two countries since Malaysia was often regarded as a place of sanctuary for Muslim separatists in southern Thailand. Relations between Malaysia and Thailand were further enhanced in April, when the two countries signed an agreement to share equally the natural gas produced in an offshore area to which both countries had made territorial claims. However, the Thai Minister of Foreign Affairs, Surin Pitsuwan, was amongst a number of international political figures who expressed concern at the arrest and detention of the former Deputy Prime Minister and Minister of Finance, Anwar Ibrahim, in September. In April 2001 the Thai Prime Minister, Thaksin Shinawatra, made his first official visit to the country on a trip intended to enhance co-operative ties. Bilateral talks were also held in January 2002 in an attempt to resolve problems arising from a planned project to build a gas pipeline between the two countries. In January 2004 new Prime Minister Abdullah Badawi visited Thailand for security discussions, following several attacks believed to have been perpetrated by separatists along the Thai side of the joint border. The two countries agreed to co-operate in efforts to bring an end to the violence and began joint border patrols. The Thai Government subsequently announced that it intended to fence off parts of the border, owing to speculation that Muslim separatists thought to be responsible for the violence might be inside Malaysia. Malaysia rejected such suggestions by the Thai Prime Minister. Amid continuing unrest in southern Thailand, Thaksin Shinawatra visited Malaysia in mid-April for further talks with Abdullah Badawi on improving security along the border. In late April Malaysia increased its border security after militants launched a series of attacks on police posts in southern Thailand; the attacks were violently suppressed by the Thai security forces. Security at the border was heightened again in October following renewed clashes in southern Thailand between government troops and Muslim protesters in which 85 people died, many of whom suffocated after being forced into army trucks. Hundreds of Malaysians demonstrated outside the Thai embassy in Kuala Lumpur in protest at the deaths. Bilateral relations were further strained in December, when the Thai Government claimed to have photographic evidence that militants in southern Thailand had received training in the Malaysian state of Kelantan. In January 2005 the Malaysian authorities arrested Abdul Rahman Ahmad, whom Thailand held responsible for organizing the separatist violence in the south. A diplomatic dispute arose between the two countries in October, concerning the fate of 131 Muslim villagers who had fled from the violence-stricken province of Narathiwat, in southern Thailand, to neighbouring Malaysia. The Malaysian authorities insisted that they would not sanction the return of the asylum-seekers to Thailand unless they received a guarantee of their safety from the Thai authorities. One of the villagers, suspected of involvement in a raid on a Thai military camp in January 2004, was subsequently relinquished to the Thai authorities, while the other 130 refugees remained in a Malaysian detention centre in Terengganu. Discussions aimed at resolving the dispute were held in November 2005 between former Prime Minister Mahathir Mohamad and Thai Prime Minister Thaksin Shinawatra; negotiations were also held between Thaksin and Prime Minister Abdullah Badawi in the same month, during the course of the APEC summit meeting in Busan, the Republic of Korea. The ongoing dispute took relations between the two countries to their lowest point in recent years. In February 2006 the Thai Government indicated that it was prepared to cease its attempts to repatriate the villagers and was to allow them to remain in Malaysia. There was some improvement in bilateral relations from October, when Gen. Surayud Chulanont was appointed as Thai Prime Minister following a coup in which Thaksin was ousted from power. Surayud visited Malaysia later that month, holding talks with Abdullah Badawi on the ongoing insurgency in Thailand's southern provinces. An official visit to Thailand by Abdullah Badawi in February 2007 was reciprocated by Surayud in August. In December Abdullah Badawi and Surayud officially opened a new bridge across the Golok River, linking the Malaysian state of Kelantan to the Thai province of Narathiwat, as part of efforts to improve the economy of the border region and, as a consequence, reduce violence.

Malaysia's relations with the People's Republic of China remained extremely cordial, with Malaysia frequently offering public support to China, particularly in response to US criticism. Mahathir paid another of a long series of official visits to China in November 2000, and the Chinese Premier, Zhu Rongji, made an official visit to Malaysia in November 1999. In May 2001 the Yang di-Pertuan Agong paid an official state visit to China at the invitation of the Chinese President, Jiang Zemin.

Malaysia forged closer ties with Japan in December 2005 with the signing of a bilateral free trade agreement, which entered into force in July 2006. Under the terms of the accord, the two countries were to eliminate tariffs on all industrial goods and on most agricultural, forestry and fishery products within a 10-year period. The agreement also covered intellectual property-rights protection, investment rules, competition policies, business facilitation and personnel training. In keeping with the spirit of invigorated relations, the Emperor and Empress of Japan paid a state visit to Malaysia in June 2006, their first official trip to the country since 1991, and Japanese Prime Minister Shinzo Abe visited Malaysia in August 2007, marking the 50th anniversary of the establishment of diplomatic relations between the two countries.

Mahathir's proposal to establish an East Asian Economic Caucus (EAEC), a trade group intended to exclude the USA, met with considerable resistance from the US Government (which continued to promote the US-dominated Asia-Pacific Economic Co-operation forum—APEC, see p. 176) and Australia. In July 1993 ASEAN agreed, despite the continuing reluctance of Japan to participate, that the EAEC should operate as an East Asian interest group within APEC. In November 1999 (although Mahathir was absent owing to the Malaysian general election) the third informal summit meeting of the 10 ASEAN countries and the People's Republic of China, Japan and the Republic of Korea (collectively known as 'ASEAN + 3') took place. At the meeting it was agreed to hold annual East Asian summits of all 13 nations and to strengthen present economic co-operation with the distant aim of forming an East Asian bloc with a common market and monetary union. This ambition was brought closer in April 2001 when, at a meeting of the ASEAN + 3 group, plans were agreed for a network of currency 'swap' arrangements to prevent a repetition of the regional financial crisis of 1997. At the annual ASEAN summit meeting held in Laos in November 2004 it was agreed to transform the ASEAN + 3 summit meeting, which was first held in 1997, into the East Asia summit, with the long-term objective of establishing an East Asian Community. In December 2005 Kuala Lumpur hosted the inaugural East Asia Summit, held during the course of the ASEAN summit meeting. At the first East Asia Summit, which was chaired by the Malaysian Prime Minister, representatives from the participating nations held discussions on a wide range of issues, including international terrorism, maritime security, the threat of avian influenza, trade and development and the promotion of human rights and democracy. It was agreed that the Summit should convene annually; the second meeting was held in Cebu, the Philippines, in January 2007.

In 1999 Mahathir objected to Australia's leadership of the UN-mandated peace-keeping mission in East Timor (now Timor-Leste, following the territory's accession to independence in May 2002), the UN Transitional Administration in East Timor (UNTAET), claiming that an ASEAN-led mission would be more appropriate. However, other ASEAN members were reluctant to assume responsibility for the peace-keeping body and Australia and East Timor both objected to the notion of Malaysia leading transitional arrangements, owing to its close relations with Indonesia. Only after the intervention of the UN Secretary-General did Malaysia finally contribute limited personnel to UNTAET. In February 2001 Malaysia announced that it would open a liaison office in Dili, East Timor, which became an embassy upon the declaration of East Timor as a fully independent state in May 2002.

Malaysia's relations with Australia, which were often strained under Mahathir, appeared to improve following the succession of Abdullah Badawi to the premiership in October 2003. In June 2004, during a visit to Malaysia by the Australian Minister for Foreign Affairs, Alexander Downer, agreement was reached to hold formal annual talks between the two countries' foreign ministers and separate regular consultations between senior security officials. At the same time Prime Minister Abdullah Badawi accepted an invitation to make a state visit to Australia. This took place in April 2005 and was the first by a Malaysian leader in more than 20 years. However, the Malaysian Government had dismissed a plan announced by the Australian Prime Minister, John Howard, in September 2004 to establish specialist counter-terrorist centres in South-East Asia and Australia, complaining that it had not been consulted about the proposal. None the less, formal negotiations on a free trade agreement between Malaysia and Australia commenced in mid-2005.

In July 1997 Mahathir (who was often regarded as the international spokesperson for developing countries) indicated that he might submit a proposal to the UN to review its 1948 Universal Declaration of Human Rights, with regard to the specific priorities of less-developed countries. While this sentiment was supported by many Asian countries, the USA reacted angrily to any suggestion of compromise on the issue of human rights. Relations with the USA were also strained by the involvement of PETRONAS in a consortium that signed an agreement during September 1997 to invest in Iran, in contravention of US sanctions against Iran. In October Mahathir paid a formal visit to Cuba, the first such visit by a Malaysian leader, and urged Malaysian firms to invest in the country, in defiance of US legislation that threatened reprisals against firms conducting business with Cuba. Bilateral relations deteriorated further in the same month following Mahathir's suggestion that the economic crisis in the South-East Asian region was due to hostile Jewish currency speculation aimed at preventing progress among Muslim nations. A resolution tabled by 34 members of the US Congress calling for the withdrawal of the remarks or Mahathir's resignation was condemned by Mahathir and the Malaysian press. Relations with the USA were further strained in 1998 following US condemnation of the detention and treatment of the former Deputy Prime Minister and Minister of Finance, Anwar Ibrahim; the Malaysian Government was particularly angered by a speech delivered at the APEC summit meeting in Kuala Lumpur in November by the US Vice-President, Albert Gore, in which Gore expressed support for the movement for political reform in Malaysia. During a speech to UMNO members in June 1999, Mahathir criticized the influence on the country of non-Malaysians (and, in particular, ethnic Europeans), who Mahathir claimed were attempting to 're-colonize' Malaysia. Relations with the USA were improved following a visit by Adm. Dennis Blair, the Commander-in-Chief of the US Pacific Command, to Kuala Lumpur in January 2001. At his meeting with Mahathir, the first between the Prime Minister and a US Pacific commander, the two countries agreed to extend military co-operation. However, the new US President, George W. Bush, insisted that any further improvement in relations would depend on better treatment for Anwar Ibrahim and other detained members of the Malaysian opposition.

In September 2001 relations with the USA were greatly strengthened when Mahathir moved quickly to condemn attacks on the US mainland thought to have been carried out by the al-Qa'ida terrorist network. However, during a meeting with the US President at an APEC summit meeting in Shanghai in October, Mahathir refused to lend his Government's support to the US-led retaliatory attacks on Afghanistan that had begun earlier that month, voicing his concerns at the large numbers of civilian casualties resulting from the raids. At a meeting of ASEAN leaders in November, Malaysia agreed to co-operate with other member nations in the fight against terrorism. In January 2002 the USA congratulated the Malaysian Government on its demonstration of support for the international coalition against terrorism, following the detention of at least 15 suspected terrorists. However, it demanded assurances that the suspects would receive a fair trial under the ISA. In October it was reported that the US Government had requested that Malaysia be the host for a regional anti-terrorism training centre.

While Mahathir made clear his opposition to the US-led campaign to remove the regime of Saddam Hussain in Iraq in 2003, relations with the USA remained generally stable, owing largely to the Government's ongoing operation against suspected domestic terrorists, which was in line with the global anti-terrorism campaign being pursued by the Bush Administration. However, in October 2003, at a summit meeting of the Organization of the Islamic Conference (OIC, see p. 369) held in Putrajaya, Prime Minister Mahathir attracted criticism from the USA, Israel and several European countries when he attacked what he described as Jewish subjugation of Islamic countries during his opening address to the meeting. The Government later issued an apology for the comments. In early 2004 relations with the USA were threatened when new Prime Minister Abdullah Badawi accused the USA of using unreliable intelligence to implicate Malaysia in a global nuclear smuggling network. (The US Government had alleged that a company owned by the Prime Minister's son had supplied components to the network.) In May the USA welcomed the arrest, under the ISA, of Buhary Syed Abu Tahir, a Sri Lankan businessman resident in Malaysia, for his alleged involvement in the network. Meanwhile, in April the Deputy Prime Minister and Minister of Defence, Najib Razak, rejected a proposal by the Commander-in-Chief of the US Pacific Command, Adm. Thomas Fargo, that US warships should patrol the Strait of Melaka between Malaysia and Indonesia to deter terrorism. In July Malaysia, Indonesia and Singapore commenced co-ordinated patrols of the Strait, a critical maritime trade route through which 50% of the world's oil passes, in an attempt to curb piracy. On his first official visit to the USA as Prime Minister in the same month, Abdullah Badawi offered to consider dispatching a medical team to Iraq. In 2006 Malaysia and the USA began negotiations on the establishment of a free trade agreement, but discussions faltered in early 2007 over disagreements in a number of contentious areas, reported to include government procurement, labour, intellectual property rights and the labelling of genetically modified foodstuffs. Opposition to a free trade agreement came from several quarters in Malaysia, including farmers fearful of competition from US imports and trade unions concerned about the impact on local livelihoods, as well as from US politicians who disapproved of Malaysia's gas agreement with Iran. Negotiations resumed in January 2008, when the US chief negotiator expressed hope that an agreement could be concluded by the middle of the year, prior to the US presidential election in November, although significant differences remained to be resolved.

In December 2006 Prime Minister Abdullah Badawi visited Venezuela. Discussions with President Hugo Chávez resulted in initial agreements in the areas of trade and energy co-operation. Meanwhile, during a meeting in November, Abdullah Badawi and the Chilean President, Michelle Bachelet, agreed to initiate bilateral negotiations on the establishment of a free trade agreement; two sessions of talks were held in 2007.

A speech by the head of the European Commission delegation in Malaysia, Thierry Rommel, in June 2007, in which he criticized policies favouring ethnic Malays, prompted considerable anger among Malaysian leaders, who accused the diplomat of interfering in the internal administration of the country. He was summoned to the Ministry of Foreign Affairs to discuss his remarks.

In June 1997 the inauguration took place of a group that aimed to foster economic co-operation among Muslim developing countries, the Developing-Eight (D-8), comprising Malaysia, Bangladesh, Egypt, Indonesia, Iran, Nigeria, Pakistan and Turkey. Malaysia continued to express its close relationship with Arab countries after it denounced US and British air strikes against Iraq in February 2001, while demanding the removal of UN sanctions. It was hoped that a D-8 agreement on preferential tariffs signed in May 2006 would further strengthen economic relations between the group's members. In November 2007, furthermore, Malaysia and Pakistan signed a bilateral free trade agreement, which entered into force in January 2008.

Government

Malaysia is a federation of 13 states. The capital, Kuala Lumpur, is a separate Federal Territory, as is the island of Labuan and the newly developed administrative capital of Putrajaya. The Head of State, or Supreme Head of Malaysia, is a monarch (Yang di-Pertuan Agong), elected for a five-year term (with a Deputy Head of State) by and from the hereditary rulers of nine of the states. The monarch acts on the advice of Parliament and the Cabinet. Parliament consists of the Dewan Negara (Senate) and the Dewan Rakyat (House of Representatives). The Senate has 70 members, including 44 appointed by the Head of State, four of which are from the Federal Territories, and 26 elected members, two chosen by each of the 13 State Legislative Assemblies. The House of Representatives consists of 222 members (increased from 219 at the March 2008 general election), elected for five years by universal adult suffrage: 165 from Peninsular Malaysia (including 11 from Kuala Lumpur and one from Putrajaya), 31 from Sarawak and 26 from Sabah (including one from Labuan). The Head of State appoints the Prime Minister and, on the latter's recommendation, other ministers. The Cabinet is responsible to Parliament. The country is divided into 137 administrative districts.

Defence

Malaysia participates in the Five-Power Defence Arrangements with Australia, New Zealand, Singapore and the United Kingdom. As assessed at November 2007, the active armed forces totalled 109,000 men: army 80,000 (although it was planned to reduce this to 60,000–70,000), navy 14,000 and air force 15,000. In February 2004 a programme of national service was introduced, initially on an experimental basis, requiring conscripts to perform three months of military service. Reserve forces numbered 51,600 (army 50,000, navy 1,000, air force 600). Paramilitary forces in 2006 included a General Operations Force (formerly the Police Field Force) of 18,000 men and a People's Volunteer Corps with about 240,000 members. Federal budget plans for 2007 allocated RM 13,360m. to defence.

Economic Affairs

In 2006, according to estimates by the World Bank, Malaysia's gross national income (GNI), measured at average 2004–06 prices, was US $141,431m., equivalent to $5,490 per head (or $11,300 per head on an international purchasing-power parity basis). During 1996–2006, it was estimated, the population increased at an annual average of 2.1%, while gross domestic product (GDP) per head increased, in real terms, by an average of 2.1% per year. Overall GDP increased, in real terms, at an average annual rate of 4.2% in 1996–2006. According to Bank Negara Malaysia (BNM) estimates, GDP increased by 5.9% in 2006 and by 6.3% in 2007.

Agriculture (including forestry and fishing) contributed 9.9% of GDP in 2007. The sector engaged 14.6% of the employed labour force in 2006. Malaysia is the world's leading producer of palm oil, exports of which contributed an estimated 5.3% of the value of total merchandise exports in 2007. Other important crops include rice, rubber, cocoa, coconuts, bananas, tea and pineapples. During 1996–2006, according to World Bank figures, agricultural GDP increased, in real terms, at an average annual rate of 2.3%. According to figures from the BNM, agricultural GDP increased by 5.2% in 2006 and by 2.2% in 2007.

Industry (including mining, manufacturing, construction and utilities) contributed 47.2% of GDP in 2007. The sector engaged 30.3% of the employed labour force in 2006. During 1996–2006, according to the World Bank, industrial GDP increased, in real terms, at an average annual rate of 4.2%. According to figures from the BNM, industrial GDP grew by 4.9% in 2006 and by 3.3% in 2007.

Mining contributed 14.3% of GDP in 2007. However, it engaged only 0.4% of the employed labour force in 2006. At the end of 2006 estimated proven gas reserves stood at 2,480,000m. cu m, and petroleum reserves at 4,200m. barrels. Petroleum production in 2006 averaged 747,000 barrels per day from Malaysia's oilfields. Exports of crude petroleum and condensates provided an estimated 5.3% of total export earnings in 2007. Malaysia is one of the world's leading producers of tin. Bauxite, copper, iron, gold and coal are also mined. The GDP of the mining sector increased at an average annual rate of 2.0% in 2000–07, according to figures from the BNM. Mining GDP contracted by 0.4% in 2006, but recovered in 2007 when it increased by 3.2%.

Manufacturing (the largest export sector) contributed 27.8% of GDP in 2007. The manufacturing sector engaged 20.3% of the employed labour force in 2006. The most important branches of manufacturing include electrical machinery and appliances, food products, metals and metal products, non-electrical machinery, transport equipment, rubber and plastic products, chemical products, wood products and furniture. According to figures from the World Bank, during 1996–2006 manufacturing GDP increased, in real terms, at an average annual rate of 5.0%. Manufacturing GDP increased by 7.1% in 2006 and by 3.1% in 2007, according to the BNM.

Energy is derived principally from Malaysia's own reserves of hydrocarbons. The country's dependence on petroleum as a source of electric energy declined from 55.9% in 1990 to 3.3% in 2004. The share contributed by natural gas increased from 22.0% to 61.8% over the same period. In 2004 hydropower and coal accounted for 7.0% and 27.9%, respectively, of the country's electricity output. Production of electricity rose from 96,214m. kWh in 2005 to 100,831m. kWh in 2006. Plans for a controversial 2,400-MW hydroelectric dam at Bakun, in Sarawak, first received government approval in 1986, but construction work has been delayed by various issues; the project was not expected to be completed before 2008. Imports of mineral products comprised 8.0% of the value of merchandise imports in 2005.

The services sector contributed 42.9% of GDP in 2007. It engaged 55.1% of the employed labour force in 2006. Tourism makes a major contribution to the economy. Revenue from this source was reported to have reached more than RM 36m. in 2006. In 2007 tourist arrivals rose to a record 21.0m. In 2007 the financial sector contributed 8.1% of GDP. The GDP of the services sector increased by an average of 4.6% per year in 1996–2006, according to the World Bank. According to the BNM, services GDP grew by 7.4% in 2006 and by 10.1% in 2007.

In 2006 Malaysia recorded a visible trade surplus of US $36,698m., with a surplus of $25,488m. on the current account of the balance of payments. In 2007 the principal sources of imports were Japan, which provided 13.0% of the total, the People's Republic of China (12.9%), Singapore (11.5%) and the USA (10.8%). Other important suppliers included Taiwan, Thailand, and the Republic of Korea. The principal market for exports (purchasing 15.6%) was the USA; other significant purchasers were Singapore (14.6%), Japan (9.1%) and China (8.8%). The principal imports in 2007 were intermediate goods, mainly parts and accessories of capital goods and miscellaneous industrial supplies. The principal exports were electrical machinery and parts (particularly electronic components and semiconductors), chemicals, palm oil, crude petroleum and condensates, and liquefied natural gas.

The 2007 budget envisaged total spending of RM 160,544m. (including net development expenditure of RM 37,460m.). Revenue reached an estimated RM 139,885m., the preliminary budgetary deficit being equivalent to 3.2% of GDP. According to the ADB, at the end of 2007 Malaysia's external debt totalled US $54,525m.; the cost of debt-servicing in that year was equivalent to 3.8% of the value of exports of goods and services. The annual rate of inflation averaged 2.4% in 1995–2005. Consumer prices increased by an average of 3.6% in 2006 and by a further 2.0% in 2007, according to the ADB. The rate of unemployment declined to 3.1% of the labour force in 2007.

Malaysia is a member of the UN Economic and Social Commission for Asia and the Pacific (ESCAP, see p. 35), the Asian Development Bank (ADB, see p. 182), the Association of South East Asian Nations (ASEAN, see p. 185), the Colombo Plan (see p. 411) and Asia-Pacific Economic Co-operation (APEC, see p. 176), all of which aim to accelerate economic progress in the region. In January 1992 the member states of ASEAN agreed to establish a free trade zone, the ASEAN Free Trade Area (AFTA). The original target for the reduction of tariffs to between 0% and 5% was 2008, but this was subsequently advanced to 2003 and then 2002, when AFTA was formally established. However, Malaysia itself was granted a three-year delay in January 2001 for the opening of its politically sensitive automotive industry to the free trade agreements, fearing competition from Thailand; this was subsequently extended until 2008.

The Malaysian economy made a rapid recovery from the regional economic crisis of the late 1990s. Following his appointment as Prime Minister in October 2003, Abdullah Badawi announced his intention to focus on the development of the country's agricultural sector and to prioritize educational reforms. The Ninth Malaysia Plan (2006–10) reiterated the aim of raising the country to the level of a developed nation by 2020. Although urban poverty had been successfully reduced, the incidence of rural poverty stood at 2.9% in 2004. An important aim of the Ninth Plan, therefore, was the eradication of poverty and the reduction of regional disparities. The Plan projected an average annual GDP growth rate of 6% during the 2006–10 period, while increasing Malaysia's global competitiveness through the development of human resources and the improvement of investment and business conditions. Foreign direct investment increased from US $3,967m. in 2005 to $6,047m. in 2006. In 2007 the rate of corporate tax was reduced from 28% (a level at which it had remained since 1988) to 27%, with a reduction of a further 1% planned for 2008. It was hoped that this would facilitate greater inflows of foreign capital. Net foreign direct investment rose by 54.4% in 2007, reaching some $9,400m. Substantial increases in public sector salaries and lower interest rates further stimulated domestic demand, engendering strong growth in most sectors of the economy (particularly services). However, moderate currency appreciation and declining foreign demand somewhat tempered growth in the external sector in 2007: while exports of commodities such as palm oil and petroleum benefited from rising international prices, which notably improved rural per caput incomes, exports of electrical goods (traditionally the strongest sector with regard to foreign sales) increased by just 1.2% in that year. Rising prices for food and fuel were likely to exert greater pressure on the fiscal deficit in 2008, given that subsidies were applied to these goods at retail level. While Malaysia's economy was perceived as being better equipped than that of other countries in the region to withstand the impact of the global credit crisis, real GDP was forecast to increase at a slightly slower rate of 5.0% in 2008.

Education

Under the Malaysian education system, free schooling is provided at government-assisted schools for children between the ages of six and 18 years, although pupils are required to pay fees for public examinations. However, in September 2006 the Government announced that, with effect from the 2007/08 academic year, these charges were to be abolished for all candidates enrolled in government schools. There are also private schools, which receive no government financial aid. Bahasa Malaysia is the main medium of instruction, while English is taught as a second language; Chinese and Tamil are used for instruction only in primary institutions. In January 2003 new legislation came into effect, requiring that all mathematics and science classes in schools be taught in English. Only primary education, which begins at six years of age and lasts for six years, is compulsory. In 2002/03 enrolment in pre-primary education included 75% of the relevant age-group (males 72%; females 79%). In the same year enrolment in primary education included 93.2% of the relevant age-group (males 93%; females 93%). Secondary education, beginning at the age of 12, lasts for seven years, comprising a first cycle of three years and a second of four. Pupils may attend vocational and technical secondary schools instead of the final four years of academic education. In 2002/03 the total enrolment at secondary schools included 75.5% of the relevant age-group (males 71%; females 81%). At January 2004 Malaysia had 48 tertiary institutions, including nine universities and 31 teacher-training colleges; in 1995 total enrolment at tertiary level was equivalent to 12% of the relevant age-group. The Ninth Malaysia Plan for the period 2006–10 proposed the creation of two new universities, in the states of Kelantan and Terengganu.

The federal budget for 2007 allocated a combined sum of RM 25,938.8m. in operating expenditure (23.0% of the total) to the Ministries of Education and of Higher Education. The 2006–10 Plan allocated RM 40,300m. (about 21% of total development expenditure) to the improvement of education and training.

Public Holidays

Each state has its own public holidays, and the following federal holidays are also observed:

2008: 10 January*† (Muharram, Islamic New Year), 7–8 February‡ (Chinese New Year), 20 March* (Mouloud, Prophet Muhammad's Birthday), 1 May (Labour Day), 19 May (Vesak Day), 5 June (Official Birthday of HM the Yang di-Pertuan Agong), 31 August (National Day), 1 October* (Hari Raya Puasa, end of Ramadan), 28 October§ (Deepavali), 8 December* (Hari Raya Haji, Feast of the Sacrifice), 25 December (Christmas Day), 29 December*† (Muharram, Islamic New Year).

2009: 26–27 January‡ (Chinese New Year), 9 March* (Mouloud, Prophet Muhammad's Birthday), 1 May (Labour Day), 2 May (Vesak Day), 5 June (Official Birthday of HM the Yang di-Pertuan Agong), 31 August (National Day), 20 September* (Hari Raya Puasa, end of Ramadan), 18 October§ (Deepavali), 27 November* (Hari Raya Haji, Feast of the Sacrifice), 18 December* (Muharram, Islamic New Year), 25 December (Christmas Day).

* These holidays are dependent on the Islamic lunar calendar and may vary by one or two days from the dates given.

† This festival occurs twice (marking the start of the Islamic years AH 1429 and 1430) within the same Gregorian year.

‡ The first two days of the first moon of the lunar calendar.

§ Except Sabah and Sarawak.

Weights and Measures

The metric system is in force. There is also a local system of weights and measures:

1 cupak = 1 quart (1.1365 litres)
1 gantang = 1 gallon (4.5461 litres)
1 tahil = 11/3 ounces (37.8 grams)
16 tahils = 1 kati = 11/3 lb (604.8 grams)
100 katis = 1 picul = 1331/3 lb (60.48 kg)
40 piculs = 1 koyan = 5,3331/3 lb (2,419.2 kg)

Statistical Survey

Sources (unless otherwise stated): Department of Statistics, Blok C6, Parcel C, Pusat Pentadbiran Kerajaan Persekutuan, 62514 Putrajaya; tel. (3) 88857000; fax (3) 88889248; e-mail jpbpo@stats.gov.my; internet www.statistics.gov.my; Bank Negara Malaysia (Central Bank of Malaysia), Jalan Dato' Onn, PO Box 10922, 50929 Kuala Lumpur; tel. (3) 26988044; fax (3) 26912990; e-mail info@bnm.gov.my; internet www.bnm.gov.my; Departments of Statistics, Kuching and Kota Kinabalu.

Note: Unless otherwise indicated, statistics refer to all states of Malaysia.

Area and Population

AREA, POPULATION AND DENSITY

Area (sq km)	
Peninsular Malaysia	131,686
Sabah (incl. Labuan)	73,711
Sarawak	124,450
Total	329,847*
Population (census results)	
14 August 1991	18,379,655
5–20 July 2000	
Males	11,853,432
Females	11,421,258
Total	23,274,690
Population (official estimate at mid-year)	
2005	26,130,000
2006	26,640,000
2007	27,170,000
Density (per sq km) at mid-2007	82.4

* 127,355 sq miles.

PRINCIPAL ETHNIC GROUPS

(at census of August 1991)*

	Peninsular Malaysia	Sabah†	Sarawak	Total
Malays and other indigenous groups	8,433,826	1,003,540	1,209,118	10,646,484
Chinese	4,250,969	218,233	475,752	4,944,954
Indians	1,380,048	9,310	4,608	1,393,966
Others	410,544	167,790	10,541	588,875
Non-Malaysians	322,229	464,786	18,361	805,376
Total	**14,797,616**	**1,863,659**	**1,718,380**	**18,379,655**

* Including adjustment for underenumeration.
† Including the Federal Territory of Labuan.

Mid-1997 (estimates, '000 persons): Malays 10,233.2; Other indigenous groups 2,290.9; Chinese 5,445.1; Indian 1,541.7; Others 685.7; Non-Malaysians 1,468.9; Total 21,665.5.

MALAYSIA

STATES
(census of 5–20 July 2000)

	Area (sq km)	Population*	Density (per sq km)	Capital
Johor (Johore)	18,987	2,740,625	144.3	Johor Bahru
Kedah	9,425	1,649,756	175.0	Alor Star
Kelantan	15,024	1,313,014	87.4	Kota Baharu
Melaka (Malacca)	1,652	635,791	384.9	Melaka
Negeri Sembilan (Negri Sembilan)	6,644	859,924	129.4	Seremban
Pahang	35,965	1,288,376	35.8	Kuantan
Perak	21,005	2,051,236	97.7	Ipoh
Perlis	795	204,450	257.2	Kangar
Pulau Pinang (Penang)	1,031	1,313,449	1,274.0	George Town
Sabah	73,619	2,603,485	35.4	Kota Kinabalu
Sarawak	124,450	2,071,506	16.6	Kuching
Selangor	7,960	4,188,876	526.2	Shah Alam
Terengganu (Trengganu)	12,955	898,825	69.4	Kuala Terengganu
Federal Territory of Kuala Lumpur	243	1,379,310	5,676.2	—
Federal Territory of Labuan	92	76,067	826.8	Victoria
Total	329,847	23,274,690	70.6	

* Including adjustment for underenumeration.

PRINCIPAL TOWNS
(population at 2000 census)

Kuala Lumpur (capital)*	1,297,526	Kuala Terengganu (Kuala Trengganu)	250,528
Ipoh	566,211	Seremban	246,441
Kelang (Klang)	563,173	Kota Baharu (Kota Bahru)	233,673
Petaling Jaya	438,084	Sandakan	220,000†
Shah Alam	319,612	Taiping‡	183,320
Kuantan	283,041	George Town (Penang)	180,573

* The new town of Putrajaya is now the administrative capital.
† Provisional.
‡ Excluding a part of Pondok Tanjong, which is in the District of Kerian.

Source: Thomas Brinkhoff, *City Population* (internet www.citypopulation.de).

Mid-2007 ('000, incl. suburbs, UN estimates): Kuala Lumpur 1,448; Kelang 956; Johore Bahru 875 (Source: UN, *World Urbanization Prospects: The 2007 Revision*).

BIRTHS AND DEATHS

	Registered live births		Registered deaths	
	Number	Rate (per 1,000)	Number	Rate (per 1,000)
1997	540,486	24.9	97,432	4.5
1998	524,696	23.7	98,219	4.4
1999	554,200	24.4	100,900*	4.4*
2000	569,500	24.5	102,100*	4.4*
2001	n.a.	22.3	n.a.	4.4
2002	n.a.	21.7	n.a.	4.5
2003*	533,600	21.3	113,900	4.5

* Provisional figures.

Sources: Ministry of Health, Kuala Lumpur; UN, *Demographic Yearbook* and *Population and Vital Statistics Report*.

2004: Birth rate 19.1 per 1,000; Death rate 4.5 per 1,000.
2005 (provisional): Birth rate 18.3 per 1,000; Death rate 4.5 per 1,000.
2006 (estimates): Birth rate 18.0 per 1,000; Death rate 4.5 per 1,000.
2007 (estimates): Birth rate 17.6 per 1,000; Death rate 4.4 per 1,000.

Expectation of life (years at birth, official estimates): 74 (males 72; females 76) in 2006.

ECONOMICALLY ACTIVE POPULATION*
(sample surveys, ISIC major divisions, '000 persons aged 15 to 64 years)

	2004	2005	2006
Agriculture, hunting and forestry	1,326.5	1,355.2	1,375.3
Fishing	126.1	115.2	128.2
Mining and quarrying	34.7	36.1	42.0
Manufacturing	2,023.0	1,989.3	2,082.8
Electricity, gas and water	57.9	56.6	75.4
Construction	890.8	904.4	908.9
Wholesale and retail trade; repair of motor vehicles, motorcycles and personal and household goods	1,607.2	1,620.3	1,650.5
Hotels and restaurants	698.2	671.8	721.3
Transport, storage and communications	532.9	544.7	539.7
Financial intermediation	236.1	247.4	242.3
Real estate, renting and business activities	458.5	459.0	508.4
Public administration and defence; compulsory social security	684.3	728.5	674.1
Education	610.7	607.1	600.1
Health and social work	198.2	212.6	223.2
Other community, social and personal service activities	231.3	234.9	247.1
Private households with employed persons	260.9	260.6	254.6
Extra-territorial organizations and bodies	2.2	1.7	1.2
Total employed	9,979.5	10,045.4	10,275.4
Unemployed	n.a.	n.a.	353.6
Total labour force	n.a.	n.a.	10,628.9

* Excluding members of the armed forces.

Source: mostly ILO.

Mid-2005 (estimates in '000): Agriculture, etc. 1,712; Total labour force 11,206 (Source: FAO).

Health and Welfare

KEY INDICATORS

Total fertility rate (children per woman, 2005)	2.8
Under-5 mortality rate (per 1,000 live births, 2005)	12
HIV/AIDS (% of persons aged 15–49, 2005)	0.5
Physicians (per 1,000 head, 2000)	0.70
Hospital beds (per 1,000 head, 2003)	1.89
Health expenditure (2004): US $ per head (PPP)	402.3
Health expenditure (2004): % of GDP	3.8
Health expenditure (2004): public (% of total)	58.8
Access to water (% of persons, 2004)	99
Access to sanitation (% of persons, 2004)	94
Human Development Index (2005): ranking	63
Human Development Index (2005): value	0.811

For sources and definitions, see explanatory note on p. vi.

MALAYSIA   *Statistical Survey*

Agriculture

PRINCIPAL CROPS
('000 metric tons)

	2004	2005	2006
Rice (paddy)	2,264	2,240	2,154
Maize*	72	75	80
Sweet potatoes	27	27	27
Cassava (Manioc)†	382	375	375
Sugar cane*	77	79	90
Coconuts	642*	573†	573†
Oil palm fruit†	69,881	75,650	75,650
Cabbages	35	35	35
Tomatoes	34	35†	35†
Cucumbers and gherkins†	49	52	52
Watermelons†	155	167	167
Bananas†	530	534	534
Pineapples	330*	340†	340†
Papayas†	72	74	74
Coffee (green)	39*	40*	40†
Cocoa beans	33	28	30†
Pepper	20	19	19
Natural rubber	1,169	1,126	1,284

* Unofficial figure(s).
† FAO estimate(s).

Aggregate production ('000 metric tons, may include official, semi-official or estimated data): Total cereals 2,336 in 2004, 2,315 in 2005, 2,234 in 2006; Total oilcrops 74,357 in 2004, 80,357 in 2005, 80,521 in 2006; Total vegetables (incl. melons) 539 in 2004, 554 in 2005, 554 in 2006; Total fruits (excl. melons) 1,305 in 2004, 1,321 in 2005, 1,321 in 2006.

Source: FAO.

LIVESTOCK
('000 head, year ending September)

	2003	2004	2005
Cattle	753	787	801
Buffaloes	133	138	137
Goats	247	264	271
Sheep	115	115	109
Pigs	2,071	2,111	2,168
Chickens*	165,000	180,000	185,000
Ducks*	16,000	16,000	16,000

* FAO estimates.

2006: Figures assumed to be unchanged from 2005 (FAO estimates).

Source: FAO.

LIVESTOCK PRODUCTS
('000 metric tons)

	2003	2004	2005
Cattle meat*	19.7	21.3	21.3
Buffalo meat*	4.3	4.7	4.5
Pig meat	198.1	203.5	205.5
Chicken meat	812.8	877.1	913.7†
Duck meat	81.6†	102.0	105.0*
Cows' milk	35.5	37.7	37.7*
Buffaloes' milk*	7.5	7.5	7.5
Hen eggs	421.3	431.0	442.0*
Other poultry eggs	10.7	11.0	11.0*

* FAO estimate(s).
† Unofficial figure.

2006: Figures assumed to be unchanged from 2005 (FAO estimates).

Source: FAO.

Forestry

ROUNDWOOD REMOVALS
('000 cubic metres, excl. bark)

	2004	2005	2006
Sawlogs, veneer logs and logs for sleepers	23,700*	23,296	21,924*
Other industrial roundwood	672	1,187	582
Fuel wood*	3,119	3,068	3,013
Total	27,491	27,551	25,519

* FAO estimate(s).

Source: FAO.

SAWNWOOD PRODUCTION
('000 cubic metres, incl. railway sleepers)

	2004	2005	2006
Total (all broadleaved)	4,934	5,173	5,129

Source: FAO.

Fishing

('000 metric tons, live weight)

	2003	2004	2005
Capture	1,287.1	1,335.8	1,214.2
Indian scad	79.1	67.3	81.0
Kawakawa	21.1	14.8	16.0
Indian mackerels	124.9	141.6	131.3
Prawns and shrimps	73.2	78.7	53.1
Squids	49.9	52.2	44.3
Aquaculture	167.2	171.3	175.8
Blood cockle	71.1	64.6	59.5
Total catch	1,454.2	1,507.0	1,390.0

Note: Figures exclude crocodiles, recorded by number rather than by weight. The number of estuarine crocodiles caught was: 307 in 2003; 1,450 in 2004; 1,058 in 2005. Also excluded are shells and corals. Catches of turban shells (metric tons, FAO estimates) were: 80 in 2003; 80 in 2004; 80 in 2005. Catches of hard corals (metric tons, FAO estimates) were: 4,000 in 2003; 4,000 in 2004; 4,000 in 2005.

Source: FAO.

Mining

PRODUCTION
(metric tons, unless otherwise indicated)

	2004	2005	2006
Tin-in-concentrates	2,745	2,857	2,398
Bauxite ('000 metric tons)	2	5	92
Iron ore ('000 metric tons)*	664	950	667
Kaolin	326,928	494,511	341,223
Gold (kg)	4,221	4,250	3,497
Hard coal	389,176	789,356	901,801
Crude petroleum ('000 barrels)	279,009	267,720	255,425
Natural gas (million cu m)†	63,165	70,471	70,191
Ilmenite*	61,471	38,196	45,649
Zirconium*	6,886	4,954	1,690

* Figures refer to the gross weight of ores and concentrates.
† Including amount reinjected, flared and lost.

Source: US Geological Survey.

MALAYSIA

Industry

SELECTED PRODUCTS
('000 metric tons, unless otherwise indicated)

	2005	2006	2007*
Canned fish, frozen shrimps/prawns	45.0	41.6	45.5
Palm oil (crude)	14,961	15,881	15,823
Refined sugar	1,411.5	1,460.3	1,597.6
Soft drinks ('000 litres)	563.7	1,424.5	2,138.4
Cigarettes (metric tons)	23,339	22,799	23,723
Woven cotton fabrics (million metres)	157.8	156.2	159.7
Veneer sheets ('000 cu metres)	1,006.1	1,138.9	1,227.4
Plywood ('000 cu metres)	4,553.5	4,923.6	4,941.2
Kerosene and jet fuel	3,149.3	3,419.5	3,306.9
Liquefied petroleum gas	3,390.7	3,437.5	3,807.3
Inner tubes and tyres ('000)	36,327	31,530	34,378
Rubber gloves (million pairs)	19,177.8	20,527.6	20,513.2
Earthen brick and cement roofing tiles (million)	1,319.6	1,265.1	1,054.5
Cement	16,659	19,456	21,910
Iron and steel bars and rods	2,668.2	3,020.6	2,743.9
Television receivers ('000)	10,528.6	7,743.8	5,752.5
Radio receivers ('000)	21,326	24,876	46,471
Semiconductors (million)	16,074	17,440	21,274
Electronic transistors (million)	27,659	29,341	30,960
Integrated circuits (million)	31,846	33,209	32,733
Passenger motor cars ('000)†	423.0	365.6	333.7
Commercial vehicles ('000)†	125.0	95.7	79.6
Motorcycles and scooters ('000)	417.8	446.1	463.4
Electric energy (million kWh)‡	96,214	100,831	n.a.

* Preliminary.
† Vehicles assembled from imported parts.
‡ Source: Asian Development Bank.

Tin (smelter production of primary metal, metric tons): 18,250 in 2003; 33,914 in 2004; 36,924 in 2005; 22,850 in 2006 (Source: US Geological Survey).

Finance

CURRENCY AND EXCHANGE RATES

Monetary Units
100 sen = 1 ringgit Malaysia (RM—also formerly Malaysian dollar).

Sterling, US Dollar and Euro Equivalents (30 November 2007)
£1 sterling = RM 6.9400;
US $1 = RM 3.3585;
€1 = RM 4.9575;
RM 100 = £14.41 = US $29.75 = €20.17.

Exchange Rate
A fixed exchange rate of RM 3.8000 = US $1 was in effect between September 1998 and July 2005. An average annual rate of exchange of RM 3.787 = US $1 was recorded for 2005, and RM 3.668 = US $1 was recorded for 2006.

FEDERAL BUDGET
(RM million)

Revenue	2005	2006	2007*
Tax revenue	80,594	86,630	95,169
Taxes on income and profits	53,543	61,572	69,396
Companies (excl. petroleum)	26,381	26,477	32,149
Individuals	8,649	10,196	11,661
Petroleum	14,566	20,674	20,453
Export duties	2,085	2,362	2,322
Import duties	3,385	2,679	2,424
Excises on goods	8,641	8,577	8,990
Sales tax	7,709	6,532	6,642
Service tax	2,582	2,685	3,013
Others	2,648	2,225	2,380
Other revenue	25,709	36,915	44,716
Total	106,304	123,546	139,885

Expenditure	2005	2006	2007*
Emoluments	25,587	28,522	32,587
Pensions and gratuities	6,809	7,008	8,251
Debt service charges	11,604	12,495	12,911
Domestic	9,875	10,990	11,485
External	1,729	1,506	1,426
Supplies and services	17,984	20,923	23,622
Subsidies	13,387	10,112	10,481
Asset acquisition	1,603	1,949	2,532
Other grants and transfers	20,427	26,294	31,501
Other expenditure	343	391	1,197
Total	97,744	107,694	123,084

* Preliminary.

FEDERAL DEVELOPMENT EXPENDITURE
(RM million)

	2005	2006	2007*
Defence and security	4,803	4,803	5,702
Social services	7,450	9,525	12,893
Education	3,736	5,349	6,271
Health	1,220	1,298	1,496
Housing	1,082	1,347	2,947
Economic services	14,957	17,404	20,116
Agriculture and rural development	2,482	3,999	3,842
Public utilities	1,481	2,244	2,358
Trade and industry	3,221	3,389	4,904
Transport	7,660	7,751	8,500
General administration	3,325	4,076	1,853
Sub-total	30,534	35,807	40,564
Less Loan recoveries	3,250	846	3,105
Total	27,284	34,961	37,460

* Preliminary.

INTERNATIONAL RESERVES
(US $ million at 31 December)

	2004	2005	2006
Gold*	64	59	62
IMF special drawing rights	199	196	214
Reserve position in IMF	776	285	195
Foreign exchange	64,906	69,369	81,724
Total	65,945	69,909	82,195

* Valued at SDR 35 per troy ounce.

Source: IMF, *International Financial Statistics*.

MONEY SUPPLY
(RM million at 31 December)

	2004	2005	2006
Currency outside banks	28,537	30,166	33,500
Demand deposits at commercial banks	84,443	92,695	104,334
Total money (incl. others)	112,980	122,861	137,834

Source: IMF, *International Financial Statistics*.

COST OF LIVING
(Consumer Price Index; base 2000 = 100)

	2003	2004	2005
Food	102.8	105.0	108.8
Beverages and tobacco	111.0	119.7	132.3
Clothing and footwear	93.3	91.6	90.7
Rent and other housing costs, heating and lighting	103.1	104.0	105.3
Furniture, domestic appliances, tools and maintenance	99.2	99.5	101.5
Medical care	107.2	108.7	110.4
Transport and communications	112.3	113.0	118.1
Education and leisure	100.7	100.6	101.1
Other goods and services	103.1	105.0	107.5
All items	104.4	105.9	109.1

MALAYSIA

NATIONAL ACCOUNTS
(RM million at current prices)

Expenditure on the Gross Domestic Product

	2005	2006	2007
Government final consumption expenditure	64,278	68,525	78,878
Private final consumption expenditure	233,305	257,868	295,685
Change in stocks	−1,868	−1,061	−2,179
Gross fixed capital formation	107,185	119,596	139,972
Total domestic expenditure	402,900	444,928	512,356
Exports of goods and services	611,081	669,776	702,905
Less Imports of goods and services	494,530	542,150	573,763
GDP in purchasers' values	519,451	572,555	641,499
GDP at constant 1987 prices	447,818	474,392	504,408

Gross Domestic Product by Economic Activity

	2005	2006	2007
Agriculture, forestry and fishing	43,361	49,865	64,515
Mining and quarrying	73,817	84,544	93,515
Manufacturing	154,740	170,559	181,814
Electricity, gas and water	14,307	15,385	16,397
Construction	15,474	15,471	17,093
Trade	55,298	60,413	69,089
Restaurants and hotels	10,890	12,021	13,841
Transport and storage	18,772	20,142	22,677
Communications	17,119	18,360	19,582
Finance and insurance	44,111	48,476	52,918
Real estate and business services	20,323	22,468	27,628
Government services	34,643	38,208	44,412
Other services	27,538	29,047	30,893
Sub-total	530,393	584,959	654,374
Import duties	6,372	5,659	5,964
Less Financial intermediation services indirectly measured	17,314	18,062	18,840
GDP in purchasers' values	519,451	572,555	641,499

BALANCE OF PAYMENTS
(US $ million)

	2004	2005	2006
Exports of goods f.o.b.	126,817	141,808	160,842
Imports of goods f.o.b.	−99,244	−108,653	−124,144
Trade balance	27,572	33,156	36,698
Exports of services	17,111	19,576	21,831
Imports of services	−19,269	−21,956	−23,720
Balance on goods and services	25,415	30,776	34,809
Other income received	4,329	5,373	8,463
Other income paid	−10,751	−11,691	−13,192
Balance on goods, services and income	18,993	24,457	30,080
Current transfers received	422	299	313
Current transfers paid	−4,335	−4,776	−4,904
Current balance	15,079	19,980	25,488
Direct investment abroad	−2,061	−2,972	−6,043
Direct investment from abroad	4,624	3,966	6,064
Portfolio investment assets	−287	−715	−2,123
Portfolio investment liabilities	8,675	−2,985	5,593
Financial derivatives assets	−1,520	−59	8
Financial derivatives liabilities	1,814	1	21
Other investment assets	−10,756	−4,877	−8,531
Other investment liabilities	4,602	−2,164	−6,883
Net errors and omissions	1,880	−6,555	−6,731
Overall balance	22,050	3,620	6,864

Source: IMF, *International Financial Statistics*.

External Trade

PRINCIPAL COMMODITIES
(RM million)

Imports c.i.f.	2005	2006	2007*
Capital goods†	60,734	65,257	69,996
Intermediate goods	308,335	335,532	358,506
Miscellaneous industrial supplies, processed	87,704	96,471	110,718
Parts and accessories of capital goods (excl. transportation equipment)	163,660	172,047	172,667
Consumption goods	24,600	27,894	28,888
Total (incl. others)‡	434,010	480,773	504,569

Exports f.o.b.	2005	2006	2007*
Palm oil	19,036	21,643	31,983
Crude petroleum and condensates	28,508	30,814	31,880
Liquefied natural gas	20,790	23,285	26,157
Semi-conductors	89,967	93,505	96,471
Electronic components	118,265	127,751	116,978
Consumer electrical products	22,632	19,099	16,469
Industrial and commercial electrical products	28,608	34,489	29,690
Electrical industrial machinery and equipment	20,476	22,844	25,183
Chemicals and chemical products	29,718	32,893	37,421
Metal manufactures	17,157	22,817	26,410
Total (incl. others)	533,788	588,965	605,193

* Preliminary.
† Figures net of re-exports.
‡ Including re-exports.

PRINCIPAL TRADING PARTNERS
(RM million)

Imports c.i.f.	2005	2006	2007
Australia	8,171	8,884	10,203
China, People's Republic	49,880	58,226	64,856
France	5,660	7,696	7,714
Germany	19,265	21,063	23,408
Hong Kong	10,797	12,650	14,676
India	4,164	4,884	7,064
Indonesia	16,566	18,166	21,370
Japan	62,982	63,568	65,495
Korea, Republic	21,604	25,911	24,917
Philippines	12,192	10,640	9,774
Singapore	50,828	56,188	57,920
Taiwan	23,974	26,220	28,706
Thailand	22,889	26,276	26,981
United Kingdom	6,522	6,809	7,264
USA	55,918	60,210	54,678
Total (incl. others)	434,010	480,773	504,569

Exports f.o.b.	2005	2006	2007
Australia	18,042	16,711	20,381
China, People's Republic	35,221	42,660	53,032
France	6,913	7,942	7,351
Germany	11,259	12,774	14,831
Hong Kong	31,205	29,144	27,966
India	14,972	18,783	20,204
Indonesia	12,580	14,916	17,739
Japan	49,918	52,215	55,239
Korea, Republic	17,945	21,291	23,026
Netherlands	17,452	21,429	23,586
Philippines	7,476	7,974	8,736
Singapore	83,333	90,751	88,509
Taiwan	14,813	16,044	16,461
Thailand	28,723	31,177	29,983
United Kingdom	9,470	10,714	9,899
USA	105,033	110,586	94,513
Total (incl. others)	533,788	588,965	605,099

MALAYSIA

Transport

RAILWAYS
(traffic, Peninsular Malaysia only)

	2002	2003	2004
Passenger-km (million)	1,138	1,031	1,152
Freight ton-km (million)	1,073	887	1,017

Source: UN, *Statistical Yearbook*.

ROAD TRAFFIC
(registered motor vehicles at 31 December)

	2000	2001	2002
Passenger cars	4,212,567	4,624,557	5,069,412
Buses and coaches	48,662	49,771	51,158
Lorries and vans	665,284	689,668	713,148
Road tractors	315,687	329,198	345,604
Motorcycles and mopeds	5,356,604	5,609,351	5,842,617

Source: International Road Federation, *World Road Statistics*.

SHIPPING

Merchant Fleet
(registered at 31 December)

	2004	2005	2006
Number of vessels	1,013	1,052	1,101
Total displacement ('000 grt)	6,056.6	5,758.7	6,389.0

Source: Lloyd's Register-Fairplay, *World Fleet Statistics*.

Sea-borne Freight Traffic*
(Peninsular Malaysia, international and coastwise, '000 metric tons)

	2001	2002	2003
Goods loaded	70,092	81,648	87,960
Goods unloaded	68,184	74,460	73,416

* Including transshipments.

Source: UN, *Monthly Bulletin of Statistics*.

CIVIL AVIATION
(traffic on scheduled services)

	2001	2002	2003
Kilometres flown (million)	217	232	247
Passengers carried ('000)	16,107	16,275	16,710
Passenger-km (million)	35,658	36,923	38,415
Total ton-km (million)	5,233	5,345	5,689

Source: UN, *Statistical Yearbook*.

Tourism

TOURIST ARRIVALS BY COUNTRY OF RESIDENCE*

	2005	2006	2007
Brunei	486,344	784,446	1,172,154
China, People's Republic	352,089	439,294	689,293
Indonesia	962,957	1,217,024	1,804,535
Japan	340,027	354,213	367,567
Singapore	9,634,506	9,634,506	10,492,692
Thailand	1,900,590	1,891,921	1,625,698
Total (incl. others)	16,431,055	17,546,863	20,972,822

* Including Singapore residents crossing the frontier by road through the Johore Causeway.

Source: Malaysia Tourism Promotion Board.

Tourism receipts (US $ million, including passenger transport): 6,799 in 2003; 9,181 in 2004; 10,389 in 2005 (Source: World Tourism Organization).

Communications Media

	2004	2005	2006
Telephones ('000 main lines in use)	4,446.3	4,365.6	4,342.1
Mobile cellular telephones ('000 subscribers)	14,611.9	19,545.0	19,463.7
Personal computers ('000 in use)	4,900	4,900	n.a.
Internet users ('000)	9,879.0	11,016.0	11,292.0
Broadband subscribers ('000)	252.5	507.1	897.3

Radio receivers ('000 in use, 1997): 9,100.

Television receivers ('000 in use, 2001): 4,773.

Facsimile machines (estimate, '000 in use): 175.0 in 1998.

Book production (incl. pamphlets, 1999): 5,084 titles (29,040,000 copies in 1996).

Daily newspapers (2004): 35 (average circulation 2,753,000 copies).

Non-daily newspapers (1997): 3 (average circulation 312,000 copies).

Periodicals (1992): 25 titles (average circulation 996,000 copies).

Sources: International Telecommunication Union; UNESCO, *Statistical Yearbook*; UN, *Statistical Yearbook*.

Education

(January 2004, unless otherwise indicated)

	Institutions	Teachers	Students
Primary	7,557	179,622	3,044,797
Secondary	1,962	130,372	2,093,645
Regular	1,751	116,006	1,979,526
Fully residential	53	3,135	29,813
Technical	88	7,224	34,710
Religious	55	3,053	37,732
Special	3	140	884
Special Model	10	688	10,437
Sports*	2	142	912
Tertiary†	48	14,960	210,724
Universities	9	7,823	97,103
Teacher training	31	3,220	46,019
MARA Institute of Technology	1	2,574	42,174

* 2003 figures.
† 1995 figures.

Source: Ministry of Education.

Pre-primary: 9,743 schools (1994); 20,352 teachers (1994); 459,015 pupils (1995) (Source: UNESCO, *Statistical Yearbook*).

Adult literacy rate (UNESCO estimates): 88.7% (males 92.0%; females 85.4%) in 2000 (Source: UNESCO Institute for Statistics).

Directory

The Constitution

The Constitution of the Federation of Malaya became effective at independence on 31 August 1957. As subsequently amended, it is now the Constitution of Malaysia. The main provisions are summarized below.

SUPREME HEAD OF STATE

The Yang di-Pertuan Agong (King or Supreme Sovereign) is the Supreme Head of Malaysia.

Every act of government is derived from his authority, although he acts on the advice of Parliament and the Cabinet. The appointment of a Prime Minister lies within his discretion, and he has the right to refuse to dissolve Parliament even against the advice of the Prime Minister. He appoints the Judges of the Federal Court and the High Courts on the advice of the Prime Minister. He is the Supreme Commander of the Armed Forces. The Yang di-Pertuan Agong is elected by the Conference of Rulers, and to qualify for election he must be one of the nine hereditary Rulers. He holds office for five years or until his earlier resignation or death. Election is by secret ballot on each Ruler in turn, starting with the Ruler next in precedence after the late or former Yang di-Pertuan Agong. The first Ruler to obtain not fewer than five votes is declared elected. The Deputy Supreme Head of State (the Timbalan Yang di-Pertuan Agong) is elected by a similar process. On election the Yang di-Pertuan Agong relinquishes, for his tenure of office, all his functions as Ruler of his own state and may appoint a Regent. The Timbalan Yang di-Pertuan Agong exercises no powers in the ordinary course, but is immediately available to fill the post of Yang di-Pertuan Agong and carry out his functions in the latter's absence or disability. In the event of the Yang di-Pertuan Agong's death or resignation he takes over the exercise of sovereignty until the Conference of Rulers has elected a successor.

CONFERENCE OF RULERS

The Conference of Rulers consists of the Rulers and the heads of the other states. Its prime duty is the election by the Rulers only of the Yang di-Pertuan Agong and his deputy. The Conference must be consulted in the appointment of judges, the Auditor-General, the Election Commission and the Services Commissions. It must also be consulted and concur in the alteration of state boundaries, the extension to the federation as a whole, of Islamic religious acts and observances, and in any bill to amend the Constitution. Consultation is mandatory in matters affecting public policy or the special position of the Malays and natives of Sabah and Sarawak. The Conference also considers matters affecting the rights, prerogatives and privileges of the Rulers themselves.

FEDERAL PARLIAMENT

Parliament has two Houses—the Dewan Negara (Senate) and the Dewan Rakyat (House of Representatives). The Senate has a membership of 70, comprising 26 elected and 44 appointed members. Each state legislature, acting as an electoral college, elects two Senators; these may be members of the State Legislative Assembly or otherwise. The Yang di-Pertuan Agong appoints the other 44 members of the Senate; these include four Senators representing the three Federal Territories—Kuala Lumpur, Labuan and Putrajaya. Members of the Senate must be at least 30 years old. The Senate elects its President and Deputy President from among its members. It may initiate legislation, but all proposed legislation for the granting of funds must be introduced in the first instance in the House of Representatives. All legislative measures require approval by both Houses of Parliament before being presented to the Yang di-Pertuan Agong for the Royal Assent in order to become law. A bill originating in the Senate cannot receive Royal Assent until it has been approved by the House of Representatives, but the Senate has delaying powers only over a bill originating from and approved by the House of Representatives. Senators serve for a period of three years, but the Senate is not subject to dissolution. Parliament can, by statute, increase the number of Senators elected from each state to three. The House of Representatives consists of 219 elected members (see Amendments). Of these, 165 are from Peninsular Malaysia (including 11 from Kuala Lumpur and one from Putrajaya), 28 from Sarawak and 26 from Sabah (including one from Labuan). Members are returned from single-member constituencies on the basis of universal adult franchise. The term of the House of Representatives is limited to five years, after which time a fresh general election must be held. The Yang di-Pertuan Agong may dissolve Parliament before then if the Prime Minister so advises.

THE CABINET

To advise him in the exercise of his functions, the Yang di-Pertuan Agong appoints the Cabinet, consisting of the Prime Minister and an unspecified number of Ministers (who must all be Members of Parliament). The Prime Minister must be a citizen born in Malaysia and a member of the House of Representatives who, in the opinion of the Yang di-Pertuan Agong, commands the confidence of that House. Ministers are appointed on the advice of the Prime Minister. A number of Deputy Ministers (who are not members of the Cabinet) are also appointed from among Members of Parliament. The Cabinet meets regularly under the chairmanship of the Prime Minister to formulate policy.

PUBLIC SERVICES

The Public Services, civilian and military, are non-political and owe their loyalty not to the party in power but to the Yang di-Pertuan Agong and the Rulers. They serve whichever government may be in power, irrespective of the latter's political affiliation. To ensure the impartiality of the service, and its protection from political interference, the Constitution provides for a number of Services Commissions to select and appoint officers, to place them on the pensionable establishment, to determine promotion and to maintain discipline.

THE STATES

The heads of nine of the 13 states are hereditary Rulers. The Ruler of Perlis has the title of Raja, and the Ruler of Negeri Sembilan that of Yang di-Pertuan Besar. The rest of the Rulers are Sultans. The heads of the States of Melaka (Malacca), Pulau Pinang (Penang), Sabah and Sarawak are each designated Yang di-Pertua Negeri and do not participate in the election of the Yang di-Pertuan Agong. Each of the 13 states has its own written Constitution and a single Legislative Assembly. Every state legislature has powers to legislate on matters not reserved for the Federal Parliament. Each State Legislative Assembly has the right to order its own procedure, and the members enjoy parliamentary privilege. All members of the Legislative Assemblies are directly elected from single-member constituencies. The head of the state acts on the advice of the State Government. This advice is tendered by the State Executive Council or Cabinet in precisely the same manner in which the Federal Cabinet tenders advice to the Yang di-Pertuan Agong.

The legislative authority of the state is vested in the head of the state in the State Legislative Assembly. The executive authority of the state is vested in the head of the state, but executive functions may be conferred on other persons by law. Every state has its own Executive Council or Cabinet to advise the head of the state, headed by its Chief Minister (Ketua Menteri in Melaka, Pulau Pinang, Sabah and Sarawak and Menteri Besar in other states), and collectively responsible to the state legislature. Each state in Peninsular Malaysia is divided into administrative districts, each with its District Officer. Sabah is divided into four residencies: West Coast, Interior, Sandakan and Tawau, with headquarters at Kota Kinabalu, Keningua, Sandakan and Tawau, respectively. Sarawak is divided into five Divisions, each in charge of a Resident—the First Division, with headquarters at Kuching; the Second Division, with headquarters at Simanggang; the Third Division, with headquarters at Sibu; the Fourth Division, with headquarters at Miri; the Fifth Division, with headquarters at Limbang.

AMENDMENTS

From 1 February 1974, the city of Kuala Lumpur, formerly the seat of the Federal Government and capital of Selangor State, is designated the Federal Territory of Kuala Lumpur. It is administered directly by the Federal Government and returns five members to the House of Representatives.

In April 1981 the legislature approved an amendment empowering the Yang di-Pertuan Agong to declare a state of emergency on the grounds of imminent danger of a breakdown in law and order or a threat to national security.

In August 1983 the legislature approved an amendment empowering the Prime Minister, instead of the Yang di-Pertuan Agong, to declare a state of emergency.

The island of Labuan, formerly part of Sabah State, was designated a Federal Territory as from 16 April 1984.

The legislature approved an amendment increasing the number of parliamentary constituencies in Sarawak from 24 to 27. The amendment took effect at the general election of 20–21 October 1990. The total number of seats in the House of Representatives, which had increased to 177 following an amendment in August 1983, was thus expanded to 180.

In March 1988 the legislature approved two amendments relating to the judiciary (see Judicial System).

MALAYSIA

In October 1992 the legislature adopted an amendment increasing the number of parliamentary constituencies from 180 to 192. The Kuala Lumpur Federal Territory and Selangor each gained three seats, Johor two, and Perlis, Kedah, Kelantan and Pahang one. The amendment took effect at the next general election (in April 1995).

In March 1993 an amendment was approved that removed the immunity from prosecution of the hereditary Rulers.

In May 1994 the House of Representatives approved an amendment that ended the right of the Yang di-Pertuan Agong to delay legislation by withholding his assent from legislation and returning it to Parliament for further consideration. Under the amendment, the Yang di-Pertuan Agong was obliged to give his assent to a bill within 30 days; if he failed to do so, the bill would, none the less, become law. An amendment was simultaneously approved restructuring the judiciary and introducing a mandatory code of ethics for judges, to be drawn up by the Government.

In 1996 an amendment was approved, increasing the number of parliamentary constituencies from 192 to 193.

In July 2001 an amendment was approved banning all discrimination on grounds of gender.

From 1 February 2001 the city of Putrajaya, formerly part of Selangor State, was designated a Federal Territory.

In 2003 the legislature approved an amendment increasing the number of parliamentary constituencies from 193 to 219. The amendments took effect at the next general election, held in March 2004.

In 2005 an amendment was approved increasing the number of parliamentary constituencies from 219 to 222, following the delineation of additional constituencies in Sarawak. The changes were implemented at the general election of March 2008.

The Government

SUPREME HEAD OF STATE

HM Yang di-Pertuan Agong: HRH Sultan Tuanku MIZAN ZAINAL ABIDIN IBNI AL-MARHUM Sultan MAHMUD (Sultan of Terengganu) (took office 13 December 2006).

Deputy Supreme Head of State

Timbalan Yang di-Pertuan Agong: HRH Tuanku Haji ABDUL HALIM MU'ADZAM SHAH IBNI AL-MARHUM Sultan BADLISHAH (Sultan of Kedah).

THE CABINET
(April 2008)

Prime Minister and Minister of Finance: Dato' Seri ABDULLAH BIN Haji AHMAD BADAWI.
Deputy Prime Minister and Minister of Defence: Dato' Seri NAJIB BIN Tun Haji ABDUL RAZAK.
Minister of Foreign Affairs: Datuk Seri Utama Dr RAIS YATIM.
Minister of Home Affairs and Internal Security: Datuk Seri SYED HAMID BIN SYED JAAFAR ALBAR.
Minister of International Trade and Industry: Tan Sri Dato' Haji MUHYIDDIN BIN MOHD YASSIN.
Minister of Domestic Trade and Consumer Affairs: Dato' SHAHRIR BIN ABDUL SAMAD.
Minister of Transport: Datuk ONG TEE KEAT.
Minister of Energy, Water and Communications: Dato' SHAZIMAN BIN ABU MANSOR.
Minister of Works: Dato' Ir MOHD ZIN BIN MOHAMED.
Minister of Education: Datuk HISHAMMUDDIN Tun HUSSEIN.
Minister of Higher Education: Dato' Seri MOHAMED KHALED BIN NORDIN.
Minister of Information: Dato' AHMAD SHABERY CHEEK.
Minister of Human Resources: Datuk Dr S. SUBRAMANIAM.
Minister of Natural Resources and the Environment: Datuk DOUGLAS UGGAH EMBAS.
Minister of Plantation Industries and Commodities: Datuk PETER CHIN FAH KUI.
Minister of Unity, Arts, Culture and Heritage: Datuk MOHD SHAFIE BIN Haji APDAL.
Minister of Tourism: Dato' Sri AZALINA BINTI Dato' OTHMAN SAID.
Minister of Science, Technology and Innovations: Datuk Dr MAXIMUS JOHNITY ONGKILI.
Minister of Health: Dato' LIOW TIONG LAI.
Minister of Agriculture and Agro-Based Industry: Dato' MUSTAPA BIN MOHAMED.
Minister of Rural and Regional Development: Tan Sri Dato' MUHAMMAD BIN MUHAMMAD TAIB.
Minister of Federal Territories: Dato' Sri Haji ZULHASNAN RAFIQUE.
Minister of Entrepreneur and Co-operative Development: Dato' Haji NOH BIN OMAR.
Minister of Women, Family and Community Development: Dato' Dr NG YEN YEN.
Minister of Finance II: NOR MOHAMED YAKCOP.
Minister of Housing and Local Government: Dato' ONG KA CHUAN.
Minister of Youth and Sports: Dato' ISMAIL SABRI BIN YAAKOB.
Ministers in the Prime Minister's Department: Tan Sri BERNARD GILUK DOMPOK, Dato' Seri MOHAMAD NAZRI BIN ABDUL AZIZ, Dato' AHMAD ZAHID BIN HAMIDI, Datuk MOHD ZAID BIN IBRAHIM, Datuk AMIRSHAM A. AZIZ.

MINISTRIES

Prime Minister's Office (Jabatan Perdana Menteri): Federal Government Administration Center, Bangunan Perdana Putra, 62502 Putrajaya; tel. (3) 88888000; fax (3) 88883444; e-mail ppm@pmo.gov.my; internet www.pmo.gov.my.

Ministry of Agriculture and Agro-Based Industry: Wisma Tani, Lot 4G1, Pusat Pentadbiran Kerajaan Persekutuan, 62624 Putrajaya; tel. (3) 88701000; fax (3) 88701845; e-mail pro@agri.moa.my; internet agrolink.moa.my.

Ministry of Defence (Kementerian Pertahanan): Wisma Pertahanan, Jalan Padang Tembak, 50634 Kuala Lumpur; tel. (3) 26921333; fax (3) 26914163; e-mail cpa@mod.gov.my; internet www.mod.gov.my.

Ministry of Domestic Trade and Consumer Affairs (Kementerian Perdagangan Dalam Negeri Dan Hal Ehwal Pengguna): Lot 2G3, Presint 2, Pusat Pentadbiran Kerajaan Persekutuan, 62623 Putrajaya; tel. (3) 88825500; fax (3) 88825762; e-mail aduan@kpdnhep.gov.my; internet www.kpdnhep.gov.my.

Ministry of Education (Kementerian Pendidikan): Kompleks Kerajaan Persekutuan, Parcel E, Pusat Pentadbiran Kerajaan Persekutuan, 62604 Putrajaya; tel. (3) 88846000; fax (3) 88895235; e-mail webmaster@moe.gov.my; internet www.moe.gov.my.

Ministry of Energy, Water and Communications (Kementerian Tenaga, Air dan Komunikasi): Blok E4–5, Parcel E, Pusat Pentadbiran Kerajaan Persekutuan, 62668 Putrajaya; tel. (3) 88836000; fax (3) 88893712; e-mail webmaster@ktak.gov.my; internet www.ktak.gov.my.

Ministry of Entrepreneur and Co-operative Development (Kementerian Pembangunan Usahawan Dan Koperasi): Lot 2G6, Presint 2, Pusat Pentadbiran Kerajaan Persekutuan, 62100 Putrajaya; tel. (3) 88805000; fax (3) 88805106; e-mail webmaster@mecd.gov.my; internet www.mecd.gov.my.

Ministry of Federal Territories (Kementerian Wilayah Persekutuan): Aras 1–4, Blok 2, Menara PJH, Presint 2, 62100 Putrajaya; tel. (3) 88897888; fax (3) 88889140; e-mail pha@kwp.gov.my; internet www.kwp.gov.my.

Ministry of Finance (Kementerian Kewangan): Kompleks Kementerian Kewangan, Presint 2, Pusat Pentadbiran Kerajaan Persekutuan, 62592 Putrajaya; tel. (3) 88823000; fax (3) 88823893; e-mail pertanyaan@treasury.gov.my; internet www.treasury.gov.my.

Ministry of Foreign Affairs (Kementerian Luar Negeri): Wisma Putra, 1 Jalan Wisma Putra, Presint 2, 62602 Putrajaya; tel. (3) 88874000; fax (3) 88891717; e-mail webmaster@kln.gov.my; internet www.kln.gov.my.

Ministry of Health (Kementerian Kesihatan): Blok E1, Parcel E, Pusat Pentadbiran Kerajaan Persekutuan, 62590 Putrajaya; tel. (3) 88833888; fax (3) 26985964; e-mail csl@moh.gov.my; internet www.moh.gov.my.

Ministry of Higher Education (Kementerian Pengajian Tinggi): Blok E3, Parcel E, Pusat Perbadanan Kerajaan Persekutuan, 62505 Putrajaya; tel. (3) 88835000; fax (3) 88893921; e-mail menteri@mohe.gov.my; internet www.mohe.gov.my.

Ministry of Home Affairs (Kementerian Hal Ehwal Dalam Negeri): Blok D2, Parcel D, Pusat Pentadbiran Kerajaan Persekutuan, 62546 Putrajaya; tel. (3) 88863000; fax (3) 88891613; e-mail azmi@mofa.gov.my; internet www.moha.gov.my.

Ministry of Housing and Local Government (Kementerian Perumahan dan Kerajaan Tempatan): Paras 3–7, Blok K, Pusat Bandar Damansara, 50782 Kuala Lumpur; tel. (3) 20947033; fax (3) 20949720; e-mail menteri@kpkt.gov.my; internet www.kpkt.gov.my.

Ministry of Human Resources (Kementerian Sumber Manusia): Level 6–9, Blok D3, Parcel D, Pusat Pentadbiran Kerajaan Persekutuan, 62530 Putrajaya; tel. (3) 88865000; fax (3) 88892381; e-mail ksm1@mohr.gov.my; internet www.mohr.gov.my.

Ministry of Information (Kementerian Penerangan): 5th Floor, Wisma TV, Angkasapuri, Bukit Putra, 50610 Kuala Lumpur; tel. (3) 22825333; fax (3) 22821255; e-mail webmaster@kempen.gov.my; internet www.kempen.gov.my.

Ministry of International Trade and Industry (Kementerian Perdagangan Antarabangsa dan Industri): Blok 10, Kompleks Pejabat Kerajaan, Jalan Duta, 50622 Kuala Lumpur; tel. (3) 62033022; fax (3) 62012337; e-mail webmiti@miti.gov.my; internet www.miti.gov.my.

Ministry of Natural Resources and the Environment (Kementerian Sumber Asli dan Alam Sekitar): Aras 14, Blok Menara 4G3, Presint 4, Pusat Pentadbiran Kerajaan Persekutuan, 62574 Putrajaya; tel. (3) 88861111; fax (3) 88892672; e-mail adenan@nre.gov.my; internet www.nre.gov.my.

Ministry of Plantation Industries and Commodities (Kementerian Perusahaan Perladangan dan Komoditi): Aras 6–13, Lot 2G4, Presint 2, Pusat Pentadbiran Kerajaan Persekutuan, 62654 Putrajaya; tel. (3) 88803300; fax (3) 88803441; e-mail pybm@kppk.gov.my; internet www.kppk.gov.my.

Ministry of Rural and Regional Development (Kementerian Kemajuan Luar Bandar dan Wilayah): Aras 5–9, Blok D9, Parcel D, Pusat Pentadbiran Kerajaan Persekutuan, 62606 Putrajaya; tel. (3) 88863500; fax (3) 88892104; e-mail info@kplb.gov.my; internet www.rurallink.gov.my.

Ministry of Science, Technology and Innovations: Aras 1–7, Blok C5, Pusat Pentadbiran Kerajaan Persekutuan, 62662 Putrajaya; tel. (3) 88858000; fax (3) 88886070; e-mail pro@mosti.gov.my; internet www.mosti.gov.my.

Ministry of Tourism (Kementerian Pelancongan): Tingkat 17, Menara Dato' Onn, Pusat Dagangan Dunia Putra, 45 Jalan Tun Ismail, 50480 Kuala Lumpur; tel. (3) 26158188; fax (3) 26935884; e-mail enquiries@tourism.gov.my; internet www.tourism.gov.my.

Ministry of Transport (Kementerian Pengangkutan): Aras 4–7, Blok D5, Parcel D, Pusat Pentadbiran Kerajaan Persekutuan, 62616 Putrajaya; tel. (3) 88866000; fax (3) 88891569; e-mail saptuyah@mot.gov.my; internet www.mot.gov.my.

Ministry of Unity, Arts, Culture and Heritage: 16th Floor, TH Perdana Tower, Maju Junction, 1001 Jalan Sultan Ismail, 50694 Kuala Lumpur; tel. (3) 26127600; fax (3) 26935114; e-mail info@heritage.gov.my; internet www.heritage.gov.my.

Ministry of Women, Family and Community Development (Kementerian Pembangunan Wanita, Keluarga dan Masyarakat): Aras 1–6, Blok E, Kompleks Petabat Kerajaan Bukit Perdana, Jalan Dato' Onn, 50515 Kuala Lumpur; tel. (3) 26930095; fax (3) 26934982; e-mail info@kpwkm.gov.my; internet www.kpwkm.gov.my.

Ministry of Works (Kementerian Kerja Raya): Tingkat 5, Blok B, Kompleks Kerja Raya, Jalan Sultan Salahuddin, 50580 Kuala Lumpur; tel. (3) 27111100; fax (3) 27112591; e-mail pro@kkr.gov.my; internet www.kkr.gov.my.

Ministry of Youth and Sports (Kementerian Belia dan Sukan): Lot 4G4, Presint 4, Pusat Pentadbiran Kerajaan Persekutuan, 62570 Putrajaya; tel. (3) 88713333; fax (3) 88888767; e-mail pa_menteri@kbs.gov.my; internet www.kbs.gov.my.

Legislature

PARLIAMENT

Dewan Negara
(Senate)

The Senate has 70 members, of whom 26 are elected. Each State Legislative Assembly elects two members. The Supreme Head of State appoints the remaining 44 members, including four from the three Federal Territories.

President: Dr ABDUL HAMID PAWANTEH.

Dewan Rakyat
(House of Representatives)

The House of Representatives has a total of 222 members: 165 from Peninsular Malaysia (including 11 from Kuala Lumpur and one from the Federal Territory of Putrajaya), 31 from Sarawak and 26 from Sabah (including one from the Federal Territory of Labuan).

Speaker: Tan Sri PANDIKAR AMIN MULIA.

Deputy Speakers: Datuk RONALD KIANDEE, Datuk Dr WAN JUNAIDI TUANKU JAAFAR.

General Election, 8 March 2008

Party	Seats
Barisan Nasional (National Front)	140
United Malays National Organization	79
Malaysian Chinese Association	15
Parti Pesaka Bumiputera Bersatu	14
Parti Rakyat Sarawak	6
Sarawak United People's Party	6
Sabah Progressive Democratic Party	4
United Kadazan People's Organization	3
Sabah Progressive Party	3
Malaysian Indian Congress	3
Parti Bersatu Sabah	3
Parti Gerakan Rakyat Malaysia	2
Parti Bersatu Rakyat Sabah	1
Liberal Democratic Party	1
Parti Keadilan Rakyat	31
Democratic Action Party	28
Parti Islam se Malaysia	23
Total	**222**

The States

JOHOR
(Capital: Johor Bahru)

Sultan: HRH Tuanku MAHMOOD ISKANDAR IBNI AL-MARHUM Sultan ISMAIL.

Menteri Besar: Datuk Haji ABDUL GHANI OTHMAN.

State Legislative Assembly: internet www.johor.gov.my; 56 seats: Barisan Nasional 50; Democratic Action Party 4; Parti Islam se Malaysia 2; elected March 2008.

KEDAH
(Capital: Alor Star)

Sultan: HRH Tuanku Haji ABDUL HALIM MU'ADZAM SHAH IBNI AL-MARHUM Sultan BADLISHAH.

Menteri Besar: AZIZAN ABDUL RAZAK.

State Legislative Assembly: internet www.kedah.gov.my; 36 seats: Parti Islam se Malaysia 16; Barisan Nasional 14; Parti Keadilan Rakyat 4; Democratic Action Party 1; Independent 1; elected March 2008.

KELANTAN
(Capital: Kota Baharu)

Sultan: HRH Tuanku ISMAIL PETRA IBNI AL-MARHUM Sultan YAHAYA PETRA.

Menteri Besar: Tuan Guru Haji Nik ABDUL AZIZ BIN Nik MAT.

State Legislative Assembly: internet www.kelantan.gov.my; 45 seats: Parti Islam se Malaysia 38; Barisan Nasional 6; Parti Keadilan Rakyat 1; elected March 2008.

MELAKA (MALACCA)
(Capital: Melaka)

Yang di-Pertua Negeri: Tan Sri KHALIL YAAKOB.

Ketua Menteri: Datuk WIRA MOHAMED ALI RUSTAM.

State Legislative Assembly: internet www.melaka.gov.my; 28 seats: Barisan Nasional 23; Democratic Action Party 5; elected March 2008.

NEGERI SEMBILAN
(Capital: Seremban)

Yang di-Pertuan Besar: Tuanku JA'AFAR IBNI AL-MARHUM Tuanku ABDUL RAHMAN.

Menteri Besar: Datuk MOHAMAD HASAN.

State Legislative Assembly: 36 seats: Barisan Nasional 21; Democratic Action Party 10; Parti Keadilan Rakyat 4; Parti Islam se Malaysia 1; elected March 2008.

PAHANG
(Capital: Kuantan)

Sultan: HRH Haji AHMAD SHAH AL-MUSTA'IN BILLAH IBNI AL-MARHUM Sultan ABU BAKAR RI'AYATUDDIN AL-MU'ADZAM SHAH.

Menteri Besar: Dato' ADNAN bin YAAKOB.

State Legislative Assembly: Unit Pengurusan Teknologi Maklumat, Pejabat Setiausaha Kerajaan, Negeri Pahang, Tingkat 6, Wisma Sri Pahang, 25503 Kuantan, Pahang Darul Makmur; tel.

MALAYSIA

(9) 5129425; fax (9) 5163490; internet www.pahang.gov.my; 42 seats: Barisan Nasional 37; Democratic Action Party 2; Parti Islam se Malaysia 2; Independent 1; elected March 2008.

PERAK
(Capital: Ipoh)

Sultan: HRH Sultan Tuanku AZLAN MUHIBUDDIN SHAH IBNI AL-MARHUM Sultan YUSUF IZUDDIN GHAFARULLAH SHAH.

Menteri Besar: MOHAMMAD NIZAR JAMALUDDIN.

State Legislative Assembly: Pejabat Setiausaha Kerajaan Negeri Perak, Bangunan Perak Darul Ridzuan, Bahagian Majlis, Jalan Panglima Bukit Gantang Wahab, 30000 Ipoh; tel. (5) 2531957; fax (5) 2414869; e-mail prosuk@perak.gov.my; internet www.perak.gov.my; 59 seats: Barisan Nasional 28; Democratic Action Party 18; Parti Keadilan Rakyat 7; Parti Islam se Malaysia 6; elected March 2008.

PERLIS
(Capital: Kangar)

Raja: HM Tuanku SYED SIRAJUDDIN IBNI AL-MARHUM SYED PUTRA JAMALULLAIL.

Menteri Besar: Datuk Dr MOHAMMAD ISA SABU.

State Legislative Assembly: e-mail sukpls@perlis.gov.my; internet www.perlis.gov.my/webperlis/welcome.html; 15 seats: Barisan Nasional 14; Parti Islam se Malaysia 1; elected March 2008.

PULAU PINANG (PENANG)
(Capital: George Town)

Yang di-Pertua Negeri: HE Datuk ABDUL RAHMAN Haji ABBAS.

Ketua Menteri: LIM GUAN ENG.

State Legislative Assembly: 40 seats: Democratic Action Party 19; Barisan Nasional 11; Parti Keadilan Rakyat 9; Parti Islam se Malaysia 1; elected March 2008.

SABAH
(Capital: Kota Kinabalu)

Yang di-Pertua Negeri: HE Datuk AHMADSHAH ABDULLAH.

Ketua Menteri: Datuk Seri MUSA AMAN.

State Legislative Assembly: Dewan Undangan Negeri Sabah, Aras 4, Bangunan Dewan Undangan Negeri Sabah, Peti Surat 11247, 88813 Kota Kinabalu; tel. (88) 427533; fax (88) 427333; e-mail pejduns@sabah.gov.my; internet www.sabah.gov.my; 60 seats: Barisan Nasional 59; Democratic Action Party 1; elected March 2008.

SARAWAK
(Capital: Kuching)

Yang di-Pertua Negeri: HE Tun Datuk Patinggi Abang Haji MUHAMMED SALAHUDDIN.

Ketua Menteri: Datuk Patinggi Tan Sri Haji ABDUL TAIB BIN MAHMUD.

State Legislative Assembly: Bangunan Dewan Undangan Negeri, Petra Jaya, 93502 Kuching, Sarawak; tel. (82) 441955; fax (82) 440628; e-mail abangof@sarawaknet.gov.my; internet www.dun.sarawak.gov.my; f. 1867; 71 seats: Barisan Nasional 62; Democratic Action Party 6; Parti Keadilan Rakyat 1; Sarawak National Party 1; Independent 1; elected May 2006.

SELANGOR
(Capital: Shah Alam)

Sultan: Tuanku IDRIS SALAHUDDIN ABDUL AZIZ SHAH.

Menteri Besar: Tan Sri Dato' ABDUL KHALID BIN IBRAHIM.

State Legislative Assembly: internet www.selangor.gov.my; 56 seats: Barisan Nasional 20; Parti Keadilan Rakyat 15; Democratic Action Party 13; Parti Islam se Malaysia 8; elected March 2008.

TERENGGANU
(Capital: Kuala Terengganu)

Yang Di-Pertuan Muda (Regent): Tuanku MUHAMMAD ISMAIL Sultan MIZAN ZAINAL ABIDIN.

Menteri Besar: Datuk AHMAD SAID.

State Legislative Assembly: internet www.terengganu.gov.my; 32 seats: Barisan Nasional 24; Parti Islam se Malaysia 8; elected March 2008.

Election Commission

Suruhanjaya Pilihan Raya (SPR): Aras 4–5, Blok C7, Parcel C, Pusat Pentadbiran Kerajaan Persekutuan, 62690 Putrajaya; tel. (3) 88856500; fax (3) 88889117; e-mail spr@spr.gov.my; internet www.spr.gov.my; f. 1957; Chair. Tan Sri Datuk RASHID BIN RAHMAN.

Political Organizations

Barisan Nasional (BN) (National Front): Suites 1–2, 8th Floor, Menara Dato' Onn, Pusat Dagangan Dunia Putra, Jalan Tun Ismail, 50480 Kuala Lumpur; tel. (3) 26920384; fax (3) 26934743; e-mail info@bn.org.my; internet www.bn2008.org.my; f. 1973; the governing multiracial coalition of 14 parties; Chair. Dato' Seri ABDULLAH BIN Haji AHMAD BADAWI; Sec.-Gen. Dato' Datuk Sri MOHAMMED RAHMAT; comprises:

Liberal Democratic Party: Tingkat 1, No. 33, Karamunsing Warehouse, POB 16033, 88868 Kota Kinabalu, Sabah; tel. (88) 218985; fax (88) 240598; e-mail ldpkk@tm.net.my; internet www.ldpsabah.com; f. 1989; Chinese-dominated; Pres. Datuk LIEW VUI KEONG; Sec.-Gen. TEO CHEE KANG.

Malaysian Chinese Association (MCA): Wisma MCA, 8th Floor, 163 Jalan Ampang, POB 10626, 50450 Kuala Lumpur; tel. (3) 21618044; fax (3) 21619772; e-mail info@mca.org.my; internet www.mca.org.my; f. 1949; 1,121,403 mems; Pres. Dato' Seri ONG KA TING; Sec.-Gen. Dato' ONG KA CHUAN.

Malaysian Indian Congress (MIC): Menara Manickavasagam, 6th Floor, 1 Jalan Rahmat, 50350 Kuala Lumpur; tel. (3) 40424377; fax (3) 40427236; e-mail michq@mic.org.my; internet www.mic.org.my; f. 1946; 401,000 mems (1992); Pres. Dato' Seri S. SAMY VELLU; Sec.-Gen. Dr S. SUBRAMANIAM.

Parti Bersatu Rakyat Sabah (PBRS) (United Sabah People's Party): POB 20148, Luyang, Kota Kinabalu, 88761 Sabah; tel. and fax (88) 269282; f. 1994; breakaway faction of PBS; mostly Christian Kadazans; Leader Datuk JOSEPH KURUP.

Parti Bersatu Sabah (PBS) (Sabah United Party): Block M, Lot 4, 2nd and 3rd Floors, Donggongon New Township, 89500 Penampang, Sabah; tel. (88) 702111; fax (88) 718067; e-mail pbshq@pbs-sabah.org; internet www.pbs-sabah.org; f. 1985; multiracial party, left the BN in 1990 and rejoined in Jan. 2002; Pres. Datuk Seri JOSEPH PAIRIN KITINGAN; Sec.-Gen. Datuk RADIN MALLEH.

Parti Gerakan Rakyat Malaysia (GERAKAN) (Malaysian People's Movement): Tingkat 5, Menara PGRM, 8 Jalan Pudu Ulu, Cheras, 56100 Kuala Lumpur; tel. (3) 92876868; fax (3) 92878866; e-mail gerakan@gerakan.org.my; internet www.gerakan.org.my; f. 1968; 300,000 mems; Pres. Tan Sri KOH TSU KOON (acting); Sec.-Gen. CHIA KWANG CHYE.

Parti Pesaka Bumiputera Bersatu (PBB) (United Traditional Bumiputra Party): Lot 401, Jalan Bako, POB 1953, 93400 Kuching, Sarawak; tel. (82) 448299; fax (82) 448294; internet www.bumiputerasarawak.org.my; f. 1983; Pres. Tan Sri Datuk Patinggi Amar Haji ABDUL TAIB MAHMUD; Dep. Pres. Datuk ALFRED JABU AK NUMPANG.

Parti Progresif Penduduk Malaysia (PPP) (People's Progressive Party): 27–29A Jalan Maharajalela, 50150 Kuala Lumpur; tel. (3) 2441922; fax (3) 2442041; e-mail info@ppp.com.my; internet www.ppp.com.my; f. 1953 as Perak Progressive Party; joined the BN in 1972; Pres. Datuk M. KAYVEAS.

Sabah Progressive Party (SAPP) (Parti Maju Sabah): Lot 23, 2nd Floor, Bornion Centre, 88300 Kota Kinabalu, Sabah; tel. (88) 242107; fax (88) 249188; e-mail sappkk@streamyx.com; internet www.sapp.org.my; f. 1994; non-racial; Pres. Datuk YONG TECK LEE; Sec.-Gen. Datuk RICHARD YONG WE KONG.

Sarawak Progressive Democratic Party (SPDP): Lot 4319–4320, Jalan Stapok, Sungai Maong, 93250 Kuching, Sarawak; tel. (82) 311180; fax (82) 311190; f. 2003 by breakaway faction of Sarawak National Party; Pres. Datuk WILLIAM MAWAN ANAK IKOM; Sec.-Gen. Agung Dr JUDSON SAKAI TAGAL.

Sarawak United People's Party (SUPP): 7 Jalan Tan Sri Ong Kee Hui, POB 454, 93710 Kuching, Sarawak; tel. (82) 246999; fax (82) 256510; e-mail supphq@yahoo.com; internet www.supp.org.my; f. 1959; Sarawak Chinese minority party; Pres. Datuk Dr GEORGE CHAN HONG NAM; Sec.-Gen. SIM KHENG HUI.

United Kadazan People's Organization (UPKO): Penampang Service Centre, Km 11, Jalan Tambunan, Peti Surat 420, 89507 Penampang, Sabah; tel. (88) 718182; fax (88) 718180; e-mail n4upko@yahoo.com; internet www.upko.org.my; f. 1994 as the Parti Demokratik Sabah (PDS—Sabah Democratic Party); formed after collapse of PBS Govt by fmr leaders of the party, represents mostly Kadazandusun, Rungus and Murut communities; Pres. Tan Sri BERNARD GILUK DOMPOK.

MALAYSIA

United Malays National Organization (Pertubuhan Kebang-saan Melayu Bersatu—UMNO Baru) (New UMNO): Menara Dato' Onn, 38th Floor, Jalan Tun Ismail, 50480 Kuala Lumpur; tel. (3) 40429511; fax (3) 40412358; e-mail email@umno.net.my; internet www.umno-online.com; f. 1988; replaced the original UMNO (f. 1946), which had been declared an illegal organization, owing to the participation of unregistered branches in party elections in April 1987; Supreme Council of 45 mems; 2.5m. mems; Pres. Dato' Seri ABDULLAH BIN Haji AHMAD BADAWI; Sec.-Gen. (vacant).

Angkatan Keadilan Insan Malaysia (AKIM) (Malaysian Justice Movement): f. 1994 by fmr members of PAS and Semangat '46; Pres. HAMBALI YAZID.

Barisan Alternatif (Alternative Front): Kuala Lumpur; f. June 1999 to contest the general election; opposition electoral alliance originally comprising the PAS, the DAP, the PKN and the PRM; the DAP left in Sept. 2001; the PKN and the PRM merged in 2003 to form the PKR.

Barisan Jama'ah Islamiah Sa-Malaysia (Berjasa) (Pan-Malaysian Islamic Front): Kelantan; f. 1977; pro-Islamic; 50,000 mems; Pres. Dato' Haji WAN HASHIM BIN Haji WAN ACHMED; Sec.-Gen. MAHMUD ZUHDI BIN Haji ABDUL MAJID.

Bersatu Rakyat Jelata Sabah (Berjaya) (Sabah People's Union): Natikar Bldg, 1st Floor, POB 2130, Kota Kinabalu, Sabah; f. 1975; 400,000 mems; Pres. Haji MOHAMMED NOOR MANSOOR.

Democratic Action Party (DAP): 24 Jalan 20/9, 46300 Petaling Jaya, Selangor; tel. (3) 79578022; fax (3) 79575718; e-mail dap.Malaysia@pobox.com; internet www.dapmalaysia.org; f. 1966; main opposition party; advocates multiracial society based on democratic socialism; 12,000 mems; Chair. KARPAL SINGH; Sec.-Gen. LIM GUAN ENG.

Kongres Indian Muslim Malaysia (KIMMA): Kuala Lumpur; tel. (3) 2324759; f. 1977; aims to unite Malaysian Indian Muslims politically; 25,000 mems; Pres. SAMMY VELLU; Sec.-Gen. MOHAMMED ALI BIN Haji NAINA MOHAMMED.

Pakatan Rakyat (People's Alliance): f. 2008; est. following the legislative election; opposition alliance of the PKR, the DAP and PAS.

Parti Hisbul Muslimin Malaysia (Hamim) (Islamic Front of Malaysia): Kota Bahru, Kelantan; f. 1983 as an alternative party to PAS; Pres. Datuk ASRI MUDA.

Parti Ikatan Masyarakat Islam (Islamic Alliance Party): Terengganu.

Parti Islam se Malaysia (PAS) (Islamic Party of Malaysia): 318A Jalan Raja Laut, 50350 Kuala Lumpur; tel. (3) 26925000; fax (3) 26938399; e-mail editor@parti-pas.org; internet www.parti-pas.org; f. 1951; seeks to establish an Islamic state; 700,000 mems; Pres. ABDUL HADI AWANG; Sec.-Gen. KAMARUDDIN JAAFAR.

Parti Keadilan Rakyat (PKR) (People's Justice Party): 110–3 Jalan Tun Sambanthan, 50470 Kuala Lumpur; tel. (3) 22723220; fax (3) 22721220; e-mail contact@partikeadilanrakyat.org; internet www.keadilanrakyat.org; f. 2003 following merger of Parti Keadilan Nasional (PKN) and Parti Rakyat Malaysia (PRM); Pres. Datin Seri Dr WAN AZIZAH WAN ISMAIL; Sec.-Gen. Datuk KAMARUL BAHRIN ABAS.

Persatuan Rakyat Malaysia Sarawak (PERMAS) (Malaysian Sarawak Party): Kuching, Sarawak; f. March 1987 by fmr mems of PBB; Leader Haji BUJANG ULIS.

Sabah Chinese Consolidated Party (SCCP): POB 704, Kota Kinabalu, Sabah; f. 1964; 14,000 mems; Pres. JOHNNY SOON; Sec.-Gen. CHAN TET ON.

Sabah Chinese Party (PCS): Kota Kinabalu, Sabah; f. 1986; Pres. Encik FRANCIS LEONG.

Sarawak National Party (SNAP): 304–305 Bangunan Mei Jun, 1 Jalan Rubber, POB 2960, 93758 Kuching, Sarawak; tel. (82) 254244; fax (82) 253562; internet sarawak-national-party.blogspot.com; f. 1961; deregistered Nov. 2002, but deregistration deferred indefinitely in April 2003 following appeal; Pres. EDWIN DUNDANG BUGAK; Sec.-Gen. STANLEY JUGOL.

Setia (Sabah People's United Democratic Party): Sabah; f. 1994.

Diplomatic Representation

EMBASSIES AND HIGH COMMISSIONS IN MALAYSIA

Afghanistan: 2nd Floor, Wisma Chinese Chamber, 258 Jalan Ampang, 50450 Kuala Lumpur; tel. (3) 42569400; fax (3) 42566400; e-mail consular@afghanembassykl.org; internet www.afghanembassykl.org; Ambassador MOHAMMAD YUNOS FARMAN.

Albania: UBN Tower 10, 31st Floor, Jalan P. Pamlee, 50250 Kuala Lumpur; tel. (3) 20788690; fax (3) 20702285; e-mail albania@streamyx.com; Chargé d'affaires a.i. DILAVER QESJA.

Algeria: 5 Jalan Mesra, off Jalan Damai, 55000 Kuala Lumpur; tel. (3) 21488159; fax (3) 21488154; e-mail enquiries@algerianembassy.org.my; internet www.algerianembassy.org.my; Ambassador AMAR BELANI.

Argentina: Suite 16-03, 16th Floor, Menara Keck Seng, 203 Jalan Bukit Bintang, 55100 Kuala Lumpur; tel. (3) 21441451; fax (3) 21441428; e-mail emsia@pd.jaring.my; Ambassador ALFREDO MORELLI.

Australia: 6 Jalan Yap Kwan Seng, 50450 Kuala Lumpur; tel. (3) 21465555; fax (3) 21415773; e-mail Public-Affairs-KLPR@dfat.gov.au; internet www.australia.org.my; High Commissioner PENNY WILLIAMS.

Austria: Suite 10.01–02, Level 10, Wisma Goldhill 67, Jalan Raja Chulan, 50200 Kuala Lumpur; tel. (3) 20570020; fax (3) 23817168; e-mail kuala-lumpur-ob@bmeia.gv.at; Ambassador Dr DONATUS KOECK.

Azerbaijan: 2nd Floor, Wisma Chinese Chamber, 258 Jalan Ampang, 50450 Kuala Lumpur; tel. (3) 42526800; e-mail azembkl@streamyx.com; Ambassador TAHIR KARIMOV.

Bangladesh: Block 1, Lorong Damai 7, Jalan Damai, 55000 Kuala Lumpur; tel. (3) 21487940; fax (3) 21413381; e-mail bddoot@streamyx.com; internet www.bangladesh-highcomkl.com; High Commissioner M. KHAIRUZZAMAN.

Belgium: Suite 10-02, 10th Floor, Menara Tan & Tan, 207 Jalan Tun Razak, 50400 Kuala Lumpur; tel. (3) 21620025; fax (3) 21620023; e-mail kualalumpur@diplobel.org; internet www.diplomatie.be/kualalumpur; Ambassador FRANK VAN DE CRAEN.

Bosnia and Herzegovina: JKR 854, Jalan Bellamy, 50460 Kuala Lumpur; tel. (3) 21440353; fax (3) 21426025; e-mail hsomun@hotmail.com; Ambassador MUSTAFA MUJEZINOVIĆ.

Brazil: Suite 20-01, 20th Floor, Menara Tan & Tan, 207 Jalan Tun Razak, 50400 Kuala Lumpur; tel. (3) 21711420; fax (3) 21711427; e-mail brazil@po.jaring.my; internet www.brazilembassy.org.my; Chargé d'affaires a.i. CESAR DE PAULA CIDADE.

Brunei: Suite 19-01, 19th Floor, Menara Tan & Tan, 207 Jalan Tun Razak, 50400 Kuala Lumpur; tel. (3) 21612800; fax (3) 2631302; High Commissioner Dato' Paduka Haji ABDUL RAHMAN.

Cambodia: 46 Jalan U Thant, 55000 Kuala Lumpur; tel. (3) 42573711; fax (3) 42571157; e-mail reckl@tm.net.my; Ambassador HRH Samdech Preah ANOCH NORODOM ARUNRASMY.

Canada: 17th Floor, Menara Tan & Tan, 207 Jalan Tun Razak, 50400 Kuala Lumpur; tel. (3) 27183333; fax (3) 27183391; e-mail klmpr@dfait-maeci.gc.ca; internet www.dfait-maeci.gc.ca/kualalumpur; High Commissioner DAVID SUMMERS.

Chile: 8th Floor, West Block, Wisma Selangor Dredging, 142-C Jalan Ampang, Peti Surat 27, 50450 Kuala Lumpur; tel. (3) 21616203; fax (3) 21622219; e-mail eochile@ppp.nasionet.net; Ambassador PATRICIO TORRES.

China, People's Republic: 229 Jalan Ampang, 50450 Kuala Lumpur; tel. (3) 21428495; fax (3) 21414552; e-mail cn@tm.net.my; internet my.china-embassy.org/eng; Ambassador CHENG YONGHUA.

Colombia: Level 28, UOA Centre, 19 Jalan Pinang, 50450 Kuala Lumpur; tel. (3) 21645488; fax (3) 21645487; e-mail emcomal@streamyx.com; internet www.embcolombia.com.my; Ambassador SILVIA CASTAÑO DE GONZÁLEZ.

Croatia: 3 Jalan Menkuang, off Jalan Ru Ampang, 55000 Kuala Lumpur; tel. (3) 42535340; fax (3) 42535217; e-mail kuala-lumpur@mvpei.hr; Ambassador ZELJKO CIMBUR.

Cuba: 10 Lorong Gurney, 54100 Kuala Lumpur; tel. (3) 26911066; fax (3) 26911141; e-mail admin@cubemb.com.my; internet www.cubaemb.com.my; Ambassador CARLOS A. AMORES.

Czech Republic: 32 Jalan Mesra, off Jalan Damai, 55000 Kuala Lumpur; tel. (3) 21427185; fax (3) 21412727; e-mail kualalumpur@embassy.mzv.cz; internet www.mzv.cz/kualalumpur; Ambassador DANA HUNÁTOVÁ.

Denmark: Wisma Denmark, 22nd Floor, 86 Jalan Ampang, 50450 Kuala Lumpur; tel. (3) 20322001; fax (3) 20322012; e-mail kulamb@um.dk; internet www.ambkualalumpur.um.dk; Ambassador BØRGE PETERSEN.

Ecuador: 10th Floor, West Block, Wisma Selangor Dredging, 142C Jalan Ampang, 50450 Kuala Lumpur; tel. (3) 21635078; fax (3) 21635096; e-mail embecua@po.jaring.my; Ambassador MANUEL PESANTES.

Egypt: 12 Jalan Rhu, off Jalan Ampang, 55000 Kuala Lumpur; tel. (3) 42568184; fax (3) 42573515; e-mail egyembkl@tm.net.my; Ambassador HANI ABDEL KADER AHMED SHASH.

Fiji: Level 2, Menara Chan, 138 Jalan Ampang, 50450 Kuala Lumpur; tel. (3) 27323335; fax (3) 27327555; e-mail fhckl@pd.jaring.my; High Commissioner (vacant).

Finland: Wisma Chinese Chamber, 5th Floor, 258 Jalan Ampang, 50450 Kuala Lumpur; tel. (3) 42577746; fax (3) 42577793; e-mail sanomat.kul@formin.fi; internet www.finland.or.my; Ambassador LAURI KORPINEN.

MALAYSIA

France: 192–196 Jalan Ampang, 50450 Kuala Lumpur; tel. (3) 20535500; fax (3) 20535501; e-mail ambassade.kuala-lumpur-amba@diplomatie.gouv.fr; internet www.ambafrance-my.org; Ambassador ALAIN DU BOISPÉAN.

Germany: 26th Floor, Menara Tan & Tan, 207 Jalan Tun Razak, 50400 Kuala Lumpur; tel. (3) 21709666; fax (3) 21619800; e-mail contact@german-embassy.org.my; internet www.kuala-lumpur.diplo.de; Ambassador HERBERT D. JESS.

Ghana: 14 Ampang Hilir, off Jalan Ampang, 55000 Kuala Lumpur; tel. (3) 42526995; fax (3) 42578698; e-mail ghcomkl@tm.net.my; High Commissioner NANA KWADWO SEINTI.

Guinea: 5 Jalan Kedondong, off Jalan Ampang Hilir, 55000 Kuala Lumpur; tel. (3) 42576500; fax (3) 42511500; e-mail mwcnakry@sotelgui.net.gn; Ambassador MOHAMED SAMPIL.

Hungary: Menara Tan & Tan, 10th Floor, Suite 10-04, Jalan Tun Razak, 50400 Kuala Lumpur; tel. (3) 21637914; fax (3) 21637918; e-mail mission.kul@kum.hu; Ambassador TAMÁS TÓTH.

India: 2 Jalan Taman Duta, off Jalan Duta, 50480 Kuala Lumpur; tel. (3) 20933510; fax (3) 20933507; e-mail highcomm@po.jaring.my; internet www.indianhighcommission.com.my; High Commissioner ASHOK K. KANTHA.

Indonesia: 233 Jalan Tun Razak, POB 10889, 50400 Kuala Lumpur; tel. (3) 21452011; fax (3) 21417908; e-mail dubresi_kul@kbrikl.org.my; internet www.kbrikl.org.my; Chargé d'affaires a.i. TATANG B. RAZAK.

Iran: 1 Lorong U Thant Satu, off Jalan U Thant, 55000 Kuala Lumpur; tel. (3) 42514824; fax (3) 42562904; e-mail ir_emb@tm.net.my; internet www.iranembassy.com.my; Ambassador MAHDI KHANDAGHABADI.

Iraq: 2 Jalan Langgak Golf, off Jalan Tun Razak, 55000 Kuala Lumpur; tel. (3) 21480555; fax (3) 21414331; Chargé d'affaires Dr HOSHIAR H. S. DAZAYI.

Ireland: Ireland House, The Amp Walk, 218 Jalan Ampang, POB 10372, 50450 Kuala Lumpur; tel. (3) 21612963; fax (3) 21613427; e-mail info@ireland-embassy.com.my; internet www.ireland-embassy.com.my; Ambassador EUGENE HUTCHINSON.

Italy: 99 Jalan U Thant, 55000 Kuala Lumpur; tel. (3) 42565122; fax (3) 42573199; e-mail embassyit@italy-embassy.org.my; internet www.ambkualalumpur.esteri.it; Ambassador ALESSANDRO BUSACCA.

Japan: 11 Pesiaran Stonor, off Jalan Tun Razak, 50450 Kuala Lumpur; tel. (3) 21427044; fax (3) 21672314; internet www.my.emb-japan.go.jp; Ambassador MASAHIKO HORIE.

Jordan: 2 Jalan Kedondong, off Jalan Ampang Hilir, 55000 Kuala Lumpur; tel. (3) 42521268; fax (3) 42528610; e-mail general@jordanembassy.org.my; internet www.jordanembassy.org.my; Ambassador HASSAN MAHMOUD MOHAMMAD AL-JAWARNEH.

Kazakhstan: 115 Jalan Ampang Hilir, 55000 Kuala Lumpur; tel. (3) 42522999; fax (3) 42523999; e-mail kuala-lumpur@kazembassy.org.my; internet www.kazembassy.org.my; Ambassador MUKHTAR TILEUBERDI.

Kenya: 8 Jalan Taman U Thant, 55000 Kuala Lumpur; tel. (3) 21461163; fax (3) 21451087; e-mail kenya@po.jaring.my; High Commissioner DAVID GACHOKI NJOKA.

Korea, Democratic People's Republic: 4 Jalan Persiaran Madge, off Jalan U Thant, 55000 Kuala Lumpur; tel. (3) 42569913; fax (3) 42569933; Ambassador PAK RYONG YON.

Korea, Republic: Lot 9 and 11, Jalan Nipah, off Jalan Ampang, 55000 Kuala Lumpur; tel. (3) 42512336; fax (3) 42521425; e-mail korem-my@mofat.go.kr; internet mys.mofat.go.kr/eng/index.jsp; Ambassador BONG RYULL-YANG.

Kuwait: 229 Jalan Tun Razak, 50400 Kuala Lumpur; tel. (3) 21410033; fax (3) 21456121; e-mail kuwait@streamyx.com; Ambassador MONTHER BADER SULAIMAN AL-EISSA.

Kyrgyzstan: 10 Lorong Damai 9, 55000 Kuala Lumpur; tel. (3) 21649862; fax (3) 21632024; e-mail kyrgyz@tm.net.my; internet www.kyrgyz.net.my; Ambassador JEENBEK KULUBAEV (designate).

Laos: 12A Persiaran Madge, off Jalan Ampang Hilir, 55000 Kuala Lumpur; tel. (3) 42511118; e-mail embassylao-kualalumpur@hotmail.com; Ambassador Dr BOUNTHEUANG MOUNLASY.

Lebanon: 56 Jalan Ampang Hilir, 55000 Kuala Lumpur; tel. (3) 42516690; fax (3) 42603426; e-mail lebanon@streamyx.com; Ambassador KHALED AL KILANI.

Libya: 6 Jalan Madge, off Jalan U Thant, 55000 Kuala Lumpur; tel. (3) 21411293; fax (3) 21413549; Chargé d'affaires a.i. AHMAD MASAOUD B. ALGHALI.

Luxembourg: Menara Keck Seng Bldg, 16th Floor, 203 Jalan Bukit Bintang, 55100 Kuala Lumpur; tel. (3) 21433134; fax (3) 21433157; e-mail emluxem@po.jaring.my; Chargé d'affaires CHARLES SCHMIT.

Maldives: Suite 07-01, Menara See Hoy Chan, 374 Jalan Tun Razak, 50400 Kuala Lumpur; tel. (3) 21637244; fax (3) 21647244; e-mail mail@maldives.org.my; High Commissioner MIDHATH HILMY.

Mauritius: 17th Floor, West Block, Wisma Selangor Dredging, Jalan Ampang, 50450 Kuala Lumpur; tel. (3) 21411870; e-mail maurhckl@streamyx.com; Chargé d'affaires a.i. D. P. GOKULSING.

Mexico: Suite 22-05, 22nd Floor, Menara Tan & Tan, 207 Jalan Tun Razak, 50400 Kuala Lumpur; tel. (3) 21646362; fax (3) 21640964; e-mail embamex@po.jaring.my; internet www.embamex.org.my; Ambassador JORGE ALBERTO LOZOYA LEGORRETA.

Morocco: Unit 9, 3rd Floor, East Block, Wisma Selangor Dredging, 142B Jalan Ampang, 50450 Kuala Lumpur; tel. (3) 21610701; fax (3) 21623081; e-mail sifmakl@po.jaring.my; Ambassador AHMED AMAZIANE.

Myanmar: 1 Lorong Ru Kedua, off Jalan Ampang Hilir, 55000 Kuala Lumpur; tel. (3) 42560280; fax (3) 42568320; e-mail mekl@tm.net.my; Ambassador U TIN LATT.

Namibia: 11 Jalan Mesra, off Jalan Damai, 55000 Kuala Lumpur; tel. (3) 21433593; e-mail namhckl@streamyx.com; High Commissioner NEVILLE MELVIN GERTZE.

Nepal: Suite 13A-01, 13th Floor, Wisma MCA, 163 Jalan Ampang, 50450 Kuala Lumpur; tel. (3) 21645934; fax (3) 21648659; e-mail mekl_88@streamyx.com; internet www.nepalembassy.com.my; Ambassador RISHIRAJ ADHIKARI.

Netherlands: The Amp Walk, 7th Floor, South Block, 218 Jalan Ampang, POB 10543, 50450 Kuala Lumpur; tel. (3) 21686200; fax (3) 21686240; e-mail kll@minbuza.nl; internet www.netherlands.org.my; Ambassador LODY EMBRECHTS.

New Zealand: Menara IMC, 21st Floor, 8 Jalan Sultan Ismail, 50250 Kuala Lumpur; tel. (3) 20782533; fax (3) 20780387; e-mail nzhckl@po.jaring.my; High Commissioner DAVID KERSEY.

Nigeria: 85 Jalan Ampang Hilir, 55000 Kuala Lumpur; tel. (3) 42517843; fax (3) 42524302; e-mail chancerykl@nigeria.org.my; internet www.nigeria.org.my; High Commissioner Dr WAHAB OLASEINDE DOSUNMU.

Norway: Suite CD, 53rd Floor, Empire Tower, Jalan Tun Razak, 50400 Kuala Lumpur; tel. (3) 21750300; fax (3) 21750308; e-mail emb.kualalumpur@mfa.no; internet www.norway.org.my; Ambassador ARILD BRAASTAD.

Oman: 6 Jalan Langgak Golf, off Jalan Tun Razak, 55000 Kuala Lumpur; tel. (3) 21452827; e-mail omanemb@po.jaring.my; Ambassador AFLAH BIN SULEIMAN ALTAEI.

Pakistan: 132 Jalan Ampang, 50450 Kuala Lumpur; tel. (3) 21618877; fax (3) 21645958; e-mail pahickl@gmail.com; internet www.pahickl.com; High Commissioner Maj.-Gen. (retd) TAHIR MAHMUD QAZI.

Papua New Guinea: 46 Jalan U Thant, 55000 Kuala Lumpur; tel. (3) 42575405; fax (3) 42576203; High Commissioner PETER P. MAGINDE.

Peru: Wisma Selangor Dredging, 6th Floor, South Block, 142A Jalan Ampang, 50450 Kuala Lumpur; tel. (3) 21633034; fax (3) 21633039; e-mail embperu@streamyx.com; Ambassador ALEJANDRO GORDILLO FERNÁNDEZ.

Philippines: 1 Changkat Kia Peng, 50450 Kuala Lumpur; tel. (3) 21484233; fax (3) 21483576; e-mail consular@philembassykl.org.my; internet www.philembassykl.org.my; Ambassador VICTORIANO M. LECAROS.

Poland: POB 10052, 50704 Kuala Lumpur; tel. (3) 42576733; fax (3) 42570123; e-mail info@ambasada.com.my; internet www.kualalumpur.polemb.net; Ambassador EUGENIOSZ SAWICKI.

Qatar: 113 Jalan Ampang Hilir, POB 13118, 55000 Kuala Lumpur; tel. (3) 42565552; fax (3) 42565553; e-mail qekll13@streamyx.com; Ambassador ABDULHAMEED MUBARAK AL-KUBAISI.

Romania: 114 Jalan Damai, off Jalan Ampang, 55000 Kuala Lumpur; tel. (3) 21423172; fax (3) 21448713; e-mail roemb@streamyx.com; Ambassador PETRU PETRA.

Russia: 263 Jalan Ampang, 50450 Kuala Lumpur; tel. (3) 42567252; fax (3) 42576091; e-mail ruemvvl@tm.net.my; internet www.malaysia.mid.ru; Ambassador ALEXANDER A. KARCHAVA.

Saudi Arabia: Level 4, Wisma Chinese Chamber, 258 Jalan Ampang, 50450 Kuala Lumpur; tel. (3) 42579433; fax (3) 42578751; e-mail saembssy@tm.net.my; Ambassador MOHAMMED REDA HUSSEIN ABU AL-HAMAYEL.

Senegal: 9 Lorong U Thant, off Jalan U Thant, 55000 Kuala Lumpur; tel. (3) 42567343; fax (3) 42563205; e-mail senamb_mal@yahoo.fr; Ambassador ABDEL KADER PIERRE FALL.

Singapore: 209 Jalan Tun Razak, 50400 Kuala Lumpur; tel. (3) 21616277; fax (3) 21616343; e-mail singhc_kul@sgmfa.gov.sg; internet www.mfa.gov.sg/kl; High Commissioner T. JASUDASEN.

Slovakia: 11 Jalan U Thant, 55000 Kuala Lumpur; tel. (3) 21150016; fax (3) 21150014; e-mail slovemb@tm.net.my; Ambassador MILAN LAJČIAK.

MALAYSIA

South Africa: Menara HLA, Suite 22-01, 3 Jalan Kia Peng, 50450 Kuala Lumpur; tel. (3) 21688663; fax (3) 21643742; e-mail sahcadm@streamyx.com; High Commissioner S. NGOMBANE.

Spain: 200 Jalan Ampang, 50450 Kuala Lumpur; tel. (3) 21484868; fax (3) 21424582; e-mail embespmy@mail.mae.es; Ambassador JOSÉ RAMÓN BARAÑANO FERNÁNDEZ.

Sri Lanka: 12 Jalan Keranji Dua, off Jalan Kedondong, Ampang Hilir, 55000 Kuala Lumpur; tel. (3) 42568987; fax (3) 42532497; e-mail slhicom@streamyx.com; internet www.slhc.com.my; High Commissioner (vacant).

Sudan: 2A Persiaran Ampang, off Jalan Ru, 55000 Kuala Lumpur; tel. (3) 42569104; fax (3) 42568107; e-mail assalamiz@hotmail.com; Ambassador ABDEL RAHMAN HAMZAH ELRAYA.

Swaziland: Suite 22-03 and 03 (A), Menara Citibank, 165 Jalan Ampang, 50450 Kuala Lumpur; tel. (3) 21632511; fax (3) 21633326; e-mail swazi@tm.net.my; High Commissioner MPUMELELO J. N. HLOPE.

Sweden: Wisma Angkasa Raya, 6th Floor, 123 Jalan Ampang, 50450 Kuala Lumpur; tel. (3) 20522550; fax (3) 21486325; e-mail ambassaden.kuala-lumpur@foreign.ministry.se; internet www.swedenabroad.se/kualalumpur; Ambassador HELENA SÅNGELAND.

Switzerland: 16 Persiaran Madge, 55000 Kuala Lumpur; tel. (3) 21480622; fax (3) 21480935; e-mail kua.vertretung@eda.admin.ch; internet www.eda.admin.ch/kualalumpur; Ambassador URS STEMMLER.

Syria: Suite 23-03, 23rd Floor, Menara Tan & Tan, 207 Jalan Tun Razak, 50400 Kuala Lumpur; tel. (3) 21634110; fax (3) 21634199; internet www.syrianembassy.com.my; Ambassador LAMIA MERIE AASI.

Thailand: 206 Jalan Ampang, 50450 Kuala Lumpur; tel. (3) 21488222; fax (3) 21486573; e-mail thaikl@pop1.jaring.my; internet www.mfa.go.th/web/1830.php?depcode=23000100; Ambassador PIYAWAT NIYOMRERKS.

Timor-Leste: 62 Jalan Ampang Hilir, 55000 Kuala Lumpur; tel. (3) 42562046; fax (3) 42562016; e-mail embaixada_tl_kl@yahoo.com; Ambassador JUVÊNCIO DE JESUS MARTINS.

Turkey: 118 Jalan U Thant, 55000 Kuala Lumpur; tel. (3) 42572225; fax (3) 42572227; e-mail turkbe@tm.net.my; Ambassador BARLAS OZENER.

Ukraine: Suite 22-02, 22nd Floor, Menara Tan & Tan, 207 Jalan Tun Razak, 50400 Kuala Lumpur; tel. (3) 21669552; fax (3) 21664371; e-mail emb_my@mfa.gov.ua; internet www.mfa.gov.ua/malaysia; Ambassador OLEKSANDR SHEVCHENKO.

United Arab Emirates: 1 Gerbang Ampang Hilir, off Persiaran Ampang Hilir, 55000 Kuala Lumpur; tel. (3) 42535221; fax (3) 42535220; e-mail uaemal@tm.net.my; Ambassador NASSER SALMAN ALABOODI.

United Kingdom: 185 Jalan Ampang, 50450 Kuala Lumpur; tel. (3) 21702200; fax (3) 21702303; e-mail political.kualalumpur@fco.gov.uk; internet www.britain.org.my; High Commissioner BOYD MCCLEARY.

USA: 376 Jalan Tun Razak, POB 10035, 50400 Kuala Lumpur; tel. (3) 21685000; fax (3) 21422207; e-mail klconsular@state.gov; internet www.usembassymalaysia.org.my; Ambassador JAMES R. KEITH.

Uruguay: 6th Floor, UBN Tower, 10 Jalan P. Ramlee, 50250 Kuala Lumpur; tel. (3) 20313669; fax (3) 20315669; e-mail urukuala@streamyx.com; Ambassador PABLO SADER.

Uzbekistan: Suite 6-03, 6th Floor, North Block The Ampang Walk, 218 Jalan Ampang, 50450 Kuala Lumpur; tel. (3) 21618100; e-mail uzbekemb@streamyx.com; Ambassador AYBEK KHASANOV.

Venezuela: Suite 20-05, 20th Floor, Menara Tan & Tan, 207 Jalan Tun Razak, 50400 Kuala Lumpur; tel. (3) 21633444; fax (3) 21636819; e-mail venezuela@po.jaring.my; internet www.embavenezmalasia.org; Ambassador MANUEL ANTONIO GUZMAN HERNÁNDEZ.

Viet Nam: 4 Jalan Persiaran Stonor, 50450 Kuala Lumpur; tel. (3) 21484036; fax (3) 21483270; e-mail daisevn@putra.net.my; internet www.mofa.gov.vn/vnemb.my; Ambassador HOANG TRONG LAP.

Yemen: 7 Jalan Kedondong, off Jalan Ampang Hilir, 55000 Kuala Lumpur; tel. (3) 42511793; fax (3) 42511794; e-mail info@yemenembassykl.com; internet yemenembassykl.com; Ambassador Dr ABDULLA MOHAMED ALI AL-MONTSER.

Zimbabwe: 124 Jalan Sembilan, Taman Ampang Utama, 68000 Ampang, Selangor Darul Ehsan; tel. (3) 42516779; fax (3) 42517252; e-mail zhck@tm.net.my; Ambassador LUCAS PANDE TAVAYA.

Judicial System

The two High Courts, one in Peninsular Malaysia and the other in Sabah and Sarawak, have original, appellate and revisional jurisdiction as the federal law provides. Above these two High Courts is the Court of Appeal, which was established in 1994; it is an intermediary court between the Federal Court and the High Court. When appeals to the Privy Council in the United Kingdom were abolished in 1985 the former Supreme Court became the final court of appeal. Therefore, at that stage only one appeal was available to a party aggrieved by the decision of the High Court. Hence, the establishment of the Court of Appeal. The Federal Court (formerly the Supreme Court) has, to the exclusion of any other court, jurisdiction in any dispute between states or between the Federation and any state; and has special jurisdiction as to the interpretation of the Constitution. The Federal Court is headed by the Chief Justice (formerly the Lord President); the other members of the Federal Court are the President of the Court of Appeal, the two Chief Judges of the High Courts and the Federal Court Judges. Members of the Court of Appeal are the President and the Court of Appeal judges, and members of the High Courts are the two Chief Judges and their respective High Court judges. All judges are appointed by the Yang di-Pertuan Agong on the advice of the Prime Minister, after consulting the Conference of Rulers. In 1993 a Special Court was established to hear cases brought by or against the Yang di-Pertuan Agong or a Ruler of State (Sultans).

The Sessions Courts, which are situated in the principal urban and rural centres, are presided over by a Sessions Judge, who is a member of the Judicial and Legal Service of the Federation and is a qualified barrister or a Bachelor of Law from any of the recognized universities. Their criminal jurisdiction covers the less serious indictable offences, excluding those that carry the death penalty. Civil jurisdiction of a Sessions Court is up to RM 250,000. The Sessions Judges are appointed by the Yang di-Pertuan Agong.

The Magistrates' Courts are also found in the main urban and rural centres and have both civil and criminal jurisdiction, although of a more restricted nature than that of the Sessions Courts. The Magistrates consist of officers from the Judicial and Legal Service of the Federation. They are appointed by the State Authority in which they officiate on the recommendation of the Chief Judge.

There are also Syariah (Shariah) courts for rulings under Islamic law. In July 1996 the Cabinet announced that the Syariah courts were to be restructured with the appointment of a Syariah Chief Judge and four Court of Appeal justices, whose rulings would set precedents for the whole country.

Prior to February 1995 trials in the High Courts for murder and kidnapping were heard with jury and assessors, respectively. The amendment to the Criminal Procedure Code abolished both the jury and the assessors systems, and all criminal trials in the High Courts are heard by a judge sitting alone. In 1988 an amendment to the Constitution empowered any federal lawyer to confer with the Attorney-General to determine the courts in which any proceedings, excluding those before a Syariah court, a native court or a court martial, be instituted, or to which such proceedings be transferred.

Federal Court of Malaysia
Palace of Justice, Presint 3, 62506 Putrajaya; tel. (3) 88803500; internet www.kehakiman.gov.my.

Chief Justice of the Federal Court: Dato' ABDUL HAMID BIN Haji MOHAMAD.

President of the Court of Appeal: Tan Sri Dato' ZAKI BIN TUN AZMI.

Chief Judge of the High Court in Peninsular Malaysia: Dato' ALAUDDIN BIN Dato' MOHD SHERIFF.

Chief Judge of the High Court in Sabah and Sarawak: Tan Sri Datuk Seri RICHARD MALANJUM.

Attorney-General: ABDUL GANI PATAIL.

Religion

Islam is the established religion. Whilst freedom of religious practice is enshrined in the Constitution, Malaysia's parallel Islamic judicial system holds great sway over the Muslim majority on religious issues. In May 2005 21 members of the controversial sect known as 'Sky Kingdom' were arrested for propagating 'devious' teachings said to humiliate Islam. Almost all ethnic Malays are Muslims, representing 60.4% of the total population in 2000. In that year 19.2% of the population followed Buddhism, 9.1% followed Christianity and 6.3% followed Hinduism.

Malaysian Consultative Council of Buddhism, Christianity, Hinduism, Sikhism and Taoism (MCCBCHST): 8 Jalan Duku, off Jalan Kasipillai, 51200 Kuala Lumpur; tel. (3) 40414669; fax (3) 40444304; f. 1981; a non-Muslim group.

MALAYSIA

ISLAM

President of the Majlis Islam: Datuk Haji MOHD FAUZI BIN Haji ABDUL HAMID (Kuching, Sarawak).

Istitut Kefahaman Islam Malaysia (IKIM) (Institute of Islamic Understanding Malaysia): 2 Langgak Tunku, off Jalan Duta, 50480 Kuala Lumpur; tel. (3) 62010889; fax (3) 62014189; internet www.ikim.gov.my.

Jabatan Kemajuan Islam Malaysia (JAKIM) (Department of Islamic Development Malaysia): Aras 4–9, Blok D7, Pusat Pentadbiran Kerajaan Persekutuan, 62519 Putrajaya; tel. (3) 88864000; e-mail faizal@islam.gov.my; internet www.islam.gov.my.

BUDDHISM

Malaysian Buddhist Association (MBA): MBA Bldg, 182 Jalan Burmah, 10050 Pinang; tel. (4) 2262690; fax (4) 2263024; e-mail email@mba.net.my; internet www.mba.net.my; f. 1959; the national body for Chinese-speaking monks and nuns and temples from the Mahayana tradition; 9 state brs and 23 other brs nation-wide; 27,115 mems; Pres. Ven. CHEK HUANG.

Buddhist Missionary Society Malaysia (BMSM): 123 Jalan Berhala, off Jalan Tun Sambanthan, 50470 Kuala Lumpur; tel. (3) 22730150; fax (3) 22740245; e-mail president@bmsm.org.my; internet www.bmsm.org.my; f. 1962 as Buddhist Missionary Society; Pres. ANG CHOO HONG.

Buddhist Tzu-Chi Merit Society (Malaysia): 24 Jesselton Ave, 10450 Pinang; e-mail mtzuchi@po.jaring.my; internet www.tzuchi.org.my.

Malaysian Fo Kuang Buddhist Association: 2 Jalan SS3/33, Taman University, 47300 Petaling Jaya, Selangor; tel. (3) 78776512; fax (3) 78776511; e-mail myfoguang@yahoo.com.

Sasana Abhiwurdhi Wardhana Society: 123 Jalan Berhala, off Jalan Tun Sambanthan, 50490 Kuala Lumpur; f. 1894; the national body for Sri Lankan Buddhists belonging to the Theravada tradition.

Young Buddhist Association of Malaysia (YBAM): 9 Jalan SS25/24, 47301 Petaling Jaya, Selangor; tel. (3) 78049154; fax (3) 78049021; e-mail ybam@streamyx.com; internet www.ybam.org.my; f. 1970; Pres. GOH TAY HOCK.

CHRISTIANITY

Majlis Gereja-Gereja Malaysia (Council of Churches of Malaysia): 26 Jalan Universiti, 46200 Petaling Jaya, Selangor; tel. (3) 7567092; fax (3) 7560353; e-mail cchurchm@streamyx.org; internet www.ccmalaysia.org; f. 1947; 18 mem. churches; 10 associate mems; Pres. Right Rev. Tan Sri Dr LIM CHENG EAN (Anglican Bishop of West Malaysia); Gen. Sec. Rev. Dr HERMEN SHASTRI.

The Anglican Communion

Malaysia comprises three Anglican dioceses, within the Church of the Province of South East Asia.

Primate: Most Rev. Datuk YONG PING CHUNG (Bishop of Sabah).

Bishop of Kuching: Rt Rev. MADE KATIB, Bishop's House, POB 347, 93704 Kuching, Sarawak; tel. (82) 240187; fax (82) 426488; e-mail bkg@pc.jaring.my; has jurisdiction over Sarawak, Brunei and part of Indonesian Kalimantan (Borneo).

Bishop of Sabah: Most Rev. Datuk YONG PING CHUNG, Rumah Bishop, Jalan Tangki, POB 10811, 88809 Kota Kinabalu, Sabah; tel. (88) 247008; fax (88) 245942; e-mail pcyong@pc.jaring.my.

Bishop of West Malaysia: Rt. Rev. Tan Sri Dr LIM CHENG EAN, Bishop's House, 16 Jalan Pudu Lama, 50200 Kuala Lumpur; tel. (3) 20312728; fax (3) 20313213; e-mail diocese@tm.net.my.

The Baptist Church

Malaysia Baptist Convention: 2 Jalan 2/38, 46000 Petaling Jaya, Selangor; tel. (3) 77823564; fax (3) 77833603; e-mail mbcpj@tm.net.my; Chair. Dr TAN ENG LEE.

The Methodist Church

Methodist Church in Malaysia: 69 Jalan 5/31, 46000 Petaling Jaya, Selangor; tel. (3) 79541811; fax (3) 79541787; e-mail bishop@methodistchurch.org.my; internet www.methodistchurch.org.my; 140,000 mems; Bishop Dr HWA YUNG.

The Presbyterian Church

Presbyterian Church in Malaysia: Joyful Grace Church, Jalan Alsagoff, 82000 Pontian, Johor; tel. (7) 711390; fax (7) 324384; Pastor TITUS KIM KAH TECK.

The Roman Catholic Church

Malaysia comprises two archdioceses and six dioceses. At 31 December 2005 approximately 3.2% of the population were adherents.

Catholic Bishops' Conference of Malaysia, Singapore and Brunei
Xavier Hall, 133 Jalan Gasing, 46000 Petaling Jaya, Selangor Darul Ehsan; tel. and fax (3) 79581371; e-mail cbcmsb@pc.jaring.my; Pres. Most Rev. NICHOLAS CHIA YECK JOO (Archbishop of Singapore).

Archbishop of Kuala Lumpur: Most Rev. MURPHY NICHOLAS XAVIER PAKIAM, Archbishop's House, 528 Jalan Bukit Nanas, 50250 Kuala Lumpur; tel. (3) 20788828; fax (3) 20313815; e-mail mpakiam@pd.jaring.my.

Archbishop of Kuching: Most Rev. JOHN HA TIONG HOCK, Archbishop's Office, 118 Jalan Tun Abang Haji Openg, POB 940, 93718 Kuching, Sarawak; tel. (82) 242634; fax (82) 425724; e-mail abcofku@pd.jaring.my.

BAHÁ'Í FAITH

Spiritual Assembly of the Bahá'ís of Malaysia: 4 Lorong Titiwangsa 5, off Jalan Pahang, 53200 Kuala Lumpur; tel. (3) 40233000; fax (3) 40226277; e-mail nsa-sec@bahai.org.my; internet www.bahai.org.my; f. 1964; mems resident in 800 localities.

The Press

PENINSULAR MALAYSIA DAILIES

English Language

Business Times: Balai Berita 31, Jalan Riong, 59100 Kuala Lumpur; tel. (3) 22822628; fax (3) 22825424; e-mail bt@nstp.com.my; internet www.btimes.com.my; f. 1976; morning; Editor ZAINUL ARIFIN; circ. 15,000.

The Edge: G501–G801, Levels 5–8, Block G, Phileo Damansara I, Jalan 16/11, off Jalan Damansara, 46350 Petaling Jaya, Selangor; tel. (3) 76603838; fax (3) 76608638; e-mail eeditor@bizedge.com; internet www.theedgedaily.com; f. 1996; weekly, with daily internet edition; business and investment news; Editor-in-Chief HO KAY TAT.

Malay Mail: Balai Berita 31, Jalan Riong, 59100 Kuala Lumpur; tel. (3) 22822829; fax (3) 22849133; e-mail malaymail@nstp.com.my; internet www.mmail.com.my; f. 1896; afternoon; Editor AHIRUDIN ATTAN; circ. 75,000.

Malaysiakini: 48 Jalan Kemuja, Bangsar Utama, 59000 Kuala Lumpur; tel. (3) 22835567; fax (3) 22892579; e-mail enquiries@malaysiakini.com; internet www.malaysiakini.com; f. 1999; Malaysia's first online newspaper; English and Malay; Editor STEVEN GAN.

New Straits Times: Balai Berita 31, Jalan Riong, 59100 Kuala Lumpur; tel. (3) 22823322; fax (3) 22821434; e-mail mailed@nstp.com.my; internet www.nst.com.my; f. 1845; morning; Group Editor-in-Chief Datuk HISHAMUDDIN AUN; circ. 190,000.

The Star: 13 Jalan 13/6, 46200 Petaling Jaya, POB 12474, Selangor; tel. (3) 7581188; fax (3) 7551280; e-mail msd@thestar.com.my; internet www.thestar.com.my; f. 1971; morning; Group Chief Editor NG POH TIP; circ. 192,059.

The Sun: Sun Media Corpn Sdn Bhd, Lot 6, Jalan 51/217, Section 51, 46050 Petaling Jaya, Selangor Darul Ehsan; tel. (3) 77846688; fax (3) 77835871; e-mail editor@thesundaily.com; internet www.thesundaily.com; f. 1993; free tabloid newspaper in print and online formats; Group Editor-in-Chief HO KAY TAT; Editor CHONG CHENG HAI; circ. 82,474.

Chinese Language

Chung Kuo Pao (China Press): 80 Jalan Riong, 59100 Kuala Lumpur; tel. (3) 2828208; fax (3) 2825327; f. 1946; Editor POON CHAU HUAY; Gen. Man. NG BENG LYE; circ. 210,000.

Guang Ming Daily: 19 Jalan Semangat, 46200 Petaling Jaya, Selangor; tel. (3) 7582888; fax (3) 7575135; licence suspended for two weeks in Feb. 2006 following the publication's reprinting of controversial cartoons depicting the Prophet Muhammad; Editor-in-Chief YE NING; circ. 87,144.

Kwong Wah Yit Poh: 19 Jalan Presgrave, 11300 Pinang; tel. (4) 2612312; fax (4) 2610510; e-mail editor@kwongwah.com.my; internet www.kwongwah.com.my; f. 1910; morning; Chief Editor WONG KWAN CHEUNG; circ. 100,000.

Nanyang Siang Pau (Malaysia): 1st Floor, 1 Jalan SS7/2, 47301 Petaling Jaya, Selangor; tel. (3) 78726829; fax (3) 78726800; e-mail info@nanyang.com; internet www.nanyang.com.my; f. 1923; morning and evening; Editor-in-Chief CHENG KHEE CHIEN; circ. 180,000 (daily), 220,000 (Sunday).

Shin Min Daily News: 31 Jalan Riong, Bangsar, 59100 Kuala Lumpur; tel. (3) 2826363; fax (3) 2821812; f. 1966; morning; Editor-in-Chief CHENG SONG HUAT; circ. 82,000.

Sin Chew Jit Poh (Malaysia): 19 Jalan Semangat, POB 367, Jalan Sultan, 46200 Petaling Jaya, Selangor; tel. (3) 7582888; fax (3)

MALAYSIA

7570527; internet www.sinchew-i.com; f. 1929; morning; Chief Editor LIEW CHEN CHUAN; circ. 227,067 (daily), 230,000 (Sunday).

Malay Language

Berita Harian: Balai Berita, 31 Jalan Riong, 59100 Kuala Lumpur; tel. (3) 22822323; fax (3) 22822425; e-mail bh@bharian.com.my; internet www.bharian.com.my; f. 1957; morning; Group Editor Datuk HISHAMUDDIN AUN; circ. 350,000.

Mingguan Perdana: 48 Jalan Siput Akek, Taman Billion, Kuala Lumpur; tel. (3) 619133; Group Chief Editor KHALID JAFRI.

Utusan Malaysia: 46M Jalan Lima, off Jalan Chan Sow Lin, 55200 Kuala Lumpur; tel. (3) 2217055; fax (3) 2220911; e-mail corpcomm@utusan.com.my; internet www.utusan.com.my; Editor ABDUL AZIZ ISHAK; circ. 239,385.

Watan: 23-1 Jalan 9A/55A, Taman Setiawangsa, 54200 Kuala Lumpur; tel. (3) 4523040; fax (3) 4523043; circ. 80,000.

Tamil Language

Malaysia Nanban: 1544-3 Batu Complex, off Jalan Ipoh, Batu 3 1/4, 51200 Kuala Lumpur; e-mail accounts@nanban.com.my; tel. (3) 62515981; fax (3) 62515986; circ. 45,000; Dir AHMAD MYDIN Dato' SIKANDAR BATCHA.

Tamil Nesan: 28 Jalan Yew, Pudu, 55100 Kuala Lumpur; tel. (3) 2216411; fax (3) 2210448; f. 1924; morning; Editor V. VIVEKANANTHAN; circ. 35,000 (daily), 60,000 (Sunday).

Tamil Thinamani: 9 Jalan Murai Dua, Batu Kompleks, off Jalan Ipoh, Kuala Lumpur; tel. (3) 66719; Editor S. NACHIAPPAN; circ. 18,000 (daily), 39,000 (Sunday).

SUNDAY NEWSPAPERS
English Language

New Sunday Times: Balai Berita 31, Jalan Riong, 59100 Kuala Lumpur; tel. (3) 2822328; fax (3) 2824482; e-mail news@nstp.com.my; f. 1931; morning; Group Editor Datuk HISHAMUDDIN AUN; circ. 191,562.

Sunday Mail: Balai Berita 31, Jalan Riong, 59100 Kuala Lumpur; tel. (3) 2822328; fax (3) 2824482; e-mail smail@nstp.com.my; f. 1896; morning; Editor JOACHIM S. P. NG; circ. 75,641.

Sunday Star: 13 Jalan 13/6, 46200 Petaling Jaya, POB 12474, Selangor Darul Ehsan; tel. (3) 7581188; fax (3) 7551280; f. 1971; Editor DAVID YEOH; circ. 232,790.

Malay Language

Berita Minggu: Balai Berita 31, Jalan Riong, 59100 Kuala Lumpur; tel. (3) 2822328; fax (3) 2824482; e-mail bharian@bharian.com.my; f. 1957; morning; Editor Dato' AHMAD NAZRI ABDULLAH; circ. 421,127.

Metro Ahad: Balai Berita 31, Jalan Riong, 59100 Kuala Lumpur; tel. (3) 22822328; fax (3) 22821482; e-mail metahad@nstp.com.my; internet www.nstp.com.my/Corporate/nstp/products/productMetroAhd.htm; f. 1995; morning; circ. 136,974.

Mingguan Malaysia: 11A The Right Angle, Jalan 14/22, 46100 Petaling Jaya; tel. (3) 7563355; fax (3) 7577755; f. 1964; Editor MOHD HASSAN MOHD NOOR; circ. 543,232.

Utusan Zaman: 11A The Right Angle, Jalan 14/22, 46100 Petaling Jaya; tel. (3) 7563355; fax (3) 7577755; f. 1939; Editor MUSTAFA FADULA SUHAIMI; circ. 11,782.

PENINSULAR MALAYSIA PERIODICALS
English Language

Her World: Berita Publishing Sdn Bhd, Balai Berita 31, Jalan Riong, 59100 Kuala Lumpur; tel. (3) 2824322; fax (3) 2828489; monthly; Editor ALICE CHEE LAN NEO; circ. 35,000.

Malaysia Warta Kerajaan Seri Paduka Baginda (HM Government Gazette): Percetakan Nasional Malaysia Berhad, Jalan Chan Sow Lin, 50554 Kuala Lumpur; tel. (3) 92212022; fax (3) 92220690; e-mail pnmb@po.jaring.my; fortnightly.

Malaysian Agricultural Journal: Ministry of Agriculture and Agro-based Industry, Publications Unit, Wisma Tani, Jalan Sultan Salahuddin, 50624 Kuala Lumpur; tel. (3) 2982011; fax (3) 2913758; f. 1901; 2 a year.

Malaysian Forester: Forestry Department Headquarters, Jalan Sultan Salahuddin, 50660 Kuala Lumpur; tel. (3) 26988244; fax (3) 26925657; e-mail skthai@forestry.gov.my; f. 1931; quarterly; Editor THAI SEE KIAM.

The Planter: Wisma ISP, 29–33 Jalan Taman U Thant, POB 10262, 50708 Kuala Lumpur; tel. (3) 21425561; fax (3) 21426898; e-mail isphq@tm.net.my; internet www.isp.org.my/index.php?id=4; f. 1919; publ. by Isp Management (M); monthly; Editor Tuan Haji DAUD Haji AMATZIN; circ. 4,000.

Young Generation: 11A The Right Angle, Jalan 14/22, 46100 Petaling Jaya, Selangor; tel. (3) 7563355; fax (3) 7577755; monthly; circ. 50,000.

Chinese Language

Mister Weekly: 2A Jalan 19/1, 46300 Petaling Jaya, Selangor; tel. (3) 7562400; fax (3) 7553826; f. 1976; weekly; Editor WONG AH TAI; circ. 25,000.

Mun Sang Poh: 472 Jalan Pasir Puteh, 31650 Ipoh; tel. (5) 3212919; fax (5) 3214006; bi-weekly; circ. 77,958.

New Life Post: 80M Jalan SS21/39, Damansara Utama, 47400 Petaling Jaya, Selangor; tel. (3) 7571833; fax (3) 7181809; f. 1972; bi-weekly; Editor LOW BENG CHEE; circ. 231,000.

New Tide Magazine: Nanyang Siang Pau Bldg, 2nd Floor, Jalan 7/2, 47301 Petaling Jaya, Selangor; tel. (3) 76202118; fax (3) 76202131; e-mail newtidemag@hotmail.com; f. 1974; monthly; Editor NELLIE OOI; circ. 39,000.

Malay Language

Dewan Masyarakat: Dewan Bahasa dan Pustaka, Jalan Wisma Putra, POB 10803, 50926 Kuala Lumpur; tel. (3) 2481011; fax (3) 2484211; f. 1963; monthly; current affairs; Editor ZULKIFLI SALLEH; circ. 48,500.

Dewan Pelajar: Dewan Bahasa dan Pustaka, Jalan Wisma Putra, POB 10803, 50926 Kuala Lumpur; tel. (3) 2481011; fax (3) 2484211; f. 1967; monthly; children's; Editor ZALEHA HASHIM; circ. 100,000.

Dewan Siswa: POB 10803, 50926 Kuala Lumpur; tel. (3) 2481011; fax (3) 2484208; monthly; circ. 140,000.

Gila-Gila: 38-1, Jalan Bangsar Utama Satu, Bangsar Utama, 59000 Kuala Lumpur; tel. (3) 22824970; fax (3) 22824967; fortnightly; circ. 70,000.

Harakah: Jabatan Penerangan dan Penyelidikan PAS, 28A Jalan Pahang Barat, Off Jalan Pahang, 53000 Kuala Lumpur; tel. (3) 40213343; fax (3) 40212422; e-mail hrkh@pc.jaring.my; internet www.harakahdaily.net; two a month; organ of the Parti Islam se Malaysia; Editor ZULKIFLI SULONG.

Jelita: Berita Publishing Sdn Bhd, 16–20 Jalan 4/109E, Desa Business Park, Taman Desa, off Jalan Klang Lama, 58100 Kuala Lumpur; tel. (3) 76208111; fax (3) 76208114; e-mail jelita@beritapub.com.my; internet www.beritapublishing.com.my; monthly; fashion and beauty magazine; Editor ROHANI PA' WAN CHIK; circ. 80,000.

Mangga: 11A The Right Angle, Jalan 14/22, 46100 Petaling Jaya, Selangor; tel. (3) 7563355; fax (3) 7577755; monthly; circ. 205,000.

Mastika: 11A The Right Angle, Jalan 14/22, 46100 Petaling Jaya, Selangor; tel. (3) 7563355; fax (3) 7577755; monthly; illustrated magazine; Editor AZIZAH ALI; circ. 15,000.

Utusan Radio dan TV: 11A The Right Angle, Jalan 14/22, 46100 Petaling Jaya, Selangor; tel. (3) 7563355; fax (3) 7577755; fortnightly; Editor NORSHAH TAMBY; circ. 115,000.

Wanita: 11A The Right Angle, Jalan 14/22, 46100 Petaling Jaya, Selangor; tel. (3) 7563355; fax (3) 7577755; monthly; women; Editor NIK RAHIMAH HASSAN; circ. 85,000.

Punjabi Language

Navjiwan Punjabi News: 52 Jalan 8/18, Jalan Toman, 46050 Petaling Jaya, Selangor; tel. (3) 7565725; f. 1950; weekly; Assoc. Editor TARA SINGH; circ. 9,000.

SABAH DAILIES

Api Siang Pau (Kota Kinabalu Commercial Press): 24 Lorong Dewan, POB 170, Kota Kinabalu; f. 1954; morning; Chinese; Editor Datuk LO KWOCK CHUEN; circ. 3,000.

Borneo Mail (Nountan Press Sdn Bhd): 1 Jalan Bakau, 1st Floor, off Jalan Gaya, 88999 Kota Kinabulu; tel. (88) 238001; fax (88) 238002; English; circ. 14,610.

Daily Express: News House, 16 Jalan Pasar Baru, POB 10139, 88801 Kota Kinabalu; tel. (88) 256422; fax (88) 238611; e-mail sph@tm.net.my; internet www.dailyexpress.com.my; f. 1963; morning; English, Bahasa Malaysia and Kadazan; Editor-in-Chief SARDATHISA JAMES; circ. 30,000.

Hwa Chiaw Jit Pao (Overseas Chinese Daily News): News House, 16 Jalan Pasar Baru, POB 10139, 88801 Kota Kinabalu; tel. (88) 256422; e-mail sph@tm.net.my; internet www.dailyexpress.com.my; f. 1936; morning; Chinese; Editor HII YUK SENG; circ. 30,000.

Merdeka Daily News: Lot 56, BDC Estate, Mile 1½ North Road, POB 332, 90703 Sandakan; tel. (89) 214517; fax (89) 275537; e-mail merkk@tm.net.my; f. 1968; morning; Chinese; Editor-in-Chief FUNG KON SHING; circ. 8,000.

New Sabah Times: Jalan Pusat Pembangunan Masyarakat, off Jalan Mat Salleh, 88100 Kota Kinabalu; POB 20119, 88758 Kota

MALAYSIA   Directory

Kinabalu; tel. (88) 230055; fax (88) 231155; internet www.newsabahtimes.com.my; English, Malay and Kadazan; Editor-in-Chief EDDY LOK; circ. 30,000.

Syarikat Sabah Times: Kota Kinabalu; tel. (88) 52217; f. 1952; English, Malay and Kadazan; circ. 25,000.

Tawau Jih Pao: POB 464, 1072 Jalan Kuhara, Tawau; tel. (89) 72576; Chinese; Editor-in-Chief STEPHEN LAI KIM YEAN.

SARAWAK DAILIES

Berita Petang Sarawak: Lot 8322, Lorong 7, Jalan Tun Abdul Razak, 93450 Kuching; POB 1315, 93726 Kuching; tel. (82) 480771; fax (82) 489006; f. 1972; evening; Chinese; Chief Editor HWANG YU CHAI; circ. 12,000.

Borneo Post: 40 Jalan Tuanku Osman, POB 20, 96000 Sibu; tel. (84) 332055; fax (84) 321255; internet www.borneopost.com.my; morning; English; Man. Dir LAU HUI SIONG; Editor NGUOI HOW YIENG; circ. 60,000.

International Times: Lot 2215, Jalan Bengkel, Pending Industrial Estate, POB 1158, 93724 Kuching; tel. (82) 482215; fax (82) 480996; e-mail news@intimes.com; internet www.intimes.com.my; f. 1968; morning; Chinese; Editor LEE FOOK ONN; circ. 37,000.

Malaysia Daily News: 7 Island Rd, POB 237, 96009 Sibu; tel. (84) 330211; tel. (84) 320540; f. 1968; morning; Chinese; Editor WONG SENG KWONG; circ. 22,735.

Sarawak Tribune and Sunday Tribune: Lot 231, Jalan Abell Utara, 93100 Kuching; tel. (82) 424411; fax (82) 415024; internet www.sarawaktribune.com.my; f. 1945; English; licence suspended indefinitely in Feb. 2006; Editor (vacant); circ. 29,598.

See Hua Daily News: 40 Jalan Tuanku Osman, POB 20, 96000 Sibu; tel. (84) 332055; fax (84) 321255; f. 1952; morning; Chinese; Man. Editor LAU HUI SIONG; circ. 80,000.

United Daily News: internet www.uniteddaily.com.my; f. 2004 following merger between Chinese Daily News and Miri Daily News; morning; Chinese; Dep. Publr WONG KEH HUONG; circ. 35,000.

SARAWAK PERIODICALS

Pedoman Rakyat: Malaysian Information Dept, Mosque Rd, 93612 Kuching; tel. (82) 240141; f. 1956; monthly; Malay; Editor SAIT BIN HAJI YAMAN; circ. 30,000.

Pemberita: Malaysian Information Services, Mosque Rd, 93612 Kuching; tel. (82) 247231; internet www.penerangan.gov.my; f. 1950; every 2 months; Iban; Editor PHILIP NYARU BUNDAK; circ. 20,000.

Sarawak Gazette: Sarawak Museum, Jalan Tun Abang Haji Openg, 93566 Kuching; tel. (82) 244232; fax (82) 246680; e-mail museum@po.jaring.my; f. 1870; 2 a year; English; Chief Editor Datu Haji SALLEH SULAIMAN.

Utusan Sarawak: Lot 231, Jalan Nipah, off Jalan Abell Utara, POB 138, 93100 Kuching; tel. (82) 424411; fax (82) 415024; internet www.utusansarawak.com.my; f. 1949; Malay; Editor Haji ABDUL AZIZ Haji MALIM; circ. 32,292.

NEWS AGENCY

Bernama (Malaysian National News Agency): Wisma Bernama, 28 Jalan 1/65A, off Jalan Tun Razak, POB 10024, 50400 Kuala Lumpur; tel. (3) 26919955; fax (3) 26919932; e-mail helpdesk@bernama.com; internet www.bernama.com; f. 1968; general and foreign news, economic features and photo services, public relations wire, screen information and data services, stock market on-line equities service, real-time commodity and monetary information services; daily output in Malay and English; in June 1990 Bernama was given the exclusive right to receive and distribute news in Malaysia; Editor-in-Chief Datuk AZMAN UJANG.

PRESS ASSOCIATION

Persatuan Penerbit-Penerbit Akhbar Malaysia (Malaysian Newspaper Publishers' Asscn): Unit 706, Blok B, Phileo Damansara 1, 9 Jalan 16/11, off Jalan Damansara, 46350 Petaling Jaya; tel. (3) 76608535; fax (3) 76608532; e-mail mnpa@macomm.com.my; Chair. MOHD NASIR ALI.

Publishers

KUALA LUMPUR

Arus Intelek Sdn Bhd: Plaza Mont Kiara, Suite E-06-06, Mont Kiara, 50480 Kuala Lumpur; tel. (3) 62011558; fax (3) 62018698; Man. Datin AZIZAH MOKHZANI.

Berita Publishing Sdn Bhd: 16–20 Jalan 4/109E, Desa Business Park, Taman Desa, off Jalan Klang Lama, 58100 Kuala Lumpur; tel. (3) 76208111; fax (3) 76208018; e-mail mbeditor@beritapub.com; internet www.beritapublishing.com.my; education, business, fiction, cookery; Chair. A. KADIR JASIN.

Dewan Bahasa dan Pustaka (DBP) (Institute of Language and Literature): Jalan Dewan Bahasa, 50460 Kuala Lumpur; tel. (3) 21481011; fax (3) 21447248; e-mail aziz@dbp.gov.my; internet www.dbp.gov.my; f. 1956; textbooks, magazines and general; Chair. Tan Sri KAMARUL ARIFFIN MOHAMED YASSIN; Dir-Gen. Dato' Haji A. AZIZ DERAMAN.

Jabatan Penerbitan Universiti Malaya (University of Malaya Press): University of Malaya, Lembah Pantai, 50603 Kuala Lumpur; tel. (3) 79574361; fax (3) 79574473; e-mail terbit@um.edu.my; internet umweb.um.edu.my/umpress; f. 1954; general fiction, literature, economics, history, medicine, politics, science, social science, law, Islam, engineering, dictionaries; Chief Editor ABDUL MANAF SAAD.

Malaya Press Sdn Bhd: Kuala Lumpur; tel. (3) 5754650; fax (3) 5751464; f. 1958; education; Man. Dir LAI WING CHUN.

Pustaka Antara Sdn Bhd: Lot UG 07 and 09, Upper Ground Floor, Kompleks Wilayah, 2 Jalan Munshi Abdullah, 50100 Kuala Lumpur; tel. (3) 26980044; fax (3) 26917997; e-mail pantara4@streamyx.com; textbooks, children's, languages, fiction; Man. Dir Datuk ABDUL AZIZ BIN AHMAD.

Utusan Publications and Distributors Sdn Bhd: 1 and 3 Jalan 3/91A, Taman Shamelin Perkasa, Cheras, 56100 Kuala Lumpur; tel. (3) 92856577; fax (3) 92856341; e-mail rose@utusan.com.my; f. 1976; school textbooks, children's, languages, fiction, general; Exec. Dir ROSELINA JOHARI.

JOHOR

Penerbitan Pelangi Sdn Bhd: 66 Jalan Pingai, Taman Pelangi, 80400 Johor Bahru; tel. (7) 89269553; fax (7) 3329201; e-mail info@pelangibooks.com; internet www.pelangibooks.com; f. 1979; children's books, guidebooks and reference; Man. Dir SAMUEL SUM KOWN CHEEK.

Textbooks Malaysia Sdn Bhd: 49 Jalan Tengku Ahmad, POB 30, 85000 Segamat, Johor; tel. (7) 9318323; fax (7) 9313323; school textbooks, children's fiction, guidebooks and reference; Man. Dir FREDDIE KHOO.

NEGERI SEMBILAN

Bharathi Press: 166 Taman AST, POB 74, 70700 Seremban, Negeri Sembilan Darul Khusus; tel. (6) 7622911; f. 1939; Mans M. SUBRAMANIA BHARATHI, BHARATHI THASAN.

PULAU PINANG

Syarikat United Book Sdn Bhd: 187–189 Lebuh Carnarvon, 10100 Pulau Pinang; tel. (4) 2626891; fax (4) 2626892; textbooks, children's, reference, fiction, guidebooks; Man. Dir CHEW SING GUAN.

SELANGOR

Federal Publications Sdn Bhd: Lot 46, Subang Hi-Tech Industrial Park, Batu Tiga, 40000 Shah Alam, Selangor; tel. (3) 56286888; fax (3) 56364620; e-mail fpsb@tpg.com.my; f. 1957; computer, children's magazines; Gen. Man. STEPHEN K. S. LIM.

FEP International Sdn Bhd: 6 Jalan SS 4c/5, POB 1091, 47301 Petaling Jaya, Selangor; tel. (3) 7036150; fax (3) 7036989; f. 1969; children's, languages, fiction, dictionaries, textbooks and reference; Man. Dir LIM MOK HAI.

International Law Book Services: 10 Jalan PJU 8/5 G, Perdana Business Centre, Bandar Damansara Perdana, 47820 Petaling Jaya, Selangor Darul Ehsan; tel. (3) 77273890; fax (3) 77273884; e-mail gbc@pc.jaring.my; internet www.malaysialawbooks.com; Man. Dr SYED IBRAHIM.

Mahir Publications Sdn Bhd: 39 Jalan Nilam 1/2, Subang Sq., Subang Hi-Tech Industrial Park, Batu Tiga, 40000 Shah Alam, Selangor; tel. (3) 7379044; fax (3) 7379043; e-mail mahirpub@tm.net.my; Gen. Man. ZAINORA BINTI MUHAMAD.

Minerva Publications (NS) Sdn Bhd: 51 Jalan SG 3/1, Tan Sri Gombak, Batu Caves, 68100 Selangor; tel. (3) 61882876; fax (3) 61883876; e-mail minerva@streamyx.com; internet www.minerva.com; f. 1974; general, children's, reference, medical, law; Dir and Chief Editor SUJAUDEEN; Man. Dir THANJUDEEN.

Pearson Education Malaysia Sdn Bhd: Lot 2, Jalan 215, off Jalan Templer, 46050 Petaling Jaya, Selangor; tel. (3) 77820460; fax (3) 77818005; e-mail inquiry@pearsoned.com.my; internet www.pearsoned.com.my; textbooks, mathematics, physics, science, general, educational materials; Dir WONG WEE WOON; Man. WONG MEI MEI.

Pelanduk Publications (M) Sdn Bhd: 12 Jalan SS 13/3E, Subang Jaya Industrial Estate, 47500 Subang Jaya, Selangor; tel. (3) 56386885; fax (3) 56386575; e-mail pelpub@tm.net.my; internet

MALAYSIA

www.pelanduk.com; f. 1984; politics, history, anthropology, religion, education, language, economics, business and management, culture, self-improvement, women's studies, law; Man. JACKSON TAN.

Penerbit Fajar Bakti Sdn Bhd: 4 Jalan U1/15, Sekseyen U1, Hicom-Glenmarie Industrial Park, 40150 Shah Alam, Selangor; tel. (3) 7047011; fax (3) 7047024; e-mail edes@pfb.po.my; school, college and university textbooks, children's, fiction, general; Man. Dir EDDA DE SILVA.

Penerbit Pan Earth Sdn Bhd: 11 Jalan SS 26/6, Taman Mayang Jaya, 47301 Petaling Jaya, Selangor; tel. (3) 7031258; fax (3) 7031262; Man. STEPHEN CHENG.

Penerbit Universiti Kebangsaan Malaysia: Universiti Kebangsaan Malaysia, 43600 UKM, Selangor; tel. (3) 8292840; fax (3) 8254375; Man. HASROM BIN HARON.

Pustaka Delta Pelajaran Sdn Bhd: Wisma Delta, Lot 18, Jalan 51A/22A, 46100 Petaling Jaya, Selangor; tel. (3) 7570000; fax (3) 7576688; economics, language, environment, geography, geology, history, religion, science; Man. Dir LIM KIM WAH.

Pustaka Sistem Pelajaran Sdn Bhd: Lot 17–22 and 17–23, Jalan Satu, Bersatu Industrial Park, Cheras Jaya, 43200 Cheras, Selangor; tel. (3) 9047558; fax (3) 9047573; Man. T. THIRU.

Sasbadi Sdn Bhd: Lot 12, Jalan Teknologi 3/4, Taman Sains Selangor 1, Kota Damansara, 47810 Petaling Jaya, Selangor; tel. (3) 61451188; fax (3) 61569080; e-mail enquiry@sasbadi.com; internet www.sasbadi.com; Man. Dir LAW KING HUI.

SNP Panpac (Malaysia) Sdn Bhd: Lot 3, Jalan Saham 23/3, Kawasan MIEL Phase 8, Section 23, 40300 Shah Alam, Selangor Darul Ehsam; tel. (3) 55481088; fax (3) 55481080; e-mail eastview@snpo.com.my; f. 1980; fmrly SNP Eastview Publications Sdn Bhd; school textbooks, children's, fiction, reference, general; Dir CHIA YAN HENG.

Times Educational Co Sdn Bhd: 22 Jalan 19/3, 46300 Petaling Jaya, Selangor; tel. (3) 79571766; fax (3) 79573607; e-mail presco@po.jaring.my; general and reference; Man. FOONG CHUI LIN.

GOVERNMENT PUBLISHING HOUSE

Percetakan Nasional Malaysia Bhd (Malaysia National Printing Ltd): Jalan Chan Sow Lin, 50554 Kuala Lumpur; tel. (3) 2212022; fax (3) 2220690; fmrly the National Printing Department, incorporated as a company under govt control in January 1993.

PUBLISHERS' ASSOCIATION

Malaysian Book Publishers' Association: 306 Block C, Glomac Business Centre, 10 Jalan SS 6/1 Kelana Jaya, 47301 Petaling Jaya, Selangor; tel. (3) 7046628; fax (3) 7046629; internet www.mabopa.com.my; f. 1968; Pres. LAW KING HUI; Hon. Sec. ZAINORA MUHAMAD; 95 mems.

Broadcasting and Communications

TELECOMMUNICATIONS

Jabatan Telekomunikasi Malaysia (JTM) (Department of Telecommunications): c/o Ministry of Energy, Water and Communications, Blok E4–5, Parcel E, Pusat Pentadbiran Kerajaan Persekutuan, 62668 Putrajaya; tel. (3) 88836000; fax (3) 88893712; e-mail webmaster@ktak.gov.my; internet www.ktkm.gov.my; regulatory body for telecommunications industry.

Celcom (Malaysia) Sdn Bhd: Menara Celcom, 82 Jalan Raja Muda Abdul Aziz, 50300 Kuala Lumpur; tel. (3) 26883939; e-mail feedback@celcom.com.my; internet www.celcom.com.my; f. 1988; private co licensed to operate mobile cellular telephone service; merged with TM Cellular Sdn Bhd in 2003; Chair. Tan Sri Dato' Ir MUHAMMAD RADZI BIN Haji MANSOR; CEO Dato' MOHAMMED SHAZALLI RAMLY.

DiGi Telecommunications Sdn Bhd: Lot 30, Jalan Delima 1/3, Subang Hi-Tech Industrial Park, 40000 Shah Alam, Selangor; tel. (3) 57211800; fax (3) 57211857; internet www.digi.com.my; private co licensed to operate mobile telephone service; Chair. Tan Sri Dato' Seri VINCENT TAN CHEE YIOUN; CEO TORE JOHNSEN.

Maxis Communications Bhd: Menara Maxis, Aras 18, Kuala Lumpur City Centre, off Jalan Ampang, 50088 Kuala Lumpur; tel. (3) 23307000; fax (3) 23300008; internet www.maxis.com.my; f. 1995; provides mobile, fixed-line and multimedia services; approx. 3.25m. subscribers in 2003; Chair. Datuk MEGAT ZAHARUDDIN BIN MEGAT MOHAMED NOR; CEO SANDIP DAS.

Technology Resources Industries Bhd (TRI): Menara TR, 23rd Floor, 161B Jalan Ampang, 50450 Kuala Lumpur; tel. (3) 2619555; fax (3) 2632018; operates mobile cellular telephone service; Chair. and Chief Exec. Tan Sri Dato' TAJUDIN RAMLI.

Directory

Telekom Malaysia Bhd: Level 51, North Wing, Menara Telekom, off Jalan Pantai Baru, 50672 Kuala Lumpur; tel. (3) 22401221; fax (3) 22832415; internet www.telekom.com.my; f. 1984; public listed co responsible for operation of basic telecommunications services; 74% govt-owned; 4.22m. fixed lines (95% of total); Chair. Haji MUHAMMAD RADZI BIN Haji MANSOR; Chief Exec. Dato' ABDUL WAHID BIN OMAR.

Time dotCom Bhd: Wisma Time, 1st Floor, 249 Jalan Tun Razak, 50400 Kuala Lumpur; tel. (3) 27208000; fax (3) 27200199; internet www.time.com.my; f. 1996 as Time Telecommunications Holdings Bhd; name changed as above in Jan. 2000; state-controlled co licensed to operate trunk network and mobile cellular telephone service; Chair. Dato' WAN MUHAMAD WAN IBRAHIM; Man. Dir Dato' BAHARUM SALLEH.

BROADCASTING

Regulatory Authority

Under the Broadcasting Act (approved in December 1987), the Minister of Information is empowered to control and monitor all radio and television broadcasting, and to revoke the licence of any private company violating the Act by broadcasting material 'conflicting with Malaysian values'.

Radio Televisyen Malaysia (RTM): Dept of Broadcasting, Angkasapuri, Bukit Putra, 50614 Kuala Lumpur; tel. (3) 22825333; fax (3) 2824735; internet www.rtm.net.my; f. 1946; television introduced 1963; supervises radio and television broadcasting; Dir-Gen. ABDUL RAHMAN HAMID; Dep. Dir-Gen. TAMIMUDDIN ABDUL KARIM.

Radio

Radio Malaysia: Radio Televisyen Malaysia (see Regulatory Authority), POB 11272, 50740 Kuala Lumpur; tel. (3) 2823991; fax (3) 2825859; f. 1946; domestic service; operates six networks; broadcasts in Bahasa Malaysia, English, Chinese (Mandarin and other dialects), Tamil and Aborigine (Temiar and Semai dialects); Dir of Radio MADZHI JOHARI.

Radio Televisyen Malaysia—Sabah: Jalan Tuaran, 88614 Kota Kinabalu; tel. (88) 213444; fax (88) 223493; f. 1955; television introduced 1971; a dept of RTM; broadcasts programmes over two networks for 280 hours a week in Bahasa Malaysia, English, Chinese (two dialects), Kadazan, Murut, Dusun and Bajau; Dir of Broadcasting JUMAT ENGSON.

Radio Televisyen Malaysia—Sarawak: Broadcasting House, Jalan P. Ramlee, 93614 Kuching; tel. (82) 248422; fax (82) 241914; e-mail pvgrtmsw@tm.net.my; f. 1954; a dept of RTM; broadcasts 445 hours per week in Bahasa Malaysia, English, Chinese, Iban, Bidayuh, Melanau, Kayan/Kenyah, Bisayah and Murut; Dir of Broadcasting NORHYATI ISMAIL.

Rediffusion Sdn Bhd: Rediffusion House, 17 Jalan Pahang, 53000 Kuala Lumpur; tel. (3) 4424544; fax (3) 4424614; f. 1949; two programmes; 44,720 subscribers in Kuala Lumpur; 11,405 subscribers in Pinang; 6,006 subscribers in Province Wellesley; 20,471 subscribers in Ipoh; Gen. Man. ROSNI B. RAHMAT.

Suara Islam (Voice of Islam): Islamic Affairs Division, Prime Minister's Department, Blok Utama, Tingkat 1–5, Pusat Pentadbiran Kerajaan Persekutuan, 62502 Putrajaya; f. 1995; Asia-Pacific region; broadcasts in Bahasa Malaysia on Islam.

Suara Malaysia (Voice of Malaysia): Wisma Radio, Angkasapuri, POB 11272, 50740 Kuala Lumpur; tel. (3) 22887824; fax (3) 22847594; f. 1963; overseas service in Bahasa Malaysia, Arabic, Myanmar (Burmese), English, Bahasa Indonesia, Chinese (Mandarin/Cantonese), Tagalog and Thai; Controller of Overseas Service STEPHEN SIPAUN.

Time Highway Radio: All Asia Broadcast Centre, Technology Park Malaysia, Bukit Jalil, 57000 Kuala Lumpur; tel. (3) 95438888; fax (3) 95439911; e-mail feedback@thr.fm; internet www.thr.fm; f. 1994; serves Kuala Lumpur region; broadcasts in English; CEO ABDUL AZIZ HAMDAN.

Television

Measat Broadcast Network Systems Sdn Bhd: All Asia Broadcast Centre, Technology Park Malaysia, Lebuhraya Puchong, Simpang Besi, Bukit Jalil, 57000 Kuala Lumpur; tel. (3) 95434188; fax (3) 95437333; e-mail custcare@astro.com.my; internet www.astro.com.my; nation-wide subscription service; Malaysia's first satellite, Measat 1, was launched in January 1996; a second satellite was launched in October of that year; Chair. T. ANANDA KRISHNAN.

Metropolitan Television Sdn Bhd (8TV): 3 Persiaran Bandar Utama, 47800 Petaling Jaya, Selangor; tel. (3) 77288282; fax (3) 77268282; e-mail izham@8tv.com.my; internet www.8tv.com.my; began broadcasting in July 1995; commercial station; operates only in Klang Valley; 44%-owned by Senandung Sesuria Sdn Bhd, 56%-owned by Metropolitan Media Sdn Bhd; COO AHMAD ISHAM OMAR.

Radio Televisyen Malaysia—Sabah: see Radio.

MALAYSIA

Radio Televisyen Malaysia—Sarawak: see Radio.

Sistem Televisyen Malaysia Bhd (TV 3): 3 Persiaran Bandar Utama, Bandar Utama, 47800 Petaling, Selangor Darul Ehsan; tel. (3) 77266333; fax (3) 77278455; e-mail enquiries@tv3.com.my; internet www.tv3.com.my; f. 1983; Malaysia's first private television network, began broadcasting in 1984; Chair. Dato' ABDUL MUTALIB BIN Datuk Seri MOHAMED RAZAK; Man. Dir Hisham Dato' ABDULLAH RAHMAN.

Televisyen Malaysia: Radio Televisyen Malaysia (see Regulatory Authority); f. 1963; operates two national networks, TV1 and TV2; Controller of Programmes ISMAIL MOHAMED JAH.

Under a regulatory framework devised by the Government, a ban on privately owned satellite dishes was ended in 1996.

Finance

(cap. = capital; auth. = authorized; res = reserves; dep. = deposits; m. = million; brs = branches; amounts in ringgit Malaysia)

BANKING

In January 2004 there were 46 domestic commercial banks, merchant banks and finance companies. In February 2000 the Government announced that it had approved plans for the creation of up to 10 banking groups to be formed through the merger of existing institutions. By August 2001 51 banks had merged under the terms of these plans. In February 2004 53 banks held 'offshore' licences in Labuan.

Central Bank

Bank Negara Malaysia: Jalan Dato' Onn, POB 10922, 50929 Kuala Lumpur; tel. (3) 26988044; fax (3) 26912990; e-mail info@bnm.gov.my; internet www.bnm.gov.my; f. 1959; bank of issue; financial regulatory authority; cap. 100.0m., res 32,549.4m., dep. 220,077.5m. (Dec. 2006); Gov. Tan Sri Dato' Sri Dr ZETI AKHTAR AZIZ; 6 brs.

Regulatory Authority

Labuan Offshore Financial Services Authority (LOFSA): Level 17, Main Office Tower, Financial Park Labuan, Jalan Merdeka, 87000 Labuan; tel. (87) 591200; fax (87) 413328; e-mail communication@lofsa.gov.my; internet www.lofsa.gov.my; regulatory body for the International Offshore Financial Centre of Labuan established in October 1990; Chair. Datuk ZETI AKHTAR AZIZ (Gov. of Bank Negara Malaysia); Dir-Gen. Dato' AZIZAN ABDUL RAHMAN.

Commercial Banks

Peninsular Malaysia

ABN Amro Bank Bhd: Levels 25–27, MNI Twins, Tower II, 11 Jalan Pinang, POB 10094, 50704 Kuala Lumpur; tel. (3) 21627888; fax (3) 21625692; e-mail info@abnamro.com.my; internet www.abnamromalaysia.com; f. 1963.

Affin Bank Bhd: Menara AFFIN, 17th Floor, 80 Jalan Raja Chulan, 50200 Kuala Lumpur; tel. (3) 20559000; fax (3) 20261415; e-mail head.ccd@affinbank.com.my; internet www.affinbank.com.my; f. 1975 as Perwira Habib Bank Malaysia Bhd; name changed to Perwira Affin Bank Bhd 1994; merged with BSN Commercial Bank (Malaysia) Bhd Jan. 2001, and name changed as above; cap. 1,290.2m., res 935.7m., dep. 22,018.0m. (Dec. 2006); Chair. Gen. Tan Sri Dato' Seri ISMAIL Haji OMAR; Pres. and CEO Dato' ABDUL HAMIDY ABDUL HAFIZ; 106 brs.

Alliance Bank Malaysia Bhd: Menara Multi-Purpose, Ground Floor, Capital Sq., 8 Jalan Munshi Abdullah, 50100 Kuala Lumpur; POB 10069, 50704 Kuala Lumpur; tel. (3) 26948800; fax (3) 26946727; e-mail info@alliancebg.com.my; internet www.alliancebank.com.my; f. 1982 as Malaysian French Bank Bhd; name changed to Multi-Purpose Bank Bhd 1996; name changed as above Jan. 2001, following acquisition of six merger partners; cap. 598.5m., res 864.3m., dep. 20,478.5m. (March 2007); Chair. LUTFIAH BINTI ISMAIL; CEO BRIDGET ANNE LAI HUNG YEE; 80 brs.

AmBank Bhd: 22nd Floor, Bangunan AmBank Group, 55 Jalan Raja Chulan, 50200 Kuala Lumpur; tel. (3) 20782633; fax (3) 20316453; e-mail customercare@ambg.com.my; internet www.ambg.com.my; f. 1994; fmrly Arab-Malaysian Bank Bhd; name changed as above 2002; cap. 505.5m., res −72.0m., dep. 9,036.3m. (March 2003); Chair. Tan Sri Dato' AZMAN HASHIM; Man. Dir KUNG BENG HONG.

Bangkok Bank Bhd (Thailand): 105 Jalan Tun H. S. Lee, 50000 Kuala Lumpur; tel. (3) 20724555; fax (3) 20788569; e-mail bbb@tm.net.my; internet www.bangkokbank.com; f. 1958; cap. 265.0m., res 98.6m., dep. 738.2m. (Dec. 2006); Chair. STAPORN KAVITANON; CEO ROBERT LOKE; 1 br.

Bank of America Malaysia Bhd: Wisma Goldhill, Jalan Raja Chulan, 50200 Kuala Lumpur; tel. (3) 20321133; fax (3) 20319087;

Directory

internet www.bankofamerica.com.my; cap. 135.8m., res 244.0m., dep. 1,005.0m. (Dec. 2006); Chair. KRISTJAN DRAKE.

Bank of Nova Scotia Bhd: POB 11056, Menara Boustead, 69 Jalan Raja Chulan, 50200 Kuala Lumpur; tel. (3) 21410766; fax (3) 21412160; e-mail bns.kualalumpur@scotiabank.com; internet www.scotiabank.com.my; f. 1973; cap. 122.4m., res 330.8m., dep. 1,580.3m. (Oct. 2006); Man. Dir RASOOL KHAN.

Bank of Tokyo-Mitsubishi UFJ (Malaysia) Bhd (Japan): Levels 9–11, Menara IMC, 8 Jalan Sultan Ismail, 50250 Kuala Lumpur; tel. (3) 20788871; fax (3) 20788870; e-mail edpbtm@tm.net.my; f. 1996 following merger of the Bank of Tokyo and Mitsubishi Bank; fmrly known as Bank of Tokyo-Mitsubishi, name changed as above following merger with UFJ; cap. 200m., res 618.9m., dep. 3,298.6m. (Dec. 2005); Chair. TETSUO TANAKA; Pres. and CEO HIROYUKI KUDO.

Bumiputra Commerce Bank Bhd: 6 Jalan Tun Perak, 50050 Kuala Lumpur; tel. (3) 26931722; fax (3) 26986628; internet www.bcb.com.my; f. 1999 following merger of Bank Bumiputra Malaysia Bhd with Bank of Commerce Bhd; cap. 2,064.0m., res 2,950.3m., dep. 59,632.6m. (Dec. 2005); Chair. Tan Sri HAIDAR MOHAMED NOOR; Group CEO Dato' MOHAMED NAZIR ABDUL RAZAK ALI; 230 brs.

Citibank Bhd (USA): 165 Jalan Ampang, POB 10112, 50450 Kuala Lumpur; tel. (3) 23830000; fax (3) 2328763; internet www.citibank.com.my; f. 1959; cap. 121.7m., res 1,195.2m., dep. 32,134.7m. (Dec. 2005); Country Officer PIYUSH GUPTA; 3 brs.

Deutsche Bank (Malaysia) Bhd (Germany): 18–20 Menara IMC, 8 Jalan Sultan Ismail, 50250 Kuala Lumpur; tel. (3) 20536788; fax (3) 20319822; f. 1994; cap. 143.0m., res 391.2m., dep. 4,193m. (Dec. 2005); Man. Dir KUAH HUN LIANG.

EON Bank Bhd: Menara EON Bank, 12th Floor, 288 Jalan Raja Laut, 50350 Kuala Lumpur; tel. (3) 26941188; fax (3) 26949588; e-mail caf@eonbank.com.my; internet www.eonbank.com.my; f. 1963; fmrly Kong Ming Bank Bhd; merged with Oriental Bank Bhd, Jan. 2001; cap. 1,329.8m., res 1,845.2m., dep. 28,584.3m. (Dec. 2006); Chair. Datin Dr UMIKALSUM BINTI MOHAMED NOH; CEO and Exec. Dir ALBERT LAU YIONG; 95 brs.

Hong Leong Bank Bhd: Wisma Hong Leong, Level 3, 18 Jalan Perak, 50450 Kuala Lumpur; tel. (3) 21642828; fax (3) 27156365; internet www.hlb.com.my; f. 1905; fmrly MUI Bank Bhd; merged with Wah Tat Bank Bhd, Jan. 2001; cap. 1,580.1m., res 2,755.2m., dep. 48,592.6m. (June 2006); Chair. Tan Sri QUEK LENG CHAN; Man. Dir YVONNE CHIA; 167 local brs, 2 overseas brs.

HSBC Bank Malaysia Bhd (Hong Kong): 2 Leboh Ampang, POB 10244, 50912 Kuala Lumpur; tel. (3) 20700744; fax (3) 20702678; e-mail manager.public.affairs@hsbc.com.my; internet www.hsbc.com.my; f. 1860; fmrly Hongkong Bank Malaysia Bhd; adopted present name in 1999; cap. 114.5m., res 2,698.4m., dep. 35,417.3m. (Dec. 2006); Chair. MICHAEL SMITH; CEO ZARIR J. CAMA.

Malayan Banking Bhd (Maybank): Menara Maybank, 14th Floor, 100 Jalan Tun Perak, 50050 Kuala Lumpur; tel. (3) 20747037; fax (3) 20789761; e-mail publicaffairs@maybank.com.my; internet www.maybank2u.com; f. 1960; acquired Pacific Bank Bhd, Jan. 2001; merged with PhileoAllied Bank (Malaysia) Bhd, March 2001; cap. 3,796.9m., res 3,896.9m., dep. 164,392.6m. (June 2006); Chair. Tan Sri MOHAMED BASIR BIN AHMAD; Pres. and CEO Datuk AMIRSHAM A. AZIZ; 327 domestic brs, 30 overseas brs.

OCBC Bank (Malaysia) Bhd: Menara OCBC, 18 Jalan Tun Perak, 50050 Kuala Lumpur; tel. (3) 83175000; fax (3) 26984363; internet www.ocbc.com.my; f. 1932; cap. 291.5m., res 1,925.8m., dep. 30,701.9m. (Dec. 2006); Group Chair. Tan Sri Dato' NASRUDDIN BIN BAHARI; CEO ALBERT YEOH BEOW TIT; 25 brs.

Public Bank Bhd: Menara Public Bank, 146 Jalan Ampang, 50450 Kuala Lumpur; tel. (3) 21638888; fax (3) 21619307; e-mail customerservice@publicbank.com.my; internet www.publicbank.com.my; f. 1965; merged with Hock Hua Bank Bhd, March 2001; cap. 3,462.8m., res 5,507.5m., dep. 121,521.9m. (Dec. 2006); Chair. Tan Sri Dato' Dr TEH HONG PIOW; 216 domestic brs, 3 overseas brs.

RHB Bank Bhd: Towers Two and Three, Menara AA, 426 Jalan Tun Razak, 50400 Kuala Lumpur; tel. (3) 92068118; fax (3) 92068088; e-mail md_ceo@rhbbank.com.my; internet www.rhbbank.com.my; f. 1997 as a result of merger between DCB Bank Bhd and Kwong Yik Bank Bhd; acquired Sime Bank Bhd in mid-1999; merged with Bank Utama (Malaysia) Bhd, May 2003; cap. 3,318.1m., res 2,407.6m., dep. 73,368.0m. (Dec. 2006); Chair. (non-exec.) Datuk AZLAN ZAINOL; CEO MICHAEL JOSEPH BARRETT; 148 brs.

Standard Chartered Bank Malaysia Bhd: 1st Floor, 2 Jalan Ampang, 50450 Kuala Lumpur; tel. (3) 20726555; fax (3) 2010621; internet www.standardchartered.com.my; 31 brs.

United Overseas Bank (Malaysia) Bhd: Menara UOB, Level 2, Jalan Raja Laut, POB 11212, 50738 Kuala Lumpur; tel. (3) 26924511; fax (3) 26913110; e-mail uob121@uob.com.my; internet www.uob.com.my; f. 1920; merged with Chung Khiaw Bank (Malaysia) Bhd in 1997 and with Overseas Union Bank (Malaysia)

MALAYSIA   Directory

Bhd in 2002; cap. 470m., res 1,902.2m., dep. 25,827.7m. (Dec. 2006); Chair. WEE CHO YAW; CEO CHAN KOK SEONG; 37 brs.

Merchant Banks

Affin Merchant Bank Bhd: Menara Boustead, 27th Floor, 69 Jalan Raja Chulan, POB 11424, 50744 Kuala Lumpur; tel. (3) 21423700; fax (3) 21423799; e-mail general@affinmerchantbank.com.my; internet www.affinmerchantbank.com.my; f. 1970 as Permata Chartered Merchant Bank Bhd; name changed as above March 2001; cap. 187.5m., res 181.6m., dep. 2,780.4m. (Dec. 2005); Chair. Tan Sri YAACOB MOHAMED ZAIN; CEO Datin ZURAIDAH ATAN-SHARARIMAN.

Alliance Investment Bank Bhd (AIB): Menara Multi-Purpose, 20th Floor, Capital Sq., 8 Jalan Munshi Abdullah, 50100 Kuala Lumpur; tel. (3) 26927788; fax (3) 26928787; e-mail ambb@allianceinvestment.com.my; internet www.allianceinvestmentbank.com.my; f. 1974 as Amanah-Chase Merchant Bank Bhd; name changed to Alliance Merchant Bank Bhd in Jan. 2001, following merger with Bumiputra Merchant Bankers Bhd; name changed as above in Aug. 2006, following merger with Kuala Lumpur City Securities (KLCS); cap. 365.0m., res 96.6m., dep. 1,904.7m. (March 2007); Chair. Dato' THOMAS MUN LUNG LEE; CEO CHUA BEE CHIN (acting).

AmInvestment Bank Bhd: 22nd Floor, Bangunan AmBank Group, 55 Jalan Raja Chulan, 50200 Kuala Lumpur; tel. (3) 20782655; fax (3) 20782842; e-mail customercare@ambg.com.my; internet www.ambg.com.my; f. 1975; fmrly Arab-Malaysian Merchant Bank Bhd, later known as AmMerchant Bank Bhd; name changed as above 2006; cap. 310.0m., res 564.4m., dep. 16,502.8m. (March 2006); Chair. Tan Sri Dato' AZMAN HASHIM; Group Man. Dir CHEAH TEK KUANG; 5 brs.

Aseambankers Malaysia Bhd: Menara Maybank, 33rd Floor, 100 Jalan Tun Perak, 50050 Kuala Lumpur; tel. (3) 20591888; fax (3) 20784194; e-mail faudziah@aseam.com.my; internet www.aseam.com.my; f. 1973; cap. 50.1m., res 499.4m., dep. 3,987.0m. (June 2006); Chair. Dato' MOHAMED BASIR AHMAD; CEO AGIL NATT; 2 brs.

CIMB Investment Bank Bhd: Bangunan CIMB, 10th Floor, Jalan Semantan, Damansara Heights, 50490 Kuala Lumpur; tel. (3) 2536688; fax (3) 2535522; e-mail info@cimb.com.my; internet www.cimbbank.com.my; f. 1974; fmrly known as Commerce International Merchant Bankers Bhd; name changed as above 2006; cap. 1,000.5m., res 667.7m., dep. 2,672.0m. (Dec. 2005); Chair. Dr ROZALI MOHAMED ALI.

MIMB Investment Bank Bhd: Menara EON Bank, 21st Floor, 288 Jalan Raja Laut, 50350 Kuala Lumpur; tel. (3) 26910200; fax (3) 26985388; internet www.mimb.com.my; f. 1970; fmrly known as Malaysian International Merchant Bankers Bhd; wholly owned subsidiary of EON Bank Berhad; cap. 75m., res 122.1m., dep. 109.5m. (Dec. 2006); Chair. Dato' ZULKIFLI BIN ALI; 2 brs.

Public Merchant Bank Bhd: 25th Floor, Menara Public Bank, 146 Jalan Ampang, 50450 Kuala Lumpur; tel. (3) 21669382; fax (3) 21669362; e-mail merchantbank@publicbank.com.my; f. 1973 as Asian International Merchant Bankers Bhd; became Sime Merchant Bankers Bhd 1996; name changed as above 2000; cap. 165.0m., res −28.9m., dep. 1,086.6m. (Dec. 2002); Chair. Tan Sri Dato' THONG YAW HONG.

RHB Investment Bank Bhd: Tower Three, 9th Floor, RHB Centre, 426 Jalan Tun Razak, 50400 Kuala Lumpur; tel. (3) 92805475; fax (3) 27118501; e-mail publicaffairs@rhb.com.my; internet www.rhb.com.my; f. 1974; fmrly known as RHB Sakura Merchant Bankers Bhd; name changed as above 2006; cap. 338.6m., res 359.5m., dep. 5,625.8m. (Dec. 2006); Chair. Encik ABDULLAH MAT NOH.

Southern Investment Bank Bhd: Menara Southern Bank, 83 Medan Setia 1, Plaza Damansara, Bukit Damansara, 50772 Kuala Lumpur; tel. (3) 62047788; fax (3) 23817198; e-mail sibb@sibb.com.my; internet www.southernbank.com.my; f. 1988; fmrly Perdana Merchant Bankers Bhd; cap. 77.9m., res 0.5m., dep. 313.6m. (Dec. 2006); Chair. Dato' Nik IBRAHIM KAMIL; CEO Tan Sri Dato' TAN TEONG HEAN.

Utama Merchant Bank Bhd: Menara Maxis, Level 33, Suite A, 50088 Kuala Lumpur; tel. (3) 20789133; fax (3) 20725511; e-mail umbb@umbb.po.my; internet www.cmsb.com.my/ubg; f. 1975 as Utama Wardley Bhd; name changed as above in 1996; cap. 156.5m., res 385.9m., dep. 8,746.2m. (Dec. 2006); Chair. Nik HASHIM BIN Nik YUSOFF; CEO DONNY KWA SOO CHUAN; 1 br.

Co-operative Bank

Bank Kerjasama Rakyat Malaysia Berhad: Bangunan Bank Rakyat, Jalan Tangsi, Peti Surat 11024, 50732 Kuala Lumpur; tel. (3) 2985011; fax (3) 2985981; f. 1954; 83,095 mems of which 823 were co-operatives (Dec. 1996); Chair. Dr YUSUF YACOB; Man. Dir Dato' ANUAR JAAFAR; 67 brs.

Development Banks

Bank Pembangunan Malaysia Bhd: Menara Bank Pembangunan, POB 12352, Jalan Sultan Ismail, 50774 Kuala Lumpur; tel. (3) 26113888; fax (3) 26928520; e-mail enq_y@bpmb.com.my; internet www.bpmb.com.my; f. 1973; govt-owned; fmrly known as Bank Pembangunana & Infrastruktur Malaysia Bhd; name changed as above following merger with Bank Industri & Teknologi Malaysia Bhd in 2005; specializes in infrastructure, maritime and high-technology sectors; cap. 2,128.7m., res 1,610.6m., dep. 3,833.8m. (Dec. 2005); Pres. and Man. Dir Datuk ABDUL RAHIM MOHAMED ZIN; Chair. Tan Sri Dr ZAINUL ARIF HUSSAIN; 14 brs.

Bank Perusahaan Kecil & Sederhana Malaysia Bhd (SME Bank): Menara SME Bank, Jalan Sultan Ismail, Peti Surat 12352, 50774 Kuala Lumpur; tel. (3) 26152020; fax (3) 26928520; e-mail enq_y@smebank.com.my; internet www.smebank.com.my; f. 2005; wholly owned subsidiary of Bank Pembangunan Malaysia Bhd; provides both financial and non-financial assistance to SMEs; cap. 1,000.0m., res 87.8m., dep 2,969.0m. (Dec. 2005); Chair. Dato' GUMURI HUSSAIN; Man. Dir Dato' AZMI ABDULLAH.

Sabah Development Bank Bhd: SDB Tower, Wisma Tun Fuad Stephens, POB 12172, 88824 Kota Kinabalu, Sabah; tel. (88) 232177; fax (88) 261852; e-mail info@sabahdevbank.com; internet www.sabahdevbank.com; f. 1977; wholly owned by State Government of Sabah; cap. 365.0m., res −111.4m., dep. 1,185.0m. (Dec. 2005); Chair. PETER SIAU WUI KEE; Man. Dir and CEO PETER LIM SIONG ENG.

Islamic Banks

Bank Islam Malaysia Bhd: Darul Takaful, 11th Floor, Jalan Sultan Ismail, 50250 Kuala Lumpur; tel. (3) 26168000; fax (3) 26980587; e-mail communications@bankislam.com.my; internet www.bankislam.com.my; f. 1983; cap. 880m., res 1,157.8m., dep. 14,449.5m. (June 2006); Chair. Tan Sri Dato' Dr ABDULLAH MOHAMED TAHIR; Man. Dir Dato' ZUKRI SAMAT; 90 brs.

Bank Muamalat Malaysia Bhd: Menara Bumiputra, 21 Jalan Melaka, 50100 Kuala Lumpur; tel. (3) 26988787; fax (3) 20325997; e-mail webmaster@muamalat.com.my; internet www.muamalat.com.my; f. 1999; CEO Tuan Haji MOHD SHUKRI HUSSIN; 40 brs.

'Offshore' Banks

ABN Amro Bank, Labuan Branch: Level 9 (A), Main Office Tower, Financial Park Labuan, Jalan Merdeka, 87000 Labuan; tel. (87) 423008; fax (87) 421078; Man. ANTHONY RAJAN.

Al-Hidayah Investment Bank (Labuan) Ltd: Level 7 (C), Main Office Tower, Financial Park Labuan, Jalan Merdeka, 87000 Labuan; tel. (87) 451660; fax (87) 583088.

AMInternational (L) Ltd: Level 12 (B), Block 4, Office Tower, Financial Park Labuan, Jalan Merdeka, 87000 Labuan; tel. (87) 413133; fax (87) 425211; e-mail felix-leong@ambg.com.my; internet www.ambg.com.my; CEO PAUL ONG.

AmMerchant Bank Bhd, Labuan Branch: Level 12 (B), Block 4, Main Office Tower, Financial Park Labuan, Jalan Merdeka, 87000 Labuan; tel. (87) 413133; fax (87) 425211; Gen. Man. PAUL ONG WHEE SEN.

Bank of America, National Trust and Savings Association, Labuan Branch: Level 13 (D), Main Office Tower, Financial Park Labuan, Jalan Merdeka, 87000 Labuan; tel. (87) 411778; fax (87) 424778; Gen. Man. Pengiran NUR FARHAH OOI ABDULLAH.

Bank of East Asia Ltd, Labuan Offshore Branch: Level 10 (C), Main Office Tower, Financial Park Labuan, Jalan Merdeka, 87000 Labuan; tel. (87) 451145; fax (87) 451148; e-mail arraisag@hkbea.com; Gen. Man. ALVIN ARRAIS.

Bank Islam (L) Ltd: Level 15 (A), Main Office Tower, Financial Park, Jalan Merdeka, 87000 Labuan; tel. (87) 451802; fax (87) 453077; e-mail engkuafandi@bankislam.com.my; Branch Man. ENGKU AFANDI TAIB.

Bank Muamalat Malaysia Bhd, Labuan Branch: Level 15 (A1), Main Office Tower, Financial Park Labuan, Jalan Merdeka, 87000 Labuan; tel. (87) 412898; fax (87) 451164; e-mail fuad@muamalat.com.my; Gen. Man. ZAINOL RASHID KHAIRUDDIN.

Bank of Nova Scotia, Labuan Branch: Level 10 (C2), Main Office Tower, Financial Park Labuan, Jalan Merdeka, 87000 Labuan; tel. (87) 451101; fax (87) 451099; Man. KWAN SING HUNG.

Bank of Tokyo-Mitsubishi UFJ Ltd, Labuan Branch: Level 12 (A & F), Main Office Tower, Financial Park Labuan, Jalan Merdeka, 87000 Labuan; tel. (87) 410487; fax (87) 410476; e-mail pulaubtm@tm.net.my; Gen. Man. WATURU TANAKA.

Barclays Bank PLC: Level 5 (A), Main Office Tower, Financial Park Labuan, Jalan Merdeka, 87000 Labuan; tel. (87) 425571; fax (87) 425575; e-mail barclay@tm.net.my; Man. MIAW SIAW LOONG.

Bayerische Landesbank Girozentrale, Labuan Branch: Level 14 (C), Block 4, Office Tower, Financial Park Labuan, Jalan Mer-

MALAYSIA

deka, 87000 Labuan; tel. (87) 422170; fax (87) 422175; e-mail blblab@tm.net.my; Exec. Vice-Pres., CEO and Gen. Man. LOUISE PAUL.

BNP Paribas, Labuan Branch: Level 9 (E), Main Office Tower, Financial Park Labuan, Jalan Merdeka, 87000 Labuan; tel. (87) 422328; fax (87) 419328; e-mail bnpkul@tm.net.my; Gen. Man. YAP SIEW YING.

Bumiputra Commerce Bank (L) Ltd: Level 14 (B), Main Office Tower, Financial Park Labuan, Jalan Merdeka, 87000 Labuan; tel. (87) 410302; fax (87) 410313; e-mail bumitrst@tm.net.my; Gen. Man. ASARAF ABU BAKAR.

Cathay United Bank, Labuan Branch: Level 3 (C), Main Office Tower, Financial Park Labuan, Jalan Merdeka, 87000 Labuan; tel. (87) 452168; fax (87) 453678; Gen. Man. YEH PIN HUNG.

CIMB (L) Ltd: Unit 11 (B1), Level 11, Main Office Tower, Financial Park Labuan, Jalan Merdeka, 87000 Labuan; tel. (87) 451608; fax (87) 451610; CEO ADHA AMIR ABDULLAH.

Citibank Malaysia (L) Ltd: Level 11 (F), Main Office Tower, Financial Park Labuan, Jalan Merdeka, 87000 Labuan; tel. (87) 421181; fax (87) 419671; Gen. Man. CLARA LIM AI CHENG.

City Credit Investment Bank Ltd: Level 11 (D1), Main Office Tower, Financial Park Labuan, Jalan Merdeka, 87000 Labuan; tel. (87) 582268; fax (87) 581268; Dir ABDUL RAHMAN ABDULLAH.

Commercial IBT Bank, Labuan Branch: 02-01, 2nd Floor, Wisma Lucas Kong Bldg, U0185 Jalan Merdeka, 87000 Labuan; tel. (87) 411868; fax (87) 416818; e-mail aong@cibtbank.com; Pres. Dir Dr ADRIAN ONG CHEE BENG.

Commerzbank AG, Labuan Branch: Level 6 (E), Main Office Tower, Financial Park Labuan, Jalan Merdeka, 87000 Labuan; tel. (87) 416953; fax (87) 413542; Prin. Officer HO KAH HENG.

Crédit Agricole Indosuez, Calyon Labuan Branch: Level 6 (B), Main Office Tower, Financial Park Labuan, Jalan Merdeka, 87000 Labuan; tel. (87) 408334; fax (87) 408335; Sr Country Officer TAN BOON EONG.

Crédit Industriel et Commercial: Level 11 (C2), Main Office Tower, Financial Park Labuan, Jalan Merdeka, 87000 Labuan; tel. (87) 452008; fax (87) 452009; Gen. Man. YEOW TIANG HUI.

Crédit Suisse First Boston, Labuan Branch: Level 10 (B), Main Office Tower, Financial Park Labuan, Jalan Merdeka, 87000 Labuan; tel. (87) 425381; fax (87) 425384; Gen. Man. RUDOLF ZAUGG.

Danaharta Managers (L) Ltd: Tingkat 10, Bangunan Setia 1, 15 Lorong Dungun, Bukit Damansara, 50490 Kuala Lumpur; tel. (3) 2531122; fax (3) 2534679; Gen. Man. (vacant).

Deutsche Bank AG, Labuan Branch: Level 9 (G2), Main Office Tower, Financial Park Labuan, Jalan Merdeka, 87000 Labuan; tel. (87) 439811; fax (87) 439866; Man. Dir KUAH HUN LIANG.

Development Bank of Singapore (DBS Bank) Ltd, Labuan Branch: Level 12 (E), Main Office Tower, Financial Park Labuan, Jalan Merdeka, 87000 Labuan; tel. (87) 423375; fax (87) 423376; Gen. Man. KEVIN WONG.

Dresdner Bank AG, Labuan Branch: Level 13 (C), Main Office Tower, Financial Park Labuan, Jalan Merdeka, 87000 Labuan; tel. (87) 419271; fax (87) 419272; Gen. Man. JAMALUDIN NASIR.

ECM Libra Investment Bank Ltd: Level 3 (I1), Main Office Tower, Financial Park Complex, Jalan Merdeka, 87000 Labuan; tel. (87) 408525; fax (87) 408527.

Hongkong & Shanghai Banking Corporation, Offshore Banking Unit: Level 11 (D), Main Office Tower, Financial Park Labuan, Jalan Merdeka, 87000 Labuan; tel. (87) 417168; fax (87) 417169; Man. PREM KUMAR.

ING Bank NV: Level 8 (B2), Main Office Tower, Financial Park Labuan, Jalan Merdeka, 87000 Labuan; tel. (87) 425733; fax (87) 425734; Gen. Man. MILLY TAN.

International Commercial Bank of China: Level 7 (E2), Main Office Tower, Financial Park Labuan, Jalan Merdeka, 87000 Labuan; tel. (87) 581688; fax (87) 581668; Gen. Man. TAI CHI-HSIEN.

J. P. Morgan Chase Bank, Labuan Branch: Level 5 (F), Main Office Tower, Financial Park Labuan, Jalan Merdeka, 87000 Labuan; tel. (87) 424384; fax (87) 424390; e-mail fauziah.hisham@chase.com; Gen. Man. LEONG KET TI.

J. P. Morgan Malaysia Ltd: Unit 5 (F), Level 5, Main Office Tower, Financial Park Labuan, Jalan Merdeka, 87000 Labuan; tel. (87) 459000; fax (87) 451328; Gen. Man. LEONG KET TI.

KBC Bank NV, Labuan Branch: Level 3 (B), Main Office Tower, Financial Park Labuan, Jalan Merdeka, 87000 Labuan; tel. (87) 581778; fax (87) 583787; Gen. Man. KONG KOK CHEE.

Lloyds TSB Bank PLC: Lot B, 11th Floor, Wisma Oceanic, Jalan OKK Awang Besar, 87007 Labuan; tel. (87) 418918; fax (87) 411928; e-mail labuan@lloydstsb.com.my; Dir and Gen. Man. BARRY FRANCIS LEA.

Macquarie Bank Ltd, Labuan Branch: Level 3 (A), Main Office Tower, Financial Park Labuan, Jalan Merdeka, 87000 Labuan; tel. (87) 583080; fax (87) 583088; Division Dir DARREN WOODWARD.

Maybank International (L) Ltd: Level 16 (B), Main Office Tower, Financial Park Labuan, Jalan Merdeka, 87000 Labuan; tel. (87) 414406; fax (87) 414806; e-mail millmit@tm.net.my; Gen. Man. LAM HEE.

Mizuho Corporate Bank Ltd, Labuan Branch: Level 9 (B and C), Main Office Tower, Financial Park Labuan, Jalan Merdeka, 87000 Labuan; tel. (87) 417766; fax (87) 419766; Gen. Man. ISAKU TANIMURA.

Natexis Banque Populaires: Level 9 (G), Main Office Tower, Financial Park Labuan, Jalan Merdeka, 87000 Labuan; tel. (87) 581009; fax (87) 583009; Gen. Man. RIZAL ABDULLAH.

National Australia Bank, Labuan Branch: Level 12 (C2), Main Office Tower, Financial Park Complex, Jalan Merdeka, 87008 Labuan; tel. (87) 426386; fax (87) 428387; e-mail natausm@po.jaring.my; Gen. Man. LIONEL LIM.

OSK Investment Bank (Labuan) Ltd: Lot 3B, Level 5, Wisma Lazenda, Jalan Kemajuan, Labuan; tel. (87) 581885; fax (87) 582885; Prin. Officer ONG LEONG HUAT.

Oversea-Chinese Banking Corporation Ltd, Labuan Branch: Level 8 (C), Main Office Tower, Financial Park Labuan, Jalan Merdeka, 87000 Labuan; tel. (87) 423381; fax (87) 423390; Gen. Man. BERNARD FERNANDO.

Public Bank (L) Ltd: Level 8 (A and B), Main Office Tower, Financial Park Labuan, Jalan Merdeka, 87000 Labuan; tel. (87) 411898; fax (87) 413220; Man. ALEXANDER WONG.

RHB Bank (L) Ltd: Level 15 (B), Main Office Tower, Financial Park Labuan, Jalan Merdeka, 87000 Labuan; tel. (87) 417480; fax (87) 417484; Gen. Man. TOH AY LENG.

RUSD Investment Bank, Inc.: Level 4 (A1), Main Office Tower, Financial Park Labuan, Jalan Merdeka, 87000 Labuan; tel. (87) 452100; fax (87) 543100; Man. Dir NASEERUDDIN A. KHAN.

Société Générale, Labuan Branch: Level 11 (B), Main Office Tower, Financial Park Labuan, Jalan Merdeka, 87000 Labuan; tel. (87) 421676; fax (87) 421669; Gen. Man. RAMZAN ABU TAHIR.

Standard Chartered Bank Offshore Labuan: Level 10 (F), Main Office Tower, Financial Park Labuan, Jalan Merdeka, 87000 Labuan; tel. (87) 417200; fax (87) 417202; Gen. Man. EDWARD NG.

Sumitomo Mitsui Banking Corpn, Labuan Branch: Level 12 (B and C), Main Office Tower, Financial Park Labuan, Jalan Merdeka, 87000 Labuan; tel. (87) 410955; fax (87) 410959; Gen. Man. JUNICHI IKENO.

UBS AG, Labuan Branch: Level 5 (E), Main Office Tower, Financial Park Labuan, Jalan Merdeka, 87000 Labuan; tel. (87) 421743; fax (87) 421746; Man. ZELIE HO SWEE LUM.

United Overseas Bank Ltd, Labuan Branch: Level 6 (A), Main Office Tower, Financial Park Labuan, Jalan Merdeka, 87000 Labuan; tel. (87) 424388; fax (87) 424389; Gen. Man. HO FONG KUN.

United World Chinese Commercial Bank: Level 3 (C), Main Office Tower, Financial Park Labuan, Jalan Merdeka, 87000 Labuan; tel. (87) 452168; fax (87) 453678; Gen. Man. PIN HUNG YEH.

Banking Associations

Association of Banks in Malaysia (ABM): UBN Tower, 34th Floor, 10 Jalan P. Ramlee, 50250 Kuala Lumpur; tel. (3) 20788041; fax (3) 20788004; e-mail banks@abm.org.my; internet www.abm.org.my; f. 1973; Chair. Dato' ABDUL HAMIDY ABDUL HAFIZ; Exec. Dir WONG SUAN LYE.

Institute of Bankers Malaysia: Wisma IBI, 5 Jalan Semantan, Damansara Heights, 50490 Kuala Lumpur; tel. (3) 20956833; fax (3) 20952322; e-mail ibbm@ibbm.org.my; internet www.ibbm.org.my; f. 1977; professional and educational body for the banking and finance industry; Chair. Tan Sri Dato' Sri Dr ZETI AKHTAR AZIZ.

Malayan Commercial Banks' Association: POB 12001, 50764 Kuala Lumpur; tel. (3) 2983991.

Persatuan Institusi Perbankan Tanpa Faedah Malaysia (Association of Islamic Banking Institutions Malaysia—AIBIM): Tingkat 9, Wisma Kraftangan, Jalan Tun Perak, 50050 Kuala Lumpur; tel. (3) 26112096; fax (3) 26112097; e-mail admin@aibim.com; internet www.aibim.com.

STOCK EXCHANGES

Bursa Malaysia: 15th Floor, Exchange Square, Bukit Kewangan, 50200 Kuala Lumpur; tel. (3) 20347000; fax (3) 27326437; e-mail enquiries@bursamalaysia.com; internet www.bursamalaysia.com; f. 1973; fmrly known as Kuala Lumpur Stock Exchange (KLSE); name changed as above in 2004; in 1988 KLSE authorized the ownership of up to 49% of Malaysian stockbroking companies by foreign interests; 988 listed cos (Jan. 2008); merged with Malaysian Exchange for Securities Dealing and Automated Quotation Bhd

MALAYSIA

(MESDAQ) in March 2002; Chair. TUN MOHAMED DZAIDDIN Haji ABDULLAH; CEO Dato' YUSLI MOHAMED YUSOFF.

Malaysia Derivatives Exchange Bhd (MDEX): 10th Floor, Exchange Sq., Bukit Kewangan, 50200 Kuala Lumpur; tel. (3) 20708199; fax (3) 20702376; e-mail info@mdex.com.my; internet www.mdex.com.my; f. 2001 as a result of merger of Kuala Lumpur Options and Financial Futures Exchange Bhd (KLOFFE) and Commodity and Monetary Exchange of Malaysia; multi-product futures exchange; Exec. Chair. Dato' ABDUL JABBAR BIN ABDUL MAJID; Gen. Man. RAGHBIR SINGH BHART.

Regulatory Authority

Securities Commission (SC): 3 Persiaran Bukit Kiara, Bukit Kiara, 50490 Kuala Lumpur; tel. (3) 62048000; fax (3) 62015078; e-mail cau@seccom.com.my; internet www.sc.com.my; f. 1993; Chair. Dato' ZARINAH ANWAR.

INSURANCE

From 1988 onwards, all insurance companies were placed under the authority of the Central Bank, Bank Negara Malaysia. In 1997 there were 69 insurance companies operating in Malaysia, including nine reinsurance companies, 11 composite, 40 general and life and two takaful (compliant with Islamic law) insurance companies.

Principal Insurance Companies

Allianz General Insurance Malaysia Bhd: Wisma UOA II, Floors 23 and 23A, 21 Jalan Pinang, 50450 Kuala Lumpur; tel. (3) 21623388; fax (3) 21626387; e-mail partner@allianz.com.my; internet www.allianz.com.my/general; f. 2001; CEO WILLIAM MEI YORK LIANG; Chair. Tan Sri RAZALI ISMAIL.

Allianz Life Insurance Malaysia Bhd: Wisma UOA II, Floors 23 and 23A, 21 Jalan Pinang, 50450 Kuala Lumpur; tel. (3) 21616001; fax (3) 21626387; e-mail partner@allianz.com.my; internet life.allianz.com.my; fmrly MBA Life Assurance Sdn Bhd; CEO CHRIS JAMES; Chief Financial Officer CHARLES ONG ENG CHOW.

Commerce Life Assurance Bhd: 338 Jalan Tunku Abdul Rahman, 50100 Kuala Lumpur; tel. (3) 26123600; fax (3) 26987035; f. 1992 as AMAL Assurance Bhd; name changed as above in 1999.

Great Eastern Life Assurance (Malaysia) Bhd: Menara Great Eastern, 303 Jalan Ampang, 50450 Kuala Lumpur; tel. (3) 42598888; fax (3) 42590500; e-mail wecare@lifeisgreat.com.my; internet www.lifeisgreat.com.my; Dir and CEO ALEX FOONG SOO HAH.

Hong Leong Assurance Sdn Bhd: Menara HLA, 26th Floor, 3 Jalan Kia Peng, 50450 Kuala Lumpur; tel. (3) 27199228; fax (3) 27101735; internet www.hla.com.my; Chair. Tan Sri QUEK LENG CHAN; Man. Dir and CEO CHARLIE ESPINOLA OROPEZA.

ING Insurance Bhd: Menara ING, 84 Jalan Raja Chulan, POB 10846, 50927 Kuala Lumpur; tel. (3) 21617255; fax (3) 21610549; internet www.ing.com.my; f. 1987; fmrly Aetna Universal Insurance Bhd; Chair. Tengku ABDULLAH IBNI AL-MARHUM Sultan ABU BAKAR.

Jerneh Insurance Corpn Sdn Bhd: Wisma Jerneh, 12th Floor, 38 Jalan Sultan Ismail, POB 12420, 50788 Kuala Lumpur; tel. (3) 2427066; fax (3) 2426672; f. 1970; general; Gen. Man. GOH CHIN ENG.

Malaysia National Insurance Sdn Bhd: Tower 1, 26th Floor, MNI Twins, 11 Jalan Pinang, 50450 Kuala Lumpur; tel. (3) 21769000; fax (3) 21769090; e-mail askme@mni.com.my; internet www.mni.com.my; f. 1970; life and general; CEO MOHAMAD SALIHUDDIN AHMAD.

Malaysian Co-operative Insurance Society Ltd: Wisma MCIS, Jalan Barat, 46200 Petaling Jaya, Selangor; tel. (3) 7552577; fax (3) 7571563; e-mail info@mcis.po.my; internet www.mcis.com.my/mcis; f. 1954; CEO L. MEYYAPPAN.

Manulife Insurance (Malaysia) Bhd: Menara Manulife RB, 12th Floor, 6 Jalan Gelenggang, Damansara Heights, 50490 Kuala Lumpur; tel. (3) 20948055; fax (3) 20935487; internet www.manulife.com.my; f. 1963; life and non-life insurance; fmrly British American Life and General Insurance Bhd; name then changed to John Hancock Life Insurance (Malaysia) Bhd; name changed as above in 2005, following 2004 merger between John Hancock Financial Services, Inc. and Manulife Financial Corpn; Chair. Tan Sri Dato' MOHAMED SHERIFF BIN MOHAMED KASSIM.

Mayban Assurance Bhd: Mayban Assurance Tower, Dataran Maybank, 1 Jalan Maarof, 50000 Kuala Lumpur; tel. (3) 22972888; fax (3) 22972828; e-mail mayassur@tm.net.my; internet www.maybank2u.com.my; Pres. and CEO Datuk AMIRSHAM A. AZIZ.

MBf Insurans Sdn Bhd: Plaza MBf, 5th Floor, Jalan Ampang, POB 10345, 50710 Kuala Lumpur; tel. and fax (3) 2613466; Man. MARC HOOI TUCK KOK.

MCIS Zürich Insurance Bhd: Wisma MCIS Zürich, Jalan Barat, 46200 Petaling Jaya, Selangor; tel. (3) 79552577; fax (3) 79574780; e-mail info@mciszurich.com.my; internet www.mciszurich.com.my;

Directory

CEO MD ADNAN MD ZAIN; Chair. Dato' BALARAM ANAK LELAKI PETHA NAIDU.

Multi-Purpose Insurans Bhd: Menara Multi-Purpose, 9th Floor, Capital Square, 8 Jalan Munshi Abdullah, 50100 Kuala Lumpur; tel. (3) 26919888; fax (3) 26945758; e-mail info@mpib.com.my; fmrly Kompas Insurans Bhd; Senior Gen. Mans WONG FOOK WAH, VISWANATH A. L. KANDASAMY.

Oriental Capital Assurance Bhd: 36 Jalan Ampang, 50450 Kuala Lumpur; tel. (3) 20702828; fax (3) 20724150; e-mail oricap@oricap.net; internet www.oricap.net; f. 2002 as a result of the merger of Capital Insurance Bhd and United Oriental Assurance Sdn Bhd; Chair. Datuk Dr K. AMPIKAIPAKAN; Exec. Dir MOHD YUSOF BIN IDRIS.

Overseas Assurance Corpn Ltd: Wisma Lee Rubber, 21st Floor, Jalan Melata, 50100 Kuala Lumpur; tel. (3) 2022939; fax (3) 2912288; Gen. Man. A. K. WONG.

Progressive Insurance Sdn Bhd: Plaza Berjaya, 9th, 10th and 15th Floors, 12 Jalan Imbi, POB 10028, 50700 Kuala Lumpur; tel. (3) 2410044; fax (3) 2418257; Man. JERRY PAUT.

RHB Insurance Bhd: Tower 1, 4th Floor, RHB Centre, Jalan Tun Razak, 50450 Kuala Lumpur; tel. (3) 9812731; fax (3) 9812729; Man. MOHAMMAD ABDULLAH.

Sime AXA Assurance Bhd: Wisma Sime Darby, 15th Floor, Jalan Raja Laut, 50350 Kuala Lumpur; tel. (3) 2937888; fax (3) 2914672; e-mail hkkang@simenet.com; Gen. Man. HAK KOON KANG.

South-East Asia Insurance Bhd: Tingkat 9, Menara SEA Insurance, 1008 Jalan Sultan Ismail, 50250 Kuala Lumpur; POB 6120 Pudu, 55916 Kuala Lumpur; tel. (3) 2938111; fax (3) 2930111; CEO HASHIM HARUN.

UMBC Insurans Sdn Bhd: Bangunan Sime Bank, 16th Floor, Jalan Sultan Sulaiman, 50000 Kuala Lumpur; tel. (3) 2328733; fax (3) 2322181; f. 1961; CEO ABDULLAH ABDUL SAMAD.

Trade and Industry

GOVERNMENT AGENCIES

Danamodal Nasional Bhd (Danamodal): 10th Floor, Bangunan Sime Bank, Jalan Sultan Sulaiman, 50000 Kuala Lumpur; tel. (3) 20312255; fax (3) 20310786; e-mail info@danamodal.com.my; f. 1998 to recapitalize banks and restructure financial institutions, incl. arranging mergers and consolidations; Chair. Raja Datuk ARSHAD Raja Tun UDA; Man. Dir MARIANUS VONG SHIN TZOI.

Federal Agricultural Marketing Authority (FAMA): Bangunan Fama Point, Lot 17304, Jalan Persiaran 1, Bandar Baru Selayang, 68100 Batu Caves, Selangor Darul Ehsan; tel. (3) 61389622; fax (3) 61365610; e-mail fama@fama.net.my; internet www.famaxchange.org; f. 1965 to supervise, co-ordinate and improve marketing of agricultural produce, and to seek and promote new markets and outlets for agricultural produce; Chair. Datuk ABDUL RAHIM B. BAKRI; Dir-Gen. Dato' Haji MOHAMED SHARIFF ABDUL AZIZ.

Federal Land Development Authority (FELDA): Wisma FELDA, Jalan Perumahan Gurney, 54000 Kuala Lumpur; tel. (3) 2935066; fax (3) 2920087; e-mail upd@felda.net.my; internet www.felda.net.my; f. 1956; govt statutory body formed to develop land into agricultural smallholdings to eradicate rural poverty; 893,150 ha of land developed (1994); involved in rubber, oil palm and sugar-cane cultivation; Chair. Tan Sri Dr MOHD YUSOF NOOR; Dir-Gen. Dato' AHMAD TARMIZI ALIAS.

Khazanah Nasional: Level 33, Tower 2, Petronas Twin Towers, 50088 Kuala Lumpur; tel. (3) 20340000; fax (3) 20340300; e-mail info@khazanah.com.my; internet www.khazanah.com.my; f. 1994; state-controlled investment co; assumed responsibility for certain assets fmrly under control of the Ministry of Finance Inc; holds 40% of Telekom Malaysia Bhd, 40% of Tenaga Nasional Bhd, 6.6% of HICOM Bhd and 17.8% of PROTON; Chair. Dato' Seri ABDULLAH BIN Haji AHMAD BADAWI; Man. Dir Dato' AZMAN BIN Haji MOKHTAR.

Malaysia External Trade Development Corpn (MATRADE): Menara MATRADE, Jalan Khidmat Usaha, off Jalan Duta, 50480 Kuala Lumpur; tel. (3) 62077077; fax (3) 62037037; e-mail info@matrade.gov.my; internet www.matrade.gov.my; f. 1993; responsible for external trade development and promotion; CEO Dato' NOHARUDDIN NORDIN.

Malaysian Institute of Economic Research: Menara Dayabumi, 9th Floor, Jalan Sultan Hishamuddin, POB 12160, 50768 Kuala Lumpur; tel. (3) 22725897; fax (3) 22730197; e-mail Admin@mier.po.my; internet www.mier.org.my; f. 1986; Exec. Dir Dr MOHAMED ARIFF; Chair. Tan Sri Dato' MOHAMED SHERIFF MOHAMED KASSIM.

Malaysian Palm Oil Board (MPOB): 6 Persiaran Institusi, Bandar Baru Bangi, 43000 Kajang, Selangor; tel. (3) 87694400; fax (3) 89259446; e-mail webmaster@mpob.gov.my; internet www.mpob.gov.my; f. 2000 by merger of Palm Oil Registration and

MALAYSIA

Licensing Authority and Palm Oil Research Institute of Malaysia; Chair. Dato' SABRI AHMAD.

Malaysian Timber Industry Board (Lembaga Perindustrian Kayu Malaysia): 13–17 Menara PGRM, 8 Jalan Pudu Ulu, 56100 Cheras, Kuala Lumpur; tel. (3) 92822235; fax (3) 92851477; e-mail info@mtib.gov.my; internet www.mtib.gov.my; f. 1973 to promote and regulate the export of timber and timber products from Malaysia; Chair. Dr MICHAEL DOSIM LUNJEW; Dir-Gen. MOHD NAZURI BIN HASHIM SHAH.

Muda Agricultural Development Authority (MADA): MADA HQ, Ampang Jajar, 05990 Alor Setar, Kedah; tel. (4) 7728255; fax (4) 7722667; internet www.mada.gov.my; Chair. Dato' Seri MAHDZIR BIN KHALID.

National Economic Action Council: NEAC-MTEN, Prime Minister's Office, Blok Utama, Tingkat 1–5, Pusat Pentadbiran Kerajaan Persekutuan, 62502 Putrajaya; tel. (3) 88882903; fax (3) 88882902; e-mail effendi@epu.jpm.my; internet www.neac.gov.my; Exec. Dir Dato' Sri MOHAMED EFFENDI NORWAWI.

National Information Technology Council (NITC): Kuala Lumpur; Sec. Datuk Tengku Dr MOHD AZZMAN SHARIFFADEEN.

National Timber Certification Council: Kuala Lumpur; Chair. CHEW LYE TENG.

Perbadanan Nasional Bhd (PERNAS): Kuala Lumpur; tel. (3) 2935177; internet www.pns.com.my; f. 1969; govt-sponsored; promotes trade, banking, property and plantation development, construction, mineral exploration, steel manufacturing, inland container transportation, mining, insurance, industrial development, engineering services, telecommunication equipment, hotels and shipping; cap. p.u. RM 116.25m.; 10 wholly owned subsidiaries, over 60 jointly owned subsidiaries and 18 assoc. cos; Chair. Datuk ISMAIL SABRI BIN YAAKOB; Man. Dir Tuan SYED KAMARULZAMAN BIN SYED ZAINOL KHODKI SHAHABUDIN.

DEVELOPMENT ORGANIZATIONS

Fisheries Development Authority of Malaysia: 7th–11th Floors, Wisma PKNS, Jalan Raja Laut, 50784 Kuala Lumpur; tel. (3) 26177000; fax (3) 26911931; e-mail info@kim.moa.my; internet lkim.gov.my; Dir-Gen. Dato' MUSTAFA BIN Haji AHMAD.

Johor Corporation: 13th Floor, Menara Johor Corporation, Kotaraya, 80000 Johor Bahru; tel. (7) 2232692; fax (7) 2233175; e-mail pdnjohor@jcorp.com.my; internet www.jcorp.com.my; development agency of the Johor state govt; Chair. Dato' Haji ABDUL GHANI BIN OTHMAN; Chief Exec. Dato' MUHAMMAD ALI HASHIM.

Kumpulan FIMA Bhd (Food Industries of Malaysia): Suite 4-1, Level 4, Block C, Plaza Damansara, 45 Jalan Medan Setia 1, Bukit Damansara, 50490 Kuala Lumpur; tel. (3) 20921211; fax (3) 20925923; e-mail enquiry@fima.com.my; internet www.fima.com.my; f. 1972; fmrly govt corpn, transferred to private sector in 1991; promotes food and related industry through investment on its own or by co-ventures with local or foreign entrepreneurs; oil palm, cocoa and fruit plantation developments; manufacturing and packaging, trading, supermarkets and restaurants; Man. Dir Encik AHMAD RIZA BIN BASIR; 1,189 employees.

Majlis Amanah Rakyat (MARA) (Trust Council for the People): Bangunan Medan MARA, 13th Floor, 21 Jalan Raja Laut, 50609 Kuala Lumpur; tel. (3) 26915111; fax (3) 26913620; e-mail webmaster@mara.gov.my; internet www.mara.gov.my; f. 1966 to promote, stimulate, facilitate and undertake economic and social development; to participate in industrial and commercial undertakings and jt ventures; Dir-Gen. Datuk ZAMANI BIN MOHD NOOR.

Malaysian Agricultural Research and Development Institute (MARDI): POB 12301, General Post Office, 50774 Kuala Lumpur; tel. (3) 89437111; fax (3) 89483664; e-mail saharan@mardi.my; internet www.mardi.my; f. 1969; research and development in food and tropical agriculture; Dir-Gen. Datuk Dr ABD. SHUKOR BIN ABD. RAHMAN.

Malaysian Industrial Development Authority (MIDA): Plaza Sentral, Block 4, 5 Jalan Stesen Sentral, 50470 Kuala Lumpur; tel. (3) 22673633; fax (3) 22747970; e-mail promotion@mida.gov.my; internet www.mida.gov.my; f. 1967; Chair. Tan Sri Datuk ZAINAL ABIDIN BIN SULONG; Dir-Gen. Datuk R. KARUNAKARAN.

Malaysian Industrial Development Finance Bhd: Level 21, Menara MIDF, 82 Jalan Raja Chulan, 50200 Kuala Lumpur; tel. (3) 21619011; fax (3) 21617580; e-mail inquiry@midf.com.my; internet www.midf.com.my; f. 1960 by the Govt; banks, insurance cos, industrial financing, advisory services, project development, merchant and commercial banking services; Chair. Tan Sri Dato' MAHMOOD TAIB; Man. Dir Dato' MOHAMED SALLEHUDDIN BIN OTHMAN.

Malaysian Pepper Board: Lot 115, Jalan Utama, 93916 Kuching, Sarawak; tel. (82) 331811; fax (82) 336877; e-mail info@mpb.gov.my; internet www.mpb.gov.my; f. 2007; responsible for the statutory grading of all Sarawak pepper for export, licensing of pepper dealers and exporters, trading and the development and promotion of pepper grading, storage and processing facilities; Chair. Datuk RICHARD RIOT JAEM; Dir-Gen. GRUNSIN AYOM.

Pinang Development Corporation: 1 Pesiaran Mahsuri, Bandar Bayan Baru, 11909 Bayan Lepas, Pinang; tel. (4) 6340111; fax (4) 6432405; e-mail enquiry@pdc.gov.my; internet www.pdc.gov.my; f. 1969; development agency of the Pinang state government; Gen. Man. ROSLI JAAFAR.

Sarawak Economic Development Corpn: Menara SEDC, 6th–11th Floors, Sarawak Plaza, Jalan Tunku Abdul Rahman, POB 400, 93902 Kuching; tel. (82) 416777; fax (82) 424330; e-mail ssedc@pop1.jaring.my; internet www.sedc.com.my; f. 1972; statutory org. responsible for commercial and industrial development in Sarawak either solely or jtly with foreign and local entrepreneurs; responsible for the development of tourism infrastructure; Chair. Datuk Haji TALIB ZULPILIP.

Selangor State Development Corporation (PKNS): Persiaran Barat, off Jalan Barat, 46505 Petaling Jaya, Selangor; tel. (3) 79572955; fax (3) 79575250; e-mail general@pkns.gov.my; internet www.pkns.gov.my; f. 1964; partially govt-owned; Corporate Man. YUSOF OTHMAN.

CHAMBERS OF COMMERCE

Associated Chinese Chambers of Commerce and Industry of Malaysia: Lot 6.05, Menara Promet, 6th Floor, Jalan Sultan Ismail, 50250 Kuala Lumpur; tel. (3) 21452503; fax (3) 21452562; e-mail acccim@acccim.org.my; internet www.acccim.org.my; Pres. Tan Sri WILLIAM CHENG; Sec.-Gen. Tan Sri Dato' SOONG SIEW HOONG.

Malay Chamber of Commerce Malaysia: 33 & 35, Jalan Medan Setia 1, Bukit Damansara, 50490 Kuala Lumpur; tel. (3) 20962233; fax (3) 20962533; e-mail wmaster@dpmm.org.my; internet www.dpmm.org.my; f. 1957 as Associated Malay Chambers of Commerce of Malaya; name changed as above 1992; Pres. SYED ALI MOHAMED ALATTAS; Sec.-Gen. ZAKI SAID.

Malaysian Associated Indian Chambers of Commerce and Industry: Megan Ave 11, Block B, 9th Floor, Unit 1, 12 Jalan Yap Kwan Seng, 50450 Kuala Lumpur; tel. (3) 21712616; fax (3) 21711195; e-mail info@maicci.org.my; internet www.maicci.org.my; f. 1950; Pres. PARDIP KUMAR KUKREJA; 8 brs.

Malaysian International Chamber of Commerce and Industry (MICCI) (Dewan Perniagaan dan Perindustrian Antarabangsa Malaysia): C-8-8, 8th Floor, Block C, Plaza Mont' Kiara, 50480 Kuala Lumpur; tel. (3) 62017708; fax (3) 62017705; e-mail micci@micci.com; internet www.micci.com; f. 1837; brs in Pinang, Perak, Johor, Melaka and Sabah; 1,000 corporate mems; Pres. G. KRISHNAN; Exec. Dir STEWART J. FORBES.

National Chamber of Commerce and Industry of Malaysia: 6A, 6th Floor, Menara BGI, Plaza Berjaya, 12 Jalan Imbi, 55100 Kuala Lumpur; tel. (3) 24190600; fax (3) 2413775; e-mail enquiry@nccim.org.my; internet www.nccim.org.my; f. 1962; Pres. Tuan SYED ALI MOHAMED ALATTAS; Hon. Sec.-Gen. Dato' SYED HUSSEIN AL-HABSHEE.

Sabah Bumiputera Chamber of Commerce (SBCC): Lot 119, 4th Floor, S.B.C.C Bldg, Locked Bag 154, Jalan Gaya, 88999 Kota Kinabalu; tel. (88) 222442; fax (88) 223454; f. 1972; Pres. Datuk Haji AHMAD ALIP LOPE ABDUL AZIZ; Sec.-Gen. Encik JURIL Haji SUDIN.

Sabah United Chinese Chambers of Commerce (SUCCC): POB 12176, 88824 Kota Kinabalu; tel. (88) 225460; fax (88) 218185; e-mail succc01@tm.net.my; internet www.succc.org; f. 1955; Pres. Datuk Seri Panglima SARI NUAR.

Sarawak Chamber of Commerce and Industry (SCCI): POB A-841, Kenyalang Park Post Office, 93806 Kuching; tel. (82) 237148; fax (82) 237186; e-mail scci@su.cmsb.com.my; internet www.cmsb.com.my/subsi/ubg/sccimain.htm; f. 1950; Chair. Datuk Haji MOHAMED AMIN Haji SATEM; Dep. Chair. Datuk Abang Haji ABDUL KARIM Tun Abang Haji OPENG.

INDUSTRIAL AND TRADE ASSOCIATIONS

Federation of Malaysian Manufacturers: Wisma FMM, 3 Persiaran Dagang, PJU 9 Bandar Sri Damansara, 52200 Kuala Lumpur; tel. (3) 62761211; fax (3) 62741266; e-mail webmaster@fmm.org.my; internet www.fmm.org.my; f. 1968; offers guidance and advice relating to trade and industry; presents problems and concerns to the Govt; 2,117 mems (Jan. 2005); Pres. Tan Sri Datuk YONG POH KON; CEO LEE CHENG SUAN.

Federation of Rubber Trade Associations of Malaysia: 138 Jalan Bandar, 50000 Kuala Lumpur; tel. (3) 2384006.

Malayan Agricultural Producers' Association: Kuala Lumpur; tel. (3) 42573988; fax (3) 42573113; e-mail mapa@myjaring.net; f. 1997; 406 mem. estates and 108 factories/mills; Pres. Dato' Dr MOHD NOOR BIN ISMAIL; Dir MOHAMAD BIN AUDONG.

Malaysian Iron and Steel Industry Federation: 28E, 30E, 5th Floor, Block 2, Worldwide Business Park, Jalan Tinju 13/50, Section 13, 40675 Shah Alam, Selangor; tel. (3) 55133970; fax (3) 55133891;

MALAYSIA

Directory

e-mail misif@po.jaring.my; internet www.misif.org.my; Chair. Tan Sri Soong Siew Hoong; 150 mems.

Malaysian Palm Oil Association (MPOA): Bangunan Getah Asli I, 12th Floor, 148 Jalan Ampang, 50450 Kuala Lumpur; tel. (3) 27105680; fax (3) 27105679; e-mail kay@mpoa.org.my; internet www.mpoa.org.my; f. 1999 as result of rationalization of plantation industry; secretariat for producers of palm oil; Chief. Exec. Dato' Mamat Salleh.

Malaysian Pineapple Industry Board: Wisma Nanas, 5 Jalan Padi Mahsuri, Bandar Baru UDA, 81200 Johor Bahru; tel. (7) 2361211; fax (7) 2365694; e-mail mpib@tm.net.my; internet www.mpib.gov.my; Dir-Gen. Tuan Haji Ismail bin Abd Jamal.

Malaysian Rubber Board: Bangunan Getah Asli, Tingkat 17 and 18, 148 Jalan Ampang, 50450 Kuala Lumpur; tel. (3) 92062000; fax (3) 21634492; e-mail general@lgm.gov.my; internet www.lgm.gov.my; f. 1998; implements policies and development programmes to ensure the viability of the Malaysian rubber industry; regulates the industry (in particular, the packing, grading, shipping and export of rubber); Dir-Gen. Dr Kamarul Baharain bin Basir.

Malaysian Rubber Products Manufacturers' Association: 1 Jalan USJ 11/1J, Subang Jaya, 47620 Petaling Jaya, Selangor; tel. (3) 56316150; fax (3) 56316152; e-mail mrpma@po.jaring.my; internet www.mrpma.com; f. 1952; Pres. Tan Sri Datuk Arshad Ayub; 144 mems.

Malaysian Timber Certification Council (MTCC): 19th Floor, Menara PGRM, 8 Jalan Pudu Ulu, Cheras, 56100 Kuala Lumpur; tel. (3) 92005008; fax (3) 92006008; e-mail mtcc@tm.net.my; internet www.mtcc.com.my; f. 1999; operates a voluntary national timber certification scheme to encourage sustainable forest management; Chair. Dato' Dr Freezailah Che Yeom.

Malaysian Wood Industries Association: 19B, 19th Floor, Menara PGRM, 8 Jalan Pudu Ulu, Cheras, 56100 Kuala Lumpur; tel. (3) 92821789; fax (3) 92821779; e-mail mwia@tm.net.my; internet www.mtc.com.my/industry/mwia/mwia.html; f. 1957; Exec. Officer Pang Suet Kum.

National Tobacco Board Malaysia (Ibu Pejabat Lembaga Tembakau Negara): Kubang Kerian, POB 198, 15720 Kota Bharu, Kelantan; tel. (9) 7652212; fax (9) 7655640; e-mail ltnm@ltn.gov.my; internet www.ltn.gov.my; Dir-Gen. Teo Hui Bek.

Northern Malaya Rubber Millers and Packers Association: 22 Pitt St, 3rd Floor, Suites 301–303, 10200 Pinang; tel. (4) 620037; f. 1919; 153 mems; Pres. Hwang Sing Lue; Hon. Sec. Lee Seng Keok.

Palm Oil Refiners' Association of Malaysia (PORAM): 801 C/802A Blok B, Executive Suites, Kelana Business Centre, 97 Jalan SS7/2, 47301 Kelana Jaya, Selangor; tel. (3) 74920006; fax (3) 74920128; e-mail poram@poram.org.my; internet www.poram.org.my; f. 1975 to promote the palm oil refining industry; Chair. Dato' Low Mong Hua (acting); CEO Frankie Wee; 80 mems.

Rubber Industry Smallholders' Development Authority (RISDA): Bangunan RISDA, Km 7, Jalan Ampang, Karung Berkunci 11067, 50990 Kuala Lumpur; tel. (3) 4564022; e-mail webmaster@risda.gov.my; internet www.risda.gov.my; Dir-Gen. Abdullah bin Abdul Kadir.

Tin Industry Research and Development Board: West Block, 8th Floor, Wisma Selangor Dredging, Jalan Ampang, POB 12560, 50782 Kuala Lumpur; tel. (3) 21616171; fax (3) 21616179; e-mail mcom@mcom.com.my; Chair. Mohamed Ajib Anuar; Sec. Muhamad Nor Muhamad.

EMPLOYERS' ORGANIZATIONS

Malaysian Employers' Federation: 3A06–3A07, Block A, Pusat Dagangan Phileo Damansara II, 15 Jalan 16/11, off Jalan Damansara, 46350 Petaling Jaya, Selangor; tel. (3) 79557778; fax (3) 79556808; e-mail mef-hq@mef.org.my; internet www.mef.org.my; f. 1959; Pres. Dato' Azman Shah Dato' Seri Harun; Exec. Dir Haji Shamsuddin Bardan; private-sector org. incorporating 13 employer organizations and 4,211 individual enterprises, including:

Association of Insurance Employers: c/o Royal Insurance (M) Sdn Bhd, Menara Boustead, 5th Floor, 69 Jalan Raja Chulan, 50200 Kuala Lumpur; tel. (3) 2410233; fax (3) 2442762; Pres. Ng Kim Hoong.

Commercial Employers' Association of Peninsular Malaysia: c/o The East Asiatic Co (M) Bhd, 1 Jalan 205, 46050 Petaling Jaya, Selangor; tel. (3) 7913322; fax (3) 7913561; Pres. Hamzah Haji Ghulam.

Malaysian Chamber of Mines: West Block, Wisma Selangor Dredging, 8th Floor, 142c Jalan Ampang, 50450 Kuala Lumpur; tel. (3) 21616171; fax (3) 21616179; e-mail mcom@mcom.com.my; internet www.mcom.com.my; f. 1914; promotes and protects interests of Malaysian mining industry; Pres. Mohamed Ajib Anuar; Exec. Dir Muhamad Nor Muhamad; 100 mems.

Malaysian Textile Manufacturers' Association: C-9-4, Megan Ave 1, 189 Jalan Tun Razak, 50400 Kuala Lumpur; tel. (3) 21621587; fax (3) 21623953; e-mail info@mtma.org.my; internet www.fashion-asia.com; Pres. Yap Fung Kong; Exec. Dir Choy Ming Bil; 230 mems.

Pan Malaysian Bus Operators' Association: 88 Jalan Sultan Idris Shah, 30300 Ipoh, Perak; tel. (5) 2549421; fax (5) 2550858; Sec. Teoh Ewe Hun.

Sabah Employers' Consultative Association: Dewan SECA, No. 4, Block A, 1st Floor, Bandar Ramai-Ramai, 90000 Sandakan, Sabah; tel. and fax (89) 272846; Chair. Ling Ah Hong.

Stevedore Employers' Association: 5 Pengkalan Weld, POB 288, 10300 Pinang; tel. (4) 2615091; Pres. Abdul Rahman Maidin.

UTILITIES

Electricity

Energy Commission of Malaysia: Levels 15, 19 and 20, Menara Dato' Onn, Putra World Centre, Jalan Tun Ismail, Kuala Lumpur; internet www.st.gov.my; f. 2002; regulatory body supervising electricity and gas supply.

Tenaga Nasional Bhd: 129 Jalan Bangsar, POB 11003, 50732 Kuala Lumpur; tel. (3) 2825566; fax (3) 2823274; e-mail webadmin@tnb.com.my; internet www.tnb.com.my; f. 1990 through the corporatization and privatization of the National Electricity Board; 53% govt-controlled; generation, transmission and distribution of electricity in Peninsular Malaysia; generating capacity of 7,621 MW (63% of total power generation); also purchases power from 12 licensed independent power producers; Chair. Tan Sri Dato' Amar Leo Moggie; Pres. and CEO Dato' Che Khalib bin Mohamad Noh.

Sabah Electricity Supply Board (SESB): Wisma SESB, Jalan Tunku Abdul Rahman, 88673 Kota Kinabalu; tel. (88) 211699; fax (88) 282314; e-mail webmaster@sesb.com.my; internet www.sesb.com.my; generation, transmission and distribution of electricity in Sabah; Man. Dir Ir Baharin bin Din.

Syarikat Sesco Bhd (SESCO): POB 149, 93700 Kuching, Sarawak; tel. (82) 441188; fax (82) 444433; e-mail public_enquiry@sesoc.com.my; internet www.sesco.com.my; fmrly known as Sarawak Electricity Supply Corpn; generation, transmission and distribution of electricity in Sarawak; Chair. Datuk Abdul Hamed Sepawi.

Gas

Energy Commission of Malaysia: see above**Gas Malaysia Sdn Bhd:** 5 Jalan Serendah 26/17, Seksyen 26, Peti Surat 7901, 40732 Shah Alam, Selangor Darul Ehsan; tel. (3) 51923000; e-mail ccu@gasmalaysia.com; internet www.gasmalaysia.com; f. 1992; Chair. Tan Sri Datuk Dr Ahmad Tajuddin Ali; CEO Muhamad Noor Hamid.

Water

Under the federal Constitution, water supply is the responsibility of the state Governments. In 1998, owing to water shortages, the National Water Resources Council was established to co-ordinate management of water resources at national level. Malaysia's sewerage system is operated by Indah Water Konsortium, owned by Prime Utilities.

National Water Resources Council: c/o Ministry of Works, Jalan Sultan Salahuddin, 50580 Kuala Lumpur; tel. (3) 2919011; fax (3) 2986612; f. 1998 to co-ordinate management of water resources at national level through co-operation with state water boards; Chair. Dato' Seri Dr Mahathir bin Mohamad.

Regulatory Authorities

Johor State Regulatory Body: c/o Pejabat Setiausaha Kerajaan Negeri Johor, Aras 1, Bangunan Sultan Ibrahim, Jalan Bukit Timbalan, 80000 Johor Bahru; tel. (7) 223850; Dir Tuan Haji Omar bin Awab.

Kelantan Water Department: Tingkat Bawah Blok 6, Kota Darul Naim, 15503 Kota Bahru, Kelantan; tel. (9) 7475240; e-mail hjabaziz@yahoo.com.my; Dir Tuan Haji Abdul Aziz bin Haji Abdul Rahman.

Water Supply Authorities

Kedah Public Works Department: Bangunan Sultan Abdul Halim, Jalan Sultan Badlishah, 05582 Alor Setar, Kedah; tel. (4) 7334041; fax (4) 7341616; internet kedah.jkr.gov.my; Dir Baharanuddin bin Che Zain.

Kelantan Water Sdn Bhd: 14 Beg Berkunci, Jalan Kuala Krai, 15990 Kota Bahru, Kelantan; tel. (10) 9022222; fax (10) 9022236; Dir Peter New Berkley.

Kuching Water Board: Jalan Batu Lintang, 93200 Kuching, Sarawak; tel. (82) 240371; fax (82) 244546; internet www.kwb.gov.my; Gen. Man. Encik Sung Siew Eng.

Labuan Public Works Department: Jalan Kg. Jawa, POB 2, 87008 Labuan; tel. (87) 414040; fax (87) 412370; Dir Ir ZULKIFLY BIN MADON.

LAKU Management Sdn Bhd: Soon Hup Tower, 6th Floor, Lot 907, Jalan Merbau, 98000 Miri; tel. (85) 442000; fax (85) 442005; e-mail chuilin@pd.jaring.my; serves Miri, Limbang and Bintulu; CEO YONG CHIONG VAN.

Melaka Water Corpn: Tingkat Bawah, 1 10–13, Graha Maju, Jalan Graha Maju, 75300 Melaka; tel. (6) 2825233; fax (6) 2837266; e-mail baharam@pamwtr.gov.my; Dir Ir Haji BAHARAM BIN Haji MOHAMED.

Negeri Sembilan Water Department: Wisma Negeri, 70990 Seremban; tel. (6) 7622314; fax (6) 7620753; Dir Ir Dr MOHD AKBAR.

Pahang Water Supply Department (Jabatan Bekalan Air Pahang): 9–10 Kompleks Tun Razak, Bandar Indera Mahkota, 25582 Kuantan, Pahang; tel. (9) 5721222; fax (9) 5721221; e-mail p-jba@pahang.gov.my; Dir Ir Haji ISMAIL BIN Haji MAT NOOR.

Perak Water Board: Jalan St John, Peti Surat 589, 30760 Ipoh, Perak; tel. (5) 2551155; fax (5) 2556397; internet www.lap.com.my; Dir Ir SANI BIN SIDIK.

Penang Water Supply Corpn: Level 32, KOMTAR, 10000 Pinang; tel. (4) 2634200; fax (4) 2613581; e-mail customer@pba.com.my; internet www.pba.com.my; f. 1973; Ir JASENI BIN MAIDINSA.

Sabah State Water Department: Wisma MUIS, Blok A, Tingkat 6, Beg Berkunci 210, 88825 Kota Kinabalu; tel. (88) 232364; fax (88) 232396; e-mail muis.air@sabah.gov.my; internet www.sabah.gov.my/air; Man. MOHAMAD TAHIR BIN MOHAMAD TALIB.

SAJ Holdings Sdn Bhd: Bangunan Ibu Pejabat SAJ Holdings, Jalan Garuda, Larkin, POB 262, 80350 Johor Bahru; tel. (7) 2244040; fax (7) 2234060; e-mail support@saj.com.my; internet www.saj.com.my; f. 1999; Exec. Chair. Tan Sri Dato' Paduka Dr SALEHUDDIN MOHAMED.

Sarawak Public Works Department: Wisma Seberkas, Jalan Tun Haji Openg, 93582 Kuching; tel. (82) 244041; fax (82) 429679; Dir MICHAEL TING KUOK NG.

Selangor Water Department: POB 5001, Jalan Pantai Baru, 59990 Kuala Lumpur; tel. (3) 2826244; fax (3) 2827535; f. 1972; Dir Ir LIEW WAI KIAT.

Sibu Water Board: Km 5, Jalan Salim, POB 405, 96007 Sibu, Sarawak; tel. (84) 211001; fax (84) 211543; e-mail swbs@swb.gov.my; internet www.swb.gov.my; Gen. Man. DANIEL WONG PARK ING.

Terengganu Water Department: Tkt 3, Wisma Negeri, Jalan Pejabat, 20200 Kuala Terengganu; tel. (9) 6222444; fax (9) 6221510; Dir Ir Haji WAN NGAH BIN WAN.

TRADE UNIONS

Congress of Unions of Employees in the Public Administrative and Civil Services (CUEPACS): internet www.cuepacs.org.my; a nat. fed. with 53 affiliates, representing 120,000 govt workers (2005); Pres. Haji OMAR BIN Haji OSMAN.

Malaysian Trades Union Congress: Wisma MTUC, 10-5, Jalan USJ 9/5T, 47620 Subang Jaya, Selangor; POB 3073, 46000 Petaling Jaya, Selangor; tel. (3) 80242953; fax (3) 80243224; e-mail mtuc@tm.net.my; internet www.mtuc.org.my; f. 1949; 247 affiliated unions, representing approx. 500,000 workers; Pres. SYED SHAHIR BIN SYED MOHAMUD; Sec.-Gen. G. RAJASEKARAN.

Principal affiliated unions:

All Malayan Estates Staff Union: 29-3, Jalan USJ 1/1A, 47620 Subang Jaya; tel. (3) 80240375; fax (3) 80247822; e-mail mes@po.jaring.my; 2,654 mems; Pres. TITUS GLADWIN; Gen. Sec. D. P. S. THAMOTHARAM.

Amalgamated Union of Employees in Government Clerical and Allied Services: 32A Jalan Gajah, off Jalan Yew, Pudu, 55100 Kuala Lumpur; tel. (3) 9859613; fax (3) 9838632; 6,703 mems; Pres. IBRAHIM BIN ABDUL WAHAB; Gen. Sec. MOHAMED IBRAHIM BIN ABDUL WAHAB.

Chemical Workers' Union: 35B, Jalan SS 15/4B, Subang Jaya, 47500 Petaling Jaya, Selangor; 1,886 mems; Pres. RUSIAN HITAM; Gen. Sec. JOHN MATHEWS.

Electricity Industry Workers' Union: 55-2 Jalan SS 15/8A, Subang Jaya, 47500 Petaling Jaya, Selangor; tel. (3) 7335243; 22,000 mems; Pres. ABDUL RASHID; Gen. Sec. P. ARUNASALAM.

Federation of Unions in the Textile, Garment and Leather Industry: c/o Selangor Textile and Garment Manufacturing Employees Union, 9D Jalan Travers, 50470 Kuala Lumpur; tel. (3) 2742578; f. 1989; four affiliates; Pres. ABDUL RAZAK HAMID; Gen. Sec. ABU BAKAR IBRAHIM.

Harbour Workers' Union, Port Kelang: 106 Persiaran Raja Muda Musa, Port Kelang; 2,426 mems; Pres. MOHAMED SHARIFF BIN YAMIN; Gen. Sec. MOHAMED HAYAT BIN AWANG.

Kesatuan Pekerja-Pekerja FELDA: 2 Jalan Maktab Enam, Melalui Jalan Perumahan Gurney, 54000 Kuala Lumpur; tel. (3) 26929972; fax (3) 26913409; 2,900 mems; Pres. INDERA PUTRA Haji ISMAIL; Gen. Sec. MOHAMAD BIN ABDUL RAHMAN.

Kesatuan Pekerja-Pekerja Perusahaan Membuat Tekstil dan Pakaian Pulau Pinang dan Seberang Prai: 23 Lorong Talang Satu, Prai Gardens, 13600 Prai; tel. (4) 301397; 3,900 mems; Pres. ABDUL RAZAK HAMID; Gen. Sec. KENNETH STEPHEN PERKINS.

Kesatuan Pekerja Tenaga Nasional Bhd: 30 Jalan Liku Bangsar, POB 10400, 59100 Kuala Lumpur; tel. (3) 2745657; 10,456 mems; Pres. MOHAMED ABU BAKAR; Gen. Sec. IDRIS BIN ISMAIL.

Malayan Technical Services Union: 3A Jalan Menteri, off Jalan Cochrane, 55100 Kuala Lumpur; tel. (3) 92851778; fax (3) 92811875; e-mail mtsu@streamyx.com; 6,000 mems; Pres. SHUHAIMI OTHMAN; Gen. Sec. SAMUEL DEVADASAN.

Malaysian Rubber Board Staff Union: POB 10150, 50908 Kuala Lumpur; tel. (3) 42565102; 850 mems; Pres. HASNAH GANI; Gen. Sec. SUBRAMANIAM SINNASAMY.

Metal Industry Employees' Union: Metalworkers' House, 5 Lorong Utara Kecil, 46200 Petaling Jaya, Selangor; tel. (3) 79567214; fax (3) 79550854; e-mail mieum@tm.net.my; 15,491 mems; Pres. SAMUSUDDIN USOP; Gen. Sec. JACOB ENGKATESU.

National Union of Bank Employees (NUBE): 12 NUBE House, 3rd Floor, Jalan Tun Sambanthan 3, Brickfield, 50470 Kuala Lumpur; tel. (3) 20789800; fax (3) 20703800; e-mail nube_hq@streamyx.com; internet www.nube.org.my; 27,000 mems; Gen. Sec. JOSEPH SOLOMON.

National Union of Commercial Workers: Bangunan NUCW, 98A-D Jalan Masjid India, 50100 Kuala Lumpur; POB 12059, 50780 Kuala Lumpur; tel. (3) 26927385; fax (3) 26925930; f. 1959; 11,937 mems; Pres. TAIB SHARIF; Gen. Sec. C. KRISHNAN.

National Union of Plantation Workers: 428 A-B, Jalan 5/46, Gasing Indah, POB 73, 46700 Petaling Jaya, Selangor; tel. (3) 77827622; fax (3) 77815321; e-mail nupw@tm.net.my; f. 1946; 29,251 mems; Pres. NADARAJA A/L KUMARAN; Gen. Sec. Dato' G. SANKARAN.

National Union of PWD Employees: 32B Jalan Gajah, off Jalan Yew, 55100 Kuala Lumpur; tel. (3) 9850149; 5,869 mems; Pres. KULOP IBRAHIM; Gen. Sec. S. SANTHANASAMY.

National Union of Telecoms Employees: Wisma NUTE, 17A Jalan Bangsar, 59200 Kuala Lumpur; tel. (3) 2821599; fax (3) 2821015; 15,874 mems; Pres. MOHAMED SHAFIE B. P. MAMMAL; Gen. Sec. MOHD JAFAR BIN ABDUL MAJID.

Non-Metallic Mineral Products Manufacturing Employees' Union: 99A Jalan SS 14/1, Subang Jaya, 47500 Petaling Jaya, Selangor; tel. (3) 56339006; fax (3) 56333863; e-mail nonmet@tm.net.my; 10,000 mems; Pres. ABDULLAH ABU BAKAR; Sec. S. SOMAHSUNDRAM.

Railwaymen's Union of Malaya: Bangunan Tong Nam, 1st Floor, Jalan Tun Sambathan (Travers), 50470 Kuala Lumpur; tel. (3) 2741107; fax (3) 2731805; 5,500 mems; Pres. ABDUL GAFFOR BIN IBRAHIM; Gen. Sec. S. VEERASINGAM.

Technical Services Union—Tenaga Nasional Bhd: Bangunan Keselamatan, POB 11003, Bangsar, Kuala Lumpur; tel. (3) 2823581; 3,690 mems; Pres. RAMLY YATIM; Gen. Sec. CLIFFORD SEN.

Timber Employees' Union: 10 Jalan AU 5C/14, Ampang, Ulu Kelang, Selangor; 7,174 mems; Pres. ABDULLAH METON; Gen. Sec. MINHAT SULAIMAN.

Transport Workers' Union: 21 Jalan Barat, Petaling Jaya, 46200 Selangor; tel. (3) 7566567; 10,447 mems; Pres. NORASHIKIN; Gen. Sec. ZAINAL RAMPAK.

Independent Federations and Unions

Kongres Kesatuan Guru-Guru Dalam Perkhidmatan Pelajaran (Congress of Unions of Employees in the Teaching Services): Johor; seven affiliates; Pres. RAMLI BIN MOHD JOHAN; Sec.-Gen. KASSIM BIN Haji HARON.

Malaysian Medical Association: MMA House, 4th Floor, 124 Jalan Pahang, 53000 Kuala Lumpur; tel. (3) 40420617; fax (3) 40418187; e-mail mma@mma.org.my; internet www.mma.org.my; 10 affiliates; Pres. Datuk Dr TEOH SIANG CHIN.

National Union of Journalists: 30B Jalan Padang Belia, 50470 Kuala Lumpur; tel. (3) 2742867; fax (3) 2744776; f. 1962; 1,700 mems; Gen. Sec. ONN EE SENG.

National Union of Newspaper Workers: 11B Jalan 20/14, Paramount Garden, 46300 Petaling Jaya, Selangor; tel. (3) 78768118; fax (3) 78751490; e-mail nunwl@tm.net.my; 3,000 mems; Pres. GAN HOE JIAN; Gen. Sec. R. CHANDRASEKARAN.

Sabah

Sabah Banking Employees' Union: POB 11649, 88818 Kota Kinabalu; internet sbeukk@tm.net.my; 729 mems; Gen. Sec. LEE CHI HONG.

MALAYSIA

Sabah Civil Service Union: Kota Kinabalu; f. 1952; 1,356 mems; Pres. J. K. K. Voon; Sec. Stephen Wong.

Sabah Commercial Employees' Union: Sinsuran Shopping Complex, Lot 3, Block N, 2nd Floor, POB 10357, 88803 Kota Kinabalu; tel. (88) 225971; fax (88) 213815; e-mail sceu-kk@tm.net.my; f. 1957; 980 mems; Gen. Sec. Rebecca Chin.

Sabah Medical Services Union: POB 11257, 88813 Kota Kinabalu; tel. (88) 242126; fax (88) 242127; e-mail smsu65@hotmail.com; 4,000 mems; Pres. Kathy Lo Nyuk Chin; Gen. Sec. Laurence Vun.

Sabah Petroleum Industry Workers' Union: POB 1087, Kota Kinabalu; tel. (88) 720737; e-mail victor.yb.sang@exxonmobil.com; internet www.sabah.org.my/spiwu; f. 1966; 168 mems; Pres. Abdullah Jamil Ahmad.

Sabah Teachers' Union: POB 10912, 88810 Kota Kinabalu; tel. (88) 420034; fax (88) 431633; f. 1962; 3,001 mems; Pres. Kwan Ping Sin; Sec.-Gen. Patrick Y. C. Chok.

Sarawak

Kepak Sarawak (Kesatuan Pegawai-Pegawai Bank, Sarawak): POB 62, Bukit Permata, 93100 Kuching, Sarawak; tel. (19) 8549372; e-mail kepaksar@tm.net.my; bank officers' union; 1,430 mems; Gen. Sec. Dominic Ch'ng Yung Ted.

Sarawak Commercial Employees' Union: POB 807, Kuching; 1,636 mems; Gen. Sec. Song Swee Liap.

Sarawak Teachers' Union: 139A Jalan Rock, 1st Floor, 93200 Kuching; tel. (82) 245727; fax (82) 245757; e-mail swktu@po.jaring.my; internet www.geocities.com/swktu; f. 1965; 12,832 mems; Pres. William Ghani Bina; Sec.-Gen. Thomas Huo Kok Sen.

Transport

RAILWAYS

Peninsular Malaysia

The state-owned Malayan Railways had a total length of 1,672 km in Peninsular Malaysia in 1996. The main railway line follows the west coast and extends 782 km from Singapore, south of Peninsular Malaysia, to Butterworth (opposite Pinang Island) in the north. From Bukit Mertajam, close to Butterworth, the Kedah line runs north to the Thai border at Padang Besar where connection is made with the State Railway of Thailand. The East Coast Line, 526 km long, runs from Gemas to Tumpat (in Kelantan). A 21-km branch line from Pasir Mas (27 km south of Tumpat) connects with the State Railway of Thailand at the border station of Sungei Golok. Branch lines serve railway-operated ports at Port Dickson and Telok Anson as well as Port Klang and Jurong (Singapore). Malaysia's first Light Rail Transit (LRT) system was opened in 1996. A second line began operating within the same system in 1998; a second LRT system, comprising one line, also commenced operations in that year. An express rail link connecting central Kuala Lumpur and the new Kuala Lumpur International Airport (KLIA) opened in 2001.

Keretapi Tanah Melayu Bhd (KTMB) (Malayan Railways): KTMB Corporate Headquarters, Jalan Sultan Hishamuddin, 50621 Kuala Lumpur; tel. (3) 22631111; fax (3) 27105706; e-mail pro@ktmb.com.my; internet www.ktmb.com.my; f. 1885; incorporated as a co under govt control in Aug. 1992; privatized in Aug. 1997; managed by the consortium Marak Unggal (Renong, DRB and Bolton); Chair. Tan Sri Dato' Lim Ah Lek.

Sabah

Sabah State Railway: Karung Berkunci 2047, 88999 Kota Kinabalu; tel. (88) 254611; fax (88) 236395; internet www.sabah.gov.my/railway; 134 track-km of 1-m gauge (2008); goods and passenger services from Tanjong Aru to Tenom, serving part of the west coast and the interior; diesel trains are used; Gen. Man. Ir Benny Wang.

ROADS

Peninsular Malaysia

Peninsular Malaysia's road system is extensive, in contrast to those of Sabah and Sarawak. In 1999 the road network in Malaysia totalled an estimated 65,877 km, of which 16,206 km were highways and 31,777 km secondary roads; 75.8% of the network was paved.

Sabah

Jabatan Kerja Raya Sabah (Sabah Public Works Department): Jalan Sembulan, Locked Bag 2032, 88582 Kota Kinabalu, Sabah; tel. (88) 244333; fax (88) 237234; e-mail pos@jkr.sabah.gov.my; internet www.jkr.sabah.gov.my; f. 1881; implements and maintains public infrastructures such as roads, bridges, buildings and sewerage systems throughout Sabah; maintains a network totalling 12,106 km, of which 3,908 km were sealed roads; Dir Angin Haji Ajik.

Sarawak

Jabatan Kerja Raya Sarawak (Sarawak Public Works Department): Tingkat 11–18, Wisma Saberkas, Jalan Tun Abg. Haji Openg, 93582 Kuching, Sarawak; tel. (82) 203100; fax (82) 429679; e-mail limkh@sarawaknet.gov.my; internet www.jkr.sarawak.gov.my; implements and maintains public infrastructures in Sarawak; road network totalling 10,979 km, of which 3,986 km were sealed roads; Dir Hubert Thian Chong Hui.

SHIPPING

The ports in Malaysia are classified as federal ports, under the jurisdiction of the federal Ministry of Transport, or state ports, responsible to the state ministries of Sabah and Sarawak.

Peninsular Malaysia

The federal ports in Peninsular Malaysia are Klang (the principal port), Pinang, Johor and Kuantan.

Johor Port Authority: 6A1–8A1 Pusat Perdagangan Pasir Gudang, Jalan Bandar, 81700 Pasir Gudang, Johor; tel. (7) 2534000; fax (7) 2517684; e-mail admin@lpj.gov.my; internet www.lpj.gov.my; f. 1976; Gen. Man. Zulfakar Rahmat.

Johor Port Bhd: POB 151, 81707 Pasir Gudang, Johor; tel. (7) 2535888; fax (7) 2510980; e-mail jpb@johorport.com.my; internet www.johorport.com.my; Exec. Chair. Dato' Mohd Taufik Abdullah.

Klang Port Authority: POB 202, Jalan Pelabuhan, 42005 Port Klang, Selangor; tel. (3) 31688211; fax (3) 31670211; e-mail onestopagency@pka.gov.my; internet www.pka.gov.my; f. 1963; Gen. Man. Datin Paduka O. C. Phang.

Kuantan Port Authority: Tanjung Gelang, POB 161, 25720 Kuantan, Pahang; tel. (9) 5858000; fax (9) 5833866; e-mail lpktn@lpktn.gov.my; internet www.lpktn.gov.my; f. 1974; Gen. Man. Khairul Anuar bin Abdul Rahman.

Penang Port Commission: 3A-6 Sri Weld Bldg, Weld Quay, Pinang; tel. (4) 2633211; fax (4) 2626211; e-mail sppp@po.jaring.my; internet www.penangport.gov.my; f. 1956; Gen. Man. Norlaila Binti Ibrahim.

Sabah

The chief ports, which are administered by the Sabah Ports Authority, are Kota Kinabalu, Sandakan, Tawau, Lahad Datu, Kudat, Semporna and Kunak. Many international shipping lines serve Sabah. Local services are operated by smaller vessels. The Sapangar Bay oil terminal, 25 km from Kota Kinabalu wharf, can accommodate oil tankers of up to 30,000 dwt.

Sabah Ports Authority: Bangunan SPA, Jalan Tun Fuad, Tanjung Lipat, Locked Bag 2005, 88617 Kota Kinabalu, Sabah; tel. (88) 538400; fax (88) 223036; e-mail sabport@tm.net.my; internet www.lpps.sabah.gov.my; f. 1968; Gen. Man. Eng. Mayong Omar.

Sarawak

There are four port authorities in Sarawak: Kuching, Rajang, Miri and Bintulu. Kuching, Rajang and Miri are state ports, while Bintulu is a federal port. Kuching port serves the southern region of Sarawak, Rajang port the central region, and Miri port the northern region.

Kuching Port Authority: Jalan Pelabuhan, Pending, POB 530, 93450 Kuching, Sarawak; tel. (82) 482144; fax (82) 481696; e-mail hq@kuport.com.my; internet www.kpa.gov.my; f. 1961; Gen. Man. Liu Moi Fong.

Rajang Port Authority: Jalan Pulau, 96000 Sibu, Sarawak; tel. (84) 319004; fax (84) 318754; e-mail rpa@rajangport.gov.my; internet www.rajangport.gov.my; f. 1970; Gen. Man. Helen Lim Hui Shyan.

Principal Shipping Companies

Archipelago Shipping (Sarawak) Sdn Bhd: Lot 267/270, Jalan Chan Chin Ann, POB 2998, 93758 Kuching; tel. (82) 412581; fax (82) 416249; Gen. Man. Michael M. Aman.

Malaysia Shipping Corpn Sdn Bhd: Office Tower, Plaza Berjaya, Suite 14c, 14th Floor, 12 Jalan Imbi, 55100 Kuala Lumpur; tel. (3) 21418788; fax (3) 21429214; Chair. Y. C. Chang.

Malaysian International Shipping Corpn Bhd (National Shipping Line of Malaysia): Menara Dayabumi, Level 25, Jalan Sultan Hishamuddin, 50050 Kuala Lumpur; tel. (3) 22738088; fax (3) 22736602; e-mail caffairs@miscbhd.com; internet www.misc.com.my; f. 1968; regular sailings between the Far East, South-East Asia, Australia, Japan and Europe; also operates chartering, tanker, haulage and warehousing and agency services; major shareholder, Petroliam Nasional Bhd (PETRONAS); Chair. Tan Sri Dato' Mohd Hassan bin Marican; Pres. and CEO Dato' Shamsul Azhar bin Abbas.

Perbadanan Nasional Shipping Line Bhd (PNSL): Kuala Lumpur; tel. (3) 2932211; fax (3) 2930493; f. 1982; specializes in bulk cargoes; Chair. Tunku Dato' Shahriman bin Tunku Sulaiman; Exec. Dep. Chair. Dato' Sulaiman Abdullah.

Persha Shipping Agencies Sdn Bhd: Bangunan Mayban Trust, Penthouse Suite, Jalan Pinang, 10200 Pinang; tel. (4) 2612400; fax (4) 2623122; Man. Dir MOHD NOOR MOHD KAMALUDIN.

Syarikat Perkapalan Kris Sdn Bhd (The Kris Shipping Co Ltd): 3A07 Block A, Kelana Centre Point, 3 Jalan SS7/19, Kelana Jaya; POB 8428, 46789 Petaling Jaya, Selangor; tel. (3) 7046477; fax (3) 7048007; domestic services; Chair. Dato' Seri SYED NAHAR SHAHABUDIN; Gen. Man. ROHANY TALIB; Dep. Gen. Man. THO TEIT CHANG.

Trans-Asia Shipping Corpn Sdn Bhd: Unit 715–718, Block A, Kelana Business Centre, 97 Jalan SS7/2, Kelana Jaya, 47301 Petaling Jaya, Selangor; tel. (3) 51018800; fax (4) 78802200; e-mail bernard@tasco.com.my; internet www.tasco.com.my; f. 1974; Man. Dir LEE CHECK POH.

CIVIL AVIATION

The new Kuala Lumpur International Airport (KLIA), situated in Sepang, Selangor (50 km south of Kuala Lumpur) began operations in June 1998, with an initial capacity of 25m.–30m. passengers a year, which was projected to rise to 45m. by 2020. It replaced Subang Airport in Kuala Lumpur (which was renamed the Sultan Abdul Aziz Shah Airport in 1996). An express rail link between central Kuala Lumpur and KLIA opened in early 2001. There are regional airports at Kota Kinabalu, Pinang, Johor Bahru, Kuching and Pulau Langkawi. In addition, there are airports catering for domestic services at Alor Star, Ipoh, Kota Bahru, Kuala Terengganu, Kuantan and Melaka in Peninsular Malaysia, Sibu, Bintulu and Miri in Sarawak and Sandakan, Tawau, Lahad Datu and Labuan in Sabah. There are also numerous smaller airstrips.

Department of Civil Aviation (Jabatan Penerbangan Awam Malaysia): Aras 1–4, Lot 4G4, Presint 4, Pusat Pentadbiran Kerajaan Persekutuan, 62570 Putrajaya; tel. (3) 88714000; fax (3) 88714331; e-mail webmaster@dca.gov.my; internet www.dca.gov.my; Dir-Gen. Dato' AZHARUDDIN ABDUL RAHMAN.

AirAsia Sdn Bhd: Asia Pacific Auction Center, 1st Floor, Sultan Abdul Aziz Shah Airport, 47200 Subang, Selangor; tel. (3) 78445555; fax (3) 78445400; e-mail tellus@airasia.com; internet www.airasia.com; f. 1993; a second national airline, budget carrier with a licence to operate domestic, regional and international flights; 85%-owned by HICOM; Chair. PAHAMIN A. RAJAB; Chief Exec. TONY FERNANDES.

Berjaya Air: ATerminal 3, Lapangan Terbang Sultan Abdul Aziz Shah, Shah Alam, Selangor, 47200 Kuala Lumpur; tel. (3) 7476828; fax (3) 7476228; e-mail berjayaa@tm.net.my; internet www.berjaya-air.com; f. 1989; scheduled and charter domestic services; Pres. Tan Sri Dato' Seri VINCENT TAN CHEE YIOUN.

Firefly: Kuala Lumpur; internet www.fireflyz.com.my; f. 2007; low-cost domestic and regional flights; 100% owned by Malaysia Airlines; Man. Dir EDDY LEONG.

Malaysia Airlines: 31st Floor, Bangunan MAS, Jalan Sultan Ismail, 50250 Kuala Lumpur; tel. (3) 21655140; fax (3) 21633178; e-mail corpcomm@mas.com.my; internet www.malaysiaairlines.com.my; f. 1971 as the Malaysian successor to the Malaysia Singapore Airlines (MSA); known as Malaysian Airline System (MAS) until Oct. 1987; 114 international routes and 118 domestic routes; Chair. Dato' Dr MOHAMED MUNIR BIN ABDUL MAJID; Man. Dir and CEO IDRIS JALA.

Transmile Air Sdn Bhd: Wisma Semantan, Mezzanine 2, Block B, 12 Jalan Gelenggang, Bukit Damansara, 50490 Kuala Lumpur; tel. (3) 2537718; fax (3) 2537719; internet www.transmile.com; f. 1992; scheduled and charter regional and domestic services for passengers and cargo; Chair. Tun Dr LING LIONG SIK.

Tourism

Malaysia has a rapidly growing tourist industry, and tourism remains an important source of foreign-exchange earnings. In 2006 a record 17.5m. tourists, of whom 9.6m. were from Singapore, visited Malaysia, and receipts exceeded RM 36m. In 2007 the number of visitors increased to 21m.

Malaysia Tourism Promotion Board: Menara Dato' Onn, 15th–18th, 24th–27th, 29th–30th Floors, Putra World Trade Centre, 45 Jalan Tun Ismail, 50480 Kuala Lumpur; tel. (3) 26158188; fax (3) 26935884; e-mail enquiries@tourism.gov.my; internet www.tourismmalaysia.gov.my; f. 1972 to co-ordinate and promote activities relating to tourism in Malaysia; Chair. Dato' Sri AZALINA Dato' OTHMAN SAID.

Sabah Tourist Association: POB 12181, 88824 Kota Kinabalu; tel. (88) 221234; fax (88) 218909; e-mail willie@tm.net.my; f. 1963; 55 mems; parastatal promotional org.; Chair. THOMAS MORE WILLIE.

Sarawak Tourism Board: Levels 6 and 7, Bangunan Yayasan Sarawak, Jalan Masjid, 93400 Kuching; tel. (82) 423600; fax (82) 416700; e-mail stb@sarawaktourism.com; internet www.sarawaktourism.com; f. 1995; CEO GRACIE GEIKIE.

THE MALDIVES

Introductory Survey

Location, Climate, Language, Religion, Flag, Capital

The Republic of Maldives (commonly referred to as 'the Maldives') is in southern Asia. The country, lying about 675 km (420 miles) south-west of Sri Lanka, consists of 1,192 small coral islands (of which 197 are inhabited), grouped in 26 natural atolls (but divided, for administrative purposes, into 20 atolls), in the Indian Ocean. The climate is warm and humid. The annual average temperature is 27°C (80°F), with little daily or seasonal variation, while annual rainfall is generally between 2,540 mm and 3,800 mm (100 ins to 150 ins). The national language is Dhivehi (Maldivian), which is related to Sinhala. Islam is the state religion, and most Maldivians are Sunni Muslims. The national flag (proportions 2 by 3) is red, with a green rectangle, containing a white crescent, in the centre. The capital is Malé.

Recent History

The Maldives, called the Maldive Islands until April 1969, formerly had an elected Sultan as head of state. The islands were placed under British protection, with internal self-government, in 1887. They became a republic in January 1953, but the sultanate was restored in February 1954. The Maldives became fully independent, outside the Commonwealth, on 26 July 1965. Following a referendum, the country became a republic again in November 1968, with Amir Ibrahim Nasir, Prime Minister since 1957, as President.

In 1956 the Maldivian and British Governments agreed to the establishment of a Royal Air Force staging post on Gan, an island in the southernmost atoll, Addu. In 1975 the British Government's decision to close the base and to withdraw British forces created a large commercial and military vacuum. In October 1977 President Nasir rejected an offer of an annual payment of US $1m. from the USSR to lease the former base on Gan, announcing that he would not lease the island for military purposes, nor lease it to a superpower. In 1981 the President announced plans to establish an industrial zone on Gan. By 1990 there were two factories (producing ready-made garments) operating on Gan. The airport on Gan, which links the capital, Malé, with the south, is now fully operational and, following construction work carried out in the first half of the 2000s, had been upgraded to international standards by 2007 in preparation for international flights, with the opening of tourist resorts in the area.

A new Constitution, promulgated in 1968, vested considerable powers in the President, including the right to appoint and dismiss the Prime Minister and the Cabinet of Ministers.

In March 1975, following rumours of a coup conspiracy, President Nasir dismissed the Prime Minister, Ahmed Zaki, and the premiership was abolished. Unexpectedly, President Nasir announced that he would not seek re-election at the end of his second term in 1978. To succeed him, the Majlis (legislature) chose Maumoon Abdul Gayoom, Minister of Transport under Nasir, who was approved by referendum in July 1978 and took office in November. President Gayoom announced that his main priority would be the development of the poor rural regions, while in foreign affairs the existing policy of non-alignment would be continued.

Ex-President Nasir left the country after his resignation, but the authorities subsequently sought his return to the Maldives, where he was required to answer charges of misappropriating government funds. In 1980 President Gayoom confirmed an attempted coup against the Government and implicated Nasir in the alleged plot. Nasir was to stand trial, in his absence, on these and other charges. In April 1981 Ahmed Naseem, former Deputy Minister of Fisheries and brother-in-law of Nasir, was sentenced to life imprisonment for plotting to overthrow President Gayoom. Nasir himself denied any involvement in the coup, and attempts to extradite him from Singapore were unsuccessful. (In July 1990, however, President Gayoom officially pardoned Nasir *in absentia*, in recognition of the role that he had played in winning national independence.) In September 1983 Gayoom was re-elected as President, for a further five years, by a national referendum (with 95.6% of the popular vote).

In September 1988 he was again re-elected unopposed, for a third five-year term, obtaining a record 96.4% of the popular vote.

Another attempt to depose President Gayoom took place in November 1988, when a sea-borne mercenary force, which was composed of around 80 alleged Sri Lankan Tamil separatists (led by a disaffected Maldivian businessman, Abdullah Luthufi), landed in Malé and endeavoured to seize control of important government installations. At the request of President Gayoom, however, the Indian Government dispatched an emergency contingent of 1,600 troops, which rapidly and successfully suppressed the attempted coup. Nineteen people were reported to have been killed in the fighting. In September 1989 the President commuted to life imprisonment the death sentences imposed on 12 Sri Lankans and four Maldivians who had taken part in the aborted coup.

In February 1990, despite alleged opposition from powerful members of the privileged élite, President Gayoom announced that, as part of proposals for a broad new policy of liberalization and democratic reform, he was planning to introduce legislation enabling him to distribute powers, currently enjoyed by the President alone, amongst other official bodies. A further sign of growing democratization in the Maldives was the holding of discussions by the President's Consultative Council, in early 1990, concerning freedom of speech (particularly in the local press). In April, however, it became apparent that some Maldivians opposed political change when three pro-reform members of the Majlis received anonymous death threats. A few months later, following the emergence of several politically outspoken magazines, including *Sangu* (The Conchshell), there was an abrupt reversal of the Government's policy regarding the liberalization of the press. All publications not sanctioned by the Government were banned, and a number of leading writers and publishers were arrested.

As part of a major cabinet reshuffle in May 1990, President Gayoom dismissed the Minister of State for Defence and National Security, Ilyas Ibrahim (who also held the Trade and Industries portfolio and headed the State Trading Corporation), following the latter's abrupt and unannounced departure from the country. The Government later disclosed that Ibrahim (Gayoom's brother-in-law) was to have appeared before a presidential special commission investigating alleged embezzlement and misappropriation of government funds. On his return to the Maldives in August, Ibrahim was placed under house arrest. In March 1991, however, the special commission concluded that there was no evidence of involvement, either direct or indirect, by Ibrahim in the alleged financial misdeeds; in the same month the President appointed Ibrahim as Minister of Atolls Administration. In April the President established an anti-corruption board, which was to investigate allegations of corruption, bribery, fraud, misappropriation of government funds and property, and misuse of government office.

In early August 1993, a few weeks before the Majlis vote on the presidential candidate, Gayoom was informed that Ibrahim, whose position as Minister of Atolls Administration had afforded him the opportunity to build a political base outside Malé (where he already enjoyed considerable popularity), was seeking the presidency and attempting to influence members of the Majlis (at that time, the Majlis nominated and elected by secret ballot a single candidate, who was presented to the country in a referendum). In the Majlis vote held in late August, the incumbent President, who had previously been unanimously nominated for the presidency by the legislature, obtained 28 votes, against 18 for his brother-in-law. For his allegedly unconstitutional behaviour, however, Ibrahim was charged with attempting to 'influence the members of the Majlis' and he promptly left the country once again. Ibrahim was subsequently tried *in absentia* and sentenced to 15 years' imprisonment. In addition, his brother, Abbas Ibrahim, was removed from his post as Minister of Fisheries and Agriculture. (Ibrahim returned to the Maldives in 1996 when he was placed under house arrest; this restriction was lifted in 1997.) In October 1993 Gayoom's re-election as President for a further five years was endorsed by a national referendum, in which he obtained 92.8% of the popular vote.

In November 1994, at an official ceremony marking Republic Day, President Gayoom outlined various measures intended to strengthen the political system and to advance the process of democratization. These included the granting of greater autonomy and responsibilities to members of the Cabinet of Ministers, the introduction of regulations governing the conduct of civil servants (in order to increase their accountability), the introduction of democratic elections to island development committees and atoll committees, and the establishment of a Law Commission to carry out reforms to the judicial system.

In November 1996 President Gayoom effected an extensive cabinet reshuffle and a reorganization of government bodies, including the establishment of a Supreme Council for Islamic Affairs, which was to be under direct presidential control and was to advise the Government on matters relating to Islam. In early 1997 President Gayoom announced that the Citizens' Special Majlis (which was established in 1980 with the specific task of amending the Constitution) had resolved to complete the revision of the Constitution during that year and to implement the amended version by 1 January 1998. The Citizens' Special Majlis finished its 17-year-long task in early November 1997. The revised Constitution was ratified by the President on 27 November and came into effect, as planned, on 1 January 1998. Under the new 156-article Constitution, a formal, multi-candidate contest was permitted for the legislature's nomination for the presidency; no restriction was placed on the number of terms a president may serve; for administrative purposes, the number of atolls was increased from 19 to 20; the Majlis, which was henceforth known as the People's Majlis, was enlarged from 48 to 50 seats; the Citizens' Special Majlis was renamed the People's Special Majlis; the rights of the people were expanded; parliamentary immunity was introduced; the office of auditor-general was created; the post of commissioner of elections was constitutionalized; ministers were afforded greater power; public officers were made more accountable; parliamentary questions were allowed; and judges and magistrates were obliged to take special oaths of loyalty.

In September 1998 five individuals declared their candidacy for the presidency; the People's Majlis unanimously voted by secret ballot for the incumbent President Gayoom to go forward to the national referendum. In the referendum, which was held in mid-October, Gayoom was re-elected as President for a fifth term in office, obtaining 90.9% of the popular vote. Following his re-election, the President carried out a cabinet reorganization. In an unexpected move, Ilyas Ibrahim was appointed to hold the new portfolio of transport and civil aviation.

In November 1999 elections for 42 members of the 50-seat People's Majlis were conducted (on a non-partisan basis). In September 2000 the Comprehensive Nuclear Test Ban Treaty was ratified by the Maldives. As part of a government initiative to promote the advancement of women in public life, President Gayoom appointed a woman as the new Island Chief of Himmafushi in June 2001. In December a woman was appointed as Atoll Chief of Vaavu Atoll (the first woman to be assigned a senior executive position of an atoll).

Meanwhile, in early 2001 an attempt by 42 prominent Maldivians, including members of the People's Majlis, former cabinet ministers and business executives, to register the newly formed Maldivian Democratic Party (MDP) was blocked by the People's Majlis on the grounds that the existence of political parties would encourage divisions among the public and, therefore, be counter-productive. It was believed by some, however, that President Gayoom had enforced the decision and, in doing so, had acted unconstitutionally.

In July 2002 three journalists were charged with defamation and inciting violence, and were sentenced to life imprisonment for writing articles criticizing the President and the Government. In early 2003 international activists demanded the release of the detainees, claiming that the journalists had not advocated violent opposition to President Gayoom or the Government, and that they had only been exercising their right to freedom of speech. In July a businessman was sentenced to life imprisonment for publishing an article via the internet urging that the Government be overthrown. Later that month the human rights group Amnesty International issued a report citing frequent cases of arbitrary detentions, unfair trials and long-term imprisonment and torture of political opponents in the Maldives. The organization urged the Government to release political prisoners, investigate allegations of torture and reform the criminal justice system. The Maldives authorities strongly rejected the allegations.

In September 2003 detainees at a prison in Malé held protests in response to the death of a fellow prisoner. Reports of the violent suppression of the rioting by the country's National Security Service (NSS), and the death of another two detainees, prompted major anti-Government protests in the capital, the first ever during President Gayoom's tenure. Large numbers of alleged demonstrators were arrested, and a curfew was imposed on the city. Gayoom appealed for calm and announced an investigation into the deaths of the prisoners (the subsequent demise of another detainee brought the number of deaths to four). Eleven members of the NSS were arrested for their alleged involvement in the over-zealous curbing of the riots, and the Deputy Chief of the NSS and Police Commissioner, Brig. Adam Zahir, was removed from office (he was appointed executive director of the Ministry of Information, Arts and Culture until his reinstatement as Police Commissioner in mid-February 2004, after the inquiry cleared him of any misconduct). Amnesty International reiterated demands for an end to widespread political repression and the violation of human rights and for reform of the judicial system.

On 25 September 2003 Gayoom was re-elected unanimously by secret ballot in the People's Majlis for a sixth presidential term, defeating three other candidates. His re-election was ratified at a public referendum on 17 October, where he secured 90.3% of the votes cast. One day after the beginning of his new term in office President Gayoom effected a cabinet reorganization, in which the Attorney-General, Dr Mohamed Munavvar, and the Minister of Planning and National Development, Ibrahim Hussain Zaki, were dismissed. Gayoom gave no reason for the dismissals, although it was alleged that the two had been removed for supporting reformers attempting to register a political party. Gayoom also announced that the judicial system, executive and legislature would be reformed over the next five years (without specifying what the changes would be) and that a human rights commission would be established in Malé. In the same month a group of political activists decided to establish the MDP (which had been prevented from registering as a political party in the Maldives in 2001—see above) in exile in Sri Lanka, in response to the rise in discontent with the Maldives Government. In mid-February 2004 members of the MDP claimed that more than 15 of the party's supporters had been arrested in Malé in an alleged attempt to disrupt a planned protest march; however, the Government asserted that the raids were aimed at criminal offenders and that only eight people had been detained.

In December 2003 a Human Rights Commission was established in Malé. At the end of that month a report by the Presidential Commission investigating the deaths of the four prisoners in September was submitted to President Gayoom. In his speech on the findings of the Commission to the People's Majlis in January 2004, Gayoom stated that the security personnel implicated in the prisoners' deaths had acted illegally and would be prosecuted. The President also announced that a programme of penal reform was under way. However, the exiled leader of the MDP, Mohamed Latheef, criticized the report, claiming that the names of those responsible for the deaths had been omitted, and demanded the President's resignation.

In May 2004 the election, by universal suffrage, of a People's Special Majlis, which was empowered to amend the Constitution, took place. Voters chose 42 members from 121 independent candidates. The President appointed an additional eight people to serve on the council; the People's Special Majlis also included members of the People's Majlis and the Cabinet of Ministers. Gayoom invited members of the public to send him proposals for constitutional reform and in early June the President himself proposed a number of radical constitutional reforms. He suggested that a President's tenure should be limited to two five-year terms and that women should be allowed to stand for the presidency. According to the proposed reforms, the President would also lose the right to appoint eight members of the People's Majlis; the People's Majlis would become independent of the executive; the post of Prime Minister would be created; the judiciary would be restructured (a Supreme Court would be created as the highest court of appeal and would be appointed by the President, on the advice of the People's Majlis), and, perhaps most importantly, the formation and functioning of political parties would be permitted. The People's Special Majlis, which was sworn in on 15 June, convened in July to discuss the proposals.

In mid-August 2004 President Gayoom declared an indefinite state of emergency after a pro-democracy protest in the capital became violent. Four police officers were reportedly stabbed and about 185 people were arrested during the protests. The Government claimed that the demonstration had been a coup attempt, a charge denied by the opposition MDP. The exiled opposition leader Latheef accused the Government of 'ruthlessly suppressing dissent'. The Government invited a European Union (EU) fact-finding team to Malé. The EU envoys, however, were denied access to the detainees and expressed concern about the continuing detention without charge of the alleged protesters and the ongoing state of emergency. By early September 122 people had been released, while about 60 people remained in detention, including former Attorney-General Dr Mohamed Munavvar and members of the People's Special Majlis. On 1 September, meanwhile, Gayoom relinquished the defence and finance portfolios as part of a cabinet reorganization, in an apparent move towards government reform. Ismail Shafeeu and Mohamed Jaleel were appointed as the new Minister of Defence and National Security and Minister of Finance and Treasury respectively.

In October 2004 the state of emergency that had been declared in August was revoked. Although a curfew remained in place, the lifting of the state of emergency meant that the opposition members who had been indefinitely detained following the August pro-democracy protest would either have to be charged or released from prison. In December four of the detained opposition members were charged with treason; later in that month, however, President Gayoom announced that all charges of treason and public order offences against those taken into custody following the August protest were to be suspended.

On 26 December 2004 a tsunami generated by a massive earthquake in the Indian Ocean, off the coast of Indonesia, devastated many of the low-lying Maldive islands. While the resultant death toll was not as high as might have been expected, several of the islands were rendered uninhabitable and an estimated 15,000 people were left homeless by the disaster. The economic consequences of the catastrophe on the Maldives were extensive, owing in large part to the significant contribution made by the tourism industry to the economy.

On 22 January 2005 149 independent candidates contested elections to the People's Majlis. The elections had been postponed from the previous month owing to the tsunami. Candidates supported by the opposition MDP reportedly won 18 of the 42 elective legislative seats. However, the Government stated that only 12 opposition candidates had done so, claiming that the results were a sign of widespread popular support for its reform policies. Following the elections President Gayoom insisted that he intended to establish a multi-party democracy in the Maldives within one year.

In May 2005 the Maldivian dissident Fathimath Nisreen, who had been sentenced to 10 years' imprisonment in July 2002 for her alleged participation in subversive activities, was freed, having received a presidential pardon. In June the People's Majlis unanimously approved a constitutional amendment permitting the registration of political parties in the Maldives, reversing its 2001 decision opposing the establishment of a multi-party democracy. The MDP was subsequently officially registered in the Maldives as a political party, together with several others, including the Dhivehi Rayyithunge Party (DRP—Maldivian People's Party) established by President Gayoom. In mid-July Gayoom instigated a major reorganization of the Cabinet in which, most notably, the long-serving Minister of Foreign Affairs, Fathulla Jameel, was dismissed and replaced by Dr Ahmed Shaheed.

In August 2005 a protest took place in Malé demanding the release of all political prisoners. Shortly afterwards the Chairman of the MDP, Mohamed Nasheed, was arrested, provoking several days of unrest in the capital and on various other atolls. Nasheed was subsequently charged with terrorism and attempting to perpetrate anti-Government actions; his trial began in October. Also in October Jennifer Latheef, daughter of the exiled Mohamed Latheef, was convicted of having incited a riot in Malé in September 2003 (see above) and was sentenced to a 10-year prison term. Amnesty International condemned the trial, describing Jennifer Latheef as a 'prisoner of conscience'. In February 2006 two dissidents who had been sentenced to lengthy prison terms in 2002 were released, having received presidential pardons.

In a significant development towards the further democratization of the Maldives, from June 2006 representatives of the Government and the MDP conducted informal talks at the British High Commission in Colombo, Sri Lanka. These negotiations resulted in what subsequently became known as the Westminster House Agreement. The reported terms of the agreement included the release of a number of opposition detainees and the advancement of constitutional reform, on the part of the Government, in return for MDP assurances that the party would curb public demonstrations and renounce violent protest. In July charges against several detainees were dropped by the Government, and in the following month 11 prisoners were released. Jennifer Latheef was also freed and received a presidential pardon, which she rejected on the grounds of her alleged innocence and the continuing imprisonment of other activists. Mohamed Nasheed, whose trial had been resumed in May, was released in September, although the charges against him were not withdrawn.

In November 2006 more than 100 members of the MDP were arrested in the run-up to a planned demonstration to demand the swifter implementation of reforms; the rally was cancelled by the MDP amid fears for the welfare of protesters. Government officials alleged that the MDP had organized the rally as an attempt to overthrow the Government, and that, if held, it would have posed a threat to public safety. In a subsequent report Amnesty International expressed concern at reports of 'repressive measures' being used by government officials. These allegations were vehemently denied by the Government, but they prompted widespread calls for the urgent introduction of a reform programme to prevent the arbitrary detention, mistreatment and torture of dissidents. In December the trial of the acting President of the MDP, Ibrahim Hussain Zaki, recommenced; the initial charge of high treason, arising from a speech that Zaki had made on Dhidhoo island in defence of fishermen's right to protest, had been amended to a charge of 'enmity, contempt and disharmony'. However, no progress was made regarding the trial in 2007 and the charges were reportedly dropped. The issue of press freedom came to the fore again in January 2007, with the commencement of the trial of Nazim Sattar, the Deputy Editor of the independent daily newspaper *Minivan News*. Sattar was charged with 'disobedience to order' for an article published in August 2005 that had quoted criticism of the Star Force unit of the Maldivian police force, resulting in the alleged persecution of the unit by the public. However, in May 2007 the Minister of Legal Reform, Information and Arts, Mohamed Nasheed, announced at the World Press Freedom Day conference in Medellin, Colombia, that charges against Sattar had been dropped.

Meanwhile, in early 2006 meetings of the People's Special Majlis, which had been established in mid-2004 to draw up and implement constitutional amendments, were obstructed by President Gayoom's refusal to permit the removal of presidential appointees from the body. The opposition MDP condemned the continued presence of representatives who had not been elected, stressing that they should be withdrawn in advance of the redrafting of the Constitution, and also proposed that the President's power to assent to the Constitution should be removed. Tensions were heightened in late February 2006 when the Speaker of the People's Special Majlis, Abbas Ibrahim, removed a scheduled debate on the matter from the legislative agenda. The MDP boycotted the opening of the People's Majlis in that month in protest at the President's alleged obstruction of the constitutional amendment process. In March, however, the Government published a 'Roadmap for the Reform Agenda', which projected the passing of a draft constitution by the People's Special Majlis by 31 May 2007 and its ratification within a month of that date; the document also forecast that multi-party elections would be held by 2008. Among the other stated aims of the agenda were judicial and electoral reforms, greater media freedom, the establishment of a Police Integrity Commission and greater autonomy for the atoll and island administrations.

A Police Integrity Commission was established in August 2006, and in November the Human Rights Commission was reconstituted as legally autonomous; however, the introduction of new regulations on press freedom and access to information was delayed indefinitely by the Government in January 2007. A referendum to determine whether to adopt a presidential or parliamentary system of government, which was originally scheduled to be held in September 2006, was postponed owing to disagreements between the Government and the opposition. In mid-February 2007 a meeting between the DRP and the MDP to address the faltering pace of constitutional reform was tentatively hailed as a positive development, although its conclusions and consequences remained unclear.

In mid-January 2007 the founder of the MDP, Mohamed Latheef, ended three years of voluntary exile in Sri Lanka with his return to the Maldives. In February the Deputy Chairman of the MDP's parliamentary group, Ibrahim Shareef, defected to the DRP, citing his disapproval of alleged militant elements within his former party. Later in the month a demonstration organized by the MDP in protest at police violence against civilians reportedly attracted an estimated 1,000 participants. In mid-April the discovery in Malé harbour of the corpse of a man who was alleged to have died in police custody prompted further demonstrations and numerous arrests; however, according to the subsequent autopsy, which was carried out in Sri Lanka, the man had not been tortured prior to his death. Meanwhile, in the same month the Minister of Higher Education, Employment and Social Security, Abdullah Yameen, resigned amid rumours of discord within the Cabinet of Ministers. Yameen also stood down as a member of the DRP, and was reported to be planning the creation of a new political party. In early May Qasim Ibrahim was elected Speaker of the People's Special Majlis, succeeding Abbas Ibrahim, who had resigned in the previous month.

The death of an inmate of Maafushi prison in the Kaafu atoll in unclear circumstances during a prison revolt in June 2007 precipitated a hunger strike by hundreds of the deceased's fellow prisoners and public outrage at the regulation and conditions of the prison. There was speculation that the subsequent cabinet reshuffle, in which Minister of Home Affairs Ahmed Thasmeen Ali was transferred to the position of Minister of Atolls Development and the home affairs portfolio was assigned to Abdullah Kamaaludheen, was related to the crisis. Further cabinet changes took place in August, when Minister of Justice Mohamed Jameel Ahmed and Attorney-General Hassan Saeed resigned, reportedly over their concerns regarding impediments and delays to the programme of democratic reforms. Minister of Foreign Affairs Dr Ahmed Shaheed resigned later in the month, and was replaced by Abdullah Shahid; Mohamed Muiz Adnan was appointed Minister of Justice. In October Azima Shakoor was sworn in as the new Attorney-General.

In August 2007 the three dissident former government members—Mohamed Jameel Ahmed, Hassan Saeed and Dr Ahmed Shaheed—launched a new body entitled the New Maldives Movement (NMM) and encouraged the formation of a united front of pro-democracy groups as the National Unity Alliance. In early January 2008 the official newspaper of the governing DRP, Hamaroalhi Daily News, accused the NMM of fostering terrorism. Later in the month the Government declared that the movement had not sought official registration and was therefore illegal. Consequently the NMM was banned by the Government, which granted a licence to two members of the DRP to operate an NGO under the name of the New Maldives Movement.

Meanwhile, in June 2007 the People's Special Majlis announced a new deadline of 30 November 2007 for the drawing up of constitutional amendments and agreed that a referendum on the system of government should be held in August. The results of the ballot, which took place on 18 August, indicated popular support for retaining the presidential system, with a reported 62% of those who participated in favour. There were doubts, however, among the opposition regarding the validity of the results and the alleged turn-out, and several complaints were lodged with the Election Commission. The November deadline for finalizing the draft constitutional amendments was not met by the People's Special Majlis and discussions on constitutional reform, including proposals with regard to new regulations on freedom of information, were continuing in early 2008. In January the People's Special Majlis voted to amend the Constitution to limit the length of a President's tenure to two five-year terms (whether consecutive or not) and to remove the gender bar on the presidency. Meanwhile, a press freedom bill was approved by the People's Majlis in August 2007, despite criticisms by Article 19, an international campaign group for freedom of expression, that it fell short of international standards.

The potential threat of terrorism to the Maldives came to the fore when a bomb exploded in Malé on 29 September 2007, injuring 12 foreign tourists. The explosion—the first recorded terrorist attack to take place in the Maldives—was widely believed to have been perpetrated by Islamic extremists. In December three Maldivian men were each sentenced to 15 years in prison for their part in the incident, which they confessed to having been planned as a deliberate attack on the country's vital tourism industry. In an attempt to combat the perceived threat of growing Islamic fundamentalism and to protect the lucrative tourism sector, the Government introduced a number of measures, including arresting suspected extremists, banning the wearing of the full veil in public, advocating the promotion of moderate Islamic views in schools and colleges, forbidding the convention of unlicensed Muslim prayer groups, and banning foreign Islamic clerics from visiting the islands unless they had been explicitly invited by the authorities. While visiting an atoll in the far north of the island chain in January 2008, President Gayoom himself escaped unhurt after an attempted knife attack by a 20-year-old Maldivian man. The Government claimed that the President's political rivals were the most likely organizers of the apparent assassination attempt, rather than Islamic extremists, as some early reports had suggested.

In November 1989, meanwhile, the Maldives hosted an international conference with delegates from other small island nations, to discuss the threat posed to low-lying island countries by the predicted rise in sea-level caused by heating of the earth's atmosphere as a result of pollution (the 'greenhouse effect'). In June 1990 an Environmental Research Unit, which was to operate under the Ministry of Planning and the Environment, was established in the Maldives. The Maldives reiterated its serious concern with regard to problems of world-wide environmental pollution when it hosted the 13th conference of the UN's Intergovernmental Panel on Climate Change (IPCC, see p. 158) in September 1997. In September 1999 a special session of the UN General Assembly was convened in New York to address the specific problems faced by the 43-member Alliance of Small Island States (see p. 422) (including the Maldives), notably climate change, rising sea levels and globalization. At the UN Millennium Summit meeting in September 2000 the President of the Maldives again took the opportunity to urge leaders to address environmental issues. The Government expressed its grave disappointment and concern at the USA's decision in April 2001 to reject the Kyoto Protocol to the UN's Framework Convention on Climate Change. A large part of the international community adopted the protocol in July after many of the emissions targets had been reduced. The USA proposed an alternative initiative in February 2002; however, most states dismissed it as potentially ineffective. In early March the Maldives, Kiribati and Tuvalu announced their decision to take legal action against the USA for refusing to sign the Kyoto Protocol and thus threatening the very survival of the low-lying island states. President Gayoom attended the South Asian Regional Conference on Ecotourism in India in January 2002. At the World Summit on Sustainable Development held in September in Johannesburg, South Africa, President Gayoom warned the international community that low-lying islands were at greater risk than ever before. He demanded urgent action, including the universal ratification and implementation of the Kyoto Protocol, to prevent a global environmental catastrophe. On his return to the Maldives, the President stated that some progress had been made in certain areas, although the decisions were not as far-reaching as desired by small island nations. The President again urged the international community to enforce the Kyoto Protocol during a television interview in August 2004, and in a speech at the Non-Aligned Movement Conference in Havana, Cuba, in September 2006, appealed for international action on climate change and environmental degradation.

The Maldives is a founder member of the South Asian Association for Regional Co-operation (SAARC, see p. 384), which was formally constituted in December 1985, and the country became a full member of the Commonwealth in June 1985. The Maldives' international standing was enhanced in November 1990, when it successfully hosted the fifth SAARC summit meeting, which was held in Malé. In November 2004 the Maldives opened its fourth resident diplomatic mission (in addition to those in Sri Lanka, at the UN headquarters in New York and in London, United Kingdom) in New Delhi, India. At the 12th SAARC Summit Conference, which was held in January 2004 in the Pakistani capital of Islamabad, the members agreed to form a South Asia Free Trade Area (SAFTA); this came into effect on 1 January 2006, but was not due to enter fully into force until 2016. In February 2008 the number of countries with which the Maldives had established diplomatic relations stood at 141.

Government

Legislative power is held by the unicameral People's Majlis, with 50 members, including 42 elected for five years by universal adult suffrage (two by the National Capital Island and two from each of the 20 atolls) and eight appointed by the President. Executive power is vested in the President, who is elected by secret ballot by the People's Majlis (under the 1998 constitutional revisions, more than one candidate may be nominated for election) and endorsed in office for five years by a national referendum. He governs with the assistance of an appointed Cabinet of Ministers, which is responsible to the People's Majlis. The country has 21 administrative districts: the capital is under direct central administration while the 20 atolls are each under an atoll chief (verin) who is appointed by the President, under the general guidance of the Minister of Atolls Administration.

Defence

There is no army, navy or air force. The voluntary National Security Service was founded in 1892 and was renamed the Maldives National Defence Force (MNDF) in April 2006 when a separate police force was established to differentiate military duties from domestic law enforcement tasks. The MNDF, which has about 2,000 members and incorporates an expanded infantry unit, undertakes paramilitary security duties (including coast-guard duties). In 2007 budgetary expenditure on defence was estimated at 480.2m. rufiyaa (equivalent to 4.1% of total spending) and expenditure on public order and internal security was projected at 662.2m. rufiyaa (5.6% of total spending).

Economic Affairs

In 2006, according to estimates by the World Bank, the Maldives' gross national income (GNI), measured at average 2004–06 prices, was US $902m., equivalent to $2,680 per head. During 1996–2006, it was estimated, the population increased at an average annual rate of 2.7%, while gross domestic product (GDP) per head grew, in real terms, by an average of 4.8% per year over the same period. Overall GDP increased, in real terms, at an average annual rate of 7.6% in 1996–2006. GDP declined by 4.1% in 2005 following the devastating tsunamis of December 2004; however, subsequent reconstruction efforts contributed to impressive growth, of 18.7%, in 2006.

Agriculture and fishing contributed an estimated 6.3% of GDP (the primary fishing sector alone accounted for 4.3%) in 2007. About 11.5% of the total working population were employed in the sector (more than 7% in fishing) at the March 2006 census. In 2007 revenue from exports of marine products totalled US $106m., thus accounting for 98% of total export earnings. The fisheries sector suffered significant damage as a result of the December 2004 tsunami disaster, with the destruction of boats and equipment contributing to the loss of many livelihoods. Small quantities of various fruits, vegetables and cereals are produced, but virtually all of the principal staple foods have to be imported. As a result of salt-water intrusion caused by the tsunamis, a significant amount of cultivable land was ruined. The dominant agricultural activity (not including fishing) in the Maldives is coconut production. The GDP of the agriculture and fisheries sector increased, in real terms, at an average annual rate of 4.8% (5.6% for the fishing sector) in 1996–2006. Real agricultural GDP grew by 12.2% in 2005 but declined by 0.7% in 2006. According to preliminary estimates, the sector's GDP declined by a massive 17.5% (23.7% for the fisheries sector alone) in 2007.

Industry (including mining, manufacturing, construction and utilities) contributed an estimated 16.5% of GDP in 2007, and employed 24.3% of the working population at the March 2006 census. Sectoral GDP increased, in real terms, at an average annual rate of 10.2% in 1996–2006. Industrial GDP grew by 3.1% in 2005, by 10.6% in 2006 and by 9.9% in 2007.

Mining and quarrying (mostly for coral and sand) contributed 0.7% of GDP in 2007, and employed 0.3% of the working population at the March 2006 census. No reserves of petroleum or natural gas have, as yet, been discovered in Maldivian waters. Mining GDP increased, in real terms, at an average annual rate of 5.7% in 1996–2006. The GDP of the mining sector grew by 5.3% in 2006 and by 2.3% in 2007.

The manufacturing sector contributed 6.3% of GDP in 2007, and employed 17.5% of the working population at the March 2006 census. There are only a small number of 'modern' manufacturing enterprises in the Maldives, including fish-canning, garment-making and soft-drink bottling. Although cottage industries (such as the weaving of coir yarn and boat-building) employ nearly one-quarter of the total labour force, there is little scope for expansion, owing to the limited size of the domestic market. Because of its lack of manufacturing industries, the Maldives has to import most essential consumer and capital goods. In the late 1980s and 1990s traditional handicrafts, such as lacquer work and shell craft, revived as a result of the expansion of the tourism sector. Manufacturing GDP increased, in real terms, at an average annual rate of 6.6% in 1996–2006. Real manufacturing GDP declined by 9.9% in 2005, but grew by 7.3% in 2006 and by 3.7% in 2007.

Energy is derived principally from petroleum, and imports of mineral fuels and oils comprised 18.5% of the cost of imports in 2007. Owing to a surge in commercial activities and a significant increase in construction projects in Malé, demand for electricity in the capital grew rapidly in the late 1980s and early 1990s. Accordingly, plans were formulated in late 1991 to augment the generating capacity of the power station in Malé and to improve the distribution network. By 2004 21 inhabited islands had been provided with electricity. In 2001 the third phase of the Malé power project, further to increase the capital's power supply, was under way. In December the Asian Development Bank (ADB) agreed to provide a loan to improve the supply of electricity to some 40 outer islands. In 2006 the ADB was to supply another loan, of US $8m., to enable the electrification of those outer islands not included in the first project.

Following the decline of the shipping industry in the 1980s, tourism gained in importance as an economic sector, and by 1989 it had overtaken the fishing industry as the Maldives' largest source of foreign exchange. In 2003 the tourism sector provided 31.5% of GDP. In 2003 tourist arrivals increased by 16.3%, compared with the previous year, to reach 563,593. In that year receipts from tourism totalled an estimated 896.2m. rufiyaa. In 2004 tourist arrivals increased by a further 9.4%, to 616,716, and receipts from tourism reached 921.6m. rufiyaa. In March 2004 the Government announced that nine more atolls would be opened for tourism and that 11 further islands would be converted into resorts. The devastating impact upon the Maldives of the massive tsunami in the Indian Ocean in December 2004 significantly affected the performance of the tourism sector in 2005, with several tourist resorts damaged and adverse publicity surrounding the disaster further discouraging prospective tourists. Tourist arrivals amounted to just 395,320 in 2005, but receipts remained strong, at 909.3m. rufiyaa. However, the contribution of the tourism sector to GDP was only 21.8% in 2005, and the sector's GDP declined, in real terms, by 33.1% in that year. The reopening by the end of 2005 of all of the resorts affected by the tsunami provided the tourism industry with a considerable boost; arrivals increased by 52.3% in 2006 to reach 601,923 and the sector's GDP grew by 42.3% to an impressive total of 1,685.9m. rufiyaa. The real GDP of the tourism sector increased, in real terms, at an average annual rate of 4.6% in 1996–2006. The services sector as a whole contributed 77.2% of GDP in 2007. The GDP of the services sector increased, in real terms, by an average of 7.1% per year in 1996–2006. Compared with the previous year, sectoral GDP declined by 8.2% in 2005, but expanded by a massive 23.8% in 2006. Growth in the services sector was sustained, at 8.6%, in 2007.

In 2006 the Maldives recorded a visible trade deficit of an estimated US $599.5m. and there was a deficit of approximately $378.6m. on the current account of the balance of payments. In 2007 the principal source of imports was Singapore (accounting for 22.5% of the total); other major sources were the United Arab Emirates, India and Malaysia. In 2007 the principal market for exports (traditionally the USA) was Thailand (accounting for 40.9% of the total); other major purchasers were Sri Lanka, France and the United Kingdom. The principal exports were marine products (tuna being the largest export commodity). The principal imports were machinery and mechanical appliances and electrical equipment, mineral products, and wood and metal manufactures.

Foreign grant aid in 2000 totalled an estimated US $17.7m. Japan has traditionally been the Maldives' largest aid donor (disbursing $11.9m. in 1997). In the aftermath of the December 2004 tsunami, the Maldives received a significant amount of international aid, in the form of both grants and concessional loans, principally from the UN, the ADB, the World Bank and Japan. A total of $88m. had been pledged in assistance by the end of April 2005, of which $75m. was to be in the form of grants. In June 2006 the Japanese Government announced a $23m. loan to aid reconstruction. In 2006, in terms of central government finance, there was an estimated fiscal deficit of 845.7m. rufiyaa (equivalent to 7.1% of GDP). The deficit for 2007 was projected to be 3,704.1m. rufiyaa. The Maldives' total external debt was $368.2m. at the end of 2005, of which $307.0m. was long-term public debt. In that year the cost of debt-servicing was equivalent to 6.9% of revenue from exports of goods and services. According to the IMF, during 1995–2005 the average annual rate of inflation was 2.8%; consumer prices increased by 3.3% in 2005, by 3.7% in 2006 and were predicted to show a sharp rise, of 7.0%, in 2007. According to the March 2006 census, 14.4% of the total labour force was unemployed at that time.

The Maldives is a member of the UN Economic and Social Commission for Asia and the Pacific (ESCAP, see p. 35), the ADB, the Colombo Plan (see p. 411) and the South Asian Association for Regional Co-operation (SAARC, see p. 384).

In response to the rapid growth and increasing importance of the tourism sector in the Maldives from the late 1990s onwards, the Government made efforts to improve the infrastructure (including the development of communication systems, sanitation and the water supply). By 1999 the Maldivian telecommunications company, Dhivehi Raajjeyge Gulhun Ltd (Dhiraagu), had provided telephone facilities to all of the inhabited islands and by March 2007 262,615 inhabitants had also subscribed to mobile cellular telephones. However, despite a recovery in fish exports and buoyant tourism receipts in the latter half of the 1990s, the current-account deficit persisted and the trade deficit continued to grow. In early 2001 the Government opened up the export of fresh and canned fish to the private sector, and in that year the Maldives Industrial Fisheries Company recorded a 13% increase in sales of fish, compared with the previous year. In 2002 the fisheries sector continued to expand and tourism gradually began to recover. The current-account deficit, however, remained high and the fiscal deficit continued to grow, largely owing to an increase in government expenditure. Furthermore, the islands continued to experience a shortage of domestic labour: in 2003 about 33,765 expatriate workers (mainly from India, Sri Lanka and Bangladesh) were employed in the Maldives, and it was estimated that in 1999 almost 20% of the country's GDP went to non-Maldivians. Development of an artificially constructed island—Hulhumalé—commenced from 1997 as a means to disperse the population, which was concentrated largely in the nearby overcrowded capital of Malé. A total of 1,500 people had been resettled in Hulhumalé by the end of December 2004 and the Government planned to move up to 45,000 people to the island by 2020. In December 2004 the tsunami generated by a massive earthquake in the Indian Ocean had a devastating effect on the Maldives, leading to widespread destruction of infrastructure and housing. An estimated 14 of the 200 inhabited islands were completely destroyed by the huge waves, which also damaged approximately 8% of the country's fishing fleet and several tourist resorts. The economic consequences of the disaster were profound; the cost of reconstruction was estimated at US $375m., the equivalent of approximately 50% of GDP. The Government was believed to have lost an estimated $40m. in revenue in 2005. In conjunction with a large increase in government expenditure, this contributed to a significant increase in both the fiscal and current-account deficits. As a direct result of the tsunami, the IMF estimated that GDP had contracted by 3.6% in 2005. The increasing levels of capital expenditure that were required to proceed with reconstruction placed considerable pressure on the budget (despite high inflows of aid from international donors) and the deficit rose from 19.5% of GDP in 2005 to 25.3% in 2006. In a report published in August 2007 the IMF warned that planned developments in the tourism sector exceeded fiscal capacity and that a more prudent budgetary outlay would safeguard the country's dwindling international reserves. Public debt rose once again in 2007, reaching 37.6% of GDP. Tourism figures for 2007 (see above) indicated that the sector had recovered and, moreover, that it remained the most dynamic subdivision of the economy. A total of 35 new resorts were opened in the Maldives during that year (a further 50 were scheduled to be opened during 2010–12) and the expansion of the international airport at Malé and the domestic airport on Gan Island—which was due to operate international flights from 2008—was expected further to increase tourist arrivals. However, the tsunami disaster highlighted the vulnerability of the economy to external events and the fact that the long-term prosperity of the Maldives required sustained growth and diversification of activities. According to the ADB, real GDP increased by 6.6% in 2007 and growth of around 8.0% was forecast for 2008.

Education

Education is not compulsory. There are three types of formal education: traditional Koranic schools (Makthab), Dhivehi-language primary schools (Madhrasa) and English-language primary and secondary schools. Schools of the third category are the only ones equipped to teach a standard curriculum. In 1984 a national curriculum was introduced in all schools. In 1989 the Government established a National Council on Education to oversee the development of education in the Maldives. Primary education begins at six years of age and lasts for five years. Secondary education, beginning at the age of 11, lasts for up to seven years, comprising a first cycle of five years and a second of two years. In 2003/04 the total enrolment at primary and secondary schools was equivalent to 91.5% of the school-age population. In 2004/05 enrolment at primary schools included 79.3% of children in the relevant age-group; the ratio for secondary enrolment of pupils in the relevant age-group was an estimated 62.6% in the same year. The construction of the first secondary school outside Malé was completed on Hithadoo Island, in Addu atoll, in 1992. By early 2005 there were 22 schools in Malé and 312 schools in the rest of the Maldives. There is a full-time vocational training centre, a teacher-training institute, an Institute of Hotel and Catering Services, an Institute of Management and Administration, a Science Education Centre, a Centre for Social Education, an Institute of Health Sciences, an Institute for Islamic Studies and a Centre for Continuing Education. The Maldives Institute of Technical Education, which was completed in late 1996, was expected to help to alleviate the problem of the lack of local skilled labour. The Maldives College of Higher Education, which was established to provide a uniform framework and policies for post-secondary education institutes, was opened in late 1998 and incorporates an Institute of Shari'a and Law. At least 116 of the country's schools were affected by the December 2004 tsunami. In the aftermath of the disaster, eight schools required complete reconstruction. A large quantity of school equipment was also lost. Projected budgetary expenditure on education by the central Government in 2007 was 1,257.1m. rufiyaa, representing 10.7% of total spending.

Public Holidays

2008: 10 January* (Islamic New Year), 9 March* (National Day), 20 March* (Birth of the Prophet Muhammad), 18 April (World Culture and Heritage Day), 26–27 July (Independence Days), 1 September* (Ramadan begins), 1 October* (Id al-Fitr, end of Ramadan), 3 November (Victory Day), 11–12 November (Republic Days), 8 December* (Id al-Adha, feast of the Sacrifice), 10 December (Fishermen's Day), 29 December* (Islamic New Year).

2009: 26 February* (National Day), 9 March* (Birth of the Prophet Muhammad), 18 April (World Culture and Heritage Day), 26–27 July (Independence Days), 22 August* (Ramadan begins), 20 September* (Id al-Fitr, end of Ramadan), 3 November (Victory Day), 11–12 November (Republic Days), 27 November* (Id al-Adha, feast of the Sacrifice), 10 December (Fishermen's Day), 18 December* (Islamic New Year).

* These holidays are dependent on the Islamic lunar calendar and may vary by one or two days from the dates given.

† This festival occurs twice (marking the start of the Islamic years AH 1429 and AH 1430) within the same Gregorian year.

Weights and Measures

The metric system is in force, but imperial units are also used.

Statistical Survey

Source (unless otherwise stated): Ministry of Planning and National Development, Ghaazee Bldg, 4th Floor, Ameer Ahmed Magu, Malé 20-05; tel. 3322919; fax 3327351; internet www.planning.gov.mv.

AREA AND POPULATION

Area: 298 sq km (115 sq miles).

Population: 270,101 at census of 31 March–7 April 2000; 298,968 (males 151,459, females 147,509) at census of 21–28 March 2006. *Mid-2007* (official estimate): 304,869.

Density (official estimate, mid-2007): 1,023 per sq km.

Administrative Divisions (population, 2006 census): *Capital City*: Malé 103,693. *Atolls*: North Thiladhunmathi 13,495; South Thiladhunmathi 16,237; North Miladhunmadulu 11,940; South Miladhunmadulu 10,015; North Maalhosmadulu 14,756; South Maalhosmadulu 9,578; Faadhippolhu 9,190; Malé 15,441; North Ari 5,776; South Ari 8,379; Felidhe 1,606; Mulakatholhu 4,710; North Nilandhe 3,765; South Nilandhe 4,967; Kolhumadulu 8,493; Hadhdhunmathi 11,990; North Huvadhu 8,262; South Huvadhu 11,013; Gnaviyani 7,636; Addu 18,026.

Births, Marriages and Deaths (2006): Registered live births 5,827 (birth rate 20 per 1,000); Marriages 5,556; Registered deaths 1,084 (death rate 4 per 1,000).

Expectation of Life (years at birth, WHO estimates): 67.9 (males 67.2; females 68.6) in 2005. Source: WHO, *World Health Statistics*.

Economically Active Population (persons aged 12 years and over, census of March 2006): Agriculture, hunting and forestry 4,236; Fishing 8,388; Mining and quarrying 339; Manufacturing 19,259; Electricity, gas and water 1,229; Construction 5,930; Wholesale and retail trade and repairs 11,711; Restaurants and hotels 12,090; Transport, storage and communications 7,098; Financing, insurance, real estate and business services 1,738; Public administration and defence 15,949; Education 9,872; Health and social work 4,182; Other community, social and personal service activities 3,248; Extra-territorial organizations and bodies 216; Activities not adequately defined 4,746; *Total employed* 110,231 (males 69,701, females 40,530); Unemployed 18,605; *Total labour force* 128,836.

HEALTH AND WELFARE
Key Indicators

Total Fertility Rate (children per woman, 2005): 4.0.

Under-5 Mortality Rate (per 1,000 live births, 2005): 45.

HIV/AIDS (% of persons aged 15–49, 2001): 0.06.

Physicians (per 1,000 head, 2004): 0.92.

Hospital Beds (per 1,000 head, 2003): 2.26.

Health Expenditure (2004): US $ per head (PPP): 494.4.

Health Expenditure (2004): % of GDP: 7.7.

Health Expenditure (2004): public (% of total): 81.4.

Access to Water (% of persons, 2004): 83.

Access to Sanitation (% of persons, 2004): 59.

Human Development Index (2005): ranking: 98.

Human Development Index (2005): value: 0.739.

For sources and definitions, see explanatory note on p. vi.

AGRICULTURE, ETC.

Principal Crops (production in long-term leased islands*, metric tons, 2006): Coconuts 78.6; Tender coconut 77.6; Aubergine 41.5; Cucumbers 30.8; Pumpkins 52.9; Bitter gourds 4.4; Ridged peppers 32.9; Papaya 478.4; Watermelons 378.1; Bananas 332.7.

*Comprising the atolls of North Thiladhunmathi, South Thiladhunmathi, North Miladhunmadulu, South Ari, Mulakatholhu, North Nilandhe, Kolhumadulu and Hadhdhunmathi.

Coconuts (number): 40.6m. in 2004; 52.4m. in 2005; 64.1m. in 2006.

Sea Fishing ('000 metric tons, 2005): Total catch 186.0 (Skipjack tuna—Oceanic skipjack 132.1; Yellowfin tuna 20.7; Sharks, rays, skates, etc. 0.8). Source: FAO.

INDUSTRY

Selected Products (metric tons, 2003): Frozen tuna 47,546; Salted, dried or smoked fish 9.2; Canned fish 7,094. Source: FAO.

Electric Energy (million kWh): 177.0 in 2004; 204.1 in 2005; 233.3 in 2006.

FINANCE

Currency and Exchange Rates: 100 laari (larees) = 1 rufiyaa (Maldivian rupee). *Sterling, Dollar and Euro Equivalents* (31 December 2007): £1 sterling = 25.654 rufiyaa; US $1 = 12.800 rufiyaa; €1 = 18.843 rufiyaa; 1,000 rufiyaa = £39.00 = $78.13 = €53.07. *Exchange Rate* (rufiyaa per US dollar): since July 2001 the mid-point rate of exchange has been fixed at US $1 = 12.80 rufiyaa.

Budget (central government finance, million rufiyaa, 2007, estimates): *Revenue*: Tax revenue 3,193.9 (Import duty 2,424.1); Other current revenue 3,912.3 (Resort lease rents 1,792.1); Capital revenue 32.4; Grants 958.9; Total 8,097.5. *Expenditure*: General administration of public services 1,892.6; Defence 480.2; Public order and internal security 662.2; Environmental protection 139.3; Education 1,257.1; Health 890.0; Social security and welfare 599.3; Community programmes 3,349.3; Economic services 2,300.1 (Agriculture and fishing 152.4, Trade and industry 149.4, Electricity, gas and water 328.6, Transport and communications 1,405.0, Tourism 111.9); Interest on public debt 305.6; Net lending −74.1; Total 11,801.6 (Current 6,797.2, Capital and net lending 5,004.4).

International Reserves (US $ million at 31 December 2006): IMF special drawing rights 0.50; Reserve position in IMF 2.34; Foreign exchange 228.54; Total 231.38. Source: IMF, *International Financial Statistics*.

Money Supply (million rufiyaa at 31 December 2006): Currency outside banks 1,067.78; Demand deposits at commercial banks 2,624.73; Total money (incl. others) 3,707.24. Source: IMF, *International Financial Statistics*.

Cost of Living (Consumer Price Index; base: 2000 = 100): All items: 98.7 in 2003; 105.0 in 2004; 108.5 in 2005; 112.5 in 2006. Source: IMF, *International Financial Statistics*.

Gross Value Added in Basic Prices (million rufiyaa at constant 1995 prices, 2007, preliminary): Agriculture 205.1; Fishing and fisheries 450.0; Mining (coral and sand) 53.3; Manufacturing 661.9; Electricity and water supply 416.4; Construction 600.1; Wholesale and retail trade 367.4; Transport and communications 1,986.0; Finance, real estate and business services 1,179.5; Tourism 2,816.6; Public administration 1,577.3; Other services 154.5; *Sub-total* 10,468.2; Financial intermediation services indirectly measured −400.9; *Gross value added in basic prices* 10,067.4.

Balance of Payments (US $ million, 2006): Exports of goods f.o.b. 215.9; Imports of goods f.o.b. −815.3; *Trade balance* −599.5; Exports of services 473.1; Imports of services −233.1; *Balance on goods and services* −359.5; Other income received 15.0; Other income paid −56.3; *Balance on goods, services and income* −400.8; Current transfers received 105.3; Current transfers paid −83.2; *Current balance* −378.6; Direct investment from abroad 13.9; Other investment assets 113.0; Other investment liabilities 163.7; Net errors and omissions 133.1; *Overall balance* 45.0. Source: IMF, *International Financial Statistics*.

EXTERNAL TRADE

Principal Commodities (million US $ million, 2007): *Imports c.i.f.*: Consumer goods 368.2 (Food items 175.0, Tobacco products 9.7, Pharmaceuticals 7.5, Other consumer goods 178.4); Petroleum products 202.9 (Motor spirit—gasoline 20.5, Diesel oil 166.5, Aviation fuel 7.2, Other petroleum products 8.7); Intermediate and capital goods 525.2 (Construction materials 172.3; Paper and paper products 2.9; Medical and surgical supplies 4.8; Computer equipment and supplies 15.3; Machinery and mechanical appliances 22.5; Textiles 8.4; Chemicals and chemical products 7.2; Transport equipment and parts 78.8); Total 1,096.3. *Exports*: Marine products 105.6 (Fresh, chilled or frozen tuna 79.5, *of which* Skipjack 42.0; Yellowfin 35.4; Dried fish 9.2; Canned fish 10.8); Other products (mostly clothing and waste and scrap of alloy steel) 2.1; Total 107.8. *Re-exports*: 120.2.

Principal Trading Partners (US $ million, 2006): *Imports*: Australia 25.5; China, People's Republic 24.5; France 11.8; Germany 23.8; India 125.9; Japan 20.7; Malaysia 93.4; Singapore 247.0; Sri Lanka 76.0; Thailand 53.0; United Arab Emirates 209.7; United Kingdom 16.1; USA 22.3; Total (incl. others) 1,096.3. *Exports*: France 7.9; Germany 1.7; Japan 4.9; Singapore 0.8; Sri Lanka 16.1; Thailand 44.1; United Kingdom 12.3; Total (incl. others) 107.8. *Re-exports*: 120.2.

TRANSPORT

Road Traffic (registered motor vehicles, 2006): Passenger cars 2,372; Buses, pick-ups and vans 1,811; Lorries and tractors 675; Motorcycles and mopeds 22,107; Total (incl. others) 28,081.

Merchant Shipping Fleet (displacement, '000 gross registered tons at 31 December): 78.1 in 2004; 87.4 in 2005; 99.9 in 2006. Source: Lloyd's Register-Fairplay, *World Fleet Statistics*.

International Shipping (freight traffic, '000 metric tons, 1990): Goods loaded 27; Goods unloaded 78. Source: UN, *Monthly Bulletin of Statistics*.

Civil Aviation (traffic at Malé International Airport, 2006): *International Flights:* Arrivals 734,733; Departures 723,758. *Domestic Flights:* Arrivals 355,015; Departures 361,191.

TOURISM

Tourist Arrivals: 395,320 in 2005; 601,923 in 2006; 675,889 in 2007.

Foreign Visitors by Country of Nationality (2007): Austria 13,673; People's Republic of China 35,976; France 45,301; Germany 72,269; India 17,327; Italy 117,246; Japan 41,121; Russia 31,845; Switzerland 26,183; United Kingdom 125,158; Total (incl. others) 675,889.

Tourism Receipts (US $ million): 286.6 in 2005; 433.7 in 2006; 493.6 in 2007.

COMMUNICATIONS MEDIA

Radio Receivers (July 2000): 29,724 registered.

Television Receivers (July 2000): 10,701 registered.

Telephones (main lines in use): 28,651 in 2002; 30,056 in 2003; 31,503 in 2004.

Mobile Cellular Telephones: 41,899 in 2002; 66,466 in 2003; 113,246 in 2004.

Personal Computers (2004): 36,000 in use.

Internet Users (registered): 1,067 in 2002; 1,155 in 2003; 1,260 in 2004.

2007: 32,513 main line telephones in use; 262,615 mobile cellular telephones; 1,326 registered internet users.

Sources: Telecommunications Authority of Maldives, Malé; International Telecommunication Union.

EDUCATION

Schools (2006): 349. Source: Ministry of Education.

Teachers (2006): Pre-primary 611; Primary 3,337; Lower secondary 2,565; Upper secondary 185. Source: Ministry of Education.

Pupils (2006): Pre-primary 14,330; Primary 54,770; Lower secondary 29,084; Upper secondary 2,214; Special needs 97. Source: Ministry of Education.

Maldives College of Higher Education (2003): Academic staff 138; Students 6,898. Source: Maldives College of Higher Education.

Adult Literacy Rate (UNESCO estimates): 96.3% (males 96.2%; females 96.4%) in 2000. Source: UNESCO Institute for Statistics.

Directory

The Constitution

Following a referendum in March 1968, the Maldive Islands (renamed the Maldives in April 1969) became a republic on 11 November 1968. On 27 November 1997 the President ratified a new 156-article Constitution, which was to replace the 1968 Constitution; the new Constitution came into effect on 1 January 1998. The main constitutional provisions are summarized below:

STATE, SOVEREIGNTY AND CITIZENS

The Maldives shall be a sovereign, independent, democratic republic based on the principles of Islam, and shall be a unitary State, to be known as the Republic of Maldives. In this Constitution, the Republic of Maldives shall hereinafter be referred to as 'the Maldives'.

The powers of the State of the Maldives shall be vested in the citizens. Executive power shall be vested in the President and the Cabinet of Ministers, legislative power shall be vested in the People's Majlis (People's Council) and the People's Special Majlis, and the power of administering justice shall be vested in the President and the courts of the Maldives.

The religion of the State of the Maldives shall be Islam. The national language of the Maldives shall be Dhivehi.

FUNDAMENTAL RIGHTS AND DUTIES OF CITIZENS

Maldivian citizens are equal before and under the law and are entitled to the equal protection of the law. No Maldivian shall be deprived of citizenship, except as may be provided by law. No person shall be arrested or detained, except as provided by law. Any Maldivian citizen subjected to oppressive treatment shall have the right to appeal against such treatment to the concerned authorities and to the President.

The following are guaranteed: inviolability of residential dwellings and premises; freedom of education; inviolability of letters, messages and other means of communication; freedom of movement; the right to acquire and hold property; protection of property rights; the right to work; and freedom of expression, assembly and association.

Loyalty to the State and obedience to the Constitution and to the law of the Maldives shall be the duty of every Maldivian citizen, irrespective of where he may be.

THE PRESIDENT

The President shall be the Head of State, Head of Government and the Commander-in-Chief of the Armed Forces and of the Police.

The President shall be elected by secret ballot by the People's Majlis (more than one candidate may be nominated for election) and endorsed in office for five years by a national referendum.

In addition to the powers and functions expressly conferred on or assigned to the President by the Constitution and law, the President shall have the power to execute the following: appointment to and removal from office of the Vice-President, Chief Justice, Speaker and Deputy Speaker of the People's Majlis, Ministers, Attorney-General, Atoll Chiefs, Judges, Auditor-General and Commissioner of Elections; appointment and dissolution of the Cabinet of Ministers; presiding over meetings of the Cabinet of Ministers; making a statement declaring the policies of the Government at the opening session of the People's Majlis every year; promulgating decrees, directives and regulations, as may be required from time to time for the purposes of ensuring propriety of the affairs of the Government and compliance with the provisions of the Constitution and law; holding public referendums on major issues; the declaration of war and peace.

While any person holds office as President, no proceedings shall be instituted or continued against him in any court or tribunal in respect of anything done or omitted to be done by him either in his official or private capacity.

A motion to remove the President from office may be considered in the People's Majlis only when one-third of the members of the Majlis have proposed it and two-thirds of the Majlis have resolved to consider it.

In the event that the presidency becomes vacant by reason of death, resignation or removal from office, the Speaker of the People's Majlis shall discharge the functions as Acting President from the time of occurrence of such vacancy. He shall continue to discharge these functions until a three-member Council is elected by a secret ballot of the People's Majlis to administer the State.

The President shall have the right to appoint at his discretion a Vice-President to discharge the duties and responsibilities assigned by the President.

THE CABINET OF MINISTERS

There shall be a Cabinet of Ministers appointed by the President, and the Cabinet shall be presided over by the President. The Cabinet of Ministers shall consist of the Vice-President (if any), Ministers charged with responsibility for Ministries and the Attorney-General.

The Cabinet of Ministers shall discharge the functions assigned to it by the President. The following shall be included in the said functions: to assist the President in formulating government policy on important national and international matters and issues; to advise the President on developing the Maldives economically and socially; to assist the President in the formulation of the annual state budget and government bills to be submitted to the People's Majlis; and to advise the President on the ratification of international treaties and agreements signed by the Maldivian Government with foreign administrations that require ratification by the State.

The President may, at his discretion, remove any Minister or the Attorney-General from office.

In the event of a vote of no confidence by the People's Majlis in a member of the Cabinet of Ministers, such member shall resign from office.

The President may dissolve the Cabinet of Ministers if, in his opinion, the Cabinet of Ministers is unable effectively to discharge its functions. Upon dissolution of the Cabinet of Ministers, the President shall inform the People's Majlis of the fact, specifying the reasons thereof, and shall appoint a new Cabinet of Ministers as soon as expedient.

THE PEOPLE'S MAJLIS

Legislative power, except the enactment of the Constitution, shall be vested in the People's Majlis. The People's Majlis shall consist of 50 members, of whom eight members shall be appointed by the President, two members elected from Malé and two members elected from each of the atolls. The duration of the People's Majlis shall be five years from the date on which the first meeting of the People's Majlis is held after its election. The Speaker and Deputy Speaker of the People's Majlis shall be appointed to and removed from office by the President. The Speaker shall not be a member of the People's Majlis, whereas the Deputy Speaker shall be appointed from among the members of the People's Majlis.

There shall be three regular sessions of the People's Majlis every year. The dates for the commencement and conclusion of these sessions shall be determined by the Speaker. An extraordinary sitting of the People's Majlis shall only be held when directed by the President. With the exception of the matters that, in accordance with the Constitution, require a two-thirds' majority for passage in the People's Majlis, all matters proposed for passage in the People's Majlis shall be passed by a simple majority.

Prior to the commencement of each financial year, the Minister of Finance shall submit the proposed state budget for approval by the People's Majlis.

A bill passed by the People's Majlis shall become law and enter into force upon being assented to by the President.

A motion expressing want of confidence in a member of the Cabinet of Ministers may be moved in the People's Majlis.

THE PEOPLE'S SPECIAL MAJLIS

The power to draw up and amend the Constitution of the Maldives shall be vested in the People's Special Majlis. The People's Special Majlis shall consist of members of the Cabinet of Ministers, members of the People's Majlis, 42 members elected from Malé and the atolls, and eight members appointed by the President.

Any article or provision of the Constitution may be amended only by a law passed by a majority of votes in the People's Special Majlis and assented to by the President.

THE JUDICIARY

The High Court shall consist of the Chief Justice and such number of Judges as may be determined by the President. The Chief Justice and the Judges of the High Court shall be appointed by the President.

All appeals from the courts of the Maldives shall, in accordance with regulations promulgated by the President, be heard by the High Court. The High Court shall hear cases determined by the President to be filed with the High Court from among the proceedings instituted by the State.

There shall be in the Maldives such number of courts at such places as may be determined by the President. The judges of the courts shall be appointed by the President.

PROCLAMATION OF EMERGENCY

Where the President has determined that the security of the Maldives or part thereof is threatened by war, foreign aggression or civil unrest, the President shall have the right to issue a Proclamation of Emergency. While the Proclamation is in force, the President shall have the power to take and order all measures expedient to protect national security and public order. Such measures may include the suspension of fundamental rights and laws. A Proclamation of Emergency shall initially be valid for a period of three months. The Proclamation may be extended, if approved by the People's Majlis, for a period determined by the People's Majlis.

GENERAL PROVISIONS

No bilateral agreement between the Government of the Maldives and the government of a foreign country and no multilateral agreement shall be signed or accepted by the Government of the Maldives unless the President has authorized in writing such signature or acceptance. In the event that such agreement requires ratification by the Maldives, such agreement shall not come into effect unless the President has ratified the same on the advice of the Cabinet of Ministers.

Note: In May 2004 a People's Special Majlis was elected to draw up and implement proposals for constitutional reform. By April 2008, however, the amendments were still under discussion and the new draft constitution had not yet been finalized and presented for approval.

The Government

HEAD OF STATE

President: MAUMOON ABDUL GAYOOM (took office 11 November 1978; re-elected 30 September 1983, 26 September 1988, 1 October 1993, 16 October 1998 and 17 October 2003).

THE CABINET OF MINISTERS
(April 2008)

Minister of Defence and National Security: ISMAIL SHAFEEU.
Minister of Finance and Treasury: QASIM IBRAHIM.
Minister of Environment, Energy and Water: AHMED ABDULLA.
Minister of Higher Education, Employment and Social Security: ABDUL RASHEED HUSSAIN.
Minister of Fisheries, Agriculture and Marine Resources: HUSSAIN HILMY.
Minister of Foreign Affairs: ABDULLAH SHAHID.
Minister of Gender and Family: AISHATH MOHAMED DIDI.
Minister of Education: ZAHIYA ZAREER.
Minister of Justice: MOHAMED MUIZ ADNAN.
Minister of Construction and Public Infrastructure: MOHAMED MAUROOF JAMEEL.
Minister of Health: ILYAS IBRAHIM.
Minister of Tourism and Civil Aviation: Dr MAHMOOD SHAUQEE.
Minister of Transport and Communication: MOHAMED SAEED.
Minister of Planning and National Development: HAMDOON HAMEED.
Minister of Home Affairs: ABDULLAH KAMAALUDHEEN.
Minister of Atolls Development: AHMED THASMEEN ALI.
Minister of Youth and Sports: MOHAMED WAHEED DEEN.
Minister of Legal Reform, Information and Arts: MOHAMED NASHEED.
Minister of Economic Development and Trade: MOHAMED JALEEL.
Minister of Housing and Urban Development: IBRAHIM RAFEEQ.
Minister of the President's Office: ANEESA AHMED.
Minister of Presidential Affairs: MOHAMED HUSSAIN.
Auditor-General: IBRAHIM NAEEM.
Minister of State and Principal Collector of Customs: IBRAHIM RASHAD.
Attorney-General: AZIMA SHAKOOR.

MINISTRIES

President's Office: Boduthakurufaanu Magu, Malé 20-05; tel. 3320701; fax 3325500; e-mail info@presidencymaldives.gov.mv; internet www.presidencymaldives.gov.mv.

Attorney-General's Office: Huravee Bldg, 3rd Floor, Ameer Ahmed Magu, Malé 20-05; tel. 3323809; fax 3314109; e-mail ashraf@agoffice.gov.mv; internet www.agoffice.gov.mv.

Ministry of Atolls Development: Faashana Bldg, Boduthakurufaanu Magu, Malé 20-05; tel. 3323070; fax 3327750; e-mail info@atolls.gov.mv; internet www.atolls.gov.mv.

Ministry of Communication, Science and Technology: Aa-ge, 4th Floor, 12 Boduthakurufaanu Magu, Malé 20-05; tel. 3331695; fax 3331694; e-mail secretariat@mcst.gov.mv; internet www.mcst.gov.mv.

Ministry of Construction and Public Infrastructure: Izzuddeenu Magu, Malé 20-01; tel. 3323234; fax 3328300; e-mail admin@construction.gov.mv; internet www.construction.gov.mv.

Ministry of Defence and National Security: Bandaara Koshi, Ameer Ahmed Magu, Malé 20-05; tel. 3322607; fax 3312800; e-mail admin@defence.gov.mv; internet www.defence.gov.mv.

Ministry of Economic Development and Trade: Ghaazee Bldg, Ameer Ahmed Magu, Malé 20-05; tel. 3323668; fax 3323840; e-mail contact@trademin.gov.mv; internet www.trademin.gov.mv.

Ministry of Education: Ghaazee Bldg, 2nd Floor, Ameer Ahmed Magu, Malé 20-05; tel. 3323262; fax 3321201; e-mail e_sec@thauleem.net; internet www.moe.gov.mv.

THE MALDIVES

Ministry of Environment, Energy and Water: Huravee Bldg, Ameer Ahmed Magu, Malé 20-05; tel. 3324861; fax 3322286; e-mail env@environment.gov.mv; internet www.environment.gov.mv.

Ministry of Finance and Treasury: Block 379, Ameenee Magu, Malé 20-379; tel. 3349200; fax 3324432; e-mail admin@finance.gov.mv; internet www.finance.gov.mv.

Ministry of Fisheries, Agriculture and Marine Resources: Ghaazee Bldg, 1st Floor, Ameer Ahmed Magu, Malé 20-05; tel. 3322625; fax 3326558; e-mail it@fishagri.gov.mv; internet www.fishagri.gov.mv.

Ministry of Foreign Affairs: Boduthakurufaanu Magu, Malé 20-307; tel. 3323400; fax 3323841; e-mail admin@foreign.gov.mv; internet www.foreign.gov.mv.

Ministry of Gender and Family: FEN Bldg, 2nd Floor, Ameene Magu, Malé 20156; tel. 3328179; fax 3316237; e-mail admin@mgf.gov.mv; internet www.mgf.gov.mv.

Ministry of Health: Ameenee Magu, Malé 20-379; tel. 3328887; fax 3328889; e-mail moh@health.gov.mv; internet www.health.gov.mv.

Ministry of Higher Education, Employment and Social Security: Haveeree Hingun, Malé 20-125; tel. 3317172; fax 3331578; e-mail admin@employment.gov.mv; internet www.employment.gov.mv.

Ministry of Home Affairs: Huravee Bldg, 3rd Floor, Ameer Ahmed Magu, Malé 20-05; tel. 3323820; fax 3324739; e-mail minhah@dhivenhinet.net.mv.

Ministry of Housing and Urban Development: MTCC Tower, 7th Floor, Boduthakurufaanu Magu, Malé 20-05; tel. 3321960; fax 3328999; e-mail admin@mhud.gov.mv; internet www.mhud.gov.mv.

Ministry of Justice: Justice Bldg, Orchid Magu, Malé 20-212; tel. 3322303; fax 3325447; e-mail admin@justice.gov.mv; internet www.justice.gov.mv.

Ministry of Legal Reform, Information and Arts: Buruzu Magu, Malé 20-04; tel. 3334333; fax 3334334; e-mail informat@dhivehinet.net.mv; internet www.maldivesinfo.gov.mv.

Ministry of Planning and National Development: Ghaazee Bldg, 3rd Floor, Ameer Ahmed Magu, Malé 20-125; tel. 3348383; fax 3325371; e-mail info@planning.gov.mv; internet www.planning.gov.mv.

Ministry of Tourism and Civil Aviation: Ghazee Bldg, 1st Floor, Ameer Ahmed Magu, Malé 20-05; tel. 3323224; fax 3322512; e-mail info@maldivestourism.gov.mv; internet www.maldivestourism.gov.mv.

Ministry of Transport and Communication: Huravee Bldg, Ameer Ahmed Magu, Malé 20-125; tel. 3343433; fax 3343434; e-mail admin@transport.gov.mv; internet www.transport.gov.mv.

Ministry of Youth and Sports: PA Complex, 5th Floor, Hilaalee Magu, Malé 20-307; tel. 3326986; fax 3327162; e-mail info@youthsports.gov.mv; internet www.youthsports.gov.mv.

Legislature

PEOPLE'S MAJLIS

The People's Majlis (People's Council) comprises 50 members, of whom eight are appointed by the President, two elected by the people of Malé and two elected from each of the 20 atolls (for a five-year term). The most recent election was held on 22 January 2005.

Speaker: AHMED ZAHIR.

Deputy Speaker: AHMED THASMEEN ALI.

PEOPLE'S SPECIAL MAJLIS

The People's Special Majlis, which holds a mandate for enacting constitutional amendments (subject to presidential assent), comprises members of the Cabinet of Ministers and the People's Majlis, 42 elected members from Malé and the atolls, and eight members appointed by the President.

President: QASIM IBRAHIM.

Election Commission

Election Commission of Maldives: PA Complex, 3rd Floor, Hilaalee Magu, Malé; tel. 3324426; fax 3323997; e-mail info@elections.gov.mv; internet www.elections.gov.mv; f. 1998; independent; appointed by the President; Commr of Elections K. D. AHMED MANIK.

Political Organizations

In June 2005 legislation was approved permitting the establishment of political parties in the Maldives for the first time since 1952. The following parties subsequently registered with the Ministry of Home Affairs, with the exception of the Maldivian National Congress, which was in August 2007 garnering signatures for the purpose of formal registration by early 2008:

Adhaalath Party (Justice Party): Malé; f. 2005; Leader Sheikh HUSSAIN RASHEED AHMED.

Dhivehi Rayyithunge Party (DRP) (Maldivian People's Party): Sinamalé 3 Galolhu, Malé; tel. 3320456; fax 3344774; e-mail info@drp.org.mv; internet www.drp.org.mv; f. 2005; Leader MAUMOON ABDUL GAYOOM.

Islamic Democratic Party: Malé; tel. 3326962; fax 3327385; e-mail info@idp.org.mv; internet www.idp.org.mv; f. 2005; Leader UMAR NASEER.

Maldivian Democratic Party (MDP): H. Sharaashaa, 1st Floor, Sosun Magu, Malé 20059; tel. 3340044; fax 3322960; e-mail secretariat@mdp.org.mv; internet www.mdp.org.mv; f. 2001; fmrly based in Colombo, Sri Lanka; official registration in Maldives permitted June 2005; Chair. MARIA AHMED DID; Pres. Dr MOHAMED MUNAVVAR; Sec.-Gen. HAMID ABDUL GHAFOOR.

Maldivian National Congress (MNC): Malé; f. 2007; Founder and Leader MOHAMED MONAZA NAEEM.

Maldivian Social Democratic Party: Malé; f. 2006; Leader IBRAHIM ('REEKO') MANIK.

People's Alliance: Malé; f. 2008; Founder and Leader ABDULLA YAMEEN.

Diplomatic Representation

HIGH COMMISSIONS IN THE MALDIVES

Bangladesh: M. Kurinbee Lodge, 5th Floor, Izzudheen Magu, Malé; tel. 3315541; fax 3315543; e-mail bdootmal@dhivehinet.net.mv; High Commissioner MOHAMED MIJARUL QUAYES.

India: H. Athireege-Aage, Ameeru Ahmed Magu, Malé; tel. 3323015; fax 3324778; High Commissioner A. K. PANDEY.

Pakistan: G. Helengely, Lily Magu, Malé; tel. 3323005; fax 3321832; e-mail pahicmale@hotmail.com; High Commissioner MUHAMMAD ANWAR CHOHAN.

Sri Lanka: H. Sakeena Manzil, Medhuziyaaraiyh Magu, Malé 20-05; tel. 3322845; fax 3321652; e-mail highcom@dhivehinet.net.mv; High Commissioner MOHAMED ALI FAROOK.

Judicial System

The administration of justice is undertaken in accordance with Islamic (*Shari'a*) law. In 1980 the Maldives High Court was established. There are four courts in Malé, and one island court in every inhabited island. All courts, with the exception of the High Court, are under the control of the Ministry of Justice.

In January 1999 the Government declared that the island court of each atoll capital would thenceforth oversee the administration of justice in that atoll. At the same time it was announced that arrangements were being made to appoint a senior magistrate in each atoll capital.

HIGH COURT

Chief Justice: Sheikh MOHAMED RASHEED IBRAHIM.

Judges: ABDUL GHANEE MOHAMED, AHMED HAMEED FAHMY, ALI HAMEED MOHAMED, ABDULLA HAMEED.

In February 1995 the President established a five-member Advisory Council on Judicial Affairs. The Council was to function under the President's Office (equivalent, in this respect, to a Supreme Court) and was to study and offer counsel to the President on appeals made to the President by either the appellant or the respondent in cases adjudicated by the High Court. The Council was also to offer such counsel as and when requested by the President on other judicial matters.

ADVISORY COUNCIL ON JUDICIAL AFFAIRS

Members: MOOSA FATHY, ABDULLA HAMEED, Dr MOHAMED MUNAVVAR, Prof. MOHAMED RASHEED IBRAHIM, ASH-SHEIKH HASSAN YOOSUF.

Religion

Islam is the state religion, and the Maldivians are Sunni Muslims. In mid-1991 there were 724 mosques and 266 women's mosques throughout the country.

In late 1996 a Supreme Council for Islamic Affairs was established, under the authority of the President's Office. The new body was to authorize state policies with regard to Islam and to advise the Government on Islamic affairs.

Musthashaaru of the Supreme Council for Islamic Affairs: (vacant).

President of the Supreme Council for Islamic Affairs: MOHAMED RASHEED IBRAHIM.

Deputy President of the Supreme Council for Islamic Affairs: MOHAMED GUBAADH ABOOBAKURU.

The Press

In 1993 the Government established a National Press Council to review, monitor and further develop journalism in the Maldives.

DAILIES

Aafathis Daily News: Feeroaz Magu, Maafannu, Malé 20-02; tel. 3318609; fax 3312425; e-mail aafathis@dhivehinet.net.mv; internet www.aafathisnews.com.mv; f. 1979; daily; Dhivehi and English; Editor AHMED ZAHIR; circ. 3,000.

Haama Daily: Ma. Night Rose, Dhilbahaaru Magu, POB 20232, Malé; tel. 3340077; fax 3343726; e-mail haama@haamadaily.com; internet www.haamadaily.com; Dhivehi and English; Chair. QASIM IBRAHIM.

Hamaroalhi Daily News: Malé; tel. 3343699; fax 3343697; e-mail editor@hamaroalhi.com.mv; internet www.hamaroalhi.com.mv; f. 2005 as weekly; daily edn commenced 2007; Dhivehi and English; organ of the Dhivehi Rayyithunge Party; politics.

Haveeru Daily: Ameenee Magu, POB 20103, Malé; tel. 3325671; fax 3323103; e-mail haveeru@haveeru.com.mv; internet www.haveeru.com.mv; f. 1979; Dhivehi and English; Chair. MOHAMED ZAHIR HUSSAIN; Editor ALI RAFEEQ; circ. 4,500.

Jazeera Daily: M. Zenthuram, Izzudheen Magu, Malé; tel. 3343738; fax 3343736; e-mail info@jazeera.com.mv; internet www.jazeera.com.mv.

Miadhu News: G. Mascot, Koimalaa Hingun, Malé 20-02; tel. 3320700; fax 3320500; e-mail miadhu@dhivehinet.net.mv; internet www.miadhu.com.mv; Propr IBRAHIM RASHEED MOOSA; Chair. AHMED ABDULLA.

Minivan News: Malé; tel. 3334888; e-mail minivan.news@gmail.com; internet www.minivannews.com; f. 2005; independent; predominantly Dhivehi, with English section; Editor AMINATH NAJEEB.

Raajje Daily: Malé; f. 2008; independent; predominantly Dhivehi with English section; Editor HASSAN SAEED.

Sangu Daily: G. Aabin, Dhonadharaadhahigun, Malé; tel. 3300065; fax 3300064; e-mail sangu@sangudaily.com; internet www.sangudaily.com; Editor IKRAM ABDUL LATHEEF.

PERIODICALS

Adduvas: Malé; f. 2000; weekly; news, entertainment, health issues and social affairs; Editor AISHATH VELEZINEE.

Dheenuge Magu (The Path of Religion): The President's Office, Boduthakurufaanu Magu, Malé 20-05; tel. 3323701; fax 3325500; e-mail info@presidencymaldives.gov.mv; f. 1986; weekly; Dhivehi; religious; publ. by the President's Office; Editor President MAUMOON ABDUL GAYOOM; Dep. Editor Sheikh MOHAMED RASHEED IBRAHIM; circ. 7,500.

Dhivehingetharika (Maldivian Heritage): National Centre for Linguistic and Historical Research, Soasun Magu, Malé 20-05; tel. 3323206; fax 3326796; e-mail nclhr@dhivehinet.net.mv; internet www.qaumiyyath.gov.mv; f. 1998; Dhivehi; Maldivian archaeology, history and language.

The Evening Weekly: Ameenee Magu, POB 20103, Malé; tel. 3325671; fax 3323103; e-mail info@eveningweekly.com.mv; internet www.haveeru.com.mv; weekly; English; owned by the Haveeru news group; Chair. MOHAMED ZAHIR HUSSAIN.

Faiythoora: National Centre for Linguistic and Historical Research, Soasun Magu, Malé 20-05; tel. 3323206; fax 3326796; e-mail nclhr@dhivehinet.net.mv; internet www.qaumiyyath.gov.mv; f. 1979; monthly magazine; Dhivehi; Maldivian history, culture and language; Editor Uz ABDULLA HAMEED; circ. 800.

Furadhaana: Ministry of Legal Reform, Information and Arts, Buruzu Magu, Malé 20-04; tel. 3321749; fax 3326211; e-mail informat@dhivehinet.net.mv; internet www.maldivesinfo.com; f. 1990; monthly; Dhivehi; Editor IBRAHIM MANIK; circ. 1,000.

Huvaas Magazine: Ameenee Magu, POB 20103, Malé; tel. 3325671; fax 3323103; e-mail huvaas@haveeru.com.mv; internet www.haveeru.com.mv/huvaas; f. 2001; fortnightly; Chair. Dr MOHAMED ZAHIR HUSSAIN.

Jamaathuge Khabaru (Community News): Centre for Continuing Education, Salahudeen Bldg, Malé 20-04; tel. 3328772; fax 3322223; monthly; Dhivehi; Editor AHMED ZAHIR; circ. 1,500.

Maldives News Bulletin: Maldives News Bureau, Ministry of Legal Reform, Information and Arts, Buruzu Magu, Malé 20-04; tel. 3323838; fax 3326211; e-mail informat@dhivehinet.net.mv; internet www.maldivesinfo.com; f. 1980; weekly; English; Editor ALI SHAREEF; circ. 350.

Marine Research Centre Bulletin: Marine Research Centre, Ministry of Fisheries, Agriculture and Marine Resources, H. White Waves, Malé 20-06; tel. 3322242; fax 3322509; e-mail info@mrc.gov.mv; f. 1984; biannual; fisheries and marine research; Exec. Dir Dr MOHAMED SHIHAM ADAM.

Monday Times: H. Neel Villa, Boduthakunufaanu Magu, Malé; tel. and fax 3315084; f. 2000; banned 2002; relaunched 2004; weekly.

Our Environment: Forum of Writers on the Environment, c/o Ministry of Planning and National Development, Ghaazee Bldg, Ameer Ahmed Magu, Malé 20-05; tel. 3324861; fax 3327351; f. 1990; monthly; Dhivehi; Editor FAROUQ AHMED.

Rasain: Ministry of Fisheries, Agriculture and Marine Resources, Ghaazee Bldg, Ameer Ahmed Magu, Malé 20-05; tel. 3322625; fax 3326558; e-mail fishagri@dhivehinet.net.mv; f. 1980; annual; fisheries devt.

Samugaa: Malé; f. 1995; publ. by the Government Employees' Club.

NEWS AGENCIES

Haveeru News Service (HNS): POB 20103, Malé; tel. 3313825; fax 3323103; e-mail haveeru@haveeru.com.mv; internet www.haveeru.com.mv; f. 1979; Chair. MOHAMED ZAHIR HUSSAIN; Man. Editor AHMED ZAHIR.

Maldives News Bureau (MNB): Ministry of Legal Reform, Information and Arts, Buruzu Magu, Malé 20-04; tel. 3323836; fax 3326211; e-mail informat@dhivehinet.net.mv; internet www.maldivesinfo.com.

Publishers

Corona Press: Feeroaz Magu, Maafannu, Malé; tel. 3310052; fax 3314741.

Cypea Printers: 25 Boduthakurufaanu Magu, Malé; tel. 3333883; fax 3323523; e-mail cyprea@dhivehinet.net.mv; f. 1984 as Cyprea Printers; Man. Dir ABDULLA SAEED.

Loamaafaanu Print: Alkariyya Bldg, Ground Floor, Ameenee Magu, Malé 20-354; tel. 3317209; fax 3313815; e-mail haveeru@netlink.net.mv.

Novelty Printers and Publishers: M. Vaarey Villa, Izzudhdheen Magu, Malé 20-317; tel. 3318844; fax 3327039; e-mail novelty@dhivehinet.net.mv; general and reference books; Man. Dir ASAD ALI.

Ummeedhee Press: M. Aasthaanaa Javaahirumagu, Malé 20-02; tel. 3325110; fax 3326412; e-mail ummpress@dhivehinet.net.mv; f. 1986; printing and publishing; Principal Officers ABDUL SHAKOOR ALI, MOHAMED SHAKOOR.

Broadcasting and Communications

TELECOMMUNICATIONS

In March 2007 a privately owned submarine fibre-optic cable link between the Maldives and India was inaugurated in an effort to provide more affordable, reliable telecommunications access to islanders and to enhance international connectivity.

Ministry of Communication, Science and Technology (Post and Telecommunication Section): Aage, 4th Floor, 12 Boduthakurufaanu Magu, Malé 20-06; tel. 3323344; fax 3320000; e-mail secretariat@mcst.gov.mv; internet www.mcst.gov.mv; policy-making authority; Dir-Gen. (Post and Telecommunication Section) HUSSAIN SHAREEF.

Telecommunications Authority of Maldives: Telecom Bldg, Husnuheena Magu, Malé 20-04; tel. 3323344; fax 3320000; e-mail secretariat@tam.gov.mv; internet www.tam.gov.mv; f. 2003; regulatory authority; Chair. Dr HASSAN HAMEED; Dir-Gen. ABDULLAH RASHEED.

THE MALDIVES

Dhivehi Raajjeyge Gulhun Ltd (Dhiraagu): 19 Medhuziyaaraiy Magu, POB 2082, Malé 20-03; tel. 3322802; fax 3322800; e-mail 123@dhiraagu.com.mv; internet www.dhiraagu.com.mv; f. 1988; jtly owned by the Maldivian Govt (55%) and by Cable and Wireless PLC of the United Kingdom (45%); functions under Ministry of Communication, Science and Technology; operates all nat. and int. telecommunications services in the Maldives (incl. internet service–Dhivehinet); Chair. IBRAHIM SHAFIU; CEO ISMAIL WAHEED.

Wataniya Telecom Maldives Pvt Ltd: 2nd Floor, Urban Development Bldg, Hulhumalé; tel. 9621111; fax 3350519; internet www.wataniya.mv; f. 2005; provides advanced cellular mobile telephone services throughout the Maldives; Chair. SOLAH FAHUD SULTAN; CEO ABRAHAM SMITH.

WARF Telecom International (Pvt) Ltd: Hulhumalé; f. 2005 by jt venture of Wattaniyya Telecom Maldives, Reliance Communications (India), and Focus Infocomm to lay fibre-optic cable between Hulhumalé and mainland India; owned by Wataniya Telecom Maldives (65%), Reliance Communications Ltd (20%) and Focus Infocomm (15%); awarded 15-year operating licence in March 2007; CEO AHMAD HALEEM.

RADIO

The Maldives Government was to permit private broadcasting by 3 May 2007 (World Press Freedom Day) under its 'Roadmap for the Reform Agenda' programme, although licences were not awarded until 21 May. Five national radio stations and a number of small local operators secured terrestrial broadcasting rights. The first private radio station commenced broadcasting operations in July.

Capital Radio: Malé; tel. 3300956; fax 3334948; e-mail info@capital956.fm; internet www.capital956.fm; f. 2007; operated by Asna Maldives Pte Ltd; broadcasts BBC news bulletins, music, current affairs and analysis programmes; Man. Dir MOHAMED NASHEED.

DhiFM 95.2: Malé; f. 2007; operated by Maldives Media Co Pvt; broadcasts news, music and general interest programmes in Dhivehi and English; anticipates operation of 24-hour nationwide service by 2008; Chief Exec. Dir IBRAHIM KHALEEL; Editorial Dir MASOOD ALI.

Radio Eke: Malé.

Voice of Islam: Malé.

Voice of Maldives (VOM) (Dhivehi Raajjeyge Adu): Voice of Maldives Bldg, Maafaanu, Malé; tel. 3322840; fax 3317273; e-mail badru@vom.gov.mv; internet www.vom.gov.mv; radio broadcasting began in 1962 under name of Malé Radio; name changed as above in 1980; two channels; home service in Dhivehi and English; Rajje FM in Dhivehi; began broadcasting 24 hrs daily from Jan. 2005; Dir-Gen. BADRU NASEER.

TELEVISION

Under the Maldivian Government's 'Roadmap for the Reform Agenda', licences for the establishment of national television stations were made available to bidders in May 2007; the only company to apply for and secure such a licence was Atoll Wave. The development represented significant progress towards the liberalization of this previously state-dominated sector.

Atoll Television: Majeediyya Alimas Ufaa, Boduthakurufaanu Magu, Henveiru, Malé; tel. 326638; fax 327143; e-mail atoll@airatoll.com; internet www.airatoll.com; f. 2007; operated by Atoll Investment Pvt Ltd.

Television Maldives: Buruzu Magu, Malé 20-144; tel. 3342200; fax 3325083; e-mail comments@tvm.gov.mv; internet www.tvm.gov.mv; television broadcasting began in 1978; two channels: TVM broadcasts for an average of 18 hrs daily and TVM Plus (f. 1994) broadcasts for 10 hrs daily; covers a 40-km radius around Malé; Exec. Dir HUSSAIN MOHAMED; CEO ALI KHALID.

Finance

(cap. = capital; res = reserves; dep. = deposits; m. = million; brs = branches; amounts in US dollars unless otherwise stated)

BANKING

Central Bank

Maldives Monetary Authority (MMA): Umar Shopping Arcade, 3rd Floor, Chandhanee Magu, Maafannu, Malé 20-156; tel. 3323783; fax 3323862; e-mail mail@mma.gov.mv; internet www.mma.gov.mv; f. 1981; bank of issue; supervises and regulates commercial bank and foreign-exchange dealings and advises the Govt on banking and monetary matters; authorized cap. 4m. rufiyaa, res 86.3m. rufiyaa, dep. 2,254.4m. rufiyaa (Dec. 2005); Gov. ABDULLAH JIHAD; Man. Dir KHADEEJA HASSAN.

Commercial Bank

Bank of Maldives PLC: 11 Boduthakurufaanu Magu, Malé 20-094; tel. 3330100; fax 3328233; e-mail bmlho@dhivehinet.net.mv; internet www.bankofmaldives.com.mv; f. 1982; 75% state-owned; cap. 36.5m., res 597.0m., dep. 4,393.9m. (Dec. 2006); Chair. ABDUL HAMEED MOHAMED; Gen. Man. and CEO SERENE HO OI KHUEN; 24 brs.

DEVELOPMENT FINANCE ORGANIZATION

Housing Development Finance Corpn: H. Fulidhooge, 5th Floor, Kalaafaanu Hingun, Malé; tel. 3338810; fax 3315138; f. 2004 to provide public housing loans; 100% state-owned; Chair. IBRAHIM NAEEM.

INSURANCE

Allied Insurance Co of the Maldives (Pte) Ltd: 04–06 STO Trade Centre, Orchid Magu, Malé 20-02; tel. 3324612; fax 3325035; internet www.alliedmaldives.com; f. 1985; all classes of non-life insurance; operated by State Trading Organization (see below); Chief Exec. MOHAMED MANIKU; Man. Dir ISMAIL RIZA.

Trade and Industry

GOVERNMENT AGENCY

Foreign Investment Services Bureau (FISB): Ministry of Economic Development and Trade, Ghazee Bldg, 1st Floor, Ameer Ahmed Magu, Malé; tel. 3323890; fax 3323756; e-mail info@investmaldives.org; internet www.investmaldives.org; under administration of Ministry of Economic Development and Trade; Dir-Gen. AHMED NASEEM.

CHAMBER OF COMMERCE AND INDUSTRY

Maldives National Chamber of Commerce and Industry (MNCCI): G. Viyafaari Hiya, Ameenee Magu, Malé 20-04; tel. 3326634; fax 3310233; e-mail mncci@dhivehinet.net.mv; internet www.mncci.com.mv; f. 1978; merged with the Maldivian Traders' Asscn in 2000; Pres. AHMED MUJUTHABA; Sec.-Gen. ABDULLAH FAIZ.

INDUSTRIAL AND TRADE ASSOCIATIONS

Maldives Association of Construction Industry (MACI): PA Complex, Ground Floor, Hilaalee Magu, Malé; tel. 3318660; fax 3318796; e-mail maci@dhivehinet.net.mv; internet www.maci.org.mv; f. 2001; Pres. ABDUL MOHAMED; Treas. AHMED ABDULLA.

Sri Lanka Trade Centre: Girithereyege Bldg, 3rd Floor, Hithaffinivaa Magu, Malé; tel. 3315183; fax 3315184; e-mail dirsltc@avasmail.com.mv; f. 1993 to facilitate and promote trade, tourism, investment and services between Sri Lanka and the Maldives; Dir M. I. SUFIYAN.

State Trading Organization PLC (STO): STO Bldg, Boduthakurufaanu Magu, Maafanau, Malé 20-345; tel. 3344333; fax 3344334; e-mail info@stomaldives.net; internet www.stomaldives.com; f. 1964 as Athirimaafannuge Trading Account, renamed as above in 1976; became public limited company in 2001; state-controlled commercial org.; under administration of independent Board of Directors; imports and distributes staple foods, fuels, pharmaceuticals and general consumer items; acts as purchaser for govt requirements; undertakes long-term devt projects; Man. Dir MOHAMED HUSSAIN MANIKU; Chair. and CEO AHMED MOHAMED.

UTILITIES

Electricity

Maldives Energy Authority: Malé; internet www.meew.gov.mv/mea; f. 2006 to replace Maldives Electricity Bureau; under administration of Ministry of Environment, Energy and Water; regulatory authority.

State Electric Co (STELCO) Ltd: Ameenee Magu, Malé; tel. 320982; fax 327036; e-mail admin@stelco.com.mv; internet www.stelco.com.mv; f. 1997 to replace Maldives Electricity Board; under administration of Ministry of Economic Development and Trade; provides electricity, consultancy services, electrical spare parts service, etc.; operates 22 power stations; installed capacity 32,921 kW (Dec. 2000); Chair. Dr ABDUL MUHSIN MOHAMED; Man. Dir ABDUL SHAKOOR; 650 employees (2006).

Gas

Maldive Gas Pvt Ltd: STO Trade Centre, 1st Floor, Orchid Magu, Malé; tel. 3335614; fax 3335615; e-mail info@maldivegas.com; internet www.maldivegas.com; f. 1999 as a jt venture between State Trading Organization and Champa Gas and Oil Co; Chair. MOHAMED MANIK.

Water

Maldives Water and Sanitation Authority (MWSA): Ameenee Magu, Malé; tel. 3317563; fax 3317569; e-mail shaheedha@mwsa.gov.mv; internet www.mwsa.gov.mv; f. 1973; Dir-Gen. Dr MOHAMED ALI.

Malé Water and Sewerage Co Pvt Ltd: Ameenee Magu, Machangolhi, POB 2148, Malé 20375; tel. 3323209; fax 3324306; e-mail mwsc@dhivehinet.net.mv; internet www.mwsc.com.mv; f. 1995; 76% govt-owned; produces approximately 7,000 metric tons of fresh, desalinated water daily, using seven plants; provides water and sewerage services to the islands of Malé, Hulhumalé and Villingili; provides water services to the island of Maafushi; Chair. Dr ABDULLA NASEER; Gen. Man. MOHAMED AHMED DIDI.

Transport

Maldives Transport and Contracting Co Ltd (MTCC): MTCC Bldg, 5th Floor, Boduthakurufaanu Magu, POB 263, Malé 20-181; tel. 3326822; fax 3323221; e-mail info@mtcc.com.mv; internet www.mtcc.com.mv; f. 1980; 60% state-owned, 40% privately owned; marine transport, civil and technical contracting, harbour devt, shipping agents for general cargo, passenger liners and oil tankers; Man. Dir IBRAHIM ATHIF SHAKOOR; Chair. Dr FAATHIN HAMEED.

SHIPPING

Vessels operate from the Maldives to Sri Lanka and Singapore at frequent intervals, also calling at points in India, Pakistan, Myanmar (formerly Burma), Malaysia, Bangladesh, Thailand, Indonesia and the Middle East. In December 2005 the merchant shipping fleet of the Maldives numbered 70 vessels, with a combined aggregate displacement of 87,402 grt. Smaller vessels provide services between the islands on an irregular basis. Malé is the only port handling international traffic. In 1986 a new commercial harbour was opened in Malé. The Malé Harbour Development Project was implemented during 1991–97, and improved and increased the capacity and efficiency of Malé Port. In July 2003 a new harbour was opened in Fuvah Mulah, on Gnaviyani atoll. Ambitious government-led plans for the construction of 60 new harbours and a transhipment port in the north of the country were under development in 2006–08.

Maldives Ports Authority (MPA): Boduthakurufaanu Magu, Maafaanu, Malé 20-250; tel. 3329339; fax 3325293; e-mail info@maldport.com.mv; internet www.maldport.com.mv; f. 1986; under administration of Ministry of Transport and Communication; Man. Dir MAHUDY IMAD; Harbour Master AHMED RASHEED.

Island Enterprises Pvt Ltd: Maaram, 1st Floor, Ameeru Ahmed Magu, Henveiru, POB 20169, Malé 20-05; tel. 3323531; fax 3325645; e-mail info@ielmaldives.com; internet www.ielmaldives.com; f. 1978; fleet of eight vessels; exporters of frozen fish, owners of processing plant, shipping agents, chandlers, cruising agents, surveyors and repairs; Man. Dir MAIZAN OMAR MANIK.

Precision Marine Pvt Ltd: H. Orchidmaage, Ground Floor, Ameeru Ahmed Magu, POB 20169, Malé 20-05; tel. 3315663; fax 3315107; e-mail info@pmlboatyard.com.mv; internet www.pmlboatyard.com.mv; subsidiary of Island Enterprises Pvt Ltd; mfrs and repairers of fibreglass boats, launches, yachts, marine sports equipment, etc.; Dir OMAR MANIK.

Maldives National Shipping Ltd: Ship Plaza, 2nd Floor, 1/6 Orchid Magu, POB 2022, Malé 20-02; tel. 3323871; fax 3324323; e-mail male@maldiveshipping.com.mv; f. 1965; 100% state-owned; fleet of three container vessels; br. in Singapore; Gen. Man. AIMON JAMEEL.

Matrana Enterprises (Pvt) Ltd: 79 Majeedhee Magu, Malé; tel. 3331166; fax 3322832; e-mail webmaster@matrana.org; internet www.matrana.org; Sr Exec. MOHAMED ABDULLA.

Villa Shipping and Trading Co (Pvt) Ltd: Villa Bldg, POB 2073, Malé 20-02; tel. 3325195; fax 3325177; e-mail info@villa.com.mv; operates five tourist resorts and owns a trading operation supported by a fleet of eight cargo vessels and tankers; Man. Dir QASIM IBRAHIM.

CIVIL AVIATION

The existing airport on Hululé Island near Malé, which was first opened in 1966, was expanded and improved to international standard with financial assistance from abroad and, as Malé International Airport, was officially opened in 1981. Charter flights from Europe subsequently began. Further expansion was completed in 2006, including the construction of the world's largest water aerodrome. Proposals have been put forward for the construction of a second runway.

In addition, there are four domestic airports covering different regions of the country. These are located on Gan Island, Addu atoll, on Kadhdhoo Island, Hadhdhummathi atoll, on Hanimaadhoo Island, South Thiladhummathi atoll, and on Kaadedhdhoo Island, South Huvadhu atoll; there are plans to build a further airport on Maamigili Island, Alif Dhaal atoll. The airport on Gan Island was to begin servicing international flights in 2008. In early 1995 there were 10 helipads in use in the Maldives.

Maldives Airport Co Ltd (MACL): Malé International Airport, Hululé 22-000; tel. 3338800; fax 3331515; e-mail info@maclnet.net; internet www.airports.com.mv; f. 2000; 100% govt-owned; under administration of Ministry of Tourism and Civil Aviation; serviced by 13 charter airlines and 12 scheduled carriers; CEO MOHAMED AMIR.

Island Aviation Services Ltd: 1st Floor, STO Aifaanu Bldg, Boduthakurufaanu Magu, Henveiru, Malé; tel. 3335544; fax 3315661; e-mail info@island.com.mv; internet www.island.com.mv; f. 2000; 100% govt-owned; operates domestic flights; commenced regional flights in Jan. 2008; Chair. MOHAMED UMAR MANIK; Man. Dir BANDHU IBRAHIM SALEEM.

Maldivian Air Taxi: Kaafu Hulhulé, POB 2023, Malé; tel. 3315201; fax 3315203; e-mail mat@mat.com.mv; f. 1993; seaplane services between Malé and outer islands; operates 15 aircraft; Chair. LARS ERIK NIELSEN; Gen. Man. AUM FAWZY.

Trans Maldivian Airways (Pvt) Ltd: Malé International Airport, POB 2079, Malé; tel. 3312444; fax 3323161; e-mail mail@tma.com.mv; internet www.transmaldavian.com; f. 1989 as Hummingbird Island Airways Pvt Ltd; name changed as above in 2000; operates 15 floatplanes; Man. Dir BRAM STELLER.

Tourism

The tourism industry brings considerable foreign exchange to the Maldives. The islands' attractions include white sandy beaches, excellent diving conditions and multi-coloured coral formations. At the end of 2004 there were 87 island resorts in operation, and some 16,858 hotel beds were available; a further 8,000 beds were to supplement capacity in 2007 when 35 new resorts were scheduled to commence operations. An additional 50 resorts were forecast to open between 2010 and 2012. The annual total of foreign visitors increased from only 29,325 in 1978 to 616,716 in 2004. Revenue from tourism amounted to 921.5m. rufiyaa in the latter year. It was feared that the devastating effect on the Maldives of the tsunami in the Indian Ocean in December 2004 would severely affect the country's tourism industry. By the end of 2005 all the resorts affected by the tsunami had reopened. However, tourist arrivals in that year totalled only 395,320, a decline of 35.9% compared with the previous year. The number of arrivals had almost completely recovered, to a reported 601,923, by the end of 2006 and estimated receipts from tourism in that year increased by an impressive 85.4%, compared with 2005, to reach 1,685.9m. rufiyaa. In 2007 a record number of visitor arrivals was achieved, at 675,889, and receipts from tourism (in US dollar terms) rose by 13.8%, compared with the previous year, to reach US $493.6m.

Maldives Association of Tourism Industry (MATI): Gadhamoo Bldg, 3rd Floor, Boduthakurufaanu Magu, POB 2056, Malé; tel. 3326640; fax 3326641; e-mail mati@dhivehinet.net.mv; internet www.mati.com.mv; f. 1984; promotes and develops tourism; Chair. MOHAMED UMAR MANIKU; Sec.-Gen. SIM I. MOHAMED.

Maldives Tourism Promotion Board: H. Aage, 3rd Floor, 12 Boduthakurufaanu Magu, Malé 20-05; tel. 3323228; fax 3323229; e-mail mtpb@visitmaldives.com; internet www.visitmaldives.com; f. 1998; Dir Dr ABDULLA MAUSOOM.

Air Maldives Travel Bureau/Tourist Information: Aifaan Bldg, Boduthakurufaanu Magu, Malé; tel. 3310917; fax 3318757; e-mail airmldvs@dhivehinet.net.mv; f. 1997.

MALI

Introductory Survey

Location, Climate, Language, Religion, Flag, Capital

The Republic of Mali is a land-locked country in West Africa, with Algeria to the north, Mauritania and Senegal to the west, Guinea and Côte d'Ivoire to the south, and Burkina Faso and Niger to the east. The climate is hot throughout the country. The northern region of Mali is part of the Sahara, an arid desert. It is wetter in the south, where the rainy season is from June to October. Temperatures in Bamako are generally between 16°C (61°F) and 39°C (103°F). The official language is French but a number of other languages, including Bambara, Fulfulde, Sonrai, Tamashek, Soninke and Dogon, are widely spoken. It is estimated that about 80% of the population are Muslims and 18% follow traditional animist beliefs; under 2% are Christians. The national flag (proportions 2 by 3) has three equal vertical stripes, of green, gold and red. The capital is Bamako.

Recent History

Mali, as the former French West African colony of Soudan, merged in April 1959 with Senegal to form the Federation of Mali, which became independent on 20 June 1960. Senegal seceded two months later, and the remnant of the Federation was proclaimed the Republic of Mali on 22 September. Its first President was Modibo Keita, the leader of the Union soudanaise—Rassemblement démocratique africain (US—RDA), who pursued authoritarian socialist policies. Mali withdrew from the Franc Zone (see p. 306) in 1962, and developed close relations with the communist bloc. Economic difficulties caused Mali to return to the Franc Zone in 1968, although the country was not fully reintegrated into the Zone's monetary union until 1984.

Following a series of purges of US—RDA and public officials, Keita was overthrown in November 1968 by a group of junior army officers, who assumed power as the Comité militaire pour la libération nationale (CMLN). The Constitution was abrogated, and all political activity was banned. Lt (later Gen.) Moussa Traoré became Head of State and President of the CMLN.

A draft Constitution, providing for the establishment of a one-party state at the end of a five-year transitional period of military rule, was approved by a national referendum in June 1974. Keita died in custody in 1977, prompting anti-Government demonstrations. The single political party, the Union démocratique du peuple malien (UDPM), was officially constituted in March 1979, and presidential and legislative elections took place in June. Traoré, the sole candidate for the presidency, was elected for a five-year term; a single list of UDPM candidates for the 82-member Assemblée nationale was elected for a four-year term.

A constitutional amendment in September 1981 increased the presidential term of office to six years and reduced that of the legislature to three years. Elections to the Assemblée nationale were thus held in June 1982 and June 1985, with UDPM candidates being elected unopposed on both occasions. In June 1985 Traoré was re-elected President, reportedly obtaining 99.9% of the votes cast. At legislative elections in June 1998 only about one-half of the incumbent deputies were returned to office, after provision was made for as many as three UDPM-nominated candidates to contest each seat.

Mali's first cohesive opposition movements began to emerge in 1990, among them the Comité national d'initiative démocratique (CNID) and the Alliance pour la démocratie au Mali (ADEMA), which together organized mass pro-democracy demonstrations in December. The security forces harshly repressed violent pro-democracy demonstrations in Bamako in March 1991: official figures later revealed that 106 people were killed, and 708 injured, in three days of unrest. On 26 March it was announced that Traoré had been arrested. A military Conseil national de réconciliation (CNR), led by Lt-Col (later Gen.) Amadou Toumani Touré, the commander of the army's parachute regiment, assumed power, and the Constitution and its institutions were abrogated. The CNR was succeeded by a 25-member Comité de transition pour le salut du peuple (CTSP), chaired by Touré. It was announced that a national conference would be convened, and that the armed forces would relinquish power to democratic institutions in January 1992. Soumana Sacko (who had briefly been Minister of Finance and Trade in 1987) returned to Mali from the Central African Republic to head a transitional, civilian-dominated government.

The transitional regime affirmed its commitment to the economic adjustment efforts of recent years, and undertook the reform of Malian political life. Among those arrested in subsequent months were Gen. Sékou Ly, Brig.-Gen. Mamadou Coulibaly (respectively, Minister of the Interior and Basic Development and Minister of Defence at the time of the violently repressed demonstrations in early 1991) and the former army Chief of Staff, Ousmane Coulibaly. In July 1991 an amnesty for most political prisoners detained under Traoré was proclaimed, and provision made for the legalization of political parties. The CNID was registered as the Congrès national d'initiative démocratique, and ADEMA adopted the additional title of Parti panafricain pour la liberté, la solidarité et la justice. Pre-independence parties, banned for many years, re-emerged, most notably the US—RDA.

The National Conference began in July 1991. Over a period of two weeks its 1,800 delegates adopted a draft Constitution, an electoral code and a charter governing the activities of political parties. In November the period of transition to democratic rule was extended until March 1992. The delay was attributed principally to the CTSP's desire to conclude a peace agreement with Tuareg rebels in the north of the country (see below). The draft Constitution was submitted to a national referendum on 12 January 1992, when it was endorsed by 99.8% of those who voted (about 43% of the registered electorate).

At municipal elections, held on 19 January 1992, ADEMA enjoyed the greatest success, winning 214 of 751 seats. At the elections to the Assemblée nationale, on 23 February and 8 March, ADEMA won 76 of the 129 seats, the CNID took nine seats, and the US—RDA eight. The date for the transition to civilian rule was again postponed, and the first round of the presidential election eventually proceeded on 12 April, contested by nine candidates. The leader of ADEMA, Alpha Oumar Konaré, won the largest share of the votes cast (some 45%). He and his nearest rival, Tiéoulé Mamadou Konaté (of the US—RDA), proceeded to a second round, on 26 April, at which Konaré secured 69% of the votes. Overall, only about 20% of the electorate were reported to have voted in the presidential election; a similar turn-out was reported in the legislative polls. Konaré was inaugurated as President on 8 June. He appointed Younoussi Touré (hitherto the national director of the Banque centrale des états de l'Afrique de l'ouest) as Prime Minister. Touré's first Council of Ministers was dominated by members of ADEMA, although a small number of portfolios were allocated to representatives of the US—RDA and of the Parti pour la démocratie et le progrès (PDP).

The trial of Traoré and his associates began in November 1992. In February 1993 Traoré, Ly, Mamadou Coulibaly and Ousmane Coulibaly were sentenced to death, having been convicted, *inter alia*, of premeditated murder at the time of the March 1991 unrest. The Supreme Court rejected appeal proceedings in May 1993; however, Konaré subsequently indicated that no death penalty would be exacted under his presidency. Charges remained against Traoré, his wife and several others in connection with the 'economic crimes' of the former administration.

Touré resigned in April 1993, following violent disturbances in Bamako, involving students and school pupils disaffected by the adverse effects of economic austerity measures. The new Prime Minister, Abdoulaye Sekou Sow (hitherto Minister of State, responsible for Defence, and who was not a member of any political party), implemented an extensive reorganization of the Government. The Council of Ministers remained dominated by ADEMA, but also included representatives of other parties, including the CNID. Following the resignation of ADEMA's Vice-President, Mohamed Lamine Traoré, from a senior government post, a major reorganization of the Council of Ministers was effected in November.

Meanwhile, a programme of austerity measures, announced in September 1993, provoked considerable political controversy and failed to prevent the suspension of assistance by the IMF and the World Bank. The 50% devaluation of the CFA franc, in January 1994, exacerbated differences regarding economic policy within the Government. Sow resigned in February, and was replaced by Ibrahim Boubacar Kéita, a member of ADEMA's 'radical' wing, which was opposed to Sow's economic policies. The withdrawal from the coalition of the CNID and the Rassemblement pour la démocratie et le progrès (RDP) prompted the appointment of a new Government, again dominated by ADEMA; the PDP in turn withdrew.

Following the election of Kéita as President of ADEMA in September 1994, Mohamed Lamine Traoré and other prominent figures resigned from the party and subsequently formed the Mouvement pour l'indépendance, la renaissance et l'intégration africaine (MIRIA). In January 1995 a party established by supporters of the UDPM, the Mouvement patriotique pour le renouveau (MPR), was granted official status. In October the Parti pour la renaissance nationale (PARENA), comprising several leading members of the CNID, who alleged excessive dominance by the party Chairman, Mountaga Tall, was registered. PARENA and ADEMA established a political alliance in February 1996, and PARENA's leaders, Yoro Diakité and Tiébilé Dramé, were appointed to the Government in July.

In early 1997 the first round of elections to the enlarged (147-seat) Assemblée nationale was postponed from 9 March until 13 April. As early results indicated that ADEMA was the only party to have won seats outright at this round, the main opposition parties denounced the results as fraudulent and announced their intention to withdraw from the second round. The opposition parties also withdrew their candidates from the forthcoming presidential and municipal elections. On 24 April the Constitutional Court invalidated the results of the first round of voting, citing irregularities in the conduct of the poll.

The presidential election was postponed, by one week, until 11 May 1997. Konaré stated that he did not wish to be the sole candidate and appealed to the opposition to participate. In early May the leader of the Parti pour l'unité, la démocratie et le progrès, Mamadou Maribatou Diaby, announced that he was prepared to contest the presidency. According to the final results, Konaré was re-elected to the presidency, securing 95.9% of the valid votes cast. Members of the radical opposition, which had campaigned for a boycott by voters, stated that the low rate of participation (28.4% of the registered electorate) effectively invalidated Konaré's victory. At the end of the month the municipal elections were postponed indefinitely.

Violent protests occurred in Bamako in June 1997, as Konaré was sworn in for a second term of office. Five opposition leaders, among them Tall (the CNID Chairman), Almamy Sylla (the RDP President and leader of the radical opposition collective) and Sogal Maïga (the MPR Secretary-General), were subsequently arrested and charged with various offences, including incitement to violence. They were released on bail in mid-June, shortly after the first round of the legislative elections (due on 6 July) had been postponed by two weeks.

A small number of opposition parties announced their intention to present candidates for the Assemblée nationale, but the radical collective, known as the Collectif des partis politiques de l'opposition (COPPO), at this time numbering 18 parties of varying political tendencies, reiterated its refusal to re-enter the electoral process. Violent disturbances, in which two deaths were reported, preceded the first round of voting on 20 July 1997, which was contested by 17 parties (including five 'moderate' opposition parties) and a number of independent candidates. COPPO again asserted that its appeal for a boycott had been heeded, and that the low rate of participation by voters (at about 12% of the registered electorate in Bamako, and 22% outside the capital) would render the new parliament illegitimate. A second round of voting was necessary for eight seats on 3 August. The final results allocated 130 of the 147 seats to ADEMA, eight to PARENA, four to the Convention démocratique et sociale (CDS), three to the Union pour la démocratie et le développement (UDD) and two to the PDP.

In September 1997 Konaré held a meeting with some 20 opposition leaders, including representatives of COPPO, at which he presented proposals for a broadly based coalition government. A new Council of Ministers, under Kéita, was appointed in mid-September. The new administration included, in addition to members of ADEMA and its allies, a small number of representatives of the moderate opposition parties (among them the UDD and PDP). Further measures intended to promote national reconciliation were implemented, and in December Konaré commuted some 21 death sentences, including those imposed on ex-President Traoré and his associates, to terms of life imprisonment. Although several parties had withdrawn from COPPO, little progress was made towards a full political reconciliation.

The municipal elections finally commenced on 21 June 1998, with voting in 19 communes, amid sporadic violence, in which one death was reported, while several members of the CNID were arrested on attempted sabotage charges. The remaining COPPO parties boycotted the elections. Elections in the majority of communes (some 682) were scheduled to take place in November 1998; however, in September it was announced that voting was to be postponed until April 1999, to allow for the resolution of outstanding administrative problems and, furthermore, for negotiations on participation by all political tendencies.

In October 1998 the trial for 'economic crimes' began in Bamako of ex-President Traoré, his wife Mariam, her brother, Abraham Douah Cissoko (the former head of customs), a former Minister of Finance and Trade, Tiénan Coulibaly, and the former representative in France of the Banque de développement du Mali, Moussa Koné. In January 1999 Traoré, his wife and brother-in-law were sentenced to death, having been convicted of 'economic crimes' to the value of some US $350,000 (the original charges had cited embezzled funds amounting to $4m.). Coulibaly and Koné were acquitted. In September Konaré commuted the death sentences to terms of life imprisonment.

In February 2000 Kéita submitted his Government's resignation. An extensively reorganized Council of Ministers was subsequently appointed. The new Prime Minister, Mandé Sidibé, was widely regarded as a supporter of economic reform. In June Choguel Kokala Maïga, the leader of the MPR, was among opposition leaders who announced their intention to participate fully in the presidential and parliamentary elections to be held in 2002, stating that conditions for electoral fairness and transparency seemed likely to be achieved.

In July 2000 the Assemblée nationale approved legislation providing for state funding of political parties. The Assemblée also adopted a revision of the Constitution proposed by Konaré, according to which some 50 articles of the 1992 document would be amended, subject to approval by referendum. Notably, people of dual nationality were to be permitted to contest presidential elections, while the Supreme Court was to be abolished. Also in July COPPO, which now comprised 15 parties and was led by Almamy Sylla of the RDP, announced that it would henceforth participate in the electoral process.

Kéita resigned from the leadership of ADEMA in October 2000, following the announcement that his opponents within the party had succeeded in calling an extraordinary congress of the party, to be held in late November. At the congress, several new members were appointed to ADEMA's executive committee, and Dioncounda Traoré was elected as the new Chairman of the party. A minor ministerial reshuffle was effected in June 2001. In July a new party led by Kéita, the Rassemblement pour le Mali (RPM), was officially registered.

In November 2001 Konaré indefinitely postponed a referendum, which had been due to take place in December, on the constitutional amendments adopted by the legislature in July 2000, following pressure from opposition parties and the judiciary. In January 2002 Soumaïla Cissé was elected as ADEMA's candidate for the forthcoming presidential election. In March Modibo Keita, hitherto Secretary-General at the presidency, was appointed as Prime Minister, following Sidibé's resignation to contest the presidency as an independent candidate. In early April 16 opposition parties, including the CNID, the RPM and the MPR, formed an electoral alliance, Espoir 2002, agreeing to support a single opposition candidate (generally expected to be Ibrahim Boubacar Kéita, who was to contest the election on behalf of the RPM) in the event of a second round of voting. Meanwhile, an alliance of 23 political parties, including MIRIA, PARENA and the US—RDA declared their support for the candidacy of Gen. (retd) Amadou Toumani Touré.

At the first round of the presidential election, which was held on 28 April 2002, contested by 24 candidates, Touré secured the largest share of the votes cast, with 28.7%, followed by Cissé, with 21.3%, and Kéita, with 21.0%. As no candidate had secured an overall majority, Touré and Cissé progressed to a second round of voting, held on 12 May. Touré, was elected to the presidency, with 65.0% of the votes cast, having obtained the support of support of more than 40 parties, including those of Espoir 2002. The electoral process was marred by allegations of fraud and incompetence, which led the Constitutional Court to annul 25% of the votes cast in the first ballot. None the less, international observers described the elections as generally free, fair and open. Touré was inaugurated as President on 8 June, and subsequently formed an interim Government, comprising 21 ministers. The new Prime Minister and Minister of African Integration, Ahmed Mohamed Ag Hamani, was regarded as a technocrat; in addition to having previously held various ministerial posts under Traoré, he had, more recently, served as ambassador to Belgium and to Morocco and as High Commissioner of the Organisation pour la mise en valeur du fleuve Sénégal (see p. 412). President Touré emphasized that he was not affiliated to any particular political party, and would be prepared to govern with any future parliamentary majority.

The elections to the Assemblée nationale in July 2002 further demonstrated the lack of any one dominant political grouping in Mali, while the rate of participation, at 25.7% nation-wide, in the second round, was low. The first round of polls was largely inconclusive. According to provisional results, ADEMA won the largest number of seats (57) in the new Assemblée, short of the overall majority that the party had held in the outgoing legislature. However, as a result of various irregularities in the conduct of the polls, several thousand votes were invalidated; following the publication, in early August, of revised results by the Constitutional Court, the RPM emerged as the single largest party, with 46 of the 147 seats (although 20 of its seats had been won in local electoral alliances with other parties of the Espoir 2002 grouping), while other parties of Espoir 2002 obtained a further 21 seats, giving a total of 67 to allies of the RPM. ADEMA secured 45 seats, while the pro-ADEMA Alliance pour la République et la démocratie won an additional six seats, giving a total of 51. The CNID received 13 seats, while parties belonging to an informal alliance supportive of President Touré, the Convergence pour l'alternance et le changement (ACC), including PARENA and the US—RDA, won a total of 10 seats. The Constitutional Court declared void the results of voting in eight constituencies in Sikasso, in the south, and Tin-Essako, in the north, owing to administrative flaws; by-elections were scheduled to be held in October. In early September 19 deputies, comprising those of the ACC parties, several independent deputies and other declared supporters of Touré, formed a grouping within the legislature, with the declared intention of forming a stable presidential majority. Later in the month Ibrahim Boubakar Kéita was elected President of the Assemblée nationale.

In mid-October 2002 Touré announced the formation of a Government of National Unity. Although many of the principal posts remained unchanged from the interim administration appointed in June, one notable appointment was that of Bassari Touré, a former official of the World Bank, as Minister of the Economy and Finance, who was expected to institute an expedited process of reform. The new Government stated that improvements to the health and education systems were among its priorities, as was the introduction of measures to alleviate the consequences of recent price rises in foodstuffs, electricity and water. Meanwhile, ADEMA increased its representation in the Assemblée nationale to 53 deputies, becoming the largest party grouping, following its victory in by-elections in all eight constituencies where elections were rerun on 20 October. A minor government reorganization was announced in mid-November.

In late April 2004 Ag Hamani tendered his resignation as Prime Minister, apparently in response to a request by President Touré. A new administration, headed by Prime Minister Ousmane Issoufi Maïga, hitherto Minister of Equipment and Transport (and not affiliated to any political party), was formed in early May. Moktar Ouane was appointed Minister of Foreign Affairs and International Co-operation, and Aboubacar Traoré became Minister of the Economy and Finance. ADEMA was the most successful party at municipal elections held on 23 May (postponed from the previous month), winning 28% of the seats contested, followed by the URD, which secured 14%, and the RPM, with 13%; the rate of participation by the electorate was relatively high, at 43.6%. ADEMA and the RPM subsequently formed an alliance, which, with ADEMA holding 44 seats and the RPM 35, gave the new grouping a majority in the 147-seat Assemblée nationale (although still short of the two-thirds majority needed to enact a motion of 'no confidence' against the head of the Government).

From mid-2004 there was considerable speculation regarding potential realignments of political organizations ahead of the presidential and legislative elections due in 2007. In February and March 2005 the President held a series of consultations with the leaders of various political organizations. However, there were signs that the political consensus that had existed since Touré's election in 2002 was likely to come to an end before the elections, as parties began to distance themselves from the President. In November 2005 the RPM announced that it would henceforth oppose the Government, stating that it had been increasingly marginalized within the ruling coalition. The victory of an RPM candidate in a legislative by-election later that month was interpreted by some observers as reflecting a decline in support for the ruling coalition, and it was subsequently reported that the RMP and URD were considering forming a common political programme. In February 2006 the executive committee of ADEMA announced that the party would support the candidacy of Touré at the presidential election due in April 2007 and that it would not, consequently, present its own candidate in the election.

The presidential election was duly held on 29 April 2007, at which 36.2% of the registered electorate participated. According to results released by the Constitutional Court in mid-May, Touré received 71.20% of the total votes cast, claiming an absolute majority and securing a second, and final, five-year term while avoiding a second round of voting. His closest rival was Kéita, who received 19.15% of the votes cast. Although a number of opposition candidates challenged the results, alleging that Touré had used public funds to finance his campaign and had manipulated the lists of voters, most independent observers believed the election to have been conducted fairly.

The first round of the legislative elections took place on 1 July 2007 and a second round followed on 22 July. According to official results, ADEMA secured 51 seats, while the URD took 34 seats and the RPM 11. Turn-out was, however, low at 12%, rising to 33% in rural areas. In total, parties supporting President Touré won 113 seats in the Assemblée nationale. In early September Dioncounda Traoré was elected President of that body

On 27 September 2007 Prime Minister Maïga tendered his resignation and that of his Government. The following day President Touré named Modibo Sidibé, hitherto Secretary-General of the Presidency, as Maïga's successor. Sidibé announced a new Council of Ministers in early October; the most notable appointments were Gen. Sadio Gassama as Minister of Internal Security and Civil Protection and a Tuareg, Mohammed El Moctar, as Minister of Culture. Ouane retained the foreign affairs portfolio and Gen. Kafougouna Koné was reappointed to head the Ministry of Territorial Administration and Local Communities. In April 2008 Ahmadou Abdoulaye Diallo replaced Bâ Fatoumata Nènè Sy as Minister of Economy, Industry and Commerce.

A predominant concern in the first half of the 1990s was the rebellion in the north of Mali, which began as large numbers of Tuareg nomads, who had migrated to Algeria and Libya at times of drought, began to return to West Africa (see also the chapter on Niger). A Tuareg attack in June 1990 on Menaka (near the border with Niger) precipitated a state of emergency in the Gao and Tombouctou regions, and the armed forces began a campaign against the nomads. A peace accord signed in January 1991 in Tamanrasset, Algeria, by representatives of the Traoré Government and delegates from two Tuareg groups, the Mouvement populaire de l'Azaouad (MPA) and the Front islamique-arabe de l'Azaouad (FIAA), failed to provide a lasting solution to the conflict. Following the overthrow of the Traoré regime, the transitional administration affirmed its commitment to the Tamanrasset accord, and Tuareg groups were represented in the CTSP. However, unrest continued. At the time of the National Conference it was reported that at least 150 members of the armed forces had been killed since 1990; meanwhile, thousands of Tuaregs, Moors and Bella (the descendants of the Tuaregs' black slaves, some of whom remained with the nomads) had fled to neighbouring countries.

In February 1992, following negotiations between representatives of the Malian Government and of the Mouvements et fronts unifiés de l'Azaouad (MFUA), comprising the MPA, the FIAA and the Armée révolutionnaire de l'Azaouad (ARLA), with Algerian mediation, a truce entered into force, and a commission of inquiry was inaugurated to examine acts of violence perpetrated and losses suffered during the conflict; the more militant Front populaire de libération de l'Azaouad (FPLA) was not reported to have attended the talks. Following further discussions, the Malian authorities and the MFUA signed a draft 'National Pact' in April. Although sporadic attacks continued, particularly against members of the northern majority Songhaï, provisions of the National Pact were implemented: joint patrols were established, and in November President Konaré visited the north to inaugurate new administrative structures. In February

1993 the Malian Government and the MFUA signed an accord facilitating the integration of an initial 600 Tuaregs into the national army. In May Rhissa Ag Sidi Mohamed, the leader of the FPLA, expressed satisfaction at the success of early efforts to repatriate refugees, and he and his supporters returned from their base in Burkina to Mali. In that month it was announced that the office of the UN High Commissioner for Refugees (UNHCR) was to oversee a two-year voluntary repatriation programme, whereby 12,000 refugees would be resettled from southern Algeria to Mali by the end of 1993. However, the assassination, in February 1994, of the MPA's military leader—now, in accordance with the Pact, a senior officer in the Malian army—resulted in several weeks of clashes between the MPA and the ARLA, which was blamed for his death.

In May 1994 the Malian authorities and Tuareg leaders reached agreement regarding the integration of 1,500 former rebels into the Malian army and of a further 4,860 Tuaregs into civilian sectors. The success of the agreement was, however, undermined by an intensification of disorder in northern Mali. Meanwhile, a Songhaï-dominated black resistance movement, the Mouvement patriotique malien Ghanda Koy ('Masters of the Land'), emerged, amid rumours of official complicity in its offensives against the Tuaregs. In June one of the leaders of the FIAA died as a result of a clash with members of the armed forces. Meeting in Tamanrasset shortly afterwards, the Malian authorities and the MFUA endorsed a reinforcement of the army presence in areas affected by the violence, and agreed procedures for the more effective integration of Tuareg fighters. Despite a serious escalation of violence in July, the ministers responsible for foreign affairs of Mali, Algeria, Burkina Faso, Libya, Mauritania and Niger met in Bamako in August to discuss the Tuareg issue, and a new agreement for the voluntary repatriation from Algeria of Malian refugees was reached. Although MFUA leaders welcomed the agreement, pledged the reconciliation of the Tuareg movements, and reiterated their commitment to the National Pact, sporadic hostilities continued.

In October 1994 both the Government and the MFUA appealed for an end to the violence, following an attack on Gao (for which the FIAA claimed responsibility) and retaliatory action, as a result of which 66 deaths were officially reported. A new Minister of the Armed Forces and Veterans was appointed shortly afterwards, and the authorities subsequently appeared to adopt a less conciliatory approach to the dissident rebel groups, with the FIAA becoming increasingly marginalized in the peace process. Further discussions involving Tuareg groups, Ghanda Koy and representatives of local communities resulted in the signing, in April 1995, of an agreement providing for co-operation in resolving hitherto contentious issues. In June the FIAA announced an end to its armed struggle, and expressed its willingness to join national reconciliation efforts. A programme for the encampment of former rebels, in preparation for their eventual integration into the national army or civilian structures, began in November and ended in February 1996, by which time some 3,000 MFUA fighters and Ghanda Koy militiamen had registered and surrendered their weapons. The MFUA and Ghanda Koy subsequently issued a joint statement affirming their adherence to Mali's Constitution, national unity and territorial integrity, urging the full implementation of the National Pact and associated accords and proclaiming the 'irreversible dissolution' of their respective movements.

In September 1997 the graduation of MFUA and Ghanda Koy contingents in the gendarmerie was reported as marking the accomplishment of the integration of all fighters within the national armed and security forces. In October the former FPLA leader, Rhissa Ag Sidi Mohamed, who had not previously been regarded as a party to the peace process, returned to Mali and expressed willingness to join efforts to consolidate peace and promote the development of the north. None the less the Ministers of Justice and of the Armed Forces and Veterans expressed concern that the continued proliferation of weapons, as well as the inadequacy of military and administrative structures in the north, could result in renewed clashes. In November 2000 it was reported that Malian government forces had been dispatched to end widespread banditry by an armed group, led by Ibrahim Bahanga, a former Tuareg rebel, in the Kidal area, near to the border with Algeria. In September 2001 Bahanga reportedly announced that his forces were to cease hostilities, following talks with a state official.

The presence of large numbers of refugees from the conflict in northern Mali dominated Mali's relations with its neighbours during the 1990s, and even after the completion of the process of repatriation in mid-1998 (and the conclusion of a UNHCR programme in June 1999) the north of the country remained vulnerable to cross-border banditry. In May 1998 the ministers responsible for the interior of Mali, Mauritania and Senegal met with a view to strengthening co-operation and border controls, and in December Mali and Senegal agreed to improve border security. In February 1999 Mali and Algeria agreed to revive their joint border committee to promote development and stability in the region. In March Konaré visited Mauritania to discuss border stability; however, in June a dispute over watering rights escalated into an armed conflict between neighbouring Malian and Mauritanian communities, in which 13 people were killed. The two Governments responded to the disturbances by increasing border controls and by sending a joint delegation to the villages involved. In August, at a meeting in Dakar, Senegal, the Malian, Mauritanian and Senegalese ministers responsible for the interior agreed to establish an operational unit drawn from the police forces of the three countries in order to ensure security in the area of their joint border. Bilateral relations between Mali and Mauritania were further strengthened by a military co-operation agreement regarding border security signed by the countries' respective Presidents in Nouakchott, Mauritania, in January 2005.

Concerns about insecurity in the region re-emerged in mid-2003, following reports, in late July, that some 15 German, Swiss and Dutch tourists, said to have been kidnapped in February by Islamist militants allegedly associated with the Groupe salafiste pour la prédication et le combat in southern Algeria, had been smuggled into Mali. Following negotiations with the kidnappers, conducted by a former rebel Tuareg leader, Iyad Ag Agaly, 14 hostages were released in mid-August (the remaining hostage had reportedly died earlier from heatstroke). In March 2004 Mali announced that it was to increase anti-terrorism co-operation with the authorities in Algeria, Chad and Niger.

Tensions arose again in May 2006 when Tuareg rebels launched an attack on the town of Kidal in the north-east of Mali. Two military bases were seized, as were two radio stations and a further military base south of Kidal, and it was reported that two government soldiers were shot and killed during army attempts to regain control of the installations. Military reinforcements were deployed to the region; however, the rebel group had taken much of the army's ammunition and weaponry and withdrawn to an area close to the Niger border, from where they demanded the commencement of negotiations with the Government over the conditions in which the Tuaregs had been forced to live since their integration into the armed forces. At a meeting between the Malian Government and the Tuareg group in June, mediated by Algerian officials, corruption and fraud were also cited among the reasons for the May attack. However, discussions were positive, including proposals for greater autonomy in the administration of the mountainous region of Kidal. In July a peace deal was signed in Algiers, Algeria, which included agreement on an investment programme for the region and the reintegration of rebels into the armed forces. There was some criticism of the Government for its relenting attitude towards the insurgents, but President Touré reiterated his determination to find a peaceful resolution to the conflict. A further reconciliation agreement was signed on 23 February 2007 between the Malian Government and the Tuareg rebels, stipulating guide-lines for the implementation of the agreement signed in July the previous year. The accord also outlined the establishment of special security units in the Kidal region, and measures for facilitating the reintegration of the Tuaregs into Malian society. In August several attacks on military personnel by Tuareg rebels were reported to have occurred near to the border with Niger. The main Tuareg group insisted that it was continuing to uphold the reconciliation agreement; however, a splinter group announced that it had formed an alliance with Tuareg militia in Niger, who had launched an offensive against the Niger Government. Following talks between the Tuareg rebels and the Malian Government in September, hostages taken in the attacks were released. Nevertheless, a US aircraft carrying aid supplies into Mali came under fire from Tuareg troops, which prompted President Touré to demand the holding of an urgent conference on peace and security in the region.

In February 1999 some 488 Malian troops joined ECOMOG (see p. 235) forces in Sierra Leone, although the Malian authorities emphasized that these troops would take on a purely peace-keeping role. However, following widespread demands in Mali for a withdrawal, during August the majority of the force departed Sierra Leone; it was later announced that seven Malian soldiers had been killed and 10 seriously injured while serving in Sierra Leone. As Chairman of ECOWAS, in March 2001 Konaré hosted a mini-summit, attended by the leaders of the three countries of the Mano River Union (see p. 413), Sierra Leone, Liberia and Guinea, in Bamako on the subject of the peace process in Sierra Leone. Konaré sought to emphasize the role of Mali in ECOWAS, and in November 2000 a 120-member ECOWAS parliament, which was to promote regional co-operation, was inaugurated in Bamako.

Mali has in recent years forged closer relations with Libya, and was a founder member of the Community of Sahel-Saharan States (see p. 411), established in Tripoli, Libya, in 1997.

Government

The Constitution of the Third Republic, which was approved in a national referendum on 12 January 1992, provides for the separation of the powers of the executive, legislative and judicial organs of state. Executive power is vested in the President of the Republic, who is elected for five years by universal suffrage. The President appoints a Prime Minister, who, in turn, appoints a Council of Ministers. Legislative power is vested in the 147-seat unicameral Assemblée nationale, elected for five years by universal suffrage. Elections take place in the context of a multi-party political system.

Mali has eight administrative regions, each presided over by a governor, and a district government in Bamako. Following a significant revision of local government structures in 1999, and a further minor revision in 2001, the number of elected mayors across Mali increased from 19 to 703. The Constitution makes provision for the establishment of a High Council of Local Communities.

Defence

As assessed at November 2007, the active Malian army numbered about 7,350 men, including a naval force of about 50 men (with patrol boats on the River Niger) and an air force of 400. Paramilitary forces comprised the gendarmerie (1,800), republican guard (2,000), militia (3,000) and national police (1,000). Military service is by selective conscription and lasts for two years. The defence budget for 2007 was estimated at 75,000m. francs CFA.

Economic Affairs

In 2006, according to estimates by the World Bank, Mali's gross national income (GNI), measured at average 2004–06 prices, was US $6,128m., equivalent to $440 per head (or $1,130 on an international purchasing-power parity basis). During 1996–2006, it was estimated, the population increased at an average annual rate of 2.9%, while gross domestic product (GDP) per head increased, in real terms, by an average of 3.0% per year. Overall GDP increased, in real terms, at an average annual rate of 6.0% in 1996–2006. According to the World Bank, real GDP increased by 5.4% in 2006.

Agriculture (including livestock-rearing, forestry and fishing) contributed 37.3% of GDP in 2006, according to figures from the Banque centrale des états de l'Afrique de l'ouest (BCEAO). An estimated 37.9% of the labour force were employed in the sector in 2004. Mali is among Africa's foremost producers and exporters of cotton (exports of which contributed an estimated 38.0% of the value of merchandise exports in 2004). Cotton production increased significantly in 2001, to a record 571,335 metric tons, reflecting a marked expansion in the area of land cultivated for the crop in that year; output declined to 439,722 tons in 2002. Output increased to a record level of 635,000 tons in 2003, before declining to 548,882 tons in 2004. According to unofficial figures 561,386 tons were produced in 2005, with an estimated 460,000 tons produced the following year. Shea-nuts (karité nuts), groundnuts, vegetables and mangoes are also cultivated for export. The principal subsistence crops are millet, rice, maize, sorghum and fonio. Cereal imports remain necessary in most years, and although a successful harvest in 2003 raised overall crop production by some 32%, according to official figures, the agricultural sector was badly damaged by the large locust swarms that affected the countries of the Sahel region in mid-2004. The livestock-rearing and fishing sectors make an important contribution to the domestic food supply and (in the case of the former) to export revenue, providing an estimated 4.7% of total exports in 2004, although both are highly vulnerable to drought. According to the World Bank, agricultural GDP increased by an average of 3.6% per year in 1996–2006; it declined by 4.9% in 2004, chiefly as a result of the locust invasion, but increased by 7.6% in 2005 and by 5.0% in 2006.

Industry (including mining, manufacturing, construction and power) contributed 25.9% of GDP in 2006, according to the BCEAO. It employed 15.1% of the labour force in 2004. Industrial GDP increased at an average annual rate of 7.3% in 1996–2006. It increased by 4.4% in 2006.

Mining contributed 9.0% of GDP in 2006, according to the BCEAO. It employed 0.4% of the labour force in 2004. The importance of the sector has increased with the successful exploitation of the country's gold reserves: exports of gold contributed an estimated 55.8% of the value of total exports in 2004, with that proportion increasing to an estimated 65% the following year. Output of gold increased significantly in the second half of the 1990s, as new mining facilities commenced operations, and by 2001 Mali had become the third largest gold producer in Africa. In 2004 exports of gold amounted to some 44.5 metric tons, yielding 270,400m. francs CFA. Two new open-pit mines, at Yalea and Loulo, operated by Randgold Resources (of South Africa), commenced operations in late 2005; underground development at the same sites was expected, in due course, to produce 1.8m. oz of gold in total over a 10-year period. Salt, diamonds, marble and phosphate rock are also mined. The future exploitation of deposits of iron ore and uranium is envisaged. According to the IMF, the GDP of the mining sector increased at an average annual rate of 46.8% in 1996–2002; growth in mining GDP reached 181.3% in 1997, before slowing to an estimated 23.1% by 2002.

The manufacturing sector, including electricity and water, contributed 10.0% of GDP in 2006, according to the BCEAO. It employed 10.5% of the labour force in 2004. The main area of activity is agro-industrial (chiefly the processing of cotton, sugar and rice). Brewing and tobacco industries are represented, and some construction materials are produced for the domestic market. According to the World Bank, manufacturing GDP declined at an average annual rate of 1.4% in 1996–2006. However, manufacturing GDP grew by 1.2% in 2005, and increased by a further 8.6% in 2006.

Of total electric energy generated in 1995, about 80% was derived from hydroelectric installations. Mali began to receive power supplies from the Manantali hydroelectric project (constructed and operated under the auspices of the Organisation pour la mise en valeur du fleuve Sénégal—OMVS) from December 2001, and there were also plans to link the Malian network with those of Côte d'Ivoire, Burkina Faso and Ghana. An agreement on energy supply was also reached with Algeria in February 1998. In July 2000 Belgium provided a loan of 2,600m. francs CFA for the construction of two high-voltage power stations in Bamako. Imports of petroleum products comprised an estimated 27.2% of the value of merchandise imports in 2004.

The services sector contributed 36.7% of GDP in 2006, according to the BCEAO. It employed 38.3% of the labour force in 2004. The GDP of the services sector increased at an average annual rate of 5.3% in 1996–2006. Services GDP increased by 6.7% in 2006.

In 2005 Mali recorded a visible trade deficit of US $144.6m., while there was a deficit of $437.7m. on the current account of the balance of payments. In 2004 the principal sources of imports were France, Senegal and Côte d'Ivoire (which supplied, respectively, 14.5%, 9.8% and 7.6% of total imports). The largest market for exports were the People's Republic of China (which accounted for 31.6% of total exports), Thailand (6.9%), Italy (6.9%) and Germany (5.1%). The principal exports in 2004 were gold and cotton, comprising, respectively, 55.8% and 38.0% of total exports. The principal imports in that year were petroleum products (accounting for 27.2% of total imports), chemical products (14.2%), foodstuffs (13.9%) and construction materials (12.3%).

In 2006, according to the IMF, Mali recorded an overall budget surplus of 1,002,400m. francs CFA. Mali's total external debt was US $2,969m. at the end of 2005, of which $2,843m. was long-term public debt. In 2004 the cost of debt-servicing was equivalent to 7.2% of the value of exports of goods and services. The annual rate of inflation averaged 1.5% in 1996–2006. Consumer prices increased by 6.3% in 2005 and by 1.6% in 2006.

Mali is a member of numerous international and regional organizations, including the Economic Community of West African States (ECOWAS, see p. 232), the West African organs of the Franc Zone (see p. 307), the African Groundnut Council (see p. 407), the Liptako-Gourma Integrated Development Authority (see p. 413), the Niger Basin Authority (see p. 413) and the OMVS (see p. 412).

MALI

Mali's economic development is hindered by its vulnerability to drought, its dependence on imports and its narrow range of exports. The country also lacks facilities for the processing of its important cotton crop; it was reported in 2002 that only 1% of Mali's cotton crop was processed in the country. In 2000 Mali was granted some US $870m. in debt-service relief under the initiative of the IMF and the World Bank for heavily indebted poor countries (HIPCs), and in September 2002 France cancelled some €80m. of bilateral debt. In March 2003 the Bretton Woods institutions announced that Mali had reached completion point under the terms of the HIPC initiative, thus becoming eligible for additional debt-relief, and in February 2005 the United Kingdom pledged to meet $45.4m. of Mali's debt to the World Bank and the African Development Bank. In late 2006 the US Millennium Challenge Corpn pledged $461m. towards poverty alleviation and in early 2007 the World Bank awarded Mali a grant of $10m. to develop infrastructure, social services and reform programmes. Meanwhile, in the first half of the 2000s the Government pursued a programme of privatization, notably transferring the railway from Bamako to Dakar, Senegal, to private management in 2003. In addition, the cotton sector underwent restructuring and a partial transfer to private ownership, having been adversely affected by a decline in international prices during the late 1990s; the privatization of a majority share of the cotton ginning company, the Compagnie Malienne pour le Développement des Textiles was, however, postponed from 2006 until 2008. GDP growth was estimated at 5.1% in 2006, driven by a strong agriculture sector, high gold prices and increased gold production. However, the country also suffered a high trade deficit as a result of rising petroleum prices. In late 2007 the IMF completed its final review under the Poverty Reduction and Growth Facility, which released a further $2.1m. in developmental assistance, bringing the total amount under the arrangement to some $14.6m. In early 2008 the European Union also pledged 366,000m. francs CFA in development aid to Mali in 2008–13. The IMF estimated GDP growth of 5.2% in 2007, with growth of 4.8% forecast for 2008. None the less, in the absence of a more diversified economic base, Mali's economy continued to remain vulnerable both to external shocks and to fluctuations in the terms of trade of its principal import and export commodities, particularly with regard to the global prices of gold and cotton.

Education
Education is provided free of charge and is officially compulsory for nine years between seven and 16 years of age. Primary education begins at the age of seven and lasts for six years. Secondary education, from 13 years of age, lasts for a further six years, generally comprising two cycles of three years. According to UNESCO estimates, in 2003/04 primary enrolment included 47% of the appropriate age-group (males 46%; females 43%), while secondary enrolment was equivalent to only 22% (males 28%; females 17%). Tertiary education facilities include the national university, developed in the mid-1990s; in 2000/01 there were some 25,000 students enrolled at that institution. Hitherto many students have received higher education abroad, mainly in France and Senegal. Estimated budgetary expenditure on education in 2000 was 64,930m. francs CFA, equivalent to 15.6% of total government expenditure in that year.

Public Holidays
2008: 1 January (New Year's Day), 20 January (Armed Forces Day), 20 March* (Mouloud, Birth of the Prophet), 24 March (Easter Monday), 25 March (Commemoration of the overthrow of Moussa Traoré), 19 April* (Baptism of the Prophet), 1 May (Labour Day), 25 May (Africa Day, anniversary of the OAU's foundation), 22 September (Independence Day), 1 October* (Korité, end of Ramadan), 9 December* (Tabaski, Feast of the Sacrifice), 25 December (Christmas Day).

2009: 1 January (New Year's Day), 20 January (Armed Forces Day), 9 March* (Mouloud, Birth of the Prophet), 25 March (Commemoration of the overthrow of Moussa Traoré), 8 April* (Baptism of the Prophet), 13 April (Easter Monday), 1 May (Labour Day), 25 May (Africa Day, anniversary of the OAU's foundation), 20 September* (Korité, end of Ramadan), 22 September (Independence Day), 27 November* (Tabaski, Feast of the Sacrifice), 25 December (Christmas Day).

* These holidays are determined by the Islamic lunar calendar and may vary by one or two days from the dates given.

Weights and Measures
The metric system is in force.

Statistical Survey

Source (unless otherwise stated): Direction Nationale de la Statistique et de l'Informatique, rue Archinard, porte 233, BP 12, Bamako; tel. 222-24-55; fax 222-71-45; e-mail cnpe.mali@afribonemali.net; internet www.dnsi.gov.ml.

Area and Population

AREA, POPULATION AND DENSITY

Area (sq km)	1,240,192*
Population (census results)†	
1–30 April 1987	7,696,348
17 April 1998	
Males	4,847,436
Females	4,943,056
Total	9,790,492
Population (UN estimates at mid-year)‡	
2005	11,611,000
2006	11,968,000
2007	12,337,000
Density (per sq km) at mid-2007	9.9

* 478,841 sq miles.
† Figures are provisional and refer to the *de jure* population.
‡ Source: UN, *World Population Prospects: The 2006 Revision*.

Ethnic Groups (percentage of total, 1995): Bambara 36.5; Peul 13.9; Sénoufo 9.0; Soninké 8.8; Dogon 8.0; Songhaï 7.2; Malinké 6.6; Diola 2.9; Bobo and Oulé 2.4; Touareg 1.7; Moor 1.2; Others 1.8 (Source: La Francophonie).

ADMINISTRATIVE DIVISIONS
(*de jure* population at 1998 census, provisional figures)

District		Mopti	1,475,274
Bamako	1,016,167	Kayes	1,372,019
Regions		Tombouctou	461,956
Sikasso	1,780,042	Gao	397,516
Ségou	1,679,201	Kidal	42,479
Koulikoro	1,565,838		

PRINCIPAL TOWNS*
(*de jure* population at 1998 census, provisional figures)

Bamako (capital)	1,016,167	Koutiala	74,153
Sikasso	113,813	Kayes	67,262
Ségou	90,898	Gao	54,903
Mopti	79,840	Kati	49,756

* With the exception of Bamako, figures refer to the population of communes (municipalities).

Mid-2007 ('000, incl. suburbs, UN estimate): Bamako 1,494 (Source: UN, *World Urbanization Prospects: The 2007 revision*).

MALI

BIRTHS AND DEATHS
(annual averages, UN estimates)

	1990–95	1995–2000	2000–05
Birth rate (per 1,000)	51.6	51.2	48.6
Death rate (per 1,000)	19.3	18.1	16.4

Source: UN, *World Population Prospects: The 2006 Revision*.

Expectation of life (years at birth, WHO estimates): 45.9 (males 44.5; females 47.2) in 2005 (Source: WHO, *World Health Statistics*).

ECONOMICALLY ACTIVE POPULATION
('000 persons, 2004, estimates)

	Males	Females	Total
Agriculture, hunting and forestry	657.7	291.7	949.4
Fishing	33.3	2.0	35.2
Mining	8.4	3.0	11.4
Manufacturing	136.1	136.4	272.5
Electricity, gas and water	5.1	—	5.1
Construction	97.5	4.7	102.1
Wholesale and retail trade; repair of motor vehicles, motorcycles and personal household goods	266.1	402.1	668.1
Hotels and restaurants	1.4	6.3	7.6
Transport, storage and communications	51.8	3.5	55.3
Financial intermediation	4.4	—	4.4
Real estate	3.5	0.6	4.0
Public administration	33.3	6.6	39.9
Education	35.6	18.3	53.9
Health and social work	11.4	9.5	20.9
Other social services	42.6	97.5	140.1
Total employed	1,388.3	982.5	2,370.8
Unemployed	107.0	120.5	227.4
Total labour force	1,495.3	1,103.0	2,598.2

Source: ILO.

Mid-2005 (estimates in '000): Agriculture, etc. 4,978; Total labour force 6,378 (Source: FAO).

Health and Welfare

KEY INDICATORS

Total fertility rate (children per woman, 2005)	6.8
Under-5 mortality rate (per 1,000 live births, 2005)	218
HIV/AIDS (% of persons aged 15–49, 2005)	1.7
Physicians (per 1,000 head, 2004)	0.08
Hospital beds (per 1,000 head, 1998)	0.24
Health expenditure (2004): US $ per head (PPP)	54.0
Health expenditure (2004): % of GDP	6.6
Health expenditure (2004): public (% of total)	49.2
Access to water (% of persons, 2004)	50
Access to sanitation (% of persons, 2004)	46
Human Development Index (2005): ranking	173
Human Development Index (2005): value	0.380

For sources and definitions, see explanatory note on p. vi.

Agriculture

PRINCIPAL CROPS
('000 metric tons)

	2004	2005	2006*
Rice (paddy)	718.1	945.8	1,018.8
Maize	459.5	634.5	587.8
Millet	974.7	1,157.8	1,060.2
Sorghum	664.1	629.1	730.0
Fonio	19.7	26.6	22.6
Sweet potatoes	49.2	133.1	60.0
Cassava (Manioc)	13.5	56.1	56.0
Yams	12.4	47.8	35.0
Sugar cane	348.0	348.0	350.0
Groundnuts (in shell)	161.0	279.5	171.5
Karité nuts (Sheanuts)	85*	n.a.	n.a.
Cottonseed	309.2	311.0	300.0
Tomatoes	47.9	64.6	70.0
Dry onions	23.1	34.9	35.0
Guavas, mangoes and mangosteens	54.8*	61.4	61.0
Cotton (lint)	239.7	250.4†	160.0

* FAO estimate(s).
† Unofficial figure.

Aggregate production ('000 metric tons, may include official, semi-official or estimated data): Total cereals 2,845 in 2004, 3,399 in 2005, 3,428 in 2006; Total pulses 120 in 2004, 112 in 2005, 112 in 2006; Total roots and tubers 132 in 2004, 314 in 2005, 216 in 2006; Total vegetables (incl. melons) 606 in 2004, 645 in 2005, 669 in 2006; Total fruits (excl. melons) 313 in 2004, 326 in 2005, 337 in 2006.

Source: FAO.

LIVESTOCK
('000 head, year ending September)

	2003	2004	2005
Cattle	7,312	7,500	7,682
Sheep	7,967*	8,364*	8,403
Goats	11,464*	12,036*	12,000
Pigs	68	68	69
Horses†	170	172	172
Asses, mules or hinnies†	700	720	720
Camels†	470	472	472
Chickens	29,000	30,000	31,000†

* Unofficial figure.
† FAO estimate(s).

2006: No data were available.

Source: FAO.

LIVESTOCK PRODUCTS
('000 metric tons, FAO estimates)

	2004	2005	2006
Cattle meat	97.8	97.8	101.4
Sheep meat	36.0	36.0	36.2
Goat meat	48.5	48.5	50.8
Chicken meat	35.1	36.0	37.1
Game meat	18.0	18.0	18.0
Pig meat	2.2	2.2	2.2
Cows' milk	183.8	188.7	191.1
Sheep's milk	124.5	126.0	127.5
Goats' milk	238.3	238.6	247.5
Camels' milk	55.2	55.2	55.5

Source: FAO.

Forestry

ROUNDWOOD REMOVALS
('000 cubic metres, excl. bark, FAO estimates)

	2004	2005	2006
Sawlogs, veneer logs and logs for sleepers	4	4	4
Other industrial wood	409	409	409
Fuel wood	4,965	5,027	5,084
Total	5,378	5,440	5,497

Source: FAO.

SAWNWOOD PRODUCTION
('000 cubic metres, incl. railway sleepers)

	1987	1988	1989
Total (all broadleaved)	11	13	13*

*FAO estimate.

1990–2006: Production assumed to be unchanged from 1989 (FAO estimates).

Source: FAO.

Fishing

('000 metric tons, live weight)

	2000	2001*	2002*
Capture	109.9	100.0	100.0
Nile tilapia	33.0	30.0	30.0
Elephantsnout fishes	7.7	7.0	7.0
Characins	5.5	5.0	5.0
Black catfishes	4.4	4.0	4.0
North African catfish	27.5	25.0	25.0
Nile perch	6.6	6.0	6.0
Other freshwater fishes	25.3	23.0	23.0
Aquaculture	0.0	0.5	1.0
Total catch	109.9	100.5	101.0

*FAO estimates.

2003–05 (FAO estimates): Data assumed to be unchanged from 2002.

Source: FAO.

Mining

(metric tons, unless otherwise indicated, estimates)

	2003	2004	2005
Gold (kg)	45,535	37,911	44,230
Gypsum	500	300	300
Salt	6,000	6,000	6,000

Source: US Geological Survey.

Industry

SELECTED PRODUCTS
('000 metric tons, unless otherwise indicated)

	1999	2000	2001
Raw sugar*	31.2†	29.1	28.0
Salted, dried or smoked fish*	6.4	8.0	7.9
Cigarettes ('000 packets)	51.4	n.a.	n.a.
Cement‡	10	10	n.a.
Electric energy (million kWh)§	404	412	415

* Data from FAO.
† Unofficial figure.
‡ Data from the US Geological Survey.
§ Provisional or estimated figures.

2002: Raw sugar ('000 metric tons) 32.0 (data from FAO).

Electrical energy (million kWh): 417 in 2002; 449 in 2003; 455 in 2004.

Source: mainly UN, *Industrial Commodity Statistics Yearbook*.

Finance

CURRENCY AND EXCHANGE RATES

Monetary Units
  100 centimes = 1 franc de la Communauté financière africaine (CFA).

Sterling, Dollar and Euro Equivalents (31 December 2007)
  £1 sterling = 892.702 francs CFA;
  US $1 = 487.592 francs CFA;
  €1 = 655.957 francs CFA;
  10,000 francs CFA = £11.20 = $20.51 = €15.24.

Average Exchange Rate (francs CFA per US $)
  2005   527.47
  2006   522.89
  2007   479.27

Note: An exchange rate of 1 French franc = 50 francs CFA, established in 1948, remained in force until January 1994, when the CFA franc was devalued by 50%, with the exchange rate adjusted to 1 French franc = 100 francs CFA. This relationship to French currency remained in effect with the introduction of the euro on 1 January 1999. From that date, accordingly, a fixed exchange rate of €1 = 655.957 francs CFA has been in operation.

BUDGET
('000 million francs CFA)*

Revenue†	2005	2006	2007‡
Budgetary revenue	461.3	504.5	534.9
Tax revenue	446.2	478.6	504.7
Non-tax revenue	15.1	25.9	30.2
Special funds and annexed budgets	45.3	49.7	47.0
Total	506.6	554.2	581.9

MALI

Statistical Survey

Expenditure§	2005	2006	2007‡
Budgetary expenditure	644.7	752.6	888.6
Current expenditure	376.6	411.8	459.0
Wages and salaries	137.8	147.9	160.3
Interest payments (scheduled)	18.3	15.5	14.1
Other current expenditure	220.5	248.4	284.6
Capital expenditure	268.1	340.8	429.6
Externally financed	170.0	228.7	268.2
Special funds and annexed budgets	45.3	49.7	47.0
Total	**690.0**	**802.3**	**935.6**

* Figures represent a consolidation of the central government budget, special funds and annexed budgets.
† Excluding grants received ('000 million francs CFA): 115.0 in 2005; 1,244.5 in 2006; 181.2 in 2007 (projected).
‡ Projected.
§ Excluding net lending ('000 million francs CFA): 22.7 in 2005; −6.0 in 2006; −49.3 in 2007 (projected).

Source: IMF, *Mali: Sixth Review Under the Three-Year Arrangement Under the Poverty Reduction and Growth Facility and Request for Waivers of Nonobservance of Performance Criteria and Request for Extension of Commitment Period - Staff Report; Press Release on the Executive Board Discussion; and Statement by the Executive Director for Mali* (March 2008).

INTERNATIONAL RESERVES
(excluding gold, US $ million at 31 December)

	2004	2005	2006
IMF special drawing rights	0.6	0.3	0.1
Reserve position in IMF	13.9	13.1	14.1
Foreign exchange	846.2	841.2	955.4
Total	**860.7**	**854.6**	**969.5**

Source: IMF, *International Financial Statistics*.

MONEY SUPPLY
('000 million francs CFA at 31 December)

	2004	2005	2006
Currency outside banks	275.4	344.9	344.4
Demand deposits	294.1	297.1	349.8
Total money (incl. others)	**569.7**	**642.4**	**694.5**

Source: IMF, *International Financial Statistics*.

COST OF LIVING
(Consumer Price Index for Bamako: base: 2000 = 100)

	2004	2005	2006
Food, beverages and tobacco	103.3	115.1	114.6
Clothing	99.5	96.3	98.2
Housing, water, electricity and gas	110.1	107.5	110.1
All items (incl. others)	**105.6**	**112.3**	**114.1**

Source: ILO.

NATIONAL ACCOUNTS
('000 million francs CFA at current prices)

Expenditure on the Gross Domestic Product

	2004	2005	2006
Final consumption expenditure	2,270.3	2,485.0	2,630.2
Households	1,797.7	1,994.6	2,122.5
General government	472.6	490.4	507.7
Gross capital formation	577.8	541.1	637.3
Gross fixed capital formation	446.6	446.7	467.3
Changes in inventories	131.2	94.4	170.0
Total domestic expenditure	**2,848.1**	**3,026.1**	**3,267.5**
Exports of goods and services	643.0	724.3	899.9
Less Imports of goods and services	859.1	952.5	1,071.3
Statistical discrepancy	—	13.6	—
GDP in market prices	**2,632.1**	**2,811.5**	**3,096.1**

Gross Domestic Product by Economic Activity

	2004	2005	2006
Agriculture, livestock-rearing, forestry and fishing	900.7	991.5	1,037.5
Mining	162.3	202.6	250.1
Manufacturing	247.7	257.7	278.8
Electricity, gas and water	42.8	50.2	63.6
Construction and public works	116.5	115.1	128.8
Trade	323.5	363.8	359.0
Transport, storage and communications	115.4	125.3	152.7
Non-market services	289.2	286.6	318.3
Other services	173.6	209.2	191.1
Sub-total	**2,371.7**	**2,601.9**	**2,779.9**
Import duties	260.4	209.6	316.2
GDP in purchasers' values	**2,632.1**	**2,811.5**	**3,096.1**

Source: Banque centrale des états de l'Afrique de l'ouest.

BALANCE OF PAYMENTS
(US $ million)

	2003	2004	2005
Exports of goods f.o.b.	927.8	976.4	1,100.9
Imports of goods f.o.b.	−988.3	−1,092.9	−1,245.5
Trade balance	**−60.5**	**−116.4**	**−144.6**
Exports of services	224.3	241.1	274.3
Imports of services	−482.2	−531.8	−588.0
Balance on goods and services	**−318.5**	**−407.1**	**−458.3**
Other income received	21.3	24.0	67.7
Other income paid	−181.2	−218.8	−274.7
Balance on goods, services and income	**−478.4**	**−601.9**	**−665.3**
Current transfers received	265.5	251.3	286.0
Current transfers paid	−58.1	−58.3	−58.5
Current balance	**−271.0**	**−409.0**	**−437.7**
Capital account (net)	113.7	151.4	148.9
Direct investment abroad	−1.4	−0.8	−34.7
Direct investment from abroad	132.3	101.0	223.8
Portfolio investment assets	−27.1	−3.2	−18.0
Portfolio investment liabilities	27.6	0.6	2.9
Other investment assets	3.7	−130.9	−109.2
Other investment liabilities	153.7	133.5	232.9
Net errors and omissions	45.2	−26.3	6.6
Overall balance	**176.5**	**−184.0**	**15.5**

Source: IMF, *International Financial Statistics*.

External Trade

PRINCIPAL COMMODITIES
('000 million francs CFA)

Imports c.i.f.	2002	2003	2004*
Foodstuffs	82.7	86.8	114.6
Cereals	27.1	28.7	17.1
Sugar	19.9	20.7	10.2
Petroleum products	112.9	108.6	224.2
Construction materials	79.7	85.5	101.2
Chemical products	129.2	122.2	116.7
Textiles and leather	19.3	20.2	12.1
Total (incl. others)	**640.0**	**564.3**	**823.8**

Exports f.o.b.	2002	2003	2004*
Cotton	158.0	144.3	184.2
Cotton fibre	155.4	140.9	181.4
Livestock	27.3	24.0	22.9
Gold	400.0	326.8	270.4
Total (incl. others)	**596.5**	**503.8**	**484.7**

* Estimates.

Source: IMF, *Mali: Statistical Appendix* (March 2006).

MALI

SELECTED TRADING PARTNERS
(US $ million)

Imports	2002	2003	2004
Belgium	32.4	32.0	49.2
China, People's Repub.	37.1	31.6	34.5
Côte d'Ivoire	197.5	107.6	141.3
France	192.1	234.1	268.8
Germany	54.4	54.9	73.7
India	27.7	42.4	29.6
Senegal	92.5	117.8	182.4
South Africa	19.3	25.6	63.0
USA	12.2	34.3	47.4
Total (incl. others)	1,382.7	1,523.1	1,857.6

Exports	2002	2003	2004
Belgium	5.1	n.a.	n.a.
China, People's Repub.	1.7	25.8	103.3
Côte d'Ivoire	1.8	0.1	0.1
France	6.5	7.7	7.4
Germany	8.5	7.3	16.5
India	14.0	25.8	15.5
Indonesia	3.8	4.1	7.3
Italy	16.9	16.1	22.4
Korea, Repub.	3.6	2.2	1.2
Spain	8.4	n.a.	n.a.
Thailand	23.9	30.0	22.7
Tunisia	3.2	4.8	2.3
United Kingdom	4.8	n.a.	n.a.
Total (incl. others)	162.3	214.5	326.7

Source: mostly IMF, *Mali: Statistical Appendix* (March 2006).

Transport

RAILWAYS
(traffic)

	1999	2000	2001
Passengers ('000)	778.7	682.3	649.0
Freight carried ('000 metric tons)	535	438	358

Passenger-km (million): 210 in 1999.

Freight ton-km (million): 241 in 1999.

ROAD TRAFFIC
(motor vehicles in use, estimates)

	1994	1995	1996
Passenger cars	24,250	24,750	26,190
Lorries and vans	16,000	17,100	18,240

1998 (motor vehicles in use): Passenger cars 29,374; Total road vehicles 47,374.

Source: IRF, *World Road Statistics*.

CIVIL AVIATION
(traffic on scheduled services)*

	1999	2000	2001
Kilometres flown (million)	3	3	1
Passengers carried ('000)	84	77	46
Passenger-km (million)	235	216	130
Total ton-km (million)	36	32	19

* Including an apportionment of the traffic of Air Afrique.

Source: UN, *Statistical Yearbook*.

Communications Media

	2004	2005	2006
Telephones ('000 main lines in use)	74.9	75.0	52.5
Mobile cellular telephones ('000 subscribers)	400.0	869.6	1,512.9
Personal computers ('000 in use)	42	45	n.a.
Internet users ('000)	50	60	70

Source: International Telecommunication Union.

Television receivers ('000 in use): 160 in 2000 (Source: UNESCO, *Statistical Yearbook*).

Radio receivers ('000 in use): 570 in 1997 (Source: UNESCO, *Statistical Yearbook*).

Daily newspapers (national estimates): 3 (total circulation 12,350 copies) in 1997; 3 (total circulation 12,600) in 1998; 9 in 2004. (Source: UNESCO Institute for Statistics).

Book production: 14 titles (28,000 copies) in 1995 (first editions only, excluding pamphlets); 33 in 1998 (Sources: UNESCO, *Statistical Yearbook*, UNESCO Institute for Statistics).

Tourism

FOREIGN VISITORS BY NATIONALITY*

	2003	2004	2005
Austria	636	1,167	2,175
Belgium, Luxembourg and the Netherlands	9,046	6,591	9,002
Canada	3,280	3,543	3,646
France	27,047	37,971	37,851
Germany	3,200	3,676	5,885
Italy	11,570	6,087	7,066
Japan	1,200	3,117	2,090
Middle Eastern states	2,712	1,524	1,064
Scandinavian states	2,728	800	1,964
Spain	4,692	4,322	7,069
Switzerland	1,345	1,236	2,384
United Kingdom	1,752	560	5,180
USA	6,113	8,951	9,641
West African states	19,000	21,993	23,972
Total (incl. others)	110,365	112,654	142,814

* Arrivals at hotels and similar establishments.

Receipts from tourism (US $ million, incl. passenger transport): 136 in 2003; 142 in 2004; 149 in 2005.

Source: World Tourism Organization.

Education

(2004/05, unless otherwise indicated)

	Institutions*	Teachers	Males	Females	Total
Pre-primary	212	1,503†	16.1†	15.7†	31.8†
Primary	2,871	27,688	852.2	653.7	1,505.9
Secondary	n.a.	8,274‡	268.6	161.1	429.7
Tertiary	n.a.	1,112	22.3	10.3	32.6

* 1998/99.
† 2002/03.
‡ 1999/2000.

Source: mainly UNESCO Institute for Statistics.

2005/06: *Pre-primary*: 412 institutions; 1,510 teachers; 51,071 students; *Primary and Secondary (lower)*: 8,079 institutions; 39,109 teachers; 1,990,765 students (1,137,787 males, 852,978 females); *Secondary (higher)*: 121 institutions; 1,904 teachers; 47,279 students (31,724 males, 15,555 females—estimates); *Secondary (technical and vocational)*: 119 institutions; 41,137 students; *Secondary (teacher training)*: 10,467 students (Source: Office of the Secretary-General of the Government, Bamako).

Adult literacy rate (UNESCO estimates): 24.0% (males 32.8%; females 15.9%) in 2003 (Source: UNESCO Institute for Statistics).

Directory

The Constitution

The Constitution of the Third Republic of Mali was approved in a national referendum on 12 January 1992. The document upholds the principles of national sovereignty and the rule of law in a secular, multi-party state, and provides for the separation of powers of the executive, legislative and judicial organs of state.

Executive power is vested in the President of the Republic, who is Head of State and is elected for five years by universal adult suffrage. The President appoints the Prime Minister, who, in turn, appoints other members of the Council of Ministers.

Legislative authority is exercised by the unicameral 147-member Assemblée nationale, which is elected for five years by universal adult suffrage.

The Constitution guarantees the independence of the judiciary. Final jurisdiction in constitutional matters is vested in a Constitutional Court.

The rights, freedoms and obligations of Malian citizens are enshrined in the Constitution. Freedom of the press and of association are guaranteed.

The Government

HEAD OF STATE

President: Gen. (retd) AMADOU TOUMANI TOURÉ (took office 8 June 2002; re-elected 29 April 2007).

COUNCIL OF MINISTERS
(March 2008)

Prime Minister: MODIBO SIDIBÉ.
Minister of Employment and Professional Training: IBRAHIMA N'DIAYE.
Minister of Health: OUMAR IBRAHIMA TOURÉ.
Minister of Crafts and Tourism: N'DIAYE BA.
Minister of Territorial Administration and Local Communities: Gen. KAFOUGOUNA KONÉ.
Minister of Stockbreeding and Fisheries: MADELEINE BA DIALLO.
Minister of Foreign Affairs and International Co-operation: MOCTAR OUANE.
Minister of Agriculture: TIÉMOKO SANGARÉ.
Minister of the Economy, Industry and Commerce: AHMADOU ABDOULAYE DIALLO.
Minister of Mining, Energy and Water Resources: AHMED SOW.
Minister of Equipment and Transport: HAMED DIANE SEMEGA.
Minister of Finance: ABOU-BAKAR TRAORÉ.
Minister of Internal Security and Civil Protection: Gen. SADIO GASSAMA.
Minister of Secondary and Higher Education and Scientific Research: AMADOU TOURÉ.
Minister of Defence and Veterans: NATIÉ PLÉAH.
Minister of Primary Education, Literacy and the National Languages: AMINATA DIALLO SIDIBÉ.
Minister of Malians Abroad and African Integration: BADRA ALOU MACALOU.
Minister for the Promotion of Women, Children and the Family: SINA DAMBA MAIGA.
Minister of Communication and New Information Technologies: MARIAM FLANTIÉ DIALLO DIARRA.
Minister of the Environment and Decontamination: AGATAM AG ALASSANE.
Minister of Labour, Civil Service and State Reform: ABDOUL WAHAB BERTHE.
Minister of Social Development, Solidarity and the Elderly: SÉKOU DIAKITE.
Minister of Justice, Keeper of the Seals: MAHARAFA TRAORÉ.
Minister of Housing, Town Planning and Land Affairs: SALIMATA GAKOU FOFANA.
Minister of Culture: MOHAMMED EL MOCTAR.
Minister of Youth and Sports: HAMANE NIANG.
Minister in charge of Relations with the Institutions and Government Spokesperson: FATOUMATA DIABATE GUINDO.

MINISTRIES

Office of the President: BP 1463, Koulouba, Bamako; tel. 222-25-72; fax 223-00-26; internet www.koulouba.pr.ml.
Office of the Prime Minister: Quartier du Fleuve, BP 790, Bamako; tel. 223-06-80; fax 222-85-83; internet www.primature.gov.ml.
Office of the Secretary-General of the Government: BP 14, Koulouba, Bamako; tel. 222-25-52; fax 222-70-50; e-mail sgg@sgg.gov.ml; internet www.sgg.gov.ml.
Ministry of Agriculture: BP 1676, Bamako; tel. 222-27-85; e-mail ministere@ma.gov.ml; internet www.maliagriculture.org.
Ministry of Communication and New Information Technologies: Quartier du Fleuve, BP 116, Bamako; tel. 222-26-47; fax 223-20-54.
Ministry of Crafts and Tourism: Badalabougou, Semagesco, BP 2211, Bamako; tel. 229-64-50; fax 229-39-17; e-mail malitourisme@afribone.net.ml; internet www.malitourisme.com.
Ministry of Culture: Quartier du Fleuve, Bamako; tel. 223-26-44; fax 490-03-46; e-mail info@culture.gov.ml; internet www.maliculture.net.
Ministry of Defence and Veterans: route de Koulouba, BP 2083, Bamako; tel. 222-50-21; fax 223-23-18.
Ministry of the Economy, Industry and Commerce: BP 234, Koulouba, Bamako; tel. 222-51-56; fax 222-01-92.
Ministry of Employment and Professional Training: Bamako; tel. 222-34-31.
Ministry of the Environment and Decontamination: Bamako; tel. 223-05-39.
Ministry of Equipment and Transport: Bamako; tel. 222-39-37.
Ministry of Finance: Bamako; internet www.finances.gov.ml.
Ministry of Foreign Affairs and International Co-operation: Koulouba, Bamako; tel. 222-83-14; fax 222-52-26.
Ministry of Health: BP 232, Koulouba, Bamako; tel. 222-53-02; fax 223-02-03.
Ministry of Housing, Town Planning and Land Affairs: Bamako; tel. 223-05-39.
Ministry of Internal Security and Civil Protection: BP E 4771, Bamako; tel. 222-00-82.
Ministry of Justice: Quartier du Fleuve, BP 97, Bamako; tel. 222-26-42; fax 223-00-63; e-mail ucprodej@afribone.net.ml; internet www.justicemali.org.
Ministry of Labour, Civil Service and State Reform: Bamako; tel. 222-31-80.
Ministry of Malians Abroad and African Integration: Cité du Niger, route de l'Hotel Mandé, Bamako; tel. 221-81-48; fax 221-25-05; e-mail info@maliensdelexterieur.gov.ml; internet www.maliensdelexterieur.gov.ml.
Ministry of Mining, Energy and Water Resources: BP 238, Bamako; tel. 222-41-84; fax 222-21-60.
Ministry of Primary Education, Literacy and the National Languages: Bamako.
Ministry for the Promotion of Women, Children and the Family: porte G9, rue 109, Badalabougou, BP 2688, Bamako; tel. 222-66-59; fax 223-66-60; e-mail mpfef@cefib.com; internet www.mpfef.gov.ml.
Ministry of Secondary and Higher Education and Scientific Research: BP 71, Bamako; tel. 222-57-80; fax 222-21-26; e-mail info@education.gov.ml; internet www.education.gov.ml.
Ministry of Social Development, Solidarity and the Elderly: Bamako; tel. 223-23-01.
Ministry of Stockbreeding and Fisheries: Bamako; tel. 223-36-96.
Ministry of Territorial Administration and Local Communities: face Direction de la RCFM, BP 78, Bamako; tel. 222-42-12; fax 223-02-47; internet www.matcl.gov.ml.
Ministry of Youth and Sports: route de Koulouba, BP 91, Bamako; tel. 222-31-53; fax 223-90-67; e-mail mjsports@mjsports.gov.ml; internet www.mjsports.gov.ml.

President and Legislature

PRESIDENT

Presidential Election, 29 April 2007

Candidate	Votes	% of votes
Gen. (retd) Amadou Toumani Touré (Independent)	1,612,912	71.20
Ibrahim Boubacar Kéita (RPM)	433,897	19.15
Tiébilé Dramé (PARENA)	68,956	3.04
Oumar Mariko (SADI)	61,670	2.72
Others	88,048	3.89
Total	**2,265,483**	**100.00**

LEGISLATURE

Assemblée nationale

BP 284, Bamako; tel. 221-57-24; fax 221-03-74; e-mail mamou@blonba.malinet.ml.
President: DIONCOUNDA TRAORÉ.

General Election, 1 and 22 July 2007

Party	Seats
Alliance pour la démocratie au Mali—Parti pan-africain pour la liberté, la solidarité et la justice (ADEMA)	51
Union pour la République et la démocratie (URD)	34
Rassemblement pour le Mali (RPM)	11
Mouvement patriotique pour le renouveau (MPR)	8
Congrès national d'initiative démocratique—Faso Yiriwa Ton (CNID)	7
Parti pour la renaissance nationale (PARENA)	4
Parti de la solidarité africaine pour la démocratie et l'indépendance (SADI)	4
Union pour la démocratie et le développement (UDD)	3
Bloc des alternances pour le renouveau, l'intégration et la coopération africaine (BARICA)	2
Mouvement pour l'indépendance, la renaissance et l'intégration africaine (MIRIA)	2
Parti de la solidarité et du progrès (PSP)	2
Bloc pour la démocratie et l'intégration africaine—Faso Jigi (BDIA)	1
Parti citoyen pour le renouveau (PCR)	1
Rassemblement national pour la démocratie (RND)	1
Union soudanaise—Rassemblement démocratique africaine (US—RDA)	1
Independents	15
Total	**147**

Election Commission

Commission électorale nationale indépendante (CENI): Bamako; Pres. FODIÉ TOURÉ.

Advisory Councils

Economic, Social and Cultural Council: BP E15, Koulouba, Bamako; tel. 222-43-68; fax 222-84-52; e-mail cesc@cefib.com; internet www.cesc.org.ml; f. 1987; Pres. MOUSSA BALLA COULIBALY.

High Council of Communities: Bamako; compulsorily advises the Govt on issues relating to local and regional devt; comprises national councillors, elected indirectly for a term of five years; Pres. OUMAROU AG MOHAMED IBRAHIM HAÏDARA.

Political Organizations

In 2007 there were 94 political parties officially registered in Mali, the most active of which included:

Alliance pour la démocratie au Mali—Parti pan-africain pour la liberté, la solidarité et la justice (ADEMA): rue Fankélé, porte 145, BP 1791, Bamako-Coura; tel. 222-03-68; f. 1990 as Alliance pour la démocratie au Mali; Pres. DIONCOUNDA TRAORÉ; Sec.-Gen. MARIMATIA DIARRA.

Bloc des alternances pour le renouveau, l'intégration et la coopération africaine (BARICA): Bamako.

Bloc pour la démocratie et l'intégration africaine—Faso Jigi (BDIA): Bolibana, rue 376, porte 83, BP E 2833, Bamako-Coura; tel. 223-82-02; f. 1993; liberal, democratic; Leader SOULEYMANE MAKAMBA DOUMBIA.

Congrès national d'initiative démocratique—Faso Yiriwa Ton (CNID): rue 426, porte 58, Niarela, BP 2572, Bamako; tel. 221-42-75; fax 222-83-21; e-mail cnid@cefib.com; f. 1991; Chair. Me MOUNTAGA TALL; Sec.-Gen. N'DIAYE BA.

Convention démocratique et sociale (CDS): Ouolofobougou-Bolibana, rue 417, porte 46, Bamako; tel. 229-26-25; f. 1996; Chair. MAMADOU BAKARY SANGARÉ.

Convention parti du peuple (COPP): Korofina nord, BP 9012, Bamako; fax 221-35-91; e-mail lawyergakou@datatech.toolnet.org; f. 1996; Pres. Me MAMADOU GACKOU.

Mouvement patriotique pour le renouveau (MPR): Quinzambougou, BP E 1108, Bamako; tel. 221-55-46; fax 221-55-43; f. 1995; Pres. Dr CHOGUEL KOKALA MAÏGA.

Mouvement pour l'indépendance, la renaissance et l'intégration africaine (MIRIA): Dravéla, Bolibana, rue 417, porte 66, Bamako; tel. 229-29-81; fax 229-29-79; e-mail miria12002@yahoo.fr; f. 1994 following split in ADEMA; Pres. MOHAMED LAMINE TRAORÉ.

Parti citoyen pour le renouveau (PCR): Bamako; f. 2005; supports administration of Pres. Touré; Pres. OUSMANE BEN FANA TRAORÉ.

Parti de la solidarité africaine pour la démocratie et l'indépendance (SADI): Djélibougou, rue 246, porte 559, BP 3140, Bamako; tel. 224-10-04; f. 2002; Leader CHEICK OUMAR SISSOKO.

Parti de la solidarité et du progrès (PSP): Bamako; Pres. OUMAR HAMMADOUN DICKO.

Parti malien pour le développement et le renouveau (PMDR): Sema I, rue 76, porte 62, BP 553, Badalabougou, Bamako; tel. 222-25-58; f. 1991; social democratic; Pres. Me ABDOUL WAHAB BERTHE.

Parti pour la démocratie et le progrès (PDP): Korofina sud, rue 96, porte 437, Bamako; tel. 224-16-75; fax 220-23-14; f. 1991; Leader MADY KONATÉ.

Parti pour la démocratie et le renouveau—Dounkafa Ton (PDR): Bamako; f. 1998; Pres. ADAMA KONÉ; Leader KALILOU SAMAKE.

Parti pour la renaissance nationale (PARENA): rue Soundiata, porte 1397, BP E 2235, Ouolofobougou, Bamako; tel. 223-49-54; fax 222-29-08; e-mail info@parena.org.ml; internet www.parena.org.ml; f. 1995 following split in CNID; Pres. TIÉBILÉ DRAMÉ; Sec.-Gen. AMIDOU DIABATÉ.

Parti pour l'indépendance, la démocratie et la solidarité (PIDS): Hippodrome, rue 250, porte 1183, BP E 1515, Bamako; tel. 277-45-75; f. 2001 by dissidents from US—RDA; Pres. DABA DIAWARA.

Rassemblement malien pour le travail (RAMAT): Marché, Hippodrome, rue 224, porte 1393, BP E 2281, Bamako; tel. 674-46-03; f. 1991; Leader ABDOULAYE MACKO.

Rassemblement national pour la démocratie (RND): Niaréla, route Sotuba, porte 1892, Hamdallaye, Bamako; tel. 229-18-49; fax 229-09-39; f. 1997 by 'moderate' breakaway group from RDP; Pres. ABDOULAYE GARBA TAPO.

Rassemblement pour la démocratie et le progrès (RDP): Niarela, rue 485, porte 11, BP 2110, Bamako; tel. 221-30-92; fax 224-67-95; f. 1991; Sec.-Gen. IBRAHIM DIAKITE (acting).

Rassemblement pour le Mali (RPM): Hippodrome, rue 232, porte 130, BP 9057, Bamako; tel. 221-14-33; fax 221-13-36; e-mail siegerpmbko@yahoo.fr; internet www.rpm.org.ml; f. 2001; Pres. IBRAHIM BOUBACAR KÉITA; Sec.-Gen. Dr BOCARY TRETA.

Union des forces démocratiques pour le progrès—Sama-ton (UFDP): Quartier Mali, BP E 37, Bamako; tel. 223-17-66; f. 1991; mem. of informal alliance supportive of Pres. Touré, the Convergence pour l'alternance et le changement (ACC), during 2002 legislative elections; Sec.-Gen. Col YOUSSOUF TRAORÉ.

Union pour la démocratie et le développement (UDD): ave OUA, porte 3626, Sogoniko, BP 2969, Bamako; tel. 220-39-71; f. 1991 by supporters of ex-Pres. Traoré; Leader Me HASSANE BARRY.

Union pour la République et la démocratie (URD): Niaréla, rue 268, porte 41, Bamako; tel. 221-86-40; e-mail urd@timbagga.com.ml; f. 2003 by fmr mems of ADEMA (q.v.) allied to 2002 presidential candidate Soumaïla Cissé; Pres. YOUNOUSSI TOURÉ.

Union soudanaise—Rassemblement démocratique africain (US—RDA): Hippodrome, porte 41, BP E 1413, Bamako; tel. and fax 221-45-22; f. 1946; sole party 1960–68, banned 1968–1991; 'moderate' faction split from party in 1998; Leader Dr BADARA ALIOU MACALOU.

MALI   *Directory*

Diplomatic Representation

EMBASSIES IN MALI

Algeria: Daoudabougou, BP 02, Bamako; tel. 220-51-76; fax 222-93-74; Ambassador ABDELKREM GHRAIEB.

Burkina Faso: ACI-2000, Commune III, BP 9022, Bamako; tel. 223-31-71; fax 221-92-66; e-mail ambafaso@experco.net; Ambassador Prof. SANNÉ MOHAMED TOPAN.

Canada: route de Koulikoro, Immeuble Séméga, Hippodrome, BP 198, Bamako; tel. 221-22-36; fax 221-43-62; e-mail bmako@international.gc.ca; internet www.bamako.gc.ca; Ambassador ISABELLE ROY.

China, People's Republic: route de Koulikoro, Hippodrome, BP 112, Bamako; tel. 221-35-97; fax 222-34-43; e-mail chinaemb_ml@mfa.gov.cn; Ambassador ZHANG GUOQING.

Côte d'Ivoire: square Patrice Lumumba, Immeuble CNAR, BP E 3644, Bamako; tel. 222-03-89; fax 222-13-76; Ambassador ABOUBACAR SIRIKI DIABATÉ.

Cuba: porte 31, rue 328, Niarela, Bamako; tel. 221-02-89; fax 221-02-93; e-mail emcuba.mali@malinet.ml; Ambassador ALBERTO MIGUEL OTERO LÓPEZ.

Egypt: Badalabougou-est, BP 44, Bamako; tel. 222-35-65; fax 222-08-91; e-mail mostafa@datatech.net.ml; Ambassador MOSTAFA ABDEL HAMID GENDY.

France: square Patrice Lumumba, BP 17, Bamako; tel. 497-57-57; fax 222-31-36; e-mail ambassade@france-mali.org.ml; internet www.ambafrance-ml.org; Ambassador MICHEL REVEYRAND DE MENTHON.

Germany: Badalabougou-est, rue 14, porte 334, BP 100, Bamako; tel. 222-32-99; fax 222-96-50; e-mail allemagne.presse@afribonemali.net; internet www.bamako.diplo.de; Ambassador Dr REINHARD SCHWARZER.

Ghana: BP 3161, Bamako; Ambassador Maj.-Gen. C. B. YAACHIE.

Guinea: Immeuble Saybou Maïga, Quartier du Fleuve, BP 118, Bamako; tel. 222-30-07; fax 221-08-06; Ambassador (vacant).

Iran: ave al-Quds, Hippodrome, BP 2136, Bamako; tel. 221-76-38; fax 221-07-31; Ambassador MOHAMMED SOLEIMANI.

Korea, Democratic People's Republic: Bamako; Ambassador KIM PONG HUI.

Libya: Badalabougou-ouest, face Palais de la Culture, BP 1670, Bamako; tel. 222-34-96; fax 222-66-97; Ambassador Dr SALAHEDDIN AHMED ZAREM.

Mauritania: route de Koulikoro, Hippodrome, BP 135, Bamako; tel. 221-48-15; fax 222-49-08; Ambassador SIDAMINE OULD AHMED CHALLA.

Morocco: Badalabougou-est, rue 25, porte 80, BP 2013, Bamako; tel. 222-21-23; fax 222-77-87; e-mail sifamali@afribone.net.ml; Ambassador MOULAY DRISS FADHILL.

Netherlands: rue 437, BP 2220, Hippodrome, Bamako; tel. 221-56-11; fax 221-36-17; e-mail bam@minbuza.nl; internet www.mfa.nl/bam; Ambassador ELLEN VAN DER LAAN.

Nigeria: Badalabougou-est, BP 57, Bamako; tel. 221-53-28; fax 222-39-74; e-mail ngrbko@malinet.ml; Ambassador MOHAMMED SANI KANGIWA.

Russia: BP 300, Niarela, Bamako; tel. 221-55-92; fax 221-99-26; Ambassador ANATOLII P. SMIRNOV.

Saudi Arabia: Villa Bal Harbour, 28 Cité du Niger, BP 81, Bamako; tel. 221-25-28; fax 221-50-64; e-mail mlemb@mofa.gov.sa; Chargé d'affaires a.i. IMAD BIN AMEEN ELIAS.

Senegal: porte 341, rue 287, angle ave Nelson Mandela, BP 42, Bamako; tel. 221-08-59; fax 216-92-68; Ambassador SAOUDATOU NDIAYE SECK.

South Africa: bât. Diarra, Hamdallaye, ACI-2000, BP 2015, Bamako; tel. 229-29-25; fax 229-29-26; e-mail bamako@foreign.gov.za; Ambassador W. T. THABETHE.

Spain: porte 81, rue 13, Badalabougou Est, BP 3230, Bamako; tel. 223-65-27; fax 223-65-24; e-mail emb.bamako@mae.es; Ambassador Dr MARTA BETANZOS ROIG.

Tunisia: Quartier du Fleuve, Bamako; tel. 223-28-91; fax 222-17-55; Ambassador FARHAT CHEOUR.

USA: ACI 2000, rue 243, porte 297, Bamako; tel. 270-23-00; fax 270-24-79; e-mail webmaster@usa.org.ml; internet mali.usembassy.gov; Ambassador TERENCE PATRICK MCCULLEY.

Judicial System

The 1992 Constitution guarantees the independence of the judiciary.

High Court of Justice: Bamako; competent to try the President of the Republic and ministers of the Government for high treason and for crimes committed in the course of their duties, and their accomplices in any case where state security is threatened; mems designated by the mems of the Assemblée nationale, and renewed annually.

Supreme Court: BP 7, Bamako; tel. 222-24-06; e-mail csupreme@afribone.net.ml; f. 1969; comprises judicial, administrative and auditing sections; judicial section comprises five chambers, administrative section comprises two chambers, auditing section comprises three chambers; Pres. DIALLO KAÏTA KAYENTAO; Sec.-Gen. ALKAÏDY SANIBIÉ TOURÉ.

President of the Bar: Me MAGATTÉ SÈYE.

Constitutional Court: BP E 213, Bamako; tel. 222-56-09; fax 223-42-41; e-mail tawatybouba@yahoo.fr; f. 1994; Pres. AMADI TAMBA CAMARA; Sec.-Gen. BOUBACAR TAWATY.

There are three Courts of Appeal, seven Tribunaux de première instance (Magistrates' Courts) and also courts for labour disputes.

Religion

According to the UN Development Programme's *Human Development Report*, around 80% of the population are Muslims, while 18% follow traditional animist beliefs and under 2% are Christians.

ISLAM

Association Malienne pour l'Unité et le Progrès de l'Islam (AMUPI): Bamako; state-endorsed Islamic governing body.

Chief Mosque: pl. de la République, Bagadadji, Bamako; tel. 221-21-90.

Haut Conseil Islamique: Bamako; f. 2002; responsible for management of relations between the Muslim communities and the State; Pres. MAHMOUD DICKO.

CHRISTIANITY

The Roman Catholic Church

Mali comprises one archdiocese and five dioceses. At 31 December 2005 there were an estimated 235,460 Roman Catholics, comprising about 1.5% of the total population.

Bishops' Conference

Conférence Episcopale du Mali, Archevêché, BP 298, Bamako; tel. 222-67-84; fax 222-67-00; e-mail cemali@afribone.net.ml.

f. 1973; Pres. Most Rev. JEAN-GABRIEL DIARRA (Bishop of San).

Archbishop of Bamako: JEAN ZERBO, Archevêché, BP 298, Bamako; tel. 222-58-42; fax 222-78-50; e-mail mgrjeanzerbo@afribone.net.ml.

Other Christian Churches

There are several Protestant mission centres, mainly administered by US societies.

BAHÁ'Í FAITH

National Spiritual Assembly: BP 1657, Bamako; e-mail ntirandaz@aol.com.

The Press

The 1992 Constitution guarantees the freedom of the press. In 2000 there were six daily newspapers, 18 weekly or twice-weekly publications and six-monthly or twice-monthly publications.

DAILY NEWSPAPERS

Les Echos: Hamdallaye, ave Cheick Zayed, porte 2694, BP 2043, Bamako; tel. 229-62-89; fax 226-76-39; e-mail lesechos@jamana.org; internet www.jamana.org/lesechos; f. 1989; daily; publ. by Jamana cultural co-operative; circ. 30,000; Dir ALEXIS KALAMBRY; Editor-in-Chief ABOUBACAR SALIPH DIARRA.

L'Essor: square Patrice Lumumba, BP 141, Bamako; tel. 222-36-83; fax 222-47-74; e-mail info@essor.gov.ml; internet www.essor.gov.ml; f. 1949; daily; pro-Govt newspaper; Editor SOULEYMANE DRABO; circ. 3,500.

Info Matin: rue 56/350, Bamako Coura, BP E 4020, Bamako; tel. 223-82-09; fax 223-82-27; e-mail redaction@info-matin.com; internet www.info-matin.com; independent; Dir SAMBI TOURÉ; Editor-in-Chief MOHAMED SACKO.

Le Républicain: 116 rue 400, Dravéla-Bolibana, BP 1484, Bamako; tel. 229-09-00; fax 229-09-33; internet www.lerepublicain.net.ml; f. 1992; independent; Dir SALIF KONÉ.

PERIODICALS

26 Mars: Badalabougou-Sema Gesco, Lot S13, BP MA 174, Bamako; tel. 229-04-59; f. 1998; weekly; independent; Dir BOUBACAR SANGARÉ.

L'Aurore: Niarela 298, rue 438, BP 3150, Bamako; tel. and fax 221-69-22; e-mail aurore@timbagga.com.ml; f. 1990; 2 a week; independent; Dir KARAMOKO N'DIAYE.

Le Canard Déchaîné: Immeuble Koumara, bloc 104, Centre Commercial, Bamako; tel. 621-26-86; fax 222-86-86; e-mail maison.presse@afribone.net.ml; weekly; satirical; Dir OUMAR BABI; circ. 3,000 (2006).

Le Carrefour: ave Cheick Zayed, Hamdallaye, Bamako; tel. 223-98-08; e-mail journalcarrefour@yahoo.fr; f. 1997; Dir MAHAMANE IMRANE COULIBALY.

Citoyen: Bamako; f. 1992; fortnightly; independent.

Le Continent: AA 16, Banankabougou, BP E 4338, Bamako; tel. and fax 229-57-39; e-mail le_continent@yahoo.fr; f. 2000; weekly; Dir IBRAHIMA TRAORÉ.

Le Courrier: 230 ave Cheick Zayed, Lafiabougou Marché, BP 1258, Bamako; tel. and fax 229-18-62; e-mail journalcourrier@webmails.com; f. 1996; weekly; Dir SADOU A. YATTARA; also *Le Courrier Magazine*, monthly.

L'Indépendant: Immeuble ABK, Hamdallaye ACI, BP E 1040, Bamako; tel. and fax 223-27-27; e-mail independant@cefib.com; 2 a week; Dir SAOUTI HAÏDARA.

L'Inspecteur: Immeuble Nimagala, bloc 262, BP E 4534, Bamako; tel. 672-47-11; e-mail inspecteurmali@yahoo.fr; f. 1992; weekly; Dir ALY DIARRA.

Jamana—Revue Culturelle Malienne: BP 2043, Bamako; BP E 1040; e-mail jamana@malinet.ml; f. 1983; quarterly; organ of Jamana cultural co-operative.

Journal Officiel de la République du Mali: Koulouba, BP 14, Bamako; tel. 222-59-86; fax 222-70-50; official gazette.

Kabaaru: Village Kibaru, Bozola, Bamako; f. 1983; state-owned; monthly; Fulbé (Peul) language; rural interest; Editor BADAMA DOUCOURÉ; circ. 5,000.

Kibaru: Village Kibaru, Bozola, BP 1463, Bamako; f. 1972; monthly; state-owned; Bambara and three other languages; rural interest; Editor NIANZÉ SAMAKÉ; circ. 5,000.

Liberté: Immeuble Sanago, Hamdallaye Marché, BP E 24, Bamako; tel. 228-18-98; e-mail ladji.guindo@cefib.com; f. 1999; weekly; Dir ABDOULAYE LADJI GUINDO.

Le Malien: rue 497, porte 277, Badialan III, BP E 1558, Bamako; tel. 223-57-29; fax 229-13-39; e-mail lemalien2000@yahoo.fr; f. 1993; weekly; Dir SIDI KEITA.

Match: 97 rue 498, Lafiabougou, BP E 3776, Bamako; tel. 229-18-82; e-mail bcissouma@yahoo.fr; f. 1997; 2 a month; sports; Dir BABA CISSOUMA.

Musow: Bamako; e-mail musow@musow.com; internet www.musow.com; women's interest.

Nyéléni Magazine: Niarela 298, rue 348, BP 13150, Bamako; tel. 229-24-01; f. 1991; monthly; women's interest; Dir MAÏMOUNA TRAORÉ.

L'Observateur: Galérie Djigué, rue du 18 juin, BP E 1002, Bamako; tel. and fax 223-06-89; e-mail belcotamboura@hotmail.com; f. 1992; 2 a week; Dir BELCO TAMBOURA.

Le Reflet: Immeuble Kanadjigui, route de Koulikoro, Boulkassoumbougou, BP E 1688, Bamako; tel. 224-39-52; fax 223-23-08; e-mail lereflet@afribone.malinet.ml; weekly; fmrly Le Carcan; present name adopted Jan. 2001; Dir ABDOUL KARIM DRAMÉ.

Royal Sports: BP 98, Sikasso; tel. 672-49-88; weekly; also *Tatou Sports*, published monthly; Pres. and Dir-Gen. ALY TOURÉ.

Le Scorpion: 230 ave Cheick Zayed, Lafiabougou Marché, BP 1258, Bamako; tel. and fax 229-18-62; f. 1991; weekly; Dir MAHAMANE HAMÈYE CISSÉ.

Le Tambour: rue 497, porte 295, Badialan III, BP E 289, Bamako; tel. and fax 222-75-68; e-mail tambourj@yahoo.fr; f. 1994; 2 a week; Dir YÉRO DIALLO.

NEWS AGENCY

Agence Malienne de Presse et Publicité (AMAP): square Patrice Lumumba, BP 141, Bamako; tel. 222-36-83; fax 222-47-74; e-mail amap@afribone.net.ml; f. 1977; Dir SOULEYMANE DRABO.

PRESS ASSOCIATIONS

Association des Editeurs de la Presse Privée (ASSEP): BP E 1002, Bamako; tel. 671-31-33; e-mail belcotamboura@hotmail.com; Pres. BELCO TAMBOURA.

Association des Femmes de la Presse Privée: porte 474, rue 428, BP E 731, Bamako; tel. 221-29-12; Pres. FANTA DIALLO.

Association des Journalistes Professionels des Médias Privés du Mali (AJPM): BP E 2456, Bamako; tel. 222-19-15; fax 223-54-78; Pres. MOMADOU FOFANA.

Association des Professionnelles Africaines de la Communication (APAC MALI): porte 474, rue 428, BP E 731, Bamako; tel. 221-29-12; Pres. MASSIRÉ YATTASSAYE.

Maison de la Presse de Mali: 17 rue 619, Darsalam, BP E 2456, Bamako; tel. 222-19-15; fax 223-54-78; e-mail maison.presse@afribone.net.ml; internet www.mediamali.org; independent media asscn; Pres. SADOU A. YATTARA.

Union Interprofessionnelle des Journalistes et de la Presse de Langue Française (UIJPLF): rue 42, Hamdallaye Marché, BP 1258, Bamako; tel. 229-98-35; Pres. MAHAMANE HAMÉYE CISSÉ.

Union Nationale des Journalistes Maliens (UNAJOM): BP 141, Bamako; tel. 222-36-83; fax 223-43-13; e-mail amap@afribone.net.ml; Pres. OUSMANE MAÏGA.

Publishers

EDIM SA: ave Kassé Keïta, BP 21, Bamako; tel. 222-40-41; f. 1972 as Editions Imprimeries du Mali; general fiction and non-fiction, textbooks; Chair. and Man. Dir ALOU TOMOTA.

Editions Donniya: Cité du Niger, BP 1273, Bamako; tel. 221-46-46; fax 221-90-31; e-mail imprimcolor@cefib.com; internet www.imprimcolor.cefib.com; f. 1996; general fiction, history, reference and children's books in French and Bambara.

Le Figuier: 151 rue 56, Semal, BP 2605, Bamako; tel. and fax 223-32-11; e-mail lefiguier@afribone.net.ml; f. 1997; fiction and non-fiction.

Editions Jamana: BP 2043, Bamako; tel. 229-62-89; fax 229-76-39; e-mail jamana@timbagga.com.ml; internet www.jamana.org; f. 1988; literary fiction, poetry, reference; Dir BA MAÏRA SOW.

Editions Teriya: BP 1677, Bamako; tel. 224-11-42; theatre, literary fiction; Dir GAOUSSOU DIAWARA.

Broadcasting and Communications

TELECOMMUNICATIONS

Orange Mali SA: Immeuble Orange Mali ACI-2000, BP E 3991, Bamako; tel. 499-90-00; fax 499-90-01; e-mail orange@orangemali.com; internet www.orangemali.com; f. 2003 as Ikatel; repackaged under brand name Orange in 2007; fixed-line and mobile cellular telecommunications; jtly owned by France Télécom and Société Nationale des Télécommunications du Sénégal; Dir-Gen. ALIOUME N'DIAYE; 100,000 subscribers (2003).

Société des Télécommunications du Mali—Malitel (SOTELMA): route de Koulikoro, Hippodrome, BP 740, Bamako; tel. 221-52-80; fax 221-30-22; e-mail segal@sotelma.ml; internet www.sotelma.ml; f. 1990; state-owned; 49% privatization proposed; operates fixed-line telephone services, also mobile and cellular telecommunications in Bamako, Kayes, Mopti, Ségou and Sikasso; 47,000 subscribers to mobile cellular telecommunications services (2003); Pres. and Dir-Gen. SIDIKI KONATE.

BROADCASTING

Radio

Office de Radiodiffusion-Télévision Malienne (ORTM): BP 171, Bamako; tel. 221-20-19; fax 221-42-05; e-mail ortm@afribone.net.ml; internet www.ortm.net; Dir-Gen. SIDIKI KONATÉ; Dir of Radio OUMAR TOURÉ.

Radio Mali–Chaîne Nationale: BP 171, Bamako; tel. 221-20-19; fax 221-42-05; e-mail ortm@spider.toolnet.org; f. 1957; state-owned; radio programmes in French, Bambara, Peulh, Sarakolé, Tamachek, Sonrai, Moorish, Wolof, English.

Chaîne 2: Bamako; f. 1993; radio broadcasts to Bamako.

In late 2003 there were an estimated 130 community, commercial and religious radio stations broadcasting in Mali.

Fréquence 3: Bamako; f. 1992; commercial.

Radio Balanzan: BP 419, Ségou; tel. 232-02-88; commercial.

Radio Bamakan: Marché de Médine, BP E 100, Bamako; tel. and fax 221-27-60; e-mail radio.bamakan@ifrance.com; f. 1991; community station; 104 hours of FM broadcasts weekly; Man. MODIBO DIALLO.

Radio Espoir—La Voix du Salut: Sogoniko, rue 130, porte 71, BP E 1399, Bamako; tel. 220-67-08; e-mail accm@mali.maf.net; f. 1998; broadcasts 16 hours of radio programming daily on topics including Christianity, devt and culture; Dir DAOUDA COULIBALY.

Radio Foko de Ségou Jamana: BP 2043, Bamako; tel. 232-00-48; fax 222-76-39; e-mail radiofoko@cefib.com.

Radio Guintan: Magnambougou, BP 2546, Bamako; tel. 220-09-38; f. 1994; community radio station; Dir RAMATA DIA.

Radio Jamana: BP 2043, Bamako; tel. 229-62-89; fax 229-76-39; e-mail jamana@malinet.net.

Radio Kayira: Djélibougou Doumanzana, BP 3140, Bamako; tel. 224-87-82; fax 222-75-68; f. 1992; community station; Dir OUMAR MARIKO.

Radio Klédu: Cité du Niger, BP 2322, Bamako; tel. 221-00-18; f. 1992; commercial; Dir FADIALA DEMBÉLÉ.

Radio Liberté: BP 5015, Bamako; tel. 223-05-81; f. 1991; commercial station broadcasting 24 hours daily; Dir ALMANY TOURÉ.

Radio Patriote: Korofina-Sud, BP E 1406, Bamako; tel. 224-22-92; f. 1995; commercial station; Dir MOUSSA KEÏTA.

Radio Rurale: Plateau, BP 94, Kayes; tel. 253-14-76; e-mail rrk@afribone.net.ml; f. 1988; community stations established by the Agence de coopération culturelle et technique (ACTT); transmitters in Niono, Kadiolo, Bandiagara and Kidal; Dir FILY KEÏTA.

Radio Sahel: BP 394, Kayes; tel. 252-21-87; f. 1991; commercial; Dir ALMAMY S. TOURÉ.

Radio Tabalé: Bamako-Coura, BP 697, Bamako; tel. and fax 222-78-70; f. 1992; independent public-service station; broadcasting 57 hours weekly; Dir TIÉMOKO KONÉ.

La Voix du Coran et du Hadit: Grande Mosquée, BP 2531, Bamako; tel. 221-63-44; f. 1993; Islamic station broadcasting on FM in Bamako; Dir El Hadj MAHMOUD DICKO.

Radio Wassoulou: BP 24, Yanfolila; tel. 265-10-97; commercial.

Radio France International, the Voix de l'Islam and the Gabonese-based Africa No. 1 began FM broadcasts in Mali in 1993; broadcasts by Voice of America and the World Service of the British Broadcasting Corpn are also transmitted via private radio stations.

Television

Office de Radiodiffusion-Télévision Malienne (ORTM): see Radio; Dir of Television BALY IDRISSA SISSOKO.

Multicanal SA: Quinzambougou, BP E 1506, Bamako; tel. 221-49-64; e-mail sandrine@multi-canal.com; internet www.multi-canal.com; private subscription broadcaster; relays international broadcasts; Pres. ISMAÏLA SIDIBÉ.

TV Klédu: 600 ave Modibo Keïta, BP E 1172, Bamako; tel. 223-90-00; fax 223-70-50; e-mail info@tvkledu.com; private cable TV operator; relays international broadcasts; Pres. MAMADOU COULIBALY.

Finance

(cap. = capital; res = reserves; dep. = deposits; m. = million; br(s). = branch(es); amounts in francs CFA)

BANKING

Central Bank

Banque centrale des états de l'Afrique de l'ouest (BCEAO): BP 206, Bamako; tel. 222-37-56; fax 222-47-86; internet www.bceao.int; f. 1962; HQ in Dakar, Senegal; bank of issue for the mem. states of Union économique et monétaire ouest-africaine (UEMOA, comprising Benin, Burkina Faso, Côte d'Ivoire, Guinea-Bissau, Mali, Niger, Senegal and Togo); cap. and res 859,313m., total assets 5,671,675m. (Dec. 2002); Gov. DAMO JUSTIN BARO (acting); Dir in Mali IDRISSA TRAORÉ; brs at Mopti and Sikasso.

Commercial Banks

Bank of Africa—Mali (BOA—MALI): 418 ave de la Marné, Bozola, BP 2249, Bamako; tel. 270-05-00; fax 270-05-60; e-mail information@boamali.net; internet www.bank-of-africa.net; f. 1983; cap. 3,000m., res 1,666m., dep. 82,402m. (March 2007); Pres. BOUREIMA SYLLA; Dir-Gen. CHRISTOPHE LASSUS-LALANNE; 7 brs.

Banque Commerciale du Sahel (BCS–SA): ave Bozola 127, BP 2372, Bamako; tel. 221-05-35; fax 221-16-60; e-mail dg@bcss.mali.com; f. 1980; fmrly Banque Arabe Libyo-Malienne pour le Commerce Extérieur et le Développement; 96.61% owned by Libyan-Arab Foreign Bank; cap. 7,500m., res 1,046m., total assets 37,953m. (Dec. 2006); Pres. KABA DIAMINATOU DIALLO; Dir-Gen. IBRAHIM ABOUJAFAR SWEAI; 1 br.

Banque de l'Habitat du Mali (BHM): ACI 2000, ave Kwamé N'Krumah, BP 2614, Bamako; tel. 222-91-90; fax 222-93-50; e-mail bhm@bhm.malinet.ml; f. 1990; present name adopted 1996; 37.1% owned by Institut National de Prévoyance Social, 25.9% by Agence Cession Immobilière; cap. and res 5,414.7m., total assets 98,237.5m. (Dec. 2003); Pres. and Dir-Gen. MAMADOU BABA DIAWARA; 1 br.

Banque Internationale pour le Commerce et l'Industrie au Mali (BICI–Mali): blvd du 22 octobre 1946, Quartier du Fleuve, BP 72, Bamako; tel. 270-07-00; fax 223-33-73; e-mail bicim-dg@africa.bnpparibas.com; f. 1998; 85% owned by BNP Paribas BDDI Participations (France); cap. and res 3,678m., total assets 40,076m. (Dec. 2003); Pres. and Dir-Gen. PIERRE BÉRÉGOVOY; 1 br.

Banque Internationale pour le Mali (BIM): ave de l'Indépendance, BP 15, Bamako; tel. 222-50-66; fax 222-45-66; e-mail bim@bim.com.ml; internet www.bim.com.ml; f. 1980; present name adopted 1995; 61.5% state-owned; privatization pending; cap. 4,255m., res 1,099m., dep. 78,806m. (Dec. 2002); total assets 91,725m. (Dec. 2003); Pres. and Dir-Gen. MAMADOU IGOR DIARRA; 7 brs.

Banque Malienne de Crédit et de Dépôts: ave Mobido Keita, BP 45, Bamako; tel. 222-53-36; fax 222-79-50; e-mail bmcd@malinet.ml; 100% state-owned; transfer to private-sector ownership proposed.

Ecobank Mali: pl. de la Nation, Quartier du Fleuve, BP E 1272, Bamako; tel. 223-33-00; fax 223-33-05; e-mail ecobank@cefib.com; f. 1998; 49.5% owned by Ecobank Transnational Inc., 17.8% by Ecobank Bénin, 14.9% by Ecobank Togo, 9.9% by Ecobank Burkina; cap. and res 2,973.9m., total assets 46,222.7m. (Dec. 2003); Pres. SEYDOU DJIM SYLLA; Dir-Gen. KASSIM ABOU KABASSI; 2 brs.

Development Banks

Banque de Développement du Mali (BDM-SA): ave Modibo Keita, Quartier du Fleuve, BP 94, Bamako; tel. 222-20-50; fax 222-50-85; e-mail info@bdm-sa.com; internet www.bdm-sa.com; f. 1968; absorbed Banque Malienne de Crédit et de Dépôts in 2001; 22.1% state-owned, 20.7% owned by Banque Marocaine du Commerce Extérieur (Morocco), 16.0% by BCEAO, 16% by Banque ouest-africaine de développement; cap. and res 15,658m., total assets 276,148m. (Dec. 2002); Pres. and Dir-Gen. ABDOULAYE DAFFÉ; 14 brs.

Banque Malienne de Solidarité (BMS): ave du Fleuve, Immeuble Dette Publique, 2e étage, BP 1280, Bamako; tel. and fax 223-50-34; fax 223-54-13; e-mail bms-sa@bms-sa.com; f. 2002; cap. 2.4m.; Dir BABALI BAH; 1 br.

Banque Nationale de Développement Agricole—Mali (BNDA—Mali): Immeuble BNDA, blvd du Mali, ACI 2000, BP 2424, Bamako; tel. 229-64-64; fax 229-25-75; e-mail bnda@bndamali.com; f. 1981; 36.8% state-owned, 22.5% owned by Agence française de développement (France), 21.3% owned by Deutsche Entwicklungsgesellschaft (Germany), 19.3% owned by BCEAO; cap. 10,988m., res 2,188m., dep. 107,896m. (Dec. 2004); Chair., Pres. and Gen. Man. MOUSSA ALASSAME DIALLO; Dir-Gen. ARNAUD BELLAMY BROWN; 22 brs.

Financial Institutions

Direction Générale de la Dette Publique: Immeuble ex-Caisse Autonome d'Amortissement, Quartier du Fleuve, BP 1617, Bamako; tel. 222-29-35; fax 222-07-93; management of the public debt; Dir NAMALA KONÉ.

Equibail Mali: rue 376, porte 1319, Niarela, BP E 566, Bamako; tel. 21-37-77; fax 21-37-78; e-mail equip.ma@bkofafrica.com; internet www.bkofafrica.net/jeux_de_cadres/equibail/equibail_mali/equibail_mali.htm; f. 1999; 50.2% owned by African Financial Holding, 17.5% by Bank of Africa—Benin; cap. 300m. (Dec. 2002); Mems of Administrative Council RAMATOULAYE TRAORÉ, PAUL DERREUMAUX, LÉON NAKA.

Société Malienne de Financement (SOMAFI): Immeuble Air Afrique, blvd du 22 octobre 1946, BP E 3643, Bamako; tel. 222-18-66; fax 222-18-69; e-mail somafi@malinet.ml; f. 1997; cap. and res 96.9m., total assets 3,844.9m. (Dec. 2002); Man. Dir ERIC LECLÈRE.

STOCK EXCHANGE

Bourse Régionale des Valeurs Mobilières (BRVM): Chambre de Commerce et de l'Industrie du Mali, pl. de la Liberté, BP E 1398, Bamako; tel. 223-23-54; fax 223-23-59; e-mail abocoum@brvm.org; f. 1998; nat. branch of BRVM (regional stock exchange based in Abidjan, Côte d'Ivoire, serving the mem. states of UEMOA); Man. AMADOU DJÉRI BOCOUM.

INSURANCE

Les Assurances Générales de France (AGF): ave du Fleuve, BP 190, Bamako; tel. 222-58-18.

Caisse Nationale d'Assurance et de Réassurance du Mali (CNAR): BP 568, square Patrice Lumumba, Bamako; tel. 221-31-17; fax 221-23-69; f. 1969; state-owned; cap. 50m.; Dir-Gen. F. KEITA; 10 brs.

Colina Mali SA: ave Modibo Keita, BP E 154, Bamako; tel. 222-57-75; fax 223-24-23; e-mail mali@groupecolina.com; internet www.colina-bd.accelance.net/fr/ml/; f. 1990; cap. 1,000m.; Dir-Gen. MARYVONNE SIDIBE.

MALI
Directory

Compagnie d'Assurance Privée—La Soutra: BP 52, Bamako; tel. 222-36-81; fax 222-55-23; f. 1979; cap. 150m.; Chair. AMADOU NIONO.

Compagnie d'Assurance et de Réassurance de Mali: BP 1822, Bamako; tel. 222-60-29.

Compagnie d'Assurance et de Réassurance Sabu Nyuman: rue 350, porte 129, Bamako-Coura, BP 1822, Bamako; tel. 222-60-29; fax 222-57-50; f. 1984; cap. 250m.; Dir-Gen. MOMADOU SANOGO.

Gras Savoye Mali: Immeuble SOGEFIH, 3ème Etage, Quartier du Fleuve, ave Moussa Travele, Bamako; tel. 222-64-75; fax 222-64-70; e-mail moussa.hiam@ml.grassavoye.com; affiliated to Gras Savoye (France); Man. FAYEZ SAMB.

Lafía Assurances: ave de la Nation, BP 1542, Bamako; tel. 222-35-51; fax 222-52-24; f. 1983; cap. 50m.; Dir-Gen. ABDOULAYE TOURÉ.

Trade and Industry

GOVERNMENT AGENCIES

Centre d'Etudes et de Promotion Industrielle (CEPI): BP 1980, Bamako; tel. 222-22-79; fax 222-80-85.

Direction Nationale des Affaires Economiques (DNAE): BP 210, Bamako; tel. 222-23-14; fax 222-22-56; involved in economic and social affairs.

Direction Nationale des Travaux Publics (DNTP): ave de la Liberté, BP 1758, Bamako; tel. and fax 222-29-02; administers public works.

Guichet Unique–Direction Nationale des Industries: rue Titi Niare, Quinzambougou, BP 96, Bamako; tel. and fax 222-31-66.

Office National des Produits Pétroliers (ONAP): Quartier du Fleuve, rue 315, porte 141, BP 2070, Bamako; tel. 222-28-27; fax 222-44-83; e-mail onap@datatech.toolnet.org; Dir-Gen. TAPA NOUGA NADIO.

Office du Niger: BP 106, Ségou; tel. 232-02-92; fax 232-01-43; f. 1932; taken over from the French authorities in 1958; restructured in mid-1990s; cap. 7,139m. francs CFA; principally involved in cultivation of food crops, particularly rice; Pres. and Man. Dir NANCOMA KEÏTA.

Office des Produits Agricoles du Mali (OPAM): BP 132, Bamako; tel. 222-37-55; fax 221-04-06; e-mail opam@datatech.toolnet.org; f. 1965; state-owned; manages National (Cereals) Security Stock, administers food aid, responsible for sales of cereals and distribution to deficit areas; cap. 5,800m. francs CFA; Pres. and Dir-Gen. YOUSSOUF MAHAMANE TOURÉ.

DEVELOPMENT ORGANIZATIONS

Agence Française de Développement (AFD): Quinzambougou, route de Sotuba, BP 32, Bamako; tel. 221-28-42; fax 221-86-46; e-mail afdbamako@ml.groupe-afd.org; internet www.afd.fr; Country Dir JEAN-FRANÇOIS VAVASSEUR.

Agence pour le Développement du Nord-Mali (ADN): Gao; f. 2005 to replace l'Autorité pour le Développement Intégré du Nord-Mali (ADIN); govt agency with financial autonomy; promotes devt of regions of Tombouctou, Gao and Kidal; br. in Bamako.

Office de Développement Intégré du Mali-Ouest (ODIMO): square Patrice Lumumba, Bamako; tel. 222-57-59; f. 1991 to succeed Office de Développement Intégré des Productions Arachidières et Céréalières; devt of diversified forms of agricultural production; Man. Dir ZANA SANOGO.

Service de Coopération et d'Action Culturelle: square Patrice Lumumba, BP 84, Bamako; tel. 221-83-38; fax 221-83-39; administers bilateral aid from France; Dir BERTRAND COMMELIN.

CHAMBER OF COMMERCE

Chambre de Commerce et d'Industrie du Mali (CCIM): pl. de la Liberté, BP 46, Bamako; tel. 222-50-36; fax 222-21-20; e-mail ccim@cimmali.org; f. 1906; Pres. JEAMILLE BITTAR; Sec.-Gen. DABA TRAORÉ.

EMPLOYERS' ASSOCIATIONS

Association Malienne des Exportateurs de Légumes (AMELEF): Bamako; f. 1984; Pres. BADARA FAGANDA TRAORÉ; Sec.-Gen. BIRAMA TRAORÉ.

Association Malienne des Exportateurs de Ressources Animales (AMERA): Bamako; tel. 222-56-83; f. 1985; Pres. AMBARKÉ YERMANGORE; Admin. Sec. ALI HACKO.

Fédération Nationale des Employeurs du Mali (FNEM): route de Sotuba, BP 2445, Bamako; tel. 221-63-11; fax 221-90-77; e-mail fnem@spider.toolnet.org; f. 1980; Pres. MOUSSA MARY BALLA COULIBALY; Permanent Sec. LASSINA TRAORÉ.

UTILITIES

Electricity

Energie du Mali (EdM): square Patrice Lumumba, BP 69, Bamako; tel. 222-30-20; fax 222-84-30; e-mail sekou.edm@cefib.com; f. 1960; 66% state-owned, 34% owned by Industrial Promotion Services (West-Africa); planning, construction and operation of power-sector facilities; cap. 7,880m. francs CFA.

Enertech GSA: marché de Lafiabougou, BP 1949, Bamako; tel. 222-37-63; fax 222-51-36; f. 1994; cap. 20m. francs CFA; solar energy producer; Dir MOCTAR DIAKITÉ.

Société de Gestion de l'Energie de Manantali (SOGEM): Parcelle 2501, ACI 2000, BP-E 4015, Bamako; tel. 223-32-86; fax 223-83-50; to generate and distribute electricity from the Manantali HEP project, under the auspices of the Organisation pour la mise en valeur du fleuve Sénégal; Dir-Gen. SALOUM CISSÉ.

Gas

Maligaz: route de Sotuba, BP 5, Bamako; tel. 222-23-94; gas distribution.

TRADE UNION FEDERATION

Union nationale des travailleurs du Mali (UNTM): Bourse du Travail, blvd de l'Indépendance, BP 169, Bamako; tel. 222-36-99; fax 223-59-45; f. 1963; 13 nat. and 8 regional unions, and 52 local orgs; Sec.-Gen. SIAKA DIAKITÉ.

There are, in addition, several non-affiliated trade unions.

Transport

RAILWAYS

Mali's only railway runs from Koulikoro, via Bamako, to the Senegal border. The line continues to Dakar, a total distance of 1,286 km, of which 729 km is in Mali. The track is in very poor condition, and is frequently closed during the rainy season. In 1995 the Governments of Mali and Senegal agreed to establish a joint company to operate the Bamako–Dakar line, and the line passed fully into private ownership in 2003. Some 358,000 metric tons of freight were handled on the Malian railway in 2001. Plans exist for the construction of a new rail line linking Bamako with Kouroussa and Kankan, in Guinea.

Transrail: Ouolofabougou, BP 4150, Bamako; tel. 222-67-77; fax 222-54-33; f. 2003 on transfer to private management of fmr Régie du Chemin de Fer du Mali; jt venture of Canac (Canada) and Getma (France); Pres. REJEAN BELANGER.

ROADS

The Malian road network in 2004 comprised 18,709 km, of which about 3,370 km were paved. A bituminized road between Bamako and Abidjan (Côte d'Ivoire) provides Mali's main economic link to the coast; construction of a road linking Bamako and Dakar (Senegal) is to be financed by the European Development Fund. The African Development Bank also awarded a US $31.66m. loan to fund the Kankan–Kouremale–Bamako road between Mali and Guinea. A road across the Sahara to link Mali with Algeria is also planned.

Compagnie Malienne de Transports Routiers (CMTR): BP 208, Bamako; tel. 222-33-64; f. 1970; state-owned; Man. Dir MAMADOU TOURÉ.

INLAND WATERWAYS

The River Niger is navigable in parts of its course through Mali (1,693 km) during the rainy season from July to late December. The River Senegal was, until the early 1990s, navigable from Kayes to Saint-Louis (Senegal) only between August and November, but its navigability was expected to improve following the inauguration, in 1992, of the Manantali dam, and the completion of works to deepen the river-bed.

Compagnie Malienne de Navigation (COMANAV): BP 10, Koulikoro; tel. 226-20-94; fax 226-20-09; f. 1968; 100% state-owned; river transport; Pres. and Dir-Gen. DEMBÉLÉ GOUNDO DIALLO.

Conseil Malien des Chargeurs (CMC): Dar-salam, Bamako; f. 1999; Pres. AMADOU DJIGUÉ.

Société Navale Malienne (SONAM): Bamako-Coura, BP 2581, Bamako; tel. 221-60-66; fax 222-60-66; f. 1981; transferred to private ownership in 1986; Chair. ALIOUNE KEÏTA.

Société Ouest-Africaine d'Entreprise Maritime (SOAEM): rue Mohamed V, BP 2428, Bamako; tel. 222-58-32; fax 222-40-24; maritime transport co.

CIVIL AVIATION

The principal airport is at Bamako-Senou. The other major airports are at Bourem, Gao, Goundam, Kayes, Kita, Mopti, Nioro, Ségou,

MALI

Tessalit and Tombouctou. There are about 40 small airfields. Mali's airports are being modernized with external financial assistance. In early 2005 the Malian Government announced the creation of a new national airline, in partnership with the Aga Khan Fund for Economic Development and Industrial Promotion Services.

Agence Nationale de l'Aéronautique Civile (ANAC): Ministère de l'Equipement et des Transports, BP 227, Bamako; tel. 229-55-24; fax 228-61-77; e-mail anacmali@hotmail.com; f. 2005 to replace Direction Nationale de l'Aéronautique Civile (f. 1990); Dir-Gen. ADAMA KONE.

Air Affaires Mali: BP E 3759, Badalabougou, Bamako; tel. 222-61-36.

Compagnie Aérienne du Mali (CAM): Bamako; f. 2005; 51% owned by Fonds Aga Khan pour le Développement Economique (AKAFED), 20% state-owned; domestic and international flights.

STA Trans African Airlines: Quartier du Fleuve, BP 775, Bamako; tel. 222-44-44; fax 221-09-81; internet www.sta-airlines.com; f. 1984 as Société des Transports Aériens; privately owned; local, regional and international services; Man. Dir MELHEM ELIE SABBAGUE.

Tourism

Mali's rich cultural heritage is promoted as a tourist attraction. In 1999 the Government launched a three-year cultural and tourism development programme centred on Tombouctou, Gao and Kidal. In 2005 142,814 tourists visited Mali, while receipts from tourism totalled some US $149m.

Ministry of Crafts and Tourism: see section on The Government.

MALTA

Introductory Survey

Location, Climate, Language, Religion, Flag, Capital

The Republic of Malta is in southern Europe. The country comprises an archipelago in the central Mediterranean Sea, consisting of the inhabited islands of Malta, Gozo and Comino, and the uninhabited islets of Cominotto, Filfla and St Paul's. The main island, Malta, lies 93 km (58 miles) south of the Italian island of Sicily and 288 km (179 miles) east of the Tunisian coast, the nearest point on the North African mainland. The climate is warm, with average temperatures of 22.6°C (72.7°F) in summer and 13.7°C (56.6°F) in winter. Average annual rainfall is 578 mm (22.8 ins). Maltese and English are the official languages, although Italian is widely spoken. About 96% of the inhabitants are Christians adhering to the Roman Catholic Church. The national flag (proportions 2 by 3) consists of two equal vertical stripes, white at the hoist and red at the fly, with a representation of the George Cross, edged with red, in the upper hoist. The capital is Valletta, on the island of Malta.

Recent History

Malta, which had been a Crown Colony of the United Kingdom since 1814, became an independent sovereign state, within the Commonwealth, on 21 September 1964. The Government, led by Dr Giorgio Borg-Olivier of the Nationalist Party (Partit Nazzjonalista—PN), negotiated defence and financial aid agreements, effective over a 10-year period, with the United Kingdom.

In June 1971 the Malta Labour Party (Partit Laburista—MLP), led by Dom Mintoff, assumed power after winning a general election. Pursuing a policy of non-alignment, the Government concluded agreements for cultural, economic and commercial co-operation with Italy, Libya, Tunisia, the USSR, several East European countries, the USA, the People's Republic of China and others, and received technical assistance, notably from Libya. The MLP Government abrogated the 1964 Mutual Defence and Assistance Agreement with the United Kingdom. This agreement was replaced in 1972 by a new seven-year agreement, under which Malta was to receive substantially increased rental payments for the use of military facilities by the United Kingdom and other members of the North Atlantic Treaty Organization (NATO, see p. 340). British troops were finally withdrawn in March 1979.

Malta became a republic in December 1974. The MLP retained power at general elections held in September 1976 and in December 1981, when it secured a majority of three seats in the 65-seat House of Representatives, although obtaining only 49.1% of the votes cast. The PN, which had received 50.9% of the votes cast, contested the result, refused to take its seats in the legislature, and organized a campaign of civil disobedience. In March 1983 the PN terminated its legislative boycott, but immediately withdrew again, in protest against a government resolution to loosen ties with the European Community (EC, now the European Union—EU, see p. 244). Although Mintoff promised constitutional amendments and weekly consultations with the opposition, these arrangements collapsed in June, when the Government blamed the PN for a bomb attack on government offices. In November a police raid on the PN headquarters was alleged to have discovered a cache of arms and ammunition.

In June 1983 the House of Representatives approved controversial legislation, under which about 75% of church property was to be expropriated to provide finance for a programme of universal free education and the abolition of fee-paying church schools. Opponents of the measure denounced it as both unconstitutional and a violation of religious liberty, and in September 1984 the courts disallowed the legislation. In April 1984 the House of Representatives approved legislation forbidding any school to accept fees (including voluntary gifts and donations). The Roman Catholic Archbishop of Malta rejected the government conditions and closed all church schools, in response to growing tensions and public unrest. A strike by state school teachers in October and November further polarized opinion, but an agreement was reached in November, when the schools were re-opened.

Mintoff retired in December 1984 and was replaced as Prime Minister by the new leader of the MLP, Dr Carmelo Mifsud Bonnici. In April 1985 the Government reached agreement with the Roman Catholic Church, providing for the phased introduction of free education in church secondary schools, and guaranteeing the autonomy of church schools. However, in July 1988 the enforced introduction of new licensing procedures for church schools led to demands by the Roman Catholic Church that the State should reduce its supervisory powers over church education.

At a general election held in May 1987 the PN obtained 50.9% of the votes cast, but won only 31 of the 65 seats in the House of Representatives, while the MLP, with 48.9% of the votes cast, won the remaining 34 seats. However, in accordance with a constitutional amendment that had been adopted in January (see Government, below), the PN was allocated four additional seats, giving it a majority of one in the legislature, thus ending the MLP's 16-year tenure in office. The leader of the PN, Dr Eddie Fenech Adami, became Prime Minister. The PN secured an increased majority of three seats over the MLP at a general election held in February 1992. This result was widely interpreted as an endorsement of the PN's pro-EC policies.

Malta has maintained a policy of non-alignment in its international relations, and has negotiated economic co-operation agreements with many countries. In 1984 the Governments of Malta and Libya signed a five-year treaty of co-operation, which included an undertaking by Libya to provide military training. The treaty signified a return to the previously close relations between the two countries, which had deteriorated in 1980, owing to a dispute over a maritime boundary (eventually resolved by the International Court of Justice in 1985). Malta also has an association agreement with the EU, originally signed in 1970 and periodically renewed until Malta's accession to the EU in 2004. On becoming Prime Minister in May 1987, Fenech Adami declared that the Government, while retaining Malta's non-aligned status and its links with Libya, would seek closer relations with the USA and other Western countries, and would apply for full membership of the EC.

A formal application for full membership of the EC was submitted by the Maltese Government in July 1990. In June 1993 the EC Commission recommended that, subject to the Government of Malta's satisfying EC requirements for regulatory reforms in financial services, competition and consumer protection, favourable consideration should be given to the future accession of Malta to the EU. In June 1995 the EU affirmed that full negotiations on Malta's accession were to begin six months after the conclusion of the 1996 Intergovernmental Conference.

Domestic opposition to Maltese accession to the EU had been led by the MLP, on the grounds that EU agricultural policies would increase the cost of living, and that integration into the EU would conflict with the Republic's traditional neutrality in its foreign relations. In September 1996 the PN Government, seeking to confirm its mandate to pursue the goal of full membership of the EU, called a general election for the following month. Although the PN contested the election on its record of economic success, the Government's introduction of value-added tax (VAT), as a precondition of Malta's admission to the EU, had proved unpopular with the electorate, and its proposed abolition by the MLP (which would concurrently disqualify Malta from EU membership) was widely regarded as the decisive factor in the election. With a participation rate of 97.1% of eligible voters, the MLP secured 50.7% of the votes cast, as against 47.8% for the PN. The MLP obtained 31 seats in the House of Representatives, with the PN receiving 34 seats. (As the MLP actually won three seats less than the PN in the election, four seats were added to its final total, giving it a one-seat majority in the legislature.) Dr Alfred Sant, the leader of the MLP, formed a new Government with the declared intention of replacing the 1970 association agreement (see above) with new arrangements providing for an eventual 'free-trade zone' between Malta and the EU. The MLP also emphasized its commitment to the advancement of Malta's financial services sector.

In February 1997 the Government announced the initiation of a 'national discussion' of proposals to legalize divorce. However, the imposition of tax increases and levies on public utilities substantially diminished the Government's popularity. Sant called a general election for September, three years earlier than constitutionally required, and in the poll, for which there was a participation rate of 95.4%, the PN, led by Fenech Adami, obtained a five-seat majority, having obtained 51.8% of votes cast, with the MLP receiving 48.0%. Immediately following the election, Fenech Adami reactivated Malta's application for full membership of the EU. In December 1999 the European Commission agreed that accession negotiations could begin in February 2000, and in the following month the President of the Commission paid an official visit to the island. In November 2000 the Commission published a report which stated that Malta was among the best-equipped economically of those countries seeking to join the EU. Further action was required in Malta to reduce state aid (notably the politically sensitive LM 15m. annual subsidy to the island's dry docks), to implement privatization plans and to strengthen tax and customs administrations. There were also some environmental issues that required attention, notably the inadequate sewerage system.

Talks over EU accession were formally concluded on 13 December 2002 in Copenhagen, Denmark. Malta had obtained 77 exemptions in the discussions, aimed largely at protecting its industrial and agricultural sectors, but also including cultural issues, such as the right to maintain the ban on divorce. A non-binding referendum was called for 8 March 2003 to determine whether the country would join the EU. Support for membership of the EU was led by the ruling PN and opposition to it by the MLP, which told voters to abstain, vote against the motion to join or spoil their ballots. Following an acrimonious campaign, 53.65% of the votes cast were in favour of EU membership, with 46.35% against. Sant refused to concede defeat, however, arguing that since the turn-out had been only 91% of the electorate the vote in support of membership of the EU did not represent an absolute majority. In accordance with the Constitution, Fenech Adami, whose mandate expired in 2004, called a general election for 12 April 2003 to confirm the referendum result, four days before the proposed signing of the EU accession treaty by 10 applicant countries, including Malta.

At the general election that took place on 12 April 2003 97.0% of the electorate participated; the PN won an absolute majority of 35 seats with 51.8% of the votes, while the MLP won 30 seats (47.5%). Fenech Adami was sworn in as Prime Minister on 14 April, announced the new Cabinet the following day (which included two new ministries with responsibility for rural affairs and the environment and for youth and the arts) and signed the EU accession treaty in Athens, Greece, on 16 April. The House of Representatives eventually ratified the treaty on 14 July by 34 votes to 25 (with six members boycotting the vote), and the President signed it on 16 July. Malta thus became a full member of the EU on 1 May 2004.

Malta's accession to the EU marked the beginning of a change in the country's politics. Since independence Malta's politics had been deeply partisan and bitterly polarized over who could best govern the archipelago, or more recently over whether to join the EU. Following the 2003 general election, however, the parties moved towards unity and consensus in order to obtain the maximum benefits for Malta from its EU membership. The MLP, which had previously been opposed outright to accession, accepted the result of the general election as a final arbiter of Maltese opinion on the question. Accordingly, following the MLP's defeat at the polls, the party leadership decided to embrace majority public opinion and work within the reality of EU membership. This decision proved divisive, and was resisted by a 'fundamentalist wing' of the MLP led by Mifsud Bonnici. However, delegates at a subsequent party conference agreed that the MLP would not withdraw Malta from the EU if the party came to power. Moreover, it was agreed that the incumbent Government would henceforth be able to rely on the MLP's support in its efforts to defend Malta's influence within the EU, particularly with regard to negotiations relating to the draft EU constitutional treaty. In January 2004 the Minister of Foreign Affairs, Dr Joe Borg, was named as Malta's first member of the European Commission.

On 7 February 2004 Fenech Adami used the occasion of his 70th birthday to announce his intention to resign as leader of the PN. He had always maintained that he would relinquish this post, and that of Prime Minister, when he reached 70 years of age, and he indicated that he would step down as Prime Minister once the party had appointed his successor. At a party conference on 29 February the Deputy Prime Minister and Minister for Social Policy, Dr Lawrence Gonzi, was elected as the PN's new leader. Gonzi won 59.3% of the delegates' votes in the first round. His nearest rival, John Dalli, the Minister for Finance and Economic Affairs, withdrew from the contest, thereby obviating the need for a second round of voting. (None the less, a second round was held as a formality; Gonzi won 94% of the votes cast.) Fenech Adami duly resigned from his seat in the House of Representatives and from his post as Prime Minister, and Gonzi was sworn in on 23 March 2004. On his assumption of the premiership he stated that his main priorities in the post would be full participation in the EU, the creation of jobs and the improvement of the economy. When naming his Cabinet, Gonzi assumed responsibility for the finance portfolio and appointed Dalli as Minister of Foreign Affairs.

On 29 March 2004 Fenech Adami was elected President by the House of Representatives, by 33 votes to 29, following his nomination by Gonzi. His appointment was controversial, as party leaders had not traditionally stood for the post, and it was bitterly opposed by the MLP. Fenech Adami was sworn in as Malta's seventh President on 4 April 2004.

On 12 June 2004 Malta participated for the first time in elections to the European Parliament. The participation rate, at 82.4%, was the third highest among the member states, surpassed only by Belgium and Luxembourg (where voting is mandatory). The MLP won three seats and the PN two.

On 3 July 2004 Dalli resigned his post as Minister of Foreign Affairs, claiming he was unable to continue amid attacks from 'different sides', which was thought to be a reference to criticism from within the PN. There were also allegations, which Dalli denied, of irregularities involving a large shipping deal and the handling of ministry travel expenses. He was replaced by his junior minister, Michael Frendo.

The Treaty establishing a Constitution for Europe was signed by the EU Heads of State and of Government on 29 October 2004, but adoption remained dependent on ratification by all 25 member states, either through a referendum or by approval of the legislature. Gonzi had confirmed in June, when the final text of the constitution was agreed, that there was no need for a referendum on the issue in Malta. On 6 July 2005 the House of Representatives unanimously ratified the constitutional treaty. However, the future of the treaty was uncertain, following its rejection at referendums in France and the Netherlands. At a meeting of the European Council in Brussels on 21–22 June 2007, a preliminary agreement was reached to replace the rejected constitutional treaty. On 13 December EU leaders signed the new Reform Treaty, which was to amend existing EU treaties, at a summit meeting in Lisbon, Portugal. The Treaty of Lisbon, as it was subsequently known, was approved by the House of Representatives in early February 2008 and was due to be ratified by all member states by the end of that year.

Following its accession to the EU, illegal immigration became an increasing problem for Malta, partly owing to its proximity to North Africa. According to the Office of the UN High Commissioner for Refugees (UNHCR, see p. 66), of all EU states Malta received the second largest number of asylum seekers per 1,000 inhabitants in 2005 (after Cyprus). Given Malta's extremely high population density the European Commission supported the Government's request in July 2005 that a proportion of the migrants arriving there be transferred to other EU states. Malta received offers of assistance from the Czech Republic, Ireland, the Netherlands and the United Kingdom. The Commission also proposed that the detention period for illegal immigrants and asylum seekers be reduced from one year to six months. The detention centres reached capacity in September, with new arrivals housed in tents. An investigation was launched in that month to determine whether the recent influx of illegal immigrants was the result of human trafficking. In October the House of Representatives adopted amendments to refugee legislation aimed at facilitating the repatriation of failed asylum seekers. In December 2005 a first group of migrants granted refugee status was transferred to the Netherlands. The USA also pledged to accept a small group in 2006. Malta also sought an agreement with Libya on the repatriation of illegal immigrants to that country. In February 2006 immigrants housed in detention centres across Malta protested, claiming that they were poorly fed and kept in insanitary conditions. Malta had been criticized by UNHCR over its treatment of asylum seekers in January 2005.

In mid-July 2006 Malta refused permission to a vessel transporting a group of 51 illegal migrants, originating mainly from sub-Saharan Africa, to enter Valletta port. The Government insisted that, as the vessel was Spanish-owned and had been rescued in Libyan waters, Malta would not accept responsibility for it, nor for its passengers. However, Spain also refused to accept responsibility for the migrants and the ship remained at sea for some eight days, during which discussions were held between Frendo, his Spanish counterpart and the Vice-President of the European Commission, responsible for Justice, Freedom and Security, Franco Frattini. Under the resulting agreement, Malta allowed the passengers to disembark at Valletta and accepted eight migrants, while Spain accepted 18; the remainder were transferred to Libya, Italy and Andorra. Later that month the EU announced its intention to deploy a police force to patrol the borders of member countries experiencing problems with illegal immigration, which would include a maritime patrol in the Mediterranean Sea between Malta and North Africa. None the less, in May 2007 there were several incidents in which the Maltese authorities refused to take responsibility for migrants arriving by sea from Africa, usually setting off from Libya, including a case in which 27 African migrants were left in the water for several days by a Maltese vessel, until they were rescued by the Italian navy. In early June Frattini accused the Maltese Government of failing to meet its international responsibilities to save lives at sea. The Deputy Prime Minister and Minister for Justice and Home Affairs, Dr Tonio Borg, subsequently defended Malta's record but insisted that Malta could not accept responsibility for all illegal immigrants rescued in the Mediterranean, particularly if they were in international and third country search and rescue areas. Borg proposed the creation of a system of shared responsibility for rescued migrants between EU member states on a quota basis. Although Frattini acknowledged Malta's predicament, immediate EU assistance was limited to the provision of an improved marine patrol force in the waters surrounding Malta, Sicily and Libya.

On 8 March 2008 Malta held its first general election since joining the EU. The Prime Minister, Gonzi, emphasized the economic achievements of the PN, while the MLP leader, Sant, campaigned on an anti-corruption platform, with pledges for greater transparency in government. The ruling PN emerged victorious with 49.3% of the votes cast, while the MLP won 48.8%; voter turn-out was 93%. However, while the PN won the popular vote, the MLP won the majority of parliamentary seats (34 seats, compared with 31 for the PN). Consequently, the PN was assigned four additional seats to ensure that it had a parliamentary majority, as required by the Constitution. Following the results of the election, Sant immediately resigned as MLP leader; a new leader was to be elected in June. After his re-election, Gonzi announced the composition of the new Cabinet, which comprised eight ministers (compared with the previous 12) and six parliamentary secretaries. The Minister for Gozo, Giovanna Debono, was the only member of the outgoing Cabinet to retain the same portfolio. Borg remained as Deputy Prime Minister but was allocated the foreign affairs portfolio in place of justice and home affairs, while the former parliamentary secretaries, Dr Tonio Fenech and Dr Carmelo Mifsud Bonnici, were appointed Minister for Finance, the Economy and Investment and Minister for Justice and Home Affairs, respectively.

Malta is a member of the Council of Europe (see p. 225) and the Organization for Security and Co-operation in Europe (see p. 354). Participation by Malta in the NATO 'Partnership for Peace' programme formally commenced in 1995, but was suspended by the MLP Government during 1996–98. In September 2005 Malta applied for full membership of the Organisation for Economic Co-operation and Development (OECD, see p. 347). On 1 January 2008 Malta adopted the single European currency, the euro, having submitted a formal application for membership of the euro area in February 2007 (see Economic Affairs, below).

In November 2005 Malta hosted the Commonwealth Heads of Government Meeting, at which leaders discussed improving co-operation in development, mass migration and combating terrorism. The British Prime Minister, Tony Blair, attended the meeting and later held talks with Gonzi on a number of issues, including illegal immigration. It was the first visit to Malta by a British Prime Minister in some 60 years.

In July 2005 Malta extended its maritime jurisdiction and established exclusive fisheries zones in response to similar measures adopted by Libya and Tunisia. Malta also requested permission from Libya for 15 vessels to operate within its unilaterally declared fisheries conservation zone at any one time during the year. In early 2006 Malta and Libya discussed reviving their 1984 co-operation agreement and agreed to consider a number of options with regard to petroleum, not limited to exploration. In February 2006 Malta and Tunisia signed an agreement on joint petroleum exploration and exploitation in zones of the continental shelf located between the two countries.

Government

Under the 1974 Constitution, legislative power is held by the unicameral House of Representatives, whose 65 members are elected by universal adult suffrage for five years (subject to dissolution) on the basis of proportional representation. The Constitution was amended in January 1987 to ensure that a party that received more than 50% of the total votes cast in a general election would obtain a majority of seats in the legislature (by the allocation—if necessary—of additional seats to that party). The President is the constitutional Head of State, elected for a five-year term by the House of Representatives, and executive power is exercised by the Cabinet. The President appoints the Prime Minister and, on the latter's recommendation, other Ministers. The Cabinet is responsible to the House of Representatives.

Defence

As assessed at November 2007, the armed forces of Malta comprised a regular army of 1,609. There was also a reserve of 90. Military service is voluntary. Budgetary expenditure on defence in 2007 was LM 13.6m.

Economic Affairs

In 2005, according to estimates by the World Bank, Malta's gross national income (GNI), measured at average 2003–2005 prices, was US $5,490.6m., equivalent to $13,590 per head (or $18,960 per head on an international purchasing-power parity basis). During 1996–2006, it was estimated, the population increased at an average annual rate of 0.6%, while gross domestic product (GDP) per head increased, in real terms, at an average annual rate of 1.4% during 1996–2005. Overall GDP increased, in real terms, at an average annual rate of 2.1% in 1996–2005. According to the IMF, GDP increased by 2.9% in 2006.

Agriculture (including hunting, forestry and fishing) contributed 2.4% of GDP and engaged 1.7% of the working population in 2005. The principal export crop is potatoes. Tomatoes and other vegetables, cereals (principally wheat and barley) and fruit are also cultivated. Livestock and livestock products are also important, and efforts are being made to develop the fishing industry. Exports of food and live animals accounted for 3.3% of total exports in 2005 (excluding re-exports). According to FAO figures, Malta's agricultural production increased at an average rate of 0.7% per year in 1995–2004. Output increased by 4.4% in 2004.

Industry (including mining, manufacturing, construction and power) provided 23.2% of GDP and engaged 26.7% of the employed labour force in 2005. According to the IMF, industrial production increased at an average rate of 3.4% per year in 1995–2004; it rose by 3.8% in 2003, but declined by 1.2% in 2004.

Mining and quarrying contributed 0.4% of GDP and engaged 0.4% of the employed labour force in 2005. The mining sector's output expanded at an average annual rate of 18.3% in 1990–96. The principal activities are stone and sand quarrying. There are reserves of petroleum in Maltese offshore waters, and petroleum and gas exploration is proceeding.

Manufacturing contributed 17.3% of GDP and engaged 17.1% of the working population in 2005. Based on the gross value of output, the principal branches of manufacturing, excluding ship-repairing, in 1999 were transport equipment and machinery (accounting for 54.7% of the total), food products and beverages (12.4%) and textiles, footwear and clothing (8.4%).

Energy is derived principally from imports of crude petroleum (the majority of which is purchased, at preferential rates, from Libya) and coal. Imports of mineral fuels comprised 11.0% of the value of total imports in 2005.

Services provided 74.4% of GDP and engaged 71.5% of the employed labour force in 2005. Tourism is a major source of foreign exchange earnings. In 2005 Malta received 1,170,610 foreign visitors, and revenue from the sector was US $923m. in the same year. In 2005 8.3% of the employed labour force were engaged in employment in the hotels and restaurants sub-sector.

In 2006 Malta recorded a visible trade deficit of US $1,221.6m., and there was a deficit of $412.0m. on the current account of the balance of payments. In 2004 the principal source of imports (accounting for 25.4% of the total value) was Italy (including San Marino); other major suppliers were France (13.1%) and the United Kingdom (12.0%). The USA was the principal market for exports (taking 15.7% of the total value); other significant purchasers of exports were France (15.5%), Singapore (14.5%), the United Kingdom (11.2%) and Germany (10.8%). The principal domestic exports in 2005 were machinery and transport equipment, accounting for 63.5% of the total, and miscellaneous manufactured articles (20.3%). The principal imports were machinery and transport equipment, accounting for 43.6% of the total, miscellaneous manufactured articles (12.5%) and basic manufactures (11.1%).

In 2006 Malta recorded a fiscal surplus of LM 28.7m. (equivalent to 1.4% of GDP in that year). According to official figures, general government debt was equivalent to 66.5% of GDP at the end of 2006. The annual rate of inflation averaged 1.5% in 1996–2006, according to the IMF; consumer prices increased by 2.8% in 2006. In 2005 5.1% of the labour force were registered as unemployed.

Malta is a member of the World Trade Organization (WTO, see p. 396) and of the European Bank for Reconstruction and Development (EBRD, see p. 239). Malta joined the European Union (EU, see p. 244) on 1 May 2004 and adopted the single European currency, the euro, on 1 January 2008.

Following the closure, in 1979, of the British military base and naval docks, on which Malta's economy had been largely dependent, successive governments pursued a policy of restructuring and diversification. The domestic market is limited, owing to the small population. There are few natural resources, and almost all raw materials have to be imported. Malta's development has therefore been based on the promotion of the island as an international financial centre and on manufacturing for export (notably in non-traditional fields, such as electronics, information technology and pharmaceuticals), together with the continuing development of tourism. From 2004 Malta's EU membership entailed a commitment on the part of the Government to reduce Malta's budgetary deficit to below 3.0% of GDP in order to comply with the convergence criteria for participation in Economic and Monetary Union (EMU). Through the implementation of strict monetary policies, institutional reform and a privatization programme, Malta reduced its deficit from more than 10% of GDP in 2003 to 2.6% in 2006 and 2.1% in 2007. The fiscal balance was projected to be in surplus by 2010. Malta joined the euro zone on 1 January 2008, with the euro becoming the sole currency by the end of that month. The benefits of membership of the euro area were expected to be evident principally in the areas of international trade and tourism. Malta confronts the same challenges as the other EU member states: modernizing the welfare state, improving flexibility in the labour market, increasing international competitiveness, and generating stronger economic growth. Pensions reform was a priority: expenditure on old-age pensions was expected to more than double during 2004–24, to about the equivalent of 11% of GDP, according to the IMF. In November 2005 the Government presented a three-year national reform programme, in the context of the EU's renewed Lisbon Agenda (a programme of reforms initially agreed in 2000 at a summit in the Portuguese capital). The programme, which entailed an investment of €228m., to be financed both nationally and with EU funds, was intended to promote the country's competitiveness, economic growth and job creation. Malta's financial sector has benefited from EU membership, with insurance and banking institutions and hedge funds moving to the Maltese Financial Centre, while restrictions have been removed on foreign financial institutions entering the domestic market. Real GDP growth was estimated at 3.2% in 2007.

Education

Education is compulsory between the ages of five and 16 years, and is available free of charge in government schools and institutions, from kindergarten to university. Kindergarten education is provided for three- and four-year-old children. In 2003/04 enrolment at pre-primary level included 88% of children in the relevant age-group (males 87%; females 89%). Primary education begins at five years of age and lasts for six years. In 2004/05 enrolment at primary level included 86% of children in the relevant age-group (males 88%; females 84%). Secondary education, beginning at 11 years of age, lasts for a maximum of seven years, but this period is extended in the case of technology and vocational courses. Enrolment at secondary level in 2004/05 included 84% of children in the relevant age-group (males 86%; females 84%). After completing five years of secondary-level education, students having the necessary qualifications may opt to follow a higher academic or technical or vocational course. The junior college, administrated by the University of Malta, prepares students specifically for a university course. About 30% of the student population attend schools administered by the Roman Catholic Church, from kindergarten to higher secondary level. The Government subsidizes the provision of free education for students in church schools. Higher education is available at the University of Malta. There are also a number of technical institutes, specialist schools and an extended skill-training scheme for trade-school leavers. Enrolment at tertiary level was equivalent to 31% of those in the relevant age-group in 2004/05 (males 27%; females 36%). The Government also provides adult education courses. Of total recurrent budgetary expenditure in 2004 LM 50.2m. (6.9%) was allocated to education. In July 2005 the Government announced its intention to reform the education system. From September state primary schools, area secondary schools and junior colleges were to be grouped together into autonomous regional colleges. The Government also proposed establishing a national commission on higher education, and the inclusion of a scholarship fund in the 2006 budget.

Public Holidays

2008: 1 January (New Year's Day), 10 February (St Paul's Shipwreck), 19 March (St Joseph), 21 March (Good Friday), 31 March (Freedom Day), 1 May (St Joseph the Worker), 7 June (Memorial of the 1919 Riot), 29 June (St Peter and St Paul), 15 August (Assumption), 8 September (Our Lady of Victories), 21 September (Independence Day), 8 December (Immaculate Conception), 13 December (Republic Day), 25 December (Christmas Day).

2009: 1 January (New Year's Day), 10 February (St Paul's Shipwreck), 19 March (St Joseph), 31 March (Freedom Day), 10 April (Good Friday), 1 May (St Joseph the Worker), 7 June (Memorial of the 1919 Riot), 29 June (St Peter and St Paul), 15 August (Assumption), 8 September (Our Lady of Victories), 21 September (Independence Day), 8 December (Immaculate Conception), 13 December (Republic Day), 25 December (Christmas Day).

Weights and Measures

The metric system is in force.

Statistical Survey

Source (unless otherwise stated): National Statistics Office, Lascaris, Valletta VLT 1921; tel. 21223221; fax 21249841; e-mail nso@magnet.mt; internet www.nso.gov.mt.

AREA AND POPULATION

Area: 315 sq km (122 sq miles).

Population: 404,962 (males 200,819, females 204,143) at census of 27 November 2005 (figures refer to *de jure* population). *2006* (estimated population at 31 December): 407,810.

Density (at 31 December 2006): 1,294.6 per sq km.

Principal Towns (total population at 31 December 2006): Birkirkara 21,658; Mosta 18,495; Qormi 16,459; Żabbar 14,671; San Ġwann 12,318; Sliema 11,890; San Pawl Il-Baħar 11,767; Valletta (capital) 6,166.

Births, Marriages and Deaths (2006): Registered live births 3,885 (birth rate 9.5 per 1,000); Marriages 2,536 (marriage rate 6.2 per 1,000); Registered deaths 3,216 (death rate 7.9 per 1,000).

Expectation of Life (years at birth, WHO estimates): 78.9 (males 76.6; females 81.1) in 2005. Source: WHO, *World Health Statistics*.

Migration (2004, unless otherwise indicated): Emigrants 70 (all to United Kingdom); Returning emigrants 459; Non-Maltese nationals settling in the islands 533 (in 2002).

Economically Active Population (at census of 27 November 2005): Agriculture and hunting 2,249; Fishing 429; Mining and quarrying 674; Manufacturing 26,201; Electricity, gas and water supply

MALTA

Statistical Survey

3,118; Construction 11,003; Wholesale and retail trade and repair of motor vehicles, motorcycles and personal and household goods 24,474; Hotels and restaurants 12,724; Transport, storage and communications 11,953; Financial intermediation 5,564; Real estate, renting and business activities 10,406; Public administration and defence and compulsory social security 13,101; Education 13,092; Health and social work 11,360; Other community, social and personal service activities 6,563; Private households with employed persons 163; Extra-territorial organizations and bodies 407; *Total employed* 153,483 (males 104,039, females 49,444); Registered unemployed 11,183; *Total labour force* 164,666. Note: figures exclude apprentices, trainees and students engaged in holiday work.

HEALTH AND WELFARE
Key Indicators

Total Fertility Rate (children per woman, 2005): 1.5.

Under-5 Mortality Rate (per 1,000 live births, 2005): 6.

HIV/AIDS (% of persons aged 15–49, 2005): 0.1.

Physicians (per 1,000 head, 2003): 3.18.

Hospital Beds (per 1,000 head, 2005): 7.50.

Health Expenditure (2004): US $ per head (PPP): 1,732.7.

Health Expenditure (2004): % of GDP: 9.2.

Health Expenditure (2004): public (% of total): 76.1.

Human Development Index (2005): ranking: 34.

Human Development Index (2005): value: 0.878.

For sources and definitions, see explanatory note on p. vi.

AGRICULTURE, ETC.

Principal Crops ('000 metric tons, 2006): Wheat 9.5*; Barley 1.6*; Potatoes 22.0; Cabbages 3.5; Tomatoes 15.9; Cauliflowers and broccoli 6.4*; Pumpkins, squash and gourds 7.1; Dry onions 7.3; Garlic 0.7; Broad beans, dry 1.0*; Melons 17.7*; Citrus fruit 0.7*; Grapes 2.7.
* FAO estimate.

Livestock ('000 head, year ending September 2006): Cattle 19.7; Pigs 73.0; Sheep 14.6; Goats 6.3; Rabbits 0.2*; Chickens 1,000*; Horses 1.0*; Asses, mules or hinnies 0.8*.
* FAO estimate.

Livestock Products ('000 metric tons, 2006): Cattle meat 1.4; Pig meat 8.2; Rabbit meat 1.8*; Chicken meat 3.9; Cows' milk 41.3; Sheep's milk 1.8; Hen eggs 7.3.
* FAO estimate.

Fishing (metric tons, live weight, 2005): Capture 1,435 (Atlantic bluefin tuna 346, Common dolphinfish 447, Swordfish 362); Aquaculture 736 (European seabass 196, Gilthead seabream 540); *Total catch* 2,171.

Source: FAO.

INDUSTRY

Production ('000 metric tons, 2001, unless otherwise indicated): Limestone flux and calcareous stones 2,000 (Limestone only); Cigarettes (1992, million) 1,475; Washing powders and detergents 9.7; Quicklime (1992, incl. other types of lime) 5; Tankers, launched (1996, number, completions) 5; Other sea-going merchant vessels launched (number, 2002) 1 (5 grt); Electricity (2004, million kWh, by public utilities) 2,216 (Source: UN, *Industrial Commodity Statistics Yearbook*).

FINANCE

Currency and Exchange Rates: 1,000 mils = 100 cents = 1 Maltese lira (LM; plural: liri). *Sterling, Dollar and Euro Equivalents* (31 December 2007): £1 sterling = 584.2 mils; US $1 = 291.6 mils; €1 = 429.3 mils; LM 10 = £17.12 = $34.29 = €23.29. *Average Exchange Rate* (Maltese lira per US $): 0.3458 in 2005; 0.3409 in 2006; 0.3117 in 2007. Note: Malta adopted the euro on 1 January 2008, and this became the sole legal tender from the end of the same month; however, most of the relevant historical data in this survey continues to be presented in terms of Maltese liri.

Budget (LM million, 2006): *Revenue:* Income tax 256.5; Customs and excise 69.2; Value-added tax 174.6; Social security 202.4; Grants 59.8; Other recurrent revenue 182.2; Non-recurrent revenue 86.6; Total 1,031.3. *Expenditure:* Recurrent expenditure 788.2 (Personal emoluments 203.1; Programmes and initiatives 474.2); Public debt servicing 77.4; Capital expenditure 137.0; Total 1,002.6.

International Reserves (US $ million at 31 December 2006): Gold (national valuation) 4.1; IMF special drawing rights 51.2; Reserve position in IMF 60.6; Foreign exchange 2,865.0; Total 2,980.9. Source: IMF, *International Financial Statistics*.

Money Supply (LM million at 31 December 2006): Currency outside banks 477.80; Demand deposits at commercial banks 955.99; Total money 1,433.79. Source: IMF, *International Financial Statistics*.

Cost of Living (Consumer Price Index; base: 2000 = 100): All items 109.5 in 2004; 112.8 in 2005; 116.0 in 2006. Source: IMF, *International Financial Statistics*.

Gross Domestic Product (LM million at constant 2000 prices): 1,719.1 in 2004; 1,775.2 in 2005; 1,833.0 in 2006. Source: IMF, *International Financial Statistics*.

Expenditure on Gross Domestic Product (LM '000 at current prices, 2006): Final consumption expenditure 1,799,575 (General government final consumption expenditure 443,186, Households 1,321,866, Non-profit institutes serving households 34,523); Gross capital formation 415,774 (Changes in stocks –2,028, Gross fixed capital formation 411,802, Acquisitions, less disposals, of valuables 6,000); *Total domestic expenditure* 2,215,349; Exports of goods and services 1,735,667; *Less* Imports of goods and services 1,851,456; *GDP in purchasers' values* 2,099,560.

Gross Domestic Product by Economic Activity (LM '000 at current prices, 2005): Agriculture, hunting and forestry 36,069; Fishing 3,897; Mining and quarrying 5,959; Manufacturing 284,784; Electricity, gas and water supply 12,438; Construction 78,146; Wholesale and retail trade, repair of motor vehicles, motorcycles and household goods 198,000; Hotels and restaurants 104,768; Transport, storage and communications 164,554; Financial intermediation 73,361; Real estate, renting and business activities 235,651; Public administration and defence, compulsory social security 130,288; Education 119,107; Health and social work 101,475; Other community, social and personal services 98,035; *Gross value added at basic prices* 1,646,530; Indirect taxes 294,456; *Less* Subsidies 13,894; *GDP in purchasers' values* 1,927,093.

Balance of Payments (US $ million, 2006): Exports of goods f.o.b. 2,908.5; Imports of goods f.o.b. –4,130.1; *Trade balance* –1,221.6; Exports of services 1,923.8; Imports of services –1,499.0; *Balance on goods and services* –796.8; Other income received 1,849.5; Other income paid –1,994.7; *Balance on goods, services and income* –941.9; Current transfers received 1,066.3; Current transfers paid –536.4; *Current balance* –412.0; Capital account (net) 191.8; Direct investment abroad –3.3; Direct investment from abroad 1,764.2; Portfolio investment assets –2,372.6; Portfolio investment liabilities –17.3; Financial derivatives assets 907.0; Financial derivatives liabilities –1,180.3; Other investment assets –4,204.4; Other investment liabilities 5,674.5; Net errors and omissions –235.7; *Overall balance* 111.8. Source: IMF, *International Financial Statistics*.

EXTERNAL TRADE

Principal Commodities (LM million, 2005, provisional): *Imports c.i.f.:* Food and live animals 128.1; Mineral fuels, lubricants, etc. 143.4; Chemicals 113.9; Basic manufactures 145.2; Machinery and transport equipment 569.0; Miscellaneous manufactured articles 163.6; Total (incl. others) 1,304.7. *Exports (excl. re-exports) f.o.b.:* Food and live animals 26.3; Chemicals 28.4; Basic manufactures 54.1; Machinery and transport equipment 509.1; Miscellaneous manufactured articles 162.6; Total (incl. others) 802.0.

Selected Trading Partners (US $ million, 2004): *Imports:* France (incl. Monaco) 498.1; Germany 338.2; Italy (incl. San Marino) 969.3; Singapore 155.2; United Kingdom 457.0; USA 197.5; Total (incl. others) 3,809.5. *Exports:* France (incl. Monaco) 409.2; Germany 283.4; Italy (incl. San Marino) 78.7; Libya 92.8; Singapore 382.5; United Kingdom 294.7; USA 412.8; Total (incl. others, of which ship stores and bunkers 133.9) 2,632.3. Source: UN, *International Trade Statistics Yearbook*.

TRANSPORT

Road Traffic (motor vehicles in use, December 2005): Private cars 206,148; Commercial vehicles 44,371; Minibuses 422; Coaches and buses 721; Motorcycles 11,905; Total (incl. others) 271,338.

Shipping: *Merchant Fleet* (31 December 2006): Vessels 1,294; Total displacement 24,849,818 grt (Source: Lloyds Register-Fairplay, *World Fleet Statistics*). *International Freight Traffic* (metric tons, 2001): Goods loaded 319,972; Goods unloaded 1,453,574.

Civil Aviation (traffic on scheduled services, 2003): Kilometres flown (million) 22; Passengers carried ('000) 1,309; Passenger-km (million) 2,174; Total ton-km (million) 209. Source: UN, *Statistical Yearbook*.

MALTA
Directory

TOURISM

Tourist Arrivals (based on departures by air and sea, revised figures): 1,118,236 in 2003; 1,157,681 in 2004; 1,170,610 in 2005.

Arrivals by Country of Origin (based on departures by air and sea, 2005): Austria 26,395; Belgium 28,731; France 82,676; Germany 138,216; Italy 92,454; Netherlands 37,149; Sweden 26,111; United Kingdom 483,171; Total (incl. others) 1,171,344.

Tourism Receipts (US $ million, incl. passenger transport): 866 in 2003; 953 in 2004; 923 in 2005.

Source: partly World Tourism Organization.

COMMUNICATIONS MEDIA

Radio Receivers (1997): 255,000 in use*.
Television Receivers (1999): 212,000 in use*.
Telephones (main lines, 2006): 202,300 in use.
Facsimile Machines (1996): 6,000 in use (estimate)†.
Mobile Cellular Telephones (2006): 346,800 subscribers.
Personal Computers (2005): 126,000 in use‡.
Internet Users (2006): 72,000.
Broadband Subscribers (2006): 42,100.
Book Production (1998): 237 titles*.
Daily Newspapers (1999): 4 titles (combined average circulation 54,000 copies per issue).
Non-daily Newspapers (1999): 10 titles.
Other Periodicals (1992): 359 titles*.

*Source: UN, *Statistical Yearbook*.
†Source: UNESCO, *Statistical Yearbook*.
‡Source: International Telecommunication Union.

EDUCATION

Pre-primary (2004/05, unless otherwise stated): 131 schools (1999/2000); 742 teachers (2001/02); 7,325 students. Source: UNESCO.

Primary (2004/05, unless otherwise stated): 126 schools (1999/2000); 2,573 teachers; 29,114 students. Source: UNESCO.

Secondary (2004/05, unless otherwise stated): *General:* 75 schools (1999/2000); 3,610 teachers; 34,603 students. *Vocational:* 23 schools (1999/2000); 310 teachers; 4,358 students. *Junior College* (1995/96): 1 school; 1,800 students. Source: UNESCO, partly *Statistical Yearbook*.

Universities, etc. (2004/05): 825 teachers; 9,441 students. Source: UNESCO.

Adult Literacy Rate (UNESCO estimates): 87.9% (males 86.4%; females 89.2%) in 1995. Source: UNESCO Institute for Statistics.

Directory

The Constitution

On 13 December 1974 the Independence Constitution of 1964 was substantially amended to bring into effect a Republican Constitution, under the terms of which Malta became a democratic republic within the Commonwealth, founded on work and on respect for the fundamental rights and freedoms of the individual. The new Constitution provided for the creation of the office of President to replace that of Governor-General.

The religion of the Maltese people is recognized to be the Roman Catholic Apostolic Religion, and the Church Authorities have the constitutional right and duty to teach according to its principles. The religious teaching of the Roman Catholic Church is provided in all state schools as part of compulsory education.

The Constitution provides that the national language and the language of the Courts is Maltese, but that both Maltese and English are official languages.

An independent Public Services Commission, consisting of three to five members, is appointed by the President, on the advice of the Prime Minister, to make recommendations to the Prime Minister concerning appointments to public office and the dismissal and disciplinary control of persons holding public office.

The Constitution also provides for an Employment Commission, consisting of a chairman and four other members, the function of which is to ensure that, in respect of employment, no distinction, exclusion or preference that is not justifiable is made or given in favour of or against any person by reason of his or her political opinion.

The Judicature is independent.

Radio and television broadcasting is controlled by an independent authority.

DECLARATION OF PRINCIPLES

The Constitution upholds the right to work and to reasonable hours of work, the safeguarding of rights of women workers, the encouragement of private economic enterprise, the encouragement of co-operatives, the provision of free and compulsory primary education, and the provision of social assistance and insurance.

FUNDAMENTAL RIGHTS AND FREEDOMS OF THE INDIVIDUAL

The Constitution provides for the protection of the right to life, freedom from arbitrary arrest or detention, protection of freedom of conscience, protection from discrimination on the grounds of race, etc.

THE PRESIDENT

Under the Constitution, the office of President becomes vacant after five years from the date of appointment made by resolution of the House of Representatives. The President appoints the Prime Minister, choosing the member of the House of Representatives who is judged to be ablest to command the confidence of a majority of the members. On the advice of the Prime Minister, the President appoints the other ministers, the Chief Justice, the Judges and the Attorney-General.

THE CABINET

The Cabinet consists of the Prime Minister and such number of other ministers as are recommended by the Prime Minister.

PARLIAMENT

The House of Representatives consists of such number of members, being an odd number and divisible by the number of divisions, as Parliament by law determines from time to time. In future the electoral divisions are not to be fewer than nine and not more than 15, as Parliament may from time to time determine. The normal life of the House of Representatives is five years, after which a general election is held. Election is by universal adult suffrage on the basis of proportional representation. The age of majority is 18 years. Under a constitutional amendment adopted in January 1987, it was ensured that a party receiving more than 50% of the total votes cast in a general election would obtain a majority of seats in the House of Representatives, by the allocation (if necessary) of additional seats to that party.

NEUTRALITY AND NON-ALIGNMENT

In January 1987 a constitutional amendment was adopted, aiming to entrench in the Constitution Malta's status of neutrality and adherence to a policy of non-alignment, and stipulating that no foreign military base was to be permitted on Maltese territory.

The Government

HEAD OF STATE

President: Dr EDWARD (EDDIE) FENECH ADAMI (took office 4 April 2004).

THE CABINET
(April 2008)

Prime Minister: Dr LAWRENCE GONZI.
Deputy Prime Minister and Minister of Foreign Affairs: Dr TONIO BORG.
Minister for Gozo: GIOVANNA DEBONO.
Minister for Communications and National Projects: Dr AUSTIN GATT.
Minister for Resources and Rural Affairs: GEORGE PULLICINO.
Minister for Education and Culture: DOLORES CRISTINA.
Minister for Social Policy: JOHN DALLI.

MALTA   Directory

Minister of Finance, the Economy and Investment: Dr TONIO FENECH.
Minister for Justice and Home Affairs: Dr CARMELO MIFSUD BONNICI.

PARLIAMENTARY SECRETARIES (ATTACHED TO MINISTRIES)

Parliamentary Secretary for Public Dialogue and Information in the Office of the Prime Minister: Dr CHRIS SAID.
Parliamentary Secretary for Tourism in the Office of the Prime Minister: Dr MARIO DE MARCO.
Parliamentary Secretary for Youth and Sport in the Ministry of Education and Culture: CLYDE PULI.
Parliamentary Secretary for Health in the Ministry for Social Policy: Dr JOE CASSAR.
Parliamentary Secretary for the Elderly and Community Care in the Ministry for Social Policy: MARIO GALEA.
Parliamentary Secretary for Revenues and Land in the Ministry of Finance, the Economy and Investment: Dr JASON AZZOPARDI.

MINISTRIES

Office of the President: The Palace, Valletta CMR 02; tel. 21221221; fax 21241241; e-mail president@gov.mt; internet www.president.gov.mt.
Office of the Prime Minister: Auberge de Castille, Valletta VLT 2000; tel. 22001400; fax 22001467; internet www.opm.gov.mt.
Ministry for Communications and National Projects: Casa Leoni, St Joseph High Rd, St Venera CMR 02; tel. 21485100; fax 23886116; e-mail info.mcmp@gov.mt; internet www.mtc.gov.mt.
Ministry of Education and Culture: Great Siege Rd, Floriana CMR 02; tel. 21223622; fax 21242759; e-mail communications.moed@gov.mt; internet www.education.gov.mt.
Ministry of Finance, the Economy and Investment: Maison Demandols, 30 South St, Valletta VLT 2000; tel. 21249640; fax 21233605; e-mail info.mfin@gov.mt; internet www.mfin.gov.mt.
Ministry of Foreign Affairs: Palazzo Parisio, Merchants St, Valletta VLT 1171; tel. 21242191; fax 21242853; e-mail info.mfa@gov.mt; internet www.mfa.gov.mt.
Ministry for Gozo: St Francis Sq., Victoria VCT 2000, Gozo; tel. 21561482; fax 21559360; e-mail info.mog@gov.mt; internet www.gozo.gov.mt.
Ministry for Justice and Home Affairs: Auberge d'Aragon, Independence Sq., Valletta VLT 2000; tel. 22957000; fax 22957348; e-mail mjha@gov.mt; internet www.mjha.gov.mt.
Ministry for Resources and Rural Affairs: Barriera Wharf, Valletta VLT 2000; tel. 22952000; fax 22952212; e-mail info.mrra@gov.mt; internet www.mrra.gov.mt.
Ministry for Social Policy: Palazzo Ferreria, 310 Republic St, Valletta VLT 2000; tel. 25903100; fax 25903121; e-mail info.mfss@gov.mt; internet www.msp.gov.mt.

Legislature

HOUSE OF REPRESENTATIVES

Speaker: ANTON TABONE.
General Election, 8 March 2008

Party	Votes	% of votes	Seats
Partit Nazzjonalista (Nationalist Party)	143,468	49.34	35
Partit Laburista (Malta Labour Party)	141,888	48.79	34
Alternattiva Demokratika (Green Party)	3,810	1.31	—
Azzjoni Nazzjonali (National Action)	1,461	0.50	—
Others	172	0.06	—
Total	290,799	100.00	69

Election Commission

Electoral Commission: Electoral Office, Evans Bldg, St Elmo Pl., Valletta VLT 2000; tel. 21221994; fax 21248457; e-mail electoral.office@gov.mt; internet www.electoral.gov.mt; independent; Chair. and Chief Electoral Commr EDWARD R. GATT; Sec. JOE CALLEJA.

Political Organizations

Alternattiva Demokratika (AD) (Green Party): 10 Manwel Dimech St, Sliema SLM 1059; tel. 21314040; fax 21314046; e-mail info@alternattiva.org.mt; internet www.alternattiva.org.mt; f. 1989; emphasizes social and environmental issues; Chair. Dr HARRY VASSALLO; Sec.-Gen. VICTOR GALEA.
Azzjoni Nazzjonali (AN) (National Action): 74 The Strand, Sliema; e-mail azzjoninazzjonali@gmail.com; internet www.azzjoninazzjonali.org; f. 2007; right-wing; Leader Dr JOSIE MUSCAT; Gen. Sec. PHILIP BEATTIE.
Partit Laburista (Malta Labour Party—MLP): National Labour Centre, Mile End Rd, Hamrun HMR 1717; tel. 21249900; fax 21244204; e-mail mlp@mlp.org.mt; internet www.mlp.org.mt; f. 1921; democratic socialist; Leader (vacant); Pres. STEFAN ZRINZO AZZOPARDI; Gen. Sec. JASON MICALLEF; 39,000 mems.
Partit Nazzjonalista (PN) (Nationalist Party): Herbert Ganado St, Pietà PTA 1541; tel. 21243641; fax 21243640; e-mail admin@pn.org.mt; internet www.pn.org.mt; f. 1880; Christian democratic; Leader Dr LAWRENCE GONZI; Sec.-Gen. JOE SALIBA; 33,000 mems.

Diplomatic Representation

EMBASSIES AND HIGH COMMISSIONS IN MALTA

Australia: Villa Fiorentina, Ta'Xbiex Terrace, Ta'Xbiex XBX 1034; tel. 21338201; fax 21344059; e-mail aushicom@onvol.net; internet www.malta.embassy.gov.au; High Commissioner JUREK JUSZCZYK.
Austria: Whitehall Mansions, 3rd Floor, Ta'Xbiex Seafront, Ta'Xbiex XBX 1034; tel. 23279000; fax 21317430; e-mail valletta-ob@bmaa.gv.at; Ambassador CAROLINE GUDENUS.
Belgium: Europa Centre, 8–9 John Lopez St., Floriana FLN 1400; tel. 21228214; fax 21243246; internet www.diplomatie.be/valletta; e-mail valletta@diplobel.be; Ambassador THOMAS BAEKELANDT.
China, People's Republic: Karmnu Court, Lapsi St, St Julian's STJ 1264; tel. 21384889; fax 21344730; e-mail chinaemb-mt@mfa.gov.cn; internet mt.chineseembassy.org; Ambassador CHAI XI.
Egypt: Villa Mon Rêve, 10 Sir Temi Zammit St, Ta'Xbiex XBX 1013; tel. 21314158; fax 21319230; e-mail embegmlt@onvol.net; Ambassador ABD AL-KARIM MAHMOUD SOLIMAN.
France: POB 408, Valletta CMR 01; 130 Melita St, Valletta CMR 01; tel. 21233430; fax 21233528; e-mail france@global.net.mt; internet www.ambafrance-mt.org; Ambassador JEAN-MARC RIVES.
Germany: 'Il-Piazzetta', Entrance B, 1st Floor, Tower Rd, Sliema SLM 1605; tel. 21336531; fax 21341271; e-mail info@valletta.diplo.de; internet www.valletta.diplo.de; Ambassador KARL ANDREAS VON STENGLIN.
Greece: Villino Fondgalland, 6 Ir-Rampa Ta'Xbiex, Ta'Xbiex XBX 1035; tel. 21320998; fax 21320788; e-mail embassy.malta@mfa.gr; Ambassador DOROTHEA TSIMBOUKELI-DOUVOS.
Holy See: V20/22 Pietru Caxaru St, Tal-Virtù, Rabat RBT 2604; tel. 21453422; fax 21453423; e-mail apost@keyworld.net; Apostolic Nuncio Most Rev. FÉLIX DEL BLANCO PRIETO (Titular Archbishop of Vannida).
Ireland: Whitehall Mansions, Ta'Xbiex Seafront, Ta'Xbiex XBX 1026; tel. 21334744; fax 21334755; e-mail vallettaembassy@dfa.ie; Chargé d'affaires GERALD O'CONNOR.
Italy: 5 Vilhena St, Floriana FRN 1111; tel. 21233157; fax 21239217; e-mail ambasciata.lavalletta@esteri.it; internet www.amblavalletta.esteri.it; Ambassador PAOLO ANDREA TRABALZA.
Libya: Dar Jamahariya, Notabile Rd, Balzan BZN 01; tel. 21486347; fax 21483939; e-mail libyanpeople@waldonet.net.mt; Sec. of People's Bureau Dr SAAD A. F. ESH-SHLMANI.
Netherlands: Whitehall Mansions, 3rd Floor, Ta'Xbiex Seafront, Ta'Xbiex XBX 1026; tel. 21313980; fax 21313990; e-mail val@minbuza.nl; internet www.mfa.nl/val; Ambassador JAN HEIDSMA.
Portugal: Whitehall Mansions, 3rd Floor, Ta'Xbiex Seafront, Ta'Xbiex XBX 1026; tel. 21322924; fax 21322927; e-mail embportmalta@sapo.pt; Ambassador ANTÓNIO AUGUSTO RUSSO DIAS.
Russia: Ariel House, 25 Anthony Schembri St, Kappara, San Ġwann SGN 08; tel. 21371905; fax 21372131; e-mail rusemb@onvol.net; internet www.malta.mid.ru; Ambassador ANDREI E. GRANOVSKII.
Spain: Whitehall Mansions, Ta'Xbiex Seafront, Ta'Xbiex XBX 1026; tel. 21317365; fax 21317362; e-mail emb.valletta@mae.es; Ambassador MARTA VILARDELL COMA.

MALTA — Directory

Tunisia: Valletta Rd, Attard ATD 9052; tel. 21417070; fax 21413414; e-mail at.lavalette@maltanet.net; Ambassador MOHAMED ALI GHANZOUI.

United Kingdom: Whitehall Mansions, Ta'Xbiex Seafront, Ta'Xbiex XBX 1026; tel. 23230000; fax 23232216; e-mail bhcvalletta@fco.gov.uk; internet www.britishhighcommission.gov.uk/malta; High Commissioner NICHOLAS ARCHER.

USA: Development House, 3rd Floor, St Anne St, Floriana FRN 9010; tel. 25614000; fax 21243229; e-mail usembmalta@state.gov; internet malta.usembassy.gov; Ambassador MOLLY HERING BORDONARO.

Judicial System

The legal system consists of enactments of the Parliament of Malta, and those of the British Parliament not repealed or replaced by enactments of the Maltese legislature. Maltese Civil Law derives largely from Roman Law, while British Law has significantly influenced Maltese public law.

The Constitutional Court, composed of three judges, is appellate in cases involving alleged violations of human rights, the interpretation of the Constitution and the invalidity of laws. It has jurisdiction to decide questions as to membership of the House of Representatives and any reference made to it relating to voting for election of members of the House of Representatives.

The Court of Appeal is composed of three judges, when it hears appeals from the judgments of the Civil Court, and of one judge, when it hears appeals from the Court of Magistrates in its civil jurisdiction. An appeal also lies to the Court of Appeal from the decisions of a number of administrative tribunals, mostly on points of law.

The Court of Criminal Appeal consists of three judges and hears appeals from persons convicted by the Criminal Court. A person convicted on indictment may appeal against his conviction in all cases or against the sentence passed on his conviction, unless the sentence is one fixed by law. An appeal can never result in a sentence of greater severity. An accused person may also appeal against a verdict of not guilty on the grounds of insanity. In certain cases the Court may also order a retrial. The Attorney-General, who is the prosecutor before the Criminal Court, cannot appeal from a verdict of acquittal or, in certain cases, against the sentence passed. This Court, when formed of one judge, hears appeals from judgments delivered by the Court of Magistrates in its criminal jurisdiction.

The Criminal Court is formed by one judge, who sits with a jury of nine persons to try, on indictment, offences exceeding the competence of the Court of Magistrates. This court may, in certain exceptional cases, sit without a jury.

The Civil Court is divided into three sections. The First Hall takes cognisance of all causes of a civil and a commercial nature, exceeding the jurisdiction of the Courts of Magistrates. The Voluntary Jurisdiction Section (formerly the Second Hall) is assigned all matters of a civil nature, such as authority to proceed the tutorship of minors, adoption, the interdiction and incapacitation of persons, the opening of successions and the confirmation of testamentary executors. The Family Section is assigned matters of a civil nature regulated by titles I, II and IV of the First Book of the Civil Code; the Maintenance Orders (Facilities for Enforcement) Ordinance; the Maintenance Ordinance (Reciprocal Enforcement) Act; the Marriage Act and the Child Abduction and Child Custody Act. One Judge presides in all three sections.

The Magistrates' Court, which is composed of one Magistrate, exercises both a civil and a criminal jurisdiction. The Court of Magistrates, in civil matters, has an inferior jurisdiction of first instance, limited to claims exceeding LM 1,500 but not exceeding LM 5,000. In criminal matters, the Court has a two-fold jurisdiction, namely, as a court of criminal judicature for the trial of offences which fall within its jurisdiction, and as a court of inquiry in respect of offences which fall within the jurisdiction of a higher tribunal.

The Court of Magistrates for Gozo, in civil matters, has a two-fold jurisdiction—an inferior jurisdiction comparable to that exercised by its counterpart Court in Malta, and a superior jurisdiction, both civil and commercial, in respect of causes which in Malta are cognisable by the First Hall of the Civil Court. Within the limits of its territorial jurisdiction, this Court has also the powers of a Court of voluntary jurisdiction.

The Small Claims Tribunal is presided over by an adjudicator who decides cases on principles of equity, according to law. Adjudicators are appointed from amongst advocates for a term of five years, and decide cases brought before them without delay. The aim is to have claims not exceeding the sum of LM 1,500 decided summarily. Sittings of this Tribunal are held in Malta or Gozo. An appeal from the decision of the Tribunal lies to the Court of Appeal on specific cases listed in the Act establishing the Tribunal.

The Juvenile Court consists of a Magistrate, as Chairman, and two members. Sittings are held in Santa Venera. The Court hears charges against, and holds other proceedings relating to, minors under the age of 16 years, and may also issue Care Orders in their regard. Given the confidential nature of such sittings, attendance to hearings is restricted to persons mentioned in the law establishing the Court.

Chief Justice and President of the Court of Appeal and the Constitutional Court: Dr VINCENT A. DE GAETANO.

Judges: CARMEL A. AGIUS, JOSEPH D. CAMILLERI, JOSEPH A. FILLETTI, ALBERTO J. MAGRI, GEOFFREY VALENZIA, GIANNINO CARUANA DEMAJO, GINO CAMILLERI, CARMELO FARRUGIA SACCO, RAYMOND PACE, DAVID P. SCICLUNA, JOSEPH R. MICALLEF, JOSEPH GALEA DEBONO, TONIO MALLIA, PHILIP SCIBERRAS, NOEL CUSCHIERI, JOSEPH AZZOPARDI, ABIGAIL LOFARO, ANNA FELICE.

Attorney-General: Dr SILVIO CAMILLERI.

Religion

CHRISTIANITY

The Roman Catholic Church

Malta comprises one archdiocese and one diocese. At 31 December 2005 adherents of the Roman Catholic Church numbered an estimated 404,786 (representing some 96.3% of the total population).

Bishops' Conference

Conferenza Episcopale Maltese, Archbishop's Curia, Floriana; tel. 21234317; fax 21223307; e-mail info@maltadiocese.org.mt; internet www.maltadiocese.org.

f. 1971; Pres. Most Rev. PAUL CREMONA (Archbishop of Malta).

Archbishop of Malta: Most Rev. PAUL CREMONA, Archbishop's Curia, Floriana; POB 29, Valletta; tel. 21235350; fax 21223307; e-mail info@maltadiocese.org.mt.

Bishop of Gozo: Rt Rev. MARIO GRECH, Chancery Office, POB 1, Republic St, Victoria VCT 1013, Gozo; tel. 21556661; fax 21551278; e-mail gozodiocese@waldonet.net.mt.

The Anglican Communion

Malta forms part of the diocese of Gibraltar in Europe.

Church of England: Pro-Cathedral of St Paul, Independence Sq., Valletta VLT 1520; tel. 21225714; fax 21225867; e-mail anglican@onvol.net; internet www.anglicanmalta.org; Bishop of Gibraltar in Europe Rt Rev. Dr GEOFFREY ROWELL (resident in England); Suffragan Bishop Rt Rev. DAVID HAMID (resident in England); Senior Chaplain and Chancellor of the Pro-Cathedral Rev. Canon TOM MENDEL.

Other Christian Churches

In 2004 there were approximately 680 Jehovah's Witnesses and 148 members of the Church of Jesus Christ of Latter-day Saints (Mormons). The Bible Baptist Church had 30 members and the Fellowship of Evangelical Churches had about 100 affiliates.

OTHER RELIGIONS

There is one Muslim mosque and a Muslim primary school. There are an estimated 3,000 Muslims in the country. There is one Jewish congregation. Zen Buddhism and the Bahá'í Faith have about 30 members each.

The Press

DAILY NEWSPAPERS

The Malta Independent: Standard House, Birkirkara Hill, St Julian's STJ 1149; tel. 21345888; fax 21344860; e-mail tmid@independent.com.mt; internet www.independent.com.mt; English; Editor STEPHEN CALLEJA.

In-Nazzjon (The Nation): Herbert Ganado St, POB 37, Pietà PTA 1450; tel. 21243641; fax 21242886; e-mail news@media.link.com.mt; internet www.media.link.com.mt; f. 1970; Maltese; publ. by Media.link Communications; Editor JOHN ZAMMIT; circ. 20,000.

L-Orizzont (The Horizon): Union Print Co, A-41 Industrial Estate, Valletta Rd, Marsa MRS 3000; tel. 21244557; fax 21238484; e-mail info@unionprint.com.mt; internet www.l-orizzont.com; f. 1962; Maltese; Editor FRANS GHIRXI; circ. 25,000.

The Times: Allied Newspapers Ltd, 341 St Paul St, Valletta VLT 1211; tel. 25594100; fax 25594116; e-mail daily@timesofmalta.com; internet www.timesofmalta.com; f. 1935; English; Editor RAY BUGEJA; circ. 23,000.

MALTA

WEEKLY NEWSPAPERS

Business Today: Vjal ir-Rihan, San Ġwann SGN 9020; tel. 21382741; fax 21385075; internet www.businesstoday.com.mt; Wednesdays; Editor MATTHEW VELLA.

Il-Gens (The People): Media Centre, National Rd, Blata il-Bajda HMR 9010; tel. 25699119; fax 25699123; e-mail gens@mediacentre.org.mt; internet www.mediacentre.org.mt; f. 1988; Maltese; Editor NICHOLAS BALDACCHINO; circ. 13,000.

Kulhadd: Centru Nazzjonali Laburista, Mile End Rd, Hamrun HMR 1717; tel. 21235313; fax 21240717; e-mail kulhadd@keyworld.net; f. 1993; Maltese; Editor FELIX AGIUS.

Lehen is-Sewwa: Catholic Institute, Floriana FLN 1600; tel. and fax 21225847; e-mail lehenissewwa@vol.net.mt; f. 1928; Roman Catholic; Editor Rev. Fr JOHN CIARLÓ; circ. 10,000.

The Malta Business Weekly: Standard House, Birkirkara Hill, St Julian's STJ 1149; tel. 21345888; fax 21344860; e-mail tmbw@independent.com.mt; internet www.maltabusinessweekly.com; f. 1994; English; Editor CHRISTOPHER SULTANA.

The Malta Independent on Sunday: Standard House, Birkirkara Hill, St Julian's STJ 1149; tel. 21345888; fax 21344884; e-mail amanduca@independent.com.mt; internet www.independent.com.mt; English; Editor NOEL GRIMA.

Malta Today: Vjal ir-Rihan, San Ġwann SGN 9020; tel. 21382741; fax 21385075; e-mail maltatoday@mediatoday.com.mt; internet www.maltatoday.com.mt; Sundays; English; Editor SAVIOUR BALZAN.

Il-Mument (The Moment): Herbert Ganado St, POB 37, Pietà PTA 1450; tel. 21243641; fax 21240839; e-mail nazzjon@mbox.vol.net.mt; f. 1972; Maltese; Editor VICTOR CAMILLERI; circ. 25,000.

The Sunday Times: Allied Newspapers Ltd, POB 328, Valletta VLT 1211; tel. 25594500; fax 25594510; e-mail sunday@timesofmalta.com; internet www.timesofmalta.com; f. 1922; English; Editor STEVE MALLIA; circ. 40,000.

It-Torca (The Torch): Union Press, A 41, Marsa Industrial Estate, Marsa MRS 3000; tel. 21244557; fax 21238484; e-mail info@unionprint.com.mt; internet www.it-torca.com; f. 1944; Maltese; Editor ALFRED BRIFFA; circ. 30,000.

SELECTED PERIODICALS

Commercial Courier: Malta Chamber of Commerce and Enterprise, Exchange Bldgs, Republic St, Valletta VLT 1117; tel. 21247233; fax 21245223; e-mail admin@chamber.org.mt; bi-monthly; Editor KEVIN J. BORG; circ. 1,500.

The Employer: Malta Employers' Asscn, 35/1 South St, Valletta VLT 1100; tel. 21222992; fax 21230227; e-mail admin@maltaemployers.com; internet www.maltaemployers.com; quarterly; Editor JOSEPH FARRUGIA.

Malta Government Gazette: Department of Information, 3 Castille Pl., Valletta VLT 2000; tel. 22001770; fax 22001775; e-mail info.doi@gov.mt; internet www.doi.gov.mt; f. 1813; official notices; Maltese and English; 2 a week; circ. 3,000.

Malta In Figures: National Statistics Office, Lascaris, Valletta VLT 1921; tel. 25997000; fax 25997205; e-mail nso@gov.mt; internet www.nso.gov.mt; official statistics; annual.

Malta This Month: Advantage Advertising Ltd, 118 St John's St, Valletta VLT 1169; tel. 21249924; fax 21249927; e-mail advantage@onvol.net; publ. by Air Malta; monthly; Editor PETER DARMANIN.

The Retailer: Association of General Retailers and Traders, Exchange Bldgs, Republic St, Valletta VLT 1117; tel. 21230459; fax 21246925; monthly; Editor VINCENT FARRUGIA.

The Teacher: Teachers' Institute, 213 Republic St, Valletta VLT 1118; tel. 21237815; fax 21244074; e-mail info@mut.org.mt; internet www.mut.org.mt; journal of the Malta Union of Teachers; 2 a year; Editor FRANKLIN BARBARA.

Xpress: 149 Archbishop St, Valletta VLT 1442; tel. 21240334; fax 21224745; publ. of the Alternattiva Demokratika; Maltese; monthly; Editor NEIL SPITERI.

Publishers

Malta University Publishers Ltd: Old University Building, St. Paul's St, Valletta VLT1216; tel. 21224067; fax 21248218; e-mail mupl@mus.com.mt; internet www.mus.com.mt; f. 1953; owned by University of Malta; Maltese folklore, history, law, bibliography and language; Admin. Officer TITA BONNICI.

Mireva: Triq Mons Carmelo Zammit St, Msida MSD 06; tel. 21312616; fax 21319311; e-mail info@mireva.com; internet www.mireva.com; academic, fiction.

Publishers Enterprises Group (PEG) Ltd: PEG Bldg, UB7 Industrial Estate, San Gwann SGN 3000; tel. 21440083; fax 21488908; e-mail contact@peg.com.mt; internet www.peg.com.mt; f. 1983; educational, children's, cookery, technical, tourism, leisure; Man. Dir EMANUEL DEBATTISTA.

Broadcasting and Communications

TELECOMMUNICATIONS

Regulatory Authority

Malta Communications Authority (MCA): Pinto Wharf, Valletta Waterfront, Valletta VLT 01; tel. 21336840; fax 21336846; e-mail info@mca.org.mt; internet www.mca.org.mt; national agency responsible for regulating telecommunications; f. 2001; Chair. and Dir-Gen. JOSEPH V. TABONE.

Service Providers

GO: Spencer Hill, POB 40, Marsa MRS 1001; tel. 21210210; fax 25945895; e-mail info@go.com.mt; internet www.go.com.mt; f. 1975; fmrly Maltacom PLC; rebranded June 2007; operates all telecommunications services; 60% owned by TECOM Investments and the Dubai Investment Group, both mems of Dubai Holding; Chair. SONNY PORTELLI; CEO DAVID KAY.

GO Mobile: Fra Diego St, Marsa MRS 1501; tel. 21246200; fax 21234314; mobile cellular subsidiary; CEO Prof. JUANITO CAMILLERI.

BROADCASTING

Regulatory Authority

Broadcasting Authority, Malta: 7 Mile End Rd, Hamrun HMR 1719; tel. 21247908; fax 21240855; e-mail info@ba-malta.org; internet www.ba-malta.org; f. 1961; statutory body responsible for the supervision and regulation of radio and television broadcasting; Chair. JOSEPH SCICLUNA; CEO Dr KEVIN AQUILINA.

Radio and Television

Bay Radio: St George's Bay, St Julian's STJ 3390; tel. 21373813; fax 21376113; e-mail 897@bay.com.mt; internet www.bay.com.mt; Station Man. TERRY FARRUGIA.

Campus FM: Old Humanities Bldg, University of Malta, Msida MSD 06; tel. 21333313; fax 21314485; e-mail campusfm@um.edu.mt; internet www.campusfm.um.edu.mt; Man. VICKY SPITERI.

Capital Radio: Media Co-op Ltd, 87 Ursula St, Valletta VLT 1234; tel. 21233078; fax 21239701; e-mail cadmin@capitalradio.com.mt; internet www.capitalradio.com.mt; Station Man. JOHN MALLIA.

Island Sound Radio: 46 Robert Samut Sq., Floriana FRN 1200; tel. 21249141; fax 21249785; News Co-ordinator BERNIE LYNCH.

Media.link Communications Co Ltd: Dar Centrali, Herbert Ganado St, Pietà PTA 1450; tel. 21243641; fax 21243640; e-mail antona@vol.net.mt; internet www.media.link.com.mt.

Net TV: Dar Centrali, Herbert Ganado St, Pietà PTA 1450; tel. 21243641; fax 21226645; CEO ANTON ATTARD.

Radio 101: Independence Point, Herbert Ganado St, Pietà PTA 1450; tel. 21241164; fax 21564111; e-mail news@media.link.com.mt; internet www.radio101.com.mt; Head of News PIERRE PORTELLI.

Melita Cable PLC: Gason Centre, Mrichel Bypass, Mrichel BKR 3000; tel. 21490006; fax 22745050; e-mail admin@melitacable.com; internet www.melitacable.com; CEO JOSEPH R. AQUILINA.

Multi Media Education and Broadcasting Centre: Maria Regina School, Mile End Rd, Hamrun HMR 1715; tel. 21239274; fax 21240701; operates television channel Education 22.

One Productions Ltd: A28B, Industrial Estate, Marsa MRS 3000; tel. 25682568; fax 25688249; e-mail onenews@one.com.mt; internet www.one.com.mt; f. 1999; owned by Malta Labour Party; Man. Dir Dr MICHAEL VELLA HABER.

Super One Radio: A28B, Industrial Estate, Marsa MRS 3000; tel. 2568 2600; fax 21231472; e-mail ray.azzopardi@one.com.mt; broadcasts 24 hours daily.

One Television: A28B Industrial Estate, Marsa MRS 3000; tel. 25682568; fax 21231472; e-mail ruth.vella@one.com.mt; broadcasts 126 hours weekly; CEO RENALD DALLI.

Public Broadcasting Services Ltd: 75 St Luke's Rd, Gwardamangia PTA 1025; tel. 21225051; fax 21244601; e-mail info@pbs.com.mt; internet www.pbs.com.mt; f. 1991; govt-owned; operates national radio and television services: Radio 'Radju Malta' and 'Radju Parlament'; Television Malta; Chair. JOE FENECH CONTI; CEO ALBERT DEBONO.

MALTA

Directory

Radio Calypso: Oasis, Mons. P. Pace St, Victoria VCT 111, Gozo; tel. 21563000; fax 21563565; e-mail info@calypso102.com; internet www.calypso102.com; News Editor PIERRE MEYLAK.

Radju MAS: 15 Old Mint St, Valletta VLT 12; tel. 21237755; fax 21247246; Editor Mgr FORTUNATO MIZZI.

RTK Radio: Media Centre, National Rd, Blata il-Bajda HMR 9010; tel. 25699145; fax 25699147; e-mail rtknews@rtk.org.mt; internet www.rtk.org.mt; f. 1992; radio station of the Catholic Church of Malta; Exec. Chair. VICTOR FORMOSA.

Smash TV and Radio: Smash Communications, Thistle Lane, Paola PLA 19; tel. 21697829; fax 21697830; f. 1992; Man. Dir JOSEPH BALDACCHINO.

Finance

(cap. = capital; res = reserves; dep. = deposits; m. = million; brs = branches; amounts in Maltese liri, unless otherwise stated)

BANKING

Central Bank

Central Bank of Malta: Pjazza Kastilja, Valletta VLT 1060; tel. 25500000; fax 25502500; e-mail info@centralbankmalta.com; internet www.centralbankmalta.com; f. 1968; bank of issue; cap. 5m., res 73m., dep. 408m. (Dec. 2006); Gov. MICHAEL C. BONELLO.

Commercial Banks

APS Bank Ltd: APS House, 24 St Anne Sq., Floriana FRN 9020; tel. 25603000; fax 21226202; e-mail headoffice@apsbank.com.mt; internet www.apsbank.com.mt; f. 1910; cap. 7m., res 5m., dep. 232m. (Dec. 2006); Chair. Prof. EMMANUEL P. DELIA; CEO EDWARD CACHIA; 6 brs.

Bank of Valletta PLC: BOV Centre, Cannon Rd. St Venera SVR 9030; tel. 21312020; fax 22753730; e-mail customercare@bov.com; internet www.bov.com; f. 1974; merged with Valletta Investment Bank Ltd in Oct. 2000; cap. 28m., res 11m., dep. 2,093m. (Sept. 2006); Chair. RODERICK CHALMERS; CEO TONIO DEPASQUALE; 46 brs.

Fortis Bank Malta Ltd: 114/5 The Strand, Gżira GZR 03; tel. 21323571; fax 21323576; internet www.fortis.com; fmrly Dişbank Malta Ltd; present name adopted 2005; 99.9% owned by Fortis Holding Malta Limited; Chair. YVAN DE COCK; Gen. Man. VEDAT KORAN.

HSBC Bank Malta PLC: 233 Republic St, Valletta VLT 1116; tel. 25970000; fax 23804923; e-mail infomalta@hsbc.com; internet www.hsbc.com.mt; f. 1975 as Mid-Med Bank; 70.03% owned by HSBC Europe BV; cap. 36m., res 11m., dep. 1,612m. (Dec. 2006); CEO ALAN RICHARDS; 43 brs.

Lombard Bank Malta PLC: Lombard House, 67 Republic St, Valletta VLT 1117; tel. 25581100; fax 25581150; e-mail mail@lombardmalta.com; internet www.lombardmalta.com; f. 1969; cap. 2m., res 7m., dep. 181m. (Dec. 2006); Chair. CHRISTIAN LEMMERICH; Dir and CEO JOSEPH SAID; 6 brs.

Principal 'Offshore' Bank

FIMBank PLC: Plaza Commercial Centre, 7th Floor, Bisazza St, Sliema SLM 1640; tel. 21322100; fax 21322122; e-mail info@fimbank.com; internet www.fimbank.com; f. 1994 as First International Merchant Bank PLC; cap. US $43m., dep. US $369m., total assets US $438m. (Dec. 2006); Chair. NAJEEB H. M. AL SALEH; Pres. MARGRITH LÜTSCHG-EMMENEGGER.

STOCK EXCHANGE

Malta Stock Exchange: Garrison Chapel, Castille Pl., Valletta VLT 1000; tel. 21244051; fax 25696316; e-mail borza@borzamalta.com.mt; internet www.borzamalta.com.mt; f. 1992; Chair. JOSEPH ZAMMIT TABONA.

INSURANCE

Aon Mediterranean Insurance Brokers (Malta) Ltd: 53 Mediterranean Bldg, Abate Rigord St, Ta'Xbiex MSD 12; tel. 23433234; fax 21341597; e-mail info@aon.com.mt; internet www.aon.com.mt; f. 1976; Man. Dir JOSEPH CUTAJAR.

Middle Sea Insurance PLC: Middle Sea House, Floriana FRN1442; tel. 21246262; fax 21248195; e-mail middlesea@middlesea.com; internet www.middlesea.com; f. 1981; Chair. MARIO C. GRECH; CEO JOSEPH M. RIZZO.

Numerous foreign insurance companies, principally British, Canadian and Italian, are represented in Malta by local agents.

Insurance Association

Malta Insurance Association: 43A/2, St Paul's Bldgs, West St, Valletta VLT 1532; tel. 21232640; fax 21248388; e-mail mia@maltainsurance.org; internet www.maltainsurance.org; Dir-Gen. Dr ANTON FELICE.

Trade and Industry

GOVERNMENT AGENCIES

Malta Enterprise: Enterprise Centre, Industrial Estate, San Gwann SGN 3000; tel. 25420000; fax 25423401; e-mail info@maltaenterprise.com; internet www.maltaenterprise.com; f. 2003 by merger of Malta External Trade Corpn Ltd (METCO), Malta Development Corpn (MDC) and Institute for the Promotion of Small Enterprise (IPSE); national agency for the promotion of inward investment, external trade and the support of enterprises; Chair. Dr ALEC MIZZI.

Malta Financial Services Authority: Notabile Rd, Attard BKR 14; tel. 21441155; fax 21441188; e-mail communications@mfsa.com.mt; internet www.mfsa.com.mt; f. 1994; supervises the financial services sector, incl. banking, insurance and investments; regulates activities of Malta Stock Exchange; houses Malta's Companies Registry; Chair. Prof. JOSEPH V. BANNISTER; COO JOSEPH DEMANUELE.

Malta Investment Management Co Ltd (MIMCOL): Trade Centre, San Gwann Industrial Estate, San Gwann SGN 3000; tel. 21497970; fax 21499568; e-mail info@mimcol.com; internet www.mimcol.com; f. 1988; manages govt investments in domestic commercial enterprises and encourages their transfer to private-sector ownership; Chair. IVAN FALZON.

CHAMBER OF COMMERCE

Malta Chamber of Commerce and Enterprise: Exchange Bldgs, Republic St, Valletta VLT 1117; tel. 21233873; fax 21245223; e-mail admin@chamber.org.mt; internet www.chamber.org.mt; f. 1848; Pres. TANCRED TABONE; 900 mems.

EMPLOYERS' ORGANIZATIONS

Malta Employers' Association: 35/1 South St, Valletta VLT 1100; tel. 21222992; fax 21230227; e-mail admin@maltaemployers.com; internet www.maltaemployers.com; f. 1965; Pres. PIERRE FAVA; Dir-Gen. JOSEPH FARRUGIA.

Malta Federation of Industry: Casa Leone, Robert Samut Sq., Floriana FRN 1200; tel. 21234428; fax 21240702; e-mail info@foi.org.mt; internet www.foi.org.mt; f. 1946; 300 corporate mems; Pres. MARTIN GALEA; Dir-Gen. RAY MUSCAT.

UTILITIES

Electricity and Gas

Enemalta Corporation: Church Wharf, Marsa HMR 01; POB 6, Hamrun HMR 01; tel. 21223601; fax 21243055; e-mail info.emc@enemalta.com.mt; internet www.enemalta.com.mt; f. 1977; state energy corpn; purchases and distributes petroleum products and operates two petroleum-fired power stations for electricity generation; distributes electricity, petroleum products and LPG; Chair. ALEXANDER J. TRANTER; CEO DAVID SPITERI GINGELL.

Water

Water Services Corporation: Qormi Rd, Luqa LQA 9043; tel. 22445566; fax 22443900; e-mail customercare@wsc.com.mt; internet www.wsc.com.mt; f. 1992; govt corpn responsible for the production and distribution of drinking water and the local sewerage system; Chair. MICHAEL FALZON; CEO MARC MUSCAT.

TRADE UNIONS

Confederation of Malta Trade Unions (CMTU): 9C Mikiel Anton Vassalli St, Valletta VLT 1310; tel. 21237313; fax 21250146; e-mail info@cmtu.org.mt; internet www.cmtu.org.mt; f. 1958; affiliated to the World Confed. of Labour, to the Commonwealth Trade Union Council and to the European Trade Union Confed; Pres. WILLIAM PORTELLI; Gen. Sec. ANTHONY MICALLEF DEBONO; 28,000 mems.

The principal affiliated unions include:

General Retailers & Traders Union (GRTU) (Asscn of General Retailers and Traders): Exchange Bldgs, Republic St, Valletta VLT 1117; tel. 21230459; fax 21246925; e-mail info@grtu.org.mt; internet www.targetltd.com/grtu; f. 1948; Pres. PAUL ABELA; Dir-Gen. VINCE FARRUGIA; 6,400 mems.

Malta Union of Teachers: Teachers' Institute, 213 Republic St, Valletta VLT 1118; tel. 21237815; fax 21244074; e-mail info@mut

.org.mt; internet www.mut.org.mt; f. 1919; Pres. JOHN BENCINI; Gen. Sec. FRANKLIN BARBARA; 6,074 mems.

Union Haddiema Maghqudin (UHM): 'Dar Reggie Miller', 69 St Thomas St, Floriana FLN 1123; tel. 21220847; fax 21246091; e-mail info@uhm.org.mt; internet www.uhm.org.mt; f. 1966; Pres. GAETANO TANTI; Sec.-Gen. GETJU VELLA; 25,793 mems.

The General Workers' Union (GWU): Workers' Memorial Bldg, South St, Valletta VLT 11; tel. 21244451; e-mail info@gwu.org.mt; internet www.gwu.org.mt; f. 1943; affiliated to the Int. Trade Union Confed. and to the European Trade Union Confed; Pres. VICTOR CARACHI; Gen. Sec. TONY ZARB; 48,758 mems.

Transport

REGULATORY BODIES

Malta Transport Authority: Sa Maison Rd, Floriana FRN 1613; tel. 25608000; fax 21255740; e-mail info@maltatransport.com; internet www.maltatransport.com; regulatory body for all land transport in Malta; Chair. JOSEPH GERADA.

Public Transport Directorate: Sa Maison Rd, Floriana FRN 1613; tel. 21255165; fax 21255175; e-mail pta@maltanet.net; internet www.maltatransport.com; f. 1989; regulatory body for public transport in Malta.

RAILWAYS

There are no railways in Malta.

ROADS

In 2004 there were 2,254 km of roads, of which 185 km were highways and 2,069 km were secondary roads. About 87.5% of roads are paved. Bus services serve all parts of the main island and most parts of Gozo.

Roads Department: Cannon Rd, St Venera SVR 9030; tel. 21483609; fax 21243753; e-mail carmel.zammit@magnet.mt; Chair. C. DEMICOLI; CEO M. FALZON.

SHIPPING

Malta's national shipping register is open to ships of all countries. At 31 December 2006 Malta's merchant fleet comprised 1,294 vessels, with a total displacement of 24,849,818 grt. The island's dry dock facilities are also an important source of revenue.

Malta Maritime Authority: Maritime Trade Centre, Triq l-Ghassara ta' l-Gheneb, Marsa MRS 1912; tel. 21222203; fax 21250365; e-mail info@mma.gov.mt; internet www.mma.gov.mt; f. 1991; govt agency supervising the administration and operation of ports and yachting centres, and of vessel registrations under the Maltese flag; Chair. Dr MARC BONELLO.

Bianchi & Co (1916) Ltd: Palazzo Marina, 143 St Christopher St, Valletta VLT 1465; tel. 21232241; fax 21232991; e-mail info@bianchi.com.mt; Man. Dir R. BIANCHI.

Cassar & Cooper Ltd: Valletta Bldgs, 54 South St, POB 311, Valletta VLT 11; tel. 25584000; fax 21237864; e-mail info@cassar-cooper.com; internet www.cassar-cooper.com; Dir MICHAEL COOPER.

O. F. Gollcher & Sons Ltd: 19 Saint Zachary St, POB 268, Valletta VLT 1133; tel. 25691100; fax 21234195; e-mail contact@gollcher.com; internet www.gollcher.com; f. 1854; Dir MARK GOLLCHER.

Malta Freeport Terminals Ltd: Freeport Centre, Port of Marsaxlokk, Kalafrana BBG 3011; tel. 21650200; fax 22251900; e-mail marketing@maltafreeport.com.mt; internet www.maltafreeport.com.mt; f. 1988; two container terminals and distribution centre; also operates petroleum products terminal and general warehousing facilities; Man. Dir UWE MALEZKI.

Malta Motorways of the Sea Ltd: 21–22 St Barbara Bastion, Valletta VLT 1961; tel. 21251564; fax 21226876; e-mail info@mmos.com.mt; internet www.mmos.com.mt; f. 2005; owned by Grimaldi Group (Italy); operates roll-on/roll-off and passenger ferry services between Malta, Italy (including Sicily) and Tunisia; Man. Dir ERNEST SULLIVAN; Gen. Man. JOE BUGEJA.

Medserv Ltd: Malta Freeport, Port of Marsaxlokk, Birzebbugia BBG 3011; tel. 22202302; fax 22202328; e-mail info@medservmalta.com; internet www.medservmalta.com; logistic and supply base for petroleum and gas extraction industry; Dirs ANTHONY S. DIACONO, ANTHONY J. DUNCAN.

Mifsud Brothers Ltd: 27 South St, Valletta VLT 11; tel. 21232157; fax 21221331; e-mail info@mbl.com.mt; internet www.mbl.com.mt; f. 1860; shipping and travel agents; Man. Dir IVAN MIFSUD.

S. Mifsud & Sons Ltd (SMS): 131 East St, Valletta VLT 06; tel. 21233127; fax 21234180; e-mail ship@sms.com.mt; internet www.sms.com.mt; cargo and ferry services between Malta and Catania, Reggio di Calabria (Italy); Dir Dr SIMON MIFSUD.

Ripard, Larvan & Ripard Ltd: 156 Ta'Xbiex Seafront, Gżira GZR 1020; tel. 21335592; fax 21344615; e-mail info@rlryachting.com; internet www.rlryachting.com; Man. Dir DARIUS GOODWIN.

Sullivan Shipping Agencies Ltd: Exchange Bldgs, Republic St, Valletta VLT 1117; tel. 21245127; fax 21233417; e-mail info@sullivanshipping.com.mt; internet www.sullivanshipping.com.mt; Dir JOHN E. SULLIVAN.

Thomas Smith & Co Ltd: 12 St Christopher St, Valletta VLT 1468; tel. 22058000; fax 22058199; e-mail info@tcsmith.com; internet www.tcsmith.com; Man. Dir JOE GERADA.

Virtu Steamship Co Ltd: 3 Princess Elizabeth Terrace, Ta'Xbiex XBX 1102; tel. 21345220; fax 21314533; f. 1945; ship-owners; ship agents; shipbrokers; Malta–Sicily (Italy) express passenger ferry service; Man. Dir F. A. PORTELLI.

CIVIL AVIATION

Malta International Airport is situated at Gudja (8 km from Valletta).

Air Malta PLC: Vjal l'Avjazzjoni, Luqa LQA 9023; tel. 21690890; fax 21692861; e-mail info@airmalta.com.mt; internet www.airmalta.com; f. 1973; national airline with a 96.4% state shareholding; scheduled passenger and cargo services to mainland Europe, the United Kingdom, Sicily (Italy), North Africa and the Middle East; charter services to the United Kingdom and mainland Europe; Chair. LAWRENCE ZAMMIT; CEO JOE CAPPELLO.

Tourism

Malta offers climatic, scenic and historical attractions, including fine beaches. Tourism forms a major sector of Malta's economy, generating foreign-exchange earnings of US $923m. in 2005; tourist arrivals totalled 1,170,610 in that year.

Malta Tourism Authority (MTA): Auberge d'Italie, Merchants St, Valletta VLT 2000; tel. 22915000; fax 22915893; e-mail info@visitmalta.com; internet www.mta.com.mt; Chair. SAM MIFSUD; CEO (vacant).

THE MARSHALL ISLANDS

Introductory Survey

Location, Climate, Language, Religion, Flag, Capital

The Republic of the Marshall Islands consists of two groups of islands, the Ratak ('sunrise') and Ralik ('sunset') chains, comprising 29 atolls (some 1,225 islets) and five islands, and covering about 180 sq km (70 sq miles) of land. The territory lies within the area of the Pacific Ocean known as Micronesia (which includes Kiribati, Tuvalu and other territories). The islands lie about 3,200 km (2,000 miles) south-west of Hawaii and about 2,100 km (1,300 miles) south-east of Guam. Rainfall decreases from south to north, with January, February and March being the driest months, although seasonal variations in rainfall and temperature are generally small. The native population comprises various ethno-linguistic groups, but English is widely understood. The principal religion is Christianity. The national flag (proportions 100 by 190) is dark blue, with a representation of a white star (with 20 short and four long rays) in the upper hoist; superimposed across the field are two progressively-wider stripes (orange above white), running from near the lower hoist corner to near the upper fly corner. The capital is the Dalap-Uliga-Darrit Municipality, on Majuro Atoll.

Recent History

The first European contact with the Marshall and Caroline Islands was by Spanish expeditions in the 16th century, including those led by Alvaro de Saavedra and Fernão de Magalhães (Ferdinand Magellan), the Portuguese navigator. The islands received their name from the British explorer, John Marshall, who visited them at the end of the 18th century. Spanish sovereignty over the Marshall Islands was recognized in 1886 by the Papal Bull of Pope Leo XIII, which also gave Germany trading rights there (German trading companies had been active in the islands from the 1850s). In 1899 Germany bought from Spain the Caroline Islands and the Northern Mariana Islands (except Guam, which had been ceded to the USA after the Spanish–American War of 1898). In 1914, at the beginning of the First World War, Japan occupied the islands, and received a mandate for its administration from the League of Nations in 1920. After the capture of the islands by US military forces in 1944 and 1945, most of the Japanese settlers were repatriated, and in 1947 the UN established the Trust Territory of the Pacific Islands (comprising the Caroline Islands, the Marshall Islands and the Northern Mariana Islands), to allow the USA to administer the region. The territory was governed by the US Navy from 1947 until 1951, when control passed to a civil administration—although the Northern Mariana Islands remained under military control until 1962.

From 1965 onwards there were increasing demands for local autonomy. In that year the Congress of Micronesia was formed; in 1967 a commission was established to examine the future political status of the islands. In 1970 it declared Micronesians' rights to sovereignty over their own lands, of self-determination, to their own constitution and to revoke any form of free association with the USA. In 1977, after eight years of negotiations, US President Jimmy Carter announced that his Administration intended to adopt measures to terminate the trusteeship agreement by 1981.

On 9 January 1978 the Marianas District achieved separate status as the Commonwealth of the Northern Mariana Islands (q.v.), but remained legally a part of the Trusteeship until 1986. The Marshall Islands District drafted its own Constitution, which came into effect on 1 May 1979, and the four districts of Yap, Truk (now Chuuk), Ponape (now Pohnpei) and Kosrae ratified a new Constitution, to become the Federated States of Micronesia (q.v.), on 10 May 1979. In the Palau District a referendum in July 1979 approved a proposed local constitution, which came into effect on 1 January 1981, when the district became the Republic of Palau (q.v.).

The USA signed a Compact of Free Association with the Republic of Palau in August 1982, and with the Marshall Islands and the Federated States of Micronesia in October of that year. The trusteeship of the islands was due to end after the principle and terms of the Compacts had been approved by the respective peoples and legislatures of the new countries, by the US Congress and by the UN Security Council. Under the Compacts, the four countries (including the Northern Mariana Islands) would be independent of each other and would manage their internal and foreign affairs separately, while the USA would be responsible for defence and security. Moreover, Marshallese citizens were granted the right to live and work in the USA. The Compacts with the Federated States of Micronesia and the Marshall Islands were approved in plebiscites in June and September 1983, respectively. The Congress of the Federated States of Micronesia ratified the country's decision in September. Under the Compact with the Marshall Islands, the USA was to retain its military bases in the Marshall Islands for at least 15 years and, over the same period, was to provide annual aid of US $30m.

The Compact between the Marshall Islands and the USA came into effect on 21 October 1986, following its approval by the islands' Government. In November President Ronald Reagan issued a proclamation formally ending US administration of Micronesia. The first President of the Republic of the Marshall Islands was Iroijlaplap (paramount chief) Amata Kabua, who was re-elected in 1984, 1988, 1992 and 1995. In December 1990 the UN Security Council finally ratified the termination of the trusteeship agreement; the Marshall Islands became a member of the UN in 1991. Prior to their scheduled expiry in 2001, the terms of Compact were extended for a further two-year period, pending negotiation of new arrangements (see below).

The Marshall Islands' atolls of Bikini and Enewetak were used by the USA for experiments with nuclear weapons: Bikini in 1946–58 and Enewetak in 1948–58. A total of 67 such tests were carried out during this period. The native inhabitants of Enewetak were evacuated before tests began, and were allowed to return to the atoll in 1980, after much of the contaminated area had supposedly been rendered safe. The inhabitants of Bikini Atoll campaigned for similar treatment, and in 1985 the US Administration agreed to decontaminate Bikini Atoll over a period of 10–15 years. In 1985 the entire population of Rongelap Atoll, which had been engulfed by radioactive fall-out from the tests at Bikini in 1954, was forced to resettle on Mejato Atoll, after surveys suggested that levels of radiation there remained dangerous. In April 2001, following the adoption by the USA of a new standard of radioactivity considered to be acceptable, some six times lower than the previous level, the Tribunal announced that Ailuk Atoll was to be evacuated and environmental studies conducted.

Under the terms of the Compact, the US Government consented to establish a US $150m. Nuclear Claims Fund to settle claims against the USA resulting from nuclear testing in the Marshall Islands during the 1940s and 1950s. Accordingly, the Marshall Islands Nuclear Claims Tribunal was established in 1988, with jurisdiction to 'render final determination upon all claims past, present and future, of the Government, citizens and nationals of the Marshall Islands' in respect of the nuclear testing programme. A compensation programme was implemented in 1991 for personal injuries deemed to have resulted from the testing programme. Following an approach defined in legislation adopted by the US Congress in 1990, which established a 'presumptive' programme of compensation for specified diseases contracted by US civilian and military personnel who had been physically present in what was termed the 'affected area' during periods of atmospheric testing in Nevada, the Marshall Islands Nuclear Claims Tribunal initially identified 25 diseases for which credible evidence demonstrated a significant statistical relationship between exposure to radiation and subsequent development of a disease; in response to the findings of later studies, the Tribunal's list had by 2003 been extended to include 11 further conditions. Compensation awards totalling $83m. had by the end of 2003 been made to, or on behalf of, 1,865 individuals who had contracted one or more of these conditions. Additionally, an award of some $578m. had been ordered in May 2000 in respect of a class action brought by the people of Enewetak for loss of and damage to property; and an award of $563m. had been made in March 2002 in settlement of a class action brought by the peoples of Bikini Atoll; settlements of similar class actions by the peoples of Rongelap and Utrik Atolls were being finalized, while a new class action had been submitted by the people of Ailuk Atoll. However, only $45.8m. had been made available for actual payment of awards decided by the Tribunal; furthermore, less than $6m. remained of the original value of the Fund. In view of the inadequacy of the Fund to meet the compensation awards made by the Tribunal, in September 2000 the Marshall Islands Government formally petitioned the US Congress for a renegotiation of the settlement agreed under the Compact; the basis of the petition, which sought additional compensation amounting to some $3,000m., was an article of the agreement providing for what were termed 'Changed Circumstances'. In early August 2004 the Tribunal declared a deadline for islanders' compensation claims of the end of that month (subsequently extended to 31 December). The reason given for the deadline was that the Tribunal's funds had diminished to some $5m., a level that not only jeopardized future compensation payments but also the very existence of the Tribunal itself. In January 2005, following the publication of a report by the US State Department's Bureau of East Asian and Pacific Affairs, the Bush Administration recommended that Congress reject the Marshall Islands' request for additional compensation payments, citing a lack of a scientific or legal basis for the request. In late February delegates from Bikini, Rongelap, Enewetak and Utrik met in Seattle, Washington, with officials of the US Senate Committee on Energy and Natural Resources in preparation for a congressional hearing on the Marshall Islands' request for additional payments. At the hearing, held in May, the Bush Administration's rejection of the appeal was reiterated, although several committee members expressed support for further consideration of the matter. At a Small Islands Summit meeting held in October in the Papua New Guinean capital of Port Moresby, the Marshall Islands' delegation demanded a further $3,000m. in compensation from the US Government. In April 2006 it was announced that the people of Bikini were suing the US Government in the Court of Federal Claims for $561m. as compensation or damages: the original award of $563m. minus the actual payment of $2.3m. The Marshall Islands Government expressed its support for the action. In April 2007 the Marshall Islands Nuclear Claims Tribunal ruled that claimants at Rongelap should receive $1,000m. in compensation; at the same time, however, the funds available to the Tribunal had decreased to $1m. In September the US Senate was examining a request for additional compensation for inhabitants of Bikini, Rongelap, Enewetak and Utrik.

In January 1994, meanwhile, several senior members of the Marshall Islands' legislature, the Nitijela, demanded that the US authorities release detailed information on the effects of its nuclear-testing programme in the islands. In July documentation released by the US Department of Energy gave conclusive evidence that Marshall Islanders had been deliberately exposed to high levels of radiation in order that its effects on their health could be studied by US medical researchers. Further evidence emerged during 1995 that the USA had withheld the medical records of islanders involved in radiation experiments (which included tritium and chromium-51 injections and genetic and bone-marrow transplant experiments).

Despite the publication of a study conducted by US scientists (in 1992) into contamination levels on Bikini atoll, which suggested that radiation levels there remained dangerous, in February 1997 a group of Bikini Islanders returned for the first time since 1946 to assist in the rehabilitation of the atoll for resettlement. The operation was to involve the removal of radioactive topsoil (although the matter of its disposal presented a serious problem) and the saturation of the remaining soil with potassium, which was believed to inhibit the absorption of radioactive material by root crops. In early 1999 the Nuclear Claims Tribunal demanded the adoption of US Environmental Protection Agency standards in the rehabilitation of contaminated islands, claiming that Marshall Islanders deserved to receive the same treatment as US citizens would in similar circumstances. The US Department of Energy, however, expressed strong resistance to the suggestion. In February 2001 a report published by an eminent Japanese scientist stated that radiation levels on Rongelap Island, according to research conducted in 1999, had now declined to such a level that human habitation of the island was again possible. In early 2004 the Marshall Islands protested that a reduction, decided upon by the US Department of Energy without consultation with Island representatives, of some US $740,000 in congressional funding allocated to nuclear test-related studies would result in the closure of a centre on Bikini Atoll used to support scientific studies at the former test site.

Another atoll in the Marshall Islands, Kwajalein, has been used since 1947 as a target for the testing of missiles fired from California, USA. The Compact as ratified in 1986 committed the US Government to provide an estimated US $170m. in rent over a period of 30 years for land used as the site of a missile-tracking station, and a further $80m. for development projects. The inhabitants of Kwajalein Atoll were concentrated on the small island of Ebeye, adjacent to the US base on Kwajalein Island, before a new programme of weapons-testing began in 1961. Consequent overcrowding reportedly led to numerous social problems on Ebeye. In 1989 the Marshall Islands Government agreed that the USA could lease a further four islands in the atoll, for five years, for the purpose of military tests. A further lease agreement was signed in 1995 for the use of Biken Island (in Aur Atoll) and Wake Island in the missile-testing programme. The issue of the Kwajalein lease proved to be one of the most controversial aspects of the renegotiated terms of the Compact, as signed in 2003 (see below). In January 2003 it was announced that the Marshall Islands Government and the USA had reached agreement on new terms extending the lease of the Kwajalein site, previously scheduled to end in 2016, until 2066 (with the USA retaining the right to extend the lease by a further 20 years). The renegotiated terms envisaged that payments for use of the site would be increased from $13.5m. annually to $16.9m. (including continued provision of $1.9m. annually in social funding for the residents of Ebeye), with a further increase, to more than $19.9m. per year, to enter into effect from 2014. However, Kwajalein landowners, who deemed the new terms unacceptable, asserted that the new arrangement was invalid, since they had not consented, as constitutionally required, to its terms. In mid-2007 the landowners had yet to accept the terms of the agreement.

Following the legislative election of November 1995, at which eight incumbent members of the 33-seat Nitijela were defeated, President Kabua was re-elected for a fifth term. Upon his death in December 1996, Iroijlaplap Imata Kabua, a cousin of the late President, was elected to succeed him in January 1997.

In 1996 the Nitijela approved legislation allowing for the introduction of gambling in the islands, in order to provide an additional source of revenue. However, income earned from the venture did not fulfil expectations. Moreover, a vociferous campaign by local church leaders to revoke the legislation led to fierce debate in the Nitijela in early 1998. Divisions within the Cabinet ensued, with three members supporting the President's pro-gambling stance and four others opposing. In April the Nitijela voted to repeal the law legalizing gambling: several influential politicians (including Imata Kabua) known to have major gambling interests were disqualified from voting. A second bill containing further measures to ensure the prohibition of all gambling activity in the islands was narrowly approved. Three ministers who had supported the anti-gambling legislation were dismissed in a cabinet reorganization in August. In the following month one of the dismissed ministers proposed a motion of 'no confidence' in Kabua. The President and his supporters boycotted subsequent sessions of the Nitijela, thereby rendering the legislature inquorate and effectively precluding the vote, as well as delaying the approval of the budget for the impending financial year. Despite opposition claims that Kabua's continued absence from the Nitijela violated the terms of the Constitution, the motion of 'no confidence' in Kabua was eventually defeated by a margin of one vote in October.

At the legislative election of November 1999 the opposition United Democratic Party (UDP) secured a convincing victory over the incumbent administration, winning 18 of the 33 seats in the Nitijela. Five senior members of the outgoing Government were defeated, including the Ministers of Finance and of Foreign Affairs and Trade—both of whom had played a prominent role in the establishment of diplomatic relations with Taiwan in 1998 (see below). The former Nitijela Speaker, Kessai Note, was elected President on 3 January 2000 (the islands' first non-traditional leader to assume the post). The UDP Chairman, Litokwa Tomeing, became Speaker of the legislature. Note subsequently appointed a 10-member Cabinet, and reiterated his administration's intention to pursue anti-corruption policies. In May a task-force was established by the Government for the purposes of investigating misconduct and corruption; it was hoped that the task-force would help to render government more accountable.

In November 2000 it was reported that finance officials had discovered that Imata Kabua had used funds granted to the Marshall Islands under the terms of the Compact of Free Association to pay off a personal loan, although the former President denied any wrongdoing. In mid-January 2001 Imata Kabua and former ministers in his Government, including the former Minister of Education, Justin DeBrum, presented a 'no confidence' motion against President Note to the Nitijela. Although it was suggested that the vote had been intended to delay the publication of a report into mismanagement and corruption on the part of the former Government, DeBrum stated that the motion resulted from a number of failings by the Note Government, including its unwillingness to renegotiate land rental payments with the USA for the use of the military base on Kwajalein Atoll and also the development of an economic relationship between the Note Government and Rev. Sun Myung Moon, the founder of the Unification Church (known as the 'Moonies'). However, the Government was successful in defeating the vote by a margin of 19 to 14.

In September 2000 the Nitijela approved legislation to ensure the closer regulation of the banking and financial sector. In May of that year the Group of Seven industrialized nations (G-7) had expressed its view that the Marshall Islands had become a significant centre for the 'laundering' of money generated by international criminal activity, and, in June the Marshall Islands was one of more than 30 countries and territories criticized by the Organisation for Economic Co-operation and Development (OECD, see p. 347) for the provision of inappropriate 'offshore' financial establishments. OECD threatened to implement sanctions against 'unco-operative tax havens' unless reforms were introduced before July 2001. The Marshall Islands remained on the OECD's list of unco-operative tax havens until 2007. In October 2002, meanwhile, following a commendation from the IMF on a series of new measures to combat fraud, including specific legislation and the establishment of a Domestic Financial Intelligence Unit, the Financial Action Task Force on Money Laundering (see p. 416) removed the Marshall Islands from its list of countries judged to be unhelpful in the combating of international financial crime.

Negotiations began between the US and Marshall Islands Governments in July 2001 to renew the provisions of the Compact of Free Association ratified in 1986, which was due to expire at the end of September 2001. A two-year extension was permitted while negotiations were under way, during which time annual assistance to the Marshall Islands was to increase by some US $5.5m. An agreement was originally scheduled for early 2002 in order to allow adequate time for the US Congress to review it and to approve the requisite legislation (by 1 October 2003), but the procedure was postponed until early May 2002 after the Marshall Islands Government submitted a proposal seeking financing of more than $1,000m. over 15 years. The Government had also objected to being allocated 25%–30% less in US grant assistance per caput than that apportioned to the Federated States of Micronesia since the year 2000. In a further attempt to increase the national income, the Government sought to raise significantly the level of taxes levied on the Kwajalein base (see above). In early November 2002 the USA and the Marshall Islands announced a programme of direct funding of $822m., to be disbursed over 20 years, in addition to the expansion of many US government services in the islands. It was envisaged that the Marshall Islands would receive some $30.5m. a year; furthermore, a trust fund would be established, to which the USA would contribute $7m. annually in order to provide a means of income after the termination of direct US assistance in 2023. The amended Compact of Free Association was signed by the Governments of the Marshall Islands and the USA in May 2003. Under the new Compact, Marshall Islanders would for the first time require passports in order to enter the USA. They would, however, retain the right to enter the USA to live, work and study, and would no longer be required to obtain work authorization documentation before taking up employment in the USA. Other than the issue of the Kwajalein lease, a principal obstacle to the negotiation of Compact amendments had been that of immigration: the USA, increasingly preoccupied by issues of homeland security, had been notably concerned to prevent future sales of Marshallese passports (a controversial programme of which had been implemented in the 1990s, although this had officially been suspended in 1997). Final terms, including the restoration of some rights of access to US health care and education programmes, were approved by the US Congress in November 2003, and ratified by President George W. Bush in December.

At a general election held on 17 November 2003 the UDP returned 20 Senators to the 33-member Nitijela. The opposition grouping Ailin Kein Ad (Our Islands), which had campaigned against the terms of the renewed Compact and which received particularly strong support from Marshall Islanders resident in the USA, secured 10 seats (the re-election of the incumbent Ailin Kein Ad Senator for Ailinglaplap Atoll was decided following a recount of votes conducted in late January 2004). Note was re-elected for a second presidential term in a vote held in the Nitijela on 4 January 2004, defeating Justin DeBrum, the candidate of Ailin Kein Ad, by 20 votes to nine. He and his new Cabinet were sworn in on 12 January.

In late March 2005 the Nitijela considered a bill providing for the establishment of a constitutional convention, to be made up of 43 representatives representing every district. Proposals for the direct election of the country's President and for the clear separation of the executive branch of government from the legislature were among the constitutional amendments to be considered. However, in February 2006 a spokesperson for Ailin Kein Ad argued that the establishment of the constitutional convention should be deferred at least until after the next legislative election, scheduled for November 2007. In April 2006, therefore, having failed to secure the requisite parliamentary majority enabling it to proceed with its programme, the ruling UDP announced that its proposals for a constitutional convention were to be submitted to the electorate in a national referendum. Voters were to be asked if they wished a constitutional convention to consider a total of 22 amendments to the country's Constitution. In January 2007 President Note confirmed that the date of the forthcoming referendum would be decided by the Speaker of the Nitijela and the Electoral Commission.

A legislative election was held on 19 November 2007. There were complaints in Majuro, where several polling stations failed to open at the appointed time; irregularities in the counting procedure were subsequently criticized. The level of participation was relatively low, at approximately 50%. According to unofficial results published in December, neither the incumbent UDP nor the opposition Ailin Kein Ad had succeeded in securing the requisite majority of 17 or more seats; both parties contested the results. While the UDP claimed that it should remain in power, Ailin Kein Ad—which had gained former Speaker and UDP leader Litokwa Tomeing as a member prior to the election—maintained that, with the support of independent candidates, its United People's Party coalition would be able to defeat the UDP. Recounts in two constituencies and negotiations between the parties and independent candidates followed. The United People's Party coalition prevailed in January 2008, when the Nitijela elected Tomeing as President by 18 votes (to 15 for the incumbent President Kessai Note), and Jurelang Zedkaia as Speaker by the same margin. Tomeing's new Cabinet included Christopher Loeak in the important position of Minister in Assistance to the President and Tony DeBrum as Minister of Foreign Affairs. In the following month the President formed a commission of inquiry into the organizational failures of the 2007 election.

In 1989 a UN report on the 'greenhouse effect' (heating of the earth's atmosphere) predicted a possible resultant rise in sea-level of some 3.7 m by 2030, which would completely submerge the Marshall Islands. The islands' Government strongly criticized the Australian Government's refusal, at the conference on climate change in Kyoto, Japan, in December 1997, to reduce its emission of pollutant gases known to contribute to the 'greenhouse effect'. Furthermore, in early 2002 the Intergovernmental Panel on Climate Change (IPCC) projected that during the 21st century global sea-level rises would submerge over 80% of Majuro atoll. However, the Marshall Islands Government has itself caused regional concerns regarding pollution, notably with regard to the possible establishment of large-scale facilities for the storage of nuclear waste. Criticism by the US Government of the plans, announced in 1994, was strongly denounced by the Marshall Islands authorities, which claimed that the project constituted the only opportunity for the country to generate sufficient income for the rehabilitation of contaminated islands and the provision of treatment for illnesses caused by the US nuclear-test programme. In mid-1997 President Imata Kabua announced the indefinite suspension of the project (despite the initiation of a feasibility study into the development of a nuclear waste storage facility). None the less, the Government approved plans for a new feasibility study on the subject in April 1998.

THE MARSHALL ISLANDS

Introductory Survey

In November 1998 the Marshall Islands established full diplomatic relations with Taiwan. The action was immediately condemned by the People's Republic of China, which in December severed diplomatic ties with the islands, closing its embassy in Majuro and suspending all intergovernmental agreements. The Marshall Islands Government insisted that it wished to maintain cordial relations with both governments. The Note administration, which took office in January 2000, emphasized its commitment to the maintenance of diplomatic relations with Taiwan. In February 2001 a proposed visit by a flotilla of Taiwanese naval vessels to the Marshall Islands was vetoed by the USA, on the grounds that the defence protocol of the Compact of Free Association prohibited such a visit. In August 2004 the Chinese Vice-Minister of Foreign Affairs, Zhou Wenzhong, expressed his country's willingness to restore normal relations, on condition that the Marshall Islands withdraw its diplomatic recognition of Taiwan. In April 2005 it was alleged that members of the ruling UDP had accepted bribes from Chinese officials hoping to expedite a return to normal diplomatic relations and the end of Marshallese recognition of Taiwan; the Government denied the allegations. Meanwhile, in September 2004 it was announced that Taiwan was to contribute more than US $40m. over a 20-year period to the Marshall Islands trust fund established in May. In June 2006 a delegation of Marshall Islands parliamentary representatives paid a visit to the mainland Chinese capital of Beijing, at the invitation of the National People's Congress, causing consternation among some government officials over the effect on the Marshall Islands' relations with Taiwan, which in April had been bolstered by President Note's third trip to Taipei, where he met Taiwanese President Chen Shui-bian for discussions. The leader of the delegation, Vice-Speaker of the Nitijela Ruben Zackhras, insisted that the Marshall Islands was simply responding to an invitation, while the Ministry of Foreign Affairs reaffirmed the country's commitment to Taiwan. In January 2008 the newly elected President, Litokwa Tomeing, who had previously expressed support for alignment with China, nevertheless confirmed that strong links with Taiwan would continue, and reinforced this position during a visit by the Taiwanese Vice-President, Annette Lu, in late January. The Minister of Foreign Affairs, Tony DeBrum, visited Taiwan in February; his visit was followed by that of President Tomeing in March. In July 2006 the Marshall Islands signed an extradition treaty with the Federated States of Micronesia and Palau, and an agreement on maritime boundaries with the Federated States of Micronesia.

Government

The Constitution of the Republic of the Marshall Islands, which became effective on 1 May 1979, provides for a parliamentary form of government, with legislative authority vested in the 33-member Nitijela. The Nitijela (members of which are elected, by popular vote, for a four-year term) elects the President of the Marshall Islands (also a four-year mandate) from among its own members. Under the terms of the Compact of Free Association, the Republic of the Marshall Islands is a sovereign, self-governing state. The first Compact was signed by the Governments of the Marshall Islands and the USA on 25 June 1983, and was effectively ratified by the US Congress on 14 January 1986. A revised Compact was signed by the Governments of the two countries on 1 May 2003; it was ratified by the US Congress in November 2003, and signed by US President George W. Bush in December of that year. Amendments to the compact were signed in May 2004.

Local governmental units are the municipalities and villages. Elected Magistrates and Councils govern the municipalities. Village government is largely traditional.

Defence

Under the terms of the Compact of Free Association as ratified in 1986 and amended in 2003, the defence of the Marshall Islands is the responsibility of the USA, which maintains a military presence on Kwajalein Atoll.

Economic Affairs

In 2006, according to estimates by the World Bank, the Marshall Islands' gross national income (GNI), measured at average 2004–06 prices, was US $196m., equivalent to $3,000 per head. During 1996–2006, it was estimated, the population increased at an average annual rate of 2.5%; gross domestic product (GDP) per head declined, in real terms, at an average rate of 1.2% per year over the same period. Overall GDP increased, in real terms, at an average annual rate of 1.3% in 1996–2006. According to the Asian Development Bank (ADB), GDP increased by 1.3% in 2005/06 and by 2.0% in 2006/07.

Agriculture is mainly on a subsistence level. The sector (including fishing and livestock-rearing) contributed an estimated 10.0% of GDP in 2006, according to the ADB. According to FAO, the sector engaged 7,000 people (mainly in subsistence fishing) in mid-2005. The principal crops are coconuts, cassava and sweet potatoes. Copra production decreased from 4,908 short tons in 2005 to an estimated 4,646 tons in 2006. In 2004/05 exports of coconut oil and copra accounted for nearly 16% of the total value of exports. The fishing sector incorporates a commercial tuna-fishing industry, including a transhipment base on Majuro. A new tuna-processing plant, employing more than 600 local workers and built by a Chinese company, was scheduled to become fully operational by 2008. The sale of fishing licences is an important source of revenue and earned the islands an estimated US $1.5m. in 2004/05. The GDP of the agricultural sector increased by 0.2% in 2005 and by 10.2% in 2006, according to the ADB.

Industrial activities (including mining, manufacturing, construction and power) engaged 18.9% of the employed labour force in 1999, and contributed an estimated 21.4% of GDP in 2006. Construction and manufacturing employed 10.1% of private-sector wage-earners in 2003/04. Between 1990 and 1999 industrial GDP declined at an average annual rate of 1.5%. The islands have few mineral resources, although there are high-grade phosphate deposits on Ailinglaplap Atoll. The GDP of the industrial sector increased by 0.2% in 2005, before declining by 5.6% in 2006, according to the ADB.

Manufacturing activity, which provided 1.9% of GDP in 2002, consists mainly of the processing of coconuts (to produce copra and coconut oil) and other agricultural products, and of fish (see above). According to the ADB, the manufacturing sector engaged a total of 800 workers in 2000.

The services sector (comprising trade, transport, storage, communications and other activities) engaged 59.8% of the employed labour force in 1999, and provided an estimated 68.6% of GDP in 2006. The international shipping registry experienced considerable expansion following political unrest in Panama in 1989, and subsequently continued to expand (largely as a result of US ships' reflagging in the islands). The number of vessels registered rose from 853 in December 2005 to 953 at the end of the following year. Tourist receipts reached US $4m. in 2002. The number of tourist arrivals rose from 9,007 in 2004 to 9,173 in 2005. According to the ADB, the GDP of the services sector grew by 2.5% in 2005 and by 3.0% in 2006.

In 2004/05 the Marshall Islands recorded an estimated trade deficit of US $69.3m., but a surplus of $0.4m. on the current account of the balance of payments. According to the ADB, there was a current account deficit equivalent to 3.8% of GDP in 2005/06. The only significant domestic exports in 2005 were coconut products. Re-exports of diesel fuel totalled $13.3m., their value greatly exceeding that of domestic exports. The principal imports in 2000 included mineral fuels and lubricants (which accounted for 37.3% of total expenditure on merchandise imports), food and live animals, and machinery and transport equipment. In 2003 the principal sources of imports were the USA (which provided 54.1% of total imports), Australia (13.4%) and Guam (11.3%). In 2000 the USA was also the principal export destination (providing 57.1% of total exports).

Financial assistance from the USA, in accordance with the terms stipulated in the Compact of Free Association, contributes a large part of the islands' revenue. Grants and military payments from the USA for use of the missile-testing site on Kwajalein, along with trust fund contributions, provide most government revenue. The 2005/06 budget provided for expenditure of US $107.3m., while revenue totalled only $36.0m. A budget deficit equivalent to 0.7% of GDP was projected for 2006/07, in comparison with a surplus equivalent to 0.9% in the previous year. The islands' external debt was estimated to have increased from $102m. in 2005/06, when the cost of debt-servicing was estimated to be the equivalent of 32.3% of revenue from the export of goods and services, to $111m. in 2006/07 Annual inflation in Majuro averaged 2.6% in 1995–2005. Consumer prices increased by 4.4% in 2006, and were estimated by the ADB to have risen by 3.4% in 2007. It was reported in early 2007 that some 35% of the work-force were unemployed. The rate of youth unemployment was estimated at 60% in 2006.

The Marshall Islands is a member of the Pacific Community (see p. 377), the Pacific Islands Forum (see p. 380), the South Pacific Regional Trade and Economic Co-operation Agreement

THE MARSHALL ISLANDS

(SPARTECA, see p. 381), the UN Economic and Social Commission for Asia and the Pacific (ESCAP, see p. 35) and the Asian Development Bank (ADB, see p. 182). In 1996 the Marshall Islands and other countries and territories of Micronesia established the Council of Micronesian Government Executives. The new body aimed to facilitate discussion of economic developments in the region, and to examine possibilities for reducing the considerable cost of shipping essential goods between the islands.

The lack of internationally marketable natural resources, the high rate of unemployment, the remote location of the islands and their susceptibility to adverse weather conditions (as demonstrated by the declaration of a drought emergency in the northern Marshall Islands in March 2007) have continued to present major challenges. A notable feature of the amended Compact of Free Association, which was signed by the Governments of the Marshall Islands and the USA in May 2003 (see Recent History), was the planned gradual decrement in grant assistance over the 20-year period of the renewed Compact. Since 1998 the islands have benefited from numerous economic agreements with Taiwan, which has financed many development projects. In September 2003 it was announced that the Taiwanese Government had agreed to make a substantial contribution to the Marshall Islands' government trust fund (see Recent History), which had been established in May with an initial investment of US $25m. and a deposit of $7m. from the USA. Taiwan planned to transfer a total of $1m. to the fund each year until 2009 and thereafter, until 2023, an annual sum of $2.4m. In March 2007, however, the Government's unauthorized withdrawal of $1.7m. from a trust fund account to which Taiwan was making regular contributions aroused renewed concerns with regard to the country's fiscal management. Futhermore, the country's external debt position and its recourse to the postponement of some loan repayments continued to cause concern. The ratio of net debt to GDP was estimated at 75% in 2007. In comparison with the previous year, capital expenditure increased by 45% in 2006/07 to reach US $21.0m., thus permitting a modest economic expansion in GDP; however, the level of government revenue remained well below that of expenditure, with the situation being exacerbated by a high degree of non-compliance in payment of taxes. The ADB forecast that GDP growth would decline to 1.0% in 2008.

Education

Education is compulsory between the ages of six and 14. In 2000/01 a total of 8,530 children attended primary schools in the Marshall Islands with 6,353 enrolled at secondary schools. In 2001/02 enrolment at pre-primary schools included 48% of pupils in the relevant age-group. In 2002/03 enrolment at primary schools included 89.6% of the relevant age-group, and enrolment at secondary schools included 74.4% of pupils. The College of the Marshall Islands (which became independent from the College of Micronesia in 1993) is based on Majuro and had 903 students enrolled in 2000/01. In 1995 the University of the South Pacific opened an extension centre on Majuro. The Fisheries and Nautical Center offers vocational courses for Marshall islanders seeking employment in the fishing industry or on passenger liners, cargo ships and tankers. Government expenditure on education in 2004/05 was US $7.4m., equivalent to 10.6% of total recurrent budgetary spending.

Public Holidays

2008: 1–2 January (New Year), 1 March (Nuclear Victims' Remembrance Day), 21 March (Good Friday), 1 May (Constitution Day), 4 July (Fishermen's Day), 5 September (Dri-Jerbal), 26 September (Manit—Culture Day), 17 November (Presidents' Day), 5 December (Kamolol—Gospel Day), 25 December (Christmas).

2009 (provisional): 1–2 January (New Year), 1 March (Nuclear Victims' Remembrance Day), 10 April (Good Friday), 1 May (Constitution Day), 3 July (Fishermen's Day), 4 September (Dri-Jerbal), 25 September (Manit—Culture Day), November (Presidents' Day), 5 December (Kamolol—Gospel Day), 25 December (Christmas).

Weights and Measures

With certain exceptions, the imperial system is in force. One US cwt equals 100 lb; one long ton equals 2,240 lb; one short ton equals 2,000 lb. A policy of gradual voluntary conversion to the metric system is being undertaken.

Statistical Survey

Source (unless otherwise indicated): Economic Policy, Planning and Statistics Office (EPPSO), Office of the President, POB 7, Majuro, MH 96960; tel. (625) 3802; fax (625) 3805; e-mail planning@ntamar.net; internet www.spc.int/prism/country/mh/stats.

AREA AND POPULATION

Area: 181.4 sq km (70.0 sq miles) (land only); two island groups, the Ratak Chain (88.1 sq km) and the Ralik Chain (93.3 sq km).

Population: 43,380 at census of 13 November 1988; 50,840 (males 26,026, females 24,814) at census of 1 June 1999. *Mid-2006:* 57,400 (Asian Development Bank estimate). *By Island Group* (1999): Ratak Chain 30,925 (Majuro Atoll 23,676); Ralik Chain 19,915 (Kwajalein Atoll 10,902).

Density (mid-2006, land area only): 316.4 per sq km.

Principal Towns (population of urban places, 1999 census): Ebeye 9,345; Darrit (Djarrot) 7,103; Delap 6,339; Rairok 3,846; Laura 2,256; Uliga 2,044. Note: The country's capital is the combined municipality of Delap-Uliga-Darrit.

Births and Deaths (2003): Registered live births 1,565 (birth rate 28.7 per 1,000); Registered deaths 294 (death rate 5.4 per 1,000). Note: Registration is incomplete.

Expectation of Life (years at birth, WHO estimates): 41.9 (males 41.5; females 42.3) in 2005. Source: WHO, *World Health Statistics*.

Economically Active Population (persons aged 15 years and over, 1999 census): Agriculture and fishery 2,114; Manufacturing 761; Electricity, gas and water 258; Construction 848; Wholesale and retail trade 788; Transport, storage and communication 763; Finance, insurance, real estate and business services 559; Community, social and personal services 3,803; Activities not reported 247; *Total employed* 10,141 (males 7,008, females 3,133); Unemployed 4,536 (males 2,671, females 1,865); Total labour force 14,677 (males 9,679, females 4,998). *Mid-2005* (estimates): Agriculture, etc. 7,000; Total labour force 29,000 (Source: FAO).

HEALTH AND WELFARE

Key Indicators

Total Fertility Rate (children per woman, 2005): 4.3.

Under-5 Mortality Rate (per 1,000 live births, 2005): 58.

Physicians (per 1,000 head, 2000): 0.47.

Hospital Beds (per 1,000 head, 1999): 2.07.

Health Expenditure (2004): US $ per head (PPP): 555.2.

Health Expenditure (2004): % of GDP: 15.2.

Health Expenditure (2004): public (% of total): 97.0.

Access to Water (% of persons, 2004): 87.

Access to Sanitation (% of persons, 2004): 82.

For sources and definitions, see explanatory note on p. vi.

AGRICULTURE, ETC.

Principal Crop ('000 metric tons, 2006, FAO estimate): Coconuts 8.0.

Livestock ('000 head, year ending September 2003): Pigs 12.9; Poultry 86.0.

Fishing ('000 metric tons, live weight, 2005): Bigeye tuna 2.5; Skipjack tuna 47.6; Yellowfin tuna 6.1; Total catch (incl. others) 56.7.

Source: FAO.

INDUSTRY

Electric Energy (million kWh, Majuro only): 81.3 in 2003; 81.0 in 2004; 81.2 in 2005. Source: Asian Development Bank, *Key Indicators of Developing Asian and Pacific Countries*.

FINANCE

Currency and Exchange Rates: United States currency is used: 100 cents = 1 United States dollar (US $). *Sterling and Euro Equivalents* (31 December 2007): £1 sterling = US $2.0034; €1 = US $1.4721; US $100 = £49.92 = €67.93.

Budget (US $ million, year ending 30 September 2006, estimates): *Revenue:* Recurrent 36.0 (Tax 25.9, Non-tax 10.1); Grants 71.4; Total 107.5. *Expenditure:* Recurrent 72.1; Capital (incl. net lending) 35.2; Total 107.3. Source: Asian Development Bank, *Key Indicators of Developing Asian and Pacific Countries*.

Cost of Living (Consumer Price Index for Majuro, average of quarterly figures; base: Jan.–March 2003 = 100): All items 103.1 in 2004; 107.7 in 2005; 112.4 in 2006.

Gross Domestic Product (US $ million at constant 2000 prices, World Bank estimates): 124.5 in 2004; 128.9 in 2005; 134.0 in 2006. Source: World Bank, *World Development Indicators*.

Gross Domestic Product by Economic Activity (US $ million at current prices, 2002): Agriculture 15; Mining, manufacturing, electricity, gas and water 5; Construction 10; Trade 19; Transport, storage and communications 7; Other activities 51; *Total* 106. Source: UN, *Statistical Yearbook for Asia and the Pacific*.

Balance of Payments (US $ million, year ending 30 September 2005, estimates): Merchandise exports f.o.b. 16.5; Merchandise imports c.i.f. −85.8; *Trade balance* −69.3; Services (net) −6.9; *Balance on goods and services* −76.2; Other income 35.6; *Balance on goods, services and income* −40.6; Private unrequited transfers (net) −12.6; Official unrequited transfers (net) 53.6; *Current balance* 0.4; Capital and financial account (net) −7.5; Net errors and omissions 1.2; *Overall balance* −5.9. Source: IMF, *Republic of the Marshall Islands: Selected Issues and Statistical Appendix* (March 2006).

EXTERNAL TRADE

Principal Commodities (US $ million, 2000, estimates): *Imports:* Food and live animals 5.0; Beverages and tobacco 6.0; Crude materials, inedible, except fuels 2.6; Mineral fuels, lubricants and related materials 20.4; Animal and vegetable oils and fats 2.4; Chemicals 0.1; Basic manufactures 3.0; Machinery and transport equipment 8.2; Miscellaneous manufactured articles 1.4; Goods not classified by kind 5.8; Total 54.7. *Exports* (year ending September 2005): Coconut oil (crude) 2.5; Copra cake 0.1; Total (incl. others) 16.4. Sources: Asian Development Bank, *Key Indicators of Developing Asian and Pacific Countries* and IMF, *Republic of the Marshall Islands: Selected Issues and Statistical Appendix* (March 2006).

Principal Trading Partners (US $ million): *Imports* (2003): Australia 10.1; Guam 8.5; Hong Kong 2.5; Japan 3.7; New Zealand 2.5; USA 40.7; Total (incl. others) 75.2. *Exports* (2000, estimates): USA 5.2; Total (incl. others) 9.1.

TRANSPORT

Road Traffic (vehicles registered, 1999): Trucks 64; Pick-ups 587; Sedans 1,404; Jeeps 79; Buses 75; Vans 66; Scooters 47; Other motor vehicles 253.

Shipping: *Merchant Fleet* (at 31 December 2006): Vessels 953; Displacement ('000 grt) 32,840.5 (Source: Lloyd's Register-Fairplay, *World Fleet Statistics*). *International Sea-borne Freight Traffic* (estimates, '000 metric tons, 1990):* Goods loaded 29; Goods unloaded 123 (Source: UN, *Monthly Bulletin of Statistics*).

* Including the Northern Mariana Islands, the Federated States of Micronesia and Palau.

Civil Aviation (traffic on scheduled services, 2002): Kilometres flown 1 million; Passengers carried 27,000; Passenger-km 36 million; Total ton-km 4 million. Source: UN, *Statistical Yearbook*.

TOURISM

Tourist Arrivals: 7,195 in 2003; 9,007 in 2004; 9,173 in 2005.

Arrivals by Country (2005): Japan 1,282; Other Asia 4,295; USA 1,650; Total (incl. others) 9,173.

Tourism Receipts (US $ million, incl. passenger transport): 4 in 2000; 4 in 2001; 4 in 2002.

Source: World Tourism Organization.

COMMUNICATIONS MEDIA

Telephones (main lines in use, estimate): 4,500 in 2006*.

Mobile Cellular Telephones (subscriptions, estimate): 600 in 2006*.

Facsimile Machines (number): 160 in 1996†.

Personal Computers: 5,000 in 2005*.

Internet Users: 2,200 in 2006*.

Non-daily Newspaper: 1 (average circulation 10,000 copies) in 1996‡.

* Source: International Telecommunication Union.
† Source: UN, *Statistical Yearbook*.
‡ Source: UNESCO, *Statistical Yearbook*.

EDUCATION

Primary (2002/03, unless otherwise indicated): 103 schools (1998); 526 teachers (estimate); 8,907 pupils enrolled (estimate).

Secondary (2002/03, unless otherwise indicated): 16 schools (1998); 387 teachers (estimate); 6,460 pupils enrolled (estimate).

Higher (2002/03, unless otherwise indicated): 1 college (1994); 49 teachers (estimate); 919 students enrolled (estimate).

Source: UNESCO Institute for Statistics.

Directory

The Constitution

On 1 May 1979 the locally drafted Constitution of the Republic of the Marshall Islands became effective. The Constitution provides for a parliamentary form of government, with legislative authority vested in the 33-member Nitijela. Members of the Nitijela are elected by a popular vote, from 25 districts, for a four-year term. There is an advisory council of 12 high chiefs, or Iroij. The Nitijela elects the President of the Marshall Islands (who also has a four-year mandate) from among its own members. The President then selects members of the Cabinet from among the members of the Nitijela. On 25 June 1983 the final draft of a Compact of Free Association was signed by the Governments of the Marshall Islands and the USA, and the Compact was effectively ratified by the US Congress on 14 January 1986. An amended Compact was signed by the Governments of the two countries on 1 May 2003; final terms were ratified by the US Congress in November, and signed by the US President in December of that year. By the terms of the Compact, free association recognizes the Republic of the Marshall Islands as an internally sovereign, self-governing state, whose policy concerning foreign affairs must be consistent with guide-lines laid down in the Compact. Full responsibility for defence lies with the USA, which undertakes to provide regular economic assistance. The economic and defence provisions of the Compact are renewable after 15 years, but the status of free association continues indefinitely.

The Government

HEAD OF STATE

President: LITOKWA TOMEING (took office 7 January 2008).

CABINET
(April 2008)

Minister in Assistance to the President: CHRISTOPHER LOEAK.
Minister of Education: NIDEL LORAK.
Minister of Finance: JACK ADING.
Minister of Transportation and Communication: DENNIS MOMOTARO.
Minister of Health: AMENTA MATTHEW.
Minister of Public Works: KEJJO BEIN.
Minister of Internal Affairs: NORMAN MATTHEW.
Minister of Justice: DAVID KRAMER.
Minister of Resources and Development: FRED MULLER.
Minister of Foreign Affairs: TONY DEBRUM.

MINISTRIES

Office of the President: Govt of the Republic of the Marshall Islands, POB 2, Majuro, MH 96960; tel. (625) 3445; fax (625) 4021; e-mail pressoff@ntamar.net; internet www.rmigovernment.org.

THE MARSHALL ISLANDS

Ministry of Education: POB 3, Majuro, MH 96960; tel. (625) 5262; fax (625) 3861; e-mail rmimoe@rmimoe.net; internet www.rmimoe.net.

Ministry of Finance: POB D, Majuro, MH 96960; tel. (625) 8320; fax (625) 3607; e-mail secfin@ntamar.net.

Ministry of Foreign Affairs: POB 1349, Majuro, MH 96960; tel. (625) 3181; fax (623) 4979; e-mail mofasec@ntamar.net.

Ministry of Health: POB 16, Majuro, MH 96960; tel. (625) 3355; fax (625) 3432; e-mail jusmohe@ntamar.net.

Ministry of Internal Affairs: POB 18, Majuro, MH 96960; tel. (625) 8240; fax (625) 5353; e-mail iasec@ntamar.net.

Ministry of Justice: c/o Office of the Attorney General, Majuro, MH 96960; tel. (625) 3244; fax (625) 5218; e-mail agoffice@ntamar.net.

Ministry of Public Works: POB 1727, Majuro, MH 96960; tel. (625) 8911; fax (625) 3005; e-mail secpw@ntamar.net.

Ministry of Resources and Development: POB 1727, Majuro, MH 96960; tel. (625) 3206; fax (625) 7471; e-mail rndsec@ntamar.net; internet rmirnd.net.

Ministry of Transportation and Communication: POB 1079, Majuro, MH 96960; tel. (625) 8869; fax (625) 3486; e-mail rmimotc@ntamar.net.

STATE TRIBUNAL

Nuclear Claims Tribunal: POB 702, Majuro, MH 96960; tel. (625) 3396; fax (625) 3389; e-mail nctmaj@ntamar.net; internet www.nuclearclaimstribunal.com; f. 1988; authorized under Section 177 of the first Compact of Free Association between the Government of the Marshall Islands and the Government of the USA to decide all claims arising from the nuclear-testing programme conducted by the USA in the Marshall Islands in 1946–58; Chair. JAMES H. PLASMAN; Defender of the Fund PHILIP A. OKNEY; Public Advocate BILL GRAHAM.

Legislature

THE NITIJELA

The Nitijela (lower house) consists of 33 elected Senators. Following the national election held on 19 November 2007, the Ailin Kein Ad (Our Islands) party, supported by independent candidates, was able to secure a parliamentary majority.

Speaker: Sen. JURELANG ZEDKAIA.

THE COUNCIL OF IROIJ

The Council of Iroij is the upper house of the bicameral legislature, comprising 12 tribal chiefs who advise the Presidential Cabinet and review legislation affecting customary law, land tenure or any traditional practice.

Chairman: Iroij KOTAK LOEAK.

Election Commission

Electoral Commission: POB 18, Majuro, MH 96900; Chief Electoral Officer CARL ALIK.

Political Organizations

Ailin Kein Ad (Our Islands): Majuro; f. 2002; formed United People's Party coalition following 2007 elections; Chair. CHRISTOPHER LOEAK.

United Democratic Party: Majuro.

Diplomatic Representation

EMBASSIES IN THE MARSHALL ISLANDS

China (Taiwan): A5-6, Lojkar Village, Long Island, POB 1229, Majuro, MH 96960; tel. (247) 4141; fax (247) 4143; e-mail eoroc@ntamar.net; Ambassador BRUCE J. D. LINGHU.

Japan: A-1 Lojkar Village, POB 300, Majuro, MH 96960; tel. (247) 7463; fax (247) 7493; Ambassador KENRO IINO.

USA: POB 1379, Majuro, MH 96960; tel. (247) 4011; fax (247) 4012; e-mail publicmajuro@state.gov; internet umajuro.usembassy.gov; Ambassador CLYDE BISHOP.

Judicial System

The judicial system consists of the Supreme Court and the High Court, which preside over District and Community Courts, and the Traditional Rights Court.

Supreme Court of the Republic of the Marshall Islands: POB 378, Majuro, MH 96960; tel. (625) 3201; fax (625) 3323; e-mail jutrep@ntamar.com; Chief Justice DANIEL CADRA.

High Court of the Republic of the Marshall Islands: Majuro; e-mail judrep@ntamar.net; Chief Justice CARL INGRAM.

District Court of the Republic of the Marshall Islands: Majuro, MH 96960; tel. (625) 3201; fax (625) 3323; Presiding Judge MILTON ZACKIOS.

Traditional Rights Court of the Marshall Islands: Majuro, MH 96960; customary law only; Chief Judge BERSON JOSEPH.

Religion

The population is predominantly Christian, mainly belonging to the Protestant United Church of Christ. The Roman Catholic Church, Assembly of God, Bukot Nan Jesus, Seventh-day Adventists, the Church of Jesus Christ of Latter-day Saints (Mormons), the Full Gospel and the Bahá'í Faith are also represented.

CHRISTIANITY

The Roman Catholic Church

The Apostolic Prefecture of the Marshall Islands included 4,601 adherents at 31 December 2005.

Prefect Apostolic of the Marshall Islands: Rev. Fr RAYMUNDO SABIO, POB 8, Majuro, MH 96960; tel. (625) 8307; fax (625) 6507; e-mail diocesemarshalls@yahoo.com.

Protestant Churches

The Marshall Islands come under the auspices of the United Church Board for World Ministries (475 Riverside Drive, New York, NY 10115, USA); Sec. for Latin America, Caribbean and Oceania Dr PATRICIA RUMER.

BAHÁ'Í FAITH

National Spiritual Assembly: POB 1017, Majuro, MH 96960; tel. (247) 3512; fax (247) 7180; e-mail nsamarshallislands@yahoo.com; internet www.mh.bahai.org; mems resident in 50 localities; Sec. Dr IRENE J. TAAFAKI.

The Press

Kwajalein Hourglass: POB 23, Kwajalein, MH 96555; tel. (355) 3539; e-mail jbennett@kls.usaka.smdc.army.mil; internet www.smdc.army.mil/KWAJ/Hourglass/Hourglass.html; f. 1954; 2 a week; Editor JIM BENNETT; circ. 2,300.

Marshall Islands Gazette: monthly; government publ.

Marshall Islands Journal: POB 14, Majuro, MH 96960; tel. (625) 8143; fax (625) 3136; e-mail journal@ntamar.net; internet www.marshallislandsjournal.com; f. 1970; weekly; Editor GIFF JOHNSON; circ. 3,700.

Broadcasting and Communications

TELECOMMUNICATIONS

National Telecommunications Authority (NTA): POB 1169, Majuro, MH 96960; tel. (625) 3676; fax (625) 3952; e-mail info@ntamar.net; internet www.ntamar.net; privatized in 1991; sole provider of local and long-distance telephone services and internet communications in the Marshall Islands; Chair. ALEX BING; Pres. and CEO ANTHONY M. MULLER.

BROADCASTING

Radio

Marshall Islands Broadcasting Co: POB 19, Majuro, MH 96960; tel. (625) 3250; fax (625) 3505; Chief Information Officer PETER FUCHS.

Radio Marshalls V7AB: POB 3250, Majuro, MH 96960; tel. (625) 8411; fax (625) 5353; govt-owned; commercial; programmes in English and Marshallese; Station Man. ANTARI ELBON.

Other radio stations include Micronesia Heatwave and V7AA.

THE MARSHALL ISLANDS

Television

Marshalls Broadcasting Co Television: POB 19, Majuro, MH 96960; tel. (625) 3413; Chief Information Officer PETER FUCHS.

The US Department of Defense operates the American Forces Radio and Television Service for the Bucholz Army Airfield on Kwajalein Atoll.

Finance

(cap. = capital; res = reserves; dep. = deposits; amounts in US dollars)

BANKING

Bank of Guam (USA): POB C, Majuro, MH 96960; tel. (625) 3322; fax (625) 3444; Man. ROMY A. ANGEL; brs in Ebeye, Kwajalein and Majuro.

Bank of the Marshall Islands: POB J, Majuro, MH 96960; tel. (625) 3636; fax (625) 3661; e-mail bankmar@ntamar.net; f. 1982; 40% govt-owned; dep. 47.5m., total assets 61.8m. (Dec. 2003); Chair. GRANT LABAUN; Pres. and Gen. Man. PATRICK CHEN; brs in Majuro, Kwajalein, Ebeye and Santo.

Marshall Islands Development Bank: POB 1048, Majuro, MH 96960; tel. (625) 3230; fax (625) 3309; f. 1989; lending suspended in 2003; Man. Dir AMON TIBON.

INSURANCE

Majuro Insurance Company: POB 60, Majuro, MH 96960; tel. (625) 8885; fax (625) 8188; Man. LUCY RUBEN.

Marshalls Insurance Agency: POB 113, Majuro, MH 96960; tel. (625) 3366; fax (625) 3189; Man. TOM LIKOVICH.

Moylan's Insurance Underwriters (Marshall) Inc: POB 727, Majuro, MH 96960; tel. (625) 3220; fax (625) 3361; e-mail marshalls@moylans.net; internet www.moylansinsurance.com; Founder, Chair. and Pres. KURT S. MOYLAN; Br. Man. STEVE PHILLIP.

Trade and Industry

DEVELOPMENT ORGANIZATIONS AND STATE AUTHORITIES

Marshall Islands Development Authority: POB 1185, Majuro, MH 96960; tel. (625) 3417; fax (625) 3158; Gen. Man. DAVID KABUA.

Marshall Islands Environmental Protection Authority: POB 1322, Majuro, MH 96960; tel. (625) 3035; fax (625) 5202; e-mail eparmi@ntamar.net; Gen. Man. JOHN BUNGITAK.

Marshall Islands Marine Resources Authority (MIMRA): POB 860, Majuro, MH 96960; tel. (625) 8262; fax (625) 5447; e-mail kiko@mimra.com; internet www.mimra.com; specializes in farming techniques and research and development; Exec. Dir GLEN JOSEPH.

Tobolar Copra Processing Authority: POB G, Majuro, MH 96960; tel. (625) 3116; fax (625) 7206; e-mail wpcandilas@ntamar.net; Plant Man. WILFREDO CANDILAS.

CHAMBER OF COMMERCE

Marshall Islands Chamber of Commerce: POB 1226, Majuro, MH 96960; tel. (625) 3177; fax (625) 2500; e-mail commerce@ntamar.net; internet marshallislandschamber.net; fmrly known as Majuro Chamber of Commerce; Pres. HIROBO OBEKETANG; Sec. JIM MCLEAN.

UTILITIES

Electricity

Marshalls Energy Company: POB 1439, Majuro, MH 96960; tel. (625) 3827; fax (625) 3397; e-mail meccorp@ntamar.net; internet www.mecrmi.net; Gen. Man. WILLIAM F. ROBERTS; Man. STEVEN WAKEFIELD.

Kwajalein Atoll Joint Utility Resource (KAJUR): POB 5819, Ebeye Island, Kwajalein, MH 96970; tel. (329) 3799; fax (329) 3722; Man. WESLEY LEMARI.

Water

Majuro Water and Sewage Services: POB 1751, Majuro, MH 96960; tel. (625) 8934; fax (625) 3837; Man. TERRY MELLAN.

CO-OPERATIVES

These include the Ebeye Co-op, Farmers' Market Co-operative, Kwajalein Employees' Credit Union, Marshall Is Credit Union, Marshall Is Fishermen's Co-operative, and the Marshall Is Handicraft Co-operative.

Transport

ROADS

Macadam and concrete roads are found in the more important islands. In 1996 there were 152 km of paved roads in the Marshall Islands, mostly on Majuro and Ebeye. Other islands have stone and coral-surfaced roads and tracks. A road improvement programme was completed in 1999.

SHIPPING

The Marshall Islands operates an 'offshore' shipping register. At the end of 2006 the merchant fleet comprised 953 vessels, with a combined displacement of some 32.8m. grt.

Vessel Registry:

Marshall Islands Maritime and Corporate Administrators Inc: 11495 Commerce Park Drive, Reston, VA 20191-1507, USA; tel. (703) 620-4880; fax (703) 476-8522; e-mail info@register-iri.com; internet www.register-iri.com; Pres. WILLIAM R. GALLAGHER; Vice-Pres. MELISSA A. HURST.

The Trust Company of the Marshall Islands Inc: Trust Company Complex, Ajeltake Island, POB 1405, Majuro, MH 96960; tel. (247) 3018; fax (247) 3017; e-mail tcmi@ntamar.net; Pres. GUY EDISON CLAY MAITLAND.

Marshall Islands Ports Authority (MIPA): Majuro; tel. 625-8269; fax 625-4269; internet rmipa-aip.org; responsible for seaports and airports; Dir JACK CHONG GUM.

CIVIL AVIATION

Continental Micronesia operates three flights a week from Honolulu and Guam to Majuro. Air Marshall Islands provides a daily domestic service; Aloha Airlines provides a weekly service from Honolulu to Kwajalein and to Majuro; and Japan Airlines operates a charter service from Tokyo to Majuro.

Air Marshall Islands (AMI): POB 1319, Majuro, MH 96960; tel. (625) 3731; fax (625) 3730; e-mail amisales@ntamar.net; internet www.airmarshallislands.com; f. 1980; internal services for the Marshall Islands; international operations ceased in early 1999; also charter, air ambulance and maritime surveillance operations; agency for Aloha airlines; Chair. KUNIO LAMARI; CFO NEIL ESCHERRA.

Continental Air Micronesia: POB 156, Majuro; tel. (625) 3209; fax (625) 3730; e-mail cmimaj@ntamar.net; international flights between Majuro, the Federated States of Micronesia, Guam and Honolulu; also internal services between Majuro and Kwajalein; based in Hagåtña, Guam; Man. LEO SION.

Tourism

The islands' attractions include excellent opportunities for diving, game-fishing and the exploration of sites and relics of Second World War battles. The Marshall Islands Visitor Authority has implemented a short-term tourism development programme focusing on special-interest tourism markets. In the longer term the Visitor Authority planned to promote the development of small-island resorts throughout the country. Tourism receipts totalled some $4m. in 2002. There were 9,173 tourist arrivals in 2005. The leading sources of vistors were the USA and Japan.

Marshall Islands Visitor Authority: POB 5, Majuro, MH 96960; tel. (625) 6482; fax (625) 6771; e-mail tourism@ntamar.net; internet www.visitmarshallislands.com; f. 1997; Gen. Man. DOLORES DE-BRUM-KATTIL.

MAURITANIA

Introductory Survey

Location, Climate, Language, Religion, Flag, Capital

The Islamic Republic of Mauritania lies in north-west Africa, with the Atlantic Ocean to the west, Algeria and the disputed territory of Western Sahara (occupied by Morocco) to the north, Mali to the east and south, and Senegal to the south. The climate is hot and dry, particularly in the north, which is mainly desert. Average annual rainfall in the capital in the 1990s was 131 mm (5.1 ins). The 1991 Constitution designates Arabic (which is spoken by the Moorish majority) as the official language, and Arabic, Poular, Wolof and Solinke as the national languages. The black population in the south is largely French-speaking, and French is widely used in commercial and business circles. Islam is the state religion, and the inhabitants are almost all Muslims. The national flag (proportions 2 by 3) comprises a green field, bearing, on the vertical median, a yellow five-pointed star between the upward-pointing horns of a yellow crescent. The capital is Nouakchott.

Recent History

Mauritania, formerly part of French West Africa, achieved full independence on 28 November 1960 (having become a self-governing member of the French Community two years earlier). Moktar Ould Daddah, leader of the Mauritanian Assembly Party (MAP) and Prime Minister since June 1959, became Head of State, and was elected President in August 1961. All parties subsequently merged with the MAP to form the Mauritanian People's Party (MPP), with Ould Daddah as Secretary-General, and Mauritania became a one-party state in 1964. In 1973 Mauritania joined the League of Arab States (see p. 332), and withdrew from the Franc Zone in the following year.

Under a tripartite agreement of November 1975, Spain ceded Spanish (now Western) Sahara to Mauritania and Morocco, to be apportioned between them. The agreement took effect in February 1976, when Mauritania occupied the southern portion of the territory. Fighting ensued between Moroccan and Mauritanian troops and the guerrilla forces of the Frente Popular para la Liberación de Saguia el-Hamra y Río de Oro (the Polisario Front), which sought independence for Western Sahara. Attacks within Mauritania by Polisario forces proved highly damaging to the economy. Diplomatic links with Algeria, which supported Polisario bases within its borders, were severed in March 1976. Meanwhile, relations with Morocco improved, following that country's renunciation of territorial claims that included Mauritania, and in mid-1977 a joint defence pact was formed.

By 1977 Mauritania was spending two-thirds of its budget on defending territory that promised no economic benefits. In July 1978 Ould Daddah was deposed in a bloodless coup, led by the armed forces Chief of Staff, Lt-Col (later Col) Moustapha Ould Mohamed Salek, who took power as Chairman of a Military Committee for National Recovery (MCNR). Polisario immediately declared a cease-fire with Mauritania, but the continuing presence of several thousand Moroccan troops in Mauritania impeded a full settlement. In April 1979 the MCNR was replaced by a Military Committee for National Salvation (MCNS). Salek continued to head the MCNS, but appointed Lt-Col Ahmed Ould Bouceif as Prime Minister. Ould Bouceif died in an air crash in May, and the MCNS appointed Lt-Col Mohamed Khouna Ould Haidalla as premier. Salek resigned in June, and was replaced as Head of State by Lt-Col Mohamed Mahmoud Ould Ahmed Louly. In July Polisario announced a resumption of hostilities against Mauritania. Later that month the Organization of African Unity (OAU, now the African Union—AU, see p. 164) recommended that a referendum be held to determine the future of the disputed region. These events provided the impetus for Mauritania's withdrawal from the war: Ould Haidalla renounced Mauritania's territorial claims in Western Sahara, and a peace treaty was signed with Polisario in August. Morocco announced its annexation of the entire territory, and diplomatic relations between Mauritania and Algeria were re-established.

Ould Haidalla succeeded Louly as Head of State in January 1980; he retained the posts of Prime Minister and Minister of Defence until December, when Sid'Ahmed Ould Bneijara was appointed premier. Although a draft Constitution, envisaging a multi-party system, was prepared, an attempted coup in March 1981 prompted Ould Haidalla to end civilian participation in the Government. The new Prime Minister, Lt-Col (later Col) Maaouiya Ould Sid'Ahmed Taya (a prominent member of the MCNS and the army Chief of Staff) assumed the defence portfolio in April, and the draft Constitution was abandoned.

In December 1984, while Ould Haidalla was temporarily absent from the country, Taya assumed the presidency in a bloodless coup and also took the defence portfolio in the new Government. An amnesty was proclaimed for all political prisoners and exiles. Ould Haidalla was detained upon his return to Mauritania, but was released, with five of his associates, in December 1988.

At a national referendum on 12 July 1991, a draft Constitution, which accorded extensive powers to the presidency and provided for the introduction of a multi-party political system, was supported by 97.9% of those who voted (85.3% of the registered electorate), according to official reports. Meanwhile, legislation permitting the registration of political parties was promulgated: among the first organizations to be accorded official status was the Democratic and Social Republican Party (DSRP), which was closely linked with Taya.

Taya was elected President on 17 January 1992, with 62.7% of the votes cast, defeating three other candidates; his nearest rival was Ahmed Ould Daddah, with 32.8%. The rate of voter participation was 51.7%.

In legislative elections, which were held on 6 and 13 March 1992, Taya's party took 67 of the 79 seats in the National Assembly, and independent candidates won 10 of the remaining 12 seats; a low rate of participation by voters was reported. Following indirect elections to the Senate, on 3 and 10 April, the new, 56-member upper house (which was elected by municipal leaders) included 36 DSRP members and 17 independents (one other party had, unsuccessfully, presented candidates for election); three seats were reserved for representatives of Mauritanians resident abroad. Taya was inaugurated as President on 18 April and appointed the hitherto Minister of Finance, Sidi Mohamed Ould Boubacar, as Prime Minister.

The DSRP secured control of 172 of Mauritania's 208 administrative districts at Mauritania's first multi-party municipal elections, held in January and February 1994. Ahmed Ould Daddah's Union of Democratic Forces—New Era (UDF—NE) won control of 17 districts, the remainder being taken by independent candidates.

In early 1995 internal tensions within the UDF—NE, including a faction that left to join the DSRP, threatened to undermine the influence of the party. In July several UDF—NE members were reported to have defected to another opposition party, the Union for Democracy and Progress (UDP).

In January 1996 Taya appointed Cheikh el Avia Ould Mohamed Khouna as Prime Minister, to head a new Council of Ministers. At legislative elections held on 11 and 18 October the DSRP won 71 of the 79 seats in the National Assembly. The Rally for Democracy and Unity (RDU), closely allied with the administration, also secured a seat. Action for Change (AC), which sought to represent the interests of Harratin (mainly dark-skinned Moors who had formerly been slaves), was the only opposition party to obtain representation in the Assembly; six independent candidates also secured election. Later in October the Prime Minister named a new Council of Ministers.

In January 1997 several opposition leaders, including Messaoud Ould Boulkheir, the AC Chairman, were arrested on charges of maintaining 'suspicious relations' with Libya. Although Ould Boulkheir and several others had been freed by February, five other opposition activists received prison sentences for conspiring to break the law; in April four of the five convicted were acquitted on appeal. In February five prominent opposition parties, including the AC and the UDF—NE, formed a coalition, the Forum of Opposition Parties (FOP).

At the presidential election, held on 12 December 1997, Taya was returned to office with 90.9% of the valid votes cast; his nearest rival, Mohamed Lemine Ch'Bih Ould Cheikh Melainine, won 7.0% of the vote. Opposition parties alleged that there had been widespread electoral fraud and disputed the official rate of voter participation, of 73.8%. Taya subsequently appointed Mohamed Lemine Ould Guig, a university academic, as Prime Minister, and a new Council of Ministers was installed. In November 1998 Khouna was again appointed Prime Minister.

Meanwhile, in March 1998 internal divisions in the UDF—NE resulted in a split in the party into two rival factions, led by Ahmed Ould Daddah and Moustapha Ould Bedreddine. In November the Government banned the pro-Iraqi Baathist National Vanguard Party (Taliaa), a constituent member of the FOP, following its criticism of the Mauritanian Government's decision to establish full diplomatic relations with Israel in the previous month.

From October 2000, following the onset of the second *intifada* (uprising) in the Palestinian Autonomous Areas, the Mauritanian Government experienced increasing pressure from opposition groups, including the UDF—NE, to break off diplomatic relations with Israel. In October several pro-Palestinian demonstrations in Nouakchott and Nouadhibou led to violent anti-Israeli protests. Arrests of members of clandestine Islamist groups and of UDF—NE activists were reported. In late October the Council of Ministers officially dissolved the UDF—NE, on the grounds that the party had incited violence and sought to damage Mauritanian national interests. Ould Daddah refused to recognize the dissolution of the party, and the UDF—NE's partners in the FOP condemned the Government's action as unconstitutional. Meanwhile, the faction of the UDF—NE led by Moustapha Ould Bedreddine, which remained authorized, restyled itself as the Union of Progressive Forces (UPF).

In December 2000 President Taya announced that an element of proportional representation would be introduced in subsequent elections to the National Assembly, and that the State would seek to facilitate funding and equal access to the media for all parties, although independent candidacies were to be prohibited. The National Assembly approved these measures in January 2001, although they were rejected as insufficient by the radical opposition, including the FOP. Also in January, a government reshuffle included the appointment of a new Minister of Foreign Affairs and Co-operation, Dah Ould Abdi.

Some 15 political parties contested legislative and municipal elections held on 19 and 26 October 2001, at which an electoral turn-out of some 55% was reported. The DSRP won 64 of the 81 seats in the enlarged National Assembly, and the RDU and the UDP, which were now both allied with the ruling party, each secured three seats. The AC was the most successful of the opposition parties, winning four seats, while the UPF and the newly formed Rally of Democratic Forces (RDF), which replaced the banned UDF—NE, also each took three seats, and the Popular Front (PF) secured the remaining seat. In November President Taya reappointed Khouna as Prime Minister, and a reshuffled Council of Ministers was appointed.

In January 2002 Ould Daddah was elected President of the RDF; four former vice-presidents of the UDF—NE were also appointed to the 12-member executive committee of the RDF. In that month the Government officially dissolved the AC, on the grounds that the party promoted racism and extremism. At partial senatorial elections, held in April, the RDF won one seat, the first time that part of the radical opposition had secured representation in the Senate, in which the DSRP enjoyed a large majority. In August the Convention for Change (CC), an organization including many former members of the AC, and led by Ould Boulkheir, was denied the right to register as a political party.

In October 2002 the UFP announced that it was to organize a series of meetings intended to promote a 'national dialogue' between the authorities and the opposition parties. However, later that month seven other opposition parties, including the CC (which remained banned), the PF and the RDF, formed a new grouping, the United Opposition Framework (UOF), which also stated as its purpose the co-ordination of dialogue between the opposition and the Government pertaining to democratic reform; the UFP was, notably, excluded from the UOF. Consequently, the initial meeting was postponed indefinitely, and, expressing discontent at the situation, in mid-November the UFP announced its withdrawal from the National Assembly. As a result of the withdrawal of the three UFP deputies from the Assembly, the group of opposition deputies was dissolved, as it was now reduced to eight members, less than the 10 required for the formation of a parliamentary group. On 27 October a government reorganization was effected. Notably, Dah Ould Abdi was replaced as Minister of Foreign Affairs and Co-operation by Mohamed Ould Tobar.

In March 2003 US-led military action in Iraq, aimed at ousting the Baathist regime of Saddam Hussain, prompted protests in Mauritania, with widespread demonstrations held to demand that the Government break off diplomatic relations with the two principal nations involved in the conflict, the United Kingdom and the USA, and also with Israel. As opposition to the Government's broadly pro-US stance intensified in early May, police raided the headquarters of a tolerated—although not officially authorized—Baathist party, the National Renaissance Party (NRP—Nouhoudh). Three leaders of the NRP, including its Secretary-General, Mohamed Ould Abdellahi Ould Eyye, were arrested on unspecified charges; 13 other Baathists were also arrested over a period of four days, including the former Secretary-General of the Taliaa party. (Ten of those arrested were later charged with attempting to re-establish Taliaa.)

In early May 2003 Taya effected a minor government reorganization, dismissing Cheyakh Ould Ely, the Minister of Communication and Relations with Parliament, who was considered a pan-Arab nationalist. The appointment of Abdellahi Ould Souleimane Ould Cheikh Sidya, reportedly a close relation of Ahmed Ould Daddah, as Minister of Economic and Development Affairs was apparently aimed at attracting supporters of the RDF to the Government, while the appointment of Lembrabott Ould Mohamed Lemine as Minister of Culture and Islamic Affairs was regarded as an attempt to reduce tensions between the Government and Islamic communities. However, at the end of May the publication of a pro-Islamist weekly journal, *Ar-Rayah*, was suspended, and nine Baathists were convicted by a Nouakchott court of engaging in illegal political activity. In early June four Islamic cultural associations were closed down, and, according to opposition reports, more than 100 alleged Islamists were detained, 36 of whom were charged with plotting against the constitutional order.

The tensions that had been escalating throughout the first half of 2003 culminated in an attempted *coup d'état*, which commenced on 8 June. Exchanges of fire were reported near the presidential palace and at other strategic locations in Nouakchott. According to official reports, 15 people (including six civilians) died in ensuing clashes between the insurgents and the security forces, including the Chief of Staff of the Armed Forces, Col Mohamed Lamine Ould Ndiayane, with a further 68 people injured. Government forces regained control of the city on 9 June. Although the exact identity and motives of the rebels were unclear, reports named the leaders of the coup as Saleh Ould Hnana, a former colonel and Baathist sympathizer, who had been expelled from the Mauritanian armed forces in 2002, and Mohammed Ould Sheikhna, a squadron leader in the national air force; Taya subsequently stated, however, that Islamists had been responsible for the rebellion. (Other sources claimed that the attempted coup had been prompted by tribal rivalries.)

In the days following the restoration of order at least 12 alleged rebel leaders were arrested, including Ould Sheikhna, although the whereabouts of Ould Hnana remained unknown. Ould Mansour fled to Senegal before later being granted political asylum in Belgium. Meanwhile, more than 30 detained Islamists, who had been freed during the disorder, were reported to have surrendered themselves to the authorities. In mid-June 2003 several senior officials, including the Chief of Staff of the National Gendarmerie, the President of the High Court of Justice and the Mayor of Nouakchott, were replaced by new appointees regarded as loyal to the President. In July another suspected coup leader, Lt Didi Ould M'Hamed, who had fled to Senegal, was extradited to Mauritania; it was subsequently announced that he would face a civil trial.

In early July 2003 Taya appointed a new Prime Minister: Sghaïr Ould M'Barek, a Harratin, was regarded as a close ally of the President. A new Government was subsequently formed. Although several of the high-ranking officials who had been arrested in mid-June had been released from custody by mid-July, it was reported that the former Prime Minister, Khouna, had been detained after having sought political asylum in Spain. Further arrests of Islamists were reported throughout the month. In early August more than 80 members of the military who had been arrested following the attempted coup were released, although many more remained in detention. At the end of the month Melainine was freed, having been granted a presidential pardon. Some 41 Islamists had also been released from detention by the end of the month, although others continued to face charges. In early September it was announced that some 30 members of the military, including 20 senior officers, were to be tried in connection with the coup attempt.

In October 2003 the Constitutional Council approved the nominations of six candidates, including Taya, Ould Daddah, Ould Boulkheir and former President Ould Haidalla, for the forthcoming presidential election. Ould Haidalla was widely regarded as the most credible challenger to Taya; the former President's campaign attracted the support of several prominent Islamists and secular Arab nationalists, as well as a number of proponents of liberal reform. According to official results of the election, held, as scheduled, on 7 November, Taya won 66.7% of the votes cast, followed by Ould Haidalla, with 18.7%, Ould Daddah, with 6.9%, and Ould Boulkheir, with 5.0%. Some 60.8% of the electorate participated in the election. Opposition candidates accused the Government of perpetrating fraud at the election, which international observers had not been permitted to monitor. On 13 November Taya announced the formation of a new Government, which included eight new appointees, among them Mohamed Vall Ould Bellal as Minister of Foreign Affairs and Co-operation, although most of the other principal posts remained unchanged.

In mid-November 2003 the trial of Ould Haidalla (who had been arrested twice in November) and 14 of his supporters, on charges of seeking to obtain power by force and by threatening the strategic interests of Mauritania, commenced. The trial concluded at the end of December, when Ould Haidalla and four of his co-defendants, including one of his sons, were convicted of plotting to overthrow the Head of State; they received five-year suspended sentences, during which time they were forbidden to engage in political activity, and were fined the equivalent of US $1,600 each. Four others received lesser sentences and fines. Ould Haidalla's conviction and sentence were upheld on appeal in April 2004.

The DSRP won 15 of the 18 seats contested at partial elections to the Senate, held on 9 and 16 April 2004, while its ally, the RDU, secured its first senatorial representation. The opposition Popular Progressive Alliance (PPA) also obtained legislative representation for the first time, winning two seats. In July Taya effected a major government reshuffle, notably replacing the ministers responsible for finance, economic affairs and trade, following a sharp rise in consumer prices and a decline in the value of the national currency, the ouguiya.

In August 2004 some 31 army officers were arrested after the security forces discovered a plot to overthrow Taya. The Mauritanian authorities accused the Governments of Libya and Burkina Faso of providing assistance to the alleged conspirators; however, both states strongly denied the allegations. In September the Government announced that it had averted another attempted coup d'état, seizing a large quantity of weapons and making a number of arrests; among those detained was Capt. Abderahmane Ould Mini, who, it was reported, had also participated in the failed coup d'état in June 2003, while Ould Hnana and Ould Sheikhna were also sought by the authorities in connection with the alleged conspiracy.

In October 2004 the Government announced that Ould Hnana had been arrested at the town of Rosso on the Senegalese border. In November the trial of more than 190 soldiers and civilians, accused of participation in the attempted coup d'état in June 2003 and in subsequent conspiracies to overthrow the Head of State, commenced at an army barracks near Ouad Naga, some 50 km east of Nouakchott. The defendants included the alleged leaders of the group, Ould Hnana, Ould Mini and Ould Sheikhna, the latter being one of 19 people tried in absentia (also among this number was Sidi Mohamed Mustapha Ould Limam Chavi, an advisor to Burkinabè President Blaise Compaoré); the civilians on trial, meanwhile, included opposition leaders Ould Haidalla, Ould Daddah and Cheikh Ould Horma. Ould Hnana pleaded guilty to the charge of conspiring to overthrow President Taya, stating that he had acted in response to the 'tribalism, clientism, discrimination against black Mauritanians and economic mismanagement' of the incumbent regime. Ould Mini also admitted conspiring to overthrow the President; the remaining accused military personnel entered pleas of not guilty. In February 2005 Ould Hnana, Ould Mini, Ould Sheikhna and a fourth officer, Capt. Mohammed Ould Salek, were sentenced to life imprisonment with hard labour, while 79 others received lesser jail sentences; Ould Haidalla, Ould Daddah and Ould Horma were among the 111 acquitted. Following his release, Ould Daddah urged the Government to initiate dialogue with the opposition.

Taya effected a government reorganization in March 2005, notably creating a new Ministry of Petroleum and Energy, headed by Zeidane Ould H'Maeyda, hitherto Minister of Mines and Industry. Other changes included the appointment of Lemrabott Sidi Mahmoud Ould Cheikh Ahmed as Minister of the Interior, Posts and Telecommunications.

In June 2005 some 15 soldiers were killed, and a further 17 injured, in an attack by some 150 assailants on a military post at Lemgheity, in north-eastern Mauritania, for which an Algerian radical Islamist militant group, the Groupe salafiste pour la prédication et le combat (GSPC), subsequently claimed responsibility. Later in June it was reported that the existence of a radical Islamist group based in Mauritania with links to the GSPC, the Mauritanian Group for Preaching and Jihad, had been uncovered, as had details of proposed targets of attack in the country. At the end of the month the Senate adopted legislation aimed at countering terrorism and money-laundering.

On 3 August 2005, while President Taya was absent from Mauritania, attending the funeral of the late King Fahd ibn Abd al-Aziz as-Sa'ud of Saudi Arabia, a group of army officers seized control of state broadcasting services and the presidential palace in a bloodless coup d'état. A 16-member Military Council for Justice and Democracy (MCJD) under the leadership of Col Ely Ould Mohamed Vall, hitherto the Director of National Security, who had been regarded as a close ally of Taya, announced that it had assumed power. The Council stated that it would preside over the country for a transitional period of up to two years, at the end of which democratic elections, in which members of the MCJD and the Government would be prohibited from participating, would be held; although the National Assembly elected in 2001 was dissolved, the 1991 Constitution and most of its institutions (including the Constitutional Council and judicial bodies) were to be retained, as supplemented and amended by the charter of the MCJD. Taya was prevented from re-entering the country and was flown initially to Niamey, Niger; he subsequently took up residence in The Gambia.

On 7 August 2005 Vall appointed Sidi Mohamed Ould Boubacar, hitherto Ambassador to France, as Prime Minister, a position that he had previously held in 1992–96; a new, civilian, government was named on 10 August, and Vall announced the intention of holding a constitutional referendum within the period of one year. None of the ministers in the outgoing Government were re-appointed, although, notably, Ahmed Ould Sid'Ahmed, who, in his former capacity as Minister of Foreign Affairs and Co-operation, had been largely responsible for Mauritania's rapprochement with Israel in 1999, was re-appointed to that position. In the immediate aftermath of the coup, which was initially widely condemned internationally, the AU announced the immediate suspension of Mauritania's membership. However, the overthrow of Taya's regime was reported to have widespread domestic support. In mid-August a delegation from the AU met members of the MCJD, subsequently announcing the willingness of the Union to co-operate with the new leadership of Mauritania, although the country was to remain suspended from the organization pending democratic elections, in accordance with the Constitutive Act of the AU.

In early September 2005 the new administration announced that it was to offer a general amnesty for political prisoners; 32 such detainees, principally from among those imprisoned in February 2005 for their role in attempted coups d'état in 2003 and 2004, were among the first to benefit from the amnesty. However, some Islamist detainees were not freed, prompting 19 such prisoners to commence a hunger strike demanding their release later in September. In mid-October, moreover, the authorities refused to recognize a recently formed Islamist political party, the Party for Democratic Convergence, on the grounds that its programme violated Mauritanian law. Indeed, Ould Vall announced that no Islamist party would be legalized. Meanwhile, Vall dismissed all 13 regional governors appointed by Taya.

In November 2005 the MCJD issued a timetable for the transition to democratic rule: a constitutional referendum was to be held in June 2006, followed by elections to municipal councils and to the National Assembly in November, elections to the Senate in January 2007 and, finally, a presidential election in March 2007. A 15-member National Independent Electoral Commission was inaugurated at the end of November 2005. Meanwhile, the former ruling DSRP, which had changed its name to the Republican Party for Democracy and Renewal (RPDR), elected Ethmane Ould Cheikh Ebi el Maali, hitherto ambassador to Kuwait, as its new President. In late December the MCJD replaced 12 of the country's regional governors, as well as most prefects and district administrators. A few days later Vall announced a 50% increase in civil servants' salaries, aimed at reducing corruption within the public sector.

An electoral census was conducted in February–April 2006. In late March the MCJD approved proposals presented by the transitional Government on constitutional amendments to be put to a national referendum on 25 June. The principal changes envisaged included: limiting the presidential term of office to five years, renewable only once; stipulating a maximum age of 75 years for presidential candidates; and prohibiting a President from holding any other official post, particularly the leadership of a political party. The proposed reforms were generally supported by most major political parties, including the RPDR. In early May the European Union (EU, see p. 244) announced the resumption of co-operation with Mauritania, which had been suspended following the coup in August 2005.

The constitutional referendum was held, as scheduled, on 25 June 2006. Several days earlier five associates of former President Taya had been arrested on suspicion of planning to sabotage the plebiscite, while a coalition of four parties critical of the Vall administration, the Bloc of Parties for Change, encouraged their supporters to boycott the referendum. None the less, observers from the AU and the Arab League declared their satisfaction with the conduct of the poll. According to official results proclaimed by the Constitutional Council at the end of the month, 96.9% of the valid votes cast were in favour of the amendments to the Constitution and a turn-out of 76.5% of the registered electorate was recorded. In late June 10 political parties, including the RDF, the PF, the PPA and the RM—TEMAM, announced the formation of the Coalition of Forces for Democratic Change (CFDC) to contest the forthcoming legislative and local elections.

At the legislative elections, which were held as scheduled on 19 November and 3 December 2006, the RDF took 15 seats, the UPF eight, the RPDR seven and the PPA five, while the Centrist Reformists and the Mauritanian Party for Union and Change—Hatem both secured four seats; 41 seats were taken by independent candidates. Indirect elections to the Senate took place on 21 January and 4 February 2007 at which independent candidates secured 34 of the 56 seats, while representatives of the CFDC took 15.

The presidential election took place as scheduled over two rounds on 11 and 25 March 2007. At the first round, which was contested by 20 candidates, Sidi Mohamed Ould Cheikh Abdellahi took 24.79% of votes cast, while Ould Daddah won 20.68%, Zeine Ould Zeidane 15.27% and Ould Boulkheir 9.80%. The rate of voter participation was recorded at 70.1%. Abdellahi and Ould Daddah thus proceeded to the second round at which, according to results proclaimed by the Constitutional Council on 29 March, Abdellahi (a government minister under both Moktar Ould Daddah and Taya) was elected President, having secured 52.85% of the valid votes cast. Some 67.5% of the electorate participated in the second round. Ould Boubacar submitted the resignation of his Government on 31 March, although the administration was to remain in office in a 'caretaker' capacity pending the inauguration of the new President, scheduled for 19 April. Abdellahi was duly inaugurated on that date, assuming executive powers in place of the MCJD, which was disbanded, and on the following day he appointed Zeidane as Prime Minister. Later in April a new Government, mainly comprising technocrats with no previous ministerial experience, was installed. The elections were largely deemed to have been fair and democratic and on 10 April Mauritania was readmitted to the AU. In June President Abdellahi effected a minor cabinet reorganization.

In late May 2007 the trial of 25 suspected Islamist militants commenced in Nouakchott; several of the accused were being tried *in absentia*. Some of the defendants were charged in connection with the attack on a military post in Lemgheity in June 2005 (see above), while others were accused of having received training from the GSPC (which had reportedly restyled itself as the al-Qa'ida Organization in the Islamic Maghreb). In early June 24 of the defendants were acquitted owing to lack of evidence, and one defendant, who had escaped from prison in April 2006, was sentenced, *in absentia*, to two years' imprisonment for falsifying identity papers. The trial of a second group of 14 alleged militants began in late June 2007. Three were charged with participating in the attack at Lemgheity, while 11 were charged with having links to the GSPC.

A long-standing border dispute with Senegal was exacerbated by the deaths, in April 1989, of two Senegalese farmers, who had been involved in a dispute regarding grazing rights with Mauritanian livestock-breeders. Mauritanian nationals resident in Senegal were attacked, and their businesses (primarily those of the retail trade) looted, while Senegalese nationals in Mauritania and black Mauritanians suffered similar aggression. By early May it was believed that several hundred people, mostly Senegalese, had been killed. Operations to repatriate nationals of both countries commenced, with international assistance. Amid allegations that the Mauritanian authorities had begun to instigate expulsions of the indigenous black population to Senegal or to Mali, a prominent human rights organization, Amnesty International, expressed concern at the reported violation of black Mauritanians' rights. Mauritania and Senegal suspended diplomatic relations in August 1989, and sporadic outbreaks of violence were reported later that year. In late 1990 the Senegalese Government denied accusations made by the Mauritanian authorities that it was implicated in an alleged attempt to overthrow Taya. In December the arrests of large numbers of black Mauritanians were reported. In early 1991 Mauritanian naval vessels were reported to have opened fire on Senegalese fishing boats, apparently in Senegal's territorial waters; in March several deaths were reported to have resulted from a military engagement on Senegalese territory, following an incursion by Senegalese troops into Mauritania.

Following renewed diplomatic activity, diplomatic relations with Senegal were resumed in April 1992, and the process of reopening the border began in May. However, Mauritanian refugees in Senegal insisted that, as long as the Taya Government refused to recognize their national identity (*mauritanité*) and land and property rights, they would not return to Mauritania. In June 2000 relations between Mauritania and Senegal deteriorated after Mauritania accused the new Senegalese administration of relaunching an irrigation project, which involved the use of joint waters from the Senegal river, in contravention of the Organisation pour la mise en valeur du fleuve Sénégal project (see p. 413). The dispute escalated when the Mauritanian authorities requested that all of its citizens living in Senegal return home and issued the estimated 100,000 Senegalese nationals living in Mauritania with a 15-day deadline by which to leave the country. In mid-June, following mediation by King Muhammad VI of Morocco and the Presidents of The Gambia and Mali, the Mauritanian Minister of the Interior announced that the decision to expel Senegalese citizens had been withdrawn and that Mauritanians living in Senegal could remain there. President Abdoulaye Wade of Senegal visited Mauritania later that month and announced that the irrigation project had been abandoned. By late 2000 the number of Mauritanian refugees in Senegal had declined to 19,800 (compared with 65,500 in mid-1995). In April 2001 President Taya's presence as guest of honour at a ceremony in Dakar to commemorate the 41st anniversary of the independence of Senegal demonstrated an improvement in relations between the countries. At the end of 2006 some 19,630 Mauritanian refugees still remained in Senegal, according to provisional figures. In January 2008 about 100 Mauritanian refugees returned from Senegal, following the conclusion of a repatriation agreement between the Senegalese and the Mauritanian authorities, which envisaged the eventual resettlement of all remaining Mauritanian refugees in Senegal.

Diplomatic relations between Mauritania and Morocco were severed in 1981, following accusations, denied by both countries, of involvement in mutual destabilization attempts. In 1983 Mauritania sought to improve relations between the Maghreb countries (Algeria, Morocco, Mauritania, Tunisia and Libya) and was a signatory of the Maghreb Fraternity and Co-operation Treaty, drafted by Algeria and Tunisia. Relations with Morocco again deteriorated from February 1984, when Mauritania announced its recognition of the Sahrawi Arab Democratic Republic (the Western Saharan state proclaimed by Polisario in 1976), although Taya restored diplomatic relations with Morocco in April 1985. In February 1989 Mauritania was a founder member, with Algeria, Libya, Morocco and Tunisia, of the Union of the Arab Maghreb (UMA, see p. 414), although relations with Libya were reported to have deteriorated from the mid-1990s; Libya was a particularly vehement critic of Mauritania's decision to establish and maintain full diplomatic relations with Israel. Diplomatic relations with Libya, severed in 1995, were none the less restored in 1997. In September 2001 King Muhammad VI of Morocco paid a three-day official visit to

Mauritania, aimed at improving bilateral relations between the two countries. In March 2004 President Taya led an official delegation to Morocco, and again met with King Muhammad. King Muhammad returned to Mauritania in March 2005 as part of a tour of West Africa. There was speculation that, during his visits to both Mauritania and Burkina Faso, the King had attempted to mediate informally between the two countries' Presidents (whose relations remained strained following Mauritania's accusation that Burkina Faso and Libya had supported an attempt to overthrow Taya), but without apparent success.

Relations with both Libya and Burkina Faso were severely strained in the wake of allegations by the Mauritanian Government that those two countries had provided support to rebel elements in the Mauritanian military, accused of participating in the failed *coup d'état* of June 2003 and of subsequently conspiring to overthrow President Taya (see above). It was alleged that Ould Hnana and Ould Sheikhna, who were held responsible by the Mauritanian authorities of leading the 2003 *coup d'état*, had been granted refuge in Burkina Faso and received weapons, money and training, while the Libyan Government was accused of supplying the rebels with weapons, vehicles and other equipment. Libya and Burkina Faso, meanwhile, strenuously denied the accusations. In March 2005 a ministerial commission appointed by the UMA to investigate the Mauritanian allegations against Libya concluded that the Libyan Revolutionary Leader Col Muammar al-Qaddafi had 'no connection' to the events in Mauritania, which it described as a 'purely Mauritanian affair'.

In November 1995 Mauritania signed an agreement to recognize and establish relations with Israel. In October 1998 Mauritania's Minister of Foreign Affairs and Co-operation visited Israel, where he held talks with the Prime Minister, Binyamin Netanyahu. The Arab League strongly criticized the visit, claiming that it contravened the League's resolutions on the suspension of the normalization of relations with Israel, and threatened to impose sanctions on Mauritania. Widespread controversy was provoked both domestically, and in Arab countries, by the establishment of full diplomatic relations between Mauritania and Israel in October 1999. (Of Arab countries, only Egypt and Jordan had taken such a step, under the terms of their respective peace treaties with Israel.) Following the resumption of the Palestinian uprising in September 2000, the Mauritanian Government came under renewed pressure to suspend diplomatic relations with Israel. A visit by the Mauritanian Minister of Foreign Affairs and Co-operation, Dah Ould Abdi, to Israel in May 2001, when he met Israeli Prime Minister Ariel Sharon and President Moshe Katsav, and entered into negotiations with the Minister of Foreign Affairs, Shimon Peres, provoked further controversy, particularly as a result of an appeal by the Arab League, issued earlier that month, for all member countries to cease political contacts with Israel. A further meeting between Peres, Taya and Ould Abdi, in Nouakchott, in October 2002, provoked further controversy. A visit to Mauritania by the Israeli Deputy Prime Minister and Minister of Foreign Affairs, Silvan Shalom, in early May 2005 was preceded, and followed, by the detention of several Islamists (see above), although the Government denied that the arrests were linked to Shalom's presence. His visit was accompanied by a number of anti-Israeli protests in Nouakchott. Although some concern was initially expressed, following the *coup d'état* of August 2005, that diplomatic relations between the two countries might be terminated, the appointment, later in the month, of Ahmed Ould Sid'Ahmed as Minister of Foreign Affairs and Co-operation (who had held that position when Mauritania re-established full diplomatic relations with Israel in 1999) appeared to indicate that the new regime intended to maintain amicable relations with Israel.

Mauritania withdrew from the Economic Community of West African States (see p. 232), with effect from 31 December 2000, owing to decisions adopted by the organization at its summit in December 1999, including the integration of the armed forces of member states and the removal of internal border controls and tariffs.

Government

Following the *coup d'état* of 3 August 2005, a 16-member Military Council for Justice and Democracy (MCJD) assumed power. The Council stated that it would preside over the country for a transitional period of up to two years, following which democratic elections would be held. The 1991 Constitution and most of its institutions, including judicial bodies, and the Constitutional Council, were to be retained, as supplemented and amended by the charter of the MCJD, although the existing legislative organs were dissolved. A referendum held on 25 June 2006 approved various amendments to the Constitution: notably, the presidential term of office was to be reduced to five years (from six), renewable only once, a maximum age of 75 years was to be stipulated for presidential candidates, and the President was to be prohibited from holding any other official post, including the leadership of a political party. Elections to the new bicameral legislature (a 95-member National Assembly, elected by universal suffrage for five years, and a 56-member Senate, elected by municipal leaders) took place during November 2006–February 2007. A presidential election took place in March 2007. Sidi Mohamed Ould Cheikh Abdellahi was inaugurated as President on 19 April, assuming executive powers in place of the MCJD, which was disbanded, and a new Government was unveiled on 28 April. All elections are conducted in the context of a multi-party political system.

For the purpose of local administration, Mauritania is divided into 13 wilayat (regions), comprising a total of 53 moughataa (counties), which are subdivided into 216 communes (districts).

Defence

As assessed at November 2007, the total armed forces were estimated to number 15,870 men: army 15,000, navy 620, air force 250. Full-time membership of paramilitary forces totalled about 5,000. Military service is by authorized conscription, and lasts for two years. The defence budget for 2007 was estimated at UM 4,800m.

Economic Affairs

In 2006, according to estimates by the World Bank, Mauritania's gross national income (GNI), measured at average 2004–06 prices, was US $2,325m., equivalent to $740 per head (or $2,600 on an international purchasing-power parity basis). During 1996–2006, it was estimated, the population increased at an average annual rate of 2.9%, while gross domestic product (GDP) per head increased, in real terms, by an average of 0.9% per year. According to the World Bank, overall GDP increased, in real terms, at an average annual rate of 3.8% in 1996–2006; GDP increased by 11.7% in 2006.

According to World Bank figures, agriculture (including forestry and fishing) contributed 17.0% of GDP in 2006. In 2005, according to FAO estimates, about 51.6% of the labour force were employed in the sector. Owing to the unsuitability of much of the land for crop cultivation, output of staple foods (millet, sorghum, rice and pulses) is insufficient for the country's needs. Livestock-rearing is the principal occupation of the rural population. Fishing, which in 2005 provided an estimated 28.6% of export earnings, supplies 5%–10% of annual GDP and a sizeable proportion of budgetary revenue, and also makes a significant contribution to domestic food requirements. During 1996–2005, according to the African Development Bank (ADB), agricultural GDP declined by an average of 3.7% per year. However, the sector's GDP increased by 4.0% in 2006.

Industry (including mining, manufacturing, construction and power) provided 43.9% of GDP in 2006, according to World Bank figures. An estimated 8% of the labour force were employed in the industrial sector in 2000. During 1996–2006, according to the ADB, industrial GDP increased at an average annual rate of 5.9%; it increased by 35.0% in 2006.

Mining contributed 15.6% of GDP in 2005, according to preliminary IMF figures. The principal activity in this sector is the extraction of iron ore, exports of which contributed an estimated 64.5% of total merchandise export earnings in 2005. Gypsum, salt, gold and copper are also mined. Other exploitable mineral resources include diamonds, phosphates, sulphur, peat, manganese and uranium. In October 1999 highly valuable blue granite deposits were discovered in the north of the country. Many international companies were involved in offshore petroleum exploration in Mauritania in the early 2000s, with reserves at the offshore Shafr el Khanjar and Chinguetti fields estimated at 450m.–1,000m. barrels; production commenced at Chinguetti in February 2006. In September 2000 a five-year programme intended to accelerate the growth of the mining sector commenced, with a US $16.5m. loan from the World Bank. According to the IMF, the GDP of the mining sector increased by an average of 8.9% per year in 1996–2005. The sector's GDP increased by an estimated 0.6% in 2005.

The manufacturing sector contributed 5.1% of GDP in 2005, according to preliminary IMF figures. Fish processing (which contributed 3.9% of GDP in 2002) is the most important activity. The processing of minerals (including imported petroleum) is also of some significance. According to the ADB, manufacturing

GDP increased at an average annual rate of 1.8% in 1996–2006; it increased by 5.0% in 2006.

Mauritania began to utilize electricity generated at hydro-electric installations constructed under the auspices of the Organisation pour la mise en valeur du fleuve Sénégal (OMVS) in late 2002, thus reducing the country's dependence on power generated at thermal stations. Imports of petroleum products comprised 14.2% of the value of merchandise imports in 2005, according to IMF figures.

According to World Bank figures, the services sector contributed 39.1% of GDP in 2006, and engaged an estimated 25.8% of the labour force in 1994. According to the ADB, the combined GDP of the services sector increased by an average rate of 7.6% per year during 1996–2006. Services GDP increased by 6.5% in 2006.

In 2006 Mauritania recorded a visible trade surplus of an estimated US $199.6m. and a deficit of an estimated $35.6m. on the current account of the balance of payments. In 2002 the principal source of imports (20.8%) was France; other major suppliers were the Belgo-Luxembourg Economic Union, Spain and Germany. The principal markets for exports in that year were Italy (14.8%), France (14.4%), Spain and the Belgo-Luxembourg Economic Union. The principal exports in 2005 were iron ore and fish, crustaceans and molluscs. The principal imports in that year were Petroleum-exploration-related machinery and equipment.

Mauritania's overall budget deficit for 2006 was UM 52,900m., equivalent to 2.4% of GDP. Mauritania's total external debt was US $2,281m. at the end of 2005, of which $2,043m. was long-term public debt. In 1998 the cost of debt-servicing was equivalent to 14.2% of the value of exports of goods and services. The annual rate of inflation averaged 6.0% in 1996–2006; consumer prices increased by an average of 6.2% in 2006. The overall rate of unemployment in 2000 was 28.9%.

Mauritania is a member of the Islamic Development Bank (see p. 329), of the OMVS (see p. 413) and of the Union of the Arab Maghreb (see p. 414).

The exploitation, from the mid-2000s, of previously untapped petroleum reserves, principally at offshore locations, was expected to have a significant impact on Mauritania's economy, and in particular on export revenues, which had hitherto been largely dependent on fishing and on the extraction of iron ore. The first major offshore field, at Chinguetti, began production, operated by Woodside Petroleum (of Australia), at a rate of around 75,000 barrels per day (b/d) in February 2006; it was estimated that output could reach 165,000 b/d by 2009, while revenue from petroleum exports was predicted to increase the Mauritanian Government's overall income by an estimated 25% by 2008. In recent years government revenue has also been bolstered by the sale of fishing licences to foreign fleets. In July 2006 the European Union (EU) revised its fishing partnership with the Mauritanian Government. The terms of this agreement span six years and, in exchange for financial aid of some €516m., Mauritania continued to allow EU vessels to fish in its waters. The Mauritanian Government planned to allocate a larger share of this revenue to the development of the indigenous fishing industry. The services sector showed strong growth in the early 2000s, and a series of road-building projects undertaken from 2002, most notably the completion in 2004 of a road linking the administrative capital, Nouakchott, with the chief commercial port, Nouadhibou, and the launch of a new partially state-owned airline (Mauritanian Airlines) in November 2007, was expected to contribute to the continuing expansion of the sector, particularly with regard to external trade and the underdeveloped tourism industry. The bloodless *coup d'état* of August 2005 and the subsequent installation of a transitional Government had little detrimental impact on the Mauritanian economy, and in mid-2007 the new Government signalled its intention to attract more foreign direct investment (recorded at only US $141m. in 2006, some 80% of which was in the mining sector), through reforms of the investment code, and improving the business environment, primarily by enabling foreign companies more easily to establish new ventures in the country. GDP growth in the first half of 2007 reached 5.7%, with the mining and telecommunications sectors in particular contributing to the strong performance. However, in late 2007 high inflation as a result of rises in food prices led to riots and threatened the stability of the economy.

Education

Primary education, which is officially compulsory, begins at six years of age and lasts for six years. In 2000/01 total enrolment at primary schools included 64% of children in the relevant age-group (66% of boys; 62% of girls), according to UNESCO estimates. Secondary education begins at 12 years of age and lasts for six years, comprising two cycles of three years each. Total enrolment at public secondary schools in 2000/01 included only 14% of children in the appropriate age-group (16% of boys; 13% of girls), according to UNESCO estimates. In 2003/04 a total of 9,292 students were enrolled at Mauritania's four higher education institutions (including the Université de Nouakchott, which was opened in 1983). In 2001 a UN project was initiated to address sexual inequality in the Mauritanian education system, which was particularly evident at higher education institutions, where only 16.6% of students were female in 1998. Total expenditure on education in 1998 was UM 6,197.8m. (equivalent to 27.5% of total government expenditure). In 1999 total expenditure on education amounted to UM 6,557.6m.

Public Holidays

2008: 1 January (New Year's Day), 10 January* (Islamic New Year), 20 March* (Mouloud, Birth of Muhammad), 1 May (Labour Day), 25 May (African Liberation Day, anniversary of the OAU's foundation), 10 July (Armed Forces Day), 30 July* (Leilat al-Meiraj, Ascension of Muhammad), 1 October* (Korité—Id al-Fitr, end of Ramadan), 28 November (Independence Day), 9 December* (Tabaski—Id al-Adha, Feast of the Sacrifice).

2009: 1 January (New Year's Day), 9 March* (Mouloud, Birth of Muhammad), 1 May (Labour Day), 25 May (African Liberation Day, anniversary of the OAU's foundation), 10 July (Armed Forces Day), 19 July* (Leilat al-Meiraj, Ascension of Muhammad), 20 September* (Korité—Id al-Fitr, end of Ramadan), 27 November* (Tabaski—Id al-Adha, Feast of the Sacrifice), 28 November (Independence Day), 18 December* (Islamic New Year).

* These holidays are determined by the Islamic lunar calendar and may vary by one or two days from the dates given.

Weights and Measures

The metric system is in force.

MAURITANIA

Statistical Survey

Source (unless otherwise stated): Office National de la Statistique, BP 240, Nouakchott; tel. 525-28-80; fax 525-51-70; e-mail webmaster@ons.mr; internet www.ons.mr.

Area and Population

AREA, POPULATION AND DENSITY

Area (sq km)	1,030,700*
Population (census results)	
5–20 April 1988	1,864,236†
1–15 November 2000‡	
Males	1,241,712
Females	1,266,447
Total	2,508,159
Population (official estimates)	
2004	2,823,062
2005	2,905,727
2006	3,162,338
Density (per sq km) at mid-2006	3.1

* 397,950 sq miles.
† Including an estimate of 224,095 for the nomad population.
‡ Figures include nomads, totalling 128,163 (males 66,007, females 62,156), enumerated during 10 March–20 April 2001.

Ethnic Groups (percentage of total, 1995): Moor 81.5; Wolof 6.8; Toucouleur 5.3; Sarakholé 2.8; Peul 1.1; Others 2.5 (Source: La Francophonie).

REGIONS
(census of November 2000)

Region	Area ('000 sq km)	Population*	Chief town
Hodh Ech Chargui	183	281,600	Néma
Hodh el Gharbi	53	212,156	Aïoun el Atrous
Assaba	37	242,265	Kiffa
Gorgol	14	242,711	Kaédi
Brakna	33	247,006	Aleg
Trarza	68	268,220	Rosso
Adrar	215	69,542	Atâr
Dakhlet-Nouadhibou	22	79,516	Nouadhibou
Tagant	95	76,620	Tidjikja
Guidimagha	10	177,707	Sélibaby
Tiris Zemmour	253	41,121	Zouïrât
Inchiri	47	11,500	Akjoujt
Nouakchott (district)	1	558,195	Nouakchott
Total	**1,030**	**2,580,159**	

* Including nomad population, enumerated during 10 March–20 April 2001.

PRINCIPAL TOWNS
(population at census of 2000*)

Nouakchott (capital)	558,195	Kiffa	32,716
Nouadhibou	72,337	Bougadoum	29,045
Rosso	48,922	Atâr	24,021
Boghé	37,531	Boutilimit	22,257
Adel Bagrou	36,007	Theiekane	22,041
Kaédi	34,227	Ghabou	21,700
Zouïrât	33,929	Mal	20,488

*With the exception of Nouakchott, figures refer to the population of communes (municipalities), and include nomads.

Mid-2007 (incl. suburbs, UN estimate): Nouakchott 673,000 (Source: UN, *World Urbanization Prospects: The 2007 Revision*).

BIRTHS AND DEATHS
(annual averages, UN estimates)

	1990–95	1995–2000	2000–05
Birth rate (per 1,000)	39.0	37.2	35.3
Death rate (per 1,000)	10.7	9.6	8.7

Source: UN, *World Population Prospects: The 2006 Revision*.

Expectation of life (years at birth, WHO estimates): 57.4 (males 55.3; females 59.5) in 2005 (Source: WHO, *World Health Statistics*).

ECONOMICALLY ACTIVE POPULATION
(census of 2000, persons aged 10 years and over, including nomads)

	Males	Females	Total
Agriculture, hunting, forestry and fishing	219,771	94,535	314,306
Mining and quarrying	5,520	249	5,769
Manufacturing	18,301	11,855	30,156
Electricity, gas and water	2,655	182	2,837
Construction	15,251	311	15,562
Trade, restaurants and hotels	83,733	24,799	108,532
Transport, storage and communications	17,225	691	17,916
Financing, insurance, real estate and business services	1,557	454	2,011
Community, social and personal services	72,137	26,583	98,720
Other and unspecified	33,350	22,608	55,958
Total	**469,500**	**182,267**	**651,767**

Mid-2005 (estimates in '000): Agriculture, etc. 705; Total labour force 1,367 (Source FAO).

Health and Welfare

KEY INDICATORS

Total fertility rate (children per woman, 2005)	5.6
Under-5 mortality rate (per 1,000 live births, 2005)	125
HIV/AIDS (% of persons aged 15–49, 2005)	0.7
Physicians (per 1,000 head, 2004)	0.11
Hospital beds (per 1,000 head, 2006)	0.60
Health expenditure (2004): US $ per head (PPP)	42.9
Health expenditure (2004): % of GDP	2.9
Health expenditure (2004): public (% of total)	69.4
Access to water (% of persons, 2004)	53
Access to sanitation (% of persons, 2004)	34
Human Development Index (2005): ranking	137
Human Development Index (2005): value	0.550

For sources and definitions, see explanatory note on p. vi.

Agriculture

PRINCIPAL CROPS
('000 metric tons)

	2004	2005	2006
Rice (paddy)	85.5	72.0	70.5
Maize	5.2*	14.4*	17.3
Sorghum	22.6*	88.0*	83.8
Millet	5.1*	0.9*	1.8
Peas, dry†	11.0	11.7	n.a.
Cow peas†	7.5	7.5	n.a.
Beans, dry†	10.0	10.0	n.a.
Dates	24.0*	22.0	n.a.

* Unofficial figure.
† FAO estimates.

Aggregate production ('000 metric tons, may include official, semi-official or estimated data): Total cereals 120 in 2004, 177 in 2005, 175 in 2006; Total pulses 34 in 2004, 37 in 2005, 37 in 2006; Total roots and tubers 6 in 2004, 6 in 2005, 6 in 2006; Total vegetables (incl. melons) 4 in 2004, 4 in 2005, 4 in 2006; Total fruits (excl. melons) 27 in 2004, 25 in 2005, 25 in 2006.

Source: FAO.

MAURITANIA

LIVESTOCK
('000 head, year ending September, FAO estimates)

	2003	2004	2005
Cattle	1,600	1,600	1,692
Goats	5,600	5,600	5,600
Sheep	8,800	8,850	8,850
Asses, mules or hinnies	158	158	158
Horses	20	20	20
Camels	1,300	1,300	1,397
Chickens	4,200	4,200	4,200

2006: Figures assumed to be unchanged from 2005 (FAO estimates).
Source: FAO.

LIVESTOCK PRODUCTS
('000 metric tons, FAO estimates)

	2003	2004	2005
Goat meat	13.8	13.8	13.8
Camel meat	23.0	23.0	23.0
Chicken meat	4.4	4.5	4.5
Camel milk	22.0	22.0	22.0
Cows' milk	120.8	120.8	120.8
Sheep's milk	96.3	96.3	96.3
Goats' milk	109.8	109.8	109.8
Hen eggs	5.3	5.3	5.3

2006: Figures assumed to be unchanged from 2005 (FAO estimates).
Source: FAO.

Forestry

ROUNDWOOD REMOVALS
('000 cubic metres, excl. bark, FAO estimates)

	2004	2005	2006
Sawlogs, veneer logs and logs for sleepers	1	1	1
Other industrial wood	5	2	2
Fuel wood	1,581	1,623	1,663
Total	1,587	1,626	1,666

Source: FAO.

Fishing

('000 metric tons, live weight)

	2003	2004	2005
Freshwater fishes*	5.0	5.0	5.0
Sardinellas	15.0*	19.2	30.5
European pilchard (sardine)	4.0	8.1	14.8
European anchovy	20.0	33.4	37.4
Jack and horse mackerels	33.5*	51.5	79.4
Chub mackerel	16.0*	23.7	14.3
Octopuses	12.0*	12.1	14.6
Total catch (incl. others)*	141.9	199.4	247.6

* FAO estimate(s).
Source: FAO.

Mining

('000 metric tons)

	2003	2004	2005
Gypsum	34.3	38.9	39.0
Iron ore: gross weight	10,377	11,000	11,000
Iron ore: metal content*	6,890	7,200	7,200

* Estimates.
Source: US Geological Survey.

Industry

SELECTED PRODUCTS
('000 metric tons, unless otherwise indicated)

	2003	2004	2005
Cement*	200	300	300
Crude steel*	5	5	5
Electric energy (million kWh)	312.0	336.0	375.5

* Data from US Geological Survey.

Finance

CURRENCY AND EXCHANGE RATES

Monetary Units
5 khoums = 1 ouguiya (UM).

Sterling, Dollar and Euro Equivalents (30 June 2006)
£1 sterling = 496.407 ouguiyas;
US $1 = 270.610 ouguiyas;
€1 = 344.027 ouguiyas;
1,000 ouguiyas = £2.01 = $3.70 = €2.91.

Average Exchange Rate (ouguiyas per US $)
2003   263.030
2004   257.190
2005   265.528

BUDGET
('000 million ouguiyas)

Revenue*	2003	2004	2005†
Tax revenue	44.9	59.2	76.0
Taxes on income and profits	12.0	16.3	26.6
Tax on business profits	6.6	9.3	15.7
Tax on wages and salaries	4.8	6.3	9.9
Taxes on goods and services	24.7	30.8	36.2
Value-added tax	16.6	21.8	26.7
Turnover taxes	3.3	2.7	2.8
Tax on petroleum products	2.4	2.8	2.5
Other excises	1.6	2.7	3.3
Taxes on international trade	7.3	11.1	10.8
Other current revenue	42.9	47.4	38.8
Fishing royalties and penalties	32.6	36.6	35.3
Revenue from public enterprises	2.1	4.2	0.6
Capital revenue	16.1	11.3	6.2
Other revenue (incl. special accounts)	8.3	6.6	2.8
Total	103.9	117.9	121.0

MAURITANIA

Expenditure‡	2003	2004	2005†
Current expenditure	105.0	96.7	126.7
Wages and salaries	16.0	17.2	22.4
Goods and services	35.3	36.9	60.6
Transfers and subsidies	26.3	9.6	8.7
Military expenditure	16.4	18.6	17.7
Interest on public debt	9.3	11.9	16.1
Capital expenditure	44.0	43.1	36.7
Domestically financed	25.4	24.6	21.4
Financed from abroad	18.6	18.5	15.2
Unidentified	9.2	9.6	0.0
Total	158.1	149.3	163.4

* Excluding grants received ('000 million ouguiyas): 15.7 in 2003; 12.5 in 2004; 10.3 (preliminary) in 2005.
† Preliminary figures.
‡ Excluding restructuring and net lending ('000 million ouguiyas): 1.4 in 2003; 0.2 in 2004; 2.9 in 2005 (preliminary).

Source: IMF, *Islamic Republic of Mauritania: Statistical Appendix* (July 2006).

2006 ('000 million ouguiyas, preliminary): Total revenue (excl. oil revenue) 153.5; Total expenditure 206.4 (Source: IMF, *Islamic Republic of Mauritania: First Review Under the Three-Year Arrangement Under the Poverty Reduction and Growth Facility - Staff Report; Press Release on the Executive Board Discussion; and Statement by the Executive Director for the Islamic Republic of Mauritania* (July 2007)).

INTERNATIONAL RESERVES
(US $ million at 31 December)

	2001	2002	2003
Gold*	3.1	3.1	4.0
IMF special drawing rights	0.2	0.2	0.1
Foreign exchange	284.3	396.0	415.2
Total	287.6	399.3	419.3

* Valued at market-related prices.

2004 (US $ million at 31 December): IMF special drawing rights 0.0.
2005 (US $ million at 31 December): IMF special drawing rights 0.1.

Source: IMF, *International Financial Statistics*.

MONEY SUPPLY
(million ouguiyas at 31 December)

	2001	2002	2003
Currency outside banks	6,688	6,282	6,412
Demand deposits at deposit money banks	21,033	22,628	25,790
Total money (incl. others)	27,721	28,910	32,202

Source: IMF, *International Financial Statistics*.

COST OF LIVING
(Consumer Price Index; base: 2000 = 100)

	2004	2005	2006
Food (incl. beverages)	131.2	149.3	157.3
Clothing (incl. footwear)	121.2	131.1	143.5
Rent	123.3	134.7	145.1
All items (incl. others)	124.2	139.3	147.9

Source: ILO.

NATIONAL ACCOUNTS
Expenditure on the Gross Domestic Product
(US $ million at current prices)

	2004	2005	2006
Government final consumption expenditure	408.30	420.84	483.86
Private final consumption expenditure	1,097.37	1,729.61	1,646.01
Gross capital formation	693.15	832.46	802.88
Total domestic expenditure	2,198.82	2,982.91	2,932.75
Exports of goods and services	462.67	666.89	1,520.55
Less Imports of goods and services	1,167.56	1,778.04	1,683.94
GDP in purchasers' values	1,493.92	1,871.75	2,769.37
GDP at constant 2000 prices	1,139.59	1,189.78	1,355.16

Source: African Development Bank.

Gross Domestic Product by Economic Activity
('000 million ouguiyas at current prices)

	2003	2004	2005*
Agriculture, hunting, forestry and fishing	84.7	91.6	105.4
Mining and quarrying	28.1	45.5	70.6
Manufacturing	18.5	21.3	22.5
Electricity, gas and water / Construction	26.0	33.9	37.3
Trade, restaurants and hotels	43.9	50.2	60.9
Transport and communications	19.8	22.5	23.8
Public administration	41.5	44.4	65.4
Other services	45.3	48.6	59.3
GDP at factor cost	307.8	358.2	445.3
Indirect taxes, *less* subsidies	30.2	38.4	51.7
GDP in purchasers' values	338.0	396.6	497.0

* Preliminary figures.

Source: IMF, *Islamic Republic of Mauritania: Statistical Appendix* (July 2006).

BALANCE OF PAYMENTS
(US $ million)

	2004	2005	2006*
Exports of goods f.o.b.	439.6	625.1	1,366.6
Imports of goods f.o.b.	−923.4	−1,428.3	−1,167.0
Trade balance	−483.8	−803.2	199.6
Exports of services	52.0	79.6	86.7
Imports of services	−259.6	−378.7	−406.3
Balance on goods and services	−691.4	−1,102.3	−120.0
Other income received	104.5	108.6	119.0
Other income paid	−38.9	−44.0	−193.3
Balance on goods, services and income	−625.8	−1,037.7	−194.3
Private unrequited transfers (net)	47.7	60.0	66.5
Official transfers	61.0	101.0	92.1
Current balance	−517.1	−876.8	−35.6
Capital account (net)	15.5	0.0	1,107.2
Direct investment (net)	391.6	814.1	154.6
Official medium- and long-term loans	19.9	−28.0	−835.7
Other capital	0.1	−22.5	−168.3
Net errors and omissions	−19.2	39.4	60.2
Overall balance	−109.7	−73.8	282.3

* Preliminary figures.

Source: IMF, *Islamic Republic of Mauritania: First Review Under the Three-Year Arrangement Under the Poverty Reduction and Growth Facility - Staff Report; Press Release on the Executive Board Discussion; and Statement by the Executive Director for the Islamic Republic of Mauritania* (July 2007).

MAURITANIA

External Trade

PRINCIPAL COMMODITIES
(US $ million)

Imports c.i.f.	1999	2000	2001
Food and live animals	160.3	112.1	77.6
Live animals chiefly for food	80.2	56.1	38.8
Cereals and cereal preparations	39.8	32.2	20.6
Sugar and honey	30.1	17.3	12.6
Mineral fuels, lubricants, etc.	41.5	35.4	94.7
Petroleum products, refined	41.5	35.4	94.7
Animal and vegetable oils, fats and waxes	18.7	8.0	5.9
Animal oils and fats	18.6	7.9	5.9
Basic manufactures	14.6	17.2	35.1
Non-metallic mineral manufactures	13.4	15.6	34.4
Machinery and transport equipment	34.9	33.0	34.9
Road vehicles	34.9	33.0	34.9
Total (incl. others)	342.8	310.2	353.0

Source: UN, *International Trade Statistics Yearbook*.

2002 (US $ million): Petroleum exploration-related machinery and equipment 48.3, Petroleum products 85.2; Total imports f.o.b. (incl. others) 431.2 (Source: IMF, *Islamic Republic of Mauritania: Statistical Appendix*—July 2006).

2003 (US $ million): Petroleum exploration-related machinery and equipment 74.5, Petroleum products 100.3; Total imports f.o.b. (incl. others) 542.1 (Source: IMF, *Islamic Republic of Mauritania: Statistical Appendix*—July 2006).

2004 (US $ million): Petroleum exploration-related machinery and equipment 298.0, Petroleum products 145.0; Total imports f.o.b. (incl. others) 923.4 (Source: IMF, *Islamic Republic of Mauritania: Statistical Appendix*—July 2006).

2005 (US $ million, provisional figures): Petroleum-exploration-related machinery and equipment 600.0, Non-petroleum mining-related machinery and equipment 69.8, Petroleum products 196.4; Total imports f.o.b. (incl. others) 1,387.4 (Source: IMF, *Islamic Republic of Mauritania: Statistical Appendix*—July 2006).

Exports f.o.b.	2003	2004	2005*
Iron ore	163.9	230.2	389.4
Fish	131.5	172.6	172.7
Total (incl. others)	318.2	439.6	604.1

*Preliminary figures.

Source: IMF, *Islamic Republic of Mauritania: Statistical Appendix* (July 2006).

PRINCIPAL TRADING PARTNERS
(US $ million)*

Imports c.i.f.	2000	2001	2002
Belgium-Luxembourg	32.9	31.4	36.8
France	94.5	89.2	86.9
Germany	17.2	21.3	23.2
Italy	21.9	22.1	17.6
Japan	9.2	9.8	16.2
Netherlands	10.0	10.7	14.0
Spain	21.8	21.5	27.9
United Kingdom	8.5	7.2	14.0
USA	9.6	16.0	14.4
Total (incl. others)	336.2	372.3	418.0

Exports c.i.f.	2000	2001	2002
Belgium-Luxembourg	30.8	28.9	33.9
France	63.5	50.7	47.6
Germany	13.2	20.8	35.7
Italy	47.4	51.0	48.8
Japan	53.0	27.1	21.0
Portugal	7.6	7.0	7.8
Spain	38.1	42.2	39.9
United Kingdom	5.4	5.4	1.5
Total (incl. others)	344.7	338.6	330.3

*Data are compiled on the basis of reporting by Mauritania's trading partners. Data detailing imports and exports of trade with developing and emerging countries were not available.

Source: IMF, *Islamic Republic of Mauritania: Statistical Appendix* (October 2003).

Transport

RAILWAYS

1984: Passengers carried 19,353; Passenger-km 7m.; Freight carried 9.1m. metric tons; Freight ton-km 6,142m.

Freight ton-km (million): 6,365 in 1985; 6,411 in 1986; 6,473 in 1987; 6,535 in 1988; 6,610 in 1989; 6,690 in 1990; 6,720 in 1991; 6,810 in 1992; 6,890 in 1993 (figures for 1988–93 are estimates) (Source: UN Economic Commission for Africa, *African Statistical Yearbook*).

ROAD TRAFFIC
('000 motor vehicles in use)

	1998	1999	2000
Passenger cars	8.6	9.9	12.2
Commercial vehicles	16.7	17.3	18.2

2001–02 ('000 motor vehicles in use): Figures assumed to be unchanged from 2000.

Source: UN, *Statistical Yearbook*.

SHIPPING

Merchant Fleet
(registered at 31 December)

	2004	2005	2006
Number of vessels	146	152	153
Total displacement ('000 grt)	49.3	51.9	51.9

Source: Lloyd's Register-Fairplay, *World Fleet Statistics*.

International Sea-borne Freight Traffic
(Port of Nouakchott, '000 metric tons)

	2003	2004	2005
Goods loaded	47.5	77.4	113.2
Goods unloaded	1,399.9	1,434.9	1,712.9

Source: Port Autonome de Nouakchott.

CIVIL AVIATION
(traffic on scheduled services)*

	2001	2002	2003
Kilometres flown (million)	2	1	1
Passengers carried ('000)	156	106	116
Passenger-km (million)	174	45	49
Total ton-km (million)	23	4	5

*Including an apportionment of the traffic of Air Afrique.

Source: UN, *Statistical Yearbook*.

Tourism

Tourist arrivals (estimates, '000): 24 in 1999.

Receipts from tourism (US $ million, excl. passenger transport): 28 in 1999 (Source: World Tourism Organization).

MAURITANIA

Communications Media

	2004	2005	2006
Telephones ('000 main lines in use)	39.0	41.0	34.9
Mobile cellular telephones ('000 subscribers)	522.4	745.6	1,060.1
Personal computers ('000 in use)	42	42	n.a.
Internet users ('000)	14	20	100
Broadband subscribers	—	200	700

Television receivers ('000 in use): 247 in 1999.

Radio receivers ('000 in use): 570 in 1997.

Facsimile machines (number in use): 3,300 in 1999.

Daily newspapers: Number 2; Estimated average circulation ('000 copies) 12 in 1996; 3 in 2004.

Sources: UNESCO, *Statistical Yearbook*; UN, *Statistical Yearbook*; International Telecommunication Union.

Education

(2004/05, unless otherwise indicated)

			Students		
	Institutions	Teachers	Males	Females	Total
Pre-primary	n.a.	251	n.a.	n.a.	4,709*
Primary	2,676†	11,001	221,838	221,777	443,615
Secondary	n.a.	2,995	50,205	42,591	92,796
Tertiary	4‡	356	6,608	2,150	8,758

* 2003/04.
† 1998/99.
‡ 1995/96.

Adult literacy rate (UNESCO estimates): 51.2% (males 59.5%; females 43.4%) in 2000 (Source: UNESCO Institute for Statistics).

Sources: mainly UNESCO Institute for Statistics and Ministry of National Education, Nouakchott.

Directory

While no longer an official language under the terms of the 1991 Constitution (see below), French is still widely used in Mauritania, especially in the commercial sector. Many organizations are therefore listed under their French names, by which they are generally known.

The Constitution

Following the *coup d'état* of 3 August 2005, the self-styled Military Council for Justice and Democracy (MCJD) introduced a Constitutional Charter that was intended to supplement and partially replace the Constitution approved by referendum in 1991 for a transitional period for up to two years, following which time democratic elections were to be held. Those provisions of the Constitution pertaining to the role of Islam, individual and collective freedoms and the prerogatives of the State were to remain in force, while certain judicial organs (namely: the High Council of Magistrates; courts and tribunals; the High Council of Islam; the Audit Court; and the Constitutional Council) were to continue to function. A number of the legislative powers previously held by a bicameral legislature (which was abolished) were transferred to the MCJD, which was also to assume executive powers. The President of the MCJD was empowered to appoint a Prime Minister and other Ministers, who were to be responsible to the MCJD and its President. The MCJD was permitted to consult with the Constitutional Council with regard to any constitutional question. A referendum held on 25 June 2006 approved various amendments to the Constitution: notably, the presidential term of office was to be reduced to five years, renewable only once, a maximum age of 75 years was to be stipulated for presidential candidates, and the President was to be prohibited from holding any other official post, including the leadership of a political party. Elections to a new bicameral legislature were held during November 2006–February 2007, while a presidential election was held over two rounds in March. Sidi Mohamed Ould Cheikh Abdellahi was inaugurated as President on 19 April, assuming executive powers in place of the MCJD, which was disbanded, and a new Government was unveiled on 28 April.

The Constitution states that the official language is Arabic, and that the national languages are Arabic, Pular, Wolof and Solinké.

The Government

HEAD OF STATE

President: SIDI MOHAMED OULD CHEIKH ABDELLAHI (inaugurated 19 April 2007).

COUNCIL OF MINISTERS
(May 2008)

Prime Minister: YAHYA OULD AHMED EL WAGHEF.

Minister of Justice: YAHYA OULD SID EL MOUSTAPH.

Minister of Foreign Affairs and Co-operation: CHEIKH EL AVIA OULD MOHAMED KHOUNA.

Minister of National Defence: MOHAMED MAHMOUD OULD MOHAMED LEMINE.

Minister of the Interior: MOHAMED YEHDHIH OULD MOCTAR EL HACEN.

Minister of the Economy and Finance: ABDERRAHMANE OULD HAMMA VEZZAZ.

Minister of Primary and Secondary Education and the Fight Against Illiteracy: NEBGHOUHA MINT HABA.

Minister of Higher Education: MOHAMED MAHMOUD OULD SEYDI.

Minister of Islamic Affairs and Original Education: DAHANE OULD AHMED MAHMOUD.

Minister of Labour, Integration and Vocational Training: HABIB OULD HEMDEIT.

Minister of Health: MOHAMED OULD MOHAMED EL HAFEDH OULD KHLIL.

Minister Petroleum and Mines: KANE MUSTAPHA.

Minister of Fisheries: ASSANE SOUMARÉ.

Minister of Trade and Industry: SALMA MINT TEGUEDDI.

Minister of Handicrafts and Tourism: MOHAMED MAHMOUD OULD BRAHIM KHLIL.

Minister of Decentralization and Land Development: YAHYA OULD KEBD.

Minister of Agriculture and Animal Resources: CORRÉRA ISSAGHA.

Minister of Equipment, Urban Development and Housing: MOHAMED OULD BILAL.

Minister of Transport: BEBAHA OULD AHMED YOURA.

Minister of Water Resources and Energy: MOHAMED OULD R'ZEIZIM.

Minister of Culture and Communication: MOHAMED OULD AMAR.

Minister of the Civil Service and the Modernization of Administration: MOUSTAPHA OULD HAMOUD.

Minister in charge of Relations with Parliament and Civil Society: SIDNEY SOKHONA.

Minister in charge of Women's, Childhood and Family Development: FATIMETOU MINT KHATTRI.

Minister in charge of Youth and Sports: MOHAMED OULD BERBESSE.

Minister-delegate to the Prime Minister, in charge of the Environment: DAHMOUD OULD MERZOUG.

Minister-delegate to the Ministry of Foreign Affairs and Co-operation, in charge of the Union of the Arab Maghreb: MOHAMED LEMINE OULD NATI.

Secretary-General of the Government: BÂ ABDOULAYE MAMADOU.

Secretary of State at the Ministry of the Economy and Finance, in charge of the Budget: SID'AHMED OULD RAYES.

Secretary of State for Mauritanians Living Abroad: MOHAMED OULD MOHAMEDOU.

Secretary of State for Information and Communications Technology: ABDALLAHI OULD ELY OULD BENANE.

MINISTRIES

Office of the President: BP 184, Nouakchott; tel. and fax 525-26-36.

Office of the Prime Minister: BP 237, Nouakchott; tel. 525-33-37.

Ministry of Capital Works and Transport: BP 237, Nouakchott; tel. 525-33-37.

Ministry of the Civil Service and Employment: BP 193, Nouakchott; tel. and fax 525-84-10.

Ministry of Communication: Nouakchott.

Ministry of Culture, Youth and Sports: BP 223, Nouakchott; tel. 525-11-30.

Ministry of Economic Affairs and Development: 303 Ilot C, BP 5150, Nouakchott; tel. 525-16-12; fax 525-51-10; e-mail nfomaed@mauritania.mr; internet www.maed.gov.mr.

Ministry of Energy and Petroleum: Nouakchott; tel. 525-71-40.

Ministry of Finance: BP 181, Nouakchott; tel. 525-20-20.

Ministry of Fisheries and the Maritime Economy: BP 137, Nouakchott; tel. 525-46-07; fax 525-31-46; e-mail ministre@mpem.mr; internet www.mpem.mr.

Ministry of Foreign Affairs and Co-operation: BP 230, Nouakchott; tel. 525-26-82; fax 525-28-60.

Ministry of Fundamental and Secondary Education: BP 387, Nouakchott; tel. 525-12-37; fax 525-12-22.

Ministry of Health and Social Affairs: BP 177, Nouakchott; tel. 525-20-52; fax 525-22-68.

Ministry of Higher Education and Scientific Research: Nouakchott.

Ministry of the Interior, Posts and Telecommunications: BP 195, Nouakchott; tel. 525-36-61; fax 525-36-40; e-mail paddec@mauritania.mr.

Ministry of Justice: BP 350, Nouakchott; tel. 525-10-83; fax 525-70-02.

Ministry of Mines and Industry: BP 199, Nouakchott; tel. 525-30-83; fax 525-69-37; e-mail mmi@mauritania.mr.

Ministry of Rural Development and the Environment: BP 366, Nouakchott; tel. 525-15-00; fax 525-74-75.

Ministry of Trade, Crafts and Tourism: BP 182, Nouakchott; tel. 525-35-72; fax 525-76-71.

Ministry of Water Resources: BP 4913, Nouakchott; tel. 525-71-44; fax 529-42-87; e-mail saadouebih@yahoo.fr.

Office of the Secretary-General of the Government: BP 184, Nouakchott.

President and Legislature

PRESIDENT

Presidential Election, First Round, 11 March 2007

Candidate	Votes	% of votes
Sidi Mohamed Ould Cheikh Abdellahi	183,743	24.79
Ahmed Ould Daddah	153,242	20.68
Zeine Ould Zeidane	113,194	15.27
Messaoud Ould Boulkheir	72,611	9.80
Ibrahim Moctar Sarr	58,818	7.94
Saleh Ould Mohamedou Ould Hanana	56,718	7.65
Mohamed Ould Maouloud	30,265	4.08
Dahane Ould Ahmed Mahmoud	15,316	2.07
Others	57,159	7.71
Total	741,066	100.00

Presidential Election, Second Round, 25 March 2007

Candidate	Votes	% of votes
Sidi Mohamed Ould Cheikh Abdellahi	373,519	52.85
Ahmed Ould Daddah	333,184	47.15
Total	706,703	100.00

Al Jamiya al-Wataniyah
(National Assembly)

ave de l'Indépendance, BP 185, Nouakchott; tel. 525-11-30; fax 525-70-78; internet www.mauritania.mr/assemblee.

President: MESSOUD OULD BOULKHEIR.

General Election, 19 November and 3 December 2006

Party	Constituency seats	National list seats	Total seats
Rally of Democratic Forces	12	3	15
Union of Progressive Forces	7	1	8
Republican Party for Democracy and Renewal	5	2	7
Popular Progressive Alliance	4	1	5
Centrist Reformists	2	2	4
Mauritanian Party for Union and Change—Hatem	3	1	4
Union for Democracy and Progress	2	1	3
Rally for Democracy and Unity	2	1	3
Democratic Renewal	1	1	2
Alternative	1	—	1
Union of the Democratic Centre	1	—	1
Popular Front	—	1	1
Independents	41	—	41
Total	81	14	95

Majlis al-Shuyukh
(Senate)

ave de l'Indépendance, BP 5838, Nouakchott; tel. 525-68-77; fax 525-73-73; internet www.senat.mr.

President: BÂ MAMADOU DIT M'BARÉ.

Election, 21 January and 4 February 2007

Party	Seats
Independents	34
Coalition of Forces for Democratic Change	15
Republican Party for Democracy and Renewal	3
Total*	52

*The total number of seats in the Senate is 56. The result from one constituency was annulled by the Constitutional Council and the remaining three seats, reserved for representatives of the Mauritanina diaspora, were yet to be allocated.

Election Commission

National Independent Electoral Commission: Nouakchott; 15 mems; Pres. Col (retd) CHEIKH SID'AHMED OULD BABAMINE.

Advisory Council

Economic and Social Council: Nouakchott.

Political Organizations

Following the *coup d'état* of August 2005, and in advance of the election of a new legislature and president, several new political parties were formed, and a number of politicians hitherto in exile returned to Mauritania. At the time of the legislative elections held in November–December 2006 some 35 political parties were legally recognized in Mauritania. The organizations listed below were among the most significant to operate at that time.

Alliance for Justice and Democracy (AJD): Nouakchott; Leader CISSÉ AMADOU CHIEKHOU.

Alternative (Al-Badil): Nouakchott; f. 2006; Leader MOHAMED YEHDHIH OULD MOKTAR EL HASSEN.

Centrist Reformists: Nouakchott; f. 2006; mem. of Coalition of Forces for Democratic Change, formed in advance of legislative and local elections in 2006; moderate Islamist grouping; Co-ordinator MOHAMED JEMIL OULD MANSOUR.

Democratic Renewal: Nouakchott; f. 2005; mem. of Coalition of Forces for Democratic Change, formed in advance of legislative and local elections in 2006; Pres. MOUSTAPHA OULD ABEIDERRAHMANE.

Mauritanian African Liberation Forces—Renovation (MALF—Renovation): Nouakchott; tel. 228-77-40; internet www.flam-renovation.org; f. 2006 in split from clandestine, exiled, Mauritanian African Liberation Forces; represents interests of Afro- (Black) Mauritanians; mem. of Coalition of Forces for

Democratic Change, formed in advance of legislative and local elections in 2006; Leader MAMADOU BOCAR BÂ.

Mauritanian Labour Party: Nouakchott; f. 2001; Leader MOHAMED EL HAFEDH OULD DENNA.

Mauritanian Party for Renewal and Agreement: Nouakchott; f. 2001; Leader MOULAY EL-HASSEN OULD JIYID.

Mauritanian Party for the Defence of the Environment (MPDE—The Greens): Nouakchott; internet pmde.hautetfort .com; ecologist; mem. of Bloc of Parties for Change, formed in advance of planned legislative and local elections in 2006; Pres. MOHAMED OULD SIDI OULD DELLAHI.

Mauritanian Party for Union and Change—Hatem: Nouakchott; f. 2005 by leadership of the fmr prohibited Knights of Change militia and reformist elements of the fmr ruling Democratic and Social Republican Party; mem. of Coalition of Forces for Democratic Change, formed in advance of legislative and local elections in 2006; Pres. SALEH OULD HNANA; Sec.-Gen. ABDERAHMANE OULD MINI.

Party for Liberty, Equality and Justice (PLEJ): Nouakchott; mem. of Bloc of Parties for Change, formed in advance of legislative and local elections in 2006; Pres. MAMADOU ALASSANE BÂ.

Popular Front (FP): Nouakchott; f. 1998; social-liberal; mem. of Coalition of Forces for Democratic Change, formed in advance of legislative and local elections in 2006; Leader MOHAMED LEMINE CH'BIH OULD CHEIKH MELAININE.

Popular Progressive Alliance (APP): Nouakchott; internet www .app-mauritanie.org; f. 1991; absorbed Convention for Change (the successor to the banned Action for Change, which sought to represent the interests of Harratin—black Moors who had frmly been slaves) in 2003; mem. of Coalition of Forces for Democratic Change, formed in advance of legislative and local elections in 2006; Pres. MESSAOUD OULD BOULKHAR.

Rally for Democracy and Unity (RDU): Nouakchott; f. 1991; supported regime of fmr Pres. Taya; Chair. AHMED OULD SIDI BABA.

Rally for Mauritania (RPM—Temam): Nouakchott; f. 2005; Islamist; mem. of Coalition of Forces for Democratic Change, formed in advance of legislative and local elections in 2006; Pres. Dr CHEIKH OULD HORMA.

Rally of Democratic Forces (RDF): Ilot K, 120, BP 4986, Nouakchott; tel. 525-67-46; fax 525-65-70; e-mail info@rfd-mauritanie.org; internet www.rfd-mauritanie.org; f. 2001 by fmr mems of the officially dissolved Union of Democratic Forces—New Era (f. 1991); mem. of Coalition of Forces for Democratic Change, formed in advance of legislative and local elections in 2006; Pres. AHMED OULD DADDAH.

Republican Party for Democracy and Renewal (RPDR): ZRB, Tevragh Zeina, Nouakchott; tel. 529-18-36; fax 529-18-00; e-mail info@prdr.mr; internet www.prdr.mr; f. 2006 to replace Democratic and Social Republican Party, the fmr ruling party, prior to *coup d'état* of August 2005; Leader Sidi Mohamed Ould Med Vall dit Ghriny.

Reward (Sawab): Nouakchott; f. 2004; social democratic; Chair. of Central Council MOHAMED MAHMOUD OULD GHOULMA; Pres. Dr CHEIKH OULD SIDI OULD HANENA.

Social Democratic Union: Nouakchott; Pres. ISSELMOU OULD HANNEFI.

Union for Democracy and Progress (UDP): Ilot V, 70, Tevragh Zeina, BP 816, Nouakchott; tel. 525-52-89; fax 525-29-95; f. 1993; Pres. NAHA HAMDI MINT.

Union of the Democratic Centre (UDC): Nouakchott; f. 2005 by fmr mems of the Democratic and Social Republican Party, the fmr ruling party; Pres. CHEIKH SID'AHMED OULD BABA.

Union of Progressive Forces (UPF) (Ittihad Quwa al-Taqaddum): Nouakchott; e-mail ufpweb2@yahoo.fr; internet www.ufpweb .org; tel. 529-32-66; fax 524-35-86; e-mail infos@ufpweb.org; f. 2000, following the enforced dissolution of the fmr Union of Democratic Forces—New Era, which it had existed as a faction thereof since 1998; mem. of Coalition of Forces for Democratic Change, formed in advance of legislative and local elections in 2006; Pres. MOHAMED OULD MAOULOUD; Sec.-Gen. MOHAMED EL MOUSTAPHA OULD BEDREDDINE.

Unauthorized, but influential, is the Islamic **Ummah Party** (the Constitution prohibits the operation of religious political organizations), founded in 1991 and led by Imam SIDI YAHYA, and the Baathist **National Vanguard Party (Taliaa)**, which was officially dissolved by the Government in 1999 and is led by AHMEDOU OULD BABANA. The clandestine **Mauritanian African Liberation Forces (MALF)** was founded in 1983 in Senegal to represent Afro-Mauritanians (Point d'ébullition, BP 5811, Dakar-Fann, Senegal; tel. +221 822-80-77; e-mail ba_demba@yahoo .fr; internet members .lycos .co .uk/flamnetPres. SAMBA THIAM); a faction broke away from this organization and returned to Mauritania in early 2006, forming the Mauritanian African Liberation Forces—Renovation. A further group based in exile is the **Arab-African Salvation Front against Slavery, Racism and Tribalism—AASF** (e-mail faas@caramail .com; internet membres .lycos .fr/faas). In August 2007 a further 18 new parties were registered: included were an Islamist party, the **National Rally for Reform and Development**, and two parties led by women, the **National Party for Development**, led by SAHLA BINT AHMAD ZAYID, and the **Mauritanian Hope Party**, led by TAHI BINT LAHBIB.

Diplomatic Representation

EMBASSIES IN MAURITANIA

Algeria: Ilot A, Tevragh Zeina, BP 625, Nouakchott; tel. 525-35-69; fax 525-47-77; Ambassador ABDELKRIM BEN HOCINE.

China, People's Republic: rue 42-133, Tevragh Zeina, BP 257, Nouakchott; tel. 525-20-70; fax 525-24-62; e-mail chinaemb_mr@mfa .gov.cn; internet mr.china-embassy.org; Ambassador ZHANG XUN.

Congo, Democratic Republic: Tevragh Zeina, BP 5714, Nouakchott; tel. 525-46-12; fax 525-50-53; e-mail ambardc.rim@caramail .com; Chargé d'affaires a.i. TSHIBASU MFUAD.

Egypt: Villa no. 468, Tevragh Zeina, BP 176, Nouakchott; tel. 525-21-92; fax 525-33-84; Ambassador BAHAA EDDIN MOKHTAR MOWAFI.

France: rue Ahmed Ould Hamed, Tevragh Zeina, BP 231, Nouakchott; tel. 529-96-99; fax 529-69-38; e-mail ambafrance .nouakchott-amba@diplomatie.gouv.fr; internet www .france-mauritanie.mr; Ambassador PATRICK NICOLOSO.

Germany: Tevragh Zeina, BP 372, Nouakchott; tel. 525-17-29; fax 525-17-22; e-mail amb-allemagne@toptechnology.mr; Ambassador EBERHARD SCHANZE.

Israel: Ilot A516, Tevragh Zeina, BP 5714, Nouakchott; tel. 525-82-35; fax 525-46-12; e-mail info@nouakchott.mfa.gov.il; Ambassador BOAZ BESMUTH BISMUTH.

Korea, Democratic People's Republic: Nouakchott; Ambassador PAK HO IL.

Kuwait: Tevragh Zeina, BP 345, Nouakchott; tel. 525-33-05; fax 525-41-45.

Libya: BP 673, Nouakchott; tel. 525-52-02; fax 525-50-53.

Mali: Tevragh Zeina, BP 5371, Nouakchott; tel. 525-40-81; fax 525-40-83; e-mail ambmali@hotmail.com; Ambassador MOUSSA KALILOU COULIBALY.

Morocco: 569 ave de Gaulle, Tevragh Zeina, BP 621, Nouakchott; tel. 525-14-11; fax 529-72-80; e-mail sifmanktt@mauritel.mr; Ambassador ABDERRAHMANE BENOMAR.

Nigeria: Ilot P9, BP 367, Nouakchott; tel. 525-23-04; fax 525-23-14; Ambassador Alhaji BALA MOHAMED SANI.

Qatar: BP 609, Nouakchott; tel. 525-23-99; fax 525-68-87; e-mail nouakchoti@mofa.gov.qa; Ambassador MOHAMMED KURDI TALEB AL-MERRI.

Russia: rue Abu Bakr, BP 221, Nouakchott; tel. 525-19-73; fax 525-52-96; e-mail ambruss@opt.mr; Ambassador LEONID V. ROGOV.

Saudi Arabia: Las Balmas, Zinat, BP 498, Nouakchott; tel. 525-26-33; fax 525-29-49; e-mail mremb@mofa.gov.sa; Ambassador MOHAMED AL FADH EL ISSA.

Senegal: Villa 500, Tevragh Zeina, BP 2511, Nouakchott; tel. 525-72-90; fax 525-72-91; Ambassador MAHMOUDOU CHEIKH KANE.

Spain: BP 232, Nouakchott; tel. 525-20-80; fax 525-40-88; e-mail emb.nouakchott@mae.es; Ambassador ALEJANDRO POLANCO MATA.

Syria: Tevragh Zeina, BP 288, Nouakchott; tel. 525-27-54; fax 525-45-00.

Tunisia: BP 681, Nouakchott; tel. 525-28-71; fax 525-18-27; Ambassador ABDEL WEHAB JEMAL.

United Arab Emirates: BP 6824, Nouakchott; tel. 525-10-98; fax 525-09-92.

USA: rue Abdallaye, BP 222, Nouakchott; tel. 525-26-60; fax 525-15-92; e-mail tayebho@state.gov; internet mauritania.usembassy.gov; Ambassador MARK M. BOULWARE.

Yemen: Tevragh Zeina, BP 4689, Nouakchott; tel. 525-55-91; fax 525-56-39.

Judicial System

The Code of Law was promulgated in 1961 and subsequently modified to incorporate Islamic institutions and practices. The main courts comprise three courts of appeal, 10 regional tribunals, two labour tribunals and 53 departmental civil courts. A revenue court has jurisdiction in financial matters. The members of the High Court of Justice are elected by the National Assembly and the Senate.

MAURITANIA

Shari'a (Islamic) law was introduced in February 1980. A special Islamic court was established in March of that year, presided over by a magistrate of Islamic law, assisted by two counsellors and two *ulemas* (Muslim jurists and interpreters of the Koran). A five-member High Council of Islam, appointed by the President, advises upon the conformity of national legislation to religious precepts, at the request of the President.

Audit Court (Cour des Comptes): Nouakchott; audits all govt institutions; Pres. SOW ADAMA SAMBA.

Constitutional Council: f. 1992; includes six mems, three nominated by the Head of State and three designated by the Presidents of the Senate and National Assembly; Pres. ABDOULLAH OULD ELY SALEM; Sec.-Gen. MOHAMED OULD M'REIZIG.

High Council of Islam (al-Majlis al-Islamiya al-A'la'): Nouakchott; f. 1992; Pres. AHMED OULD NEINI.

High Court of Justice: Nouakchott; f. 1961; comprises an equal number of appointees elected from their membership by the National Assembly and the Senate, following each partial or general renewal of those legislative bodies; competent to try the President of the Republic in case of high treason, and the Prime Minister and members of the Government in case of conspiracy against the state.

Supreme Court: BP 201, Palais de Justice, Nouakchott; tel. 525-21-63; f. 1961; comprises an administrative chamber, a civil and commercial chamber, a social and employment chamber and a criminal chamber; also functions as the highest court of appeal; Pres. KABR OULD ELEWA.

Religion

ISLAM

Islam is the official religion, and the population are almost entirely Muslims of the Malekite rite. The major religious groups are the Tijaniya and the Qadiriya. Chinguetti, in the region of Adrar, is the seventh Holy Place in Islam. A High Council of Islam supervises the conformity of legislation to Muslim orthodoxy.

CHRISTIANITY

Roman Catholic Church

Mauritania comprises the single diocese of Nouakchott, directly responsible to the Holy See. The Bishop participates in the Bishops' Conference of Senegal, Mauritania, Cape Verde and Guinea-Bissau, based in Dakar, Senegal. At 31 December 2005 there were an estimated 4,500 adherents, mainly non-nationals, in the country.

Bishop of Nouakchott: Most Rev. MARTIN ALBERT HAPPE, Evêché, BP 5377, Nouakchott; tel. 525-04-27; fax 525-37-51; e-mail mgr-martin-happe@mauritel.mr.

The Press

Of some 400 journals officially registered in Mauritania in mid-2004, some 30 were regular, widely available publications, of which the following were among the most important:

Al-Akhbar: BP 5346, Nouakchott; tel. 525-08-94; fax 525-37-57; e-mail fr.redaction@alakhbar.info; internet fr.alakhbar.info; f. 1995; weekly; Arabic.

Al-Qalam/Le Calame: BP 1059, Nouakchott; tel. 529-02-34; fax 525-75-55; e-mail calame@compunet.mr; internet www.calame.8k.com; f. 1994; weekly; Arabic and French; independent; Editors-in-Chief RIYAD OULD AHMED EL-HADI (Arabic edn), HINDOU MINT AININA (French edn).

Le Carrefour: Nouakchott; Dir MOUSSA OULD SAMBA SY.

Châab: BP 371, Nouakchott; tel. 525-29-40; fax 525-85-47; daily; Arabic; also publ. in French *Horizons*; publ. by Agence Mauritanienne de l'Information; Dir-Gen. MOHAMED EL-HAFED OULD MAHAM.

Challenge: BP 1346, Nouakchott; tel. and fax 529-06-26.

Ech-tary: BP 1059, Nouakchott; tel. 525-50-65; fortnightly; Arabic; satirical.

L'Essor: BP 5310, Nouakchott; tel. 630-21-68; fax 525-88-90; e-mail sidiel2000@yahoo.fr; monthly; the environment and the economy; Dir SIDI EL-MOCTAR CHEÏGUER; circ. 2,500.

El-Anba: BP 3901, Nouakchott; tel. and fax 525-99-27.

L'Eveil-Hebdo: BP 587, Nouakchott; tel. 525-67-14; fax 525-87-54; e-mail symoudou@yahoo.fr; f. 1991; weekly; independent; Dir of Publication SY MAMADOU.

Inimich al-Watan: Nouakchott; independent; Arabic; Dir of Publication MOHAMED OULD ELKORY.

Journal Officel: BP 188, Nouakchott; tel. 525-33-37; fax 525-34-74; fortnightly.

Maghreb Hebdo: BP 5266, Nouakchott; tel. 525-98-10; fax 525-98-11; f. 1994; weekly; Dir KHATTRI OULD DIÈ.

Nouakchott-Info: Immeuble Abbas, Tevragh Zeina, BP 1905, Nouakchott; tel. 525-02-71; fax 525-54-84; e-mail jedna@mapeci.com; internet www.akhbarnouakchott.com; f. 1995; daily; independent; Arabic and French; Dir of Publication and Editor-in-Chief CHEIKHNA OULD NENNI.

L'Opinion Libre: Nouakchott; weekly; Editor ELY OULD NAFA.

Rajoul Echarée: Nouakchott; e-mail rajoul_echaree@toptechnology.mr; weekly; independent; Arabic; Dir SIDI MOHAMED OULD YOUNÈS.

Ar-Rayah (The Banner): Nouakchott; e-mail team@rayah.info; internet www.rayah.info; f. 1997; independent; weekly; pro-Islamist; publication prohibited in May 2003; Editor AHMED OULD WEDIAA.

Le Rénovateur: Nouakchott; every 2 months; f. 2001; Editor Chiekh TIDIANE DIA.

La Tribune: BP 6227, Nouakchott; tel. 525-44-92; fax 525-02-09; Editor-in-Chief MOHAMMED FALL OULD OUMÈRE.

NEWS AGENCY

Agence Mauritanienne de l'Information (AMI): BP 371, Nouakchott; tel. 525-29-40; fax 525-45-87; e-mail ami@mauritania.mr; internet www.ami.mr; fmrly Agence Mauritanienne de Presse; state-controlled; news and information services in Arabic and French; Dir MOHAMED CHEIKH OULD SIDI MOHAMED.

Publishers

Imprimerie Commerciale et Administrative de Mauritanie: BP 164, Nouakchott; textbooks, educational.

Imprimerie Nationale: BP 618, Nouakchott; tel. 525-44-38; fax 525-44-37; f. 1978; state-owned; Pres. RACHID OULD SALEH; Man. Dir ISSIMOU MAHJOUB.

GOVERNMENT PUBLISHING HOUSE

Société Nationale d'Impression: BP 618, Nouakchott; Pres. MOUSTAPHA SALECK OULD AHMED BRIHIM.

Broadcasting and Communications

TELECOMMUNICATIONS

Mauritel: BP 7000, Nouakchott; tel. 525-23-40; fax 525-17-00; e-mail webmaster@mauritel.mr; internet www.mauritel.mr; fmrly Société Mauritanienne des Télécommunications; 46% state-owned, 34% owned by Maroc Télécom (Morocco), 20% owned by Abdallahi Ould Noueigued group; Dir Col AHMEDOUL OULD MOHAMED EL KORY

El-Jawel Mauritel Mobiles: ave du Roi Fayçal, BP 5920, Nouakchott; tel. 529-80-80; fax 529-81-81; e-mail mminfos@mauritel.mr; internet www.mauritelmobiles.mr; f. 2000; operates a mobile cellular telephone network (El Jawal) in Nouakchott and more than 27 other locations and three highways nation-wide; more than 350,000 subscribers (2005).

Société Mauritano-Tunisienne de Télécommunications (Mattel): BP 3668, Nouakchott; tel. 529-53-54; fax 529-81-03; e-mail mattel@mattel.mr; internet www.mattel.mr; f. 2000; privately owned Mauritanian-Tunisian co; operates mobile cellular communications network in Nouakchott and more than 10 other locations nation-wide.

BROADCASTING

Radio

Radio de Mauritanie (RM): ave Gamal Abdel Nasser, BP 200, Nouakchott; tel. and fax 525-21-64; e-mail rm@radiomauritanie.com; f. 1958; state-controlled; five transmitters; radio broadcasts in Arabic, French, Sarakolé, Toucouleur and Wolof; Dir SID BRAHIM OULD HAMDINOU.

Television

Télévision de Mauritanie (TVM): BP 5522, Nouakchott; tel. 525-40-67; fax 525-40-69; e-mail dg@tvmsat.mr; internet www.tvm.mr; f. 1982; Dir-Gen. HAMOUD OULD M'HAMED.

Finance

(cap. = capital; res = reserves; dep. = deposits; m. = million; br(s).= branch(es); amounts in ouguiyas)

BANKING

Central Bank

Banque Centrale de Mauritanie (BCM): ave de l'Indépendance, BP 623, Nouakchott; tel. 525-22-06; fax 525-27-59; e-mail info@bcm.mr; internet www.bcm.mr; f. 1973; bank of issue; total assets 200m. (2001); Gov. KANE OUSMANE; 4 brs.

Commercial Banks

Banque El Amana pour le développement et l'Habitat (BADH): BP 5559, Nouakchott; tel. 525-34-90; fax 525-34-95; e-mail badh@opt.mr; f. 1997; 73% privately owned, 27% owned by Société Nationale Industrielle et Minière; cap. and res 1,297.4m., total assets 7,248.4m. (Dec. 2001); cap. 1,500m. (Dec. 2005); Pres. AHAMED SALEM OULD BOUNA MOKHTAR; Dir-Gen. MOHAMMED OULD OUMAROU; 6 brs.

Banque Internationale d'Investissement (BII): Nouakchott; tel. 529-70-00; fax 524-53-00; internet www.bii.mr; f. 2005; cap. 4,000m. (Jan. 2006); Pres. and Dir-Gen. JEAN-PHILLIPE EQUILBECQ; 1 br.

Banque pour le Commerce et l'Industrie (BCI): ave Nasser, BP 5050, Nouakchott; tel. 529-28-76; fax 529-28-77; e-mail bci@bci-banque.com; internet www.bci-banque.com; f. 1999; privately owned; cap. 2,040m. (Dec. 2005); Pres. and Dir-Gen. ISSELMOU OULD DIDI OULD TAJEDINE; 9 brs.

Banque pour le Commerce et l'Investissement en Mauritanie (Bacim-Bank): BP 1268, Nouakchott; tel. 529-19-00; fax 529-13-60; e-mail bacim-bank@mauritel.mr; internet www.bacim.mr; f. 2002; privately owned; cap. 1,500m. (Dec. 2005); Pres. and Dir-Gen. AHMED OULD EL WAFI; 6 brs.

Banque Mauritanienne pour le Commerce International (BMCI): Immeuble Afarco, ave Nasser, BP 622, Nouakchott; tel. 525-28-26; fax 525-20-45; e-mail info@bmci.mr; internet www.bmci.mr; f. 1974; privately owned; cap. 3,000m. (Dec. 2005); res 801m., dep. 19,066m. (Dec. 2003); Pres. and Dir-Gen. MOULAY SIDI OULD HACEN OULD ABASS; 24 brs.

Banque Nationale de Mauritanie (BNM): ave Nasser, BP 614, Nouakchott; tel. 525-26-02; fax 525-33-97; e-mail bnm10@bnm.mr; f. 1989; privately owned; cap. 2,500m., res 977m., dep. 20,659m. (Dec. 2003); cap. 6,000m. (Dec. 2005); Pres. and Dir-Gen. MOHAMED OULD NOUEIGUED; 14 brs.

Chinguitty Bank: ave Gamal Abdel Nasser, BP 626, Nouakchott; tel. 525-21-73; fax 525-33-82; e-mail chinguittybank@mauritel.mr; f. 1972; 51% owned by Libyan Arab Foreign Bank, 49% state-owned; cap. and res 4,002.9m., total assets 11,428.7m. (Dec. 2007); cap. 3,500m. (Dec. 2007); Pres. MOHAMED OULD DIDI; Gen. Man. YOUNIS TAHER AL SOUDI; 2 brs.

Générale de Banque de Mauritanie pour l'Investissement et le Commerce SA (GBM): ave de l'Indépendance, BP 5558, Nouakchott; tel. 525-36-36; fax 525-46-47; e-mail gbm@gbm.mr.com; f. 1995; 70% privately owned; cap. 5,100m., res 2,941.6m., dep. 12,989.1m. (Dec. 2003); cap. 7,200m. (Dec. 2005); Pres. and Dir-Gen. MOHAMED HMAYEN OULD BOUAMATOU; 2 brs.

Islamic Bank

Banque al-Wava Mauritanienne Islamique (BAMIS): 758, rue 22–018, ave du Roi Fayçal, BP 650, Nouakchott; tel. 525-14-24; fax 525-16-21; e-mail bamis@bamis.mr; internet www.bamis.mr; f. 1985; fmrly Banque al-Baraka Mauritannienne Islamique; majority share privately owned; cap. 2,000m., res 2,821m., dep. 13,778m. (Dec. 2005); Pres. MOHAMED ABDELLAHI OULD ABDELLAHI; Dir-Gen. MOHAMED ABDELLAHI OULD SIDI; Exec. Dir MOHAMED OULD TAYA; 2 brs.

INSURANCE

Assurances Générales de Mauritanie: BP 2141, ave de Gaulle, TZA Ilot A 667, Nouakchott; tel. 529-29-00; fax 529-29-11; Man. MOULAYE ELY BOUAMATOU.

Compagnie Nationale d'Assurance et de Réassurance (NASR): 12 ave Nasser, BP 163, Nouakchott; tel. 525-26-50; fax 525-18-18; e-mail nasr@nasr.mr; internet www.nasr.mr; f. 1994; state-owned; Pres. MOHAMED ABDALLAHI OULD SIDI; Dir-Gen. AHMED OULD SIDI BABA.

Société Anonyme d'Assurance et de Réassurance (SAAR): ave J. F. Kennedy, Immeuble El-Mamy, BP 2841, Nouakchott; tel. 525-30-56; fax 525-25-36; e-mail saar@infotel.mr; f. 1999; Pres. and Dir-Gen. AHMED BEZEID OULD MED LEMINE.

TAAMIN: BP 5164, Nouakchott; tel. 529-40-00; fax 529-40-02; e-mail taamin@toptechnology.mr; Pres. and Dir-Gen. MOULAYE EL HASSEN OULD MOCTAR EL HASSEN.

Trade and Industry

DEVELOPMENT ORGANIZATIONS

Agence Française de Développement (AFD): rue Mamadou Kouaté prolongée, BP 5211, Nouakchott; tel. 525-25-25; fax 525-49-10; e-mail afdnouakchott@groupe-afd.org; internet www.afd.fr; Country Dir GILLES CHAUSSE.

Mission Française de Coopération et d'Action Culturelle: BP 203, Nouakchott; tel. 525-21-21; fax 525-20-50; e-mail mcap.coop.france@opt.mr; administers bilateral aid from France; Dir MAURICE DADOUCHE.

Société Nationale pour le Développement Rural (SONADER): BP 321, Nouakchott; tel. 521-18-00; fax 525-32-86; e-mail sonader@toptechnology.mr; f. 1975; Dir AHMED OULD BAH OULD CHEIKH SIDIA.

CHAMBER OF COMMERCE

Chambre de Commerce, d'Industrie et d'Agriculture de Mauritanie: BP 215, Nouakchott; tel. 525-22-14; fax 525-38-95; f. 1954; Pres. MAHMOUD OULD AHMEDOU; Dir HABIB OULD ELY.

EMPLOYERS' ORGANIZATION

National Confederation of Mauritanian Employers (CNPM): 824 ave de Roi Fayçal, Ksar, BP 383, Nouakchott; tel. 525-33-01; fax 525-91-08; e-mail germe@opt.mr; f. 1960; professional asscn for all employers active in Mauritania; Pres. MOHAMED OULD BOUAMATOU; Sec.-Gen. SEYID OULD ABDALLAHI.

UTILITIES

Electricity

Société Mauritanienne d'Electricité (SOMELEC): BP 355, Nouakchott; tel. 525-23-08; fax 525-39-95; f. 2001; state-owned; transfer to majority private sector ownership proposed; production and distribution of electricity; Dir-Gen. Col AHMEDOU OULD MOHAMED EL-KORI.

Gas

Société Mauritanienne des Gaz (SOMAGAZ): POB 5089, Nouakchott; tel. 525-18-71; fax 529-47-86; e-mail somagaz@compunet.mr; production and distribution of butane gas; Dir-Gen. MOHAMED YAHYA OULD MOHAMED EL-MOCTAR.

Water

Société Nationale d'Eau (SNDE): ave 42-096, no. 106, Tevragh Zeina, BP 796, Nouakchott; tel. 525-52-73; fax 525-19-52; e-mail mfoudail@infotel.mr; f. 2001; Dir-Gen. THIAM SAMBA.

TRADE UNIONS

Confédération Générale des Travailleurs de Mauritanie: BP 6164, Nouakchott; tel. 525-80-57; e-mail admin@cgtm.org; internet cgtm.org; f. 1992; obtained official recognition in 1994; Sec.-Gen. ABDALLAHI OULD MOHAMED, dit NANA.

Confédération Libre des Travailleurs de Mauritanie: BP 6902, Nouakchott; fax 525-23-16; f. 1995; Sec.-Gen. SAMORI OULD BEYI.

Union des Travailleurs de Mauritanie (UTM): Bourse du Travail, BP 630, Nouakchott; f. 1961; Sec.-Gen. ABDERAHMANE OULD BOUBOU; 45,000 mems.

Transport

RAILWAYS

A 670-km railway connects the iron-ore deposits at Zouérate with Nouadhibou; a 40-km extension services the reserves at El Rhein, and a 30-km extension those at M'Haoudat. Motive power is diesel-electric. The Société Nationale Industrielle et Minière (SNIM) operates one of the longest (2.4 km) and heaviest (22,000 metric tons) trains in the world.

SNIM—Direction du Chemin de Fer et du Port: BP 42, Nouadhibou; tel. 574-51-74; fax 574-53-96; e-mail m.khalifa.beyah@zrt.snim.com; internet www.snim.com; f. 1963; Gen. Man. MOHAMED SALECK OULD HEYINE.

MAURITANIA

ROADS

In 1999 there were about 7,891 km of roads and tracks, of which only 2,090 km were paved. The 1,100-km Trans-Mauritania highway, completed in 1985, links Nouakchott with Néma in the east of the country. Plans exist for the construction of a 7,400-km highway, linking Nouakchott with the Libyan port of Tubruq (Tobruk). In August 1999 the Islamic Development Bank granted Mauritania a loan worth US $9.4m. to help finance the rebuilding of the Chouk–Kiffa road. The construction of a 470-km highway between Nouakchott and Nouadhibou was completed in 2004.

Société Mauritanienne des Transports (SOMATRA): Nouakchott; tel. 525-29-53; f. 1975; Pres. CHEIKH MALAININE ROBERT; Dir-Gen. MAMADOU SOULEYMANE KANE.

INLAND WATERWAYS

The River Senegal is navigable in the wet season by small coastal vessels as far as Kayes (Mali) and by river vessels as far as Kaédi; in the dry season as far as Rosso and Boghé, respectively. The major river ports are at Rosso, Kaédi and Gouraye.

SHIPPING

The principal port, at Point-Central, 10 km south of Nouadhibou, is almost wholly occupied with mineral exports. In 1998 the port handled 11.6m. metric tons of cargo and cleared 3,804 vessels. There is also a commercial and fishing port at Nouadhibou. The deep-water Port de l'Amitié at Nouakchott, built and maintained with assistance from the People's Republic of China, was inaugurated in 1986. The port, which has a total capacity of about 1.5m. tons annually, handled 843,000 tons in 1998 (compared with 479,791 tons in 1990); the port cleared 453 vessels in 1998 (compared with 244 in 1990). In 2006 Mauritania's merchant fleet consisted of 153 vessels and had a total displacement of 51,870 grt.

Port Autonome de Nouakchott (Port de l'Amitié): BP 5103, El Mina, Nouakchott; tel. 525-14-53; fax 525-17-94; e-mail ouldmohamedna@yahoo.fr; f. 1986; deep-water port; Dir-Gen. AHMEDOU OULD HAMED.

Port Autonome de Nouadhibou: BP 236, Nouadhibou; tel. 525-21-34; f. 1973; state-owned; Pres. BAL MOHAMEDED EL HABIB; Dir-Gen. BÉBAHA OULD AHMED YOURA.

Shipping Companies

Cie Mauritanienne de Navigation Maritime (COMAUNAM): 119 ave Nasser, BP 799, Nouakchott; tel. 525-36-34; fax 525-25-04; f. 1973; 51% state-owned, 49% owned by Govt of Algeria; nat. shipping co; forwarding agent, stevedoring; Chair. MOHAND TIGHILT; Dir-Gen. KAMIL ABDELKADER.

Société d'Acconage et de Manutention en Mauritanie (SAMMA): BP 258, Nouadhibou; tel. 574-52-63; fax 574-52-37; internet www.samma.mr; f. 1960; freight and handling, shipping agent, forwarding agent, stevedoring; Man. Dir DIDI OULD BIHA.

Société Générale de Consignation et d'Entreprises Maritimes (SOGECO): 1765 rue 22-002, Commune du Ksar, BP 351, Nouakchott; tel. 525-22-02; fax 525-39-03; e-mail sogeco@sogeco.sa.mr; internet www.sogecosa.com; f. 1973; shipping agent, forwarding, stevedoring; Man. Dir SID'AHMED ABEIDNA.

Société Mauritanienne pour la Pêche et la Navigation (SMPN): BP 40254, Nouakchott; tel. 525-36-38; fax 525-37-87; e-mail smpn@toptechnology.mr; Dir-Gen. ABDALLAHI OULD ISMAIL.

VOTRA: Route de l'Aéroport, BP 454, Nouakchott; tel. 525-24-10; fax 525-31-41; e-mail votra@mauritel.mr; internet www.votra.net; Dir-Gen. MOHAMED MAHMOUD OULD MAYE.

CIVIL AVIATION

There are international airports at Nouakchott, Nouadhibou and Néma, and 23 smaller airstrips.

Mauritania Airways: Nouakchott; internet www.fly-mauritaniaairways.com; f. 2006; 10% state-owned, 51% owned by Tunisair (Tunisia); Gen. Man. MONCEF BADIS.

Tourism

Mauritania's principal tourist attractions are its historical sites, several of which have been listed by UNESCO under its World Heritage Programme, and its game reserves and national parks. Some 24,000 tourists visited Mauritania in 1999. Receipts from tourism in that year totalled an estimated US $28m.

Office National du Tourisme: BP 2884, Nouakchott; tel. 529-03-44; fax 529-05-28; e-mail ont@tourisme-mauritanie.com; f. 2002; Dir KHADIJÉTOU MINT BOUBOU.

SOMASERT: BP 42, Nouadhibou; tel. 574-29-91; fax 574-90-43; subsidiary of SNIM; responsible for promoting tourism, managing hotels and organizing tours; Dir-Gen. MOHAMED OULD BIYAH.

MAURITIUS

Introductory Survey

Location, Climate, Language, Religion, Flag, Capital

The Republic of Mauritius lies in the Indian Ocean. The principal island, from which the country takes its name, lies about 800 km (500 miles) east of Madagascar. The other main islands are Rodrigues, the Agalega Islands and the Cargados Carajos Shoals (St Brandon Islands). The climate is maritime sub-tropical and generally humid. The average annual temperature is 23°C (73°F) at sea-level, falling to 19°C (66°F) at an altitude of 600 m (about 2,000 ft). Average annual rainfall varies from 890 mm (35 ins) at sea-level to 5,080 mm (200 ins) on the highest parts. Tropical cyclones, which may be severe, occur between September and May. Most of the population are of Indian descent. The most widely spoken languages in 2000 were Creole (38.6%) and Bhojpuri (30.6%). English is the country's official language, and Creole (derived from French) the lingua franca. The principal religious group are Hindus, who comprise more than 50% of the population. About 30% are Christians and 17% are Muslims. The national flag (proportions 2 by 3) has four equal horizontal stripes, of red, blue, yellow and green. The capital is Port Louis.

Recent History

The islands of Mauritius and Rodrigues, formerly French possessions, passed into British control in 1810. Subsequent settlement came mainly from East Africa and India, and the European population has remained largely French-speaking.

A ministerial form of government was introduced in 1957. The first elections under universal adult suffrage, held in 1959, were won by the Mauritius Labour Party (MLP), led by Dr (later Sir) Seewoosagur Ramgoolam. Mauritius became independent, within the Commonwealth, on 12 March 1968, with Ramgoolam as Prime Minister.

In November 1965 the United Kingdom transferred the Chagos Archipelago (including the atoll of Diego Garcia), a Mauritian dependency about 2,000 km (1,250 miles) north-east of the main island, to the newly created British Indian Ocean Territory (BIOT, q.v.). Mauritius has subsequently campaigned for the return of the islands, which have been developed as a major US military base. Mauritius also claims sovereignty of the French-held island of Tromelin, about 550 km (340 miles) to the north-west.

During the 1970s political opposition to successive coalition governments formed by Ramgoolam was led by a radical left-wing group, the Mouvement Militant Mauricien (MMM), founded by Paul Bérenger. Although the MMM became the largest single party in the Legislative Assembly following a general election in December 1976, Ramgoolam was able to form a new coalition Government with the support of the Parti Mauricien Social Démocrate (PMSD). However, social unrest and rising unemployment undermined popular support for the Government, and at a general election in June 1982 the MMM, in alliance with the Parti Socialiste Mauricien (PSM), won all 60 contested seats on the main island. Aneerood (later Sir Aneerood) Jugnauth, the leader of the MMM, became Prime Minister, and Bérenger Minister of Finance.

The MMM/PSM coalition collapsed in March 1983, when Bérenger and his supporters resigned, following differences concerning economic policy. Jugnauth formed a new Government and a new party, the Mouvement Socialiste Militant (MSM), which subsequently merged with the PSM. A general election took place in August, at which an electoral alliance of the MSM, the MLP and the PMSD, led by Sir Gaëtan Duval, gained a legislative majority. Jugnauth formed a new coalition Government, in which Duval became Deputy Prime Minister. The MLP, however, withdrew from the coalition in February 1984.

Following a general election in August 1987, the MSM again formed an electoral alliance with the PMSD and the MLP; the three parties obtained 39 of the 62 elective seats. Bérenger, who failed to secure a seat, transferred his functions as leader of the opposition in the Legislative Assembly to Dr Paramhansa Nababsingh (while Bérenger himself replaced Nababsingh as Secretary-General of the MMM). A new coalition, led by Jugnauth, took office in September, and the Government subsequently announced plans to make Mauritius a republic within the Commonwealth. In August 1988, following a disagreement over employment policies, the PMSD withdrew from the coalition.

In July 1990 the MSM and the MMM agreed to form an alliance to contest the next general election, and to promote constitutional measures allowing Mauritius to become a republic within the Commonwealth. This proposal, however, was jointly opposed by the MLP and the PMSD, prompting Jugnauth to dismiss the MLP leader, Sir Satcam Boolell, from the Government, together with two dissident ministers from the MSM. A further three ministers representing the MLP resigned, leaving only one MLP member in the Government. Boolell subsequently relinquished the leadership of the MLP to Dr Navinchandra Ramgoolam (the son of the late Sir Seewoosagur Ramgoolam). In September Jugnauth formed a new coalition Government.

Jugnauth dissolved the Legislative Assembly in August 1991. At the subsequent general election, which took place on 15 September, an alliance of the MSM, the MMM and the small Mouvement des Travaillistes Démocrates (MTD), won 57 of the 62 directly elected seats, while the MLP/PMSD alliance obtained three seats. The two remaining seats were secured by the Organisation du Peuple Rodriguais (OPR). Four 'additional' seats were subsequently allocated to members of the MLP/PMSD alliance. Jugnauth formed a new government coalition, to which nine representatives of the MMM (including Bérenger, who became Minister of External Affairs) and one representative of the MTD were appointed.

In December 1991 the Legislative Assembly approved the constitutional framework for the country's transition to a republic within the Commonwealth. Following the proclamation of the Republic of Mauritius on 12 March 1992, the Legislative Assembly was redesignated as the National Assembly, and the incumbent Governor-General, Sir Veerasamy Ringadoo, became interim President. Later in March the Government announced its choice of Cassam Uteem, the Minister of Industry and Industrial Technology and a member of the MMM, to assume the presidency in June. Uteem was duly elected President by the National Assembly; Sir Rabindrah Ghurburrun, a member of the MMM, took office as Vice-President.

The government coalition came under increasing pressure during 1993, amid intensifying disputes between the MSM and the MMM. In August, following an unexpected success by the PMSD in municipal by-elections in a constituency that traditionally supported the MMM, a meeting between Bérenger and Ramgoolam prompted speculation that an MMM/MLP alliance was contemplated. Shortly afterwards Jugnauth dismissed Bérenger from the Council of Ministers, on the grounds that he had repeatedly criticized government policy.

The removal of Bérenger precipitated a serious crisis within the MMM, whose political bureau decided that the other nine members of the party who held ministerial portfolios should remain in the coalition Government. Led by Nababsingh, the Deputy Prime Minister, and Jean-Claude de l'Estrac, the Minister of Industry and Industrial Technology, supporters of the pro-coalition faction announced in October 1993 that Bérenger had been suspended as Secretary-General of the MMM. Bérenger and his supporters responded by expelling 11 MMM officials from the party, and seeking a legal ban on Nababsingh and de l'Estrac from using the party name. The split in the MMM led in November to a government reshuffle, in which the remaining two MMM ministers supporting Bérenger were replaced by members of the party's pro-coalition faction.

In April 1994 the MLP and the MMM announced that they had agreed terms for an alliance to contest the next general elections. Under its provisions, Ramgoolam was to be Prime Minister and Bérenger the Deputy Prime Minister, with ministerial portfolios allocated on the basis of 12 ministries to the MLP and nine to the MMM. In the same month, three deputies from the MSM, who had been close associates of a former Minister of Agriculture dismissed two months earlier, withdrew their support from the Government.

Nababsingh and the dissident faction of the MMM, having lost Bérenger's legal challenge for the use of the party name, formed a new party, the Renouveau Militant Mauricien (RMM), which formally commenced political activity in June 1994. In the same month Jugnauth declared that the Government, which retained a cohesive parliamentary majority, would remain in office to the conclusion of its mandate in September 1996.

During the course of a parliamentary debate in November 1994, Bérenger and de l'Estrac accepted a mutual challenge to resign their seats in the National Assembly and to contest by-elections. In the following month the MSM indicated that it would not oppose RMM candidates in the two polls. In January 1995, however, Jugnauth unsuccessfully sought to undermine the MLP/MMM alliance by offering electoral support to the MLP. The by-elections, held in February, were both won by MLP/MMM candidates, and Bérenger was returned to the National Assembly. Following these results, Jugnauth opened political negotiations with the PMSD, whose leader, Charles Gaëtan Xavier-Luc Duval (the son of Sir Gaëtan Duval), entered the coalition as Minister of Industry and Industrial Technology and Minister of Tourism. The post of Attorney-General and Minister of Justice was also allocated to the PMSD, and Sir Gaëtan Duval agreed to act as an economic adviser to the Prime Minister. As a result, however, of widespread opposition within the PMSD to participation in the coalition, Xavier-Luc Duval left the Government in October, and Sir Gaëtan Duval subsequently resumed the leadership of the party. The Minister for Rodrigues, representing the OPR, also left the Government.

In November 1995 the Government was defeated in a parliamentary vote, requiring a two-thirds' majority, to introduce a constitutional requirement for instruction in oriental languages to be provided in primary schools. Jugnauth dissolved the National Assembly, and at the subsequent general election in December the MLP/MMM alliance won a decisive victory: of the 62 elected seats, the MLP secured 35 seats, the MMM obtained 25 seats and the OPR two seats. Under constitutional arrangements providing representation for unsuccessful candidates attracting the largest number of votes, Sir Gaëtan Duval re-entered the National Assembly, together with two members of the Mouvement Rodriguais and one representative of Hizbullah, an Islamist fundamentalist group. Ramgoolam became Prime Minister of the new MLP/MMM coalition, with Bérenger as Deputy Prime Minister with responsibility for foreign and regional relations. Sir Gaëtan Duval died in May 1996 and was succeeded in the National Assembly and as leader of the PMSD by his brother, Hervé Duval, although Xavier-Luc Duval continued to command a significant following within the party.

Serious divisions began to emerge within the coalition Government in late 1996, when differences were reported between Ramgoolam and Bérenger over the allocation of ministerial responsibilities and the perception by the MMM of delays in the implementation of social and economic reforms. In January 1997 rumours had begun to circulate of a possible political alliance between the MMM and the MSM, and in March it was reported that Ramgoolam intended to seek support from certain members of the PMSD should the MMM decide to withdraw from the Government. Bérenger's criticism of the coalition's performance intensified in the following months, and culminated in June in his dismissal from the Government and the consequent withdrawal of the MMM from the coalition. Following unsuccessful efforts by Ramgoolam to draw the PMSD into a new administration, an MLP Council of Ministers was formed by Ramgoolam, who additionally assumed Bérenger's former responsibilities for foreign affairs. Ramgoolam emphasized his determination to remain in office for the full legislative term to December 2000. On 28 June 1997 the National Assembly re-elected Cassam Uteem to a second five-year term as President. A prominent supporter of the MLP, Angidi Verriah Chettiar, was elected Vice-President.

Following the dissolution of the MLP/MMM alliance, Bérenger sought to assume the leadership of a consolidated political opposition to the Government. In August 1997 two small parties, the Mouvement Militant Socialiste Mauricien (MMSM) and the Rassemblement pour la Réforme (RPR), agreed to support Bérenger in this aim. The alliance was extended to include a breakaway faction of the PMSD, known as the 'Vrais Bleus', under the leadership of Hervé Duval, who had been replaced as party leader by Xavier-Luc Duval, an opponent of co-operation with the MMM.

In April 1998 the MMM, the MMSM, the RPR and the 'Vrais Bleus' formed an electoral coalition, the Alliance Nationale, to contest a by-election for a vacant seat in the National Assembly. The seat, which was retained by the MLP, had also been sought by Jugnauth on behalf of the MSM, which remained unrepresented in the National Assembly. Jugnauth, seeking to revitalize his party's prospects in preparation for the next general election (which was constitutionally required to take place by December 2000), subsequently entered negotiations with Bérenger for an electoral alliance, and in December 1998 both parties agreed terms for a joint list of candidates. Ramgoolam, following a reshuffle of the Council of Ministers in October, announced proposals in the following month for an all-party review of the electoral system, with a view to considering the adoption of proportional representation.

The MLP announced in mid-1999 its endorsement of the candidature of Xavier-Luc Duval for a legislative by-election to be held in September. Xavier-Luc Duval, after obtaining the vacant seat, joined the Government as Minister of Industry, Commerce, Corporate Affairs and Financial Services, following an extensive government reshuffle completed at the end of the month. The selection in October of Pravind Jugnauth, the son of Sir Aneerood Jugnauth, as Deputy Leader of the MSM gave rise to speculation that Sir Aneerood was contemplating retirement from politics and intended his son to be his successor.

In August 2000 the MSM/MMM formed an alliance, in advance of the imminent general election, on the basis that Jugnauth would lead as Prime Minister for three years in the event of victory, before assuming the more honorary role of President, thus allowing Bérenger to become Prime Minister for the remaining two years.

A general election was held on 11 September 2000, with 81% of the 790,000 registered electors casting their ballots. The MSM/MMM alliance achieved an overwhelming victory, winning 54 of the 62 directly elected seats in the National Assembly, while the MLP/PMSD alliance gained only six seats and the OPR two seats. As agreed, Sir Aneerood Jugnauth became Prime Minister again, while Paul Bérenger was appointed Deputy Prime Minister and Minister of Finance. A new Council of Ministers was appointed one week later.

In November 2000 the British High Court of Justice ruled that the eviction of several thousand inhabitants of the Chagos Archipelago between 1967 and 1973, to allow the construction of a US military base on the atoll of Diego Garcia, had been unlawful, and overturned a 1971 ordinance preventing the islanders from returning to the Archipelago. (The majority of the displaced islanders had been resettled in Mauritius, which had administered the Chagos Archipelago until its transfer to BIOT in 1965.) Following the ruling, the Mauritian Government declared its right to sovereignty over the islands to be indisputable and sought international recognition as such. Jugnauth stated that he would be prepared to negotiate with the USA over the continued presence of the military base. The United Kingdom responded that it would return the islands if, as had been maintained for many years, the USA was prepared to move out of the base on Diego Garcia. India declared its support for the Mauritian Government's claim to sovereignty, as part of the close relationship being encouraged between the two countries.

In November 2001 exiled Chagos islanders demonstrated outside the British High Commission in Port Louis, in support of their demands for compensation from the British Government. In February 2002 legislation allowing the displaced islanders to apply for British citizenship received royal assent in the United Kingdom. At that time the British Government was also examining the feasibility of a return to the Chagos Archipelago for the islanders, who continued to seek compensation.

In January 2002 a commission on constitutional and electoral reform presented its proposals at a series of public forums, before submitting them to the Government for consideration. Recommendations included the introduction of a system of proportional representation in legislative elections and a reinforcement of presidential powers. In mid-February controversial legislation on the prevention of terrorism was finally promulgated by the Chief Justice of the Supreme Court, Arianga Pillay, acting as interim President, following the resignations of both President Uteem and his successor, Vice-President Chettiar, over the issue. The legislation had been rejected by opposition parties and proved unpopular with many sections of society for arrogating excessive powers to the authorities and infringing on citizens' rights. On 25 February Karl Offman was elected as President by an extraordinary session of the National Assembly, which was boycotted by opposition deputies. Although formally elected for five years, Offman was to relinquish the presidency to Jugnauth in October 2003; in preparation for this, in April 2003 Jugnauth announced his resignation from the leadership of the MSM, to be succeeded by his son, Pravind.

In August 2003, in preparation for the transfer of governing roles, a constitutional amendment was approved by the National Assembly to increase the powers of the President, giving the incumbent the right to refuse a request from the Prime Minister to dissolve the legislature following a vote of 'no confidence'. As agreed, on 1 October Offman resigned as President and was replaced, in an acting capacity, by the Vice-President, Raouf Bundhun, pending the election by the National Assembly of Sir Aneerood Jugnauth as his successor one week later. Jugnauth had resigned as Prime Minister on 30 September and was immediately replaced by Paul Bérenger, who appointed a new Council of Ministers. On 23 December Bérenger effected a government reshuffle, notably appointing Jaya Krishna Cuttaree as Minister of Foreign Affairs, International Trade and Regional Co-operation. During his first months in office Bérenger conducted a premiership active in international diplomacy, visiting two of the country's principal trading partners, India and France, and signing co-operation agreements with Madagascar. In early 2004 he also renewed the campaign to reclaim sovereignty of the Chagos Archipelago from the United Kingdom, on the basis that international law does not allow the dismemberment of a country before independence, and of Tromelin from France. It was established in 2004 that Mauritius had the right to pursue the case of the Chagos islands at the International Court of Justice, in spite of British objections on the basis of restrictions imposed by membership of the Commonwealth. In mid-December a minor reorganization of the Cabinet of Ministers took place.

In early February 2005 the Minister of Public Infrastructure, Land Transport and Shipping, Anil Bachoo, resigned, to be replaced by Govindranath Gunness; the Minister of Local Government and Solid Waste Management, Mookhesswur Choonee, also left office the following week and was succeeded by Prithvirajsing Roopun. The two erstwhile ministers formed a new opposition party the following month, the Mouvement Sociale Démocrate (MSD), having also resigned from the MSM alleging poor leadership of that party by Pravind Jugnauth. Bachoo and Choonee reportedly disapproved of an apparent pre-electoral agreement between the parties of the ruling coalition, whereby, should they successfully be re-elected to office, Bérenger would relinquish the premiership in mid-term in favour of Pravind Jugnauth, just as the incumbent President (Pravind Jugnauth's father) had in September 2003. The MSD announced the formation of an electoral alliance with the MLP, known as the Social Alliance, thus creating a credible rival political force to the governing parties for the forthcoming legislative elections.

At the elections, which were held on 3 July 2005, the Social Alliance bloc defeated the incumbent coalition, winning 38 of the 62 directly elected mandates. The MSM/MMM alliance took 22 seats while the OPR secured two. The rate of voter participation was 81.5%. Ramgoolam was appointed as Prime Minister and a new 19-member Council of Ministers was sworn into office later that month. At local elections held in early October the Social Alliance won 122 of the 126 seats contested, including many long-term MSM/MMM strongholds. Following the elections the PMSD withdrew from the opposition alliance in which it had participated with the MSM and MMM. Tensions between the politically opposed premier and President initially proved somewhat obstructive to the functioning of the Government, however, they subsequently eased.

The Social Alliance Government continued with efforts to regain sovereignty over the Chagos Archipelago. A group of 102 Chagossians was permitted to visit the Archipelago in late March 2006, accompanied by Deputy Prime Minister Duval and two other government ministers, principally in order to visit the graves of relatives. In May the British High Court of Justice overturned the Orders in Council issued by the British Government under the royal prerogative in June 2004, ruling them to be unlawful, and confirmed the right of the islanders to return to the Archipelago without any conditions. In February 2007 the British Government commenced proceedings in the Court of Appeal to overturn the May 2006 ruling. However, in May that court confirmed that the residents of the Chagos Archipelago had been unlawfully removed and upheld the displaced islanders' immediate right to return.

Meanwhile, in April 2006 the opposition was further weakened when the MSM/MMM alliance collapsed following weeks of increasing tension between Pravind Jugnauth and Bérenger, and the PMSD announced that it was joining the government coalition. The MSM withdrew its support from Bérenger as official leader of the opposition and he was succeeded by Nando Bodha, the Secretary-General of the MSM and a close ally of Pravind Jugnauth (who had failed to retain his seat in the legislature in July 2005), since the MSM held 11 seats in the National Assembly to the MMM's 10. Bodha's nomination was rejected by Ashock Jugnauth, a senior member of the MSM (and uncle of Pravind), who resigned from the party and established a new opposition party, the Union Nationale. In August 2007 Chettiar resumed the position of Vice-President, replacing Bundhun. In September Bodha resigned as leader of the opposition and in October Bérenger once again assumed the role. Prime Minister Ramgoolam dismissed Minister of Foreign Affairs, International Trade and Co-operation Madan Murlidhar Dulloo in March 2008, assuming responsibility for that portfolio himself.

Government

Constitutional amendments, which were approved by the Legislative Assembly (henceforth known as the National Assembly) in December 1991 and came into effect on 12 March 1992, provided for the establishment of a republic. The constitutional Head of State is the President of the Republic, who is elected by a simple majority of the National Assembly for a five-year term of office. Legislative power is vested in the unicameral National Assembly, which comprises the Speaker, 62 members elected by universal adult suffrage for a term of five years, up to eight 'additional' members (unsuccessful candidates who receive the largest number of votes at a legislative election, to whom seats are allocated by the Electoral Supervisory Commission to ensure a balance in representation of the different ethnic groups), and the Attorney-General (if not an elected member). Executive power is vested in the Prime Minister, who is appointed by the President and is the member of the National Assembly best able to command a majority in the Assembly. The President appoints other ministers, on the recommendation of the Prime Minister.

Defence

The country has no standing defence forces, although as assessed at November 2007 paramilitary forces were estimated to number 2,000, comprising a special mobile force of 1,500, to ensure internal security, and a coastguard of 500. Projected budgetary expenditure on defence for 2007 was Rs 599m.

Economic Affairs

In 2006, according to estimates by the World Bank, Mauritius' gross national income (GNI), measured at average 2004–06 prices, was US $6,833m., equivalent to $5,450 per head (or $13,510 per head on an international purchasing-power parity basis). During 1996–2006, it was estimated, the population increased at an average annual rate of 1.0%, while gross domestic product (GDP) per head increased, in real terms, by an average of 3.5% per year. Overall GDP increased, in real terms, at an average annual rate of 4.6% in 1996–2006; growth in 2006 was 3.5%.

Agriculture (including hunting, forestry and fishing) contributed 4.5% of GDP in 2007, according to provisional estimates, and engaged 9.3% of the employed labour force in 2006. The principal cash crops are sugar cane (sugar accounted for 18.4% of domestic export earnings in 2007, according to provisional figures), tea and tobacco. Food crops include potatoes and vegetables. Chicken farming is also practised. During 1996–2006, according to the World Bank, the GDP of the agricultural sector decreased, in real terms, at an average rate of 0.1% per year; it declined by 4.8% in 2006.

Industry (including mining, manufacturing, construction and utilities) contributed 26.5% of GDP in 2007, according to provisional estimates, and engaged 33.5% of the employed labour force in 2006. During 1996–2006, according to the World Bank, industrial GDP increased, in real terms, at an average annual rate of 3.0%; however, it declined by 1.8% in 2006. Mining is negligible, accounting for less than 0.1% of employment in 2006 and less than 0.1% of GDP in 2007.

Manufacturing contributed 18.8% of GDP in 2007, according to provisional estimates, and engaged 23.5% of the employed labour force in 2006. The principal branches of manufacturing are clothing and food products, mainly sugar. Clothing (excluding footwear) provided 31.9% of export earnings in 2006, according to official figures. Factories in the Export Processing Zone (EPZ) import raw materials to produce goods for the export market. Clothing and apparel firms accounted for 75.8% of total EPZ employment in September 2005. Other important products include fish preparations, textiles, and precious stones. Export receipts from EPZ products provisionally represented 46.1% of total export earnings (and 16.6% of import earnings) in 2005. During 1996–2006, according to the World Bank, the GDP of the manufacturing sector increased, in real terms, at an average annual rate of 2.1%; manufacturing GDP decreased by 2.1% in 2005 and by 3.2% in 2006.

Electric energy is derived principally from thermal (oil-fired) and hydroelectric power stations. Bagasse (a by-product of sugar cane) is also used as fuel for generating electricity and in 2006 it accounted for 19.0% of electricity produced (93% of indigenous production; 20% of electricity was produced locally). Imports of mineral fuels comprised 19.7% of the value of merchandise imports in 2007, according to provisional figures. Thermal energy accounted for 96.7% of electricity generated in 2006.

The services sector contributed 69.0% of GDP in 2007, according to provisional estimates, and engaged 57.2% of the employed labour force in 2006. Tourism is the third most important source of revenue, after manufacturing and agriculture. The number of foreign tourist arrivals increased to 906,970 in 2007 from 422,000 in 1995. Gross receipts from tourism were estimated to total Rs 40,687m. in 2007. An 'offshore' banking sector and a stock exchange have operated since 1989. According to the World Bank, the real GDP of the services sector increased at an average annual rate of 5.6% in 1996–2006; growth in 2006 was 2.0%.

In 2006 Mauritius recorded a visible trade deficit of US $1,079.0m., and there was a deficit of $610.9m. on the current account of the balance of payments. In 2006 the principal source of imports (14.2%) was France; other major suppliers were India (13.6%), the People's Republic of China (8.6%) and South Africa (7.3%). The principal market for exports in that year (32.4%) was the United Kingdom; other significant purchasers were France (12.6%), the United Arab Emirates (11.4%) and the USA (8.3%). The principal exports (excluding re-exports) in 2007 were miscellaneous manufactured articles, food and live animals (in particular sugar) and basic manufactures. The principal imports in that year were machinery and transport equipment (21.8%), basic manufactures, mineral fuels and lubricants, and food and live animals.

In 2006/07 there was an estimated budgetary deficit of Rs 8,659.8m. (equivalent to 3.7% of GDP). Mauritius' external debt totalled US $2,160m. at the end of 2005, of which $731m. was long-term public debt. In that year the cost of debt-servicing was equivalent to 7.2% of the value of exports of goods and services. The annual rate of inflation averaged 5.9% in 1996–2006. Consumer prices increased by an average of 8.9% in 2006. About 8.5% of the labour force were unemployed in 2007.

Mauritius is a member of the Common Market for Eastern and Southern Africa (COMESA, see p. 205), the Southern African Development Community (SADC, see p. 386) and the Indian Ocean Commission (IOC, see p. 412), which aims to promote regional economic co-operation. Mauritius was among the founder members of the Indian Ocean Rim Association for Regional Co-operation (IOR—ARC, see p. 413) in 1997.

From the 1980s the Mauritius Government pursued a successful policy of economic diversification away from its traditional dependence on sugar production, encouraging labour-intensive manufacturing (particularly of clothing) in the export promotion zone (EPZ), and implemented extensive reforms with IMF support. The geographical location of Mauritius, as well as a number of incentive measures implemented by the Government, has contributed to its successful establishment as an international financial centre. By the late 1990s the island had become a significant provider of 'offshore' banking and investment services for a number of south Asian countries (particularly India), as well as for members of SADC. Mauritius has also been promoted as a future hub of information and communications technology, with the aim of encouraging the next stage of economic development and transferring the emphasis towards services. The expiry of the preferential Multi-Fibre Arrangement (subsequently known as the Agreement on Textiles and Clothing) with the European Union (EU, see p. 244) in December 2004 posed a threat to the textiles industry, exposing it to direct competition from countries with lower labour costs, particularly those in Asia, while the decision of the EU to reduce preferential trade terms for countries of the African, Caribbean and Pacific resulted in a reduction of 36% from 2005 in the price paid for sugar. (European countries represent the biggest importers of Mauritian sugar.) Nevertheless, the Government was reluctant to close down the sugar sector altogether, and it was hoped that companies could develop more specialized, high-value products and the further production of bagasse. The authorities began to focus on the development of the high-end tourist sector, the most important result of which was the liberalization of international air routes, and the introduction of favourable terms for those wishing to purchase holiday homes, and also offered foreigners more opportunities to invest in Mauritius. Further to this aim, the Business Facilitation Act was introduced before the National Assembly in late 2006, as a result of which Mauritius saw foreign investment grow at a record 19.0% in 2006, followed by a more modest 8.6% in 2007. The budgetary deficit, however, remained a concern, as did the high level of unemployment. GDP growth of 5.4% was recorded in 2007, and it was forecast to increase to 6.0% in 2008, according to official sources.

Education

Education is officially compulsory for seven years between the ages of five and 12. Primary education begins at five years of age and lasts for six years. Secondary education, beginning at the age of 11, lasts for up to seven years, comprising a first cycle of three years and a second of four years. Primary and secondary education are available free of charge and became compulsory in 2005. According to UNESCO estimates, in 2004/05 enrolment at primary schools included 95% of pupils in the relevant age group (males 94%; females 95%), while the comparable ratio for secondary schools was 83% (males 82%; females 83%). The education system provides for instruction in seven Asian languages (71% of primary school children and 30% of secondary school children were studying at least one of these in 2005). The Government exercises indirect control of the large private sector in secondary education (in 2005 only 70 of 188 schools were state administered). The University of Mauritius had 6,602 students in 2005/06 (35% of whom were part-time students); in addition, many students receive further education abroad. Of total expenditure by the central Government in 2006/07, Rs 6,291.1m. (13.4%) was for education.

Public Holidays

2008: 1–2 January (New Year), 1 February (Abolition of Slavery Commemoration), 7 February (Chinese New Year), 6 March (Maha Shivaratree), 12 March (National Day), 5 April (Ougadi), 1 May (Labour Day), 15 August (Assumption), 3 September (Ganesh Chathurti), 1 October* (Id al-Fitr, end of Ramadan), 28 October (Diwali), 2 November (Arrival of Indentured Labourers), 25 December (Christmas Day).

2009: 1–3 January (New Year), 1 February (Abolition of Slavery Commemoration), 7 February (Chinese New Year), 23 February (Maha Shivaratree), 12 March (National Day), 25 March (Ougadi), 1 May (Labour Day), 15 August (Assumption), 23 August (Ganesh Chathurti), 20 September* (Id al-Fitr, end of Ramadan), 17 October (Diwali), 2 November (Arrival of Indentured Labourers), 25 December (Christmas Day).

Thaipoosam Cavadee is also celebrated in late January or early February. However, the exact date is dependent on the appearance of a full moon.

* This holiday is dependent on the Islamic lunar calendar and may vary by one or two days from the dates given.

Weights and Measures

The metric system is in standard use.

MAURITIUS

Statistical Survey

Source (unless otherwise stated): Central Statistics Office, LIC Bldg, President John F. Kennedy St, Port Louis; tel. 212-2316; fax 211-4150; e-mail cso@mail.gov.mu; internet statsmauritius.gov.mu.

Area and Population

AREA, POPULATION AND DENSITY

Area (sq km)	2,040*
Population (census results)	
1 July 1990	1,058,942†
2 July 2000‡	
Males	583,949
Females	595,188
Total	1,179,137
Population (official estimates at 31 December)	
2005	1,248,592
2006	1,256,739
2007	1,264,866
Density (per sq km) at 31 December 2007	620.0

* 788 sq miles.
† Including an adjustment of 2,115 for underenumeration.
‡ Excluding an adjustment for underenumeration.

ISLANDS

		Population	
	Area (sq km)	2000 census	Official estimates 31 December 2007
Mauritius	1,865	1,143,069	1,227,078
Rodrigues	104	35,779	37,499
Other islands	71	289	289

Ethnic Groups: Island of Mauritius, mid-1982: 664,480 Indo-Mauritians (507,985 Hindus, 156,495 Muslims), 264,537 general population (incl. Creole and Franco-Mauritian communities), 20,669 Chinese.

LANGUAGE GROUPS
(census of 2 July 2000)*

Arabic	806	Marathi		16,587
Bhojpuri	361,250	Tamil		44,731
Chinese	16,972	Telegu		18,802
Creole	454,763	Urdu		34,120
English	1,075	Other languages		169,619
French	21,171	Not stated		3,170
Hindi	35,782	**Total**		1,178,848

* Figures refer to the languages of cultural origin of the population of the islands of Mauritius and Rodrigues only. The data exclude an adjustment for underenumeration.

POPULATION BY DISTRICT
(estimates at mid-2006)

Plaine Wilhems	378,499	Riv du Rempart	106,360
Flacq	136,649	Moka	79,953
Pamplemousses	133,315	Black River	71,063
Port Louis	130,189	Savanne	69,729
Grand Port	113,451	Rodrigues	37,230

PRINCIPAL TOWNS
(mid-2006)

Port Louis (capital)	148,872	Curepipe	83,198
Beau Bassin/Rose Hill	108,921	Quatre Bornes	80,136
Vacoas/Phoenix	106,011		

BIRTHS, MARRIAGES AND DEATHS*

	Registered live births		Registered marriages		Registered deaths	
	Number	Rate (per 1,000)	Number	Rate (per 1,000)	Number	Rate (per 1,000)
2000	20,205	17.0	10,963	9.2	7,982	6.7
2001	19,696	16.4	10,635	8.9	7,983	6.7
2002	19,983	16.5	10,484	8.6	8,310	6.9
2003	19,343	15.8	10,812	8.8	8,520	7.0
2004	19,230	15.5	11,385	9.2	8,475	6.8
2005	18,829	15.1	11,294	n.a.	8,648	7.0
2006	17,605	14.1	11,471	n.a.	9,162	7.3
2007	17,034	13.5	12,471	n.a.	8,495	6.7

* Figures refer to the islands of Mauritius and Rodrigues only. The data are tabulated by year of registration, rather than by year of occurrence.

Expectation of life (WHO estimates, years at birth, WHO estimates): 72.4 (males 69.2; females 75.7) in 2005 (Source: WHO, *World Health Statistics*).

ECONOMICALLY ACTIVE POPULATION
('000 persons aged 15 years and over, incl. foreign workers)

	2004	2005	2006
Agriculture, forestry and fishing	49.0	48.7	48.1
Sugar cane	19.1	18.6	18.2
Mining and quarrying	0.3	0.3	0.3
Manufacturing	125.2	120.1	121.0
EPZ	71.6	65.5	65.0
Electricity and water	3.0	3.0	3.0
Construction	49.1	47.0	48.4
Wholesale and retail trade, repair of motor vehicles and household goods	74.8	76.5	78.8
Hotels and restaurants	28.4	31.1	31.8
Transport, storage and communications	35.9	36.4	36.9
Financial intermediation	7.9	8.8	9.4
Real estate, renting and business activities	18.1	20.0	21.1
Public administration and defence	39.0	39.4	39.6
Education	26.2	27.1	28.4
Health and social work	14.5	15.0	15.0
Other services	33.1	33.6	34.0
Total employed	504.5	507.0	515.8
Males	336.9	338.2	340.8
Females	167.6	168.8	175.0
Unemployed	45.1	52.1	50.1
Total labour force	549.6	559.1	565.9

Health and Welfare

KEY INDICATORS

Total fertility rate (children per woman, 2005)	2.0
Under-5 mortality rate (per 1,000 live births, 2005)	15
HIV/AIDS (% of persons aged 15–49, 2005)	0.6
Physicians (per 1,000 head, 2004)	1.06
Hospital beds (per 1,000 head, 2005)	3.0
Health expenditure (2004): US $ per head (PPP)	516.1
Health expenditure (2004): % of GDP	4.3
Health expenditure (2004): public (% of total)	54.7
Access to sanitation (% of persons, 2004)	94
Human Development Index (2005): ranking	65
Human Development Index (2005): value	0.804

For sources and definitions, see explanatory note on p. vi.

MAURITIUS

Agriculture

PRINCIPAL CROPS
('000 metric tons)

	2004	2005	2006
Potatoes	11.2	12.8	11.3
Sugar cane	5,280.4	4,984.1	4,748.9
Coconuts*	1.9	1.7	1.7
Cabbages and other brassicas	6.5	4.8	4.5
Lettuce and chicory	1.9	1.7	1.6
Tomatoes	14.4	12.8	15.1
Cauliflowers and broccoli	3.0	2.0	1.4
Pumpkins, squash and gourds	17.8	14.1	17.6
Cucumbers and gherkins	12.6	8.7	10.8
Aubergines (Eggplants)*	2.8	2.1	2.8
Dry onions	4.7	5.6	4.5
Carrots and turnips	5.8	3.9	4.1
Bananas	12.0	11.6	10.8
Pineapples	4.5	4.9	5.6
Tea (made)	1.5	1.4	1.6
Tobacco (leaves)	0.4	0.3	0.3

* FAO estimates.

Aggregate production ('000 metric tons, may include official, semi-official or estimated data): Total cereals 0.4 in 2004, 0.59 in 2005, 0.5 in 2006; Total roots and tubers 12.4 in 2004, 13.9 in 2005, 12.3 in 2006; Total vegetables (incl. melons) 92.1 in 2004, 77.6 in 2005, 84.6 in 2006; Total fruits (excl. melons) 17.7 in 2004, 17.7 in 2005, 17.6 in 2006.

Source: FAO.

LIVESTOCK
('000 head, year ending September)

	2001	2002	2003
Cattle*	28	28	28
Pigs	14*	12*	13
Sheep*	12	12	12
Goats*	95	93	93
Poultry*	8,900	9,800	9,800

* FAO estimate(s).

2004–06: Production as in 2003 (FAO estimates).
Source: FAO.

LIVESTOCK PRODUCTS
('000 metric tons)

	2004	2005	2006
Cattle meat	2	2	2
Chicken meat	33	33	36
Cows' milk	4	4	4
Hen eggs*	5	5	5

* FAO estimates.
Source: FAO.

Forestry

ROUNDWOOD REMOVALS
('000 cubic metres, excl. bark)

	2004	2005	2006
Sawlogs, veneer logs and logs for sleepers	5	6	7
Other industrial wood	3	2	2
Fuel wood	6	5	7
Total	14	13	15

Source: FAO.

SAWNWOOD PRODUCTION
('000 cubic metres, incl. railway sleepers)

	2004	2005	2006
Coniferous (softwood)	2	2	4
Broadleaved (hardwood)	1	1	1
Total	3	3	4

Source: FAO.

Fishing

(metric tons, live weight)

	2003	2004	2005
Capture	11,136	10,627	10,168
Groupers and seabasses	879	794	633
Snappers and jobfishes	1,806	1,595	2,584
Emperors (Scavengers)	3,955	3,374	2,534
Goatfishes	537	425	456
Spinefeet (Rabbitfishes)	404	319	345
Swordfish	601	1,011	1,001
Tuna-like fishes	745	736	730
Octopuses	327	307	293
Aquaculture	33	350	400
Red drum	n.a.	326	368
Total catch	11,169	10,977	10,568

Source: FAO.

Industry

SELECTED PRODUCTS
('000 metric tons, unless otherwise indicated)

	2003	2004	2005*
Fish	37.5	40.7	46.0
Frozen	6.3	5.7	5.9
Canned	30.5	34.2	38.9
Raw sugar	537.2	572.3	519.8
Molasses	160.0	155.8	145.4
Beer and stout (hectolitres)	400.8	363.7	339.0
Cigarettes (million)	938	918	900
Iron bars and steel tubes	58.7	59.9	60.5
Fertilizers	89.4	89.4	85.0
Electric energy (million kWh)	2,057	2,138	2,242

* Estimates.

Finance

CURRENCY AND EXCHANGE RATES

Monetary Units
100 cents = 1 Mauritian rupee.

Sterling, Dollar and Euro Equivalents (31 October 2007)
£1 sterling = 61.62 rupees;
US $1 = 29.71 rupees;
€1 = 42.93 rupees;
1,000 Mauritian rupees = £16.23 = $33.65 = €23.29.

Average Exchange Rate (Mauritian rupees per US $)
2004 29.499
2005 29.496
2006 31.708

MAURITIUS

BUDGET
(million rupees, year ending 30 June)

Revenue*

	2004/05	2005/06	2006/07†
Current revenue	35,192.4	38,508.7	42,193.0
Tax revenue	32,718.6	35,381.5	38,562.0
Taxes on income, profits and capital gains	5,829.0	7,468.9	7,800.0
Individual income tax	2,553.2	2,767.9	2,525.0
Corporate tax	3,275.8	4,701.0	5,275.0
Taxes on property	1,680.2	1,939.5	2,509.0
Domestic taxes on goods and services	17,464.7	18,762.0	21,473.0
Excise duties	2,838.4	2,467.8	3,360.0
Taxes on services	1,235.1	n.a.	n.a.
Value-added tax	12,529.3	13,709.5	15,000.0
Taxes on international trade	7,730.5	7,195.4	6,745.0
Other tax revenue	14.2	15.7	35.0
Non-tax revenue	2,473.8	3,127.2	3,631.0
Property income	1,234.7	1,804.8	2,036.0
Other non-tax revenue	1,239.1	1,322.4	1,595.0
Capital revenue	383.2	221.7	110.0
Total	**35,575.6**	**38,730.4**	**42,303.0**

EXPENSE/OUTLAYS

Expense by economic type	2004/05	2005/06	2006/07†
Current expenditure	38,042.3	41,915.3	44,089.7
Wages and salaries	11,670.3	12,298.7	12,278.8
Other purchases of goods and services	3,658.0	4,593.6	3,958.7
Interest payments	7,184.4	7,354.7	9,409.9
Subsidies and other current transfers	15,529.6	17,668.3	18,442.3
Transfer to non-profit institutions and households	12,776.1	14,130.9	15,491.9
Capital expenditure	6,344.8	6,959.9	7,663.1
Acquisition of fixed capital assets	5,354.6	5,159.2	5,445.6
Capital transfers	940.6	1,653.0	2,147.5
Total	**44,387.1**	**48,875.2**	**51,752.8**

Outlays by function of government	2004/05	2005/06	2006/07†
General government services	6,755.5	7,419.0	7,608.3
General public services	3,105.5	3,439.3	3,532.8
Defence	292.3	345.4	385.5
Public order and safety	3,357.7	3,634.3	3,690.0
Community and Social Services	19,225.5	21,110.7	21,767.1
Education	5,834.3	6,127.7	6,291.1
Health	3,597.0	4,049.0	3,817.0
Social security and welfare	8,568.7	9,578.8	10,293.2
Housing and community amenities	771.0	869.6	875.5
Recreational, cultural and religious services	454.5	485.6	490.3
Economic services	2,828.1	3,884.8	3,211.6
Agriculture, forestry, fishing and hunting	1,212.4	1,187.6	1,238.0
Transportation and communications	357.3	822.3	954.1
Other economic services	1,098.4	1,714.4	811.9
Other current expenditure	9,233.2	9,500.8	11,502.7
Public debt interest	7,184.4	7,354.7	9,409.9
Capital expenditure	6,344.8	6,959.9	7,663.1
Total expenditure	**44,387.1**	**48,875.2**	**51,752.8**

*Excluding grants received (million rupees): 444.0 in 2004/05; 489.2 in 2005/06; 790.0 in 2006/07 (estimate).
† Budget estimates.

Statistical Survey

INTERNATIONAL RESERVES
(US $ million at 31 December)

	2004	2005	2006
Gold (market prices)	23.9	25.9	31.3
IMF special drawing rights	27.2	25.7	27.5
Reserve position in IMF	34.0	25.0	15.8
Foreign exchange	1,544.7	1,298.2	1,226.3
Total	**1,629.8**	**1,374.8**	**1,300.9**

Source: IMF, *International Financial Statistics*.

MONEY SUPPLY
(million rupees at 31 December)

	2004	2005	2006
Currency outside banks	10,651.5	11,664.1	13,028.3
Demand deposits at deposit money banks	22,588.5	24,711.2	26,780.5
Total money (incl. others)	**33,330.3**	**36,702.8**	**40,206.6**

Source: IMF, *International Financial Statistics*.

COST OF LIVING
(Consumer Price Index; base: July 2001–June 2002 = 100)

	2004	2005	2006
Food and non-alcoholic beverages	112.5	119.1	131.0
Alcoholic beverages and tobacco	119.8	127.0	143.6
Clothing and footwear	105.0	106.3	113.4
Housing, fuel and electricity	107.1	110.8	123.6
Household operations	107.6	112.8	120.3
All items (incl. others)	**112.1**	**117.6**	**128.1**

NATIONAL ACCOUNTS
(million rupees in current prices, revised estimates)

National Income and Product

	2005	2006	2007
Compensation of employees	68,877	74,572	83,715
Operating surplus / Consumption of fixed capital	91,690	105,654	121,112
Gross domestic product (GDP) at factor cost	**160,567**	**180,226**	**204,827**
Taxes on production and imports / Less Subsidies	24,781	26,061	30,656
GDP in purchasers' values	**185,348**	**206,287**	**235,483**
Primary incomes received from abroad / Less Primary incomes paid abroad	−239	1,633	7,491
Gross national income	**185,109**	**207,920**	**242,974**
Current transfers from abroad / Less Current transfers paid abroad	1,797	2,269	3,693
Gross national disposable income	**186,906**	**210,189**	**246,667**

Expenditure on the Gross Domestic Product

	2005	2006	2007
Private final consumption expenditure	127,349	145,491	165,790
Government final consumption expenditure	27,368	29,355	30,743
Gross fixed capital formation	39,731	50,048	59,170
Increase in stocks	2,027	4,694	3,461
Total domestic expenditure	**196,475**	**229,588**	**259,164**
Exports of goods and services	110,940	127,128	138,236
Less Imports of goods and services	122,067	150,429	161,917
GDP in purchasers' values	**185,348**	**206,287**	**235,483**

MAURITIUS

Gross Domestic Product by Economic Activity

	2005	2006	2007
Agriculture, hunting, forestry, and fishing	9,790	10,130	9,785
Mining and quarrying	88	101	96
Manufacturing	32,187	36,356	41,060
Electricity, gas and water	3,355	3,521	3,674
Construction	9,099	10,205	13,145
Wholesale and retail trade, repair of motor vehicles and personal goods	19,571	22,534	25,598
Hotels and restaurants	12,423	15,500	19,517
Transport, storage and communications	20,447	22,173	24,826
Financial intermediation	16,766	18,850	21,607
Real estate, renting and business activities	16,609	19,026	22,539
Public administration and defence; compulsory social security	11,460	12,199	12,674
Education	7,780	8,440	9,136
Health and social work	5,580	6,266	6,824
Other services	6,007	6,784	7,981
Sub-total	171,162	192,085	218,462
Less Financial intermediation services indirectly measured	8,991	10,117	11,528
Gross value added in basic prices	162,171	181,968	206,934
Taxes, less subsidies, on products	23,177	24,319	28,549
GDP in market prices	185,348	206,287	235,483

BALANCE OF PAYMENTS
(US $ million)

	2004	2005	2006
Exports of goods f.o.b.	1,993.1	2,138.4	2,332.8
Imports of goods f.o.b.	−2,572.6	−2,935.2	−3,411.9
Trade balance	−579.5	−796.8	−1,079.0
Exports of services	1,455.6	1,618.1	1,671.0
Imports of services	−1,023.3	−1,197.7	−1,324.0
Balance on goods and services	−147.2	−376.5	−732.1
Other income received	51.7	142.9	373.9
Other income paid	−65.7	−151.3	−323.7
Balance on goods, services and income	−161.1	−385.0	−681.9
Current transfers received	168.1	162.3	179.2
Current transfers paid	−118.7	−101.3	−108.2
Current balance	−111.8	−324.0	−610.9
Capital account (net)	−1.6	−1.8	−2.7
Direct investment abroad	−31.8	−47.0	−9.6
Direct investment from abroad	13.9	41.8	106.8
Portfolio investment assets	−52.4	−41.6	−110.5
Portfolio investment liabilities	15.3	25.4	77.2
Other investment assets	−49.4	−230.9	−371.0
Other investment liabilities	112.4	394.3	367.4
Net errors and omissions	77.9	18.7	413.2
Overall balance	−27.5	−165.0	−140.1

Source: IMF, *International Financial Statistics*.

External Trade

PRINCIPAL COMMODITIES
(million rupees)

Imports c.i.f.	2004	2005	2006
Food and live animals	11,947	13,820	17,276
Fish and fish preparations	3,170	4,266	6,687
Mineral fuels, lubricants, etc.	10,020	15,394	19,321
Refined petroleum products	8,791	13,471	17,025
Chemicals	6,412	7,386	8,157
Basic manufactures	19,806	19,297	21,811
Textile yarn, fabrics, etc	4,189	3,167	4,097
Cotton fabrics	2,210	1,751	1,875
Machinery and transport equipment	17,916	26,110	35,931
Machinery specialized for particular industries	3,451	3,046	3,350
General industrial machinery, equipment and parts	2,368	2,795	3,049
Telecommunications and sound equipment	2,666	9,739	10,676
Other electrical machinery, apparatus, etc.	2,796	2,996	2,926
Road motor vehicles	4,028	4,216	4,505
Miscellaneous manufactured articles	6,624	7,257	8,208
Total (incl. others)	76,387	93,282	115,502

Exports f.o.b.*	2004	2005	2006
Food and live animals	13,277	15,437	17,876
Sugar	9,631	10,536	11,198
Fish and fish preparations	2,250	3,168	5,016
Basic manufactures	3,371	3,438	3,739
Textile yarn, fabrics, etc.	1,453	1,325	1,502
Pearls, precious and semi-precious stones	1,252	1,379	1,375
Miscellaneous manufactured articles	26,136	22,330	24,970
Clothing and accessories (excl. footwear)	23,386	19,534	21,999
Total (incl. others)	43,676	59,095	68,966

* Excl. re-exports (million rupees): 9,028 in 2004; 16,991 in 2005; 21,328 in 2006. Also excluded are stores and bunkers for ships and aircraft (million rupees): 2,201 in 2004; 4,124 in 2005; 5,071 in 2006.

2007 (provisional): *Imports:* Food and live animals 17,926; Mineral fuels, lubricants etc. 22,170; Chemicals 8,576; Basic manufactures 23,927; Machinery and transport equipment 24,457; Miscellaneous manufactured articles 9,092. Total (incl. others) 112,343. *Exports* (excl. re-exports): Food and live animals 17,029 (Sugar 9,268); Basic manufactures 4,100; Miscellaneous manufactured articles 27,907; Total (incl. others) 50,289.

PRINCIPAL TRADING PARTNERS
(million rupees)*

Imports c.i.f.	2004	2005	2006
Argentina	910	1,137	994
Australia	2,845	2,699	3,105
Bahrain	4,021	5,086	1,349
Belgium	1,368	1,488	1,758
China, People's Repub.	7,068	9,166	9,988
Denmark	196	1,010	240
Finland	822	4,485	2,784
France	6,818	6,958	16,440
Germany	2,852	3,794	4,613
Hong Kong	771	652	597
Hungary	226	2,141	4,007
India	6,989	6,461	15,687
Indonesia	1,558	2,112	2,346
Italy	2,431	2,402	2,950
Japan	3,083	3,333	3,254
Korea, Repub.	797	906	1,081
Madagascar	932	436	478
Malaysia	2,285	2,670	2,978
Pakistan	1,182	1,011	1,239
Saudi Arabia	1,418	3,409	4,000

MAURITIUS

Imports c.i.f.—continued	2004	2005	2006
Singapore	1,175	1,586	1,103
South Africa	8,562	8,066	8,433
Spain	1,475	2,091	2,325
Switzerland	1,444	1,121	1,296
Taiwan	1,246	1,718	2,340†
Thailand	1,168	1,532	1,677
United Arab Emirates	1,737	3,588	3,309
United Kingdom	2,377	2,589	2,894
USA	1,651	1,972	2,328
Total (incl. others)	76,387	93,282	115,502

Exports f.o.b.	2004	2005	2006
Belgium	1,363	1,559	1,851
France	9,084	8,391	8,704
Germany	1,268	1,070	1,295
Italy	2,156	3,308	2,754
Madagascar	2,689	3,373	3,288
Netherlands	914	723	870
Portugal	732	558	187
Réunion	1,485	1,561	1,652
South Africa	775	788	1,488
Spain	860	1,589	2,447
Switzerland	640	644	662
United Arab Emirates	778	4,903	7,882
United Kingdom	17,356	19,215	22,362
USA	7,768	5,640	5,754
Total (incl. others)	52,704	59,095	68,966

* Imports by country of origin; exports by country of destination (including re-exports, excluding ships' stores and bunkers).
† Provisional figure.

Transport

ROAD TRAFFIC
(motor vehicles registered at 31 December)

	2005	2006	2007
Private vehicles:			
Cars	120,046	128,272	144,405
Motorcycles and mopeds	133,430	138,174	142,606
Commercial vehicles:			
Buses	2,560	2,612	2,753
Taxis	6,798	6,860	6,885
Goods vehicles	36,036	36,794	37,470

SHIPPING

Merchant Fleet
(registered at 31 December)

	2004	2005	2006
Number of vessels	50	47	45
Total displacement ('000 grt)	79.0	70.6	68.6

Source: Lloyd's Register-Fairplay, *World Fleet Statistics*.

Sea-borne Freight Traffic
('000 metric tons)

	2004	2005	2006*
Goods unloaded	4,696	4,709	4,619
Goods loaded†	1,773	1,197	1,226

* Provisional.
† Excluding ships' bunkers.

CIVIL AVIATION
(traffic)

	2004	2005	2006*
Aircraft landings†	9,316	9,705	8,791
Freight unloaded (metric tons)‡	22,400	23,900	21,200
Freight loaded (metric tons)‡	26,000	25,200	23,800

* Provisional.
† Commercial aircraft only.
‡ Figures are rounded.

Tourism

FOREIGN TOURIST ARRIVALS

Country of residence	2005	2006	2007
France	220,421	182,295	240,028
Germany	55,983	57,251	65,165
India	29,755	37,498	42,974
Italy	43,458	69,407	69,510
Réunion	99,036	89,127	95,823
South Africa	58,446	70,796	81,733
Switzerland	15,773	16,161	17,546
United Kingdom	95,407	102,333	107,297
Total (incl. others)	761,063	788,276	906,970

Tourism earnings (gross, million rupees): 25,704 in 2005; 31,942 in 2006; 40,687 in 2007.

Communications Media

	2004	2005	2006
Telephones ('000 main lines in use)	353.8	357.5	357.3
Mobile cellular telephones ('000 subscribers)	547.7	656.8	772.4
Personal computers ('000 in use)	200	200	n.a.
Internet users ('000)	240	300	n.a.
Broadband subscribers ('000)	2.6	3.1	21.9
Television sets licensed ('000)	260.3	275.8	277.4
Daily newspapers	7	9	8
Non-daily newspapers	35	37	38

1996: Book production: titles 80, copies ('000) 163.

1997: Facsimile machines (number in use) 28,000.

Sources: partly UNESCO, *Statistical Yearbook*; UN, *Statistical Yearbook*; International Telecommunication Union.

Education

(March 2007)

	Institutions	Personnel	Students*
Pre-primary	1,076	3,386	36,421
Primary	289	6,679†	119,310
Secondary	186	7,423	116,706
Technical and vocational	153	701	9,573

* By enrolment.
† Excluding instruction in oriental language.

Adult literacy rate (official estimates): 84.3% (males 88.2%; females 80.5%) in 2000 (Source: UNESCO Institute for Statistics).

Directory

The Constitution

The Mauritius Independence Order, which established a self-governing state, came into force on 12 March 1968, and was subsequently amended. Constitutional amendments providing for the adoption of republican status were approved by the Legislative Assembly (henceforth known as the National Assembly) on 10 December 1991, and came into effect on 12 March 1992. The main provisions of the revised Constitution are listed below:

HEAD OF STATE

The Head of State is the President of the Republic, who is elected by a simple majority of the National Assembly for a five-year term of office. The President appoints the Prime Minister (in whom executive power is vested) and, on the latter's recommendation, other ministers.

COUNCIL OF MINISTERS

The Council of Ministers, which is headed by the Prime Minister, is appointed by the President and is responsible to the National Assembly.

THE NATIONAL ASSEMBLY

The National Assembly, which has a term of five years, comprises the Speaker, 62 members elected by universal adult suffrage, a maximum of eight additional members and the Attorney-General (if not an elected member). The island of Mauritius is divided into 20 three-member constituencies for legislative elections. Rodrigues returns two members to the National Assembly. The official language of the National Assembly is English, but any member may address the Speaker in French.

The Government

HEAD OF STATE

President: Sir ANEROOD JUGNAUTH (took office 7 October 2003).
Vice-President: ANGIDI VERRIAH CHETTIAR.

COUNCIL OF MINISTERS
(March 2008)

Prime Minister, Minister of Defence and Home Affairs, Civil Service and Administrative Reforms and Rodrigues and Outer Islands and Minister of Foreign Affairs, International Trade and Co-operation: NAVINCHANDRA RAMGOOLAM.
Deputy Prime Minister and Minister of Public Infrastructure, Land Transport and Shipping: AHMED RASHID BEEBEEJAUN.
Deputy Prime Minister and Minister of Tourism, Leisure and External Communications: CHARLES GAËTAN XAVIER-LUC DUVAL.
Deputy Prime Minister and Minister of Finance and Economic Development: RAMA KRISHNA SITHANEN.
Minister of the Environment and the National Development Unit: ANIL KUMAR BACHOO.
Minister of Education and Human Resources: DHARAMBEER GOKHOOL.
Minister of Public Utilities: ABU TWALIB KASENALLY.
Minister of Local Government: JAMES BURTY DAVID.
Minister of Agro-industry and Fisheries: ARVIN BOOLELL.
Minister of Labour, Industrial Relations and Employment: VASANT KUMAR BUNWAREE.
Minister of Social Security, National Solidarity and Senior Citizens' Welfare and Reform Institutions: SHEILABAI BAPPOO.
Minister of Women's Rights, Child Development, Family Welfare and Consumer Protection: INDRANEE SEEBUN.
Minister of Labour, Industrial Relations and Employment: VASANT KUMAR BUNWAREE.
Attorney-General and Minister of Justice and Human Rights: JAYARAMA VALAYDEN.
Minister of Health and Quality of Life: SATYA VEYASH FAUGOO.
Minister of Industry, Small and Medium Enterprises, Commerce and Co-operatives: RAJESHWAR JEETAH.
Minister of Arts and Culture: MAHENDRA GOWRESSOO.
Minister of Housing and Land: MOHAMMED ASRAF ALLY DULULL.
Minister of Information Technology and Telecommunications: JOSEPH NOËL-ETIENNE GHISLAIN SINATAMBOU.
Minister of Youth and Sports: SYLVIO HOCK SHEEN TANG WAH HING.

MINISTRIES

Office of the President: State House, Le Réduit, Port Louis; tel. 454-3021; fax 464-5370; e-mail president@mail.gov.mu; internet president.gov.mu.
Office of the Prime Minister: New Treasury Bldg, Port Louis; tel. 201-1003; fax 208-8619; e-mail primeminister@mail.gov.mu; internet pmo.gov.mu.
Ministry of Agro-industry and Fisheries: Renganaden Seeneevassen Bldg, 8th and 9th Floor, cnr Jules Koenig and Maillard Sts, Port Louis; tel. 212-2335; fax 212-4427; e-mail moa-headoffice@mail.gov.mu; internet agriculture.gov.mu.
Ministry of Arts and Culture: Renganaden Seeneevassen Bldg, 7th Floor, cnr Pope Hennessy and Maillard Sts, Port Louis; tel. 212-9993; fax 208-0315; e-mail minoac@intnet.mu; internet culture.gov.mu.
Ministry of Civil Service Affairs and Administrative Reform: New Government Centre, 7th Floor, Port Louis; tel. 201-2886; fax 212-9528; e-mail civser@mail.gov.mu; internet www.civilservice.gov.mu.
Ministry of Defence and Home Affairs: New Government Centre, 4th Floor, Port Louis; e-mail pmo@mail.gov.mu; internet pmo.gov.mu/dha.
Ministry of Education and Human Resources: IVTB House, Pont Fer, Phoenix; tel. 601-5200; fax 698-2550; e-mail moeps@mail.gov.mu; internet ministry-education.gov.mu.
Ministry of the Environment and the National Development Unit: Ken Lee Tower, Barracks St, Port Louis; tel. 212-3363; fax 212-8324; e-mail admenv@intnet.mu; internet environment.gov.mu.
Ministry of Finance and Economic Development: Government House, Ground Floor, Port Louis; tel. 201-1146; fax 211-0096; e-mail mof@mail.gov.mu; internet mof.gov.mu.
Ministry of Foreign Affairs, International Trade and Co-operation: New Government Centre, 5th Floor, Port Louis; tel. 201-1648; fax 208-8087; e-mail mfa@mail.gov.mu; internet foreign.gov.mu.
Ministry of Health and Quality of Life: 5th Floor, Emmanuel Anquetil Bldg, Sir Seewoosagur Ramgoolam St, Port Louis; tel. 201-1912; fax 208-0376; e-mail moh@mail.gov.mu; internet health.gov.mu.
Ministry of Housing and Land: Moorgate House, Port Louis; tel. 212-6022; fax 212-7482; internet housing.gov.mu.
Ministry of Industry, Small and Medium Enterprises, Commerce and Co-operatives: Air Mauritius Centre, 7th Floor, John F. Kennedy St, Port Louis; tel. 210-7100; fax 212-8201; e-mail mind@mail.gov.mu; internet industry.gov.mu.
Ministry of Information Technology and Telecommunications: Air Mauritius Centre, Level 9, John F. Kennedy St, Port Louis; tel. 210-0201; fax 212-1673; e-mail mtel@mail.gov.mu; internet telecomit.gov.mu.
Ministry of Justice and Human Rights: Renganaden Seeneevassen Bldg, 2nd Floor, Port Louis; tel. 212-2139; fax 212-6742; e-mail ago@intnet.mu; internet attorneygeneral.gov.mu.
Ministry of Labour, Industrial Relations and Employment: Victoria House, cnr St Louis and Barracks Sts, Port Louis; tel. 207-2600; fax 212-3070; e-mail mol@mail.gov.mu; internet labour.gov.mu.
Ministry of Local Government: Emmanuel Anquetil Bldg, 3rd Floor, cnr Sir Seewoosagur Ramgoolam and Jules Koenig Sts, Port Louis; tel. 201-1216; fax 208-9729; e-mail mlg@mail.gov.mu; internet localgovernment.gov.mu.
Ministry of Public Infrastructure, Land Transport and Shipping: Moorgate House, 9th Floor, Sir William Newton St, Port Louis; tel. 210-7270; fax 212-8373; internet publicinfrastructure.gov.mu.
Ministry of Public Utilities: Medcor Bldg, 10th Floor, John F. Kennedy St, Port Louis; tel. 210-3994; fax 208-6497; e-mail minpuuti@intnet.mu; internet publicutilities.gov.mu.
Ministry of Rodrigues and Outer Islands: Fon Sing Bldg, 1st floor, Edith Cavell St, Port Louis; tel. 208-8472; fax 212-6329; internet shipping.gov.mu.
Ministry of Social Security, National Solidarity and Senior Citizens' Welfare and Reform Institutions: Renganaden Seeneevassen Bldg, Jules Koenig St, Port Louis; tel. 207-0625; fax 212-8190; e-mail mss@mail.gov.mu; internet socialsecurity.gov.mu.

MAURITIUS

Directory

Ministry of Tourism, Leisure and External Communications: Air Mauritius Centre, Level 12, John F. Kennedy St, Port Louis; tel. 211-7930; fax 208-6776; e-mail mtou@mail.gov.mu; internet tourism.gov.mu.

Ministry of Women's Rights, Child Development, Family Welfare and Consumer Protection: CSK Bldg, cnr Remy Ollier and Emmanuel Anquetil Sts, Port Louis; tel. 206-3700; fax 240-7717; e-mail mwfwcd@mail.gov.mu; internet women.gov.mu.

Ministry of Youth and Sports: Emmanuel Anquetil Bldg, 3rd Floor, Sir Seewoosagur Ramgoolam St, Port Louis; tel. 201-2543; fax 210-7554; e-mail mys@mail.gov.mu; internet youthsport.gov.mu.

Legislature

National Assembly

Port Louis; tel. 201-1414; fax 212-8364; e-mail themace@intnet.mu; internet mauritiusassembly.gov.mu.

Speaker: KAILASH PURRYAG.

General Election, 3 July 2005

Party	Directly elected	Additional*	Total
Social Alliance†	38	4	42
Mouvement Socialiste Militant (MSM)/Mouvement Militant Mauricien (MMM)	22	2	24
Organisation du Peuple Rodriguais (OPR)	2	2	4
Total	62	8	70

* Awarded to those among the unsuccessful candidates who attracted the largest number of votes, in order to ensure that a balance of ethnic groups are represented in the Assembly.
† Alliance primarily comprising the Mauritius Labour Party, the Parti Mauricien Xavier-Luc Duval, the Mouvement Républicain and the Mouvement Militant Socialiste Mauricien.

Election Commission

Electoral Commissioner's Office (ECO): 4th Floor, Max City Bldg, cnr Louis Pasteur and Remy Ollier Sts, Port Louis; tel. 241-7000; fax 241-0967; e-mail elec@mail.gov.mu; internet www.gov.mu/portal/site/eco; under the aegis of the Prime Minister's Office; Commissioner appointed by the Judicial and Legal Service Commission; Electoral Commissioner M. I. ABDOOL RAHMAN.

Political Organizations

Mauritius Labour Party (MLP) (Parti Travailliste): 7 Guy Rozemont Sq., Port Louis; tel. 212-6691; fax 210-0189; e-mail labour@intnet.mu; internet labour.intnet.mu; f. 1936; formed part of the Social Alliance for the 2005 election and subsequently a govt; Leader Dr NAVINCHANDRA RAMGOOLAM; Chair. ETIENNE SINATAMBOU; Sec.-Gen. DEVENAND VIRAHSAWMY.

Mouvement Militant Mauricien (MMM): 21 Poudrière St, Port Louis; tel. 212-6553; fax 208-9939; internet mmm.mmmonline.org; f. 1969; socialist; formed an alliance with the Mouvement Socialiste Militant for both the 2000 and the 2005 elections; Pres. SAM LAUTHAN; Leader PAUL BÉRENGER; Sec.-Gen. STEVEN OBEEGADOO, RAJESH BHAGWAN.

Mouvement Militant Socialiste Mauricien (MMSM): Port Louis; forms part of the incumbent Social Alliance, elected in 2005; Leader MADUN DULLOO.

Mouvement Rodriguais (MR): Port Mathurin, Rodrigues; tel. 831-1876 (Port Mathurin); tel. and fax 831-2648 (Port Louis); e-mail numally@intnet.mu; f. 1992; represents the interests of Rodrigues; Leader LOUIS JOSEPH (NICHOLAS) VON-MALLY.

Mouvement Sociale Démocrate (MSD) (Social Democratic Movement): Port Louis; f. 2005; Leader ANIL BACHOO.

Mouvement Socialiste Militant (MSM): Sun Trust Bldg, 31 Edith Cavell St, Port Louis; tel. 212-8787; fax 208-9517; e-mail request@msmsun.com; internet www.msmsun.com; f. 1983; by fmr mems of the MMM; dominant party in subsequent coalition govts until Dec. 1995 and again from 2000–05; Leader (vacant); Chair. JOE LESJONGARD; Sec.-Gen. VISHWANATH SAJADAH.

Organisation du Peuple Rodriguais (OPR): Port Mathurin, Rodrigues; represents the interests of Rodrigues; Leader LOUIS SERGE CLAIR.

Parti Mauricien Social Démocrate (PMSD): Melville, Grand Gaube; centre-right; participated in an alliance with the MSM and MMM for the 2005 legislative and municipal elections; Leader MAURICE ALLET; Sec.-Gen. JACQUES PANGLOSE.

Parti Mauricien Xavier-Luc Duval (PMXD): Port Louis; f. 1998; forms part of the Social Alliance; Leader CHARLES GAËTAN XAVIER-LUC DUVAL.

Union Nationale (Mauritian National Union): Port Louis; f. 2006; Chair. ASHOCK JUGNAUTH.

Some of the blocs and parties that participated in the 2005 election include the **Front Solidarité Mauricienne (FSM)**, **Les Verts Fraternels/The Greens** (Leader SYLVIO MICHEL), the **Mouvement Républicain** (Leader RAMA VALAYDEV), the **Parti du Peuple Mauricien (PPM)**, the **Mouvement Démocratique National Raj Dayal (MDN Raj Dayal)**, the **Rezistans ek Alternativ** (Secretary ASHOK SUBRON), **Lalit** (lalitmauritius.com) and the **Tamil Council**.

Diplomatic Representation

EMBASSIES AND HIGH COMMISSIONS IN MAURITIUS

Australia: Rogers House, 2nd Floor, John F. Kennedy St, POB 541, Port Louis; tel. 202-0160; fax 208-8878; e-mail ahc.portlouis@dfat.gov.au; internet www.mauritius.embassy.gov.au; High Commissioner CATHERINE JOHNSTONE.

China, People's Republic: Royal Rd, Belle Rose, Rose Hill; tel. 454-9111; fax 464-6012; e-mail chinaemb_mu@mfa.gov.cn; internet www.ambchine.mu; Ambassador GAO YUCHEN.

Egypt: Sun Trust Bldg, 2nd floor, Edith Cavell St, Port Louis; tel. 213-1765; fax 213-1768; Ambassador BAKRY ROSHDY EL-AMARY.

France: 14 St George St, Port Louis; tel. 202-0100; fax 202-0110; e-mail ambafr@intnet.mu; internet www.ambafrance-mu.org; Ambassador JACQUES MAILLARD.

India: Life Insurance Corpn of India Bldg, 6th Floor, John F. Kennedy St, POB 162, Port Louis; tel. 208-3775; fax 208-6859; e-mail hicom.ss@intnet.mu; internet indiahighcom.intnet.mu; High Commissioner BONDAL JAISHANKAR.

Madagascar: Guiot Pasceau St, Floreal, POB 3, Port Louis; tel. 686-5015; fax 686-7040; e-mail madmail@intnet.mu; Ambassador BRUNO RANARIVELO.

Pakistan: 9A Queen Mary Ave, Floreal, Port Louis; tel. 698-8501; fax 698-8405; e-mail pareportlouis@hotmail.com; High Commissioner SYED HASAN JAVED.

Russia: Queen Mary Ave, POB 10, Floreal, Port Louis; tel. 696-1545; fax 696-5027; e-mail rusemb.mu@intnet.mu; Ambassador OLGA IVANOVA.

South Africa: BAI Bldg, 4th Floor, 25 Pope Hennessy St, POB 908, Port Louis; tel. 212-6925; fax 212-6936; e-mail sahc@intnet.mu; High Commissioner MADUMANE M. MATABANE.

United Kingdom: Les Cascades Bldg, 7th Floor, Edith Cavell St, POB 1063, Port Louis; tel. 202-9400; fax 202-9408; e-mail bhc@intnet.mu; High Commissioner Dr JOHN MURTON.

USA: Rogers House, 4th Floor, John F. Kennedy St, POB 544, Port Louis; tel. 208-4400; fax 208-9534; e-mail usembass@intnet.mu; internet mauritius.usembassy.gov; Ambassador CESAR BENITO CABRERA.

Judicial System

The laws of Mauritius are derived both from the French Code Napoléon and from English Law. The Judicial Department consists of the Supreme Court, presided over by the Chief Justice and such number of Puisne Judges as may be prescribed by Parliament (currently nine), who are also Judges of the Court of Criminal Appeal and the Court of Civil Appeal. These courts hear appeals from the Intermediate Court, the Industrial Court and 10 District Courts (including that of Rodrigues). The Industrial Court has special jurisdiction to protect the constitutional rights of the citizen. There is a right of appeal in certain cases from the Supreme Court to the Judicial Committee of the Privy Council in the United Kingdom.

Supreme Court: Jules Koenig St, Port Louis; tel. 212-0275; tel. 212-9946; internet supremecourt.intnet.mu.

Chief Justice: ARIANGA PILLAY.

Senior Puisne Judge: B. YEUNG SIK YUEN.

Religion

Hindus are estimated to comprise more than 50% of the population, with Christians accounting for some 30% and Muslims 17%. There is also a small Buddhist community.

CHRISTIANITY

The Anglican Communion

Anglicans in Mauritius are within the Church of the Province of the Indian Ocean, comprising six dioceses (four in Madagascar, one in Mauritius and one in Seychelles). The Archbishop of the Province is the Bishop of Antananarivo, Madagascar. In 1983 the Church had 5,438 members in Mauritius.

Bishop of Mauritius: Rt Rev. IAN ERNEST, Bishop's House, Phoenix; tel. 686-5158; fax 697-1096; e-mail dioang@intnet.mu.

The Presbyterian Church of Mauritius

Minister: Pasteur ANDRÉ DE RÉLAND, cnr Farquhar and Royal Rds, Coignet, Rose Hill; tel. 464-5265; fax 395-2068; e-mail embrau@bow.intnet.mu; f. 1814.

The Roman Catholic Church

Mauritius comprises a single diocese, directly responsible to the Holy See, and an apostolic vicariate on Rodrigues. At 31 December 2005 there were an estimated 278,251 adherents in the country, representing about 24.3% of the total population.

Bishop of Port Louis: Rt Rev. MAURICE PIAT, Evêché, 13 Mgr Gonin St, Port Louis; tel. 208-3068; fax 208-6607; e-mail eveche@intnet.mu.

BAHÁ'Í FAITH

National Spiritual Assembly: Port Louis; tel. 212-2179; mems resident in 190 localities.

ISLAM

Mauritius Islamic Mission: Noor-e-Islam Mosque, Port Louis; Imam S. M. BEEHARRY.

The Press

DAILIES

China Times: 24 Emmanuel Anquetil St, POB 325, Port Louis; tel. 240-3067; f. 1953; Chinese; Editor-in-Chief LONG SIONG AH KENG; circ. 3,000.

Chinese Daily News: 32 Rémy Ollier St, POB 316, Port Louis; tel. 240-0472; f. 1932; Chinese; Editor-in-Chief WONG YUEN MOY; circ. 5,000.

L'Express: 3 Brown Sequard St, POB 247, Port Louis; tel. 202-8200; fax 208-8174; internet www.lexpress-net.com; f. 1963; owned by La Sentinelle Ltd; English and French; Editor-in-Chief RAJ MEETARBHAN; circ. 35,000.

Maurice Soir: Port Louis; f. 1996; Editor SYDNEY SELVON; circ. 2,000.

Le Matinal: AAPCA House, 6 La Poudrière St, Port Louis; tel. 207-0909; fax 213-4069; e-mail editorial@lematinal.com; internet www.lematinal.com; f. 2003; in French and English; AAPCA (Mauritius) Ltd; Dir SIDHARTH BHATIA.

Le Mauricien: 8 St George St, POB 7, Port Louis; tel. 208-3251; fax 208-7059; e-mail redaction@lemauricien.com; internet www.lemauricien.com; f. 1907; English and French; Editor-in-Chief GILBERT AHNEE; circ. 35,000.

Le Quotidien: Pearl House, 4th Floor, 16 Sir Virgile Naz St, Port Louis; tel. 208-2631; fax 211-7479; e-mail quotidien@bow.intnet.mu; f. 1996; English and French; Dirs JACQUES DAVID, PATRICK MICHEL; circ. 30,000.

Le Socialiste: Manilall Bldg, 3rd Floor, Brabant St, Port Louis; tel. 208-8003; fax 211-3890; English and French; Editor-in-Chief VEDI BALLAH; circ. 7,000.

The Tribune: Port Louis; f. 1999; Publr HARISH CHUNDUNSING.

WEEKLIES AND FORTNIGHTLIES

5-Plus Dimanche: 3 Brown Sequard St, Port Louis; tel. 213-5500; fax 213-5551; e-mail comments@5plusltd.com; internet www.5plusltd.com; f. 1994; English and French; Editor-in-Chief FINLAY SALESSE; circ. 30,000.

5-Plus Magazine: 3 Brown Sequard St, Port Louis; tel. 213-5500; fax 213-5551; e-mail comments@5plusltd.com; f. 1990; English and French; Editor-in-Chief PIERRE BENOÎT; circ. 10,000.

Bollywood Massala: Le Défi Bldg, Royal Rd, Port Louis; tel. 211-8131; fax 213-0959; e-mail ledefi.plus@intnet.mu; internet www.defimedia.info.

Business Magazine: TN Tower, 2nd Floor, 13 St George St, Port Louis; tel. 211-1925; fax 211-1926; e-mail businessmag@intnet.mu; internet www.businessmag.mu; f. 1993; owned by La Sentinelle Ltd; English and French; Editor-in-Chief LINDSAY RIVIÈRE; circ. 6,000.

Le Croissant: cnr Velore and Noor Essan Mosque Sts, Port Louis; tel. 240-7105; English and French; Editor-in-Chief RAYMOND RICHARD NAUVEL; circ. 25,000.

Le Défi-Plus: Le Défi Bldg, Royal Rd, Port Louis; tel. 211-8131; fax 213-0959; e-mail ledefi.plus@intnet.mu; internet www.defimedia.info; Saturdays.

Le Dimanche: 5 Jemmapes St, Port Louis; tel. 212-5887; fax 212-1177; e-mail ledmer@intnet.mu; f. 1961; English and French; Editor RAYMOND RICHARD NAUVEL; circ. 25,000.

L'Hèbdo: Le Défi Bldg, Royal Rd, Port Louis; tel. 211-8131; fax 213-0959; e-mail ledefi.plus@intnet.mu; internet www.defimedia.info.

Impact News: 10 Dr Yves Cantin St, Port Louis; tel. 211-5284; fax 211-7821; e-mail farhadr@wanadoo.mu; internet www.impactnews.info; English and French; Editor-in-Chief FARHAD RAMJAUN.

Lalit de Klas: 153B Royal Rd, G.R.N.W., Port Louis; tel. 208-2132; e-mail lalitmail@intnet.mu; internet www.lalitmauritius.org; English, French and Mauritian Creole; Editor RADA KISTNASAMY.

Mauritius Times: 23 Bourbon St, Port Louis; tel. and fax 212-1313; e-mail mtimes@intnet.mu; internet www.mauritiustimes.com; f. 1954; English and French; Editor-in-Chief MADHUKAR RAMLALLAH; circ. 15,000.

Mirror: 39 Emmanuel Anquetil St, Port Louis; tel. 240-3298; Chinese; Editor-in-Chief NG KEE SIONG; circ. 4,000.

News on Sunday: Dr Eugen Laurent St, POB 230, Port Louis; tel. 211-5902; fax 211-7302; e-mail newsonsunday@news.intnet.mu; internet newsonsunday.150m.com; f. 1996; owned by Le Défi Group; weekly; in English; Editor NAGUIB LALLMAHOMED; circ. 10,000.

Le Nouveau Militant: 21 Poudrière St, Port Louis; tel. 212-6553; fax 208-2291; f. 1979; publ. by the Mouvement Militant Mauricien; English and French; Editor-in-Chief J. RAUMIAH.

Le Rodriguais: Saint Gabriel, Rodrigues; tel. 831-1613; fax 831-1484; f. 1989; Creole, English and French; Editor JACQUES EDOUARD; circ. 2,000.

Star: 38 Labourdonnais St, Port Louis; tel. 212-2736; fax 211-7781; e-mail starpress@intnet.mu; internet www.mauriweb.com/star; English and French; Editor-in-Chief REZA ISSACK.

Sunday: Port Louis; tel. 208-9516; fax 208-7059; f. 1966; English and French; Editor-in-Chief SUBASH GOBIN.

Turf Magazine: 8 George St, POB 7, Port Louis; tel. 207-8200; fax 208-7059; e-mail bdlm@intnet.mu; internet www.lemauricien.com/turfmag; owned by Le Mauricien Ltd.

La Vie Catholique: 28 Nicolay Rd, Port Louis; tel. 242-0975; fax 242-3114; e-mail viecatho@intnet.mu; internet pages.intnet.mu/lavie; f. 1930; weekly; English, French and Creole; Editor-in-Chief (vacant); circ. 8,000.

Week-End: 8 St George St, POB 7, Port Louis; tel. 207-8200; fax 208-3248; e-mail redaction@lemauricien.com; internet www.lemauricien.com/weekend; f. 1966; owned by Le Mauricien Ltd; French and English; Editor-in-Chief GÉRARD CATEAUX; circ. 80,000.

Week-End Scope: 8 St George St, POB 7, Port Louis; tel. 207-8200; fax 208-7059; e-mail wes@lemauricien.com; internet www.lemauricien.com/wes; owned by Le Mauricien Ltd; English and French; Editor-in-Chief JACQUES ACHILLE.

OTHER SELECTED PERIODICALS

CCI–INFO: 3 Royal St, Port Louis; tel. 208-3301; fax 208-0076; e-mail mcci@intnet.mu; internet www.mcci.org; English and French; f. 1995; quarterly; publ. of the Mauritius Chamber of Commerce and Industry.

Ciné Star Magazine: 64 Sir Seewoosagur Ramgoolam St, Port Louis; tel. 240-1447; English and French; Editor-in-Chief ABDOOL RAWOOF SOOBRATTY.

Education News: Edith Cavell St, Port Louis; tel. 212-1303; English and French; monthly; Editor-in-Chief GIAN AUBEELUCK.

Le Message de L'Ahmadiyyat: c/o Ahmadiyya Muslim Asscn, POB 6, Rose Hill; tel. 464-1747; fax 454-2223; e-mail darussalaam@intnet.mu; French; monthly; Editor-in-Chief MOHAMMAD AMEEN JOWAHIR; circ. 3,000.

Le Progrès Islamique: 51B Solferino St, Rose Hill; tel. 467-1697; fax 467-1696; f. 1948; English and French; monthly; Editor DEVINA SOOKIA.

La Voix d'Islam: Parisot Rd, Mesnil, Phoenix; f. 1951; English and French; monthly.

Publishers

Boukié Banané (The Flame Tree): 5 Edwin Ythier St, Rose Hill; tel. 454-2327; fax 465-4312; e-mail limem@intnet.mu; internet pages.intnet.mu/develop; f. 1979; Morisien literature, poetry and drama; Man. Dir DEV VIRAHSAWMY.

Business Publications Ltd: TN Tower, 2nd Floor, St George St, Port Louis; tel. 211-3048; fax 211-1926; internet www.businessmag.mu; f. 1993; English and French; Dir LYNDSAY RIVIÈRE.

Editions du Dattier: 82 Goyavier Ave, Quatre Bornes; tel. 466-4854; fax 446-3105; e-mail dattier@intnet.mu; English and French; Dir JEAN-PHILIPPE LAGESSE.

Editions de l'Océan Indien: Stanley, Rose Hill; tel. 464-6761; fax 464-3445; e-mail eoibooks@intnet.mu; internet www.eoi-info.com; f. 1977; general, textbooks, dictionaries, literature; English, French and Asian languages; Gen. Man. DEVANAND DEWKURUN.

Editions Le Printemps: 4 Club Rd, Vacoas; tel. 696-1017; fax 686-7302; e-mail elp@bow.intnet.mu; Man. Dir A. I. SULLIMAN.

Editions Vizavi: 9 St George St, Port Louis; tel. 211-3047; e-mail vizavi@intnet.mu; Dir PASCALE SIEW.

Broadcasting and Communications

TELECOMMUNICATIONS

Information and Communication Technologies Authority (ICTA): The Celicourt, 12th Floor, 6 Sir Celicourt Antelme St, Port Louis; tel. 211-5333; fax 211-9444; e-mail icta@intnet.mu; internet www.icta.mu; f. 1999; regulatory authority; Chair. TRILOK DWARKA.

Mauritius Telecom Ltd: Telecom Tower, Edith Cavell St, Port Louis; tel. 203-7000; fax 208-1070; e-mail ceo@mauritiustelecom.com.mu; internet www.mauritiustelecom.com; f. 1992; 60% owned by Govt of Mauritius, State Bank of Mauritius and National Pensions Fund, 40% owned by France Télécom through RIMCOM; privatized in 2000; provides all telecommunications services, including internet and digital mobile cellular services; Chair. APPALSAMY (DASS) THOMAS; CEO SARAT LALLAH.

Cellplus Mobile Communications Ltd: Telecom Tower, 9th Floor, Edith Cavell St, Port Louis; tel. 203-7500; fax 211-6996; e-mail cellplus@intnet.mu; internet www.cellplus.mu; f. 1996; introduced the first GSM cellular network in Mauritius and recently in Rodrigues (Cell-Oh); a wholly owned subsidiary of Mauritius Telecom.

Emtel: 1 Boundary Road, Rose Hill; tel. 454-5400; fax 454-1010; e-mail emtel@emtelnet.com; internet www.emtel-ltd.com; f. 1989; CEO SHYAM ROY.

BROADCASTING

In 1997 the Supreme Court invalidated the broadcasting monopoly held by the Mauritius Broadcasting Corporation.

Independent Broadcasting Authority: 5 de Courson St, Curepipe Rd, Curepipe; tel. 670-4621; fax 670-2335; e-mail iba@intnet.mu; internet iba.gov.mu; Dir PIERRE AH-FAT.

Radio

Mauritius Broadcasting Corpn: Broadcasting House, Louis Pasteur St, Forest Side; tel. 602-1200; fax 674-0488; e-mail customercare@mbc.intnet.mu; internet www.mbcradio.tv; f. 1964; independent corpn operating eight national radio services and nine television channels; Chair. FAREED JANGEER-KHAN; Dir-Gen. BIJAYE COOMAR MADHOU.

Radio One: Port Louis; tel. 211-4555; fax 211-4142; e-mail sales@r1.mu; internet www.r1.mu; f. 2002; owned by Sentinelle media group; news and entertainment; Dir-Gen. JEAN-MICHEL FONTAINE.

Radio Plus: 4B, Labourdonnais St, Port-Louis; tel. 208-6002; fax 212-0042; e-mail radioplus@intnet.mu; internet www.defimedia.info.

Top FM: The Peninsula, Caudan Bldg, 7th Floor, 2A Falcon ST, Caudan, Port Louis; tel. 213-2121; fax 213-2222; e-mail topfm@intnet.mu; internet www.topfmradio.com; f. 2003; part of the International Broadcasting Group, in partnership with the Sunrise Group; Chair. BALKRISHNA KAUNHYE.

Television

Independent television stations were to commence broadcasting from 2002, as part of the liberalization of the sector.

Mauritius Broadcasting Corpn: see Radio.

Finance

(cap. = capital; res = reserves; dep. = deposits; m. = million; brs = branches; amounts in Mauritian rupees, unless otherwise stated)

BANKING

Central Bank

Bank of Mauritius: Sir William Newton St, POB 29, Port Louis; tel. 208-4164; fax 208-9204; e-mail governor.office@bom.intnet.mu; internet bom.intnet.mu; f. 1966; bank of issue; cap. 1,000.0m., res 16,653.5m., dep. 8,867.2m. (June 2005); Gov. RUNDHEERSING BHEENICK.

Principal Commercial Banks

Bank of Baroda: 32 Sir William Newton St, POB 553, Port Louis; tel. 208-1504; fax 208-3892; e-mail info@bankofbaroda-mu.com; internet www.bankofbaroda-mu.com; f. 1962; total assets 2,655,000m. (June 2007); Vice-President (Mauritius Operations) PRABHAT AGARWAL; 7 brs.

Barclays Bank PLC, Mauritius: Harbour Front Bldg, 8th Floor, John F. Kennedy St, POB 284, Port Louis; tel. 208-2685; fax 208-2720; e-mail barclays.mauritius@barclays.com; f. 1919; absorbed Banque Nationale de Paris Intercontinentale in 2002; cap. 100.0m., res 616.1m., dep. 6,886.7m. (Dec. 2001); Dir Gen. KARL STUMKE; 16 brs.

First City Bank Ltd: 16 Sir William Newton St, POB 485, Port Louis; tel. 208-5061; fax 208-5388; e-mail info@firstcitybank-mauritius.com; f. 1991 as the Delphis Bank Ltd; merged with Union International Bank in 1997; private bank; taken over by consortium in 2002; 51.6% owned by the Development Bank of Mauritius Ltd; cap. 450.0m., res 98.9m., dep. 4,361.0m. (June 2005); Chair. B. CHOORAMUN; Chief Exec. ROHIT AUKLE.

Hongkong and Shanghai Banking Corpn Ltd (HSBC): pl. d'Armes, POB 50, Port Louis; tel. 208-1801; fax 210-0400; e-mail hsbcmauritius@hsbc.co.mu; internet www.hsbc.co.mu; f. 1916; CEO PHILLIP DAWE.

Indian Ocean International Bank Ltd (IOIB): 34 Sir William Newton St, POB 863, Port Louis; tel. 208-0121; fax 208-0127; e-mail ioibltd@intnet.mu; internet www.ioib.intnet.mu; f. 1978; 51% owned by the State Bank of India; cap. 100.5m., res 305.7m., dep. 2,934.4m. (June 2005); Pres. VISWANATHEN VALAYDON; Chief Exec. A. K. SINGH; 8 brs.

Mauritius Commercial Bank Ltd: MCB Centre, 9–15 Sir William Newton St, POB 52, Port Louis; tel. 202-5000; fax 208-7054; e-mail mcb@mcb.co.mu; internet www.mcb.mu; f. 1838; cap. 2,503m., res 6,791m., dep. 75,437m. (June 2007); Pres. GERARD J. HARDY; CEO PIERRE-GUY NOEL; 42 brs.

Mauritius Post and Co-operative Bank Ltd: 1 Sir William Newton St, Port Louis; tel. 207-9999; fax 208-7270; e-mail mpcb@mpcb.mu; internet www.mpcb.mu; f. 2003; 44.3% owned by The Mauritius Post Ltd, 35.7% state owned, 10% owned by the Sugar Investment Trust; cap. 384.0m., res 39.5m., dep. 4,516.1m. (Dec. 2005); CEO RAJIV KUMAR BEEHARRY; Gen. Man. PAVADAY THONDRAYON.

South East Asian Bank Ltd (SEAB): Max City Bldg, 2nd Floor, cnr Rémy Ollier and Louis Pasteur Sts, POB 13, Port Louis; tel. 208-8826; fax 211-4900; internet www.seab.mu; f. 1989; 60% owned by Bumiputra-Commerce Bank Berhad (Malaysia); cap. 200.0m., res 16.4m., dep. 2,423.4m. (Dec. 2005); Chair. Tan Sri Dato' MOHD DESA PACHI; 5 brs.

Standard Chartered Bank (Mauritius) Ltd: Happy World House, Level 8, 37 Sir William Newton St, Port Louis; tel. 213-9000; fax 208-5992; e-mail scbmauritius@intnet.mu; internet www.standardchartered.com/mu; wholly owned subsidiary of Standard Chartered Bank Plc; offshore banking unit.

State Bank of Mauritius Ltd: State Bank Tower, 1 Queen Elizabeth II Ave, POB 152, Port Louis; tel. 202-1111; fax 202-1234; e-mail sbm@sbm.intnet.mu; internet www.sbmonline.com; f. 1973; cap. 325.1m., surplus and res 7,857.8m., dep. 32,930.9m. (June 2005); Chair. RAJA RAMDAURSING; Chief Exec. CHAITLALL GUNNESS; 43 brs.

Development Bank

Development Bank of Mauritius Ltd: La Chaussée, POB 157, Port Louis; tel. 208-0241; fax 208-8498; e-mail dbm@intnet.mu; internet www.dbm.mu; f. 1964; name changed as above in 1991; 65% govt-owned; cap. 125m., res 1,507.6m., dep. 3,240.8m. (June 2004); Chair. CHANDAN KHESWAR JANKEE; Man. Dir B. CHOORAMUN; 6 brs.

MAURITIUS

Principal 'Offshore' Banks

Mascareignes International Bank Ltd: 1 Cathedral Square, Level 8, 16 Jules Koenig St, POB 489, Port Louis; tel. 207-8700; fax 212-4983; e-mail mib@mib.mu; internet www.mib.mu; f. 1991; name changed as above 2004; 65% owned by Banque de la Réunion (65%), 35% owned by Financière Océor (France); cap. 423.7m., res 43.3m., dep. 6,546.2m. (Dec. 2005); Chair. BERNARD BOBROWSKI; CEO CHRISTIAN MONTAGARD.

SBI International (Mauritius) Ltd: Harbour Front Bldg, 7th Floor, John F. Kennedy St, POB 376, Port Louis; tel. 212-2054; fax 212-2050; e-mail sbilmaur@intnet.mu; f. 1989; 98% owned by the State Bank of India; cap. US $10.0m., res $13.3m., dep. $120.0m. (June 2007); Chair. S. K. HARIHARAN; Man. Dir V. SRINIVASAN.

Bank of Baroda, Barclays Bank PLC, African Asian Bank, PT Bank International Indonesia, Investec Bank (Mauritius) and HSBC Bank PLC also operate 'offshore' banking units.

STOCK EXCHANGE

Financial Services Commission: 4th Floor, Harbour Front Bldg, President John Kennedy St, Port Louis; tel. 210-7000; fax 208-7172; e-mail fscmauritius@intnet.mu; internet www.fscmauritius.org; f. 2001; regulatory authority for securities, insurance and global business activities; Chief Exec. MILAN J.N. MEETARBHAN.

Stock Exchange of Mauritius Ltd: 1 Cathedral Sq. Bldg, 4th Floor, 16 Jules Koenig St, Port Louis; tel. 212-9541; fax 208-8409; e-mail stockex@sem.intnet.mu; internet www.stockexchangeofmauritius.com; f. 1989; 11 mems; Chair. P. GOPALLEN MOOROOGEN; CEO SUNIL BENIMADHU.

INSURANCE

Albatross Insurance Co Ltd: 22 St George St, POB 116, Port Louis; tel. 207-9007; fax 208-4800; e-mail headoffice@albatross-insurance.mu; internet www.albatross-insurance.com; f. 1975; Chair. TIMOTHY TAYLOR.

Anglo-Mauritius Assurance Society Ltd: Swan Group Centre, 10 Intendance St, POB 837, Port Louis; tel. 202-8600; fax 208-8956; e-mail anglomtius@intnet.mu; internet www.groupswan.com; f. 1951; Chair. CYRIL MAYER; CEO LOUIS RIVALLAND.

British American Insurance Co (Mauritius) Ltd: BAI Bldg, 25 Pope Hennessy St, POB 331, Port Louis; tel. 202-3600; fax 208-3713; e-mail bai@intnet.mu; f. 1920; Chair. DAWOOD RAWAT; Man. Dir HEINRICH K. DE KOCK.

Ceylinco Stella Insurance Co Ltd: 36 Sir Seewoosagur Ramgoolam St, POB 852, Port Louis; tel. 208-0056; fax 208-1639; e-mail stellain@intnet.mu; internet www.stellain.com; f. 1977; Chair. and Man. Dir R. KRESHAN JHOBOO.

Indian Ocean General Assurance Ltd: 35 Corderie St, POB 865, Port Louis; tel. 212-4125; fax 212-5850; e-mail iogaltd@intnet.mu; f. 1971; Chair. SAM M. CUNDEN; Man. Dir SHRIVANA CUNDEN.

Island Insurance Co Ltd: Labourdonnais Court, 5th Floor, cnr Labourdonnais and St George Sts, Port Louis; tel. 212-4860; fax 208-8762; f. 1998; Chair. CARRIM A. CURRIMJEE; Man. Dir OLIVIER LAGESSE.

Jubilee Insurance (Mauritius) Ltd: PCL Bldg, 4th Floor, 43 Sir William Newton St, POB 301, Port Louis; tel. 210-3678; fax 212-7970; f. 1998; Chair. and CEO AUGUSTINE J. HATCH.

Lamco International Insurance Ltd: 12 Barracks St, Port Louis; tel. 212-4494; fax 208-0630; e-mail lamco@intnet.mu; internet www.lamcoinsurance.com; f. 1978; Chair. A. B. ATCHIA; Gen. Man. N. C. ADIA.

Life Insurance Corpn of India: LIC Centre, John F. Kennedy St, Port Louis; tel. 212-5316; fax 208-6392; e-mail liccmm@intnet.mu; f. 1956; Chief Man. NAVIN SINHA.

Mauritian Eagle Insurance Co Ltd: 1st Floor, IBL House, Caudan Waterfront, POB 854, Port Louis; tel. 203-2200; fax 203-2299; e-mail caudan@mauritianeagle.com; internet www.mauritianeagle.com; f. 1973; Chair. P. D'HOTMAN DE VILLIERS; Man. Dir ERIC A. VENPIN.

Mauritius Union Assurance Co Ltd: 4 Léoville L'Homme St, POB 233, Port Louis; tel. 207-5500; fax 212-2962; e-mail mua@mua.mu; internet www.mauritiusunion.com; f. 1948; Chair. BERNARD MARIE JOSEPH MAYER; Man. Dir JACQUES DE NAVACELLE.

The New India Assurance Co Ltd: Bank of Baroda Bldg, 3rd Floor, 15 Sir William Newton St, POB 398, Port Louis; tel. 208-1442; fax 208-2160; e-mail niasurance@intnet.mu; internet www.niacl.com; f. 1935; general insurance; Chief Man. A. K. JAIN.

La Prudence Mauricienne Assurances Ltée: Le Caudan Waterfront, 2nd Floor, Barkly Wharf, POB 882, Port Louis; tel. 207-2500; fax 208-8936; e-mail prudence@intnet.mu; Chair. ROBERT DE FROBERVILLE; Man. Dir FÉLIX MAUREL.

Rainbow Insurance Co Ltd: 23 Edith Cavell St, POB 389, Port Louis; tel. 212-5767; fax 208-8750; f. 1976; Chair. B. GOKULSING; Man. Dir PREVIN RENBURG.

State Insurance Co of Mauritius Ltd (SICOM): SICOM Bldg, Sir Célicourt Antelme St, Port Louis; tel. 203-8400; fax 208-7662; e-mail email@sicom.intnet.mu; internet www.sicom.mu; f. 1975; Chair. A. F. HO CHAN FONG; Man. Dir K. BHOOJEDHUR-OBEEGADOO.

Sun Insurance Co Ltd: 2 St George St, Port Louis; tel. 208-0769; fax 208-2052; f. 1981; Chair. Sir KAILASH RAMDANEE; Man. Dir A. MUSBALLY.

Swan Insurance Co Ltd: Swan Group Centre, 10 Intendance St, POB 364, Port Louis; tel. 211-2001; fax 208-6898; e-mail swan@intnet.mu; f. 1955; Chair. J. M. ANTOINE HAREL; CEO LOUIS RIVALLAND.

L. and H. Vigier de Latour Ltd: Les Jamalacs Bldg, Old Council St, Port Louis; tel. 212-2034; fax 212-6056; Chair. and Man. Dir L. J. D. HENRI VIGIER DE LATOUR.

Trade and Industry

GOVERNMENT AGENCIES

Agricultural Marketing Board (AMB): Dr G. Leclézio Ave, Moka; tel. 433-4025; fax 433-4837; e-mail agbd@intnet.mu; internet amb.intnet.mu; f. 1964; operates under the aegis of the Ministry of Agro-industry and Fisheries; markets certain locally produced and imported food products (such as potatoes, onions, garlic, spices and seeds); also collects raw milk and distributes pasteurized milk; provides storage facilities to importers and exporters; Gen. Man. PARMANAND RAMNAWAZ.

Mauritius Meat Authority: Abattoir Rd, Roche Bois, POB 612, Port Louis; tel. 242-5884; fax 217-1077; e-mail mauritiusmeat@intnet.mu; f. 1974; licensing authority; controls and regulates sale of meat and meat products; also purchases and imports livestock and markets meat products; Gen. Man. A. BALGOBIN.

Mauritius Sugar Authority: Ken Lee Bldg, 2nd Floor, Edith Cavell St, Port Louis; tel. 208-7466; fax 208-7470; e-mail msa@intnet.mu; regulatory body for the sugar industry; Chair. S. HANOOMANJEE; Exec. Dir Dr G. RAJPATI.

Mauritius Tea Board: Wooton St, Curepipe Rd, Curepipe; POB 28, Eau Coulée; tel. 675-3497; fax 676-1445; e-mail teaboard@intnet.mu; internet www.gov.mu/portal/site/teaboard; f. 1975; regulates and controls the activities of the tea industry; Gen. Man. A. SEEPERGAUTH.

Mauritius Tobacco Board: Plaine Lauzun, Port Louis; tel. 212-2323; fax 208-6426; e-mail tobaco@intnet.mu; internet agriculture.gov.mu/tobacco; Chair. N. MAUDARBACCUS.

DEVELOPMENT ORGANIZATIONS

Board of Investment—Mauritius (BOI): Cathedral Square Bldg 1, 10th Floor, 16 Jules Koenig St, Port Louis; tel. 211-4190; fax 208-2924; e-mail invest@boi.intnet.mu; internet www.boimauritius.com; f. 2001 to promote international investment, business and services; Chair. of Bd MAURICE LAM; Gen. Man. RAJU JADDOO.

Enterprise Mauritius: 7th Floor, Saint James Court, Saint Denis St, Port-Louis; tel. 212-9760; fax 212-9767; e-mail info@em.intnet.mu; internet www.enterprisemauritius.biz; f. 2004 from parts of the Mauritius Industrial Development Authority, the Export Processing Zones Development Authority and the Sub-contracting and Partnership Exchange—Mauritius; comprises a Corporate Services Unit, a Strategic Direction Unit, a Business Development Unit, a Client-Services Unit and a Special Support Unit (estd from the former Clothing and Textile Centre); Chair. AMÉDÉE DARGA; CEO PRAKESH BEEHARRY.

Joint Economic Council (JEC): Plantation House, 3rd Floor, pl. d'Armes, Port Louis; tel. 211-2980; fax 211-3141; e-mail jec@intnet.mu; internet www.jec-mauritius.org; f. 1970; the co-ordinating body of the private sector of Mauritius, including the main business organisations of the country; Pres. ARIF CURRIMJEE; Dir RAJ MAKOOND.

Mauritius Freeport Authority (MFA): Trade and Marketing Centre, 1st Floor, Freeport Zone 6, Mer Rouge; tel. 206-2500; fax 206-2600; e-mail mfa@freeport.gov.mu; internet www.efreeport.com; f. 1990; Chair. KAVYDASS RAMANO; Dir-Gen. RAJAKRISHNA CHELLAPERMAL.

National Productivity and Competitiveness Council (NPCC): 4th Floor, Alexander House, Cybercity, Reduit; tel. 467-7700; fax 467-3838; e-mail natpro@intnet.mu; internet www.npccmauritius

MAURITIUS

.com; f. 2000; represents the Government, the private sector and trade unions; Exec. Dir Dr KRISHNALALL COONJAN.

Small Enterprises and Handicraft Development Authority (SEHDA): Industrial Zone, Coromandel; tel. 233-0500; fax 233-5545; e-mail smido@intnet.mu; internet www.sehda.org; f. 2006 following the merger of the Small and Medium Industries Development Organization and the National Handicraft Promotion Agency; provides support to potential and existing small entrepreneurs.

State Investment Corpn Ltd (SIC): Air Mauritius Centre, 15th Floor, John F. Kennedy St, Port Louis; tel. 202-8900; fax 208-8948; e-mail contactsic@stateinvestment.com; internet www.stateinvestment.com; f. 1984; provides support for new investment and transfer of technology, in agriculture, industry and tourism; Man. Dir IDBAL MALLAM-HASHAM; Chair. RAJ RINGADOO.

CHAMBERS OF COMMERCE

Chinese Chamber of Commerce: Suite 206, Jade Court, Jummah Mosque St, Port Louis; tel. and fax 242-0156; e-mail admin@cccmauritius.org; f. 1908; Pres. ANNABELLE KOK SHUN.

Mauritius Chamber of Commerce and Industry: 3 Royal St, Port Louis; tel. 208-3301; fax 208-0076; e-mail mcci@intnet.mu; internet www.mcci.org; f. 1850; 400 mems; Pres. AZIM CURRIMJEE; Sec.-Gen. MAHMOOD CHEEROO.

INDUSTRIAL ASSOCIATIONS

Association of Mauritian Manufacturers (AMM): c/o The Mauritius Chamber of Commerce and Insdustry, 3 Royal St, Port Louis; tel. 208-3301; fax 208-0076; e-mail mcci@intnet.mu; f. 1995; Pres. PATRICK RIVALLAND.

Mauritius Export Processing Zone Association (MEPZA): Unicorn House, 6th Floor, 5 Royal St, Port Louis; tel. 208-5216; fax 212-1853; internet www.mepza.org; f. 1976; consultative and advisory body; Chair. LOUIS LAI FAT FUR.

Mauritius Sugar Producers' Association (MSPA): Plantation House, 2nd Floor, pl. d'Armes, Port Louis; tel. 212-0295; fax 212-5727; Chair. ARNAUD LAGESSE; Dir PATRICE LEGRIS.

EMPLOYERS' ORGANIZATION

Mauritius Employers' Federation: Cernée House, 1st Floor, Chaussée St, Port Louis; tel. 212-1599; fax 212-6725; e-mail info@mef-online.org; internet www.mef-online.org; f. 1962; Chair. MOOKHESHWARSING GOPAL; Dir Dr AZAD JEETUN.

UTILITIES

Electricity

Central Electricity Board: Royal Rd, POB 40, Curepipe; tel. 601-1100; fax 675-7958; internet cebweb.intnet.mu; f. 1952; state-operated; Chair. PATRICK ASSIRVADEN; Gen. Man. KRISHNANAND GUPTAR.

Water

Central Water Authority: Royal Rd, St Paul-Phoenix; tel. 601-5000; fax 686-6264; e-mail cwa@intnet.mu; internet ncb.intnet.mu/putil/cwa; corporate body; scheduled for privatization; f. 1973; Gen. Man. H. K. BOOLUCK; Chair. Prof. ANWAN HUSSEIN SUBRATTY.

Waste Water Management Authority: Sir Celicourt Antelme St, Port Louis; tel. 206-3000; fax 211-7007; e-mail wma@intnet.mu; internet wma.gov.mu; f. 2000; Chair. KHUSHAL LOBINE.

TRADE UNIONS

Federations

Federation of Civil Service and Other Unions (FCSOU): Jade Court, Rm 308, 3rd Floor, 33 Jummah Mosque St, Port Louis; tel. 216-1977; fax 216-1475; e-mail f.c.s.u@intnet.mu; internet www.fcsu.org; f. 1957; 72 affiliated unions with 30,000 mems (2006); Pres. TOOLSYRAJ BENYDIN; Sec. AWADHKOOMARSINGH BALLUCK.

General Workers' Federation: 13 Brabant St, Port Louis; tel. 212-3338; Pres. FAROOK AUCHOYBUR; Sec.-Gen. DEVANAND RAMJUTTUN.

Mauritius Federation of Trade Unions: Arc Bldg, 3rd Floor, cnr Sir William Newton and Sir Seewoosagur Ramgoolam Sts, Port Louis; tel. 208-9426; f. 1958; four affiliated unions; Pres. FAROOK HOSSENBUX; Sec.-Gen. R. MAREEMOOTOO.

Mauritius Labour Congress (MLC): 8 Louis Victor de la Faye St, Port Louis; tel. 212-4343; fax 208-8945; e-mail mlcongress@intnet.mu; f. 1963; 55 affiliated unions with 70,000 mems (1992); Pres. NURDEO LUCHMUN ROY; Gen. Sec. JUGDISH LOLLBEEHARRY.

Mauritius Trade Union Congress (MTUC): Emmanuel Anquetil Labour Centre, James Smith St, Port Louis; tel. 210-8567; internet www.mtucmauritius.org; f. 1946.

Trade Union Trust Fund: Richard House, 2nd Floor, cnr Jummah Mosque and Remy Ollier Sts, Port Louis; tel. and fax 217-2073; internet www.gov.mu/portal/site/tradeuniontf; f. 1997 to receive and manage funds and other property obtained from the Govt and other sources; to promote workers' education and provide assistance to workers' orgs; Chair. RADHAKRISNA SADIEN.

Principal Unions

Government Servants' Association: 107A Royal Rd, Beau Bassin; tel. 464-4242; fax 465-3220; e-mail gsa@intnet.mu; internet www.gsa.mauritius.org; f. 1945; Pres. R. SADIEN; Sec.-Gen. P. RAMJUG.

Government Teachers' Union: 3 Mgr Gonin St, POB 1111, Port Louis; tel. 208-0047; fax 208-4943; f. 1945; Pres. JUGDUTH SEEGUM; Sec. MOHAMMAD SALEEM CHOOLUN; 4,550 mems (2005).

Nursing Association: 159 Royal Rd, Beau Bassin; tel. and fax 464-5850; e-mail nur.ass@intnet.mu; f. 1955; Pres. CASSAM KUREEMAN; Sec.-Gen. FRANCIS SUPPARAYEN.

Organization of Artisans' Unity: 42 Sir William Newton St, Port Louis; tel. and fax 212-4557; f. 1973; Pres. AUGUSTE FOLLET; Sec. ROY RAMCHURN; 2,874 mems (1994).

Plantation Workers' Union: 8 Louis Victor de la Faye St, Port Louis; tel. 212-1735; f. 1955; Pres. C. BHAGIRUTTY; Sec. N. L. ROY; 13,726 mems (1990).

Port Louis Harbour and Docks Workers' Union: Port Louis; tel. 208-2276; Pres. M. VEERABADREN; Sec.-Gen. GERARD BERTRAND.

Sugar Industry Staff Employees' Association: 1 Rémy Ollier St, Port Louis; tel. 212-1947; f. 1947; Chair. T. BELLEROSE; Sec.-Gen. G. CHUNG KWAN FANG; 1,450 mems (1997).

Textile, Clothes and Other Manufactures Workers' Union: Thomy d'Arifat St, Curepipe; tel. 676-5280; Pres. PADMATEE TEELUCK; Sec.-Gen. DÉSIRÉ GUILDAREE.

Union of Bus Industry Workers: Port Louis; tel. 212-3338; f. 1970; Pres. M. BABOOA; Sec.-Gen. F. AUCHOYBUR.

Union of Employees of the Ministry of Agriculture and other Ministries: 28 Hennessy Ave, Quatre-Bornes; tel. 465-1935; e-mail bruno5@intnet.mu; f. 1989; Sec. BRUNEAU DORASAMI; 2,500 mems (Dec. 2003).

Union of Labourers of the Sugar and Tea Industry: Royal Rd, Curepipe; f. 1969; Sec. P. RAMCHURN.

Transport

RAILWAYS

There are no operational railways in Mauritius.

ROADS

In 2004 there were 2,015 km of paved roads, of which 70 km were motorways, 950 km were other main roads, and 592 km were secondary roads. An urban highway links the motorways approaching Port Louis. A motorway connects Port Louis with Plaisance airport.

SHIPPING

Mauritius is served by numerous foreign shipping lines. In 1990 Port Louis was established as a free port to expedite the development of Mauritius as an entrepôt centre. In 1995 the World Bank approved a loan of US $30.5m. for a programme to develop the port. At 31 December 2006 Mauritius had a merchant fleet of 45 vessels, with a combined displacement of 68,608 grt.

Mauritius Ports Authority: H. Ramnarain Bldg, Mer Rouge, Port Louis; tel. 206-5400; fax 240-0856; e-mail info@mauport.com; internet www.mauport.com; f. 1976; Chair. Dr M. S. CHADY; Dir-Gen. S. SUNTAH.

Ireland Blyth Ltd: IBL House, Caudan, Port Louis; tel. 203-2000; fax 203-2001; e-mail iblinfo@iblgroup.com; internet www.iblgroup.com; Chair. THIERRY LAGESSE; CEO P. D'HOTMAN DE VILLIERS; 2 vessels.

Islands Services Ltd: Rogers House, 5 John F. Kennedy St, POB 60, Port Louis; tel. 208-6801; fax 208-5045; services to Indian Ocean islands; Chair. Sir RENÉ MAINGARD; Exec. Dir Capt. RENÉ SANSON.

Mauritius Freeport Development Co Ltd: Freeport Zone 5, Mer Rouge; tel. 206-2000; fax 206-2025; e-mail info@mfd.mu; internet www.mfd.mu; f. 1997; manages and operates Freeport Zone 5, more than 40,000 sq m of storage facility; facilities include dry warehouses, cold warehouses, processing and transformation units, open storage container parks and a container freight station; largest logistics centre in the Indian Ocean region; CEO DOMINIQUE DE FROBERVILLE.

Mauritius Shipping Corpn Ltd: St James Court, Suite 417/418, St Denis St, Port Louis; tel. 208-5900; fax 210-5176; internet www.mauritiusshipping.mu; f. 1985; state-owned; operates two passenger-cargo vessels between Mauritius, Rodrigues, Reunion and Madagascar; Man. Dir Capt. J. PATRICK RAULT.

Société Mauricienne de Navigation Ltée: 1 rue de la Reine, POB 53, Port Louis; tel. 208-3241; fax 208-8931; Man. Dir Capt. FRANÇOIS DE GERSIGNY.

CIVIL AVIATION

Sir Seewoosagur Ramgoolam International Airport is at Plaisance, 4 km from Mahébourg. From 2006 air routes with France and the United Kingdom were to be liberalized, allowing new carriers to operate on the routes.

Civil Aviation Department: Sir Seewoosagur Ramgoolam International Airport, Plaine Magnien; tel. 603-2000; fax 637-3164; e-mail civil-aviation@mail.gov.mu; internet civil-aviation.gov.mu; overseen by the Ministry of Training, Skills Development, Productivity and External Communications; Dir SARUPANAND KINNOO.

Air Mauritius: Air Mauritius Centre, John F. Kennedy St, POB 441, Port Louis; tel. 207-7070; fax 208-8331; e-mail mkcare@airmauritius.intnet.mu; internet www.airmauritius.com; f. 1967; 51% state-owned; services to 28 destinations in Europe, Asia, Australia and Africa; Chair. SANJAY BUCKHORY; Man. Dir MANOJ R. K. UJOODHA.

Tourism

Tourists are attracted to Mauritius by its scenery and beaches, the pleasant climate and the blend of cultures. Accommodation capacity totalled 21,072 beds in 2005. The number of visitors increased from 300,670 in 1990 to 788,276 in 2006, when the greatest numbers of visitors were from France (23.1%), the United Kingdom (13.0%) and Réunion (11.3%). Gross revenue from tourism in 2006 was estimated at Rs 31,942m. The Government sought to increase the volume of tourists visiting the country (to some 2m. people by 2015) by improving the jetty facilities in the port in order to welcome cruise ships and by liberalizing air transit routes.

Mauritius Tourism Promotion Authority: Victoria House, 4th and 5th Floor, St Louis St, Port Louis; tel. 210-1545; fax 212-5142; e-mail mtpa@intnet.mu; internet www.tourism-mauritius.mu; Chair. ROBERT DESVAUX.

Tourism Authority (TA): Victoria House, 1st and 2nd Floor, St Louis St, Port Louis; tel. 213-1740; fax 213-1745; e-mail tourism.authority@intnet.mu; f. 2003; parastatal; issues licences for and monitors compliance of the regulation of the tourism industry; Dir JOËL RAULT.

MEXICO

Introductory Survey

Location, Climate, Language, Religion, Flag, Capital

The United Mexican States is bordered to the north by the USA, and to the south by Guatemala and Belize. The Gulf of Mexico and the Caribbean Sea lie to the east, and the Pacific Ocean and Gulf of California to the west. The climate varies with altitude. The tropical southern region and the coastal lowlands are hot and wet, with an average annual temperature of 18°C (64°F), while the highlands of the central plateau are temperate. Much of the north and west is arid desert. In Mexico City, which lies at about 2,250 m (nearly 7,400 ft) above sea-level, temperatures are generally between 5°C (42°F) and 25°C (78°F). The country's highest recorded temperature is 58°C (136°F). The principal language is Spanish, spoken by more than 90% of the population, while about 8% speak indigenous languages, of which Náhuatl is the most widely spoken. Almost all of Mexico's inhabitants profess Christianity, and about 87% are adherents of the Roman Catholic Church. The national flag (proportions 4 by 7) has three equal vertical stripes from hoist to fly, of green, white and red, with the state emblem (a brown eagle, holding a snake in its beak, on a green cactus, with a wreath of oak and laurel beneath) in the centre of the white stripe. The capital is Mexico City.

Recent History

Conquered by Hernán Cortés in the 16th century, Mexico was ruled by Spain until the wars of independence of 1810–21. After the war of 1846, Mexico ceded about one-half of its territory to the USA. Attempts at political and social reform by the anti-clerical Benito Juárez precipitated civil war in 1857–60, and the repudiation of Mexico's external debts by Juárez in 1860 led to war with the United Kingdom, the USA and France. The Austrian Archduke Maximilian, whom France tried to install as Emperor of Mexico, was executed, on the orders of Juárez, in 1867. Order was restored during the dictatorship of Porfirio Díaz, which lasted from 1876 until the Revolution of 1910. The Constitution of 1917 embodied the aims of the Revolution by revising land ownership, drafting a labour code and curtailing the power of the Roman Catholic Church. From 1929–2000 the country was dominated by the Partido Revolucionario Institucional (PRI), for much of that time in an effective one-party system, although a democratic form of election was maintained. However, allegations of widespread electoral malpractice persistently arose in connection with PRI victories.

In a presidential election held in July 1976 the PRI candidate, José López Portillo, was elected with almost 95% of the votes cast. In 1977 López Portillo initiated reforms to increase minority party representation in the legislature and to widen democratic participation. The high level of political participation in the presidential election of July 1982 (held amid a financial crisis) was without precedent, with left-wing groups taking part for the first time; however, the PRI's candidate, Miguel de la Madrid Hurtado, was successful. The concurrent elections to the Cámara Federal de Diputados (Federal Chamber of Deputies) resulted in another overwhelming victory for the PRI. On taking office in December, the new President embarked on a programme of major economic reform, giving precedence to the repayment of Mexico's debts, a policy which imposed severe financial constraints upon the middle and lower classes and which led to growing disaffection among traditional PRI supporters. Notably, the Partido Acción Nacional (PAN), an opposition party, made important gains at municipal elections in two state capitals in mid-1983. The PRI's effective response ensured success at the remaining elections, but provoked opposition allegations of widespread electoral fraud. Contrary to expectations, at gubernatorial and congressional elections conducted in July 1985, the PRI secured all seven of the available state governorships and won 288 of the 300 directly elective seats in the Cámara Federal de Diputados.

The formation of a major left-wing alliance, the Partido Mexicano Socialista—PMS (comprising six parties), in 1987 and, in particular, the emergence of a dissident faction, the Corriente Democrática (CD), within the PRI in 1986 were disturbing political developments for the ruling party. In early 1988 the CD and four left-wing parties (including the PMS coalition) formed an electoral alliance, the Frente Democrático Nacional (FDN), headed by CD leader Cuauhtémoc Cárdenas Solórzano. The legitimacy of the PRI victory at the presidential and congressional elections, conducted in July, was fiercely challenged by the opposition groups, following a delay in the publication of official results, reports of widespread electoral fraud and the failure of the Federal Electoral Commission to release details of results from almost 50% of polling stations. Moreover, Cárdenas claimed victory on behalf of the broad-left coalition; for the first time ever, the opposition secured seats in the Senado (Senate), while the PRI suffered defeats in the Distrito Federal and at least three other states.

In August 1988 the new Congreso de la Unión (Congress) was installed and immediately assumed the function of an electoral college, in order to investigate the claims of both sides. In September the allocation of 200 seats in the Cámara Federal de Diputados by proportional representation afforded the PRI a congressional majority and effective control of the electoral college. Opposition members withdrew from the Cámara in protest at the PRI's obstruction of the investigation, enabling the ruling party to ratify Carlos Salinas de Gortari as the new President. The results, although widely regarded as having been manipulated by the PRI, revealed a considerable erosion in support for the party, particularly among the traditional bastions of the trade unions, peasant groups and bureaucracy.

Agreements on rescheduling Mexico's vast foreign debts were reached with the 'Paris Club' of official creditors in 1989, and with some 450 commercial banks in early 1990. Success for the Government in financial negotiations with creditors was largely dependent upon its ability to provide evidence of a stable and developing domestic economy. In January 1989 a Pact for Economic Stability and Growth was implemented, with the agreement of employers' organizations and trade unions, and was subsequently extended until the end of 1994. None the less, the country experienced severe labour unrest in 1989 in support of greater pay increases and in protest at the Government's divestment programme.

During 1989 political opposition to the PRI was strengthened by success in gubernatorial and municipal elections, and by further accusations against the PRI of electoral fraud. In October proposed constitutional amendments were approved with the unexpected support of the PAN. A 'governability clause', whereby an absolute majority of seats in the Cámara Federal de Diputados would be awarded to the leading party, should it receive at least 35% of the votes at a general election, was criticized by the Partido de la Revolución Democrática (PRD), the successor party to the FDN.

In July 1991 the Federal Electoral Code was approved by the Cámara Federal de Diputados with support from all represented parties, except the PRD. The legislation contained provisions for the compilation of a new electoral roll, the issue of more detailed identification cards for voters, the modification of the Instituto Federal Electoral (IFE—Federal Electoral Institute), and the creation of a Tribunal Federal Electoral (Federal Electoral Tribunal, which, in 1996, became the Tribunal Electoral del Poder Judicial de la Federación). The PRD was highly critical of many of the provisions, including alleged procedural obstacles to the formation of political alliances, and the power given to the President to appoint the head of the IFE (the Secretary of the Interior) and to nominate six 'independent' lawyers to its executive. Further constitutional reform, with regard to agriculture, education and religion, were adopted in 1992.

Meanwhile, in June 1990, in response to continuing allegations of federal police complicity in abuses of human rights, President Salinas announced the creation of a national commission for human rights. In October the Government proposed legislation transferring responsibility for the interrogation of suspected criminals from the federal judicial police to the public magistrate's office. The proposed legislation also sought to undermine the validity of confession alone (often allegedly extracted under torture) as sufficient grounds for conviction.

The PRI continued to secure disputed electoral success at municipal and state level in 1991. At mid-term congressional elections in August, the party won almost all of the 300 directly elective seats in the Cámara Federal de Diputados (plus 30 of the 200 seats awarded by proportional representation) and 31 of the 32 contested seats in the Senado. The return to the level of support that the PRI had enjoyed prior to the 1988 elections was largely attributed to the success of the Government's programme of economic reform. The election results were less encouraging for the opposition; the PAN secured 10 directly elective seats in the Cámara and its first seat in the Senado, but the PRD failed to win a directly elective seat in either congressional house.

PRI victories at gubernatorial and legislative elections in several states during 1993 were denounced by the opposition as fraudulent. In September the Congreso approved electoral reforms that included provisions for greater access to the media for all parties, restrictions on party funding, and improved impartiality of supervision. Other measures sought to increase the representation of minority parties in the Senado, and to end over-representation of larger parties in the Cámara Federal de Diputados. The 'governability clause' introduced in 1989 was to be removed. Divisions within the PRI emerged in November, following the selection of Luis Donaldo Colosio, the Secretary of Social Development, as the party's candidate in the presidential elections. Additional electoral reforms, which claimed to end PRI control of the IFE, received congressional approval in March 1994, but failed to appease PRD leaders, who demanded that the incumbent head of the IFE should be replaced by an impartial president elected by the IFE's newly created six-member commission.

In March 1994 Colosio was assassinated at a campaign rally. Mario Aburto Martínez, arrested at the scene of the murder, was later identified as the apparently motiveless assassin. However, speculation that Colosio had been the victim of a conspiracy within the PRI establishment increased following the arrest, in connection with the incident, of a number of party members associated with police and intelligence agencies. The PRI subsequently named Ernesto Zedillo Ponce de León, a former cabinet minister who had most recently been acting as Colosio's campaign manager, as the party's presidential candidate. Zedillo was elected President on 21 August, with 49% of the votes, ahead of the PAN candidate, Diego Fernández de Cevallos (26%), and the PRD candidate, Cuauhtémoc Cárdenas (17%). The PRI also achieved considerable success at the concurrent congressional elections. Despite the participation of some 70,000 impartial monitors and the attendance of a UN advisory technical team, numerous incidents of electoral malpractice were reported.

Zedillo identified the immediate aims of his administration as the promotion of the independence of the judiciary, the separation of party political activity from the functions of federal government and the further reform of the electoral system. Public confidence in the impartiality and ability of the judiciary had been seriously undermined by the inconsistency and confusion surrounding recent investigations into the deaths of Colosio and José Francisco Ruiz Massieu (see below). Zedillo's appointment of a senior member of the PAN to the post of Attorney-General in a new Cabinet announced in November 1994, together with the disclosure, in December, of more detailed plans for judicial reform, sought to restore the prestige of the judiciary.

The report of a special investigation into Colosio's murder, published in July 1994, concluded that Aburto Martínez had acted alone in the assassination, reversing the findings of a preliminary investigation which had suggested the existence of a number of conspirators. The report provoked incredulity, and President Salinas commissioned a further independent investigation. Speculation that Colosio had been the first victim of a politically motivated campaign of violence, conducted by a cabal of senior PRI traditionalists in order to check the advance of the party's reformist wing, intensified following the murder, in September, of the PRI Secretary-General, José Francisco Ruiz Massieu. In February 1995, however, a report issued by the Attorney-General was highly critical of all previous investigations of the Colosio assassination, concluding that the assassination had involved at least two gunmen. (An alleged second gunman was acquitted in August 1996.) Meanwhile, in November 1994 Ruiz Massieu's brother, Mario, resigned his post as Deputy Attorney-General, claiming that senior PRI officials, including the party's President and Secretary-General, had impeded his investigation into his brother's death, in an attempt to protect the identities of those responsible for the assassination. In February 1995 Raúl Salinas de Gortari, brother of former President Salinas, was arrested on charges of complicity in Ruiz Massieu's murder, and in April Fernando Rodríguez González (a former employee at the Cámara Federal de Diputados, who was charged with hiring the assassins) implicated several new conspirators, including five state Governors. Mario Ruiz Massieu was subsequently detained in the USA. In October two men were each sentenced to 18 years' imprisonment for perpetrating the murder of the PRI Secretary-General. In October 1996 the case against Raúl Salinas was prejudiced further by the discovery of a body buried in the grounds of his property in Mexico City.

In March 1995, following the arrest of his brother, former President Salinas began a public campaign to discredit the new administration and to defend himself from accusations of responsibility for the country's economic crisis and from allegations that he had obstructed attempts to bring to justice those responsible for Colosio's death. Salinas's efforts culminated in a highly publicized but brief hunger strike which prompted the Attorney-General to issue a statement confirming that there was no evidence that Salinas had impeded the Colosio murder inquiry. Raúl Salinas was convicted of murder and, in January 1999, sentenced to 50 years' imprisonment (later reduced to almost 28 years); in August 2002 he was additionally charged with the embezzlement of up to 209m. new pesos from a secret presidential fund under his brother's control. In September 1999 Mario Ruiz Massieu committed suicide in the USA while awaiting trial on charges of 'laundering' money gained from drugs-trafficking; he left a note repeating his earlier accusations against the PRI and blaming Zedillo and other senior officials for his own death and the assassination of Colosio.

The Government's ongoing attempts to effect political reform were reactivated in January 1996 at a meeting of some 50 civil and political groups. In July the PRI, the PAN, the PRD and the Partido del Trabajo (PT, a labour party) reached consensus on reforms that would include introducing a directly elected governor of the Distrito Federal, increasing and regulating public financing for political parties, employing proportional representation in elections to the Senado, granting a right of vote to Mexican citizens resident abroad, and allowing the IFE greater independence. The reforms received congressional approval in August. However, in November, in apparent response to their diminishing share of the vote in recent municipal elections, PRI traditionalists secured the adoption by the Cámara Federal de Diputados of a series of amendments to the electoral reform bill, increasing public funding in 1997 for political parties by some 476%, pronouncing that to exceed campaign finance limits would no longer be a criminal or electoral offence, expanding the Government's access to the media, and restricting the right of opposition parties to form coalitions.

In May 1996 President Zedillo dismissed Mexico City's chief of police following public outcry at the violent tactics employed by his officers to disperse a group of striking teachers in the capital. In the following months hundreds of police employees throughout the country were dismissed for incompetence or corruption, while army officers were increasingly appointed to positions within the police force. In March 1997 some 2,500 members of Mexico City's police force were replaced by army personnel, and in October an élite police unit was disbanded after accusations that as many as 35 of its members were implicated in the torture and murder of three youths in September. Several officers at the anti-abduction unit in the state of Morelos were also accused of torture and murder in early 1998, precipitating the resignation of the state's PRI Governor in May.

At elections held in July 1997 for all 500 members of the Cámara Federal de Diputados the PRI lost its overall majority for the first time, while the PRD and the PAN made substantial gains. At concurrent elections held for one-quarter of the seats in the Senado the PRI retained its overall majority, albeit significantly reduced, while the PAN and the PRD increased their representation. An informal congressional alliance between the PAN, the PRD, the Partido Verde Ecologista de México (PVEM) and the PT meant that opposition parties were able to take control of important legislative committees. In addition to the poor legislative electoral performance, the PRI was defeated by the PAN in two of six gubernatorial elections conducted at the same time. Most significant, however, was the election of Cárdenas, the PRD candidate, as Head of Government of the Distrito Federal. The electoral defeats suffered by the PRI exacerbated tensions within the party and several party members defected to the PRD, some of whom were selected as candidates in gubernatorial elections.

In mid-1998 the PRI encountered strong opposition in the Congreso to its proposals to convert into public debt liabilities to the value of some US $65,000m. assumed by the bank rescue agency, the Fondo Bancario de Protección al Ahorro (FOBAPROA), after the financial crisis of late 1994. In December revised legislation establishing a successor to the FOBAPROA was approved by the Cámara Federal de Diputados, and the Government was forced to concede that FOBAPROA's liabilities would not automatically become public debt. FOBAPROA's successor, the Instituto de Protección al Ahorro Bancario, was created in May 1999.

A presidential election was held on 2 July 2000. The PRI's candidate was the former Secretary of the Interior, Francisco Labastida Ochoa, while the former Governor of Guanajuato state, Vicente Fox Quesada, represented a PAN-PVEM alliance known as the Alianza por el Cambio (AC), and Cárdenas was once again the PRD's nominee (officially he stood for the PRD-dominated Alianza por México—AM). Fox secured 43% of the votes cast, while Labastida attracted 37% and Cárdenas 17%. Fox was thus elected President, ending the PRI's 71-year hegemony in Mexican government. In the concurrent elections to the Congreso the AC secured 223 of the 500 seats, compared with 209 won by the PRI and 68 by the parties of the AM. The PRI remained the largest grouping in the Senado, however, with 60 seats. Fox took office as President on 1 December, stating that his priorities were a reduction in poverty, improved relations with the USA and peace and reconciliation within Mexico. His first Cabinet contained members of the PAN, PRI and other parties, in addition to a number of prominent figures from commerce and academia. The PRD declined an offer of three cabinet portfolios.

In October 2001 the Government announced that eight parties, including the PRI and the PRD, had signed the Acuerdo Político para el Desarrollo Nacional (Political Agreement for National Development), designed to facilitate law-making. Under the terms of the Agreement, the parties promised to support government measures to improve public finances and to deregulate the energy and telecommunications sectors. Nevertheless, the Government continued to encounter congressional opposition to its proposed fiscal reforms.

In January 2002 the Government announced that an investigation was to be held into allegations that the state petroleum company, Petróleos de México (PEMEX), had covertly funded Labastida's presidential election campaign. The affair centred on the alleged diversion of PEMEX funds into PRI accounts by two leaders of the petroleum workers' union, the Sindicato de Trabajadores Petroleros de la República Mexicana. In May a former director of PEMEX, Manuel Gómez-Peralta, was detained in connection with the allegations; furthermore, a former PEMEX President, Rogelio Montemayor, was arrested in Houston, Texas, USA, in October. In that month opposition parties demanded that President Fox allow the re-opening of investigations into allegations that the PAN organization Amigos de Fox, responsible for Fox's presidential campaign, had received substantial illegal foreign funding. (The investigation had been suspended on grounds of banking secrecy, but had been ordered to recommence by the electoral tribunal in May.) The PRI threatened to initiate a congressional investigation unless the Amigos de Fox accounts were made public. In October 2003 the IFE fined both the PAN and the PVEM for receiving illegal campaign funding from Amigos de Fox.

In May 2002 27 Zapotec Indians were killed in suspicious circumstances at Agua Fría, in Santiago Textitlán, Oaxaca; state authorities arrested 17 villagers, but local Indian organizations claimed that paramilitary groups had been involved in the attacks. Following the incident, an official from the human rights organization Amnesty International denounced the state Attorney-General's office for abuses.

In early November 2003 the Supreme Court ruled that prosecution for murder could proceed even in cases where no body had been found. The ruling enabled prosecutions to proceed for human rights abuses committed during the 'guerra sucia' ('dirty war') of the late 1970s; in February 2004 Miguel Nazar Haro, former director of the covert Dirección General de Seguridad, was arrested in connection with the disappearance of left-wing activist Jesús Piedra Ibarra in 1975. In mid-2004 the Supreme Court made a further ruling that cases concerning disappearance could be brought in connection with the suppression of dissent in the 1970s and 1980s. Meanwhile, a special prosecutor, Ignacio Carrillo, was appointed to investigate the role of, among others, the former President Luis Echeverría in the 'guerra sucia'; however, Carrillo's request that Echeverría be arrested was rejected. In February 2005 the Supreme Court ruled that the Vienna Convention on genocide, which came into force in 2002, could not be applied retrospectively, while in July 2005 the case against Echeverría was dismissed on the grounds that there was no evidence of genocide. This dismissal, however, was itself overruled on appeal in November 2006, thereby reopening the possibility of a prosecution.

In November 2003 the Government's budget proposals were rejected by the Cámara Federal de Diputados. The PRI, the largest congressional party, subsequently presented its own budget proposals to the legislature. However, divisions appeared within that party, ostensibly over the alternative proposals. In December 118 PRI deputies voted to replace Elba Esther Gordillo Morales, the party's Secretary-General, as leader of the PRI legislative bloc. Gordillo, who had originally supported the Government's proposed budget, initially refused to accept her dismissal and continued to rely on the support of 104 PRI deputies. It was widely believed that the underlying reason for the split was an ongoing feud between Gordillo and party President Roberto Madrazo Pintado over who would secure the PRI nomination for the presidential election due in 2006.

In March 2004 a scandal emerged surrounding the PRD Head of Government of the Distrito Federal, Andrés Manuel López Obrador, who was a popular and likely candidate in the 2006 presidential election. A videotape appeared to show López Obrador's finance chief, Gustavo Ponce Meléndez, gambling large amounts at a casino in the USA (Ponce was arrested in October). A further video recording came to light that apparently showed the Head of Government's former private secretary accepting money from a prominent Argentine businessman, Carlos Ahumada, who was accused of corruption. López Obrador denied any knowledge of either incident and claimed that a 'dirty tricks' campaign was being waged against him. In June 2004 the Attorney-General's office announced it was to prosecute López Obrador for allegedly ignoring an injunction against a compulsory purchase order and disregarding a federal ruling to re-employ numerous dismissed city officials; as a result, a formal request was made to the Congreso to rescind López Obrador's immunity from prosecution. In an indication of his popularity in Mexico City, however, in early August thousands of supporters attended a march in the capital against the move to impeach him. Following much deliberation, in April 2005 a four-member committee of the Cámara Federal de Diputados voted to recommend that López Obrador be stripped of his immunity; the lower house concurred with the committee's recommendation, in order that charges might be brought against López Obrador. Following the vote López Obrador took a leave of absence from office, although the Distrito Federal assembly approved a motion confirming him in office. Later in April as many as 1.2m. people participated in a demonstration in Mexico City in support of their mayor, who returned to his post the following day. The federal Attorney-General was subsequently dismissed; this was widely interpreted as an admission by the Government that its plan to prevent López Obrador from contesting the forthcoming presidential election had failed (people facing criminal charges were prohibited from running for office); indeed, in early May the new Attorney-General dismissed all charges against López Obrador. In July López Obrador resigned as Head of Government of the Distrito Federal and, in the following month, secured the PRD's presidential nomination.

Discord continued within the PRI during 2005 between the supporters of Gordillo and Madrazo in their respective campaigns to secure the party's nomination for the presidential election. In January Gordillo and the powerful teachers' union, the Sindicato Nacional de Trabajadores de la Educación, of which she was President, launched the Nueva Alianza (NA) in order to consolidate support for her candidacy. Madrazo had been due to resign as President of the party in mid-2005 to contest the party's primary election; traditionally, he would have been succeeded by the Secretary-General, Gordillo, but the rivalry between the two meant that Madrazo delayed his departure until August. At the end of that month the party's national political council elected Mariano Palacios Alcocer, who had previously served as party President, as Madrazo's successor; Gordillo resigned as Secretary-General in September. In early August a third faction, Unidad Democrática, more commonly known as Todos Unidos Contra Madrazo (TUCOM—Everyone United against Madrazo) elected Arturo Montiel, the outgoing Governor of the Estado de México, as its nominee for the PRI's presidential candidate. However, in October, following allegations of corruption regarding his use of public money during his time as Governor, Montiel suddenly withdrew from the primary contest. It was widely assumed that Madrazo had been behind the allegations. A series of defections in late 2005 by prominent members of the PRI opposed to Madrazo further highlighted the divisions within the party. None the less, in November Madrazo won an overwhelming victory in the election for the PRI's presidential nomination.

Meanwhile, in October 2005 the former Secretary of Energy, Felipe Calderón Hinojosa, from the traditional, clericist wing of the PAN, unexpectedly won the election to decide that party's 2006 presidential nomination, defeating Santiago Creel Miranda, who had enjoyed the support of President Fox. In December the PRI and the PVEM announced an alliance, Alianza por México, in advance of the 2006 elections. The PRD also formed an alliance, named Por el Bien de Todos (For the Good of Everyone), with two smaller left-wing parties, Convergencia and the PT, to contest the ballots.

At the presidential election, held on 2 July 2006, the PAN's Calderón secured an extremely narrow margin of victory, of just 0.6% (243,934 votes out of almost 42m. cast), over López Obrador. According to official results, Calderón polled 35.9% of the total votes cast, compared with López Obrador's 35.3%. Madrazo, the PRI nominee, trailed in third place with 22.3%, an historic low for the party. López Obrador did not accept the results, alleging that electoral irregularities, combined with the narrow margin of defeat, undermined their legitimacy. He demanded that the votes be recounted and called on supporters to take to the streets in peaceful protest to put pressure on the electoral authorities. A rally was held in the capital by López Obrador's supporters on 8 July to demand a recount. The close election results were an important test of the autonomy of the IFE. Control of the IFE had been removed from the Secretariat of the Interior under President Zedillo, and the federal electoral body had secured an unprecedented degree of popular trust by overseeing the end to the PRI's monopoly on the presidency in 2000. However, there were fears that the official election result, with its echoes of Cuauhtémoc Cárdenas's defeat in 1988, would undermine the recent gains in legitimacy and lead to instability and institutional crisis. Calderón was inaugurated as President on 1 December in a ceremony notable for its lack of celebration and ostentation. A week earlier López Obrador had held a ceremony in Mexico City's main square, declaring himself to be Mexico's legitimate President in front of a large crowd.

Results of elections to the Congreso, also held on 2 July 2006, were evenly distributed among the three leading parties, ensuring that the new President would face a legislature dominated by the opposition. The PAN secured 206 of the 500 seats in the Cámara Federal de Diputados, with the PRI-led Alianza por México winning 159 seats and the PRD's Por el Bien de Todos alliance garnering 122 seats. In the 128-seat Senado, the PAN won 52 seats, the Alianza por México 39 seats and Por el Bien de Todos alliance 36 seats. Political obstacles in the Congreso threatened to undermine the new Government's ability to introduce reforms to the state sector, just as they had during President Fox's administration.

One of the first major challenges that the new Government faced was the increasing unrest in Oaxaca. In June 2006 some 70,000 teachers had begun industrial action in support of salary increases. This had been accompanied by demonstrations, which became violent when police and protesters clashed, leaving around 100 people injured. Indigenous Indian rights activists and local farmers' co-operatives joined the protests, swelling their numbers to some 50,000. By September protesters had started to demand the resignation of the state Governor Ulises Ruiz Ortiz, accusing him of violently suppressing dissent and of winning the state election in April 2004 by fraudulent means; five of these people were shot dead by police. A further three protesters were shot dead in October and by the end of that month President-elect Calderón had dispatched 5,000 security personnel supported by armoured trucks and helicopters to retake control of the centre of the city. More that 150 people were subsequently arrested for their part in the protests and many more were injured during violent confrontations. In total some 14 people were killed during the disturbances. A series of bomb explosions in Mexico City in early November, which caused severe damage to property but no loss of life, were reportedly in response to 'repression in Oaxaca'; although no particular group claimed responsibility for the attacks, the Ejército Popular Revolucionario (EPR), a left-wing guerrilla group hitherto active only in the southern states, was believed to have been linked to them. The EPR did claim responsibility for a series of bomb attacks affecting petroleum and gas pipelines belonging to PEMEX in central Mexico in early July, as well as another similar series of explosions in September, both of which caused severe disruption to major industries.

A series of substantial increases in the price of tortillas and other food staples, such as milk and eggs, prompted demonstrations by over 100,000 people in Mexico City in January 2007. The protests were led by the self-declared 'parallel President' López Obrador. Calderón responded by negotiating an agreement between producers and retailers to attempt to fix the price of tortillas for the remainder of 2007.

A law to reform the electoral system by reducing the influence of money in elections was approved with the votes of all three main parties in the Senado in September 2007 and entered into law in November. The provisions of the reform, *inter alia*, reduced from 270m. to 40m. new pesos the amount that a party could spend on an election campaign, granted each party a limited amount of publicity in the broadcast media and prohibited the diffusion of propaganda that denigrated parties or candidates; the latter provision was in response to the negative campaign conducted by opponents of López Obrador that had preceded the 2006 presidential election.

The first change to Calderón's Government also occurred in September 2007 following the resignation of the Secretary of Public Function, Germán Martínez Cázares, in order to campaign for election to the presidency of the PAN. He was replaced by his deputy, Salvador Vega Casillas. Martínez Cázares, who was regarded as politically close to Calderón, was elected unopposed as the party's President in December. In January 2008 Calderón dismissed the Secretary of the Interior, Francisco Javier Ramírez Acuña, and the Secretary of Social Development, María Beatriz Zavala Peniche, appointing in their stead Juan Camilo Mouriño Terrazo and Ernesto Cordero Arroyo, respectively. The appointment of Mouriño, hitherto Chief of the Office of the President, caused controversy, with the PRD alleging that as the holder of dual Mexican and Spanish nationality he was constitutionally ineligible for ministerial office. (Mouriño was born in Spain to a Spanish father and obtained Mexican citizenship at the age of 18; his mother's nationality, and thus his eligibility for naturalization, was disputed.) In March the opposition further accused the minister of having taken advantage of his position as head of the congressional energy commission in the early 2000s and, later, adviser to the then Secretary of Energy, Calderón, to sign a series of contracts between his family's transportation company and PEMEX. Mouriño denied any wrongdoing and resisted demands for his resignation.

In late March 2008 an election to choose the President of the PRD highlighted the divisions in the party between a faction that supported López Obrador's continued claim to the presidency, refusing to deal with what it considered to be an illegitimate Government, and those who favoured a more pragmatic approach. Preliminary indications suggested that Alejandro Encinas, representing the pro-López Obrador faction, had defeated the moderate candidate, Jesús Ortega; however, counting of ballots was suspended in several states following allegations of irregularities by both sides. The official result of the election had still not been declared by early April.

Mexico's poor human rights record was highlighted in late 2001 by the assassination in October of a leading civil liberties lawyer, Digna Ochoa, and by the publication, in December, of an Amnesty International report alleging that Mexican security forces were involved in widespread human rights violations. In response, President Fox, whose electoral campaign had made the elimination of corruption and an improvement in human rights a priority, announced an official inquiry into the 'disappearance' of 532 people detained by security forces in the 1970s and 1980s. In February 2002 Fox ordered the immediate release of Gen. José Francisco Gallardo, who had been sentenced to 28 years' imprisonment in 1993 after being convicted of misappropriating military property. Human rights groups and supporters of Gallardo had maintained that the charges were fabricated and that he had been incarcerated after demanding a reform of the military justice system. However, in August 2003 Amnesty International published a report that accused the Government of inefficiency and negligence in investigating the rape and murder of an estimated 307 women (and the disappearance of a further 500) in Ciudad Juárez over the previous 10 years. In 2004 some 130 government officials were investigated for negligence in the ongoing murder investigations. In mid-2004 a further Amnesty International report asserted that widespread abuse of human rights persisted. The report alleged that the police and military routinely abused peasants, and that torture was commonly used by police and in the justice system. According to official figures, 531 kidnappings occurred in Mexico in 2003; however, other sources estimated that the real figure was 3,000. In December 2004 President Fox unveiled a National Plan for Human Rights, aimed at eliminating torture and abuse. A report commissioned by Fox in 2002, which was published in November 2006, acknowledged government responsibility in the massacres, torture and 'disappearances' of the 1970s. In March 2007 the investigating magistrate ordered the murder case of Digna Ochoa to be reopened. In December of the same year the Supreme Court concluded an investigation into allegations that the PRI Governor of Puebla, Mario Marín Torres, had violated the human rights of the investigative journalist Lydia Cacho. A recording of a telephone conversation implied that Marín had ordered Cacho's illegal arrest and torture in December 2005, in retaliation for a book published by the journalist that had implicated him in a child abuse scandal; however, after ruling the evidence inadmissible, the court absolved Marín of responsibility. The ruling was strongly condemned by left-wing critics.

An anti-narcotics effort by the Fox administration led to an increased number of arrests in 2002–04, including the leaders of the Tijuana and Golfo cocaine cartels. However, the anti-drugs programme was itself the subject of an anti-corruption drive in 2002, leading to a number of specialized army units being dismantled. Meanwhile, in November the investigation into the 'guerra sucia' of the late 1970s resulted in the conviction of Brig.-Gen. Mario Acosta and Gen. Francisco Quirós on charges of protecting the operations of the Juárez cartel; they also faced charges over the disappearance of 143 activists. Despite efforts by President Fox to address the crime problem, drugs-related crime continued to escalate as the amount of narcotics crossing the Mexican–US border increased. It appeared that an internecine war between the Tijuana, Golfo and Sinaloa cartels was taking place in the north of Mexico. During 2005 more than 180 people were killed in Nuevo Laredo, Tamaulipas, in what appeared to be an ongoing conflict between two drugs cartels. In November Ricardo García Urquiza, alleged to be the leader of the Juárez cartel, was arrested in Mexico City.

Upon his election in mid-2006 President Calderón announced that law enforcement would form one of his priorities in office. A major offensive was subsequently launched in December against the activities of the drugs cartels in Michoacán state with the deployment of 7,000 troops and federal police officers. The federal budget approved in December included an increase in security expenditure of 24%. A second major operation was launched in Tijuana, Baja California, in early January 2007, while later in the same month some 9,000 troops were sent into the states of Sinaloa, Durango and Chihuahua. Meanwhile, Calderón was highly commended by the US authorities for his decision in January to allow the extradition of 15 drugs-trafficking suspects to the USA. The extradition of the individuals (who included the head of the Golfo cartel and senior figures from the Sinaloa and Tijuana cartels) represented a significant change in policy from previous administrations, which had refused to allow extradition until suspects had faced a Mexican court. By mid-May the army and federal police had been deployed in a law-enforcement role in 10 states. Although these offensives against organized crime appeared to have little immediate impact (according to official figures, at least 2,500 people were killed by gangsters in 2007, compared with 2,350 in 2006), the Government emphasized that its strategy would take several years to accomplish. In January 2008 the arrest, in Culiacán, Sinaloa, of Alfredo Beltrán Leyva, a senior leader of the Sinaloa cartel, was one of a number of important successes in the offensive; however, it appeared that the cartels were attempting to move into Mexico City, which had previously been little affected by drugs-related crime, and a bomb explosion in the capital in mid-February (which killed only the bomb's carrier) was attributed to the Sinaloa cartel.

On 1 January 1994 armed Indian groups numbering 1,000–3,000 took control of four municipalities of the southern state of Chiapas. The rebels issued the Declaration of the Lacandona Jungle, identifying themselves as the Ejército Zapatista de Liberación Nacional—EZLN (after Emiliano Zapata, who championed the land rights of Mexican peasants during the 1910–17 Revolution), and detailed a series of demands for economic and social change in the region, culminating in a declaration of war against the Government and a statement of intent to depose the 'dictator', President Salinas. A charismatic rebel spokesman, identified as 'subcomandante Marcos' (later tentatively identified as Rafael Sebastián Guillén Vicente, a former professor at the Universidad Autónoma Metropolitana), stated that the insurgency had been timed to coincide with the implementation of the North American Free Trade Agreement (NAFTA—see below), which the rebels considered to be the latest in a series of segregative government initiatives adopted at the expense of indigenous groups. Negotiations between the Zapatistas and government representatives concluded with the publication of a document detailing 34 demands of the EZLN, and the Government's response to them. A preliminary accord was reached following the Government's broad acceptance of many of the rebels' stipulations, including an acceleration of the wide-ranging anti-poverty programme in the region, the incorporation of traditional Indian structures of justice and political organization, and a commitment from the Government to investigate the impact of NAFTA and recent land reform legislation on Indian communities. Official figures suggested that 100–150 guerrillas, soldiers and civilians had been killed during the conflict, while the Roman Catholic Church estimated that there had been as many as 400 casualties. In June the EZLN announced that the Government's peace proposal had been rejected by an overwhelming majority of the movement's supporters. However, a similar majority had rejected the resumption of hostilities with the security forces, and had endorsed the extension of the ceasefire pending renewed bilateral discussions. Tensions, however, continued over the following years, with attempts to reach an accord between the Zapatistas and the Government proving unsuccessful. In February 1996 the ELZN and the Government signed an agreement guaranteeing the cultural, linguistic and local government rights of indigenous groups. However, the ELZN withdrew from negotiations in September on the grounds that the agreement had not been implemented. In September 1997 several thousand Zapatistas and their sympathizers staged a peaceful demonstration in Mexico City, during which the EZLN inaugurated the Frente Zapatista de Liberación Nacional, a political movement that embodied the Zapatistas' ideology. In December there was widespread disquiet at the killing of 45 Indians in a church in the village of Acteal, in the municipality of Chenalhó, Chiapas. Emilio Chuayffet, the Secretary of the Interior, and Julio César Ruiz Ferro, the Governor of Chiapas, were forced to resign, following criticism of their roles in the events leading to the Acteal massacre. In April 1998 Gen. Julio César Santiago Díaz, who had been acting chief of staff of Chiapas state police at the time of the massacre, was arrested and charged with failing to intervene to prevent the bloodshed. In September 1999 Jacinto Arias, mayor of Chenalhó at the time of the massacre, was convicted on charges of supplying the weapons used in the massacre and sentenced to 35 years' imprisonment. In November 2002 18 people were each sentenced to 36 years' imprisonment for their involvement in the deaths as part of a paramilitary group with links to the PRI; they joined 70 others previously convicted.

In February 2001 subcomandante Marcos and other Zapatista leaders began a tour of Mexico which culminated in Mexico City in early March, where a rally in the capital's main square, attended by an estimated 150,000 people, was held in support of congressional approval of the proposed indigenous rights legislation. Following a congressional vote four EZLN leaders were permitted to address both legislative chambers and, in March, the EZLN announced that formal dialogue with the Government would recommence. Subcomandante Marcos successfully negotiated the dismantling of the remaining three garrisons in Chiapas, and in April the Congreso approved amendments to six articles of the Constitution, which recognized and guaranteed indigenous political, legal, social and economic rights, and prohibited discrimination against Indians based on race and tribal affiliation. However, the legislation fell short of granting indigenous peoples the right to autonomy over land and natural resources; in response, the EZLN suspended all contact with the Government. In August 2003 the EZLN declared that 30 municipalities in Chiapas, hitherto under Zapatista control, were to be granted autonomy. 'Councils of Good Government' (Juntas de Buen Gobierno) would oversee the transition from military to civilian control in these areas. The transformation of the EZLN into a political force was underlined in August 2005, when subcomandante Marcos announced his plans to create a left-wing alliance of peasants' organizations. In early 2006 the Zapatistas began an alternative presidential election campaign, although it failed to gather significant support.

Mexico's foreign policy has been determined largely by relations with the USA. The rapid expansion of petroleum production from the mid-1970s onwards gave Mexico a new independence, empowering it to favour the left-wing regimes in Cuba and Nicaragua, opposed by the USA, during the 1980s. In February 1985 relations between Mexico and the USA deteriorated following the murder of an agent of the US Drug Enforcement Administration (DEA) by Mexican drugs-traffickers. The situation worsened in April 1990, when a Mexican physician was abducted, in Mexico, by agents employed by the DEA, and transported to the USA to be arrested on charges relating to the murder. Meanwhile, relations between Mexico and the USA remained tense, largely because of disagreement over the problem of illegal immigration from Mexico into the USA and Mexico's failure to take effective action against the illegal drugs trade. This situation improved following the deportation to the USA in 1996 of Juan García Abrego, the alleged head of the Golfo drugs cartel. In February 1997 Mexico's credibility in combating drugs-trafficking was seriously undermined when Gen. Jesús Gutiérrez Rebollo, the head of the counter-narcotics agency, was dismissed and charged with receiving payment from Amado Carrillo Fuentes, the head of the Juárez drugs cartel. (He was later sentenced to more than 30 years' imprisonment.) Nevertheless, in March the USA 'certified' Mexico as a country co-operating in its campaign against drugs-trafficking. In May Mexico's discredited counter-narcotics agency was disbanded and replaced with a specially trained anti-drugs unit. Bilateral relations were strained in May 1998, when a major US counter-narcotics operation was conducted in Mexico, without Mexican authorization. None the less, additional co-operation agreements were signed by the two countries in early 1999, and Mexico continued to be 'certified' by the USA. Although President Fox advocated abolition of the certification practice, it was reaffirmed in March 2001.

NAFTA, comprising Mexico, the USA and Canada, took effect from 1 January 1994. Among the Agreement's provisions are the gradual reduction of tariffs on 50% of products over a period of 10–15 years (some 57% of tariffs on agricultural trade between the USA and Mexico was removed immediately), and the establishment, by Mexico and the USA, of a North American Development Bank (NADBank) charged with the funding of initiatives for the rehabilitation of the two countries' common border. From January 2003 tariffs on a number of agricultural products were reduced or removed entirely, provoking widespread discontent among Mexico's 25m.-strong rural community. In particular, they pointed to the greater subsidies received by US farmers and to a poor transport infrastructure, which resulted in higher costs. A pledge by President Fox in May 2002 to repay Mexico's 'water debt' to the USA had also angered Mexican farmers. Following the collapse, in September 2003, of the fifth Ministerial Conference of the World Trade Organization (WTO) in Cancún, Mexico joined the group of developing countries led by Brazil that opposed US-European Union (EU, see p. 244) subsidies of agricultural products. At a summit meeting in March 2005 between President Fox, US President George W. Bush and Canadian Prime Minister Paul Martin, the three leaders announced an accord to increase regional co-operation on economic and security issues.

The Fox Government sought to persuade the US Administration of George W. Bush, which took office in 2001, to adopt a more liberal position on Mexican immigrants to the USA. However, progress on immigration policy was suspended following the terrorist attacks in the USA on 11 September 2001, and proposals to tighten security on the US–Mexican border were approved by the US Congress in 2002. In March of that year, nevertheless, following a summit meeting in Monterrey, the two Presidents announced a 'smart border' partnership agreement, intended to facilitate the legal entry of Mexican people and goods into the USA while, at the same time, securing the frontier against possible acts of terrorism. In September, however, Fox requested that the emphasis in US-Mexican relations be shifted back to bilateral issues, which had been neglected in favour of border security. In the same month Mexico unilaterally withdrew from the Inter-American Treaty of Reciprocal Assistance (the Rio Treaty), the defence pact linking Mexico to the USA, resulting in a downturn in relations with the USA.

In March 2003, with Mexican public opinion strongly against armed intervention to remove the regime of Saddam Hussain in Iraq, President Fox risked a deterioration of relations with both the USA and Spain by stating his opposition to war. His stance was all the more significant owing to Mexico's place as one of the 10 non-permanent members of the UN Security Council. In January 2004 the announcement of a revised US immigration initiative, which offered significantly less to Mexican immigrants in the USA than had been hoped, was met with disappointment by the Mexican Government, which had hoped to increase freedom of movement between the two countries. In the same month US officials began managing the security arrangements for US-bound flights leaving Mexico City's airport.

Throughout 2005 tensions remained high between Mexico and the USA over border security, specifically regarding illegal immigration from Mexico to the USA, and also escalating drugs-related violence in Mexico (see above). However, in October a Mexican-US joint effort to reduce lawlessness in the border area was announced: a bilateral agreement was signed in March 2006. None the less, the Mexican Government expressed strong opposition to a US plan, announced in late 2005, to build security fences along some 1,600 km of the most accessible sections of the border in order to deter illegal immigrants. By September 2006, despite the objections of the Mexican authorities, the proposal, involving the construction of a triple barrier, monitored by look-out towers, sensors and cameras, had been approved by the US Congress. The Mexican Government appealed directly to President Bush to veto the bill, claiming that it would harm bilateral relations and be contrary to the spirit of co-operation necessary in guaranteeing the security of the common border. Various indigenous groups whose territories straddled the border also expressed concern at the proposal. Other commentators speculated on the possibility that, by forcing Mexicans to take more dangerous routes into US territory, there would be an increase in the death rate of migrants.

US-Mexican relations deteriorated somewhat in 2007 following Calderón's accession to the presidency, as a result not only of the USA's continued uncompromising stance on border security but also of Mexico's improved relations with Cuba and Venezuela (see below). None the less, as a result of negotiations between Presidents Bush and Calderón in March in Mérida, Yucatán, in October Bush promised the Mexican Government some US $500m. per year in order to combat drugs-related crime. The so-called 'Mérida Initiative' would require approval by the US Congress.

In April 2004 Mexico's relations with Cuba were strained after Mexico voted in favour of a UN motion to censure Cuba for human rights abuses. In early May the Cuban leader, Fidel Castro Ruz, criticized Mexico's stance and accused the Fox Government of interference in the island's affairs. In response, President Fox expelled the Cuban ambassador from the country and recalled the Mexican ambassador in Havana; the ambassadors returned to their posts in July. Under President Calderón Mexico effected a rapprochement towards Cuba, and in June 2007 Mexico voted in favour of a UN Human Rights Council resolution to end UN scrutiny of human rights in Cuba. In late 2005 Mexico and Venezuela recalled their respective ambassadors, after left-wing President Lt-Col (retd) Hugo Chávez Frías of Venezuela criticized President Fox for being subservient to the USA. Full diplomatic relations between the two countries were restored in August 2007.

In January 1991 a preliminary free trade agreement was signed with Honduras, Guatemala, El Salvador, Nicaragua and Costa Rica, in order to facilitate the negotiation of bilateral agreements between Mexico and each of the five countries, leading to free trade in an increasing range of products over a six-year period. During the 1990s Mexico concluded agreements for greater economic co-operation and increased bilateral trade with Colombia and Venezuela as the Group of Three (see p. 412), with Bolivia, Costa Rica and with the EU (see p. 244). A free trade accord with Nicaragua came into force in 1998; a similar accord with Chile was signed in 1998 and came into force in the following year. A further trade agreement with Guatemala, Honduras and El Salvador (the Northern Triangle) was concluded in 2000. In March 2000 Mexico and the EU signed a free trade agreement, the first to be signed between the EU and a Latin American country. The accord provided for the gradual elimination of tariffs on industrial and agricultural products, the progressive liberalization of trade in services, and preferential access to public procurement; it also obliged the signatories to respect democratic principles and human rights. In October 2003 Mexico signed an Organization of American States agreement on regional security, which was also aimed at increasing co-operation on social and environmental issues. In April 2004 the Secretary of Foreign Affairs, Luis Ernesto Derbez, announced Mexico's aim of becoming a full member of Mercosur (Mercado Común del Sur, or Southern Common Market, see p. 391), and in late 2004 he declared Mexico's intention of seeking permanent representation on the UN Security Council.

Government

Mexico is a federal republic comprising 31 states and a Distrito Federal (Federal District, comprising the capital). Under the 1917 Constitution, legislative power is vested in the bicameral Congreso de la Unión, elected by universal adult suffrage. The Senado has 128 members (four from each state and the Distrito Federal), serving a six-year term. The Cámara Federal de Diputados, directly elected for three years, has 500 seats, of which 300 are filled from single-member constituencies. The remaining 200 seats, allocated so as to achieve proportional representation, are filled from parties' lists of candidates. Executive power is held by the President, directly elected for six years at the same time as the Senado. He governs with the assistance of an appointed Cabinet. Each state has its own constitution and is administered by a Governor (elected for six years) and an elected chamber of deputies. The Distrito Federal is administered by a Head of Government.

Defence

Military service, on a part-time basis (four hours per week), is compulsory for conscripts selected by lottery, for one year. As assessed in November 2007, the active armed forces totalled 236,100: 178,000 in the army, 46,400 in the navy (including naval air force—1,250—and marines—12,600) and 11,700 in the air force. Paramilitary forces numbered 30,700, comprising a federal preventive police force of 12,700 and a rural defence militia numbering 18,000. The reserve numbered 39,899. Defence expenditure for 2007 was budgeted at 43,400m. new pesos, an increase of some 23% on the previous year.

Economic Affairs

In 2006, according to estimates by the World Bank, Mexico's gross national income (GNI), measured at average 2004–06 prices, was US $820,319.m., equivalent to $7,870 per head (or $11,410 per head on an international purchasing-power parity basis). During 1996–2006, it was estimated, the population increased at an average annual rate of 1.2%, while gross domestic product (GDP) per head increased, in real terms, by an average of 2.3% per year. Overall GDP increased, in real terms, at an average annual rate of 2.9% in 1999–2006; GDP increased by 4.8% in 2006.

Agriculture (including forestry and fishing) contributed 3.9% of GDP and engaged about 13.5% of the employed labour force in 2007. The staple food crops are maize, wheat, sorghum, barley, rice, beans and potatoes. The principal cash crops are coffee, cotton, sugar cane, and fruit and vegetables (particularly tomatoes). Livestock-raising and fisheries are also important. During 1996–2006, according to World Bank estimates, agricultural GDP increased at an average annual rate of 1.8%; agricultural GDP increased by 4.8% in 2006. The reduction and eventual removal of import tariffs proposed under the North American Free Trade Agreement (NAFTA) was a significant blow to Mexico's agriculture sector, which had lower subsidies and higher overhead costs than in the USA. In late 2004 the Congreso approved a law regulating the use of genetically modified seeds.

Industry (including mining, manufacturing, construction and power) engaged 25.7% of the employed labour force in 2007 and provided an estimated 26.2% of GDP in the same year. According to the World Bank, during 1996–2006 industrial GDP increased by an average of 3.3% per year; industrial GDP increased by 5.0% in 2006.

Mining contributed 1.6% of GDP in 2007, and, together with electricity production and distribution, engaged 0.9% of the employed labour force in the same year. During 2000–07 the GDP of the mining sector increased by an average of 1.9% per year; mining GDP increased by 0.2% in 2007. Mexico has large reserves of petroleum and natural gas (mineral products accounted for an estimated 16.3% of total export earnings in 2007). Zinc, salt, silver, copper, celestite and fluorite are also major mineral exports. In addition, mercury, bismuth, antimony, cadmium, manganese and phosphates are mined, and there are significant reserves of uranium.

Manufacturing provided 17.6% of GDP and engaged 16.4% of the employed labour force in 2007. According to the World Bank, manufacturing GDP increased by an annual average of 3.2% in 1996–2006; the sector increased by 4.7% in 2006. In the 1990s the *maquila* sector (where intermediate materials produced on US territory are processed or assembled on the Mexican side of the border) grew in importance. By December 2000 Mexico had 3,703 *maquila* export plants, providing an estimated 1.3m. jobs and making a significant contribution to the manufacturing sector; however, the sector suffered a downturn in the early 2000s, and the number of plants fell to 2,810 in 2004, before increasing again in 2005 to an estimated 2,860. *Maquila* exports were valued at an estimated 214,430.2m. new pesos in 2006, an increase of 4.5% from 2005 and equivalent to 45.3% of total revenue from manufacturing exports. In 2005 an estimated 1.2m. people were employed in the *maquila* sector.

Energy is derived principally from mineral fuels and lubricants and hydroelectric power. In 2004, according to the World Bank, some 31.1% of total output of electricity production was derived from petroleum, 38.8% came from natural gas, and 10.7% came from coal-powered plants. The Fox Government's planned liberalization of the energy sector, including the troubled state-run Petróleos Mexicanos (PEMEX), ran into difficulties owing to congressional opposition. In late 2004 the IMF recommended that Mexico further open its energy sector to private investment. In 2006, according to PEMEX, oil production was an estimated 3,256,000 barrels per day, while production of natural gas was 5,356m. cu ft per day. In 2007 mineral imports were estimated at 7.3% of total merchandise imports, while exports of petroleum accounted for an estimated 14.9% of the total export value in 2005. In late 2001 the Governments of Mexico and Guatemala reached agreement, under the regional 'Plan Puebla-Panamá' (a series of joint transport, industry and tourism projects intended to integrate the Central American region), to link their electricity grids.

The services sector contributed 69.8% of GDP and engaged 60.1% of the employed labour force in 2007. According to World Bank figures, the GDP of the sector increased by an average of 3.8% per year in 1996–2006; the sector experienced growth of 4.7% in 2006. Tourism is one of Mexico's principal sources of foreign exchange. In 2006 there were an estimated 21.4m. foreign visitors to Mexico (mostly from the USA and Canada), providing revenue of US $12,177m.

In 2006 Mexico recorded a visible trade deficit of an estimated US $6,133m., and there was a deficit of $2,008m. on the current account of the balance of payments. In 2007 the principal source of imports (49.6%) was the USA, which was also the principal market for exports (82.1%). The principal exports in 2007 were machinery and mechanical appliances, electric and electronic products and transport equipment; the principal imports were electric and electronic products, industrial machinery and transport equipment.

In 2007 there was an estimated budgetary deficit of 771,435m. new pesos, equivalent to 7.9% of GDP. Mexico's external debt totalled US $167,228m. at the end of 2005, of which $108,786m. was long-term public debt. In that year the cost of debt-servicing was equivalent to 17.2% of the value of exports of goods and services. The average annual rate of inflation was 7.3% in 1996–2006. Consumer prices increased by an average of 3.9% in 2007. An estimated 3.4% of the total labour force were officially recorded as unemployed in 2007. In that year remittances from Mexicans living abroad totalled US $23,979m., a 1.0% increase on 2006. It was estimated that remittances were Mexico's second largest source of foreign income, after petroleum exports.

Mexico is a member of the Inter-American Development Bank (IDB, see p. 308), and of the Latin American Integration Association (see p. 331). Mexico was admitted to the Asia-Pacific Economic Co-operation group (APEC, see p. 176) in 1993, and joined the Organisation for Economic Co-operation and Development (OECD, see p. 347) in 1994. Mexico is also a signatory nation to NAFTA (see p. 338). In September 2004 Mexico concluded a free trade agreement with Japan.

Mexico's economic development, centred on the expansion of the petroleum industry, was impeded from the mid-1980s by the decrease in international petroleum prices, in addition to the persistent problems of the flight of capital, the depreciation of the peso, a shortage of foreign exchange and vast foreign debt. A programme of tax reform and economic liberalization was undertaken from the late 1980s, but in late 1994 and early 1995 a sharp devaluation of the peso provoked a financial crisis, necessitating a stringent policy of economic adjustment and the procurement of substantial international credit facilities. Strong export performance in the latter half of the decade, particularly in the *maquila* industries, prompted an economic recovery, and annual economic growth reached 6.6% in 2000. An economic slowdown occurred in the early 2000s, caused by the sluggish economy of Mexico's largest trading partner, the USA, particularly in the *maquila* sector. The USA was estimated to contribute as much as 30% of Mexico's GDP (albeit indirectly) and the economy as a

MEXICO

whole benefited from the steady growth of that country in 2004–06. The manufacturing sector, in particular, attracted substantial foreign investment (mainly from the USA), particularly into the automotive sector. However, a significant decline in US growth in 2007, which worsened during early 2008, prompted the Central Bank of Mexico to revise its projections for the year. Real GDP growth of 2.8% was envisaged for 2008, in comparison to an earlier forecast of 3.7%. Inflows of foreign investment and remittances were identified as being especially vulnerable; exports of automobiles and electronics (of which the USA was a key purchaser) were also expected to decrease. Recent diversification of external markets was likely to moderate the decline, particularly following the implementation of the Dominican Republic-Central American Free Trade Agreement, which had stimulated demand in the Central American region for textiles (of which Mexico was a major supplier). The Government of Vicente Fox, which left office in late 2006, was considered to have failed to implement the economic reforms necessary to sustain consistent growth. Although the administration of President Felipe Calderón intended to accelerate reform, the President's weak mandate prompted concern that he too might encounter difficulties in gaining approval for his legislative agenda. However in September 2007 Congress approved a comprehensive programme of tax reforms devised by Calderón: considerable revisions to the system of revenue collection were expected and a new minimum income tax was to be applied to companies at a rate of 16.5%. Mexico had, hitherto, relied largely upon revenues from oil production to finance budgetary operations and it was hoped that the reforms would engender diversification of the tax base, thereby allowing the state petroleum concern (PEMEX) to reinvest a greater portion of its profits into oil exploration; output of crude petroleum was estimated to have declined by 5.6% in 2007.

Education

Education in state schools is provided free of charge and is officially compulsory. It covers six years of primary education, beginning at six years of age, and three years of secondary education, either general or technical, from the age of 12. This can then be followed by another three-year cycle of higher or specialized secondary education. In 2005 enrolment at primary schools included 98.0% of pupils in the relevant age-group, while in the same year enrolment at secondary schools included 65.0% of pupils in the relevant age-group. In 2006 there were an estimated 4,977 institutes of higher education, attended by some 2,446,700 students. In 2002 there were 56 universities in Mexico. In 2001/02 nursery schools for the indigenous population numbered 8,487, while there were 9,065 primary schools for the indigenous population. However, in spite of the existence of more than 80 indigenous languages in Mexico, there were few bilingual secondary schools. Federal expenditure on education in 2003 was an estimated 265,238.1m. new pesos (equivalent to 21.4% of total central government expenditure).

Public Holidays

2008: 1 January (New Year's Day), 4 February (for Constitution Day), 17 March (for Birthday of Benito Juárez), 20 March (Maundy Thursday)*, 21 March (Good Friday*), 1 May (Labour Day), 5 May (Anniversary of the Battle of Puebla)*, 16 September (Independence Day), 2 November (All Souls' Day)*, 17 November (for Anniversary of the Revolution), 12 December (Day of Our Lady of Guadalupe)*, 25 December (Christmas).

2009: 1 January (New Year's Day), 2 February (for Constitution Day), 16 March (for Birthday of Benito Juárez), 9 April (Maundy Thursday)*, 10 April (Good Friday*), 1 May (Labour Day), 5 May (Anniversary of the Battle of Puebla)*, 16 September (Independence Day), 2 November (All Souls' Day)*, 16 November (for Anniversary of the Revolution), 12 December (Day of Our Lady of Guadalupe)*, 25 December (Christmas).

* Widely celebrated unofficial holidays.

Weights and Measures

The metric system is in force.

Statistical Survey

Sources (unless otherwise stated): Dirección General de Estadística, Instituto Nacional de Estadística, Geografía e Informática (INEGI), Edif. Sede, Avda Prolongación Héroe de Nacozari 2301 Sur, 20270 Aguascalientes, Ags; tel. (14) 918-1948; fax (14) 918-0739; e-mail webmaster@inegi.gob.mx; internet www.inegi.gob.mx; Banco de México, Avda 5 de Mayo 1, Col. Centro, Del. Cuauhtémoc, 06059 México, DF; tel. (55) 5237-2000; fax (55) 5237-2370; internet www.banxico.org.mx.

Area and Population

AREA, POPULATION AND DENSITY

Area (sq km)	
Continental	1,959,248
Islands	5,127
Total	1,964,375*
Population (census and by-census results)†	
14 February 2000	97,483,412
29 October 2005	
Males	50,249,955
Females	53,013,433
Total	103,263,388
Population (projected mid-year estimates)‡	
2006	104,874,282
2007	105,790,725
2008	106,682,518
Density (per sq km) at mid-2008	54.3

* 758,449 sq miles.
† Including adjustment for underenumeration (1,730,016 in 2000).
‡ Source: Consejo Nacional de Población, *Proyecciones de la Población de México 2005–2050*.

ADMINISTRATIVE DIVISIONS
(at by-census of October 2005)

States	Area (sq km)*	Population	Density (per sq km)	Capital
Aguascalientes (Ags)	5,623	1,065,416	189.5	Aguascalientes
Baja California (BC)	71,540	2,844,469	36.8	Mexicali
Baja California Sur (BCS)	73,937	512,170	6.9	La Paz
Campeche (Camp.)	57,718	754,730	13.1	Campeche
Chiapas (Chis)	73,680	4,293,459	58.3	Tuxtla Gutiérrez
Chihuahua (Chih.)	247,490	3,241,444	13.1	Chihuahua
Coahuila (de Zaragoza) (Coah.)	151,447	2,495,200	16.5	Saltillo
Colima (Col.)	5,629	567,996	100.9	Colima
Distrito Federal (DF)	1,485	8,720,916	5,87.7	Mexico City
Durango (Dgo)	123,364	1,509,117	12.2	Victoria de Durango
Guanajuato (Gto)	30,617	4,893,812	159.8	Guanajuato
Guerrero (Gro)	63,618	3,115,202	50.0	Chilpancingo de los Bravos
Hidalgo (Hgo)	20,855	2,345,514	112.5	Pachuca de Soto
Jalisco (Jal.)	78,624	6,752,113	85.9	Guadalajara
México (Méx.)	22,332	14,007,495	627.2	Toluca de Lerdo

MEXICO

Statistical Survey

States— continued	Area (sq km)*	Population	Density (per sq km)	Capital
Michoacán (de Ocampo) (Mich.)	58,672	3,966,073	67.6	Morelia
Morelos (Mor.)	4,894	1,612,899	329.6	Cuernavaca
Nayarit (Nay.)	27,861	949,684	34.1	Tepic
Nuevo León (NL)	64,206	4,199,292	65.4	Monterrey
Oaxaca (Oax.)	93,348	3,506,821	37.6	Oaxaca de Juárez
Puebla (Pue.)	34,246	5,383,133	157.2	Heroica Puebla de Zaragoza
Querétaro (de Arteaga) (Qro)	11,659	1,598,139	137.1	Querétaro
Quintana Roo (Q.Roo)	42,544	1,135,309	26.7	Ciudad Chetumal
San Luis Potosí (SLP)	61,165	2,410,414	39.4	San Luis Potosí
Sinaloa (Sin.)	57,334	2,608,442	45.5	Culiacán Rosales
Sonora (Son.)	179,527	2,394,861	13.3	Hermosillo
Tabasco (Tab.)	24,747	1,989,969	80.4	Villahermosa
Tamaulipas (Tam.)	80,155	3,024,238	37.7	Ciudad Victoria
Tlaxcala (Tlax.)	3,988	1,068,207	267.8	Tlaxcala de Xicohténcatl
Veracruz-Llave (Ver.)	71,856	7,110,214	99.0	Jalapa Enríquez
Yucatán (Yuc.)	39,675	1,818,948	45.8	Mérida
Zacatecas (Zac.)	75,412	1,367,692	18.1	Zacatecas
Total	1,959,248	103,263,388	52.7	—

* Excluding islands.

PRINCIPAL TOWNS
(population at census of 14 February 2000)

Ciudad de México (Mexico City, capital)	8,605,239	Querétaro	536,463
Guadalajara	1,646,183	Torreón	502,964
Ecatepec de Morelos (Ecatepec)	1,621,827	San Nicolás de los Garzas	496,879
Heroica Puebla de Zaragoza (Puebla)	1,271,673	Santa María Chimalhuacán (Chimalhuacán)	482,530
Nezahualcóyotl	1,225,083	Atizapán de Zaragoza	467,544
Ciudad Juárez	1,187,275	Tlaquepaque	458,674
Tijuana	1,148,681	Toluca de Lerdo (Toluca)	435,125
Monterrey	1,110,909	Cuautitlán Izcalli	433,830
León	1,020,818	Victoria de Durango (Durango)	427,135
Zapopan	910,690	Tuxtla Gutiérrez	424,579
Naucalpan de Juárez (Naucalpan)	835,053	Veracruz Llave (Veracruz)	411,582
Tlalnepantla de Baz (Tlalnepantla)	714,735	Reynosa	403,718
Guadalupe	669,842	Benito Juárez (Cancún)	397,191
Mérida	662,530	Matamoros	376,279
Chihuahua	657,876	Jalapa Enríquez (Xalapa)	373,076
San Luis Potosí	629,208	Villahermosa	330,846
Acapulco de Juárez (Acapulco)	620,656	Mazatlán	327,989
Aguascalientes	594,092	Cuernavaca	327,162
Saltillo	562,587	Valle de Chalco (Xico)	322,784
Morelia	549,996	Irapuato	319,148
Mexicali	549,873	Tonalá	315,278
Hermosillo	545,928	Nuevo Laredo	308,828
Culiacán Rosales (Culiacán)	540,823		

Mid-2007 ('000, incl. suburbs, UN estimates): Ciudad de México 19,028; Guadalajara 4,198; Monterrey 3,712; Puebla 2,195; Tijuana 1,553; Toluca de Lerdo 1,531; León de los Aldamas 1,488; Ciudad Juárez 1,343; Torreón 1,144 (Source: UN, *World Urbanization Prospects: The 2007 Revision*).

BIRTHS, MARRIAGES AND DEATHS

	Registered live births		Registered marriages		Registered deaths	
	Number	Rate (per 1,000)	Number	Rate (per 1,000)	Number	Rate (per 1,000)
1999	2,769,089	24.2	743,856	n.a.	443,950	n.a.
2000	2,798,339	24.5	707,422	7.2	437,667	4.9
2001	2,767,610	22.9	665,434	6.7	443,127	4.8
2002	2,699,084	21.7	616,654	6.1	459,687	4.8
2003	2,655,894	20.6	584,142	5.7	472,140	4.8
2004	2,625,056	19.8	600,563	5.8	473,417	4.8
2005	2,567,906	19.3	595,713	5.7	495,240	4.8
2006	2,505,939	19.0	586,978	5.6	494,471	4.8

Expectation of life (years at birth, UN estimates): 74.3 (males 71.8; females 76.9) in 2005 (Source: WHO *World Health Statistics*).

ECONOMICALLY ACTIVE POPULATION
(sample surveys, '000 persons aged 14 years and over, April–June)

	2005	2006	2007
Agriculture, hunting, forestry and fishing	6,059.8	6,033.0	5,772.4
Mining, quarrying and electricity	379.6	350.3	406.3
Manufacturing	6,845.1	7,000.3	7,041.3
Construction	3,181.5	3,452.5	3,585.8
Trade	8,020.8	8,211.6	8,502.3
Hotels and restaurants	2,438.3	2,514.9	2,670.6
Transport and communications	2,018.4	2,222.7	2,133.1
Finance and business services	2,221.4	2,365.9	2,530.4
Social services	3,317.3	3,413.7	3,531.9
Other services	4,141.2	4,288.2	4,371.9
Public sector	1,920.5	2,034.9	2,048.5
Activities not adequately defined	248.2	309.7	312.2
Total employed	40,791.8	42,197.8	42,906.7
Unemployed	1,482.5	1,377.7	1,505.2
Total labour force	42,274.3	43,575.5	44,411.9
Males	26,770.9	27,409.4	27,726.2
Females	15,503.4	16,166.1	16,685.6

Health and Welfare

KEY INDICATORS

Total fertility rate (children per woman, 2005)	2.3
Under-5 mortality rate (per 1,000 live births, 2005)	27
HIV/AIDS (% of persons aged 15–49, 2005)	0.3
Physicians (per 1,000 head, 2002)	1.5
Hospital beds (per 1,000 head, 2004)	1.0
Health expenditure (2004): US $ per head (PPP)	655.4
Health expenditure (2004): % of GDP	6.5
Health expenditure (2004): public (% of total)	46.4
Access to water (% of persons, 2004)	97
Access to sanitation (% of persons, 2004)	79
Human Development Index (2005): ranking	52
Human Development Index (2005): value	0.829

For sources and definitions, see explanatory note on p. vi.

MEXICO

Statistical Survey

Agriculture

PRINCIPAL CROPS
('000 metric tons)

	2004	2005	2006
Wheat	2,321	3,015	3,336
Rice (paddy)	279	291	339
Barley	932	761	874
Maize	21,670	18,012	21,765
Oats	103	127	153
Sorghum	7,004	5,524	5,487
Potatoes	1,506	1,635	1,543
Sugar cane	48,373	45,195	50,597
Dry beans	1,163	1,200*	1,375
Chick-peas	105	134	163
Soybeans (Soya beans)	132	187	81
Groundnuts (in shell)	99	73	68
Coconuts	907	1,062	1,022
Safflower seed	231	944	724
Cottonseed	212	215*	215*
Cabbages	196	221	204
Lettuce and chicory	247	275	274
Tomatoes	2,969	2,800	2,878
Cauliflower and broccoli	356	359	305
Pumpkins, squash and gourds	69	86	79
Cucumbers and gherkins	518	475	496
Chillies and green peppers	1,431	1,617	1,681
Dry onions	1,241	1,115	1,151
Carrots and turnips	389	376	382
Bananas	2,361	2,250	2,197
Oranges	3,977	4,113	3,980
Tangerines, mandarins, clementines and satsumas	421	403	337
Lemons and limes	1,928	1,807	1,866
Grapefruit and pomelos	409	350	380
Apples	573	584	602
Peaches and nectarines	202	208	223
Strawberries	177	163	192
Grapes	305	323	244
Watermelons	1,003	866	969
Cantaloupes and other melons	534	580	570
Guavas, mangoes and mangosteens	1,573	1,679	2,050
Avocados	987	1,022	1,137
Pineapples	669	552	628
Papayas	788	709	806
Coffee (green)	311	288*	288*
Cocoa beans	44	36	38
Cotton (lint)	138†	138†	138*
Tobacco (leaves)	22	16	19

* FAO estimate(s).
† Unofficial figure.

Aggregate production ('000 metric tons, may include official, semi-official or estimated data): Total cereals 32,311.7 in 2004, 27,733.0 in 2005, 31,959.2 in 2006; Total fruits (excl. melons) 15,116.8 in 2004, 14,902.6 in 2005, 15,384.7 in 2006; Total sugarcrops 48,374.1 in 2004, 45,196.4 in 2005, 50,596.7 in 2006; Total vegetables (incl. melons) 11,372.4 in 2004, 11,240.6 in 2005, 11,486.0 in 2006.

Source: FAO.

LIVESTOCK
('000 head, year ending September)

	2004	2005	2006
Horses*	6,260	6,260	6,260
Asses, mules or hinnies*	6,540	6,540	6,540
Cattle	31,248	28,763	28,649
Pigs	15,177	15,342	15,370
Sheep	7,083	7,624	7,484
Goats	8,853	8,887	8,897
Chickens	432,084	287,612	289,663
Ducks*	8,100	8,100	8,100
Turkeys	4,770	4,451	4,236

* FAO estimates.

Source: FAO.

LIVESTOCK PRODUCTS
('000 metric tons)

	2004	2005	2006
Cattle meat	1,543	1,557	1,602
Sheep meat	42	46	48
Goat meat	42	42	42
Pig meat	1,058	1,103	1,103
Horse meat*	79	79	79
Chicken meat	2,225	2,437	2,411
Cows' milk	9,874	9,868	10,029
Goats' milk	154	164	163
Hen eggs	1,906	2,025	2,014
Honey	57	51	52

* FAO estimates.

Source: FAO.

Forestry

ROUNDWOOD REMOVALS
('000 cubic metres, excl. bark)

	2004	2005	2006
Sawlogs, veneer logs and logs for sleepers	5,737	5,022	5,115
Pulpwood	954	975	937
Other industrial wood	221	184	141
Fuel wood*	38,269	38,448	38,521
Total	45,181	44,629	44,714

* FAO estimates.

Source: FAO.

SAWNWOOD PRODUCTION
('000 cubic metres, incl. railway sleepers)

	2004	2005	2006
Coniferous (softwood)	2,716	2,222	2,280
Broadleaved (hardwood)	246	452	549
Total	2,962	2,674	2,829

Source: FAO.

Fishing

('000 metric tons, live weight)

	2003	2004	2005
Capture	1,387.4	1,287.2	1,332.7*
Tilapias	62.4	68.7	64.6
California pilchard (sardine)	561.9	475.7	548.4
Yellowfin tuna	134.1	132.1	143.2
Marine shrimps and prawns	61.5	58.1	—
American cupped oyster	45.3	45.0	43.7
Jumbo flying squid	97.3	87.2	49.7
Aquaculture	84.5	104.4	117.5
Whiteleg shrimp	45.9	62.4	72.3
Total catch (incl. others)	1,471.9	1,391.5	1,450.4*

* FAO estimate.

Note: Figures exclude aquatic plants ('000 metric tons, capture only): 29.0 in 2003; 27.4 in 2004; 27.0 in 2005. Also excluded are aquatic mammals and crocodiles (recorded by number rather than by weight), shells and corals. The number of Morelet's crocodiles caught was: 1,037 in 2003; 609 in 2004; 855 in 2005. The catch of marine shells (metric tons) was: 170 in 2003; 183 in 2004; 190 in 2005.

Source: FAO.

MEXICO

Mining

(metric tons, unless otherwise indicated)

	2003	2004	2005
Antimony*	434	503	565
Arsenic*	1,729	1,828	1,664
Barytes	287,451	306,668	268,657
Bismuth*	1,064	1,014	970
Cadmium*	1,639	1,618	1,627
Coal	6,648,257	6,450,594	7,096,555
Coke	1,462,106	1,445,052	1,491,847
Copper*	303,765	352,286	373,252
Crude petroleum ('000 barrels per day)	3,371	3,383	3,333
Celestite	130,329	87,610	110,833
Diatomite	53,395	59,818	62,132
Dolomite	565,896	1,158,929	1,308,977
Feldspar	346,315	364,166	373,411
Flourite	756,258	842,698	875,450
Gas (million cu ft per day)	4,498	4,573	4,818
Gold (kg)*	22,177	21,818	26,762
Graphite	8,730	14,769	12,357
Gypsum	3,779,659	4,840,099	5,087,849
Kaolin	28,272	16,241	32,648
Iron*	6,759,198	6,889,538	7,012,306
Lead*	144,297	110,931	121,669
Manganese*	114,550	135,893	132,872
Molybdenum*	3,524	3,731	4,245
Salt	7,546,987	8,565,520	9,057,623
Silica	1,689,042	2,055,940	2,120,878
Silver*	2,945,710	2,452,872	2,565,586
Sulphur	1,051,968	1,121,546	1,016,822
Wollastonite	31,234	28,224	27,132
Zinc*	412,255	374,428	427,061

* Figures for metallic minerals refer to metal content of ores.

Industry

SELECTED PRODUCTS
('000 metric tons, unless otherwise indicated)

	2002	2003	2004
Wheat flour	2,619	2,647	2,609
Other cereal flour	1,614	1,588	n.a.
Raw sugar	2,736	2,852	3,094
Beer ('000 hectolitres)	63,530	65,462	67,575
Soft drinks ('000 hectolitres)	126,933	132,642	138,289
Cigarettes (million units)	54,704	41,856	40,752
Cotton yarn (pure and mixed)	17	29	n.a.
Tyres ('000 units)*	11,628	13,868	n.a.
Cement	33,372	33,594	34,992
Gas stoves—household ('000 units)	4,510	4,304	n.a.
Refrigerators—household ('000 units)	2,222	2,162	2,291
Washing machines—household ('000 units)	1,657	1,547	n.a.
Lorries, buses, tractors, etc. ('000 units)	504	516	n.a.
Passenger cars ('000 units)	1,247	1,028	n.a.
Electric energy (million kWh)	235,158	217,867	224,077

* Tyres for road motor vehicles.

Source: UN, *Industrial Commodity Statistics Yearbook*.

Finance

CURRENCY AND EXCHANGE RATES

Monetary Units
100 centavos = 1 Mexican nuevo peso.

Sterling, Dollar and Euro Equivalents (31 December 2007)
£1 sterling = 21.769 nuevos pesos;
US $1 = 10.866 nuevos pesos;
€1 = 15.996 nuevos pesos;
1,000 Mexican nuevos pesos = £45.94 = $92.03 = €62.52.

Average Exchange Rate (nuevos pesos per US $)
2005   10.8979
2006   10.8992
2007   10.9282

Note: Figures are given in terms of the nuevo (new) peso, introduced on 1 January 1993 and equivalent to 1,000 former pesos.

BUDGET*
(million new pesos)

Revenue	2005	2006	2007
Taxation	810,511	890,078	1,001,013
Income taxes	384,522	448,100	526,694
Value-added tax	318,432	380,576	409,079
Excise tax	49,627	−5,242	−6,732
Import duties	26,820	31,726	32,311
Other tax revenue	31,109	34,917	39,662
Other revenue	601,994	668,730	710,526
Total revenue	1,412,505	1,558,808	1,711,539

Expenditure	2005	2006	2007
Programmable expenditure	1,458,540	1,656,938	1,895,106
Current expenditure	1,171,190	1,321,397	1,491,414
Personal services	557,422	610,652	653,948
Transfers, subsidies and aid	202,606	223,592	292,264
Other current expenditure	411,163	487,153	545,203
Capital expenditure	287,350	335,541	403,692
Non-programmable expenditure	499,472	598,283	587,868
Interest and fees	210,186	250,065	238,955
Revenue sharing	278,892	329,337	332,563
Other	10,393	18,881	16,350
Total expenditure	1,958,012	2,255,221	2,482,974

* Figures refer to the consolidated accounts of the central Government, including government agencies and the national social security system. The budgets of state and local governments are excluded.

INTERNATIONAL RESERVES*
(US $ million at 31 December)

	2004	2005	2006
IMF special drawing rights	465	445	482
Reserve position in the Fund	898	594	340
Foreign exchange	62,778	73,015	75,448
Total	64,141	74,054	76,270

* Excluding gold reserves.

Source: IMF, *International Financial Statistics*.

MONEY SUPPLY
(million new pesos at 31 December)

	2004	2005	2006
Currency outside banks	300,982	335,904	389,282
Demand deposits at deposit money banks	442,239	529,988	599,188
Total money	743,221	865,891	988,470

Source: IMF, *International Financial Statistics*.

MEXICO

Statistical Survey

COST OF LIVING
(Consumer Price Index; base: 2000 = 100)

	2004	2005	2006
Food, beverages and tobacco	122.9	129.4	134.1
Clothing and footwear	110.9	112.1	113.5
Electricity, gas and other fuel	149.1	160.6	173.1
Rent	125.2	129.1	133.2
All items (incl. others)	122.3	127.2	131.8

Source: ILO.

NATIONAL ACCOUNTS
(million new pesos at current prices)

National Income and Product

	2002	2003	2004
Compensation of employees*	2,039,094	2,184,544	2,341,996
Operating surplus*	3,660,762	4,022,863	4,580,602
Taxes on production and imports	583,552	712,221	819,276
Less Subsidies	20,271	27,636	32,778
GDP in purchasers' values	6,263,137	6,891,992	7,709,096
Net factor income received from abroad	−14,829	23,375	74,464
Gross national product (GNP)	6,248,308	6,915,367	7,783,560

*Including consumption of fixed capital.

Expenditure on the Gross Domestic Product

	2005	2006	2007
Government final consumption expenditure	965,931	1,074,923	1,144,781
Private final consumption expenditure	5,704,780	6,191,714	6,723,612
Increase in stocks	208,225	140,611	42,121
Gross fixed capital formation	1,616,445	1,867,356	2,030,503
Total domestic expenditure	8,495,381	9,274,604	9,941,017
Exports of goods and services	2,508,403	2,916,551	3,176,101
Less Imports of goods and services	2,637,578	3,033,590	3,354,255
GDP in purchasers' values	8,366,205	9,157,565	9,762,864
GDP at constant 1993 prices	1,753,595	1,837,926	1,898,398

Gross Domestic Product by Economic Activity

	2005	2006	2007
Agriculture, forestry and fishing	287,344	319,598	350,955
Mining and quarrying	112,312	129,083	143,781
Manufacturing	1,333,950	1,480,974	1,579,198
Electricity, gas and water	101,067	117,190	127,480
Construction	401,478	470,617	500,366
Trade, restaurants and hotels	1,585,987	1,739,110	1,888,211
Transport, storage and communications	788,525	865,075	944,649
Finance, insurance, real estate and business services	982,256	1,063,896	1,151,034
Community, social and personal services	1,994,288	2,136,693	2,274,628
Sub-total	7,587,207	8,322,236	8,960,302
Less Imputed bank service charge	90,419	101,621	113,824
GDP at factor cost	7,496,787	8,220,615	8,846,477
Indirect taxes, *less* subsidies	869,418	936,950	916,387
GDP in purchasers' values	8,366,205	9,157,565	9,762,864

BALANCE OF PAYMENTS
(US $ million)

	2004	2005	2006
Exports of goods f.o.b.	187,999	214,233	249,997
Imports of goods f.o.b.	−196,810	−221,820	−256,131
Trade balance	−8,811	−7,587	−6,133
Exports of services	14,047	16,137	16,393
Imports of services	−19,779	−21,440	−22,833
Balance on goods and services	−14,543	−12,890	−12,574
Other income received	5,617	5,359	6,406
Other income paid	−14,811	−18,378	−19,950
Balance on goods, services and income	−23,738	−25,909	−26,118
Current transfers received	17,226	20,774	24,197
Current transfers paid	−80	−57	−88
Current balance	−6,592	−5,191	−2,008
Direct investment abroad	−4,432	−6,474	−5,759
Direct investment from abroad	22,777	20,960	19,212
Portfolio investment assets	1,718	—	—
Portfolio investment liabilities	5,238	8,366	1,296
Other investment assets	−9,051	−7,719	−11,913
Other investment liabilities	−3,939	−1,124	−4,999
Net errors and omissions	−1,615	−1,854	2,868
Overall balance	4,104	6,965	−1,303

Source: IMF, *International Financial Statistics*.

External Trade

PRINCIPAL COMMODITIES
(distribution by Harmonized System, US $ million)

Imports f.o.b.*	2005	2006	2007†
Live animals and products thereof	4,028.9	4,193.9	5,159.1
Vegetable products	5,177.0	6,155.5	7,581.0
Animal and vegetable oils and fats	761.8	755.2	1,065.5
Prepared food, beverages, spirits and tobacco	3,950.9	4,479.6	5,166.0
Mineral products	13,072.1	15,879.0	20,650.2
Chemicals and related industries	16,625.7	18,617.9	20,886.2
Plastics, rubber and articles thereof	17,500.9	19,547.1	20,144.9
Raw hides, skins, leather and furs	1,636.6	1,481.7	1,309.4
Wood, charcoal, cork, straw, etc.	1,353.1	1,436.1	1,517.4
Paper-making material; paper and paperboard and articles thereof	5,522.2	6,134.9	6,496.0
Textiles and textile articles	9,046.0	9,062.3	8,681.3
Footwear, headgear, umbrellas, etc.	517.7	586.9	643.4
Articles of stone, plaster, cement, asbestos, etc.; glass and glassware	2,027.5	2,219.6	2,427.0
Pearls, precious stones and metals and articles thereof; imitation jewelry and coins	752.9	1,032.4	1,226.8
Base metals and articles thereof	19,312.5	23,752.5	24,758.1
Machinery and mechanical appliances; electrical equipment, parts and accessories	84,202.6	96,375.4	103,492.0
Vehicles, aircraft, vessels and associated transport equipment	22,898.6	26,026.0	28,604.2
Optical, photographic, measuring, precision and medical apparatus; clocks and watches; musical instruments	7,283.5	10,258.5	13,068.4
Arms and ammunitions, parts and accessories	38.0	41.0	47.0
Miscellaneous manufactured articles	3,495.4	4,488.4	6,024.9
Works of art, collectors pieces, antiques	13.2	13.0	19.8
Other (incl. unclassified)	2,279.4	3,182.6	3,906.5
Total	221,819.5	256,058.4	283,233.4

*Figures include data for the *maquila* sector (US $ million): 74,903.1 in 2005; 86,527.3 in 2006; n.a. in 2007.
† Preliminary.

MEXICO

Exports f.o.b.*	2005	2006	2007†
Live animals and products thereof	1,515.7	1,729.6	1,790.7
Vegetable products	5,205.5	5,851.0	6,815.5
Animal and vegetable oils and fats	80.7	91.5	115.8
Prepared food, beverages, spirits and tobacco	4,878.2	5,982.7	6,303.2
Mineral products	33,162.0	40,042.4	44,286.7
Chemicals and related industries	6,261.0	6,894.3	7,127.8
Plastics, rubber and articles thereof	5,688.3	6,173.5	6,716.0
Raw hides, skins, leather and furs	526.9	549.1	565.9
Wood, charcoal, cork, straw, etc.	433.0	491.8	434.6
Paper-making material; paper and paperboard and articles thereof	1,714.8	1,862.8	1,920.8
Textiles and textile articles	9,555.2	8,451.1	7,318.2
Footwear, headgear, umbrellas, etc.	365.6	380.4	394.6
Articles of stone, plaster, cement, asbestos, etc.; glass and glassware	2,566.8	2,850.8	2,848.9
Pearls, precious stones and metals and articles thereof; imitation jewelry and coins	1,728.9	3,064.1	3,824.9
Base metals and articles thereof	10,889.6	13,267.1	15,073.5
Machinery and mechanical appliances; electrical equipment, parts and accessories	81,072.5	94,340.6	104,177.6
Vehicles, aircraft, vessels and associated transport equipment	33,087.3	40,889.0	43,937.2
Optical, photographic, measuring, precision and medical apparatus; clocks and watches; musical instruments	7,887.9	8,922.9	8,954.1
Arms and ammunitions, parts and accessories	17.0	17.5	17.6
Miscellaneous manufactured articles	7,074.1	7,393.1	8,060.7
Works of art, collectors pieces, antiques	9.7	10.9	8.2
Other (incl. unclassified)	511.9	696.9	677.0
Total	214,233.0	249,925.1	272,044.3

*Figures include data for the *maquila* sector (US $ million): 97,401.4 in 2005; 111,823.8 in 2006; n.a. in 2007.
† Preliminary.

PRINCIPAL TRADING PARTNERS*
(US $ million)

Imports c.i.f.	2005	2006	2007†
Argentina	1,302.8	1,798.5	1,610.2
Brazil	5,214.2	5,557.8	5,581.9
Canada	6,169.3	7,376.2	7,975.3
Chile	1,754.1	2,469.8	2,594.0
China, People's Republic	17,696.3	24,438.3	29,791.9
France	2,564.6	2,661.5	3,100.9
Germany	8,670.4	9,437.0	10,699.3
Italy	3,498.2	4,108.5	5,560.5
Japan	13,077.8	15,295.2	16,360.2
Korea, Republic	6,495.9	10,621.4	12,615.5
Malaysia	3,658.3	4,474.4	4,773.0
Philippines	1,322.9	1,232.3	1,198.5
Singapore	2,225.7	1,955.2	2,087.1
Spain	3,324.6	3,638.2	3,833.4
Switzerland	1,019.9	1,121.9	1,246.8
Taiwan	4,066.0	4,973.7	5,898.5
Thailand	1,557.8	1,783.9	2,106.1
United Kingdom	1,866.1	2,140.3	2,300.9
USA	118,973.6	130,854.2	140,569.9
Total (incl. others)	221,819.5	256,130.4	283,233.4

Exports f.o.b.	2005	2006	2007†
Aruba	1,447.6	1,469.4	1,517.8
Canada	4,234.5	5,176.2	6,494.4
China, People's Republic	1,135.6	1,688.1	1,895.9
Colombia	1,548.3	2,132.1	2,943.4
Germany	2,289.4	2,972.6	4,104.8
Japan	1,470.0	1,594.0	1,919.9
Spain	2,954.1	3,270.1	3,583.7
United Kingdom	1,188.3	924.9	1,563.2
USA	183,562.8	211,799.4	223,403.7
Venezuela	1,288.7	1,783.2	2,333.0
Total (incl. others)	214,233.0	249,925.1	272,044.3

* Imports by country of origin; exports by country of destination.
† Preliminary.

Transport

RAILWAYS
(traffic)

	2002	2003	2004
Passengers carried ('000)	237	270	253
Passenger-kilometres (million)	69	78	74
Freight carried ('000 tons)	80,451	85,168	88,097
Freight ton-kilometres (million)	51,616	54,132	54,387

Source: Dirección General de Planeación, Secretaría de Comunicaciones y Transportes.

ROAD TRAFFIC
('000 vehicles in use at 31 December, estimates)

	2002	2003	2004
Passenger cars	12,931	14,007	14,713
Lorries and vans	5,951	6,492	6,860
Buses	700	299	298
Motorcycles	385	442	n.a.

Source: IRF, *World Road Statistics*.

SHIPPING

Merchant Fleet
(registered at 31 December)

	2004	2005	2006
Number of vessels	687	718	753
Total displacement ('000 grt)	1,008.0	1,099.8	1,161.9

Source: Lloyd's Register-Fairplay, *World Fleet Statistics*.

Sea-borne Shipping
(domestic and international freight traffic, '000 metric tons)

	2002	2003	2004
Goods loaded	160,894	175,923	177,915
Goods unloaded	87,203	88,816	88,093

Source: Coordinación General de Puertos y Marina Mercante.

CIVIL AVIATION
(traffic on scheduled services)

	2002	2003	2004
Passengers carried ('000)	33,190	35,287	39,422
Freight carried ('000 tons)	389.0	410.0	466.7

Sources: Dirección General de Planeación, Secretaría de Comunicaciones y Transportes.

Tourism

	2004	2005	2006
Tourist arrivals ('000)	20,618	21,915	21,353
Border tourists ('000)	81,204	83,905	78,577
Total expenditure (US $ million)	10,796	11,803	12,177

Source: Secretaría de Turismo de México.

Communications Media

	2004	2005	2006
Telephone ('000 main lines in use)	18,073.2	19,512.0	19,860.9
Mobile cellular telephones ('000 subscribers)	38,451.1	47,141.0	57,016.4
Personal computers ('000 in use)	11,210	14,000	n.a.
Internet users ('000)	14,036.5	18,091.8	n.a.
Broadband subscribers ('000)	1,057.3	1,922.4	3,728.2

Radio receivers ('000 in use): 31,000 in 1997.

Television receivers ('000 in use): 28,000 in 2000.

Facsimile machines ('000 in use): 285 in 1997.

Daily newspapers (2000): Number 311; Average circulation 9,251,000.

Non-daily newspapers (2000): Number 26; Average circulation 614,000.

Books published (titles): 15,542 in 2002.

Sources: partly International Telecommunication Union; UNESCO Institute for Statistics; UNESCO, *Statistical Yearbook*; UN, *Statistical Yearbook*.

Education

(2005/06)

	Institutions	Teachers	Students ('000)
Pre-primary	84,337	197,841	4,452.2
Primary	98,045	561,342	14,548.2
Secondary (incl. technical)	32,012	348,235	5,979.3
Intermediate: professional/technical	1,561	31,040	357.2
Intermediate: Baccalaureate	11,280	224,889	3,301.6
Higher (incl. post-graduate)	4,977	261,889	2,446.7

Adult literacy rate (UNESCO estimates): 91.6% (males 93.2%; females 90.2%) in 2005 (Source: UNESCO Institute for Statistics).

Directory

The Constitution

The present Mexican Constitution was proclaimed on 5 February 1917, at the end of the revolution, which began in 1910, against the regime of Porfirio Díaz. Its provisions regarding religion, education and the ownership and exploitation of mineral wealth reflect the long revolutionary struggle against the concentration of power in the hands of the Roman Catholic Church and the large landowners, and the struggle which culminated, in the 1930s, in the expropriation of the properties of the foreign petroleum companies. It has been amended from time to time.

GOVERNMENT

The President and Congress

The President of the Republic, in agreement with the Cabinet and with the approval of the Congreso de la Unión (Congress) or of the Permanent Committee when the Congreso is not in session, may suspend constitutional guarantees in case of foreign invasion, serious disturbance, or any other emergency endangering the people.

The exercise of supreme executive authority is vested in the President, who is elected for six years and enters office on 1 December of the year of election. The presidential powers include the right to appoint and remove members of the Cabinet and the Attorney-General; to appoint, with the approval of the Senado (Senate), diplomatic officials, the higher officers of the army, and ministers of the supreme and higher courts of justice. The President is also empowered to dispose of the Armed Forces for the internal and external security of the federation.

The Congreso is composed of the Cámara Federal de Diputados (Federal Chamber of Deputies) elected every three years, and the Senado whose members hold office for six years. There is one deputy for every 250,000 people and for every fraction of over 125,000 people. The Senado is composed of two members for each state and two for the Distrito Federal. Regular sessions of the Congreso begin on 1 September and may not continue beyond 31 December of the same year. Extraordinary sessions may be convened by the Permanent Committee.

The powers of the Congreso include the right to: pass laws and regulations; impose taxes; specify the criteria on which the Executive may negotiate loans; declare war; raise, maintain and regulate the organization of the Armed Forces; establish and maintain schools of various types throughout the country; approve or reject the budget; sanction appointments submitted by the President of the Supreme Court and magistrates of the superior court of the Distrito Federal; approve or reject treaties and conventions made with foreign powers; and ratify diplomatic appointments.

The Permanent Committee, consisting of 29 members of the Congreso (15 of whom are deputies and 14 senators), officiates when the Congreso is in recess, and is responsible for the convening of extraordinary sessions of the Congreso.

The States

Governors are elected by popular vote in a general election every six years. The local legislature is formed by deputies, who are changed every three years. The judicature is specially appointed under the Constitution by the competent authority (it is never subject to the popular vote).

Each state is a separate unit, with the right to levy taxes and to legislate in certain matters. The states are not allowed to levy interstate customs duties.

The Federal District

The Distrito Federal (DF) consists of Mexico City and several neighbouring small towns and villages. The first direct elections for the Head of Government of the Distrito Federal were held in July 1997; hitherto a Regent had been appointed by the President.

EDUCATION

According to the Constitution, the provision of educational facilities is the joint responsibility of the federation, the states and the municipalities. Education shall be democratic, and shall be directed to developing all the faculties of the individual students, while imbuing them with love of their country and a consciousness of international solidarity and justice. Religious bodies may not provide education, except training for the priesthood. Private educational institutions must conform to the requirements of the Constitution with regard to the nature of the teaching given. The education provided by the states shall be free of charge.

RELIGION

Religious bodies of whatever denomination shall not have the capacity to possess or administer real estate or capital invested therein. Churches are the property of the nation; the headquarters of bishops, seminaries, convents and other property used for the propagation of a religious creed shall pass into the hands of the state, to be dedicated to the public service of the federation or of the respective state. Institutions of charity, provided they are not connected with a religious body, may hold real property. The establishment of monastic orders is prohibited. Ministers of religion must be Mexican; they may not criticize the fundamental laws of the country in a public or private meeting; they may not vote or form associations for political purposes. Political meetings may not be held in places of worship.

A reform proposal, whereby constitutional restrictions on the Catholic Church were formally ended, received congressional approval in December 1991 and was promulgated as law in January 1992.

LAND AND MINERAL OWNERSHIP

Article 27 of the Constitution vests direct ownership of minerals and other products of the subsoil, including petroleum and water, in the nation, and reserves to the Federal Government alone the right to grant concessions in accordance with the laws to individuals and companies, on the condition that they establish regular work for the exploitation of the materials. At the same time, the right to acquire ownership of lands and waters belonging to the nation, or concessions for their exploitation, is limited to Mexican individuals and companies, although the State may concede similar rights to foreigners who agree not to invoke the protection of their governments to enforce such rights.

The same article declares null all alienations of lands, waters and forests belonging to towns or communities made by political chiefs or other local authorities in violation of the provisions of the law of 25 June 1856*, and all concessions or sales of communally held lands, waters and forests made by the federal authorities after 1 December 1876. The population settlements which lack ejidos (state-owned smallholdings), or cannot obtain restitution of lands previously held, shall be granted lands in proportion to the needs of the population. The area of land granted to the individual may not be less than 10 hectares of irrigated or watered land, or the equivalent in other kinds of land.

The owners affected by decisions to divide and redistribute land (with the exception of the owners of farming or cattle-rearing properties) shall not have any right of redress, nor may they invoke the right of amparo† in protection of their interests. They may, however, apply to the Government for indemnification. Small properties, the areas of which are defined in the Constitution, will not be subject to expropriation. The Constitution leaves to the Congreso the duty of determining the maximum size of rural properties.

In March 1992 an agrarian reform amendment, whereby the programme of land-distribution established by the 1917 Constitution was abolished and the terms of the ejido system of tenant farmers were relaxed, was formally adopted.

Monopolies and measures to restrict competition in industry, commerce or public services are prohibited.

A section of the Constitution deals with work and social security.

POLITICAL ORGANIZATIONS AND ELECTORAL PROCEDURE

In December 1977 a Federal Law on Political Organizations and Electoral Procedure was promulgated. It includes the following provisions:

Legislative power is vested in the Congreso de la Unión which comprises the Cámara Federal de Diputados and the Senado. The Cámara shall comprise 300 deputies elected by majority vote within single-member electoral districts and up to 100 deputies (increased to 200 from July 1988) elected by a system of proportional representation from regional lists within multi-member constituencies. The Senado comprises two members for each state and two for the Distrito Federal, elected by majority vote.

Executive power is exercised by the President of the Republic of the United Mexican States, elected by majority vote.

Ordinary elections will be held every three years for the federal deputies and every six years for the senators and the President of the Republic on the first Sunday of July of the year in question. When a vacancy occurs among members of the Congreso elected by majority vote, the house in question shall call extraordinary elections, and when a vacancy occurs among members of the Cámara elected by proportional representation it shall be filled by the candidate of the same party who received the next highest number of votes at the last ordinary election.

Voting is the right and duty of every citizen, male or female, over the age of 18 years.

A political party shall be registered if it has at least 3,000 members in each one of at least half the states in Mexico or at least 300 members in each one of at least half of the single-member constituencies. In either case the total number of members must be no less than 65,000. A party can also obtain conditional registration if it has been active for at least four years. Registration is confirmed if the party obtains at least 1.5% of the popular vote. All political parties shall have free access to the media.

In September 1993 an amendment to the Law on Electoral Procedure provided for the expansion of the Senado to 128 seats, representing four members for each state and the Distrito Federal, three to be elected by majority vote and one by proportional representation.

* The Lerdo Law against ecclesiastical privilege, which became the basis of the Liberal Constitution of 1857.
† The Constitution provides for the procedure known as *juicio de amparo*, a wider form of habeas corpus, which the individual may invoke in protection of his constitutional rights.

The Government

HEAD OF STATE

President: Felipe Calderón Hinojosa (took office 1 December 2006).

CABINET
(March 2008)

Secretary of the Interior: Juan Camilo Mouriño Terrazo.
Secretary of Foreign Affairs: Patricia Espinosa Cantellano.
Secretary of Finance and Public Credit: Agustín Carstens Carstens.
Secretary of National Defence: Gen. Guillermo Galván Galván.
Secretary of the Navy: Adm. Mariano Francisco Saynez Mendoza.
Secretary of the Economy: Eduardo Sojo Garza-Aldape.
Secretary of Social Development: Ernesto Cordero Arroyo.
Secretary of Public Security: Genaro García Luna.
Secretary of Public Function: Salvador Vega Casillas.
Secretary of Communications and Transport: Luis Téllez Kuenzler.
Secretary of Labour and Social Welfare: Javier Lozano Alarcón.
Secretary of the Environment and Natural Resources: Juan Rafael Elvira Quesada.
Secretary of Energy: Georgina Kessel Martínez.
Secretary of Agriculture, Livestock, Rural Development, Fisheries and Food: Alberto Cárdenas Jiménez.
Secretary of Public Education: Josefina Vázquez Mota.
Secretary of Health: José Angel Córdova Villalobos.
Secretary of Tourism: Rodolfo Elizondo Torres.
Secretary of Agrarian Reform: Abelardo Escobar Prieto.
Procurator-General: Eduardo Medina-Mora Icaza.

SECRETARIATS OF STATE

Office of the President: Los Pinos, Col. San Miguel Chapultepec, 11850 México, DF; tel. (55) 5091-1100; fax (55) 5277-2376; e-mail felipe.calderon@presidencia.gob.mx; internet www.presidencia.gob.mx.

Secretariat of State for Agrarian Reform: Edif. de Avda Heroica, 1°, Escuela Naval Militar 701, Col. Presidentes Ejidales, Del. Coyoacán, 04470 México, DF; tel. (55) 5695-6776; fax (55) 5695-6368; e-mail sra@sra.gob.mx; internet www.sra.gob.mx.

Secretariat of State for Agriculture, Livestock, Rural Development, Fisheries and Food: Avda Municipio Libre 377, Col. Santa Cruz Atoyac, Del. Benito Juárez, 03310 México, DF; tel. (55) 9183-1000; fax (55) 9183-1018; e-mail ofsec@sagarpa.gob.mx; internet www.sagarpa.gob.mx.

Secretariat of State for Communications and Transport: Avda Xola y Universidad, Col. Narvarte, Del. Benito Juárez, 03020 México, DF; tel. (55) 5723-9300; fax (55) 5530-0093; e-mail buzon_ucg@sct.gob.mx; internet www.sct.gob.mx.

Secretariat of State for the Economy: Alfonso Reyes 30, Col. Hipódromo Condesa, 06170 México, DF; tel. (55) 5729-9100; fax (55) 5729-9320; internet www.economia.gob.mx.

Secretariat of State for Energy: Insurgentes Sur 890, 17°, Col. del Valle, 03100 México, DF; tel. (55) 5000-6000; fax (55) 5000-6222; e-mail acastellanos@energia.gob.mx; internet www.energia.gob.mx.

Secretariat of State for the Environment and Natural Resources: Blvd Adolfo Ruíz Cortines 4209, Col. Jardines en la Montaña, Tlalpan, 14210 México, DF; tel. (55) 5628-0602; fax (55) 5628-0643; e-mail contactodgeia@semarnat.gob.mx; internet www.semarnat.gob.mx.

Secretariat of State for Finance and Public Credit: Palacio Nacional, Primer Patio Mariano, 3°, Of. 3045, Col. Centro, Del. Cuauhtémoc, 06000 México, DF; tel. (55) 9158-2000; fax (55) 9158-1142; e-mail secretario@hacienda.gob.mx; internet www.hacienda.gob.mx.

Secretariat of State for Foreign Affairs: Avda Ricardo Flores Magón 2, Col. Guerrero, Del. Cuauhtémoc, 06995 México, DF; tel. (55) 5063-3000; fax (55) 5063-3195; e-mail comentario@sre.gob.mx; internet www.sre.gob.mx.

Secretariat of State for Health: Lieja 7, 1°, Col. Juárez, Del. Cuauhtémoc, 06600 México, DF; tel. (55) 5286-2383; fax (55) 5553-7917; e-mail afrias@salud.gob.mx; internet www.salud.gob.mx.

Secretariat of State for the Interior: Bucareli 99, Col. Juárez, 06069 México, DF; tel. (55) 5592-1141; fax (55) 5546-5350; internet www.gobernacion.gob.mx.

Secretariat of State for Labour and Social Welfare: Edif. A, 4°, Anillo Periférico Sur 4271, Col. Fuentes del Pedregal, 14149 México, DF; tel. (55) 5645-3965; fax (55) 5645-5594; e-mail correo@stps.gob.mx; internet www.stps.gob.mx.

Secretariat of State for National Defence: Blvd Manuel Avila Camacho, esq. Avda Industria Militar, 3°, Col. Lomas de Sotelo, Del.

MEXICO

Miguel Hidalgo, 11640 México, DF; tel. (55) 5557-5571; fax (55) 5395-2935; e-mail ggalvang@mail.sedena.gob.mx; internet www.sedena.gob.mx.

Secretariat of State for the Navy: Eje 2 oriente, Tramo Heroica, Escuela Naval Militar 861, Col. Los Cipreses, Del. Coyoacán, 04830 México, DF; tel. (55) 5624-6500; e-mail srio@semar.gob.mx; internet www.semar.gob.mx.

Secretariat of State for Public Education: Dinamarca 84, 5°, Col. Juárez, 06600 México, DF; tel. (55) 5510-2557; fax (55) 5329-6873; e-mail educa@sep.gob.mx; internet www.sep.gob.mx.

Secretariat of State for Public Function: Insurgentes Sur 1735, 10°, Col. Guadalupe Inn, Del. Alvaro Obregón, 01020 México, DF; tel. (55) 1454-3000; e-mail sactel@funcionpublica.gob.mx; internet www.funcionpublica.gob.mx.

Secretariat of State for Public Security: Londres 102, 7°, Col. Juárez, 06600 México, DF; e-mail enlace@ssp.gob.mx; internet www.ssp.gob.mx.

Secretariat of State for Social Development: Avda Reforma 116, Col. Juárez, Del. Cuauhtémoc, 06600 México, DF; tel. (55) 5328-5000; e-mail secretariadelramo@sedesol.gob.mx; internet www.sedesol.gob.mx.

Secretariat of State for Tourism: Presidente Masaryk 172, Col. Chapultepec Morales, 11587 México, DF; tel. (55) 3002-6300; fax (55) 1036-0789; internet www.sectur.gob.mx.

Office of the Procurator-General: Avda Paseo de la Reforma 211–213, Col. Cuauhtémoc, Del. Cuauhtémoc, 06500 México, DF; tel. (55) 5346-0114; fax (55) 5346-0908; e-mail ofproc@pgr.gob.mx; internet www.pgr.gob.mx.

State Governors
(March 2008)

Aguascalientes: Luis Armando Reynoso (PAN).
Baja California: José Guadalupe Osuna Millán (PAN).
Baja California Sur: Narciso Agúndez (PRD).
Campeche: Jorge Carlos Hurtado Valdez (PRI).
Chiapas: Juan José Sabines Guerrero (PRD).
Chihuahua: José Reyes Baeza (PRI).
Coahuila (de Zaragoza): Humberto Moreira Valdes (PRI).
Colima: Jesús Silverio Cavazos Ceballos (PRI-PT-PVEM).
Durango: Ismael Hernández Deras (PRI).
Guanajuato: Juan Manuel Oliva Ramírez (PAN).
Guerrero: Zeferino Torreblanco (PRD).
Hidalgo: Miguel Angel Osorio Chong (PRI).
Jalisco: Emilio González Márquez (PAN).
México: Enrique Peña Nieto (PRI).
Michoacán (de Ocampo): Leonel Godoy Rangel (PRD).
Morelos: Marco Antonio Adame Castillo (PAN).
Nayarit: Ney González Sánchez (PRI).
Nuevo León: José Natividad González Parás (PRI-PVEM-PLM-Fuerza Ciudadana).
Oaxaca: Ulises Ruíz (PRI).
Puebla: Mario Marín Torres (PRI).
Querétaro (de Arteaga): Francisco Garrido Patrón (PAN).
Quintana Roo: Félix González Canto (PRI).
San Luis Potosí: Marcelo de los Santos Fraga (PAN).
Sinaloa: Jesús Aguilar Padilla (PRI).
Sonora: José Eduardo Robinson Bours Castelo (PRI-PVEM).
Tabasco: Andrés Rafael Granier Melo (PRI).
Tamaulipas: Eugenio Hernández Flores (PRI).
Tlaxcala: Mariano González Zarur (PRI).
Veracruz-Llave: Fidel Herrera (PRI).
Yucatán: Ivonne Ortega Pacheco (PRI).
Zacatecas: Amalia García Medina (PRD).
Head of Government of the Distrito Federal: Marcelo Luis Ebrard Casaubon (PRD).

President and Legislature

PRESIDENT

Election, 2 July 2006

Candidate	Number of votes	% of votes
Felipe Calderón Hinojosa (PAN)	14,916,927	35.89
Andrés Manuel López Obrador (Por el Bien de Todos*)	14,683,096	35.33
Roberto Madrazo Pintado (Alianza por México†)	9,237,000	22.23
Patricia Mercado Castro (PASC‡)	1,124,280	2.71
Roberto Campa Cifrián (Nueva Alianza)	397,550	0.96
Total§	41,557,430	100.00

* An alliance of the PRD, the PT and Convergencia.
† An alliance of the PRI and the PVEM.
‡ The Partido Alternativa Socialdemócrata y Campesina, subsequently renamed the Partido Socialdemócrata.
§ Including 900,373 invalid votes and 298,204 votes for unregistered candidates.

CONGRESO DE LA UNIÓN

Senado

Senate: Xicoténcatl 9, Centro Histórico, 06010 México, DF; tel. (55) 5130-2200; internet www.senado.gob.mx.

President: Santiago Creel Miranda (PAN).

Elections, 2 July 2006

Party	Seats
Partido Acción Nacional (PAN)	52
Partido Revolucionario Institucional (PRI)*	33
Partido de la Revolución Democrática (PRD)†	29
Partido Verde Ecologista de México (PVEM)*	6
Convergencia†	5
Partido del Trabajo (PT)†	2
Nueva Alianza	1
Total	128

* Part of the Alianza por México.
† Part of the Por el Bien de Todos alliance.

Cámara Federal de Diputados

Federal Chamber of Deputies: Avda Congreso de la Unión 66, Col. El Parque, Del. Venustiano Carranza, 15969 México, DF; tel. (55) 5628-1300; internet www.diputados.gob.mx.

President: Ruth Zavaleta Salgado (PRD).

Elections, 2 July 2006

Party	Seats
Partido Acción Nacional (PAN)	206
Partido de la Revolución Democrática (PRD)*	126
Partido Revolucionario Institucional (PRI)†	104
Partido Verde Ecologista de México (PVEM)†	19
Convergencia*	16
Partido del Trabajo (PT)*	16
Nueva Alianza	9
Partido Alternativa Socialdemócrata y Campesina (PASC)‡	4
Total	500

* Part of the Por el Bien de Todos alliance.
† Part of the Alianza por México.
‡ Subsequently renamed the Partido Socialdemócrata.

Election Commission

Instituto Federal Electoral (IFE): Viaducto Tlalpan 100, Col. Arenal Tepepan, Del. Tlalpan, 14610 México, DF; e-mail info@ife.org.mx; internet www.ife.org.mx; f. 1990; independent; Pres. Leonardo Valdés Zurita.

MEXICO

Political Organizations

To retain legal political registration, parties must secure at least 1.5% of total votes at two consecutive federal elections. In 2006 eight national political parties were registered.

Convergencia: Louisiana 113, Col. Nápoles, Del. Benito Juárez, 03810 México, DF; tel. (55) 5543-8517; e-mail convergencia@prodigy.net.mx; internet www.convergencia.org.mx; f. 1995 as Convergencia por la Democracia; part of the Por el Bien de Todos alliance formed to contest 2006 presidential election, later renamed the Frente Amplio Progresista; Pres. LUIS VENEGAS MALDONADO; Sec.-Gen. PEDRO JIMÉNEZ LEÓN.

Partido Acción Nacional (PAN): Avda Coyoacán 1546, Col. del Valle, Del. Benito Juárez, 03100 México, DF; tel. (55) 5200-4000; e-mail correo@cen.pan.org.mx; internet www.pan.org.mx; f. 1939; democratic party; 150,000 mems; Pres. GERMÁN MARTÍNEZ CÁZARES; Sec.-Gen. GUILLERMO ANAYA LLAMAS.

Partido Socialdemócrata (PSD): Avda Insurgentes Sur 1942, Col. Florida, Del. Alvaro Obregón, 01030 México, DF; tel. (55) 9150-5191; fax (55) 9150-5190; e-mail info@alternativa.org.mx; internet www.alternativa.org.mx; f. 2005 as Partido Alternativa Socialdemócrata y Campesina; adopted current name 2008; progressive and peasants' rights; Pres. ALBERTO BEGNÉ GUERRA.

Partido Popular Socialista de México (PPS): Avda Alvaro Obregón 185, Col. Roma, Del. Cuauhtémoc, 06797 México, DF; tel. (55) 5672-2057; fax (55) 5609-1896; e-mail ppsm@ppsm.org.mx; internet www.ppsm.org.mx; f. 1948; Marxist-Leninist; First Sec. CUAUHTÉMOC AMEZCUA DROMUNDO.

Partido de la Revolución Democrática (PRD): Avda Benjamín Franklin 84, Col. Escandón, 11800 México, DF; tel. (55) 1085-8000; fax (55) 1085-8144; e-mail comunicacion@prd.org.mx; internet www.prd.org.mx; f. 1989; centre-left; leading mem. of the Por el Bien de Todos alliance formed to contest 2006 presidential election, later renamed the Frente Amplio Progresista; factions include Izquierda Unida (supporters of Andrés Manuel López Obrador's claim to the presidency) and Nueva Izquierda; Pres. LEONEL COTA MONTAÑO; Sec.-Gen. GUADALUPE ACOSTA NARANJO.

Partido Revolucionario Institucional (PRI): Edif. 2, Insurgentes Norte 59, Col. Buenavista, Del. Cuauhtémoc, 06359 México, DF; tel. (55) 5729-9600; internet www.pri.org.mx; f. 1929 as the Partido Nacional Revolucionario; regarded as the natural successor to the victorious parties of the revolutionary period; broadly based and centrist; formed Alianza por el México alliance with PVEM to contest 2006 presidential election; Pres. BEATRIZ ELENA PAREDES RANGEL; Sec.-Gen. JESÚS MURILLO KARAM; groups within the PRI include: the Corriente Crítica Progresista, the Corriente Crítica del Partido, la Corriente Constitucionalista Democratizadora, Corriente Nuevo PRI XIV Asamblea, Democracia 2000, México Nuevo and Galileo.

Partido del Trabajo (PT): Avda Cuauhtémoc 47, Col. Roma Norte, 06700 México, DF; tel. and fax (55) 5525-6287; internet www.partidodeltrabajo.org.mx; f. 1990; labour party; part of the Por el Bien de Todos alliance formed to contest 2006 presidential election, later renamed the Frente Amplio Progresista; Leader ALBERTO ANAYA GUTIÉRREZ.

Partido Verde Ecologista de México (PVEM): Loma Bonita 18, Col. Lomas Altas, 11950 México, DF; tel. and fax (55) 5257-0188; internet www.pvem.org.mx; f. 1987; ecologist party; formed Alianza por el México alliance with PRI to contest 2006 presidential election; Pres. JORGE EMILIO GONZÁLEZ MARTÍNEZ; Sec.-Gen. NATALIA ESCUDERO BARRERA.

The following parties are not officially registered but continue to be politically active:

Fuerza Ciudadana: Rochester 94, Col. Nápoles, 03810 México, DF; tel. (55) 5534-4628; e-mail info@fuerzaciudadana.org.mx; internet www.fuerzaciudadana.org.mx; f. 2002; citizens' ascn; Pres. JORGE ALCOCER VILLANUEVA; Dir-Gen. KARYNA GARCÍA CASTILLO URDIALES.

Nueva Alianza: Durango 199, Col. Roma, Del. Cuauhtémoc, 06700 México, DF; tel. (55) 3685-8485; e-mail contacto@nueva-alianza.org.mx; internet www.nueva-alianza.org.mx; f. 2005 by dissident faction of the PRI; includes mems of the Sindicato Nacional de Trabajadores de la Educación (SNTE, see Trade Unions) and supporters of Elba Esther Gordillo Morales; Pres. JORGE KAHWAGI MACARI; Sec.-Gen. SONIA RINCÓN CHANONA.

Partido Democrático Popular Revolucionario: f. 1996; political grouping representing the causes of 14 armed peasant orgs, including the EPR and the PROCUP.

Partido Revolucionario Obrerista y Clandestino de Unión Popular (PROCUP): peasant org.

Illegal organizations active in Mexico include the following:

Ejército Popular Revolucionario (EPR): e-mail pdprepr@hotmail.com; internet www.pdpr-epr.org; f. 1994; left-wing guerrilla group active mainly in southern states, linked to the Partido Democrático Popular Revolucionario (q.v.).

Ejército Revolucionario Popular Insurgente (ERPI): f. 1996; left-wing guerrilla group active in Guerrero, Morelos and Oaxaca; Leader JACOBO SILVA NOGALES.

Ejército Zapatista de Liberación Nacional (EZLN): e-mail laotra@ezln.org.mx; internet www.ezln.org.mx; f. 1993; left-wing guerrilla group active in the Chiapas region; Leader 'Subcomandante MARCOS'.

Frente Democrático Oriental de México Emiliano Zapata (FDOMEZ): peasant org.

Other armed groups include the Tendencia Democrática Revolucionaria-Ejército del Pueblo and the Comando Popular Revolucionario—La Patria es Primero.

Diplomatic Representation

EMBASSIES IN MEXICO

Algeria: Sierra Madre 540, Col. Lomas de Chapultepec, Del. Miguel Hidalgo, 11000 México, DF; tel. (55) 5520-6950; fax (55) 5540-7579; e-mail embajadadeargelia@yahoo.com.mx; Ambassador MERZAK BELHIMEUR.

Angola: Gaspar de Zúñiga 226, Col. Lomas de Chapultepec, Sección Virreyes, Del. Miguel Hidalgo, 11000 México, DF; tel. (55) 5202-4421; fax (55) 5540-5928; e-mail info@embangolamex.org; Ambassador JOSÉ JAIME FURTADO GONÇALVEZ.

Argentina: Avda Palmas 910, Col. Lomas de Chapultepec, Del. Miguel Hidalgo, 11000 México, DF; tel. (55) 5520-9430; fax (55) 5540-5011; e-mail embajadaargentina@prodigy.net.mx; Ambassador JORGE RAÚL YOMA.

Australia: Rubén Darío 55, Col. Polanco, Del. Miguel Hidalgo, 11580 México, DF; tel. (55) 1101-2200; fax (55) 1101-2201; e-mail dima-mexico.city@dfat.gov.au; internet www.mexico.embassy.gov.au; Ambassador KATRINA ANNE COOPER.

Austria: Sierra Tarahumara 420, Col. Lomas de Chapultepec, Del. Miguel Hidalgo, 11000 México, DF; tel. (55) 5251-1606; fax (55) 5245-0198; e-mail mexiko-ob@bmaa.gv.at; internet www.embajadadeaustria.com.mx; Ambassador Dr WERNER DRUML.

Belgium: Alfredo Musset 41, Col. Polanco, Del. Miguel Hidalgo, 11550 México, DF; tel. (55) 5280-0758; fax (55) 5280-0208; e-mail mexico@diplobel.org; internet www.diplomatie.be/mexico; Ambassador GUSTAVUS J. M. DIERCKX.

Belize: Bernardo de Gálvez 215, Col. Lomas de Chapultepec, Del. Miguel Hidalgo, 11000 México, DF; tel. (55) 5520-1274; fax (55) 5520-6089; e-mail embelize@prodigy.net.mx; Ambassador SALVADOR AMÍN FIGUEROA.

Bolivia: Goethe 104, Col. Anzures, Del. Miguel Hidalgo, 11590 México, DF; tel. and fax (55) 5255-3620; e-mail embajada@embol.org.mx; internet www.embol.org.mx; Ambassador JORGE MANSILLA TORRES.

Brazil: Lope de Armendáriz 130, Col. Lomas Virreyes, Del. Miguel Hidalgo, 11000 México, DF; tel. (55) 5201-4531; fax (55) 5520-4929; e-mail embrasil@brasil.org.mx; internet www.brasil.org.mx; Ambassador IVÁN OLIVEIRA CANNABRAVA.

Bulgaria: Paseo de la Reforma 1990, Col. Lomas de Chapultepec, Del. Miguel Hidalgo, 11000 México, DF; tel. (55) 5596-3283; fax (55) 5596-1012; e-mail ebulgaria@yahoo.com; Ambassador SERGEY PENCHEV MICHEV.

Canada: Schiller 529, Col. Polanco, Del. Miguel Hidalgo, 11560 México, DF; tel. (55) 5724-7900; fax (55) 5724-7980; e-mail embajada@canada.org.mx; internet www.canada.org.mx; Ambassador GUILLERMO E. RISHCHYNSKI.

Chile: Andrés Bello 10, 18°, Col. Polanco, Del. Miguel Hidalgo, 11560 México, DF; tel. (55) 5280-9681; fax (55) 5280-9703; e-mail echilmex@prodigy.net.mx; internet www.embajadadechile.com.mx; Ambassador GERMÁN GUERRERO PAVEZ.

China, People's Republic: Avda San Jerónimo 217B, Del. Alvaro Obregón, 01090 México, DF; tel. (55) 5616-0609; fax (55) 5616-0460; e-mail embchina@adetel.net.mx; internet www.embajadachina.org.mx; Ambassador YIN HENGMIN.

Colombia: Paseo de la Reforma 379, 1°, 5° y 6°, Col. Cuauhtémoc, Del. Cuauhtémoc, 06500 México, DF; tel. (55) 5525-0277; fax (55) 5208-2876; e-mail emcolmex@prodigy.net.mx; internet www.colombiaenmexico.org; Ambassador LUIS CAMILO OSORIO ISAZA.

Costa Rica: Río Po 113, Col. Cuauhtémoc, Del. Cuauhtémoc, 06500 México, DF; tel. (55) 5525-7764; fax (55) 5511-9240; e-mail embcrica@ri.redint.com; Ambassador GIOCONDA UBEDA RIVERA.

Côte d'Ivoire: Tennyson 67, Col. Polanco, Del. Miguel Hidalgo, 11560 México, DF; tel. 5280-8573; fax 5282-2954; Ambassador ANNE GNAHOURET TATRET.

MEXICO

Cuba: Presidente Masaryk 554, Col. Polanco, Del. Miguel Hidalgo, 11560 México, DF; tel. and fax (55) 5280-8039; e-mail cancilleria@embacuba.com.mx; internet www.embacuba.com.mx; Ambassador Manuel Francisco Aguilera de la Páz.

Cyprus: Sierra Gorda 370, Col. Lomas de Chapultepec, Del. Miguel Hidalgo, 11000 México, DF; tel. (55) 5202-7600; fax (55) 5520-2693; e-mail chipre@att.net.mx; Ambassador Antonis Grivas.

Czech Republic: Cuvier 22, Col. Nueva Anzures, Del. Miguel Hidalgo, 11590 México, DF; tel. (55) 5531-2777; fax (55) 5531-1837; e-mail mexico@embassy.mzv.cz; internet www.mzv.cz/mexico; Ambassador Jiří Havlík.

Denmark: Tres Picos 43, Col. Chapultepec Morales, Del. Miguel Hidalgo, 11580 México, DF; tel. (55) 5255-3405; fax (55) 5545-5797; e-mail mexamb@um.dk; internet www.ambmexicocity.um.dk; Ambassador Johannes Dahl-Hansen.

Dominican Republic: Bahía Magdalena 148, Of. 307, (entre Bahía de Caracas y Bahía de las Palmas), Col. Verónica Anzures, Del. Miguel Hidalgo, 11300 México, DF; tel. and fax (55) 5260-7262; e-mail embajada@ambadom.org.mx; internet www.embadom.org.mx; Ambassador Pablo A. Mariñez Alvarez.

Ecuador: Tennyson 217, Col. Polanco, Del. Miguel Hidalgo, 11560 México, DF; tel. (55) 5545-3141; fax (55) 5254-2442; e-mail mecuamex@prodigy.net.mx; Ambassador Galo Galarza Dávila.

Egypt: Alejandro Dumas 131, Col. Polanco, Del. Miguel Hidalgo, 11560 México, DF; tel. (55) 5281-0823; fax (55) 5282-1294; e-mail embofegypt@prodigy.net.mx; Ambassador Aly Hosussam Eldin Elhefny Mahmoud.

El Salvador: Temístocles 88, Col. Polanco, Del. Miguel Hidalgo, 11560 México, DF; tel. (55) 5281-5725; fax (55) 5280-0657; e-mail embesmex@webtelmex.net.mx; Ambassador Hugo Roberto Carrillo Corleto.

Finland: Monte Pelvoux 111, 4°, Col. Lomas de Chapultepec, Del. Miguel Hidalgo, 11000 México, DF; tel. (55) 5540-6036; fax (55) 5540-0114; e-mail finmex@prodigy.net.mx; internet www.finlandia.org.mx; Ambassador Ulla Marianna Vaisto.

France: Campos Elíseos 339, Col. Polanco, Del. Miguel Hidalgo, 11560 México, DF; tel. (55) 9171-9700; fax (55) 9171-9703; e-mail prensa@ambafrance-mx.org; internet www.ambafrance-mx.org; Ambassador Alain Le Gourriérec.

Germany: Horacio 1506, Col. Los Morales, Del. Miguel Hidalgo, 11530 México, DF; tel. (55) 5283-2200; fax (55) 5281-2588; e-mail info@mexi.diplo.de; internet www.mexiko.diplo.de; Ambassador Dr Roland Michael Wegener.

Greece: Sierra Gorda 505, Col. Lomas de Chapultepec, Del. Miguel Hidalgo, 11010 México, DF; tel. (55) 5520-2070; fax (55) 5202-4080; e-mail grecemb@prodigy.net.mx; Ambassador Alexander Migliaressis.

Guatemala: Explanada 1025, Col. Lomas de Chapultepec, Del. Miguel Hidalgo, 11000 México, DF; tel. (55) 5540-7520; fax (55) 5202-1142; e-mail embaguatemx@minex.gob.gt; Chargé d'affaires a.i. Eduardo Antonio Escobedo Sanabria.

Haiti: Presa Don Martín 53, Col. Irrigación, Del. Miguel Hidalgo, 11500 México, DF; tel. (55) 5557-2065; fax (55) 5395-1654; e-mail ambadh@mail.internet.com.mx; Ambassador Idalbert Pierre-Jean.

Holy See: Juan Pablo II 118, Col. Guadalupe Inn, Del. Alvaro Obregón, 01020 México, DF; tel. (55) 5663-3999; fax (55) 5663-5308; Apostolic Nuncio Most Rev. Christophe Pierre (Titular Archbishop of Gunela).

Honduras: Alfonso Reyes 220, Col. Condesa, Del. Cuauhtémoc, 06170 México, DF; tel. (55) 5211-5747; fax (55) 5211-5425; e-mail emhonmex@prodigy.net.mx; Ambassador Rosalinda Bueso Asfura.

Hungary: Paseo de las Palmas 2005, Col. Lomas de Chapultepec, Del. Miguel Hidalgo, 11000 México, DF; tel. (55) 5596-0523; fax (55) 5596-2378; internet www.mfa.gov.hu/kulkepviselet/MX/hu; Ambassador György Tibor Herczsg.

India: Musset 325, Col. Polanco, Del. Miguel Hidalgo, 11550 México, DF; tel. (55) 5531-1050; fax (55) 5254-2349; e-mail indembmx@prodigy.net.mx; internet www.indembassy.org; Ambassador Rinzing Wangdi.

Indonesia: Julio Verne 27, Col. Polanco, Del. Miguel Hidalgo, 11560 México, DF; tel. (55) 5280-6363; fax (55) 5280-7062; e-mail kbrimex@prodigy.net.mx; Ambassador Andung Abdullah Nitimihardja.

Iran: Paseo de la Reforma 2350, Col. Lomas Altas, Del. Miguel Hidalgo, 11950 México, DF; tel. (55) 9172-2691; fax (55) 9172-2694; e-mail iranembmex@hotmail.com; Ambassador Mohammad Hassan Ghadiri Abyaneh.

Iraq: Paseo de la Reforma 1875, Col. Lomas de Chapultepec, Del. Miguel Hidalgo, 11000 México, DF; tel. (55) 5596-0933; fax (55) 5596-0254; Chargé d'affaires a.i. Sabir Mahmoud Abdulrazzak al-Ani.

Ireland: Cerrada Blvd Manuel Avila Camacho 76, 3°, Col. Lomas de Chapultepec, Del. Miguel Hidalgo, 11000 México, DF; tel. (55) 5520-5803; fax (55) 5520-5892; e-mail emexicoembassy@dfa.ie; Ambassador Dermot Brangan.

Israel: Sierra Madre 215, Col. Lomas de Chapultepec, Del. Miguel Hidalgo, 11000 México, DF; tel. (55) 5201-1500; fax (55) 5201-1555; e-mail embisrael@prodigy.net.mx; internet mexico-city.mfa.gov.il; Ambassador Yosef Livne.

Italy: Paseo de las Palmas 1994, Col. Lomas de Chapultepec, Del. Miguel Hidalgo, 11000 México, DF; tel. (55) 5596-3655; fax (55) 5596-2472; e-mail segreteria.messico@esteri.it; internet www.ambcittadelmessico.esteri.it; Ambassador Felice Scauso.

Jamaica: Schiller 326, 8°, Col. Chapultepec Morales, Del. Miguel Hidalgo, 11570 México, DF; tel. (55) 5250-6804; fax (55) 5250-6160; e-mail embajadadejamaica@prodigy.net.mx; Ambassador Sheila Ivoline Sealy-Monteith.

Japan: Paseo de la Reforma 395, Apdo 5-101, Col. Cuauhtémoc, Del. Cuauhtémoc, 06500 México, DF; tel. (55) 5211-0028; fax (55) 5207-7743; e-mail embjapmx@mail.internet.com.mx; internet www.mx.emb-japan.go.jp; Ambassador Masaaki Ono.

Korea, Democratic People's Republic: Eugenio Sue 332, Col. Polanco, Del. Miguel Hidalgo, 11550 México, DF; tel. (55) 5545-1871; fax (55) 5203-0019; e-mail dpkoreaemb@prodigy.net.mx; Ambassador So Jae Myong.

Korea, Republic: Lope de Armendáriz 110, Col. Lomas Virreyes, Del. Miguel Hidalgo, 11000 México, DF; tel. (55) 5202-9866; fax (55) 5540-7446; e-mail coremex@prodigy.net.mx; internet mex.mofat.go.kr; Ambassador Won Jong-Chan.

Lebanon: Julio Verne 8, Col. Polanco, Del. Miguel Hidalgo, 11560 México, DF; tel. (55) 5280-5614; fax (55) 5280-8870; e-mail embalib@prodigy.net.mx; Ambassador Nouhad Mahmoud.

Libya: Horacio 1003, Col. Polanco, Del. Miguel Hidalgo, 11550 México, DF; tel. (55) 5545-5725; fax (55) 5545-5677; e-mail libia.mexico@yahoo.com.

Malaysia: Sierra Nevada 435, Col. Lomas de Chapultepec, Del. Miguel Hidalgo, 11000 México, DF; tel. (55) 5202-4923; fax (55) 5282-4910; e-mail mwmexico@prodigy.net.mx; Chargé d'affaires a.i. Harris bin Alwi.

Morocco: Paseo de las Palmas 2020, Col. Lomas de Chapultepec, Del. Miguel Hidalgo, 11000 México, DF; tel. (55) 5245-1786; fax (55) 5245-1791; e-mail sifamex@infosel.net.mx; internet www.marruecos.org.mx; Ambassador Mahmoud Rmiki.

Netherlands: Edif. Calakmul 7°, Avda Vasco de Quiroga 3000, Col. Santa Fe, Del. Alvaro Obregón, 01210 México, DF; tel. (55) 5258-9921; fax (55) 5258-8138; e-mail nlgovmex@nlgovmex.com; internet www.paisesbajos.com.mx; Ambassador Cornelia Minderhoud.

New Zealand: Edif. Corporativo Polanco 4°, Jaime Balmes 8, Col. Polanco, Del. Miguel Hidalgo, 11510 México, DF; tel. (55) 5283-9460; fax (55) 5283-9480; e-mail kiwimexico@prodigy.net.mx; Ambassador Cecile Hillyer.

Nicaragua: Prado Norte 470, Col. Lomas de Chapultepec, Del. Miguel Hidalgo, 11000 México, DF; tel. (55) 5540-5625; fax (55) 5520-6961; e-mail embanic@prodigy.net.mx; Ambassador Horacio Brenes Icabalceta.

Nigeria: Paseo de las Palmas 1880, Col. Lomas de Chapultepec, Del. Miguel Hidalgo, 11000 México, DF; tel. (55) 5245-1487; fax (55) 5245-0105; e-mail nigembmx@att.net.mx; Chargé d'affaires a.i. Clement Onoja Aduku.

Norway: Avda de los Virreyes 1460, Col. Lomas Virreyes, Del. Miguel Hidalgo, 11000 México, DF; tel. (55) 5540-3486; fax (55) 5202-3019; e-mail emb.mexico@mfa.no; internet www.noruega.org.mx; Ambassador Knut Solem.

Pakistan: Hegel 512, Col. Chapultepec Morales, Del. Miguel Hidalgo, 11570 México, DF; tel. (55) 5203-3636; fax (55) 5203-9907; Ambassador Zehra Akbari.

Panama: Sócrates 339, Col. Polanco, Del. Miguel Hidalgo, 11560 México, DF; tel. (55) 5280-7857; fax (55) 5280-7586; e-mail informes@embpanamamexico.com; internet www.embpanamamexico.com; Ambassador Ricardo José Alemán Alfaro.

Paraguay: Homero 415, 1°, esq. Hegel, Col. Polanco, Del. Miguel Hidalgo, 11570 México, DF; tel. (55) 5545-0405; fax (55) 5531-9905; e-mail embapar@prodigy.net.mx; Ambassador José Félix Fernández Estigarribia.

Peru: Paseo de la Reforma 2601, Col. Lomas Reforma, Del. Miguel Hidalgo, 11000 México, DF; tel. (55) 5570-2443; fax (55) 5259-0530; e-mail embaperu@prodigy.net.mx; Ambassador Carlos Berninzón Devéscovi.

Philippines: Sierra Gorda 175, Col. Lomas de Chapultepec, Del. Miguel Hidalgo, 11000 México, DF; tel. (55) 5202-8456; fax (55) 5202-8403; e-mail ambamexi@att.net.mx; Ambassador Antonio Manuel Lagdameo Revilla.

Poland: Cracovia 40, Col. San Angel, Del. Alvaro Obregón, 01000 México, DF; tel. (55) 5550-4700; fax (55) 5616-0822; e-mail embajada@polonia.org.mx; internet www.polonia.org.mx; Chargé d'affaires a.i. JACEK GAWRYSZEWSKI.

Portugal: Avda Alpes 1370, Lomas de Chapultepec, Del. Miguel Hidalgo, 11000 México, DF; tel. (55) 5520-7897; fax (55) 5520-4688; e-mail embpomex@prodigy.net.mx; internet www.portugalenmexico.com.mx; Ambassador FRANCISCO DOMINGOS GARCÍA FALCÃO MACHADO.

Romania: Sófocles 311, Col. Polanco, Del. Miguel Hidalgo, 11560 México, DF; tel. (55) 5280-0197; fax (55) 5280-0343; e-mail secretariat@rumania.org.mx; internet www.rumania.org.mx; Ambassador MANUELA VULPE.

Russia: José Vasconcelos 204, Col. Hipódromo Condesa, Del. Cuauhtémoc, 06140 México, DF; tel. (55) 5273-1305; fax (55) 5273-1545; e-mail embrumex@mail.internet.com.mx; Ambassador VALERY I. MOROZOV.

Saudi Arabia: Paseo de las Palmas 2075, Col. Lomas de Chapultepec, Del. Miguel Hidalgo, 11000 México, DF; tel. (55) 5596-0173; fax (55) 5020-3160; e-mail saudiemb@prodigy.net.mx; Ambassador MUNEER IBRAHIM AL-BENJABI.

Serbia: Montañas Rocallosas Oeste 515, Col. Lomas de Chapultepec, Del. Miguel Hidalgo, 11000 México, DF; tel. (55) 5520-0524; fax (55) 5520-9927; e-mail embajadaserbia@att.net.mx; Ambassador MILISAV PAIC.

Slovakia: Julio Verne 35, Col. Polanco, Del. Miguel Hidalgo, 11560 México, DF; tel. (55) 5280-6669; fax (55) 5280-6294; e-mail eslovaquia@prodigy.net.mx; Ambassador MARIÁN ADAMEC.

South Africa: Edif. Forum, 9°, Andrés Bello 10, Col. Polanco, Del. Miguel Hidalgo, 11560 México, DF; tel. and fax (55) 5282-9260; e-mail safrica@prodigy.net.mx; Ambassador MPHAKAMA NYANGWENI MBETE.

Spain: Galileo 114, esq. Horacio, Col. Polanco, Del. Miguel Hidalgo, 11550 México, DF; tel. (55) 5282-2271; fax (55) 5282-1520; e-mail embaes@prodigy.net.mx; Ambassador CARMELO ANGULO BARTUREN.

Sweden: Paseo de las Palmas 1375, Col. Lomas de Chapultepec, Del. Miguel Hidalgo, 11000 México, DF; tel. (55) 9178-5010; fax (55) 5540-3253; e-mail info@suecia.com.mx; internet www.suecia.com.mx; Ambassador ANNA LINDSTEDT.

Switzerland: Paseo de las Palmas 405, 11°, Torre Óptima, Col. Lomas de Chapultepec, Del. Miguel Hidalgo, 11000 México, DF; tel. (55) 5520-3003; fax (55) 5520-8685; e-mail vertretung@mex.rep.admin.ch; internet www.eda.admin.ch/mexico_emb/s/home.html; Ambassador URS BREITER.

Thailand: Paseo de las Palmas 1610, Col. Lomas de Chapultepec, Del. Miguel Hidalgo, 11000 México, DF; tel. (55) 5540-4551; fax (55) 5540-4817; e-mail thaimex@prodigy.net.mx; internet www.thaiembmexico.co.nr; Ambassador RAVEE HONGSAPRABHAS.

Turkey: Monte Líbano 885, Col. Lomas de Chapultepec, Del. Miguel Hidalgo, 11000 México, DF; tel. (55) 5282-5446; fax (55) 5282-4894; e-mail turkem@mail.internet.com.mx; Ambassador AHMET SEDAT BANGUOGLU.

Ukraine: Paseo de la Reforma 730, Col. Lomas de Chapultepec, Del. Miguel Hidalgo, 11000 México, DF; tel. (55) 5282-4085; fax (55) 5282-4768; e-mail ukrainembasy@mexis.com; Ambassador OLEKSII BRANASHKO.

United Kingdom: Río Lerma 71, Col. Cuauhtémoc, Del. Cuauhtémoc, 06500 México, DF; tel. (55) 5242-8500; fax (55) 5242-8517; e-mail ukinmex@att.net.mx; internet www.embajadabritanica.com.mx; Ambassador GILES PAXMAN.

USA: Paseo de la Reforma 305, Del. Cuauhtémoc, 06500 México, DF; tel. (55) 5080-2000; fax (55) 5080-2150; internet www.usembassy-mexico.gov; Ambassador ANTONIO O. GARZA, Jr.

Uruguay: Hegel 149, 1°, Col. Chapultepec Morales, Del. Miguel Hidalgo, 11560 México, DF; tel. (55) 5531-4029; fax (55) 5545-3342; e-mail uruazte@ort.org.mx; Ambassador JOSÉ IGNACIO KORZENIAK PASTORINO.

Venezuela: Schiller 326, Col. Chapultepec Morales, Del. Miguel Hidalgo, 11570 México, DF; tel. (55) 5203-4233; fax (55) 5203-5072; e-mail embemve.mxmdf@mre.gob.ve; Ambassador ROY CHADERTON MATOS.

Viet Nam: Sierra Ventana 255, Col. Lomas de Chapultepec, Del. Miguel Hidalgo, 11000 México, DF; tel. (55) 5540-1632; fax (55) 5540-1612; e-mail vietnam.mx@mofa.gov.vn; Ambassador PHAM VAN QUE.

Judicial System

The principle of the separation of the judiciary from the legislative and executive powers is embodied in the 1917 Constitution. The judicial system is divided into two areas: the federal, dealing with federal law, and the local, dealing only with state law within each state.

The federal judicial system has both ordinary and constitutional jurisdiction and judicial power is exercised by the Supreme Court of Justice, the Electoral Court, Collegiate and Unitary Circuit Courts and District Courts. The Supreme Court comprises two separate chambers: Civil and Criminal Affairs, and Administrative and Labour Affairs. The Federal Judicature Council is responsible for the administration, surveillance and discipline of the federal judiciary, except for the Supreme Court of Justice.

In 2006 there were 172 Collegiate Circuit Courts (Tribunales Colegiados), 62 Unitary Circuit Courts (Tribunales Unitarios) and 285 District Courts (Juzgados de Distrito). Mexico is divided into 29 judicial circuits. The Circuit Courts may be collegiate, when dealing with the derecho de amparo (protection of constitutional rights of an individual), or unitary, when dealing with appeal cases. The Collegiate Circuit Courts comprise three magistrates with residence in the cities of México, Toluca, Naucalpan, Guadalajara, Monterrey, Hermosillo, Puebla, Boca del Río, Xalapa, Torreón, Saltillo, San Luis Potosí, Villahermosa, Morelia, Mazatlán, Oaxaca, Mérida, Mexicali, Guanajuato, León, Chihuahua, Ciudad Juárez, Cuernavaca, Ciudad Victoria, Ciudad Reynosa, Tuxtla Gutiérrez, Tapachula, Acapulco, Chilpancingo, Querétaro, Zacatecas, Aguascalientes, Tepic, Durango, La Paz, Cancún, Tlaxcala and Pachuca. The Unitary Circuit Courts comprise one magistrate with residence mostly in the same cities as given above.

SUPREME COURT OF JUSTICE

Suprema Corte de Justicia de la Nación: Pino Suárez 2, Col. Centro, 06065 México, DF; tel. (55) 5522-0096; fax (55) 5522-0152; e-mail administrator@mail.scjn.gob.mx; internet www.scjn.gob.mx.

Chief Justice: GUILLERMO I. ORTÍZ MAYAGOITIA.

First Chamber—Civil and Criminal Affairs

President: SERGIO ARMANDO VALLS HERNÁNDEZ.

Second Chamber—Administrative and Labour Affairs

President: JOSÉ FERNANDO FRANCO GONZÁLEZ SALAS.

ELECTORAL TRIBUNAL OF THE FEDERAL JUDICIARY

Tribunal Electoral del Poder Jucicial de la Federación (TEPJF): Carlota Amero 5000, Col. Culhuacán, Del. Coyoacán, 04480 México, DF; tel. (55) 5728-2300; fax (55) 5728-2400; internet www.trife.gob.mx; Pres. MARÍA DEL CARMEN ALANIS FIGUEROA.

Religion

CHRISTIANITY

The Roman Catholic Church

The prevailing religion is Roman Catholicism, but the Church, disestablished in 1857, was for many years, under the Constitution of 1917, subject to state control. A constitutional amendment, promulgated in January 1992, officially removed all restrictions on the Church. For ecclesiastical purposes, Mexico comprises 18 archdioceses, 65 dioceses, five territorial prelatures and two eparchies (both directly subject to the Holy See). An estimated 87% of the population are adherents.

Bishops' Conference

Conferencia del Episcopado Mexicano (CEM), Edif. S. S. Juan Pablo II, Prolongación Ministerios 26, Col. Tepeyac Insurgentes, Apdo 118-055, 07020 México, DF; tel. (55) 5781-8462; fax (55) 5577-5489; e-mail segcem@cem.org.mx; internet www.cem.org.mx; Pres. CARLOS AGUIAR RETES (Bishop of Texcoco); Sec.-Gen. JOSÉ LEOPOLDO GONZÁLEZ GONZÁLEZ.

Archbishop of Acapulco: FELIPE AGUIRRE FRANCO, Arzobispado, Quebrada 16, Apdo 201, Centro, 39300 Acapulco, Gro; tel. and fax (744) 482-0763; e-mail arzobispadoaca@aca.cableonline.com.mx; internet www.arquidiocesisacapulco.org.mx.

Archbishop of Antequera, Oaxaca: JOSÉ LUIS CHÁVEZ BOTELLO, García Virgil 600, Anexos de Catedral, Col. Centro, 68000 Oaxaca, Oax.; tel. (951) 516-4822; fax (951) 514-1348; e-mail arzobispadoaxaca@hotmail.com; internet arquidiocesisoaxaca.org.mx.

Archbishop of Chihuahua: JOSÉ FERNÁNDEZ ARTEAGA, Arzobispado, Avda Cuauhtémoc 1828, Apdo 7, Col. Cuauhtémoc, 31020 Chihuahua, Chih.; tel. (614) 410-3202; fax (614) 410-5621; e-mail ferar@megalink.com.mx; internet www.arquichi.org.mx.

Archbishop of Durango: HÉCTOR GONZÁLEZ MARTÍNEZ, Arzobispado, 20 de Noviembre 306, Poniente Centro, 34000 Durango, Dgo; tel. (618) 811-4242; fax (618) 812-8881; e-mail arqdgo@prodigy.net.mx.

MEXICO

Archbishop of Guadalajara: Cardinal JUAN SANDOVAL IÑIGUEZ, Arzobispado, Liceo 17, Apdo 1-331, Col. Centro, 44100 Guadalajara, Jal.; tel. (33) 3614-5504; fax (33) 3658-2300; e-mail arzgdl@arquinet.com.mx; internet www.arquidiocesisgdl.org.mx.

Archbishop of Hermosillo: JOSÉ ULISES MACÍAS SALCEDO, Arzobispado, Dr Paliza y Ocampo, Ala Sur de la Catedral, Col. Centenario, 83260 Hermosillo, Son.; tel. (662) 213-2138; fax (662) 213-1327; e-mail arzohmo@hotmail.com; internet www.iglesiahermosillo.com.mx.

Archbishop of Jalapa: HIPÓLITO REYES LARIOS, Arzobispado, Avda Manuel Avila Camacho 73, Apdo 359, Col. Centro, 91000 Jalapa, Ver.; tel. (228) 812-0579; fax (228) 817-5578; e-mail arzobispadoalxal@prodigy.net.mx.

Archbishop of León: JOSÉ GUADALUPE MARTÍN RÁBAGO, Arzobispado, Pedro Moreno 312, Apdo 108, 37000 León, Gto; tel. (477) 713-2747; fax (477) 713-1286; e-mail canciller@arquidiocesisleon.org.mx; internet www.arquidiocesisdeleon.org.mx.

Archbishop of Mexico City: Cardinal NORBERTO RIVERA CARRERA, Curia del Arzobispado de México, Durango 90, 5°, Col. Roma, Apdo 24433, 06700 México, DF; tel. (55) 5208-3200; fax (55) 5208-5350; e-mail arzobisp@arquidiocesismexico.org.mx; internet www.arzobispadomexico.org.mx.

Archbishop of Monterrey: Cardinal FRANCISCO ROBLES ORTEGA, Zuazua 1100 Sur con Ocampo Centro, Apdo 7, 64000 Monterrey, NL; tel. (81) 1158-2450; fax (81) 1158-2488; e-mail cancilleria@arquidiocesismty.org; internet www.arquidiocesismty.org.mx.

Archbishop of Morelia: ALBERTO SUÁREZ INDA, Arzobispado, Costado Catedral, Frente Avda Madero, Apdo 17, 58000 Morelia, Mich.; tel. (443) 313-2493; fax (443) 312-0919; e-mail asuarexi@prodigy.net.mx; tel. www.arquimorelia.com.

Archbishop of Puebla de los Angeles: ROSENDO HUESCA PACHECO, Avda 2 Sur 305, Apdo 235, Col. Centro, 72000 Puebla, Pue.; tel. (222) 232-4591; fax (222) 246-2277; e-mail rhuesca@mail.cem.org.mx.

Archbishop of San Luis Potosí: LUIS MORALES REYES, Arzobispado, Francisco Madero 300, Apdo 1, Col. Centro, 78000 San Luis Potosí, SLP; tel. (444) 812-4555; fax (444) 812-7979; e-mail arqsanluis@iglesiapotosina.org; internet www.iglesiapotosina.org.

Archbishop of Tijuana: RAFAEL ROMO MUÑOZ, Arzobispado, Calle Décima y Avda Ocampo 8525, Apdo 226, 22000 Tijuana, BCN; tel. (664) 684-8411; fax (664) 684-7683; internet www.iglesiatijuana.org.

Archbishop of Tlalnepantla: RICARDO GUÍZAR DÍAZ, Arzobispado, Avda Juárez 42, Apdo 268, Col. Centro, 54000 Tlalnepantla, Méx.; tel. (55) 5565-3944; fax (55) 5565-2751; e-mail curia@arqtlalnepantla.org; internet www.arqtlalnepantla.org.

Archbishop of Tulancingo: PEDRO ARANDA DÍAZ-MUÑOZ, Arzobispado, Plaza de la Constitución, Apdo 14, 43600 Tulancingo, Hgo; e-mail sgamitra@netpac.net.mx.

Archbishop of Tuxtla Gutiérrez: ROGELIO CABRERA LÓPEZ, Uruguay 500A, Col. El Retiro, Apdo 365, 29040 Tuxtla Gutiérrez, Chis; e-mail casaepiscopal@prodigy.net.mx.

Archbishop of Yucatán: EMILIO CARLOS BERLIE BELAUNZARÁN, Arzobispado, Calle 58 501, Col. Centro, 97000 Mérida, Yuc.; tel. (999) 924-7777; fax (999) 923-7983; e-mail aryu@prodigy.net.mx; internet www.arquidiocesisdeyucatan.org.

The Anglican Communion

Mexico is divided into five dioceses, which form the Province of the Anglican Church in Mexico, established in 1995.

Bishop of Cuernavaca: RAMIRO DELGADO VERA, Minerva 1, Col. Delicias, 62431 Cuernavaca, Mor.; tel. and fax (777) 315-2870; e-mail adoc@cableonline.com.mx; internet www.cuernavaca-anglican.org.

Bishop of Mexico City and Primate of the Anglican Church in Mexico: CARLOS TOUCHÉ PORTER, La Otra Banda 40, Avda San Jerónimo 117, Col. San Ángel, 01000 México, DF; tel. and fax (55) 5616-2205; e-mail contacto@iglesiaanglicandemexico.org; internet www.iglesiaanglicanademexico.org.

Bishop of Northern Mexico: MARCELINO RIVERA DELGADO, Simón Bolívar 2005 Nte, Col. Mitras Centro, 64460 Monterrey, NL; tel. (81) 8333-0922; fax (81) 8348-7362; e-mail diocesisdelnorte@att.net.mx.

Bishop of South-Eastern Mexico: BENITO JUÁREZ MARTÍNEZ, Avda de las Américas 73, Col. Aguacatl, 91130 Jalapa, Ver.; tel. and fax (228) 814-6951; e-mail dioste99@aol.com.

Bishop of Western Mexico: LINO RODRÍGUEZ-AMARO, Francisco Javier Gamboa 255, Col. Barrera, 45150 Guadalajara, Jal; tel. (33) 3615-5070; fax (33) 3615-4413; e-mail iamoccidente@prodigy.net.mx; internet www.iamoccidente.org.mx.

Protestant Churches

Iglesia Luterana Mexicana: POB 1-1034, 44101 Guadalajara, Jal.; tel. (33) 3639-7253; e-mail dtrejocoria@hotmail.com; f. 1951; Pres. DANIEL TREJO CORIA; 1,500 mems.

Iglesia Metodista de México, Asociación Religiosa: Miravelle 209, Col. Albert, 03570 México, DF; tel. (55) 5539-3674; e-mail prenapro@iglesia-metodista.org.mx; internet www.iglesia-metodista.org.mx; f. 1930; 55,000 mems; Pres. Rev MOISÉS VALDERRAMA GÓMEZ; 370 congregations; comprises six episcopal areas.

National Baptist Convention of Mexico: Tlalpan 1035-A, Col. Américas Unidas, 03610 México, DF; tel. and fax (55) 5539-7720; e-mail comunicacion@cnbm.org.mx; internet www.cnbm.org.mx; f. 1903; Pres. Rev. JOSÉ TRINIDAD BONILLA MORALES.

BAHÁ'Í FAITH

National Spiritual Assembly of the Bahá'ís of Mexico: Emerson 421, Col. Chapultepec Morales, 11570 México, DF; tel. (55) 5545-2155; fax (55) 5255-5972; e-mail info@bahaimexico.org; internet www.bahaimexico.org; mems resident in 978 localities.

JUDAISM

The Jewish community numbered some 40,000 in 2004.

Comité Central de la Comunidad Judía de México: Cofre de Perote 115, Lomas Barrilaco, 11010 México, DF; tel. (55) 5520-9393; fax (55) 5540-3050; e-mail comitecentral@prodigy.net.mx; internet www.tribuna.org.mx; Pres. OSCAR GORODZINSKY.

The Press
DAILY NEWSPAPERS
México, DF

La Afición: Ignacio Mariscal 23, Apdo 64 bis, Col. Tabacalera, 06030 México, DF; tel. (55) 5546-4780; fax (55) 5546-5852; internet www.laaficion.com; f. 1930; sport; Pres. FRANCISCO A. GONZÁLEZ; circ. 85,000.

La Crónica de Hoy: Grupo Editorial Convergencia, SA de CV, Balderas 33, 6°, Col. Centro, 06040 México, DF; tel. and fax (52) 5512-3429; e-mail suscripciones@cronica.com.mx; internet www.cronica.com.mx; Pres. JORGE KAHWAGI GASTINE; Editorial Dir PABLO HIRIART LE BERT.

Cuestión: Laguna de Mayrán 410, Col. Anáhuac, 11320 México, DF; tel. (55) 5260-0499; fax (55) 5260-3645; e-mail contacto@cuestion.com.mx; internet www.cuestion.com.mx; f. 1980; midday; Dir-Gen. Lic. ALBERTO GONZÁLEZ PARRA; circ. 48,000.

Diario de México: Chimalpopoca 38, Col. Obrera, 06800 México, DF; tel. (55) 5442-6501; fax (55) 5588-4289; e-mail dirgral@diariodemexico.com.mx; internet www.diariodemexico.com.mx; f. 1948; morning; Dir-Gen. FEDERICO BRACAMONTES GÁLVEZ; Dir ABRAHAM SHEIMBERG; circ. 76,000.

El Economista: Avda Coyoacán 515, Col. del Valle, 03100 México, DF; tel. (55) 5326-5454; fax (55) 5687-3821; e-mail jppadilla@eleconomista.com.mx; internet www.economista.com.mx; f. 1988; financial; Pres. JOSÉ GÓMEZ CAÑIBE; Editor-in-Chief DAVID CUEN; circ. 37,448.

Esto: Guillermo Prieto 7, 1°, Col. San Rafael, Del. Cuauhtémoc, 06470 México, DF; tel. and fax (55) 5566-1511; e-mail esto@oem.com.mx; internet www.esto.com.mx; f. 1941; published by Organización Editorial Mexicana; morning; sport; Dir CARLOS TRAPAGA BARRIENTOS; circ. 400,000, Mondays 450,000.

Excélsior: Paseo de la Reforma 18 y Bucareli 1, Apdo 120 bis, Col. Centro, 06600 México, DF; tel. (55) 5705-4444; fax (55) 5566-0223; e-mail foro@excelsior.com.mx; internet www.excelsior.com.mx; f. 1917; morning; independent; Dir DANIEL MORENO; Gen. Man. JUVENTINO OLIVERA LÓPEZ; circ. 200,000.

El Financiero: Lago Bolsena 176, Col. Anáhuac entre Lago Peypus y Lago Onega, 11320 México, DF; tel. (55) 5227-7600; fax (55) 5254-6427; internet www.elfinanciero.com.mx; f. 1981; financial; Dir-Gen. PILAR ESTANDÍA DE CÁRDENAS; circ. 119,000.

El Heraldo de México: Dr Lucio, esq. Dr Velasco, Col. Doctores, 06720 México, DF; tel. (55) 5578-7022; fax (55) 5578-9824; e-mail heraldo@iwm.com.mx; internet www.heraldo.com.mx; f. 1965; morning; Dir-Gen. GABRIEL ALARCÓN VELÁZQUEZ; circ. 209,600.

La Jornada: Avda Cuauhtémoc 1236, Col. Santa Cruz Atoyac, Del. Benito Juárez, 03310 México, DF; tel. (55) 9183-0300; internet www.jornada.unam.mx; f. 1984; morning; Dir-Gen. Lic. CARMEN LIRA SAADE; Gen. Man. Lic. JORGE MARTÍNEZ JIMÉNEZ; circ. 86,275.

Milenio Diario: México, DF; internet www.mileniodiario.com.mx; publishes México, DF, and regional editions, and a weekly news magazine, *Milenio Semanal* (www.milenio.com/semanal); Pres. FRANCISCO A. GONZÁLEZ; Dir-Gen. CARLOS MARÍN.

Novedades: Balderas 87, esq. Morelos, Col. Centro, 06040 México, DF; tel. (55) 5518-5481; fax (55) 5521-4505; internet www.novedades.com.mx; f. 1936; morning; independent; Pres. and Editor-in-Chief

MEXICO

Romulo O'Farrill, Jr; Vice-Pres. José Antonio O'Farrill Avila; circ. 42,990, Sundays 43,536.

Ovaciones: Lago Zirahuén 279, 20°, Col. Anáhuac, 11320 México, DF; tel. (55) 5328-0700; fax (55) 5260-2219; e-mail ovaciones@ova.com.mx; internet www.ovaciones.com; f. 1947; morning and evening editions; Pres. and Dir-Gen. Mauricio Vázquez Ramos; circ. 130,000; evening circ. 100,000.

La Prensa: Basilio Badillo 40, Col. Tabacalera, 06030 México, DF; tel. (55) 5228-8981; fax (55) 5521-8209; e-mail bmedina@la-prensa.com.mx; internet www.la-prensa.com.mx; f. 1928; published by Organización Editorial Mexicana; morning; Pres. and Dir-Gen. Lic. Mario Vázquez Raña; Dir Mauricio Ortega Camberos; circ. 270,000.

Reforma: Avda México Coyoacán 40, Col. Santa Cruz Atoyac, 03310 México, DF; tel. (55) 5628-7777; fax (55) 5628-7188; internet www.reforma.com; f. 1993; morning; Pres. and Dir-Gen. Alejandro Junco de la Vega Elizondo; circ. 94,000.

El Sol de México: Guillermo Prieto 7, 20°, Col. San Rafael, 06470 México, DF; tel. (55) 5566-1511; fax (55) 5535-5560; e-mail enlinea@elsoldemexico.com.mx; internet www.elsoldemexico.com.mx; f. 1965; published by Organización Editorial Mexicana; morning and midday; Pres. and Dir-Gen. Lic. Mario Vázquez Raña; Dir Isabel Zamorano Ramos; circ. 76,000.

El Universal: Bucareli 8, Apdo 909, Col. Centro, Del. Cuauhtémoc, 06040 México, DF; tel. (55) 5709-1313; fax (55) 5510-1269; e-mail rdirgral@eluniversal.com.mx; internet www.eluniversal.com.mx; f. 1916; morning; independent; centre-left; Pres. Juan Francisco Ealy Ortiz; Dir-Gen. Juan Francisco Ealy, Jr; circ. 165,629, Sundays 181,615.

Unomásuno: Gabino Barreda 86, Col. San Rafael, México, DF; tel. (55) 1055-5500; fax (55) 5598-8821; e-mail cduran@servidor.unam.mx; internet www.unomasuno.com.mx; f. 1977; morning; left-wing; Pres. Naim Libien Kaui; Dir José Luis Rojas Ramírez; circ. 40,000.

PROVINCIAL DAILY NEWSPAPERS

Baja California

El Sol de Tijuana: Rufino Tamayo 4, Zona del Río, 22320 Tijuana, BC; tel. (664) 634-3232; fax (664) 634-2234; e-mail soltij@oem.com.mx; internet www.oem.com.mx/elsoldetijuana; f. 1989; published by Organización Editorial Mexicana; morning; Dir Arturo González Pérez; circ. 50,000.

La Voz de la Frontera: Avda Madero 1545, Col. Nueva, Apdo 946, 21100 Mexicali, BC; tel. (686) 562-4545; fax (686) 562-6912; e-mail ramondiaz@lavozdelafrontera.com.mx; internet www.oem.com.mx/lavozdelafrontera; f. 1964; morning; published by Organización Editorial Mexicana; Dir Felipe de Jesús López Rodríguez; Gen. Man. Lic. Mario Valdés Hernández; circ. 65,000.

Chihuahua

El Diario: Publicaciones Paso del Norte, Avda Paseo Triunfo de la República 2505, Zona Pronaf, 32310 Ciudad Juárez, Chih.; tel. (656) 629-6900; internet www.diario.com.mx; f. 1976; Pres. Osvaldo Rodríguez Borunda.

El Heraldo de Chihuahua: Avda Universidad 2507, Apdo 1515, 31240 Chihuahua, Chih.; tel. (614) 413-9339; fax (614) 413-5625; e-mail elheraldo@buzon.online.com.mx; internet www.oem.com.mx/elheraldodechihuahua; f. 1927; published by Organización Editorial Mexicana; morning; Dir Lic. Javier H. Contreras; circ. 27,520, Sundays 31,223.

El Mexicano de Ciudad Juárez: Ciudad Juárez, Chih.; e-mail director@pesquisasenlinea.org; internet www.pesquisasenlinea.org/elmexicano; f. 1959; published by Organización Editorial Mexicana; morning; Dir Rafael Navarro; Editor-in-Chief Jaime Núñez; circ. 80,000.

Coahuila

La Opinión: Blvd Independencia 1492 Oeste, Apdo 86, 27010 Torreón, Coah.; tel. (871) 559-8777; fax (871) 759-8164; internet www.opinion.com.mx; f. 1924; morning; Dir-Gen. Oscar López Morales; circ. 40,000.

El Siglo de Torreón: Avda Matamoros 1056 Pte, Col. Centro, 27000 Torreón, Coah.; tel. (871) 759-1200; e-mail internet@elsiglodetorreon.com.mx; internet www.elsiglodetorreon.com.mx; f. 1922; morning; Pres. Olga De Juambelz y Horcasitas; Dir-Gen. Antonio Irazoqui y de Juambelz; circ. 38,611, Sundays 38,526.

Vanguardia: Blvd Venustiano Carranza 1918, esq. con Chiapas, República Oriente, 25280 Saltillo, Coah.; tel. (844) 450-1000; e-mail hola@vanguardia.com.mx; internet www.vanguardia.com.mx; Dir-Gen. Diana María Galindo de Castilla.

Colima

Diario de Colima: Avda 20 de Noviembre 380, 28060 Colima, Col.; tel. (312) 312-5688; internet www.diariodecolima.com; f. 1953; Dir-Gen. Héctor Sánchez de la Madrid; Man. Dir Enrique Zárate Canseco.

Guanajuato

Correo de Guanajuato: Carreterra Guanajuato—Juventino Rosas Km 9.5, 36260 Guanajuato, Gto; tel. (477) 733-1263; fax (477) 733-0057; e-mail magana@correo-gto.com.mx; internet www.correo-gto.com.mx; Dir-Gen. Arnaldo Cuéllar.

El Sol de Salamanca: Faro de Oro 800, 36700 Salamanca, Gto; tel. (464) 647-0144; e-mail aherrera@elsoldeirapuato.com.mx; internet www.elsoldesalamanca.com.mx; published by Organización Editorial Mexicana; Dir-Gen. Lic. Alejandro Herrera Sánchez.

Jalisco

El Informador: Independencia 300, Apdo 3 bis, 44100 Guadalajara, Jal.; tel. (33) 3678-7700; e-mail webmanager@informador.com.mx; internet www.informador.com.mx; f. 1917; morning; Editor Jorge Álvarez del Castillo; circ. 50,000.

El Occidental: Calzada Independencia Sur 324, Apdo 1-699, 44100 Guadalajara, Jal.; tel. (33) 3613-0690; fax (33) 3613-6796; e-mail silvia@eloccidental.com.mx; internet www.eloccidental.com.mx; f. 1942; published by Organización Editorial Mexicana; morning; Pres. and Dir-Gen. Lic. Mario Vásquez Raña; circ. 49,400.

México

ABC: Avda Hidalgo Oriente 1339, Centro Comercial, Col. Ferrocarriles Nacionales, 50070 Toluca, Méx.; tel. (722) 217-9880; fax (722) 217-8402; e-mail miled1@mail.miled.com; internet www.miled.com; f. 1984; morning; Pres. and Editor Miled Libien Kaui; circ. 65,000.

Diario de Toluca: Allende Sur 209, 50000 Toluca, Méx.; tel. (722) 215-9105; fax (722) 214-1523; e-mail eldiario@netspace.com.mx; f. 1980; also publishes *Siete Dias* and *El Noticiero*; morning; Pres. Anuar Maccise Dib; circ. 22,200.

El Heraldo de Toluca: Salvador Díaz Mirón 700, Col. Sánchez Colín, 50150 Toluca, Méx.; tel. (722) 217-3542; fax (722) 212-2535; e-mail editotol@prodigy.net.mx; f. 1955; morning; Editor Alberto Barraza Sánchez; circ. 90,000.

El Sol de Toluca: Santos Degollado 105, Apdo 54, Col. Centro, 50050 Toluca, Méx.; tel. (722) 214-7077; fax (722) 215-2564; internet www.oem.com.mx/elsoldetoluca; f. 1947; published by Organización Editorial Mexicana; morning; Dir Rafael Vilchis Gil de Arévalo; circ. 42,000.

Michoacán

La Voz de Michoacán: Blvd del Periodismo 1270, Col. Arriaga Rivera, Apdo 121, 58190 Morelia, Mich.; tel. (443) 327-3712; fax (443) 327-3728; e-mail jcgonzalez@voznet.com.mx; internet www.voznet.com.mx; f. 1948; morning; Dir-Gen. Lic. Miguel Medina Robles; circ. 50,000.

Morelos

El Diario de Morelos: Morelos Sur 132, Col. Las Palmas, 62050 Cuernavaca, Mor.; tel. and fax (777) 362-0220; e-mail redaccion@diariodemorelos.com; internet www.diariodemorelos.com; f. 1978; Propr Grupo BRACA de Comunicación; morning; CEO and Editor-in-Chief Miguel Bracamontes; circ. 35,000.

Nayarit

Meridiano de Nayarit: E. Zapata 73 Pte, Apdo 65, 63000 Tepic, Nay.; internet www.meridiano.com.mx; f. 1942; morning; Dir Dr David Alfaro; circ. 60,000.

Nuevo León

ABC: Platón Sánchez Sur 411, 64000 Monterrey, NL; tel. (81) 8344-2510; fax (81) 8344-5990; e-mail abcnuevo@hotmail.com; f. 1985; morning; Dir-Gen. Gonzalo Estrado Torres; circ. 40,000, Sundays 45,000.

El Norte: Washington 629 Oeste, Apdo 186, 64000 Monterrey, NL; tel. (81) 8345-3388; fax (81) 8343-2476; internet www.elnorte.com.mx; f. 1938; morning; Man. Dir Lic. Alejandro Junco de la Vega; circ. 133,872, Sundays 154,951.

El Porvenir: Galeana Sur 344, Apdo 218, 64000 Monterrey, NL; tel. (81) 8345-4080; fax (81) 8345-7795; internet www.elporvenir.com.mx; f. 1919; morning; Dir-Gen. José Gerardo Cantú Escalante; circ. 75,000.

MEXICO

Oaxaca

El Imparcial: Armenta y López 312, Apdo 322, 68000 Oaxaca, Oax.; tel. (951) 516-2812; fax (951) 514-7020; e-mail el_imparcial@infosel.net.mx; internet www.imparoax.com.mx; f. 1951; morning; Dir-Gen. Lic. BENJAMÍN FERNÁNDEZ PICHARDO; circ. 17,000, Sundays 20,000.

Puebla

El Sol de Puebla: Avda 3 Oeste 201, Apdo 190, 72000 Puebla, Pue.; tel. (222) 242-4560; fax (222) 246-0869; e-mail elsoldepuebla@elsoldepuebla.com.mx; internet www.oem.com.mx/elsoldepuebla; f. 1944; published by Organización Editorial Mexicana; morning; Dir MARCO A. PONCE DE LEÓN; circ. 67,000.

San Luis Potosí

El Heraldo: Villerías 305, 78000 San Luis Potosí, SLP; tel. (444) 812-3312; fax (444) 812-2081; e-mail redaccion@elheraldoslp.com.mx; internet www.elheraldoslp.com.mx; f. 1954; morning; Dir-Gen. ALEJANDRO VILLASANA MENA; circ. 60,620.

Pulso: Galeana 485, Centro, 78000 San Luis Potosí, SLP; tel. (444) 812-7575; fax (444) 812-3525; internet www.pulsoslp.com.mx; morning; Dir-Gen. PABLO VALLADARES GARCÍA; circ. 60,000.

El Sol de San Luis: Avda Universidad 565, Apdo 342, 78000 San Luis Potosí, SLP; tel. and fax (444) 812-4412; internet www.elsoldesanluis.com.mx; f. 1952; published by Organización Editorial Mexicana; morning; Dir JOSÉ ANGEL MARTÍNEZ LIMÓN; circ. 60,000.

Sinaloa

El Debate de Culiacán: Madero 556 Pte, 80000 Culiacán, Sin.; tel. (667) 716-6353; fax (667) 715-7131; internet www.debate.com.mx; f. 1972; morning; Dir ROSARIO I. OROPEZA; circ. 23,603, Sundays 23,838.

Noroeste Culiacán: Grupo Periódicos Noroeste, Angel Flores 282 Oeste, Apdo 90, 80000 Culiacán, Sin.; tel. (667) 713-2100; fax (667) 712-8006; e-mail cschmidt@noroeste.com.mx; internet www.noroeste.com.mx; f. 1973; morning; Pres. MANUEL J. CLOUTHIER; Editor RODOLFO DIAZ; circ. 35,000.

El Sol de Sinaloa: Blvd G. Leyva Lozano y Corona 320, Apdo 412, 80000 Culiacán, Sin.; tel. (667) 713-1621; fax (667) 713-1800; internet www.elsoldesinaloa.com.mx; f. 1956; published by Organización Editorial Mexicana; morning; Dir JORGE LUIS TÉLLEZ SALAZAR; circ. 30,000.

Sonora

Expreso: Hermosillo, Son.; tel. (662) 108-3000; e-mail holguin@expreso.com.mx; internet www.expreso.com.mx; Dir-Gen. MARTÍN HOLGUÍN ALATORRE; circ. 17,000, Sundays 18,000.

El Imparcial: Sufragio Efectivo y Mina 71, Col. Centro, Apdo 66, 83000 Hermosillo, Son.; tel. (662) 259-4700; fax (662) 217-4483; e-mail lector@elimparcial.com.; internet www.imparcial.com.mx; f. 1937; morning; Pres. and Dir-Gen. JUAN HEALY; circ. 32,083, Sundays 32,444.

Tabasco

Tabasco Hoy: Avda de los Ríos 206, Col. Tabasco 2000, 86035 Villahermosa, Tab.; tel. (993) 310-0229; internet www.tabascohoy.com.mx; f. 1987; morning; Dir-Gen. MIGUEL CANTÓN ZETINA; circ. 50,000.

Tamaulipas

El Bravo: Morelos y Primera 129, Apdo 483, 87300 Matamoros, Tamps; tel. (871) 816-0100; fax (871) 816-2007; e-mail comenta@elbravo.com.mx; internet www.elbravo.com.mx; f. 1951; morning; Pres. and Dir-Gen. JOSÉ CARRETERO BALBOA; circ. 60,000.

El Diario de Nuevo Laredo: González 2409, Apdo 101, 88000 Nuevo Laredo, Tamps; tel. (867) 711-5500; fax (867) 712-8221; internet www.diario.net; f. 1948; morning; Editor RUPERTO VILLARREAL MONTEMAYOR; circ. 68,130, Sundays 73,495.

Expresión: Calle 3 y Novedades 3, Col. Periodistas, 87457 Matamoros, Tamps; tel. (868) 817-9555; fax (868) 817-3307; e-mail xpresion@prodigy.net.mx; morning; Dir-Gen. MIGUEL GARAY AVILA; circ. 50,000.

El Mañana: Juárez y Perú, Col. Juárez, Nuevo Laredo, Tamps; tel. (867) 711-9900; fax (867) 715-0405; e-mail ramon.cantu@elmanana.com.mx; internet www.elmanana.com.mx; f. 1932; morning; Pres. NINFA DEÁNDAR MARTÍNEZ; Editor RAMÓN CANTÚ DEANDAR; circ. 16,473, Sundays 20,957.

El Mañana de Reynosa: Prof. Lauro Aguirre con Matías Canales, Apdo 14, Col. Ribereña, 88620 Ciudad Reynosa, Tamps; tel. (899) 921-9950; fax (899) 924-9348; internet www.elmananarey.com; f. 1949; morning; Dir-Gen. HERIBERTO DEANDAR MARTÍNEZ; circ. 52,000.

Prensa de Reynosa: Matamoros y González Ortega, Zona Centro, 88500 Reynosa, Tamps; tel. (899) 922-0299; fax (899) 922-2412; e-mail prensa_88500@yahoo.com; internet www.prensadereynosa.com; f. 1963; morning; Dir-Gen. FÉLIX GARZA ELIZONDO; circ. 60,000.

El Sol de Tampico: Altamira 311 Pte, Apdo 434, 89000 Tampico, Tamps; tel. (833) 212-3566; fax (833) 212-6986; internet www.elsoldetampico.com.mx; f. 1950; published by Organización Editorial Mexicana; morning; Dir-Gen. Lic. RUBÉN DÍAZ DE LA GARZA; circ. 77,000.

Veracruz

Diario del Istmo: Avda Hidalgo 1115, Col. Centro, 96400 Coatzacoalcos, Ver.; tel. (921) 211-8000; e-mail info@istmo.com.mx; internet www.diariodelistmo.com; f. 1979; morning; Dir-Gen. HÉCTOR ROBLES BARAJAS; circ. 64,600.

El Dictamen: 16 de Septiembre y Arista, 91700 Veracruz, Ver.; tel. (229) 931-1745; fax (229) 931-5804; internet www.eldictamen.com.mx; f. 1898; morning; Pres. CARLOS ANTONIO MALPICA MARTÍNEZ; circ. 38,000, Sundays 39,000.

La Opinión: Poza Rica de Hidalgo, Ver.; e-mail publicidad@laopinion.com.mx; internet www.laopinion.com.mx; Dir ABEL ANDRADE LICONA.

Yucatán

Diario de Yucatán: Calle 60 521, 97000 Mérida, Yuc.; tel. (999) 942-2222; fax (999) 942-2204; internet www.yucatan.com.mx; f. 1925; morning; Dir-Gen. CARLOS R. MENÉNDEZ NAVARRETE; circ. 54,639, Sundays 65,399.

Por Esto!: Calle 60, No 576 entre 73 y 71, 97000 Mérida, Yuc.; tel. (999) 24-7613; fax (999) 28-6514; e-mail redaccion@poresto.net; internet www.poresto.net; f. 1991; morning; Dir-Gen. MARIO RENATO MENÉNDEZ RODRÍGUEZ; circ. 26,985, Sundays 28,727.

Zacatecas

Imagen: Calzada Revolución 24, Col. Tierra y Libertad, Guadalupe, Zac.; tel. and fax (492) 923-8898; e-mail buzon@imagenzac.com.mx; internet www.imagenzac.com.mx; Dir-Gen. EUGENIO MERCADO.

SELECTED WEEKLY NEWSPAPERS

El Heraldo Bajio: Hermanos Aldama 222, Apdo 299, Zona Centro, 37000 León, Gto; tel. (477) 719-8800; e-mail heraldo@el-heraldo-bajio.com.mx; internet www.el-heraldo-bajio.com.mx; f. 1957; Pres. and Dir-Gen. MAURICIO BERCÚN LÓPEZ; circ. 85,000.

Segundamano: Insurgentes Sur 619, Col. Nápoles, Del. Benito Juárez, 03810 México, DF; tel. (55) 5350-7070; e-mail soporte@segundamano.com.mx; internet www.segundamano.com.mx; f. 1986; Dir-Gen. LUIS MAGAÑA MAGAÑA; circ. 105,000.

Zeta: Avda las Américas 4633, Fraccionamiento El Paraíso, Tijuana, BC; e-mail zeta@zetatijuana.com; internet www.zetatijuana.com; f. 1980; news magazine; Dir JESÚS BLANCORNELOS.

SELECTED PERIODICALS

Boletín Industrial: Goldsmith 37-403, Col. Polanco, 11550 México, DF; tel. (55) 5280-6463; fax (55) 5280-3194; e-mail bolind@viernes.iwm.com.mx; internet www.bolind.com.mx; f. 1983; monthly; Dir-Gen. HUMBERTO VALADÉS DÍAZ; circ. 22,000.

Casas & Gente: Amsterdam 112, Col. Hipódromo Condesa, 06100 México, DF; tel. (55) 5286-7794; fax (55) 5211-7112; e-mail informac@casasgente.com; internet www.casasgente.com; 10 a year; interior design; Dir-Gen. IGNACIO DÍAZ SÁNCHEZ.

Conozca Más: Vasco de Quiroga 2000, Col. Santa Fe, Del. Alvaro Obregón, 01210 México, DF; tel. (55) 5261-2000; fax (55) 5261-2704; internet www.esmas.com.conozcamas; f. 1990; monthly; scientific; Dir EUGENIO MENDOZA; circ. 90,000.

Contenido: Darwin 101, Col. Anzures, 11590 México, DF; tel. (55) 5531-3162; fax (55) 5545-7478; e-mail contenido@contenido.com.mx; internet www.contenido.com.mx; f. 1963; monthly; popular appeal; Dir ARMANDO AYALA ANGUIANO; circ. 124,190.

Cosmopolitan México: Vasco de Quiroga 2000, Col. Santa Fe, Del. Alvaro Obregón, 01210 México, DF; tel. (55) 5261-2600; fax (55) 5261-2704; internet www.esmas.com/editorialtelevisa; f. 1973; fortnightly; women's magazine; Dir SARA MARÍA CASTANY; circ. 260,000.

Expansión: Avda Constituyentes 956, Col. Lomas Altas, 11950 México, DF; tel. and fax (55) 9177-4100; e-mail quien@expansion.com.mx; internet www.expansion.com.mx; fortnightly; business and financial; Editor ALBERTO BELLO.

Fama: Avda Eugenio Garza Sada 2245 Sur, Col. Roma, Apdo 3128, 64700 Monterrey, NL; tel. (81) 8359-2525; internet www.revistafama.com; fortnightly; show business; Pres. JESÚS D. GONZÁLEZ; Dir RAÚL MARTÍNEZ; circ. 350,000.

MEXICO

Gaceta Médica de México: Academia Nacional de Medicina, Unidad de Congresos del Centro Médico Nacional Siglo XXI, Bloque B, Avda Cuauhtémoc 330, Col. Doctores, 06725 México, DF; tel. (55) 5578-2044; fax (55) 5578-4271; e-mail gaceta@medigraphic.com; internet www.medigraphic.com; f. 1864; every 2 months; journal of the Academia Nacional de Medicina de México; Editor ALFREDO ULLOA AGUIRRE; circ. 20,000.

Kena Mensual: Río Balsas 101, Col. Cuauhtémoc, 06500 México, DF; tel. (55) 5442-9600; e-mail corporativo@grupoarmonia.com.mx; f. 1977; fortnightly; women's interest; Editor GINA URETA; circ. 100,000.

Letras Libres: Presidente Carranza 210, Col. Coyoacán, 04000 México, DF; tel. (55) 5554-8810; fax (55) 5658-0074; e-mail suscripciones@letraslibres.com; internet www.letraslibres.com; monthly; culture; Editor-in-Chief JULIO TRUJILLO.

Manufactura: Avda Constituyentes 956, esq. Rosaleda, Col. Lomas Altas, 11950 México, DF; tel. (55) 9177-4100; e-mail dluna@expansion.com.mx; internet www.manufacturaweb.com; f. 1994; monthly; industrial; Dir-Gen. DAVID LUNA ARELLANO; circ. 25,000.

Marie Claire: Editorial Televisa, SA de CV, Avda Vasco de Quiroga 2000, Col. Santa Fe, 01210 México, DF; tel. (55) 5261-2600; fax (55) 5261-2704; f. 1990; monthly; women's interest; Editor FERNANDA GONZÁLEZ VILCHIS; circ. 70,000.

Mecánica Popular (Popular Mechanics en Español): Vasco de Quiroga 2000, Col. Santa Fe, Del. Alvaro Obregón, 01210 Mexico, DF; tel. (55) 5447-4711; fax (55) 5261-2705; internet www.mimecanicapopular.com; f. 1947; monthly; crafts and home improvements; Dir ANDRÉS JORGE; circ. 55,000.

Men's Health: Vasco de Quiroga 2000, Col. Santa Fe, Del. Alvaro Obregón, 01210 México, DF; tel. (55) 5261-2645; fax (55) 5261-2733; e-mail mens.health@editorial.televisa.com.mx; internet www.esmas.com/editorialtelevisa; f. 1994; monthly; health; Editor JUAN ANTONIO SEMPERE; circ. 130,000.

Muy Interesante: Vasco de Quiroga 2000, Col. Santa Fe, Del. Alvaro Obregón, 01210 México, DF; tel. (55) 5261-2600; fax (55) 5261-2704; internet www.esmas.com/editorialtelevisa; f. 1984; monthly; scientific devt; Dir PILAR S. HOYOS; circ. 250,000.

Negocios y Bancos: Bolívar 8-103, Apdo 1907, Col. Centro, 06000 México, DF; tel. (55) 5510-1884; fax (55) 5512-9411; e-mail nego_bancos@mexico.com; f. 1951; fortnightly; business, economics; Dir ALFREDO FARRUGIA REED; circ. 10,000.

Proceso: Fresas 7, Col. del Valle, 03100 México, DF; tel. (55) 5636-2028; internet www.proceso.com.mx; f. 1976; weekly; news analysis; Pres. JULIO SCHERER GARCÍA; circ. 98,784.

Quién: Avda Constituyentes 956, Col. Lomas Altas, CP 11950, México, DF; tel. (55) 9177-4100; e-mail aguien@expansion.com.mx; internet www.quien.com; fortnightly; celebrity news, TV, radio, films; Editor BLANCA GÓMEZ MORERA.

La Revista Peninsular: Calle 35, 489 x 52 y 54, Zona Centro, Mérida, Yuc.; tel. and fax (999) 926-3014; e-mail direccion@larevista.com.mx; internet www.larevista.com.mx; f. 1988; weekly; news and politics; Dir-Gen. RODRIGO MENÉNDEZ CÁMARA.

Selecciones del Reader's Digest: Avda Prolongación Paseo de la Reforma 1236, 10°, Col. Santa Fe, Del. Alvaro Obregón, 05348 México, DF; tel. (55) 5351-2200; internet www.selecciones.com.mx; f. 1940; monthly; Editor AUDÓN CORIA; circ. 611,660.

Siempre!: Vallarta 20, Col. Tabacalera, 06030 México, DF; tel. and fax (55) 5566-1804; e-mail suscripciones@siempre.com.mx; internet www.siempre.com.mx; f. 1953; weekly; left of centre; Dir Lic. BEATRIZ PAGÉS REBOLLAR DE NIETO; circ. 100,000.

Tele-Guía: Vasco de Quiroga 2000, Col. Santa Fe, Del. Alvaro Obregón, 01210 México, DF; tel. (55) 5261-2600; fax (55) 5261-2704; internet www.esmas.com/editorialtelevisa; f. 1952; weekly; television guide; Editor MARÍA EUGENIA HERNÁNDEZ; circ. 375,000.

Tiempo Libre: Holbein 75 bis, Col. Nochebuena Mixcoac, Del. Benito Juárez, 03720 México, DF; tel. (55) 5611-2884; fax (55) 5611-3982; e-mail buzon@tiempolibre.com.mx; internet www.tiempolibre.com.mx; f. 1980; weekly; entertainment guide; Dir-Gen. ANGELES AGUILAR ZINSER; circ. 95,000.

Tú: Vasco de Quiroga 2000, Col. Santa Fe, Del. Alvaro Obregón, 01210 México, DF; tel. (55) 5261-2600; fax (55) 5261-2730; internet www.esmas.com/editorialtelevisa; f. 1980; monthly; teenage; Editor MARÍA ANTONIETA SALAMANCA; circ. 250,000.

TV y Novelas: Vasco de Quiroga 2000, Col. Santa Fe, Del. Alvaro Obregón, 01210 México, DF; tel. (55) 5261-2600; fax (55) 5261-2704; f. 1982; weekly; television guide and short stories; Dir JESÚS GALLEGOS; circ. 460,000.

Ultima Moda: Morelos 16, 6°, Col. Centro, 06040 México, DF; tel. (55) 5518-5481; fax (55) 5512-8902; e-mail revista_ultimamoda@yahoo.com.mx; f. 1966; monthly; fashion; Pres. ROMULO O'FARRILL, Jr; Gen. Man. Lic. SAMUEL PODOLSKY RAPOPORT; circ. 110,548.

Vanidades: Vasco de Quiroga 2000, Col. Santa Fe, Del. Alvaro Obregón, 01210 México, DF; tel. (55) 5261-2600; fax (55) 5261-2704; e-mail vanidades@editorialtelevisa.com; internet www.esmas.com/vanidades; f. 1961; fortnightly; women's magazine; Dir JAQUELINE BLANCO; circ. 290,000.

Vogue (México): Condé Nast México, México, DF; tel. (55) 5095-8076; fax (55) 5245-7109; e-mail suscrip@condenast.com.mx; internet www.vogue.com.mx; f. 1999; monthly; women's fashion; circ. 208,180.

ASSOCIATIONS

Asociación Nacional de Periodistas y Comunicadores, A.C.: Luis G. Obregón 17, Of. 209, Col. Centro, 06020 México, DF; tel. (55) 5341-1523; Pres. MOISÉS HUERTA.

Federación de Asociaciones de Periodistas Mexicanos (Fapermex): Humboldt 5, Col. Centro, 06030 México, DF; tel. (55) 5510-2679; e-mail fapermex@fapermex.com; internet www.fapermex.com; Pres. JOSÉ ANTONIO CALCÁNEO COLLADO; Sec.-Gen. AURORA SANSORES SERRANO; 88 mem. asscns; 9,000 mems.

Federación Latinoamericana de Periodistas (FELAP): Nuevo Leon 144, 1°, Col. Hipódromo Condesa, 06170 México, DF; tel. (55) 5286-6055; fax (55) 5286-6085; Pres. JUAN CARLOS CAMAÑO; Sec.-Gen. JOSÉ RAFAEL VARGAS.

Fraternidad de Reporteros de México (FREMAC): Avda Juárez 88, Col. Centro, Del. Cuauhtémoc, México, DF; e-mail info@fremac.org.mx; internet www.fremac.org.mx; f. 1995; Sec.-Gen. MARCELA YARCE VIVEROS.

NEWS AGENCIES

Agencia de Información Integral Periodística (AIIP): Tabasco 263, Col. Roma, Del. Cuauhtémoc, 06700 México, DF; tel. (55) 8596-9643; fax (55) 5235-3468; e-mail aiipsa@axtel.net; internet www.aiip.com.mx; f. 1987; Dir-Gen. MIGUEL HERRERA LÓPEZ.

Agencia Mexicana de Información (AMI): Avda Cuauhtémoc 16, Col. Doctores, 06720 México, DF; tel. (55) 5761-9933; e-mail info@red-ami.com; internet www.ami.com.mx; f. 1971; Dir-Gen. JOSÉ LUIS BECERRA LÓPEZ; Gen. Man. EVA VÁZQUEZ LÓPEZ.

Notimex, SA de CV: Morena 110, 3°, Col. del Valle, 03100 México, DF; tel. (55) 5420-1172; fax (55) 5420-1188; e-mail ventas@notimex.com.mx; internet www.notimex.com.mx; f. 1968; services to press, radio and television in Mexico and throughout the world; Dir-Gen. Dr JORGE MEDINA VIEDAS.

Publishers

MÉXICO, DF

Aguilar, Altea, Taurus, Alfaguara, SA de CV: Avda Universidad 767, Col. del Valle, 03100 México, DF; tel. (55) 5688-8966; fax (55) 5604-2304; e-mail sealtiel@santillana.com.mx; f. 1965; general literature; Dir SEALTIEL ALATRISTE.

Arbol Editorial, SA de CV: Avda Cuauhtémoc 1430, Col. Santa Cruz Atoyac, 03310 México, DF; tel. (55) 5688-4828; fax (55) 5605-7600; e-mail editorialpax@maxis.com; f. 1979; health, philosophy, theatre; Man. Dir GERARDO GALLY TEOMONFORD.

Artes de México y del Mundo, SA de CV: Cordoba 69, Col. Roma, 06700 México, DF; tel. (55) 5525-5905; fax (55) 5525-5925; e-mail artesdemexico@artesdemexico.com; internet www.artesdemexico.com; f. 1988; art, design, poetry.

Editorial Avante, SA de CV: Luis G. Obregón 9, 1°, Apdo 45-796, Col. Centro, 06020 México, DF; tel. (55) 5510-8804; fax (55) 5521-5245; e-mail editorialavante@editorialavante.com.mx; internet www.editorialavante.com.mx; f. 1948; educational, drama, linguistics; Man. Dir Lic. MARIO A. HINOJOSA SAENZ.

Editorial Azteca, SA: Calle de la Luna 225–227, Col. Guerrero, 06300 México, DF; tel. (55) 5526-1157; fax (55) 5526-2557; f. 1956; religion, literature and technical; Man. Dir ALFONSO ALEMÓN JALOMO.

Cía Editorial Continental, SA de CV (CECSA): Renacimiento 180, Col. San Juan Tlihuaca, Azcapotzalco, 02400 México, DF; tel. (55) 5561-8333; fax (55) 5561-5231; e-mail info@patriacultural.com.mx; f. 1954; business, technology, general textbooks; Pres. CARLOS FRIGOLET LERMA.

Ediciones de Cultura Popular, SA: Odontología 76, Copilco Universidad, México, DF; f. 1969; history, politics, social sciences; Man. Dir URIEL JARQUÍN GALVEZ.

Editorial Diana, SA de CV: Arenal 24, Edif. Norte, Ex-Hacienda Guadalupe, Chimalistac, Del. Alvaro Obregón, 01050 México, DF; tel. (55) 5089-1220; fax (55) 5089-1230; e-mail jlr@diana.com.mx; internet www.editorialdiana.com.mx; f. 1946; general trade and technical books; Pres. and CEO JOSÉ LUIS RAMÍREZ.

MEXICO

Edamex, SA de CV: Heriberto Frias 1104, Col. del Valle, 03100 México, DF; tel. (55) 5559-8588; fax (55) 5575-0555; e-mail octaviocolmenares@edamex.com; internet www.edamex.com; arts and literature, sport, journalism, education, philosophy, food, history, children's, health, sociology; Dir-Gen. MONICA COLMENARES.

Ediciones Era, SA de CV: Calle del Trabajo 31, Col. La Fama, Tlalpan, 14269 México, DF; tel. (55) 5528-1221; fax (55) 5606-2904; e-mail edicionesera@laneta.apc.org; internet www.edicionesera.com.mx; f. 1960; general and social science, art and literature; Gen. Man. NIEVES ESPRESATE XIRAU.

Editorial Everest Mexicana, SA: Calzada Ermita Iztapalapa 1631, Col. Barrio San Miguel del Iztapalapa, 09360 México, DF; tel. (55) 5685-1966; fax (55) 5685-3433; f. 1980; general textbooks; Gen. Man. JOSÉ LUIS HUIDOBRO LEÓN.

Fernández Editores, SA de CV: Eje 1 Pte México-Coyoacán 321, Col. Xoco, 03330 México, DF; tel. (55) 5605-6557; fax (55) 5688-9173; f. 1943; children's literature, textbooks, educational toys; Man. Dir LUIS GERARDO FERNÁNDEZ PÉREZ.

Editorial Fondo de Cultura Económica, SA de CV: Carretera Picacho-Ajusco 227, Col. Bosques del Pedregal, 14200 México, DF; tel. (55) 5227-4672; fax (55) 5227-4640; e-mail editorial@fce.com.mx; f. 1934; economics, history, philosophy, children's books, science, politics, psychology, sociology, literature; Dir Lic. MIGUEL DE LA MADRID.

Editorial Grijalbo, SA de CV: Calzada San Bartolo-Naucalpan 282, Col. Argentina, Apdo 17-568, 11230 México, DF; tel. (55) 5358-4355; fax (55) 5576-3586; e-mail diredit@grijalbo.com.mx; internet www.randomhousemondadori.com.mx; f. 1954; owned by Mondadori (Italy); general fiction, history, sciences, philosophy, children's books; Man. Dir AGUSTÍN CENTENO RÍOS.

Nueva Editorial Interamericana, SA de CV: Cedro 512, Col. Atlampa, Apdo 4-140, 06450 México, DF; tel. (55) 5541-6789; fax (55) 5541-1603; f. 1944; medical publishing; Man. Dir RAFAEL SÁINZ.

Distribuidora Intermex, SA de CV: Lucio Blanco 435, Azcapotzalco, 02400 México, DF; tel. (55) 5230-9500; fax (55) 5230-9516; e-mail pmuhechi@televisa.com.mx; f. 1969; romantic fiction; Gen. Dir Lic. ALEJANDRO PAILLÉS.

Editorial Jus, SA de CV: Avda Constituyentes 647, 3°, Col. 16 de Septiembre, 11810 México, DF; tel. (55) 5093-1925; fax (55) 5529-0951; e-mail webmaster@dsc.com.mx; internet www.jus.com.mx; f. 1938; history of Mexico, law, philosophy, economy, religion; Man. TOMÁS G. REYNOSO.

Ediciones Larousse, SA de CV: Londres 247, Col. Juárez, Del. Cuauhtémoc, 06600 México, DF; tel. (55) 1102-1300; fax (55) 5208-6225; e-mail larousse@larousse.com.mx; internet www.larousse.com.mx; f. 1965; Dir-Gen. FARID AOURAGH.

Editorial Limusa, SA de CV: Balderas 95, 1°, Col. Centro, 06040 México, DF; tel. (55) 5521-2105; fax (55) 5512-2903; e-mail limusa@noriega.com.mx; internet www.noriega.com.mx; f. 1962; science, general, textbooks; Pres. CARLOS NORIEGA MILERA.

McGraw-Hill Interamericana de México, SA de CV: Cedro 512, Col. Atlampa Cuauhtémoc, 06450 México, DF; tel. (55) 5576-7304; fax (55) 5628-5367; e-mail mcgraw-hill@infosel.net.mx; internet www.mcgraw-hill.com.mx; education, business, science; Man. Dir CARLOS RIOS.

Editorial Nuestro Tiempo, SA: Avda Universidad 771, Despachos 103–104, Col. del Valle, 03100 México, DF; tel. (55) 5688-8768; fax (55) 5688-6868; f. 1966; social sciences; Man. Dir ESPERANZA NACIF BARQUET.

Editorial Oasis, SA: Avda Oaxaca 28, 06700 México, DF; tel. (55) 5528-8293; f. 1954; literature, pedagogy, poetry; Man. MARÍA TERESA ESTRADA DE FERNÁNDEZ DEL BUSTO.

Editorial Orión: Sierra Mojada 325, 11000 México, DF; tel. (55) 5520-0224; f. 1942; archaeology, philosophy, psychology, literature, fiction; Man. Dir SILVIA HERNÁNDEZ BALTAZAR.

Editorial Patria, SA de CV: Renacimiento 180, Col. San Juan Tlihuaca, Del. Azcapotzalco, 02400 México, DF; tel. (55) 5354-9100; fax (55) 5354-9109; e-mail info@patriacultural.com.mx; internet www.patriacultural.com.mx; f. 1933; fiction, general trade, children's books; Pres. CARLOS FRIGOLET LERMA.

Editorial Planeta Mexicana, SA de CV: Clavijero 70, Col. Esperanza, México, DF; tel. (55) 5533-1250; internet www.editorialplaneta.com.mx; general literature, non-fiction; part of Grupo Planeta (Spain); Grupo Planeta incorporates Ariel, Crítica, Destino, Deusto, Ediciones del Bronce, Editorial Joaquín Mortiz, Emecé, Espasa, Martínez Roca, Seix Barral and Temas de Hoy; Man. Dir JOAQUIN DIEZ-CANEDO.

Editorial Porrúa Hnos, SA: Argentina 15, 5°, 06020 México, DF; tel. (55) 5702-4574; fax (55) 5702-6529; e-mail servicios@porrua.com; internet www.porrua.com; f. 1944; general literature; Dir JOSÉ ANTONIO PÉREZ PORRÚA.

Editorial Posada, SA de CV: Eugenia 13, Despacho 501, Col. Nápoles, 03510 México, DF; tel. (55) 5682-0660; f. 1968; general; Dir-Gen. CARLOS VIGIL ZUBIETA.

Editorial Quetzcoatl, SA: Medicina 37, Local 1 y 2, México, DF; tel. (55) 5548-6180; Man. Dir ALBERTO RODRÍGUEZ VALDÉS.

Medios Publicitarios Mexicanos, SA de CV: Eugenia 811, Eje 5 Sur, Col. del Valle, 03100 México, DF; tel. (55) 5523-3342; fax (55) 5523-3379; e-mail editorial@mpm.com.mx; internet www.mpm.com.mx; f. 1958; advertising media rates and data; Gen. Man. FERNANDO VILLAMIL.

Reverté Ediciones, SA de CV: Río Pánuco 141A, Col. Cuauhtémoc, 06500 México, DF; tel. (55) 5533-5658; fax (55) 5514-6799; e-mail reverte@reverte.com.mx; internet www.reverte.com; f. 1955; science, technical, architecture; Man. RAMÓN REVERTÉ MASCÓ.

Salvat Mexicana de Ediciones, SA de CV: Presidente Masaryk 101, 5°, 11570 México, DF; tel. (55) 5250-6041; fax (55) 5250-6861; medicine, encyclopaedic works; Dir GUILLERMO HERNÁNDEZ PÉREZ.

Siglo XXI Editores, SA de CV: Avda Cerro del Agua 248, Col. Romero de Terreros, Del. Coyoacán, 04310 México, DF; tel. (55) 5658-7999; fax (55) 5658-7599; e-mail informes@sigloxxieditores.com.mx; internet www.sigloxxieditores.com.mx; f. 1966; art, economics, education, history, social sciences, literature, philology and linguistics, philosophy and political science; Dir-Gen. Lic. JAIME LABASTIDA OCHOA; Gen. Man. Ing. JOSÉ MARÍA CASTRO MUSSOT.

Editorial Trillas, SA: Avda Río Churubusco 385 Pte, Col. Xoco, Apdo 10534, 03330 México, DF; tel. (55) 5688-4233; fax (55) 5601-1858; e-mail trillas@ovinet.com.mx; internet www.trillas.mx; f. 1954; science, technical, textbooks, children's books; Man. Dir FRANCISCO TRILLAS MERCADER.

Universidad Nacional Autónoma de México: Dirección General de Fomento Editorial, Avda del Imán 5, Ciudad Universitaria, 04510 México, DF; tel. (55) 5622-6572; internet www.unam.mx; f. 1935; publications in all fields; Dir-Gen. ARTURO VELÁZQUEZ JIMÉNEZ.

ESTADO DE MÉXICO

Pearson Educación de México, SA de CV: Calle 4, 25, Fraccionamiento Industrial Alce Blanco, 53370 Naucalpan de Juárez, Méx.; tel. (55) 5387-0700; fax (55) 5358-6445; internet www.pearson.com.mx; f. 1984; educational books under the imprints Addison-Wesley, Prentice Hall, Allyn and Bacon, Longman and Scott Foresman; Pres. STEVE MARBAN.

ASSOCIATIONS

Cámara Nacional de la Industria Editorial Mexicana: Holanda 13, Col. San Diego Churubusco, 04120 México, DF; tel. (55) 5688-2011; fax (55) 5604-3147; e-mail cepromex@caniem.com; internet www.caniem.com; f. 1964; Pres. JOSÉ ANGEL QUINTANILLA; Gen. Man. GUILLERMO COCHRAN.

Instituto Mexicano del Libro, AC: México, DF; tel. (55) 5535-2061; Pres. KLAUS THIELE; Sec.-Gen. ISABEL RUIZ GONZÁLEZ.

Broadcasting and Communications

TELECOMMUNICATIONS

Regulatory Authorities

Comisión Federal de Telecomunicaciones (Cofetel): Bosque de Radiatas 44, 4°, Col. Bosques de las Lomas, Del. Cuajimalpa, 05120 México, DF; tel. and fax (55) 5261-4000; e-mail nuevaimagen@cft.gob.mx; internet www.cofetel.gob.mx; Pres. HÉCTOR OSUNA.

Dirección General de Política de Telecomunicaciones: Avda Xola y Universidad s/n, Col. Narvarte, Del. Benito Juárez, 03020 México, DF; tel. (55) 5519-1993; fax (55) 5530-1816; e-mail llcelaya@sct.gob.mx; internet www.sct.gob.mx; part of Secretariat of State for Communications and Transport; Dir Ing. LEONEL LÓPEZ CELAYA.

Principal Operators

Alestra: Paseo de las Palmas 405, Col. Lomas de Chapultepec, 11000 México, DF; internet www.alestra.com.mx; 49% owned by AT&T; Dir-Gen. ROLANDO ZUBIRÁN SHETLER.

AT&T México: Montes Urales 470, Col. Lomas de Chapultepec, 11000 México, DF; internet www.att.com.

América Móvil, SA de CV: Lago Alberto 366, Edif. Telcel 2, Col. Anáhuac, 11320 México, DF; tel. (55) 2581-3947; fax (55) 2581-3948; e-mail patricia.ramirez@americamovil.com; internet www.americamovil.com; f. 2000; subsidiaries operate mobile telephone services in 17 countries in the Americas; CEO DANIEL HAJJ ABOUMRAD.

Telcel: internet www.telcel.com; subsidiary of above, providing mobile services in Mexico; COO PATRICIA RAQUEL HEVIA COTO.

MEXICO

Avantel: Liverpool 88, Col. Juárez, 06600 México, DF; e-mail servicioaclientes@avantel.com.mx; internet www.avantel.net.mx; f. 1994; Dir-Gen. OSCAR RODRÍGUEZ MARTÍNEZ.

Axtel: Blvd Díaz Ordáz km 3.33, Zona Industrial, 66215 San Pedro Garza García, NL; tel. (81) 8114-0000; e-mail contacto@axtel.com.mx; internet www.axtel.com.mx; f. 1993; fixed-line operator.

Carso Global Telecom, SA de CV: Insurgentes Sur 3500, Col. Peña Pobre, 14060 México, DF; tel. (55) 5726-3686; fax (55) 5238-0601; internet www.cgtelecom.com.mx; f. 1996; subsidiaries include Telmex and Global Telecom; Pres. JAIME CHICO PARDO.

Teléfonos de México, SA de CV (Telmex): Parque Vía 198, Of. 701, Col. Cuauhtémoc, 06599 México, DF; tel. (55) 5222-5462; fax (55) 5545-5500; e-mail ri@telmex.com; internet www.telmex.com.mx; Pres. CARLOS SLIM DOMIT; Dir-Gen. HÉCTOR SLIM SEADE.

Grupo Iusacell, SA de CV: Avda Prolongación Paseo de la Reforma 1236, Col. Santa Fe, 05438 México, DF; tel. (55) 5109-0611; e-mail webmaster@iusacell.com.mx; internet www.iusacell.com.mx; f. 1992; a merger with Unefon was announced in Sept. 2006; operates mobile cellular telephone network; 74% owned by Móvil Access; Dir-Gen. GUSTAVO GUZMÁN SEPÚLVEDA.

Maxcom: Guillermo González Camarena 2000, Col. Centro Ciudad Santa Fe, 01210 México, DF; tel. (55) 5147-1111; internet www.maxcom.com.mx; f. 1996; fixed-line operator.

Telecomunicaciones de México (TELECOMM): Torre Central de Telecomunicaciones, Eje Central Lázaro Cárdenas 567, 11°, Ala Norte, Col. Narvarte, Del. Benito Juárez, 03020 México, DF; tel. (55) 5090-1166; fax (55) 1035-2408; internet figueroa@telecomm.net.mx; internet www.telecomm.net.mx; govt-owned; Dir-Gen. ANDRÉS FIGUEROA COBIÁN.

Telefónica México: Prolongación Paseo de la Reforma 1200, Lote B-2, Col. Santa Fe, Cruz Manca, 05348 México, DF; tel. (55) 1616-5000; internet www.telefonicamoviles.com.mx; operates mobile telephone service Telefónica Móviles México (MoviStar), telecommunications co Telefónica Data; controls Pegaso, Cedetel, Norcel, Movitel and Baja Celular; owned by Telefónica, SA (Spain); Pres. FRANCISCO GIL DÍAZ; CEO MIGUEL MENCHEN.

Unefon: Periférico Sur 4119, Col. Fuentes del Pedregal, 14141 México, DF; tel. (55) 8582-5000; e-mail ainfante@unefon.com.mx; internet www.unefon.com.mx; mobile operator; a merger with Grupo Iusacell was announced in Sept. 2006.

BROADCASTING

Regulatory Authority

Dirección General de Radio, Televisión y Cine (RTC): Roma 41, Col. Juárez, Del. Cuauhtémoc, 06600 México, DF; tel. (55) 5140-8000; e-mail buzonrtc@segob.gob.mx; internet www.rtc.gob.mx; Dir-Gen. EDUARDO GARZÓN VALDEZ.

Radio

There were 1,423 radio stations in Mexico in 2004. Among the most important commercial networks are:

ARTSA: Avda de Los Virreyes 1030, Col. Lomas de Chapultepec, 11000 México, DF; tel. (55) 5202-3344; fax (55) 5202-6940; Dir-Gen. Lic. GUSTAVO ECHEVARRÍA ARCE.

Corporación Mexicana de Radiodifusión: Tetitla 23, esq. Calle Coapa, Col. Toriello Guerra, 14050 México, DF; tel. (55) 5424-6380; fax (55) 5666-5422; e-mail comentarios@cmr.com.mx; internet www.cmr.com.mx; Pres. ENRIQUE BERNAL SERVÍN; Dir-Gen. OSCAR BELTRÁN.

Firme, SA: Gauss 10, Col. Nueva Anzures, 11590 México, DF; tel. and fax (55) 5250-7788; Dir-Gen. LUIS IGNACIO SANTIBÁNEZ.

Grupo Acir, SA: Monte Pirineos 770, Col. Lomas de Chapultepec, 11000 México, DF; tel. (55) 5540-4291; fax (55) 5540-4106; f. 1965; comprises 140 stations; Pres. FRANCISCO IBARRA LÓPEZ.

Grupo Radio Centro, SA de CV: Constituyentes 1154, Col. Lomas Atlas, Del. Miguel Hidalgo, 11950 México, DF; tel. (55) 5728-4947; fax (55) 5259-2915; f. 1965; comprises 100 radio stations; Pres. ADRIÁN AGUIRRE GÓMEZ; Dir-Gen. Ing. GILBERTO SOLIS SILVA.

Grupo Siete Comunicación: Montecito 38, 31°, Of. 33, México, DF; tel. (55) 5488-0887; e-mail jch@gruposiete.com.mx; internet www.gruposiete.com.mx; f. 1997; Pres. Lic. FRANCISCO JAVIER SÁNCHEZ CAMPUZANO.

Instituto Mexicano de la Radio (IMER): Mayorazgo 83, 2°, Col. Xoco, 03330 México, DF; tel. (55) 5628-1730; f. 1983; Dir-Gen. CARLOS LARA SUMANO.

MVS Radio Stereorey y FM Globo: Mariano Escobedo 532, Col. Anzures, 11590 México, DF; tel. (55) 5203-4574; fax (55) 5255-1425; e-mail vargas@data.net.mx; f. 1968; Pres. Lic. JOAQUÍN VARGAS G.; Vice-Pres. Lic. ADRIÁN VARGAS G.

Núcleo Radio Mil: Prolongación Paseo de la Reforma 115, Col. Paseo de las Lomas, Santa Fe, 01330 México, DF; tel. (55) 5258-1200; e-mail radiomil@rnm.com.mx; internet www.nrm.com.mx; f. 1942; comprises seven radio stations; Pres. and Dir-Gen. Lic. E. GUILLERMO SALAS PEYRÓ.

Organización Radio Centro: Artículo 123, No 90, Col. Centro, 06050 México, DF; tel. (55) 5709-2220; fax (55) 512-8588; nine stations in Mexico City; Pres. MARÍA ESTHER GÓMEZ DE AGUIRRE.

Organización Radiofónica de México, SA: Tuxpan 39, 8°, Col. Roma Sur, 06760 México, DF; tel. (55) 5264-2025; fax (55) 5264-5720; Pres. JAIME FERNÁNDEZ ARMENDÁRIZ.

Radio Cadena Nacional, SA (RCN): Lago Victoria 78, Col. Granada, 11520 México, DF; tel. (55) 2624-0401; e-mail loregonzalez@rcn.com.mx; internet www.rcn.com.mx; f. 1948; Pres. RAFAEL C. NAVARRO ARRONTE; Dir-Gen. SERGIO FAJARDO ORTIZ.

Radio Educación: Angel Urraza 622, Col. del Valle, 03100 México, DF; tel. (55) 1500-1050; fax (55) 1500-1053; e-mail direccion@radioeducacion.edu.mx; internet www.radioeducacion.edu.mx; f. 1968; Dir-Gen. VIRGINIA BELLO MÉNDEZ.

Radio Fórmula, SA: Privada de Horacio 10, Col. Polanco, 11560 México, DF; tel. (55) 5282-1016; Dir Lic. ROGERIO AZCARRAGA.

Radiodifusoras Asociadas, SA de CV (RASA): Durango 341, 2°, Col. Roma, 06700 México, DF; tel. (55) 5286-1222; fax (55) 5211-6159; f. 1956; Exec. Pres. JOSÉ LARIS RODRÍGUEZ.

Radiodifusores Asociados de Innovación y Organización, SA: Emerson 408, Col. Chapultepec Morales, 11570 México, DF; tel. (55) 5203-5577; fax (55) 5545-2078; Dir-Gen. Lic. CARLOS QUIÑONES ARMENDÁRIZ.

Radiópolis, SA de CV: owned by Grupo Televisa and Grupo Prisa; owns 5 radio stations; affiliated to Radiorama, SA de CV (q.v.) in 2004; Dir-Gen. RAÚL RODRÍGUEZ GONZÁLEZ.

Radiorama, SA de CV: Reforma 56, 5°, 06600 México, DF; tel. (55) 5566-1515; fax (55) 5566-1454; Dir JOSÉ LUIS C. RESÉNDIZ.

Representaciones Comerciales Integrales: Avda Chapultepec 431, Col. Juárez, 06600 México, DF; tel. (55) 5533-6185; Dir-Gen. ALFONSO PALMA V.

Sistema Radio Juventud: Pablo Casals 567, Prados Providencia, 44670 Guadalajara, Jal.; tel. (33) 3641-6677; fax (33) 3641-3413; f. 1975; network of several stations including Estereo Soul 89.9 FM; Dirs ALBERTO LEAL A., J. JESÚS OROZCO G., GABRIEL ARREGUI V.

Sistema Radiofónico Nacional, SA: Baja California 163, Of. 602, 06760 México, DF; tel. (55) 5574-0298; f. 1971; represents commercial radio networks; Dir-Gen. RENÉ C. DE LA ROSA.

Sociedad Mexicana de Radio, SA de CV (SOMER): Gutenberg 89, Col. Anzures, 11590 México, DF; tel. (55) 5255-5297; fax (55) 5545-0310; Dir-Gen. EDILBERTO HUESCA PERROTIN.

Radio Insurgente, the underground radio station of the Ejército Zapatista de Liberación Nacional (EZLN—Zapatistas), is broadcast from south-eastern Mexico. Programmes can be found on www.radioinsurgente.org.

Television

There were 658 television stations in 2004. Among the most important are:

Asesoramiento y Servicios Técnicos Industriales, SA (ASTISA): México, DF; tel. (55) 5585-3333; commercial; Dir ROBERTO CHÁVEZ TINAJERO.

MVS (Multivisión): Blvd Puerto Aéreo 486, Col. Moctezuma, 15500 México, DF; tel. (55) 5764-8100; e-mail orivas@mvs.com; internet www.mvs.com; subscriber-funded; Pres. JOAQUÍN VARGAS GUAJARDO; Vice-Pres. ERNESTO VARGAS.

Once TV: Carpio 475, Col. Casco de Santo Tomás, 11340 México, DF; tel. (55) 5356-1111; fax (55) 5396-8001; e-mail canal11@vmredipn.ipn.mx; f. 1959; Dir-Gen. ALEJANDRA LAJOUS VARGAS.

Tele Cadena Mexicana, SA: Avda Chapultepec 18, 06724 México, DF; tel. (55) 5535-1679; commercial, comprises about 80 stations; Dir Lic. JORGE ARMANDO PIÑA MEDINA.

Televisa, SA de CV: Edif. Televicentro, Avda Chapultepec 28, Col. Doctores, 06724 México, DF; tel. (55) 5709-3333; fax (55) 5709-3021; e-mail webmaster@televisa.com.mx; internet www.televisa.com; f. 1973; commercial; began broadcasts to Europe via satellite in Dec. 1988 through its subsidiary, Galavisión; 406 affiliated stations; Chair. and CEO EMILIO AZCÁRRAGA JEAN.

Televisión Azteca, SA de CV: Anillo Periférico Sur 4121, Col. Fuentes del Pedregal, 14141 México, DF; tel. (55) 5420-1313; fax (55) 5645-4258; e-mail webtva@tvazteca.com; internet tvazteca.todito.com; f. 1992; assumed responsibility for fmr state-owned channels 7 and 13; Pres. RICARDO B. SALINAS PLIEGO; CEO PEDRO PADILLA LONGORIA.

Televisión de la República Mexicana: Mina 24, Col. Guerrero, México, DF; tel. (55) 5510-8590; cultural; Dir EDUARDO LIZALDE.

MEXICO

Association

Cámara Nacional de la Industria de Radio y Televisión (CIRT): Avda Horacio 1013, Col. Polanco Reforma, Del. Miguel Hidalgo, 11550 México, DF; tel. (55) 5726-9909; fax (55) 5545-6767; e-mail cirt@cirt.com.mx; internet www.cirt.com.mx; f. 1942; Pres. ENRIQUE PEREDA GÓMEZ; Dir-Gen. ANDRÉS MASSIEU FERNÁNDEZ.

Finance

(cap. = capital; res = reserves; dep. = deposits; m. = million; amounts in new pesos unless otherwise stated)

BANKING

The Mexican banking system is comprised of the Banco de México (the central bank of issue), multiple or commercial banking institutions and development banking institutions. Banking activity is regulated by the Federal Government.

Commercial banking institutions are constituted as *Sociedades Anónimas*, with wholly private social capital. Development banking institutions exist as *Sociedades Nacionales de Crédito*, participation in their capital is exclusive to the Federal Government, notwithstanding the possibility of accepting limited amounts of private capital. In 2005 there were 34 commercial and development banks operating in Mexico and 71 foreign banks maintained offices.

All private banks were nationalized in September 1982. By July 1992, however, the banking system had been completely returned to the private sector. Legislation removing all restrictions on foreign ownership of banks received congressional approval in 1999.

Supervisory Authority

Comisión Nacional Bancaria y de Valores (CNBV) (National Banking and Securities Commission): Avda Insurgentes Sur 1971, Torre Norte, Sur y III, Col. Guadalupe Inn, Del. Alvaro Obregón, 01020 México, DF; tel. and fax (55) 5724-6000; e-mail info@cnbv.gob.mx; internet www.cnbv.gob.mx; f. 1924; govt commission controlling all credit institutions in Mexico; Pres. GUILLERMO ENRIQUE BABATZ TORRES.

Central Bank

Banco de México (BANXICO): Avda 5 de Mayo 2, Col. Centro, Del. Cuauhtémoc, 06059 México, DF; tel. (55) 5237-2000; fax (55) 5237-2070; e-mail comsoc@banxico.org.mx; internet www.banxico.org.mx; f. 1925; currency issuing authority; became autonomous on 1 April 1994; cap. 5,995m., res −96,843m., dep. 687,906m. (Dec. 2006); Gov. Dr GUILLERMO ORTIZ MARTÍNEZ; 6 brs.

Commercial Banks

Banco del Bajío, SA: Avda Manuel J. Clouthier 508, Col. Jardines del Campestre, 37128 León, Gto; tel. (477) 710-4600; fax (477) 710-4693; e-mail internacional@bancobajio.com.mx; internet www.bancobajio.com.mx; f. 1994; cap. 1,656.6m., res 3,007.4m., dep. 40,476.0m. (Dec. 2006); Pres. SALVADOR OÑATE.

Banco Mercantil del Norte, SA (BANORTE): Avda Revolución 3000, Col. Primavera, 64830 Monterrey, NL; tel. (81) 3319-7200; fax (81) 3319-5216; internet www.banorte.com; f. 1899; merged with Banco Regional del Norte in 1985; cap. 11,463m., res 6,902m., dep. 181,795m. (Dec. 2006); Chair. ROBERTO GONZÁLEZ BARRERA; CEO LUIS PEÑA KEGEL; 457 brs.

Banco Nacional de México, SA (Banamex): Avda Isabel la Católica 44, 06089 México, DF; tel. (55) 5720-7091; fax (55) 5920-7323; internet www.banamex.com; f. 1884; transferred to private ownership in 1991; merged with Citibank México, SA in 2001; cap. 28,882m., res 42,983m., dep. 379,318m. (Dec. 2006); CEO MANUEL MEDINA MORA; 1,260 brs.

Banca Santander, SA: Mod 401, 4°, Prolongación Paseo de la Reforma 500, Col. Lomas de Santa Fe, Del. Alvaro Obregon, 01219 México, DF; tel. (55) 5261-1543; fax (55) 5261-5549; internet www.santander.com.mx; f. 1864 as Banco Serfin; acquired by Banco Santander Central Hispano (Spain) in Dec. 2000; adopted current name 2006; cap. 8,942m., res 32,253m., dep. 312,640m. (Dec. 2006); Chair. and Pres. CARLOS GÓMEZ; CEO and Gen. Man. ADOLFO LAGOS ESPINOSA; 554 brs.

BBVA Bancomer, SA: Centro Bancomer, Avda Universidad 1200, Col. Xoco, 03359 México, DF; tel. (55) 5621-3434; fax (55) 5621-3230; internet www.bancomer.com.mx; f. 2000 by merger of Bancomer (f. 1864) and Mexican operations of Banco Bilbao Vizcaya Argentaria (Spain); privatized in 2002; cap. 15,247.9m., res 31,795.5m., dep. 455,671.6m. (Dec. 2005); Chair. HÉCTOR RANGEL DOMENE; Vice-Chair. and CEO IGNACIO DESCHAMPS GONZÁLEZ.

Dresdner Bank Mexico, SA: Bosque de Alisos 47A, 4°, Col. Bosques de las Lomas, 05120 México, DF; tel. (55) 5258-3170; fax (55) 5258-

Directory

3199; e-mail mexico@dbla.com; f. 1995; Man. Dir LUIS NIÑO DE RIVERA.

HSBC México: Paseo de la Reforma 156, Col. Juárez, Del. Cuauhtémoc, 06600 México, DF; tel. (55) 5721-2222; fax (55) 5721-2393; internet www.hsbc.com.mx; f. 1941; bought by HSBC (United Kingdom) in 2002; name changed from Banco Internacional, SA (BITAL) in 2004; cap. 3,929.6m., res 16,214.7m., dep. 239,916.6m. (Dec. 2006); CEO PAUL THURSTON; 1,400 brs.

Scotiabank Inverlat, SA: Blvd Miguel Avila Camacho 1, 18°, Col. Lomas de Chapultepec, Del. Miguel Hidalgo, 11009 México, DF; tel. (55) 5728-1000; fax (55) 5229-2019; internet www.scotiabankinverlat.com; f. 1977 as Multibanco Comermex, SA; changed name to Banco Inverlat, SA 1995; 55% holding acquired by Scotiabank Group (Canada) and adopted current name 2001; cap. 4,039m., surplus and res 11,526m., dep. 102,499m. (Dec. 2006); CEO ANATOL VON HANN; 476 brs.

Development Banks

Banco Nacional de Comercio Exterior, SNC (BANCOMEXT): Periférico Sur 4333, Col. Jardines en la Montaña, Del. Tlalpan, 14210 México, DF; tel. (55) 5449-9100; fax (55) 5652-9342; internet www.bancomext.com; f. 1937; cap. 4,667m., res 3,619m., dep. 80,433m. (Dec. 2006); Dir-Gen. MARIO MARTÍN LABORÍN GÓMEZ.

Banco Nacional del Ejército, Fuerza Aérea y Armada, SNC (BANJERCITO): Avda Industria Militar 1055, Col. Lomas de Sotelo, 11200 México, DF; tel. and fax (55) 5626-0500; fax (55) 5557-8821; internet www.banjercito.com.mx; f. 1947; Dir-Gen. Brig.-Gen. FERNANDO MILLÁN VILLEGAS; 52 brs.

Banco Nacional de Obras y Servicios Públicos, SNC (BANOBRAS): Avda Javier Barros Sierra 515, Col. Lomas de Santa Fe, 01219 México, DF; tel. (55) 5270-1552; fax (55) 5270-1564; internet www.banobras.gob.mx; f. 1933; govt-owned; cap. 11,503m., res 282m., dep. 87,238m. (Dec. 2006); Dir-Gen. ALONSO GARCÍA TAMÉS.

Financiera Rural: Agrarismo 227, Col. Escandón, Del. Miguel Hidalgo, CP 11800, México, DF; tel. (55) 5230-1600; internet www.financierarural.gob.mx; f. 2004; state-run devt bank, concerned with agricultural, forestry and fishing sectors; Dir-Gen. ENRIQUE DE LA MADRID CORDERO.

Nacional Financiera, SNC (NAFIN): Insurgentes Sur 1971, Torre IV, 13°, Col. Guadalupe Inn, 01020 México, DF; tel. (55) 5325-6700; fax (55) 5661-8418; e-mail info@nafin.gob.mx; internet www.nafin.com; f. 1934; cap. 7,661m., res 3,528m., dep. 178,860m. (Dec. 2006); Dir-Gen. MARIO MARTÍN LABORÍN GÓMEZ; 32 brs.

BANKERS' ASSOCIATION

Asociación de Bancos de México: 16 de Setiembre 27, Col. Centro Histórico, 06000 México, DF; tel. (55) 5722-4305; internet www.abm.org.mx; f. 1928; Pres. ENRIQUE CASTILLO; Dir-Gen. JUAN CARLOS JIMÉNEZ ROJAS; 52 mems.

STOCK EXCHANGE

Bolsa Mexicana de Valores, SA de CV: Paseo de la Reforma 255, Col. Cuauhtémoc, 06500 México, DF; tel. (55) 5726-6000; fax (55) 5726-6836; e-mail cinformas@bmv.com.mx; internet www.bmv.com.mx; f. 1894; Pres. GUILLERMO PRIETO DE CASTILLA; Dir-Gen. Ing. GERARDO FLORES DEUCHLER.

INSURANCE

México, DF

ACE Seguros: Bosques de Alisos, 47A, 1°, Col. Bosques de las Lomas, 5120 México, DF; tel. (5) 258-5800; fax (5) 258-5899; e-mail info@acelatinamerica.com; f. 1990; fmrly Seguros Cigna.

Aseguradora Cuauhtémoc, SA: Manuel Avila Camacho 164, 11570 México, DF; tel. (55) 5250-9800; fax (55) 5540-3204; f. 1944; general; Exec. Pres. JUAN B. RIVEROLL; Dir-Gen. JAVIER COMPEÁN AMEZCUA.

Aseguradora Hidalgo, SA: Presidente Masaryk 111, Col. Polanco, Del. Miguel Hidalgo, 11570 México, DF; f. 1931; life; Dir-Gen. JOSÉ GÓMEZ GORDOA; Man. Dir HUMBERTO ROQUE VILLANUEVA.

ING Comercial América—Seguros: Insurgentes Sur 3900, Col. Tlalpan, 14000 México, DF; tel. (55) 5169-2500; internet www.comercialamerica.com.mx; f. 1936 as La Comercial; acquired by ING Group in 2000; life, etc.; Pres. GLENN HILLIARS; Dir-Gen. Ing. ADRIÁN PÁEZ.

La Nacional, Cía de Seguros, SA: México, DF; f. 1901; life, etc.; Pres. CLEMENTE CABELLO; Chair. Lic. ALBERTO BAILLERES.

Pan American de México, Cía de Seguros, SA: México, DF; f. 1940; Pres. Lic. JESS N. DALTON; Dir-Gen. GILBERTO ESCOBEDA PAZ.

Royal & SunAlliance Mexico: Blvd Adolfo López Mateos 2448, Col. Altavista, 01060 México, DF; tel. (55) 5723-7999; fax (55) 5723-7941; e-mail omar.antonio@mx.royalsun.com; internet www

.royalsun.com.mx; f. 1941; acquired Seguros BBV-Probursa in 2001; general, except life.

Seguros Azteca, SA: Insurgentes 102, México, DF; f. 1933; general including life; Pres. JUAN CAMPO RODRÍGUEZ.

Seguros Banamex, SA: Isabel la Católica 44, Col. Centro Histórico, Del. Cuauhtémoc, 06000 México, DF; e-mail sbainternet@banamex.com; internet www.segurosbanamex.com; f. 1994; life, accident and health; Pres. AGUSTÍN F. LEGORRETA; Dir-Gen. JUAN OROZCO GÓMEZ PORTUGAL.

Seguros Constitución, SA: Avda Revolución 2042, Col. La Otra Banda, 01090 México, DF; tel. (55) 5550-7910; f. 1937; life, accident; Pres. ISIDORO RODRÍGUEZ RUIZ; Dir-Gen. ALFONSO DE ORDUÑA Y PÉREZ.

Seguros el Fénix, SA: México, DF; f. 1937; Pres. VICTORIANO OLAZÁBAL E.; Dir-Gen. JAIME MATUTE LABRADOR.

Seguros Internacional, SA: Abraham González 67, México, DF; f. 1945; general; Pres. Lic. GUSTAVO ROMERO KOLBECK.

Seguros de México, SA: Insurgentes Sur 3496, Col. Peña Pobre, 14060 México, DF; tel. (55) 5679-3855; f. 1957; life, etc.; Dir-Gen. Lic. ANTONIO MIJARES RICCI.

Seguros La Provincial, SA: México, DF; f. 1936; general; Pres. CLEMENTE CABELLO; Chair. ALBERTO BAILLERES.

Seguros La República, SA: Paseo de la Reforma 383, México, DF; f. 1966; general; 43% owned by Commercial Union (United Kingdom); Pres. LUCIANO ARECHEDERRA QUINTANA; Gen. Man. JUAN ANTONIO DE ARRIETA MENDIZÁBAL.

Monterrey, NL

Seguros Monterrey Aetna, SA: Avda Diagonal Santa Engracia 221 Oeste, Col. Lomas de San Francisco, 64710 Monterrey, NL; tel. (81) 8319-1111; fax (81) 8363-0428; f. 1940; casualty, life, etc.; Dir-Gen. FEDERICO REYES GARCÍA.

Seguros Monterrey del Círculo Mercantil, SA, Sociedad General de Seguros: Padre Mier Pte 276, Monterrey, NL; f. 1941; life; Gen. Man. CARMEN G. MASSO DE NAVARRO.

Insurance Association

Asociación Mexicana de Instituciones de Seguros, AC (AMIS): Fco I Madero 21, Col. Tlacopac, San Angel, 01040 México, DF; tel. (55) 5662-6161; fax (55) 5662-8036; e-mail amis@mail.internet.com.mx; internet www.amis.com.mx; f. 1946; all insurance cos operating in Mexico are mems; Pres. ROLANDO VEGA SAÉNZ; Dir-Gen. RECAREDO ARIAS JIMÉNEZ.

Trade and Industry

GOVERNMENT AGENCIES

Comisión Federal de Protección Contra Riesgos Sanitarios (COFEPRIS): Monterrey 33, esq. Oaxaca, Col. Roma, Del. Cuauhtémoc, 06700 Mexico, DF; tel. (55) 5080-5200; e-mail mgallegos@salud.gob.mx; internet www.cofepris.gob.mx; f. 2003; pharmaceutical regulatory authority; Sec.-Gen. MARIO GALLEGOS DUARTE.

Comisión Nacional Forestal (CONAFOR): Carretera a Nogales s/n, Esq. Periférico Poniente 5360, 5°, San Juan de Ocotán, 45019 Zapopan, Jal.; tel. (33) 3777-7047; fax (33) 3777-7028; e-mail cgonzalez@conafor.gob.mx; internet www.conafor.gob.mx; f. 2001; Dir-Gen. JOSÉ CIBRIÁN TOVAR.

Comisión Nacional de Inversiones Extranjeras (CNIE): Dirección General de Inversión Extranjera, Insurgentes Sur 1940, 8°, Col. Florida, 01030 México, DF; tel. (55) 5229-6100; fax (55) 5229-6507; f. 1973; govt commission to co-ordinate foreign investment; Exec. Sec. Dr CARLOS CAMACHO GAOS.

Comisión Nacional de los Salarios Mínimos (CNSM): Avda Cuauhtémoc 14, 2°, Col. Doctores, 06720 México 7, DF; tel. (55) 5588-9844; fax (55) 5578-5775; e-mail cnsm1@conasami.gob.mx; internet www.conasami.gob.mx; f. 1962; in accordance with Section VI of Article 123 of the Constitution; national commission on minimum salaries; Pres. Lic. BASILIO GONZÁLEZ NÚÑEZ.

Instituto Nacional de Investigaciones Nucleares (ININ): Centro Nuclear de México, Carretera México–Toluca Km 36.5, La Marquesa, 52750 Ocoyoacac, Méx.; tel. (55) 5329-7200; e-mail webmastr@nuclear.inin.mx; internet www.inin.mx; f. 1979 to plan research and devt of nuclear science and technology; also researches the peaceful uses of nuclear energy, for the social, scientific and technological devt of the country; administers the Secondary Standard Dosimetry Laboratory, the Nuclear Information and Documentation Centre, which serves Mexico's entire scientific community; operates a tissue culture laboratory for medical treatment; the 1 MW research reactor which came into operation, in 1967, supplies part of Mexico's requirements for radioactive isotopes; also operates a 12 MV Tandem van de Graaff. Mexico has two nuclear reactors, each with a generating capacity of 654 MW; the first, at Laguna Verde, became operational in 1989 and is administered by the Comisión Federal de Electricidad (CFE); Dir-Gen. JOSÉ RAÚL ORTÍZ MAGAÑA.

Instituto Nacional de Pesca (National Fishery Institute): Pitágoras 1320, Col. Santa Cruz Atoyac, Del. Benito Juárez, 03310 México, DF; tel. (55) 5688-1469; fax (55) 5604-9169; e-mail compean@inp.sagarpa.gob.mx; internet inp.sagarpa.gob.mx; f. 1962; Dir GUILLERMO COMPEAN JIMÉNEZ.

Procuraduría Federal del Consumidor (Profeco): Dr Carmona y Valle 11, Col. Doctores, 06720 México, DF; tel. (55) 5761-3021; internet www.profeco.gob.mx; f. 1975; consumer protection; Procurator ANTONIO MORALES DE LA PEÑA.

Servicio Geológico Mexicano (SGM): Blvd Felipe Angeles, Carretera México–Pachuca, km 93.5, Col. Venta Prieta, 42080 Pachuca, HI; tel. (771) 711-4266; fax (771) 711-4204; e-mail fescandon@coremisgm.gob.mx; internet www.coremisgm.gob.mx; f. 1957; govt agency for the devt of mineral resources; Dir-Gen. Ing. FRANCISCO JOSÉ ESCANDÓN VALLE.

DEVELOPMENT ORGANIZATIONS

Centro de Investigación para el Desarollo, AC (CIDAC) (Centre of Research for Development): Jaime Balmes 11, Edif. D, 2°, Col. Los Morales Polanco, 11510 México, DF; tel. (55) 5985-1010; fax (55) 5985-1030; e-mail info@cidac.org.mx; internet www.cidac.org; f. 1984; researches economic and political devt.

Comisión Nacional de las Zonas Aridas (CONAZA): Blvd Isidro Lopez Zertuche 2513, Col. Los Maestros, 25260 Saltillo, Coah.; e-mail uenlace@conaza.gob.mx; internet www.conaza.gob.mx; f. 1970; commission to co-ordinate the devt and use of arid areas; Dir-Gen. Lic. EDUARDO TERRAZAS RAMOS.

Fideicomiso de Fomento Mineiro (FIFOMI): Puente de Tecamachalco 26, 2°, Col. Lomas de Chapultepec, Del. Miguel Hidalgo, 11000 México, DF; tel. (55) 5249-9500; e-mail pguerra@fifomi.gob.mx; internet www.fifomi.gob.mx; trust for the devt of the mineral industries; Dir-Gen. PEDRO GUERRA MENÉNDEZ.

Fideicomisos Instituídos en Relación con la Agricultura (FIRA): Km 8, Antigua Carretera Pátzcuaro, 58341 Morelia, Mich.; tel. (443) 322-2399; fax (443) 327-6338; e-mail webmaster@correo.fira.gob.mx; internet www.fira.gob.mx; Dir FRANCISCO MERÉ PALAFOX; a group of devt funds to aid agricultural financing, under the Banco de México, comprising Fondo de Garantía y Fomento para la Agricultura, Ganadería y Avicultura (FOGAGA); Fondo Especial para Financiamientos Agropecuarios (FEFA); Fondo Especial de Asistencia Técnica y Garantía para Créditos Agropecuarios (FEGA); Fondo de Garantía y Fomento para las Actividades Pesqueras (FOPESCA).

Fondo de Operación y Financiamiento Bancario a la Vivienda (FOVI): Ejército Nacional 180, Col. Anzures, 11590 México, DF; tel. (55) 5263-4500; fax (55) 5263-4541; e-mail jmartinez@fovi.gob.mx; internet www.fovi.gob.mx; f. 1963 to promote the construction of low-cost housing through savings and credit schemes; devt fund under the Banco de México; Dir-Gen. MANUEL ZEPEDA PAYERAS.

Instituto Mexicano del Petróleo (IMP): Eje Central Lázaro Cárdenas 152, Col. San Bartolo Atepehuacan, Del. Gustavo A. Madero, 07730 México, DF; tel. (55) 9175-6000; fax (55) 9175-8000; e-mail jalim@imp.mx; internet www.imp.mx; f. 1965 to foster devt of the petroleum, chemical and petrochemical industries; Dir Lic. JUAN ARTURO LIM MEDRANO.

CHAMBERS OF COMMERCE

American Chamber of Commerce of Mexico (Amcham): Lucerna 78, Col. Juárez, 06600 México, DF; tel. (55) 5141-3800; fax (55) 5703-3908; e-mail amchammx@amcham.com.mx; internet www.amcham.com.mx; f. 1917; brs in Guadalajara and Monterrey; Chair. SIMON DÍAZ; Exec. Vice-Pres. LARRY D. RUBIN.

Confederación de Cámaras Nacionales de Comercio, Servicios y Turismo (CONCANACO-SERVYTUR) (Confederation of National Chambers of Commerce, Services and Tourism): Balderas 144, 3°, Col. Centro, 06079 México, DF; tel. (55) 5722-9300; e-mail comentarios@concanacored.com; internet www.concanacored.com; f. 1917; Pres. LUIS ANTONIO MAHBUB SARQUIS; Dir-Gen. Lic. EDUARDO GARCÍA VILLASEÑOR; comprises 283 regional Chambers.

Cámara de Comercio, Servicios y Turismo Ciudad de México (CANACO) (Chamber of Commerce, Services and Tourism of Mexico City): Paseo de la Reforma 42, 3°, Col. Centro, Apdo 32005, 06048 México, DF; tel. (55) 5592-2677; fax (55) 5592-2279; internet www.ccmexico.com.mx; f. 1874; 50,000 mems; Pres. LORENZO YSASI MARTÍNEZ.

Cámara Nacional de la Industria de Transformación (CANACINTRA): Avda San Antonio 256, Col. Ampliación Nápoles, Del. Benito Juárez, México, DF; tel. (55) 5563-5100; fax 5598-8044; internet mmaron@canacintra.org.mx; internet www.canacintra

MEXICO

Directory

.org.mx; represents majority of smaller manufacturing businesses; Pres. MIGUEL MARON MANZUR.

Chambers of Commerce exist in the chief town of each state as well as in the larger centres of commercial activity. There are also other international Chambers of Commerce.

CHAMBERS OF INDUSTRY

The 47 national chambers, 15 regional chambers, 3 general chambers and 42 associations, many of which are located in the Federal District, are representative of the major industries of the country.

Central Confederation

Confederación de Cámaras Industriales de los Estados Unidos Mexicanos (CONCAMIN) (Confed. of Industrial Chambers): Manuel María Contreras 133, 4°, Col. Cuauhtémoc, Del. Cuauhtémoc, 06500 México, DF; tel. (55) 5140-7800; fax 5140-7831; e-mail webmaster@concamin.org.mx; internet www.concamin.org.mx; f. 1918; represents and promotes the activities of the entire industrial sector; Pres. ISMAEL PLASCENCIA NÚÑEZ; Dir-Gen. FRANCISCO JAVIER JIMÉNEZ ROJAS; 108 mem. orgs.

INDUSTRIAL AND TRADE ASSOCIATIONS

Asociación Nacional de Importadores y Exportadores de la República Mexicana (ANIERM) (National Association of Importers and Exporters): Monterrey 130, Col. Roma, Del. Cuauhtémoc, 06700 México, DF; tel. (55) 5584-9522; fax (55) 5584-5317; e-mail anierm@anierm.org.mx; internet www.anierm.org.mx; f. 1944; Pres. RODRIGO GUERRA B.; Vice-Pres. HUMBERTO SIMONEEN ARDILA.

Asociación Nacional de la Industria Química (ANIQ): Angel Urraza 505, Col. del Valle, 03100 México, DF; tel. (55) 5230-5100; internet www.aniq.org.mx; f. 1959; chemicals asscn; Dir-Gen. Ing. MIGUEL BENEDETTO; c. 200 mem. cos.

Comisión Nacional de Seguridad Nuclear y Salvaguardias (CNSNS): Dr José María Barragán 779, Col. Narvarte, Del. Benito Juárez, 03020 México, DF; tel. (55) 5095-3200; fax (55) 5095-3295; e-mail swaller@cnsns.gob.mx; internet www.cnsns.gob.mx; f. 1979; nuclear regulatory agency; Dir-Gen. JUAN EIBENSCHUTZ HARTMAN.

Comisión Petroquímica Mexicana: México, DF; promotes the devt of the petrochemical industry; Tech. Sec. Ing. JUAN ANTONIO BARGÉS MESTRES.

Consejo Empresarial Mexicano para Asuntos Internacionales (CEMAI): Homero 527, 7°, Col. Polanco, 11570 México, DF; tel. (55) 5250-7033; fax (55) 5531-1590.

Consejo Mexicano del Café (CMCAFE): José María Ibarrarán 84, 1°, Col. San José Insurgentes, Del. Benito Juárez, 03900 México, DF; tel. and fax (55) 5611-9075; e-mail cmc@sagar.gob.mx; f. 1993; devt of coffee sector; Pres. ROBERTO GIESEMANN.

Consejo Mexicano de Comercio Exterior (COMCE): Lancaster 15, 2° y 3°, Col. Juárez, 06600 México, DF; tel. (52) 5231-7100; fax (55) 5321-7109; e-mail comce@comce.org.mx; internet www.comce.org.mx; f. 1999 to promote international trade; Pres. VALENTÍN DIEZ MORODO.

Consejo Nacional de la Industria Maquiladora de Exportación (CNIME): Ejército Nacional 418, 12°, Of. 1204, Col. Chapultepec Morales, Del. Miguel Hidalgo, 11570 México, DF; tel. and fax (55) 5250-6093; internet www.cnime.org.mx; f. 1975; Pres. JOSÉ DE JESÚS CALLEROS; Sec. MÓNICA GONZÁLEZ.

Instituto Nacional de Investigaciones Forestales y Agropecuarios (INIFAP) (National Forestry and Agricultural Research Institute): Serapio Rendón 83, Col. San Rafael, Del. Cuauhtémoc, 06470 México, DF; tel. (55) 5140-1674; fax (55) 5566-3799; e-mail productosyservicios@inifap.gob.mx; internet www.inifap.gob.mx; f. 1985; conducts research into plant genetics, management of species and conservation; Dir-Gen. PEDRO BRAJCICH GALLEGOS.

EMPLOYERS' ORGANIZATIONS

Consejo Coordinador Empresarial (CCE): Lancaster 15, Col. Juárez, 06600 México, DF; tel. (55) 5229-1100; fax (55) 5592-3857; e-mail sistemas@cce.org.mx; internet www.cce.org.mx; f. 1976; co-ordinating body of private sector; Pres. ARMANDO PAREDES ARROYO; Dir-Gen. LUIS MIGUEL PANDO.

Consejo Mexicano de Hombres de Negocios (CMHN): México, DF; f. 1963; represents leading businesspeople; affiliated to CCE; Pres. ANTONIO DEL VALLE RUIZ.

STATE HYDROCARBONS COMPANY

Petróleos Mexicanos (PEMEX): Avda Marina Nacional 329, Col. Huasteca, 11311 México, DF; tel. (55) 1944-2500; fax (55) 5531-6354; internet www.pemex.com; f. 1938; govt agency for the exploitation of Mexico's petroleum and natural gas resources; Dir-Gen. JESÚS REYES HEROLES GONZÁLEZ GARZA; 106,900 employees.

UTILITIES

Regulatory Authorities

Comisión Nacional del Agua (CNA): Avda Insurgentes Sur 2146, Col. Copilco el Bajo, Del. Coyoacán, 04340 México, DF; tel. (55) 5550-7607; fax (55) 5550-6721; e-mail direccion@cna.gob.mx; internet www.cna.gob.mx; commission to administer national water resources; Dir-Gen. JOSÉ LUIS LUEGE TAMARGO.

Comisión Reguladora de Energía (CRE): Horacio 1750, Col. Morales Polanco, Del. Miguel Hidalgo, 11510 México, DF; tel. (55) 5283-1500; internet www.cre.gob.mx; f. 1994; commission to control energy policy and planning; Pres. FRANCISCO XAVIER SALAZAR DIEZ DE SOLLANO; Exec. Sec. CARLOS HANS VALADEZ MARTÍNEZ.

Secretariat of State for Energy: see section on The Government (Secretariats of State).

Electricity

Comisión Federal de Electricidad (CFE): 2 Sec. del Bosque de Chapultepec, Museo Tecnológico, Del. Miguel Hidalgo, México, DF; tel. (55) 5229-4400; fax (55) 5553-5321; e-mail alfredo.elias@cfe.gob.mx; internet www.cfe.gob.mx; state-owned power utility; Dir-Gen. ALFREDO ELÍAS AYUB.

Luz y Fuerza del Centro: Melchor Ocampo 171, Col. Tlaxpana, Del. Miguel Hidalgo, 11379 México, DF; tel. (55) 5140-0040; fax (55) 5140-0300; e-mail cin@inter01.lfc.gob.mx; internet www.lfc.gob.mx; state-owned; operates electricity network in the centre of the country; Dir-Gen. JORGE GUTIÉRREZ VERA.

Gas

Gas Natural México (GNM): Jaime Blames 8-703, Col. Los Morales Polanco, 11510 México, DF; e-mail sugerencias@gnm.com.mx; internet www.gasnaturalmexico.com.mx; f. 1994 in Mexico; distributes natural gas in the states of Tamaulipas, Aguascalientes, Coahuila, San Luis Potosí, Guanajuato, Nuevo León and México and in the Distrito Federal; subsidiary of Gas Natural (Spain); Pres. JAVIER HERNÁNDEZ SINDE.

Petróleos Mexicanos (PEMEX): see State Hydrocarbons Company; distributes natural gas.

TRADE UNIONS

Congreso del Trabajo (CT): Avda Ricardo Flores Magón 44, Col. Guerrero, 06300 México 37, DF; tel. (55) 5583-3817; internet www.congresodeltrabajo.org.mx; f. 1966; trade union congress comprising trade union federations, confederations, etc.; Pres. Lic. HÉCTOR VALDÉS ROMO.

Confederación Regional Obrera Mexicana (CROM) (Regional Confederation of Mexican Workers): República de Cuba 60, México, DF; f. 1918; Sec.-Gen. IGNACIO CUAUHTÉMOC PALETA; 120,000 mems, 900 affiliated syndicates.

Confederación Revolucionaria de Obreros y Campesinos de México (CROC) (Revolutionary Confederation of Workers and Farmers): Hamburgo 250, Col. Juárez, Del. Cuauhtémoc, 06600 México, DF; tel. (55) 5208-5449; e-mail crocmodel@hotmail.com; internet www.croc.org.mx; f. 1952; Sec.-Gen. ISIAS GONZÁLEZ CUEVAS; 4.5m. mems in 32 state federations and 17 national unions.

Confederación Revolucionaria de Trabajadores (CRT) (Revolutionary Confederation of Workers): Dr Jiménez 218, Col. Doctores, México, DF; f. 1954; Sec.-Gen. MARIO SUÁREZ GARCÍA; 10,000 mems; 10 federations and 192 syndicates.

Confederación de Trabajadores de México (CTM) (Confederation of Mexican Workers): Vallarta 8, Col. Tabacalera, Del. Cuauhtémoc, 06030 México, DF; tel. (55) 5703-3130; e-mail ctmorganizacion@prodigy.net.mx; internet ctmorganizacion.org.mx; f. 1936; admitted to ICFTU; Sec.-Gen. JOAQUÍN GAMBOA; 5.5m. mems.

Federación Obrera de Organizaciones Femeniles (FOOF) (Workers' Federation of Women's Organizations): Vallarta 8, México, DF; f. 1950; women workers' union within CTM; Sec.-Gen. HILDA ANDERSON NEVÁREZ; 400,000 mems.

Federación Nacional de Sindicatos Independientes (National Federation of Independent Trade Unions): Isaac Garza 311 Oeste, 64000 Monterrey, NL; tel. (81) 8375-6677; e-mail fnsi@prodigy.net.mx; internet www.fnsi.org.mx; f. 1936; Sec.-Gen. JACINTO PADILLA VALDEZ; 230,000 mems.

Federación de Sindicatos de Trabajadores al Servicio del Estado (FSTSE) (Federation of Unions of Government Workers): Gómez Farías 40, Col. San Rafael, 06470 México, DF; internet www.fstse.com; f. 1938; Sec.-Gen. JOEL AYALA ALMEIDA; 2.5m. mems; 80 unions.

Frente Unida Sindical por la Defensa de los Trabajadores y la Constitución (United Union Front in Defence of the Workers and

MEXICO

Directory

the Constitution): f. 1990 by more than 120 trade orgs to support the implementation of workers' constitutional rights.

Unión General de Obreros y Campesinos de México, Jacinto López (UGOCM-JL) (General Union of Workers and Farmers of Mexico, Jacinto López): José María Marroquí 8, 2°, 06050 México, DF; tel. (55) 5518-3015; f. 1949; admitted to WFTU/CSTAL; Sec.-Gen. José Luis González Aguilera; 7,500 mems, over 2,500 syndicates.

Unión Nacional de Trabajadores (UNT) (National Union of Workers): Villalongen 50, Col. Cuauhtémoc, México, DF; tel. (55) 5140-1425; fax (55) 5703-2583; e-mail secretariageneral@strm.org.mx; internet www.unt.org.mx; f. 1998; Sec.-Gen. Francisco Hernández Juárez.

A number of major unions are non-affiliated, including:

Federación Democrática de Sindicatos de Servidores Públicos (Democratic Federation of Public Servants): México, DF; f. 2005.

Frente Auténtico de los Trabajadores (FAT).

Pacto de Unidad Sindical Solidaridad (PAUSS): comprises 10 independent trade unions.

Sindicato Nacional de Trabajadores Mineros, Metalúrgicos y Similares de la República Mexicana (SNTMM) (Mine, Metallurgical and Related Workers): Avda Dr Vertiz 668, Col. Narvarte, 03020 México, DF; tel. (55) 5519-5690; f. 1933; Sec.-Gen. Napoleón Gómez Urrutia; 86,000 mems.

Sindicato Nacional de Trabajadores de la Educación (SNTE) (Education Workers): Venezuela 44, Col. Centro, México, DF; tel. (55) 5702-0005; fax (55) 5702-6303; f. 1943; Pres. Elba Esther Gordillo Morales; Sec.-Gen. Tomás Vázquez Vigil; 1.4m. mems.

Coordinadora Nacional de Trabajadores de la Educación (CNTE): dissident faction; Leader Teodoro Palomino.

Sindicato de Trabajadores Petroleros de la República Mexicana (STPRM) (Union of Workers): Zaragoza 15, Col. Guerrero, 06300 México, DF; tel. (55) 5546-0912; close links with PEMEX; Sec.-Gen. Carlos Romero Deschamps; 110,000 mems; includes:

Movimiento Nacional Petrolero: reformist faction; Leader Hebraícaz Vásquez.

Sindicato de Trabajadores Ferrocarrileros de la República Mexicana (STFRM) (Railway Workers): Avda Ricardo Flores Magón 206, Col. Guerrero, México 3, DF; tel. (55) 5597-1011; f. 1933; Sec.-Gen. Víctor F. Flores Morales; 100,000 mems.

Sindicato Unico de Trabajadores Electricistas de la República Mexicana (SUTERM) (Electricity Workers): Río Guadalquivir 106, Col. Cuauhtémoc, 06500 México, DF; tel. (55) 5207-0578; Sec.-Gen. Leonardo Rodríguez Alcaine.

Sindicato Unico de Trabajadores de la Industria Nuclear (SUTIN) (Nuclear Industry Workers): Viaducto Río Becerra 139, Col. Nápoles, 03810 México, DF; tel. (55) 5523-8048; fax (55) 5687-6353; e-mail exterior@sutin.org.mx; internet www.sutin.org.mx; Sec.-Gen. Arturo Delfín Loya.

Unión Obrera Independiente (UOI) (Independent Workers' Union): non-aligned.

The major agricultural unions are:

Confederación Nacional Campesina (CNC) (National Peasant Confederation): Mariano Azuela 121, Col. Santa María de la Ribera, México, DF; Sec.-Gen. Lic. Beatriz Paredes Rangel.

Confederación Nacional de Organizaciones Ganaderas (National Confederation of Stockbreeding Organizations): Calzada Mariano Escobedo 714, Col. Anzures, México, DF; tel. (55) 5203-3506; e-mail sistemas@cnog.com.mx; internet www.cnog.com.mx; Pres. Oswaldo Cházaro Montalvo; 300,000 mems.

Consejo Agrarista Mexicano (Mexican Agrarian Council): 09760 Iztapalapa, México, DF; Sec.-Gen. Humberto Serrano.

Unión Nacional de Trabajadores Agriculturas (UNTA) (National Union of Agricultural Workers).

Transport

Road transport accounts for about 98% of all public passenger traffic and for about 80% of freight traffic. Mexico's terrain is difficult for overland travel. As a result, there has been an expansion of air transport and there were 61 international and national airports in 2004. In 2002 plans to build a new airport in the capital were postponed after conflict over the proposed site. International flights are provided by a large number of national and foreign airlines. Mexico has 140 seaports, 29 river docks and a further 29 lake shelters. More than 85% of Mexico's foreign trade is conducted through maritime transport. In the 1980s the Government developed the main industrial ports of Tampico, Coatzacoalcos, Lázaro Cárdenas, Altamira, Laguna de Ostión and Salina Cruz in an attempt to redirect growth and to facilitate exports. The port at Dos Bocas, on the Gulf of Mexico, was one of the largest in Latin America when it opened in 1999. A 300-km railway link across the isthmus of Tehuantepec connects the Caribbean port of Coatzacoalcos with the Pacific port of Salina Cruz.

Secretariat of State for Communications and Transport: see section on The Government (Secretariats of State).

Aeropuertos y Servicios Auxiliares (ASA): Avda 602 161, Edif. B, Col. San Juan de Aragón, Del. Venustiano Carranza, 15620 México, DF; tel. (55) 5133-1000; fax (55) 5786-9709; internet www.asa.gob.mx; Dir-Gen. Ernesto Valesco León.

Caminos y Puentes Federales (CAPUFE): Calzada de los Reyes 24, Col. Tetela del Monte, 62130 Cuernavaca, Mor.; tel. (55) 5200-2000; e-mail contacto@capufe.gob.mx; internet www.capufe.gob.mx; Dir-Gen. Manuel Zubiria Maqueo.

RAILWAYS

In 2004 there were 26,662 km of main line track. In that year the railway system carried an estimated 253,000 passengers and 54,387m. freight ton-km. Ferrocarriles Nacionales de México (FNM), government-owned since 1937, was liquidated in 2001 following a process of restructuring and privatization. A suburban train system for the Valle de México was due to become operational in 2008. In that year plans were under way for the construction of a high-speed rail link between Mexico City and Guadalajara, and a new line from Manzanillo, Aguascalientes to Mexico City.

Ferrocarril Mexicano, SA de CV (Ferromex): Bosque de Curuelos 99, Col. Bosques de la Loma, 11700 México, DF; tel. (55) 5246-3700; internet www.ferromex.com.mx; 50-year concession awarded to Grupo Ferroviario Mexicano, SA, (GFM) commencing in 1998; owned by Grupo México, SA de CV; 8,500 km of track and Mexico's largest rail fleet; links from Mexico City to Guadalajara, Hermosillo, Monterrey, Chihuahua and Pacific ports; Exec. Pres. Alfredo Casar Pérez; Dir-Gen. Rogelio Vélez López de la Cerda.

Ferrocarril del Sureste (Ferrosur): Jaime Balmes 11, Torre C, 4°, Col. Los Morales Polanco, 11510 México, DF; tel. (55) 5387-6500; internet www.ferrosur.com.mx; 50-year concession awarded to Grupo Tribasa in 1998; 66.7% sold to Empresas Frisco, SA de CV, in 1999, owned by Grupos Carso, SA de CV; Dir Guillermo Muñoz Lara.

Kansas City Southern de México (KCSM): Avda Manuel L. Barragán 4850, Col. Hidalgo, 64281 Monterrey, NL; tel. (81) 8305-7800; fax (81) 8305-7766; e-mail tfm@tfm.com.mx; internet www.tfm.com.mx; formerly Ferrocarril del Noreste; 4,242 km of line, linking Mexico City with the ports of Lázaro Cárdenas, Veracruz, Tampico/Altamira and north-east Mexico; Dir-Gen. M. Mohar.

Servicio de Transportes Eléctricos del Distrito Federal (STE): Avda Municipio Libre 402, Col. San Andrés Tetepilco, México, DF; tel. (55) 5539-2800; fax (55) 5672-4758; e-mail sugiere@ste.df.gob.mx; internet www.ste.df.gob.mx; suburban tram route with 17 stops upgraded to light rail standard to act as a feeder to the metro; also operates bus and trolleybus networks; Dir-Gen. Martín López Delgado.

Sistema de Transporte Colectivo (Metro) (STC): Delicias 67, 06070 México, DF; tel. (55) 5709-1133; fax (55) 5512-3601; internet www.metro.df.gob.mx; f. 1967; the first stage of a combined underground and surface railway system in Mexico City was opened in 1969; 10 lines, covering 158 km, were operating, in 1998, and five new lines, bringing the total distance to 315 km, are to be completed by 2010; the system is wholly state-owned and the fares are partially subsidized; Dir-Gen. Florencia Serranía Soto.

ROADS

In 2004 there were 352,072 km of roads, of which 34.5% were paved.

Long-distance buses form one of the principal methods of transport in Mexico, and there are some 600 lines operating services throughout the country.

Dirección General de Autotransporte Federal: Calzada de las Bombas 411, 11°, Col. Los Girasoles, Del. Goyoacán, 04920 México, DF; tel. (55) 5677-3561; internet dgaf.sct.gob.mx; co-ordinates long distance bus services.

SHIPPING

At the end of 2006 Mexico's registered merchant fleet numbered 753 vessels, with a total displacement of 1,161,900 grt. The Government operates the facilities of seaports. In 1994–95 management of several ports were transferred to the private sector.

Coordinación General de Puertos y Marina Mercante (CGPMM): Avda Nuevo León 210, Col. Hipódromo, 03310 México, DF; tel. (55) 5723-9300; e-mail cgpmmweb@sct.gob.mx; internet cgpmm.sct.gob.mx; Dir-Gen. de Puertos Angel González Rul y Avidrez; Dir-Gen. de Marina Mercante José Tómas Lozano y Pardinas.

MEXICO

Port of Acapulco: Puertos Mexicanos, Malecón Fiscal s/n, Acapulco, Gro; Harbour Master Capt. RENÉ F. NOVALES BETANZOS.

Port of Coatzacoalcos: Administración Portuaria Integral de Coatzacoalcos, SA de CV, Interior recinto portuario s/n Coatzacoalcos, 96400 Ver.; tel. (921) 214-6744; fax (921) 214-6758; e-mail lvenegas@apicoatza.com; internet www.apicoatza.com; Dir-Gen. Ing. GILBERTO ANTÓNIO RIOS RUÍZ.

Port of Dos Bocas: Administración Portuaria Integral de Dos Bocas, SA de CV, Carretera Federal Puerto Ceiba–Paraíso 414, Col. Quintín Arzuz, 86600 Paraíso, Tab.; tel. (933) 353-2744; e-mail dosbocas@apidosbocas.com; internet www.apidosbocas.com; Dir-Gen. ROBERTO DE LA GARZA LICÓN.

Port of Manzanillo: Administración Portuaria Integral de Manzanillo, SA de CV, Avda Tte Azueta 9, Col. Burócrata, 28250 Manzanillo, Col.; tel. (314) 331-1400; fax (314) 332-1005; e-mail comercializacion@apimanzanillo.com.mx; internet www.apimanzanillo.com.mx; Dir-Gen. Capt. HÉCTOR MORA GÓMEZ.

Port of Tampico: Administración Portuaria Integral de Tampico, SA de CV, Edif. API de Tampico, 1°, Recinto Portuario, 89000 Tampico, Tamps; tel. (833) 212-4660; fax (833) 212-5744; e-mail apitam@puertodetampico.com.mx; internet www.puertodetampico.com.mx; Gen. Dir Ing. MANUEL FLORES GUERRA.

Port of Veracruz: Administración Porturia Integral de Veracruz, SA de CV, Avda Marina Mercante 210, 7°, Col. Centro, 91700 Veracruz, Ver.; tel. (229) 932-2170; fax (229) 932-3040; e-mail sperez@apiver.com; internet apiver.com; privatized in 1994; Dir-Gen. JORGE ALEJANDRO GONZÁLEZ OLIVIERI.

Transportación Marítima Mexicana, SA de CV (TMM): Avda de la Cúspide 4755, Col. Parque del Pedregal, Del. Tlalpan, 14010 México, DF; tel. (55) 5629-8866; fax (55) 5629-8899; e-mail grupotmm@tmm.com.mx; internet www.tmm.com.mx; f. 1955; cargo services to Europe, the Mediterranean, Scandinavia, the USA, South and Central America, the Caribbean and the Far East; Pres. JUAN CARLOS MERODIO; Dir-Gen. JAVIER SEGOVIA.

CIVIL AVIATION

There were 61 airports in Mexico in 2004, of which 47 were international. Of these, México, Cancún, Guadalajara, Monterrey and Tijuana registered the highest number of operations.

Aeropuertos y Servicios Auxiliares (ASA): Edif. B, Avda 602 161, Col. San Juan de Aragón, Del. Venustiano Carranza, 15620 México, DF; tel. (55) 5133-1000; fax (55) 5133-2985; e-mail evelasco@asa.gob.mx; internet www.asa.gob.mx; oversees airport management and devt; Dir-Gen. ERNESTO VELASCO LEÓN.

Dirección General de Aeronáutica Civil (DGAC): Avda Xola y Universidad, Col. Narvarte, Del. Benito Juárez, 03020 México, DF; tel. (55) 5723-9300; fax (55) 5530-0093; internet dgac.sct.gob.mx; subdivision of Secretariat of State for Communications and Transport; regulates civil aviation; Dir-Gen. GILBERTO LÓPEZ MEYER.

Aerocalifornia: Aquiles Serdán 1955, 23000 La Paz, BCS; e-mail aeroll@aerocalifornia.uabcs.mx; f. 1960; services suspended in 2006 over safety concerns; regional carrier with scheduled passenger and cargo services in Mexico and the USA; Chair. PAUL A. ARECHIGA.

Aerocancún: Edif. Oasis 29, Avda Kukulcan, esq. Cenzontle, Zona Hotelera, 77500 Cancún, Q. Roo; charter services to the USA, South America, the Caribbean and Europe; Dir-Gen. JAVIER MARANÓN.

Aeroliteral: e-mail comentarios@aerolitoral.com; internet www.aerolitoral.com.mx; owned by state holding co Consorcio Aeroméxico, SA; operates internal flights in central and northern Mexico, and flights to the USA.

Aeromar, Transportes Aeromar: Hotel María Isabel Sheraton, Paseo de la Reforma 325, Local 10, México, DF; tel. (55) 5514-2248; e-mail web.aeromar@aeromar.com.mx; internet www.aeromar.com.mx; f. 1987; scheduled domestic passenger and cargo services; Dir-Gen. JUAN I. STETA.

Aeromexpress Cargo: Avda Texococo s/n esq., Avda Tahel, Col. Peñón de los Baños, 15620 México, DF; tel. (55) 5133-0203; internet www.aeromexpress.com.mx; owned by state holding co Consorcio Aeroméxico, SA; cargo airline.

Aerovías de México (Aeroméxico): Paseo de la Reforma 445, 3°, Torre B, Col. Cuauhtémoc, 06500 México, DF; tel. (55) 5133-4000; fax (55) 5133-4619; internet www.aeromexico.com; f. 1934 as Aeronaves de México, nationalized 1959; sold by state holding co Consorcio Aeroméxico, SA, to private investors in 2007; services between most principal cities of Mexico and the USA, Chile, Brazil, Peru, France and Spain; Pres. and Dir-Gen. ANDRÉS CONESA LABASTIDA.

Aviacsa: Aeropuerto Internacional, Zona C, Hangar 1, Col. Aviación General, 15520 México, DF; tel. (55) 5716-9005; fax (55) 5758-3823; internet www.aviacsa.com; f. 1990; operates internal flights, and flights to the USA.

Azteca Lineas Aéreas: e-mail info@aazteca.com; internet www.aazteca.com.mx; f. 2000; domestic flights.

Click Mexicana: Avda Xola 535, Col. del Valle, 03100 México, DF; tel. (55) 5284-3132; e-mail servicio.cliente@clickmx.com; internet www.clickmx.com; f. 2005; owned by Mexicana; fmrly known as Aerocaribe; budget airline operating internal flights; CEO ISAAC VOLIN BOLOK.

Interjet (ABC Aerolíneas, SA de CV): Aeropuerto Internacional de Toluca, Toluca, Méx.; tel. (55) 1102-5555; e-mail atencionaclientes@interjet.com.mx; internet www.interjet.com.mx; f. 2005; budget airline operating internal flights; Pres. MIGUEL ALEMÁN MAGNANI.

Mexicana (Compañía Mexicana de Aviación, SA de CV): Avda Xola 535, Col. del Valle, 03100 México, DF; tel. (55) 5448-3000; fax (55) 5448-3129; e-mail dirgenmx@mexicana.com.mx; internet www.mexicana.com; f. 1921; fmrly state-owned; sold to Grupo Posadas in 2005; international services between Mexico City and the USA, Central America and the Caribbean; domestic services; Pres. GASTÓN AZCARRAGA ANDRADE; Dir-Gen. MANUEL BORJA CHICO.

Volaris: Aeropuerto Internacional de la Ciudad de Toluca, 50500 Toluca, DF; tel. (55) 1102-8000; e-mail comentarios@volaris.com.mx; internet www.volaris.com.mx; f. 2006; operated by Vuela Compañía de Aviación; budget airline operating internal flights; Pres. PEDRO ASPE ARMELLA; Dir-Gen. ENRIQUE BELTRANENA.

Tourism

Tourism remains one of Mexico's principal sources of foreign exchange. Mexico received 21.4m. foreign visitors in 2006, as well as 78.6m. excursionists, and receipts from tourism in that year were estimated at US $12,177m. More than 90% of visitors come from the USA and Canada. The country is famous for volcanoes, coastal scenery and the great Sierra Nevada (Sierra Madre) mountain range. The relics of the Mayan and Aztec civilizations and of Spanish Colonial Mexico are of historic and artistic interest. Zihuatanejo, on the Pacific coast, and Cancún, on the Caribbean, were developed as tourist resorts by the Government. In 2004 an estimated 1.8m. people were employed in the tourism sector. In October 2005 'Hurricane Wilma' inflicted heavy damage on some tourist areas, notably Cancún. The government tourism agency, FONATUR, encourages the renovation and expansion of old hotels and provides attractive incentives for the industry. FONATUR is also the main developer of major resorts in Mexico.

Secretariat of State for Tourism: see section on The Government (Secretariats of State).

Asociación Mexicana de Agencias de Viajes (AMAV): Guanajuato 128, México, DF; tel. (55) 5584-9300; e-mail amavcun@prodigy.net.mx; internet www.amavnacional.com.mx; f. 1945; asscn of travel agencies; Pres. JORGE HERNÁNDEZ DELGADO.

Fondo Nacional de Fomento al Turismo (FONATUR): Tecoyotitla 100, Col. Florida, 01030 México, DF; tel. (55) 5090-4200; fax (55) 5090-4469; e-mail jmccarthy@fonatur.gob.mx; internet www.fonatur.gob.mx; f. 1956 to finance and promote the devt of tourism; Dir-Gen. MIGUEL GÓMEZ-MONT URUETA.

THE FEDERATED STATES OF MICRONESIA

Introductory Survey

Location, Climate, Language, Religion, Flag, Capital

The Federated States of Micronesia forms (with Palau, q.v.) the archipelago of the Caroline Islands, about 800 km east of the Philippines. The Federated States of Micronesia comprises 607 islands and includes (from west to east) the states of Yap, Chuuk (formerly Truk), Pohnpei (formerly Ponape) and Kosrae. The islands are subject to heavy rainfall, although precipitation decreases from east to west. January, February and March are the driest months, although seasonal variations in rainfall and temperature are generally small. Average annual temperature is 27°C (81°F). The native population consists of various ethno-linguistic groups, but English is widely understood. The principal religion is Christianity, much of the population being Roman Catholic. The national flag (proportions 10 by 19) consists of four five-pointed white stars, arranged as a circle, situated centrally on a light blue field. The capital is Kolonia, on Pohnpei.

Recent History

The Federated States of Micronesia was formerly part of the US-administered Trust Territory of the Pacific Islands (for history up to 1965, see the chapter on the Marshall Islands).

From 1965 there were increasing demands for local autonomy within the Trust Territory of the Pacific Islands. In that year the Congress of Micronesia was formed, and in 1967 a commission was established to examine the future political status of the islands. In 1970 it declared Micronesians' rights to sovereignty over their own lands, to self-determination, to devise their own constitution and to revoke any form of free association with the USA. In May 1977, after eight years of negotiations, US President Jimmy Carter announced that his administration intended to adopt measures to terminate the trusteeship agreement by 1981. Until 1979 the four districts of Yap, Truk (Chuuk since 1990), Ponape (Pohnpei since 1984) and Kosrae were governed by a local Administrator, appointed by the President of the USA. However, on 10 May 1979 the four districts ratified a new Constitution to become the Federated States of Micronesia. The Constitution was promulgated in 1980.

The USA signed the Compact of Free Association with the Republic of Palau in August 1982, and with the Marshall Islands and the Federated States of Micronesia in October. Under the Compacts, the four countries (including the Northern Mariana Islands) became independent of each other and took charge of both their internal and foreign affairs separately, while the USA remained responsible for defence and security. The Compact was approved by plebiscite in the Federated States of Micronesia in June 1983, and was ratified by the islands' Congress in September.

In May 1986 the UN Trusteeship Council endorsed the US Government's request for the termination of the existing trusteeship agreement with the islands. US administration of the Federated States of Micronesia was formally ended in November of that year. The UN Security Council ratified the termination of the trusteeship agreement in December 1990. Ponape was renamed Pohnpei in November 1984, when its Constitution came into effect. Truk was renamed Chuuk in January 1990, when its new Constitution was proposed (being later adopted). The Federated States of Micronesia was admitted to the UN in September 1991.

The incumbent President (since 1987), John Haglelgam, was replaced by Bailey Olter, a former Vice-President, in May 1991. At congressional elections in March 1995 Olter was re-elected to the Pohnpei Senator-at-Large seat, and in early May he was re-elected to the presidency unopposed. Similarly, Jacob Nena was re-elected as Vice-President. Allegations that financial mismanagement by the Governor of Chuuk, Sasao Gouland, had resulted in state debts of some US $20m. led to his resignation in June 1996, in order to avoid impeachment proceedings. In July Olter suffered a stroke. Jacob Nena served as acting President during Olter's absence from office, and in May 1997 was sworn in as President of the country. (Olter died in February 1999.)

Congressional elections took place in early March 1997 for the 10 Senators elected on a two-yearly basis, at which all of the incumbents were returned to office. A referendum held concurrently on a proposed amendment to the Constitution (which envisaged increasing the allocation of national revenue to the state legislatures from 50% to 80% of the total budget) was approved in Chuuk and Yap, but rejected in Pohnpei and Kosrae.

Allegations of government interference in the media became widespread when the editor of the country's principal newspaper, *FSM News*, was refused permission to re-enter the islands in June 1997. The Government had sought to deport the editor (who was a Canadian national) following publication in the periodical of reports on government spending, which the authorities claimed were false and malicious. It was also thought that by enforcing the exclusion order, the Government hoped to suppress the publication in the newspaper of information relating to alleged corruption among public officials. The newspaper ceased publication in late 1997.

In February 1998 Congress approved proposals to restructure and reorganize the Cabinet. Several ministerial portfolios were consequently merged or abolished, with the aim of reducing government expenditure. Congressional elections took place on 2 March 1999, at which President Nena was re-elected to the Kosrae Senator-at-Large seat and Vice-President Leo Falcam to the Pohnpei Senator-at-Large seat. On 11 May Congress elected Falcam as President and the Chuuk Senator-at-Large, Redley Killion, as Vice-President.

A first round of renegotiations of the Compact of Free Association (certain terms of which were due to expire in 2001) was completed in late 1999. The USA and the Federated States of Micronesia pledged to maintain defence and security relations. It was also agreed that the USA would continue to provide economic aid to the islands and assist in the development of the private sector, as well as in promoting greater economic self-sufficiency. In July 2001 the USA offered annual assistance of US $61m. and a trust fund of $13m., and expressed concern that the $2,600m. it had given to Micronesia and the Marshall Islands since 1986 had been mismanaged. The Compact's funding terms for Micronesia were originally due to expire on 3 November 2001, but negotiations regarding a new Compact were not completed by this time. Funding was, nevertheless, continued at the Compact's 15-year average level while negotiations remained in progress. Following a proposal by the USA in April 2002 to extend economic assistance for a period of 20 years, a new draft funding structure was agreed, and in March the US budget projections for 2004 granted Micronesian citizens access to private health care resources in the USA as part of the Federated States' continued entitlement to US federal programmes. On 1 May 2003 the amended Compact of Free Association was signed by representatives of the two countries in Pohnpei. The new Compact envisaged direct annual grants of $76.2m. in 2004, in addition to a further $16m. annually, which was to be paid into a Trust Fund for Micronesia. From 2007, direct grants were to decrease by some $800,000, with this amount being transferred to the trust fund. (The total amount to be paid prior to the expected termination of US assistance in 2023 amounted, in 2004 terms, to some $1,760m.) Furthermore, the Micronesian Government also undertook to provide frequent, strictly monitored audit information on all US funding in order to ensure greater accountability. In October 2003 final agreement was reached on some outstanding security and immigration issues, and the US Congress approved the amended Compact in November. President George W. Bush signed the pact in December, and representatives of both Governments signed a document of implementation in June 2004. Nevertheless, there remained widespread concern in the Federated States of Micronesia that the new Compact represented a substantial overall reduction in annual income over the long term. Moreover, the formula for the distribution of Compact funds to each of Micronesia's states and the removal of certain US subsidies remained the subject of considerable controversy. In August representatives of Micronesia and the USA met to review the management of Compact funds in the first session of the Joint Economic Management Committee.

In September 2002 unrest occurred on the Faichuk islands, part of Chuuk, where the Faichuk Commission for Statehood continued its campaign to secede from Chuuk and gain equal status within the Federation. The secessionists believed that independence would bring more goods, services, medical treatment and capital improvement projects. Local dissatisfaction worsened in September following allegations of electoral manipulation against the village mayor of Udot island, with a large crowd appearing to support attempts by local security forces to prevent the mayor's arrest. In March 2005 Congressman Twiter Aritos introduced to the national Congress legislation to grant Faichuk the status of the Federation's fifth state.

Also in September 2002 a referendum was held on a number of proposed amendments to the Constitution. The prospective changes included a provision for the direct election of presidential candidates, the extension of the right of islanders to hold dual citizenship and changes to the distribution formula for Compact of Free Association funds. However, the measures did not receive the required three-quarters' majority of votes and were thus rejected.

At the congressional elections of 6 March 2003 President Leo Falcam unexpectedly failed to achieve re-election to a further four-year term as Senator-at-Large for Pohnpei. In mid-May Congress appointed the Senator-at-Large for Yap, Joseph J. Urusemal, to the presidency. The elections were the subject of some controversy, as it appeared that elected officials had disbursed a portion of the 2002 US funding for Micronesia in order to enhance their electoral prospects. The alleged misallocation of funds was reportedly a significant factor in the worsening fiscal positions of Chuuk, Pohnpei and Kosrae. Moreover, perceptions of official accountability continued to deteriorate in 2003; in November three serving Congressmen were indicted for their role in an alleged fraud involving some $1.2m. in public funds. In January 2004 the national Congress approved a resolution to dismiss the judge assigned to the case. President Urusemal lodged a petition against the dismissal on the grounds that it infringed the constitutionally guaranteed separation of powers. In August the Supreme Court ruled in favour of the petition and overturned the judge's dismissal. Also in January 2004, members of the national Congress attempted to introduce legislation effectively absolving public officials from corruption allegations relating to Compact of Free Association funds. The proposals aroused widespread public hostility, and several representatives of state legislatures threatened to secede from the federation unless the measure were withdrawn. In March the so-called 'amnesty bill' was returned to a congressional subcommittee for further discussion.

At congressional elections held on 7 March 2005 all but one of the incumbent Senators-at-Large were re-elected, with results from Chuuk awaiting confirmation in early April. At congressional elections held on the following day eight of the 10 incumbent Senators with two-year mandates were re-elected. (Results from Chuuk were annulled, owing to alleged voting irregularities, and in late April a new round of voting was held in this state, at which, amid further allegations of electoral malpractice, Peter S. Sitan was elected.) Concurrent to the second round of congressional elections, a referendum was held over three proposed amendments to the Constitution, including the question of whether each state should recognize and uphold the laws and judicial rulings of other states, and whether to allow dual citizenship. Although a majority of voters favoured the proposed amendments, these could not be implemented because the majority of 75% or more of the votes, as required by the Constitution, had not been obtained.

In April 2006 the national Congress filed a lawsuit against President Urusemal in protest at his use of the presidential veto against certain items of proposed legislation. In June the Supreme Court approved the Department of Justice's decision, on behalf of the President, to dismiss the lawsuit, on the basis that the judicial system was not authorized to examine the reasons for a presidential veto. Urusemal had argued that these bills were unconstitutional because relevant first and second readings had been held on the same day; he later urged the Congress to resubmit them. At the end of July the Chinese Minister of Foreign Affairs, Li Zhaoxing, became the highest-ranking official of the People's Republic of China ever to visit the Federated States of Micronesia, meeting President Urusemal and Sebastian Anefal, the Secretary of the Department of Foreign Affairs. In September residences built by the Chinese for the President, Vice-President, Speaker of Congress and Chief Justice of the Federated States of Micronesia were presented to the Government at a ceremony that highlighted the strong links between the two countries.

At congressional elections held on 6 March 2007 for all 14 seats of the chamber, the incumbent Senators-at-Large for Kosrae, Pohnpei and Yap were re-elected, while Immanuel Mori defeated Vice-President Redley Killion to become Senator-at-Large for Chuuk. On 11 May 2007, in a congressional vote, Mori was elected President of the Federated States of Micronesia, taking office on the same day; Alik L. Alik of Kosrae succeeded Redley Killion as Vice-President. 'Special' congressional elections were conducted in July to fill the seats vacated by Mori and Alik. In a protracted confirmation process, members of Mori's Government were individually nominated and sworn in during the latter half of 2007 and early 2008. A reorganization of ministries was also instigated, including the creation of a Department of Education. Meanwhile, relations between the Federated States of Micronesia and China were bolstered with the opening of a Micronesian embassy in Beijing in May. In December President Mori paid a visit to Japan, attending a meeting with the Japanese Prime Minister, Yasuo Fukuda. Fukuda reportedly acknowledged the challenge posed by global warming to island nations such as the Federated States of Micronesia, and confirmed that the Japanese embassy in Kolonia would soon benefit from the presence of a resident ambassador.

Periodic extreme weather formations have caused loss of life and severe damage to crops, property and infrastructure in Micronesia. Following a severe typhoon in December 2002, President George W. Bush of the USA declared Micronesia a federal disaster area and ordered emergency US funding and resources to be allocated to the relief effort. A further typhoon which struck Yap in April 2004 left 1,200 people homeless; the US Government offered to assume 75% of the cost of the recovery effort.

In late 2000 marine biologists issued a warning regarding the erosion of the islands' coastlines, caused by the destruction of the coral reefs by pollution, overfishing and increasing sea temperatures. Furthermore, in late 2003 concerns over environmental pollution increased, owing to the environmental damage caused by former US and Japanese military equipment submerged in Micronesian waters. A former US Navy oil tanker submerged off the remote Ulithi Atoll was reported at this time to be leaking. Meanwhile, in September 2003 President Urusemal urged the UN General Assembly to work towards halting climate change and its consequent effects on sea-levels and weather systems.

In February 2003 Pohnpei hosted the first Summit of Micronesian Leaders. At the second summit, held in Koror, Palau, in March 2004, President Urusemal and the leaders of Palau, the Northern Mariana Islands and Guam undertook to increase co-operation among the Pacific island states in the areas of tourism and the environment. Further co-operation in the fields of health, the economy and labour were discussed at a summit meeting in late 2007.

Government

On 10 May 1979 the locally drafted Constitution of the Federated States of Micronesia, incorporating the four states of Kosrae, Yap, Ponape (later Pohnpei) and Truk (later Chuuk), became effective. The federal legislature, the Congress, comprises 14 members (Senators). The four states each elect one 'Senator-at-Large', for a four-year term. The remaining 10 Senators are elected for two-year terms: their seats are distributed in proportion to the population of each state. Each of the four states also has its own Constitution, Governor and legislature. The federal President and Vice-President are elected by the Congress from among the four Senators-at-Large; the offices rotate among the four states. (By-elections are then held for the seats to which the President and Vice-President had been elected.) In November 1986 the Compact of Free Association was signed by the Governments of the Federated States of Micronesia and the USA. Certain of its terms, due to expire in 2001, were renegotiated in late 1999, and an amended Compact was signed by the Governments of both countries on 1 May 2003. By the terms of the Compact, the Federated States of Micronesia is a sovereign, self-governing state.

Local government units are the municipalities and villages. Elected Magistrates and Councils govern the municipalities. Village government is largely traditional.

THE FEDERATED STATES OF MICRONESIA

Defence
The USA is responsible for the defence of the Federated States of Micronesia.

Economic Affairs
In 2006, according to estimates by the World Bank, gross national income (GNI) in the Federated States of Micronesia, measured at average 2004–06 prices, was US $264m., equivalent to $2,380 per head (or $7,830 per head on an international purchasing–power parity basis). During 1996–2006, it was estimated, the population increased at an average annual rate of 0.3%, while gross domestic product (GDP) per head decreased, in real terms, by an average of 0.4% per year. Overall GDP decreased, in real terms, at an average annual rate of 0.1% in 1996–2006. According to the Asian Development Bank (ADB), real GDP decreased by 2.3% in 2006 and by 2.5% in 2007.

Agriculture is mainly on a subsistence level, although its importance is diminishing. The principal crops are coconuts, bananas, betel nuts, cassava and sweet potatoes. White peppercorns are produced on Pohnpei. The sector (including forestry and fishing) contributed 27.6% of the GDP of defined activities in 2002 and engaged about 24% of the employed labour force in 2005. In the year to September 2005 fishing access fees, mainly from Japanese fleets, totalled US $13.3m. (some 25% of total government current revenue). Exports of fish are a major source of revenue.

Industry (including mining, manufacturing, utilities and construction) provided 21.1% of the GDP of defined activities in 2002. There is little manufacturing, other than the production of buttons using trochus shells. A garment factory in Yap, staffed mainly by Asian migrant workers, made a significant contribution to exports prior to its closure in 2005. The islands are dependent on imported fuels, with imports of mineral products accounting for 22.4% of the value of total imports in 2006.

The services sector provided an estimated 51.2% of the GDP of defined activities in 2002. A total of 6,524 people were employed by the national and state Governments in 2005/06. Tourism is an important industry, with receipts for 2005 totalling some US $17m. The number of tourist arrivals decreased from 19,260 in 2004 to 18,958 in 2005, rising to 19,136 in 2006. Remittances from overseas emigrants are a significant source of income support.

In the financial year ending September 2006 there was a visible trade deficit of an estimated US $128.9m., with a deficit of $38.4m. on the current account of the balance of payments. The principal sources of imports in 2006 were the USA (which supplied 39.7% of the total), Guam (18.8%) and Japan (9.5%). Japan was the principal market for exports in 2005, purchasing 15.5% of the total, while Guam accounted for 7.3%. The principal imports in 2006 were mineral products (22.4% of the total), prepared foodstuffs, beverages and tobacco (18.8%) and machinery, mechanical appliances and electrical equipment (10.6%). Fish is the major export commodity, accounting for 94.0% of total exports in 2005. Other exports in that year included betel nuts.

In 2005/06 the Government (including the four state governments) incurred an estimated budget deficit of US $13.0m., despite receiving grants totalling $85.3m. The budget deficit was estimated to be the equivalent of 5.4% of GDP in 2005/06, decreasing to 2.7% in 2006/07. The Federated States of Micronesia relies heavily on financial assistance, particularly from the USA, with funding made available under the Compact of Free Association (see Recent History). The USA's proposed budget for 2006/07 provided $97.6m. of Compact funding to Micronesia. Bilateral grants have been provided by the People's Republic of China and Japan. At the end of the 2006/07 financial year, according to the ADB, the islands' total external debt stood at $60m., and in that year the cost of debt-servicing was equivalent to 6.0% of the value of exports of goods and services. The annual rate of inflation averaged 1.9% in 2000–06. According to the ADB, the inflation rate decreased from an annual average of 4.8% in 2006 to 2.8% in 2007. Some 22% of the labour force were unemployed at the 2000 census.

The Federated States of Micronesia is a member of the Pacific Community (see p. 377), the Pacific Islands Forum (see p. 380), the South Pacific Regional Trade and Economic Co-operation Agreement (SPARTECA, see p. 381), the UN Economic and Social Commission for Asia and the Pacific (ESCAP, see p. 35) and the Asian Development Bank (ADB, see p. 182). In November 2002 the Federated States of Micronesia was announced as the location of the headquarters for the Tuna Commission, a new multilateral agency to manage migratory fish stocks in the central and western Pacific region. The Council of Micronesian Government Executives, of which the Federated States of Micronesia was a founder member in 1996, aims to facilitate discussion of economic developments in the region and to examine possibilities for reducing the considerable cost of shipping essential goods between the islands.

Economic development has been constrained by the islands' remote position, the high rate of emigration, the lack of marketable commodities and vulnerability to adverse climatic conditions. The expansion of the private sector has been restricted by the disproportionately high cost of domestic labour, rates of pay in the public sector having risen substantially. It was hoped that Micronesia would have achieved financial self-sufficiency by 2023, but concerns continued with regard to the lack of progress in restructuring the economy in preparation for the potentially serious impact of the eventual withdrawal of direct US aid in that year, upon the expiry of the Compact of Free Association (see Recent History). Some considered that the amendments made to the Compact in 2003 represented a substantial real reduction in Micronesia's grant income. Gross financial contributions from the USA were to total $104.9m. annually from September 2005. Under the amended Compact, instead of general budgetary grants, US aid was to be targeted more towards specific projects and government departments. Also, aid was to be conditional upon the efficiency of its management and use, and was to be reviewed annually. Meanwhile, the Trust Fund for Micronesia, established to support the economy upon the expiry of the Compact, was expected to remain vulnerable to international economic performance, the majority of this capital being invested in US stock markets. In September 2005, in an attempt to increase government revenue, a radical programme of tax reform was approved. In the longer term, another area identified as being in need of reform was that of public enterprises. Measures to encourage the development of the private sector were also required. Although the number of citizens resident overseas was estimated to total 30,000, in 2004/05 gross receipts of private transfers reached only $6.0m., equivalent to less than 2.5% of GDP in that year. The economy contracted for the fourth successive year in 2007, partly owing to the limitations placed on government expenditure by the reductions in US funding. The ADB forecast that the decline would accelerate in 2008, with GDP expected to contract by 3.5% in that year.

Education
Primary education, which begins at six years of age and lasts for eight years, is compulsory. Secondary education, beginning at 14 years of age, comprises two cycles, each of two years. The Micronesia Maritime and Fisheries Academy, which was opened in Yap in 1990, provides education and training in fisheries technology at secondary and tertiary levels. The College of Micronesia offers two- and three-year programmes leading to a degree qualification. A summit meeting was held in September 2000 to discuss the improvement and reform of the education sector. In 1997 Micronesia had a student-teacher ratio of 17. An average of 37% of students remained in education from first grade to graduation. In 2005/06 there were 24,601 pupils enrolled in primary education and 8,246 pupils enrolled in secondary education. In the same year approximately 2,283 were studying at college level.

Public Holidays
2008: 1 January (New Year's Day), 21 March (Good Friday, Pohnpei only), 9 May (Constitution Day), 24 October (United Nations Day), 3 November (Independence Day), 25 December (Christmas Day).

2009: 1 January (New Year's Day), 10 April (Good Friday, Pohnpei only), 11 May (Constitution Day), 23 October (United Nations Day), 3 November (Independence Day), 25 December (Christmas Day).

Weights and Measures
With certain exceptions, the imperial system is in force. One US cwt equals 100 lb; one long ton equals 2,240 lb; one short ton equals 2,000 lb. A policy of gradual voluntary conversion to the metric system is being undertaken.

Statistical Survey

Source (unless otherwise indicated): Statistics Unit, Office of Statistics, Budget and Economic Management, Overseas Development Assistance and Compact Management (SBOC), POB PS-12, Palikir, Pohnpei, FM 96941; tel. (691) 320-2820; fax (691) 320-5854; e-mail fsmstat@sboc.fm; internet www.spc.int/prism/country/fm/stats.

AREA AND POPULATION

Area: 700.8 sq km (270.6 sq miles): Chuuk (Truk, 294 islands) 127.4 sq km; Kosrae (5 islands) 109.6 sq km; Pohnpei (Ponape, 163 islands) 345.2 sq km; Yap (145 islands) 118.6 sq km.

Population: 105,506 (males 53,923, females 51,583) at census of 18 September 1994; 107,008 (males 54,191, females 52,817) at census of 1 April 2000. *By State* (2000): Chuuk 53,595; Kosrae 7,686; Pohnpei 34,486; Yap 11,241. *2007* (official estimate at 1 April): 108,031 (males 54,403, females 53,628).

Density (estimate at 1 April 2007): 154.2 per sq km.

Principal Towns (population of municipalities at 2000 census): Weno (Moen) 13,802; Palikir (capital) 6,444; Nett 6,158; Kitti 6,007. Source: Thomas Brinkhoff, *City Population* (internet: www.citypopulation.de).

Births and Deaths (1999/2000, official estimates): Birth rate 28.1 per 1,000; Death rate 6.7 per 1,000. *2003* (incomplete registration): Live births 2,483; Deaths 427 (Source: UN, *Population and Vital Statistics Report*). *2000–05* (annual averages, UN estimates): Birth rate 29.7 per 1,000; Death rate 6.3 per 1,000 (Source: UN, *World Population Prospects: The 2006 Revision*).

Expectation of Life (years at birth, WHO estimates): 68.3 (males 66.7; females 69.9) in 2005. Source: WHO, *World Health Statistics*.

Economically Active Population (persons aged 15 years and over, 2000 census): Agriculture, forestry and fishing (excl. paid employees) 15,216; *Total employed* (incl. others) 29,175 (males 16,957, females 12,218); Unemployed 8,239 (males 4,419, females 3,820); *Total labour force* 37,414 (males 21,376, females 16,038). *Mid-2005* (estimates in '000): Agriculture, etc. 11; Total labour force 46 (Source: FAO).

HEALTH AND WELFARE
Key Indicators

Total Fertility Rate (children per woman, 2005): 4.3.
Under-5 Mortality Rate (per 1,000 live births, 2005): 42.
Physicians (per 1,000 head, 2000): 0.60.
Hospital Beds (per 1,000 head, 2000): 2.8.
Health Expenditure (2004): US $ per head (PPP): 291.7.
Health Expenditure (2004): % of GDP: 7.6.
Health Expenditure (2004): public (% of total): 85.7.
Access to Water (% of persons, 2004): 94.
Access to Sanitation (% of persons, 2004): 28.

For sources and definitions, see explanatory note on p. vi.

AGRICULTURE, ETC.

Principal Crops ('000 metric tons, 2006, FAO estimates): Coconuts 40; Cassava 12; Sweet potatoes 3; Vegetables 3; Bananas 2.

Livestock ('000 head, year ending September 2006, FAO estimates): Pigs 32; Cattle 14; Goats 4; Chickens 185.

Livestock Products (metric tons, 2006, FAO estimates): Cattle meat 244; Pig meat 873; Chicken meat 135; Hen eggs 174.

Fishing ('000 metric tons, live weight, 2005): Skipjack tuna 23.2; Yellowfin tuna 3.7; Bigeye tuna 1.0; Total catch (incl. others) 29.5. Source: FAO.

FINANCE

Currency and Exchange Rates: United States currency is used: 100 cents = 1 United States dollar (US $). *Sterling and Euro Equivalents* (31 December 2007): £1 sterling = US $2.0034; €1 = US $1.4721; US $100 = £49.92 = €67.93.

Budget (US $ million, year ending 30 September 2006, estimates): *Revenue:* Current 54.7 (Tax 29.7, Non-tax 25.0); Grants 85.3; Total 140.0. *Expenditure:* Current 146.4; Capital 6.5; Total 153.0. Note: Figures represent a consolidation of the accounts of the national Government and the four state governments.

International Reserves (US $ '000 at 31 December 2006): IMF special drawing rights 1,943; Reserve position in IMF 1; Foreign exchange 44,679; Total 46,623. Source: IMF, *International Financial Statistics*.

Money Supply (US $ '000 at 31 December 2006): Demand deposits at banking institutions 20,225. Source: IMF, *International Financial Statistics*.

Cost of Living (Consumer Price Index, average of quarterly figures; base: 1999 = 100): All items 105.1 in 2004; 109.6 in 2005; 114.7 in 2006.

Gross Domestic Product (US $ million at constant 1998 prices, year ending 30 September: 209.9 in 2004; 208.7 in 2005; 203.9 in 2006.

Gross Domestic Product by Economic Activity (US $ million at current prices, 2002): Agriculture, hunting, forestry and fishing 34; Manufacturing 2; Mining, electricity, gas and water 3; Construction 21; Wholesale and retail trade, hotels and restaurants 34; Transport, storage and communications 29; Other activities 117; *GDP in purchasers' values* 240. Source: UN, *Statistical Yearbook for Asia and the Pacific*.

Balance of Payments (US $ million, year ending 30 September 2006, estimates): Merchandise exports f.o.b. 17.0; Merchandise imports f.o.b. –145.9; *Trade balance* –128.9; Exports of services 20.1; Imports of services –57.5; *Balance on goods and services* –166.2; Other income received 20.5; Other income paid –5.3; *Balance on goods, services and income* –151.0; Private unrequited transfers (net) 5.3; Official unrequited transfers (net) 107.3; *Current balance* –38.4; Capital account (net) 12.0; Other long-term capital (net) 1.9; Other short-term capital (net) 0.8; *Overall balance* (incl. errors and omissions) –23.6.

EXTERNAL TRADE

Principal Commodities (US $'000): *Imports c.i.f.* (2006): Mineral products 30,845; Prepared foodstuffs, beverages and tobacco 25,960; Machinery, mechanical appliances and electrical equipment 14,671; Vegetable products 9,466; Animals and animal products 8,261; Transportation equipment 8,240; Chemicals 8,086; Base metals and articles thereof 7,796; Total (incl. others) 137,993. *Exports f.o.b.* (2005): Fish 12,199; Betel nuts 403; Kava 135; Total (incl. others) 12,984.

Principal Trading Partners (US $'000): *Imports* (2006): Australia 5,777; China, People's Republic 4,399; Guam 25,970; Hong Kong 5,024; Japan 13,158; Korea, Republic 8,055; Philippines 6,003; Singapore 6,353; USA 54,754; Total (incl. others) 137,993. *Exports* (2005): Guam 942; Japan 2,010; Total (incl. others) 12,984.

TRANSPORT

Shipping: *Merchant Fleet* (registered at 31 December 2006): Vessels 28; Total displacement ('000 grt) 11.8. Source: Lloyd's Register-Fairplay, *World Fleet Statistics*.

TOURISM

Foreign Tourist Arrivals: 19,260 in 2004; 18,958 in 2005; 19,136 in 2006.

Tourist Arrivals by Country or Region of Residence (2006): Europe 2,398; Japan 3,071; Philippines 1,347; Other Asia 1,525; USA 8,053; Total (incl. others) 19,136.

Tourism Receipts (US $ million, incl. passenger transport): 17 in 2003; 17 in 2004; 17 in 2005 (provisional).

Source: World Tourism Organization.

COMMUNICATIONS MEDIA

Telephones ('000 main lines in use, 2006, estimate): 12.4*.
Facsimile Machines (number in use, 1998): 539*.
Mobile Cellular Telephones (2006, estimate): 14,100 subscribers.
Radio Receivers (1996): 22,000 in use.
Internet Users ('000, 2006): 16.0*.

THE FEDERATED STATES OF MICRONESIA

Television Receivers (1996): 19,800 in use.
*Source: International Telecommunication Union.

EDUCATION

Primary (1995): 174 schools; 1,051 teachers (1984); 27,281 pupils (Sources: UN, *Statistical Yearbook for Asia and the Pacific* and UNESCO Institute for Statistics).

Secondary (1995): 24 schools; 314 teachers (1984); 6,898 pupils (Sources: UN, *Statistical Yearbook for Asia and the Pacific* and UNESCO Institute for Statistics).

Tertiary (1998/99): 1,510 students (Sources: UN, *Statistical Yearbook for Asia and the Pacific* and UNESCO Institute for Statistics).

Adult Literacy Rate (population aged 10 years and over, 2000 census): 92.4% (males 92.9%, females 91.9%).

Directory

The Constitution

On 10 May 1979 the locally drafted Constitution of the Federated States of Micronesia, incorporating the four states of Kosrae, Yap, Ponape (formally renamed Pohnpei in November 1984) and Truk (renamed Chuuk in January 1990), became effective. Each of the four states has its own Constitution, elected legislature and Governor. The Constitution guarantees fundamental human rights and establishes a separation of the judicial, executive and legislative powers. The federal legislature, the Congress of the Federated States of Micronesia, is a unicameral parliament with 14 members, popularly elected. The executive consists of the President, elected by the Congress, and a Cabinet. The Constitution provides for a review of the governmental and federal system every 10 years.

In November 1986 the Compact of Free Association was signed by the Governments of the Federated States of Micronesia and the USA. By the terms of the Compact, the Federated States of Micronesia is an internally sovereign, self-governing state, whose policy concerning foreign affairs must be consistent with guide-lines laid down in the Compact. Full responsibility for defence lies with the USA, and the security arrangements may be terminated only by mutual agreement. Furthermore, the Compact guaranteed exclusivity to US military forces in Micronesia's waters. The Governments of the Federated States of Micronesia and the USA signed an amended Compact on 1 May 2003, whereby its terms were renewed until 2023. The agreement was approved by the US Congress in November 2003 and ratified by President George W. Bush in December. The amended Compact came into force in June 2004 and was due to expire in 2023.

The Government

HEAD OF STATE

President: IMMANUEL (MANNY) MORI (took office 11 May 2007).
Vice-President: ALIK L. ALIK.

THE CABINET
(April 2008)

Secretary of the Department of Finance and Administration: FINLEY S. PERMAN.

Secretary of the Department of Foreign Affairs: LORIN S. ROBERT.

Secretary of the Department of Economic Affairs: (vacant).

Secretary of the Department of Resources and Development: PETER M. CHRISTIAN.

Secretary of the Department of Health and Social Affairs: Dr VITA AKAPITO SKILLING.

Secretary of the Department of Justice: MAKETO ROBERT.

Secretary of the Department of Transportation, Communications and Infrastructure: FRANCIS I. ITIMAI.

Secretary of the Department of Education: CASIANO SHONIBER.

Public Defender: JULIUS JOEY SAPELALUT.

Postmaster-General: Rev. MIDION G. NETH.

GOVERNMENT OFFICES

Office of the President: POB PS-53, Palikir, Pohnpei, FM 96941; tel. 320-2228; fax 320-2785; e-mail ppetrus@mail.fm; internet www.fsmpio.fm.

Department of Economic Affairs: POB PS-12, Palikir, Pohnpei, FM 96941; tel. 320-2646; fax 320-5854; e-mail fsmdea@mail.fm; internet www.fsminvest.fm.

Department of Education: POB PS-87, Palikir, Pohnpei, FM 96941; tel. 320-2643; fax 320-5500.

Department of Finance and Administration: POB PS-158, Palikir, Pohnpei, FM 96941; tel. 320-2640; fax 320-2380; e-mail fsmsofa@mail.fm.

Department of Foreign Affairs: POB PS-123, Palikir, Pohnpei, FM 96941; tel. 320-2641; fax 320-2933; e-mail foreignaffairs@mail.fm; internet www.fsmgov.org/ovmis.html.

Department of Health and Social Affairs: POB PS-70, Palikir, Pohnpei, FM 96941; tel. 320-2872; fax 320-5263; e-mail fsmhesa@mail.fm.

Department of Justice: POB PS-105, Palikir, Pohnpei, FM 96941; tel. 320-2644; fax 320-2234; e-mail doj@mail.fm.

Department of Resources and Development: POB PS-12, Palikir, Pohnpei, FM 96941; tel. 320-2646; fax 320-5854; e-mail fsmrd@dea.fm.

Department of Transportation, Communication and Infrastructure: POB PS-2, Palikir, Pohnpei, FM 96941; tel. 320-2865; fax 320-5853; e-mail transfsm@mail.fm; internet www.ict.fm.

Office of the Public Auditor: POB PS-05, Palikir, Pohnpei, FM 96941; tel. 320-2863; fax 320-5482; e-mail hhainrick@mail.fm; internet www.fsmpublicauditor.fm.

Office of the Public Defender: POB PS-174, Palikir, Pohnpei, FM 96941; tel. 320-2648; fax 320-5775.

Public Information Office: POB PS-34, Palikir, Pohnpei, FM 96941; tel. 320-2548; fax 320-4356; e-mail fsmpio@mail.fm; internet www.fsmpio.fm/pio.htm.

The Legislature

CONGRESS OF THE FEDERATED STATES OF MICRONESIA

The Congress comprises 14 members (Senators), of whom four are elected for a four-year term and 10 for a two-year term. The most recent election, for all 14 seats, was held on 6 March 2007.

Speaker: ISAAC V. FIGIR.

STATE LEGISLATURES

Chuuk State Legislature: POB 189, Weno, Chuuk, FM 96942; tel. 330-2234; fax 330-2233; Senate of 10 mems and House of Representatives of 28 mems elected for four years; Gov. WESLEY W. SIMINA.

Kosrae State Legislature: POB 187, Tofol, Kosrae, FM 96944; tel. 370-3002; fax 370-3162; e-mail kosraelc@mail.fm; unicameral body of 14 mems serving for four years; Gov. ROBERT J. WEILBACHER.

Pohnpei State Legislature: POB 39, Kolonia, Pohnpei, FM 96941; tel. 320-2235; fax 320-2505; internet www.fm/pohnpeileg; 27 representatives elected for four years (terms staggered); Gov. JOHN EHSA.

Yap State Legislature: POB 39, Colonia, Yap, FM 96943; tel. 350-2108; fax 350-4113; 10 mems, six elected from the Yap Islands proper and four elected from the Outer Islands of Ulithi and Woleai, for a four-year term; Gov. SEBASTIAN L. ANEFAL.

Election Commission

National Election Commission: POB PS-355, Palikir, Pohnpei 96941; tel. 320-4283; fax 320-7534; e-mail ned@mail.fm; Dir Rev. KIMEUO KIMIUO.

THE FEDERATED STATES OF MICRONESIA

Diplomatic Representation

EMBASSIES IN THE FEDERATED STATES OF MICRONESIA

Australia: POB S, Kolonia, Pohnpei, FM 96941; tel. 320-5448; fax 320-5449; e-mail australia@mail.fm; internet www.australianembassy.fm; Ambassador SUSAN COX.

China, People's Republic: POB 1530, Kolonia, Pohnpei, FM 96941; tel. 320-5575; fax 320-5578; e-mail chinaemb@mail.fm; internet fm.chineseembassy.org/eng; Ambassador LIU FEI.

Japan: Pami Bldg, 3rd Floor, POB 1847, Kolonia, Pohnpei, FM 96941; tel. 320-5465; fax 320-5470; Chargé d'affaires a.i. TOSHIO OMURA.

USA: POB 1286, Kolonia, Pohnpei, FM 96941; tel. 320-2187; fax 320-2186; e-mail usembassy@mail.fm; internet www.fm/usembassy; Ambassador MIRIAM K. HUGHES.

Judicial System

Supreme Court of the Federated States of Micronesia: POB PS-J, Palikir Station, Pohnpei, FM 96941; tel. 320-2357; fax 320-2756; internet www.fsmlaw.org; Chief Justice ANDON L. AMARAICH. State Courts and Appellate Courts have been established in Yap, Chuuk, Kosrae and Pohnpei.

Religion

The population is predominantly Christian, mainly Roman Catholic. The Assembly of God, Jehovah's Witnesses, Seventh-day Adventists, the Church of Jesus Christ of Latter-day Saints (Mormons), the United Church of Christ, Baptists and the Bahá'í Faith are also represented.

CHRISTIANITY

The Roman Catholic Church

The Federated States of Micronesia forms a part of the diocese of the Caroline Islands, suffragan to the archdiocese of Agaña (Guam). The Bishop participates in the Catholic Bishops' Conference of the Pacific, based in Fiji. At 31 December 2005 there were 68,500 adherents in the diocese.

Bishop of the Caroline Islands: Most Rev. AMANDO SAMO, Bishop's House, POB 939, Weno, Chuuk, FM 96942; tel. 330-2399; fax 330-4585; e-mail diocese@mail.fm; internet www.dioceseofthecarolines.org.

Other Churches

Calvary Baptist Church: Kolonia, Pohnpei, POB 2179, FM 96941; tel. 320-2830; fax 320-3887; e-mail cca_pohnpei@yahoo.com; Pastor ISAMO WELLES.

Liebenzell Mission: Rev. Seigbert Betz, POB 9, Weno, Chuuk, FM 96942; tel. 330-3869; e-mail missions@liebenzellusa.org; internet www.liebenzellusa.org.

Truth Independent Baptist Church: Kolonia, Pohnpei, POB 65, FM 969410065; tel. 320-3643; fax 320-6769; Pastor RICARDO P. VERACRUZ.

United Church of Christ in Pohnpei: Kolonia, Pohnpei, POB 864, FM 96941; tel. 320-2271; fax 320-4404; Pres. BERNELL EDWARD.

The Press

Da Rohng: Jano News Service, POB 510, Kolonia, Pohnpei FM 96941; tel. 320-6494; fax 320-4200; e-mail darohng2005@yahoo.com; Editor MARTIN JANO.

The Island Tribune: Pohnpei, FM 96941; f. 1997; fortnightly.

Kaselehlie Press: POB 2222, Pohnpei, FM 96941; tel. 320-6547; fax 320-6571; e-mail kpress@mail.fm; internet www.bild-art.de/kpress; fortnightly; Man. Editor BILL JAYNES.

Micronesian Alliance: POB 543, Tofol, Kosrae, FM 96944; tel. 370-6131; e-mail equatormedia@yahoo.com.

Yap Networker: PB 1266, Yap, FM 96943; tel. 350-2937; fax 350-4525; e-mail microtech@mail.fm; internet www.yapnetworker.com; Editor BERNA GORONG.

Directory

Broadcasting and Communications

TELECOMMUNICATIONS

FSM Telecommunication Corporation: POB 1210, Kolonia, Pohnpei, FM 96941; tel. 320-2740; fax 320-2745; e-mail customerservice@telecom.fm; internet www.fm; provides domestic and international services; Gen. Man. TAKURO AKINAGA.

BROADCASTING

Radio

Federated States of Micronesia Public Information Office: POB PS-34, Palikir, Pohnpei, FM 96941; tel. 320-2548; fax 320-4356; e-mail fsmpio@mail.fm; internet www.fsmpio.fm/pio.htm; govt-operated; four regional stations, each broadcasting 18 hours daily; Information Officer KESTER JAMES.

Station V6AH: POB 1086, Kolonia, Pohnpei, FM 96941; programmes in English and Pohnpeian; Man. JOSEPH C. P. ALANNZO.

Station V6AI: POB 117, Colonia, Yap, FM 96943; tel. 350-2174; fax 350-4426; programmes in English, Yapese, Ulithian and Satawalese; Man. SEBASTIAN F. TAMAGKEN.

Station V6AJ: POB 147, Tofol, Kosrae, FM 96944; tel. 370-3040; fax 370-3880; e-mail v6aj@.mail.fm; programmes in English and Kosraean; Man. MCDONALD ITTU.

Station V6AK: Wenn, Chuuk, FM 96942; tel. 330-2596; programmes in Chuukese and English; Man. JOE COMMOR.

WSZA Yap: Dept of Youth and Civic Affairs, POB 30, Colonia, Yap 96943; tel. 350-2174; Media Dir PETER GARAMFEL.

WSZD Pohnpei: POB 1086, Kolonia, Pohnpei 96941; tel. 320-2296; programmes in English and Pohnpeian; Man. JOSEPH C. P. ALANNZO.

Television

Island Cable TV—Pohnpei: POB 1628, Pohnpei, FM 96941; tel. 320-2671; fax 320-2670; e-mail ictv@mail.fm; f. 1991; Pres. BERNARD HELGENBERGER; Gen. Man. DAVID O. CLIFFE.

TV Station Chuuk (TTTK): Wenn, Chuuk, FM 96942; commercial.

TV Station Pohnpei (KPON): Central Micronesia Communications, POB 460, Kolonia, Pohnpei, FM 96941; f. 1977; commercial; Pres. BERNARD HELGENBERGER; Tech. Dir DAVID CLIFFE.

TV Station Yap (WAAB): Colonia, Yap, FM 96943; tel. 350-2160; fax 350-4113; govt-owned; Man. LOU DEFNGIN.

Finance

BANKING

Regulatory Authority

Federated States of Micronesia Banking Board: POB 1887, Kolonia, Pohnpei, FM 96941; tel. 320-2015; fax 320-5433; e-mail fsmbb@mail.fm; e-mail wfwbb_gov@mail.fm; f. 1980; Chair. LARRY RAIGETAL; Commissioner WILSON F. WAGUK.

Banks are also supervised by the US Federal Deposit Insurance Corporation.

Commercial Banks

Bank of the Federated States of Micronesia: POB BF, Tofol, Kosrae, FM 96944; tel. 370-3225; e-mail bofsmhq@mail.fm; brs in Kosrae, Yap, Pohnpei and Chuuk.

Bank of Guam (USA): POB 367, Kolonia, Pohnpei, FM 96941; tel. 320-2550; fax 320-2562; e-mail bogpohn@mail.fm; internet www.bankofguam.com; Br. Mans JOANNE H. AKINAGA, VIDA B. RICAFRENTE; brs in Chuuk and Pohnpei.

Yap Credit Union: POB 610, Colonia, Yap; tel. 350-2142.

Development Bank

Federated States of Micronesia Development Bank: POB M, Kolonia, Pohnpei, FM 96941; tel. 320-2840; fax 320-2842; e-mail fsmdb@mail.fm; f. 1979; total assets US $31.7m. (2004); Chair. IHLEN JOSEPH; Pres. ANNA MENDIOLA; 4 brs.

Banking services for the rest of the islands are available in Guam, Hawaii and on the US mainland.

INSURANCE

Actouka Executive Insurance: POB 55, Kolonia, Pohnpei; tel. 320-5331; fax 320-2331; e-mail mlamar@mail.fm.

Caroline Insurance Underwriters: POB 37, Chuuk; tel. 330-2705; fax 330-2207.

FSM Insurance Group: Kosrae; tel. 370-3788; fax 370-2120.

THE FEDERATED STATES OF MICRONESIA   *Directory*

Islands Insurance: POB K, Kolonia, Pohnpei; tel. 320-3422; fax 320-3424.
Moylan's Insurance Underwriters: POB 1448, Kolonia, Pohnpei; tel. 320-2118; fax 320-2519; e-mail pohnpei@moylansinsurance.com; Pres. and Gen. Man. LOREN PETERSON.
Oceania Insurance Co: POB 1202, Weno, Chuuk, FM 96942; tel. 330-3036; fax 330-2334; e-mail oceanpac@mail.fm; also owns and manages Pacific Basin Insurance.
Pacific Islands Insurance Underwriters: POB 386, Colonia, Yap; tel. 350-2340; fax 350-2341.
Transpacific Insurance: POB 510, Kolonia, Pohnpei; tel. 320-5525; fax 320-5524.
Yap Insurance Agency: POB 386, Colonia, Yap; tel. 350-2340; fax 350-2341; e-mail tachelioyap@mail.fm.

Trade and Industry

GOVERNMENT AGENCIES

Coconut Development Authority: POB 297, Kolonia, Pohnpei, FM 96941; tel. 320-2892; fax 320-5383; e-mail fsmcda@mail.fm; responsible for all purchasing, processing and exporting of copra and copra by-products in the islands; Gen. Man. NAMIO NANPEI.
FSM National Fisheries Corporation: POB R, Kolonia, Pohnpei, FM 96941; tel. 320-2529; fax 320-2239; e-mail nfcairfreight@mail.fm; internet www.fsmgov.org/nfc; f. 1984; established in 1990, with the Economic Devt Authority and an Australian co, the Caroline Fishing Corpn (three vessels); promotes fisheries development; Pres. NICK SOLOMON.
Micronesian Fisheries Authority: PS122, Palikir, Pohnpei State, FM 96941; tel. 320-2700; fax 320-2383; e-mail fsmfish@mail.fm; name changed as above from Micronesian Maritime Authority in 2000.
National Oceanic Resource Management Authority (NORMA): POB PS-122, Palikir, Pohnpei, FM 96941; tel. 320-2700; fax 320-2383; e-mail info@norma.fm; internet norma.fm; fmrly Micronesian Fisheries Authority; name changed 2002; responsible for conservation, management and development of tuna resources and for issue of fishing licences; Exec. Dir BERNARD THOULAG; Deputy Dir EUGENE PANGELINAN.
Office of Compact Management: 253 Palikir Station, Pohnpei FM 96941; tel. 320-8375; fax 320-8377; Exec. Dir EHPEL ILON.
Pohnpei Economic Development Authority: POB 738, Kolonia, Pohnpei, FM 96941; tel. 320-2298; fax 320-2775; e-mail eda@mail.fm; chaired by the President of the Federated States of Micronesia; Exec. Dir SHELTEN NETH.

CHAMBERS OF COMMERCE

Chuuk Chamber of Commerce: POB 700, Weno, Chuuk, FM 96941; tel. 330-2318; fax 330-2314; e-mail larry.bruton@mail.fm; Pres. LARRY J. BRUTON.
Kosrae Chamber of Commerce: POB 1075, Tofol, Kosrae, FM 96944; tel. 370-2044; fax 370-2066; e-mail info@kosraechamberofcommerce.org; internet www.kosraechamberofcommerce.org; Chair. GEOFF RASCHOU.
Pohnpei Chamber of Commerce: POB 405, Kolonia, Pohnpei, FM 96941; tel. 320-2452; fax 320-5277; e-mail amc@mail.fm; Pres. AMBROS SENDA.
Yap Chamber of Commerce: Colonia, Yap, FM 96943; tel. 350-2298.

UTILITIES

Chuuk Public Works (CPW): POB 248, Weno, Chuuk, FM 96942; tel. 330-2242; fax 320-4815; e-mail chkpublicworks@mail.fm.
Kosrae Utility Authority: POB 277, Tofol, Kosrae, FM 96944; tel. 370-3799; fax 370-3798; e-mail kua@mail.fm; corporatized in 1994; Gen. Man. ROBERT NELSON.
Pohnpei Utilities Corporation: POB C, Kolonia, Pohnpei, FM 96941; tel. 320-2374; fax 320-2422; e-mail info@puc.fm; internet www.puc.fm; f. 1992; provides electricity, water and sewerage services; Gen. Man. MARCELINO ACTOUKA.
Yap Public Services Corporation: POB 621, Colonia, Yap, FM 96943; tel. 350-2175; fax 350-2331; f. 1996; provides electricity, water and sewerage services.

CO-OPERATIVES

Chuuk: Chuuk Co-operative, Faichuk Cacao and Copra Co-operative Asscn, Pis Fishermen's Co-operative, Fefan Women's Co-operative.
Pohnpei: Pohnpei Federation of Co-operative Asscns (POB 100, Pohnpei, FM 96941), Kapingamarangi Copra Producers' Asscn, Kitti Minimum Co-operative Asscn, Kolonia Consumers' and Producers' Co-operative Asscn, Kosrae Island Co-operative Asscn, Metalanim Copra Co-operative Asscn, Mokil Island Co-operative Asscn, Ngatik Island Co-operative Asscn, Nukuoro Island Co-operative Asscn, PICS Co-operative Asscn, Pingelap Consumers' Co-operative Asscn, Pohnpei Fishermen's Co-operative, Pohnpei Handicraft Co-operative, Uh Soumwet Co-operative Asscn.
Yap: Yap Co-operative Asscn, POB 159, Colonia, Yap, FM 96943; tel. 350-2209; fax 350-4114; e-mail yca@mail.fm; f. 1952; Pres. FAUSTINO YANGMOG; Gen. Man. TONY GANNGIYAN; 1,832 mems.

Transport

ROADS

Macadam and concrete roads are found in the more important islands. Other islands have stone and coral-surfaced roads and tracks.

SHIPPING

Pohnpei, Chuuk, Yap and Kosrae have deep-draught harbours for commercial shipping. The ports provide warehousing and transhipment facilities.
Caroline Fisheries Corporation (CFC): POB 7, Kolonia, Pohnpei, FM 96941; tel. 320-3926; fax 320-4733; e-mail cfc@mail.fm; Gen. Man. MILAN KAMBER.
Pacific Shipping Agency: POB 154, Lelu, Kosrae FM 96944; tel. 350-2475; Gen. Man. THEODORE SIGRAH.
Pohnpei Transfer & Storage, Inc: POB 340, Kolonia, Pohnpei FM 96941; tel. 320-2552; fax 320-2389; e-mail fsmlinejv@mail.fm; Gen. Man. JOE VITT.
Truk Transportation Company (TRANSCO): POB 99, Weno, Chuuk FM 96942; tel. 330-2143; fax 330-2726; e-mail transco@mail.fm; Pres. NYRON HACHIGUCHI; Gen. Man. GIDEON BISALEN.
Waab Transportation Company: POB 177, Colonia, Yap FM 96943; tel. 350-2301; fax 350-4110; e-mail waabtrans@mail.fm; agents for PM & O Lines (USA); Man. LOUIS GAW.

CIVIL AVIATION

The Federated States of Micronesia is served by Continental Micronesia, Our Airline (formerly Air Nauru) and Continental Airlines (USA). Pacific Missionary Aviation, based in Pohnpei and Yap, provides domestic air services. There are international airports on Pohnpei, Chuuk, Yap and Kosrae, and airstrips on the outer islands of Onoun and Ta in Chuuk.

Tourism

The tourist industry is a significant source of revenue, although it has been hampered by the lack of infrastructure. Visitor attractions include excellent conditions for scuba-diving (notably in Chuuk Lagoon), Second World War battle sites and relics (many underwater) and the ancient ruined city of Nan Madol on Pohnpei. The number of tourist arrivals totalled 19,136 in 2006. According to provisional estimates, tourist receipts totalled US $17m. in 2005.
Federated States of Micronesia Visitors Board: Dept of Economic Affairs, National Government, PO Box PS-12, Palikir, Pohnpei, FM 96941; tel. 320-5133; fax 320-3251; e-mail fsminfo@visit-fsm.org; internet www.visit-fsm.org.
Chuuk Visitors Bureau: POB FQ, Weno, Chuuk, FM 96942; tel. 330-4133; fax 330-4194; e-mail cvb@mail.fm.
Kosrae Visitors Bureau: POB 659, Tofol, Kosrae, FM 96944; tel. 370-2228; fax 370-3000; e-mail kosrae@mail.fm; internet www.kosrae.com.
Pohnpei Department of Tourism and Parks: POB 66, Kolonia, Pohnpei, FM 96941; tel. 320-2421; fax 320-6019; e-mail tourismparks@mail.fm; Deputy Chief BUMIO SILBANUZ.
Pohnpei Visitors Bureau: POB 1949, Kolonia, Pohnpei, FM 96941; tel. 320-4851; fax 320-4868; e-mail pohnpeiVB@mail.fm; internet www.visit-pohnpei.fm.
Yap Visitors Bureau: POB 988, Colonia, Yap, FM 96943; tel. 350-2298; fax 350-7015; e-mail yvb@mail.fm; internet www.visityap.com; Chair. ALPHONSO GANANG; Gen. Man. LAURENCE KENBAROY.

MOLDOVA

Introductory Survey

Location, Climate, Language, Religion, Flag, Capital

The Republic of Moldova is a small, land-locked country situated in south-eastern Europe. The republic is bounded to the north, east and south by Ukraine. To the west it borders Romania. The climate is favourable for agriculture, with long, warm summers and relatively mild winters. Average temperatures in Chişinău range from 21°C (70°F) in July to −4°C (24°F) in January. The 1994 Constitution describes the official language as Moldovan, a Romance language that is widely considered to be identical to Romanian. Most of the inhabitants of Moldova profess Eastern Orthodox Christianity. The national flag (proportions 1 by 2) consists of three equal vertical stripes, of light blue, yellow and red; the yellow stripe has at its centre the arms of Moldova (a shield bearing a stylized bull's head in yellow, set between an eight-pointed yellow star, a five-petalled yellow flower, and a yellow crescent, the shield being set on the breast of an eagle, in gold and red, which holds a green olive branch in its dexter talons, a yellow sceptre in its sinister talons, and a yellow cross in its beak). The capital is Chişinău.

Recent History

The area of the present-day Republic of Moldova corresponds to only part of the medieval principality of Moldova (Moldavia), which emerged as an important regional power in the 15th century. In the following century, however, the principality came under Ottoman (Osmanlı) domination. Following a period of conflict between the Ottoman and Russian Empires in the late 18th century, Moldova was divided into two parts under the Treaty of Bucharest of 1812: the eastern territory of Bessarabia, situated between the Prut and Dniester (Dnestr or Nistru) rivers (which roughly corresponds to modern Moldova), was ceded to Russia, while the Ottomans retained control of western Moldova. A Romanian nationalist movement evolved in western Moldova and the neighbouring region of Wallachia during the 19th century, culminating in the proclamation of a Romanian state in 1877, which became a kingdom in 1881. In June 1918, after the collapse of the Russian Empire, Bessarabia was proclaimed an independent republic, although in November it voted to become part of Romania. This union was recognized in the Treaty of Paris (1920). However, the USSR (established in 1922) refused to recognize Romania's claims to the territory, and in October 1924 formed a Moldovan Autonomous Soviet Socialist Republic (ASSR) on the eastern side of the Dniester, within the Ukrainian Soviet Socialist Republic (SSR). In June 1940 Romania was forced to cede Bessarabia and northern Bucovina to the USSR, under the terms of the Treaty of Non-Aggression (the 'Molotov-Ribbentrop Pact'), concluded with Nazi Germany in August 1939. Northern Bucovina, southern Bessarabia and the Kotovsk-Balţa region of the Moldovan ASSR were incorporated into the Ukrainian SSR. The remaining parts of the Moldovan ASSR and of Bessarabia were merged to form the Moldovan SSR, which formally joined the USSR on 2 August 1940. Political power in the republic was vested in the Communist Party of Moldova (CPM), part of the Communist Party of the Soviet Union (CPSU).

Between July 1941 and August 1944 the Moldovan SSR was reunited with Romania. However, the Soviet Army reannexed the region in 1944, and the Moldovan SSR was re-established. Soviet policy in Moldova concentrated on isolating the region from its historical links with Romania: cross-border traffic virtually ceased, the Cyrillic script was imposed on the Romanian language (which was referred to as Moldovan) and Russian and Ukrainian immigration was encouraged. In the 1950s thousands of ethnic Romanians were deported to Central Asia.

In May 1989 a number of independent cultural and political groups, which had recently emerged, but were denied legal status by the authorities, allied to form the Popular Front (PF). In June some 70,000 people attended a protest demonstration, organized by the PF, on the anniversary of the Soviet annexation of Bessarabia in 1940. In August 1989 mass demonstrations were convened in the capital, Chişinău, in support of proposals by the Moldovan Supreme Soviet (Supreme Council—legislature) to declare Romanian the official language of the republic. Following protests by non-ethnic Romanians, the proposals were amended: legislation was enacted providing for Russian to be retained as a language of inter-ethnic communication, but the official language was to be Romanian, written in the Latin script. Following disturbances in Chişinău, during the celebrations of the anniversary of the Bolshevik Revolution on 7 November, the First Secretary of the CPM, Semion Grossu, was dismissed. He was replaced by Petru Lucinschi.

The increasing influence of the Romanian-speaking population was strongly opposed by other inhabitants of the republic (who, at the 1989 census, comprised some 35% of the total population). In the areas east of the Dniester, Transnistria or Pridnestrovie, where Russians and Ukrainians predominated (and which had mostly constituted the Moldovan ASSR in 1924–40), the local authorities refused to implement the language law. Opposition to growing Moldovan nationalism was led by the Unity Movement (Yedinstvo), dominated by leading CPM members, and the Slav-dominated United Work Collectives. Both organizations had strong links with Gagauz Halky (Gagauz People), the most prominent of the political groups representing the 150,000-strong Gagauz minority (a Turkic, Orthodox Christian people, resident mostly in southern regions of Moldova). In January 1990 a referendum took place in the eastern town of Tiraspol, in which the predominantly Russian-speaking population voted to seek greater autonomy for Transnistria.

None of the independent political groups was officially allowed to endorse candidates in elections to the Moldovan Supreme Soviet in February 1990. About 80% of the 380 deputies elected were members of the CPM, but many were also sympathetic to the aims of the PF. The new Supreme Soviet convened in April, whereupon Mircea Snegur, a CPM member supported by the PF, was elected Chairman. In the following month the Government resigned after losing a vote of 'no confidence'. A new Council of Ministers, chaired by an economist, Mircea Druc, implemented far-reaching political changes. The CPM's constitutional right to power was revoked, and media organizations belonging to the CPM were transferred to state control. On 23 June the Supreme Soviet adopted a declaration of sovereignty asserting the supremacy of Moldova's Constitution and laws throughout the republic. The Supreme Soviet also declared the 1940 annexation of Bessarabia to have been illegal. In September Snegur was elected to the newly instituted post of President of the Republic.

The actions of the increasingly radical Romanian majority in the legislature provoked further anxiety among the country's minority ethnic groups during 1990. In August the Gagauz proclaimed a separate 'Gagauz SSR' in the southern region around Comrat (Komrat), and in September east-bank Slavs proclaimed their secession from Moldova and the establishment of the 'Transdnestrian SSR', with its self-styled capital at Tiraspol (this territory contained much of Moldova's industry, as well as three of Moldova's five largest cities). Both declarations were immediately annulled by the Moldovan Supreme Soviet. In October Moldovan nationalists sought to thwart elections to a Gagauz Supreme Soviet by sending some 50,000 armed volunteers to the area. Violence was prevented only by the dispatch of Soviet troops to the region. The new Gagauz Supreme Soviet convened in Comrat and elected Stepan Topal as its President. Further inter-ethnic violence occurred east of the Dniester in November, when elections were announced to a Transnistrian Supreme Soviet. Negotiations in Moscow, the Russian and Soviet capital, involving the Moldovan Government, the east-bank Slavs and the Gagauz, failed to resolve the crisis, but the elections proceeded without further violence.

In mid-December 1990 around 800,000 people, attending a 'Grand National Assembly', voted to reject any new union treaty (which was being negotiated by other Soviet republics), and in February 1991 the Moldovan Supreme Soviet resolved not to participate in the all-Union referendum on the future of the USSR. Despite the official boycott, in March some 650,000 people (mostly ethnic Russians, Ukrainians and Gagauz) did take part, voting almost unanimously for the preservation of the USSR. Nevertheless, the ethnic-Romanian-dominated Government and legislature continued the process of *de facto* secession. In May the designation 'Soviet Socialist' was removed from the republic's name and the Supreme Soviet was renamed Parlamentul (the Parliament). In the same month, following a vote of 'no confidence' by the legislature, Druc was removed as Prime Minister.

Following the attempted coup by conservative communists in Moscow in August 1991, the commanders of the USSR's South-Western Military District sought to impose a state of emergency in Moldova. However, the republican leadership immediately announced its support for the Russian President, Boris Yeltsin, in his opposition to the coup. On 27 August, after the coup had collapsed, Moldova proclaimed its independence from the USSR. In September President Snegur ordered the creation of national armed forces, and assumed control of the republican KGB (state security service), transforming it into a Ministry of National Security, while the CPM was proscribed.

At the election to the republican presidency on 8 December 1991 Snegur, the sole candidate, received 98.2% of the votes cast. On 21 December Moldova was among the 11 signatories to the Alma-Ata (Almaty) Declaration establishing the Commonwealth of Independent States (CIS, see p. 215). Moldovan affairs during the first half of 1992 were dominated by the armed conflict in Transnistria (see below) and by the question of possible unification with Romania, strongly advocated by the ruling PF (which in February was re-formed as the Christian Democratic Popular Front—CDPF). Moreover, a National Council for Reintegration had been established in December 1991, comprising legislators from both Moldova and Romania who were committed to the idea of a unified Romanian state. Within Moldova, however, popular support for unification remained insubstantial. In June 1992 the CDPF-dominated Government announced its resignation. Andrei Sangheli was appointed Prime Minister, and a new Government 'of national accord' was formed, led by the Agrarian Democratic Party (ADP), which largely comprised members of the former communist leadership. Several portfolios that had been reserved for representatives from Transnistria and Gagauz-Yeri (Gagauzia, as the Gagauz-majority area around Comrat was known) were refused. The CDPF became the main opposition party. The ADP declared its commitment to consolidating Moldovan statehood, rejecting any future union with Romania in favour of a closer alignment with Russia and the CIS. The ADP's anti-unification policies were strongly supported by President Snegur, who in January 1993 proposed that the issue be resolved in a referendum. Snegur's proposal was narrowly rejected by Parlamentul, but the ensuing political crisis led to several resignations, including that of the Chairman of Parlamentul, Alexandru Moşanu. Moşanu was replaced in February by Lucinschi.

During 1993 the ADP made substantial progress with the drafting of a new Moldovan constitution, which was to be ratified following the election of a new parliament. The draft constitution provided, *inter alia*, for a reduced, 104-member legislature. Moldova's first multi-party elections were held on 27 February 1994, with the participation of more than 73% of the electorate. In Transnistria the local leadership did not open polling stations, although residents were able to vote on the west bank of the Dniester. In all, 13 parties and blocs contested the elections. The ADP obtained an overall majority in Parlamentul (56 seats). The successor party to the CPM, the Socialist Party (SP), in alliance with the Unity Movement, won 28 seats. Two pro-unification groups shared the remaining 20 seats: the Peasants' Party of Moldova/Congress of Intelligentsia alliance (11) and the CDPF (nine). In a national referendum held on 6 March, more than 95% of the votes cast by 75% of the electorate were in favour of continued independence. In late March Sangheli and Lucinschi were re-elected as premier and legislative Chairman, respectively. A new Council of Ministers, solely comprising members of the ADP, was appointed in April. In May the CPM was permitted to re-form, as the Party of Communists of the Republic of Moldova (Partidul Comuniştilor din Republica Moldova—PCRM).

The new Constitution, adopted by Parlamentul in July 1994, entered into force in August. As well as establishing the country's permanent neutrality, the Constitution provided for a 'special autonomous status' for Transnistria and Gagauz-Yeri within Moldova, the exact terms of which were to be determined at a later date. The state language was specified as Moldovan (rather than Romanian). In March–April 1995 thousands of students participated in rallies in Chişinău, demanding that the state language be redesignated as Romanian, prompting the establishment of a special committee to examine the matter. In June, following the rejection by the ADP and its allies in Parlamentul of the proposal that the state language be constitutionally described as Romanian, Snegur resigned his membership of the ADP (which he had joined in 1994) and in August 1995 established the Party of Rebirth and Conciliation (PRC), with the support of several disaffected ADP deputies. In February 1996 Parlamentul again rejected the proposed redesignation of the state language as Romanian.

At the presidential election, held on 17 November 1996, Snegur received the largest share of the votes cast (39%) of any of the nine candidates, his failure to win an absolute majority necessitated a second round of voting, in which his opponent was Lucinschi, now supported by the ADP (who had secured 28%). In the second round of polling, held on 1 December, Lucinschi emerged as the winner, with 54% of the votes cast. The authorities in Transnistria again boycotted the poll, and there were reports that residents were prevented from leaving the region to vote on the west bank of the Dniester. Lucinschi was inaugurated as President on 15 January 1997, and a new Government was announced later that month, headed by Ion Ciubuc, a non-party economist. In March the leader of the ADP, Dumitru Moţpan, was elected as Chairman of Parlamentul.

Parliamentary elections took place on 22 March 1998. In an apparent rejection of Lucinschi's economic reform programme, the elections were won by the PCRM, led by Vladimir Voronin, which took 30.1% of the votes cast (40 seats). The Democratic Convention of Moldova (CDM), an alliance led by Snegur, won 19.2% (26 seats), while the Movement for a Democratic and Prosperous Moldova (MDPM) received 18.2% (24 seats) and the Moldovan Party of Democratic Forces 8.8% (11 seats). The remaining 11 parties (including the ADP) failed to secure the 4% of the votes required for representation. The elections were again boycotted in Transnistria, but voters were permitted to cross the Dniester to vote.

At the first session of the new legislature, convened in April 1998, Dumitru Diacov was elected Chairman. The Government resigned shortly afterwards. Since none of the political parties had secured an overall parliamentary majority, the new Government, appointed in May (with Ciubuc retaining his post as Prime Minister), was a coalition of the MDPM, the CDM and the Moldovan Party of Democratic Forces known as the Alliance for Democracy and Reforms and led within Parlamentul by Snegur.

Ciubuc resigned as Prime Minister in February 1999. Snegur resigned as parliamentary leader of the government coalition one day later, after his nominee for the premiership was rejected. Shortly afterwards Lucinschi nominated the Mayor of Chişinău, Serafim Urechean, as Prime Minister. He was, however, unable to obtain the support of the parliamentary majority. Consequently, Lucinschi nominated Ion Sturza, the Deputy Prime Minister and Minister of the Economy and Reforms, as Prime Minister. Although Parlamentul twice failed to endorse his proposed government, Lucinschi nominated Sturza a third time. Confronted with a choice between acceptance or the constitutional requirement to hold an early general election, Parlamentul narrowly approved Sturza's Government in March.

Local elections were held on 23 May 1999, after which the country was reorganized into nine provinces and two autonomous entities (Gagauz-Yeri and Transnistria). A referendum held on the same day, approving increased presidential powers was initially invalidated because of the low rate of electoral participation, and was subsequently ruled to have been illegal, as it had not been announced and organized by Parlamentul.

In October 1999 the creation of a new, independent political bloc, principally comprising members of the MDPM, weakened the Government's support in Parlamentul. In the following month Sturza lost a vote of confidence in the legislature, after the defeat of legislation on the privatization of the wine and tobacco industries; the IMF and the World Bank subsequently suspended credits to Moldova (the bill was finally approved in October 2000). Following the failure of two candidates for the premiership (including Voronin) to secure the necessary support in the legislature, the President's nomination of Dumitru Braghiş, hitherto Deputy Minister of Economy and Reform, as Prime Minister was approved in December.

In July 2000 Parlamentul voted in favour of amending the Constitution to permit the legislature to elect the Head of State. Parlamentul swiftly overturned President Lucinschi's decision to veto the proposed amendment, which duly took effect. In

October Parlamentul announced that a presidential election would be contested within the legislature in December.

Neither of the two candidates in the presidential election—Voronin, for the PCRM, and Pavel Barbalat, the Chairman of the Constitutional Court, who had been proposed by a coalition of the Democratic Party of Moldova (PDM, as the MDPM had been renamed in April), the CDM, the People's Christian Democratic Party (PPCD, formerly the CDPF) and the Moldovan Party of Democratic Forces—obtained the requisite number of votes to secure an overall victory after three rounds of voting. The PDM, the CDM, the PPCD and the Moldovan Party of Democratic Forces boycotted a fourth round of voting on 21 December 2000, preventing it from taking place, thereby permitting the President to dissolve the legislature and schedule early parliamentary elections.

At the legislative elections, held on 25 February 2001, the PCRM won an overall majority in Parlamentul, securing 49.9% of the votes cast and 71 seats. The Braghiş Alliance, formed by the incumbent Prime Minister, obtained 19 seats, while the PPCD obtained 11 seats. The elections were described as free and fair by observers from the Organization for Security and Co-operation in Europe (OSCE, see p. 354). The rate of voter participation was some 70%. In the presidential election, which took place on 4 April, Voronin secured 71 votes, Braghiş obtained 15 and another communist candidate, Valerian Cristea, won three; the 11 PPCD deputies abstained from voting. Following his inauguration as President on 7 April, Voronin nominated Vasile Tarlev, a former businessman without party affiliation, as premier.

Proposals by the Minister of Education, Ilie Vancea, for the introduction of the compulsory teaching of Russian language and history to the national curriculum from 2002, were confirmed in December 2001. A demonstration, organized by the PPCD and involving an estimated 3,000 people, took place in Chişinău in early January 2002 to protest against these measures; large-scale, daily protests continued throughout the month. In late January the Ministry of Justice suspended the PPCD from participation in political activities for a period of one month, thus preventing it from organizing further protests. However, in February, following intervention by the Council of Europe, the PPCD's suspension was annulled in order to allow the party to campaign for local elections, due to be held in April. In mid-February, however, the Constitutional Court ruled that the scheduling of early local elections for April, was unconstitutional.

Meanwhile, in February 2002 the Deputy Prime Minister and Minister of the Economy, Andrei Cucu, and the reformist Minister of Finance, Mihai Manole, the only two non-PRCM members of the Council of Ministers, tendered their resignations. Following further protests against the proposed reform of the education system, Vancea announced that the proposed legislation would be retracted; he was consequently dismissed on 26 February. The following day Vasile Draganel resigned as Minister of the Interior, amid reports that he had been unwilling to dispel protesters by force. Draganel was replaced by Gheorghe Papuc, a long-serving member of the security forces. Despite a ruling by the Supreme Court declaring the ongoing protests to be illegal and demanding that they be halted, in February 2002 demonstrators began to protest outside the headquarters of the national television company against state censorship and misinformation. In March the Deputy Chairman of the PPCD, Vlad Cubreacov, who had been involved in organizing the anti-Government protests, was declared missing; thousands of demonstrators subsequently gathered to protest against Cubreacov's disappearance. At the end of the month the PPCD announced that it had discontinued its anti-Government protests. In May Cubreacov was discovered alive, although his kidnappers remained unidentified. In June judicial proceedings against members of the opposition involved in the organization of public protests (including Cubreacov) were suspended indefinitely.

A number of government changes were made in late 2002, including the creation of the new post of Minister of Reintegration, with responsibility for, inter alia, the resolution of the status of Transnistria. Local elections took place on 25 May and 8 June 2003, in which the PCRM won the majority of seats, followed by the newly formed Our Moldova alliance, comprising the Alliance of Independents of Moldova, the National Liberal Party and the Social Democratic Alliance of Moldova. Following the elections, new legislation on administrative reform, approved by the Government in January, came into effect, according to which the nine provinces and two autonomous regions introduced in 1999 were replaced with a structure comprising 33 municipalities and two municipalities (Balţi and Chişinău). In July 2003 the parties of the Our Moldova bloc formally merged, together with the Popular Democratic Party of Moldova, to form the Our Moldova Alliance, led by Braghiş, Urechean and Veaceslav Untilă.

Thousands of protesters took part in opposition demonstrations in November 2003, against the Government's initial support for a Russian proposal for the federalization of Moldova (see below). The proposals, rejected in late November, had envisaged the installation of a popularly elected president and new, bicameral legislature, with an upper house comprising nine representatives elected from Transnistria, four from Gagauz-Yeri and 13 from the remainder of Moldova; Transnistria and Gagauz-Yeri were to have been represented at federal level by deputy prime ministers. In early December the Prosecutor-General, Vasile Rusu, resigned, following criticism of his response to the protests; he was replaced by Valeriu Balaban. New legislation, which was approved on 19 December, which sought to promote the use of Russian as a language of inter-ethnic communication (while retaining Moldovan as an official language), was a further source of demonstrations.

In February 2004 Andrei Strătan replaced Nicolae Dudău as Minister of Foreign Affairs. In the same month Parlamentul withdrew the immunity from prosecution of three members of the PPCD, including the party's Chairman, Iurie Roşca, at the request of the Prosecutor-General, to permit their prosecution on charges of organizing and participating in unauthorized protests. From April the PDM and the Social Liberal Party agreed to co-operate with Our Moldova, as the Democratic Moldova bloc, in preparation for parliamentary elections scheduled to be held in 2005. In October the Minister of Defence, Victor Gaicuc, was dismissed from office following the theft of substantial quantities of military ordnance from army depots. In December Strătan was appointed as Deputy Prime Minister, retaining the foreign affairs portfolio.

In the legislative elections, held on 6 March 2005, the PCRM won 46.0% of the votes cast and 56 seats, the Democratic Moldova bloc obtained 28.5% (34 seats) and the PPCD received 9.1% (11 seats). No other party or grouping obtained legislative representation. Although the PCRM held an absolute majority of seats in Parlamentul, it did not hold the quorum of 61 necessary for the election of a president. At the inaugural session of Parlamentul the PDM withdrew from the Democratic Moldova bloc, forming its own eight-member faction, and three members of the Social Liberal Party subsequently also left the bloc, which was renamed the Our Moldova Alliance faction in the legislature. Despite declarations that opposition deputies would boycott the presidential vote, in the event only Our Moldova did so. The election was held on 4 April, contested by the incumbent, Voronin, and another PCRM-nominated candidate, Gheorghe Duca, the President of the Moldovan Academy of Sciences (in order to comply with the constitutional requirement that presidential elections be contested). Voronin secured 75 of the 101 votes available (some 95 legislators were present); Duca received only one vote. Voronin was inaugurated as President on 7 April, and on 19 April Parlamentul approved a new Government, again led by Tarlev and retaining many members of the previous Council of Ministers.

In April 2005 Urechean resigned as Mayor of Chişinău, announcing that the role was incompatible with his leadership of Our Moldova. In October members of the PCRM voted in Parlamentul to remove the parliamentary immunity of Urechean and two other deputies, following allegations of abuse of office. In the same month Mihai Pop was appointed Minister of Finance, in succession to Zinaida Grecianii, who became First Deputy Prime Minister. In November Braghiş left the Our Moldova Alliance, of which Urechean remained the sole leader, in order to form the Party of Social Democracy of Moldova.

In January 2006 a former Minister of Defence, Valeriu Pasat, was sentenced to 10 years' imprisonment, after being convicted of defrauding the state when selling redundant fighter aircraft to the USA in 1997. In February 2006 Pasat was indicted on further, unrelated charges of having organized protests during the 2005 legislative elections in an attempt to overthrow Voronin and of conspiring to murder PPCD leader Iurie Roşca. (However, in July 2007 Pasat was unexpectedly released by the Court of Appeal.)

In September 2006 Voronin replaced the Minister of Justice, appointing the hitherto government representative to the European Court of Human Rights to the post. In the same month the Minister of the Economy and Trade was also replaced. In June 2007 local elections were conducted throughout Moldova; voter turnout was recorded at 52.3% nationwide and about 37.2% in Chișinău. Overall, the PCRM secured 334 mayoralties, 465 seats in district and municipal councils, and 4,040 seats in city and village councils; the Our Moldova Alliance won 157 mayoralties, 220 seats in district and municipal councils, and 1,987 seats in city and village councils. The PCRM won 16 seats on Chișinău Municipal Council; however, Dorin Chrtoaca of the Liberal Party, which had obtained 11 seats in the Council, was elected Mayor. Also in June Voronin dismissed the Minister of Defence, Valeriu Plesca, after a civilian was killed when journalists were permitted to participate in a military training exercise; it was announced that criminal proceedings were to be taken against Plesca. In July he was replaced by Vitalie Vrabie, hitherto Deputy Prime Minister and Minister of Local Public Administration; Vrabie's deputy, Valentin Guznac, succeeded him as Minister of Local Public Administration. In August the newly elected mayor of Drasliceni (in the district of Căușeni), who had planned to make public allegations of corrupt practices at the mayoralty, was killed by unknown assailants. In late 2007 a number of new political organizations, including a pro-Russian party, known as Patriots of Moldova, were established in preparation for legislative elections due in early 2009. In December 2007 the Party of Social Democracy of Moldova merged with the Social Democratic Party of Moldova.

In January 2008 Voronin appointed a prominent member of the PCRM, Victor Stepaniuc, as a Deputy Prime Minister. On 19 March 2008 Tarlev submitted his resignation and that of his Government; Tarlev announced that he intended to leave political life. Vorinin subsequently nominated Grecianîi to the premiership. On 31 March a new Government formed by Grecianîi (the country's first female Prime Minister) was approved by Parlamentul by 56 votes, with opposition deputies abstaining from voting; Igor Dodon, the Minister of Economy and Trade, succeeded Grecianîi as First Deputy Prime Minister.

Following the proclamation of Transnistria's secession in September 1990, relations with the central Government in Chișinău remained tense. Armed conflict broke out in December 1991, as the leadership of the self-proclaimed republic, opposed to the Government's objective of reunification with Romania, launched a campaign to gain control of Transnistria (with the ultimate aim of unity with Russia). Over six months of military conflict ensued, as Moldovan government troops were dispatched to combat the local Slav militia. The situation was complicated by the presence (and alleged involvement in support of the east-bank Slavs) of the former Soviet 14th Army, which was still stationed in the region and jurisdiction over which had been transferred to Russia. Although peace negotiations were held at regular intervals, with the participation of Moldova, Russia, Ukraine and Romania, none of the agreed cease-fires was observed. By June 1992 some 700 people were believed to have been killed in the conflict, with an estimated 50,000 people forced to take refuge in Ukraine. On 21 July, however, a peace agreement was finally negotiated by Presidents Snegur and Yeltsin, whereby Transnistria was accorded 'special status' within Moldova (the terms of which were to be formulated later). Later in July Russian, Moldovan and Transnistrian peace-keeping troops were deployed in the region to monitor the cease-fire.

Transnistria continued to demand full statehood, and in January 1994 the Moldovan Government accepted proposals by the Conference on Security and Co-operation in Europe (CSCE—later OSCE) for greater autonomy for Transnistria, within a Moldovan confederation. The Transnistrian leadership expressed approval of the proposals, and the result of the Moldovan parliamentary elections of the following month (which eliminated the possibility of Moldova's future unification with Romania) further enhanced the prospects for a settlement. In April President Snegur and the Transnistrian leader, Igor Smirnov, pledged their commitment to holding negotiations for a peaceful resolution of the conflict, based on the CSCE recommendations.

In July 1994, following the adoption of the new Moldovan Constitution, which provided for a 'special autonomous status' for Transnistria, negotiations commenced on the details of the region's future status within Moldova. Progress was obstructed, in particular, by disagreement over the future of the 15,000-strong 14th Army, since the Transnistrian leadership demanded the continued presence of the Army in the region as a guarantor of security. In October, however, the Moldovan and Russian Governments reached an agreement, under which Russia was gradually to withdraw the 14th Army, whereupon Transnistria's negotiated 'special autonomous status' would take effect. A referendum (declared illegal by President Snegur) was held in Transnistria in March 1995, in which some 91% of participants voted against the withdrawal of the 14th Army. In December two further referendums were held in Transnistria: 82.7% of the electorate endorsed a new constitution (which proclaimed the region's independence), while 89.7% voted for Transnistria to join the CIS as a sovereign state. In February 1996, however, the CIS rejected admittance for Transnistria on such terms.

In July 1996 the executive and legislative authorities of Moldova and Transnistria initialled a memorandum, drafted with the aid of Russian, Ukrainian and OSCE mediators, on normalizing relations; this was viewed as an important stage towards defining the 'special status' of Transnistria within a future Moldovan confederation. Smirnov was re-elected as 'President' of Transnistria in December. In May 1997 the memorandum was signed in Moscow by the new Moldovan President, Lucinschi, and Smirnov, with Russia and Ukraine acting as guarantors of the document. Representatives of the Moldovan and Transnistrian sides, meeting in Moscow in October, subsequently reached agreement on a number of 'confidence-building measures'. On 20 March 1998 a further agreement (the Odesa Accords) was signed in Odesa, Ukraine, by Lucinschi, Smirnov, Russian Prime Minister Viktor Chernomyrdin and President Leonid Kuchma of Ukraine, which envisaged a reduction in Moldovan and Transnistrian peace-keeping forces, while Russian troops were to remain in Transnistria until a final political settlement was reached.

In June 1998 Russian and Moldovan delegations to the joint commission monitoring the Odesa Accords agreed proposals for the composition of peace-keeping forces in the Transnistrian security zone, and Moldova's peace-keeping troops were gradually reduced in number. From late May 1999, following local elections in Moldova (in which the region refused to participate), Transnistria was designated an autonomous entity. In July Lucinschi met Smirnov, along with Russian Prime Minister Sergei Stepashin and an OSCE representative in Kyiv, Ukraine, and a joint declaration on the normalization of relations between Moldova and Transnistria was signed; however, Smirnov declared that differences remained.

In June 2000 the 'Transdnestrian Supreme Soviet' was converted to a reduced, unicameral legislature and in July Smirnov introduced a form of presidential rule. The Moldovan President elected in April 2001, Voronin, declared the pursuit of a final political settlement for Transnistria to be a priority but no substantive progress was made. A deterioration in Transnistria's relations with the Moldovan Government took place in September, following the Government's introduction of new customs procedures, in accordance with World Trade Organization (WTO) specifications, leading to claims by Transnistria that the Moldovan Government was attempting to impose an 'economic blockade' on the region. Smirnov was re-elected as 'President' of the region in December, although the election was recognized by neither the Moldovan Government nor the international community. In December 2002 the OSCE amended a deadline agreed in 1999 for the removal of Russian forces from Moldova, extending it for a further year, until December 2003; however, Russia indicated that some troops might remain, with a possible mandate for maintaining peace and stability in the event of a final settlement.

In July 2002 mediators from Russia, Ukraine and the OSCE submitted a new draft agreement (the 'Kyiv agreement'), according to which Moldova would become a federal state, in which the autonomous territories would maintain their own legislature and constitution; however, Smirnov insisted that recognition of Transnistria's 'independence' was a fundamental prerequisite. On 27 February 2003 the European Union (EU, see p. 244) and the USA, and subsequently other countries, imposed a travel ban on those Transnistrian officials considered to be 'primarily responsible for a lack of co-operation in promoting a political settlement'. In mid-November the Russian President, Vladimir Putin, announced new proposals for a political settlement. Drafted by the deputy head of the presidential administration, Dmitrii Kozak, the plan envisaged the establishment of an 'asymmetrical federation', comprising Moldova and Transnistria, with unified defence, customs and finance systems. The leaders of both Transnistria and Moldova initially responded positively to the proposals, but Voronin withdrew his support in late November, following opposition protests and reservations expressed by the OSCE. Although new proposals for Moldova's federalization were submitted to OSCE mediators in February 2004, the Transnistrian authorities argued that they offered the region insufficient autonomy, and representatives of the Moldovan Government also criticized the draft for its failure to clarify the issue of the continued presence of Russian troops and military equipment in Transnistria. In mid-2004 controversy arose over the closure by the Transnistrian authorities of Moldovan-language schools teaching a Moldovan syllabus, in the Latin script. The Moldovan Government responded by withdrawing from the OSCE-mediated negotiation process and imposing economic sanctions on the separatist region, which retaliated in kind. The EU, the USA and other international parties condemned the closure of the schools as an infringement of human rights, adding a further 10 Transnistrian officials to the list of those prohibited from travelling to their countries, and a case was submitted to the European Court of Human Rights.

In December 2004, at an OSCE meeting held in Sofia, Bulgaria, the Russian delegation obstructed the adoption of a final statement containing a reference to the Russian commitment to withdraw troops and ammunition from Moldova. Russian representatives also refused to sign a Moldovan-drafted Declaration of Stability and Security, which proposed the inclusion of the EU and the USA in talks for the resolution of the Transnistrian conflict.

In April 2005 President Viktor Yushchenko of Ukraine presented a plan for the resolution of the Transnistrian conflict during a summit meeting in Chișinău. The plan envisaged that Transnistria would be awarded 'special status', as an autonomous entity within the Republic of Moldova, would provide for a Transnistrian constitution (to comply with the Moldovan Constitution) and symbols, and would permit Transnistria to participate in foreign-policy decisions affecting its interests. In June Parlamentul endorsed the Yushchenko Plan, while noting that it made no mention of either the withdrawal of Russian troops or the establishment of border controls along the Transnistrian section of the border with Ukraine. At the end of July the Moldovan Government removed the trade sanctions imposed against Transnistria in the previous year. In late September all five parties to the negotiations on the status of Transnistria agreed to invite the EU and the USA (but not Romania) to participate in the process as observers, as suggested in the Yushchenko plan; however, talks in late 2005 failed to record any substantive progress. Legislative elections (recognized by neither the Moldovan Government nor the international community) were held in Transnistria in December. Notably, the reformist Renewal bloc won the most seats in the region's Supreme Soviet.

At the end of November 2005 the EU launched a Border Assistance Mission to help secure the Transnistrian–Ukrainian border, following appeals from Presidents Voronin and Yushchenko. As part of the same initiative, at the end of December the Prime Ministers of Moldova and Ukraine signed a joint declaration on external trade, whereby Ukraine agreed not to recognize Transnistria's customs regime and to deal only in goods processed through the Moldovan customs system, in an attempt to combat smuggling. The new measures came into force in March 2006. In response, the Transnistrian authorities, which interpreted the new regulations as an economic blockade, withdrew from the internationally mediated negotiations. The Transnistrian authorities subsequently introduced legislation banning all foreign-financed non-governmental organizations, and Smirnov appealed to Russia to dispatch more troops to the region. (In February Russia had reportedly confirmed that it did not intend to complete the withdrawal of its troops from Transnistria before a final settlement on the region's status had been reached.) In late March Russia suspended the import of Moldovan wine and other agricultural products, ostensibly owing to safety concerns. At a CIS summit held in Minsk, Belarus, in November President Putin declared an end to the trade ban against Moldova (reportedly in an effort to secure the support of the Moldovan Government for a Russian application to join the WTO). In early 2007 the Russian authorities announced that the import of fruit and vegetables from Moldova had resumed. In October the Russian Government announced that Moldovan wineries that had received approval for their output following safety assessments were permitted to resume exports.

At the end of March 2006, following the initiation in February of formal negotiations to determine the final status of the Serbian UN-administered province of Kosovo (see the chapter on Kosovo), Transnistrian officials declared their intention to schedule a referendum on future relations with Moldova, stating that the eventual secession of Kosovo from Serbia could set a precedent for the granting of statehood to other separatist territories in Europe. On 17 September the Transnistrian authorities conducted an internationally unrecognized referendum on the territory's independence and potential options for eventual integration, at which some 97% voted for a continuation of *de facto* independence from Moldova and an objective of eventual unification with Russia, while some 95% voted against the territory being ruled as part of Moldova. On 10 December a presidential election in Transnistria (which was unrecognized by the international community) was won by Smirnov, with 82.4% of votes cast. Some 65.4% of registered voters participated in the election. Shortly after Kosovo's unilateral declaration of independence on 17 February 2008, Transnistria (together with Abkhazia and South Ossetia—see the chapter on Georgia) requested that the Russian legislature, the UN and other organizations recognize their independence. In March, following strong indications that Russia was not prepared to recognize Transnistria, Smirnov announced that he was willing to enter into discussions with the Moldovan Government. In April he and Voronin met for the first time since 2001 in Tighina (Bender), Transnistria; the discussions, which followed between Moldovan and Transnistrian delegations in Odesa, Ukraine, were regarded as preparatory to the resumption of official negotiations on a political resolution of the status of Transnistria.

During the Transnistrian conflict in 1991–92, the situation in Gagauz-Yeri (which, unlike Transnistria, constitutes several non-contiguous territories) remained peaceful, although the region continued to demand full statehood. The Moldovan Constitution adopted in 1994, provided for a 'special autonomous status' for Gagauz-Yeri, as for Transnistria, and negotiations duly commenced on the details of this status. Agreement was quickly reached between the Government and the Gagauz authorities, and in December Parlamentul adopted legislation on the status of Gagauz-Yeri. The regions of southern Moldova populated by the Gagauz were to enjoy broad self-administrative powers, and Gagauz was to be one of three official languages (with Moldovan and Russian). Legislative power was to be vested in a regional assembly, and a directly elected Başkan (Governor) was to hold a quasi-presidential position. The law entered into force in February 1995, and in March a referendum was held in the region to determine which settlements would form part of the region. Elections to the 35-seat Halk Toplusu (Popular Assembly) took place in May–June. Concurrent elections held to the post of Başkan were won by Gheorghe Tabunscic, the First Secretary of the Comrat branch of the PCRM. Under the new Constitution, Tabunscic, as Gagauz leader, became a member of the Council of Ministers of Moldova. Following local elections in Moldova in late May 1999, Gagauz-Yeri, like Transnistria, was designated an autonomous entity. Elections to the Halk Toplusu and to the post of Başkan were held in late August. Following a second round of voting in early September, Dumitru Croitor was elected as Başkan, with 61.5% of the votes cast. In mid-February 2002 the Halk Toplusu passed a vote of 'no confidence' in Croitor, and scheduled a referendum in the hope of securing his dismissal. On 24 February, the date that the referendum was scheduled to take place, the regional security forces reportedly seized the offices of the regional Election Commission, declaring its mandate to have expired and the plebiscite to be illegal. President Voronin subsequently visited the region and demanded the resignations of both Croitor and the Chairman of the Halk Toplusu. Croitor finally resigned at the end of June. At a second round of voting in an election held on 11 October, Tabunscic regained the position of Başkan. On 25 July 2003 Parlamentul officially recognized the autonomous status of Gagauz-Yeri through an amendment to the national Constitution, which awarded the Halk Toplusu the right to self-determination and to propose its own legislation. Legislative elections were held in the region in November and December, in which the PCRM and independent candidates each won almost one-half of the seats contested. On 17 December 2006 an independent candidate, Mihail Formuzal, was elected Başkan at a second round of voting. Further elections to the Halk Toplusu took place on 16 and 31 March 2008, with voter turnout estimated at 60.5%. Independent candidates won 21 seats, the PCRM 10 seats, the PDM two seats and a pro-Russian Equal Rights (Ravnopravie) Socio-political Republican Movement two seats in the Assembly; it was reported that the PCRM, in coalition with independent candidates, commanded the greatest representation.

Owing to the changing domestic situation, Moldova's membership of the CIS was equivocal from its signature of the Alma-Ata Declaration in December 1991 until early 1994. In August 1993 Parlamentul failed by four votes to ratify the Alma-Ata Declaration, largely owing to the influence of deputies favouring unification with Romania, thus technically removing Moldova from the CIS. However, in September President Snegur signed a treaty to join the new CIS economic union. Following Moldova's parliamentary elections of February 1994 and the referendum in March, which strongly endorsed continued independence, Parlamentul reversed its earlier decision, and in April it finally ratified membership of the CIS.

The communist Government elected in 2001 initially undertook a policy of rapprochement with Russia, and in late December Parlamentul ratified a treaty on friendship and co-operation, which had been signed by the two countries' respective Presidents in the previous month. The treaty was ratified by the Russian Gosudarstvennaya Duma (State Duma) in April 2002. However, in 2004 relations deteriorated, largely owing to developments associated with Transnistria (see above). From the beginning of 2006 Russia attempted to increase two-fold the price charged to Moldova for supplies of natural gas (from US $80 to $160 per 1,000 cu m). Gas supplies from Russia temporarily ceased in January, after Moldova refused to sign a new contract with the Russian state-controlled gas supplier, Gazprom. In mid-January a compromise agreement was reached, covering the first three months of the year; in return for agreeing to relinquish the Transnistrian assets of the joint-venture company Moldovagaz to Gazprom (which already held a majority stake in the company), Moldova was be charged $110 per cu m for its gas supplies from Russia. At the end of December Moldova withdrew objections to Russia's accession to the WTO, on condition that value added taxes on Russian gas deliveries to Moldova were levied in the country of destination rather than in Russia, in accordance with WTO regulations. Leading officials of Moldovagaz and Gazprom also signed a five-year agreement, providing for staged increases in the price of gas supplied to Moldova, while the Moldovan Government was to transfer control of its gas distribution system to Gazprom.

Since gaining independence Moldova has sought to develop good relations with the neighbouring countries of Ukraine and Romania. Agreement on the delimitation of the Moldovan–Ukrainian border, apart from the Transnistrian section, was reached in November 1997, and the two countries finally defined their border in May 1999. In November 2004 Moldova dissociated itself from the countries in Russia's sphere of influence by condemning suspected electoral malpractice in Ukraine during the presidential election there. The Government subsequently established cordial relations with the new administration of President Viktor Yushchenko in Ukraine. Moldova had also established good relations with the new, western-orientated Government in Georgia, under President Mikheil Saakashvili, who was inaugurated in early 2004. In December 2005 Moldova attended a meeting in Kyiv, Ukraine, to launch the new Community of Democratic Choice, originally conceived by Ukraine and Georgia. The nine-member alliance aimed to remove divisions and resolve conflicts in the Baltic, Black Sea and Caspian regions, and observers in Russia expressed concern that the grouping might serve to weaken its influence. In May 2006 the leaders of Georgia, Ukraine, Azerbaijan and Moldova met in Kyiv, Ukraine, to revive the regional GUAM organization, renaming it the Organization for Democracy and Economic Development—GUAM.

Relations with Romania were subject to tensions. A basic political treaty, in preparation for six years, was agreed in May 1999 and initialled in April 2000; however, it was not signed, and in late 2003 the Romanian Prime Minister, Adrian Năstase, indicated that the country no longer considered the treaty to be relevant to the political situation. In February 2000 many Moldovans applied to obtain Romanian citizenship as formal negotiations on Romania's accession to the EU commenced. The Romanian Government subsequently introduced measures to simplify the application process, angering the Moldovan authorities, since the Constitution did not permit dual citizenship. The situation was resolved when President Lucinschi drafted a new law, allowing Moldovans to hold dual citizenship with Israel, Romania and Russia, which was enacted in August. In March 2002 a Romanian diplomat was expelled from Moldova, after having reportedly met organizers of opposition protests (see above); Romania responded by expelling a Moldovan diplomat. From April 2003 ministerial co-operation between Moldova and Romania was resumed, together with discussions on the initiation of negotiations regarding a border agreement; it was confirmed that Romania would not require Moldovan citizens to possess entry visas until its accession to the EU. None the less, in October the Moldovan Government appealed to the Council of Europe for assistance with its deteriorating relations with Romania, after that country failed to sign a bilateral treaty confirming Moldova's borders. In 2004 the apparent realignment of Moldovan foreign policy towards the West provided a greater convergence of interests. In January 2005 the new President of Romania, Traian Băsescu, visited Moldova and declared his support for the country's desire to achieve eventual membership of the EU, which had begun to formulate an official policy towards Moldova. In March 2007 the Moldovan Government strongly criticized Romania for granting Romanian citizenship to large numbers of Moldovans (with an estimated 800,000 applications pending), on the grounds that the policy undermined Moldova's statehood. Romania's accession to full EU membership, which took effect in January 2007, resulted in Moldovan citizens being required to possess entry visitors to enter that country; in protest at this decision, the Moldovan authorities reversed a decision to allow Romania to open two new consulates in the country. In December Moldova expelled two Romanian diplomats, who had allegedly supplied funds to opposition newspapers, for activities 'incompatible with their status'.

Government

Under the Constitution of 1994, supreme legislative power is held by the unicameral Parlamentul (Parliament), which is directly elected every four years. Parlamentul comprises 101 members. The President is Head of State and holds executive power in conjunction with the Council of Ministers, led by the Prime Minister. According to constitutional amendments introduced in July 2000, the President is elected by the legislature for a four-year term. Following local elections in May 1999 the country was reorganized into nine provinces and two autonomous entities—Gagauz-Yeri and Transnistria. However, in January 2003 the Government approved new legislation on administrative reform, replacing the structure introduced in 1999 with one based upon 33 districts (rayons) and two municipalities, although the two autonomous entities retained that status.

Defence

Following independence from the USSR in 1991, the Moldovan Government initiated the creation of national armed forces. As assessed at November 2007, these numbered 6,750, with an army of 5,150 (including conscripts) and an air force of 850. In addition, reserves totalled 66,000. There were an estimated 3,279 paramilitary forces, attached to the Ministry of Internal Affairs. Military service is compulsory (with exemptions for students) and lasts for one year. Under an agreement concluded by the Moldovan and Russian Governments in late 1994, the former Soviet 14th Army (under Russian jurisdiction) was to have been withdrawn from Transnistria within three years, but in March 1998 it was announced that Russian forces would remain in Transnistria until a political settlement for the region was reached. Despite subsequent agreements providing for a withdrawal, Russian troops, numbering some 2,500, remained in Transnistria in 2008. In early 1994 Moldova joined the North Atlantic Treaty Organization's (NATO) 'Partnership for Peace' (see p. 342) programme. The 2007 budget allocated 194m. Moldovan lei to defence.

Economic Affairs

In 2006, according to estimates by the World Bank, Moldova's gross national income (GNI), measured at average 2004–06 prices, was US $3,743.8m., equivalent to $1,100 per head (or $2,880 per head on an international purchasing-power parity basis). During 1996–2006, it was estimated, the population decreased by an annual average of 1.2%, while gross domestic product (GDP) per head increased, in real terms, at an average rate of 4.5% per year. Overall GDP increased, in real terms, at an average annual rate of 3.2% in 1996–2006; GDP increased by 4.0% in 2006.

As a result of its extremely fertile land and temperate climate, Moldova's economy is dominated by agriculture and related industries. Some 85% of the country's terrain is cultivated. In 2006 agriculture (including hunting, forestry and fishing) contributed some 17.6% of GDP, and the sector provided 33.6% of employment in 2006. Principal crops include wine grapes and other fruit, tobacco, vegetables and grain. The wine industry has traditionally occupied a central role in the economy. The private ownership of land was legalized in 1991, although the sale of agricultural land was not permitted until 2001. In 2004 some 73.1% of agricultural land was privately owned and the private sector accounted for some 99% of production. According to the World Bank, the GDP of the agricultural sector increased, in real terms, at an average rate of 1.3% per year during 1996–2006. Agricultural GDP increased, in real terms, by 2.0% in 2006, according to World Bank estimates, although official estimates for the same year suggested a decline of 4.1%.

In 2006 industry (including mining, manufacturing, power and construction) contributed 21.4% of GDP. The sector provided 18.2% of employment in 2006. In 1996–2006, according to the World Bank, industrial GDP increased at an average rate of 0.8% per year. However, industrial GDP declined by 10.0% in 2006, owing, in part, to import restrictions imposed by Russia and increased production costs engendered by the rise in fuel prices.

Mining and quarrying employed just 0.3% of the working population in 2006, and contributed 0.4% of GDP in 2004. Moldova has extremely limited mineral resources, and there is no domestic production of fuel or non-ferrous metals. Activity is focused primarily on the extraction and processing of industrial minerals such as gypsum, limestone, sand and gravel. Deposits of petroleum and natural gas were discovered in southern Moldova in the early 1990s; total reserves of natural gas have been estimated at 22,000m. cu m.

The manufacturing sector provided 10.7% of employment in 2006, and contributed 16.4% of GDP in 2004. The sector is dominated by food-processing, wine and tobacco production, machine-building and metal-working, and light industry. In 2005 the principal branches, measured by gross value of output, were food-processing and beverages (62.6%), non-metallic mineral products (11.6%) and clothing and furs (3.3%). According to the World Bank, manufacturing GDP increased, in real terms, by an annual average of 0.4% in 1996–2006. Manufacturing GDP declined by 10.0% in 2006.

Moldova relies heavily on imported energy—primarily natural gas and petroleum products—from Russia, Romania and Ukraine (such imports accounted for 76.7% of consumption in 2004). In the mid 2000s Moldova announced its intention to diversify its gas suppliers, and to increase domestic energy production substantially; domestic production represented 23.3% of consumption in 2004. A large proportion of natural gas imports supply the Moldoveneasca power station, located in Transnistria, which contributes much of the country's electricity generating capacity. In February 2005 an Azerbaijani company purchased the unfinished Giurgiulesti petroleum terminal in southern Moldova, with plans for its further development; completion was scheduled for 2006. In 2004 natural gas accounted for 92.2% of electricity production, and coal accounted for just 5.4% (compared with 43.8% in 1994). Mineral products comprised 21.2% of the value of total merchandise imports in 2005, according to the World Bank.

Services accounted for 61.0% of GDP in 2006, and the sector provided 48.2% of total employment in that year. The GDP of the services sector increased, in real terms, by an annual average of 4.2% in 1996–2006. Services GDP increased by 12.3% in 2006.

In 2006 Moldova recorded a visible trade deficit of US $1,591.5m., while there was a deficit of $391.6m. on the current account of the balance of payments. In 2005 the principal source of imports was Ukraine (accounting for 20.9% of the value of total imports). Other major suppliers were Russia (11.7%), Romania (11.2%), Germany and Italy. The main market for exports in that year was Russia (accounting for 31.8% of the value of total exports). Other important purchasers were Italy, Romania, Ukraine and Belarus. In 2005 the principal imports were mineral products, machinery and mechanical appliances, chemicals and related products, textiles and base metals. The main exports in that year were food products, beverages and tobacco, textiles and vegetable products.

In 2006 the consolidated state budget recorded a deficit of 1,368m. Moldovan lei (equivalent to 3.1% of GDP). At the end of 2005 Moldova's total external debt totalled US $2,053m., of which $700m. was long-term public debt. In that year the cost of debt-servicing was equivalent to 10.2% of the value of exports of goods and services. Consumer prices increased by an annual average of 15.0% during 1996–2006. The average rate of inflation was 12.8% in 2006. The average rate of unemployment was 7.4% in 2005.

Moldova became a member of the IMF and the World Bank in 1992. It also joined the European Bank for Reconstruction and Development (EBRD, see p. 239), as a 'Country of Operations'. Moldova subsequently became a member of the Organization of the Black Sea Economic Co-operation (see p. 367), and it joined the World Trade Organization (see p. 396) in 2001.

After independence, economic performance was adversely affected by disruptions in inter-republican trade, as well as the armed conflict in Transnistria (the main industrial centre) in the 1992 and the region's subsequent effective de facto secession from Moldova (see Recent History). After 1998 the reform process stalled, and from 1999 the IMF repeatedly suspended lending. Although the economy had recorded continued growth since 2000, by the mid-2000s the country was the poorest in Europe, and remittances from workers seeking employment abroad accounted for some 30% of GDP in 2005. The IMF had suspended lending under its Poverty Reduction and Growth Facility (PRGF) in mid-2003, but agreement was reached on a new three-year PRGF in mid-2006. Economic growth in 2006, at an estimated 4.0%, was slower than had previously been forecast, largely due to external shocks such as an increase in prices charged for Russian gas prices, and the blocking, for much of the calendar year, of wine exports to Russia, ostensibly on safety grounds (the ban was subsequently repealed in October 2007). The economy fared better in 2007, during which GDP was estimated to have expanded by 5.0%. Investment increased notably in that year, superseding remittances as the primary source of growth. However, the agricultural sector was impeded by drought in the early part of the year, and an associated downturn in production of staple crops contributed to an overall increase in consumer prices, which rose by 13% in 2007 according to IMF estimates. Continued adherence to fiscal austerity invited praise from the IMF, which disbursed funds of US $18.6m. to the authorities following completion of a third review of the PRGF arrangement in March 2008. Legislation devised to rationalize budgetary operations was approved by Parlamentul in mid-2007, with the Government intending that the additional revenues thereby generated would offset increased expenditure on public sector salaries (which were scheduled to increase sharply in 2008, following concerns that low wages were precipitating emigration). Growth of 7.0% was projected for 2008, while the budget deficit was expected to decline to only 0.5% of GDP. Improvements to the regulatory system guiding business activities were likely to engender further investment, but further problems in the energy sector were expected in the absence of structural reform.

Education

Education is officially compulsory in Moldova between seven and 16 years of age. Primary education begins at seven years of age and lasts for four years. Secondary education, beginning at 11, lasts for a maximum of seven years, comprising a first cycle of five years and a second of two years. Primary enrolment in 2004 included 86% of children in the relevant age-group, and the comparable ratio for secondary education was 77%. In 2004 consolidated budgetary expenditure on education was 1,689m. lei (equivalent to 15.1% of GDP).

Public Holidays

2008: 1 January (New Year's Day), 7–8 January (Orthodox Christmas), 8 March (International Women's Day), 27–28 April (Orthodox Easter), 1 May (Labour Day), 9 May (Victory and Commemoration Day), 27 August (Independence Day), 31 August ('Limbă Noastră', National Language Day).

2009: 1 January (New Year's Day), 7–8 January (Orthodox Christmas), 8 March (International Women's Day), 19–20 April (Orthodox Easter), 1 May (Labour Day), 9 May (Victory and Commemoration Day), 27 August (Independence Day), 31 August ('Limbă Noastră', National Language Day).

Weights and Measures

The metric system is in force.

MOLDOVA

Statistical Survey

Principal sources (unless otherwise indicated): State Department for Statistics and Sociology, 2028 Chişinău, şos. Hînceşti 53D; tel. (22) 73-37-74; fax (22) 22-61-46; e-mail dass@statistica.md; internet www.statistica.md.

Note: Most of the figures from 1993 onwards exclude the Transnistria (Pridnestrovie) region, which remained outside central government control.

Area and Population

AREA, POPULATION AND DENSITY

Area (sq km)	33,800*
Population (census results)†	
12 January 1989	4,335,360
5–12 October 2004 (preliminary)	
Males	1,632,519
Females	1,755,552
Total	3,388,071
Population (official estimates at 1 January)‡§	
2004	3,606,800
2005	3,386,000
2006	3,395,600
Density (per sq km) at January 2006‡	100.5

* 13,050 sq miles.
† Figures refer to the *de jure* population. The *de facto* total at the 1989 census was 4,337,592 (males 2,058,160, females 2,279,432).
‡ Excluding Transnistria.
§ Rounded figures calculated on the basis of preliminary census data.

POPULATION BY ETHNIC GROUP*
(permanent inhabitants, 2004 census)

	Number	%
Moldovan	2,564,849	75.8
Ukrainian	282,406	8.4
Russian	201,218	5.9
Gagauz	147,500	4.4
Romanian	73,276	2.2
Bulgarian	65,662	1.9
Others and unknown	48,421	1.4
Total	3,383,332	100.0

* According to official declaration of nationality.

ADMINISTRATIVE DIVISIONS
(population estimates at 1 January 2006)

Districts (raione)			
Anenii Noi	81,500	Nisporeni	64,900
Basarabeasca	28,900	Ocniţa	56,400
Briceni	77,300	Orhei	115,800
Cahul	119,200	Rezina	50,800
Cantemir	61,300	Rîşcani	68,900
Călăraşi	74,800	Sîngerei	87,000
Căuşeni	90,400	Soroca	100,900
Cimişlia	60,800	Străşeni	88,700
Criuleni	72,000	Şoldăneşti	41,900
Donduşeni	45,900	Ştefan Vodă	70,500
Drochia	86,400	Taraclia	43,000
Dubăsari	35,100	Teleneşti	69,900
Edineţ	83,500	Ungheni	110,700
Făleşti	89,800	*Municipalities*	
Floreşti	88,600	Bălţi	127,600
Glodeni	60,500	Chişinău	717,900
		Autonomous Territory	
Hînceşti	119,600		
Ialoveni	97,800	Gagauz-Yeri	155,700
Leova	51,600	**Total**	3,395,600

Population of Transnistria (Pridnestrovie) (estimated figure obtained as residual from total country population estimates at 1 January 2003): 601,088.

PRINCIPAL TOWNS
(estimated population at 1 January 1996)

Chişinău (capital)	655,000	Tighina (Bender)	128,000
Tiraspol	187,000	Râbnita (Rybnitsa)	62,900
Bălţi	153,500		

2006 (1 January, estimates): Chişinău 593,800; Bălţi 122,700.

BIRTHS, MARRIAGES AND DEATHS

	Registered live births		Registered marriages		Registered deaths	
	Number	Rate (per 1,000)	Number	Rate (per 1,000)	Number	Rate (per 1,000)
1998	46,755	10.9	25,793	6.0*	47,691	11.1
1999†	38,501	9.0	23,524	5.5	41,315	9.6
2000†	36,939	8.7	21,684	5.1	41,224	9.7
2001	36,448	10.0	21,200‡	5.8	40,100‡	11.0
2002	35,705	9.9	21,700‡	6.0	41,900‡	11.6
2003	36,471	10.1	n.a.	6.9	43,079	11.9
2004	38,272	11.3	n.a.	7.0	41,700‡	12.3
2005	37,695	10.5	27,187	7.6	44,689	12.4

* Estimate.
† Numbers exclude, but rates include, Transnistria.
‡ Rounded figures.

2006: Live births 37,587 (birth rate 10.5 per 1,000).

Sources: partly UN, *Population and Vital Statistics Report*.

Expectation of life (years at birth, WHO estimates): 68.5 (males 64.6; females 72.3) in 2005 (Source: WHO, *World Health Statistics*).

ECONOMICALLY ACTIVE POPULATION
('000 persons aged 15 years and over)

	2004	2005	2006
Agriculture, hunting and forestry	531.9	534.0	421.6
Fishing	1.0	1.5	0.8
Mining and quarrying	0.8	1.8	3.4
Manufacturing	135.4	131.8	134.5
Electricity, gas and water supply	25.6	25.8	23.5
Construction	52.0	51.6	67.3
Wholesale and retail trade; repair of motor vehicles, motorcycles and personal and household goods	159.6	159.9	174.1
Hotels and restaurants	19.1	23.0	21.8
Transport, storage and communications	73.4	71.0	65.3
Financial intermediation	13.6	13.4	15.0
Real estate, renting and business activities	28.9	28.7	31.0
Public administration and defence; compulsory social security	64.1	61.5	71.9
Education	107.9	108.2	120.4
Health and social work	68.7	69.4	64.3
Other community, social and personal service activities	30.3	32.1	36.5
Private households with employed persons	3.3	3.3	4.7
Extra-territorial organizations and bodies	0.4	0.5	1.1
Total employed	1,316.0	1,318.7	1,257.3
Unemployed	116.5	103.7	99.9
Total labour force	1,432.5	1,422.3	1,357.2
Males	701.6	689.5	690.3
Females	731.0	732.9	666.9

Source: ILO.

MOLDOVA

Health and Welfare

KEY INDICATORS

Total fertility rate (children per woman, 2005)	1.2
Under-5 mortality rate (per 1,000 live births, 2005)	16
HIV/AIDS (% of persons aged 15–49, 2005)	1.1
Physicians (per 1,000 head, 2004)	2.64
Hospital beds (per 1,000 head, 2005)	6.4
Health expenditure (2004): US $ per head (PPP)	138.2
Health expenditure (2004): % of GDP	7.4
Health expenditure (2004): public (% of total)	56.8
Access to water (% of persons, 2004)	92
Human Development Index (2005): ranking	111
Human Development Index (2005): value	0.708

For sources and definitions, see explanatory note on p. vi.

Agriculture

PRINCIPAL CROPS
('000 metric tons)

	2004	2005	2006
Wheat	861.0	1,056.7	691.4
Barley	268.3	212.0	200.1
Maize	1,794.5	1,492.0	1,322.2
Potatoes	317.7	378.2	377.0
Sugar beet	911.3	991.2	1,177.3
Dry beans	20.3	27.4	26.6
Dry peas	28.9	33.9	33.8
Sunflower seed	335.2	331.1	379.9
Cabbages and other brassicas	40.9	53.2	64.9
Tomatoes	74.2	84.6	104.4
Cucumbers and gherkins	21.3	28.0	38.1
Chillies and green peppers	20.5	32.1	46.0
Aubergines (Eggplants)	4.8	7.2	8.6
Dry onions	42.3	52.3	54.4
Carrots and turnips	15.6	19.3	2.4
Watermelons	54.8	36.8	89.0
Apples	310.1	278.4	202.8
Plums and sloes	55.6	41.4	75.9
Grapes	685.6	518.5	466.1
Tobacco (leaves)	7.9	6.7	4.9

Source: FAO.

LIVESTOCK
('000 head at 1 January)

	2004	2005	2006
Horses	77.4	72.5	69.1
Cattle	372.8	330.6	310.5
Pigs	445.9	398.0	460.7
Sheep	817.1	822.8	818.3
Goats	120.9	119.4	119.4
Chickens	15,755*	17,522*	22,100

* FAO estimate.
Source: FAO.

LIVESTOCK PRODUCTS
('000 metric tons)

	2004	2005	2006
Cattle meat	16.0	15.6	15.0
Sheep meat	2.6	2.4	2.3
Pig meat	41.3	39.7	48.0
Chicken meat	24.4	28.0	30.9
Cows' milk	604.0	627.1	595.3
Sheep's milk	17.7	21.1	19.9
Goats' milk	6.0	10.4	12.3
Hen eggs	23.4	26.7	26.8
Honey	2.1	2.4	2.7
Wool: greasy	2.0	2.1	2.1*

* FAO estimate.
Source: FAO.

Forestry

ROUNDWOOD REMOVALS
('000 cubic metres, excl. bark)

	1999	2000	2001
Sawlogs, veneer logs and logs for sleepers	3	5	3
Other industrial wood	9	24	24*
Fuel wood	36	30	30*
Total	48	59	57

* FAO estimate.

2002–06: Annual production as in 2001 (FAO estimates).
Source: FAO.

SAWNWOOD PRODUCTION
('000 cubic metres, incl. railway sleepers)

	1998	1999	2000
Coniferous (softwood)	25	—	—
Broadleaved (hardwood)	5	6	5
Total	30	6	5

2001–06: Annual production as in 2000 (FAO estimates).
Source: FAO.

Fishing

(metric tons, live weight)

	2003	2004	2005
Capture	343	487	531
Common carp	125	128	160
Crucian carp	139	152	156
Aquaculture	2,638	4,470	4,470*
Common carp	197	1,660	1,660*
Grass carp (White amur)	115	21	21*
Silver carp	2,291	2,780	2,780*
Total catch	2,981	4,957	5,001*

* FAO estimate.
Source: FAO.

Mining

('000 metric tons)

	2003	2004	2005
Gypsum	116.1	102.5	110.0
Peat*	475	475	475
Sand and gravel*	300.0	300.0	300.0

* Estimated production.
Source: US Geological Survey.

MOLDOVA

Industry

SELECTED PRODUCTS
('000 metric tons, unless otherwise indicated)

	2002	2003	2004
Vegetable oil	51.7	72.8	85.3
Flour	151.4	116.7	45.3
Raw sugar	165.5*	107.1	112.0
Wine ('000 hectolitres)†	1,480	1,900	3,060
Mineral water ('000 hectolitres)	535	n.a.	n.a.
Soft drinks ('000 hectolitres)†	420	600	550
Cigarettes (million)	6,310	7,126	7,300
Carpets ('000 sq m)	2,444	3,537	4,467
Footwear ('000 pairs, excl. rubber)	1,925	2,738	2,877
Cement	279.0	255.4	439.7
Washing machines ('000 units)	40.1	47.7	53.8
Television receivers ('000 units)	7.6	10.3	0.5
Electric energy (million kWh)	1,180	1,046	1,022

* Including production in Transnistria.
† Rounded figures.

Finance

CURRENCY AND EXCHANGE RATES

Monetary Units
100 bani (singular: ban) = 1 Moldovan leu (plural: lei).

Sterling, Dollar and Euro Equivalents (31 December 2007)
£1 sterling = 22.677 lei;
US $1 = 11.319 lei;
€1 = 16.663 lei;
1,000 Moldovan lei = £44.10 = $88.35 = €60.01.

Average Exchange Rate (Moldovan lei per US$)
2005   12.600
2006   13.131
2007   12.140

Note: The Moldovan leu was introduced (except in Transnistria) on 29 November 1993, replacing the Moldovan rouble at a rate of 1 leu = 1,000 roubles. The Moldovan rouble had been introduced in June 1992, as a temporary coupon currency, and was initially at par with the Russian (formerly Soviet) rouble.

STATE BUDGET
(million lei)*

Revenue†	2004	2005	2006‡
Tax revenue	9,545	11,888	14,889
Taxes on profits	780	709	1,079
Taxes on personal incomes	797	962	1,128
Value-added tax	3,428	4,623	6,194
Excises	910	1,172	1,071
Taxes on international trade	496	681	828
Social Fund contributions	2,493	2,972	3,691
Health Fund contributions	326	442	558
Other taxes	317	327	342
Non-tax revenue	617	935	1,154
Total	10,162	12,823	16,044

Expenditure§	2004	2005	2006‡
Current expenditure	9,537	11,641	14,223
Wages	2,507	3,000	4,183
Goods and services	2,485	2,899	3,635
Health insurance fund	927	1,108	1,485
Interest payments	612	471	455
Transfers	3,727	5,012	5,935
Other current expenditure	206	259	16
Capital expenditure	1,613	2,335	3,567
Total	11,150	13,976	17,790

* Figures refer to a consolidation of the operations of central (republican) and local governments, including the Social Fund.
† Excluding grants received (million lei): 125 in 2004; 460 in 2005; 315 in 2006 (preliminary).
‡ Preliminary.
§ Excluding net lending (million lei): −57 in 2004; −39 in 2005; −63 in 2006 (preliminary).

Source: IMF, *Republic of Moldova: Second Review Under the Three-Year Arrangement Under the Poverty Reduction and Growth Facility and Request for Waiver of Nonobservance of Performance Criterion—Staff Report; Staff Statement; Staff Supplement; Press Release on the Executive Board Discussion; and Statement by the Executive Director for the Republic of Moldova* (August 2007).

INTERNATIONAL RESERVES
(US $ million at 31 December)

	2004	2005	2006
IMF special drawing rights	0.07	0.01	0.19
Reserve position in IMF	0.01	0.01	0.01
Foreign exchange	470.18	597.43	775.28
Total (excl. gold)	470.26	597.45	775.48

Source: IMF, *International Financial Statistics*.

MONEY SUPPLY
(million lei at 31 December)

	2004	2005	2006
Currency outside banks	3,699.91	4,571.22	5,145.81
Demand deposits at commercial banks	1,869.86	2,760.86	3,122.03
Total money (incl. others)	5,571.55	7333.21	8,268.34

Source: IMF, *International Financial Statistics*.

COST OF LIVING
(Consumer Price Index; base: 2000 = 100)

	2004	2005	2006
Food	147.9	168.0	183.4
All items (incl. others)	145.3	162.7	183.5

Source: ILO.

NATIONAL ACCOUNTS
(million lei at current prices, excl. Transnistria)

Expenditure on the Gross Domestic Product

	2004	2005	2006
Government final consumption expenditure	5,172.5	6,674.3	8,646.8
Private final consumption expenditure	28,125.2	34,694.1	41,319.1
Changes in inventories	1,656.5	2,348.5	2,791.2
Gross fixed capital formation	6,786.9	9,257.9	12,315.8
Total domestic expenditure	41,741.1	52,974.8	65,072.9
Exports of goods and services	16,398.4	19,264.1	20,590.7
Less Imports of goods and services	26,107.7	34,587.1	41,594.8
GDP in market prices	32,031.8	37,651.9	44,068.8

MOLDOVA

Gross Domestic Product by Economic Activity

	2004	2005	2006
Agriculture, hunting, forestry and fishing	5,633.4	6,174.9	6,635.5
Industry	6,569.6	7,192.8	8,057.3
Construction	1,101.2	1,257.0	1,730.3
Services	16,044.4	19,005.1	22,968.9
Wholesale and retail trade, and repairs of vehicles and personal and household goods	3,383.9	3,928.6	4,583.0
Transport, storage and communications	3,780.2	4,603.9	5,342.6
Sub-total	28,247.4	32,372.8	37,661.7
Less Financial intermediation services indirectly measured	729.8	756.9	993.0
Gross value added in basic prices	27,517.6	31,615.9	36,668.7
Taxes, *less* subsidies, on products and imports	4,514.2	6,036.0	7,400.1
GDP in market prices	32,031.8	37,651.9	44,068.8

Source: National Bank of Moldova.

BALANCE OF PAYMENTS
(US $ million)

	2004	2005	2006
Exports of goods f.o.b.	994.1	1,104.6	1,053.0
Imports of goods f.o.b.	−1,748.2	−2,296.1	−2,644.4
Trade balance	−754.2	−1,191.5	−1,591.5
Exports of services	332.1	398.9	488.6
Imports of services	−353.1	−419.7	−484.4
Balance on goods and services	−775.1	−1,212.2	−1,587.2
Other income received	490.0	539.3	605.8
Other income paid	−133.0	−129.0	−205.2
Balance on goods, services and income	−418.1	−802.0	−1,186.6
Current transfers received	406.8	596.8	854.9
Current transfers paid	−35.8	−43.2	−60.0
Current balance	−47.1	−248.4	−391.6
Capital account (net)	−18.3	−16.9	−22.8
Direct investment abroad	−3.2	0.2	0.7
Direct investment from abroad	87.7	197.4	241.9
Portfolio investment assets	−1.5	−1.2	−0.2
Portfolio investment liabilities	−8.3	−5.8	−4.6
Financial derivatives assets	−0.5	−1.7	−0.1
Financial derivatives liabilities	1.0	0.1	0.3
Other investment assets	−31.6	−77.9	−73.2
Other investment liabilities	69.3	91.4	153.3
Net errors and omissions	100.6	178.0	105.2
Overall balance	148.2	115.2	8.9

Source: IMF, *International Financial Statistics*.

External Trade

PRINCIPAL COMMODITIES
(US $ million)

Imports c.i.f.	2003	2004	2005
Vegetable products	82.3	73.5	67.1
Foodstuffs, beverages and tobacco	92.0	105.3	150.6
Mineral products	297.7	384.9	505.2
Mineral fuels, mineral oils and related materials	287.2	370.6	n.a.
Chemicals and related products	132.7	161.8	232.6
Medicinal and pharmaceutical products	51.0	48.2	n.a.
Plastics, rubber and articles thereof	69.3	101.1	140.2
Plastics	53.3	79.4	n.a.
Raw hides, skins, leather and articles thereof	36.3	72.5	n.a.
Pulp of wood, paper and paperboard and articles thereof	56.4	63.4	69.6
Textiles and textile articles	118.4	150.6	180.0
Articles of stone, plaster, cement, ceramic or glass	52.7	64.4	69.1
Base metals and articles of base metals	70.3	111.9	161.1
Machinery and mechanical appliances	214.0	239.7	322.2
Vehicles and associated transport equipment	75.2	96.0	130.2
Total (incl. others)	1,402.3	1,768.5	2,311.8

Exports f.o.b.	2003	2004	2005
Live animals and animal products	28.6	20.2	17.2
Vegetable products	91.2	120.0	131.9
Edible fruit	54.5	64.7	n.a.
Animal or vegetable fats	28.9	41.2	37.8
Foodstuffs, beverages and tobacco	314.3	345.9	396.2
Preparations of vegetables or fruits	38.4	40.3	n.a.
Mineral products	20.6	30.3	20.1
Raw hides, skins and leather	44.8	77.9	71.6
Textiles and textile articles	129.7	170.1	193.9
Articles of apparel and clothing accessories, not knitted	70.6	89.6	n.a.
Base metals and articles of base metals	19.4	29.9	48.8
Machinery and mechanical appliances	30.3	39.3	46.3
Total (incl. others)	789.9	985.2	1,091.3

MOLDOVA

PRINCIPAL TRADING PARTNERS
(US $ million)

Imports c.i.f.	2003	2004	2005
Belarus	50.6	64.3	84.3
Belgium	18.4	21.7	30.1
Bulgaria	30.1	29.6	29.0
China, People's Repub.	21.5	37.7	73.9
Czech Republic	19.0	21.5	28.8
France	35.2	52.7	64.4
Germany	135.6	150.2	191.1
Hungary	19.6	22.9	33.8
Italy	116.6	131.6	152.0
Kazakhstan	48.3	50.3	67.0
Netherlands	13.2	17.5	31.0
Poland	39.5	44.8	65.1
Romania	97.9	164.1	257.3
Russia	182.9	212.3	268.2
Turkey	48.2	69.1	93.0
Ukraine	309.2	436.3	479.8
USA	34.5	29.4	40.8
Total (incl. others)	1,402.3	1,768.5	2,293.0

Exports f.o.b.	2003	2004	2005
Austria	11.3	10.0	11.7
Belarus	41.1	58.7	71.2
Belgium	7.2	11.8	14.6
France	9.3	11.4	16.5
Germany	56.2	71.2	47.4
Hungary	8.0	14.5	14.7
Italy	82.4	136.4	133.4
Kazakhstan	9.2	15.4	17.3
Poland	4.5	6.6	25.3
Romania	90.2	98.9	111.7
Russia	308.4	353.3	347.5
Slovakia	1.2	1.7	15.1
Turkey	7.2	12.3	24.7
Ukraine	56.1	64.7	99.9
USA	33.6	42.7	37.5
Total (incl. others)	789.9	985.2	1,091.3

Transport

RAILWAYS
(traffic, incl. Transnistria)

	2002	2003	2004
Passenger journeys (million)	5.1	5.3	5.1
Passenger-km (million)	355	352	346
Freight transported (million metric tons)	12.6	14.7	13.3
Freight ton-km (million)	2,748	3,019	3,006

ROAD TRAFFIC
(motor vehicles in use)

	1997	1998	1999
Passenger cars	205,973	222,769	232,278
Buses and coaches	11,169	12,917	13,582
Lorries and vans	56,924	57,404	52,430

2004 (motor vehicles in use): Passenger cars 274,472; Buses and coaches 19,741; Lorries and vans 73,855; Motorcycles and mopeds 15,700.

Source: IRF, *World Road Statistics*.

INLAND WATERWAYS
(traffic, '000 metric tons)

	2002	2003	2004
Freight transported	107.5	120.0	119.7

CIVIL AVIATION
(traffic)

	2002	2003	2004
Passengers carried ('000)	240	250	310
Passenger-km (million)	324	304	365
Freight transported ('000 metric tons)	0.9	0.75	0.72
Freight ton-km (million)	1.3	0.9	1.0

Tourism

FOREIGN VISITOR ARRIVALS
(incl. excursionists)

Country of origin	2003	2004	2005
Belarus	750	1,072	1,161
Bulgaria	625	471	448
Germany	717	632	703
Italy	702	1,019	1,141
Netherlands	529	223	268
Poland	320	428	443
Romania	2,381	2,350	3,496
Russia	3,270	3,952	3,294
Turkey	3,965	3,521	3,038
Ukraine	3,283	3,173	3,406
United Kingdom	219	3,054	365
USA	2,494	2,494	3,088
Total (incl. others)	23,598	26,045	25,073

Receipts from tourism (US $ million, incl. passenger transport): 83 in 2003; 134 in 2004; 163 in 2005.

Source: World Tourism Organization.

Communications Media

	2004	2005	2006
Telephones ('000 main lines in use)	863.4	929.4	1,018.1
Mobile cellular telephones ('000 subscribers)	787.0	1,089.8	1,358.2
Personal computers ('000 in use)	112	112	n.a.
Internet users ('000)	406.0	550.0	727.7
Broadband subscribers ('000)	2.4	10.4	21.8

Television receivers ('000 in use): 1,300 in 2000.

Radio receivers ('000 in use): 3,220 in 1997.

Book production (including pamphlets): 921 titles (2,779,000 copies) in 1996.

Facsimile machines ('000 in use): 716 in 1999.

Daily newspapers: 4 (average circulation 261,000) in 1996.

Non-daily newspapers: 206 (estimated average circulation 1,350,000) in 1996.

Other periodicals: 76 (average circulation 196,000) in 1994.

Sources: UNESCO, *Statistical Yearbook*; International Telecommunication Union.

Education

(2005/06 unless otherwise indicated)

	Institutions	Teachers	Students
Primary	104	40,877	13,954
Secondary: general	1,454		505,073
Secondary: vocational	78	2,200*	25,005
Higher: colleges	51	1,898*	27,060
Higher: universities	35	5,909*	126,132

* 2004/05.

Adult literacy rate (UNESCO estimates): 99.1% (males 99.6%; females 98.6%) in 2004 (Source: UNESCO Institute for Statistics).

Directory

The Constitution

The Constitution of the Republic of Moldova, summarized below, was adopted by the Moldovan Parliament on 28 July 1994 and entered into force on 27 August. In 2000 amendments to the Constitution were enacted, which transformed Moldova into a parliamentary republic. The Constitution was further amended, to recognize the autonomous status of Gagauz-Yeri (Gagauzia) in July 2003.

GENERAL PRINCIPLES

The Republic of Moldova is a sovereign, independent, unitary and indivisible state. The rule of law, the dignity, rights and freedoms of the people, and the development of human personality, justice and political pluralism are guaranteed. The Constitution, the supreme law, upholds democracy and political pluralism, the separation and co-operation of the legislative, executive and judicial powers, respect for international law and treaties, fundamental principles regarding property, free economic initiative and the right to national identity. The national language of the republic is Moldovan and its writing is based on the Latin alphabet, although the right to use other languages spoken within the country is acknowledged.

FUNDAMENTAL RIGHTS, FREEDOMS AND DUTIES

All citizens are equal before the law and are presumed innocent until proven guilty.

The State guarantees the right to life and to the freedoms of movement, conscience, expression, assembly and political association, and the enfranchisement of Moldovan citizens aged over 18 years. Moldovan citizens have the right of access to information and education, of health security, of establishing and joining a trade union, of working and of striking. Obligations of the citizenry include the payment of taxes and the defence of the motherland.

PARLAMENTUL

Parlamentul (The Parliament) is the sole legislative authority of Moldova, comprising 101 members, who are directly elected for a four-year term. The Chairman of Parlamentul is elected by members. Parlamentul's basic powers include: the enactment of laws, the calling of referendums, the approval of state policy, the approval or suspension of international treaties, the election of state officials and the declaration of the states of national emergency, martial law and war.

THE PRESIDENT OF THE REPUBLIC

The President of the Republic is the Head of State and is elected by the legislature for a four-year term. A candidate must be aged at least 40 years, be a Moldovan citizen and a speaker of the official language. The candidate must be in good health and must submit the written support of a minimum of 15 parliamentarians. A decision on the holding of a presidential election is taken by parliamentary resolution, and the election must be held no fewer than 45 days before the expiry of the outgoing President's term of office. To be elected President, a candidate must obtain the support of three-fifths of the parliamentary quorum. If necessary, further ballots must then be conducted, contested by the two candidates who received the most votes. The candidate who receives more votes becomes President. The post of President may be held by the same person for not more than two consecutive terms.

The President's main responsibilities include the promulgation of laws, the issue of decrees, the scheduling of referendums, the conclusion of international treaties and the dissolution of Parlamentul. The President is allowed to participate in parliamentary proceedings. The President, after consultation with the parliamentary majority, is responsible for nominating a Prime Minister-designate and a Government. The President may preside over government meetings and may consult the Government on matters of special importance and urgency. On proposals submitted by the Prime Minister, the President may revoke or renominate members of the Government in cases of vacancies or the reallocation of portfolios. The President is Commander-in-Chief of the armed forces.

If the President has committed a criminal or constitutional offence, the votes of two-thirds of the members of Parlamentul are required to remove the President from office; the removal must be confirmed by the Supreme Court of Justice, for a criminal offence, and by a national referendum, for a constitutional offence.

THE COUNCIL OF MINISTERS

The principal organ of executive government is the Council of Ministers, which supervises state policy and public administration of the country. The Council of Ministers is headed by a Prime Minister, who co-ordinates the activities of the Government. The Council of Ministers must resign if Parlamentul votes in favour of a motion of 'no confidence' in the Council.

LOCAL ADMINISTRATION

For administrative purposes, the Republic of Moldova is divided into districts, towns and villages. At village and town level, elected local councils and mayors operate as autonomous administrative authorities. At district level, an elected council co-ordinates the activities of village and town councils.

The area on the left bank of the Dniester (Dnestr or Nistru) river, as well as certain other places in the south of the republic (i.e. Gagauz-Yeri) may be granted special autonomous status, according to special statutory provisions of organic law.

JUDICIAL AUTHORITY

Every citizen has the right to free access to justice. Justice shall be administered by the Supreme Court of Justice, the Court of Appeal, tribunals and courts of law. Judges sitting in the courts of law and the Supreme Court of Justice are appointed by the President following proposals by the Higher Magistrates' Council. They are elected for a five-year term, and subsequently for a 10-year term, after which their term of office expires on reaching the age limit. The Higher Magistrates' Council is composed of 11 magistrates, who are appointed for a five-year term. It is responsible for the appointment, transfer and promotion of judges, as well as disciplinary action against them.

The Prosecutor-General, who is appointed by Parlamentul, exercises control over the enactment of law, as well as defending the legal order and the rights and freedoms of citizens.

THE CONSTITUTIONAL COURT

The Constitutional Court is the sole authority of constitutional judicature in Moldova. It is composed of six judges, who are appointed for a six-year term. The Constitutional Court's powers include: the enforcement of constitutionality in laws, decrees and governmental decisions, as well as international treaties endorsed by the Republic; the confirmation of the results of elections and referendums; the explanation and clarification of the Constitution; and decisions over matters of the constitutionality of parties. The decisions of the Constitutional Court are final and are not subject to appeal.

CONSTITUTIONAL REVISIONS

A revision of the Constitution may be initiated by one of the following: a petition signed by at least 200,000 citizens from at least one-half of the country's districts and municipalities; no less than one-third of the members of Parlamentul; the President of the Republic; the Government. Provisions regarding the sovereignty, independence, unity and neutrality of the State may be revised only by referendum.

The Government

HEAD OF STATE

President: VLADIMIR VORONIN (indirectly elected 4 April 2001; indirectly re-elected 4 April 2005).

COUNCIL OF MINISTERS
(April 2008)

Prime Minister: ZINAIDA GRECIANÎI.
First Deputy Prime Minister and Minister of the Economy and Trade: IGOR DODON.
Deputy Prime Minister: VICTOR STEPANIUC.
Deputy Prime Minister and Minister of Foreign Affairs and European Integration: ANDREI STRĂTAN.
Minister of Local Public Administration: VALENTIN GUZNAC.
Minister of Agriculture and the Food Industry: ANATOLIE GORODENCO.
Minister of Finance: MARIANA DURLESTEANU.
Minister of Information Development: PAVEL BUCEATCHI.
Minister of Transport and Road Management: VASILE URSU.
Minister of Construction and Territorial Development: VLADIMIR BALDOVICI.
Minister of Ecology and Natural Resources: VIOLETA IVANOV.
Minister of Education and Youth: LARISA SAVGA.
Minister of Health: LARISA CATRINICI.
Minister of Social Protection, the Family and Children: GALINA BALMOS.
Minister of Culture and Tourism: ARTUR COZMA.

MOLDOVA

Minister of Justice: VITALIE PÎRLOG.
Minister of Internal Affairs: VALENTIN MEJINSCHI.
Minister of Defence: VITALIE VRABIE.
Minister of Reintegration: VASILE ŞOVA.

Note: the President of the Moldovan Academy of Sciences, GHEORGHE DUCA, and the Başkan (Governor) of the Autonomous Territory of Gagauz-Yeri (Gagauzia) are also members of the Government. MIHAIL FORMUZAL was elected to the latter position in December 2006.

MINISTRIES

Office of the President: 2073 Chişinău, bd Ştefan cel Mare 154; tel. (22) 23-47-93; e-mail president@prm.md; internet www.president.md.

Office of the Council of Ministers: 2033 Chişinău, Piaţa Marii Adunări Naţionale 1; tel. (22) 25-01-04; fax (22) 24-26-96; e-mail anteprim@moldova.md; internet www.gov.md.

Ministry of Agriculture and the Food Industry: 2012 Chişinău, bd Ştefan cel Mare 162; tel. (22) 23-34-27; fax (22) 23-23-68; e-mail adm_maia@moldova.md; internet www.maia.gov.md.

Ministry of Construction and Territorial Development: Chişinău.

Ministry of Culture and Tourism: 2033 Chişinău, Piaţa Marii Adunări Naţionale 1, Of. 326; tel. (22) 22-76-20; fax (22) 23-23-88; e-mail culture@turism.md; internet www.turism.md.

Ministry of Defence: 2021 Chişinău, şos. Hînceşti 84; tel. (22) 25-22-22; fax (22) 23-26-31; e-mail ministru@army.md; internet www.army.md.

Ministry of Ecology and Natural Resources: 2005 Chişinău, str. Cosmonauţilor 9; tel. and fax (22) 21-45-33; e-mail cima@moldova.md; internet www.cim.moldova.md.

Ministry of the Economy and Trade: 2033 Chişinău, Piaţa Marii Adunări Naţionale 1; tel. (22) 23-74-48; fax (22) 23-40-64; e-mail mineconcom@mec.gov.md; internet www.mec.gov.md.

Ministry of Education and Youth: 2033 Chişinău, Piaţa Marii Adunări Naţionale 1; tel. (22) 23-33-48; fax (22) 23-35-15; e-mail consilier@edu.md; internet www.edu.md.

Ministry of Finance: 2005 Chişinău, str. Cosmonauţilor 7; tel. (22) 23-35-75; fax (22) 22-13-07; e-mail protocol@minfin.moldova.md; internet www.minfin.md.

Ministry of Foreign Affairs and European Integration: 2012 Chişinău, str. 31 August 80; tel. (22) 57-82-07; fax (22) 23-23-02; e-mail secdep@mfa.md; internet www.mfa.md.

Ministry of Health: 2009 Chişinău, str. Vasile Alecsandri 2; tel. (22) 72-99-07; fax (22) 73-87-81; e-mail cancelaria@mednet.md; internet www.ms.md.

Ministry of Information Development: Chişinău, str. Puşkin 42; tel. (22) 22-91-23; fax (22) 22-80-20; internet www.mdi.gov.md.

Ministry of Internal Affairs: 2012 Chişinău, bd Ştefan cel Mare 75; tel. (22) 22-45-47; fax (22) 22-27-43; e-mail mai@mai.md; internet www.mai.md.

Ministry of Justice: 2012 Chişinău, str. 31 August 1989 82; tel. (22) 23-47-95; fax (22) 23-47-97; e-mail secretariat@justice.gov.md; internet www.justice.gov.md.

Ministry of Local Public Administration: 2033 Chişinău, Piaţa Marii Adunări Naţionale 1; tel. (22) 20-01-70; fax (22) 23-89-22; e-mail info@mapl.gov.md; internet www.mapl.gov.md.

Ministry of Reintegration: Chişinău, str. A. Mateevici 109/1; tel. (22) 25-01-46; fax (22) 25-08-72; e-mail reintegrarea@moldova.md; internet www.reintegrarea.gov.md.

Ministry of Social Protection, the Family and Children: 2009 Chişinău, str. Vasile Alecsandri 1; tel. (22) 28-07-92; fax (22) 73-75-72; e-mail secretariat@mpsfc.gov.md; internet www.mpsfc.gov.md.

Ministry of Transport and Road Management: 2012 Chişinău, bd Ştefan cel Mare 134; tel. (22) 25-11-17; fax (22) 54-65-64; e-mail secretary@mci.gov.md; internet mci.gov.md.

President

The President of the Republic is elected by parliamentary deputies, and is required to receive the support of at least 61 of the 101 members of Parlamentul. VLADIMIR VORONIN was re-elected President on 4 April 2005, receiving 75 votes. His sole opponent, GHEORGHE DUCA, obtained one vote.

Legislature

Parlamentul (Parliament)

2073 Chişinău, bd Ştefan cel Mare 105; tel. (22) 23-33-52; fax (22) 23-30-12; e-mail info@parlament.md; internet www.parliament.md.
Chairman: MARIAN LUPU.

General Election, 6 March 2005

Parties and alliances	Votes	%	Seats
Party of Communists of the Republic of Moldova	716,336	45.98	56
Democratic Moldova*	444,377	28.53	34
People's Christian Democratic Party	141,341	9.07	11
Other parties, alliances and independents	255,774	16.42	—
Total	1,557,828	100.00	101

* An electoral bloc, comprising: the Democratic Party of Moldova; the Our Moldova Alliance; and the Social Liberal Party.

Election Commission

Comisia Electorală Centrală a Republicii Moldova (Central Electoral Commission of the Republic of Moldova): Chişinău, str. Vasile Alecsandri 119; tel. (22) 25-14-51; fax (22) 25-14-50; e-mail cec@molddata.md; internet www.cec.md; Pres. EUGENIU ŞTIRBU.

Political Organizations

In March 2007 27 political parties were registered with the Ministry of Justice; the following were among the most important.

Agrarian Party of Moldova (APM) (Partidul Agrar din Moldova): Chişinău, str. Teatrului 15; tel. (22) 22-22-74; fax (22) 22-60-50; f. 1991 by moderates from both the Popular Front of Moldova and the Communist Party of Moldova; supports economic and agricultural reform; Chair. ANATOL POPUŞOI.

Centrist Union of Moldova (Uniunea Centristă din Moldova): Chişinău, str. Tricolorului 35; tel. (22) 21-13-26; fax (22) 22-46-71; f. 2000; Chair. MIHAI PETRACHE.

Democratic Party of Moldova (Partidul Democrat din Moldova—PDM): 2001 Chişinău, str. Tighina 32; tel. (22) 27-82-29; fax (22) 27-82-30; e-mail secretariat@pdm.md; internet www.pdm.md; f. 1997; centrist; fmrly Movement for a Democratic and Prosperous Moldova, name changed in April 2000; contested 2005 legislative elections as mem. of the Democratic Moldova bloc; merged with Social Liberal Party in Feb. 2008; Chair. DUMITRU DIACOV.

Equal Rights (Ravnopravie) Socio-political Movement (Mişcarea social-politică Ravnopravie'—RSPMR): Chişinău, str. Sarmisegetuza 90/2/201; tel. (22) 27-12-71; f. 1998; Chair. VALERIU CLIMENCO.

Liberal Party (Partidul Liberal): Chişinău, str. Bucureşti 87; tel. (22) 23-26-89; fax (22) 22-80-97; e-mail liberal@pl.md; internet www.pl.md; f. 1993 as Party of Reform; renamed as above 2005; Chair. MIHAI GIMPU; 12,000 mems.

National Liberal Party (Partidul Naţional Liberal): Chişinău, str. Puşkin 62 A; tel. (22) 54-85-27; fax (22) 54-85-28; e-mail vitlaia@ch.moldpac.md; f. 2006 in split from Our Moldova Alliance; Pres. VITALIA PAVLICENCO.

Our Moldova Alliance (Alianţa 'Moldova Noastră'—AMN): 2012 Chişinău, str. M. Eminescu 68A; tel. (22) 26-00-07; fax (22) 21-13-94; e-mail alianta@amn.md; internet www.amn.md; f. 2003 by merger of the Alliance of Independents of Moldova, the Liberal Party (which left the Alliance in Dec. 2006), the Social Democratic Alliance of Moldova and the Popular Democratic Party of Moldova; supports Moldova's integration into Europe, a market economy and interethnic harmony; contested 2005 legislative elections as mem. of the Democratic Moldova bloc; Chair. SERAFIM URECHEAN; c. 100,000 mems (2007).

Party of Communists of the Republic of Moldova (Partidul Comuniştilor din Republica Moldova—PCRM): 2012 Chişinău, str. N. Iorga 11; tel. (22) 23-46-14; fax (22) 23-36-73; e-mail info@pcrm.md; internet www.pcrm.md; fmrly the Communist Party of Moldova (banned Aug. 1991); revived as above 1994; First Sec. VLADIMIR VORONIN.

People's Christian Democratic Party (Partidul Popular Creştin Democrat—PPCD): 2009 Chişinău, str. N. Iorga 5; tel. (22) 28-25-34; fax (22) 23-86-66; e-mail echipa@ppcd.md; internet www.ppcd.md; f. 1989 as the People's Front of Moldova, renamed 1992, and as above

MOLDOVA

1999; advocates Moldova's entry into the EU and NATO; Chair. IURIE ROŞCA.

Republican Party of Moldova (Partidul Republican din Moldova—PRM): Chişinău, str. Cuza-Voda 35/2, ap. 21; tel. and fax (22) 76-94-22; e-mail acurteanma@yahoo.com; f. 1999; Chair. ION CURTEAN.

Social Democratic Party of Moldova (Partidul Social Democrat din Moldova—PSDM): 2005 Chişinău, str. Petru Rareş 33/1; tel. (22) 29-64-67; fax (22) 29-03-09; e-mail info@psdm.md; internet www.psdm.md/ro; f. 1990; merged with Party of Social Democracy in Dec. 2007; Pres. EDUARD MUŞUC; Chair. of National Council LORETTA HANDRABURA.

Socialist Party of Moldova (Partidul Socialist din Moldova): Chişinău, str. V. Alecsandri 35 A; tel. (22) 73-12-96; f. 1992; successor to the former Communist Party of Moldova; favours socialist economic and social policies, defends the rights of Russian and other minorities and advocates continued CIS membership; contested 2005 legislative election as mem. of the Fatherland-Motherland (Patria-Rodina) electoral bloc; Pres. VICTOR MOREV.

Parties and organizations in Transnistria include: **Renewal** (Obnovleniye), led by YEVGENII SHEVCHUK; **Transnistrian Communist Party** (Pridnestrovskaya Kommunisticheskaya Partiya—PKP), led by OLEG KHORZHAN; **Patriotic Party of Transnistria** (Patrioticheskaya Partiya Pridnestroviya—PPP), led by OLEG SMIRNOV; and **Republic** (Respublica), led by YURII SUKHOV.

Parties and organizations in Gagauz-Yeri include: **Fatherland** (Vatan), led by ANDREI CHESHMEJI; **Gagauz People** (Gagauz Halky), led by KONSTANTIN TAUSHANDJI; and **People's Republican Party**, (Respublika Halk Partiyasi), led by, *inter alia*, MIHAIL FORMUZAL.

Diplomatic Representation

EMBASSIES IN MOLDOVA

Austria: 2009 Chişinău, Mateevici 23B; tel. (22) 73-93-70; fax (22) 72-14-11; e-mail chisinau@ada.gv.at.

Azerbaijan: 2012 Chişinău, str. Kogelnichanu 64; tel. (22) 23-22-77; fax (22) 22-75-58; e-mail chisinau@mission.mfa.gov.az; Ambassador ISFENDIYAR VAHABZADEH.

Belarus: 2012 Chişinău, str. Mateevici 35; tel. (22) 23-83-02; fax (22) 23-83-00; e-mail moldova@belembassy.org; internet www.belembassy.org/moldova; Ambassador VASILIY A. SAKOVICH.

Bulgaria: 2012 Chişinău, str. Bucureşti 92; tel. (22) 23-79-83; fax (22) 23-79-78; e-mail ambasada-bulgara@meganet.md; internet www.mfa.bg/kishinev; Ambassador NIKOLAI ILIYEV.

China, People's Republic: 2004 Chişinău, str. Mitropolit Dosoftei 124; tel. (22) 24-85-51; fax (22) 29-59-60; e-mail chinaembassy@mtc.md; internet md.chineseembassy.org; Ambassador REN MINGGONG.

Czech Republic: 2005 Chişinău, str. Moara Roşie 23; tel. (22) 29-65—04; fax (22) 29-64-37; e-mail chisinau@embassy.mzv.cz; internet www.mzv.cz/chisinau; Ambassador PETR KYPR.

France: Chişinău, str. Vlaicu Pîrcălab 6; tel. (22) 20-04-00; fax (22) 20-04-01; e-mail amb-fr@cni.md; internet www.ambafrance.md; Ambassador PIERRE ANDRIEU.

Germany: 2012 Chişinău, str. Maria Cibotari 35; tel. (22) 20-06-00; fax (22) 23-46-80; e-mail info@chisinau.diplo.de; internet www.chisinau.diplo.de; Ambassador NIKOLAUS VON DER WENGE GRAF LAMBSDORFF.

Hungary: 2004 Chişinău, bd Ştefan cel Mare 131; tel. (22) 22-34-04; fax (22) 22-45-13; e-mail hu.emb@cni.md; Ambassador MIHÁLY BAYER.

Lithuania: 2001 Chişinău, str. I. Valilenco 24/1; tel. (22) 54-31-94; fax (22) 23-42-87; e-mail amb.md@urm.lt; Ambassador VYTAUTAS ŽALYS.

Poland: 2019 Chişinău, str. Grenoble 126; tel. (22) 28-59-50; fax (22) 28-90-00; e-mail polemb@mtc.md; internet www.kiszyniow.polemb.net; Ambassador KRZYSZTOF SUPROWICZ.

Romania: Chişinău, str. Bucureşti 66/1; tel. (22) 21-30-37; fax (22) 22-81-29; e-mail ambrom@moldnet.md; internet chisinau.mae.ro; Ambassador FILIP TEODORESCU.

Russia: 2004 Chişinău, bd Ştefan cel Mare 153; tel. (22) 23-49-43; fax (22) 23-51-07; e-mail domino@mtc.md; internet www.moldova.mid.ru; Ambassador VALERII I. KUZMIN.

Turkey: Chişinău, str. Valeriau Cupcea 60; tel. (22) 50-91-00; fax (22) 22-55-28; e-mail tremb@moldova.md; Ambassador FATMA FIRAT TOPÇUOĞLU.

Ukraine: 2008 Chişinău, bul. Vasile Lupu 17; tel. (22) 58-21-51; fax (22) 58-51-08; e-mail emb_md@mfa.gov.ua; internet www.mfa.gov.ua/moldova; Ambassador SERHIY I. PYROZHKOV.

United Kingdom: 2012 Chişinău, str. N. Iorga 18; tel. (22) 22-59-02; fax (22) 25-18-59; e-mail enquiries.chisinau@fco.gov.uk; internet www.britishembassy.md; Ambassador JOHN BEYER.

USA: 2009 Chişinău, str. Mateevici 103; tel. (22) 40-83-00; fax (22) 23-30-44; e-mail IRCChisinau@state.gov; internet moldova.usembassy.gov; Ambassador MICHAEL D. KIRBY.

Judicial System

Supreme Court of the Republic of Moldova (Curtea Supremă de Justiţie a Republicii Moldova): 2009 Chişinău, str. M. Kogălniceanu 70; tel. and fax (22) 22-15-47; internet www.scjustice.md; Pres. ION MURUIANU.

Constitutional Court of the Republic of Moldova (Curtea Constitutionala a Republicii Moldova): 2004 Chişinău, str. A. Lapuşneanu 28; tel. (22) 25-37-08; fax (22) 25-37-46; e-mail curtea@constcourt.md; internet www.constcourt.md; f. 1994; Chair. DUMITRU PULBERE.

Prosecutor-General: VALERIU GURBULEA, 2005 Chişinău, str. Mitropolit Bănulescu-Bodoni 26; tel. (22) 22-50-75; fax (22) 21-20-32; internet www.procuratura.md.

Religion

The majority of the inhabitants of Moldova profess Christianity, the largest denomination being the Eastern Orthodox Church. The Gagauz, of Turkic descent, are also adherents of Orthodox Christianity.

CHRISTIANITY

Eastern Orthodox Church

In December 1992 the Patriarch of Moscow and All Russia issued a decree altering the status of the Eparchy of Chişinău and Moldova to that of a Metropolitan See. In 2002 the Government permitted the registration of an Autonomous Metropolitate of Bessarabia. The recognition of the this church, an exarchate of the Romanian Orthodox Church, was confirmed by the Supreme Court in late 2004. In late 2007 the Romanian Orthodox Church announced that three dioceses in Moldova, which had been abolished in 1944 following the Soviet occupation of the territory, were to be reactivated.

Metropolitanate of Bessarabia, Archbishop of Chişinău: 2004 Chişinău, Str. 31 August 161; e-mail gbadea2006@yahoo.com; internet www.mitropoliabasarabiei.ro; Metropolitan of Bessarabia PETRU (PĂDURARU).

Russian Orthodox Church (Moscow Patriarchate): 2004 Chişinău, str. Bucureşti 119; tel. (22) 23-78-78; e-mail sec@mitropolia.md; internet www.mitropolia.md; 1,520 parishes (2004); Metropolitan of Chişinău and all-Moldova VLADIMIR (KANTARYAN).

Roman Catholic Church

In October 2001 the diocese of Chişinău, covering the whole country, was established. At 31 December 2005 there were an estimated 20,000 Roman Catholics in Moldova.

Bishop of Chişinău: Rt Rev. ANTON COŞA, 2012 Chişinău, str. Mitropolit Dosoftei 85; tel. (22) 22-34-70; fax (22) 22-52-10; e-mail episcopia@starnet.md.

The Press

The publications listed below are in Moldovan, except where otherwise indicated.

PRINCIPAL NEWSPAPERS

Accente Libere: Chişinău, str. Renasterii 22/1, bir. 48; tel. (22) 23-86-28; e-mail accente@rambler.ru; weekly; Editor-in-Chief SERGIU AFANASIU.

Dnestrovskaya Pravda (Dnestr Truth): Tiraspol, str. 25 October 101; tel. and fax (533) 3-46-86; f. 1941; 3 a week; in Russian; Editor TATYANA M. RUDENKO; circ. 7,000.

Ekonomicheskoye Obozreniye (Economic Review): Chişinău, bd Ştefan cel Mare 180; tel. (22) 24-69-52; fax (22) 24-69-50; e-mail red@logos.press.md; internet logos.press.md; f. 1990; weekly; in Russian; Editor-in-Chief SERGEI MIŞIN.

Glasul Naţiunii (The Voice of the Nation): Chişinău, str. 31 August 15; tel. and fax (22) 54-31-37; e-mail glasul_natiunii@hotmail.com; 4 a month; Editors VASILE NĂSTASE, EMANUELA JORGA.

MOLDOVA

GP Flux: Chișinău, str. Corobceanu 17; tel. (22) 23-22-14; fax (22) 24-75-29; e-mail secretar@flux.press.md; internet flux.press.md; daily; Editor-in-Chief Igor Burciu.

Jurnal de Chișinău: 2012 Chișinău, str. Pușkin 22/444; tel. (22) 23-40-41; fax (22) 23-42-30; e-mail cotidian@jurnal.md; internet www.jurnal.md; f. 1999; daily; Editor-in-Chief Rodica Mahu; circ. 13,400.

Kishinevskii Obozrevatel (Chișinău Correspondent): Chișinău, bd Ștefan cel Mare 162/604/7; tel. (22) 21-02-34; fax (22) 21-02-64; e-mail oboz@molodvacc.md; weekly; in Russian; Editor-in-Chief Irina Astakhova.

Kishinevskiye Novosti (Chișinău News): Chișinău, str. Pușkin 22; tel. (22) 23-39-18; fax (22) 23-42-40; e-mail kn@kn.md; internet www.kn.md; weekly; in Russian; Editor-in-Chief Maia Fililovna Ionko.

Kommersant Moldovy (Businessman of Moldova): 2012 Chișinău, str. Pușkin 22/601; tel. (22) 23-36-94; fax (22) 23-33-31; e-mail info@commert.press.md; internet www.km.press.md; weekly; in Russian; also known as *Kommersant Plus*; Editor-in-Chief Artem Varenița.

Komsomolskaya Pravda—v Moldove (Young Communist League Truth—in Moldova): Chișinău, str. Vlaicu Pîrcălab 45; tel. (22) 22-96-62; fax (22) 22-12-74; e-mail ser@kp.md; internet www.kp.md; daily; owned by Komsomolskaya Pravda (Basarabia), a subsidiary of Komsomolskaya Pravda (Russia); in Russian; Editor-in-Chief Sergei Ciuricov.

Moldavskiye Vedomosti (Moldovan Gazette): 2012 Chișinău, str. Bănulescu-Bodoni 21; tel. and fax (22) 23-86-18; e-mail editor@mv.net.md; internet vedomosti.md; f. 1995; weekly; in Russian; Editor-in-Chief Dmitrii A. Ciubasenko; circ. 5,100 (2004).

Moldova Suverană (Sovereign Moldova): 2012 Chișinău, str. Pușkin 22, 3rd Floor; tel. (22) 23-35-38; fax (22) 23-31-96; e-mail cotidian@moldova-suverana.md; internet www.moldova-suverana.md; f. 1924; daily; fmrly organ of the Govt; Editor Ion Berlinschi; circ. 105,000.

Nezavisimaya Moldova (Independent Moldova): 2012 Chișinău, str. Pușkin 22, 303; tel. (22) 23-36-05; fax (22) 23-31-41; e-mail admin@nm.mldnet.com; internet www.nm.md; f. 1991; daily; fmrly organ of the Govt; in Russian; Editor Iurii Tiscenco; circ. 60,692.

Tinerimya Moldovei/Molodezh Moldovy (Youth of Moldova): Chișinău; f. 1928; 3 a week; editions in Romanian (circ. 12,212) and Russian (circ. 4,274); Editor V. Botnaru.

Trudovoi Tiraspol (Working Tiraspol): Tiraspol, str. 25 October 101; tel. (533) 3-04-12; f. 1989; in Russian; Editor Dima Kondratovich.

Viață Satului (Life of the Village): 2612 Chișinău, str. Pușkin 22, Casa presei, 4th Floor; tel. (22) 23-03-68; f. 1945; weekly; govt publ; Editor V. S. Spiney.

Vremya (Time): 2068 Chișinău, str. Alecu Russo 1, 166; tel. (22) 44-09-41; fax (22) 44-73-33; e-mail nata@vremea.md; internet www.vremea.net; f. 1999; daily; in Russian; Editor Natalia Uzun.

PRINCIPAL PERIODICALS

Basarabia (Bessarabia): 2004 Chișinău, str. 31 August 98, 401; tel. (22) 21-05-13; e-mail libr@mnc.md; f. 1931; fmrly *Nistru*; monthly; journal of the Union of Writers of Moldova; fiction; Editor-in-Chief D. Matkovsky.

Chipăruș (Peppercorn): 2612 Chișinău, str. Pușkin 22; tel. (22) 23-38-16; f. 1958; fortnightly; satirical; Editor-in-Chief Ion Vikol.

Democratia (Democracy): 2012 Chișinău, str. Pușkin 22, 516–518; tel. (22) 24-32-53; fax (22) 24-35-85; e-mail democratia@cfem.md; internet www.democratia.cfem.md; f. 2001; weekly; political; Editor-in-Chief Cornel Ciurea.

Femeia Moldovei (Moldovan Woman): 2470 Chișinău, str. 28 June 45; tel. (22) 23-31-64; f. 1951; monthly; popular; for women.

Lanterna Magică (Magic Lantern): Chișinău, str. Pușkin 24, 49; tel. (22) 74-86-43; fax (22) 23-23-88; e-mail lung_ro@yahoo.com; internet www.iatp.md/lanternamagica; f. 1990; publ. by the Ministry of Culture and Tourism; 6 a year; art, culture.

Literatură și Artă: 2009 Chișinău, str. Sfatul Țării 2; tel. (22) 23-82-12; fax (22) 23-82-17; e-mail literatura@moldnet.md; f. 1954; weekly; organ of the Union of Writers of Moldova; literary; Editor Nicolae Dabija.

Moldova si Lumea (Moldova and the World): 2012 Chișinău, str. Pușkin 22, 510; tel. (22) 23-75-81; fax (22) 23-40-32; f. 1991; monthly; state-owned; international socio-political review; Editor Boris Stratulat.

Noi (Us): Chișinău; tel. (22) 23-31-91; f. 1930; fmrly *Scînteia Leninista* (Leninist Sparks); monthly; fiction; for 12-to-18 year-olds; Man. Valeriu Volontir; circ. 5,000.

Politica: 2033 Chișinău, bd Ștefan cel Mare 105; tel. (22) 23-74-03; fax (22) 23-32-10; e-mail vppm@cni.md; f. 1991; monthly; political issues.

Săptămîna (The Week): Chișinău, str. 31 August 107; tel. (22) 22-44-61; fax (22) 21-37-07; e-mail saptamin@mom.mldnet.com; internet www.net.md/saptamina; weekly magazine; Editor-in-Chief Viorel Mihail.

Sud-Est Cultural (South-East Cultural): Chișinău, str. 31 August 78; tel. (22) 23-21-03; fax (22) 76-55-80; e-mail vtazlauanu@dnt.md; internet www.sud-est.md; f. 2004; quarterly; art, culture; Editor-in-Chief Valentina Tazlauanu.

Timpul de Dimineața (The Morning Times): Chișinău, str. Mitropolitul Dosoftei 95; tel. (22) 29-40-45; fax (22) 29-24-28; e-mail timpul@mdl.net; internet www.timpul.md; weekly; independent; Editor-in-Chief Constantin Tanase.

NEWS AGENCIES

AP Flux Press Agency: Chișinău, str. Corobceanu 17; tel. (22) 24-92-72; fax (22) 24-91-51; e-mail flux@cni.md; internet flux.press.md; f. 1995; Dir Nadine Gogu.

BASA-press—Moldovan Information and Advertising Agency: 2012 Chișinău, str. Vasile Alecsandri 72; tel. and fax (22) 22-03-90; e-mail basa@basa.md; internet www.basa.md; f. 1992; independent; co-operates with Mediafax News Agency (Romania); Gen. Dir Valeriu Renita.

DECA Press Agency: Bălți, str. M. Viteazul 18, 3rd Floor; tel. (231) 60-744; fax (231) 61-385; e-mail info@deca.md; internet www.deca-press.net; f. 1996; local news; non-profit; Dir Vitalie Cazacu.

InfoMarket.MD (Denimax Grup): Chișinău; tel. (22) 27-76-26; e-mail redactor@infomarket.md; internet www.infomarket.md; on-line business news; Editor Alecsandru Burdeinii.

Infotag News Agency: 2014 Chișinău, str. Kogâlniceanu 76; tel. (22) 23-49-30; fax (22) 23-49-33; e-mail office@infotag.md; internet www.infotag.md; f. 1993; leading private news agency; Dir Alexandru Tanas.

Interlic News Agency: 2012 Chișinău, str. M. Cibotari 37, bir. 306; tel. and fax (22) 25-16-49; fax (22) 23-20-67; e-mail info@interlic.md; internet www.interlic.md; f. 1995; independent; Dir Ivan Sveatcenko.

Olvia-Press: 3300 Tiraspol, str. Pravda 31; tel. (3022) 8-24-97; fax (3022) 8-20-04; e-mail olvia@idknet.com; internet www.olvia.idknet.com; f. 1992; sole press agency of the 'Transnistrian Moldovan Republic'; reports political, economic and cultural developments in the region; Editor-in-Chief Oleg A. Yelkov.

Reporter.md: 2012 Chișinău, str. V. Alecsandri 90/1; tel. (22) 81-57-46; fax (22) 21-15-35; e-mail info@reporter.md; internet www.reporter.md; f. 2000 as an online journal; began operating as an independent news agency from 2002.

State Information Agency—Moldpres: 2012 Chișinău, str. Pușkin 22; tel. (22) 23-37-26; fax (22) 23-26-98; e-mail inform@moldpres.md; internet www.moldpres.md; f. 1940 as ATEM, reorganized 1990 and 1994; Dir Valeriu Renita.

PRESS ASSOCIATIONS

Association of Independent Press (API): 2012 Chișinău, str. Bucuresti 77; tel. and fax (22) 22-09-96; e-mail api@api.md; internet www.api.md; f. 1997; Pres. Ion Mititelu; Exec. Dir Petru Macovei.

Independent Journalism Centre (IJC): 2012 Chișinău, str. Sciusev 53; tel. (22) 21-36-52; fax (22) 22-66-81; e-mail editor@ijc.md; internet www.ijc.md; f. 1994; non-governmental org.

Publishers

Editura Cartea Moldovei: 2004 Chișinău, bd Ștefan cel Mare 180; tel. (22) 24-65-10; fax (22) 24-64-11; f. 1977; fiction, non-fiction, poetry, art books; Dir Dumitru Furdui; Editor-in-Chief Raisa Suveica.

Editura Hyperion: 2004 Chișinău, bd Ștefan cel Mare 180; tel. (22) 24-40-22; f. 1976; fiction, literature, arts; Dir Valeriu Matei.

Editura Lumina (Light): 2004 Chișinău, bd Ștefan cel Mare 180; tel. (22) 24-63-95; f. 1966; educational textbooks; Dir Victor Stratan; Editor-in-Chief Anatol Malev.

Editura Știința (Science): 2028 Chișinău, str. Academiei 3; tel. (22) 73-96-16; fax (22) 73-96-27; e-mail prini@stiinta.asm.md; f. 1959; textbooks, encyclopedias, dictionaries, children's books and fiction in various languages; Dir Gheorghe Prini.

MOLDOVA   *Directory*

Broadcasting and Communications

TELECOMMUNICATIONS

Regulatory Authority

National Regulatory Agency in Telecommunications and Informatics (ANRTI) (Agenția Națională pentru Reglementare în Telecomunicații și Informatica): 2012 Chișinău, bd Ștefan cel Mare 134; tel. (22) 25-13-17; fax (22) 22-28-85; internet www.anrti.md; f. 2000; Dir STANISLAV GORDEA.

Service Providers

Eventis: Chișinău, Str. V. Pircalab 52; tel. (22) 30-05-00; internet www.eventismobile.md; f. 2007; 51% owned by Eventis Telecom Holdings (Cyprus); mobile cellular telecommunications.

Moldcell: 2060 Chișinău, str. Belgrad 3; tel. (22) 20-62-06; fax (22) 20-62-07; e-mail moldcell@moldcell.md; internet www.moldcell.md; f. 1999; mobile telecommunications; owned by Fintur Holdings b.v. (Netherlands).

Moldtelecom: 2001 Chișinău, bd Ștefan cel Mare 10; tel. (22) 57-01-01; fax (22) 57-01-11; e-mail office@moldtelecom.md; internet www.moldtelecom.md; f. 1993; telephone communication and internet service provider; scheduled for partial privatization; Gen. Dir STELA SCOLA.

Orange Moldova: 2071 Chișinău, str. Alba-Iulia 75; tel. (22) 57-50-10; e-mail orange@orange.md; internet www.orange.md; f. 1998 as Voxtel SA; present name adopted 2007; mobile cellular telecommunications; 56.7% owned by France Telecom Mobiles (France), 33.4% by MMT-BIS; Dir.-Gen. BRUNO DUTOIT.

Unité: 2001 Chișinău, bd. Ștefan cel Mare 10; tel. (22); e-mail marketing@unite.md; internet www.unite.md; f. 2007; mobile cellular communications; 100% owned by Moldtelecom.

BROADCASTING

Regulatory Authorities

Radio and Television Co-ordinating Council (Consiliul Coordonator al Audiovizualului): 2012 Chișinău, str. Mihai Eminescu 28; tel. (22) 27-74-70; fax (22) 27-74-71; e-mail office@cca.md; internet www.cca.md; f. 1995; state owned; regulatory and licensing body; Pres. GHEORGHE ION GORINCIOI.

State Communication Inspectorate (Inspectoratul de Stat al Comunicatiilor): 2021 Chișinău, str. Drumul Viilor 28/2; tel. (22) 73-53-64; fax (22) 73-39-41; e-mail ciclicci@isc.net.md; internet www.mdi.gov.md/main_gis_md; f. 1993; responsible for frequency allocations and monitoring, certification of post and communications equipment and services; Dir TEODOR CICLICCI.

Radio

State Radio and Television Company of Moldova (Teleradio) (Televiziunea de Stat a Republicii Moldova): 2028 Chișinău, str. Miorița 1; tel. (22) 72-10-77; fax (22) 72-33-52; e-mail info@trm.md; internet www.trm.md; f. 1994; Pres. VALENTIN TODERCAN; Exec. Dir (Radio) SERGIU PATOC.

Radio Moldova: 2028 Chișinău, str. Miorița 1; tel. (22) 72-13-88; fax (22) 72-35-37; f. 1930; broadcasts in Romanian, Russian, Ukrainian, Gagauz and Yiddish; Exec. Dir VICTOR TABARTA.

Television

State Radio and Television Company of Moldova (Teleradio) (Televiziunea de Stat a Republicii Moldova): 2028 Chișinău, str. Miorița 1; tel. (22) 72-10-77; fax (22) 72-33-52; e-mail info@trm.md; internet www.trm.md; f. 1994; Pres. VALENTIN TODERCAN; Exec. Dir (TV) ADELA RAILEANU.

Finance

(cap. = capital; res = reserves; dep. = deposits; m. = million; brs = branches; amounts in Moldovan lei, unless otherwise stated)

BANKING

The National Bank of Moldova, established in 1991, is independent of the Government (but responsible to Parlamentul) and has the power to regulate monetary policy and the financial system. At February 2006 there were 16 commercial banks in operation.

Central Bank

National Bank of Moldova (Banca Națională a Moldovei): 2006 Chișinău, bd Renașterii 7; tel. (22) 40-90-06; fax (22) 22-05-91; e-mail official@bnm.org; internet www.bnm.org; f. 1991; cap. 288.9m., res 711.1m., dep. 3,639.4m. (Dec. 2006); Gov. LEONID TALMACI.

Commercial Banks

Banca de Economii a Moldovei: 2012 Chișinău, str. Columna 115; tel. (22) 24-47-22; fax (22) 24-47-31; e-mail bem@bem.md; internet www.bem.md; f. 1992; cap. 29.3m., res 15.6m., dep. 2,992.6m. (Dec. 2005); Pres. GRIGORE GACIKEVICI; 37 brs.

Banca de Finanțe și Comerț (FinComBank SA—Finance and Trade Bank JSC): 2012 Chișinău, str. Pușkin 26; tel. (22) 22-74-35; fax (22) 23-73-08; e-mail fincom@fincombank.com; internet www.fincombank.com; f. 1993; cap 179.7m., dep. 854.7m., total assets 1,229.8m. (June 2007); Chair. VICTOR KHVOROSTOVSKY; 13 brs.

Banca Socială: 2005 Chișinău, str. Bănulescu-Bodoni 61; tel. (22) 22-14-94; fax (22) 22-42-30; e-mail office@socbank.md; internet www.socbank.md; f. 1991; jt-stock commercial bank; cap. 57.6m., res 27.5m., dep. 1,005.6m. (Dec. 2005); Pres. VLADIMIR SUETNOV; Chair. VALENTIN CUNEV; 20 brs.

Comerțbank (Commercebank): 2001 Chișinău, str. Hîncești 38A; tel. (22) 73-99-91; fax (22) 73-99-81; e-mail comertbank@mdl.net; internet www.comertbank.md; f. 1991; cap. 96.0m., total assets 149.9m. (Jan. 2003); Chair. NATALIA ULIYANOVA.

Energbank: 2012 Chișinău, str. Vasile Alecsandri 78; tel. (22) 54-43-77; fax (22) 25-34-09; e-mail office@energbank.com; internet www.energbank.com; f. 1997; cap. 80.0m., dep. 263.9m., total assets 390.3m. (June 2005); Chair. MIHAIL OGORODNICOV; 48 brs.

EuroCreditBank: 2001 Chișinău, str. Ismail 33; tel. (22) 50-01-01; fax (22) 54-88-27; e-mail info@ecb.md; internet www.ecb.md; f. 1992; jt-stock co; commercial investment bank; cap. 108.0m., res 8.4m., dep. 59.6m. (Mar. 2007); Pres. AURELIU CINCILEI; 3 brs.

Eximbank: 2001 Chișinău, bd Ștefan cel Mare și Sfânt 6; tel. (22) 27-25-83; fax (22) 54-62-34; e-mail info@eximbank.com; internet www.eximbank.com; Chair. MARCEL CHIRCĂ.

Investprivatbank: 2001 Chișinău, str. Sciusev 34; tel. (22) 27-43-86; fax (22) 54-05-10; internet www.ipb.md; f. 1994; cap. 70m., dep. 92.8m., total assets 186.3m. (Jul. 2004); Chair. IVAN CHIRPALOV; 3 brs.

Mobiasbanca: 2012 Chișinău, bd Ștefan cel Mare și Sfânt 81A; tel. and fax (22) 54-19-74; e-mail office@mobiasbanca.md; internet www.mobiasbanca.md; f. 1990; acquired Bancoop in 2001; commercial bank; cap. 71.1m., res 10.7m., dep. 1,322.1m. (Dec. 2006); Chair. of Bd VICTOR POPUSOI; 11 brs.

Moldindconbank (Moldovan Bank for Industry and Construction): 2012 Chișinău, str. Armeneasca 38; tel. (22) 57-67-82; fax (22) 27-91-95; e-mail info@moldinconbank.com; internet www.moldindconbank.com; f. 1991; jt-stock commercial bank; cap. 29.4m., res 4.8m., dep. 1,863.1m. (Dec. 2006); Chair. of Bd VALERIAN MIRZAC; 21 brs.

Moldova Agroindbank: 2006 Chișinău, str. Cosmonauților 9; tel. (22) 21-28-28; fax (22) 22-80-58; e-mail aib@maib.md; internet www.maib.md; f. 1991; joint-stock commercial bank; cap. 207.5m., res 31.0m., dep. 3,028.7m. (Dec. 2005); Chair. of Bd VICTOR MICULEȚ; Chair. NATALIA VRABIE; 45 brs.

Unibank: 2012 Chișinău, str. Mitropolit G. Bănulescu-Bodoni 45; tel. (22) 22-55-86; fax (22) 22-05-30; e-mail welcome@unibank.md; internet www.unibank.md; f. 1993; jt-stock commercial bank; cap. 95.0m., res 8.5m., dep. 240.6m. (June 2005); Pres. CLAUDIA MELNIK; 5 brs.

Universalbank: 2004 Chișinău, bd Ștefan cel Mare 180; tel. (22) 29-59-00; fax (22) 29-59-06; e-mail ub@mail.universalbank.md; internet www.universalbank.md; f. 1994; cap. 86.8m., res 10.0m., dep. 143.4m. (Aug. 2007); Chair. of Bd DIANA MOTOLOGA; 7 brs.

Victoriabank: 2004 Chișinău, str. 31 August 141; tel. (22) 23-30-65; fax (22) 23-39-33; e-mail mail@victoriabank.md; internet www.victoriabank.md; f. 1989; cap. 32.0m., res 13.1m., dep. 2,055.8m. (Dec. 2006); Pres. VICTOR ȚURCANU; 12 brs.

STOCK EXCHANGE

Moldovan Stock Exchange (Bursa de Valori a Moldovei SA): 2001 Chișinău, bd Ștefan cel Mare 73; tel. (22) 27-75-94; fax (22) 27-73-56; e-mail dodu@moldse.md; internet www.moldse.md; f. 1994; Chair. Dr CORNELIU DODU.

INSURANCE

In April 2007 there were 32 insurance companies operating in Moldova.

State Inspectorate for the Supervision of Insurance and Non-state Pension Funds (Inspectoratul de Stat pentru Supravegherea Asigurarilor si Fondurilor Nestatale de Pensii—ISSA): 2001 Chișinău, bd Ștefan cel Mare si Sfânt 124; tel. (22) 27-86-53; e-mail issa@tmg.md; internet www.issa.md; f. 1996; Dir ALEXANDRU MUNTEANU.

Asito: 2005 Chișinău, str. Bănulescu-Bodoni 57/1; tel. (22) 22-62-12; fax (22) 22-11-79; e-mail asito@qbe-asito.com; internet www.qbe-asito.com; f. 1991; 48.3% owned by Moldova Investment Group (United Kingdom); fmrly QBE Asito; Gen. Man. EUGEN SHLOPAK.

Donaris Group: 2012 Chișinău, Str. Columna 72; tel. (22) 22-82-33; fax (22) 27-83-94; e-mail office@donaris.md; internet www.donaris.md; life and non-life, insurance and reinsurance.

Moldasig: 2009 Chișinău, str. Eminescu 2; tel. (22) 23-81-61; fax (22) 23-83-46; e-mail moldasig@dnt.md; internet www.moldasig.md; f. 2002; 51% owned by Banca de Economii SA, 25% owned by Calea Ferată din Moldova, 24% owned by Poșta Moldovei; 25% market share in Moldova in 2006; Gen. Dir VITALI I. BODYA.

Moldcargo: 2012 Chișinău, Str. V. Alecsandri 97; tel. (22) 24-55-67; fax (22) 23-36-70; e-mail office@moldcargo.md; internet www.moldcargo.md; f. 1999; life and non-life; Pres. VLADIMIR FLOREA.

Victoria Asigurari: tel. (22) 22-83-53; fax (22) 22-83-52; e-mail office@victoria-asiguari.md; Dir.-Gen. OCTAVIAN LUNGU.

Trade and Industry

GOVERNMENT AGENCIES

State Department for Privatization (Departamentul Privatizarii al Republicii Moldova): 2012 Chișinău, str. Pușkin 26; tel. (22) 23-43-50; fax (22) 23-43-36; e-mail dep.priv@moldtelecom.md; Dir.-Gen. ALEXANDR BANNICOV.

Moldovan Investment and Export Promotion Organization (MEPO) (Organizația de Atragere a Investițiilor și Promovare a Exportului din Moldova): 2009 Chișinău, str. Mateevici 65; tel. (22) 27-36-54; fax (22) 22-43-10; e-mail office@miepo.md; internet www.miepo.md; f. 1999; assists enterprises in increasing exports and improving business environment; Dir.-Gen. LILIA RUSSU.

CHAMBER OF COMMERCE

Chamber of Commerce and Industry of the Republic of Moldova (Camera de Comerț și Industrie a Republicii Moldova): 2012 Chișinău, str. M. Eminescu 28; tel. (22) 22-15-52; fax (22) 24-14-53; e-mail inform@chamber.md; internet www.chamber.md; f. 1969; Chair. GHEORGHE CUCU.

UTILITIES

Regulatory Authority

National Energy Regulatory Agency (ANRE): 2012 Chișinău, str. Columna 90; tel. (22) 54-13-84; fax (22) 22-46-98; e-mail anre@anre.md; internet www.anre.md; f. 1997; autonomous public institution; Dir ANATOL BURLACOB; Gen. Dir NICOLAE TRIBOI.

Electricity

The sector comprises one transmission company, five distribution companies and four power generation plants.

MoldElectrica IS: 2012 Chișinău, str. V. Alecsandri 78; tel. (22) 22-22-70; fax (22) 25-31-42; e-mail disp@moldelectrica.md; internet www.moldelectrica.md; f. 2000 to assume the transmission and distribution functions of Moldtranselectro; Dir MARC RÎMIȘ.

Rețelele Electrice (mun. Chișinău) SA: 2024 Chișinău, str. A. Doga 4; tel. (22) 42-16-55; privatized in 2000; wholly owned by Unión Eléctrica Fenosa (Spain); distribution co supplying electricity to Chișinău.

Gas

MoldovaGaz SA: 2005 Chișinău, str. Albișoara 38; tel. (22) 57-80-02; fax (22) 22-00-02; f. 1999; national gas pipeline and distribution networks; comprises 2 transmission companies and 18 distribution companies; 64% owned by Gazprom (Russia), 35% owned by Govt of Moldova; Gen. Dir GHENADIE ABAȘCHIN (acting).

TRADE UNIONS

Confederation of Trade Unions of the Republic of Moldova (Confederația Sindecatelor din Republica Moldova): 2012 Chișinău, str. 31 August 129; tel. (22) 23-76-74; fax (22) 23-76-98; e-mail cfsind@cni.md; f. 1990; Pres. PETRU CHIRIAC.

Transport

RAILWAYS

Plans for the reconstruction and upgrading to European gauge of the rail link connecting Chișinău with Iași, Romania, were announced in mid-2002 and resumed in 2005.

Calea Ferată din Moldova: 2012 Chișinău, str. Vlaicu Pîrcălab 48; tel. (22) 25-44-08; fax (22) 22-13-80; internet www.railway.md; f. 1992; total network 1,075 km; Dir.-Gen. MIRON GAGAUZ.

ROADS

In 2000 Moldova's network of roads totalled 12,691 km (86.1% of which was hard-surfaced), including 3,328 km of main roads.

INLAND WATERWAYS

In 1997 the total length of navigable waterways in Moldova was 424 km. The main river ports are located within the separatist territory of Transnistria, at Tighina (Bendery), Râbnița.

CIVIL AVIATION

The refurbishment of Chișinău International Airport was completed in 2000. Moldova has four civilian airports, in Chișinău, Tiraspol, Bălți and Mărculești.

Civil Aviation Administration (Administrația de stat a Aviației Civile): 2026 Chișinău, Aeroportul Chișinău; tel. (22) 52-40-64; fax (22) 52-91-18; e-mail info@caa.md; internet www.caa.md; f. 1993; Dir.-Gen. VALENTIN VIZANT.

Air Moldova (Compania Aeriana Moldova): 2026 Chișinău, bd Dacia 80/2, Aeroportul Chișinău; tel. (22) 52-55-02; fax (22) 52-60-09; e-mail info@airmoldova.md; internet www.airmoldova.md; f. 1993; wholly state-owned; scheduled and charter passenger and cargo flights to destinations in Europe and the CIS; Dir.-Gen. VASILE BOTNARI.

Moldavian Airlines: 2026 Chișinău, Aeroportul Chișinău; tel. (22) 52-93-56; fax (22) 52-50-64; e-mail sales@mdv.md; internet www.mdv.md; f. 1994; scheduled flights to Budapest (Hungary) and to Timisoara (Romania); also charter passenger and cargo flights; Pres. and Chief Exec. NICOLAE PETROV.

Tourism

There were 25,073 tourist arrivals in 2005, in which year tourist receipts (including passenger transport) totalled US $163m. in 2005.

Department of Tourism Development: 2004 Chișinău, bd Ștefan cel Mare și Sfânt 180, bir. 901; tel. (22) 21-07-74; fax (22) 23-26-26; e-mail dept@turism.md; internet www.turism.md.

MONACO

Introductory Survey

Location, Climate, Language, Religion, Flag

The Principality of Monaco lies in western Europe. The country is a small enclave in south-eastern France, about 15 km east of Nice. It has a coastline on the Mediterranean Sea but is otherwise surrounded by French territory. The climate is Mediterranean, with warm summers and very mild winters. The official language is French, but Monégasque (a mixture of the French Provençal and Italian Ligurian dialects), Italian and English are also spoken. Most of the population profess Christianity, with about 91% belonging to the Roman Catholic Church. The national flag (proportions 4 by 5) has two equal horizontal stripes, of red and white. The state flag (proportions 4 by 5) displays the princely arms of Monaco (a white shield, held by two monks and superimposed on a pavilion of ermine) on a white background.

History

The Principality of Monaco is an hereditary monarchy, which has been ruled by the Grimaldi dynasty since 1297. It was abolished during the French Revolution but re-established in 1814. In 1861 Monaco became an independent state under the protection of France. The Constitution, promulgated in January 1911, vested legislative power jointly in the Prince and an 18-member Conseil national (National Council), selected for a term of five years by a panel comprising nine delegates of the municipality and 21 members elected by universal suffrage. Agreements in 1918 and 1919 between France and Monaco provided for Monaco's incorporation into France should the reigning prince die without leaving a male heir. Prince Louis II, the ruler of Monaco since 1922, died in May 1949, and was succeeded by his grandson, Prince Rainier III. A new Constitution, introduced in December 1962, abolished the principle of the divine right of the ruler, and stipulated that the Conseil national be elected by universal adult suffrage.

Supporters of Prince Rainier, grouped in the Union nationale et démocratique (UND), dominated at five-yearly elections in 1963–88, on all but two occasions taking all 18 seats on the Conseil national. In January 1993, however, two lists of candidates, the Liste Campora (led by Jean-Louis Campora, the President of the football team, AS Monaco) and the Liste Médecin, secured 15 and two seats, respectively, while an independent candidate won the remaining seat. At legislative elections in February 1998 UND candidates secured all 18 seats.

Controversy surrounding the use of Monaco's financial sector for the transfer of funds derived from criminal activities intensified in 1998 with the culmination of an investigation into the deposit of US $5.5m. in cash, suspected of originating from the illegal drugs trade, at a bank in Monaco in 1995. The affair led to a crisis in relations between France and the Principality, with the French Government overruling Prince Rainier by refusing to extend the mandate of Monaco's Chief Prosecutor, whom it suspected of not conducting a sufficiently thorough investigation of the scandal. Following further criticisms of Monégasque banking practice in a report by the Organisation for Economic Co-operation and Development (OECD, see p. 347) in 2000, the French Government recommended a rapid revision of the bilateral treaties between Monaco and France, proposing that Monégasque institutions be brought into greater conformity with French excise, fiscal and banking regulations. In a list published in April 2002, OECD defined Monaco as an 'unco-operative tax haven'; in early 2008 Monaco was one of three jurisdictions that remained on the list. In December 2004 the EU signed an agreement with Monaco on the taxation of savings income. Under the agreement, savings income, in the form of interest payments made in Monaco to residents of the EU, was to be subject to a withholding tax from 1 July 2005. Monaco also agreed to exchange information on request with EU member states in criminal or civil cases of tax fraud or comparable offences.

In March 2002 the electoral law was amended, and in April the Conseil national approved a number of significant constitutional amendments. Both measures were in part intended to expedite Monaco's application for full membership of the Council of Europe (see p. 225), which had been submitted in October 1998. The age of majority was lowered from 21 years to 18 years, and several executive powers of the Prince were transferred to the Conseil national, the size of which was to be increased to 24 members following the elections in 2003. Additionally, the law of succession was modified, to permit succession through the female line.

In late 2002 discontent was reported at a proposal, supported by Campora, to sell AS Monaco to a Russian investment company based in the Principality, Fedcominvest, which was also the football club's principal sponsor. Following a report in *Le Monde*, in December 2002, which alleged that Fedcominvest was involved in money-laundering, Prince Rainier, who, on behalf of the Principality, retained ultimate control over the club, prohibited the proposed sale. The ensuing scandal appeared to be a significant factor in appreciably reducing support for Campora's UND at the legislative elections, held on 9 February 2003, when the UND secured only three seats on the enlarged Conseil national; the remaining 21 seats were awarded to the Union pour Monaco list, led by a former member of the UND, Stéphane Valéri.

In April 2004 the Parliamentary Assembly of the Council of Europe (PACE) ruled that Monaco was entitled to receive special 'guest status' at PACE but that further reforms were required before the Principality could be considered for full membership; among the principal requirements were the extension of eligibility for several senior government positions, including the Minister of State (who, under the terms of a 1930 treaty, was required to be a French civil servant), to Monégasque citizens, and an enhancement of fiscal regulation. Following the decision of the Joint Committee of the Council of Europe (comprising representatives of the Parliamentary Assembly and the Committee of Ministers) that talks between France and Monaco had demonstrated significant progress towards the eventual reform of the 1930 convention, Monaco was admitted as the 46th member of the Council of Europe on 5 October.

In early 2005 a reorganization of the Council of Government took place. The number of Government Councillors was increased from three to five, with the creation of Government Councillors for Social Affairs and Health and for External Relations, and it was announced that Jean-Paul Proust was to replace Patrick Leclercq as Minister of State from the beginning of May.

On 6 April 2005, following a protracted period of ill health, Prince Rainier died at the age of 81. He was succeeded by his son, Prince Albert II, who had acted as Regent of the Principality since 31 March. In early July, several days before his formal inauguration as Head of State, it was confirmed that Prince Albert, who was unmarried and had no legal heir, had fathered an illegitimate child in 2003. It was announced, however, that the Prince's son would neither bear the name Grimaldi nor be eligible to inherit the throne. (In June 2006 Prince Albert formally acknowledged paternity of a second illegitimate child, a 14-year-old girl, who also would not take the family name or be eligible to inherit the throne.) Albert II was formally enthroned in mid-November 2005, marking the conclusion of the formal transfer of power.

A number of changes to the Council of Government were effected in mid-2006. In April Paul Masseron was appointed as Government Councillor for the Interior. In July the Government Councillor for Finance and the Economy, Franck Biancheri, assumed the newly created role of Head of Mission at the Ministry of State, responsible for International Financial Dossiers, and was replaced in his former post by Gilles Tonelli, hitherto Government Councillor for Capital Works, the Environment and Town Planning. Tonelli was, in turn, replaced by Robert Cavagno. In August Henri Fissore, hitherto ambassador to Italy, replaced Rainer Imperti as Government Councillor for External Relations. In early April 2007 the death was announced of the Government Councillor for Social Affairs and Health, Denis Ravera. He was replaced on 1 May by Jean-Jacques Campana.

At legislative elections held on 3 February 2008, the UND retained its 21 seats in the Conseil national. The remaining three seats were won by the Rassemblement et Enjeux pour Monaco list.

Monaco participates in the work of a number of international organizations, and in 1993 became a member of the UN. In February 2006 France upgraded the status of its diplomatic representation in Monaco from consular to ambassadorial level, becoming the first country to operate an embassy in the Principality. Italy also opened an embassy in Monaco later in the year.

Government

Legislative power is vested jointly in the Prince, an hereditary ruler, and the 24-member Conseil national (National Council), which is elected by universal adult suffrage, partly under a system of proportional representation, for a term of five years. The electorate comprises only Monégasque citizens aged 18 years or over. Executive power is exercised, under the authority of the Prince, by the five-member Council of Government, headed by the Minister of State (a French civil servant selected by the Prince from a list of three candidates presented by the French Government). The Prince represents the Principality in its relations with foreign powers, and signs and ratifies treaties. There is, additionally, a consultative Conseil communal (Communal Council), comprising 15 members elected for a term of four years, headed by a mayor.

Economic Affairs

In 2001, according to World Bank estimates, Monaco's gross national income (GNI), measured at average 1999–2001 prices, was equivalent to approximately US $24,700 per head. In 2000, according to World Bank estimates, GNI, measured at average 1998–2000 prices, was equivalent to approximately $25,200 per head, or approximately $25,700 on an international purchasing-power parity basis. According to UN estimates, Monaco's gross domestic product (GDP) was $847m. in 1995 (equivalent to $26,470 per head). During 1990–95 GDP increased, in real terms, at an average annual rate of 1.1%. GDP grew by 2.2% in 1995. The annual rate of population increase averaged 0.6% in 1990–2000. Monaco has the highest population density of all the independent states in the world.

There is no agricultural land in Monaco. In 1990 a Belgian enterprise established an offshore fish farm for sea bass and sea bream. In 2005 there were just 28 private sector employees working in the primary sector.

Industry (including construction and public works) contributed 13.9% of the Principality's turnover in 2006. The sector engaged 16.0% of those employed in the private sector in 2006. Industry is mainly light in Monaco. The principal sectors, measured by gross value of output, are chemicals, pharmaceuticals and cosmetics (which together accounted for 43.4% of all industrial revenue in 2004), plastics (29.1%), electrical and electronic goods, paper and textile production.

Service industries represent the most significant sector of the economy in Monaco, contributing 86.1% of total turnover in 2006, and providing employment to 83.9% of those working in the private sector in the same year. Banking and finance accounted for more than 38% of the services sector and employed some 1,400 people in the late 1990s. At the end of 2006 the total value of deposits in Monaco's private banking sector was estimated at €23,450m. Trade accounted for 44.7% of national turnover in 2006, while banking and financial activities accounted for 16.0%.

Tourism is also an important source of income, providing an estimated 25% of total government revenue in 1991 and engaging some 20% of the employed labour force in the late 1990s, while the hotel business alone contributed 3.3% of the Principality's total turnover in 2006, and (together with restaurants and associated activities) engaged 16.2% of those employed in the private sector in the same year. In 2006 some 313,070 tourists (excluding excursionists) visited Monaco. The greatest number of visitors (excluding excursionists) in 2005 were from Italy (20.5%), France (18.4%), the United Kingdom (14.4%) and the USA (8.6%).

Monaco's external trade is included in the figures for France. Excluding trade within the association with France, in 2006 Monaco's principal merchandise imports were professional and business apparatus and road vehicles and machinery. The most significant exports were semi-finished non-metallic goods, consumer goods and processed agricultural manufactures. Excluding France, the most important source of imports in 2006 was the People's Republic of China (27.3% of the total value), followed by Italy and Germany. Germany was the most important market for exports (excluding France), contributing 17.2% of total export earnings. Italy, Spain and the United Kingdom were also important markets for exports.

In 2006 there was a budgetary deficit of €61.2m.; expenditure amounted to €789.1m. In 2000 value-added tax (VAT) contributed 52.8% of total government revenue. In the early 2000s it was estimated that less than 3% of the population were unemployed in the Principality.

Monaco is largely dependent on imports from France, owing to its lack of natural resources. There is a severe labour shortage in the Principality, and the economy is reliant on migrant workers (many of whom remain resident in France and Italy). Following the establishment of a casino in the 1860s, tourism became the dominant sector in the economy. In particular, the Principality has sought to establish itself as a major centre of the conference industry: about one-quarter of the nights spent at Monaco's hotels in 2004 were connected with this sector, compared with one-10th in the early 1970s. From the 1980s, however, the industry and real estate sectors expanded, as a series of land reclamation projects increased Monaco's area by 20%. A number of foreign companies and banks are registered in Monaco in order to take advantage of the low rates of taxation on company profits. Since the removal of French restrictions on foreign exchange in 1987, Monaco's banking industry (which includes an 'offshore' sector) has expanded. In February 2008 Monaco came under scrutiny when the German Federal Chancellor, Angela Merkel, called for more transparency in the Principality's banking sector. She criticized foreign nationals who avoid paying taxes in their own country by holding secret bank accounts in the Principality. A new state-owned company, the Société d'Exploitation des Ports de Monaco, was formed in 2003 to oversee the operations and future development of Monaco's two principal ports, at La Condamine (Port Hercule) and Fontvieille. The shipping sector is also significant, contributing some 4% of business revenue and providing employment for around 1,300 people. The telecommunications sector was also a focus of expansion in the Principality in the early 2000s.

Education

Education follows the French system, and is compulsory for 10 years for children aged six to 16 years. Primary education begins at six years of age and lasts for five years. Secondary education begins at 11 years of age and lasts for seven years. In 2004 expenditure on education was equivalent to 4.4% of GDP.

Public Holidays

2008: 1 January (New Year's Day), 27 January (Feast of St Dévote, Patron Saint of the Principality), 24 March (Easter Monday), 1 May (Labour Day and Ascension Day), 12 June (Whit Monday), 15 August (Assumption), 1 November (All Saints' Day), 19 November (National Day/Fête du Prince), 8 December (Immaculate Conception), 25–26 December (Christmas).

2009: 1 January (New Year's Day), 27 January (Feast of St Dévote, Patron Saint of the Principality), 13 April (Easter Monday), 1 May (Labour Day), 21 May (Ascension Day), 1 June (Whit Monday), 15 August (Assumption), 1 November (All Saints' Day), 19 November (National Day/Fête du Prince), 8 December (Immaculate Conception), 25–26 December (Christmas).

Weights and Measures

The metric system is in force.

Statistical Survey

Source: (unless otherwise stated): Direction de l'expansion économique, division des statistiques et des études économiques, 9 rue du Gabian, MC 98000; tel. 93-15-41-59; fax 93-15-87-59.

AREA AND POPULATION

Area: 1.95 sq km.

Population: 29,972 at census of 23 July 1990; 32,020 (males 15,544, females 16,476) at census of July 2000.

Density (July 2000): 16,435 per sq km.

Population by Nationality (2000): French 10,229; Italian 6,410; Monégasque 6,089; Other 9,292. *2004* (official estimate at 31 December): Monégasque 7,716 (males 3,318, females 4,398).

Districts (population at 2000 census): Monte-Carlo 15,507; Condamine 12,187; Fontvieille 3,292; Monaco-Ville (capital) 1,034.

Births, Marriages and Deaths (2006 unless otherwise indicated): Live births 880; Marriages 171 (2004); Deaths 535.

Expectation of Life (years at birth, WHO estimates): 81.8 (males 78.4; females 85.1) in 2005. Source: WHO, *World Health Statistics*.

Employment (private sector only, December 2006): Agriculture, hunting, forestry and fishing 27; Mining and quarrying 4; Manufacturing 3,503; Construction 3,479; Electricity and gas 140; Services 37,273 (Hotels, restaurants and associated activities 7,213; Real estate, renting and business services 10,968); *Total* 44,426 (males 25,224, females 19,202).

HEALTH AND WELFARE

Key Indicators

Total Fertility Rate (children per woman, 2005): 1.8.

Under-5 Mortality Rate (per 1,000 live births, 2005): 4.

Physicians (per 1,000 head, 1995): 5.81.

Hospital Beds (per 1,000 head, 1995): 19.6.

Health Expenditure (2004): US $ per head (PPP): 4,743.9.

Health Expenditure (2004): % of GDP: 9.9.

Health Expenditure (2004): public (% of total): 75.7.

For sources and definitions, see explanatory note on p. vi.

FINANCE

Currency and Exchange Rates: French currency: 100 cent = 1 euro (€). *Sterling and Dollar Equivalents* (31 December 2007): £1 sterling = 1.3609 euros; US $1 = 0.6793 euros; €10 = £7.35 = $14.72. *Average Exchange Rate* (euros per US dollar): 0.8041 in 2005; 0.7971 in 2006; 0.7306 in 2007. *Note:* The local currency was formerly the French franc, although some Monégasque currency, at par with the French franc, also circulated. From the introduction of the euro, with French participation, on 1 January 1999, a fixed exchange rate of €1 = 6.55957 French francs was in operation. Euro notes and coins were introduced on 1 January 2002. The euro and local currency circulated alongside each other until 17 February, after which the euro became the sole legal tender.

Budget (€ million, 2006): Revenue 727.9; Expenditure 789.1 (Current expenditure 519.3, Capital expenditure 269.9).

Turnover of the Principality (official figures, private sector only, € million, 2006): Industry 861.7; Public works and real estate 965.6; Hotel business 428.3; Banking and finance 2,102.5; Wholesale and retail trade 5,876.5; Transport 298.4; Other activities 2,615.4; Total 13,148.5.

EXTERNAL TRADE

Note: Monaco's imports and exports are included in the figures for France, and separate figures for Monaco's trade with France are not included here.

Principal Commodities (€ million, 2006): *Imports:* 751.7 (Professional and business apparatus 270.4; Road vehicles and machinery 38.3; Consumer goods 119.5; Semi-finished non-metallic goods 116.3). *Exports:* 678.6 (Semi-finished non-metallic goods 243.8; Consumer goods 82.6; Processed agricultural products 80.6).

Principal Trading Partners (€ million, 2006): *Imports:* Belgium 50.2; China, People's Republic 205.4; Germany 40.3; Italy 143.8; Japan 76.9; Madagascar 31.1; Spain 16.6; Switzerland 13.0; United Kingdom 37.7; USA 29.6; Total (incl. others) 751.7. *Exports:* Australia 11.3; Belgium 11.4; Germany 116.5; Italy 69.8; Japan 28.7; Mauritania 11.1; Portugal 11.1; Spain 68.3; Switzerland 15.2; United Kingdom 61.5; USA 23.0; Total (incl. others) 678.6.

TRANSPORT

Road Traffic (vehicles in use at 31 December 1996, estimates): Passenger cars 21,120; Buses and coaches 70; Lorries and vans 2,700; Road tractors 80; Motorcycles and mopeds 5,400. Source: IRF, *World Road Statistics*.

TOURISM

Tourist Arrivals (excluding excursionists): 250,159 in 2004; 285,675 in 2005; 313,070 in 2006. Figures refer to arrivals of foreign visitors at hotels and similar establishments.

Tourist Arrivals by Country (2006): France 57,660; Germany 12,593; Italy 64,287; Japan 6,370; Russia 7,234; Spain 7,620; Switzerland 8,661; United Kingdom 44,994; USA 26,772; Total (incl. others) 313,070.

COMMUNICATIONS MEDIA

Radio Receivers (1997): 34,000 in use.

Television Receivers (1997): 25,000 in use.

Daily Newspapers (1996): 1 title (estimated circulation 8,000 copies—1995). *2004:* 1 title.

Non-daily Newspapers (1996): 5 titles (estimated circulation 50,000 copies).

Telephones (2005): 34,000 main lines in use.

Facsimile Machines (1992): 1,880 in use.

Book production (1999): 72 titles.

Mobile Cellular Telephones (2005): 17,200 subscribers.

Internet Users (2006): 20,000.

Broadband Subscribers (2005): 9,400 (Sources: mostly International Telecommunication Union; UN, *Statistical Yearbook*; UNESCO Institute for Statistics).

EDUCATION

(2004/05)

Pre-primary: 40 teachers (33 public, 7 private); 903 pupils (736 public, 167 private).

Elementary: 133 teachers (108 public, 25 private); 1,827 pupils (1,365 public, 462 private).

Secondary: 330 teachers (277 public, 53 private); 3,095 pupils (2,399 public, 696 private).

Note: Educational establishments in Monaco in 2004/05 comprised the following: three public pre-primary schools; four primary schools (three public, one private), which integrate pre-primary and elementary age groups; one public elementary school; three public secondary schools, comprising one lower secondary school, one general upper secondary school, and one vocational secondary school; and one private school integrating primary and secondary age groups. There was also one private higher educational establishment, the International University of Monaco, a business school where instruction is conducted in English.

Source: Direction de l'éducation nationale, de la jeunesse et des sports.

Directory

The Constitution

The Constitution of 17 December 1962, as amended on 2 April 2002, vests legislative power jointly in the Ruling Prince and the 24-member Conseil national (National Council), which is elected by universal adult suffrage, partly under a system of proportional representation, for a term of five years. Executive power is exercised, under the authority of the Ruling Prince, by the Council of Government, headed by the Minister of State, who is appointed by the Ruling Prince and is assisted by five Government Councillors. The Constitution maintains the traditional hereditary monarchy, although the principle of the divine right of the ruler is renounced. The law of succession was modified to permit succession through the female line in April 2002. The right of association, trade union freedom and the right to strike are guaranteed. The Supreme Tribunal safeguards fundamental liberties. Constitutional amendments have to be submitted for approval by the Conseil national.

The Government

HEAD OF STATE

Ruling Prince: HSH Prince ALBERT II (succeeded 6 April 2005).

COUNCIL OF GOVERNMENT
(April 2008)

Minister of State: JEAN-PAUL PROUST.
Government Councillor for Finance and the Economy: GILLES TONELLI.
Government Councillor for the Interior: PAUL MASSERON.
Government Councillor for External Relations: JEAN PASTORELLI.
Government Councillor for Capital Works, the Environment and Town Planning: ROBERT CALCAGNO.
Government Councillor for Social Affairs and Health: JEAN-JACQUES CAMPANA.

MINISTRY OF STATE AND DEPARTMENTS

Ministry of State: place de la Visitation, MC 98000; tel. 98-98-80-00; fax 98-98-82-17; e-mail sgme@gouv.mc; internet www.gouv.mc.
Department of Capital Works, the Environment and Town Planning: Ministère d'Etat, place de la Visitation, MC 98000; tel. 98-98-85-67.
Department of External Relations: Ministère d'Etat, place de la Visitation, BP 522, MC 98015 Cedex; tel. 98-98-89-04; fax 98-98-85-54; e-mail relext@gouv.mc; internet www.diplomatie.gouv.mc.
Department of Finance and the Economy: Ministère d'Etat, place de la Visitation, MC 98000; tel. 98-98-82-56; e-mail dfin@troisseptsept.mc.
Department of the Interior: Ministère d'Etat, place de la Visitation, MC 98000; tel. 98-98-84-56; fax 93-50-82-45.
Department of Social Affairs and Health: Ministère d'Etat, place de la Visitation, MC 98000; tel. 98-98-19-19; fax 98-98-19-99; e-mail afss@gouv.mc.

Legislature

Conseil national

12 rue Col Bellando de Castro, MC 98000; tel. 93-30-41-15; fax 93-25-31-90; e-mail vviora@conseil-national.mc; internet www.conseilnational.mc.

The Conseil national (National Council) has 24 members. At the most recent elections, which took place on 3 February 2008, the Union pour Monaco (UpM) list secured 21 seats, with the Rassemblement et Enjeux pour Monaco controlling the remaining three.

President: STÉPHANE VALÉRI.
Vice-President: BERNARD MARQUET.

Advisory Councils

Conseil d'état: Palais de Justice, Monte-Carlo; advises on proposed laws or ordinances submitted for its approval by the Ruling Prince or by the Government, or on any other matter; 12 mems, appointed by the Ruling Prince, following the advice of the Minister of State and the Director of Judicial Services; Pres. PHILIPPE NARMINO; Sec. BRIGITTE GRINDA-GAMBARINI.
Conseil de la Couronne: Monte-Carlo; f. 1942; advises the Ruling Prince on matters of state, and must be consulted by the Ruling Prince prior to the implementation of certain constitutional matters, including the signature or ratification of treaties, the dissolution of the Conseil national, questions of naturalization or reintegration, the issuing of pardons or amnesties; seven mems, appointed for renewable terms of three years; Pres. and three mems are appointed by free choice of the Ruling Prince, the remaining three mems are nominated by the Ruling Prince on the recommendation of the Conseil national; all mems must hold Monégasque nationality; Pres. CHARLES BALLERIO; Sec. PATRICK SOMMER.
Conseil économique et social: Centre Administratif, 8 rue Louis-Notari, MC 98000; tel. 97-97-77-91; fax 93-50-05-96; f. 1945; advises on economic matters; 36 mems, appointed for a term of three years; 12 mems directly appointed by Govt, 12 appointed by Govt from list prepared by Union des Syndicats de Monaco, 12 appointed by Govt from list prepared by the Fédération Patronale Monégasque; the Ruling Prince appoints Pres. and two Vice-Pres from among the mems; Pres. ANDRÉ GARINO; Vice-Pres ANDRÉ THIBAULT, JACQUES WOLZOK.

Political Organizations

There are no political parties as such in Monaco; however, candidates are generally grouped into lists to contest elections to the Conseil national. Between 1963 and 1992, and 1998 and 2003 the Conseil national was dominated by representatives of the Union Nationale et Démocratique (UND). At the 1993 elections, however, the two main groupings were the Liste Campora, led by Jean-Louis Campora, and the Liste Médecin, led by Jean-Louis Médecin. The majority of seats at the 2003 elections were secured by the Union pour Monaco list, which comprised members of the Union pour la Principauté and of the Union Nationale pour l'Avenir de Monaco. At the 2008 elections the Union pour Monaco list again secured the majority of seats, with the Rassemblement et Enjeux pour Monaco winning the remainder. Monaco Ensemble failed to win representation.

Diplomatic Representation

In February 2006 France opened an embassy in Monaco, becoming the first country to institute ambassadorial-level diplomatic relations with the Principality. Italy opened an embassy in Monaco later in the year. By May 2007 ambassadors from 18 countries were accredited to Monaco.

France: Le Roc fleuri, 1 rue du Tenao, BP 345, MC 98006 Cedex; tel. 92-16-54-60; fax 92-16-54-64; e-mail courrier@ambafrance.mc; internet www.ambafrance.mc; Ambassador ODILE REMIK-ADIM.
Italy: L'Annonciade, 17 ave de l'Annonciade, MC 98000; tel. 93-50-22-71; fax 93-50-06-89; e-mail ambasciata.montecarlo@esteri.it; internet www.ambprincipatomonaco.esteri.it; Ambassador MARIO POLVERINI.

Judicial System

The organization of the legal system is similar to that of France. There is one Justice of the Peace, a Tribunal de Première Instance (Tribunal of First Instance), a Cour d'Appel (Court of Appeal), a Cour de Révision (High Court of Appeal), a Tribunal Criminel (Criminal Tribunal) and finally the Tribunal Suprême (Supreme Tribunal), which deals with infringements of the rights and liberties provided by the Constitution, and also with legal actions aiming at the annulment of administrative decisions for abusive exercise of power.

Palais de Justice

5 rue Col Bellando de Castro, MC 98000; tel. 98-98-88-11; fax 98-98-85-89.

Director of Judicial Services: PHILIPPE NARMINO.
President of the Supreme Tribunal: HUBERT CHARLES.
President of the Court of Revision: JEAN APOLLIS.
First President of the Court of Appeal: MONIQUE FRANÇOIS.
President of the Tribunal of First Instance: BRIGITTE GRINDA-GAMBARINI.
Attorney-General: ANNIE BRUNET FUSTER.

Religion

CHRISTIANITY

The Roman Catholic Church

Monaco comprises a single archdiocese, directly responsible to the Holy See. At 31 December 2005 there were an estimated 29,000 adherents in the Principality, representing about 90.6% of the total population.

Archbishop of Monaco: Most Rev. BERNARD BARSI, Archevêché, 1 rue de l'Abbaye, BP 517, MC 98015 Cedex; tel. 93-30-88-10; fax 92-16-73-88; e-mail archeveche-mc@libello.com; internet www.eglise-catholique.mc.

The Anglican Communion

Within the Church of England, Monaco forms part of the diocese of Gibraltar in Europe.

Chaplain: Fr WALTER RAYMOND, St Paul's Church House, 22 ave de Grande Bretagne, Monte-Carlo, MC 98000; tel. 93-30-71-06; fax 93-30-50-39; e-mail stpauls@monaco.mc; internet www.stpauls.monaco.mc.

The Principality also has two Protestant churches and a synagogue.

The Press

Gazette Monaco-Côte d'Azur: 1 ave Princesse Alice, MC 98000; tel. 97-97-61-20; fax 93-50-68-27; e-mail lagazette@aip.mc; f. 1976; monthly; regional information; Dir-Gen. MAX POGGI; Editor-in-Chief NOËLLE BINE-MULLER; circ. 10,000.

Journal de Monaco: Ministère d'Etat, place de la Visitation, BP 522, MC 98015; tel. 93-15-83-15; fax 93-15-82-17; e-mail journaldemonaco@gouv.mc; internet www.gouv.mc/DataWeb/jourmon.nsf; f. 1858; edited at the Ministry of State; official weekly; contains texts of laws and decrees; Editor ROBERT COLLE.

Monaco Actualité: 2 rue du Gabian, MC 98000; tel. 92-05-75-36; fax 92-05-75-34; e-mail actualite@monaco.mc; internet www3.monaco.mc/actualite; Dir-Gen. MAURICE RICCOBONO; circ. 15,000.

Monaco Hebdo: 27 blvd d'Italie, MC 98000; tel. 93-50-56-52; fax 93-50-19-22; internet monacohebdo.free.fr; Man. Editor ROBERTO TESTA.

Monte-Carlo Méditerranée: tel. 92-05-67-67; fax 92-05-37-01; Dir-Gen. GÉRARD COMMAN; Editor-in-Chief CAROLE CHABRIER.

French newspapers are widely read, and a special Monaco edition of the daily *Nice-Matin* is published in Nice, France.

NEWS AGENCY

Monte-Carlo Press: Le Beverly Palace, 13 blvd de Belgique, MC 98000; tel. 97-70-74-24; e-mail mcpress@monaco.net; internet www.mcpress.mc; f. 1987.

Publishers

EDIPROM: Monte-Carlo; tel. 92-05-67-67; fax 92-05-37-01; advertising material, official publications; Pres. GÉRARD COMMAN.

Editions Alphée: 28 rue Comte Félix Gastaldi, BP 524, MC 98015; tel. 93-30-40-06; fax 97-70-37-00; e-mail editions_alphee@libello.com; internet www.editions-alphee.com; f. 1963; spirituality, personal devt; Dir JEAN-PAUL BERTRAND.

Editions EGC: 9 ave Albert II, BP 438, MC 98011 Cedex; e-mail multiprint@multiprintmc.com; economics, history, literature; Gen. Man. GÉRARD COMMAN.

Editions Victor Gadoury: 57 rue Grimaldi, MC 98000; tel. 93-25-12-96; fax 93-50-13-39; e-mail contact@gadoury.com; internet www.gadoury.com; f. 1967; numismatics.

Marsu Productions: 9 ave des Castelans, MC 98000; tel. 92-05-61-11; fax 92-05-76-60; e-mail marsuproductions@libello.com; internet www.marsupilami.com; comic strips, children's entertainment.

Editions de l'Oiseau-Lyre SAM: Les Remparts, BP 515, MC 98015 Cedex; tel. 93-30-09-44; fax 93-30-19-15; e-mail oiseaulyre@monaco.mc; internet www.oiseaulyre.com; f. 1932; owned by The Lyrebird Trust; classical music publishers; Pres. and Man. Dir KENNETH GILBERT.

Editions de Radio Monte Carlo SAM: Monte-Carlo; tel. 93-15-17-57; general; Pres. JEAN PASTORELLI.

Editions Regain S.N.C. Boy et Cie: Monte-Carlo; tel. 93-50-62-04; f. 1946; fiction, essays, autobiography, travel, religion, philosophy, poetry; Dir-Gen. MICHÈLE G. BOY.

Editions du Rocher: 28 rue Comte Félix Gastaldi, BP 521, MC 98015; tel. 99-99-67-17; fax 99-99-67-18; internet www.editionsdurocher.fr; f. 1943; fiction, history, sciences; Pres. and Dir-Gen. BÉATRICE GARETTE.

Editions André Sauret SAM: Monte-Carlo; tel. 93-50-67-94; fax 93-30-71-04; art, fiction; Dir RAYMOND LEVY.

Broadcasting and Communications

TELECOMMUNICATIONS

Direction du Controle des Concessions et des Télécommunications: 23 ave Albert II, MC 98000; tel. 98-98-88-00; fax 97-98-56-57; e-mail rviora@gouv.mc; Dir RAOUL VIORA.

Monaco Telecom: 25 blvd de Suisse, MC 98000 Cedex; tel. 99-66-63-00; fax 99-66-63-01; e-mail communication@monaco-telecom.mc; internet www.monaco-telecom.mc; f. 1997; 49% owned by Cable & Wireless (United Kingdom), 45% by the Société Nationale de Financement (wholly owned by Govt of Monaco), 6% by the Compagnie Monégasque de Banque; incorporates the wholly owned subsidiaries Monaco Telecom International, Société Monégasque de Services de Telecoms (SMST), Société Monégasque de Télédistribution (SMT) and Divona; Pres. ETIENNE FRANZI; Dir-Gen. DENIS MARTIN.

BROADCASTING

Radio

Monte-Carlo Doualiya: 1 ave Henri Dunant, MC 98000; internet www.mc-doualiya.com; fmr subsidiary of RMC, transferred to Radio-France Internationale in 1996; in French and Arabic; Pres. ANTOINE SCHWARZ; Dir-Gen. PHILIPPE BEAUVILLARD.

Riviera Radio: 10 quai Antoine 1er, MC 98000; tel. 97-97-94-94; fax 97-97-94-95; e-mail info@rivieraradio.mc; internet www.rivieraradio.mc; owned by Morris Communications Co (USA); broadcasts in English; Man. Dir PAUL KAVANAGH.

Trans World Radio SC: BP 349, MC 98007; tel. 92-16-56-00; fax 92-16-56-01; internet www.twr.org; f. 1955; evangelical Christian broadcaster; Pres. THOMAS J. LOWELL (acting).

Television

TVI Monte-Carlo: 8 quai Antoine 1er, MC 98000; tel. 92-16-88-20; fax 93-25-46-39; e-mail tvimc@frateschi.mc; programmes in Italian; CEO LUIGI FRATESCHI.

Société Spéciale d'Entreprises Télé Monte-Carlo: 16 blvd Princesse Charlotte, BP 279, MC 98090; tel. 93-50-59-40; fax 93-25-01-09; f. 1954; Pres. JEAN-LOUIS MÉDECIN.

Finance

(cap. = capital, res = reserves, dep. = deposits, m. = million, br(s) = branch(es), amounts in euros)

BANKING

In 2008 a total of 41 banks, including major British, French, Italian and US banks, were represented in the Principality.

Banque de Gestion Edmond de Rothschild: BP 317, Les Terrasses, 2 ave de Monte-Carlo, MC 98000; tel. 93-10-47-47; fax 93-25-75-57; e-mail bger@lcf-rothschild.mc; internet www.lcf-rothschild.com; f. 1986; present name adopted 1993; cap. 12.0m., res 14.9m., dep. 696.4m. (Dec. 2006); Chair. LEONARDO P. A. POGGI; Gen. Man. GIAMPAOLO BERNINI.

Banque J. Safra (Monaco): La Belle Epoque, 15–17 bis ave d'Ostende, MC 98000; tel. 93-10-66-55; fax 93-50-60-71; internet www.safra.com; f. 1994 as Banque du Gothard (Monaco); present name adopted 2006; 100% owned by Banque Jacob Safra (Switzerland); cap. 40.0m., res 21.3m., dep. 849.9m. (Dec. 2004); Pres. JOSEPH SAFRA; Gen. Man. YVES BRACCALENTI.

BNP Paribas Private Bank Monaco: 15–17 ave d'Ostende, MC 98000; tel. 93-15-68-00; fax 93-15-68-01; e-mail privatebank.monaco@bnpparibas.com; internet www.privatebank.bnpparibas.mc; f. 2003 by merger of United European Bank—Monaco and BNP Paribas Private Bank Monaco; acquired Société Monégasque de Banque Privée and Bank Von Ernst (Monaco) 2005; private banking; cap. 13.0m. (April 2007); Dir-Gen. ERIC GEORGES.

Compagnie Monégasque de Banque: 23 ave de la Costa, BP 149, MC 98007; tel. 93-15-77-77; fax 93-25-08-69; e-mail cmb@cmb.mc; internet www.cmb.mc; f. 1976; 100% owned by Mediobanca—Banca di Credito Finanziario SpA (Italy); cap. 111.1m., res 142.2m., dep. 1,750.1m. (Dec. 2006); Chair. ETIENNE FRANZI; Deputy Chair. and Man. Dir EDOARDO LOEWENTHAL; 2 brs.

Crédit Foncier de Monaco (CFM Monaco): 11 blvd Albert 1er, BP 499, MC 98012 Cedex; tel. 93-10-20-00; fax 93-10-23-50; internet

MONACO

www.cfm.mc; f. 1922; 77.1% owned by Calyon (France); cap. 35.0m., res 113.5m., dep. 2,595.1m. (Dec. 2006); Chair. YVES BARSALOU; Gen. Man. HERVÉ CATALA.

Crédit Suisse (Monaco): 27 ave de la Costa, BP 155, MC 98003; tel. 93-15-27-27; fax 93-25-27-99; e-mail alain.ucari@credit-suisse.com; f. 1987; cap. 12.0m., res 9.7m., dep. 1,042.8m. (Dec. 2006); Chair. FRANCO MULLER; Man ALAIN UCARI.

EFG Eurofinancière d'Investissements: Villa Les Aigles, 15 ave d'Ostende, MC 98000; tel. 93-15-11-11; fax 93-15-11-12; e-mail enquiries_mco@efgbank.com; internet www.efggroup.com; f. 1990; owned by Private Financial Investments Holding Ltd (Jersey); private banking; cap. 16.0m., res 3.3m., dep. 341.4m. (Dec. 2005); Dir-Gen. GEORGE CATSIAPIS.

HSBC Private Bank (Monaco): 17 ave d'Ostende, MC 98000; tel. 93-15-25-25; fax 93-15-25-00; internet www.hsbcprivatebank.com; f. 1997 as Republic National Bank of New York (Monaco) SA; present name adopted 2004; owned by HSBC Private Banking Holdings (Suisse) SA (Switzerland); private banking; cap. 131.0m., dep. 5,540.5m., total assets 5,798.4m. (Dec. 2006); Chief Exec. and Dir-Gen. GÉRARD COHEN.

KB Luxembourg (Monaco): 8 ave de Grande Bretagne, BP 262, MC 98005; tel. 92-16-55-55; fax 92-16-55-99; internet www.europeanprivatebankers.com; f. 1996; owned by Kredietbank SA Luxembourgeoise (Luxembourg); cap. 7.2m., res 1.7m., dep. 328.8m. (Dec. 2005); Chair. of Bd JEAN-PAUL LOOS; Man. Dir PAUL-MARIE JACQUES.

UBS (Monaco): 2 ave de Grande Bretagne, BP 189, MC 98007; tel. 93-15-58-15; fax 93-15-58-00; e-mail pierre.meylan@ubs.com; internet www.ubs.com/monaco; f. 1956; present name adopted 1998; owned by UBS AG (Switzerland); cap. 9.2m., res 28.6m., dep. 1,709.6m. (Dec. 2006); Chair. DIETER KIEFER; CEO CHRISTIAN GRÜTTER; 1 br.

INSURANCE

Assurances J.P. et C. Sassi AXA: Le Suffren, 7 rue Suffren-Reymond, BP 25, MC 98001; tel. 93-30-45-88; fax 93-25-86-07; e-mail agence.sassi@axa.fr; f. 1968; Dir JEAN-PIERRE SASSI.

The Eric Blair Network: 33 blvd Princesse Charlotte, BP 265, MC 98005 Cedex; tel. 93-50-99-66; fax 97-70-72-00; e-mail eric@insure.monaco.mc; internet www.ericblairnet.com; Chief Exec. ERIC BLAIR.

Gramaglia Assurances: 14 blvd des Moulins, BP 153, MC 98003 Cedex; tel. 92-16-59-00; fax 92-16-59-16; e-mail assur@gramaglia.mc; internet www.gramaglia.mc; Dir ANTOINE GRAMAGLIA.

Monaco Insurance Services: 9 rue de Millo, MC 98000; tel. 97-97-39-39; fax 93-25-74-37; e-mail maoun@monaco377.com; Dir PIERRE AOUN.

Mourenon et Giannotti: 22 blvd Princesse Charlotte, MC 98000; tel. 97-97-08-88; fax 97-97-08-80; f. 1975; Dirs JEAN-PHILIPPE MOURENON, JOSÉ GIANNOTTI.

Silvain Assurances: 33 blvd Princesse Charlotte, BP 267, MC 98005; tel. 93-25-54-45; fax 93-50-39-05; Dir FRANÇOIS SILVAIN.

Société Française de Recours Cie d'Assurances: 28 blvd Princesse Charlotte, MC 98000; tel. 93-50-52-63; fax 93-50-54-49; Dir FLORIANO CONTE.

Trade and Industry

GOVERNMENT AGENCIES

Direction de l'Environnement: 3 ave de Fontvieille, MC 98000; tel. 98-98-80-00; fax 92-05-28-91; e-mail environnement@gouv.mc; Dir CYRIL GOMEZ.

Direction de l'Expansion Economique: 9 rue du Gabian, MC 98000; tel. 93-15-88-12; fax 92-05-75-20; comprises five divisions: General Administration; Economic Development; Economic and Financial Enquiries; Intellectual Property; and Statistics and Economic Studies; Dir CATHERINE ORECCHIA-MATTHYSSENS.

Direction de la Prospective, de l'Urbanisme et de la Mobilité: 23 ave Albert II, MC 98000; tel. 98-98-22-99; fax 98-98-88-02; e-mail prospective@gouv.mc; Dir PATRICE CELLARIO.

Direction des Services Fiscaux: 'Le Panorama', 57 rue Grimaldi, BP 475, MC 98000; tel. 98-98-80-00; fax 93-15-81-55; Dir ANTOINE DINKEL.

CHAMBER OF COMMERCE

Jeune Chambre Economique de Monaco: 1 ave des Castelans, MC 98000; tel. 92-05-20-19; fax 92-05-31-29; e-mail jcemonaco@jcemonaco.mc; internet www.jcemonaco.mc; f. 1963; 102 mems; Pres. BÉATRICE BOISSON.

EMPLOYERS' ASSOCIATION

Fédération Patronale Monégasque (FPM) (Employers' Fed. of Monaco): 'Le Coronado', 20 ave de Fontvieille, MC 98000; tel. 92-05-38-92; fax 92-05-20-04; e-mail info@federation-patronale.mc; internet www.federation-patronale.mc; f. 1944; Pres. PHILIPPE ORTELLI; Sec.-Gen. ALBERTE ESCANDE; 25 mem. orgs, with 1,200 individual mems.

UTILITIES

Electricity and Gas

Société Monégasque de l'Electricité et du Gaz (SMEG): 10 ave de Fontvieille, BP 633, MC 98013 Cedex; tel. 92-05-05-00; fax 92-05-05-92; e-mail smeg@smeg.mc; internet www.smeg.mc; f. 1890; 64% owned by Groupe Suez (France); 20% owned by the Govt of Monaco; Dir-Gen. GUY MAGNAN.

Water

Société Monégasque des Eaux (SME): 29 ave de Fontvieille, MC 98000; tel. 97-98-51-00; fax 92-05-23-83; e-mail sme@sme.mc; internet www.sme.mc; f. 1983; Pres. STÉPHANE GIACCARDI.

TRADE UNION FEDERATION

Union des Syndicats de Monaco (USM): 28 blvd Rainier III, MC 98000; tel. 93-30-19-30; fax 93-25-06-73; e-mail usm@usm.mc; internet www.usm.mc; f. 1944; Sec.-Gen. ANGÈLE BRAQUETTI; 41 mem. unions.

Transport

RAILWAYS

The 1.7 km of railway track in Monaco, running from France to Monte-Carlo, is operated by the French state railway, the Société Nationale des Chemins de fer Français (SNCF). As part of the Government's policy of land reclamation, an underground railway station was opened in 1999.

ROADS

In 2007 there were an estimated 50 km of major roads in the Principality.

SHIPPING

Direction des Affaires Maritimes: quai Jean-Charles Rey, BP 468, MC 98012 Cedex; tel. 98-98-22-80; fax 98-98-22-81; e-mail marine@gouv.mc; Dir JEAN-LOUIS BISSUEL.

Société d'Exploitation des Ports de Monaco (SEPM): 6 quai Antoine 1er, BP 453, MC 98011 Cedex; tel. 97-77-30-00; fax 97-77-30-01; e-mail info@ports-monaco.com; internet www.ports-monaco.com; f. 2002; state-owned; responsible for management and devt of the two principal ports in Monaco, at La Condamine (Port Hercule) and Fontvieille; Pres. ALECO KEUSSEOGLOU; Gen. Man. GIANBATTISTA BOREA D'OLMO.

Shipping Companies

D'Amico Dry Ltd: 20 blvd de Suisse, MC 98000 Cedex; tel. 93-10-31-05; fax 93-10-56-07; e-mail info@damicoship.com; internet www.cogema-sam.com; owned by d'Amico Società di Navigazione SpA (Italy); Group CEO CESARE D'AMICO.

MC Shipping Inc.: Gildo Pastor Center, 7 rue du Gabian, MC 98000; tel. 97-97-49-90; fax 97-97-49-99; e-mail contact@mcshipping.com; internet www.mcshipping.com; f. 1989; Chair. of Bd CHARLES LONGBOTTOM; Pres. and CEO TONY CRAWFORD.

Société Anonyme Monégasque d'Administration Maritime et Aérienne (SAMAMA): L'Estoril, Bloc B, 1er étage, 31 ave Princesse Grace, MC 98000; tel. 99-99-51-00; fax 99-99-51-09; e-mail general@samama-monaco.com; Pres. FRANK O. WALTERS; Dir-Gen. J. F. MEGGINSON.

CIVIL AVIATION

There is a helicopter shuttle service between the international airport at Nice, France, and Monaco's heliport at Fontvieille.

Heli-Air Monaco SAM: Héliport de Monaco, MC 98000; tel. 92-05-00-50; fax 92-05-00-51; e-mail helico@heliairmonaco.com; internet www.heliairmonaco.com; Pres. JACQUES CROVETTO.

Tourism

Tourists are attracted to Monaco by the Mediterranean climate, dramatic scenery and numerous entertainment facilities, including a casino. In 2006 313,070 tourists (excluding excursionists) visited Monaco. There were 2,555 hotel rooms available in that year.

Direction du Tourisme et des Congrès: 2A blvd des Moulins, MC 98030 Cedex; tel. 92-16-61-16; fax 92-16-60-00; e-mail dtc@gouv.mc; internet www.visitmonaco.com; Dir-Gen. of Tourism MICHEL BOUQUIER.

Monte-Carlo SBM: place du Casino, BP 139, MC 98007; tel. 92-16-25-25; fax 92-16-26-26; e-mail resort@sbm.mc; internet www.montecarloresort.com; f. 1863; corpn in which the Govt holds a 69.5% interest; controls the entertainment facilities of Monaco, including the casino and numerous hotels, clubs, restaurants and sporting facilities; Chair. JEAN-LUC BIAMONTI; Gen. Man. BERNARD LAMBERT.

MONGOLIA

Introductory Survey

Location, Climate, Language, Religion, Flag, Capital

Mongolia is a land-locked country in central Asia, with the Russian Federation to the north and the People's Republic of China to the south, east and west. The climate is dry, with generally mild summers but very cold winters. Temperatures in Ulan Bator (traditional spelling; Ulaanbaatar in transcription from Mongolian Cyrillic) range between −32°C (−26°F) and 22°C (71°F). The principal language is Khalkha Mongolian. Kazakh is spoken in the province of Bayan-Ölgii. There is no state religion, but Buddhist Lamaism is being encouraged once again. The national flag (proportions 1 by 2) has three equal vertical stripes, of red, blue and red, with the 'soyombo' symbol (a combination of abstract devices) in gold on the red stripe at the hoist. The capital is Ulan Bator.

Recent History

The country was formerly the Manchu province of Outer Mongolia. In 1911, following the republican revolution in China, Mongolian princes declared the province's independence. With support from Tsarist Russia, Outer Mongolia gained autonomy, as a feudal Buddhist monarchy, but Russia accepted Chinese suzerainty over the province in 1915. Following the Russian revolution of 1917, China began to re-establish control in Mongolia in 1919. In 1920 Mongol nationalists appealed to the new Soviet regime for assistance, and in March 1921 they met on Soviet territory to found the Mongolian People's Party (called the Mongolian People's Revolutionary Party—MPRP—from 1924) and established a Provisional People's Government. After nationalist forces, with Soviet help, drove anti-Bolshevik troops from the Mongolian capital, the People's Government was proclaimed on 11 July 1921. Soviet Russia recognized the People's Government in November of that year. In November 1924, after the death of Bogd Khan (King) Javzandamba Khutagt VIII, the Mongolian People's Republic was proclaimed.

The Mongolian People's Republic became increasingly dependent on the USSR's support. The Government conducted campaigns to collectivize the economy and to destroy the power of the nobility and Buddhist priests. In 1932 an armed uprising was suppressed with Soviet assistance. Following his reorganization of the MPRP and army leadership in 1936–39, power was held by Marshal Khorloogiin Choibalsan as Prime Minister and MPRP leader. The dictatorship of Choibalsan closely followed the model of the regime of Stalin (Iosif Dzhugashvili, 1924–53) in the USSR. Its thousands of victims included eminent politicians, military officers, religious leaders and intellectuals. In 1939 a Japanese invasion from Manchuria was repelled by Soviet and Mongolian forces at Khalkhyn Gol (Nomonhan). In keeping with the Yalta agreement to preserve the status quo in Mongolia, war was declared on Japan in August 1945, four days before the Japanese surrender, and northern China was invaded. In a Mongolian plebiscite in October, it was reported that 100% of the votes were cast in favour of independence, and this was recognized by China in January 1946.

Choibalsan died in January 1952 and was succeeded as Prime Minister by Yumjaagiin Tsedenbal, who had been the MPRP's First Secretary since 1940. Dashiin Damba became First Secretary of the MPRP in April 1954. In 1955 India became the first non-communist country to recognize Mongolia. Tsedenbal replaced Damba as First Secretary of the MPRP in November 1958, and a new Constitution was adopted in July 1960. Mongolia became a member of the UN in October 1961 and was subsequently accorded diplomatic recognition by the United Kingdom (1963), other Western European states and developing countries. By January 1987, when Mongolia was finally granted diplomatic recognition by the USA, it maintained diplomatic relations with more than 100 states.

Jamsrangiin Sambuu, Head of State since July 1954, died in May 1972. He was replaced in June 1974 by Tsedenbal, who remained First Secretary of the MPRP (restyled General Secretary in 1981) but relinquished the post of Chairman of the Council of Ministers to Jambyn Batmönkh. In August 1984 Tsedenbal was removed from the party leadership and state presidency, apparently owing to ill health, and Batmönkh replaced him as General Secretary of the MPRP. In December Batmönkh also became Head of State, while Dumaagiin Sodnom, hitherto a Deputy Chairman of the Council of Ministers and the Chairman of the State Planning Commission, was appointed Chairman of the Council of Ministers.

By the end of 1988 the MPRP Political Bureau was obliged to admit that economic renewal was not succeeding because of the need for social reforms. Batmönkh advocated greater openness and offered the prospect of multi-candidate elections. He criticized Tsedenbal for the country's 'stagnation', also stating that the former leader had belittled collective leadership.

Between December 1989 and March 1990 there was a great increase in public political activity, as several newly formed opposition movements organized a series of peaceful demonstrations in Ulan Bator, demanding political and economic reforms. The most prominent of the new opposition groups was the Mongolian Democratic Union (MDU), founded in December 1989. In January 1990 dialogue was initiated between MPRP officials and representatives of the MDU, including its chief co-ordinator, Sanjaasürengiin Zorig (a lecturer at the Mongolian State University). The emergence of further opposition groups, together with escalating public demonstrations (involving as many as 20,000 people), led to a crisis of confidence within the MPRP. At a party plenum in mid-March Batmönkh announced the resignation of the entire Political Bureau as well as of the Secretariat of the Central Committee. Gombojavyn Ochirbat, a former head of the Ideological Department of the Central Committee and a former Chairman of the Central Council of Mongolian Trade Unions, was elected the new General Secretary of the party, replacing Batmönkh. A new five-member Political Bureau was formed. The plenum voted to expel the former MPRP General Secretary, Yumjaagiin Tsedenbal, from the party and to rehabilitate several prominent officials who had been removed by Tsedenbal in the 1960s.

At a session of the People's Great Khural (legislature), held shortly after the MPRP plenum, Punsalmaagiin Ochirbat, hitherto the Minister of Foreign Economic Relations and Supply, was elected Chairman of the Presidium (Head of State), replacing Batmönkh, and other senior positions in the Presidium were reallocated. Dumaagiin Sodnom was dismissed from his post as Chairman of the Council of Ministers and was replaced by Sharavyn Gungaadorj, a Deputy Chairman and Minister of Agriculture and the Food Industry. The Khural also adopted amendments to the Constitution, including the deletion of references to the MPRP as the 'guiding force' in Mongolian society, and approved a new electoral law. It was decided that the next elections to the Khural would be held in mid-1990, and not in 1991 as originally planned. Meanwhile, all limits on personal livestock holdings were removed, and new regulations were introduced to encourage foreign investment in Mongolia. However, in late March 1990 an estimated 13,000 people, dissatisfied with the results of the Khural's session, demonstrated in Ulan Bator to demand the dissolution of the Khural. Opposition leaders declared that the changes introduced by the legislature were insufficient, and demanded the introduction of a multi-party electoral law.

In April 1990 the MPRP held an extraordinary congress, at which more than three-quarters of the membership of the Central Committee was renewed. General Secretary Gombojavyn Ochirbat was elected to the restyled post of Chairman of the party. The Political Bureau was renamed the Presidium, and a new, four-member Secretariat of the Central Committee was appointed. In May the People's Great Khural adopted a law on political parties, which legalized the new 'informal' parties through official registration, and also adopted further amendments to the Constitution, introducing a presidential system with a standing legislature called the State Little Khural, elected by proportional representation of parties.

At the July 1990 legislative election and consequent re-elections, 430 deputies were elected to serve a five-year term: 357 from the MPRP (in some instances unopposed), 16 from the Mongolian Democratic Party (MDP, the political wing of the MDU), 19 shared among the Mongolian Revolutionary Youth

League, the Mongolian National Progress Party (MNPP), and the Mongolian Social-Democratic Party (MSDP), and 39 without party affiliation. Under constitutional amendments adopted in May, the People's Great Khural was required to convene at least four times in the five years of its term.

In September 1990 the People's Great Khural elected Punsalmaagiin Ochirbat to be the country's first President, with a five-year term of office; the post of Chairman of the Presidium was abolished. Dashiin Byambasüren was appointed Prime Minister (equivalent to the former post of Chairman of the Council of Ministers) and began consultations on the formation of a multi-party government. The newly restyled Cabinet was elected by the State Little Khural in September and October. Under the amended Constitution, the President, Vice-President and Ministers were not permitted to remain concurrently deputies of the People's Great Khural; therefore, re-elections of deputies to the legislature were held in November.

The 20th Congress of the MPRP, held in February 1991, elected a new 99-member Central Committee, which, in turn, appointed a new Presidium. The Central Committee also elected a new Chairman, Büdragchaagiin Dash-Yondon, the Chairman of the Ulan Bator City Party Committee, who had become a Presidium member in November 1990.

A new Constitution was adopted by an almost unanimous vote of the Great Khural in January 1992, and entered into force in the following month. It provided for a unicameral Mongolian Great Khural, comprising 76 members, to replace the People's Great Khural, following elections to be held in June. (The State Little Khural was abolished.) The country's official name was changed from the Mongolian People's Republic to Mongolia, and the communist gold star was removed from the national flag.

At the elections to the Mongolian Great Khural in June 1992, contested by the MPRP, an alliance of the MDP, the MNPP and the United Party (UP), the MSDP, and six other parties and another alliance, a total of 293 candidates stood for 76 seats in 26 constituencies, comprising the 18 *aimag* (provinces), the towns of Darkhan and Erdenet, and Ulan Bator City (six). A total of 95.6% of the electorate participated in the elections. Candidates were elected by a simple majority, provided that they obtained the support of at least 50% of the electorate in their constituency. The MPRP candidates received some 57% of the total votes, while the candidates of the other parties (excluding independents) achieved a combined total of 40%. However, the outcome of the election was disproportionate, with the MPRP winning 70 seats (71 including a pro-MPRP independent). The remaining seats were taken by the MDP (two, including an independent), the MSDP, MNPP and UP (one each).

The first session of the Mongolian Great Khural opened in July 1992 with the election of officers, the nomination of Puntsagiin Jasrai (who had served as a Deputy Chairman of the Council of Ministers in the late 1980s) to the post of Prime Minister, and the approval of his Cabinet. Natsagiin Bagabandi, a Vice-Chairman of the MPRP Central Committee, was elected Chairman of the Great Khural. Jambyn Gombojav (Chairman of the People's Great Khural from late 1990 to late 1991) was elected Vice-Chairman of the new Khural. Meanwhile, a National Security Council was established, with the country's President as its Chairman, and the Prime Minister and Chairman of the Great Khural as its members.

In October 1992 the MDP, MNPP, UP and the Mongolian Renewal Party amalgamated to form the Mongolian National Democratic Party (MNDP), with a General Council headed by the MNPP leader, Davaadorjiin Ganbold, and including Sanjaasürengiin Zorig and other prominent opposition politicians. In the same month the MPRP Central Committee was renamed the MPRP Little Khural, and its membership was increased to 169 (and subsequently to 198). The Presidium was replaced by a nine-member Party Leadership Council, headed by Büdragchaagiin Dash-Yondon as its General Secretary.

The Great Khural adopted a Presidential Election Law in March 1993, and direct elections to the presidency were scheduled for June. Lodongiin Tüdev, a member of the Party Leadership Council and Editor-in-Chief of the MPRP organ, *Ünen*, was chosen as the MPRP's candidate, while President Ochirbat was nominated by a coalition of the MNDP and the MSDP. The result of the election was a convincing popular victory for Ochirbat: he received 57.8% of the votes cast, compared with 38.7% for Tüdev.

The MPRP in early 1996 forced through the Great Khural the passage of amendments that increased the number of constituencies from 26 to 76, making them all single-seat constituencies, while preserving the majority vote system. To be declared elected, a candidate was required to have received only 25% of the constituency votes. In response, opposition parties formed an election coalition, the Democratic Alliance, which received support from the Mongolian Green Party and the MDU.

At the legislative election, held at the end of June 1996, a resounding victory was achieved by the Democratic Alliance, which won 50 of the 76 seats in the Great Khural, receiving some 46.7% of the total votes cast. The MPRP took only 25 seats (40.6%), while one seat was won by a candidate of the United Heritage Party (UHP). Electoral turn-out was 92.2%. At the legislature's inaugural session, in mid-July, the leader of the MSDP, Radnaasümbereliin Gonchigdorj, was elected to the post of Chairman of the Great Khural. Mendsaikhany Enkhsaikhan, the leader of the Democratic Alliance and the group's choice for Prime Minister, was nominated by President Ochirbat and voted into office. Following the rejection of MPRP demands concerning the allocation of positions in the Great Khural, MPRP members organized a three-day boycott of the legislature, leaving it inquorate and unable to function. After the boycott ended, the MNDP leader, Tsakhiagiin Elbegdorj, was elected Vice-Chairman of the Great Khural; a new Government was formed at the end of July.

Following their election defeat, and amid growing evidence of a rift between supporters of tradition and advocates of the reform process, in July 1996 the MPRP Little Khural elected a new Leadership Council and General Secretary of the party, Nambaryn Enkhbayar. Indications of a division in the party increased in February 1997, when the leaders of the MPRP sought to enforce their uncompromising policies on the party congress. Several prominent dissenting members resigned from the party, and Natsagiin Bagabandi, who had been Chairman of the Great Khural in 1992–96, was elected Chairman of the party.

With a date in May 1997 set for the presidential election, the MNDP and the MSDP proposed a joint candidate for the post of President—the incumbent, Ochirbat. The MPRP nominated the party Chairman, Bagabandi, while the UHP adopted Jambyn Gombojav, a former Vice-Chairman of the Great Khural. The election was won convincingly by Bagabandi, with some 60.8% of the total votes cast. In a severe set-back to the democratic movement, Ochirbat received only 29.8%, a reflection of popular dissatisfaction at the rigorous economic reform policies implemented by the ruling Democratic Alliance. Gombojav obtained 6.6% of the votes. Following Bagabandi's success in the presidential election, Enkhbayar was elected Chairman of the MPRP in his place. In August he won a by-election for Bagabandi's former seat in the Great Khural.

In April 1998 the Democratic Alliance decided that, henceforth, the Cabinet was to comprise members of the Great Khural, headed by the leader of the Alliance. Tsakhiagiin Elbegdorj, leader of the MNDP, was thus appointed Prime Minister, and a new Cabinet was formed in May. The Government became embroiled in a dispute over the amalgamation of the state-owned Reconstruction Bank, declared bankrupt after over-extending its credit, with the private Golomt Bank. Amid accusations that Democratic Alliance leaders had obtained loans from the bank shortly before its failure, the MPRP effected a boycott of the Great Khural. The party rejected the Government's reinstatement of Reconstruction Bank and returned to the Great Khural in late July to pursue a motion of no confidence in the Government. The vote was carried by 42 votes to 33, with the support of 15 members of the Democratic Alliance.

In August 1998 the Democratic Alliance nominated as its candidate for Prime Minister Davaadorjiin Ganbold, Chairman of the Economic Standing Committee of the Great Khural (who had been chief Deputy Prime Minister in 1990–92 and President of the MNDP in 1992–96). President Bagabandi rejected Ganbold's nomination, on the grounds of his failure to act to resolve the bank merger crisis in his capacity as Chairman of the Committee. Ganbold was nominated a second time, and again rejected by Bagabandi, who proposed Great Khural member Dogsomyn Ganbold. The Democratic Alliance persisted, and by the end of the month Davaadorjiin Ganbold had been nominated and rejected five times. The Democratic Alliance then proposed Rinchinnyamyn Amarjargal, acting Minister of External Relations and a member of the MNDP General Council. President Bagabandi accepted the nomination, but it was rejected by one vote in the Great Khural in September. Two other candidates were subsequently rejected by Bagabandi.

In October 1998 Sanjaasürengiin Zorig, the Minister of Infrastructure Development and founder of the Mongolian Democratic Movement, was murdered. Although not nominated for the post, Zorig had been widely regarded as a potential prime ministerial candidate. Following Zorig's state funeral, Bagabandi named six more candidates of his own, including Dogsomyn Ganbold and the Mayor of Ulan Bator, Janlavyn Narantsatsralt. The Democratic Alliance disregarded the presidential list and for the sixth time nominated Davaadorjiin Ganbold. Although the nomination was supported by all 48 Democratic Alliance members of the Great Khural, Bagabandi once again rejected him. The political crisis was then deepened by a new Constitutional Court ruling that members of the Great Khural could not serve concurrently in the Government. Two months later the Democratic Alliance finally nominated Bagabandi's candidate, Narantsatsralt, who was appointed Prime Minister in December. The formation of his Government was completed in January 1999.

Narantsatsralt's Government remained in power for just over six months. In July 1999 the Prime Minister was challenged in the Great Khural over a letter that he had written in January to Yurii Maslyukov, First Deputy Chairman of the Russian Government, in which he seemingly acknowledged Russia's right to privatize its share in the Erdenet copper-mining joint venture without reference to Mongolia. Unable to offer a satisfactory explanation, in late July Narantsatsralt lost a vote of confidence, in which MSDP members of the Great Khural voted with the opposition MPRP. The Democratic Alliance nominated Rinchinnyamyn Amarjargal for the post of Prime Minister, but the proposal was immediately challenged by Bagabandi. The President insisted that, following the Constitutional Court ruling of late 1998, he could consider Amarjargal's suitability for nomination in the Great Khural only after the candidate had resigned his seat. After several days of arguments, representatives of the Democratic Alliance and the President adopted a formula that allowed the Great Khural's approval of the prime ministerial nomination and the nominee's resignation of his Great Khural seat to take place simultaneously. Amarjargal was elected Prime Minister at the end of July. The ministers of Narantsatsralt's Government remained in office in an acting capacity until early September, when all but one (the Minister of Law) were reappointed. The formation of the Government was completed in late October with the appointment of Dashpuntsagiin Ganbold as Minister of Law. In November 1999 Amarjargal assumed the presidency of the MNDP, replacing Narantsatsralt.

The 1992 Constitution was amended for the first time in December 1999 by a Great Khural decree supported by all three parliamentary parties, which simplified the procedure for the appointment of the Prime Minister and allowed members of the Great Khural to serve as government ministers while retaining their seats in the legislature. An attempt by the President to veto the decree was defeated by the Great Khural in January 2000, but the Constitutional Court ruled in March that the decree had been illegal. When the Great Khural opened its spring session in April, members rejected the ruling and refused to discuss it. The Constitutional Court's demand for a statement on the issue was disregarded by the Great Khural.

As the legislative election approached, a breakaway grouping of the MNDP re-established the Mongolian Democratic Party, and a faction of the MSDP founded the Mongolian New Social Democratic Party. Sanjaasürengiin Oyuun, the sister of the murdered minister, Zorig, established the Civil Courage Party (or Irgenii Zorig Nam), drawing away from the MNDP several more members of the Great Khural, and formed an electoral alliance with the Green Party. The MNDP, unable to reconstitute the previously successful Democratic Alliance with the MSDP, therefore formed a new Democratic Alliance with the Mongolian Believers' Democratic Party.

At the election, held in early July 2000, three coalitions and 13 parties were represented by a total of 603 candidates, including 27 independents. The MPRP won 72 of the 76 seats in the Great Khural. Prime Minister Rinchinnyamyn Amarjargal and his entire Cabinet lost their seats. The MPRP received 50.2% of the votes cast. The level of participation was 82.4% of the electorate. The MPRP's main support lay in rural constituencies, where it was widely seen as willing and able to halt the economic and social stagnation of the countryside. The Democratic Alliance won 13% of the votes cast, while the Mongolian Democratic New Socialist Party (MDNSP, which had amalgamated with the Mongolian Workers' Party in 1999) received 10.7% of the votes; each of them won one seat. The MSDP received 8.9% of the votes cast but won no seats.

When the Great Khural opened, Lkhamsürengiin Enebish, the MPRP General Secretary, was elected Chairman (Speaker) of the chamber. However, the nomination of the MPRP Chairman, Nambaryn Enkhbayar, for the post of Prime Minister was rejected by President Bagabandi, on the grounds that priority be given to the constitutional amendments. After a week of discussions a compromise was reached whereby Enkhbayar's nomination was presented to the Great Khural, while the amendments remained in force pending a Great Khural debate and a full nine-member session of the Constitutional Court. In July 2000 the Great Khural approved Enkhbayar's appointment as Prime Minister by 67 MPRP members' votes to three. Enkhbayar's Cabinet was approved in August.

At a conference in early December 2000 five parties—the MNDP, the MSDP, the Mongolian Democratic Party, the Believers' Democratic Party and the Democratic Renewal Party—decided to dissolve themselves and form a new Democratic Party (DP). Dambyn Dorligjav, a former Minister of Defence and director of the Erdenet copper enterprise, was elected Chairman, while Janlavyn Narantsatsralt and the former Minister of the Environment, Sonomtserengiin Mendsaikhan, were elected as Vice-Chairmen. The party's National Advisory Committee was formed in February 2001 and comprised two members from each of the Great Khural's 76 constituencies.

In mid-December 2000 the Great Khural readopted, unchanged and for immediate implementation, the decree of December 1999 amending the 1992 Constitution. The President's veto of the decree was rejected. However, the Constitutional Court was unable to meet in full session because the election of replacements for time-expired members was delayed in the Great Khural. President Bagabandi finally approved the amendments in May 2001.

In February 2001 the 23rd Congress of the ruling MPRP re-elected Prime Minister Nambaryn Enkhbayar as its Chairman, approved the establishment of a new Little Khural of 244 members and enlarged the Party Leadership Council from 11 to 15 members. At the end of September Lkhamsürengiin Enebish, Chairman of the Great Khural and recently re-elected as General Secretary of the MPRP, died; he was succeeded in the latter post by Doloonjingiin Idevkhten and as Chairman of the Great Khural by Sanjbegziin Tömör-Ochir, Secretary of the MPRP.

The presidential election of May 2001 was won by the MPRP's candidate, Natsagiin Bagabandi, who received 57.95% of the votes cast. Radnaasümbereliin Gonchigdorj of the DP won 36.58% of votes, and Luvsandambyn Dashnyam of the Civil Courage Party received 3.54%.

In January 2001, meanwhile, during one of Mongolia's most severe winters ever, a helicopter carrying 23 people, who were investigating the *zud* (livestock starvation owing to frozen fodder) in western Mongolia, crashed, killing eight. The dead included several UN staff and Shagdaryn Otgonbileg, a member of the Great Khural and former director of the Erdenet copper enterprise. Later that month the UN appealed for humanitarian aid to help Mongolian herders, whose animals were dying in huge numbers. In May Otgonbileg was replaced by his widow Tuyaa as Great Khural MPRP member, who was elected unopposed.

In March 2002 Sanjaasürengiin Oyuun's Civil Courage Party merged with Bazarsadyn Jargalsaikhan's Mongolian Republican Party (MRP) to form the Civil Courage Republican Party, under Oyuun's leadership. However, in June 2003 the MRP leader Bazarsadyn Jargalsaikhan withdrew from the merger after disagreement about the formation of a coalition with the DP. Attempts in December to oust Oyuun from the party leadership failed, and in March 2004 she agreed to join the Motherland Democracy (MD) coalition comprising Erdenebat's MDNSP and the DP (see below).

In June 2002 the Great Khural approved the Law on Land and the Law on Land Privatization. Although less than 1% of the country's total territory was to be available for privatization, the laws generated much controversy. From November there were several demonstrations farmers who were arrested for parking their tractors on Sükhbaatar Square in central Ulan Bator. The demonstrators, led by DP leader Erdeniin Bat-Üül, protested that the poor would be denied land by the 'oligarchy'. The privatization law duly entered into force in May 2003.

Meanwhile, an effective protest against the Government's silencing of the opposition was made by Lamjavyn Gündalai, a DP member of the Great Khural, who interrupted the Prime Minister's televised address and disrupted the opening ceremony of the autumn 2002 session of the Great Khural by displaying to television cameras a series of placards on which he demanded the right to speak, condemned the imprisonment of journalists and criticized the land privatization programme. When the 2003 spring session opened at the beginning of April Gündalai again displayed a range of slogans; the President and the Prime Minister were unable to deliver their speeches, and the televised session was suspended.

At the end of May 2003 Gündalai made a public allegation that there existed 'top secret' information that the Minister of Justice and Home Affairs, Tsendiin Nyamdorj, had links with the special services of a foreign country. Nyamdorj denied the allegations. In July Gündalai was removed from an aircraft at Ulan Bator airport, while on his way via the Republic of Korea to a conference in Singapore, and arrested for 'violation of the border'. This provoked an uproar regarding the breaching of Gündalai's parliamentary immunity, and the DP sought an investigation by the human rights committee of the Inter-Parliamentary Union (a non-governmental organization based in Geneva, Switzerland). In late July, on the same day as the newspaper *Önöödör* published extracts from the 'top secret' material relating to Nyamdorj, Gündalai was released. In August the charges against him were abandoned on the instructions of the Deputy Chief Prosecutor. In October Gündalai succeeded, for a third time, in disrupting the opening of the Great Khural's autumn session, with the result that the Prime Minister was once again unable to deliver his report to the cameras.

The National Human Rights Commission's 2003 annual report was highly critical of bureaucracy, corruption and cronyism, and the police were accused of numerous cases of brutality. The National Human Rights Programme was adopted in December. Also in 2003, Damirangiin Enkhbat, who had been suspected of the murder of Sanjaasürengiin Zorig in 1998 and had since been resident in France, was reported to have been abducted by Mongolian secret agents and subsequently imprisoned in Mongolia. In early 2004 reports from Amnesty International, the human rights organization, suggested that he had been tortured during interrogation. In June 2005 the UN's Special Rapporteur on torture, and other cruel, inhuman or degrading treatment or punishment, Manfred Nowak, carried out a prison inspection and met Enkhbat and his lawyer. Nowak's report, which was published in December but did not appear in the Mongolian press until a year later, condemned torture in Mongolian prisons and criticized the provisions of the Law on State Secrets for preventing dissemination of information about death sentences. (Enkhbat was released from prison in February 2006 on the grounds of ill health, and subsequently died.)

In the spring of 2004 political campaigning began for the election to the Mongolian Great Khural, which was held in late June. The new General Election Committee (GEC) incorporated many MPRP nominees. The electorate was calculated to total nearly 1.3m. persons, but there was no provision for the 70,000 people who were resident abroad to vote. The opposition MD election pact, formed by Mendsaikhany Enkhsaikhan's DP and Badarchiin Nyamdorj's 'Motherland' MDNSP, was joined by Sanjaasürengiin Oyuun's Civil Courage Republican Party, minus the followers of Bazarsadyn Jargalsaikhan, who left to re-establish the Republican Party.

After the registration of participating political parties and coalitions, the GEC examined the official lists, rejecting all Mongolian Youth Party candidates. Before polling day three candidates withdrew, leaving the final number at 241: 76 each for the MPRP and the MD coalition, 33 for the Republican Party, 23 for the National Solidarity Party, nine for the Mongolian Traditional United Party (also known as the United Heritage Party), five for the Green Party, four for the Liberal Party and 15 Independents.

The initial results of the election of 27 June 2004 (compiled as percentages of the total ballot in each constituency) left the political scene in disarray: the MPRP and the MD coalition had each won about one-half of the seats, leaving neither with the necessary majority of 39 (one-half of the Great Khural seats plus one seat). The three Independents elected, although all DP members, were ruled as not counting in this process. The Republican Party won one seat. The rate of participation was 82.2% of registered voters. In 25 constituencies there was a straight contest between the MPRP and the MD coalition. Amid mutual accusations of bribery and electoral fraud in a number of constituencies, efforts to form a government soon became embroiled in disputes at the GEC and the recently established City Administrative Court.

The GEC submitted the results in 74 of the 76 constituencies to President Bagabandi in early July 2004, at the first session of the newly elected Great Khural, which was boycotted by the MPRP. The President stated that it was right to convene the first session, despite the fact that two results had yet to be confirmed, because of the need to address many important issues. However, the MD members were not allowed to take the oath. Meeting separately, 70 of the MPRP members elected in 2000 filed a lawsuit against the President on the grounds that he had contravened the Constitution and allowed the Great Khural to meet without a quorum (57 members being present) before the final session of the outgoing Great Khural had taken place. The closing session of the previous legislature was held in late July 2004. Among other decisions, it released the Great Khural's Deputy Chairman Jamsrangiin Byambadorj (who had lost his parliamentary seat in the recent election) to take up a vacant seat in the Constitutional Court and accused the President of acting unconstitutionally in convening the first session of the incoming legislature. All these decisions were vetoed by President Bagabandi in late July as unconstitutional. (Byambadorj was elected a member, then the Chairman, of the Constitutional Court in January 2005.)

Postponed after another MPRP boycott, the first plenary session of the new Great Khural was held in late July 2004, when 74 members were sworn in. The first business was the election of the new Chairman of the chamber. The MPRP group supported the candidature of the MPRP leader and acting Prime Minister, Nambaryn Enkhbayar, but protracted discussion of this proposal with the MD members of the Khural continued for days without resolution. The MPRP members of the Great Khural proposed that the MD members should nominate the next Prime Minister, while the MD members proposed the formation of a joint working group to draw up a programme for a government of 'national accord'.

Eventually, at the end of August 2004, former Prime Minister Nambaryn Enkhbayar of the MPRP was appointed Chairman of the Great Khural, and Tsakhiagiin Elbegdorj of the MD coalition was appointed Prime Minister. Although the newly elected members of the Mongolian Great Khural agreed on the formation, chairmanship and membership of the Khural's standing committees and sub-committees, discussion of the basic principles for the establishment of a coalition government were protracted. In mid-September Prime Minister Elbegdorj forwarded to President Bagabandi proprosals for the composition of a new Cabinet, and in late September the new Government was appointed. The deputy ministers, one-half nominated by the MD coalition and one-half by the MPRP, were appointed in November and December respectively. The Government Action Programme 2004–2008, approved by the Great Khural in November 2004, included provision for a monthly grant of 3,000 tögrög from January 2005 to each child under the age of 18 in families with more than three children and a per caput income below the national minimum—a compromise of MPRP and MD election pledges.

The National Human Rights Commission's annual report for 2004 noted the need for the rights of vulnerable groups and the human rights activities of legal organizations to remain the 'centre of attention'. The report also noted that torture and severe punishment were still common activities and that many police officers equated punishment with physical torture. Provisions of the Convention against Torture and other Cruel, Inhumane or Degrading Treatment or Punishment, which Mongolia joined in 2000, were not widely known, and effective measures were not being taken to curb illegal acts, the report stated.

At the end of December 2004 Radnaasümbereliin Gonchigdorj took the chairmanship of the DP at a meeting of the executive of its National Consultative Committee (NCC) and installed his supporters in other senior posts. His predecessor, Mendsaikhany Enkhsaikhan, seemed to retain the support of the DP's National Assembly. Although a court ruled that the leadership change was contrary to the party's rules, it declined to intervene. Badarchiin Erdenebat, the Minister of Defence and leader of the MDNSP, then withdrew from the MD coalition, which collapsed. The Civil Courage Republican Party leader, Sanjaasürengiin Oyuun, was obliged to relinquish her post of Deputy Chairwoman of the Great Khural in January 2005. Prime Minister Elbegdorj took over the defence portfolio from Erdenebat in February, and a new Minister of Defence, Tserenkhüügiin Sharavdorj, was appointed in March. The MD coalition's parliamentary group in the Great Khural disbanded, and many DP members, including Gonchigdorj (but not Enkhsaikhan), joined the Khural's MPRP group members to form a parliamentary 'combined group', of which Gonchigdorj was elected Deputy Chairman. Meanwhile, Doloonjingiin Idevkhten was replaced as General Secretary of the MPRP by Sanjaagiin (Sanjiin) Bayar, the Mongolian ambassador to Russia. In February Jügderdemidiin Gürragchaa (MPRP) and in September Zandaakhüügiin Enkhbold (MD) were declared the winners in the two constituencies where the results of the 2004 election to the Great Khural election had been contested. Gürragchaa was duly sworn in, but Enkhbold had already accepted the post of Chairman of the State Property Committee in the previous December.

In March 2005, in the fourth demonstration since January by the Healthy Society Citizens' Movement, protesters broke through a police cordon to enter Ulan Bator's central Sükhbaatar Square and forced their way onto the Sükhbaatar-Choibalsan mausoleum on the south side of the Government Palace. The demonstrators demanded the resignations of the Great Khural Chairman and MPRP leader Nambaryn Enkhbayar, of Prime Minister Elbegdorj and of the DP 'turncoats' in the Great Khural who had joined the MPRP's parliamentary group. Four of the five parliamentary political parties presented candidates for the forthcoming presidential election, scheduled for late May, and they were registered in early April. The candidates were Nambaryn Enkhbayar (of the MPRP), Bazarsadyn Jargalsaikhan (Republican Party), Badarchin Erdenebat (Motherland Party, the recently renamed MDNSP) and Mendsaikhany Enkhsaikhan (DP). The election, held on 22 May, was won by Enkhbayar, who secured more than 53% of the votes cast, thereby receiving more votes than the other three candidates combined.

Enkhbayar's victory led to personnel changes in the MPRP and in the Great Khural. At the MPRP's congress in June 2005 the Mayor of Ulan Bator, Miyeegombyn Enkhbold, was chosen to replace Enkhbayar as the new party Chairman. The party's Leadership Council was enlarged to 21 members: nine re-elected (with four failing to secure re-election) and 10 new members, including Party Secretary Yondongiin Otgonbayar, the Ministers of Foreign Affairs, of Food and Agriculture, and of Health, and six MPRP Great Khural members. Two vacancies were held open, including one for a new head of the Presidential Secretariat. Enkhbayar was inaugurated as President of Mongolia on 24 June. At the beginning of July the Great Khural elected the Minister of Justice and Home Affairs, Tsendiin Nyamdorj (of the MPRP), to replace Enkhbayar as Chairman of the Great Khural.

After an attempt by the MPRP to force the Prime Minister to resign, including the expulsion of DP members from the 'combined' MPRP parliamentary group (the 'group of 62'), shortly before the closing of its spring 2005 session the Great Khural voted in favour of the formation of a DP parliamentary group, which 25 party members (headed by Gonchigdorj) joined. The by-election in Enkhbayar's former constituency was to be held at the end of August. The MPRP chose its Chairman, Miyeegombyn Enkhbold, as its candidate, and the DP nominated Prime Minister Tsakhiagiin Elbegdorj. However, Elbegdorj's nomination was withdrawn at the beginning of August, a coalition accord having been signed by the DP and the MPRP to 'respect the results of the 2004 election and maintain the stability of the coalition government', and the by-election was subsequently won by Miyeegombyn Enkhbold.

Rebuilding of the south front of the State Palace (which houses the Great Khural and government offices) to accommodate a Genghis Khan Memorial, Ceremony and Worship Complex, began in August 2005, in accordance with presidential and government decrees adopted in May 2001, with a view to celebrating in August 2006 the 800th anniversary of the founding of the Mongolian state by Genghis Khan. Plans drawn up in March 2003 provided for the demolition of the mausoleum of revolutionary leaders Sükhbaatar and Choibalsan, which stood where the complex was being built, and for the removal of their remains for burial at the main Altan-Ölgii cemetery in Ulan Bator. The Government claimed that it had the consent of the relatives to transfer the remains of Sükhbaatar and Choibalsan. In an overnight operation in August 2005, the remains were removed from the mausoleum and cremated. There was widespread public dissatisfaction that they had been disposed of in such an 'undignified' manner. Meanwhile, construction of the complex (by Chinese builders) continued, with completion due in May 2006. The partly completed south façade of the complex, with a 5.4 m bronze seated statue of Genghis Khan, was inaugurated by President Enkhbayar at a grand ceremony in July 2006. In November the finished façade was declared open.

In January 2006 a Motherland Party deputy defected to the MPRP, thereby giving the latter its 38th seat in the Great Khural. Following demands by the MPRP for Prime Minister Elbegdorj's resignation, the 10 MPRP ministers in his Cabinet resigned and the 'grand coalition' Government was voted out of office. Miyeegombyn Enkhbold, MPRP Chairman and Mayor of Ulan Bator, was elected Prime Minister. He formed a new 'national solidarity' Government that included the Motherland and Republican Party leaders Erdenebat and Jargalsaikhan, ex-DP member Gündalai, who had recently established a new party, the Party of the People, and three DP members—Enkhsaikhan, Narantsatsralt and Sonompil—who were subsequently expelled from the rump DP, now excluded from the MPRP's new coalition. One newspaper described these politicians as 'unscrupulous'; another claimed that the MPRP's abandonment of its coalition with the DP was intended to halt the progress of a new anti-corruption bill that would focus on corruption within its ranks. The new Anti-Corruption Law was finally adopted in July, eight years after the first legislation.

Following his appointment in January 2006 to the post of Deputy Prime Minister, Mendsaikhany Enkhsaikhan and his supporters began forming a new party, which was named the National New Party at its first congress in May. After the death of Great Khural member Onomoogiin Enkhsaikhan in March, the resultant by-election was delayed (possibly unconstitutionally) until early September, when it was won by the Minister of Education, Culture and Science, Ölziisaikhany Enkhtüvshin (MPRP).

The political upheaval of early 2006 also delayed a decision on amendments to the 1997 Minerals Law, introduced at the end of December 2005, which caused disquiet among foreign investors in Mongolia's mining industry. Amid much public debate about the merits of state control of the country's resources and various protests, the Great Khural discussed the amendments, consolidated them in committee and finally adopted a new redaction of the 1997 law in July 2006. According to initial reports of the text prior to publication, mining licences were to be granted only to companies, not to individuals; foreign and domestic investors in mining were to be taxed at the same rate; stability agreements were to be replaced by investment contracts; and local people in proposed mining areas would be granted greater rights with regard to decisions on exploitation licences. Also, the Government would have the right to acquire up to 50% of the resources of deposits discovered with the help of state funds and to control up to 34% of resources obtained from privately funded deposits. Royalties were to be raised from 2.5% to 5.0%, severe penalties were envisaged for serious environmental damage and the size of foreign work-forces would be limited to 10%.

In October 2006 a parliamentary motion of no confidence was submitted against the Government: Enkhbold was accused of misconduct in relation to land sales during his tenure of the post of Mayor of Ulan Bator, while the Government was criticized for alleged incompetence and its failure to improve the living standards of the population. However, the motion failed to garner sufficient votes to succeed. In February 2007 Danzandarjaagiin Tuyaa of the MPRP was appointed Minister of Health, to replace Lamjavyn Gündalai of the Party of the People, who had been dismissed. The Minister of Social Welfare and Labour, Luvsangiin Odonchimed of the MPRP, resigned and was replaced by another MPRP member, Damdingiin Demberel. In April Tserengiin Davaadorj was appointed to succeed Bazaryn Jargalsaikhan as Minister of Industry and Trade.

Meanwhile, in preparation for the legislative election of June 2008, the Great Khural approved amendments to the Law on Elections, restoring 26 large multi-candidate constituencies similar to those prevailing at the time of the 1992 legislative election.

In early 2007 it emerged that Tsendiin Nyamdorj, the Chairman (Speaker) of the Great Khural, had re-edited legislation, including the Election Law and the Minerals Law, after the final texts had been approved by the Great Khural. Nyamdorj's explanation was accepted by some of his MPRP colleagues, but, following a Constitutional Court ruling that his actions were unconstitutional, in June he was obliged to resign from his post. He was replaced by the Deputy Chairman, Danzangiin Lündeejantsan. DP Chairman Tsakhiagiin Elbegdorj was injured in a car accident in July, but was able to resume his normal duties later in the year.

At the MPRP's 25th Congress in October 2007, delegates expressed their dissatisfaction with Miyeegombyn Enkhbold's performance by voting to remove him from the chairmanship of the party, in favour of General Secretary Sanjiin Bayar. The members of a new 255-member MPRP Little Khural and 23-member Leadership Council were later announced; in total, 13 of the 19 Leadership Council members elected in 2005 were replaced and three were re-elected. Former MPRP secretary Yondongiin Otgonbayar was elected General Secretary and six new secretaries were approved, including Enkhbold and Nyamdorj. For the first time intra-party political movements and factions were represented by three Leadership Council members; also of note was the inclusion of four women, one of them a Mongolian Kazakh. The reorganization of the Little Khural had been the subject of wide speculation and was regarded as an important stage in the preparation of the final list of MPRP candidates for the legislative election scheduled for June 2008.

An important consequence of these events was Enkhbold's resignation as Prime Minister in early November 2007, thus allowing Bayar's election to the position later in the month. Bayar's first acts included the appointment of Ravdangiin Bold, ambassador to the USA, to the post of head of the Main Directorate of Intelligence and the dismissal of the ministers for disaster reduction and professional inspection, their portfolios passing to the new Deputy Prime Minister, Enkhbold. After the signing of co-operation agreements with the Civil Courage Party and the National New Party, Bayar formed a new Cabinet in December. Among the three female appointees was Civil Courage Party leader Sanjaasürengiin Oyuun, who assumed the role of Minister of Foreign Affairs. Meanwhile, the Mayor and Governor of Ulan Bator, Tsogtyn Batbayar, was replaced in December by Tüdeviin Bilegt, head of the Presidential Secretariat.

Janlavyn Narantsatsralt, Minister of Construction and Urban Development and a former Prime Minister, was killed in a car accident in November 2007. He was replaced by Tserendashiin Tsolmon, who also became Chairman of the National New Party in February 2008. In the same month a new political organization was registered, the Mongolian Democratic Movement Party.

In foreign relations, two important documents outlining Mongolian policy objectives were published in July 1994. Advocating 'political realism', *The Mongolian National Security Concept* emphasized the importance of maintaining a 'balanced relationship' with Russia and the People's Republic of China, while 'strengthening trust and developing all-round good-neighbourly relations and mutually beneficial co-operation with both'. *The Mongolian Foreign Policy Concept* also described as the 'foremost objective' of the country's foreign policy the pursuit of 'friendly relations with Russia and China, and without favouring one or the other to develop co-operation with them in complete equality'. Traditional features and specific aspects of economic co-operation were to be safeguarded. Other priorities listed were: good relations with the USA, Japan, Germany and other highly developed nations of West and East; consolidation of political and economic integration in the Asian region; co-operation with the UN and its various bodies; and sound relations with the newly independent states of eastern Europe and the CIS, as well as with developing countries.

Following the dissolution of the USSR in 1991, co-operation with Russia, the largest of the successor states, continued. During an official visit to Russia in January 1993, President Ochirbat and the Russian President, Boris Yeltsin, issued a joint statement expressing regret at the execution and imprisonment of Mongolian citizens in the USSR during the Stalinist period. Ochirbat and Yeltsin also signed a new 20-year Mongolian-Russian Treaty of Friendship and Co-operation to replace the defunct Mongolian-Soviet treaty of 1986. A similar treaty had been signed with Ukraine in November 1992, during the official visit to Mongolia by Ukrainian President Leonid Kravchuk. In November 2000 the Russian President, Vladimir Putin, stayed overnight in Ulan Bator en route to an Asia-Pacific Economic Co-operation (APEC) conference in Brunei. He was the most senior Russian or Soviet visitor to Mongolia since 1974. Presidents Bagabandi and Putin issued a joint declaration on bilateral co-operation and the protection of each other's national interests. Russia affirmed its commitment to guaranteeing Mongolia's security in connection with its nuclear weapons-free status. Russian Prime Minister Mikhail Kasyanov officially visited Mongolia in late March 2002, to discuss economic and military co-operation, and also the issue of Mongolia's outstanding debt of 11,400m. transferable roubles that the Russian Government claimed it was owed for Soviet aid granted during 1947–91, which the Mongolian Government referred to as the 'big debt'. The two countries had been unable to agree terms for the previous 10 years. Mongolia disagreed with Russia's position that the debt should be paid in full at par value with the US dollar, and there was also Mongolian opposition pressure to offset the cost of damage done to the environment by Soviet military activity. The disagreement disrupted Mongolian-Russian discussions in early 2003 on a new contract for the Erdenet copper-mining joint venture.

However, when the two Prime Ministers did eventually meet in the Russian capital of Moscow in July 2003, a new five-year agreement on the operation of the Erdenet copper enterprise was reached, preserving Mongolia's 51% ownership of stock. Russia agreed that Mongolia had already repaid the cost of building the Erdenet plant. Otherwise, Mongolia's main concern was to reduce Russian taxes on imports of Mongolian goods. At the end of December Russia announced that it had received Mongolia's payment in settlement of the 'big debt'. Russia had waived 98% of the total debt and accepted US $250m. Prime Minister Nambaryn Enkhbayar celebrated a political and diplomatic victory for the MPRP Government, but the details of the settlement remained unclear. DP leader and ex-Prime Minister Enkhsaikhan pointed out that under the Constitution international agreements required approval by the Great Khural. Former Prime Minister Byambasüren revived charges of Soviet price-fixing, stating that from 1976 Mongolia had been paid only 0.39 roubles for every one rouble of the value of its exports to the USSR but had been charged 1.5 roubles for its imports of Soviet goods. In March 2005 the Great Khural established a parliamentary working group to investigate the circumstances of the repayment of the 'big debt'.

Relations with China were good until the onset of the Sino-Soviet dispute in the 1960s. In 1986, however, Sino-Mongolian relations improved significantly when the Chinese Vice-Minister of Foreign Affairs visited Ulan Bator, and the two countries signed agreements on consular relations and trade. In June 1987 a delegation from the Chinese National People's Congress visited Ulan Bator. A treaty concerning the resolution of border disputes was subsequently initialled by representatives of the two Governments.

A new Treaty of Friendship and Co-operation was concluded during a visit to Ulan Bator by Chinese Premier Li Peng in April 1994. An agreement on cultural, economic and technical co-operation was also signed. Mongolia continued to protest in 1995 at the ongoing series of nuclear tests being carried out in China (in the Xinjiang Uygur Autonomous Region). Mongolian human rights groups and the Ulan Bator press supported protests in Inner Mongolia against the arrest by the Chinese authorities of Inner Mongolian human rights activists in December. Prime Minister Jasrai's official visit to China in March 1996, focusing on trade and co-operation, appeared not to have been affected by these events. Relations with China were further consolidated in 1997 by the visits to Ulan Bator of Qiao Shi, the Chairman of the National People's Congress Standing Committee, in April, and of Qian Qichen, the Chinese Deputy Premier and Minister of Foreign Affairs, in August.

In June 2003 Chinese President Hu Jintao visited Ulan Bator, where he had discussions with President Bagabandi and Prime Minister Enkhbayar and addressed the Great Khural on the subject of 'neighbourly partnership of mutual trust' which, besides reiterating respect for each other's independence, sovereignty and territorial integrity, embodied in the handling of bilateral relations 'a spirit of consultation, co-operation and friendship'. China granted Mongolia 50m. yuan for the purposes of building a road across their border from Zamyn-Üüd to Erlian.

Mongolia received three important foreign visitors in mid-1999: President Kim Dae-Jung of the Republic of Korea visited in May, and in July official visits were paid by Prime Minister Keizo Obuchi of Japan and President Jiang Zemin of China. In November Prime Minister Amarjargal visited both North and South Korea and also China. In March 2000 he paid an official visit to the United Kingdom. Nambaryn Enkhbayar's first overseas trip as Prime Minister was to the World Economic Forum in Davos, Switzerland, in January 2001. He subsequently travelled to Japan.

During an official visit to the USA in November 2001, Prime Minister Enkhbayar addressed the UN General Assembly in New York and also had a meeting with President George W. Bush. Enkhbayar reaffirmed the strategic partnership with the USA and urged greater investment in Mongolia. Having condemned the terrorist attacks of 11 September against the USA, he informed President Bush of Mongolia's readiness to allow the use of its air space to help combat terrorism. Following the US military intervention in Iraq in March 2003, soldiers of the Mongolian army's élite battalion were sent to Iraq for tours of duty with the Polish contingent stationed north of Baghdad.

The Secretary-General of the UN, Kofi Annan, paid a brief visit to Mongolia in October 2002. The Dalai Lama visited Ulan Bator in November, travelling via Japan after Russia refused him a visa and Korean Air, the national carrier of South Korea, banned him on the grounds that he posed a security threat. Although his visit was at the invitation of Mongolia's Buddhist leaders rather than of the Government, the Chinese authorities indicated their displeasure by halting rail traffic on their mutual border for 36 hours.

President Natsagiin Bagabandi paid a state visit to China in July 2004, visiting Hainan and the Special Administrative Region of Macao, and discussing economic co-operation with President Hu Jintao. Later in the same month Bagabandi visited the USA, where he met President Bush and signed a Trade and Investment Framework Agreement. US Assistant Secretary of State James Kelly and the Japanese Minister of Foreign Affairs, Yoriko Kawaguchi, visited Ulan Bator in August. Also in October, President Bagabandi paid a state visit to Canada, after a brief stop in the South Korean capital of Seoul. At the invitation of the Chairman of the Presidium of the Supreme People's Assembly, Kim Yong Nam, President Bagabandi visited North Korea in December to promote bilateral co-operation. In January 2005 President Bagabandi visited Viet Nam and Laos. Meanwhile, Great Khural Chairman Nambaryn Enkhbayar was received by Queen Elizabeth and Prince Philip of the United Kingdom in November 2004 during his visit to London for a conference of the Alliance of Religion and Conservation, of which he was President.

The US Secretary of Defense, Donald Rumsfeld, visited Ulan Bator briefly in October 2005. Rumsfeld informed Minister of Defence Sharavdorj that the USA was 'anxious and willing' to help Mongolia enhance its peace-keeping capabilities. In 2005 the USA provided Mongolia with US $18m. in military assistance, including regular training exchanges and bilateral peace-keeping exercises.

Nambaryn Enkhbayar's first official foreign travel after his inauguration as President of Mongolia was in July 2005 to Astana, the capital of Kazakhstan, where he attended a meeting of the Shanghai Co-operation Organization with Russian President Vladimir Putin, Chinese President Hu Jintao and other leaders (Mongolia had been granted observer status). Shortly afterwards he welcomed Turkish Prime Minister Reçep Erdoğan to Ulan Bator. Mongolia's relations with Turkey had been developing on the basis of a co-operation agreement concluded in 1995, which incorporated investment in Mongolia's mining sector.

On the first visit to Mongolia by a sitting US President, in November 2005 George W. Bush spent four hours in Ulan Bator where he had discussions with President Enkhbayar. A joint statement noted that President Bush welcomed Mongolia's progress towards becoming a mature and stable democracy and the country's development of a free market economy, led by the private sector. The two Presidents also emphasized their commitment to combating terrorism.

In February 2006, following a closed meeting in Ulan Bator with foreign donors (the World Bank, the Asian Development Bank (ADB), the IMF, the UN, Japan, the USA and Germany), which urged greater accountability, the US Administration issued a statement noting that the US Agency for International Development had found that corruption in Mongolia was increasing at all levels. The Mongolian Government was to be required to draw up lists of specific actions to combat corruption and to detail all the changes needed within existing law in order that Mongolia might comply with the UN Convention Against Corruption (UNCAC).

Prime Minister Miyeegombyn Enkhbold's first foreign trip was to Japan, in March 2006. President George W. Bush sent a message in February to Mongolia's Kazakhs on the occasion of Kurban Ait (Id al-Adha), the first time a US President had done so. The South Korean President, Roh Moo-Hyun, visited Mongolia in May, and Russian Prime Minister Mikhail Fradkov visited in July. In August Mongolia received Japanese Prime Minister Junichiro Koizumi, who discussed joint efforts to develop energy resources in Mongolia, as well as issues relating to North Korea. During the same month the Dalai Lama paid his seventh visit to Mongolia at the invitation of local Buddhists and presided over religious ceremonies in Ulan Bator.

In November 2006 Enkhbold signed a trade and economic co-operation agreement with China, during his first official visit to Beijing since becoming Prime Minister in January. He also visited Urumqi, in the Xinjiang Uygur Autonomous Region, where Mongolia hoped to open a consulate. At the beginning of December President Enkhbayar toured the Republics of Buryatiya and Kalmykiya, before flying to Moscow for the first state visit by a Mongolian president in 13 years. Following a meeting with President Putin, a treaty on the border regime and trade and economic agreements were signed.

President Enkhbayar's travels in 2007 took him to France, Japan and the United Kingdom, which he visited in April; he met the Duke of Edinburgh, the Queen's husband, and had discussions with Prime Minister Tony Blair. In July visitors to Mongolia included Kim Yong Nam, President of the Presidium of the Supreme People's Assembly of North Korea, and the Amir of Kuwait, Sheikh Sabah al-Ahmad al-Jaber as-Sabah. Other visitors to Mongolia in 2007 included the Presidents of Bulgaria and Laos, the Commander of US Pacific Command and the Chief of Staff of the Armed Forces of Qatar. In January 2008 the Canadian Minister of International Trade, David Emerson, visited Mongolia to discuss the development of bilateral trade and investment, especially in the mining sector.

In August 2007 President Nambaryn Enkhbayar travelled to a summit meeting of the Shanghai Co-operation Organization in Astana, where he had discussions with President Putin, President Nursultan Nazarbayev of Kazakhstan, and other leaders. In October President Enkhbayar visited the USA, meeting the UN General Secretary and President George W. Bush; Enkhbayar and Bush signed a Millennium Challenge contract, which pledged US $285m. in funds for Mongolia. In the following month Enkhbayar visited Kuwait, Qatar and the United Arab Emirates. Meanwhile, Prime Minister Enkhbold paid a visit to Austria in September and to Luxembourg in October. Speaker Lündeejantsan visited Canada in December.

Government

Supreme legislative power is vested in the 76-member Mongolian Great Khural (Assembly), elected by universal adult suffrage for four years. The Great Khural recognizes the President on his election and appoints the Prime Minister and members of the Cabinet, which is the highest executive body. The President, who is directly elected for a term of four years, is Head of State and Commander-in-Chief of the Armed Forces. The revised Law on Elections to the Mongolian Great Khural, which was adopted in December 2005 and published in February 2006, provided for the replacement of the 76 single-seat constituencies with 26 multi-seat constituencies.

In August 2002 the Great Khural approved the reorganization of government agencies, reducing the number of regulatory agencies to eight and executive agencies to 33. Those subordinated to the Prime Minister included the Chief Directorate of Intelligence, State Property Committee, National Radio and Television, and the Montsame News Agency. The coalition Government formed in 2004 increased the number of ministries to 13 and began restructuring the agencies.

Mongolia is divided into 21 provinces (*aimag*) and one municipality (Ulan Bator), with appointed governors and elected local assemblies. However, plans to reduce the number of *aimag* to four (the original pre-revolutionary divisions) and to develop the town of Kharkhorin (the ancient Karakorum) as the future capital were under consideration in 2005.

Defence

Under the 1992 Constitution, the President of Mongolia is, ex officio, Commander-in-Chief of the Armed Forces. The defence roles of the President, the Mongolian Great Khural, the Government and local administrations are defined by the Mongolian Law on Defence (November 1993). Mongolia's *Military Doctrine*, a summary of which was issued by the Great Khural in July 1994, defines the armed forces as comprising general purpose troops, air defence troops, construction troops and civil defence troops. The border troops and internal troops, which are not part of the armed forces, are responsible for protection of the borders and of strategic installations, respectively. As assessed at November 2007 by the International Institute for Strategic Studies, Mongolia's defence forces numbered 8,600, comprising an army of 7,500 (of whom 3,300 were thought to be conscripts), 800 air defence personnel and 300 construction troops. There was a paramilitary force of about 7,200, comprising 1,200 internal security troops and 6,000 border guards. Military service is for 12 months (for males aged 18–25 years), but a system of alternative service is being introduced. In September 2003 the first contingent of Mongolian soldiers was dispatched to serve with coalition forces in Iraq. Defence spending for 2008 was projected at 59,686.9m. tögrög, some 3.1% of total expenditure.

Economic Affairs

In 2006, according to estimates by the World Bank, Mongolia's gross national income (GNI), measured at average 2004–06 prices, was US $2,284m., equivalent to $880 per head (or $2,280 per head on an international purchasing-power parity basis). During 1996–2006, it was estimated, the population increased at an average annual rate of 1.2%, while gross domestic product (GDP) per head increased, in real terms, at an average of 3.7% per year. Overall GDP increased, in real terms, at an average annual rate of 4.9% in 1996–2006. According to revised Asian Development Bank (ADB) estimates published in early 2008, real GDP growth was 8.6% in 2006 and 9.9% in 2007.

Agriculture (including forestry) contributed 18.2% of GDP in 2006. The sector engaged 38.8% of the employed labour force in that year. Animal herding is the main economic activity and is practised throughout the country. Most livestock is privately owned. Following exceptionally severe weather, livestock numbers (sheep, goats, horses, cattle and camels) declined sharply in 2002, to fewer than 23.7m., before steadily recovering to reach some 40m. by the end of 2007. The principal crops are cereals, potatoes and vegetables. Annual grain production reached 138,600 metric tons in 2006, before declining to 114,800 tons in 2007. During 1996–2006, according to figures from the World Bank, the GDP of the agricultural sector increased, in real terms, at an average annual rate of 0.4%. According to the ADB, agricultural GDP increased by 7.5% in 2006 and by an estimated 15.8% in 2007.

Industry (comprising mining, manufacturing, construction and utilities) provided 39.3% of GDP in 2006 and the sector (excluding printing and publishing, but including fishing and logging) engaged 17.3% of the employed labour force in the same year. According to the World Bank, during 1996–2006 industrial GDP increased, in real terms, at an average rate of 4.9% per year. According to the ADB, the industrial sector's GDP increased by 6.9% in 2006 and by 7.1% by 2007.

Mining contributed 29.2% of GDP in 2006, and some 13,700 workers were engaged in the sector in January 2007. Mongolia has significant, largely unexplored, mineral resources and is a leading producer and exporter of copper, gold, molybdenum and fluorspar concentrates. In 2006 the value of exports of copper concentrate increased by more than 90% to US $635.4m., reflecting the rise in world market prices for the commodity, and this trend continued in 2007, with a similar export volume valued at $811m. The copper-molybdenum works at Erdenet, a Mongolian-Russian joint venture, is the most important mining operation in the country. A Canadian company, Ivanhoe Mines, continued to develop the Oyu Tolgoi (Turquoise Hill) mineral deposits at Khanbogd, South Gobi, not only raising its estimates of copper and gold content but also, in 2003, finding plentiful supplies of underground water. Further commitments by Ivanhoe, in strategic partnership with the multinational Rio Tinto group, to develop the site were reported during 2007. Production was scheduled to begin in 2008. Other mineral resources include coal, tungsten, tin, uranium and lead. In 2000 Mongolia's coal reserves were estimated at 150,000m. metric tons. Output of coal rose from 7.5m. tons in 2005 to 8.1m. tons in 2006. Petroleum reserves were discovered in 1994. Extraction of crude petroleum, from the Tamsag basin, commenced in 1997. Mongolia's production of crude petroleum rose from 200,700 barrels in 2005 to 366,800 barrels in 2006. Increased production of both coal and petroleum was reported in 2007. Gold production rose to 24.1 metric tons in 2005, but output declined marginally to 22.6 tons in 2006. According to the ADB, the GDP of the mining sector expanded by an average annual rate of 13.1% in 1995–2006, increasing by 11.0% in 2005 alone. The ADB estimated real growth of 2.7% in the sector's GDP in 2006.

The manufacturing sector accounted for 5.7% of GDP in 2006. Manufacturing industries are based largely on the products of the agricultural and animal husbandry sector. The principal branches of manufacturing include food products, textiles and non-metallic mineral products. However, major reductions in textile output followed the expiry of the World Trade Organization's (WTO's) Multi-Fibre Arrangement (MFA) in December 2004. According to preliminary figures for 2007, production of food products, leather and hides increased during the year, while there was a decline in timber and paper production. Mongolia is one of the world's foremost producers of cashmere, and also manufactures garments, leather goods and carpets. According to figures from the World Bank, manufacturing GDP increased by an annual average of 2.0% in 1996–2006. The sector's GDP contracted by 22.0%, in real terms, in 2005, but a real growth rate of 21.6% was recorded in the sector in 2006.

Energy is derived principally from thermal power stations, fuelled by coal. Most provincial centres have thermal power stations or diesel generators, while minor rural centres generally rely on small diesel generators. In more isolated areas wood, roots, bushes and dried animal dung are used for domestic fuel. The Ulan Bator No. 4 power station, the largest in the country, went into operation in 1985. Its capacity of 380 MW doubled Mongolia's generating capacity. Mongolia imports from Russia electricity and petroleum products, including liquid petroleum gas. In 2006 the cost of Mongolia's imports of fuels and lubricants rose to US $434.6m., thus accounting for 29.3% of the total cost of merchandise imports. According to preliminary reports, the cost of fuel imports increased to more than $500m. in 2007, with more than 95% of this amount allocated to imports of Russian petroleum products.

The services sector contributed 41.5% of GDP in 2006 and engaged an estimated 30.6% of the employed labour force in the same year. During 1996–2006, according to figures from the World Bank, the GDP of the sector increased, in real terms, by an average of 6.0% annually. According to the ADB, the GDP of the services sector increased by 6.1% in 2006 and by 8.9% in 2007. Receipts from tourism were estimated to have increased from US $205m. in 2004 to $223m. in 2005. The number of visitor arrivals reached 385,989 in 2006 (about 46% of arrivals being visitors from the People's Republic of China), rising to an estimated 451,000 in 2007.

In 2006 Mongolia recorded its first ever visible trade surplus, amounting to some US $189m., according to the ADB, and there was an estimated surplus of $218m. (equivalent to 6.9% of GDP in that year) on the current account of the balance of payments. The ADB estimated a visible trade deficit of $25m. for 2007, with a current account surplus ($69m.) equivalent to 1.8% of GDP in that year. In 2007 the principal source of imports was Russia, supplying 34.6% of the total, with the People's Republic of China providing 31.7%. Other significant suppliers were Japan, the Republic of Korea and the Germany. China was the principal market for exports, purchasing 74.4% of the total. Other important purchasers were Canada, the USA, Italy, Russia and the Republic of Korea. The principal imports in 2005 were fuels and lubricants (29.3%) and machinery and vehicles (28.3%). The principal exports in 2005 were copper concentrate (41.2%) and gold.

In 2006 a budget surplus of some 123,000m. tögrög (equivalent to 3.9% of GDP) was achieved, and although a deficit of some 109,000m. tögrög was indicated by provisional budget figures for 2007, a fiscal surplus equivalent to 2.2% of GDP was forecast by the ADB. Mongolia's external debt totalled US $1,327m. at the end of 2005, of which $1,267m. was long-term public debt. In 2004 the cost of debt-servicing was equivalent to 2.9% of the value of exports of goods and services. According to the IMF, the annual rate of inflation averaged 13.7% during 1995–2005; consumer prices rose by 6.0% in 2006, and were reported to have increased by some 9% during 2007. The number of registered unemployed persons decreased from 32,900 (equivalent to some 3.3% of the labour force) in 2006, to 29,900 in 2007. However, the number of unregistered unemployed persons was believed to be far greater.

In 1989 Mongolia joined the Group of 77 (an organization of developing countries, founded under the auspices of UNCTAD, see p. 55, to promote economic co-operation). In February 1991 Mongolia became a member of the Asian Development Bank (ADB, see p. 182) as well as of the IMF and World Bank. In 1994 the European Union (EU, see p. 244) announced the inclusion of Mongolia in TACIS, the EU's programme of technical assistance to the Commonwealth of Independent States. In 1997 Mongolia became a member of the World Trade Organization (WTO, see p. 396). In July 1998 Mongolia was admitted to the ASEAN Regional Forum (ARF, see p. 188), and in May 2000 the country became a member of the European Bank for Reconstruction and Development (EBRD, see p. 239). Mongolia is also a member of the UN Economic and Social Commission for Asia and the Pacific (ESCAP, see p. 35).

The national development plan announced in 2001 aimed to end Mongolia's dependency on nomadic herding. The plan envisaged the building of new towns and the urbanizing of

MONGOLIA

90% of the population during the next 30 years. These towns would be linked by a 2,400-km east–west highway ('the Millennium Road'), which would serve as a development corridor across the country. Following the enactment of legislation to permit the privatization of various state industries, a land privatization law was approved in 2002 (see Recent History). In July 2006 Mongolia became a 'country of operations' of the EBRD. Attention was to focus on support for the country's transition to a market economy. An External Partners Technical Meeting, organized jointly with the World Bank, was convened in Ulan Bator in January 2008. At the end of January the Mongolian legislature approved a draft National Development Policy, encompassing the period to 2021. Meanwhile, higher tax revenues, boosted by a windfall tax on the copper and gold sectors imposed in 2006, enabled a continued improvement in the Government's fiscal balance (although this was also due, in part, to logistical limitations on the Government's ability to enact its capital expenditure programmes). Higher prices for food (especially imported products) contributed to an increase in the rate of inflation, which was reported to have reached 15% at the end of 2007. Despite suggestions that the imposition of the 2006 windfall tax had curtailed growth in production in 2007 and had even encouraged a resurgence in smuggling, strong international prices for gold and copper sustained the performance of the mining sector in 2005–07, while relatively mild winters greatly benefited the agricultural sector. GDP growth was expected to remain close to 10% in 2008, provided that international commodity prices remained buoyant and investor interest in mining projects was maintained. With the incidence of poverty having been estimated at 32.6% in 2006, and with the standards of health care and of education reported to be deteriorating, in the longer term the continued development of the private sector and the improvement of national infrastructure, along with the implementation of sound monetary and fiscal policies, remained essential if high levels of growth were to be sustained.

Education

Ten-year general education is compulsory, beginning at six years of age, and 11-year schooling was being introduced as of early 2005. Pupils may attend vocational-technical schools from the ages of 16 to 18 years. In 2004/05 enrolment in primary schools included 93.3% of pupils in the relevant age-group, while enrolment in secondary schools included 91.8% of pupils. In 2006/07 724 general education schools, with a total enrolment of 596,500 pupils, employed 22,900 teachers. The 44 vocational training schools (some of them private) had a total enrolment of 24,800 in that year. In higher education, in 2006/07 there were 48 state-owned universities and colleges with 93,500 students, and 116 private universities and colleges with 48,500 students. Many Mongolian students continue their academic careers at universities and technical schools in Russia, Germany the United Kingdom and the USA. Government expenditure on education in 2005 amounted to 147,792.2m. tögrög (19.3% of budgetary expenditure). The state budget allocation to the Ministry of Education, Culture and Science for 2008 was 387,271.7m. tögrög (19.8% of planned budgetary expenditure).

Public Holidays

2008: 1 January (New Year), 8–9 February (Tsagaan Sar, lunar new year), 8 March (International Women's Day), 1 June (Children's Day), 11–13 July (Naadam, national sports festival), 26 November (Republic Day).

2009: 1 January (New Year), 25–26 February (Tsagaan Sar, lunar new year), 8 March (International Women's Day), 1 June (Children's Day), 11–13 July (Naadam, national sports festival), 26 November (Republic Day).

Weights and Measures

The metric system is in force.

Statistical Survey

Unless otherwise indicated, revised by Alan J. K. Sanders

Area and Population

AREA, POPULATION AND DENSITY

Area (sq km)	1,564,116*
Population (census results)	
5 January 1989	2,043,400
5 January 2000	
Males	1,177,981
Females	1,195,512
Total	2,373,493
Population (official estimates at 31 December)	
2004	2,533,100
2005	2,562,400
2006	2,594,800
2007	2,635,100
Density (per sq km) at 31 December 2007	1.7

* 603,909 sq miles.

ADMINISTRATIVE DIVISIONS
(estimates at 31 December 2006)

Province (Aimag)	Area ('000 sq km)	Estimated population ('000)	Provincial centre
Arkhangai	55.3	93.3	Tsetserleg
Bayankhongor	116.0	83.8	Bayankhongor
Bayan-Ölgii	45.7	100.1	Ölgii
Bulgan	48.7	60.3	Bulgan
Darkhan-Uul	3.3	87.5	Darkhan
Dornod (Eastern)	123.6	73.6	Choibalsan
Dornogobi (East Gobi)	109.5	54.5	Sainshand
Dundgobi (Central Gobi)	74.7	49.2	Mandalgobi
Gobi-Altai	141.4	60.3	Altai
Gobi-Sümber	5.5	12.3	Choir
Khentii	80.3	71.0	Öndörkhaan
Khovd	76.1	88.5	Khovd
Khövsgöl	100.6	122.1	Mörön
Orkhon	0.8	79.4	Erdenet
Ömnögobi (South Gobi)	165.4	46.5	Dalanzadgad
Övörkhangai	62.9	114.9	Arvaikheer
Selenge	41.2	100.1	Sükhbaatar
Sükhbaatar	82.3	55.6	Baruun Urt
Töv (Central)	74.0	86.4	Zuun mod
Ulan Bator (Ulaanbaatar)*	4.7	994.3	(capital city)
Uvs	69.6	80.5	Ulaangom
Zavkhan	82.5	80.6	Uliastai
Total	**1,564.1**	**2,594.8**	

* Ulan Bator, including Nalaikh, and Bagakhangai and Baganuur districts beyond the urban boundary, has special status as the capital city.

MONGOLIA

ETHNIC GROUPS
(January 2000 census)

	Number	%
Khalh (Khalkha)	1,934,700	81.5
Kazakh (Khasag)	103,000	4.3
Dörvöd (Durbet)	66,700	2.8
Bayad (Bayat)	50,800	2.1
Buryat (Buriat)	40,600	1.7
Dariganga	31,900	1.3
Zakhchin	29,800	1.3
Uriankhai	25,200	1.1
Other ethnic groups	82,600	3.5
Foreign citizens	8,100	0.3
Total	**2,373,500**	**100.0**

PRINCIPAL TOWNS
(December 1999 unless otherwise indicated, estimated population)

Ulan Bator (capital)	1,050,779*	Erdenet	65,700
Darkhan	72,600	Choibalsan	40,900†

* December 2007.
† January 2000 census.

BIRTHS, MARRIAGES AND DEATHS

	Registered live births Number	Rate (per 1,000)	Registered marriages* Number	Rate (per 1,000)	Registered deaths Number	Rate (per 1,000)
1999	49,461	21.0	13,722	10.1	16,105	6.8
2000	48,721	20.4	12,601	9.0	15,472	6.5
2001	49,658	20.5	12,393	8.6	15,999	6.6
2002	46,922	19.1	13,514	9.2	15,857	6.4
2003	45,723	18.4	14,572	9.6	16,006	6.4
2004	45,501	18.1	11,242	7.2	16,404	6.5
2005	45,326	17.8	14,993	9.3	16,480	6.5
2006	49,092	19.0	48,996	19.0	16,682	6.5
2007	55,800	22.0	n.a.	n.a.	n.a.	6.6

* Persons aged 18 years and over.

Expectation of life (years at birth): 65.85 (males 62.59; females 69.38) in 2006 (Source: *Mongolian Statistical Yearbook*).

EMPLOYMENT
('000 employees at 31 December)

	2004	2005	2006
Agriculture and forestry	381.8	386.2	391.4
Industry*	114.2	113.9	118.9
Transport and communications	42.2	42.4	41.2
Construction	39.2	48.9	56.3
Trade	133.7	141.9	160.6
Public administration	46.2	46.7	46.9
Education			
Science, research and development	57.8	58.8	62.0
Health	39.4	39.5	39.3
Total (incl. others)	**950.5**	**968.3**	**1,009.9**

* Comprising manufacturing (except printing and publishing), mining and quarrying, electricity, water, logging and fishing.

Source: *Mongolian Statistical Yearbook*.

Unemployed ('000 registered at 31 December): 35.6 in 2004; 32.9 in 2005; 32.9 in 2006; 29.9 in 2007 (Sources: Asian Development Bank, *Key Indicators of Developing Asian and Pacific Countries*; Mongolian Statistical Directorate).

Health and Welfare

KEY INDICATORS

Total fertility rate (children per woman, 2005)	2.3
Under-5 mortality rate (per 1,000 live births, 2005)	49
HIV/AIDS (% of persons aged 15–49, 2005)	<0.1
Physicians (per 1,000 head, 2003)	2.7
Hospital beds (per 1,000 head, 2003)	7.3
Health expenditure (2004): US $ per head (PPP)	140.9
Health expenditure (2004): % of GDP	6.0
Health expenditure (2004): public (% of total)	66.6
Access to water (% of persons, 2004)	62
Access to sanitation (% of persons, 2004)	59
Human Development Index (2005): ranking	114
Human Development Index (2005): value	0.700

For sources and definitions, see explanatory note on p. vi.

Agriculture

PRINCIPAL CROPS
(metric tons)

	2005	2006	2007
Cereals*	75,500	138,600	114,800
Potatoes	82,800	109,100	114,500
Other vegetables	64,100	70,400	76,500
Hay	845,100	983,300	930,400

* Mostly wheat, but also small quantities of barley and oats.

LIVESTOCK
(at December census)

	2005	2006	2007
Sheep	12,884,500	14,815,100	16,990,100
Goats	13,267,400	15,451,700	18,347,800
Horses	2,029,100	2,114,800	2,239,500
Cattle	1,963,600	2,167,900	2,425,800
Camels	254,200	253,500	260,600
Pigs	22,677	32,761	n.a.
Poultry	141,701	211,700	n.a.

LIVESTOCK PRODUCTS
('000 metric tons, unless otherwise indicated)

	2004	2005	2006
Meat	195.2	183.9	170.7
Beef	53.8	45.3	44.2
Mutton and goat meat	96.2	93.4	88.4
Sheep's wool	13.4	14.2	15.2
Cashmere	3.2	3.7	4.0
Hides and skins ('000)	6,655.2	6,927.1	6,374.0
Milk	406.3	425.9	479.4
Eggs (million)	16.0	21.3	19.0

Source: *Mongolian Statistical Yearbook*.

Forestry

ROUNDWOOD REMOVALS
('000 cubic metres)

	2001	2002	2003
Total	609.9	568.3	576.5

Source: *Mongolian Statistical Yearbook*.

MONGOLIA

SAWNWOOD PRODUCTION
('000 cubic metres, incl. railway sleepers)

	2004	2005	2006
Total	38.7	32.6	28.4

Source: *Mongolian Statistical Yearbook*.

Fishing

(metric tons, live weight)

	2003	2004	2005
Total catch (freshwater fishes)	382	305	366

Source: FAO.

Mining

(metric tons, unless otherwise indicated)

	2004	2005	2006
Salt	258	196	166
Coal	6,865,000	7,517,100	8,074,100
Fluorspar concentrate	148,200	134,100	137,600
Copper concentrate*	371,400	361,600	370,500
Molybdenum concentrate*	2,428	2,528	2,987
Iron ore	33,500	167,700	180,000
Zinc ore	—	22,800	109,900
Gold (kilograms)	19,418	24,122	22,561
Crude petroleum (barrels)	215,700	200,700	366,800

* Figures refer to the gross weight of concentrates. Copper concentrate has an estimated copper content of 35%, while the metal content of molybdenum concentrate is 47%.

Source: *Mongolian Statistical Yearbook*.

Industry

SELECTED PRODUCTS

	2004	2005	2006
Flour ('000 metric tons)	57.8	58.3	63.6
Bread ('000 metric tons)	23.4	22.6	20.4
Confectionery ('000 metric tons)	7.1	8.3	10.2
Sheep's guts ('000 bunches)	385.4	612.3	700.4
Vodka and wine ('000 litres)	9,161.0	7,956.4	10,719.6
Beer ('000 litres)	7,980.7	7,996.9	7,393.0
Soft drinks ('000 litres)	34,032.7	42,260.6	38,813.2
Cashmere (combed) (metric tons)	357.0	581.9	1,064.4
Wool, scoured (metric tons)	1,782.1	900.0	1,100.0
Felt ('000 metres)	67.8	69.1	68.8
Camelhair blankets ('000 metres)	36.8	33.5	34.4
Spun thread (metric tons)	57.4	69.7	38.5
Knitwear ('000 garments)	7,989.9	3,448.5	4,529.3
Trousers ('000)	9,379.9	7,116.3	5,910.9
Shirts ('000)	12,042.4	10,366.0	7,208.9
Carpets ('000 sq metres)	690.4	586.9	606.3
Leather footwear ('000)	3.0	3.0	4.9
Felt footwear ('000 pairs)	4.9	10.5	7.8
Surgical syringes (million)	24.4	20.9	21.9
Bricks (million)	12.5	14.6	22.2
Lime ('000 metric tons)	30.0	81.2	60.4
Cement ('000 metric tons)	61.9	111.9	140.8
Ferroconcrete ('000 cu metres)	2.4	4.8	2.7
Copper (metric tons)	2,376.1	2,474.5	2,618.4
Electricity (million kWh)	3,303.4	3,418.9	3,544.2

Sources: *Mongolian Statistical Yearbook*; Ministry of Industry and Trade (Ulan Bator).

Finance

CURRENCY AND EXCHANGE RATES

Monetary Units
100 möngö = 1 tögrög (tughrik).

Sterling, Dollar and Euro Equivalents (31 December 2007)
£1 sterling = 2,344.00 tögrög;
US $1 = 1,170.00 tögrög;
€1 = 1,722.36 tögrög;
10,000 tögrög = £4.27 = $8.55 = €5.81.

Average Exchange Rate (tögrög per US $)
2005   1,205.22
2006   1,165.37
2007   1,170.97

BUDGET
(million tögrög)

Revenue	2004	2005	2006
Tax revenue	537,490.7	635,564.4	1,056,570.5
Income tax	136,176.8	168,078.0	462,911.3
Excise duty	70,283.2	78,959.2	100,131.8
Taxes on goods and services	229,638.1	254,017.5	331,315.2
Value-added tax	153,247.5	169,118.5	225,146.4
Other current revenue	111,589.0	128,797.8	213,703.0
Social insurance	84,471.9	98,343.2	115,498.6
Grants and transfers	22,828.7	28,147.6	29,159.3
Foreign aid	6,051.8	4,290.7	4,685.2
Total	671,908.4	792,509.8	1,299,432.7

Expenditure	2004	2005	2006
Current expenditure	511,400.7	566,169.9	938,053.3
Goods and services	323,867.3	350,310.1	646,160.6
Wages and salaries	119,428.2	132,476.2	182,819.4
Interest payments	22,069.6	20,682.8	18,081.7
Subsidies and transfers	165,463.8	195,176.9	273,811.1
Capital expenditure	90,944.5	77,145.0	159,618.7
Foreign financed	22,176.4	10,418.3	8,684.1
Lending (net)	108,900.4	74,490.3	78,986.9
Total	711,245.5	717,805.2	1,176,658.9

Source: *Mongolian Statistical Yearbook*.

2007 (million tögrög, revised forecasts): Total revenue 1,617,213.0; Total expenditure 1,725,971.7 (Source: *Töriin Medeelel*—State Information).

2008 (million tögrög, forecasts): Total revenue 1,718,115.4; Total expenditure 1,946,579.2 (Source: *Töriin Medeelel*—State Information).

INTERNATIONAL RESERVES
(US $ million at 31 December)

	2005	2006	2007
Gold (national valuation)	—	134.57	198.96
IMF special drawing rights	0.02	0.01	0.02
Reserve position in IMF	0.19	0.20	0.21
Foreign exchange	430.10	925.81	1,195.40
Total	430.31	1,060.59	1,394.59

Source: IMF, *International Financial Statistics*.

MONEY SUPPLY
(million tögrög at 31 December)

	2005	2006	2007
Currency outside banks	152,369	185,127	283,325
Demand deposits at deposit money banks	116,755	146,777	307,146
Total money	269,124	331,903	590,472

Source: IMF, *International Financial Statistics*.

MONGOLIA

COST OF LIVING
(Consumer Price Index at December; base: December 2005 = 100)

	2003	2004	2006
Foods	74.2	86.0	103.3
Clothing and footwear	99.1	100.4	107.5
Rent and utilities	92.3	95.9	108.7
All items (incl. others)	82.3	91.4	106.0

Source: *Mongolian Statistical Yearbook*.

NATIONAL ACCOUNTS

Expenditure on the Gross Domestic Product
('000 million tögrög at current prices, unless otherwise indicated)

	2004	2005	2006
Government final consumption expenditure	322.0	354.4	467.4
Private final consumption expenditure	1,187.3	1,398.5	1,482.4
Increase in stocks	81.4	61.0	90.9
Gross fixed capital formation	753.9	987.4	1,052.0
Total domestic expenditure	2,344.6	2,801.3	3,092.7
Exports of goods and services } *Less* Imports of goods and services	−230.3	−108.8	135.4
Sub-total	2,114.3	2,692.5	3,228.1
Statistical discrepancy*	−168.7	−168.1	−55.6
GDP in purchasers' values	1,945.6	2,524.3	3,172.4
GDP at constant 2000 prices	1,256.8	1,346.1	1,459.0

* Referring to the difference between the sum of the expenditure components and official estimates of GDP, compiled from the production approach.

Source: Asian Development Bank, *Key Indicators of Developing Asian and Pacific Countries*.

Gross Domestic Product by Economic Activity
(million tögrög at current prices)

	2004	2005	2006
Agriculture	422,503.7	525,464.6	594,817.6
Fishing	68.1	105.8	105.8
Mining	365,682.3	615,735.0	952,985.7
Manufacturing	99,579.6	130,581.2	185,509.7
Electricity, heating and water supply	61,187.3	76,024.1	79,432.8
Construction	51,713.1	60,288.4	64,725.7
Trade	455,030.5	534,253.4	601,024.0
Hotels and restaurants	14,749.8	19,165.9	26,812.9
Transport and communications	241,881.9	303,982.1	345,738.5
Finance	81,484.9	99,503.1	109,638.2
Real estate	28,385.3	28,818.9	34,201.8
Public administration, defence and social security	70,806.8	79,597.0	101,884.1
Education, health and other services	117,506.2	130,665.1	170,568.9
Sub-total	2,010,579.5	2,604,184.6	3,267,445.6
Less Financial intermediation services indirectly measured	64,930.0	79,858.5	95,000.0
Total	1,945,649.5	2,524,326.1	3,172,445.6

Source: *Mongolian Statistical Yearbook*.

BALANCE OF PAYMENTS
(US $ million)

	2004	2005	2006
Exports of goods f.o.b.	872.1	1,068.6	1,545.2
Imports of goods f.o.b.	−901.0	−1,097.4	−1,356.7
Trade balance	−28.9	−28.8	188.5
Exports of services	338.4	414.5	485.8
Imports of services	−503.7	−476.0	−523.2
Balance on goods and services	−194.2	−90.8	151.0
Other income received	16.5	10.7	17.4
Other income paid	−27.7	−61.4	−161.9
Balance on goods, services and income	−205.3	−141.5	6.5
Current transfers received	230.9	177.6	179.8
Current transfers paid	−50.2	−41.2	−77.4
Current balance	−24.6	−5.1	108.9
Direct investment from abroad	92.9	184.6	344.0
Portfolio investment assets	−2.5	n.a.	n.a.
Portfolio investment liabilities	−50.0	n.a.	n.a.
Other investment assets	−132.2	−124.8	−223.4
Other investment liabilities	68.6	−14.2	60.8
Net errors and omissions	1.4	−74.9	−7.8
Overall balance	−46.3	−34.4	282.5

Source: IMF, *International Financial Statistics*.

External Trade

PRINCIPAL COMMODITIES
(US $ million, distribution by SITC)

Imports c.i.f.	2004	2005	2006
Food and live animals	125.2	121.5	142.6
Raw materials	7.7	8.7	9.8
Fuels and lubricants	227.6	314.7	434.6
Chemical products	50.6	59.7	81.0
Manufactured goods, classified chiefly by material	210.7	206.9	222.7
Machinery and vehicles	303.7	371.3	419.7
Miscellaneous manufactured articles	61.7	69.7	138.1
Total (incl. others)	1,021.1	1,184.3	1,485.6

Exports f.o.b.	2004	2005	2006
Food and live animals	16.1	12.7	26.6
Raw materials	400.0	515.9	997.4
Copper concentrate	284.3	326.2	635.4
Fuels and lubricants	25.6	40.2	70.4
Chemical products	1.0	1.1	1.6
Manufactured goods, classified chiefly by material	38.3	46.7	66.6
Machinery and vehicles	3.0	8.0	17.1
Miscellaneous manufactured articles	142.2	108.2	92.1
Gold, unwrought or in semi-manufactured forms	243.3	331.6	270.5
Total (incl. others)	869.7	1,064.9	1,542.8

Source: *Mongolian Statistical Yearbook*.

PRINCIPAL TRADING PARTNERS
(US $ million)

Imports c.i.f.	2004	2005	2006
China, People's Republic	257.2	307.3	415.0
Japan	75.0	75.5	97.6
Kazakhstan	26.3	40.5	49.8
Korea, Republic	61.2	63.7	82.5
Russia	341.9	417.9	547.8
USA	46.5	40.1	44.1
Total (incl. others)	1,021.1	1,184.3	1,485.6

MONGOLIA

Exports f.o.b.	2004	2005	2006
Canada	14.7	122.1	171.2
China, People's Republic	413.9	514.2	1,050.2
Italy	17.3	24.8	40.4
Russia	20.6	27.2	45.1
United Kingdom	137.4	87.1	38.6
USA	156.3	152.5	119.0
Total (incl. others)	869.7	1,064.9	1,542.8

2007 (US $ million): Total imports 2,117.3; total exports 1,888.9.

Source: *Mongolian Statistical Yearbook*.

Transport

FREIGHT CARRIED
('000 metric tons)

	2005	2006	2007
Rail	15,586.3	14,779.8	14,100.0
Road	9,617.4	9,189.4	9,198.1
Air	2.0	2.1	1.9
Total (incl. other)	25,206.2	23,971.3	23,300.0

Source: Mongolian Statistical Directorate.

PASSENGERS CARRIED
(million)

	2005	2006	2007
Rail	4.2	4.3	4.5
Road	188.2	190.7	205.0
Air*	0.3	0.4	0.4
Total	192.7	195.4	209.9

* MIAT only.

Source: *Mongolian Statistical Yearbook*.

RAILWAYS
(traffic)

	2005	2006	2007
Passengers carried ('000)	4,227.1	4,322.8	4,500.0
Freight carried ('000 metric tons)	15,586.3	14,779.8	14,100.0
Freight ton-km (million)	9,947.7	9,225.6	n.a.

Source: Mongolian Statistical Directorate.

ROAD TRAFFIC
(motor vehicles in use)

	2004	2005	2006
Passenger cars	79,691	87,792	94,442
Buses and coaches	10,645	11,067	11,726
Lorries, special vehicles and tankers	30,082	32,325	34,704

2007: Total vehicles 162,000.

Source: Mongolian Statistical Directorate.

CIVIL AVIATION
(traffic on scheduled services)

	2005	2006	2007
Passengers carried ('000)	335.3	364.8	388.3
Freight carried (tons)	2,015.5	2,117.5	1,900.0

Source: Mongolian Statistical Directorate.

Tourism

FOREIGN ARRIVALS BY NATIONALITY

Country	2004	2005	2006
China, People's Republic	139,283	170,345	178,941
France	5,545	5,822	5,237
Germany	8,769	8,168	8,576
Japan	13,092	12,952	16,707
Korea, Republic	26,602	30,787	39,930
Russia	53,917	57,926	79,163
United Kingdom	4,948	5,206	5,893
USA	9,431	10,153	11,377
Total (incl. others)	300,538	338,715	385,989

Source: *Mongolian Statistical Yearbook*.

Tourism receipts (US $ million, incl. passenger transport): 154 in 2003; 205 in 2004; 223 in 2005 (Source: World Tourism Organization).

Communications Media

	2004	2005	2006
Television receivers ('000 in use)	290.0	320.0	362.5
Cable television subscribers ('000)	64.1	77.3	81.8
Telephones ('000 main lines in use)	152.6	160.5	156.6
Mobile cellular telephones ('000 subscribers)	445.1	570.9	770.1
Internet users ('000)	20.4	22.0	26.0
Personal computers ('000 in use)	60.0	85.0	99.6
Books (million printers' sheets)	34.8	n.a.	n.a.
Newspapers (million printers' sheets)	68.7	n.a.	n.a.

2007: 150,000 main telephone lines in use; 1,175,100 mobile cellular telephone subscribers.

Book production (1994): 128 titles; 640,000 copies.

Newspapers (titles): 170 in 2004 (daily 6, non-daily 164).

Periodicals (titles): 60 in 2004.

Sources: mainly *Mongolian Statistical Yearbook*.

Education

(2006/07)

	Institutions	Teachers	Students ('000)
General education schools:			
Primary (grades 1–3)	71		239.3
Incomplete secondary (grades 4–8)	172	22,900	216.9
Complete secondary (grades 9–10)	499		86.3
Vocational schools			
State-owned	40	1,300	23.9
Private	4		0.9
Universities			
State-owned	11		66.3
Private	3	6,800	8.1
Other higher education			
State-owned	37		27.2
Private	113		40.4

Note: In addition, 700 students were studying abroad through inter-governmental agreements.

Pre-school institutions (2007): 768 kindergartens attended by 100,400 infants.

Source: Ministry of Education, Culture and Science (Ulan Bator).

Adult literacy rate (UNESCO estimates): 97.8% (males 98.0%; females 97.5%) in 2000 (Source: UNESCO Institute for Statistics).

Directory

The Constitution

The Constitution was adopted on 13 January 1992 and came into force on 12 February of that year. It proclaims Mongolia (*Mongol Uls*), with its capital at Ulan Bator (Ulaanbaatar), to be an independent sovereign republic which ensures for its people democracy, justice, freedom, equality and national unity. It recognizes all forms of ownership of property, including land, and affirms that a 'multi-structured economy' will take account of 'universal trends of world economic development and national conditions'.

The 'citizen's right to life' is qualified by the death penalty for serious crimes, and the law provides for the imposition of forced labour. Freedom of residence and travel within the country and abroad may be limited for security reasons. The citizens' duties are to respect the Constitution and the rights and interests of others, pay taxes, and serve in the armed forces, as well as the 'sacred duty' to work, safeguard one's health, bring up one's children and protect the environment.

Supreme legislative power is vested in the Mongolian Great Khural (Assembly), a single chamber with 76 members elected by universal adult suffrage for a four-year term, with a Chairman and Vice-Chairman elected from amongst the members. The Great Khural recognizes the President on his election and appoints the Prime Minister and members of the Cabinet. A presidential veto of a decision of the Great Khural can be overruled by a two-thirds majority of the Khural. Decisions are taken by a simple majority.

The President is Head of State and Commander-in-Chief of the Armed Forces. He must be an indigenous citizen at least 45 years old who has resided continuously in Mongolia for the five years before election. Presidential candidates are nominated by parties with seats in the Great Khural; the winning candidate in general presidential elections is President for a four-year term.

The Cabinet is the highest executive body and drafts economic, social and financial policy, takes environmental protection measures, strengthens defence and security, protects human rights and implements foreign policy for a four-year term.

The Supreme Court, headed by the Chief Justice, is the highest judicial organ. Judicial independence is protected by the General Council of Courts. The Procurator General, nominated by the President, serves a six-year term.

Local administration in the 21 *aimag* (provinces) and Ulan Bator is effected on the basis of 'self-government and central guidance', comprising local khurals of representatives elected by citizens and governors (*zasag darga*), nominated by the Prime Minister to serve four-year terms.

The Constitutional Court, which guarantees 'strict observance' of the Constitution, consists of nine members nominated for a six-year term, three each by the Great Khural, the President and the Supreme Court. It accepts petitions from the public.

The first amendments to the Constitution, adopted by the Mongolian Great Khural in December 2000, despite opposition over procedure from the Constitutional Court, were finally approved by President Bagabandi in May 2001. The main effects of the amendments were to clarify the method of appointment of Prime Ministers, enable decision-making by a simple majority vote, and shorten the minimum length of sessions of the Khural from 75 days to 50.

The Government

PRESIDENCY

President and Commander-in-Chief of the Armed Forces: NAMBARYN ENKHBAYAR (elected 22 May 2005; inaugurated 24 June 2005).
Head of Presidential Secretariat: (vacant).

NATIONAL SECURITY COUNCIL

The President heads the National Security Council; the Prime Minister and the Chairman of the Mongolian Great Khural are its members. The Secretary is the President's national security adviser.
Chairman: NAMBARYN ENKHBAYAR.
Secretary: PALAMYN SÜNDEV.
Members: DANZANGIIN LÜNDEEJANTSAN, SANJAAGIIN (SANJIIN) BAYAR.

CABINET
(April 2008)

Prime Minister: SANJAAGIIN (SANJIIN) BAYAR.
Deputy Prime Minister: MIYEEGOMBYN ENKHBOLD.

General Ministries
Minister of Foreign Affairs: SANJAASÜRENGIIN OYUUN.
Minister of Finance: CHÜLTEMIIN ULAAN.
Minister of Justice and Home Affairs: TSENDIIN MÖNKH-ORGIL.

Sectoral Ministries
Minister of Nature and the Environment: GANJKHUYAGIIN SHIILEGDAMBA.
Minister of Defence: JAMYANDORJIIN BATKHUYAG.
Minister of Education, Culture and Science: NORDOVYN BOLORMAA.
Minister of Construction and Urban Development: TSERENDASHIIN TSOLMON.
Minister of Roads, Transport and Tourism: RADNAABAZARYN RASH.
Minister of Social Welfare and Labour: DAMDINGIIN DEMBEREL.
Minister of Industry and Trade: KHALZKHÜÜGIIN NARANKHÜÜ.
Minister of Fuel and Power: CHIMEDIIN KHÜRELBAATAR.
Minister of Food and Agriculture: TSERENDORJIIN GANKHUYAG.
Minister of Health: BAYAMBAAGIIN BATSEREEDEN.
Head of Government Affairs Directorate: NYAMAAGIIN ENKHBOLD.

MINISTRIES AND GOVERNMENT DEPARTMENTS

All Ministries and Government Departments are in Ulan Bator.
Prime Minister's Office: Government Palace, Sükhbaataryn Talbai 1, Ulan Bator; tel. (11) 322356; fax (11) 328329.
Ministry of Construction and Urban Development: Government Bldg 12, Barilgachdyn Talbai 3, Chingeltei District, Ulan Bator; tel. (11) 261718; fax (11) 322904; e-mail web@mcud.pmis.gov.mn; internet www.mcud.gov.mn.
Ministry of Defence: Government Bldg 7, Dandaryn Gudamj 51, Bayanzürkh District, Ulan Bator; tel. (11) 458495; fax (11) 451727; e-mail mdef@mdef.pmis.gov.mn; internet www.mdef.pmis.gov.mn.
Ministry of Education, Culture and Science: Government Bldg 3, Baga Toiruu 44, Sükhbaatar District, Ulan Bator; tel. (11) 262480; fax (11) 323158; e-mail mecs@mecs.pmis.gov.mn; internet www.mecs.pmis.gov.mn.
Ministry of Finance: Government Bldg 2, Negdsen Ündestnii Gudamj 5/1, Chingeltei District, Ulan Bator; tel. and fax (11) 264891; internet www.mof.gov.mn.
Ministry of Food and Agriculture: Government Bldg 9, Enkh Taivny Örgön Chölöö 16A, Bayanzürkh District, Ulan Bator; tel. (11) 262376; fax (11) 453121; e-mail mofa@mofa.gov.mn; internet www.mofa.gov.mn.
Ministry of Foreign Affairs: Enkh Taivny Örgön Chölöö 7A, Sükhbaatar District, Ulan Bator; tel. (11) 262788; fax (11) 322127; e-mail mongmer@magicnet.mn; internet www.mongolia-foreign-policy.net.
Ministry of Fuel and Power: Government Bldg 2, Negdsen Ündestnii Gudamj 5/2, Chingeltei District, Ulan Bator; tel. and fax (11) 330627.
Ministry of Health: Government Bldg 8, Olimpiin Gudamj 2, Sükhbaatar District, Ulan Bator; tel. (11) 261742; fax (11) 320916; e-mail moh@moh.mng.net; internet www.moh.mn.
Ministry of Industry and Trade: Block A, Government Bldg 2, Negdsen Ündestnii Gudamj 5/1, Chingeltei District, Ulan Bator; tel. (11) 261529; fax (11) 322595; e-mail mit@mit.pmis.gov.mn; internet www.mit.pmis.gov.mn.
Ministry of Justice and Home Affairs: Government Bldg 5, Khudaldaany Gudamj 6/1, Chingeltei District, Ulan Bator; tel. (11) 267014; fax (11) 325225; e-mail admin@mojha.gov.mn; internet www.mojha.gov.mn.
Ministry of Nature and the Environment: Government Bldg 3, Baga Toiruu 44, Sükhbaatar District, Ulan Bator; tel. (11) 265615; fax (11) 321401; internet www.mne.mn.
Ministry of Roads, Transport and Tourism: Government Bldg 2, Negdsen Ündestnii Gudamj 5/2, Chingeltei District, Ulan Bator; tel. (11) 310597; fax (11) 310612; e-mail info@mrtt.pmis.gov.mn; internet www.mrtt.pmis.gov.mn.
Ministry of Social Welfare and Labour: Government Bldg 2, Negdsen Ündestnii Gudamj 5/1, Chingeltei District, Ulan Bator; tel. (11) 324918; fax (11) 328634; e-mail obaigalmaa@mswl.gov.mn; internet www.mswl.pmis.gov.mn.

MONGOLIA

Government Affairs Directorate (Cabinet Secretariat): Government Palace, Sükhbaataryn Talbai 1, Ulan Bator; tel. and fax (11) 310011; internet www.pmis.gov.mn/cabinet.

President and Legislature

PRESIDENT

Office of the President: Government Palace, Sükhbaataryn Talbai, Ulan Bator; fax (11) 311121; internet www.president.mn.

Election, 22 May 2005

Candidate	Votes	%
Nambaryn Enkhbayar (MPRP)	495,975	53.46
Mendsaikhany Enkhsaikhan (Democratic Party)	182,990	19.73
Bazarsadyn Jargalsaikhan (Republican Party)	129,278	13.94
Badarchiin Erdenebat (Motherland Party)	106,762	11.51

MONGOLIAN GREAT KHURAL

Under the fourth Constitution, which came into force in February 1992, the single-chamber Mongolian Great Khural is the State's supreme legislative body. With 76 members elected for a four-year term, the Great Khural must meet for at least 50 working days in every six months. Its Chairman may act as President of Mongolia when the President is indisposed.

Chairman: DANZANGIIN LÜNDEEJANTSAN.
Vice-Chairman: DOLOONJINGIIN IDEVTKHEN.
General Secretary: NAMSRAIJAVYN LUVSANJAV.

General Election, 27 June 2004

Party	Seats
Mongolian People's Revolutionary Party (MPRP)	36
Motherland Democracy (MD) coalition*	34
Mongolian Republican Party	1
Independents†	3
Undeclared‡	2
Total	76

* Comprising the Democratic Party (DP), the 'Motherland' Mongolian Democratic New Socialist Party (MDNSP) and the Civil Courage Republican Party.
† All three candidates were DP members who stood independently.
‡ In two constituencies the declaration of the final results of voting was delayed. The result in one constituency was declared in February 2005, the seat being awarded to the MPRP; the final result in the other seat was confirmed in favour of the MD at the end of September 2005. As of August 2007, the Great Khural membership included members of the National New Party and the Party of the People who had resigned from the DP.

Election Commission

General Election Committee: Government Bldg 11, Sambuugiin Gudamj 11, Ulan Bator 38; tel. (11) 263383; e-mail gecm@mongol.net; internet www.gec.gov.mn; f. 1992; Chair. BATAAGIIN BATTULGA.

Political Organizations

Civil Courage Party (CCP): Rm 1, Altai College, Sükhbaatar District, Ulan Bator (CPOB 37); tel. and fax (11) 319006; e-mail oyun@mail.parl.gov.mn; f. 2002; est. by merger of the Civil Courage Party and Mongolian Republican Party; merged with Mongolian National Solidarity Party in April 2008; also known as Citizens' Will; 53,000 mems (2008); Chair. SANJAASÜRENGIIN OYUUN; Sec.-Gen. MÖNKHCHULUUNY ZORIGT.

Democratic Party (DP): Sükhbaataryn Talbai, Ulan Bator; internet www.demparty.mn; f. 2000; est. by amalgamation of the Mongolian National Democratic Party, Mongolian Social-Democratic Party, Mongolian Democratic Party, Mongolian Democratic Renewal Party and the Mongolian Believers' Democratic Party; Mongolian Social-Democratic Party re-established as an independent party in Dec. 2004; c. 170,000 mems. (May 2002); Chair. TSAKHIAGIIN ELBEGDORJ; Sec.-Gen. DAMBYN DORLIGJAV.

Mongolian Democratic Party (MDP): Ulan Bator; f. 1990; merged in Oct. 1992 with other parties to form the Mongolian National Democratic Party (MNDP); reconstituted in Jan. 2000, the party won no seats in the 2000 elections, and in Dec. 2000 most members merged with the MDNP and other parties to form the Democratic Party (DP); a splinter group opposed to the merger tried unsuccessfully to challenge the legal status of the DP and then elected a new MDP leadership; Chair. DAMDINDORJIIN NINJ.

Mongolian Green Party: Erkh Chölöönii Gudamj 11, Ulan Bator (POB 38/51); tel. (11) 323871; fax (11) 458859; f. 1990; political wing of the Alliance of Greens; 5,000 mems (March 1997); Chair. D. ENKHBAT.

Mongolian Liberal Party: internet www.liberal.mn; f. 1999 as Mongolian Civil Democratic New Liberal Party, renamed 2004; ruling body Little Khural of 90 mems with Leadership Council of nine; Chair. D. BANZRAGCH.

Mongolian People's Revolutionary Party (MPRP): Baga Toiruu 37/1, Ulan Bator; tel. (11) 320432; fax (11) 320432; e-mail contact@mprp.mn; internet www.mprp.mn; f. 1921; est. as Mongolian People's Party; c. 161,000 mems (2006); ruling body Party Baga Khural (255 mems at Oct. 2007), which elects the Leadership Council; Chair. SANJAAGIIN (SANJIIN) BAYAR; Gen. Sec. YONDONGIIN OTGONBAYAR.

Mongolian Republican Party: c/o The Mongolian Great Khural, Ulan Bator; this party was re-registered in 2004 after the split in the leadership of the Civil Courage Party (see above); Chair. BAZARSADYN JARGALSAIKHAN.

Mongolian Social-Democratic Party (MSDP): Ulan Bator; re-formed and registered January 2005; Chair. ARYAAGIIN GANBAATAR; Gen. Sec. TS. SAINBAYAR.

Mongolian Traditional United Party: Huvisgalchdyn Örgön Chölöö 26, Ulan Bator; tel. (11) 325745; fax (11) 342692; also known as the United Heritage (conservative) Party; f. 1993; est. as an amalgamation of the United Private Owners' Party and the Independence Party; 14,000 mems (1998); ruling body General Political Council; Gen. Sec. BATDELGERIIN BATBOLD.

Motherland Party: Erel Co, Bayanzürkh District, Ulan Bator; f. 1998; fmrly Mongolian Democratic New Socialist Party, name changed as above Jan. 2005; amalgamated with Mongolian Workers' Party 1999; 110,000 mems (May 2002); Chair. BADARCHIIN ERDENEBAT.

National New Party: NNP Bldg, Baga Toiruu 26, 6th Sub-district, Sükhbaatar District, Ulan Bator (POB 46/252); tel. and fax (11) 321819; f. 2006; est. after a split in the leadership of the Democratic Party upon the formation of the national solidarity government; Chair. TSERENDASHIIN TSOLMON.

Party of the People: c/o The Mongolian Great Khural, Ulan Bator; tel. 99681212; e-mail info@ardtumen.mn; f. Dec. 2005 by fmr member of Democratic Party; 3,000 mems; Pres. LAMJAVYN GÜNDALAI.

Diplomatic Representation

EMBASSIES IN MONGOLIA

Bulgaria: Olimpiin Gudamj 8, Ulan Bator (CPOB 702); tel. (11) 322841; fax (11) 324841; e-mail posolstvobg@magicnet.mn; Ambassador MIRCHO IVANOV.

China, People's Republic: Zaluuchuudyn Örgön Chölöö 5, Ulan Bator (CPOB 672); tel. (11) 320955; fax (11) 311943; internet mn.chineseembassy.org; Ambassador YU HONGYAO.

Cuba: Negdsen Ündestnii Gudamj 18, Ulan Bator (CPOB 710); tel. (11) 323778; fax (11) 327709; Ambassador EDUARDO CASTELLANOS SOTO.

Czech Republic: Olimpiin Gudamj 12, Ulan Bator (CPOB 665); tel. (11) 321886; fax (11) 323791; e-mail czechemb@magicnet.mn; internet www.mzv.cz/ulaanbaatar; Ambassador (vacant).

France: 3 Peace Ave, Ulan Bator (CPOB 687); tel. (11) 324519; fax (11) 319176; e-mail ambafrance@magicnet.mn; internet www.ambafrance-mn.org; Ambassador PATRICK CHRISMANT.

Germany: Negdsen Ündestnii Gudamj 7, Ulan Bator (CPOB 708); tel. (11) 323325; fax (11) 323905; internet www.ulan-bator.diplo.de; Ambassador PIUS A. FISCHER.

India: Zaluuchuudyn Örgön Chölöö 10, Ulan Bator (CPOB 691); tel. (11) 329522; fax (11) 329532; e-mail indembmongolia@magicnet.mn; Ambassador YOGESHWAR VARMA.

Japan: Olimpiin Gudamj 8, Ulan Bator (CPOB 1011); tel. (11) 320777; fax (11) 313332; e-mail eojmongol@magicnet.mn; internet www.eojmongolia.mn; Ambassador YASUYOSHI ICHIHASHI.

Kazakhstan: Diplomatic Corps Bldg 95, Apartment 2-11, Chingeltei District, Ulan Bator (CPOB 291); tel. (11) 312240; fax (11) 312204; e-mail kzemby@mbox.mn; Ambassador ORMAN NURBAYEV.

MONGOLIA   *Directory*

Korea, Democratic People's Republic: Khuvisgalchdyn Gudamj, Ulan Bator (CPOB 1015); tel. (11) 326153; fax (11) 330529; Ambassador PAK JONG DO.

Korea, Republic: Olimpiin Gudamj 10, Ulan Bator (CPOB 1039); tel. (11) 321548; fax (11) 311157; Ambassador PARK JIN-HO.

Laos: Ikh Toiruu 59, Ulan Bator (CPOB 1030); tel. (11) 322834; fax (11) 321048; Ambassador PENG INTARAT.

Poland: Diplomatic Corps Bldg 95, Apartment 66, Ulan Bator (CPOB 1049); tel. (11) 320641; fax (11) 320576; e-mail polkonsulat@magicnet.mn; Ambassador ZBIGNIEW JERZY KULAK.

Russia: Enkh Taivny Gudamj 6-A, Ulan Bator (CPOB 661); tel. (11) 327191; fax (11) 327018; Ambassador BORIS ALEKSANDROVICH GOVORIN.

Turkey: Enkh Taivny Örgön Chölöö 5, Ulan Bator (CPOB 1009); tel. (11) 311200; fax (11) 313992; Ambassador AHMET ASIM ARAR.

United Kingdom: Enkh Taivny Gudamj 30, Ulan Bator 13 (CPOB 703); tel. (11) 458133; fax (11) 458036; Ambassador (vacant).

USA: Ikh Toiruu 59/1, Ulan Bator (CPOB 1021); tel. (11) 329095; fax (11) 320776; e-mail webmaster@us-mongolia.com; internet mongolia.usembassy.gov; Ambassador MARK C. MINTON.

Viet Nam: Enkh Taivny Örgön Chölöö 47, Ulan Bator (CPOB 670); tel. (11) 458917; fax (11) 458923; Ambassador UONG HUY THANH.

Judicial System

Under the fourth Constitution, judicial independence is protected by the General Council of Courts, consisting of the Chief Justice (Chairman of the Supreme Court), the Chairman of the Constitutional Court, the Procurator General, the Minister of Justice and Home Affairs and others. The Council nominates the members of the Supreme Court for approval by the Great Khural. The Chief Justice is chosen from among the members of the Supreme Court and approved by the President for a six-year term. Routine civil, criminal and administrative cases are handled by 30 rural district and inter-district courts and eight urban district courts. There are 22 appellate courts at provincial and capital city level. Some legal cases are required by law to be dealt with by the Supreme Court, appellate courts or special courts (military, railway etc.). The Procurator General and his deputies, who play an investigatory role, are nominated by the President and approved by the Great Khural for six-year terms.

Chief Justice: SODNOMDARJAAGIIN BATDELGER.

Procurator General: MONGOLYN ALTANKHUYAG.

Religion

The 1992 Constitution maintains the separation of Church and State. The Law on State-Church Relations (of November 1993) sought to make Buddhism the predominant religion and restricted the dissemination of beliefs other than Buddhism, Islam and shamanism. During the early years of communist rule Mongolia's traditional Mahayana Buddhism was virtually destroyed. In the early 1990s some 2,000 lamas established small communities at the sites of 120 former monasteries, temples and religious schools, some of which were being restored. The Kazakhs of western Mongolia are nominally Sunni Muslims. Mosques, also destroyed in the 1930s or closed subsequently, are only now being rebuilt or reopened. Traces of shamanism from the pre-Buddhist period still survive. In recent years there has been an increase in Christian missionary activity in Mongolia.

BUDDHISM

At the end of 2006 there were 150 Buddhist temples and monasteries in Mongolia, including 29 in Ulan Bator with 2,461 lamas (monks), 3,117 employees and 1,076 students in religious schools. It is estimated that about 70% of the adult population (975,600) are Buddhists, that is, some 39% of the total population.

Living Buddha: The Ninth Javzandamba Khutagt (Ninth Bogd), Jambalnamdolchoijinjaltsan (resident in Dharamsala, India).

Asian Buddhists' Peace Assembly: Mongolian Office, Ulan Bator; Sec.-Gen. T. BULGAN.

Gandantegchinlen Monastery: Zanabazaryn Gudamj, Bayangol District, Ulan Bator; tel. (11) 360354; Centre of Mongolian Buddhists; Khamba Lama (Abbot) DEMBERELIIN CHOIJAMTS.

'Good Merit' Buddhist Society: Ulan Bator; Pres. Lama A. ERDENEBAT.

Karmapa Monastery: Khamba Lama (Abbot) DAVAASAMBUUGIIN TAIVANSAIKHAN.

Pethub Buddhist Institute: Ikh Toiruu, Chingeltei District, Ulan Bator (POB 38/105); tel. (11) 321867; fax (11) 320676; e-mail pethubmongolia@magicnet.mn; internet www.pethubmonastery.com; f. 2001 by Ven. Kushok Bakula Rinpoche (Indian Ambassador to Mongolia 1990–2000).

CHRISTIANITY

At the end of 2006 there were 125 Christian congregations in Mongolia, including 97 in Ulan Bator, with 712 employees and 3,086 students attending Christian studies.

Roman Catholic Church

The Church is represented in Mongolia by a single mission. At April 2005 there were 264 Catholics in the country.

Catholic Mission: 18th Sub-District, Bayanzürkh District, Ulan Bator (CPOB 694); tel. (11) 458825; fax (11) 458027; e-mail info@ccmvatican.mn; internet www.ccmvatican.mn; f. 1992; Apostolic Prefect Bishop WENCESLAO PADILLA.

Cathedral of St. Peter and St. Paul: Bayanzürkh District, Ulan Bator.

Protestant Church

Association of Mongolian Protestants: f. 1990; Pastor M. BOLDBAATAR.

Mongolian Evangelical Alliance: Kseni Bldg, Baga Toiruu, Chingeltei District, Ulan Bator; tel. (11) 312771; e-mail mea@magicnet.mn; f. 1998; a branch of the World Evangelical Alliance.

Other Christian Churches

Church of Jesus Christ of Latter-Day Saints (Mormon): Khudaldaany Gudamj, Chingeltei District, Ulan Bator; tel. (11) 312761.

Jesus Reigns Assembly: Ulan Bator; Pastor D. NARANMANDAKH.

Russian Orthodox Church: Holy Trinity Church, Jukovyn Gudamj 55, Ulan Bator; e-mail fatheraleksei@hotmail.com; internet www.pravoslavie.mn; opened in 1864, closed in 1927; services recommenced 1997 for Russian community; Head Father ALEKSEI TRUBACH.

Seventh-day Adventist Church: 5th Sub-District, Bayangol District, Ulan Bator; tel. (11) 688031; fax (11) 688032.

ISLAM

At the end of 2006 there were seven Muslim congregations, all in western Mongolia, with 60 clergy, 27 employees and 759 students. It is assumed that the majority of Mongolia's ethnic Kazakh population (numbering 103,000 at the January 2000 census) are Muslim. It was stated in March 2005 that Mongolia had 32 mosques in Bayan-Ölgii and Khovd provinces and in the towns of Darkhan and Nalaikh.

Chief Imam (Ölgii): KH. BATYRBEK.

Imam of Gümyr shrine (Ölgii): DÖITENGIIN SHERKHAN.

Muslim Society: f. 1990; Hon. Pres. K. SAIRAAN; Chair. of Central Council M. AZATKHAN; Exec. Dir KH. BATYRBEK.

BAHÁ'Í FAITH

Bahá'í Society: Ulan Bator; tel. (11) 321867; f. 1989; Leader A. ARIUNAA.

SHAMANISM

Darkhad Shamanist Study Centre: Ulan Bator; Leader CH. TSERENBAAVAI.

Tengeriin Süld Shamanist Union: Ulan Bator; Pres. CH. CHINBAT.

The Press

PRINCIPAL NATIONAL NEWSPAPERS

State-owned publications in Mongolia were denationalized with effect from 1 January 1999, although full privatization could not proceed immediately. The number of newspapers published annually decreased from 134.1m. copies in 1990 to 18.5m. copies in 2003.

Ardchilal (Democracy): Democracy Palace, 11th Sub-District, Sükhbaatar District, Ulan Bator; tel. 70110187; 260 a year.

Ardyn Erkh (People's Power): Internom Shop Bldg, Amarsanaagiin Gudamj, Amaryn Gudamj 2, Ulan Bator; tel. and fax (11) 330116; e-mail ardiin_erkh@mongolnet.mn; f. 2004; original title ceased publication in 1999 (see *Ödriin Sonin*, below); subsequently assumed by new publr; 256 a year; Editor-in-Chief BAYARMAGNAIN TEMÜÜLEN; Sec. SOSORBARAMYN GANTOGOO.

MONGOLIA

Khödölmör (Labour): Sükhbaataryn Talbai 3, Ulan Bator; tel. (11) 323026; f. 1928; publ. by Confederation of Mongolian Trade Unions; 260 a year; Editor-in-Chief TSOODOLYN KHULAN; circ. 64,920.

Mongolyn Medee (Mongolian News): Jigjidjavyn Gudamj 6-1, Chingeltei District, Ulan Bator; tel. (11) 322005; fax (11) 311215; e-mail news-of-mon@mongolnet.mn; internet www.mongolmedia.com; 256 a year; Editor-in-Chief YO. GERELCHULUUN; circ. 2,900.

Montsame-giin Medee (Montsame News): Montsame News Agency, Jigjidjavyn Gudamj 8, Ulan Bator (CPOB 1514); tel. (11) 321324; e-mail localnews@montsame.mn; internet www.montsame.mn; daily news digest primarily for govt depts; 252 a year; Editor B. ZANDANKHÜÜ.

Ödriin Sonin (Daily News): Mongol News Co Bldg, Ikh Toiruu, Ulan Bator; tel. 99030027; fax (11) 353897; internet www.dailynews.mn; f. 1924; restored 1990; fmrly Ardyn Erkh, Ardyn Ündesnii Erkh, Ündesnii Erkh and Ödriin Toli; 312 a year; Editor-in-Chief JAMBALYN MYAGMARSÜREN; circ. 14,200.

Öglöö Oroi (Morning and Evening): 1st Sub-District, Sükhbaatar District, Ulan Bator; tel. 99108810; e-mail ugluu_oroi2007@yahoo.com; 252 a year; Editor-in-Chief B. BOLOR-ERDENE.

Öglöönii Sonin (Morning News): No. 1 Bldg, 4th Sub-District, Chingeltei District, Ulan Bator (POB 46/411); tel. (11) 319386; fax (11) 315695; e-mail ugluuniisonin@yahoo.com; 260 a year.

Önöödör (Today): Mongol News Co Bldg, Juulchny Gudamj 40, Ulan Bator; tel. (11) 330797; fax (11) 330798; e-mail mntoday@mobinet.mn; internet www.mongolnews.mn; f. 1996; 300 a year; Editor-in-Chief B. NANDINTÜSHIG; circ. 5,500.

Önöödriin Mongol (Mongolia Today): Erkhüügiin Gudamj, Sükhbataar District, Ulan Bator (POB 20/374); tel. (11) 350345; fax (11) 354440; e-mail mongoliatoday@chinggis.com; 260 a year; Editor-in-Chief Do. TSENDJAV.

Ulaanbaatar Taims (Ulan Bator Times): A. Amaryn Gudamj 1, Ulan Bator; tel. (11) 311187; fax (11) 322215; e-mail info@ubtimes.mn; internet www.ubtimes.mn; f. 1990; est. as Ulaanbaatar; publ. by Ulan Bator City Govt; 264 a year; Editor-in-Chief J. SARUULBUYAN; circ. 2,000.

Ünen (Truth): Baga Toiruu 11, Ulan Bator; tel. (11) 321287; fax (11) 323223; internet www.unen.mongolmedia.com; f. 1920; publ. by MPRP; 256 a year; Editor-in-Chief TSERENSODNOMYN GANBAT; circ. 8,330.

Zuuny Medee (Century's News): Amaryn Gudamj 1, Ulan Bator; tel. (11) 313499; fax (11) 321279; e-mail zuuniimedee@yahoo.com; internet www.zuuniimedee.mn; f. 1991; previously titled Zasgiin Gazryn Medee; 312 a year; Editor-in-Chief DAMDINSÜRENGIIN BOLDKHUYAG; circ 8,000.

Zuuny Shuudan (Century Post): Former Ardyn Erkh Bldg, Ikh Toiruu, Ulan Bator; tel. (11) 354632; fax (11) 354631; e-mail zuuniishuudan@yahoo.com; 312 a year; Editor-in-Chief BAASANJAVYN GANBOLD.

OTHER NEWSPAPERS AND PERIODICALS

4 dekh Zasaglal (Fourth Estate): Mongol Sonin Co, Gazar Holding Bldg, Variete Centre, Ulan Bator (POB 46A/81); tel. 99188125; e-mail dorovdekhzasaglal@yahoo.com; internet www.mongolmedia.com/4thEstate; 36 a year; Editor A. ENKHBAYAR.

81-r Suvag (Channel 81): Söüliin Gudamj, Bayangol District, Ulan Bator (POB 46A/81); tel. 96003992; fax (11) 460718; e-mail channel81@mongolmedia.com; internet www.channel81.mongolmedia.com; publishes views of the Mongolian Newspaper Asscn; 36 a year; Editor-in-Chief T. TSOGT-ERDENE.

Alag Shagai (Ankle-Bones): Bldg XVIII, Baga Toirog, Chingeltei District, Ulan Bator; tel. (11) 322005; fax (11) 311215; publ. by Mongolyn Medee; 300 a year; Editor-in-Chief YO. GERELCHULUUN.

Altangadas (Pole Star): AG Töv, Söüliin Gudamj, Bayanzürkh District, Ulan Bator (CPOB 430); tel. (11) 319411; fax (11) 319414; e-mail info@altangadas.mn; internet www.altangadas.mn; monthly political magazine; Editor NOROVYN ALTANKHUYAG.

Anagaakh Arga Bilig (The Healthy Way of Yin and Yang): Ulan Bator (CPOB 1053); tel. (11) 321367; e-mail arslny7144@magicnet.mn; twice monthly; Editor YA. ARSLAN.

Bagsh (Teacher): Rm 106, Teachers' College, Ulan Bator; tel. 99183398; f. 1989; by Ministry of Education; 24 a year.

Biznesiin Medee (Business News): Democratic Party Bldg, Sükhbaatar District, Ulan Bator (POB 20/335); tel. (11) 350541; fax (11) 350548; e-mail info@businessnews.mn; 48 a year; Editor-in-Chief S. KHÜREL.

Biznes, Uls Töriin Toim (Business and Political Review): Inforum Marketing and PR Centre, Ulan Bator; tel. (11) 319235; fax (11) 319236; e-mail toim@publicist.com; internet www.inforum.mn; monthly magazine; Editor-in-Chief A. BATPÜREV.

Bolson Yavdal (Events): Söüliin Gudamj, Sükhbaatar District, Ulan Bator (POB 36/346); e-mail bolsonyavdal@yahoo.com; 36 a year; Editor T. SANGAA.

Business Times: Chamber of Commerce and Industry, Government Bldg 11, Rm 712, Erkh Chölöönii Talbai, Ulan Bator; tel. and fax (11) 325374; e-mail marketing@mongolchamber.mn; internet www.businesstimes.mn; 36 a year; Editor BATSÜKHIIN SARANTUYAA.

Chansaa (Quality): Tergüün Chansaa Co, Jamyan Günii Gudamj, Ulan Bator; tel. (11) 335000; e-mail chansaa2005@yahoo.com; 36 a year; Editor-in-Chief DAVAADORJIIN AMARTÜVSHIN.

Deed Shüükhiin Medeelel (Supreme Court Information): Mongolian Supreme Court, Ulan Bator; quarterly journal.

Deedsiin Amidral (Elite's Life): Bldg 4, Rm 514, A. Amaryn Gudamj, Ulan Bator (CPOB 356); tel. 91189699; fax (11) 323847; e-mail deedsiinamidral@mongol.mn; internet www.elitslife.mongolmedia.com; 36 a year; Editor-in-Chief B. OTGONBAYAR.

Deedsiin Khüreelen (Elite's Forum): Ulan Bator (CPOB 1114); tel. and fax (11) 450602; e-mail deed_huree@yahoo.com; 36 a year; Publr M. SÜKHBAATAR; Editor KH. UYANGA; circ. 12,000.

Emiin Medeelel (Drug Newsletter): National Health Development Centre, Ministry of Health, Ulan Bator; tel. (11) 321485; fax (11) 320633; e-mail zorig@nchd.mn; bi-monthly magazine published by the National Health Development Centre; Editor T. ZORIG.

Erüül Mend (Health): Super Zuun Co, Ulan Bator (POB 20/412); tel. 99192239; fax (11) 321278; e-mail dr_jargal_d@yahoo.com; internet www.erul_mend.net; publ. by Ministry of Health; monthly; Editor D. JARGALSAIKHAN; circ. 5,600.

Il Tovchoo (Clear Summary): Chölööt Mongol Co Bldg, 8th Sub-District, Chingeltei District, Ulan Bator; tel. 91918674; Editor TSEND-AYUUSHIIN BUYANZAYAA.

Khani (Spouse): National Agricultural Co-operative Members' Association Bldg, Rm 201, Enkh Taivny Gudamj 18A, Bayanzürkh District, Ulan Bator (POB 49/600); tel. (11) 460698; fax (11) 458550; e-mail khani_sonin@yahoo.com; women and family issues; 36 a year; Editor-in-Chief G. BATTSETSEG; circ. 64,920.

Khiimori (Wind-Horse): Rm 305, Mongol News Co Bldg, Ikh Toiruu 20, Sükhbaatar District, Ulan Bator; tel. (11) 354565; 36 a year; Editor-in-Chief A. ERDENETUYAA.

Khökh Tolbo (Blue Spot): Mon-Azi Co Bldg, Ulan Bator (POB 24/306); tel. (11) 313405; fax (11) 312794; 36 a year; Publr BATYN ERDENEBAATAR; Editor-in-Chief E. ENKHTSOLMON; circ. 3,500.

Khöröngiin Zakh Zeel (Capital Market): Mongolian Stock Exchange, Sükhbaataryn Talbai 2, Ulan Bator; tel. (11) 313511; fax (11) 325170; e-mail info@mse.mn; monthly; Editor RENTSENGIIN SODKHÜÜ.

Khümüün Bichig (People and Script): Montsame News Agency, Jigjidjavyn Gudamj 8, Ulan Bator (CPOB 1514); tel. (11) 329486; fax (11) 327857; e-mail khumuun@montsame.mn; current affairs in Mongolian classical script; 48 a year; Editor T. GALDAN; circ. 15,000.

Khümüüs (People): Central Palace of Culture South Bldg, Rm 206, Ulan Bator (POB 46/411); tel. and fax 70118363; fax (11) 314147; e-mail humuus2006@yahoo.com; 48 a year; Editor O. MÖNKH-ERDENE; circ. 21,500.

Khümüüsiin Amidral (People's Life): Central Palace of Culture South Bldg, Rm 206, Ulan Bator (CPOB 2348); tel. 70118363; e-mail peoples_life@yahoo.com; 48 a year; Editor B. AMGALAN.

Khuuli Züin Medee (Legal News): Ministry of Justice and Home Affairs, Ulan Bator; f. 1990; 24 a year.

Khuviin Soyol (Personal Culture): Rm 2, Block 39, behind No. 5 School, Baga Toiruu, Ulan Bator (CPOB 1254); 24 a year; Editor BEKHBAZARYN BEKHSÜREN.

Leaders: Ulan Bator (POB 46A/455); tel. (11) 311322; magazine about political and business leaders; Editor AYUURBUMYAAGIIN LKHAGVA.

Mash Nuuts (Top Secret): Mongol Shaazan Bldg, Ulan Bator (POB 49/113); tel. (11) 328675; fax (11) 330690; e-mail tsecret@mongolnet.mn; 32 a year; Editor-in-Chief ONONGIIN CHINZORIG.

Mongolian Business Review: Green House, Baga Toiruu 29, Ulan Bator; tel. (11) 321312; Editor BADARALYN ZULBAYAR.

Mongoljin Goo (Mongolian Beauty): Mongolian Women's Federation, Ulan Bator (POB 44/717); tel. (11) 320790; fax (11) 367406; e-mail monwofed@magicnet.mn; f. 1990; monthly; Editor J. ERDENECHIMEG; circ. 3,000.

Mongolyn Anagaakh Ukhaan (Mongolian Medicine): Ulan Bator (CPOB 696); tel. (11) 112306; fax (11) 451807; e-mail nymadawa@hotmail.com; publ. by Scientific Society of Mongolian Physicians and Mongolian Academy of Sciences; quarterly; Editor-in-Chief Prof. PAGVAJAVYN NYAMDAVAA.

Mongolyn Khödöö (Mongolian Countryside): Agricultural University, Zaisan, Ulan Bator; tel. (11) 345211; e-mail haaint@magicnet.mn; publ. by Mongolian State University of Agriculture and

MONGOLIA
Directory

Academy of Agricultural Sciences; 24 a year; Editor-in-Chief Prof. BEGZIIN DORJ.

Mongolyn Neg Ödör (One Day of Mongolia): Bldg 31, Bayanzürkh District, Ulan Bator (POB 44/764); tel. (11) 450103; fax (11) 460718; e-mail oneday@mongolmedia.com; 48 a year; Editor-in-Chief SH. OTGONSETSEG.

Myangany Zuuch (Millennium Messenger): Mönkh Press Co, West side of Choijin Lama Temple, Sükbataar District, Ulan Bator (POB 46/390); tel. and fax (11) 319745; e-mail monkh@mobinet.mn; internet www.newspapers.mn; 36 a year; Deputy Editor G. ENKHJARGAL.

Notstoi Medee (Important News): Maximus Press Co, Ulan Bator (POB 20/359); tel. (11) 316953; 36 a year; Publr B. MÖNKHZUL; Editor B. OIDOV.

Nyam Garig (Sunday): Mongol News Co Bldg, Juulchny Gudamj, Ulan Bator; tel. (11) 330797; fax (11) 330798; e-mail weekend@mongolnews.mn; supplement of *Önöödör*; Editor-in-Chief B. BOLD-KHÜÜ.

Odoo Tsag (The Present): Baga Toiruu, Sükbataar District, Ulan Bator (POB 46A/161); tel. 88181260; 24 a year; Editor D. ÖRNÖKH.

Onigoo (Jokes): Konsulyn Gudamj 5-13, Bayanzürkh District, Ulan Bator (POB Sky Post 46/50); tel. 70150001; e-mail onigoosonin@yahoo.com; Editor S. SARANCHIMEG.

Önöögiin Törkh (Present Image): Rm 107, Mongolian Red Cross Society Bldg, Sükbataar District, Ulan Bator (POB 48/282); tel. and fax (11) 319007; 24 a year; Editor-in-Chief D. BADAMGARAV.

Sankhüügiin Medee (Financial News): Ulan Bator; 36 a year; Editor L. DONDOG.

Serüüleg (Alarm Clock): Business Plaza Bldg 2, Enkh Taivny Örgön Chölöö, Ulan Bator (CPOB 1094); tel. (11) 455570; fax (11) 459182; e-mail a.tsaschikher@yahoo.com; 48 a year; Editor-in-Chief BAYANMÖNKHIIN TSOOJCHULUUNTSETSEG; circ. 28,600.

Setgüülch (Journalist): Ulan Bator (POB 46/600); tel. (11) 325388; fax (11) 313912; f. 1982; publ. by Union of Journalists; journalism, politics, literature, art, economy; quarterly; Editor TSENDIIN ENKHBAT.

Shar Sonin (Yellow Newspaper): Ulan Bator (POB 46A/225); tel. (11) 313984; e-mail thesharsonin@yahoo.com; 36 a year; Editor B. NAMUUN.

Shine Erkh Chölöö (New Freedom): Ödriin Sonin Bldg, Ikh Toiruu, Ulan Bator (CPOB 2590); tel. and fax 70137010; e-mail erkhchoıoo2007@yahoo.com; quarterly; social and political affairs; Editor-in-Chief Ts. OYUUNCHIMEG.

Shine Yörtönts (New World): Empathy Centre, Baga Toiruu, 6th Sub-District, Ulan Bator; tel. (11) 313019; fax (11) 324657; quarterly; popular science magazine; Editor B. SARNAI.

Shinjlekh Ukhaany Akademiin Medee (Academy of Sciences News): Yörönkhii Said Amaryn Gudamj 1, Ulan Bator; tel. (11) 321993; fax (11) 261993; e-mail mas@mas.ac.mn; internet www.mas.ac.mn; f. 1961; publ. by Academy of Sciences; quarterly; Editor-in-Chief L. TSEDENDAMBA.

Shuurkhai Zar (Quick Advertisement): Ulan Bator Bank Bldg, Rm 104, 1st Floor, Ulan Bator (POB 46A/151); tel. (11) 313778; e-mail shirevger@mobinet.mn; 100 a year; Editor E. TSEYENKHORLOO.

Solongo (Rainbow): Baruunselbe Service Centre, Ulan Bator (POB 23/628); tel. 99860276; f. 1992; monthly; Deputy Editor-in-Chief T. BAYANJARGAL.

Soyombo: Ministry of Defence, Ulan Bator; tel. 91177221; f. 1924; est. as *Ardyn Tsereg* (People's Soldier); renamed *Ekh Orny Tölöö* (For the Motherland), then *Ulaan Od* (Red Star); Dep. Editor-in-Chief Lt-Col G. NYAMDORJ.

Strategi Sudlal (Strategic Studies): Institute of Strategic Studies, Ulan Bator (CPOB 870); tel. (11) 260710; fax (11) 324055; f. 1991; 4 a year; owned by National Security Council; Editor D. MYAGMAR.

Tavan Tsagarig (Five Rings): National Olympic Committee, Ikh Toiruu 20, Ulan Bator; tel. (11) 352487; fax (11) 343541; e-mail t_ts_sport@yahoo.com; noc@olympic.mn; 100 a year; Editor-in-Chief SODNOMDARJAAGIIN BATBAATAR.

Tengerleg Khümüüs (Heavenly People): Soyombo Press Co, Partizany Gudamj 17, Sükbataar District, Ulan Bator (POB 44/716); tel. (11) 325250; fax (11) 330383; internet www.soyomboprinting.com; 36 a year; Dir-Gen D. AMBARBAYASGALAN; Editor P. JARGALSAIKHAN.

Tonshuul (Woodpecker): Enkh Taivny Örgön Chölöö 4, Rm 148, Bayanzürkh District (CPOB 322); tel. 99118668; fax (11) 459265; e-mail ariun_tonshuul@yahoo.com; fortnightly magazine of cartoons, humour and satire; Editor Ts. ARIUNAA.

Töriin Medeelel (State Information): Secretariat of the Mongolian Great Khural, Government Palace, Ulan Bator; tel. (11) 265958; fax (11) 322866; e-mail luvsanjav@mail.parl.gov.mn; internet www.parl.gov.mn; f. 1990; presidential and governmental decrees, state laws; 48 a year; circ. 5,000.

Tsenkher Delgets (Light Blue Screen): Ulan Bator; tel. (11) 312010; fax (11) 311850; e-mail bsnews@magicnet.mn; weekly guide to TV and radio programmes; Editor-in-Chief GALIGAAGIIN BAYARSAIKHAN.

Tsonkh (Window): Chingisiin Örgön Chölöö 1, Ulan Bator (CPOB 1085); tel. (11) 310717; publ. by the Democratic Party's Political Department; 24 a year.

Tsog (Ember): Mongolian Union of Writers, Ulan Bator; literary quarterly.

Üg (The Word): Bldg 86, Chingeltei District, Ulan Bator; tel. 55152675; fax (11) 329795; e-mail ugsonin@mol.mn; fmrly the journal of the Mongolian Social Democratic Party (until 2000); Editor-in-Chief A. GANBAATAR.

Uls Töriin Sonin (Political Newspaper): Delta Centre, Juulchny Gudamj, Chingeltei District, Ulan Bator (POB 46/796); tel. 99095040; fax (11) 312608; e-mail political_newspaper@yahoo.com; internet pnews.delhii.net; f. 2005 following closure of the *Mongol Times*; 48 a year; Editor GANTÖMÖRIIN UYANGA.

Utga Zokhiol Urlag (Literature and Art): Mongolian Union of Writers, Sükhbaataryn Gudamj 11, Ulan Bator (POB 46A/555); tel. (11) 318035; fax (11) 320817; e-mail info@utgazokhiol.mn; f. 1955; 36 a year; Editor J. BAYARAA; circ. 3,000.

Zar Medee (Advertisement News): Government Bldg 5, 1st Floor, Rm 130, Juulchny Gudamj, Chingeltei District, Ulan Bator; tel. and fax (11) 312379; e-mail advertisement-news@yahoo.com; personal and company advertisements; 100 a year; Editor D. BAYASGALAN.

Zindaa (Ranking): Room 305, former Ardyn Erkh Bldg, Sükhbaatar District, Ulan Bator; tel. (11) 354545; fax (11) 354555; internet www.zindaa.mongolmedia.com; wrestling news; 48 a year; Editor-in-Chief KH. MANDAKHBAYAR.

FOREIGN LANGUAGE PUBLICATIONS

Inspiring Mongolia: Mongolian National Chamber of Commerce and Industry, Sambuugiin Gudamj 11, Ulan Bator 38; tel. (11) 312501; fax (11) 324620; e-mail marketing@mongolchamber.mn; internet www.mongolchamber.mn; magazine in English, publ. twice a year; Editor-in-Chief SAMBUU DEMBEREL.

Menggu Xiaoxi Bao (News of Mongolia): Montsame News Agency, Ulan Bator (CPOB 1514); tel. (11) 320077; e-mail mgxxbao@chinggis.com; f. 1929; weekly; in Chinese; Sec. P. OYUUNTSETSEG.

Mongolian Magazine: Interpress Publishers, Ulan Bator; f. 2004; English-language monthly illustrated magazine about Mongolian history, culture, nature, life and customs.

Mongolia This Week: Ulan Bator; tel. and fax (11) 318339; e-mail mongoliathisweek@mobinet.mn; internet www.mongoliathisweek.mn; weekly in English, online daily; Editor-in-Chief D. NARANTUYAA; English Editor ERIC MUSTAFA.

Mongolia Today: Montsame News Agency, Jigjidjavyn Gudamj 8, Ulan Bator (CPOB 1514); quarterly; in English; Editor-in-Chief G. PÜREVSAMBUU.

Mongoliya Segodnya (Mongolia Today): Zoos Goyol Co Bldg, Chingeltei District, Ulan Bator (POB 46/609); tel. and fax (11) 324141; weekly; in Russian; Editor-in-Chief DÜNGER-YAICHILIIN SOLONGO.

The Mongol Messenger: Montsame News Agency, Jigjidjavyn Gudamj 8, Ulan Bator (CPOB 1514); tel. and fax (11) 325512; e-mail monmessenger@magicnet.mn; internet www.mongolmessenger.mn; f. 1991; weekly newspaper in English; owned by Montsame national news agency; Editor-in-Chief BORKHONDOIN INDRA; circ. 2,000.

Mongoru Tsushin (Mongolia News): Montsame News Agency, Jigjidjavyn Gudamj 8, Ulan Bator (CPOB 1514); weekly; in Japanese.

Montsame Daily News: Montsame News Agency, Jigjidjavyn Gudamj 8, Ulan Bator (CPOB 1514); tel. (11) 314574; fax (11) 327857; e-mail montsame@magicnet.mn; daily English news digest for embassies, etc.; Editor-in-Chief BAYANBATYN BAYASGALAN.

Novosti Mongolii (News of Mongolia): Montsame News Agency, Jigjidjavyn Gudamj 8, Ulan Bator (CPOB 1514); tel. (11) 310157; fax (11) 327857; e-mail novosty_mongolii@yahoo.co.uk; f. 1942; weekly; in Russian; Editor-in-Chief DÜGERSÜRENGIIN ARIUNBOLD.

The UB Post: Mongol News Co, Juulchny Gudamj, Ulan Bator; tel. (11) 330397; fax (11) 330798; e-mail ubpost@mongolnews.mn; internet ubpost.mongolnews.mn; f. 1996; weekly; in English; Editor-in-Chief CH. SUMYAABAZAR; circ. 4,000.

NEWS AGENCIES

Montsame (Mongol Tsakhilgaan Medeenii Agentlag) (Mongolian News Agency): Jigjidjavyn Gudamj 8, Ulan Bator (CPOB 1514); tel. (11) 266904; fax (11) 327857; e-mail montsame@magicnet.mn; internet www.montsame.mn; f. 1921; govt-controlled; Gen. Dir D. ARIUNBOLD; Editor-in-Chief BAYANBATYN BAYASGALAN.

MONGOLIA

Mongolyn Medee (Mongolian News): Public Radio and Television, Khuvisgalyn Zam, Ulan Bator; Dir Ts. SÜKHBAATAR.

PRESS ASSOCIATIONS

Mongolian Newspaper Association: Ulan Bator; Pres. R. KHADBAATAR; Vice-Pres. D. BATSÜKH.

United Association of National Daily Newspapers: c/o Önöödör, Mongol News Co, Juulchny Gudamj, Ulan Bator; f. 2006; Pres. (vacant).

Publishers

The ending of the state monopoly has led to the establishment of several small commercial publishers, including Shuvuun Saaral (Ministry of De-fence), Mongol Khevlel and Soyombo Co, Mongolpress (Montsame), Erdem (Academy of Sciences), Süülenkhüü children's publishers, Sudaryn Chuulgan, Interpress, Sükhbaatar Co, Öngöt Khevlel, Admon, Odsar, Khee Khas Co, etc.

Admon Co: Amaryn Gudamj 2, Sükhbaatar District, Ulan Bator (CPOB 92); tel. (11) 329253; fax (11) 327251; e-mail admon@magicnet.mn; Dir R. ENKHBAT.

Darkhan Sergelen Co: Naadamchdyn Gudamj, Darkhan; tel. (37) 23049; fax (37) 24741; internet www.munkhiin-useg.mn.

Chölööt Khevlel San (Free Press Foundation): Ikh Toiruu 11B, Ulan Bator (POB 20/357); tel. (11) 350016; e-mail mpfnph@magicnet.mn; f. 1996; the country's largest printer of newspapers and the biggest pre-press service provider; Man. Dir BAASTYN GALSANDORJ.

Khevleliin Khüreelen (Press Institute NGO): Ikh Toiruu 11, Sükhbaatar District, Ulan Bator; tel. and fax (11) 350012; e-mail ts_byambaa12@yahoo.com; internet www.owc.org.mn/pressinstitute; Chair. Ts. ENKHBAT.

Mongol News Group: Mongol News Group Bldg, Juulchny Gudamj, Ulan Bator; tel. (11) 330797; fax (11) 330798; e-mail mntoday@mobinet.mn; f. 1996; owns newspapers *MN-Önöödör*, *Tavan Tsagarig*, *Nyam Garig* and *The UB Post*, TV Channel 25 and ABM Co printers; Pres. B. NANDINTÜSHIG.

Mönkhiin Üseg Group: Teeverchdiin Gudamj, Songinokhairkhan District, Ulan Bator; tel. (11) 320807; fax (11) 321318; e-mail munuseg@mbox.mn; internet www.munkhiin-useg.mn; Chair. G. BATMÖNKH.

Novum Co: Migma Bldg, Ulan Bator; tel. (11) 319140; fax (11) 319319; e-mail print@mynovum.com; internet www.mynovum.com.

Öngöt Khevlel Co: Amaryn Gudamj 2, Sükhbaatar District, Ulan Bator; tel. (11) 323121; fax (11) 329519; e-mail ungut_khevlel@mongolnet.mn.

Soyombo Printing Co: Natsagdorjiin Gudamj, Sükhbaatar District, Ulan Bator; tel. (11) 325052.

Sükhbaatarprint Co: Amaryn Gudamj 2, Sükhbaatar District, Ulan Bator; tel. and fax (11) 320504; e-mail sukhprint@magicnet.mn.

Zurag Züi Co (Cartography): Ikh Toiruu 15, Ulan Bator; tel. (11) 322164; e-mail cart@magicnet.mn; publisher and retailer of maps and atlases.

PUBLISHERS' ASSOCIATIONS

Local Press and Information Association: Ulan Bator; f. 2006; Pres. S. SHARAVDORJ.

Mongolian Book Publishers' Association: Ulan Bator; Exec. Dir S. TSERENDORJ.

Mongolian Free Press Publishers' Association: POB 306, Ulan Bator 24; tel. and fax (11) 313405; Pres. BATYN ERDENEBAATAR.

Broadcasting and Communications

TELECOMMUNICATIONS

Digital exchanges have been installed in Ulan Bator, Darkhan, Erdenet, Sükhbaatar, Bulgan and Arvaikheer, while radio-relay lines have been digitalized between: Ulan Bator–Darkhan–Sükhbaatar; Ulan Bator–Darkhan–Erdenet; and Dashinchilen–Arvaikheer. Mobile telephone companies operate in Ulan Bator and other central towns, in addition to Arvaikheer, Sainshand and Zamyn-Üüd. By May 2005 a total of 1,776 km of fibre optic cable had been installed in Mongolia, with plans to lay another 1,400 km by the end of the year. The Ulan Bator–Bulgan cable was under construction.

Bodicom: Ulan Bator; tel. (11) 325144; fax (11) 318486; e-mail bodicom@mongolnet.mn; internet www.bodicom.mn.

Datacom: Rm 112, Mongolian Technology National Park, Baga Toiruu, Sükhbaatar District, Ulan Bator; tel. (11) 329688; fax (11) 320210; internet www.datacom.mn; service provider for Magicnet connection to internet; Dir DANGAASÜRENGIIN ENKHBAT.

G-Mobile: Gem International Co., 1st Sub-District, Chingeltei District, Ulan Bator; tel. (11) 333636; e-mail info@g-mobile.mn; internet www.g-mobile.mn; Dir-Gen. R. GANZORIG.

Incomnet: Enkh Taivny Örgön Chölöö, Bayanzürkh District, Ulan Bator (CPOB 582); tel. (11) 480606; fax (11) 480808; e-mail info@icn-mn.net; internet www.icn-mn.net; internet service provider, cable TV, satellite communications.

MagicNet Co: Rm 222, Ground Floor, Science and Technology Information Centre, Ulan Bator; tel. (11) 312061; fax (11) 311496; e-mail info@magicnet.mn; internet www.magicnet.mn; internet service provider.

MCSCom: MCS Plaza, 3rd Floor, Baga Toiruu 49, Ulan Bator; tel. (11) 327854; fax (11) 311323; e-mail mcscom@mcs.mn; internet www.mcscom.mn; internet service provider.

Micom: Mongol Tsakhilgaan Kholboo Co Bldg, Sükhbaataryn Talbai, Ulan Bator (CPOB 1124); tel. (11) 313229; fax (11) 322473; internet www.micom.mn; Dir CH. NARANTUNGALAG.

MobiCom: Mobicom Corp. Bldg, Enkh Taivny Örgön Chölöö 3/1, Ulan Bator; tel. (11) 318115; fax (11) 310411; e-mail feedback@mobicom.mn; internet www.mobicom.mn; mobile telephone service provider; Exec. Dir FUMIAKI SHIGA; Dir-Gen. R. ARVINTSOGT.

Moncom: Ulan Bator (POB 51/207); tel. (11) 329409; e-mail ch.enkhmend@hotmail.com; pager services.

Mongolia Telecom: Mongol Tsakhilgaan Kholboo Co Bldg, Sükhbaataryn Talbai, Ulan Bator (CPOB 1166); tel. (11) 320597; fax (11) 325412; e-mail mt@mtcone.net; internet www.mongol.net; 54.6% state-owned, 40.0% owned by Korea Telecom; Pres. and CEO OONOIGIIN SHAALUU.

Newcom LLC: Enkh Taivny Örgön Chölöö 3/1, Bayanzürkh District, Ulan Bator; tel. (11) 313183; fax (11) 318521; e-mail secretary@newcom.mn; internet www.newcom.mn.

Newtel Co: Sambuugiin Gudamj 36, Chingeltei District, Ulan Bator; tel. and fax (11) 311581; e-mail marketing@ntc.mn; internet www.ntc.mn; Exec. Dir D. BOLOR.

Orbitnet: New Horizon Bldg, Olimpiin Gudamj 6, Sükhbaatar District, Ulan Bator; tel. (11) 323705; fax (11) 312699; e-mail orbitnet@mcs.mn; internet www.orbitnet.mcs.mn.

Railcom: Mongolian Railways (MTZ), Zamchny Gudamj 1, Ulan Bator (CPOB 376); tel. (11) 252525; e-mail info@railcom.mn; internet www.railcom.mn; telephone, TV and internet service provider.

Skynetcom: 1st Sub-District, Chingeltei District, Ulan Bator; tel. 77007700; e-mail info@skynet.com; internet www.skynetcom.mn; mobile telephone service provider.

Skytel: Skytel Plaza Centre, Chingisiin Örgön Chölöö, Ulan Bator; tel. (11) 319191; fax (11) 318487; e-mail skytel@mongol.net; internet www.skytel.mn; mobile telephone and voice mail service provider; Mongolia-Republic of Korea jt venture; Dir-Gen. R. GANBOLD; Marketing Man. G. TÜVSHINTÖGS.

Unitel: Rokmon Bldg, Ündsen Khuuliin Gudamj 24, Ulan Bator; tel. (11) 328888; fax (11) 330708; e-mail info@unitel.mn; internet www.unitel.mn; f. 2005 by MBSB Telecom, Uangel Corpn (Republic of Korea) and Dream Choice Co (Canada); mobile telephone service provider; Dir-Gen. Ts. AMARAA.

Ulusnet: TEDY Centre, Sambuugiin Gudamj 18, Chingeltei District, Ulan Bator; tel. (11) 322686; e-mail service@ulusnet.mn; internet www.ulusnet.mn; Mongolia's first Wimax service provider.

BROADCASTING

A 1,900-km radio relay line from Ulan Bator to Altai and Ölgii provides direct-dialling telephone links as well as television services for western Mongolia. New radio relay lines have been built from Ulan Bator to Choibalsan, and from Ulan Bator to Sükhbaatar and Sainshand. Most of the population is in the zone of television reception, following the inauguration of relays via satellites operated by the International Telecommunications Satellite Organization (INTELSAT). In 2004 Mongolia had 30 radio stations and 35 television stations.

All provincial centres receive two channels of Mongolian national television; and all district centres can receive television, although only one-third can receive Mongolian television. At the beginning of 2005 the first legislative measures were taken to end state control, with the passing of the Law on Public Broadcasting, the provisions of which entered into force on 1 July 2005, creating an independent public service broadcaster to be known as Public Radio and Television. Also in 2005 it was planned to extend television coverage (UBS, TV-5, TV-9 and Channel 25) to outlying areas of Ulan Bator, including Partizan, Songino and Gachuurt, by installing additional local transmitters.

Public Radio and Television (ONRT): Khuvisgalyn Zam 3, Bayangol District, Ulan Bator; f. 2006; replaced the govt-run Direc-

MONGOLIA

Directory

torate of Radio and Television Affairs; Chair. of National Council Khaidavyn Chilaajav; Dir-Gen. M. Naranbaatar.

Radio

Mongolradio: Khuvisgalyn Zam 3, Bayangol District, Ulan Bator; tel. (11) 323096; f. 1934; operates for 17 hours daily on three long-wave and one medium-wave frequency, and VHF; programmes in Mongolian (two) and Kazakh; part of Public Radio and Television; Dir B. Pürevdash; Dep. Dir B. Khanddolgor.

  Voice of Mongolia: Ulan Bator; e-mail radiomongolia@magicnet .mn; external service of Mongolradio; broadcasts in Russian, Chinese, English and Japanese on short wave; Dir B. Narantuyaa.

AE and JAAG Studio: Amryn Gudamj 2, Ulan Bator (POB 20/126); tel. (11) 352463; fax (11) 326545; e-mail aejaag@magicnet.mn; f. 1996; broadcasts for 4.5–5 hours daily; CEO Z. Altai.

FM 98.9 Hi Fi (Hit First): Khair Tokhoi Co Bldg, Chingisiin Örgön Chölöö 10/1, Ulan Bator; tel. and fax (11) 330989; e-mail hifi@hi-fi .mn; internet www.hi-fi.mn.

FM 99.3 Ineemseglel (Smile): Central Palace of Culture, Sükhbaatar District, Ulan Bator; e-mail 99147994; internet (11) 319789; Dir Kh. Ikhbayar.

FM 100.1 Kiss: Ulan Bator; tel. (11) 312234.

FM 100.5 Minii Mongol (My Mongolia): Central Palace of Culture, Sükhbaatar District, Ulan Bator; tel. (11) 323599.

FM 100.9 Khökh Tenger (Blue Sky Radio): Mongolian National Television Bldg, Chingeltei District, Ulan Bator; tel. (11) 320522; broadcasts for 12 hours Mon. to Sat. and shorter hours on Sun; short-wave transmitter on 4,850 kHz; Dir L. Amarzayaa.

FM 101.7: Narny Titem, 5th Sub-District, Chingeltei District, Ulan Bator; tel. 70110981; fax (11) 322472; Dir U. Bulgan.

FM 102.1 Ekh Oron (Homeland): Central Palace of Culture, Sükhbaatar District, Ulan Bator; tel. (11) 327383; fax (11) 322472; operated by the Open Information Foundation.

FM 102.5 Radio Ulan Bator: Ulan Bator; tel. (11) 329269.

FM 103.1: Ulan Bator; BBC World Service Relay.

FM 103.6: Amaryn Gudamj, Sükhbaatar District, Ulan Bator; tel. 70110632; TV-9's radio station.

FM 104 Life: Alaska Centre, 13th Sub-District, Bayanzürkh District, Ulan Bator; tel. (11) 463782.

FM 104.5 Ger Büliin Radio (Family Radio): Mamba Datsan, Bayanzürkh District, Ulan Bator; tel. (11) 461045; fax (11) 452987.

FM 105 Tany Derged (Near You): Central Palace of Culture, Sükhbaatar District, Ulan Bator; tel. (11) 319789.

FM 105.5 Info Radio: Russian Foundation, Od Plaza, Sükhbaatar District, Ulan Bator; tel. (11) 319492; fax (11) 313687; internet www .inforadio.mn.

FM 106.6: Democratic Party Bldg, Chingisiin Örgön Chölöö, Ulan Bator; tel. (11) 329353; Voice of America news and information in Mongolian, English lessons and music.

FM 107 New Century Radio: Media Group Co Bldg, Chingisiin Öörgön Chölöö, Khan-Uul District, Ulan Bator; tel. (11) 312011.

FM 107.5 Shine Dolgion (New Wave): Namyanjügiin Gudamj 40, Bayanzürkh District, Ulan Bator; tel. and fax (11) 452444; e-mail info@fm1075.mn; internet www.fm1075.mn; relays of Voice of America broadcasts in English and Russian, entertainment programmes; Dir Ts. Ariunaa.

There are seven long- and short-wave radio transmitters and 49 FM stations in 23 towns.

Television

Channel 25: Mongol News Bldg, Juulchny Gudamj, Chingeltei District, Ulan Bator; tel. (11) 321989; broadcasts entertainment in the evening from Tue. to Sun; 50 hours a week; Dir-Gen. B. Nandintüshig; Gen. Man. Ayuushiin Avirmed.

Eagle Broadcasting System: Erkhüüd Centre, 5th Sub-District, Bayanzürkh District, Ulan Bator; tel. (11) 463088; fax (11) 463087; internet www.eagle-tv.mn; programmes broadcast by Sansar cable TV company; evening audience est. at 64,500; first broadcast in 1996; restarted 2005 after two years off air; Exec. Dir B. Bayarsaikhan.

Khiimori Co: Bldg 3A, No. 2 Combined Clinical General Hospital, Ulan Bator; tel. (11) 458531; fax (11) 458569; f. 1995; cable TV service provider.

Mongolteleviz (MNTV): Mongolian National Television, Khuvisgalyn Zam 3, Bayangol District, Ulan Bator (CPOB 365); tel. (11) 327214; fax (11) 328939; e-mail mrtv@magicnet.mn; f. 1967; daily morning and evening transmissions of locally originated material relayed by land-line and via INTELSAT satellites; short news bulletins in English Mon., Wed. and Fri; state-owned; part of Public Radio and Television; Dir A. Ganbaatar.

Sansar (STV): 2nd Sub-District, Chingeltei District, Ulan Bator; tel. (11) 315674; fax (11) 313770; e-mail stv_zar@yahoo.com; cable television equipment and services, reaches 220,000 households; f. 1994; Dir-Gen. A. Enkhbat.

Supervision: Enkhtaivny Örgön Chölöö, 3rd Sub-District, Bayanzürkh District, Ulan Bator; tel. (11) 455082; fax (11) 320396; internet www.supervisiontv.mn; cable supplier of international programmes.

TV-5: Sapporo Centre, 1st Sub-District, Songinokhairkhan District; tel. (11) 680327; fax (11) 680326; e-mail feedback@tv5.mn; internet www.tv5.mn; evening broadcasts from 6 p.m., repeated the following morning.

TV-9: Yörönkhii Said Amaryn Gudamj, Sükhbaatar District, Ulan Bator; tel. 70110630; fax (11) 343647; e-mail programm@tv9.mn; internet www.tv9.mn; f. 2003; broadcaster for the Ulan Bator area, general entertainment, with 20% religious content; Dir Ts. Enkhbat.

UBS (Ulan Bator Broadcasting System): Khuvisgalchdyn Gudamj 3, Bayangol District, Ulan Bator (POB 24/983); tel. (11) 368987; e-mail info@ubs.mn; internet www.ubs.mn; f. 1992; operated by Ulan Bator City Government; evening broadcasts repeated the following morning except Mondays; Dir-Gen. L. Balkhjav.

Cable television companies (29 in total) operate in 19 towns. There are local television stations in Ulan Bator (three), Darkhan, Sükhbaatar and Baganuur. Chinese, Kazakh, Russian, German and French television services are among those that can also be received.

Finance

(cap. = capital; res = reserves; dep. = deposits; m. = million; brs = branches; amounts in tögrög, unless otherwise stated)

BANKING

Before 1990 the State Bank was the only bank in Mongolia, responsible for issuing currency, controlling foreign exchange and allocating credit. With the inauguration of market reforms in Mongolia in the early 1990s, the central and commercial functions of the State Bank were transferred to the newly created specialized commercial banks: the Bank of Capital Investment and Technological Innovation and the State Bank International. In May 1991 the State Bank became an independent central bank, and the operation of private, commercial banks was permitted. In November 1996 amendments were made to banking legislation to improve the regulation and supervision of commercial banks, and two major insolvent banks were liquidated. Restructuring of the banking sector subsequently continued.

Central Bank

Bank of Mongolia (Mongolbank): Baga Toiruu 9, Ulan Bator; tel. (11) 310413; fax (11) 311471; e-mail ad@mongolbank.mn; internet www.mongolbank.mn; f. 1924; est. as the State Bank of the Mongolian People's Republic; cap. 5,000m., res 23,555m., dep. 775,149m. (Dec. 2006); Pres. Alagiin Batsükh; Chief Vice-Pres. Batsükhiin Enkhkhuyag.

Other Banks

Anod Bank: Juulchny Gudamj 18, Chingeltei District, Ulan Bator (CPOB 361); tel. (11) 315315; fax (11) 315431; e-mail anod@anodbank .com; internet www.anod.com; cap. 11,504.2m., res 60.8m., dep. 178,512.3m. (Dec. 2006); Dir-Gen. D. Enkhtör; Exec. Dir L. Ulambayar; Pres. N. Davaa.

Capital Bank: Sambuugiin Gudamj 48, Ulan Bator; tel. (11) 315500; fax (11) 310833; e-mail info@capitalbank.mn; internet www .capitalbank.mn; cap. 8,000m., res 806m., dep. 14,397m. (June 2007); f. 1990; Bishrelt Holding; CEO Agvaanjambyn Ariunbold; Deputy CEO Damdingiin Düger; 24 brs.

Capitron Bank: Capitron Bank Bldg, Usny Gudamj 4, Enkhtaivny Örgön Chölöö, Sükhbaatar District, Ulan Bator; tel. (11) 328373; fax (11) 328372; e-mail info@capitronbank.mn; internet www .capitronbank.mn; f. 2001; cap. 8,000.5m., res 3.4m., dep. 74,746.7m. (Dec. 2006); CEO Balbaryn Medree.

Chinggis Khaan Bank: New Century Plaza, Chingisiin Örgön Chölöö 15, Sükhbaatar District, Ulan Bator; tel. (11) 317178; fax (11) 318367; e-mail bank@ckbank.mn; internet www.ckbank.mn; f. 2001; est. by Millennium Securities Management Ltd and Coral Sea Holdings Ltd (British Virgin Islands); cap. 39,696.1m., dep. 2,972.4m. (Dec. 2005); Chair. S. B. Gromov; CEO Chimidiin Saintsogt.

Credit Bank: Government Palace Bldg (east side), Sükhbaataryn Talbai, Sükhbaatar District, Ulan Bator; tel. (11) 326053; fax (11) 321897; e-mail creditbk@creditbank.mn; internet www.creditbank .mn; f. 1997; owned by Russian interests; cap. 8,090m., res 20,594m., dep. 12,363m. (July 2006); Exec. Dir B. Tsengel.

MONGOLIA

Erel Bank: Erel Co No. 2 Bldg, Chingisiin Örgön Chölöö, Khan-Uul District, Ulan Bator (POB 36/500); tel. (11) 344550; fax (11) 343387; e-mail info@erelbank.mn; internet www.erelbank.mn; f. 1997; cap. 4,000m., res 45.9m., dep. 3,163.4m. (Dec. 2005); Owner BADARCHIIN ERDENEBAT; CEO GOMBOJAVYN DORJ.

Golomt Bank of Mongolia: Bodi Tower, Sükhbaataryn Talbai 3, 4th Floor, Ulan Bator; tel. (11) 311530; fax (11) 311958; e-mail mail@golomtbank.com; internet www.golomtbank.com; f. 1995; est. by Mongolian-Portuguese IBH Bodi International Co Ltd; cap. 21,934.1m., dep. 303,944.3m. (Dec. 2006); Chair. DANZANDORJIIN BAYASGALAN; Exec. Dir JOHN FINIGAN; 14 brs.

Khadgalamjiin Bank (Savings Bank): Khudaldaany Gudamj 6, Chingeltei District, Ulan Bator; tel. (11) 327329; fax (11) 310621; e-mail savbank@magicnet.mn; internet www.savingsbank.mn; f. 1996; est. as Ardyn Bank; owned by MD Securities Co, a consortium of Chinggis Khaan Bank, Mongol Daatgal and Bratsk People's Bank (Russian Federation); cap. 4,000.0m., res 1,243.7m., dep. 51,364.0m. (Dec. 2004); CEO TSEDEVDAMBYN MÖNKHBAT; 43 brs.

Khan Bank (KhAAN or Agricultural Bank): Söüliin Gudamj 25, Sükhbaatar District, Ulan Bator (POB 44/192); tel. (11) 332333; fax (11) 70117023; e-mail info@khanbank.com; internet www.khanbank.com; f. 1991; purchased by H and S Securities (Japan) in Feb. 2003; cap. 14,307m., dep. 179,098m. (June 2005); Chair. HIDEO SAWADA; CEO J. PETER MORROW; 380 brs.

Mongol Shuudan Bank (Post Bank): Kholboochdyn Gudamj 4, Ulan Bator (CPOB 874); tel. (11) 310103; fax (11) 328501; e-mail post_bank@mongol.net; internet www.postbank.mn; f. 1993; cap. 8,017.9m., res 1,732.0m., dep. 128,964.6m. (Dec. 2006); 100% in private ownership; Exec. Dir D. OYUUNJARGAL.

Trade and Development Bank of Mongolia (Khudaldaa Khögjliin Bank): Cnr of Juulchny Gudamj 7 and Baga Toiruu 12, Ulan Bator; tel. (11) 312362; fax (11) 327028; e-mail tdbank@tdbm.mn; internet www.tdbm.mn; f. 1991; carries out Mongolbank's foreign operations; cap. 6,610.1m., res. 12,171.8m., dep. 360,710.7m. (Dec. 2006); 76% equity bought by Banca Commerciale (Lugano) and Gerald Metals (Stanford, CT), May 2002; Pres. RANDOLPH KOPPA; CEO B. MEDREE.

Transport and Development Bank (Trans Bank): Juulchny Gudamj, 1st Sub-District, Chingeltei District, Ulan Bator; tel. (11) 319580; fax (11) 319591; internet www.transbank.mn; owned by Russian interests; CEO A. E. NOVOZHILOV.

Ulaanbaatar City Bank: Sükhbaataryn Gudamj 16, Ulan Bator (POB 46/370); tel. (11) 319041; fax (11) 330508; e-mail info@ubcbank.mn; internet www.ubcbank.mn; f. 1998; est. by Capital City with assistance from the Bank of Taipei (Taiwan); cap. 5,349m., dep. 50,064m. (June 2005); CEO DASHDORJIN BADRAA.

XacBank: Yörönkhii Said Amaryn Gudamj, Sükhbaatar District, Ulan Bator (POB 46/721); tel. (11) 312218; fax (11) 328701; e-mail centralbranch.cs@xacbank.org; internet www.xacbank.org; f. 2001; cap. 8,034.2m., res 1,061.3m., dep. 47,088.0m. (Dec. 2006); Pres. MAGVANY BOLD; CEO CH. GANKHUYAG.

Zoos Bank: Baga Toiruu 7/1, Ulan Bator (POB 44/304); tel. (11) 312107; fax (11) 329537; e-mail secretary@zoosbank.mn; internet www.zoosbank.mn; f. 1999; cap. 5,612m., dep. 64,803m. (March 2005); Exec. Dir SHARAVYN CHUDANJII.

Banking Associations

Mongolian Banks Association: Ulan Bator; e-mail monba@mongolnet.mn; Pres. SHARAVYN CHUDANJII; Exec. Dir GOTOVYN TSERENPÜREV.

STOCK EXCHANGE

At the end of 2006 there were 387 listed companies (compared with 392 at the end of 2005), of which 60 were wholly or partly state-owned. In 2006 a total of 74.6m. shares were traded, 48.3m. more than in the previous year. The value of transactions rose by more than 6,000m. to reach 18,000m. tögrög.

Stock Exchange: Sükhbaataryn Talbai 2, Ulan Bator; tel. (11) 310501; fax (11) 325170; internet www.mse.mn; f. 1991; Dir RENTSENGIIN SODKHÜÜ.

INSURANCE

Ard Daatgal: Tavan Bogd Plaza, Amaryn Gudamj 8, Ulan Bator; tel. (11) 331185; fax (11) 330083; est. with Omni Whittington Guernsey.

Bodi Daatgal Co: Bodi Tower, Sükhbaataryn Talbai, Ulan Bator; tel. 70110280; fax (11) 326535; e-mail bodi@bodiinsurance.mn; internet www.bodiinsurance.mn; Dir L. BOLDKHUYAG.

Ganzam Insurance: Mongolian Railways (MTZ), Zamchdyn Gudamj, Ulan Bator; tel. and fax (11) 242643.

Mongol Daatgal: Enkh Taivny Örgön Chölöö 13, Ulan Bator; tel. (11) 313615; fax (11) 310347; e-mail insurance@mongoldaatgal.mn; internet www.mongoldaatgal.mn; f. 1934; sold Dec. 2003 to consortium formed by Angara-SKB and Chinggis Khan Bank; Chair. and CEO BADARCHIIN ENKHBAT; Sr Vice-Pres. CHIMIDYN BATTSOGT.

Nomin Daatgal: State Department Store, Enkhtaivny Örgön Chölöö, Ulan Bator; tel. (11) 330023; fax (11) 325528; e-mail insurance@nomin.net; internet www.insurance.nomin.net.

Ochir Undraa Daatgal: Söüliin Gudamj 15/2, 4th Sub-District, Sükhbaatar District, Ulan Bator (POB 44/398); tel. (11) 324248; fax (11) 324666; e-mail insurance@ochir-undraa.com; internet www.ochir-undraa.com.

UB Daatgal Co: Baga Toiruu 37B, Sükbataar District, Ulan Bator (POB 46/385); tel. (11) 324828; fax (11) 322362; e-mail sanal_huselt@ubdaatgal.mn; internet www.ubdaatgal.mn.

Trade and Industry

GOVERNMENT AGENCIES

Foreign Investment and Foreign Trade Agency (FIFTA): Government Bldg 11, J. Sambuugiin Gudamj 11, Ulan Bator; tel. (11) 326040; fax (11) 324076; e-mail fifta@investmongolia.com; internet www.investmongolia.com; f. 1996; Chair. BAASANKHÜÜGIIN GANZORIG.

Labour Migration Co-ordination Directorate: Khuvisgalchdyn Gudamj 14, Ulan Bator; tel. and fax (11) 327906; Dir GOMBOSÜRENGIIN BILEGSAIKHAN.

Minerals and Petroleum Affairs Directorate (Agency): Central Bldg, Government Bldg 12, Ulan Bator; tel. (11) 263707; e-mail petromon@magicnet.mn; fmrly Mongol Gazryn Tos (Petroleum Authority of Mongolia) and Mineral Resources Authority—amalgamated Dec. 2004; Dir LUVSANVANDANGIIN BOLD.

State Industry and Trade Control Service: Barilgachdyn Talbai, Ulan Bator (POB 38/66); tel. and fax (11) 328049; e-mail chalkhaajavd@mongolnet.mn; f. 2000; enforces laws and regulations relating to trade and industry, services, consumer rights, and geology and mining; Dir DAMBADARJAAGIIN CHILKHAAJAV.

State Property Committee: Government Bldg 4, Ulan Bator; tel. (11) 263911; fax (11) 312798; internet odmaa@spc.gov.mn; supervision and privatization of state property; Chair. DULAMYN SUGAR.

DEVELOPMENT ORGANIZATIONS

Economics and Market Research Center: Government Bldg 1, J. Sambuugiin Gudamj 11, Ulan Bator; tel. (11) 324258; fax (11) 324620; e-mail emrc@mongolchamber.mn; internet www.mongolchamber.mn; Dir J. BOZKHÜÜKHEN.

Mongolian Business Development Agency: Yörönkhii Said Amaryn Gudamj, Ulan Bator (CPOB 458); tel. (11) 311094; fax (11) 311092; internet www.mbda-mongolia.org; f. 1994; Gen. Man. D. BAYARBAT.

Mongolian Development Research Centre: Rm 50, Baga Toiruu 13, Chingeltei District, Ulan Bator (POB 20A/63); tel. and fax (11) 315686; internet www.mdrc.mn; f. 1998; Chair. TSEDENDAMBYN BATBAYAR.

CHAMBERS OF COMMERCE

Junior Chamber of Commerce: Youth Union Bldg, Ulan Bator; tel. (11) 328694; Chair NATSAGDORJ.

Mongolian National Chamber of Commerce and Industry: Sambuugiin Gudamj 11, Ulan Bator 38; tel. (11) 312501; fax (11) 324620; e-mail chamber@mongolchamber.mn; internet www.mongolchamber.mn; f. 1960; responsible for establishing economic and trading relations, contacts between trade and industrial organizations, both at home and abroad, and for generating foreign trade; organizes commodity inspection, press information, and international exhbns and fairs at home and abroad; registration of trademarks and patents; issues certificates of origin and of quality; Chair. and CEO SAMBUUGIIN DEMBEREL.

INDUSTRIAL AND TRADE ASSOCIATIONS

Association of Exporters of Livestock, Raw Materials and Semi-Processed Products: Ulan Bator; Exec. Dir B. TÖRMÖNKH.

Association of Mongolian Sewn Goods and Knitwear Products Manufacturers: Ulan Bator; Pres. N. DASH-ÖLZII.

Building Materials Industry Association: Ulan Bator; Exec. Dir O. LKHAGVADORJ.

Financial Market Association: Ulan Bator; Pres. Ö. GANZORIG.

Grain Producers' Association: Ulan Bator; Pres. TSEVEENJAVYN ÖÖLD.

Mongolian Air Traffic Controllers' Association: National Air Traffic Services, Chinggis Khaan International Airport, Buyant-

MONGOLIA

Ukhaa 210634, Ulan Bator; tel. (11) 282008; fax (11) 282108; e-mail monatca@mcaa.gov.mn.

Mongolian Association of Container and Packaging Makers and Users: Ulan Bator; Pres. DEMBERELIIN OTGONBAATAR.

Mongolian Builders' Association: Block 3, Urt Tsagaan, Chingeltei District, Ulan Bator; tel. 99112636; fax (11) 318685; Pres. MÖNKHBAYARYN BATBAATAR.

Mongolian Coal Association: Ulan Bator; Exec. Dir T. NARAN.

Mongolian Export Association: Ulan Bator; Exec. Dir D. GALSANDORJ.

Mongolian Farmers and Flour Producers' Association: Agro-Pro Business Centre, 19th Sub-District, Bayangol District, Ulan Bator; tel. (11) 300114; fax (11) 362875; e-mail agropro@magicnet.mn; f. 1997; research and quality inspection services in domestic farming and flour industry; Pres. SHARAVYN GUNGAADORJ.

Mongolian Foodstuffs Traders' Association: Ulan Bator; Exec. Dir KH. GIIMAA.

Mongolian Franchising Council of the Mongolian National Chamber of Commerce and Industry: Ulan Bator; tel. (11) 327178; fax (11) 324620; e-mail tecd@mongolchamber.mn; Head J. BATZANDAN.

Mongolian Institute of Internal Auditors: Ulan Bator; tel. (11) 312773; e-mail miia@bizcon.mn; internet www.bizcon.mn/miia; Pres. L. OTGONBAYAR.

Mongolian Marketing Association: Ulan Bator; Pres. D. DAGVADORJ.

Mongolian Metallurgists' Association: School of Technology, Darkhan-Uul Province; tel. (37) 24723; Pres. DO. GANBOLD; Exec. Dir TS. MÖNKHJARGAL.

Mongolian National Industrialists' Association: Ulan Bator; Pres. NAMJAAGIIN DASHZEVEG.

Mongolian National Mining Association: 501 Geosan Company Bldg, Ikh Surguuliin Gudamj 8, Ulan Bator; tel. (11) 314877; fax (11) 330032; e-mail info@miningmongolia.mn; internet www.miningmongolia.mn; f. 1994; provides members of the mining sector with legal protection, and reflects their views in Government mining policy and mineral sector development; Pres. DOGSOMYN GANBOLD; Exec. Dir NAMGARYN ALGAA.

Mongolian PR Association: Ulan Bator; Chair. D. BOLDKHUYAG.

Mongolian Printing Works Association: Ulan Bator; Pres. G. KHAVCHUUR.

Mongolian Timber Industry Association: Mon-Frukt Co, 1st Sub-District, Bayangol District, Ulan Bator (POB 36/51); tel. 91111191; fax (11) 343145.

Mongolian Wool and Cashmere Federation: Khan-Uul District, Ulan Bator; tel. (11) 341871; fax (11) 342814; Pres. D. GANKKHUYAG.

Petroleum Gas Association: Ulan Bator; f. 2005; Pres. SH. GUNGAADORJ.

EMPLOYERS' ORGANIZATIONS

Employers' and Owners' United Association: Rm 401, 4th Floor, Mongolian Youth Association 'B' Bldg, Ulan Bator; tel. (11) 326513; Exec. Dir. B. SEMBEEJAV.

Federation of Professional Business Women of Mongolia: Ulan Bator; tel. and fax (11) 315638; e-mail mbpw@mongolnet.mn; f. 1992; provides education, training, and opportunities for women to achieve economic independence, and the running of businesses; Pres. OCHIRBATYN ZAYAA; 7,000 mems, 14 brs.

Immovable Property (Real Estate) Business Managers' Association: Ulan Bator; Pres. J. BYAMBADORJ.

Mongolian Employers' Federation: Baga Toiruu 44A, Ulan Bator 48; tel. and fax (11) 325635; e-mail monef@magicnet.mn; internet www.monef.mn; f. 1990; fmrly Private Industry Owners' Association; 7,900 mems; Pres. LUVSANBALDANGIIN NYAMSAMBUU.

Mongolian Management Association: Ulan Bator; Chair. Exec. Council DAGVADORJIIN TSERENDORJ.

Private Business Owners' Association: Tsatsral Mon Bldg, 1st Sub-District, Songinokhairkhan District, Ulan Bator; tel. (11) 682905; Pres. T. NYAMDORJ.

Private Employers' Association: Ulan Bator; Pres. O. NATSAGDORJ.

Refuse Disposal Business Managers' Association: Ulan Bator; Chair. SH. BAASANJAV.

Scrap Business Managers' Association: Ulan Bator; Dir S. ALTANTSETSEG.

UTILITIES
Electricity

Central Zone Power Distribution Network: Chingisiin Örgön Chölöö 45, Ulan Bator.

Dulaan Tsakhilgaan Stants-IV Co: 20th Sub-District, Bayangol District, Ulan Bator; tel. (11) 631768; Mongolia's biggest power station; Exec. Dir TS. BAYARBAATAR.

TsTS Co: Ulan Bator; tel. (11) 41294; supervision of electric power network in Ulan Bator; Exec. Dir D. BATTULGA.

Water

Dulaany Süljee Co: Ulan Bator; tel. (11) 343047; e-mail engineer@dhc.mn; internet www.dhc.mn; supervision of hot water district heating network in Ulan Bator; Exec. Dir D. BYAMBA-OCHIR.

USAG: Khökh Tengeriin Gudamj 5, Ulan Bator; tel. (11) 455055; fax (11) 450120; e-mail usag@magicnet.mn; supervision of water supply network in Ulan Bator; Chair. OSORYN ERDENEBAATAR.

IMPORT AND EXPORT ORGANIZATIONS

Agrotekhimpeks: Ulan Bator; imports agricultural machinery and implements, seed, fertilizer, veterinary medicines and irrigation equipment.

Altjin: Ulan Bator; company importing and distributing oil and oil products and also running distilleries, a spin-off from APU; Dir G. ALTAN.

Arisimpex: Ulan Bator; tel. (11) 343007; fax (11) 343008; exports hides and skins, fur and leather goods; imports machinery, chemicals and accessories for leather, fur and shoe industries; Pres. A. TSERENBALJID.

Avtoimpeks: Ulan Bator; f. 1934; state-owned; international trader in motor vehicles; Exec. Dir S. CHULUUNBAT.

Barter and Border: Khuvisgalchdyn Gudamj, Ulan Bator; tel. (11) 324848; barter and border trade operations.

Böönii Khudaldaa: Songinokhairkhan District, Ulan Bator; wholesale trader; privately owned; Dir-Gen. OCHBADRAKHYN BALJINNYAM.

Khorshoololimpeks: Tolgoit, Ulan Bator (CPOB 262); tel. (11) 332926; fax (11) 331128; f. 1964; exports sub-standard skins, hides, wool and furs, handicrafts and finished products; imports equipment and materials for housing, and for clothing and leather goods; Dir L. ÖLZIIBUYAN.

Kompleksimport: Enkh Taivny Gudamj 7, Ulan Bator; tel. and fax (11) 688948; f. 1963; imports consumer goods, foodstuffs, sets of equipment and turnkey projects; training of Mongolians abroad; state-owned pending planned privatization; cap. 3,500m. tögrög.

Makhimpeks: 4th Sub-District, Songinokhairkhan District, Ulan Bator; tel. (11) 632471; fax (11) 632517; f. 1946; abattoir, meat processing, canning, meat imports and exports; 51% share privatized in 1999; cap. 7,800m. tögrög; Exec. Dir B. BÜDRAGCHAA.

Materialimpex: Teeverchdiin Gudamj, Ulan Bator; tel. (11) 365143; fax (11) 367904; e-mail matimpex@magicnet.mn; internet www.materialimpex.com; f. 1957; exports cashmere, wool products, animal skins; imports glass, roofing material, dyes, sanitary ware, metals and metalware, wallpaper, bitumen, wall and floor tiles; partially privatized Feb. 1999, but most shares still state-owned; Gen. Dir B. ZORIG; 126 employees.

Metallimpeks (Metalimpex): Ulan Bator; tel. (11) 331154; Dir D. GANBAT.

Monfa Trade: Monfarma Trade Co, Bldg 69, First 40,000, 4th Sub-District, Sükhbaatar District, Ulan Bator; tel. and fax (11) 324420; e-mail monfatrade@mongol.net; procurement and distribution of pharmaceuticals.

Mongoleksport Co Ltd: Government Bldg 7, 8th Fl., Erkh Chölöönii Talbai, Ulan Bator; tel. (11) 329234; fax (11) 327884; exports wool, hair, cashmere, mining products, antler, skins and hides; Dir-Gen. D. CHIMEDDAMBAA.

Mongolemimpex: Khuvisgalchdyn Gudamj, Ikh Toiruu 39, Ulan Bator; tel. (11) 323961; fax (11) 323877; e-mail moemim@magicnet.mn; internet www.mongolemimpex.mn; f. 1923; procurement and distribution to hospitals and pharmacies of drugs and surgical appliances; Dir-Gen. BATBAYARYN BOLORMAA.

Mongolimpeks: Khuvisgalchdyn Örgön Chölöö, Ulan Bator; tel. (11) 326081; exports cashmere, camels' wool, hair, fur, casings, powdered blood and horn, antler, wheat gluten, alcoholic drinks, cashmere and camels' wool knitwear, blankets, copper concentrate, souvenirs, stamps and coins; imports light and mining industry machinery, scientific instruments, chemicals, pharmaceuticals and consumer goods; state-owned; Dir-Gen. DORJPALAMYN DÖKHÖMBAYAR.

MONGOLIA

Mongol Safari Co Ltd: Baigal Ordon 38, Ulan Bator; tel. (11) 360267; fax (11) 360067; e-mail monsafari@magicnet.mn; internet www.monsafari.com; f. 1990; exports hunting products; imports hunting equipment and technology; organizes hunting and trekking tours; Dir-Gen. U. BUYANDELGER.

Monnoos: Ulan Bator (POB 36/450); tel. (11) 343201; fax (11) 342591; e-mail monnoos@mongolnet.mn; wool trade enterprise; Dir SANJIIN BAT-OYUUN.

Monos Cosmetics: Monos Group, Bldg 25, II-40,000, 2nd Sub-District, Chingeltei District, Ulan Bator; tel. and fax (11) 315908; fax (11) 320967; e-mail info@monoscosmetics.mn; internet www.monoscosmetics.mn; f. 1990; production, export and import of cosmetics; Chair. and CEO BALDANDORJIIN ERDENEKHISHIG; Exec. Dir KH. SOLONGO; 90 employees.

Monos Pharm Trade: Monos Group, Namyaanjugiin Gudamj 23, 18th Sub-District, Bayanzürkh District, Ulan Bator; tel. and fax (11) 450054; fax (11) 463158; internet www.monos.mn; f. 1990; production, export and import of medicine, medical equipment and health food; Dir-Gen. LUVSANGIIN KHÜRELBAATAR; 280 employees.

Noosimpeks: Ulan Bator; tel. (11) 341577; exports scoured sheep's wool, yarn, carpets, fabrics, blankets, mohair and felt boots; imports machinery and chemicals for wool industry.

Nüürs: Ulan Bator; tel. (11) 327428; exports and imports in coal-mining field; Man. D. DÜGERJAV.

Packaging: Tolgoit, Ulan Bator; tel. (11) 31053; exports raw materials of agricultural origin, sawn timber, consumer goods, unused spare parts and equipment, and non-ferrous scrap; imports machinery and materials for packaging industry, and consumer goods.

Petrovis: Ulan Bator; tel. (11) 330153; fax (11) 320426; e-mail info@petrovis.mn; internet www.petrovis.mn; oil products importer and distributor; in Feb. 2004 acquired the 80% state-owned shares in the country's biggest distributor NIK (Neft Import Kontsern) for US $8.5m; CEO and Pres. J. OYUUNGEREL.

Raznoimpeks: 3rd Sub-District, Bayangol District, Ulan Bator; tel. (11) 329465; fax (11) 329901; f. 1933; exports wool, cashmere, hides, canned meat, powdered bone, alcoholic drinks, macaroni and confectionery; imports cotton and woollen fabrics, silk, knitwear, shoes, fresh and canned fruit, vegetables, tea, milk powder, acids, paints, safety equipment, protective clothing, printing and packaging paper; state-owned pending planned privatization; cap. 6,100m. tögrög; Exec. Dir Ts. BAT-ENKH.

Tekhnikimport: Ulan Bator; tel. (11) 685149; imports machinery, instruments and spare parts for light, food, wood, building, power and mining industries, road-building and communications; state-owned; Dir-Gen. G. GANTULGA.

Tüshig Trade Co Ltd: Enkh Taivny Örgön Chölöö, Ulan Bator (POB 44/481); tel. (11) 314062; fax (11) 314052; exports sheep and camel wool, and cashmere goods; imports machinery for small enterprises, foodstuffs and consumer goods; Dir-Gen. D. GANBAATAR.

CO-OPERATIVES

Association of Private Herders' Co-operatives: Ulan Bator (POB 21/787); tel. (11) 633601; fax (11) 325935; e-mail mongolherder@magicnet.mn; f. 1991; Pres. R. ERDENE; Exec. Dir Ts. MYAGMAR-OCHIR.

Central Association of Consumer Co-operatives: Ulan Bator; tel. and fax (11) 329025; f. 1990; wholesale and retail trade; exports animal raw materials; imports foodstuffs and consumer goods; Chair. G. MYANGANBAYAR.

Mongolian Association of Production Co-operatives: Urt Tsagaan, Khudaldaany Gudamj 12, Chingeltei District, Ulan Bator; tel. (11) 310956; e-mail cumic@mol.mn.

Mongolian Association of Savings and Credit Co-operatives: Bldg 2, State Property Committee, Chingeltei District, Ulan Bator; tel. (11) 313665; Pres. SH. GOOKHÜÜ.

Mongolian Co-operatives Development Centre: Ulan Bator; Dir DANZANGIIN RADNAARAGCHAA.

National Association of Mongolian Agricultural Co-operative Members: Enkhtayvny Örgön Chölöö, 18 A/1, Ulan Bator; tel. (11) 453535; fax (11) 458899; e-mail namac63@mongolnet.mn; internet www.namac.mn; f. 1992; Pres. NADMIDYN BAYARTSAIKHAN.

Union of Mongolian Production and Services Co-operatives: Bldg 16, II-40,000, 3rd Sub-District, Chingeltei District, Ulan Bator (POB 46/470); tel. (11) 327583; fax (11) 328446; e-mail umpscoop@hotmail.com; f. 1990; Pres. SAMDANY ENKHTUYAA.

TRADE UNIONS

Confederation of Mongolian Trade Unions: Sükhbaataryn Talbai 3, Ulan Bator; tel. (11) 327253; fax (11) 322128; e-mail mpcd@cmtu.mn; internet www.cmtu.mn; brs throughout the country; Chair. S. GANBAATAR; Sec.-Gen. M. GANAA.

Mongolian United Confederation of Trade Unions: Ulan Bator; Chair. D. TSEYEN-OIDOV.

Transport

MTT (Mongol Transport Team): MTT Bldg, 5th Sub-District, Bayangol District, Ulan Bator; tel. (11) 689000; fax (11) 684953; e-mail mtt@mtteam.mn; internet www.mtteam.mn; international freight forwarding by air, sea, rail and road; offices in Beijing, Berlin, Moscow and Prague.

Tuushin Co Ltd: Tuushin Bldg, Yörönkhii Said Amaryn Gudamj, Sükhbaatar District, Ulan Bator; tel. (11) 312092; fax (11) 325570; e-mail tuushin@magicnet.mn; internet www.tuushin.mn; f. 1990; international freight forwarders; transport and forwarding policy and services, warehousing, customs agent; tourism; offices in Beijing, Moscow and Prague; Dir-Gen. N. ZORIGT.

RAILWAYS

In 2004 the total track length was 2,083 km, of which 1,815 km was the main-line track.

Mongolian Railway Affairs Directorate: Zamchdyn Gudamj, Ulan Bator; internet www.gate1.pmis.gov.mn/tzheg; Dir DAVAADORJIIN GANBOLD.

Ulan Bator Railway: Zamchdyn Gudamj, Ulan Bator (CPOB 376); tel. (21) 944409; fax (11) 328360; internet www.mtz.mn; f. 1949; jt-stock co with Russian Federation; Dir VANCHIGDORJIIN OTGONDEMBEREL; Chair. I. V. ROMASHOV.

External Lines: from the Russian frontier at Naushki/Sükhbaatar (connecting with the Trans-Siberian Railway) to Ulan Bator and on to the Chinese frontier at Zamyn-Üüd/Erenhot, connecting with Beijing (total length 1,110 km).

Branches: from Darkhan to Sharyn Gol coalfield (length 63 km); branch from Salkhit near Darkhan, westwards to Erdenet (Erdenetiin-ovoo open-cast copper mine) in Bulgan Province (164 km); from Bagakhangai to Baganuur coal-mine, south-east of Ulan Bator (96 km); from Khar Airag to Bor-Öndör fluorspar mines (60 km); from Sainshand to Züünbayan oilfield (63 km).

Eastern Railway, linking Mongolia with the Trans-Siberian and Chita via Borzya; from the Russian frontier at Solovyevsk to Choibalsan (238 km), with branch from Chingis Dalan to Mardai uranium mine near Dashbalbar (110 km), possibly inactive.

IFFC (International Freight-forwarding Centre of Mongolian Railways): Mongolian Railway Headquarters, Zamchdyn Gudamj 1, Bayangol District, Ulan Bator (CPOB 376); tel. (11) 312509; fax (11) 313165; e-mail iffc@railcom.mn; internet www.iffc.mn; international freight forwarding.

ROADS

Main roads link Ulan Bator with the Chinese frontier at Zamyn Üüd/Erenhot and with the Russian frontier at Altanbulag/Kyakhta. A road from Chita in Russia crosses the frontier in the east at Mangut/Onon (Ölzii) and branches for Choibalsan and Öndörkhaan. In the west and north-west, roads from Biisk and Irkutsk in Russia go to Tsagaannuur, Bayan-Ölgii aimag, and Khankh, on Lake Khövsgöl, respectively. The total length of the road network was 45,000 km in 2005, of which asphalted roads comprised 1,500 km (incl. 400 km in Ulan Bator), gravel roads comprised 1,400 km, and improved earth roads comprised 1,300 km. The first section of a hard-surfaced road between Ulan Bator and Bayankhongor was completed in 1975. The road from Darkhan to Erdenet was also surfaced. Construction has been focused on the routes from Ulan Bator southwards to Choir and Sainshand and eastward to Öndörkhaan. In 2005 a further 389 km of hard-surfaced road was built, and 747 km of gravel road. The length of hard-surfaced roads increased from 2,278.6 km in 2005 to 2,392.8 km in 2006. In 2007 a further 268.4 km of hard-surfaced road and 75.4 km of gravel road were put into operation. Mongolia divides its road system into state-grade and country-grade roads. State-grade roads (of which there were 11,000 km in 2005) run from Ulan Bator to provincial centres and from provincial centres to the border. Country-grade roads account for the remaining roads, but they are mostly rough cross-country tracks.

To mark the millennium, the Government decided to construct a new east–west road, linking the Chinese and Russian border regions via Ölgii, Lake Khar Us, Zavkhan and Arkhangai provinces, Dashinchilen, Lün, Ulan Bator, Nalaikh, Baganuur, Öndörkhaan and Sümber (Khalkh Gol). Construction was expected to take about 10 years, but because of the cost, the road was not expected to be surfaced for the whole length.

There are bus services in Ulan Bator and other large towns, and road haulage services throughout the country on the basis of motor transport depots, mostly situated in provincial centres.

MONGOLIA

CIVIL AVIATION

Civil aviation in Mongolia, including the provision of air traffic control and airport management, is the responsibility of the Main Directorate of Civil Aviation, which provides air traffic and airport management services. It also supervises the Mongolian national airline (MIAT) and smaller operators such as Khangarid and Tengeriin Ulaach, which operate local flights. Aeroflot (Russia) and Air China operate flights to Ulan Bator (Chinggis Khaan International Airport).

Main Directorate of Civil Aviation: Chinggis Khaan International Airport, Buyant-Ukhaa, Ulan Bator; tel. (11) 282004; fax (11) 282102; e-mail webmaster@mcaa.gov.mn; internet internet www.mcaa.gov.mn; Dir-Gen. SANJAAJAVYN BATMÖNKH.

A-Jet Aviation: Olimpiin Gudamj, 1st Sub-District, Sükhbaatar District, Ulan Bator (POB 46/202); tel. (11) 318480; fax (11) 319780; e-mail flt_ops@jetmongol.com; internet www.jetmongol.com; f. 2000; fmrly Central Mongolia Airways; 3 Mi-8 helicopters for tourist travel; Exec. Dir LHAMJAV NYAMBAYAR.

Aero Mongolia Co Ltd: Chinggis Khaan International Airport, Buyant-Ukhaa, Ulan Bator (POB 34/105); tel. (11) 283212; e-mail management@aeromongolia.mn; internet www.aeromongolia.mn; f. 2001; began operations June 2003; scheduled international flights to Irkutsk and Hohhot and scheduled internal flights to five provincial centres and Juulchin's South Gobi tourist camp by Fokker-50 aircraft; twice-weekly flights by Fokker-100 to the Republic of Korea inaugurated in Feb. 2006; Dir B. CHULUUNBAATAR.

Blue Sky Aviation: Door 2, Apt S-61, 1st Sub-District, Sükhbaatar District, Ulan Bator; tel. (11) 312085; fax (11) 322857; e-mail bsa@maf-europe.org; internet www.blueskyaviation.mn; jt venture of Mission Aviation Fellowship and Exodus International; operates charter flights and medical emergency services; f. 1999; Dir NIRI LID; Operations Man. JAN TORE FOLDØY.

Eznis (Easiness) Airways: Naiman Zokhis Bldg, Söüliin Gudamj, Sükhbaatar District, Ulan Bator; tel. (11) 313689; fax (11) 314258; internet www.eznis.com; f. 2006; operates two SAAB 340B aircraft on internal routes; Exec. Dir L. OYUUNBAT.

Khangarid: Room 210, MPRP Bldg, Baga Toiruu 37/1, Ulan Bator; tel. (11) 320138; fax (11) 311333; e-mail hangard_air_co@magicnet.mn; domestic and international passenger and freight services; Dir L. SERGELEN.

Mongolian Civil Air Transport (MIAT): MIAT Bldg, Chinggis Khaan International Airport, Buyant-Ukhaa, Khan-Uul District, Ulan Bator; tel. (11) 379935; fax (11) 379919; e-mail contact@miat.com; internet www.miat.com; f. 1956; scheduled services to Moscow, Irkutsk, Beijing, Seoul, Osaka, Berlin, Hohhot, and to some Mongolian provincial centres; carried 303,500 passengers in 2004; Pres. LUTYN SANDAG; Exec. Dir B. ERDENEBILEG.

Tengeriin Ulaach (Sky Horse Aviation): Chinggis Khaan International Airport, Buyant-Ukhaa, Khan-Uul District, Ulan Bator (POB 34/17); tel. (11) 282023; fax (11) 379765; e-mail skyhorsenew@mbox.mn; internal helicopter transport for tourists and businesspeople; Dir L. TÖMÖR.

Trans-Ölgii: Ölgii, Bayan-Ölgii Province; f. 2006; operates one leased An-24 on Ölgii–Ulan Bator route twice a week.

Tourism

A foreign tourist service bureau was established in 1954, but tourism is not very developed. In 2003 Mongolia had 132 tourist camps with 6,400 beds and 260 hotels with 7,000 beds. By 2005 the numbers of camps and hotels had increased to around 160 and 300 respectively. Of the 30 or more hotels in Ulan Bator, all but four are relatively small, and in the peak summer season there is a shortage of rooms. The outlying tourist centres (Terelj, South Gobi, Öndör-Dov and Khujirt) have basic facilities. The country's main attractions are its scenery, wildlife and historical relics. According to the Soros Foundation, there were 344,635 foreign visitors to Mongolia in 2005, of whom 234,352 described the purpose of their visit as leisure or holiday. Total arrivals in 2006 numbered 385,980, rising to some 451,000 in 2007. Tourism revenue in 2005 reportedly reached US $223m.

Juulchin World Tours Corporation: Olimpiin Gudamj, 1st Sub-District, Sükhbaatar District; tel. (11) 312091; fax (11) 320246; e-mail info@juulchin.com; internet www.juulchin.com; f. 1954; offices in Berlin, New Jersey, Beijing, Tokyo, Osaka and Seoul; tours, trekking, safaris, jeep tours, expeditions; Exec. Dir SH. NERGÜI.

Mongolian Adventure Tourism Association: Ulan Bator; Sec.-Gen. B. JIYAANDORJ.

Mongolian Tourism Association: 3/F, Rm 318, Building of the Mongolian Trade Unions Confederation, Sükhbaataryn Talbai, Ulan Bator; tel. (11) 327820; fax (11) 323026; e-mail info@travelmongolia.org; internet www.travelmongolia.org; Pres. BAYARSAIKHANY TSEVELMAA.

MONTENEGRO

Introductory Survey

Location, Climate, Language, Religion, Flag, Capital

The Republic of Montenegro is situated in the central Balkan peninsula, in south-eastern Europe. Montenegro has frontiers with Bosnia and Herzegovina to the west and north-west, Serbia to the north, Kosovo (a former Serbian province, which made a declaration of independence on 17 February 2008) to the east, and Albania to the south-east, as well as a short frontier with the Dubrovnik exclave of Croatia in the south-west. There is a western coastline along the Adriatic Sea (part of the Mediterranean). Montenegro has a rugged mountainous terrain, being dominated by the Black Mountains (Crna Gora), from which the country takes its name. The climate is Mediterranean near the coast, and continental inland. Mountainous areas have a colder climate with heavy snowfall in winter. Average temperatures range from between −7°C (19.4°F) and 23°C (73.4°F) inland, and between 11°C (51.8°F) and 28°C (84.2°F) on the coast. Montenegro's mountainous regions receive some of the highest amounts of rainfall in Europe. The Constitution, adopted in October 2007, defined the principal language as Montenegrin, with the Cyrillic and Latin alphabets in equal use. The Serbian, Bosnian, Albanian and Croatian languages are also in official use. The principal religion is Orthodox Christianity, and there are significant Roman Catholic and Muslim communities. The national flag (proportions 1 by 2) is red, with a golden coat of arms depicting a double-headed eagle. Podgorica is the capital of Montenegro. The historical capital is Cetinje.

Recent History

After the Second World War, Montenegro became one of the six constituent republics of the federal Yugoslavia established by the Communist Party of Yugoslavia (known as the League of Communists of Yugoslavia—LCY—from 1952) under Josip Broz (Tito). The Montenegrins were, traditionally, close to the Serbs and adherents of the Orthodox Church. Montenegrins were strongly represented among the ranks of the LCY and of the Yugoslav People's Army (YPA). Montenegro generally supported the Serbian reassertion of dominance within Yugoslavia after the death of Tito in the 1980s. Institutionally, this was helped by the installation of a new party leadership in the republic, following demonstrations during 1988 in favour of the Serbian leader, Slobodan Milošević. Subsequent reforms transformed the Skupština Republike Crne Gore (Assembly of the Republic of Montenegro) into a unicameral body of 125 members and replaced Montenegro's collective Presidency with a directly elected state President. The elections, in December 1990, represented a victory for the ruling League of Communists of Montenegro (subsequently renamed the Democratic Party of Montenegrin Socialists—DPMS), which secured 83 seats in the new legislature, while its presidential candidate, Momir Bulatović, became President, after a second round of voting. In February 1991 Bulatović invited one of his party colleagues, Milo Đukanović, to head the republican Government. The third member of the new Montenegrin leadership was Svetozar Marović (who was later to serve three terms as parliamentary Speaker).

The onset of armed conflict in Yugoslavia prompted Montenegro to adopt a pragmatic response to the disintegration of the federation and ensure its proper representation in any negotiations. Although the republic supported Serbia in the crises of the early 1990s, Montenegro nevertheless adopted a declaration of state sovereignty on 18 October 1991 and a new Constitution in November. However, Montenegro remained committed to the federation with Serbia, confirming this conclusively in a referendum in March 1992. As a result, the two republics announced a new federal Constitution, which was a continuation of the old state, but effectively acknowledged the secession of the other four federal units. The Federal Republic of Yugoslavia (FRY) came into effect on 27 April. On 12 October a new Montenegrin Constitution declared the republic to be part of the FRY and, early in 1993, the disposition of power was confirmed by the re-election of Bulatović as State President and the continuation of Đukanović as premier. Meanwhile, another Montenegrin, Radoje Kontić, became the federal Prime Minister.

Relations between Montenegro and Serbia deteriorated from the mid-1990s. The Montenegrins were generally committed to the federal union, but resisted encroachments on their autonomy. The attempts of Serbian leader Milošević to disassemble separate republican defence and foreign policy structures were particularly resisted. Montenegro also wished to obtain international aid, which entailed its pursuit of a distinct foreign policy, often at variance with that of the central authorities. The divergence in economic interests had mainly stemmed from Serbia's introduction in mid-1993 of an export-import licensing system, which had prompted Montenegro to enact similar inter-republican trade controls. The central authorities also tried to assert control over some state assets in Montenegro, which was a contentious issue when privatization and the structures of a free market were further advanced in Montenegro than Serbia. Increasingly, however, the principal dichotomy in Montenegrin politics was not so much a simple split between Serbia and Montenegro, but between the presidency and the premiership. Bulatović became more and more identified by his support for Milošević, who was attempting to control all opposition within the FRY, thereby threatening Montenegrin autonomy. Đukanović was more reform-minded than those in power at the centre, and resistant to Milošević's dominance of republican as well as federal politics, but in May 1996 the premier still maintained that most Montenegrins favoured the union with Serbia. Đukanović and Bulatović appeared united in their pursuit of separate negotiation of Montenegro's status in the international economic community, but relations between the two were strained by the premier's expressed support for Serbian anti-Government protesters later that year. In February 1997 Đukanović publicly declared Milošević unfit to hold public office, the one in question being the federal presidency, while in the following month he resisted the demands of Bulatović that he dismiss all anti-Milošević ministers in the republican Government. The ruling DPMS (the parliamentary dominance of which had been conclusively confirmed in legislative elections in November 1996) split into two factions during 1997, as a result of Bulatović's support for the Serbian leader (who became the federal President in July). In July supporters of Đukanović within the DPMS voted to remove Bulatović from the leadership of the party. Bulatović and Đukanović became the leading candidates in the Montenegrin presidential election of October. Đukanović won the second round of voting, with 50.8% of votes cast, although his opponent refused to accept the result as legitimate.

Đukanović was inaugurated as the President of Montenegro in January 1998, amid violent protests from supporters of Bulatović. A compromise agreement on early legislative elections in May was reached, pending which a transitional Government, led by the Đukanović faction of the DPMS, was formed in February. Bulatović's faction refused to participate and renamed itself the Socialist People's Party of Montenegro (SPPM). However, support for the anti-Milošević stance of Đukanović and his party was confirmed in the elections of May, when the DPMS won an outright majority (it formed a coalition Government, led by Filip Vujanović, in July). Montenegro had become increasingly suspicious of Serbia's intentions, particularly with the appointment of Bulatović as federal Prime Minister in May (in succession to Kontić). He proceeded to purge many Montenegrin officials from federal institutions, in response to the DPMS appointing its own nominees to the federal chamber of the Yugoslav parliament in June; the republican authorities were anxious to resist institutional reforms that would enhance the powers of the federal presidency. Montenegro refused to acknowledge the administration of Bulatović, suspending all links with the federal Government in August.

Relations between the federal partners of the FRY increasingly deteriorated during 1999. Despite the wishes of President Milošević in the previous year, significant elements of the Serbian and federal establishments had resisted using the military to resolve the disputes in Montenegro, and in 1999 the armed forces were otherwise occupied. Escalating civil conflict in the Serbian province of Kosovo, a majority of the population of which comprised ethnic Albanians, led to aerial bombardment of the FRY by forces of the North Atlantic Treaty Organization (NATO, see p. 340) in March–June. Despite Montenegro's appeals to be spared such damage, the republic suffered during the action that was attempting to force Yugoslav compliance with the international community's protection of the Albanian population. None the less, Montenegro continued to distance itself from Serbian military actions; in March Montenegro refused to recognize the state of war declared by the federal Government at the commencement of the NATO bombardment and disassociated itself from the severing of diplomatic relations with several NATO countries, while in April Đukanović refused to place Montenegrin security forces under federal military command, as ordered by President Milošević.

In the aftermath of the open conflict in Kosovo, the Yugoslav federation became increasingly unstable, as internal wrangling and external forces combined to drive the two constituent republics apart. Politically, in mid-1999 the Government of Montenegro proposed the replacement of the federal system with an association of two states, threatening a referendum on full independence if Milošević did not agree; in October the Skupština Republike Crne Gore enacted a citizenship law, which was viewed as progress towards such an arrangement. Economically, Montenegro attempted to insulate itself from the isolated Serbian economy, provoking reactions that further distanced the partners; inter-republican talks having foundered, in November Montenegro replaced the depreciating Yugoslav dinar as its official currency with the German Deutsche Mark (the federal Constitutional Court declared the measure illegal in January 2000, to little effect). Serbia confirmed the economic rupture by imposing a partial blockade and then, in January 2000, a ban on the export of foodstuffs to Montenegro and a full economic embargo in March. By May premier Vujanović was saying that the Yugoslav federation had ceased to exist, and had already effectively been replaced with a looser confederation. Most of the Montenegrin Government preferred such a solution, rather than outright independence, but fears of Milošević increasing his political influence or of Serbian military action (such as the federal army's seizure of control over Montenegro's main airport in December 1999) escalated tensions.

Partial municipal elections in Montenegro in mid-2000 indicated the divided state of public opinion and were a disappointment to the Đukanović administration. In the capital, the DPMS-led ruling coalition commanded an overall majority, but the Bulatović-led alliance remained strong, while the pro-independence Liberal Alliance of Montenegro (LAM) did not perform strongly. In some parts of the republic, such as Herceg Novi, the opposition parties achieved a majority. Attempts to reform federal institutions in a way that would weaken the influence of the smaller partner in the federation were viewed with alarm in Montenegro, and the Skupština Republike Crne Gore voted against the proposals in July. However, the anti-Milošević stance of Đukanović was to prove less useful once there had been a change of regime in Serbia in October (the ruling Montenegrin coalition had boycotted the federal polls of the previous month), which included Bulatović resigning as federal Prime Minister. Đukanović began to advocate full independence for Montenegro, urging a referendum on the issue. This prompted the pro-federation People's Party of Montenegro to withdraw from the ruling republican coalition, precipitating legislative elections in April 2001. The DPMS-led pro-independence coalition won 36 of the 77 seats, the SPPM-led alliance 33 and the LAM six. Vujanović was reappointed as premier. Meanwhile, negotiations about a new form of federal association were ongoing, and, from November, were mediated by the European Union (EU, see p. 244). The federal and republican leaderships signed a framework agreement on confederation on 14 March 2002, which provided for Serbia and Montenegro to maintain separate economies and state structures, but to be united by a shared presidency and legislature in charge of foreign and defence policies. Crucially, Montenegro had the right to refer the issue of independence to a referendum after three years. However, despite the appeals of other pro-independence groups, later in March the LAM resigned from the Government in protest at the agreement. None the less, the Assembly approved the accord on 9 April, although further resignations from the Government forced Vujanović to seek a new coalition, which he was unable to achieve by July.

On 20 October 2002 the DPMS-led, pro-independence ruling coalition, now known as the Democratic List for a European Montenegro, won 39 of the 75 seats in the republican legislature. Together for Changes, which had opposed looser union with Serbia and was led by the SPPM (which had a new leadership), retained 30 seats. Vujanović, who continued to act as premier until a new coalition was formed, was elected Speaker of the Skupština Republike Crne Gore on 5 November. Vujanović became acting President of the Republic of Montenegro 20 days later, when Đukanović resigned, so that he could be nominated to form a government. A dispute over the allocation of ministerial portfolios with the DPMS's ally, the Social Democratic Party of Montenegro (SDP), delayed the formalization of the coalition, but the new Government headed by Đukanović was finally approved by the legislature on 8 January 2003. Meanwhile, the pro-federation SPPM and the pro-independence LAM had organized a boycott of the presidential election, held on 22 December 2002, which was consequently won by Vujanović, with 83.7% of the votes cast, but with those votes cast amounting to less than the one-half of the total electorate required for a victory. Vujanović was the Democratic List candidate, but, owing to the boycott, the election was not contested by the main opposition group, Together for Change. He won 82.0% of votes in the repeated poll held on 9 February 2003, but with only 47% of the electorate participating, prompting the Skupština Republike Crne Gore to abolish the regulation on participation, in advance of a further attempt to elect a President. Vujanović was duly elected President on 11 May, with 62.9% of the votes cast (about 48% of the electorate participated). His nearest rival was Miodrag Živković of the LAM, who received 30.7%

Prior to the final election of Vujanović (who was pro-independence, but had been induced by the EU to support the compromise of a looser union with Serbia), on 29 January 2003 the Skupština Republike Crne Gore approved the new arrangements for confederation with Serbia. On 4 February the federal parliament formally adopted a Constitutional Charter, thereby transforming the FRY into a new State Union of Serbia and Montenegro. A Skupština, President (former Montenegrin parliamentary Speaker and DPMS leader, Marović) and Prime Minister of the State Union were elected in late February and March. Nevertheless, the republican Government continued to work towards the referendum on independence after three years, which was announced by Vujanović upon his election in May. Further preparations for potential independence were enacted in July, when the Skupština Republike Crne Gore adopted a new flag and anthem, as well as making 13 July a national holiday (being the anniversary of the 1878 recognition of Montenegrin independence by the Congress of Berlin and of the 1941 start of a popular revolt against the occupying Axis powers).

Politicians in Serbia and Montenegro agreed that the EU should set the conditions for and supervise the conduct of any referendum on Montenegrin independence. In February 2006, amid much controversy, the EU announced that any proposal to make Montenegro independent of its Union with Serbia would require the approval of 55% of those voting, with at least 50% participating in the referendum, to secure international recognition. The Government, which favoured a simple majority, reluctantly agreed to the conditions. Legislation providing for a referendum to be held on 21 May was duly enacted on 1 March (with the support of 60 of the 75 deputies). In April the Government formally presented to the Serbian Government a guarantee of equal status for Serbian citizens within Montenegro in the event of independence.

Two days after the referendum of 21 May 2006 the electoral authorities declared Montenegro to have voted in favour of independence. With a participation rate of over 86%, some 55.5% of votes cast at the referendum were in favour of independence and 44.5% against, thereby narrowly fulfilling the EU criteria for a successful vote. The pro-Union parties denounced the result, but the EU and other international organizations declared the vote to have been free and fair. The Skupština Republike Crne Gore duly declared the country independent on 3 June, and international recognition followed. Some two weeks later, Serbia acknowledged the dissolution of the Union and adopted its own independence. A new Ministry of Defence formally assumed responsibility for all military units of the Union on Montenegrin territory, while in July the respective finance ministers and central bank governors agreed the division of the financial rights and obligations of the former State Union (Montenegro was to receive 5.9% of the convertible currency and gold reserves of Serbia and Montenegro). On 11 July President Vujanović announced that legislative and local elections had been scheduled for September.

The general election of 10 September 2006 was won outright by the ruling coalition of the DPMS and the SDP, which secured 41 of the 81 seats in an expanded Skupština Republike Crne Gore. The SPPM alliance, no longer fuelled by the struggle against independence, only obtained 11 seats (eight for the SPPM itself), being displaced as the largest opposition grouping by the more overt Serbian List, led by Andrija Mandić of the Serb People's Party of Montenegro, which won 12 seats. A new party, the Movement for Changes (established on the basis of a reformist group founded by academics and economists in 2002), which was pro-European and anti-corruption, also obtained 11 seats. The Liberal Party of Montenegro (the only surviving successor to the LAM, which split in 2004), in alliance with the Bosniak Party of Montenegro, secured two seats. Other groups to secure a seat mainly represented the Muslim minorities. In early October 2006 Đukanović announced that he would not seek to continue his premiership, as he wished to develop his business interests (although he would remain leader of the DPMS). (Đukanović had been accused of involvement with organized crime, and was under investigation by the Italian authorities, mainly in connection with large-scale illicit tobacco trade in the Balkans.) He reportedly favoured Minister of Finance Igor Lukšić as his nominated successor, but a compromise was agreed with another senior party leader, Marović, and the Minister of Justice, Željko Šturanović, became the DPMS candidate. Once the new Skupština Republike Crne Gore met, Šturanović and his Government were duly installed, despite the delaying tactics of the pro-Serbian bloc, on 10 November. The legislature was subsequently also to act as a constituent assembly and to debate a new constitution.

Montenegro was admitted to the Organization for Security and Co-operation in Europe (see p. 354) on 22 June 2006 and to the UN as the 192nd member state on 28 June. The country then proceeded to seek membership of other international organizations. (Owing to the disintegrating association with Serbia, Montenegro already had links with many international organizations, usually informal, but had, for instance, sought membership of the World Trade Organization since 2004.) Montenegro has ambitions to join NATO and the EU (the last of which, in July 2006, agreed to adapt negotiations for a Stabilization and Association Agreement—SAA—with the former Union to the new situation). Iceland was the first country to recognize the newly independent state, followed by Switzerland and Russia. The EU recognized Montenegro on 12 June, and the USA recognized it on the following day. Serbia, which had declared its own independence from the defunct Union with Montenegro on 5 June, extended recognition on 15 June, establishing diplomatic relations one week later. Montenegro acceded to the Geneva Conventions on 2 August. On 14 December Montenegro (together with Serbia, and Bosnia and Herzegovina) was admitted to NATO's 'Partnership for Peace' (see p. 342) programme. On 18 January 2007 Montenegro officially became the 185th member of the World Bank, also joining the IMF and the other associated institutions.

Following a February 2007 ruling by the International Court of Justice (see p. 20) that the Serbian state was not directly responsible for genocide in Bosnia and Herzegovina in 1992–95 (see the chapter on Serbia), it was expected that Croatia would abandon a case submitted to the Court in 1999 against the FRY (devolved on Montenegro), in favour of a financial settlement with Montenegro (the military of which had played a leading role in the attack on Dubrovnik, Croatia, in 1991). Montenegro initialled the SAA with the EU on 15 March 2007. (The adoption of a new constitution in accordance with EU standards was required for the official signing of the SAA and its ratification by EU member states.) On 2 April the Skupština Republike Crne Gore approved a new draft Constitution, which, however, included several alternative amendments regarding the regulation of state symbols, official languages and religious communities, owing to the failure of the ruling coalition and the opposition to reach agreement in these areas. On 11 May Montenegro was admitted to the Council of Europe (see p. 225).

On 19 October 2007, after prolonged acrimonious debate, a new Constitution was finally approved by 55 of the 76 deputies present in the Skupština Republike Crne Gore, narrowly achieving the requisite two-thirds' majority of votes; the Constitution was officially promulgated on 22 October. Serbian parties denounced the new Constitution (in which Montenegrin replaced Serbian as the main official language) as being discriminatory to Serbs, and the Serbian List issued a declaration repudiating its ratification. The adoption of the Constitution allowed the official signature of the SAA at a meeting of EU foreign ministers in the same month.

In mid-January 2008 the parliamentary Speaker announced that the forthcoming presidential election would take place on 6 April. On 31 January Šturanović tendered his resignation from his position as Prime Minister, on grounds of ill health. On 6 February the DPMS nominated Đukanović to return to the prime ministerial office; Vujanović was selected as the party's presidential candidate in the forthcoming election. On 29 February the appointment of Đukanović as premier and of his Government (which remained unchanged from the previous administration) was narrowly approved, with 41 votes cast in the Skupština Republike Crne Gore. (Although the Italian investigation into organized crime allegations continued, Đukanović's immunity from prosecution was restored by his return to office.)

Following Kosovo's declaration of independence from Serbia on 17 February 2008, the Montenegrin Government announced that it would only extend diplomatic recognition to Kosovo after ensuring that this would not endanger national security. In March Đukanović and his Croatian counterpart, meeting in Zagreb, agreed to refer the issue of demarcation of the maritime boundary between the two countries to the International Court of Justice at The Hague, the Netherlands. At a NATO summit meeting, which took place in Bucharest, Romania, in early April, Montenegro (together with Bosnia and Herzegovina) was invited to enter into an intensified dialogue towards membership.

Vujanović's re-election to the presidency on 6 April 2008, with 52.3% of the votes cast, further consolidated the strength of the DPMS. Mandić won 19.3% of the votes; the reformist leader of the Movement for Changes, Nebojša Medojević, won 17.3%; and Srđan Milić of the SPPM won 11.1%. The rate of voter participation was estimated at about 69% (considerably higher than in 2003). Vujanović, who was scheduled to be inaugurated on 21 May, pledged to work towards EU accession.

Government

In accordance with the provisions of the Constitutional Charter of February 2003, Montenegro became independent of the former State Union of Serbia and Montenegro on 3 June 2006, following a national referendum held on 21 May. The Constitution of the Republic of Montenegro was adopted by the legislature on 19 October 2007 and was officially promulgated on 22 October. Legislative power is vested in the 81-member Skupština Republike Crne Gore (Assembly of the Republic of Montenegro), which is directly elected for a period of four years. Executive power is vested in the Government and judicial power in the courts of law. The President of the Republic is directly elected for a term of five years, and is restricted to two terms in office. Constitutionality and legality are protected by the Constitutional Court. The President nominates the Prime Minister for approval by the Skupština. The Prime Minister proposes the composition of the Government to the Skupština.

Defence

Following Montenegro's declaration of independence on 3 June 2006, the Montenegrin Government established a Ministry of Defence and revoked compulsory military service. In December Montenegro was admitted to the 'Partnership for Peace' (see p. 342) programme of the North Atlantic Treaty Organization (NATO). In May 2007 Montenegro and the USA signed a Status of Forces Agreement, providing for increased military co-operation and allowing US military personnel to operate in Montenegro. As assessed at November, Montenegro's total armed forces numbered 5,800, comprising an army of 2,500 and a navy of 3,300. There was, in addition, a paramilitary force of 10,100, which included 6,000 personnel of the Ministry of Internal Affairs and Public Administration. The Government planned to reduce the size of the army to about 2,400. The budget for 2006 allocated an estimated €257m. to defence.

Economic Affairs

In 2006, according to estimates by the World Bank, Montenegro's gross national income (GNI), measured at average 2004–06 prices, was US $2,317m., equivalent to $3,860 per head. During 1996–2006, it was estimated, the population decreased at an average annual rate of 0.5%, while gross domestic product (GDP) per head increased, in real terms, by an average of 2.7% per year during 1997–2006. Overall GDP increased, in real terms, at an average annual rate of 1.8% in 1997–2006. According to official figures, real GDP increased by 6.5% in 2006.

Agriculture (including hunting, forestry and fishing) contributed 10.1% of GDP in 2006, when it accounted for some 1.8% of the total employed labour force. Montenegro's principal crops are potatoes, maize and wheat. The cultivation of fruit (particularly grapes, plums, oranges and tangerines) and vegetables is also important. Agricultural output increased by an annual average of 2.2% during 2002–06; output increased by 5.5% in 2006.

Industry (including mining, manufacturing, construction and power) contributed 20.4% of GDP in 2006, and engaged 28.3% of the employed labour force in the same year. Industrial production declined by an annual average of 1.0% during 1996–2001, and increased by an annual average of 3.7% during 2002–06. Industrial output increased by 6.0% in 2006.

The mining and quarrying sector contributed an estimated 1.6% of GDP in 2006, and engaged 2.8% of the employed labour force. The principal minerals extracted are lignite, red bauxite and sea salt. Production in the sector declined by an annual average of 2.0% during 2002–06. Output decreased by 6.1% in 2005, but increased by 5.4% in 2006.

The manufacturing sector contributed an estimated 9.4% of GDP in 2006, and engaged 17.3% of the employed labour force. In 2005 the principal branches of manufacturing were metals, building materials, chemicals, woodworking, and food and tobacco products. Production in the sector remained constant during 2002–06; output increased by 2.1% in 2006.

Energy in Montenegro is derived principally from hydroelectric power (which provided about 65.2% of total electricity generated in 2005) and thermoelectric power (34.8%). Imports of mineral fuels accounted for 19.7% of the value of total imports (excluding trade with Serbia) in 2005.

Services contributed an estimated 69.5% of GDP in 2006, when the sector employed some 69.9% of the population. Total foreign tourist arrivals increased from 272,005 in 2005 to 377,798 in 2006.

In 2006 Montenegro recorded a trade deficit of €938m., and there was a deficit of €601m. on the current account of the balance of payments. In 2005 the principal source of imports was Serbia (30.0%); other major sources were Germany, Italy and Greece. The principal market for exports in that year was Serbia (34.3%); other important purchasers were Italy, Greece and Slovenia. The main exports in 2005 were basic manufactures and miscellaneous manufactured articles. The principal imports in that year were machinery and transport equipment, mineral fuels and lubricants, and basic manufactures.

In 2005, according to preliminary figures, the overall budgetary surplus was €38m., which was equivalent to 2.1% of GDP. The rate of unemployment was estimated at 30.3% in 2005.

Following the official declaration of independence from the Union with Serbia on 3 June 2006, Montenegro was recognized as an independent state by the European Union (EU, see p. 244) on 12 June, admitted to the Organization for Security and Cooperation in Europe (OSCE, see p. 354) on 22 June, and became the 192nd member state of the UN on 28 June. Montenegro joined the IMF and World Bank on 18 January 2007.

The pro-independence Government of Montenegro adopted the German currency, the Deutsche Mark (DM), as its official currency in November 1999, and the European common currency, the euro, on 1 January 2002. Under an EU-mediated agreement for the establishment of the State Union, reached in March (and formalized in February 2003), the economies, currencies and customs services of Montenegro and Serbia were to be separate. In early July 2006, following independence, the respective Ministers of Finance and central bank Governors signed an agreement to divide financial rights and obligations of the two republics, whereby Montenegro was to receive about 5.9% of the hard currency and gold reserves of the former State Union. In early November the EU issued a progress report on Montenegro's first months of independence, which emphasized the need for economic reform to combat a continuing over-reliance on certain sectors of the economy, high unemployment and regulatory obstacles. Agreements on bilateral economic relations were signed with neighbouring and other European countries. Montenegro initialled a Stabilization and Association Agreement with the EU in March 2007; it was officially signed on 15 October (shortly before a new Constitution entered into effect). The EU subsequently urged the Government to further integration prospects with the continuation of judicial reforms and measures to combat corruption. The Government announced in December that GDP growth was expected to reach 7.0% in 2008, with the rate of inflation anticipated to be 4.0%. In February 2008 former Prime Minister Milo Đukanović was returned to the premiership (see Recent History); the restructuring of public enterprises prior to privatization and improvement of state administration to meet EU requirements were priorities for his administration. The Government also planned to initiate infrastructural projects in order to benefit from the country's tourism potential, and to construct a number of small-scale hydroelectric installations to improve its capacity to meet energy requirements.

Education

Elementary education is free and compulsory for all children between the ages of seven and 15, when children attend the 'eight-year school'. Various types of secondary education are available to all who qualify, but the vocational and technical schools are the most popular. Alternatively, children may attend a general secondary school (gymnasium), where they follow a four-year course. At the secondary level there are also a number of art schools, apprentice schools and teacher-training schools. Higher education is offered at the University of Montenegro, which was established in 1974, and at post-secondary schools. Some 12,903 students were enrolled in higher education in 2005/06.

Public Holidays

2008: 1–2 January (New Year), 7–8 January (Christmas), 25–28 April (Orthodox Easter), 27 April (Statehood Day), 1–2 May (Labour Day), 9 May (Victory Day), 13 July (National Day).

2009: 1–2 January (New Year), 7–8 January (Christmas), 17–20 April (Orthodox Easter), 27 April (Statehood Day), 1–2 May (Labour Day), 9 May (Victory Day), 13 July (National Day).

Weights and Measures

The metric system is in force.

Statistical Survey

Sources: Statistical Office of Montenegro, 81000 Podgorica, IV Proleterske 2; tel. (81) 241206; fax (81) 241270; e-mail statistika@cg.yu; internet www.monstat.cg.yu.

AREA AND POPULATION

Area: 13,812 sq km (5,333 sq miles). *By Municipality* (sq km): Andrijevica 283; Bar 598; Berane 717; Bijelo Polje 924; Budva 122; Cetinje 910; Danilovgrad 501; Herceg Novi 235; Kolašin 897; Kotor 335; Mojkovac 367; Nikšić 2,065; Plav 486; Pljevlja 1,346; Plužine 854; Podgorica 1,441; Rožaje 432; Šavnik 553; Tivat 46; Ulcinj 255; Žabljak 445.

Population: 620,145 (males 305,225, females 314,920) at census of 31 October 2003. *2006* (official estimate on 1 January) 624,000.

Density (1 January 2006, official estimate): 45.2 per sq km.

Population by Municipality (census of 31 October 2003): Andrijevica 5,785; Bar 40,037; Berane 35,068; Bijelo Polje 50,284; Budva 15,909; Cetinje 18,482; Danilovgrad 16,523; Herceg Novi 33,034; Kolašin 9,949; Kotor 22,947; Mojkovac 10,066; Nikšić 75,282; Plav 13,805; Pljevlja 35,806; Plužine 4,272; Podgorica 169,132; Rožaje 22,693; Šavnik 2,947; Tivat 13,630; Ulcinj 20,290; Žabljak 4,204; Total 620,145.

Ethnicity (population as declared at 2003 census): Montenegrin 267,669; Serb 198,414; Bosniak 48,184; Albanian 31,163; Muslim 24,625; Croat 6,811.

Principal Towns (population in '000, official estimates on 1 January 2006): Podgorica 173; Nikšić 75; Bijelo Polje 50; Bar 41; Berane 35; Rožaje 23.

Births, Marriages and Deaths (2006): Live births 7,531 (birth rate 12.1 per 1,000); Marriages 3,462 (marriage rate 5.5 per 1,000); Deaths 5,968 (death rate 9.6 per 1,000).

Expectation of life (WHO estimates, years at birth): 74.2 (males 71.3; females 77.0) in 2005 (Source: WHO, *World Health Statistics*).

MONTENEGRO

Employment (persons aged 15 years and over, October 2006): Agriculture, hunting, forestry and fishing 2,722; Mining and quarrying 4,159; Manufacturing 26,065; Electricity, gas and water supply 5,627; Construction 6,853; Wholesale and retail trade, repair of motor vehicles, motorcycles, and personal and household goods 29,602; Hotels and restaurants 10,928; Transport, storage and communications 12,133; Financial intermediation 3,114; Real estate, renting and business activities 5,905; Public administration and defence, and compulsory social security 10,345; Education 12,846; Health and social work 12,012; Other community, social and personal service activities 8,489; *Total employed* 150,800.

HEALTH AND WELFARE
Key Indicators

Total Fertility Rate (children per woman, 2005): 1.8.

Under-5 Mortality Rate (per 1,000 live births, 2005): 10.

Physicians (per 1,000 head, 2005): 2.0.

Hospital Beds (per 1,000 head, 2005): 4.2.

AGRICULTURE, ETC.

Principal Crops (metric tons, 2006, FAO estimates): Wheat 2,450; Maize 8,100; Barley 1,400; Potatoes 126,000; Tobacco 395; Plums 13,000; Olives 1,800; Oranges and tangerines 4,500; Grapes 50,000. Source: FAO.

Livestock ('000 head, 2006): Cattle 117.8; Horses 7.1; Pigs 10.7; Sheep 254.9; Poultry 462.1. Source: FAO.

Livestock Products (metric tons unless otherwise indicated, 2005): Cattle meat 11,756; Pigmeat 2,573; Sheep meat 5,887; Chicken meat 375; Milk 185.8m. litres; Eggs 55.8m. units; Honey 610.

Forestry ('000 cubic metres, 2006): *Timber Removals:* 631.3 (Broadleaved 280.8, Coniferous 350.5); *Assortments:* 513.3 (Broadleaved 232.6, Coniferous 280.7).

Fishing (metric tons, 2005): Total catch 1,235 (marine 443, freshwater 792).

MINING

Selected Products ('000 metric tons, 2006): Lignite 1,502.3; Red bauxite 659.4; Sea salt 5.0.

INDUSTRY

Selected Products ('000 metric tons unless otherwise indicated, 2006): Wheat flour 16.7; Wines ('000 hl) 121.7; Beer ('000 hl) 516.7; Spruce and fir lumber ('000 cu metres) 70.1; Oxygen, nitrogen and acetylene 13.0; Cut marble panels ('000 sq metres) 43.1; Steel ingots 50.0; Steel castings 143.2; Aluminium oxide 236.7; Aluminium ingots 118.4; Electric energy (kWh) 2,951.6m.

FINANCE

Currency and Exchange Rates: 100 cent = 1 euro (€). *Sterling and Dollar Equivalents* (31 December 2007): £1 sterling = 1.3609 euros; US $1 = 0.6793 euros; €10 = £7.35 = $14.72. *Average Exchange Rate* (euros per US dollar): 0.8041 in 2005; 0.7971 in 2006; 0.7306 in 2007.

Budget (€ million, 2005, preliminary): Total revenues (incl. revenues from privatizations) 581; Total expenditure 543. Source: Central Bank of Montenegro.

International Reserves (US $ million at 31 December 2006): Gold (national valuation) 24.15; Foreign exchange 432.91; Total 457.06. Source: IMF, *International Financial Statistics*.

Money Supply (€ million at 31 December 2006): Demand deposits 488.2. Source: IMF, *International Financial Statistics*.

Cost of Living (Consumer Price Index for 2006; base: 2005=100): Food 104.5; Tobacco and beverages 101.2; Clothing and footwear 101.0; Housing 101.5; Fuel and light 100.7; All items (incl. others) 103.0.

Expenditure on the Gross Domestic Product (€ million at current prices, 2006): Government final consumption expenditure 580.1; Private final consumption expenditure 1,660.9; Gross fixed capital formation 469.8; Changes in inventories 77.0; *Total domestic expenditure* 2,787.8; Exports of goods and services 1,061.0; *Less* Imports of goods and services 1,699.8; *GDP in purchasers' values* 2,149.0.

Gross Domestic Product by Economic Activity (€ million at current prices, 2006): Agriculture, hunting, forestry and fishing 178.2; Mining and quarrying 28.6; Manufacturing 164.7; Electricity, gas and water supply 88.5; Construction 76.0; Wholesale and retail trade, repair of motor vehicles, motorcycles, and personal and household goods 237.9; Hotels and restaurants 64.1; Transport, storage and communications 208.3; Financial intermediation 65.0; Real estate, renting and business activities 245.1; Public administration and defence, and compulsory social security 174.3; Education 87.5; Health and social work 84.6; Other community, social and personal service activities 54.1; *Sub-total* 1,756.9; Financial intermediation services indirectly measured –4.1; *Gross value added in basic prices* 1,752.8; Taxes, less subsidies, on products 396.2; *GDP in purchasers' values* 2,149.0.

Balance of Payments (€ million, 2006, estimates): Exports of goods 559; Imports of goods f.o.b. –1,498; *Trade balance* –938; Exports of services 434; Imports of services –217; *Balance on goods and services* –722; Net factor income –26; *Balance on goods, services and income* –748; Net current transfers received 147; *Current balance* –601. Source: Central Bank of Montenegro.

EXTERNAL TRADE

Principal Commodities (excluding trade with Serbia, € million, 2005): *Imports:* Food and live animals 88.2; Mineral fuels, lubricants, etc. 134.5; Chemicals products 56.7; Basic manufactures 109.1; Machinery and transport equipment 200.8; Total (incl. others) 681.9. *Exports:* Crude materials (except fuels) 18.6; Basic manufactures 229.6; Machinery and transport equipment 20.8; Miscellaneous manufactured articles 162.6; Total (incl. others) 302.5.

Principal Trading Partners (€ million, 2005): *Imports:* Austria 38.7; China, People's Republic 30.4; Germany 96.9; Greece 52.9; Italy 91.4; Serbia 292.4; Switzerland 48.2; Total (incl. others) 974.3. *Exports:* Bosnia and Herzegovina 22.1; Greece 50.2; Italy 146.3; Serbia 158.2; Slovenia 26.4; Total (incl. others) 460.6.

TRANSPORT

Road Transport (2005): 118,930 passenger cars in use.

Railways (traffic, 2006): Passengers carried ('000) 1,067; Passenger-km ('000) 131,500; Freight carried ('000 metric tons) 2,494; Total ton-km ('000) 182,163.

Shipping (freight handled, '000 metric tons, 2005): Goods loaded 1,167; Goods unloaded 851.2.

Civil Aviation (2006): Passenger movements 833,715; Freight carried 1,067 metric tons.

TOURISM

Foreign Tourist Arrivals: 272,005 in 2005; 377,798 in 2006.

Arrivals by Nationality (2006): Albania 25,925; Bosnia and Herzegovina 55,553; Croatia 17,702; Czech Republic 28,674; Germany 20,252; Italy 17,702; Russia 14,469; Slovakia 61,092; Slovenia 17,607; USA 5,982; Total (incl. others) 377,798.

COMMUNICATIONS MEDIA

Telephones (main lines in use, 2006): 175,794.

Mobile Cellular Telephones (subscribers, 2006): 703,053.

EDUCATION

Pre-primary (2006/07): Schools 88; Pupils 10,511; Teaching staff 693.

Primary (2007/08): Schools 444; Pupils 75,038; Teaching staff 4,889.

Secondary (2007/08): Schools 47; Students 31,557; Teaching staff 2,254.

Higher (incl. faculties, art academies and private institutions, 2005/06): Schools 21; Students 12,903.

Adult Literacy Rate: 97.65% at 2003 census.

Directory

Constitution

Following a national referendum on 21 May 2006, Montenegro became independent from the State Union of Serbia and Montenegro on 3 June. The Constitution of the Republic of Montenegro was adopted by the Constitutional Assembly on 19 October 2007 and was officially proclaimed, replacing the Constitution of 1992, on 22 October. The Constitution's main provisions are summarized below.

BASIC PROVISIONS

Montenegro is an independent and sovereign state, with a republican form of government. Sovereignty is vested in Montenegrin citizens, who exercise it directly and through the freely elected representatives. The territory of Montenegro is unified and inalienable. Human rights and liberties are guaranteed and protected. Ratified international agreements and generally accepted rules of international law have supremacy over national legislation and are directly applicable when they regulate relations differently from internal legislation. The official language in Montenegro is Montenegrin. The Cyrillic and Latin alphabets are equal. The Serbian, Bosnian, Albanian and Croatian languages are also in official use. Religious communities, which are equal and free in the exercise of religious affairs, are separated from the state. Montenegro will co-operate and develop friendly relations with other states, and regional and international organizations, based on the principles and rules of international law. The Skupština Republike Crne Gore (Assembly of the Republic of Montenegro) shall decide on the manner of accession to the European Union. Montenegro shall not enter into a union with another state by which it loses its independence and full international personality.

HUMAN RIGHTS AND LIBERTIES

Rights and liberties are exercised on the basis of the Constitution and confirmed international agreements. The right to local self-government is guaranteed. The death penalty is prohibited. Elections, which are free and direct, are conducted by secret ballot. The freedom of the press and other forms of public information are guaranteed. The freedom to operate political, trade union and other associations is guaranteed. The rights and liberties of persons belonging to minority national communities are guaranteed.

LEGISLATURE

The Skupština comprises 81 members, who are elected for a term of four years. The first session of a new Skupština will be held within 15 days of the date of publication of the final results of the legislative elections. The Skupština adopts decisions by majority vote of members at a session attended by more than one-half of the total number of members, unless otherwise regulated by the Constitution. The Skupština decides by a two-thirds' majority of the total number of members on the laws regulating the electoral system and property rights of foreign nationals. The Skupština decides by a two-thirds' majority of the total number of members in the first round of voting and by a majority of the total number of members in the second round of voting, on the laws regulating the manner of exercising obtained minority rights and the use of military units in international forces. The Skupština will be dissolved if it fails to elect a Government within 90 days of the President having nominated a candidate for Prime Minister.

PRESIDENT

The President of Montenegro is directly elected for a term of five years. The same person may be elected President for a maximum of two terms. A Montenegrin citizen who has resided in Montenegro for a minimum of 10 years in the previous 15 years may be elected President. The President proposes to the Skupština the President and judges of the Constitutional Court and, after consultations with the representatives of the political parties represented in the Skupština, the candidate for the office of Prime Minister.

THE GOVERNMENT

The Government comprises the Prime Minister, one or more Deputy Prime Ministers, and ministers. The President nominates a Prime Minister within 30 days of the Skupština being convened. The nominated candidate presents a programme to the Skupština and proposes the composition of the Government. The resignation of the Prime Minister is regarded as marking the resignation of the Government. The right to local self-government includes the right of citizens and local bodies of self-government to regulate and manage certain public and other affairs. The basic form of local self-government is the municipality.

JUDICIARY

The judiciary is independent. The Supreme Court is the highest court in Montenegro. The President of the Supreme Court is elected and dismissed by the Skupština, at the joint proposal of the President of Montenegro, the Speaker of the Skupština and the Prime Minister. The Judicial Council comprises a President and nine members, and the President of the Judicial Council is the President of the Supreme Court. Judges and Presidents of lower courts are elected and dismissed by the Judicial Council.

ECONOMIC SYSTEM

The economic system of Montenegro is based on a free and open market and the protection and equality of all forms of property. The Central Bank Council governs the Central Bank of Montenegro. The National Audit Institution of Montenegro is an independent and supreme authority of the national audit.

THE CONSTITUTIONAL COURT

The Constitutional Court monitors the enforcement of constitutionality and legality. The Constitutional Court comprises seven judges, who are elected by the Skupština for a period of nine years, and adopts decisions by a majority vote of judges. The President of the Constitutional Court is elected from amongst the judges for three years. A proposal to change the Constitution may be submitted by the President, the Government, or a minimum of 25 members of the Skupština. A proposal to change the Constitution may be adopted in the Skupština by a vote of two-thirds of the members of the Skupština. Constitutional legislation providing for the enforcement of the Constitution may be adopted by the Skupština with a majority vote of all members thereof.

The Government

HEAD OF STATE

President: FILIP VUJANOVIĆ (elected 11 May 2003; took office 13 June 2003; re-elected 6 April 2008).

COUNCIL OF MINISTERS
(April 2008)

The Government comprises members of the Democratic Party of Montenegrin Socialists (DPMS), the Social Democratic Party of Montenegro (SDP) and the Democratic Union of Albanians (DUA).

Prime Minister: MILO ĐUKANOVIĆ (DPMS).

Deputy Prime Minister, with responsibility for European Integration: GORDANA ĐUROVIĆ (DPMS).

Deputy Prime Minister, with responsibility for Economic Policy: VUJICA LAZOVIĆ (SDP).

Minister of Justice: MIRAŠ RADOVIĆ (DPMS).

Minister of Finance: Dr IGOR LUKŠIĆ (DPMS).

Minister of Foreign Affairs: MILAN ROĆEN (DPMS).

Minister of Education and Science: Prof. SRETEN ŠKULETIĆ (DPMS).

Minister of Culture, Sports and Media: BRANISLAV MIĆUNOVIĆ (DPMS).

Minister of Defence: BORO VUČINIĆ (DPMS).

Minister of Economic Development: BRANIMIR GVOZDENOVIĆ (DPMS).

Minister of Maritime Affairs, Transportation and Telecommunications: Dr ANDRIJA LOMPAR (SDP).

Minister of Agriculture, Forestry and Water Management: MILUTIN SIMOVIĆ (DPMS).

Minister of Internal Affairs and Public Administration: JUSUF KALAMPEROVIĆ (SDP).

Minister of Tourism and Environmental Protection: PREDRAG NENEZIĆ (DPMS).

Minister of Health, Labour and Social Welfare: Dr MIODRAG RADUNOVIĆ (DPMS).

Minister for the Protection of Human and Minority Rights: FUAD NIMANI (DUA).

Minister without Portfolio: SUAD NUMANOVIĆ (DPMS).

MONTENEGRO

MINISTRIES

Office of the President: 81000 Podgorica, Sveti Petar Cetinjski 3; tel. (81) 242388; fax (81) 246608; e-mail predsjednik@cg.yu; internet www.predsjednik.cg.yu.

Office of the Prime Minister: 81000 Podgorica, Jovana Tomaševića bb; tel. (81) 242530; fax (81) 242329; e-mail kabinet.premijera@mn.yu; internet www.vlada.cg.yu.

Ministry of Agriculture, Forestry and Water Management: 81000 Podgorica, Poslovni centar Vektra, Cetinjski put bb; tel. (81) 482109; fax (81) 234306; e-mail milutins@mn.yu; internet www.minpolj.vlada.cg.yu.

Ministry of Culture, Sports and Media: 81000 Podgorica, Vuka Karadžića 3; tel. (81) 231561; fax (81) 231540; e-mail min.kulture.rcg@cg.yu; internet www.ministarstvokulture.vlada.cg.yu.

Ministry of Economic Development: 81000 Podgorica, Rimski trg 46; tel. (81) 234156; fax (81) 234131; internet www.minekon.vlada.cg.yu.

Ministry of Education and Science: 81000 Podgorica, Rimski trg bb; tel. (81) 405301; fax (81) 405343; e-mail mpin@cg.yu; internet www.mpin.vlada.cg.yu.

Ministry of Finance: 81000 Podgorica, Stanka Dragojevića 2; tel. (81) 242835; fax (81) 224450; e-mail mf@mn.yu; internet www.ministarstvo-finansija.vlada.cg.yu.

Ministry of Foreign Affairs: 81000 Podgorica, Stanka Dragojevića 2; tel. (81) 224609; fax (81) 224670; e-mail mip@mn.yu; internet www.mip.vlada.cg.yu.

Ministry of Health, Labour and Social Welfare: 81000 Podgorica, Rimski trg 46; tel. (81) 242276; fax (81) 242762; e-mail mzdravlja@mn.yu; internet www.mzdravlja.vlada.cg.yu.

Ministry of Internal Affairs and Public Administration: 81000 Podgorica, bul. Svetog Petra Cetinjskog 6; tel. (81) 241252; fax (81) 9821; e-mail mup.kabinet@cg.yu; internet www.mup.vlada.cg.yu.

Ministry of Justice: 81000 Podgorica, Vuka Karadžića 3; tel. and fax (81) 248541; e-mail zeljkos@cg.yu; internet www.pravda.vlada.cg.yu.

Ministry of Maritime Affairs, Transportation and Telecommunications: 81000 Podgorica, Rimski trg 46; tel. (81) 234179; fax (81) 234331; e-mail angelinaz@mn.yu; internet www.minsaob.vlada.cg.yu.

Ministry for the Protection of Human and Minority Rights: 81000 Podgorica, Cetinjski put bb; tel. (81) 482126; fax (81) 234198; e-mail min.manj@cg.yu; internet www.minmanj.vlada.cg.yu.

Ministry of Tourism and Environmental Protection: 81000 Podgorica, Rimski trg 46; tel. (81) 482329; fax (81) 234168; e-mail ministarstvo.turizma@mn.yu; internet www.mturizma.vlada.cg.yu.

President

Presidential Election, 6 April 2008

Candidate	% of votes
Filip Vujanović (Democratic Party of Montenegrin Socialists)	52.3
Andrija Mandić (Serb People's Party of Montenegro)	19.3
Nebojša Medojević (Movement for Changes)	17.3
Srđan Milić (Socialist People's Party of Montenegro)	11.1
Total	**100.0**

Legislature

Skupština Republike Crne Gore
(Assembly of the Republic of Montenegro)

81000 Podgorica, Svetog Petra Cetinjskog 2; tel. (81) 242182; fax (81) 242192; e-mail ranko.krivokapic@skupstina.cg.yu; internet www.skupstina.cg.yu.

Speaker: Ranko Krivokapić.

Election, 10 September 2006

Party	Votes	% of votes	Seats
Coalition for A European Montenegro*	164,737	48.62	41
Serbian List†	49,698	14.67	12
Socialist People's Party of Montenegro/People's Party of Montenegro/Democratic Serbian Party of Montenegro	47,683	14.07	11
Movement for Changes	44,483	13.13	11
Liberal Party of Montenegro/ Bosniak Party of Montenegro	12,748	3.76	3
Democratic League of Montenegro/Party of Democratic Prosperity	4,373	1.29	1
Democratic Union of Albanians	3,693	1.09	1
Albanian Alternative	2,656	0.78	1
Others	8,764	2.59	—
Total	**338,835**	**100.00**	**81**

* Comprising the Democratic Party of Montenegrin Socialists, the Social Democratic Party of Montenegro and the Croat Civic Initiative.
† Coalition led by the Serb People's Party of Montenegro.

Political Organizations

Albanian Alternative: Leader Vaselj Sinistaj.

Bosniak Party of Montenegro (Bošnjačka Stranka Crna Gore): 84310 Rožaje; e-mail info@bosnjackastranka.org; internet www.bosnjackastranka.org; Leader Rafet Husović.

Croat Civic Initiative (Hrvatska građanska inicijativa—HGI): 85320 Tivat; f. 2002; joined Democratic Party of Socialists of Montenegro coalition 2006; Pres. Dalibor Burić.

Democratic League of Montenegro (Demokratski Savez Crne Gore): Podgorica; ethnic Albanian party; Leader Mehmet Barhdi.

Democratic Party of Montenegrin Socialists (DPMS) (Demokratska Partija Socijalista Crne Gore): 81000 Podgorica, Jovana Tomaśevića 33; tel. (81) 225830; fax (81) 242101; e-mail webmaster@dps.cg.yu; internet www.dps.cg.yu; name changed from League of Communists of Montenegro in 1991; Chair. Milo Đukanović.

Democratic Serbian Party of Montenegro (Demokratska Srpska Stranka Crne Gore—DSS): Leader Ranko Kadić.

Democratic Union of Albanians (DUA) (Demokratska Unija Albanaca): 85360 Ulcinj; tel. (81) 242261; e-mail dscg@skupstina.mn.yu; Leader Ferhat Dinoša.

Liberal Party of Montenegro (Liberalna Partija Crne Gore—LPCG): 81000 Podgorica, Slobode 78; tel. (81) 232364; e-mail info@lpcg.org; internet www.lpcg.org; f. 2004; Leader Miodrag Živković.

Movement for Changes (Pokret za Promjene—PZP): 81000 Podgorica, Dalmatinska 130D; tel. and fax (81) 269336; e-mail gzpkotor@cg.yu; internet www.promjene.org; f. 2002 as non-governmental org.; became political party in 2006; supports European integration; Leader Nebojša Medojević.

Party of Democratic Prosperity (Partija Demokratskog Prospertiteta): ethnic Albanian party; Leader Mehmet Barhdi.

People's Party (Narodna Stranka): 81000 Podgorica, Vasa Raichovića bb; tel. (81) 238715; fax (81) 238712; e-mail narodna@cg.yu; internet www.narodnastranka.cg.yu; conservative; supports close relations with Serbia; Chair. Predrag Popović.

Serb People's Party of Montenegro (SPP) (Srpska Narodna Stranka Crne Gore): 81000 Podgorica, Vojislava Grujića 4; tel. (81) 652149; e-mail sns@cg.yu; internet www.sns.cg.yu; seeks to represent the interests of ethnic Serbs in Montenegro; Pres. Andrija Mandić.

Social Democratic Party of Montenegro (SDP) (Socijaldemokratska Partija Crne Gore): 81000 Podgorica, Jovana Tomasévića bb; tel. (81) 248648; fax (81) 612133; e-mail sdp@cg.yu; internet www.sdp.cg.yu; Pres. Ranko Krivokapić.

Socialist People's Party of Montenegro (SPPM) (Socijalistička Narodna Partija Crne Gore—SNP): 81000 Podgorica, Vaka Đurovića 5; tel. (81) 272420; e-mail snp@cg.yu; internet www.snp.cg.yu; Leader Srđan Milić.

Diplomatic Representation

Albania: 81000 Podgorica, Zmaj Jovina br. 30, Stari Aerodrom; tel. (81) 652796; fax (81) 652798; Chargé d'affaires Saimir Bala.

MONTENEGRO

Austria: 81000 Podgorica, Kralja Nikole 104; tel. (81) 601580; fax (81) 624344; e-mail podgorica-ob@bmeia.gv.at; Ambassador FLORIAN RAUNIG.

Bosnia and Herzegovina: 81000 Podgorica, Atinska 58; tel. (81) 618105; fax (81) 618016; Ambassador BRANIMIR JUKIĆ.

Bulgaria: 81000 Podgorica, Vukice Mitrovića 10; tel. (81) 655009; fax (81) 655008; e-mail bg.embassy.me@abv.bg; Ambassador SNEZHANA NAYDENOVA.

China, People's Republic: 81000 Podgorica, Radosava Burića 4A; tel. and fax (81) 609275; Ambassador LI MANCHANG.

Croatia: 81000 Podgorica, Vladimira Ćetkovića 2; tel. (81) 269760; fax (81) 269810; Ambassador PETAR TURČINOVIĆ.

France: 81000 Podgorica, Atinska 35; tel. (81) 665348; e-mail france@cg.yu; Ambassador BERNARD GARANCHER.

Germany: 81000 Podgorica, Hercegovačka 10; tel. and fax (81) 667285; e-mail l@podg.diplo.de; internet www.beograd.diplo.de; Ambassador THOMAS SCHMITT.

Greece: 81000 Podgorica, Atinska 4; tel. (81) 655544; fax (81) 655543; Chargé d'affaires a.i. NIKOLAOS KAYMENAKIS.

Hungary: 81000 Podgorica, Kralja Nikole 104; tel. (81) 602910; fax (81) 625243; e-mail mission.pdg@kum.hu; Ambassador Dr ZOLTÁN SOMOGYI.

Italy: 81000 Podgorica, Džordža Vašingtona 83; tel. (81) 234661; fax (81) 234663; e-mail segreteria.podgorica@esteri.it; internet www.conspodgorica.esteri.it; Ambassador GABRIELE MEUCCI.

Macedonia, former Yugoslav republic: 81000 Podgorica, Hercegovačka 49/III; tel. (81) 667415; fax (81) 667205; e-mail mkgkpodgorica@cg.yu; Ambassador STEFAN NIKOLOVSKI.

Poland: 81000 Podgorica, 8 Marta 72; tel. (81) 662442; fax (81) 662397; e-mail ambaspol@cg.yu; Chargé d'affaires JAROSŁAW LINDENBERG.

Romania: 81000 Podgorica, Vukice Mitrovića 40; tel. (81) 618040; fax (81) 655081; Ambassador MIHAIL FLOROVICI.

Russia: 81000 Podgorica, Veliše Mugoše 1; tel. and fax (81) 272460; e-mail gencons.ru@cg.yu; Ambassador YAKOV F. GERASIMOV.

Serbia: 81000 Podgorica, Bulevar Svetog Petra Cetinjskog 1, Hotel Podgorica; tel. (81) 402500; fax (81) 402500; Ambassador ZORAN LUTOVAC.

Slovenia: 81000 Podgorica, 13 Jula bb, PC Čelebić; tel. (81) 208020; fax (81) 237095; e-mail kpg@gov.si; Ambassador JERNEJ VIDETIČ.

United Kingdom: 81000 Podgorica, bul. Svetog Petra Cetinjskog 149; tel. (81) 205460; fax (81) 205441; Ambassador KEVIN LYNE.

USA: 81000 Podgorica, Ljubljanska bb; tel. (81) 225417; fax (81) 241358; e-mail podgorica@state.gov; internet podgorica.usembassy.gov; Ambassador RODERICK V. MOORE.

Judicial System

Constitutional Court of the Republic of Montenegro: 81000 Podgorica, Lenjina 3; tel. (81) 41846; 5 judges; Pres. MLADEN VUKČEVIĆ.

Supreme Court: 81000 Podgorica, Njegoševa 6; tel. (81) 43070; 13 judges; Pres. VESNA MEDENICA.

Office of the Public Prosecutor: 81000 Podgorica, Njegoševa 6; tel. (81) 43053; Public Prosecutor VESNA MEDENICA.

Religion

CHRISTIANITY

The Eastern Orthodox Church

Montenegrin Orthodox Church (Crnogorska Pravoslavna Crkva): 81250 Cetinje, Gruda bb; tel. and fax (86) 31310; e-mail crkva@moc-cpc.org; internet www.moc-cpc.org; autocephalous until 1920, when it was dissolved and annexed to the Serbian Orthodox Church; restored 1993; Archbishop of Cetinje and Metropolitan of Montenegro His Excellency MIHAILO (DEDEIĆ).

Orthodox Metropolitanate of Montenegro and the Littoral—Serbian Orthodox Church (Pravoslavna Mitropolitija Crnogorsko Primorska—Srpska Pravoslavna Crkva): 81250 Cetinje; e-mail mitropolija@cg.yu; internet www.mitropolija.cg.yu; Metropolitan of Montenegro and the Littoral AMFILOHIJE (RADOVIĆ).

The Roman Catholic Church

At 31 December 2005 there were an estimated 11,512 adherents in the archdiocese of Bar (which is directly answerable to the Holy See) and an estimated 10,000 adherents in the Diocese of Kotor (which is suffragan to the archdiocese of Split-Makarska, based in Croatia).

Archbishop of Bar: Most Rev. ZEF GASHI, 85000 Bar, Popovići 98; tel. (85) 344236; fax (85) 344233; e-mail zega_bar@cg.yu.

Bishop of Kotor: Most Rev ILIJA JANJIĆ, 85330 Kotor, Stari grad 336; tel. (82) 322315; fax (82) 322175; e-mail carbicot@cg.yu.

ISLAM

Almost 20% of the Montenegrin population profess Islam as their faith, many being ethnic Slav Muslims (Bosniaks) of the Sandžak region (which was partitioned between Montenegro and Serbia in 1913).

The Press

PRINCIPAL DAILIES

Dan (The Day): 81000 Podgorica, 13 Jula 10; tel. (81) 239106; fax (81) 239102; e-mail dan@cg.yu; internet www.dan.cg.yu; f. 1999; Chief Editor MLADEN MILUTINOVIĆ.

Pobjeda (Victory): 81000 Podgorica, bul. Revolucije 11, POB 101; tel. (81) 245955; fax (81) 224901; e-mail direktor@pobjeda.cg.yu; internet www.pobjeda.co.yu; f. 1944; morning; Editor-in-Chief ANDRIJA RACKOVIĆ; circ. 18,000 (2003).

Republika (The Republic): 81000 Podgorica, Crnogorskih serdara 8; tel. (81) 601430; fax (81) 625123; e-mail direktor@republika.cg.yu; internet www.republika.cg.yu; Editor-in-Chief MILOŠ PAVIĆEVIĆ.

Vijesti (The News): 81000 Podgorica, bul. Revolucije 9; tel. (81) 406901; fax (81) 242306; e-mail vijesti@cg.yu; internet www.vijesti.cg.yu; f. 1997; Editor-in-Chief SLAVOLJUB SĆEKIĆ.

PERIODICALS

Crnogorski Književni List (Montenegrin Literary Paper): 81000 Podgorica, trg Božane Vucinić 1; tel. (81) 623552; fax (81) 623285; e-mail ckl@cg.yu; internet www.ckl.cg.yu; f. 2000; literature, culture, science, politics; Editor-in-Chief JEVREM BRKOVIĆ.

Monitor: 81000 Podgorica, ul 19 Decembra 19; tel. (81) 242479; fax (81) 243739; e-mail monitor@cg.yu; internet www.monitor.cg.yu; f. 1990; weekly; independent; politics, general; Editor-in-Chief ESAD KOČAN.

PRESS ASSOCIATION

Asscn of Professional Journalists of Montenegro: 81000 Podgorica, 13 Jula 25; tel. and fax (81) 243169; e-mail publika@cg.yu; Pres DANILO BURZAN, RADOVAN MILJANIĆ.

Publishers

Obod: 81250 Cetinje, Njegoševa 3; tel. (86) 21331; fax (86) 21953; general literature; Dir VASKO JANKOVIĆ.

Pobjeda (Victory) Publishing House: 81000 Podgorica, Južni bul. bb; tel. (81) 44433; f. 1974; poetry, fiction, lexicography and scientific works.

Broadcasting and Communications

TELECOMMUNICATIONS

Regulatory Agency

Agency for Telecommunications: 81000 Podgorica, bul. Revolucije 1; tel. (81) 246786; fax (81) 241805; e-mail agentel@cg.yu; internet www.agentel.cg.yu; f. 2001; independent regulatory body; Dir ZORAN SEKULIĆ.

Service Providers

Crnogorski Telekom: 81000 Podgorica, Moskovska 29; tel. (81) 433433; fax (81) 432400; e-mail office@telekom-cg.com; internet www.telekom-cg.com; 76.53% owned by Magyar Telekom (Hungary); Chair. of Bd of Dirs BENCE MAKAI.

ProMonte: 81000 Podgorica, bul. Džordža Vašingtona 83; tel. (81) 235400; fax (81) 235035; e-mail info@promonte.com; internet www.promonte.com; f. 1996; 100% owned by Telenor (Norway); mobile cellular telecommunications services; Gen. Dir KARE GUSTAD.

T-Mobile Crna Gora: 81000 Podgorica, bul. Svetog Petra Cetinjskog bb; tel. (81) 400801; fax (81) 225752; e-mail office@monetcg.com; internet www.t-mobile-cg.com; f. 2000; fmrly Monet; present name adopted 2006; subsidiary of Crnogorski Telekom; mobile cellular telecommunications services.

MONTENEGRO

BROADCASTING

Regulatory Agency

Montenegro Broadcasting Agency (Agencija za radio-diffuziu Crne Gore): 81000 Podgorica, bul. Svetog Petra Cetinjskog 9; fax (81) 201440; e-mail sard@ard.mn.yu; internet www.ard.cg.yu; Dir ABAZ BELI DŽAFIĆ.

Television and Radio

Radiotelevizija Crne Gore (Radio and Television of Montenegro): 81000 Podgorica, Cetinjski put bb; tel. (81) 225602; fax (81) 225108; internet www.rtcg.org; f. 1944 (radio) and 1971 (television); 2 terrestrial television channels and 1 satellite channel; 2 radio channels—Prvi program (Channel 1) and Radio 98; Dir-Gen. RADOVAN MILJANIĆ; Dir of Television VELJO JAUKOVIĆ; Dir of Radio BUDIMIR RAIČEVIĆ.

Radio D: 81000 Podgorica, 13 Jula bb; tel. (81) 238909; e-mail mladenm@cg.yu; f. 2000; independent; Dir SVETLANA VUČELJIĆ.

Finance

(cap. = capital; res = reserves; dep. = deposits; m. = million; amounts in euros; br. = branch)

BANKING

Central Bank

The Central Bank of Montenegro was established in 2001.

Central Bank of Montenegro (Centralna Banka Crne Gore—CBCG): 81000 Podgorica, bul. Petra Cetinjskog 7; tel. (81) 403191; fax (81) 664140; e-mail info@cb-cg.org; internet www.cb-mn.org; f. 2001; cap. 2.6m., res 36.8m., dep. 295.3m. (Dec. 2006); Gov. LJUBIŠA KRGOVIĆ.

Selected Banks

In 2006 some 11 banks were operating in Montenegro, six of which were foreign-owned.

Crnogorska komercjalna banka a.d. Podgorica (CKB): 81000 Podgorica, Moskovska bb; tel. (81) 404232; fax (81) 404277; e-mail info@ckb.cg.yu; internet www.ckb.cg.yu; f. 1997; 100% owned by National Savings and Commercial Bank—OTP Bank (Hungary); cap. 15.3m., total assets 303.3m. (Dec. 2005); Pres. JOZSEF WINDHEIM; 33 brs.

NLB Montenegrobanka a.d. Podgorica: 81000 Podgorica, Dragojevića 46; tel. (81) 402000; fax (81) 402133; e-mail info@montenegro-banka.com; internet www.montenegrobanka.com; f. 1905; frmly MNB Crnogorska banka—Banque de Montenegro; present name adopted Jan. 2006; 86.97% owned by Nova Ljubljanska Banka d.d. (Slovenia); cap. 4.1m., dep. 60.9m. (Dec. 2005); Pres. ANDREJ HAZABENT; Gen. Man. CRTOMIR MESARIĆ.

Opportunity Bank a.d. Podgorica: 81000 Podgorica, Marka Miljanova 46; tel. (81) 625615; fax (81) 625997; e-mail info@opportunitybank.cg.yu; internet www.opportunitybank.cg.yu; f. 2002; cap. 7.0m., res 0.3m., dep. 108.7m. (Dec. 2006); Pres. KEITH FLINTHAM.

STOCK EXCHANGE

Montenegro Stock Exchange (Montenegroberza): 81000 Podgorica, Moskovska 77; tel. and fax (81) 244422; e-mail mberza@cg.yu; internet www.montenegroberza.com; f. 1993; CEO DEJANA ŠUŠKAVČEVIĆ.

INSURANCE

Lovćen Osiguranje a.d. Podgorica (Lovćen Insurance Co Podgorica): 81000 Podgorica, ul. Slobode 13 A; tel. (81) 404400; fax (81) 245482; e-mail lovosig@cg.yu; internet www.lovcenosiguranje.cg.yu; insurance and reinsurance; Sec. PURIĆ RADENKO.

Trade and Industry

CHAMBER OF COMMERCE

Chamber of Commerce of Montenegro (Privredna Komora Crne Gore): 81000 Podgorica, Novaka Miloševa 29; tel. (81) 31071; fax (81) 34926; e-mail pkcg@cg.yu; internet www.pkcg.org; Pres. VOJIN ĐUKANOVIĆ.

UTILITIES

Electricity

Elektroprivreda Crne Gore a.d. Nikšić (EPCG) (Montenegro Electricity Co): 81400 Nikšić, Vuka Karadžića 2; tel. and fax (83) 214252; e-mail Listepcg@cg.yu; internet www.epcg.cg.yu; production, transmission and distribution of electric power.

Transport

RAILWAYS

Željeznica Crne Gore: 81000 Podgorica, trg Golootočkih žrtava 13; tel. (81) 441302; fax (81) 633957; e-mail zcg-uprava@cg.yu; internet www.zeljeznica.cg.yu; 60.1% state-owned; Chair. of Bd of Dirs RANKO MEDENICA; Gen. Man. REŠAD NUHODŽIĆ.

SHIPPING

The principal coastal outlet is the port of Bar, which is linked to the Italian ports of Ancona and Bari by a regular ferry service.

CIVIL AVIATION

Montenegro Airlines: 81000 Podgorica, Beogradska 10; tel. (81) 405501; fax (81) 405548; e-mail contact@mgx.cg.yu; internet www.montenegroairlines.com; f. 1994; operations commenced 1997; direct flights between Podgorica and: Tivat (Montenegro); Belgrade and Niš (Serbia); Frankfurt (Germany); Ljubljana (Slovenia); Paris (France); Rome (Italy); Vienna (Austria); and Zurich (Switzerland); Pres. ZORAN DURIŠIĆ.

Tourism

National Tourism Organization of Montenegro: 81000 Podgorica, Omladinskih brigada 7; tel. (81) 230959; fax (81) 230979; e-mail tourism@cg.yu; internet www.visit-montenegro.com; Man. Dir PREDRAG JELUSIĆ.

MOROCCO

Introductory Survey

Location, Climate, Language, Religion, Flag, Capital

The Kingdom of Morocco is situated in the extreme north-west of Africa. It has a long coastline on the shores of the Atlantic Ocean and, east of the Strait of Gibraltar, on the Mediterranean Sea, facing southern Spain. Morocco's eastern frontier is with Algeria, while to the south lies the disputed territory of Western Sahara (under Moroccan occupation), which has a lengthy Atlantic coastline and borders Mauritania to the east and south. Morocco's climate is semi-tropical. It is warm and sunny on the coast, while the plains of the interior are intensely hot in summer. Average temperatures are 27°C (81°F) in summer and 7°C (45°F) in winter for Rabat, and 38°C (101°F) and 4°C (40°F), respectively, for Marrakesh. The rainy season in the north is from November to April. The official language is Arabic, but a large minority speak Berber. Spanish is widely spoken in the northern regions, and French in the rest of Morocco. The established religion is Islam, and most of the country's inhabitants are Muslims. There are small minorities of Christians and Jews. The national flag (proportions 2 by 3) is red, with a green pentagram (intersecting lines in the form of a five-pointed star), known as 'Solomon's Seal', in the centre. The capital is Rabat.

Recent History

In 1912, under the terms of the Treaty of Fez, most of Morocco became a French protectorate, while a smaller Spanish protectorate was instituted in the north and far south of the country. Spain also retained control of Spanish Sahara (now Western Sahara), and Tangier became an international zone in 1923. A nationalist movement developed in Morocco during the 1930s and 1940s, led by the Istiqlal (Independence) grouping, and on 2 March 1956 the French protectorate achieved independence as the Sultanate of Morocco. Sultan Muhammad V, who had reigned since 1927 (although he had been temporarily removed from office by the French authorities between 1953 and 1955), became the first Head of State. The northern zone of the Spanish protectorate joined the new state in April 1956, and Tangier's international status was abolished in October. The southern zone of the Spanish protectorate was ceded to Morocco in 1958, but no agreement was reached on the enclaves of Ceuta and Melilla, in the north, the Ifni region in the south, or the Saharan territories to the south of Morocco, which all remained under Spanish control. The Sultan was restyled King of Morocco in August 1957, and became Prime Minister in May 1960. He died in February 1961, and was succeeded by his son, Moulay Hassan, who took the title of Hassan II.

Elections to Morocco's first House of Representatives took place in May 1963, and six months later King Hassan relinquished the post of Prime Minister. In June 1965, however, increasing political fragmentation prompted Hassan to declare a 'state of exception', and to resume full legislative and executive powers. The emergency provisions remained in force until July 1970, when a new Constitution was approved. Elections in the following month resulted in a pro-Government majority in the new Majlis an-Nuab (Chamber of Representatives).

In July 1971 an attempted *coup d'état* was suppressed by forces loyal to the King. Among those subsequently arrested were numerous members of the left-wing Union nationale des forces populaires (UNFP), five of whom were sentenced to death. Although a revised Constitution was approved in March 1972 by popular referendum, a general election did not take place until June 1977. Two-thirds of the deputies in the Chamber of Representatives were directly elected, the remainder being elected by local government councils, professional associations and labour organizations. Supporters of the King's policies won a majority of seats in the new legislature. A Government of national unity was formed, including opposition representatives from Istiqlal and the Mouvement populaire (MP) in addition to the pro-monarchist independents.

In October 1981, when it was announced that the term of office of the Chamber of Representatives was to be extended from four to six years, all 14 deputies belonging to the Union socialiste des forces populaires (USFP) withdrew from the assembly. Elections to the legislature were postponed and an interim Government of national unity was appointed, headed by Muhammad Karim Lamrani (Prime Minister in 1971–72). The new Government included members of the six main political parties: Istiqlal, the MP, the Parti national démocrate (PND), the Rassemblement national des indépendants (RNI), the Union constitutionnelle (UC) and the USFP. The postponed legislative elections took place in September and October 1984. Despite significant gains by the USFP, the Chamber of Representatives was again dominated by the centre-right parties. A new Cabinet, appointed in April 1985, included members of the MP, the PND, the RNI and the UC. Lamrani resigned in September 1986, on the grounds of ill health, and was replaced by Az ad-Dine Laraki (hitherto Deputy Prime Minister and Minister of National Education).

In March 1992 King Hassan announced that the Constitution was to be revised and submitted for approval in a national referendum, in preparation for legislative elections (which had been postponed since 1990, pending settlement of the Western Sahara dispute). The King indicated in July that the elections would take place in November, and that voting would be extended to include Western Sahara—irrespective of the UN's progress in organizing a referendum on the territory's status (see below). In August the King dissolved the Government, and named Lamrani as Prime Minister in an interim, non-partisan Government. According to official results, the revised Constitution was overwhelmingly endorsed by 99.96% of voters in the national referendum, which was held in September; approval was officially reported to be unanimous in the major cities and in three of the four provinces of Western Sahara. Under the terms of the new Constitution, the King would retain strong executive powers, including the right to appoint the Prime Minister, although government members would henceforth be nominated by the premier. The Government would be required to reflect the composition of the Chamber of Representatives, and was obliged to submit its legislative programme for the Chamber's approval; new legislation would automatically be promulgated one month after having been endorsed by parliament, regardless of whether royal assent had been received. Provision was also made for the establishment of a Constitutional Council and of an Economic and Social Council, and guarantees of human rights were enshrined in the document.

Legislative elections eventually took place on 25 June 1993. Parties of the Bloc démocratique (also known as the Koutla démocratique)—grouping Istiqlal, the USFP, the Parti du progrès et du socialisme (PPS), the Organisation de l'action démocratique et populaire (OADP) and the UNFP—won a combined total of 99 of the 222 directly elective seats in the enlarged chamber. (Within the Bloc, the USFP won 48 seats and Istiqlal 43.) The MP won 33 seats, the RNI 28 and the UC 27. The indirect election (by an electoral college) of the remaining 111 members of the Chamber, which followed on 17 September, was less favourable to the Bloc démocratique, which won only 21 further seats. Of the 333 seats in the Chamber, the USFP now controlled 56, the UC 54, Istiqlal 52, the MP 51 and the RNI 41. In November the King reappointed Lamrani as premier. The new Government comprised technocrats and independents, and did not include any representatives of the parties that had contested the legislative elections. (By-elections took place in April 1994 in 14 constituencies—in all but one of which the Constitutional Council had annulled results of the previous year's elections.)

In May 1994 Hassan replaced Lamrani with Abd al-Latif Filali, hitherto Minister of State for Foreign Affairs and Co-operation. Although the new Prime Minister held consultations with the political groupings represented in parliament, the composition of the new Government (in which he retained the foreign affairs portfolio) was effectively unchanged. In July the King appealed to all political parties to participate in a government of national unity, and in October he announced his intention to select a premier from the ranks of the opposition. However, negotiations on the formation of a coalition government failed, apparently owing to the Bloc démocratique's refusal to join an administration in which Driss Basri (a long-serving government member and close associate of the King) remained as Minister of the Interior and Information, and in January 1995 Hassan instructed Filali to form a new cabinet. The interior and information portfolios were, notably, separated in the new Government: Basri remained Minister of the Interior, while Driss Alaoui M'Daghri assumed responsibility for the restyled Ministry of Communication.

Muhammad Basri, a prominent opposition figure (sentenced to death *in absentia* in 1974) and founder member of both the UNFP and the USFP, returned to Morocco from France in June 1995, after 28 years in exile. It was widely believed that his rehabilitation had been precipitated by the royal amnesty of July 1994 and by the return to Morocco (also from France) in May 1995 of the First Secretary of the USFP, Abd ar-Rahman el-Youssoufi, both of which seemed to indicate a greater level of political tolerance on the part of the Moroccan authorities. In December Abdessalam Yassine, the leader of the unauthorized Islamist movement Al-Adl wal-Ihsan (Justice and Charity), was briefly released after six years of house arrest, but restrictions on his movement were reinstated after Yassine criticized the Government. Despite the King's assertion that there were no longer any political detainees in Morocco, a report published by the Association marocaine des droits humains (AMDH) in February 1996 claimed that 58 political prisoners (primarily radical Islamists, supporters of independence for Western Sahara and left-wing activists) remained in detention.

In August 1996 the King presented further constitutional amendments, including the creation of an indirectly elected second parliamentary assembly, the Majlis al-Mustasharin (Chamber of Advisers), and the introduction of direct elections for all members of the Chamber of Representatives. Most political parties supported the reforms; however, an appeal by the OADP leadership for a boycott of a planned referendum on the amendments led to a split in the party and the subsequent creation of the Parti socialiste démocratique (PSD). According to official results of the referendum, held in September, the reforms were approved by 99.6% of voters. Legislation regarding the new bicameral parliament was promulgated in August 1997: the Chamber of Representatives was to comprise 325 members, directly elected for a five-year term; the 270 members of the Chamber of Advisers would be indirectly elected, for a nine-year term, by local councils (which would chose 162 members), chambers of commerce (81) and trade unions (27).

At elections to the Chamber of Representatives held on 14 November 1997, the Bloc démocratique won a combined total of 102 seats (of which the USFP took 57 and Istiqlal 32); the centre-right Entente nationale took 100 (50 secured by the UC, 40 by the MP), and centrist parties 97 (including 46 obtained by the RNI). The Mouvement populaire constitutionnel et démocratique (MPCD), which earlier in the year had formally absorbed members of the Islamist Al Islah wa Attajdid, won nine seats, securing parliamentary representation for the first time. (In October 1998 the MPCD changed its name to the Parti de la justice et du développement—PJD.) At indirect elections to the Chamber of Advisers, which followed on 5 December, centrist parties won 90 of the seats (42 secured by the RNI, 33 by the Mouvement démocratique et social), the Entente nationale 76 (28 obtained by the UC, 27 by the MP) and the Bloc démocratique 44 (21 won by Istiqlal). In February 1998 the King appointed el-Youssoufi as the new Prime Minister, in an apparent attempt to appease opposition parties dissatisfied with the outcome of the legislative elections. This was the first time since independence that a socialist had been appointed to the Moroccan premiership. In March a new Cabinet was formed, including members of the USFP, the RNI, Istiqlal, the PPS, the Mouvement national populaire (MNP), the Front des forces démocratiques and the PSD.

King Hassan died on 23 July 1999, after several years of ill health. His eldest son, Crown Prince Sidi Muhammad, succeeded as King Muhammad VI. At the end of July the new King decreed an amnesty whereby some 8,000 prisoners were freed and more than 38,000 had their sentences reduced. In August the King ordered the creation within the Conseil Consultatif des Droits de l'Homme (CCDH)—established by King Hassan in April 1990—of an independent commission to determine levels of compensation for families of missing political activists and for those subjected to arbitrary detention. In April 1999 the CCDH had announced that it had been agreed to compensate the families of 112 people who were now officially acknowledged as having 'disappeared' between 1960 and 1990. However, independent Moroccan human rights organizations asserted that the number of missing people amounted to almost 600. In September 1999 King Muhammad approved the return to Morocco of Abraham Serfaty, a left-wing dissident who had been deported to France in 1991; Serfaty had been granted a passport by the el-Youssoufi administration in 1998, but his return had not been authorized. The family of former opposition activist and UNFP leader Mehdi Ben Barka, who had been abducted and apparently murdered in Paris, France, in 1965, was also permitted to return to Morocco in November 1999.

Meanwhile, in November 1999 King Muhammad dismissed the long-serving Minister of State for the Interior, Driss Basri. Basri's removal from office, apparently in response to the violent suppression of protests in Western Sahara in September (see below), was interpreted as a particularly important step towards the modernization of Moroccan society. The new Minister of the Interior, Ahmed Midaoui (a former Director of National Security), immediately pledged to work towards the strengthening of democracy and the reconciliation of the administration and the people of Morocco. Victims of repression and their families, together with left-wing political parties and non-governmental organizations, subsequently formed a 'Justice and Trust' organization, which aimed to investigate human rights abuses in Morocco since independence. In April 2000 the Government commenced payments, reportedly totalling 40m. dirhams, in respect of the cases of an initial 40 victims of arbitrary detention, from the fund established in the previous year. Abdessalam Yassine of Al-Adl wal-Ihsan was again released from house arrest in May.

In March 2001 King Muhammad announced the establishment of a royal commission to revise the country's laws on personal rights and responsibilities; the commission was to be chaired by the First President of the Supreme Court and included leading Islamic scholars and jurists. Meanwhile, the King demonstrated a commitment to greater rights for Moroccan women by appointing women as royal advisers, ambassadors and to other senior public offices. In September King Muhammad appointed Driss Jettou, a former Minister of Finance and Industry, as Minister of the Interior; Ahmed Midaoui became an adviser to the King. In October Muhammad established a royal institute charged with preserving the language and culture of the country's Berber population; the institute would also work towards integrating the Berber language into the education system.

In June 2001 the Moroccan authorities granted Jean-Baptiste Parlos, the French judge leading the inquiry into the disappearance of Mehdi Ben Barka (see above), permission to visit Morocco as part of his investigation. Later that month Ahmed Boukhari, a former member of the Moroccan special services, alleged in a newspaper article that Ben Barka had been kidnapped in Paris by French police officers in the employ of the Moroccan secret service and had been tortured to death by Morocco's then Minister of the Interior, Gen. Muhammad Oufkir. In July Boukhari received a summons to appear before the French investigation into Ben Barka's disappearance; however, the Moroccan authorities refused to grant Boukhari a passport, and in the following month he was arrested on charges of financial irregularity. Boukhari's detention was condemned by human rights organizations, which claimed that the Moroccan Government was attempting to prevent Boukhari from testifying at the Parlos inquiry. In December 2002 the Moroccan authorities announced that they would co-operate fully with the French investigation into the Ben Barka affair, and in January 2003 a French judge travelled to Rabat where he interviewed Boukhari about the disappearance of Ben Barka. The investigation was still ongoing in October 2007, when French magistrate Patrick Ramaël issued arrest warrants for five Moroccan officials suspected of involvement in Ben Barka's disappearance.

Meanwhile, in January 2002 el-Youssoufi stated that he would stand down as Prime Minister after the legislative elections scheduled for September, but would remain as First Secretary of the USFP. In March the Government agreed a number of changes to the electoral system, including the abandonment of the simple majority system in favour of proportional representation. The Government insisted that the new system would reduce fraudulent practices and increase public confidence in the electoral process; at least 10% of the 325 seats in the lower house were to be reserved for women. The general election took place on 27 September 2002. According to official figures, the USFP won the largest number of seats, although its representation in the

Chamber of Representatives was reduced from 57 to 50 seats. Istiqlal increased its parliamentary representation to 48 members, while the PJD took 42 seats, the RNI 41, the MP 27, the MNP 18 and the UC 16. The rate of voter participation was recorded at just 51.6% of the electorate. In October King Muhammad appointed Jettou as the new Prime Minister, and a new Government was announced in the following month. Despite securing the third highest number of seats in the Chamber of Representatives, the PJD was not allocated any ministerial portfolios. The new Cabinet comprised members of the USFD, Istiqlal, the RNI, the MNP, the MP and the PPS, as well as a number of non-affiliated technocrats—one of whom, Al Mustapha Sahel, replaced Jettou as Minister of the Interior. Three women were appointed to the Government. In early May 2003 King Muhammad marked the occasion of the birth of a son and heir to the throne, Prince Moulay Hassan, by ordering the release of an estimated 9,000 prisoners and reducing the gaol terms of a further 38,000.

In mid-May 2003 45 people died and more than 100 others were injured in a series of suicide bomb attacks in central Casablanca, which targeted the Belgian consulate, a Spanish restaurant and a Jewish cultural centre. Among those killed were reported to be 12 suicide bombers, and two other suspected attackers were detained by the security forces along with some 30 others thought to have been involved in the bombings. The Moroccan authorities believed that the bombers were linked to a small Moroccan-based militant Islamist group, al-Assirat al-Moustaquim (Righteous Path), but that the attacks had been orchestrated by an international terrorist network operating in Europe, possibly the al-Qa'ida (Base) organization of the fugitive Saudi Arabian-born Islamist Osama bin Laden. In late May the suspected co-ordinator of the attacks, who had been arrested in Fez, died in police custody as a result of ill health. Later in May stricter anti-terrorism measures were approved by the legislature, which broadened the definition of terrorism and increased the number of offences punishable by the death sentence.

In mid-July 2003 10 of the alleged 31 members of the radical Islamist group Salafia Jihadia, who had been arrested during police operations against Islamist networks in mid-2002, were sentenced to death by a court in Casablanca, having been convicted of murder and attempted murder. The remainder of the accused received lengthy prison terms. Later in July 2003 it was announced that more than 700 people would be tried in connection with the bomb attacks; 52 defendants subsequently appeared before Casablanca's criminal court. In August four men, including the two suspected surviving suicide bombers, received death sentences for their roles in the violence; 39 others were sentenced to life imprisonment for plotting further attacks in Essaouira, Agadir and Marrakesh. Some 50 Islamists received various prison sentences during September for their alleged roles in attempting to carry out further bomb attacks within Morocco, and in February 2005 10 men were imprisoned for eight years for membership of Salafia Jihadia. Two members of Salafia Jihadia were sentenced to death in July, having been convicted of the murders in Casablanca of five people, including an official of the Ministry of the Interior. In early April 2008 nine of the men convicted for their links to the suicide bombings in Casablanca tunnelled their way out of Kenitra prison, north of Rabat. Seven of the fugitives were reportedly serving life sentences, while the other two were serving terms of 20 years. According to Abderrahim Mahtade, President of the prisoner rights advocacy group Annasir, the men left behind a letter criticizing the alleged injustices of the Moroccan legal system. One of the escaped prisoners was apprehended by Moroccan police less than a month later, but the search for the eight remaining fugitives was still ongoing in early May.

Despite the clampdown on Islamist activity in the wake of the Casablanca bombings, King Muhammad continued to pursue his policies of reform and modernization of Moroccan society, including provision for the teaching of the Berber language in schools. In October 2003 King Muhammad announced major revisions to the *mudawana* (family code), which he claimed would promote female equality and protect children's rights. The reforms (originally outlined in 2000) would raise the legal age of marriage for women from 15 to 18 and simplify the procedure for women seeking a divorce from their husband. Although polygamy was not to be outlawed under the new legislation, women would be able to prevent their husbands from taking a second wife and would also be provided with equal authority and property rights within the marriage. In January 2004 the changes to the *mudawana* were approved by the legislature.

In February 2004 an earthquake measuring 6.4 on the Richter scale hit the province of Al-Hoceima in the north of the country, killing more than 600 people and leaving thousands more homeless. While international aid organizations were quick to respond to the disaster, relief efforts were hampered by a reported lack of organization on the part of the Moroccan authorities, leading to angry demonstrations by hundreds of people demanding food, medical assistance and tents.

In June 2005 Nadia Yassine, the daughter of Abdessalam Yassine and spokesperson for Al-Adl wal-Ihsan, was charged with attacking the monarchy following the publication of an interview in which she stated that the monarchy was no longer relevant for Morocco. Along with Abdelaziz Koukas, the editor of the magazine in which the interview appeared, Yassine faced up to five years' imprisonment if found guilty. However, the trial was immediately postponed, and was still pending, following several further adjournments, in April 2008. Meanwhile, in late March 2008 a Moroccan computer engineer, Fouad Mourtada, was sentenced to three years in prison and fined 10,000 dirhams for creating a false profile of Prince Mourlay Rachid on a popular social networking internet site. However, following complaints from international human rights groups, Mourtada was given a royal pardon and released from prison.

A series of attempts by large organized groups of African migrants to scale fences along the border between Morocco and the Spanish enclaves of Ceuta and Melilla resulted in the deaths of at least 11 people in late September and early October 2005. Moroccan troops later admitted to shooting dead four of the victims and seven others were reported to have been crushed. In mid-October the Government denied allegations that groups of migrants sent back to Morocco from Spain had been transported to the country's southern desert region and abandoned without food or water. Later the same month the Moroccan authorities repatriated more than 1,000 migrants by air to various sub-Saharan African countries. Illegal immigration from Morocco in 2006 was reported to have fallen sharply compared with 2005, owing in part to tighter border controls by Morocco and Spain. However, in July 2006 another attempt by some 70 migrants to scale the six-metre-high fence surrounding Melilla resulted in two deaths, at least one of which, according to the Spanish authorities, was likely to have been the result of a gunshot.

In February 2006 King Muhammad appointed Chakib Benmoussa, a non-affiliate, as Minister of the Interior to replace Sahel, who became Morocco's ambassador to the UN. In May–June the police arrested more than 500 members of Al-Adl wal-Ihsan, most of whom were quickly released, after unconfirmed reports that the Islamist movement was planning an uprising. Al-Adl wal-Ihsan, which is unauthorized but generally tolerated by the Moroccan authorities, had launched an 'open doors' campaign earlier in 2006 to disseminate information among the general public and recruit new members outside its traditional areas of support such as mosques and universities. Indications of a possible threat from militant Islamism surfaced in August, when 56 members of a group called Ansar al-Mahdi were arrested on suspicion of planning a campaign of violence against the monarchy. According to Benmoussa, the group possessed the capability to carry out a more destructive attack than the series of bombings in Casablanca in 2003. Among those detained were several members of the police and armed forces as well as three women, two of whom were married to pilots of the national airline, Royal Air Maroc. In January 2008 the leader of Ansar al-Mahdi, Hassan Khattab, was sentenced to 25 years in prison, while 49 other members of the group were given prison terms of between two and 20 years, having been convicted of various crimes including plotting to attack government buildings and stealing funds to enable them to pursue militant activities.

In March 2007 a suicide bomb attack at an internet café in Casablanca resulted in three people being injured. In April, during a police operation in Casablanca in connection with the previous month's suicide attack, three suspected Islamist militants detonated explosive belts and a fourth was shot dead by police as he attempted to do so. Four days later two suicide bombers targeted the US consulate and a US cultural centre in the city. The series of attacks coincided with two large explosions in Algiers that were claimed by al-Qa'ida in the Islamic Maghreb (formerly the Groupe salafiste pour la prédication et le combat—see the chapter on Algeria). Although a statement on the internet

MOROCCO

purporting to be from al-Qa'ida claimed responsibility for the explosions in Casablanca, Moroccan police insisted that they were the work of a group with no links to external organizations. In late February 2008 32 members of the small Islamist party al-Badil al-Hadari (Alternative Civilization) were arrested in Morocco on suspicion of being involved in plans to carry out politically motivated attacks such as assassinations of senior officials. The Secretary-General of the party, Mustapha Moatassim, was among those detained. The party was subsequently banned by the Moroccan authorities following the discovery of weapons at the houses of suspects and allegations of links with international terrorist networks, including having maintained contacts with al-Qa'ida in Afghanistan in 2001. Moroccan police claimed to have dismantled at least 50 terrorist cells and to have made nearly 3,000 arrests since the Casablanca suicide bombings in 2003.

Meanwhile, in April 2006 one of Morocco's principal weekly newspapers, Le Journal Hebdomadaire, was ordered by the Court of Appeal to pay damages of 3m. dirhams for defamation to the Belgium-based European Strategic Intelligence and Security Centre (ESISC), while the publication's editor and one of its journalists were fined 50,000 dirhams each. The newspaper had questioned the impartiality of a report published by the ESISC that had been highly critical of the separatist Polisario Front (see below), claiming that it had been guided by the Moroccan authorities. The damages were the highest ever awarded in a defamation case in the country. In January 2007 the editor and a reporter of the news magazine Nichane were each given a three-year suspended prison sentence and fined 80,000 dirhams for publishing jokes deemed to have denigrated Islam. The magazine was also banned from circulation for two months. Mustapha Hormatallah, a journalist for the Al Watan Al An weekly, was sentenced to eight months' imprisonment in August for publishing 'confidential documents' pertaining to anti-terrorism operations in Morocco. An appeals court in Casablanca subsequently reduced Hormatallah's sentence to a term of seven months, but granted him a provisional release. The editor of the newspaper, Abderrahim Ariri, was given a five-month suspended sentence, and both men were fined 1,000 dirhams.

At the general election held on 7 September 2007, Istiqlal won a majority of seats (52) in the Chamber of Representatives. The PJD came in second place with 46 seats, followed by the MP (which had merged with the MNP and the Union démocratique in 2006) with 41, and the RNI with 39. The USFP, which previously held the majority of seats in the legislature, only managed to secure 38. Voter turn-out for the election was at a record low of 37% of eligible participants. On 19 September Abbas el-Fassi, the leader of Istiqlal and Minister of State in the outgoing Government, was appointed as the new Prime Minister by King Muhammad. In mid-October a new Government made up of a coalition of four parties (Istiqlal, the RNI, the USFP and the PPS), along with several independent ministers, was sworn into office. Chakib Benmoussa retained his position as Minister of the Interior, while former Minister of Industry Salaheddine Mezouar was named as Minister of the Economy and Finance and the Deputy Minister of Foreign Affairs and Co-operation, Taieb Fassi Fihri, was promoted to head the foreign affairs portfolio. Cognisant with King Muhammad's commitment to cautious social reforms, the new Cabinet included seven women (two of these becoming deputy ministers).

Following the cession of the Spanish enclave of Ifni to Morocco in 1969, political opinion in Morocco was united in opposing the continued occupation by Spain of areas considered to be historically parts of Moroccan territory: namely Spanish Sahara and Spanish North Africa (q.v.)—a number of small enclaves on Morocco's Mediterranean coast. A campaign to annex Spanish Sahara, initiated in 1974, received active support from all Moroccan political parties. In October 1975 King Hassan ordered a 'Green March' by more than 300,000 unarmed Moroccans to occupy the territory. The marchers were stopped by the Spanish authorities when they had barely crossed the border, but in November Spain agreed to cede the territory to Morocco and Mauritania, to be apportioned equally between them. Spain formally relinquished sovereignty of Spanish Sahara in February 1976. Moroccan troops moved into the territory to confront a guerrilla uprising led by the Frente Popular para la Liberación de Saguia el-Hamra y Río de Oro (the Polisario Front), a national liberation movement supported by Algeria and (later) Libya which aimed to achieve an independent Western Saharan state. On 27 February the Polisario Front declared the 'Sahrawi Arab Democratic Republic' (SADR), and shortly afterwards established a 'Government-in-exile' in Algeria. In protest, Morocco severed diplomatic relations with Algeria.

Moroccan troops inflicted heavy casualties on the insurgents, and ensured the security of Western Sahara's main population centres, but they failed to prevent constant infiltration, harassment and sabotage by Polisario forces. Moreover, Polisario had considerable success against Mauritanian troops, and in August 1979 Mauritania renounced its claim to Saharan territory and signed a peace treaty with the Polisario Front. Morocco immediately asserted its claim to the whole of Western Sahara and annexed the region.

In July 1980 the SADR applied to join the Organization of African Unity (OAU—now African Union, see p. 164) as a sovereign state. Although 26 of the 50 members then recognized the Polisario Front as the rightful government of Western Sahara, Morocco insisted that a two-thirds' majority was needed to confer membership. Morocco rejected an OAU proposal for a cease-fire and a referendum on the territory, and in 1981 heavy fighting resumed in the region. The SADR was accepted as the OAU's 51st member in early 1982, but a threat by 18 members to leave the organization in protest necessitated a compromise whereby the SADR, while remaining a member, agreed not to attend OAU meetings. In late 1984 a SADR delegation did attend a summit meeting of the OAU with little opposition from other states, causing Morocco to resign from the organization. Meanwhile, fighting continued in Western Sahara; decisive victories for Polisario proved impossible, however, as Morocco constructed a 2,500-km defensive wall of sand, equipped with electronic detectors, to surround Western Sahara.

In October 1985 Morocco announced a unilateral cease-fire in Western Sahara, and invited the UN to supervise a referendum to be held there the following January. A series of indirect talks between the two sides, arranged by the UN and the OAU in 1986–87, failed to achieve a solution, and in January 1988 Polisario forces renewed their offensive against Moroccan positions in Western Sahara. In August, however, it was announced that the Polisario Front and Morocco had provisionally accepted a peace plan proposed by the UN Secretary-General, Javier Pérez de Cuéllar, which envisaged the conclusion of a formal cease-fire, a reduction in Moroccan military forces in Western Sahara and the withdrawal of Polisario forces to their bases, to be followed by a referendum on self-determination in Western Sahara. A list of eligible voters was to be based on the Spanish census of 1974. A meeting in Marrakesh in January 1989 between King Hassan and officials of the Polisario Front and the SADR—the first direct contact for 13 years—was apparently limited to exchanges of goodwill, but was followed, in February, by the announcement of a unilateral cease-fire by Polisario. A further meeting was postponed by Hassan, who in September rejected the possibility of official negotiations with the SADR; later that month Polisario renewed its military attacks on Moroccan positions.

UN Security Council Resolution No. 690 of April 1991 established a peace-keeping force, the UN Mission for the Referendum in Western Sahara (MINURSO, see p. 81), which was to implement the 1988 plan for a referendum on self-determination. In June 1991 Polisario agreed to a formal cease-fire, with effect from 6 September, from which date the 2,000-strong MINURSO delegation would undertake its duties in the region. Reports in September suggested that some 30,000 people had entered Western Sahara from Morocco, prompting claims that the Moroccan authorities were attempting to alter the region's demography in advance of the referendum. It was also reported that more than 170,000 Sahrawis who had fled the region since 1976 were being repatriated in order that they might participate in the referendum. By November 1991 only 200 MINURSO personnel had been deployed in Western Sahara, and the peace process was undermined further by Morocco's failure to withdraw any of its forces from the region (under the terms of the cease-fire agreement, Morocco was to have withdrawn one-half of its 130,000 troops from Western Sahara by mid-September). In May 1992 Pérez de Cuéllar's successor as UN Secretary-General, Dr Boutros Boutros-Ghali, announced that Morocco and Polisario representatives were to begin indirect talks under his auspices. In the same month, however, Morocco appeared to prejudge the result of the proposed referendum by including the population of Western Sahara in the voting lists for its own regional and local elections. In June the SADR Government, which by this time was recognized by 75 countries, appealed to the international community and the UN to condemn alleged Moroccan violations of the cease-fire and to exert pressure for the implementation of the UN peace plan. UN-sponsored negotiations in the USA in September failed to formulate acceptable criteria for the drafting of lists of eligible voters at an eventual referendum.

In March 1993 the UN Security Council approved plans for the holding of the referendum on Western Sahara by the end of the year. In July the first direct negotiations took place between the Moroccan Government and Polisario, although little progress was achieved. In March 1994 Boutros-Ghali submitted a report to the UN Security Council detailing possible procedures for overcoming the impasse on the Western Saharan issue, including the effective withdrawal of the UN from the peace process. (It had been reported in September 1993 that only 360 of the proposed 2,000 UN military personnel were in place.) The Security Council subsequently agreed to a continuation of negotiations for a further three months, and undertook to review the future of MINURSO if a referendum was not organized before the end of the year. In April Polisario accepted the UN programme for the registration of voters. However, the work of a UN voter identification commission, which had been due to commence in June, was delayed by the Moroccan Government's objection to the inclusion of OAU observers in the process.

In mid-1995 Polisario withdrew from the voter identification process, in protest at the severity of sentences placed upon pro-independence Sahrawi protesters by the Moroccan authorities and at alleged Moroccan violations of the cease-fire. In September the SADR announced the formation of a new 14-member Government, headed by Mahfoud Ali Beïba, and in October the first elected Sahrawi National Assembly was inaugurated at a refugee camp in Tindouf, Algeria.

The UN Security Council voted periodically to extend MINURSO's mandate on a short-term basis, noting in January 1996 that it was improbable that the referendum would take place during that year. In May the Security Council voted to suspend the registration of voters in Western Sahara until 'convincing proof' was offered by the Moroccan Government and the Sahrawi leadership that they would not further obstruct preparations for the referendum. The mandate of MINURSO was extended, but its personnel was to be reduced by 20%.

In March 1997 the new UN Secretary-General, Kofi Annan, appointed James Baker (a former US Secretary of State) as his Personal Envoy to Western Sahara. In June Baker mediated in talks in Portugal between representatives of Morocco and the SADR. The process of voter identification resumed in December for a referendum scheduled to be held one year later. However, disagreement between Morocco and Polisario regarding the eligibility of voters delayed the identification process and led the UN to revise the proposed date for the referendum on several occasions. By September 1998 a total of 147,350 voters had been identified since the commencement of the process in August 1994, but the issue of the disputed tribes remained unresolved. In June 1998, meanwhile, as Morocco intensified its efforts to rejoin the OAU, several OAU member states debated the expulsion from the organization of the SADR; only a minority of member countries continued to recognize its independent status.

During talks with Moroccan and SADR officials in November 1998, the UN Secretary-General warned that the UN would withdraw from Western Sahara if the two parties failed to show political will towards resolving the conflict. Annan presented proposals regarding the disputed tribes, the publication of a list of voters not contested by either party, and the repatriation of refugees under the auspices of the UN High Commissioner for Refugees. Although the proposals were accepted by Polisario, the Moroccan authorities expressed reservations. Morocco delayed the signing of a technical agreement with the UN (defining the legal status of MINURSO troops in Western Sahara) until February 1999: Algeria and Mauritania had signed similar accords with the UN in November 1998. In July 1999 MINURSO published a list of 84,251 people provisionally entitled to vote in the referendum, which was scheduled to be held on 31 July 2000.

In February 1999, meanwhile, the SADR announced the formation of a new Government, led by Beïba's predecessor, Bouchraya Hammoudi Bayoune. In September the Polisario Front congress re-elected the President of the SADR, Muhammad Abd al-Aziz, as Secretary-General of the organization. In October a delegation comprising several ministers of the Moroccan Government was dispatched to el-Aaiún (the principal city in Western Sahara, also known as Laâyoune) for consultations with the Sahrawi population at the behest of King Muhammad—who had in September established a royal commission to monitor affairs in Western Sahara.

In response to indications by UN officials in November 1999 that the referendum was likely to be subject to a further postponement, Polisario stated that it could not rule out a return to an armed struggle. Nevertheless, in late November Polisario released 191 Moroccan prisoners. In December the mandate of MINURSO was once again extended to enable it to complete its work on the identification of possible voters in the referendum. However, the UN Secretary-General subsequently announced that it would be impossible to organize the referendum before 2002, owing to the large number of appeals lodged by those deemed ineligible to vote. In January 2000 it was announced that 86,381 out of a total of 198,481 people identified in Western Sahara would be eligible to vote in the referendum. In February, however, Annan postponed the referendum indefinitely, and warned, furthermore, of the possibility that it might never take place, owing to the persistent differences regarding criteria for eligibility to vote. By March the number of appeals lodged had reached over 130,000, and Abd al-Aziz reiterated the threat of the resumption of armed hostilities if Morocco continued to obstruct the UN peace plan.

In April 2000 Baker toured Morocco and Western Sahara, and in London, United Kingdom, in May he chaired the first direct talks between representatives of Morocco and Polisario for three years. Algeria and Mauritania also sent delegations, but the meeting failed to make any substantive progress. In October Annan urged Morocco partially to devolve authority in Western Sahara, stating that if no such concessions were granted, the UN would reactivate plans to hold a referendum in the territory. In February 2001 Annan announced that if Morocco failed to offer or support some devolution of governmental authority, MINURSO would be directed to begin the process of hearing appeals regarding eligibility to vote in the referendum. A further report issued by the Secretary-General in April declared that 'substantial progress' had been made towards determining whether Morocco was prepared to countenance some measure of devolution.

In June 2001 the UN Security Council unanimously approved a compromise resolution (No. 1359), formulated by Baker, which encouraged Polisario and Morocco to discuss an autonomy plan for Western Sahara without abandoning the delayed referendum. Under the terms of the autonomy proposal the inhabitants of Western Sahara would have the right to elect their own legislative and executive bodies and have control over most areas of local government for a period of at least five years, during which Morocco would retain control over defence and foreign affairs. A referendum on the final status of the territory would take place within this five-year period. In August Baker hosted talks in Wyoming, USA, attended by representatives from Polisario, Mauritania and Algeria; however, Polisario subsequently accused the UN of ceding to Moroccan pressure and in September Polisario announced its formal rejection of Baker's proposal. In the following month King Muhammad visited Western Sahara for the first time since his accession to the throne, and in early November he granted an amnesty to 56 prisoners in Western Sahara.

In February 2002 Annan outlined four possible measures to be considered by the UN Security Council in order to attempt to resolve the continuing impasse over Western Sahara: to resume attempts to implement the 1988 settlement plan, with or without the agreement of Polisario and the Moroccan Government; to charge Baker with revising his earlier draft framework agreement; to commence discussions regarding the division of the territory; or to terminate MINURSO's mandate, which had continued to be extended by Security Council resolutions for periods of between two and six months. In July 2002 the UN Security Council admitted that it had been unable to agree on the resolution of the Western Sahara issue, since none of the four proposals had secured the required support, but had voted unanimously to allow Baker to pursue efforts to find a political solution which would provide for self-determination.

Following exploratory negotiations held between Baker and government officials in Mauritania and Algeria, as well as with Abd al-Aziz and King Muhammad, in late May 2003 Annan formally released details of a new peace plan aimed at ending the Western Sahara dispute and urged Morocco, Polisario and

Algeria to accept the proposals. The new plan, known as 'Baker Plan II', proposed immediate self-government for Western Sahara for a period of four to five years, after which time a referendum would be held in order to give all bona fide residents the opportunity to decide the long-term future of the territory. The Security Council approved Annan's proposals at the beginning of June. At the end of June Polisario, under strong pressure from Algeria, accepted the Baker plan as a basis for negotiation. Morocco, however, refused to accept any 'imposed decision' on Western Sahara.

On 31 July 2003 the UN Security Council unanimously adopted Resolution 1495, which supported Baker Plan II and called on parties and states of the region to co-operate fully with the Secretary-General and his Personal Envoy in working towards the implementation of the peace plan. (However, following strong opposition from France, the resolution did not demand that Morocco and Polisario comply with the plan.) It also called on Polisario to release without further delay all remaining Moroccan prisoners of war, and for Morocco and Polisario to co-operate with the International Committee of the Red Cross (ICRC) to resolve the fate of persons unaccounted for since the beginning of the conflict. In September Polisario released 243 Moroccan prisoners of war, although the ICRC maintained that a further 914 Moroccans were still being held captive. Polisario released another 300 Moroccan prisoners of war in November, and a further 100 in February 2004. In April, having urged Morocco to accept and implement Baker Plan II on several occasions, Annan stated that he required a 'final response' from Morocco with regard to the plan.

In late April 2004 the UN Security Council unanimously adopted Resolution 1541, which urged the two sides to accept the UN plan to grant Western Sahara immediate self-government and which extended MINURSO's mandate until October. (The Security Council continued to extend MINURSO's mandate at six-monthly intervals, most recently on 31 October 2007.) Morocco, however, continued to reject this proposal, maintaining that it could not accept a plan for a referendum that included independence as an option, and remained insistent on granting the territory 'autonomy within the framework of Moroccan sovereignty'. In June 2004 James Baker resigned as Annan's Personal Envoy for Western Sahara; at the request of Annan, he was replaced by Alvaro de Soto, a former Peruvian diplomat who had hitherto been the Secretary-General's Special Representative for the region. In September de Soto commenced talks with the Moroccan authorities and Polisario to attempt to resolve the impasse, and a resolution (No. 1570) adopted by the Security Council in late October calling for an end to the deadlock and an advancement towards a political solution was welcomed by the Moroccan authorities. Protests against Moroccan policy towards the region took place in several cities in Western Sahara towards the end of 2004, and in December King Muhammad expressed his country's readiness to find a suitable political solution, while emphasizing that he was not prepared to jeopardize Morocco's sovereignty. Following the transfer of a Sahrawi prisoner from el-Aaiún to a gaol in Morocco in May 2005, pro-independence demonstrations took place in el-Aaiún, during which 50 people were reportedly injured. Meanwhile, in early May de Soto left his role of Special Representative and immediately assumed the position of UN Special Co-ordinator for the Middle East Peace Process. In July Annan appointed Peter van Walsum of the Netherlands as his new Personal Envoy for Western Sahara, and in August it was announced that Francesco Bastagli of Italy would replace de Soto as Special Representative of the Secretary-General and MINURSO Chief of Mission. Later in August the Polisario Front released the remaining 408 Moroccan prisoners of war, some of whom had been held in Tindouf for more than 20 years, one month after Abd al-Aziz had urged Morocco to release 150 Sahrawis he claimed were still in detention. In November one person was killed during further violent confrontations in el-Aaiún, which preceded celebrations to mark the 30th anniversary of the Green March, between protesters demanding independence and Moroccan security forces. In a televised address on the anniversary, King Muhammad announced his intention to consult with Morocco's political parties on the issue of autonomy for Western Sahara 'within the sovereignty of the kingdom'. However, Polisario immediately rejected the plan and stated that a referendum was the only viable solution.

In March 2006 King Muhammad visited Western Sahara for the third time since his accession to the throne in 1999, and royal pardons were granted to 216 Sahrawi prisoners. (In April the King ordered the release of all the remaining 48 Sahrawi prisoners held by Morocco.) During the visit Muhammad also announced the appointment of a revised Royal Advisory Council for Saharan Affairs (CORCAS), a body that had been originally established in 1981 by King Hassan II. The 140 newly appointed members were to assist with the formulation of draft proposals for Sahrawi autonomy. In mid-April 2006 Annan submitted a report to the UN Security Council in which he noted the demise of Baker Plan II, which had not been mentioned in any of the relevant Security Council resolutions since Morocco rejected the proposal in 2004, and called on all parties in the dispute, including Algeria, to engage in direct negotiations with no preconditions in order to reach a consensual solution to the impasse. In February 2007 the new UN Secretary-General, Ban Ki-Moon, appointed Julian Harston of the United Kingdom as his Special Representative.

The 'Moroccan initiative for negotiating an autonomy statute for the Sahara region', which had been formulated over the course of 2006, was finally presented to the UN Security Council in April 2007. It proposed the granting of extensive legislative, executive and judicial autonomy to the region, with Morocco retaining sovereignty and control of borders, national security, foreign and religious affairs, among other areas. The plan was rejected by Polisario, which described it as 'null and void' and on the same day offered the UN a rival plan for a referendum with three options—full independence, autonomy within Morocco or full integration—including proposals for a special political and economic relationship with Morocco in the event of a vote for independence. On 30 April the Security Council unanimously adopted Resolution 1754, which described Morocco's plan as 'serious and credible', while also noting the Polisario proposal, and again called on both sides to enter into direct negotiations without preconditions under the aegis of the Secretary-General. Following the adoption of the resolution, both Morocco and Polisario agreed to begin negotiations, and UN-mediated talks between the two sides (attended by representatives of Algeria and Mauritania) took place in June and again in August in the New York suburb of Manhasset, USA. There was a setback in mid-December when the Polisario held its 12th congress in Tifariti, at which it suggested preparing for the resumption of war with Morocco. None the less, two further rounds of negotiations between Moroccan officials and Polisario were held in January and March 2008. While the talks failed to achieve any significant progress, the two sides agreed to consider relaxing restrictions on people travelling by road to visit families in the disputed territory. At the conclusion of the fourth round of talks, Morocco and Polisario agreed to meet again, although there was no immediate indication as to the timing or format of the talks.

Relations with other North African states, which had been strained due to the situation in Western Sahara, improved significantly in the late 1980s. In May 1988 Algeria and Morocco agreed to re-establish diplomatic relations. (Relations with Mauritania had been suspended in 1981 and resumed in April 1985.) In February 1989 North African heads of state, meeting in Marrakesh, signed a treaty establishing the Union du Maghreb arabe (UMA—Union of the Arab Maghreb, see p. 414). The new body, grouping Morocco, Algeria, Libya, Mauritania and Tunisia, aimed to promote trade by allowing the free movement of goods, services and workers. During 1990 bilateral agreements on economic co-operation were concluded by Morocco with Algeria and Libya, and there were further discussions within the UMA on the formation of a North African free trade area. However, there were political disagreements particularly concerning Algeria's continued support for the Polisario Front, and over Moroccan condemnation of Iraq's invasion of Kuwait in August 1990. In early 1993 it was announced that the five UMA members had decided there should be a 'pause' in the development of a closer union; of 15 conventions signed since the inauguration of the UMA, none had as yet been fully applied. However, the organization continued to hold meetings on an annual basis. In December 1995 King Hassan expressed disapproval at Algeria's continued support for the independence of Western Sahara, and demanded that UMA activities be suspended. An impending UMA summit was subsequently postponed.

In March 1999 President Zine al-Abidine Ben Ali of Tunisia made his first official visit to Morocco, during which he pledged to improve bilateral relations and to reactivate the UMA. At bilateral meetings during 2000 with other Maghreb heads of state King Muhammad also pledged to take measures to revive the UMA. A summit meeting of ministers responsible for foreign affairs of the five UMA states proceeded in the Algerian capital in March 2001. However, the meeting, which was to have made preparations for the first summit meeting of UMA heads of state since 1995, quickly broke down following disagreements between Moroccan and Algerian representatives. Libya assumed the chairmanship of the UMA in December 2003, and Libyan leader Col Muammar al-Qaddafi pledged to host a summit meeting of the UMA heads of state following the presidential election in Algeria, due to be held in April of the following year. The meeting was subsequently scheduled to take place in Tripoli, Libya, in May 2005. However, a statement of renewed support for the Polisario Front by the Algerian President, Abdelaziz Bouteflika, provoked a fresh dispute between Morocco and Algeria days before the summit meeting was due to begin and King Muhammad declined to attend. Following a further postponement, the summit meeting eventually took place in Tangiers in late April 2008. The meeting was attended by both Prime Minister Abbas el-Fassi and the Prime Minister of Algeria, Abdelaziz Belkhadem, along with delegates from the three other UMA member states. In spite of a dispute between Belkhadem and the Minister of State and leader of the Moroccan USFP, Muhammad el-Yazghi, over the situation in Western Sahara, the summit ended peacefully, with renewed calls for regional co-operation.

Relations with Algeria had been further undermined in mid-1994 by the murder, apparently by radical Islamists, of two Spanish tourists in Marrakesh, which the Moroccan authorities attributed in part to Algerian nationals. The imposition by Morocco of entry restrictions on Algerian citizens prompted the Algerian Government to introduce reciprocal visa restrictions and to close its border with Morocco. Tensions eased somewhat in September, when Algeria announced the appointment of a new ambassador to Morocco, and in October a Moroccan minister attended ceremonies in Algeria to mark the commencement of work on a Maghreb–Europe gas pipeline. In January 1995 three people, including one Algerian, were sentenced to death for their part in acts of terrorism, including the murders in Marrakesh; three others were sentenced to life imprisonment. The French security forces made further arrests in connection with the murder of the two Spaniards during 1995–96, and in early 1997 a French court sentenced another 29 alleged conspirators (two Moroccans, the remainder French citizens of Maghreb origin) to terms of imprisonment ranging from one to eight years. The Western Sahara issue remained a source of tension between Morocco and Algeria, but in mid-1998 the Moroccan authorities indicated their desire to normalize relations with Algeria and to reopen the common border. In September 1999, however, Algeria's new President, Abdelaziz Bouteflika, claimed that radical Islamist rebels were launching attacks on Algeria from Morocco, and accused Morocco of ignoring the increasing trade in illicit drugs between the two countries. Bouteflika also criticized Morocco for negotiating a separate trade agreement with the European Union (EU, see p. 244), claiming that this was not in the interests of the UMA. None the less, both Morocco and Algeria subsequently reiterated their commitment to reviving the activities of the UMA.

Although relations remained generally co-operative, Bouteflika was vocal in opposing the UN proposals for Western Sahara in mid-2001, which he claimed favoured Morocco. In February 2002, furthermore, Morocco asserted that Algerian support for the partition of Western Sahara risked destabilizing the region; for its part, Algeria accused Morocco of blocking a UN-sponsored solution to the Western Sahara issue. During a visit to Algiers by the Moroccan Minister of Foreign Affairs and Co-operation in June 2003, it was agreed to establish three bilateral commissions to consider political, economic and social matters. Following talks in July 2004 between the Moroccan Minister of the Interior, Al Mustapha Sahel, and his Algerian counterpart, Noureddine Yazid Zerhouni, the two countries signalled their desire to improve diplomatic relations. In May 2005, however, Bouteflika issued a statement renewing Algeria's support for the Polisario Front, and in October allegations by Polisario that Morocco had abandoned African migrants in the Western Saharan desert further increased tensions between the two countries. Jettou accused Algeria of instigating the allegations, and claimed that Algeria had exacerbated the problem by allowing some illegal immigrants to establish camps close to their joint border.

From the late 1990s Morocco was actively involved in wider regional integration efforts, as a member of the Community of Sahel-Saharan States (CEN-SAD, see p. 411), and also through bilateral and multilateral free trade arrangements; in May 2001, notably, the Governments of Morocco, Iraq, Jordan and Tunisia agreed, at a meeting in Agadir, to establish a free trade zone. In October of that year Morocco and Mauritania took steps to improve bilateral relations after King Muhammad visited that country.

A visit to Rabat by the Israeli Prime Minister, Itzhak Rabin, in September 1993 was regarded as an indication of improved relations between Morocco and Israel, and of the role played by King Hassan in the Middle East peace process. In September 1994 Morocco became only the second Arab country (after Egypt) to establish direct links with Israel; liaison offices were subsequently opened in Rabat and Tel-Aviv. In March 1997, however, in condemnation of recent Israeli settlement policy, ministers of foreign affairs of the League of Arab States (the Arab League, see p. 332) recommended a number of sanctions against Israel, including the closure of representative missions. In January 2000 Morocco and Israel agreed in principle to upgrade diplomatic relations to ambassadorial level, although no indication was given as to when embassies would be established. In October, however, as the crisis in Israeli–Palestinian relations deepened, Morocco announced that it had closed down Israel's liaison office in Rabat and its own representative office in Tel-Aviv. There was widespread outrage in Morocco in response to the Israeli military offensive in Palestinian-controlled areas of the West Bank from March 2002. A national march in solidarity with the Palestinian people took place in Rabat in April, attracting more than 1m. people—the biggest demonstration in the Arab world.

Morocco has generally maintained close relations with France. However, the French Government expressed considerable concern following the imposition of death sentences on three defendants in January 1995 (see above), all of whom had been resident in France prior to their arrest. As the development of a Maghreb union slowed, Morocco attempted to improve relations with the EU, which had been critical of Morocco's human rights record. In February 1996, after two years of negotiations, Morocco signed an association agreement with the EU, which provided for greater political and economic co-operation, financial aid and the eventual establishment of a free trade zone. In March 2000 King Muhammad made his first state visit abroad since acceding to the throne to attend talks with President Chirac in France. During the visit Muhammad expressed his hope that Morocco would be accorded partnership status with the EU and, ultimately, full membership of the union. A fisheries agreement between Morocco and the EU entered into force in July 2006, despite opposition from Sweden, which claimed that Morocco had no right to include the territorial waters of Western Sahara in the agreement.

In February 1995, following the approval by the Spanish parliament of statutes of autonomy for the enclaves of Ceuta and Melilla, Morocco intensified its diplomatic campaign to obtain sovereignty over the territories. Relations between Morocco and Spain deteriorated further in April, when responsibility for two bomb explosions in Ceuta was claimed by a guerrilla group suspected by the Spanish authorities of receiving clandestine support from Morocco. Prime Minister Filali made an official visit to Spain in mid-1997, and in January 1998 the two countries established a joint commission to examine security issues including illegal immigration (to Spain) and drugs-trafficking. In August 1999 Prime Minister el-Youssoufi urged a review of the statutes of Ceuta and Melilla; however, Spain asserted that no Moroccan sovereignty claims with regard to this issue would be considered. The Spanish premier, José María Aznar, visited Morocco in May 2000, and in September, during King Muhammad's first visit to Spain since his accession, two economic co-operation agreements were signed. Nevertheless, relations remained strained owing to lack of progress in negotiations with the EU regarding a new fisheries accord and attacks by Spanish fishermen on lorries carrying Moroccan products through Spanish ports.

In July 2001, in an attempt to limit the increasing number of Moroccans entering Spain illegally, the two countries signed an agreement that would allow as many as 20,000 Moroccans to enter Spain each year in search of employment. In September, however, Spain refuted allegations made by King Muhammad that Spanish criminal associations were responsible for the large increase in numbers of Moroccan economic migrants attempting illegally to cross the Straits of Gibraltar, asserting that collusion between Moroccan police and the smugglers was ongoing. Later that month Morocco recalled its ambassador from Spain. The Moroccan Government was critical of border controls introduced by the Spanish authorities for Moroccans entering the Spanish enclaves of Ceuta and Melilla, and the breakdown, in April 2002, of talks on renewing the EU fisheries accord also contributed to strained bilateral relations. Moroccan–Spanish relations were further strained in mid-July, when a small detachment of Moroccan troops occupied the uninhabited rocky islet of Perejil (known as Leila to Morocco), west of the Spanish enclave of Ceuta and close to the Moroccan coastline. Morocco claimed that it was establishing a surveillance post on the island as part of its campaign against illegal emigration and drugs-smuggling. However, Spain insisted that there had been since 1990 an agreement that neither Morocco nor Spain would occupy Perejil, and, with the support of the EU and NATO, demanded the immediate evacuation of Moroccan troops from the island. A few days later Spain's ambassador to Morocco was recalled, and Spanish special forces intervened and forcibly removed Moroccan troops from Perejil. Spanish officials insisted that their troops would be withdrawn if King Muhammad gave assurances that Moroccan forces would not reoccupy the island, and the Spanish Minister of Foreign Affairs, Ana Palacio, stated that Spain had no interest in maintaining a permanent military presence on the island. Following mediation by the US Secretary of State, Colin Powell, Spanish forces withdrew from the island. Talks held later in July 2002 in Rabat between Palacio and her Moroccan counterpart Muhammad Benaïssa resulted in an accord whereby both states agreed to return to the *status quo ante*. In January 2003 Muhammad temporarily allowed Spanish boats to fish in Moroccan waters, and in the following month the two countries agreed to the return of their respective ambassadors. In December Morocco and Spain announced plans to construct a 39-km underwater rail tunnel between the two countries.

In March 2004 a series of bomb attacks on commuter trains in the Spanish capital, Madrid, killed 191 people. A number of Moroccans from the Groupe islamique combattant marocain (GICM), who had also been linked with the Casablanca bombings of 2003, were among a group of suspected militant Islamists detained by the Spanish authorities in connection with the attacks, and in December 2004 a Moroccan man, Hassan al-Haski, was charged with having planned the bombings. The Moroccan authorities were quick to show their commitment to fighting terrorism, and in April 2004, following an official visit to Morocco by the new Spanish Prime Minister, José Luis Rodríguez Zapatero, the two countries announced renewed diplomatic ties. In May the two Governments revealed plans to establish a joint task force to tackle terrorism and organized crime. Diplomatic relations between Morocco and Spain remained stable into early 2005, following a visit by King Juan Carlos of Spain to Morocco in January. However, during June–July six delegations of Spanish politicians and journalists, seeking to conduct investigations following demonstrations in Western Sahara, were accused by Morocco of supporting Sahrawi independence and were refused permission to enter the disputed territory (see above).

In September–October 2005 at least 11 African migrants were reported to have died while attempting to enter Ceuta and Melilla illegally. Four were shot dead by Moroccan troops as the migrants scaled fences constructed to protect the borders between Morocco and the Spanish enclaves. The Spanish Government urged its Moroccan counterpart to increase its efforts to prevent illegal border crossings but later ended the practice of returning unsuccessful migrants to Morocco, amid claims by human rights organizations that migrants had been taken to the southern Moroccan desert and abandoned by the authorities. In January 2006 Zapatero visited Ceuta and Melilla in an apparent show of support for the enclaves; the visit was the first by an incumbent Spanish premier for 25 years. At a summit meeting held between Spain and Morocco in March 2007 and attended by Zapatero, the two countries reached an agreement on the prevention of unaccompanied child migrants. Zapatero also welcomed Morocco's plan for autonomy in Western Sahara (see above) as a means to the opening of dialogue within the framework of the UN, while maintaining that Spain was committed to a consensual solution to the issue that respected the principles laid down by the UN. However, diplomatic relations between Morocco and Spain deteriorated in November, when it was announced that King Juan Carlos would pay his first royal visit to Ceuta and Melilla. The trip provoked criticism from the Moroccan Government and the country recalled its ambassador to Spain, Omar Azziman, in protest. Azziman returned to his post in January 2008.

The Moroccan Government was swift to condemn the September 2001 attacks on New York and Washington, DC, USA, for which the al-Qa'ida network was believed to be responsible. In June 2002 the Moroccan authorities announced that they had arrested three Saudi nationals who were alleged to be members of an Islamist cell linked to al-Qa'ida that was preparing terrorist attacks on US and British warships in the Strait of Gibraltar. Seven Moroccans, including two of the suspects' wives, had also been arrested for allegedly acting as couriers between the Saudis in Morocco and al-Qa'ida, which had provided them with funds and logistical support. In February 2003 the three Saudis were sentenced to 10 years' imprisonment by a court in Casablanca; six of the Moroccans received sentences ranging from four months to one year for their roles in the plot. Also in February a Moroccan student, Mounir al-Motassadek, who was alleged to have been a member of the cell that had planned and executed the September 2001 attacks, was convicted by a court in Hamburg, Germany, of belonging to a terrorist group and of aiding and abetting the murder of 3,066 people. He was sentenced to 15 years' imprisonment. In August 2003 the trial commenced in Hamburg of a second Moroccan student charged with identical offences; however, he was acquitted of all charges in February 2004. In March al-Motassadek's conviction was quashed by the German Federal Criminal Court and he was released from detention in April. A retrial began in August, and al-Motassadek was acquitted in August 2005 of involvement in the September 2001 attacks; he was nevertheless convicted of belonging to a terrorist organization and sentenced to seven years' imprisonment. In November 2006 the German Federal Court of Justice overturned al-Motassadek's acquittal on charges of accessory to murder, and he was again sentenced to 15 years' imprisonment in January 2007.

In June 2004 Morocco became only the second Arab country (after Jordan in 2001) to sign a free trade agreement with the USA. Both the Moroccan Chamber of Representatives and Chamber of Advisers ratified the accord in January 2005. Meanwhile, in April 2008 Morocco and France signed a number of agreements aimed at consolidating their economic and social cooperation. The agreements were a result of decisions reached during the ninth Franco-Moroccan intergovernmental seminar in October 2007, when President Nicolas Sarkozy visited Morocco. Part of the collaboration was to involve France loaning Morocco €150m. to construct a tram network in Rabat. Morocco was also expected to achieve 'advanced status' with the EU by 2009.

Government

The 1992 Constitution (amended by referendum in 1996) provides for a modified constitutional monarchy, with an hereditary King as Head of State. Legislative power is vested in the Majlis an-Nuab (Chamber of Representatives), with 325 members directly elected, on the basis of universal adult suffrage, for five years, and in the Majlis al-Mustasharin (Chamber of Advisers), with 270 members chosen by electoral colleges (representing mainly local councils, with the remainder selected from professional associations and trade unions) for a nine-year term. Executive power is vested in the King, who appoints (and may dismiss) the Prime Minister and (on the latter's recommendation) other members of the Cabinet. The King may also dissolve the legislature.

Defence

As assessed at November 2007, Morocco's active armed forces numbered 195,800, consisting of an army of an estimated 175,000 (including some 100,000 conscripts), a navy of 7,800 and an air force of 13,000. In addition, there was a paramilitary 'gendarmerie royale' of 20,000, and a paramilitary 'force auxiliaire' of 30,000 men (including a mobile intervention corps of 5,000). Army reserve forces totalled 150,000. Military service of 18 months is by authorized conscription. The defence budget for 2007 was 19,700m. dirhams.

Economic Affairs

In 2006, according to estimates by the World Bank, Morocco's gross national income (GNI), measured at average 2004–06 prices, was US $57,977m., equivalent to $1,900 per head (or $5,000 per head on an international purchasing-power parity basis). During 1996–2006, it was estimated, the population increased at an average annual rate of 1.3%, while gross domestic product (GDP) per head increased, in real terms, by an average of 2.1% per year. Overall GDP increased, in real terms, at an average annual rate of 3.4% in 1996–2006; it increased by 7.3% in 2006.

Agriculture (including forestry and fishing) contributed 15.7% of GDP in 2006, according to provisional figures, and engaged 43.4% of the employed labour force in that year. The principal crops are cereals (mainly wheat and barley), potatoes, sugar beet and sugar cane, tomatoes, melons and citrus fruit. Almost all of Morocco's meat requirements are produced within the country. The sale of licences to foreign fishing fleets is an important source of revenue. In 2006 seafoods and seafood products accounted for 7.5% of total exports, according to provisional data. During 1996–2006 agricultural GDP increased at an average annual rate of 1.3%; sectoral GDP decreased by 11.8% in 2005, but grew by 21% in 2006.

Industry (including mining, manufacturing, construction and power) provided 27.8% of GDP in 2006, according to provisional figures, and engaged 20.3% of the employed labour force in the same year. During 1996–2006 industrial GDP increased by an average of 3.9% per year; it grew by 4.7% in 2006.

Mining and quarrying contributed 2.0% of GDP in 2006, according to provisional figures; the sector engaged 0.6% of the employed labour force in 2000. The major mineral exports are phosphate rock and phosphoric acid, which together earned 11.9% of export revenues in 2006, according to provisional data. Morocco is the world's largest exporter of phosphate rock. Petroleum exploration activity was revived at the end of the 1990s, and the discovery of major oil and natural gas reserves in the Talsinnt region of eastern Morocco was announced in August 2000. Coal, salt, iron ore, barytes, lead, copper, zinc, silver, gold and manganese are mined. Deposits of nickel, cobalt and bauxite have been discovered. During 1990–2002 mining GDP increased at an average annual rate of 1.3%. According to official estimates, mining GDP increased by 1.8% in 2006.

Manufacturing contributed 16.8% of GDP in 2006, according to provisional figures, and employed 12.3% of the employed labour force in 2000. The most important branches, measured by gross value of output, are oil refining and energy products, food-processing, textiles, and chemicals. In 2006 manufactured garments accounted for 18.7% of export revenues. During 1996–2006 manufacturing GDP increased at an average annual rate of 3.2%; the sector's GDP expanded by 4.7% in 2006.

In 2004 electric energy was derived principally from coal (67.4%), petroleum (23.2%) and hydroelectric power stations (8.4%). Facilities for generating wind power have also been developed. According to provisional data, imports of energy and lubricants comprised an estimated 21.7% of the value of total merchandise imports in 2006.

The services sector contributed an estimated 56.5% of GDP, according to provisional figures, and engaged 36.3% of the employed labour force in 2006. The tourism industry is generally a major source of revenue, and tourist arrivals totalled some 3.8m. in 2006. The GDP of the services sector increased by an average of 3.8% per year during 1996–2006, and by 5.3% in 2006.

In 2006 Morocco recorded a visible trade deficit of US $9,416m., but there was a surplus of $1,778m. on the current account of the balance of payments. According to provisional data, in 2006 the principal source of imports was France (which provided an estimated 17.1% of merchandise imports); other major suppliers in that year included Spain, Saudi Arabia, Italy and the People's Republic of China. France was also the principal market for exports (28.4%) in 2006; Spain and the United Kingdom were also important purchasers of Moroccan exports. According to provisional data, the principal exports in 2006 were finished consumer products (notably manufactured garments and hosiery), semi-finished products (including phosphoric acid and electronic components) and foodstuffs, beverages and tobacco (particularly seafoods and seafood products). The principal imports in that year were semi-finished products, and fuel and energy products (notably crude petroleum).

In 2006 there was a budget deficit of 9,800m. dirhams, equivalent to an estimated 1.9% of GDP. Morocco's total external debt in 2005 was US $16,846m., of which $13,113m. was long-term public debt. The cost of debt-servicing in that year was equivalent to 11.3% of exports of goods and services. The annual rate of inflation averaged 1.7% in 1996–2006, and was recorded at 3.3% in 2006. According to official figures, some 9.7% of the labour force were unemployed in 2006; however, certain sources reported the rate to be closer to 20%.

Morocco is a member of the African Development Bank (ADB, see p. 162), the Islamic Development Bank (see p. 329) and of the Arab Fund for Economic and Social Development (see p. 174). It is a founder member of the Union du Maghreb arabe (Union of the Arab Maghreb, see p. 414).

Since 1980 the Moroccan authorities have undertaken a series of economic reforms under IMF auspices, including the reduction of taxes, tariffs and subsidies, and the introduction of a more efficient tax system. Efforts to stimulate foreign investment have had considerable success, while a programme of privatization has bolstered government revenue. In March 2000 a trade and co-operation agreement with the European Union (EU) came into effect, which provided for the establishment of a free trade zone with the EU within 10 years. The Government was able to compensate for the loss of revenue from the fisheries accord with the EU, which expired in 2001, with the sale, for US $1,100m., of Morocco's second mobile cellular telephone operating licence and the partial privatization of Maroc Télécom—35% of which was sold to the French telecommunications company Vivendi Universal for $2,330m.; this share was subsequently increased to 51%. A free trade agreement was also signed between Morocco and the USA in June 2004, making 95% of trade between the two countries duty-free. The first terminal of a new port complex located some 35 km to the east of Tangier—and just 14 km from the Spanish coast on the Strait of Gibraltar—was inaugurated in July 2007, with a second terminal scheduled to open in mid-2008. It was hoped that the port, which formed part of the Tangier Mediterranean Project launched in 2002, would become a trading hub between Europe and Africa, creating more than 100,000 new jobs and encouraging industrial development in northern Morocco through its planned network of industrial and trade zones, roads and railways. The tourism sector was adversely affected by the volatile situation in the Middle East from 2002 and the suicide bombings launched against Western targets in Casablanca in May 2003. Nevertheless, the Government continued with ambitious plans—under the so-called 'Vision 2010' strategy—to raise the number of tourist visitors to Morocco to 10m., and significantly to increase tourism revenues from an estimated 8% of GDP per year to nearer 20%, by 2010. Vision 2010 provides for the creation of around 600,000 new jobs in the tourism industry. Although reasonable economic growth occurred in Morocco during 2000–04, high international petroleum prices, a decline in agricultural output and the abolition of the World Trade Organization quota system in the textile industry contributed to slower growth, of some 1.7%, in 2005. A number of high-profile privatizations took place in 2004, including the sale in November of a further 16% stake in Maroc Télécom to Vivendi Universal; another 4% of the company was divested in June 2007. In an effort to reduce poverty levels, a project initiated in late 2006 involved plans to eradicate slums in the principal cities by removing inadequate housing and providing incentives for developers to build more affordable accommodation for people on low incomes. Moreover, the Government appointed in October 2007 under Prime Minister Abbas el-Fassi set out ambitious plans with regard to state expenditure on social and infrastructural projects. A severe drought in 2007 destroyed much of that year's cereal harvest, leading to poor overall GDP growth and some 18,000 job losses in the agricultural sector. A recovery was expected for 2008, however, although a three-week-long strike by employees in the fishing industry caused concerns for the sector early in the year.

Education

Morocco has state-controlled primary, secondary and technical schools, and there are also private schools. Education (at the primary level) is compulsory for seven years, to be undertaken between the ages of six and 13 years. Secondary education, beginning at the age of 13, lasts for up to six years (comprising two cycles of three years). Primary enrolment in 2004/05 included 86.1% of children in the relevant age-group, while in 2002/03, according to UNESCO estimates, secondary enrolment included 35.1% of the relevant age-group. The Government has recently taken steps to expand the teaching of the Berber language in primary schools (see Recent History). There were 277,442 students enrolled at state universities and equivalent-level institutions in 2003/04. Under the 2004 budget, expenditure on education by the central Government was 28,485m. dirhams (20.8% of total spending).

MOROCCO

Public Holidays

2008: 1 January (New Year), 10 January*† (Muharram, Islamic New Year), 11 January (Independence Manifesto), 19 January* (Ashoura), 20 March* (Mouloud, Birth of the Prophet), 1 May (Labour Day), 23 May (National Day), 30 July (Festival of the Throne, anniversary of King Muhammad's accession), 14 August (Oued ed-Dahab Day, anniversary of the 1979 annexation), 2 September* (Ramadan begins), 1 October* (Eid es-Seghir—Id al-Fitr, end of Ramadan), 6 November (Anniversary of the Green March), 18 November (Independence Day), 9 December* (Eid el-Kebir—Id al-Adha, Feast of the Sacrifice), 29 December*† (Muharram, Islamic New Year).

2009: 1 January (New Year), 7 January*‡ (Ashoura), 11 January (Independence Manifesto), 9 March* (Mouloud, Birth of the Prophet), 1 May (Labour Day), 23 May (National Day), 30 July (Festival of the Throne, anniversary of King Muhammad's accession), 14 August (Oued ed-Dahab Day, anniversary of the 1979 annexation), 22 August* (Ramadan begins), 20 September* (Eid es-Seghir—Id al-Fitr, end of Ramadan), 6 November (Anniversary of the Green March), 18 November (Independence Day), 27 November* (Eid el-Kebir—Id al-Adha, Feast of the Sacrifice), 18 December* (Muharram, Islamic New Year), 27 December*‡ (Ashoura).

* These holidays are dependent on the Islamic lunar calendar and may vary by one or two days from the dates given.
† This festival occurs twice (marking the start of the Islamic years AH 1429 and 1430) within the same Gregorian year.
‡ This festival occurs twice (in the Islamic years AH 1430 and 1431) within the same Gregorian year.

Weights and Measures

The metric system is in force.

Statistical Survey

Sources (unless otherwise stated): Haut Commissariat au Plan, Direction de la Statistique, rue Muhammad Belhassan el-Ouazzani, BP 178, Rabat 10001; tel. (3) 7773606; fax (3) 7773217; e-mail statguichet@statistic.gov.ma; internet www.hcp.ma; Bank Al-Maghrib, 277 ave Muhammad V, BP 445, Rabat; tel. (3) 7702626; fax (3) 7706677; e-mail dai@bkam.gov.ma; internet www.bkam.ma.

Note: Unless otherwise indicated, the data exclude Western (formerly Spanish) Sahara, a disputed territory under Moroccan occupation.

Area and Population

AREA, POPULATION AND DENSITY

Area (sq km)	710,850*
Population (census results)†	
2 September 1994	
Males	12,944,517
Females	13,074,763
Total	26,019,280
2 September 2004	29,891,708
Population (UN estimate at mid-year)‡	
2005	30,495,000
2006	30,853,000
2007	31,224,000
Density (per sq km) at mid-2007	43.9

* 274,461 sq miles. This area includes the disputed territory of Western Sahara, which covers 252,120 sq km (97,344 sq miles).
† Including Western Sahara, with an estimated population of 417,000 at the 2004 census.
‡ Source: UN, *World Population Prospects: The 2006 Revision*.

REGIONS
(population at 2004 census)

	Population
Oued ed-Dahab Lagouira*	99,367
El-Aaiún Boujdour*	256,152
Guelmim es-Semara†	462,410
Souss Massa-Draa	3,113,653
Gharb Chrarda Beni-Hsen	1,859,540
Chaouia Ouardigha	1,655,660
Marrakech Tensift al-Haou	3,102,652
Oriental	1,918,094
Grand Casablanca	3,631,061
Rabat Salé Zemmour Zaer	2,366,494
Doukkala Abda	1,984,039
Tadla Azilal	1,450,519
Meknès Tafilalet	2,141,527
Fès Boulemane	1,573,055
Taza al-Hoceima Taounate	1,807,113
Tanger Tétouan	2,470,372
Total	**29,891,708**

* Regions situated in Western Sahara.
† Region partly situated in Western Sahara.

PRINCIPAL TOWNS
(population at 2004 census)

Casablanca	2,933,684		Tétouan	320,539
Rabat (capital)*	1,622,860		Safi	284,750
Fès (Fez)	946,815		Mohammedia	188,619
Marrakech (Marrakesh)	823,154		El-Aaiún†	183,691
Agadir	678,596		Khouribga	166,397
Tanger (Tangier)	669,685		Beni-Mellal	163,286
Meknès	536,232		El-Jadida	144,440
Oujda	400,738		Taza	139,686
Kénitra	359,142			

* Including Salé and Temara.
† Town situated in Western Sahara.

Source: Thomas Brinkhoff, *City Population* (internet www.citypopulation.de).

Mid-2007 ('000, incl. suburbs, UN estimates): Casablanca 3,181; Rabat 1,705; Fès 1,002; Marrakech 872 (Source: UN, *World Urbanization Prospects: The 2007 Revision*).

BIRTHS AND DEATHS
(annual averages, UN estimates)

	1990–95	1995–2000	2000–05
Birth rate (per 1,000)	27.3	23.4	20.9
Death rate (per 1,000)	7.2	6.4	6.0

Source: UN, *World Population Prospects: The 2006 Revision*.

Expectation of life (years at birth, WHO estimates): 71.2 (males 69.0; females 73.5) in 2005 (Source: WHO, *World Health Statistics*).

MOROCCO

ECONOMICALLY ACTIVE POPULATION
(sample surveys, '000 persons aged 15 years and over)

	2004	2005	2006
Agriculture, hunting, forestry and fishing	4,498	4,352	4,303
Mining and quarrying; manufacturing; electricity, gas and water	1,250	1,203	1,225
Construction	662	683	790
Wholesale and retail trade	1,247	1,247	1,233
Transport, storage and communications	347	369	395
General administration and community services	916	1,061	1,214
Other services	895	706	758
Activities not adequately defined	7	6	11
Total employed	**9,822**	**9,628**	**9,928**
Unemployed	1,193	1,197	1,062
Total labour force	**11,015**	**10,825**	**10,990**

Health and Welfare

KEY INDICATORS

Total fertility rate (children per woman, 2005)	2.7
Under-5 mortality rate (per 1,000 live births, 2005)	40
HIV/AIDS (% of persons aged 15–49, 2005)	0.1
Physicians (per 1,000 head, 2004)	0.51
Hospital beds (per 1,000 head, 2004)	0.90
Health expenditure (2004): US $ per head (PPP)	233.9
Health expenditure (2004): % of GDP	5.1
Health expenditure (2004): public (% of total)	34.3
Access to water (% of persons, 2004)	81
Access to sanitation (% of persons, 2004)	73
Human Development Index (2005): ranking	126
Human Development Index (2005): value	0.646

For sources and definitions, see explanatory note on p. vi.

Agriculture

PRINCIPAL CROPS
('000 metric tons)

	2004	2005	2006
Wheat	5,540	3,043	6,300*
Rice (paddy)	30*	43	30†
Barley	2,760	1,102	2,500*
Maize	224	50	200*
Potatoes	1,482	1,479	1,569
Sugar cane	872	782	997
Sugar beet	3,190	3,302	2,252
Dry broad beans	109	73	181
Dry peas	26	14	24
Chick-peas	42	33	66
Lentils	33	15	34
Almonds	60	71	83
Groundnuts (in shell)	52	47	45*
Olives	500	750	750
Sunflower seed	49	18	8
Cabbages and other brassicas	49	46	44
Artichokes	54	53	55
Tomatoes	1,214	1,206	1,245
Cauliflowers and broccoli	36	37	73
Pumpkins, squash and gourds	184	150	169
Cucumbers and gherkins	41	54	70
Aubergines (Eggplants)	39	50	57
Chillies and green peppers	182	190	236
Dry onions	879	716	882
Green peas	145	65	147
String beans	129	142	163
Carrots and turnips	311	373	373
Carobs†	26	26	26
Watermelons	684	402	712
Cantaloupes and other melons	665	649	649
Figs	60	83	77

—continued	2004	2005	2006
Grapes	315	334	356
Dates	69	48	55
Apples	396	309	374
Pears	45	42	35
Quinces	39	30	28
Peaches and nectarines	54	55	55†
Plums and sloes	48	61	61†
Strawberries	106	119	112
Oranges	719	835	788
Tangerines, mandarins, clementines and satsumas	408	463	454
Apricots	85	104	129
Bananas	189	190	203
Anise, badian, fennel and coriander†	23	23	23

* Unofficial figure.
† FAO estimate(s).

Aggregate production ('000 metric tons, may include official, semi-official or estimated data): Total cereals 8,604 in 2004, 4,284 in 2005, 9,091 in 2006; Total pulses 278 in 2004, 182 in 2005, 361 in 2006; Total roots and tubers 1,494 in 2004, 1,486 in 2005, 1,573 in 2006; Total vegetables (incl. melons) 5,336 in 2004, 4,765 in 2005, 5,504 in 2006; Total fruits (excl. melons) 2,644 in 2004, 2,794 in 2005, 2,851 in 2006.

Source: FAO.

LIVESTOCK
('000 head, year ending September)

	2004	2005	2006*
Cattle	2,729	2,722	2,722
Sheep	17,026	16,872	16,872
Goats	5,359	5,332	5,332
Camels*	36	36	36
Horses	157	159	159
Asses and mules or hinnies	1,506	1,522	1,522
Chickens*	137	137	140

* FAO estimates.

Source: FAO.

LIVESTOCK PRODUCTS
('000 metric tons)

	2004	2005	2006
Cattle meat	140	150	150
Sheep meat	105	108	112
Goat meat	18	16	17
Chicken meat	325	350	340
Cows' milk	1,375	1,400	1,500
Sheep's milk*	27	27	27
Goats' milk*	34	34	34
Hen eggs	n.a.	195*	168*
Honey	2	3	3*
Wool: greasy*	40	40	40

* FAO estimate(s).

Source: FAO.

Forestry

ROUNDWOOD REMOVALS
('000 cubic metres, excl. bark)

	2004	2005	2006
Sawlogs, veneer logs and logs for sleepers	185	259	215
Pulpwood	378	315	384
Fuel wood	298	383	345
Total	**861**	**957**	**944**

Source: FAO.

MOROCCO

SAWNWOOD PRODUCTION
('000 cubic metres, incl. railway sleepers)

	1987*	1988	1989
Coniferous (softwood)	40	26*	43*
Broadleaved (hardwood)	40	27	40
Total	80	53	83

* FAO estimate(s).

1990–2006: Production assumed to be unchanged from 1989 (FAO estimates).

Source: FAO.

Fishing

('000 metric tons, live weight)

	2003	2004	2005
Capture	896.3	907.7	945.5
European pilchard (sardine)	659.2	644.7	629.5
Chub mackerel	40.7	68.1	67.9
Marine fishes	20.1	37.2	42.0
Octopuses	28.9	19.2	44.9
Aquaculture	1.5	1.7	2.3
Total catch (incl. others)	897.8	909.5	947.8

Source: FAO.

Mining

('000 metric tons)

	2004	2005	2006*
Crude petroleum	32.3	32.3	11.2
Iron ore†	9.9	8.1	4.6
Copper concentrates†	14.2	12.7	17.8
Lead concentrates†	44.7	59.9	59.1
Manganese ore†	9.0	11.3	4.8
Zinc concentrates†	146.2	151.3	148.7
Phosphate rock‡	25,369.0	27,254.0	27,386.0
Fluorspar (acid grade)	112.1	114.7	98.1
Barytes	355.8	475.7	612.8
Salt (unrefined)	253.8	319.9	319.9
Bentonite	85.4	54.4	34.0

* Preliminary figures.
† Figures refer to the gross weight of ores and concentrates.
‡ Including production in Western Sahara.

Industry

SELECTED PRODUCTS
('000 metric tons, unless otherwise indicated)

	2002	2003	2004
Wine*	33	34	n.a.
Olive oil (crude)	66	75	97
Motor spirit—petrol	377	132	257
Naphthas	527	553	625
Kerosene	80	52	12
Distillate fuel oils	2,323	1,535	2,254
Residual fuel oils	1,999	1,747	2,264
Jet fuel	137	108	174
Petroleum bitumen—asphalt	131	58	141
Liquefied petroleum gas ('000 barrels)†	2,690	1,000‡	3,000‡
Cement	8,057	9,276	9,828
Phosphate fertilizers§	432	n.a.	n.a.
Carpets and rugs ('000 sq m)	407	384‡	n.a.
Electric energy (million kWh)	16,680	18,109	18,241

* Source: FAO.
† Source: US Geological Survey.
‡ Provisional figure.
§ Estimated production in terms of phosphoric acid.

Source: partly UN, *Industrial Commodity Statistics Yearbook*.

Finance

CURRENCY AND EXCHANGE RATES

Monetary Units
100 centimes (santimat) = 1 Moroccan dirham.

Sterling, Dollar and Euro Equivalents (31 December 2007)
£1 sterling = 15.45 dirhams;
US $1 = 7.71 dirhams;
€1 = 11.35 dirhams;
100 Moroccan dirhams = £6.47 = $12.96 = €8.81.

Average Exchange Rate (dirhams per US $)
2005   8.865
2006   8.796
2007   8.192

GENERAL BUDGET
(million dirhams)

Revenue*	2002	2003	2004
Tax revenue	91,020	94,229	100,762
Taxes on income and profits	30,378	33,145	36,467
Individual	16,353	17,783	19,583
Corporate	12,917	14,536	15,857
Taxes on international trade	14,231	12,578	13,292
Indirect taxes	40,056	41,890	43,901
Value-added tax	23,951	26,010	29,070
Excises	16,105	15,880	14,831
Registration and stamps	4,999	5,296	5,505
Revenue accruing to the road fund	1,356	1,320	1,597
Non-tax revenue	7,241	8,631	10,553
Dividend and licence income	4,244	5,038	7,132
Total	98,261	102,860	111,315

MOROCCO

Statistical Survey

Expenditure	2002	2003	2004
General public services	6,885	6,870	7,136
Defence	16,994	17,476	17,632
Public order	10,096	9,199	10,026
Education	25,894	27,810	28,485
Health, social security and welfare	5,183	5,189	5,495
Housing	969	791	784
Recreation, culture, etc.	930	579	591
Agriculture, mines and energy	5,107	4,505	4,173
Transport and communications	3,604	2,193	1,685
General expenditure	11,355	12,540	13,253
Transfers to local governments	6,989	7,185	7,803
Other	24,793	32,635	39,986
Total	**118,799**	**126,973**	**137,049**

* Excluding receipts from privatization (621 in 2002; 11,957 in 2003; 10,416 in 2004).

Source: IMF, *Morocco, Statistical Appendix* (November 2005).

2005 (million dirhams): Total revenue 140,206; Total expenditure 160,052 (Source: IMF, *International Financial Statistics*).

2006 (million dirhams): Total revenue 157,100; Total expenditure 166,900 (Source: IMF, *International Financial Statistics*).

INTERNATIONAL RESERVES
(US $ million at 31 December)

	2004	2005	2006
Gold (national valuation)	239	280	307
IMF special drawing rights	120	79	53
Reserve position in IMF	109	101	106
Foreign exchange	16,107	16,008	20,182
Total	**16,575**	**16,468**	**20,648**

Source: IMF, *International Financial Statistics*.

MONEY SUPPLY
(million dirhams at 31 December)

	2004	2005	2006
Currency outside banks	79,715	89,304	108,564
Demand deposits at deposit money banks	247,310	283,997	326,418
Total money (incl. others)	**328,689**	**375,663**	**437,068**

Source: IMF, *International Financial Statistics*.

COST OF LIVING
(Consumer Price Index for urban areas; base: 1989 = 100)

	2004	2005	2006
Food	169.0	169.5	176.1
Clothing	169.2	170.4	172.3
Shelter	169.8	172.0	175.7
Household equipment	140.6	142.0	144.9
All items (incl. others)	**167.1**	**168.7**	**174.3**

NATIONAL ACCOUNTS
(million dirhams at current prices)

Expenditure on the Gross Domestic Product

	2004	2005	2006*
Government final consumption expenditure	94,112	100,580	105,207
Private final consumption expenditure	288,243	295,998	319,127
Change in inventories	10,342	9,078	16,714
Gross fixed capital formation	133,404	149,054	165,301
Total domestic expenditure	**526,101**	**554,710**	**606,349**
Exports of goods and services	145,953	165,382	189,921
Less Imports of goods and services	171,973	197,443	220,998
GDP in purchasers' values	**500,081**	**522,649**	**575,271**

* Provisional figures.

Gross Domestic Product by Economic Activity

	2004	2005	2006*
Agriculture, hunting, forestry and fishing	73,672	62,650	80,475
Mining and quarrying	7,704	8,646	10,271
Manufacturing	75,467	82,516	85,993
Oil refining and energy products	969	1,750	1,465
Electricity and water	13,047	14,624	14,580
Construction	28,822	30,563	31,694
Commerce	54,438	57,277	63,177
Hotels and restaurants	11,129	12,424	12,759
Transport and communications	34,117	36,631	39,251
Public administration and social security	43,729	47,899	50,102
Other services	107,219	116,475	124,886
Sub-total	**449,345**	**469,705**	**513,188**
Taxes, less subsidies, on imports	50,737	52,944	62,082
GDP in purchasers' values	**500,081**	**522,649**	**575,271**

* Provisional figures.

BALANCE OF PAYMENTS
(US $ million)

	2004	2005	2006
Exports of goods f.o.b.	9,922	10,690	11,916
Imports of goods f.o.b.	–16,408	–18,894	–21,332
Trade balance	**–6,487**	**–8,204**	**–9,416**
Exports of services	6,710	8,098	9,835
Imports of services	–3,451	–3,845	–4,479
Balance on goods and services	**–3,228**	**–3,951**	**–4,060**
Other income received	505	689	747
Other income paid	–1,176	–1,003	–1,169
Balance on goods, services and income	**–3,898**	**–4,266**	**–4,482**
Current transfers received	4,974	5,441	6,439
Current transfers paid	–154	–158	–179
Current balance	**922**	**1,018**	**1,778**
Capital account (net)	–8	–5	–3
Direct investment abroad	–31	–78	–438
Direct investment from abroad	787	1,552	2,699
Portfolio investment assets	—	2	2
Portfolio investment liabilities	597	64	–309
Other investment assets	–454	–891	–813
Other investment liabilities	–797	–803	–1,702
Net errors and omissions	–282	–414	–498
Overall balance	**733**	**445**	**717**

Source: IMF, *International Financial Statistics*.

External Trade

PRINCIPAL COMMODITIES
(million dirhams)

Imports c.i.f.	2004	2005	2006*
Foodstuffs, beverages and tobacco	13,606	15,617	15,112
Wheat	4,941	4,155	3,087
Energy and lubricants	26,214	39,510	44,890
Crude petroleum	14,539	23,947	25,172
Crude products	10,794	12,017	12,402
Semi-finished products	37,000	41,162	48,861
Chemical products	4,768	5,223	6,022
Finished industrial capital goods	33,678	37,177	43,059
Finished consumer products	35,400	37,559	40,560
Pharmaceutical products	2,168	2,382	2,526
Textile and cotton fabrics	7,585	7,222	7,174
Total (incl. others)	**157,921**	**184,379**	**206,997**

MOROCCO

Exports f.o.b.	2004	2005	2006*
Foodstuffs, beverages and tobacco	15,582	19,431	21,057
Crustaceans and molluscs	2,657	3,945	4,197
Prepared and preserved fish	3,148	3,626	4,212
Energy and lubricants	1,762	2,359	1,978
Crude mineral products	6,053	7,122	8,499
Phosphates	3,729	4,593	4,753
Semi-finished products	23,286	27,041	31,885
Phosphoric acid	6,320	7,641	8,592
Natural and chemical fertilizers	3,822	3,939	4,476
Electronic components (transistors)	5,511	5,492	6,194
Finished industrial capital goods	6,649	8,442	9,663
Electric wire and cable	3,649	5,155	4,692
Finished consumer products	31,985	31,490	34,963
Manufactured garments	18,676	17,899	20,922
Hosiery	7,641	6,847	7,033
Total (incl. others)	87,896	99,265	111,688

* Provisional data.

PRINCIPAL TRADING PARTNERS
(million dirhams)*

Imports c.i.f.	2004	2005	2006†
Algeria	1,430	3,169	4,021
Argentina	2,234	2,287	2,541
Belgium-Luxembourg	2,889	3,350	4,377
Brazil	3,961	4,014	4,028
Canada	1,402	1,881	1,505
China, People's Republic	6,602	9,399	11,069
France	29,148	33,483	35,464
Germany	9,329	8,866	9,595
India	1,090	1,341	1,616
Iran	2,454	5,008	8,311
Italy	10,312	11,103	13,267
Japan	3,174	3,219	3,558
Netherlands	2,621	3,510	4,616
Russia	9,263	12,653	9,417
Saudi Arabia	8,468	12,186	13,947
Spain	19,246	21,448	23,836
United Kingdom	5,217	4,127	4,304
USA	6,501	6,104	9,134
Total (incl. others)	157,921	184,379	206,997

Exports f.o.b.	2004	2005	2006†
Belgium-Luxembourg	2,068	2,755	3,140
Brazil	2,312	2,198	2,514
France	29,521	29,829	31,738
Germany	3,004	3,177	3,021
India	3,001	3,939	4,643
Italy	4,100	4,962	5,399
Japan	647	1,012	877
Netherlands	2,025	2,511	2,982
Russia	772	1,249	1,612
Spain	15,358	19,844	23,672
United Kingdom	6,710	6,289	6,638
USA	3,419	2,535	2,099
Total (incl. others)	87,896	99,265	111,688

* Imports by country of production; exports by country of last consignment.
† Provisional data.

Transport

RAILWAYS
(traffic)*

	2002	2003	2004
Passengers carried ('000)	14,685	16,516	18,543
Passenger-km (million)	2,145	2,374	2,645
Freight ('000 metric tons)	29,945	30,552	32,901
Freight ton-km (million)	4,974	5,146	5,563

* Figures refer to principal railways only.

ROAD TRAFFIC
('000 motor vehicles in use at 31 December)

	1999	2000	2001
Passenger cars	1,161.9	1,211.1	1,253.0
Commercial vehicles	400.3	415.7	431.0

Motorcycles and scooters: 20,388 in 2000; 20,569 in 2001.
Passenger cars: 1,326,108 passenger cars in 2003.
Sources: IRF, *World Road Statistics*; UN, *Statistical Yearbook*.

SHIPPING

Merchant Fleet
(registered at 31 December)

	2004	2005	2006
Number of vessels	497	514	513
Total displacement ('000 grt)	522.6	544.0	526.8

Source: Lloyd's Register-Fairplay, *World Fleet Statistics*.

International Sea-borne Freight Traffic
('000 metric tons)

	2002	2003	2004*
Goods loaded	24,891	24,355	27,355
Goods unloaded	32,097	31,785	34,149

* Provisional figures.

CIVIL AVIATION
(traffic on Royal Air Maroc scheduled services)

	2001	2002	2003*
Kilometres flown (million)	62.8	61.6	63.6
Passengers carried ('000)	3,677	3,517	3,457
Passenger-km (million)	6,642	6,605	6,547

* Estimates.

Total ton-km (million): 718.5 in 2000.

Passengers carried ('000, estimate): 4,675 in 2004.

Tourism

FOREIGN TOURIST ARRIVALS*

Country of nationality	2004	2005	2006
France	1,167,088	1,337,204	1,481,610
Germany	141,210	144,200	151,396
Italy	112,807	120,955	140,923
Spain	317,119	367,811	467,956
United Kingdom	150,353	193,552	265,536
Other European countries	112,564	117,383	143,438
Maghreb countries	81,969	93,549	107,164
USA	76,889	82,980	93,646
Total (incl. others)	2,987,101	3,289,010	3,790,256

* Excluding Moroccans resident abroad (2,769,132 in 2004; 2,787,825 in 2005; n.a. in 2006).

Cruise-ship passengers: 259,937 in 2003; 255,663 in 2004; 233,458 in 2005.

Receipts from tourism (US $ million, incl. passenger transport): 3,369 in 2003.

Communications Media

	2004	2005	2006
Telephones ('000 main lines in use)	1,308.6	1,341.2	1,266.1
Mobile cellular telephones ('000 subscribers)	9,336.9	12,392.8	16,004.7
Personal computers ('000 in use)	620	740	n.a.
Internet users ('000)	3,500	4,600	6,100
Broadband subscribers ('000)	64.7	249.1	390.8

1997: Radio receivers ('000 in use) 6,640; Telefax stations (number in use) 18,000 (estimate).

1999: Book production (titles) 386.

2000: Television receivers ('000 in use) 4,700; Daily newspapers 23 (average circulation 846,000 copies); Other newspapers 507 (average circulation 4,108,000 copies); Periodicals 364 (average circulation 4,956,000 copies).

Sources: UNESCO, *Statistical Yearbook*; UN, *Statistical Yearbook*; and International Telecommunication Union.

Education

(1999/2000, unless otherwise indicated)

	Institutions	Teachers	Males	Females	Total
Pre-primary	33,577*	43,952	532,076	284,978	817,054
Primary:					
public	5,940	121,763	1,932,806	1,565,120	3,497,926
private	625	5,819	92,595	79,084	171,679
Secondary:					
general (public)	1,446	84,024†	785,550	610,346	1,393,896
general (private)	218	4,277	26,834	18,258	45,092
vocational	69	n.a.	12,810	9,981	22,791
University level*‡	68	9,667	154,314	112,193	266,507

* 1997/98 figure(s).
† Including vocational teachers.
‡ Provisional; state institutions only.

2001/02 (pupils/students): Primary 4,029,112 (public 3,832,356; private 196,756); Secondary 1,610,753 (public 1,561,686; private 49,067); University level 266,621.

2002/03 (pupils/students): Primary 4,101,157 (public 3,884,638; private 216,519); Secondary 1,679,077 (public 1,628,490; private 50,587); University level 280,599.

2003/04 (pupils/students): Primary 4,070,182 (public 3,846,950; private 223,232); Secondary 1,764,787 (public 1,707,871; private 56,916); University level 277,442.

2004/05 (pupils/students, estimates): Primary 4,022,600; Secondary 1,952,456.

Source: Ministry of National Education, Higher Education, Training and Scientific Research; UNESCO Institute for Statistics.

Adult literacy rate (UNESCO estimates): 52.3% (males 65.7%; females 39.6%) in 2004 (Source: UNESCO Institute for Statistics).

Directory

The Constitution

The following is a summary of the main provisions of the Constitution, as approved in a national referendum on 4 September 1992, and as amended by referendum on 13 September 1996.

PREAMBLE

The Kingdom of Morocco, a sovereign Islamic State whose official language is Arabic, constitutes a part of the Great Arab Maghreb. As an African State, one of its aims is the realization of African unity. It adheres to the principles, rights and obligations of those international organizations of which it is a member and works for the preservation of peace and security in the world.

GENERAL PRINCIPLES

Morocco is a constitutional, democratic and social monarchy. Sovereignty pertains to the nation and is exercised directly by means of the referendum and indirectly by the constitutional institutions. All Moroccans are equal before the law, and all adults enjoy equal political rights including the franchise. Freedoms of movement, opinion and speech and the right of assembly are guaranteed. Islam is the state religion. All Moroccans have equal rights in seeking education and employment. The right to strike, and to private property, is guaranteed. All Moroccans contribute to the defence of the Kingdom and to public costs. There shall be no one-party system.

THE MONARCHY

The Crown of Morocco and its attendant constitutional rights shall be hereditary in the line of HM King Hassan II, and shall be transmitted to the oldest son, unless during his lifetime the King has appointed as his successor another of his sons. The King is the symbol of unity, guarantees the continuity of the state, and safeguards respect for Islam and the Constitution. The King appoints, and may dismiss, the Prime Minister and other Cabinet Ministers (appointed upon the Prime Minister's recommendation), and presides over the Cabinet. He shall promulgate adopted legislation within a 30-day period, and has the power to dissolve the Chamber of Representatives and/or the Chamber of Advisers. The Sovereign is the Commander-in-Chief of the Armed Forces; makes appointments to civil and military posts; appoints Ambassadors; signs and ratifies treaties; presides over the Supreme Council of the Magistracy, the Supreme Council of Education and the Supreme Council for National Reconstruction and Planning; and exercises the right of pardon. In cases of threat to the national territory or to the action of constitutional institutions, the King, having consulted the President of the Chamber of Representatives, the President of the Chamber of Advisers and the Chairman of the Constitutional Council, and after addressing the nation, has the right to declare a State of Emergency by royal decree. The State of Emergency shall not entail the dissolution of Parliament and shall be terminated by the same procedure followed in its proclamation.

LEGISLATURE

This consists of a bicameral parliament: the Chamber of Representatives and the Chamber of Advisers. Members of the Chamber of Representatives are elected by direct universal suffrage for a five-year term. Three-fifths of the members of the Chamber of Advisers are elected by electoral colleges of local councils; the remainder are elected by electoral colleges representing chambers of commerce and trade unions. Members of the Chamber of Advisers are elected for a nine-year term, with one-third renewable every three years. Deputies in both chambers enjoy parliamentary immunity. Parliament shall adopt legislation, which may be initiated by members of either chamber or by the Prime Minister. Draft legislation shall be examined consecutively by both parliamentary chambers. If the two chambers fail to agree on the draft legislation the Government may request that a bilateral commission propose a final draft for approval by the chambers. If the chambers do not then adopt the draft, the Government may submit the draft (modified, if need be) to the Chamber of Representatives. Henceforth the draft submitted can be definitively adopted only by absolute majority of the members of the Chamber of Representatives. Parliament holds its meetings during two sessions each year, commencing on the second Friday in October and the second Friday in April.

GOVERNMENT

The Government, composed of the Prime Minister and his Ministers, is responsible to the King and Parliament and ensures the execution of laws. The Prime Minister is empowered to initiate legislation and to exercise statutory powers except where these are reserved to the

King. He presents to both parliamentary chambers the Government's intended programme and is responsible for co-ordinating ministerial work.

RELATIONS BETWEEN THE AUTHORITIES

The King may request a second reading, by both Chambers of Parliament, of any draft bill or proposed law. In addition, he may submit proposed legislation to a referendum by decree; and dissolve either Chamber or both if a proposal that has been rejected is approved by referendum. He may also dissolve either Chamber by decree after consulting the Chairman of the Constitutional Council, and addressing the nation, but the succeeding Chamber may not be dissolved within a year of its election. The Chamber of Representatives may force the collective resignation of the Government either by refusing a vote of confidence or by adopting a censure motion. The election of the new Parliament or Chamber shall take place within three months of its dissolution. In the interim period the King shall exercise the legislative powers of Parliament, in addition to those conferred upon him by the Constitution. A censure motion must be signed by at least one-quarter of the Chamber's members, and shall be approved by the Chamber only by an absolute majority vote of its members. The Chamber of Advisers is competent to issue 'warning' motions to the Government and, by a two-thirds' majority, force its resignation.

THE CONSTITUTIONAL COUNCIL

The Constitutional Council consists of six members appointed by the King (including the Chairman) for a period of nine years, and six members appointed for the same period—three selected by the President of the Chamber of Representatives and three by the President of the Chamber of Advisers. One-third of each category of the Council is renewed every three years. The Council is empowered to judge the validity of legislative elections and referendums, as well as that of organic laws and the rules of procedure of both parliamentary chambers, submitted to it.

JUDICIARY

The Judiciary is independent. Judges are appointed on the recommendation of the Supreme Council of the Magistracy presided over by the King.

THE ECONOMIC AND SOCIAL COUNCIL

An Economic and Social Council shall be established to give its opinion on all matters of an economic or social nature. Its constitution, organization, prerogatives and rules of procedure shall be determined by an organic law.

THE HIGH AUDIT COUNCIL

The High Audit Council exercises the general supervision of the implementation of fiscal laws. It ensures the regularity of revenues and expenditure operations of the departments legally under its jurisdiction, as it assesses the management of the affairs thereof. It is competent to penalize any breach of the rules governing such operations. Regional audit councils exercise the supervision of the accounts of local assemblies and bodies, and the management of the affairs thereof.

LOCAL GOVERNMENT

Local government in the Kingdom consists of establishing regions, governorships, provinces and communes.

REVISING THE CONSTITUTION

The King, the Chamber of Representatives and the Chamber of Advisers are competent to initiate a revision of the Constitution. The King has the right to submit the revision project he initiates to a national referendum. A proposal for a revision by either parliamentary chamber shall be adopted only if it receives a two-thirds' majority vote by the chamber's members. Revision projects and proposals shall be submitted to the nation for referendum by royal decree; a revision of the Constitution shall be definitive after approval by referendum. Neither the state, system of monarchy nor the prescriptions related to the religion of Islam may be subject to a constitutional revision.

The Government

HEAD OF STATE

Monarch: HM King MUHAMMAD VI (acceded 23 July 1999).

CABINET
(April 2008)

A coalition of Istiqlal, the Union socialiste des forces populaires (USFP), the Rassemblement national des indépendants (RNI), the Parti du progrès et du socialisme (PPS) and independents (Ind.).

Prime Minister: ABBAS EL-FASSI (Istiqlal).

Minister of State: MUHAMMAD EL-YAZGHI (USFP).
Minister of Justice: ABDELWAHAD RADI (USFP).
Minister of the Interior: CHAKIB BENMOUSSA (Ind.).
Minister of Foreign Affairs and Co-operation: TAIEB FASSI FIHRI (Ind.).
Minister of Habous (Religious Endowments) and Islamic Affairs: AHMED TOUFIQ (Ind.).
Secretary-General of the Government: ABDESSADEK RABIAÂ (Ind.).
Minister in charge of Relations with Parliament: MUHAMMAD SAÂD EL-ALAMI (Istiqlal).
Minister of the Economy and Finance: SALAHEDDINE MEZOUAR (RNI).
Minister of Agriculture and Fisheries: AZIZ AKHENOUCH (RNI).
Minister of Employment and Vocational Training: JAMAL AGHMANI (USFP).
Minister of National Education, Higher Education, Staff Training and Scientific Research: AHMED AKHCHICHINE (Ind.).
Minister of Culture: TOURIYA JABRANE (Ind.).
Minister of Tourism and Handicrafts: MUHAMMAD BOUSSAID (RNI).
Minister of Equipment and Transport: KARIM GHELLAB (Istiqlal).
Minister of Housing, Town Planning and Development: AHMED TAOUFIQ HEJIRA (Istiqlal).
Minister of Industry, Trade and New Technologies: AHMED REDA CHAMI (USFP).
Minister of Health: YASMINA BADDOU (Istiqlal).
Minister of Youth and Sports: NAWAL EL-MOUTAWAKIL (RNI).
Minister of Energy, Mining, Water and the Environment: AMINA BENKHADRA (RNI).
Minister of Communication and Government Spokesperson: KHALID NACIRI (PPS).
Minister of Foreign Trade: ABDELLATIF MAÂZOUZ (Istiqlal).
Minister of Social Development, the Family and Solidarity: NOUZHA SKALLI (PPS).
Minister-delegate to the Prime Minister, in charge of Economic and General Affairs: NIZAR BARAKA (Istiqlal).
Minister-delegate to the Prime Minister, in charge of National Defence: ABDERRAHMANE SBAI (Ind.).
Minister-delegate to the Prime Minister, in charge of the Modernization of the Public Sector: MUHAMMAD ABBOU (RNI).
Minister-delegate to the Prime Minister, in charge of Moroccans Resident Abroad: MUHAMMAD AMEUR (USFP).

There are also seven Secretaries of State.

MINISTRIES

Office of the Prime Minister: Palais Royal, Touarga, Rabat; tel. (3) 7219400; fax (3) 7768656; e-mail courrier@pm.gov.ma; internet www.pm.gov.ma.

Ministry of Agriculture and Fisheries: Quartier Administratif, pl. Abdellah Chefchaouni, BP 607, Rabat; tel. (3) 7760933; fax (3) 7776411; e-mail info@mardrpm.gov.ma; internet www.madrpm.gov.ma.

Ministry of Communication: ave Allal al-Fassi, Madinat al-Irfane Souissi, 10000 Rabat; tel. (3) 7772412; fax (3) 7767815; e-mail webmaster@mincom.gov.ma; internet www.mincom.gov.ma.

Ministry of Culture: 1 rue Ghandi, Rabat; tel. (3) 7209494; fax (3) 7209400; e-mail webmaster@minculture.gov.ma; internet www.minculture.gov.ma.

Ministry of the Economy and Finance: blvd Muhammad V, Quartier Administratif, Chellah, Rabat; tel. (3) 7677501; fax (3) 7677527; e-mail daag@daag.finances.gov.ma; internet www.finances.gov.ma.

Ministry of Employment and Vocational Training: ave Muhammad V, Hassan, Rabat; tel. (3) 7760521; fax (3) 7765312; e-mail communication@emploi.gov.ma; internet www.emploi.gov.ma.

Ministry of Energy, Mining, Water and the Environment: rue Abou Marouane Essaadi, BP 6208, Agdal, Rabat; tel. (3) 7688857; fax (3) 7688863; e-mail dsi@mem.gov.ma; internet www.mem.gov.ma.

Ministry of Equipment and Transport: Quartier Administratif, Chellah, Rabat; tel. (3) 7762811; fax (3) 7766633; internet www.mtpnet.gov.ma.

Ministry of Foreign Affairs and Co-operation: ave Franklin Roosevelt, Rabat; tel. (3) 7761583; fax (3) 7765508; e-mail mail@maec.gov.ma; internet www.maec.gov.ma.

Ministry of Foreign Trade: 63 ave Moulay Youssef, Rabat; e-mail ministere@mce.gov.ma; internet www.mce.gov.ma.

MOROCCO

Ministry of Habous (Religious Endowments) and Islamic Affairs: Al-Mechouar Essaid, Rabat; tel. (3) 7766801; fax (3) 7765282; e-mail infos@habous.gov.ma; internet www.habous.gov.ma.

Ministry of Health: 335 blvd Muhammad V, Rabat; tel. (3) 7761025; fax (3) 7768401; e-mail inas@sante.gov.ma; internet www.sante.gov.ma.

Ministry of Housing, Town Planning and Development: rues al-Jouaze and al-Joumaize, Hay Ryad, Secteur 16, 10000 Rabat; tel. (3) 7577000; fax (3) 7577373; e-mail zerrad@mhuae.gov.ma; internet www.mhuae.gov.ma.

Ministry of Industry, Trade and New Technologies: Quartier Administratif, Chellah, Rabat; tel. (3) 7761868; fax (3) 7766265; e-mail leministre@mcinet.gov.ma; internet www.technologies.gov.ma.

Ministry of the Interior: Quartier Administratif, Chellah, Rabat; tel. (3) 7761868; fax (3) 7762056.

Ministry of Justice: pl. Mamounia, Rabat; tel. (3) 7732941; fax (3) 7730772; e-mail kourout@justice.gov.ma; internet www.justice.gov.ma.

Ministry of the Modernization of the Public Sector: Quartier Administratif, rue Ahmed Cherkaoui, Agdal, BP 1076, Rabat; tel. (3) 7773106; fax (3) 7778438; e-mail info@mmsp.gov.ma; internet www.mmsp.gov.ma.

Ministry of National Education, Higher Education, Staff Training and Scientific Research: Bab Rouah, Rabat; tel. (3) 7771822; fax (3) 7201385; e-mail divcom@men.gov.ma; internet www.men.gov.ma.

Ministry in charge of Relations with Parliament: Nouveau Quartier Administratif, Agdal, Rabat; tel. (3) 7775159; fax (3) 7777719; e-mail mirepa@mcrp.gov.ma; internet www.mcrp.gov.ma.

Ministry of Social Development, the Family and Solidarity: 47 ave Ibn Sina, Agdal, Rabat; tel. (3) 7684060; fax (3) 7671967; e-mail mdsfs@mdsfs.ma; internet www.social.gov.ma.

Ministry of Youth and Sports: blvd ibn Sina, Rabat; tel. (3) 7680028; fax (3) 7680145.

Legislature

MAJLIS AN-NUAB
(Chamber of Representatives)

President: MUSTAPHA MANSOURI (RNI).

General Election, 7 September 2007

Party	Votes*	% of votes*	Seats
Istiqlal	494,256	10.7	52
Parti de la justice et du développement (PJD)	503,396	10.9	46
Mouvement populaire (MP)	426,849	9.3	41
Rassemblement national des indépendants (RNI)	447,244	9.7	39
Union socialiste des forces populaires (USFP)	408,945	8.9	38
Union constitutionnelle (UC)	335,116	7.3	27
Parti du progrès et du socialisme (PPS)	248,103	5.4	17
Parti national démocrate (PND)/Parti Al Ahd	253,816	5.5	14
Front des forces démocratiques (FFD)	207,982	4.5	9
Mouvement démocratique et social (MDS)	168,960	3.7	9
Parti de l'avant-garde démocratique socialiste (PADS)/Congrès national ittihadi (CNI)/Parti socialiste unifié (PSU)	123,897	2.7	6
Parti travailliste (PT)	140,224	3.0	5
Parti de l'environnement et du développement (PED)	131,524	2.9	5
Parti du renouveau et de l'équité (PRE)	83,516	1.8	4
Other parties	552,301	12.0	8
Independents	81,364	1.8	5
Total	**4,607,493**	**100.00**	**325†**

* Excluding votes for the seats reserved for women (see below).

† 30 of the 325 seats were reserved for women. Of these, the PJD and Istiqlal each won six seats; the RNI, the MP and the USFP all secured five; and the PPS received three.

MAJLIS AL-MUSTASHARIN
(Chamber of Advisers)

President: MUSTAPHA OKACHA.

Election, 5 December 1997*

	Seats
Rassemblement national des indépendants (RNI)	42
Mouvement démocratique et social (MDS)	33
Union constitutionnelle (UC)	28
Mouvement populaire (MP)	27
Parti national démocrate (PND)	21
Istiqlal	21
Union socialiste des forces populaires (USFP)	16
Mouvement national populaire (MNP)	15
Parti de l'action (PA)	13
Front des forces démocratiques (FFD)	12
Parti du progrès et du socialisme (PPS)	7
Parti social et démocratique (PSD)	4
Parti démocratique pour l'indépendance (PDI)	4
Trade unions	
Confédération Démocratique du Travail (CDT)	11
Union Marocaine du Travail (UMT)	8
Union Générale des Travailleurs Marocains (UGMT)	3
Others	5
Total	**270**

* Of the Chamber of Advisers' 270 members, 162 were elected by local councils, 81 by chambers of commerce and 27 by trade unions.

Note: Elections were conducted in September 2000, October 2003 and September 2006, with one-third of the membership of the Chamber of Advisers being renewed at each. At the 2006 elections the seats were allocated as follows: Istiqlal 17, MP 14, RNI 13, USFP 11, UC 6, PPS 4, Parti Al Ahd 4, PND 4, Parti de l'environnement et du développement (PED) 2, FFD 2, Parti de la Choura et de l'Istiqlal 1, MDS 1, Parti des forces citoyennes (PFC) 1, Parti du renouveau et de l'équité 1.

Political Organizations

Congrès national ittihadi (CNI): 209 blvd Strasbourg, Résidence C, 2ème étage, Casablanca; tel. and fax (2) 2447664; f. 2001 by dissident mems of USFP; Sec.-Gen. ABDELMAJID BOUZOUBÂA.

Front des forces démocratiques (FFD): 13 ave Tariq ibn Ziad, Hassan, Rabat; tel. (3) 7661625; fax (3) 7660621; e-mail forces@menara.ma; internet www.ffd.ma; f. 1997 after split from PPS; Sec.-Gen. THAMI EL-KHYARI.

Istiqlal (Independence): 4 ave Ibnou Toumert, Bab el-Had, 50020 Rabat; tel. (3) 7730951; fax (3) 7729107; e-mail istiqlal@istiqlal.ma; internet www.istiqlal.ma; f. 1944; aims to raise living standards and to confer equal rights on all; emphasizes the Moroccan claim to Western Sahara; Sec.-Gen. ABBAS EL-FASSI.

Mouvement démocratique et social (MDS): 4 ave Imam Malik, route des Zaërs, Rabat; tel. (7) 3834771; fax (3) 7764767; f. 1996 as Mouvement national démocratique et social after split from Mouvement national populaire (MNP); adopted current name in Nov. 1996; Leader MAHMOUD ARCHANE.

Mouvement populaire (MP): 66 rue Patrice Lumumba, Rabat; tel. (3) 7766431; fax (3) 7767537; internet www.harakamp.ma; f. 1958; merged with the MNP and Union démocratique in 2006; liberal; Sec.-Gen. MOHAND LAENSER.

Parti de l'action (PA): 113 ave Allal ben Abdallah, Rabat; tel. (3) 7206661; f. 1974; advocates democracy and progress; Sec.-Gen. MUHAMMAD EL-IDRISSI.

Parti Al Ahd: 14 rue Idriss al-Akbar, rue Tafraout, Hassan, Rabat; tel. (3) 7204816; fax (3) 7204786; e-mail alhakika@iam.net.ma; f. 2002; Chair. NAJIB EL-OUAZZANI.

Parti de l'avant-garde démocratique socialiste (PADS): BP 2091, 54 ave de la Résistance Océan, Rabat; tel. (3) 7200559; fax (3) 7708491; an offshoot of USFP; legalized in April 1992; Sec.-Gen. AHMAD BENJELLOUNE.

Parti démocratique et de l'indépendance (PDI): 9 Lalla Yakout, rue Araar, Apt 11, 2ème étage, blvd d'Anfa, Casablanca; tel. (2) 2200949; fax (2) 2200928; f. 1946; Sec.-Gen. ABD AL-WAHID MAÂCH.

Parti de l'environnement et du développement (PED): 3 rue Azilal, Hassan, Rabat; tel. and fax (3) 7702174; e-mail alamiahmed@hotmail.com; internet www.geocities.com/ped_maroc; f. 2002; Sec.-Gen. AHMAD AL-ALAMI.

Parti des forces citoyennes (PFC): 353 blvd Muhammad V, 9ème étage, Casablanca; tel. (2) 2400608; fax (2) 2400613; e-mail citoyennes@iam.net.ma; f. 2001; Sec.-Gen. ABDERRAHIM LAHJOUJI.

MOROCCO

Parti de la justice et du développement (PJD): ave Abdelwahed Elmorakechi, rue Elyafrani, 4 les Orangers, Rabat; tel. (3) 7208862; fax (3) 7208854; e-mail info@pjd.ma; internet www.pjd.ma; f. 1967 as Mouvement populaire constitutionnel et démocratique; breakaway party from MP; formally absorbed mems of the Islamic asscn Al Islah wa Attajdid in June 1996; adopted current name in Oct. 1998; Sec.-Gen. SAÂDEDDINE OTHMANI.

Parti marocain libéral (PML): 114 ave Allal ben Abdellah, 2ème étage, Rabat; tel. (3) 7733670; fax (3) 7733611; e-mail pml@menara.ma; f. 2002; Nat. Co-ordinator MUHAMMAD ZIANE.

Parti national démocrate (PND): 18 rue de Tunis, Hassan, Rabat; tel. (3) 7732127; fax (3) 7720170; e-mail annidal@menara.ma; internet www.pnd.ma; f. 1981 from split within RNI; Sec.-Gen. ABDULLAH KADIRI.

Parti du progrès et du socialisme (PPS): 29 ave John Kennedy, Youssoufia, Rabat; tel. (3) 7759464; fax (3) 7759476; e-mail sg@pps.maroc.org; internet www.pps-maroc.com; f. 1974; successor to Parti communiste marocain (banned in 1952) and Parti de la libération et du socialisme (banned in 1969); left-wing; advocates modernization, social progress, nationalization and democracy; 35,000 mems; Sec.-Gen. ISMAÏL ALAOUI.

Parti de la réforme et du développement (PRD): 34 ave Pasteur, Rabat; tel. and fax (3) 7703801; f. 2001 by fmr mems of RNI; Leader ABD AR-RAHMANE EL-KOUHEN.

Parti de la renaissance et de la vertu (Renaissance and Virtue Party): Bouznika; f. 2005; national democratic party based on the principles of Islam; Sec.-Gen. MUHAMMAD KHALIDI.

Parti du renouveau et de l'équité (PRE): 16 rue Sebou, Apt 5, Agdal, Rabat; tel. (3) 7777266; fax (3) 7777452; f. 2002; Pres. CHAKIR ACHAHBAR.

Parti socialiste unifié (PSU): Casablanca; f. 2005 by merger of Parti de la gauche socialiste unifieé and Fidélité à la démocratie; Sec.-Gen. MUHAMMAD MOUJAHID.

Parti travailliste (PT): 9 rue Ksar Essouk, Hassan, Rabat; f. 2005; centre-left; Sec.-Gen. ABDELKRIM BENATIQ.

Rassemblement national des indépendants (RNI): 6 rue Laos, ave Hassan II, Rabat; tel. (3) 7721420; fax (3) 7733824; internet rni.leguide.ma; f. 1978 from the pro-Govt independents' group that then formed the majority in the Chamber of Representatives; Leader MUSTAPHA MANSOURI.

Union constitutionnelle (UC): 158 ave des Forces Armées Royales, Casablanca; tel. (2) 2441144; fax (2) 2441141; e-mail union_constit@menara.ma; internet www.unionconstitutionnelle.org; f. 1983; 25-mem. Political Bureau; Sec.-Gen. MUHAMMAD ABIED.

Union Marocaine pour la démocratie (UMD): Rabat; f. 2006; Sec.-Gen. ABDELLAH AZMANI.

Union socialiste des forces populaires (USFP): 9 ave al-Araâr, Hay Riad, Rabat; tel. (3) 7565511; fax (3) 7565510; e-mail webmaster@usfp.ma; internet www.usfp.ma; f. 1959 as Union nationale des forces populaires (UNFP); became USFP in 1974 after UNFP split into two separate entities; merged with Parti socialiste démocratique in 2005; left-wing progressive party; 160,000 mems; First Sec. MUHAMMAD EL-YAZGHI.

The following movement is not authorized as a political party by the Government, but is generally tolerated:

Al-Adl wal-Ihsan (Justice and Charity): internet www.aljamaa.net; advocates an Islamic state based on *Shari'a* law; rejects violence; Leader ABDESSALAM YASSINE.

The following group is active in the disputed territory of Western Sahara:

Frente Popular para la Liberación de Saguia el-Hamra y Río de Oro (Frente Polisario) (Polisario Front): BP 10, el-Mouradia, Algiers; tel. (2) 747907; fax (2) 747206; e-mail dgmae@mail.wissal.dz; f. 1973 to gain independence for Western Sahara, first from Spain and then from Morocco and Mauritania; signed peace treaty with Mauritanian Govt in 1979; supported by Algerian Govt; in February 1976 proclaimed the Sahrawi Arab Democratic Republic (SADR); admitted as the 51st mem. of the OAU in Feb. 1982 and currently recognized by more than 75 countries worldwide; its main organs are a 33-mem. National Secretariat, a 101-mem. Sahrawi National Assembly (Parliament) and a 13-mem. Govt; Sec.-Gen. of the Polisario Front and Pres. of the SADR MUHAMMAD ABD AL-AZIZ; Prime Minister of the SADR ABDELKADER TALEB OUMAR.

Diplomatic Representation

EMBASSIES IN MOROCCO

Algeria: 46–48 blvd Tariq ibn Ziad, BP 448, 10001 Rabat; tel. (3) 7661574; fax (3) 7762237; e-mail algerabat@iam.net.ma; Ambassador LARBI BELKHEIR.

Angola: km 5, 53 Ahmed Rifaï, BP 1318, Souissi, Rabat; tel. (3) 7659239; fax (3) 7653707; e-mail amb.angola@iam.net.ma; Ambassador Dr LUIS JOSÉ DE ALMEIDA.

Argentina: 4 ave Mehdi Ben Barka, Souissi, 10000 Rabat; tel. (3) 7755120; fax (3) 7755410; e-mail emarr@mrecic.gov.ar; Ambassador ALBERTO DE NÚÑEZ.

Austria: 2 rue Tiddas, BP 135, 10000 Rabat; tel. (3) 7761698; fax (3) 7765425; e-mail rabat-ob@bmeia.gv.at; Ambassador Dr GEORG MAUTNER-MARKHOF.

Azerbaijan: rue 3 Abu Hanifa, Aqdal, Rabat; tel. (3) 7671915; fax (3) 7671918; e-mail azembma@menara.ma; Ambassador SABIR AGHA-BAYOV.

Bahrain: rue beni Hassan, km 6.5, route des Zaêrs, Souissi, Rabat; tel. (3) 7633600; fax (3) 7633732; e-mail bahrain@mtds.com; Ambassador KHALID BIN SALMAN AL-KHALIFA.

Bangladesh: 25 ave Tarek ibn Ziad, BP 1468, Rabat; tel. (3) 7766731; fax (3) 7766729; e-mail bdoot@mtds.com; Ambassador MOHAMMAD AL-HAROON.

Belgium: 6 ave de Muhammad el-Fassi, Tour Hassan, Rabat; tel. (3) 7268060; fax (3) 7767003; e-mail rabat@diplobel.org; internet www.diplomatie.be/rabat; Ambassador PATRICK VERCAUTEREN DRUBBEL.

Benin: 30 ave Mehdi ben Barka, BP 5187, Souissi, 10105 Rabat; tel. (3) 7754158; fax (3) 7754156; e-mail benin@menara.ma; Ambassador ISSIRADJOU IBRAHIM GOMINA.

Brazil: 10 ave el-Jacaranda, Secteur 2, Hay Riad, 10000 Rabat; tel. (3) 7714663; fax (3) 7714808; e-mail brabat@menara.ma; internet www.ambassadedubresil.org; Ambassador CARLOS ALBERTO SIMAS MAGALHÃES.

Bulgaria: 4 ave Ahmed el-Yazidi, BP 1301, 10000 Rabat; tel. (3) 7765477; fax (3) 7763201; e-mail bulemrab@wanadoo.net.ma; Ambassador KATIA PETROVA TODOROVA.

Burkina Faso: 7 rue al-Bouziri, BP 6484, Agdal, 10101 Rabat; tel. (3) 7675512; fax (3) 7675517; e-mail ambfrba@smirt.net.ma; Ambassador Brig.-Gen. IBRAHIM TRAORÉ.

Cameroon: 20 rue du Rif, BP 1790, Souissi, Rabat; tel. (3) 7754194; fax (3) 7750540; e-mail ambacamrabat@ifrance.com; Ambassador MAHAMAT PABA SALÉ.

Canada: 13 bis rue Jaâfar as-Sadik, BP 709, Agdal, Rabat; tel. (3) 7687400; fax (3) 7687430; e-mail rabat@dfait-maeci.gc.ca; internet www.dfait-maeci.gc.ca/morocco; Ambassador MICHÈLE LÉVESQUE.

Central African Republic: Villa No 4, ave Souss, Cité Saâda, Quartier Administratif, BP 770, Agdal, 10000 Rabat; tel. (3) 7631654; fax (3) 7631655; e-mail centrafricaine@iam.net.ma; Ambassador ISMAÏLA NIMAGA.

Chile: 35 ave Ahmed Balafrej, Souissi, Rabat; tel. (3) 7636065; fax (3) 7636067; e-mail echilema@menara.net.ma; Ambassador MARCIA COVARRUBIAS.

China, People's Republic: 16 ave Ahmed Balafrej, 10000 Rabat; tel. (3) 7754056; fax (3) 7757519; e-mail chinaemb_ma@mfa.gov.cn; internet ma.china-embassy.org; Ambassador CHENG TAO.

Congo, Democratic Republic: 34 ave de la Victoire, BP 553, 10000 Rabat; tel. and fax (3) 7262280; Chargé d'affaires a.i. WAWA BAMIALY.

Congo, Republic: 197 ave Général Abdendi Britel, Souissi II, Rabat; tel. (3) 7659966; fax (3) 7659959; Ambassador JEAN-MARIE EWENGUE.

Côte d'Ivoire: 21 rue de Tiddas, BP 192, 10001 Rabat; tel. (3) 7763151; fax (3) 7762792; e-mail ambcim@clam.net.ma; Ambassador AKE CHARLES DARIUS ATCHIMON.

Croatia: 73 rue Marnissa, Souissi, Rabat; tel. (3) 7638824; fax (3) 7638827; e-mail croamb@menara.ma; Ambassador DARKO BEKIĆ.

Czech Republic: Villa Merzaa, km 4.5, route des Zaêrs, BP 410, Zankat Aït Melloul, Souissi, 10200 Rabat; tel. (3) 7755421; fax (3) 7755493; e-mail rabat@embassy.mzv.cz; internet www.mzv.cz/rabat; Ambassador ELEONORA URBANOVÁ.

Egypt: 31 rue al-Jazair, 10000 Rabat; tel. (3) 7731833; fax (3) 7706821; e-mail embegypt@mtds.com; Ambassador ACHRAF YOUSUF ABDELHALIM ZAÂZAÂ.

Equatorial Guinea: ave President Roosevelt, angle rue d'Agadir 9, Rabat; tel. and fax (3) 7769454; Ambassador JUAN NDONG NGUEMA MBENGONO.

Finland: 145 rue Soufiane Ben Wahb, BP 590, 10002 Rabat; tel. (3) 7658775; fax (3) 7658904; e-mail sanomat.rab@formin.fi; Ambassador SAULI ERIK FEODOROW (resident in Lisbon, Portugal).

France: 3 rue Sahnoun, BP 602, Rabat; tel. (3) 7689700; fax (3) 7689701; internet www.ambafrance-ma.org; Ambassador JEAN-FRANÇOIS THIBAULT.

Gabon: km 3.5, route des Zaêrs, BP 1239, 10100 Rabat; tel. (3) 7751950; fax (3) 7757550; Ambassador FRANÇOIS BANGA EBOUMI.

Gambia: 11 rue Cadi ben Hammadi Senhaji, Souissi, Rabat; tel. (3) 7638045; fax (3) 7638189; Ambassador MAUDO HARLEY NURU TOURAY.

MOROCCO

Germany: 7 Zankat Madnine, BP 235, 10001 Rabat; tel. (3) 7709662; fax (3) 7706851; e-mail amballma@mtds.com; internet www.rabat.diplo.de; Ambassador Dr Gottfried Haas.

Ghana: 27 rue Ghomara, La Pinede, Souissi, Rabat; tel. (3) 7757620; fax (3) 7757630; Ambassador Kobina Annan.

Greece: km 5, route des Zaêrs, Villa Chems, Souissi, 10000 Rabat; tel. (3) 7638964; fax (3) 7638990; e-mail ambagrec@iam.net.ma; Ambassador Michel Cambanis.

Guinea: 15 rue Hamzah, Agdal, 10000 Rabat; tel. (3) 7674148; fax (3) 7672513; Ambassador Mahmadou Saliou Syla.

Holy See: rue Béni M'tir, BP 1303, Souissi, Rabat (Apostolic Nunciature); tel. (3) 7772277; fax (3) 7756213; e-mail nuntius@iam.net.ma; Apostolic Nuncio Most Rev. Antonio Sozzo (Titular Archbishop of Concordia).

Hungary: route des Zaêrs, 17 Zankat Aït Melloul, BP 5026, Souissi, Rabat; tel. (3) 7750757; fax (3) 7754123; e-mail ambhongrie@menara.ma; internet www.mfa.gov.hu/emb/rabat; Ambassador László Váradi.

India: 13 ave de Michlifen, Agdal, 10000 Rabat; tel. (3) 7671339; fax (3) 7671269; e-mail india@menara.ma; internet www.indianembassymorocco.ma; Ambassador Prabhu Dayal.

Indonesia: 63 rue Béni Boufrah, km 5.9, route des Zaêrs, BP 576, 10105 Rabat; tel. (3) 7757860; fax (3) 7757859; e-mail kbrirabat@iam.net.ma; internet www.indonesie.ma; Ambassador Sjachwien Adenan.

Iran: ave Imam Malik, BP 490, 10001 Rabat; tel. (3) 7752167; fax (3) 7659118; e-mail iranembassy@iam.net.ma; Ambassador Wahid Ahmadi.

Iraq: 39 blvd Mehdi ben Barka, 10100 Rabat; tel. (3) 7754466; fax (3) 7759749; e-mail rbtemb@iraqmofamail.net; Ambassador Abd al-Muhsin Muhammad Said.

Italy: 2 rue Idriss al-Azhar, BP 111, 10001 Rabat; tel. (3) 7219730; fax (3) 7706882; e-mail ambassade.rabat@esteri.it; internet www.ambrabat.esteri.it; Ambassador Umberto Lucchesi Palli.

Japan: 39 ave Ahmed Balafrej, Souissi, 10100 Rabat; tel. (3) 7631782; fax (3) 7750078; e-mail amb-japon@fusion.net.ma; internet www.ma.emb-japan.go.jp; Ambassador Haruku Hirose.

Jordan: 65 Villa al-Wafaa, Souissi, 10000 Rabat; tel. (3) 7759270; fax (3) 7758722; Ambassador (vacant).

Korea, Republic: 41 ave Mehdi ben Barka, Souissi, 10100 Rabat; tel. (3) 7756791; fax (3) 7750189; e-mail morocco@mofat.go.kr; internet mar.mofat.go.kr; Ambassador Yoo Jung-Hee.

Kuwait: km 4.3, route des Zaêrs, BP 11, 10001 Rabat; tel. (3) 7631111; fax (3) 7753591; Ambassador Salah Muhammad al-Bijan.

Lebanon: 19 ave Abd al-Karim ben Jalloun, 10000 Rabat; tel. (3) 7760728; fax (3) 7766667; Ambassador Ahmad Othmane Abdellah.

Liberia: Lot no 7, Napabia, rue Ouled Frej, Souissi, Rabat; tel. (3) 7638426; Ambassador (vacant).

Libya: 1 rue Chouaïb Doukkali, BP 225, 10000 Rabat; tel. (3) 7769566; fax (3) 7705200; Ambassador Muhammad Belkacem Ezzaoui.

Malaysia: 17 ave Bir Kacem, Souissi, Rabat; tel. (3) 7658324; fax (3) 7658363; e-mail malrabat@kln.gov.my; internet www.kln.gov.my/perwakilan/rabat; Ambassador Othman Samin.

Mali: 58 cité Olm, Souissi, Rabat; tel. (3) 7759125; fax (3) 7754742; Ambassador Moussa Coulibaly.

Mauritania: 6 rue Thami Lamdour, BP 207, Souissi, 10000 Rabat; tel. (3) 7656678; fax (3) 7656680; e-mail ambassadeur@mauritanie.org.ma; Ambassador Chaikh Ould Aâl.

Mexico: 6 rue Cadi Mohamed Brebi, BP 1789, Souissi, Rabat; tel. (3) 7631969; fax (3) 7631971; e-mail embamexmar@smirt.net.ma; Ambassador Juan Antonio Mateos Cicero.

Netherlands: 40 rue de Tunis, BP 329, Hassan, 10001 Rabat; tel. (3) 7219600; fax (3) 7219665; e-mail nlgovrab@mtds.com; internet www.ambassadepaysbasrabat.org; Ambassador Sjoerd Leenstra.

Niger: 14 bis, rue Jabal al-Ayachi, Agdal, Rabat; tel. (3) 7674615; fax (3) 7674629; Ambassador Diori Hamani Ramatou.

Nigeria: 70 ave Omar ibn al-Khattab, BP 347, Agdal, Rabat; tel. (3) 7671857; fax (3) 7672739; e-mail nigerianrabat@menara.ma; Ambassador Alhaji Abubakar Shehu Wurno.

Norway: 9 rue Khénifra, BP 757, Agdal, 10006 Rabat; tel. (3) 7764084; fax (3) 7764088; e-mail emb.rabat@mfa.no; internet www.norvege.ma; Ambassador Arne Aasheim.

Oman: 21 rue Hamza, Agdal, 10000 Rabat; tel. (3) 7673788; fax (3) 7674567; Ambassador Abdullah bin Muhammad bin Abdullah al-Farissi.

Pakistan: 37 ave Ahmed Balafrej, Souissi, Rabat; tel. (3) 7631367; fax (3) 7631243; e-mail pareprabat@iam.net.ma; Ambassador Qazi Rizwan-ul-Haq Mahmood.

Peru: 16 rue d'Ifrane, 10000 Rabat; tel. (3) 7723236; fax (3) 7702803; e-mail embajadadelperuenmarruecos@msn.com; Ambassador Jorge Abarca del Carpio.

Poland: 23 rue Oqbah, Agdal, BP 425, 10000 Rabat; tel. (3) 7771173; fax (3) 7775320; e-mail apologne@menara.ma; internet www.ambpologne.ma; Ambassador Joanna Wronecka.

Portugal: 5 rue Thami Lamdouar, Souissi, 10100 Rabat; tel. (3) 7756446; fax (3) 7756445; e-mail embport-rabat@hotmail.com; Ambassador João Rosa La.

Qatar: 4 ave Tarik ibn Ziad, BP 1220, 10001 Rabat; tel. (3) 7765681; fax (3) 7765774; e-mail rabat@mofa.gov.qa; Ambassador Saqr Mubarak al-Mansouri.

Romania: 10 rue d'Ouezzane, Hassan, 10000 Rabat; tel. (3) 7724694; fax (3) 7700196; e-mail amb.roumanie@menara.ma; internet rabat.mae.ro; Ambassador Vasile Popovici.

Russia: km 4 route des Zaêrs, 10100 Rabat; tel. (3) 7753509; fax (3) 7753590; e-mail ambrus@iam.net.ma; internet www.morocco.mid.ru; Ambassador Alexander Tokovinin.

Saudi Arabia: 322 ave Imam Malik, km 6, route des Zaêrs, Rabat; tel. (3) 657789; fax (3) 7768587; e-mail ambassd@goodinfo.net.ma; Ambassador Dr Muhammad Abd ar-Rahman bin Abd al-Aziz Bachar.

Senegal: 17 rue Cadi ben Hamadi Senhaji, Souissi, BP 365, 10000 Rabat; tel. (3) 7754171; fax (3) 7754149; e-mail ambassene@iam.net.ma; Ambassador Ibou Ndiaye.

Serbia: BP 5014, 23 ave Mehdi ben Barka, Souissi, 10105 Rabat; tel. (3) 7752201; fax (3) 753258; e-mail sermont@menara.ma; Ambassador Mehmed Becović.

South Africa: 34 rue Saâdiens, Rabat; tel. (3) 7706760; fax (3) 7724550; e-mail sudaf@menara.ma; Chargé d'affaires C. Moller.

Spain: 3 rue Aïn Khalouiya, km 5.3, route des Zaêrs, Souissi, 10000 Rabat; tel. (3) 7633900; fax (3) 7630600; e-mail emb.rabat@maec.es; internet www.mae.es/Embajadas/Rabat; Ambassador D. Luis Planas Puchades.

Sudan: 5 ave Ghomara, Souissi, Rabat; tel. (3) 7752863; fax (3) 7752865; e-mail soudanirab@maghrebnet.net.ma; Ambassador Yahia Abdeljalil Mahmoud.

Sweden: 159 ave John Kennedy, BP 428, Souissi, Rabat; tel. (3) 7633210; fax (3) 7758048; e-mail ambassaden.rabat@foreign.ministry.se; internet www.swedenabroad.com/rabat; Ambassador Klas Gierow.

Switzerland: square de Berkane, BP 169, 10001 Rabat; tel. (3) 7268030; fax (3) 7268040; e-mail rab.vertretung@eda.admin.ch; internet www.eda.admin.ch/rabat; Ambassador Christian Dunant.

Syria: km 5.2, route des Zaêrs, BP 5158, Souissi, Rabat; tel. (3) 7755551; fax (3) 7757522; Ambassador Nabih Ismail.

Thailand: 11 rue de Tiddes, BP 4436, Rabat; tel. (3) 7763328; fax (3) 7763920; e-mail thaima@menara.ma; Ambassador Akrasid Amatayakul.

Tunisia: 6 ave de Fès et 1 rue d'Ifrane, 10000 Rabat; tel. (3) 7730636; fax (3) 7730637; Ambassador Salah Baccari.

Turkey: 7 ave Abdelkrim Benjelloun, 10000 Rabat; tel. (3) 7661522; fax (3) 7660476; e-mail amb-tur-rabat@iam.net.ma; Ambassador Haluk Ilicak.

Ukraine: rue Mouaouya ben Houdaig, Villa 212, Cité OLM, Souissi II, Rabat; tel. (3) 7657840; fax (3) 7754679; Ambassador Vitaliy Yokhna.

United Arab Emirates: 11 ave des Alaouines, 10000 Rabat; tel. (3) 7702085; fax (3) 7724145; e-mail emirabat@iam.net.ma; Ambassador Issaa Hamad Bushahab.

United Kingdom: 28 ave S.A.R. Sidi Muhammad, Souissi, Rabat; tel. (3) 72633333; fax (3) 7704531; e-mail generalenquiries.rabat@fco.gov.uk; internet www.britishembassy.gov.uk/morocco; Ambassador Charles Gray.

USA: 2 ave de Muhammad el-Fassi, Rabat; tel. (3) 7762265; fax (3) 7765661; e-mail ircrabat@usembassy.ma; internet rabat.usembassy.gov; Ambassador Thomas T. Riley.

Venezuela: 58 Lot OLM, Villa Yasmine, rue Capitaine Abdeslam el-Moudden el-Alami, Souissi, Rabat; tel. (3) 7650315; fax (3) 7650372; e-mail emvenez@menara.ma; Ambassador Luisa Rebeca Sánchez Bello.

Yemen: 11 rue Abou-Hanifa, Agdal, 10000 Rabat; tel. (3) 7674306; fax (3) 7674769; e-mail yemenembassy@iam.net.ma; Ambassador Ahmad A. al-Basha.

MOROCCO

Judicial System

SUPREME COURT

Al-Majlis al-Aala
Hay Ryad, Ave an-Nakhil, Rabat; tel. (3) 7714931; fax (3) 7715106; e-mail coursupreme@coursupreme.ma; internet www.coursupreme.ma.

Responsible for the interpretation of the law and regulates the jurisprudence of the courts and tribunals of the Kingdom. The Supreme Court sits at Rabat and is divided into six Chambers.

First President: DRISS DAHAK.

Attorney-General: TAÏEB CHARKAOUI.

The 21 Courts of Appeal hear appeals from lower courts and also comprise a criminal division.

The 65 Courts of First Instance pass judgment on offences punishable by up to five years' imprisonment. These courts also pass judgment, without possibility of appeal, in personal and civil cases involving up to 3,000 dirhams.

The Communal and District Courts are composed of one judge, who is assisted by a clerk or secretary, and hear only civil and criminal cases.

The seven Administrative Courts pass judgment, subject to appeal before the Supreme Court pending the establishment of administrative appeal courts, on litigation with Government departments.

The nine Commercial Courts pass judgment, without the possibility of appeal, on all commercial litigations involving up to 9,000 dirhams. They also pass judgment on claims involving more than 9,000 dirhams, which can be appealed against in the commercial appeal courts.

The Permanent Royal Armed Forces' Court tries offences committed by the armed forces and military officers.

Religion

ISLAM

About 99% of Moroccans are Muslims (of whom about 90% are of the Sunni sect), and Islam is the state religion.

CHRISTIANITY

There are about 69,000 Christians, mostly Roman Catholics.

The Roman Catholic Church

Morocco (excluding the disputed territory of Western Sahara) comprises two archdioceses, directly responsible to the Holy See. At 31 December 2005 there were an estimated 23,099 adherents in the country, representing less than 0.1% of the population. The Moroccan archbishops participate in the Conférence Episcopale Régionale du Nord de l'Afrique (f. 1985).

Bishops' Conference: Conférence Episcopale Régionale du Nord de l'Afrique, 1 rue Hadj Muhammad Riffaï, BP 258, 10001 Rabat; tel. (37) 709239; fax (37) 706282; e-mail archev.rabat@wanadoo.net.ma; f. 1985; Pres. Most Rev. VINCENT LANDEL (Archbishop of Rabat).

Archbishop of Rabat: Most Rev. VINCENT LANDEL, Archevêché, 1 rue Hadj Muhammad Riffaï, BP 258, 10001 Rabat; tel. (3) 7709239; fax (3) 7706282; e-mail landel@wanadoo.net.ma.

Archbishop of Tangier: Most Rev. JOSÉ ANTONIO PETEIRO FREIRE, Archevêché, 55 rue Sidi Bouabid, BP 2116, 9000 Tangier; tel. (3) 9932762; fax (3) 9949117; e-mail igletanger@wanadoo.net.ma.

Western Sahara comprises a single Apostolic Prefecture, with an estimated 140 Catholics (2005).

Prefect Apostolic of Western Sahara: Fr ACACIO VALBUENA RODRIGUEZ, Misión Católica, BP 31, 70001 el-Aaiún; tel. 893270; e-mail omisahara@menara.ma.

The Anglican Communion

Within the Church of England, Morocco forms part of the diocese of Gibraltar in Europe. There are Anglican churches in Casablanca and Tangier.

Protestant Church

Evangelical Church: 33 rue d'Azilal, 20000 Casablanca; tel. (2) 2302151; fax (2) 2444768; e-mail eeam@lesblancs.com; f. 1920; established in eight towns; Pres. Pastor JEAN-LUC BLANC; 1,000 mems.

JUDAISM

It is estimated that there are fewer than 7,000 Jews in Morocco, of whom approximately 5,000 reside in Casablanca, with smaller communities in Rabat and other cities.

Conseil des Communautés Israélites du Maroc: 52 Bne-Snassen, Souissi, Rabat; tel. (2) 222861; fax (2) 266953; Pres. SERGE BERDUGO.

The Press

DAILIES

Casablanca

Al-Ahdath al-Maghribia (Moroccan Events): 5 rue Saint-Emilion, Casablanca; tel. (2) 2443038; fax (2) 2442976; e-mail y.benjelloun@alahdath.info; internet www.ahdath.info; f. 1998; Arabic; Dir MUHAMMAD AL-BRINI; circ. 38,559 (2006).

Assabah (The Morning): Groupe Ecomedia, 70 blvd al-Massira al-Khadra, Casablanca; tel. (2) 2953660; fax (2) 2364358; e-mail assabah@assabah.press.ma; internet www.assabah.press.ma; Arabic; Dir-Gen. KHALID BELYAZID; circ. 61,737 (2006).

Assahra al-Maghribia: 17 rue Othman ben Affan, Casablanca; tel. (2) 2489120; fax (2) 2203935; e-mail h.elattafi@almaghribia.ma; internet www.almaghribia.ma; f. 1989; Arabic; Dir HASSAN EL-ATTAFI.

Aujourd'hui le Maroc: 213 Rond-Point d'Europe, Casablanca; tel. (2) 2262674; fax (2) 2262718; e-mail kidrissi@aujourdhui.ma; internet www.aujourdhui.ma; French; Dir KHALIL HACHIMI IDRISSI; Editor-in-Chief OMAR DAHBI; circ. 12,262 (2006).

Al-Bayane (The Manifesto): blvd Emile Zola, 8ème étage, BP 13152, Casablanca; tel. (2) 2307882; fax (2) 2308080; internet www.albayane.ma; Arabic and French; organ of the Parti du progrès et du socialisme; Dir ISMAÏL ALAOUI; Editor AHMED ZAKI; circ. 3,239 (2006).

L'Economiste: Groupe Ecomedia, 70 blvd al-Massira al-Khadra, Casablanca; tel. (2) 2953600; fax (2) 2365926; e-mail info@leconomiste.com; internet www.leconomiste.com; f. 1991; French; Pres. ABDELMOUNAÏM DILAMI; Dir-Gen. KHALID BELYAZID; Editor-in-Chief NADIA SALAH; circ. 17,254 (2006).

Al-Ittihad al-Ichtiraki (Socialist Unity): 33 rue Amir Abdelkader, BP 2165, Casablanca; tel. (2) 2407385; fax (2) 2619405; e-mail contact@alittihadalichtiraki.press.ma; internet www.alittihad.press.ma; Arabic; f. 1983; organ of the Union socialiste des forces populaires; Dir MUHAMMAD EL-YAZGHI; Editor MUSTAPHA LAÂRAKI; circ. 14,669 (2006).

Libération: 33 rue Amir Abdelkader, BP 2165, Casablanca; tel. (2) 2619404; fax (2) 2620972; e-mail liberation@mis.net.ma; internet www.liberation.press.ma; f. 1964; French; organ of the Union socialiste des forces populaires; Dir ABDELHADI KHAÏRAT; circ. 3,735 (2006).

Al-Massae (The Evening): 10 ave des Forces Armées Royales, 2ème étage, Casablanca; tel. (2) 2275918; fax (2) 2275597; e-mail chaouki.samir@gmail.com; f. 2006; Arabic; independent; Dir RACHID NINI; circ. 41,085 (2006).

Le Matin du Sahara et du Maghreb: 17 rue Othman ben Affan, Casablanca; tel. (2) 2489100; fax (2) 2203048; e-mail m.jouahri@lematin.ma; internet www.lematin.ma; f. 1971; French; Dir-Gen. MUHAMMAD JOUAHRI; circ. 22,762 (2006).

Rissalat al-Oumma (The Message of the Nation): 152 ave des Forces Armées Royales, BP 20005, Casablanca; tel. (2) 2901925; fax (2) 2901926; Arabic; weekly edn in French; organ of the Union constitutionnelle; Dir MUHAMMAD TAMALDOU.

Rabat

Al-Alam (The Flag): ave Hassan II, rue Casablanca, Lot Vita, BP 141, Rabat; tel. (3) 7293002; fax (3) 7292639; e-mail alalam@alalam.ma; internet www.alalam.ma; f. 1946; Arabic; literary supplement on Saturdays; organ of the Istiqlal party; Dir HASSAN ABDELKHALEK; circ. 11,943.

Attajdid (Reform): 3 blvd al-Moukawama, BP 9173, Rabat; tel. (3) 7705854; fax (3) 7705852; e-mail attajdid@attajdid.ma; internet www.attajdid.ma; f. 1999; Arabic; associated with the Parti de la justice et du développement; Dir ABDELILLAH BENKIRAN; circ. 4,581 (2006).

Al-Haraka (Progress): 66 rue Patrice Lumumba, BP 1317, Rabat; tel. (3) 7768667; fax (3) 7768677; e-mail harakamp@menara.ma; internet www.harakamp.ma; Arabic; organ of the Mouvement populaire; Dir ALI ALAOUI; circ. 1,034 (2006).

Al-Mithaq al-Watani (The National Charter): 6 rue Laos, BP 469, Rabat; tel. (3) 7722708; fax (3) 7722765; f. 1977; Arabic; organ of the Rassemblement national des indépendants; Dir MUHAMMAD AUAJJAR.

An-Nahar al-Maghribia (The Moroccan Day): 12 pl. des Alaouites, 2ème étage, Rabat; tel. (3) 7737568; fax (3) 7737547; e-mail annaharalmaghribia@menara.fr; internet www.annahar.ma; Arabic; circ. 11,221 (2006).

MOROCCO

L'Opinion: ave Hassan II, Lot Vita, Rabat; tel. (3) 7293002; fax (3) 7292639; e-mail lopinion@lopinion.ma; internet www.lopinion.ma; f. 1965; French; organ of Istiqlal; Dir MUHAMMAD IDRISSI KAÏTOUNI; Editor-in-Chief JAMAL HAJJAM; circ. 20,662 (2006).

SELECTED PERIODICALS

Casablanca

Al-Ayam (The Days): Espace Paquet, 508 rue Muhammad Smiha, Casablanca; tel. (2) 2442694; fax (2) 2441173; e-mail alayam@menara.com; f. 2001; Arabic; weekly; circ. 24,399 (2006).

CGEM Infos: 23 blvd Muhammad Abdou, Palmiers, Casablanca; tel. (2) 2997000; fax (2) 2983971; e-mail cgem@cgem.ma; internet www.cgem.ma; weekly; French; organ of the Confédération Générale des Entreprises du Maroc; Dir MOULAY HAFID ELALAMY.

Challenge Hebdo: Tour des Habous, 13ème étage, 58 ave des Forces Armées Royales, Casablanca; tel. (2) 2548153; fax (2) 2300990; e-mail redaction@challengehebdo.com; internet www.challengehebdo.com; weekly; French; business; Dir ADIL LAHLOU; circ. 5,151 (2006).

Construire: 744 rue Boukraâ, Résidence Hanane Jassim I, Bourgogne, Casablanca; tel. (2) 2220273; fax (2) 2273627; e-mail nlleconstruire@menara.ma; f. 1940; weekly; French; Dir ABDELKRIM TALAL.

Femmes du Maroc: Immeuble Zénith I, Lot Attaoufik, route de Nouaceur, Sidi Maârouf, Casablanca; tel. (2) 2973949; fax (2) 2973929; internet www.femmesdumaroc.com; monthly; French; lifestyle magazine for women; Dir AÏCHA ZAÏMI SAKHRI; Editor-in-Chief GÉRALDINE DULAT; circ. 15,368 (2006).

La Gazette du Maroc: ave des Forces Armées Royales, Tour des Habous, 13ème étage, Casablanca; tel. (2) 2548150; fax (2) 2318094; e-mail info@lagazettedumaroc.com; internet www.lagazettedumaroc.com; weekly; French; Dir KAMAL LAHLOU; circ. 9,291 (2006).

Le Journal Hebdomadaire: 61 ave des Forces Armées Royales, BP 20000, Casablanca; tel. (2) 2546670; fax (2) 2446185; e-mail courrier@lejournal-hebdo.com; internet www.lejournal-hebdo.com; weekly; French; news, politics, economics; Dir ALI AMAR; circ. 14,832 (2006).

Maroc Fruits: 283 blvd Zerktouni, Casablanca; tel. (2) 2363946; fax (2) 2363996; f. 1958; fortnightly; Arabic and French; organ of the Association des Producteurs d'Agrumes du Maroc; Pres. LYOUSSI HASSAN; circ. 6,000.

Maroc Hebdo International: 4 rue des Flamants, Casablanca; tel. (2) 2238176; fax (2) 2981346; e-mail mhi@maroc-hebdo.press.ma; internet www.maroc-hebdo.com; f. 1991; weekly; French; Dir MUHAMMAD SELHAMI; 11,848 (2006).

Al-Mountakhab (The Team): 42 bis rue de Madagascar, Rabat; tel. (2) 2261951; fax (2) 2264638; e-mail almocom.j@menara.ma; internet www.almountakhab.com; f. 1986; fortnightly; Arabic; sport; Dir BADREDDINE IDRISSI; circ. 21,876 (2006).

Nissae min al-Maghrib (Women of Morocco): Immeuble Zénith I, Lot Attaoufik, route de Nouaceur, Sidi Maârouf, Casablanca; tel. (2) 2973949; fax (2) 2973929; e-mail y.guennoun@akwagroup.com; monthly; Arabic edn of *Femmes du Maroc*; circ. 32,564 (2006).

La Nouvelle Tribune: 320 blvd Zerktouni, angle rue Bouardel, Casablanca; tel. (2) 2424670; fax (2) 2200031; e-mail courrier@lanouvelletribune.com; internet www.lanouvelletribune.com; f. 1996; weekly (Thurs.); French; Dir FAHD YATA.

Parade: Immeuble Zénith I, Lot Attaoufik, route de Nouaceur, Sidi Maârouf, Casablanca; tel. (2) 2973949; fax (2) 2973929; e-mail y.guennoun@akwagroup.com; monthly; French; circ. 4,716 (2006).

Perspectives du Maghreb: 8 blvd Yacoub el Mansour, Maârif, Casablanca; tel. (2) 2257617; fax (2) 2257738; e-mail popmedia@menara.ma; internet www.perspectives-online.com; f. 2005; monthly; French; circ. 4,973 (2006).

La Quinzaine du Maroc: 53 rue Dumont d'Urville, Casablanca; tel. (2) 2440033; fax (2) 2440426; e-mail mauro@wanadopro.ma; internet quinzainedumaroc.com; f. 1951; fortnightly; English and French; visitors' guide; Dir HUBERT MAURO.

Le Reporter: 1 Sahat al-Istiqlal, 2ème étage, Casablanca; tel. (2) 2541103; fax (2) 2541105; e-mail redaction@lereporter.ma; internet www.lereporter.ma; f. 1998; weekly; French; Dir BAHIA AMRANI.

Assahifa al Maghribiya (The Moroccan Newspaper): 61 ave des Forces Armées Royales, Casablanca; e-mail ibargach2@yahoo.fr; tel. (2) 2546671; fax (2) 2446185; weekly; Arabic; Dir ISSAM BARGACH.

TelQuel: 28 ave des Forces Armées Royales, Casablanca; fax (2) 220563; e-mail courrier@telquel.info; internet www.telquel-online.com; weekly; French; Dir AHMAD BENCHEMSI; Editor-in-Chief KARIM BOUKHARI; circ. 21,747 (2006).

Directory

La Vérité: 174 blvd Zerktouni, 6ème étage, Casablanca; tel. (2) 2206411; fax (2) 2206423; e-mail elamrani321@yahoo.fr; internet www.laverite.ma; weekly (Fri.); French; Dir ABDALLAH EL-AMRANI.

Version Homme: ave des Forces Armées Royales, Tour des Habous, 13ème étage, Casablanca; tel. (2) 2450089; fax (2) 2442213; e-mail redaction@versionhomme.com; internet www.versionhomme.com; monthly; lifestyle magazine for men; Dir ADIL LAHLOU; circ. 5,745 (2006).

La Vie éco: 5 blvd Abdallah ben Yassine, 20300 Casablanca; tel. (2) 2450555; fax (2) 2304542; e-mail vieeco@marocnet.net.ma; internet www.lavieeco.com; f. 1921; weekly; French; economics; Dir FADEL AGOUMI; Editor-in-Chief SAÂD BEN MANSOUR; circ. 14,671 (2006).

La Vie Touristique Africaine: 17 rue El Houcine Ben Ali, Casablanca; tel. (2) 2227643; fax (2) 2275319; e-mail vietouristique@wanadoo.net.ma; internet www.vietouristique.ma; fortnightly; French; tourist information; Dir AHMED ZEGHARI.

Al-Watan al-An (The Nation Now): 33 rue Muhammad Bahi, Casablanca; tel. (2) 2251295; fax (2) 2251325; e-mail alwatanpress@menara.ma; internet www.alwatan.press.ma; weekly; Arabic; news; Editor ABDERRAHIM ARIRI; circ. 12,195 (2006).

Rabat

Al-Alam al-Amazighi: Éditions Amazigh, 5 rue Dakar, BP 477, Rabat; tel. (6) 1767073; fax (3) 7727283; e-mail lemondeamazigh@hotmail.com; weekly; Berber.

Asdae (Echoes): 30 ave Okba, Rabat; tel. (3) 7773706; e-mail asdae@menara.ma; internet www.asdae.com; weekly; Arabic; Dir EL-HASSAN ARBAI.

Ach-Chorta (The Police): BP 437, Rabat; tel. (3) 7652087; monthly; Arabic; Dir MUHAMMAD AD-DRIF.

Da'ouat al-Haqq (Call of the Truth): al-Michwar as-Said, Rabat; tel. (3) 7766851; e-mail direction_haq@habous.gov.ma; internet www.daouatalhaq.ma; publ. by Ministry of Habous (Religious Endowments) and Islamic Affairs; f. 1957; monthly; Arabic.

An-Nidal ad-Dimokrati (The Democratic Struggle): 18 rue de Tunis, Hassan, Rabat; tel. (3) 7732127; fax (3) 7720170; e-mail annidal@menara.ma; internet www.pnd.ma; f. 1984; weekly; Arabic; organ of the Parti national démocrate; Dir ABDELHAMID KHATIR.

At-Tadamoun (Solidarity): 6 rue Aguensous, BP 1740, Rabat; tel. (3) 7730961; fax (3) 7738851; e-mail amdh1@mtds.com; internet www.amdh.org.ma; monthly; Arabic; organ of the Association marocaine des droits humains; Dir ABD AL-MAJID SEMLALI EL-HASANI.

La Voix du Centre: 4 ave Imam Malik, route des Zaërs, Rabat; tel. (7) 3834771; fax (3) 7764767; weekly; French; organ of the Mouvement démocratique et social; Editor-in-Chief MUSTAPHA SHIMI.

Tangier

Achamal 2000: 137 ave Prince Héritier, Tangier; tel. (3) 9373927; fax (3) 9944216; e-mail ashamal@menara.ma; weekly; Arabic; Editor-in-Chief KHALID MECHBAL.

Le Journal de Tanger: 7 bis rue Omar Ben Abdelaziz, Tangier; tel. (3) 9943008; fax (3) 9945709; e-mail direct@lejournaldetanger.com; internet www.lejournaldetanger.com; f. 1904; weekly; French, English, Spanish and Arabic; Dir ABDELHAK BAKHAT; Editor-in-Chief MUHAMMAD ABOUABDILLAH; circ. 10,000.

NEWS AGENCY

Maghreb Arabe Presse (MAP): 122 ave Allal ben Abdallah, BP 1049, 10000 Rabat; tel. (3) 7279464; fax (3) 7279465; e-mail mapweb@map.co.ma; internet www.map.ma; f. 1959; Arabic, French, English and Spanish; state-owned; Dir-Gen. MUHAMMAD KHABBACHI.

PRESS ASSOCIATIONS

Fédération Marocaine des Editeurs de Journaux (FMEJ): Groupe Ecomedia, 70 blvd al-Massira al-Khadra, Casablanca; tel. (2) 2953600; fax (2) 2365926; f. 2005; Pres. ABDELMOUNAIM DILAMI.

Organisme de Justification de la Diffusion (OJD Maroc): 4 rue des Flamants, Casablanca; tel. (2) 2238176; fax (2) 2981346; e-mail asmae@maroc-hebdo.press.ma; internet www.ojd.ma; f. 2004; compiles circulation statistics; Pres. MUHAMMAD SELHAMI; Dir ASMAE HASSANI.

Publishers

Afrique Orient: 159 bis blvd Yacoub el-Mansour, Casablanca; tel. (2) 2259813; fax (2) 2440080.

Belvisi: 17 rue Abbas Ibnou Farnass, BP 8044, Casablanca; tel. (2) 2250973; fax (2) 2986258; f. 1986.

Dar el-Kitab: place de la Mosquée, Quartier des Habous, BP 4018, Casablanca; tel. (2) 2305419; fax (2) 3026630; f. 1948; philosophy, history, Africana, general and social science; Arabic and French; Dir BOUTALEB ABDOU ABD AL-HAY; Gen. Man. KHADIJA EL-KASSIMI.

Editions Le Fennec: 89B blvd d'Anfa, 14ème étage, Casablanca; tel. (2) 2209314; fax (2) 2277702; e-mail info@lefennec.com; internet www.lefennec.com; f. 1987; fiction, social sciences; Dir LAYLA B. CHAOUNI.

Editions La Porte: 281 blvd Muhammad V, BP 331, Rabat; tel. (3) 7709958; fax (3) 7706476; e-mail la_porte@meganet.net.ma; law, guides, economics, educational books.

Les Editions Maghrébines: Quartier Industriel, blvd E, N 15, Sin Sebaâ, Casablanca; tel. (2) 2351797; fax (2) 2357892; f. 1962; general non-fiction.

Les Editions Toubkal: Immeuble I.G.A, pl. de la Gare Voyageurs, Bélvèdere, 20300 Casablanca; tel. and fax (2) 22342323; e-mail contact@toubkal.ma; internet www.toubkal.ma; f. 1985; economy, history, social sciences, literature, educational books; Dir ABDELJALIL NADEM.

Malika Editions: 60 blvd Yacoub el-Mansour, 20100 Casablanca; tel. (2) 2235688; fax (2) 2251651; e-mail edmalika@connectcom.net.ma; internet www.malikaedition.com; art publications.

Tarik Editions: 321 route el-Jadida, 20000 Casablanca; tel. (2) 2259007; fax (2) 2232550; e-mail tarik.editions@wanadoo.net.ma; f. 2000; history and social sciences; Dir BICHR BENNANI.

Yomad: rue Boronia, secteur 17, Hay Riad, Rabat; tel. (3) 7717590; fax (3) 7717589; e-mail yomadeditions@yahoo.com; f. 1998; children's literature; Dir NADIA ES-SALMI.

GOVERNMENT PUBLISHING HOUSE

Imprimerie Officielle: ave Yacoub el-Mansour, Rabat-Chellah; tel. (3) 7765024; fax (3) 7765179.

Broadcasting and Communications

TELECOMMUNICATIONS

Regulatory Authority

Agence Nationale de Réglementation des Télécommunications (ANRT): Centre d'Affaires, blvd ar-Ryad, BP 2939, Hay Ryad, 10100 Rabat; tel. (3) 7718400; fax (3) 7203862; e-mail con@anrt.net.ma; internet www.anrt.net.ma; f. 1998; Dir-Gen. MUHAMMAD BENCHAÂBOUN.

Principal Operators

Itissalat al-Maghrib—Maroc Télécom: ave Annakhil Hay Riad, Rabat; tel. (3) 7719000; fax (3) 7714860; e-mail webmaster@iam.ma; internet www.iam.ma; f. 1998 to take over telephone services from the ONPT; privatized in 2004; Vivendi Universal (France) holds a 51% stake; Chair. ABDESLAM AHIZOUNE.

Méditel: Twin Centre, angle blvd Zerktouni et blvd Massira al-Khadra, Casablanca; internet www.meditel.ma; f. 1999; subsidiary of Telefónica SA and Portugal Telecom; provides national mobile telecommunications services; Dir-Gen. IÑIGO SERRANO.

BROADCASTING

Morocco can receive broadcasts from Spanish radio stations, and the main Spanish television channels can also be received in northern Morocco.

Radio

Radio Casablanca: c/o Loukt s.a.r.l, BP 16011, Casa Principal, 20001 Casablanca; e-mail i-RC@maroc.net; internet www.maroc.net/rc; f. 1996; Gen. Man. AMINE ZARY.

Radio Méditerranée Internationale: 3 rue Emsallah, BP 2055, 9000 Tangier; tel. (3) 9936363; fax (3) 9935755; e-mail medi1@medi1.com; internet www.medi1.com; Arabic and French; Man. Dir PIERRE CASALTA.

Voice of America Radio Station in Tangier: c/o US Consulate-General, chemin des Amoureux, Tangier.

Television

Radiodiffusion-Télévision Marocaine: 1 rue el-Brihi, BP 1042, 1000 Rabat; tel. (3) 7766885; fax (3) 7766888; internet www.rtm.ma; govt station; transmission commenced 1962; 45 hours weekly; French and Arabic; carries commercial advertising; Dir-Gen. and Dir Television FAIÇAL LARAICHI.

SOREAD 2M: Société d'études et de réalisations audiovisuelles, km 7.3 route de Rabat, Aïn-Sebaâ, Casablanca; tel. (2) 2667373; fax (2) 2667392; e-mail portail@tv2m.co.ma; internet www.2m.tv; f. 1988; transmission commenced 1989; public television channel, owned by Moroccan Govt (72%) and by private national foreign concerns; broadcasting in French and Arabic; Man. Dir SAMI EL-JAI.

Finance

(cap. = capital; res = reserves; dep. = deposits; m. = million; brs = branches; amounts in dirhams)

BANKING

Central Bank

Bank Al-Maghrib: 277 ave Muhammad V, BP 445, Rabat; tel. (3) 7702626; fax (3) 7706667; e-mail deri@bkam.gov.ma; internet www.bkam.gov.ma; f. 1959 as Banque du Maroc; name changed as above in 1987; bank of issue; cap. 500m., res 5,001.3m., dep. 65,951.7m. (Dec. 2006); Gov. ABDELLATIF JOUAHRI.

Other Banks

Attijariwafa Bank: 2 blvd Moulay Youssef, BP 11141, 20000 Casablanca; tel. (2) 2298888; fax (2) 2294125; e-mail contact@attijariwafa.com; internet www.attijariwafabank.com; f. 2005 by merger between Banque Commerciale du Maroc SA and Wafabank; 33.2% owned by Groupe ONA, 14.6% by Grupo Santander (Spain); cap. 1,930.0m., res 9,629.5m., dep. 126,140.0m. (Dec. 2006); Chair. and CEO MUHAMMAD EL-KETTANI.

Banque Centrale Populaire (Crédit Populaire du Maroc): 101 blvd Muhammad Zerktouni, BP 10622, 21100 Casablanca; tel. (2) 2202533; fax (2) 2229699; e-mail bcp@banquepopulairemorocco.ma; internet www.cpm.co.ma; f. 1961; 51% state-owned, 49% privately owned; merged with Société Marocaine de Dépot et Crédit in 2003; cap. 1,684.1m., res 6,568.6m., dep. 99,691.2m. (Dec. 2005); Pres. and Gen. Man. NOUREDDINE OMARY; 530 brs.

Banque Marocaine du Commerce Extérieur SA (BMCE): 140 ave Hassan II, BP 13425, 20000 Casablanca; tel. (2) 2200496; fax (2) 2200512; e-mail communicationfinanciere@bmcebank.co.ma; internet www.bmcebank.ma; f. 1959; transferred to majority private ownership in 1995; cap. 1,587.5m., res 3,943.6m., dep. 59,362.8m. (Dec. 2005); Chair. and CEO OTHMAN BENJELLOUN; 412 brs.

Banque Marocaine pour le Commerce et l'Industrie SA (BMCI): 26 pl. des Nations Unies, BP 15573, Casablanca; tel. (2) 22461000; fax (2) 22299406; e-mail adiba.lahbabi@africa.bnpparibas.com; internet www.bmcinet.com; f. 1964; 65.05% owned by BNP Paribas (France); cap. 1,000.3m., res 1,818.1m., dep. 38,350.8m. (Dec. 2006); Chair. MOURAD CHERIF; CEO JOËL SIBRAC; Gen. Man. RACHID MARRAKCHI; 200 brs.

Citibank-Maghreb: Zénith Millenium, Immeuble 1, Lot Attaoufik, Sidi Maârouf, BP 13362, Casablanca; tel. (2) 2489600; fax (2) 2974197; f. 1967; total assets 1,211.0m.; cap. and res 194.0m. (Dec. 2003); Pres. NUHAD SALIBA; 2 brs.

Crédit Agricole du Maroc SA: 29 rue Abou Faris al-Marini, BP 49, 10000 Rabat; tel. (3) 7208219; fax (3) 7445063; e-mail m_kettani@creditagricole.ma; internet www.creditagricole.ma; f. 1961 as Caisse Nationale de Crédit Agricole; became a limited co and adopted present name in 2003; 78% owned by Ministry of the Economy and Finance; cap. 1,820.5m., res 840.7m., dep. 33,055.0m. (Dec. 2005); Man. Dir KARIM BELMAACHI.

Crédit Immobilier et Hôtelier: 187 ave Hassan II, Casablanca; tel. (2) 2479000; fax (2) 2479363; e-mail info-client@cih.co.ma; internet www.cih.co.ma; f. 1920; transferred to majority private ownership in 1995; cap. 3,323.4m., res –4,443.9m., dep. 19,502.7m. (Dec. 2005); Pres. KHALID ALIOUA; Gen. Mans GILLES THERRY, SAID LAFTIT; 91 brs.

Crédit du Maroc SA: 48–58 blvd Muhammad V, BP 13579, 20000 Casablanca; tel. (2) 2477477; fax (2) 2477127; e-mail mohammadine.menjra@ca-cdm.ma; internet www.cdm.co.ma; f. 1963 as Crédit Lyonnais Maroc; name changed as above in 1966; 52.6% owned by Crédit Agricole (France); cap. 833.8m., res 933.3m., dep. 21,453.7m. (Dec. 2005); Chair. and CEO FRANCIS SAVOYE; 163 brs.

Société Générale Marocaine de Banques SA: 55 blvd Abdelmoumen, BP 13090, 21100 Casablanca; tel. (2) 2438888; fax (2) 2234931; e-mail contact@sgmaroc.com; internet www.sgmaroc.com; f. 1962; cap. 1,170.0m., res 1,335.2m., dep. 29,008.6m. (Dec. 2005); Pres. ABDELAZIZ TAZI; 132 brs.

Bank Organizations

Association Professionnelle des Sociétés de Bourse du Maroc: angle rue Muhammad Errachid et ave des Forces Armées Royales, 20000 Casablanca; tel. (2) 2542333; fax (2) 2542336; e-mail apsb@apsb.org.ma; internet www.apsb.org.ma; f. 1995; groups all brokers in the stock exchange of Casablanca for studies, inquiries of general interest and contacts with official authorities; 12 mems;

MOROCCO

Pres. Yousuf Benkirane; Vice-Pres. Omar Amine; Exec. Dir Sanaâ Laroui.

Groupement Professionnel des Banques du Maroc: 71 ave des Forces Armées Royales, Casablanca; tel. (2) 2314824; fax (2) 2314903; f. 1967; groups all commercial banks for studies, inquiries of general interest, and contacts with official authorities; 18 mems; Pres. Othman Benjelloun.

STOCK EXCHANGE

Bourse de Casablanca: angle ave des Forces Armées Royales et rue Muhammad Errachid, Casablanca; tel. (2) 2452626; fax (2) 2452625; e-mail contact@casablanca-bourse.com; internet www.casablanca-bourse.com; f. 1929; Chair. Houssine Sahib; CEO Amine Benabdesslem.

INSURANCE

Assurances Al-Amane: 122 ave Hassan II, 20000 Casablanca; tel. (2) 2267272; fax (2) 2265664; f. 1975; cap. 120m.; Pres. and Dir-Gen. Muhammad Boughaleb.

Atlanta Assurances: 181 blvd d'Anfa, BP 13685, 20001 Casablanca; tel. (2) 2957676; fax (2) 2369929; e-mail info@atlanta.ma; internet www.atlanta.ma; f. 1947; cap. 591.6m.; Dir-Gen. Muhammad Hassan Bensalah.

AXA Assurance Maroc: 120–122 ave Hassan II, 21000 Casablanca; tel. (2) 2224185; fax (2) 2260150; cap. 900m.; Dir-Gen. Daniel Antunès.

Compagnie d'Assurances et de Réassurances SANAD: 181 blvd d'Anfa, Tours Balzac, Casablanca; tel. (2) 2957878; fax (2) 2360406; e-mail contact@sanad.ma; internet www.sanad.ma; f. 1975; cap. 125m.; Chair. Muhammad Hassan Bensalah; Dir-Gen. Abdeltif Tahiri.

CNIA Assurance: 216 blvd Muhammad Zerktouni, 20000 Casablanca; tel. (2) 2474040; fax (2) 2206081; internet www.cnia.ma; f. 1949; cap. 30m.; Pres. and Dir-Gen. Moulay Hafid Elalamy.

La Marocaine Vie: 37 blvd Moulay Youssef, Casablanca; tel. (2) 2206320; fax (2) 2261971; f. 1978; 83% owned by Société Générale Marocaine de Banques SA; Pres. Marc Duval; Gen. Man. Karim Moultaki.

Mutuelle Centrale Marocaine d'Assurances (MCMA): 16 rue Abou Inane, BP 27, Rabat; tel. (3) 7766960; Pres. Abed Yacoubi Soussane; Man. Dir Annie Guerrawi.

Mutuelle d'Assurances des Transporteurs Unis (MATU): 215 blvd Muhammad Zerktouni, Casablanca; tel. (2) 2367097; Dir-Gen. Benyamna Muhammad.

RMA Watanya: 83 ave des Forces Armées Royales, 20000 Casablanca; tel. (2) 2312163; fax (2) 2313137; e-mail info@rmawatanya.com; internet www.rmawatanya.com; f. 2005 by merger of Al-Wataniya and La Royale Marocaine d'Assurances; cap. 1,774m.; Pres. Sébastien Castro.

Es-Saâda, Compagnie d'Assurances et de Réassurances: 123 ave Hassan II, BP 13860, 20000 Casablanca; tel. (2) 2497100; fax (2) 2262655; e-mail es-saada@techno.net.ma; internet www.essaada.com; f. 1961; cap. 107.6m.; Pres. Mehdi Ouazzani; Man. Dir Abdelfettah Alami.

Société Centrale de Réassurance (SCR): Tour Atlas, pl. Zallaqa, BP 13183, Casablanca; tel. (2) 2460400; fax (2) 2460460; e-mail scr@scrmaroc.com; internet www.scrmaroc.com; f. 1960; cap. 30m.; Chair. Mustapha Bakkoury; Man. Dir Ahmad Zinoun.

Société Marocaine d'Assurance à l'Exportation (SMAEX): 24 rue Ali Abderrazak, BP 15953, Casablanca; tel. (2) 2982000; fax (2) 2252070; e-mail smaex@smaex.com; internet www.smaex.com; f. 1988; insurance for exporters in the public and private sectors; assistance for export promotion; Pres. and Dir-Gen. Nezha Lahrichi; Asst Dir-Gen. Abderrazak M'Haimdat.

WAFA Assurance: 1–3 blvd Abd al-Moumen, BP 13420, 20001 Casablanca; tel. (2) 2224575; fax (2) 2209103; e-mail webmaster@wafaassurance.com; internet www.attijariwafabank.com; subsidiary of Attijariwafa Bank; Pres. Saâd Kettani; Dir-Gen. Jaouad Kettani.

Zurich Compagnie Marocaine d'Assurances: Residence City Park Centre, 106 rue Abderrahmane Sahraoui, 20000 Casablanca; tel. (2) 2279015; fax (2) 2276718; e-mail customerservice@zurich.com; f. 1954; cap. 90m.; all kinds of insurance; Pres. and Dir-Gen. Berto Fisler.

INSURANCE ASSOCIATION

Fédération Marocaine des Sociétés d'Assurances et de Réassurances: 154 blvd d'Anfa, Casablanca; tel. (2) 2391850; fax (2) 2391854; e-mail a.boughaleb@fmsar.ma; internet www.fmsar.org.ma; f. 1958; 15 mem. cos; Pres. Mustapha Bakhoury.

Trade and Industry

GOVERNMENT AGENCIES

Agence Nationale pour la Promotion de la Petite et Moyenne Entreprise (ANPME): 10 rue Ghandi, BP 211, Rabat; tel. (3) 7708460; fax (3) 7707695; e-mail anpme@anpme.ma; internet www.anpme.ma; f. 2002; Dir-Gen. Latifa Echihabi.

Centre Marocain de Promotion des Exportations (CMPE): 23 blvd Bnou Majid el-Bahar, BP 10937, 20000 Casablanca; tel. (2) 2302210; fax (2) 2301793; e-mail cmpe@cmpe.org.ma; internet www.cmpe.org.ma; f. 1980; state org. for promotion of exports; Sec.-Gen. Ali el-Alaoui.

Direction des Entreprises Publiques et de la Privatisation (DEPP): rue Haj Ahmed Cherkaoui, Quartier Administratif, Agdal, Rabat; tel. (3) 7689303; fax (3) 7689347; e-mail talbi@depp.finances.gov.ma; part of the Ministry of the Economy and Finance; in charge of regulation, restructuring and privatization of state enterprises; Dir Abdelaziz Talbi.

Office National des Hydrocarbures et des Mines (ONHYM): 5 ave Moulay Hassan, BP 99, 10050 Rabat; tel. (3) 7239898; fax (3) 7709411; e-mail benkhadra@onhym.com; internet www.onhym.com; f. 2003 to succeed Bureau de Recherches et de Participations Minières and Office National de Recherches et d'Exploitations Pétrolières; state agency conducting exploration, valorization and exploitation of hydrocarbons and mineral resources; Dir-Gen. Amina Benkhadra.

Société de Gestion des Terres Agricoles (SOGETA): 35 rue Daïet-Erroumi, BP 731, Agdal, Rabat; tel. (3) 7772778; fax (3) 7772765; f. 1973; oversees use of agricultural land; Man. Dir Bachir Saoud.

DEVELOPMENT ORGANIZATIONS

Agence National pour la Promotion de Petite et Moyenne Entreprise (ANPME): 10 rue Gandhi, BP 211, 10001 Rabat; tel. (3) 7708460; fax (3) 7707695; e-mail anpme@anpme.ma; internet www.anpme.ma; f. 1973 as the Office pour le Développement Industriel; name changed as above in 2002; state agency to develop industry; Dir-Gen. Latifa Echihabi.

Caisse de Dépôt et de Gestion: pl. Moulay el-Hassan, BP 408, 10001 Rabat; tel. (3) 7765520; fax (3) 7763849; internet www.cdg.ma; f. 1959; finances small-scale projects; Dir-Gen. Mustapha Bakkouri; Sec.-Gen. Hassan Boubrik.

Caisse Marocaine des Marchés (Marketing Fund): Résidence el-Manar, 52 blvd Abd al-Moumen, 20100 Casablanca; tel. (2) 2259118; fax (2) 2252316; e-mail y.chraibi@cmm.ma; internet www.cmm.ma; f. 1950; cap. 10m. dirhams; Man. Hassan Kissi.

Société de Développement Agricole (SODEA): ave Hadj Ahmed Cherkaoui, BP 6280, Rabat; tel. (3) 7770825; fax (3) 7774798; internet www.sodea.com; f. 1972; state agricultural devt org.; Man. Dir Ahmed Hajjaji.

Société Nationale d'Investissement (SNI): 60 rue d'Alger, BP 38, 20000 Casablanca; tel. (2) 2224102; fax (2) 2484303; f. 1966; transferred to majority private ownership in 1994; cap. 10,900m. dirhams; Pres. Hassan Bouhemou; Sec.-Gen. Saâd Bendidi.

CHAMBERS OF COMMERCE

Fédération des Chambres de Commerce et d'Industrie du Maroc (FCCIM): 6 rue d'Erfoud, BP 218, Hassan, Rabat; tel. (3) 7767078; fax (3) 7767076; f. 1962; groups the 28 Chambers of Commerce and Industry; Pres. Driss Houat; Dir-Gen. Muhammad Larbi el-Harras.

Chambre de Commerce, d'Industrie et de Services de la Wilaya de Rabat-Salé: 1 rue Gandhi, BP 131, Rabat; tel. (3) 7706442; fax (3) 7706768; e-mail ccisrs@ccisrs.org.ma; Pres. Omar Derraji; Dir Mounji Zniber.

Chambre de Commerce, d'Industrie et de Services de la Wilaya du Grand Casablanca: 98 blvd Muhammad V, BP 423, Casablanca; tel. (2) 2264327; fax (2) 2268436; Pres. Lahcen el-Wafi.

INDUSTRIAL AND TRADE ASSOCIATIONS

Office National Interprofessionnel des Céréales et des Légumineuses (ONICL): 3 ave Moulay Hassan, BP 154, Rabat; tel. (3) 7217300; fax (3) 7709626; e-mail directeur@onicl.org.ma; internet www.onicl.org.ma; f. 1937; Dir-Gen. Abdellatif Guedira.

Office National des Pêches: 15 rue Lieutenant Mahroud, BP 16243, 20300 Casablanca; tel. (2) 2242084; fax (2) 2242305; e-mail onp@onp.co.ma; internet www.onp.co.ma; f. 1969; state fishing org.; Man. Dir Majid Kaissar el-Ghaib.

MOROCCO

EMPLOYERS' ORGANIZATIONS

Association Marocaine des Exporteurs (ASMEX): 36B blvd Anfa, Casablanca; tel. (2) 2261033; fax (2) 2484191; e-mail asmex@asmex.org; internet www.asmex.org; f. 1982; Pres. ABDELLATIF BEN MADANI.

Association Marocaine des Industries Textiles et de l'Habillement (AMITH): 92 blvd Moulay Rachid, Casablanca; tel. (2) 2942085; fax (2) 2940587; e-mail mtazi@amith.org.ma/amith; internet www.textile.org.ma; f. 1958; 700 mems; textile, knitwear and ready-made garment manufacturers; Pres. MUHAMMAD TAMER; Dir-Gen. MUHAMMAD TAZI.

Association des Producteurs d'Agrumes du Maroc (ASPAM): 283 blvd Zerktouni, Casablanca; tel. (2) 2363946; fax (2) 2364041; f. 1958; links Moroccan citrus growers; has its own processing plants; Pres. LYOUSSI HASSAN.

Association Professionnelle des Agents Maritimes, Consignataires de Navires, et Courtiers d'Affrètement du Maroc (APRAM): 219 blvd des Forces Armées Royales, 5ème étage, 20000 Casablanca; tel. (2) 2541112; fax (2) 2541415; e-mail apram@wanadoopro.ma; internet www.apram.ma; f. 1999; 37 mems; Pres. ABDELAZIZ MANTRANCH.

Association Professionnelle des Cimentiers (APC): 239 blvd Moulay Ismaïl, Casablanca; tel. (2) 2401342; fax (2) 2248208; internet www.apc.ma; 4 mems; cement manufacturers; Pres. MUHAMMAD CHAIBI.

Confédération Générale des Entreprises du Maroc (CGEM): angle ave des Forces Armées Royales et rue Muhammad Errachid, 20100 Casablanca; tel. (2) 2997000; fax (2) 2983971; e-mail cgem@cgem.ma; internet www.cgem.ma; 25 affiliated feds; Pres. MOULAY HAFID ELALAMY.

UTILITIES

Electricity and Water

Office National de l'Eau Potable (ONEP): Station de Traitement ONEP, ave Muhammad Belhassan El Ouazzani, BP 10002 Rabat-Chellah, Rabat; tel. (3) 7759600; fax (3) 7759106; e-mail onepbo@onep.ma; internet www.onep.org.ma; f. 1972; responsible for drinking-water supply; Dir ALI FASSI-FIHRI.

Office National de l'Electricité (ONE): 65 rue Othman ben Affan, BP 13498, 20001 Casablanca; tel. (2) 2668080; fax (2) 2220038; e-mail offelec@one.org.ma; internet www.one.org.ma; f. 1963; state electricity authority; Dir-Gen. YOUNÈS MAÂMAR.

Gas

Afriquia Gaz: 139 blvd Moulay Ismail, Aïn Sebaâ, Casablanca; tel. (2) 2352144; fax (2) 2352239; e-mail r.idrissi@akwagroup.com; internet www.akwagroup.com; f. 1992; Morocco's leading gas distributor; Pres. ALI WAKRIM; Dir-Gen. TAWFIK HAMOUMI.

TRADE UNIONS

Confédération Démocratique du Travail (CDT): 64 rue al-Mourtada, Quartier Palmier, BP 13576, Casablanca; tel. (2) 2994470; fax (2) 2994473; e-mail cdtmaroc@cdt.ma; internet www.cdt.ma; f. 1978; Sec.-Gen. NOUBIR EL-AMAOUI.

Fédération Démocratique du Travail (FDT): 12 rue Muhammad Diouri, Sidi Belyoute, Casablanca; tel. (2) 2446362; fax (2) 2444764; internet www.fdt.ma; f. 2003 by fmr mems of CDT associated with USFP; Sec.-Gen. TAYEB MOUNCHID.

Union Générale des Travailleurs du Maroc (UGTM): 9 rue du Rif, blvd Muhammad VI, Casablanca; tel. (2) 2281788; fax (2) 2282144; e-mail info@ugtm.ma; internet www.ugtm.ma; f. 1960; associated with Istiqlal; supported by unions not affiliated to UMT; Sec.-Gen. MUHAMMAD BENJELLOUN ANDALOUSSI.

Union Marocaine du Travail (UMT): Bourse du Travail, 232 ave des Forces Armées Royales, Casablanca; tel. (2) 2302292; fax (2) 2307854; f. 1955; left-wing; most unions are affiliated; Sec. MAHJOUB BENSEDDIQ.

Union Nationale du Travail du Maroc (UNTM): 352 ave Muhammad V, immeuble Saâda, Rabat; tel. (3) 7793196; fax (3) 7263546; f. 1976; Islamist, associated with the PJD; Sec.-Gen. MUHAMMAD YATIM.

Transport

Société Nationale des Transports et de la Logistique (SNTL): rue al-Fadila, Quartier Industriel, BP 114, Chellah, Rabat; tel. (3) 7289300; fax (3) 7797850; internet www.sntl.ma; f. 1958; Dir-Gen. MUHAMMAD LAHBIB EL-GUEDDARI.

RAILWAYS

In 2005 there were 1,907 km of railways, of which 418 km were double track; 1,022 km of lines were electrified and diesel locomotives were used on the rest. In that year the network carried some 18.5m. passengers and 32.7m. metric tons of freight. All services are nationalized. A feasibility study took place in 1998 into the construction of a 28-km metro system in Casablanca. In 2007 another feasibility study was begun into plans for a 40-km railway tunnel under the Straits of Gibraltar linking Morocco and Spain.

Office National des Chemins de Fer (ONCF): 8 bis rue Abderrahmane el-Ghafiki, Rabat-Agdal; tel. (3) 7774747; fax (3) 7774480; e-mail ketary@oncf.ma; internet www.oncf.ma; f. 1963; administers all Morocco's railways; Dir-Gen. MUHAMMAD RABIE KHLIE.

ROADS

In 2004 there were 57,493 km of classified roads, of which 56.9% were paved. The motorway network covered 640 km in 2007, and was due to be extended to 1,420 km by 2010.

Autoroutes du Maroc (ADM): Hay Riad, Rabat; tel. (3) 7711056; fax (3) 7711059; e-mail naitbrahim.ismail@adm.co.ma; internet www.adm.co.ma; responsible for the construction and upkeep of Morocco's motorway network.

Compagnie de Transports au Maroc (CTM—SA): km 13.5, autoroute Casablanca–Rabat, Casablanca; tel. (2) 2762100; fax (2) 2765428; e-mail webmaster@ctm.co.ma; internet www.ctm.co.ma; agencies in Tangier, Rabat, Meknès, Oujda, Marrakesh, Agadir, El Jadida, Safi, Casablanca, Essaouira, Fez and Ouarzazate; privatized in 1993, with 40% of shares reserved for Moroccan citizens; Pres. and Dir-Gen. MUHAMMAD BOUDA.

SHIPPING

According to official figures, Morocco's 21 ports handled 61.5m. metric tons of goods in 2004. The most important ports, in terms of the volume of goods handled, are Casablanca, Jorf Lasfar, Safi and Mohammadia. Tangier is the principal port for passenger services. Construction work on new ports at Tangier (to handle merchandise traffic) and Agadir commenced in 2000.

Office d'Exploitation des Ports (ODEP): 175 blvd Muhammad Zerktouni, 20100 Casablanca; tel. (2) 2232324; fax (2) 2232325; e-mail administrateur@odep.org.ma; internet www.odep.org.ma; f. 1985; port management and handling of port equipment; Gen. Man. MUSTAPHA BARROUG.

Principal Shipping Companies

Agence Med SARL: 3 rue ibn Rochd, 90000 Tangier; tel. (3) 9935875; fax (3) 9933239; e-mail agencemed@menara.ma; f. 1904; owned by the Bland Group; also at Agadir, Casablanca, Jorf Lasfar, Nador and Safi; Operations Man. MUHAMMAD CHATT.

Compagnie Chérifienne d'Armement: 5 blvd Abdallah ben Yacine, 21700 Casablanca; tel. (2) 2309455; fax (2) 2301186; f. 1929; regular services to Europe; Man. Dir MAX KADOCH.

Compagnie Marocaine d'Agences Maritimes (COMARINE): 45 ave des Forces Armées Royales, BP 60, 20000 Casablanca; tel. (2) 2548510; fax (2) 2548570; e-mail comarine@comarine.co.ma.

Compagnie Marocaine de Navigation (COMANAV): 7 blvd de la Résistance, BP 628, Casablanca 20300; tel. (2) 2303012; fax (2) 2308455; e-mail comanav@comanav.co.ma; internet www.comanav.ma; f. 1946 as Cie Franco-Chérifienne de Navigation; name changed as above in 1959; privatization pending; regular services to Mediterranean, North-west European, Middle Eastern and West African ports; tramping; Pres. and Dir-Gen. TOUFIQ IBRAHIMI; Sec.-Gen. MEHDI BELGHITI; 12 agencies.

Intercona SA: 7 rue Hariri, 4ème étage, Tangier; tel. (3) 9945907; fax (3) 9945909; e-mail intercona-sa@menara.ma; f. 1943; daily services from Algeciras (Spain) to Tangier and Ceuta (Spanish North Africa); Pres. VICENTE JORRO.

Limadet-ferry: 3 rue ibn Rochd, Tangier; tel. (3) 933639; fax (3) 937173; e-mail headoffice@limadet.com; f. 1966; daily services between Algeciras (Spain) and Tangier; Dir-Gen. RACHID BEN MANSOUR.

Société Marocaine de Navigation Atlas: 81 ave Houmane el-Fatouaki, 21000 Casablanca; tel. (2) 2224190; fax (2) 2200164; e-mail atlas@marbar.co.ma; f. 1976; Chair. HASSAN CHAMI; Man. Dir MUHAMMAD SLAOUI.

Union Maritime Maroc-Scandinave (UNIMAR): 12 rue de Foucauld, BP 746, Casablanca; tel. (2) 2279590; fax (2) 2223883; f. 1974; chemicals; Dir-Gen. ABD AL-WAHAB BEN KIRANE.

Voyages Paquet: 65 ave des Forces Armées Royales, 20000 Casablanca; tel. (2) 2761941; fax (2) 2442108; f. 1970; Pres. MUHAMMAD ELOUALI ELALAMI; Dir-Gen. NAÏMA BAKALI ELOUALI ELALAMI.

CIVIL AVIATION

The main international airports are at Casablanca (King Muhammad V), Rabat, Tangier, Marrakesh, Agadir Inezgane, Fez, Oujda, Al-Hocima, el-Aaiún, Ouarzazate, Agadir al-Massira and Nador. The completion of a second runway at King Muhammad V airport was followed by the inauguration, in September 2007, of a second terminal, which increased the airport's annual passenger capacity from 5m. to 11m.

Atlas Blue: Aéroport Marrakesh Ménara, BP 440, Medina, Marrakesh; fax (2) 44424222; e-mail contact@atlas-blue.com; internet www.atlas-blue.com; f. 2004; wholly owned by Royal Air Maroc (RAM); low-cost airline; domestic flights and services to six European countries; Chair ZOUHAIR MUHAMMAD EL-AOUFIR.

Office Nationale des Aéroports: Siège Social Nouasseur, BP 8101, Casablanca; tel. (2) 2539040; fax (2) 2539901; e-mail onda@onda.ma; internet www.onda.ma; f. 1990; Dir-Gen. MUHAMMAD NOURI.

Regional Air Lines: Aéroport de Muhammad V, BP 83, 20240 Casablanca; tel. (2) 2538020; fax (2) 2538411; e-mail customer-service@regionalmaroc.com; internet www.regionalmaroc.com; f. 1997; privately owned; domestic flights and services to southern Spain, Portugal and the Canary Islands; Pres. MUHAMMAD HASSAN BENSALAH; CEO HICHAM NECHAD.

Royal Air Maroc (RAM): Aéroport de Casablanca-Anfa; tel. (2) 2912000; fax (2) 2912087; e-mail callcenter@royalairmaroc.com; internet www.royalairmaroc.com; f. 1953; 94.4% state-owned; scheduled for partial privatization; domestic flights and services to countries in Western Europe, Scandinavia, the Americas, North and West Africa, the Canary Islands and the Middle East; CEO DRISS BENHIMA.

Tourism

Tourism is Morocco's second main source of convertible currency. The country's tourist attractions include its sunny climate, ancient sites (notably the cities of Fez, Marrakesh, Meknès and Rabat) and spectacular scenery. There are popular holiday resorts on the Atlantic and Mediterranean coasts. In 2006 foreign tourist arrivals totalled 3.79m., compared with 1.63m. in 1996. Tourism receipts, including passenger transport, totalled US $3,369m. in 2003.

Office National Marocain du Tourisme: 31 angle ave al-Abtal et rue Oued Fès, Agdal, Rabat; tel. (3) 7674013; fax (3) 7674015; e-mail website@onmt.org.ma; internet www.tourisme-marocain.com/onmt; f. 1918; Dir-Gen. FATHIA BENNIS.

MOZAMBIQUE

Introductory Survey

Location, Climate, Language, Religion, Flag, Capital

The Republic of Mozambique lies on the east coast of Africa, bordered to the north by Tanzania, to the west by Malawi, Zambia and Zimbabwe, and to the south by South Africa and Swaziland. The country has a coastline of about 2,470 km (1,535 miles) on the shores of the Indian Ocean, and is separated from Madagascar, to the east, by the Mozambique Channel. Except in a few upland areas, the climate varies from tropical to sub-tropical. Rainfall is irregular, but the rainy season is usually from November to March, when average temperatures in Maputo are between 26°C (79°F) and 30°C (86°F). In the cooler dry season, in June and July, the average temperatures are 18°C (64°F) to 20°C (68°F). Portuguese is the official language, while there are 39 indigenous languages, the most widely spoken being Makhuwa, Tsonga, Sema and Lomwe. Many of the inhabitants follow traditional beliefs. There are about 5m. Christians, the majority of whom are Roman Catholics, and 4m. Muslims. The national flag (proportions 2 by 3) has three equal horizontal stripes, of green, black and yellow, separated by narrow white stripes. At the hoist is a red triangle containing a five-pointed yellow star, on which are superimposed an open book, a hoe and a rifle. The capital is Maputo (formerly Lourenço Marques).

Recent History

Mozambique became a Portuguese colony in the 19th century and an overseas province in 1951. Nationalist groups began to form in the 1960s. The Frente de Libertação de Moçambique (Frelimo—Mozambique Liberation Front) was formed in 1962 and launched a military campaign for independence in 1964. After the coup in Portugal (q.v.) in April 1974, negotiations between Frelimo and the new Portuguese Government resulted in a period of rule in Mozambique by a transitional Government, followed by full independence on 25 June 1975. The leader of Frelimo, Samora Machel, became the first President of Mozambique. Between September and December 1977 elections took place to local, district and provincial assemblies and, at national level, to the Assembléia Popular (People's Assembly).

In March 1976 Mozambique closed its border with Rhodesia (now Zimbabwe) and applied economic sanctions against that country. Mozambique was the principal base for Rhodesian nationalist guerrillas, and consequently suffered considerable devastation as a result of offensives launched by Rhodesian government forces against guerrilla camps. The border was reopened in January 1980.

After Zimbabwean independence in April 1980, South Africa adopted Rhodesia's role as supporter of the Mozambican opposition guerrilla group, Resistência Nacional Moçambicana (Renamo), also known as the Movimento Nacional da Resistência de Moçambique. The activities of Renamo subsequently increased, causing persistent disruption to road, rail and petroleum pipeline links from Mozambican ports, which were vital to the economic independence of southern African nations from South Africa. In March 1984 Mozambique and South Africa signed a formal joint non-aggression pact, known as the Nkomati accord, whereby each Government undertook to prevent opposition forces on its territory from launching attacks against the other, and a Joint Security Commission was established. The accord effectively implied that South Africa would withdraw its covert support for Renamo in return for a guarantee by Mozambique that it would prevent any further use of its territory by the then banned African National Congress of South Africa (ANC). However, following an intensification of Renamo activity, in 1985 the Frelimo Government appealed to foreign powers for increased military assistance, and in June it was agreed that Zimbabwe would augment its military presence in Mozambique. A major military offensive against Renamo in July resulted in the capture, in August, of the rebels' national operational command centre. Mozambique subsequently alleged that South Africa had repeatedly violated the Nkomati accord by providing material support for the rebels. The Joint Security Commission ceased to meet in 1985.

General elections were scheduled to take place in 1982, but were postponed several times because of the security situation. Legislative elections eventually began in August 1986, but were delayed, owing to the internal conflict. The post of Prime Minister was created in July and allocated to Mário Machungo. President Machel died in an air crash in South Africa in October. The causes of the incident were unclear, and the Mozambican Ministry of Information declared that it did not exclude the possibility of South African sabotage. (In May 1998 it was announced that South Africa's Truth and Reconciliation Commission—TRC—was to examine evidence relating to the crash. The TRC final report stated that the evidence was inconclusive, but a number of questions merited further investigation. In early 2006 the South African Government announced that it was to reopen the inquiry into Machel's death.) In November 1986 the Central Committee of Frelimo appointed Joaquim Alberto Chissano, hitherto Minister for Foreign Affairs, as President. The elections were then resumed. In contrast to the 1977 elections, the voters were given a choice of candidates; nevertheless, all government and party leaders had been re-elected when the poll was completed in December 1986.

In June 1988, following six months of negotiations, Mozambique, South Africa and Portugal signed an agreement to rehabilitate the Cahora Bassa hydroelectric plant in Mozambique (potentially one of the greatest sources of electricity in southern Africa). In May Mozambican and South African officials had agreed to reactivate the Nkomati accord and to re-establish the Joint Security Commission; subsequently a joint commission for co-operation and development was established.

At Frelimo's fifth congress, held in July 1989, the party's exclusively Marxist-Leninist orientation was renounced, and party membership was opened to Mozambicans from all sectors of society. In January 1990 Chissano announced the drafting of a new constitution.

In mid-1989 Presidents Daniel arap Moi of Kenya and Robert Mugabe of Zimbabwe agreed to mediate between the Mozambique Government and Renamo. In August Renamo rejected the Government's peace proposals, and demanded recognition as a political entity, the introduction of multi-party elections and the withdrawal of Zimbabwean troops from Mozambique as preconditions for peace. However, further talks between the Government and the rebels resulted in an agreement, in December 1990, for a partial cease-fire. Under the terms of the agreement, all Zimbabwean troops present in Mozambique were required to retire to the Beira and Limpopo transport 'corridors' linking Zimbabwe to the Mozambican ports of Beira and Maputo. The cease-fire was confined to these areas.

The agreement followed the introduction, on 30 November 1990, of a new Mozambican Constitution, formally ending Frelimo's single-party rule and committing the State to political pluralism and a free-market economy, and enshrining private property rights and guarantees of press freedom. The official name of the country was changed from the People's Republic of Mozambique to the Republic of Mozambique. Renamo refused to recognize the new Constitution, declaring that it had been drafted without democratic consultation. The President was henceforth to be elected by direct universal suffrage, and the legislature was renamed the Assembléia da República (Assembly of the Republic). A new law concerning the formation, structure and function of political parties came into effect in February 1991. In accordance with the Constitution, Renamo would not be recognized as a legitimate political party until it had renounced violence completely.

In December 1990 negotiations between the Government and Renamo resumed in Rome, Italy, and a Joint Verification Commission, comprising independent representatives from 10 nations, in addition to those of the Mozambican Government and Renamo, was established to monitor the partial cease-fire. Further talks took place in Rome in January 1991, but collapsed following the presentation of a report by the Joint Verification Commission containing accusations that Renamo had violated the cease-fire agreement, and did not resume until May.

In October 1991 Renamo and the Government signed a protocol agreeing fundamental principles and containing a set of mutual guarantees as a basis for a peace accord. Throughout the discussions Renamo continued guerrilla attacks, many of which were launched (despite the Nkomati accord) from South Africa. Under the terms of the protocol, Renamo effectively recognized the legitimacy of the Government and agreed to enter the multi-party political framework. In return, the Government pledged not to legislate on any of the points under negotiation in Rome until a general peace accord had been signed. In November a second protocol was signed by both parties, enabling Renamo to begin functioning as a political party immediately after the signing of a general peace accord.

In March 1992, following discussions conducted in Rome, a third protocol was signed establishing the principles for the country's future electoral system. Under its terms, the elections, to be held under a system of proportional representation, were to be supervised by international observers. An electoral commission was to be established, with one-third of its members to be appointed by Renamo. On 7 August, following three days of discussions in Rome, Chissano and the Renamo leader, Afonso Macacho Marceta Dhlakama, signed a joint declaration committing the two sides to a total cease-fire by 1 October, as part of an Acordo Geral de Paz (General Peace Agreement—AGP). In September Chissano and Dhlakama met in Gaborone, Botswana, to attempt to resolve the deadlocked military and security issues. Chissano offered to establish an independent commission to monitor and guarantee the impartiality of the Serviço de Informação e Segurança do Estado (SISE—State Information and Security Service). In addition, the figure of 30,000 was agreed upon as the number of troops to comprise the joint national defence force.

The AGP was finally signed on 4 October 1992. Under the terms of the agreement, a general cease-fire was to come into force immediately after ratification of the treaty by the legislature. Both the Renamo troops and the government forces were to withdraw to assembly points within seven days of ratification. The new national defence force, the Forças Armadas de Defesa de Moçambique (FADM), would then be created, drawing on equal numbers from each side, with the remaining troops surrendering their weapons to a UN peace-keeping force within six months. A Cease-fire Commission, incorporating representatives from the Government, Renamo and the UN, was to be established to assume responsibility for supervising the implementation of the truce regulations. Overall political control of the peace process was to be vested in a Comissão de Supervisão e Controle (CSC—Supervision and Control Commission), comprising representatives of the Government, Renamo and the UN. In addition, Chissano was to appoint a Comissão Nacional de Informação (National Information Commission—COMINFO), with responsibilities including supervision of the SISE. Presidential and legislative elections were to take place, under UN supervision, one year after the signing of the AGP, provided that it had been fully implemented and the demobilization process completed. The AGP was duly ratified by the Assembléia da República and came into force on 15 October. On that day UN observers arrived in Maputo to supervise the first phase of the cease-fire. However, shortly afterwards the Government accused Renamo of systematically violating the accord. Dhlakama subsequently claimed that Renamo's actions had been defensive manoeuvres and, in turn, accused government forces of violating the accord by advancing into Renamo territory.

In November 1992, owing to considerable delays in the formation of the various peace commissions envisaged in the AGP, the timetable for the cease-fire operations was redrafted. In December the UN Security Council finally approved a plan for the establishment of the UN Operation in Mozambique (ONUMOZ), providing for the deployment of some 7,500 troops, police and civilian observers to oversee the process of demobilization and formation of the FADM, and to supervise the forthcoming elections. However, there were continued delays in the deployment of ONUMOZ. In March the peace process was effectively halted when Renamo withdrew from the CSC and the Cease-fire Commission, protesting that proper provisions had not been made to accommodate its officials, and in April Dhlakama announced that his forces would begin to report to assembly points only when Renamo received US $15m. to finance its transition into a political party. Meanwhile, the first UN troops became operational on 1 April.

In June 1993 Renamo rejoined the CSC. The commission subsequently agreed to a formal postponement of the election date to October 1994. A meeting in Maputo of international aid donors, also in June 1993, produced promises of additional support for the peace process, bringing the total pledged by donors to US $520m., including support for the repatriation of 1.5m. refugees from neighbouring countries, the resettlement of 4m.–5m. displaced people and the reintegration of some 80,000 former combatants into civilian life. The UN also agreed to establish a trust fund of $10m. to finance Renamo's transformation into a political party, with the disbursement of funds dependent on UN approval.

Renamo announced new preconditions to the advancement of the peace process in July 1993, insisting initially on the recognition of its own administration, to operate parallel to that of the Government, and later on the appointment of its members to five of the country's 11 provincial governorships. Under the terms of an agreement signed in September, Renamo was to appoint three advisers to each of the incumbent provincial governors to make recommendations relating to the reintegration of areas under Renamo control into a single state administration. In October 1993 the CSC approved a new timetable covering all aspects of the peace process, including the elections in October 1994. In November 1993 the UN Security Council renewed the mandate of ONUMOZ for a further six months. In addition, it acceded to the joint request by the Government and Renamo for a UN police corps. In the same month consensus was finally reached on the text of the electoral law, which was promulgated at the end of December. At a meeting of the CSC in mid-November an agreement was signed providing for the confinement of troops, to be concluded by the end of the year.

In February 1994 the UN Security Council announced that, in response to demands made by Renamo, it would be increasing the membership of the UN police corps monitoring the confinement areas from 128 to 1,144. By the end of February only 50% of troops had entered designated assembly points, and none had officially been demobilized. In March, in an effort to expedite the confinement process, the Government announced that it was to commence the unilateral demobilization of its troops. Renamo began the demobilization of its troops shortly afterwards. In April Lt-Gen. Lagos Lidimo, the nominee of the Government, and the former Renamo guerrilla commander, Lt-Gen. Mateus Ngonhamo, were inaugurated as the high command of the FADM. In the same month Chissano issued a decree scheduling the presidential and legislative elections for 27–28 October, and in May the UN Security Council renewed the mandate of ONUMOZ for the final period, ending on 15 November.

On 16 August 1994, in accordance with the provisions of the AGP, the government Forças Armadas de Moçambique were formally dissolved and their assets transferred to the FADM, which was inaugurated as the country's official armed forces on the same day. In December the Cease-fire Commission issued its final report, according to which ONUMOZ had registered a combined total of 91,691 government and Renamo troops during the confinement process, of whom 11,579 had enlisted in the FADM (compared with the 30,000 envisaged in the AGP).

In August 1994 Renamo formally registered as a political party. In the same month the Partido Liberal e Democrático de Moçambique, the Partido Nacional Democrático and the Partido Nacional de Moçambique formed an electoral coalition, the União Democrática (UD). The presidential and legislative elections took place on 27–29 October. The extension of voting to a third day had become necessary following the withdrawal of Renamo from the elections only hours before the beginning of the poll, claiming that conditions were not in place to ensure free and fair elections. However, following concerted international pressure, Renamo abandoned its boycott after the first day. In the presidential election Chissano secured an outright majority (53.3%) of the votes. His closest rival was Dhlakama, who received 33.7% of the votes. In the legislative elections Frelimo also secured an overall majority, winning 129 of the 250 seats in the Assembléia da República; Renamo obtained 112 seats, and the UD the remaining nine. Later in November the UN Security Council extended the mandate of ONUMOZ until the end of January 1995.

Chissano was inaugurated as President on 9 December 1994, and the new Government, in which all portfolios were assigned to members of Frelimo, was sworn in on 23 December. Demands by Renamo that it be awarded governorships in the five provinces where it won a majority of the votes in the legislative elections were rejected by Chissano. At the first session of the new legislature, which began on 8 December, a dispute resulted in the withdrawal of the Renamo and UD deputies, although both groups abandoned their boycott by the end of December.

By the end of March 1995 only a small unit of ONUMOZ officials remained in the country. In February 1996 the Government proposed that municipal elections, which the Constitution stipulated must be conducted no later than October 1996, be held in 1997. Delays in the election process had resulted from a dispute between the parliamentary opposition, which demanded simultaneous local elections throughout Mozambique, and the Government, which sought to hold elections only in those areas that had attained municipal status. In October 1996 the Assembléia da República approved a constitutional amendment differentiating between municipalities and administrative posts. In August 1997 the Government postponed the elections until 1998, owing to delays in the disbursement by international donors of funding for the voter registration process. In January 1998 Renamo alleged that the voter registration process had been fraudulent, and threatened to boycott the elections unless a further registration of voters was conducted. In April Renamo was among 16 opposition parties that officially withdrew from the elections. Renamo subsequently campaigned vigorously to dissuade the electorate from participating in the ballot. At the elections, which took place on 30 June, Frelimo secured all the mayoral posts and won control of all the municipal authorities contested. Very few opposition parties contested the election, and Frelimo's main competition came from independent candidates. Moreover, the voter turn-out was only 14.6%, prompting Renamo to demand the annulment of the elections.

Under the Constitution, presidential and legislative elections were to take place by November 1999. However, political disputes and administrative delays threatened to force a postponement of the elections. A principal cause of the delay was Renamo's insistence on the need to re-register the entire electorate. In June Frelimo announced that Chissano would stand as its presidential candidate. In the following month 11 opposition parties, led by Renamo, signed an agreement to contest the forthcoming elections as a coalition, styled Renamo—União Eleitoral (Renamo—UE). The coalition was to present a single list of legislative candidates, with Dhlakama as its presidential candidate.

Presidential and legislative elections took place on 3–5 December 1999. In the presidential contest, Chissano defeated Dhlakama (his sole challenger), taking 52.3% of the valid votes cast. Frelimo secured an outright majority in the legislative elections, winning 133 of the 250 seats in the Assembléia da República; Renamo—UE obtained the remaining seats. Renamo rejected the outcome, claiming that the vote had been fraudulent. However, international monitors declared that the vote had been free and fair. In January 2000 the Supreme Court—exercising the functions of the Constitutional Council, which had yet to be established—rejected the appeal by Renamo against the results of the elections. On 15 January Chissano was sworn in for a further five-year presidential term. Renamo boycotted the election of the new Comissão Nacional de Eleições (CNE—National Elections Commission), officially inaugurated in July, on the grounds that it did not recognise the legitimacy of the current Government, and that a review of the current electoral law was needed. Frelimo appointed eight representatives to the 15-member CNE.

In November 2000 one of the country's most influential journalists, Carlos Cardoso, was killed in Maputo. It was alleged by Dhlakama that Cardoso had been murdered as a result of an article, published in his newspaper Metical, in which he had criticized the Government's involvement in protests over the 1999 election earlier in November 2000; however, it was announced in March 2001 that three people, including the former manager of a branch of the Banco Comercial de Moçambique—BCM, had been arrested in connection with Cardoso's murder; shortly before his death Cardoso had apparently uncovered details relating to the theft of some 144,000m. meticais from a branch of the BCM in 1996.

In late December 2000 Dhlakama and Chissano held talks (the first since the disputed election of December 1999) in an attempt to resolve the growing tension between their two parties. The two leaders agreed to hold further talks in 2001, and to establish inquiries into the violence of November 2000. Moreover, Dhlakama stated that he was prepared to accept the results of the 1999 elections, and Chissano pledged to consult Renamo about future state appointments. However, comments by Dhlakama, accusing Frelimo of violence and intimidation towards Renamo, subsequently jeopardized the future of talks between the two parties. In a second meeting between the two leaders in January 2001 it was agreed that a number of working groups (including groups on defence and security, constitutional and parliamentary affairs, and the media) would be established in February. At a further meeting, in March, Chissano referred Dhlakama's demand for the appointment of Renamo state governors to the Assembléia da República, whose Frelimo representatives were strongly opposed to accommodating Renamo demands. In protest, Dhlakama ceased negotiations in April.

President Chissano announced in May 2001 that he would not stand for re-election on the expiry of his term in 2004. At the long-postponed Renamo congress, held in October 2001, Dhlakama was re-elected party President, obtaining over 95% of votes cast; Joaquim Vaz was elected Secretary-General. The holding of a party congress by Renamo for the first time since the end of the civil war, as well as the establishment of a 10-member Political Committee, were regarded as confirmation of the movement's decision to establish itself as a full political party, and to decentralize the party leadership and structure.

In June 2002, at the party's eighth congress, Frelimo elected Armando Guebuza as its Secretary-General, and thus also its candidate for the 2004 presidential election. During July Renamo's attempt to establish itself as a legitimate opposition party was threatened after Dhlakama dismissed Vaz as Secretary-General, assuming the position himself, and dissolved the party's Political Committee. In October Renamo announced its intention to contest municipal elections (due in 2003) alone, rather than in coalition, while in November 2002 the party regained some stability with the appointment of Viana Magalhaes as Secretary-General. In December, however, further controversy arose when Renamo demanded the exclusion from the Assembléia da República of five deputies who had resigned or been expelled from the party, including Raul Domingos, formerly a senior member of Renamo, who had been expelled from the party in 2000. Renamo protesters caused an estimated US $11,000 of damage to the Assembléia. The former Renamo deputies retained their right to participate in the Assembléia.

Meanwhile, in November 2002, during the trial of six men for Cardoso's murder in 2000, President Chissano's eldest son, Nyimpine Chissano, was accused by three of the defendants of having ordered or paid for the assassination; Nyimpine Chissano denied any involvement in the murder. It was additionally claimed that one of the accused, Aníbal António dos Santos, who had escaped from custody in suspicious circumstances at the beginning of September, was making secret threats against key figures in the trial. In January 2003 all six accused were found guilty of Cardoso's murder; dos Santos, who had been tried in absentia, was arrested in South Africa at the end of January, and extradited to Mozambique to serve a prison term of 28 years and six months. He escaped custody again in May 2004 but was subsequently arrested in Canada and extradited to Mozambique in January 2005. The Supreme Court ruled in December 2004 that he should be retried; dos Santos was sentenced to 30 years' imprisonment in January 2006. Nyimpine Chissano continued to deny any involvement in the murder. In June 2004 seven people, including three who were serving prison sentences for Cardoso's murder, were convicted of charges relating to the disappearance of funds from the BCM and were sentenced to terms of imprisonment.

In February 2003, in response to Renamo's decision to run alone in the municipal elections, 10 opposition parties announced the formation of a new coalition, the União Eleitoral, led by Domingos, who had previously announced his intention of standing as an independent in the presidential election. In October Domingos founded his own party, the Partido para a Paz, Democracia e Desenvolvimento (PPDD). From mid-2003 divisions became apparent within Frelimo between supporters of its presidential candidate, Guebuza, and Chissano loyalists. The Conselho Constitucional (Constitutional Council), which was to supervise elections and determine the constitutionality of new legislation, was inaugurated in early November, with Rui Baltazar dos Santos Alves as its first Chairman. Municipal elections were held on 19 November. Despite allegations by Renamo of irregularities, the elections proceeded smoothly, and their conduct was later commended by an observer mission from the European Union (EU, see p. 244), although voter turn-out, at 24.2%, was low. Frelimo won a majority in 29 municipalities, while Renamo won a majority in four, including Beira. The results were verified by the Constitutional Council in January 2004.

In mid-February 2004 Luísa Dias Diogo was appointed as Prime Minister, to replace Mocumbi, who resigned the premiership to take up an executive post in an EU-sponsored initiative specializing in clinical research. Diogo retained the responsibilities of Minister of Planning and Finance, the post she had held under Mocumbi.

By the deadline for submissions in October 2004, eight candidates, five of whom were subsequently approved by the Conselho Constitucional, had registered their intention to contest the presidential election. Three candidates were rejected on the grounds that they had not gathered the requisite 10,000 signatures to support their nominations. The five candidates were Guebuza, Dhlakama, Domingos, Yaqub Sabindy of the Partido Independente de Moçambique, reportedly an Islamist party (although the Constitution prohibited religious affiliations in political organizations), and Carlos Alexandre dos Reis, the leader of the União Nacional Moçambicana. A total of 25 political organizations and coalitions registered to contest the legislative elections, although there were serious misgivings regarding the credibility of a number of the parties. In mid-November the Assembléia da República approved changes to the Constitution, which were to take effect on the day following the declaration of the results of the elections. Notably, the President would no longer be afforded immunity from prosecution and a Council of State was to be created. It was also envisaged that elections to provincial assemblies, which were to mirror in structure those to the Assembléia, would take place in 2008. In March 2007 the Assembléia approved the first reading of legislation that was to govern the provincial elections. The first phase of voter registration for the provincial elections began in September, followed by a second that commenced in December; however, the process was hampered by severe flooding that affected the country in January 2008. Nevertheless, the registration of the electorate was scheduled to be completed by March, although the Assembléia enforced its right to extraordinary powers of amendment to the Constitution and altered the date for the holding of provincial elections to 2009; having been amended in 2004, under normal circumstances the Constitution should not have undergone further review for at least five years.

Meanwhile, the presidential and legislative elections took place as scheduled on 1–2 December 2004, and proceeded without notable incident, although 37 voting stations did not open, reportedly owing to bad weather. For the first time Mozambicans living abroad were able to vote. Although national and international observers stated that the elections had been generally free and fair, they did express concern at the lack of access that they had been granted to the counting process and about the low rate of voter participation, which was recorded at just 36.3%. Renamo, later joined by other opposition parties, announced that it would not recognize the results, due to alleged irregularities produced by the computer system used to tabulate the votes and demanded that the elections be rerun. Official results, which were released on 21 December, revealed that Guebuza had won 63.7% of the votes cast at the presidential election, while Dhlakama took 31.7% and Domingos 2.7%. In the legislative elections, Frelimo won 62.0% of the votes, securing 160 of the available 250 seats, while Renamo took 29.7% and 90 seats (a significant decline compared with the 117 seats it had won in the 1999 elections). No other party achieved the minimum of 5% of total votes cast required to secure parliamentary representation. Protests lodged by Renamo with the CNE and the Constitutional Council were rejected in January 2005, and Renamo announced that it would accept the election results and participate in the new legislature.

In mid-January 2005 the election results were approved by the Constitutional Council. The new Assembléia da República was inaugurated on 31 January, and Eduardo Mulémbue was re-elected to the post of Chairman. Guebuza was sworn in as President on 2 February and in his inauguration speech pledged to promote rural development and to take measures to combat corruption and poverty. The new Government, featuring a number of new appointees, was announced the following day. Diogo retained her position as Prime Minister; however, in a reorganization of ministerial functions, Manuel Chang became Minister of Finance, while Aiuba Cuereneia headed the newly created Ministry of Planning and Development. Alcinda Abreu was appointed Minister of Foreign Affairs and Co-operation, while José Pacheco became Minister of the Interior. In mid-February a further three ministers were appointed to the justice, science and technology and veterans' affairs portfolios. In March Chissano resigned as President of Frelimo and was replaced by Guebuza.

Meanwhile, in February 2005 it was reported that members of Dhlakama's guard, protesting against the non-payment of wages and poor living conditions, had taken five Renamo officials hostage. The following month the Government announced plans to integrate the guards (estimated to number 100–150), who had been maintained by Dhlakama as his personal guard following the end of the civil war in 1992, into the state security forces, however such attempts were consistently stalled by Dhlakama. In September 2005 conflict between Frelimo and Renamo supporters led to the deaths of 12 people in Mocímboa da Praia, in Cabo Delgado province, following a disputed by-election earlier in the year.

In November 2005 the Assembléia da República passed legislation providing for the formation of the Council of State, as envisaged in changes to the Constitution approved in late 2004. Members of the Council, including Dhlakama, were subsequently appointed by Guebuza and the Assembléia da República, and took office in late December 2005.

In December 2006 the Assembléia da República passed the final reading of amendments to the electoral legislation. Among the amendments were provisions for the restructuring of the CNE, which had been reduced in size to 13 members. Five members were henceforth to be nominated by the Assembléia in proportion to the number of seats held by each political party, while the remaining eight members were to be nominated by legally constituted civil society bodies. A 14th member was to be appointed by the Government, but would not have the right to vote. The procedure for voter registration was also amended with the electorate required to re-register every five years. Further changes to the election procedure included the abolition of the 5% 'barrier clause', whereby parties must secure at least 5% of votes cast in order to win seats in the Assembléia.

In February 2007 President Guebuza effected a minor reorganization of the Council of Ministers; the Minister of Agriculture, Tomás Mandlate, was dismissed and replaced by Erasmo Muhate, hitherto the Director of the Instituto de Algodão de Moçambique. In December Guebuza removed Muhate from office, replacing him with Soares Nhaca, who had previously served as Governor of Manica.

In March 2007 an explosion at a munitions storage facility in a residential area of Maputo resulted in the deaths of more than 100 people and left over 500 others injured. A commission of inquiry was established in April to investigate the incident. The Government admitted that it had been storing equipment since the end of the civil war and weapons experts were later deployed to dispose of obsolete military equipment. In June a munitions expert from South Africa was killed in an explosion whilst assisting with the destruction of unexploded missiles. A further explosion was reported in October, after which the Government agreed to relocate weapons stores away from residential areas.

In March 2008 Minister of National Defence Gen. (retd) Tobias Joaquim Dai was dismissed and replaced by Filipe Nhussi; no official reason was given for the change. Earlier that month President Guebuza effected a reorganization of the Council of Ministers in which Oldemiro Baloi replaced Alcinda Abreu as Minister of Foreign Affairs and Co-operation, the latter having been demoted to the role of Minister of Environmental Co-ordination. Maria Benvida Levy became Minister of Justice, while Paulo Zucula assumed responsibility for the transport and communications portfolio.

During 1995 the activities, principally in the border province of Manica, of a group of mainly Zimbabwean dissidents, known as Chimwenje, came under increasing scrutiny. The group, which was alleged to have links with Renamo, was believed to be preparing for military incursions into Zimbabwe, where it sought the overthrow of President Mugabe. In early 1996 the Chissano Government announced its intention to expel the dissidents from Mozambique. In June, following a series of armed attacks on both sides of the Mozambique–Zimbabwe border, which were believed to have been perpetrated by Chimwenje, the Governments of Mozambique and Zimbabwe agreed to combine and intensify efforts to combat the activities of the dissidents. The group was suppressed in late 1996. During late 2002 and early 2003 Mozambique resettled a number of white Zimbabwean farmers whose land had been appropriated by the Mugabe regime.

After stepping down as President following the election of December 2004, Chissano increasingly took on an international role. In mid-2005, as the UN Secretary-General's special envoy, he monitored the presidential election in Guinea-Bissau, while in August he was appointed mediator for the African Union (see p. 164) in Zimbabwe.

After independence, Mozambique developed strong international links with the USSR and other countries of the communist

MOZAMBIQUE

Introductory Survey

bloc, and with neighbouring African states: it is a member of the Southern African Development Community (SADC, see p. 386), founded in 1979, as the Southern African Development Co-ordination Conference, then with the aim of reducing the region's economic dependence on South Africa, principally by developing trade routes through Mozambique. In December 1996 Mozambique, Malawi, Zambia and Zimbabwe (also SADC members) formally agreed to establish the Beira Development Corridor as a trading route avoiding South Africa's ports. In 1993 full diplomatic relations were established with South Africa. In July 1994 Mozambique and South Africa established a new Joint Defence and Security Commission, replacing the Joint Security Commission originally established in 1984. In November 1995 Mozambique was admitted, by special dispensation, as a full member of the Commonwealth (see p. 206). In 2006 Mozambique was admitted as an observer member of the Organisation Internationale de la Francophonie (see p. 425).

Government

The Constitution of 30 November 1990 (amended in 1996 and 2004) provides for a multi-party political system. Legislative power is vested in the Assembléia da República, with 250 members, who are elected for a five-year term. Members are elected by universal, direct adult suffrage in a secret ballot, according to a system of proportional representation. The President of the Republic, who is Head of State, is directly elected for a five-year term; the President holds executive power and governs with the assistance of an appointed Council of Ministers. A Council of State advises the President, who, however, has no obligation to follow its advice. Provincial governors, appointed by the President, have overall responsibility for the functions of government within each of the 11 provinces. For the purposes of local government, Mozambique is divided into 33 municipalities. The 2004 amendments to the Constitution provided for the creation of provincial assemblies, scheduled to be elected in 2008.

Defence

As assessed at November 2007, total active armed forces were estimated at 11,200 (army 10,000, navy 200, air force 1,000). At that time Mozambican forces were deployed in two overseas peace-keeping missions. Military service is compulsory and lasts for two years. Expenditure on defence was budgeted at an estimated 1,480,000m. meticais in 2007.

Economic Affairs

In 2006, according to estimates by the World Bank, Mozambique's gross national income (GNI), measured at average 2004–06 prices, was US $6,924m., equivalent to $340 per head (or $1,220 per head on an international purchasing-power parity basis). During 1996–2006, it was estimated, the population increased at an average annual rate of 2.1%, while gross domestic product (GDP) per head increased, in real terms, by an average of 6.2% per year. Overall GDP increased, in real terms, at an average annual rate of 8.4% in 1996–2006; growth in 2006 was 8.5%.

Agriculture (including forestry and fishing) contributed 26.8% of GDP in 2006. In mid-2005 an estimated 79.9% of the economically active population were employed in the sector. Fishing is the principal export activity: fish, crustaceans and molluscs accounted for 9.2% of total export earnings in 2003. The principal cash crops are fruit and nuts, cotton, sugar cane and copra. After production fell sharply in the 1990s, the Government attempted to increase revenue from the cashew crop by promoting production and improving processing facilities. The main subsistence crop is cassava. During 1996–2006, according to official figures, agricultural GDP increased by an average of 5.7% per year. Growth in 2006 was 10.9%.

Industry (including mining, manufacturing, construction and power) employed 5.6% of the economically active population in 1997, and provided 21.6% of GDP in 2006. During 1996–2006, according to official figures, industrial GDP increased at an average annual rate of 16.9%; growth in 2006 was 9.1%.

Mining contributed 1.0% of GDP in 2006, and employed 0.5% of the economically active population in 1997. Only coal, bauxite, marble, gold and salt are exploited in significant quantities, although gravel and crushed rocks are also mined. In November 2004 the Companhia Vale do Rio Doce (Brazil) was granted a coal mining concession in Moatize; production was expected to begin in 2010. There are reserves of other minerals, including high-grade iron ore, precious and semi-precious stones, and natural gas. Plans began in 1994 to exploit natural gas reserves at Pande, in the province of Inhambane, which were estimated at 55,000m. cu m. A South African company, SASOL Ltd, was granted a 25-year concession to develop gasfields at Pande and Temane (also in Inhambane province); it was anticipated that the Government would receive revenues of some US $900m. from the project, and the construction of a pipeline to transport the gas to South Africa was completed in early 2004. A gas-processing centre opened in Temane in early 2004. In 2003 the Government announced that it was to invest $20m. in gas prospecting in Sofala province. In 1999 the largest reserve of titanium in the world (estimated at 100m. metric tons) was discovered in the district of Chibuto, in the province of Gaza; production from the Limpopo Corridor Sands Project in Chibuto was expected to begin in 2007 and last for some 35 years, providing up to 1m. tons of titanium per year. In mid-2007 the British company Pan African Resources plc was investigating the viability of developing a new gold mine in Manica province. Preliminary estimates suggested that production could amount to 2,600 kg per year. According to official figures, mining GDP increased at an average annual rate of 20.6% in 1996–2006; growth in 2006 was 4.5%.

Manufacturing contributed 15.8% of GDP in 2006, and employed 3.0% of the economically active population in 1997. A large aluminium smelter, Mozal, was opened in 2000 and expanded in 2003, with the completion of Mozal 2, which was expected to double capacity, to some 506,000 metric tons of aluminium ingots per year. Aluminium production was valued at 19,067,000m. meticais in 2003, equivalent to 16.8% of GDP. In 2004 unwrought aluminium and alloys accounted for 60.8% of total export earnings. During 1996–2006, according to official figures, manufacturing GDP increased at an average annual rate of 15.4%; growth in 2006 was 6.0%.

Electrical energy is derived principally from hydroelectric power, which provided some 99.7% of total electricity production in 2004. Mozambique's important Cahora Bassa hydroelectric plant on the Zambezi River supplies electricity to South Africa and Zimbabwe. By 2004 an extended power supply from Cahora Bassa to Zambézia, Manica and Sofala was in operation. From 1999 a consortium involving Mozambican, French and German companies financed a feasibility study for the construction of a hydroelectric power plant at Mepanda Uncua, some 70 km downstream of Cahora Bassa, which would help to support the 900-MW energy requirement of the Mozal smelter. Construction of the plant, which would have a generating capacity of 2,500 MW, was projected to cost some US $1,500m. It was envisaged that power from the plant, which would not be completed before 2007, would also be exported to South Africa. Mozambique currently imports all of its petroleum requirements. Imports of mineral fuels and lubricants comprised 1.6% of the value of total imports in 2005.

The services sector engaged 12.3% of the economically active population in 1997, and contributed 47.3% of GDP in 2006. By the end of the 1990s tourism was the fastest growing sector of the economy, and in 2004 receipts from tourism totalled US $96m. It was hoped that the formal opening, in April 2002, of the Great Limpopo Transfrontier Park, comprising South Africa's Kruger National Park, Zimbabwe's Gonarezhou National Park and Mozambique's Limpopo National Park, would attract additional tourists; in 2005 some 950,000 tourists visited Mozambique, compared with about 711,000 in the previous year. The GDP of the services sector increased by an average of 7.7% per year in 1996–2006, according to official figures; services GDP increased by 7.8% in 2006.

In 2006 Mozambique recorded a trade deficit of US $267.7m., and there was a deficit of $643.3m. on the current account of the balance of payments. In 2004 the principal source of imports was South Africa (41.4%). In the same year the Netherlands was the principal market for exports (receiving 60.9%); South Africa was the other significant purchaser. The principal exports in 2003 were unwrought aluminium and alloys, food, live animal and tobacco, and mineral fuels and lubricants. The principal imports in 2003 were machinery and transport equipment, mineral fuels and lubricants, food and live animals, and chemicals. Production from the Mozal aluminium smelter provided around 50% the value of total exports in that year.

In 2005 there was an overall budgetary deficit of 5,487,000m. meticais. Mozambique's total external debt was US $5,121m. at the end of 2005, of which $3,727m. was long-term public debt. In that year the cost of debt-servicing was equivalent to 4.2% of the total value of exports of goods and services. The average annual rate of inflation was 9.5% in 1996–2006; consumer prices increased by an average of 6.5% in 2005, and by 13.2% in 2006. The number of unemployed was 118,000 at the end of 1996.

Mozambique is a member of the Southern African Development Community (SADC, see p. 386). In November 2000 Mozambique was invited by the Common Market for Eastern and Southern Africa (COMESA, see p. 205) to rejoin the organization (Mozambique left COMESA in 1993, when it joined SADC).

During the 1980s economic development was severely frustrated by the effects of the civil war; however, since 1990 there has been considerable progress in liberalizing the economy. Increased production in rural areas, continued structural reform and the partial restoration of the infrastructure contributed to significant GDP growth from 1993, and in 1994–98 Mozambique's economy was one of the fastest growing in the world. In June 1999 the Bretton Woods institutions reduced Mozambique's public debt by almost two-thirds, significantly decreasing the country's annual servicing obligations for the period 1999–2005, and, following severe flooding in southern and central Mozambique, much of Mozambique's foreign debt was deferred and later cancelled. In June 2002 the IMF commended Mozambique's rapid post-flood recovery, extending the Poverty Reduction and Growth Facility (PRGF) arrangement approved in 1999 by three years, and in December 2005 it announced that Mozambique's outstanding debt to the Fund, worth an estimated US $153m., would be cancelled. In February 2006 the IMF completed a review of Mozambique's PRGF facility, and again praised the Government's economic policies, while encouraging the Government to implement policies to raise domestic revenue and decentralize expenditure. (A new tax authority was created in 2007, and fiscal revenues exceeded budget projections during that year.) Development of Mozambique's considerable mineral wealth continued in 2006–07 and the Government signalled its intention to join the Extractive Industrial Transparency Initiative in anticipation of increased revenues from the mining sector (particularly petroleum, of which large scale exploration was expected to ensue following the allocation of concessions to foreign companies). The IMF supported this action and again praised the authorities for their prudent development strategy. According to the Fund, Mozambique's GDP increased by 7% in 2007, while inflation slowed to 8.2%. Government expenditure increased in that year owing to damage inflicted by 'Cyclone Favio' and the explosion of a military arsenal in Maputo (see Recent History). Infrastructure repairs that followed the flooding of the Zambezi river in January 2008 were expected to increase expenditure further. While the Government maintained its commitment to the country's Action Plan for the Reduction of Absolute Poverty (an estimated 50% of the population were living below the poverty line in 2004, compared with 69% in 1997) unemployment remained extremely high and it was estimated that 16% of the adult population was infected with HIV/AIDS.

Education

Education is officially compulsory for seven years from the age of six. Primary schooling begins at six years of age and lasts for seven years. It is divided into two cycles, of five and two years. Secondary schooling, from 13 years of age, lasts for six years and comprises two cycles, each lasting three years. According to UNESCO estimates, in 2003/04 71% of children in the relevant age-group were enrolled at primary schools (males 75%; females 67%), while secondary enrolment included only 4% of children in the relevant age-group (males 5%; females 4%). There were 11,619 students in higher education in 1999. Two privately owned higher education institutions, the Catholic University and the Higher Polytechnic Institute, were inaugurated in 1996. In late 2003 it was announced that education would no longer take place solely in Portuguese, but also in some Mozambican dialects. In 2005 an estimated 5,000 new teachers were to be recruited. In 2006 some US $39m. was granted by international donors to develop educational resources. Education was allocated 20.2% of total current expenditure in that year.

Public Holidays

2008: 1 January (New Year's Day), 3 February (Heroes' Day, anniversary of the assassination of Eduardo Mondlane), 7 April (Day of the Mozambican Woman), 1 May (Workers' Day), 25 June (Independence Day), 7 September (Victory Day—anniversary of the end of the Armed Struggle), 25 September (Anniversary of the launching of the Armed Struggle for National Liberation, and Day of the Armed Forces of Mozambique), 4 October (Peace and National Reconciliation Day), 25 December (National Family Day).

2009: 1 January (New Year's Day), 3 February (Heroes' Day, anniversary of the assassination of Eduardo Mondlane), 7 April (Day of the Mozambican Woman), 1 May (Workers' Day), 25 June (Independence Day), 7 September (Victory Day—anniversary of the end of the Armed Struggle), 25 September (Anniversary of the launching of the Armed Struggle for National Liberation, and Day of the Armed Forces of Mozambique), 4 October (Peace and National Reconciliation Day), 25 December (National Family Day).

Weights and Measures

The metric system is in force.

Statistical Survey

Source (unless otherwise stated): Instituto Nacional de Estatística, Comissão Nacional do Plano, Av. Ahmed Sekou Touré 21, CP 493, Maputo; tel. 21491054; fax 21490384; e-mail webmaster@ine.gov.mz; internet www.ine.gov.mz.

Area and Population

AREA, POPULATION AND DENSITY

Area (sq km)	799,380*
Population (census results)	
1 August 1997	16,099,246
1 August 2007 (preliminary)	
Males	9,787,135
Females	10,743,579
Total	20,530,714
Density (per sq km) at 1 August 2007	20.1

* 308,641 sq miles. The area includes 13,000 sq km (5,019 sq miles) of inland water.

PROVINCES
(at census of 1 August 2007)

Province	Area (sq km)	Population (preliminary)	Density (per sq km)
Cabo Delgado	82,625	1,632,809	19.8
Gaza	75,709	1,219,013	16.1
Inhambane	68,615	1,267,035	18.5
Manica	61,661	1,418,927	23.0
City of Maputo	300	1,099,102	3,663.7
Maputo Province	26,058	1,259,713	48.3
Nampula	81,606	4,076,642	50.0
Niassa	129,056	1,178,117	9.1
Sofala	68,018	1,654,163	24.3
Tete	100,724	1,832,339	18.2
Zambézia	105,008	3,892,854	37.1
Total	799,380	20,530,714	25.7

MOZAMBIQUE

PRINCIPAL TOWNS
(at 2007 census, preliminary)

Maputo (capital)	1,099,102	Nacala-Porto	207,894
Matola	675,422	Quelimane	192,876
Nampula	477,900	Tete	152,909
Beira	436,240	Xai-Xai	116,343
Chimoio	238,976		

BIRTHS AND DEATHS

	2004	2005	2006
Crude birth rate (per 1,000)	39.3	38.8	38.2
Crude death rate (per 1,000)	20.1	20.0	19.9

Source: African Development Bank.

Expectation of life (years at birth, WHO estimates): 45.6 (males 45.9; females 45.4) in 2005 (Source: WHO, *World Health Statistics*).

ECONOMICALLY ACTIVE POPULATION
(persons aged 12 years and over, 1980 census)

	Males	Females	Total
Agriculture, forestry, hunting and fishing	1,887,779	2,867,052	4,754,831
Mining and quarrying			
Manufacturing	323,730	23,064	346,794
Construction	41,611	510	42,121
Commerce	90,654	21,590	112,244
Transport, storage and communications	74,817	2,208	77,025
Other services*	203,629	39,820	243,449
Total employed	2,622,220	2,954,244	5,576,464
Unemployed	75,505	19,321	94,826
Total labour force	2,697,725	2,973,565	5,671,290

* Including electricity, gas and water.

Source: ILO, *Yearbook of Labour Statistics*.

1997 (percentage distribution of economically active population at census of 1 August): Agriculture, forestry and hunting: 91.3% of females, 69.6% of males; Mining: 0.0% of females, 1.0% of males; Manufacturing: 0.8% of females, 5.5% of males; Energy: 0.0% of females, 0.3% of males; Construction: 0.3% of females, 3.9% of males; Transport and communications: 0.1% of females, 2.3% of males; Commerce and finance: 4.3% of females, 9.7% of males; Services: 2.2% of females, 3.4% of males; Unknown: 0.9% of females, 1.4% of males.

Mid-2005 (estimates in '000): Agriculture, etc. 8,250; Total labour force 10,321 (Source: FAO).

Health and Welfare

KEY INDICATORS

Total fertility rate (children per woman, 2005)	5.3
Under-5 mortality rate (per 1,000 live births, 2005)	145
HIV/AIDS (% of persons aged 15–49, 2005)	16.1
Physicians (per 1,000 head, 2004)	0.03
Hospital beds (per 1,000 head, 1990)	0.87
Health expenditure (2004): US $ per head (PPP)	42.0
Health expenditure (2004): % of GDP	4.0
Health expenditure (2004): public (% of total)	68.4
Access to water (% of persons, 2004)	43
Access to sanitation (% of persons, 2004)	32
Human Development Index (2005): ranking	172
Human Development Index (2005): value	0.384

For sources and definitions, see explanatory note on p. vi.

Agriculture

PRINCIPAL CROPS
('000 metric tons)

	2004	2005	2006
Rice (paddy)	177*	174*	174†
Maize	1,437*	1,403*	1,300†
Millet	53*	36*	49†
Sorghum	337*	307*	307†
Potatoes†	81	82	82
Sweet potatoes†	67	68	68
Cassava (Manioc)†	6,413	11,458	11,458
Cashew nuts†	64	68	68
Groundnuts (in shell)*	127	100	104
Coconuts†	269	266	266
Copra*	50	48	46
Sunflower seed†	12	12	12
Cottonseed*	47	65	67
Tomatoes†	8	8	8
Bananas†	92	93	93
Oranges†	12	12	12
Grapefruits and pomelos†	14	14	14
Guavas, mangoes and mangosteens†	25	25	25
Pineapples†	14	15	15
Papayas†	40	40	40
Cotton (lint)*	26	26	25
Tobacco†	12	12	12

* Unofficial figure(s).
† FAO estimate(s).

Aggregate production ('000 metric tons, may include official, semi-official or estimated data): Total cereals 2,006 in 2004, 1,921 in 2005, 1,831 in 2006; Total roots and tubers 6,567 in 2004, 11,615 in 2005, 11,615 in 2006; Total vegetables (incl. melons) 116 in 2004, 116 in 2005, 116 in 2006; Total fruits (excl. melons) 335 in 2004, 336 in 2005, 336 in 2006.

Source: FAO.

LIVESTOCK
('000 head, year ending September, FAO estimates)

	1998	1999	2000
Asses, mules or hinnies	22	23	23
Cattle	1,300	1,310	1,320
Pigs	176	178	180
Sheep	123	124	125
Goats	388	390	392
Chickens	26,000	27,000	28,000

2001–06: Figures assumed to be unchanged from 2000 (FAO estimates).

Source: FAO.

LIVESTOCK PRODUCTS
('000 metric tons, FAO estimates)

	2003	2004	2005
Cattle meat	38	38	38
Goat meat	2	2	2
Pig meat	13	13	13
Chicken meat	40	43	44
Cows' milk	60	60	60
Goats' milk	8	8	8
Hen eggs	14	14	14

2006: Figures assumed to be unchanged from 2005 (FAO estimates).

Source: FAO.

Forestry

ROUNDWOOD REMOVALS
('000 cubic metres, excl. bark)

	2003	2004	2005
Sawlogs, veneer logs and logs for sleepers	128	123	113
Other industrial wood	1,191	1,191	1,191
Fuel wood	16,724	16,724	16,724
Total	18,043	18,038	18,028

2006: Figures assumed to be unchanged from 2005 (FAO estimates).
Source: FAO.

SAWNWOOD PRODUCTION
('000 cubic metres, incl. railway sleepers)

	2004	2005	2006
Total	32	38	43

Source: FAO.

Fishing

(metric tons, live weight)

	2003	2004	2005
Dagaas	10,948	18,759	13,007
Tuna-like fishes	1,728	n.a.	n.a.
Penaeus shrimps	13,551	12,403	13,005
Knife shrimp	1,413	992	1,774
Total catch (incl. others)	44,342*	45,129*	45,018

* FAO estimate.

Note: Figures exclude crocodiles, recorded by number rather than by weight. The number of Nile crocodiles caught was: 5,130 in 2003; n.a. in 2004; 1,323 in 2005.
Source: FAO.

Mining

('000 metric tons, unless otherwise indicated)

	2004	2005	2006*
Bauxite	6.7	9.5	12.0
Coal	16.5	3.4	10.0
Gold (kilograms)†	56	63	68
Quartz (metric tons)	173.5	n.a.	n.a.
Gravel and crushed rock ('000 cubic metres)	779.9	850.9	880.0
Marble (slab) ('000 square metres)	13.7	12.3	16.0
Salt (marine)*	80	80	80
Natural gas (million cu m)	1,295	2,316	2,330

* Estimates.
† Figures exclude artisanal gold production; total gold output is estimated at 360 kg–480 kg per year.
Source: US Geological Survey.

Industry

SELECTED PRODUCTS
('000 metric tons, unless otherwise indicated)

	2002	2003	2004
Flour (cereals other than wheat)	1	1	n.a.
Wheat flour	145	163	160
Raw sugar	35	225	199
Groundnut oil ('000 metric tons)*	13.8	15.8	20.2
Beer ('000 hl)	779	1,044	1,025
Soft drinks ('000 hl)	547	30	1,224
Cigarettes (million)	1,255	1,390	n.a.
Footwear (excl. rubber, '000 pairs)	12†	17†	n.a.
Cement	274	582	484
Electric energy (million kWh)	12,713	10,602	11,714

* FAO estimates.
† Estimate.

Sources: FAO; UN, *Industrial Commodity Statistics Yearbook*.

2005 ('000 metric tons): Groundnut oil 16.9 (FAO estimate) (Source: FAO).

Finance

CURRENCY AND EXCHANGE RATES

Monetary Units
100 centavos = 1 metical (plural: meticais).

Sterling, Dollar and Euro Equivalents (31 December 2007)
£1 sterling = 48.08 meticais;
US $1 = 24.00 meticais;
€1 = 35.33 meticais;
1,000 meticais = £2.08 = $4.17 = €2.83.

Average Exchange Rate (meticais per US $)
2004 22.58
2005 23.06
2006 25.40

Note: Between April 1992 and October 2000 the market exchange rate was the rate at which commercial banks purchased from and sold to the public. Since October 2000 it has been the weighted average of buying and selling rates of all transactions of commercial banks and stock exchanges with the public. A devaluation of the metical, with 1 new currency unit becoming equivalent to 1,000 of the former currency, was implemented on 1 July 2006.

BUDGET
('000 million meticais)

Revenue*	2003	2004	2005
Taxation	13,695	18,993	16,721
Taxes on income	3,235	4,445	4,469
Domestic taxes on goods and services	7,799	11,522	8,936
Customs duties	2,229	2,398	2,816
Other taxes	432	627	500
Non-tax revenue	1,019	1,476	3,662
Total	14,714	20,469	20,383

Expenditure†	2003	2004	2005
Current expenditure	16,342	21,890	20,365
Compensation of employees	7,734	11,045	10,358
Goods and services	2,991	4,908	4,407
Interest on public debt	1,319	1,244	1,248
Transfer payments	3,075	3,778	3,730
Other	1,223	915	622
Capital expenditure	13,369	17,026	13,101
Unallocated	252	—	170
Total	29,963	38,917	33,636

* Excluding grants received ('000 million meticais): 10,590 in 2003; 9,992 in 2004; 9,937 in 2005.
† Excluding net lending ('000 million meticais): 481 in 2003; 1,826 in 2004; 2,171 in 2005.

Source: Banco de Moçambique.

MOZAMBIQUE

Statistical Survey

INTERNATIONAL RESERVES
(US $ million at 31 December)

	2004	2005	2006
IMF special drawing rights	0.08	0.23	0.23
Reserve position in IMF	0.01	0.01	0.01
Foreign exchange	1,130.86	1,053.58	1,155.49
Total	**1,130.96**	**1,053.82**	**1,155.73**

Source: IMF, *International Financial Statistics*.

MONEY SUPPLY
('000 million meticais at 31 December)

	2004	2005	2006
Currency outside banks	5,487.8	6,417.9	7,152.0
Demand deposits at commercial banks	10,240.9	12,809.4	17,095.4
Total money (incl. others)	**15,728.7**	**19,227.4**	**24,247.5**

Source: IMF, *International Financial Statistics*.

COST OF LIVING
(Consumer Price Index; base: 1998 = 100)

	2002	2003	2004
Food, beverages and tobacco	151	175	187
Clothing and footwear	126	122	125
Firewood and furniture	190	215	263
Health	119	133	134
Transportation and communications	205	232	234
Education, recreation and culture	145	150	151
Other goods and services	136	154	159
All items	**157**	**179**	**195**

Source: IMF, *Republic of Mozambique: Selected Issues and Statistical Appendix* (August 2005).

NATIONAL ACCOUNTS
('000 million meticais at current prices)

National Income and Product

	2001	2002	2003
Compensation of employees	20,446.5	27,012.5	36,346.7
Net operating surplus	11,059.2	11,282.6	11,239.4
Net mixed income	31,949.0	42,114.9	47,406.5
Domestic primary incomes	**63,454.8**	**80,410.1**	**94,992.6**
Consumption of fixed capital	10,401.4	13,865.7	15,079.6
Gross domestic product (GDP) at factor cost	**73,856.1**	**94,275.8**	**110,072.2**
Taxes on production and imports	4,634.2	5,050.1	6,145.3
Less Subsidies	1,945.5	2,442.4	2,314.9
GDP in market prices	**76,544.9**	**96,883.5**	**113,902.5**

Expenditure on the Gross Domestic Product

	2004	2005	2006*
Government final consumption expenditure	17,729.4	19,662.9	22,228.5
Private final consumption expenditure	109,881.2	126,354.4	139,338.0
Change in stocks	–392.0	–1,543.6	1,222.7
Gross capital formation	23,996.6	28,360.7	32,559.1
Total domestic expenditure	**151,215.2**	**172,834.4**	**195,348.3**
Exports of goods and services	38,340.8	46,212.6	52,748.5
Less Imports of goods and services	60,887.6	67,340.0	71,292.7
GDP in purchasers' values	**128,668.3**	**151,706.9**	**176,804.0**
GDP at constant 2003 prices	**119,721.6**	**129,763.5**	**140,845.5**

*Preliminary estimates.

Gross Domestic Product by Economic Activity

	2004	2005	2006
Agriculture, livestock and forestry	29,634.5	34,837.9	41,721.1
Fishing	2,244.2	2,284.0	2,830.5
Mining	1,160.8	1,476.4	1,709.2
Manufacturing	20,528.8	21,304.1	26,233.0
Electricity and water	6,358.7	7,605.6	9,579.0
Construction	3,835.2	4,506.8	5,356.1
Wholesale and retail trade	11,360.7	17,656.6	20,696.3
Repairs	558.8	556.7	630.5
Restaurants and hotels	1,792.3	2,141.7	2,692.1
Transport and communications	12,415.1	14,559.6	16,077.0
Financial services	4,544.4	6,748.8	8,355.3
Real estate and business services	11,176.0	11,307.1	11,647.2
Public administration and defence	5,005.2	5,658.9	6,639.6
Education	4,705.8	5,613.7	6,521.5
Health	1,514.5	1,846.0	2,241.4
Other services	2,539.2	2,725.1	3,067.8
Sub-total	**119,374.1**	**140,828.9**	**165,997.6**
Less Financial services indirectly measured	3,084.5	3,137.3	4,731.8
Gross value added in basic prices	**116,289.6**	**137,691.6**	**161,265.8**
Taxes on products / *Less* Subsidies on products	12,378.6	14,015.3	15,538.1
GDP in market prices	**128,668.3**	**151,706.9**	**176,804.0**

BALANCE OF PAYMENTS
(US $ million)

	2004	2005	2006
Exports of goods f.o.b.	1,503.9	1,745.3	2,381.1
Imports of goods f.o.b.	–1,849.7	–2,242.3	–2,648.8
Trade balance	**–345.8**	**–497.1**	**–267.7**
Exports of services	255.6	341.9	386.4
Imports of services	–531.4	–648.6	–758.1
Balance on goods and services	**–621.7**	**–803.8**	**–639.5**
Other income received	74.5	98.9	159.8
Other income paid	–374.0	–458.8	–655.4
Balance on goods, services and income	**–921.2**	**–1,163.6**	**–1,135.0**
Current transfers received	370.5	479.0	574.5
Current transfers paid	–56.7	–76.0	–73.8
Current balance	**–607.4**	**–760.7**	**–643.3**
Capital account (net)	578.1	187.9	488.5
Direct investment (net)	244.7	107.9	153.3
Portfolio investment (net)	–25.4	–88.5	–123.8
Other investment assets	–88.7	–78.5	–13.8
Other investment liabilities	–177.1	154.3	–1,656.6
Errors and omissions (net)	216.4	281.0	143.8
Overall balance	**140.7**	**–196.6**	**–1,642.6**

Source: IMF, *International Financial Statistics*.

MOZAMBIQUE   *Statistical Survey*

External Trade

PRINCIPAL COMMODITIES
(US $ million)

Imports c.i.f.	2002	2003
Food and live animals	187.4	215.7
Cereals	113.1	126.7
Mineral fuels, lubricants etc.	159.6	288.5
Chemicals and related products	86.6	117.1
Plastic and related products	56.9	21.6
Metals and related products	107.6	87.6
Iron and steel	20.7	22.9
Wood pulp and related products	28.1	50.5
Books, magazines, etc.	12.0	27.6
Textiles and related products	29.2	35.7
Machinery and transport equipment	405.6	476.7
General industrial machinery, equipment and parts	89.4	140.4
Electrical machinery, apparatus, etc.	85.4	144.2
Road vehicles and parts	194.9	157.7
General optical and photographic material, etc.	18.4	26.4
Miscellaneous manufactured articles	24.2	27.4
Commodities and transactions not classified elsewhere	402.2	318.5
Total (incl. others)	1,543.0	1,753.0

Exports f.o.b.	2002	2003
Food, live animals and tobacco	204.1	179.8
Fish, crustaceans, molluscs and other seafood	122.4	95.9
Textiles	25.2	45.4
Cotton	16.0	30.8
Mineral fuels, lubricants, etc.	136.0	136.1
Basic manufactures	367.1	574.2
Aluminium and alloys, unwrought	361.4	568.1
Machinery and transport equipment	32.5	44.8
Total (incl. others)	809.8	1,043.9

PRINCIPAL TRADING PARTNERS
(US $ million)

Imports c.i.f.	2002	2003	2004
Australia	7.5	211.3	2.7
France-Monaco	22.5	35.3	34.5
Germany	10.2	36.6	18.9
India	53.6	72.9	62.8
Japan	42.4	29.8	16.6
Malawi	2.3	19.2	n.a.
Pakistan	6.8	14.3	n.a.
Portugal	77.5	62.4	67.0
Saudi Arabia	25.0	18.4	n.a.
South Africa	342.2	654.4	842.0
Spain	5.8	27.6	24.6
Taiwan	16.9	40.6	n.a.
United Kingdom	12.5	19.9	n.a.
USA	55.6	104.3	48.3
Total (incl. others)	1,262.9	1,753.0	2,034.7

Exports f.o.b.	2002	2003	2004
Belgium	282.6	454.5	8.6
Italy	1.5	30.4	0.8
Malawi	10.4	32.8	49.9
Netherlands	1.9	29.6	916.6
Portugal	29.8	38.9	42.0
South Africa	120.4	169.6	211.4
Spain	19.0	70.0	38.0
Swaziland	0.5	17.4	2.7
United Kingdom	0.7	30.6	2.9
USA	10.7	15.7	n.a.
Zimbabwe	39.2	29.5	35.0
Total (incl. others)	682.0	1,043.9	1,503.9

Transport

RAILWAYS
(traffic)

	2002	2003	2004
Freight ton-km (million)	808	778	794
Passenger-km (million)	138	82	106

Source: UN, *Statistical Yearbook*.

ROAD TRAFFIC
(motor vehicles in use at 31 December)

	1999	2000	2001
Passenger cars	78,600	81,600	81,600
Lorries and vans	46,900	76,000	76,000

Source: UN, *Statistical Yearbook*.

SHIPPING

Merchant Fleet
(registered at 31 December)

	2004	2005	2006
Number of vessels	128	126	129
Total displacement ('000 grt)	36.1	35.4	36.5

Source: Lloyd's Register-Fairplay, *World Fleet Statistics*.

Freight Handled
('000 metric tons)

	2001	2002	2003
Goods loaded and unloaded	7,423	8,201	8,421

International Sea-borne Freight Traffic
('000 metric tons)

	2001	2002	2003
Goods loaded	2,962	2,780	2,982
Goods unloaded	3,144	4,062	3,837

CIVIL AVIATION
(traffic on scheduled services)

	2001	2002	2003
Kilometres flown (million)	7.5	6.6	6.5
Passengers carried ('000)	266.5	284.2	285.3
Passenger-km (million)	354.7	402.4	410.8

MOZAMBIQUE

Tourism

TOURIST ARRIVALS BY COUNTRY OF RESIDENCE

Country	2003	2004	2005
Malawi	121,267	74,933	100,580
Portugal	25,392	11,898	15,970
South Africa	335,426	288,104	306,177
Swaziland	20,018	17,773	23,856
United Kingdom	5,798	6,700	8,993
USA	5,035	5,647	7,878
Zimbabwe	114,936	65,896	88,450
Total (incl. others)	726,099	711,060	954,433

Tourism receipts (US $ million, excl. passenger transport): 98 in 2003; 96 in 2004; n.a. in 2005.

Source: World Tourism Organization.

Communications Media

	2004	2005	2006
Telephones ('000 main lines in use)	69.7	69.7	67.0
Mobile cellular telephones ('000 subscribers)	708.0	1,503.9	2,339.3
Personal computers ('000 in use)	138	138	n.a.
Internet users ('000)	112	178	n.a.

1998: Daily newspapers 12 (average circulation 43,099); Non-daily newspapers 40 (estimated average circulation 205,800); Periodicals 32 (average circulation 83,000).

Television receivers ('000 in use): 230 in 2001.

Radio receivers ('000 in use): 730 in 1997.

Facsimile machines ('000 in use): 7.2 in 1996.

Sources: International Telecommunication Union; UN, *Statistical Yearbook*; UNESCO Institute for Statistics.

Education

(2003, unless otherwise indicated)

	Institutions	Teachers	Students
Pre-primary*†	5,689	28,705	1,745,049
Primary	9,027	51,912	3,177,586
Secondary	154	4,112	160,093
Technical	36	924	20,086
Teacher training‡	18	n.a.	9,314

* Public education only.
† 1997 figures.
‡ 2002 figures.

Source: mainly Ministry of Education.

Adult literacy rate (UNESCO estimates): 38.7% (males 54.8%; females 25.0%) in 1997 (Source: UNESCO Institute for Statistics).

Directory

The Constitution

The Constitution came into force on 30 November 1990, replacing the previous version, introduced at independence on 25 June 1975 and revised in 1978. Its main provisions, as amended in 1996 and 2004, are summarized below. There are 306 articles in the Constitution.

GENERAL PRINCIPLES

The Republic of Mozambique is an independent, sovereign, unitary and democratic state of social justice. Sovereignty resides in the people, who exercise it according to the forms laid down in the Constitution. The fundamental objectives of the Republic include:

the defence of independence and sovereignty;

the defence and promotion of human rights and of the equality of citizens before the law; and

the strengthening of democracy, of freedom and of social and individual stability.

POLITICAL PARTICIPATION

The people exercise power through universal, direct, equal, secret, personal and periodic suffrage to elect their representatives, by referendums and through permanent democratic participation. Political parties are prohibited from advocating or resorting to violence.

FUNDAMENTAL RIGHTS AND DUTIES OF CITIZENS

All citizens enjoy the same rights and are subject to the same duties, irrespective of colour, race, sex, ethnic origin, place of birth, religion, level of education, social position or occupation. In realizing the objectives of the Constitution, all citizens enjoy freedom of opinion, assembly and association. All citizens over 18 years of age are entitled to vote and be elected. Active participation in the defence of the country is the duty of every citizen. Individual freedoms are guaranteed by the State, including freedom of expression, of the press, of assembly, of association and of religion. The State guarantees accused persons the right to a legal defence. No Court or Tribunal has the power to impose a sentence of death upon any person.

STATE ORGANS

Public elective officers are chosen by elections through universal, direct, secret, personal and periodic vote. Legally recognized political parties may participate in elections.

THE PRESIDENT

The President is the Head of State and of the Government, and Commander-in-Chief of the armed forces. The President is elected by direct, equal, secret and personal universal suffrage on a majority vote, and must be proposed by at least 10,000 voters, of whom at least 200 must reside in each province. The term of office is five years. A candidate may be re-elected on only two consecutive occasions, or again after an interval of five years between terms. The President is advised by a Council of State, but is not obliged to follow its advice.

THE ASSEMBLY OF THE REPUBLIC

Legislative power is vested in the Assembléia da República (Assembly of the Republic). The Assembléia is elected by universal direct adult suffrage on a secret ballot, and is composed of 250 Deputies. The Assembléia is elected for a maximum term of five years, but may be dissolved by the President before the expiry of its term. The Assembléia holds two ordinary sessions each year. The Assembléia, with a two-thirds majority, may impeach the President.

THE COUNCIL OF MINISTERS

The Council of Ministers is the Government of the Republic. The Prime Minister assists and advises the President in the leadership of the Government and presents the Government's programme, budget

MOZAMBIQUE

and policies to the Assembléia da República, assisted by other ministers.

LOCAL STATE ORGANS

The Republic is administered in provinces, municipalities and administrative posts. The highest state organ in a province is the provincial government, presided over by a governor, who is answerable to the central Government. There shall be assemblies at each administrative level.

THE JUDICIARY

Judicial functions shall be exercised through the Supreme Court and other courts provided for in the law on the judiciary, which also subordinates them to the Assembléia da República. Courts must safeguard the principles of the Constitution and defend the rights and legitimate interests of citizens. Judges are independent, subject only to the law.

The Government

HEAD OF STATE

President of the Republic and Commander-in-Chief of the Armed Forces: ARMANDO EMÍLIO GUEBUZA (took office 2 February 2005).

COUNCIL OF MINISTERS
(March 2008)

Prime Minister: LUÍSA DIAS DIOGO.
Minister of Foreign Affairs and Co-operation: OLDEMIRO BALOI.
Minister of National Defence: FILIPE NHUSSI.
Minister of Finance: MANUEL CHANG.
Minister of Justice: MARIA BENVIDA LEVY.
Minister of the Interior: JOSÉ PACHECO.
Minister of Development and Planning: AIUBA CUERENEIA.
Minister of State Administration: LUCAS CHOMERA.
Minister of Agriculture: SOARES NHACA.
Minister of Fisheries: CADMIEL FILIANE MUTHEMBA.
Minister of Industry and Trade: ANTÓNIO FERNANDO.
Minister of Energy: SALVADOR NAMBURETE.
Minister of Mineral Resources: ESPERANÇA BIAS.
Minister of Transport and Communications: PAULO ZUCULA.
Minister of Education and Culture: AIRES BONIFÁCIO ALI.
Minister of Health: PAULO IVO GARRIDO.
Minister of Environmental Co-ordination: ALCINDA ABREU.
Minister of Labour: MARIA HELENA TAIPO.
Minister of Public Works and Housing: FELÍCIO ZACARIAS.
Minister of Youth and Sport: DAVID SIMANGO.
Minister of Women's Affairs and Social Welfare Co-ordination: VIRGÍLIA BERNARDA NETO ALEXANDRE SANTOS MATABELE.
Minister of Tourism: FERNANDO SUMBANA, Jr.
Minister of Veterans' Affairs: FELICIANO SALOMÃO GUNDANA.
Minister of Science and Technology: VENÂNCIO MASSINGUE.
Minister in the Presidency with responsibility for Parliamentary Affairs: ISABEL MANUEL NKAVANDEKA.
Minister in the Presidency with responsibility for Diplomatic Affairs: FRANCISCO CAETANO MADEIRA.

MINISTRIES

Office of the President: Av. Julius Nyerere 1780, Maputo; tel. 21491121; fax 21492065; e-mail gabimprensa@teldata.mz; internet www.presidencia.gov.mz.
Office of the Prime Minster: Praça da Marinha Popular, Maputo; tel. 21426861; fax 21426881; internet www.govmoz.gov.mz.
Ministry of Agriculture: Praça dos Heróis Moçambicanos, CP 1406, Maputo; tel. 21460011; fax 21460055.
Ministry of Development and Planning: Av. Ahmed Sekou Touré 21, CP 4087, Maputo; tel. 21490006; fax 21495477; internet www.mpd.gov.mz.
Ministry of Education and Culture: Av. 24 de Julho 167, CP 34, Maputo; tel. 21492006; fax 21492196; internet www.mec.gov.mz.
Ministry of Energy: Av. 25 de Setembro, 1218 3° andar, CP 1831, Maputo; tel. 21303265; fax 21313971; e-mail asi@me.gov.mz.
Ministry of Environmental Co-ordination: Rua Kassoende 167, Maputo; tel. 21492403; e-mail jwkacha@virconn.com; internet www.micoa.gov.mz.

Directory

Ministry of Finance: Praça da Marinha Popular, CP 272, Maputo; tel. 21315000; fax 21306261.
Ministry of Fisheries: Rua Consiglieri Pedroso 347, CP 1723, Maputo; tel. 21431266; fax 21425087.
Ministry of Foreign Affairs and Co-operation: Av. 10 de Novembro, 640, Maputo; tel. 21327000; fax 21327020; e-mail minec@zebra.uem.mz.
Ministry of Health: Avs Eduardo Mondlane e Salvador Allende 1008, CP 264, Maputo; tel. 21427131; fax 21427133; internet www.misau.gov.mz.
Ministry of Industry and Trade: Praça 25 de Junho 300, CP 1831, Maputo; tel. 21352600; fax 214262301; e-mail infomic@mic.gov.mz; internet www.mic.gov.mz.
Ministry of the Interior: Av. Olof Palme 46/48, CP 290, Maputo; tel. 21303510; fax 21420084.
Ministry of Justice: Av. Julius Nyerere 33, Maputo; tel. 21491613; fax 21494264.
Ministry of Labour: Av. 24 de Julho 2351, CP 281, Maputo; tel. 21428301; fax 21421881; internet www.mitrab.gov.mz.
Ministry of Mineral Resources: Av. Fernão de Magalhães 34, CP 294, Maputo; tel. 21314843; fax 21427103; internet www.mireme.gov.mz.
Ministry of National Defence: Av. Mártires de Mueda 280, CP 3216, Maputo; tel. 21492081; fax 21491619.
Ministry of Public Works and Housing: Av. Karl Marx 606, CP 268, Maputo; tel. 21430028; fax 21421369.
Ministry of Science and Technology: Av. Patrice Lumumba 770, Maputo; tel. 21352800; fax 21352860; e-mail secretariado@mct.gov.mz; internet www.mct.gov.mz.
Ministry of State Administration: Rua da Rádio Moçambique 112, CP 4116, Maputo; tel. 21426666; fax 21428565.
Ministry of Tourism: Av. 25 de Setembro 1018, CP 4101, Maputo; tel. 21306210; fax 21306212; internet www.moztourism.gov.mz.
Ministry of Transport and Communications: Av. Mártires de Inhaminga 336, CP 276, Maputo; tel. 21430152; fax 21431028.
Ministry of Veterans' Affairs: Rua General Pereira d'Eça 35, CP 3697, Maputo; tel. 21490601.
Ministry of Women's Affairs and Social Welfare Co-ordination: Rua de Tchamba 86, CP 516, Maputo; tel. 21490921; fax 21492757.
Ministry of Youth and Sport: Av. 25 de Setembro 529, CP 2080, Maputo; tel. 21312172; fax 21300040; e-mail mjd@tvcabo.co.mz; internet www.mjd.gov.mz.

PROVINCIAL GOVERNORS
(March 2008)

Cabo Delgado Province: LÁZARO MATHE.
Gaza Province: DJALMA LOURENÇO.
Inhambane Province: FRANCISCO MEQUE.
Manica Province: RAIMUNDO DIOMBO.
Maputo Province: TELMINA PEREIRA.
Nampula Province: FELISMINO ERNESTO TOCOLE.
Niassa Province: ARNALDO VICENTE BIMBE.
Sofala Province: ALBERTO CLEMENTINO VAQUINA.
Tete Province: ILDEFONSO MUANANTAPHA.
Zambézia Province: CARVALHO MUÁRIA.
City of Maputo: ROSA MANUEL DA SILVA.

President and Legislature

PRESIDENT

Presidential Election, 1–2 December 2004

Candidate	Votes	% of votes
Armando Guebuza (Frelimo)	2,004,226	63.74
Afonso Macacho Marceta Dhlakama (Renamo—União Eleitoral)	998,059	31.74
Raul Domingos (PPDD)	85,815	2.73
Yaqub Sabindy (PIMO)	28,656	0.91
Carlos Alexandre dos Reis (FMBG)	27,412	0.87
Total*	**3,144,168**	**100.00**

*Excluding 96,684 blank votes and 81,315 spoilt votes.

MOZAMBIQUE

LEGISLATURE

Assembléia da República: CP 1516, Maputo; tel. 21400826; fax 21400711; e-mail cdi@sortmoz.com.
Chair.: EDUARDO MULÉMBUE.
General Election, 1–2 December 2004

Party	Votes	% of votes	Seats*
Frente de Libertação de Moçambique (Frelimo)	1,889,054	62.03	160
Resistência Nacional Moçambicana—União Eleitoral (Renamo—UE)	905,289	29.73	90
Partido para a Paz, Democracia e Desenvolvimento (PPDD)	60,758	2.00	—
Partido para a Liberdade e Solidariedade (PAZS)	20,686	0.68	—
Partido de Reconciliação Nacional (PARENA)	18,220	0.60	—
Partido Independente de Moçambique (PIMO)	17,960	0.59	—
Partido Social de Moçambique (PASOMO)	15,740	0.52	—
Others	117,722	3.87	—
Total (incl. others)†	3,045,429	100.00	250

* Parties must obtain a minimum of 5% of the vote in order to gain representation in the Assembléia da República.
† Excluding 166,540 blank votes and 109,957 spoilt votes.

Election Commission

Comissão Nacional de Eleições (CNE): Maputo; f. 1997; 13 mems; Chair. ARAO LITSURE.

Political Organizations

In mid-2004 there were five coalitions and 42 parties registered with the Comissão Nacional de Eleiçoes. The parties listed below secured votes in the December 2004 legislative elections.

Congresso dos Democratas Unidos (CDU): Maputo; f. 2001; Leader ANTÓNIO PALANGE.

Frente de Libertação de Moçambique (Frelimo): Rua Pereira do Lago 10, Bairro de Sommerschield, Maputo; tel. 21490181; fax 21490008; e-mail info@frelimo.org.mz; internet www.frelimo.org.mz; f. 1962 by merger of three nationalist parties; reorg. 1977 as a 'Marxist-Leninist vanguard movement'; in 1989 abandoned its exclusive Marxist-Leninist orientation; Pres. ARMANDO GUEBUZA.

Frente de Mudança e Boa Governa (FMBG): f. 2004; comprises:

Partido de Todos os Nativos Moçambicanos (Partonamo): f. 1996; Pres. MUSSAGY ABDUL REMANE.

União Nacional Moçambicana (Unamo): f. 1987; breakaway faction of Renamo; social democratic; obtained legal status 1992; fmr mem. of União Eleitoral; Pres. CARLOS ALEXANDRE DOS REIS; Sec.-Gen. FLORENCIA JOÃO DA SILVA.

Partido Democrático de Libertação de Moçambique (Padelimo): based in Kenya; Pres. JOAQUIM JOSÉ NHOTA.

Partido Independente de Moçambique (PIMO): f. 1993; Islamist; Leader YAQUB SABINDY; Sec.-Gen. MAGALHÃES BRAMUGY.

Partido Liberal e Democrático de Moçambique (Palmo): f. 1991; obtained legal status 1993; Pres. ANTÓNIO MUEDO.

Partido para a Paz, Democracia e Desenvolvimento (PPDD): Quelimane; f. 2003; liberal; Leader RAUL DOMINGOS.

Partido Popular Democrático (PPD): f. 2004; Leader MARCIANO FIJAMA.

Partido de Reconciliação Nacional (PARENA): Maputo; f. August 2004; Leader ANDRÉ BALATE.

Partido Social, Liberal e Democrático (Sol): breakaway faction of Palmo; Leader CASIMIRO MIGUEL NHAMITHAMBO.

Partido Social de Moçambique (Pasomo): Maputo; Leader FRANCISCO CAMPIRA.

Partido do Trabalho (PT): f. 1993; breakaway faction of PPPM; Pres. MIGUEL MABOTE; Sec.-Gen. LUÍS MUCHANGA.

Partido Verde de Moçambique (PVM): Leader BRUNO SAPEMBA.

Resistência Nacional Moçambicana-União Eleitoral (Renamo-UE): f. 1999; coalition comprising Renamo and the União Eleitoral which, in late 2004, consisted of 10 minor parties.

Constituent members include:

Resistência Nacional Moçambicana (Renamo): Av. Julius Nyerere 2541, Maputo; tel. 21493107; also known as Movimento Nacional da Resistência de Moçambique (MNR); f. 1976; fmr guerrilla group, in conflict with the Govt between 1976 and Oct. 1992; obtained legal status in 1994; Pres. AFONSO MACACHO MARCETA DHLAKAMA; Sec.-Gen. OSSUFO MOMADE.

Aliança Independente de Moçambique (Alimo): Maputo; f. 1998; Sec.-Gen. ERNESTO SERGIO.

Frente de Ação Patriótica (FAP): Maputo; f. 1991; Pres. JOSÉ CARLOS PALAÇO.

Frente Democrática Unida—United Democratic Front (UDF): Maputo; Pres. JANEIRO MARIANO.

Frente Unida de Moçambique (Fumo): Av. Mao Tse Tung 230, 1° andar, Maputo; tel. 21494044; in early 2005 the party was reported to have split, with the faction led by Simeão Cuamba and Pedro Loforte supporting a withdrawal from the UE; Sec.-Gen. JOSÉ SAMO GUDO.

Partido de Convenção Nacional (PCN): Av. de 25 Setembro 1123, 3° andar, Maputo; tel. 21426891; obtained legal status in 1992; Chair. LUTERO CHIMBIRIMBIRI SIMANGO; Sec.-Gen. Dr GABRIEL MABUNDA.

Partido Ecologista de Moçambique (PEMO): Maputo.

Partido do Progresso do Povo de Moçambique (PPPM): Av. de 25 Setembro, 1123, 4° andar, Maputo; tel. 21426925; f. 1991; obtained legal status 1992; Pres. Dr PADIMBE MAHOSE KAMATI; Sec.-Gen. CHE ABDALA.

Partido Renovador Democrático (PRD): obtained legal status 1994; Pres. MANECA DANIEL.

Partido de Unidade Nacional (PUN): TV Sado 9, Maputo; tel. 21419204; Pres. HIPOLITO COUTO.

União para a Salvação de Moçambique (Usamo): f. 2004; coalition comprising the União para a Mudança (UM), PADRES, PSDM, and the PSM; Chair. JULIO NIMUIRE.

Partido Socialista de Moçambique (PSM): Leader JOÃO NKALAMBA.

Other parties obtaining votes at the December 2004 legislative elections were the **Frente do Amplo Oposicão (FAO)** (f. 2004), the **Partido Ecologista—Movimento da Terra** (f. 2002), the **Partido para a Liberdade e Solidariedade (PAZS)** (f. 2004), the **Partido para a Reconciliação Democrática (PAREDE)**, and the **União Democrática (UD)** (f. 1994, coalition). In 2005 a coalition comprising 18 small parties, including the **Partido Popular Democrático (PPD)**, the **Partido Nacional de Moçambique (Panamo)** and the **Partido Progressivo e Liberal de Moçambique (PPLM)**, was formed.

Diplomatic Representation

EMBASSIES AND HIGH COMMISSIONS IN MOZAMBIQUE

Algeria: Rua de Mukumbura 121–125, CP 1709, Maputo; tel. 21492070; fax 21490582; e-mail ab220261@virconn.com; Ambassador FOUAD BOUTTOURA.

Angola: Av. Kenneth Kaunda 783, CP 2954, Maputo; tel. 21493139; fax 21493930; Ambassador JOÃO GARCIA BIRES.

Brazil: Av. Kenneth Kaunda 296, CP 1167, Maputo; tel. 21484800; fax 21484806; e-mail ebrasil@teledata.mz; Ambassador LEDA CAMARGO.

China, People's Republic: Av. Julius Nyerere 3142, CP 4668, Maputo; tel. 21491560; fax 21491196; e-mail emb.chi@tvcabo.co.mz; Ambassador TIAN GUANGFENG.

Congo, Democratic Republic: Av. Kenneth Kaunda 127, CP 2407, Maputo; tel. 21497154; fax 21494929; Chargé d'affaires a.i. MULUMBA TSHIDIMBA MARCEL.

Congo, Republic: Av. Kenneth Kaunda 783, CP 4743, Maputo; tel. 21490142; Chargé d'affaires a.i. MONSEGNO BASHA OSHEFWA.

Cuba: Av. Kenneth Kaunda 492, CP 387, Maputo; tel. 21492444; fax 21491905; e-mail residcuba.mozambique@tvcabo.co.mz; Ambassador MARCELINA EVANGELINA SEOANE DOMÍNGUEZ.

Denmark: Av. Julius Nyerere 1162, CP 4588, Maputo; tel. 21480000; fax 21480010; e-mail mpmamb@um.dk; internet www.ambmaputo.um.dk; Ambassador MADS SANDAU-JENSEN.

Egypt: Av. Mao Tse Tung 851, CP 4662, Maputo; tel. 21491118; fax 21491489; e-mail egypt2@tropical.co.mz; Ambassador HAMDY ABD ELWAHAB SALEH.

Finland: Av. Julius Nyerere 1128, CP 1663, Maputo; tel. 21482400; fax 21491662; e-mail sanomat.map@formin.fi; Ambassador KARI ALANKO.

MOZAMBIQUE

France: Av. Julius Nyerere 2361, CP 4781, Maputo; tel. 21484600; fax 21484680; e-mail ambafrancemz@tvcabo.co.mz; internet www.ambafrance-mz.org; Ambassador THIERRY VITEAU.

Germany: Rua Damião de Góis 506, CP 1595, Maputo; tel. 21492700; fax 21492888; e-mail germaemb@tvcabo.co.mz; internet www.maputo.diplo.de; Ambassador KLAUS-CHRISTIAN KRAEMER.

Holy See: Av. Kwame Nkrumah 224, CP 2738, Maputo; tel. 21491144; fax 21492217; Apostolic Nuncio Most Rev. GEORGE PANIKULAM (Titular Archbishop of Caudium).

Iceland: Av. Zimbabwe 1694, Maputo; tel. 21483509; fax 21483511; e-mail mozambique@iceida.is; internet www.iceland.org/mo; Chargé d'affaires a.i. JÓHANN PÁLSSON.

India: Av. Kenneth Kaunda 167, CP 4751, Maputo; tel. 21492437; fax 21492364; e-mail hicomind@tvcabo.co.mz; internet www.hicomind-maputo.org; High Commissioner RAJINDER BHAGAT.

Ireland: Av. Julius Nyerere 3332, Maputo; tel. 21491440; fax 21493023; e-mail maputoembassy@dfa.ie; Ambassador FRANK SHERIDAN.

Italy: Av. Kenneth Kaunda 387, CP 976, Maputo; tel. 21492229; fax 21492046; e-mail ambasciata.maputo@esteri.it; internet www.ambmaputo.esteri.it; Ambassador GUIDO LARCHER.

Japan: Av. Julius Nyerere 2832, CP 2494, Maputo; tel. 21499819; fax 21498957; Ambassador TATSUYA MIKI.

Korea, Democratic People's Republic: Rua da Kaswende 167, Maputo; tel. 21491482; Ambassador PAK KUN GWANG.

Malawi: Av. Kenneth Kaunda 75, CP 4148, Maputo; tel. 21492676; fax 21490224; High Commissioner MARTIN O. KANSICHI.

Mauritius: Rua Dom Carlos 42, Av. de Zimbabwe, Sommerscheid, Maputo; tel. 21494624; fax 21494729; e-mail mhcmoz@intra.co.mz; High Commissioner ALAIN LARIDON.

Netherlands: Av. Kwame Nkrumah 324, CP 1163, Maputo; tel. 21484200; fax 21484248; e-mail map@minbuza.nl; internet www.hollandinmozambique.org; Ambassador FRANS BIJVOET.

Nigeria: Av. Kenneth Kaunda 821, CP 4693, Maputo; tel. and fax 21490991; High Commissioner ALBERT G. PIUS OMOTAIO.

Norway: Av. Julius Nyerere 1162, CP 828, Maputo; tel. 21480100; fax 21480107; e-mail emb.maputo@mfa.no; internet www.norway.org.mz; Ambassador THORBJØRN GAUSTADSÆTHER.

Portugal: Av. Julius Nyerere 720, CP 4696, Maputo; tel. 21490316; fax 21491172; e-mail embaixada@embpormaputo.org.mz; Ambassador JOSÉ JOAQUIM ESTEVES DOS SANTOS DE FREITAS FERRAZ.

Russia: Av. Vladimir I. Lénine 2445, CP 4666, Maputo; tel. 21417372; fax 21417515; e-mail embrus@tvcabo.co.mz; internet www.mozambique.mid.ru; Ambassador IGOR V. POPOV.

South Africa: Av. Eduardo Mondlane 41, CP 1120, Maputo; tel. 21493030; fax 21493029; e-mail sahc@tropical.co.mz; High Commissioner THANDI LUJABE-RANKOE.

Spain: Rua Damião de Góis 347, CP 1331, Maputo; tel. 21492048; fax 21494769; e-mail emb.maputo@mae.es; Ambassador JUAN MANUEL MOLINA LAMOTHE.

Swaziland: Av. Kwame Nkrumah, CP 4711, Maputo; tel. 21491601; fax 21492117; High Commissioner Prince TSHEKEDI.

Sweden: Av. Julius Nyerere 1128, CP 338, Maputo; tel. 21480300; fax 21480390; e-mail ambassaden.maputo@foreign.ministry.se; internet www.swedenabroad.com/maputo; Ambassador TORVALD ÅKESSON.

Switzerland: Av. Ahmed Sekou Touré 637, CP 135, Maputo; tel. 21315275; fax 21315276; e-mail map.vertretung@eda.admin.ch; internet www.eda.admin.ch/maputo; Ambassador RUDOLF BAERFUSS.

Tanzania: Ujamaa House, Av. dos Mártires da Machava 852, CP 4515, Maputo; tel. 21490110; fax 21494782; e-mail ujamaa@zebra.eum.mz; High Commissioner ISSA MOHAMED ISSA.

Timor-Leste: Maputo; Chargé d'affaires a.i. MARINA ALKATIRI.

United Kingdom: Av. Vladimir I. Lénine 310, CP 55, Maputo; tel. 21356000; fax 21356060; e-mail bhc.consular@tvcabo.co.mz; internet www.britishhighcommission.gov.uk/mozambique; High Commissioner ANDREW SOPER.

USA: Av. Kenneth Kaunda 193, CP 783, Maputo; tel. 21492797; fax 21490114; e-mail consularmaputo@state.gov; internet www.usembassy-maputo.gov.mz; Ambassador WILLIAM R. STEIGER (designate).

Zambia: Av. Kenneth Kaunda 1286, CP 4655, Maputo; tel. 21492452; fax 21491893; e-mail zhcmmap@zebra.uem.mz; High Commissioner SIMON GABRIEL MWILA.

Zimbabwe: Av. Kenneth Kaunda 816, CP 743, Maputo; tel. 21490404; fax 21492237; e-mail maro@isl.co.mz; Ambassador AGRIPA MUTAMBARA.

Judicial System

The Constitution of November 1990 provides for a Supreme Court and other judicial courts, an Administrative Court, courts-martial, customs courts, maritime courts and labour courts. The Supreme Court consists of professional judges, appointed by the President of the Republic, and judges elected by the Assembléia da República. It acts in sections, as a trial court of primary and appellate jurisdiction, and in plenary session, as a court of final appeal. The Administrative Court controls the legality of administrative acts and supervises public expenditure.

President of the Supreme Court: MÁRIO MANGAZE.
Attorney-General: AUGUSTO PAULINO.

Religion

There are an estimated 5m. Christians and 4m. Muslims, as well as small Hindu, Jewish and Bahá'í communities. In 2004 over 100 religious groups were officially registered.

CHRISTIANITY

There are many Christian organizations registered in Mozambique.

Conselho Cristão de Moçambique (CCM) (Christian Council of Mozambique): Av. Agostino Neto 1584, CP 108, Maputo; tel. 21322836; fax 21321968; f. 1948; 22 mems; Pres. Rt Rev. ARÃO MATSOLO; Gen. Sec. Rev. DINIS MATSOLO.

The Roman Catholic Church

Mozambique comprises three archdioceses and nine dioceses. At 31 December 2005 it was estimated that there were some 4,380,842 adherents, representing some 21.4% of the total population.

Bishops' Conference

Conferência Episcopal de Moçambique (CEM), Secretariado Geral da CEM, Av. Paulo Samuel Kankhomba 188/RC, CP 286, Maputo; tel. 21490766; fax 21492174.

f. 1982; Pres. Most Rev. TOMÉ MAKHWELIHA (Archbishop of Nampula).

Archbishop of Beira: Most Rev. JAIME PEDRO GONÇALVES, Cúria Arquiepiscopal, Rua Correia de Brito 613, CP 544, Beira; tel. 23322313; fax 23327639; e-mail arquidbeira@teledata.mz.

Archbishop of Maputo: Most Rev. FRANCISCO CHIMOIO, Paço Arquiepiscopal, Avda Eduardo Mondlane 1448, CP 258, Maputo; tel. 21326240; fax 21321873.

Archbishop of Nampula: Most Rev. TOMÉ MAKHWELIHA, Paço Arquiepiscopal, CP 84, 70100 Nampula; tel. 26213024; fax 26214194; e-mail arquidiocesenpl@teledata.mz.

The Anglican Communion

Anglicans in Mozambique are adherents of the Anglican Church of Southern Africa (formerly the Church of the Province of Southern Africa). There are two dioceses in Mozambique. The Metropolitan of the Province is the Archbishop of Cape Town, South Africa.

Bishop of Lebombo: Rt Rev. DINIS SALOMÃO SENGULANE, CP 120, Maputo; tel. 21734364; fax 21401093; e-mail libombo@zebra.uem.mz.

Bishop of Niassa: Rev. MARK VAN KOEVERING, CP 264, Lichinga, Niassa; tel. 27112735; fax 27112336; e-mail anglican-niassa@maf.org.

Other Churches

Baptist Convention of Mozambique: Av. Maguiguane 386, CP 852, Maputo; tel. 2126852; Pres. Rev. BENTO BARTOLOMEU MATUSSE; 78 churches, 25,000 adherents.

The Church of Jesus Christ of the Latter-Day Saints: Maputo; 9 congregations, 1,975 mems.

Free Methodist Church: Pres. Rev. FRANISSE SANDO MUVILE; 214 churches, 21,231 mems.

Igreja Congregational Unida de Moçambique: Rua 4 Bairro 25 de Junho, CP 930, Maputo; tel. 21475820; Pres., Sec. of the Synod A. A. LITSURE.

Igreja Maná: Rua Francisco Orlando Magumbwe 528, Maputo; tel. 21491760; fax 21490896; e-mail adm_mocambique@igrejamana.com; Bishop DOMINGOS COSTA.

Igreja Reformada em Moçambique (IRM) (Reformed Church in Mozambique): CP 3, Vila Ulongue, Anogonia-Tete; f. 1908; Gen. Sec. Rev. SAMUEL M. BESSITALA; 60,000 mems.

Presbyterian Church of Mozambique: Av. Ahmed Sekou Touré 1822, CP 21, Maputo; tel. 21421790; fax 21428623; e-mail ipmoc@zebra.uem.mz; 100,000 adherents; Pres. of Synodal Council Rev. MÁRIO NYAMUXWE.

MOZAMBIQUE

Seventh-Day Adventist Church: Av. Maguiguana 300, CP 1468, Maputo; tel. and fax 21427200; e-mail victormiconde@teledata.co.mz; 937 churches, 186,724 mems (2004).

Other denominations active in Mozambique include the Church of Christ, the Church of the Nazarene, the Greek Orthodox Church, the United Methodist Church of Mozambique, the Wesleyan Methodist Church, the Zion Christian Church, and Jehovah's Witnesses.

ISLAM

Comunidade Mahometana: Av. Albert Luthuli 291, Maputo; tel. 21425181; fax 21300880; internet www.paginaislamica.8m.com/pg1.htm; Pres. ABDUL ASSIZ OSMAN LATIF.

Congresso Islâmico de Moçambique (Islamic Congress of Mozambique): represents Sunni Muslims; Chair. ASSANE ISMAEL MAQBUL.

Conselho Islâmico de Moçambique (Islamic Council of Mozambique): Leader Sheikh AMINUDDIN MOHAMAD.

The Press

DAILIES

Correio da Manha: Av. Filipe Samuel Magaia 528, CP 1756, Maputo; tel. 21305322; fax 21305321; e-mail refi@virconn.com; f. 1997; published by Sojornal, Lda; also publishes weekly Correio Semanal; Dir REFINALDO CHILENGUE.

Diário de Moçambique: Av. 25 de Setembro 1509, 2° andar, CP 2491, Beira; tel. and fax 23427312; f. 1981; under state management since 1991; Dir EZEQUIEL AMBRÓSIO; Editor FARUCO SADIQUE; circ. 5,000 (2003).

Expresso da Tarde: Av. Patrice Lumumba 511, 1° andar, Maputo; tel. 21314912; subscription only; distribution by fax; Dir SALVADOR RAIMUNDO HONWANA.

Mediafax: Av. Amílcar Cabral 1049, CP 73, Maputo; tel. 21301737; fax 21302402; e-mail mediafax@tvcabo.co.mz; f. 1992 by co-operative of independent journalists Mediacoop; news-sheet by subscription only, distribution by fax and internet; Editor BENEDITO NGOMANE.

Notícias de Moçambique: Rua Joaquim Lapa 55, CP 327, Maputo; tel. 21420119; fax 21420575; f. 1926; morning; f. 1906; under state management since 1991; Dir BERNARDO MAVANGA; Editor HILÁRIO COSSA; circ. 12,793 (2003).

Further newspapers available solely in email or fax format include Diário de Notícias and Matinal.

WEEKLIES

Campeão: Av. 24 de Julho 3706, CP 2610, Maputo; tel. and fax 21401810; sports newspaper; Dir RENATO CALDÉIRA; Editor ALEXANDRE ZANDAMELA.

Correio Semanal: Av. Filipe Samuel Magaia 528, CP 1756, Maputo; tel. 21305322; fax 21305312; Dir REFINALDO CHILENGUE.

Desafio: Rua Joaquim Lapa 55, Maputo; tel. 21305437; fax 21305431; Dir ALMIRO SANTOS; Editor BOAVIDA FUNJUA; circ. 3,890 (2003).

Domingo: Rua Joaquim Lapa 55, CP 327, Maputo; tel. 21431026; fax 21431027; f. 1981; Sun.; Dir JORGE MATINE; circ. 15,000 (2007).

Fim de Semana: Rua da Resistência 1642, 1° andar, Maputo; tel. and fax 21417012; e-mail fimdomes@tvcabo.co.mz; internet www.fimdesemana.co.mz; f. 1997; independent.

Savana: Av. Amílcar Cabral 1049, CP 73, Maputo; tel. 21301737; fax 21302402; e-mail savana@mediacoop.co.mz; internet www.mediacoop.odline.com; f. 1994; owned by mediacoop, SA; CEO FERNANDO LIMA; Dir KOK NAM; Editor FERNANDO GONÇALVES; circ. 15,000 (2007).

Tempo: Av. Ahmed Sekou Touré 1078, CP 2917, Maputo; tel. 21426191; f. 1970; magazine; under state management since 1991; Dir ROBERTO UAENE; Editor ARLINDO LANGA; circ. 40,000.

Zambeze: Rua José Sidumo, Maputo; tel. 21302019; Dir SALOMÃO MOYANE; circ. 2,000 (2003).

PERIODICALS

Agora: Afrisurvey, Lda, Rua General Pereira d'Eça 200, 1° andar, CP 1335, Maputo; tel. 21494147; fax 21494204; internet www.agora.co.mz; f. 2000; monthly; economics, politics, society; Pres. MARIA DE LOURDES TORCATO; Dir JOVITO NUNES; Editor-in-Chief ERCÍLIA SANTOS; circ. 5,000.

Agricultura: Instituto Nacional de Investigação Agronómica, CP 3658, Maputo; tel. 2130091; f. 1982; quarterly; publ. by Centro de Documentação de Agricultura, Silvicultura, Pecuária e Pescas.

Aro: Av. 24 de Julho 1420, CP 4187, Maputo; f. 1995; monthly; Dir POLICARTO TAMELE; Editor BRUNO MACAME, Jr.

Arquivo Histórico: Av. Filipe Samuel Magaia 715, CP 2033, Maputo; tel. 21421177; fax 21423428; f. 1934; Editor JOEL DAS NEVES TEMBE.

Boletim da República: Av. Vladimir I. Lénine, CP 275, Maputo; govt and official notices; publ. by Imprensa Nacional da Moçambique.

Maderazinco: Maputo; e-mail maderazinco@yahoo.com; f. 2002; quarterly; literature.

Moçambique–Novos Tempos: Av. Ahmed Sekou Touré 657, Maputo; tel. 21493564; fax 21493590; f. 1992; Dir J. MASCARENHAS.

Mozambiquefile: c/o AIM, Rua da Radio Moçambique, CP 896, Maputo; tel. 21313225; fax 21313196; e-mail aim@aim.org.mz; internet www.sortmoz.com/aimnews; monthly; Dir GUSTAVO MAVIZ; Editor PAUL FAUVET.

Mozambique Inview: c/o Mediacoop, Av. Amílcar Cabral 1049, CP 73, Maputo; tel. 21430722; fax 21302402; e-mail inview@mediacoop.co.mz; internet www.mediacoop.odline.com; f. 1994; 2 a month; economic bulletin in English; Editor FRANCES CHRISTIE.

Portos e Caminhos de Ferro: CP 276, Maputo; English and Portuguese; ports and railways; quarterly.

Revista Médica de Moçambique: Instituto Nacional de Saúde, Ministério da Saúde e Faculdade de Medicina, Universidade Eduardo Mondlane, CP 264, Maputo; tel. 21420368; fax 21431103; e-mail mdgedge@malarins.uem.mz; f. 1982; 4 a year; medical journal; Editor MARTINHO DGEDGE.

NEWS AGENCY

Agência de Informação de Moçambique (AIM): Rua da Rádio Moçambique, CP 896, Maputo; tel. 21313225; fax 21313196; e-mail aim@aim.org.mz; internet www.sortmoz.com/aimnews; f. 1975; daily reports in Portuguese and English; Dir GUSTAVO LISSETIANE MAVIE.

Publishers

There are an estimated 30 printing and publishing companies in Mozambique.

Arquivo Histórico de Moçambique (AHM): Av. Filipe Samuel Magaia 715, CP 2033, Maputo; tel. 21421177; fax 21423428; internet www.ahm.uem.mz; Dir JOEL DAS NEVES TEMBE.

Central Impressora: c/o Ministério da Saúde, Avs Eduardo Mondlane e Salvador Allende 1008, CP 264, Maputo; tel. 21427131; fax 21427133; owned by the Ministry of Health.

Centro de Estudos Africanos: Universidade Eduardo Mondlane, CP 1993, Maputo; tel. 21490828; fax 21491896; f. 1976; social and political science, regional history, economics; Dir Col SERGIO VIEIRA.

Editora Minerva Central: Rua Consiglieri Pedroso 84, CP 212, Maputo; tel. 2122092; f. 1908; stationers and printers, educational, technical and medical textbooks; Man. Dir J. F. CARVALHO.

Editorial Ndjira, Lda: Av. Ho Chi Minh 85, Maputo; tel. 21300180; fax 21308745; f. 1996.

Empresa Moderna Lda: Av. 25 de Setembro, CP 473, Maputo; tel. 21424594; f. 1937; fiction, history, textbooks; Man. Dir LOUIS GALLOTI.

Fundo Bibliográfico de Língua Portuguesa: Av. 25 de Setembro 1230, 7° andar, Maputo; tel. 21429531; fax 21429530; e-mail palop@zebra.uem.mz; f. 1990; state owned; Pres. LOURENÇO ROSÁRIO.

Imprensa Universitária: Universidade Eduardo Mondlane, Praça 19 de Maio, Maputo; internet www.uem.mz/imprensa_universitaris; university press.

Instituto Nacional do Livro e do Disco: Av. 24 de Julho 1921, CP 4030, Maputo; tel. 21434870; govt publishing and purchasing agency; Dir ARMÉNIO CORREIA.

Moçambique Editora: Rua Armando Tivane 1430, Bairro de Polana, Maputo; tel. 21495017; fax 21499071; e-mail info@me.co.mz; internet www.me.co.mz; f. 1996; educational textbooks, dictionaries.

Plural Editores: Av. 24 de Julho 414, Maputo; tel. 21486828; fax 21486829; e-mail plural@pluraleditores.co.mz; internet www.pluraleditores.co.mz; f. 2003; educational textbooks; part of the Porto Editora Group.

GOVERNMENT PUBLISHING HOUSE

Imprensa Nacional de Moçambique: Rua da Imprensa, CP 275, Maputo; tel. 21427021; fax 21424858; internet www.imprensanac.gov.mz; part of Ministry of State Administration; Dir VENÂNCIO T. MANJATE.

MOZAMBIQUE
Directory

Broadcasting and Communications

TELECOMMUNICATIONS

Regulatory Authority

Instituto Nacional das Comunicações de Moçambique (INCM): Av. Eduardo Mondlane 123–127, CP 848, Maputo; tel. 21490131; fax 21494435; e-mail info@incm.gov.mz; internet www.incm.gov.mz; regulates post and telecommunications systems.

Major Telecommunications Companies

TDM currently has a monopoly on fixed lines; however, plans were announced in 2004 to open this sector to competition in the late 2000s.

Telecomunicações de Moçambique, SARL (TDM): Rua da Sé 2, CP 25, Maputo; tel. 21431921; fax 21431944; e-mail jcarvalho@tdm.mz; internet www.tdm.mz; f. 1993; Chair. JOAQUIM RIBEIRO PEREIRA DE CARVALHO; Man. Dir SALVADOR ADRIANO.

Moçambique Celular (mCel): Edif. Mcel, Esquina Av. 25 de Setembro e Rua Belmiro Obede Muianga, CP 1463, Maputo; tel. 21351111; fax 21351119; internet www.mcel.co.mz; f. 1997 as a subsidiary of TDM; separated from TDM in 2003; mobile cellular telephone provider.

Vodacom Moçambique: Time Square Complex, Bloco 3, Av. 25 de Setembro, Maputo; tel. 21084111; internet www.vm.co.mz; f. 2002; owned by Vodacom (South Africa); Chair. HERMENGILDO GAMITO; Man. Dir CLIVE TARR.

BROADCASTING

Radio

Rádio Encontro: Av. Francisco Manyanga, CP 366, Nampula; tel. 26215588.

Rádio Feba Moçambique: Av. Julius Nyerere 441, Maputo; tel. 21440002.

Rádio Maria: Rua Igreja 156A, Machava Sede, Matola, Maputo; tel. 21750505; fax 21752124; e-mail ramamo@virconn.com; f. 1995; evangelical radio broadcasts; Dir Fr JOÃO CARLOS H. NUNES.

Rádio Miramar: Rede de Comunicação, Av. Julius Nyerere 1555, Maputo; tel. and fax 21488613; e-mail jose.guerra@tvcabo.co.mz; owned by Brazilian religious sect, the Universal Church of the Kingdom of God.

Rádio Moçambique: Rua da Rádio 2, CP 2000, Maputo; tel. 21431687; fax 21321816; e-mail sepca_mz@yahoo.com.br; internet www.rm.co.mz; f. 1975; programmes in Portuguese, English and vernacular languages; Chair. RICARDO MADAUANE MALATE.

Rádio Terra Verde: fmrly Voz da Renamo; owned by former rebel movement Renamo; transmitters in Maputo and Gorongosa, Sofala province.

Rádio Trans Mundial Moçambique: Av. Eduardo Mondlane 2998, Maputo; tel. 21407358; fax 21407357.

Television

The Portuguese station RTP-Africa also broadcasts in Mozambique.

Rádio Televisão Klint (RTK): Av. Agostinho Neto 946, Maputo; tel. 21422956; fax 21493306; Dir CARLOS KLINT.

Televisão Miramar: Rua Pereira Lago 221, Maputo; owned by Brazilian religious sect, the Igrega Universal do Reino de Deus (Universal Church of the Kingdom of God).

Televisão de Moçambique, EP (TVM): Av. 25 de Setembro 154, CP 2675, Maputo; tel. 21308117; fax 21308122; e-mail tvm@tvm.co.mz; internet www.tvm.co.mz; f. 1981; Chair. and CEO SIMÃO JORDÃO ANGUILAZE.

TV Cabo Moçambique: Av. dos Presidentes 68, CP 1750, Maputo; tel. 21480500; fax 21480501; e-mail tvcabo@tvcabo.co.mz; internet www.tvcabo.co.mz; cable television and internet services in Maputo.

Finance

(cap. = capital; res = reserves; dep. = deposits; m. = million; brs = branches; amounts in meticais, unless otherwise stated)

BANKING

Central Bank

Banco de Moçambique: Av. 25 de Setembro 1679, CP 423, Maputo; tel. 21318000; fax 21323247; e-mail cdi@bancomoc.mz; internet www.bancomoc.mz; f. 1975; bank of issue; cap. 248,952m., res 532,697m., dep. 17,360m. (Dec. 2006); Gov. ERNESTO GOUVEIA GOVE; 4 brs.

National Banks

Banco Austral: Av. 25 de Setembro 1184, CP 757, Maputo; tel. 21308800; fax 21301094; internet www.bancoaustral.co.mz; f. 1977; fmrly Banco Popular de Desenvolvimento (BPD); renationalized in 2001; 80% owned by Amalgamated Banks of South Africa, 20% owned by União, Sociedade e Participacões, SARL, which represents employees of the bank; cap. 315,000m., res –550m., dep. 2,047,081m. (Dec. 2003); Chair. CASIMIRO FRANCISCO; Man. Dir GERALD JORDAAN; 52 brs and agencies.

BCI Fomento (BCI) (Banco Comercial e de Investimentos, SARL): Edif. John Orr's, Av. 25 de Setembro 1465, CP 4745, Maputo; tel. 21307777; fax 21307762; e-mail bci@bci.co.mz; internet www.bci.co.mz; f. 1996; renamed as above following 2003 merger between Banco Comercial e de Investimentos and Banco de Fomento; 42% owned by Caixa Geral de Depósitos (Portugal), 30% Banco Português de Investimento; dep. US $360.0m. (Dec. 2004); Chair. ABDUL MAGID OSMAN; 34 brs.

Banco de Desenvolvimento e de Comércio de Moçambique, SARL (BDCM): Av. 25 de Setembro 420, 1° andar, sala 8, Maputo; tel. 21313040; fax 21313047; f. 2000; 42% owned by Montepio Geral (Portugal).

BIM—Investimento (Banco Internacional de Moçambique—Investimento): Av. Kim Il Sung 961, Maputo; tel. 21354896; fax 21354897; e-mail mpinto@bim.co.mz; internet www.bimnet.co.mz; f. 1998; 50% owned by Millennium bim, 25% by BCP Investimento and 15% by International Finance Corpn; total assets US $2.7m. (Dec. 2003); Chair. Dr MÁRIO FERNANDES DA GRAÇA MACHUNGO; Gen. Dir Dr JOSÉ A. FERREIRA GOMES.

Banco Mercantil e de Investimento, SARL (BMI): Av. 24 de Julho 3549, Maputo; tel. 21407979; fax 21408887.

ICB-Banco Internacional de Comércio, SARL: Av. 25 de Setembro 1915, Maputo; tel. 21311111; fax 21314797; e-mail icbm@teledata.mz; internet www.icbank-mz.com; f. 1998; cap. and res 44,923,748m., total assets 164,773,569m. (Dec. 2003); Chair. JOSEPHINE SIVARETNAM; CEO LEE SANG HUAT.

Millennium bim: Av. 25 de Setembro 1800, CP 865, Maputo; tel. 21351500; fax 21354808; e-mail fxavier@millenniumbim.co.mz; internet www.millenniumbim.co.mz; f. 1995; name changed from Banco Internacional de Moçambique in 2005; 66.7% owned by Banco Comercial Português, 17.8% by the state; cap. 741,000m. (Dec. 2007); Pres. MÁRIO FERNANDES DA GRAÇA MACHUNGO; CEO JOÃO FILIPE DE FIGUEIREDO JÚNIOR; 86 brs.

Novo Banco, SARL: Av. do Trabalho 750, Maputo; tel. and fax 21407705; f. 2000; cap. and res 51,995m., total assets 108,847m. (Dec. 2003).

Standard Bank, SARL (Moçambique): Praça 25 de Junho 1, CP 2086, Maputo; tel. 21352500; fax 21426967; e-mail camal.daude@standardbank.co.mz; internet www.standardbank.co.mz; f. 1966 as Banco Standard Totta de Mozambique; 96.0% owned by Stanbic Africa Holdings, UK; cap. 174,000m., res 173,295m., dep. 6,080,437m. (Dec. 2003); Man. Dir ANTONIO COUTINHO; 24 brs.

Foreign Banks

African Banking Corporation (Moçambique), SA: ABC House, Av. Julius Nyerere 999, Polana, CP 1445, Maputo; tel. 21482100; fax 21487474; e-mail abcmoz@africanbankingcorp.com; internet www.africanbankingcorp.com; f. 1999; 100% owned by African Banking Corpn Holdings Ltd (Botswana); fmrly BNP Nedbank (Moçambique), SARL; changed name as above after acquisition in 2002; cap. 148m., res 173m., dep. 1,094m. (Dec. 2007); Chair. BENJAMIM ALFREDO; Man. Dir JOHN MCGUFOG; 2 brs.

African Banking Corporation Leasing, SARL: Rua da Imprensa 256, 7° andar, CP 4447, Maputo; tel. 21300451; fax 21431290; e-mail ulcmoz@mail.tropical.co.mz; 66% owned by African Banking Corpn Holdings Ltd (Botswana); fmrly ULC (Moçambique); changed name as above in 2002; total assets US $1.8m. (Dec. 1998); Chair. ANTÓNIO BRANCO; Gen. Man. VICTOR VISEU.

União Comercial de Bancos (Moçambique), SARL: Av. Friedrich Engels 400, Maputo; tel. 21481900; fax 21498675; e-mail contact@mcbmozambique.com; f. 1999; 81.24% owned by Mauritius Commercial Bank Group; total assets US $46,777m. (Dec. 2006); Chair. PIERRE GUY NOEL; Gen. Man. ROBERT CANTIN.

DEVELOPMENT FUND

Fundo de Desenvolvimento Agrícola e Rural: CP 1406, Maputo; tel. 21460349; fax 21460157; f. 1987 to provide credit for small farmers and rural co-operatives; promotes agricultural and rural devt; Sec. EDUARDO OLIVEIRA.

STOCK EXCHANGE

Bolsa de Valores de Moçambique: Av. 25 de Setembro 1230, Prédio 33, 5° andar, Maputo; tel. 21308826; fax 21310559; Chair. Dr JUSSUB NURMAMAD.

INSURANCE

In December 1991 the Assembléia da República approved legislation terminating the state monopoly of insurance and reinsurance activities. In 2005 five insurance companies were operating in Mozambique.

Companhia de Seguros de Moçambique, IMPAR: Rua da Imprensa 625, Prédio 33, Maputo; tel. 21429695; fax 21430640; f. 1992; Pres. INOCÊNCIO A. MATAVEL; Gen. Man. MANUEL BALANCHO.

Empresa Moçambicana de Seguros, EE (EMOSE): Av. 25 de Setembro 1383, CP 1165, Maputo; tel. 21356300; fax 21424526; f. 1977 as state insurance monopoly; took over business of 24 fmr cos; 80% govt-owned, 20% private; cap. 150m.; Chair. VENÂNCIO MONDLANE.

Seguradora Internacional de Moçambique: Av 25 Setembro 1800, Maputo; tel. 21430959; fax 21430241; e-mail simseg@zebra.uem.mz; Pres. MÁRIO FERNANDES DA GRAÇA MACHUNGO.

Trade and Industry

GOVERNMENT AGENCIES

Centro de Promoção de Investimentos (CPI) (Investment Promotion Centre): Rua da Imprensa 332, CP 4635, Maputo; tel. 21313295; fax 21313325; e-mail cpi@cpi.co.mz; internet www.cpi.co.mz; f. 1987; encourages domestic and foreign investment and IT ventures with foreign firms; evaluates and negotiates investment proposals; Dir MAHOMED RAFIQUE JUSOB MAHOMED.

Instituto de Algodão de Moçambique (IAM): Av. Eduardo Mondlane 2221, 1° andar, CP 806, Maputo; tel. 21424264; fax 21430679; e-mail iampab@zebra.uem.mz; responsible for promotion and devt of the cotton industry; Dir (vacant).

Instituto do Fomento do Cajú (INCAJU): Maputo; national cashew institute; Dir CLEMENTINA MACHUNGO.

Instituto Nacional de Açúcar (INA): Rua da Gávea 33, CP 1772, Maputo; tel. 21326550; fax 21427436; e-mail gpsca.ina@tvcabo.co.mz; Chair. ARNALDO RIBEIRO.

Instituto Nacional de Petróleo (INP): Av. Fernão de Magalhães 34, CP 4724, Maputo; tel. 21320935; fax 21430850; e-mail info@inp.gov.mz; internet www.inp.gov.mz; f. 2005; regulates energy sector; Dir ARSÉNIO MABOTE.

Instituto para a Promoção de Exportações (IPEX): Av. 25 de Setembro 1008, 3° andar, CP 4487, Maputo; tel. 21307257; fax 21307256; e-mail ipex@tvcabo.co.mz; internet www.ipex.gov.mz; f. 1990 to promote and co-ordinate national exports abroad; Pres. Dr JOÃO MACARINGUE.

Unidade Técnica para a Reestruturação de Empresas (UTRE): Rua da Imprensa 256, 7° andar, CP 4350, Maputo; tel. 21426514; fax 21421541; implements restructuring of state enterprises; Dir MOMADE JUMAS.

CHAMBERS OF COMMERCE

Câmara de Comércio de Moçambique (CCM): Rua Mateus Sansão Muthemba 452, CP 1836, Maputo; tel. 21491970; fax 21490428; e-mail cacomo@teledata.nz; internet www.teledata.mz/cacomo; f. 1980; Pres. JACINTO VELOSO; Sec.-Gen. MANUEL NOTIÇO.

Mozambique-USA Chamber of Commerce: Rua Matheus Sansão Muthemba 452, Maputo; tel. 21492904; fax 21492739; e-mail ccmusa@tvcabo.co.mx; internet www.ccmusa.co.mz; f. 1993; Sec. PETER VAN AS.

South Africa-Mozambique Chamber of Commerce (SAMOZACC): e-mail info@samozacc.co.za; internet www.samozacc.co.za; f. 2005; Chair. (Mozambique) ANTÓNIO MATOS.

TRADE ASSOCIATIONS

Associação das Indústrias do Cajú (AICAJU): Maputo; cashew processing industry assen; Chair. CARLOS COSTA; 12 mem. cos.

Confederação das Associações Económicas de Moçambique (CTA): Rua de Castanheda, CP 2975, Maputo; tel. 21491914; fax 21493094; internet www.cta.org.mz; Pres. SALIMO ABDULA; Exec. Dir SÉRGIO CHITARÁ; 58 mem. cos.

STATE INDUSTRIAL ENTERPRISES

Empresa Nacional de Carvão de Moçambique (CARBOMOC): Rua Joaquim Lapa 108, CP 1773, Maputo; tel. 21427625; fax 21424714; f. 1948; mineral extraction and export; transfer to private ownership pending; Dir JAIME RIBEIRO.

Empresa Nacional de Hidrocarbonetos de Moçambique (ENH): Av. Fernão de Magalhães 34, CP 4787, Maputo; tel. 21429456; fax 21421608; controls concessions for petroleum exploration and production; Dir MÁRIO MARQUES.

Petróleos de Moçambique (PETROMOC): Praça dos Trabalhadores 9, CP 417, Maputo; tel. 21427191; fax 21430181; internet www.petromoc.co.mz; f. 1977 to take over the Sonarep oil refinery and its associated distribution co; formerly Empresa Nacional de Petróleos de Moçambique; state directorate for liquid fuels within Mozambique, incl. petroleum products passing through Mozambique to inland countries; CEO CASIMIR FRANCISCO.

UTILITIES

Electricity

Electricidade de Moçambique (EDM): Av. Agostinho Neto 70, CP 2447, Maputo; tel. 21490636; fax 21491048; e-mail ligacaoexpresso@edm.co.mz; internet www.edm.co.mz; f. 1977; 100% state-owned; production and distribution of electric energy; in 2004 plans were announced to extend EDM grid to entire country by 2020, at an estimated cost of US $700m; Pres. MANUEL JOÃO CUAMBE; Dir PASCOAL BACELA; 2,700 employees.

Companhia de Transmissão de Moçambique, SARL (MOTRACO) (Mozambique Transmission Co): Prédio JAT, 4° andar, Av. 25 de Setembro 420, Maputo; tel. 21313427; fax 21313447; e-mail asimao@motraco.co.mz; internet www.motraco.co.mz; f. 1998; jt venture between power utilities of Mozambique, South Africa and Swaziland; electricity distribution; Gen. Man. FRANCIS MASAWI.

Water

Direcção Nacional de Águas: Av. 25 de Setembro 942, 9° andar, CP 1611, Maputo; tel. 21420469; fax 21421403; e-mail watco@zebra.uem.mz; internet www.dna.mz; Dir AMÉRICO MUIANGA.

TRADE UNIONS

Freedom to form trade unions, and the right to strike, are guaranteed under the 1990 Constitution.

Confederação de Sindicatos Livres e Independentes de Moçambique (CONSILMO): Sec.-Gen. JEREMIAS TIMANE.

Organização dos Trabalhadores de Moçambique—Central Sindical (OTM—CS) (Mozambique Workers' Organization—Trade Union Headquarters): Rua Manuel António de Sousa 36, Maputo; tel. 21426786; fax 21421671; internet www.otm.org.mz; f. 1983; Pres. AMÓS JÚNIOR MATSIUHE; Sec.-Gen. (vacant); 15 affiliated unions with over 94,000 mems including:

Sindicato Nacional dos Empregadores Bancários (SNEB): Av. Fernão de Magalhães 785, 1° andar, CP 1230, Maputo; tel. 21428627; fax 21303274; e-mail snebmoz@tvcabo.co.mz; internet www.snebmoz.co.mz; f. 1992; Sec.-Gen. CARLOS MELO.

Sindicato Nacional da Função Pública (SNAPF): Av. Ho Chi Min 365, Maputo; Sec.-Gen. MANUEL ABUDO MOMAD.

Sindicato Nacional dos Profissionais da Estiva e Ofícios Correlativos (SINPEOC): Av. Paulo Samuel Kakhomba 1568, Maputo; tel. and fax 21309535; Sec.-Gen. BENTO MADALA MAUNGUE.

Sindicato Nacional dos Trabalhadores Agro-Pecuários e Florestais (SINTAF): Av. 25 de Setembro 1676, 1° andar, CP 4202, Maputo; tel. 21306284; f. 1987; Sec.-Gen. EUSÉBIO LUÍS CHIVULELE.

Sindicato Nacional dos Trabalhadores da Aviação Civil, Correios e Comunicações (SINTAC): Rua de Silves 24, Maputo; tel. 21309574; Sec.-Gen. LUCAS LUCAZE.

Sindicato Nacional dos Trabalhadores do Comércio, Seguros e Serviços (SINECOSSE): Av. Ho Chi Minh 365, 1° andar, CP 2142, Maputo; tel. 21428561; Sec.-Gen. AMÓS JÚNIOR MATSINHE.

Sindicato Nacional dos Trabalhadores da Indústria do Açúcar (SINTIA): Av. das FPLM 1912, Maputo; tel. 21461772; fax 21461975; f. 1989; Sec.-Gen. ALEXANDRE CÂNDIDO MUNGUAMBE.

Sindicato Nacional dos Trabalhadores da Indústria Alimentar e Bebidas (SINTIAB): Av. Eduardo Mondlane 1267, CP 394, Maputo; tel. 21324709; fax 21324123; f. 1986; Gen. Sec. SAMUEL FENIAS MATSINHE.

Sindicato Nacional dos Trabalhadores da Indústria de Cajú (SINTIC): Rua do Jardim 574, 4° andar, Maputo; tel. 21477732; Sec.-Gen. BOAVENTURA MONDLANE.

Sindicato Nacional dos Trabalhadores da Indústria Metalúrgica, Metalomecânica e Energia (SINTIME): Av. Samora Machel 30, 6°, Maputo; Sec.-Gen. SIMIÃO NHATUMBO.

MOZAMBIQUE

Sindicato Nacional dos Trabalhadores da Indústria Química, Borracha, Papel e Gráfica (SINTIQUIGRA): Av. Olof Palme 255, CP 4439, Maputo; tel. 21320288; fax 21321096; f. 1987; chemical, rubber, paper and print workers' union; due to merge with SINTEVEC in 2007; Co-ordinator JESSICA GUNE; 4,970 mems.

Sindicato Nacional dos Trabalhadores da Indústria Têxtil Vestuário, Couro e Calçado (SINTEVEC): Av. do Trabalho 1276, 1° andar, CP 2613, Maputo; tel. 21404669; fax 21409295; clothing, leather and footwear workers' union; due to merge with SINTIQUIGRA in 2007; Sec.-Gen. MARIO RAIMUNDO SITOE; 1,700 mems.

Sindicato Nacional dos Trabalhadores da Marinha Mercante e Pesca (SINTMAP): Rua Joaquim Lapa 22, 5° andar, No. 6, Maputo; tel. 21305593; Sec.-Gen. DANIEL MANUEL NGOQUE.

Sindicato Nacional dos Trabalhadores dos Portos e Caminhos de Ferro (SINPOCAF): Av. Guerra Popular, esquina 24 de Setembro, CP 2158, Maputo; tel. 21403912; fax 21303839; Sec.-Gen. SAMUEL ALFREDO CHEUANE.

Sindicato Nacional de Jornalistas (SNJ): Av. 24 de Julho 231, Maputo; tel. 21492031; fax 823015912; f. 1978; Sec.-Gen. EDUARDO CONSTANTINO.

Transport

Improvements to the transport infrastructure since the signing of the Acordo Geral de Paz (General Peace Agreement) in 1992 have focused on the development of 'transport corridors', which include both rail and road links and promote industrial development in their environs. The Beira Corridor, with rail and road links and a petroleum pipeline, runs from Manica, on the Zimbabwean border, to the Mozambican port of Beira, while the Limpopo Corridor joins southern Zimbabwe and Maputo. Both corridors form a vital outlet for the land-locked southern African countries, particularly Zimbabwe. The Maputo Corridor links Ressano Garcia in South Africa to the port at Maputo, and the Nacala Corridor runs from Malawi to the port of Nacala. Two further corridors were planned: the Mtwara Development Corridor was to link Mozambique, Malawi, Tanzania and Zambia, while the Zambezi Corridor was to link Zambézia province with Malawi. In February 2000 much of the country's infrastructure in the southern and central provinces was devastated as the result of massive flooding. Railway lines, roads and bridges suffered considerable damage.

RAILWAYS

In 2003 the total length of track was 3,114 km, of which 2,072 km was operational. There are both internal routes and rail links between Mozambican ports and South Africa, Swaziland, Zimbabwe and Malawi. During the hostilities many lines and services were disrupted. Improvement work on most of the principal railway lines began in the early 1980s. In the early 2000s work began on upgrading the railway system and private companies were granted non-permanent concessions to upgrade and run the railways.

Empresa Portos e Caminhos de Ferro de Moçambique (CFM): Praça dos Trabalhadores, CP 2158, Maputo; tel. 21327173; fax 21427746; e-mail cfmnet@cfmnet.co.mz; internet www.cfmnet.co.mz; fmrly Empresa Nacional dos Portos e Caminhos de Ferro de Moçambique; privatized and restructured in 2002; Chair. RUI FONSECA; comprises four separate systems linking Mozambican ports with the country's hinterland, and with other southern African countries, including South Africa, Swaziland, Zimbabwe and Malawi:

CFM—Centro (CFM—C): Largo dos CFM, CP 236, Beira; tel. 23321000; fax 23329290; lines totalling 994 km linking Beira with Zimbabwe and Malawi, as well as link to Moatize (undergoing rehabilitation); Exec. Dir JOAQUIM VERÍSSIMO.

CFM—Norte: Av. do Trabalho, CP 16, Nampula; tel. 26214320; fax 26212034; lines totalling 872 km, including link between port of Nacala with Malawi; management concession awarded to Nacala Corridor Development Co (a consortium 67% owned by South African, Portuguese and US cos) in January 2000; Dir FILIPE NHUSSI; Dir of Railways MANUEL MANICA.

CFM—Sul: Praça dos Trabalhadores, CP 2158, Maputo; tel. and fax 21430894; lines totalling 1,070 km linking Maputo with South Africa, Swaziland and Zimbabwe, as well as Inhambane–Inharrime and Xai-Xai systems; Exec. Dir JOAQUIM ZUCULE.

CFM—Zambézia: CP 73, Quelimane; tel. 24212502; fax 24213123; 145-km line linking Quelimane and Mocuba; Dir ORLANDO J. JAIME.

Beira Railway Co: Dondo; f. 2004; 51% owned by Rites & Ircon (India), 49% owned by CFM; rehabilitating and managing Sena and Zimbabwe railway lines.

ROADS

In 1999 there were an estimated 30,400 km of roads in Mozambique, of which 5,685 km were paved. Although the road network was improved in the 1990s, the severe floods in February 2000 meant that much of the construction would have to be repeated. In 2001 the Government announced plans to invest US $1,700m. in upgrading and maintaining the road network. In 2003 827 km of road were built or upgraded. Road and bridge construction projects were ongoing in the mid-2000s.

Administraçao Nacional de Estradas (ANE): Av. de Moçambique 1225, CP 1294, Maputo; tel. 21475157; fax 21475290; internet www.dnep.gov.mz; f. 1999 to replace the Direcção Nacional de Estradas e Pontes; implements government road policy through the Direcção de Estradas Nacionais (DEN) and the Direcção de Estradas Regionais (DER); Pres. Eng. CARLOS FRAGOSO; Dir-Gen. IBRAIMO REMANE.

SHIPPING

Mozambique has three main sea ports, at Nacala, Beira and Maputo, while inland shipping on Lake Niassa and the river system was underdeveloped. At December 2006 Mozambique's registered merchant fleet consisted of 129 vessels, totalling 36,478 grt.

Empresa Portos e Caminhos de Ferro de Moçambique (CFM-EP): Praça dos Trabalhadores, CP 2158, Maputo; tel. 21427173; fax 21427746; e-mail cfmnet@cfmnet.co.mz; internet www.cfmnet.co.mz; fmrly Empresa Nacional dos Portos e Caminhos de Ferro de Moçambique; privatized and restructured in 2002; Port Dir CFM-Sul BOAVENTURA CHAMBAL; Port Dir CFM-Norte AGOSTINHO LANGA, Jr; Port Dir CFM-Centro CHINGUANE MABOTE.

Agência Nacional de Frete e Navegação (ANFRENA): Rua Consiglieri Pedroso 396, CP 492, Maputo; tel. 21427064; fax 21427822; Dir FERDINAND WILSON.

Empresa Moçambicana de Cargas, SARL (MOCARGO): Rua Consiglieri Pedroso 430, 1°–4° andares, CP 888, Maputo; tel. 21428318; fax 21302067; e-mail msamaral@teledata.mz; internet www.mocargo.co.mz; f. 1982; shipping, chartering and road transport; Man. Dir MANUEL DE SOUSA AMARAL.

Manica Freight Services, SARL: Praça dos Trabalhadores 51, CP 557, Maputo; tel. 21356500; fax 21431084; e-mail fdimande@manica.co.mz; internet www.manica.co.mz; international shipping agents; Man. Dir A. Y. CHOTHIA.

Maputo Port Development Co, SARL (MPDC): Port Director's Building, Porto de Maputo, CP 2841, Maputo; tel. 21313920; fax 21313921; e-mail info@portmaputo.com; internet www.portmaputo.com; f. 2002; private-sector international consortium with concession (awarded 2003) to develop and run port of Maputo until 2018; CEO PETER LOWE.

Mozline, SARL: Av. Karl Marx 478, 2° andar, Maputo; tel. 21303078; fax 21303073; e-mail mozline1@virconn.com; shipping and road freight services.

Navique, SARL: Av. Mártires de Inhaminga 125, CP 145, Maputo; tel. 21312705; fax 21426310; e-mail smazoi@navique.co.mz; internet www.navique.com; f. 1985; Chair. J. A. CARVALHO; Man. Dir PEDRO VIRTUOSO.

CIVIL AVIATION

In 2006 there were five international airports.

Instituto de Aviação Civil de Moçambique (IACM): Maputo; civil aviation institute; Dir ANÍBAL SAMUEL.

Air Corridor, SARL: Av. Eduardo Mondlane 945, Nampula; tel. 26213333; fax 26213355; e-mail fagadit@aircorridor.com.mz; internet www.aircorridor.co.mz; f. 2004; domestic carrier and cargo transport; Chair. MOMADE AQUI RAJAHUSSEN; Commercial Dir FARUK ALY GADIT.

Linhas Aéreas de Moçambique, SARL (LAM): Aeroporto Internacional de Maputo, CP 2060, Maputo; tel. 21465137; fax 21422936; e-mail flamingoclub@lam.co.mz; internet www.lam.co.mz; f. 1980; 80% state-owned; operates domestic services and international services to South Africa, Tanzania, Mayotte, Zimbabwe and Portugal; Chair. and Dir-Gen. JOSÉ RICARDO ZUZARTE VIEGAS.

Sociedade de Transportes Aéreos/Sociedade de Transporte e Trabalho Aéreo, SARL (STA/TTA): Rua da Tchamba 405, CP 665, Maputo; tel. 21492022; fax 21491763; e-mail dido@mail.tropical.co.mz; internet www.sta.co.mz; f. 1991; domestic airline and aircraft charter transport services; acquired Empresa Nacional de Transporte e Trabalho Aéreo in 1997; Chair. ROGÉRIO WALTER CARREIRA; Man. Dir JOSÉ CARVALHEIRA.

Other airlines operating in Mozambique include Serviço Aéreo Regional, South African Airlines, Moçambique Expresso, SA—Airlink International, Transairways (owned by LAM) and TAP Air Portugal.

MOZAMBIQUE

Tourism

Tourism, formerly a significant source of foreign exchange, ceased completely following independence, and was resumed on a limited scale in 1980. There were 1,000 visitors in 1981 (compared with 292,000 in 1972 and 69,000 in 1974). With the successful conduct of multi-party elections in 1994 and the prospect of continued peace, there was considerable scope for development of this sector. By the late 1990s tourism was the fastest growing sector of the Mozambique economy, and in 2000 it was announced that a comprehensive tourism development plan was to be devised, assisted by funding from the European Union. In 2005 there were 5,030 hotels in Mozambique. The opening of the Great Limpopo Transfrontier Park, linking territories in Mozambique with South Africa and Zimbabwe, was expected to attract additional tourists. Further national parks were planned. Foreign tourist arrivals in 2005 were 954,433; tourism receipts totalled US $96m. in 2004.

Fundo Nacional do Turismo: Av. 25 de Setembro 1203, CP 4758, Maputo; tel. 21307320; fax 21307324; internet www.futur.org.mz; f. 1993; hotels and tourism; CEO ZACARIAS SUMBANA.

MYANMAR

Introductory Survey

Location, Climate, Language, Religion, Flag, Capital

The Union of Myanmar (Myanma Naing-ngan—formerly Burma) lies in the north-west region of South-East Asia, between the Tibetan plateau and the Malay peninsula. The country is bordered by Bangladesh and India to the north-west, by the People's Republic of China and Laos to the north-east and by Thailand to the south-east. The climate is tropical, with an average temperature of 27°C (80°F) and monsoon rains from May to October. Average annual rainfall is between 2,500 mm and 5,000 mm in the coastal and mountainous regions of the north and east, but reaches a maximum of only 1,000 mm in the lowlands of the interior. Temperatures in Yangon (Rangoon) are generally between 18°C (65°F) and 36°C (97°F). The official language is Myanmar (Burmese), and there are also a number of tribal languages. About 87% of the population are Buddhists. There are animist, Muslim, Hindu and Christian minorities. The national flag (proportions 5 by 9) is red, with a blue canton, in the upper hoist, bearing two ears of rice within a cog-wheel and a ring of 14 five-pointed stars (one for each state), all in white. In 2006 the functions of the capital city were transferred from Yangon to the new administrative centre of Nay Pyi Taw.

Recent History

Burma (now Myanmar) was annexed to British India during the 19th century, and became a separate British dependency, with a limited measure of self-government, in 1937. Japanese forces invaded and occupied the country in 1942, and Japan granted nominal independence under a Government of anti-British nationalists. The Burmese nationalists later turned against Japan and aided Allied forces to reoccupy the country in 1945. They formed a resistance movement, the Anti-Fascist People's Freedom League (AFPFL), led by Gen. Aung San, which became the main political force after the defeat of Japan. Aung San was assassinated in July 1947 and was succeeded by U Nu. On 4 January 1948 the Union of Burma became independent, outside the Commonwealth, with U Nu as the first Prime Minister.

During the first decade of independence Burma was a parliamentary democracy, and the Government successfully resisted revolts by communists and other insurgent groups. In 1958 the ruling AFPFL split into two wings, the 'Clean' AFPFL and the 'Stable' AFPFL, and U Nu invited the Army Chief of Staff, Gen. Ne Win, to head a caretaker Government. Elections to the Chamber of Deputies in February 1960 gave an overwhelming majority to U Nu, leading the 'Clean' AFPFL (which was renamed the Union Party in March), and he resumed office in April. Despite its popularity, the U Nu administration proved ineffective, and in March 1962 Gen. Ne Win staged a coup to depose U Nu (who was subsequently detained until 1966). The new Revolutionary Council suspended the Constitution and instituted authoritarian control through the government-sponsored Burma Socialist Programme Party (BSPP). All other political parties were outlawed in March 1964.

During the next decade a more centralized system of government was created, in an attempt to win popular support and to nationalize important sectors of the economy. A new Constitution, aiming to transform Burma into a democratic socialist state, was approved in a national referendum in December 1973. The Constitution of the renamed Socialist Republic of the Union of Burma, which came into force in January 1974, confirmed the BSPP as the sole authorized political party, and provided for the establishment of new organs of state. Elections to a legislative People's Assembly took place in January 1974, and in March the Revolutionary Council was dissolved. U Ne Win (who, together with other senior army officers, had become a civilian in 1972) was elected President by the newly created State Council. Burma's economic problems increased, however, and in 1974 there were riots over food shortages and social injustices. Student demonstrations took place in 1976, as social problems increased. Following an attempted coup by members of the armed forces in July, the BSPP reviewed its economic policies, and in 1977 a new economic programme was adopted in an attempt to quell unrest.

An election in January 1978 gave U Ne Win a mandate to rule for a further four years, and in March he was re-elected Chairman of the State Council. In May 1980 a general amnesty was declared for political dissidents, including exiles (as a result of which U Nu, who had been living abroad since 1969, returned to Burma). Gen. San Yu, formerly the Army Chief of Staff, was elected Chairman of the State Council in November 1981. In August 1985 U Ne Win was re-elected Chairman of the BSPP. Elections for a new People's Assembly were held in November.

In August 1987, owing to the country's increasing economic problems, an unprecedented extraordinary meeting, comprising the BSPP Central Committee, the organs of the State Council and other state bodies, was convened. U Ne Win proposed a review of the policies of the past 25 years. In September the announcement of the withdrawal from circulation of high-denomination banknotes, coupled with rice shortages, provoked student riots (the first civil disturbances since 1976). Owing to continued economic deprivation, further student unrest in Rangoon (now Yangon) in March 1988 culminated in major protests, which were violently suppressed by riot police under the direct command of U Sein Lwin, the BSPP Joint General Secretary. Further demonstrations started in June. The Government's response was again extremely brutal, and many demonstrators were killed. In July vain attempts were made to counter the growing unpopularity of the Government, including the removal from office of the Minister of Home and Religious Affairs and the head of the People's Police Force in Rangoon. (The Prime Minister, also, was subsequently dismissed.) Finally, at an extraordinary meeting of the BSPP Congress, U Ne Win resigned as party Chairman and asked the Congress to approve the holding of a national referendum on the issue of a multi-party political system. The Congress rejected the referendum proposal and the resignation of four other senior members of the BSPP, including that of U Sein Lwin, but accepted the resignation of U San Yu, the BSPP Vice-Chairman.

The subsequent election of U Sein Lwin to the chairmanship of the BSPP, and his appointment as Chairman of the State Council and as state President, provoked further student-led riots. Martial law was imposed on Rangoon, and thousands of unarmed demonstrators were reportedly massacred by the armed forces throughout the country. In August 1988 U Sein Lwin was forced to resign after only 17 days in office. He was replaced by the more moderate Dr Maung Maung, hitherto the Attorney-General, whose response to the continued rioting was conciliatory. Martial law was revoked; Brig.-Gen. Aung Gyi (formerly a close colleague of U Ne Win, now an outspoken critic of the regime), who had been detained under U Sein Lwin, was released; and permission was given for the formation of the All Burma Students' Union. Demonstrations continued, however, and by September students and Buddhist monks had assumed control of the municipal government of many towns. In that month U Nu requested foreign support for his formation of an 'alternative government'. The emerging opposition leaders, Aung Gyi, Aung San Suu Kyi (daughter of Gen. Aung San) and Gen. (retd) Tin Oo (a former Chief of Staff and Minister of Defence), then formed the National United Front for Democracy, which was subsequently renamed the League for Democracy and later the National League for Democracy (NLD).

At an emergency meeting of the BSPP Congress in September 1988 it was decided that free elections would be held within three months and that members of the armed forces, police and civil service could no longer be affiliated to a political party. Now distanced from the BSPP, the armed forces, led by Gen. (later Senior Gen.) Saw Maung, seized power on 18 September, ostensibly to maintain order until multi-party elections could be arranged. A State Law and Order Restoration Council (SLORC) was formed, all state organs (including the People's Assembly, the State Council and the Council of Ministers) were abolished, demonstrations were banned and a night-time curfew was imposed nation-wide. Despite these measures, opposition movements demonstrated in favour of an interim civilian government, and it was estimated that more than 1,000 demonstrators were killed in the first few days following the coup. The SLORC announced the formation of a nine-member Government, with Saw Maung as Minister of Defence and of Foreign Affairs and subsequently also Prime Minister. Although ostensibly in retirement, it was widely believed that U Ne Win retained a controlling influence over the new leaders. The new Government changed the official name of the country to the Union of Burma (as it had been before 1973). The law maintaining the BSPP as the sole party was abrogated, and new parties were encouraged to register for the forthcoming elections. The BSPP registered as the National Unity Party (NUP). In December 1988, owing to disagreements with Suu Kyi, Aung Gyi was expelled from the NLD after he had founded the Union National Democracy Party. Tin Oo was elected as the new NLD Chairman. U Nu returned to prominence as the leader of a new party, the League for Democracy and Peace (LDP), and also commanded the support of the new Democracy Party.

From October 1988 to January 1989 Suu Kyi campaigned in townships and rural areas across the nation, and elicited much popular support, despite martial law regulations banning public gatherings of five or more people. In March 1989 there were anti-Government demonstrations in many cities, in protest at the increasing harassment of Suu Kyi and the arrest of many NLD supporters and activists. In July Suu Kyi cancelled a rally to commemorate the anniversary of the assassination of her father, owing to the threat of government violence; two days later, both she and Tin Oo were placed under house arrest, accused of 'endangering the State'.

In May 1989 electoral legislation was ratified, providing for multi-party elections to be held on 27 May 1990, and permitting campaigning only in the three months prior to the election date. In June 1989 the SLORC changed the official name of the country to the Union of Myanmar (Myanma Naing-ngan), on the grounds that the previous title conveyed the impression that the population consisted solely of ethnic Burmans. The transliteration to the Roman alphabet of many other place-names was changed, to correspond more closely with pronunciation.

In December 1989 Tin Oo of the NLD was sentenced by a military tribunal to three years' imprisonment, with hard labour, for his part in the anti-Government uprising in 1988. In the same month U Nu was disqualified from contesting the forthcoming general election, owing to his refusal to dissolve the 'alternative government' that he had proclaimed in September 1988. In January 1990 U Nu and 13 members of the 'alternative government' were placed under house arrest. Five members subsequently resigned and were released. Later in January, Suu Kyi was barred from contesting the election, owing to her 'entitlement to the privileges of a foreigner' (a reference to her marriage to a British citizen) and her alleged involvement with insurgents.

Martial law was revoked in eight townships in November 1989, and in a further 10 in February 1990. It was reported that during 1989 tens of thousands of residents had been forcibly evicted from densely populated areas in major cities, where anti-Government demonstrations had received much support, and resettled in rural areas. In January and April 1989 a prominent human rights organization, Amnesty International, published information regarding violations of human rights in Myanmar, including the torture and summary execution of dissident students. This was followed by criticism from the UN later in the year.

In May 1990 93 parties presented a total of 2,296 candidates to contest 492 seats at the general election for the new assembly; there were also 87 independent candidates. Despite previous efforts to weaken the influence of known leaders and to eliminate dissidents, the voting was reported to be free and orderly. The NLD received 59.9% of the total votes and won 396 of the 485 seats that were, in the event, contested; the NUP obtained 21.2% of the votes, but won only 10 seats. The NLD demanded the immediate opening of negotiations with the SLORC, and progress towards popular rule. However, the SLORC announced that the election had been intended to provide not a legislature but a Constituent Assembly, which was to draft a constitution establishing a 'strong government', and was to be under the direction of a national convention to be established by the SLORC. The resulting draft constitution would have to be endorsed by referendum, and subsequently approved by the SLORC. In July the SLORC announced Order 1/90, stating that the SLORC would continue as the de facto Government until a new constitution was drafted. Elected members of the NLD responded (independently of their leadership) with the 'Gandhi Hall Declaration', urging that an assembly of all elected representatives be convened by September.

In August 1990, at an anti-Government protest held in Mandalay to commemorate the killing of thousands of demonstrators in 1988, troops killed four protesters, including two Buddhist monks. In September the SLORC arrested six members of the NLD, including the acting Chairman, Kyi Maung, and acting Secretary-General, Chit Hlaing, on charges of passing state secrets to unauthorized persons. Kyi Maung was replaced as acting NLD Chairman by U Aung Shwe. Also in September NLD representatives discussed plans to declare a provisional government in Mandalay, without the support of the party's Central Executive Committee. Influential monks agreed to support the declaration, but the plan was abandoned after government troops surrounded monasteries. The SLORC subsequently ordered the dissolution of all Buddhist organizations involved in anti-Government activities (all except nine sects) and empowered military commanders to impose death sentences on rebellious monks. More than 50 senior members of the NLD were arrested, and members of all political parties were required to endorse Order 1/90: in acquiescing, the NLD effectively nullified its demand for an immediate transfer of power.

In December 1990 a group of candidates who had been elected to the Constituent Assembly fled to Manerplaw, on the Thai border, and announced a 'parallel government', the National Coalition Government of the Union of Burma (NCGUB), with the support of the Democratic Alliance of Burma (DAB), a broadly based organization uniting ethnic rebel forces with student dissidents and monks. The self-styled Prime Minister of the NCGUB was Sein Win, the leader of the Party for National Democracy (PND) and a cousin of Suu Kyi. The NLD leadership expelled members who had taken part in the formation of the 'parallel government', despite broad support for the move in the NLD. The SLORC subsequently annulled the registration as a political party of the PND, the LDP and two other parties and the elected status of the eight members of the NCGUB. In April 1991 Gen. (later Senior Gen.) Than Shwe, the Vice-Chairman of the SLORC and the Deputy Chief of Staff of the armed forces, officially announced that the SLORC would not transfer power to the Constituent Assembly, as the political parties involved were 'subversive' and 'unfit to rule'. In response to continued pressure from the SLORC, the NLD carried out a complete reorganization of the party's Central Executive Committee, replacing Suu Kyi as General Secretary with the previously unknown U Lwin, and Tin Oo with the former acting Chairman, U Aung Shwe.

In July 1991 the SLORC retroactively amended electoral legislation adopted in May 1989, extending the grounds on which representatives of the Assembly could be disqualified or debarred from contesting future elections to include convictions for breaches of law and order. More than 80 elected representatives had already died, been imprisoned or been forced into exile since the election in May 1990. In September 1991 the SLORC declared its intention to remain in charge of state administration for a further five to 10 years. In that month U Ohn Gyaw was appointed Minister for Foreign Affairs in place of Saw Maung, becoming the first civilian in the Cabinet.

In October 1991 Suu Kyi was awarded the Nobel Peace Prize. Sein Win attended the presentation of the award to Suu Kyi's family in Oslo, Norway, in December, gaining the Norwegian Government's de facto recognition of the NCGUB. In Myanmar students who staged demonstrations (the first since 1989) to coincide with the ceremony were dispersed by security forces. It was subsequently announced that Suu Kyi had been expelled from the NLD. In January 1992 Tin Oo's expulsion from the NLD was announced in a broadcast.

Three additional members were appointed to the SLORC in January 1992, and the Cabinet was expanded to include seven new ministers, four of whom were civilians. The changes, together with a reorganization of senior ministers in February, were widely perceived to benefit the Chief of Military Intelligence, Maj.-Gen. (later Lt-Gen.) Khin Nyunt (First Secretary of the SLORC). Khin Nyunt was widely regarded as the most powerful member of the SLORC, owing to U Ne Win's continued patronage. Divisions within the ruling junta between Khin Nyunt and the more senior officers were becoming increasingly evident. In March Than Shwe replaced Saw Maung as Minister of Defence, and in April Saw Maung retired as Chairman of the SLORC and Prime Minister for reasons of ill health. Than Shwe was subsequently appointed to both these posts. The SLORC promptly ordered the release of several political prisoners, including U Nu, and announced that Suu Kyi could receive a visit from her family. Than Shwe indicated that he was prepared to meet Suu Kyi personally to discuss her future. In June the first meeting took place between members of the SLORC and opposition representatives from the remaining 10 legal parties, in preparation for the holding of a national convention to draft a new constitution.

In January 1993 the National Convention finally assembled, but was adjourned several times during the year, owing to the objections of the opposition members to SLORC demands for a leading role in government for the armed forces. The SLORC reacted to what it regarded as opposition intransigence by suspending any conciliatory gestures (which had included the revocation of two martial law decrees and amnesties for a total of 534 political prisoners), and many arrests were reported. Towards the end of the year the Chairman of the National Convention's Convening Committee, U Aung Toe (the Chief Justice), announced (seemingly without grounds) that a consensus existed in favour of the SLORC's demands, which comprised: the inclusion, in both the lower and upper chambers of a proposed parliament, of military personnel (to be appointed by the Commander-in-Chief of the Armed Forces); the election of the President by an electoral college; the independent self-administration of the armed forces; and the right of the Commander-in-Chief to exercise state power in an emergency (effectively granting legitimate status to a future coup).

In September 1993 an alternative mass movement to the NUP (which had lost credibility through its election defeat) was formed to establish a civilian front through which the armed forces could exercise control. The Union Solidarity and Development Association (USDA), the aims of which were indistinguishable from those of the SLORC, was not officially registered as a political party, thus enabling civil servants to join the organization, with the incentive of considerable privileges.

In January 1994 the National Convention reconvened, and in April it was adjourned, having adopted guidelines for three significant chapters of the future Constitution. Accordingly, Myanmar was to be renamed the Republic of the Union of Myanmar, comprising seven states (associated with some of the country's minority ethnic groups) and seven divisions in central and southern Myanmar (largely representing the areas populated by the ethnic Bamars—Burmans). The Republic would be headed by an executive President, elected by the legislature for five years; proposals for the disqualification of any candidate with a foreign spouse or children would prevent Suu Kyi from entering any future presidential election. Reconvening in September, the Convention again stressed that the central role of the military (as 'permanent representatives of the people') be enshrined in the new Constitution. It was proposed that legislative power be shared between a bicameral Pyidaungsu Hluttaw (Union Parliament) and divisional and state assemblies, all of which were to include representatives of the military. The Pyidaungsu Hluttaw was to comprise the Pyithu Hluttaw (House of Representatives) and the Amyotha Hluttaw (House of Nationalities): the former would comprise 330 elected deputies and 110 members of the armed forces, and would be elected for five years. The latter would be constituted with equal numbers of representatives from the proposed seven regions and seven states of the Republic, as well as members of the military, and was to comprise a maximum of 224 deputies. A general election was provisionally scheduled for 2 September 1997 (although it was not actually held). The session was adjourned in April 1995.

In September 1994, following mediation by a senior Buddhist monk between Suu Kyi and leading members of the SLORC, Suu Kyi was permitted to leave her home to meet Than Shwe and Khin Nyunt. In October Suu Kyi held a second meeting with senior SLORC members. In November it was reported that Suu Kyi had met other detained members of the NLD, including Tin Oo. In January 1995 the SLORC announced that Suu Kyi would be freed only when the new constitution had been completed; Suu Kyi simultaneously rejected suggestions that she might reach a compromise with the SLORC on the terms for her release. In February leading members of the SLORC held talks in Yangon with an envoy of the UN Secretary-General. In March the Government released 31 political prisoners, including Tin Oo and Kyi Maung.

In July 1995 Suu Kyi was unexpectedly granted an unconditional release from house arrest. The SLORC, which thus hoped to attract greater foreign investment, was in a powerful position: the armed forces were united; political dissent had been effectively suppressed; and cease-fire accords had been reached with nearly all the ethnic insurgent groups. On her release Suu Kyi made a conciliatory speech, urging negotiations with the SLORC and a spirit of compromise. Suu Kyi swiftly reconciled the early leaders of the NLD with the new leadership, which had compromised with the SLORC. Hundreds of supporters gathered daily to hear Suu Kyi speak outside her house in Yangon without being dispersed by security forces. Suu Kyi was reinstated as General Secretary of the NLD in October, in a reorganization of the party's executive committee; Tin Oo and Kyi Maung were named Vice-Chairmen. Aung Shwe, who had led the 'legal' NLD and represented the party at the National Convention, was retained as party Chairman.

In November 1995 the National Convention reconvened. The NLD attended the opening session of the Convention, but later withdrew when the SLORC ignored its requests to expand the Convention to make it truly representative. (Suu Kyi was, of course, not a member of the National Convention.) Denouncing the Convention as illegitimate and undemocratic, the NLD for the first time appealed for international support for its cause. The SLORC, which had already begun to imprison NLD supporters for petty crimes, reacted strongly to the NLD boycott, officially expelling the party from the Convention and threatening to 'annihilate' anyone threatening national interests.

In May 1996 more than 260 members of the NLD (mostly delegates elected to the Constituent Assembly in 1990) were arrested prior to the opening of the party's first congress. The majority were detained for the duration of the congress, which only 18 NLD members were able to attend. The congress resolved to draft an alternative constitution. In June the SLORC intensified its action against the NLD with an order banning any organization that held illegal gatherings or obstructed the drafting of the new Constitution by the National Convention; members of a proscribed party could be liable to between five and 20 years' imprisonment. In September police erected road-blocks around Suu Kyi's house, and again detained NLD activists, in order to prevent the holding of a further congress. Suu Kyi's telephone line was disconnected, and she was unable to deliver her weekly speech for the first time since her release from house arrest. From October the road-block was resumed each week with the purpose of preventing access to Suu Kyi's speech. The SLORC recommenced talks with NLD officials later that month. However, relations quickly deteriorated following an attack on vehicles in which Suu Kyi and other NLD leaders were travelling.

In October 1996 student action in Yangon, in protest against the detention and brutal treatment of fellow students, prompted further repression and numerous arrests (among those detained was Kyi Maung). This was followed in early December by the largest pro-democracy demonstration since 1988, involving more than 2,000 students. The gathering was dispersed peacefully, although some 600 demonstrators were temporarily detained. Smaller student demonstrations continued sporadically until mid-December, when Suu Kyi was briefly confined to her home (although she denied involvement), and tanks were deployed in Yangon; university establishments were closed indefinitely. At the end of December some 50 members of the Communist Party of Burma (CPB) and of the NLD were arrested in connection with the protests. In January 1997 14 people, including at least five NLD members, were convicted of involvement in the unrest and sentenced to seven years' imprisonment.

In January 1997 Suu Kyi was allowed to deliver her weekly speech for the first time in three months. However, the SLORC imposed new restrictions on media access to Suu Kyi, and barricades remained outside her home. In March there were further arrests of NLD members, together with an increased army presence in several towns. Also in March a series of attacks on Muslim targets by Buddhist monks took place across the country. These attacks were rumoured to have been organized by opponents within the regime of Myanmar's application to join the Association of South East Asian Nations (ASEAN, see p. 185), in an attempt to alienate Muslim-dominated members of the grouping.

In April 1997 a bomb attack at the home of the Second Secretary of the SLORC, Tin Oo, resulted in the death of his daughter. The Government attributed the bombing to anti-Government groups based in Japan; however, major opposition groups in exile denied involvement in the attack, which was denounced by the NLD. The attack was rumoured to be related to a power struggle between Khin Nyunt, who was increasingly regarded as a moderate, and the more conservative Commander-in-Chief of the Army and Vice-Chair of the SLORC, Gen. Maung Aye, who commanded the support of Tin Oo. The detention of NLD members increased during 1997, while government propaganda vilifying the opposition grew more frequent and Suu Kyi's freedom of movement and association remained restricted. In July, however, Khin Nyunt invited the NLD Chairman, Aung Shwe, to a meeting, which constituted the first high-level contact between the SLORC and the NLD since the release of Suu Kyi from house arrest in July 1995. A further meeting between the SLORC leadership and the NLD was due to take place in September, but was cancelled by the opposition, who insisted that future discussions required the participation of Suu Kyi in her capacity as General Secretary of the NLD. The SLORC granted permission for an NLD congress to be held in September.

On 15 November 1997 the ruling junta unexpectedly announced the dissolution of the SLORC and its replacement with the State Peace and Development Council (SPDC). The 19-member SPDC comprised exclusively military personnel; younger regional military commanders were included (largely to prevent them from developing local power bases), while the four most senior members of the SLORC retained their positions at the head of the new junta: Than Shwe was appointed Chairman, Maung Aye Vice-Chairman, Khin Nyunt First Secretary and Tin Oo Second Secretary. A number of former members of the SLORC were ostensibly promoted to an 'Advisory Group', which was, however, subsequently abolished; five members of this group, who had also held positions in the Cabinet, were placed under house arrest in December, pending investigations into allegations of corruption. The SPDC immediately implemented a reorganization of the Cabinet. The new 40-member Cabinet included 25 former ministers, but, in contrast to the SLORC (the members of which had virtually all held cabinet portfolios), only one member of the SPDC, Than Shwe, was appointed to serve concurrently as a cabinet minister. Among the more junior members of the Cabinet were an increased number of civilian appointees, largely selected from the USDA. The restructuring of the junta and the Cabinet appeared to benefit Khin Nyunt, as several supporters of Maung Aye were removed from power. In December the SPDC announced a further cabinet reorganization and the appointment of a new Chairman (the Minister of Hotels and Tourism, Maj.-Gen. Saw Lwin) and Vice-Chairmen of the National Convention Convening Commission; however, the Convention, which had adjourned in March 1996, remained in recess.

Harassment and persecution of members of the NLD and other opposition movements continued throughout 1998. In March 40 people were arrested on charges of complicity in a conspiracy allegedly led by the exiled All-Burma Students Democratic Front (ABSDF, an armed movement formed in 1988 by students within the DAB, which had officially renounced its armed struggle in 1997) to assassinate leaders of the military junta and initiate terrorist attacks on government offices and foreign embassies. The ABSDF, which rejected the allegations, was accused of complicity with the NLD. Six of the accused were sentenced to death at the end of April. However, the SPDC unexpectedly authorized an NLD party congress, attended by 400 delegates, at the end of May to celebrate the eighth anniversary of the general election. In June the NLD demanded that the SPDC reconvene the Pyithu Hluttaw, in accordance with the results of the 1990 election, by 21 August. Some 40 elected NLD representatives were detained at the end of June, and others were forced to sign pledges restricting their freedom of movement. In July the SPDC ordered NLD elected representatives to report to their local police station twice a day and confined them to their townships. During July and August Suu Kyi attempted to visit NLD members outside the city, in an effort to exert pressure on the SPDC to comply with the NLD's demands. On four separate occasions the opposition leader was prevented from continuing her journey by road-blocks set up by the ruling junta. On one such occasion in July Suu Kyi was forcibly returned to her home by security forces after a six-day protest in her car, following government refusals to comply with her demands for the release of detained opposition members and the commencement of substantive dialogue with the NLD. In a further incident in August, she was returned to her home by ambulance after spending 13 days in her car, prompting considerable international criticism of the SPDC. During Suu Kyi's protest in August Khin Nyunt held a reportedly cordial meeting with the NLD Chairman, Aung Shwe.

Shortly before the NLD's prescribed deadline for convening the Pyithu Hluttaw, the SPDC published an official rejection of the NLD's demands. The NLD responded by declaring its intention unilaterally to convene a 'People's Parliament', which would include elected representatives of all the ethnic minority groups. On the day that Suu Kyi abandoned her protest at the road-block, student demonstrations took place in Yangon (for the first time since December 1996), in support of the NLD's demands. In September 1998 thousands of students staged anti-Government demonstrations, which were dispersed by security forces. Arrests of opposition activists increased dramatically, and by early September 193 elected NLD members of the Pyithu Hluttaw and hundreds of party supporters had been detained. In the same month a 10-member Representative Committee, led by Suu Kyi and Aung Shwe, was established by the NLD to act on behalf of the 'People's Parliament' until a legislature could be convened under the 1990 election law. The Committee (which claimed a mandate based on the authorization of more than one-half of the representatives of the Pyithu Hluttaw elected in 1990, many of whom were in detention) asserted that all laws passed by the military junta over the previous 10 years had no legal authority, and also demanded the immediate and unconditional release of all political prisoners. Four parties representing Shan, Mon, Arakanese and Zomi ethnic groups expressed their support for the 'People's Parliament', together with the ABSDF. In the same month 15 senior military officers were reportedly arrested for allegedly planning to meet with Suu Kyi, and a number of large pro-Government rallies were held in Yangon. The NLD condemned the alleged use of coercion, intimidation and threats by government military intelligence units to secure the involuntary resignations of vast numbers of NLD members and the closure of a number of regional party headquarters. Following the death in custody in October of a member of the NLD, detained by the SPDC since early the previous month, the NLD also formally condemned the junta's treatment of detained opposition party members in a letter to Than Shwe. (In August of the same year an elected representative of the NLD, Saw Win, had died in prison while serving an 11-year term of imprisonment, the third NLD member of the Pyithu Hluttaw to die in custody.) In October UN Assistant Secretary-General Alvaro de Soto met with SPDC leaders and also with Suu Kyi during a visit to Myanmar. He reportedly offered large-scale financial and humanitarian aid to the junta in exchange for the initiation of substantive dialogue with the NLD. During October and November about 300 opposition members were released by the Government; however, a further 500 were believed to remain in detention.

In March 1999, despite requests from several foreign Governments, the ruling junta refused to grant a visa to Suu Kyi's terminally ill husband, Michael Aris. The junta instead encouraged Suu Kyi to visit Aris in the United Kingdom; however, Suu Kyi declined to leave the country for fear that she would not be permitted to return. Following Aris's death later the same month, more than 1,000 supporters of Suu Kyi were permitted to attend a Buddhist ceremony at Suu Kyi's home marking her husband's demise.

In April 1999 the UN adopted a unanimous resolution deploring the escalation in the persecution of the democratic opposition in Myanmar. Nevertheless, the harassment and intimidation of NLD members continued, with the resignations from the party of nearly 300 members reported in July; further resignations were reported in November and in January 2000. In December 1999 it was reported that an elected representative of the People's Assembly, U Maung Maung Myint, had been forced to resign by the ruling SPDC. The lack of political progress by the NLD in 1999 led to the formation of a breakaway faction of the party by a prominent party member, Than Tun, who was subsequently expelled from the NLD.

In August 1999 a series of protests was staged by opposition supporters to mark the anniversary of the massacre of thousands of pro-democracy demonstrators by the military Government in 1988. In October the Supreme Court rejected a claim by the NLD that its activities had been 'continuously disrupted, prevented and destroyed' and that hundreds of its members had been illegally detained. In April 2000 Suu Kyi alleged that more than 40 youth members of the NLD had been arrested by the SPDC for their involvement in party activities.

Opposition radio sources continued to give details of small-scale protests throughout 2000 and 2001. A rare bomb explosion in May 2001 reportedly killed 12 people and injured eight others in a market in Mandalay. In the same month it was reported that religious riots in Toungoo, Bago Division, had led to the deaths of 24 Buddhist monks. The disturbances spread to other towns, prompting allegations that the SPDC had instigated the riots in an attempt to divert public attention from political and economic problems.

Suu Kyi also continued her persistent opposition to the SPDC. In August 2000 Suu Kyi and 14 NLD colleagues attempted to visit members of the party in Kunyangon, a town just outside Yangon. The group was stopped by a military road-block, but refused to return home. A nine-day stand-off finally ended with Suu Kyi and the NLD members being forcibly returned to Yangon. Suu Kyi and eight others were kept under house arrest for the next two weeks. In early September the SPDC raided the NLD headquarters, and detained a number of other party leaders in their homes. Undeterred, the NLD announced that it was to draft a new constitution for the country, an act declared illegal in 1996 and punishable by 20 years' imprisonment. Later in the month Suu Kyi attempted to leave Yangon again, this time by train to Mandalay, only to be told that all trains were full. The NLD leader was once again returned home and placed under house arrest, while NLD Vice-Chairman Tin Oo and eight other party workers were taken to a government 'guest house'. Pressure on the NLD increased in October 2000, when a deadline for an eviction order for the party to vacate its premises expired. The landladies responsible for the eviction order had been incarcerated by the SPDC for allowing the NLD to use loudspeakers, but claimed that their decision to evict had not been influenced by external coercion.

Despite the sustained suppression of the opposition party and the prevention of protest, the SPDC's treatment of its political rivals became markedly more liberal from mid-2000. In July the SPDC reportedly allowed 60,000 university students to resume their education. The undergraduate universities, however, were relocated in the suburbs, in order to avoid demonstrations in the city centres that might draw in other civilians. Razali Ismail, a Malaysian diplomat newly appointed as the UN Secretary-General's Special Envoy to Myanmar, was allowed access to Suu Kyi during a four-day visit in October 2000, and in the same month James Mawdsley, a British human rights activist sentenced to 17 years' imprisonment in Myanmar in September 1999, was released (see below).

Conciliation between the SPDC and the NLD was confirmed in January 2001, when it was announced that the two parties had been holding secret talks since October, the first high-level discussions between the opponents since 1994. Lt-Gen. Khin Nyunt met with Suu Kyi several times, although the details of the talks remained closely guarded. Some analysts feared that the resumption of discussions was merely a cynical ploy by the Government to attract foreign investment and curb economic sanctions, a view supported by the fact there was little initial evidence of progress.

In January 2001, in a further placatory gesture, the SPDC ordered the media to stop the regular acrimonious attacks on Suu Kyi and the NLD. In the same month the government-controlled Yangon division court dismissed a lawsuit brought by Suu Kyi's US-based brother, Aung San Oo, who claimed ownership of half of Suu Kyi's house. Although foreigners cannot buy or transfer property in Myanmar, San Oo had been granted an exemption from the Government in July 2000, and thus requested half the family property according to Myanma inheritance law. In October 2001, however, the court rejected Suu Kyi's application to have her brother's claim dismissed. The hearing was subsequently adjourned on several occasions and in December 2003 was postponed until February 2004. At the end of January 2001 the SPDC released NLD Vice-Chairman Tin Oo and 84 other party supporters, who had been detained since Suu Kyi's attempted train journey in September 2000. A few days later a delegation of the European Union (EU, see p. 244) was permitted to meet with Suu Kyi, as was Dr Paulo Sérgio Pinheiro, UN human rights envoy to Myanmar, in April 2001.

In February 2001 Lt-Gen. Tin Oo, the army chief of staff and, as the Council's Second Secretary, the SPDC's fourth most powerful member, was killed in a helicopter crash. While the accident was officially attributed to bad weather and mechanical failure, there were rumours of an assassination, as Lt-Gen. Tin Oo had survived two previous attempts on his life, in 1996 and 1997.

In mid-2001, as discussions continued, the Government ordered the release of a number of NLD members from prison and permitted the reopening of the NLD headquarters and several branch offices in Yangon. In August the release of Aung Shwe, Chairman of the NLD, and of Vice-Chairman Tin Oo, was hailed as an indication of progress. Shortly afterwards Ismail held further discussions with Suu Kyi during a visit to Yangon.

In November 2001 two senior army generals—Lt-Gen. Win Myint (widely regarded as the fourth most powerful individual in the country) and Deputy Prime Minister Tin Hla—were dismissed. While no official explanation was given, the two men were under investigation for corruption. As both had expressed only muted support for the ongoing talks with Suu Kyi, there was also speculation that their replacement would be more conducive to the attainment of a political settlement. Two days later the SPDC announced that five government ministers were to retire. While two Deputy Prime Ministers, Rear Adm. Maung Maung Khin and Lt-Gen. Tin Tun, had been expected to relinquish their positions, the other departures had not been foreseen. No official explanation was given for the changes. However, it was thought that their removal constituted an attempt to improve the Government's corrupt and anti-democratic image. In the same month Razali Ismail visited the country again. Upon his departure, Ismail expressed satisfaction with the progress that had been made.

In January 2002 it was reported that Suu Kyi had met privately with Gen. Than Shwe for the first time since 1994, raising hopes that the two sides might be close to reaching a breakthrough. However, in February 2002 international pressure on the SPDC to release all remaining political prisoners (an estimated 1,500, according to Amnesty International) and begin a more substantive dialogue with the NLD increased, prompted by the release of a critical report by the US Government (see below). The Myanma Government responded by releasing five further detainees and expressing its confidence that a successful conclusion to the negotiation process was imminent.

In March 2002 the son-in-law and three grandsons of U Ne Win were arrested on charges of plotting to overthrow the Government. It was alleged that they had intended to abduct three government leaders and force them to form a figurehead government under U Ne Win's influence. Four senior military officials—the Commander-in-Chief of the Air Force, Maj.-Gen. Myint Swe, the Chief of Police, Maj.-Gen. Soe Win, and two regional commanders—were dismissed and questioned in connection with the attempted coup. Ne Win and his daughter, Sandar Win, were placed under house arrest. Despite suspicions that the coup allegations were linked to internal conflicts within the military, owing to the insubstantial nature of the evidence gathered to support the charges, in September U Ne Win's four relatives were convicted of high treason and sentenced to death. They entered appeals against the sentences. In December U Ne Win himself died while under house arrest.

In May 2002 Aung San Suu Kyi was finally released from house arrest. The SPDC stated that her release was unconditional and that it would not attempt to impose any restrictions upon her travel. Shortly afterwards Suu Kyi urged the immediate resumption of dialogue with the junta, which had ceased following her liberation. In June she travelled to Mandalay on her first political trip since she was freed; the journey passed without incident. In August Razali Ismail returned to the country with the intention of promoting further political dialogue between the NLD and the SPDC, but made little progress. Meanwhile, Suu Kyi challenged the SPDC to prove its commitment to the achievement of democracy by ordering the release of all political prisoners. In the following month a delegation from the EU visited Myanmar and met with Suu Kyi, but failed to secure a meeting with any members of the SPDC. In November the junta announced the release of 115 prisoners, the largest number to have been freed since negotiations began. However, the releases were dismissed by both the USA and human rights groups as inadequate.

In early 2003 representatives from Amnesty International were permitted to enter Myanmar for the first time and to hold talks with Suu Kyi. Following the visit, the human rights organization condemned Myanmar's judicial system. Meanwhile, 12 political activists in the country were arrested on suspicion of planning anti-Government activities. In February it was reported that Suu Kyi wanted economic sanctions to be maintained against the Myanma Government until it began a meaningful dialogue with the opposition. In the same month it was announced that Lt-Gen. Soe Win would assume the previously vacant post of Second Secretary of the SPDC. Meanwhile, the Minister of Health, Maj.-Gen. Ket Sein, and the Minister of Finance and Revenue, U Khin Maung Thein, were permitted to retire. They were replaced, respectively, by Dr Kyaw Myint and Maj.-Gen. Hla Tun. In the following month UN envoy Paulo

Sérgio Pinheiro restated a UN demand that the junta release all remaining political prisoners, estimated to number 1,200, and enter into serious dialogue with the opposition. Later that month a bomb exploded in Yangon, killing one person, during celebrations being held to commemorate Armed Forces Day. An unexploded bomb was also discovered near the US embassy on the same day.

In April 2003 Suu Kyi issued a rare criticism of the SPDC for refusing to enter into any substantive dialogue with the opposition. In May 10 members of the NLD were imprisoned on charges that they had organized public protests and participated in clandestine activities. Later in the same month the political situation in Myanmar deteriorated further when violent confrontations occurred in the town of Ye-u, in the north of the country, between government supporters and opposition members travelling with an entourage carrying Suu Kyi. While the SPDC insisted that the violence had been provoked by the opposition, it was subsequently reported that the clashes had occurred when Suu Kyi and her supporters were ambushed and attacked by pro-Government forces. It was estimated that around 80 members of the entourage had died as a result. On the following day it was reported that Suu Kyi had been taken into 'protective custody' by the SPDC; meanwhile, the headquarters of the NLD, together with NLD offices across the country, were closed down, 17 other members of the NLD were also detained, and all universities under the control of the Ministry of Education were shut indefinitely. In June UN envoy Razali Ismail proceeded with a planned visit to Myanmar. Ismail was permitted to meet with Suu Kyi and confirmed that she had not sustained any injuries during the recent violence. The junta's detention of Suu Kyi prompted widespread international criticism. At a meeting of ASEAN ministers of foreign affairs held later in that month the organization transgressed its traditional policy of non-interference in the affairs of other member states, calling for Suu Kyi to be freed and for Myanmar to make a peaceful transition to democratic practices. Later in June, following the failure of its appeal to the SPDC for the liberation of Suu Kyi, the country's largest aid donor, Japan, announced that it had suspended all economic aid. In July the Government announced that it had freed 91 of the NLD activists detained after the violence of May and permitted a delegation from the International Committee of the Red Cross (ICRC) to visit Suu Kyi; the delegates subsequently confirmed that she was in good health, contradicting reports from the US Department of State, which claimed that she had gone on a hunger strike.

In July 2003 it was reported that three cabinet Ministers—Minister of Industry (No. 1) U Aung Thaung, Minister of Forestry Aung Phone and Minister of Agriculture and Irrigation Maj.-Gen. Nyunt Tin—had all been dismissed. In late August a major reorganization of the Government was announced, during which the former First Secretary of the SPDC, Gen. Khin Nyunt, replaced Field Marshal Than Shwe as Prime Minister. Than Shwe retained the defence portfolio, however. Lt-Gen. Soe Win became First Secretary and was replaced as Second Secretary by Lt-Gen. Thein Sein. Khin Nyunt subsequently announced that the Government intended to reconvene the National Convention, which had been in recess since 1996, in order to draw up a new constitution and move towards the holding of new elections. However, no schedule was announced for the proposed developments, leading to criticism that the announcement was merely an attempt to encourage the removal of international sanctions against the country and the resumption of aid.

In September 2003 it was announced that Aung San Suu Kyi had returned to her home and was being held under house arrest, having undergone major surgery in hospital. A visit to Myanmar by Razali Ismail in the following month failed to secure her release or to end the political deadlock. Paulo Sérgio Pinheiro returned to the country in late October. In November five members of the NLD's Central Executive Committee, who had been held in connection with the violence in May, were released. In December nine people were sentenced to death, having been convicted of high treason; they were among 12 people arrested in July for allegedly plotting to overthrow the ruling junta. (Four of the nine people subsequently had their sentences commuted to two years on appeal, and that of another was reduced to five years, while the remaining four were to face life imprisonment.) In January 2004 the release of a further 26 members of the NLD was announced and, in the following month, Vice-Chairman of the NLD Tin Oo was released into house arrest, having been imprisoned since May 2003. Also in January 2004, following a meeting with government officials, representatives from 25 ethnic groups and alliances rejected the proposed 'road map' to democracy outlined by Prime Minister Gen. Khin Nyunt in August 2003 and reiterated demands for the Government to begin talks with the opposition. However, following a visit to the country in March 2004, Razali Ismail expressed confidence that the SPDC would adhere to the 'road map' and proclaimed his trip to have been a success. In April the SPDC released the NLD's Chairman, Aung Shwe, and its Secretary, U Lwin, who had both been under house arrest since May 2003, and reopened the party's headquarters.

The National Convention was reconvened in mid-May 2004, despite a boycott by some ethnic minority groups and the NLD, which demanded that the SPDC release Suu Kyi and Tin Oo from house arrest and reopen the party's branch offices. (It was reported that Khin Nyunt had favoured freeing Suu Kyi to allow her to participate in the Convention, but that Than Shwe had ordered that she be excluded.) More than 1,000 delegates attended the opening session, which was chaired by Lt-Gen. Thein Sein, the SPDC Second Secretary. It was emphasized that the Convention was to be a continuation of the discussions held between 1993 and 1996, at which a number of constitutional provisions had already been drafted (see above). Strict regulations governing the conduct of the delegates were imposed by the SPDC. Criticism of the proceedings could lead to up to 20 years' imprisonment, distribution of unauthorized information from the talks was banned, and delegates were forbidden from expressing disloyalty to the state or discussing any issues not included in the official agenda. The National Convention was adjourned in July. In August courts in Yangon and Mandalay refused to accept petitions from the NLD for the release of Suu Kyi and Tin Oo, and for the reopening of the party's branch offices. Shortly afterwards the UN Secretary-General, Kofi Annan, released a statement urging the Myanma Government to free Suu Kyi and to hold substantive talks with the NLD and other political parties, noting that the National Convention would otherwise lack credibility. Meanwhile, Razali Ismail had been unable to return to Myanmar since his visit in March, as the authorities had rejected his requests for a visa. In September four members of the NLD were reportedly convicted of threatening national security and sentenced to seven years' imprisonment.

In mid-September 2004 a cabinet reorganization took place. Most notably, the civilian Minister of Foreign Affairs, U Win Aung, and his deputy, Khin Maung Win, were replaced by senior military officers Maj.-Gen. Nyan Win and Col Maung Myint, respectively. The changes appeared to reinforce Than Shwe's authority over the Government, as Win Aung was reported to be an ally of Prime Minister Khin Nyunt, who was perceived to be considerably more committed to reform than the SPDC Chairman. Amid reports of a power struggle within the SPDC, Khin Nyunt was removed from the premiership and from his position as Chief of Military Intelligence in October, and was placed under house arrest, apparently owing to his alleged involvement in corruption related to smuggling by military intelligence staff. Lt-Gen. Soe Win was appointed as Prime Minister, while Lt-Gen. Thein Sein replaced Soe Win as First Secretary of the SPDC. The National Intelligence Bureau was abolished, and associates of Khin Nyunt, including several members of his family and many military intelligence officers, were subsequently arrested. In November it was reported that three senior military intelligence officers had been convicted of corruption charges and sentenced to 22 years' imprisonment, and that 12 senior judicial officials, who were either linked to Khin Nyunt or had resisted the purge of those loyal to the former Prime Minister, had been dismissed. Meanwhile, in early November the SPDC announced that the Minister of Home Affairs, Col Tin Hlaing, the Minister of Science and Technology and of Labour, Tin Win, and four deputy ministers had been permitted to retire. It was reported that Tin Hlaing, an ally of Khin Nyunt, had also been placed under house arrest.

In late November 2004 the SPDC ordered the release of 9,248 prisoners who, it claimed, had been wrongly imprisoned owing to improper conduct by the dissolved National Intelligence Bureau. According to the opposition, however, the mass amnesty included only 43 of an estimated 1,300 political prisoners held by the authorities. Moreover, the NLD announced that Aung San Suu Kyi's detention under house arrest had been extended for at least a further year. In mid-December the SPDC freed a further 5,070 prisoners, 11 of whom were reported to be political prisoners, including the Chairman of the Democracy Party, U Thu Wai. However, a number of NLD members were arrested in the same month for allegedly inciting public unrest. In January 2005 widespread rumours of a gun battle involving Maung Aye, Than Shwe, Soe Win and their aides, which were prompted by the unexplained death of Maung Aye's personal assistant, Lt-Col Bo Win Tun, appeared to be unfounded, although speculation about tension within the leadership continued. In the same month it was reported that four associates of Khin Nyunt who had been arrested in October 2004 had died in detention, while the closed trials of some 300 others on corruption charges had commenced in a prison in Yangon. The National Convention resumed in mid-February 2005, again without the participation of the NLD and several ethnic minority groups and amid criticism from the EU, the UN and the USA. A few days earlier Tin Oo's detention under house arrest had been extended for a further year.

Following months of speculation, in July 2005 it was announced at the ASEAN Ministerial Meeting held in the Laotian capital of Vientiane that Myanmar was to relinquish the chair of ASEAN, which it had been due to assume in 2006. Myanmar had recently come under increasing pressure from the international community, and in particular from the other member states of ASEAN (a notable departure from the organization's usual policy of non-interference in the internal affairs of members), to forgo its turn to assume the rotating chair in order to enable the Myanma Government instead to focus its attention on addressing the country's human rights situation. Also in July former Prime Minister Khin Nyunt was convicted on eight charges, including corruption and bribery, and was given a suspended prison sentence of 44 years; his two sons were also convicted and sentenced to prison terms. In the same month the Government authorized the release of dozens of political prisoners; however, in September the UN Special Rapporteur for human rights in Myanmar, Paulo Sérgio Pinheiro, stated in an address to the UN General Assembly that approximately 1,100 dissidents remained in detention in Myanmar. Pinheiro's report was based on information derived from various independent sources, as Pinheiro himself had been repeatedly refused entry to Myanmar since November 2003. In August 2005 UN Special Envoy to Myanmar Ali Alatas had been allowed to visit the country, the first special envoy to be granted entry since Razali Ismail in March 2004.

Meanwhile, in August 2005 the World Food Programme (WFP) published a report stating that one-third of young children in Myanmar were malnourished; in some border areas afflicted by fighting between rival ethnic rebel groups, the figure was believed to be as high as 60%. The report also noted with concern the high number of Myanma children who received little or no formal education. In September Amnesty International released a report detailing the 'unacceptable' use by the military of tens of thousands of ethnic minority citizens to carry out forced labour; the report also drew attention to the military's use of physical abuse against such labourers.

In November 2005 the Government announced that it had initiated the first phase of a relocation of the country's administrative capital from Yangon to Pyinmana, a sparsely populated mountainous region approximately 400 km (nearly 250 miles) to the north of Yangon. Minister of Information Brig.-Gen. Kyaw Hsan announced that the decision to move to Pyinmana had been made owing to its central location and resultant ease of access to and from other parts of the country. However, various popular theories abounded about alternative motives for the transfer, including a fear of invasion by the USA. (The new administrative centre was officially named Nay Pyi Taw in March 2006.) Also in November the NLD announced that Aung San Suu Kyi's detention under house arrest had again been extended by an additional 12 months.

In January 2006, after having being refused access to the country for almost two years, Razali Ismail, the UN Secretary-General's Special Envoy to Myanmar, relinquished his post. In a statement announcing his decision to resign, Ismail urged ASEAN to adopt a more forceful role in exerting pressure for democratic reform in Myanmar. Earlier that month the US-based organization Human Rights Watch had dismissed the junta's pledges of democratic reform as 'empty rhetoric'. In late January the junta adjourned a session of the National Convention, with a view to reconvening towards the end of 2006. Critics continued to denounce the proceedings as worthless, given that the delegates in attendance had all been selected by the country's military rulers. In February U Win Aung went on trial in Yangon, charged with corruption and bribery; in April the former Minister of Foreign Affairs was convicted and sentenced to seven years' imprisonment. Meanwhile, in February the detention under house arrest of Tin Oo was again extended by a further year. In May UN envoy Ibrahim Gambari was permitted to enter the country, holding discussions with Than Shwe and attending a brief meeting with Suu Kyi. The visit was regarded by many as a positive development, partly because Gambari had been allowed access to Suu Kyi but also owing to Gambari's conclusion that SPDC leaders seemed willing to strengthen links with the international community. Later in the month UN Secretary-General Kofi Annan urged Than Shwe to free Suu Kyi; on the following day, however, her term of house arrest was extended for a further year. At the end of September the UN Security Council reviewed the human rights situation in Myanmar for the first time. Gambari paid a second visit to Myanmar in November and was again allowed to hold a brief meeting with Suu Kyi, who, according to Gambari, welcomed discourse between the UN and the Government of Myanmar. In January 2007 a draft resolution urging the Myanma Government to release all political prisoners and end its violation of human rights was submitted to the UN Security Council, sponsored by the USA and the United Kingdom. However, the resolution was defeated when, in an unusual development, both China and Russia, two of the five permanent members of the Security Council, exercised their right of veto.

Meanwhile, in April 2006 the ABSDF, the Federation of Trade Unions—Burma (FTUB), the NCGUB and the National League for Democracy—Liberated Area (NLD—LA) were denounced as terrorist organizations by the Government, in relation to bomb attacks and attempted bombings in 2000–06. Several cabinet changes were implemented in May 2006: the Minister of Culture, Maj.-Gen. Kyi Aung, retired and was replaced by Khin Aung Myint, while the Minister of Immigration and Population and of Social Welfare, Relief and Resettlement, Maj.-Gen. Sein Htwa, was replaced by Maj.-Gen. Maung Maung Swe. Col Zaw Min, hitherto Minister of Co-operatives, became Minister of Electric Power (No. 1), succeeding Maj.-Gen. Tin Htut, who assumed responsibility for the co-operatives portfolio; the hotels and tourism portfolio was allocated to Maj.-Gen. Soe Naing, a new appointee to the Cabinet. In June a Supreme Court judge and several deputy ministers were said to have retired, prompting speculation that they had been dismissed. The National Convention reconvened in October. The admission of the foreign press to the proceedings represented progress to some observers, but the absence of the NLD and the relatively small number of delegates from other political parties did not bode well for democratic reform. In early January 2007 it was reported that the SPDC had released 2,831 prisoners, including some 30 political prisoners, in an amnesty to mark Independence Day. However, the detention under house arrest of Tin Oo was extended for a further year in the following month, as was that of Suu Kyi in late May, despite ongoing international pressure for their release. More than 50 people were arrested in mid-May while attending prayer vigils in support of Suu Kyi; most of the detainees had been freed by late June.

In May 2007 Lt-Gen. Thein Sein, the First Secretary of the SPDC, assumed the role of Prime Minister in an acting capacity, amid conjecture about Lt-Gen. Soe Win's health. The final session of the National Convention commenced in July and was formally closed in September. Thein Sein announced that the Convention had adopted detailed principles for a new constitution. As proposed in the 1994 sessions (see above), legislative power was to be vested in a bicameral Pyidaungsu Hluttaw, comprising the Pyithu Hluttaw and the Amyotha Hluttaw, with 25% of the seats to be allocated to representatives of the military nominated by the Commander-in-Chief of the Armed Forces. The principles approved by the Convention provided for the election of the President by members of the Pyidaungsu Hluttaw, from among three Vice-Presidents selected by an electoral college. The Commander-in-Chief of the Armed Forces was also to designate the government ministers responsible for defence, security, home affairs and border affairs, and was to assume executive, legislative and judicial power in the event of a state of emergency being declared. A 54-member commission, chaired by Chief Justice U Aung Toe, was appointed by the SPDC in October to draft the new constitution and commenced work in December without the participation of the opposition.

Meanwhile, substantial unexpected increases in fuel prices in mid-August 2007 provoked a series of anti-Government protests in Yangon and other towns. More than 60 demonstrators had been arrested by the end of the month; those detained included leaders of the '88 Generation' students' group who had participated in the 1988 pro-democracy uprising. The protests escalated in September with the involvement of Buddhist monks. In early September, during two days of demonstrations in Pakokku, in central Myanmar, monks held some 20 government officials captive for several hours after the security forces had forcibly dispersed some 300–400 monks, detaining around 10 and injuring several. On 9 September the Alliance of All Burmese Buddhist Monks, a previously unknown group, made a series of demands to the SPDC—an apology for the force used in Pakokku, a reduction in commodity and fuel prices, the release of all political prisoners and those detained for participating in the recent protests, and the initiation of a dialogue with pro-democracy forces—threatening to withdraw all religious services from the authorities if they did not comply by 17 September. The SPDC accused the NLD and 'external groups' of instigating the unrest. Some of the marches were allowed to proceed peacefully, but on 18 September tear gas was used to disperse a rally of some 1,000 monks and civilians in the western town of Sittwe. Meanwhile, with the monks' demands unfulfilled, daily marches commenced in Yangon. The Alliance of All Burmese Buddhist Monks issued a statement describing the military Government as 'the enemy of the people' and pledging to continue protesting until the Government was removed from office. On 22 September, the sixth consecutive day of demonstrations in Yangon, Suu Kyi made a brief public appearance when the monks were permitted to pass the house in which she was confined. On the same day up to 10,000 monks were reported to have marched in Mandalay. Around 150 Buddhist nuns joined some 5,000 monks on 23 September in Yangon, and on the following day the largest protest yet was held in the city, attended by an estimated 50,000–100,000 monks and civilians, including NLD leaders, while demonstrations also took place in more than 20 other towns.

Having thus far exercised relative restraint in response to the protests, on 25 September 2007 the SPDC imposed a night-time curfew in Yangon and Mandalay, banned gatherings of more than five people and deployed armed troops on the streets. On the following day, as up to 10,000 monks and other protesters defied government warnings to halt the marches, troops fired live ammunition, reportedly killing up to five people. Some 200 monks were later reportedly detained in overnight raids on several monasteries, during which many were allegedly beaten. Two NLD members were also arrested. The UN Security Council expressed concern at the situation in an emergency meeting, but China, Myanmar's closest ally, rejected a US proposal to consider the imposition of sanctions against the Myanma authorities. Despite the rising tension, anti-Government protests continued on 27–28 September, but were violently suppressed. The Government claimed that 10 people had died as a result of the violence (later increasing this figure to 15), but diplomats and witnesses reported that the death toll was much higher, with some estimating that up to 200 had been killed. As international condemnation of the military action mounted, the Myanma authorities sought to block telecommunications networks. By the end of the month the uprising had been largely quashed, with many monks in detention, while others were reportedly being prevented from leaving their monasteries. During October the security forces continued to arrest those suspected of involvement in the street protests, and reports emerged of ill-treatment in detention centres, including claims that an NLD member had died as a result of being tortured in custody. In mid-October the authorities announced that 2,927 protesters (including 596 monks) had been arrested since 26 September, 2,459 of whom had been released after pledging not to participate in further demonstrations. However, other estimates suggested that some 6,000 people had been detained, including 2,400 monks. (In December the UN human rights envoy to Myanmar, Paulo Sérgio Pinheiro, reported that at least 31 people had died and that 3,000–4,000 people had been arrested in September and October, 500–1,000 of whom were still in detention; according to the security forces, only 80 people, including 21 monks, remained in custody at this time.) Meanwhile, the curfew in Yangon and Mandalay was removed on 20 October. At the end of the month more than 100 monks marched through Pakokku, their progress reportedly unimpeded by the security forces.

UN envoy Ibrahim Gambari visited Myanmar in late September 2007, initially holding discussions with acting Prime Minister Thein Sein and other government ministers, as well as with Suu Kyi, and in early October he was finally permitted to meet Than Shwe and Maung Aye. The SPDC agreed to Gambari's recommendation that a government official be appointed to enter into dialogue with Suu Kyi, assigning this role (Minister of Relations) to the Deputy Minister of Labour, U Aung Kyi. Than Shwe had reportedly told Gambari that he would be willing to meet Suu Kyi personally, but only if she withdrew her support for international sanctions against his regime and abandoned her 'confrontational attitude'. In mid-October the UN Security Council unanimously adopted a statement deploring the use of violence against peaceful demonstrators, calling for the early release of all political prisoners and remaining detainees, and urging the Government to create the necessary conditions for a 'genuine dialogue' with Suu Kyi; it was reported that the original statement (drafted by France, the United Kingdom and the USA) had been modified in order to secure China's support. Later that month WFP reported that it was able to assist only 500,000 of some 5m. people who were suffering food shortages in Myanmar, and urged the Myanma Government to pursue reforms aimed at reducing poverty.

Thein Sein was formally appointed Prime Minister in late October 2007, following Soe Win's death earlier that month, and was replaced as First Secretary of the SPDC by Lt-Gen. Thiha Thura Tin Aung Myint Oo. At the same time U Aung Kyi was promoted to the position of Minister of Labour, while retaining responsibility for liaising with Suu Kyi. On the following day Aung Kyi and Suu Kyi held their first talks.

In early November 2007 the Myanma Government announced the expulsion of Charles Petrie, the most senior UN official resident in the country. Petrie had recently publicly linked the pro-democracy protests to economic hardship and a 'deteriorating humanitarian situation'. Shortly afterwards Gambari arrived for a further visit, during which he held discussions with the Prime Minister and Suu Kyi, although not with Than Shwe. It was reported by the Myanma state media that the SPDC had rejected an offer by Gambari to mediate in the dialogue between Suu Kyi and Aung Kyi. However, following the visit, Gambari issued a statement on behalf of Suu Kyi, in which she declared her willingness to co-operate with the SPDC 'in the interest of the nation'. A second meeting subsequently took place between Aung Kyi and Suu Kyi, who was also permitted to meet other members of the NLD for the first time in more than three years. In mid-November the UN Secretary-General, Ban Ki-Moon, urged the SPDC to conduct a 'meaningful and substantive dialogue' with the opposition, amid some scepticism among diplomats and other observers regarding the junta's commitment to genuine dialogue aimed at democratic reform. In early December the Government announced that it had granted amnesty to 8,585 prisoners since mid-November to mark the conclusion of the National Convention, although it was reported that only 10 were political detainees. Suu Kyi held two rounds of talks with Aung Kyi in January 2008, and was also permitted to meet NLD colleagues again at the end of the month, after which the party announced that its General Secretary was not satisfied with her meetings with Aung Kyi, mainly because no time-frame had been established for them. Meanwhile, in mid-January the Security Council expressed regret at the slow rate of progress towards meeting the 'objectives' outlined in its October statement (i.e. the release of political prisoners and dialogue with Suu Kyi), and urged Myanmar to allow another visit by Gambari. In late January Amnesty International claimed that 96 pro-democracy activists had been arrested since November 2007, increasing the total number in detention to 1,850, of whom 700 were accused of participating in the August and September protests. A few days later 10 activists, including Min Ko Naing and Ko Ko Gyi of the '88 Generation' students' group, were reportedly charged with making illegal statements.

In February 2008 the SPDC unexpectedly announced that a constitutional referendum would be held in May, followed by multi-party elections in 2010. Chief Justice Aung Toe subsequently confirmed that his commission had completed the draft constitution. The NLD expressed surprise that elections had been planned before the results of the constitutional referendum were known. A few days later the detention under house arrest of Tin Oo was again extended by a further year. Ibrahim Gambari returned to Myanmar in March, meeting Suu Kyi and several government officials, the most senior of whom was the Minister of Information, Brig.-Gen. Kyaw Hsan. However, no apparent progress was made during the visit, with the Government rejecting Gambari's proposal that independent observers be allowed to monitor the forthcoming referendum and refusing to consider amending the draft constitution to allow Suu Kyi to contest elections.

In early May 2008 a major cyclone struck southern Myanmar. Although initial reports suggested that there had been hundreds of fatalities, subsequent news releases indicated that the death toll was significantly higher. Yangon and four other regions, including the Ayeyarwady (Irrawaddy) Delta, suffered the most serious devastation and were declared disaster areas. The Government was criticized for its weak response to the developing crisis and for the restrictions it imposed on international aid efforts, which exacerbated the risks faced by survivors, many of whom had no access to clean drinking water, food or shelter. Within days the official death toll had risen to 22,000, although some international estimates were closer to 100,000. Although some provisions supplied by the UN and foreign donors were eventually allowed into the country, the Government refused entry to foreign aid workers. In mid-May the UN Secretary-General, Ban Ki-Moon stated that the Government's reaction to the disaster had been 'unacceptably slow'. While the Government's calculation of the number of fatalities had reached approximately 38,500 by this point, the ICRC suggested that the figure might be as high as 128,000, while the UN estimated that 2.5m. people had been affected by the disaster.

Despite the widespread destruction caused by the cyclone, which prompted the Government to postpone the constitutional referendum in the affected regions, the poll proceeded as scheduled in other areas on 10 May. According to preliminary reports, turn-out was high, at 99%, while 92.4% of voters endorsed the new Constitution.

After Burma gained independence in 1948, various groups conducted armed insurgency campaigns against government forces. The most effective of the ethnic-based insurgency groups was the Karen (Kayin) National Union (KNU), founded in 1948, which led a protracted campaign for the establishment of an independent state for the Karen ethnic group (restyled Kayin in the transliteration changes of 1989), partly through the activities of its military wing, the Karen (Kayin) National Liberation Army (KNLA). The KNU was a member of the National Democratic Front (NDF), an organization which at one time comprised 11 ethnic minority groups—including Kachin, Karenni (Kayinni), Mon, Shan, Pa-O, Palaung, Wa, Arakanese (Rakhine) and Lahu parties—formed in 1975 (by five groups, originally) with the aim of making Burma a federal union and opposing both the Government and, initially, the CPB. The CPB was one of the most well-organized insurgent movements, in military terms, and gained control of significant areas in northern Burma. By May 1986 the various minority groups in the NDF had agreed to relinquish their individual demands for autonomy, in favour of a unified demand for a federal system of government. At the same time, the CPB withdrew its demand for a 'one-party' government and entered into an alliance with the NDF. At the second NDF Congress in June 1987, Maj.-Gen. Bo Mya, the President of the KNU and Chief of Staff of the KNLA, was replaced as NDF President by Saw Maw Reh, a former Chairman of the Karenni (Kayinni) National Progressive Party (KNPP), and further leadership changes removed all KNU representatives from senior NDF positions. The new NDF leaders advocated the establishment of autonomous, ethnic-based states within a Burmese union.

The insurgent groups were sympathetic to anti-Government movements in the major cities. Continued attacks throughout 1988 engaged the government forces in the border areas, leaving fewer of them to impose order in the towns. In September the Karens announced plans to co-operate with protesting students and Buddhist monks to work towards the achievement of democracy. After the armed forces seized power, insurgents intensified operations, aided by at least 3,000 students whom the Karen rebels agreed to train and arm. In November 22 anti-Government groups, led by members of the NDF, formed the DAB. Bo Mya was elected President.

In April 1989 dissatisfaction with the leadership of the CPB led to a mutiny by Wa tribesmen, who constituted an estimated 80%–90% of the CPB's membership. Rebellious Wa soldiers captured the CPB headquarters, and the party's leaders were forced into exile in the People's Republic of China. The leaders of the mutiny subsequently accepted SLORC proposals for the former forces of the CPB army to become government-controlled militia forces in exchange for supplies of rice, financial support and development aid. The former CPB troops agreed to use their main forces against the 25,000-strong rebel separatist Mong Tai (Shan State) Army (formerly the Shan United Army), whose leader, Khun Sa, controlled much of the drug trade in the 'Golden Triangle', the world's major opium-producing area, where the borders of Myanmar, Laos and Thailand meet. The SLORC also approached members of the NDF, and was successful in securing agreements with the Shan State Progressive Party in September 1989, the Pa-O National Organization in March 1991 and the Palaung State Liberation Organization in May of that year. In July, at the third NDF Congress, these three movements were expelled, reducing the NDF's membership to eight organizations, and Nai Shwe Kyin was elected as the NDF's new President.

In December 1988, following a visit by the Prime Minister of Thailand, the SLORC granted licences to Thai business interests to exploit raw materials in Burma, in return for much-needed foreign exchange. Although there was no announcement of any official Thai-Burmese agreement, subsequent offensives by government forces against rebel groups achieved unprecedented success, with troops frequently attacking insurgent bases from Thai territory. By December 1989 six KNU bases along the Thai border had been captured, and in January 1990 two more camps, harbouring a large number of student dissidents, were seized. In January 1990 the armed forces launched an offensive against Mon separatists. In February they succeeded in capturing Three Pagodas Pass, a principal 'black market' trade route between Thailand and Myanmar, and the headquarters of the New Mon State Party.

Intense fighting between government and rebel forces continued as the KNLA advanced into the lower central Ayeyarwady Delta in late 1991. This potentially diversionary tactic failed to prevent a concerted attempt by government troops to seize control of the KNU and DAB headquarters, which was also the seat of the NCGUB. However, despite the use of sophisticated weaponry purchased from the People's Republic of China, government troops failed to capture the camp at Manerplaw. In March 1992 the Thai Government fulfilled prior threats of strong retaliation, forcing hundreds of Myanma troops out of entrenched positions taken up in order to attack the KNU headquarters from the rear. In April the SLORC officially suspended its offensive against the KNU, 'in the interests of national unity'. In October, however, government troops resumed hostilities, making several incursions into Thai territory. In December the Thai and Myanma Governments agreed to 'relocate' the Myanma armed forces, and in February 1993 they resolved to demarcate their common border.

In February and March 1993 the Kachin Independence Organization (KIO) attended peace talks with the Government in the Kachin state capital of Myitkyina. The Kachins were in a vulnerable position, since they were no longer able to obtain arms from the practically defunct CPB or through Thailand (as the Mong Tai Army controlled the territory between Kachin encampments and the Thai border). The SLORC was anxious to reach an accommodation with the Kachins, as the NCGUB would be severely weakened by the loss of their support (although a de facto national cease-fire had been in effect since October 1992). The KIO appeared to have signed a peace agreement in April but, owing to attempts by the Kachins to persuade other members of the DAB to enter discussions with the SLORC, the cease-fire was not announced until October. The agreement was ratified in Yangon in February 1994. The KIO was suspended from the DAB in October 1993 for negotiating separately with the SLORC, and the DAB reiterated its conditions for discussions with the SLORC in a series of open letters. Its stipulations included: the recognition of the DAB as a single negotiating body (the SLORC insisted on meeting each ethnic group separately); the location of the negotiating process in a neutral country; an immediate end to the forcible mass relocation of villagers; a new body to draft a constitution; and the release of all political detainees, beginning with Suu Kyi. Under Thai pressure, however, the DAB policy of negotiating as a front was unofficially abandoned. In February 2001 there were rumours of a coup within the KIO, as Chairman Lt-Gen. Zau Mai was replaced by his deputy, Maj.-Gen. Tu Jai. The rumours were swiftly denied, the reason for the replacement being given as Zau Nai's ill health.

In May 1994 the Karenni (Kayinni) National People's Liberation Front concluded a cease-fire agreement with the SLORC, reportedly the 11th insurgent group to do so. This was followed in July by the declaration of a cease-fire by the Kayan New Land Party, and in October by the declaration of a cease-fire by the Shan State Nationalities Liberation Organization. In December government forces launched a new offensive against the KNU, recapturing its headquarters at Manerplaw in January 1995 (and forcing many hundreds of KNU fighters across the border into Thailand). The virtual defeat of the KNU forces was attributed to their reportedly severe lack of ammunition and funds and also to the recent defection from the Christian-led KNU of a mainly Buddhist faction, which established itself as the

Democratic Karen (Kayin) Buddhist Army (DKBA). The DKBA, which had comprised about 10% of the strength of the KNLA, allegedly supported the government forces in their offensive. In February 1995 the Myanma army captured the KNU's last stronghold, and in the following month Bo Mya resigned as the Commander-in-Chief of the KNLA (although he remained the leader of the KNU). In March the KNU declared a unilateral cease-fire, with the aim of initiating negotiations with the SLORC. Earlier in the month the KNPP reportedly became the 14th ethnic insurgent group to abandon its armed struggle against the SLORC. This agreement collapsed in June, however, as government troops entered areas designated in the accord to be under KNPP control. In August 5,000 troops were dispatched to suppress the KNPP rebellion. Clashes continued throughout the year, and in January 1996 government forces captured a major Kayinni stronghold. The KNPP continued fighting, however, with support from the ABSDF. In February 1996 talks between the KNU and the SLORC in Mawlamyine (Moulmein), calling for tripartite negotiations between the NLD, the NCGUB (which had re-elected Sein Win as its head in Sweden in July 1995) and the SLORC, were inconclusive.

Further talks between the SLORC and the KNU began in November 1996, but had collapsed by December. In January 1997 the DKBA, allegedly supported by government forces, attacked Kayin refugee camps in Thailand. The KNU claimed that requests in late January for further peace negotiations were rejected by the SLORC, which then initiated a new offensive against the KNU. Fighting between the KNU and government forces continued in March, forcing several thousand Kayins across the border into Thailand. As a result of the forcible relocation of tens of thousands of Kayins away from KNU bases in Myanmar during 1997, further refugees fled to Thailand. The Thai armed forces denied collusion with the Myanma troops in the process of forced repatriations of Kayin refugees, who were believed to number more than 100,000 in mid-1997. In March 1998 the DKBA, supported by government troops, launched two further attacks on Kayin refugee camps in Thailand, prompting a retaliatory attack by the KNU on DKBA forces. In April 1999 the KNU issued a statement confirming the deaths of seven members of a group of 13 government officials whom they had abducted in February; the remaining six were said to have been released unharmed.

In January 2000 it was reported that 800–1,000 Kayins had fled across the border into Thailand, following clashes between government forces and the KNU. In the same month Gen. Bo Mya was succeeded as the leader of the KNU by the former Secretary-General of the organization, Saw Ba Thin. Following his appointment as leader, Ba Thin announced that, while the KNU intended to continue its struggle against the ruling SPDC, the movement was prepared to negotiate a political settlement with the military regime. It was subsequently reported by both government and independent sources that an initial but inconclusive round of talks between the KNU and the SPDC was held in February, followed by further discussions in March. However, in late 2000 the Government began to use 'scorched-earth' tactics to deprive the KNU of its support base, displacing up to 30,000 people in eastern Myanmar.

In January 2001 Johnny and Luther Htoo, teenage leaders of the Karen rebel group, God's Army, surrendered with 12 of their followers to the Thai authorities. While much smaller than the KNU or the KNLA, God's Army had gained international notoriety owing to the leadership of the twin boys, thought to be aged 13 or 14. Two of the 12 members who surrendered were believed to have been involved in a raid on a Thai village that had left six civilians dead in December 2000.

In April 2003 the KNU claimed responsibility for a series of explosions that had destroyed sections of a gas pipeline in Karen State over the previous two months, declaring that they had intended to draw the attention of the international community to the human rights abuses being perpetrated by government troops in the area. Several bombings along the border with Thailand in the following month were also attributed to the KNU. In December, however, Vice-Chairman of the KNU Bo Mya led a personal delegation to Yangon to explore the possibility of a potential cease-fire arrangement with the Government. In January 2004, having unified the KNU behind his initiative, Bo Mya and other KNU officials held talks with government representatives in Yangon, which resulted in the conclusion of an informal cease-fire arrangement between the two sides. Bo Mya had previously made any peace agreement conditional both on the release of Aung San Suu Kyi and other NLD detainees and on the Government's adherence to UN resolutions delineating a return to democracy for the country. At further talks, held in Mawlamyine in February, the KNU and the Government discussed the demarcation of KNU territory, the relocation of the armed forces and the resettlement of some 200,000 internally displaced civilians in Karen State. However, despite the informal cease-fire, sporadic fighting continued between government troops and the KNLA. Further negotiations in Yangon in October were curtailed at the Government's request following the dismissal of Prime Minister Khin Nyunt. Bo Mya retired as Vice-Chairman of the KNU in December because of ill health; he was replaced by Gen. Tamalabaw. In January 2005 10 government troops were reportedly killed in clashes with the KNU after attacking one of the group's bases near the border with Thailand. Later that month the KNU demanded a resumption of the peace talks, which remained stalled. In the mean time, government forces were reported to have launched an offensive against a KNPP stronghold in Yamu, again close to the Thai border. In March 2006 it was reported that an army offensive was being conducted against the KNU in Karen state, resulting in the displacement of several hundred people. In May reports emerged of a military campaign against the KNU in another part of the state, following which an estimated 15,000 Karen people were reported to have fled from the violence. Bo Mya died in a Thai hospital in December 2006. In February 2007 a relatively small breakaway faction of the KNU led by Htain Maung negotiated a peace agreement with the Government, but the goals of the KNU itself were said to be unaffected. In April it was reported that DKBA and government forces had captured four KNU bases near the Thai border. In June 27 people were killed in two separate ambushes on buses in Kayah and Kayin states; the KNU and the KNPP claimed responsibility for the attacks, but insisted that the victims were armed troops and not civilians. Three people were killed in four minor bomb explosions in January 2008, which the authorities attributed to the KNU and other ethnic insurgent groups. The KNU suffered a reverse in February, when its Secretary-General, Pado Mahn Sha, was killed by two unknown gunmen at his home in the Thai border town of Mae Sot; it was speculated that the DKBA was responsible for the assassination.

Meanwhile, in December 1993 the SLORC initiated a major offensive against Khun Sa's Mong Tai Army encampments on the Thai border. During that month Khun Sa convened a Shan 'parliament' in his base of Homong, which was attended by hundreds of delegates. This was followed, in May 1994, by Khun Sa's declaration of an independent Shan State, of which he declared himself 'President'. In the same month fighting intensified between government forces and the Mong Tai Army near the Thai border, with heavy losses reported on both sides. However, Khun Sa claimed that his army retained control of two-thirds of the Shan State. In July he was reported to have offered to end opium cultivation and to surrender to the government forces, in exchange for their withdrawal from the Shan State and a guarantee of Shan independence. In March 1995 government forces launched an intensive campaign, lasting several months, against the Mong Tai Army. In August a faction calling itself the Shan State National Army broke away from the Mong Tai Army, accusing Khun Sa of using Shan nationalism as a 'front' for drugs-trafficking. Khun Sa subsequently offered to relinquish areas under his control to an international force that could ensure the safety of the Shan while eradicating illicit drugs. Khun Sa's position was considerably weakened in September, as improving relations between Thailand and Myanmar led to a Thai pledge to close the common border, thus obstructing his supply routes, and cease-fires with neighbouring ethnic groups allowed the Government to deploy troops in hitherto inaccessible areas. Certain ethnic groups, notably the Wa, were also actively engaged in fighting the Mong Tai Army to gain control of the opium trade. In November Khun Sa announced his retirement from all political and military positions, citing his betrayal by the breakaway group. In January 1996 government troops entered Homong without resistance, and thousands of his former supporters surrendered. Although no formal agreement with the SLORC was announced, it was widely believed that Khun Sa had previously negotiated a settlement with the authorities since he was not detained and it was officially announced that he would not be extradited to the USA on drugs-trafficking charges. (Khun Sa was, moreover, later accorded the status of an honoured elder. He died in Yangon in October 2007.) The Mong Tai Army was subsequently transformed into a militia volunteer unit under the command of the armed forces.

Between November 1996 and February 1997 there were reports of clashes between the Shan United Revolutionary Party (a faction of the Mong Tai Army that had not surrendered in January 1996) and government forces. In September 1997 the alliance between three of the major Shan groups who continued their resistance—including the Shan State National Army (SSNA), remnants of the MTA, and the Shan State Peacekeeping Council (SSPC) and its military wing, the Shan State Army (SSA)—was formalized, and the groups joined together in an enlarged SSA. In November it was reported that Shan separatist groups had launched a further offensive against government troops. In May 1999 it was reported that at least 300,000 Shan had been forced from their villages into resettlement camps by government troops. Clashes between SSA units and government forces were reported in December. In March 2000, following the group's announcement that it wished to seek a peaceful settlement with the ruling junta, the SSA issued a statement outlining cease-fire terms. It was later claimed by the SSA that these terms had been misinterpreted by the Government. In May several senior army officers died in an SSA ambush. In the following month more than 60 Shan and hill tribespeople, who had been forcibly relocated and had then attempted to return to their village, were reportedly killed by the Myanma military in a retaliatory attack. In similar incidents in the region in June, as many as 50 other villagers were believed to have been murdered. In 2001 the Government launched several offensives against SSA border camps, causing hundreds more Shan to flee the area. In September 2001 the leader of the SSA, Col Yodsuek, stated that the group would be willing to enter into peace talks with the SPDC.

In late 1996 Gen. Maung Aye ordered that the forces of the United Wa State Army (UWSA—who reached an accommodation with the SLORC in 1989) should withdraw from its principal base or surrender to the Government by the end of 1997. As the deadline approached, tension between the two sides increased until the UWSA was given permission to remain at the base for a further year. In January 2000 it was reported that the SPDC was to launch an operation to relocate 50,000 people from UWSA-controlled opium-growing areas with the alleged intention of eradicating the production of drugs in the areas by 2005. The relocation programme began to cause ethnic tension early in 2001, as the Shan complained that the Wa tribespeople were occupying land that they had previously owned. It was also claimed that the Wa were still growing opium, in spite of the fact that the scheme had been introduced supposedly to prevent heroin production. In February 2001 the office of the UN High Commissioner for Refugees (UNHCR) investigated reports that 300,000 Shan had fled over the border to Thailand as a result of the Wa influx.

In late 1989 the SLORC began resettling Bamar (Burman) Buddhists in the predominantly Muslim areas of Arakan (renamed Rakhine), displacing the local Rohingya Muslims. In April 1991 Rohingya refugees were forced over the border into Bangladesh, as a result of the brutal operations of the Myanma armed forces, including the destruction of villages, widespread killings and pillaging. The Rohingyas had been similarly persecuted in 1976–78, when more than 200,000 of them had sought refuge in Bangladesh. The Rohingyas had finally been repatriated, only to lose their citizenship following the introduction of new nationality legislation in 1982. In November 1991 the SLORC pledged to repatriate genuine Myanma citizens, but claimed that many of the refugees were illegal Bengali immigrants. In April 1992 the Myanma and Bangladeshi Governments signed an agreement providing for the repatriation of those Rohingya refugees in possession of official documentation. The repatriation programme was delayed, however, owing to the continuing flow of refugees to Bangladesh (reaching an estimated 270,000 by the end of June). The first Rohingya refugees were returned to Myanmar in September, without the supervision of UNHCR. Despite demonstrations by Rohingyas in Bangladesh against forced repatriation, refugees continued to be returned to Myanmar. The SLORC's agreement, in November 1993, to allow UNHCR access to repatriated Rohingyas was expected to accelerate the programme. In April 1994 guerrillas of the Rohingya Solidarity Organization carried out attacks in the Maungdaw area of Rakhine. By May 1995 more than 216,000 refugees had been repatriated. In July 1999, however, about 20,000 Rohingya refugees remained in camps in Bangladesh, despite the expiry of the official deadline for their repatriation in August 1997. In April 2000 the International Federation of Human Rights Leagues (FIDH) issued a report condemning the treatment of Rohingya Muslims by the Myanma Government, including forced labour, punitive taxes and extrajudicial killings. The FIDH claimed that the regime was attempting to force the exodus of Rohingyas from their native Rakhine and criticized UNHCR for its effective complicity with the Myanma regime in designating the more recent refugees as economic migrants. In February 2001 violence between Buddhist and Muslim communities in the state capital, Sittwe, was reported to have resulted in at least 12 deaths, prompting the Government to regulate further the movement of Rohingya and other Muslims in and out of Rakhine. In 2003 UNHCR assisted more than 3,000 refugees to return to Myanmar from Bangladesh, following the removal of technical restrictions on their repatriation. Nevertheless, more than 27,000 remained in two camps in Bangladesh in early 2008, many of whom were reportedly unwilling to return to Myanmar. In addition, it was estimated that some 200,000 Rohingyas were residing in Bangladesh without refugee status.

The People's Republic of China restored diplomatic relations with Burma in 1978. From 1988, as Burma's international isolation deepened, China assumed an increasingly important role. It became Myanmar's principal aid donor, arms supplier and source of consumer goods, and delayed the passage of UN resolutions that were strongly critical of the SLORC's violations of human rights. In May 1997 an agreement was reached to establish a trade route through Myanmar to provide the Chinese province of Yunnan with access to the Indian Ocean. In the same year the Chinese Government signed a 30-year agreement with Myanmar that allowed for more than 200 Chinese fishing boats to operate in Myanma waters; the agreement was widely perceived as an indication of increasing Chinese influence in Myanmar. Furthermore, China announced the construction in Myanmar of two liquefied petroleum gas plants in October 2000 and also of a dry dock in February 2001. In December 2001 the Chinese President, Jiang Zemin, travelled to Myanmar, becoming the first Chinese Head of State to visit the country since 1985. Before his arrival the Government announced that it had ordered the release of more than 200 Chinese prisoners as a gesture of goodwill. Following successful discussions, the two Governments signed a series of bilateral agreements intended to enhance co-operative ties. It was reported that China had offered Myanmar US $100m. in aid and investment, although this was thought to be linked to Chinese demands that the ruling junta increase its efforts to eradicate the drug trade between the two countries. Relations between the two countries were further strengthened in March 2004, during a visit to Yangon by Chinese Vice-Premier Wu Yi, by the signing of 24 agreements on economic and technical co-operation and, in February 2006, by a visit to Beijing by the Prime Minister of Myanmar, Lt-Gen. Soe Win, during which the two heads of states agreed further to promote cordial bilateral relations.

In April 2007 Myanmar and the Democratic People's Republic of Korea (North Korea) agreed to restore diplomatic relations, which had been severed in 1983 after the latter was held responsible for a bomb attack in Yangon during a visit by the President of the Republic of Korea (South Korea). It was speculated that North Korea hoped to gain access to Myanmar's energy resources, while Myanmar would benefit from North Korean military co-operation.

Japan and the member states of ASEAN were anxious to halt Myanmar's excessive dependence on China for aid and trade. Myanmar, in its turn, applied to join ASEAN (which maintained a policy of 'constructive engagement' in relation to Myanmar) in an attempt to end its isolation, accelerate economic growth and gain protection from Western criticism of its internal affairs. In July 1994 Myanmar was invited to attend the annual meeting of ASEAN ministers responsible for foreign affairs, and in July 1995 it signed the organization's founding Treaty of Amity and Co-operation, a precursor to full membership. In July 1996 Myanmar was granted observer status, and in July 1997 the country was admitted as a full member of the organization. In May 1996 Myanmar joined the ASEAN Regional Forum (ARF, see p. 188) and in May 2000 the country hosted a high-level meeting of the economic ministers of the ASEAN member countries; the meeting, which was also attended by ministers from the People's Republic of China, Japan and the Republic of Korea, attracted strong criticism from the NLD. Myanmar enjoyed particularly cordial relations with Indonesia, and the military regime aspired to Indonesia's internationally accepted political system, in which the dominant role of the armed forces was enshrined in the Constitution. ASEAN links were strengthened by official visits from the Prime Minister of Cambodia, Hun Sen, in February 2000, and the Vietnamese Minister of Foreign Affairs, Nguyen Dy Nien, in October of the same year. In January 2001 Dr Mahathir Mohamad, Prime Minister of Malaysia and an integral figure in gaining entry for Myanmar into ASEAN, visited Yangon. Gen. Than Shwe and Gen. Khin Nyunt paid a reciprocal visit in September. Mahathir visited the country again in August 2002. In March 2006 the Malaysian Minister of Foreign Affairs, Syed Hamid Albar, was denied a meeting with Aung San Suu Kyi by the military junta. Albar, acting as an ASEAN envoy to assess the progress of political reform, had held a meeting with Lt-Gen. Soe Win, the Myanma Prime Minister, and was initially positive about the visit. However, he claimed in July that ASEAN's development was being impeded by Myanmar, and that ASEAN could no longer defend Myanmar as it was 'not making an attempt to co-operate or help itself'. In late September 2007, in a rare departure from the Association's policy of non-interference in member states' internal affairs, ASEAN ministers responsible for foreign affairs, meeting in New York, USA, issued a statement in which they declared that they had expressed their 'revulsion' to their Myanma counterpart over reports that anti-Government protests (see above) were being suppressed violently, and had urged the Myanma Government to resume efforts at national reconciliation and release all political detainees. ASEAN came under pressure to take action against Myanmar in advance of its summit meeting in November, at which member states signed a new charter committing themselves *inter alia* to strengthening democracy and promoting and protecting human rights, with the US Senate notably approving a resolution urging the Association to suspend Myanmar. However, ASEAN's Secretary-General rejected this suggestion, deeming it confrontational, and the Myanma Government also succeeded in forcing the cancellation of a planned address by UN envoy Ibrahim Gambari. None the less, the President of the Philippines warned that her country's legislature was unlikely to ratify the new ASEAN charter unless Myanmar agreed to release Suu Kyi.

In the late 1990s bilateral relations between Myanmar and Thailand were rather less cordial than previously, with the Thai Government advocating a more limited 'flexible engagement' with Myanmar, in place of the ASEAN policy of 'constructive engagement' formerly endorsed by the country. Relations between the two countries were placed under some strain in late 1999 when a group of armed Myanma student activists, styled the Vigorous Burmese Student Warriors, seized control of the Myanma embassy in Bangkok in early October, demanding the release of all political prisoners in Myanmar and the opening of a dialogue between the military Goverment and the opposition. All 89 hostages were released by the activists within 24 hours, in exchange for the Thai Government's provision of helicopter transport to the Thai–Myanma border. The Thai Government's release of the perpetrators angered the ruling junta in Myanmar, and Myanmar closed its border with Thailand immediately after the incident. The border was re-opened to commerce in late November, although relations between the two countries remained strained. In January 2000 Thai troops shot dead 10 armed Myanma rebels who had taken control of a hospital in Ratchaburi, holding hundreds of people hostage. The rebels, who were reported by some sources to be linked to the Kayin insurgent group, God's Army, had issued several demands, including that the shelling of their base on the Thai–Myanma border by the Thai military be halted, that co-operation between the Thai and Myanma armies against the Kayins should cease, and that Kayin tribespeople be allowed to seek refuge in Thailand. While the Thai Government denied reports that the perpetrators had been summarily executed after handing over their weapons, the brutal resolution of the incident was praised by the military Government in Myanmar.

There was renewed tension on the Thai–Myanma border in October 2000 when a Thai soldier was killed and two others were injured. It was unclear whether the clash was with Myanma troops or a faction allied to the Government. Tension was further heightened in November as 2,000 Myanma troops were deployed along the border, in preparation for an offensive against the KNU. In January 2001 it was reported that a Thai F-16 fighter aircraft had intruded into Myanma airspace, prompting the Government to announce the building of air defence systems along the border. Another border transgression occurred in February, when five Myanma soldiers were arrested by the Thai Border Patrol Police (BPP). The soldiers claimed that they were searching for food, whereas the BPP believed them to be gathering intelligence on Thai positions. On the previous day an offensive had been launched against the KNU, involving 300 Myanma troops, of whom five were killed. In mid-February there was a major incursion into Thai territory by some 200 Myanma troops, in pursuit of 100 SSA rebels. The troops clashed with Thai soldiers and occupied a hill that was within Thai territory for two days. At least two Thai villagers were killed, and officially 14 Myanma soldiers and two civilians also died. A cease-fire was signed, but this did not prevent Myanmar from ordering all SPDC troops on the border to be placed on full combat-ready status. By the end of February Thailand had detained 40 Myanma nationals for spying, according to Myanma figures, while the SPDC accused Thailand of providing support to the SSA.

In May 2001 Thai-Myanma relations deteriorated further when the Thai Government lodged a formal protest over an incident in which members of the DKBA had allegedly attacked a military unit situated in a Thai border village, causing the deaths of three civilians. A further protest was made several days later when the UWSA captured a hill believed to lie within Thai territory; the hill was later recaptured by Thai troops. In response, the Myanma Government demanded the withdrawal of Thai troops from 35 border outposts and claimed that the Thai army had launched air strikes into its territory, an accusation denied by the Thai authorities. The situation was further exacerbated by the publication of an article in a Myanma newspaper that Thailand claimed was insulting to its monarchy. In June Thai Prime Minister Thaksin Shinawatra arrived in Yangon for discussions, which defused the tensions, although the two sides failed to reach any firm agreement as to how they would overcome the problems affecting their relations. In the following month the Thai Minister of Defence, Chavalit Yongchaiyudh, visited Myanmar and agreed to work with the SPDC to aid the forced repatriation of refugees on the Thai–Myanma border. In September Gen. Khin Nyunt made a three-day trip to Thailand, which was seen by many to constitute a starting point for a new era of improved bilateral relations. In January 2002 a joint Thai-Myanma commission (meeting for the first time since 1999) agreed to establish a task force to assist in the repatriation of illegal workers. In February the Thai Minister of Foreign Affairs, Surakiart Sathirathai, visited Yangon. During his stay both countries agreed to co-operate in controlling the cross-border drugs trade.

In mid-2002 relations with Thailand deteriorated sharply when fighting broke out on the border between government troops, allied with the UWSA, and the SSA. It was alleged that Thai troops had fired shells into the country, in the belief that the fighting had encroached upon Thai territory. In response, the Myanma Government again accused Thailand of lending its support to the SSA. The joint border was closed shortly afterwards as tensions escalated. Border incursions continued as the bilateral relationship worsened. In August Surakiart Sathirathai met with leaders of the SPDC in an attempt to defuse the tensions; the border subsequently reopened in October. Relations continued to improve, owing in large part to the adaptation of a policy of 'soft engagement' by the Thai Government and, in early 2003, the two countries signed an unprecedented agreement pledging that future military exercises would be conducted at a suitable distance from the border.

In December 2003 Thailand hosted an international forum, called the 'Bangkok Process', at which the Myanma Minister for Foreign Affairs, U Win Aung, presented the 'road map' to government representatives from 10 other Asian and European countries. In early 2004, in a reflection of the improved relationship between Myanmar and Thailand, Myanmar announced that it was to award Thailand fishing concessions in its waters for one year. Fishing rights had been terminated in May 2001 following tensions on the joint border. A second 'Friendship Bridge' linking the two countries opened in January 2006. However, a second round of talks in the 'Bangkok Process', scheduled for late April 2004, was postponed indefinitely earlier that month at Myanmar's request. Prime Minister Khin Nyunt visited Thailand in June, and discussed various economic, development and border issues with Prime Minister Thaksin Shinawatra. In December the Thai Prime Minister paid a visit to Myanmar, his first since the ousting of Khin Nyunt, and held talks with the new Prime Minister, Lt-Gen. Soe Win. In January 2005 Thailand increased security along the border with Myanmar, amid renewed concerns that fighting between Myanma troops and KNPP rebels might encroach upon Thai territory. In April Thailand again intensified security along its border with Myanmar in response to renewed fighting between the UWSA and the SSA close to Thai territory. In December the Thai Government announced that it was not prepared to host the delayed second meeting of the 'Bangkok Process' since Myanmar had not kept it sufficiently informed of its progress towards democracy; it was unclear whether any future efforts would be made to revive the initiative. In December 2007 UNHCR reported that 124,300 Myanma refugees remained resident in nine camps in Thailand, while a total of 20,878 had been resettled in third countries since January 2005, more than one-half having been accepted by the USA.

In October 2002 the Australian Minister of Foreign Affairs, Alexander Downer, arrived in Myanmar; he was the most senior Australian politician to have visited the country for 20 years. During his stay he met with senior members of the SPDC and with Aung San Suu Kyi. However, following his departure Suu Kyi reportedly claimed that she would prefer Australia to lend its support to the international sanctions against the country rather than attempt to engage with its leaders. In October 2007 the Australian Government imposed financial sanctions on more than 400 Myanma leaders and associates.

Despite the killing of three Indian soldiers in a clash with Myanma troops in October 2000, relations between the two countries subsequently improved. Gen. Maung Aye paid a seven-day visit to India in November 2000, meeting both the country's President and Prime Minister. In mid-February 2001 India's Minister of External Affairs, Jaswant Singh, visited Myanmar, the first Indian cabinet minister to do so since the SLORC's assumption of power in 1988. While there, Singh officially opened the Tamu–Kalewa highway, a road built by India at a cost of US $22m. in order to increase bilateral trade with Myanmar. In January 2003 Minister of Foreign Affairs U Win Aung paid a visit to India, during which he met with the Prime Minister and several cabinet ministers. The two Governments agreed to hold regular consultations and to co-operate in counter-terrorism activities. In October 2004 the Chairman of the SPDC, Than Shwe, paid the first visit to India by a Myanma Head of State in 24 years, agreeing to further bilateral co-operation at meetings with the Indian President and Prime Minister. Following discussions between the two countries' respective Ministers of Home Affairs in October 2005, Myanmar and India agreed to a policy of joint interrogation of persons arrested for militant activities and on charges of smuggling drugs or weapons. In March 2006 President Aavul Pakkiri Jainulabidin Abdul Kalam visited Yangon, the first ever state visit to Myanmar by an Indian President. In September senior officials of the Myanma and Indian Ministries of Home Affairs signed an agreement to increase security co-operation. A claim by Amnesty International that India intended to sell a military helicopter to Myanmar provoked controversy in July 2007 because many of the components of the helicopter had been developed or manufactured in EU member states, meaning that such a sale would infringe the Union's arms embargo against Myanmar. However, the Indian Government rejected Amnesty's allegations.

Following the release of Suu Kyi from house arrest in July 1995, Japan resumed substantial economic aid to Myanmar, which had been halted in 1988. In November 1999 the Japanese Prime Minister met with Senior Gen. Than Shwe during an ASEAN summit meeting in Manila; the meeting was the first between the leader of a major world power and a senior member of the military Government since the junta's suppression of the democratic opposition in 1988. In April 2001 Japan accelerated its policy of engagement, promising a US $28m. aid programme intended to facilitate the upgrading of a hydroelectric power plant in Kayah (see Economic Affairs). The renewal of aid to the country was widely perceived to be a political gesture intended to reward the SPDC for its efforts to reach a settlement with the NLD. The international community criticized Japan's decision to resume aid as being premature in the light of Myanmar's failure to end forced labour and other human rights abuses in the country. In June 2003, following the junta's reimprisonment of Suu Kyi in May of that year, the Japanese Government suspended all economic aid to Myanmar. However, in early 2004 it was announced that Japan was to resume aid once again, having been satisfied that the release of some political prisoners by the SPDC constituted adequate progress towards democracy in the country. Tension arose between Japan and Myanmar in late September 2007, when a Japanese journalist was killed during the violent suppression of anti-Government protests in Yangon (see above). After evidence emerged that suggested that the journalist might have been deliberately targeted by the security forces, the Japanese Deputy Minister of Foreign Affairs visited Myanmar to investigate the incident. In the following month Japan cancelled some $4.7m. in funding for an educational centre at Yangon University, as Myanmar continued to maintain that the journalist had been accidentally shot.

In July 1996, as repression increased, Suu Kyi for the first time urged the imposition of international economic sanctions against Myanmar. From March 1997 the EU withdrew Myanmar's special trading status, in response to concerns over Myanmar's human rights record; later that year a meeting scheduled to take place in November between the EU and ASEAN was cancelled by the EU, owing to its objection to the representation of Myanmar at the talks. In early 1999 a further meeting between the EU and ASEAN, scheduled to be held in February, was postponed indefinitely as a result of continued disagreement between the two organizations regarding the proposed representation of Myanmar. However, an agreement was subsequently reached by the two sides to allow Myanmar to take a 'passive role' in the Joint Co-operation Committee meeting between the EU and ASEAN scheduled to take place in May. The SPDC became more open to the development of external relations when it allowed an EU delegation to visit Myanmar and hold talks with Suu Kyi in January 2001. Despite this, the EU extended its sanctions against Myanmar for a further six months in April 2001, owing to the human rights situation. However, in October the EU announced that it had decided to ease its sanctions. After Razali Ismail's fourth visit to Myanmar in November 2001, plans for a US $16m. HIV/AIDS prevention programme were mooted. Several countries, particularly Japan and the EU, indicated that they would be willing to support a carefully monitored international aid programme, and it was hoped that the prospect of the resumption of limited aid would encourage the Government to release more political prisoners. In January 2003 the Myanma Deputy Minister of Foreign Affairs, Khin Maung Win, was permitted to attend an EU-ASEAN summit meeting for the first time since Myanmar's suspension from the meetings in 1997. However, in April the EU elected to extend its sanctions against the country and to increase the list of SPDC officials subject to visa sanctions and 'freezing' of their assets. These sanctions were subsequently renewed annually.

Relations between the EU and ASEAN were strained by pressure from some EU member states to exclude ASEAN's three newest members (Cambodia, Laos and Myanmar) from an Asia-Europe Meeting of heads of government (ASEM) in Viet Nam in October 2004. The EU initially insisted that the SPDC should release Aung San Suu Kyi from house arrest and commit to a number of other reforms before Myanmar be allowed to attend. However, ASEAN responded that if its new members were not allowed to participate, then the EU's 10 new members should also be excluded. The result was that Myanmar was represented at the summit meeting by a lower-level delegation, led by the newly appointed Minister of Foreign Affairs, Maj.-Gen. Nyan Win. Two days after the ASEM summit EU ministers responsible for foreign affairs implemented an earlier threat to broaden sanctions against Myanmar if the country did not make progress towards democratization in time for the meeting. The ministers agreed to widen the list of Myanma officials subject to visa sanctions and to co-ordinate international bans on investment in the country (although France secured an exclusion from such a ban for European countries that had already invested in Myanmar). In November 2007, in response to the use of force to quell anti-Government protests in Myanmar in September, the EU formally increased the number of officials subject to visa sanctions and asset 'freezing', expanded the scope of an investment ban on state-owned enterprises and imposed a new ban on some Myanma exports, including timber, metals and gemstones.

In September 1999, meanwhile, a diplomatic dispute began between Myanmar and the United Kingdom after British consular staff were refused permission to visit two Britons in detention in Myanmar for their separate involvement in pro-democracy protest action. The British Government expressed its grave concern over their treatment. One of the two Britons was released in November. The second detainee, James Mawdsley, who had received a prison sentence of 17 years for entering the country illegally and carrying pro-democracy leaflets, was released in October 2000, following international pressure; he confirmed that he had been beaten heavily while in captivity.

MYANMAR

In May 1997 the USA imposed trade sanctions in protest at persistent and large-scale repression by the SLORC. The sanctions prohibited further investment in Myanmar, but did not affect existing US interests in the country. In July, at a ministerial meeting that followed the ASEAN conference, the US Secretary of State, Madeleine Albright, denounced Myanmar publicly for its poor human rights record and the country's lack of progress towards democracy. During 1998 the USA criticized the military junta in Myanmar for its treatment of Suu Kyi and also demanded the release of hundreds of political prisoners. In March 1999 Albright publicly criticized the regime for taking insufficient action to combat the production of and trade in narcotics within Myanmar. The USA showed its support for the SPDC-NLD talks with a visit by a senior Department of State official to Suu Kyi in February 2001. However, while welcoming the discussions, the US Government renewed its sanctions later in the year. In December pro-democracy activists in Myanmar accused the USA of neglecting their cause after a reappraisal of its foreign policy in the wake of the terrorist attacks on the country in September 2001 (see the chapter on the USA). They claimed that the US Government had moderated its criticism of the ruling military junta on the grounds that it suspected the international terrorist network, al-Qa'ida, had a presence in the country. In February 2002 a report issued by the US Government offered the prospect of an easing of sanctions, but only if the military junta released all remaining political prisoners and made further tangible progress towards democracy. However, following the detention of Aung San Suu Kyi in May 2003, in July the US President, George W. Bush, approved the Burmese Freedom and Democracy Act, already passed by Congress, banning all imports from Myanmar for three years and extending visa sanctions already imposed on SPDC officials. The USA extended economic sanctions against Myanmar for another year in May 2004 and again in subsequent years. In August 2006 President Bush renewed the Burmese Freedom and Democracy Act of 2003 for a further three years. In September 2007 the US Department of State expanded its visa ban to more than 35 additional government and military officials; a further 14 senior officials were also designated subject to 'freezing' of their assets. In October Bush announced the imposition of stricter controls on imports from Myanmar, as well as sanctions affecting the property interests of senior Myanma leaders. At the beginning of May 2008, furthermore, the US Treasury was ordered to 'freeze' the assets of state-owned companies in Myanmar.

In November 1998 the SPDC strongly denied claims made by the UN that the Myanma Government was responsible for the widespread abuse of human rights within the country. However, a report published in August by the International Labour Organization (ILO, see p. 107), following an investigation into the alleged use of forced labour and the suppression of trade unions in Myanmar, found the use of forced labour to be 'pervasive' throughout the whole country, and accused the military regime of using beatings, torture, rape and murder in the exaction of its forced labour policy, constituting a 'gross denial of human rights'. In June 1999 a resolution condemning Myanmar for its widespread use of forced labour was adopted by the member countries of the ILO, and the country was barred from participating in any ILO activities. (In the same month the ruling junta was accused by the human rights organization Amnesty International of perpetrating widespread abuses against ethnic minority groups.) Following the failure of the military Government to carry out the recommendations made by the ILO Commission of Inquiry in 1998 after the organization's initial investigation, in March 2000 the governing body of the ILO recommended that at its meeting in June the International Labour Conference take action to secure compliance by the ruling junta with the ILO's recommendations. In a statement issued in late March, the SPDC categorically rejected the governing body's decision and recommendations. Despite the Government's assurance in November 2000 that it would accept ILO monitors to verify the cessation of forced labour practices, the UN labour body voted to proceed with sanctions against Myanmar. This was the first time such action, the strongest available to the ILO, had been undertaken in the organization's 81-year history. The ILO subsequently requested its members to review their relations with Myanmar and to adopt sanctions. China, India, Malaysia and Russia voted against the action.

In September 2001 an ILO contingent arrived in Myanmar for a three-week visit intended to ascertain whether the military junta had honoured its promise to bring about the abolition of forced labour. In November the ILO issued a report concluding that, while some progress had been made, the practice was still endemic in many parts of the country. It recommended that a permanent ILO presence be established in Myanmar to monitor continued efforts to end forced labour in the region; discussions as to how this could be implemented headed the agenda during a further visit by the ILO in February 2002. The ILO delegation, however, was not permitted to see the NLD leader, Suu Kyi, during its visit and, upon departure, the head of the delegation expressed disappointment at the lack of co-operation it had received from the Myanma authorities. Despite this, in March the ILO agreed to establish a liaison office in the country and, in October, an ILO mission visited the country to assist further in the development of good labour practices. In early 2004, following a visit by an ILO envoy, the SPDC agreed to allow ILO representatives to work freely towards the elimination of forced labour practices in the country. At the ILO's annual International Labour Conference in June, it was reported that the use of forced labour remained widespread in Myanmar, particularly on local infrastructure projects and by the army, although there had been some improvement since the 1990s, with forced labour no longer routinely used on national infrastructure projects. In February 2007 the ILO announced that the Myanma authorities had tentatively agreed to allow investigations into submitted forced labour cases without negative repercussions for alleged victims.

In October 1999 the UN Secretary-General's Special Envoy for Myanmar, Alvaro de Soto, arrived in the country to attempt, for the fifth time, to promote a dialogue between the military Government and the NLD; de Soto's efforts were, however, fruitless. In April 2000 de Soto was replaced as Special Envoy for Myanmar by Razali Ismail, a Malaysian diplomat, who subsequently arranged the secret dialogue between Suu Kyi and Lt-Gen. Khin Nyunt in October. In November the UN human rights envoy to Myanmar, Rajsoomer Lallah, resigned from his position, citing lack of financial and administrative assistance. Lallah had previously produced a damning report of Myanmar's human rights situation, but had not been granted a visa throughout his four-year term. His successor, Dr Paulo Sérgio Pinheiro, was able to visit Myanmar in April 2001, within six months of taking office. He returned for a further visit in October, but was criticized by the NLD for his failure to spend enough time consulting with local communities. His visit had to be curtailed for reasons of ill health. In February 2002 Pinheiro visited the country for a third time and held further discussions with senior members of the SPDC and with Suu Kyi and other political prisoners. The Government released 11 political prisoners during his stay and, upon leaving, he declared his visit to have been a success. In October Pinheiro travelled to the country again; during his time there he investigated allegations, made by several human rights groups, that members of the Myanma armed forces routinely raped ethnic women along the border with Thailand. He also met with Suu Kyi. In March 2003 he paid a further visit to the country but curtailed his stay, having discovered a hidden microphone in a room where he was interviewing NLD prisoners. He later urged the SPDC to release all remaining political prisoners and enter into a serious dialogue with the opposition. In the first half of 2004 Pinheiro was twice denied entry to Myanmar, and in June he described the ongoing National Convention as a 'meaningless and undemocratic exercise' owing to the restrictions imposed on free discussion and to the absence of the NLD. In early October 2007 the UN Human Rights Council adopted a resolution deploring the violent repression of peaceful demonstrations in the previous month and calling for the release of peaceful protesters and all other political detainees. In November, during his first visit to Myanmar since 2003, Pinheiro held talks with government ministers and several prominent political prisoners, although he was not permitted to meet Suu Kyi. Following his visit, Pinheiro stated that the Myanma authorities had admitted that 15 people had been killed during the suppression of the anti-Government protests in September (five more than previously acknowledged), and in the following month he reported that his investigations indicated that at least a further 16 people had died, that 500–1,000 people were still being detained by the authorities (far more than claimed by the Government) and that 74 people were missing. Pinheiro also reported that the ill-treatment of detainees and the poor conditions in which they were being held had resulted in several deaths in custody.

In May 1999 the ICRC, which had withdrawn from Myanmar in 1995 but reopened its office there in October 1998, regained permission from the ruling junta to visit a limited number of prisons in the country. Despite having been initially critical of the ICRC for reaching an agreement with the SPDC, Suu Kyi was reported subsequently to have expressed her support for the Committee's work with political prisoners. The ICRC sent a delegation to the country in July 2003, in order to ascertain that Suu Kyi was in good health following her recent imprisonment by the SPDC. In June 2007, in an unusual departure from its policy of neutrality, the ICRC issued a statement severely criticizing the Myanma authorities, claiming that human rights violations in Myanmar were causing 'immense suffering' for thousands of people. The Committee explained that the continued refusal of Myanma officials to discuss the alleged abuses had prompted it to make its concerns public.

In May 2007 it was announced that Russia was to assist with the construction of a 10-MW nuclear research reactor in Myanmar. An earlier agreement (concluded in 2002) had reportedly faltered over Russian payment concerns.

Government

Following the military coup of September 1988, all state organs, including the People's Assembly, the State Council and the Council of Ministers, were abolished by the State Law and Order Restoration Council (SLORC), and the country was placed under martial law. Legislative elections took place in May 1990, but the SLORC subsequently announced that the opposition-dominated elected body was a Constituent Assembly, which was accorded no legislative power. During September 1992 a night curfew, imposed in 1988, and two martial law decrees, in force for three years, were revoked. A ban remained, however, on gatherings of more than five people. In early 1993 a National Convention, comprising members of the SLORC and representatives of the opposition parties, met to draft a new constitution; discussions continued until March 1996, when the National Convention was adjourned. In November 1997 the ruling military junta announced the dissolution of the SLORC and its replacement by the newly created State Peace and Development Council (SPDC). In August 2003 the SPDC announced its intention to reconvene the National Convention, which had remained in recess since 1996, in order that proceedings for the drafting of a new constitution could begin. The Convention entered its final session in mid-2007, and in October a 54-member constitution-drafting committee was established. The resultant document was officially published in April 2008, to be submitted to a national referendum in May. The SPDC envisaged that the promulgation of the new Constitution would be followed by multi-party elections in 2010.

Defence

Myanmar maintains a policy of neutrality and has no external defence treaties. The armed forces are largely engaged in internal security duties. As assessed at November 2007, the armed services totalled some 406,000 men, of whom a reported 375,000 were in the army, an estimated 16,000 in the navy and 15,000 in the air force. Paramilitary forces included the People's Police Force of 72,000 men and the People's Militia of 35,000 men. In 2006 the defence budget was an estimated US $6,900m.

Economic Affairs

In 1986, according to estimates by the World Bank, Myanmar's gross national income (GNI), measured at average 1984–86 prices, was US $7,450m., equivalent to $200 per head. In 1996–2006, it was estimated, the population increased at an annual average rate of 1.2%, while gross domestic product (GDP) per head increased, in real terms, by an average of 8.9% per year. Overall GDP increased, in real terms, by an annual average of 11.3% between 1996 and 2006. According to the Asian Development Bank (ADB), real GDP expanded by 12.7% in 2006/07.

According to figures from the ADB, agriculture (including forestry and fishing) contributed an estimated 48.4% of GDP in 2004/05. The sector engaged an estimated 68.6% of the employed labour force in mid-2005, according to FAO. Rice is the staple crop, and production reached an estimated 25.2m. metric tons in 2006. In 2006/07 pulses and beans accounted for an estimated 11.6% of total exports. Other crops include sugar cane, maize, dry beans, groundnuts, sesame seed, tobacco and rubber. The fishing sector is also important. The total catch reached an estimated 2,217.5m. metric tons in 2005. Sales of teak and other hardwood provided an estimated 9.8% of total export revenue in 2006/07. In 2007 Myanmar remained one of the world's largest sources of illicit opium. According to a survey conducted by the UN Office on Drugs and Crime (see p. 47) (formerly the UN Office of Drug Control and Crime Prevention), the area under opium poppy cultivation expanded by 29% in 2007 to reach an estimated 27,700 ha. Production of opium was believed to have increased from an estimated 315 metric tons in 2006 to 460 tons in 2007. Between 1990/91 and 2000/01, according to figures from the ADB, the real GDP of the agricultural sector increased by an annual average of 5.8%. Having reached 8.7% in 2001/02 and 6.0% in 2002/03, annual agricultural GDP growth reportedly exceeded 11.0% in subsequent years, to reach 12.1% in 2005/06. According to the ADB, the GDP of the agricultural sector increased, in real terms, by 9.2% in the following year. Much slower growth, of 3.3%, was projected for 2007/08.

Industry (including mining, manufacturing, construction and utilities) provided an estimated 16.2% of GDP in 2004/05, according to the ADB. The industrial sector engaged 22.0% of the employed labour force (excluding activities not adequately defined) in 2005. Between 1990/91 and 2000/01, according to figures from the ADB, industrial GDP increased by an annual average of 10.7%. The GDP of the industrial sector was reported to have expanded strongly during 2003/04–2006/07; growth remained within a range of 19.9%–21.9% during those years. However, this sector appeared unable to maintain such a high rate of increase and, according to the ADB, industrial GDP rose by a more modest 9.8% in 2007/08.

Mining and quarrying contributed an estimated 0.6% of GDP in 2004/05 and engaged 0.7% of the employed labour force in 1997/98. Significant new onshore and offshore discoveries of natural gas and petroleum resulted from exploration and production-sharing agreements with foreign companies, the first of which was signed in 1989. In March 2005, however, the Government announced that henceforth all onshore oil and gas blocks would be exclusively operated by the Myanma Oil and Gas Enterprise under the Ministry of Energy. Other important minerals that are commercially exploited include tin, zinc, copper, tungsten, coal, lead, jade, gemstones, silver and gold; some of Myanmar's potentially lucrative mineral resources remain largely unexploited. According to the ADB, the GDP of the mining sector increased by an annual average of 18.3% between 1990/91 and 2000/01. Growth in the GDP of the mining sector rose from 8.7% in 2003/04 to 13.4% in 2004/05.

Manufacturing contributed an estimated 11.6% of GDP in 2004/05 and engaged 9.1% of the employed labour force in 1998. The most important branches are food and beverage processing, the production of industrial raw materials (cement, plywood and fertilizers), petroleum refining and textiles. The sector is adversely affected by shortages of electricity and the high price of machinery and spare parts. From mid-2003 a US ban on imports from Myanmar had a serious impact upon the textile sector; and revenue from garment exports subsequently declined. However, alternative external markets for these products were rapidly established, and the revenue from garment exports rose from 1,586.0m. kyats in 2005/06 to an estimated 1,601.8m. kyats in 2006/07. The real GDP of the manufacturing sector increased, according to the ADB, at an average rate of 8.4% per year between 1990/91 and 2000/01. Manufacturing GDP reportedly rose by 22.0% in 2003/04 and by 24.8% in 2004/05.

Energy is derived principally from natural gas, which accounted for 57.0% of electricity production in 2004; hydroelectric power contributed 36.2% and petroleum 6.8%. In 2005 a 280-MW hydropower plant, financed by a Chinese company, was opened at Paung Laung. The same Chinese company was also involved in the ongoing construction of the 790-MW Yeywa hydropower station in Mandalay, and the Shweli Hydel hydroelectric power project in northern Shan State, which was expected to generate 3,042m. kWh annually. Imports of mineral oils accounted for 23.6% of total imports in 2006/07.

The services sector contributed 35.4% of GDP in 2004/05, according to the ADB, and engaged 25.1% of the employed labour force in 1997/98. Tourism revenue is an important source of foreign exchange. Receipts from tourism (including passenger transport) totalled US $98m. in 2004. However, the number of tourist arrivals declined from 241,938 in 2004 to 232,218 in 2005. According to figures from the ADB, the GDP of the services sector increased by an average of 7.3% per year between 1990/91 and 2000/01. GDP growth in the sector was reported to have reached 14.6% in 2003/04, declining slightly in the two subsequent years, before increasing to an estimated 13.9% in 2006/07. The ADB estimated that the GDP of this sector increased by 6.5% in 2007/08.

In 2006 Myanmar recorded a visible trade surplus of US $2,211.3m., and there was a surplus of $802.0m. on the current account of the balance of payments. In 2006/07 the principal sources of imports were Singapore (which supplied 35.2% of the total), the People's Republic of China (which supplied 24.9% of the total) and Thailand (10.4%); other major suppliers were India, Japan and Malaysia. The principal market for exports (45.1%) was Thailand; other significant purchasers were India (14.0%), China (11.8%), Hong Kong and Singapore. According to preliminary figures, the principal imports in 2006/07 were refined mineral oils, machinery and transport equipment and base metals and manufactures. The principal exports in that year included gas, dried pulses, teak and other hardwoods and also garments.

In the financial year ending 31 March 2003 there was an estimated budgetary deficit of 74,012m. kyats. The budget deficit was estimated by the ADB to have decreased from the equivalent of 6.0% of GDP in 2004 to 4.0% in 2005. Myanmar's external debt at the end of 2005 totalled US $6,645m., of which $5,196m. was long-term public debt; in 2004 the cost of servicing external debt was equivalent to 3.8% of exports of goods and services. The annual rate of inflation averaged 20.6% in 1997–2006. According to the ADB, consumer prices increased by 36.9% in 2007. The ADB estimated the rate of unemployment in 2003 at 4.0% of the labour force.

Myanmar is a member of the UN Economic and Social Commission for Asia and the Pacific (ESCAP, see p. 35), the Asian Development Bank (ADB, see p. 182) and the Colombo Plan (see p. 411), which promote economic development in the region. In July 1997 Myanmar acceded to the Association of South East Asian Nations (ASEAN, see p. 185). Myanmar was granted a 10-year period from 1 January 1998 to comply with the tariff reductions (to between 0% and 5%) required under the ASEAN Free Trade Area (AFTA), which was formally established on 1 January 2002.

Weaknesses in data, compounded by the vast disparity between the official and market values of the country's currency, have impeded accurate assessments of Myanmar's economy. Although official statistics continued to indicate strong growth in most sectors of the economy in the mid-2000s, other sources suggested that progress was more modest. The Government's ambitious development plan for 2006–10 projected annual GDP growth of 10%, and while growth was officially estimated to have exceeded this level in 2007, some sources placed the figure closer to 5.9%. Some analysts concluded that, without considerable adjustment to economic policy, the Myanma people would experience little improvement in their standard of living, regardless of the rate of GDP growth. According to unofficial sources, the IMF advised the Myanma authorities to curb expenditure on the state sector and to take measures to consolidate the exchange rate mechanism. The IMF's review document (which was reportedly compiled in mid-2007 and was still awaiting publication in May 2008, pending approval from the Myanma Government) argued that such reforms would help reduce inflation and improve economic growth; moreover, that the partial liberalization of the agricultural sector and the provision of targeted subsidies would greatly improve socio-economic conditions for the general population. While the official exchange rate remained at an average of less than six kyats to the US dollar in 2004–07, the ratio of the parallel rate to the official rate was believed to have reached 1,140 kyats to the dollar in May 2008. Strong investment in the natural gas sector ensured that exports of mineral fuels continued to increase in 2007, thereby strengthening Myanmar's balance of payments situation. While the hydrocarbons sector was likely to perform well in 2008, the imposition of further trade sanctions on Myanmar by both the European Union and the USA (see Recent History) was expected to curtail the performance of other merchandise exports. In August 2007 the Government withdrew fuel subsidies, thereby precipitating massive increases in the prices of petrol, diesel and natural gas, which were estimated to have doubled the cost of public transport. Furthermore, international rice prices were reported to have increased by 50% in the first four months of 2008 alone. Prices for this staple food item rose sharply in May 2008 as a result of the damage caused to the country's rice-growing areas by a major cyclone. The disaster was expected to have a serious impact on the country's entire economy.

Education

Education is provided free of charge, where available, and is compulsory at primary level. Primary education begins at five years of age and lasts for five years. Primary enrolment was equivalent to 100% of children in the relevant age-group in 2005/06 (males 99%; females 101%). Secondary education, beginning at 10 years of age, lasts for a further six years, comprising a first cycle of four years and a second of two years. In 2005/06 enrolment at secondary schools was equivalent to 40% of children in the relevant age-group (males 41%; females 40%). In 1994 total enrolment at tertiary level was equivalent to 5.4% of the relevant age-group (males 4.2%; females 6.7%). In 2001/02 an estimated 587,300 students were enrolled at a total of 958 tertiary level institutions. Emphasis is placed on vocational and technical training. Current expenditure on education by the central Government in 2000/01 was 31,345m. kyats, representing 14.2% of total expenditure.

Public Holidays

2008: 4 January (Independence Day), 12 February (Union Day), 2 March (Peasants' Day, anniversary of the 1962 coup), 21 March* (Full Moon of Tabaung), 27 March (Armed Forces' Day), 13–16 April* (Maha Thingyan—Water Festival), 17 April* (Myanma New Year), 1 May (Workers' Day), 19 May* (Full Moon of Kason), 17 July* (Full Moon of Waso and beginning of Buddhist Lent), 19 July (Martyrs' Day), 14 October* (Full Moon of Thadingyut and end of Buddhist Lent), 28 October* (Deepavali), 12 November* (Tazaungdaing Festival), 22 November* (National Day), 23 December* (Kayin New Year), 25 December (Christmas Day).

2009: 4 January (Independence Day), 12 February (Union Day), 2 March (Peasants' Day, anniversary of the 1962 coup), March* (Full Moon of Tabaung), 27 March (Armed Forces' Day), 13–16 April* (Maha Thingyan—Water Festival), April* (Myanma New Year), April* (Full Moon of Kason), 1 May* (Workers' Day), 19 July (Martyrs' Day), July* (Full Moon of Waso and beginning of Buddhist Lent), October* (Full Moon of Thadingyut and end of Buddhist Lent), 17 October* (Deepavali), November* (Tazaungdaing Festival), November/December* (National Day), 23 December* (Kayin New Year), 25 December (Christmas Day).

* A number of holidays depend on lunar sightings.

Weights and Measures

The imperial system is in force.

Statistical Survey

Source (unless otherwise stated): Central Statistical Organization, Ministry of National Planning and Economic Development, Building 32, Nay Pyi Taw; tel. (67) 406325; fax (67) 407265; e-mail cso.stat@mptmail.net.mm; internet www.csostat.gov.mm.

Area and Population

AREA, POPULATION AND DENSITY

Area (sq km)	676,552*
Population (census results)	
31 March 1973	28,885,867
31 March 1983†	
Males	17,507,837
Females	17,798,352
Total	35,306,189
Population (UN estimates at mid-year)‡	
2005	47,967,000
2006	48,379,000
2007	48,798,000
Density (per sq km) at mid-2007	72.1

* 261,218 sq miles.
† Figures exclude adjustment for underenumeration. Also excluded are 7,716 Myanma citizens (males 5,704, females 2,012) abroad.
‡ Source: UN, *World Population Prospects: The 2006 Revision*.

PRINCIPAL TOWNS
(population at census of 31 March 1983)

Yangon (Rangoon)	2,513,023	Pathein (Bassein)	144,096
Mandalay	532,949	Taunggyi	108,231
Mawlamyine (Moulmein)	219,961	Sittwe (Akyab)	107,621
Bago (Pegu)	150,528	Manywa	106,843

Source: UN, *Demographic Yearbook*.

Mid-2007 ('000, incl. suburbs, UN estimates): Yangon 4,088; Mandalay 961 (Source: UN, *World Urbanization Prospects: The 2007 Revision*).

BIRTHS AND DEATHS
(annual averages, UN estimates)

	1990–95	1995–2000	2000–05
Birth rate (per 1,000)	25.3	22.1	19.5
Death rate (per 1,000)	10.3	9.8	10.2

Source: UN, *World Population Prospects: The 2006 Revision*.

Expectation of life (years at birth, WHO estimates): 58.8 (males 55.9; females 62.1) in 2005 (Source: WHO, *World Health Statistics*).

ECONOMICALLY ACTIVE POPULATION*
('000 persons, official estimates)

	1997	1998
Agriculture, hunting, forestry and fishing	11,381	11,507
Mining and quarrying	132	121
Manufacturing	1,573	1,666
Electricity, gas and water	21	48
Construction	378	400
Trade, restaurants and hotels	1,746	1,781
Transport, storage and communications	470	495
Financing, insurance, real estate and business services	577	597
Community, social and personal services†	1,686	1,744
Total employed	**17,964**	**18,359**
Unemployed‡	535	452
Total labour force	**18,499**	**18,811**

* Excludes members of the armed forces.
† Includes activities not adequately defined.
‡ Persons aged 18 years and over.

Unemployed ('000 persons aged 18 years and over): 326.5 in 2003; 291.3 in 2004; 189.7 in 2005 (Source: ILO).

Mid-2005 (estimates in '000): Agriculture, etc. 19,479; Total labour force 28,390 (Source: FAO).

Health and Welfare

KEY INDICATORS

Total fertility rate (children per woman, 2005)	2.2
Under-5 mortality rate (per 1,000 live births, 2005)	104
HIV/AIDS (% of persons aged 15–49, 2005)	1.3
Physicians (per 1,000 head, 2004)	0.36
Hospital beds (per 1,000 head, 2000)	0.63
Health expenditure (2004): US $ per head (PPP)	37.9
Health expenditure (2004): % of GDP	2.2
Health expenditure (2004): public (% of total)	12.9
Access to water (% of persons, 2004)	78
Access to sanitation (% of persons, 2004)	77
Human Development Index (2005): ranking	132
Human Development Index (2005): value	0.583

For sources and definitions, see explanatory note on p. vi.

Agriculture

PRINCIPAL CROPS
('000 metric tons)

	2004	2005	2006
Wheat*	130	145	148
Rice (paddy)	24,718	25,364	25,200*
Maize*	771	820	950
Millet*	160	160	163
Potatoes	457	478	500†
Sweet potatoes	57†	52	56†
Cassava	188	202	207†
Sugar cane	7,310	7,187	7,300†
Dry beans	1,659	n.a.	1,700†
Dry peas†	36	37	37
Chick-peas	220	172†	172†
Dry cow peas	129	n.a.	130†
Pigeon peas	525	530†	530†
Areca (Betel) nuts†	57	57	57
Soybeans (Soya beans)*	117	118	120
Groundnuts (in shell)	916	910*	910*
Coconuts†	364	362	362
Sunflower seed	369	353*	350*
Sesame seed	555	570*	580*
Cottonseed†	137	121	123
Dry onions†	720	720	720
Garlic†	105	104	104
Plantains	602	602†	602†
Tea (made)	25*	25†	25†
Jute	26	26†	26†
Tobacco (leaves)	33	33†	33†
Cotton (lint)*	60	59	59
Natural rubber	40	40*	40†

* Unofficial figure(s).
† FAO estimate(s).

Aggregate production ('000 metric tons, may include official, semi-official or estimated data): Total cereals 25,791 in 2004, 26,501 in 2005, 26,474 in 2006; Total roots and tubers 701 in 2004, 732 in 2005, 763 in 2006; Total vegetables (incl. melons) 3,825 in 2004, 3,824 in 2005, 3,824 in 2006; Total fruits (excl. melons) 1,742 in 2004, 1,752 in 2005, 1,752 in 2006.

Source: FAO.

MYANMAR

LIVESTOCK
('000 head, year ending September)

	2003	2004	2005
Horses*	120	120	120
Cattle	11,728	11,939	12,123
Buffaloes	2,600	2,650	2,705
Pigs	4,840	5,217	5,677
Sheep	454	479	517
Goats	1,622	1,711	1,846
Chickens	62,986	71,274	81,518
Ducks	7,683	8,393	9,112
Geese*	620	650	660

* FAO estimates.
2006: Figures assumed to be unchanged from 2005 (FAO estimates).
Source: FAO.

LIVESTOCK PRODUCTS
('000 metric tons)

	2003	2004	2005
Cattle meat	97.4	93.7	105.7
Buffalo meat	17.6	20.8	23.6
Goat meat	11.6	14.9	16.5
Pig meat	220.8	261.0	327.8
Chicken meat	379.6	456.6	560.7
Cows' milk	679.0	732.2	807.8
Buffaloes' milk	150.5	162.8	170.6
Goats' milk	8.5*	8.2*	n.a.
Hen eggs	134.6	157.4	186.6
Other poultry eggs*	12.5	13.5	14.2

* FAO estimate(s).
2006: Figures assumed to be unchanged from 2005 (FAO estimates).
Source: FAO.

Forestry

ROUNDWOOD REMOVALS
('000 cubic metres, excl. bark)

	2003	2004	2005
Sawlogs, veneer logs and logs for sleepers	2,885	2,816	2,849
Other industrial wood	1,353	1,380	1,413
Fuel wood	37,954	37,560	38,286
Total	42,192	41,756	42,548

2006: Figures assumed to be unchanged from 2005 (FAO estimates).
Source: FAO.

SAWNWOOD PRODUCTION
('000 cubic metres, incl. railway sleepers)

	2003	2004	2005
Total (all broadleaved)	1,001	1,056	1,530

2006: Figures assumed to be unchanged from 2005 (FAO estimates).
Source: FAO.

Fishing
('000 metric tons, live weight)

	2003*	2004*	2005
Capture	1,343.9	1,586.7	1,743.0
Freshwater fishes	290.1	454.3	538.7
Marine fishes	1,015.7	1,091.8	1,181.9
Aquaculture	252.0	400.4	474.5*
Common carp	50.0	50.0	50.0*
Roho labeo	100.0	100.0	100.0*
Total catch	1,595.9	1,987.0	2,217.5

* FAO estimate(s).
Source: FAO.

Mining
(metric tons, unless otherwise indicated)

	2003	2004	2005
Coal and lignite	109,214	237,949	229,647
Crude petroleum ('000 barrels)	7,204	7,160	8,133
Natural gas (million cu m)*	9,799	10,277	11,648
Copper ore†	27,870	31,756	34,500
Lead ore†	2,000	2,000	2,000
Zinc ore†	127	196	78
Tin concentrates†	434	330	402
Chromium ore (gross weight)‡	3,000	3,000	3,000
Silver ore (kilograms)†	778	1,120	2,302
Gold ore (kilograms)†§	90	90‡	90‡
Feldspar‡§	10,000	10,000	10,000
Barite (Barytes)	4,850	2,224	2,058
Salt (unrefined, excl. brine)‡	35,000	35,000	35,000
Gypsum (crude)	66,069	71,155	67,522
Rubies, sapphires and spinel ('000 metric carats)§	4,379	6,199	5,220
Jade	10,693	12,408	19,446

* Marketed production.
† Figures refer to the metal content of ores and concentrates (including mixed concentrates).
‡ Estimated production.
§ Twelve months beginning 1 April of year stated.
Source: US Geological Survey.

MYANMAR

Industry

SELECTED PRODUCTS
('000 metric tons, unless otherwise indicated)

	2001	2002	2003
Raw sugar*	103	126	100
Refined sugar*†	101	89	88
Cigarettes (million)†	2,650	2,657	2,806
Cotton yarn†	5.5	4.1	n.a.
Plywood ('000 cu m)	53	80	81
Printing and writing paper	15	15	13
Nitrogenous fertilizers‡	28	20	n.a.
Petroleum refinery products ('000 barrels)§‖	5,286	5,500	n.a.
Cement*	384	462	581
Tin—unwrought (metric tons)§	212	210	n.a.
Electric energy (million kWh, net)*	4,689	5,864	6,213

* Data from UN, *Industrial Commodity Statistics Yearbook*.
† Production by government-owned enterprises only.
‡ Production in terms of nitrogen during 12 months ending 30 September of stated year.
§ Twelve months beginning 1 April of year stated. Data from US Geological Survey.
‖ Figure includes gasoline, jet fuel, kerosene, diesel, distillate fuel oil and residual fuel oil.

Beer (government-owned enterprises only, year ending 31 March, '000 gallons): 1,856 in 2003/04; 2,492 in 2004/05; 2,728 in 2005/06.

Petroleum refinery products ('000 barrels): 6,028 in 2003; 5,835 in 2004; 5,133 in 2005 (Source: US Geological Survey).

Cement ('000 metric tons): 519 in 2004; 543 in 2005 (Source: US Geological Survey).

Plywood ('000 cu m): 128 in 2003; 118 in 2004; 110 in 2005 (Source: FAO).

Printing and writing paper ('000 metric tons): 13 in 2003; 13 in 2004; 14 in 2005 (Source: FAO).

Woven cotton fabrics (million sq m): 13 in 1998; 21 in 1999; 26 in 2000 (Source: UN, *Industrial Commodity Statistics Yearbook*).

Source (unless otherwise specified): UN, *Statistical Yearbook for Asia and the Pacific*.

Finance

CURRENCY AND EXCHANGE RATES

Monetary Units
100 pyas = 1 kyat.

Sterling, Dollar and Euro Equivalents (31 December 2007)
£1 sterling = 10.9069 kyats;
US $1 = 5.4420 kyats;
€1 = 8.0144 kyats;
100 kyats = £9.17 = $18.37 = €12.48.

Average Exchange Rate (kyats per US $)
2005   5.7610
2006   5.7838
2007   5.6121

Note: Since January 1975 the value of the kyat has been linked to the IMF's special drawing right (SDR). Since May 1977 the official exchange rate has been fixed at a mid-point of SDR 1 = 8.5085 kyats. On 1 June 1996 a new customs valuation exchange rate of US $1 = 100 kyats was introduced. In September 2001 the free market exchange rate was $1 = 450 kyats.

CENTRAL GOVERNMENT BUDGET
(million kyats, year ending 31 March, excl. capital account)

Current revenue and grants	2000/01	2001/02	2002/03
Tax revenue	75,727	80,094	112,564
Taxes on income, profits and capital gains	26,140	28,287	45,589
Domestic taxes on goods and services	44,101	45,506	61,680
General sales, turnover or value-added tax	32,961	32,460	46,782
Taxes on international trade and transactions	5,486	6,301	5,295
Other revenue	58,324	82,152	166,455
Grants	242	288	358
Total	134,293	162,534	279,377

Current expenditure	2000/01	2001/02	2002/03
General public services, incl. public order	44,910	75,684	82,572
Defence	63,453	64,015	76,082
Education	31,345	35,266	51,711
Health	7,388	8,818	18,852
Social security and welfare	4,993	6,299	7,189
Recreational, cultural and religious affairs	2,668	1,646	2,382
Economic affairs and services	66,132	78,117	111,058
Agriculture, forestry, fishing and hunting	38,447	25,917	37,004
Transportation and communication	25,917	48,789	65,041
Housing and community amenities	366	1,526	3,543
Total	221,255	271,371	353,389

Source: IMF, *Government Finance Statistics Yearbook*.

Tax revenue (million kyats, year ending 31 March): 161,844 in 2003/04; 265,192 in 2004/05; 447,964 in 2005/06.

INTERNATIONAL RESERVES
(US $ million at 31 December)

	2004	2005	2006
Gold (national valuation)	12.6	11.6	12.2
IMF special drawing rights	0.0	0.2	0.2
Foreign exchange	672.1	770.5	1,235.4
Total	684.7	782.3	1,247.8

Source: IMF, *International Financial Statistics*.

MONEY SUPPLY
(million kyats at 31 December)

	2003	2004	2005
Currency outside banks	1,102,940	1,347,600	1,743,654
Demand deposits at deposit money banks	82,948	139,880	209,324
Total money (incl. others)	1,186,100	1,487,650	1,953,375

Source: IMF, *International Financial Statistics*.

COST OF LIVING
(Consumer Price Index; base: 2000 = 100)

	2004	2005	2006
Food (incl. beverages)	277.5	303.2	365.7
Fuel and light	258.1	281.6	370.0
Clothing (incl. footwear)	300.5	299.6	337.6
Rent	272.2	333.0	388.8
All items (incl. others)	271.6	297.1	356.5

Source: ILO.

MYANMAR

NATIONAL ACCOUNTS
(million kyats at current prices, year ending 31 March)

National Income and Product
Expenditure on the Gross Domestic Product

	2002/03	2003/04	2004/05
Final consumption expenditure	5,049,366	6,865,352	7,979,598
Increase in stocks	19,095	418	33,934
Gross fixed capital formation	551,749	850,124	1,060,038
Total domestic expenditure	5,620,210	7,715,894	9,073,570
Exports of goods and services	19,955	14,119	16,697
Less Imports of goods and services	14,910	13,398	11,339
GDP in purchasers' values	5,625,255	7,716,616	9,078,929
GDP at constant 2000/01 prices	3,184,117	3,624,926	4,119,435

Source: Asian Development Bank, *Key Indicators of Developing Asian and Pacific Countries*.

Gross Domestic Product by Economic Activity

	2002/03	2003/04	2004/05
Agriculture, hunting, forestry and fishing	3,067,357	3,906,194	4,389,837
Mining and quarrying	25,163	34,583	56,636
Manufacturing	516,243	756,183	1,050,447
Electricity, gas and water	4,654	5,992	7,470
Construction	185,611	303,496	356,770
Wholesale and retail trade	1,326,615	1,743,643	2,022,045
Transport, storage and communications	358,124	776,704	933,588
Finance	4,799	5,297	6,602
Government services	50,724	64,742	103,890
Other services	85,965	119,782	151,644
GDP in purchasers' values	5,625,255	7,716,616	9,078,929

Source: Asian Development Bank, *Key Indicators of Developing Asian and Pacific Countries*.

BALANCE OF PAYMENTS
(US $ million)

	2004	2005	2006
Exports of goods f.o.b.	2,926.6	3,787.8	4,554.7
Imports of goods f.o.b.	−1,998.7	−1,759.4	−2,343.4
Trade balance	927.9	2,028.4	2,211.3
Exports of services	254.7	259.1	279.5
Imports of services	−459.6	−502.0	−562.9
Balance on goods and services	723.0	1,785.5	1,928.0
Other income received	40.4	55.5	97.8
Other income paid	−785.8	−1,427.3	−1,346.2
Balance on goods, services and income	−22.4	413.8	679.6
Current transfers received	160.6	197.8	161.4
Current transfers paid	−26.7	−23.8	−39.0
Current balance	111.5	587.7	802.0
Direct investment from abroad	213.5	237.2	278.6
Other investment liabilities	−88.3	−71.1	−25.6
Net errors and omissions	−142.7	−610.3	−632.1
Overall balance	94.0	143.6	422.9

Source: IMF, *International Financial Statistics*.

External Trade

PRINCIPAL COMMODITIES
(distribution by SITC, million kyats, year ending 31 March)

Imports c.i.f.	2004/05	2005/06	2006/07*
Edible vegetable oil and other hydrogenated oils	474.0	571.1	478.2
Pharmaceutical products	314.8	362.1	554.9
Base metals and manufactures	899.3	1,164.0	1,183.9
Machinery and transport equipment	2,164.9	1,786.2	2,718.2
Electrical machinery and apparatus	874.4	645.8	707.6
Paper, paperboard and manufactures	314.6	295.8	302.8
Refined mineral oils	1,361.0	1,560.9	3,966.6
Fabric of artificial materials and synthetics	823.2	917.2	1,059.7
Plastic	457.4	574.3	719.7
Total (incl. others)	11,338.5	11,514.2	16,835.0

Exports f.o.b.	2004/05	2005/06	2006/07*
Dried beans, peas, etc. (shelled)	1,282.5	1,875.8	3,497.9
Fresh and dried prawns	597.2	576.1	608.0
Fish and fish products	409.8	544.4	725.4
Teak	1,515.3	1,723.1	1,750.1
Other hardwood	726.8	1,027.2	1,189.0
Base metals and ores	547.5	646.2	637.8
Gas	5,812.2	6,234.7	11,676.2
Garments	1,237.7	1,586.0	1,601.8
Total (incl. others)	16,697.3	20,646.6	30,026.1

*Preliminary.

PRINCIPAL TRADING PARTNERS
(million kyats, year ending 31 March)

Imports	2004/05	2005/06	2006/07*
China, People's Republic	2,818.9	2,716.0	4,185.8
Hong Kong	129.5	119.0	135.0
India	480.1	465.2	916.5
Indonesia	288.7	336.1	539.8
Japan	920.4	610.7	896.3
Korea, Republic	514.6	498.6	486.9
Malaysia	666.1	810.8	634.5
Singapore	3,471.5	3,240.2	5,928.0
Thailand	1,054.2	1,376.2	1,749.4
Total (incl. others)	11,338.5	11,514.2	16,835.0

Exports	2004/05	2005/06	2006/07*
China, People's Republic	1,658.8	2,125.2	3,530.4
Hong Kong	656.1	1,488.1	2,316.6
India	1,956.3	2,841.6	4,217.2
Indonesia	308.9	380.5	506.4
Japan	737.3	790.4	952.4
Malaysia	620.5	540.4	507.6
Singapore	807.3	1,532.7	1,047.9
Thailand	7,219.2	7,868.6	13,533.8
United Kingdom	316.2	356.1	290.7
Total (incl. others)	16,697.3	20,646.6	30,026.1

*Preliminary.

Transport

RAILWAYS
(traffic, million)

	2004/05	2005/06	2006/07
Passenger-miles	2,604	2,969	3,298
Freight ton-miles	545	570	551

ROAD TRAFFIC
(registered motor vehicles at 31 March)

	2004/05	2005/06	2006/07
Passenger cars	188,240	196,314	206,020
Trucks	52,748	54,801	55,382
Buses	17,973	18,038	18,857
Motorcycles	638,519	641,777	646,872
Others	66,789	68,358	69,625
Total	964,269	979,288	996,756

INLAND WATERWAYS
(traffic by state-owned vessels)

	2004/05	2005/06	2006/07
Passenger-miles (million)	516	589	655
Freight ton-miles (million)	453	455	520

SHIPPING

Merchant Fleet
(registered at 31 December)

	2004	2005	2006
Number of vessels	127	125	126
Displacement ('000 grt)	444.3	435.5	397.3

Source: Lloyd's Register-Fairplay, *World Fleet Statistics*.

International Sea-Borne Traffic
('000 metric tons)

	2004/05	2005/06	2006/07
Goods loaded	788	1,173	1,479
Goods unloaded	2,811	3,252	3,582

CIVIL AVIATION
(traffic on scheduled services)

	2002	2003
Kilometres flown (million)	15	16
Passengers carried ('000)	1,186	1,117
Passenger-km (million)	1,154	1,083
Total ton-km (million)	106	100

Source: UN, *Statistical Yearbook*.

2005/06 (million): Passenger-miles 73.1.

2006/07 (million): Passenger-miles 75.3.

Tourism

TOURIST ARRIVALS BY COUNTRY OF NATIONALITY

	2003	2004	2005
Australia	4,950	6,069	6,342
China, People's Republic	15,564	17,890	15,596
France	13,125	13,372	15,295
Germany	13,341	14,112	13,689
India	6,291	8,357	7,679
Italy	6,129	7,924	7,083
Japan	18,799	20,296	19,584
Korea, Republic	8,399	10,405	10,934
Malaysia	10,003	12,478	9,858
Singapore	10,373	11,292	9,674
Taiwan	19,645	20,424	17,600
Thailand	22,214	32,735	27,199
United Kingdom	7,848	7,720	8,126
USA	13,256	16,432	16,598
Total (incl. others)	205,610	241,938	232,218

Tourism receipts (US $ million, incl. passenger transport): 70 in 2003; 98 in 2004; n.a. in 2005.

Source: World Tourism Organization.

Communications Media

	2004	2005	2006
Telephones ('000 main lines in use)	424.9	503.9	n.a.
Mobile cellular telephones ('000 subscribers)	92.5	128.7	214.2
Personal computers ('000 in use)	325	400	n.a.
Internet users ('000)	12	32	94
Broadband subscribers ('000)	n.a.	0.2	0.8

Book production (1999): 227 titles.

Newspapers (1998): 4 dailies (average circulation 400,000).

Facsimile machines (number in use): 2,540 in 1999.

Radio receivers ('000 in use): 3,157 in 1999.

Television receivers ('000 in use): 344.3 in 2000.

Sources: International Telecommunication Union; UNESCO, *Statistical Yearbook*; UN, *Statistical Yearbook*.

Education

(1994/95, provisional)

	Institutions	Teachers	Students
Primary schools*	35,856	169,748	5,711,202
Middle schools	2,058	53,859	1,390,065
High schools	858	18,045	389,438
Vocational schools	86	1,847	21,343
Teacher training	17	615	4,031
Higher education	45	6,246	247,348
Universities	6	2,901	62,098

* Excluding 1,152 monastic primary schools with an enrolment of 45,360.

2001/02 (provisional): *Primary:* Institutions 36,010, Teachers 143,490, Students ('000) 4,793.5; *General Secondary:* Institutions 2,110, Teachers 53,896, Students ('000) 1,600.9; *Tertiary:* Institutions 958, Teachers 15,947, Students ('000) 587.3 (Source: UN, *Statistical Yearbook for Asia and the Pacific*).

Adult literacy rate (UNESCO estimates): 89.9% (males 93.9%; females 86.4%) in 2000 (Source: UNESCO Institute for Statistics).

MYANMAR   *Directory*

Directory

The Constitution

On 18 September 1988 a military junta, the State Law and Order Restoration Council (SLORC), assumed power and abolished all state organs created under the Constitution of 3 January 1974. The country was placed under martial law. The state organs were superseded by the SLORC at all levels with the Division, Township and Village State Law and Order Restoration Councils. The SLORC announced that a new constitution was to be drafted by the 485-member Constituent Assembly that was elected in May 1990. In early 1993 a National Convention, comprising members of the SLORC and representatives of opposition parties, met to draft a new constitution; however, the Convention was adjourned in March 1996 and remained in recess in early 2004. In November 1997 the SLORC was dissolved and replaced by the newly formed State Peace and Development Council (SPDC). In August 2003 the SPDC announced that it planned to reconvene the National Convention in 2004 in order that it could commence the drafting of a new constitution. The National Convention met in May 2004 and several times thereafter.

The Government

HEAD OF STATE

Chairman of the State Peace and Development Council: Field Marshal THAN SHWE (took office as Head of State 23 April 1992).

STATE PEACE AND DEVELOPMENT COUNCIL
(April 2008)

Chairman: Field Marshal THAN SHWE.
Vice-Chairman: Dep. Senior Gen. MAUNG AYE.
First Secretary: Lt-Gen. Thiha Thura TIN AUNG MYINT OO.
Other members: Rear-Adm. KYI MIN, Lt-Gen. KYAW THAN, Lt-Gen. AUNG HTWE, Lt-Gen. YE MYINT, Lt-Gen. KHIN MAUNG THAN, Maj.-Gen. KYAW WIN, Maj.-Gen. Thura SHWE MANN, Maj.-Gen. MYINT AUNG, Lt-Gen. MAUNG BO, Lt-Gen. TIN AYE.

CABINET
(April 2008)

Prime Minister: Lt-Gen. THEIN SEIN.
Minister of Defence: Field Marshal THAN SHWE.
Minister of Military Affairs: Lt-Gen. Thiha Thura TIN AUNG MYINT OO.
Minister of Agriculture and Irrigation: Maj.-Gen. HTAY OO.
Minister of Industry (No. 1): U AUNG THAUNG.
Minister of Industry (No. 2): Maj.-Gen. SAW LWIN.
Minister of Foreign Affairs: Maj.-Gen. NYAN WIN.
Minister of National Planning and Economic Development: U SOE THA.
Minister of Transport: Maj.-Gen. THEIN SHWE.
Minister of Culture: Maj.-Gen. KHIN AUNG MYINT.
Minister of Co-operatives: Maj.-Gen. TIN HTUT.
Minister of Rail Transportation: Maj.-Gen. AUNG MIN.
Minister of Energy: Brig.-Gen. LUN THI.
Minister of Education: CHAN NYEIN.
Minister of Health: Dr KYAW MYINT.
Minister of Commerce: Brig.-Gen. TIN NAING THEIN.
Minister of Communications, Posts and Telegraphs: Brig.-Gen. THEIN ZAW.
Minister of Finance and Revenue: Maj.-Gen. HLA TUN.
Minister of Religious Affairs: Brig.-Gen. THURA MYINT MAUNG.
Minister of Construction: Maj.-Gen. SAW TUN.
Minister of Science and Technology: U THAUNG.
Minister of Labour and of Relations with Aung San Suu Kyi: U AUNG KYI.
Minister of Immigration and Population and of Social Welfare, Relief and Resettlement: Maj.-Gen. MAUNG MAUNG SWE.
Minister of Information: Brig.-Gen. KYAW HSAN.
Minister of Progress of Border Areas, National Races and Development Affairs: Col THEIN NYUNT.
Minister of Electric Power (No. 1): Col ZAW MIN.
Minister of Electric Power (No. 2): Maj.-Gen. KHIN MAUNG MYINT.
Minister of Sports: Brig.-Gen. THURA AYE MYINT.
Minister of Forestry: Brig.-Gen. THEIN AUNG.
Minister of Home Affairs: Maj.-Gen. MAUNG OO.
Minister of Mines: Brig.-Gen. OHN MYINT.
Minister of Livestock and Fisheries: Brig.-Gen. MAUNG MAUNG THEIN.
Minister of Hotels and Tourism: Maj.-Gen. SOE NAING.
Minister at the Office of the Prime Minister: U KO LAY.

MINISTRIES

Office of the Chairman of the State Peace and Development Council: 15–16 Windermere Park, Yangon; tel. (1) 282445.
Prime Minister's Office: Minister's Office, Theinbyu St, Botahtaung Township, Yangon; tel. (1) 283742.
Ministry of Agriculture and Irrigation: Bldg 15, Nay Pyi Taw; tel. (67) 410004; fax (67) 140130; e-mail dap.moai@mptmail.net.mm; internet www.moai.gov.mm.
Ministry of Commerce: Bldg 3, Nay Pyi Taw; tel. (67) 408002; fax (67) 408007; e-mail moc@commerce.gov.mm; internet www.commerce.gov.mm.
Ministry of Communications, Posts and Telegraphs: Bldg 2, Nay Pyi Taw; tel. (67) 407037; internet www.mcpt.gov.mm.
Ministry of Construction: Office No 11, Nay Pyi Taw; tel. (67) 407073; fax (67) 407181; e-mail pwscon@constuction.gov.mm; internet www.construction.gov.mm.
Ministry of Co-operatives: Bldg 16, Nay Pyi Taw; tel. (67) 410032; fax (67) 410036; e-mail mcop@mptmail.net.mm; internet www.myancoop.gov.mm.
Ministry of Culture: Bldg 35, Nay Pyi Taw; tel. (67) 408023; fax (1) 283794; internet www.myanmar.com/Ministry/culture.
Ministry of Defence: Ahlanpya Phaya St, Yangon; tel. (1) 281611.
Ministry of Education: Bldg 13, Nay Pyi Taw; tel. (67) 407131; internet www.myanmar-education.edu.mm.
Ministry of Electric Power: Bldg 38, Nay Pyi Taw; tel. (67) 411083; internet www.energy.gov.mm/MEP_1.htm.
Ministry of Energy: Bldg 6, Nay Pyi Taw; tel. (67) 411060; e-mail myanmoe@mptmail.net.mm; internet www.energy.gov.mm.
Ministry of Finance and Revenue: Bldg 26, Nay Pyi Taw; tel. (67) 410046; internet www.myanmar.com/Ministry/finance.
Ministry of Foreign Affairs: Bldg 19, Nay Pyi Taw; tel. (67) 412009; e-mail mofa.aung@mptmail.net.mm; internet www.mofa.gov.mm.
Ministry of Forestry: Bldg 28, Nay Pyi Taw; tel. (67) 405004; internet www.energy.gov.mm/MOF_1.htm.
Ministry of Health: Bldg 4, Nay Pyi Taw; tel. (67) 411358; internet www.moh.gov.mm.
Ministry of Home Affairs: Bldg 10, Nay Pyi Taw; tel. (67) 412079; internet www.moha.gov.mm.
Ministry of Hotels and Tourism: Bldg 33, Nay Pyi Taw; tel. (67) 406056; fax (67) 406057; e-mail dg.dht@mptmail.net.mm; internet www.hotel-tourism.gov.mm.
Ministry of Immigration and Population: Bldg 23, Nay Pyi Taw; tel. (67) 404026; internet www.myanmar.com/Ministry/imm&popu.
Ministry of Industry (No. 1): Bldg 37, Nay Pyi Taw; tel. (67) 408080; e-mail moi1@myanmar.com.mm; internet www.myanmar.com/Ministry/MOI-1.
Ministry of Industry (No. 2): Bldg 30, Nay Pyi Taw; tel. (67) 405042; e-mail dmip@mptmail.net.mm; internet www.industry2.gov.mm.
Ministry of Information: Bldg 7, Nay Pyi Taw; tel. (67) 412321.
Ministry of Labour: Bldg 21, Nay Pyi Taw; tel. (67) 404339.
Ministry of Livestock and Fisheries: Bldg 36, Nay Pyi Taw; tel. (67) 408045; e-mail dolf@mptmail.net.mm; internet www.livestock-fisheries.gov.mm.
Ministry of Military Affairs: Nay Pyi Taw.
Ministry of Mines: Bldg 19, Nay Pyi Taw; tel. (67) 409001; internet www.energy.gov.mm/MOM_1.htm.
Ministry of National Planning and Economic Development: Bldg 1, Nay Pyi Taw; tel. (67) 407023; e-mail ministry.nped@mptmail.net.mm; internet www.mnped.gov.mm.
Ministry of Progress of Border Areas, National Races and Development Affairs: Bldg 14, Nay Pyi Taw; tel. (67) 409022.
Ministry of Rail Transportation: Bldg 29, Nay Pyi Taw; tel. (67) 405034.

MYANMAR

Ministry of Religious Affairs: Bldg 31, Nay Pyi Taw; tel. (67) 406008; internet www.mora.gov.mm.

Ministry of Science and Technology: Bldg 21, Nay Pyi Taw; tel. (67) 404451.

Ministry of Social Welfare, Relief and Resettlement: Bldg 23, Nay Pyi Taw; tel. (67) 404021; e-mail social-wel-myan@mptmail.net.mm; internet www.myanmar.gov.mm/ministry/MSWRR/index.htm.

Ministry of Sports: Bldg 31, Nay Pyi Taw; tel. (67) 406028; e-mail MOCYGN.MYA@mptmail.net.mm.

Ministry of Transport: Bldg 5, Nay Pyi Taw; tel. (67) 411039; fax (67) 411038; e-mail minotran@mptmail.net.mm; internet www.mot.gov.mm.

Legislature

CONSTITUENT ASSEMBLY

Following the military coup of 18 September 1988, the 489-member Pyithu Hluttaw (People's Assembly), together with all other state organs, was abolished. A general election was held on 27 May 1990. It was subsequently announced, however, that the new body was to serve as a constituent assembly, responsible for the drafting of a new constitution, and that it was to have no legislative power. The next legislative election was provisionally scheduled for September 1997, but did not take place.

General Election, 27 May 1990

Party	% of Votes	Seats
National League for Democracy	59.9	392
Shan Nationalities League for Democracy	1.7	23
Arakan (Rakhine) League for Democracy	1.2	11
National Unity Party	21.2	10
Mon National Democratic Front	1.0	5
National Democratic Party for Human Rights	0.9	4
Chin National League for Democracy	0.4	3
Kachin State National Congress for Democracy	0.1	3
Party for National Democracy	0.5	3
Union Pa-O National Organization	0.3	3
Zomi National Congress		2
Naga Hill Regional Progressive Party		2
Kayah State Nationalities League for Democracy		2
Ta-ang (Palaung) National League for Democracy		2
Democratic Organization for Kayan National Unity		2
Democracy Party		1
Graduates' and Old Students' Democratic Association		1
Patriotic Old Comrades' League		1
Shan State Kokang Democratic Party	12.8	1
Union Danu League for Democracy Party		1
Kamans National League for Democracy		1
Mara People's Party		1
Union Nationals Democracy Party		1
Mro (or) Khami National Solidarity Organization		1
Lahu National Development Party		1
United League of Democratic Parties		1
Karen (Kayin) State National Organization		1
Independents		6
Total	**100.0**	**485**

Political Organizations

A total of 93 parties contested the general election of May 1990. By October 1995 the ruling military junta had deregistered all except nine political parties:

Kokang Democracy and Unity Party: Yangon.

Mro (or) Khami National Solidarity Organization: Kyauktaw; f. 1988; Leader U SAN THA AUNG.

National League for Democracy (NLD): 97B West Shwegondine Rd, Bahan Township, Yangon; f. 1988; initially known as the National United Front for Democracy, and subsequently as the League for Democracy; present name adopted in Sept. 1988; central exec. cttee of 10 mems; Gen. Sec. Daw AUNG SAN SUU KYI; Chair. U AUNG SHWE; Vice-Chair. U TIN OO.

National Unity Party (NUP): 93C Windermere Rd, Kamayut, Yangon; tel. (1) 278180; f. 1962 as the Burma Socialist Programme Party; sole legal political party until Sept. 1988, when present name was adopted; 15-mem. Cen. Exec. Cttee and 280-mem. Cen. Cttee; Chair. U THA KYAW; Gen. Secs U TUN YI, U THAN TIN.

Shan Nationalities League for Democracy (SNLD): f. 1988; Chair. KHUN HTUN OO; Sec.-Gen. SAI NYUNT LWIN.

Shan State Kokang Democratic Party: 140 40 St, Kyauktada; f. 1988; Leader U YANKYIN MAW.

Union Karen (Kayin) League: Saw Toe Lane, Yangon.

Union Pa-O National Organization: f. 1988; Leader U KHUN SEIN WIN HLA.

Wa National Development Party: Byuhar St, Yangon.

The following parties contested the general election of March 1990 but subsequently had their legal status annulled:

Anti-Fascist People's Freedom League: Bo Aung Kyaw St, Bahan Township, Yangon; f. 1988; assumed name of wartime resistance movement that became Myanmar's major political force after independence; Chair. BO KYAW NYUNT; Gen. Sec. CHO CHO KYAW NYEIN.

Democracy Party: f. 1988; comprises supporters of fmr Prime Minister U NU; Chair. U THU WAI; Vice-Chair. U KHUN YE NAUNG.

Democratic Front for National Reconstruction: Yangon; f. 1988; left-wing.

Lahu National Development Party: f. 1988; deregistered 1994; Leader U DANIEL AUNG.

League for Democracy and Peace: 10 Wingaba Rd, Bahan Township, Yangon; f. 1988; Gen. Sec. U THEIN SEIN.

Party for National Democracy: Yangon; f. 1988; Chair. Dr SEIN WIN.

Union National Democracy Party (UNDP): 2–4 Shin Saw Pu Rd, Sanchaung Township, Yangon; f. 1988; est. by Brig.-Gen. AUNG GYI (fmr Chair. of the National League for Democracy); Chair. U KYAW MYINT LAY.

United League of Democratic Parties: 875 Compound 21, Ledauntkan St, Sa-Hsa Ward, Thingangyun Township, Yangon; f. 1989.

United Nationalities League for Democracy: Yangon; an alliance of parties representing non-Bamar nationalities; won a combined total of 65 seats at the 1990 election.

Other deregistered parties included the Arakan (Rakhine) League for Democracy, the Mon National Democratic Front, the National Democratic Party for Human Rights, the Chin National League for Democracy, the Kachin State National Congress for Democracy, the Zomi National Congress, the Naga Hill Regional Progressive Party, the Kayah State Nationalities League for Democracy, the Ta-ang (Palaung) National League for Democracy, the Democratic Organization for Kayan National Unity, the Graduates' and Old Students' Democratic Association, the Patriotic Old Comrades' League, the Union Danu League for Democracy, the Kamans National League for Democracy, the Mara People's Party and the Karen (Kayin) State National Organization.

The following groups are, or have been, in armed conflict with the Government:

Burma Democratic Alliance (BDA): f. 2004; opposition alliance composed of several dissident organizations; Leader Dr NAING AUNG.

Chin National Army: Chin State.

Chin National Front: f. 1988; forces trained by Kachin Independence Army 1989–91; first party congress 1993; conference in March 1996; carried out an active bombing campaign in 1996–97, mainly in the Chin State; Pres. THOMAS TANG NO.

Communist Party of Burma (CPB): f. 1939; reorg. 1946; operated clandestinely after 1948; participated after 1986 in jt military operations with sections of the NDF; in 1989 internal dissent resulted in the rebellion of about 80% of CPB members, mostly Wa hill tribesmen and Kokang Chinese; the CPB's military efficacy was thus completely destroyed; Chair. of Cen. Cttee Thakin BA THEIN TIN (exiled).

Democratic Alliance of Burma (DAB): Manerplaw; f. 1988; formed by members of the NDF to incorporate dissident students, monks and expatriates; Pres. Maj.-Gen. BO MYA; Gen. Sec. U TIN MAUNG WIN; remaining organizations include:

All-Burma Student Democratic Front (ABSDF): Dagwin; f. 1988; in 1990 split into two factions, under U MOE THI ZUN and U NAING AUNG; the two factions reunited in 1993; Chair. THAN KHE; Sec.-Gen. MYO WIN.

MYANMAR

Karen (Kayin) National Union (KNU): f. 1948; Chair. SAW BA THIN; Vice-Chair. Gen. TAMALABAW; Sec.-Gen. TU TU LAY; military wing: Karen (Kayin) National Liberation Army (KNLA); c. 6,000 troops; Chief of Staff SAW BO MYA.

Karenni (Kayinni) National Progressive Party: agreement with the SLORC signed in March 1995 but subsequently collapsed; resumed fighting in June 1996; Chair. Gen. AUNG THAN LAY; military wing: Karenni (Kayinni) Revolutionary Army.

God's Army: breakaway faction of the KNU; Leaders JOHNNY HTOO, LUTHER HTOO (surrendered to the Thai authorities in Jan. 2001).

National Democratic Front (NDF): f. 1975; aims to establish a federal union based on national self-determination; largely defunct.

National Socialist Council of Nagaland: Sagaing Division; comprises various factions.

Shan State Army (SSA): enlarged in Sept. 1997 through formal alliance between the following:

Shan State National Army (SSNA): Shan State; f. 1995; breakaway group from Mong Tai Army (MTA); Shan separatists; 5,000–6,000 troops; Leader KARN YORD.

Shan State Peace Council (SSPC): fmrly Shan State Progressive Party; Pres. HSO HTEN; Gen. Sec. KARN YORD; cease-fire agreement signed in Sept. 1989, but broken by SSA elements following establishment of above alliance in Sept. 1997; military wing: original **Shan State Army** (5,000 men); Leaders SAI NONG, KAI HPA, PANG HPA.

Other MTA remnants also participated in the alliance.

Vigorous Burmese Student Warriors (VBSW): f. 1999.

Most of the following groups have signed cease-fire agreements, or reached other means of accommodation, with the ruling military junta (the date given in parentheses indicates the month in which agreement with the junta was concluded):

Democratic Karen (Kayin) Buddhist Organization: Manerplaw; breakaway group from the KNU; military wing: Democratic Karen (Kayin) Buddhist Army.

Kachin Democratic Army: (Jan. 1991); fmrly the 4th Brigade of the Kachin Independence Army; Leader U ZAW MAING.

Kachin Independence Organization (KIO): (Oct. 1993); Chair. U LAMON TU JAI; military wing: Kachin Independence Army.

Karen (Kayin) Solidarity Organization (KSO): f. 1997; fmrly All Karen Solidarity and Regeneration Front; breakaway group from the KNU; 21-mem. exec. cttee; advocates nation-wide cease-fire and the settlement of all national problems through negotiations; Pres. SAW W. P. NI; Sec.-Gen. MAHN AUNG HTAY.

Karenni (Kayinni) National People's Liberation Front: (May 1994); Leader U TUN KYAW.

Kayan National Guard: (Feb. 1992).

Kayan New Land Party: (July 1994); Leader U THAN SOE NAING.

Myanmar National Democracy Alliance: (March 1989).

National Democracy Alliance Army: (June 1989).

New Democratic Army: Kachin; (Dec. 1989).

New Mon State Party: (June 1995); Chair. (vacant); military wing: Mon National Liberation Army.

Palaung State Liberation Organization: (April 1991); military wing: Palaung State Liberation Army; 7,000–8,000 men.

Pa-O National Organization: (Feb. 1991); Chair. AUNG KHAM HTI; military wing: Pa-O National Army.

Shan State Nationalities People's Liberation Organization: (Oct. 1994); Chair. U THA KALEI.

United Wa State Party: (May 1989); fmrly part of the Communist Party of Burma; military wing: **United Wa State Army** (10,000–15,000 men); Leaders CHAO NGI LAI, PAO YU CHANG.

Since 1991 the National Coalition Government of the Union of Burma, constituted by representatives elected in the general election of 1990, has served as a government-in-exile:

National Coalition Government of the Union of Burma (NCGUB): 77 South Washington Street, Suite 308, Rockville, Maryland 20850, USA; tel. (301) 424-4810; fax (301) 424-4812; e-mail ncgub@ncgub.net; internet www.ncgub.net; Prime Minister Dr SEIN WIN.

Diplomatic Representation

EMBASSIES IN MYANMAR

Australia: 88 Strand Rd, Yangon; tel. (1) 251810; fax (1) 246159; internet www.burma.embassy.gov.au; Ambassador BOB DAVIS.

Bangladesh: 11B Than Lwin Rd, Yangon; tel. (1) 515275; fax (1) 515273; e-mail bdootygn@mptmail.net.mm; Ambassador Maj.-Gen. ABU ROSHDE ROKONUDDAWLA.

Brunei: 317/319 U Wisara Rd, Sanchaung Township, Yangon; tel. (1) 524285; fax (1) 512854; Ambassador Brig.-Gen. Dato' Paduka Haji MOHAMAD YUSOF BIN ABU BAKAR.

Cambodia: 34 Kaba Aye Pagoda Rd, Yangon; tel. (1) 549609; fax (1) 546156; e-mail recyangon@mptmail.net.mm; Ambassador HUL PHANY.

China, People's Republic: 1 Pyidaungsu Yeiktha Rd, Yangon; tel. (1) 221281; fax (1) 227019; e-mail chinaemb_mm@mfa.gov.cn; internet mm.china-embassy.org; Ambassador GUAN MU.

Egypt: 81 Pyidaungsu Yeiktha Rd, Yangon; tel. (1) 222886; fax (1) 222865; Ambassador YOUSSEF KAMAL BOUTROS HANNA.

France: 102 Pyidaungsu Yeiktha Rd, POB 858, Yangon; tel. (1) 212523; fax (1) 212527; e-mail ambafrance-rangoun@diplomatie.gouv.fr; internet www.ambafrance-mm.org; Ambassador JEAN-PIERRE LAFOSSE.

Germany: 9 Bogyoke Aung San Museum Rd, POB 12, Yangon; tel. (1) 548951; fax (1) 548899; e-mail info@rangun.diplo.de; internet www.rangun.diplo.de; Ambassador DIETRICH ANDREAS.

India: 545–547 Merchant St, POB 751, Yangon; tel. (1) 282552; fax (1) 254086; e-mail amb.indembygn@mptmail.net.mm; internet www.indiaembassy.net.mm; Ambassador BHASKAR KUMAR MITRA.

Indonesia: 100 Pyidaungsu Yeiktha Rd, POB 1401, Yangon; tel. (1) 254465; fax (1) 254468; e-mail kbriygn@indosat.net.id; internet www.indonesia.com.mm; Ambassador WYOSO PROJOWARSITO.

Israel: 15 Khabaung Road, Hlaing Township, Yangon; tel. (1) 515115; fax (1) 515116; e-mail info@yangon.mfa.gov.il; internet yangon.mfa.gov.il; Ambassador RUTH SCHATZ.

Italy: 3 Inya Myaing Rd, POB 866, Golden Valley, Bahan Township, Yangon 11201; tel. (1) 527100; fax (1) 514565; e-mail ambitaly@ambitaly.net.mm; internet www.italian-embassy.org.ae/ambasciata_yangon; Ambassador GIUSEPPE CINTI.

Japan: 100 Natmauk Rd, POB 841, Bahan Township, Yangon 11021; tel. (1) 549644; fax (1) 549643; e-mail jembassy@baganmail.net.mm; internet www.mm.emb-japan.go.jp; Ambassador YASUAKI NOGAWA.

Korea, Republic: 97 University Ave, Yangon; tel. (1) 515190; fax (1) 513286; e-mail hankuk@koremby.net.mm; internet mmr.mofat.go.kr; Ambassador PARK GI-JONG.

Laos: A1 Diplomatic Quarters, Franser Rd, Yangon; tel. (1) 222482; fax (1) 227446; Ambassador KOUILY SOUPHAKET.

Malaysia: 82 Pyidaungsu Yeiktha Rd, Dagon Township, Yangon; tel. (1) 220249; fax (1) 221840; e-mail mwkyangon@mptmail.net.mm; internet www.kln.gov.my/perwakilan/yangon; Ambassador Datuk MAZLAN MUHAMMAD.

Nepal: 16 Natmauk Yeiktha Rd, POB 84, Tamwe, Yangon; tel. (1) 545880; fax (1) 549803; e-mail nepemb@mptmail.net.mm; Ambassador GUNA LAXMI SHARMA BISWAKARMA.

Pakistan: A4 Diplomatic Quarters, Pyay Rd, Dagon Township, Yangon; tel. (1) 222881; fax (1) 221147; e-mail parepygn@myanmar.com.mm; Ambassador QAZI M. KHALILULLAH.

Philippines: 50 Saya San Rd, Bahan Township, Yangon; tel. (1) 558149; fax (1) 558154; e-mail phyangon@mptmail.net.mm; Ambassador PHOEBE ABAYA GOMEZ.

Russia: 38 Sagawa Rd, Yangon; tel. (1) 241955; fax (1) 241953; e-mail rusinmyan@mptmail.net.mm; internet www.rusembmyanmar.org; Ambassador MIKHAIL M. MGELADZE.

Serbia: 114A Inya Rd, POB 943, Yangon; tel. (1) 515282; fax (1) 504274; e-mail serbemb@yangon.net.mn; Chargé d'affaires a.i. DRAGAN JANEKOVIĆ.

Singapore: 238 Dhamazedi Rd, Bahan Township, Yangon; tel. (1) 559001; fax (1) 559002; e-mail singemb_ygn@sgmfa.gov.sg; internet www.mfa.gov.sg/yangon; Ambassador ROBERT CHUA.

Sri Lanka: 34 Taw Win Rd, POB 1150, Yangon; tel. (1) 222812; fax (1) 221509; e-mail srilankaemb@mpt.net.mm; Ambassador P. A. D. SAMARASEKERA.

Thailand: 73 Manawhari St, Dagon Township, Yangon; tel. (1) 224647; fax (1) 225929; e-mail thaiygn@mfa.go.th; Ambassador BANSARN BUNNAG.

United Kingdom: 80 Strand Rd, Kyauktada Township, Yangon; tel. (1) 370863; fax (1) 370866; e-mail chancery.Rangoon@fco.gov.uk; Ambassador MARK CANNING.

USA: 581 Merchant St, POB 521, Yangon; tel. (1) 379880; fax (1) 256018; e-mail info.rangoon@state.gov; internet rangoon.usembassy.gov; Chargé d'affaires SHARI VILLAROSA.

Viet Nam: 317–319 U Wisara Rd, Sanchaung Township, Yangon; tel. (1) 524656; fax (1) 524285; e-mail vnembmyr@bertech.net.mm;

MYANMAR   Directory

internet www.vietnamembassy-myanmar.org; Ambassador TRAN VAN TUNG.

Judicial System

A new judicial structure was established in March 1974. Its highest organ, composed of members of the People's Assembly, was the Council of People's Justices, which functioned as the central Court of Justice. Below this Council were the state, divisional, township, ward and village tract courts formed with members of local People's Councils. These arrangements ceased to operate following the imposition of military rule in September 1988, when a Supreme Court with five members was appointed. A chief justice, an attorney-general and a deputy attorney-general were also appointed. In March 2003 a deputy chief justice, four more justices and two further deputy attorney-generals were appointed.

Office of the Supreme Court
Bldg 24, Nay Pyi Taw; tel. (67) 404140.
Chief Justice: U AUNG TOE.
Attorney-General: AYE MAUNG.

Religion

Freedom of religious belief and practice is guaranteed. In 1992 an estimated 87.2% of the population were Buddhists, 5.6% Christians, 3.6% Muslims, 1.0% Hindus and 2.6% animists or adherents of other religions.

BUDDHISM

State Sangha Maha Nayaka Committee: c/o Dept of Promotion and Propagation of the Sasana, Kaba Aye Pagoda Precinct, Mayangone Township, Yangon; tel. (1) 660759.

CHRISTIANITY

Myanmar Naing-ngan Khrityan Athin-dawmyar Kaung-si (Myanmar Council of Churches): Myanmar Ecumenical Sharing Centre, 601 Pyay Rd, University PO, Yangon 11041; tel. (1) 537957; fax (1) 296848; e-mail oikom@yangon.net.mm; f. 1914 as Burma Representative Council of Mission; reconstituted as Burma Council of Churches in 1974; 13 mem. nat. churches, 9 mem. nat. Christian orgs; Pres. Rev. SAW MAR GAY GYI; Gen. Sec. Rt Rev. SMITH N. ZA THAWNG.

The Roman Catholic Church
Myanmar comprises three archdioceses and 10 dioceses. At 31 December 2005 an estimated 1.2% of the total population were adherents.

Catholic Bishops' Conference of Myanmar
292 Pyay Rd, POB 1080, Sanchaung PO, Yangon 11111; tel. (1) 525868; fax (1) 527198; e-mail clspcbcm@mptmail.net.mm.
f. 1982; Pres. Most Rev. CHARLES MAUNG BO (Archbishop of Yangon).
Archbishop of Mandalay: Most Rev. PAUL ZINGTUNG GRAWNG, Archbishop's House, 81st and 25th St, Mandalay 06011; tel. (2) 33916; e-mail paulgrawng@mandalay.net.mm.
Archbishop of Taunggyi: Most Rev. MATTHIAS U SHWE, Archbishop's Office, Bayint Naung Rd, Taunggyi 06011; tel. (81) 21689; fax (81) 22164; e-mail matthias@myanmar.com.mm.
Archbishop of Yangon: Most Rev. CHARLES MAUNG BO, Archbishop's House, 289 Theinbyu St, Botataung, 11161 Yangon; tel. (1) 246710; fax (1) 379059.

The Anglican Communion
Anglicans are adherents of the Church of the Province of Myanmar, comprising six dioceses. The Province was formed in February 1970, and contained an estimated 45,000 adherents in 1985.
Archbishop of Myanmar and Bishop of Yangon: Most Rev. SAMUEL SAN SI HTAY, Bishopscourt, 140 Pyidaungsu Yeiktha Rd, Dagon PO (11191), Yangon; tel. (1) 285379; fax (1) 251405.

Protestant Churches
Lutheran Bethlehem Church: 181–183 Theinbyu St, Mingala Taung Nyunt PO 11221, POB 773, Yangon; tel. (1) 246585; Pres. Rev. JENSON RAJAN ANDREWS.
Myanmar Baptist Convention: 143 Minye Kyawswa Rd, POB 506, Yangon; tel. (1) 223231; fax (1) 221465; e-mail mbc@mptmail.net.mm; internet www.mbc1813.org; f. 1865; est. as Burma Baptist Missionary Convention; present name adopted 1954; 650,293 mems (2003); Pres. Rev. Dr HONOR NYO; Gen. Sec. Rev. K. D. TU LOM.

Myanmar Methodist Church: 47 Baho Rd, Thazin Lane, Ah Lone Township 65, Alanpya Pagoda Rd, Dagon, Yangon; Pres. Bishop ZOTHAN MAWIA.
Presbyterian Church of Myanmar: Synod Office, Falam, Chin State; 22,000 mems; Pres. Rev. SUN KANGLO.
Other denominations active in Myanmar include the Lisu Christian Church and the Salvation Army.

The Press

DAILIES

Botahtaung (The Vanguard): 22–30 Strand Rd, Botahtaung PO, POB 539, Yangon; tel. (1) 274310; Myanmar.
Guardian: 392–396 Merchant St, Botahtaung PO, POB 1522, Yangon; tel. (1) 270150; English.
Kyahmon (The Mirror): 77 52nd St, Dazundaung PO, POB 819, Yangon; tel. (1) 282777; internet www.myanmar.com/newspaper/kyaymon/index.html; Myanmar.
Myanmar Alin (New Light of Myanmar): 58 Komin Kochin Rd, Bahan PO, POB 21, Yangon; tel. (1) 544309; internet www.myanmar.com/newspaper/myanmarahlin/index.html; f. 1963; fmrly Loktha Pyithu Nezin (Working People's Daily); organ of the SPDC; morning; Myanmar; Chief Editor U WIN TIN; circ. 400,000.
New Light of Myanmar: 22–30 Strand Rd, Yangon; tel. (1) 297028; e-mail webmaster@myanmar.com; internet www.myanmar.com/newspaper/nlm/index.html; f. 1963; fmrly Working People's Daily; organ of the SPDC; morning; English; Chief Editor U KYAW MIN; circ. 14,000.

PERIODICALS

A Hla Thit (New Beauty): 46 90th St, Yangon; tel. (1) 287106; international news.
Dana Business Magazine: 72 8th St, Lanmadaw Township, Yangon; tel. and fax (1) 224010; e-mail dana@mptmail.net.mm; economic; Editor-in-Chief WILLIAM CHEN.
Do Kyaung Tha: Myawaddy Press, 184 32nd St, Yangon; tel. (1) 274655; f. 1965; monthly; Myanmar and English; circ. 17,000.
Gita Padetha: Yangon; journal of Myanma Music Council; circ. 10,000.
Guardian Magazine: 392–396 Merchant St, Botahtaung PO, POB 1522, Yangon; tel. (1) 296510; f. 1953; nationalized 1964; monthly; English; literary; circ. 11,600.
Kyee Pwar Yay (Prosperity): 296 Bo Sun Pat St, Yangon; tel. (1) 278100; economic; Editor-in-Chief U MYAT KHINE.
Moethaukpan (Aurora): Myawaddy Press, 184 32nd St, Yangon; tel. (1) 274655; f. 1980; monthly; Myanmar and English; circ. 27,500.
Myanma Dana (Myanmar's Economy): 210A 36th St, Kyauktada PO, Yangon; tel. (1) 284660; economic; Editor-in-Chief U THIHA SAW.
Myanmar Morning Post: Yangon; f. 1998; weekly; Chinese; news; circ. 5,000.
Myanmar Times & Business Review: 379–383 Bo Aung Kyaw St, Kyauktada Township, Yangon; tel. (1) 253646; fax (1) 392706; e-mail management@myanmartimes.com.mm; internet www.mmtimes.com; f. 2000; Editor-in-Chief ROSS DUNKLEY.
Myawaddy Journal: Myawaddy Press, 184 32nd St, Yangon; tel. (1) 274655; f. 1989; fortnightly; news; circ. 8,700.
Myawaddy Magazine: Myawaddy Press, 184 32nd St, Yangon; tel. (1) 274655; f. 1952; monthly; literary magazine; circ. 4,200.
Ngwetaryi Magazine: Myawaddy Press, 184 32nd St, Yangon; tel. (1) 274655; f. 1961; monthly; cultural; circ. 3,400.
Pyinnya Lawka Journal: 529 Merchant St, Yangon; tel. (1) 283611; publ. by Sarpay Beikman Management Board; quarterly; circ. 18,000.
Shwe Thwe: 529 Merchant St, Yangon; tel. (1) 283611; weekly; bilingual children's journal; publ. by Sarpay Beikman Management Board; circ. 100,000.
Taw Win Journal (Royal Journal): 149 37th St, Yangon; news; Editor-in-Chief SOE THEIN.
Teza: Myawaddy Press, 184 32nd St, Yangon; tel. (1) 274655; f. 1965; monthly; English and Myanmar; pictorial publication for children; circ. 29,500.
Thwe Thauk Magazine: Myawaddy Press, 184 32nd St, Yangon; f. 1946; monthly; literary.
Ya Nant Thit (New Fragrance): 186 39th St, Yangon; tel. (1) 276799; international news; Editor-in-Chief U CHIT WIN MG.

NEWS AGENCY

Myanmar News Agency (MNA): 212 Theinbyu Rd, Botahtaung, Yangon; tel. (1) 270893; f. 1963; govt-controlled; Chief Editors U Zaw Min Thein (domestic section), U Kyaw Min (external section).

Publishers

Hanthawaddy Press: 157 Bo Aung Kyaw St, Yangon; f. 1889; textbooks, multilingual dictionaries; Man. Editor U Zaw Win.

Knowledge Publishing House: 130 Bo Gyoke Aung San St, Yegyaw, Yangon; art, education, religion, politics and social sciences.

Kyipwaye Press: 84th St, Letsaigan, Mandalay; tel. (2) 21003; arts, travel, religion, fiction and children's.

Myawaddy Press: 184 32nd St, Yangon; tel. (1) 276889; journals and magazines; CEO U Thein Sein.

Sarpay Beikman Management Board: 529 Merchant St, Yangon; tel. (1) 283611; f. 1947; encyclopaedias, literature, fine arts and general; also magazines and translations; Chair. Aung Htay.

Shumawa Press: 146 West Wing, Bogyoke Aung San Market, Yangon; mechanical engineering.

Shwepyidan: 12A Haiaban, Yegwaw Quarter, Yangon; politics, religion, law.

Smart and Mookerdum: 221 Sule Pagoda Rd, Yangon; arts, cookery, popular science.

Thu Dhama Wadi Press: 55–56 Maung Khine St, POB 419, Yangon; f. 1903; religious; Propr U Tin Htoo; Man. U Pan Maung.

GOVERNMENT PUBLISHING HOUSE

Printing and Publishing Enterprise: 365–367 Bo Aung Kyaw St, Kyauktada Township, Yangon; tel. (1) 294645; f. 1880 as the Government Printing Office; Man. Dir U Aung Nyein.

PUBLISHERS' ASSOCIATION

Myanma Publishers' Union: 146 Bogyoke Market, Yangon.

Broadcasting and Communications

TELECOMMUNICATIONS

Posts and Telecommunications Department: Block 68, Ayeyar Wun Rd, South Dagon Township, Yangon; tel. (1) 591388; fax (1) 591383; e-mail dg.ptd@mptmail.net.mm; internet www.mcpt.gov.mm/ptd/index.htm; regulatory authority responsible for supervising radio communication, telephone, telegraph and post operations; Dir-Gen. U Tin Htwe.

Myanma Posts and Telecommunications (MPT): 839 Bogyoke Aung San Rd, Ahlone Township, Yangon; tel. (1) 297722; fax (1) 251911; internet www.mpt.net.mm; fmrly the Posts and Telecommunications Corpn; Man. Dir Col Maung Maung Tin.

BROADCASTING

Radio

Myanma TV and Radio Department (MTRD): 426 Pyay Rd, Kamayut 11041, Yangon; POB 1432, Yangon 11181; tel. (1) 531850; fax (1) 530211; f. 1946; broadcasts in Bamar, Arakanese (Rakhine), Shan, Karen (Kayin), Kachin, Kayah, Chin, Mon and English; Dir-Gen. U Khin Maung Htay; Dir of Radio Broadcasting U Ko Ko Htway.

In 1992 the National Coalition Government of the Union of Burma (NCGUB) began broadcasting daily to Myanmar from Norway under the name Democratic Voice of Burma (DVB). In 1995 it was believed that the DVB was being operated by Myanma student activists from the Norway-Burma Council, without any formal control by the NCGUB.

Television

Myanma TV and Radio Department (MTRD): 426 Pyay Rd, Kamayut 11041, Yangon; tel. (1) 535553; fax (1) 525428; f. 1946; colour television transmissions began in 1980; Dir-Gen. U Khin Maung Htay; Dir of Television Broadcasting U Myint Oo.

TV Myawaddy: Hmawbi, Hmawbi Township, Yangon; tel. (1) 620270; f. 1995; military broadcasting station transmitting public information, education and entertainment programmes via satellite.

In 2005 the Democratic Voice of Burma (DVB) began broadcasting Myanmar-language news and educational programmes via satellite from Norway. At the start of operations, the DVB broadcast two hours of transmissions per week, but planned to expand operations over the latter half of 2005. Despite the existence of strict regulations concerning ownership of satellite receiver equipment in Myanmar, it was believed that a considerable number of Myanma households owned a satellite dish without a licence.

Finance

(cap. = capital; res = reserves; dep. = deposits; m. = million; brs = branches; amounts in kyats)

BANKING

In July 1990 new banking legislation was promulgated, reorganizing the operations of the Central Bank, establishing a state-owned development institution, the Myanma Agricultural and Rural Development Bank, and providing for the formation of private sector banks and the opening of branches of foreign banks.

Central Bank

Central Bank of Myanmar: 26A Settmu Rd, POB 184, Yankin Township, Yangon; tel. (1) 285300; fax (1) 543621; e-mail cbm.ygn@mptmail.net.mm; f. 1947 as People's Bank of the Union of Burma; name changed as above in 1990; bank of issue; cap. 350m., dep. 13,545m.; Gov. U Kyaw Kyaw Maung; 37 brs.

State Banks

Myanma Economic Bank (MEB): 564 Merchant St, Yangon; tel. (1) 289345; fax (1) 283679; f. 1975; provides domestic banking network throughout the country; Man. Dir U Myat Maw.

Myanma Foreign Trade Bank: 80–86 Maha Bandoola Garden St, POB 203, Kyauktada Township, Yangon; tel. (1) 284911; fax (1) 289585; e-mail mftb-hoygn@mptmail-net.mm; f. 1976; handles all foreign exchange and international banking transactions; Chair. and Man. Dir U Than Ye; Man. and Sec. U Htin Kyaw Thein.

Development Banks

Myanma Agricultural Development Bank (MADB): 1–7 cnr of Latha St and Kanna Rd, Yangon; tel. (1) 226734; f. 1953; est. as State Agricultural Bank, reconstituted as Myanma Agricultural and Rural Development Bank 1990 and as above 1996; state-owned; Man. Dir U Chit Swe.

Myanma Investment and Commercial Bank (MICB): 170/176 Bo Aung Kyaw St, Botahtaung Township, Yangon; tel. (1) 256871; fax (1) 250518; e-mail micb.hoygn@mptmail.net.mm; f. 1989; state-owned; cap. 400m., res 786m., dep. 7,035m. (March 2000); Chair. and Man. Dir U Mya Than; 1 br.

Private Banks

In 2003 a crisis in Myanmar's private banking sector forced the closure of six of the country's 20 private banks. Following government intervention, three subsequently reopened in early 2004, having been cleared of committing banking irregularities. In 2005, however, the licences of a further two private banks were revoked following a government investigation into allegations of money-laundering.

Asian Yangon Bank Ltd: 319–321 Maha Bandoola St, Botahtaung Township, Yangon; tel. (1) 245825; fax (1) 245865; f. 1994 as Asian Yangon International Bank Ltd; name changed as above in 2000; Gen. Man. Tun Nyunt.

Co-operative Bank Ltd: 334–336 Kanna Rd, Yangon; tel. (1) 272641; fax (1) 283063; e-mail cbbank@mptmail.net.mm; f. 1992; Gen. Man. U Nyunt Hlaing.

First Private Bank Ltd (FPB): 619–621 Merchant St, Pabedan Township, Yangon; tel. (1) 251750; fax (1) 242320; e-mail myintzaw@fpbank-myanmar.com; internet www.fpb-myanmar.com; f. 1992; est. as the first publicly subscribed bank; fmrly the Commercial and Development Bank Ltd; provides loans to private business and small-scale industrial sectors; cap. 1,132.05m. (March 2005); Chair. Dr Sein Maung; 15 brs.

Innwa Bank Ltd: 554–556 Merchant St, Cnr of 35th and 36th Streets, Kyauktada Township, Yangon; tel. (1) 254642; fax (1) 254431; f. 1997.

Kanbawza Bank Ltd: 615/1 Pyay Rd, Kamayut Township, Yangon; tel. (1) 538075; fax (1) 538069; e-mail kbz@mptmail.net.mm; internet www.kbzbank.com; f. 1994; Chair. U Aung Ko Win; 22 brs.

Myanma Citizens Bank Ltd (MCB): 383 Maha Bandoola St, Kyauktada Township, Yangon; tel. (1) 273512; fax (1) 245932; f. 1991; Chair. U Hla Tin.

Myanma Oriental Bank Ltd (MOB): 166–168 Pansodan St, Kyauktada Township, Yangon; tel. (1) 246594; fax (1) 253217; e-mail mobl.ygn@mptmail.net.mm; f. 1993; Chair. U Myat Kyaw; Man. Dir and CEO U Win Myint.

MYANMAR
Directory

Myanma Universal Bank (MUB): 81 Theinbyu Rd, Yangon; tel. (1) 297339; fax (1) 201428; f. 1995.

Myanmar Industrial Development Bank Ltd: 26–42 Pansodan St, Kyauktada Township, Yangon; tel. (1) 249536; fax (1) 249529; f. 1996; cap. US $335m.

Myawaddy Bank Ltd: 24–26 Sule Pagoda Rd, Kyauktada Township, Yangon; tel. (1) 283665; fax (1) 250093; e-mail mwdbankygn@mtpt400.stems.com; f. 1993; Gen. Mans U TUN KYI, U MYA MIN.

Tun Foundation Bank Ltd: 165–167 Bo Aung Kyaw St, Yangon; tel. (1) 240710; e-mail tfbbank@mptmail.net.mm; f. 1997; Chair. U THEIN TUN.

Yadanabon Bank Ltd: 58A 26th St, cnr of 84th and 85th Sts, Aung Myay Thar Zan Township, Mandalay; tel. (2) 23577; f. 1992.

Yangon City Bank Ltd: 12–18 Sepin St, Kyauktada Township, Yangon; tel. (1) 289256; fax (1) 289231; f. 1993; auth. cap. 500m.; 100% owned by the Yangon City Development Committee; Chair. Col MYINT AUNG.

Yoma Bank Ltd: 1 Kungyan St, Mingala Taung Nyunt Township, Yangon; tel. (1) 242138; fax (1) 246548; f. 1993; Chair. SERGE PUN.

Foreign Banks

By November 2003 18 foreign banks had opened representative offices in Yangon.

STOCK EXCHANGE

Myanmar Securities Exchange Centre: 1st Floor, 21–25 Sule Pagoda Rd, Yangon; tel. (1) 283984; f. 1996; jt venture between Japan's Daiwa Institute of Research and Myanma Economic Bank; Man. Dir EIJI SUZUKI.

INSURANCE

At the end of November 2003 there were three representative offices of foreign insurance companies in Myanmar.

Myanma Insurance: 627–635 Merchant St, Yangon; tel. (1) 256244; fax (1) 250275; e-mail myansure@mptmail.net.com; internet www.soft-comm.com/myanma_insurance/index.html; f. 1976; govt-controlled; Man. Dir Col THEIN LWIN.

Trade and Industry

GOVERNMENT AGENCIES

Inspection and Agency Services: 383 Maha Bandoola St, Yangon; tel. (1) 284821; fax (1) 284823; works on behalf of state-owned enterprises to promote business with foreign companies; Man. Dir U OHN KHIN.

Myanmar Investment Commission: Ministry of National Planning and Economic Development, 653–691 Merchant St, Pabedan Township, Yangon; tel. (1) 241918; fax (1) 282101; Chair. U THAUNG; Vice-Chair. Maj.-Gen. TIN HTUT.

Union of Myanmar Economic Holdings: 72–74 Shwadagon Pagoda Rd, Yangon; tel. (1) 78905; f. 1990; public holding co; auth. cap. 10,000m. kyats; 40% of share capital subscribed by the Ministry of Defence and 60% by members of the armed forces.

CHAMBER OF COMMERCE

Union of Myanmar Federation of Chambers of Commerce and Industry (UMFCCI): 29 Min Ye Kyawswa Rd, Lanmadaw Township, Yangon; tel. (1) 214344; fax (1) 214484; e-mail umcci@mptmail.net.mm; internet www.umfcci.com.mm; f. 1919 as Burmese Chamber of Commerce; name changed as above in 1999; Pres. U WIN MYINT; Gen. Sec. U SEIN WIN HLAING.

UTILITIES

Electricity

Myanma Electric Power Enterprise (MEPE): 197–199 Lower Kyimyindine Rd, Yangon; tel. (1) 220918; fax (1) 221006; e-mail mepe@mptmail.net.mm; Man. Dir U ZAW WIN.

Water

Mandalay City Development Committee (Water and Sanitation Dept): cnr of 26th and 72nd Sts, Mandalay; tel. (2) 36173; f. 1992; Head of Water and Sanitation Dept U TUN KYI.

Water Resources Utilization Department (WRUD): Ministry of Agriculture and Irrigation, Thiri Mingala Lane, off Kaba Aye Pagoda Rd, Yangon; tel. (1) 666359; fax (1) 667456; f. 1995.

Yangon City Development Committee (Water and Sanitation Dept): City Hall, cnr of Maha Bandoola Rd and Sule Pagoda Rd, Kyauktada Township, Yangon; tel. (1) 248112; fax (1) 246016; e-mail priycdc@mptmail.net.mm; internet www.yangoncity.com.mm/ycdc/index.asp; f. 1992; Head of Water and Sanitation Dept U ZAW WIN.

CO-OPERATIVES

In 1993/94 there were 22,800 co-operative societies, with a turnover of 23,603m. kyats. In 2003, according to official reports, there were 18,041 co-operative societies.

Central Co-operative Society (CCS) Council: 334–336 Strand Rd, Yangon; tel. (1) 274550; Chair. U THAN HLANG; Sec. U TIN LATT.

Co-operative Department: 259–263 Bogyoke Aung San Rd, Yangon; tel. (1) 277096; Dir-Gen. U MAUNG HTI.

WORKERS' AND PEASANTS' COUNCILS

Conditions of work are stipulated in the Workers' Rights and Responsibilities Law, enacted in 1964. Regional workers' councils ensure that government directives are complied with, and that targets are met on a regional basis. In January 1985 there were 293 workers' councils in towns, with more than 1.8m. members. They are co-ordinated by a central workers' organization in Yangon, formed in 1968 to replace trade union organizations, which had been abolished in 1964. The Myanma Federation of Trade Unions operates in exile.

Peasants' Asiayone (Organization): Yangon; tel. (1) 82819; f. 1977; peasants' representative org.; Chair. Brig.-Gen. U THAN NYUNT; Sec. U SAN TUN.

Workers' Unity Organization: Central Organizing Committee, 61 Thein Byu St, Yangon; tel. (1) 284043; f. 1968; workers' representative org.; Chair. U OHN KYAW; Sec. U NYUNT THEIN.

Transport

All railways, domestic air services, passenger and freight road transport services and inland water facilities are owned and operated by state-controlled enterprises.

RAILWAYS

The railway network comprised 3,955 km of track in 1996/97, most of which was single track.

Myanma Railways: 361 Theinbyu Rd, Botataung Township, Yangon; tel. (1) 298585; fax (1) 284220; f. 1877; govt-operated; Man. Dir U MIN SWE; Gen. Man. U HLA YI.

ROADS

In 1996 the total length of the road network in Myanmar was an estimated 28,200 km, of which an estimated 3,440 km were paved. In 2001/02 the total length of road accessible to motor vehicles was 28,598 km.

Road Transportation Department: 375 Bogyoke Aung San St, Yangon; tel. (1) 284426; fax (1) 289716; f. 1963; controls passenger and freight road transport; in 1993/94 operated 1,960 haulage trucks and 928 passenger buses; Man. Dir U OHN MYINT.

INLAND WATERWAYS

The principal artery of traffic is the River Ayeyarwady (Irrawaddy), which is navigable as far as Bhamo, about 1,450 km inland, while parts of the Thanlwin and Chindwinn rivers are also navigable.

Inland Water Transport: 50 Pansodan St, Yangon; tel. (1) 222399; fax (1) 286500; govt-owned; operates cargo and passenger services throughout Myanmar; Man. Dir U KHIN MAUNG.

SHIPPING

Yangon is the chief port. Vessels with a displacement of up to 15,000 grt can be accommodated. In 2006 the Myanma merchant fleet totalled 126 vessels, with a combined displacement of 397,300 grt.

Myanma Port Authority: 10 Pansodan St, POB 1, Yangon; tel. (1) 280094; fax (1) 295134; internet www.mot.gov.mm/mpa/index.html; f. 1880; general port and harbour duties; Man. Dir U HTIEN HTAY; Gen. Man. U HLAING SOON.

Myanma Five Star Line: 132–136 Theinbyu Rd, POB 1221, Yangon; tel. (1) 295279; fax (1) 297669; e-mail mfslhq@mptmail.net.mm; internet www.mfsl-shipping.com; f. 1959; cargo services to the Far East and Australia; Man. Dir MAUNG MAUNG NYEIN; Gen. Man. WIN PE; fleet of 26 coastal and ocean-going vessels.

CIVIL AVIATION

Mingaladon Airport, near Yangon, is equipped to international standards. The newly built Mandalay International Airport was inaugurated in September 2000. In 2002 plans for the construction of the country's third international airport, Hanthawaddy International Airport in Bago (Pegu), were finally approved.

Department of Civil Aviation: Mingaladon Airport, Yangon; tel. (1) 665144; fax (1) 665124; e-mail dca.myanmar@mpt.mail.net.mm; internet www.mot.gov.mm/dca/index.html; Dir-Gen. U WIN MAUNG.

Air Bagan Ltd: 56 Shwe Taung Gyar St, Bahan Township, Yangon; tel. (1) 514861; fax (1) 515102; e-mail info@airbagan.com.mm; internet www.airbagan.com; f. 2004; domestic services to 14 destinations; Chair. TAY ZA; Man. Dir SOE WIN.

Air Mandalay: 146 Dhammazedi Rd, Bahan Township, Yangon; tel. (1) 501520; fax (1) 525937; e-mail info@airmandalay.com; internet www.airmandalay.com; f. 1994; Myanmar's first airline; jt venture between Air Mandalay Holding and Myanma Airways; operates domestic services and regional services to Chiang Mai and Phuket, Thailand, and Siem Reap, Cambodia; Chair. Dr TUN CHIN; Man. Dir ERIC KANG TIAN LYE; 242 employees.

Myanmar Airways (MA): 104 Kanna Rd, Yangon; tel. (1) 284566; fax (1) 89583; e-mail 8mpr@maiair.com.mm; internet www.mot.gov.mm/ma/index.html; f. 1993; govt-controlled; internal network operates services to 21 airports; Man. Dir TIN MAUNG TUN.

Myanmar Airways International (MAI): 08–02 Sakura Tower, 339 Bogyoke Aung San Rd, Yangon; tel. (1) 255260; fax (1) 255305; e-mail management@maiair.com; internet www.maiair.com; f. 1993; govt-owned; established by Myanmar Airways in jt venture with Highsonic Enterprises of Singapore to provide international services; operates services to Bangkok, Dhaka, Hong Kong, Kuala Lumpur and Singapore; Man. Dir AUNG GYI.

United Myanmar Air: Summit Parkview Hotel, Yangon; internet www.unitedmyanmar.com; f. 2003; jt venture between Myanmar Airways and Sunshine Strategic Investments Holdings of Hong Kong; international services to Bangkok, Hong Kong, Kuala Lumpur and Singapore; CEO EDWARD TAN.

Yangon Airways: MMB Tower, Level 5, 166 Upper Pansodan Rd, Mingalar Taungnyunt Township, Yangon; tel. (1) 383100; fax (1) 383127; e-mail info@yangonair.com; internet www.yangonair.com; f. 1996; domestic services to 13 destinations; Man. Dir U KYAW WIN.

Tourism

Yangon, Mandalay, Taunggyi and Pagan possess outstanding palaces, Buddhist temples and shrines. The number of foreign visitors to Myanmar declined severely following the suppression of the democracy movement in 1988. In the early 1990s, however, the Government actively promoted the revival of the tourism industry, and between 1995 and 1998 alone the number of hotel rooms almost doubled, reaching a total of nearly 14,000. In 2005 there were 232,218 foreign tourist arrivals (compared with only 5,000 in 1989); revenue from tourism (including passenger transport) totalled an estimated US $98m. in 2004.

Myanmar Hotels and Tourism Services: 77–91 Sule Pagoda Rd, Yangon 11141; tel. (1) 282013; fax (1) 254417; e-mail mtt.mht@mptmail.net.mm; govt-controlled; manages all hotels, tourist offices, tourist department stores and duty-free shops; Gen. Man. U TIN HTAY.

Myanmar Tourism Promotion Board: Level 3, Business Centre, 223 Signal Pagoda Rd, Yangon; tel. (1) 242828; fax (1) 242800; e-mail mtpb@mptmail.net.mm; internet www.myanmar-tourism.com; Chair. U AUNG MYAT KYAW.

Myanmar Travels and Tours: 77–91 Sule Pagoda Rd, POB 559, Yangon 11141; tel. (1) 382243; fax (1) 254417; e-mail mtt.mht@mptmail.net.mm; internet www.myanmartravelsandtours.com; f. 1964; govt tour operator and travel agent; handles all travel arrangements for groups and individuals; Gen. Man. U HTAY AUNG.

Union of Myanmar Travel Association (UMTA): Bldg 69, No 609B, 6th Floor, Yuzana Condo Tower, cnr Shwegonedaing Rd and Kabaraye Pagoda Rd, Bahan Township, Yangon; tel. (1) 559673; fax (1) 545707; e-mail UMTA@mptmail.net.mm; internet www.umtanet.org; f. 2002; organizes private travel agencies and tour operators; promotes Myanmar as a tourist destination; Chair. U KHIN ZAW.

NAMIBIA

Introductory Survey

Location, Climate, Language, Religion, Flag, Capital

The Republic of Namibia (formerly known as South West Africa) lies in south-western Africa, with South Africa to the south and south-east, Botswana to the east and Angola to the north. The country has a long coastline on the Atlantic Ocean. The narrow Caprivi Strip, between Angola and Botswana in the north-east, extends Namibia to the Zambezi river, giving it a border with Zambia. The climate is generally hot, although coastal areas have relatively mild temperatures. Most of the country is subject to drought and unreliable rainfall. The average annual rainfall varies from about 50 mm (2 ins) on the coast to 550 mm (22 ins) in the north. The arid Namib Desert stretches along the west coast, while the easternmost area is part of the Kalahari Desert. The official language is English; however, most of the African ethnic groups have their own languages. At the 2001 census the most widely spoken African languages were Oshiwambo (used in 48% of households), Nama/Damara (11%), Rukavango (10%) and Otjiherero (8%). In addition, Afrikaans is spoken (11%) and German is also used. About 90% of the population are Christians. The national flag (proportions 2 by 3) comprises a blue triangle in the upper hoist corner, bearing a yellow sun (a blue-bordered disc, surrounded by 12 triangular rays), separated from a green triangle in the lower fly corner by a white-bordered, broad red stripe. The capital is Windhoek.

Recent History

South West Africa became a German possession in 1884. The territory excluded the port of Walvis Bay and 12 small offshore islands, previously annexed by the United Kingdom and subsequently incorporated into South Africa. During the First World War South African forces occupied South West Africa in 1914, and in 1915 Germany surrendered the territory. In 1920 the League of Nations entrusted South Africa with a mandate to administer South West Africa. In 1925 South Africa granted a Constitution giving limited self-government to European (white) inhabitants only. No trusteeship agreement was concluded with the UN after the Second World War, and in 1946 the UN refused South Africa's request for permission to annex South West Africa. In 1949 the territory's European voters were granted representation in the South African Parliament. The following year the International Court of Justice (ICJ, see p. 20) issued a ruling that the area should remain under international mandate and that South Africa should submit it to UN control. South Africa refused to comply with this judgment. In October 1966 South Africa's security and apartheid laws were extended to South West Africa, retrospective to 1950.

Opposition within South West Africa to South African rule led to the establishment of two African nationalist organizations, the South West Africa People's Organisation (SWAPO—founded in 1957 as the Ovamboland People's Congress) and the South West African National Union (SWANU—formed in 1959). During 1966 SWAPO's military wing, the People's Liberation Army of Namibia (PLAN), launched an armed struggle for the liberation of the territory. PLAN operated from bases in Angola and Zambia, and was controlled by the external wing of SWAPO (led by Sam Nujoma—the organization's President from 1959). SWAPO also had a legal wing, which was tolerated in South West Africa.

South Africa was consistently criticized at the UN over its extension of apartheid to the territory. The UN General Assembly voted to terminate South Africa's mandate in October 1966, established a UN Council for South West Africa in May 1967, and changed the name of the territory to Namibia in June 1968. In 1971 the ICJ ruled that South Africa's presence was illegal. In 1973 the UN General Assembly recognized SWAPO as 'the authentic representative of the Namibian people', and appointed a UN Commissioner for Namibia to undertake 'executive and administrative tasks'.

A multiracial constitutional conference on the territory's future, organized by the all-white South West Africa Legislative Assembly, was convened in Windhoek in September 1975, attended by representatives of the territory's 11 main ethnic groups. However, neither the UN nor the Organization of African Unity (OAU, now the African Union, see p. 164) recognized this so-called Turnhalle Conference, owing to its ethnic and non-democratic basis. In 1976 and 1977 proposals for procedures whereby Namibia was to achieve independence and formulate a constitution were made by the Turnhalle Conference, but rejected by SWAPO, the UN and the OAU. In September 1977 South Africa appointed an Administrator-General to govern the territory. In November the Turnhalle Conference was dissolved, and the Democratic Turnhalle Alliance (DTA), a coalition of conservative political groups representing the ethnic groups involved in the Turnhalle Conference, was formed.

In early 1978 talks were held between South Africa, SWAPO and a 'contact group' comprising Canada, France, the Federal Republic of Germany, the United Kingdom and the USA. In September the contact group's proposals for a Namibian settlement, including the holding of UN-supervised elections, were conditionally accepted by both South Africa and SWAPO and were incorporated in UN Security Council Resolution 435. However, South Africa continued to implement its own internal solution for Namibia with an election for a Constituent Assembly in December. The election was contested by five parties, but boycotted notably by SWAPO. Of the 50 seats in the Assembly, 41 were won by the DTA. In May 1979 South Africa unilaterally established a legislative National Assembly, without executive powers, from the existing Constituent Assembly.

All-party negotiations, held under UN auspices in Geneva, Switzerland, in January 1981, failed in their aim of arranging a cease-fire and eventual UN-supervised elections. Later in 1981 the contact group attempted to secure support for a three-phase independence plan. However, South Africa's insistence (supported by the USA) that any withdrawal of South African forces must be linked to the withdrawal of Cuban troops from Angola was rejected by Angola and the UN. Meanwhile, the Ministerial Council, formed in 1980 and chaired by Dirk Mudge (also Chairman of the DTA), assumed much of the Administrator-General's executive power in September 1981. However, the Ministerial Council was dissolved in January 1983, when, after several months of disagreement with the South African Government regarding the future role of the DTA in the territory, Mudge resigned as Council Chairman. South Africa disbanded the National Assembly and resumed direct rule of Namibia, with Willem van Niekerk as Administrator-General.

The Multi-Party Conference (MPC) was established in November 1983, grouping, initially, seven internal political parties. Boycotted by SWAPO, it appeared to be promoted by South Africa as a means of settling the independence issue outside the framework of Resolution 435, and of reducing SWAPO's dominance in any future post-independence government for Namibia. None the less, South Africa continued to negotiate on the independence issue with SWAPO and Angola. In February 1984 South Africa and Angola agreed to a cease-fire on the Angola–Namibia border, and set up a joint commission to monitor the withdrawal of all South African troops from Angola. Angola undertook to ensure that neither Cuban nor SWAPO forces would move into the areas vacated by the South African troops. Discussions on the independence issue in mid-1984, involving van Niekerk, SWAPO and the MPC, ended inconclusively, as did negotiations in 1984–86 between the South African Government and the US Assistant Secretary of State for African Affairs.

In April 1985 the South African Government accepted a proposal by the MPC for a 'Transitional Government of National Unity' (TGNU) in Namibia. This was formally established in Windhoek in June, although the arrangement was condemned in advance by the contact group and was declared 'null and void' by the UN Secretary-General. The TGNU consisted of an executive Cabinet, drawn from a National Assembly of 62 members who were appointed from among the parties constituting the MPC. Its establishment was accompanied by the proclamation of a 'bill of rights', drafted by the MPC, which prohibited racial discrimination. A Constitutional Council was also established to prepare a constitution for an independent Namibia. The South African Government retained responsibility for foreign affairs, defence and internal security, and all legislation was to be subject to approval by the Administrator-General. Louis Pienaar replaced van Niekerk in this post in July.

During 1987, following the liberalization of labour laws and the legalization of trade unions for black workers in 1986, the trade union movement became increasingly active. In mid-1987 the Constitutional Council published a draft document; however, South Africa indicated that it could not accept the lack of a guarantee of minority rights in the proposal. In March 1988 the Namibian Supreme Court declared the 'AG8' law of 1980 (providing for the election of 'second-tier' legislative assemblies and for the administration of education and health facilities on an ethnic, rather than a geographical, basis) to be in conflict with the 1985 'bill of rights'.

Both Angola and Cuba were reported in January 1988 to have accepted, in principle, the US demand for a complete withdrawal of Cuban troops from Angola, but they reiterated that this would be conditional on the cessation of South African support for the insurgent União Nacional para a Independência Total de Angola (UNITA). In July Angola, Cuba and South Africa reached agreement on 14 'essential principles' for a peaceful settlement, and in August it was agreed that the implementation of Resolution 435 would begin on 1 November. Also in August the Governments of South Africa, Cuba and Angola announced a cease-fire, to which SWAPO agreed, and South Africa undertook to withdraw all its forces from Angola. The November deadline was not met, owing to failure to agree on an exact schedule for the evacuation of Cuban troops from Angola. In December Angola, Cuba and South Africa signed a formal treaty designating 1 April 1989 as the implementation date for Resolution 435 and establishing a joint commission to monitor the treaty's implementation. (A further agreement was signed by Angola and Cuba, requiring the evacuation of all Cuban troops from Angola by July 1991.) A Constituent Assembly was to be elected in Namibia on 1 November 1989. South African forces in Namibia were to be confined to their bases, and their numbers reduced to 1,500 by July 1989; all South African troops were to have been withdrawn from Namibia one week after the November election. SWAPO forces were to be confined to bases in Angola in April, before being disarmed and repatriated. A multinational military observer force, the UN Transition Assistance Group (UNTAG), was to monitor the South African withdrawal, and civilian administrators and an international police force were to supervise the election. At the end of February the TGNU was formally disbanded, and on 1 March the National Assembly voted to dissolve itself: until independence the territory was governed by the Administrator-General, in consultation with a Special Representative of the UN Secretary-General, Martti Ahtisaari. Pienaar and Ahtisaari were to be jointly responsible for arranging the November election.

Implementation of Resolution 435 was disrupted by large-scale movements, from April 1989, of SWAPO guerrillas into Namibia from Angola, as a result of which the South African security forces, with the consent of the UN, suspended the cease-fire. About 280 SWAPO troops were reported to have been killed in the subsequent conflict. Following negotiations by the joint monitoring commission, conditions were arranged for an evacuation of the SWAPO forces to Angola, and in May the commission certified the cease-fire to be once more in force. In June most racially discriminatory legislation was repealed, and an amnesty was granted to Namibian refugees and exiles: by late September nearly 42,000 people, including Nujoma, had returned to Namibia. Meanwhile, South Africa completed its troop reduction ahead of schedule.

Voting proceeded peacefully on 7–11 November 1989, with the participation of more than 95% of the electorate. SWAPO received 57.3% of all votes cast and won 41 of the Constituent Assembly's 72 seats, while the DTA, with 28.6% of the votes, secured 21 seats. (In 1991 the South African Government admitted that it had contributed funds to the electoral campaigns of the DTA and several other political parties opposed to SWAPO.) Following the election, South Africa's remaining troops were evacuated from Namibia, while SWAPO's bases in Angola were decommissioned. The SWAPO Government subsequently reached an agreement with South Africa that no legal action would be taken for atrocities committed by either side. The agreement also precluded the establishment of a truth and reconciliation commission.

In February 1990 the Constituent Assembly adopted a draft Constitution, providing for a multi-party democracy based on universal adult suffrage. Later in the month the Constituent Assembly elected Nujoma as Namibia's first President. On 21 March Namibia finally achieved independence; the Constituent Assembly was redesignated the National Assembly, and Nujoma assumed executive power. A Cabinet, headed by the Constituent Assembly Chairman, Hage Geingob (a long-serving SWAPO activist), was also sworn in.

Following Namibia's independence, the port of Walvis Bay, its surrounding territory of 1,124 sq km and the 12 offshore Penguin Islands remained under South African jurisdiction. In September 1991 the Namibian and South African Governments agreed to administer the disputed territories jointly, pending a final settlement on sovereignty, and in August 1992 the two countries announced the forthcoming establishment of a joint administration authority. In August 1993, however, South Africa's multi-party constitutional negotiating committee instructed the Government to prepare legislation for the transfer of sovereignty over Walvis Bay to Namibia. Accordingly, negotiations between Namibia and South Africa resulted in bilateral agreements regarding the future of South African interests in the Walvis Bay area. Namibia formally took control of Walvis Bay and its islands from 1 March 1994. In August SWAPO won eight seats, and the DTA two, in Walvis Bay's first non-racial local elections.

Namibia's first post-independence presidential and legislative elections in December 1994 resulted in overwhelming victories for Nujoma and SWAPO. Nujoma was elected for a second term as President, securing 76.3% of the votes cast, while SWAPO secured 53 of the elective seats in the National Assembly, with 73.9% of the valid votes cast. The DTA won 15 seats (with 20.8% of the votes), and the United Democratic Front (UDF) two. The remaining two seats were won by the Democratic Coalition of Namibia (an alliance of the National Patriotic Front and the German Union) and the Monitor Action Group (MAG).

At the SWAPO Congress in May 1997 Nujoma was re-elected unopposed as party President. Among the resolutions endorsed by the Congress was a proposal that Nujoma should seek re-election for a third term as national President. It was agreed that the Constitution, which stipulates that a President may serve no more than two consecutive terms, could be exceptionally amended to allow Nujoma to seek a further mandate, since the incumbent had initially been appointed by the Constituent Assembly, and had only once been elected President on a popular mandate. In August 1998 a senior SWAPO official, Ben Ulenga, resigned as Namibia's High Commissioner to the United Kingdom, in protest at the proposed arrangement to allow Nujoma to seek a renewed mandate. In October the exceptional constitutional amendment was approved by the requisite two-thirds' majority in the National Assembly, having received the support of SWAPO's members; the amendment was similarly endorsed by the National Council in November. In March 1999 it was reported that Ulenga was to establish a new political party, the Congress of Democrats (CoD), with a view to contesting the presidential and legislative elections due later in the year.

In August 1998 the DTA's executive announced the suspension of Mishake Muyongo as party President, and dissociated the party from Muyongo's overt support for the secession of the Caprivi Strip—a narrow area of land extending in the north-east, between Angola and Botswana, as far as the Zambezi river (Namibia's border with Zambia). In November it emerged that Muyongo, leading the so-called Caprivi Liberation Movement (CLM), was among more than 100 people who, apparently armed, had crossed into Botswana in October, and who were now seeking asylum in that country. The Namibian Government stated that it had discovered plans for a secessionist rebellion, led by Muyongo and a chief of the Mafwe tribe, Boniface Mamili, in Caprivi. Representatives of the office of the UN High Commissioner for Refugees (UNHCR) subsequently advised the Botswana authorities that the secessionists' fears of persecution, should they be returned to Namibia, were 'plausible'. In subsequent weeks many more people crossed into Botswana, claiming to be fleeing harassment and persecution by the Namibian security forces: among those who left the country were many San, who were not believed to be associated with the secessionist movement. (In mid-2001 it was reported that many more San were considering leaving Namibia, again alleging harassment by the security forces.) During a visit to Botswana in March 1999 Nujoma reached an agreement with President Festus Mogae of that country, whereby the separatist leaders (whose extradition had hitherto been sought by Namibia in order that they could be tried on terrorist charges) would be accorded refugee status, on condition that they be resettled in a third country. Muyongo and Mamili were subsequently granted asylum in Denmark. The agreement also provided for the return to Namibia, under the auspices of UNHCR and without fear of prosecution or persecution, of the estimated 2,500 refugees who had crossed into Botswana since late 1998.

A period of apparent calm in the Caprivi region ended abruptly in early August 1999 with an armed attack by members of an organization styling itself the Caprivi Liberation Army (CLA), who targeted a military base at Mpacha airport and the police headquarters and offices of the Namibian Broadcasting Corpn in the regional capital, Katima Mulilo. At least eight members of the Namibian security forces and five CLA fighters were killed during the attack and its suppression. Nujoma responded by declaring a state of emergency in the region. While there was support within Namibia for the declaration, the CoD, as well as church leaders and human rights organizations, expressed concern at evidence of the ill-treatment of detainees. Several members of the Government were subsequently reported to have admitted that 'mistakes' were made in the aftermath of the attack; however, the army Chief of Staff maintained that the decisive response of the forces under his command had been justified. Visiting Katima Mulilo in late August, Nujoma announced an end to the state of emergency, although army and police reinforcements were to remain in Caprivi. Initially, 12 alleged rebels were remanded on charges of high treason, murder, public violence and illegal possession of firearms; the prosecution asserted that 17 known leaders of the CLA remained at large. Meanwhile, a further 47 suspects were charged with aiding and abetting the rebels. Repatriations of refugees from Botswana were halted following the attack on Katima Mulilo, although UNHCR expressed the hope that voluntary repatriations would resume as soon as the security situation in Caprivi was adequate to guarantee the safe return of refugees. In early 2000, however, following an escalation of instability in the region of the Namibia–Angola border, a further 400 Namibian nationals were reported to have fled to Botswana. In late 2001 officials from Botswana and Namibia held talks regarding the repatriation of about 500 Namibian refugees. In September of that year, in response to a request from the Namibian Government, the Gaborone Magistrates' Court in Botswana ordered the extradition of a group of suspected Caprivi separatists who were wanted to stand trial for high treason in connection with the attack on Katima Mulilo. The Namibian Government was also seeking to extradite Muyongo from Denmark to answer similar charges; the Danish Government stated that it was awaiting advice from UNHCR before making a decision. In October 2003, after numerous delays, the trial commenced of 121 Namibians charged with offences related to the attack on Katima Mulilo. In February 2004 the trial judge ruled that 13 of the defendants were 'irregularly before the court', as a result of a process of 'disguised extradition' whereby they had been removed from Zambia and Botswana, and ordered their release. The Government indicated that it would seek permission to appeal to the Supreme Court against this ruling. It was reported that the 13 defendants thus acquitted had been immediately rearrested on their release. In August 2007 10 individuals were convicted in relation to the rebellion and given sentences of up to 32 years' imprisonment. The trial of the remaining defendants was ongoing in early 2008.

Meanwhile, presidential and legislative elections, which were held on 30 November and 1 December 1999, resulted in an overwhelming victory for Nujoma and SWAPO, with Ulenga and the CoD apparently winning support at the expense of the DTA. In the presidential election Nujoma was returned for a third (and final) term of office with 76.8% of the votes cast, while Ulenga took 10.5% and Katuutire Kaura (Muyongo's successor as President of the DTA) 9.6%. SWAPO won 55 of the elective seats in the National Assembly, with 76.1% of the votes cast (thus ensuring that it retained the two-thirds' majority required to amend the Constitution); the CoD and the DTA each won seven seats (taking, respectively, 9.9% and 9.5% of the total votes cast).

Geingob was reappointed Prime Minister in a reorganization of the Cabinet announced by Nujoma in March 2000. A further cabinet reshuffle was effected in January 2001. In November Nujoma announced that he would not be standing for a fourth term as President on the expiry of his current mandate in 2004.

In August 2002 Nujoma reorganized his Cabinet; Theo-Ben Gurirab was appointed Prime Minister, replacing Geingob, who resigned from the Government, having declined the position of Minister of Regional and Local Government and Housing. It was reported that Nujoma considered Geingob a threat to his authority. Hidipo Hamutenya became Minister of Foreign Affairs, Information and Broadcasting. In May 2003, in a further reallocation of portfolios, Nangolo Mbumba was replaced as Minister of Finance by Saarah Kuugongelwa-Amadhila, while Mbumba became Minister of Information and Broadcasting. Hamutenya was dismissed without explanation in late May 2004, although many observers regarded the decision as part of a plan by the President to manoeuvre his own choice of successor, the Minister of Lands, Resettlement and Rehabilitation, Hifikepunye Pohamba, into a stronger position. Pohamba was duly selected as the presidential candidate of the SWAPO party later that month. Meanwhile Hamutenya was replaced by the Minister of Labour, Marco Hausiku, and the labour portfolio was awarded to Marlene Mungunda.

At national elections held on 15–16 November 2004 Pohamba was elected President with, according to official results, 76.44% of the votes cast; his nearest rival, Ulenga, secured 7.28%. SWAPO also recorded a decisive victory in the elections to the National Assembly, retaining 55 of the 72 seats with 76.1% of the national vote. The CoD increased its share of the vote but won only five seats, compared with seven in the 1999 elections. The DTA took four seats, the UDF three and the MAG one seat, while two newly reactivated parties, the National Unity Democratic Organization and the Republican Party, won three seats and one seat, respectively. The Electoral Commission of Namibia recorded voter turn-out at 85%. (Following claims of electoral irregularities by members of the opposition a recount was held in March 2005: with the exception of the CoD all parties received a smaller number of votes; however, the overall allocation of seats remained the same.) Pohamba was due to take office in March 2005, upon the expiry of Samuel Nujoma's third term as President.

Nujoma duly stood down as President on 21 March 2005, but was expected to remain as leader of SWAPO until 2007. Following his swearing in as President that day, Pohamba unveiled his Cabinet, which included six new appointees. The former Minister of Higher Education, Training and Employment Creation, Nahas Angula, and the former Minister of Health and Social Services, Dr Libertina Amathila, were appointed as Prime Minister and Deputy Prime Minister, respectively. The overall structure of the ministries was reorganized and several were renamed to reflect their changed remits. Responsibility for prisons and correctional services was transferred to the newly created Ministry of Safety and Security under Peter Tshirumbu-Tsheehama, who was also appointed acting Minister of Defence. (Maj.-Gen. (retd) Charles Namoloh was appointed Minister of Defence in April 2005.) Albert Kawana was awarded the newly created post of Minister of Presidential Affairs, while the new Ministry of Education, headed by Nangolo Mbumba, assumed the functions of the former ministries of Higher and Basic Education. The incumbent Attorney-General, Pendukeni Ivula-Ithana, assumed the justice portfolio. Despite the structural changes, the composition of the new Government was interpreted as an indication that it would continue with the policies set down under the previous administration. The National Assembly subsequently unanimously elected Gurirab as Speaker.

Meanwhile, in April 2001 the Government announced that it had allocated N $100m. to acquire land for redistribution on a voluntary basis over a five-year period. At that time approximately 4,000 (mainly white-owned) farms occupied 52% of the total land area, while the Government had acquired only some 6% of the land required for resettlement. In October 2002 the Government announced that it was considering the seizure of white-owned farms for redistribution to the landless black population, and criticized white farmers for taking advantage of the voluntary basis for land redistribution by charging excessively high prices for their land. In March 2004 the Government estimated that it would cost more than US $150m. over a five-year period to redistribute some 9m. ha of land among an estimated 243,000 applicants. (It was reported that land prices had increased three-fold between 1990 and 2005.) By September the Government had bought just over 140 farms at a cost of N $131m.—under the 'willing buyer, willing seller' scheme—and resettled 9,156 people. The expropriation of the first white-owned commercial farm was carried out in November 2005; a further 19 farms were listed for expropriation under compulsory purchase orders. However, an independent report, issued by the Legal Assistance Centre, criticized the Government programme, concluding that the resettlement targets were 'logistically impossible' and 'economically unrealistic'. In early December 2005 the National Assembly approved legislation granting former President Nujoma the title of 'Founding Father'.

In November 2007 a new political party, the Rally for Democracy and Progress (RDP), was registered under the leadership of two former cabinet ministers and members of SWAPO. Jesaya Nyamu, who was named as acting Chairman of the party, had been Minister of Trade and Industry until 2004 and Hidipo Hamutenya, acting President of the RDP, was formerly Minister of Foreign Affairs. Both had resigned from SWAPO a week prior to the RDP's registration. The resignations appeared to have instigated a crisis of legitimacy for the party, which subsequently proposed to abolish the role of the Prime Minister and introduce the position of Vice-President. The constitutional amendment required to implement the proposal was to be discussed at the party's congress in late 2007. A second new opposition party—the All People's Party of Namibia, founded by Herbert and Ignatius Shixwameni—was registered in January 2008 following a split within the CoD.

In April 2008 President Pohamba announced a major reorganization of the Cabinet. The most notable appointment was that of former Prime Minister Geingob to the post of Minister of Trade and Industry, while the Minister of Security, Peter Tshirumbu-Tsheehama, was replaced by Dr Nickey Iyambo, hitherto the Minister of Agriculture, Water and Forestry.

In March 1993 UNITA alleged that members of the Namibia Defence Force (NDF) had crossed the border into southern Angola to assist Angolan government forces in offensives against UNITA, and subsequently claimed that some 2,000 Cuban troops had landed at Namibia's southern port of Lüderitz, from where they had been transferred to Angola to assist government forces. The Namibian authorities denied any involvement in the Angolan conflict, however. A 550-km stretch of the Okavango river border was closed from September 1994, following the deaths of three Namibians in an attack attributed by the Namibian authorities to UNITA. In September 1995 the Namibian Government announced the formation of a border control unit to assist police and NDF troops deployed along the Okavango. In November the two countries' defence and security commission agreed new measures aimed at facilitating the work of border patrols. Namibia subsequently announced that the Government was to contribute 200 NDF troops to the UN peace-keeping mission in Angola.

Following the attack on Katima Mulilo by Caprivi separatists in August 1999, the Namibian Government alleged that UNITA was lending military and logistical support to the CLA. (Links were also reported with the separatist Barotse Patriotic Front in Zambia, and the Namibian authorities alleged that the CLA had received training on Zambian territory.) There was considerable speculation that not only was Caprivi an important supply route for UNITA, but also that the Angolan rebel movement was attempting to divert resources of the Namibian armed forces away from the conflict in the Democratic Republic of the Congo (DRC, q.v.).

Tensions in the region of the Namibia–Angola border escalated from late 1999, after the two countries began joint patrols targeting UNITA, and the Namibian Government authorized the Angolan armed forces to launch attacks against UNITA from Namibian territory. In February 2000 it was announced that Nujoma and President José Eduardo dos Santos of Angola had agreed to implement measures to restore security in the border region; by June, when a curfew was imposed on the north-eastern border with Angola, more than 50 Namibians had been killed in cross-border raids by the Angolan rebels. Continuing conflict in southern Angola resulted in a large number of refugees entering Namibia (some 6,000 arrived from Angola between November 1999 and August 2000, although increased border security subsequently reduced the flow). In March 2001 President Nujoma ordered a further reinforcement of the Namibian military presence in Caprivi. In October UNITA rebels were reported to have destroyed an electricity substation in the Kavango region, and in November a group of unidentified gunmen killed four people in western Caprivi before escaping to Angola.

In April 2002 the Namibian Government welcomed the signing of a formal cease-fire agreement by the Angolan Government and UNITA, some six weeks after the death of Jonas Savimbi, the UNITA leader. Some stability was restored in the Kavango and Caprivi regions in mid-2002, and in August a number of Angolan refugees were repatriated; the majority of them, estimated at around 20,000, were due to return home in mid-2003, under the auspices of UNHCR. In February 2005 Namibia and Angola reached agreement on a maritime border; negotiations had begun in 1993 but were not formalized until 2003 when a joint commission for delimitation and demarcation was established.

Following independence, Namibia became a member of the UN, the Commonwealth, the OAU and the Southern African Development Co-ordination Conference—now the Southern African Development Community (SADC, see p. 386). Despite expressed concerns at South African dominance of the regional economy, the Nujoma regime has forged close links with post-apartheid South Africa, and in 1994 SWAPO contributed funds to the electoral campaigns of the African National Congress of South Africa and the Pan-Africanist Congress. In February 1997 legislation providing for the cancellation of the debt (now amounting to N $1,200m.) was formally approved by the South African Parliament. In August 2001 the foreign ministers of Namibia and South Africa held talks regarding their 400 km border; Namibia claimed its southern border extended to the middle of the Orange river, while South Africa claimed that its territory stretched to the northern bank. (When South Africa's borders were reassessed in 1994, following its first democratic elections, the Surveyors-General of both Namibia and South Africa had agreed to place the border in the middle of the river, but the agreement was never signed.) The confusion over the location of the border has led to differences over mineral and fishing rights in the river, as well as grazing rights on its islands.

In February 1995 it was announced that Namibia and Botswana were to refer a dispute regarding the demarcation of their joint border on the Chobe river (specifically, the issue of the sovereignty of the small, uninhabited island of Kasikili-Sedudu) for adjudication by the ICJ. The dispute was formally submitted to the Court in mid-1996. The ICJ ruled in December 1999 that the island formed part of the territory of Botswana; the judgment further ruled that nationals of (and vessels flying the flags of) Botswana and Namibia should enjoy equal treatment in the two channels around the island. In January 1998 the two countries' Joint Commission on Defence and Security held an emergency meeting, following allegations by Namibia that troops from Botswana had taken control of a further island in disputed border territory—Situngu Island in the Caprivi Strip. The Joint Commission agreed to expedite the establishment of a Joint Technical Commission for the demarcation of the border. Relations were complicated by the issue of Caprivi secessionism (see above). Situngu is claimed as Mafwe land; furthermore, Namibia's representative in discussions regarding the island, said to be a member of the secessionist movement, was reported to have fled to Angola. In 2003 Botswana and Namibia accepted the demarcation by a joint commission of their joint border along the Kwando, Linyanti and Chobe rivers.

From August 1998 Namibia, which was participating in regional efforts to resolve the conflict in the DRC, supported a Zimbabwean-led initiative by members of SADC (notably excluding South Africa) for military intervention in support of the regime of President Laurent-Désiré Kabila; as many as 2,000 Namibian troops were subsequently dispatched to the DRC, provoking vociferous criticism by opponents of Nujoma. Namibia's continuing military commitments in the DRC following the failure of the 1999 Lusaka accord (to which Namibia was a signatory), together with the need for additional army resources in north-east Namibia as a result of the Caprivi rebellion and the intensification of operations against UNITA (see above), necessitated the allocation of an additional N $173m. to defence in the supplementary budget for 1999/2000, announced in early 2000.

President Laurent-Désiré Kabila was assassinated in January 2001, and was succeeded by his son, Maj.-Gen. Joseph Kabila. Efforts to resolve the conflict in the DRC were accelerated, and in February proposals for the withdrawal of troops involved in the regional military intervention, including the estimated 2,000 Namibians, were approved by the participating countries, under the aegis of the UN Security Council. In March it was announced that Namibian forces would remain in the DRC until the specified date for withdrawal in May. All but an estimated 150 Namibian troops eventually withdrew from the DRC in September, although other foreign forces were still deployed in large numbers; at least 30 Namibian troops were reported to have been killed in three years of service. All Namibian troops had been withdrawn by the end of 2002.

Germany has been a major aid donor to Namibia since independence, and relations are generally close. In September 1995, none the less, during a visit by the German Chancellor, Helmut Kohl, some 300 members of the Herero ethnic group staged a demonstration outside the German embassy in Windhoek to demand compensation for suffering inflicted on the Herero under German rule. In June 2001 the Herero filed a lawsuit in Washington, DC, USA, against three German companies (Deutsche Bank AG, Woermann Line and Terex Corporation), claiming US $2,000m. in reparation for the alleged exploitation and eventual extermination of some 65,000 Herero in 1904–07; a second lawsuit, for a further US $2,000m., was filed against the German Government in September 2001. The case against Terex Corpn was subsequently withdrawn, after the company claimed that it was under different management at the time of the atrocities. In October 2003 it was reported that the Federal Court in Washington, DC, had ruled that it did not have jurisdiction over the Herero case, and that the Herero were consequently considering filing a lawsuit in New York. In January 2004, at a commemoration of the Herero uprising against German rule in 1904, the Government of Germany expressed its regret for the extermination of Herero, but declared itself unwilling to pay compensation to descendants of the victims. During a visit to Namibia in August 2004 the German Minister of Economic Co-operation and Development, Heidemarie Wieczorek-Zeul, apologized to the Herero Community for the atrocities carried out during 1904–07. During a visit to Germany in early December 2005 President Pohamba rejected an offer of reparations valued at N $160m. Bilateral consultations were scheduled to take place in May 2006 and would include a German proposal to invest N $150m., over a 10-year period, in regions inhabited by descendants of populations that suffered during the colonial occupation. The money would be made available in addition to existing aid commitments, which were reported to amount to some €11m. per year. However, the German Government denied that the additional money was intended as war reparations.

Government

On 21 March 1990 Namibia became independent, and the Constitution took effect. Executive authority is held by the President, who is the Head of State. According to the Constitution, the President shall be directly elected by universal adult suffrage for a term of five years, and permitted to hold office for a maximum of two terms. (In late 1998 legislation was approved whereby the Constitution was to be exceptionally amended to allow the incumbent President to seek a third term of office.) Legislative power is vested in the National Assembly, comprising 72 members directly elected by universal adult suffrage and as many as six non-voting members nominated by the President. The National Assembly has a maximum term of five years. An advisory National Council, comprising two representatives from each of the country's 13 regional councils, elected for a six-year period, operates as the second chamber of parliament. Each region has its own Governor.

Defence

As assessed at November 2007, the Namibian Defence Force numbered an estimated 9,000 men; there was also a 200-strong navy, operating as part of the Ministry of Fisheries and Marine Resources, and a paramilitary force of 6,000. Projected budgetary expenditure on defence for 2007 was N $1,680m.

Economic Affairs

In 2006, according to estimates by the World Bank, Namibia's gross national income (GNI), measured at average 2004–06 prices, was US $6,617m., equivalent to US $3,230 per head (or US $8,110 per head on an international purchasing-power parity basis). During 1996–2006, it was estimated, the population increased at an average annual rate of 1.9% per year, while gross domestic product (GDP) per head increased, in real terms, by an average of 2.2% per year. Overall GDP increased, in real terms, at an average annual rate of 4.2% in 1996–2006. Real GDP increased by 4.6% in 2006.

Agriculture (including hunting, forestry and fishing) contributed 11.3% of GDP in 2006, according to the Bank of Namibia. About 37.4% of the labour force were employed in the sector in 2005. Government revenue from sales of fishing concessions was projected at N $70m. in the financial year ending 31 March 1999, and exports of fish and fish products provided 24.5% of total export earnings in 2003. The principal agricultural activity is beef production; the production of karakul sheepskins is also important. In addition, sealing and ostrich farming are practised on a commercial basis. The main subsistence crops are root crops, millet and maize, although Namibia remains highly dependent on imports of basic foods, especially in drought years. Plantations of seedless grapes were developed on the banks of the Orange river in the late 1990s, and projected growth in production was expected to increase significantly their contribution to export revenue. In recent years Namibia's traditionally rich fisheries have suffered a reverse and in February 2006 fishing quotas were further lowered and a five-year moratorium was declared on new fishing rights. Legislation aimed at developing aquaculture was adopted in 2003 and a number of fish farms were established. Agricultural GDP increased at an average annual rate of 1.9% in 1996–2006; it increased by 10.9% in 2006.

Industry (including mining, manufacturing, construction and power) contributed 32.6% of GDP in 2006, and engaged 14.8% of the employed labour force in 2004. During 1996–2006 industrial GDP increased by an average of 5.0% per year. Industrial GDP increased by 5.8% in 2006.

Mining and quarrying contributed 12.8% of GDP in 2006 and engaged 2.0% of the employed labour force in 2004. Namibia has rich deposits of many minerals, and is among the world's leading producers of gem diamonds (some 98% of diamonds mined in Namibia are of gem quality). Diamond-mining contributed 73.5% of the sector's GDP in 2006, and diamonds are the principal mineral export, accounting for 10.8% of export earnings in 2003. Total production was 1.9m. carats in 2005. In July 2004 the Israeli company Lev Leviev Diamonds established a diamond-cutting and -polishing factory in Windhoek, the first in Namibia and the largest of its kind in Africa. Copper production, which ceased in 1998, following the liquidation of the Tsumeb Corpn, resumed at the former Tsumeb sites in September 2000. In 2005 the smelter at Tsumeb, operated by Ongopolo, remained the only one in the country; imports of foreign ore accounted for around 40% of its production. The Skorpion zinc mine and refinery near Rosh Pinah, opened in mid-2003 by Anglo American plc, was expected to contribute some 4% of GDP on reaching full production in the second half of 2004. Production of an estimated 150,000 metric tons of zinc per year was anticipated over a period of 15 years. Despite health and environmental concerns, a new uranium mine was expected to begin production at Langer Heinrich in 2007, making Namibia the third largest producer in the world of that commodity; the mine was expected to contribute some N $1,400m. to the economy. In addition, zinc, lead, gold, salt, fluorspar, marble and semi-precious stones are extracted, and there are also considerable deposits of hydrocarbons, lithium, manganese, tungsten, cadmium and vanadium. Namibia is also believed to have substantial reserves of coal, iron ore and platinum. Mining GDP increased at an average annual rate of 5.7% in 1996–2006; the sector's GDP decreased by 1.4% in 2005 and by 15.4% in 2006.

Manufacturing contributed 13.0% of GDP in 2006 and engaged 6.2% of the employed labour force in 2004. The sector has hitherto remained underdeveloped, largely owing to Namibia's economic dependence on South Africa. The principal manufacturing activities are the processing of fish and minerals for export; brewing, meat processing and the production of chemicals are also significant. Manufacturing GDP increased by an average of 4.2% per year in 1996–2006; however the sector declined by 8.3% in 2006.

In 2004 96.9% of Namibia's electricity production was derived from hydroelectric power. There is a hydroelectric station at Ruacana, on the Cunene river at the border with Angola, and a second hydroelectric power station was planned at Divundu on the Okavango river; a project to construct a power station at Epupa remained stalled in 2005, following a disagreement between the Namibian and Angolan Governments over the most appropriate site. Final agreement was reached on developing the Kudu offshore gasfield in early 2006. An 800-MW 'gas-to-power' plant would supply the domestic market and the surplus would be exported to South Africa under an agreement with that country's Electricity Supply Commission. Construction of the plant was scheduled to begin in 2007, for completion by 2009. The construction of a further 400-MW gas fired plant at Walvis Bay was proposed in late 2006, and it was envisaged that Namibia would become a significant exporter of electric power. Imports of mineral fuels and lubricants accounted for 10.4% of the value of total merchandise imports in 2003. South Africa supplies all of Namibia's petroleum requirements.

The services sector contributed 56.0% of GDP in 2006. Tourism is expanding rapidly, and has been the focus of a major privatization initiative. The acquisition of Walvis Bay in March 1994, and subsequent establishment there of a free-trade zone, was expected to enhance Namibia's status as an entrepôt for regional trade. By March 2004 it was estimated that the free-trade zone had attracted some N $80m. of direct foreign investment. In 2006 the Government remained the largest employer, accounting for some 70,000 jobs. The GDP of the services sector increased at an average annual rate of 4.5% in 1996–2006. Services GDP increased by 0.3% in 2006.

In 2006 Namibia recorded a visible trade surplus of US $103.6m., and there was a surplus of US $998.5m. on the current account of the balance of payments. South Africa was the dominant source of imports in 2003, providing 80.5% of the total. In that year South Africa was also the principal market for Namibian exports (31.5%), followed by Angola (24.9%), Spain (12.8%) and the United Kingdom (10.4%). The principal exports were food and live animals (notably fish and meat), manufactured goods and diamonds. The principal import groups in that year included machinery and transport equipment, manufactured goods, food and live animals and mineral fuels and lubricants.

In the financial year ending 31 March 2008 Namibia recorded an estimated overall budget deficit of N $747.6m. In 1997 South Africa officially cancelled the external public debt inherited by Namibia at independence. Namibia's external debt was estimated at US $716m. in 2003. The annual rate of inflation averaged 5.5% in 2002–07; consumer prices increased by 6.7% in 2007. According to the 2001 census some 31% of the labour force were unemployed.

Namibia is a member of the Common Market for Eastern and Southern Africa (see p. 205), of the Southern African Development Community (see p. 386), and of the Southern African Customs Union (with Botswana, Lesotho, South Africa and Swaziland); and is also a signatory to the Cotonou Agreement with the European Union.

Namibia's potential for economic prosperity remains high, given its abundant mineral reserves and well-developed infrastructure, both of which were enhanced in 1994 by the acquisition of sovereignty over Walvis Bay and of important diamond-mining rights. The mining of offshore diamond deposits is of increasing importance: the leading diamond producer in the country, Namdeb (a joint venture between the Government and De Beers), accounts for some 10% of national GDP and 30% of export earnings. However, Namibia's economic progress continues to be largely influenced by its dependence on South Africa. (The Namibian dollar, introduced in 1993, is at par with the rand.) The 1995 Export Processing Zones (EPZ) Act aimed to industrialize the economy, which was dominated by primary sector industries and by mid-2005 companies in the EPZ were reported to have attracted more than N $5,200m. in foreign direct investment and contributed N $11,600m. to the economy. Some 7,000 workers were directly employed within the EPZ, principally in the manufacturing industry, which included automotive parts and rebuilding and reconditioning motor vehicles; zinc and copper refinery; and the production of textiles, garments and leatherwear. The Government hoped that the Namibia Diamond Trading Company (established in January 2007) would stimulate production in the country's diamond cutting industry; preliminary estimates suggested that around N $2,000m. of locally excavated rough diamonds would be processed in Namibia by 2009. Restructuring had reduced growth in the minerals sector during 2007; however, rising output of uranium and metals was expected to enable strong recovery in 2008. The central bank forecast real GDP growth of 4.7% for 2008, compared with 3.8% in 2007. High rates of poverty and unemployment (the latter estimated at 36.7% in June 2006) and that fact that more than 20% of the population was infected with HIV/AIDS, remained causes for serious concern, while investment was largely concentrated in the mining sector, which employed capital intensive production techniques and provided relatively few employment opportunities. In a report published in February 2008, the IMF recommended that further measures be implemented to increase job creation in other areas of the private sector and suggested that a 60% increase in capacity would be required to utilize the unemployed labour force.

Education

Under the Constitution, education is compulsory between the ages of six and 16 years, or until primary education has been completed (whichever is the sooner). Primary education consists of seven grades, and secondary education of five. According to UNESCO estimates, in 2002/03 enrolment at primary schools included 74% of children in the relevant age-group (males 71%; females 76%), while the comparable ratio for secondary enrolment in that year was 38% (males 32%; females 44%). In that year there were some 455,077 children enrolled in pre-primary and primary education, and 138,099 in secondary education. Higher education is provided by the University of Namibia, the Technicon of Namibia, a vocational college and four teacher-training colleges. In 2002/03 13,536 students were enrolled in tertiary education. Various schemes for informal adult education are also in operation in an effort to combat illiteracy. Under the 2004/05 budget N $2,613.2m. was allocated to education (20.6% of total government expenditure).

Public Holidays

2008: 1 January (New Year's Day), 21 March (Independence Day), 21–24 March (Easter), 1 May (Workers' Day), 1 May (Ascension Day), 4 May (Cassinga Day), 25 May (Africa Day, anniversary of the OAU's foundation), 26 August (Heroes' Day), 10 December (Human Rights Day), 25–26 December (Christmas), 26 December (Family Day).

2009: 1 January (New Year's Day), 21 March (Independence Day), 10–13 April (Easter), 1 May (Workers' Day), 4 May (Cassinga Day), 21 May (Ascension Day), 25 May (Africa Day, anniversary of the OAU's foundation), 26 August (Heroes' Day), 10 December (Human Rights Day), 25–26 December (Christmas), 26 December (Family Day),

Weights and Measures

The metric system is in use.

Statistical Survey

Source (unless otherwise indicated): Central Bureau of Statistics, National Planning Commission, Government Office Park, Block D2, Luther St, Windhoek; Private Bag 13356, Windhoek; tel. (61) 2834056; fax (61) 237620; e-mail info@npc.gov.na; internet www.npc.gov.na.

Area and Population

AREA, POPULATION AND DENSITY*

Area (sq km)	824,292†
Population (census results)	
21 October 1991	1,409,920
28 August 2001	
Males	936,718
Females	890,136
Total	1,826,854
Population (UN estimates at mid-year)‡	
2005	2,020,000
2006	2,047,000
2007	2,074,000
Density (per sq km) at mid-2007	2.5

* Including data for Walvis Bay, sovereignty over which was transferred from South Africa to Namibia with effect from March 1994. Walvis Bay has an area of 1,124 sq km (434 sq miles) and had a population of 22,999 in 1991.
† 318,261 sq miles.
‡ Source: UN, *World Population Prospects: The 2006 Revision*.

ETHNIC GROUPS
(population, 1988 estimate)

Ovambo	623,000	Caprivian	47,000
Kavango	117,000	Bushmen	36,000
Damara	94,000	Baster	31,000
Herero	94,000	Tswana	7,000
White	80,000	Others	12,000
Nama	60,000	**Total**	1,252,000
Coloured	51,000		

PRINCIPAL TOWNS
(population at 2001 census)

Windhoek	233,529	Rehoboth	21,300
Rundu	44,413	Otjiwarongo	19,614
Walvis Bay	42,015	Keetmanshoop	15,543
Oshakati	28,255	Gobabis	13,856
Katima Mulilo	22,694	Tsumeb	13,108

Mid-2007 (including suburbs, UN estimate): Windhoek (capital) 313,000 (Source: UN, *World Urbanization Prospects: The 2007 Revision*).

BIRTHS AND DEATHS
(annual averages, UN estimates)

	1990–95	1995–2000	2000–05
Birth rate (per 1,000)	39.2	32.7	27.4
Death rate (per 1,000)	8.5	9.4	12.9

Source: UN, *World Population Prospects: The 2006 Revision*.

Expectation of life (WHO estimates, years at birth): 51.8 (males 51.6; females 51.8) in 2005 (Source: WHO, *World Health Statistics*).

EMPLOYMENT
(persons aged 15 to 69 years, 2004 labour force survey)

	Males	Females	Total
Agriculture, hunting, and forestry	64,991	37,645	102,636
Fishing	7,933	4,787	12,720
Mining and quarrying	5,909	1,653	7,562
Manufacturing	12,082	11,673	23,755
Electricity, gas and water	5,031	1,120	6,151
Construction	18,296	1,309	19,605
Wholesale and retail trade, repair of motor vehicles, motorcycles and personal and household goods	27,004	26,891	53,895
Restaurants and hotels	5,889	7,243	13,132
Transport, storage and communications	12,744	3,117	15,861
Financial intermediation	3,506	4,076	7,582
Real estate, renting and business activities	5,280	4,095	9,375
Public administration and defence; compulsory social security	20,216	10,469	30,685
Education	12,313	18,855	31,168
Health and social work	3,533	10,477	14,010
Other community, social and personal services	7,480	5,152	12,632
Private households with employed persons	4,067	20,014	24,081
Extra-territorial organizations and bodies	72	—	72
Not classifiable by economic activity	305	102	407
Total employed	216,651	168,678	385,329

Source: ILO.

Mid-2005 ('000 persons, FAO estimates): Agriculture, etc. 311; Total labour force 832 (Source: FAO).

Health and Welfare

KEY INDICATORS

Total fertility rate (children per woman, 2005)	3.7
Under-5 mortality rate (per 1,000 live births, 2005)	62
HIV/AIDS (% of persons aged 15–49, 2005)	19.60
Physicians (per 1,000 head, 2004)	0.30
Health expenditure (2004): US $ per head (PPP)	407.4
Health expenditure (2004): % of GDP	6.8
Health expenditure (2004): public (% of total)	69.0
Access to water (% of persons, 2004)	87
Access to sanitation (% of persons, 2004)	25
Human Development Index (2005): ranking	125
Human Development Index (2005): value	0.650

For sources and definitions, see explanatory note on p. vi.

NAMIBIA

Agriculture

PRINCIPAL CROPS
('000 metric tons)

	2004	2005	2006
Wheat	8.3	11.0	12.9
Maize	28.2	40.7	60.9
Millet	74.4	47.9	49.0
Sorghum*	6.0	5.8	6.0
Cottonseed*	4.1	4.5	4.5
Grapes*	8.9	9.5	9.5

* FAO estimates.

Aggregate production ('000 metric tons, may include official, semi-official or estimated data): Total cereals 116.9 in 2004, 105.5 in 2005, 128.7 in 2006; Total roots and tubers 295.0 in 2004, 295.0 in 2005, 295.0 in 2006; Total vegetables (incl. melons) 14.8 in 2004, 14.9 in 2005, 14.7 in 2006; Total fruits (excl. melons) 23.4 in 2004, 24.0 in 2005, 24.0 in 2006.

Source: FAO.

LIVESTOCK
('000 head, year ending September)

	2004	2005	2006
Horses	62.7	47.4	46.2
Asses, mules or hinnies*	141.7	147.0	147.0
Cattle	2,309.4	3,133.9	2,384.0
Sheep	2,619.4	2,663.8	2,660.3
Goats	1,997.2	2,043.5	2,061.4
Chickens*	3,500	3,500	3,500

* FAO estimates.
Source: FAO.

LIVESTOCK PRODUCTS
('000 metric tons)

	2004	2005	2006
Cattle meat	42.9	38.6	36.2
Sheep meat	6.6	6.7*	6.7*
Chicken meat*	5.8	6.2	6.2
Cows' milk*	109	109	109
Hen eggs*	1.9	1.9	1.9
Wool (greasy)*	2.2	2.2	2.2

* FAO estimate(s).
Source: FAO.

Forestry

Separate figures are not yet available. Data for Namibia are included in those for South Africa.

Fishing

('000 metric tons, live weight)*

	2003	2004	2005
Capture†	671.6	605.7	588.1
Cape hakes (Stokvisse)	192.3	173.9	158.1
Kingklip	7.2	7.5	5.6
Devil anglerfish	12.9	9.0	11.1
Southern African pilchard	22.3	28.6	27.3
Cape horse mackerel (Maasbanker)	366.9	314.5	324.5
Aquaculture†	0.0	0.0	0.0
Total catch†	671.7	605.8	588.1

* Figures include quantities caught by licensed foreign vessels in Namibian waters and processed in Lüderitz and Walvis Bay. The data exclude aquatic mammals (whales, seals, etc.). The number of South African fur seals caught was: 35,000 in 2003–05 (FAO estimates). The number of Nile crocodiles caught was: 400 in 2005.
† FAO estimates.

Source: FAO.

Mining

(metric tons, unless otherwise indicated)

	2003	2004	2005
Copper ore*	16,175	11,174	10,157
Lead concentrates*	18,782	14,338	14,320
Zinc concentrates*	60,500	66,028	68,000†
Silver ore (kilograms)*	45,100	27,153	30,003
Uranium oxide	2,401	3,583	3,711
Gold ore (kilograms)*	2,508	2,205	2,703
Fluorspar (Fluorite)‡	79,349	104,785	84,211
Salt (unrefined)	697,914	754,351	573,248
Diamonds ('000 metric carats)	1,481	2,004	1,902

* Figures refer to the metal content of ores and concentrates.
† Estimate.
‡ Figures (on a wet-weight basis) refer to acid-grade material.
Source: US Geological Survey.

Industry

SELECTED PRODUCTS
(metric tons)

	2003	2004	2005
Unrefined (blister) copper (unwrought)	26,036	24,704	23,551

Source: US Geological Survey.

Finance

CURRENCY AND EXCHANGE RATES

Monetary Units
100 cents = 1 Namibian dollar (N $).

Sterling, US Dollar and Euro Equivalents (31 December 2007)
£1 sterling = N $13.643;
US $1 = N $6.810;
€1 = N $10.025;
N $100 = £7.33 = US $14.68 = €9.98.

Average Exchange Rate (N $ per US $)
2005   6.3593
2006   6.7716
2007   7.0454

Note: The Namibian dollar was introduced in September 1993, replacing (at par) the South African rand. The rand remained legal tender in Namibia.

NAMIBIA

CENTRAL GOVERNMENT BUDGET
(N $ million, year ending 31 March)

Revenue*	2005/06	2006/07	2007/08†
Taxation	11,963.5	14,591.5	12,982.0
Taxes on income and profits	4,575.7	4,689.0	4,872.0
Taxes on property	110.1	122.0	140.0
Domestic taxes on goods and services	3,272.4	3,186.1	3,296.0
Taxes on international trade and transactions	3,891.9	6,471.4	4,538.0
Other taxes	113.4	123.0	136.0
Non-tax revenue	1,105.3	1,545.5	953.0
Entrepreneurial and property income	542.9	1,048.9	531.4
Fines and forfeitures	17.6	23.5	23.5
Administrative fees and charges	512.4	407.1	364.1
Return on capital from lending and equity	32.4	66.0	34.0
Total	13,068.8	16,137.0	13,935.0

Expenditure	2005/06	2006/07	2007/08†
Current expenditure	11,541.7	12,538.8	12,587.1
Personnel expenditure	5,888.3	6,139.4	6,183.2
Expenditure on goods and other services	1,922.4	2,198.5	2,208.0
Interest payments	1,186.3	1,478.1	1,477.7
Subsidies and other current transfers	2,544.7	2,722.8	2,718.2
Capital expenditure	1,650.9	2,749.0	2,143.5
Capital investment	1,337.4	1,848.2	1,462.5
Capital transfers	106.0	248.8	247.1
Total lending and equity participation	207.5	652.4	433.9
Total	13,192.6	15,287.8	14,730.6

* Excluding grants received from abroad (N $ million): 153.2 in 2005/06; 72.0 in 2006/07; 48.0 in 2007/08 (estimate).
† Estimates.
Source: Bank of Namibia, *Quarterly Bulletin* (December 2007).

INTERNATIONAL RESERVES
(US $ million at 31 December, excl. gold)

	2004	2005	2006
IMF special drawing rights	0.03	0.03	0.03
Reserve position in IMF	0.09	0.10	0.11
Foreign exchange	344.94	311.98	449.44
Total	345.06	312.10	449.58

Source: IMF, *International Financial Statistics*.

MONEY SUPPLY
(N $ million at 31 December)

	2004	2005	2006
Currency outside banks	632.7	680.0	763.4
Demand deposits at deposit money banks	8,898.0	8,728.8	12,915.6
Total money	9,530.7	9,408.8	13,678.9

Source: IMF, *International Financial Statistics*.

COST OF LIVING
(Consumer Price Index; base: December 2001 = 100)

	2005	2006	2007
Food and non-alcoholic beverages	124.4	132.5	148.7
Alcoholic beverages and tobacco	130.1	139.7	149.9
Clothing and footwear	108.2	105.0	108.5
Housing, fuel and power	124.3	128.3	132.7
Health	112.6	110.1	115.2
Transport	132.3	143.0	151.5
Communications	108.5	109.2	110.8
Recreation and culture	111.1	113.9	119.1
Education	140.6	149.9	158.8
All items (incl. others)	122.9	129.1	137.7

NATIONAL ACCOUNTS
(N $ million at current prices)

National Income and Product

	2004	2005	2006
Compensation of employees	13,903	14,973	16,473
Operating surplus	12,863	14,023	19,594
Domestic factor incomes	26,766	28,996	36,067
Consumption of fixed capital	5,913	6,585	6,300
Gross domestic product (GDP) at factor cost	32,680	35,581	42,367
Indirect taxes	4,030	4,367	4,847
Less Subsidies	213	238	244
GDP in purchasers' values	36,496	39,710	46,971
Factor income received from abroad	1,483	955	1,185
Less Factor income paid abroad	944	1,670	1,674
Gross national income	37,035	38,995	46,481
Less Consumption of fixed capital	5,913	6,585	6,300
National income in market prices	31,122	32,410	40,181
Other current transfers from abroad	4,529	4,548	6,771
Less Other current transfers paid abroad	225	286	306
National disposable income	35,426	36,672	46,646

Expenditure on the Gross Domestic Product

	2004	2005	2006
Government final consumption expenditure	9,027	9,734	10,554
Private final consumption expenditure	21,031	20,882	23,204
Increase in stocks	175	530	321
Gross fixed capital formation	9,190	9,727	12,235
Total domestic expenditure	39,423	40,873	46,313
Exports of goods and services	16,757	18,901	24,534
Less Imports of goods and services	18,992	20,261	24,676
Statistical discrepancy	–693	197	799
GDP in purchasers' values	36,496	39,711	46,971
GDP in constant 1995 prices	18,201	19,077	19,854

Gross Domestic Product by Economic Activity

	2004	2005	2006
Agriculture and forestry	1,873	2,398	2,909
Fishing	1,547	1,916	1,958
Mining and quarrying	3,489	3,391	5,518
Diamond mining	3,048	2,782	4,054
Manufacturing	4,001	4,055	5,628
Electricity and water	1,197	1,344	1,250
Construction	1,100	1,247	1,743
Wholesale and retail trade, repairs, etc.	3,985	4,235	5,191
Hotels and restaurants	653	670	724
Transport, storage and communications	2,671	3,019	3,341
Financial intermediation	1,213	1,455	1,562
Real estate and business services	3,542	3,764	4,073
Government services	7,124	7,752	8,269
Other community, social and personal services	282	320	354
Other services	647	673	721
Sub-total	33,324	36,238	43,242
Less Financial services indirectly measured	394	440	544
GDP at basic prices	32,930	35,798	42,698
Taxes, less subsidies, on products	3,567	3,913	4,273
GDP in purchasers' values	36,496	39,711	46,971

NAMIBIA

BALANCE OF PAYMENTS
(US $ million)

	2004	2005	2006
Exports of goods f.o.b.	1,827.5	2,069.9	2,647.9
Imports of goods f.o.b.	−2,110.3	−2,326.2	−2,544.2
Trade balance	−282.8	−256.3	103.6
Exports of services	475.4	413.5	528.9
Imports of services	−420.2	−368.8	−429.7
Balance on goods and services	−227.7	−211.5	202.8
Other income received	216.2	225.3	234.4
Other income paid	−212.1	−352.6	−318.9
Balance on goods, services and income	−223.6	−338.7	118.3
Current transfers received	642.1	651.1	925.6
Current transfers paid	−34.9	−44.7	−45.4
Current balance	383.6	267.6	998.5
Capital account (net)	77.2	79.6	83.3
Direct investment abroad	22.7	12.3	12.8
Direct investment from abroad	88.2	166.1	−30.9
Portfolio investment assets	−824.6	−1,052.7	−1,066.3
Portfolio investment liabilities	4.5	5.1	4.7
Other investment assets	44.6	43.0	−354.1
Other investment liabilities	−113.6	−48.6	−25.0
Net errors and omissions	115.3	163.5	133.7
Overall balance	−202.1	−364.1	−243.1

Source: IMF, *International Financial Statistics*.

External Trade

PRINCIPAL COMMODITIES
(US $ million)

Imports c.i.f.	2001	2002	2003
Food and live animals	172.4	138.6	163.7
Mineral fuels and lubricants	160.4	158.8	147.0
Petroleum and petroleum products	158.5	149.4	142.6
Chemicals and related products	166.4	116.3	113.7
Basic manufactures	267.5	224.0	268.3
Non-metallic mineral manufactures	51.0	41.0	52.0
Metal products	86.2	75.9	68.5
Machinery and transport equipment	533.5	447.4	460.0
Machinery specialized for particular industries	89.9	60.6	57.7
General industrial machinery, equipment and parts	51.3	60.9	57.4
Telecommunications and sound equipment	38.2	27.0	44.0
Telecommunications equipment, parts and accessories	28.1	17.4	27.9
Electrical machinery, apparatus, etc.	71.1	62.0	69.8
Road vehicles	180.9	132.2	163.3
Passenger motor vehicles (excl. buses)	119.7	83.2	103.1
Other transport equipment	44.4	51.8	14.9
Miscellaneous manufactured articles	185.5	154.1	164.2
Clothing and accessories	46.0	37.1	35.5
Total (incl. others)	1,552.9	1,310.1	1,427.9

Exports f.o.b.	2001	2002	2003
Food and live animals	438.0	391.4	479.8
Fish, shellfish and preparations thereof	315.9	270.8	318.9
Fresh or frozen fish	293.8	253.6	305.2
Beverages and tobacco	67.2	77.7	139.7
Beverages	65.5	74.3	136.9
Alcoholic beverages	49.0	52.4	68.0
Beer made from malt	43.5	41.0	55.2
Crude materials (inedible) except fuels	132.5	146.7	84.2
Metal ores and scrap	103.6	116.8	49.3
Ores and concentrates of uranium and thorium	102.2	115.8	47.1
Basic manufactures	485.2	471.3	229.4
Non-metallic mineral manufactures	450.3	430.5	151.6
Pearl, precious and semi-precious stones	448.1	425.4	141.3
Diamonds	447.8	424.3	141.0
Machinery and transport equipment	54.6	74.5	112.3
Miscellaneous manufactured articles	176.8	66.4	197.2
Printed matter	154.8	31.0	147.8
Total (incl. others)	1,404.5	1,282.9	1,303.7

Source: UN, *International Trade Statistics Yearbook*.

PRINCIPAL TRADING PARTNERS
(US $ million)

Imports c.i.f.	2001	2002	2003
China, People's Repub.	16.9	11.7	18.2
Germany	30.6	41.1	33.4
South Africa	1,335.9	1,013.3	1,148.9
Spain	13.0	16.3	19.4
United Kingdom	18.2	34.3	17.5
USA	14.0	26.3	14.2
Total (incl. others)	1,552.9	1,310.1	1,427.9

Exports f.o.b.	2001	2002	2003
Angola	82.1	186.5	324.8
Belgium	7.7	7.5	7.1
Canada	0.5	4.1	12.9
Congo, Republic	5.0	9.1	33.8
France	25.2	82.4	23.4
Germany	12.2	14.7	14.5
Italy	24.5	23.3	23.0
Netherlands	19.4	17.3	13.9
South Africa	433.5	326.1	410.6
Spain	184.5	155.8	167.0
United Kingdom	495.5	315.1	135.7
USA	41.6	40.4	35.2
Total (incl. others)	1,404.5	1,282.9	1,303.7

Source: UN, *International Trade Statistics Yearbook*.

Transport

RAILWAYS

	2002/03	2003/04
Freight (million net ton-km)	1,244.6	1,247.4
Passengers carried	125,656	112,033

Source: TransNamib Holdings Ltd, *2004 Annual Report*.

NAMIBIA

ROAD TRAFFIC
(motor vehicles in use at 31 December)

	1994*	1995*	1996
Passenger cars	61,269	62,500	74,875
Buses and coaches	5,098	5,200	10,175
Lorries and vans	60,041	61,300	59,352
Motorcycles and mopeds	1,450	1,480	1,520

* Estimates.

Total vehicles in use (excl. motorcycles and mopeds): 146,999 in 2000; 152,794 in 2001; 166,998 in 2002.

2002: Passenger cars 82,580; Buses and coaches 4,922; Lorries and vans 79,496; Motorcycles and mopeds 3,416.

Source: International Road Federation, *World Road Statistics*.

SHIPPING

Merchant Fleet
(at 31 December)

	2004	2005	2006
Number of vessels	157	178	173
Displacement (gross registered tons)	92,299	106,350	102,901

Source: Lloyd's Register-Fairplay, *World Fleet Statistics*.

Sea-borne Freight Traffic
('000 freight tons*, year ending 30 August, unless otherwise indicated)

	1999/2000†	2000/01	2001/02
Port of Lüderitz:			
Goods loaded	93.6	143.3	171.2
Goods unloaded	39.5	105.1	101.7
Goods transhipped	14.1	10.0	4.6
Containers handled (total TEUs)	2,311	2,320	2,480
Port of Walvis Bay:			
Goods loaded	723.4	720.7	915.8
Goods unloaded	1,460.3	1,452.1	1,443.1
Goods transhipped	40.0	56.6	60.3
Containers handled (total TEUs)	24,859	25,768	31,569

* One freight ton = 40 cu ft (1.133 cu m) of cargo capacity.
† Year ending 30 September 2000.

Source: Namibian Ports Authority.

CIVIL AVIATION
(traffic on scheduled services)

	2001	2002	2003
Kilometres flown (million)	9	9	11
Passengers carried ('000)	215	222	266
Passenger-km (million)	754	760	930
Total ton-km (million)	151	98	139

Source: UN, *Statistical Yearbook*.

Tourism

FOREIGN TOURIST ARRIVALS*

Country of origin	2002	2003	2005†
Angola	278,816	222,752	281,365
Botswana	29,328	22,679	22,333
Germany	61,236	58,036	61,222
South Africa	243,894	222,009	230,949
United Kingdom	19,560	19,291	20,978
Zimbabwe	19,145	17,795	22,765
Total (incl. others)	757,201	695,221	777,890

* Excluding same-day visitors: 947,778 in 2002; 917,000 in 2003; 973,168 in 2005.
† Figures for 2004 were not available.

Tourism receipts (US $ million, excl. passenger transport): 333 in 2003; 405 in 2004; 348 in 2005.

Source: World Tourism Organization.

Communications Media

	2004	2005
Telephones ('000 main lines in use)	127.9	138.9
Mobile cellular telephones ('000 subscribers)	286.1	495
Personal computers ('000 in use)	220	n.a.
Internet users ('000)	75.0	n.a.

Television receivers ('000 in use): 67 in 2000.

Source: International Telecommunication Union.

Radio receivers ('000 in use): 232 in 1997 (Source: UNESCO, *Statistical Yearbook*).

Daily newspapers (2004): 4 (average circulation 55,800) (Source: UNESCO, *Statistical Yearbook*).

Non-daily newspapers (2004): 3 (average circulation 240,000) (Source: UNESCO, *Statistical Yearbook*).

Education

(2004/05, unless otherwise indicated)

	Teachers	Males	Females	Total
Pre-primary	1,314*	23,442†	25,740†	49,182†
Primary	13,113	202,832	201,366	404,198
Secondary	5,896	69,456	78,648	148,104
Tertiary	898†	5,709‡	6,488‡	12,197‡

* Estimate for 1999/2000.
† 2002/03.
‡ 2003/04.

Institutions (1998/99): Primary 1,362.

Source: UNESCO, Institute for Statistics.

Adult literacy rate (UNESCO estimates): 85.0% (males 83.5%; females 86.8%) in 2001 (Source: UNESCO Institute for Statistics).

Directory

The Constitution

The Constitution of the Republic of Namibia took effect at independence on 21 March 1990. Its principal provisions are summarized below:

THE REPUBLIC

The Republic of Namibia is a sovereign, secular, democratic and unitary State and the Constitution is the supreme law.

FUNDAMENTAL HUMAN RIGHTS AND FREEDOMS

The fundamental rights and freedoms of the individual are guaranteed regardless of sex, race, colour, ethnic origin, religion, creed or social or economic status. All citizens shall have the right to form and join political parties. The practice of racial discrimination shall be prohibited.

THE PRESIDENT

Executive power shall be vested in the President and the Cabinet. The President shall be the Head of State and of the Government and

NAMIBIA

the Commander-in-Chief of the Defence Force. The President shall be directly elected by universal and equal adult suffrage, and must receive more than 50% of the votes cast. The term of office shall be five years; one person may not hold the office of President for more than two terms.*

THE CABINET

The Cabinet shall consist of the President, the Prime Minister and such other ministers as the President may appoint from members of the National Assembly. The President may also appoint a Deputy Prime Minister. The functions of the members of the Cabinet shall include directing the activities of ministries and government departments, initiating bills for submission to the National Assembly, formulating, explaining and assessing for the National Assembly the budget of the State and its economic development plans, formulating, explaining and analysing for the National Assembly Namibia's foreign policy and foreign trade policy and advising the President on the state of national defence.

THE NATIONAL ASSEMBLY

Legislative power shall be vested in the National Assembly, which shall be composed of 72 members elected by general, direct and secret ballots and not more than six non-voting members appointed by the President by virtue of their special expertise, status, skill or experience. Every National Assembly shall continue for a maximum period of five years, but it may be dissolved by the President before the expiry of its term.

THE NATIONAL COUNCIL

The National Council shall consist of two members from each region (elected by regional councils from among their members) and shall have a life of six years. The functions of the National Council shall include considering all bills passed by the National Assembly, investigating any subordinate legislation referred to it by the National Assembly for advice, and recommending legislation to the National Assembly on matters of regional concern.

OTHER PROVISIONS

Other provisions relate to the administration of justice (see under Judicial System), regional and local government, the public service commission, the security commission, the police, defence forces and prison service, finance, and the central bank and national planning commission. The repeal of, or amendments to, the Constitution require the approval of two-thirds of the members of the National Assembly and two-thirds of the members of the National Council; if the proposed repeal or amendment secures a majority of two-thirds of the members of the National Assembly, but not a majority of two-thirds of the members of the National Council, the President may make the proposals the subject of a national referendum, in which a two-thirds' majority is needed for approval of the legislation.

* In late 1998 the National Assembly and National Council approved legislation whereby the Constitution was to be exceptionally amended to allow the incumbent President to seek a third term of office.

The Government

HEAD OF STATE

President and Commander-in-Chief of the Defence Force: HIFIKEPUNYE POHAMBA (elected by direct suffrage 15–16 November 2004; took office 21 March 2005).

THE CABINET
(April 2008)

President: HIFIKEPUNYE POHAMBA.
Prime Minister: NAHAS ANGULA.
Deputy Prime Minister: Dr LIBERTINA AMATHILA.
Minister of Presidential Affairs: ALBERT KAWANA.
Minister of Home Affairs and Immigration: ROSALIA NGHIDINWA.
Minister of Safety and Security: Dr NICKEY IYAMBO.
Minister of Defence: Maj.-Gen. (retd) CHARLES NAMOLOH.
Minister of Foreign Affairs: MARCO HAUSIKO.
Minister of Information and Communication Technology: JOEL KAAPANDA.
Minister of Education: NANGOLO MBUMBA.
Minister of Mines and Energy: ERRKI NGHIMTINA.
Minister of Justice and Attorney-General: PENDUKENI IVULA-ITHANA.
Minister of Trade and Industry: Dr HAGE GEINGOB.

Minister of Agriculture, Water and Forestry: JOHN MUTORWA.
Minister of Finance: SAARA KUUGONGELWA-AMADHILA.
Minister of Health and Social Services: RICHARD KAMWI.
Minister of Labour and Social Welfare: IMMANUEL NGATJIZEKO.
Minister of Regional and Local Government and Housing and Rural Development: JERRY EKANDJO.
Minister of Environment and Tourism: NETUMBO NANDI-NDAITWAH.
Minister of Works, Transport and Communications: HELMUT ANGULA.
Minister of Lands, Resettlement and Rehabilitation: ALPHEUS NARUSEB.
Minister of Fisheries and Marine Resources: Dr ABRAHAM IYAMBO.
Minister of Gender Equality and Child Welfare: MARLENE MUNGUNDA.
Minister of Youth, National Service, Sport and Culture: WILLEM KONJORE.
Minister of War Veterans: Dr NGARIKUTUKE TJIRIANGE.

Also attending Cabinet

Dir-Gen. of the Namibia Central Intelligence Agency: Lt-Gen. LUCAS HANGULA.
Dir-Gen. of the National Planning Commission: PETER KATJAVIVI.

MINISTRIES

Office of the President: State House, Robert Mugabe Ave, PMB 13339, Windhoek; tel. (61) 2707111; fax (61) 221780; e-mail angolo@op.gov.na; internet www.op.gov.na.

Office of the Prime Minister: Robert Mugabe Ave, PMB 13338, Windhoek; tel. (61) 2879111; fax (61) 230648; internet www.opm.gov.na.

Ministry of Agriculture, Water and Forestry: Government Office Park, PMB 13184, Windhoek; tel. (61) 2087111; fax (61) 221733; internet www.mawf.gov.na.

Ministry of Defence: PMB 13307, Windhoek; tel. (61) 2042055; fax (61) 232518; e-mail psecretary@mod.gov.na; internet www.mod.gov.na.

Ministry of Education: Government Office Park, PMB 13186, Windhoek; internet www.mec.gov.na; tel. (61) 2933358; fax (61) 2933368.

Ministry of Environment and Tourism: Swabou Bldg, Post St Mall, PMB 13346, Windhoek; tel. (61) 2842111; fax (61) 221930; e-mail kshangula@met.gov.na; internet www.met.gov.na.

Ministry of Finance: Fiscus Bldg, John Meinert St, PMB 13185, Windhoek; tel. (61) 2092931; fax (61) 227702; internet www.mof.gov.na.

Ministry of Fisheries and Marine Resources: Uhland and Goethe Sts, Private Bag 13355, Windhoek; tel. (61) 2059111; fax (61) 233286; e-mail mfmr@mfmr.gov.na; internet www.mfmr.gov.na.

Ministry of Foreign Affairs: Govt Bldgs, Robert Mugabe Ave, PMB 13347, Windhoek; tel. (61) 2829111; fax (61) 223937; e-mail headquarters@mfa.gov.na; internet www.mfa.gov.na.

Ministry of Gender Equality and Child Welfare: Private Bag 13359, Windhoek; tel. (61) 2833111; fax (61) 238941; e-mail genderequality@mgecw.gov.na; internet www.mgecw.gov.na.

Ministry of Health and Social Services: Old State Hospital, Harvey St, PMB 13198, Windhoek; tel. (61) 2039111; fax (61) 227607; internet www.mhss.gov.na.

Ministry of Home Affairs and Immigration: Cohen Bldg, Kasino St, PMB 13200, Windhoek; tel. (61) 2922111; fax (61) 2922185; internet www.mha.gov.na.

Ministry of Information and Communication Technology: Windhoek.

Ministry of Justice: Justitia Bldg, Independence Ave, PMB 13248, Windhoek; tel. (61) 2805111; fax (61) 221615; includes the office of the Attorney-General.

Ministry of Labour and Social Welfare: 32 Mercedes St, Khomasdal, PMB 19005, Windhoek; tel. (61) 2066111; fax (61) 212323; internet www.mol.gov.na.

Ministry of Lands, Resettlement and Rehabilitation: Brendan Simbwaye Bldg, Goethe St, PMB 13343, Windhoek; tel. (61) 2852111; fax (61) 254240.

Ministry of Mines and Energy: 1st Aviation Rd, PMB 13297, Windhoek; tel. (61) 2848111; fax (61) 238643; e-mail info@mme.gov.na; internet www.mme.gov.na.

NAMIBIA

Ministry of Presidential Affairs: Windhoek.

Ministry of Regional and Local Government and Housing and Rural Development: PMB 13289, Windhoek; tel. (61) 2975111; fax (61) 226049; internet www.mrlgh.gov.na.

Ministry of Safety and Security: Brendan Simbwaye Bldg, Goethe St, PMB 13323; tel. (61) 2846111; fax (61) 233879.

Ministry of Trade and Industry: Uhland St, cnr Goethe St, Private Bag 13340, Windhoek; tel. (61) 2837111; fax (61) 220227; internet www.mti.gov.na.

Ministry of War Veterans: Windhoek.

Ministry of Works, Transport and Communications: PMB 13341, Windhoek; tel. (61) 2088111; fax (61) 228560.

Ministry of Youth, National Service, Sport and Culture: Windhoek.

President and Legislature

PRESIDENT

Presidential Election, 15–16 November 2004

Candidate	Votes	% of votes
Hifikepunye Pohamba (SWAPO)	625,605	76.44
Ben Ulenga (CoD)	59,547	7.28
Katuutire Kaura (DTA)	41,905	5.12
Kuaima Riruako (NUDO)	34,616	4.23
Justus Garoeb (UDF)	31,354	3.83
Henk Mudge (RP)	15,955	1.95
Kosie Pretorius (MAG)	9,738	1.15
Total	**818,360**	**100.00**

NATIONAL ASSEMBLY*

Speaker: Theo-Ben Gurirab.

General Election, 15–16 November 2004

Party	Votes	% of votes	Seats
South West Africa People's Organisation of Namibia (SWAPO)	620,787	76.11	55
Congress of Democrats (CoD)	59,465	7.29	5
Democratic Turnhalle Alliance of Namibia (DTA)	41,714	5.11	4
National Unity Democratic Organisation (NUDO)	33,874	4.15	3
United Democratic Front (UDF)	29,336	3.60	3
Republican Party	15,965	1.96	1
Monitor Action Group (MAG)	6,920	0.85	1
Namibia Movement for Democratic Change (NMDC)	4,138	0.51	—
South West African National Union (SWANU)	3,438	0.42	—
Total	**815,637**	**100.00**	**72**

* In addition to the 72 directly elected members, the President of the Republic is empowered to nominate as many as six non-voting members.

NATIONAL COUNCIL

Chairman: Asser Kuveri Kapere.

The second chamber of parliament is the advisory National Council, comprising two representatives from each of the country's 13 Regional Councils, elected for a period of six years.

Election Commission

Electoral Commission of Namibia (ECN): Daniel Munamava St, POB 13352 Windhoek; tel. (61) 220337; fax (61) 224174; internet www.ecn.gov.na; f. 1992; independent; Chair. Victor L. Tonchi; Dir of Elections and CEO Philemon H. Kanime.

Political Organizations

All People's Party of Namibia (APP): f. 2008 in Kavango region; splinter group of the CoD, which split in late 2007; Chair. Ignatius Shixwameni.

Congress of Democrats (CoD): 8 Storch St, POB 40905, Windhoek; tel. (61) 256954; fax (61) 256980; internet www.cod.org.na; f. 1999 after split from SWAPO; Leader Ben Ulenga; Nat. Chair. Tsudao Gurirab; Sec.-Gen. Kala Gertze.

Democratic Turnhalle Alliance of Namibia (DTA): POB 173, Windhoek 9000; tel. 238530; fax 226494; e-mail m.venaani@parliament.gov.na; f. 1977 as a coalition of 11 ethnically based political groupings; reorg. in 1991 to allow dual membership of coalition groupings and the main party; Pres. Katuutire Kaura; Chair. Johan de Waal; Sec.-Gen. Alois Gende.

Monitor Action Group (MAG): POB 80808, Olympia, Windhoek; tel. (61) 252008; fax (61) 229242; e-mail monitor@cyberhost.com.na; f. 1991 by mems of the National Party of South West Africa alliance; Leader and Chair. J. W. F. (Kosie) Pretorius.

Namibia Democratic Movement for Change (NDMC): POB 60043, Katutura; tel. and fax (61) 297795; f. 2004; Pres. Frans Goagoseb; Sec.-Gen. Claudia Namises.

National Unity Democratic Organisation (NUDO): POB 60043, Katutura; tel. and fax (61) 297795; f. 1964 by the Herero Chiefs' Council; joined the DTA in 1977; broke away from the DTA in 2003; Pres. Chief Kuaima Riruako; Sec.-Gen. Joseph Kauandenge.

Rally for Democracy and Progress (RDP): f. 2007 by fmr mems of ruling SWAPO party; Chair. Jesaya Nyamu (acting); Pres. Hidipo Hamutenya (acting).

Republican Party: 6 Hügel St, POB 20020, Windhoek; tel. (61) 225632; fax (61) 225636; f. 1977 after breaking away from the National Party; joined the DTA later in 1977; dissolved in 1991; reactivated in 2003 after breaking away from the DTA; Pres. Henk Mudge; Sec.-Gen. Carola Engelbrecht.

SWAPO Party of Namibia (SWAPO): POB 1071, Windhoek; tel. (61) 238364; fax (61) 232368; f. 1957 as the Ovamboland People's Congress; renamed South West Africa People's Organisation in 1960; adopted present name in 1997; Pres. Dr Samuel Daniel Nujoma; Vice-Pres. Hifikepunye Pohamba; Sec.-Gen. Ngarikutuke Tjiriange.

South West African National Union (SWANU): Windhoek; f. 1959 by mems of the Herero Chiefs' Council; formed alliance with the Workers' Revolutionary Party in 1999; Pres. Rihupisa Kandando.

United Democratic Front (UDF): POB 20037, Windhoek; tel. (61) 230683; fax (61) 237175; f. 1989 as a centrist coalition of eight parties; reorg. as a single party in 1999; Nat. Chair. Eric Biwa; Pres. Justus Garoeb.

Workers' Revolutionary Party: Windhoek; f. 1989; Trotskyist; Leaders Werner Mamugwe, Hewat Beukes.

The **Caprivi Liberation Army (CLA)**, f. 1998 as the Caprivi Liberation Movement, seeks secession of the Caprivi Strip; conducts military operations from bases in Zambia and Angola; political wing operates from Denmark as the **Caprivi National Union**, led by Mishake Muyongo and Boniface Mamili.

Diplomatic Representation

EMBASSIES AND HIGH COMMISSIONS IN NAMIBIA

Algeria: 111A Gloudina St, Ludwigsdorf, POB 3079, Windhoek; tel. (61) 221507; fax (61) 236376; Chargé d'affaires a.i. Youcef Delileche.

Angola: Angola House, 3 Dr Agostinho Neto St, Ausspannplatz, PMB 12020, Windhoek; tel. (61) 227535; fax (61) 221498; Ambassador Manuel A. D. Rodriguez.

Botswana: 101 Nelson Mandela Ave, POB 20359, Windhoek; tel. (61) 221942; fax (61) 221948; High Commissioner Norman Moleboge.

Brazil: 52 Bismarck St, POB 24166, Windhoek; tel. (61) 237368; fax (61) 233389; e-mail brasemb@mweb.com.na; Ambassador Christiano Windhoek.

China, People's Republic: 13 Wecka St, POB 22777, Windhoek; tel. (61) 222089; fax (61) 225544; e-mail chinaemb@iafrica.com.na; internet na.chineseembassy.org; Ambassador Ren Xiaoping.

Congo, Republic: 9 Korner St, POB 22970, Windhoek; tel. (61) 257517; fax (61) 240796; Ambassador Patrice Ndounga.

Cuba: 31 Omuramba Rd, Eros, POB 23866, Windhoek; tel. (61) 227072; fax (61) 231584; Ambassador Ana Vilma Vallejera Rodríguez.

Egypt: 10 Berg St, POB 11853, Windhoek; tel. (61) 221501; fax (61) 228856; Ambassador Mohamed Hadi Mostafa El-Tonsi.

Finland: 2 Crohn St (cnr Bahnhof St), POB 3649, Windhoek; tel. (61) 221355; fax (61) 221349; e-mail sanomat.win@formin.fi; internet www.finland.org.na; Chargé d'affaires a.i. Seija Kinni-Huttunen.

NAMIBIA

France: 1 Goethe St, POB 20484, Windhoek; tel. (61) 2276700; fax (61) 231436; e-mail frambwdk@iafrica.com.na; internet www.ambafrance-na.org; Ambassador PHILIPPE BOSSIÈRE.

Germany: Sanlam Centre, 6th Floor, 154 Independence Ave, POB 231, Windhoek; tel. (61) 273100; fax (61) 222981; e-mail germany@iway.na; internet www.windhuk.diplo.de; Ambassador ARNE FREIHERR VON KITTLITZ UND OTTENDORF.

Ghana: 5 Nelson Mandela Ave, POB 24165, Windhoek; tel. (61) 221341; fax (61) 221343; High Commissioner MAUREEN A. AMEMA-TEKPOR.

India: 97 Nelson Mandela Ave, POB 1209, Windhoek; tel. (61) 226037; fax (61) 237320; e-mail hicomind@mweb.com.na; internet www.highcommissionofindia.web.na; High Commissioner TSEWANG TOPDEN.

Indonesia: 103 Nelson Mandela Ave, POB 20691, Windhoek; tel. (61) 2851000; fax (61) 2851231; e-mail kbri@iafrica.com.na; internet www.indonesiawindhoek.org; Ambassador (vacant).

Kenya: Kenya House, 5th Floor, 134 Robert Mugabe Ave, POB 2889, Windhoek; tel. (61) 226836; fax (61) 221409; e-mail rboit@mfa.go.ke; High Commissioner ROSE BOIT.

Libya: 69 Burg St, Luxury Hill, POB 124, Windhoek; tel. (61) 234454; fax (61) 234471; Ambassador SALAM MOHAMMED KRAYEM; (designate).

Malawi: 56 Bismarck St, POB 13254, Windhoek 9000; tel. (61) 221391; fax (61) 227056; e-mail mhc@mweb.co.na; High Commissioner F. CHIKUTA.

Malaysia: 12 Babs Street, Ludwigsdorf, POB 312, Windhoek; tel. (61) 259344; fax (61) 259343; e-mail malwdhoek@kln.gov.my; High Commissioner HAYATI BT ISMAIL.

Mexico: Southern Life Tower, 3rd Floor, 39 Post St Mall, POB 13220, Windhoek; tel. (61) 229082; fax (61) 229180; Ambassador MAURICIO DE MARÍA Y CAMPOS.

Nigeria: 4 Omuramba Rd, Eros Park, POB 23547, Windhoek; tel. (61) 232103; fax (61) 221639; High Commissioner OKUN AYODEJI.

Russia: 4 Christian St, POB 3826, Windhoek; tel. (61) 228671; fax (61) 229061; Ambassador NIKOLAI M. GRIBKOV.

South Africa: RSA House, cnr Jan Jonker and Nelson Mandela Aves, POB 23100, Windhoek; tel. (61) 229765; fax (61) 224140; Chargé d'affairs a.i. P. J. COETZEE.

Spain: 58 Bismarck St, POB 21811, Windhoek-West; tel. (61) 223066; fax (61) 223046; e-mail emb.windhoek@mae.es; Ambassador MARÍA VICTORIA SCOLA PLIEGO.

Sweden: Sanlam Centre, 9th Floor, POB 23087, Windhoek; tel. (61) 2859111; fax (61) 2859222; e-mail ambassaden.windhoek@sida.se; Chargé d'affaires a.i. LENA JOHANSSON BLOMSTRAND.

United Kingdom: 116 Robert Mugabe Ave, POB 22202, Windhoek; tel. (61) 274800; fax (61) 228895; e-mail general.windhoek@fco.gov.uk; internet www.britishhighcommission.gov.uk/namibia; High Commissioner MARK BENSBERG.

USA: 14 Lossen St, Ausspannplatz, PMB 12029, Windhoek 9000; tel. (61) 221601; fax (61) 229792; internet windhoek.usembassy.gov; Ambassador GAIL DENNISE MATHIEU.

Venezuela: Southern Life Tower, 3rd Floor, 39 Post St Mall, PMB 13353, Windhoek; tel. (61) 227905; fax (61) 227804; Chargé d'affaires a.i. JORGE JIMÉNEZ.

Zambia: 22 Sam Nujoma Dr., cnr Mandume Ndemufayo Rd, POB 22882, Windhoek; tel. (61) 237610; fax (61) 228162; e-mail zahico@iway.na; internet www.zahico.iway.na; High Commissioner GRIFFIN NYIRONGO.

Zimbabwe: cnr Independence Ave and Grimm St, POB 23056, Windhoek; tel. (61) 228134; fax (61) 226859; Ambassador CHIPO ZINDOGA.

Judicial System

Judicial power is exercised by the Supreme Court, the High Court and a number of Magistrate and Lower Courts. The Constitution provides for the appointment of an Ombudsman.

Chief Justice: PETER SHIVUTE.

Religion

It is estimated that about 90% of the population are Christians.

CHRISTIANITY

Council of Churches in Namibia: 8 Mont Blanc St, POB 41, Windhoek; tel. (61) 374054; fax (61) 62786; e-mail ccn.gensec@mweb.com.na; f. 1978; eight mem. churches; Pres. Bishop JOHANNES SINDANO; Gen. Sec. Rev. PHILLIP STRYDOM.

The Anglican Communion

Namibia comprises a single diocese in the Anglican Church of Southern Africa (formerly the Church of the Province of Southern Africa). The Metropolitan of the Province is the Archbishop of Cape Town, South Africa. In 2006 there were an estimated 110,000 Anglicans in the country.

Bishop of Namibia: Rt Rev. NATHANIEL NDAXUMA NAKWATUMBAH, POB 57, Windhoek; tel. (61) 238920; fax (61) 225903; e-mail bishop@anglicanchurchnamibia.com.

Dutch Reformed Church

Dutch Reformed Church in Namibia (Nederduitse Gereformeerde Kerk): 34 Feldstreet, POB 389, Windhoek; tel. (61) 374350; fax (61) 227287; e-mail clem@ngkn.com.na; internet www.ngkn.com.na; f. 1898; Sec. Rev. CLEM MARAIS; 22,500 mems in 44 congregations (2006).

Evangelical Lutheran

Evangelical Lutheran Church in Namibia (ELCIN): PMB 2018, Ondangwa; tel. (65) 240241; fax (65) 240472; e-mail head.office@elcin.org.na; f. 1870; became autonomous in 1954; Presiding Bishop Dr THOMAS SHIVUTE; Gen. Sec. Rev. ELIKAIM N. K. SHAANIKA; 663,338 mems (2005).

Evangelical Lutheran Church in the Republic of Namibia (ELCRN) (Rhenish Mission Church): POB 5069, Windhoek; tel. (61) 224531; fax (61) 226775; f. 1957; became autonomous in 1972; Pres. Bishop Dr ZEPHANIA KAMEETA; 250,000 mems in 55 congregations.

German Evangelical-Lutheran Church in Namibia (ELCIN—GELC): POB 233, Windhoek; tel. (61) 224294; fax (61) 221470; e-mail delk@namibnet.com; Pres. Bishop REINHARD KEDING; 5,000 mems.

Methodist

African Methodist Episcopal Church: POB 798, Keetmanshoop; tel. (63) 222347; fax (63) 223026; e-mail erikke5@hotmail.com; bishop resident in Cape Town, South Africa; Rep. Rev. Dr ANDREAS BIWA; c. 8,000 mems in 33 churches.

Methodist Church of Southern Africa: POB 143, Windhoek; tel. (61) 228921; fax (61) 229202; e-mail central@iway.na; Rep. Rev. EDGAR LUKEN.

The Roman Catholic Church

Namibia comprises one archdiocese, one diocese and one apostolic vicariate. At 31 December 2005 there were 404,269 adherents of the Roman Catholic Church, representing some 17.5% of the total population.

Bishops' Conference

Namibian Catholic Bishops' Conference, POB 11525, Windhoek 9000; tel. (61) 224798; fax (61) 228126; e-mail ncbc@windhoek.org.na.

f. 1996; Pres. (vacant).

Archbishop of Windhoek: LIBORIUS NDUMBUKUTI NASHENDA, POB 272, Windhoek 9000; tel. (61) 227595; fax (61) 229836; e-mail rcarch@iafrica.com.na; internet www.rcchurch.na.

Other Christian Churches

Among other denominations active in Namibia are the Evangelical Reformed Church in Africa, the Presbyterian Church of Southern Africa, Seventh Day Adventists and the United Congregational Church of Southern Africa. At mid-2000 there were an estimated 820,000 Protestants and 192,000 adherents professing other forms of Christianity.

JUDAISM

Windhoek Hebrew Congregation: POB 563, Windhoek; tel. (61) 221990; fax (61) 226444.

BAHÁ'Í FAITH

National Spiritual Assembly: POB 20372, Windhoek; tel. (61) 250890; fax (61) 272745; e-mail zayanih@potentia.com.na; Sec. ZAYANIH DENNIS; mems resident in 215 localities.

The Press

The African Magazine: NCCI, 2 Jenner St, POB 1770, Windhoek; tel. and fax (61) 255018; e-mail info@theafricanmagazin.org; internet www.theafricanmagazin.org.

NAMIBIA

AgriForum: 114 Robert Mugabe Ave, POB 86641, Windhoek; tel. (61) 256023; fax (61) 256035; quarterly; Afrikaans and English; publ. by the Namibia Agricultural Union; Editor RICHTER ERASMUS; circ. 5,000.

Allgemeine Zeitung: Omurambaweg 11, POB 86695, Eros, Windhoek; tel. (61) 225822; fax (61) 220225; e-mail azinfo@az.com.na; internet www.az.com.na; f. 1916; publ. by Newsprint Namibia; daily; German; Editor-in-Chief STEFAN FISCHER; circ. 5,300 (Mon.–Thurs.), 6,500 (Fri.).

The Big Issue Namibia: 37 Bahnhof St, POB 97140 Maerua Park, Windhoek; tel. (61) 242216; fax (61) 242232; e-mail jo@bigissue.com.na; internet www.bigissuenamibia.org; f. 2002; monthly; Man. Dir JO ROGGE; Editor CATHERINE SASMAN.

Insight Namibia: 34 Sam Nujoma Dr., POB 86058, Windhoek; tel. (61) 301437; fax (61) 240385; e-mail editor@insight.com.na; internet www.insight.com.na; f. 2004; monthly; business and current affairs; Editor ROBIN SHERBOURNE.

Namib Times: Sam Nujoma Ave, POB 706, Walvis Bay; tel. (64) 205854; fax (64) 204813; e-mail ntimes@iway.na; 2 a week; Afrikaans, English, German and Portuguese; Editor FLORIS STEENKAMP; circ. 4,300.

Namibia Brief: Independence Ave, POB 2123, Windhoek; tel. and fax (61) 251044; quarterly; English; Editor CATHY BLATT; circ. 7,500.

Namibia Economist: 7 Schuster St, POB 49, Windhoek 9000; tel. (61) 221925; fax (61) 220615; e-mail daniel@economist.com.na; internet www.economist.com.na; f. 1986; weekly; English; business, finance and economics; Editor DANIEL STEINMANN; circ. 7,000.

Namibia Magazin: POB 6870, Windhoek; tel. and fax (61) 224929; e-mail evonwiet@iafrica.com.na; publ. by Klaus Hess Verlag; German; politics, tourism and culture; Rep. ERIKA VON WIETERSHEIM.

Namibia Review: Directorate Print Media and Regional Offices, Regular Publications, Turnhalle Bldg, Bahnhof St, PMB 13344, Windhoek; tel. (61) 222246; fax (61) 224937; e-mail bupe@webmail.co.za; f. 1992; publ. by the Ministry of Information and Broadcasting; monthly; information on govt policy and developmental issues; Editor ELIZABETH KALAMBO-M'ULE; circ. 5,000.

Namibia Sport: POB 1246, Windhoek; tel. (61) 224132; fax (61) 224613; e-mail editor@namibiasport.com.na; internet www.namibiasport.com.na; f. 2002; monthly; Editor HELGE SCHUTZ; circ. 2,500.

Namibia Today: 21 Johan Albrecht St, POB 24669, Windhoek; tel. (61) 276730; fax (61) 276381; 2 a week; Afrikaans, English, Oshiherero and Oshiwambo; publ. by SWAPO; Editor KAOMO-VIJINDA TJOMBE; circ. 5,000.

The Namibian: 42 John Meinert St, POB 20783, Windhoek; tel. (61) 279600; fax (61) 279602; e-mail editor@namibian.com.na; internet www.namibian.com.na; daily; English; Editor GWEN LISTER; circ. 23,000 (Mon.–Thurs.), 32,000 (Fri.).

The Namibian Worker: POB 50034, Bachbrecht, Windhoek; tel. (61) 215037; fax (61) 215589; e-mail nunw@mweb.com.na; newsletter publ. by National Union of Namibian Workers; revived in 2003; Afrikaans, English and Oshiwambo; Editor-in-Chief C. RANGA HAIKALI; circ. 1,000.

NCCI Namibia Business Journal: NCCI Head Office, 2 Jenner St, POB 9355, Windhoek; tel. (61) 228809; fax (61) 228009; publ. by the Namibia Chamber of Commerce and Industry; 6 a year; English; CEO TARAH SHAANIKA; Editor CHARITY MWIYA; circ. 4,000.

New Era: Daniel Tjongarero House, cnr Kerby and W. Kulz Sts, Private Mail Bag 13364, Windhoek; tel. (61) 273300; fax (61) 220583; internet www.newera.com.na; e-mail editor@newera.com.na; f. 1991; daily; publ. by the Ministry of Information and Broadcasting; English; Chair. VILBARD USIKU; CEO SYLVESTER BLACK; Editor RAJAH MUNAMAVA; circ. 10,000.

Plus Weekly: POB 21506, Windhoek; tel. (61) 233635; fax (61) 230478; e-mail info@namibiaplus.com; internet www.namibiaplus.com; publ. by Federsen Publications; Afrikaans, English and German.

Republikein: 11 Omuramba Rd, POB 3436, Eros, Windhoek; tel. (61) 2972000; fax (61) 223721; e-mail republkn@republikein.com.na; internet www.republikein.com.na; f. 1977; daily; Afrikaans and English; publ. by Newsprint Namibia; Group Gen. Man. CHRIS JACOBIE; circ. 17,500 (Mon.–Wed.), 21,000 (Thurs.–Fri.).

Sister Namibia: POB 40092, Ausspanplatz, Windhoek; tel. (61) 230618; fax (61) 236371; e-mail sister@iafrica.com.na; 6 a year; publ. by Sister Namibia human rights org.; women's issues; Editor LIZ FRANK.

The Southern Times: cnr Dr W Külz and Kerby Sts, POB 32235, Windhoek; tel. (61) 301094; fax (61) 301095; e-mail tstnews@newera.com.na; internet www.southerntimesafrica.com; f. 2004; weekly (Sun.); owned by New Era and Zimpapers, Zimbabwe; printed in Namibia and Zimbabwe; regional; CEO PETER MIETZNER; Editor INNOCENT GORE.

Space Magazine: Sanlam Centre, 3rd Floor, POB 3717, Windhoek; tel. (61) 225155; e-mail space@mweb.com.na; monthly; English; family life; Publr ESTER SMITH; Editor YANNA SMITH.

Windhoek Observer: 6 Schuster St, POB 2255, Windhoek; tel. (61) 221737; fax (61) 226098; e-mail whkob@africaonline.com.na; f. 1978; weekly; English; Editor HANNES SMITH; circ. 14,000.

NEWS AGENCY

Namibia Press Agency (Nampa): cnr Keller and Eugene Marais Sts, POB 61354, Windhoek 9000; tel. (61) 374000; fax (61) 221713; e-mail admin@nampa.org; internet www.nampa.org; f. 1990; Chair. MAUREEN HINDA; CEO NGHIDINUA HAMUNIME; Editor TOMMY KATAMILA.

PRESS ASSOCIATION

Press Club Windhoek: POB 2032, Windhoek; tel. (61) 2796000; fax (61) 279602; e-mail carmen@namibian.com.na; Chair. CARMEN HONEY.

Publishers

ELOC Printing Press: PMB 2013, Oniipa, Ondangwa; tel. and fax (6756) 40211; f. 1901; Rev. Dr KLEOPAS DUMENI.

Gamsberg Macmillan Publishers (Pty) Ltd: 19 Faraday St, POB 22830, Windhoek; tel. (61) 232165; fax (61) 233538; e-mail gmp@iafrica.com.na; internet www.macmillan-africa.com; imprints incl. New Namibia Books and Out of Africa; Man. Dir HERMAN VAN WYK.

Longman Namibia: POB 9251, Eros, Windhoek; tel. (61) 231124; fax (61) 224019; Publr LINDA BREDENKAMP.

National Archives of Namibia: 1–9 Eugène Marais St, PMB 13250, Windhoek; tel. (61) 2935213; fax (61) 2935217; e-mail natarch@mec.gov.na; f. 1939; Chief Archivist WERNER HILLEBRECHT.

PUBLISHERS' ASSOCIATION

Association of Namibian Publishers: POB 40219, Windhoek; tel. (61) 228284; fax (61) 231496; f. 1991; Chair. Dr H. MELBER.

Broadcasting and Communications

TELECOMMUNICATIONS

Telecom Namibia Ltd (Telecom): POB 297, Windhoek; tel. (61) 2019211; fax (61) 248723; internet www.telecom.na; f. 1992; state-owned; Chair. T. HAIMBILI; Man. Dir FRANS NDOROMA.

Mobile Telecommunications Ltd (MTC): cnr Malcolm Spence and Reginald Walker Sts, Olympia, Windhoek; POB 23051, Windhoek; tel. (61) 249570; fax (61) 249571; e-mail aaochamub@mtc.com.na; f. 1995 as jt venture between Namibia Post and Telecommunications Holdings (NPTH), Telia and Swedfund; 34% owned by Portugal Telecom, 64% by NPTH; Chair. STEVE MOTINGA; Man. Dir JOSE A. FERREIRA.

BROADCASTING

Radio

In 2004 there were a total of 19 radio stations broadcasting from Windhoek including:

Namibian Broadcasting Corpn (NBC): POB 321, Windhoek; tel. (61) 2913133; fax (61) 215767; e-mail tnandjaa@nbc.com.na; internet www.nbc.com.na; f. 1990; runs 10 radio stations, broadcasting daily to 90% of the population in English (24 hours), Afrikaans, German and eight indigenous languages (10 hours); Chair. PONHELE YA FRANCE; Dir-Gen. VEZERA BOB KANDETU.

Channel 7/Kanaal 7: POB 20500, Windhoek; tel. (61) 235815; fax (61) 240190; e-mail channel7@k7.com.na; internet www.k7.com.na; Christian community radio station; English and Afrikaans; Man. NEAL VAN DEN BERGH.

Katutura Community Radio: POB 22355, Windhoek; tel. (61) 263768; fax (61) 262786; f. 1995 by non-governmental orgs; Dir FREDERICK GOWASEB.

Kudu FM: 158 Jan Jonker St, POB 5369, Windhoek; tel. (61) 247262; fax (61) 247259; e-mail radiokudu@radiokudu.com.na; internet www.radiokudu.com.na; f. 1998; commercial station affiliated to Omulunga Radio; English, Afrikaans and German.

Omulunga Radio: POB 40789, Windhoek; tel. (61) 239706; fax (61) 247259; e-mail omulunga@omulunga.com.na; internet www.omulunga.com.na; f. 2002; Ovambo interest station affiliated to Kudu FM; Oshiwambo and English.

NAMIBIA

Directory

Radio Antenna Namibia (Pty) Ltd (Namibia FM 99): 6 Teinert St, POB 11849, Windhoek; tel. (61) 223634; fax (61) 230964; e-mail radio99@namfm99.com; f. 1994; Man. Dir GERT JACOBIE.

Radio Energy (Radio 100): 17 Bismarck St, Windhoek West; POB 676, Windhoek; tel. (61) 256380; fax (61) 256379; internet www.energy100fm.com; commercial radio station; Man. Dir MARIO AITA.

Other radio stations included: Kosmos Radio, Radio France International (via relay), Radio 99, and Radio Wave. There were six community radio stations including: Radio Ecclesia (Catholic), Live FM (in Rehoboth), Ohangwenga Community Radio, and UNAM Radio (University of Namibia). A further four community stations were planned in 2005 at Oshakti, Gobabis, Keetmanshoop and Swakopmund.

Television

Namibian Broadcasting Corpn (NBC): POB 321, Windhoek; tel. (61) 2913111; fax (61) 216209; internet www.nbc.com.na; f. 1990; broadcasts television programmes in English to 45% of the population, 18 hours daily; Chair. UAZUVA KAUMBI; Dir-Gen. GERRY MUNYAMA.

Multi-Choice Namibia: POB 1752, Windhoek; tel. (61) 222222; fax (61) 227605; commercial television channels; Gen. Man. KOBUS BEZUIDENHOUT.

Finance

(cap. = capital; res = reserves; dep. = deposits; m. = million; brs = branches; amounts in Namibian dollars)

BANKING

Central Bank

Bank of Namibia: 71 Robert Mugabe Ave, POB 2882, Windhoek; tel. (61) 2835111; fax (61) 2835228; internet www.bon.com.na; f. 1990; cap. 40.0m., res 1,048.7m., dep. 1,270.5m. (Dec. 2002); Gov. TOM K. ALWEENDO; Dep. Gov. P. HARTMAN.

Commercial Banks

Bank Windhoek Ltd: Bank Windhoek Bldg, 262 Independence Ave, POB 15, Windhoek; tel. (61) 2991122; fax (61) 2991620; e-mail info@bankwindhoek.com.na; internet www.bankwindhoek.com.na; f. 1982; cap. 4.7m., res 283.2m., dep. 2,939.0m. (March 2002); Chair. J. C. 'KOOS' BRANDT; Man. Dir JOHAN J. SWANEPOEL; 22 brs.

First National Bank of Namibia Ltd: 209–211 Independence Ave, POB 195, Windhoek; tel. (61) 2992016; fax (61) 2220979; e-mail info@fnbnamibia.com.na; internet www.fnbnamibia.com.na; f. 1987 as First Nat. Bank of Southern Africa Ltd; present name adopted 1990; total assets 4,731.9m. (June 2003); Chair. H. DIETER VOIGTS; CEO VEKUII RUKORO; 28 brs and 12 agencies.

Namibian Banking Corpn: Carl List Haus, Independence Ave, POB 370, Windhoek; tel. (61) 225946; fax (61) 223741; Chair. J. C. WESTRAAT; Man. Dir P. P. NIEHAUS; 3 brs.

Nedbank Namibia: 12–20 Dr Frans Indongo St, POB 1, Windhoek; tel. (61) 2959111; fax (61) 2952120; e-mail serviceplus@nedbank.com; internet www.nedbank.com.na; f. 1973; fmrly Commercial Bank of Namibia Ltd; subsidiary of Nedbank Ltd, South Africa; total assets 3,000.0m. (June 2005); Chair. T. J. FRANK; Man. Dir ERASTUS HOVEKA; 17 brs and 4 agencies.

Standard Bank Namibia Ltd: Standard Bank Centre, cnr Werner List St and Post St Mall, POB 3327, Windhoek; tel. (61) 2942126; fax (61) 2942583; e-mail info@standardbank.com.na; internet www.standardbank.com.na; f. 1915; controlled by Standard Bank Africa; total assets 10,400.2m. (Dec. 2006); Chair. LEAKE S. HANGALA; Man. Dir MPUMZI PUPUMA; 23 brs.

Agricultural Bank

Agricultural Bank of Namibia (AgriBank): 10 Post St Mall, POB 13208, Windhoek; tel. (61) 2074111; fax (61) 2074289; e-mail agribank@iafrica.com.na; f. 1922; state-owned; total assets 739.1m. (March 2001); Chair. HANS-GUENTHER STIER; Acting CEO S. E. NDJABA.

Development Bank

Development Bank of Namibia (DBN): POB 235, Windhoek; tel. (61) 2908000; fax (61) 2908049; e-mail info@dbn.com.na; internet www.dbn.com.na; f. 2004; Chair. SVEN THIEME; CEO DAVID NUYOMA.

STOCK EXCHANGE

Namibian Stock Exchange (NSX): Kaiser Krone Centre, Shop 8, Post St Mall, POB 2401, Windhoek; tel. (61) 227647; fax (61) 248531; e-mail loiden@nsx.com.na; internet www.nsx.com.na; f. 1992; Chair. Exec. Cttee P. HANGO; Gen. Man. HEIKO NIEDERMEIER.

INSURANCE

Corporate Guarantee and Insurance Co of Namibia Ltd (CGI): Corporate House, Ground Floor, 17 Lüderitz St, POB 416, Windhoek; tel. (61) 259525; fax (61) 255213; e-mail info@corporateguarantee.com; internet www.corporateguarantee.com; f. 1996; wholly owned subsidiary of Nictus Group Ltd since 2001; Chair. J. L. OLIVER; Man. Dir and Principal Officer F. R. VAN STADEN.

Insurance Co of Namibia (INSCON): POB 2877, Windhoek; tel. (61) 275900; fax (61) 233808; f. 1990; short-term insurance; Chair. CHARLES KAURAISA; Man. Dir FERDINAND OTTO.

Legal Shield: 140–142 Robert Mugabe Ave, POB 11363, Windhoek; tel. (61) 2754200; fax (61) 2754090; internet www.legalshield.com.na; f. 2000; legal, funeral and medical insurance; Man. Dir QUINTON VAN ROOYEN.

Metropolitan Namibia: Metropolitan Pl., 1st Floor, cnr Bülow and Stubel Sts, POB 3785, Windhoek; tel. (61) 2973000; fax (61) 248191; internet www.metropolitan.com.na; f. 1996; subsidiary of Metropolitan Group, South Africa; acquired Channel Life in 2004; Chair. M. L. SMITH; Man. Dir LEEBA FOUCHÉ.

Mutual and Federal Insurance Co Ltd: Mutual and Federal Centre, 5th–7th Floors, 227 Independence Ave, POB 151, Windhoek; tel. (61) 2077111; fax (61) 2077205; f. 1990; subsidiary of Mutual and Federal, South Africa; acquired CGU Holdings Ltd in 2000 and FGI Namibia Ltd in 2001; Man. Dir G. KATJIMUNE; Gen. Man. J. W. B. LE ROUX.

Namibia National Reinsurance Corpn Ltd (NamibRE): Capital Centre, 2nd Floor, Levinson Arcade, POB 716 Windhoek; tel. (61) 256905; fax (61) 256904; e-mail administrator@namibre.com; f. 2001; 100% state-owned; Man. Dir ANNA NAKALE-KAWANA.

Old Mutual Life Assurance Co (Namibia) Ltd: Mutual Platz, 5th Floor, Post St Mall, POB 165, Windhoek; tel. (61) 2993999; fax (61) 2993520; e-mail nambusdev@oldmutual.com; internet www.oldmutual.com.na; Chair. G. S. VAN NIEKERK; Chief Exec. BERTIE VAN DER WALT.

Sanlam Namibia: 154 Independence Ave, POB 317, Windhoek; tel. (61) 2947418; fax (61) 2947416; e-mail marketing@sanlam.com.na; internet www.sanlam.com.na; f. 1928; subsidiary of Sanlam Ltd, South Africa; merged with Regent Life Namibia, Capricorn Investments and Nam-Mic Financial Services in Dec. 2004; Chair. ROY ANDERSEN; CEO Dr JOHAN VAN ZYL.

Santam Namibia Ltd: Ausspanplaza Complex, Ausspanplatz POB 204, Windhoek; tel. (61) 2928000; fax (61) 235225; 60% owned by Santam, South Africa; 33.3% owned by Bank Windhoek Holdings Ltd; acquired Allianz Insurance of Namibia Ltd in 2001; Chief Exec. NAMA SIMON GOABAB.

Swabou Insurance Co Ltd: Swabou Bldg, Post St Mall, POB 79, Windhoek; tel. (61) 2997528; fax (61) 2997551; internet www.swabouinsurance.com.na; f. 1990; acquired by FNB Namibia Holdings Ltd in 2004; short-term insurance; Man. Dir RENIER TALJAARD.

Swabou Life Assurance Co Ltd: 209–211 Independence Ave, POB 79, Windhoek; tel. (61) 2997502; fax (61) 2997550; e-mail tgurirab@fnbnamibia.com.na; internet www.swaboulife.com.na; f. 1990; acquired by FNB Namibia Holdings Ltd in 2004; life assurance; CEO GERHARD MANS.

Trade and Industry

GOVERNMENT AGENCIES

Karakul Board of Namibia—Swakara Fur Producers and Exporters: Private Bag 13300, Windhoek; tel. (61) 235168; fax (61) 2909300; e-mail swakara@agra.com.na; internet www.swakara.net; Chair. H. J. VAN WYK; Man. W. H. VISSER.

Meat Board of Namibia: POB 38, Windhoek; tel. (61) 275830; fax (61) 228310; f. 1935; Chair. JOHN LE ROUX; Gen. Man. PAUL STRYDOM.

Meat Corpn of Namibia (Meatco Namibia): POB 3881, Windhoek; tel. (61) 3216400; fax (61) 3216401; e-mail hoffice@meatco.com.na; internet www.meatco.com.na; f. 1986; processors of meat and meat products at four abattoirs and one tannery; CEO KOBUS DU PLESSIS.

Namibian Agronomic Board: 30 Hochland Rd, POB 5096, Ausspannplatz, Windhoek; tel. (61) 379500; fax (61) 225371; internet www.nab.com.na; e-mail nabdesk@nammic.com.na; f. 1985; CEO CHRISTOF BROCK.

National Petroleum Corpn of Namibia (NAMCOR): Petroleum House, 1 Aviation Rd, Private Bag 13196, Windhoek; tel. (61) 2045000; fax (61) 221785; internet www.namcor.com.na; f. 1965 as Southern Oil Exploration Corpn (South-West Africa) (Pty) Ltd—SWAKOR; present name adopted 1990; state petroleum co;

responsible for importing 50% of national oil requirements; Chair. F. KISTING; Man. Dir SAM BEUKES (acting).

DEVELOPMENT ORGANIZATIONS

Namibia Investment Centre (NIC): Ministry of Trade and Industry, Brendan Simbwaye Sq., Block B, 6th Floor, Goethe St, Private Bag 13340, Windhoek; tel. (61) 2837335; fax (61) 220278; e-mail nic@mti.gov.na; f. 1990; promotes foreign and domestic investment; Exec. Dir BERNADETTE ARTIVOR.

Namibia Non-Governmental Organisation Forum (NANGOF): 18 Axalie Doeseb St, POB 70433 Khomasdal, Windhoek; tel. (61) 239469; fax (61) 239471; e-mail nangof@iafrica.com.na; f. 1991; umbrella body representing 95 community-based orgs; Chair. SANDY TJARONDA.

National Housing Enterprise: 7 Omuramba Rd, Eros, POB 20192, Windhoek; tel. (61) 2927111; fax (61) 2927271; internet www.nhe.com.na; f. 1983; replaced Nat. Building and Investment Corpn; provides low-cost housing; manages Housing Trust Fund; 100% state-owned; total assets N $496.4m. (Dec. 2001); Chair. V. R. RUKORO; CEO VINCENT HAILULU.

CHAMBERS OF COMMERCE

Chamber of Mines of Namibia (CoM): Channel Life Tower, 4th Floor, Post St Mall, 2895, Windhoek; tel. (61) 237925; fax (61) 222638; e-mail malango@iway.na; f. 1979; Pres. OTTO SHILOONGO; Gen. Man. VESTON MALANGO; 59 mems (2005).

Namibia National Chamber of Commerce and Industry (NNCCI): 2 Jenner St, cnr Simpson and Jenner Sts, POB 9355, Windhoek; tel. (61) 228809; fax (61) 228009; e-mail ncciinfo@ncci.org.na; internet www.ncci.org.na; f. 1990; Chair. INGE K. ZAAMWANI-KAMWI; CEO TARAH SHAANIKA; c. 2,000 mems (2007).

Windhoek Chamber of Commerce and Industries: SWA Building Society Bldg, 3rd Floor, POB 191, Windhoek; tel. (61) 222000; fax (61) 233690; f. 1920; Pres. H. SCHMIDT; Gen. Man. T. D. PARKHOUSE; 230 mems.

EMPLOYERS' ORGANIZATIONS

Construction Industries Federation of Namibia: 22 Stein St, POB 1479, Klein Windhoek; tel. (61) 230028; fax (61) 224534; e-mail info@cif.namibia.na; internet www.cif.namibia.na; Pres. RENATE SCHMIDT; Sec. RICKI WILSON; 60 contracting mems, 12 trade mems, 5 affiliated mems.

Namibia Agricultural Union (NAU): PMB 13255, Windhoek; tel. (61) 237838; fax (61) 220193; e-mail nau@agrinamibia.com.na; internet www.agrinamibia.com.na; f. 1947; represents commercial farmers; Pres. RAIMAR VON HASE; Exec. Man. SAKKIE COETZEE.

Namibia National Farmers' Union (NNFU): 4 Axalie Doeseb St, Windhoek West; POB 3117, Windhoek; tel. (61) 271117; fax (61) 271115; e-mail info@nnfu.org.na; represents communal farmers; Pres. MANFRED RUKORO.

Namibia Professional Hunting Association (NAPHA): 318 Sam Nujoma Dr., Klein Windhoek; POB 11291, Windhoek; tel. (61) 234455; fax (61) 222567; internet www.natron.net/napha; f. 1974; represents hunting guides and professional hunters; Pres. FRANK HEGER; c. 400 mems.

Retail Motor Industry of Namibia (RMI Namibia): POB 2110, Windhoek; tel. (61) 240280; fax (61) 240276; fmrly Motor Industries Federation of Namibia; present name adopted 2002; affiliated to RMI South Africa; Chair. HAROLD PUPKEWITZ; Pres. NEELS SWIEGERS; 40 mems (2003).

UTILITIES

Namibia Power Corpn (Pty) Ltd (NamPower): NamPower Centre, 15 Luther St, POB 2864, Windhoek; tel. (61) 2054111; fax (61) 232805; e-mail register@nampower.com.na; internet www.nampower.com.na; Chair. ANDRIES LEEVI HUNGAMO; Man. Dir Dr LEAKE S. HANGALA.

Northern Electricity: POB 891, Tsumeb; tel. (67) 222243; fax (67) 222245; private electricity supply co; first regional electricity distributor in Namibia, operating in the north of the country; Man. Dir C. G. N. HUYSEN.

TRADE UNIONS

In 2004 there were 27 unions representing more than 100,000 workers.

Trade Union Federations

National Union of Namibian Workers (NUNW): Mungunda St, Katutura; POB 50034, Windhoek; tel. (61) 215037; fax (61) 215589; f. 1972; affiliated to the SWAPO party; Pres. RISTO KAPENDA; Sec.-Gen. EVILASTUS KAARONDA; c. 70,000 mems.

The NUNW has 10 affiliates which include:

Metal and Allied Namibian Workers' Union (MANWU): Mingunda St, POB 22771, Windhoek 9000; tel. (61) 263100; fax (61) 264300; e-mail manwu@mweb.com.na; f. 1987; affiliated to the Building and Wood Workers Int. and Int. Metalworkers' Fed.; Pres. J. NAOBEB; Gen. Sec. MOSES SHIIKWA (acting); 5,500 mems.

Mineworkers' Union of Namibia (MUN): POB 1566, Windhoek; tel. (61) 261723; fax (61) 217684; f. 1986; Pres. ANDRIES EISEB; 12,500 mems.

Namibia Farm Workers' Union (NAFWU): NUNW Centre, Mungunda Street, Katutura, POB 21007, Windhoek; tel. (61) 218653; fax (61) 263714; e-mail nafwu@iafrica.com.na; internet www.nunw.org.na/nafwu.htm; f. 1994; Pres. ASSER HENDRICKS; Sec.-Gen. ALFRED ANGULA.

Namibia Financial Institutions Union (NAFINU): POB 61791, Windhoek; tel. (61) 239917; fax (61) 215589; f. 2000; Pres. ALEX KAMAUNDJU; Gen. Sec. ASNATH ZAMUEE.

Namibia Food and Allied Workers' Union (NAFAU): Mungunda St, Katutura; POB 1553, Windhoek; tel. (61) 218213; fax (61) 263714; e-mail nafau@mweb.com.na; f. 1986; affiliated to the Int. Textile, Garment and Leather Workers' Fed. and Int. Union of Food, Agricultural, Hotel, Restaurant, Catering, Tobacco and Allied Workers' Asscns; Pres. DAVID NAMALENGA; Gen. Sec. KIROS SACARIAS; 12,000 mems.

Namibia National Teachers' Union (NANTU): POB 61009, Windhoek; tel. (61) 262247; fax (61) 261926; e-mail nantu@nantu.org.na; f. 1989; affiliated to Education Int.; Pres. NDAPEWA NGHIPANDULWA; Gen. Sec. MIRIAM HAMUTENYA-KATONYALA; 13,000 mems (2002).

Namibia Public Workers' Union (NAPWU): POB 50035, Bachbrecht, Windhoek; tel. (61) 261961; fax (61) 263100; e-mail napwu@namibnet.com; f. 1987; affiliated to the Public Services Int.; Pres. ELIPHAS NDINGARA; Sec.-Gen PETRUS NEVONGA; 11,000 mems.

Namibia Transport and Allied Workers' Union (NATAU): POB 7516, Katutura, Windhoek; tel. (61) 218514; fax (61) 263767; f. 1988; affiliated to the Int. Transport Workers' Fed.; Pres. DAWID TJOMBE; Gen. Sec. JOHN KWEDHI; 7,500 mems.

Trade Union Congress of Namibia (TUCNA): POB 2111, Windhoek; tel. (61) 246143; fax (61) 212828; f. 2002 following the merger of the Namibia People's Social Movement (f. 1992 as the Namibia Christian Social Trade Unions) and the Namibia Fed. of Trade Unions (f. 1998); Pres. PAULUS HANGO; c. 45,000 mems (2005).

TUCNA has 14 affiliates including:

Local Authorities Union of Namibia (LAUN): Frans Indongo St, Windhoek; POB 22060, Windhoek; tel. (61) 234625; fax (61) 230035; Pres. FRANCOIS ADONIS.

Namibia Building Workers' Union (NABWU): 3930 Verbena St, Khomasdal; POB 22679, Windhoek; tel. (61) 212828.

Namibia Seamen and Allied Workers Union (NASAWU): Nataniel Maxuilli St, Walvis Bay; POB 1341, Walvis Bay; tel. (64) 204237; fax (64) 205957; Pres. PAULUS HANGO.

Namibia Wholesale and Retail Workers Union (NWRWU): 19 Verbena St, Khomasdal; POB 22769, Windhoek; tel. (61) 212378; fax (61) 212828; Sec.-Gen. JOSHUA MABUKU.

Public Service Union of Namibia (PSUN): 45–51 Kroon Rd, Khomasdal; POB 21662, Windhoek; tel. (61) 213083; fax (61) 213047; e-mail psun@namibnet.com; f. 1991; successor to the Govt Service Staff Asscn; Pres. AWEBAHE HOESEB; Sec.-Gen. VICTOR KAZONJATI.

Teachers Union of Namibia (TUN): PSUN Bldg, Dollar St 4551, Khomasdal, POB 30800, Windhoek; tel. (61) 229115; fax (61) 246360; e-mail tun@mweb.com.na; Pres. CHANVILLE GREGORY MACKRILL.

Transport

RAILWAYS

The main line runs from Nakop, at the border with South Africa, via Keetmanshoop to Windhoek, Kranzberg, Tsumeb, Swakopmund and Walvis Bay. There are three branch lines, from Windhoek to Gobabis, Otavi to Grootfontein and Keetmanshoop to Lüderitz. The total rail network covers 2,382 route-km. There are plans for a railway line connecting Namibia with Zambia, as part of a programme to improve transport links among the members of the Common Market for Eastern and Southern Africa; plans to extend the northern railway line by 248 km, from Tsumeb to Ondangwa, were announced in 2001. In 2006 the Namibian and Botswana Governments commenced discussions regarding a proposed railway linking the two countries.

TransNamib Holdings Ltd: TransNamib Bldg, cnr Independence Ave and Bahnhof St, PMB 13204, Windhoek; tel. (61) 2981111; fax (61) 227984; e-mail pubrelation@transnamib.com.na; internet www.transnamib.com.na; state-owned; Chair. FOIBE JACOBS; CEO JOHN M. SHAETONHODI.

ROADS

Between 2000 and 2002 the total road network decreased from 66,467 km to 42,237 km of roads, of which 12.8% was paved in 2002. A major road link from Walvis Bay to Jwaneng, northern Botswana, the Trans-Kalahari Highway, was completed in 1998, along with the Trans-Caprivi Highway, linking Namibia with northern Botswana, Zambia and Zimbabwe. The Government is also upgrading and expanding the road network in northern Namibia. In 2001 total spending on the road network was equivalent to US $17.7m.

SHIPPING

The ports of Walvis Bay and Lüderitz are linked to the main overseas shipping routes and handle almost one-half of Namibia's external trade. Walvis Bay has a container terminal, built in 1999, and eight berths; it is a hub port for the region, serving land-locked countries such as Botswana, Zambia and Zimbabwe. In 2005 NAMPORT added a N 30m. floating dock to the Walvis Bay facilities with a view to servicing vessels used in the region's expanding petroleum industry. Traditionally a fishing port, a new quay was completed at Lüderitz in 2000, with two berths, in response to growing demand from the offshore diamond industry. At the end of 2006 Namibia's merchant fleet comprised 173 vessels, with a combined displacement of 102,901 gross registered tons.

African Portland Industrial Holdings (APIH): Huvest Bldg, 1st Floor, AE/Gams Centre, Sam Nujoma Dr., POB 40047, Windhoek; tel. (61) 248744; fax (61) 239485; e-mail jacques@apiholdings.com; f. 1994; 80% owned by Grindrod (South Africa); bulk port terminal operator; Man. Dir ATHOL EMERTON; Sec. JACQUES CONRADIE.

Namibian Ports Authority (NAMPORT): 17 Rikumbi Kandanga Rd, POB 361, Walvis Bay; tel. (64) 2082207; fax (64) 2082320; e-mail jerome@namport.com.na; internet www.namport.com; f. 1994; Chair. SHAKESPEARE MASIZA; Man. Dir SEBBY KANKONDI.

Pan-Ocean Shipping Services Ltd: POB 2613, Walvis Bay; tel. (64) 203959; fax (64) 204199; f. 1995; Man. Dir JÜRGEN HEYNEMANN; Gen. Man. GEORGE KIROV.

CIVIL AVIATION

There are international airports at Windhoek (Hosea Kutako) and Walvis Bay (Rooikop), as well as a number of other airports throughout Namibia, and numerous landing strips.

Air Namibia: TransNamib Bldg, cnr Independence Ave and Bahnhof St, POB 731, Windhoek; tel. (61) 2996000; fax (61) 2996101; e-mail aarickerts@airnamibia.com.na; internet www.airnamibia.com.na; f. 1946 as South West Air Transport; present name adopted in 1991; state-owned; part-privatization postponed indefinitely in 2003; services to Angola, Botswana, South Africa and Zimbabwe, Germany and the United Kingdom; Chair. H. PIUS ASHEEKE; Man. Dir KOSMOS EGUMBO.

Kalahari Express Airlines (KEA): POB 40179, Windhoek; tel. (61) 245665; fax (61) 245612; f. 1995; domestic and regional flights; Exec. Dir PEINGONDJABI SHIPOH.

Tourism

Namibia's principal tourist attractions are its game parks and nature reserves, and the development of 'eco-tourism' is being promoted. Tourist arrivals in Namibia in 2005 totalled 777,890. In 2003 tourism receipts amounted to US $333m.

Namibia Tourism Board: 1st Floor, Channel Life Towers, 39 Post Street Mall, Private Bag 13244, Windhoek; tel. (61) 2906000; fax (61) 254848; e-mail info@namibiatourism.com.na; internet www.namibiatourism.com.na; Chair. ERICKA AKUENJE; CEO DIGU NAOBEB.

NAURU

Introductory Survey

Location, Climate, Language, Religion, Flag, Capital

The Republic of Nauru is a small island in the central Pacific Ocean, lying about 40 km (25 miles) south of the Equator and about 4,000 km (2,500 miles) north-east of Sydney, Australia. Its nearest neighbour is Banaba (Ocean Island), in Kiribati, about 300 km (186 miles) to the east. The climate is tropical, with a westerly monsoon season from November to February. The average annual rainfall is about 2,060 mm (80 ins), but actual rainfall is extremely variable. Day temperatures vary between 24°C and 34°C (75°–93°F). Of the total resident population in 2002, 77% were Nauruans. Their language is Nauruan, but English is also widely understood. The majority of Nauruans are Christians, mostly adherents of the Nauruan Protestant Church. The national flag (proportions 1 by 2) is royal blue, divided by a narrow horizontal yellow stripe, with a 12-pointed white star at the lower hoist. The island state has no official capital, but the seat of the legislature and most government offices are in Yaren district.

Recent History

Nauru, inhabited by a predominantly Polynesian people, organized in 12 clans, was annexed by Germany in 1888. In 1914, shortly after the outbreak of the First World War, the island was captured by Australian forces. It continued to be administered by Australia under a League of Nations mandate (granted in 1920), which also named the United Kingdom and New Zealand as co-trustees. Between 1942 and 1945 Nauru was occupied by the Japanese, who deported 1,200 islanders to Truk (now Chuuk), Micronesia, where many died in bombing raids or from starvation. In 1947 the island was placed under UN Trusteeship, with Australia as the administering power on behalf of the Governments of Australia, New Zealand and the United Kingdom. The UN Trusteeship Council proposed in 1964 that the indigenous people of Nauru be resettled on Curtis Island, off the Queensland coast. This offer was made in anticipation of the progressive exhaustion of the island's phosphate deposits, and because of the environmental devastation resulting from the mining operations. However, the Nauruans elected to remain on the island. Between 1906 and 1968 41m. metric tons of phosphate were mined. Nauru was accorded a considerable measure of self-government in January 1966, with the establishment of Legislative and Executive Councils, and proceeded to independence on 31 January 1968 (exactly 22 years after the surviving Nauruans returned to the island from exile in Micronesia). In early 1998 Nauru announced its intention to seek UN membership and full Commonwealth membership (Nauru had hitherto been a 'special member' of the Commonwealth, not represented at meetings of Heads of Government). The decision was largely based on the islanders' desire to play a more prominent role in international policies relating to issues that affect them, most notably climate change (see below). Nauru became a full member of the Commonwealth in May 1999, and a member of the UN in September of that year.

The Head Chief of Nauru, Hammer DeRoburt, was elected President in May 1968 and re-elected in 1971 and 1973. Dissatisfaction with his increasingly personal rule led to the election of Bernard Dowiyogo (leader of the recently-established, informal Nauru Party) to the presidency in 1976. Dowiyogo was re-elected President after a general election in late 1977. However, DeRoburt's supporters adopted tactics of obstruction in Parliament, and in December 1977 Dowiyogo resigned, in response to Parliament's refusal to approve budgetary legislation; he was re-elected shortly afterwards, but was again forced to resign in April 1978, following the defeat of a legislative proposal concerning phosphate royalties. Lagumot Harris, another member of the Nauru Party, succeeded him, but resigned three weeks later when Parliament rejected a finance measure, and DeRoburt was again elected President. He was re-elected in December of that year, in December 1980 and in May and December 1983.

In September 1986 DeRoburt resigned, following the defeat of a government budget proposal; he was replaced as President by Kennan Adeang, who was elected in Parliament by nine votes to DeRoburt's eight. However, after holding office for only 14 days, Adeang was defeated in a parliamentary vote of no confidence, and DeRoburt subsequently resumed the presidency. Following a general election in December, Adeang was again narrowly elected President. However, he was subsequently ousted by another vote of no confidence, and DeRoburt was reinstated as President. The atmosphere of political uncertainty generated by the absence of a clear majority in Parliament led DeRoburt to dissolve Parliament in preparation for another general election in January 1987, following which which the incumbent was re-elected to the presidency by 11 votes to six. In February Adeang announced the establishment of the Democratic Party of Nauru, essentially a revival of the Nauru Party. Eight members of Parliament subsequently joined the new party, which declared that its aim was to curtail the extension of presidential powers and to promote democracy. In August 1989 a parliamentary motion of no confidence in DeRoburt (proposed by Adeang) was approved by 10 votes to five, and Kenas Aroi, a former Minister for Finance, was subsequently elected President. Aroi resigned in December, owing to ill health, and after a general election in the same month Bernard Dowiyogo was re-elected President, defeating DeRoburt by 10 votes to six. The next presidential election, held shortly after a general election in November 1992, resulted in victory for Dowiyogo, by 10 parliamentary votes to seven, over Buraro Detudamo.

At a general election held in November 1995, when a total of 67 candidates contested the 18 parliamentary seats, all cabinet members were re-elected. A subsequent presidential election resulted in Lagumot Harris's defeat of the incumbent Dowiyogo by nine votes to eight. The resignation of the Chairman of Air Nauru, following allegations of misconduct, prompted Parliament to vote on a motion of no confidence in the Government in November 1996. The motion was narrowly approved and Harris was replaced by Dowiyogo as President. Later that month, however, Dowiyogo's new Government was itself defeated in a parliamentary vote of no confidence, and Kennan Adeang was elected to the presidency. A widespread perception that the new Government lacked experience was thought to be a major factor prompting a further motion of 'no confidence' in December, at which Adeang was similarly removed from office. At a subsequent presidential contest Reuben Kun, a former Minister for Finance, defeated Adeang by 12 votes to five, on the understanding that his administration would organize a general election. An election duly took place in February 1997, at which four new members were elected to Parliament, following an apparent agreement between the supporters of Harris and those of Dowiyogo to end the political manoeuvring that had resulted in several months of instability in Nauru. At the subsequent election to the presidency Kinza Clodumar (nominated by Dowiyogo) defeated Harris by nine parliamentary votes to eight.

In early 1998 five members of Parliament (including former President Lagumot Harris) were dismissed by Adeang, the Speaker, for refusing to apologize for personal remarks about him that had been published in an opposition newsletter. At the resultant by-elections, held in late February 1998, three of the five members were re-elected. A motion expressing no confidence in the President was approved in June, and Dowiyogo was consequently elected to replace Clodumar. In a further vote of no confidence, in late April 1999 Dowiyogo was defeated by 10 votes to seven; his replacement was Rene Harris, previously Chairman of the Nauru Phosphate Corporation. Former President Lagumot Harris died in September 1999.

Following the legislative election held on 8 April 2000, Rene Harris was re-elected President, narrowly defeating Dowiyogo by nine parliamentary votes to eight. Ludwig Scotty was elected Speaker of Parliament. However, Scotty and his deputy, Ross Cairn, subsequently resigned, stating only that they were unable to continue under the 'current political circumstances'. Harris therefore tendered his resignation and was replaced by Dowiyogo, whereupon Scotty and Cairn were re-elected to their posts in the legislature. Observers attributed the manoeuvring to shifting political allegiances within the legislature.

In early 2001, in another reversal to Dowiyogo's leadership, Anthony Audoa, the Minister for Home Affairs, Culture, Health and Women's Affairs, resigned and requested that Parliament be recalled. He claimed that Dowiyogo had squandered Nauru's wealth during his various tenures as President and that in promoting the island as a tax haven he had allowed Nauru to be used by Russian criminal gangs to 'launder' their illegal funds, prompting speculation that he intended to mount a challenge for the presidency.

In late March 2001 Dowiyogo was ousted from the presidency in a parliamentary vote of no confidence while he was undergoing hospital treatment in Australia. The motion, which was adopted by two votes, led to Rene Harris regaining the presidency. In October, however, Harris was flown to Australia for emergency medical treatment for a diabetes-related illness, during which time Remy Namaduk performed the role of acting President. Allegations that Nauru's 'offshore' financial centre was being used extensively by Russian criminal organizations for 'laundering' the proceeds of their illegal activities had led Dowiyogo to order a full review of the industry in March 1999. In early 2000 President Rene Harris announced that Nauru was to suspend its 'offshore' banking services and improve the accountability of existing banks on the island, as part of the Government's efforts to bring Nauru's financial services regulations into conformity with international standards. Dowiyogo similarly reaffirmed his commitment to reform the 'offshore' sector, following his election in April 2000. However, in February 2001 11 members of Nauru's 18-member legislature signed a petition requesting that Dowiyogo attend a special session of Parliament to answer questions relating to the island's alleged role in 'laundering' significant funds from Russian criminal organizations. The allegations originated in claims by Russia's central bank that some US $70,000m. of illegal funds had been processed in 'offshore' banks in Nauru. It was estimated that 400 such banks existed on the island in early 2001. The Government subsequently drew up an Anti-Money Laundering Act in August 2001, but the Paris-based Financial Action Task Force (FATF, see p. 416) found that the new laws contained several deficiencies and imposed sanctions in December. (The FATF had been established in 1989 on the recommendation of the Group of Seven (G-7) industrialized nations.) The Government announced revised anti-money-laundering legislation in the same month, and was considering legal action against the FATF in early 2002. Meanwhile, following Islamist attacks on New York and Washington, DC, on 11 September 2001, Nauru's financial system was subject to international scrutiny, amid suspicion that it might have been used as a conduit for the terrorists' funds.

As a result of continued US pressure, Nauru's Parliament approved a new law in February 2004 to address the problem of 'money-laundering', along with legislation to close down the country's 'offshore' banks. In October 2004 the FATF withdrew counter-measures against the country, and in October 2005, following the implementation of the requisite legislation, Nauru became the last of the Pacific islands to be removed from the FATF list of non-co-operative countries and territories. Nauru's removal from the list coincided with the final preparations for the presentation of the National Sustainable Development Strategy, announced at the international donor meeting held in Nauru at the end of November (see below). In December 2003 following the island's commitment to improve transparency and to exchange information on tax matters with other countries, Nauru had been removed from a list of unco-operative tax havens, issued in April 2002 by the Organisation for Economic Co-operation and Development (OECD, see p. 347).

In January 2003 meanwhile, President Rene Harris was defeated in a motion of no confidence by eight votes to three and was replaced by Bernard Dowiyogo. The vote followed a political crisis resulting from the defeat of the Government's budget proposals at the end of December 2002, as well as reports of increasing dissatisfaction with Harris's alleged economic mismanagement of the country. Nauru's deteriorating financial situation, in addition to the Government's decision to accept more than 1,000 asylum-seekers in return for aid from Australia, were believed to be major factors in the loss of confidence in Harris, which had led to the defection to the opposition of two cabinet ministers, two backbenchers and the Speaker in late 2002. However, Harris applied to the Supreme Court, and on 10 January 2003 an injunction was issued against Dowiyogo accepting the presidency. This decision had been based on the fact that only 11 of the 18 members of Parliament had attended the session when the vote took place, thus rendering it invalid; Harris and his Cabinet had staged a boycott of Parliament when the motion was to be proposed. Despite the injunction, Dowiyogo maintained his position and appointed a new Cabinet. Several days of confusion and political instability ensued. Finally, Harris was reinstated as President, following the intervention of Nauru's Melbourne-based Chief Justice. However, he resigned from the presidency the following day. In the resultant contest Dowiyogo defeated Kinza Clodumar by nine votes to eight to become the new President on 20 January. A lack of support for Dowiyogo within Parliament continued to create problems, however, amid appeals for an early election to resolve the impasse.

Meanwhile, a complete collapse of Nauru's telecommunications system in early January 2003 increased the problems experienced by the island. Nauru, thus, effectively became cut off from the rest of the world with external contact only possible when ships equipped with satellite telephones were calling. A speech by Dowiyogo claiming that Nauru was on the verge of bankruptcy, unable to pay its public servants or to send its sick citizens to Australia for treatment, and appealing to donor countries for emergency assistance, could not be transmitted for almost a month. Telecommunications services were restored in early March following a visit from a technician supplied by Australia's government aid agency, AusAID.

In early March 2003 Dowiyogo travelled to Washington, DC, at the request of the US Government, which had threatened to impose harsh economic sanctions on the island and to repossess Air Nauru's only aircraft, if Nauru did not discontinue its 'offshore' banking services. The administration of George W. Bush was reported to have been angered by the possibility that individuals with links to terrorist organizations might have used the island's financial services to 'launder' their funds; some 400 'offshore' banks were registered on the island in the early 2000s. Consequently, Dowiyogo agreed to sign executive orders not to renew any banking licences or to issue any further so-called 'investor passports'. Shortly after the meeting, however, Dowiyogo collapsed and, following emergency heart surgery, died on 9 March. Derog Gioura was appointed acting Head of State and on 20 March was elected President by nine parliamentary votes to seven. Legislation providing for the expiry of most 'offshore' banking licences within 30 days (and for the remainder within six months) was approved by Parliament in late March, in accordance with the agreement that Dowiyogo had signed in the USA. At the end of March acting President Derog Gioura himself suffered a heart attack and was flown to Australia for treatment.

A general election took place on 3 May 2003, at which six new members were elected to the legislature. However, the new Speaker resigned one day after his election, and with no further nominations for the position, Parliament was unable to proceed to a presidential election. The impasse was resolved when a Speaker was finally elected in late May and Ludwig Scotty won the subsequent presidential election, defeating Kinza Clodumar with 10 parliamentary votes to seven. Scotty, who named a new six-member Cabinet in June, stated his Government's intention to focus on 'prudent management and financial stability'. However, on 8 August Scotty was ousted from office by a no confidence motion and replaced by Rene Harris, who became the fourth President of 2003. The reasons for Scotty's removal were not clear, although concerns had been expressed about his plans to close the recently opened embassies in Washington, DC, and Beijing, and there had been speculation that he intended to switch Nauru's diplomatic allegiance from the People's Republic of China back to Taiwan (see below).

In August 2003 workers at the Nauru Phosphate Corporation began a strike in support of demands for almost six months of unpaid salaries. Opposition politicians claimed that the dispute was an indication of more widespread dissatisfaction with corruption and mismanagement in the industry and within the Government.

In January 2004 President Rene Harris was flown to Australia amid rumours that he had suffered a physical collapse and was in a poor state of health. Officials declined to respond to queries surrounding the President, merely stating that Derog Gioura would be acting President in his absence. In the following month the Minister for Justice resigned, precipitating a vote of no confidence in the President. The country faced a further political crisis when the motion received an equal number of votes in favour and against. Moreover, when Parliament was unable to agree on the election of a new Speaker, following the resignation of the incumbent in early April, the resulting impasse meant that Parliament could not be formally convened. As the country's financial crisis deepened, President Harris travelled to Australia in mid-April to request assistance in averting imminent bankruptcy for the island. On his return to Nauru Harris faced angry demonstrations by hundreds of government employees protesting at the hardship imposed on them as a result of their salaries having been unpaid for 12 months. Reports indicated that government employees (who constituted the majority of paid employees on the island) were surviving on subsistence diets of fish and coconuts. In the same month receivers were appointed to manage the assets of the Nauru Phosphate Royalties Trust (including Nauru's extensive property portfolio in Australia) which was unable to pay off debts of some $A230m. to US interests. Nauruans working in government-owned buildings in Melbourne and Sydney were served with eviction notices. Meanwhile, with neither the Government nor the opposition willing to nominate a Speaker from among its members (thereby giving the other side a majority in Parliament), the legislature was unable to produce a budget. In May, however, during another of Harris's overseas trips, the opposition elected one of its members as Speaker and immediately approved legislation making it illegal for a government to operate without a budget. In the following month, and before the Supreme Court had ruled on the matter, Kinza Clodumar, the Minister of Finance, crossed the floor, thereby allowing the opposition to approve a motion of no confidence in Harris. Ludwig Scotty was subsequently elected to the presidency. In late July Australian Treasury official Peter Depta arrived in Nauru to take up the post of Financial Secretary, effectively assuming control of the country's finances.

Nauru's precarious political situation deteriorated during September 2004, and by the end of the month President Ludwig Scotty had dissolved Parliament and declared a state of emergency. His action had been prompted by the Speaker Russell Kun's suspension of the Minister of Health, Kieren Keke, on the grounds that he held dual Nauruan and Australian nationality. Keke's suspension had resulted in the loss of the Government's one-seat majority and a consequent stalemate in Parliament, during which budget legislation had been unable to be approved. Scotty assumed sole responsibility over the government of the country until a general election took place on 23 October. At the election all nine members of Scotty's Government retained their seats in the legislature, while seven of the nine opposition members of parliament were not re-elected. The result thus gave President Scotty an ample majority in Parliament. Within days of its election the new Government approved a budget that included a reduction in public-sector salaries and increased import duties. In the following month legislation aimed at discouraging criminals, particularly terrorists, from using the country's financial sector was approved, in addition to the establishment of a procedure for conducting possible future referendums and of reviewing the Constitution. The sudden death of the Speaker, Vassal Gadoengin, from a heart attack in December 2004 led to the election of Valdon Dowiyogo, a new member of Parliament and son of the former President, to the position in the following month.

In January 2005 a committee of members of Parliament began a review of Nauru's Constitution, motivated partly by a desire to achieve greater political stability in the country. In 2006 the committee formed the Independent Commission on Constitutional Review, and in mid-2007 a Constitutional Convention, comprising 18 directly elected members and 18 appointees, met to discuss the Commission's conclusions.

At the legislative election held on 25 August 2007 several members and supporters of the Scotty Government were re-elected to Parliament. Later in that month Scotty was re-elected as the island's President, defeating Marcus Stephen by a considerable margin of parliamentary votes. Scotty's new Cabinet retained all the ministers of the previous Government. In December, however, Scotty was removed from office in a vote of no confidence, amid allegations of corruption against the Minister of Foreign Affairs and of Finance, David Adeang, and the withdrawal of support of several members of the Government. Marcus Stephen was subsequently elected to replace Scotty, appointing a Cabinet that included Kieren Keke (who had served as a minister under Scotty) as Minister of Foreign Affairs, Trade, Telecommunications and Transport.

The new Government's progress was hampered by increasing discord and its lack of a majority in the legislature, and in April Speaker David Adeang, a member of the opposition, announced the suspension of all nine government members of Parliament. Stephen subsequently declared a state of emergency and dissolved Parliament, setting in motion the procedure for the holding of an early election. At the election, held on 26 April 2008, the incumbent Government was able to increase its representation in Parliament to 12 of the 18 legislators, at the expense of three members of the opposition who lost their seats. Riddell Akua was elected Speaker, while Stephen's Cabinet was expected to remain largely unchanged.

In September 2001 Nauru agreed to accept 310 of 460 predominantly Afghan asylum-seekers who were on board a Norwegian freighter, the *MV Tampa*, unable to disembark on Christmas Island as Australia refused to grant them entry into its territory (see the chapter on Christmas Island). The Australian Government agreed to fund the processing of the asylum-seekers and to pay an undisclosed sum to Nauru, which was to accommodate the asylum-seekers for three months while their claims for asylum were assessed. Following the interception of several other boats carrying asylum-seekers in Australian waters later the same month, Nauru received a pledge of $A20m. from the Australian Government for agreeing to host 800 asylum-seekers. In December 2001 Nauru signed an agreement with Australia's Minister for Foreign Affairs to accommodate a total of 1,200 at any one time, in return for a further $A10m. of aid, to be allocated to education, health and infrastructure programmes. Local residents and owners of the land upon which the camps were located expressed concern over the delays in processing the asylum-seekers' claims, which were due to be completed by July 2002. In May Australia offered monetary assistance to Afghan asylum-seekers as an incentive to return to their homeland, and in the following month the President announced that he anticipated that all the asylum-seekers would have left Nauru by the end of the year. However, in December some 700 people remained in the camps, despite the deportation of more than 100 Afghan asylum-seekers to Kabul. In the same month the President signed a new agreement with Australia's Minister for Foreign Affairs to extend the duration of the camps' operations and to accommodate up to 1,500 asylum-seekers.

In mid-2003 the Australian Government was accused of cruelty for detaining some 100 children in the camps on Nauru and for failing to reunite families held in separate camps for extended periods. The Nauruan Government was subject to further criticism when the visa of a Catholic priest and prominent human rights activist was withdrawn hours before he was due to visit refugees detained on the island. It was believed that Nauruan officials had been instructed to cancel the visa by the Australian Government. Concerns about the conditions at the camps and the welfare of the detainees increased during 2003, and in December some of those held began a hunger strike in order to attract attention to their situation. A reported 40 asylum-seekers participated in the strike, some of whom stitched their lips together. The Nauruan Government's subsequent appeals for medical assistance from Australia to care for the hunger strikers, many of whom required hospital treatment during the following weeks, were refused. The emerging rift between the two countries intensified when Nauru's Minister of Finance, Kinza Clodumar, condemned remarks made by Australia's Minister for Immigration, Amanda Vanstone, who had said that the health of the hunger strikers was of no concern to Australia. Clodumar, who stated that his country's limited medical resources could not cope with a problem of this scale, accused Australia of failing to recognize its obligations in continuing to ignore the plight of the asylum-seekers on Nauru. The strike ended about one month after it had begun, and in mid-January 2004 the Australian Government sent a delegation to inspect medical facilities available to asylum-seekers on the island. The resultant report, however, which found services for those held in detention to be adequate, was widely regarded as flawed, as it had failed to examine any of the detainees and had been compiled solely by Australian government officials. In late June 2004 the first of 146 Afghan refugees, approved to enter Australia, left the detention centre. In November 2005, after four years of detention on the island, a total of 25 asylum-seekers were transferred to Melbourne. It was reported that only two detainees, who had failed to meet security requirements, remained on Nauru; their departure from the centre was finally arranged in late 2006. In early 2007 the claims of 82 Sri Lankan asylum-seekers, who had been intercepted by the Australian navy in February, were being processed on Nauru, along with those of seven detainees from Myanmar. In February 2008 the 21 remaining detainees left Nauru, marking the end of Australia's policy of accommodating asylum-seekers on the island. The Australian Government's decision was not welcomed by all Nauruans, in view of its likely impact on the island's economy.

In February 1987 representatives of the British, Australian and New Zealand Governments signed documents effecting the official demise of the British Phosphate Commissioners, who from 1919 until 1970 had overseen the mining of Nauru's phosphate deposits. President DeRoburt subsequently expressed concern about the distribution of the Commissioners' accumulated assets, which were estimated to be worth $A55m. His proposal that part of this sum be spent on the rehabilitation of areas of the island that had been mined before independence was rejected by the three Governments involved. DeRoburt subsequently established a commission of inquiry to investigate proposals for rehabilitation. The commission proposed that the three Governments provide one-third ($A72m.) of the estimated rehabilitation costs. In 1989 Australia's refusal to contribute to the rehabilitation of former phosphate-mining areas prompted Nauru to institute proceedings, claiming compensation from Australia for damage to its environment, at the International Court of Justice. However, in 1993, following negotiations between President Dowiyogo and the Australian Prime Minister, Paul Keating, a Compact of Settlement was signed, under which the Australian Government was to pay some $A107m. to Nauru. New Zealand and the United Kingdom subsequently agreed to contribute $A12m. each towards the settlement. An investigation into methods for the rehabilitation of the damaged areas of the island included plans to use landfill to encourage the restoration of vegetation to the mined areas, and the re-establishment of many of the species of flora and fauna that had previously been abundant on the island. In mid-1995 a report commissioned by the Government published details of a rehabilitation programme extending over the next 20–25 years and costing $A230m. The success of the rehabilitation scheme, however, was dependent on the co-operation of landowners, some of whom were expected to continue to allow areas to be mined for residual ore once phosphate reserves had been exhausted. In mid-1997 Parliament approved the Nauru Rehabilitation Corporation (NRC) Act, providing for the establishment of a corporate body to manage the rehabilitation programme. The NRC held its inaugural meeting in May 1999. The rehabilitation programme (which was to be partly financed from the Compact of Settlement with Australia) was expected to transform the mined areas into sites suitable for agriculture, new housing and industrial units. The project, however, was hampered considerably by delays, and in early 2004 the chair of the NRC resigned, reportedly in frustration at problems regarding the implementation of a feasibility study into the mining of residual phosphate. Results published in September 2004 from a series of test sites on the island indicated that the potential for residual phosphate mining might be greater than had been previously thought. A major refurbishment of the island's mining plant was subsequently undertaken, and exports of phosphates resumed in 2006 (see Economic Affairs). In March 2008 protests reportedly related to the export of phosphates escalated into violence, with a group of approximately 100 demonstrators setting fire to a police station. A team of volunteers was appointed by local Australian police officers to maintain stability on the island.

As a result of a strike by pilots of Air Nauru, begun in 1988, the Governments of Australia and New Zealand withdrew certification of the airline, concerned that it was not complying with safety standards. Air Nauru resumed operations in 1989, and diplomatic relations with Australia (which had been suspended in the previous year) were restored. In July 1998 the airline was transferred to the Australian aviation register in order to achieve improved surveillance and safety standards. In February 2001 Nauru's transport links with the rest of the world were severed when Air Nauru temporarily suspended all its operations, following a report by the Civil Aviation Safety Authority in Australia.

In December 2005 Air Nauru faced the prospect of closure following a court order for the seizure of the carrier's only aircraft, on account of the airline's non-payment of loan instalments to the Export-Import Bank of the United States. Discussions with Taiwan began in the hope that Air Nauru, which had consistently operated at a loss, might be revived, and in January 2006 Nauru's Minister of Civil Aviation announced that Taiwan had agreed to offer support. Meanwhile, Air Pacific (of Fiji), Air Vanuatu and Air Marshall Islands (which had hitherto provided only domestic services) were operating on sectors of the routes formerly serviced by Air Nauru. In September 2006 Air Nauru was relaunched under the new name of Our Airline after Taiwan provided sufficient funding for the Government's acquisition of an aircraft with which it could resume services. The future of the airline was discussed at a meeting held in the Marshall Islands later in the year, and it was resolved that a task force be established to analyse the possibility of Our Airline becoming a sub-regional carrier, jointly owned by Nauru, the Federated States of Micronesia, Kiribati, Solomon Islands, the Marshall Islands and Tuvalu.

Nauru was persistently critical of France's use of the South Pacific region for nuclear-weapons testing, and was one of the most vociferous opponents of the French Government's decision in mid-1995 to resume its nuclear-testing programme. Diplomatic relations, suspended between the two countries in 1995, were formally resumed in early 1998.

In early 2001 Nauru voiced strong opposition to the US Government's plans to develop a missile defence system, in which missiles are deployed to shoot down other missiles in flight. Government officials in Nauru expressed fears that testing of the system in the region could result in missile debris landing on the Pacific islands.

The President of Nauru met the Cuban Minister of Foreign Affairs in November 2001 at a UN meeting, where they agreed to establish diplomatic relations between their two countries and discussed a proposed technical and economic co-operation agreement whereby Nauru would be provided with health experts from Cuba.

In 1989 a UN report on the 'greenhouse effect' (the heating of the earth's atmosphere and a resultant rise in sea-level) listed Nauru as one of the countries that might disappear beneath the sea in the 21st century, unless drastic action were taken. The Government of Nauru strongly criticized Australia's refusal, at the December 1997 Conference of the Parties to the Framework Convention on Climate Change (see UN Environment Programme, see p. 62), in Kyoto, Japan, to reduce its emission of pollutant gases known to contribute to the 'greenhouse effect'.

In August 2001 Nauru hosted the Pacific Islands Forum summit meeting, despite a problematic shortage of accommodation, caused by the presence of contingents of officials from Australia, refugee agencies, the UN and Eurest (the company subcontracted to operate Nauru's refugee camp). Fiji had been expected to perform this role, but its participation had been opposed owing to its failure to reinstate democratic rule following the coup of the previous year.

In July 2004 President Ludwig Scotty held emergency discussions with the Presidents of Kiribati and Tuvalu regarding at least US $2m. in outstanding salary payments owed to their nationals employed in Nauru by the Nauru Phosphate Corporation. Nauru's financial crisis (see above) led it to appeal for assistance from the Pacific region and the international community. Consequently, in September 2004 the Pacific Islands Forum offered to help pay the salaries of Nauruan government employees (which had been unpaid for many months, resulting in considerable hardship), while the Cuban Government responded to an appeal for healthcare workers (as discussed in a co-operation agreement in late 2001—see above) by sending 11 doctors to Nauru to alleviate an increasingly serious situation, in which only three doctors were available to sick Nauruans. In May 2006 the Government embarked upon a programme to improve the health of the population, having developed a draft national strategy for addressing the high prevalence of obesity and lifestyle diseases such as diabetes.

In July 2002 a political crisis had emerged after President Rene Harris decided unilaterally to recognize the People's Republic of China, thus ending 22 years of diplomatic relations with Taiwan. Several cabinet ministers opposed the shift in policy, and the controversy increased after Harris immediately accepted US $60m. in aid and $77m. in debt annulment from the People's Republic of China. Following the switch in allegiance, Taiwan announced that it would take legal action to recover a loan of $12.5m., which it had arranged to make available to Nauru.

In March 2005 President Ludwig Scotty made an official visit to mainland China where he took part in discussions on bilateral aid and economic and technical co-operation. However, in May the Chinese Government announced that Nauru had severed its diplomatic relations with the People's Republic by switching its allegiance back to Taiwan. In July it was reported that Taiwan was to pay the outstanding salaries of some 1,000 workers from Kiribati and Tuvalu, who had remained stranded on Nauru since the island's financial crisis had resulted in the Government's inability to pay their wages. In March 2006 it was announced that Taiwan was providing US $3m. in overdue salary payments to the former phosphate miners from Kiribati and Tuvalu.

In February 2003 two diplomatic missions were opened, in Washington, DC, and in Beijing, primarily to address US concerns over 'money-laundering' and international terrorism (fears regarding the latter increased when, in the same month, two members of al-Qa'ida were found to be travelling on Nauruan passports). However, in July President Scotty announced plans to close the missions, citing economic constraints and his belief that they were not serving their intended purpose. Representatives in China and the USA expressed surprise at the announcement and queried the President's motives, in particular his commitment to ending the lucrative sale of Nauruan passports.

Nauru attracted considerable controversy in June 2005 when, at a meeting of the International Whaling Commission (IWC) in the Republic of Korea, it voted with Japan to remove the moratorium on commercial whaling introduced in 1986. Japan was accused by some observers of encouraging small, developing countries to join the IWC and then of attempting to influence their voting with financial incentives. However, Nauru denied that it had been subjected to any form of manipulation by the Japanese Government, stating that it had voted to remove the ban on whaling in order to preserve its tuna stocks.

Government

Legislative power is vested in the unicameral Parliament, with 18 members elected by universal adult suffrage for up to three years. Executive authority is vested in a Cabinet, which consists of the President of the Republic, elected by the Parliament, and ministers appointed by him. The Cabinet is collectively responsible to Parliament. Responsibilities for administration are divided between the Nauru Local Government Council and the Government. The Council, an elected body of nine members from the country's 14 districts, elects one of its members to be Head Chief.

Defence

Nauru has no defence forces: under an informal arrangement, Australia is responsible for the country's defence.

Economic Affairs

In 2006, according to official sources, Nauru's gross domestic product (GDP), measured at current prices, was $A37m., equivalent to $A3,742 per head. In 1995–2004, it was estimated, GDP decreased, in real terms, at an average annual rate of 1.5%. The population increased by an annual average of about 0.1% per year in 1995–2006. Real GDP expanded by 6.3% in 2006, according to the Asian Development Bank (ADB), but in 2007 the economy was estimated to have contracted by 27.3%.

Agricultural activity comprises mainly the small-scale production of tropical fruit, vegetables and livestock, although the production of coffee and copra for export is increasingly significant. According to FAO, agriculture and fishing engaged some 33% of the economically active population in mid-2005. The sector provided 11.7% of GDP in 2005/06. Following a period of decline, agricultural GDP increased, in real terms, by 25.5% in 2003. Coconuts are the principal crop. Bananas, pineapples and the screw-pine (*Pandanus*) are also cultivated as food crops, while the islanders keep pigs and chickens. However, almost all Nauru's requirements are imported. Increased exploitation of the island's marine resources was envisaged following the approval by Parliament of important fisheries legislation in the late 1990s, but the sector has continued to be constrained by lack of equipment. Revenue from fishing licence fees totalled an estimated $A7m. in 2005/06.

Industrial activity (mining, manufacturing, construction and utilities) accounted for 6.8% of GDP in 2005/06. In real terms, industrial GDP declined by 7.5% in 2002 and by 9.8% in 2003. Until the early 1990s Nauru's economy was based on the mining of phosphate rock, which constituted four-fifths of the island's surface area. Phosphate extraction was conducted largely by indentured labour, notably by I-Kiribati and Tuvaluan workers. Revenue from phosphate sales was invested in a long-term trust fund (the Nauru Phosphate Royalties Trust (NPRT—see below) and the Nauru Local Government Council. As the depletion of primary deposits continued, in 2004 an Australian engineering company undertook a detailed survey of the island's potential for secondary phosphate mining (see Recent History). The discovery of substantial new deposits of high-grade phosphate was announced in 2005. An agreement with an Australian fertilizer company was signed in late 2005, and in early 2006 it was announced that a Thai company was also to become involved in phosphate-mining operations on Nauru. In September, following the upgrading of processing facilities, the first major shipment of phosphate for nearly 10 years was exported to India. The mining of secondary phosphate resources, which was expected to sustain the industry for about 30 years, was to commence in 2007. However, operations in that year were disrupted when the island's port facilities were damaged.

Energy is derived principally from imported petroleum. Output of electrical energy totalled 32m. kWh in 2004, the same production level as in the previous year.

The services sector, accounting for 81.6% of Nauru's GDP in 2005/06, comprises mainly those employed in public service. The real GDP of services rose by 3.4% in 2002, but decreased by 0.4% in 2003. The sector recorded no growth in 2004, with many salaries remaining in arrears (see Recent History). According to official estimates, public administration accounted for an estimated 44.5% of GDP in 2005/06. There is no tourism sector. Commercial banking services are not widely available.

The country's trade balance deteriorated significantly in the year to June 2005, when the deficit rose to US $28.7m. Imports increased from US $24.3m. in 2003/04, to $33.7m. in 2004/05. This was accompanied by a substantial decline in exports, which decreased from US $43.2m. in 2003/04 to $19.7m. in the following year and to only $5.0m. in 2004/05. The principal imports are manufactured goods, machinery and transport equipment, food and live animals, and chemical products. Phosphates have traditionally been the most important export, earning $38.1m. in 1995; exports of crude fertilizers to Australia totalled $A8.5m. in 2001. The main exports in 2005 included manufactured goods and crude materials. The principal export markets in 2005 were the Republic of Korea (which purchased about 23% of the total) and Canada (20%). The principal sources of imports in that year were the Republic of Korea (supplying 43%) and Australia (36%).

The 2006/07 budget envisaged revenue of $A22,288m. and expenditure of $A22,226m., a modest surplus of $A62,000 thus being forecast. Development assistance from Australia was projected at $A8.7m. for 2007/08. Nauru's external debt was estimated by the ADB at US $A310m. in 2007. In that year the level of international and domestic debt was reported to be the equivalent of 30 times the country's GDP. Consumer prices increased by 17.9% in 2000, but subsequently moderated. The annual rate of inflation was estimated by the ADB at 3.2% in 2006 and 2.9% in 2007. The rate of unemployment in 2002 was estimated at 22.7% of the labour force.

Nauru is a member of the Pacific Community (see p. 377), of the Pacific Islands Forum (see p. 380) and of the UN Economic and Social Commission for Asia and the Pacific (ESCAP, see p. 35), all of which aim to promote regional development. Nauru is also a member of the Asian Development Bank (ADB, see p. 182).

After gaining independence in 1968, Nauru benefited from sole control of earnings from phosphate mining, and as a result its income per head was among the highest in the world. However, this had serious repercussions for the country, which became excessively dependent on expatriate labour, imports of consumer goods and convenience foods, causing environmental, health and social problems. The assets of the NPRT, meanwhile, became seriously depleted, being estimated to total only $A300m. in 2003, compared with $A1,300m. in 1991. In November 2005 Nauru hosted an international donor meeting, attended by representatives of about 20 donor nations and agencies, at which it requested support for its National Sustainable Development Strategy. The aims of this programme included an increase in revenue from phosphate production, better use of fish resources and the encouragement of agricultural activities, with particular emphasis on local food production. While the resumption of phosphate mining in 2006 was to provide the Government with additional revenue, a considerable fiscal adjustment was expected. Many public departments had continued to function inefficiently; therefore, the planned abolition of the Computer Bureau and of the Department of Works, as the Government sought to contract out such services, in addition to the removal of subsidies for public enterprises, were signs of positive action towards the reform of the public sector. The substantial contraction in the economy during 2006/07 was primarily due to a decline in the public sector, concomitant with the completion of the construction of new processing facilities for the phosphate sector (see above). Owing to adverse weather conditions and the resultant damage to export facilities, phosphate mining was temporarily suspended during 2007, but the ADB anticipated a subsequent improvement in the situation and that the economy would contract by only 2.4% in 2007/08. Despite the sharp decrease in GDP and the reduction in government expenditure, the inflation rate remained steady in 2006/07, partly owing to the moderate level of inflation in Australia (Nauru uses the Australian dollar as its official currency). However, the closure of a refugee-processing centre (see Recent History) was expected to have an adverse impact on the island's economy in 2008.

Education

Education is compulsory for Nauruan children between six and 16 years of age. Primary education begins at the age of six and lasts for seven years. Secondary education, beginning at 13 years of age, lasts for up to four years. In 2002/03 enrolment at pre-primary schools was equivalent to 71% of the relevant age-group. In 2003/04 enrolment at primary level was equivalent to 83.7% and enrolment at secondary level was equivalent to 47.8%. In 2007 there were four pre-primary schools, two primary schools and four secondary schools with a total of 134 teachers. In 2003 there were four vocational level teachers with 38 students. In 2001 Nauruans studying overseas at secondary and tertiary levels numbered 85. There is a university extension centre, linked with the University of the South Pacific in Suva, Fiji. The education sector was particularly badly affected by the country's economic crisis during 2004. With payment of their salaries in arrears, many expatriate teachers left the country. The sector also continued to be constrained by the lack of adequate teaching materials.

Public Holidays

2008: 1 January (New Year's Day), 31 January (Independence Day), 21–24 March (Easter), 17 May (Constitution Day), 26 October (Angam Day), 25–26 December (Christmas).
2009: 1 January (New Year's Day), 31 January (Independence Day), 10–13 April (Easter), 17 May (Constitution Day), 26 October (Angam Day), 25–26 December (Christmas).

Weights and Measures

The imperial system is in force.

Statistical Survey

Source (unless otherwise indicated): Bureau of Statistics, Ministry of Finance, Government Offices, Yaren District; tel. (674) 444-3142; fax (674) 444-3125; e-mail bos@cenpac.net.nr; fax www.spc.int/prism/country/nr/stats.

AREA AND POPULATION

Area: 21.3 sq km (8.2 sq miles).

Population: 8,042 (Nauruan 4,964, Other Pacific Islanders 2,134, Asians 682, Caucasians—mainly Australians and New Zealanders—262) at census of 13 May 1983; 9,919 (males 5,079, females 4,840) at census of 17 April 1992; 10,065 (males 5,136, females 4,929) at census of 23 September 2002. *Mid-2007* (projected estimate): 8,777.

Density (mid-2007): 412.1 per sq km.

Principal Districts (population, 1992 census): Denigomudu 2,548; Meneng 1,269; Aiwo 1,072; Boe 750; Yaren (capital) 672; Buada 661. Source: Thomas Brinkhoff, *City Population* (internet www.citypopulation.de).

Births, Marriages and Deaths (1995): Registered live births 203 (birth rate 18.8 per 1,000); Registered marriages 57 (marriage rate 5.3 per 1,000); Registered deaths 49 (death rate 4.5 per 1,000). *2002:* Registered live births 219; Registered deaths 75.

Expectation of Life (years at birth, WHO estimates): 61.3 (males 58.1; females 65.1) in 2005. Source: WHO, *World Health Statistics*.

Economically Active Population (census of 17 April 1992): 2,007 (Elementary occupations 401, Clerks and office workers 355, Craft and related workers 299, Service, shop and market sales workers 250, Professionals 208, Plant, machine operators and assemblers 136, Technicians and associate professionals 115, Legislators, senior officials and managers 18, Agriculture and related workers 2, Not classified 223). *Mid-2005* (estimates): Agriculture, etc. 2,000; Total labour force 6,000 (Source: FAO).

HEALTH AND WELFARE
Key Indicators

Total Fertility Rate (children per woman, 2005): 3.8.
Under-5 Mortality Rate (per 1,000 live births, 2005): 30.
Physicians (per 1,000 head, 1995): 1.45.
Hospital Beds (per 1,000 head, 2004): 6.0.
Health Expenditure (2004): US $ per head (PPP): 399.3.
Health Expenditure (2004): % of GDP: 8.1.
Health Expenditure (2004): public (% of total): 73.0.

For sources and definitions, see explanatory note on p. vi.

AGRICULTURE, ETC.

Principal Crop and Livestock (2006, FAO estimates): Coconuts 1,600 metric tons; Pigs 2,800 head; Chickens 5,000 head.

Livestock Products (metric tons, 2006, FAO estimates): Pig meat 71; Chicken meat 3; Hen eggs 16.

Fishing (metric tons, live weight of capture, 2005): Yellowfin tuna 12; Bigeye tuna 3; Skipjack tuna 13; Total catch (incl. other marine fishes) 39.

Source: FAO.

MINING

Phosphate Rock ('000 metric tons, estimates): 84 in 2003; 22 in 2004; 11 in 2005. The phosphoric acid content ('000 metric tons, estimates) was: 26 in 2003; 7 in 2004; 3 in 2005. Source: US Geological Survey.

INDUSTRY

Electric Energy (million kWh): 30 in 2002; 32 in 2003; 32 in 2004. Source: Asian Development Bank, *Key Indicators of Developing Asian and Pacific Countries*.

FINANCE

Currency and Exchange Rates: Australian currency: 100 cents = 1 Australian dollar ($A). *Sterling, US Dollar and Euro Equivalents* (31 December 2007): £1 sterling = $A2.2725; US $1 = $A1.1343; €1 = $A1.6698; $A100 = £44.01 = US $88.16 = €59.89. *Average Exchange Rate* (Australian dollars per US $): 1.3095 in 2005; 1.3280 in 2006; 1,1951 in 2007.

Budget ($A '000, year ending 30 June 2007, provisional figures): *Total Revenue:* 22,288 (Tax revenue 8,646, Non-tax revenue 13,643); *Total Expenditure:* 22,226 (Employee expenses 5,890, Operating expenses 8,543, Property expenses 505, Current transfers 2,150, Gross fixed capital formation 4,682, Other 457).

Gross Domestic Product ($A '000, year ending 30 June at current prices): 34,009 in 2005; 36,881 in 2006; 26,897 in 2007 (projection).

EXTERNAL TRADE

Principal Commodities (US $ '000, year ending 30 June 2005): *Imports:* Food and live animals 4,548; Beverages and tobacco 1,891; Crude materials (except food and fuel) 1,741; Mineral fuels and lubricants 1,528; Animal fats and vegetable oils 1,698; Chemical products 3,300; Manufactured goods 11,898; Machinery and transport equipment 5,375; Miscellaneous manufacture articles 1,705; Total (incl. others) 33,683. *Exports:* Food and live animals 293; Crude materials (except food and fuel) 1,489; Chemical products 408; Manufactured goods 2,039; Machinery and transport equipment 616; Miscellaneous manufacture articles 113; Total (incl. others) 4,959.

Principal Trading Partners (US $ million, year ending 31 December 2005): *Imports:* Australia 10.7; Fiji 0.7; Germany 1.3; Republic of Korea 13.0; USA 1.8; Total (incl. others) 29.9. *Exports:* Canada 0.9; Germany 0.4; India 0.5; Republic of Korea 1.0; Total (incl. others) 4.4. Source: Asian Development Bank, *Key Indicators of Developing Asian and Pacific Countries*.

NAURU

Trade Totals (US $ '000, year ending 30 June): *Imports c.i.f.*: 37,196 in 2003; 24,292 in 2004; 33,683 in 2005. *Exports f.o.b.*: 43,221 in 2003; 19,656 in 2004; 4,959 in 2005.

TRANSPORT

Road Traffic (1989): 1,448 registered motor vehicles.

Shipping: *Merchant Fleet* (displacement, '000 grt at 31 December): 15 in 1991 (at 30 June); 5 in 1992; 1 in 1993. Source: Lloyd's Register of Shipping. *International Freight Traffic* (estimates, '000 metric tons, 1990): Goods loaded 1,650; Goods unloaded 59. Source: UN, *Monthly Bulletin of Statistics*.

Civil Aviation (traffic on scheduled services, 2003): Kilometres flown (million) 3; Passengers carried ('000) 156; Passenger-km (million) 275; Total ton-km (million) 28. Source: UN, *Statistical Yearbook*.

COMMUNICATIONS MEDIA

Radio Receivers (1997): 7,000 in use*.

Television Receivers (1997): 500 in use*.
Telephones (main lines, 2001): 2,000 in use†.
Mobile Cellular Telephones (2001): 1,500 subscribers†.
Internet Users (2001): 300†.

* Source: UNESCO, *Statistical Yearbook*.
† Source: International Telecommunication Union.

EDUCATION

Pre-primary (2007): 4 schools; 38 teachers; 669 pupils.
Primary (2007): 2 schools; 53 teachers; 1,235 pupils.
Secondary (2007): 4 schools; 43 teachers; 689 pupils.
Vocational (2003, unless otherwise indicated): 2 schools (2004); 4 teachers; 38 students.

Note: Nauruans studying at secondary and tertiary levels overseas in 2001 numbered 85.

Source: Department of Education, Yaren, Nauru.

Directory

The Constitution

The Constitution of the Republic of Nauru came into force at independence on 31 January 1968, having been adopted two days previously. It protects fundamental rights and freedoms, and vests executive authority in the Cabinet, which is responsible to a popularly elected Parliament. The President of the Republic is elected by Parliament from among its members. The Cabinet is composed of five or six members, including the President, who presides. There are 18 members of Parliament, including the Cabinet. Voting is compulsory for all Nauruans who are more than 20 years of age, except in certain specified instances.

The highest judicial organ is the Supreme Court and there is provision for the creation of subordinate courts with designated jurisdiction.

There is a Treasury Fund from which monies may be taken by Appropriation Acts.

A Public Service is provided for, with the person designated as the Chief Secretary being the Commissioner of the Public Service.

Special mention is given to the allocation of profits and royalties from the sale of phosphates.

The Government

HEAD OF STATE

President: MARCUS STEPHEN (elected 19 December 2007).

CABINET
(April 2008)

President and Minister of Public Service, Home Affairs, Police, Prisons and Emergency Services, and the Nauru Phosphate Royalties Trust: MARCUS STEPHEN.

Minister of Finance, Economic Planning, Foreign Affairs and Trade, responsible for assisting the President: Dr KIEREN KEKE.

Minister of Commerce, Industry and Resources: FREDERICK PITCHER.

Minister of Education and Fisheries: ROLAND KUN.

Minister of Health, Sports and Justice: MATTHEW BATSIUA.

Minister of Telecommunications and Transport: SPRENT DABWIDO.

MINISTRIES

Office of the President: Yaren; tel. 444-3772; fax 444-3776; e-mail the.president@naurugov.nr.

Ministry of Commerce, Industry and Resources: Yaren; e-mail minister.cir@naurugov.nr.

Ministry of Education: Yaren; tel. 444-3130; fax 444-3718; e-mail minister.education@naurugov.nr.

Ministry of Finance: Government Treasury Bldg, Aiwo; tel. 444-3140; fax 555-4477; e-mail minister.finance@naurugov.nr.

Ministry of Fisheries: e-mail minister.fisheries@naurugov.nr.

Ministry of Foreign Affairs: e-mail minister.foreignaffairs@naurugov.nr.

Ministry of Health: ; tel. 444-3133; fax 444-3188; e-mail minister.health@naurugov.nr.

Ministry of Home Affairs: e-mail minister.homeaffairs@naurugov.nr.

Ministry of Justice: Yaren; tel. 444-3160; fax 444-3108; e-mail minister.justice@naurugov.nr.

Ministry for Nauru Phosphate Royalties Trust: e-mail minister.nprt@naurugov.nr.

Ministry of Police: e-mail minister.police@naurugov.nr.

Ministry of Public Service: e-mail minister.publicservice@naurugov.nr.

Ministry of Sport: e-mail minister.sport@naurugov.nr.

Ministry of Telecommunications: e-mail minister.telecommunications@naurugov.nr.

Ministry of Transport: e-mail minister.transport@naurugov.nr.

Ministry of Utilities: e-mail minister.utilities@naurugov.nr.

Ministry of Youth Affairs: e-mail minister.youthaffairs@naurugov.nr.

Legislature

PARLIAMENT

Parliament comprises 18 members. The most recent general election took place on 26 April 2008.

Speaker: RIDDELL AKUA.

Political Organizations

Democratic Party of Nauru: c/o Parliament House, Yaren; f. 1987; revival of Nauru Party (f. 1975); Leader KENNAN ADEANG.

Naoero Amo (Nauru First): c/o Parliament House, Yaren; e-mail visionary@naoeroamo.com; f. 2001; Co-Leaders DAVID ADEANG, KIEREN KEKE.

Diplomatic Representation

EMBASSY IN NAURU

China (Taiwan): Civic Center, 1st Floor, Aiwo; tel. 444-3239; fax 444-3846; e-mail nru@mofa.gov.tw.

Judicial System

The Chief Justice presides over the Supreme Court, which exercises original, appellate and advisory jurisdiction. The Resident Magistrate presides over the District Court, and he also acts as Coroner under the Inquests Act 1977. The Supreme Court is a court of record.

NAURU

The Family Court consists of three members, one being the Resident Magistrate as Chairman, and two other members drawn from a panel of Nauruans. The Chief Justice is Chairman of the Public Services Appeals Board and of the Police Appeals Board.

Supreme Court
Yaren; tel. 444-3163; fax 444-3104.
Chief Justice: BARRY CONNELL (non-resident).

DISTRICT COURT
Resident Magistrate: G. N. SAKSENA.

FAMILY COURT
Chairman: G. N. SAKSENA.

Religion

Nauruans are predominantly Christians, adhering either to the Nauruan Protestant Church or to the Roman Catholic Church.
Nauruan Protestant Church: Head Office, Nauru; Moderator (vacant).
Roman Catholic Church: POB 16, Nauru; tel. and fax 444-3708; Nauru forms part of the diocese of Tarawa and Nauru, comprising Kiribati and Nauru. The Bishop resides on Tarawa Atoll, Kiribati.

The Press

Central Star News: Nauru; f. 1991; fortnightly.
Nasero Bulletin: Nauru; tel. 444-3847; fax 444-3153; e-mail bulletin@cenpac.net.nr; fortnightly; English; local and overseas news; Editor SEPE BATSIUA; circ. 500.
The Nauru Chronicle: Nauru; Editor RUBY DEDIYA.

Broadcasting and Communications

TELECOMMUNICATIONS
Nauru Telecommunications Service: Nauru; tel. 444-3324; fax 444-3111; Dir EDWARD W. R. H. DEYOUNG.

BROADCASTING
Radio
Nauru Broadcasting Service: Information and Broadcasting Services, Chief Secretary's Department, POB 77, Nauru; tel. 444-3133; fax 444-3153; e-mail director.media@naurugov.nr; f. 1968; state-owned and non-commercial; broadcasts in the mornings in English and Nauruan; operates Radio Nauru; Station Man. RIN TSITSI; Man. Dir GARY TURNER.

Television
Nauru Television (NTV): Nauru; tel. 444-3133; fax 444-3153; e-mail ntvmanager@cenpac.net.nr; began operations in June 1991; govt-owned; broadcasts 24 hrs per day on 3 channels; most of the programmes are supplied by foreign television companies via satellite or on videotape; a weekly current affairs programme is produced locally; Man. MICHAEL DEKARUBE; Dir of Media GARY TURNER.

Finance

(cap. = capital; res = reserves; dep. = deposits; m. = million; amounts in Australian dollars unless otherwise stated)

BANKING
State Bank
Bank of Nauru: Civic Centre, POB 289, Nauru; tel. 444-3238; fax 444-3203; e-mail bonauru@yahoo.com; f. 1976; state-owned; Chair. NAGENDRA GOSWAMI.

INSURANCE
Nauru Insurance Corporation: POB 82, Nauru; tel. 444-3346; fax 444-3731; f. 1974; sole licensed insurer and reinsurer in Nauru; Chair. NIMES EKWONA.

Trade and Industry

GOVERNMENT AGENCIES
Nauru Agency Corporation: POB 300, Aiwo; tel. 444-3782; fax 444-3730; e-mail info@nauruoffshore.com; internet nauruoffshore.com; f. 1972; management service to assist entrepreneurs in the incorporation of holding and trading corpns and the procurement of trust and insurance licences; CEO R. MOSES.
Nauru Corporation: Civic Centre, Yaren; f. 1925; operated by the Nauru Council; the major retailer in Nauru; Gen. Man. A. EPHRAIM.
Nauru Fisheries and Marine Resources Authority: POB 449, Nauru; tel. 444-3733; fax 444-3812; e-mail nfmra@cenpac.net.nr; f. 1997.
Nauru Phosphate Corporation: Aiwo; tel. 444-3839; fax 444-2752; f. 1970; has operated the phosphate industry and several public services of the Republic of Nauru (including provision of electricity and fresh water) on behalf of the Nauruan people; responsibility for phosphate-mining operations assumed by Republic of Nauru Phosphate Company (Ronphos), overseen from 2005 by Astro Pacific Group (New Zealand); Chair. RIDDELL AKUA; Gen. Man. LESI OLSSON.
Nauru Phosphate Royalties Trust (NPRT): Nauru; e-mail nprtnau@cenpac.net.nr; statutory corpn; invests phosphate royalties to provide govt revenue; extensive international interests, incl. hotels and real estate; Sec. NIRAL FERNANDO.
Nauru Rehabilitation Corporation (NRC): Civic Centre, Aiwo; tel. 444-3200; fax 444-3272; e-mail nrcadm@cenpac.net.nr; f. 1999; manages and devises programmes for the rehabilitation of those parts of the island damaged by the over-mining of phosphate; Chair. ALI AMWANO.

UTILITIES
Nauru Phosphate Corporation: Aiwo; tel. 444-3839; fax 444-2752; operates generators for the provision of electricity and water supplies; Chair. RIDDELL AKUA; Gen. Man. LESI OLSSON.

Transport

RAILWAYS
There are 5.2 km of 0.9-m gauge railway serving the phosphate workings.

ROADS
A sealed road, 16 km long, circles the island, and another serves Buada District.

SHIPPING
As Nauru has no wharves, passenger and cargo handling are operated by barge. In late 1998 finance was secured from the Japanese Government for the construction of a harbour in Anibare district. Work on the project began in 1999, and the harbour was opened in 2000.
Nauru Pacific: Government Bldg, Yaren; tel. 444-3133; f. 1969; operates cargo charter services to ports in Australia, New Zealand, Asia, the Pacific and the west coast of the USA; Man. Dir (vacant).

CIVIL AVIATION
Our Airline: Directorate of Civil Aviation, Government of Nauru Offices, POB 40, Yaren; tel. 444-3746; fax 444-3705; e-mail info@ourairline.com.au; internet www.ourairline.com.au; f. 1970; corporatized in 1996 and moved to Australian aviation register in mid-1997; operates passenger and cargo services to Kiribati, Solomon Islands and Australia; fmrly Air Nauru; name changed as above in 2006; Chair. KEN MCDONALD; CEO GEOFFREY BOWMAKER.

NEPAL

Introductory Survey

Location, Climate, Language, Religion, Flag, Capital

Nepal is a land-locked Asian country in the Himalaya mountain range, with India to the east, south and west, and Tibet (the Xizang Autonomous Region), in the People's Republic of China, to the north. The climate varies sharply with altitude, from arctic on the higher peaks of the Himalaya mountains (where the air temperature is permanently below freezing point) to humid subtropical in the central valley of Kathmandu, which is warm and sunny in summer. Temperatures in Kathmandu, which is 1,337 m (4,386 ft) above sea-level, are generally between 2°C (35°F) and 30°C (86°F), with an annual average of 11°C (52°F). The rainy season is between June and October. Average annual rainfall varies from about 1,000 mm (40 ins) in western Nepal to about 2,500 mm (100 ins) in the east. The official language is Nepali, which was spoken by 48.6% of the population in 2001. Other languages include Maithir (12.3% in 2001) and Bhojpuri (7.5%). Some 80.6% of the population were Hindus in 2001, with 10.7% Buddhists and 4.2% Muslims. The national flag (proportions 4 by 3) is composed of two crimson pennants, each with a blue border. The upper section contains a white crescent moon (horns upwards and surmounted by a disc with eight rays) and the lower section a white sun in splendour. The capital is Kathmandu.

Recent History

Although Nepal was an hereditary monarchy, for more than 100 years, until 1951, effective power was held by the Rana family, who created the post of hereditary Prime Minister. A popular revolution, led by the Nepali Congress Party (NCP), ousted the Ranas and restored King Tribhuvan to power. A limited constitutional monarchy was established in 1951. During most of the 1950s government was controlled by the monarchy, first under Tribhuvan and then, after his death in 1955, under his son, Mahendra. In February 1959 King Mahendra promulgated Nepal's first Constitution, providing for a bicameral parliament, including a popularly elected lower house. Elections held later that month resulted in victory for the NCP, led by Bisweswor Prasad (B. P.) Koirala, who became Prime Minister. However, the King retained a certain degree of power, and persistent differences between the King and the Prime Minister led to a royal coup in December 1960: Nepal's first brief period of democracy was thus brought to an abrupt end. The King dismissed the Council of Ministers and dissolved Parliament. A royal decree of January 1961 banned political parties. King Mahendra accused the Koirala administration of corruption, and in December 1962 he introduced a new Constitution, reasserting absolute royal power and providing for a 'partyless' system of government, based on the Panchayat (village council), with a Prime Minister appointed by the King. This office was filled successively by Dr Tulsi Giri (1962–65), Surya Bahadur Thapa (1965–69) and Kirti Nidhi Bista (1969–70, 1971–73). King Mahendra himself was Prime Minister from April 1970 to April 1971. In January 1972 King Mahendra died and was succeeded by his son, Birendra. Nagendra Prasad Rijal became Prime Minister in July 1973, and held office until December 1975, when Dr Giri was reappointed. The new Government made major changes to the Constitution, which allowed for a widening of the franchise and more frequent elections to the Rashtriya Panchayat (National Assembly), but in no way were the King's powers eroded. In September 1977 Dr Giri resigned and was succeeded by Bista.

B. P. Koirala, the former Prime Minister and an advocate of parliamentary democracy, was acquitted of treason in February 1978. Returning from abroad a year later, he was placed under house arrest in April 1979, but then released, partly to appease students who had been demonstrating for reforms. National unrest grew and, after King Birendra announced in May that there would be a national referendum on whether to restore multi-party democracy, Bista resigned and was succeeded as Prime Minister by Thapa. In the referendum, held in May 1980, 54.8% of the voters supported the Panchayat system with reforms. As a result, the King formed a Constitutional Reforms Commission, and in December he issued a decree under which amendments to the Constitution were made, including the proviso that the appointment of the Prime Minister by the King would henceforth be on the recommendation of the Rashtriya Panchayat. In accordance with the new provisions, direct legislative elections were held in May 1981, the first of their kind since 1959, although still on a non-party basis. Thapa was re-elected by the Rashtriya Panchayat as Prime Minister in June 1981, and the King installed a new Council of Ministers (on the recommendation of the Prime Minister). An extensive ministerial reshuffle took place in October 1982, but this failed to stem increasing official corruption and economic mismanagement. In July 1983, for the first time in the 23-year history of the Panchayat system, the incumbent Prime Minister, Surya Bahadur Thapa, was ousted, and a new Council of Ministers was formed by a former Chairman of the Rashtriya Panchayat, Lokendra Bahadur Chand, who had successfully introduced a motion expressing no confidence in Thapa.

In March 1985 the NCP held a convention in Kathmandu, and in May it embarked upon a campaign of civil disobedience, aimed at restoring a multi-party political system and parliamentary rule under a constitutional monarchy. In June there was a series of bomb explosions, resulting in loss of life. The explosions were apparently co-ordinated by two newly formed anti-monarchist and anti-Government groups, the Janawadi Morcha (Democratic Front) and the Samyukta Mukti Bahini (United Liberation Torch-bearers). These bombings united an otherwise seriously divided legislature against the terrorists, and forced the predominantly moderate opposition to abandon the campaign of civil disobedience and to disclaim any responsibility for the explosions. In August the Rashtriya Panchayat approved a stringent anti-terrorist law, and more than 1,000 people were arrested in connection with the unrest.

In May 1986 a general election was held. About 64% of the electorate voted, in spite of appeals by the NCP and the pro-China faction of the Communist Party of Nepal (CPN) (neither of which presented candidates) for a boycott of the polls. All the candidates in the election were nominally independents, but it was reported that among the 72 new entrants to the Rashtriya Panchayat (40 members retained their seats) were at least 16 members of the Marxist-Leninist faction of the CPN. In June the King nominated 25 additional members of the new Rashtriya Panchayat, and Marich Man Singh Shrestha (previously Chairman of the Rashtriya Panchayat) was elected unopposed by the Assembly as the new Prime Minister. In late 1986, to counter the growing influence of the communist faction in the Rashtriya Panchayat, several senior figures (including Jog Meher Shrestha, a former government minister, and Chand) established a 'Democratic Panchayat Forum', which expressed full support for the non-party system.

In June 1987, in an apparent attempt to improve the image of the Panchayat system, the Government initiated an anti-corruption campaign, during the course of which several senior officials were arrested for drugs-trafficking and other offences. In early 1988 the Government continued its policy of suppressing opposition. In January the President of the NCP was arrested, and in February more than 100 people, who were planning to demonstrate in support of the NCP mayor of Kathmandu (who had been suspended from office for his anti-Panchayat stance), were also detained.

In September 1989 the Government arrested more than 900 NCP supporters, in an apparent effort to prevent them from celebrating the anniversary of the birth of Nepal's first elected Prime Minister, B. P. Koirala (who died in 1982). During these celebrations the NCP demonstrated in protest against the failings of the country's non-party political system. In November the leaders of the NCP held a meeting in Kathmandu with members of several other left-wing and communist political groups, to discuss the proposed formation of a country-wide peaceful 'movement for the restoration of democracy'; the movement's aims would be the alleviation of Nepal's severe economic problems (including the trade dispute with India, see below), the restoration of full democracy, the transfer from absolute to constitutional monarchy, the immediate replacement of the Panchayat Government by an interim national government, the removal of the ban on political activities, and the introduction of a multi-party system. In January 1990 a co-ordination committee to conduct the Jana Andolan (People's Movement) was formed by the NCP and the newly formed United Left Front (ULF, which was led by Sahana Pradhan and comprised six factions of the CPN and a labour group), despite the Government's efforts to pre-empt its inauguration by arresting hundreds of activists (including many students) and by banning, or heavily censoring, more newspapers. During the consequent violent confrontations between protesters and police that took place in February, it was officially estimated that 12 people were killed and hundreds more arrested. Violent demonstrations, strikes and mass arrests continued throughout March. At the end of the month the Minister of Foreign Affairs, Shailendra Kumar Upadhayaya, resigned from his post, following differences with the Prime Minister regarding the Government's management of the crisis. A few days later there was an extensive government reshuffle, including the dismissal of nine ministers who allegedly opposed the Government's acts of repression against the pro-democracy movement. In an effort to end the political unrest, the King dismissed Shrestha's Government on 6 April and nominated a restricted four-member Council of Ministers, under the leadership of the more moderate Chand. King Birendra also offered to establish a body that would examine the possibility of altering the Constitution and to hold discussions with the opposition, and he promised to initiate an official inquiry into the 20 deaths that had occurred during demonstrations since February. Despite these concessions, the situation worsened later the same day. A temporary curfew was imposed on the capital, and many political agitators were arrested. The Government immediately initiated talks with the opposition, and on 8 April the King announced that the 30-year ban on political parties was to be ended, thus enabling the future holding of multi-party elections, and that a commission to study constitutional reform was to be established. At the same time, the Jana Andolan suspended its campaign of demonstrations. Many political activists continued to agitate, however, demanding the removal of the formal structure of the Panchayat system. A week later, the King accepted the resignation of Chand from his post as Prime Minister, dismissed the Council of Ministers and announced the dissolution of the Rashtriya Panchayat. King Birendra then invited the opposition alliance of the NCP and the ULF to form an interim government. On 19 April a new 11-member coalition Council of Ministers (including two ministers nominated by the King and two independents), under the premiership of the President of the NCP, Krishna Prasad (K. P.) Bhattarai, was sworn in. The new Prime Minister announced that a general election would be held, on a multi-party basis, within a year. The principal task of the interim Government was to prepare a new constitution in accordance with the spirit of multi-party democracy and constitutional monarchy. King Birendra stated that he was committed to transforming his role into that of a constitutional monarch, and, following further violent clashes in Kathmandu between anti-royalists and police, he ordered the army and the police to comply with the orders of the interim Government in order to facilitate a smooth transition to democracy.

In mid-May 1990 King Birendra announced a general amnesty for all religious and political prisoners. On 21 May he delegated the legislative powers of the dissolved Rashtriya Panchayat to the new Council of Ministers, so that the Council was empowered to enact, amend and repeal legislation in order to bring about the introduction of a multi-party democracy. At the end of the month the King formed a nine-member Constitutional Recommendation Commission, based on the suggestions of the Prime Minister, which, after consulting the various parties, was to prepare a draft constitution and present it to the King within three months. In July the death sentence was abolished and the laws restricting freedom of the press and freedom of association were repealed. In addition, the King suspended almost one-half of the articles in the Constitution to enable the interim Government to function smoothly. The draft of the new Constitution, which was published at the end of August, recommended the introduction of a constitutional monarchy; a democratic multi-party system and a bicameral legislature, composed of a 205-member House of Representatives (Pratinidhi Sabha) and a 60-member National Assembly (Rashtriya Sabha); the official guarantee of fundamental rights (including freedom of expression); an independent judiciary; and the placing of the army under the control of a three-member National Defence Council, headed by the Prime Minister. The draft Constitution recognized Hinduism as the country's dominant religion. It also, however, guaranteed freedom for religious minorities to practise their beliefs (although restrictions on proselytizing were to remain in force). Under the draft Constitution, the King would be allowed to declare a state of emergency on the advice of the Council of Ministers, but such declarations would have to be approved by the House of Representatives within three months. A crucial clause in the new Constitution required the King 'to obey and protect' the Constitution: under the old regime, the King was considered to be above the Constitution. The draft Constitution was approved by the Council of Ministers on 15 October and sent to the King for his endorsement. King Birendra, however, amended the draft in a final effort to retain sovereign authority and full emergency powers. This retrograde action provoked violent protests. The Council of Ministers rejected most of the proposed amendments in the royal counter-draft, but agreed to the King's proposal to establish a Council of State (Raj Parishad), with a standing committee headed by a royal appointee. The 15-member committee was to be composed of eight royal appointees and seven other members, including the Prime Minister, the Ministers of Defence and Foreign Affairs, the Chief Justice of the Supreme Court and the Chief of Army Staff. Bhattarai stressed, however, that the formation of this committee would not alter the democratic nature of the new Constitution, since it would not function as a parallel body to the Council of Ministers. He also emphasized that the King would only be permitted to act on judicial, executive and legislative matters on the advice of the Council of Ministers. The new Constitution was officially promulgated by the King on 9 November.

The communist movement in Nepal suffered a set-back in December 1990, when four of the seven constituent members of the ULF broke away from the front, citing their lack of representation in the interim coalition Council of Ministers. Sahana Pradhan stated, however, that the three remaining factions would continue to operate as the ULF. In January 1991 two major factions of the CPN (the Marxist and Marxist-Leninist factions) merged to form the CPN (Unified Marxist-Leninist—UML).

The general election was held on 12 May 1991. Of the 44 political parties that had been registered by the Election Commission, however, only 20 actually participated. The NCP decided to contest the election alone and not on the basis of an electoral alignment with any of its former Jana Andolan partners. The communists interpreted the NCP's move as the result of an increased understanding between the palace and the NCP on the basis that both wanted to forestall the rise of communism in the country. Consequently, relations between the NCP and the UML became strained and competitive. The general election was not only peaceful, but was also characterized by a good turn-out (65.2% of the electorate). The NCP won a comfortable majority, but it was soundly defeated by the UML in the eastern hill districts and in some parts of the Terai. In Kathmandu, supposedly an NCP stronghold, the party lost all of the seats but one. The UML established itself as the second largest party in the House of Representatives, followed by the United People's Front (UPF), an amalgam of radical, Maoist groups. The Rashtriya Prajatantra Party (Chand) and the Rashtriya Prajatantra Party (Thapa), led by the former Prime Ministers of those names, fared badly in the election, winning only four seats between them. Acting Prime Minister Bhattarai lost his seat in the capital, and was replaced in the premiership by Girija Prasad (G. P.) Koirala, the General Secretary of the NCP and brother of the late B. P. Koirala.

By the end of 1991 unity within the ruling NCP was threatened by growing internal dissent amongst its leadership, particularly between the senior leader, Ganesh Man Singh, and G. P. Koirala. The Government suffered a further set-back in April 1992 when a *bandh* (general strike), organized by the communist and other opposition parties in Kathmandu in protest against price rises, water shortages and alleged government corruption, resulted in the deaths of at least seven demonstrators following violent clashes with the police. Despite the consequent imposition of curfews in the capital and in the neighbouring town of Lalitpur, the opposition staged a number of anti-Government protest marches and demonstrations during the following week. The success of a second general strike, which was held in early May, demonstrated the continuing strength of the radical left. It brought Kathmandu to a standstill and, unlike the earlier general strike, passed off without violent incidents. Despite the strikes and the rising cost of living, the NCP performed well in the local elections held throughout the country in May and June. There were, however, widespread reports of corruption and electoral malpractice.

Under the leadership of G. P. Koirala, the centrist NCP Government shifted to the right. The public image of the monarchy and leading members of the former Panchayat regime were rehabilitated with government support. No charges were brought against senior officials of the former administration for corruption or human rights violations. Replicating the patronage system of the Panchayat regime, the NCP rapidly began to dominate the public administration structure. The ruling party's persistent failure to democratize its internal bodies and the absence of open election to posts in the party leadership met with criticism both within and outside the NCP.

In addition to opposition from the leadership of his own party, G. P. Koirala faced increasing criticism from the opposition parties themselves, which focused on an agreement drawn up by the Prime Minister in December 1991 granting India access to water from the Tanakpur barrage on the Mahakali River, the terms of which were only subsequently revealed to the Nepalese House of Representatives. Alleging that the agreement constituted a treaty affecting national sovereignty, and therefore requiring a two-thirds' majority in the House of Representatives, the opposition launched a campaign calling for the resignation of Koirala on the grounds of unconstitutional behaviour. An indeterminate Supreme Court ruling in December 1992 on Koirala's action only intensified the protest.

In January–February 1993 the national UML congress abandoned much of the party's Marxist dogma and tacitly acknowledged its commitment to working within a democratic multi-party system. However, the untimely deaths of the party's General Secretary, Madan Bhandari, and Politburo member Jiv Raj Ashrit, following a road accident in mid-May, threw the UML into disarray. The rejection by the UML of the findings of a government inquiry, which concluded that the deaths had been accidental, provoked nation-wide protests in support of demands for an independent inquiry into the so-called 'Dhasdunga Incident'. In late May Madhav Kumar Nepal was appointed as the new General Secretary of the UML.

In the mean time, the rehabilitation of officials of the former Panchayat regime continued. In January 1993 the King appointed senior figures of the old administration, including former Prime Ministers Chand and Shrestha, to the 121-member Council of State (Raj Parishad), in a move designed both to rehabilitate former Panchayat officials and to reassert his leadership role over them. In June the right-wing Rashtriya Prajatantra Party (RPP, formed in February 1992, following a merger of the Chand and Thapa factions) held its first national conference in Kathmandu, an event that would have been inconceivable three years previously, when its leaders were forced into hiding by the democracy movement.

In August 1993 the UML signed an agreement with the NCP, providing for the permanent withdrawal of the UML from anti-Government agitation in return for the ruling party's pledge to establish an independent commission to investigate the 'Dhasdunga Incident'. The UPF and other left-wing groups, however, continued their campaign of nation-wide general strikes and demonstrations. Further serious rifts became apparent within the ruling NCP when the party's President, K. P. Bhattarai, lost a legislative by-election to the UML candidate in Kathmandu in February 1994; his defeat was widely attributed to G. P. Koirala's public opposition to his candidature. In March the Government survived a vote of no confidence (by 113 votes to 81) presented to the House of Representatives by the UML. The opposition itself suffered from internal dissension in mid-1994 when both the UPF and the CPN (Unity Centre) split into competing factions, while the UML continued to be divided between radical and conservative camps. The crisis within the NCP culminated on 10 July when followers of Ganesh Man Singh withdrew their support for Koirala, who thereby lost his parliamentary majority. Consequently the Prime Minister offered his resignation, and on the following day the King dissolved the House of Representatives. Koirala was appointed as interim Prime Minister pending the holding of a general election, which was brought forward from mid-1996 to 15 November 1994. At the general election, which attracted a turn-out of 58%, the UML unexpectedly emerged as the single largest party, winning 88 of the 205 seats in the House of Representatives, while the NCP won 85 seats. At the end of the month the UML formed a minority Government under the premiership of its moderate Chairman, Man Mohan Adhikari. In late December the communist Government won a vote of confidence in the House of Representatives (as required by the Constitution for a new administration to continue in power).

On 11 June 1995 the NCP registered a parliamentary motion of no confidence against the communist Government and, in conjunction with the RPP and the Nepali Sadbhavana Party (NSP), submitted a memorandum to King Birendra, staking their claim to form an alternative government. On the recommendation of the Prime Minister, who wished to avert the passage of the motion, the King dissolved the legislature on 13 June and announced that fresh elections were to be held on 23 November. Adhikari and his Council of Ministers were to function as a caretaker Government, pending the general election. In an apparent attempt to win popular support in the run-up to the election, Adhikari's interim administration substantially increased budgetary expenditure and implemented a number of welfare programmes. The opposition, angered by the communists' mode of electioneering, challenged the dissolution of the House of Representatives in the Supreme Court. In a controversial ruling, declared on 28 August, the Supreme Court decided that the dissolution of the lower house on the advice of a minority administration (when a majority coalition was ready to assume power) had, indeed, been unconstitutional. The House of Representatives was consequently reconvened and the election abandoned. The UML Government was defeated in a vote of no confidence on 10 September, by 107 votes to 88. On 12 September a coalition Government, composed of members of the NCP, the RPP and the NSP, and headed by the NCP's parliamentary leader, Sher Bahadur Deuba, was formed.

In early March 1996 the Government introduced a number of security measures following a series of violent clashes between a group of Maoist activists and the police in western Nepal, which resulted in the deaths of at least 11 people (by the end of the year more than 100 people had been killed as a result of the insurgency). The left-wing extremists (many of whom were members of the underground Communist Party of Nepal—Maoist and the UPF) had launched a 'people's revolutionary war' in the hills of Nepal in February, demanding the abolition of the constitutional monarchy and the establishment of a republic. In May G. P. Koirala was elected to replace Bhattarai as President of the NCP; for the first time since its foundation, the party elected its leader by ballot. In early December seven RPP members of the Council of Ministers resigned from their posts and the faction of the party led by Chand withdrew from the ruling coalition; the Government, however, which continued to enjoy the support of the RPP faction led by Thapa, narrowly survived a legislative vote of no confidence (presented by the UML) later that month. In early January 1997 five of the former RPP ministers who had resigned from the Government in the previous month reversed their position and pledged their support for Deuba's administration; a few days later four of these politicians were reinstated in the Government as part of a ministerial reshuffle. The Government suffered a set-back at the end of the month when the UML, already the largest party in the House of Representatives, increased its strength from 87 to 90 deputies, following its success in three by-elections. Deuba's administration finally collapsed in early March when it lost a vote of confidence in the House of Representatives. Chand was appointed as the new Prime Minister (for the fourth time) at the head of a coalition Government composed of members of the RPP, the UML, the NSP and the Nepal Workers' and Peasants' Party. The new Government, however, seemed unstable from the outset, since the members of the Thapa faction of the RPP refused to support Prime Minister Chand and the ideological differences between the communists and the former pro-monarchists appeared insuperable. Although Chand held the premiership, the UML, as the largest component of the coalition, was responsible for more ministerial posts than the RPP. In May and June the communists replaced the NCP as the country's dominant force in local government, following resounding successes in local elections. These elections were marred, however, by violent clashes between supporters of the main political parties in which about 30 people were killed. In mid-June more than 10,000 NCP supporters demonstrated in Kathmandu in protest over alleged electoral irregularities on the part of the UML during the recent polls. During 1997 the UML suffered from factional infighting, with a major rift developing between Deputy Prime Minister Bam Dev Gautam and the General Secretary of the party, Madhav Kumar Nepal. This factionalism served to destabilize the coalition Government further. In August a strike organized by an alliance of left-wing groups (known as the National Democratic Front) in protest at the rise in the price of fuel and a proposed anti-terrorist law brought Kathmandu and surrounding towns to a standstill. In the following month an anti-defection bill, the aim of which was to prevent politicians from deserting their own party and thus to bring stability to Nepal's politics, was unanimously approved by the House of Representatives.

On 4 October 1997 the Government lost a parliamentary vote of no confidence tabled by the NCP. A few days later King Birendra appointed Thapa, the President of the RPP, to replace Chand as Prime Minister. A new coalition Government, comprising members of the RPP and the NSP, took office on the following day. In December Prime Minister Thapa expanded the Council of Ministers in a reshuffle that introduced members of the NCP and a number of independents into the coalition. In January 1998 Nepal was once again faced with political upheaval when Thapa recommended to the King that he dissolve the House of Representatives and set a date for mid-term elections. The Prime Minister presented the petition for fresh polls following a decision by the UML and dissident members of the RPP (including Chand) to introduce a parliamentary vote of no confidence against the Government. Uncertain as to how to act in this political impasse, the King referred the matter to the Supreme Court (the first time a Nepalese monarch had ever done so). In early February the Court advised King Birendra to convene a special session of the House of Representatives to discuss a no confidence motion against Thapa's Government. Although the Supreme Court's advice was not binding, the King called the parliamentary session. The no confidence motion, which was presented on 20 February, was, however, narrowly defeated. Meanwhile, in mid-January Chand and nine other rebel deputies were expelled from the RPP; they immediately re-established a breakaway faction known as the RPP (Chand). In March the UML suffered a serious reverse when about one-half of the party's parliamentary deputies formed a breakaway faction entitled the Communist Party of Nepal (Marxist-Leninist) (ML). Bam Dev Gautam was unanimously elected as the new party's leader. The creation of the new party left the UML with 49 deputies, while the ML claimed the support of 40 deputies.

Under an agreement reached in October 1997 when Thapa assumed power, the Prime Minister was to transfer the leadership of the coalition Government to the NCP within an agreed time frame. By early April 1998, however, Thapa appeared reluctant to relinquish his post, and the NCP threatened to withdraw support for the Government unless the Prime Minister resigned immediately. Thapa tendered his resignation, and the President of the NCP, G. P. Koirala, was appointed Prime Minister in mid-April, taking office with only two other ministers. After obtaining a parliamentary vote of confidence, by 144 votes to four, the Prime Minister substantially expanded his Council of Ministers. Koirala stated that among the top priorities of the one-party minority Government would be the tackling of the Maoist insurgency (which had escalated in recent months). In August, in a seeming attempt to strengthen his own precarious administration and to encourage the UML's communist rivals, the Prime Minister invited the ML to join in alliance with the NCP and to form a coalition government. A new coalition administration was consequently established on 26 August (with the NCP retaining the most important ministries), giving Prime Minister Koirala an adequate parliamentary majority. Meanwhile, the 'people's war' waged by the Maoist activists in the hills of west Nepal gathered momentum. In May the Government launched a large-scale police operation in an effort to curb the guerrilla violence.

In December 1998 the ML withdrew from the coalition Government, alleging that its ruling partner, the NCP, had failed to implement a number of agreements drawn up between the two parties and other political groups in August. Prime Minister G. P. Koirala tendered his resignation, but was asked to head a new coalition Council of Ministers, which was to hold power in an acting capacity pending the holding of a general election. On the recommendation of the Prime Minister, the King appointed a new coalition administration, comprising members of the NCP, the UML and the NSP, and, for the first time in eight years, a nominee of the King, on 25 December. In mid-January 1999 the acting Government won a convincing vote of confidence in the House of Representatives, and on the following day the King dissolved the legislature in preparation for the forthcoming general election.

In late April 1999 the UML suffered a set-back when its veteran leader and former Prime Minister, Man Mohan Adhikari, died during the electoral campaign. In May the NCP won an outright majority in the general election (held over two rounds), securing 110 of the 205 seats in the lower house; the UML obtained 68 seats and the RPP (Thapa) took 11 seats, while the ML and the RPP (Chand) both failed to win a single seat. Voting was conducted relatively peacefully, according to government sources, despite threats by the Maoist insurgents to disrupt the electoral process. A new Council of Ministers, headed by the veteran NCP leader, K. P. Bhattarai, and composed solely of NCP members, was appointed at the end of the month. In late June the UML won all six seats in elections to the National Assembly, and in August Dr Mohammad Mohasin of the RPP was elected Chairman of the upper house.

In late November 1999, in an effort to resolve the Maoist insurgency, which, according to government sources, now affected (moderately to severely) 31 of Nepal's 75 districts and had led to the deaths of more than 1,000 people, the Prime Minister offered to grant the guerrillas an amnesty and various rehabilitation measures if they surrendered their arms and entered into negotiations with the Government. In response, the insurgents (who were estimated to number 5,000–6,000 and to have the support of about 8,000 sympathizers) stated that they were not prepared to enter into peace talks until arrest warrants issued against their leaders were withdrawn, official investigations were carried out into alleged extrajudicial killings of suspected militants by the police, and imprisoned activists were released. In an attempt to facilitate the peace process, the Government established a six-member high-level negotiation commission under the convenorship of former Prime Minister Sher Bahadur Deuba, which was charged with finding a solution to the Maoist situation that met with the approval of all political parties (including the insurgents themselves).

In mid-December 1999 the ruling NCP, despite a number of by-election victories, was once again beset by internecine strife when about 80 pro-Koirala legislators initiated an attempt to oust (by means of a petition) the Prime Minister from his position as the NCP's parliamentary party leader (which would automatically lead to his removal from the premiership). Koirala had initially been supportive of Bhattarai's premiership, but had since become a vociferous critic of his rival's administration, particularly with regard to the Government's perceived mismanagement of the Maoist crisis. In February 2000 a minor reorganization of the Council of Ministers took place, which included the appointment of Ram Chandra Poudel, a former Speaker of the lower house, as Deputy Prime Minister; the ministerial reshuffle was prompted by the earlier resignation of the Minister of Finance, Mahesh Acharya, following a disagreement with the Prime Minister over the appointment of the new Governor of the Central Bank. A few days after the government reorganization, the Minister of Education, Yog Prasad Upadhyaya, resigned in protest at the appointment of Poudel as Deputy Prime Minister. The political unrest culminated in the registration of a vote of no confidence by 58 dissident NCP legislators against Prime Minister Bhattarai; this move led to the immediate resignation of 11 government ministers. The NCP's parliamentary party was scheduled to vote on the no-confidence motion in late February; however, following the reaching of a secret agreement between the Prime Minister and the NCP President, G. P. Koirala, including Bhattarai's reported assurance that he would stand down voluntarily within two weeks, the proposal was withdrawn. A second motion of no confidence in Bhattarai was registered by 69 predominantly pro-Koirala legislators in the NCP secretariat in mid-March. Under such pressure, Bhattarai tendered his resignation to the King. It was announced that G. P. Koirala was to be the new Prime Minister (for the fourth time), following his election as parliamentary party leader of the NCP; this election process replaced the party's traditional method of choosing a parliamentary leader through consensus. Koirala and a new Council of Ministers were sworn in by the King on 22 March, and vowed to continue the basic programmes and policies that the previous NCP Government had adopted. In May a Human Rights Commission was formed following accusations by various bodies that both the security forces and the Maoist guerrillas had committed human rights violations, including murder and torture.

In early April 2000 Prime Minister Koirala activated the National Defence Council, which, according to the Constitution, comprised the Prime Minister, the Minister of Defence and the Commander-in-Chief of the Royal Nepal Army, to resolve the Maoist crisis. In comparison to the inadequately trained and poorly armed police force, which had suffered numerous casualties, the army was much better equipped to deal with the insurgency, and Koirala expressed his wish to mobilize the armed forces in the ongoing fight against militant activity. The possibility of the deployment of the armed forces met with immediate criticism from various Nepalese human rights groups, which claimed that mobilization of the army would lead to an escalation in corruption.

At the end of August 2000 the Maoist crisis worsened. During two Maoist attacks in Dolpa and Lamjung, 24 police officers were killed and 44 were injured. The Royal Nepal Army was criticized for failing to intervene to protect the police from insurgents. The Minister of Home Affairs, Govinda Raj Joshi, resigned after admitting his failure to 'maintain law and order in the country'. The Prime Minister responded to the confusion over the command and control structure of the army by giving Mahesh Acharya, the Minister of Finance, the additional portfolio of defence. G. P. Koirala had hitherto held charge of this portfolio, but it had become clear that the Government and army needed an independent defence minister, clarification of the army's ambiguous role and the development of a procedure for mobilizing the army (such matters not being incorporated in the 1991 Constitution). It was later decided that the Government would employ a dual approach: using the army, as well as encouraging negotiations, in order to resolve the Maoist crisis. In the mean time, the RPP (Chand) merged with the RPP (Thapa); the former was officially closed down in late 2000.

At the end of October 2000 the first direct unofficial negotiations began between the Government and the Communist Party of Nepal (Maoist)—CPN (M); however, they were short-lived, and the violence resumed in early November. In the same month the high-level commission charged with finding a solution to the Maoist crisis (see above) produced a report advising the Government and Maoist insurgents to cease violence and participate in negotiations. The report also recommended that the Government improve and modernize its security forces. The UML leader, who had earlier held negotiations with the insurgents, ruled out any alliance with the CPN (M) until it abandoned the use of force.

In January 2001 the Minister for Tourism and Civil Aviation, Tarani Datta Chataut, resigned following a controversial agreement to lease an Austrian aircraft to the Royal Nepal Airlines Corporation. In early February leading opposition parties issued a memorandum to the Prime Minister, demanding his resignation over the aircraft deal and also the worsening security situation. Koirala strongly denied his involvement in the leasing of the Austrian aircraft. The King then approved a reorganization of the Council of Ministers, on the recommendation of Prime Minister Koirala. However, shortly after the new administration was announced, two ministers withdrew their names, criticizing Koirala for making decisions without consulting other senior leaders. Palten Gurung later reneged on his decision, but Khum Bahadur Khadka refused to join the Council of Ministers. In March the Prime Minister faced increasing opposition from within and outside his party. Further ministerial resignations followed. The opposition continued to disrupt parliamentary proceedings, and, as a result, the King prorogued the National Assembly and House of Representatives in early April. At the end of the month the anti-corruption commission cleared the Prime Minister of involvement in the controversial aircraft agreement, but filed cases against 10 other people, including the former minister, Chataut. At the same time, Koirala was accused of accepting bribes in another aircraft deal. The opposition continued to demand his resignation and organized a nation-wide strike in protest against the Government's alleged misuse of power.

On 1 June 2001 King Birendra, Queen Aishwarya and six other members of the royal family were shot dead; the heir to the throne, Crown Prince Dipendra, was gravely wounded. Another family member, Dhirendra Shah, died later in hospital. Initial reports suggested that Prince Dipendra had shot members of his family before shooting himself, following a dispute between himself and his mother, regarding his intentions to marry Devyani Rani (the daughter of a prominent Nepalese politician), of whom the Queen disapproved. Prince Gyanendra, the deceased King Birendra's brother, however, issued a statement claiming that the deaths were the result of an accidental discharge of an automatic weapon. Immediately after the incident Prince Dipendra was pronounced King, and Prince Gyanendra was appointed regent. On 4 June King Dipendra died and was succeeded by Prince Gyanendra. These events caused considerable unrest in Kathmandu, and a curfew was imposed. In the mean time, rumours about the killings began to spread. Few believed the statement given by Gyanendra. Some suggested that Maoist insurgents were to blame, while others claimed that India was responsible. Following his accession, King Gyanendra established a commission to investigate the deaths. The commission, comprising the Chief Justice, K. P. Upadhyaya, and the Speaker of the House of Representatives, T. Ranabhat, duly concluded that Dipendra had been responsible for the shootings and that at the time had been under the influence of drugs and alcohol. King Gyanendra bestowed the title of Queen on his wife, Princess Komal, but did not declare his son the Crown Prince until the end of October, owing to the latter's unpopularity among the public, caused by his profligate behaviour.

In late June 2001 elections to 16 seats in the National Assembly took place. The UML won eight seats, bringing its total to 23 and rendering it the largest bloc in the chamber. In June–July Maoist leaders, taking advantage of the discontent in Nepal, intensified their activities. On 13 July the Deputy Prime Minister, Ram Chandra Poudel, resigned, owing to disagreements with the Prime Minister over government policy towards the insurgency. Several days later a senior Maoist leader declared that he would enter negotiations with the Government on the condition that the Prime Minister resigned. On 19 July Prime Minister Koirala resigned, citing his failure to curb the Maoist insurgency and long-standing corruption allegations. A few days later the NCP elected former premier Sher Bahadur Deuba as its new leader; King Gyanendra appointed Deuba as Prime Minister on the same day and a new Council of Ministers was sworn in on 26 July. Prime Minister Deuba retained a number of Koirala's former ministers in an effort to ensure stability and initially took personal charge of many of the more important portfolios.

Immediately after his appointment Prime Minister Deuba persuaded the Maoist leaders to reciprocate his offer of a cease-fire and agree to enter into dialogue. Prior to the negotiations, both sides took part in a series of confidence-building measures: the Maoist activists released 31 kidnapped police officers, and the Government set free more than 30 Maoist leaders and published the names of 273 guerrillas who remained in prison. At the same time Parliament passed legislation to establish an armed police force and to develop the co-ordination of regional development and security. The Government released a further 68 insurgents after the first two rounds of negotiations in August and September 2001. Despite the cease-fire, however, Maoist insurgents continued to carry out violent acts. During the peace talks tens of thousands of people held demonstrations against the fighting. The third round of negotiations, which took place in November, ended in failure, owing to the Maoists' continued demand for the dissolution of the Constitution, the establishment of an interim government, the election of a constituent assembly and, ultimately, a republic. The Government, in contrast, was prepared to offer a much less radical set of changes. Two days later the leader of the CPN (M), Pushpa Kamal Dahal (better known under his pseudonym, 'Prachanda'—'The Fierce One'), announced the end of the cease-fire. The Maoists established a parallel central government, the 'United People's Revolutionary Government', and resumed their violent campaign. The Maoists set up parallel governments in 40 of the country's 75 districts, and established direct rule in 22 districts in western Nepal. The violence escalated; on 26 November the King declared a state of emergency and authorized, for the first time, the deployment of the army to curb the insurgency. The King termed the Maoists as 'terrorists' and promulgated the Terrorist and Disruptive Activities Ordinance 2001, which sanctioned a number of counter-terrorist measures, including the suspension of civil liberties and the imposition of media restrictions. In mid-December Prime Minister Deuba declared that he would not resume negotiations with the Maoists until they had surrendered their arms.

Meanwhile, in early September 2001 the Government implemented a radical land reform programme, which was designed to help poor, landless farmers. The programme was supported by the UML, but opposed by smaller parties. Major landowners who risked losing part of their land because of the programme opposed the limit to the size of individual landholdings. In mid-August Deuba announced that discrimination against Dalits (or 'untouchables') would henceforth be illegal and pledged to pass legislation ending the caste system. A national commission for Dalit welfare and a National Women's Commission were also to be established.

In January 2002 the Nepal Rastra Bank 'froze' the bank accounts of individuals and organizations associated with Maoist militants. In mid-February Maoist insurgents launched their heaviest-ever offensive against government outposts. More than 150 people, mainly soldiers and police officers, were killed in the fighting. In response to the attacks, the army was instructed to use offensive as well as defensive measures to combat the insurgency. On 21 February the legislature voted to extend the state of emergency for three months. Although the opposition criticized the Government for its handling of the insurgency and for failing to react to warnings that major attacks were imminent, it voted for the extension after the Prime Minister agreed to establish social and economic development programmes in poor rural areas where Maoists were active, and ensured the fair use of the emergency powers.

In the mean time, in mid-February 2002 the UML and its breakaway faction, the ML, merged. The merger of the more moderate communist parties was regarded largely as a move to counter the influence of the Maoist insurgents. Strikes occurred in March, severely affecting businesses and schools. In its first annual report, the Human Rights Commission of Nepal accused the Maoist insurgents of committing serious human rights abuses. The commission also criticized the Government for allegedly violating human rights. In early April the Government reduced the controversial restrictions it had imposed on the media and political parties as part of the state of emergency. The violent campaign escalated in mid-April, leading to hundreds of fatalities. In May Deuba tabled a parliamentary motion proposing an extension of the six-month state of emergency (which was due to expire on 25 May), prompting strong opposition from within and outside his party. Members of the governing NCP, led by former premier G. P. Koirala, accused Deuba of not consulting them before recommending an extension and urged the Government to withdraw its parliamentary motion. The rift in the party led King Gyanendra to dissolve unexpectedly the House of Representatives on 22 May, on the recommendation of the Prime Minister. A general election was scheduled to take place on 13 November, and the incumbent Government was instructed to rule the country in the interim. Political leaders strongly condemned this decision. On 23 May Deuba was suspended from his party and three days later was expelled from the NCP for three years. In the mean time, three ministers, including the Minister of Finance, resigned in protest at the calling of early elections. In late May King Gyanendra extended the state of emergency by three months. Meanwhile, in early May the army launched a heavy attack against Maoist insurgents in Rolpa district, resulting in the deaths of more than 500 guerrillas, according to government sources. A series of counter-attacks and attacks ensued, leading to further hundreds of fatalities; by the end of May some reports estimated that more than 4,000 people had been killed since the beginning of the insurgency. On 9 May the Maoist leader made an offer of a one-month cease-fire by e-mail to newspapers in Kathmandu; Deuba promptly rejected the proposal, repeating his request for the insurgents to renounce violence.

In mid-June 2002 the NCP officially split during a 'general convention' held by the Deuba faction. Eventually, in mid-September the Election Commission recognized the faction led by G. P. Koirala as the official NCP. Several days later Deuba's minority breakaway faction registered as a new political party, the Nepali Congress Party—Democratic (NCP—D). Meanwhile, in April the Nepal Sadbhavana Party split into two factions and in July two communist parties, the National People's Front and the UPF, merged to form the People's Front Nepal (Janamorcha Nepal).

In the mean time, the state of emergency expired in late August 2002 and the Maoists consequently intensified their violent campaign. In mid-September the Government rejected Prachanda's offer of a cease-fire, on the grounds that it lacked credibility. In early October Deuba requested King Gyanendra to postpone the general election by one year, citing the deteriorating law and order situation. However, King Gyanendra dismissed the Prime Minister and the interim Council of Ministers for reportedly failing to organize the election. The King assumed executive power and postponed indefinitely parliamentary elections scheduled for November. In October King Gyanendra appointed a nine-member interim Government, headed by the former premier and monarchist Lok Bahadur Chand. The NCP, UML and legal experts condemned the dismissal of Deuba and his Government and the establishment of a new Council of Ministers as unconstitutional. In mid-November the King disregarded demands by political parties to create a new government composed of their members, instead reorganizing and expanding the interim Council of Ministers to include a former UML member, businessmen and independents. At the same time, amid continuing violence and disruption, the Deputy Prime Minister stated that the interim Government was prepared to enter negotiations with the CPN (M) and would consider the latter's demand for an elected constituent assembly. In December the human rights organization Amnesty International issued a damning report on the human rights situation in Nepal since the collapse of peace talks in November 2001. The army and Armed Police Force were severely criticized for the reported 'unprecedented levels' of human rights abuses, including torture, arbitrary detention and deaths in custody. In addition, the report accused Maoist insurgents of torturing and killing captives, taking hostages and recruiting children. The report claimed that nearly one-half of the 4,366 people who had died in the conflict since late 2001 were civilians, killed by both security forces and Maoists.

In January 2003 suspected Maoist militants shot dead the chief of the Armed Police Force, Inspector-General Krishna Mohan Shrestha, in Kathmandu; his wife and bodyguard were also killed. Three days later the CPN (M) and the Government announced an immediate cease-fire and agreed to resume peace negotiations after the Government agreed to declassify Maoist activists as terrorists, to withdraw rewards offered for the arrest of Maoist leaders and to cancel international police warrants issued for the guerrilla leaders. In February a series of informal talks took place; at the end of the month the Maoists presented two conditions for the resumption of formal negotiations: the release of Maoist prisoners and the return of the army to barracks. A 22-point code of conduct was signed by the chief government negotiator and Minister of Physical Planning and Construction, Narayan Singh Pun, and the Maoist leader, Baburam Bhattarai, in mid-March. According to the code, the Government would release prisoners gradually and give Maoists equal access to the state-controlled media; there was no mention of the army moving back to barracks, however. Both sides also agreed formally to cease hostilities. The following day a Maoist negotiator declared that, while a communist republic continued to be the CPN (M)'s goal, the militant group would comply with the public's decision on the future of the monarchy. In the mean time, Chand continued to prove unsuccessful in his attempts to involve political parties in the peace process and therefore to form a broad-based negotiating team. The country's political parties and the Maoists questioned the interim Government's authority to negotiate with the Maoists.

The interim Government and Maoist representatives commenced formal negotiations at the end of April 2003; it was reported that the CPN (M) demanded the release of Maoist prisoners, participation in an interim government and the creation of a constituent assembly, but did not include the abolition of the monarchy in its agenda. At the second round of peace talks, which took place in May, the Government agreed to release several Maoist detainees and to restrict army troops to within 5 km of their barracks. Both sides also achieved consensus on the composition of a committee to monitor the code of conduct guiding the cease-fire. The third round of negotiations, which eventually took place on 17–19 August, ended in impasse over the Maoists' demand for an elected assembly to draft a new constitution. Although the two sides agreed to meet again the following week, on 27 August Prachanda ended the seven-month cease-fire and withdrew from the peace process. On the following day the Government reclassified the insurgents as 'terrorists' after violent activity resumed. Thousands of people marched in Kathmandu at the end of August to urge the Government and the CPN (M) to resume peace talks.

In the mean time, at the end of May 2003 Prime Minister Chand resigned in response to pressure from leaders of the major political parties. The parties (the NCP, UML, Nepal Workers' and Peasants' Party, Nepali Sadbhavan Party—Anandi Devi, and People's Front Nepal), with the support of students, had held frequent demonstrations against the Chand Government and the King. On 4 June the King appointed the monarchist and former premier Surya Bahadur Thapa as Prime Minister, rejecting the nomination by the five opposition parties of Madhav Kumar Nepal, the General Secretary of the UML. One week later the King appointed a new interim Council of Ministers, which was composed entirely of members of the monarchist RPP. Thapa had invited M. K. Nepal and Deuba to join the Government, but the leading politicians refused, maintaining that Thapa's appointment had been unconstitutional. Opposition parties held a large demonstration in Kathmandu, demanding

Thapa's resignation, the reinstatement of the legislature and the establishment of an all-party government. In late August Nepal's major political parties refused Thapa's appeal for co-operation, instead pledging to launch a new series of nation-wide protests demanding the return of parliamentary democracy. On 1 September, however, the Government banned all demonstrations or public gatherings of five or more people in the Kathmandu valley, citing fears of infiltration by Maoist guerrillas. None the less, about a week later more than 1,000 pro-democracy protesters, including former premier G. P. Koirala, were arrested for defying the ban and taking part in a demonstration.

The CPN (M) fully resumed its violent campaign in September 2003. In the same month it organized a three-day general strike, which severely affected businesses, transport services and schools throughout most of the country. In mid-September the police filed charges against 21 members of the CPN (M), including Prachanda and Baburam Bhattarai, for the murder in January of the Inspector-General of the Armed Police Force and two others (see above). According to a report published at the end of October by the Nepal human rights group the Informal Sector Service Centre (INSEC), more than 1,000 people had died in the violence since the collapse of the cease-fire. Meanwhile, Prachanda had issued a statement declaring that the CPN (M) would, henceforth, target US-supported organizations instead of infrastructure targets. In response, the US Administration announced at the end of the month that it had proscribed the CPN (M), listing the group as a threat to national security (the USA was already providing the Nepalese army with military assistance for its campaign against the Maoist insurgents).

In mid-November 2003 it was reported that a high-ranking Nepalese army officer had died in the violence. At the end of the month the international police agency Interpol issued arrest warrants for 11 senior CPN (M) officials, including Prachanda and Baburam Bhattarai. In mid-December the Government announced that it would grant an amnesty to anyone who surrendered by mid-February 2004; this message was dismissed by Maoist leaders. In January the Maoists announced the formation of autonomous people's governments in 10 districts under their control. At the end of the month the CPN (M) stated that it would give priority to development in these areas, and that representatives of the King and the USA were banned from operating in districts under Maoist influence. At the same time, the Nepalese army announced that 15 soldiers had been convicted of human rights violations and other criminal activities, and had been sentenced to up to six years' imprisonment; six other soldiers had been dismissed from the army for illegal activity committed during military operations against Maoist guerrillas. It was reported in mid-February that more than 500 Maoist militants had surrendered to security forces since the launch of the amnesty in December 2003; the deadline of the amnesty was extended to mid-April 2004. The violence increased, meanwhile, and the Maoists organized a further number of disruptive nation-wide general strikes. The number of people killed in the eight-year 'people's war' had risen sharply to more than 9,130 by mid-March, of whom more than 1,500 had died since the collapse of the cease-fire in August 2003. It was also reported that more than 250 people had 'disappeared' since August.

Meanwhile, it was reported in mid-November 2003 that the central committee of the RPP had requested Prime Minister Thapa to resign for failing to form an all-party government following his appointment. Thapa, however, maintained the support of the King and was thus able to remain in his position. In January 2004 there were almost daily student-led pro-republic protests held in Kathmandu. At the end of the month the five main opposition parties issued a joint statement offering formal support to the student movement. This action provided evidence that the NCP, a committed supporter of the constitutional monarchy, and the UML were reconsidering their views towards the monarchy. In early February, as part of a two-week tour around the troubled mid-western region, King Gyanendra gave a public address in the city of Nepalganj. During the speech, the King appealed for an end to the insurgency and appeared to seek an active role in governing democracy. Opposition parties criticized the King, claiming that he was not committed to multi-party democracy and the constitutional monarchy, and pledged to intensify their protests against 'regression'. Prime Minister Thapa, meanwhile, announced that the interim Government was preparing to hold a general election in the near future. The opposition, however, maintained that the Thapa Government was illegitimate and should be replaced by an all-party government, which would, in turn, hold elections and enter a peace process with the Maoist militants. In March the leaders of the five main opposition parties announced that a constitutional monarchy had not been successful and that, henceforth, their movement would be directed at achieving the establishment of a republic. Meanwhile, in the same month King Gyanendra reorganized and expanded the Council of Ministers. In early May the Prime Minister tendered his resignation as a result of the continuing political impasse. The resignation prompted the collapse of the entire Government; King Gyanendra authorized Thapa to remain in office in an acting capacity pending the formation of a new administration. Later in the same month the CPN (M) called a three-day general strike, which disrupted communications throughout the country and brought Kathmandu to a standstill. Violence during the strike resulted in the deaths of at least 45 people.

In June 2004 King Gyanendra appointed Sher Bahadur Deuba as Prime Minister for the third time. Several days later the King appointed two members of the NCP—D to the new Council of Ministers, in which Deuba held the majority of portfolios. The Council was expanded to 31 members in the following month and incorporated ministers from the four-party coalition (comprising the NCP—D, the UML, the RPP and the NSP) that had been formed following the resignation of Prime Minister Thapa.

In August 2004, for the first time since it had launched its campaign in 1996, the CPN (M) instigated a blockade of Kathmandu, stating that it would be of indefinite duration and would last until the Government released all remaining Maoist prisoners and initiated an investigation into the fates of Maoist activists who had reportedly died while in custody. The blockade was lifted after a week, reportedly in response to pleas from ordinary people, who were suffering significant hardship as the prices of food and other essential items had risen steeply. In response, at the end of the month the Government announced the formation of a peace committee, headed by Prime Minister Deuba, which, it was hoped, would commence peace talks with the Maoists in an attempt to end the ongoing insurgency. However, the rebels rejected a subsequent offer of peace negotiations. In September a riot in Kathmandu resulted in the deaths of two protesters, who were shot dead by police attempting to control the demonstrations (an estimated 3,000 demonstrators had gathered to protest against the murder of 12 Nepalese hostages by Iraqi insurgents during the US-led campaign in Iraq).

In October 2004 the Government agreed to observe a cease-fire that had been proposed by the CPN (M) for the duration of the Hindu religious festival of Dasain. Both sides were reported to have adhered, for the most part, to the halt in military operations during the nine-day festival. In the following month Prime Minister Deuba set the rebels a deadline of 13 January 2005 to commence peace talks with the Government. Deuba stated that if the Maoists did not agree to begin discussions, he would ensure that legislative elections were held by mid-April 2005, using the mandate that had been granted to him by King Gyanendra. However, Prachanda later rejected the proposed deadline. The rejection reportedly led to disagreement within the Government over the feasibility of holding elections amidst the ongoing insurgency. The violence had intensified following the expiry of the short-lived cease-fire in late October 2004. The Government was destabilized further in November when the founding President of the RPP, former Prime Minister Thapa, announced that he intended to launch a new political party, effectively creating a split within the RPP.

In February 2005 the political situation in Nepal seriously deteriorated when King Gyanendra abruptly dismissed Prime Minister Deuba and his Government, declared an indefinite state of emergency in the kingdom and announced that, henceforth, he would rule Nepal directly. All communications links into and out of Nepal were severed temporarily, censorship was imposed on the media and former ministers were placed under house arrest. The King claimed that his actions were a result of the Prime Minister's failure to halt the Maoist insurgency and to hold legislative elections in the country. In an attempt to prevent protests, the King ordered the detention of large numbers of political activists. Maoist rebels subsequently instigated a two-week blockade of national highways in protest at the King's actions. Shortly after he had assumed supreme power, the King appointed a new, 10-member Council of Ministers, under his chairmanship. Former Prime Ministers Dr Tulsi Giri and Kirti Nidhi Bista were appointed to serve as Vice-Chairmen. King Gyanendra's assumption of power met with an unfavourable international response, with Nepal's key allies, India and the United Kingdom, suspending military aid to the country and several nations recalling their ambassadors from Nepal in protest.

In March 2005 Thapa announced the foundation of his new political party, the Rashtriya Jana Shakti Party (RJP—National People's Power Party). In the same month several political leaders who had been detained following the royal coup were released from house arrest, including former Prime Minister Deuba. Meanwhile, protests against the King's actions, orchestrated by an opposition alliance comprising five of the country's main political parties, gathered momentum. At the same time, the Maoist insurgency intensified, with several clashes taking place between rebels and government troops. The state of emergency was lifted at the end of April, although there were few indications that normal political activity would be able to resume. Public meetings and demonstrations continued to be prohibited, and police powers of arrest and detention were extended. Meanwhile, former Prime Minister Deuba was re-arrested and charged with corruption offences by the newly established Royal Commission for Corruption Control (RCCC). Deuba refused to acknowledge the legitimacy of the body.

In May 2005 seven political parties, including the NCP, announced a joint agenda for the restoration of democracy in Nepal, calling for King Gyanendra to end his period of direct rule and for the House of Representatives, which had been dissolved in 2002, to be recalled. Later that month the alliance organized a demonstration in Kathmandu in protest against the King. In June Maoist rebels were responsible for the detonation of a landmine under a bus in the southern district of Chitwan, which resulted in the deaths of 39 civilians. The Maoists subsequently apologized for the attack, claiming that the bomb had been intended to target security forces, and announced that, henceforth, all attacks on unarmed civilians would be suspended.

In June 2005 Deuba and six of his former government colleagues were cleared by the RCCC of charges relating to the misappropriation of money from the Prime Minister's Relief Fund. However, Deuba remained in custody pending a further judgment against him. In the following month Deuba, along with four other defendants, was convicted of charges of embezzlement relating to the issuing of a water contract and sentenced to a two-year prison term. Meanwhile, a reorganization and expansion of the Council of Ministers was carried out.

In August 2005, as opposition to King Gyanendra's ongoing direct rule intensified, it was announced that the seven-party alliance had decided to begin talks with the CPN (M) and to plan joint protests against the King. It cited positive gestures by the Maoist group, such as its suspension of attacks on unarmed civilians, as the reason for co-operation, having consistently maintained that it would be willing to hold discussions with the rebels only if they renounced violence. In September the Maoists announced a three-month unilateral cease-fire, an offer welcomed by the international community but one to which the Government responded cautiously. By the middle of that month, according to the INSEC, 12,809 people had been killed since the beginning of the 'people's war' in 1996. In October 2005 the Government announced that elections would take place to Nepal's 58 municipal councils in February 2006. The seven-party alliance announced that it intended to boycott the polls, although two of its members, the RPP and the RJP, later announced that they had not yet decided whether to participate. Shortly afterwards King Gyanendra stated that elections to the House of Representatives would take place in April 2007. In November 2005, following talks with the CPN (M), the opposition alliance announced that it had reached a 12-point agreement with the rebels intended to attempt to restore democracy to Nepal. The agreement included a boycott of the February 2006 municipal elections and the election of a constituent assembly, the latter being a long-standing Maoist demand.

In December 2005 an extensive reorganization of the Council of Ministers took place, in which eight ministers were dismissed and several ministers from the RPP and RJP were appointed. In the same month the CPN (M) announced that it would extend its cease-fire by one month. However, in January 2006 the Maoists stated that the cease-fire had come to an end, owing to the lack of response from the Government, which had continued to authorize offensive operations against them. The insurgency subsequently intensified. In the following month the municipal elections were held, taking place in only 36 of the 58 municipal councils owing to an insufficient number of candidates and against the background of a four-day general strike, which was co-ordinated by the Maoists and was intended to disrupt the polls. Turn-out reached an estimated 20% of registered voters, according to official figures, although the major opposition parties, which boycotted the polls, claimed that the figure was significantly lower. Later that month the RCCC was outlawed after the Supreme Court ruled that its orders were not valid. Former Prime Minister Deuba was subsequently freed from prison, having been convicted of corruption offences by the body in the previous year. In March the Maoists instigated an indefinite blockade of Kathmandu in another attempt to force King Gyanendra to end his period of direct rule. Meanwhile, the Government offered an amnesty to any Maoist rebels who surrendered before a mid-June 2006 deadline.

In April 2006 the opposition alliance called a nation-wide general strike. Mass demonstrations followed, in response to which the Government announced the imposition of a 'shoot on sight' curfew. As thousands of protesters defied the curfew and violent clashes ensued, King Gyanendra's position appeared increasingly untenable. Following almost three weeks of popular demonstrations, the King offered to permit the opposition alliance to name a new Prime Minister. However, this offer was rejected and the protests continued to escalate. Several days later, in accordance with opposition demands, the King announced that he would reinstate Parliament, thus quelling the unrest. The CPN (M), however, rejected the royal offer and vowed to continue their insurgency, accusing the political parties of betraying the 12-point agreement. They did, none the less, agree to observe a three-month cease-fire. The opposition alliance subsequently nominated former Prime Minister G. P. Koirala to lead a new Government. The House of Representatives formally convened later in that month and approved legislation enabling the establishment of a constituent assembly to redraft the country's Constitution. The formation of a complete Council of Ministers, announced by Koirala at the beginning of May, was delayed for three weeks owing to disagreement over the distribution of ministerial portfolios among the political parties. Appointments included K. P. Sharma Oli of the UML as Deputy Prime Minister and Minister of Foreign Affairs, and the NCP's Krishna Sitaula and Dr Ram Sharan Mahat as Minister of Home Affairs and Minister of Finance respectively; Koirala himself assumed responsibility for the portfolios of defence, health and population, and industry, commerce and supplies. In June Koirala expanded the Council of Ministers to include representatives of a further two members of the seven-party alliance—namely the People's Front Nepal and the NSP. At this stage all of the seven-party alliance members were represented in the Government, with the exception of the Nepal Workers' and Peasants' Party.

On 3 May 2006 the Council of Ministers had announced a cease-fire with the CPN (M), offering to declassify the group as a terrorist organization and to abandon terrorism charges in exchange for the holding of peace talks. According to government figures, 467 of an estimated 1,000 Maoist prisoners had been freed by 25 May. Despite the Maoists' assertions that they would not enter into negotiations until all their prisoners had been released, and their insistence that the formation of a constituent assembly was subject to the abolition of the existing Constitution, legislature and monarchy, the Government and the CPN (M) engaged in a preliminary round of discussions on 26 May, establishing a code of conduct for the duration of peace talks. Meanwhile, on 12 May four former ministers, including Kamal Thapa, the former Minister of Home Affairs, and Ramesh Nath Pandey, the former Minister of Finance, were arrested and charged with use of excessive force in containing the April pro-democracy protests (three of the four detainees were later released on the orders of the Supreme Court). On 18 May the House of Representatives passed a resolution divesting the King of his role as Commander-in-Chief of the Army, his authority to make military appointments and nominate an heir, and his legal immunity and exemption from taxes. Nepal was pronounced a secular state in an attempt to extricate the concept of a divinely instituted monarchy from the national ideology. The transfer of power away from the monarchy continued in June: the King was no longer able to veto legislation, he was not required to open and close parliamentary sessions, and he lost the authority to announce government policy.

In mid-June 2006 talks between Koirala and Prachanda in Kathmandu led to the announcement that the CPN (M) would be included in a new interim government, which was to oversee elections for a constituent assembly. At Koirala's request, a UN team arrived in Nepal at the end of July to determine weapons management strategies for the Nepalese army and the People's Liberation Army (PLA) of the Maoists; Koirala reportedly deemed the decommissioning of weapons as a prerequisite of the entry of the CPN (M) into government. Also at the end of July, Prachanda extended the cease-fire by three months. On 9 August Koirala and Prachanda agreed to a system of management for the Nepalese army and the PLA, which stipulated that the former would remain in barracks, while the latter would reside in holding camps. Two days later Lt-Gen. Rukmangad Katuwal assumed the post of Chief of Army Staff in an acting capacity, replacing Gen. Pyar Jung Thapa, who had been among those accused of using excessive force to quell the April uprising. In October further talks between the negotiating teams of the Government and the Maoists produced a tentative schedule for elections to the constituent assembly, which was to draw up a new constitution, with a deadline of the end of June 2007 for the assembly's first session. Prachanda reiterated his demand for the declaration of a republic, stating that an agreement to this effect would ensure the disarmament of Maoist forces. He announced a further three-month extension of the cease-fire in October 2006. The Comprehensive Peace Agreement (CPA), which was signed by Koirala and Prachanda on 21 November, provided for the establishment of an interim constitution, assembly and council of ministers by 1 December, and was hailed as the end of a civil war that had claimed the lives of more than 13,000 people. A disarmament agreement soon followed, the terms of which included the complete cessation of hostilities by both sides. The Maoist military forces were to be contained in cantonments, their weapons registered and impounded under UN supervision, while the Nepalese army, which was to remain in barracks, would also have its arms locked away. With the signing of an Interim Constitution in December 2006, constitutional powers of governance were reassigned from the monarchy to the Prime Minister. The National Assembly and House of Representatives were dissolved with the promulgation of the Interim Constitution in mid-January 2007. In their place an Interim Parliament, or 'Legislature-Parliament' was established; this body included members of the original 1999 Parliament as well as appointees selected by the seven-party alliance and the CPN (M) (which itself controlled 83 seats in its first parliamentary participation). A few days later the Maoists announced the closure of their 'People's Governments' and 'People's Courts'.

Tensions among the Madhesi people in southern Nepal, however, threatened to slow the peace process in 2007. Madhesi groups, who were demanding increased independence for their region and greater representation in government, organized demonstrations and called strikes to draw attention to their campaign. The protests were at times violent and clashes with police resulted in several fatalities. At the end of January Koirala, reportedly in response to Madhesi demands, asserted that, under the terms of the forthcoming permanent constitution, Nepal would become a federal state. However, the ethnic unrest continued into the following month amid claims that the Government had not adequately addressed Madhesi needs. A government committee was subsequently established to negotiate with Madhesi groups. Constitutional amendments approved by the Interim Parliament in March provided for proportional representation and a federal style of government, and the revision of constituency boundaries to grant one-half of parliamentary seats to the southern plains, where an estimated 50% of the population resided. Despite these concessions, an element of dissatisfaction remained, with the Madhesi People's Rights Forum calling for total autonomy.

Progress in other areas of reform was halting. Conditions in the PLA holding camps were reported to be poor, with hundreds of troops departing, in contravention of the peace agreement. As late as March 2007, Prachanda commented that the arms decommissioning process had not been completed, and large numbers of Maoist troops had yet to move into the camps. Meanwhile, in February the King's image was removed from bank notes as part of a general move to eradicate symbols of the monarchy from public life; nationalization of the monarchy's assets was also proposed. In the following month Koirala suggested that the voluntary abdication of the King and the Crown Prince would be a positive outcome. According to the Interim Constitution, the future of the monarchy was to be decided at the inaugural session of the constituent assembly.

At the beginning of April 2007 an Interim Council of Ministers was approved by the Interim Parliament. G. P. Koirala was reappointed interim Prime Minister, heading an administration that included five members of the CPN (M), who assumed responsibility for information and communications, among other portfolios. Sahana Pradhan and Ram Chandra Poudel, both of the UML, were assigned the key portfolios of foreign affairs and peace and reconstruction respectively; the latter post was a newly created position that reflected the stated primary objective of the interim Government to promote domestic concord and tolerance. Later in April the Chief Election Commissioner expressed doubt that preparations for the constituent assembly elections, scheduled for 20 June, would be completed on time; at the end of May the Government decided to postpone the elections until November. In July the CPN (M) registered itself as a political party with the Election Commission of Nepal.

Although it had been agreed that the fate of the monarchy lay with the constituent assembly, demands for the declaration of a republic continued to be made. In June 2007 the Interim Parliament approved a constitutional amendment giving the legislature power to vote on the issue should the King be involved in attempts to influence the constituent assembly election process. Seven royal palaces were nationalized by the Government in August. In September the NCP and the NCP—D announced their merger. In the same month the CPN (M) withdrew from the Government, citing the continuing existence of the monarchy and disagreement over the composition of the constituent assembly—contrary to the dictates of the Interim Constitution, the CPN (M) demanded that constituent assembly members be determined solely through proportional representation—as major obstacles to co-operation with its coalition partners. As a result, the CPN (M) members of the Interim Council of Ministers tendered their resignations. A period of intense negotiations ensued, during which the CPN (M)'s numerous demands were considered by the remaining parties of the governing alliance, amid fears for the future of the peace process. In early October the elections were postponed indefinitely. In November the Interim Parliament approved a motion that reiterated the CPN (M)'s key stipulations: the declaration of a republic and the utilization of the proportional representation system for all constituent assembly seats. The Maoists had gained the support of the UML but not the NCP, and the motion, although approved, was consequently unable to garner the two-thirds' majority required for a constitutional amendment. However, at the end of December an amended version of the motion secured the requisite two-thirds of the vote, specifying that, although the monarchy was to be abolished, this change would only come into effect upon the approval of the constituent assembly. More than one-half of the assembly was to be determined by a system of proportional representation, with the bulk of the remainder directly elected and several appointees; elections were scheduled for April 2008. A few days later, the CPN (M) returned to government, with five of its members resuming their positions in the Interim Council of Ministers.

Meanwhile, in the latter half of 2007 tensions remained and the security situation deteriorated in the Terai region where the Madhesi People's Rights Forum and numerous other groups continued to campaign for autonomy. In December the Minister of Environment, Science and Technology, Mahantha Thakur, resigned, together with several Madhesi members of the Interim Parliament, citing the Government's unwillingness to address the ongoing unrest in the Terai. Shortly after these resignations, the United Democratic Madhesi Front (UDMF), an alliance of three political organizations—the Madhesi People's Rights Forum, the NSP and the Terai-Madhes Democratic Party—was established. In February blockades orchestrated by the UDMF caused widespread disruption in the south of the country and led to fuel shortages in Kathmandu and elsewhere. Later in the month, the Government and the UDMF signed an agreement ending the blockade and allowing for increased autonomy and representation of Madhesis on party lists and institutions such as the Nepal Army. Concerns remained, however, regarding the campaigns of more hardline Madhesi groups operating outside the negotiations.

At the constituent assembly elections, which were held on 10 April 2008, the CPN (M) won 220 out of a total of 575 elected seats, twice as many as the NCP, which came second. The UML expressed disappointment at its election to only 103 seats, putting it in third place, while the Madhesi People's Rights Forum won 52. Prachanda declared victory on behalf of the CPN (M) and indicated that he would lead a coalition government. The CPN (M) also urged the King to abdicate voluntarily in advance of the inevitable declaration of a republic. The Constituent Assembly, which was to include an additional 26 members nominated by the Interim Government, was scheduled to hold its inaugural session on 28 May, following which the Interim Parliament was to be dissolved in accordance with the Interim Constitution.

In 1978 the old Trade and Transit Treaty between Nepal and India was replaced by two treaties (renewed in the mid-1980s), one concerning bilateral trade between the two countries, the other allowing Nepal to develop trade with other countries via India. Relations with India deteriorated considerably in March 1989, however, when India decided not to renew the treaties, insisting that a common treaty covering both issues be negotiated. Nepal refused, stressing the importance of keeping the treaties separate, on the grounds that trade issues are negotiable, whereas the right of transit is a recognized basic right of land-locked countries. In response, India closed 13 of the 15 transit points through which most of Nepal's trade was conducted. Severe shortages of food and fuel ensued. It was widely believed that a major issue aggravating the dispute was Nepal's purchase of weapons (including anti-aircraft guns) from the People's Republic of China in 1988, which, according to India, violated the Treaty of Peace and Friendship concluded by India and Nepal in 1950. Diplomatic relations between Nepal and India remained strained throughout 1989, with trade at a virtual standstill. Following several rounds of senior-level talks, a joint communiqué was signed by the two countries in June 1990, restoring trade relations and reopening the transit points, and assuring mutual consultations on matters of security. A few days earlier, as an apparent gesture of goodwill to India, the Nepalese Government had told the Chinese Government to defer indefinitely the delivery of the final consignment of weapons destined for Nepal. The visit to Kathmandu by the Indian Prime Minister in February 1991 (the first official visit to Nepal by an Indian head of government since 1977) helped to reaffirm the traditionally amicable ties between the two countries. Separate trade and transit treaties (valid for five and seven years respectively) were signed during a visit by Prime Minister Koirala to India in December 1991; these treaties were both subsequently renewed. A major breakthrough in Indo-Nepalese relations was achieved in February 1996, when the Prime Ministers of the two countries formally signed a treaty in New Delhi regarding the shared utilization of the waters of the Mahakali River basin (for irrigation, general consumption and the production of hydroelectric power). The costs and benefits of the project, which involved the construction of a massive hydroelectric power plant, were to be divided between Nepal and India, although not, some critics claimed, to Nepal's benefit. During a visit to Nepal by the Indian Prime Minister in June 1997, the Mahakali Treaty was formally endorsed, and India granted Nepal access to Bangladeshi ports through a new transit facility across Indian territory via the Karkavita-Phulbari road (this facility was extended and improved in 1998). Some tension in Indo-Nepalese relations, nevertheless, remained; this centred on border demarcation disputes and, in particular, on the Indian border police's use of territory that Nepal claimed as its own in the far west of the country (namely the strategically-situated Kalapani junction between India, Nepal and China, which covers an area of about 35 sq km). In late 2001 India supplied Nepal with two helicopters and arms to assist its neighbour in its struggle against the Maoist insurgency. In early 2002 the Nepalese and Indian Governments held talks on the civil disorder problem in Nepal and India repeated its offer of financial assistance. From early 2003, however, the Indian Government became increasingly concerned about King Gyanendra's perceived disregard for democracy. In February 2005 its concerns were realized when the King dismissed the Government and assumed executive power. India condemned the King's actions and suspended military aid to Nepal. It also intensified security along the shared border, owing to increased fears of infiltration by Maoist insurgents and their possible co-operation with rebels operating in India's fractious north-eastern states. In July India resumed non-lethal military aid to Nepal. In June 2007 Prime Minister Koirala paid an official visit to India, during which the Indian Prime Minister, Manmohan Singh, pledged Rs 10,000m. in developmental and infrastructural aid to Nepal.

The People's Republic of China has contributed a considerable amount to the Nepalese economy. The first meeting of a joint committee on economic co-operation took place in 1984. This committee met for a second time (and thenceforth annually) in Kathmandu in 1986, when China agreed to increase its imports from Nepal in order to minimize trade imbalances. Relations between Nepal and China improved further during the late 1980s and 1990s, as indicated by reciprocal visits made by high-ranking Nepalese and Chinese officials (notably, a state visit to Nepal was conducted by the Chinese President, Jiang Zemin, in 1996). In May 2001 the leaders of Nepal and China signed a six-point co-operation agreement to improve cross-border trade, increase road and aviation links and promote tourism.

In 1985 it was agreed that Nepal's border with Tibet (the Xizang Autonomous Region) should be opened. Following the outbreak of ethnic violence in Tibet in 1989, however, the border between Nepal and Tibet was closed indefinitely. The Nepalese authorities have been consistent in their commitment to the 'One China' policy and in their efforts to repatriate refugees fleeing from Tibet. In 1993 G. P. Koirala paid an informal visit to Tibet—the first visit to the region by a Nepalese Premier since the 1950s. In 1995, however, the Nepalese authorities banned a proposed peace march by Tibetans through Nepalese territory. During a visit to China by the Nepalese Minister of Foreign Affairs in August 2000, an agreement was reached to allow Nepal increased use of a new road in Tibet. Greater technological and economic co-operation was also achieved, therefore noticeably increasing bilateral trade. Nepal provoked strong criticism from the UN and Western governments in late May 2003, after it helped Chinese officials to deport 18 Tibetan refugees from Kathmandu to Tibet (Nepal's usual policy was to transfer Tibetan refugees to officials of the UN High Commissioner for Refugees—UNHCR). It was reported in late June that a further 19 Tibetans had been arrested in the western Nepalese district of Accham. In March and April 2008 regular demonstrations were held by Tibetan refugees in Kathmandu, as the approach of the Beijing Olympic Games drew international attention to the Tibet issue. The Nepalese police force was widely criticized for its reportedly violent suppression of the protests and the arrests of hundreds of activists.

Ties with Bangladesh are also significant, particularly regarding the utilization of joint water resources. Large-scale migration from Bangladesh has resulted in a notable demographic transformation in Nepal, with the Muslim population increasing from around 4% of the total in the early 1990s to, unofficially, about 10% by the end of the decade. In January 2001 the Nepalese Minister of Foreign Affairs visited Bangladesh, where agreements on greater economic and transport co-operation were reached. In December 1982 Nepal and Pakistan strengthened their trade links by renewing a 1962 agreement, and in 1983 they established a joint economic commission and a regular air link. In March 2005 the joint economic commission met for the first time in 10 years, when a delegation of Pakistani economic officials visited Nepal.

In late 1991 thousands of Bhutanese of Nepalese origin began to arrive at refugee camps in eastern Nepal, following the outbreak of political and ethnic unrest in Bhutan. By early 1996 nearly 100,000 refugees were living in eight camps in the districts of Jhapa and Morang. In the first half of 1993 talks were held between Bhutanese and Nepalese government officials regarding proposals to resolve the issues at stake. The Nepalese Government steadfastly refused to consider any solution that did not include the resettlement in Bhutan of all ethnic Nepalese refugees living in the camps. This proposal was rejected by the Bhutanese Government, which claimed that the majority of the camp population were not actually Bhutanese. The deadlock was apparently broken, however, when a joint statement was signed by the Ministers of Home Affairs of Bhutan and Nepal in July, which committed each side to establishing a 'high-level joint committee' to work towards a settlement (including the categorization of the refugees). In a notable shift in strategy, in January 1996 the Nepalese Government transferred the responsibility of handling the Bhutanese refugee problem from the Ministry of Home Affairs to the Ministry of Foreign Affairs. In April 1997 more than 10,000 Bhutanese refugees gathered at a mass demonstration in the eastern Nepalese town of Damak to call for UN intervention in the crisis. They also demanded that the Nepal Government either resolve the refugee problem or, failing that, 'internationalize' it. Nepal and Bhutan finally achieved a breakthrough at the 10th round of negotiations in December 2000. Both countries agreed that nationality would be verified on the basis of the head of the refugee family for those over 25 years of age; refugees under 25 years of age would be verified on an individual basis. By the end of January 2001 a Joint Verification Team (JVT) had concluded the inspection of refugee camps, and by late 2001 the verification of individuals in the Khudanabari camp had been completed. However, despite two further rounds of negotiations, the process reached a standstill in early 2002, with Bhutan reluctant to accept the individuals already verified, and both Governments undecided over the most suitable way to continue the verification process. In January 2003 Nepal and Bhutan finally harmonized their positions on the categorization of the refugees into four different groups and arrangements were commenced to conduct the repatriation to Bhutan of about 70 families (comprising around 300 people who were in the category of being Bhutanese nationals who had been forcefully evicted—Category I) by the end of the year. The majority of residents of the Khudanabari camp were categorized as either Bhutanese nationals who had left Bhutan voluntarily (Category II) or as non-Bhutanese (Category III); the remainder were classified as Bhutanese who had committed criminal acts (Category IV). It was agreed that the JVT would review the remaining appeals from people in the Khudunabari camp in November and then begin verification of the Sanischare camp. The two countries also decided that Bhutan would be fully responsible for any Category I persons, while Category II people could apply for either Bhutanese or Nepalese citizenship, in accordance with the respective laws. However, in December the Bhutanese members of the JVT were attacked in the Khudanabari camp by several thousand refugees protesting against the terms and conditions of the agreement. The JVT members were subsequently withdrawn to Thimphu and talks between Bhutan and Nepal were suspended. In March 2004 Teknath Rizal, Chairman of the Human Rights Council of Bhutan, began a hunger strike in Nepal, with the intention of drawing international attention to the plight of the refugees. Rizal ended his strike in the following month after receiving assurances from the Nepalese Government that it would attempt to enlist the involvement of UNHCR and India in restarting the stalled repatriation process. In September Rizal led a Nepalese delegation to the headquarters of UNHCR in Geneva, Switzerland, in a further attempt to raise the international profile of the refugees. In the following month the US Assistant Secretary of State for Population, Refugees and Migration, Arthur Dewey, visited the area and held discussions on how to end the stalemate. In October 2006 the US Government offered to resettle as many as 60,000 of the refugees. This met with a mixed response: some argued that third-country resettlement would amount to an exoneration of Bhutan's actions, while others welcomed the proposal. In the following month Australia, Canada and New Zealand also offered asylum to the refugees, although proposed intake numbers were not supplied. Bhutan reacted negatively to the Nepalese assertion, made at the UN General Assembly, that the refugee problem was a Bhutanese rather than a bilateral issue. UNHCR, which had urged Bhutan to allow repatriation, and the Nepalese Government began a census of the estimated 106,000 refugees in the Jhapa and Morang districts of Nepal in mid-November. In the same month much anticipated negotiations between the Bhutanese and Nepalese Governments were postponed indefinitely—once at the request of Bhutan and a second time owing to the unsettled political situation in Nepal. In March 2008 the resettlement of refugees in the USA and New Zealand began. In the same month a fire devastated one of the camps in Nepal, leaving some 10,000 refugees homeless.

Nepal pursues a non-aligned foreign policy, and had diplomatic relations with 128 countries in early 2008. Nepal (with seven other countries) is a member of the South Asian Association for Regional Co-operation (SAARC, see p. 384), which was formally established in 1985; the Association's permanent secretariat was established in Kathmandu in 1987. Kathmandu hosted a SAARC summit meeting in January 2002, despite rising tension in the region. Nepal is a signatory to the organization's agreement on the South Asian Free Trade Area (SAFTA), which came into force in January 2006 (SAFTA, however, was not due to enter fully into force until 2016).

Government

Under the provisions of the Constitution promulgated in November 1990, Nepal was a constitutional monarchy. The Constitution provided for a bicameral Parliament, comprising a 205-member House of Representatives (Pratinidhi Sabha) and a 60-member National Assembly (Rashtriya Sabha), as the supreme legislative body. The House of Representatives was elected for a five-year term, and members of the National Assembly held office for a six-year term. Executive power was vested in the King and the Council of Ministers, which was answerable to the House of Representatives. The King appointed the leader of the party that commanded a majority in the House of Representatives as Prime Minister, while other ministers were appointed, from among the members of Parliament, on the recommendation of the Prime Minister.

On 15 January 2007 the bicameral legislature instituted by the 1990 Constitution was dissolved upon the promulgation of a new Interim Constitution, and a 330-member Interim Parliament, or 'Legislature-Parliament', was convened by agreement of the seven-party alliance and the Maoists. In accordance with articles stipulated in the Interim Constitution, constitutional powers of governance were reassigned from the monarchy to the acting Prime Minister and the temporary legislature was to facilitate preparations for the democratic election of a constituent assembly by the end of June of that year. The constituent assembly would be responsible for drawing up a new permanent constitution. According to the Interim Constitution, the future of the monarchy was to be decided at the first official sitting of the constituent assembly. In December 2007 a parliamentary resolution declaring Nepal a republic received the requisite two-thirds' majority for a constitutional amendment, but this decision was due to come into effect only upon the approval of the Constituent Assembly, which was elected in April 2008 and was scheduled to hold its inaugural session on 28 May.

For the purposes of local administration, Nepal is divided into five development regions, 14 zones, 75 districts, 3,913 village development committees and 58 municipalities.

Defence

As assessed at November 2007, Nepal's total armed forces numbered 69,000 men. Paramilitary forces numbered 62,000 men. Military service is voluntary. An Armed Police Force was formed in 2001 and numbered 15,000 in November 2007. The defence budget for 2007 was projected at NRs 10,900m.

Economic Affairs

In 2006, according to estimates by the World Bank, Nepal's gross national income (GNI), measured at average 2004–06 prices, was US $8,051.1m., equivalent to $290 per head (or $1,630 per head on an international purchasing-power parity basis). During 1996–2006, it was estimated, the population increased at an average annual rate of 2.2%, while gross domestic product (GDP) per head increased, in real terms, by an average of 1.3% per year. Overall GDP increased, in real terms, at an average annual rate of 3.5% in 1996–2006. According to official figures, real GDP grew by 2.5% in 2006/07.

Agriculture (including forestry and fishing) contributed an estimated 33.1% of GDP in the fiscal year ending 15 July 2007. The sector engaged an estimated 92.9% of the economically active population in mid-2005, according to FAO figures. The principal crops are rice, maize, millet, wheat, sugar cane, potatoes and vegetables, and melons. According to the World Bank, during 1996–2006 agricultural GDP increased by an average of 3.2% per year. The agricultural sector grew by 0.7% in 2006/07.

Industry (comprising mining, manufacturing, construction and utilities) employed only 9.8% of the labour force in 1999, but provided an estimated 16.4% of GDP in 2006/07, according to the Asian Development Bank (ADB, see p. 182). About 60% of Nepal's industrial output comes from traditional cottage industries, and the remainder from modern industries. During 1996–2006 industrial GDP increased at an average annual rate of 3.3%. Industrial production rose by 3.5% in 2006.

Mining employed only 0.08% of the labour force in 1999, and contributed an estimated 0.5% of GDP in 2005/06. Mining GDP increased at an average annual rate of 4.1% in 1995–2004. Mica is mined east of Kathmandu, and there are also small deposits of lignite, copper, talc, limestone, cobalt and iron ore. Geophysical investigations have indicated that the Siwalik range and the Terai belt are potential prospective areas for petroleum.

Manufacturing contributed an estimated 7.5% of GDP in 2005/06, and employed about 5.8% of the labour force in 1999. Manufacturing GDP increased by an average annual rate of 2.4% in 1996–2006. Manufacturing production rose by 2.2% in 2006. The principal branches of the sector include textiles, particularly carpets and rugs, food products, wearing apparel and tobacco products. Traditional cottage industries include basket-making and the production of cotton fabrics and edible oils.

Energy is derived principally from traditional sources (particularly fuelwood). Imports of mineral fuel and lubricants (mainly for the transport sector), however, comprised an estimated 20.8% of the cost of total imports in 2005/06. In addition, Nepal's rivers are exploited for hydroelectric power (HEP) production, but in July 2002 it was estimated that only about 1% of the country's huge potential generating capacity (83m. kW) was being utilized. In January 2004 the 144,000-kW Kali Gandaki A HEP plant was officially inaugurated. The project, the country's largest, began generating electricity in 2002. Nepal was hoping to export excess electricity to India. Several other HEP projects were under construction in the early 2000s. In August 2004 Cairn Energy Co of the United Kingdom signed an agreement with the Nepalese Government to explore for petroleum and gas in a 22,000-sq km area in the Terai plain, near the border with India.

The services sector employed 14.0% of the labour force in 1999. The sector contributed an estimated 50.6% of GDP in 2006/07. The GDP of the services sector increased at an average annual rate of 3.1% in 1996–2006. Sectoral GDP grew by 2.4% in 2005 before declining by 5.9% in 2006. By 1996 tourism had emerged as Nepal's major source of foreign exchange; in 1999/2000 revenue from tourism amounted to 12.9% of total foreign-exchange earnings. The Maoist insurgency affected visitor levels in the first half of the 2000s. In 2003 tourist arrivals showed some improvement, with 338,132 tourists visiting Nepal in that year. Arrivals increased further in 2004, reaching 385,297. However, in 2005 arrivals declined by 2.6% to 375,398, owing to the King's assumption of power in February and a concomitant deterioration in the domestic security situation, reflected in a particularly significant decrease in arrivals in the first five months of that year. The cessation of Maoist hostilities in 2006 and the subsequent peace agreement between the former insurgents and the political parties' alliance were expected to aid recovery in the tourism sector. Tourism industry reports for the first months of 2007 indicated significant growth in arrivals, particularly from Bangladesh, the People's Republic of China and the Republic of Korea, which was attributed to the introduction of additional airline services between Nepal and these countries.

In 2006 Nepal recorded a visible trade deficit of US $1,592.2m. and there was a deficit of $10.4m. on the current account of the balance of payments. In 2005/06 India was the principal source of imports (supplying 62.4% of the total) and the principal market for exports (67.1%). Other major trading partners were the People's Republic of China, the USA and Germany. The principal exports in 2005/06 were basic manufactures, manufactured goods and articles and garments. The principal imports were basic manufactures, machinery and transport equipment, and mineral fuels and lubricants.

In 2006/07 there was an estimated overall budget deficit of NRs 58,536m. (equivalent to 10.8% of GDP). Foreign aid plays a vital role in the Nepalese economy. Nepal's total external debt was US $3,285m. at the end of 2005, of which $3,217m. was long-term public debt. In that year the cost of debt-servicing was equivalent to 4.6% of receipts from exports of goods and services. The annual rate of inflation averaged 5.3% in 1996–2006. Inflation increased by 7.6% in 2006. According to the ADB, in 1999/2000 47% of Nepali workers were underemployed, while urban unemployment, a major problem, particularly among educated youths, stood at 7%. According to the ADB, the total unemployment rate in 2002 was 5.0%.

Nepal is a member of the UN Economic and Social Commission for Asia and the Pacific (ESCAP, see p. 35), the ADB, the Colombo Plan (see p. 411) and the South Asian Association for Regional Co-operation (SAARC, see p. 384), all of which seek to encourage regional economic development. Nepal became the 147th member of the World Trade Organization (WTO, see p. 396) in April 2004.

With an inhospitable terrain comprising isolated valleys and very high mountains, Nepal is among the least developed countries in the world. Successive administrations since 1991 have followed a policy of economic liberalization: many state enterprises have been privatized (although there have been numerous delays in the process), and there have been attempts to reduce the fiscal deficit, to increase revenue mobilization, to restructure and improve the financial sector, and to institute and operate open trade and investment policies. In February 1993, as part of a series of economic reforms introduced in an attempt to develop industry further and to increase exports to countries other than India, the Nepalese rupee was made fully convertible for current-account transactions. In 2001/02, for the first time in 19 years, Nepal's GDP registered a negative growth rate: the economy contracted by 0.6%. Tourism and foreign trade fared particularly poorly, owing to a worsening internal security situation, regional tension and the terrorist attacks on the USA. In 2002 the interim Government launched the Tenth Five-Year Plan, which aimed for a 4.3%–6.2% growth rate during 2002–07. One of the objectives of the plan was to reduce the level of poverty to 30% of the population from 42%. In November 2003 the IMF approved a three-year US $72m. Poverty Reduction and Growth Facility for Nepal, in support of the country's poverty reduction strategies. By 2003/04 the level of poverty had declined to 31%, owing in part to an increase in remittances from Nepalese workers overseas. The country's accession to the WTO in April 2004 would, it was hoped, lead to the further integration of Nepal into the global economy. However, the expiry at the beginning of 2005 of the WTO's Multi-fibre Arrangement, which imposed quotas upon textile exports from developing countries, had a significant impact upon the country's garment industry; garment exports declined sharply over the course of the year. Meanwhile, foreign investment in Nepal remained negligible, with significant reforms needed if the country's attractiveness as an investment destination was to increase. In August 2005 Unilever Nepal was forced to close its soap-making factory in the country, having been unable to meet demands from Maoists and trade unions for wage rises for its employees. The peace process that was instigated by the political party alliance and the Maoists in 2006 (see Recent History) was expected to ensure a more stable economy. The fiscal year ending July 2006 saw GDP increase by 3.1%, with the economy continuing to be undermined by political and financial insecurity. Minor improvements in the industrial sector were offset by weak conditions in the agricultural sector, mainly owing to poor weather conditions. The rate of GDP growth declined to 2.3% in 2006/07, according to the ADB, primarily due to adverse weather conditions in conjunction with continuing political unrest. With the agricultural sector accounting for some 36% of GDP, the economy suffered the detrimental impact of contracted output in important crops such as rice paddy, potatoes and oil seeds. Despite subsequent rises in food prices, average inflation fell to 6.4% in 2006/07, compared with 8.0% in the previous financial year. GDP growth was forecast to increase to 3.8% in 2007/08, with the rate of inflation moving back up towards 7.0%.

Education

Primary education, beginning at six years of age and lasting for five years, is officially compulsory and is provided free of charge in government schools. Secondary education, beginning at the age of 11, lasts for a further seven years, comprising a first cycle of three years (lower secondary), a second of two years (secondary) and a third of two years (higher secondary). In 2005/06 the total enrolment at primary and secondary schools was equivalent to an estimated 79% of the school-age population. In 2003/04 enrolment at primary schools included an estimated 79% of children in the relevant age-group (boys 84%, girls 74%). In 2005/06 secondary enrolment was equivalent to an estimated 43% of pupils in the relevant age-group (boys 46%, girls 40%). There are four state universities: the Tribhuvan University in Kathmandu, the Mahendra Sanskrit Viswavidyalaya in Beljhundi, Dang, the Purbanchal University and the Pokhara University. In addition, there is one private university in Banepa. Altogether, the universities had more than 120,000 students in 1999/2000. Expenditure on education by the central Government in the 2003/04 budget was NRs 14,317m. (18.6% of total spending).

Public Holidays

The public holidays observed in Nepal vary locally. The dates given below apply to Kathmandu.

2008: 16 January (Day of Reconciliation), 30 January (Martyrs' Day), 8 February (Lhosar, Tibetan New Year), 11 February (Vasant Panchami—Advent of Spring Day), 19 February (Rashtriya Prajatantra Divas—National Democracy Day), March (Ghode Jatra—Horse Festival), 6 March (Maha Shivaratri—in honour of Lord Shiva), 20 March (Phagu Purnima—Holi Festival Day), 13 April (Navabarsha—New Year's Day), 14 April (Ram Nawami—Lord Ram's Birthday), 1 May (Labour Day), 20 May (Lord Gautam Buddha's Birthday), 16 August (Janai Purnima—Sacred Thread Ceremony), 20 August (Children's Day), 24 August (Janmashtami—Lord Krishna's Birthday), 2 September (Haritalika Teej—Women's Festival), 30 September (Ghatasthapana and, over nine days, Dasain), 9 October (Durga Puja Festival), 27 October (Laxmi Puja), 28 October (Diwali—Festival of Lights, over three days), 29 October (Bhai Tika—Brothers' Day), September/October/November (Indra Jatra—Festival of Rain God), 9 November (Constitution Day).

2009: 16 January (Day of Reconciliation), 27 January (Lhosar, Tibetan New Year), 30 January (Martyrs' Day), 31 January (Vasant Panchami—Advent of Spring Day), 19 February (Rashtriya Prajatantra Divas—National Democracy Day),

NEPAL

March (Ghode Jatra—Horse Festival), 11 March (Phagu Purnima—Holi Festival Day), 23 February (Maha Shivaratri—in honour of Lord Shiva), 3 April (Ram Nawami—Lord Ram's Birthday), 14 April (Navabarsha—New Year's Day), 1 May (Labour Day), 9 May (Lord Gautam Buddha's Birthday), 5 August (Janai Purnima—Sacred Thread Ceremony), 14 August (Janmashtami—Lord Krishna's Birthday), 20 August (Children's Day), September (Haritalika Teej—Women's Festival), September/October/November (Indra Jatra—Festival of Rain God), October (Ghatasthapana and, over nine days, Dasain), October (Durga Puja Festival), October/November (Bhai Tika—Brothers' Day), 17 October (Diwali—Festival of Lights, over three days), November (Laxmi Puja), 9 November (Constitution Day).

Weights and Measures

The metric system has been officially adopted but traditional local and Indian systems of weights and measures are widely used.

Statistical Survey

Source (unless otherwise stated): National Planning Commission Secretariat, Singha Durbar, POB 1284, Kathmandu; tel. (1) 4225879; fax (1) 4226500; e-mail npcs@wlink.com.np; internet www.npc.gov.np.

Area and Population

AREA, POPULATION AND DENSITY

Area (sq km)	147,181*
Population (census results)	
22 June 1991	18,491,097
22 June 2001†‡	
Males	11,563,921
Females	11,587,502
Total	23,151,423
Population (estimates at mid-year)§	
2005	27,094,000
2006	27,641,000
2007	28,196,000
Density (per sq km) at mid-2007	191.6

* 56,827 sq miles.
† Population is *de jure*.
‡ Includes estimates for certain areas in 12 districts where the census could not be conducted, owing to violence and disruption.
§ Source: UN, *World Population Prospects: The 2006 Revision*.

PRINCIPAL TOWNS
(population at 2001 census)

Kathmandu*	671,846	Mahendranagar	80,839
Biratnagar	166,674	Butawal	75,384
Lalitpur	162,991	Janakpur	74,192
Pokhara	156,312	Bhaktapur	72,543
Birgunj	112,484	Hetaunda	68,482
Dharan	95,332	Dhangadhi	67,447
Bharatpur	89,323		

* Total for urban agglomeration 1,081,845.

Mid-2007 (incl. suburbs, UN estimate): Kathmandu 895,000 (Source: UN, *World Urbanization Prospects: The 2007 Revision*).

BIRTHS AND DEATHS
(annual averages, UN estimates)

	1990–95	1995–2000	2000–05
Birth rate (per 1,000)	38.1	34.5	30.2
Death rate (per 1,000)	12.0	9.8	8.7

Source: UN, *World Population Prospects: The 2006 Revision*.

2001 (estimates): Birth rate 33.1 per 1,000; Death rate 9.6 per 1,000.

Expectation of life (years at birth, WHO estimates): 61.1 (males 60.8; females 61.2) in 2005 (Source: WHO, *World Health Statistics*).

ECONOMICALLY ACTIVE POPULATION
(1999 labour force survey, '000 persons aged 15 years and over)

Agriculture, hunting and forestry	7,190
Fishing	13
Mining and quarrying	8
Manufacturing	553
Electricity, gas and water	26
Construction	344
Wholesale and retail trade	408
Hotels and restaurants	114
Transport, storage and communications	135
Financial intermediation	19
Real estate, renting and business activities	32
Public administration and defence	70
Education	164
Health and social work	34
Other community, social and personal services	57
Private households with employed persons	289
Extra-territorial organizations and bodies	8
Total employed	**9,463**

Source: Central Bureau of Statistics, Kathmandu.

Mid-2005 (official estimates in '000): Agriculture, etc. 12,078; Total labour force 12,998 (Source: FAO).

Health and Welfare

KEY INDICATORS

Total fertility rate (children per woman, 2005)	3.5
Under-5 mortality rate (per 1,000 live births, 2005)	74
HIV/AIDS (% of persons aged 15–49, 2005)	0.5
Physicians (per 1,000 head, 2004)	0.21
Hospital beds (per 1,000 head, 2001)	0.15
Health expenditure (2004): US $ per head (PPP)	71.0
Health expenditure (2004): % of GDP	5.6
Health expenditure (2004): public (% of total)	26.3
Access to water (% of persons, 2004)	90
Access to sanitation (% of persons, 2004)	35
Human Development Index (2005): ranking	142
Human Development Index (2005): value	0.534

For sources and definitions, see explanatory note on p. vi.

Agriculture

PRINCIPAL CROPS
('000 metric tons)

	2004	2005	2006
Wheat	1,387	1,442	1,394
Rice (paddy)	4,456	4,290	4,209
Barley	31	29	28
Maize	1,590	1,716	1,734
Millet	283	290	291
Potatoes	1,643	1,739	1,975
Sugar cane	2,305	2,376	2,463
Beans, dry*	30	30	30
Pigeon peas	19	18	19
Lentils	159	161	158
Mustard seed	133	142	139
Garlic	28	29	29
Oranges	34	35	36
Apples	34	35	33
Ginger	152	154	154
Jute and jute-like fibres	17	16	17
Tobacco (leaves)	3	3	3

*FAO estimate(s).

Aggregate production ('000 metric tons, may include official, semi-official or estimated data): Total cereals 7,747 in 2004, 7,767 in 2005, 7,657 in 2006; Total roots and tubers 1,753 in 2004, 1,849 in 2005, 2,085 in 2006; Total vegetables (incl. melons) 1,930 in 2004, 2,106 in 2005, 2,233 in 2006; Total fruits (excl. melons) 511 in 2004, 519 in 2005, 536 in 2006.

Source: FAO.

LIVESTOCK
('000 head, year ending September)

	2004	2005	2006
Cattle	6,966	6,994	7,003
Buffaloes	3,953	4,081	4,203
Pigs	935	948	961
Sheep	824	817	812
Goats	6,980	7,154	7,422
Chickens	23,024	22,790	23,221

Source: FAO.

LIVESTOCK PRODUCTS
('000 metric tons)

	2004	2005	2006
Cattle meat*	48.5	48.9	48.9
Buffalo meat	133.6	139.0	142.0
Sheep meat	2.8	2.7	2.7
Goat meat	40.5	41.7	42.8
Pig meat	15.4	15.7	15.8
Chicken meat	16.1	15.5	15.6
Cows' milk	368.5	380.0	385.3
Buffaloes' milk	863.3	894.6	926.9
Goats' milk*	65.0	65.0	65.0
Ghee*	20.2	n.a.	n.a.
Hen eggs*	26.2	26.0	26.0

*FAO estimates.
Source: FAO.

Forestry

ROUNDWOOD REMOVALS
('000 cubic metres, excl. bark, FAO estimates)

	2004	2005	2006
Sawlogs, veneer logs and logs for sleepers	1,260	1,260	1,260
Fuel wood	12,702	12,692	12,595
Total	13,962	13,952	13,855

Source: FAO.

SAWNWOOD PRODUCTION
('000 cubic metres, incl. railway sleepers)

	1999	2000	2001
Coniferous (softwood)*	20	20	20
Broadleaved (hardwood)	610	610	610
Total	630	630	630

*FAO estimates.

2002–06: Production as in 2001 (FAO estimates).

Source: FAO.

Fishing

('000 metric tons, live weight)

	2003	2004	2005
Capture	18.9	19.9	20.0
Aquaculture	17.7	20.0	22.5
Common carp	3.6	4.1	4.6
Bighead carp	2.7	3.0	3.4
Silver carp	5.3	6.0	6.0
Other cyprinids	5.1	n.a.	n.a.
Total catch	36.6	39.9	42.5

Source: FAO.

Industry

SELECTED PRODUCTS
('000 metric tons unless otherwise indicated, year ending 15 July)

	2003/04	2004/05	2005/06
Cement	279.4	610.0	613.6
Iron rods	169.3	166.5	n.a.
Jute goods	35.7	32.8	n.a.
Raw sugar	96.2	97.7	98.5
Tea	11.4	11.5	11.6
Vegetable ghee	72.1	199.6	179.2
Beer and liquor (million litres)	29.4	39.6	n.a.
Soft drinks (million litres)	32.5	46.3	n.a.
Paper	42.8	29.0	29.9
Cigarettes ('000 million)	7.3	9.4	9.5
Cotton clothing (million metres)	1.5	1.5	n.a.
Synthetic clothing (million metres)	31.2	11.8	n.a.
Soap	53.8	44.3	44.8

Source: Federation of Nepalese Chambers of Commerce and Industry, Kathmandu.

Finance

CURRENCY AND EXCHANGE RATES

Monetary Units
100 paisa (pice) = 1 Nepalese rupee (NR).

Sterling, Dollar and Euro Equivalents (31 December 2007)
£1 sterling = NRs 127.32;
US $1 = NRs 63.6;
€1 = NRs 93.55;
1,000 Nepalese rupees = £7.85 = $15.74 = €10.69.

Average Exchange Rate (rupees per US $)
2005   71.368
2006   72.756
2007   66.415

NEPAL

Statistical Survey

BUDGET
(NRs million, year ending 15 July)*

Revenue†	2001/02	2002/03	2003/04
Taxation	39,331	42,587	48,173
Taxes on income and profits	8,920	8,132	9,515
Taxes on property	1,134	1,414	1,698
Domestic taxes on goods and services	16,618	18,804	21,406
Taxes on international trade and transactions	12,659	14,236	15,555
Other revenue	9,226	12,103	12,307
Charges, fees, fines, etc.	1,987	2,368	3,377
Sales of goods and services	1,143	1,274	1,322
Dividends	2,513	2,498	2,661
Interest receipts	1,220	925	1,657
Total	48,556	54,690	60,480

Expenditure	2001/02	2002/03	2003/04
Regular expenditure‡	42,155	45,414	47,657
General administration	7,283	7,283	7,283
Defence	5,860	7,381	8,520
Social services	13,070	13,459	14,038
Education	10,258	10,440	10,921
Health	1,980	2,032	2,121
Economic services	2,948	3,097	3,238
Agriculture-related	508	678	679
Infrastructure	1,121	1,127	1,118
Interest payments	5,770	6,622	6,544
Other purposes	7,224	5,806	6,235
Development expenditure§	29,495	27,493	29,140
Social services	9,410	10,501	11,507
Education	2,755	2,730	3,396
Health	1,877	1,620	1,847
Provision of drinking water	1,904	2,139	2,569
Economic services	20,085	16,992	17,633
Agriculture-related	6,132	4,188	4,352
Infrastructure	9,338	9,446	9,413
Total	71,650	72,907	76,797

*Figures refer to the regular and development budgets of the central Government.
† Excluding grants received (NRs million, estimates): 5,800 in 2001/02; 9,600 in 2002/03; 11,300 in 2003/04.
‡ Excluding amortization payments on domestic and foreign loans.
§ Including net lending and excluding principal repayment from corporations.

Source: IMF, *Nepal: Selected Issues and Statistical Appendix* (February 2006).

2004/05 (NRs million): *Revenue:* Total 70,123. *Expenditure:* Recurrent 61,686; Capital 27,341; Total (incl. others) 102,560 (Source: Federation of Nepalese Chambers of Commerce and Industry, Kathmandu).

2005/06 (NRs million, estimates): *Revenue:* Total 73,500. *Expenditure:* Recurrent 69,067; Capital 28,802; Total (incl. others) 112,075 (Source: Federation of Nepalese Chambers of Commerce and Industry, Kathmandu).

2006/07 (NRs million, estimates): *Revenue:* Total 85,376. *Expenditure:* Recurrent 83,768; Capital 44,976; Total (incl. others) 143,912 (Source: Federation of Nepalese Chambers of Commerce and Industry, Kathmandu).

INTERNATIONAL RESERVES
(US $ million at mid-December)

	2003	2004	2005
Gold*	6.5	6.5	5.4
IMF special drawing rights	0.8	9.7	8.8
Reserve position in IMF	8.6	—	—
Foreign exchange	1,213.1	1,452.5	1,490.2
Total	1,229.0	1,468.7	1,504.4

*Valued at US $42.5 per troy ounce in 2003 and 2004, and at $41.9 in 2005.

Source: IMF, *International Financial Statistics*.

MONEY SUPPLY
(NRs million at mid-December)*

	1998	1999	2000
Currency outside banks	32,244	36,929	44,526
Private sector deposits with monetary authorities	2,287	4,346	3,160
Demand deposits at commercial banks	10,979	13,832	15,343
Total money	45,509	55,107	63,028

2001: Currency outside banks 51,699; Private sector deposits 3,570.
2002: Currency outside banks 56,022; Private sector deposits 2,350.
2003: Currency outside banks 58,076; Private sector deposits 2,557.
2004: Currency outside banks 65,767; Private sector deposits 3,315.
2005: Currency outside banks 71,525; Private sector deposits 3,603.
2006: Currency outside banks 79,016; Private sector deposits 5,356.

*Excluding Indian currency in circulation.

Source: IMF, *International Financial Statistics*.

COST OF LIVING
(Consumer Price Index; base: 2000 = 100)

	2002	2003	2004
Food (incl. beverages)	104.4	110.1	112.9
Fuel and light	106.3	122.8	130.0
Clothing (excl. footwear)	104.4	106.3	108.4
Rent	110.9	116.4	120.9
All items (incl. others)	105.9	112.0	115.2

Source: ILO.

All items (Consumer Price Index; base: 2000 = 100): 122.9 in 2005; 132.2 in 2006 (Source: IMF, *International Financial Statistics*).

NATIONAL ACCOUNTS
(NRs million at current prices, year ending 15 July)

Expenditure on the Gross Domestic Product

	2003/04	2004/05*	2005/06†
Government final consumption expenditure	50,381	54,426	59,245
Private final consumption expenditure	383,978	412,776	458,991
Increase in stocks	35,869	53,038	68,859
Gross fixed capital formation	95,124	101,094	107,624
Total domestic expenditure	565,352	621,334	694,719
Exports of goods and services	89,543	85,957	108,142
Less Imports of goods and services	158,150	173,753	219,914
GDP in purchasers' values	496,745	533,538	582,948
GDP at constant 1994/95 prices	312,267	320,729	326,743

* Revised estimates.
† Preliminary estimates.

Gross Domestic Product by Economic Activity

	2003/04	2004/05*	2005/06†
Agriculture, forestry and fishing	183,117	194,363	212,827
Mining and quarrying	2,377	2,530	2,669
Manufacturing	36,634	39,286	41,768
Electricity, gas and water	11,355	11,892	12,508
Construction	49,029	52,922	56,558
Trade, restaurants and hotels	49,718	50,168	56,139
Transport, storage and communications	43,668	48,724	55,919
Finance and real estate	51,940	58,335	64,937
Community and social services	47,081	50,431	54,544
Sub-total	474,919	508,651	557,869
Less Imputed bank service charges	15,135	17,027	18,764
Gross value added in basic prices	459,784	491,624	539,105
Indirect taxes, *less* subsidies	36,961	41,914	43,842
GDP in market prices	496,745	533,538	582,948

* Revised estimates.
† Preliminary estimates.

NEPAL

BALANCE OF PAYMENTS
(US $ million)

	2004	2005	2006
Exports of goods f.o.b.	773.1	902.9	848.8
Imports of goods f.o.b.	−1,908.0	−2,276.5	−2,441.0
Trade balance	−1,134.9	−1,373.6	−1,592.2
Exports of services	460.9	380.3	385.7
Imports of services	−385.0	−434.7	−492.8
Balance on goods and services	−1,059.1	−1,428.0	−1,699.4
Other income received	63.0	139.9	158.2
Other income paid	−78.0	−91.6	−96.1
Balance on goods, services and income	−1,074.1	−1,379.7	−1,637.3
Current transfers received	1,091.8	1,441.3	1,695.7
Current transfers paid	−62.8	−60.5	−68.9
Current balance	−45.0	1.1	−10.4
Capital account (net)	15.7	40.3	46.3
Direct investment from abroad	−0.4	2.5	−6.6
Other investment assets	−348.0	−242.4	−250.9
Investment liabilities	−140.0	−36.5	260.3
Net errors and omissions	415.9	139.0	108.5
Overall balance	−101.9	−96.1	147.2

Source: IMF, *International Financial Statistics*.

OFFICIAL DEVELOPMENT ASSISTANCE
(US $ million)

	1998	1999	2000
Bilateral donors	218.8	212.3	234.7
Multilateral donors	189.4	138.8	155.1
Total	408.2	351.1	389.8
Grants	255.1	255.0	251.6
Loans	153.1	96.1	138.2
Per caput assistance (US $)	18.7	15.7	17.0

Source: UN, *Statistical Yearbook for Asia and the Pacific*.

External Trade

PRINCIPAL COMMODITIES
(NRs million, year ending 15 July)

Imports c.i.f.	2003/04	2004/05	2005/06
Food and live animals	8,554	9,821	13,549
Crude materials (inedible) except fuels	10,551	11,207	11,180
Mineral fuels and lubricants	21,904	29,927	36,457
Animal and vegetable oils and fats	8,634	6,016	10,205
Chemicals and pharmaceuticals	16,545	19,180	24,850
Basic manufactures	36,511	37,047	42,574
Machinery and transport equipment	25,694	26,262	26,271
Miscellaneous manufactured articles	5,104	7,552	8,602
Total (incl. others)	136,277	149,474	175,109

Exports f.o.b.	2003/04	2004/05	2005/06
Food and live animals	6,277	6,994	7,463
Animal and vegetable oils and fats	3,376	5,070	4,255
Chemicals and pharmaceuticals	3,866	3,678	3,810
Basic manufactures	23,602	28,591	28,997
Miscellaneous manufactured articles	15,380	13,240	14,104
Total (incl. others)	53,911	58,706	61,167

Source: Asian Development Bank.

Exports of carpets (US $ million, year ending 15 July): 80.8 in 2001/02; 68.4 in 2002/03; 76.9 in 2003/04.

Exports of garments (US $ million, year ending 15 July): 101.8 in 2001/02; 152.8 in 2002/03; 129.4 in 2003/04.

Source: IMF, *Nepal: Selected Issues and Statistical Appendix* (February 2006).

PRINCIPAL TRADING PARTNERS
(NRs million, year ending 15 July)

Imports	2003/04	2004/05	2005/06
Australia	1,271.4	1,521.1	1,415.3
Belgium	1,125.6	824.0	240.2
China, People's Republic	9,299.9	12,859.2	12,083.5
France	675.5	668.5	909.9
Germany	1,977.9	1,570.9	2,761.8
Hong Kong	1,641.6	1,286.4	930.9
India	78,739.5	88,675.5	109,305.9
Indonesia	3,253.8	5,222.7	5,647.8
Japan	1,690.4	2,565.2	1,935.1
Korea, Republic	3,080.6	2,784.6	1,788.9
Malaysia	3,676.4	2,820.9	2,474.7
New Zealand	1,283.7	1,229.7	1,018.8
Saudi Arabia	2,547.9	3,138.5	2,329.7
Singapore	8,698.6	7,746.8	3,375.3
Taiwan	1,175.1	825.7	567.9
Thailand	4,320.2	3,117.5	2,602.1
United Kingdom	1,035.5	1,452.2	961.4
USA	1,433.3	1,763.8	1,677.5
Total (incl. others)	136,277.1	149,473.6	175,108.0

Exports	2003/04	2004/05	2005/06
China, People's Republic	2,348.2	1,888.5	892.6
France	581.8	617.8	129.7
Germany	3,567.0	3,121.7	284.4
India	30,777.1	38,916.9	41,012.6
Italy	589.4	582.8	712.3
United Kingdom	1,677.1	1,050.0	1,184.1
USA	9,696.0	7,570.7	6,993.4
Total (incl. others)	53,910.7	58,705.7	61,167.1

Source: Federation of Nepalese Chambers of Commerce and Industry, Kathmandu.

Transport

ROAD TRAFFIC
(vehicles registered)

	2000/01	2001/02	2002/03
Cars, jeeps and vans	5,152	4,374	2,906
Buses and minibuses	1,453	1,343	730
Tractors	3,519	3,189	2,485
Other agro-industrial vehicles	1,271	1,798	1,212
Motorcycles	29,291	38,522	29,404
Total (incl. others)	40,995	49,560	37,610

Source: Department of Transport Management, Kathmandu.

Civil Aviation

Royal Nepal Airlines Corporation
(traffic on scheduled services)

	2001	2002	2003
Kilometres flown (million)	9	10	8
Passengers carried ('000)	641	681	356
Passenger-km (million)	1,153	1,211	663
Total ton-km (million)	119	127	64

Source: UN, *Statistical Yearbook*.

Tourism

FOREIGN TOURIST ARRIVALS

Country of residence	2003	2004	2005
Australia	7,916	9,839	7,093
Bangladesh	5,215	14,640	19,206
China, People's Republic	5,677	12,733	21,092
France	15,730	18,992	14,108
Germany	14,875	16,031	14,345
India	86,578	89,861	95,685
Italy	8,201	12,121	8,785
Japan	27,267	24,196	18,239
Korea, Republic	13,769	10,654	10,121
Netherlands	8,339	11,064	8,890
Sri Lanka	13,960	16,045	18,686
Thailand	11,392	14,680	13,614
United Kingdom	21,550	24,644	24,950
USA	18,871	20,584	18,476
Total (incl. others)	338,132	385,297	375,398

Tourism receipts (US $ million, incl. passenger transport): 233 in 2003; 260 in 2004; 160 in 2005.

Source: World Tourism Organization.

Communications Media

	2004	2005	2006
Telephones ('000 main lines in use)	417.9	484.6	595.8
Mobile cellular telephones ('000 subscribers)	116.8	227.3	1,041.8
Personal computers ('000 in use)	116	116	n.a.
Internet users ('000)	120	225	249.4

2003: Daily newspapers 251 titles; Non-daily newspapers 3,490 titles.

Facsimile machines ('000 in use, year ending 15 July): 8 in 1999.

Radio receivers ('000 in use): 840 in 1997.

Television receivers ('000 in use): 170 in 2000; 193 in 2001.

Sources: UNESCO, *Statistical Yearbook*; International Telecommunication Union.

Education

(2004)

	Institutions*	Teachers	Students
Primary	24,746	101,483	4,030,045
Lower Secondary	7,436	25,962	1,444,997
Secondary	4,547	20,232	543,764

* Including duplication, since many schools offer education at more than one level. The total number of primary, lower secondary and secondary institutions was 26,277.

Pre-primary: 1,471 institutions, 257,121 students in 2003.

Source: Ministry of Education and Sports, Kathmandu.

Adult literacy rate (UNESCO estimates): 48.6% (males 62.7%; females 34.9%) in 2001 (Source: UNESCO Institute for Statistics).

Directory

Interim Constitution

In May 2006, prior to the convening of a Constituent Assembly, the House of Representatives approved a provisional proclamation significantly curtailing the powers of the King. All existing constitutional provisions that contradicted the proclamation were to be nullified. The most significant declarations of the proclamation were: that Nepal would henceforth be designated a secular state; that all legislative powers in the country would be exercised by the House of Representatives; that all executive authority in Nepal would reside with the Council of Ministers; that the Council of State (Raj Parishad) would be abolished; that the 'Royal Nepal Army' would be renamed the 'Nepal Army'; that the monarch would no longer hold the position of Supreme Commander-in-Chief of the Royal Nepal Army; that the monarch would no longer possess the authority to enact laws concerning the royal succession; that the monarch's acts could henceforth be challenged by both the House of Representatives and the courts; and that henceforth sessions of the House of Representatives would no longer be convened by the monarch, but by the Speaker, on the advice of the Prime Minister. In addition, in June, following a unanimous parliamentary vote, King Gyanendra was stripped of his right to veto laws, and in July his mandate to appoint judges was also taken away. The proclamation of May 2006 effectively overrode the Constitution promulgated by the King on 9 November 1990.

Following extensive negotiations between members of the seven-party alliance (a political coalition demanding an end to autocratic governance in Nepal), the Communist Party of Nepal (Maoist) and a UN peace delegation to Nepal, an Interim Constitution was presented in December 2006 and subsequently endorsed on 15 January 2007. (Maoist inclusion in the interim legislature was agreed according to the conditions of a Comprehensive Peace Agreement, which was signed on 21 November 2006 and which promised the disarmament of the Maoist militant groups and the containment of insurgent military personnel in government-supervised camps.) The enactment of the Interim Constitution effected the dissolution of the National Assembly and the House of Representatives and instituted a 330-member Interim Parliament, or 'Legislature-Parliament', which was mandated to formulate a model for the election of a Constituent Assembly, which would draft a permanent Constitution. All constitutional powers of governance formerly commanded by King Gyanendra were transferred to Prime Minister Girija Prasad Koirala, who was nominated Head of State. Executive power was conferred upon the Council of Ministers.

Further requested amendments to the Interim Constitution were confirmed in February 2007, particularly with respect to proportional and comprehensive representation of the Madhesi people and federal governance structure; following the submission of concerns from international observers in the USA, the process of judicial appointments and the administration of justice were also highlighted as issues for revision. A two-thirds' majority parliamentary vote was required to initiate all constitutional amendments. In December the Interim Parliament endorsed a constitutional amendment providing for the abolition of the monarchy; however, the change was to come into effect only upon the approval of the Constituent Assembly. At the same time, the membership of the Constituent Assembly was increased, with a significant number to be elected under the system of proportional representation.

The preamble to the Interim Constitution of Nepal, 2063 (2007), envisages the guarantee of the fundamental and human rights of every citizen and the protection of his civil liberty; the rights of the Nepalese people to structure their own Constitution and to engage in the unrestricted, impartial election of a Constituent Assembly; the resolution of class, caste, gender and regional tensions through systematic state restructure; universal adult suffrage and the multi-party system; complete freedom of press; and the provision of an independent judicial system. Democracy, peace, prosperity, economic and social progress, integrity and independence are national priorities. Sovereignty and state governance reside in the Nepalese people. The Constitution is the fundamental law of the land and nullifies any other extraneous laws that it may be attempted to introduce.

Nepal is a multi-ethnic, multi-lingual, religiously multi-denominational, independent, indivisible, sovereign, secular and inclusive democratic state. Nepali is recognized as the national language; Nepali in the Devnagari representation is the official language.

CITIZENSHIP AND FUNDAMENTAL RIGHTS

At the effective implementation of the Constitution, persons domiciled in Nepal who are eligible to apply for or have acquired citizenship are regarded as Nepali citizens. Honorary or naturalized citizenship may be endowed by the Government in accordance with legal provisions, and shall not be acquired or revoked unless dictated by law. Part Three of the Constitution provides for the fundamental rights of the citizen: all citizens are equal before the law and shall be awarded equal protection from the law; no discrimination is to be practised on the basis of religion, race, sex, caste, tribe, origin, language or ideology; acts of racial discrimination or untouchability shall be punishable by law and the victim eligible for compensation; no person can be deprived of his liberty except in accordance with the law; capital punishment remains abolished; freedom of expression and opinion, freedom to assemble peaceably and without arms, freedom to form political parties or organizations, freedom to form trade unions and associations, freedom of profession, and freedom of movement are also guaranteed. Similarly, pre-censorship of publications and impediment to communication media is prohibited and, thus, the right to press and publications is ensured. In the sphere of criminal justice, the following rights are specified in the Constitution: no person is to be regarded as an offender unless proven so by law, nor punished unless made punishable by law; any indicted person is entitled to confidential legal counsel at the time of arrest and may be represented by their chosen legal practitioner; those persons with insufficient financial means are to be entitled to free legal aid; no person may be tried more than once for the same offence; no one is compelled to testify against himself; no one is to be given punishment greater than that which the law at the time of the offence has prescribed; torture of detainees is prohibited; no person is to be detained without having first been informed about the grounds for such an action; and the detainee must appear before the judicial authorities within 24 hours of his arrest. In addition, provision has also been made to compensate any person who is wrongfully detained. Every citizen is entitled to a clean living environment and state-funded basic health care. A person's right to property and compensation for land reclaimed by the State under national programmes is ensured, and the right to protect and promote one's own language, script and culture have been safeguarded. The right to state-funded education up to secondary level (provided in the child's mother tongue up to primary level) is similarly ensured, while all persons are guaranteed the right to employment, and social security is to benefit all social groups. Exploitation and exile are guarded against. The rights of women to inheritance, protection from violence and sexual discrimination are assured, as are those of children to protection, nurture and state privileges in the case of disadvantaged birth. Additionally, social justice is guaranteed for women and tribal, oppressed and deprived social groups, and all citizens are to be permitted access to information pertaining to themselves or matters of national importance. The right to practise religion and to manage and protect religious places and trusts has been granted to the country's various religious groups. The right to secrecy and inviolability of the person, residence, property, documents, letters and other information is also guaranteed. The right to constitutional resolution secures the enforcement of all other rights designated by the Constitution.

GOVERNMENT AND LEGISLATURE

The executive powers of the country are vested in the Council of Ministers. The direction, supervision and conduct of the general administration of Nepal are the responsibility of the Council of Ministers. The Prime Minister and Council of Ministers are appointed according to political consensus. In the absence of a consensus the Legislature-Parliament elects a Prime Minister by a two-thirds' majority. The Prime Minister selects ministers from the Legislature-Parliament upon the recommendation of the relevant party, but may also appoint ministers and deputy ministers who are not members of the Legislature-Parliament. The Prime Minister and other ministers are answerable to the Legislature-Parliament. The Legislature-Parliament is unicameral and has 330 members, that is: 209 members of the political organizations in the seven political parties (Nepali Congress Party, Communist Party of Nepal (Unified Marxist-Leninist), Nepali Congress Party—Democratic, Janamorcha Nepal, Nepali Sadbhavana Party (Anadidevi), Nepal Majdur Kisan Party and Samyukta Bam Morcha) and of the most recent House of Representatives and National Assembly, which were dissolved with the introduction of the Interim Constitution; 73 members or representatives of the Communist Party of Nepal (Maoist); and 48 members nominated from the Samyukta Bam Morcha, selected organizations, disadvantaged and oppressed groups and others. Membership is denied to those who 'were against' the 'people's movement'. The Legislature-Parliament's term ends following the inaugural meeting of the Constituent Assembly (sched-uled to be held on 28 May 2008). All persons aged 18 years by 15 December 2006 will be eligible to vote. The Constituent Assembly was to comprise 601 members, of whom 335 were to be elected using the system of proportional representation, 240 directly elected and 26 nominated. The Constituent Assembly was to be responsible for drafting a new Constitution; the tenure of office of its members was to be two years.

GOVERNANCE

Part Four of the Constitution details the responsibilities, policies and regulatory tenets of the State, particularly citing the objectives of electoral reform to provide for free and impartial election of the Constituent Assembly, the institution of a multi-party democratic and inclusive political system adherent to citizens' fundamental and human rights, the restructuring of the State to eliminate discrimination against or marginalization of any social group and actively promote full social and economic integration, the promotion of a national socio-economic development programme and prohibition of assets procurement by corrupt means, provision for the relief and rehabilitation of victims of the conflict, including the institution of an investigatory Truth and Reconciliation Commission, and prevention of further violence and conflict through institutionalized peace. In addition, the promotion of national economic independence and growth, enhancement of the people's basic quality of life and state infrastructure, and the adoption of a co-operative and equality driven foreign policy are ensured. No legal challenge may be submitted as to the implementation or otherwise of any such policies.

Part 17 of the Constitution makes provision for local self governance through the institution of district, municipal and village interim organizations. The State, through national and local government, is empowered to marshal revenue and resources in the interests of fulfilling such state policies.

THE JUDICIARY

The judicial system has three tiers: the Supreme Court, the Appellate Courts and the District Courts. The Supreme Court is the principal court and is also a Court of Record. The Supreme Court consists of a Chief Justice and a maximum of 14 other judges. The Chief Justice is appointed by the Prime Minister on the recommendation of the Constitutional Council; other Supreme Court, Appellate Court and District Court judges are nominated by the Chief Justice on the recommendation of the Judicial Council. A Constituent Assembly Court was established in February 2008 to address election issues.

OTHER INSTITUTIONS

The Interim Constitution also makes provisions for the establishment of a Constitutional Council, Public Service Commission, Election Commission, National Human Rights Commission, Commission for the Investigation of Abuse of Authority, Auditor General and Attorney-General.

POLITICAL PARTIES

Political parties are required to register with the Election Commission, and must be non-discriminatory, have democratic aims, and produce the signatures of at least 10,000 voters in support of their application. It has been specifically provided that no law that bans, or imposes restrictions on, political parties may be enacted. Parties whose aims run 'contrary' to the Preamble of the Interim Constitution will be disqualified from registering.

EMERGENCY PROVISIONS

If and when there is a grave emergency in the country, caused by a threat to the sovereignty, integrity or security of the country or any of its parts (owing to war, armed revolt or extreme economic depression), the Council of Ministers may declare a state of emergency in the country or its relevant part. The proclamation must be approved by a two-thirds' majority in the Legislature-Parliament to stay in force for a three-month period; the Legislature-Parliament may then approve an extension. During the period of emergency, fundamental rights, with several exceptions including the right of recourse to *habeas corpus*, may be suspended.

AMENDMENTS

The Constitution may be amended by a two-thirds' majority in each House of Parliament.

DEFENCE

The Commander-in-Chief of the Nepal Army is appointed by the Council of Ministers. The Council of Ministers shall work towards the democratization and human rights awareness of the Nepal Army. The Nepal Army is administered and deployed by the Council of Ministers on the recommendation of the National Defence Council, which consists of the Prime Minister, the Minister of Defence, three other ministerial nominees and the Commander-in-Chief. The Council of Ministers shall establish a committee to oversee the assimila-

NEPAL

tion and rehabilitation of Maoist combatants. Certain other procedures are governed by agreements between the (former) Government of Nepal and the Communist Party of Nepal (Maoist).

TRANSITIONAL PROVISIONS

No executive power shall be vested in the King. The future of the monarchy will be decided by a simple majority vote at the inaugural meeting of the Constituent Assembly. Property belonging to the King (in his capacity as monarch) shall be nationalized.

The Government

HEAD OF STATE

Prime Minister GIRIJA PRASAD KOIRALA.

INTERIM COUNCIL OF MINISTERS
(April 2008)

Prime Minister and Minister of Defence: GIRIJA PRASAD KOIRALA.
Minister of Foreign Affairs: SAHANA PRADHAN.
Minister of Peace and Reconstruction: RAM CHANDRA POUDEL.
Minister of Finance: Dr RAM SHARAN MAHAT.
Minister of Law, Justice and Parliamentary Affairs: NARENDRA BIKRAM NEMBANG.
Minister of Environment, Science and Technology: PHARMULLAH MANSUR.
Minister of Agriculture and Co-operatives: CHHABILAL BISWOKARMA.
Minister of Forests and Soil Conservation: MATRIKA YADAV.
Minister of Home Affairs: KRISHNA PRASAD SITAULA.
Minister of Land Reforms and Management: JAGAT BAHADUR BOGATI.
Minister of Physical Planning and Works: HISILA YAMI.
Minister of Local Development: DEV GURUNG.
Minister of Culture, Tourism and Civil Aviation: PRITHVI SUBBA GURUNG.
Minister of Education and Sports: PRADEEP NEPAL.
Minister of Industry, Commerce and Supplies: SHYAM SUNDAR GUPTA.
Minister of Information and Communications: KRISHNA BAHADUR MAHARA.
Minister of Women, Children and Social Welfare: PAMPHA BHUSAL.
Minister of Health and Population: GIRIRAJMANI POKHAREL.
Minister of Labour and Transport Management: RAMESH LEKHAK.
Minister of Water Resources: GYANENDRA BAHADUR KARKI.
Minister of General Administration: RAM CHANDRA YADAV.
Minister without Portfolio: SUJATA KOIRALA.
In addition, there are eight State Ministers.

MINISTRIES

Prime Minister's Office: Singha Durbar, POB 43312, Kathmandu; tel. (1) 421000; e-mail info@opmcm.gov.np; internet www.opmcm.gov.np.
Ministry of Agriculture and Co-operatives: Singha Durbar, Kathmandu; tel. (1) 4228371; fax (1) 4229139; e-mail memoac@moac.gov.np; internet www.moac.gov.np.
Ministry of Culture, Tourism and Civil Aviation: Bhrikutimandap, Kathmandu; tel. (1) 4256217; fax (1) 4227281; e-mail info@tourism.gov.np; internet www.tourism.gov.np.
Ministry of Defence: Singha Durbar, Kathmandu; tel. (1) 4211290; fax (1) 4211294.
Ministry of Education and Sports: Keshar Mahal, Kantipath, Kathmandu; tel. (1) 4418784; fax (1) 412199; e-mail infomoe@most.gov.np; internet www.moe.gov.np.
Ministry of Environment, Science and Technology: Singha Durbar, Kathmandu; tel. (1) 4244609; fax (1) 4225474; e-mail info@most.gov.np; internet www.most.gov.np.
Ministry of Finance: Singha Durbar, Kathmandu; tel. (1) 4211809; fax (1) 4211831; e-mail admindivision@mof.gov.np; internet www.mof.gov.np.
Ministry of Foreign Affairs: Shital Niwas, Maharajganj, Kathmandu; tel. (1) 4416011; fax (1) 4416016; e-mail adm@mofa.gov.np; internet www.mofa.gov.np.

Ministry of Forests and Soil Conservation: Singha Durbar, Kathmandu; tel. (1) 4220067; fax (1) 4223868; e-mail info@mosc.gov.np; internet www.mofsc.gov.np.
Ministry of General Administration: Singha Durbar, Kathmandu; tel. (1) 4245367; fax (1) 4242138; e-mail moga@most.gov.np; internet www.moga.gov.np.
Ministry of Health and Population: Singha Durbar Plaza, Ramshah Path, Kathmandu; tel. (1) 4262862; fax (1) 4262896; e-mail info@moh.gov.np; internet www.moh.gov.np.
Ministry of Home Affairs: Singha Durbar, Kathmandu; tel. (1) 4211224; e-mail moha@wlink.com.np; internet www.moha.gov.np.
Ministry of Industry, Commerce and Supplies: Singha Durbar, Kathmandu; tel. (1) 4211967; fax (1) 4211619; e-mail info@moics.gov.np; internet www.moics.gov.np.
Ministry of Information and Communications: Singha Durbar, Kathmandu; tel. (1) 4211556; fax (1) 4221729; e-mail moicppme@ntc.net.np; internet www.moic.gov.np.
Ministry of Labour and Transport Management: Singha Durbar, Kathmandu; tel. (1) 4247842; fax (1) 4256877; e-mail info@moltm.gov.np; internet www.moltm.gov.np.
Ministry of Land Reform and Management: Singha Durbar, Kathmandu; tel. (1) 4225366; fax (1) 4220108; e-mail lrm@most.gov.np; internet www.molrm.gov.np.
Ministry of Law, Justice and Parliamentary Affairs: Singha Durbar, Kathmandu; tel. (1) 4223727; fax (1) 4220684; e-mail info@moljpa.gov.np; internet www.moljpa.gov.np.
Ministry of Local Development: Sri Mahal, Pulchowk, Lalitpur; tel. (1) 5521727; fax (1) 5522045; e-mail info@mld.gov.np; internet www.mld.gov.np.
Ministry of Physical Planning and Works: Singha Durbar, Kathmandu; tel. (1) 4228285; fax (1) 4228420; e-mail info@moppw.gov.np; internet www.moppw.gov.np.
Ministry of Water Resources: Singha Durbar, Kathmandu; tel. (1) 4211511; e-mail mowr@most.gov.np; internet www.mowr.gov.np.
Ministry of Women, Children and Social Welfare: Singha Durbar, Kathmandu; tel. (1) 4241728; fax (1) 4241516; internet www.mowcsw.gov.np.

Legislature

INTERIM PARLIAMENT

On 15 January 2007 the legislature instituted by the 1990 Constitution, comprising the Rashtriya Sabha (National Assembly) and the Pratinidhi Sabha (House of Representatives), was dissolved upon the promulgation of a new Interim Constitution (see Interim Constitution), and a 330-member Interim Parliament, or 'Legislature-Parliament', was convened by agreement of a seven-party political coalition and the Maoist former insurgents. In accordance with articles stipulated in the Interim Constitution, the temporary legislature facilitated preparations for a democratically elected Constituent Assembly (see below), and was to be dissolved following the first meeting of the Assembly on 28 May 2008.

Speaker: SUBAS NEMBANG.
Chairman: BAL BAHADUR RAI.

Interim Parliament constituted by multi-party agreement, 15 January 2007

Party	Seats
Nepali Congress Party (NCP)*	85
Communist Party of Nepal (Unified Marxist-Leninist—UML)	83
Communist Party of Nepal (Maoist—M)	83
Nepali Congress Party—Democratic (NCP—D)*	48
Rashtriya Prajatantra Party (RPP)	9
People's Front Nepal†	9
Nepali Sadbhavana Party (Anandi Devi)‡	5
Nepal Workers' and Peasants' Party	4
United Left Front	3
Rashtriya Jana Shakti Party	1
Total	**330**

* Merged in September 2007.
† Split into three factions in December 2006, each operating under the ensign of the People's Front Nepal (Jana Morcha Nepal); representation includes seats secured by all three organizations.
‡ Split into two factions, Anandi Devi and Mandal, in 2003; the latter group is not represented in the Interim Parliament.

NEPAL   *Directory*

CONSTITUENT ASSEMBLY

The Constituent Assembly, which is responsible for drafting a new Constitution, comprises 601 members, of whom 575 were elected (using the mixed electoral system) and 26 nominated by the incumbent Interim Parliament. The term of office of its members is two years. The Constituent Assembly was due to hold its inaugural meeting on 28 May 2008, upon which the Interim Parliament would be disbanded.

Election, 10 April 2008

Party	Seats*
Communist Party of Nepal (Maoist—M)	220
Nepali Congress Party (NCP)	110
Communist Party of Nepal (Unified Marxist-Leninist—UML)	103
Madhesi People's Rights Forum Nepal	52
Terai Madhes Loktantrik Party	20
Sadbhavana Party	9
Communist Party of Nepal (Marxist-Leninist)	8
Rashtriya Prajatantra Party (RPP)	8
Janamorcha Nepal	7
Communist Party of Nepal (United)	5
Nepal Workers' and Peasants' Party	4
Rashtriya Prajatantra Party Nepal	4
Rastriya Janamorcha	4
Rashtriya Janshakti Party	3
Communist Party of Nepal (Unified)	2
Nepali Janata Dal	2
Nepali Sadbhavana Party (Anandi Devi)	2
Rastriya Janamukti Party	2
Sanghiya Loktantrik Rastriya Manch	2
Churevawar Rastriya Ekata Party Nepal	1
Dalit Janajati Party	1
Nepal Loktantrik Samajbadi Dal	1
Nepal Pariwar Dal	1
Nepal Rastriya Party	1
Samajwadi Prajatantrik Janata Party Nepal	1
Independents	2
Nominated	26
Total	**601**

* Includes seats determined by proportional representation and 'first past the post' systems.

Election Commission

Election Commission of Nepal: Bahadur Bhawan, Kantipath, Kathmandu; tel. (1) 4228663; fax (1) 4229227; e-mail info@election.gov.np; internet www.election.gov.np; independent; appointed by the Prime Minister, on recommendation of a Constitutional Council, for a six-year term; Chief Election Commr BHOJ RAJ POKHAREL.

Political Organizations

According to the Interim Constitution (which was formally endorsed in January 2007), political parties are required to register with the Election Commission, and must be non-discriminatory, have democratic aims, and produce the signatures of at least 10,000 voters supporting them. No law that bans or imposes restrictions on political parties may be enacted. Parties whose aims run 'contrary' to the Preamble of the Interim Constitution will not be permitted to register. By mid-2007 11 major political parties of the interim Parliament had been registered as official national parties with the Election Commission and confirmed as eligible to contest the forthcoming constituent assembly elections, which were held in April 2008.

Communist Party of Nepal (Maoist) (CPN(M)): internet www.cpnm.org; f. 1990 as Communist Party of Nepal (Unity Centre), renamed as above in 1995; fmr underground political movement, represented in Interim Parliament in 2007; orchestrated 'people's war' in hills of west Nepal (1996–2006); advocates abolition of constitutional monarchy and establishment of people's republic; merged with Communist Party of Nepal (Unified Marxist-Leninist-Maoist) Sept. 2007; merged with Communist Party of Nepal (Marxist) in Feb. 2008; Leader PUSHPA KAMAL DAHAL ('Prachanda').

Communist Party of Nepal (Unified): Kathmandu; f. 2007; Gen. Sec. RAJ SINGH SHRIS.

Communist Party of Nepal (United): Kathmandu; f. 2007 following a split in the Communist Party of Nepal (United Marxist); Gen. Sec. GANESH SHAH.

Green Nepal Party: Kalikasthan, POB 890, Kathmandu; tel. and fax (1) 4438402; e-mail greennepal@htp.com.np; internet www.nepalgreenparty.com; f. 1997; Pres. PUSP PRASAD LUINTEL; Chair. KUBER SHARMA.

Madhesi Jana Adhikar Forum Nepal (Madhesi People's Rights Forum Nepal): f. 2006; Chair. UPENDRA YADAV.

Nepali Janata Dal: Tripureshwor, Kathmandu; tel. (1) 4212389; f. 1990; advocates the consolidation of the multi-party democratic system and supports the campaign against corruption; Leader KESHAR JUNG RAYAMAJHI.

Rashtriya Janshakti Party (National People's Power Party): Ramalphokhari, Kathmandu; tel. (1) 4437063; fax (1) 4437064; e-mail rjpnepal@info.com.np; f. 2005; Leader SURYA BAHADUR THAPA.

Rashtriya Prajatantra Party (RPP) (National Democratic Party—NDP): Charumati Bahal, Chabahil, Kathmandu; tel. (1) 4471071; fax (1) 4423384; e-mail info@rppnepal.com; internet www.rppnepal.org; liberal democratic party; Pres. PASHUPATI SHUMSHERE J. B. RANA; Sec.-Gen. DEEPAK BOHARA.

Rashtriya Prajatantra Party Nepal: Kathmandu; tel. (1) 4375455; f. 2008; Pres. RABINDRA NATH SHARMA.

Rastriya Janamorcha: Kathmandu; tel. (1) 4420226; Pres. CHITRA BAHADUR K. C.

Rastriya Janamukti Party: Maha Laxmisthan, Lagan Khel, POB 5569, Kathmandu; tel. (1) 5542212; fax (1) 5525531; e-mail zhedi43@yahoo.com; internet www.janamuktiparty.com; f. 1990; Pres. MALBAR SINGH THAPA.

Sadbhavana Party: Kathmandu.

Sanghiya Loktantrik Rastriya Manch: Kathmandu; Pres. KAMAL CHARAHANG.

Terai Madhes Loktantrik Party: Kathmandu; tel. (1) 4462398; Pres. MAHANTH THAKUR.

Seven-party alliance (SPA): coalition of left-wing parties.

Communist Party of Nepal (Unified Marxist-Leninist) (UML): Madan Nagar, Balkhu, POB 5471, Kathmandu; tel. (1) 4278081; fax (1) 4278084; e-mail uml@ntc.net.np; internet www.cpnuml.org; f. 1991 when two major factions of the Communist Party of Nepal (CPN; f. 1949; banned 1960; legalized 1990)—the Marxist and Marxist-Leninist factions—merged; the Communist Party of Nepal (Marxist-Leninist—ML) seceded in 1998 and rejoined the UML in 2002; the Communist Party of Nepal (Verma) merged with the UML in 2001; Gen. Sec. AMRIT KUMAR BOHARA (acting).

Nepali Congress Party (NCP): B. P. Smriti Bhawan, B. P. Nagar, Sanepa, Lalitpur; tel. (1) 5555263; fax (1) 5555188; e-mail ncparty@wlink.com.np; internet www.nepalicongress.org; f. 1947; banned 1960; legalized 1990; Nepali Congress Party—Democratic formed as breakaway faction in 2002, rejoined Sept. 2007; Pres. SUSHIL KOIRALA (acting); Gen. Secs K. B. GURUNG, BIMALENDRA NIDHI, Dr RAM BARAN YADAV; 101,000 active members, 500,000 ordinary members.

Nepali Sadbhavana Party (NSP) (Nepal Goodwill Party): Shantinagar, New Baneshwor, Kathmandu; tel. (1) 4488068; fax (1) 4470797; f. 1990; promotes the rights of the Madhesiya community, who are of Indian origin and reside in the Terai; demands that the Government recognize Hindi as an official language, that constituencies in the Terai be allocated on the basis of population, and that the Government grant citizenship to those who settled in Nepal before April 1990; in 2003 the party split into two factions, one led by Babri Prasad Mandal, known as the Mandal Group, and the other led by Anandi Devi Singh, known as the Anandi Devi group (the NSP member of the SPA).

Nepal Workers' and Peasants' Party: Golmadhi Tole-7, Bhaktapur, Kathmandu; tel. (1) 6610974; fax (1) 6613207; e-mail nwpp@ntc.net.np; Chair. NARAYAN MAN BIJUKCHHEN (Comrade Rohit).

People's Front Nepal (Janamorcha Nepal): Kathmandu; f. 2002 following merger of Rashtriya Jana Morcha (National People's Front) and United People's Front; split into three factions in Dec. 2006; Pres. AMIK SHERCHAN; Vice-Chair. LILAMANI POKHAREL.

United Left Front: coalition of Nepali communist parties; f. 2002.

Communist Party of Nepal (Marxist-Leninist) (CPN—ML): Kathmandu; f. 2002 following the reunification of the Communist Party of Nepal (Marxist-Leninist) with the Communist Party of Nepal (Unified Marxist–Leninist); C. P. Mainali, co-founder of the original CPN(ML) as a break-away faction of the CPN(UML) in 1998, had opposed the merger and formed a separate party under the CPN(ML) title; Leader C. P. MAINALI.

Other parties elected to the Constituent Assembly in April 2008 were Churevawar Rastriya Ekata Party Nepal, Dalit Janajati Party, Nepal Loktantrik Samajbadi Dal, Nepal Pariwar Dal, Nepal Rastriya Party, and Samajwadi Prajatantrik Janata Party Nepal.

Diplomatic Representation

EMBASSIES IN NEPAL

Australia: Suraj Niwas, Bansbari, POB 879, Kathmandu; tel. (1) 4371678; fax (1) 4371533; internet www.nepal.embassy.gov.au; Ambassador GRAEME LADE.

Bangladesh: Maharajgunj Ring Rd, POB 789, Kathmandu; tel. (1) 4372843; fax (1) 4373265; e-mail bdootktm@wlink.com.np; Ambassador IMTIAZ AHMED.

China, People's Republic: Baluwatar, POB 4234, Kathmandu; tel. (1) 4419053; fax (1) 4414045; e-mail chinaemb_np@mfa.gov.cn; internet www.fmprc.gov.cn/ce/cenp; Ambassador ZHENG XIANGLIN.

Denmark: 761 Neel Saraswati Marg, Lazimpat, POB 6332, Kathmandu; tel. (1) 4413010; fax (1) 4411409; e-mail ktmamb@um.dk; internet www.ambkathmandu.um.dk; Ambassador FINN THILSTED.

Egypt: Pulchowk, Lalitpur, POB 792, Kathmandu; tel. (1) 5524812; fax (1) 5522975; Ambassador ABDUL HAMEED MAHMOUD SOLIMAN.

Finland: Bishalnagar, POB 2126, Kathmandu; tel. (1) 4416636; fax (1) 4416703; e-mail sanomat.kat@formin.fi; internet www.finland.org.np; Chargé d'affaires a.i. PIRKKO-LIISA KYÖSTILÄ.

France: Lazimpat, POB 452, Kathmandu; tel. (1) 4412332; fax (1) 4419968; e-mail consulat@ambafrance-np.org; internet www.ambafrance-np.org; Ambassador GILLES-HENRY GARAULT.

Germany: Gyaneshwar, POB 226, Kathmandu; tel. (1) 4412786; fax (1) 4416899; e-mail info@kathmandu.diplo.de; internet www.kathmandu.diplo.de; Ambassador FRANZ RING.

India: 336 Kapurdhara Marg, POB 292, Kathmandu; tel. (1) 4410900; fax (1) 4428279; e-mail pic@eoiktm.org; internet www.south-asia.com/embassy-India; Ambassador SHIV SHANKAR MUKHERJEE.

Israel: Bishramalaya House, Lazimpat, POB 371, Kathmandu; tel. (1) 4411811; fax (1) 4413920; e-mail info@kathmandu.mfa.gov.il; internet kathmandu.mfa.gov.il; Ambassador DAN STAV.

Japan: Panipokhari, POB 264, Kathmandu; tel. (1) 4426680; fax (1) 4414101; e-mail comjpn@mos.com.np; internet www.np.emb-japan.go.jp; Ambassador TATSUO MIZUNO.

Korea, Democratic People's Republic: Jhamsikhel, Lalitpur, Kathmandu; tel. (1) 5521855; fax (1) 5525394; Ambassador JANG YONG CHOL.

Korea, Republic: Red Cross Marg, Tahachal, POB 1058, Kathmandu; tel. (1) 4270172; fax (1) 4272041; e-mail koreaemb@mos.com.np; Ambassador NAM SANG-JUNG.

Malaysia: Block B, 2nd Floor, Karmachari Sanchaya Kosh Bldg, Pulchowk, POB 24372, Lalitpur, Kathmandu; tel. (1) 5010004; fax (1) 5010492; e-mail malkatmandu@kln.gov.my; internet www.kln.gov.my/perwakilan/kathmandu; Ambassador MAHINDER SINGH.

Myanmar: Chakupath, Patan Gate, Lalitpur, POB 2437, Kathmandu; tel. (1) 5521788; fax (1) 5523402; Ambassador U AUNG KHIN SOE.

Norway: Surya Court, Pulchowk, Lalitpur, POB 20765, Kathmandu; tel. (1) 5545307; fax (1) 5545226; e-mail emb.kathmandu@mfa.no; internet www.norway.org.np; Ambassador TORE TORENG.

Pakistan: Pushpanjali, Maharajgunj, Chakrapath, POB 202, Kathmandu; tel. (1) 4374024; fax (1) 4374012; e-mail parepktm@wlink.com.np; Ambassador SOHAIL AMIN.

Russia: Baluwatar, POB 123, Kathmandu; tel. (1) 4412155; fax (1) 4416571; e-mail ruspos@info.com.np; internet www.nepal.mid.ru; Ambassador ANDREI LEONIDOVICH TROFIMOV.

Sri Lanka: 'Shah Villa', Chundevi Rd, Maharajgunj, POB 8802, Kathmandu; tel. (1) 4720623; fax (1) 4720128; e-mail embassy@srilanka.info.com.np; Ambassador SUMITH NAKANDALA.

Thailand: 167/4 Ward No. 3, Maharajgunj-Bansbari Rd, POB 3333, Kathmandu; tel. (1) 4371410; fax (1) 4371409; e-mail thaiemb@wlink.com.np; internet www.thaiembassy.org/kathmandu; Ambassador VANVISA THAMRONGNAVASAWAT.

United Kingdom: Lainchaur, POB 106, Kathmandu; tel. (1) 4410583; fax (1) 4411789; e-mail britemb@wlink.com.np; internet www.britishembassy.gov.uk/nepal; Ambassador Dr ANDREW HALL.

USA: Panipokhari, POB 295, Kathmandu; tel. (1) 4411179; fax (1) 4419963; e-mail usembktm@state.gov; internet nepal.usembassy.gov; Ambassador NANCY J. POWELL.

Judicial System

According to the Interim Constitution (which was officially endorsed in January 2007), the judicial system has three tiers: the Supreme Court (which is also a Court of Record), the Appellate Courts and the District Courts. The Supreme Court consists of a Chief Justice and a maximum of 14 other judges. The Chief Justice is appointed by the Prime Minister on the recommendation of the Constitutional Council; other Supreme Court, Appellate Court and District Court judges are nominated by the Chief Justice on the recommendation of the Judicial Council. A Constituent Assembly Court was established in February 2008 to deal with election matters.

Supreme Court: Ramashah Path, Kathmandue-mail info@supremecourt.gov.np; internet www.supremecourt.gov.np.

Chief Justice: KEDAR PRASAD GIRI.

Judges of the Supreme Court: MIN BAHADUR RAYAMAJHEE, ANUP RAJ SHARMA, RAM PRASAD SHRESTHA, KHIL RAJ REGMI, SHARDA SHRESTHA, BALA RAM K. C., TAP BAHADUR MAGAR, DAMODAR PRASAD SHARMA, RAM KUMAR PRASAD SHAH, KALYAN SHRESTHA, GAURI DHAKAL, TAHIR ALI ANSARI, RAJENDRA KOIRALA.

Registrar: Dr RAM KRISHNA TIMALSENA.

Attorney-General: YAGYAMURTI BANJADE.

Religion

At the 2001 census, an estimated 80.6% of the population professed Hinduism (the religion of the royal family), while 10.7% were Buddhists and 4.2% Muslims. The actual number of Muslims in the country was considered to be much higher, owing to immigration from Bangladesh. There were an estimated 101,976 Christians in Nepal in 2001.

BUDDHISM

All Nepal Bhikkhu Association: Vishwa Shanti Vihara (World Peace Temple), 465 Ekadantamarga, Minbhawan, New Baneshwar, POB 8973 NPC-327, Kathmandu; tel. (1) 4482984; fax (1) 4482250; e-mail vishwa@ntc.net.np; Treas. BHIKSHU BODHIJNANA.

Nepal Buddhist Council: Nahtole, Lalitpur 20; tel. (1) 5534277; e-mail nepal_bp@hotmail.com; Contact MAHISWOR RAJ BAJRACHARYA.

United Trungram Buddhist Foundation: Hattigauda, Bansbari, POB 3157, Kathmandu; tel. (1) 4370089; fax (1) 4370292; e-mail utbfnp@hotmail.com; Information Officer GANGJA SINGH GURUNG.

CHRISTIANITY

Protestant Church

Presbyterian Church of the Kingdom of Nepal: POB 3237, Kathmandu; tel. and fax (1) 4524450.

The Roman Catholic Church

The Church is represented in Nepal by a single apostolic prefecture. At 31 December 2005 there were an estimated 6,935 adherents in the country.

Apostolic Prefecture: Church of the Assumption, Everest Postal Care P. Ltd, POB 8975 EPC-343, Kathmandu; tel. (1) 5542802; fax (1) 5521710; e-mail anath@wlink.com.np; f. 1983 as Catholic Mission; Prefect Apostolic Fr ANTHONY FRANCIS SHARMA.

The Press

PRINCIPAL DAILIES

The Commoner: Naradevi, POB 203, Kathmandu; tel. (1) 4228236; f. 1956; English; Publr and Chief Editor GOPAL DASS SHRESTHA; circ. 7,000.

Daily News: Bhimsensthan, POB 171, Kathmandu; tel. (1) 4279147; fax (1) 4279544; e-mail manju_sakya@hotmail.com; f. 1983; Nepali and English; Chief Editor MANJU RATNA SAKYA; Publr SUBHA LAXMI SAKYA; circ. 20,000.

Dainik Nirnaya: Bhairawa; tel. (71) 520117; Nepali; Editor P. K. BHATTACHAN.

Gorkhapatra: Dharma Path, POB 23, Kathmandu; tel. (1) 4221478; fax (1) 4222921; internet www.gorkhapatra.org.np/gopa.php; f. 1901; Nepali; govt-owned; Chair. TEJ PRAKASH PANDIT; Editor-in-Chief SHIVA PRASAD BHATTARAI; circ. 75,000.

The Himalayan Times: International Media Network Nepal (Pvt) Ltd, APCA House, Baidya Khana Rd, Anam Nagar, POB 11651, Kathmandu; tel. (1) 4770504; fax (1) 4770701; internet www.thehimalayantimes.com; English; Editor RAM PRADHAN.

Janadoot: Ga 2-549, Kamal Pokhari (in front of the Police Station), Kathmandu; tel. (1) 4412501; f. 1970; Nepali; Editor GOVINDA BIYOGI; circ. 6,500.

Kantipur: Kantipur Complex, Subhidhanagar, POB 8559, Kathmandu; tel. (1) 4480100; fax (1) 4470178; e-mail narayan@kantipur.com.np; internet www.kantipuronline.com; f. 1993; Nepali; Chief Exec. HEM RAJ GYAWALI; Editor NARAYAN WAGLE; circ. 210,000.

NEPAL

Kathmandu Post: Kantipur Complex, Subhidhanagar, POB 8559, Kathmandu; tel. (1) 4480100; fax (1) 4466320; e-mail kpost@kantipur.com.np; internet www.kantipuronline.com; f. 1993; English; Editor PRATEEK PRAHAN; circ. 40,000.

Motherland: POB 1184, Kathmandu; English; Editor MANINDRA RAJ SHRESTHA; circ. 5,000.

Nepal Samacharpatra: Sagarmatha Press, Ramshah Path, Kathmandu; e-mail sadhana@mail.com.np; internet newsofnepal.com; f. 1945; Nepali; Editor NARENDRA BILAS PANDEY; circ. 1,000.

Nepali Hindi Daily: 72 Kalinchok Marg, Maitidevi, POB 49, Kathmandu; tel. (1) 4436374; fax (1) 4435931; e-mail das@ntc.net.np; f. 1954; evening; Hindi; Publr UMA KANT DAS; Chief Editor VIJOY KUMAR DAS; circ. 100,000.

Rajdhani: Kathmandu; internet www.rajdhani.com.np; Editor KAPIL KAFLE; circ. 50,000.

Rising Nepal: Dharma Path, POB 1623, Kathmandu; tel. (1) 4222279; fax (1) 4224381; e-mail trn@gorkhapatra.org.np; internet www.gorkhapatra.org.np/trn.php; f. 1965; English; Editor-in-Chief AJAY SHUMSHER RANA; circ. 20,000.

Samaj: National Printing Press, Dillibazar, Kathmandu; f. 1954; Nepali; Editor MANI RAJ UPADHYAYA; circ. 5,000.

Samaya: Kamal Press, Ramshah Path, Kathmandu; f. 1954; Nepali; Editor MANIK LALL SHRESTHA; circ. 18,000.

Space Time Dainik: Iceberg Bldg, 3rd Floor, Putali Sadak, Kathmandu; tel. (1) 4419133; fax (1) 4419504; e-mail info@spacetimenetwork.com; internet www.spacetimenetwork.com; f. 2000; Nepali; Man. Dir JAMIM SHAH; circ. 60,000.

Swatantra Samachar: Kathmandu; tel. (1) 4419285; f. 1957; Editor MADAN DEV SHARMA; circ. 2,000.

SELECTED PERIODICALS

Agricultural Credit: Agricultural Training and Research Institute, Agricultural Development Bank, Head Office, Ramshah Path, Panchayat Plaza, Kathmandu; tel. (1) 4220756; fax (1) 4225329; 2 a year; publ. by the Agricultural Development Bank; Chair. Dr NARAYAN N. KHATRI; Editor RUDRA PD DAHAL.

Arpan: Bhimsensthan, POB 285, Kathmandu; tel. (1) 4244450; fax (1) 4279544; e-mail manju_sakya@hotmail.com; internet www.nepalnews.com.arpan.php; f. 1964; weekly; Nepali; Publr and Chief Editor MANJU RATNA SAKYA; circ. 18,000.

Awake Weekly Chronicle: Kathmandu; English.

Commerce: Bhimsensthan, POB 171, Kathmandu; tel. (1) 4279636; fax (1) 4279544; e-mail manju_sakya@hotmail.com; f. 1971; monthly; English; Publr and Chief Editor MANJU RATNA SAKYA; Editor SUBHA LAXMI SAKYA; circ. 12,000.

Current: Gautam Marg, Kamalpokhari, Kathmandu; tel. (1) 4419484; fax (1) 4445406; e-mail current@namche.com; internet www.current.com.np; f. 1982; weekly; Nepali; publ. by private limited co; Man. Editor KIRAN GAUTAM; Chief Editor DEVENDRA GAUTAM; circ. 10,000.

Cyber Post: Kathmandu; fortnightly; computers, electronics.

Foreign Affairs Journal: 5/287 Lagon, Kathmandu; f. 1976; 3 a year; articles on Nepalese foreign relations and diary of main news events; Publr and Editor BHOLA BIKRUM RANA; circ. 5,000.

Himal Southasian: POB 24393, Kathmandu; tel. (1) 5547279; fax (1) 5552141; e-mail info@himalmag.com; internet www.himalmag.com; f. 1987; monthly; political, business, social and environmental issues throughout South Asia; Editor-in-Chief KANAK MANI DIXIT; Marketing Man. KOMAL MORE.

The Independent: Shankher Deep Bldg, Khichhapokhari, POB 3543, Kathmandu; tel. (1) 4249256; fax (1) 4226293; e-mail independ@mos.com.np; internet www.nepalnews.com/independent.htm; f. 1991; weekly; English; Editor SUBARNA B. CHHETRI.

Janadharana (People's Opinion): Kathmandu; e-mail janadharana@gmail.com; internet www.nepalnews.com.np/janadharana; weekly; independent; Editor NIMKANT PANDEY.

Janmabhumi: Janmabhumi Press, Tahachal, Kathmandu; tel. (1) 4280979; fax (1) 4274795; e-mail sirishnp@hotmail.com; f. 1970; weekly; Nepali; Publr and Editor SHIRISH BALLABH PRADHAN.

Koseli: Kathmandu; weekly; Nepali.

Madhuparka: Dharmapath, POB 23, Kathmandu; tel. (1) 4222278; f. 1986; monthly; Nepali; literary; Editor-in-Chief KRISHNA BHAKTA SHRESTHA; circ. 20,000.

Matribhoomi (Nepali Weekly): Ga 2-549, Kamal Pokhari (in front of the Police Station), Kathmandu; tel. (1) 4412501; weekly; Nepali; Editor GOVINDA BIYOGI.

Mulyankan: Kathmandu; monthly; left-wing; Editor SHYAM SHRESTHA.

Nepal: Kantipur Complex, Subhidhanagar, POB 8559, Kathmandu; tel. (1) 4480100; fax (1) 4470178; e-mail feedback@kantipuronline.com; internet www.kantipuronline.com/Nepal; f. 2000; fortnightly; Nepali; Editor KISHORE NEPAL.

Nepal Chronicle: Maruhiti; weekly; English; Publr and Editor CHANDRA LAL JHA.

Nepal Overseas Trade Statistics: Trade and Export Promotion Centre, Pulchowk, Lalitpur, POB 825, Kathmandu; tel. (1) 5525348; fax (1) 5525464; e-mail info@tepc.gov.np; internet www.tepc.gov.np; annual; English.

Nepal Trade and Export Bulletin: Trade and Export Promotion Centre, Pulchowk, Lalitpur, POB 825, Kathmandu; tel. (1) 5532642; fax (1) 5525464; e-mail info@tepc.gov.np; internet www.tepc.gov.np; 3 a year; English; Editor BADRI ADHIKARY.

Nepali Times: Himalmedia Pvt Ltd, POB 7251, Kathmandu; tel. (1) 5543333; fax (1) 5521013; e-mail editors@nepalitimes.com; internet www.nepalitimes.com; f. 2000; weekly; English; publ. by Himalmedia Private Ltd; Publr and Chief Editor KUNDA DIXIT; Exec. Editor ANAGHA NEELAKANTAN; circ. 15,000.

People's Review: Pipalbot, Dillibazar, POB 3052, Kathmandu; tel. (1) 4417352; fax (1) 4438797; e-mail preview@ntc.net.np; internet www.peoplesreview.com.np; weekly; English; Editor-in-Chief PUSHPA RAJ PRADHAN; circ. 15,000.

Rastrabani: Kathmandu; tel. (1) 4410339; weekly; Nepali; Chief Editor HARI LAMSAL.

Sanghu Weekly: Kathmandu; weekly; Editor GOPAL BUDHATHOKI.

Sanibariya: Kathmandu; weekly.

Saptahik Weekly: Kantipur Complex, Subhidhanagar, POB 8559, Kathmandu; tel. (1) 4480100; fax (1) 4470178; internet www.kantipuronline.com/saptahic_html/saptahik; f. 1997; weekly; Nepali; news and entertainment; Editor SUBASH DHAKAL.

Spotlight: POB 7256, Kathmandu; tel. (1) 4410772; e-mail spotlight@mos.com.np; f. 1991; weekly; English; Editor MADHAV KUMAR RIMAL.

Swatantra Manch Weekly: POB 49, Kathmandu; tel. (1) 4436374; fax (1) 4435931; e-mail das@ntc.net.np; f. 1985; independent; weekly; Nepali; Publr and Chief Editor VIJOY KUMAR DAS; circ. 30,000.

The Telegraph: Ghattekulo, Dillibazar, POB 4063, Kathmandu; tel. (1) 4419370; e-mail tgw@ntc.net.np; weekly; English; Chief Editor NARENDRA P. UPADHYAYA.

Vashudha: Makhan, Kathmandu; monthly; English; social, political and economic affairs; Publr and Editor T. L. SHRESTHA.

NEWS AGENCY

Rastriya Samachar Samiti (RSS): Singa Darbar Plaza, Kathmandu; tel. (1) 4262724; fax (1) 4262744; e-mail info@rss.com.np; internet www.rss.com.np; f. 1962; state-operated; Gen. Man. JAYA SHANKAR MAHATO; Chair. MITHARAM BISWOKARMA DUKHI.

PRESS ASSOCIATIONS

Federation of Nepalese Journalists (FNJ): Media Village, Sinamangal, Kathmandu; tel. (1) 4490063; fax (1) 4490085; e-mail fnjnepal@mail.com.np; internet www.fnjnepal.org; f. 1956; Pres. DHARMENDRA JHA; Gen. Sec. K. C. POSHAN.

Nepal Journalists' Association (NJA): Maitighar, POB 285, Kathmandu; tel. (1) 4262426; fax (1) 4279544; e-mail manju_sakya@hotmail.com; internet www.nja.org.np; 5,400 mems; Pres. MANJU RATNA SAKYA; Gen. Sec. NIRMAL KUMAR ARYAL.

Press Council: Sanchargram, Tilganga, POB 3077, Kathmandu; tel. (1) 4469799; fax (1) 4469894; e-mail prescoun_mdf@wlink.com.np; internet www.presscouncilnepal.org; f. 1970; Chair. RAJENDRA DAHAL; Sec. MUKUNDA PRASAD ACHARYA.

Publishers

Educational Enterprise (Pvt) Ltd: Mahankalsthan, POB 1124, Kathmandu; tel. (1) 4223749; e-mail ishwarbshrestha@yahoo.com; f. 1962; educational and technical; Dir MOHAN SHRESTHA.

Himal Books: Himal Association, Patan Dhoka, POB 166, Lalitpur, Kathmandu; tel. (1) 5542544; fax (1) 5541196; e-mail books@himalassociation.org; internet www.himalassociation.org/himalbooks; f. 1992; subsidiary operation of Himal Association; general interest and academic publications in English and Nepali; Exec. Dir BASANTA THAPA.

International Standards Books and Periodicals (Pvt) Ltd: Bhotahity Bazaar, Chowk Bhitra, POB 3000, Kathmandu 44601; tel. (1) 4262815; fax (1) 4264179; e-mail u2@ccsl.com.np; f. 1991; Chief Man. Dir YOGYNDRA LALL CHHIPA; Chief Exec. and Man. Dir GANESH LALL SINGH CHHIPA.

Lakoul Press: Palpa-Tansen, Kathmandu; educational and physical sciences.

NEPAL

Mahabir Singh Chiniya Main: Makhan Tola, Kathmandu.

Mandass Memorials Publications: Kathmandu; Man. BASANT RAJ TULADHAR.

Pilgrims Book House: Thamel, POB 3872, Kathmandu; tel. (1) 4700942; fax (1) 4700943; e-mail pilgrims@wlink.com.np; internet www.pilgrimsbooks.com; f. 1986; Asian studies, religion and travel; Propr PUSHPA TIWARI.

Pilgrims Publishing Nepal (Pvt) Ltd: Goldhunga, POB 21646, Kathmandu; tel. (1) 4356764; e-mail johnsnepal@wlink.com.np; internet www.pilgrimsbooks.com; f. 2000; Exec. Dir JOHN SNYDER; Man. Dir BISHOW BHATTA.

Ratna Pustak Bhandar: 71 'Ga' Bank Marg, POB 98, Kathmandu; tel. (1) 4223026; fax (1) 4248421; e-mail rpb@wlink.com.np; f. 1945; textbooks, general, non-fiction and fiction; Propr RATNA PRASAD SHRESTHA.

Royal Nepal Academy: Kamaladi, Kathmandu; tel. (1) 4221241; fax (1) 4221175; f. 1957; languages, literature, social sciences, art and philosophy; Dep. Admin. Chief T. D. BHANDARI.

Sajha Prakashan: Pulchowk, Lalitpur, POB 20259, Kathmandu; tel. (1) 5521118; fax (1) 5544236; e-mail sajhap@wlink.com.np; internet www.sajha.org.np; f. 1964; educational, literary and general; Chair. BISHNU PRASAD GHIMIRE; Gen. Man. Dr DHRUBA CHANDRA GAUTAM.

Trans Asian Media Pvt Ltd: Thapathali Crossing, POB 5320, Kathmandu; tel. (1) 4242895; fax (1) 4223889; Man. Editor SHYAM GOENKA.

GOVERNMENT PUBLISHING HOUSE

Department of Information: Ministry of Information and Communications, Singha Durbar, Kathmandu; tel. (1) 4220150; fax (1) 4221729; internet www.moic.gov.np/Departments/Printing.

Broadcasting and Communications

TELECOMMUNICATIONS

Nepal Telecommunications Authority: 768/12 Thir Bam Sadhak, POB 9754, Baluwatar, Kathmandu; tel. (1) 4446001; fax (1) 4446006; e-mail info@nta.gov.np; internet www.nta.gov.np; telecommunications regulatory body; f. 1998; Chair. DINESH KUMAR SHARMA.

Nepal Telecom (Nepal Doorsanchar Co Ltd): Bhadrakali Plaza, POB 11803, Kathmandu; tel. (1) 4210202; fax (1) 4222424; e-mail rkt@ntc.net.np; internet www.ntc.com.np; f. 1975; operates landline and mobile services; 85% state-owned, 10% owned by Nepalese public, 5% owned by Nepal Telecom employees; Man. Dir SUGAT RATNA KANSAKAR.

Spice Nepal (Pvt) Ltd (SNPL): Krishna Tower, Buddhanagar, New Baneshwor, Kathmandu; tel. (1) 5554444; fax (1) 5554538; e-mail info@spicenepal.com; internet www.spicenepal.com; f. 2002; jt venture between Kazakhstan-based Group VISOR (75%), Raj Group (20%) and India-based Spice Cell (5%); operates GSM mobile network; Chair. RAJ BAHADUR SINGH; CEO DMITRY ZAIKA.

STM Telecom Sanchar: 768/47 Thirbam Sadak, Baluwatar, Kathmandu; tel. (1) 4445981; fax (1) 44419366; e-mail marketing@stmnetworks.com; internet www.stmi.com; f. 2003 as jt venture between the USA, Thailand and Nepal; awarded World Bank-funded project to provide rural telecommunication services to eastern region of Nepal; CEO ABHINAV PURI.

United Telecom: Ground Floor, Triveni Complex, Putali Sadak, Kathmandu; tel. (1) 2000050; fax (1) 2499999; e-mail info@utlnepal.com; internet www.utlnepal.com; f. 2003; jt venture between Indian-owned Mahanagar Telephone Nigam Ltd, Videsh Sanchar Nigam Ltd, Telecom Consultants India, and Nepal Venture (Pvt) Ltd; Chair. Shri S. K. GUPTA.

BROADCASTING

Radio

In July 2005 there were 47 commercial and community radio stations in Nepal. A media ordinance adopted by the King in October of that year banned private radio stations in the country from broadcasting news or information-related programmes. Following the April 2006 uprising and revocation of the King's direct rule, the seven-party alliance Government resumed issuing licences to independent broadcasters; by February 2008 licences had been granted to 254 FM operators.

Radio Nepal: Radio Broadcasting Service, HM Government of Nepal, Singha Durbar, POB 634, Kathmandu; tel. (1) 4241923; fax (1) 4221952; e-mail radio@engg.wlink.com.np; internet www.radionepal.org; f. 1951; broadcasts on short wave, medium wave and FM frequencies in 20 regional languages, incl. Nepali and English, for 18 hours daily (incl. two hours of regional broadcasting in the morning and evening); short-wave station at Khumaltar and medium-wave stations at Bhainsepati, Pokhara, Surkhet, Dipayal, Bardibas and Dharan; FM stations at Kathmandu, Kanchanpur, Rupandehi, Chitwan, Makawanpur, Bara, Jumla, Mustang, Jlam, Simikot and Humla; Exec. Dir R. S. KARKI.

Himalaya Broadcasting Co (Radio HBC 94 FM): POB 8974, CPC 94, Kathmandu; tel. (1) 4489618; fax (1) 4499788; e-mail hbc94fm@hbc.com.np; internet www.hbc.com.np; f. 1999.

Hits FM: POB 21912, Baneshwor, Kathmandu; tel. (1) 4780534; fax (1) 4780543; e-mail info@hitsfm.com.np; internet www.hitsfm.com.np; f. 1996; broadcasts 24 hrs daily; Exec. Dir JEEVAN SHRESTHA.

Image FM (Kath FM): POB 5566, Kathmandu; tel. (1) 4230368; fax (1) 4241260; e-mail kath979@wlink.com.np; internet www.imagechannels.com; f. 1999; Station Man. BHARAT SHAKYA.

Kantipur FM: Kantipur Complex, Subhidhanagar, POB 8559, Kathmandu; tel. (1) 4480100; fax (1) 4470178; e-mail kfm@kanti.mos.com.np; f. 1998; broadcasts 24 hrs daily; Man. Dir BINOD RAJ GYAWALI; Station Man. PRABHAT RIMAL.

Radio Lumbini: Aanandabane VDC, Ward No. 3, Manigram, Rupandehi, Lumbini; tel. (71) 561003; fax (71) 561545; e-mail lumbinifm@mos.com.np; internet www.radiolumbini.org; f. 2000; Station Man. MOHAN CHAPAGAIN.

Radio Sagarmatha: Bakhundol, Lalitpur, GPOB 6958, Kathmandu; tel. (1) 5528091; fax (1) 5530227; e-mail stationmanager@radiosagarmatha.org; internet www.radiosagarmatha.org; f. 1997; independent; Chair. LAXMAN UPRETI; Station Man. MOHAN BISTA.

Times FM: GPOB 8975, EPC 906, Jawalakhel, Lalitpur, Kathmandu; tel. and fax (1) 5539171; e-mail timesfm@hotnepal.com; Man. Dir R. K. SHRESTHA.

Television

In 1986 Nepal's first television station began broadcasting within the Kathmandu valley.

Nepal Television Corpn: Singha Durbar, POB 3826, Kathmandu; tel. (1) 4220348; fax (1) 4228312; internet neptv.com.np; f. 1985; operates NTV and NTV2; programmes in Nepali (50%), English (25%) and Hindi/Urdu (25%); regional station at Kohalpur; Chair. and Gen. Man. Dr RISHI RAJ BARAL.

Avenues TV: 11 Avenues Plaza, Teku Rd, Ganeshman Marga, Kathmandu; tel. (1) 4227222; fax (1) 4248811; e-mail atv@avenues.tv; f. 2003; news service.

Image Channel: 369 Narayan Gopal Sadak, POB 9581, Lazimpat, Kathmandu; tel. (1) 4433141; fax (1) 4432707; e-mail ichannel@wlink.com.np; internet www.imagechannels.com; f. 2003; privately owned; Chair. R. K. MANANDHAR.

Kantipur Television Network (KTV): Kantipur Complex, Subhidhanagar, POB 8559, Kathmandu; tel. (1) 4480100; fax (1) 4470178; f. 2003; Chair. HEM RAJ GYAWALI; Man. Dir JEEWA LAMICHHANE.

Finance

(auth. = authorized; cap. = capital; m. = million; dep. = deposits; res = reserves; brs = branches; amounts in Nepalese rupees)

BANKING

Central Bank

Nepal Rastra Bank: Central Office, Baluwatar, POB 73, Kathmandu; tel. (1) 4411834; fax (1) 4414955; e-mail gsd@nrb.org.np; internet www.nrb.org.np; f. 1956; bank of issue; 100% state-owned; cap. 3,000.0m., res 29,191.1m., dep. 27,745.7m. (July 2004); Gov. KRISHNA BAHADUR MANANDHAR (acting); 9 brs.

Domestic Commercial Banks

Kumari Bank Ltd: Putalisadak, POB 21128, Kathmandu; tel. (1) 4232112; fax (1) 4231960; e-mail info@kbl.com.np; internet www.kumaribank.com; f. 2001; auth. cap. 625m., res 218.6m., dep. 8,020.4m. (July 2006); Chair. NOOR PRATAP RANA.

Nepal Bank Ltd: Nepal Bank Bldg, Dharmapath, New Rd, POB 36, Kathmandu; tel. (1) 4222397; fax (1) 4220414; e-mail craigmca@nepalbank.com.np; internet www.nepalbank.com.np; f. 1937; 40% state-owned, 60% owned by Nepalese public; CEO CRAIG McALLISTER; 96 brs.

Nepal Industrial and Commercial Bank Ltd (NIC Bank): Kamaladi, Ganeshthan, POB 7367, Kathmandu; tel. (1) 4222336; fax (1) 4241865; e-mail kamaladi@nicbank.com.np; internet www.nicbank.com.np; f. 1998; privately owned; cap. 600.0m., res 141.5m., dep. 9,515.2m. (July 2006); Chair. JAGDISH PRASAD AGRAWAL; CEO SASHIN JOSHI; 10 brs.

NEPAL

Rastriya Banijya Bank (National Commercial Bank): POB 8368, Singha Durbar Plaza, Kathmandu; tel. (1) 4252595; fax (1) 4252931; e-mail secretary@rbb.com.np; internet www.rbb.com.np; f. 1966; 100% state-owned; Chair. Dr BHOLA NATH CHALISE; CEO JANARDAN ACHARYA; 114 brs, 4 regional offices.

Joint-venture Banks

Bank of Kathmandu Ltd: Kamal Pokhari, POB 9044, Kathmandu; tel. (1) 4414541; fax (1) 4418990; e-mail info@bok.com.np; internet www.bok.com.np; f. 1993; 58% owned by Nepalese public, 42% by local promoters; cap. 463.6m., res 376.2m., dep. 10,485.4m. (July 2006); Chair. SANJAY B. SHAH; Man. Dir RADHESH PANT.

Everest Bank Ltd: POB 13384, EBL House, Lazimpat, Kathmandu; tel. (1) 4443377; fax (1) 4443160; e-mail ebl@mos.com.np; internet www.everestbankltd.com; f. 1994; 50% owned by directors, 20% by Punjab National Bank (India) and 30% by the Nepalese public; cap. 518.0m., res 336.2m., dep. 14,118.3m. (July 2006); Chair. BISHNU KRISHNA SHRESTHA; Exec. Dir JASPAL SINGH JASS; 22 brs.

Global Bank Ltd: Adarshanagar, Birgunj 13, POB 45, Parsa; tel. (1) 530337; fax (1) 530339; internet www.globalbanknepal.com; f. 2006; Chair. CHANDRA PRASAD DHAKAL; CEO SUMAN NEUPANE.

Himalayan Bank Ltd: Karmachari Sanchaya Kosh Bldg, Tridevi Marg, Thamel, POB 20590, Kathmandu; tel. (1) 4227749; fax (1) 4222800; e-mail hbl@hbl.com.np; internet www.himalayanbank.com; f. 1993; 20% owned by Habib Bank Ltd (Pakistan); cap. 772.2m., res 837.4m., dep. 26,924.4m. (July 2006); Chair. MANOJ BAHADUR SHRESTHA; CEO ASOKE S. J. B. RANA; 8 brs.

Laxmi Bank Ltd: Hattisar, POB 19593, Kathmandu; tel. (51) 530394; fax (51) 530393; e-mail info@laxmibank.com; internet www.laxmibank.com; f. 2001; cap. 609.9m., res 15.7m., dep. 4,449.1m. (July 2006); Chair. MOHAN GOPAL KHETAN; CEO SUMAN JOSHI.

Nabil Bank Ltd (Nabil): Nabil House, Kamaladi, POB 3729, Kathmandu; tel. (1) 4429546; fax (1) 4429548; e-mail nabil@nabilbank.com; internet www.nabilbank.com; f. 1984 as Nepal Arab Bank Ltd, name changed as above Jan. 2000; 50% owned by National Bank of Bangladesh, 30% by the Nepalese public and 20% by Nepalese govt financial institutions; cap. 491.7m., res 2,068.7m., dep. 23,342.3m. (July 2007); Chair. SATYENDRA PYARA SHRESTHA; Chief. Exec. ANIL SHAH; 27 brs.

Nepal Bangladesh Bank Ltd: Bijuli Bazar, New Baneshwor, POB 9062, Kathmandu; tel. (1) 4783976; fax (1) 4780316; e-mail nbblho@nbbl.com.np; internet www.nbbl.com.np; f. 1994; 50% owned by International Finance Investment and Commerce Bank Ltd (Bangladesh), 20% by Nepalese promoters and 30% public issue; cap. 359.9m., res 324.0m., dep. 10,580.7m. (July 2003); CEO SHOVAN DEV PANT; Chair. JEET BAHADUR SHRESTHA; 15 brs.

Nepal Credit and Commerce Bank Ltd: NB Bldg, Bagh Bazar, Kathmandu; tel. (1) 4246991; fax (1) 4244610; e-mail nccb@nccbank.com.np; internet www.nccbank.com.np; f. as Nepal Bank of Ceylon, reconstituted as above in Sept. 2002 after Bank of Ceylon (Sri Lanka) sold its shares to NB Group (Nepal); Chair. PRITHIVI RAJ LIGAL; CEO RATNA RAJ BAJRACHARYA; 17 brs.

Nepal Investment Bank Ltd: Durbar Marg, POB 3412, Kathmandu; tel. (1) 4228229; fax (1) 4226349; e-mail info@nibl.com.np; internet www.nibl.com.np; f. 1986 as Nepal Indosuez Bank Ltd, name changed as above in June 2002; 50% owned by a consortium of Nepalese investors, 20% by general public, 15% by Rastriya Banijya Bank and 15% by Rastriya Beema Sansthan; cap. 590.6m., res 778.9m., dep. 19,496.1m. (July 2006); Chair. and Chief Exec. PRITHIVI BAHADUR PANDE; 12 brs.

Nepal SBI Bank Ltd: Corporate Office, Hattisar, POB 6049, Kathmandu; tel. (1) 4435516; fax (1) 4435612; e-mail nsblco@nsbl.com.np; internet www.nsbl.com.np; f. 1993; 50% owned by State Bank of India, 30% by Nepalese public, 15% by Employees' Provident Fund (Nepal) and 5% by Agricultural Development Bank (Nepal); Chair. B. K. SHRESTHA; Man. Dir V. P. DANI.

Nepal Sri Lanka Merchant Bank Ltd: NSLMB Bldg, Kalamadi, POB 12248, Kathmandu; tel. (1) 4440300; fax (1) 4441034; e-mail nslmb@info.com.np; Exec. Dir VED MAN SINGH MALLA.

Standard Chartered Bank Nepal Ltd: Grindlays Bhavan, Naya Baneshwor, POB 3990, Kathmandu; tel. (1) 4246753; fax (1) 4226762; internet www.standardchartered.com/np; f. 1986 as Nepal Grindlays Bank; name changed in July 2001; 75% owned by Standard Chartered Bank (United Kingdom) and 25% by the Nepalese public; cap. 374.6m., res 1,008.9m., dep. 23,061m. (July 2006); Chair. CHRISTOPHER LOW; CEO SUJIT MUNDUL; 7 brs.

Banking Organization

Nepal Bankers' Association (NBA): Heritage Plaza, C and D Block, 2nd Floor, Kamaladi, Kathmandu; e-mail info@nepalbankers.com; internet www.nepalbankers.com; Pres. RADHESH PANT.

Directory

Development Finance Organizations

Agricultural Development Bank: Ramshah Path, Kathmandu; tel. (1) 4262885; fax (1) 4262616; e-mail info@adbn.gov.np; internet www.adbn.gov.np; f. 1968; 93.6% state-owned, 2.1% owned by the Nepal Rastra Bank, and 4.3% by co-operatives and private individuals; specialized agricultural credit institution providing credit for agricultural development to co-operatives, individuals and asscns; receives deposits from individuals, co-operatives and other asscns to generate savings in the agricultural sector; acts as Government's implementing agency for small farmers' group development project, assisted by the Asian Development Bank and financed by the UN Development Programme; operational networks include 14 zonal offices, 37 brs, 92 sub-brs, 52 depots and 160 small farmers' development projects, three Zonal Training Centres, two Appropriate Technology Units; Chair. MUKUNDA PRASAD ARJYAL; Gen. Man. YOGESWOR PANT.

Nepal Development Bank: Heritage Plaza, POB 11017, Kamaladi, Kathmandu; tel. (1) 4254639; fax (1) 4245753; e-mail ndevbank@ndbl.com.np; internet www.ndevbank.com; f. 1998; Chair. AMAR GURUNG; CEO SUNANDA B. SHRESTHA.

Nepal Housing Development Finance Co Ltd: New Baneswor, POB 5624, Kathmandu; tel. (1) 4780259; fax (1) 4792753; e-mail info@nepalhousing.com; internet www.nepalhousing.com; Chair. BINOD KUMAR GURAGAI; Gen. Man. ACHUT RAJ SAPKOTA.

Nepal Industrial Development Corpn (NIDC): NIDC Bldg, Durbar Marg, POB 10, Kathmandu; tel. (1) 4228322; fax (1) 4227428; e-mail nidc@wlink.com.np; internet www.nidc.org.np; f. 1959; state-owned; holds investments of 5,609.9m. in 1,125 industrial enterprises (2000/01); offers financial and technical assistance to private-sector industries; in 2000/01 approved a total of 9.41m. in loans and working capital, and disbursed 8.17m.; Gen. Man. UTTAM NARAYAN SHRESTHA.

STOCK EXCHANGE

Nepal Stock Exchange Ltd (NEPSE): Singha Durbar Plaza, POB 1550, Kathmandu; tel. (1) 4250735; fax (1) 4262538; e-mail info@nepalstock.com; internet www.nepalstock.com; f. 1976; reorg. 1984; converted in 1993 from Securities Exchange Centre Ltd to Nepal Stock Exchange Ltd; 147 listed cos, 139 scripts; Chair. BIMAL PRADAD WAGLE; Gen. Man. REWAT BAHADUR KARKI.

INSURANCE

Alliance Insurance Co Ltd: Durbar Marg, POB 10811, Kathmandu; tel. (1) 4222836; fax (1) 4241411; e-mail sk@aic.wlink.com.np.

Everest Insurance Co Ltd: Hattisar, POB 10675, Kathmandu; tel. (1) 4444717; fax (1) 4444366; e-mail eveinsco@mos.com.np; internet www.everestinsurance.com; Chair. RAJENDRA K. KHETAN.

Himalayan General Insurance Co Ltd: Durbar Marg, POB 148, Kathmandu; tel. (1) 4231581; fax (1) 4223906; e-mail info@thamel.com; internet www.thamel.com/hgi; f. 1993; CEO MAHENDRA KRISHNA SHRESTHA.

National Insurance Co Ltd: Tripureswor, POB 376, Kathmandu; tel. (1) 4250710; fax (1) 4261289; e-mail natinsur@ccsl.com.np; Man. A. S. KOHLI.

National Life and General Insurance Co Ltd: Lazimpat, POB 4332, Kathmandu; tel. (1) 4412625; fax (1) 4416427; e-mail nlgi@mail.com.np; Chief Exec. S. K. SINGH; Pres. OM SINGH.

Neco Insurance Ltd: Hattisar, POB 12271, Lal Durbar, Kathmandu; tel. (1) 4427354; fax (1) 4418761; e-mail info@necoins.com.np; f. 1994; Chair. JANARDAN AACHARYA; CEO ANIL SHARMA.

Nepal Insurance Co Ltd: NIC Bldg, Kamaladi, POB 3623, Kathmandu; tel. (1) 4221353; fax (1) 4225446; e-mail info@nepalinsurance.com; internet www.nepalinsurance.com; Chair. BHARAT KARKI; Man. Dir NIRMAL KUMAR BARAL.

The Oriental Insurance Co Ltd: Jyoti Bhavan, POB 165, Kathmandu; tel. (1) 4221448; fax (1) 4223419; e-mail oriental@wlink.com.np; CEO Dr MADHUSUDAN KUMAR.

Premier Insurance Co (Nepal) Ltd: Tripureswor Plaza, Tripureswor, POB 9183, Kathmandu; tel. (1) 4259567; fax (1) 4249708; e-mail premier@picl.com.np; internet www.premier-insurance.com.np; f. 1994; Pres. RADHE SHYAM GORKHALI.

Rastriya Beema Sansthan (National Insurance Corpn): RBS Bldg, Ramshah Path, POB 527, Kathmandu; tel. (1) 4213882; fax (1) 4262610; e-mail beema@wlink.com.np; internet www.beema.com.np; f. 1967; Gen. Man. BIR BIKRAM RAXAMAJHI.

Sagarmatha Insurance Co Ltd: Kathmandu Plaza, Block Y, 4th Floor, Kamaladi, POB 12211, Kathmandu; tel. (1) 4240896; fax (1) 4247947; e-mail sagarmatha@insurance.wlink.com.np; Exec. Dir K. B. BASNYAT.

United Insurance Co (Nepal) Ltd: I. J. Plaza, Durbar Marg, POB 9075, Kathmandu; tel. (1) 4246686; fax (1) 4246687; e-mail uic@mail

NEPAL

.com.np; internet www.unitedinsurance.com.np; Chair. Ravi Bhakta Shrestha; Gen. Man. Rabi Man Joshi.

Trade and Industry

GOVERNMENT AGENCY

National Planning Commission (NPC): Singha Durbar, POB 1284, Kathmandu; tel. (1) 4225879; fax (1) 4226500; e-mail npcs@npcnepal.gov.np; internet www.npc.gov.np; Vice-Chair. Jagadish Chandra Pokharel.

DEVELOPMENT ORGANIZATIONS

National Productivity and Economic Development Centre: Balaju Industrial District, POB 1318, Kathmandu; tel. (1) 4350566; fax (1) 4350530; e-mail npedc@wlink.com.np; internet www.npedc-nepal.org; functions as secretariat of National Productivity Council; provides services for industrial promotion and productivity improvement through planning research, consultancy, training, seminars and information services; Gen. Man. Shambhu Nath Pant (acting).

National Tea and Coffee Development Board (NTCDB): New Baneshwor, POB 9683, Kathmandu; tel. (1) 4495792; fax (1) 4497941; e-mail ntcdb@hons.com.np; internet teacoffee.gov.np; f. 1992 to promote and expand the Nepalese tea industry; Vice-Chair. Suraj Vaidya.

National Trading Ltd: Teku, POB 128, Kathmandu; tel. (1) 4225799; fax (1) 4225151; e-mail info@nationaltrading.com.np; internet www.nationaltrading.com.np; f. 1962; govt-owned; imports and distributes construction materials and raw materials for industry; also machinery, vehicles and consumer goods; operates bonded warehouse, duty-free shop and related activities; brs in all major towns; Chair. Sonafi Yadav.

Nepal Foreign Trade Association: Bagmati Chamber, 1st Floor, Milan Marg, Teku, POB 541, Kathmandu; tel. (1) 4223784; fax (1) 4247159; e-mail nfta@mos.com.np; f. 1972; Pres. Akhil Kumar Chapagain; Vice-Pres. Satish Kumar More; 431 mems.

Nepal Tea Development Corpn Ltd: Triveni Complex, Putali Sadak, Kathmandu; tel. (1) 4224074; fax (1) 4266133; e-mail ntdc@trivenionline.com; internet www.ntdcltd.com; f. 1966; privatized in early 2000s; commercial production of tea; Contact Subhash C. Shanghai.

Trade and Export Promotion Centre (TPC): Na Tole, Pulchowk, Lalitpur, POB 825, Kathmandu; tel. (1) 5525898; fax (1) 5525464; e-mail info@tepc.gov.np; internet www.tepc.gov.np; f. 1971 to encourage exports; govt-owned; Chair. Purshottam Ojha.

CHAMBERS OF COMMERCE

Federation of Nepalese Chambers of Commerce and Industry (FNCCI): Pachali Shahid Shukra FNCCI Milan Marg, Teku, POB 269, Kathmandu; tel. (1) 4262061; fax (1) 4261022; e-mail fncci@mos.com.np; internet www.fncci.org; f. 1965; comprises 90 District Municipality Chambers (DCCIs), 64 Commodity Associations, 367 leading industrial and commercial undertakings in both the public and private sector, and 10 Bi-national Chambers; publishes annual *Nepal and the World: A Statistical Profile* and tri-annual directory of members; Pres. Chandi Raj Dhakal; Dir-Gen. Megh Nath Neupane (acting).

Birganj Chamber of Commerce and Industries: Hospital Rd, Birganj; tel. (51) 522290; fax (51) 526049; e-mail bicci@atcnet.com.np; 605 mems; Pres. Vijay Kumar Sarawagi.

Lalitpur Chamber of Commerce and Industry: Mangal Bazar, Patan Durbar Sq., POB 26, Lalitpur; tel. (1) 5521740; fax (1) 5530661; e-mail lcci@mos.com.np; f. 1967; Pres. Umesh Lal Amatya; Sec.-Gen. Naresh Kumar Shrestha.

Nepal Chamber of Commerce: Chamber Bhavan, Kantipath, POB 198, Kathmandu; tel. (1) 4230947; fax (1) 4229998; e-mail chamber@wlink.com.np; internet www.nepalchamber.org; f. 1952; non-profit org. promoting industrial and commercial development; 8,000 regd cos and 1,600 ordinary mems; Pres. Surendra Bir Malakar; Sec.-Gen. Bhakta Bahadur Malla.

INDUSTRIAL AND TRADE ASSOCIATIONS

Association of Craft Producers: Ravi Bhawan Mode, POB 3701, Kathmandu; tel. (1) 4275108; fax (1) 4272676; e-mail craftacp@mos.com.np; internet acp.org.np; f. 1984; local non-profit org. providing technical, marketing and management services for craft producers; manufacturer, exporter and retailer of handicraft goods; Exec. Dir Meera Bhattarai; Programme Dir Revita Shrestha.

Association of Forest-based Industries and Trade: Thapathali, POB 2798, Kathmandu; tel. (1) 4216020.

Directory

Association of Nepalese Rice, Oil and Pulses Industries: POB 20782, Radha Bhawvan, Tripureswor, Kathmandu; tel. (1) 4215676; e-mail nfma@mcmail.com.np; Pres. Tola Ram Dugar; Gen. Sec. Chandra Krishna Karmacharya.

Association of Pharmaceutical Producers of Nepal: Babar Mahal, POB 21721, Maitighar, Kathmandu; tel. and fax (1) 4231871; e-mail appon@wlink.com.np; Pres. Pradeep Man Vaidya; Sec.-Gen. Umesh Lal Shrestha.

Cargo Agents Association of Nepal: Thamel, POB 5355, Kathmandu; tel. (1) 4419019; fax (1) 4419858.

Central Carpet Industries Association of Nepal: Maitighar, Babar Mahal, POB 2419, Kathmandu; tel. (1) 4259400; fax (1) 4262458; e-mail ccia@enet.com.np; internet www.nepalcarpet.org; Pres. A. G. Sherpa; Gen. Sec. Kapil Prasad Bazgain.

Computer Association of Nepal: 453 Maitidevi, Kathmandu; tel. (1) 4432700; fax (1) 4441998; e-mail info@can.org.np; internet www.can.org.np; f. 1992; asscn of the IT Businessmen's Organization; Pres. Biplav Man Singh.

Federation of Handicrafts Associations of Nepal: Upma Marg, Thapathali, POB 784, Kathmandu; tel. (1) 4244231; fax (1) 4222940; e-mail han@wlink.com.np; internet www.nepalhandicraft.org.np; f. 1972; Pres. Puskar Man Shakya.

Federation of Nepal Cottage and Small Industries (FNCSI): Chabahil, POB 6530, Kathmandu; tel. (1) 4491528; fax (1) 4468337; e-mail fncsi@ntc.net.np; internet www.fncsi.org.np; business networks in 70 districts; represents interests and promotes development of nation's micro, cottage and small industries; 30,000 general mems (2007); Pres. Ang Dendi Sherpa.

Garment Association of Nepal: Shankhamul Rd, New Baneshwor, POB 21332, Kathmandu; tel. (1) 4780691; fax (1) 4780173; e-mail gan@ntc.net.np; internet www.ganasso.org; Pres. Kiran P. Saakha.

Himalayan Orthodox Tea Producers' Association of Nepal: Kathmandu; f. 1998; non-profit making org.; represents and promotes the Himalayan tea sector; Chair. Suraj Vaidya.

Leather Footwear and Goods Manufacturers' Association of Nepal: Bag Bazar, POB 19732, Kathmandu; tel. (1) 4219349; e-mail lfgman@ntc.net.np; Pres. Ram Krishna Prasai.

Nepal Association of Tour and Travel Agents: Gairidhara Rd, Goma Ganesh, Naxal, POB 362, Kathmandu; tel. (1) 4419409; fax (1) 4418684; e-mail nata@mail.com.np; internet www.nata.org.np; f. 1966; 280 mems; Pres. Ram Kaji Koney.

Nepal Forest Industries Association: Naxal, Nag Pokhari, POB 5623, Kathmandu; tel. (1) 4411865; fax (1) 4413838; e-mail padmasri@ccsl.com.np; Pres. Hari Prasad Giri; Sec.-Gen. Rohini Thapaliya.

Nepal Leather Industries Association: POB 9944, Anamnagar, Kathmandu; tel. (1) 4265248; fax (1) 4228978; e-mail giris@atcnet.com.np; Pres. Sanjay Giri; Sec.-Gen. Ramesh Raj Pokharel.

Nepal Plastic Manufacturers' Association: Kandevsthan, Kupandol, POB 2350, Lalitpur; tel. and fax (1) 5528185; Pres. Shailendra Lal Pradhan; Sec.-Gen. Rajeswor Lal Joshi.

Nepal Tea Planters' Association: Bhadrapur-4, Jhapa; tel. (23) 520059; fax (23) 420679; Pres. Chandi Prasad Parajuli; Sec.-Gen. Mal Chand Goyal.

Nepal Textile Industries Association: Krishna Galli, Lalitpur; tel. (1) 5529290; fax (1) 5520291; Pres. Gopal P. Kshatriya; Sec.-Gen. Ram K. Maharjan.

Nepal Trans-Himalayan Trade Association: Jyoti Bhawan, Kantipath, POB 133, Kathmandu; tel. (1) 4225490; fax (1) 4254048; e-mail syamukapu@unilever.wlink.com.np; Pres. Tribhuwan D. Tuladhar; Gen. Sec. Mahesh Tuladhar.

UTILITIES

Electricity

Butwal Power Co Ltd: 313 Ganga Devi Marga, Buddha Nagar, POB 11728, Kathmandu; tel. (1) 4781776; fax (1) 4780994; e-mail service@bpc.com.np; internet www.bpc.com.np; f. 1966; partially privatized in 2003; principal shareholders: 68.95% owned by Shangri-La Energy Ltd, 9.09% by Ministry of Water Resources and 6.05% by Interkraft Norway; 5.91% divided between Nepalese energy orgs and employees; public sector retains 10% ownership; owns and operates Jhimruk and Andhi Khola Hydropower Plants; supplies electricity to the national grid; 326 employees; Chair. Gyanendra Lal Pradhan.

Chilime Hydropower Co Ltd: Kalikasthan, POB 25210, Kathmandu; tel. (1) 4443077; fax (1) 4443076; e-mail chpcl@wlink.com.np; 51% owned by Nepal Electricity Authority; Dir Damber Bahadur Nepali.

Department of Electricity Development: 576 Bhakti Thapa Sadak-4, POB 2507, Anamnagar, Kathmandu; tel. (1) 4479507; fax

(1) 4480257; e-mail info@doed.gov.np; internet www.doed.gov.np; f. 1993; fmrly Electricity Development Centre; name changed as above 1999; under Ministry of Water Resources; Dir-Gen. SRIRANJAN LACOUL.

Nepal Electricity Authority: Durbar Marga, Kathmandu; tel. (1) 4252835; fax (1) 4256091; e-mail sapkota.pawan@gmail.com; internet www.nea.org.np; f. 1985 following merger; govt-owned; Chair. GYANENDRA BAHADUR KARKI; Man. Dir and CEO ARJUN KUMAR KARKI.

Water

Nepal Water Supply Corpn: Tripureswor Marg, POB 5349, Kathmandu; tel. (1) 4262202; fax (1) 4262229; e-mail info@nwsc.com.np; internet www.nwsc.gov.np; f. 1990; govt-owned; Gen. Man. GAUTAM BAHADUR AMATYA.

TRADE UNIONS

Trade unions were banned in Nepal in 1961, but were legalized again in 1990, following the success of the pro-democracy movement and the collapse of the Panchayat system.

Nepal Trade Union Congress—I (NTUC—I): POB 5507, Kathmandu; tel. (1) 5527443; fax (1) 5527469; e-mail ntuc@mos.com.np; internet www.ntuc.org.np; f. 1947 as the Nepal Trade Union Congress; 28 affiliated unions; affiliated to ICFTU; operates in association with Nepali Congress Party; merged with Democratic Confederation of Nepalese Trade Unions in March 2008 and name changed to the above; Co-Pres. LAXMAN BASNET; Co-Pres. KHILA NATH DAHAL; 192,000 mems.

General Federation of Nepalese Trade Unions (GEFONT): Man Mohan Labour Bldg, GEFONT Plaza, Putali Sadak, POB 10652, Kathmandu; tel. (1) 4248072; fax (1) 4248073; e-mail dfa@gefont.org; internet www.gefont.org; f. 1989; 19 affiliated unions; Chair. MUKUNDA NEUPANE.

Transport

Ministry of Labour and Transport Management: Singha Durbar, Kathmandu; tel. (1) 4247842; fax (1) 4256877; e-mail info@moltm.gov.np; internet www.moltm.gov.np; Sec. SHYAM PRASAD MAINALI.

Interstate Multi-Modal Transport (Pvt) Ltd: Shiva Sabitri Sadan, 240 Red Cross Marg, Kalimati, Kathmandu; tel. (1) 4271473; fax (1) 4271570; e-mail rauniar@mos.com.np; f. 1975; provides freight forwarding, transport contracting, customs clearance, warehousing and shipping services, transport consultancy, terminal operations, logistics solutions; Gen. Man. ANAND S. RAUNIAR.

RAILWAYS

Nepal Railways Corpn Ltd (NRC): Khajuri, Janakpur; tel. (41) 52082; HQ Jayanagar, India; f. 1937 as Janakpur-Jayanagar Railways; name changed as above June 2004; 53 km open, linking Jayanagar with Janakpur and Bijalpura; narrow gauge; 11 steam engines, 25 coaches and vans, and 20 wagons; Gen. Man. MADAN SINGH MAHAT.

Nepal Government Railway: Birganj; f. 1927; 7 steam engines, 12 coaches and 82 wagons; Man. D. SINGH (acting).

ROADS

In 2007 there were 17,609 km of roads, of which 5,222 km were black-topped and 4,738 km gravel-covered. Around Kathmandu there are short sections of roads suitable for motor vehicles, and there is a 28-km ring road round the valley. A 190-km mountain road, Tribhuwana Rajpath, links the capital with the Indian railhead at Raxaul. The Siddhartha Highway, constructed with Indian assistance, connects the Pokhara valley, in mid-west Nepal, with Sonauli, on the Indian border in Uttar Pradesh. The 114-km Arniko Highway, constructed with Chinese help, connects Kathmandu with Kodari, on the Chinese border. In the early 1990s the final section of the 1,030-km East–West Highway was under construction. A number of north–south roads were also being constructed to connect the district headquarters with the East–West Highway.

A fleet of container trucks operates between Kolkata and Raxaul in India and other points in Nepal for transporting exports to, and imports from, third countries. Trolley buses provide a passenger service over the 13 km between Kathmandu and Bhaktapur.

ROPEWAY

A 42-km ropeway links Hetauda and Kathmandu and can carry 22 metric tons of freight per hour throughout the year. Food grains, construction goods and heavy goods on this route are transported by the ropeway.

CIVIL AVIATION

Tribhuvan International Airport is situated about 6 km from Kathmandu. In 2007 Nepal had 47 airports, of various standards; in mid-2007, however, only 33 of these airports were in operation.

Nepal Airlines Corpn (NAC): RNAC Bldg, Kantipath, POB 401, Kathmandu 711000; tel. (1) 4220757; fax (1) 4225348; e-mail info@nac.com.np; internet www.royalnepal-airlines.com; f. 1958; fmrly Royal Nepal Airlines Corpn (RNAC); 100% state-owned (scheduled for transfer to private ownership); scheduled services to 30 domestic airfields, international scheduled flights to 10 destinations in Europe, the Middle East and the Far East, charter flights; Chair. MADHAV GHIMERE; Man. Dir GAUTAM DAS SHRESTHA.

The monopoly of the RNAC in domestic air services came to an end in 1992. By 2007 there were about 16 private airlines in Nepal providing domestic cargo and passenger services. (The Government of Nepal announced in August 2007 that foreign airlines operating services to Nepal would be permitted to increase flight frequencies during the height of the tourist season that year—between September and December—in order to ease pressure on existing services and those provided by the national NAC.)

Buddha Air: Jawalakhal, Lalitpur, POB 2167, Kathmandu; tel. (1) 5521015; fax (1) 5537726; e-mail buddhaair@buddhaair.com; internet www.buddhaair.com; f. 1997; domestic passenger services; Man. Dir BIRENDRA B. BASNET; Chair. SURENDRA B. BASNET.

Cosmic Air: Kalimatidole, Sinamangal, POB 3488, Kathmandu; tel. (1) 4490146; fax (1) 4497569; e-mail soi@wlink.com.np; internet www.cosmicair.com; f. 1997; operates domestic cargo, passenger and mountain flights; began operating flights to a limited no. of Indian destinations in 2004; Exec. Chair. SANJAYA PRADHAM; Man. Dir M. B. MATHEMA.

Gorkha Airlines: Maharajgunj, POB 9451, Kathmandu; tel. (1) 4435122; fax (1) 4444525; e-mail gorkha@mos.com.np; internet www.gorkhaairlines.com; f. 1996; scheduled and charter passenger and cargo flights to domestic destinations; Gen. Man. RABINDRA SILWAL.

Yeti Airlines: Tilganga, POB 20011, Kathmandu; tel. (1) 4465888; fax (1) 4464977; e-mail yetiair@wlink.com.np; internet www.yetiairlines.com; f. 1998; operates scheduled and chartered domestic flights; Chair. LHAKPA SONAM SHERPA; Man. Dir ANG TSHERING SHERPA.

Tourism

Tourism is being developed through the construction of new tourist centres in the Kathmandu valley, Pokhara valley and Chitwan. Regular air services link Kathmandu with Pokhara and Chitwan. Major tourist attractions include Lumbini, the birthplace of Buddha, the lake city of Pokhara and the Himalaya mountain range, including Mt Everest, the world's highest peak. In 1989, in an effort to increase tourism, the Government abolished travel restrictions in 18 areas of north-western Nepal that had previously been inaccessible to foreigners. Following the restoration of parliamentary democracy in 1990, tourist arrivals in Nepal rose considerably. Further travel restrictions in the remote areas of the country were abolished in 1991, and efforts were made to attract foreign investment in the Nepalese tourism industry, but the insurgency in the west hindered development in the early 2000s. Hotel bed capacity increased from 32,214 in 1999 to an estimated 36,163 in 2001. Nepal received an estimated 463,646 tourists in 2000. The number of visitor arrivals declined to 361,237 in 2001 and to 275,468 in 2002. In 2003 the number of arrivals rose again, to 338,132, and in 2004 arrivals increased further, to 385,297. However, a deterioration in the domestic security situation in 2005 resulted in a decline in arrivals to 375,398. Tourism receipts declined from US $191m. in 2001 to $135m. in 2002, but increased to $233m. in 2003 and to $260m. in 2004 before falling significantly in 2005, to $160m. The cessation of Maoist hostilities in 2006 and the subsequent peace agreement between the former insurgents and the political parties' alliance appeared to have aided recovery in the tourism sector as visitor arrivals in that year totalled 383,926. Tourism industry reports for 2007 indicated significant growth in arrivals, particularly from Bangladesh, the People's Republic of China and the Republic of Korea, which was attributed to the introduction of additional airline services between Nepal and these countries. Since 2005 access has been granted to a further 175 mountains, raising the total number of mountains open to climbers to 326, in an effort further to promote tourism.

Nepal Tourism Board: Tourist Service Centre, Bhrikuti Mandap, POB 11018, Kathmandu; tel. (1) 4256909; fax (1) 4256910; e-mail info@ntb.org.np; internet www.welcomenepal.com; f. 1998; Chair. LEELA MANI POUDEL; CEO PRACHANDA MAN SHRESTHA.

NEPAL

Hotel Association Nepal (HAN): Subarna Shamsher Marg, Gairidhara, POB 2151, Kathmandu; tel. (1) 4412705; fax (1) 4424914; e-mail info@hotelassociation.org.np; internet www.hotelassociation.org.np; f. 1966; Pres. NARENDRA BAJRACHARYA.

Nepal Association of Tour and Travel Agents (NATTA): Gairidhara Rd, Goma Ganesh, Naxal, POB 362, Kathmandu; tel. (1) 4419409; fax (1) 4418661; e-mail natta@mail.com.np; internet www.natta.org.np; f. 1966 to promote and regulate development in the tourism industry; non-governmental org.; 340 mems; CEO Dr HARI SARMAH.

Tourist Guide Association of Nepal (TURGAN): POB 5344, Kamaladi, Kathmandu; tel. (1) 4225102; fax (1) 4423939.

Trekking Agents Association of Nepal: Maligaun Ganesthan, POB 3612, Kathmandu; tel. (1) 4427473; fax (1) 4419245; e-mail info@taan.org.np; internet www.taan.org.np; Pres. B. C. NARENDRA; Sec.-Gen. SITA RAM SAPKOTA.

THE NETHERLANDS

Introductory Survey

Location, Climate, Language, Religion, Flag, Capital

The Kingdom of the Netherlands is situated in western Europe, bordered to the east by Germany and to the south by Belgium. Its northern and western shores face the North Sea. The climate is temperate: the average temperature in January is 0°C (32°F), and the summer average is 21°C (70°F). The national language is Dutch. There is a Frisian-speaking minority (numbering about 400,000). About one-third of the inhabitants are Roman Catholics and about one-quarter are Protestants, while most of the remainder do not profess any religion. The national flag (proportions 2 by 3) has three equal horizontal stripes, of red, white and blue. The capital is Amsterdam, but the seat of government is The Hague (Den Haag or 's-Gravenhage).

Recent History

The Netherlands was occupied by Germany during the Second World War. Following its liberation in 1945, the country chose to abandon its traditional policy of neutrality, subsequently becoming a member of Western European Union (WEU, see p. 426) and the North Atlantic Treaty Organization (NATO, see p. 340). The Treaty establishing the Benelux Economic Union (see p. 411) between the Netherlands, Belgium and Luxembourg was signed in 1958 and came into force in 1960. The Netherlands was a founder member of the European Community (EC, now European Union—EU, see p. 244). Indonesia, formerly the Netherlands East Indies, was granted independence in 1949, except for West New Guinea, which was transferred to Indonesia in 1963. In 1975 Suriname became independent, leaving the Netherlands Antilles as the only remaining Dutch dependency. Aruba, formerly part of the Netherlands Antilles, was granted separate status within the Kingdom of the Netherlands in 1986. A commission, established jointly by the Governments of the Netherlands and the Netherlands Antilles, recommended in October 2004 that the islands of Curaçao and St Maarten (in the Netherlands Antilles) should be given autonomous status within the Kingdom of the Netherlands (i.e. have *status aparte*, like that of Aruba), while the three other islands of the dependency, Saba, Bonaire and St Eustatius, should be placed under direct rule. In a series of non-binding referendums between 2000 and 2005 a majority of voters in St Maarten and Curaçao favoured obtaining *status aparte*, while the electorates of both Bonaire and Saba strongly favoured direct rule. St Eustatius was the only island to favour remaining part of the Netherlands Antilles. None the less, in late October 2005 the Dutch Minister of Government Reform and Kingdom Relations, Alexander Pechtold, concluded an outline agreement on constitutional reform with all five islands. Curaçao and St Maarten were to be granted *status aparte*, while Bonaire, Saba and St Eustatius would become *koninkrijkseilanden* (kingdom islands) with direct ties to the Netherlands. The future status of Bonaire, Saba and St Eustatius was subsequently refined to that of *bijzondere gemeente* (special municipalities), similar in most ways to other metropolitan Netherlands municipalities, although with separate social security and currency arrangements, for example. However, the populations of the Antillean municipalities would be able to vote in Dutch and European elections (the province of Noord-Holland offered to include the three territories). Following the negotiation of further details, the reforms were due to take effect on 15 December 2008.

Queen Juliana, who had reigned since 1948, abdicated in favour of her eldest daughter, Beatrix, in April 1980, following the adoption in February of a constitutional amendment that allowed for the accession of the reigning monarch's eldest child, regardless of sex.

All post-war administrations have been formed by various coalitions between the several 'confessional' Roman Catholic and Protestant and 'progressive' Socialist and Liberal parties. At a general election held in 1971 left-wing parties made substantial gains. In July 1972 the Government was forced to resign after losing its working majority in the Second Chamber of the States-General (see Government, below). Another general election took place in November, at which the 'confessional' parties suffered a major reverse, and in May 1973 a new Government was formed by a left-of-centre coalition under the leadership of Dr Joop den Uyl of the Partij van de Arbeid (PvdA—Labour Party).

The coalition collapsed in March 1977; a general election followed in May. Attempts to form a left-of-centre coalition between the PvdA, the Christen Democratisch Appèl (CDA—Christian Democratic Appeal)—an alliance of 'confessional' groupings, which united in 1980 to form a single party—and Democraten '66 were unsuccessful, and in December 1977 Andries van Agt (of the CDA) formed a centre-right coalition Government of the CDA and the right-wing Volkspartij voor Vrijheid en Democratie (VVD—People's Party for Freedom and Democracy). Despite retaining only a narrow majority in the Second Chamber and several ministerial disagreements, the Government survived its full term in office. A general election was held in May 1981, and a centre-left coalition Government was formed in September, led by van Agt and comprising the CDA, the PvdA and Democraten '66. The Council of Ministers resigned after only five weeks in office, owing to its failure to agree on economic strategy. In November the coalition partners accepted a compromise economic programme, but deep divisions within the Government continued. The coalition collapsed again in May 1982, when all six PvdA ministers resigned, after which van Agt led a minority interim Government of the CDA and Democraten '66.

Although at a general election held in September 1982 the PvdA became the largest party in the Second Chamber (with 47 of 150 deputies), the election produced a significant swing to the right. Talks on the formation of a new administration continued until November, when a centre-right CDA-VVD coalition was established under the leadership of Ruud Lubbers, who had recently succeeded van Agt as Chairman of the CDA. The CDA-VVD coalition was returned to power at a general election in May 1986, having retained its majority in the Second Chamber. A loss of nine seats by the VVD was offset by a corresponding gain by the CDA, which, with 54 seats, became the party with the largest representation in the Second Chamber. The election did, none the less, produce a shift towards the centrist parties, with the PvdA and Democraten '66 (D66, as the party was restyled) both gaining seats at the expense of smaller radical groups. Following the election, Wim Kok replaced den Uyl as parliamentary leader of the PvdA. A new CDA-VVD coalition was formed in July.

In May 1989 the VVD caused the collapse of the Government by refusing to support Lubbers' proposals for the financing of a 20-year National Environment Policy (NEP), which was to involve a reduction in government spending in sectors such as defence and housing, an increase in taxes on motor fuels and the abolition of tax concessions for commuters using private transport. A general election was called for September, at which the CDA again secured 54 seats in the Second Chamber, while the PvdA took 49 seats. The VVD lost five seats. An alliance of left-wing organizations, GroenLinks, won six seats. In October negotiations between the CDA and the PvdA culminated in the formation of a centre-left coalition, again led by Lubbers. The coalition accord envisaged increased welfare provision, to be funded by a reduction in defence expenditure, as well as a programme of job creation and reductions in certain categories of taxation. Kok was appointed Deputy Prime Minister and Minister of Finance. In August 1990 the Government introduced an amended version of the NEP, designated the National Environment Policy Plus (NEPP), which was to be financed by both the Government and the industrial sector. The NEPP was to be implemented at a faster pace than its predecessor, and placed strong emphasis on energy conservation and improvements in waste disposal and recycling.

In November 1992 the Second Chamber ratified the Treaty on European Union, which had been signed by EC Heads of Government at Maastricht in December 1991; the First Chamber similarly approved the Treaty in December 1992.

The CDA lost its leading position in the Government at the May 1994 general election, winning only 34 seats in the Second Chamber. The PvdA, which had focused its election manifesto on unemployment and reductions in social welfare, became the party with the largest representation in the Chamber, with 37 seats. Both the VVD and D66 improved upon their performances at the previous general election, securing 31 and 24 seats respectively. The remaining 24 seats were distributed among eight smaller parties and special issue groups. Negotiations on a three-party coalition agreement between the PvdA, the VVD and D66 were initially retarded by deeply entrenched disagreement between the VVD and PvdA over the latter's reluctance to sanction severe reductions in social welfare spending. Following several concessions by the PvdA (including the proposed privatization of some social benefits), a tripartite coalition, with Kok as Prime Minister, was eventually agreed in August. The CDA (now led by Enneüs Heerma) was thus excluded from the Council of Ministers for the first time since 1917.

In April 1996 the Government agreed that its liberal policy on the personal consumption of recreational 'soft' drugs should be subject to stricter controls, in response to protests by neighbouring states that drugs-trafficking from the Netherlands would be facilitated by the withdrawal of EU border controls under the Schengen Agreement.

The PvdA won increased representation at the general election to the Second Chamber held on 6 May 1998, taking 45 seats. The VVD secured 38 seats, while the CDA's representation was further reduced, to 29 seats. D66 won only 14 seats, having lost votes to GroenLinks and the Socialistische Partij (SP—Socialist Party). None the less, the PvdA, VVD and D66 agreed to renew their coalition (it was considered that D66 would be useful as an intermediary in conflicts of policy between the two leading partners), and a new Government, led by Kok, was inaugurated in August.

A parliamentary committee was established in October 1998 to investigate the Government's response to the crash, six years earlier, of a cargo aircraft belonging to El Al, the Israeli national carrier, into a densely populated suburb of Amsterdam, in which 43 people had died. The inquiry was ordered after the Israeli Government had confirmed reports published in a Dutch newspaper that the cargo on the flight had included depleted uranium and chemical components of sarin nerve gas. The inquiry investigated claims that residents and workers who had been in contact with the wreckage had suffered ill health since the disaster, as well as allegations that Dutch ministers had been aware of the nature of the cargo. The committee's report, published in April 1999, found that there was a direct link between the accident and the high incidence of ill health around the site of the crash, and was severely critical of the failure of the Prime Minister to co-ordinate government action with respect to the disaster. El Al was accused of failing to co-operate with accident investigators. The report, none the less, concluded that there was no evidence of attempts by the Netherlands Government to conceal details of the flight's cargo.

In May 1999 the First Chamber rejected the Government's proposal to allow the use of referendums on policy issues, a key demand of D66, after the refusal of a prominent member of the VVD to support the measure. D66 subsequently announced that it could no longer work with the VVD, and withdrew from the ruling coalition, prompting the resignation of the Council of Ministers. However, following a series of talks between the three parties, in early June the Government formally withdrew its resignation. In January 2001 the three coalition parties reached a new agreement on the introduction of the use of referendums. The new proposals were for a judicially non-binding referendum and would not require a change to the Constitution. The temporary referendum law entered into force on 1 January 2002 and expired three years later. Legislation was subsequently adopted to allow a national referendum to be held exceptionally on the proposed EU constitutional treaty in June 2005 (see below).

In September 2000 the First Chamber approved laws giving same-sex couples the same legal status as heterosexuals, including the right to marriage and adoption (the legislation took effect in April 2001). Legal recognition of homosexual partnerships had been granted in 1998.

During 1992–93 parliament debated and approved legislation codifying a procedure for the practice of euthanasia in circumstances where it was repeatedly requested by an incurably ill patient. In April 2001 the First Chamber passed a bill legalizing euthanasia by 46 votes to 28. (In November 2000 the Second Chamber had passed the bill by 104 votes to 40.) The practice was to be subject to strict criteria. The key conditions according to which life could lawfully be ended were that the patient was terminally ill and in unbearable pain with no prospect of improvement. Euthanasia became legal in April 2002. In October 2005 the practice was extended to include terminally ill infants in acute suffering, with the express consent of the parents.

In August 2001 Kok announced that he would not seek re-election for a further term in office at the general election, scheduled for May 2002. He also announced that he would step down as Party Leader of the PvdA and subsequently endorsed the appointment of Ad Melkert, the Parliamentary Leader of the party, as his successor. Jaap de Hoop Scheffer, the Parliamentary Leader of the CDA, resigned in September 2001. He was replaced by Jan Peter Balkenende in the following month.

In April 2002 the entire Council of Ministers resigned following the publication of a report by the Netherlands Institute for War Documentation into the massacre of some 7,000 Bosnian Muslims by Bosnian Serb troops in Srebrenica, Bosnia and Herzegovina, in 1995. The report blamed the Dutch Government, the Dutch military and the UN for their respective roles in failing to prevent the atrocity and claimed that the 100 lightly armed Dutch peace-keeping troops who had been stationed in the town at the time had been ill-trained and had no clear mandate. At the request of Queen Beatrix, the Government agreed to remain in office in a caretaker capacity pending the forthcoming general election, which was scheduled to be held on 15 May 2002. In addition, the Chief of Staff of the army, Gen. Ad van Baal, who had been the second highest ranking officer in the army at the time of the massacre, resigned.

Further investigations by a parliamentary commission, in November 2002, into the failure of the Dutch authorities to prevent the massacre at Srebrenica in 1995 revealed that the former Government had been aware of the likelihood of atrocities occurring in the UN camp, and that the possibility of such killings had, in fact, been discussed in a meeting of the Council of Ministers on 11 July 1995, the very day the mass murders had occurred. In January 2003 the commission concluded that the Netherlands bore responsibility for the massacre, that the Government had failed adequately to plan the mission and that the Netherlands army had suppressed details of its failures. In September 2004 about 50 women who had survived the massacre held a demonstration outside the States-General to demand compensation from the Government for the failure of Dutch peace-keepers to protect Srebrenica. In November 2007 a court in The Hague ruled that a case against both the UN and the Netherlands Government brought by a group of relatives of those killed at Srebrenica in 1995 was admissible under Dutch law.

On 6 May 2002 the controversial politician Pim Fortuyn was shot dead in Hilversum, in the central Netherlands, just days before the general election, in which his newly established party, the populist and anti-immigration Lijst Pim Fortuyn (LPF—Pim Fortuyn List), was expected to secure a substantial proportion of votes. Fortuyn had formed the movement following his dismissal in January as leader of the Leefbaar Nederland (LN—Livable Netherlands) party for his anti-immigration rhetoric. In November Volkert van der Graaf, an animal-rights activist who had been arrested shortly after Pim Fortuyn's murder, confessed to the murder. At his trial, which began in late March 2003, van der Graaf claimed that he believed Fortuyn had presented a threat to vulnerable members of society. He was convicted in April and received a prison sentence of 18 years. Appeals were lodged by van der Graaf and by the prosecution, which demanded life imprisonment; in mid-July, however, the original sentence was upheld.

At the general election of 15 May 2002 the CDA won 43 of the 150 seats in the Second Chamber, with 27.9% of the valid votes cast. The LPF took 26 seats (with 17.0% of the votes), the VVD 24 (15.4%) and the PvdA 23 (15.1%). In the light of their electoral defeats, both the PvdA and the VVD changed their Parliamentary Leaders, to Jeltje van Nieuwenhoven and Gerrit Zalm, respectively.

Balkenende was inaugurated as Prime Minister on 21 July 2002, leading a coalition Government comprising the CDA, the LPF and the VVD. However, the same day, a Suriname-born LPF minister in the Ministry of Emancipation and Family Affairs, Philomena Bijhout, resigned when it was confirmed that she had been linked to a Surinamese militia group involved in political killings in the former Dutch colony in December 1982. The LPF suffered a further reverse when allegations were made by a newspaper that their new leader, Mat Herben, had tried unfairly to influence the selection procedure for the LN's electoral candidates when Fortuyn was still leader and Herben a party member. Herben resigned at the end of July 2002 and was subsequently replaced by Harry Wijnschenk.

The new Government detailed policies to reform the health insurance and social security system and reduce the number of illegal immigrants to the Netherlands. In early October 2002 the Minister of Immigration and Integration opened a new college for the instruction of Muslim religious leaders (*imams*) in Dutch values and social conventions. The course was compulsory for new *imams*, who faced deportation if they practised without passing the exam.

Meanwhile, the LPF was riven by factionalism and personal acrimony. In addition to the expulsion of two party members who objected to Wijnschenk's leadership style, in early October 2002 a feud developed between two ministers. Herman Heinsbroek, the Minister of Economic Affairs, articulated his ambition to assume the deputy premiership, which resulted in a dispute with the incumbent Deputy Prime Minister and Minister of Public Health, Welfare and Sport, Dr Eduard Bomhoff. Despite the subsequent resignations of Heinsbroek and Bomhoff from the Council of Ministers, the LPF's coalition partners refused to co-operate further with the party and the Government resigned on 16 October, after just 87 days in power. Balkenende presided over a minority Government, comprising the CDA and the VVD, pending a general election, which was scheduled for January 2003.

In the general election of 22 January 2003, in which 79.9% of the electorate participated, the CDA won 44 seats in the Second Chamber (securing 28.6% of total votes cast), while the PvdA increased its number of seats from 23 to 42 (27.3%), under its new leader, Wouter Bos. The LPF, again led by Herben, following the resignation of Wijnschenk in late 2002, secured only eight seats, while the D66 obtained six. Although the popularity of the right-wing LPF had declined sharply, the electoral manifestos of the mainstream parties addressed the issues raised by the movement. Of these, immigration became a prominent subject of debate, the VVD echoing Fortuyn's statement that the Netherlands was already 'full'. In late January 2003 negotiations began regarding the formation of a coalition administration under Balkenende. Disagreements between the CDA and the PvdA over Dutch support for an impending US-led military campaign to remove the regime of Saddam Hussein in Iraq hindered progress. In March, in his capacity as Prime Minister of the interim administration, Balkenende announced that, while Dutch troops would not assist in the campaign, some units of the armed forces and weapons would be supplied to help defend Turkey, should the conflict escalate. Negotiations resumed in late March and, as the US-led coalition entered Iraq, both parties expressed their support for the military operation. In early April, however, talks collapsed following the failure of the two sides to agree on reductions in budgetary expenditure necessary to revive a stagnant economy. The following month the CDA negotiated the formation of a centre-right coalition with the VVD and the D66, thereby gaining a slender majority of six in the 150-seat Second Chamber. The coalition Government, under the renewed premiership of Balkenende, was formally sworn in on 27 May.

In late May 2003 the provincial councils elected a new First Chamber in which the CDA-VVD-D66 coalition also obtained a majority, securing 41 of the 75 seats. The new Council of Ministers largely resembled the caretaker administration formed in October 2002. The CDA held eight portfolios, the VVD six and the D66 two. Two new Deputy Prime Ministers were appointed: Zalm of the VVD, who was also assigned the post of Minister of Finance, and Thom de Graaf of the D66, who was also named as Minister of Government Reform and Kingdom Relations. One of the stated priorities of the incoming Government was a pledge to tackle the problems of illegal drugs and crime. The new administration proposed the extension of police powers to stop and search people and the introduction of compulsory identity cards for citizens from the age of 14 years.

Legislation was passed by Parliament in September 2003 providing for the prescription of cannabis for medicinal purposes by the national health service. The drug was to be produced by two authorized growers and rigorously controlled for quality. In the same month the Government announced its intention to reform the Netherlands' generous social security system, which had been rendered increasingly expensive by the combination of a rapidly increasing, ageing population and a decline in the work-force. The proposed reforms included the reduction of hospital budgets by 5%, the limitation of free dental care to those aged 18 years or under and the introduction of charges for non-prescription drugs. The Government planned to increase the involvement of the private sector in health care, thereby transferring certain costs from the State to the individual. Under the proposed reforms, in 2006 the public and private health care systems would merge and a standard insurance scheme would be offered by the various private health insurance companies. In an effort to encourage more people to work (the rate of unemployment had risen from only 3% in 2001 to 6.5% in 2004), the Government planned to make the eligibility criteria for disability and unemployment benefits more stringent; in addition, incentives for early retirement were to be abolished.

In December 2003 Rotterdam City Council adopted a highly controversial policy paper that aimed to restore the city's socio-economic balance by building expensive rather than affordable housing and by restricting the issue of residence permits to those who earned at least 20% more than the minimum wage and who spoke a good level of Dutch. A parliamentary report published the following month highlighted a perceived unwillingness to integrate on the part of some immigrants and judged that the tolerant and multiculturalist policies practised over the previous 30 years had generally failed.

The Government also introduced a number of stringent new policies regarding immigrants and asylum seekers. In late January 2004 the Government announced that, in order to prevent the destabilization of the employment market, a maximum of 22,000 immigrants from the 10 new EU member states (which were scheduled to join the EU on 1 May) would be permitted to settle in the Netherlands. In mid-February parliament approved a bill that would permit the deportation of 26,000 failed asylum seekers over the following three years. The legislation applied to asylum seekers who had arrived in the Netherlands before 1 April 2001 and who had exhausted their appeals. It authorized the removal of their welfare benefits, and the provision of a repatriation payment and a free flight to their country of origin. The law was condemned by human rights groups and considered too severe by left-wing groups, but was welcomed by certain sectors of society (particularly among those with low rates of pay) that threatened by the rising level of unemployment. The 'voluntary returns' policy came into effect in June 2003. By early 2005 some 8,636 cases had been processed, of which an estimated 41% were granted residence permits. Of the remainder, the majority had returned to their country of origin of their own volition, while 519 people were compulsorily repatriated. Moreover, emigration from the Netherlands rose by 8.9% in 2004, while the number of immigrants entering the country declined by 10.0% overall and by 33.7% among those from outside Europe.

At elections on 10 June 2004 to the enlarged European Parliament, in which 39.1% of the electorate participated, the CDA and the opposition PvdA each won seven of the 27 Dutch seats, while the VVD obtained four. A new party called Europa Transparant (Transparent Europe) won two seats by campaigning against corruption within the EU. The decline in support for the CDA and the VVD (which had previously held nine and six seats, respectively) was interpreted as a protest against the stagnant economy and the deployment of troops to Iraq. None the less, Balkenende subsequently extended the mandate of the troops by eight months to March 2005.

In September 2004 the Government announced proposals for an austerity budget for 2005, in an attempt to reduce the budget deficit and prepare for the economic effects of an ageing population. The proposed measures included reforms to unemployment and disability benefits, reductions in health care expenditure and the elimination of tax benefits for those saving for early retirement. The proposals provoked widespread industrial action in September and October, culminating in a demonstration in Amsterdam in early October attended by some 200,000 protesters. However, as a result of negotiations with representatives of the Government, a compromise was reached in November whereby the trade union leaders accepted the proposed disincentive to early retirement and the restriction of eligibility for disability benefits, and agreed to demand only minimal wage increases over the forthcoming year.

The murder in November 2004 of Theo van Gogh, who had made a controversial film about Islamic culture, raised concerns regarding the threat to the Netherlands' liberalism presented by the country's failure to assimilate ethnic minorities. Mohammed Bouyeri, who was convicted of van Gogh's murder and sentenced to life imprisonment in late July 2005, was suspected of membership of a militant Islamic organization, known as the Hofstad group. Other members of this group were arrested in connection with threats to kill prominent politicians who were openly critical of Islam, including the writer of van Gogh's screenplay and VVD deputy in the Second Chamber, Ayaan Hirsi Ali. Following van Gogh's murder, a number of arson attacks and acts of vandalism took place, damaging Islamic schools and mosques and other Muslim community buildings. Arson attacks, presumed to be have been committed by Islamists, also took place at five churches. The trial of another alleged member of the Hofstad group, Samir Azzouz, began in February 2005 on charges of planning bomb attacks on Schiphol airport (Amsterdam), the parliament building and a nuclear power station. Azzouz was acquitted of these charges in April on the grounds of a lack of direct evidence, although he was sentenced to three months' imprisonment for the illegal possession of weapons; his acquittal was confirmed on appeal in December. Meanwhile, in October Azzouz was one of seven people arrested on suspicion of attempting to procure heavy firearms and planning terrorist attacks against national politicians and public buildings. In December the trial began of Bouyeri and 13 other alleged members of the Hofstad group on charges of membership of a terrorist organization. In March 2006 nine of the defendants were convicted and sentenced to terms of imprisonment ranging from one year to 15 years; Bouyeri was found guilty of leading the organization. In an attempt to improve security, parliament adopted legislation in January 2005 requiring all citizens and foreigners to carry official identification.

In March 2005 de Graaf tendered his resignation as Deputy Prime Minister and Minister of Government Reform. His resignation followed the rejection by parliament of an electoral reform bill that would have introduced direct election of mayors. The governing coalition was further destabilized when the two remaining D66 cabinet members announced that they were also reconsidering their positions. However, following negotiations between representatives of the coalition partners, an agreement was reached that ensured the continuance of the incumbent Government. Pechtold, the Chairman of the D66 and the Mayor of Wageningen, was appointed Minister of Government Reform and Kingdom Relations, while the D66 Minister of Economic Affairs, Laurens Jans Brinkhorst, assumed the additional role of Deputy Prime Minister.

In October 2005 the Minister of Immigration and Integration, Rita Verdonk, announced proposals that would prohibit the wearing of traditional Islamic dress, such as the burka and other face veils, in certain public places. Despite criticism by Muslim and human rights organizations, a motion in support of such measures was narrowly approved by the Second Chamber in December. In March 2006, however, following an investigation into the implications of human rights law on such a ban, the Government failed to reach agreement on the issue, and the proposals were to be reconsidered. In the same month further measures to control immigration were introduced, requiring potential immigrants from the majority of non-EU countries to pass an examination in their country of origin on their knowledge of Dutch culture and language.

In May 2006 the Secretary of State for Education, Culture and Science, Mark Rutte, defeated Verdonk in a contest for the VVD leadership, which had emphasized deep divisions within the party, particularly regarding immigration and the integration of ethnic minorities into Dutch society. (Rutte was widely regarded as holding moderate views on such issues, in contrast to Verdonk.) During the leadership election campaign, Verdonk had publicly questioned the right to Dutch citizenship of her Somali-born parliamentary colleague, Hirsi Ali, and threatened to revoke Hirsi Ali's passport after irregularities were discovered in her original application. The intervention of Verdonk was unfavourably received, not only by opposing political parties and the electorate, but within the VVD itself. None the less, later that month Hirsi Ali admitted to falsifying elements of her application for citizenship and announced that she would resign as a member of the Second Chamber. On 27 June, however, Verdonk announced that an inquiry into Hirsi Ali's original application for citizenship had found that her claim was legitimate. Two days later Verdonk survived a motion of censure in the Second Chamber urging her departure from office. The motion had been supported by the D66, the three Government members of which subsequently resigned. On 30 June the remaining members of the Government followed suit. Owing to the timing of the resignations, just prior to the parliamentary summer recess, an early election in September was considered undesirable. Consequently, following discussions between party leaders, a minority interim administration comprising the CDA and the VVD was sworn in on 7 July, with a general election scheduled for November.

In September 2006 the Minister of Justice, Piet Hein Donner, and the Minister of Housing, Spatial Planning and the Environment, Sybilla Dekker, resigned, following the conclusion of an inquiry into a fire at a detention centre for illegal immigrants near Schiphol airport in October 2005, in which 11 people had died. The inquiry found that state bodies under the jurisdiction of the two ministers had failed to ensure that safety procedures at the detention centre were followed adequately.

A general election was held on 22 November 2006. The three largest parties all suffered a reduction in support among the electorate (80.1% of whom voted). The CDA emerged as the largest party in the Second Chamber, with 26.5% of the valid votes cast (41 seats, a decrease of three on 2003). The PvdA won 21.2% of the valid votes cast (33 seats, from 42 in 2003) and the VVD 14.7%, (22 seats, from 28). The SP achieved the largest electoral gain, winning some 16.6% of the votes (25 seats, from eight) and the 'confessional' ChristenUnie (CU—Christian Union) party also increased its representation, achieving 4.0% of the vote (six seats, from three in the previous parliament). The nationalist Partij voor de Vrijheid (PVV—Freedom Party), which was formed in February 2006 by former VVD parliamentarian Geert Wilders, won 5.9% of the valid votes cast (nine seats).

Following protracted negotiations between the main parties, in late February 2007 a centre-left coalition of the CDA, the PvdA and the CU was formed under the renewed premiership of Balkenende. The PvdA leader, Bos, became Deputy Prime Minister and Minister of Finance, and the CU leader, André Rouvoet, Deputy Prime Minister and Minister of Youth and the Family. In total, the CDA held eight portfolios, the PvdA six and the CU two. The appointment of two foreign-born Muslim Secretaries of State, Ahmed Aboutaleb and Nebahat Albayrak, both of the PvdA, provoked some controversy. Wilders strongly criticized Aboutaleb and Albayrak after it was revealed that they, respectively, retained Moroccan and Turkish nationality in addition to their Dutch citizenship. The PVV and some VVD representatives, including Verdonk, demanded that the two ministers renounce their foreign nationality—despite the fact that this was not legally possible—and proposed legislation to prevent government members from holding dual nationality. The proposal was later withdrawn. In a television interview in late February Verdonk also urged Princess Máxima, the Argentine-born wife of Prince Willem-Alexander, Queen Beatrix's eldest child and thus heir to the throne, to give up her Argentine citizenship. The new coalition agreement signalled the Government's intention to reverse some of the policies of the previous administration, including a slowing in the reduction of disability payments and a relaxation of restrictions on immigration. However, its programme was criticized by some observers as lacking substantial measures for economic reform. In June the Second Chamber approved a government-proposed amnesty for asylum seekers whose applications had been rejected. Under the legislation, around 30,000 asylum seekers who had arrived in the Netherlands before April 2001 would be eligible for the scheme, reversing legislation approved in February 2004 that allowed for their voluntary repatriation (see above). However, later that month negotiations between the Government, trade union federations and employers' organizations ended with only a minor agreement over plans to create 200,000 new jobs, while more contentious proposals for the deregulation of dismissal procedures remained unresolved.

The limited progress of the Government in implementing its reform programme allowed nationalist groups to dominate the political agenda in late 2007. In October Verdonk resigned her membership of the VVD, following her expulsion from the party's parliamentary group in September for criticizing the leadership. None the less, Verdonk retained her seat in the Second Chamber and a week later she announced the formation of a new political movement, Trots op Nederland (Proud of the Netherlands), under her leadership; Trots op Nederland was formally inaugurated in April 2008. Meanwhile, in late March 2008 Wilders provoked controversy when a film he had produced, entitled *Fitna* (an Arabic word commonly translated as strife), which was critical of the Islamic religion, was broadcast on an internet site. Following the broadcast, the Government accused Wilders of attempting deliberately to cause offence, having previously expressed its fears that the film's release would provoke acts of violence and economic boycotts of Dutch interests, citing the reaction to the publication in 2005 of cartoons depicting the Islamic Prophet Muhammad, initially in a Danish newspaper (and their circulation, by a group of *imams*, alongside several more inflammatory images, in various countries of the Middle

East), which were deemed to be offensive towards Islam (see the Recent History of Denmark). However, despite limited criticism from politicians in some Islamic countries, initial reaction to Wilders' film was calm.

Government plans to commit troops to a NATO peace-keeping mission to southern Afghanistan prompted fierce opposition in late 2005. (Some 350 soldiers from the Netherlands were already stationed in the provinces of Baghlan and Kabul, in the north and east of Afghanistan, while a further 250 were engaged in counter-terrorism operations.) Opponents of further participation in the International Security Assistance Force referred to events in Srebrenica (see above), and claimed that Afghanistan's southern provinces were not sufficiently stable for peace-keeping exercises. However, following a debate in the Second Chamber, in early February 2006 the Minister of Defence, Henk Kamp, announced that 1,200 military personnel were to join the mission in the province of Uruzgan, in central Afghanistan, from August. (Dutch troops had been withdrawn from Iraq in March 2005.) In December 2007 the Second Chamber voted to extend the mandate of Dutch troops in Uruzgan province until December 2010.

The EU Treaty establishing a Constitution for Europe was signed by the EU heads of state and of government in October 2004. It required ratification by all 25 EU member countries, either through a referendum or by a vote in the national legislature, before it could come into force. In February 2005 the Council of Ministers confirmed that a non-binding referendum on the treaty would take place on 1 June. As the referendum was consultative, the States-General would still be competent to ratify the constitutional treaty even if it were rejected in the popular vote. However, the Government pledged to abide by a clear result. At the referendum, which was held, as scheduled, on 1 June, 61.6% of those who voted (63% of the electorate) were opposed to the treaty's ratification. On the following day the Government formally withdrew the proposed legislation. This decisive rejection of the treaty by Dutch voters, and by French voters a few days earlier, prompted several other member countries to postpone indefinitely their own referendums. In March 2007 Balkenende expressed his new coalition Government's opposition to proposals by Germany and some other EU member countries to introduce a new treaty that would contain some of the main elements of the constitutional treaty. Following a meeting with his British counterpart, Tony Blair, in April Balkenende reiterated his opposition to a new EU constitutional treaty, instead favouring a new treaty similar to those signed in Maastricht in 1992 and Amsterdam in 1997. In late June 2007, at a meeting of the European Council in Brussels, Belgium, EU heads of state and of government reached a preliminary agreement for a comprehensive reform treaty. In September Balkenende announced that the new treaty would be approved by parliamentary vote, thus avoiding the prospect of a further defeat at a national referendum. The treaty was formally signed by EU leaders on 13 December at a summit meeting in Lisbon, Portugal, and was expected to be approved by parliament by late 2008.

Government

The Netherlands is a constitutional and hereditary monarchy. Legislative power is held by the bicameral States-General (Staten-Generaal). The First Chamber (Eerste Kamer) or Senate (Senaat) has 75 members and is indirectly elected for four years by members of the 12 Provincial Councils. The Second Chamber (Tweede Kamer) comprises 150 members and is directly elected by universal adult suffrage for four years (subject to dissolution), on the basis of proportional representation. The Head of State has mainly formal prerogatives, and executive power is exercised by the Council of Ministers, which is led by the Prime Minister and is responsible to the States-General. The monarch appoints the Prime Minister and, on the latter's recommendation, other ministers. Each of the 12 provinces is administered by a directly elected Provincial Council, a Provincial Executive and a Sovereign Commissioner, who is appointed by Royal Decree.

Defence

The Netherlands is a member of the North Atlantic Treaty Organization (NATO, see p. 340). Conscription to the armed forces was ended in August 1996, and a gradual reduction in the number of military personnel is ongoing. The total strength of the armed forces, as assessed at November 2007, was 45,608: army 18,266; navy 10,401; air force 10,141; and military police 6,800. Total reserves stood at 32,200 (army 22,200; navy 5,000; air force 5,000). In August 1995 a joint Dutch-German army corps, numbering 28,000 men, was inaugurated, and in January 1996 the operational units of the Royal Netherlands Navy merged with the Belgian navy under the command of the Admiral of the Benelux. Budgeted defence expenditure in 2007 totalled €8,130m. By November 2004 the Netherlands was committed to contributing troops to two of 13 European Union (see p. 244) battle groups, one with the participation of Germany and Finland and one with the United Kingdom.

Economic Affairs

In 2006, according to estimates by the World Bank, the Netherlands' gross national income (GNI), measured at average 2004–06 prices, was US $698,555m., equivalent to $42,670 per head (or $37,580 per head on an international purchasing-power parity basis). During 1996–2006, it was estimated, the population grew at an average annual rate of 0.5%, while gross domestic product (GDP) per head increased, in real terms, at an average annual rate of 1.7% over the same period. Overall GDP increased, in real terms, at an average annual rate of 2.3% in 1996–2006; real GDP increased by 2.9% in 2006.

Agriculture (including hunting, forestry and fishing) contributed 2.1% of GDP in 2007, although only 3.1% of the employed labour force were engaged in the sector in 2005. According to provisional figures, the Netherlands is a net exporter of agricultural products: in 2007 exports of food and live animals provided 11.0% of total export earnings. The principal crops are potatoes, sugar beet, wheat and onions. The main agricultural activity is horticulture; market gardening is highly developed, and the production of cut flowers and bulbs has traditionally been a significant industry, although its contribution to export earnings showed some decline in the early years of the 21st century (partly compensated for by re-exports from other growers to European markets). Livestock farming is also an important activity. According to the Central Bureau of Statistics, during 1997–2007 agricultural GDP increased, in real terms, at an average annual rate of 0.5%; the sector's GDP declined by 1.9% in 2006 but rose by 1.1% in 2007.

Industry (including mining, manufacturing, construction and power) contributed 24.2% of GDP in 2007 and engaged 20.9% of the employed labour force in 2005. The Central Bureau of Statistics put the increase in industrial GDP, in real terms, at an average annual rate of 1.6% in 1997–2007; real industrial GDP rose by 2.0% in 2006 and by a further 3.0% in 2007.

Mining and quarrying provided 3.5% of GDP in 2007 and engaged 0.1% of the employed labour force in 2005. The principal mineral resource is natural gas. Total extraction in 2005 was an estimated 75,000m. cu m. Reserves of petroleum and salts are also exploited. The GDP of the mining sector declined, in real terms, at an average annual rate of 0.6% in 1997–2007; it declined by 3.3% in 2006, before increasing by 1.3% in 2007.

Manufacturing contributed 13.2% of GDP in 2007 and accounted for 13.7% of the employed labour force in 2005. Several multinational companies are domiciled in the Netherlands, including the electrical firm Philips, the brewer Heineken, and two British-Dutch firms, the food industry company Unilever and the petroleum firm Royal Dutch Shell. According to the Central Bureau of Statistics, manufacturing GDP increased at an average annual rate of 1.0% in 1997–2007; it rose by 2.3% in 2006 and by a further 2.5% in 2007.

In 2004 natural gas provided 60.5% of total electricity production and coal 26.0%. Imports of mineral fuels and lubricants comprised 10.4% of the value of total imports in 2003; by 2007 this figure had increased to 15.8%. In recent years the gradual depletion of the Groningen natural gas field has prompted the exploration of investment possibilities in smaller fields, while successive Governments have sought to promote the utilization of renewable energy resources.

The services sector contributed 73.7% of GDP in 2007 and engaged 76.0% of the employed labour force in 2005. Within the sector, financial services, tourism and transport are of considerable importance. The GDP of the services sector increased, in real terms, at an average annual rate of 2.9% in 1997–2007; it increased by 3.8% in 2007.

In 2006 the Netherlands recorded a visible trade surplus of €45,195m. and there was a surplus of €55,795m. on the current account of the balance of payments. In 2007 the principal source of imports was Germany (contributing 20.1% of the total); other major suppliers were Belgium (10.8%), the People's Republic of China (8.6%), the USA (7.9%), the United Kingdom (6.4%) and France (4.9%). Germany was also the principal market for exports (accounting for 23.6% of the total); other major purchasers in 2006 were Belgium (11.9%), the United Kingdom (9.1%), France (8.2%) and the USA (5.0%). The principal exports in 2007 were machinery and transport equipment, chemicals and related products, food and live animals and petroleum. The principal imports in that year were also machinery and transport equipment, followed by mineral fuels and lubricants, chemicals and related products and basic manufactures.

In 2006 the Netherlands recorded an overall budgetary surplus of €4,054m., equivalent to 0.8% of GDP. In 2006 government debt, according to IMF figures, was estimated to be equivalent to 53.2% of GDP. In 1996–2006 the annual rate of inflation averaged 2.2%. Consumer prices increased by 1.1% in 2006. The annual average rate of registered unemployment was 6.5% in 2005.

The Netherlands is a founder member of the European Union (EU, see p. 244), of the Benelux Economic Union (see p. 411), of the Organisation for Economic Co-operation and Development (OECD, see p. 347) and of the European Bank for Reconstruction and Development (EBRD, see p. 239).

In the early 1990s the hitherto buoyant, export-led growth of the Dutch economy was undermined by a series of budget deficits, a high level of unemployment and fluctuations in international prices for natural gas. The administration of Wim Kok (1994–2002), pursuing a policy of economic consensus, sought to reduce public expenditure, to restrain labour costs and to deregulate commercial activity. In 1999 the Netherlands recorded its first budgetary surplus for some 25 years. However, the state of the economy deteriorated sharply in 2001–03. The Netherlands was particularly vulnerable to the global economic downturn, as a result of the country's small size, dependence on trade (exports and imports of goods and services were equivalent to around 75% and 65% of GDP, respectively, in 2006), decreasing industrial production and increasing labour costs. Moreover, demographic ageing and rising levels of unemployment increased demands for state-funded pensions, health care and welfare benefits. In an attempt to reduce the budget deficit in order to comply with the limit of 3% of GDP imposed by the EU's Stability and Growth Pact, the Government announced plans for a comprehensive reform of the health system, measures to encourage labour participation by restricting access to unemployment and disability payments, and the planned abolition of early retirement tax benefits. As a result, the Government succeeded in reducing the budget deficit to the equivalent of 2.2% of GDP in 2004; and small surpluses of 0.1% and 0.8% were achieved in 2005 and 2006, respectively. A fiscal surplus of 0.5% was estimated for 2007 and the economy was observed to have performed well overall: real GDP increased by 3.5% (amongst the highest rates achieved by EU member countries during that year and the highest rate recorded in the Netherlands since 2000) owing to the strengthening of exports and higher investment. However, the economy's reliance on external partners meant that worsening global conditions were expected to engender slower growth in 2008, particularly in the event of further appreciation of the euro. None the less, the IMF forecast growth of around 2.3% in 2008.

Education

There are two types of school in the Netherlands: public schools, which are maintained by municipalities, and attended by about 35% of all school children; and private schools, which are, for the most part, denominational and are attended by almost 65% of the school-going population. Both types of school are fully subsidized by the State. Schools are administered by school boards, responsible to the local authorities or to the private organizations that operate them, thus providing teachers with considerable freedom. The Minister of Education, Culture and Science, advised by an education council, is responsible for educational legislation and its enforcement.

Full-time education is compulsory in the Netherlands from five to 16 years of age, and part-time education is compulsory for a further two years. Some 98% of four-year-old children also attend primary schools. Primary education lasts for eight years and is followed by various types of secondary education. In 2005 enrolment in primary education included 98.5% of children in the relevant age-group, while enrolment in secondary education included 87.1% of children in the relevant age-group. Pre-university schools provide various six-year courses that prepare pupils for university education. General secondary education comprises senior and junior secondary schools, providing five- and four-year courses that prepare pupils for higher vocational institutes and senior secondary vocational education respectively. In all types there is latitude in the choice of subjects taken. In 2004/05 199,350 students were enrolled at the Netherlands' 13 universities, while some 346,210 students were enrolled at the 54 institutes of higher vocational education. In addition, 21,004 students were registered with the Open University at 31 December 2003. Education, culture and science were allocated €32,500m. (equivalent to some 19.3% of total expenditure) by the central Government in the 2008 budget.

Public Holidays

2008: 1 January (New Year's Day), 21 March (Good Friday), 24 March (Easter Monday), 30 April (Queen's Day), 1 May (Ascension Day), 12 May (Whit Monday), 25–26 December (Christmas).

2009: 1 January (New Year's Day), 10 April (Good Friday), 13 April (Easter Monday), 30 April (Queen's Day), 21 May (Ascension Day), 1 June (Whit Monday), 25–26 December (Christmas).

Weights and Measures

The metric system is in force.

THE NETHERLANDS

Statistical Survey

Source: Netherlands Central Bureau of Statistics, Prinses Beatrixlaan 428, POB 959, 2270 AZ Voorburg; tel. (70) 3373800; fax (70) 3877429; e-mail infoservice@cbs.nl; internet www.cbs.nl.

Area and Population

AREA, POPULATION AND DENSITY

Area (sq km)	
Land	33,873
Inland waters	3,479
Coastal water	4,175
Total	41,528*
Population (census results)†	
1 January 1991‡	15,010,445
1 January 2001‡	
Males	7,909,855
Females	8,077,220
Total	15,987,075
Population (official estimate at 1 January)†	
2006	16,334,210
2007	16,357,992
2008	16,404,282
Density (per sq km of land) at 1 January 2008	484.3§

* 16,034 sq miles.
† Population is *de jure*.
‡ Based on a compilation of continuous accounting and sample surveys.
§ Land area only.

PROVINCES

	Land area (sq km)*	Population (1 January 2007)†	Density (per sq km)
Groningen	2,340	573,614	245
Friesland	3,356	642,209	191
Drenthe	2,649	486,197	184
Overijssel	3,337	1,116,374	335
Flevoland	1,421	374,424	263
Gelderland	4,983	1,979,059	397
Utrecht	1,363	1,190,604	874
Noord-Holland	2,657	2,613,070	983
Zuid-Holland	2,867	3,455,097	1,205
Zeeland	1,805	380,497	211
Noord-Brabant	4,929	2,419,042	491
Limburg	2,164	1,127,805	522
Total	33,871	16,357,992	483

* Figures refer to area at 1 January 2000.
† Provisional.

PRINCIPAL TOWNS
(population of municipalities at 1 January 2007)*

Amsterdam (capital)†	742,884	Arnhem	142,569
Rotterdam	584,058	Zaanstad	141,402
's-Gravenhage/Den Haag (The Hague)†	473,941	Amersfoort	139,054
Utrecht	288,401	Haarlemmermeer	138,255
Eindhoven	209,699	's-Hertogenbosch/Den Bosch	135,648
Tilburg	201,259	Maastricht	119,038
Groningen	181,613	Dordrecht	118,541
Almere	180,924	Zoetermeer	118,024
Breda	170,349	Leiden	117,485
Nijmegen	160,907	Zwolle	114,635
Apeldoorn	155,564	Emmen	108,832
Enschede	154,476	Ede	107,500
Haarlem	146,960		

* Provisional figures.
† Amsterdam is the capital, while The Hague is the seat of government.

BIRTHS, MARRIAGES AND DEATHS

	Live births*		Marriages		Deaths*	
	Number	Rate (per 1,000)	Number	Rate (per 1,000)	Number	Rate (per 1,000)
1999	200,445	12.7	89,428	5.7	140,487	8.9
2000	206,619	13.0	88,074	5.5	140,527	8.8
2001	202,603	12.6	82,091	5.0	140,270	8.7
2002	202,083	12.5	85,808	5.3	142,355	8.8
2003	200,297	12.3	80,427	5.0	141,936	8.7
2004	194,007	11.9	72,231	4.5	136,553	8.4
2005	187,910	11.5	72,263	4.4	136,402	8.4
2006	185,057	11.3	72,369	4.4	135,372	8.3

* Including residents outside the country if listed in a Netherlands population register.

Expectation of life (years at birth, WHO estimates): 79.2 (males 76.9; females 81.3) in 2005 (Source: WHO, *World Health Report*).

IMMIGRATION AND EMIGRATION

Immigrants from*	2002	2003	2004
Europe	59,500	54,892	54,461
Belgium	2,039	1,952	1,710
France	1,770	1,677	1,621
Germany	4,933	4,719	5,103
Turkey	6,181	6,703	4,580
United Kingdom	4,476	3,779	3,419
Americas	18,023	15,537	12,964
Netherlands Antilles	5,992	4,273	3,043
Suriname	3,413	3,433	2,857
USA	2,181	2,785	2,495
Asia	21,013	18,039	14,849
Afghanistan	2,824	1,838	865
Iraq	1,535	1,311	1,165
Africa	21,410	14,939	10,759
Morocco	5,192	4,894	3,655
Oceania	1,304	1,107	986
Total	121,250	104,514	94,019

Emigrants to†	2002	2003	2004
Europe	50,142	50,585	54,815
Belgium	1,519	1,512	1,255
France	1,552	1,551	950
Germany	4,387	4,142	3,205
Spain	1,230	1,268	914
Turkey	1,601	2,148	1,789
United Kingdom	3,788	3,842	2,310
Americas	7,366	7,972	8,533
Netherlands Antilles	3,772	4,593	3,940
Suriname	1,668	1,805	1,044
USA	2,665	2,686	1,646
Asia	5,033	5,535	6,088
Africa	3,500	4,064	4,907
Oceania	687	729	706
Total	66,728	68,885	75,049

* Including Dutch nationals returning to the Netherlands: 21,442 in 2002; 19,828 in 2003; 21,911 in 2004.
† Excluding estimates for underenumeration.

THE NETHERLANDS

ECONOMICALLY ACTIVE POPULATION
('000 persons aged 15–64, labour force survey)

	2003	2004	2005
Agriculture, hunting, forestry and fishing	214	236	234
Mining and quarrying	8	8	8
Manufacturing	1,035	1,051	1,021
Electricity, gas and water supply	32	42	44
Construction	460	462	483
Wholesale and retail trade and repair	1,232	1,108	1,134
Hotels and restaurants	297	311	308
Transport, storage and communications	464	486	484
Financial intermediation	273	258	260
Real estate, renting and business activities	995	895	913
Public administration, social security and defence	536	546	538
Education	510	513	518
Health and social work	1,175	1,149	1,207
Other community, social and personal service activities	358	306	307
Private households with employed persons	4	3	3
Activities not adequately defined	236	408	323
Total employed	7,830	7,782	7,784
Unemployed	357	419	430
Total labour force	8,187	8,201	8,214
Males	4,563	4,533	4,491
Females	3,624	3,668	3,723

Source: ILO.

Health and Welfare

KEY INDICATORS

Total fertility rate (children per woman, 2005)	1.7
Under-5 mortality rate (per 1,000 live births, 2005)	5
HIV/AIDS (% of persons aged 15–49, 2005)	0.2
Physicians (per 1,000 head, 2003)	3.15
Hospital beds (per 1,000 head, 2003)	5.0
Health expenditure (2004): US $ per head (PPP)	3,092.0
Health expenditure (2004): % of GDP	9.2
Health expenditure (2004): public (% of total)	62.4
Human Development Index (2005): ranking	9
Human Development Index (2005): value	0.953

For sources and definitions, see explanatory note on p. vi.

Agriculture

PRINCIPAL CROPS
('000 metric tons)

	2004	2005	2006
Wheat	1,224	1,175	1,207
Barley	288	307	269
Maize	265	253	237*
Rye	17	11	12
Triticale (wheat-rye hybrid)	19	20	20
Potatoes	7,488	6,777	6,500
Sugar beet	6,292	5,931	5,500*
Cabbages	207	209	209*
Lettuce	73	74	74*
Spinach	40	43	43*
Tomatoes	655	660	660*
Cauliflower	42	41	41*
Cucumbers and gherkins	435	440	440*
Aubergines (Eggplants)	41	42	42*
Chillies and green peppers	318	345	345*

—continued	2004	2005	2006
Green shallots and onions*	24	24	24
Dry onions	1,225	983	983*
Leeks and other alliaceous vegetables	104	82	82*
Green beans	73	70	70*
Green peas*	80	84	84
Carrots	471	487	487*
Mushrooms	260	245	245*
Apples	436	359	365*
Pears	210	195	222
Strawberries	37†	39	39

* FAO estimate(s).
† Unofficial figure.

Aggregate production ('000 metric tons, may include official, semi-official or estimated data): Total cereals 1,822 in 2004, 1,775 in 2005, 1,755 in 2006; Total roots and tubers 7,488 in 2004, 6,777 in 2005, 6,500 in 2006; Total vegetables (incl. melons) 4,406 in 2004, 4,149 in 2005, 4,149 in 2006; Total fruits (excl. melons) 698 in 2004, 678 in 2005, 650 in 2006.

Source: FAO.

LIVESTOCK
('000 head, year ending September)

	2004	2005	2006
Horses	129	129*	129
Cattle	3,767	3,799	3,746
Chickens	85,816	92,914	90,000*
Sheep	1,236	1,363	1,725
Goats	290	300	310
Pigs	11,153	11,312	11,300

* FAO estimate.

Source: FAO.

LIVESTOCK PRODUCTS
('000 metric tons)

	2004	2005	2006
Cattle meat	386	396	355
Sheep meat	16	13	14*
Pig meat	1,289	1,297	1,230
Chicken meat	615	628	635*
Turkey meat*	67	62	62
Cows' milk	10,905†	10,531*	10,532*
Hen eggs	595	595*	595*

* FAO estimate(s).
† Unofficial figure.

Source: FAO.

Forestry

ROUNDWOOD REMOVALS
('000 cubic metres, excl. bark)

	2004	2005	2006
Sawlogs, veneer logs and logs for sleepers	393	448	443
Pulpwood	310	328	343
Other industrial wood	33	44	33
Fuel wood	290	290	290
Total	1,026	1,110	1,109

Source: FAO.

SAWNWOOD PRODUCTION
('000 cubic metres, incl. railway sleepers)

	2004	2005	2006
Coniferous (softwood)	175	176	179
Broadleaved (hardwood)	98	103	86
Total	273	279	265

Source: FAO.

THE NETHERLANDS

Fishing

('000 metric tons, live weight)

	2003	2004	2005
Capture*	526.3	521.6	549.2
European plaice	28.9	25.1	23.1
Blue whiting	57.3	77.2	128.4
Atlantic herring	95.1	129.6	128.0
Round sardinella	102.0	55.6	70.9
European pilchard	47.4	46.8	31.8
Atlantic horse mackerel	68.1	66.7	67.8
Chub mackerel	25.2	7.5	3.5
Atlantic mackerel	29.2	28.0	23.5
Aquaculture	66.6	75.7	68.2
Blue mussel	56.2	67.2	59.5
Total catch*	**592.9**	**597.4**	**617.4**

* FAO estimates.

Note: Figures exclude aquatic plants and aquatic mammals. Aquatic mammals are recorded by number rather than by weight. The number of porpoises caught was: 100 in 2004 and 150 in 2005.

Source: FAO.

Mining

	2001	2002	2003
Crude petroleum ('000 barrels)*	16,490	16,790	18,000
Natural gas (million cu metres)†	74,232	75,000*	75,000*
Salt ('000 metric tons)*	5,000	5,000	5,000

* Estimated production.

† Figures refer to gross volume of production. Marketed output (in million cu m) was: 73,296 in 2001; 74,000 in 2002 (estimate); 74,000 in 2003 (estimate).

2003–05: Production assumed to be unchanged from 2003 (US Geological Survey estimates).

Source: US Geological Survey.

Industry

SELECTED PRODUCTS
('000 metric tons, unless otherwise indicated)*

	2001	2002	2003
Sand and quartz	8,593	8,317	n.a.
Gravel and crushed stone	5,847	5,569	5,412
Margarine	252	274	307
Raw sugar	1,036	1,112	n.a.
Refined sugar	953	1,023	n.a.
Cocoa powder (metric tons)	187,979	191,769	179,241
Cocoa butter (metric tons)	206,581	204,048	192,932
Prepared animal feeds	13,118	13,030	12,482
Beer ('000 hectolitres)	24,605	24,774	25,699
Mineral waters ('000 hectolitres)	1,858	1,993	1,732
Soft drinks ('000 hectolitres)	18,039	15,239	15,823
Cigars (million)	2,241	2,379	n.a.
Veneer sheets ('000 cubic metres)	18	11	n.a.
Mechanical wood pulp	130	118	124
Newsprint	399	357	427
Other printing and writing paper	846	890	n.a.
Wrapping and packaging paper and paperboard	1,800	1,971	n.a.
Packing containers of paper or paperboard	1,155	1,174	1,190
Soda ash	400	400	n.a.
Synthetic dyestuffs†	23,993	19,642	n.a.
Nitrogenous fertilizers (a)‡	1,013	1,068	n.a.
Phosphate fertilizers (b)‡	174	71	n.a.
Synthetic rubber†	97	104	n.a.
Washing powders and detergents	384	371	441
Jet fuels	6,655	6,174	6,669
Kerosene	413	484	498

—continued	2001	2002	2003
Motor spirit (petrol) and other light oils	14,423	15,767	15,730
Naphthas	12,116	8,655	10,222
Gas-diesel (distillate fuel) oil	22,167	19,583	20,787
White spirit	386	287	294
Residual fuel oils	10,730	12,654	12,333
Lubricating oils	574	609	578
Petroleum bitumen (asphalt)	714	606	297
Liquefied petroleum gas	3,974	4,664	4,780
Coke	2,305	2,213	2,249
Coke-oven gas (terajoules)	19,268	17,983	19,054
Clay building bricks ('000 cu metres)	1,394	1,369	n.a.
Cement§	3,400	3,400	3,400
Pig-iron	5,305	5,000||	5,000
Crude steel§	6,037	6,117	6,587
Aluminium (unwrought):§			
primary	294	284	278
secondary	120||	120||	50
Refined lead: secondary§	24	22	22
Zinc (unwrought): primary	205	203	223
Merchant vessels launched ('000 grt)	32	33	n.a.
Bicycles ('000)	1,042	1,086	1,058
Electricity (million kWh)	93,781	96,066	96,763

* Official figures refer to activity by establishments employing 20 or more persons. For manufactured goods, except for cement, petroleum, coal and basic metal products, such data relate to sales (rather than production) by the relevant establishments.
† Refers to amounts sold.
‡ Output during 12 months ending 30 June of the year stated. Figures are in terms of (a) nitrogen or (b) phosphoric acid.
§ Data from US Geological Survey.
\|\| Estimate.

Sources: partly UN, *Industrial Commodity Statistics Yearbook* and *Monthly Bulletin of Statistics*; FAO; IRF, *World Road Statistics*.

Finance

CURRENCY AND EXCHANGE RATES

Monetary Units
100 cent = 1 euro (€).

Sterling and Dollar Equivalents (31 December 2007)
£1 sterling = 1.3609 euros;
US $1 = 0.6793 euros;
€10 = £7.35 = $14.72.

Average Exchange Rate (euros per US $)
2005   0.8041
2006   0.7971
2007   0.7306

Note: The national currency was formerly the guilder. From the introduction of the euro, with the Netherlands' participation, on 1 January 1999, a fixed exchange rate of €1 = 2.20371 guilders was in operation. Euro notes and coins were introduced on 1 January 2002. The euro and local currency circulated alongside each other until 28 January, after which the euro became the sole legal tender.

THE NETHERLANDS

BUDGET
(€ million)

Revenue	2002	2003	2004
Taxation	110,900	111,700	106,300
Wage and income taxes	28,300	27,500	26,100
Company tax	19,100	18,100	15,900
Dividend tax	3,700	3,800	3,300
Inheritance tax	1,700	1,600	1,400
Gambling tax	200	200	200
Value-added tax	35,000	36,200	35,500
Motor vehicle taxes	9,300	10,100	9,800
Excise duties	8,000	8,500	9,200
Environmental taxes	3,600	4,000	3,200
Import duties	1,800	1,500	1,500
Consumer tax	200	200	200
Other revenue	18,700	17,600	17,400
Total	129,600	129,300	123,700

Expenditure	2002	2003	2004
Education, culture and science	23,100	24,800	25,700
Social security and employment	19,500	20,600	22,700
General public services	13,300	14,200	13,300
Housing and community amenities	11,900	12,600	11,900
Public health, welfare and sport	8,300	9,500	11,100
Foreign affairs and development co-operation	10,400	9,900	9,400
Transport and public works	8,000	8,700	8,200
Defence	7,000	7,300	7,700
Home affairs	4,500	4,900	5,000
Justice	4,800	4,600	5,000
Finance	3,400	3,700	3,800
Housing, planning regulation and environmental management	3,400	3,500	3,500
Agriculture, nature and food quality	2,100	2,100	1,900
Economic affairs	1,800	1,700	1,600
Other	4,200	4,700	3,600
Total	125,700	132,800	134,400

2005 (€ million): *Revenue:* Current 127,790 (Taxes on income and wealth 54,693, Taxes on production and imports 59,581, Other revenue 13,516); Capital revenue 5,474; Total 133,263. *Expenditure:* Current 122,451 (Personnel 33,400, Subsidies on products 2,412, Taxes on production and imports 44, Social transfers 86,595); Capital 10,310; Total 132,760.

2006 (€ million, provisional): *Revenue:* Current 139,447 (Taxes on income and wealth 59,486, Taxes on production and imports 63,740, Other revenue 16,221); Capital revenue 5,618; Total 145,065. *Expenditure:* Current 130,414 (Personnel 34,434, Taxes paid on production and imports 45, Subsidies on products 2,438, Social transfers 93,495); Capital 10,597; Total 141,011.

INTERNATIONAL RESERVES
(US $ million at 31 December)

	2004	2005	2006
Gold (market prices)	10,948	11,462	13,100
IMF special drawing rights	778	716	785
Reserve position in IMF	2,667	1,192	691
Foreign exchange	7,210	7,078	9,327
Total	21,603	20,448	23,903

Source: IMF, *International Financial Statistics*.

MONEY SUPPLY
(€ '000 million at 31 December)

	2004	2005	2006
Currency issued*	26.45	29.70	32.93
Demand deposits at banking institutions	162.25	182.92	197.14

* Currency put into circulation by De Nederlandsche Bank: €23,140m. in 2004; €23,900m. in 2005; €24,420m. in 2006.

Source: IMF, *International Financial Statistics*.

COST OF LIVING
(Consumer Price Index; base: 2000 = 100)

	2004	2005	2006
Food	107.8	106.5	108.3
Electricity, gas and other fuels	134.6	153.5	168.2
Clothing (incl. footwear)	99.9	97.3	97.8
Rent	112.2	115.1	117.8
All items (incl. others)	111.2	113.1	114.4

Source: ILO.

NATIONAL ACCOUNTS
(€ million at current prices)

National Income and Product

	2004	2005	2006
Compensation of employees	251,030	253,363	263,127
Net operating surplus/mixed income	111,614	121,297	129,716
Domestic primary incomes	362,644	374,660	392,843
Consumption of fixed capital	73,498	75,651	78,360
Gross domestic product (GDP) at factor cost	436,142	450,311	471,203
Taxes on production and imports	63,301	66,301	70,815
Less Subsidies on production and imports	8,259	7,648	7,694
GDP in market prices	491,184	508,964	534,324
Net primary income from abroad	13,149	3,198	8,792
Gross national income (GNI)	504,333	512,162	543,116
Less Consumption of fixed capital	73,498	75,651	78,360
Net national income	430,835	436,511	464,756
Net current transfers from abroad	−7,492	−8,168	−8,141
Net national disposable income	423,343	428,343	456,615

Expenditure on the Gross Domestic Product

	2005	2006	2007
Government final consumption expenditure	121,720	135,694	141,305
Private final consumption expenditure	249,735	253,482	263,150
Increase in stocks	521	114	−1,244
Gross fixed capital formation	96,494	105,283	111,625
Total domestic expenditure	468,470	494,573	514,836
Exports of goods and services	355,326	391,346	421,342
Less Imports of goods and services	314,832	351,595	376,641
GDP in purchasers' values	508,964	534,324	559,537
GDP at constant 2000 prices	443,937	457,278	473,203

THE NETHERLANDS

Gross Domestic Product by Economic Activity

	2005	2006	2007
Agriculture, hunting, forestry and fishing	9,647	10,410	10,546
Mining and quarrying	13,572	16,960	17,403
Manufacturing	63,295	63,087	65,496
Electricity, gas and water supply	6,895	7,948	8,998
Construction	24,437	26,278	28,115
Wholesale and retail trade; repair of motor vehicles, motorcycles and personal household goods	57,771	61,389	64,444
Hotels and restaurants	8,328	8,646	9,209
Transport and storage	20,513	21,725	23,137
Post and telecommunications	12,231	12,049	12,036
Financial activities	34,509	31,331	28,457
Real estate activities	33,809	37,925	41,731
Activities of employment agencies	10,642	12,585	14,923
Other business activities	46,001	49,371	53,388
General government	52,467	53,718	55,552
Care and other service activities	57,769	60,188	63,280
GDP at basic prices	451,886	473,610	496,715
Taxes, less subsidies, on imports	56,388	60,806	64,161
Value-added tax, *less* imputed bank service charge	690	–92	–1,339*
GDP in purchasers' values	508,964	534,324	559,537

*Figure obtained as a residual.

BALANCE OF PAYMENTS
(€ million)

	2004	2005	2006
Exports of goods f.o.b.	313,429	343,726	386,923
Imports of goods f.o.b.	–272,590	–298,684	–341,728
Trade balance	40,839	45,042	45,195
Exports of services	73,772	80,092	82,271
Imports of services	–69,444	–73,313	–79,539
Balance on goods and services	45,167	51,821	47,928
Other income received	80,671	98,837	131,087
Other income paid	–69,306	–93,529	–110,715
Balance on goods, services and income	56,533	57,129	68,299
Current transfers received	9,764	11,144	12,392
Current transfers paid	–20,197	–22,550	–24,897
Current balance	46,100	45,723	55,795
Capital account (net)	–1,614	–1,764	–2,792
Direct investment abroad	–28,849	–133,929	–46,474
Direct investment from abroad	4,379	47,235	7,197
Portfolio investment assets	–105,084	–81,845	–43,830
Portfolio investment liabilities	74,104	159,993	59,482
Financial derivatives assets	165,590	150,955	133,924
Financial derivatives liabilities	–167,108	–155,136	–140,862
Other investment assets	–67,053	–52,628	–185,690
Other investment liabilities	77,840	29,609	162,461
Net errors and omissions	785	–10,003	1,567
Overall balance	–911	–1,790	778

Source: IMF, *International Financial Statistics*.

OFFICIAL ASSISTANCE TO DEVELOPING COUNTRIES
(net disbursements, US $ million)

	2001	2002	2003
Total	3,172	3,338	3,981

Source: OECD.

External Trade

PRINCIPAL COMMODITIES
(distribution by SITC, € '000)

Imports c.i.f.	2005	2006	2007*
Food and live animals	19,195	20,886	23,835
Crude materials (inedible) except fuels	9,768	11,134	12,896
Mineral fuels, lubricants, etc.	36,956	47,553	48,386
Petroleum, petroleum products, etc.	30,670	38,564	39,533
Crude petroleum	18,971	22,893	22,461
Chemicals and related products	32,502	36,030	41,469
Organic chemicals	8,399	9,750	11,172
Basic manufactures	28,323	34,365	39,141
Machinery and transport equipment	89,066	97,608	102,560
Office machines and automatic data-processing equipment	29,045	33,547	25,738
Telecommunications and sound equipment	13,518	13,893	22,260
Other electrical machinery, apparatus, etc.	16,044	14,939	14,964
Road vehicles (incl. air-cushion vehicles) and parts (excl. tyres, engines, and electrical parts)	14,319	15,776	17,458
Passenger motor vehicles (excl. buses)	7,142	7,490	7,796
Miscellaneous manufactured articles	29,162	32,487	33,149
Total (incl. others)	249,845	285,370	307,012

Exports f.o.b.	2005	2006	2007*
Food and live animals	32,430	34,568	38,171
Vegetables and fruit	8,647	9,755	10,950
Crude materials (inedible) except fuels	15,414	17,602	18,667
Mineral fuels, lubricants, etc.	30,813	41,430	41,733
Petroleum, petroleum products, etc.	20,905	28,067	28,652
Chemicals and related products	47,678	53,072	60,001
Organic chemicals	12,509	14,166	16,556
Plastics in primary form	9,764	10,770	11,421
Basic manufactures	27,063	32,310	36,878
Machinery and transport equipment	90,731	97,936	113,126
Office machines and automatic data-processing equipment	30,557	32,974	29,063
Automatic data-processing machines	17,245	17,646	12,206
Telecommunications and sound equipment	11,841	13,193	21,026
Other electrical machinery, apparatus, etc.	17,688	17,028	17,688
Thermionic tubes, transistors, etc.	7,944	6,423	6,748
Road vehicles (incl. air-cushion vehicles) and parts (excl. tyres, engines, and electrical parts)	11,044	12,070	13,323
Miscellaneous manufactured articles	28,875	32,384	28,916
Total (incl. others)†	281,300	318,953	347,958

*Preliminary figures.
†Including victuals and stores supplied to foreign ships and aircraft.

THE NETHERLANDS

PRINCIPAL TRADING PARTNERS
(€ million)

Imports c.i.f.	2005	2006	2007*
Belgium	26,960	31,036	33,090
Brazil	3,978	2,972	2,801
China, People's Republic	19,056	23,007	26,363
Denmark	2,724	3,308	3,140
France	12,808	14,266	15,009
Germany	47,563	55,504	61,624
Hong Kong	1,776	1,928	1,613
Ireland	3,569	3,524	3,688
Italy	6,592	7,121	7,655
Japan	6,109	6,479	7,184
Korea, Republic	2,315	2,620	2,270
Malaysia	4,146	4,571	4,965
Norway	4,133	3,839	4,310
Russia	8,342	10,969	10,404
Saudi Arabia	4,092	4,389	3,295
Singapore	2,977	3,209	3,093
Spain	4,843	5,380	5,985
Sweden	4,187	4,975	5,507
Switzerland	2,175	2,209	2,217
Taiwan	3,325	2,962	2,571
United Kingdom	15,571	18,136	19,566
USA	19,674	23,757	24,110
Total (incl. others)	249,845	285,370	307,012

Exports f.o.b.	2005	2006	2007*
Austria	3,780	4,359	4,913
Belgium	32,899	39,613	41,393
Denmark	4,276	4,338	4,773
France	25,734	26,285	28,551
Germany	66,957	78,917	81,949
Italy	16,087	16,007	17,226
Japan	2,217	2,206	2,541
Poland	3,998	4,826	6,259
Spain	10,900	11,371	12,559
Sweden	5,812	6,059	6,324
Switzerland	4,070	4,825	4,738
United Kingdom	25,907	28,427	31,694
USA	13,596	16,166	17,397
Total (incl. others)	281,300	318,953	347,958

* Figures are provisional.

Transport

RAILWAYS
(traffic)

	1996	1997	1998
Passenger-km (million)	14,131	14,485	14,879
Freight ton-km (million)	3,123	3,406	3,778

Passenger-km (million): 14,730 in 2005; 15,414 in 2006; 15,546 in 2007 (Source: Nederlandse Spoorwegen NV, *Annual Report 2007*).

ROAD TRAFFIC
('000 motor vehicles)

	2001	2002	2003
Passenger vehicles	6,539	6,711	6,855
Commercial passenger vehicles	753	788	780
Buses and coaches	11	11	11
Vans	756	798	856
Lorries	143	145	144
Motorcycles	438	461	494

SHIPPING
Inland Waterways
(transport fleet at 1 January)

	1997	1998	1999
Number of vessels	5,067	5,003	4,577
Carrying capacity ('000 metric tons)	5,859	5,589	5,212

Inland Waterways
(freight traffic, million metric tons)

	1996	1997	1998
Internal transport: Commercial	61.2	75.7	79.3
Internal transport: Private	28.2	20.9	19.3
International transport	201.1	224.5	219.7

Merchant Fleet
(at 31 December)

	2004	2005	2006
Number of vessels	1,276	1,257	1,258
Displacement ('000 grt)	5,622.9	5,669.0	5,818.4

Source: Lloyd's Register-Fairplay, *World Fleet Statistics*.

Sea-borne Freight Traffic
('000 metric tons)

	1997	1998	1999
Goods loaded	88,667	85,137	92,000
Goods unloaded	312,864	319,684	305,000

CIVIL AVIATION*
(Netherlands scheduled air services)

	2001	2002	2003
Kilometres flown (million)	425	424	429
Passengers carried ('000)	19,261	22,119	22,590
Passenger-km (million)	68,793	68,979	68,688
Total ton-km (million)	11,154	11,244	11,331

* Figures include data for airlines based in the territories and dependencies of the Netherlands.

Source: UN, *Statistical Yearbook*.

Tourism

FOREIGN TOURIST ARRIVALS
('000)*

Country of origin	2003	2004	2005
Belgium	779	811	917
France	465	510	527
Germany	2,803	2,649	2,570
Italy	339	369	374
Spain	275	298	322
United Kingdom	1,646	1,760	1,853
Total (incl. others)	9,181	9,647	10,012

* Arrivals at all accommodation establishments.

Tourism receipts (US $ million, excl. passenger transport): 9,164 in 2003; 10,311 in 2004; 10,383 in 2005 (Source: World Tourism Organization).

Communications Media

	2004	2005	2006
Telephones ('000 main lines in use)	7,861	7,600	n.a.
Mobile cellular telephones ('000 subscribers)	14,800	15,834	n.a.
Internet users ('000)	10,000	12,060	14,544
Broadband subscribers ('000)	3,206	4,100	5,192

Personal computers ('000 in use): 11,110 in 2004.

Daily newspapers: 35 in 2000 (circulation 4,443,000).

Non-daily newspapers (regional or local): 49 in 2000 (circulation 317,000).

Book production (1993): 34,067 titles, excluding pamphlets.

Radio receivers ('000 in use): 15,300 in 1997.

Television receivers ('000 in use): 8,600 in 1997.

Facsimile machines ('000 in use): 600 in 1997.

Sources: UNESCO, *Statistical Yearbook*; UN, *Statistical Yearbook*; International Telecommunication Union.

Education

(2004/05)

	Institutions	Students ('000)
Primary	7,314	1,599.2
Secondary	668	937.9
Higher vocational	54	346.2
University	13	199.4

Directory

The Constitution

The Netherlands' first Constitution was adopted in 1814–15. The present Constitution, the first new one since 1848, came into force on 17 February 1983. Its main provisions are summarized below:

THE KINGDOM OF THE NETHERLANDS

The Kingdom of the Netherlands consists of territories in Europe (the Netherlands) and in the Caribbean (the Netherlands Antilles and Aruba). Under the Charter for the Kingdom of the Netherlands, signed by Queen Juliana in 1954, these territories constitute a single realm, ruled by the House of Orange-Nassau.

THE MONARCHY

The Netherlands is a constitutional monarchy with a parliamentary system of government. The Constitution regulates the royal succession and the regency in great detail. A successor to the Throne may be appointed by Act of Parliament if it appears that there will otherwise be no successor. The Bill for this purpose shall be discussed and decided upon in a joint session of the two Chambers of the States-General (Staten-Generaal). The Sovereign is succeeded by his or her eldest child. The age of majority of the Sovereign is 18 years. Until the Sovereign has attained that age, the royal prerogative shall be exercised by a Regent.

ELECTORAL SYSTEM

The Parliament of the Netherlands is the Staten-Generaal and is composed of two Chambers, a First and a Second Chamber. The Second Chamber (Tweede Kamer), which is the more important politically, consists of 150 members, and is directly elected for four years on the basis of proportional representation. The First Chamber (Eerste Kamer), or Senate (Senaat), comprises 75 members and is elected by the (directly elected) members of the Provincial Councils.

Nearly all Dutch nationals who have attained the age of 18 years are entitled to take part in the election for the Second Chamber. Those not entitled to vote are certain groups of non-resident nationals, mentally disordered and legally incompetent persons.

To be eligible for membership of the Staten-Generaal, a person must be a Dutch national, must have attained the age of 18 years and must not have been disqualified from voting.

MINISTERIAL RESPONSIBILITY

The Ministers, led by the Prime Minister, are responsible to the Staten-Generaal for all acts of government. This means, for example, that the power of the Government (Sovereign and Ministers) to dissolve one or both Chambers of the Staten-Generaal is ultimately subject to the judgment of the Staten-Generaal. The right to declare war and conclude treaties can, in principle, only be exercised subject to prior parliamentary approval. The Constitution contains provisions concerning the transferral of legislative, executive and judicial power to international institutions and on the legal supremacy of self-executing provisions of treaties.

The Prime Minister and the other Ministers are appointed and dismissed by Royal Decree. Ministries are established by Royal Decree.

A Council of Ministers is formed by a so-called 'formateur' (usually the future Prime Minister), who will have been assured of the support of a majority in the Second Chamber of the Staten-Generaal.

A Minister may not be a member of the Staten-Generaal. However, Ministers have the right to attend sittings of the Chambers and may take part in the deliberations. They must supply the Chambers, either orally or in writing, with any information requested, provided that this cannot be deemed to conflict with the interests of the State.

A statement of the policy that is to be pursued by the Government is given by the Sovereign every year on the third Tuesday in September before a joint session of the two Chambers of the Staten-Generaal.

Acts of Parliament are passed jointly by the Government and the Staten-Generaal. Bills, including the draft budget, must be introduced into the Second Chamber. The Second Chamber has the right to amend bills; the First Chamber can only accept or reject a bill. Revision of the Constitution requires two parliamentary readings of the bills that contain the proposed changes. In between the two readings, the Staten-Generaal must be dissolved and elections held.

THE COUNCIL OF STATE

The Council of State is the Government's oldest and most important advisory body. It must be consulted on all bills and draft general administrative orders. The Council is also an important court for administrative disputes.

The Sovereign is President of the Council of State, but the day-to-day running of the Council is the responsibility of its Vice-President. Its other members—usually former politicians, scholars, judges and business executives—are appointed for life.

LOCAL GOVERNMENT

The Netherlands is divided into 12 provinces. Provinces may be dissolved and established by Act of Parliament. The provincial administrative organs are the Provincial Council, the Provincial Executive and the Sovereign's Commissioner. The Provincial Council—directly elected on the basis of proportional representation—forms the provincial equivalent of the Parliament. Each Provincial Council elects, from among its members, a Provincial Executive.

The Sovereign's Commissioner is appointed and dismissed by Royal Decree. Each Commissioner presides over both the Provincial Council and the Provincial Executive. The provincial administrative organs have the constitutionally guaranteed power to regulate and administer their own internal affairs. They may also be required by, or pursuant to, Act of Parliament to provide regulation and administration. In April 2008 there were 443 municipalities in the Netherlands. The municipal administrative organs are the Municipal Council (directly elected by the local inhabitants), the Municipal Executive (chosen by the Council from among its members) and the Burgemeester (appointed and dismissed by Royal Decree). The Burgemeester (Mayor) presides over both the Municipal Council and the Municipal Executive. The Municipal Council has the power to make local regulations.

THE NETHERLANDS

The Government

HEAD OF STATE

Queen of the Netherlands: HM Queen BEATRIX WILHELMINA ARMGARD (succeeded to the throne 30 April 1980).

COUNCIL OF MINISTERS
(April 2008)

A coalition comprising the Christen Democratisch Appèl (CDA—Christian Democratic Appeal), the Partij van de Arbeid (PvdA—Labour Party) and the ChristenUnie (CU—Christian Union).

Prime Minister, Minister of General Affairs: Dr JAN PIETER (JAN PETER) BALKENENDE (CDA).
Deputy Prime Minister, Minister of Finance: WOUTER JACOB BOS (PvdA).
Deputy Prime Minister, Minister of Youth and the Family: ANDRÉ ROUVOET (CU).
Minister of Economic Affairs: MARIA JOSEPHINA ARNOLDINA VAN DER HOEVEN (CDA).
Minister of Foreign Affairs: MAXIME JACQUES MARCEL VERHAGEN (CDA).
Minister of the Interior and Kingdom Relations: Dr GUUS (GUUSJE) TER HORST (PvdA).
Minister of Defence: EIMERT VAN MIDDELKOOP (CU).
Minister of Housing, Communities and Integration: CATHARINA PIETERNELLA (ELLA) VOGELAAR (PvdA).
Minister of Justice: Dr ERNST MAURITS HENRICUS HIRSCH BALLIN (CDA).
Minister of Agriculture, Nature and Food Quality: GERRITJE (GERDA) VERBERG (CDA).
Minister of Education, Culture and Science: Dr RONALD HANS ANTON PLASTERK (PvdA).
Minister of Social Affairs and Employment: JAN PIET HEIN (PIET HEIN) DONNER (CDA).
Minister of Health, Welfare and Sport: Dr ABRAHAM (AB) KLINK (CDA).
Minister of the Environment and Spatial Planning: Dr JACQUELINE MARIAN CRAMER (PvdA).
Minister of Development Co-operation: ALBERT GERARD (BERT) KOENDERS (PvdA).
Minister of Transport, Public Works and Water Management: CAMIEL MARTINUS PETRUS STEPHANUS EURLINGS (CDA).
Minister Plenipotentiary for the Netherlands Antilles: PAUL RALSTON JOSEPH COMENENCIA.
Minister Plenipotentiary for Aruba: Dr FRANCISCO WALFRIDO (FRIDO) CROES.

There are, in addition, 11 Secretaries of State.

MINISTRIES

Office of the Prime Minister, Ministry of General Affairs: Binnenhof 20, POB 20001, 2500 EA The Hague; tel. (70) 3564100; fax (70) 3564683; internet www.minaz.nl.
Ministry of Agriculture, Nature and Food Quality: Bezuidenhoutseweg 73, POB 20401, 2500 EK The Hague; tel. (70) 3786868; fax (70) 3786100; e-mail webredactie@minlnv.nl; internet www.minlnv.nl.
Ministry of Defence: Plein 4, POB 20701, 2500 ES The Hague; tel. (70) 3188188; fax (70) 3187888; e-mail defensievoorlichting@mindef.nl; internet www.mindef.nl.
Ministry of Economic Affairs: Bezuidenhoutseweg 30, POB 20101, 2500 EC The Hague; tel. (800) 6463951; internet www.ez.nl.
Ministry of Education, Culture and Science: Rijnstraat 50, POB 16375, 2500 BJ The Hague; tel. (70) 4123456; fax (70) 4123450; e-mail ocwinfo@postbus51.nl; internet www.minocw.nl.
Ministry of the Environment and Spatial Planning: Rijnstraat 8, POB 20951, 2500 EZ The Hague; tel. (70) 3393939; internet www.vrom.nl.
Ministry of Finance: Prinses Beatrixlaan 512, POB 20201, 2500 EE The Hague; tel. (70) 3428000; fax (70) 3427900; e-mail webmaster@minfin.nl; internet www.minfin.nl.
Ministry of Foreign Affairs: Bezuidenhoutseweg 67, POB 20061, 2500 EB The Hague; tel. (70) 3486486; fax (70) 3484848; e-mail minbuza@buza.minbuza.nl; internet www.minbuza.nl; incorporates Development Co-operation.
Ministry of Housing, Communities and Integration: operates under Ministry of the Environment and Spatial Planning (see above).

Ministry of the Interior and Kingdom Relations: Schedeldoekshaven 200, POB 20011, 2500 EA The Hague; tel. (70) 4266426; fax (70) 3639153; e-mail info@minbzk.nl; internet www.minbzk.nl.
Ministry of Justice: Schedeldoekshaven 100, POB 20301, 2500 EH The Hague; tel. (70) 3707911; fax (70) 3707900; e-mail voorlichting@minjus.nl; internet www.justitie.nl.
Ministry of Public Health, Welfare and Sport: Parnassusplein 5, POB 20350, 2500 EJ The Hague; tel. (70) 3407911; fax (70) 3407834; internet www.minvws.nl.
Ministry of Social Affairs and Employment: Anna van Hannoverstraat 4, POB 90801, 2509 LV The Hague; tel. (70) 3334444; fax (70) 3334033; internet www.szw.nl.
Ministry of Transport, Public Works and Water Management: Plesmanweg 1–6, POB 20901, 2500 EX The Hague; tel. (70) 3516171; fax (70) 3517895; e-mail venwinfo@postbus51.nl; internet www.minvenw.nl.
Ministry of Youth and the Family: operates under the Ministry of Public Welfare, Health and Sport (see above).
Office of the Minister Plenipotentiary for Aruba: R. J. Schimmelpennincklaan 1, 2517 JN The Hague; tel. (70) 3566200; fax (70) 3451446; e-mail info@arubahuis.nl; internet www.arubahuis.nl.
Office of the Minister Plenipotentiary for the Netherlands Antilles: Badhuisweg 173–175, POB 90706, 2509 LS The Hague; tel. (70) 3066111; fax (70) 3066110; e-mail info@antillenhuis.nl; internet www.antillenhuis.nl.

Legislature

STATEN-GENERAAL
(States-General)

Eerste Kamer
(First Chamber)

Binnenhof 22, 2513 AA The Hague; tel. (70) 3129200; fax (70) 3129390; e-mail postbus@eerstekamer.nl; internet www.eerstekamer.nl.

President: YVONNE TIMMERMAN-BUCK (CDA).

Election, 29 May 2007

	Seats
Christen Democratisch Appèl	21
Volkspartij voor Vrijheid en Democratie	14
Partij van de Arbeid	14
Socialistische Partij	12
GroenLinks	4
ChristenUnie	4
Democraten 66	2
Staatkundig Gereformeerde Partij	2
Partij voor de Dieren	1
Independent	1
Total	**75**

Tweede Kamer
(Second Chamber)

Binnenhof 4, 2513 AA Den Haag; tel. (70) 3183040; internet www.tweedekamer.nl.

President: GERDI A. VERBEET (PvdA).

General Election, 22 November 2006

	Votes	%	Seats
Christen Democratisch Appèl	2,608,573	26.51	41
Partij van de Arbeid	2,085,077	21.19	33
Socialistische Partij	1,630,803	16.58	25
Volkspartij voor Vrijheid en Democratie	1,443,312	14.67	22
Partij voor de Vrijheid	579,490	5.89	9
GroenLinks	453,054	4.60	7
ChristenUnie	390,969	3.97	6
Democraten 66	193,232	1.96	3
Partij voor de Dieren	179,988	1.83	2
Staatkundig Gereformeerde Partij	153,266	1.56	2
Others	120,919	1.23	—
Total	**9,838,683**	**100.00**	**150**

THE NETHERLANDS

Election Commission

Kiesraad (Dutch Electoral Council): Herengracht 21, POB 20011, 2500 EA The Hague; tel. (70) 4266266; fax (70) 4266489; e-mail kiesraad@kiesraad.nl; internet www.kiesraad.nl; f. 1989; independent; Chair. Prof. HENK KUMMELING.

Advisory Councils

Raad van State (Council of State): Paleisstraat 3, POB 20019, 2500 EA The Hague; tel. (70) 4264426; fax (70) 3651380; e-mail voorlichting@raadvanstate.nl; internet www.raadvanstate.nl; comprises a Vice-Pres. and up to 28 mems nominated by the Sovereign, who formally presides over the Council; advises on legislation, constitutional issues, international treaties and all matters of national importance; Vice-Pres. H. D. TJEENK WILLINK; Sec. R. VAN DER BRUG.

Sociaal-Economische Raad (Social and Economic Council): Bezuidenhoutseweg 60, POB 90405, 2509 LK The Hague; tel. (70) 3499499; fax (70) 3832535; internet www.ser.nl; f. 1950; tripartite advisory body; to advise Govt on social and economic policy; monitors commodity and industrial boards; 33 mems, of which 11 belong to the Netherlands trade union federations, 11 belong to the employers' organizations, and 11 are independent experts in social and economic affairs appointed by the Crown; Chair. Dr ALEXANDER RINNOOY KAN; Sec.-Gen. Dr VÉRONIQUE TIMMERHUIS.

Political Organizations

Christen Democratisch Appèl (CDA) (Christian Democratic Appeal): Buitenom 18, POB 30453, 2500 GL The Hague; tel. (70) 3424888; fax (70) 3643417; e-mail cda@cda.nl; internet www.cda.nl; f. 1980; by merger of three 'confessional' parties; Chair. PETER VAN HEESWIJK; Party Leader JAN PIETER (JAN PETER) BALKENENDE; Parliamentary Leader PETRUS LEONARDUS BASTIAAN ANTONIUS (PIETER) VAN GEEL; 69,000 mems.

ChristenUnie (CU) (Christian Union): Puntenburgerlaan 91, POB 439, 3800 AK Amersfoort; tel. (33) 4226969; fax (33) 4226968; e-mail bureau@christenunie.nl; internet www.christenunie.nl; f. 2000 by merger of two 'evangelical' parties, the Gereformeerd Politiek Verbond and the Reformatorische Politieke Federatie; interdenominational, based on biblical precepts; mem. of European Christian Political Movement; Chair. PETER BLOKHUIS; Party Leader ANDRÉ ROUVOET; Parliamentary Leader ARIE SLOB; c. 25,000 mems (2005).

Democraten 66 (D66) (Democrats 66): Laan van Meerdervoort 50, POB 660, 2501 CR The Hague; tel. (70) 3566066; fax (70) 3641917; e-mail info@d66.nl; internet www.d66.nl; f. 1966; Chair. INGRID VAN ENGELSHOVEN; Parliamentary Leader ALEXANDER PECHTOLD; 12,500 mems.

EénNL (One NL): Rotterdam; tel. (10) 2085971; e-mail info@eennl.nl; internet www.eennl.nl; f. 2006 by fmr mems of Leefbaar Rotterdam and List Pim Fortuyn; right-wing, nationalist; agenda broadly similar to that of Pim Fortuyn; Leaders MARCO PASTORS, JOOST EERDMANS.

Europa Transparant (Transparent Europe): POB 3196, 4800 DD Breda; tel. (76) 5317946; fax (76) 5397701; e-mail paul.vanbuitenen-assistant@europarl.europa.eu; internet www.europatransparant.nl; f. 2004; aims to encourage openness within the European Union; Pres. PAUL VAN BUITENEN.

Fryske Nasjonale Partij (FNP) (Frisian National Party): FNP-hûs, Obrechtstrjitte 32, 8916 EN Ljouwert; tel. (58) 2131422; fax (58) 2131420; e-mail fnphus@globalxs.nl; internet www.fnp.nl; f. 1962; promotes federalism and greater regional autonomy; Leader JOHANNES KRAMER; c. 1,300 mems.

De Groenen (Green Party): POB 1251, 3500 BG Utrecht; tel. (71) 5762027; e-mail info@degroenen.nl; internet www.degroenen.nl; f. 1983; Chair. JACQUES DE COO, PAUL FRERIKS.

GroenLinks (GL) (Green Left): Oudegracht 312, POB 8008, 3503 RA Utrecht; tel. (30) 2399900; fax (30) 2300342; e-mail info@groenlinks.nl; internet www.groenlinks.nl; f. 1990 by merger of Communistische Partij van Nederland, Evangelische Volkspartij, Pacifistisch-Socialistische Partij and Politieke Partij Radicalen; Chair. HENK NIJHOF; Parliamentary Leader FEMKE HALSEMA; c. 20,000 mems.

Leefbaar Nederland (LN) (Liveable Netherlands): POB 18581, 2502 EN The Hague; tel. and fax (47) 5410205; e-mail info@leefbaar.nl; internet www.leefbaar.nl; Chair. FONS ZINKEN.

Nieuwe Communistische Partij Nederland (NCPN) (New Communist Party of the Netherlands): Haarlemmerweg 177, 1051 LB Amsterdam; tel. (20) 6825019; fax (20) 6828276; e-mail manifest@wanadoo.nl; internet www.ncpn.nl; f. 1992; Chair. JOB PRUIJSER.

Nieuwe Midden Partij (NMP) (New Centre Party): POB 2087, 8203 AB Lelystad; tel. and fax (320) 281412; e-mail info@nmp.nl; internet www.sdnl.nl/nmp.htm; f. 1970; campaigns on economic issues; Leader MARTIN DESSING.

Partij van de Arbeid (PvdA) (Labour Party): Herengracht 54, POB 1310, 1000 BH Amsterdam; tel. (20) 5512155; fax (20) 5512250; e-mail voorzitter@pvda.nl; internet www.pvda.nl; f. 1946 by merger of progressive and liberal organizations; social democratic; Chair. RUUD KOOLE (acting); Party Leader WOUTER BOS; Parliamentary Leader MARIËTTE HAMER; c. 65,000 mems.

Partij voor de Dieren (Party for the Animals): POB 16698, 1001 RD Amsterdam; tel. (20) 5203870; e-mail info@partijvoordedieren.nl; internet www.partijvoordedieren.nl; f. 2002; promotes animal rights and animal welfare; Chair. MARIANNE THIEME; Sec. PETER BOOGAARD.

Partij voor de Vrijheid (PVV) (Freedom Party): POB 20018, 2500 EA The Hague; internet www.pvv.nl; f. 2004 as Groep Wilders; present name adopted 2006; populist, anti-immigration; Leader GEERT WILDERS.

Socialistische Alternatieve Politiek (SAP) (Socialist Political Alternative): Postbus 2096, 3000 CB Rotterdam; tel. (20) 6259272; e-mail redactie@grenzloos.nl; internet www.grenzeloos.org; f. 1974; Trotskyist.

Socialistische Partij (SP) (Socialist Party): Vijverhofstraat 65, 3032 SC Rotterdam; tel. (10) 2435555; fax (10) 2435566; e-mail sp@sp.nl; internet www.sp.nl; f. 1972; Chair. JAN MARIJNISSEN; Gen. Sec. HANS VAN HEIJNINGEN; 51,366 mems (2007).

Staatkundig Gereformeerde Partij (SGP) (Reformed Political Party): Burgemeester van Reenensingel 101, 2803 Gouda; tel. (82) 696900; fax (82) 573222; e-mail info@sgp.nl; internet www.sgp.nl; f. 1918; Calvinist; female membership banned in 1996; Chair. Rev. A. VAN HETEREN; Parliamentary Leader B. J. (BAS) VAN DER VLIES; Gen. Sec. V. A. SMIT; 25,900 mems (2005).

Verenigde Senioren Partij (VSP) (United Senior Citizens' Party): Israëlslaan 37, 3431 AS Nieuwegein; tel. (30) 6300208; fax (30) 6300209; e-mail secretariaat@verenigdeseniorenpartij.nl; internet www.verenigdeseniorenpartij.nl; Chair. HERMAN TROOST; Sec. JACK KOEHORST.

Volkspartij voor Vrijheid en Democratie (VVD) (People's Party for Freedom and Democracy—Netherlands Liberal Party): Laan Copes van Cattenburch 52, POB 30836, 2500 GV The Hague; tel. (70) 3613061; fax (70) 3608276; e-mail alg.sec@vvd.nl; internet www.vvd.nl; f. 1948; advocates free enterprise, individual freedom and responsibility, but its programme also supports social security and recommends the participation of workers in profits and management; Chair. JAN VAN ZANEN; Parliamentary Leader MARK RUTTE; 48,000 mems.

Diplomatic Representation

EMBASSIES IN THE NETHERLANDS

Albania: Anna Paulownastraat 109B, 2518 BD The Hague; tel. (70) 4272101; fax (70) 4272083; e-mail embalba@xs4all.nl; Ambassador ROLAND BIMO.

Algeria: Van Stolklaan 1–3, 2585 JS The Hague; tel. (70) 3522954; fax (70) 3061961; e-mail ambalg1@wanadoo.nl; internet www.embalgeria.nl; Ambassador BENCHAÂ DANI.

Argentina: Javastraat 20, 2585 AN The Hague; tel. (70) 3118411; fax (70) 3118410; e-mail argentina@xs4all.nl; internet www.embassyargentina.nl; Ambassador SANTOS GOÑI MARENCO.

Australia: Carnegielaan 4, 2517 KH The Hague; tel. (70) 3108200; fax (70) 3107863; e-mail austemb_thehague@dfat.gov.au; internet www.netherlands.embassy.gov.au; Ambassador LYDIA MORTON.

Austria: Van Alkemadelaan 342, 2597 AS The Hague; tel. (70) 3245470; fax (70) 3282066; e-mail den-haag-ob@bmeia.gv.at; internet www.bmeia.at/denhaag; Ambassador WOLFGANG PAUL.

Azerbaijan: Laan Copes van Cattenburch 127, 2585 EZ The Hague; tel. (70) 3538205; fax (70) 3469604; e-mail info@azembassy.nl; Ambassador FUAD ISKANDAROV.

Bangladesh: Wassenaarseweg 39, 2596 CG The Hague; tel. (70) 3283722; fax (70) 3283524; e-mail amb.vanbangladesh@wanadoo.nl; internet www.bangladeshembassy.nl; Ambassador MIZANUR RAHMAN.

Belarus: Anna Paulownastraat 34, 2518 BE The Hague; tel. (70) 3631566; fax (70) 3640555; e-mail info@witrusland.com; internet www.witrusland.com; Ambassador VLADIMIR GERASIMOVICH.

Belgium: Alexanderveld 97, 2585 DB The Hague; tel. (70) 3123456; fax (70) 3645579; e-mail thehague@diplobel.org; internet www.diplomatie.be/thehague; Ambassador LUC CARBONEZ.

THE NETHERLANDS

Bolivia: Nassaulaan 5, 2514 JS The Hague; tel. (70) 3616707; fax (70) 3620039; e-mail embolned@xs4all.nl; Ambassador ROBERTO CALZADILLA SARMIENTO.

Bosnia and Herzegovina: Bezuidenhoutseweg 223, 2495 AL The Hague; tel. (70) 3588505; fax (70) 3584367; e-mail fuad.sabeta@mfa.gov.ba; internet www.xs4all.nl/~bih; Ambassador FUAD SABETA.

Brazil: Mauritskade 19, 2514 HD The Hague; tel. (70) 3023959; fax (70) 3023950; e-mail brasil@brazilianembassy.nl; internet www.brazilianembassy.nl; Ambassador GILBERTO VERGNE SABOIA.

Bulgaria: Duinrooseweg 9, 2597 KJ The Hague; tel. (70) 3503051; fax (70) 3584688; e-mail info@embassy-bulgaria.nl; internet www.embassy-bulgaria.nl; Ambassador ZLATIN V. TRAPKOV.

Cameroon: Amaliastraat 14, 2514 JC The Hague; tel. (70) 3469715; fax (70) 3652979; e-mail ambacam-la-haye@planet.nl; internet www.cameroon-embassy.nl; Chargé d'affaires a.i. MATHIEU BLAISE BANOUM.

Canada: Sophialaan 7, POB 30820, 2500 GV The Hague; tel. (70) 3111600; fax (70) 3111620; e-mail info@canada.nl; internet www.canada.nl; Ambassador JAMES CORNELIUS WALL.

Chile: Mauritskade 51, 2514 HG The Hague; tel. (70) 3123640; fax (70) 3616227; e-mail echilenl@echile.nl; internet www.echile.nl; Ambassador CECILIA MACKENNA ECHAURREN.

China, People's Republic: William Lodewijklaan 10, 2517 JT The Hague; tel. (70) 3065091; fax (70) 3551651; e-mail chinaemb_nl@mfa.gov.cn; internet www.chinaembassy.nl; Ambassador ZHANG JUN.

Colombia: Groot Hertoginnelaan 14, 2517 EG The Hague; tel. (70) 3614545; fax (70) 3614636; e-mail info@colombiaemb.nl; internet www.colmbiaemb.nl; Chargé d'affaires a.i. SONIA MARINA PEREIRA PORTILLA.

Congo, Democratic Republic: Violenweg 2, 2597 KL The Hague; tel. (70) 3547904; fax (70) 3541373; Ambassador JACQUES MASANGU-A-MWANZA.

Costa Rica: Laan Copes van Cattenburch 46, 2585 GB The Hague; tel. (70) 3540780; fax (70) 3584754; e-mail embajada@embacrica.demon.nl; Ambassador FRANCISCO JOSÉ AGUILAR URBINA.

Croatia: Amaliastraat 16, 2514 JC The Hague; tel. (70) 3623638; fax (70) 3623195; e-mail croemb.haag@mvp.hr; internet nl.mfa.hr; Ambassador FRANE KRNIĆ.

Cuba: Scheveningseweg 9, 2517 KS The Hague; tel. (70) 3606061; fax (70) 3647586; e-mail embacuba@cistron.nl; internet www.embacuba.nl; Ambassador OSCAR DE LOS REYES RAMOS.

Cyprus: Surinamestraat 15, 2585 GG The Hague; tel. (70) 3466499; fax (70) 3924024; e-mail cyprus@xs4all.nl; internet www.mfa.gov.cy/embassythehague; Ambassador JAMES DROUSHIOTIS.

Czech Republic: Paleisstraat 4, 2514 JA The Hague; tel. (70) 3130031; fax (70) 3563349; e-mail hague@embassy.mzv.cz; internet www.mfa.cz/hague; Ambassador PETR MAREŠ.

Denmark: Koninginnegracht 30, 2514 AB The Hague; tel. (70) 3025959; fax (70) 3025950; e-mail haaamb@um.dk; internet www.ambhaag.um.dk; Ambassador KIRSTEN BIERING.

Dominican Republic: Raamweg 21–22, 2596 HL The Hague; tel. (70) 3317553; fax (70) 4049890; e-mail embajada@embajadadominicana.nl; Ambassador GUIDO D'ALESSANDRO.

Ecuador: Koninginnegracht 84, 2514 AJ The Hague; tel. (70) 3463763; fax (70) 3658910; e-mail ambassade@ambassadevanecuador.nl; internet www.embajadaecuador.nl; Ambassador Dr RODRIGO GUILLERMO RIOFRÍO MACHUCA.

Egypt: Badhuisweg 92, 2587 CL The Hague; tel. (70) 3542000; fax (70) 3543304; e-mail ambegnl@wanadoo.nl; Ambassador AHMED AMIN FATHALLAH.

El Salvador: Riouwstraat 137, 2585 HP The Hague; tel. (70) 3249855; fax (70) 3247842; Ambassador EDGAR HERNÁN VARELA ALAS.

Eritrea: Nassauplein 13, 2585 EB The Hague; tel. (70) 4276812; fax (70) 4277236; e-mail eritrea@xs4all.nl; Ambassador MOHAMMED SULEIMAN AHMED.

Estonia: Zeestraat 92, 2518 AD The Hague; tel. (70) 3029050; fax (70) 3029051; e-mail embassy.haag@mfa.ee; internet www.estemb.nl; Ambassador GITA KALMET.

Finland: Groot Hertoginnelaan 16, 2517 EG The Hague; tel. (70) 3469754; fax (70) 3107174; e-mail info.haa@formin.fi; internet www.finlande.nl; Ambassador MIKKO JOKELA.

France: Smidsplein 1, 2514 BT The Hague; tel. (70) 3125800; fax (70) 3125824; e-mail info@ambafrance-nl.org; internet www.ambafrance-nl.org; Ambassador JEAN-MICHEL GAUSSOT.

Georgia: Groot Hertoginnelaan 28, 2517 EG The Hague; tel. (70) 3029081; fax (70) 3029080; e-mail thehague.emb@mfa.gov.ge; internet www.netherlands.mfa.gov.ge; Ambassador Dr MAIA PANJIKIDZE.

Germany: Groot Hertoginnelaan 18–20, 2517 EG The Hague; tel. (70) 3420600; fax (70) 3651957; e-mail ambduits@euronet.nl; internet www.den-haag.diplo.de; Ambassador Dr THOMAS LÄUFER.

Ghana: Laan Copes van Cattenburch 70, 2585 GD The Hague; tel. (70) 3384380; fax (70) 3062800; e-mail gaababio@ghanaembassy.nl; internet www.ghanaembassy.nl; Ambassador Dr GRACE AMPONSAH-ABABIO.

Greece: Amaliastraat 1, 2514 JC The Hague; tel. (70) 3638700; fax (70) 3563040; e-mail grembhag@planet.nl; internet www.greekembassy.nl; Ambassador CONSTANTINOS IOANNIS RALLIS.

Guatemala: Javastraat 44, 2585 AP The Hague; tel. (70) 3020253; fax (70) 3602270; e-mail embpaisesbajos@minex.gob.gt; Ambassador CARLA MARÍA RODRÍGUEZ MANCÍA.

Honduras: Burgemeester Patijnlaan 1932, 2585 CB The Hague; tel. (70) 3641684; fax (70) 3649134; e-mail eholan@honduras.demon.nl; Ambassador JULIO ANTONIO RENDÓN BARNICA.

Holy See: Carnegielaan 5 (Apostolic Nunciature), 2517 KH The Hague; tel. (70) 3503363; fax (70) 3521461; e-mail apost.nuntiatuur@inter.nl.net; Apostolic Nuncio Most Rev. FRANÇOIS BACQUÉ (Titular Archbishop of Gradisca).

Hungary: Hogeweg 14, 2585 JD The Hague; tel. (70) 3500404; fax (70) 3521749; e-mail mission.hga@kum.hu; internet www.hungarianembassy.nl; Ambassador IVÁN UDVARDI.

India: Buitenrustweg 2, 2517 KD The Hague; tel. (70) 3469771; fax (70) 3617072; e-mail ambassador@indianembassy.nl; internet www.indianembassy.nl; Ambassador NEELAM D. SABHARWAL.

Indonesia: Tobias Asserlaan 8, 2517 KC The Hague; tel. (70) 3108100; fax (70) 3643331; e-mail bidpen@indonesia.nl; internet www.indonesia.nl; Ambassador JUNUS EFFENDI HABIBIE.

Iran: Duinweg 20–22, 2585 JX The Hague; tel. (70) 3548483; fax (70) 3503224; e-mail info@iranembassy.nl; internet www.iranianembassy.nl; Ambassador BOZORGMEHR ZIARAN.

Iraq: Johan de Wittlaan 16, 2517 JR The Hague; tel. (70) 3101260; fax (70) 3924958; e-mail info@embassyofiraq.nl; internet www.embassyofiraq.nl; Ambassador SIAMAND BANAA.

Ireland: Dr Kuyperstraat 9, 2514 BA The Hague; tel. (70) 3630993; fax (70) 3617604; e-mail thehagueembassy@dfa.ie; internet www.irishembassy.nl; Ambassador RICHARD RYAN.

Israel: Buitenhof 47, 2513 AH The Hague; tel. (70) 3760500; fax (70) 3760555; e-mail info@hague.mfa.gov.il; internet thehague.mfa.gov.il; Ambassador HARRY KNEY-TAL.

Italy: Alexanderstraat 12, 2514 JL The Hague; tel. (70) 3021030; fax (70) 3614932; e-mail ambitaly.denhaag@esteri.it; internet www.amblaja.esteri.it; Ambassador GAETANO CORTESE.

Japan: Tobias Asserlaan 2, 2517 KC The Hague; tel. (70) 3469544; fax (70) 3106341; e-mail japan.cultural@planet.nl; internet www.nl.emb-japan.go.jp; Ambassador MINORU SHIBUYA.

Jordan: Badhuisweg 79, 2587 CD The Hague; tel. (70) 4167200; fax (70) 4167209; e-mail info@jordanembassy.nl; internet www.jordanembassy.nl; Ambassador AHMAD S. AL-HASSAN.

Kazakhstan: Nieuwe Parklaan 69, 2597 LB The Hague; tel. (70) 3634757; fax (70) 3657600; e-mail info@kazakhembassy.nl; internet www.kazakhembassy.nl; Ambassador MAINURA S. MURZAMADIYEVA.

Kenya: Nieuwe Parklaan 21, 2597 LA The Hague; tel. (70) 3504215; fax (70) 3553594; e-mail info@kenya-embassy.nl; Ambassador Prof. RUTHIE CHEPKOECH RONO.

Korea, Republic: Verlengde Tolweg 8, 2517 JV The Hague; tel. (70) 3586076; fax (70) 3504712; e-mail koremb@euronet.nl; internet www.mofat.go.kr/netherlands; Ambassador JONG-MOO CHOI.

Kuwait: Carnegielaan 9, 2517 KH The Hague; tel. (70) 3123400; fax (70) 3924858; e-mail info@kuwaitembassy.nl; Ambassador YOUSEF ABDULLAH AHMAD AL-ONAIZI AL-QENAEI.

Latvia: Balistraat 88, 2585 XX The Hague; tel. (70) 3063934; fax (70) 3062858; e-mail embassy.netherlands@mfa.gov.lv; Ambassador BAIBA BRAŽE.

Lebanon: Frederikstraat 2, 2514 LK The Hague; tel. (70) 3658906; fax (70) 3620779; e-mail amb.lib@wanadoo.nl; Ambassador ZEIDAN AS-SAGHIR.

Libya: 15 Parkweg, 2585 JH The Hague; tel. (70) 355886; fax (70) 3559075; e-mail libyanembassy@wanadoo.nl; Sec. of the People's Bureau ZAKIA ABDUSSALAM M. SAHLI.

Lithuania: Laan van Meerdervoort 20, 2517 AK The Hague; tel. (70) 3855418; fax (70) 3853940; e-mail amb.nl@urm.lt; internet nl.mfa.lt; Ambassador VAIDOTAS VERBA.

Luxembourg: Nassaulaan 8, 2514 JS The Hague; tel. (70) 3647589; fax (70) 3462000; e-mail lahaye.amb@mae.etat.lu; Ambassador JEAN GRAFF.

Macedonia, former Yugoslav republic: Laan van Meerdervoort 50C, 2517 AM The Hague; tel. (70) 4274464; fax (70) 4274469; e-mail repmak@wanadoo.nl; Ambassador Dr DOBRINKA TASKOVSKA.

Malaysia: Rustenburgweg 2, 2517 KE The Hague; tel. (70) 3506506; fax (70) 3506536; e-mail malaysia@euronet.nl; internet www.kln.gov.my/perwakilan/thehague; Chargé d'affaires a.i. MOHAMAD RAZDAN BIN JAMIL.

Malta: Carnegielaan 4–14, 2517 KH The Hague; tel. (70) 3561252; fax (70) 3648789; e-mail maltaembassy.thehague@gov.mt; Ambassador Dr IVAN FSADNI.

Mexico: Nassauplein 28, 2585 EC The Hague; tel. (70) 3602900; fax (70) 3560543; e-mail embamex@embamex-nl.com; internet www.embamex-nl.com; Ambassador JORGE LOMÓNACO TONDA.

Morocco: Oranjestraat 9, 2514 JB The Hague; tel. (70) 3469617; fax (70) 3562829; e-mail ambamar.lahaye@wanadoo.nl; Ambassador ALI AL-MHAMDI.

New Zealand: Eisenhowerlaan 77N, 2517 KK The Hague; tel. (70) 3469324; fax (70) 3632983; e-mail nzemb@xs4all.nl; internet www.nzembassy.com/netherlands; Ambassador RACHEL FRY.

Nicaragua: Statenlaan 81, 2582 GE, The Hague; tel. (70) 3225063; fax (70) 3508331; e-mail embajador@embanic.nl; Ambassador CARLOS ARGÜELLO GÓMEZ.

Nigeria: Wagenaarweg 5, 2597 LL The Hague; tel. (70) 3501703; fax (70) 3551110; e-mail nigembassy@nigerianembassy.nl; internet www.nigerianembassy.nl; Chargé d'affaires a.i. NICHOLAS OLUSHEYE DAVIES.

Norway: Lange Vijverberg 11, 2513 AC The Hague; tel. (70) 3117611; fax (70) 3659630; e-mail emb.hague@mfa.no; internet www.noorwegen.nl; Ambassador EVA BUGGE.

Oman: Nieuwe Parklaan 9, LA The Hague; tel. (70) 3615800; fax (70) 3605364; e-mail info@embassyofoman.nl; Ambassador KHADIJA HASSAN SALMAN AL-LAWATI.

Pakistan: Amaliastraat 8, 2514 JC The Hague; tel. (70) 3648948; fax (70) 3106047; e-mail info@embassyofpakistan.com; internet www.embassyofpakistan.com; Ambassador SIBTE YAHYA NAQVI.

Peru: Nassauplein 4, 2585 EA The Hague; tel. (70) 3653500; fax (70) 3651929; e-mail info@embassyofperu.nl; Chargé d'affaires a.i. PEDRO ROBERTO REATEGUI GAMARRA.

Philippines: Laan Copes van Cattenburch 125, 2585 EZ The Hague; tel. (70) 3604820; fax (70) 3560030; e-mail ph@bart.nl; internet www.philembassy.nl; Ambassador ROMEO A. ARGUELLES.

Poland: Alexanderstraat 25, 2514 JM The Hague; tel. (70) 7990100; fax (70) 7990137; e-mail ambhaga@polamb.nl; internet www.haga.polamb.net; Ambassador Dr JANUSZ STAŃCZYK.

Portugal: Bazarstraat 21, 2518 AG The Hague; tel. (70) 3630217; fax (70) 3615589; e-mail info@portembassy.nl; Ambassador JÚLIO FRANCISCO DE SALES MASCARENHAS.

Qatar: Borweg 7, 2597 LR The Hague; tel. (70) 4166666; fax (70) 4166660; e-mail info@embassyofqatar.nl; internet www.embassyofqatar.nl; Ambassador SALEH ABDULLAH AL-BOUANIN.

Romania: Catsheuvel 55, 2517 KA The Hague; tel. (70) 3543796; fax (70) 3541587; e-mail sicrned@tip.nl; internet haga.mae.ro; Ambassador CĂLIN FABIAN.

Russia: Andries Bickerweg 2, 2517 JP The Hague; tel. (70) 3451300; fax (70) 3617960; e-mail ambrusnl@euronet.nl; internet www.netherlands.mid.ru; Ambassador KIRILL G. GEVORGIYAN.

Saudi Arabia: Alexanderstraat 19, 2514 JM The Hague; tel. (70) 3614391; fax (70) 4276183; e-mail saudiembassy@casema.nl; Ambassador WALID A. AL-KHEREIJI.

Serbia: Groot Hertoginnelaan 30, 2517 EG The Hague; tel. (70) 3632397; fax (70) 3602421; e-mail yuambanl@bart.nl; internet users.bart.nl/~yuambanl; Ambassador RADOSLAV STOJANOVIĆ.

Slovakia: Parkweg 1, 2585 JG The Hague; tel. (70) 4167777; fax (70) 4167783; e-mail embassy@haag.mfa.sk; internet www.haag.mfa.sk; Ambassador OKSANA TOMOVÁ.

Slovenia: Anna Paulownastraat 11, 2518 BA The Hague; tel. (70) 3108690; fax (70) 36266008; e-mail vhg@mzz-dkp.gov.si; internet hague.embassy.si; Ambassador Dr TEA PETRIN.

South Africa: Wassenaarseweg 40, 2596 CJ The Hague; tel. (70) 3924501; fax (70) 3460669; e-mail info@zuidafrika.nl; internet www.zuidafrika.nl; Ambassador HLENGIWE BUHLE MKHIZE.

Spain: Lange Voorhout 50, 2514 EG The Hague; tel. (70) 3024999; fax (70) 3617959; e-mail ambassade.spanje@worldonline.nl; internet www.mae.es/embajadas/lahaya; Ambassador JUAN PRAT Y COLL.

Sri Lanka: Jacob de Graefflaan 2, 2517 JM The Hague; tel. (70) 3655910; fax (70) 3465596; e-mail mission@infolanka.nl; Ambassador PAMELA JAYASEKERA DEEN.

Sudan: Laan Copes van Cattenburch 81, 2585 EW The Hague; tel. (70) 3620939; fax (70) 3617975; e-mail sudan@tiscali.nl; Ambassador ABUELGASIM ABDELWAHID SHEIKH IDRIS.

Suriname: Alexander Gogelweg 2, 2517 JH The Hague; tel. (70) 3650844; fax (70) 3617445; e-mail ambassade.suriname@wxs.nl; Ambassador URMILA JOELLA.

Sweden: Jan Willem Frisolaan 3, 2517, JS The Hague; tel. (70) 4120200; fax (70) 4120211; e-mail ambassaden.haag@foreign.ministry.se; internet www.swedenabroad.com/thehague; Ambassador HANS OSCAR MAGNUSSON.

Switzerland: Lange Voorhout 42, 2514 EE The Hague; tel. (70) 3642831; fax (70) 3561238; e-mail hay.vertretung@eda.admin.ch; internet www.eda.admin.ch/denhaag; Ambassador DOMINIK MATTHIAS ALDER.

Thailand: Laan Copes van Cattenburch 123, 2585 EZ The Hague; tel. (70) 3450766; fax (70) 3451929; e-mail thaihag@thaihag.demon.nl; internet www.thaiembassy.org/hague; Ambassador SUCHITRA HIRANPRUECK.

Tunisia: Gentsestraat 98, 2587 HX The Hague; tel. (70) 3512251; fax (70) 3514323; e-mail ambassadetunisie@wanadoo.nl; Ambassador MUHAMMAD SALAH TEKAYA.

Turkey: Jan Evertstraat 15, 2514 BS The Hague; tel. (70) 3604912; fax (70) 3617969; e-mail turkishembassy@euronet.nl; Ambassador SELAHATTIN ALPAR.

Ukraine: Zeestraat 78, 2518 AD The Hague; tel. (70) 3626095; fax (70) 3615565; e-mail embukr@wxs.nl; internet www.oekraine.com; Ambassador (vacant).

United Arab Emirates: Eisenhowerlaan 130, 2517 KN The Hague; tel. (70) 3384370; fax (70) 3384373; e-mail info@uae-embassy.nl; internet www.uae-embassy.nl; Ambassador ALI THANI AS-SUWAIDI.

United Kingdom: Lange Voorhout 10, 2514 ED The Hague; tel. (70) 4270427; fax (70) 4270345; internet www.britain.nl; Ambassador LYN PARKER.

USA: Lange Voorhout 102, 2514 EJ The Hague; tel. (70) 3102209; fax (70) 3102307; e-mail ircthehague@state.gov; internet thehague.usembassy.gov; Chargé d'affaires a.i. MICHAEL GALLAGHER.

Uruguay: Mauritskade 33, 2514 HD The Hague; tel. (70) 3609815; fax (70) 3562826; e-mail uruholan@wxs.nl; Ambassador Dr CARLOS ANTONIO MORA MEDERO.

Venezuela: Nassaulaan 2, 2514 JS The Hague; tel. (70) 3651256; fax (70) 3656954; e-mail embvene@xs4all.nl; internet www.embven.nl; Ambassador AUGUSTÍN PÉREZ CELIS.

Viet Nam: Nassauplein 12, 2585 EB The Hague; tel. (70) 3648917; fax (70) 3648656; e-mail emviet@wanadoo.nl; Ambassador HÀ HUY THÔNG.

Yemen: Nassaulaan 2A, 2514 JS The Hague; tel. (70) 3653936; fax (70) 3563312; e-mail yemenembassy@planet.nl; internet www.yemenembassy.nl; Ambassador NAGUIB AHMED OBEID OBEID.

Judicial System

Justices and judges must have graduated in law at a Dutch university, and are nominated for life by the Crown. The justices of the Supreme Court are nominated from a list of three compiled by the Second Chamber of the States-General.

SUPREME COURT

De Hoge Raad der Nederlanden

Kazernestraat 52, POB 20303, 2500 EH The Hague; tel. (70) 3611311; fax (70) 3658700; internet www.rechtspraak.nl/Gerechten/HogeRaad.

For appeals in cassation against decisions of courts of lower jurisdiction. As a court of first instance, the Supreme Court tries offences committed in their official capacity by members of the States-General and Ministers. Dealing with appeals in cassation a court is composed of five or, in more straightforward cases, of three justices (Raadsheren).

President of the Supreme Court: W. J. M. DAVIDS.
Procurator-General: J. W. FOKKENS.
Secretary of the Court: E. HARTOGS.

COURTS OF APPEAL

Gerechtshoven: Five courts: Amsterdam, Arnhem, 's-Hertogenbosch, Leeuwarden, The Hague. A court is composed of three judges (Raadsheren); appeal is from decisions of the District Courts of Justice. Fiscal Divisions (Belastingkamers) of the Courts of Appeal deal with appeals against decisions relating to the enforcement of the fiscal laws (administrative jurisdiction). The court of Arnhem has a Tenancy Division (Pachtkamer), composed of three judges and two assessors (a tenant and a landlord), and a Penitentiary Division (Penitentiaire Kamer), composed of three judges and two experts. The Tenancy Division hears appeals from decisions of all Canton Tenancy Divisions. The Penitentiary Division hears appeals against refusals of release on license, which is usually granted after two-thirds of a prison sentence longer than one year, unless there are special objections from the Minister of Justice. A Companies Division

THE NETHERLANDS

(Ondernemingskamer) is attached to the court at Amsterdam, consisting of three judges and two experts as assessors

DISTRICT COURTS OF JUSTICE

Arrondissementsrechtbanken: There are 19 courts for important civil and penal cases and for appeals from decisions of the Canton Judges. A court is composed of three judges (Rechter); no jury; summary jurisdiction in civil cases by the President of the Court; simple penal cases, including economic offences, generally by a single judge (Politierechter). Offences committed by juveniles are (with certain exceptions) tried by a specialized judge (Kinderrechter), who is also competent to take certain legal steps when the upbringing of a juvenile is endangered. Economic offences, and in particular environmental offences, are also dealt with by a specialized judge sitting alone.

CANTON COURTS

Kantongerechten: There are 62 courts for civil and penal cases of minor importance. A court consists of a single judge, the Canton Judge (Kantonrechter). Each Canton Court has a Tenancy Division (Pachtkamer), presided over by the Canton Judge who is assisted by two assessors (a landlord and a tenant).

ADMINISTRATIVE COURTS

The administrative courts regulate relations between the authorities and citizens according to the provisions of the General Administrative Law Act. The majority of cases are heard by the Administrative Law Sections of the District Courts, while appeals are heard by the Administrative Law Division of the Council of State (Afdeling Bestuursrechtspraak van de Raad van State), which also acts as the court of sole and last instance in the majority of cases concerning education, the environment and spatial planning. In addition, cases relating to certain areas of administrative law are heard by the following bodies:

Centrale Raad van Beroep (Central Appeals Council): Graadt van Roggenweg 200–250, POB 16002, 3500 DA Utrecht; tel. (30) 8502100; fax (30) 8502198; e-mail crvb@rechtspraak.nl; internet www.rechtspraak.nl/gerechten/crvb; hears appeals against decisions of the District Courts in matters concerning the public service and social security; Pres. T. G. M. SIMONS.

College van Beroep voor het Bedrijfsleven (Trade and Industry Appeals Tribunal): Prins Clauslaan 60, POB 20021, 2500 EA The Hague; tel. (70) 3813910; fax (70) 3813999; internet www.rechtspraak.nl/gerechten/cbb; hears in first and last instance appeals against decisions enforcing socio-economic and agricultural legislation made by certain bodies, such as regulatory bodies and Chambers of Commerce, and by certain ministers; Pres. R. R. WINTER.

Administration Law Section, Aliens Division, District Court of The Hague: court of sole and last instance in cases involving immigration; brs in Zwolle, 's-Hertogenbosch, Amsterdam and Haarlem. The introduction of a limited right of further appeal is pending.

Tariefcommissie (Tariff Commission): court of sole and last instance for all customs and excise disputes.

Religion

CHRISTIANITY

Raad van Kerken in Nederland (Council of Churches in the Netherlands): Koningin Wilhelminalaan 5, 3818 HN Amersfoort; tel. (33) 4633844; e-mail rvk@raadvankerken.nl; internet www.raadvankerken.nl; f. 1968; 12 mem. churches; Pres. Prof. Dr A. H. C. VAN EIJK; Gen. Sec. Drs H. J. BAKKER.

The Roman Catholic Church

The Netherlands comprises one archdiocese and six dioceses. At 31 December 2005 there were an estimated 4,875,252 adherents in the country (32.0% of the population).

Bishops' Conference

Nederlandse Bisschoppenconferentie, Biltstraat 121, POB 13049, 3507 LA Utrecht; tel. (30) 2334244; fax (30) 2332103; e-mail secrbk@rkk.nl; internet www.katholieknederland.nl/rkkerk.
f. 1986; Pres. (vacant).

Archbishop of Utrecht: Most Rev. WILLEM JACOBUS (WIM) EIJK, Aartsbisdom, Maliebaan 40, POB 14019, 3508 SB Utrecht; tel. (30) 2338030; fax (30) 2311962; e-mail secretariaat@aartsbisdom.nl; internet www.de-oase.nl.

Protestant Churches

Christelijke Gereformeerde Kerken in Nederland (Christian Reformed Churches in the Netherlands): Vijftien Morgen, POB 334, 3900 AH Veenendaal; tel. (318) 582350; e-mail lkb@cgk.nl; internet www.cgk.nl; f. 1834; Relations Dir Rev. J. G. H. VAN DER VINNE; c. 73,400 mems; 180 churches.

First Church of Christ, Scientist: Andries Bickerweg 1B, 2517 JP The Hague; tel. (70) 3636652; e-mail peter.faas@hccnet.nl; churches at Amsterdam, Haarlem and The Hague.

Deutsche Evangelische Gemeinde (German Evangelical Church): Bleijenburg 3B, 2511 VC, The Hague; tel. (70) 3465727; e-mail deg.haag@tiscali.nl; internet www.evangelischekirche-denhaag.nl; Leaders Pastor E. BENZ-WENZLAFF, Pastor B. WENZLAFF.

Dutch Mennonites: Algemene Doopsgezinde Sociëteit, Singel 454, 1017 AW Amsterdam; tel. (20) 6230914; fax (20) 6278919; e-mail dn@ads.nl; internet www.doopsgezind.nl; f. 1811; Pres. OTTO BLEKER; Sec.-Gen. H. W. STENVERS; 9,000 mems; 118 parishes.

Evangelische Broedergemeente (Hernhutters): Zusterpl. 20, 3703 CB Zeist; tel. (30) 6424833; fax (30) 6919639; e-mail provinciaalbestuur@ebg.nl; internet www.ebg.nl; f. 1746; Pres. RITA HARRY; 3,000 mems in Holland; six parishes.

Hersteld Apostolische Zendingkerk (Restored Apostolic Missionary Church): Hogerbeetsstraat 32, 2242 TR Wassenaar; tel. and fax (70) 5113995; e-mail s.de.jong.hazk@hazknederland.org; internet www.hazknederland.org; f. 1863; Pres. Apostle for the Netherlands H. F. RIJNDERS; Sec. J. L. M. STRAETEMANS; 500 mems; 10 parishes.

Protestante Kerk in Nederland (Protestant Church in the Netherlands): Joseph Haydnlaan 2A, POB 8504, 3503 RM Utrecht; tel. (30) 8801880; fax (30) 8801300; e-mail info@pkn.nl; internet www.pkn.nl; f. 2004; unification of the Nederlandse Hervormde Kerk with the Gereformeerde Kerken in Nederland and the Evangelisch-Lutherse Kerk; 2.5m. mems, 3,000 parishes in 77 districts; Pres. Rev. G. DE FIJTER; Sec.-Gen. Rev. Dr B. PLAISIER; 1.9m. mems.

Remonstrantse Broederschap (Remonstrant Brotherhood): Nieuwe Gracht 27A, 3512 LC Utrecht; tel. (30) 2316970; fax (30) 2311055; e-mail info@remonstranten.org; internet www.remonstranten.org; f. 1619; Pres. J. W. VAN DER KAMP; Gen. Sec. M. A. BOSMAN-HUIZINGA; 10,000 mems; 46 parishes.

Unie van Baptistengemeenten in Nederland (Union of Baptist Churches in The Netherlands): Biltseweg 10, 3735 MC Bosch en Duin; tel. (30) 2255660; fax (30) 2251798; e-mail administratie@baptisten.nl; internet www.baptisten.nl; f. 1881; Pres. J. HOFMAN; 11,500 mems.

Other Christian Churches

Anglikaans Kerkgenootschap (Anglican Church): Ary van der Spuyweg 1, 2585 HA The Hague; tel. (70) 3555359; e-mail churchoffice@stjohn-stphilip.org; internet www.stjohn-stphilip.org; f. 1698; Chaplain Rev. TONY ROAKE.

Katholiek Apostolische Gemeenten (Catholic Apostolic Church): 1E De Riemerstraat 3, 2513 CT The Hague; tel. (70) 3555018; f. 1867; seven parishes in the Netherlands and three in Belgium.

Oud-Katholieke Kerk van Nederland (Old Catholic Church): Koningin Wilhelminalaan 3, 3818 HN Amersfoort; tel. (33) 4620875; e-mail info@okkn.nl; internet www.okkn.nl; f. 1723 in the Netherlands with Jansenist influence; refuses to accept papal infallibility and other 'new' dogmas of the Roman Catholic Church; full communion with the Anglican Churches since 1931; Leader Archbishop of Utrecht Mgr JORIS A. O. L. VERCAMMEN (18 parishes), Bishop of Haarlem Mgr JAN LAMBERT WIRIX-SPEETJENS (10 parishes); 10,000 mems; also churches in the rest of Europe.

Vrij-Katholieke Kerk (Liberal Catholic Church): Diedenweg 29, 6703 GS Wageningen; tel. (31) 7413679; e-mail frank.den.outer@freeler.nl; internet www.vkk.nl; f. 1916; Regionary Bishop Rt Rev. FRANK R. DEN OUTER; Auxiliary Bishop Rt Rev. PETER BAAIJ; 10 congregations; 2 bishops; 25 priests; 1,000 mems.

ISLAM

At 1 January 2004 there were around 944,000 Muslims in the Netherlands, representing some 5.8% of the total population.

Contactorgaan Moslims en Overheid (CMO) (Contact Group for Muslims and the Government): POB 85518, 2506 CE The Hague; tel. (70) 3028224; internet www.islamenburgerschaap.nl; f. 2004; promotes dialogue between Muslim community and the Government; includes eight Muslim groups.

JUDAISM

Portugees-Israëlietische Gemeente (Portuguese-Israelite Community): Mr. Visserplein 3, 1011 RD Amsterdam; tel. (20) 6245351;

fax (20) 6254680; e-mail info@esnoga.com; internet www.esnoga.com; Gen. Sec. NATHAN MOKED.

BAHÁ'Í FAITH

National Spiritual Assembly (Bahá'í Community of the Netherlands): Riouwstraat 27, 2585 GR The Hague; tel. (70) 3554017; fax (70) 3506161; e-mail nsa@bahai.nl; internet www.bahai.nl; f. 1962; mems resident in 179 locations (2008).

The Press

PRINCIPAL DAILIES

Alkmaar

Noordhollands Dagblad: Edisonweg 10, POB 2, 1800 AA Alkmaar; tel. (72) 5196196; fax (72) 5124152; e-mail redactie@nhd.hdc.nl; internet www.nhd.nl; morning; eight regional editions; Editors GEERT TEN DAM, JAN-GEERT MAJOOR; circ. 147,064 (2006).

Amersfoort

AD Amersfoortse Courant: POB 1262, 3800 BG Amersfoortse; tel. (33) 4647911; fax (33) 4647334; e-mail ac.redactie@ad.nl; internet www.amersfoortsecourant.nl; f. 1887; publ. by AD NieuwsMedia; evening; Editor-in-Chief ARJEH KALMANN.

Amsterdam

Het Financieele Dagblad (Financial Daily): Weesperstraat 85–87, POB 216, 1000 AE Amsterdam; tel. (20) 5928888; fax (20) 5928700; e-mail redsec@fd.nl; internet www.fd.nl; f. 1796; morning; Editor ULKO JONKER; circ. 58,350 (2006).

Metro: Metro Holland BV, Delflandlaan 4, POB 90009, 1006 BA Amsterdam; tel. (20) 5114000; fax (20) 5114090; e-mail info@metronieuws.nl; internet www.metronieuws.nl; f. 2004 in Rotterdam; separate Amsterdam edition since 2005; morning; owned by Metro International SA (Sweden); Editor ROBERT VAN BRANDWIJK (from 1 July 2008); circ. 465,224 (2006).

Het Parool: Jacob Bontiusplaats 9, POB 433, 1000 AK Amsterdam; tel. (20) 5584444; fax (20) 5584351; e-mail redactie@parool.nl; internet www.parool.nl; f. 1940; evening; Editor BARBARA VAN BEUKERING; circ. 86,656 (2006).

Sp!ts: POB 2620, 1000 CP Amsterdam; tel. (20) 5853045; fax (20) 5853065; e-mail redactie@spitsnieuws.nl; internet www.spitsnieuws.nl; f. 1998; morning; distributed free of charge; publ. by BasisMedia BV; Editor T. WOLTERS; circ. 401,553 (2006).

De Telegraaf: POB 376, 1000 EB Amsterdam; tel. (20) 5859111; fax (20) 5858017; e-mail redactie@telegraaf.nl; internet www.telegraaf.nl; f. 1893; morning; Editor EEF BOS; circ. 714,563 (2006).

Trouw (Loyalty): Jacob Bontiusplaats 9, POB 859, 1000 AW Amsterdam; tel. (20) 5629444; e-mail redactie@trouw.nl; internet www.trouw.nl; f. 1943; morning; Editor WILLEM SCHOONEN; circ. 108,435 (2006).

De Volkskrant (The People's Journal): Jacob Bontiusplaats 9, POB 1002, 1000 BA Amsterdam; tel. (20) 5626222; fax (20) 5626289; e-mail redactie@volkskrant.nl; internet www.volkskrant.nl; f. 1919; morning; Editor PIETER I. BROERTJES; circ. 284,801 (2006).

Apeldoorn

Reformatorisch Dagblad: Laan van Westenenk 12, POB 670, 7300 AR Apeldoorn; tel. (55) 5390222; fax (55) 5412288; e-mail redactie@refdag.nl; internet www.refdag.nl; f. 1971; evening; publ. by Erdee Media Groep; Editor-in-Chief WIM B. KRANENDONK; circ. 57,427 (2006).

De Stentor: Laan van Westenenk 6, POB 99, 7336 AZ Apeldoorn; tel. (55) 5388388; fax (55) 5388200; e-mail redactiesecretariaat@destentor.wegener.nl; internet www.destentor.nl/apeldoorn; f. 2003; evening; publishes nine regional versions; Editor ALEX ENGBERS; circ. 140,757 (2006).

Barneveld

Nederlands Dagblad: Hermesweg 20, POB 111, 3770 AC Barneveld; tel. (342) 411711; fax (342) 411611; e-mail redactie@nd.nl; internet www.nd.nl; f. 1944; morning; Editor-in-Chief P. A. BERGWERFF; circ. 33,200 (2006).

Breda

BN/De Stem (The Voice): Spinveld 55, POB 3229, 4800 MB Breda; tel. (76) 5312311; fax (76) 5312355; e-mail l.krijneni@uitg-zwn.nl; internet www.bndestem.nl; f. 1998 by merger of Brabants Nieuwsblad and De Stem; owned by Koninklijke Wegener NV; morning; Editor JOHAN VAN UFFELEN; circ. 124,213 (2006).

Dordrecht

AD De Dordtenaar: POB 54, 3300 AB Dordrecht; tel. (78) 6324705; fax (78) 6324729; e-mail dd.redactie@ad.nl; internet www.ad.nl; f. 1946; morning; Editor BART VERKADE.

Eindhoven

Eindhovens Dagblad (ED): Wal 2, POB 534, 5600 AM Eindhoven; tel. (40) 2336336; fax (40) 2436244; e-mail redactie@eindhovensdagblad.nl; internet www.ed.nl; owned by Wegener; Editor HENK VAN WEERT; circ. 116,901 (2006).

Enschede

De Twentsche Courant Tubantia: Getfertsingel 41, POB 28, 7500 AA Enschede; tel. (53) 4842842; fax (53) 4842200; e-mail lezers@tubantia.wegener.nl; internet www.tctubantia.nl; f. 1844; publ. by Koninklijke Wegener NV; Editor ANDRÉ VIS; circ. 124,070 (2006).

's-Gravenhage/Den Haag
(The Hague)

AD Haagsche Courant: POB 16050, 2500 AA The Hague; tel. (70) 3190911; fax (70) 3954783; e-mail hc.lezers@ad.nl; internet www.ad.nl; evening; Editor DENNIS MULKENS.

Nederlandse Staatscourant: Prinses Margrietplantsoen 88, POB 20020, 2500 EA The Hague; tel. (70) 3789639; fax (70) 3855505; e-mail staatscourant@sdu.nl; internet www.staatscourant.nl; f. 1814; morning; Editor W. M. C. DE JONG; circ. 5,913 (2006).

Groningen

Dagblad van het Noorden: Lübeckweg 2, POB 60, 9700 MC Groningen; tel. (50) 5844444; fax (50) 5844209; e-mail redactie@dvhn.nl; internet www.dvhn.nl; f. 1888; morning; Editor PIETER SIJPERSMA; circ. 156,247 (2006).

Haarlem

Haarlems Dagblad: Stationsplein 86, POB 507, 2003 PA Haarlem; tel. (88) 8241200; fax (88) 8241212; e-mail stadsredactie@haarlemsdagblad.nl; internet www.haarlemsdagblad.nl; f. 1656; evening; Editors GEERT TEN DAM, JAN GEERT MAJOOR; circ. 44,123 (2006).

IJmuider Courant: Marktplein 1, 1972 GA IJmuiden; tel. (255) 561800; fax (255) 561888; e-mail redactie@ijmuidercourant.nl; internet www.ijmuidercourant.nl; evening; Editors GEERT TEN DAM, JAN GEERT MAJOOR.

's-Hertogenbosch/Den Bosch

Brabants Dagblad: Emmaplein 25, POB 235, 5201 HB 's-Hertogenbosch; tel. (73) 6157157; fax (73) 6157105; e-mail redactiesecretariaat@brabantsdagblad.nl; internet www.brabantsdagblad.nl; f. 1771; morning; publ. by Koninklijke Wegener NV; Editor ANNEMIEKE BESSELING; circ. 136,068 (2006).

Hilversum

De Gooi- en Eemlander: Seinstraat 14, 1223 DA Hilversum; tel. (35) 6477000; fax (35) 6477108; e-mail redactie@gooieneemlander.nl; internet www.gooieneemlander.nl; f. 1871; evening; Editors GEERT TEN DAM, JAN-GEERT MAJOOR; circ. 29,752 (2006).

Leeuwarden

Leeuwarder Courant: Sixmastraat 15, POB 394, 8901 BD Leeuwarden; tel. (58) 2845655; fax (58) 2845419; e-mail redactie@leeuwardercourant.nl; internet www.leeuwardercourant.nl; f. 1752; evening; Editor RIMMER MULDER; circ. 103,489 (2006).

Leiden

Leidsch Dagblad: 3e Binnenvestgracht 23, POB 54, 2300 AB Leiden; tel. (71) 5356356; fax (71) 5356415; e-mail stadsredactie@leidschdagblad.nl; internet www.leidschdagblad.nl; f. 1860; publ. by HDC Media; evening; Editors GEERT TEN DAM, JAN-GEERT MAJOOR; circ. 34,781 (2006).

Nijmegen

De Gelderlander: Voorstadslaan 2, POB 36, 6500 DA Nijmegen; tel. (24) 3650611; fax (24) 3650479; e-mail redactie@gelderlander.nl; internet www.gelderlander.nl; f. 1848; owned by Koninklijke Wegener NV; morning; Editor K. PIJNAPPELS; circ. 163,780 (2006).

Rotterdam

AD: Marten Meesweg 35, POB 8983, 3009 TC Rotterdam; tel. (10) 4067211; e-mail ad@ad.nl; internet www.ad.nl; f. 1946; fmrly

THE NETHERLANDS

Algemeen Dagblad; morning; Editor JAN BONJER; circ. 524,974 (2006, incl. regional editions).

AD Rotterdams Dagblad: Westblaak 180, POB 2999, 3000 CZ Rotterdam; tel. (10) 4004400; fax (10) 4128509; e-mail rd.redactie@ad.nl; internet www.ad.nl; f. 1991; evening; Editor BART VERKADE.

NRC Handelsblad: Marten Meesweg 35, POB 8987, 3009 TH Rotterdam; tel. (10) 4066111; fax (10) 4066967; e-mail nrc@nrc.nl; internet www.nrc.nl; f. 1970; evening; Editor BIRGIT DONKER; circ. 239,211 (2006).

Sittard

Dagblad De Limburger: POB 1056, 6201 MK Maastricht; tel. (43) 3502000; fax (43) 3501879; e-mail nieuwsdienst@ld.mgl.nl; internet www.limburger.nl; f. 1845; morning; Editor FONS VELDERSEN; circ. 180,000.

Limburgs Dagblad: Mercator 3, 6135 KW Sittard; tel. (46) 4116000; fax (46) 4116471; e-mail marketing@mgl.nl; internet www.limburger.nl; f. 1918; morning; Editor JOS ADRIAENS; circ. 53,904 (2006).

Utrecht

AD Utrechts Nieuwsblad: Essenkade 2, POB 500, 3990 DM Houten; tel. (30) 6399911; fax (30) 6399937; e-mail un.lezers@ad.nl; internet www.ad.nl; f. 1993; evening; Editor-in-Chief ARJEH KALMANN.

Vlissingen

Provinciale Zeeuwse Courant: POB 31, 4460 AA Goes; tel. (113) 315600; fax (113) 315669; e-mail redactie@pzc.nl; internet www.pzc.nl; f. 1758; morning; Editor PETER JANSEN; circ. 56,868 (2006).

SELECTED WEEKLIES

Adformatie: POB 75462, 1070 AL Amsterdam; tel. (20) 5733644; fax (20) 6793581; e-mail redactie@adformatie.nl; internet www.adformatie.nl; advertising, marketing and media; Editor-in-Chief LÉON BOUWMAN; circ. 40,000.

Avrobode: 's-Gravelandseweg 52, 1217 ET Hilversum; tel. (35) 6717911; fax (35) 717443; internet www.avrobode.nl; publ. by Algemene Omroepvereniging; radio and TV guide; circ. 791,986.

Boerderij: Hanzestraat 1, POB 4, 7000 BA Doetinchem; tel. (314) 349446; fax (314) 344397; e-mail boerderij@reedbusiness.nl; internet www.boerderij.nl; f. 1915; farming; Editor-in-Chief MARCEL HENST; circ. 65,000.

Donald Duck: Haaksbergsweg 75, 1101 BR Amsterdam; tel. (20) 4300300; fax (20) 4300315; internet www.donaldduck.nl; f. 1952; children's interest; weekly; Publr SUZAN SCHOUTEN HAAGMANS; Editor JESSICA HAAGMANS; circ. 62,784.

Elsevier: POB 152, 1000 AD Amsterdam; tel. (20) 5159944; fax (20) 5159900; e-mail redactie.elsevier@elsevier.nl; internet www.elsevier.nl; f. 1945; current affairs; Chief Editor ARENDO JOUSTRA; circ. 160,000.

Fancy: POB 1610, 2130 JA Hoofddorp; tel. (23) 5565117; fax (23) 5565116; e-mail fancy@sanoma-uitgevers.nl; internet www.fancy.nl; teenage girls' interest; Editor ANNET NITERINK; circ. 120,000.

HP/De Tijd (The Times): Amsterdam; tel. (20) 5734811; fax (20) 5734406; f. 1845 as daily; changed to weekly in 1974; Christian progressive; current affairs; Dir A. VISSER; circ. 37,580.

Libelle: POB 1742, 2130 JC Hoofddorp; tel. (23) 5564002; fax (23) 5564003; e-mail libelle@libelle.nl; internet www.libelle.nl; f. 1934; women's interest; Editor-in-Chief FRANSKA STUY; circ. 587,754.

Margriet: POB 1640, 2130 JA Hoofddorp; tel. (23) 5564200; e-mail redactie@margriet.nl; internet www.margriet.nl; f. 1939; women's interest; Editor ELSA HINTZPETER; circ. 499,868.

Mikro-Gids: Zeverijnstraat 6, 1216 GK Hilversum; tel. (35) 6726751; fax (35) 6726752; internet www.mikrogids.nl; f. 1974; radio and TV guide; Dir H. SCHEENSTRA; circ. 468,280.

NCRV-Gids: POB 25900, 1202 HW Hilversum; tel. (35) 6726801; fax (35) 6726863; internet www.ncrvgids.nl; f. 1966; publ. by Nederlandse Christelijke Radio Vereniging; radio and TV guide; Dir C. ABBENHUIS; circ. 419,363.

Nederlands Tijdschrift voor Geneeskunde (Dutch Journal of Medicine): POB 75971, 1070 AZ Amsterdam; tel. (20) 6620150; fax (20) 6735481; e-mail redacfie@ntvg.nl; internet www.ntvg.nl; f. 1856; Editors Prof. Dr J. VAN GIJN, Prof. Dr F. W. A. VERHEUG, Prof. Dr A. J. P. M. OVERBEKE, Dr H. VEEKEN; circ. 30,000.

Nieuwe Revu: Haaksbergsweg 75, POB 23059, 1100 DN Amsterdam; tel. (20) 7518380; fax (20) 7518381; e-mail redactie@revu.nl; internet www.revu.nl; f. 1968; general interest; Editor-in-Chief FRED SENGERS; circ. 127,802.

Panorama: Ceylonpoort 5–25, 2037 AA Haarlem; tel. (23) 5304304; fax (23) 5361624; internet www.panorama.nl; f. 1913; general interest; Dir R. VAN VUURE; circ. 194,466.

Privé: POB 1980, 1000 BZ Amsterdam; tel. (20) 5853375; fax (20) 5854225; e-mail redactie@prive.nl; internet www.prive.nl; f. 1977; women's interest; Editor EVERT SANTEGOEDS; circ. 490,000.

Story: POB 1760, 2130 JD Hoofddorp; tel. (23) 5564894; fax (23) 5564911; internet www.story.nl; f. 1974; women's interest; Editor PETRA BAKKER-SCHUT; circ. 272,700.

TeleVizier: Zeverijnstraat 6, POB 20002, 1202 AB Hilversum; tel. (35) 6726834; fax (35) 6726712; e-mail redactie@televizier.nl; internet www.televizier.nl; publ. by Algemene Omroepvereniging; radio and TV guide; circ. 258,487.

Tina: Ceylonpoort 5–25, 2037 AA Haarlem; tel. (23) 5304304; fax (23) 5352554; f. 1967; teenage interest; circ. 112,191.

TrosKompas: POB 28600, 1202 LR Hilversum; tel. (35) 6728798; fax (35) 6728631; internet www.troskompas.nl; f. 1966; radio and TV guide; Editor EDGER HAMER.

TV Krant: POB 28600, 1202 LR Hilversum; tel. (35) 6728798; fax (35) 6728631; f. 1990; radio and TV guide; Editor EDGER HAMER.

Vara TV Magazine: POB 175, 1200 AD Hilversum; tel. (35) 6711445; fax (35) 6711429; e-mail tv.magazine@vara.nl; internet omroep.vara.nl; radio and TV guide; circ. 500,000.

Veronica: POB 22000, 1202 CA Hilversum; tel. (35) 6463333; fax (35) 6463300; e-mail bladredactie@veronicapublishing; internet www.veronica.nl; f. 1971; radio and TV guide; Editor PETER CONTANT; circ. 1,250,000.

Viva: POB 1630, 2130 JA Hoofddorp; tel. (23) 5565165; fax (23) 5565200; e-mail redactie@viva.nl; internet www.viva.nl; women's interest; Editor KARIN VAN GILST; circ. 149,461.

VNU: Ceylonpoort 5–25, 2037 AA Haarlem; POB 1, 2000 MA Haarlem; tel. (23) 5463463; fax (23) 5463912; e-mail vnupr@hq.vnu.com; circ. 174,250.

VPRO-Gids: POB 11, 1200 JC Hilversum; tel. (35) 6712665; fax (35) 6712285; e-mail gids@vpro.nl; internet www.vpro.nl/gids; radio and TV guide; Dir H. VAN DALFSEN; circ. 254,000.

Vrij Nederland: Raamgracht 4, POB 1254, 1000 BG Amsterdam; tel. (20) 5518711; fax (20) 6247476; e-mail redactie@vn.nl; f. 1940; current affairs; Editor EMILE FALLAUX; circ. 80,000.

SELECTED PERIODICALS

Art, History and Literature

De Architect: POB 34, 2501 AG The Hague; tel. (70) 3045833; fax (70) 3045806; e-mail architect@wkths.nl; internet www.deArchitect.nl; Dir HARM TILMAN; circ. 8,000.

Kunstbeeld: POB 256, 1110 AG Diemen; tel. (20) 5310900; fax (20) 5310971; e-mail redactie@kunstbeeld.nl; internet www.kunstbeeld.nl; monthly; art, sculpture; Editor ROBBERT ROOS; circ. 11,000 (2007).

Spiegel Historiael: Molukkenstraat 200, E5, 1098 TW Amsterdam; tel. (20) 6652759; fax (20) 6657831; e-mail s.h@inter.nl.net; f. 1966; monthly; history and archaeology; circ. 8,000.

Tableau Fine Arts Magazine: Capellalaan 65, 2132 JL Hoofddorp; tel. (23) 5565377; fax (23) 5565376; e-mail tableau@sanoma-uitgevers.nl; every 2 months; Editor RONALD KRAAYEVELD; circ. 17,000.

Tijdschrift voor Geschiedenis (Historical Review): Instituut Geschiedenis UU, Kromme Drift 10, 3512 BS Utrecht; tel. (30) 2537868; e-mail tvg@let.uu.nl; f. 1886; quarterly; Chair. M. GREVER.

Economics and Business

Computable: POB 1905, 2003 BA Haarlem; tel. (23) 5463413; fax (23) 5465526; e-mail computable@bp.vnu.com; internet www.computable.nl; Editor ALEX BESHUIZEN; circ. 96,636.

Elektronica: POB 23, 7400 GA Deventer; tel. (570) 648699; fax (570) 610918; e-mail hdevries@kluwer.nl; internet elektronica.profpages.nl; f. 1953; 11 a year; electronics design; Editor HENK DE VRIES; circ. 7,000.

Intermediair: POB 1900, 2003 BA Haarlem; tel. (23) 5463455; fax (23) 5465530; e-mail redactie@intermediair.nl; internet www.intermediair.nl; f. 1965; weekly; business recruitment; Editor PETER TER HORST; circ. 240,678.

Management Team: VNU Business Publications, POB 1907, 2003 BA Haarlem; tel. (318) 521422; fax (318) 523136; internet www.mt.nl; f. 1980; monthly; management; Editor BEN KUIKEN; circ. 142,000 (2001).

PCM (Personal Computer Magazine): Ceylonpoort 5–25, 2037 AA Haarlem; tel. (23) 5463704; fax (23) 5465524; internet www.pcmweb.nl; f. 1982; monthly; computing; Editor-in-Chief EDWIN AMMERLAAN; circ. 94,997.

THE NETHERLANDS   *Directory*

Trade Channel: Holland Business Press BV, Sophiastraat 1, 2011 VT Haarlem; tel. (23) 5319022; fax (23) 5317974; e-mail pvroom@tradechannel.com; internet www.tradechannel.com; f. 1945; monthly, 2 edns: Trade Channel Consumer Goods and Trade Channel Industrial & Technical Products; promote imports and exports; Editor HENK VAN CAPELLE; circ. 13,286 (consumer edn), 55,000 (technical edn).

Home, Fashion and General

Ariadne at Home: Capellalaan 65, POB 1919, 2130 YM Hoofddorp; tel. (23) 5566770; fax (23) 5361624; internet www.ariadneathome.nl; f. 1946; monthly; home decoration; Editor BRIGITTE SPEEKMAN; circ. 169,198.

Het Beste uit Reader's Digest: POB 23330, 1100 DV Amsterdam; tel. (20) 56789111; fax (20) 6976422; e-mail hetbeste@readersdigest.nl; internet www.readersdigest.nl; f. 1957; monthly; general interest; Man. Dir OELE STEENKS; circ. 304,453.

Cosmopolitan: Capellalaan 65, POB 1730, 2132 JL Hoofddorp; fax (23) 5565259; e-mail h.mulder@sanoma-uitgevers.nl; internet www.cosmopolitan.nl; f. 1982; monthly; women's interest; Editor H. MULDER; circ. 108,406.

Kijk: Ceylonpoort 5–25, 2037 AA Haarlem; tel. (20) 4300455; fax (20) 4300450; sports, science, technology and adventure; circ. 92,993.

Knipmode: Capellalaan 65, POB 1900, 2130 JL Hoofddorp; tel. (23) 5565006; fax (23) 5566771; internet www.knipmode.nl; monthly; DIY fashion; Editor-in-Chief MARGREET HAGDORN; Publr GERT JAAP SCHOPPINK; circ. 124,000.

Nouveau: Ceylonpoort 5–25, 2037 AA Haarlem; tel. (23) 304304; fax (23) 350621; f. 1986; women's interest; Dir K. P. M. VAN DE PAS; circ. 134,669.

Opzij: POB 2748, 1000 CS Amsterdam; tel. (20) 5518525; fax (20) 6227265; e-mail opzij@redactie.weekbladpers.nl; internet www.opzij.nl; f. 1972; monthly; feminist themes; Editor CISCA DRESSELHUYS; circ. 80,000.

Ouders van Nu: POB 740, 2400 AS Alphen Aan Den Ryn; tel. (23) 5565066; fax (23) 5565095; e-mail ouders@jongezinnen.nl; internet www.oudersvannu.nl; f. 1967; monthly; childcare; Editor K. KROONSTUIVER; circ. 156,720.

Playboy: POB 1662, 2130 JB Hoofddorp; tel. (23) 5463369; fax (23) 5463924; e-mail playboy@tidjschriften.vnu.com; internet www.playboy.nl; f. 1983; monthly; Editor JAN HEEMSKERK; circ. 85,348.

SEN: Mathenesserlaan 179, 3014 HA Rotterdam; fax (102) 092629; e-mail info@senmagazine.com; internet www.senmagazine.com; f. 2004; monthly; women's interest; Publr SENAY OZDEMIR; circ. 20,000.

TIP Culinair: POB 1632, 2130 JA Hoofddorp; tel. (23) 5565466; fax (23) 5565488; e-mail tipculinair@sanoma-uitgevers.nl; internet www.tipculinair.nl; f. 1977; monthly; cookery; Editor-in-Chief DOSIA BREWER; circ. 120,000.

VT-Wonen: Ceylonpoort 5-25, 2037 AA Haarlem; tel. (30) 822511; fax (30) 898388; internet www.vtwonen.nl; f. 1964; monthly; home-owning and decorating, circ. 210,374; Editor MAKKIE MULDER.

Leisure Interests and Sport

Autokampioen: POB 93200, 2509 BA The Hague; tel. (70) 3146688; fax (70) 3146279; e-mail autokampioen@anwb.nl; internet www.autokampioen.nl; f. 1908; publ. by Royal Dutch Touring Club (ANWB); motoring; fortnightly; Chief Editor JOS VROOMANS; circ. 70,000.

Grasduinen (Browsing): POB 23209, 1100 DT Amsterdam; tel. (20) 7510110; fax (20) 7510111; e-mail grasduinen@smm.nl; internet www.grasduinen.nl; monthly; leisure, healthy living, art; Editor LIEES LOOGMAN KANNEKENS; circ. 51,000.

Kampeer en Caravankampioen: POB 93200, 2509 BA The Hague; tel. (70) 3146691; fax (70) 3146692; e-mail kck@anwb.nl; internet www.kck-online.nl; f. 1941; monthly; camping and caravanning; publ. by Royal Dutch Touring Club (ANWB); Editor-in-Chief F. VOORBERGEN; circ. 139,601.

Kampioen: POB 93200, 2509 BA The Hague; tel. (70) 3146285; fax (70) 3146983; e-mail kampioen@anwb.nl; internet www.kampioen.nl; f. 1885; monthly; recreation and tourism; publ. by Royal Dutch Touring Club (ANWB); Editor E. LODEWYKS; circ. 3,700,000.

101 Woonideeën: POB 1702, 2130 JC Hoofddorp; tel. (23) 5564590; fax (23) 5564505; e-mail 101woonideeen@sanoma-uitgevers.nl; internet www.101woonideeen.nl; f. 1957; monthly; home ideas; Editor M. WIEMEYER; circ. 95,000.

Reizen Magazine: POB 93200, 2509 BA The Hague; tel. (88) 2696670; fax (88) 2697610; e-mail reizen@anwb.nl; internet www.reizen.nl; monthly; tourism, travel; publ. by Royal Dutch Touring Club (ANWB); Editor-in-Chief HARRI THEIRLYNCK; circ. 48,000.

Sport International: POB 225, 2800 AE Gouda; tel. (182) 599366; fax (182) 516650; f. 1981; five a year; Editor J. LINSE; circ. 47,350.

Voetbal International: WP Sport Media BV, POB 764, 1000 AT Amsterdam; tel. (20) 5518510; e-mail webmaster@vi.nl; internet www.vi.nl; weekly; football; Editor-in-Chief JOHAN DERKSEN.

Waterkampioen: POB 93200, 2509 BA The Hague; tel. (70) 3145796; fax (70) 3147356; e-mail waterkampioen@anwb.nl; internet www.waterkampioen.nl; f. 1927; fortnightly; water sports and yachting; publ. by Royal Dutch Touring Club (ANWB); Editor INGEBORG BERGHUIJS; circ. 54,000.

Scientific and Medical

Huisarts en Wetenschap: POB 3231, 3502 GE Utrecht; tel. (30) 2881700; fax (30) 2870668; e-mail redactie@nhg-nl.org; monthly; medical; Editor Dr JOOST VAAT; circ. 8,500.

Natuur & Techniek: Segment Special Interest Media, POB 75, 6190 AB Beek (L); tel. (46) 4389444; fax (46) 4370161; e-mail natutech@xs4all.nl; internet www.natutech.nl; f. 1932; monthly; Editor R. DOBBELAER; circ. 47,360.

Technische Revue: POB 4, 7000 BA Doetinchem; tel. (314) 349911; fax (314) 361522; internet www.ebi.nl; monthly; review of new products; Chief Editor M. L. MATSER; circ. 28,000.

NEWS AGENCY

Algemeen Nederlands Persbureau (ANP) (Netherlands News Agency): POB 1, 2501 AA The Hague; tel. (70) 4141414; fax (70) 4140560; e-mail redactie@anp.nl; internet www.anp.nl; f. 1934; official agency of the Netherlands Daily Press Asscn; Man. Dir LUC VAN GOMPEL; Editor-in-Chief ERIK VAN GRUIJTHUIJSEN.

PRESS ORGANIZATIONS

Buitenlandse Persvereniging in Nederland (Foreign Press Asscn in the Netherlands): Oudezijds Voorburgwal 129, 1012 EP Amsterdam; tel. (20) 4221209; e-mail tsterling@ap.org; internet www.bpv-fpa.nl; f. 1925; Pres. KERSTIN SCHWEIGHÖFER; 120 mems.

Nederlandse Dagbladpers (NDP) (Dutch Asscn of Daily Newspaper Publrs): Hogehilweg 6, POB 12040, 1100 AA Amsterdam-Zuidoost; tel. (20) 6763366; fax (20) 6766777; f. 1908; affiliated to Nederlands Uitgeversverbond; Chair. C. G. G. SPAAN; Gen. Sec. T. NAUTA; 34 mems.

De Nederlandse Nieuwsbladpers (NNP) (Organization of Local News Media in the Netherlands): Hogebrinkerweg 23C, 3871 KM Hoevelaken; tel. (33) 4481650; fax (33) 4481652; e-mail nnpnl@nnp.nl; internet www.nnp.nl; f. 1945; asscn of publrs of non-daily local newspapers and other local news media; Pres. M. C. BOOM; Dir J. P. BOS; 131 mems.

Nederlandse Vereniging van Journalisten (Netherlands Union of Journalists): Johannes Vermeerstraat 22, POB 75997, 1070 AZ Amsterdam; tel. (20) 6766771; fax (20) 6624901; e-mail vereniging@nvj.nl; internet www.villamedia.nl/n/nvj; f. 1884; publ. *De Journalist* (fortnightly); Chair. (vacant); Sec. T. BRUNING; 9,000 mems.

Publishers

Uitgeverij Altamira BV: Blekersvaartweg 19A, Heemstede; tel. (23) 5286882; e-mail altamira@tip.nl; internet www.altamira-becht.nl; f. 1985; philosophy, psychology, New Age, health and spirituality.

Uitgeverij Ankh-Hermes BV: Smyrnastraat 5, POB 125, 7400 AC Deventer; tel. (57) 0678900; fax (57) 0624632; e-mail info@ankh-hermes.nl; internet www.ankh-hermes.nl; health, eastern and western religions, astrology, alternative medicine, psychology, esoterics; Dir A. STEENBERGEN; Publrs E. TEN SELDAM, W. DE VEER.

Ambo Anthos: Herengracht 435–437, 1017 BR Amsterdam; tel. (20) 5245411; fax (20) 4200422; e-mail info@amboanthos.nl; internet www.amboanthos.nl; literature, cultural history, biographies, history, politics; Dir R. AMMERLAAN.

APA (Academic Publishers Associated): POB 806, 1000 AV Amsterdam; tel. (20) 6265544; fax (20) 5285298; e-mail apa@apa-publishers.com; internet www.apa-publishers.com; f. 1966; subsidiaries: Holland University Press, Fontes Pers, Oriental Press, Philo Press, van Heusden, Hissink & Co; new and reprint edns in the arts, humanities and science; Man. Dir G. VAN HEUSDEN.

BV Uitgeverij De Arbeiderspers: Herengracht 370–372, POB 2877, 1000 CW Amsterdam; tel. (20) 5247500; fax (20) 6224937; e-mail info@arbeiderspers.nl; internet www.ap-archipel.nl; participant in Weekbladpers holdings group; general, fiction and non-fiction; Dir R. C. HAANS.

A. Asher & Co BV: Zeeweg 264, POB 258, 1970 AG Ijmuiden; tel. (25) 5523839; fax (25) 5510352; e-mail info@asherbooks.com;

internet www.asherbooks.com; f. 1830; natural history; Dirs M. J. ROOS, J. W. STEINER.

Bert Bakker BV: Herengracht 507, POB 1662, 1000 BV Amsterdam; tel. (20) 6241934; fax (20) 6225461; e-mail pbo@pbo.nl; internet www.pbo.nl; f. 1893; Dutch and international literature, sociology, history, politics, science; Dir MAI SPIJKERS.

John Benjamins BV: Klaprozenweg 105, POB 36224, 1020 ME Amsterdam; tel. (20) 6304747; fax (20) 6739773; e-mail customer.services@benjamins.nl; internet www.benjamins.com; f. 1964; linguistics, philology, psychology and art history; antiquarian scholarly periodicals; Man. Dirs J. L. BENJAMINS, C. L. BENJAMINS-SCHALEKAMP, SELINE BENJAMINS.

Uitgeverij De Bezige Bij BV: Van Mireveldstraat 1, POB 75184, 1070 AD Amsterdam; tel. (20) 3059810; fax (20) 3059824; e-mail info@debezigebij.nl; internet www.debezigebij.nl; f. 1945; Publr MICHIEL GAAF.

Erven J. Bijleveld: Janskerkhof 7, 3512 BK Utrecht, POB 1238, 3500 BE Utrecht; tel. (30) 2317008; fax (30) 2368675; e-mail bijleveld.publishers@wxs.nl; internet www.bijleveldbooks.nl; f. 1865; psychology, sociology, philosophy, religion and history; computer books (as Bijleveld Press); Mans J. B. BOMMELJÉ, L. S. BOMMELJÉ.

Boekencentrum Uitgevers: Goudstraat 50, POB 29, 2700 AA Zoetermeer; tel. (79) 3615481; fax (79) 3615489; e-mail info@boekencentrum.nl; internet www.boekencentrum.nl; bibles, books and magazines; Dir N. A. DE WAAL.

Bohn Stafleu Van Hoghum BV: Het Spoor 2, POB 246, 3990 GA Houten; tel. (30) 6385838; fax (30) 6383839; e-mail klantenservice@bsl.nl; internet www.bsl.nl; mem. of Wolters Kluwer NV holdings group; social sciences, humanities, medical, dental and nursing; Dir P. J. A. SNAKKERS.

Boom Uitgeverij BV: Prinsengracht 747–751, 1017 JX Amsterdam; tel. (20) 6226107; fax (20) 6253327; e-mail info@virgeverijboom.nl; internet www.uitgeverijboom.nl; f. 1842; fmrly Boom Pers BV, Meppel; philosophy, educational and social sciences, environment, history; Man. Dir DRIES VAN INGEN.

Brill Academic Publishers: Plantijnstraat 2, POB 9000, 2300 PA Leiden; tel. (71) 5353500; fax (71) 5317532; e-mail cs@brill.nl; internet www.brill.nl; f. 1683; academic books and periodicals (mainly in English); classics, medieval, renaissance and oriental studies, comparative religion, biology; CEO HERMAN PABBRUWE.

A. W. Bruna Uitgevers BV: Kobaltweg 23–25, POB 40203, 3504 AA Utrecht; tel. (30) 2470411; fax (30) 2410018; e-mail info@awbruna.nl; internet www.awbruna.nl; f. 1868; general fiction and non-fiction; Dir J. A. A. BOEZEMAN.

Uitgeverij Cantecleer BV: Julianalaan 11, POB 309, 3740 AM Baarn; tel. (35) 5486600; fax (35) 5486645; e-mail cantecleer@worldonline.nl; internet www.cantecleer.nl; f. 1948; mem. of Bosch & Keuning Uitgevers group; Man. Dir H. SCHWURMANS.

Uitgeverij De Fontein BV: Prinses Marielaan 8, POB 1, 3740 AA Baarn; tel. (35) 5486311; fax (35) 5423855; f. 1981; mem. of Bosch & Keuning holding group; commercial fiction, non-fiction and children's books; Dir T. AKUELD.

Uitgeverij van Gennep BV: Keizersgracht 524, 1017 EK Amsterdam; tel. (20) 6247033; fax (20) 6247035; e-mail vangennep@wxs.nl; history, social theory, political science, biographies, literature.

Uitgeverij J. H. Gottmer/H. J. W. Becht BV: Wilhelminapark 6, POB 317, 2000 AH Haarlem; tel. (23) 5411190; fax (23) 5274404; e-mail info@gottmer.nl; internet www.gottmer.nl; f. 1937; fiction, non-fiction, children's books, religion, spirituality, travel guides; imprints incl. Aramith, Becht, Dominicus and Hollandia; Dir C. G. A. VAN WIJK.

Uitgeverij Hollandia BV: e-mail info@hollandia-boeken.nl; internet www.hollandia-boeken.nl; f. 1899; travel, yachting and nautical books; Dir TONNIS MUNTINGA.

Uitgeverij Holland BV: Spaarne 110, 2011 CM Haarlem; tel. (23) 5323061; fax (23) 5342908; e-mail info@uitgeverijholland.nl; internet www.uitgeverijholland.nl; f. 1922; literature, reference, science, children's books; Publr J. B. VAN ULZEN.

Uitgeefmaatschappij J. H. Kok: Ijsseldijk 31, POB 5019, 8260 GA Kampen; tel. (38) 3392555; fax (38) 3327331; e-mail algemeen@kok.nl; internet www.kok.nl; f. 1894; theology, belles-lettres, science, periodicals; mem. of Veen Bosch & Keuning Uitgevers; nine subsidiaries; Dir B. A. ENDEDIJK.

Ten Have BV: Ijsseldijk 31, POB 5018, 8266 DA Kampen; tel. (38) 3328912; fax (38) 3392500; e-mail info@uitgeverijtenhave.nl; internet www.uitgeverijtenhave.nl; f. 1831; imprint of Uitgeefmaatschappij J. H. Kok; religious; Dir B. A. ENDEDIJK; Editor P. DE BOER.

Uitgeverij Voorhoeve: Stationsplein 62, POB 133, 3740 AC Baarn; tel. (35) 5418855; fax (35) 5413174; f. 1876; imprint of Uitgeversmaatschappij J. H. Kok; general non-fiction, children's books; Dir B. A. ENDEDIJK.

Kosmos-Z&K Uitgevers: Maliebaan 74, POB 13288, 3507 LG Utrecht; tel. (30) 2349211; fax (30) 2349247; e-mail info@kosmoszk.nl; internet www.kosmoszk.nl; f. 1992; mem. of Veen Bosch & Keuning Uitgevers; Dir ROBBERT SCHUURMANS.

Lemniscaat BV: Vijverlaan 48, POB 4066, 3006 AB Rotterdam; tel. (10) 2062929; fax (10) 4141560; e-mail info@lemniscaat.nl; internet www.lemniscaat.nl; f. 1963; philosophy, psychology, care of the disabled and mentally handicapped, books for juveniles and young adults, picture books; Dir J. C. BOELE VAN HENSBROEK.

Uitgeverij Leopold BV: Singel 262, POB 3879, 1001 AR Amsterdam; tel. (20) 5511250; fax (20) 4204699; e-mail info@leopold.nl; internet www.leopold.nl; f. 1923; mem. Weekbladpers BV; children's books; Dir MARTINE SCHAAP.

Uitgeverij Luitingh-Sijthoff BV: Leidsegracht 105A, 1017 ND Amsterdam; tel. (20) 5307340; fax (20) 626251; e-mail info@luitingh-sijthoff.nl; Luitingh; f. 1946; Sijthoff; f. 1851; merged in 1989; mem. of Veen Bosch en Keuning Uitgevers publishing group; fiction and popular non-fiction; Man. Dir J. A. B. LEPPINK.

Malmberg BV: Leeghwaterlaan 16, POB 233, 5201 AE Den Bosch; tel. (73) 6288811; fax (73) 6210512; e-mail malmberg@malmberg.nl; internet www.malmberg.nl; f. 1885; part of SanomaWSOY Group (Finland); educational; Dir J. DRIESSEN.

J. M. Meulenhoff BV: Nieuwe Spiegelstraat 26, POB 100, 1000 AC Amsterdam; tel. (20) 5533500; fax (20) 6251135; e-mail info@meulenhoff.nl; internet www.meulenhoff.nl; f. 1895; literature, historical, political, social/cultural, art, paperbacks and pocket books; Dir ROB HOGENES.

Nienhuis Montessori International BV: Industriepark 14, POB 16, 7020 AA Zelhem; tel. (314) 627127; fax (314) 627128; e-mail info@nienhuis.nl; internet www.nienhuis.nl; f. 1800; holdings group; publrs and printers specializing in scientific books and periodicals; Dir A. J. NIENHUIS.

Uitgeverij Ploegsma BV: Keizersgracht 616, POB 19857, 1000 GW Amsterdam; tel. (20) 6262907; fax (20) 6242994; internet www.ploegsma.nl; subsidiary: Uitgeverij De Brink; Dir M. BRINKMAN.

Em. Querido's Uitgeverij BV: Singel 262, POB 3879, 1001 AR Amsterdam; tel. (20) 5511262; fax (20) 6391968; internet www.querido.nl; f. 1915; subsidiary: Uitgeverij Nijgh & van Ditmar; participant in 'Singel 262' holdings group; general fiction, history, children's books, translations from Latin and Greek texts; Dir ARY T. LANGBROEK.

Reed Elsevier NV: Van de Sande Bakhuyzenstraat 4, 1061 AG Amsterdam; POB 470, 1000 AL Amsterdam; tel. (20) 5159111; fax (20) 6832617; internet www.elsevier.nl; f. 1979 by merger; subholdings include some 60 subsidiaries in the Netherlands and abroad specializing in: reference works, handbooks, weekly magazines, newspapers, trade and technical pubs, (postgraduate) scientific books and journals, audiovisual materials, further education study courses, databases; CEO CRISPIN DAVIS.

Excerpta Medica Medical Communications: Radarweg 29, 1043 NX Amsterdam; tel. (20) 4853975; fax (20) 4853188; e-mail excerptamedica@elsevier.com; internet www.excerptamedica.com; Man. Dir GERARD STOIA.

Editions Rodopi BV: Tijnmuiden 7, 1046 AK Amsterdam; tel. (20) 6114821; fax (20) 4472979; e-mail info@rodopi.nl; internet www.rodopi.nl; f. 1966; Dir F. A. VAN DER ZEE.

SDU: Prinses Beatrixlaan 116, POB 20025, 2500 EA The Hague; tel. (70) 3789911; fax (70) 3854321; e-mail sdu@sdu.nl; internet www.sdu.nl; Chair. Dr L. JONGSMA.

Springer: Van Godewijckstraat 30, POB 989, 3311 GX Dordrecht; tel. (78) 6576050; fax (78) 6576467; internet www.springeronline.com; merged with Kluwer Academic Publrs in 2004; publrs of books and journals in the fields of science, technology and medicine, incl., inter alia, natural sciences, mathematics, engineering, computer science and psychology; CEO DERK HAANK.

Uitgeverij Strengholt: Hofstede Oud-Bussem, Flevolaan 41, POB 338, 1400 AH Bussum; tel. (35) 6958411; fax (35) 6946173; e-mail tanya.jansen@strengholt.nl; internet www.uitgeverijstrengholt.nl; f. 1928; health, biography, music, current affairs, psychology, parapsychology, sports, cookery; Dir T. M. JANSEN.

Taylor & Francis The Netherlands (T&F NL): Schipholweg 107C, POB 447, 2300 AK Leiden; tel. (71) 5243080; fax (71) 5234571; e-mail pub.nl@tandf.co.uk; internet www.taylorandfrancis.com; f. 1901 as Swets & Zeitlinger Publishers; acquired by Taylor & Francis (United Kingdom) in 2003; publr of books in civil engineering, water, environment and earth sciences; Sr Publr JANJAAP BLOM.

Uitgeverij De Tijdstroom BV: Janskerkhof 26, POB 775, 3500 AT Utrecht; tel. (30) 2364450; fax (30) 23699354; e-mail info@tijdstroom.nl; internet www.tijdstroom.nl; f. 1921; educational and professional publications on health and welfare, periodicals in these fields; Dir N. F. VAN 'T ZET.

THE NETHERLANDS

Unieboek BV: Onderdoor 7, POB 97, 3990 DB Houten; tel. (30) 7998300; fax (30) 7998398; e-mail info@unieboek.nl; internet www.unieboek.nl; f. 1890; holding group incorporating 10 publishing houses; general and juvenile literature, fiction, popular science, history, art, social, economics, religion, textbooks, etc.; Dir W. VAN GILS.

Veen Bosch en Keuning Uitgevers NV: St Jacobsstraat 125, POB 8049, 3503 RA Utrecht; tel. (30) 2349211; fax (30) 2349208; e-mail algemeen@veenboschenkeuning.nl; internet www.veenboschenkeuning.nl; f. 2001; merger between Veen Uitgevers Groep and Bosch & Keuning; Dirs A. DE GROOT, J. ATEMA.

VNU Business Publications BV: Ceylonpoort 5–25, POB 4020, 2031 EA Haarlem; tel. (23) 5463463; fax (23) 5463931; e-mail info@bp.vnu.com; internet www.vnubp.nl; trade and fashion, careers, IT, personal computer, management, training.

West Friesland BV: Slijksteeg 4, POB 2308, 1620 EH Hoorn; tel. (22) 9248820; fax (22) 9218944; f. 1943; novels, biographies, children's books, paperbacks, young adults; Man. Dir B. E. ENDEDIJK; Editor-in-Chief F. H. JONKERS.

Wolters Kluwer NV: Apollolaan 153, POB 75248; 1070 AE Amsterdam; tel. (20) 6070400; fax (20) 6070490; e-mail info@wolterskluwer.com; internet www.wolterskluwer.com; health, accounting, finance, legal; Chair. ADRI BAAN; CEO NANCY MCKINSTRY.

Wolters-Noordhoff BV: Damsport 157, POB 58, 9700 MB Groningen; tel. (50) 5226922; fax (50) 5277599; e-mail info@wolters.nl; internet www.wolters-noordhoff.nl; f. 1836; educational and scientific books, educational software, geographical and historical atlases and maps; Man. Dir Dr A. M. W. HOLL.

PUBLISHERS' ASSOCIATIONS

Koninklijke Vereniging van het Boekenvak (KVB) (Royal Asscn for the Book Trade): Frederiksplein 1, POB 15007, 1001 MA Amsterdam; tel. (20) 6240212; fax (20) 6208871; e-mail info@kvb.nl; internet www.kvb.nl; f. 1815; Chair. E. BRINKMAN; Exec. Dir CONNIE VERBERNE; 1,500 mems.

Nederlands Uitgeversverbond (NUV) (Dutch Publrs' Asscn): Hogehilweg 6, POB 12040, 1100 AA Amsterdam Zuidoost; tel. (20) 4309150; fax (20) 4309179; e-mail info@nuv.nl; internet www.nuv.nl; Chair. L. M. L. H. A. HERMANS; Dir J. BOMMER; 142 mems.

Broadcasting and Communications

TELECOMMUNICATIONS

Regulatory Authority

Onafhankelijke Post en Telecommunicatie Autoriteit (OPTA): Babylon Bldg, Tower B, Koningin Julianaplein 30, POB 90420, 2509 LK The Hague; tel. (70) 3153500; fax (70) 3153501; e-mail mail@opta.nl; internet www.opta.nl; f. 1997; supervises compliance with legislation, settles disputes, manages the telephone number database; Chair. CHRIS A. FONTEIJN.

Service Providers

debitel Nederland BV: POB 6700, 2130 LT Hoofddorp; internet www.debitel.nl; f. 1993; mobile cellular telecommunications; subsidiary of debitel AG (Germany); CEO HUIB KLOOSTERHUIS.

Enertel NV: Toren op Zuid, Wilhelminakade 123, POB 70024, 3000 LE Rotterdam; tel. (10) 8803800; fax (10) 8803700; e-mail info@enertel.nl; internet www.enertel.nl; f. 1994; fixed-line telecommunications and internet access; acquired by Koninklijke KPN NV in 2006.

Koninklijke KPN NV: Maanplein 55, POB 30000, 2500 GA The Hague; tel. (70) 3434343; fax (70) 3436568; e-mail webmaster@kpn.com; internet www.kpn.com; privatized 1989; fmrly Koninklijke PTT NV, present name adopted 1998; operates KPN Mobile; fixed-line operator and internet access provider; CEO ADRIANUS (AD) SCHEEPBOUWER.

Orange Nederland NV: Groenhovenstr. 2, POB 95313, 2509 CH The Hague; tel. (06) 48999000; e-mail info@dutchtone.nl; internet www.orange.nl; mobile cellular telecommunications and internet access; owned by Deutsche Telekom; Man. Dir NIEK JAN VAN DAMME.

T-Mobile: Rijswijkseweg 60, POB 16272, 2500 BG The Hague; tel. (61) 4095000; internet www.t-mobile.nl; owned by Deutsche Telekom; mobile telephone operator.

Telfort BV: POB 23079, 1100 DN Amsterdam Zuid-Oost; tel. 0800-1771; internet www.telfort.com; f. 1996; mobile cellular telecommunications and internet access; owned by Koninklijke KPN NV; Man. Dir MARCO VISSER.

UPC Nederland NV: POB 80900, 1005 DA Amsterdam; tel. (20) 7755731; fax (20) 7756724; e-mail mediarelations@upc.nl; internet www.upc.nl; subsidiary of UPC Broadband; broadband internet, telephone, digital television and radio service provider; Man. Dir DIEDERIK KARSTEN.

Vodafone: POB 1500, 6201 BM Maastricht; e-mail press.nl@vodafone.com; internet www.vodafone.nl; f. 1999; owned by Vodafone Group PLC (United Kingdom); CEO GUY LAURENCE.

BROADCASTING

Under the Netherlands public broadcasting system the two co-ordinating bodies work with the seven licensed broadcasters to provide a complete range of programmes.

Co-ordinating Bodies

Nederlandse Programma Stichting (NPS) (Dutch National Broadcasting Service): Sumatralaan 49, POB 29000, 1202 MA Hilversum; tel. (35) 6779333; fax (35) 6774959; e-mail publiek@nps.nl; internet www.nps.nl; Dir CAREL KUYL.

Nederlandse Publieke Omroep (NPO) (Netherlands Public Broadcasting): POB 26444, 1202 JJ Hilversum; tel. (35) 6779222; fax (35) 6772649; e-mail npo.communicatie@omroep.nl; internet www.omroep.nl; f. 1969; co-ordination of Dutch national public broadcasting and news, sports and teletext programmes on six national public radio and three television channels; fmrly Nederlandse Omroep Stichting; Chair. HARM BRUINS SLOT.

Broadcasting Associations

Algemene Omroepvereniging AVRO: 's-Gravelandseweg 80, POB 2, 1200 JA Hilversum; tel. (35) 6717911; fax (35) 6717439; e-mail info@avro.nl; internet www.avro.nl; f. 1923; independent; general broadcaster; 800,000 mems; Pres. Dr ROB NEUTELINGS (acting).

Evangelische Omroep (EO): Oude Amersfoortseweg 79, POB 21000, 1202 BA Hilversum; tel. (35) 6474747; fax (35) 6474727; e-mail eo@eo.nl; internet www.eo.nl; f. 1967; Protestant; Chair. ARIE VAN DER VEER; Man. Dir HENK HAGOORT.

Katholieke Radio Omroep (KRO): 's-Gravelandseweg 80, POB 23000, 1202 EA Hilversum; tel. (35) 6713911; fax (35) 6713666; internet www.kro.nl; f. 1925; Catholic; 615,000 mems; Pres. Dr F. C. H. SLANGEN; Sec.-Gen. Dr H. A. M. HOOFT.

Nederlandse Christelijke Radio Vereniging (NCRV): 's-Gravelandseweg 80, POB 25000, 1202 HB Hilversum; tel. (35) 6719911; fax (35) 6719285; e-mail info@ncrv.nl; internet www.ncrv.nl; f. 1924; Protestant; more than 550,000 mems; Chair. LEO BORN; Dir COEN ABBENHUIS.

Omroepvereniging VARA: Sumatralaan 49, POB 175, 1200 AD Hilversum; tel. (35) 6711911; fax (35) 6711333; e-mail vara@vara.nl; internet www.vara.nl; f. 1925; social-democratic and progressive; 515,000 mems; Pres. VERA M. M. KEUR.

Omroepvereniging VPRO: Villa VPRO, Mediapark, Sumatralaan 49, POB 11, 1200 JC Hilversum; tel. (35) 6712911; fax (35) 6712220; e-mail info@vpro.nl; internet www.vpro.nl; f. 1926; progressive; 344,000 mems; Pres. PETER VAN LIESHOUT; Gen. Dir PETER SCHRURS; Dir of Radio KEES SCHAEPMAN; Dirs of Television BREGTJE VAN DER HAAK, FRANK WIERING.

TROS: Lage Naarderweg 45–47, POB 28450, 1202 LL Hilversum; tel. (35) 6715715; fax (35) 6715236; e-mail publiekservice@tros.nl; internet www.tros.nl; f. 1964; independent; general broadcaster; 573,664 mems; Chair. K. VAN DOODEWAERD.

Radio

There are six privately owned national radio stations that are operated on a public-service basis, as well as 13 regional stations and about 330 local stations.

Radio 1: internet www.radio1.nl; 24-hour news and sports programming.

Radio 2: internet www.radio2.nl; broadcasts popular music.

3FM: internet www.3fm.nl; broadcasts contemporary music.

Radio 4: internet www.radio4.nl; broadcasts popular classical music.

Radio 5: internet www.radio5.nl; broadcasts popular music, current affairs and cultural programmes; aimed at people aged over 55.

Radio 6: internet www.radio6.nl; broadcasts Americana, electronica, folk, jazz and 'world' music.

Television

Television programmes are transmitted on three public channels, each of which is allocated to a different combination of broadcasting associations and other organizations, and on the commercially funded channels operated by RTL Nederland.

RTL Nederland: Sumatralaan 47, Postbus 15016, 1200 TV Hilversum; tel. (35) 6718711; fax (35) 6236892; e-mail info@rtl.nl; internet www.rtl.nl; f. 1996 as Holland Media Groep; present name adopted

THE NETHERLANDS

2004; operates four television channels: RTL 4, RTL 5, RTL 7 and RTL 8; subsidiary of RTL Group (Luxembourg); CEO FONS VAN WESTERLOO.

SBS 6/NET5: Plantage Middenlaan 14, POB 18179, 1001 ZB Amsterdam; e-mail info@sbs6.nl; internet www.sbs6.nl; private broadcaster; Man. JORIS BOUMAN.

United Pan-Europe Communications NV: POB 80900, 1005 DA Amsterdam; tel. (20) 7729729; fax (20) 7729988; e-mail service@upc.nl; internet www.upc.nl; cable broadcaster; Chair. MICHAEL T. FRIES.

Overseas Broadcasting

BVN TV: Witte Kruislaan 55, POB 222, 1200 JG Hilversum; tel. (35) 6724333; fax (35) 6724343; e-mail bvn@rnw.nl; internet www.bvn.nl; f. 1998; by Radio Nederland Wereldomroep, VRT and Nederlandse Omroep Stichting (NOS); daily international transmissions of news and cultural programmes from public-service broadcasters in Flanders and the Netherlands; Dir of Programmes P. LANDMAN.

Radio Nederland Wereldomroep (Radio Netherlands International): Witte Kruislaan 55, POB 222, 1200 JG Hilversum; tel. (35) 6724211; fax (35) 6724352; e-mail wereldomroep@rnw.nl; internet www.rnw.nl; f. 1947; public-service broadcaster; daily transmissions in Arabic, Dutch, English, Indonesian, Papiamento, Portuguese, Sarnami Hindi and Spanish; programme and transcription services for foreign radio and TV stations; Radio Nederland Training Centre (for students from developing countries); Dir-Gen. JAN HOEK.

Finance

(cap. = capital; res = reserves; dep. = deposits; m. = million; br(s). = branch(es); amounts in euros)

BANKING

Central Bank

De Nederlandsche Bank NV: Westeinde 1, POB 98, 1000 AB Amsterdam; tel. (20) 5249111; fax (20) 5242500; e-mail info@dnb.nl; internet www.dnb.nl; f. 1815; nationalized 1948; merged with Pensioen- en Verzekeringskamer (Chamber of Insurance and Pensions) in 2004; cap. 500m., res 15,134m., dep. 17,900m. (Dec. 2006); Pres. A. H. E. M. (NOUT) WELLINK; Exec. Dirs HENK BROUWER, ARNOLD SCHILDER, JOANNE KELLERMANN, FLIP KLOPPER.

Principal Commercial Banks

ABN AMRO Bank NV: Gustav Mahlerlaan 10, POB 283, 1082 PP Amsterdam; tel. (20) 6289393; fax (20) 6287740; e-mail postbox@abnamro.com; internet www.abnamro.com; f. 1991 by merger of Algemene Bank Nederland NV and Amsterdam-Rotterdam Bank NV; acquisition by consortium comprising Royal Bank of Scotland PLC (United Kingdom), Grupo Santander (Spain) and Fortis Bank NV (Belgium) agreed in October 2007; cap. 1,085m., res 3,913m., dep. 897,782m. (Dec. 2006); Chair., Management Bd MARK FISHER; 915 brs nationally.

Amsterdam Trade Bank NV: Herengracht 475, 1017 BS Amsterdam; tel. (20) 5209209; fax (20) 5209219; e-mail info@atbank.nl; internet www.atbank.nl; f. 1994 as Stolichny Bank International NV; present name adopted 1999; 100% owned by Alfa-Bank (Russia); cap. 117.3m., res 18.2m., dep. 2,032.1m. (Dec. 2006); Chair., Supervisory Bd P. SMIDA; Man. Dirs ALEXEI V. DROVOSSEKOV, J. P. J. KONIJN, ANTON H. DEN HELD.

Bank Nederlandse Gemeenten NV (BNG): Koninginnegracht 2, POB 30305, 2500 GH The Hague; tel. (70) 3750750; fax (70) 3454743; e-mail info@bng.nl; internet www.bng.nl; f. 1914 as NV Gemeentelijke Creditbank; present name adopted 1992; 50% Govt-owned, 50% by provincial and municipal authorities; cap. 139m., res 2,238m., dep. 80,759m. (Dec. 2006); Pres. P. O. VERMEULEN.

Banque Artesia Nederland NV (GE Artesia Bank): Herengracht 539–543, POB 274, 1000 AG Amsterdam; tel. (20) 5204911; fax (20) 6247502; e-mail info@artesia.nl; internet www.artesia.nl; f. 1863 as the Nederlandsche Credit & Depositobank; became Banque Paribas Nederland in 1984; present name adopted 1998; acquired by GE Commercial Finance (USA) in 2006; cap. 73.7m., res 134.8m., dep. 4,339.6m. (Dec. 2005); Chair. S. W. PRINS; Man. Dirs V. SNEYDERS, D. E. A. WAEBENS, J. H. M. EVERY; 9 brs.

Dexia Bank Nederland NV: Piet Heinkade 55, POB 808, 1000 AV Amsterdam; tel. (20) 3485000; fax (20) 5571414; e-mail klantenservie@dexiabank.nl; internet www.dexiabank.nl; f. 2001 by merger of Bank Labouchere NV (f. 1990) and Kempen and Co NV; owned by Dexia banking group; dep. 5,398.1m., total assets 7,290.1m. (Dec. 2001); Chair. B. F. M. KNÜPPE; 1 br.

Fortis Bank (Nederland) NV: Blaak 555, POB 1045, 3000 BA Rotterdam; tel. (10) 2701010; fax (10) 4148391; e-mail info@fortis.com; internet www.fortisbank.nl; f. 1999 by merger of VSB Bank and Generale Bank Nederland; cap. 566m., res 3,333m., dep. 3,314m. (Dec. 2004); Chair. C. J. BEUVING.

Friesland Bank NV: Beursplein 1, POB 1, 8900 AA Leeuwarden; tel. (58) 2994499; fax (58) 2994591; e-mail service@frieslandbank.nl; internet www.frieslandbank.nl; f. 1913 as Coöperatieve Zuivel-Bank; present name adopted 1995; dep. 7,834.3m., total assets 9,346.8m. (Dec. 2006); Chair. Dr W. F. C. CRAMER; Dirs T. BRANBERGEN, A. VLASKAMP; 36 brs.

Indonesische Overzeese Bank NV (Indover Bank): Stadhouderskade 84, POB 526, 1000 AM Amsterdam; tel. (20) 5700700; fax (20) 6626119; e-mail info@indover.com; internet www.indoverbank.com; f. 1965; owned by Bank Indonesia; cap. 48.0m., res 117.0m., dep. 590.1m. (Dec. 2006); Chair. SUBARJO JOYOSUMARTO.

ING Bank NV: Amstelveenseweg 500, 1081 KL Amsterdam; tel. (20) 5415411; fax (20) 5415444; e-mail ing@ing.com; internet www.ing.com; f. 1990 by merger of Nationale-Nederlanden and NMB Postbank Groep; cap. 525m., res 21,288m., dep. 770,895m. (Dec. 2005); Chair. and CEO MICHEL TILMANT; more than 400 brs.

KAS BANK NV: Spuistraat 172, POB 24001, 1000 DB Amsterdam; tel. (20) 5575911; fax (20) 5576100; e-mail info@kasbank.com; internet www.kasbank.com; f. 1806 by merger; present name adopted 2002; cap. 15.7m., res 182.3m., dep. 6,106.9m. (Dec. 2006); Chair., Managmement Bd ALBERT A. RÖELL.

F. van Lanschot Bankiers NV: Hooge Steenweg 29, POB 1021, 5200 HC 's-Hertogenbosch; tel. (73) 5483548; fax (73) 5483648; e-mail vanlanschot@vanlanschot.nl; internet www.vanlanschot.nl; f. 1737; merger with CenE Bankiers NV completed 2005; cap. 32.4m., res 837.7m., dep. 16,436.2m. (Dec. 2006); Chair. F. G. H. DECKERS; 32 brs.

Mizuho Corporate Bank Nederland NV: Apollolaan 171, POB 7075, 1007 JB Amsterdam; tel. (20) 5734343; fax (20) 5734372; f. 2000 by merger of Dai Ichi Kangyo Bank Europe NV and Fuji Bank Nederland NV; cap. 141.8m., res 18.5m., dep. 1,447.8m. (Dec. 2006); Man. Dir A. UJITA.

NIBC Bank NV: Carnegieplein 4, POB 380, 2501 BH The Hague; tel. (70) 3425425; fax (70) 3651071; e-mail info@nibc.com; internet www.nibc.com; f. 1945 as Herstelbank; present name adopted 2005; cap. 1,363m., res 448m., dep. 28,272m. (Dec. 2006); Chair., Management Bd JEROEN DROST; 1 br.

Postbank NV: Haarlemmerweg 506, POB 21009, 1000 EX Amsterdam; tel. (20) 5846133; fax (20) 5846132; internet www.postbank.nl; f. 1985; retail bank operating through post offices; 100% owned by ING Group NV; Chair. MICHEL TILMANT.

Rabobank Nederland (Coöperatieve Centrale Raiffeisen-Boerenleenbank BA): Croeselaan 18, POB 17100, 3500 HG Utrecht; tel. (30) 2160000; fax (30) 2162672; e-mail rabocomm@rn.rabobank.nl; internet www.rabobank.nl; f. 1972 by merger of Coöperatieve Centrale Raiffeisenbank of Utrecht and Coöperatieve Centrale Boerenleenbank of Eindhoven; dep. 521,222m., total assets 556,455m. (Dec. 2006); Chair. H. HEEMSKERK; 1,727 brs.

SNS Bank NV: Croeselaan 1, 3503 BJ Utrecht; tel. (30) 2915100; fax (30) 2915300; e-mail info@snsbank.nl; internet www.sns.nl; f. 1971 as Bank der Bondsspaarbanken NV; present name adopted 2002; cap. 383m., res 2,498m., dep. 59,642m. (Dec. 2006); Group Chair. and CEO S. VAN KEULEN; 256 brs.

Staalbankiers NV: Lange Houtstraat 8, POB 327, 2501 CH The Hague; tel. (70) 3101510; fax (70) 3650819; e-mail info@staalbankiers.nl; internet www.staalbankiers.nl; f. 1916 as Bankierskantoor Staal & Co NV; present name adopted 2005; mem. of Achmea Groep; dep. 2,136.6m., total assets 2,518.4m. (Dec. 2006); Chair. and CEO P. A. DE RUIJTER; Man. Dirs P. J. HUURMAN, D. BECK.

Bankers' Association

Nederlandse Vereniging van Banken (NVB) (Netherlands Bankers' Asscn): Singel 236, POB 3543, 1001 AH Amsterdam; tel. (20) 5502888; fax (20) 6239748; e-mail info@nvb.nl; internet www.nvb.nl; f. 1989; Chair. B. STAAL; Dir HEIN G. M. BLOCKS; 91 mems.

STOCK EXCHANGES

A supervisory authority, the Netherlands Securities Board, commenced activities in 1989.

Euronext Amsterdam: Beursplein 5, POB 19163, 1000 GD Amsterdam; tel. (20) 5505555; fax (20) 5504899; e-mail info@euronext.nl; internet www.euronext.com; subsidiary of NYSE Euronext; Euronext NV was formed by merger of Amsterdam, Paris and Brussels exchanges and joined in 2002 by the London futures exchange Liffe and the Lisbon stock exchange; merged with New York Stock Exchange 2007 to form NYSE Euronext; unitary stock and options exchange; Chair. JOOST VAN DER DOES DE WILLEBOIS.

There are also financial futures, grain, citrus fruits and insurance bourses in the Netherlands; a 'spot' market for petroleum operates from Rotterdam.

THE NETHERLANDS

INSURANCE

AEGON Nederland: AEGONplein 50, POB 202, 2501 CE The Hague; tel. (70) 3443210; fax (70) 3475238; internet www.aegon.nl; f. 1983 by merger; life, accident, health, general and linked activities; Chair. JOHAN VAN DER WERF.

Delta Lloyd Verzekeringsgroep NV: Spaklerweg 4, POB 1000, 1000 BA Amsterdam; tel. (20) 5949111; fax (20) 937968; internet www.deltalloyd.nl; f. 1807; Chair. JACQUES VAN DIJK.

De Eerste Nederlandsche: POB 325, 1170 AH Badhoevedorp; tel. (20) 6143340; fax (20) 6696556; e-mail info@eerste.nl; internet www.eerste.nl; all branches.

Fiducia BV: Ruysdaelplein 42, 2282 BJ Rijswijk; tel. (70) 4140404; fax (70) 4140405; e-mail info@fiducia.nl; internet www.fiducia.nl; f. 1990.

Fortis ASR Verzekeringsgroep NV: Weena 70, POB 100, 3000 AC Rotterdam; tel. (10) 4017465; fax (10) 4125490; internet www.asr.nl; f. 2000 by merger of ASR Verzekeringsgroep NV (f. 1720) and AMEV Nederland NV (f. 1883); owned by the Fortis group; Chair. J. C. VAN EK.

Generali Verzekeringsgroep: Diemerhof 42, 1112 XN Diemen; tel. (20) 6604444; fax (20) 3983000; e-mail info@generali.nl; internet www.generali.nl; f. 1870; life and non-life; Gen. Dir FREEK WANSINK.

ING Groep NV: Amstelveenseweg 500, 1081 KL Amsterdam; tel. (70) 5415433; fax (70) 5415412; e-mail mediarelations@ing.com; internet www.ing.com; f. 1963; Chair. C. A. J. HERKSTRÖTER.

   Nationale-Nederlanden NV: Weena 505, 3013 AL Rotterdam; tel. (10) 45130303; f. 1863; Chair. LUDO WIJNGAARDEN.

RVS Levensverzekering NV: Weena 505, 3013 AL Rotterdam; tel. (10) 4012911; fax (10) 4012933; e-mail rvs@rvs.nl; internet www.rvs.nl; f. 1838; subsidiary of ING Groep NV; mem. of Internationale-Nederlanden group; life; Chair. H. W. SMID.

Insurance Association

Verbond van Verzekeraars (Asscn of Insurers): Bordewijklaan 2, POB 93450, 2509 AL The Hague; tel. (70) 3338500; fax (70) 338510; e-mail info@verzekeraars.nl; internet www.verzekeraars.nl; f. 1978; Chair. P. F. M. OVERMARS; Gen. Man. Prof. Dr E. J. FISCHER.

Trade and Industry

GOVERNMENT AGENCY

Netherlands Foreign Investment Agency: Bezuidenhoutseweg 16A, POB 20101, 2500 EC The Hague; tel. (70) 3798818; fax (70) 3796322; e-mail info@nfia.nl; internet www.nfia.nl; govt agency; facilitates foreign direct investment.

CHAMBERS OF COMMERCE

There are 12 autonomous Chambers of Commerce and Industry in the Netherlands. The most important are:

Kamer van Koophandel Amsterdam (Chamber of Commerce and Industry for Amsterdam): De Ruyterkade 5, 1013 AA Amsterdam; POB 2852, 1000 CW Amsterdam; tel. (20) 5314000; fax (20) 5314799; e-mail info@amsterdam.kvk.nl; internet www.amsterdam.kvk.nl; f. 1811; Dir-Gen. H. E. VAN BAARSBANK.

Kamer van Koophandel Rotterdam (Chamber of Commerce for Rotterdam): Blaak 40, 3011 TA Rotterdam; POB 450, 3000 AL Rotterdam; tel. (10) 4027777; fax (10) 4145754; e-mail post@rotterdam.kvk.nl; internet www.rotterdam.kvk.nl; f. 1803; Pres. (vacant).

EMPLOYERS' ORGANIZATIONS

LTO-Nederland (Netherlands Agricultural Organization): Bezuidenhoutseweg 225, 2594 AL The Hague; POB 29773, 2502 LT The Hague; tel. (70) 3382700; fax (70) 3382810; e-mail info@lto.nl; internet www.lto.nl; f. 1995; Chair. A. J. MAAT; 50,000 mems.

NERG (Nederlands Elektronica- en Radiogenootschap): POB 39, 2260 AK Leidschendam; tel. (70) 3325112; fax (70) 3326477; internet www.nerg.nl; f. 1921; Chair. Prof. Dr N. H. G. BAKEN; Sec. E. BOTTELIER; c. 500 mems.

Nederlands Centrum voor Handelsbevordering (NCH) (Netherlands Council for Trade Promotion): Juliana van Stolberglaan 148, POB 10, 2501 CA The Hague; tel. (70) 3441544; fax (70) 3853531; e-mail info@nchnl.nl; internet www.handelsbevordering.nl; Man. Dir G. C. VAANDRAGER; 800 mem. cos.

Nederlandsche Maatschappij voor Nijverheid en Handel (NMNH) (Netherlands Society for Industry and Trade): Jan van Nassaustraat 75, 2596 BP The Hague; tel. (70) 3141940; fax (70) 3247515; e-mail info@nmnh.nl; internet www.nmnh.nl; f. 1777; Pres. R. J. A. DE LANGE; Dir-Gen. GEERT VAN DER TANG; more than 5,500 mems.

De Nederlandse Tuinbouwraad (NTR) (Netherlands Horticultural Council): Schipholweg 1, 2316 XB Leiden; tel. (71) 5659596; fax (71) 5659610; e-mail informatie@tuinbouwraad.nl; internet www.tuinbouwraad.nl; f. 1908; Chair. Dr N. C. A. (NICO) KOOMEN; Sec. JAN WILLEM GRIEP.

Vereniging VNO-NCW (Confederation of Netherlands Industry and Employers): Bezuidenhoutseweg 12, POB 93002, 2509 AA The Hague; tel. (70) 3490349; fax (70) 3490300; e-mail informatie@vno-ncw.nl; internet www.vno-ncw.nl; f. 1997 as merger of Verbond van Nederlandse Ondernemingen (VNO) and Nederlands Christelijk Werkgeversverbond (NCW); represents almost all sectors of the Dutch economy; Pres. B. E. M. (BERNARD) WIENTJES; mems: 160 asscns representing more than 115,000 enterprises.

UTILITIES

Electricity

E.ON Benelux BV: POB 909, 2270 AX Voorburg; tel. (70) 3820028; fax (70) 3383901; e-mail info@eon-benelux.com; internet www.eon-benelux.com; f. 2000; replaced Electriciteitsbedrijf Zuid Holland (f. 1941); supplies energy to large-volume customers and distributors.

ENECO: POB 96, 2900 AB Capelle a/d Ijssel; tel. (10) 4576979; fax (10) 4577784; internet www.eneco.nl; Chair. R. BLOM; 5,000 employees.

Essent: Nieuwe Stationsstraat 20, 6811 KS Arnhem; internet www.essent.nl; f. 1999 by merger of Edon Group and Pnem Mega Group; electricity generation and supply, also supplier of gas; Chair., Management Bd MICHIEL BOERSMA.

Nuon NV: Spaklerweg 20, POB 41920, 1009 DC Amsterdam; tel. (20) 5972729; e-mail nuon@nuon.com; internet www.nuon.com; f. 1999; energy and water; Chair. W. MEIJER; CEO LUDO M. J. VAN HALDEREN.

Tennet BV: Utrechtseweg 310, POB 718, 6812 AS Arnhem; tel. (26) 3731111; fax (26) 3731112; e-mail servicedesk@tennet.org; internet www.tennet.org; f. 1999; independent; Dutch Transmission System operator; manages 220/380-kW national grid and supplies electricity to direct suppliers; Dir MEL KROON.

Gas

Full liberalization of the gas market in the Netherlands took effect from the beginning of July 2004. Although retaining ownership of the main transport network, NV Nederlandse Gasunie passed the legal tasks of the national transmission system operator to a new, state-owned organization, Gas Transport Services BV, founded on 2 July 2004.

ENECO: see above.

Essent: see above.

Gas Transport Services BV: POB 181, 9700 AD Groningen; tel. (50) 3626000; fax (50) 3626100; e-mail info@gastransport.nl; internet www.gastransportservices.nl; f. 2004; independent; transmission system operator; CEO GEERT H. GRAAF.

NV Nederlandse Gasunie: Concourslaan 17, POB 19, 9700 MA Groningen; tel. (50) 5219111; fax (50) 5211999; e-mail communicatie@gasunie.nl; internet www.gasunie.nl; f. 2005; CEO MARCEL P. KRAMER.

RWE Obragas NV: POB 300, 5700 AH Helmond; tel. (49) 2594888; fax (49) 2594990; internet www.rwe.nl.

Water

Nuon: see above.

Vewin: POB 1019, 2280 CA Rijswijk; tel. (70) 4144750; fax (70) 4144420; e-mail info@vewin.nl; internet www.vewin.nl; Man. Dir J. J. SCHMITZ.

TRADE UNIONS

Central federations and affiliated unions are mainly organized on a religious, political or economic basis. The most important unions are those of the transport, metal, building and textile industries, the civil service and agriculture.

Central Federations

Christelijk Nationaal Vakverbond in Nederland (CNV) (Christian National Federation of Trade Unions): Tiberdreef 4, POB 2475, 3500 GL Utrecht; tel. (30) 7511100; fax (30) 7511109; e-mail cnvinfo@cnv.nl; internet www.cnv.nl; f. 1909; affiliated to ITUC and European Trade Union Confederation; Pres. RENÉ PAAS; Gen. Sec. BERT VAN BOGGELEN; 330,000 mems.

Eleven affiliated unions, of which the principal unions are:

CNV Bedrijvenbond (Industry, Food and Transport): Tiberdreef 4, POB 2525, 3500 GM Utrecht; tel. (30) 7511007; e-mail info@cnv.net;

internet www.cnvbedrijvenbond.nl; Chair. Jaap Jongejan; 85,000 mems.

CNV Dienstenbond (Service Industries, Media and Printing): Polarisave 175, POB 3135, 2130 KC Hoofddorp; tel. (23) 5651052; fax (23) 5650150; e-mail cnvdienstenbond@cnvdibo.nl; internet www .cnvdienstenbond.nl; f. 1894; Pres. D. Swagerman; Sec. R. J. Rotshuizen; 36,500 mems.

CNV Hout en Bouw (Wood and Building): Oude Haven 1, 3984 KT Odijk; tel. (30) 6597711; fax (30) 6571101; e-mail info@cnvhb.nl; internet www.cnvhb.nl; f. 1900; Chair. A. A. van Wijngaarden; Gen. Sec. J. T. Slok; 48,000 mems.

CNV Onderwijs (Education): Tiberdreef 4, POB 2510, 3500 ZC Utrecht; tel. (30) 75117000; fax (30) 7511709; e-mail info@cnvo.nl; internet www.cnvo.nl; f. 2000; Pres. Marleen Barth.

CNV Publieke Zaak (Public Sector Union): Carnegielaan 1, POB 84500, 2508 AM The Hague; tel. (70) 4160600; fax (70) 4160690; e-mail denhaag@cnvpubliekezaak.nl; internet www .cnvpubliekezaak.nl; Pres. P. J. Koeslag; Sec. K. Kruithof; 79,000 mems.

Federatie Nederlandse Vakbeweging (FNV) (Netherlands Trade Union Confederation): Naritaweg 10, POB 8456, 1005 AL Amsterdam; tel. (20) 5816300; fax (20) 6844541; e-mail persvoorlichting@vc.fnv.nl; internet www.fnv.nl; f. 1975 as confederation of the Netherlands Federation of Trade Unions (f. 1906) and the Netherlands Catholic Trade Union Federation (f. 1909); Pres. Agnes Jongerius; Vice-Pres. Peter Gortzak; Gen. Sec. Wilna Wind; 1,234,361 mems.

Seventeen affiliated unions, of which the principal are:

ABVAKABO FNV (Government Personnel, Civil Servants, Private Health Workers, Social Workers, Post and Telecom Workers, Public Utility Workers): Boerhaavelaan 1, POB 3010, 2700 KT Zoetermeer; tel. (79) 3536161; fax (79) 3521226; e-mail post@abvakabo.nl; internet www.abvakabofnv.nl; f. 1982; Pres. Edith Snoey; Gen. Sec. Xander den Uyl; 365,000 mems.

Algemene Onderwijsbond (AOb) (Education): Jaarbeursplein 22, POB 2875, 3500 GW Utrecht; tel. (30) 2989898; fax (30) 2989862; e-mail info@aob.nl; internet www.aob.nl; f. 1997 as merger between Algemene Bond van Onderwijspersoneel and NGL—Dordrecht; Pres. Walter Dresscher; Gen. Sec. Martin Knoop; 76,000 mems.

FNV Bondgenoten (Transport, Metal and Steel, Information Technology, Electrotechnical, Textiles, Financial Services, Retail, Wholesale, Foods, Agriculture): Varrolaan 100, POB 9208, 3506 GE Utrecht; tel. (30) 2738222; fax (30) 2738225; internet www .bondgenoten.fnv.nl; f. 1998 by merger; Pres. Henk van der Kolk; Sec. Ellen Dekkers; 460,000 mems.

FNV Bouw (Building): Houttuinlaan 3, POB 520, 3440 AM Woerden; tel. (348) 575575; fax (348) 423610; e-mail info@fnvbouw.nl; internet www.fnvbouw.nl; f. 1917; Pres. Dick van Haaster; 150,000 mems.

FNV KIEM (Printing and Allied Trades): J. Tooropstraat, POB 9354, 1006 AJ Amsterdam; tel. (20) 3553636; fax (20) 3553737; e-mail algemeen@fnv-kiem.nl; internet www.fnv.nl/kiem; Chair. Herman Leisink; Gen. Sec. Bea van den Bosch; 41,000 mems.

Nederlandse Politiebond (NPB) (Police): Steinhagenseweg 2D, POB 68, 3440 AB Woerden; tel. (34) 8707444; fax (34) 8707411; e-mail info@politiebond.nl; internet www.politiebond.nl; f. 1946; Pres. Hans van Duijn; Gen. Sec. Frans van der Heiden; 22,500 mems.

Vakcentrale voor Middengroepen en Hoger Personeel (MHP) (Federation for Middle Groups and Higher Personnel): Multatulilaan 12, POB 575, 4100 AN Culemborg; tel. (345) 851900; fax (345) 851915; e-mail info@vc-mhp.nl; internet www.vakcentralemhp.nl; f. 1974; mem. of the European Trade Union Confederation; Pres. Ad Verhoeven; 160,000 mems.

Four affiliated unions, of which the following is the largest:

Unie van Onafhankelijke Vakorganisaties (UoV) (United Independent Trade Unions): Multatulilaan 12, POB 400, 4100 AK Culemborg; tel. (345) 851851; fax (345) 851500; e-mail info@unie .nl; internet www.uov.nl; 16 affiliated independent trade unions, including De Unie; 93,900 mems.

Consultative Organization

Stichting van de Arbeid (Labour Foundation): Bezuidenhoutseweg 60, 2594 AW The Hague; tel. (70) 3499577; fax (70) 3499796; internet www.stvda.nl; f. 1945; central organ of co-operation and consultation between employers and employees; 16 bd mems; Jt Pres B. E. M. Wientjes, A. M. Jongerius.

Land Reclamation and Development

Without intensive land-protection schemes, nearly the whole of the north and west of the Netherlands (about one-half of the total area of the country) would be inundated by sea-water twice a day. A large part of the country (including a section of the former Zuiderzee, now the IJsselmeer) has already been drained.

The Delta Plan, which was adopted in 1958 and provided for the construction of eight dams, a major canal, several locks and a system of dykes, aimed to shorten the southern coastline by 700 km and to protect the estuaries of Zeeland and Southern Holland. The final cost of the delta works project, which had originally been projected at 2,500m. guilders, totalled around 14,000m. guilders, as the result of a complex adaptation to ensure the preservation of the delta's ecological balance.

The Ministry of Transport, Public Works and Water Management is responsible for land reclamation and waterways.

Transport

RAILWAYS

About 70% of the Dutch railway network is electrified; the remaining track carries diesel electric and diesel stock. There were approximately 6,500 km of railways in 2007, providing mainly passenger services. The infrastructure of the Dutch railway network remains wholly under public ownership. Until early 2002 the main railway operator, Nederlandse Spoorwegen (NS), was partially privatized, but, following a sharp deterioration in the quality of service, it was taken back under government control. NS retains a majority of the passenger and freight rolling stock, and station premises, while there is a small number of additional, privately owned network service providers.

Nederlandse Spoorwegen NV (NS): Laan van Puntenberg 100, POB 2025, 3500 HA Utrecht; tel. (30) 2359111; fax (30) 2332458; internet www.ns.nl; f. 1937; partially privatized until early 2002, when the Govt reasserted management control; operates most railway lines in the Netherlands; Pres. and Man. Dir Aad W. Veenman (until 31 December 2008), Bert Meerstadt (from 1 January 2009).

NoordNed Personenvervoer BV: Stationsplein 4, POB 452, 8901 BG Leeuwarden; tel. (58) 2335646; fax (58) 2335636; e-mail t .degnua@noordned.com; internet www.noordned.com; f. 1999; subsidiary of Arriva Nederland; operates train and bus services in North and South-West Friesland.

ProRail: POB 2038, 3500 GA Utrecht; tel. (30) 2357104; fax (30) 2359056; internet www.prorail.nl; f. 2003; manages and maintains railway infrastructure, and controls passenger and freight traffic; independent; Chair. Bert Klerk.

Railion Benelux NV: POB 2060, 3500 GB Utrecht; tel. (30) 2354004; fax (30) 2354334; e-mail info@railion.nl; internet www .railion.nl; international goods transport by rail; Man. Dir Carel P. H. Robbeson.

ROADS

In 2003 there were 2,500 km of motorway, 6,700 km of main roads, 57,500 km of secondary roads and 59,400 km of other roads in the Netherlands.

INLAND WATERWAYS

An extensive network of rivers and canals navigable for ships of 50 metric tons and over, totalling 5,046 km, has led to the outstanding development of Dutch inland shipping. About one-third of goods transported inside the Netherlands are carried on the canals and waterways. Dutch inland shipping has access to Germany and France along the Rhine and its branch rivers, and to France and Belgium along the Meuse and Scheldt (including the Rhine-Scheldt link). Ocean traffic reaches Rotterdam via the New Waterway, and the 21-km long North Sea Canal connects Amsterdam to the North Sea.

SHIPPING

The Netherlands is one of the world's leading shipping countries. At the end of 2006 the merchant fleet comprised 1,258 vessels, with a combined displacement of 5.8m. gross registered tons. The Port of Rotterdam complex, incorporating Europoort (for large oil tankers and bulk carriers), is the main European Union port and the busiest in the world, handling over 350m. metric tons of cargo per year.

Principal Companies

Amasus Chartering BV: Zijlvest 26, Farmsum, POB 250, 9930 Delfzijl; tel. (596) 610744; fax (596) 616551; e-mail chartering@amasus.nl; internet www.amasus.nl; shipowners, managers and operators.

Hudig Freight Services: Debussystraat 2, POB 1030, 3160 AE Rhoon; tel. (10) 5066550; fax (10) 5012827; e-mail info@hudig.nl; internet www.hudig.com; f. 1795; international freight services; Man. Dir A. D. FONTEIN.

Koninklijke Vopak NV: Westerlaan 10, POB 863, 3000 AW Rotterdam; tel. (10) 4002911; fax (10) 4139829; e-mail info@vopak.com; internet www.vopak.com; f. 1999; Chair. JOHN PAUL BROEDERS.

Koninklijke Wagenborg BV: Marktstraat 10, POB 14, 9930 AA Delfzyl; tel. (596) 636911; fax (596) 636250; e-mail info@wagenborg.com; internet www.wagenborg.com; shipowners, managers and operators; Man. Dirs Dr E. VUURSTEEN, Dr G. R. WAGENBORG.

Seatrade Groningen BV: Laan Corpus den Hoorn 200, POB 858, 9700 AW Groningen; tel. (50) 5215300; fax (50) 5215399; e-mail info@seatrade.nl; internet www.seatrade.nl; shipowners, managers and operators; Man. Dir Capt. MARK JANSEN.

Spliethoff's Bevrachtingskantoor BV: Radarweg 36, POB 409, 1000 AK Amsterdam; tel. (20) 4488400; fax (20) 4488500; e-mail gogracht@spliethoff.com; internet www.spliethoff.nl; shipowners, managers and operators; Man. ROLF G. W. ERIKSSON.

Stena Line: Stationsweg 10, POB 2, 3150 AA Hoek van Holland; tel. (17) 4389333; fax (17) 4389309; e-mail info.nl@stenaline.net; internet www.stenaline.com; operates daily (day and night) ferry services for accompanied private cars, commercial freight vehicles and trailers between Hoek van Holland and Harwich (UK); Man. Dir GUNNAR BLOMDAHL.

Van Uden Maritime BV: POB 1123, 3000 BC, Rotterdam; tel. (10) 2973100; fax (10) 4851044; e-mail group@van-uden.nl; internet www.van-uden.nl; f. 1848; agencies in Rotterdam, Amsterdam; liner operators and representatives; international chartering; Man. D. P. F. DUTILH.

Vroon BV: Haven Westzijde 21, POB 28, 4510 AA Breskens; tel. (117) 384910; fax (117) 384218; e-mail office@vroon.nl; internet www.vroon.nl; shipowners, managers and operators; Man. Dir F. D. VROON.

Wijnne & Barends' Cargadoors- en Agentuurkantonen BV: Handelskade Oost 5, POB 123, 9930 AC Delfzyl; tel. (596) 637777; fax (596) 637790; e-mail info@wijnne-barends.nl; internet www.wijnne-barends.nl; f. 1855; became part of Spliethoff Group in 2003; shipowners, managers and operators; cargo services and agents; Man. Dir D. P. MAKKINJE.

Shipping Associations

Federatie van Werknemers in de Zeevaart (Dutch Seafarers' Federation): Heemraadssingel 323, POB 25131, 3001 HC Rotterdam; tel. (10) 4771188; fax (10) 4773846; e-mail fwz.nl@wxs.nl; internet www.fnv.nl/zeevaart.

Koninklijke Vereniging van Nederlandse Reders (KVNR) (Royal Asscn of Netherlands' Shipowners): Wijnhaven 65B, POB 2442, 3000 CK Rotterdam; tel. (10) 4146001; fax (10) 2330081; e-mail kvnr@kvnr.nl; internet www.kvnr.nl; f. 1905; Chair. A. KORTELAND; Man. Dir G. X. HOLLAAR; 300 mems.

Vereniging Nederlandse Scheepsbouw Industrie (Netherlands Shipbuilding Industry Asscn): Boerhaavelaan 40, POB 138, 2700 AC Zoetermeer; tel. (79) 3531165; fax (79) 3531155; e-mail info@vnsi.nl; internet www.vnsi.nl; promotes Dutch shipbuilding on a national basis; Man. Dir R. J. SCHOUTEN; 95 mems.

CIVIL AVIATION

The main Dutch airport is at Schiphol, near Amsterdam. There are also international airports at Zestienhoven for Rotterdam, Beek for Maastricht and at Eelde for Groningen. Schiphol has expanded rapidly since the late 1990s, from 25.3m. passengers in 1995 to 47.7m. in 2007. A fifth runway was opened in early 2003, while the planned privatization of Schiphol was abandoned in February 2007.

KLM (Koninklijke Luchtvaart Maatschappij) NV (Royal Dutch Airlines): Amsterdamseweg 55, 1182 GP Amstelveen; tel. (20) 6499123; fax (20) 6488069; internet www.klm.com; f. 1919; world's oldest commercial airline; regular international air services; merged with Air France in 2004 to create Europe's largest airline; subsidiaries: KLM cityhopper, transavia.com; Pres. and CEO PETER F. HARTMAN.

Martinair Holland NV: Havenmeesterweg 201, POB 7507, 1118 ZG Schiphol Airport; tel. (20) 6011767; fax (20) 6011303; internet www.martinair.nl; f. 1958; world-wide passenger and cargo services; Pres. and CEO ARIE VERBERK.

transavia.com: Westelijke Randweg 3, POB 7777, 1118 ZM Schiphol Airport; tel. (20) 6046555; fax (20) 6015093; internet transavia.com; f. 1965 as Transavia Limburg N.V.; scheduled and charter services to leisure destinations; subsidiary of KLM; Pres. and CEO ONNO P. M. VAN DEN BRINK.

Tourism

The principal tourist attractions in the Netherlands are the cosmopolitan city of Amsterdam, which receives nearly one-half of all tourist visits, the historic towns, the canals, the cultivated fields of spring flowers, the outlying islands, the art galleries and modern architecture. Some 10.0m. foreign tourists stayed in hotels and boarding houses in the Netherlands in 2005. Receipts from tourism totalled an estimated US $10,383m. in the same year.

Toerisme Recreatie Nederlands (Netherlands Board of Tourism): Vlietweg 15, POB 458, 2260 MG Leidschendam; tel. (70) 3705705; fax (70) 3201654; e-mail info@holland.com; internet www.holland.com; f. 1968; Man. Dir HANS VAN DRIEM.

Royal Dutch Touring Club ANWB: POB 93200, 2596 EC The Hague; tel. (70) 3147147; fax (70) 3146969; e-mail info@anwb.nl; internet www.anwb.nl; f. 1883; CEO GUIDO H. N. L. VAN WOERKOM; 55 brs in Europe; 3.9m. mems.

NETHERLANDS DEPENDENCIES

ARUBA

Introductory Survey

Location, Climate, Language, Religion, Flag, Capital

Aruba is one of the group of Benedenwindse Eilands or 'Leeward Islands', which it forms with part of the Netherlands Antilles (q.v.), and lies in the southern Caribbean Sea, 25 km north of Venezuela and 68 km west of the island of Curaçao (Netherlands Antilles). The climate is tropical, with an average annual temperature of 28°C (82°F), but is tempered by north-easterly winds. Rainfall is very low, averaging only about 426 mm (16.8 ins) annually. The official language is Dutch, but the dominant language is Papiamento (a mixture of Dutch, Spanish, English, Arawak Indian and several West African dialects). Spanish and English are also spoken. Most of the inhabitants profess Christianity and belong to the Roman Catholic Church, although a wide variety of other denominations are represented. The national flag (proportions 2 by 3) is blue, with two narrow yellow horizontal stripes in the lower section and a white-bordered four-pointed red star in the upper hoist. The capital is Oranjestad.

Recent History

The Caribbean island of Aruba was claimed for Spain in 1499, but was first colonized by the Dutch in 1636 and subsequently formed part of the Dutch possessions in the West Indies. Administered from Curaçao after 1845, in 1954 Aruba became a member of the autonomous federation of the Netherlands Antilles. The establishment in 1929 of a large petroleum refinery on the island, at San Nicolaas, led to the rapid expansion of the economy and a high standard of living for the islanders. However, many Arubans resented the administrative dominance of Curaçao, and what they regarded as the excessive demands made upon Aruban wealth and resources by the other five islands within the Netherlands Antilles. The island's principal political party, the Movimentu Electoral di Pueblo (MEP), campaigned, from its foundation in 1971 onwards, for Aruban independence and separation from the other islands. In a referendum held in Aruba in March 1977 82% of voters supported independence and withdrawal from the Antillean federation. The MEP used its position in the coalition Government of the Netherlands Antilles, formed in 1979, to press for concessions from the other islands towards early independence for Aruba. In 1981 (after the MEP had withdrawn from the Government of the Netherlands Antilles) a provisional agreement regarding Aruba's future was reached between the Dutch and Antillean Governments. Following further discussions, it was agreed in March 1983 that Aruba should receive separate status (*status aparte*), within the Kingdom of the Netherlands, from 1 January 1986, achieving full independence in 1996. The Dutch Government would remain responsible for defence and external relations until independence, while Aruba was to form a co-operative union with the Netherlands Antilles (the Antilles of the Five) in economic and monetary affairs.

At local elections in April 1983 the MEP increased its representation to 13 of the 21 seats in the Staten (parliament), and the leader of the MEP, Gilberto F. (Betico) Croes, remained as leader of the island Government. Austerity measures, introduced in an attempt to alleviate the adverse effects of the closure (announced in October 1984) of the San Nicolaas petroleum refinery, provoked a series of strikes and demonstrations by civil servants in protest at wage reductions and price rises. The MEP consequently lost popular support and, following elections to the Staten in November 1985, was succeeded in government by a coalition of four opposition parties led by the Arubaanse Volkspartij (AVP). Aruba achieved separate status, as planned, on 1 January 1986, and Jan Hendrik Albert (Henny) Eman, leader of the AVP, became its first Prime Minister. Croes died in November 1986; he was succeeded as leader of the MEP by Nelson O. Oduber.

From 1988 Aruba began to enjoy an economic recovery, based on tourism. However, the MEP claimed that the benefits to the whole community were limited, and also criticized Eman's stated reservations about independence in 1996 and his refusal to negotiate with the Netherlands about transitional arrangements. At a general election in January 1989 the MEP came within 28 votes of securing an absolute majority in the Staten. The number of seats held by the MEP increased from eight to 10, and in February Oduber formed a Government in coalition with the Partido Patriótico Arubano (PPA) and the Acción Democrático Nacional (ADN). (Both these parties had been in the previous Government, and retained one seat each at the election.)

The MEP and the AVP each secured nine seats in the Staten at the January 1993 general election, while the three remaining seats were won by the ADN, the PPA and the Organisacion Liberal Arubano (OLA). Despite gaining fewer votes than the AVP, the MEP administration remained in office, renewing the coalition with the ADN and the PPA. In April 1994, however, Oduber announced the Government's resignation, following the withdrawal of the ADN and the PPA from the coalition. In May, following lengthy inter-party negotiations, it was agreed that a fresh general election would be held. Government functions were to be undertaken in the interim by the MEP. The general election was held on 29 July: the AVP secured 10 seats, while the MEP won nine seats and the OLA the remaining two. In late August Eman formed a Government in coalition with the OLA.

In March 1994 the Governments of Aruba, the Netherlands and the Netherlands Antilles convened in The Hague, the Netherlands, and decided to cancel plans for Aruba's transition to full independence, due to take place in 1996. The possibility of a transition to full independence at a later date was not excluded, but was not considered a priority, and would, moreover, require the approval of the Aruban people, by referendum, as well as the support of a two-thirds' majority in the Staten.

In September 1997 the Staten was dissolved after the OLA withdrew from the coalition. A general election was thus held on 12 December; this resulted in a political composition identical to that of the 1993 polls. Following protracted negotiations, the AVP and the OLA renewed their coalition in mid-1998, and a new Council of Ministers, headed by Eman, was appointed.

In June 2001 the governing coalition collapsed, following the withdrawal of the OLA's support for the AVP's plan to privatize the Aruban Tourism Authority. As a result, the legislative elections that had been scheduled to be held in December were brought forward to 28 September. The MEP comfortably defeated the incumbent AVP in the elections, securing 52% of the votes cast and 12 seats in the Staten. The AVP legislative representation was reduced to six seats. The three remaining seats were shared between the PPA (two) and the OLA (one). Oduber was once again appointed Prime Minister and a new single-party Government, with an unprecedented opportunity to pass legislation through the Staten, took office in November.

In early 2004 after several months of discussion, the Aruban and Dutch Governments agreed to appoint Fredis Refunjol, hitherto Minister of Education, as Governor. The Dutch Government objected to the fact that there was only one candidate for the position and argued that the appointment was overtly political. Nevertheless, since Refunjol's candidature had strong cross-party support in the Staten, he was duly sworn in on 7 May. The erstwhile President of the Staten, Francisco Walfrido Croes, assumed the vacant education portfolio. Meanwhile, in January the Staten voted against becoming an Ultra Periphery Area of the European Union (EU, see p. 244). The island thus remained an Overseas Territory of the EU.

At a general election on 23 September 2005 the MEP again won a majority of seats (11, from 43% of the popular vote) in the 21-seat Staten. The victory came in spite of broad public criticism of the Government's unwillingness to defend wage levels from the downward pressure caused by large-scale immigration from South America. Notably, the minimum wage had not been adjusted for five years. The AVP won eight seats, an improvement on its result in the 2001 election, and the PPA and Network each won one legislative seat. The electoral turn-out among those eligible to vote was 85%. Oduber, who continued as Prime Minister, defended his economic policies and pledged to continue to develop the tourism sector and to balance the budget, which is heavily dependent on external creditors, by 2009.

Aruba's relations with the Antilles of the Five improved after 1986. In 1987 Aruba agreed to undertake economic co-operation, and in 1988 the three Dutch 'Leeward Islands' initiated a joint project for the development of tourism. Aruba's relations with the 'metropolitan' Netherlands were dominated at this time by the latter's pressure for more control to be exercised over the large amount of aid that it gave to Aruba, and by the issue of independence, in particular the future arrangements for the island's security: Aruba's strategic position, close to the South American mainland, and the possibility of its being used as a base for drugs-trafficking, were matters of particular concern. In September 1990 Aruba announced that it was to adopt the 1988 UN Convention on measures to combat trade in illegal drugs; a joint Dutch and Aruban team was formed to conduct investigations. In December 1996, however, the USA included Aruba on its list of major drugs-producing or transit countries. New legislation to facilitate the extradition of suspected drugs-traffickers and money-launderers took effect in October 1997. US naval and air force patrols began operating from a base in Aruba in May 1999 in an effort to counter the transport of illicit drugs. In 2001 the Caribbean Financial Action Task Force commended the Government on its efforts in combating money-laundering. In the same year the territory was removed from the list of so-called 'un-co-operative tax havens' drawn up by the Organisation for Economic Co-operation and Development (OECD, based in Paris, France), after the Government pledged to reform the territory's financial sector in order to conform to OECD's guidelines by 2005. In October the Minister of Justice, Rudy Croes, visited The Hague to discuss the issue of independence with the Dutch Government. Relations between Aruba and the Netherlands deteriorated, however, when the Dutch Government forced Aruba to introduce a more stringent policy on visa conditions. In November 2003 Aruba signed an agreement with the USA to exchange tax information in order to combat illegal financial activities, such as money-laundering, that are associated with international terrorism and drugs-trafficking. The issue of immigration arose again in late 2004: in the first 10 months of the year Aruba deported 864 Colombians, most of whom arrived on the island from Venezuela. In late 2006 Aruba was collaborating with the Netherlands towards drafting its first anti-corruption legislation, which would equip the Caribbean state with the legislative means to ratify international anti-corruption treaties.

In May 2005 the disappearance of a US teenager, Natalee Holloway, on the island and the attendant negative publicity in her home country led to tension in the relationship between Aruba and the USA and placed severe strain on the island's crucial tourism industry, which is heavily dependent upon US custom. Later in the year the Governor of Alabama, the missing girl's home state, blamed the Aruban Government for the failure to discover her whereabouts and, backed by overwhelming US public support (and, in January 2006, by the Alabama Senate), unsuccessfully requested that the US Government impose sanctions on Aruba. Several arrests were made during 2006 but suspects were subsequently released, exacerbating criticism of the investigation's perceived mismanagement. In early 2007 legal representatives for two of the original suspects (resident in Aruba) applied to the Superior Court in Los Angeles for the dismissal of a 'wrongful death' action filed by Holloway's parents against the defendants in December 2006. The case continued to feature in the Aruban media in early 2008, when a Dutch journalist released video footage of the main suspect apparently confessing to dumping Holloway's body at sea after she allegedly collapsed while the two were together on a beach. However, the whereabouts of the US teenager remained unknown despite extensive ground and sea searches.

Amendments to the Western Hemisphere Travel Initiative, ratified by the US Congress on 4 October 2006, requiring all US citizens and foreign nationals travelling to and from the Caribbean to hold a valid passport, were implemented from 8 January 2007. The initiative precipitated myriad travel incentives within Aruba and other Caribbean states in an attempt to offset the anticipated decline in tourism. Unified by the perceived threat, several of the Caribbean states' tourism officials lobbied for the deadline to be extended to June 2009, when the legislation would also become applicable to cruise-ship passengers. The new visa requirements were, however, enacted as scheduled but in June delays experienced in the processing of applications prompted the US Department of State to issue a limited extension of existing regulations until September 2007. Reports from the Aruba Airport Authority suggested that the feared collapse in tourist arrivals had not materialized in the first 11 months of 2007, with a 9.8% growth in arrivals at airports.

After acquiring separate status, Aruba fostered relations with some of its Caribbean neighbours and with countries in Latin America. This included the development of ties with Venezuela, which had traditionally laid claim to the Dutch 'Leeward Islands', including Aruba, and the signing of a memorandum of understanding with Brazil in September 2006, which sought to promote more extensive air transport links.

Government

Aruba has separate status within the Kingdom of the Netherlands. Legislative power is held by the unicameral Staten (parliament) of 21 members, elected by universal adult suffrage for four years (subject to dissolution). Executive power in all domestic affairs is vested in the Council of Ministers (led by the Prime Minister), responsible to the Staten. The Governor, appointed by the Dutch Crown for a term of six years, represents the monarch of the Netherlands on Aruba and holds responsibility for external affairs and defence. The Governor is assisted by an advisory council.

Defence

The Netherlands is responsible for Aruba's defence and military service is compulsory. The Governor is Commander-in-Chief of the armed forces on the island. A Dutch naval contingent is stationed in Aruba, primarily to combat drugs-trafficking and organized crime. In May 1999 the USA began air force and navy patrols from a base on Aruba as part of efforts to prevent the transport of illegal drugs.

Economic Affairs

In 2000, according to the UN, Aruba's gross national income (GNI), was US $1,756m. During 1995–2004 the population increased at an average annual rate of 2.3% per year, while in 2003–06 it increased at an average annual rate of 0.7%. According to the UN, gross domestic product (GDP) per head increased, in real terms, by an average of 3.6% per year in 1996–2006. Overall GDP increased, in real terms, at an average annual rate of 2.5% in 1996–2006. Real GDP increased by an estimated 2.4% in 2006.

Owing to the poor quality of the soil and the prohibitive cost of desalinated water, the only significant agricultural activity is the cultivation of aloes (used in the manufacture of cosmetics and pharmaceuticals); aloe-based products are exported. Some livestock is raised, and there is a small fishing industry (although in the mid-1990s fishing production contributed only some 12.5% of Aruba's annual consumption of fish and fish products). In 2000 the agricultural sector engaged 0.6% of the employed labour force, although FAO estimated that it employed 20.8% of the employed labour force in mid-2005. The sector contributed 0.4% of total GDP in 2006, according to UN estimates.

The industrial sector, and the island's economy, was formerly based on the refining and transhipment of imported petroleum and petroleum products. In the early 1980s this sector accounted for one-quarter of GDP and provided almost all Aruba's exports. The San Nicolaas petroleum refinery ceased operations in 1985; however, in 1990 the plant partially reopened, following renovation; after more construction and revision works, production reached an estimated 202,000 barrels per day (b/d) in 1999, an increase of 26% on the previous year's total. Following a further US $250m. renovation in 2000, production increased to 280,000 b/d. In March 2004 the refinery was purchased by the US-based Valero Energy Corporation, which, in 2005, announced that it was considering a US $6,000m. expansion of the plant in order to increase production to as much as 800,000 b/d by about 2012. In 2005 Aruba refined 78.2m. barrels of crude petroleum; imports of crude petroleum were valued at A. Fl. 5,910m. and exports at A. Fl. 7,602m. (total exports excluding mineral fuels and free-trade zone transactions amounted to just A. Fl. 36.1m. in the same year). There is a large petroleum transhipment terminal on Aruba, and a small petrochemicals industry. An advanced-technology coker plant opened in 1995 to supply liquefied petroleum gas, largely for export to the USA. There are believed to be exploitable reserves of hydrocarbons within Aruban territory, and Aruba also has reserves of salt. The industrial sector contributed an estimated 10.2% of GDP in 2006, and engaged 16.4% of the employed labour force in 2000.

Light industry is engaged in the production of beverages, building materials, paints and solvents, paper and plastic products, candles, detergents, disinfectants, soaps and aloe-based cosmetics. There is a 'free zone', and the ports of Oranjestad and Barcadera provide bunkering and repair facilities for ships. In 1996 a ports development initiative was announced, proposing the relocation (over a 20-year period) of all cargo operations to Barcadera, leaving Oranjestad's port to accommodate commercial, recreation and resort activities. The construction sector, which grew steadily in the 1980s, declined in importance following a moratorium on the construction of new hotels in 1992. In 2005–07, however, some US $150m. was to be invested in the renovation and expansion of existing hotels and resorts, thereby reinvigorating the construction sector. Manufacturing, meanwhile, contributed an estimated 3.4% of GDP in 2006 and, along with electricity, gas and water, engaged 7.0% of the employed labour force in 2000.

The service industries are Aruba's principal economic activity, employing 83.1% of the active labour force in 2000, and contributing an estimated 84.2% of the island's GDP in 2006. Financial services are well established in Aruba, particularly the data-processing sector, an important service to US companies in particular. Aruba's principal source of income is tourism; the hotels and restaurants sector alone was estimated to provide 10.5% of Aruba's GDP in 2002. In 2001 there was a slight decrease in the number of visitor arrivals, attributed mainly to the global economic slowdown and to the effects on tourism of the terrorist attacks on the USA in September of that year. In 2004 the sector finally recorded positive growth again when the number of stop-over arrivals increased by 13.4%, to 728,157. The number of cruise-ship passengers also increased significantly in that year (by 6.3% to 567,320) and receipts from tourism increased by 23.3% to a total of A. Fl. 1,875.8m. The sector continued to perform well in 2005 and revenues increased by 4.3% to A. Fl. 1,956.8m., although there was a slight decline in total visitor numbers to 1,285,333. Total visitor numbers increased slightly to 1,285,846 (694,372 stop-over visitors and 591,474 cruise-ship passengers) in 2006. Total tourist expenditure reached A. Fl. 2,244.3m. in 2007.

Aruba is obliged to import most of its requirements, particularly machinery and electrical equipment, chemical products and foodstuffs; in 2006 the island recorded a visible trade surplus of US $113.9m., and there was also a surplus on the current account of the balance of payments of US $213.4m. In 2007 the principal source of imports, excluding the petroleum sector and the 'free zone', was the USA (58.1% of the total value); other major sources were the Netherlands, Venezuela and the Netherlands Antilles. The principal export commodity is refined petroleum (see above). Excluding the petroleum sector and the 'free zone', the principal market for exports in 2007 was also the USA (accounting for 34.9% of the total value of exports), followed by the Netherlands Antilles, the Netherlands and Venezuela.

In 2007 the budget deficit was A Fl. 42.1m., equivalent to 0.9% of GDP in that year. At the end of 2007 total government debt was A Fl. 2,143.3m. (equivalent to 45.6% of GDP), of which 45.8% was owed to external creditors, primarily the Government of the Netherlands. The average annual rate of inflation was 3.0% in 1996–2006; consumer prices increased by 2.5% in 2004, by 3.4% in 2005 and by 3.6% in 2006. Some 6.9% of the labour force were unemployed in 2005.

As part of the Kingdom of the Netherlands, Aruba is classed as an Overseas Territory in association with the European Union (see p. 244). It forms a co-operative union with the Antilles of the Five in monetary and economic affairs. Aruba also has observer status with the Caribbean Community and Common Market (CARICOM, see p. 196).

The closure of the San Nicolaas petroleum refinery in 1985 and Aruba's separation from the rest of the Netherlands Antilles in 1986 prompted the Aruban administration to institute a policy of retrenchment and austerity, except for investment in tourism development. In 1992, following six consecutive years of rapid economic growth, a moratorium was imposed on construction in the tourism industry, partly in recognition of the adverse environmental impact on the island and also to preserve the island's reputation as an exclusive holiday destination for the wealthy. Economic growth subsequently slowed to a more sustainable level during the remainder of the decade. Aruba also maintained reasonably low levels of inflation and of unemployment, and was considered to be one of the most prosperous islands in the Caribbean. Concern, however, has been expressed that Aruba's high public-sector wage bill and the generous nature of the island's social welfare system, combined with its ageing population, would threaten the future stability of public finance, already hindered by a narrow taxation base and poor revenue collection. The budgetary deficit increased markedly during the early 2000s and in May 2005 the IMF re-emphasized the need for the Government to gain control of the worsening ratio of public debt to GDP. Government efforts to address the current account deficit in 2006 included a review of the Civil Servants Pension Fund and its universal health scheme. It was hoped that an increase of the import duty tariffs on a more comprehensive range of goods would help to redress the fiscal deficit. Increased efficiency in tax administration and greater discipline over fiscal expenditure were also pursued during 2006. The disappearance in May 2005 of a US teenager on the island generated large amounts of negative publicity in North America, jeopardizing tourism revenue. Tourist occupancy rates in September 2005 were 6.2% lower than the comparative figure in 2004. While tourist arrivals to the island increased only marginally in 2006, a significant growth in cruise-ship passengers provided an indication that the sector was beginning to recover; cruise-ship arrivals were estimated to have increased by 15%, and cruise-ship passengers by 87%, since 1996. It was hoped that investments of over US $350m. to be implemented during 2007 (including the renovation and upgrade of the island's cruise-ship terminals, facility improvements at Queen Beatrix International Airport, the inauguration of a new private jet terminal, and extensive hotel and resort renovation and expansion) would reinvigorate the tourism industry and further advance its economic performance. In the fist six months of 2007 tourism arrivals were up by a reported 6.9%, compared with the previous year. The largest increases were in visitors from Venezuela, Colombia and Brazil, while US visitor numbers were also higher than they were in 2006. However, concerns remained about the territory's growing public debt, its vulnerability to the economic slowdown in the USA and the higher oil prices, and its dependence on the tourism sector. In late 2007 the Government announced measures to balance Aruba's budget and reduce debt to under 40% of GDP by 2009. While GDP growth in 2006 was estimated at just 0.6% by the IMF, the economy grew by 2.1% in 2007 as a result of increased revenue from tourism. The IMF projected similar growth for 2008.

Education

A Compulsory Education Act was introduced in 1999, to cover the four-to-16 age group. Kindergarten begins at four years of age. Primary education begins at six years of age and lasts for six years. Secondary education, beginning at the age of 12, lasts for up to six years. In 2004/05 enrolment at primary schools included 99.4% of pupils in the relevant age-group, while the comparable enrolment ratio at secondary schools was 76.3%. The main language of instruction is Dutch, but Papiamento (using a different spelling system from that of the Antilles of the Five) is used in kindergarten and primary education and in the lower levels of technical and vocational education. Papiamento is also being introduced onto the curriculum in all schools. In Aruba there are two institutes of higher education: the University of Aruba, comprising the School of Law and the School of Business Administration, which had 208 students in 1999/2000; and the Teachers' College, which had 180 students in 2000/01. There is also a community college. The majority of students, however, continue their studies abroad, generally in the Netherlands. The Government allocated a planned 12.6% of budget expenditure to education in 1999, equivalent to an estimated 3.4% of GDP; the Ministry of Education, Social Affairs and Infrastructure invested A. Fl. 13m. in education projects in 2006.

Public Holidays

2008: 1 January (New Year's Day), 25 January (Gilberto F. (Betico) Croes' Birthday), 4 February (Lenten Carnival), 18 March (National Anthem and Flag Day), 21–24 March (Easter), 30 April (Queen's Day), 1 May (Labour Day), 1 May (Ascension Day), 25–26 December (Christmas).

2009: 1 January (New Year's Day), 25 January (Gilberto F. (Betico) Croes' Birthday), 23 February (Lenten Carnival), 18 March (National Anthem and Flag Day), 10–13 April (Easter), 30 April (Queen's Day), 1 May (Labour Day), 21 May (Ascension Day), 25–26 December (Christmas).

Weights and Measures

The metric system is in force.

Statistical Survey

Sources (unless otherwise stated): Department of Economic Affairs, Commerce and Industry (Direktie Economische Zaken, Handel en Industrie), Sun Plaza Bldg, L. G. Smith Blvd 160, Oranjestad; tel. 5821181; fax 5834494; e-mail deaci@setarnet.aw; internet www.arubaeconomicaffairs.aw; Centrale Bank van Aruba, J. E. Irausquin Blvd 8, POB 18, Oranjestad; tel. 5822509; fax 5832251; e-mail cbaua@setarnet.aw; internet www.cbaruba.org.

AREA AND POPULATION

Area: 193 sq km (74.5 sq miles).

Population: 66,687 (males 32,821, females 33,866) at census of 6 October 1991; 102,817 at mid-2006.

Density (mid-2006): 532.7 per sq km.

Principal Towns (population estimates, 2002): Oranjestad (capital) 20,700; Sint Nicolaas 17,400. Source: Stefan Helders, *World Gazetteer* (internet www.world-gazetteer.com). *Mid-2007* (UN estimate, incl. suburbs): Oranjestad 32,000 (Source: UN, *World Urbanization Prospects: The 2007 Revision*).

Births and Deaths (2006): Live births 1,227 (birth rate 11.9 per 1,000); Deaths 537 (death rate 5.2 per 1,000). Source: UN, *Population and Vital Statistics Report*.

Expectation of Life (years at birth, 2007): 74.2 (males 71.3; females 77.1). Source: Pan American Health Organization.

Economically Active Population (persons aged 15 years and over, 2000): Agriculture, hunting and forestry 251; Manufacturing electricity, gas and water 2,940; Construction 3,892; Wholesale and retail trade, repairs 7,112; Hotels and restaurants 7,651; Transport, storage and communications 2,905; Financial intermediation 1,485; Real estate, renting and business activities 3,722; Public administration, defence and social security 3,573; Education 1,431; Health and social work 1,986; Other community, social and personal services 2,776; Private households with employed persons 1,870; Other 324; Total employed 41,918; Unemployed 3,118; Total labour force 45,036. *September 2005* (estimate): Total employed 47,350; Unemployed 3,114; Total labour force 50,464.

HEALTH AND WELFARE

Under-5 Mortality Rate (per 1,000 live births, 2006): 20.0.

Physicians (per 1,000 head, 1999): 1.28.

Hospital Beds (per 1,000 head, 2003): 3.2.

Health Expenditure (% of GDP, 1998): 2.5.

Source: partly Pan American Health Organization.

For definitions, see explanatory note on p. vi.

FISHING

Total catch (metric tons, live weight, 2005, FAO estimates): 162 (Groupers 17, Snappers and jobfishes 50, Wahoo 50, Other marine fishes 45). Source: FAO.

INDUSTRY

Electric Energy (million kWh, 2006): 909.5.

FINANCE

Currency and Exchange Rates: 100 cents = 1 Aruban gulden (guilder) or florin (A Fl.). *Sterling, Dollar and Euro Equivalents* (31 December 2007): £1 sterling = A Fl. 3.586; US $1 = A Fl. 1.790; €1 = A Fl. 2.635; A Fl. 100 = £27.89 = $55.87 = €37.95. Note: The Aruban florin was introduced in January 1986, replacing (at par) the Netherlands Antilles guilder or florin (NA Fl.). Since its introduction, the currency has had a fixed exchange rate of US $1 = A Fl. 1.79.

Budget (A Fl. million, 2007, preliminary): *Revenue:* Tax revenue 882.2; Non-tax revenue 145.9 (incl. grants 28.2); Total 1,028.1. *Expenditure:* Wages 300.9; Goods and services 186.9; Interest payments 106.9; Investments 18.9; Transfer to the General Health Insurance (AZV) 85.1; Other 109.6; Total (incl. others) 1,070.2.

International Reserves (US $ million at 31 December 2006): Gold 70.6; Foreign exchange 337.8; Total 408.4. Source: IMF, *International Financial Statistics*.

Money Supply (A Fl. million at 31 December 2006): Currency outside banks 157.36; Demand deposits at commercial banks 883.59; Total money (incl. others) 1,055.45. Source: IMF, *International Financial Statistics*.

Cost of Living (Consumer Price Index; base: 2000 = 100): All items 113.0 in 2004; 116.8 in 2005; 121.0 in 2006. Source: IMF, *International Financial Statistics*.

Gross Domestic Product (A. Fl. million at constant 1995 prices): 2,836 in 2003; 2,936 in 2004; 3,004 in 2005.

Expenditure on the Gross Domestic Product (A. Fl. million at current prices, 2007, preliminary): Final consumption expenditure 3,588; Gross capital formation 1,582; *Total domestic expenditure* 5,170; Exports of goods and services 3,111; *Less* Imports of goods and services 3,555; Statistical discrepancy –30; *GDP in purchasers' values* 4,696.

Gross Domestic Product by Economic Activity (A. Fl. million at current prices, 2000): Agriculture, hunting, forestry and fishing, and mining and quarrying 14; Manufacturing 91; Electricity, gas and water (incl. petroleum refining) 212; Construction 202; Trade 440; Restaurants and hotels 355; Transport, storage and communications 287; Finance, insurance, real estate and business services 877; Government services 390; Other community, social and personal services 365; *Sub-total* 3,234; *Less* Imputed bank service charges 163; Indirect taxes, *less* subsidies 255; *GDP in purchasers' values* 3,326. *2003* (A. Fl. million at current prices): Agriculture, hunting, forestry and fishing 15; Mining, manufacturing and utilities 331 (Manufacturing 99); Construction 248; Wholesale and retail trade, restaurants and hotels 851; Transport, storage and communications 298; Activities not adequately defined 1,735; *Total value added* 3,478. Source: UN, mostly *National Accounts Statistics*.

Balance of Payments (US $ million, 2006): Exports of goods f.o.b. 3,951.5; Imports of goods f.o.b. –3,837.5; *Trade balance* 113.9; Exports of services 1,314.2; Imports of services –985.4; *Balance on goods and services* 442.7; Other income received 57.7; Other income paid –161.5; *Balance on goods, services and income* 338.9; Current transfers received 56.6; Current transfers paid –182.1; *Current balance* 213.4; Capital account (net) 20.9; Direct investment abroad 0.4; Direct investment from abroad 326.0; Portfolio investment assets –78.9; Portfolio investment liabilities 40.5; Financial derivatives assets –2.0; Other investment assets –425.1; Other investment liabilities –42.5 Net errors and omissions 2.3; *Overall balance* 55.1. Source IMF, *International Financial Statistics*.

EXTERNAL TRADE

Principal Commodities (A Fl. million, 2007): *Imports c.i.f.:* Live animals and animal products 109.7; Food products 199.2; Chemical products 184.1; Base metals and articles thereof 156.1; Machinery and electrical equipment 320.3; Transport equipment 125.9; Total (incl. others) 1,875.5. *Exports f.o.b.:* Live animals and animal products 1.1; Machinery and electrical equipment 7.9; Transport equipment 5.1; Art objects and collectors' items 9.4; Total (incl. others) 55.8. Note: Figures exclude transactions involving mineral fuels and those of the Free Trade Zone of Aruba.

Principal Trading Partners (A Fl. million, 2007): *Imports c.i.f.:* Japan 34.2; Netherlands 238.8; Netherlands Antilles 56.1; USA 1,089.3; Venezuela 42.4; Total (incl. others) 1,875.5. *Exports f.o.b.:* Colombia 0.9; Netherlands 13.7; Netherlands Antilles 8.9; USA 19.5; Venezuela 3.2; Total (incl. others) 55.8. Note: Figures exclude transactions of the petroleum sector and those of the Free Trade Zone of Aruba.

TRANSPORT

Road Traffic (motor vehicles registered, December 2005): Passenger cars 49,521; Lorries 907; Buses 300; Taxis 398; Rental cars 3,514; Other cars 578; Motorcycles 1,499; Total 56,717.

Shipping: *Arrivals* (2006): 1,971 vessels. *Merchant Fleet* (vessels registered at 31 December 2006): Number of vessels 2; Total displacement 400 grt (Source: Lloyd's Register-Fairplay, *World Fleet Statistics*).

Civil Aviation: *Aircraft Landings:* 17,866 in 2004; 16,270 in 2005; 16,842 in 2006. *Passenger Arrivals:* 875,021 in 2004; 860,212 in 2005; 810,322 in 2006.

TOURISM

Tourist Arrivals: 1,304,477 (728,157 stop-over visitors, 576,320 cruise-ship passengers) in 2004; 1,285,333 (732,514 stop-over visitors, 552,819 cruise-ship passengers) in 2005; 1,285,846 (694,372 stop-over visitors, 591,474 cruise-ship passengers) in 2006.

Tourism Receipts: A. Fl. 1,953.0m. in 2005; A. Fl. 1,917.0m. in 2006; A. Fl. 2,244.3 in 2007.

COMMUNICATIONS MEDIA

Radio Receivers (1997): 50,000 in use.

Television Receivers (1997): 20,000 in use.

Telephones (2005): 38,300 main lines in use.

Facsimile Machines (1996): 3,600 in use.

Mobile Cellular Telephones (2005): 108,200 subscribers.

Internet Users (2001): 7,912.

Broadband Subscribers (2005): 12,300.

Daily Newspapers (1996): 13 titles (estimated circulation 73,000 copies per issue).

Sources: mainly UNESCO, *Statistical Yearbook*; International Telecommunication Union; UN, *Statistical Yearbook*.

EDUCATION

Pre-primary (2000/01): 23 schools; 2,737 pupils; 105 teachers.

Primary (2000/01): 33 schools; 8,849 pupils; 415 teachers.

General Secondary (2000/01): 10 schools; 4,251 pupils; 242 teachers.

Technical-Vocational (2000/01): 2 schools; 3,237 pupils; 263 teachers.

Community College (1999/2000): 1 school; 1,187 pupils; 106 teachers.

University (1999/2000): 1 university; 208 students; 24 tutors.

Teacher Training (2000/01): 1 institution; 180 students; 25 teachers.

Special Education (2000/01): 4 schools; 272 pupils; 56 teachers.

Private, Non-aided (1999/2000): 4 schools; 553 pupils; 58 teachers.

International School (2000/01): 154 pupils; 25 teachers.

2004/05: *Pre-primary:* 2,760 pupils, 144 teachers; *Primary:* 10,250 pupils, 567 teachers; *Lower Secondary:* 3,438 pupils, 243 teachers (estimate); *Upper Secondary:* 3,678 pupils, 259 teachers (estimate); *Tertiary:* 2,106 students, 228 teachers (Source: UNESCO Institute for Statistics).

Adult Literacy Rate (official estimates, 2000): Males 97.6%; Females 97.1%.

Directory

The Constitution

On 1 January 1986 Aruba acquired separate status (*status aparte*) within the Kingdom of the Netherlands. The form of government is similar to that for the Netherlands Antilles, and is embodied in the Charter of the Kingdom of the Netherlands (operational from 20 December 1954). The Netherlands, the Netherlands Antilles (Antilles of the Five) and Aruba each enjoy full autonomy in domestic and internal affairs, and are united on a basis of equality for the

NETHERLANDS DEPENDENCIES

Aruba

protection of their common interests and the granting of mutual assistance. In economic and monetary affairs there is a co-operative union between Aruba and the Antilles of the Five, known as the 'Union of the Netherlands Antilles and Aruba'.

The Governor, who is appointed by the Dutch Crown for a term of six years, represents the monarch of the Netherlands in Aruba. The Government of Aruba appoints a minister plenipotentiary to represent it in the Government of the Kingdom. Whenever the Netherlands Council of Ministers is dealing with matters coming under the heading of joint affairs of the realm (in practice mainly foreign affairs and defence), the Council assumes the status of Council of Ministers of the Kingdom. In that event, Aruba's Minister Plenipotentiary takes part, with full voting powers, in the deliberations.

A legislative proposal regarding affairs of the realm and applying to Aruba as well as to the metropolitan Netherlands is sent, simultaneously with its submission, to the Staten Generaal (the Netherlands parliament) and to the Staten (parliament) of Aruba. The latter body can report in writing to the Staten Generaal on the draft Kingdom Statute and designate one or more special delegates to attend the debates and furnish information in the meetings of the Chambers of the Staten Generaal. Before the final vote on a draft the Minister Plenipotentiary has the right to express an opinion on it. If he disapproves of the draft, and if in the Second Chamber a three-fifths' majority of the votes cast is not obtained, the discussions on the draft are suspended and further deliberations take place in the Council of Ministers of the Kingdom. When special delegates attend the meetings of the Chambers this right devolves upon the delegates of the parliamentary body designated for this purpose.

The Governor has executive power in external affairs, which he exercises in co-operation with the Council of Ministers. He is assisted by an advisory council which consists of at least five members appointed by him.

Executive power in internal affairs is vested in a nominated Council of Ministers, responsible to the Staten. The Aruban Staten consists of 21 members, who are elected by universal adult suffrage for four years (subject to dissolution), on the basis of proportional representation. Inhabitants have the right to vote if they have Dutch nationality and have reached 18 years of age. Voting is not compulsory.

The Government

HEAD OF STATE

Queen of the Netherlands: HM Queen BEATRIX.
Governor: FREDIS J. REFUNJOL (took office 7 May 2004).

COUNCIL OF MINISTERS
(April 2008)

Prime Minister and Minister of General Affairs and Utilities: NELSON ORLANDO ODUBER.
Deputy Prime Minister and Minister of Education, Social Affairs and Infrastructure: MARISOL J. LOPEZ-TROMP.
Minister of Finance and Economic Affairs: NILO J. J. SWAEN.
Minister of Justice: HYACINTHO RUDY CROES.
Minister of Labour, Culture, Integration, Community Development and Sports: TAI FOO RAMON LEE.
Minister of Public Health and the Environment: CANDELARIO A. S. D. (BOOSHI) WEVER.
Minister of Tourism and Transportation: EDISON BRIESEN.
Minister Plenipotentiary and Member of the Council of Ministers of the Realm for Aruba in the Netherlands: FRANCISCO WALFRIDO CROES.
Minister Plenipotentiary of the Realm for Aruba in Washington, DC (USA): (vacant).

MINISTRIES

Office of the Governor: Plaza Henny Eman 3, Oranjestad; tel. 834445; fax 834930.
Office of the Prime Minister: Government Offices, L. G. Smith Blvd 76, Oranjestad; tel. 5880300; fax 5880024.
Ministry of Education, Social Affairs and Infrastructure: Caya Betico Croes 38, Oranjestad; tel. 5226700; fax 5880032; e-mail minszi@setarnet.aw; internet www.minszi.aw.
Ministry of Finance and Economic Affairs: Cumana 69, Oranjestad; tel. 5880269; fax 5880347; internet www.aruba.com/extlinks/govs/governm.html.
Ministry of General Affairs and Utilities: L. G. Smith Blvd 76, Oranjestad; tel. 5839022; fax 5838958.
Ministry of Justice: L. G. Smith Blvd 76, Oranjestad; tel. 5824900; fax 5825388.
Ministry of Labour, Culture, Integration, Community Development and Sports: Victor Hugostraat 10, Oranjestad; tel. 5880900; fax 5880331; e-mail macs@setarnet.aw.
Ministry of Public Health and the Environment, Administrative Affairs and Immigration: Bernardstraat 75, San Nicolas; tel. 5841199; fax 5849744.
Ministry of Tourism and Transportation: Arnold Schuttestraat 2, Oranjestad; tel. 5880114; fax 5880121.
Office of the Minister Plenipotentiary for Aruba: R. J. Schimmelpennincklaan 1, 2517 JN The Hague, Netherlands; tel. (70) 3566200; fax (70) 3451446; e-mail info@arubahuis.nl; internet www.arubahuis.nl.

Legislature

STATEN

President: MERVIN WYATT-RAS, Staten, L. G. Smith Blvd 72, Oranjestad.

General Election, 23 September 2005

Party	Seats
Movimentu Electoral di Pueblo	11
Arubaanse Volkspartij	8
Movimentu Patriótico Arubano	1
RED Eternal Democratico	1
Total	**21**

Political Organizations

Acción Democratico Nacional (ADN) (National Democratic Action): Oranjestad; f. 1985; Leader PEDRO CHARRO KELLY.
Aliansa Democratico Arubano (Aruban Democratic Alliance): Oranjestad; Leader ROBERT FREDERICK WEVER.
Arubaanse Volkspartij (AVP) (Aruba People's Party): Oranjestad; tel. 5833500; fax 5837870; f. 1942; advocates Aruba's separate status; Leader MICHIEL GODFRIED EMAN.
Conscientisacion y Liberacion Arubano (CLA) (Concentration for the Liberation of Aruba): Oranjestad; Leader MARIANO DUVERT BLUME.
Movimentu Electoral di Pueblo (MEP) (People's Electoral Movement): Santa Cruz 74D, Oranjestad; tel. 5854495; fax 5850768; e-mail mep@setarnet.aw; f. 1971; socialist; 1,200 mems; Pres. and Leader NELSON ORLANDO ODUBER.
Movimentu Patriótico Arubano (MPA) (Aruban Patriotic Movement): Oranjestad; Leader MONICA KOCK ARENDS.
Organisacion Liberal Arubano (OLA) (Aruban Liberal Organization): Oranjestad; f. 1991; Leader GLENBERT FRANCOIS CROES.
Partido Patriótico Arubano (PPA) (Patriotic Party of Aruba): Oranjestad; internet www.ppa-aruba.org; f. 1949; social democratic; opposed to complete independence for Aruba; Leader BENEDICT (BENNY) JOCELYN MONTGOMERY NISBETT.
RED Democratico (RED Democratic Network): Oranjestad; internet www.red.aw; f. 2003; Leader Fr RUDY LAMPE.

Judicial System

Legal authority is exercised by the Court of First Instance. Appeals are heard by the Joint High Court of Justice of the Netherlands Antilles and Aruba.

Attorney-General of Aruba: THERESA CROES-FERNANDES PEDRA.
Solicitor-General of Aruba: NICO JÖRG.
Courts of Justice: J. G. Emanstraat 51, Oranjestad; tel. 5822294; fax 5821241; e-mail griffiekopie@setarnet.aw.

Religion

Roman Catholics form the largest religious community, numbering more than 80% of the population. The Anglicans and the Methodist, Dutch Protestant and other Protestant churches have a total membership of about 6,500. There are approximately 130 Jews.

CHRISTIANITY

The Roman Catholic Church

Aruba forms part of the diocese of Willemstad, comprising the Netherlands Antilles and Aruba. At 31 December 2005 there were an estimated 224,809 adherents in the diocese. The Bishop resides in Willemstad (Curaçao, Netherlands Antilles).

NETHERLANDS DEPENDENCIES

Aruba

Roman Catholic Church: J. Yrausquin Plein 3, POB 702, Oranjestad; tel. 5821434; fax 5821409.

The Anglican Communion

Within the Church in the Province of the West Indies, Aruba forms part of the diocese of the North Eastern Caribbean and Aruba. The Bishop is resident in The Valley, Anguilla.

Anglican Church: Holy Cross, Weg Seroe Pretoe 31, Sint Nicolaas; tel. 5845142; fax 5843394; e-mail holycross@setarnet.aw.

Protestant Churches

Baptist Church: Aruba Baptist Mission, SBC, Paradera 98-C; tel. 5883893.

Church of Christ: Pastoor Hendrikstraat 107, Sint Nicolaas; tel. 5848172.

Church of Jesus Christ Latter Day Saints: Dadelstraat 16, Oranjestad; tel. 5823507.

Dutch Protestant Church: Wilhelminastraat 1, Oranjestad; tel. 5821435.

Evangelical Church: Jasmijnstraat 7, Sint Nicolaas; tel. 5848973.

Faith Revival Center: Rooi Afo 10, Paradera; tel. 5831010; fax 5833070.

Iglesia Evangelica Pentecostal: Asamblea di Dios, Reamurstraat 2, Oranjestad; tel. 5831940.

Jehovah's Witnesses: Guyabastraat 3, Oranjestad; tel. 5828963.

Methodist Church: Longfellowstraat, Oranjestad; tel. 5845243.

New Apostolic Church: Goletstraat 5A, Oranjestad; tel. 5833762.

Pentacostal Apostolic Assembly: Bernhardstraat 185; tel. 5848710; fax 5845699.

Seventh-day Adventist: Weststraat, Oranjestad; tel. 5845896.

JUDAISM

Beth Israel Synagogue: Adriaan Laclé Blvd, Oranjestad; tel. 5823272; fax 5823534.

BAHÁ'Í FAITH

Spiritual Assembly: Bucutiweg 19, Oranjestad; tel. 5823104; Contact M. CHRISTIAN.

The Press

DAILIES

Amigoe di Aruba: Patriastraat 13, POB 323, Oranjestad; tel. 5824333; fax 5822368; e-mail amigoearuba@setarnet.aw; internet www.amigoe.com; f. 1884; Dutch; Man. BRENDA BOUWMAN; circ. 12,000 (in Aruba and Netherlands Antilles).

Aruba Today: Weststraat 22, Oranjestad; tel. 5827800; fax 5827093; e-mail news@arubatoday.com; internet www.arubatoday.com; Editor-in-Chief JULIA C. RENFRO.

Bon Dia Aruba: Weststraat 22, Oranjestad; tel. 5827800; fax 5827044; e-mail noticia@cspnv.com; internet www.bondia.com; Dirs JOHN CHEMALY, JOHN CHEMALY, Jr.

Diario: Engelandstraat 29, POB 577, Oranjestad; tel. 5826747; fax 5828551; e-mail diario@setanet.aw; internet www.diarioaruba.com; f. 1980; Papiamento; morning; Editor and Man. JOSSY M. MANSUR; circ. 15,000.

Extra: Dominicanessenstraat 17, Oranjestad; tel. 58834034; fax 5821639; Papiamento; Dir C. FRANKEN.

The News: Italiestraat 5, POB 300, Oranjestad; tel. 5824725; fax 5889430; e-mail thenewsaruba@setarnet.aw; f. 1951; English; Dir SONIA WEVER-SCHOUTEN; Editor-in-Chief MARGARET BONARRIVA-WEVER; circ. 6,900.

La Prensa: Bachstraat 6, POB 566 Oranjestad; tel. 5821199; fax 5828634; e-mail laprensa@laprensacur.com; internet www.laprensacur.com; f. 1929; Papiamento; Editor THOMAS C. PIETERSZ.

NEWS AGENCIES

Algemeen Nederlands Persbureau (ANP) (The Netherlands): Caya G. F. (Betico) Croes 110, POB 323, Oranjestad; tel. 5824333; fax 5822368; internet www.anp.nl.

Aruba News Agencies: Bachstraat 6, Oranjestad; tel. 5821243.

Publishers

Aruba Experience Publications NV: Verbindingsweg 2, POB 634, Oranjestad; tel. 5834467; fax 5384520; e-mail info@arubaexperience.com; internet www.arubaexperience.com; f. 1985; Gen. Man. MICHEL J. M. JANSSEN.

Caribbean Publishing Co Ltd (CPC): L. G. Smith Blvd 116, Oranjestad; tel. 5820485; fax 5820484.

De Wit Stores NV: L. G. Smith Blvd 110, POB 386, Oranjestad; tel. 5823500; fax 5821575; e-mail dewitstores@setarnet.aw; f. 1948; Gen. Man. LYANNE BEAUJON.

Editorial Charuba: Lagoenweg 31, Oranjestad; tel. 7301512; fax 5884574; e-mail alivaro@hotmail.com; f. 1982; Pres. ALICE VAN ROMONDT.

Gold Book Publishing: L. G. Smith Blvd 116, Oranjestad; tel. 5820485; fax 5820484; e-mail drosario@caribbeanhotels.org; internet www.caribbeanhotels.org; a division of the Caribbean Hotel Asscn, based in the Cayman Islands.

Oranjestad Printing NV: Italiestraat 5, POB 300, Oranjestad; Man. Dir GERARDUS J. SCHOUTEN.

ProGraphics Inc: Italiestraat 5, POB 201, Oranjestad; tel. 5824550; fax 5833072; e-mail prographics@setarnet.aw; f. 2001; fmrly VAD Printers Inc; Publr WILBERT WEVER.

Publicidad Aruba NV: Emanstraat 110, POB 295, Oranjestad; tel. 5835139.

Publicidad Exito Aruba SA: Domenicanessenstraat 17, POB 142, Oranjestad; tel. 5822020; fax 5824242; f. 1958.

Van Dorp Aruba NV: Caya G. F. (Betico) Croes 77, POB 596, Oranjestad; tel. 5823076; fax 5823573.

Broadcasting and Communications

TELECOMMUNICATIONS

Digicel Aruba: Marisol Bldg, L.G. Smith Blvd 60, POB 662, Oranjestad; tel. 5222222; fax 5222223; e-mail customercare@digicelaruba.com; internet www.digicelaruba.com; f. 2003; owned by an Irish consortium; established a mobile cellular telephone network connecting Aruba with Bonaire and Curaçao in July 2006; Chair. DENIS O'BRIEN; CEO (Dutch Caribbean) HANS LUTE.

Servicio di Telecomunicacion di Aruba NV (SETAR): Seroe Blanco z/n, POB 13, Oranjestad; tel. 5251000; fax 5251515; e-mail sysop@setarnet.aw; internet www.setar.aw; f. 1986; Man. Dir ROLAND CROES.

BROADCASTING

Radio

Canal 90 FM Stereo: Van Leeuwenhoekstraat 26, Oranjestad; tel. 5828952; fax 837340; e-mail info@canal90fm.aw.

Cristal Sound 101.7 FM: J. G. Emanstraat 124A, Oranjestad; tel. 5827726; fax 5820144.

Hit 94 FM: Oranjestad; e-mail hit94fm@hotmail.com; internet www.hit94fm.com; f. 1993; Dir JOHNNY HABIBE.

Magic 96.5 FM: Oranjestad; internet www.magic965.com.

Radio 1270: Bernardstraat 138, POB 28, Sint Nicolaas; tel. 5845602; fax 5827753; commercial station; programmes in Dutch, English, Spanish and Papiamento; Dir F. A. LEAUER; Station Man. J. A. C. ALDERS.

Radio Carina FM: Datustraat 10A, Oranjestad; tel. 5821450; fax 5831955; commercial station; programmes in Dutch, English, Spanish and Papiamento; Dir-Gen. ALBERT R. DIEFFENTHALER.

Radio Caruso Booy FM: G. M. de Bruynewijk 49, Savaneta; tel. 5847752; fax 5843351; e-mail sira@setarnet.aw; internet www.geocities.com/carusobooy; commercial station; broadcasts for 24 hrs a day; programmes in Dutch, English, Spanish and Papiamento; Pres. HUBERT ERQUILLES ANTONIO BOOY; Gen. Man. SIRA BOOY.

Radio Galactica FM: J. G. Emanstraat 120, Oranjestad; tel. 5830999; fax 5838999; e-mail radiogalactica@hotmail.com; internet www.galactica999fm.aw; f. 1990; Dir MODESTO J. ODUBER; Station Man. MAIKEL J. ODUBER.

Radio Kelkboom: Bloemond 14, POB 146, Oranjestad; tel. 5821899; fax 5834825; e-mail radiokelkboom@setarnet.aw; internet www.watapana-aruba.com; f. 1954; commercial radio station; programmes in Papiamento, Dutch, English, Spanish, Portuguese and Creole; Owners CARLOS A. KELKBOOM, E. A. M. KELKBOOM; Dir EMILE A. M. KELKBOOM.

Radio Victoria: Washington 23A, POB 5291, Oranjestad; tel. 5873444; fax 5873444; e-mail radiovictoria@setarnet.aw; internet www.radiovictoriaaruba.org; f. 1958; religious and cultural FM radio station owned by the Radio Victoria Foundation; programmes in Dutch, English, Spanish and Papiamento; Pres. N. J. F. ARTS.

Voz di Aruba (Voice of Aruba): Van Leeuwenhoekstraat 26, POB 219, Oranjestad; tel. 5823355; fax 5837340; commercial radio station; programmes in Dutch, English, Spanish and Papiamento; also operates Canal 90 on FM; Dir A. M. ARENDS, Jr.

NETHERLANDS DEPENDENCIES
Aruba

Television

ABC Aruba Broadcasting Co NV (ATV): Royal Plaza Suite 223, POB 5040, Oranjestad; tel. 5838150; fax 5838110; e-mail 15atv@setarnet.aw.

Telearuba NV: Pos Chiquito 1A, POB 392, Oranjestad; tel. 5857302; fax 5851683; e-mail telearuba@hotmail.com; internet www.telearuba.aw; f. 1963; fmrly operated by Netherlands Antilles Television Co; commercial; acquired by SETAR in March 2005; Gen. Man. M. MARCHENA.

Finance

(cap. = capital; res = reserves; dep. = deposits; m. = million; brs = branches; amounts in Aruban florin, unless otherwise stated)

BANKING

Central Bank

Centrale Bank van Aruba: J. E. Irausquin Blvd 8, POB 18, Oranjestad; tel. 5252100; fax 5252101; e-mail cbaua@setarnet.aw; internet www.cbaruba.org; f. 1986; cap. 10.0m., res 174.1m., dep. 379.1m. (Dec. 2006); Pres. HASSANALI MEHRAN; Exec. Dirs K. A. H. POLVLIET, J. R. FIGAROA-SEMELEER.

Commercial Banks

Aruba Bank NV: Camacuri 12, POB 192, Oranjestad; tel. 5277777; fax 5277715; e-mail info@arubabank.com; internet www.arubabank.com; f. 1925; acquired Interbank Aruba NV in Dec. 2003; total assets US $260m. (Dec. 2004); Man. Dir and CEO EDWIN TROMP; 5 brs.

Banco di Caribe NV: Vondellaan 31, POB 493, Oranjestad; tel. 5232000; fax 5832422; e-mail bdcaua@setarnet.aw; internet www.bancodicaribe.com; f. 1987; Gen. Man. EDUARDO A. (DITO) DE KORT; 1 br.

Caribbean Mercantile Bank Aruba: Caya G. F. (Betico) Croes 53, POB 28, Oranjestad; tel. 5823118; fax 5830919; e-mail executive_office@cmbnv.com; internet www.cmbnv.com; f. 1963; cap. 4.0m., res 86.7m., dep. 932.1m. (Dec. 2006); Pres. LIONEL CAPRILES, II; Gen. Man. Dir W. G. CARSON; 6 brs.

RBTT Bank Aruba NV: Italiestraat 36, Sasakiweg, Oranjestad; tel. 5233100; fax 58821576; e-mail info@tt.rbtt.com; internet www.rbtt.com; f. 2001; fmrly First National Bank of Aruba NV (f. 1985 and acquired by Royal Bank of Trinidad and Tobago Ltd in 1998); total assets US $111.5m. (Dec. 2003); Chair. PETER J. JULY; 6 brs.

Investment Bank

AIB NV: Wilhelminastraat 34–36, POB 1011, Oranjestad; tel. 5827327; fax 5827461; e-mail info@aib-bank.com; internet www.aib-bank.com; f. 1987 as Aruban Investment Bank; name changed as above in April 2004; total assets 149.0m. (Dec. 2005); Man. Dir FRENDSEL W. GIEL; Asst Man. Dir HERRY M. KOOLMAN.

Mortgage Bank

Fundacion Cas pa Comunidad Arubano (FCCA): Sabana Blanco 66, Oranjestad; tel. 5238800; fax 5836272; internet www.fcca.com; f. 1979; Man. Dir PETER VAN POPPEL.

'Offshore' Bank

Citibank Aruba NA: Arulex Bldg, Punta Bravo z/n, Oranjestad; tel. 5822138; fax 5832363; e-mail fred.aarons@citicorp.com.

INSURANCE

There were eight life insurance companies and 14 non-life insurance companies active in Aruba in December 2005.

Association

Insurance Association of Aruba (IAA): L. G. Smith Blvd 160, Oranjestad; tel. 5821111; fax 5826138; 10 mems.

Trade and Industry

DEVELOPMENT ORGANIZATIONS

Department of Agriculture, Husbandry, and Fisheries: Piedra Plat 114A, Oranjestad; tel. 5858102; fax 5855639; e-mail dlvv@aruba.gov.aw; internet www.overheid.aw; f. 1976; Dir T. G. DAMIAN.

Department of Economic Affairs, Commerce and Industry (Directie Economische Zaken, Handel en Industrie): Sun Plaza Bldg, L. G. Smith Blvd 160, Oranjestad; tel. 5821181; fax 5834494; e-mail deaci@setarnet.aw; internet www.arubaeconomicaffairs.aw; f. 1986; Dir MARIA DIJKHOFF-PITA.

CHAMBER OF COMMERCE AND INDUSTRY

Chamber of Commerce and Industry Aruba: J. E. Irausquin Blvd 10, POB 140, Oranjestad; tel. 5821120; fax 5883200; e-mail secretariat@arubachamber.com; internet www.arubachamber.com; f. 1930; Pres. EDWIN A. ROOS; Exec. Dir LORRAINE C. DE SOUZA.

TRADE ASSOCIATION

Aruba Trade and Industry Association (ATIA): ATIA Bldg, Pedro Gallegostraat 6, POB 562, Oranjestad; tel. 5827593; fax 5833068; e-mail atiaruba@setarnet.aw; internet www.atiaruba.org; f. 1945; Pres. JUAN YRAUSQUIN; 230 mems.

UTILITIES

Electricity and Water

Utilities Aruba NV: Arulex Center, Punta Brabo z/n; tel. 5828277; fax 5828682; e-mail utilities@setarnet.aw; govt-owned holding co.; Man. Dir HAROLD HENRIQUEZ.

Electriciteit-Maatschappij Aruba (ELMAR) NV: Wilhelminastraat 110, POB 202, Oranjestad; tel. 5237100; fax 5828991; e-mail info@elmar.aw; internet www.elmar.aw; independently managed co, residing under Utilities Aruba NV; electricity distribution; Man. Dir ING. A. O. RAFINÉ; 167 employees.

Water en Energiebedrijf Aruba (WEB) NV: Balashi 76, POB 575, Oranjestad; tel. 5254600; fax 5857681; e-mail info@webaruba.com; internet www.webaruba.com; f. 1991; independently managed co, residing under Utilities Aruba NV; production and distribution of industrial and potable water, and electricity generation; Man. Dir JOSSY M. LACLÉ.

Gas

Aruba Gas Supply Company Ltd (ARUGAS): Barcadera z/n, POB 190, Oranjestad; tel. 5851198; fax 5852187; e-mail webmaster@arugas.com; internet www.arugas.com.

BOC Gases Aruba NV: Balashi z/n, POB 387, Oranjestad; tel. 5852624; fax 5852823; e-mail bocaruba@setarnet.aw; internet www.boc-gases.com; acquired by the Linde Group global industrial gases and engineering org. in Sept. 2006.

TRADE UNIONS

Federacion di Trahadornan di Aruba (FTA) (Aruban Workers' Federation): Bernhardstraat 23, Sint Nicolaas; tel. 5845448; fax 5845504; e-mail fetraua@setarnet.aw; f. 1964; independent; affiliated with the International Trade Union Confederation; Pres. JOSÉ RUDOLF (RUDY) GEERMAN; Vice-Pres. JANE ANASTACIA BRAAFHART.

There are also several unions for government and semi-government workers and employees.

Transport

There are no railways, but Aruba has a network of all-weather roads.

Arubus NV: Sabana Blanco 67, Oranjestad; tel. 5882300; fax 5828633; e-mail info@arubus.com; internet www.arubus.com; f. 1979; state-owned company providing public transport services; runs a fleet of 48 buses; Dir FRANKLIN KUIPERI.

SHIPPING

The island's principal seaport is Oranjestad, whose harbour can accommodate ocean-going vessels. There are also ports at Barcadera and Sint Nicolaas, the latter administered by the Valero Aruba Refining Company.

Aruba Ports Authority NV: Port Administration Bldg, L. G. Smith Blvd 23, Oranjestad; tel. 5826633; fax 5832896; e-mail info@arubaports.com; internet www.arubaports.com; f. 1981; responsible for the administration of the ports of Oranjestad and Barcadera; Man. Dir JUAN ALFONSO BOEKHOUDT.

Valero Aruba Refining Co NV: Lagoweg 5, POB 2150, Sint Nicolaas; tel. 5894904; fax 5849087; internet www.valero.com; f. 1989; petroleum refinery, responsible for the administration of the port of Sint Nicolaas; acquired by Valero in 2004; Gen. Man. RAYMOND A. BUCKLEY.

Principal Shipping Companies

Anthony Veder & Co (Aruba) NV: Frankrijkstraat 1, Oranjestad; tel. 5821953; fax 5825988; e-mail anveder@setarnet.aw.

Beng Lian Shipping S. de R. L. A. V. V.: Dominicanessenstraat 22, Oranjestad.

NETHERLANDS DEPENDENCIES

Rodoca Shipping and Trading SA: Parkietenbos 30, Barcadera Harbour; tel. 5850096; fax 5850097; fmrly Aruba Shipping and Chartering Co NV.

Valero Aruba Marine Services: Lagoweg, POB 2150, Sint Nicolaas; tel. 5894742; fax 5894554.

Windward Island Agencies: Heyligerweg, POB 66, Oranjestad.

CIVIL AVIATION

The Queen Beatrix International Airport (Aeropuerto Internacional Reina Beatrix), about 2.5 km from Oranjestad, is served by numerous airlines (including Dutch Antilles Express, based in Curaçao, Netherlands Antilles), linking the island with destinations in the Caribbean, Europe, the USA and Central and South America. After renovation and expansion, the airport was expected to be able to handle 2.6m. passengers per year by 2010. In November 2000 the national carrier, Air Aruba, was declared bankrupt.

Aruba Airport Authority NV: Queen Beatrix International Airport, Wayaca z/n, Oranjestad; tel. 5242424; fax 5834229; internet www.airportaruba.com; handled 1,638.1m. passengers (incl. transfers) in 2006; Man. Dir PETER STEINMETZ.

Tourism

Aruba's white sandy beaches, particularly along the southern coast, are an attraction for foreign visitors, and tourism is a major industry. The number of hotel rooms totalled 7,226 in 2004. In that year most stop-over visitors came from the USA (73.5%), Venezuela (8.1%) and the Netherlands (5.2%). In 2006 694,372 stop-over visitors and 591,474 cruise-ship passengers visited Aruba. Receipts from tourism totalled A. Fl. 2,244.3m. in 2007.

Aruba Cruise Tourism: Suite 230, Royal Plaza Mall, L. G. Smith Blvd 94, POB 5254, Oranjestad; tel. 5833648; fax 5835088; e-mail info@arubabycruise.com; internet www.arubabycruise.com; f. 1995 as the Cruise Tourism Authority—Aruba; name changed as above in 2005; non-profit government organization; Exec. Dir KATHLEEN ROJER.

Aruba Hotel and Tourism Association (AHATA): L. G. Smith Blvd 174, POB 542, Oranjestad; tel. 5822607; fax 5824202; e-mail info@ahata.com; internet www.ahata.com; f. 1965; 101 mems; Pres. and CEO JORGE PESQUERA; Chair. EWALD BIEMANS.

Aruba Tourism Authority (ATA): L. G. Smith Blvd 172, Eagle, Oranjestad; tel. 5823777; fax 5834702; e-mail ata.aruba@aruba.com; internet www.aruba.com; f. 1953; Man. Dir MYRNA JANSEN-FELICIANO.

THE NETHERLANDS ANTILLES

Introductory Survey

Location, Climate, Language, Religion, Flag, Capital

The Netherlands Antilles (Antilles of the Five) consists of two groups of islands in the Caribbean Sea, about 800 km (500 miles) apart. The main group, lying off the coast of Venezuela, consists of Bonaire and Curaçao which (together with Aruba, 68 km to the east of Curaçao) are known as the Benedenwindse Eilands or 'Leeward Islands'; to the north-east lie the small volcanic islands of St (Sint) Eustatius (also known as Statia), Saba and St (Sint) Maarten (the northern half of the last island being a dependency of the French overseas department of Guadeloupe), known as the Bovenwindse Eilands or 'Windward Islands' (although actually in the Leeward group of the Lesser Antilles). The climate is tropical, moderated by the sea, with an average annual temperature of 27.5°C (81°F) and little rainfall. The official languages are Dutch and Papiamento (a mixture of Dutch, Spanish, Portuguese, English, Arawak Indian and several West African dialects), which is the dominant language of the 'Leeward Islands'. English is the official and principal language of the 'Windward Islands'. Spanish is also widely spoken. Almost all of the inhabitants profess Christianity: the people of the 'Leeward Islands' and Saba are predominantly Roman Catholics, while those of St Eustatius and St Maarten are predominantly Protestants. The state flag (proportions 2 by 3) is white, with a red vertical stripe in the centre, crossed by a horizontal blue stripe on which there are five white five-pointed stars (one for each of the main islands) arranged in an oval. The capital is Willemstad, on the island of Curaçao.

Recent History

The 'Leeward Islands', already settled by communities of Arawak Indians, were discovered by the Spanish in 1499 and were seized by the Dutch in the 1630s. Curaçao became prosperous in the late 17th and 18th centuries as an entrepôt for trade in the Caribbean. The Dutch settled the 'Windward Islands', once settled by Carib Indians, in the mid-17th century. After frequent changes in possession, the islands (including Aruba) were finally confirmed as Dutch territory in 1816. The two groups were administered as Curaçao and Dependencies between 1845 and 1948. Slavery was abolished in 1863, and the islands suffered from an economic decline until the establishment of petroleum refineries on Curaçao and Aruba, in 1918 and 1929, respectively. During the Second World War Queen Wilhelmina of the Netherlands promised independence, and in 1954 a Charter gave the federation of six islands full autonomy in domestic affairs, and declared it to be an integral part of the Kingdom of the Netherlands.

Divisions of political allegiance within the territory have been along island, rather than policy, lines, and a series of coalition Governments has frequently paralysed decision-making. In 1969 serious rioting and looting broke out in Willemstad after a demonstration by workers in the petroleum industry. Troops had to be sent from the Netherlands to quell the disturbances and to restore order. In February 1970 the socialist Government of Ciro Kroon resigned over the nomination of a new Governor, and in 1971 the Government of E. Petronia resigned over the rejection by the Staten (parliament) of new financial measures.

Following elections to the Staten in June 1977, a coalition Government was formed, with the leader of the Democratische Partij (DP), Silvio Rozendal, as Prime Minister. After a boycott of the session by the Movimentu Electoral di Pueblo (MEP) of Aruba and the Frente Obrero i Liberashon 30 di mei (FOL), the Staten was eventually convened by a Governor's decree in October. Rozendal resigned in April 1979, and elections were held in July. A coalition administration was formed by the Movimentu Antiyas Nobo (MAN), the MEP and the Unión Patriótico Bonairiano (UPB), with Dominico (Don) Martina, the leader of the MAN, as Prime Minister. The DP joined the coalition Government in December 1980.

In Aruba resentment of the administrative dominance of Curaçao resulted, in 1971, in the establishment of the pro-independence MEP. In 1981 a series of talks regarding Aruba's future began with the Netherlands Government. However, in September the MEP representatives in the Staten withdrew their support for the Government on the question of Aruba's rights to possible discoveries of petroleum off its coast. The Government's majority was restored by the inclusion of the DP—St Maarten (DP—StM) member for the 'Windward Islands' in the coalition, but a DP resignation in January 1982 precipitated a further crisis. A general election in June failed to resolve the situation, and it was not until October that agreement was reached on the formation by Martina of a new coalition, which excluded the MEP.

In March 1983 agreement was finally reached whereby Aruba would be given separate status (*status aparte*) within the Kingdom of the Netherlands from January 1986, with the prospect of full independence in 1996 (for further details, see Aruba, q.v.). Arguments persisted regarding the division of the Antilles' financial reserves, and over rights to explore for petroleum and other minerals. In June 1984 Martina's coalition Government resigned. A five-party coalition was eventually formed in September, with Maria Liberia-Peters of the conservative Partido Nashonal di Pueblo (PNP) as Prime Minister.

At a general election in November 1985 the PNP gained the largest number of seats in the Staten for the Antilles of the Five (six out of 22), but was unable to secure enough support from other parties to form a government. Martina once again became Prime Minister and formed a coalition Government. During 1986–87 the Government was forced to introduce a series of economic austerity measures, following Aruba's separation from the Netherlands Antilles and the decline of both the petroleum-refining industry and 'offshore' financial services. The Government resigned in March 1988, after losing the support of the DP—StM and the FOL. In May Liberia-Peters formed a coalition with all the parties represented in the Staten except for the MAN and the DP—Curaçao (DP—C).

In January 1989 Martina revealed that successive Curaçao administrations had diverted revenues from the 'offshore' financial sector into a fund that had not been declared to The Hague, the Netherlands, during negotiations for budgetary support. The Netherlands had recently exerted pressure for more control to be exercised over the large amount of aid that it provided for the Netherlands Antilles. By the early 1990s it appeared that, while the 'metropolitan'

Government was unwilling to allow the complete disintegration of the federation, it was prepared to consider a less centralized system or the creation of two federations in the separate island groups.

At a general election in March 1990 the PNP increased the number of its seats (all on Curaçao) to seven, again making it the largest single party in the Staten, and, after some weeks of negotiations, Liberia-Peters assumed the leadership of a broadly based coalition. In March 1992 the FOL and its partner at the 1990 election, the Social Independiente, withdrew from the Government. Liberia-Peters formed a new coalition with the DP—StM, the UPB and the DP—C. In September 1993 the DP—StM withdrew, although the Government maintained its majority in the Staten with the support of an independent deputy and subsequently that of the Windward Islands People's Movement (WIPM).

A referendum was conducted on Curaçao in November 1993 regarding its constitutional status; 74% of the electorate voted for a continuance of the island's status as a member of the Antillean federation. The option of *status aparte* within the Kingdom of the Netherlands, favoured by the Government, received only 18% of the votes cast. As a result of this defeat, the WIPM and the UPB withdrew their support, leaving the Government without a majority in the Staten. Liberia-Peters resigned, and Alejandro Felippe Paula, a professor at the University of the Netherlands Antilles, subsequently agreed to head an interim Government. A general election took place in February 1994, at which a new, Curaçao-based party, the Partido Antía Restrukturá (PAR), led by Miguel A. Pourier, became the largest single party in the Staten. Pourier assumed the leadership of a broadly based coalition Government, which was inaugurated in March.

Referendums on status were conducted on St Maarten, St Eustatius, Saba and Bonaire in October 1994. On St Maarten 60% of the electorate voted to remain within the Antillean federation, while the option of *status aparte* received 32% of the vote. On St Eustatius 86% of voters opted for continued membership of the Antillean federation, while the equivalent vote on Saba was 91%. On Bonaire (where voting took place one week later) some 88% of voters favoured continued federation.

A general election was held on 30 January 1998, at which the PAR lost four of its eight seats in the Staten. The PNP retained its three seats, while a new party, the Partido Laboral Krusada Popular (PLKP), also took three seats. The loss of support for the PAR was attributed to the unpopularity of austerity measures imposed by the outgoing Government. Pourier failed in his attempts to form a new coalition, largely owing to opposition to the PAR's economic policies. A new coalition Government, with Susanne F. C. Camelia-Römer of the PNP as Prime Minister, was finally agreed in early May, only to collapse later in the month, when it was revealed that a designated cabinet member was under criminal investigation. A new Government was sworn in on 1 June. The coalition comprised six parties, with the support of 13 of the 22 members of the Staten.

In late 1998 the Government adopted a National Recovery Plan, which aimed both to reduce the fiscal deficit and also to generate growth in the economy through the introduction of measures intended to stimulate investment. However, the Government's subsequent attempts to reduce state expenditure proved to be highly controversial, and proposals to reduce the public sector work-force by some 2,400—principally through cuts in the civil service of the central Government and of the island Government of Curaçao—caused great tension between Camelia-Römer's PNP and its fellow Curaçao-based coalition partners, the PLKP and the FOL, which led, in October 1999, to the collapse of both the central Government and the island Government of Curaçao. In the following month former Prime Minister Pourier formed a new broad-based coalition Government, which had the support of 18 of the 22 members of the Staten. Concerns were, however, expressed that Pourier's Government would face the same problems as the previous administration in its attempt fully to implement the National Recovery Plan, and this was, to some extent, anticipated by the appointment of Camelia-Römer as Minister for the National Recovery Plan and Economic Affairs.

A referendum on the constitutional future of St Maarten took place on 23 June 2000. Only 4% of participants in St Maarten favoured maintaining the *status quo*. Some 69% favoured obtaining *status aparte* within the Kingdom of the Netherlands, 14% favoured complete independence and 12% preferred a restructuring of the Antilles of the Five. Although the Dutch Government indicated that it would not support a request by St Maarten to receive *status aparte*, it supported the establishment of a commission to explore the possibilities of St Maarten adopting *status aparte*. In February 2003 Johan Remkes, the Dutch Minister of Interior and Kingdom Relations, confirmed that the Netherlands would not permit St Maarten to leave the federation. Despite this set-back, St Maarten had signed an agreement with the central Government in August 2002, which would permit the island's executive council to take out loans on its own initiative, without seeking permission from the central bank. Furthermore, in late 2002 the executive council proposed to the central bank that discussions should begin on a separate monetary system for St Maarten.

The elections of 18 January 2002 were won by the FOL, led by Anthony Godett, which had campaigned against the stringent measures imposed by the IMF. Despite the party's victory, attempts by the FOL to form a coalition Government failed because of allegations of corruption and mismanagement of funds by party leaders. Eventually, in June 2002 a coalition Government that included representatives of the PAR, the PNP, the PLKP, the DP—StM, the UPD and the Democratische Partij—Statia (DP—StE) took office, under the leadership of the new PAR leader, Etienne Ys, replacing Pourier's caretaker Government.

Local elections in Curaçao in May 2003 were won by the FOL under the leadership of Anthony Godett, who had been detained by the police in April for alleged corrupt activities. The victory of Godett's party, known for its independent and assertive attitude towards the Netherlands and the IMF, was expected to impact negatively on the implementation of IMF measures and the island's political relationship with the Netherlands, which had improved under the PAR leadership. Later in the same month Prime Minister Ys' cabinet resigned to allow the FOL to form a fresh governing coalition (comprised of the FOL, the PNP, the PLKP, the UPB, the DP—StE and the WIPM), based on new local political alliances. In late July Ben Komproe of the FOL was sworn in as Prime Minister on a temporary basis, as Godett could not be approved for the post while he faced corruption charges. In August Mirna Luisa Godett, the sister of the FOL leader, was elected by the party to the post of Prime Minister, despite not being a member of the Staten. Komproe, meanwhile, was appointed Minister of Justice. Following the conviction in December of Anthony Godett (and 16 other party members, business leaders and officials) for fraud, embezzlement and corruption charges, in January 2004 the governing coalition almost lost control of the legislature when the WIPM and the UPB withdrew their support. The Government managed to retain its majority, however, when the Democratische Partij—Bonaire (DP—B) agreed to join the coalition later in the same month. In February the Staten rejected a motion proposed by the opposition (and directed at Anthony Godett) that legislators found guilty of corruption be prevented from retaining their parliamentary seats.

Meanwhile, as anticipated, relations between the Netherlands Antilles and the Dutch Government worsened following the advent of the FOL-dominated Government. In August 2003 Mirna Luisa Godett announced that a delegation of Dutch MPs would not be officially received when they visited the territory. Godett's administration further alienated the Dutch Government by its support of a proposal to remove a body scanner at Curaçao's international airport, which had been installed in an attempt to combat the increasing drugs trade between Amsterdam and the Caribbean. Relations continued to worsen during the remainder of 2003 and in January 2004 Godett accused Dutch officials of spying on her Government after it emerged that local justice officials had met two visiting Dutch ministers without her knowledge. Tension was further exacerbated by Godett's rejection of a Dutch proposal to ban known drugs-traffickers from Antillean airlines.

The Government lost its parliamentary majority in early April 2004 after four parties (the PNP, the PLKP, DP—B and the DP—StE) withdrew from the FOL-led coalition, having failed to effect the resignation of the Minister of Justice, Ben Komproe. The coalition partners accused Komproe of allowing the FOL's main political donor, Nelson Monte, who was serving a custodial sentence for corruption, to stay in a luxury hospital rather than be jailed. After the Staten voted in favour of a 'no confidence' motion against the Government, the Prime Minister submitted her resignation on 6 April; Komproe, along with two ministers, also resigned. Komproe's position had already been weakened by his failure to reverse the rising crime rate on Curaçao and by his brother's alleged involvement in fraud. In the wake of the resignations, the Governor, Fritz Goedgedrag, assumed the task of forming a new government; a seven-party coalition (consisting of the PAR, the PNP, the PLKP, the UPB, the DP—StM, the DP—StE and the WIPM) led by Etienne Ys was duly appointed in June and charged with the responsibility of repairing the territory's relationship with the Netherlands and reducing the huge national debt. Meanwhile, in July Anthony Godett was sentenced to 15 months' imprisonment on corruption-related charges; the sentence was confirmed by the High Court in The Hague. However, five of the original 15 months were suspended, and the FOL leader—who had retained his parliamentary and Island Council membership owing to anomalies in existing legislation—was released in March 2007.

In November 2005 Ys announced that the PAR-led Government had lost its slim majority following the withdrawal from the coalition of the UPB. (The UPB was reportedly dissatisfied with the central Government's financial support for Bonaire's San Francisco Hospital and Flamingo Field Airport.) A general election, intended to be the final election to the Netherlands Antilles Staten, was consequently held on 27 January 2006. The PAR, led by Ys, secured the largest number of seats (five) in the 22-seat legislature. In addition, the MAN won three seats, the PNP, the National Alliance (NA—comprising the National Progressive Party and the St Maarten Patriotic Alliance), the UPB, the FOL and Forsa Kòrsou each won two seats and the DP—StM, the WIPM, the DP—StE and the DP—B each secured one legislative seat. In total, 27 parties contested the election. Negotiations to form a new coalition government were, as usual, protracted. Eventually, on 26 March, a coalition Government comprising representatives of the PAR, the MAN, the PNP, the NA, the UPB, the DP—StE and the WIPM, and headed by the PAR leader, Emily de Jongh-Elhage, was sworn into office. (The DP—StE and the WIPM had representatives at the rank of State Secretary rather than at full ministerial level.) De Jongh-Elhage pledged to ensure that the best interests of all the constituent parts of the federation would be considered during the transition period, and that education and the eradication of poverty would be her Government's main concerns.

On 8 October 2004 the Jesurun Commission, established by the Dutch and Antillean Governments and headed by Edsel Jesurun—a former Governor of the territory—recommended the dissolution of the Netherlands Antilles; support for the federation had, it was argued, virtually disintegrated on most of the islands. In particular, changes were needed to combat the rise in unemployment, poverty, violent crime and drugs-smuggling in the territory. The Commission proposed that Curaçao and St Maarten should become autonomous states within the Netherlands (i.e., have *status aparte*), while Saba, Bonaire and St Eustatius should be directly administered by the Dutch Government. In September and November, respectively, in official referendums, a majority of voters on both Bonaire (59%) and Saba (86%) strongly favoured becoming part of the Netherlands. Further referendums on the constitutional futures of Curaçao and St Eustatius took place on 8 April 2005: 68% of participants in Curaçao favoured *status aparte*, in line with the recommendations of the Commission, 23% voted for closer ties with the Netherlands and 5% voted for complete independence—there was a 54% voter turn-out. In St Eustatius, from a voter turn-out of 55%, 76% of the electorate favoured remaining part of the Netherlands Antilles, while 20% voted for closer ties with the Netherlands and 1% preferred to seek complete independence for the tiny island. Taking into account the results of the referendum on St Maarten in 2000 (see above), since St Eustatius was the only island of the dependency to favour the *status quo*, the future of the Antillean federation appeared to be limited. On 3 December 2005 a preliminary agreement with the Dutch Government that the extant federation be dissolved by 1 July 2007 was duly signed in Curaçao. Under the new structure, Curaçao and St Maarten were, as expected, to become autonomous members of the Kingdom of the Netherlands, while Saba, Bonaire and St Eustatius were to become 'Kingdom Islands', a status that was likely to be equivalent to that of a Dutch province.

Arrangements towards effecting the proposed dissolution of the Netherlands Antilles federation advanced considerably in 2006. An agreement confirming the three smaller islands' impending accession to 'special municipality' status was signed in The Hague on 12 October 2006, and included provisions for citizens of Saba, Bonaire and St Eustatius to participate in Dutch national and local elections and for election of candidates to the European Parliament. On 2 November the Dutch Government granted St Maarten and Curaçao independent governance within the Kingdom of the Netherlands; endorsement of this latter agreement was contingent upon the two larger islands ceding authority for the administration of defence, foreign policy and law enforcement matters to the Dutch Government. Responsibility for the Netherlands Antilles' substantial collective debt, estimated at NA Fl. 5,000m., was to be assumed by the Dutch administration, assuming comprehensive ratification of the 2 November accord by the respective heads of Island Councils. The Common Court of Justice of the Netherlands Antilles and Aruba was to be retained as the islands' principal judicial authority.

However, while St Maarten acceded to the agreement on 28 November 2006, Curaçao's Island Council voted by a decisive 13–6 majority against the accord, averring that further negotiations were required in order to safeguard the interests of the island's citizens, specifically over the administration of justice (over which they regarded the Dutch Government as having too great an influence). Particular concern had been expressed by the detractors with regard to stipulations for the management of the islands' respective budgets—entailing submission to a joint central bank—and the supervision of their judicial and police departments by the Dutch Government; furthermore, potential deficiencies had been identified within the Dutch system regarding the regulation of political practices, freedom of expression, the synthesis of European Union (see p. 244) directives with national democratic tenets, and the integration of foreign nationals into Dutch society. Representatives of the PAR and PNP, who had voted in favour of the final agreement, left the Island Council in protest at the decision. Their departure left Curaçao without a legitimate government. Furthermore, in January 2007 the Netherlands Government rejected the island's request for a renegotiation of the 2 November accord. Curaçao's abstention was regarded as having jeopardized certain provisions of the agreement that were dependent upon all five islands becoming signatories and provoked polarized responses from the island's people. The urgency of addressing Curaçao's already burdensome public debt, estimated as constituting approximately one-half of the entire federation's total obligation, was rendered more acute in light of the fact that the island would no longer benefit from the debt relief awarded by the Netherlands to signatories of the 2 November agreement.

A further 'transition accord' was signed by the Netherlands Antilles central Government, the Island Councils of Saba, Bonaire, St Eustatius, St Maarten and the Netherlands on 12 February 2007, envisaging the islands' complete secession from the federation and commencement of their respective new orders of governance on 15 December 2008, a day customarily celebrated as 'Kingdom Day'. Curaçao was conspicuously absent from the provisions of the agreement and consequently attended the signing ceremony in an observer capacity only. Under the terms of this covenant, the Netherlands was to pledge over NA Fl. 1,000m. (in addition to existing financial assistance) to facilitate the process of disintegration; of this sum, NA Fl. 224m. was designated specifically for debt relief, while the remaining funds were to be disseminated through social and economic development programmes and budgetary aid, with each of the four participating islands receiving individual allocations. Curaçao's exclusion from the restructured Netherlands Antilles precipitated serious concerns for the island's pursuit of autonomy and its future status and relations with the Dutch Government and, consequently, on 9 July the Curaçao Island Council signed the November accord's 'closing statement', although its late accession to the arrangement precluded the island from the Netherlands Government's debt-restructuring provisions.

In early 2007 the Curaçao Island Council—now comprised of the FOL, the Liste Ni'un Paso Atras (LNPA), the MAN and the Movimentu Sosial Laboral (MSL)—was reportedly exploring the possibility of greater involvement in the Caribbean Community through the regional organization, CARICOM, while St Maarten, Saba and St Eustatius had expressed an interest in acceding to the Organization of Eastern Caribbean States (OECS). State Secretary of Finance Alex Rosaria reaffirmed the islands' commitment to the Caribbean Community after an official visit by the Secretary-General of the OECS, Edwin Carrington, in September.

Local government elections were staged on all five islands of the federation on 20 April 2007, representing the final elections prior to dissolution of the Netherlands Antilles, anticipated before the end of the following year. The PAR received the greatest number of votes and obtained seven seats in the Curaçao Island Council. The MAN won five seats and the FOL's representation was reduced to two seats, along with the PNP and the LNPA.

Opposition-led protests took place in late 2007 in Curaçao in response to the continuing constitutional negotiations with the Dutch Government. On 12 November riot police were deployed to disperse a crowd of around 300 protesters when violence broke out. A week later the Island Council formally ratified the results of the 2005 referendum: at a second peaceful demonstration held in early December and attended by several thousand people, opposition parties called for an end to the negotiations and for the Government to seek to achieve the autonomous status of Curaçao, in accordance with the results of the ballot. The Dutch Government expressed concern that the target date of 15 December 2008 for constitutional reform on each of the islands would not be met and advised that the deadline should be revised to December 2010.

In December 2000 an agreement was reached with the Dutch Government on the compulsory acculturation of Antillean migrants to the Netherlands. The high level of unemployment, particularly among the younger members of the Antillean community in the Netherlands, and the steady influx of new migrants in recent years had led the Dutch Government to propose that the Netherlands Antilles adopt legislation whereby those under 25 years of age would be granted permission to emigrate to the Netherlands only after attending acculturation classes designed to facilitate their integration into Dutch society. In May 2005 the Netherlands announced plans to introduce legislation to require citizens of the Netherlands Antilles aged between 16 and 24 years to find work or begin studies within three months of arriving in the Netherlands, or face deportation; it was estimated by the Dutch Government that immigrants from the Netherlands Antilles aged under 25 years were four times more likely to turn to crime than the general Dutch population. Prime Minister Ys described the policy as discriminatory and threatened to take the Dutch Government to court.

In December 2004 the Dutch Government pledged to send 60 police officers to the Netherlands Antilles, primarily Curaçao, to combat the increase in crime on the islands. In addition, 25 Dutch customs and military officials were sent to Curaçao and Bonaire airports in January 2005 to improve security against drugs-transshipment between the Netherlands and its dependent territory. Proposals announced by the Dutch Ministry of Immigration and Integration in September 2006 for the forcible return of Antillean juvenile offenders to the Caribbean, even if they held Dutch citizenship, were condemned as being in violation of European Human Rights legislation (by discriminating in favour of Netherlands-born nationals). In

January 2007 draft legislation was submitted to the Island Council of St Maarten for the proposed repatriation of persons who had assumed illegal residence on the island since 2005. It was estimated that over 25,000 people were living in the territory at that time, although the proportion of this number to which compulsory expulsion would apply was unclear. The measure appeared to coincide with requirements for immigration and security reforms ahead of the proposed redesignation of St Maarten within the Kingdom of the Netherlands (see above).

Efforts by the Netherlands Antilles Government to improve its regulation of financial transactions and tax administration—and to attain recognition as an international financial centre—were bolstered by the formation of a 'double taxation task force' in October 2006. One of the new organization's stated principal objectives was to extend its network of Double Taxation Agreements (DTA); to this end, the Government announced plans to negotiate such agreements with Mexico, Spain, Suriname, the United Arab Emirates and Colombia in 2008. The Staten approved a series of amendments to the national tax legislation in November 2006 which would render the Netherlands Antilles compliant with requirements for the establishment of a Tax Information and Exchange Agreement with the USA and facilitate future discussions towards a bilateral DTA; a similar agreement for the exchange of tax information was reached with New Zealand in March 2007.

Government

The Governor of the Netherlands Antilles, appointed by the Dutch Crown for a term of six years, represents the monarch of the Netherlands in the territory, and has executive power over external affairs. The Governor is assisted by an advisory council. Executive power in internal affairs is vested in the Council of Ministers. The Council is responsible to the Staten (parliament), which has 22 members elected by universal adult suffrage for four years (subject to dissolution). The administration of each island is conducted by its own Island Council, Executive Council and Lieutenant-Governor.

Defence

Although defence is the responsibility of the Netherlands, compulsory military service is laid down in an Antilles Ordinance. The Governor is the Commander-in-Chief of the armed forces in the islands, and a Dutch contingent is stationed in Willemstad, Curaçao. The Netherlands also operates a Coast Guard Force (to combat organized crime and drugs-smuggling), based at St Maarten and Aruba. In May 1999 the US air force and navy began patrols from a base on Curaçao to combat the transport of illegal drugs.

Economic Affairs

In 1994 the gross national income (GNI) of the Netherlands Antilles, measured at current prices, was an estimated US $1,550m., equivalent to some $8,800 per head. Gross domestic product (GDP) was some $3,352m. in 2006 (equivalent to $17,904.2 per head), according to UN estimates. In 1996–2006 the population decreased at a negligible rate, while GDP per head increased, in real terms, by an average of 0.9% per year during 1995–2005. According to UN estimates, GDP decreased, in real terms, by an annual average rate of 0.03% in 1996–2006; real GDP increased by 0.9% in 2006.

Agriculture, together with forestry, fishing and mining, contributed only 0.7% of GDP in 2004. The sector employed an average of 1.0% of the working population on Curaçao in 2004–06. Some 8% of the total land area is cultivated. The chief products are aloes (Bonaire is a major exporter), sorghum, divi-divi, groundnuts, beans, fresh vegetables and tropical fruit. A bitter variety of orange is used in the production of Curaçao liqueur. There is also some fishing.

Industry (comprising manufacturing, construction, power and water, but excluding mining) contributed 16.5% of GDP in 2004, and employed an average of 15.7% of the working population on Curaçao in 2004–06.

The mining and quarrying sector employed only 0.3% of the working population on Curaçao in 2000. Apart from some phosphates on Curaçao (exploited until the mid-1980s), and some limestone and salt on Bonaire, the islands have no other significant mineral reserves. Aggregate is quarried on St Maarten and consumed primarily by the local construction industry.

Manufacturing contributed 5.9% of GDP in 2004, and employed an average of 6.7% of the working population on Curaçao in 2004–06; activities include food-processing, production of Curaçao liqueur, and the manufacture of paint, paper, soap and cigarettes. Bonaire has a textile factory, and Curaçao's 'free zone' is of considerable importance in the economy, but the 'Windward Islands' have very few manufacturing activities. Petroleum-refining (using petroleum imported from Venezuela) is the islands' principal industrial activity, with the Curaçao refinery leased to the Venezuelan state petroleum company. Production capacity at the refinery was 116.8m. barrels per year in 2001, according to the US Geological Survey; however, industrial action in Venezuela led to the closure of the refinery during December 2002–March 2003, impacting heavily upon the islands' economy. Petroleum transshipment is also important, and ship repairs at the Curaçao dry dock make a significant contribution to the economy. In 2002 petroleum imports comprised 68.4% of total merchandise imports.

The services sector contributed 82.9% of GDP in 2004, and engaged an average of 83.2% of the employed labour force on Curaçao in 2004–06. The Netherlands Antilles is a major 'offshore' financial centre. In June 2000 the Netherlands Antilles was urged by the Organisation for Economic Co-operation and Development (OECD) to improve the accountability and transparency of its financial services; in response, the Government announced that it was to review its taxation legislation to comply more closely with OECD's standards. In April 2002 the Netherlands Antilles was removed from the list of those countries deemed to be 'un-co-operative tax havens' after OECD favourably assessed the Government's legislative amendments. In the same month an agreement was signed with the USA, pledging to share information on tax matters, with the aim of combating money-laundering and associated criminal activities. A 'double taxation task force' was established in October 2006 (see Recent History) and a Tax Information and Exchange Agreement signed with New Zealand in March 2007; it was hoped that amendments to national tax legislation approved by the Staten in November 2006 would enable the establishment of a similar agreement with the USA and lead to a bilateral Double Taxation Agreement to improve regulation of financial transactions between the two countries. The financial and business services sector contributed 31.6% of GDP in 2004, and employed an average of 17.1% of the Curaçao working population in 2004–06. Operational income from the 'offshore' sector increased significantly from the 1990s. A major industry for all the islands (particularly St Maarten) is tourism, which is the largest employer after the public sector. Significant improvements in the number of stop-over tourists, the number of cruise-ship passengers and the level of tourism revenue were recorded in 2003 and 2004. Figures for the whole of the latter year were the best since 1994. Tourism continued to improve in 2004–06. The number of cruise-ship passengers visiting Bonaire, Curaçao and St Maarten alone increased further, to 1,805,040, in 2006. In addition to tourism, Curaçao, in particular, has sought to establish itself as a centre for regional trade, exploiting its excellent harbours. In 1998 a free trade zone was established at the island's airport, which further enhanced Curaçao's entrepôt status.

In 2005 the Netherlands Antilles recorded a visible trade deficit of US $1,314.1m., and there was a deficit of $148.3m. on the current account of the balance of payments. The petroleum industry dominates the trade figures of the Netherlands Antilles, particularly of the 'Leeward Islands'. In 2002 the principal source of imports (60.4%) was Venezuela (which provides crude petroleum), and the principal market for exports (22.1%) was the USA. The USA is an important trading partner for all the islands of the Netherlands Antilles, as are the Netherlands and other Caribbean countries. Petroleum is the principal commodity for both import and export, and accounted for 68.4% of imports and 94.7% of exports in 2002. The Netherlands Antilles also imports machinery and transport equipment, manufactured goods, and chemicals and related products, while it exports aloes, Curaçao liqueur and some light manufactures.

In 2006 the general Government (including island governments) recorded a budgetary deficit of NA Fl. 153.7m., which was equivalent to 2.7% of GDP in 2004. In 2006 the central Government recorded a deficit of NA Fl. 88.0m. on its budget. The administrations of the islands tend to operate with deficits. At the end 2006 the combined public domestic debts of the central Government and the island Government of Curaçao were NA Fl. 4,369.0m. (71.1% of GDP). Total foreign debt stood at NA Fl. 742.3m. (12.1% of GDP). The average annual rate of inflation was 2.3% in 1996–2006; consumer prices increased by an average of 3.8% in 2005 and by 3.3% in 2006. The rate of unemployment in the labour force was an estimated 15.1% for the Netherlands Antilles as a whole in June 2005. According to a sample survey of the labour force, 14.7% of the Curaçao work-force were unemployed in 2004–06. Figures from the 2001 census showed that the rate of unemployment in St Maarten stood at 12.2%, with the rate of youth unemployment at 24.1%.

The Netherlands Antilles, as part of the Kingdom of the Netherlands, has the status of an Overseas Territory in association with the European Union (see p. 244). The Netherlands Antilles enjoys observer status in the Caribbean Community and Common Market (CARICOM, see p. 196).

The relative isolation of the individual islands has led to the development of semi-independent economies, and economic conditions vary considerably between them. Notwithstanding, the Netherlands Antilles experienced relatively strong economic growth in the early 1990s, but, owing mainly to a decline in both the financial services and the petroleum-refining sectors, the past decade witnessed a progressive weakening of the economy, leading to a prolonged recession, high unemployment and increasing rates of emigration. Under the terms of the structural adjustment programme (SAP), undertaken from 1996 in consultation with the IMF, which aimed to eliminate the fiscal deficit over a period of four years, the civil service was to be rationalized, public sector wages were to be 'frozen' and pension arrangements reviewed, while new indirect taxes were to be introduced. Successive administrations, however, recorded only limited success in implementing the terms of the SAP and its successor, the National Recovery Plan, which was adopted in late 1998, in part owing to the great unpopularity of both programmes. Following stringent measures announced by the Pourier Government in 2001, the Dutch Government released NA Fl. 153m. (to be spent in 2002–06) to encourage sustained economic development and to support the Netherlands Antilles Government in improving the quality of its administration and education systems. The Netherlands approved the release of €125m. in additional funds in 2003, and the Dutch and Netherlands Antillean Governments agreed on a more prominent role for the Central Bank in the monitoring and implementation of the IMF targets. In 2002–05 the long formation periods of four successive Governments and the consequent lack of a central programme, coupled with the effects of the weak US dollar and, in the earlier part of the period, an under-performing international tourism market, damaged confidence, leading to only small increases in real GDP, according to central bank figures. An expansion of 2.4% was recorded for 2007. Growth was forecast to reach 2.6% in 2008, though inflation was also expected to rise to 3.5% that year, as a result of higher oil prices. Some optimism was engendered by the improving tourism industry: the addition of a new US $87m. terminal at the Princess Juliana International Airport on St Maarten in October 2006, expanding the airport's passenger handling capabilities by 2.5m., was expected to result in increased visitor numbers. However, amendments to the US Western Hemisphere Travel Initiative, requiring all US citizens travelling to and from Caribbean destinations to hold a valid passport from January 2007 (although cruise-ship passengers were to be exempted until 1 January 2009) was expected to have a negative impact upon all tourism markets in the region. Growth in activity in Curaçao's free trade zone and a consequent increase in arrivals from Venezuela and the Dominican Republic was reportedly an important boost for the tourism and retail sectors. The tourism industry continued to expand in 2007, particularly in Curaçao, where six new resorts were being constructed and five existing ones expanded, increasing room capacity by 1,241. Under the agreement to dissolve the Netherlands Antilles by July 2007 (see Recent History), the Dutch Government agreed to help restructure the islands' public debt, a large proportion of which was owed to the Netherlands. However, subsequent covenants signed by the Netherlands Antilles and the Dutch administration towards secession from the federation during 2006 and early 2007 resulted in changes to the debt-relief provisions offered: Curaçao's decision to abstain from the 2 November accord, under which the Netherlands Government was to adopt the federation's estimated NA Fl. 5,000m. collective debt, necessitated a revision of the concession in February 2007. The three islands to gain municipal status (Bonaire, St Eustatius and Saba) following secession, now postponed until 15 December 2008, were expected to start to benefit from an enhanced association with the Netherlands from 2009. In February 2008 it was announced that the Netherlands Antilles would begin to move away from tax policies that promote transparency and the exchange of information in tax matters, and instead opt for Double Taxation Agreements (DTA), which it was hoped would stimulate growth in the financial services sector. In March that year officials met with Surinamese delegates to negotiate a DTA between the territories.

Education

Education was made compulsory in 1992. The islands' educational facilities are generally of a high standard. The education system is the same as that of the Netherlands. Dutch is used as the principal language of instruction in schools on the 'Leeward Islands', while English is used in schools on the 'Windward Islands'. Instruction in Papiamento (using a different spelling system from that adopted by Aruba) has been introduced in primary schools. Primary education begins at six years of age and lasts for six years. Secondary education lasts for a further five years. In 2003/04 enrolment in all levels of education, with the exception of primary schools, was equivalent to 88% of students in the relevant age categories. The University of the Netherlands Antilles, sited on Curaçao, had 2,032 students in 2006/07. In April 2002 the Netherlands Government made more than €12.7m. available for improvements to education provision in the Netherlands Antilles. In 1995 local government expenditure on education in the Antilles of the Five was NA Fl. 178.9m. (19.3% of total spending by the island governments).

Public Holidays

2008: 1 January (New Year's Day), 19 January (Bonaire only: Carnival Rest Day), 4 February (Curaçao and Bonaire only: Lenten Carnival), 21–24 March (Easter), 30 April (Queen's Day), 1 May (Labour Day and Ascension Day), 8 May (St Maarten, Saba and St Eustatius only: Celebration of World War II Victory), 12 May (St Maarten, Saba and St Eustatius only: Whit Monday), 1 June (Emancipation Day), 2 July (Curaçao Day), 21 July (St Maarten, Saba and St Eustatius only: Schoelcher Day), 31 July (Carnival), 6 September (Bonaire Day), 21 October (Antillian Day), 1 November (St Maarten, Saba and St Eustatius only: All Saints' Day), 11 November (St Maarten Day), 16 November (St Eustatius Day), 6 December (Saba Day), 15 December (St Maarten, Saba and St Eustatius only: Kingdom Day), 25–26 December (Christmas).

2009: 1 January (New Year's Day), 19 January (Bonaire only: Carnival Rest Day), 23 February (Curaçao and Bonaire only: Lenten Carnival), 10–13 April (Easter), 30 April (Queen's Day), 1 May (Labour Day), 8 May (St Maarten, Saba and St Eustatius only: Celebration of World War II Victory), 21 May (Ascension Day), 1 June (St Maarten, Saba and St Eustatius only: Whit Monday), 1 July (Emancipation Day), 2 July (Curaçao Day), 21 July (St Maarten, Saba and St Eustatius only: Schoelcher Day), 31 July (Carnival), 6 September (Bonaire Day), 21 October (Antillian Day), 1 November (St Maarten, Saba and St Eustatius only: All Saints' Day), 11 November (St Maarten Day), 16 November (St Eustatius Day), 6 December (Saba Day), 15 December (St Maarten, Saba and St Eustatius only: Kingdom Day), 25–26 December (Christmas).

Weights and Measures

The metric system is in force.

Statistical Survey

Sources (unless otherwise stated): Centraal Bureau voor de Statistiek, Fort Amsterdam, Willemstad, Curaçao; tel. (9) 461-1031; fax (9) 461-1696; internet www.central-bureau-of-statistics.an; Bank van de Nederlandse Antillen, Simon Bolivar Plein 1, Willemstad, Curaçao; tel. (9) 434-5500; fax (9) 461-5004; e-mail info@centralbank.an; internet www.centralbank.an.

AREA AND POPULATION

Area (sq km): Curaçao 444; Bonaire 288; St Maarten (Dutch sector) 34; St Eustatius 21; Saba 13; Total 800 (309 sq miles).

Population: 189,474 at census of 27 January 1992 (excluding adjustment for underenumeration, estimated at 3.2%); 175,653 (males 82,521, females 93,132) at census of 29 January 2001; 191,780 at 1 January 2007 (estimate). *By Island* (at 1 January 2007, estimates): Curaçao 137,094; Bonaire 11,537; St Maarten (Dutch sector) 38,959; St Eustatius 2,699; Saba 1,491.

Density (per sq km, 1 January, estimates): *2007:* Curaçao 308.8; Bonaire 40.1; St Maarten (Dutch sector) 1,145.9; St Eustatius 128.5; Saba 114.7; Total 239.7.

Principal Town: Willemstad (capital), population (incl. suburbs, UN estimate) 120,000 at mid-2007. Source: UN, *World Urbanization Prospects: The 2007 Revision.*

Births, Marriages and Deaths (2004): Registered live births 2,357; Registered marriages 710 (marriage rate 3.9 per 1,000); Registered deaths 1,412 (death rate 7.7 per 1,000). *2007:* Birth rate 12.5 per 1,000; death rate 7.9 per 1,000 (Source: Pan American Health Organization).

Expectation of Life (years at birth): 75.1 (males 71.3; females 78.8) in 2007. Source: Pan American Health Organization.

Economically Active Population (sample survey, Curaçao only, persons aged 15 years and over, average 2004–06): Agriculture, forestry, fishing and mining 550; Manufacturing 3,592; Electricity, gas and water 820; Construction 4,061; Wholesale and retail trade, repairs 10,160; Hotels and restaurants 4,267; Transport, storage and communications 3,105; Financial intermediation 3,958; Real estate, renting and business activities 5,221; Public administration, defence and social security 4,755; Education 2,564; Health and social work 4,555; Other community, social and personal services 3,859; Private households with employed persons 2,253; Extra-territorial organizations and bodies 77; *Total employed* 53,797 (males 27,033, females 26,764); Unemployed 9,241 (males 3,469, females 5,772); *Total labour force* 63,038 (males 30,502, females 32,536).

HEALTH AND WELFARE

Total Fertility Rate (children per woman, 2007): 1.9.

Under-5 Mortality Rate (per 1,000 live births, 2006): 16.8.

Physicians (per 1,000 head, 1999): 1.4.

Hospital Beds (per 1,000 head, 2002): 7.24.

Health Expenditure (% of GDP, 2005): 4.8.

Source: mostly Pan American Health Organization.

For other sources and definitions, see explanatory note on p. vi.

AGRICULTURE, ETC.

Livestock ('000 head, year ending September 2005, FAO estimates): Asses 2.6; Cattle 0.6; Pigs 2.5; Goats 13.5; Sheep 9.0; Chickens 135. Note: Data were not available for 2006.

Livestock Products (metric tons, 2005, FAO estimates): Pig meat 156; Chicken meat 697; Cows' milk 410; Hen eggs 510. Note: data were not available for 2006.

Fishing (metric tons, live weight, 2004): Skipjack tuna 8,708; Yellowfin tuna 4,161; Bigeye tuna 1,822; *Total catch* (incl. others) 15,765 (FAO estimate). *2005* (FAO estimate): Total catch (excl. tuna) 2,422.

Source: FAO.

MINING

Production ('000 metric tons, 2003, estimate): Salt 500. Source: US Geological Survey.

INDUSTRY

Production ('000 metric tons, 2004, unless otherwise indicated): Jet fuel 790; Kerosene 46; Residual fuel oils 4,188; Lubricating oils 384; Petroleum bitumen (asphalt) 994; Liquefied petroleum gas 118; Motor spirit (petrol) 1,716; Aviation gasoline 21; Distillate fuel oils (gas-diesel oil) 2,202; Sulphur (recovered) 30 (2002); Electric energy (million kWh) 1,248 (2005).

Sources: mainly UN, *Industrial Commodity Statistics Yearbook*, and US Geological Survey.

FINANCE

Currency and Exchange Rates: 100 cents = 1 Netherlands Antilles gulden (guilder) or florin (NA Fl.). *Sterling, Dollar and Euro Equivalents* (31 December 2007): £1 sterling = NA Fl. 3.586; US $1 = NA Fl. 1.790; €1 = NA Fl. 2.635; NA Fl. 100 = £27.89 = $55.87 = €37.95. *Exchange Rate:* In December 1971 the central bank's midpoint rate was fixed at US $1 = NA Fl. 1.80. In 1989 this was adjusted to $1 = NA Fl. 1.79. The US dollar also circulates on St Maarten.

Central Government Budget (NA Fl. million, 2006): *Revenue:* Tax revenue 649.3 (Taxes on property 37.3, Taxes on goods and services 461.4, Taxes on international trade and transactions 143.9, Other taxes 6.7); Non-tax revenue 83.5 (Entrepreneurial and property income 68.5, Administrative fees and charges, non-industrial and incidental sales 13.2, Other 1.8); Grants (from other levels of government, excluding overseas development aid) 89.8; Total 822.6. *Expenditure:* Wages and salaries 295.5; Other goods and services 117.7; Interest payments 147.0; Subsidies 0.0; Current transfers 348.2; Capital expenditure (incl. transfers and net lending) 2.2; Total 910.6.

International Reserves (US $ million at 31 December 2006): Gold (national valuation) 204; Foreign exchange 495; Total 699. Source: IMF, *International Financial Statistics*.

Money Supply (NA Fl. million at 31 December 2006): Currency outside banks 263.7; Demand deposits at commercial banks 1,270.0; Total (incl. others) 1,558.7. Source: IMF, *International Financial Statistics*.

Cost of Living (Consumer Price Index; base: 2000 = 100): All items 105.7 in 2004; 109.3 in 2005; 112.7 in 2006. Source: IMF, *International Financial Statistics*.

Gross Domestic Product (US $ million at constant 1990 prices): 3,115 in 2004; 3,204 in 2005; 3,352 in 2006. Source: UN Statistics Division, National Accounts Main Aggregates Database.

Expenditure on the Gross Domestic Product (million NA Fl. at current prices, 2006): Final consumption expenditure 4,594 (Government 1,292, Households and non-profit institutions serving households 3,302); Gross fixed capital formation 1,482; Change in inventories 8; *Total domestic expenditure* 6,084; Exports of goods and services 5,520; *Less* Imports of goods and services 5,598; Statistical discrepancy (relating to the disparity between the expenditure and production approaches to GDP) –6; *GDP in market prices* 6,000. Source: UN Statistics Division, National Accounts Main Aggregates Database.

Gross Domestic Product (million NA Fl. at current prices, 2004): Agriculture, fishing, mining, etc. 35.7; Manufacturing 311.7; Electricity, gas and water 263.7; Construction 286.8; Wholesale and retail trade 678.8; Hotels and restaurants 219.5; Transport, storage and communications 553.7; Financial intermediation 808.0; Real estate, renting and business activities 848.1; Public administration, defence, etc. 444.9; Education 194.0; Health care and social services 266.4; Other community, social and personal services 305.8; Private households with employed persons 21.8; *Sub-total* 5,238.9; *Less* Financial intermediation services indirectly measured 123.1; *Gross value added at basic prices* 5,115.8; Taxes, less subsidies, on products 549.0; *Gross domestic product in market prices* 5,665.0.

Balance of Payments (US $ million, 2005): Exports of goods f.o.b. 971.1; Imports of goods f.o.b. –2,285.2; *Trade balance* –1,314.1; Exports of services 1,847.3; Imports of services –813.2; *Balance on goods and services* –280.0; Other income received 103.5; Other income paid –107.5; *Balance on goods, services and income* –284.1; Current transfers received 401.0; Current transfers paid –265.2; *Current balance* –148.3; Capital account (net) 95.6; Direct investment abroad –72.4; Direct investment from abroad 73.5; Portfolio investment assets –25.7; Portfolio investment liabilities 1.6; Financial derivatives assets 0.9; Financial derivatives liabilities 0.6; Other investment assets 44.1; Other investment liabilities –1.2; Net errors and omissions 80.3; *Overall balance* 48.9. Source: IMF, *International Financial Statistics*.

EXTERNAL TRADE

Principal Commodities (US $ million, 2002): *Imports c.i.f.:* Food and live animals 145.5; Petroleum, petroleum products, etc. 1,552.1 (Crude petroleum 1,354.4); Basic manufactures 110.4; Machinery and transport equipment 126.3 (Road vehicles 72.9); Total (incl. others) 2,268.5. *Exports f.o.b.:* Refined petroleum products 1,609.0; Total (incl. others) 1,699.2. Source: UN, *International Trade Statistics Yearbook*.

Principal Trading Partners (US $ million, 2002): *Imports c.i.f.:* Colombia 30.3; Germany 39.0; Iraq 151.1; Japan 36.7; Netherlands 187.4; USA 305.1; Venezuela 1,370.9; Total (incl. others) 2,268.5. *Exports f.o.b.:* Antigua and Barbuda 22.0; Aruba 22.7; Bahamas 129.9; Belize 26.1; Canada 68.6; Colombia 18.2; Cuba 61.5; El Salvador 80.0; Guatemala 66.5; Guyana 69.7; Haiti 34.2; Honduras 74.2; Netherlands 73.7; Nicaragua 36.3; Panama 68.0; Suriname 24.1; United Arab Emirates 40.6; USA 375.0; Venezuela 169.9; Total (incl. others) 1,699.2. Source: UN, *International Trade Statistics Yearbook*.

TRANSPORT

Road Traffic (Curaçao and Bonaire, motor vehicles registered, excl. government-owned vehicles, 2004): Passenger cars 64,729; Lorries 14,873; Buses 462; Taxis 218; Other cars 207; Motorcycles 1,498.

Shipping: *International Sea-borne Freight Traffic* (Curaçao, TEUs moved, 2004): 82,087. *Merchant Fleet* (registered at 31 December 2006): Number of vessels 185; Total displacement 1,411,551 grt (Source: Lloyd's Register-Fairplay, *World Fleet Statistics*).

Civil Aviation (aircraft landings): *Bonaire* (2005): 15,900 (Commercial 13,577). *Curaçao* (2003): 20,902 (Commercial 18,066).

TOURISM

Tourist Arrivals: *Stop-overs:* 779,974 in 2004; 770,187 in 2005; 782,161 in 2006. *Cruise-ship Passengers:* (Bonaire, Curaçao and St Maarten only) 1,629,327 in 2004; 1,804,495 in 2005; 1,805,040 in 2006.

Tourism Receipts (NA Fl. million, incl. passenger transport): 1,683.5 in 2002; 1,761.0 in 2003; 1,906.5 in 2004.

COMMUNICATIONS MEDIA

Radio Receivers (1997): 217,000 in use.

Television Receivers (1999): 71,000 in use.

Telephones (2004): 81,000 main lines in use.

Mobile Cellular Telephones (2005): 200,000 subscribers.

Internet Users (1999, UN estimate): 2,000.

Daily Newspapers: 6 titles (estimated circulation 70,000 copies per issue) in 1996; 5 in 2004.

Sources: UNESCO, *Statistical Yearbook*; UNESCO Institute for Statistics; UN, *Statistical Yearbook*; International Telecommunication Union.

EDUCATION

Pre-primary (2002/03): 5,972 pupils; 309 teachers.

Primary (2002/03): 22,667 pupils; 1,145 teachers.

General Secondary (2002/03): 9,180 pupils; 639 teachers.

Vocational (2002/03): 6,088 pupils; teachers 542.

Tertiary (2001/02): 2,285 students; 340 teachers.

English Language Secondary (2000/01): 377 pupils.

Special Education (2000/01): 2,337 pupils; 178 teachers.

Teacher Training (2000/01): 133 students; 22 teachers.

NETHERLANDS DEPENDENCIES

The Netherlands Antilles

Adult Literacy Rate (2005): 96.9% (males 96.9%; females 97.0%) (Source: Pan American Health Organization).

Source: partly UNESCO Institute for Statistics.

Directory

The Constitution

The form of government for the Netherlands Antilles is embodied in the Charter of the Kingdom of the Netherlands, which came into force on 20 December 1954. The Netherlands, the Netherlands Antilles and, since 1986, Aruba each enjoy full autonomy in domestic and internal affairs and are united on a basis of equality for the protection of their common interests and the granting of mutual assistance.

The monarch of the Netherlands is represented in the Netherlands Antilles by the Governor, who is appointed by the Dutch Crown for a term of six years. The central Government of the Netherlands Antilles appoints a Minister Plenipotentiary to represent the Antilles in the Government of the Kingdom. Whenever the Netherlands Council of Ministers is dealing with matters coming under the heading of joint affairs of the realm (in practice mainly foreign affairs and defence), the Council assumes the status of Council of Ministers of the Kingdom. In that event, the Minister Plenipotentiary appointed by the Government of the Netherlands Antilles takes part, with full voting powers, in the deliberations.

A legislative proposal regarding affairs of the realm and applying to the Netherlands Antilles as well as to the 'metropolitan' Netherlands is sent, simultaneously with its submission, to the Staten Generaal (the Netherlands parliament) and to the Staten (parliament) of the Netherlands Antilles. The latter body can report in writing to the Staten Generaal on the draft Kingdom Statute and designate one or more special delegates to attend the debates and furnish information in the meetings of the Chambers of the Staten Generaal. Before the final vote on a draft the Minister Plenipotentiary has the right to express an opinion on it. If he disapproves of the draft, and if in the Second Chamber a three-fifths' majority of the votes cast is not obtained, the discussions on the draft are suspended and further deliberations take place in the Council of Ministers of the Kingdom. When special delegates attend the meetings of the Chambers this right devolves upon the delegates of the parliamentary body designated for this purpose.

The Governor has executive power in external affairs, which he exercises in co-operation with the Council of Ministers. He is assisted by an advisory council, which consists of at least five members appointed by him.

Executive power in internal affairs is vested in the nominated Council of Ministers, responsible to the Staten. The Netherlands Antilles Staten consists of 22 members, who are elected by universal adult suffrage for four years (subject to dissolution). Each island forms an electoral district. Curaçao elects 14 members, Bonaire three members, St Maarten three members and Saba and St Eustatius one member each. In the islands where more than one member is elected, the election is by proportional representation. Inhabitants have the right to vote if they have Dutch nationality and have reached 18 years of age. Voting is not compulsory. Each island territory also elects its Island Council (Curaçao 21 members, Bonaire 9, St Maarten 7, St Eustatius and Saba 5), and its internal affairs are managed by an executive council, consisting of the Gezaghebber (Lieutenant-Governor), and a number of commissioners. The central Government of the Netherlands Antilles has the right to annul any local island decision which is in conflict with the public interest or the Constitution. Control of the police, communications, monetary affairs, health and education remain under the jurisdiction of the central Government.

On 1 January 1986 Aruba acquired separate status (*status aparte*) within the Kingdom of the Netherlands. However, in economic and monetary affairs there is a co-operative union between Aruba and the Antilles of the Five, known as the 'Union of the Netherlands Antilles and Aruba'.

The islands of Saba, Bonaire and St Eustatius ratified an agreement with the Government of the Netherlands on 12 October 2006 under which they would be redesignated as 'special municipalities' of the Kingdom of the Netherlands. A further accord was signed by St Maarten and Curaçao on 28 November 2006 and 9 July 2007, respectively, confirming these islands' secession from the federation to achieve a degree of independent governance and status similar to that enjoyed by Aruba. While the transition process was well advanced by mid-2007, final dissolution of the Netherlands Antilles was not expected until 15 December 2008.

The Government

HEAD OF STATE

Queen of the Netherlands: HM Queen BEATRIX.
Governor: Dr FRITZ M. DE LOS SANTOS GOEDGEDRAG.

COUNCIL OF MINISTERS
(April 2008)

A coalition of the Partido Antía Restrukturá (PAR), the Movimentu Antiyas Nobo (MAN), Partido Nashonal di Pueblo (PNP), the National Alliance (NA), the Unión Patriótico Bonairiano (UPB), the Democratic Partij—Statia (DP—StE) and the Windward Islands People's Movement (WIPM).

Prime Minister and Minister of General Affairs and Foreign Relations: EMILY DE JONGH-ELHAGE (PAR).
Deputy Prime Minister and Minister of Finance and of Public Health and Social Development: ERSILIA T. M. DE LANNOOY (PNP).
Minister of Economic Affairs and Labour: BURNEY F. EL HAGE (UPB).
Minister of Constitutional Affairs and the Interior: ROLAND E. DUNCAN (NA).
Minister of Justice: DAVID A. DICK (PAR).
Minister of Education, Culture, Youth and Sports and of Transport and Telecommunications: OMAYRA VICTORIA ELISABETH LEEFLANG (PAR).
State Secretary of Constitutional Affairs and the Interior, with responsibility for the Transfer of Tasks and Authority: HUBERT MARTIS.
State Secretary of Finance with responsibility for Tax Affairs: ALEX ROSARIA.
State Secretary of Finance, with responsibility for the Solidarity Fund: SHAMARA A. NICHOLSON.
State Secretary of Justice with responsibility for Police Affairs and the Penal Institution of the Windward Isles: E. C. SIMMONS.
State Secretary of Health with responsibility for Medical Care in the Windward Isles and Bonaire: R. E. SAMUEL.
Minister Plenipotentiary and Member of the Council of Ministers of the Realm of the Netherlands Antilles in the Netherlands: PAUL R. J. COMENENCIA (PAR).
Minister Plenipotentiary of the Realm of the Netherlands Antilles in Washington, DC (USA): NORBERTO V. RIBEIRO.
Attorney-General of the Netherlands Antilles: DICK A. PIAR.

MINISTRIES

Office of the Governor: Fort Amsterdam 2, Willemstad, Curaçao; tel. (9) 461-1289; fax (9) 461-1412; e-mail rojer@kgna.an; internet www.gouverneur.an.
Ministry of Constitutional Affairs and the Interior: Willemstad, Curaçao.
Ministry for Economic Affairs and Labour: Directorate of Labour, Schouwburgweg 22, Willemstad, Curaçao; tel. (9) 461-9999; fax (9) 461-5553; e-mail info@diraz.an; internet www.diraz.an.
Ministry of Education and Culture: Schouwburgweg 24–26 (APNA gebouw), Willemstad, Curaçao; tel. (9) 434-3711; fax (9) 462-4471; e-mail minoc@gov.an; internet www.minoc.an.
Ministry of Finance: Pietermaai 17, Willemstad, Curaçao; tel. (9) 432-8000; fax (9) 461-3339; e-mail g.d.dirfin@curinfo.an.
Ministry of Foreign Affairs: Plasa Horacio Hoyer 9, Willemstad, Curaçao; tel. (9) 461-1866; fax (9) 461-1268.
Ministry of Justice: Willhelminaplein, Willemstad, Curaçao; tel. (9) 463-0650; fax (9) 465-8083.
Ministry of Public Health and Social Development: Santa Rosaweg 122, Willemstad, Curaçao; tel. (9) 736-3530; fax (9) 736-3531; e-mail vornil@cura.net.
Ministry of Transport: Fort Amsterdam 17, Willemstad, Curaçao; tel. (9) 461-3988.
Office of the Minister Plenipotentiary of the Netherlands Antilles: Kabinet van de Gevolmachtigde Minister van de Nederlanse Antillen, Badhuisweg 175, POB 90706, 2597 JP's-Gravenhagen, The Hague, the Netherlands; tel. (70) 3066111; fax (70) 3066110; e-mail info@antillenhuis.nl; internet www.antillenhuis.nl.

GEZAGHEBBERS
(Lieutenant-Governors)

Bonaire: HERBERT F. DOMACASSE, Wilhelminaplein 1, Kralendijk, Bonaire; tel. 717-5330; fax 717-5100; e-mail gezag@bonairelive.com.

NETHERLANDS DEPENDENCIES   The Netherlands Antilles

Curaçao: Lizanne M. Richards-Dindial, Voorlichtingscentrum 'Bentana di informashon', Johan van Walbeeckplein 11, Willemstad, Curaçao; tel. (9) 433-3131; fax (9) 433-3130; e-mail info@curacao-gov.an; internet www.curacao-gov.an.

Saba: Sydney A. E. Sorton, The Bottom, Saba; tel. 416-3215; fax 416-3274.

St Eustatius: Hyden C. I. Gittens, Oranjestad, St Eustatius; tel. 318-2552; fax 318-2324; e-mail lt.governor@statiagovernment.com; internet www.statiagovernment.com.

St Maarten: Franklyn E. Richards, Government Administration Bldg, Clem Labega Sq., POB 943, Philipsburg, St Maarten; tel. 542-6085; fax 542-4172; e-mail hodge@governorsxm.com; internet www.governorsxm.com.

Legislature

STATEN

Speaker: Dwigno Puriel.

General Election, 27 January 2006

Party	Seats
Partido Antía Restrukturá	5
Movimentu Antiyas Nobo	3
Frente Obrero i Liberashon 30 di mei	2
Partido Nashonal di Pueblo	2
Forsa Kòrsou	2
National Alliance	2
Unión Patriótico Bonairiano	2
Democratic Party—St Maarten	1
Democratische Partij—Bonaire	1
Democratic Party—Statia	1
Windward Islands People's Movement	1
Partido Laboral Krusado Popular	—
Pueblo Soberano	—
Democratische Partij—Curaçao	—
Total (incl. others)	**22**

Political Organizations

Democratische Partij—Bonaire (DP—B) (Democratic Party—Bonaire): Kaya America 13A, POB 294, Kralendijk, Bonaire; tel. 717-8903; fax 717-5923; f. 1954; also known as Partido Democratico Boneriano; liberal; Leader Jopie Abraham.

Democratische Partij—Curaçao (DP—C) (Democratic Party—Curaçao): Neptunusweg 28, Willemstad, Curaçao; f. 1944; Leader Norbert George.

Democratische Partij—Sint Maarten (DP—StM): Tamarind Tree Dr. 4, Union Rd, Cole Bay, St Maarten; tel. 543-1166; fax 542-4296; Leader Sarah Wescott-Williams.

Democratische Partij—Statia (DP—StE): Oranjestad, St Eustatius; Leader Julian Woodley.

Forsa Kòrsou: Willemstad, Curaçao; Leader Nelson Navarro.

Frente Obrero i Liberashon 30 di mei (FOL) (Workers' Liberation Front of 30 May): Mayaguanaweg 16, Willemstad, Curaçao; tel. (9) 461-8105; f. 1969; socialist; Leaders Anthony Godett, Rignald Lak, Editha Wright.

Liste Ni'un Paso Atras (LNPA): Willemstad, Curaçao; Leader Nelson Pierre.

Movimentu Antiyas Nobo (MAN) (Movement for a New Antilles): Landhuis Morgenster, Willemstad, Curaçao; tel. (9) 468-4781; f. 1971; socialist; Leader Dominico (Don) F. Martina.

Movimentu Sosial Laboral (MSL): Willemstad, Curaçao; Leader César Prince.

National Alliance (NA): Philipsburg, St Maarten; internet www.sxmnationalalliance.org; Leader William Marlin.

National Progressive Party: Willemstad, Curaçao; contested the 2002 and 2006 elections as the National Alliance with the St Maarten Patriotic Alliance (q.v.).

St Maarten Patriotic Alliance (SPA): Frontstraat 69, Philipsburg, St Maarten; tel. 543-1064; fax 543-1065; contested the 2002 and 2006 elections as the National Alliance with the National Progressive Party (q.v.); Leader (vacant).

Partido Antía Restrukturá (PAR) (Restructured Antilles Party): Fokkerweg 26, Unit 3, Willemstad, Curaçao; tel. (9) 465-2566; fax (9) 465-2622; e-mail omi7@ibm.net; internet www.cura.net/archives/par/frame.html; f. 1993; social-Christian ideology; Leader Miguel Archangel Pourier.

Partido Laboral Krusado Popular (PLKP): Winston Churchillweg 57, Willemstad, Curaçao; tel. (9) 868-1924; internet www.plkp.an; f. 1997; progressive; Leader Errol A. Cova.

Partido Nashonal di Pueblo (PNP) (National People's Party): Winston Churchillweg 133, Willemstad, Curaçao; tel. (9) 869-6777; fax (9) 869-6688; f. 1948; also known as Nationale Volkspartij; social christian party; Pres. Faroe Metry; Leader Ersilia De Lannooy.

People's Democratic Party (PDP): Philipsburg, St Maarten; tel. 542-2696; Leader Millicent de Weever.

People's Progressive Alliance: Philipsburg, St Maarten; Leader Gracita Arrindell.

Pueblo Soberano: Willemstad, Curaçao; Leader Herman Wiels.

Saba United Democratic Party (SUDP): Saba; tel. 416-3311; fax 416-3434; Leader Steve Hassell.

Saint Eustatius Alliance (SEA): Oranjestad, St Eustatius; Leader Ingrid Whitfield-Houtman.

Unión Patriótico Bonairiano (UPB) (Patriotic Union of Bonaire): Kaya Sabana 22, Kralendijk, Bonaire; tel. 717-8906; fax 717-5552; 2,134 mems; Christian democratic; Leader Ramonsito T. Booi; Sec.-Gen. C. V. Winklaar.

Windward Islands People's Movement (WIPM): Windwardside, POB 525, Saba; tel. 416-2244; Chair. and Leader Ray Hassell; Sec.-Gen. Dave Levenstone.

Judicial System

Legal authority is exercised by the Court of First Instance (which sits in all the islands) and in appeal by the Joint High Court of Justice of the Netherlands Antilles and Aruba. The members of the Joint High Court of Justice sit singly as judges in the Courts of First Instance. The Chief Justice of the Joint High Court of Justice, its members (a maximum of 30) and the Attorneys-General of the Netherlands Antilles and of Aruba are appointed for life by the Dutch monarch, after consultation with the Governments of the Netherlands Antilles and Aruba. The Supreme Court of the Netherlands (based in The Hague) is the court of Final Instance for any appeal. Under a provision of the agreement for the dissolution of the five-island federation by December 2008, reforms to the judicial system were to be implemented from 2007.

Joint High Court of Justice

Wilhelminaplein 4, Willemstad, Curaçao; tel. (9) 463-4111; fax (9) 461-8341; e-mail hofcur@cura.net.

Chief Justice of the Joint High Court: Lisbeth Hoefdraad.

Secretary-Executive of the Joint High Court: M. E. N. Rojer-de Freitas (acting).

Religion

CHRISTIANITY

Most of the population were Christian, the predominant denomination being Roman Catholicism. According to the 1992 census, Roman Catholics formed the largest single group on four of the five islands: 82% of the population of Bonaire, 81% on Curaçao, 65% on Saba and 41% on St Maarten. On St Eustatius the Methodists formed the largest single denomination (31%). Of the other denominations, the main ones were the Anglicans and the Dutch Reformed Church. There were also small communities of Jews, Muslims and Bahá'ís.

Curaçaose Raad van Kerken (Curaçao Council of Churches): Periclesstraat 6, Willemstad, Curaçao; tel. (9) 465-3207; fax (9) 461-0733; e-mail ddtic@yahoo.com; f. 1958; six mem. churches; Chair. Ida Visser; Exec. Sec. Paul van der Waal.

The Roman Catholic Church

The Netherlands Antilles and Aruba together form the diocese of Willemstad, suffragan to the archdiocese of Port of Spain (Trinidad and Tobago). At 31 December 2005 the diocese numbered an estimated 224,809 adherents (about 78% of the total population). The Bishop participates in the Antilles Episcopal Conference, currently based in Trinidad and Tobago.

Bishop of Willemstad: Rt Rev. Luigi Antonio Secco, Bisdom, Breedestraat 31, Otrobanda, Willemstad, Curaçao; tel. (9) 462-5857; fax (9) 462-7437; e-mail bisdomwstad@curinfo.an.

The Anglican Communion

Saba, St Eustatius and St Maarten form part of the diocese of the North Eastern Caribbean and Aruba, within the Church in the Province of the West Indies. The Bishop is resident in The Valley, Anguilla.

NETHERLANDS DEPENDENCIES

Other Churches

Iglesia Protestant Uni (United Protestant Church): Fortkerk, Fort Amsterdam, Willemstad, Curaçao; tel. (9) 461-1139; fax (9) 465-7481; e-mail vpg-cur@curlink.com; internet www.vpg-curacao.com; f. 1825 by union of Dutch Reformed and Evangelical Lutheran Churches; associated with the World Council of Churches; Pres. MARITZA BEAUJON-BAKHUIS; 3 congregations; 11,280 adherents; 3,200 mems.

Methodist Church: Oranjestad, St Eustatius.

Other denominations active in the islands include the Moravian, Apostolic Faith, Wesleyan Holiness and Norwegian Seamen's Churches, the Baptists, Calvinists, Jehovah's Witnesses, Evangelists, Seventh-day Adventists, the Church of Christ and the New Testament Church of God.

JUDAISM

Reconstructionist Shephardi Congregation Mikvé Israel-Emanuel: Hanchi di Snoa 29, POB 322, Willemstad, Curaçao; tel. (9) 461-1067; fax (9) 465-4141; e-mail information@snoa.com; internet www.snoa.com; f. 1732 on present site; about 350 mems.

Congregation 'Shaarei Tsedek' Ashkenazi Orthodox Jewish Community: 37 Magdalenaweg, Willemstad, Curaçao; tel. and fax (9) 738-5949; e-mail ariel@cura.net; 100 mems; Rabbi ARIEL YESHURUN.

The Press

Algemeen Dagblad: ADCARIBBEAN NV, Kaya Flamboyan 3C, Willemstad, Curaçao; tel. (9) 747-2200; fax (9) 747-2257; e-mail algemeen@antilliaansdagblad.com; internet www.antilliaansdagblad.com; daily; Dutch; Editor NOUD KÖPER.

Amigoe: Kaya Fraternan di Skèrpenè z/n, POB 577, Curaçao; tel. (9) 767-2000; fax (9) 767-4084; e-mail management@amigoe.com; internet www.amigoe.com; f. 1884; Christian; daily; evening; Dutch; Dir INGRID DE MAAIJER-HOLLANDER; Editor-in-Chief MICHAEL WILLEMSE; circ. 12,000.

Bala: Noord Zapateer nst 13, Willemstad, Curaçao; tel. (9) 467-1646; fax (9) 467-1041; e-mail bala@cura.net; daily; Papiamento.

Beurs- en Nieuwsberichten: A. M. Chumaceiro Blvd 5, POB 741, Willemstad, Curaçao; tel. (9) 465-4544; fax (9) 465-3411; f. 1935; daily; evening; Dutch; Editor L. SCHENK; circ. 8,000.

Bonaire Holiday: POB 569, Curaçao; tel. (9) 767-1403; fax (9) 767-2003; f. 1971; tourist guide; English; 3 a year; circ. 95,000.

Bonaire Reporter: Kaya Gob. Debrot 200-6, POB 407, Bonaire; tel. and fax 717-8988; e-mail info@bonairereporter.com; internet bonairereporter.com; English; weekly.

The Business Journal: Indjuweg 30A, Willemstad, Curaçao; tel. (9) 461-1367; fax (9) 461-1955; monthly; English.

Colors: Liberty Publications, Curaçao; tel. and fax (9) 869-6066; e-mail colors@curacao-online.net; internet www.curacao-online.net/colors; f. 1998; general interest magazine; 4 a year; Publr TIRZAH Z. B. LIBERT.

Curaçao Holiday: POB 569, Curaçao; tel. (9) 767-1403; fax (9) 767-2003; f. 1960; tourist guide; English; 3 a year; circ. 300,000.

De Curaçaosche Courant: Frederikstraat 123, POB 15, Willemstad, Curaçao; tel. (9) 461-2766; fax (9) 462-6535; f. 1812; weekly; Dutch; Editor J. KORIDON.

Daily Herald: Bush Rd 22, POB 828, Philipsburg, St Maarten; tel. 542-5253; fax 542-5913; e-mail editorial@thedailyherald.com; internet www.thedailyherald.com; daily; English.

Extra: W. I. Compagniestraat 41, Willemstad, Curaçao; tel. (9) 462-4595; fax (9) 462-7575; e-mail redactie@extra.an; daily; morning; Papiamento; Man. R. YRAUSQUIN; Editor MIKE OEHLERS; circ. 20,000.

Newsletter of Curaçao Trade and Industry Association: Kaya Junior Salas 1, POB 49, Willemstad, Curaçao; tel. (9) 461-1210; fax (9) 461-5422; f. 1972; monthly; English and Dutch; economic and industrial paper.

Nobo: Scherpenheuvel w/n, POB 323, Willemstad, Curaçao; tel. (9) 467-3500; fax (9) 467-2783; daily; evening; Papiamento; Editor CARLOS DAANTJE; circ. 15,000.

Nos Isla: Refineria Isla (Curazao) SA, Emmastad, Curaçao; 2 a month; Papiamento; circ. 1,200.

La Prensa: W. I. Compagniestraat 41, Willemstad, Curaçao; tel. (9) 462-3850; fax (9) 462-5983; e-mail laprensa@laprensacur.com; internet www.laprensacur.com; f. 1929; daily; evening; Papiamento; Man. R. YRAUSQUIN; Editor SIGFRIED RIGAUD; circ. 10,750.

Saba Herald: The Level, Saba; tel. 416-2244; f. 1968; monthly; news, local history; Editor WILL JOHNSON; circ. 500.

St Maarten Guardian: Vlaun Bldg, Pondfill, POB 1046, Philipsburg, St Maarten; tel. 542-6022; fax 542-6043; e-mail guardian@sintmaarten.net; f. 1989; daily; English; Man. Dir RICHARD F. GIBSON; Man. Editor JOSEPH DOMINIQUE; circ. 4,000.

St Maarten Holiday: POB 569, Curaçao; tel. (9) 767-1403; fax (9) 767-2003; f. 1968; tourism guide; English; 3 a year; circ. 175,000.

Teen Times: c/o The Daily Herald, Bush Rd 22, POB 828, Philipsburg, St Maarten; tel. 542-5597; e-mail info@teentimes.com; for teenagers by teenagers; sponsored by The Daily Herald; English; Editor-in-Chief MICHAEL GRANGER.

Ultimo Noticia: Frederikstraat 123, Willemstad, Curaçao; tel. (9) 462-3444; fax (9) 462-6535; daily; morning; Papiamento; Editor A. A. JONCKHEER.

La Unión: Rotaprint NV, Willemstad, Curaçao; weekly; Papiamento.

NEWS AGENCIES

Algemeen Nederlands Persbureau (ANP) (Netherlands): Panoramaweg 5, POB 439, Willemstad, Curaçao; tel. (9) 461-2233; fax (9) 461-7431; Representative RONNIE RENS.

Publishers

Curaçao Drukkerij en Uitgevers Maatschappij: Willemstad, Curaçao.

Ediciones Populares: W. I. Compagniestraat 41, Willemstad, Curaçao; f. 1929; Dir RONALD YRAUSQUIN.

Drukkerij Scherpenheuvel NV: Scherpenheuvel, POB 60, Willemstad, Curaçao; tel. (9) 467-1134.

Drukkerij de Stad NV: W. I. Compagniestraat 41, Willemstad, Curaçao; tel. (9) 462-3566; fax (9) 462-2175; e-mail kenrick@destad.an; internet www.destad.an; f. 1929; Dir KENRICK A. YRAUSQUIN.

Holiday Publications: POB 569, Curaçao; tel. (9) 767-1403; fax (9) 767-2003.

Offsetdrukkerij Intergrafia NV: Essoweg 54, Willemstad, Curaçao; tel. (9) 464-3180.

Broadcasting and Communications

TELECOMMUNICATIONS

Digicel Curaçao: Schottegatweg Oost 19, Willemstad, Curaçao; tel. (9) 736-1056; fax (9) 736-1057; internet www.curacaotelecom.com; f. 1999; bought by Digicel (Ireland) in 2005; bought into Bonaire market through majority shareholding of Antilliano Por NV in April 2006; known as Curaçao Telecom until 2006; telephone and internet services; Digicel acquired mobile business of TELBO (Bonaire) in Dec. 2006; also operates in Aruba; Chair. DENIS O'BRIEN; CEO (Dutch Caribbean) HANS LUTE.

East Caribbean Cellular NV (ECC): 13 Richardson St, Philipsburg, St Maarten; tel. 542-4100; fax 542-5675; e-mail info@eastcaribbeancellular.com; internet www.eastcaribbeancellular.com; f. 1989.

SMITCOMS NV (St Maarten International Telecommunications Services): Falcon Dr. No. 3, Harbor View, Philipsburg, St Maarten; tel. 542-9140; fax 542-9141; e-mail Sales@smitcoms.com; internet www.smitcoms.com; f. 2000; international telephone network provider; affiliated with TelEm group in Jan. 2006; Man. Dir ELDERT LOUISA (acting).

St Maarten Telephone Co (TelEm): C. A. Cannegieter St 17, POB 160, Philipsburg, St Maarten; tel. 542-2278; fax 543-0101; e-mail webmaster@sintmaarten.net; internet www.sintmaarten.net; f. 1975; local landline and value-added services, also operates TelCell digital cellular service and TelNet internet service provider; sister company Smitcoms; 15,000 subscribers; Man. Dir CURTIS K. HAYNES.

Telefonia Bonairiano NV (TELBO NV): Kaya Libertador Simon Bolivar 8, POB 94, Bonaire; tel. 717-7000; fax 717-5007; e-mail telbo@telbo.an; internet www.telbo.net; f. 1983; land-line telecommunications and internet service provider; Telbo's mobile operations on Bonaire were purchased by Digicel in December 2006; Gen. Man. EDSEL WINKLAAR.

United Telecom Services (UTS): UTS Headquarters, Rigelweg 2, Willemstad, Curaçao; tel. (9) 777-0101; fax (9) 777-1284; e-mail info@uts.an; internet www.uts.an; f. 1999 following merger of Antelecom NV (f. 1908) and SETEL (f. 1979); Antelecom and SETEL still operate under own names; Chair. DAVID DICK; Man. Dir HENDRIK J. EIKELENBOOM.

    Servicio de Telekomunikashon (UTS Wireless Curaçao) (SETEL): UTS Headquarters, Rigelweg 2, Willemstad, Curaçao; tel. (9) 777-0101; fax (9) 777-1284; e-mail info@uts.an; internet www.uts.an; f. 1979; telecommunications equipment and network provider; forms part of UTS; state-owned, but privatization pending; Pres. ANGEL R. KOOK; Man. Dir JULIO CONSTANCIA; 400 employees.

NETHERLANDS DEPENDENCIES

BROADCASTING

Radio

Curom Broadcasting Inc: Roodeweg 64, POB 2169, Willemstad, Curaçao; tel. (9) 462-2020; fax (9) 462-5796; f. 1933; broadcasts in English, Papiamento, Dutch and Spanish; Dir ORLANDO CUALES.

Mi 95: f. 1988; FM; music station, aimed at adults.

Z-86: news station.

88 Ròckòrsou: rock music station, aimed at young people.

Easy 97.9 FM: Arikokweg 19A, Willemstad, Curaçao; tel. (9) 462-3162; fax (9) 462-8712; e-mail radio@easyfm.com; internet www.easyfm.com; f. 1995; Dir KEVIN CARTHY.

Laser 101 (101.1 FM): Suite 2, 106 A. T. Illidge Rd, Philipsburg, St Maarten; tel. 543-2200; fax 543-2229; e-mail master@laser101.com; internet www.laser101.fm; 24 hours a day; music; English and Papiamento.

Radio Caribe: Ledaweg 35, Brievengat, Willemstad, Curaçao; tel. (9) 736-9555; fax (9) 736-9569; f. 1955; commercial station; programmes in Dutch, English, Spanish and Papiamento; Dir-Gen. C. R. HEILLEGGER.

Radiodifusión Boneriana NV: Kaya Gobernador Debrot 2, Kralendijk, Bonaire; tel. 717-8273; fax 717-8220; e-mail vdb@vozdibonaire.com; internet www.vozdibonaire.com; f. 1980; Owner FELICIANO DA SILVA PILOTO.

Alpha FM: broadcasts in Spanish.

Mega FM: broadcasts in Dutch.

Voz di Bonaire (PJB2) (Voice of Bonaire): broadcasts in Papiamento.

Radio Exito: Julianaplein 39, Curaçao; tel. (9) 462-5577; fax (9) 462-5580.

Radio Hoyer NV: Plasa Horacio Hoyer 21, Willemstad, Curaçao; tel. (9) 461-1678; fax (9) 461-6528; e-mail radio1@radiohoyer.com; internet www.radiohoyer.com; f. 1954; commercial; two stations: Radio Hoyer I (mainly Papiamento, also Spanish) and II (mainly Dutch, also English) in Curaçao; Man. Dir HELEN HOYER.

Radio Korsou FM: Bataljonweg 7, POB 3250, Willemstad, Curaçao; tel. (9) 737-3012; fax (9) 737-2888; e-mail master@korsou.com; internet www.korsou.com; f. 1976; 24 hrs a day; programmes in Papiamento and Dutch; Gen. Man. ALAN H. EVERTSZ.

Radio Tropical: Kaya W. F. G. Mensing, Willemstad, Curaçao; tel. (9) 465-0190; fax (9) 465-2470; e-mail tropi@cura.net; Dir DWIGHT RUDOLPHINA.

Trans World Radio (TWR): Kaya Gobernador N. Debrot 64, Kralendijk, Bonaire; tel. 717-8800; fax 717-8808; e-mail 800am@twr.org; internet www.twr.org; f. 1964; religious, educational and cultural station; programmes to South, Central and North America, Caribbean in five languages; Pres. Dr DAVID G. TUCKER, Jr; Station Dir JOSEPH BARKER.

Voice of St Maarten (PJD2 Radio): Plaza 21, Backstreet, POB 366, Philipsburg, St Maarten; tel. 542-2580; fax 542-4905; also operates PJD3 on FM (24 hrs); commercial; programmes in English; Gen. Man. DON R. HUGHES.

Voice of Saba (PJF1): The Bottom, POB 1, Saba; studio in St Maarten; tel. 546-3213; also operates The Voice of Saba FM; Man. MAX W. NICHOLSON.

There is a relay station for Radio Nederland on Bonaire.

Television

Antilliaanse Televisie Maatschappij NV (TeleCuraçao): Berg Ararat z/n, POB 415, Willemstad, Curaçao; tel. (9) 461-1288; fax (9) 461-4138; e-mail web@telecuracao.com; internet www.telecuracao.com; f. 1960; fmrly operated Tele-Aruba; commercial; owned by United Telecommunication Services; also operates cable service, offering programmes from US satellite television and two Venezuelan channels; Dir PAUL DE GEUS; Gen. Man. HUGO LEW JEN TAI.

Leeward Broadcasting Corporation—Television: Postbus 375, Philipsburg, St Maarten; tel. (5) 23491; transmissions for approx. 10 hours daily.

Five television channels can be received on Curaçao in total. Relay stations provide Bonaire with programmes from Curaçao, St Maarten with programmes from Puerto Rico, and Saba and St Eustatius with programmes from St Maarten and neighbouring islands. Curaçao has a publicly owned cable television service, TDS.

The Netherlands Antilles

Finance

(cap. = capital; res = reserves; dep. = deposits; m. = million; br(s) = branch(es); amounts in Netherlands Antilles guilders unless otherwise stated)

BANKING

Central Bank

Bank van de Nederlandse Antillen (Bank of the Netherlands Antilles): Simon Bolivar Plein 1, Willemstad, Curaçao; tel. (9) 434-5500; fax (9) 461-5004; e-mail info@centralbank.an; internet centralbank.an; f. 1828 as Curaçaosche Bank, name changed as above Jan. 1962; cap. 30.0m., res 339.8m., dep. 1,320.7m. (Dec. 2006); Chair. RALPH PALM; Pres. Dr EMSLEY D. TROMP; 2 brs on St Maarten and Bonaire.

Commercial Banks

Banco di Caribe NV: Schottegatweg Oost 205, POB 3785, Willemstad, Curaçao; tel. (9) 432-3000; fax (9) 461-5220; e-mail info@bancodicaribe.com; internet www.bancodicaribe.com; f. 1973; dep. 963.4m., total assets 1,067.2m. (Dec. 2005); Chair. WILFRED J. CURIEL; CEO and Gen. Man. Dir EDUARDO DE KORT; Man. Dirs KENNETH ABRAHAM, PERCIVAL VIRGINIA; 5 brs.

CITCO Banking Corporation NV: Kaya Schottengatweg Oost 44, POB 707, Willemstad, Curaçao; tel. (9) 732-2322; fax (9) 732-2330; e-mail curacao-bank@citco.com; f. 1980 as Curaçao Banking Corpn NV; Man. Dir and Gen. Man. RONALD F. IRAUSQUIN; Man. Dirs CHARLES RUND, GLENDA E. C. SOON-TRAPENBERG, RUPERT E. WALLÉ.

FirstCaribbean International Bank (Curaçao) NV: De Ruyterkade 61, POB 3144, Willemstad, Curaçao; tel. (9) 433-8000; fax (9) 433-8198; e-mail bank.curacao@firstcaribbeanbank.com; internet www.firstcaribbeanbank.an; f. 1964 as ABN AMRO Bank NV; part of FirstCaribbean Group, based in Barbados; 83% CIBC, Canada; Man. Dir W. M. VAN DER BERG; 6 brs.

Fortis Bank (Curaçao) NV: Berg Arrarat 1, POB 3889, Willemstad, Curaçao; tel. (9) 433-9200; fax (9) 461-3769; internet www.fortisbank.com; f. 1952 as Pierson, Heldring and Pierson (Curaçao) NV; became Meespierson (Curaçao) NV in 1993, name changed as above in 2000; international banking/trust co; Man. Dir GREGORY ELIAS.

Girobank NV: Scharlooweg 35, Willemstad, Curaçao; tel. (9) 433-9999; fax (9) 461-7861; e-mail info@gironet.com; internet www.girobank.net; Man. Dir ERIC GARCIA.

Maduro & Curiel's Bank NV: Plaza Jojo Correa 2–4, POB 305, Willemstad, Curaçao; tel. (9) 466-1100; fax (9) 466-1122; e-mail info@mcb-bank.com; internet www.mcb-bank.com; f. 1916 as NV Maduro's Bank; merged with Curiel's Bank in 1931; affiliated with Bank of Nova Scotia NV, Toronto; br. in Bonaire; cap. 50.5m., res 127.5m., dep. 3,884.2m. (Dec. 2006); Chair. LIONEL CAPRILES; Man. Dirs WILLIAM H. L. FABRO, RON GOMES CASSERES; 31 brs.

Orco Bank NV: Dr Henry Fergusonweg 10, POB 4928, Willemstad, Curaçao; tel. (9) 737-2000; fax (9) 737-6741; internet www.orcobank.com; f. 1986; cap. 30.7m., res 27.5m., dep. 523.9m. (Dec. 1999); Chair. E. L. GARCIA; Man. Dirs R. KOELEWIJN, K. R. CANWORD; 1 br.

Rabobank Curaçao NV: Zeelandia Office Park, Kaya W. F. G. (Jombi), Mensing 14, POB 3876, Willemstad, Curaçao; tel. (9) 465-2011; fax (9) 465-2066; e-mail l.an.curacao.ops@rabobank.com; internet www.rabobank.com; f. 1978; cap. US $53.0m., res $17.8m., dep. $4,535.2m. (Dec. 2003); Chair. LENSE KOOPMANS; Gen. Man. J. S. KLEP.

RBTT Bank NV: Kaya Flamboyan 1, Willemstad; tel. (9) 763-8000; fax (9) 763-8449; e-mail info@tt.rbtt.com; internet www.rbtt.com; f. 1997 as Antilles Banking Corpn; name changed to RBTT Bank Antilles in 2001; name changed as above in 2002; cap. 114.5m., res 118.5m., dep. 2,433.7m. (Dec. 2005); Pres. RODNEY S. PRASAD; Chair. PETER J. JULY; 4 brs.

Windward Islands Bank Ltd: Clem Labega Sq. 7, POB 220, Philipsburg, St Maarten; tel. 542-2313; fax 542-4761; e-mail info@wib-bank.net; affiliated to Maduro and Curiel's Bank NV; f. 1960; cap. and res 53.2m., dep. 662.2m. (Dec. 2006); Man. Dir JAN J. BEAUJON.

'Offshore' Banks

Abu Dhabi International Bank NV: Kaya W. F. G. (Jombi), Mensing 36, POB 3141, Willemstad, Curaçao; tel. (9) 461-1299; fax (9) 461-5392; internet www.nbad.com; f. 1981; cap. US $20.0m., res $30.0m., dep. $112.2m. (Dec. 2006); Pres. QAMBAR AL MULLA; Man. Dir NAGY S. KOLTA.

FirstCaribbean International Wealth Management (Curaçao) NV: De Ruyterkade 61, Curaçao; tel. (9) 433-8000; fax (9) 433-8198; f. 1976 as ABN AMRO Bank Asset Management (Curaçao) NV; acquired by FirstCaribbean Bank in Dec. 2005; Man. Dir E. J. W. HERMENS.

3317

NETHERLANDS DEPENDENCIES

F. Van Lanschot Bankiers (Curaçao) NV: Schottegatweg Oost 32, POB 4799, Willemstad, Curaçao; tel. (9) 737-1011; fax (9) 737-1086; e-mail info@vanlanschot.an; f. 1962; wholly owned by F. Van Lanschot Bankiers NV (Netherlands); Man. A. VAN GEEST.

Development Banks

Ontwikkelingsbank van de Nederlandse Antillen NV: Schottegatweg Oost 3C, POB 267, Willemstad, Curaçao; tel. (9) 747-3000; fax (9) 747-3320; e-mail obna@obna-bank.com; f. 1981; Man. Dir DENNIS CIJNTJE.

Stichting Korporashon pa Desaroyo di Korsou (Curaçao Development Corporation—KORPDEKO): Schottegatweg Oost 369, Willemstad, Curaçao; tel. (9) 738-1799; fax (9) 738-1766; e-mail info@korpodeko.an; internet www.korpodeko.an.

Savings Banks

Postspaarbank van de Nederlandse Antillen: Waaigatplein 1, Willemstad, Curaçao; tel. (9) 433-1100; fax (9) 461-7561; e-mail info@postpaarbank.com; f. 1905; post office savings bank; Chair. H. J. J. VICTORIA; cap. 21m.; 20 brs.

Spaar- en Beleenbank van Curaçao NV: MCB Salinja Bldg, Schottegatweg Oost 130, Willemstad, Curaçao; tel. (9) 466-1585; fax (9) 466-1590; e-mail chbsbb@mcb-bank.com.

There are also several mortgage banks and credit unions.

Banking Associations

Association of International Bankers in the Netherlands Antilles (IBNA): Chumaceiro Blvd 3, POB 220, Curaçao; tel. (9) 461-5367; fax (9) 461-5369; e-mail info@ibna.an; internet www.ibna.an; f. 1980; 32 mems; Pres. HANS F. C. BLANKVOORT.

Bonaire Bankers' Association: Maduro & Curiel's Bank (Bonaire) NV, Kaya L. D. Gerharts 1, POB 366, Kralendijk, Bonaire; tel. 717-5520; fax 717-5884; Pres. R. GOMEZ.

Curaçao Bankers' Association (CBA): Banco di Caribe NV, Schottegatweg Oost 205, POB 3785, Willemstad, Curaçao; tel. (9) 432-3000; fax (9) 432-3343; e-mail florisela.bentoera@an.rbtt.com; f. 1972; Pres. E. A. DE KORT; Sec. FLORISELA BENTOERA.

Federashon di Kooperativanan di Spar i Kredito Antiyano (Fekoskan): Curaçaostraat 50, Willemstad, Curaçao; tel. (9) 462-3676; fax (9) 462-4995; e-mail fekoskan@attglobal.net; Vice-Pres. R. FRANS.

International Bankers' Association in the Netherlands Antilles: SA. M. Chumaceiro Blvd 3, Willemstad, Curaçao; tel. (9) 461-5367; fax (9) 461-5369; Pres. F. GIRIGORI.

The Windward Islands Bankers' Association: Clem Labega Sq., Philipsburg, St Maarten; tel. 542-2313; fax 542-6355; Pres. J. BEAUJON.

INSURANCE

Amersfoortse Antillen NV: Kaya W. F. G. Mensing 19, Willemstad, Curaçao; tel. (9) 461-6399; fax (9) 461-6709.

Aseguro di Kooperativa Antiyano (ASKA) NV: Scharlooweg 15, Willemstad, Curaçao; tel. (9) 461-7765; fax (9) 461-5991; accident and health, motor vehicle, property.

Ennia Caribe Schaden NV: J. B. Gorsiraweg 6, POB 581, Willemstad, Curaçao; tel. (9) 434-3800; fax (9) 434-3873; e-mail mail@ennia.com; f. 1948; general; life insurance as Ennia Caribe Leven NV; Pres. DONALD BAKHUIS; Man. Dir ALBARTUS WILLEMSEN.

ING Fatum: Cas Coraweg 2, Willemstad, Curaçao; tel. (9) 777-7777; fax (9) 461-2023; f. 1904; property insurance.

MCB Group Insurance NV: MCB Bldg Scharloo, Scharloo, Willemstad, Curaçao; tel. (9) 466-1370; fax (9) 466-1327.

Netherlands Antilles and Aruba Assurance Company (NA&A) NV: Pietermaai 135, Willemstad, Curaçao; tel. (9) 465-7146; fax (9) 461-6269; accident and health, motor vehicle, property.

Seguros Antilliano NV: S. b. N. Doormanweg/Reigerweg 5, Willemstad, Curaçao; tel. (9) 736-6877; fax (9) 736-5794; general.

A number of foreign companies also have offices in Curaçao, mainly British, Canadian, Dutch and US firms.

Insurance Association

Insurance Association of the Netherlands Antilles (NAVV): c/o Ing Fatum, Cas Coraweg 2, POB 3002, Willemstad, Curaçao; tel. (9) 777-7777; fax (9) 736-9658; Pres. R. C. MARTINA-JOE.

Trade and Industry

DEVELOPMENT ORGANIZATIONS

Curaçao Industrial and International Trade Development Company NV (CURINDE): Emancipatie Blvd 7, Landhuis Koningsplein, Curaçao; tel. (9) 737-6000; fax (9) 737-1336; e-mail info@curinde.com; internet www.curinde.com; f. 1980; state-owned; manages the harbour free zone, the airport free zone and the industrial zone; Man. Dir ERIC R. SMEULDERS.

Foreign Investment Agency Curaçao (FIAC): Luchthavenweg 55, 5657 EA Eindhoven, Netherlands, Curaçao; tel. (40) 2518674; fax (40) 2572098.

World Trade Center Curaçao: POB 6005, Piscadera Bay, Curaçao; tel. (9) 463-6271; fax (9) 462-4408; e-mail info@wtccuracao.com; internet www.wtccuracao.com; Man. Dir JOSÉ VICENTE SANCHES PIÑA.

CHAMBERS OF COMMERCE

Bonaire Chamber of Commerce and Industry: Princess Mariestraat, POB 52, Kralendijk, Bonaire; tel. 717-5595; fax 717-8995.

Curaçao Chamber of Commerce and Industry: Kaya Junior Salas 1, POB 10, Willemstad, Curaçao; tel. (9) 461-1451; fax (9) 461-5652; e-mail management@curacao-chamber.an; internet www.curacao-chamber.an; f. 1884; Chair. RUUD THUIS; Exec. Dir PAUL R. J. COMENENCIA.

St Maarten Chamber of Commerce and Industry: Cannegieterstraat 11, POB 454, Philipsburg, St Maarten; tel. 542-3590; fax 542-3512; e-mail info@sintmaartenchamber.org; internet www.sintmaartenchamber.org; f. 1979; Pres. HURBERT PANTOPHLET; Exec. Dir (vacant).

INDUSTRIAL AND TRADE ASSOCIATIONS

Curaçao Exporters' Association (CEA): c/o Seawings NV, Maduro Plaza z/n CEA, POB 6049, Curaçao; tel. (9) 733-1591; fax (9) 733-1599; e-mail albert.elens@seawings-curacao.com; f. 1993; Dir ALBERT ELENS.

Curaçao International Financial Services Association (CIFA): Chumaceiro Blvd 3, POB 220, Curaçao; tel. (9) 461-5371; fax (9) 461-5378; e-mail info@cifa.an; internet www.cifa.an; Chair. HERMAN J. BEHR.

Curaçao Trade and Industry Association (Vereniging Bedrijfsleven Curaçao—VBC): Kaya Junior Salas 1, POB 49, Willemstad, Curaçao; tel. (9) 461-1210; fax (9) 461-5422; e-mail vbc1@cura.net; f. 1944; Pres. B. KOOYMAN; Exec. Dir R. P. J. LIEUW.

St Maarten Hospitality and Trade Association (SHTA): 33A WJA Nisbeth Rd, POB 486, Philipsburg; tel. 542-0108; fax 542-0107; e-mail info@shta.com; internet www.shta.com; Pres. EMIL LEE.

UTILITIES

Electricity and Water

Aqualectra Production NV (KAE): Rector Zwijsenstraat 1, POB 2097, Curaçao; tel. (9) 433-2200; fax (9) 462-6685; e-mail mgmt@aqualectra.com; internet www.aqualectra.com; present name adopted in 2001 following the restructuring of Curaçao's energy sector; Dir S. MARTINA.

EcoPower Bonaire BV: Bonaire; f. 2007; consortium of Econcern (Germany), MAN (Germany) and Enercon (Netherlands); sustainable energy producer.

GEBE NV: Pond Fill, W. J. A. Nisbeth Rd 35, POB 123, St Maarten; tel. 542-2213; fax 542-4810; e-mail gebesxm@sintmaarten.net; f. 1961; generates and distributes electricity via island network; operates island water supply system; Man. Dir WILLIAM GODFREY BROOKS.

Water & Energiebedrijf Bonaire (WEB) NV: Carlos Nicolaas 3, Kralendijk; tel. 717-8244.

TRADE UNIONS

Algemene Bond van Overheidspersoneel (ABVO) (General Union of Civil Servants): POB 3604, Willemstad, Curaçao; tel. (9) 737-6097; fax (9) 737-3145; e-mail abvo_na@cura.net; internet www.abvo-informa.org; f. 1936; Pres. ROLAND H. IGNACIO; Sec. R. C. SAEZ; 4,000 mems.

Central General di Trahado di Corsow (CGTC) (General Headquarters for Workers of Curaçao): POB 2078, Willemstad, Curaçao; tel. (9) 737-6097; fax (9) 737-3145; e-mail abvo_na@cura.net; f. 1949; Sec.-Gen. ROLAND H. IGNACIO.

Curaçaosche Federatie van Werknemers (Curaçao Federation of Workers): Schouwburgweg 44, Willemstad, Curaçao; tel. (9) 737-6300; fax (9) 737-1426; f. 1964; Pres. WILFRED SPENCER; Sec.-Gen. GILBERT POULINA; 204 affiliated unions; about 2,000 mems.

Federashon Bonaireana di Trabou (FEDEBON): Kaya Krabè 6, Nikiboko, POB 324, Bonaire; tel. and fax 717-8845; Pres. GEROLD BERNABELA.

Petroleum Workers' Federation of Curaçao: Willemstad, Curaçao; tel. (9) 737-0255; fax (9) 737-5250; affiliated to Int. Petroleum and Chemical Workers' Fed; f. 1955; Pres. R. G. GIJSBERTHA; approx. 1,500 mems.

Sentral di Sindikatonan di Korsou (SSK) (Central Trade Unions of Curaçao): Schouwburgweg 44, POB 3036, Willemstad; tel. (9) 737-0255; fax (9) 737-5250; Pres. PABLO COVA; 6,000 mems.

Sindikato di Trahado den Edukashon na Korsou (SITEK) (Curaçao Schoolteachers' Trade Union): Landhuis Stenen Koraal, POB 3545, Willemstad, Curaçao; tel. (9) 468-2902; fax (9) 469-0552; 1,234 mems.

Windward Islands' Federation of Labour (WIFOL): Pond Fill, Long Wall Rd, POB 1097, St Maarten; tel. 542-2797; fax 542-6631; e-mail wifol@sintmaarten.net; Pres. THEOPHILUS THOMPSON.

Transport

RAILWAYS

There are no railways.

ROADS

All the islands have a good system of all-weather roads. There were 845 km of roads in 2004, of which 31% were paved.

SHIPPING

Curaçao is an important centre for the refining and transshipment of Venezuelan and Middle Eastern petroleum. Willemstad is served by the Schottegat harbour, set in a wide bay with a long channel and deep water. Facilities for handling containerized traffic at Willemstad were inaugurated in 1984. A Mega Cruise Facility, with capacity for the largest cruise ships, has been constructed on the Otrobanda side of St Anna Bay. Ports at Bullen Bay and Caracas Bay also serve Curaçao. St Maarten is one of the Caribbean's leading ports for visits by cruise ships and in January 2001 new pier facilities were opened which could accommodate up to four cruise ships and add more cargo space. Each of the other islands has a good harbour, except for Saba, which has one inlet, equipped with a large pier. In May 2002 the Netherlands provided NA Fl. 9.6m. for the repair of Saba's port, which sustained severe hurricane damage in 1999. Many foreign shipping lines call at ports in the Netherlands Antilles.

Curaçao Ports Authority: Werf de Wilde z/n, POB 689, Willemstad, Curaçao; tel. (9) 443-5999; fax (9) 461-3907; e-mail cpamanag@curports.com; internet curports.com; Man. Dir RICHARD LÓPEZ-RAMÍREZ.

Curaçao Shipping Association (SVC): c/o Dammers & van der Heide (Antilles) Inc, Kaya Flamboyan 11, Willemstad, Curaçao; tel. (9) 737-0600; fax (9) 737-3875; Pres. K. PONSEN.

St Maarten Ports Authority: J. Yrausquin Blvd, POB 146, Philipsburg, St Maarten; tel. 542-2307; fax 542-5048; e-mail kfranca@smpanv.com; internet www.portofstmaarten.com; Man. Dir KEITH FRANCA.

Principal Shipping Companies

Caribbean Moving Services NV: Caracasbaaiweg 328, POB 442, Willemstad, Curaçao; tel. (9) 767-2588; fax 747-1155; internet www.ccs.an; fmrly Caribbean Cargo Services NV; Ma. Dir LOES VAN DER WOUDE.

Curaçao Dry-dock Co Inc: POB 3012, Curaçao; tel. (9) 733-0000; fax (9) 736-5580; e-mail info@cdmnv.com; internet www.curacao-drydock.com; f. 1958; Man. Dir MARIO RAYMOND EVERTSZ.

Curaçao Ports Services Inc NV (CPS): Curaçao Container Terminal, POB 170, Curaçao; tel. (9) 461-5177; fax (9) 461-6536; e-mail cps@cps.an; Man. Dir KAREL JAN O. ASTER.

Dammers & van der Heide, Shipping and Trading (Antilles) Inc: Dammers Bldg, Kaya Flamboyan 11, POB 3018, Willemstad, Curaçao; tel. (9) 737-0600; fax (9) 737-3875; e-mail general@dammers-curacao.com; internet www.dammers-curacao.com; f. 1964; Man. Dir J. J. PONSEN.

Gomez Transport NV: Zeelandia z/n, Willemstad, Curaçao; tel. (9) 461-5900; fax (9) 461-3358; e-mail info@gomezshipping.an; Man. FERNANDO DA COSTA GÓMEZ.

Hal Antillen NV: De Ruyterkade 63, POB 812, Curaçao.

Intermodal Container Services NV: Salinja Galleries, 1st Floor Unit 201, POB 3747, Curaçao; tel. (9) 461-3330; fax (9) 461-3432; Mans A. R. BEAUJON, N. N. HARMS.

Kroonvlag/Maduro Shipping: Dokweg 19, Maduro Plaza, Curaçao; tel. (9) 733-1510; fax (9) 733-1538; e-mail maduroship@madurosons.com; internet www.madurosons.com.

Lagendijk Maritime Services: POB 3481, Curaçao; tel. (9) 465-5766; fax (9) 465-5998; e-mail ims@ibm.net.

S. E. L. Maduro & Sons (Curaçao) Inc: Maduro Plaza, POB 3304, Willemstad, Curaçao; tel. (9) 733-1501; fax (9) 733-1539; e-mail maduroship@madurosons.com; internet www.madurosons.com; Man. Dir H. MEIJER; Vice-Pres. R. CORSEN.

St Maarten Port Services: POB 270, Philipsburg, St Maarten; tel. 542-2304.

Anthony Veder & Co NV: Zeelandia z/n, POB 3677, Curaçao; tel. (9) 461-4700; fax (9) 461-2576; e-mail anveder@vrshipping.com; Man. Dir JOOP VAN VLIET.

CIVIL AVIATION

There are international airports at Curaçao (Dr Albert Plesman, or Hato, 12 km from Willemstad), Bonaire (Flamingo Field) and St Maarten (Princess Juliana, 16 km from Philipsburg); and airfields for inter-island flights at St Eustatius and Saba. In 1998 a free trade zone was inaugurated at the international airport on Curaçao. The second phase of a US $118m. project to expand Princess Juliana Airport, which commenced in June 2004, was completed in November 2006. The development comprised a new terminal enhancing the airport's passenger handling capacity by 2.5m. Financing was secured for the construction of new passenger terminal building at Dr Albert Plesman Airport in September 2003. The national carrier of the Netherlands Antilles, known as Dutch Caribbean Airlines (DCA) from 2002, was declared bankrupt in late 2004.

Dutch Antilles Express: Flamingo Field, Bonaire; tel. 717-0808; fax 717-0880; e-mail reservations@flydae.com; internet www.flydae.com; f. 2005; scheduled passenger flights within the Netherlands Antilles and to other Caribbean and South American destinations.

Windward Express Airways: Princess Juliana International Airport; tel. 545-2001; fax 545-2224; e-mail windwardexpress@hotmail.com; internet www.windwardexpress.com; domestic and limited Caribbean island charter flights, including destinations with restricted access; passenger and cargo flights; Man. Dir CURLETTA HALLEY.

Windward Islands Airways International (WIA—Winair) NV: Princess Juliana Airport, POB 2088, Philipsburg, St Maarten; tel. 545-4237; fax 545-2002; e-mail info@fly-winair.com; internet www.fly-winair.com; f. 1961; govt-owned since 1974; scheduled and charter flights throughout north-eastern Caribbean; Man. Dir EDWIN HODGE.

Tourism

Tourism is a major industry on all the islands. The principal attractions for tourists are the white, sandy beaches, marine wildlife and diving facilities. There are marine parks in the waters around Curaçao, Bonaire and Saba. The numerous historic sites are of interest to visitors. The largest number of tourists visit St Maarten, Curaçao and Bonaire. In 2006 stop-over visitors totalled some 781,890. In the same year 1,805,014 cruise-ship passengers visited St Maarten, Curaçao and Bonaire. Tourism generated earnings of NA Fl. 1,906.5m. in 2004.

Tourism Corporation Bonaire (TCB): Kaya Grandi 2, Kralendijk, Bonaire; tel. 717-8322; fax 717-8408; e-mail info@tourismbonaire.com; internet www.infobonaire.com; Gen. Man. RONELLA CROES.

Curaçao Tourist Board: Pietermaai 19, POB 3266, Willemstad, Curaçao; tel. (9) 434-8200; fax (9) 461-5017; e-mail ctdbcur@ctdb.net; internet www.ctb.an; f. 1989; supervised by the Curaçao Tourism Development Bureau; Marketing Dir E. NITA.

Saba Tourist Office: Windwardside, POB 527, Saba; tel. 416-2231; fax 416-2350; e-mail tourism@sabagov.com; internet www.sabatourism.com; Dir GLENN C. HOLM.

St Eustatius Tourist Office: St Eustatius Tourism Development Foundation, Fort Oranje, Oranjestad, St Eustatius; tel. and fax 318-2433; e-mail info@statiatourism.com; internet www.statiatourism.com; Dir ALIDA FRANCIS.

St Maarten Tourist Bureau: Vineyard Office Park, W. G. Buncamper Rd 33, Philipsburg, St Maarten; tel. 542-2337; fax 542-2734; e-mail info@st-maarten.com; internet www.st-maarten.com; Commr THEO HEYLIGER; Dir REGINA LA BEGA.

HOTEL ASSOCIATIONS

Bonaire Hotel and Tourism Association: Kaya Soeur Bartola 15B, Kralendijk, Bonaire; tel. 717-5134; fax 717-8534; e-mail info@bonhata.org; internet www.ilovebonaire.com; f. 1980; Pres. SARA MATERA; Vice Pres. MARTIN VAN BEKKUM.

Curaçao Hospitality and Tourism Association (CHATA): POB 6115, Kurason Komèrsio, Curaçao; tel. (9) 465-1005; fax (9) 465-1052; e-mail information@chata.org; internet www.chata.org; f. 1967 as Curaçao Hotel Asscn; Pres. PAUL KOK.

St Maarten Hospitality and Trade Association: W. J. A. Nisbeth Rd 33A, POB 486, Philipsburg, St Maarten; tel. 542-0108; fax 542-0107; e-mail info@shta.com; internet www.shta.com; Pres. EMIL LEE.

NEW ZEALAND

Introductory Survey

Location, Climate, Language, Religion, Flag, Capital

The Dominion of New Zealand lies in the South Pacific Ocean, about 1,750 km (1,100 miles) south-east of Australia. It consists of North Island and South Island, separated by the narrow Cook Strait, and several smaller islands, including Stewart Island (or Rakiura) in the south. The climate is temperate and moist, with an average temperature of 12°C (52°F), except in the far north, where higher temperatures are reached. The official languages are English and Maori. At the 2001 census, 15.7% of respondents professed adherence to the Anglican Church, 13.0% being Roman Catholics and 11.5% Presbyterians. At the 2006 census, 55.6% of respondents professed adherence to the Christian religion. The national flag (proportions 1 by 2) is dark blue, with a representation of the United Kingdom flag as a canton in the upper hoist. In the fly are four five-pointed red stars, edged in white, in the form of the Southern Cross constellation. The capital is Wellington, on North Island.

Recent History

New Zealand is a former British colony. It became a dominion, under the British Crown, in 1907 and achieved full independence by the Statute of Westminster, adopted by the British Parliament in 1931 and accepted by New Zealand in 1947.

In 1962 Western Samoa (now Samoa, q.v.), formerly administered by New Zealand, achieved independence, and in 1965 the Cook Islands attained full internal self-government, but retained many links, including common citizenship, with New Zealand. In October 1974 Niue, one of New Zealand's island territories, obtained similar status 'in free association with New Zealand'. New Zealand retains two Dependent Territories, Ross Dependency and Tokelau (see the chapter on New Zealand's Dependent Territories).

In December 1972 the first Labour Government for more than 12 years came to power, under the leadership of Norman Kirk, after a succession of New Zealand National Party administrations. The New Zealand Labour Party took office at a time when the economy was thriving, mainly as a result of a sharp increase in international prices for agricultural commodities. However, this prosperity was accompanied by inflation. Higher domestic demand and the international energy crisis of 1973–74 led to a rapid rise in imports, a reduction in exchange reserves and a severe balance-of-payments problem. The Labour Government's foreign policy was more independent than that of its predecessors. It phased out New Zealand's military commitments under the South-East Asia Treaty Organization and established diplomatic relations with the People's Republic of China.

Norman Kirk died in August 1974, and Wallace Rowling, hitherto Minister of Finance, became Prime Minister in September. The economic recession worsened, and in November 1975 a general election resulted in victory for the National Party, which won 55 of the 87 seats in the House of Representatives, while the Labour Party took the remaining 32 seats. The new Government, under Robert (later Sir Robert) Muldoon, who had led the National Party since July 1974, introduced austere economic policies, and in 1976 reduced the annual intake of migrants from 30,000 to 5,000, while conducting a campaign against illegal immigrants.

Popular dissatisfaction with Muldoon's sometimes controversial leadership was reflected at the general election in November 1978. The National Party retained power, with 50 of the 92 seats in the enlarged House of Representatives, but its share of the total vote fell from 47.2% in 1975 to 39.8%. Labour won more votes (40.4% of the total) but fewer seats (41). The Social Credit Party received 17.1% of the total votes, compared with only 7.4% in 1975, but obtained only one seat. In the November 1981 election Muldoon's majority was further reduced. The National Party won 47 of the 92 seats in the House, while Labour, which again received more votes, won 43 seats and Social Credit (despite obtaining 20.6% of votes cast) only two.

In February 1984 Muldoon's Government antagonized New Zealand's trade unions by effecting legislation to ban 'closed shop' agreements with employers, thus giving employees the right to choose whether or not to join a trade union. Further legislation was used in June to compel striking construction workers to return to work. In the same month, faced with dissent within his own party, Muldoon called an early general election for July. The Labour Party obtained 43% of the total votes and secured 56 of the 95 seats in an enlarged House of Representatives, while the National Party, with 36% of the votes, took 37 seats: it was thought that the National Party had lost considerable support to the newly formed New Zealand Party, a right-wing party which won 12.3% of the votes (but no seats) after campaigning for a minimum of government intervention in the economy. David Lange (the leader of the Labour Party since February 1983) became Prime Minister. James McLay, who had been deputy leader of the National Party since March 1984, defeated Muldoon in an election for the leadership of the party in November 1984, but he was replaced as party leader by his deputy, James (Jim) Bolger, in March 1986.

The Labour Government introduced controversial deregulatory measures to improve the country's economic situation. The initial success of these measures, together with widespread popular support for the Government's anti-nuclear policy (see below), contributed to a second victory for the Labour Party in a general election in August 1987. Of the 97 seats in the enlarged House of Representatives, the Labour Party secured 58, and the National Party 39. (The Democratic Party lost both the seats that its predecessor, the Social Credit Party, had won at the 1984 election.) Of the votes cast, the Labour Party received 47.4%, and the National Party 42.8%.

In 1987 Lange's Government initiated a controversial policy of 'privatization' of state-owned enterprises. In November 1988 policy disagreements prompted Lange to dismiss the minister responsible for the privatization programme, Richard Prebble. Lange was accused by cabinet colleagues of acting without consultation, and in December Roger (later Sir Roger) Douglas, the Minister of Finance, declared that he would not serve another term under Lange. Douglas was promptly dismissed from office, and later that month unsuccessfully challenged Lange for the leadership of the Labour Party. In May 1989 the formation of the NewLabour Party (led by a former president of the Labour Party, Jim Anderton) was announced: the party aimed to appeal to disillusioned Labour supporters. In early August Douglas was elected by Labour MPs to a vacant cabinet post, thus prompting Lange to resign. Shortly afterwards, Geoffrey Palmer, hitherto the deputy leader of the Labour Party, was elected the Labour Party's parliamentary leader and Prime Minister.

In January 1990 Palmer undertook a wide-ranging government reorganization. The return of Richard Prebble to the Cabinet, in his former post as Minister for State-Owned Enterprises, provoked considerable anger within the Labour Party. The Government aroused further hostility by its introduction of a substantial fee for tertiary-level students. The continued sale of state assets, especially that of the telecommunications company, Telecom, was also unpopular. In September 1990, less than eight weeks before the next general election, Palmer resigned as Prime Minister. Public opinion polls had indicated that Labour, under his leadership, had lost support to the National Party, and members of the Cabinet had consequently urged him to resign. Michael Moore, the Minister of External Relations and Trade (who had also contested the August 1989 leadership election), replaced Palmer as Prime Minister and Labour Party leader. Moore promised to act promptly to avert the enormous budget deficit forecast for 1991/92 and, two weeks later, he secured an agreement with the country's trade union leaders regarding restricted pay settlements. In October 1990, none the less, the National Party won 47.8% of the votes at the general election, taking 67 of the 97 seats in the House of Representatives. The Labour Party, with 35.1% of the votes, won 29 seats, while the NewLabour Party retained its sole seat, obtaining 5.2% of the votes. Jim Bolger, as leader of the National Party, thus became Prime Minister at the head of a Government that promised to continue Labour's strict budgetary and monetary controls. The sale of state assets would also continue.

In November 1990 the new Government's first economic proposals were outlined. They included the repeal of legislation on equal pay for women, and envisaged reductions in public spending, particularly in the field of social welfare. In December the Government announced measures that entailed proposed reductions in unemployment benefit, family benefits, and in medical and sickness payments, and prepared for the introduction of a system whereby users of medical and educational services (hitherto provided free of charge) would be required to pay, according to a means test. These measures were received with anger by social and church groups. Protest marches took place in April 1991, and plans for a 'freeze' in the levels of old-age pensions prompted groups representing the elderly unsuccessfully to petition the British monarch (through the Governor-General) to dismiss the Government. Two National Party members of the House of Representatives resigned from the party in August, in protest against the proposals, and the Minister of Maori Affairs, Winston Peters (who had openly criticized the Government's economic strategy), was dismissed in October. In November Sir Robert Muldoon announced that he would resign from the legislature in early 1992, in protest against the Government's economic policies. Earlier in the month criticism had prompted the Government to withdraw its stringent means-testing measures for the allocation of state pensions, but the overall level of payments remained lower than previously.

In December 1991 a coalition was formed by minor parties as a challenge to the two main parties. The grouping, known as the Alliance, consisted of the NewLabour Party, the New Zealand Democratic Party, the Green Party of Aotearoa—New Zealand and Mana Motuhake. In its first electoral test (the by-election in February 1992 that had been precipitated by Muldoon's resignation) the Alliance campaigned for the provision of education and health care free of charge and the return to the public sector of 'privatized' state assets. The National Party retained the seat in the by-election, but with a greatly reduced majority. The Alliance secured 38% of the votes, only 5% less than the National Party.

In September 1992 a preliminary referendum on proposed electoral reform was held. The electorate voted overwhelmingly in favour of the abolition of the 'first-past-the-post' system and for its replacement by a form of proportional representation; of the four alternatives offered, the mixed member proportional (MMP) system (similar to that used in Germany) received the greatest support. The new rules were to be implemented at the 1996 election, following a second, binding referendum.

In March 1993 the outspoken Winston Peters, who had continued to embarrass the Government, resigned from his parliamentary seat in order to stand for re-election as an independent candidate. The by-election in April resulted in an overwhelming victory for Peters, the major political parties having declined to present candidates. In July Peters established New Zealand First, and announced that the party would contest all 99 seats at the forthcoming general election.

At the election, held on 6 November 1993, the National Party, which had campaigned mainly on the Government's record of economic recovery, was narrowly returned to office, receiving 35.2% of the total votes cast and securing 50 seats in the House of Representatives. The Labour Party, with 34.7% of the votes, won 45 seats, the Alliance two and New Zealand First two. At a concurrent, second referendum on electoral reform, 54% of voters favoured the adoption of the MMP system. A new Government was appointed in late November.

In October 1994 Peter Dunne, a former cabinet minister, resigned from the Labour Party, following differences over the party's policy on taxation, and declared his intention to remain in the House of Representatives as an independent member. He subsequently established a new party, Future New Zealand. The traditional two-party system was further challenged in early 1995, when support for ACT New Zealand, co-founded by Sir Roger Douglas (reformist Minister of Finance in 1984–88), who had recently announced his return to politics, began to increase rapidly. In June 1995, however, the position of the ruling party was strengthened by the formation of United New Zealand by seven members of the House of Representatives (four National, two Labour and the leader of Future New Zealand, Peter Dunne). The new grouping pledged its support for the Government on issues of confidence. In February, for the first time since the early 1930s, a formal coalition Government was established when the National Party formed an official alliance with United New Zealand. In the ensuing government reorganization, Peter Dunne joined the Cabinet as Minister of Revenue and Internal Affairs. As a result of a number of parliamentary defections and realignments, by April 1996 the number of parliamentary seats held by the National Party had been reduced to 41. In March, meanwhile, Sir Michael Hardie Boys replaced Dame Catherine Tizard as Governor-General.

The first general election under the MMP system was held on 12 October 1996. No party achieved an outright majority. The National Party, with 34.1% of the votes, won 44 of the 120 seats in the expanded House of Representatives, the Labour Party (28.3%) secured 37 seats and New Zealand First (13.1%) garnered 17 seats, while the Alliance won 13 seats, ACT New Zealand eight and United New Zealand one. A notable development was the increase in the number of Maori MPs from six to 15, a figure almost equivalent to the proportion of Maori (the country's aboriginal inhabitants) in the population as a whole. Although the election result initially appeared to favour the formation of a centre-left coalition under the leadership of Helen Clark, complex negotiations finally led to the establishment in December of an alliance between the National Party and New Zealand First, led by Winston Peters.

Jim Bolger thus continued as Prime Minister, while Winston Peters was appointed Deputy Prime Minister and Treasurer, the latter newly created post carrying responsibility for the drafting of the country's budget. Although Peters had previously discounted the possibility of a reconciliation and of entering into a coalition with the National Party, he had unexpectedly altered his stance in exchange for concessions on economic policy. The incoming Cabinet incorporated a total of five members of New Zealand First. Don McKinnon of the National Party retained the foreign affairs portfolio, and Bill Birch continued to hold nominal responsibility for finance.

In September 1997 proposals for the introduction of a compulsory retirement savings scheme were overwhelmingly rejected by the electorate in a referendum. The holding of the referendum had been a condition of New Zealand First's participation in the ruling coalition, but the Prime Minister had also actively supported the proposed pension reforms. In the following month thousands of protesters took to the streets to demand the resignation of the Government, the latter's policies on health and education having drawn particular criticism.

In November 1997, following a leadership challenge from Jenny Shipley, a cabinet minister whose portfolios now included transport and women's affairs, the Prime Minister announced his intention to resign. Shipley was thus sworn in as New Zealand's first woman Prime Minister in December, reiterating the National Party's commitment to a continuation of the partnership with New Zealand First. In the ensuing government reorganization, most supporters of Jim Bolger retained their portfolios but were downgraded. Winston Peters continued as Deputy Prime Minister, while other members of New Zealand First also remained in the Cabinet.

In November 1997, meanwhile, following the Alliance's rejection of a Greens' proposal to establish a coalition arrangement, the Green Party of Aotearoa decided that at the next general election it would stand as a separate political party but would remain a member of the Alliance until that time. In January 1998 the Liberal Party announced that it was to be dissolved and would merge with the Alliance.

In May 1998 the outcome of a parliamentary by-election to fill the seat vacated by Jim Bolger confirmed the electorate's growing disillusionment with the coalition Government. Although the seat was retained by the National Party, its majority was greatly reduced. In August, following an acrimonious dispute regarding the sale of the Government's stake in Wellington airport, Winston Peters was dismissed from the post of Deputy Prime Minister and Treasurer and the dissolution of the coalition Government was announced. Rejecting demands for an early general election, Jenny Shipley reallocated many cabinet portfolios. Although Tau Henare (who in late 1998 founded a new party, Mauri Pacific, having been removed as deputy leader of New Zealand First in July), the Minister of Maori Affairs, was the only former New Zealand First minister to retain his post within the Cabinet, three other erstwhile members of the National Party's former coalition partner remained as ministers outside the Cabinet. Despite the defection of Winston Peters to the opposition, the Prime Minister was able to secure the support of eight of the 16 New Zealand First representatives in the legislature, and in September she survived a vote of confidence in the House. In the same month, in an attempt to raise public concern over the social effects of government policy, in particular the plight of low-income families, the Anglican Church initiated an ecumenical 'Hikoi of Hope', in which protesters from both ends of the country marched to Wellington and converged upon the House of Representatives.

In December 1998 the minority Government's position was further weakened by the unexpected resignation of a supporting independent (and former New Zealand First) MP, following the administration's decision to proceed with its acquisition of 28 F-16 fighter aircraft from the USA. (However, the contract to lease the aircraft was cancelled in March 2000 by the new Labour Government.) The Prime Minister was placed under further pressure in early 1999, when it was alleged that the Minister of Tourism, Murray McCully, had acted inappropriately with regard to the handling of a major contract for the advertising business of the New Zealand Tourism Board. In February, as the Prime Minister became personally implicated in the affair and as opposition MPs accused her of deliberately misleading the legislature over her association with the head of the advertising agency in question, the Government won a motion of no confidence by 61 votes to 59. Claiming that the ruling party had intended to exploit its links with the agency during the next general election campaign, the Labour Party demanded an inquiry into the Government's alleged payments to departing members of the New Zealand Tourism Board and into the Board's expenditure on overseas promotions. In March the $NZ53m. marketing contract with the agency was terminated. McCully relinquished the tourism portfolio in April.

At the general election, conducted on 27 November 1999, the opposition Labour Party won the largest share of votes cast. A recount of votes in one constituency, where the Green Party candidate then unexpectedly took the seat from the incumbent National MP, combined with the incorporation of 'special votes' (which included those cast by New Zealanders overseas), led to a substantial modification of the initial results. Having secured 38.7% of the votes cast, the Labour Party was finally allocated 49 of the 120 seats in the House of Representatives, while the National Party, which had won 30.5% of the votes, received 39 seats. The Alliance was allocated 10 seats and ACT New Zealand nine seats. Under the recently-introduced system of proportional representation, the Green Party's victory in the one constituency automatically entitled the movement to a further six seats in the legislature. New Zealand First's representation declined to five seats; the party's leader, Winston Peters, only narrowly retained his seat. United New Zealand took the one remaining seat. Having previously discounted any co-operation with the Green Party, the Labour Party was thus obliged to seek the support not only of the Alliance but also of the seven Green MPs.

The leader of the Labour Party, Helen Clark (who had served as Deputy Prime Minister in 1989–90), thus became Prime Minister. The minority Government, which incorporated several members of the Alliance, took office in December 1999. Jim Anderton, the leader of the Alliance, was appointed Deputy Prime Minister, Minister for Economic Development and Minister for Industry and Regional Development. The treasury and finance portfolios were assigned to Dr Michael Cullen, while Phil Goff became Minister of Foreign Affairs and Trade and also assumed responsibility for the justice portfolio.

In a non-binding, citizen-initiated referendum held on the same day as the general election, a majority of voters favoured a reduction in the number of members of the House of Representatives from 120 to 99; voters also favoured a reform of the criminal justice system, including the placing of greater emphasis on the needs of victims of crime.

One of the new Government's stated priorities was the 'Closing the Gaps' initiative, which aimed to address the socio-economic disparities between the Maori and non-Maori communities, particularly in health, housing, education, income and the incidence of crime. Among its first actions were the repeal of the Employment Contracts Act, the restoration of the state monopoly in the provision of accident compensation and the cancellation of the contract to lease 28 F-16 fighter aircraft from the USA. The new Government was strongly criticized by opposition politicians and accused of racism, following its decision in mid-2000 to sell a 25% share of a lucrative radiowaves company (which auctions high frequency radio positions to telecommunications companies) to a Maori trust under its 'Closing the Gaps' policy.

In June 2000 the Prime Minister was obliged to dismiss the Minister of Maori Affairs, Dover Samuels, following allegations of sexual misconduct. On 4 April 2001 Dame Silvia Cartwright (New Zealand's first female High Court Judge) took office as Governor-General. Her appointment represented a significant achievement for women in New Zealand public life, and created an unprecedented situation in which the five most important public roles in the country (those of Prime Minister, Leader of the Opposition, Attorney-General, Chief Justice and Governor-General) were all occupied by women.

In October 2001 Jenny Shipley resigned as leader of the National Party and was replaced by Bill English, a former Minister of Health. The incoming leader renamed the party the New National Party. In December Jim Anderton was placed under considerable pressure from left-wing members of the Alliance to withdraw his support for the Government's military involvement in Afghanistan, following the Prime Minister's confirmation that New Zealand Hercules transport aircraft had landed in Afghanistan, to assist in the US-led military campaign there (see the chapter on Afghanistan). In early April 2002, after months of wrangling, the Alliance split. Anderton and six other members of the party agreed to form a breakaway party, later named the Progressive Coalition, but continued to support the ruling coalition. The seven members of the legislature were expelled from the Alliance in late April. At the same time Laila Harré, Minister of Women's Affairs, Youth Affairs and Statistics, succeeded Anderton as leader of the Alliance and confirmed her support for the Government until the next legislative elections. In June the Prime Minister announced that the next general election was to be held earlier than planned, in late July, largely owing to the collapse of the Alliance, and a dispute between the Labour Party and the Greens over the Government's decision not to renew a moratorium banning the commercial release of genetically modified organisms (which expired in October 2003).

In April 2002, following extensive consultations, the Government announced the proposed replacement of the monarch's Privy Council (based in London, United Kingdom) as New Zealand's court of final appeal by an independent Supreme Court, consisting of five judges headed by the Chief Justice. The requisite legislation was approved in October 2003; the new court began functioning in July 2004.

Some 77% of the registered voters participated in the general election, which took place on 27 July 2002. The Labour Party won 41% of the party votes, thereby securing a second term in office. However, the party failed to secure an overall majority in the House of Representatives, winning 52 of the 120 seats. New Zealand First received 10% of the vote (13 seats); ACT New Zealand 7% (nine seats); the Greens 7% (nine seats) and United Future New Zealand 7% (eight seats). The Progressive Coalition won 1.7% of the party votes and secured two seats, while the Alliance failed to secure any parliamentary representation. The National Party performed badly at the election, winning only 21% of the party votes; its representation declined by 12 seats to 27. Clark, unable to reach an agreement with the Greens on the issue of genetically modified organisms, formed a minority coalition Government with the Progressive Coalition. The Labour Party leader secured the support of United Future New Zealand. In May 2003 the Prime Minister carried out a government reorganization.

In June 2003 Clark announced that the Government intended to draw up new legislation to ensure that the country's coastline and seabed were owned by the Crown, following a ruling by the Court of Appeal that Maori tribes could pursue their own claims to ownership of the Marlborough Sands foreshore and seabed in South Island. Maori attacked the Government's 'draconian' and 'colonialist' actions. In late June the House of Representatives approved the Prostitution Reform Bill, which decriminalized prostitution and provided a legal framework for the sex industry. In October the legislature voted overwhelmingly in favour of the Anti-Terrorism Act, which extended the powers of the police force. The act, an extension of the 2002 Terrorism Suppression Act, created new offences including: improperly dealing with nuclear and radioactive materials; causing the infection of animals; contaminating products, such as food and water; and harbouring a terrorist. The Green Party opposed the legislation, claiming that the law would infringe upon civil liberties.

In February 2004 the Minister of Commerce and of Immigration, Lianne Dalziel, was forced to resign after it transpired that she had lied over the disclosure to the media of a document relating to the deportation of a Sri Lankan youth. The Prime Minister ordered an inquiry into the obtaining by Dalziel of a confidential legal document and into officials' involvement in its subsequent circulation. A cabinet reorganization was subsequently effected. Meanwhile, in the same month the new leader of the opposition National Party, Don Brash, a former governor of the central bank, announced that if he won power he would discontinue all forms of positive discrimination for Maori, considering 'special privileges' to be unnecessary and divisive. Brash also pledged to abolish the parliamentary seats reserved for Maori and to repeal 'divisive, race-based' legislation. Clark accused Brash of creating disharmony by breaking the national consensus on dealing with Maori affairs; nevertheless, two days later she promised a review of state assistance for Maori, agreeing that policies should be based on need and not on any perceived privilege. In the February government reorganization, Clark also created the post of Co-ordinating Minister for Race Relations after opinion polls showed a decline in support for her administration over its policies towards the Maori. The portfolio was assigned to the Minister of Education, of State Services, and for Sport and Recreation, Trevor Mallard; he was given the immediate responsibility of conducting a full review of government policy.

In April 2004 the Progressive Coalition renamed itself the Progressive Party. In the same month Clark dismissed the Associate Minister of Maori Affairs, Tariana Turia, after Turia stated that she intended to vote against the Government's Seabed and Foreshore Bill, which ensured that coastal areas were owned by the Crown, on the grounds that the new legislation was in contravention of the rights of indigenous Maori. Following her dismissal, in the following month Turia resigned from the Labour Party and the House of Representatives. In May the Prime Minister secured a narrow victory in a vote of no confidence precipitated by Turia's resignation. Meanwhile, a two-week hikoi (protest march) against the planned legislation, which had commenced in mid-April, arrived outside the Parliament building in Wellington.

In July 2004 Tariana Turia secured victory in a by-election to the seat of Te Tai Hauauru on North Island, necessitated by her resignation from the House of Representatives in the previous month. Turia was the candidate of the newly formed Maori Party. In November the controversial Seabed and Foreshore Bill was finally approved by the House of Representatives, with the Government securing a narrow victory in the vote owing to the support of New Zealand First. In the same month the Minister of Youth Affairs, for Land Information and of Statistics, John Tamihere, resigned following the revelation that a report on his activities had been sent to the Serious Fraud Office for investigation. In the following month a major government reorganization was announced, in which Tamihere's portfolios were reassigned. The appointments came into effect in February 2005, when Attorney-General Margaret Wilson left the Cabinet in order to succeed Jonathan Hunt as Speaker of the House of Representatives. Deputy Prime Minister Michael Cullen became the new Attorney-General, while retaining his existing portfolios. In March the Serious Fraud Office announced that, following its investigation, it did not intend to charge Tamihere with any offence.

In May 2005 Minister of Fisheries David Benson-Pope resigned from his cabinet post, following the commencement of a police inquiry into allegations that he had abused children during his former career as a teacher. However, he was reinstated to the Cabinet in the following month. In July Prime Minister Helen Clark announced that a general election would take place in September. At the election, which was held on 17 September, Clark's Labour Party secured victory by a narrow margin, winning 41.1% of the vote and 50 seats, compared with 39.1% of the vote and 48 seats for the National Party, which had improved significantly on its performance at the 2002 election. The newly formed Maori Party secured 2.1% of the vote, winning four of the seven seats reserved for Maoris. As the Labour Party had failed to gain an overall majority, it subsequently entered into a coalition with the Progressive Party, which had won only one seat. With the support of New Zealand First and United Future New Zealand, secured on a more informal basis, this brought the total number of seats controlled by the Government in the new legislature to 61.

In October 2005 the new Government was sworn in. Controversial New Zealand First leader Winston Peters was appointed Minister of Foreign Affairs, while Peter Dunne was allocated the revenue portfolio, but with the unusual provision that both would remain outside the Cabinet. The appointment of Peters met with widespread criticism, owing largely to his anti-immigration views. In March 2006 David Parker, who had been appointed to the post of Attorney-General in the new Government, resigned from the position, having admitted that he had made an error while filing an annual return for a company with which he was involved. However, he retained the cabinet portfolios of energy and transport. Deputy Prime Minister Michael Cullen subsequently became Attorney-General for the second time, holding the post concurrently with the finance and tertiary education portfolios. In the same month Maj.-Gen. Jerry Mateparae, hitherto Chief of the Army, became the first Maori to be appointed Chief of the New Zealand Defence Force; he took up the position in May. In mid-August 2006 Te Arikinui (Dame Te Atairangikaahu, the Maori Queen) died, bringing to an end her 40-year reign. Te Arikinui's son, Tuheitia Paki, took the throne, shortly before a traditional Maori funeral ceremony for Dame Te Ata, which was attended by thousands of mourners, including Prime Minister Clark. Also in August Anand Satyanand, a retired judge of Indo-Fijian descent, replaced Dame Silvia Cartwright as Governor-General upon the expiry of her term of office. While Dame Silvia used her farewell speech to highlight the pressing issue of domestic and other violence in New Zealand society, Satyanand, who was sworn in on 23 August, emphasized the country's diversity and the importance of greater cohesion among the various communities. In October the Auditor-General, Kevin Brady, published a report on an investigation into campaign funding during the 2005 legislative election, a controversy that had led to a dispute between the Government and the opposition. Brady found that the Labour Party had improperly spent $NZ768,000 of taxpayers' money on its election campaign; several other parties, including New Zealand First and the Green Party, were similarly implicated in breaches of regulations, albeit for smaller sums. Although Labour promptly announced that it was to reimburse the funds, Helen Clark's public reputation was believed to have been damaged. Legislation retrospectively validating the relevant election campaign expenditure was swiftly enacted by the House of Representatives, but controversy continued. In November 2006 Don Brash resigned as leader of the National Party, citing concerns that increased speculation about his position was having a negative effect on the party. Brash had applied for an injunction against the publication of his e-mails in a book that attempted to prove a link between himself and the Exclusive Brethren, a business-orientated Christian group that had allegedly been involved in improperly influencing the outcome of the 2005 election, although he denied allegations of irregular campaign practices and maintained that his resignation was not related to the impending publication of the book. John Key, hitherto the National Party's finance spokesman, was subsequently elected unopposed to the National Party leadership.

In July 2007 the Minister for Social Development and Employment and for the Environment, David Benson-Pope, resigned in connection with the allegedly unfair dismissal of an employee of the Ministry for the Environment. Amid opinion poll results suggesting an increase in support for the National Party, Prime Minister Clark announced a ministerial reorganization in October 2007, referring to the changes as part of the Government's preparations for the general election due to be held in the latter part of 2008. Steve Chadwick was appointed Minister of Conservation and of Women's Affairs, Maryan Street Minister for the Accident Compensation Corporation and of Housing, and Shane Jones Minister for Building and Construction. Another notable change was the allocation of the justice portfolio to Annette King, in addition to her existing responsibilities for transport and police.

In October 2007 a nation-wide police operation, carried out in various cities as well as in a remote part of North Island, resulted in the arrest of 17 people under the Terrorism Suppression Act. Some of the detainees were reported to be activists for causes including Maori independence and the environment, and were alleged to have been involved in illegal training camps where firearms and other weapons were found. Tame Iti, a well-known Maori campaigner, was among those arrested. Hundreds of people took part in demonstrations to protest against the police action, while the development prompted a wide debate about the possibility of an insurgency within the country. In early November the Solicitor-General concluded that the detainees could not be charged under the Terrorism Suppression Act, but charges such as the illegal possession of weapons were not ruled out.

During 1987, meanwhile, there were protests by the Maori concerning their cultural and economic rights and, in particular, their claims to land in accordance with the Treaty of Waitangi, concluded in 1840 by the British Government and Maori leaders, whereby sovereignty had been ceded to the United Kingdom in return for the Maori people's retention of hunting and fishing grounds. In November 1987 a ruling by the Waitangi Tribunal, reconvened in 1975 to consider retrospectively the claims of

Maori land rights activists, recommended the restoration of an Auckland harbour headland to the Maori people. By 1994 about 75% of the country was subject to land claims by Maori groups. In December of that year the Government offered the sum of $NZ1,000m., payable over a 10-year period from September 1992, in full and final settlement of outstanding claims for compensation. However, the condition that all future land claims be renounced was rejected by most Maori groups. In the same month a historic agreement between the Government and the Tainui people of Waikato provided for the return of land confiscated in 1863 and for the deposit over a period of five years of $NZ65m. in a land acquisition trust.

In May 1995 the Prime Minister and the Queen of the Tainui people signed an agreement relating to a full and final settlement, valued at $NZ170m., of land grievances dating back to 1863. However, increasing ethnic tension was demonstrated by the destruction in September 1995 of an old school building by Maori protesters involved in a land dispute and by the burning down in October of a historic church, known as the 'Maori Cathedral', at Otaki, in an apparent retaliatory arson attack by white extremists. In November, in a significant ceremony in Wellington, Queen Elizabeth II gave her personal assent to the legislation ending the Tainui grievances when she signed the Waikato Raupatu Claims Settlement Act, which implemented the $NZ170m. agreement, including the return of 15,780 ha of land, and which incorporated an apology from the Crown for the loss of lives and for the confiscation of property. A final settlement payment of $NZ13m. was made to the Tainui tribe in late 2000. In October 1996, as more modest agreements continued to be reached, the Government announced a $NZ170m. provisional settlement with the South Island's Ngai Tahu (one of New Zealand's smallest Maori tribes) regarding the group's long-standing claim for compensation. In early 1997 Maori leaders, pursuing a claim first lodged by tribal advocates in 1991, embarked upon a lawsuit aimed at the official alteration of New Zealand's name to Aotearoa ('Land of the Long White Cloud').

In July 1997 a Maori tribe that had been driven off its land in the 1840s lodged a claim to the site of the Parliament building in Wellington. The Ngati Tama also presented claims to other areas of the capital, while declaring their willingness to negotiate. At a ceremony in Wellington in September 1997, following six years of negotiations, the Government and the Ngai Tahu reached a formal agreement, subject to approval by the tribe's members, regarding the compensation of $NZ170m. The Government's offer also included the right to name mountains and rivers, often in combination with the English equivalents, and incorporated a full apology from the Crown. In November, the tribal beneficiaries having voted overwhelmingly in favour of the arrangements, the historic deed of full and final settlement was signed by the Prime Minister and representatives of the Ngai Tahu. In March 1998 the Ngai Tahu Claims Settlement Bill was duly submitted to the House of Representatives, where it received approval six months later. In July, exercising for the first time its power of compulsory recommendation, the Waitangi Tribunal ordered the Government to return to the Ngati Turangitukua land (now valued at $NZ6.1m.) which had been confiscated from its Maori owners more than 30 years previously to permit the construction of housing for workers engaged on an electric power project in the central North Island. In early 2000 a joint land claim was lodged by five Maori tribes of the central North Island. With the forestry claim alone worth an estimated $NZ588m., the application was potentially the largest ever submitted to the Waitangi Tribunal. In March 2001 the Ngati Ruanui became the first Taranaki tribe to conclude a deed of settlement with the Government, amounting to $NZ41m. In early 2003 the Ngati Awa voted in favour of a treaty settlement with the Government, which included an apology from the Crown, the return of 64 ha of land and $NZ42m. In August 2005 Prime Minister Helen Clark announced that all Maori land claims under the Treaty of Waitangi would have to be filed by 1 September 2008, in order that they could be settled by 2020. The announcement constituted one of the Labour Party's pledges in advance of the general election. According to reports, by 2007 the Waitangi Tribunal had been able to settle only about 20 claims.

In response to Maori grievances over fishing rights, the Government introduced, in 1988, a Maori Fisheries Bill, under the provisions of which 2.5% of current fishing quotas were to be restored to the Maori people annually for the following 19 years. However, Maori activists alleged that the proposed legislation was racially discriminatory, since it stipulated that no other Maori fishing claim would be considered by the Waitangi Tribunal until the 19 years had elapsed. The bill was also condemned by some white New Zealanders, as, if implemented as proposed, it would guarantee the Maori people about 50% of the country's entire fishing rights by the year 2008. In August 1992, finding that the Government had failed to honour its obligations under the Treaty of 1840, the Waitangi Tribunal recommended that ownership of most of the fisheries of South Island be transferred to the Ngai Tahu. In November 1992, in the hope of reaching a permanent settlement, the Government advanced the sum of $NZ150m. to a Maori consortium to enable the latter's purchase of a 50% stake in the country's biggest inshore fishing company. In early 1996 the Treaty of Waitangi Fisheries Commission, established to resolve the issue of the allocation among Maori of resources valued at $NZ200m., had yet to deliver its recommendations. In April the Court of Appeal declared that, despite having no coastline, urban Maori constituted an *iwi* (tribe) and were therefore directly entitled to a share of these fishery assets. The case was subsequently referred to the Privy Council in London. Its decision, announced in January 1997, overruled the Court of Appeal's definition of an *iwi*. In mid-1998 the Waitangi Tribunal ruled that urban Maori without blood ties should be accorded similar negotiating rights to those of traditional *iwi*. The historic decision thus acknowledged urban Maori trusts as modern tribes. In August, however, a High Court judge ruled in favour of traditional Maori tribes, effectively declaring that urban Maori groups had no claim to fishery assets. In October 1999, furthermore, the urban Maori claim was rejected by the Court of Appeal. In June 2004 it was reported that Maori tribes had been offered 20% of all new aquaculture or marine farming areas and 20% of aquaculture areas that had been allocated since 1992 in an attempt to resolve the 1992 fisheries settlement. The offer was believed to be, in part, an inducement to Maori to accept the controversial Seabed and Foreshore Bill (see above).

In April 1997 urban Maori were outraged at a proposal by the Treaty of Waitangi Fisheries Commission to allocate up to $NZ300m. of fishery assets on a tribal basis, rather than according to *iwi* size as the populous northern tribes demanded. The Ngai Tahu and other *iwi*, meanwhile, argued that the length of coastline and traditional fishing grounds should determine the allocation of assets. In early 1998, following an incident in late 1997 when a fishing boat reportedly landed several metric tons of snapper without commercial quota rights, it was announced that new regulations were to govern the management of 'customary' fishing by *tangata whenua* (people of the land), whereby Maori are permitted to take an unlimited amount of seafood provided that it is not for pecuniary gain. Meanwhile, in October 2007 the Government instigated a campaign to persuade Maoris living in Australia to return to New Zealand.

From 1984 the Lange Government's pledge to ban from New Zealand's ports all vessels believed to be carrying nuclear weapons or powered by nuclear energy caused considerable strain in the country's relations with Australia and the USA, its partners in the ANZUS military pact (see p. 422). The ban was duly imposed in February 1985. In July 1986 the US Government announced its intention to devise new, bilateral defence arrangements with Australia, and in August the USA's military obligations to New Zealand under the ANZUS Treaty were formally suspended. In February 1987 the US Government announced its decision not to renew a 1982 memorandum of understanding (due to be renegotiated in June of that year), whereby New Zealand was able to purchase military equipment from the USA at favourable prices. The Lange Government subsequently defined a new defence strategy, based on increased self-reliance for the country's military forces. In June 1987 legislation banning nuclear-armed ships was formally enacted by the House of Representatives, despite strong opposition from the National Party. In September 1989 New Zealand agreed the terms for a joint venture with Australia to build as many as 12 naval frigates to patrol the South Pacific. The decision proved to be very contentious because of the high costs and because of allegations that the Government was succumbing to political pressure from Australia to return to the ANZUS alliance and abandon its independent anti-nuclear stance. In March 1990 the opposition National Party announced its support for the anti-nuclear policy, a position that it retained after its election to office in October.

Following the US Government's decision, in September 1991, to remove nuclear weapons from surface naval vessels, Bolger announced that his administration would reconsider the law banning visits from nuclear-armed and nuclear-propelled warships. The review would focus on the nuclear propulsion ban, which was seen as the obstacle to a renegotiated alliance with Australia and the USA. In July 1992 the USA announced that its warships no longer carried tactical nuclear weapons. In December the report commissioned by the Prime Minister was released. The committee of scientists concluded that the dangers of permitting nuclear-powered vessels to enter New Zealand waters were minimal. Despite these findings, no immediate change to the anti-nuclear legislation was envisaged. In February 1994 the Prime Minister welcomed the US decision to resume senior-level contacts with New Zealand, suspended since 1985. As relations continued to improve, in December 1994 the USA announced that nuclear-armed warships would not be dispatched to New Zealand, thus acknowledging the latter's ban. In August 1998, during a visit by the US Secretary of State, the Prime Minister of New Zealand strongly reiterated her country's long-standing ban on visits by nuclear-armed or nuclear-powered vessels. In July 2005 a private member's bill proposing the removal of the ban was rejected by a large majority by the House of Representatives. Following his attendance at the summit meeting of the Asia-Pacific Economic Co-operation (APEC) forum held in Auckland in September 1999, President Bill Clinton announced the end of the 14-year ban on New Zealand's participation in military exercises with the USA, in preparation for the dispatch of a multinational peace-keeping force to East Timor (now Timor-Leste—q.v.), of which New Zealand troops were to form part.

Meanwhile, New Zealand's trading relations with the USA were strained during 1999 by the latter's imposition of tariffs on imports of New Zealand lamb. However, in December 2000 the World Trade Organization (WTO, see p. 396) ruled in favour of New Zealand's case against the tariffs, and upheld the decision when the USA appealed against the ruling. The Prime Minister visited the USA in March 2002 for a series of meetings with the US President, Secretary of State and other senior officials, raising hopes among members of New Zealand's business community that a free trade agreement between the two nations could be achieved, despite New Zealand's adherence to its antinuclear policy.

The Government quickly expressed support for the USA following the suicide attacks of 11 September 2001 and offered to share intelligence in the effort to combat terrorism. In October the administration provided troops from the Special Air Service (SAS) for the US-led military campaign against the al-Qa'ida (Base) organization, held principally responsible for the attacks, and its Taliban hosts in Afghanistan. However, US policy in the 'war on terror' was a source of concern in New Zealand. In 2003, during the build-up to the US-led military campaign to remove the regime of Saddam Hussain in Iraq, the Government stated that it would favour action in Iraq only through the UN, a stance that was popularly supported in New Zealand. Relations with the US Administration were affected as a result. This was unlikely to help New Zealand's attempts to achieve a free trade agreement between the two nations. In May Prime Minister Clark warned the USA and the United Kingdom that by invading Iraq without the endorsement of a UN resolution, they had set a dangerous precedent, and that they might later regret unleashing the 'law of the jungle', particularly as China was set to become a dominant world power. However, New Zealand decided to provide humanitarian support for Iraq and sent a team of army engineers and defence force staff to assist in the rehabilitation of the country once the UN authorized reconstruction efforts following the ousting of Saddam Hussain. The Government had already sent forces to Afghanistan to assist in the reconstruction there and in March 2004 agreed to send SAS troops back to the South Asian country to take part in the search for senior al-Qa'ida leaders. In February 2005 the Prime Minister announced an extension to the New Zealand Defence Force's deployment in Afghanistan, and in March 2007 it was stated that an expanded force would remain in Afghanistan until at least September 2008. Meanwhile, in June 2006 New Zealand deported Rayed Mohammed Abdullah Ali, a Saudi-born Yemeni citizen who was alleged to have links with one of the perpetrators of the 11 September suicide attacks on the USA. In August 2007 it emerged that earlier in the year Air New Zealand had flown Australian soldiers to Kuwait and the United Arab Emirates, en route to military service in Iraq; the revelation was reported to have appalled Prime Minister Clark.

In July 1985 the *Rainbow Warrior*, the flagship of the antinuclear environmentalist group, Greenpeace (which was to have led a flotilla to Mururoa Atoll, in French Polynesia, to protest against France's testing of nuclear weapons in the South Pacific), was blown up and sunk in Auckland Harbour. One member of the crew was killed as a result of the explosion. Two agents of the French secret service were tried for manslaughter in November and sentenced to 10 years' imprisonment, initially in Auckland. The French Government made repeated requests for the release or repatriation of the agents, and in July 1986 the two Governments eventually reached an agreement, whereby the agents were to be transferred to detention on Hao Atoll, in French Polynesia, for three years. The French Government made a formal apology for its part in the sabotage operation, and paid the New Zealand Government $NZ7m. in compensation. By May 1988, however, both the agents had been taken back to France, ostensibly for medical reasons. When neither agent was returned to the atoll, Lange referred the matter to the UN: in May 1990 an arbitration panel ruled that France's repatriation of the agents constituted a substantial violation of the 1986 agreement, but it announced that the agents would not be required to return to Hao Atoll. France agreed to pay an initial US $2m. into a joint fund intended to foster close and friendly relations between the two countries. In April 1991 the French Prime Minister, Michel Rocard, visited New Zealand and again apologized for the sinking of the *Rainbow Warrior*, while reiterating that French testing of nuclear weapons in the Pacific was to continue. However, relations between the two countries deteriorated in July, following the French Government's announcement that it had conferred an honour for distinguished service on one of the two agents responsible for the sabotage of the *Rainbow Warrior*. The issue re-emerged in November, when a third French agent, also suspected of involvement in the 1985 incident, was arrested, at New Zealand's instigation, in Switzerland. In December 1991, however, the New Zealand Government decided against seeking the man's extradition, on the grounds that the case was now considered to be closed. In October 2006 the New Zealand Government responded in a similar manner to the naming of another French agent allegedly involved in the incident. In July 2005 an article in a French newspaper confirmed that the sinking of the *Rainbow Warrior* had been authorized by the then French President, François Mitterrand. France announced the suspension of its nuclear testing in the South Pacific in April 1992. In May 1993 the first French warship to visit New Zealand since 1985 entered Auckland Harbour. (Similarly, in June 1995 the first British warship to visit New Zealand for 12 years arrived in Wellington.)

In June 1995 President Chirac's announcement that France was to resume its nuclear-testing programme in the South Pacific aroused international condemnation. New Zealand suspended military relations with France, and the New Zealand ambassador to Paris was recalled. In August, in response to public pressure, the New Zealand Government dispatched a naval research vessel to the test area. The first in the new series of tests was carried out in early September. Later in the month the International Court of Justice ruled that it could not reopen New Zealand's case against France, brought in 1973. France's continuation of its testing programme, in defiance of world opinion, was a major issue at the Commonwealth heads of government meeting held in Auckland in November 1995. New Zealand's relations with the United Kingdom were strained by the British Prime Minister's apparent support for France's position; upon his arrival in Auckland, thousands of anti-nuclear demonstrators took to the streets to express their outrage. In March 1996 (the French tests having been concluded) France, the United Kingdom and the USA finally acceded to the South Pacific Nuclear-Free Zone Treaty (Treaty of Rarotonga—Pacific Islands Forum, see p. 380), thus opening the way to improved relations with New Zealand and other Pacific nations. In October 1997, following a two-day official visit to Paris by the New Zealand Prime Minister, the resumption of normal relations with France was declared.

Although New Zealand's trade with the People's Republic of China is of increasing significance, relations have been strained by the issue of China's nuclear-testing programme. Relations were further strained in September 1996 when the Dalai Lama, the exiled spiritual leader of Tibet, paid a four-day visit to New Zealand, where he was welcomed by the Prime Minister. In September 1997, however, the New Zealand Deputy Prime Minister expressed support for China's bid to join the WTO. In November 1998 New Zealand's decision to accord Taiwanese government officials similar privileges to those granted to representatives of the People's Republic provoked serious concern in China. During a visit to China in July 1999, however, the

Prime Minister of New Zealand reaffirmed her country's support for the 'one China' policy. An official visit to China by the Prime Minister in April 2001 was intended to improve New Zealand's trading position with the country, prior to its accession to the WTO. A senior Chinese official, on a diplomatic tour of the Asia-Pacific region, met with New Zealand's Deputy Prime Minister in April 2002, when New Zealand reconfirmed its 'one China' policy. The Chinese Prime Minister, Wen Jiabao, paid an official visit to New Zealand in April 2006. In March 2008 it was reported that China had agreed to grant 'most favoured nation' status to New Zealand as part of a free trade agreement between the two countries, which was signed in the following month.

New Zealand remained committed to its aim of the global elimination of all nuclear weapons, and in November 1996 was a co-sponsor of a UN resolution, overwhelmingly adopted by the General Assembly, to promote the establishment of a nuclear-weapons-free southern hemisphere. In December the Deputy Prime Minister of New Zealand announced that the Government was to finance a lawsuit against the United Kingdom that was being prepared by former servicemen (and veterans' widows) who had long campaigned for compensation for their exposure to the effects of British hydrogen bomb tests conducted in the South Pacific region in the late 1950s. In January 1997 New Zealand lodged a strong protest with the Japanese Government regarding the proposed route of a ship transporting nuclear waste to Japan from France. In March 1998 the New Zealand Prime Minister travelled to Japan, the first official visit by the country's head of government for 22 years. Relations with Japan, however, continued to be strained by a fishing dispute relating to Japan's perceived failure to conserve stocks of southern bluefin tuna, as agreed in a treaty of 1993, of which Australia was also a signatory. In July 1998, following a protest to Japan's ambassador in Wellington, New Zealand closed its ports to all Japanese tuna-fishing vessels. In August 1999 an international tribunal ruled in favour of New Zealand and Australia. In early 2000, the Labour Party's commitment to the protection of the environment having been reaffirmed, the new Government of New Zealand became embroiled in a further dispute with Japan, this time relating to the latter's controversial whaling programme. The Prime Minister, Helen Clark, announced her intention to raise the issue with Japan on an official visit to that country in April 2001, and expressed her Government's desire to pursue proposals for a southern seas whale sanctuary through the International Whaling Commission (see p. 404). In December 2000 New Zealand reiterated its opposition to nuclear waste shipments in response to the news that a shipment of high-level waste had left the United Kingdom for Japan, warning that the vessel must not enter New Zealand's exclusive economic zone. In October of that year New Zealand had ratified the Waigani Convention (signed by all South Pacific Forum members in 1995, except Marshall Islands and Tuvalu), which bans the export of hazardous and radioactive waste to the Pacific Islands.

Meanwhile, New Zealand continued to play an active role in Pacific island affairs. In 1997, in the quest for peace in Papua New Guinea, it participated in a peace-keeping force on the secessionist island of Bougainville. New Zealand hosted discussions between the Papua New Guinea Government and representatives of the secessionist movement, and in January 1998 a permanent ceasefire agreement was signed in Christchurch. The agreement was successfully implemented at the end of April. New Zealand strongly condemned the coup in Fiji in May 2000, which led to the overthrow of the Indian-led, elected Government of the country and prompted outbreaks of racially-motivated violence throughout the islands. New Zealand's Minister of Foreign Affairs and Trade, Phil Goff, led a Commonwealth delegation, together with his Australian counterpart, to negotiate with the ethnic militias involved in a coup in Solomon Islands in June 2000. The New Zealand naval frigate, Te Kaha, was dispatched to the islands to serve as a venue for peace talks, and the country pledged to contribute to a group of international peace-keepers following the signing of a ceasefire agreement in October. In mid-2003 New Zealand troops joined forces from Australia and several Pacific Islands to provide a peace-keeping force in Solomon Islands. New Zealand, together with Australia, deployed security forces to Tonga in November 2006 to restore stability following violent pro-reform demonstrations. In December Prime Minister Clark condemned the military coup in Fiji as an 'outrage'; the Government subsequently imposed defence, travel and development sanctions. Further sanctions were announced in June 2007 after New Zealand's high commissioner to Fiji was expelled because of his alleged interference in the country's internal affairs.

In September 2001 relations with Australia were strained by the failure of Ansett, the Melbourne-based airline. Ansett's owner, Air New Zealand, had been unable to find a purchaser for the loss-making company, which was therefore placed in receivership. In Melbourne irate Ansett staff blockaded an aircraft upon which the New Zealand Prime Minister was due to travel, and the Australian media demanded a boycott of New Zealand products. Nevertheless, in the same month the New Zealand Government helped Australia to resolve an international crisis, when it agreed to accept up to 150 of the refugees stranded aboard the Norwegian vessel, the MV Tampa (see the chapter on Christmas Island). Despite international pressure, neither Australia nor Indonesia (where they had embarked) were willing to accept the asylum-seekers for the duration of the processing of their claims. The Indonesian President, meanwhile, had paid a historic official visit to New Zealand in June 2001.

In July 2004 New Zealand's relations with Israel were strained when two alleged agents from the Israeli secret service, Mossad, were fined and sentenced to six-month prison terms by the Auckland High Court, having been convicted of fraudulently attempting to obtain New Zealand passports. Prime Minister Helen Clark stated that the available evidence strongly suggested that the men were acting as Israeli agents, but that no explanation had been forthcoming from the Israeli Government. New Zealand subsequently suspended senior-level diplomatic contact with Israel, demanding an apology for the incident. In connection with the deterioration in bilateral relations, in July several graves in a Jewish cemetery in Wellington were desecrated, in what was believed to have been the first anti-Semitic attack to take place in the country. In September, having been released from prison early, the Israelis were deported from the country. Relations remained strained into 2005. However, in June of that year the Israeli Government issued a formal apology for the incident, following which cordial diplomatic relations were restored.

As part of her golden jubilee tour of the Commonwealth, Queen Elizabeth II visited New Zealand in February 2002. Having previously stated that New Zealand's eventual transition to a republic was inevitable, the Prime Minister attracted some criticism for her absence from the country on the day of the Queen's arrival. In response to the international condemnation of the conduct of Zimbabwe's presidential election of March 2002, which subsequently led to that country's suspension from the Commonwealth, New Zealand followed the European Union, Canada and the USA in imposing a travel ban on senior members of the Zimbabwe Government in April. New Zealand also announced a ban on sales of armaments to Zimbabwe and declared that any New Zealand-based assets and investments found to belong to the Zimbabwean President or his associates would be 'frozen'.

Government

Executive power is vested in the British monarch, as Head of State, and is exercisable by an appointed representative, the Governor-General, who must be guided by the advice of the Executive Council (Cabinet), led by the Prime Minister. Legislative power is vested in the unicameral House of Representatives, elected for three years by universal adult suffrage. A system of mixed member proportional representation was introduced in 1996. At the 2005 election the legislature was expanded to 121 seats: 69 electorate members, including seven seats reserved for Maori, and 52 being chosen from party lists. The Governor-General appoints the Prime Minister and, on the latter's recommendation, other Ministers. The Cabinet is responsible to the House.

Defence

The ANZUS Security Treaty (see p. 422) was signed by New Zealand in 1951. New Zealand also participates in the Five-Power Defence Arrangements with Australia, Malaysia, Singapore and the United Kingdom. The total strength of active forces as assessed at November 2007 was 9,051: army 4,580, navy 2,034, air force 2,437. Reserves totalled 2,243. The defence budget for 2006/07 was estimated at $NZ2,170m.

Economic Affairs

In 2006, according to estimates by the World Bank, New Zealand's gross national income (GNI), measured at average 2004–06 prices, was US $112,416m., equivalent to US $27,250 per head (or US $27,220 per head on an international purchasing-power parity basis). During 1996–2006, it was estimated, the population increased at an average annual rate of 1.0%, while gross domestic product (GDP) per head increased, in real terms, by an average of 1.8% per year. Overall GDP increased, in real terms, at an average annual rate of 2.9% in 1996–2006. According to official figures, GDP growth reached 1.5% in 2006 and 3.1% in 2007.

Agriculture (including fishing, forestry and logging) contributed, along with mining, 6.2% of GDP in the year ending March 2005. About 7.1% of the employed labour force were engaged in the sector in 2006. The principal crops are barley, maize and wheat. Fruit (particularly kiwi fruit, apples and pears) and vegetables are also cultivated. New Zealand is a major producer of wool, although its significance as a source of export earnings has declined in recent years. Meat and dairy products are important, contributing 13.5% and 18.1% of export earnings, respectively, in 2006. The forestry industry showed strong expansion in the early 1990s. In 2006 exports of logs, wood and wood articles totalled $NZ2,136m. (equivalent to 6.2% of total export earnings). The fisheries sector is of increasing significance, exports in 2006 being worth $NZ1,195m. (equivalent to 3.5% of total export earnings). Between 1999/2000 and 2006/07 agricultural GDP (including fishing and forestry), together with mining, increased by an average of 1.3% per year. Compared with the previous year, the combined GDP of these sectors increased by 2.8% in 2005/06 but declined by 0.6% in 2006/07.

Industry (including mining, manufacturing, construction and utilities) engaged 22.3% of the employed labour force in 2006. The industrial sector provided 24.6% of GDP in the year ending March 2005. Between 1999/2000 and 2006/07 industrial GDP (excluding mining) increased at an average annual rate of 2.3%. Compared with the previous year, industrial GDP decreased by 0.6% in 2005/06 and by 2.0% in 2006/07.

Mining contributed only 1.1% of GDP in the year ending March 2005. New Zealand has substantial coal reserves; petroleum, natural gas, iron, gold and silica are also exploited. A considerable amount of natural gas is used to produce synthetic petrol.

Manufacturing contributed an estimated 15.3% of GDP in the year ending March 2005. The sector engaged 13.0% of the employed labour force in 2006. The principal branches of manufacturing are food products, printing and publishing, wood and paper products, chemicals, metals and metal products, machinery and transport equipment. Between 1999/2000 and 2006/07 manufacturing GDP increased by an average of 1.9% per year. Manufacturing GDP contracted by 1.6% in 2005/06 and by 2.1% in 2006/07.

Energy is derived mainly from domestic supplies of natural gas, coal and petroleum. Hydroelectric power supplied about 64.6% of total electricity output in 2004, gas 16.7% and coal 9.9%. Imports of petroleum and its products comprised 14.8% of the total value of merchandise imports in 2006.

The services sector provided 69.1% of GDP in 2004/05. This sector engaged 70.4% of the employed labour force in 2006. Tourism became the single largest source of foreign exchange in 1987/88. Receipts rose to $NZ6,377m. in 2006. In 2007 international visitor arrivals reached almost 2.5m. Between 1999/2000 and 2006/07 the GDP of the services sector increased at an average annual rate of 3.8%. Compared with the previous year, the sector's GDP expanded by 2.8% in 2006/07.

In 2006 New Zealand recorded a visible trade deficit of US $2,112m., and there was a deficit of US $9,381m. on the current account of the balance of payments. In 2006 the principal sources of imports were Australia (20.1%), the People's Republic of China (12.2%) and the USA (12.1%). Australia was also the principal market for exports in that year (20.4%), followed by the USA (13.1%) and Japan (10.3%). The principal exports in 2006 were dairy products, meat, logs, wood and wood articles, machinery and equipment and fruit. The principal imports were petroleum and petroleum products, boilers and mechanical appliances, vehicles, parts and accessories and electrical machinery and equipment.

In the year ending June 2008 a budgetary surplus of $NZ4,958m. was projected. Overseas debt was officially estimated to have reached a total of $NZ192,770m. in March 2007, when it represented 118% of GDP. The average rate of unemployment decreased to 3.6% of the labour force in 2007. Annual inflation averaged 2.1% in 1996–2006. Consumer prices increased by 2.4% in 2007.

New Zealand is a member of the Organisation for Economic Co-operation and Development (see p. 347), Asia-Pacific Economic Co-operation (APEC, see p. 176), the Pacific Community (see p. 377), the Pacific Islands Forum (see p. 380) and of the Cairns Group (see p. 464). New Zealand is also a member of the Colombo Plan (see p. 411) and the UN Economic and Social Commission for Asia and the Pacific (ESCAP, see p. 35). In 1982 New Zealand signed an agreement for a 'closer economic relationship' (CER) with Australia; trade barriers between the two countries were eliminated in July 1990.

Upon taking office in late 1999, the minority Labour Government embarked upon a programme of reforms in the health, education and housing sectors, in addition to focusing on projects aimed at benefiting the Maori population. The Government also curtailed the previous administration's programme of transferring state assets to the private sector. Upon its return to power at the election of September 2005, the minority Labour Government undertook to increase spending on health and education. However, following several consecutive years of steady expansion, in 2005 the rate of economic growth began to decelerate. New Zealand's external deficit had continued to increase, although as a percentage of GDP the current account deficit was estimated to have declined from the equivalent of 8.7% in 2006 to 7.9% in 2007 and was expected to decrease further, to 7.4% of GDP, in 2008. Nevertheless, by 2007 concerns with regard to the very low rates of household saving and rising levels of personal debt were increasingly being expressed, and in early 2008 the housing market was reported to be decelerating more quickly than anticipated. In 2007 New Zealand and Australia confirmed their intention to continue negotiations on the establishment of a single economic market in Australasia, and New Zealand's trade prospects were greatly enhanced by the signing of a free trade agreement with the People's Republic of China in April 2008. In 2007/08, however, exports were adversely affected by the strength of the New Zealand dollar, which in mid-2007 reached its highest level for 22 years against the US dollar. Inflationary pressures also became a cause for concern in late 2007, and by March 2008 the annual rate of inflation had reached 3.4%. Furthermore, following two consecutive years of contraction in the manufacturing sector, in April 2008 the Government conceded that its principal long-term economic challenge was to raise the country's productivity levels.

Education

State education is free and, for children between six and 16 years of age, compulsory. Primary education lasts from five to 11 years of age, after which children transfer to secondary schools until a maximum age of 18. As a proportion of children in the relevant age-groups, the enrolment ratios in 2005 were equivalent to 93% in pre-primary schools and 99% in primary schools. In 2002 enrolment at secondary level included 92% of the relevant age-group. In July 2004 a total of 450,196 students were enrolled in primary schools and 264,522 in secondary schools. In addition, 39,268 pupils attended composite schools, providing both primary and secondary education. There are eight universities, as well as 20 polytechnics, offering education at the post-secondary level. Changes introduced in 1991 obliged most students to pay part of their fees: parental income is tested to determine the level of allowances. Projected budgetary expenditure on education by the central Government in the financial year ending 30 June 2008 was $NZ10,321m., representing 14.4% of total spending.

Public Holidays

2008: 1–2 January (New Year), 6 February (Waitangi Day, anniversary of 1840 treaty), 21–24 March (Easter), 25 April (ANZAC Day, anniversary of 1915 landing at Gallipoli), 2 June (Queen's Official Birthday), 27 October (Labour Day), 25 December (Christmas Day), 26 December (Boxing Day).

2009: 1–2 January (New Year), 6 February (Waitangi Day, anniversary of 1840 treaty), 10–13 April (Easter), 25 April (ANZAC Day, anniversary of 1915 landing at Gallipoli), 1 June (Queen's Official Birthday), 26 October (Labour Day), 25 December (Christmas Day), 26 December (Boxing Day).

In addition to these national holidays, each region celebrates an anniversary day.

Weights and Measures

The metric system is in force.

Statistical Survey

Source (unless otherwise stated): Statistics New Zealand, Aorangi House, 85 Molesworth St, POB 2922, Wellington 1; tel. (4) 495-4600; fax (4) 472-9135; e-mail info@stats.govt.nz; internet www.stats.govt.nz.

Area and Population

AREA, POPULATION AND DENSITY

Area (sq km)	270,534*
Population (census results)†	
6 March 2001	3,737,277
7 March 2006	
Males	1,965,618
Females	2,062,329
Total	4,027,947
Population (official estimate at mid-year)	
2007	4,228,300
Density (per sq km) at mid-2007	15.6

* 104,454 sq miles.
† Figures refer to the population usually resident. The total population (including foreign visitors) was: 3,820,749 in 2001; 4,143,282 in 2006.

ADMINISTRATIVE REGIONS
(census of March 2006)

	Area (sq km)	Population	Density (per sq km)
North Island			
Northland	13,296	148,470	11.2
Auckland	5,048	1,303,068	258.1
Waikato	26,170	382,713	14.6
Bay of Plenty	11,428	257,379	22.5
Gisborne	8,355	44,499	5.3
Hawke's Bay Region	13,764	147,783	10.7
Taranaki	7,227	104,124	14.4
Manawatu-Wanganui	22,687	222,423	9.8
Wellington	8,056	448,959	55.7
Total North Island	116,031	3,059,418	26.4
South Island			
Tasman	14,538	44,625	3.1
Nelson	444	42,891	96.6
Marlborough	12,493	42,558	3.4
West Coast	23,351	31,326	1.3
Canterbury	45,845	521,832	11.4
Otago	31,476	193,800	6.2
Southland	25,392	90,876	3.6
Total South Island	153,540	967,908	38.1
Area outside regions	963	618	0.6
Total	270,534	4,027,947	14.9

Note: Totals may not be equal to the sum of components, owing to rounding.

PRINCIPAL CENTRES OF POPULATION
(population at census of 7 March 2006, enumerated totals, incl. visitors)

Auckland city	404,658	Palmerston North	75,543
Christchurch	348,435	Hastings district	70,842
Wellington (capital)	179,466	Rotorua district	65,901
Hamilton	129,249	Napier	55,359
Dunedin	118,683	Nelson	42,888
Tauranga	103,635		

BIRTHS, MARRIAGES AND DEATHS

	Live births*		Marriages†		Deaths*	
	Number	Rate (per '000)	Number	Rate (per '000)	Number	Rate (per '000)
2000	56,605	14.7	20,655	5.4	26,660	7.0
2001	55,799	14.4	19,972	5.1	27,825	7.2
2002	54,021	13.7	20,690	5.2	28,065	7.1
2003	56,134	13.9	21,419	5.3	28,010	7.0
2004	58,073	14.2	21,006	5.1	28,419	7.0
2005	57,745	14.0	20,470	5.0	27,034	6.5
2006	59,193	14.1	21,461	5.1	28,245	6.8
2007	64,044	15.1	n.a.	n.a.	28,522	6.7

* Data for births and deaths are tabulated by year of registration rather than by year of occurrence.
† Based on the resident population concept, replacing the previous de facto concept.

Expectation of life (years at birth, WHO estimates): 79.7 (males 77.5; females 81.9) in 2005 (Source: WHO, *World Health Statistics*).

IMMIGRATION AND EMIGRATION

	2004	2005	2006
Long-term immigrants*	80,479	78,963	82,732
Long-term emigrants†	65,371	71,992	68,123

* Figures refer to persons intending to remain in New Zealand for 12 months or more, and New Zealand citizens returning after an absence of 12 months or more.
† Figures refer to New Zealand citizens intending to remain abroad for 12 months or more, and overseas migrants departing after a stay of 12 months or more.

ECONOMICALLY ACTIVE POPULATION
('000 persons aged 15 years and over, excl. armed forces)

	2004	2005	2006
Agriculture, hunting, forestry	148.5	145.3	149.2
Fishing	3.1	2.7	1.7
Mining and quarrying	3.9	4.0	4.8
Manufacturing	292.1	282.5	275.8
Electricity, gas and water	9.5	8.1	8.2
Construction	152.3	161.6	184.1
Wholesale and retail trade; repair of motor vehicles, motorcycles and personal and household goods	359.3	363.3	368.4
Restaurants and hotels	94.2	99.6	96.6
Transport, storage and communications	118.5	118.8	116.7
Financial intermediation	60.6	65.8	70.7
Real estate, renting and business activities	218.1	234.8	246.9
Public administration and defence; compulsory social security	114.2	126.8	134.5
Education	161.1	163.1	163.0
Health and social work	180.3	187.1	193.4
Other community, social and personal service activities	94.9	101.7	92.0
Private households with employed persons	2.6	2.5	3.2
Activities not adequately defined	3.9	5.4	8.1
Total employed	2,017.1	2,072.9	2,117.2
Unemployed	82.0	79.3	82.6
Total labour force	2,099.1	2,152.2	2,199.8
Males	1,134.3	1,157.9	1,184.0
Females	964.7	994.3	1,015.8

Source: ILO.

NEW ZEALAND

Health and Welfare

KEY INDICATORS

Total fertility rate (children per woman, 2005)	2.0
Under-5 mortality rate (per 1,000 live births, 2005)	6
HIV/AIDS (% of persons aged 15–49, 2005)	0.1
Physicians (per 1,000 head, 2002)	2.1
Hospital beds (per 1,000 head, 2002)	6.0
Health expenditure (2004): US $ per head (PPP)	2,080.9
Health expenditure (2004): % of GDP	8.4
Health expenditure (2004): public (% of total)	77.4
Human Development Index (2005): ranking	19
Human Development Index (2005): value	0.943

For sources and definitions, see explanatory note on p. vi.

Agriculture

PRINCIPAL CROPS
('000 metric tons)

	2004	2005	2006
Wheat	319	256	256*
Barley	303	273	350*
Maize	168	162	162*
Oats	29	25	25*
Potatoes	500	500	500*
Dry peas	30	38*	32*
Cabbages and other brassicas	34*	40	40*
Lettuce and chicory*	35	38	38
Tomatoes	95	90	90
Cauliflowers and broccoli*	67	73	73
Pumpkins, squash and gourds	108	124	124
Green onions and shallots	250	165	165
Green peas	63	63	63
Carrots and turnips	65	65	65
Green corn*	112	n.a.	105
Grapes	166	142	142
Apples	546	524	524*
Pears*	40	32	32
Kiwi fruit	309	318	318

* FAO estimate(s).

Aggregate production ('000 metric tons, may include official, semi-official or estimated data): Total cereals 829 in 2004, 726 in 2005, 803 in 2006; Total roots and tubers 520 in 2004, 518 in 2005, 518 in 2006; Total vegetables (incl. melons) 1,008 in 2004, 940 in 2005, 938 in 2006; Total fruits (excl. melons) 1,165 in 2004, 1,131 in 2005, 1,131 in 2006.

Source: FAO.

LIVESTOCK
('000 head at 30 June)

	2004	2005	2006
Cattle	9,600	9,501	9,651
Sheep	39,271	39,928	40,107*
Goats	153	155*	155*
Pigs	389	341	341*
Horses	77	n.a.	77*
Chickens	20,000	20,939	20,939*
Ducks*	180	180	180
Geese and guinea fowls*	70	70	70
Turkeys*	75	75	75

* FAO estimate(s).
Source: FAO.

LIVESTOCK PRODUCTS
('000 metric tons)

	2004	2005	2006
Cattle meat	709.1	651.8	700.0
Sheep meat	518.2	542.8	500.0
Pig meat	51.9	50.5	50.5*
Chicken meat	155.9	165.0	149.0
Game meat	36.7	41.8	41.8*
Cows' milk	15,030	14,498	14,498*
Hen eggs	47.9†	50.9†	50.9*
Other poultry eggs*	2.4	2.5	2.5
Honey	8.9	9.7	9.7*
Wool: greasy	217.7	209.3	209.3*

* FAO estimate(s).
† Unofficial figure.
Source: FAO.

Forestry

ROUNDWOOD REMOVALS
('000 cubic metres)

	2004	2005	2006
Sawlogs, veneer logs and logs for sleepers	9,239	8,801	8,894
Pulpwood	3,315	3,317	3,110
Other industrial roundwood	7,207	6,887	7,250
Total	19,761	19,005	19,254

Source: FAO.

SAWNWOOD PRODUCTION
('000 cubic metres, year ending 31 March)

Species	2004/05	2005/06	2006/07
Radiata pine	4,193	4,018	4,171
Other introduced pines	6	5	6
Douglas fir	167	156	155
Rimu and miro	5	n.a.	3
Total (incl. others)	4,407	4,215	4,369

Source: Forestry Statistics Section, Ministry of Agriculture and Forestry, Wellington.

Fishing

('000 metric tons, live weight)

	2003	2004	2005
Capture*	550.9	545.9	535.4
Southern blue whiting	28.1	21.6	30.3
Blue grenadier (Hoki)	181.1	134.4	127.6
Pink cusk-eel	19.5	18.7	16.0
Oreo dories	15.3	19.6	17.4
Jack and horse mackerels	37.7	43.2	45.7
Snoek (Barracouta)	21.7	22.5	31.1
Wellington flying squid	43.7	84.4	87.8
Aquaculture	84.6	92.2	105.3†
New Zealand mussel	78.0	85.0	95.0
Total catch	635.6	638.2	640.7†

* Excluding catches made by chartered vessels and landed outside New Zealand.
† FAO estimate.

Note: Figures exclude aquatic mammals (recorded by number rather than by weight) and sponges. The number of whales and dolphins caught was: 33 in 2003; 31 in 2004; 12 in 2005.

Source: FAO.

Mining

('000 metric tons, unless otherwise indicated)

	2004	2005	2006
Coal (incl. lignite)	5,154	5,267	5,768
Gold (kg)	10,151	10,583	10,618
Crude petroleum ('000 barrels)	7,625	7,032	7,000*
Gross natural gas (million cu m)	4,500	4,223	4,100*
Liquid petroleum gas ('000 barrels)	1,710	1,946	1,900*
Iron sands	2,329	2,207	2,146
Silica sand	60.1	65.4	58.7
Limestone	4,312	5,226	5,032

* Estimate.

Source: US Geological Survey.

Industry

SELECTED PRODUCTS
(metric tons, unless otherwise indicated)

	2002	2003	2004
Wine (million litres)	89.0	55.0	119.2
Beer (sales, '000 hectolitres)	3,093	3,127	2,902
Chemical wood pulp*	711,361	623,437	743,671
Mechanical wood pulp*	838,963	795,394	852,787
Newsprint*	351,585	362,130	379,913
Other paper and paperboard*	518,155	447,512	537,350
Fibre board (cu m)*	880,301	868,539	873,408
Particle board (cu m)*	204,650	221,855	243,798
Veneer (cu m)*	552,738	637,556	680,687
Plywood (cu m)*	299,056	343,715	402,147
Jet fuels ('000 metric tons)	869	832	930
Motor spirit—petrol ('000 metric tons)	1,530	1,520	1,627
Gas-diesel (Distillate fuel) oils ('000 metric tons)	2,049	2,018	1,763
Residual fuel oils ('000 metric tons)	427	359	350
Cement ('000 metric tons)	1,090	1,100	1,110
Aluminium—unwrought ('000 metric tons):			
primary	335.0	342.0	351.4
secondary†	21.5	21.5	21.5
Electric energy (million kWh)	40,346	40,441	41,813

* Source: Ministry of Agriculture and Forestry, Wellington.
† Estimates.

Sources (unless otherwise stated): UN, *Industrial Commodity Statistics Yearbook* and *Monthly Bulletin of Statistics*; US Geological Survey; New Zealand Wine Online.

2005: Wine (million litres) 102.0; Chemical wood pulp (metric tons, provisional) 747,768; Mechanical wood pulp (metric tons, provisional) 852,961; Newsprint (metric tons) 379,628; Other paper and paperboard (metric tons) 541,711; Fibre board (cu m) 845,663; Particle board (cu m) 229,971; Veneer (cu m) 694,301; Plywood (cu m) 408,635 (Sources: New Zealand Wine Online; Ministry of Agriculture and Forestry, Wellington).

2006: Wine (million litres) 133.2; Chemical wood pulp (metric tons, provisional) 751,349; Mechanical wood pulp (metric tons, provisional) 749,679; Newsprint (metric tons) 367,064; Other paper and paperboard (metric tons) 573,396; Fibre board (cu m) 906,938; Particle board (cu m) 238,205; Veneer (cu m) 665,206; Plywood (cu m) 403,808 (Sources: New Zealand Wine Online; Ministry of Agriculture and Forestry, Wellington).

2007: Wine (million litres) 147.6; Newsprint (metric tons) 292,015; Other paper and paperboard (metric tons) 579,931; Fibre board (cu m) 836,755 (provisional); Particle board (cu m) 256,239 (provisional); Veneer (cu m) 688,312; Plywood (cu m) 421,794 (provisional) (Sources: New Zealand Wine Online; Ministry of Agriculture and Forestry, Wellington).

Finance

CURRENCY AND EXCHANGE RATES

Monetary Units
100 cents = 1 New Zealand dollar ($NZ).

Sterling, US Dollar and Euro Equivalents (31 December 2007)
£1 sterling = $NZ2.588;
US $1 = $NZ1.292;
€1 = $NZ1.902;
$NZ100 = £38.63 = US $77.40 = €52.58.

Average Exchange Rate (New Zealand dollars per US $)
2005   1.4203
2006   1.5421
2007   1.3601

BUDGET
($NZ million, year ending 30 June)

Revenue	2005/06	2006/07*	2007/08*
Taxation	51,973	51,658	54,173
Compulsory fees, fines, penalties and levies	3,411	3,691	3,693
Sales of goods and services	13,337	12,563	13,253
Interest revenue and dividends	5,828	3,072	3,366
Other	2,032	2,406	2,387
Total	76,581	73,390	76,872

Expenditure	2005/06	2006/07*	2007/08*
Social security and welfare	18,969	20,142	21,271
GSF pension expenses	1,671	645	629
Health	9,262	10,658	11,699
Education	10,430	10,204	10,321
Core government services	2,046	2,982	2,132
Law and order	2,420	2,800	3,076
Defence	1,339	1,489	1,597
Transport and communications	5,986	7,150	7,671
Economic and industrial services	6,334	4,994	5,879
Primary services	1,219	1,316	1,319
Heritage, culture and recreation	2,361	2,091	2,218
Housing and community development	758	908	961
Other	48	113	79
Finance costs	2,652	2,781	2,748
Total (incl. others)	65,084	67,853	71,914

* Forecasts.

Source: New Zealand Treasury, Wellington.

INTERNATIONAL RESERVES
(US $ million at 31 December)

	2004	2005	2006
IMF special drawing rights	34	34	33
Reserve position in IMF	474	165	119
Foreign exchange	6,439	8,694	13,916
Total	6,947	8,893	14,068

Source: IMF, *International Financial Statistics*.

MONEY SUPPLY
($NZ million at 31 December)

	2004	2005	2006
Currency outside banks	2,188	3,020	3,136
Demand deposits at banking institutions	19,578	18,957	19,610
Total money (incl. others)	21,789	22,471	31,784

Source: IMF, *International Financial Statistics*.

NEW ZEALAND

Statistical Survey

COST OF LIVING
(Consumer Price Index; base: 2000 = 100)

	2004	2005	2006
Food (incl. beverages)	110.3	113.1	116.2
Fuel and light	122.7	131.8	n.a.
Clothing (incl. footwear)	101.8	101.6	n.a.
Rent	97.6	100.0	n.a.
All items (incl. others)	109.7	113.0	116.8

Source: ILO.

NATIONAL ACCOUNTS
($NZ million at current prices, year ending 31 March)

Expenditure on the Gross Domestic Product

	2004/05	2005/06	2006/07
Government final consumption expenditure	26,335	28,542	30,890
Private final consumption expenditure	87,544	93,394	98,683
Change in inventories	1,646	848	−459
Gross fixed capital formation	35,571	38,084	38,568
Total domestic expenditure	151,095	160,869	167,682
Exports of goods and services	43,353	43,786	48,199
Less Imports of goods and services	44,512	47,444	50,528
GDP in market prices	149,936	157,210	165,353
GDP at constant 1995/96 prices	125,124	128,520	130,463

Gross Domestic Product by Economic Activity

	2002/03	2003/04	2004/05
Agriculture	6,924	7,539	7,656
Fishing	274	268	261
Forestry and logging	1,217	1,021	1,016
Mining and quarrying	1,489	1,339	1,581
Manufacturing	20,048	20,374	22,044
Electricity, gas and water	3,318	3,812	4,032
Construction	5,809	6,623	7,803
Wholesale and retail trade	17,292	18,560	19,271
Hotels and restaurants	2,418	2,585	2,844
Transport, storage and communications	9,445	10,011	10,615
Financial intermediation (incl. insurance)	8,033	8,651	9,041
Property and business activities	18,645	20,161	21,728
Ownership of dwellings	8,780	9,280	9,669
Public administration and defence	5,487	5,842	6,344
Education	5,170	5,624	6,087
Health and community services	6,761	7,371	8,108
Cultural and recreational services	3,105	3,407	3,545
Personal and other services	1,911	2,042	2,248
Sub-total	126,128	134,512	143,892
Less Financial intermediation services indirectly measured	4,725	4,875	5,108
Gross value added at basic prices	121,403	129,637	138,784
Goods and services tax on production	8,851	9,571	10,282
Import duties	742	719	870
GDP in market prices	130,996	139,928	149,936

BALANCE OF PAYMENTS
(US $ million)

	2004	2005	2006
Exports of goods f.o.b.	20,466	21,956	22,491
Imports of goods f.o.b.	−21,894	−24,615	−24,602
Trade balance	−1,428	−2,659	−2,112
Exports of services	7,898	8,306	7,874
Imports of services	−7,215	−8,209	−7,774
Balance on goods and services	−746	−2,562	−2,012
Other income received	1,530	1,451	1,430
Other income paid	−7,404	−9,021	−9,308
Balance on goods, services and income	−6,619	−10,132	−9,890
Current transfers received	901	1,243	1,291
Current transfers paid	−781	−867	−782
Current balance	−6,499	−9,756	−9,381
Capital account (net)	156	−197	−217
Direct investment abroad	884	1,130	−737
Direct investment from abroad	2,780	1,690	7,941
Portfolio investment assets	−2,002	−587	−944
Portfolio investment liabilities	8,072	447	−377
Other investment assets	−52	4,577	−1,196
Other investment liabilities	−1,162	3,955	8,927
Net errors and omissions	−1,555	1,149	242
Overall balance	620	2,410	4,258

Source: IMF, *International Financial Statistics*.

External Trade

PRINCIPAL COMMODITIES
($NZ million)

Imports (c.i.f.)	2004	2005	2006
Vehicles, parts and accessories	5,439	5,407	4,771
Nuclear reactors, boilers, machinery and mechanical appliances	4,785	5,055	5,157
Petroleum, petroleum products, etc.	3,682	4,525	6,029
Electrical machinery and equipment	3,252	3,289	3,554
Textiles and textile articles	1,602	1,669	1,846
Plastic and plastic articles	1,322	1,406	1,543
Iron and steel and articles	1,212	1,302	738
Optical, medical and measuring equipment	1,076	1,104	1,216
Total (incl. others)	34,915	37,279	40,716

Exports f.o.b.	2004	2005	2006
Dairy produce; birds' eggs; natural honey; edible products or animal origin, not elsewhere specified or included	5,007	5,198	6,255
Meat and edible offal	4,576	4,655	4,668
Logs, wood and wood articles	2,101	1,913	2,136
Nuclear reactors, boilers, machinery and mechanical appliances; parts thereof	1,603	1,683	1,886
Fruit and nuts; peel of citrus fruit or melons	1,391	1,168	1,202
Fish, crustaceans and molluscs	1,130	1,132	1,195
Aluminium and aluminium articles	1,061	1,085	1,484
Electrical machinery and equipment	1,026	1,010	1,099
Total (incl. others)*	30,712	30,817	34,634

* Including re-exports.

NEW ZEALAND

PRINCIPAL TRADING PARTNERS
($NZ million)

Imports (c.i.f.)*	2004	2005	2006
Australia	7,812	7,682	8,194
Belgium	331	314	295
Canada	622	479	681
China, People's Republic	3,376	4,033	4,964
France	1,038	1,005	778
Germany	1,817	1,804	1,801
Indonesia	422	586	674
Italy	836	874	832
Japan	3,895	4,082	3,709
Korea, Republic	993	1,024	1,191
Malaysia	839	945	1,196
Netherlands	286	386	296
Singapore	973	1,240	1,850
Sweden	354	366	343
Taiwan	798	880	729
Thailand	662	951	1,030
United Arab Emirates	343	513	576
United Kingdom	1,172	1,192	1,112
USA	3,916	4,065	4,924
Total (incl. others)	34,915	37,279	40,716

* Excluding specie and gold.

Exports*	2004	2005	2006
Australia	6,400	6,589	7,076
Belgium	519	515	627
Canada	521	524	553
China, People's Republic	1,745	1,566	1,875
Fiji	341	353	371
France	373	387	387
Germany	727	789	882
Hong Kong	560	524	560
Indonesia	411	465	613
Italy	439	446	513
Japan	3,443	3,260	3,556
Korea, Republic	1,165	1,081	1,358
Malaysia	523	468	497
Mexico	394	437	424
Philippines	500	504	512
Saudi Arabia	326	379	411
Singapore	362	428	540
Taiwan	704	773	768
Thailand	365	338	438
United Kingdom	1,456	1,432	1,694
USA	4,436	4,373	4,540
Total (incl. others)	30,712	30,817	34,634

* Including re-exports, but excluding specie and gold.

Transport

RAILWAYS
(traffic, year ending 30 June)

	2000/01	2001/02	2002/03
Freight ('000 metric tons)	14,461	14,330	14,822
Passengers ('000)	12,714	12,521	12,300*

* Excludes passengers on the Tranz Scenic network.

Source: Tranz Rail Ltd, Wellington.

ROAD TRAFFIC
(vehicles licensed at June)

	2005	2006	2007
Passenger cars	2,211,791	2,254,669	2,300,094
Taxis	8,172	8,011	8,069
Buses and service coaches	15,671	16,486	17,198
Trailers and caravans	408,982	420,289	435,633
Motorcycles and mopeds	47,999	57,684	65,658
Tractors	26,521	27,124	27,510
Trucks	399,843	408,757	417,886

Source: Land Transport New Zealand.

Statistical Survey

SHIPPING
Merchant Fleet
(registered at 31 December)

	2004	2005	2006
Number of vessels	173	174	171
Displacement (grt)	206,415	215,705	206,573

Source: Lloyd's Register-Fairplay, *World Fleet Statistics*.

Vessels Handled
(international, '000 grt)

	1993	1994	1995
Entered	37,603	39,700	48,827
Cleared	35,128	37,421	42,985

Source: UN, *Statistical Yearbook*.

International Sea-borne Freight Traffic
('000 metric tons, year ending 30 June)

	2004/05	2005/06	2006/07*
Goods loaded	21,894	21,840	22,986
Goods unloaded	19,164	18,119	18,499

* Provisional.

CIVIL AVIATION
(domestic and international traffic on scheduled services)

	2001	2002	2003
Kilometres flown (million)	190	180	164
Passengers carried ('000)	11,467	11,285	10,334
Passenger-km (million)	23,079	23,323	23,280
Total metric ton-km (million)	2,846	2,787	3,203

Source: UN, *Statistical Yearbook*.

Tourism

VISITOR ARRIVALS

Country of residence	2005	2006	2007
Australia	874,738	903,504	950,206
China, People's Republic	87,850	105,716	120,804
Germany	57,549	59,353	59,765
Japan	154,925	136,401	121,652
Korea, Republic	112,005	111,361	99,453
United Kingdom	306,815	294,812	292,717
USA	214,507	225,629	216,027
Total (incl. others)	2,382,950	2,421,561	2,465,680

Tourism receipts ($NZ million): 6,298.4 in 2004; 6,134.7 in 2005; 6,377.1 in 2006.

Source: partly Tourism Research Council, Wellington.

Communications Media

	2003	2004	2005
Telephones ('000 main lines in use)	1,798.0	1,800.5	1,729.0
Mobile cellular telephones ('000 subscribers)	2,599	3,027	3,530
Personal computers ('000 in use)	1,771	1,924	1,924
Internet users ('000)	2,110	2,350	2,754
Broadband subscribers ('000)	83.0	191.7	331.0

2006 ('000): Internet users 3,200; Broadband subscribers 576.1.

Television receivers ('000 in use): 2,130 in 2001.

Radio receivers ('000 in use): 3,750 in 1997.

Facsimile machines ('000 in use, year ending 31 March 1996): 65.

Daily newspapers: 23 (circulation 739,000 copies) in 2004.

Non-daily newspapers: 2 (circulation 311,380 copies) in 2002.

Book production (1999): 4,800 titles.

Sources: partly International Telecommunication Union; UNESCO, *Statistical Yearbook*; UN, *Statistical Yearbook*.

Education

(July 2004)

	Institutions	Teachers (full-time equivalent)	Students
Early childhood services	4,374	11,485[2]	184,513[3]
Primary schools[4]	2,124	26,011[2]	450,196
Composite schools[5]	147	2,403[2]	39,268
Secondary schools[6]	352	19,180[2]	264,522
Special schools	47	945[2]	2,672
Polytechnics	20[7]	4,223[7]	117,514
Colleges of education	4[7]	491[7]	11,107
Universities	8[7]	6,562[7]	138,583
Wananga[8]	3[7]	781[7]	41,644
Private training establishments receiving government grants	522[7]	4,177[7]	59,158

[1] Excludes 1,205 play-centre teaching staff and Te Kohanga Reo personnel (responsible for Maori 'Language Nests').
[2] Teachers employed in state schools at 1 March 2004.
[3] Includes children on the regular roll of the Correspondence School, kindergartens, playcentres, Te Kohanga Reo, Early Childhood Development Unit funded playgroups, Early Childhood Development Unit funded Pacific Islands language groups, education and care centres (incl. home-based childcare).
[4] Primary schools include Full Primary Years 1–8, Contributing Years 1–6, Intermediate Years 7–8.
[5] Composite schools provide both primary and secondary education (includes area schools and the Correspondence School).
[6] Secondary schools include Years 7–15, Years 9–15.
[7] 2003 figure.
[8] Tertiary institutions providing polytechnic and university level programmes specifically for Maori students, with an emphasis on Maori language and culture.

Source: Ministry of Education, Wellington.

Directory

The Constitution

New Zealand has no written constitution. The political system is closely modelled on that of the United Kingdom (with an element of proportional representation introduced to the legislature in 1996). As in the United Kingdom, constitutional practice is an accumulation of convention, precedent and tradition. A brief description of New Zealand's principal organs of government is given below:

HEAD OF STATE

Executive power is vested in the monarch and is exercisable in New Zealand by the monarch's personal representative, the Governor-General.

In the execution of the powers and authorities vested in him or her, the Governor-General must be guided by the advice of the Executive Council.

EXECUTIVE COUNCIL

The Executive Council consists of the Governor-General and all the Ministers. Two members, exclusive of the Governor-General or the presiding member, constitute a quorum. The Governor-General appoints the Prime Minister and, on the latter's recommendation, the other Ministers.

HOUSE OF REPRESENTATIVES

Parliament comprises the Crown and the House of Representatives. At the 1996 general election, a system of mixed member proportional representation was introduced. The House of Representatives comprises 120 members: 67 electorate members (five seats being reserved for Maoris) and 53 members chosen from party lists. They are designated 'Members of Parliament' and are elected for three years, subject to the dissolution of the House before the completion of their term.

Everyone over the age of 18 years may vote in the election of members for the House of Representatives. Since August 1975 any person, regardless of nationality, ordinarily resident in New Zealand for 12 months or more and resident in an electoral district for at least one month is qualified to be registered as a voter. Compulsory registration of all electors except Maoris was introduced at the end of 1924; it was introduced for Maoris in 1956. As from August 1975, any person of the Maori race, which includes any descendant of such a person, may enrol on the Maori roll for the particular Maori electoral district in which that person resides.

By the Electoral Amendment Act 1937, which made provision for a secret ballot in Maori elections, Maori electors were granted the same privileges, in the exercise of their vote, as general electors.

In local government the electoral franchise is the same.

The Government

Head of State: HM Queen ELIZABETH II (acceded to the throne 6 February 1952).

Governor-General and Commander-in-Chief: Judge ANAND SATYANAND (assumed office 23 August 2006).

CABINET
(April 2008)

A coalition of the Labour Party and the Progressive Party.

Prime Minister and Minister for Arts, Culture and Heritage: HELEN CLARK.

Deputy Prime Minister, Attorney-General, Minister of Finance, Minister in charge of Treaty of Waitangi Negotiations, and Leader of the House: Dr MICHAEL CULLEN.

Minister of Agriculture, for Biosecurity, of Fisheries and of Forestry: JIM ANDERTON.

Minister of Defence, of Corrections, of Trade and for Disarmament and Arms Control: PHIL GOFF.

Minister of Justice, of Police and of Transport: ANNETTE KING.

Minister for Economic Development, for Tertiary Education and of Research, Science and Technology: PETE HODGSON.

Minister of Maori Affairs: PAREKURA HOROMIA.

Minister of Education: CHRIS CARTER.

NEW ZEALAND

Minister of Health and for Communications and Information Technology: DAVID CUNLIFFE.
Minister for the Environment, of Labour, of Broadcasting and for State Owned Enterprises: TREVOR MALLARD.
Minister for Social Development and Employment, for Senior Citizens and for the Community and Voluntary Sector: RUTH DYSON.
Minister of Commerce and for Food Safety: LIANNE DALZIEL.
Minister of State Services, of Energy and for Land Information: DAVID PARKER.
Minister of Customs, of Local Government and of Youth Affairs: NANAIA MAHUTA.
Minister of Immigration and for Sport and Recreation: CLAYTON COSGROVE.
Minister of Internal Affairs, of Civil Defence, for Courts and of Veterans' Affairs: RICK BARKER.
Minister of Tourism: DAMIEN O'CONNOR.
Minister of Conservation and of Women's Affairs: STEVE CHADWICK.
Minister for the Accident Compensation Corporation and of Housing: MARYAN STREET.
Minister for Building and Construction: SHANE JONES.

MINISTERS OUTSIDE CABINET
(April 2008)

Minister of Foreign Affairs and for Racing: WINSTON PETERS.
Minister of Revenue: PETER DUNNE.
Minister of Consumer Affairs: JUDITH TIZARD.
Minister for Transport Safety: HARRY DUYNHOVEN.
Minister of Pacific Island Affairs: Luamanuvao WINNIE LABAN.
Minister of Statistics: DARREN HUGHES.
Ministers of State: MITA RIRINUI, MAHARA OKEROA.

MINISTRIES AND GOVERNMENT DEPARTMENTS

Department of the Prime Minister and Cabinet: Executive Wing, Parliament Bldgs, Wellington; tel. (4) 817-9700; fax (4) 472-3181; e-mail admin@dpmc.govt.nz; internet www.dpmc.govt.nz.
Ministry of Agriculture and Forestry: 25 The Terrace, POB 2526, Wellington; tel. (4) 894-0100; fax (4) 894-0720; e-mail info@maf.govt.nz; internet www.maf.govt.nz.
Department of Building and Housing: Level 6, 86 Customhouse Quay, POB 10-729, Wellington; tel. (4) 494-0260; fax (4) 494-0290; internet www.dbh.govt.nz.
Ministry of Civil Defence and Emergency Management: Level 9, 22 The Terrace, POB 5010, Wellington; tel. (4) 473-7363; fax (4) 473-7369; e-mail emergency.management@dia.govt.nz; internet www.civildefence.govt.nz.
Department of Conservation: POB 10420, Wellington 1643; tel. (4) 471-0726; fax (4) 471-1082; e-mail tsmith@doc.govt.nz; internet www.doc.govt.nz.
Ministry for Culture and Heritage: POB 5364, Wellington; tel. (4) 499-4229; fax (4) 499-4490; e-mail info@mch.govt.nz; internet www.mch.govt.nz.
Ministry of Defence: POB 12703, Molesworth St, Wellington; tel. (4) 496-0999; fax (4) 496-0859; e-mail info@defence.govt.nz; internet www.defence.govt.nz.
Ministry of Economic Development: POB 1473, 33 Bowen St, Wellington; tel. (4) 472-0030; fax (4) 473-4638; e-mail info@med.govt.nz; internet www.med.govt.nz.
Ministry of Education: 45–47 Pipitea St, Thorndon, Wellington; tel. (4) 463-8000; fax (4) 463-8001; e-mail enquiries.national@minedu.govt.nz; internet www.minedu.govt.nz.
Ministry for the Environment: 23 Kate Sheppard Place, POB 10-362, Wellington; tel. (4) 439-7400; fax (4) 439-7700; e-mail library@mfe.govt.nz; internet www.mfe.govt.nz.
Ministry of Fisheries: ASB Bank House, 101–103 The Terrace, POB 1020, Wellington; tel. (4) 470-2600; fax (4) 819-4601; e-mail info@fish.govt.nz; internet www.fish.govt.nz.
Ministry of Foreign Affairs and Trade: Private Bag 18901, Wellington; tel. (4) 439-8000; fax (4) 472-9596; e-mail enquiries@mfat.govt.nz; internet www.mfat.govt.nz.
Ministry of Health: 133 Molesworth St, POB 5013, Wellington; tel. (4) 496-2000; fax (4) 496-2340; e-mail emailmoh@moh.govt.nz; internet www.moh.govt.nz.
Department of Internal Affairs: 46 Waring Taylor St, POB 805, Wellington; tel. (4) 495-7200; fax (4) 495-7222; e-mail info@dia.govt.nz; internet www.dia.govt.nz.

Ministry of Justice: POB 180, Wellington; tel. (4) 918-8800; fax (4) 918-8820; e-mail reception@justice.govt.nz; internet www.justice.govt.nz.
Department of Labour: POB 3705, Wellington; tel. (4) 915-4000; fax (4) 915-40151; e-mail info@dol.govt.nz; internet www.dol.govt.nz.
Ministry of Maori Development (Te Puni Kokiri): POB 3943, Wellington 6015; tel. (4) 819-6000; fax (4) 819-6299; e-mail tpkinfo@tpk.govt.nz; internet www.tpk.govt.nz.
Ministry of Pacific Island Affairs: POB 833, Wellington; tel. (4) 473-4493; fax (4) 473-4301; e-mail contact@minpac.govt.nz; internet www.minpac.govt.nz.
Ministry of Research, Science and Technology: POB 5336, Wellington 6145; tel. (4) 917-2900; fax (4) 471-1284; e-mail info@morst.govt.nz; internet www.morst.govt.nz.
Ministry of Social Development: Bowen State Bldg, Bowen St, POB 1556, Wellington 6140; tel. (4) 916-3300; fax (4) 918-0099; e-mail information@msd.govt.nz; internet www.msd.govt.nz.
State Services Commission: POB 329, Wellington; tel. (4) 495-6600; fax (4) 495-6686; e-mail commission@ssc.govt.nz; internet www.ssc.govt.nz.
Statistics New Zealand (Tatauranga Aotearoa): POB 2922, Wellington; tel. (4) 931-4600; fax (4) 931-4030; e-mail info@stats.govt.nz; internet www.stats.govt.nz.
Ministry of Tourism: POB 5640, Wellington; tel. (4) 498-7440; fax (4) 498-7445; e-mail info@tourism.govt.nz; internet www.tourism.govt.nz.
Ministry of Transport: POB 3175, Wellington; tel. (4) 439-9000; fax (4) 439-9001; e-mail info@transport.govt.nz; internet www.transport.govt.nz.
Treasury: POB 3724, Wellington 6140; tel. (4) 472-2733; fax (4) 473-0982; e-mail info@treasury.govt.nz; internet www.treasury.govt.nz.
Ministry of Women's Affairs: POB 10-049, Wellington; tel. (4) 915-7112; fax (4) 916-1604; e-mail mwa@mwa.govt.nz; internet www.mwa.govt.nz.
Ministry of Youth Development: POB 1556, Wellington; tel. (4) 916-3300; fax (4) 918-0091; e-mail mydinfo@myd.govt.nz; internet www.myd.govt.nz.

Legislature

HOUSE OF REPRESENTATIVES

Speaker: MARGARET WILSON.
General Election, 17 September 2005

Party	Number of votes	% of votes	Party seats	List seats	Total seats
NZ Labour Party	935,319	41.10	31	19	50
NZ National Party	889,813	39.10	31	17	48
New Zealand First	130,115	5.72	—	7	7
Green Party	120,521	5.30	—	6	6
Maori Party	48,263	2.12	4	—	4*
United Future NZ	60,860	2.67	1	2	3
ACT New Zealand	34,469	1.51	1	1	2
Progressive Party	26,441	1.16	1	—	1
Total (incl. others)	2,286,190	100.00	69	52	121

* Includes two guaranteed seats.

Election Commission

Electoral Commission of New Zealand: POB 3050, Wellington; tel. (4) 474-0670; fax (4) 474-0674; e-mail info@elections.govt.nz; internet www.elections.org.nz; independent; Pres. Justice ANDREW MCGECHAN; Chief Exec. Dr HELENA CATT.

Political Organizations

In March 2008 16 political parties were registered.

ACT New Zealand: Unit A, 11–13 Clovernook Rd, POB 99-651, Newmarket, Auckland; tel. (9) 523-0470; fax (9) 523-0472; e-mail info@voteact.org.nz; internet www.act.org.nz; f. 1994; supports free enterprise, tax reform and choice in education and health; Pres. GARRY MALLETT; Leader RODNEY HIDE.

Direct Democracy Party: POB 43146, Mangere, Auckland; tel. (7) 286-8789; e-mail secretary@ddp.co.nz; internet www.ddp.co.nz; f. 2005; Leader KELVYN ALP.

NEW ZEALAND

Green Party of Aotearoa—New Zealand: POB 11-652, Wellington; tel. (4) 801-5102; fax (4) 801-5104; e-mail greenparty@greens.org.nz; internet www.greens.org.nz; f. 1989; fmrly Values Party, f. 1972; Co-Leaders JEANETTE FITZSIMONS, RUSSEL NORMAN.

Maori Party: POB 50-271, Porirua; tel. (4) 471-9900; fax (4) 499-7269; e-mail hekeretari2@maoriparty.com; internet www.maoriparty.com; f. 2004; Co-Leaders Dr PITA SHARPLES, Hon. TARIANA TURIA; Pres. Dr WHATARANGI WINIATA.

The New Zealand Democratic Party for Social Credit: POB 18-907, New Brighton, Christchurch 8641; tel. (7) 829-5157; fax (3) 382-9544; e-mail naitchison@xtra.co.nz; internet www.democrats.org.nz; f. 1953 as Social Credit Political League; subsequently known as New Zealand Democratic Party Inc; liberal; Pres. NEVILLE AITCHISON; Leader STEPHNIE DE RUYTER.

New Zealand First: Parliament Bldgs, Wellington; tel. (4) 471-9292; fax (4) 472-8557; e-mail info@nzfirst.org.nz; internet www.nzfirst.org.nz; f. 1993 by fmr National Party mems; Leader WINSTON PETERS; Pres. DAIL JONES.

New Zealand Labour Party: Fraser House, POB 784, Wellington; tel. (4) 384-7649; fax (4) 384-8060; e-mail labour@labour.org.nz; internet www.labour.org.nz; f. 1916; advocates an organized economy guaranteeing an adequate standard of living to every person able and willing to work; Pres. MIKE WILLIAMS; Parl. Leader HELEN CLARK; Gen. Sec. MIKE SMITH.

New Zealand National Party: Willbank House, 14th Floor, 57 Willis St, POB 1155, Wellington 6001; tel. (4) 472-5211; fax (4) 478-1622; e-mail hq@national.org.nz; internet www.national.org.nz; f. 1936; centre-right; supports private enterprise and competitive business, together with maximum personal freedom; Pres. JUDY KIRK; Parl. Leader JOHN KEY.

Progressive Party: POB 33-243, Christchurch 8030; tel. (3) 377-7679; fax (3) 377-7673; e-mail contact@progressive.org.nz; internet www.progressive.org.nz; f. 2002 as the Progressive Coalition to contest the general election; name changed as above April 2004; Leader JIM ANDERTON; Gen. Sec. PHIL CLEARWATER.

United Future New Zealand (UFNZ): Bowen House, Parliament Bldgs, Wellington; tel. (4) 471-9410; e-mail unitedfuture@parliament.govt.nz; internet www.unitedfuture.org.nz; f. 1995 by four mems of National Party, two mems of Labour Party and leader of Future New Zealand; Leader PETER DUNNE; Pres. DENISE KRUM.

Other parties registered in 2008 included the Alliance, the Aotearoa Legalise Cannabis Party, Libertarianz, the Family Party and the Republic of New Zealand Party.

Diplomatic Representation

EMBASSIES AND HIGH COMMISSIONS IN NEW ZEALAND

Argentina: Sovereign Assurance House, 14th Floor, 142 Lambton Quay, POB 5430, Lambton Quay, Wellington; tel. (4) 472-8330; fax (4) 472-8331; e-mail enzel@arg.org.nz; internet www.arg.org.nz; Ambassador PEDRO R. HERRERA.

Australia: 72–76 Hobson St, Thorndon, POB 4036, Wellington; tel. (4) 473-6411; fax (4) 498-7135; e-mail nzinbox@dfat.gov.au; internet www.australia.org.nz; High Commissioner JOHN DAUTH.

Brazil: Level 9, Deloitte House, 10 Brandon St, Wellington 6011; tel. (4) 473-3516; fax (4) 473-3517; e-mail brasemb@brazil.org.nz; internet www.brazil.org.nz; Ambassador MANOEL GOMES-PEREIRA.

Canada: Level 11, 125 The Terrace, POB 8047, Wellington; tel. (4) 473-9577; fax (4) 471-2082; e-mail wlgtn@international.gc.ca; internet www.wellington.gc.ca; High Commissioner PENNY REEDIE.

Chile: 19 Bolton St, POB 3861, Wellington; tel. (4) 471-6270; fax (4) 472-5324; e-mail echile@xtra.co.nz; internet www.embchile.co.nz; Ambassador JUAN A. SALAZAR SPARKS.

China, People's Republic: 2–6 Glenmore St, POB 17-257, Karori, Wellington; tel. (4) 472-1382; fax (4) 499-0419; e-mail administration@chinaembassy.org.nz; internet www.chinaembassy.org.nz; Ambassador ZHANG YUANYUAN.

Cuba: 35 Hobson St, Thorndon, Wellington; tel. (4) 472-3748; fax (4) 473-2958; e-mail embajada@xtra.co.nz; Ambassador JOSÉ LUIS ROBAINA GARCÍA.

Fiji: 31 Pipitea St, Thorndon, POB 3940, Wellington; tel. (4) 473-5401; fax (4) 499-1011; e-mail viti@paradise.net.nz; internet www.fiji.org.nz; High Commissioner SAKIUSA RAKAI (acting).

France: Sovereign House, 13th Floor, 34–42 Manners St, POB 11-343, Wellington; tel. (4) 384-2555; fax (4) 384-2579; e-mail amba.france@actrix.co.nz; internet www.ambafrance-nz.org; Ambassador MICHEL LEGRAS.

Germany: 90–92 Hobson St, POB 1687, Wellington; tel. (4) 473-6063; fax (4) 473-6069; e-mail german.embassy@iconz.co.nz; internet www.wellington.diplo.de; Ambassador JÖRG HANS ZIMMERMANN.

Greece: 5–7 Willeston St, 10th Floor, POB 24-066, Wellington; tel. (4) 473-7775; fax (4) 473-7441; e-mail info@greece.org.nz; Ambassador EVANGELOS DAMIANAKIS.

Holy See: Apostolic Nunciature, 112 Queen's Drive, Lyall Bay, POB 14-044, Wellington 6041; tel. (4) 387-3470; fax (4) 387-8170; e-mail nuntius@ihug.co.nz; Apostolic Nuncio Most Rev. CHARLES D. BALVO (Titular Archbishop of Castello).

India: 180 Molesworth St, POB 4045, Wellington 1; tel. (4) 473-6390; fax (4) 499-0665; e-mail hicomind@hicomind.org.nz; internet www.hicomind.org.nz; High Commissioner K. P. ERNEST.

Indonesia: 70 Glen Road, Kelburn, POB 3543, Wellington; tel. (4) 475-8698; fax (4) 475-9374; e-mail kbriwell@ihug.co.nz; internet www.indonesianembassy.org.nz; Ambassador AMRIS HASSAN.

Iran: POB 14733, Kilbirnie, Wellington; tel. (4) 386-2983; fax (4) 386-3065; e-mail info@iranembassy.org.nz; internet www.iranembassy.org.nz; Ambassador MORTEZA RAHMANI-MOVAHED.

Italy: 34–38 Grant Rd, Thorndon, POB 463, Wellington 1; tel. (4) 473-5339; fax (4) 472-7255; e-mail ambasciata.wellington@esteri.it; internet www.ambwellington.esteri.it/ambasciata_wellington; Ambassador Dr GIOACCHINO TRIZZINO.

Japan: Majestic Centre, Levels 18–19, 100 Willis St, POB 6340, Wellington 1; tel. (4) 473-1540; fax (4) 471-2951; e-mail japan.emb@eoj.org.nz; internet www.nz.emb-japan.go.jp; Ambassador TAKAHASHI TOSHIHIRO.

Korea, Republic: ASB Bank Tower, Level 11, 2 Hunter St, POB 11-143, Wellington; tel. (4) 473-9073; fax (4) 472-3865; e-mail info@koreanembassy.org.nz; internet www.koreanembassy.org.nz; Ambassador LEE JOON-GYU.

Malaysia: 10 Washington Ave, Brooklyn, POB 9422, Wellington; tel. (4) 385-2439; fax (4) 385-6973; e-mail mwwelton@xtra.co.nz; internet www.kln.gov.my/perwakilan/wellington; High Commissioner Dato' SOPIAN BIN AHMAD.

Mexico: AMP Chambers, Level 2, 185–187 Featherston St, POB 11-510, Wellington; tel. (4) 472-0555; fax (4) 496-3559; e-mail mexico@xtra.co.nz; internet www.sre.gob.mx/nuevazelandia; Ambassador MARÍA ANGÉLICA ARCE MORA.

Netherlands: Investment House, 10th Floor, cnr Featherston and Ballance Sts, POB 840, Wellington; tel. (4) 471-6390; fax (4) 471-2923; e-mail wel@minbuza.nl; internet www.netherlandsembassy.co.nz; Ambassador HENRICA E. C. M. TER BRAACK.

Pakistan: 182 Onslow Rd, Khandallah, Wellington; tel. (4) 479-0026; fax (4) 479-4315; e-mail pakhcwellington@xtra.co.nz; High Commissioner MUNAWAR SAEED BHATTI.

Papua New Guinea: 279 Willis St, POB 197, Wellington; tel. (4) 385-2474; fax (4) 385-2477; e-mail pngnz@globe.net.nz; High Commissioner BERNARD NAROKOBI.

Peru: Cigna House, Level 8, 40 Mercer St, POB 2566, Wellington; tel. (4) 499-8087; fax (4) 499-8057; e-mail embassy.peru@xtra.co.nz; internet www.embassyofperu.org.nz; Ambassador CARLOS ZAPATA LÓPEZ.

Philippines: 50 Hobson St, Thorndon, POB 12-042, Wellington; tel. (4) 472-9848; fax (4) 472-5170; e-mail embassy@wellington-pe.co.nz; Ambassador Dr BIENVENIDO V. TEJANO.

Poland: 17 Upland Rd, Kelburn, POB 10211, Wellington; tel. (4) 475-9453; fax (4) 475-9458; e-mail polishembassy@xtra.co.nz; internet poland.org.nz; Ambassador LECH MASTALERZ.

Russia: 57 Messines Rd, Karori, Wellington; tel. (4) 476-6113; fax (4) 476-3843; e-mail info@rus.co.nz; internet www.rus.co.nz; Ambassador MIKHAIL LYSENKO.

Samoa: 1A Wesley Rd, Kelburn, POB 1430, Wellington; tel. (4) 472-0953; fax (4) 471-2479; e-mail shc@paradise.net.nz; High Commissioner ASI TUIATAGA J. F. BLAKELOCK.

Singapore: 17 Kabul St, Khandallah, POB 13140, Wellington; tel. (4) 470-0850; fax (4) 479-4066; e-mail singhc_wlg@sgmfa.gov.sg; internet www.mfa.gov.sg/wellington; High Commissioner SEETOH HOY CHENG.

Switzerland: Panama House, 22 Panama St, POB 25004, Wellington; tel. (4) 472-1593; fax (4) 499-6302; e-mail vertretung@wel.rep.admin.ch; Ambassador Dr BEAT NOBS.

Thailand: 2 Cook St, Karori, POB 17-226, Wellington; tel. (4) 476-8616; fax (4) 476-3677; e-mail thaiembassynz@xtra.co.nz; internet www.thaiembassynz.org.nz; Ambassador OUM MOALANON.

Turkey: 15–17 Murphy St, Level 8, POB 12-248, Wellington; tel. (4) 472-1292; fax (4) 472-1277; e-mail turkem@xtra.co.nz; Ambassador UGUR ERGUN.

United Kingdom: 44 Hill St, POB 1812, Wellington; tel. (4) 924-2888; fax (4) 473-4982; e-mail ppa.mailbox@fco.gov.uk; internet www.britain.org.nz; High Commissioner GEORGE FERGUSSON.

NEW ZEALAND

USA: 29 Fitzherbert Terrace, POB 1190, Wellington; tel. (4) 462-6000; fax (4) 499-0490; internet wellington.usembassy.gov; Ambassador WILLIAM P. MCCORMICK.

Viet Nam: Level 2, Grand Plimmer Tower, 2–6 Glimer Terrace, Wellington; tel. (4) 473-5912; fax (4) 473-5913; e-mail embassyvn@paradise.net.nz; Ambassador VUONG HAI NAM.

Judicial System

The Judicial System of New Zealand comprises a Supreme Court, a Court of Appeal, a High Court and District Courts, all of which have civil and criminal jurisdiction, and the specialist courts, the Employment Court, the Family Court, the Youth Court and the Maori Land Court. Until the establishment of the Supreme Court on 1 January 2004, final appeal was to the Judicial Committee of the Privy Council in the United Kingdom. After 1 January 2004 the Supreme Court replaced the Privy Council as the final appellate court. The right to appeal to the Supreme Court was granted only if the Court was satisfied that the case involved a matter of general or public importance or commercial significance, or in order to correct or prevent a substantial miscarriage of justice.

The Court of Appeal hears appeals from the High Court and from District Court Jury Trials, although it does have some original jurisdiction. Its decisions are final, except in cases that may be appealed to the Supreme Court. Appeals regarding convictions and sentences handed down by the High Court or District Trial Courts are by leave only.

The High Court has jurisdiction to hear cases involving crimes, admiralty law and civil matters. It hears appeals from lower courts and tribunals, and reviews administrative actions.

District Courts have an extensive criminal and civil law jurisdiction. They hear civil cases, while Justices of the Peace can hear minor criminal and traffic matters. The Family Court, which is a division of the District Courts, has the jurisdiction to deal with dissolution of marriages, adoption, guardianship applications, domestic actions, matrimonial property, child support, care and protection applications regarding children and young persons, and similar matters.

The tribunals are as follows: the Employment Tribunal (administered by the Department of Labour), Disputes Tribunal, Complaints Review Tribunal, Residential Tenancies Tribunal, Waitangi Tribunal, Environment Court, Deportation Review Tribunal and Motor Vehicles Disputes Tribunal.

In criminal cases involving indictable offences (major crimes), the defendant has the right to a jury. In criminal cases involving summary offences (minor crimes), the defendant may elect to have a jury if the sentence corresponding to the charge is three months or greater.

Attorney-General: Dr MICHAEL CULLEN.
Chief Justice: Dame SIAN ELIAS.

THE SUPREME COURT

Judges: Dame SIAN ELIAS, PETER BLANCHARD, ANDREW PATRICK CHARLES TIPPING, JOHN MCGRATH, NOEL ANDERSON, WILLIAM WILSON.

THE COURT OF APPEAL

President: WILLIAM YOUNG.
Judges: SUSAN GLAZEBROOK, ROBERT GRANT HAMMOND, ROBERT CHAMBERS, MARK O'REGAN, BRUCE ROBERTSON, TERENCE ARNOLD, ELLEN FRANCE, DAVID BARAGWANATH.

THE HIGH COURT

Permanent Judges: Chief Justice Dame SIAN ELIAS (ex officio), Chief High Court Judge ANTHONY RANDERSON, JOHN HANSEN, HUGH WILLIAMS, LOWELL GODDARD, GRAHAM PANCKHURST, LESTER CHISHOLM, WARWICK GENDALL, JUDITH POTTER, JOHN WILD, RODNEY HANSEN, JOHN PRIESTLEY, RONALD YOUNG, RHYS HARRISON, PAUL HEATH, GEOFFREY VENNING, PATRICK KEANE, JOHN FOGARTY, ALAN MACKENZIE, FORREST MILLER, MARK COOPER, HELEN WINKELMANN, CHRISTOPHER ALLAN, PATRICIA COURTNEY, SIMON FRANCE, RAYNOR ASHER, GRAHAM LANG, DENIS CLIFFORD, PAMELA ANDREWS, LYNTON STEVENS, JILLIAN MALLON, PETER WOODHOUSE, AILSA DUFFY, ROBERT ANDREW DOBSON.

Religion

CHRISTIANITY

Te Runanga Whakawhanaunga i Nga Hahi o Aotearoa (Maori Council of Churches in New Zealand): Private Bag 11903, Ellerslie, Auckland, Aotearoa-New Zealand; tel. (9) 525-4179; fax (9) 525-4346; f. 1982; four mem. churches; Administrator TE RUA GRETHA.

The Anglican Communion

The Anglican Church in Aotearoa, New Zealand and Polynesia comprises Te Pihopatanga o Aotearoa and eight dioceses (one of which is Polynesia). In 1996 the Church had an estimated 631,764 members in New Zealand.

Primate of the Anglican Church in Aotearoa, New Zealand and Polynesia, and Bishop of Auckland: Rt Rev. BROWN TUREI, POB 37-242, Parnell, Auckland; tel. (9) 302-7201; fax (9) 377-6962.

General Secretary and Treasurer of the Anglican Church in Aotearoa, New Zealand and Polynesia: ROBIN NAIRN, POB 885, Hastings; tel. (6) 878-7902; fax (6) 878-7905; e-mail gensec@hb.ang.org.nz; internet www.anglican.org.nz.

The Roman Catholic Church

For ecclesiastical purposes, New Zealand comprises one archdiocese and five dioceses. At 31 December 2005 there were an estimated 487,456 adherents.

Bishops' Conference

New Zealand Catholic Bishops' Conference, Catholic Communications, Private Bag 47904, Ponsonby, Auckland 1144; tel. (9) 378-8017; fax (9) 360-3061; e-mail communications@catholic.org.nz; internet www.catholic.org.nz.

f. 1974; Pres. Most Rev. DENIS BROWNE (Bishop of Hamilton); Sec. Archbishop JOHN A. DEW (Archbishop of Wellington); Exec. Officer ANNE DICKINSON.

Archbishop of Wellington: Most Rev. JOHN A. DEW, POB 1937, Wellington 6015; tel. (4) 496-1777; fax (4) 496-1330; e-mail j.dew@wn.catholic.org.nz; internet www.wn.catholic.org.nz.

Other Christian Churches

Baptist Churches of New Zealand: 8 Puhinui Rd, Manukau City, POB 97543, South Auckland; tel. (9) 278-7494; fax (9) 278-7499; e-mail info@baptist.org.nz; internet www.baptist.org.nz; f. 1882; 22,456 mems; Pres. KEN EDKINS; Nat. Leader Rev. RODNEY MACAAN.

Congregational Union of New Zealand: POB 2937, Auckland 1140; tel. and fax (9) 620-8290; fax (9) 620-8291; e-mail cunz@xtra.co.nz; f. 1884; 600 mems, 14 churches; Sec. ROGER FROST; Chair. PETER ECCLES.

Methodist Church of New Zealand: Connexional Office, POB 931, Christchurch; tel. (3) 366-6049; fax (3) 364-9439; e-mail info@methodist.org.nz; internet www.methodist.org.nz; 18,548 mems; Gen. Sec. Rev. JILL VAN DE GEER.

Presbyterian Church of Aotearoa New Zealand: 275 Cuba St, POB 9049, Wellington; tel. (04) 801-6000; fax (04) 801-6001; e-mail assemblyoffice@presbyterian.org.nz; internet www.presbyterian.org.nz; 30,000 mems; Moderator Rt Rev. PAMELA TANKERSLEY; Assembly Exec. Sec. Rt Rev. Dr MARTIN BAKER.

There are several Maori Churches in New Zealand, with a total membership of over 30,000. These include the Ratana Church of New Zealand, Ringatu Church, Church of Te Kooti Rikirangi, Absolute Maori Established Church, Destiny Church and United Maori Mission. The Antiochian Orthodox Church, the Assemblies of God, the Greek Orthodox Church of New Zealand, the Liberal Catholic Church and the Society of Friends (Quakers) are also active.

BAHÁ'Í FAITH

National Spiritual Assembly of the Bahá'ís of New Zealand: POB 21-551, Henderson, Auckland 1231; tel. (9) 837-4866; fax (9) 837-4898; e-mail natsec@nsa.org.nz; internet www.bahai.org.nz; f. 1957; CEO MURRAY R. SMITH.

The Press

NEWSPAPERS AND PERIODICALS

Principal Dailies

In 2006 there were 28 daily newspapers in New Zealand.

Bay of Plenty Times: 108 Durham St, Private Bag 12002, Tauranga; tel. (7) 577-7770; fax (7) 578-0047; e-mail editor@bopp.co.nz; internet www.bayofplentytimes.co.nz; f. 1872; evening; Mon.–Sat.; Gen. Man. ROD HALL; Editor CRAIG NICHOLSON; circ. 24,038 (2006).

The Daily Post: 1143 Hinemoa St, POB 1442, Rotorua; tel. (7) 348-6199; fax (7) 346-0153; e-mail daily@dailypost.co.nz; internet www.dailypost.co.nz; f. 1885; evening; Gen. Man. MIKE FLETCHER; Editor CRAIG COOPER; circ. 12,056 (2006).

Dominion Post: Dominion Post House, 40 Boulcott St, POB 3740, Wellington; tel. (4) 474-0185; fax (4) 474-0350; e-mail editor@dompost.co.nz; internet www.dompost.co.nz; f. 2002 following merger of *The Evening Post* and *The Dominion*; morning; Gen. Man. PAUL ELENIO; Editor TIM PANKHURST; circ. 98,229.

NEW ZEALAND

Gisborne Herald: 64 Gladstone Rd, POB 1143, Gisborne; tel. (6) 869-0600; fax (6) 869-0643; e-mail info@gisborneherald.co.nz; internet www.gisborneherald.co.nz; f. 1874; evening; Man. Dir M. C. Muir; Editor Iain Gillies; circ. 9,587.

Hawke's Bay Today: 113 Karamu Rd, POB 180, Hastings; tel. (6) 873-0800; fax (6) 873-0812; e-mail editor@hbtoday.co.nz; internet www.hbtoday.co.nz; f. 1999; evening; conservative; Gen. Man. Ron D. Hall; Editor Louis Pierard; circ. 28,037 (2006).

Manuwatu Standard: POB 3, Palmerston North; tel. (6) 356-9009; fax (6) 350-9545; e-mail editor@msl.co.nz; internet www.manawatustandard.co.nz; f. 1880; evening; Gen. Man. Gerard Watt; Editor Paul Taggart; circ. 20,566.

Marlborough Express: 62–64 Arthur St, POB 242, Blenheim; tel. (3) 577-2950; fax (3) 577-2953; internet www.marlboroughexpress.co.nz; f. 1866; Gen. Man. Roger G. Rose; Editor Lance Dodd; circ. 10,431.

The Nelson Mail: 15 Bridge St, POB 244, Nelson; tel. (3) 548-7079; fax (3) 546-2802; e-mail billm@nelsonmail.co.nz; internet www.stuff.co.nz/nelsonmail; f. 1866; evening; Gen. Man. Craig Dennis; Editor Bill Moore; circ. 18,445 (2006).

New Zealand Herald: 46 Albert St, POB 32, Auckland; tel. (9) 379-5050; fax (9) 373-6421; internet www.nzherald.co.nz; f. 1863; morning; Editor (print edn) Tim Murphy; Editor (multi-media) Jeremy Rees; circ. 215,000.

The Northern Advocate: 88 Robert St, POB 210, Whangarei; tel. (9) 470-2899; fax (9) 470-2869; e-mail daily@northernadvocate.co.nz; internet www.northernadvocate.co.nz; f. 1875; evening; Gen. Man. Tony Verdon; Editor Laura Franklin; circ. 14,987 (2006).

Otago Daily Times: 52 Stuart St, POB 517, Dunedin; tel. (3) 477-4760; fax (3) 474-7422; e-mail odt.editor@alliedpress.co.nz; internet www.odt.co.nz; f. 1861; morning; Man. Dir Julian C. S. Smith; Editor Robin Charteris; circ. 44,500.

The Press: Cathedral Sq., Private Bag 4722, Christchurch; tel. (3) 379-0940; fax (3) 364-8492; e-mail editorial@press.co.nz; internet www.press.co.nz; f. 1861; morning; Gen. Man. Chris Jagusch; Editor Paul Thompson; circ. 92,000.

Southland Times: 67 Esk St, POB 805, Invercargill; tel. (3) 218-1909; fax (3) 214-9905; e-mail editor@stl.co.nz; internet www.southlandtimes.co.nz; f. 1862; morning; Gen. Man. Barry Appleby; Editor Fred Tulett; circ. 29,928.

Taranaki Daily News: 49–65 Currie St, New Plymouth; tel. (6) 759-0800; fax (6) 758-4653; e-mail dailynews@newszone.co.nz; internet www.stuff.co.nz/dailynews; f. 1857; morning; Editor Lance Girling-Butcher; circ. 26,754.

Timaru Herald: 52 Bank St, POB 46, Timaru; tel. (3) 684-4129; fax (3) 688-1042; e-mail editor@timaruherald.co.nz; internet www.timaruherald.co.nz; f. 1864; morning; Man. Chris McAuslin; Editor Dave Wood; circ. 14,141.

Waikato Times: Private Bag 3086, Hamilton; tel. (7) 849-6180; fax (7) 849-9603; e-mail andrew.boyle@waikatotimes.co.nz; internet www.stuff.co.nz/waikatotimes; f. 1872; evening; independent; Gen. Man. Andrew Boyle; Editor Bryce Johns; circ. 41,000.

Wanganui Chronicle: 59 Taupo Quay, POB 433, Wanganui; tel. (6) 349-0710; fax (6) 349-0722; e-mail news@wanganuichronicle.co.nz; internet www.wanganuichronicle.co.nz; f. 1856; morning; Gen. Man. Andy Jarden; Editor Kirsty Macnicol; circ. 13,000.

Weeklies and Other Newspapers

Best Bets: POB 1327, Auckland; fax (9) 366-4565; e-mail alan.caddy@friday-flash.co.nz; Sun. and Thur.; horse-racing, trotting and greyhounds; Editor Alan Caddy; circ. 10,000.

Christchurch Star: 293 Tuam St, POB 1467, Christchurch; tel. (3) 379-7100; fax (3) 366-0180; e-mail bob_cotton@christchurchstar.co.nz; f. 1868; 2 a week; Chief Reporter Bob Cotton; circ. 118,170.

Herald on Sunday: 58 Albert St, POB 32, Auckland; tel. (9) 373-9323; fax (9) 373-9372; internet www.heraldonsunday.co.nz; f. 2004; Editor Shayne Currie.

MG Business: 8 Sheffield Cres., Christchurch 8005; tel. (3) 358-3219; fax (3) 358-4490; f. 1876; fmrly Mercantile Gazette; fortnightly; Mon; economics, finance, management, stock market, politics; Editor Bill Horsley; circ. 16,300.

The National Business Review: Bank of New Zealand Tower, Level 26, 125 Queen St, POB 1734, Auckland; tel. (9) 307-1629; fax (9) 307-5129; e-mail editor@nbr.co.nz; internet www.nbr.co.nz; f. 1970; weekly; Editor-in-Chief Nevil Gibson; circ. 14,328.

New Zealand Gazette: Dept of Internal Affairs, POB 805, Wellington; tel. (4) 470-2930; fax (4) 470-2932; e-mail gazette@parliament.govt.nz; internet www.gazette.govt.nz; official government publication; f. 1840; weekly; Man. Janet Gootjes; circ. 1,000.

New Zealand Truth Weekly: Truth Publications Ltd, POB 9613, Newmarket, Auckland 1149; tel. (9) 909-3660; fax (9) 373-5410; e-mail editor@truth.co.nz; internet www.truth.co.nz; f. 1905; Friday; local news and features, TV and entertainment, sports; owned by Truth Publications Ltd; Editor Wayne Butler; circ. 13,000.

North Shore Times: POB 33-235, Takapuna, Auckland; tel. (9) 489-4189; fax (9) 486-1950; e-mail janet.ainsworth@snl.co.nz; 3 a week; Man. Janet Ainsworth; Editor Peter Ely; circ. 75,000.

Sunday News: POB 1327, Auckland; tel. (9) 302-1300; fax (9) 358-3003; e-mail editor@sunday-news.co.nz; internet www.sundaynews.co.nz; Editor Chris Baldock; circ. 113,422.

Sunday Star-Times: POB 1409, Auckland; tel. (9) 302-1300; fax (9) 309-0258; e-mail feedback@star-times.co.nz; internet www.sundaystartimes.co.nz; f. 1994 by merger; Editor Cate Brett; circ. 210,510.

Taieri Herald: POB 105, Mosgiel; tel. (3) 489-7123; fax (3) 489-7668; e-mail taieri.herald@stl.co.nz; f. 1962; weekly; Editor Maria Cobden; circ. 12,500.

Wairarapa News: POB 902, Masterton; tel. (6) 370-5690; fax (6) 379-6481; e-mail editor@wainews.co.nz; f. 1869; Editor Walt Dickson; circ. 19,920 (2006).

Other Periodicals

AA Directions: AA Centre, cnr Albert and Victoria Sts, Auckland; tel. (9) 966-8800; fax (9) 966-8975; e-mail editor@aa.co.nz; internet www.aa.co.nz/Online; quarterly; official magazine of The New Zealand Automobile Association; Editor Kathryn Webster; circ. 546,968.

Air New Zealand Inflight Magazine: Private Bag 47-920, Ponsonby, Auckland; tel. (9) 379-8822; fax (9) 379-8821; e-mail nzsales@pol.net.nz; monthly; in-flight magazine of Air New Zealand; circ. 61,000.

Architecture New Zealand: AGM Publishing Ltd, Private Bag 99-915, Newmarket, Auckland; tel. (9) 846-4068; fax (9) 846-8742; e-mail johnw@agm.co.nz; f. 1987; every 2 months; Editor John Walsh; circ. 10,000.

Australian Women's Weekly (NZ edition): Private Bag 92-512, Wellesley St, Auckland; tel. (9) 308-2735; fax (9) 302-0667; monthly; Editorial Dir Louise Wright; circ. 90,651.

Computer Buyer New Zealand: 246 Queen St, Level 8, Auckland; tel. (9) 377-9902; fax (9) 377-4604; every 2 months; Man. Editor Don Hill; circ. 120,968.

Dairying Today: POB 3855, Auckland; tel. (9) 307-0399; fax (9) 307-0122; e-mail editor@ruralnews.co.nz; internet www.ruralnews.co.nz; monthly; Editor Adam Fricker; circ. 25,979.

Fashion Quarterly: ACP Media Centre, Private Bag 92-512, Auckland; tel. (9) 308-2735; fax (9) 302-0667; e-mail fq@acpmedia.co.nz; f. 1982; 5 a year; Editor Leonie Barlow; circ. 31,500.

Friday Flash: 155 New North Rd, POB 1327, Auckland; tel. (9) 302-1300; fax (9) 366-4565; e-mail editor@friday-flash.co.nz; weekly; racing; Editor Mike Brown; circ. 7,926.

Grapevine: Private Bag 92-124, Auckland; tel. (9) 813-4956; fax (9) 813-4957; e-mail info@grapevine.org.nz; internet www.grapevine.org.nz; monthly; family magazine; Editor John Cooney; circ. 149,658.

Info-Link: AGM Publishing Ltd, Private Bag 99-915, Newmarket, Auckland; tel. (9) 846-4068; fax (9) 846-8742; e-mail pengelly@agm.co.nz; internet www.info-link.co.nz; quarterly; Editors Sally Lindsay, Rebecca Wood; circ. 22,000.

Inwood Magazine: POB 89-027, 7 Tipau St, Torbay; tel. (9) 473-1901; fax (9) 473-1853; e-mail magazines@npl.net.nz; internet www.inwoodmag.com; f. 1993; monthly; forestry; Publr Tony Neilson; circ. 8,000.

Landfall: Otago University Press, POB 56, Dunedin; tel. (3) 479-8807; fax (3) 479-8385; e-mail landfall@otago.ac.nz; internet www.otago.ac.nz/press/landfall; f. 1947; 2 a year; new fiction, poetry, biographical and critical essays, cultural commentary; circ. 1,200.

Mana Magazine: POB 1101, Rotorua; tel. (7) 349-0260; fax (7) 349-0258; e-mail editor@manaonline.co.nz; internet www.manaonline.co.nz; Maori news magazine; Editor Derek Fox.

Management: Wellesley St, POB 5544, Auckland; tel. (9) 630-8940; fax (9) 630-1046; e-mail editor@management.co.nz; internet www.profile.co.nz; f. 1954; monthly; business; Editor Reg Birchfield; circ. 12,000.

New Idea New Zealand: 48 Greys Ave, 4th Floor, Auckland; tel. (9) 979-2700; fax (9) 979-2721; weekly; women's interest; Editor (vacant); circ. 59,039.

New Truth: 155 New North Rd, Auckland 1; tel. (9) 302-1300; fax (9) 307-0761; e-mail editor@truth.co.nz; weekly; Editor Clive Nelson; circ. 22,000.

New Zealand Dairy Exporter: POB 5544, Wellesley St, Auckland; tel. (9) 630-1624; fax (9) 630-1046; e-mail glenys@dairymag.co.nz;

NEW ZEALAND

internet www.dairymag.co.nz; f. 1925; monthly; Editor GLENYS CHRISTIAN; circ. 22,739.

New Zealand Gardener: POB 6341, Wellesley St, Auckland; tel. (4) 293-4495; internet www.nzgardener.co.nz; f. 1944; monthly; Editor LYNDA HALLINAN; circ. 77,077.

New Zealand Horse and Pony: POB 12965, Penrose, Auckland; tel. (9) 634-1800; fax (9) 634-2948; e-mail editor@horse-pony.co.nz; internet www.horse-pony.co.nz; f. 1959; monthly; Editor ROWAN DIXON; circ. 11,941.

New Zealand Medical Journal: Department of Surgery, Christchurch Hospital, POB 4345, Christchurch; tel. (3) 364-1277; fax (3) 364-1683; e-mail frank.frizelle@cdhb.govt.nz; internet www.nzma.org.nz; 2 a month; Editor Prof. FRANK A. FRIZELLE; circ. 5,000.

New Zealand Science Review: POB 1874, Wellington; fax (4) 389-5095; e-mail mberridge@malaghan.org.nz; internet nzas.rsnz.org/publish.html; f. 1942; 4 a year; reviews, policy and philosophy of science; Editor M. V. BERRIDGE.

New Zealand Woman's Day: Wellesley St, Private Bag 92-512, Auckland; tel. (9) 308-2700; fax (9) 357-0978; e-mail wdaynz@acp.nz.co.nz; weekly; Editor-in-Chief LOUISE WRIGHT; circ. 143,420.

New Zealand Woman's Weekly: NZ Magazines Ltd, POB 90-119, Auckland Mail Centre, Auckland; tel. (9) 360-3820; fax (9) 360-3826; e-mail editor@nzww.co.nz; internet www.on-line.co.nz; f. 1932; Mon.; women's issues and general interest; Editor NICKY PELLEGRINO; circ. 130,706.

Next: Level 4, cnr Fanshawe and Beamont Sts, Westhaven, Private Bag 92-512, Auckland 1036; tel. (9) 308-2773; fax (9) 377-6725; e-mail next@acpmagazines.co.nz; internet www.acpmedia.co.nz; f. 1991; monthly; home and lifestyle; owned by ACP Media; Editor SUSANNAH WALKER; circ. 60,277.

North & South: Wellesley St, Private Bag 92-512, Auckland; tel. (9) 308-2700; fax (9) 308-9498; e-mail northsouth@acpmedia.co.nz; f. 1986; monthly; current affairs and lifestyle; Editor ROBYN LANGWELL; circ. 35,959.

NZ Catholic: POB 147-000, Ponsonby, Auckland 1144; tel. (9) 360-3067; fax (9) 360-3065; e-mail contact@nzcatholic.org.nz; internet www.nzcatholic.org.nz; f. 1996; fortnightly; Roman Catholic; Editor GAVIN ABRAHAM; circ. 6,700.

NZ Home and Entertaining: ACP Media Centre, cnr Fanshawe and Beaumont Sts, Private Bag 92-512, Auckland; tel. (9) 308-2700; f. 1936; bi-monthly, design, architecture, lifestyle; Editor JEREMY HANSEN; circ. 23,000.

NZ House and Garden: 317 New North Rd, Eden Terrace, Auckland; tel. (9) 909-6800; fax (9) 909-6802; internet www.nzhouse-garden.co.nz; monthly; circ. 62,975.

NZ Listener: POB 90-783, Auckland Mail Centre, Level 4, APN Bldg, 46 Albert St, Auckland; tel. (9) 373-9400; fax (9) 373-9406; internet www.listener.co.nz; f. 1939; weekly; current affairs and entertainment; Editor PAMELA STIRLING; Publr and Chief Exec. RICK NEVILLE; circ. 73,404.

Otago Southland Farmer: POB 805, Invercargill; tel. (3) 211-1082; fax (3) 211-1098; e-mail julie.hayward@stl.co.nz; fortnightly; Editor MARIA COBDEN; Reg. Man. JULIE HAYWARD; circ. 22,322.

Pacific Wings: NZ Wings Ltd, Harewood, POB 39-099, Christchurch; tel. (3) 359-0256; fax (3) 982-3595; e-mail editor@nzwings.co.nz; internet www.nzwings.co.nz; f. 1932; monthly; Editor CALLUM MACPHERSON; circ. 20,000.

Prodesign: AGM Publishing Ltd, Private Bag 99-915, Newmarket, Auckland; tel. (9) 846-4068; fax (9) 846-8742; e-mail greg@agm.co.nz; f. 1993; every 2 months; publ. of the Designers' Institute of New Zealand; Editor GREG FRAME; circ. 8,000.

PSA Journal: PSA House, 11 Aurora Terrace, POB 3817, Wellington 6015; tel. (4) 917-0333; fax (4) 917-2051; e-mail enquiries@psa.org.nz; internet www.psa.org.nz; f. 1913; 4 a year; journal of the NZ Public Service Asscn; circ. 52,000.

Reader's Digest: POB 90-489, Auckland; e-mail editors.au@readersdigest.com; internet www.readersdigest.co.nz; f. 1950; monthly; Editor TONY SPENCER-SMITH; circ. 85,036.

RSA Review: 181 Willis St, POB 27-248, Wellington; tel. (6) 867-7248; fax (6) 867-73655; e-mail rsareview@rnzrsa.org.nz; internet www.rsa.org.nz; quarterly; official magazine of the Royal New Zealand Returned and Services' Asscn; Editor BARRY ALLISON; circ. 95,000.

Rural News: POB 3855, Auckland; tel. (9) 307-0399; fax (9) 307-0122; e-mail hamishc@ruralnews.co.nz; fortnightly; Editor HAMISH CARNACHAN; circ. 88,366.

Spanz: POB 9049, Wellington; tel. (4) 801-6000; fax (4) 801-6001; e-mail commsmanager@presbyterian.org.nz; internet www.presbyterian.org.nz; f. 1987; bi-monthly; magazine of Presbyterian Church; circ. 21,500.

Straight Furrow: c/o Rural Press, POB 4233, Auckland; tel. (9) 376-9786; fax (9) 376-9780; e-mail straightfurrow@ruralpress.com; internet www.straightfurrow.co.nz; f. 1933; fortnightly; Editor SUSAN TOPLESS; circ. 85,000.

Time New Zealand: Hopetoun St, Level 3, Newton; fax (9) 366-4706; internet www.time.com; weekly; circ. 27,859.

TV Guide (NZ): POB 1327, Auckland; tel. (9) 302-1300; fax (9) 373-3036; e-mail editor@tv-guide.co.nz; f. 1986; weekly; Editor JULIE ELEY; circ. 207,894.

UNANewZ: UN Asscn of NZ, POB 24494, Wellington; tel. (4) 473-0441; fax (4) 473-2339; e-mail office@unanz.org.nz; internet www.unanz.org.nz; f. 1945; quarterly; Editor (vacant).

NEWS AGENCIES

New Zealand Press Association: Newspaper House, 93 Boulcott St, POB 1599, Wellington; tel. (4) 472-7910; fax (4) 473-7480; e-mail news@nzpa.co.nz; internet www.nzpa-online.co.nz; f. 1879; non-political; Chair. JULIAN SMITH.

South Pacific News Service Ltd (Sopacnews): Lambton Quay, POB 5026, Wellington; tel. and fax (3) 472-8329; f. 1948; Man. Editor NEALE MCMILLAN.

PRESS COUNCIL

New Zealand Press Council: The Terrace, POB 10879, Wellington; tel. (4) 473-5220; fax (4) 471-1785; e-mail presscouncil@asa.co.nz; internet www.presscouncil.org.nz; f. 1972; Chair. BARRY PATERSON; Sec. M. E. MAJOR.

PRESS ASSOCIATIONS

Commonwealth Press Union (New Zealand Section): POB 1066, Wellington; tel. (4) 472-6223; fax (4) 471-0987; Chair. T. PANKHURST; Sec. L. GOULD.

Newspaper Publishers' Association of New Zealand (Inc): Newspaper House, 93 Boulcott St, POB 1066, Wellington 1; tel. (4) 472-6223; fax (4) 471-0987; e-mail npa@npa.co.nz; internet wwww.npa.gov.nz; f. 1898; 31 mems; Pres. J. SANDERS; CEO L. GOULD; Corporate Affairs Man. H. SOUTER.

Publishers

Auckland University Press: Private Bag 92-019, University of Auckland, Auckland; tel. (9) 373-7528; fax (9) 373-7465; e-mail aup@auckland.ac.nz; internet www.auckland.ac.nz/aup; f. 1966; scholarly; Dir ELIZABETH CAFFIN.

The Caxton Press Ltd: 113 Victoria St, POB 25-088, Christchurch 1; tel. (3) 366-8516; fax (3) 365-7840; e-mail peter@caxton.co.nz; internet www.caxton.co.nz; f. 1935; human and general interest, local and NZ history, tourist pubs; Man. Dir BRUCE BASCAND.

Dunmore Publishing Ltd: POB 250-80, Wellington; tel. (4) 472-2705; fax (4) 471-0604; e-mail books@dunmore.co.nz; internet www.dunmore.co.nz; f. 1975; non-fiction, educational; Publrs MURRAY GATENBY, SHARMIAN FIRTH.

Hachette Livre NZ Ltd: POB 100-749, North Shore Mail Centre, Auckland 0745; tel. (9) 478-1000; fax (9) 478-1010; e-mail admin@hachette.co.nz; f. 1971; fmrly Hodder Moa Beckett Publishers Ltd; Man. Dir KEVIN CHAPMAN.

HarperCollins Publishers (New Zealand) Ltd: 31 View Rd, Glenfield, Auckland; tel. (9) 443-9400; fax (9) 443-9403; e-mail editors@harpercollins.co.nz; internet www.harpercollins.co.nz; f. 1888; general and educational; CEO ROBERT GORMAN; Man. Dir TONY FISK.

Learning Media Ltd: POB 3293, Wellington; tel. (4) 472-5522; fax (4) 472-6444; e-mail info@learningmedia.co.nz; internet www.learningmedia.co.nz; f. 1947 as School Publications; state-owned enterprise; educational products in a range of media and languages; also publishing and professional devt services; Marketing and Sales Man. TIM ALLEN.

Legislation Direct: POB 12357, Wellington; tel. (4) 568-0005; fax (4) 568-0003; internet www.legislationdirect.co.nz; general publishers and leading distributor of government pubs; fmrly Govt Printing Office/GP Publications; Publications Man. WENDY CAYLOR.

LexisNexis NZ Ltd: Level 1, 181 Wakefield St, POB 472, Wellington; tel. (4) 385-1479; fax (4) 385-1598; internet www.lexisnexis.co.nz; legal; Exec. Dir SHARON BENNETT.

McGraw-Hill Book Co, New Zealand Ltd: Private Bag 11904, Ellerslie, Auckland 1005; tel. (9) 526-6200; fax (9) 526-6216; e-mail cservice_auckland@mcgraw-hill.com; f. 1974; educational; Man. FIRGAL ADAMS.

New Zealand Council for Educational Research: POB 3237, Wellington; tel. (4) 384-7939; fax (4) 384-7933; e-mail sales@nzcer

NEW ZEALAND

.org.nz; internet www.nzcer.org.nz; f. 1934; scholarly, research monographs, educational, academic, periodicals; Chair. PETER ALLEN; Dir ROBYN BAKER.

Otago University Press: POB 56, Dunedin; tel. (3) 479-8807; fax (3) 479-8385; e-mail university.press@otago.ac.nz; internet www.otago.ac.nz/press; f. 1958; publishes titles on New Zealand, the Pacific and Asia, with special emphasis on history, literature, the arts and natural and social sciences; also educational titles and journals; Publr WENDY HARREX.

Pearson Education New Zealand Ltd: Private Bag 102-908, North Shore Mail Centre, Glenfield, Auckland 10; tel. (9) 414-9980; fax (9) 414-9981; e-mail rosemary.stagg@pearsoned.co.nz; internet www.pearsoned.co.nz; f. 1968; fmrly Addison Wesley Longman; educational; Dirs ROSEMARY STAGG, P. FIELD.

Penguin Group (NZ) Ltd: Private Bag 102-902, North Shore Mail Centre, Auckland 0745; tel. (9) 442-7400; fax (9) 442-7401; e-mail publishing@penguin.co.nz; internet www.penguin.co.nz; f. 1973; Publ. Dir GEOFF WALKER; Man. Dir TONY HARKINS.

Wendy Pye Ltd: Private Bag 17-905, Greenlane, Auckland; tel. (9) 525-3575; fax (9) 525-4205; e-mail admin@sunshine.co.nz; children's fiction and educational; Man. Dir WENDY PYE.

Random House New Zealand Ltd: Private Bag 102-950, North Shore Mail Centre, Glenfield, Auckland; tel. (9) 444-7197; fax (9) 444-7524; e-mail admin@randomhouse.co.nz; internet www.randomhouse.co.nz; f. 1977; general; Man. Dir MICHAEL MOYNAHAN.

Reed Publishing (NZ) Ltd: Private Bag 34-901, Birkenhead, Auckland 0626; tel. (9) 441-2960; fax (9) 480-4999; e-mail info@reed.co.nz; internet www.reed.co.nz; children's and general non-fiction; Heinemann Education primary, secondary, tertiary and library; Man. Dir DAVID O'BRIEN.

Whitcoulls Ltd: 210 Queen St, 3rd Floor, Private Bag 92-098, Auckland 1; tel. (9) 356-5410; fax (9) 356-5423; NZ, general and educational; Gen. Man. S. PRESTON.

PUBLISHERS' ASSOCIATION

Book Publishers' Association of New Zealand Inc: POB 36-477, Northcote, Auckland 1309; tel. (9) 480-2711; fax (9) 480-1130; e-mail bpanz@copyright.co.nz; internet www.bpanz.org.nz; f. 1977; Pres. MICHAEL MOYNAHAN.

Broadcasting and Communications

TELECOMMUNICATIONS

Compass Communications Ltd: POB 2533, Auckland; tel. (9) 965-2200; fax (9) 965-2270; internet www.compass.net.nz; f. 1995; CEO KARIM HUSSONA.

Kordia: POB 2495, Auckland; tel. (9) 916-6400; fax (9) 916-6403; internet www.kordiasolutions.com; fmrly known as THL Group; name changed as above 2006; telecommunications, broadcasting and converged solutions; operates in New Zealand and Australia; Chair. WAYNE BROWN; CEO GEOFF HUNT.

NewCall Group Ltd: POB 8703, Level 2, NewCall Tower, Symonds St, 44 Khyber Pass, Auckland; tel. (9) 917-6572; fax (9) 917-8338; internet www.newcall.co.nz; Man. Dir G. JAMES BRACKNELL, Jr.

Singtel Optus Ltd: ASB Centre, Level 14, 135 Albert St, Auckland; tel. (9) 356-2660; fax (9) 356-2669.

Telecom Corpn of New Zealand Ltd: Telecom Networks House, 68 Jervois Quay, POB 570, Wellington; tel. (4) 801-9000; fax (4) 385-3469; internet www.telecom.co.nz; Chair. WAYNE BOYD; Chief Exec. PAUL REYNOLDS.

TelstraClear: TelstraClear Centre, cnr Northcote and Taharoto Rds, Takapuna, Private Bag 92-143, Auckland; tel. (9) 912-4200; fax (9) 912-4442; e-mail webmaster@telstraclear.co.nz; internet www.telstraclear.co.nz; f. 1990 as Clear Communications Ltd; merged with TelstraSaturn Ltd 2001; business solutions, local and toll services, enhanced internet, etc.; Chair. DAVID THODEY; CEO Dr ALLAN FREETH.

Vodafone New Zealand Ltd: 21 Pitt St, Private Bag 92-161, Auckland; tel. (9) 355-2007; fax (9) 355-2001; internet www.vodafone.co.nz; fmrly Bell South; cellular network; CEO RUSSELL STANNERS.

Woosh Wireless Ltd: 11–15 Railway St, POB 9635, Newmarket, Auckland; tel. (9) 522-3699; fax (9) 520-3447; internet www.woosh.com; f. 1999 as Walker Wireless Ltd; name changed as above 2003; provides internet and telephony services; Chair. ROD INGLIS; CEO KEVIN WILEY.

WorldxChange Communications Ltd: Level 9, Tower Two, 55–65 Shortland St, POB 3296, Auckland; tel. (9) 308-1300; e-mail info@wxc.co.nz; internet www.wxc.co.nz; CEO CECIL ALEXANDER.

Directory

Regulatory Authority

Telecommunications Policy Section, Ministry of Economic Development: 33 Bowen St, POB 1473, Wellington; tel. (4) 472-0030; fax (4) 473-4638; e-mail info@med.govt.nz; internet www.med.govt.nz.

BROADCASTING

In December 1995 Radio New Zealand Commercial (RNZC) and New Zealand Public Radio Ltd (NZPR) became independent entities, having assumed responsibility for, respectively, the commercial and non-commercial activities of Radio New Zealand. RNZC was sold to the New Zealand Radio Network Consortium in 1996, and NZPR, which remained a Crown-owned company, assumed the name of its now-defunct parent company, to become Radio New Zealand Ltd. In late 1999 there were 190 radio stations broadcasting on a continuous basis, of which 170 were operating on a commercial basis.

Radio

Radio Broadcasters' Association (NZ) Inc: POB 3762, Auckland; tel. (9) 378-0788; fax (9) 378-8180; e-mail info@rba.co.nz; internet www.rba.co.nz; represents commercial radio industry; Exec. Council Chair. JOHN MCELHINNEY; Exec. Dir DAVID INNES; 13 mems.

Radio New Zealand Ltd: RNZ House, 155 The Terrace, POB 123, Wellington; tel. (4) 474-1999; fax (4) 474-1459; e-mail rnz@radionz.co.nz; internet www.radionz.co.nz; f. 1936; Crown-owned entity, operating non-commercial national networks: Radio New Zealand National and Radio New Zealand Concert; parliamentary broadcasts on AM Network; Radio New Zealand News and Current Affairs; the short-wave service, Radio New Zealand International; and Radio New Zealand Sound Archives; Chair. BRIAN CORBAN; Dep. Chair. ALISON TIMMS.

The Radio Network of New Zealand Ltd: 54 Cook St, Private Bag 92-198, Auckland; tel. (9) 373-0000; e-mail enquiry@radionetwork.co.nz; internet www.radionetwork.co.nz; operates 120 commercial stations, reaching 1.3m. people; Chief Exec. JOHN MCELHINNEY.

Television

Television New Zealand (TVNZ) Ltd: Television Centre, 100 Victoria St West, POB 3819, Auckland; tel. (9) 916-7000; fax (9) 916-7934; internet www.tvnz.co.nz; f. 1960; the television service is responsible for the production of programmes for two TV networks, TV One and 2; networks are commercial all week and transmit in colour; both channels broadcast 24 hours a day, seven days a week, and reach 99.9% of the population; Chair. Sir JOHN ANDERSON.

Maori Television: 9–15 Davis Crescent, POB 113-017, Newmarket, Auckland; tel. (9) 539-7000; fax (9) 539-7199; e-mail info@maoritelevision.com; internet www.maoritelevision.com; f. 2003; broadcasts Maori- and English-language programmes for 7.5 hrs daily; Chair. GARRY MURIWAI; CEO JIM MATHER.

Private Television

Auckland Independent Television Services Ltd: POB 1629, Auckland.

Bay Satellite TV Ltd: Hastings; tel. (6) 878-9081; fax (6) 878-5994; Man. Dir JOHN LYNAM.

Sky Network Television Limited: 10 Panorama Rd, POB 9059, Newmarket, Auckland; tel. (9) 579-9999; fax (9) 579-0910; internet www.skytv.co.nz; f. 1990; UHF service on six channels, satellite service on 18 channels; 667,270 subscribers (Aug. 2006); Chair. PETER MACOURT; CEO JOHN FELLET.

TV3 Network Services Ltd: Symonds St, Private Bag 92-624, Auckland; tel. (9) 377-9730; fax (9) 366-5999; internet www.tv3.co.nz; f. 1989; operated by TV Works; Man. Dir RICK FRIESEN.

Finance

(cap. = capital; res = reserves; dep. = deposits; m. = million; br(s). = branch(es); amounts in New Zealand dollars)

BANKING

Central Bank

Reserve Bank of New Zealand (RBNZ): 2 The Terrace, POB 2498, Wellington; tel. (4) 472-2029; fax (4) 473-8554; e-mail rbnz-info@rbnz.govt.nz; internet www.rbnz.govt.nz; f. 1934; res 1,421.4m., dep. 11,621.0m. (June 2006); Gov. ALAN BOLLARD; Dep. Gov. GRANT SPENCER.

Registered Banks

As a result of legislation which took effect in April 1987, several foreign banks were incorporated into the domestic banking system.

ANZ National Bank Ltd: Level 14, ANZ Tower, 215–229 Lambton Quay, Wellington; tel. (4) 496-7000; fax (4) 494-4000; internet www.anz.com/nz; f. 1979; subsidiary of Australia and New Zealand Banking Group Ltd of Melbourne, Australia; fmrly ANZ Banking Group (New Zealand) Ltd; name changed as above 2004 following merger with National Bank of New Zealand Ltd; cap. 5,943m., res 55m., dep. 84,348m. (Sept. 2006); Chair. Sir DRYDEN SPRING; Chief Exec. GRAHAM HODGES; 143 brs and sub-brs.

ASB Bank Ltd: ASB Bank Centre, cnr Wellesley and Albert Sts, POB 35, Auckland 1; tel. (9) 377-8930; fax (9) 358-3511; e-mail helpdesk@asbbank.co.nz; internet www.asbbank.co.nz; f. 1847 as Auckland Savings Bank, name changed 1988; cap. 1,563m., res 1,126m., dep. 41,307m. (June 2006); Chair. G. J. JUDD; Man. Dir G. HUGH BURRETT; 123 brs.

Bank of New Zealand (BNZ): BNZ Tower, 125 Queen St, Auckland; tel. (9) 302-4955; fax (9) 375-9537; internet www.bnz.co.nz; f. 1861; owned by National Australia Bank; cap. 1,451m., res –5m., dep. 45,400m. (Sept. 2006); Chair. T. K. MCDONALD; Man. Dir and CEO CAMERON CLYNE; 179 domestic brs and 1 overseas br.

Citibank NA (USA): Citibank Centre, Level 11, 23 Customs Street East, POB 3429, Auckland; tel. (9) 307-1902; fax (9) 308-9928; internet www.citibank.com.au; CEO ANDREW AU; 2 brs.

Deutsche Bank New Zealand: Wellesley St, POB 6900, Auckland; tel. (9) 351-1000; fax (9) 351-1001; e-mail christine.cutler@db.com; internet www.deutsche-bank.co.nz; f. 1986; fmrly Bankers Trust New Zealand; Chief Exec. BRETT SHEPHERD.

Hongkong and Shanghai Banking Corporation Ltd (Hong Kong): 1 Queen St, Level 9, POB 5947, Auckland; tel. (9) 308-8888; fax (9) 308-8997; e-mail hsbcplb@clear.net.nz; internet www.hsbc.co.nz; CEO NORMAN A. WILSON; 6 brs.

Kiwibank Ltd: Private Bag 39888, Wellington; tel. (4) 473-1133; fax (4) 462-7996; internet www.kiwibank.co.nz; f. 2001; 100% New Zealand-owned; savings bank for small depositors; Chair. JIM BOLGER; Chief Exec. SAM KNOWLES.

Rabobank (New Zealand): POB 38-396, Wellington Mail Centre, Wellington; tel. (4) 819-2700; fax (4) 819-2706; e-mail wellington.enquiry@rabobank.com; internet www.rabobank.co.nz; f. 1996; full subsidiary of Rabobank Nederland; CEO BRUCE DICK.

TSB Bank Ltd: POB 240, New Plymouth; tel. (6) 968-3810; fax (6) 968-3815; internet www.tsbbank.co.nz; f. 1850; dep. 2,300m. (March 2006); Man. Dir K. W. RIMMINGTON; 15 brs.

Westpac New Zealand: 318 Lambton Quay, POB 691, Wellington; tel. (4) 498-1000; fax (4) 498-1350; e-mail customer_support@westpac.co.nz; internet www.westpac.co.nz; acquired Trust Bank New Zealand; New Zealand division of Westpac Banking Corpn (Australia); Chief Exec. ANN SHERRY; 196 brs.

Association

New Zealand Bankers' Association: POB 3043, Wellington; tel. (4) 472-8838; fax (4) 473-1698; e-mail nzba@nzba.org.nz; internet www.nzba.org.nz; f. 1891; Chief Exec. ALAN YATES.

STOCK EXCHANGES

Dunedin Stock Exchange: POB 298, Dunedin; tel. (3) 477-5900; Chair. E. S. EDGAR; Sec. R. P. LEWIS.

New Zealand Exchange Ltd (NZX): Level 2, NSX Centre, 11 Cable St, POB 2959, Wellington 6140; tel. (4) 472-7599; fax (4) 496-2893; e-mail info@nzx.com; internet www.nzx.com; Chair. SIMON ALLEN; CEO MARK WELDON.

Supervisory Body

New Zealand Securities Commission: POB 1179, Wellington; tel. (4) 472-9830; fax (4) 472-8076; e-mail seccom@seccom.govt.nz; internet www.seccom.govt.nz; f. 1979; Chair. JANE DIPLOCK.

INSURANCE

ACE Insurance NZ Ltd: POB 734, Auckland; tel. (9) 377-1459; fax (9) 303-1909; e-mail michael.poole@ace-ina.com; internet www.aceinsurance.co.nz; Man. Dir MICHAEL POOLE.

AMI Insurance Ltd: 29–35 Latimer Sq., POB 2116, Christchurch 8001; tel. (3) 371-9000; fax (3) 371-8314; internet www.ami.co.nz; f. 1926; Chair. KERRY G. L. NOLAN; CEO JOHN B. BALMFORTH.

ANZ Life Assurance Co Ltd: POB 1492, Wellington; tel. (4) 496-7000; fax (4) 470-5100; Man. R. A. DEAN.

Atradius: Level 8, Deloitte House, 10 Brandon St, Wellington 6011; tel. (4) 474-4142; fax (4) 472-6966; e-mail info.nz@atradius.com; internet www.atradius.com/nz; fmrly known as Gerling NCM; name changed as above following acquisition by Deutsche Bank and Swiss Re; trade credit insurance services.

AXA New Zealand Ltd: POB 1692, Wellington; tel. (4) 474-4500; fax (4) 472-5069; internet www.axa.co.nz; CEO RALPH STEWART.

BNZ Life Insurance Ltd: POB 1299, Wellington; tel. (4) 382-2577; fax (4) 474-6883; internet www.bnz.co.nz; Man. Dir and CEO CAMERON CLYNE.

Farmers' Mutual Group: 68 The Square, POB 1943, Palmerston North 5330; tel. (6) 356-9456; fax (6) 356-4603; e-mail enquiries@fmg.co.nz; internet fmg.co.nz; comprises Farmers' Mutual Insurance Asscn, Farmers' Mutual Insurance Ltd and other cos; fire, accident, motor vehicle, marine, life; Chair. GREG GENT.

ING Life (NZ) Ltd: 205 Wairau Rd, Glenfield, Auckland 1310; tel. (9) 442-4800; fax (9) 442-4801; e-mail enquiries@inglife.co.nz; internet www.inglife.co.nz; CEO MARC LIEBERMAN.

New Zealand Insurance: IAG House, 151 Queen St, Private Bag 92130, Auckland 1030; tel. (9) 309-7000; fax (9) 309-7097; internet www.nzi.co.nz; owned by Insurance Australia Group New Zealand Ltd; Head IAN FOY.

New Zealand Local Government Insurance Corporation Ltd (Civic Assurance): Civic Assurance House, 114–118 Lambton Quay, POB 5521, Wellington; tel. (4) 978-1250; fax (4) 978-1260; e-mail tim.sole@civicassurance.co.nz; internet www.civicassurance.co.nz; f. 1960; fire, motor, all risks, accident; Chief Exec. TIM SOLE; Gen. Man. GEOFF MERCER.

Promina Group: 48 Shortland St, Auckland; tel. (9) 363-2222; internet www.promina.co.nz; f. 1878; fmrly Royal & SunAlliance; subsidiary of Suncorp-Metway Ltd; comprises AA Insurance, Vero Insurance New Zealand Ltd and other cos; fire, accident, marine, general.

QBE Insurance (International) Ltd: Level 6, Quay Tower, 29 Customs St West, Auckland; tel. (9) 366-9920; fax (9) 366-9930; f. 1890; Gen. Man. GRAEME EVANS.

Sovereign Ltd: Private Bag Sovereign, Auckland Mail Centre 1020; tel. (9) 487-9000; fax (9) 486-9501; e-mail enquire@sovereign.co.nz; internet www.sovereign.co.nz; f. 1989; life insurance and investment.

State Insurance Ltd: Microsoft House, 3–11 Hunter St, POB 5037, Wellington 1; tel. (9) 969-1150; fax (4) 476-9664; internet www.state.co.nz; f. 1905; mem. NRMA Insurance Group; Man. Dir T. C. SOLE.

Tower Insurance Ltd: 22 Fanshawe St, POB 90-347, Auckland; tel. (9) 369-2200; fax (9) 369-2128; internet www.towerlimited.com; f. 1873; fmrly National Insurance Co of New Zealand; CEO ROB FLANNAGAN.

Associations

Insurance Council of New Zealand: POB 474, Wellington; tel. (4) 472-5230; fax (4) 473-3011; e-mail icnz@icnz.org.nz; internet www.icnz.org.nz; CEO CHRISTOPHER RYAN.

Investment Savings and Insurance Association of New Zealand Inc: POB 1514, Wellington; tel. (4) 473-8730; fax (4) 471-1881; e-mail isi@isi.org.nz; internet www.isi.org.nz; f. 1996 from Life Office Asscn and Investment Funds Asscn; represents cos that act as manager, trustee, issuer, insurer, etc. of managed funds, life insurance and superannuation; Chief Exec. VANCE ARKINSTALL; Exec. Officer DEBORAH KEATING.

Trade and Industry

GOVERNMENT AGENCY

New Zealand Trade and Enterprise: POB 2878, Wellington; tel. (4) 816-8100; fax (4) 816-8101; e-mail info@nzte.govt.nz; internet www.nzte.govt.nz; f. 2003; national government development agency with global network of 48 offices; provides businesses, organizations and investors with access to quality New Zealand goods and services and acts as a gateway to partnerships with New Zealand businesses and to investment opportunities in New Zealand; CEO TIM GIBSON; Chair. PHIL LOUGH.

CHAMBERS OF COMMERCE

Auckland Regional Chamber of Commerce and Industry: POB 47, Auckland 1020; tel. (9) 309-6100; fax (9) 309-0081; e-mail mbarnett@chamber.co.nz; internet www.chamber.co.nz; CEO MICHAEL BARNETT; Chair. JOHN LINDSAY.

Canterbury Employers' Chamber of Commerce: 57 Kilmore St, POB 359, Christchurch; tel. (3) 366-5096; fax (3) 379-5454; e-mail info@cecc.org.nz; internet www.cecc.org.nz; f. 1859; formed through merger of Employers' Fed. and Chamber of Commerce; employment and business support services including legal consultancy and international trade advice, business performance and training, networking and advocacy; Chief Exec. PETER TOWNSEND.

Otago Chamber of Commerce Inc: Ground Floor, Burns House, 10 George St, Dunedin; tel. (3) 477-0341; fax (3) 643-0341; e-mail

NEW ZEALAND

office@otagochamber.co.nz; internet www.otagochamber.co.nz; f. 1861; CEO J. A. CHRISTIE; Pres. C. STAYNES.

Wellington Regional Chamber of Commerce: 28th Level, Majestic Centre, 100 Willis Street, Wellington; tel. (4) 914-6500; fax (4) 914-6524; e-mail info@wellingtonchamber.co.nz; internet www.wellingtonchamber.co.nz; f. 1856; Chief Exec. CHARLES FINNY; Pres. JOHN LUMSDEN; 1,000 mems.

INDUSTRIAL AND TRADE ASSOCIATIONS

Canterbury Manufacturers' Association: POB 13-152, Armagh, Christchurch; tel. (3) 353-2540; fax (3) 353-2549; e-mail cma@cma.org.nz; internet www.cma.org.nz; f. 1879; CEO JOHN WALLEY; 500 mems.

Employers' and Manufacturers' Association (Central Inc): 2nd Floor, Lumley House, 3-11 Hunter St, Wellington, POB 1087, Wellington 6140; tel. (4) 473-7224; fax (4) 473-4501; e-mail ema@emacentral.org.nz; internet www.emacentral.org.nz; f. 1997 by merger of Wellington Manufacturers' Asscn and Wellington Regional Employers' Asscn; CEO PAUL WINTER; 2,200 mems.

Employers' and Manufacturers' Association (Northern Inc): 159 Khyber Pass Rd, Grafton, Private Bag 92066, Auckland; tel. (9) 367-0900; fax (9) 367-0902; e-mail ema@ema.co.nz; internet www.ema.co.nz; f. 1886; fmrly Auckland Manufacturers' Asscn; Pres. C. MARTIN; 5,000 mems.

ENZA: POB 56, Auckland; tel. (9) 573-8700; fax (9) 573-8879; e-mail info@enza.co.nz; internet www.enza.co.nz; fmrly New Zealand Apple and Pear Marketing Board; Man. Dir JEFF WESLEY; Gen. Man. DAWN GRAY.

Federated Farmers of New Zealand (Inc): POB 715, Wellington; tel. (4) 473-7269; fax (4) 473-1081; e-mail receptionwgton@fedfarm.org.nz; internet www.fedfarm.org.nz; f. 1946; Pres. CHARLIE PEDERSEN; CEO ANNABEL YOUNG; 16,000 mems.

Horticulture New Zealand: POB 10232, Wellington 1; tel. (4) 472-3795; fax (4) 471-2861; internet www.hortnz.co.nz; formed through merger of New Zealand Fruitgrowers' Federation, New Zealand Berryfruit Federation and New Zealand Vegetable and Potato Growers' Federation; 7,000 mems; Pres. ANDREW FENTON; CEO PETER SILCOCK.

Kiwifruit New Zealand: POB 4683, Mt Maunganui South 3149; tel. (7) 572-3685; fax (7) 572-5934; e-mail richard.procter@knz.co.nz; f. 2000; Chair. Sir BRIAN ELWOOD.

Meat and Wool New Zealand: POB 121, Wellington 6015; tel. (4) 473-9150; fax (4) 474-0800; e-mail help@meatandwoolnz.com; internet www.meatnz.co.nz; Chair. MIKE PETERSEN.

National Beekeepers' Association of New Zealand (Inc): 10 Nikau Lane, RD 1, Otaki 5581; tel. (6) 363-6301; fax (6) 362-6302; e-mail secretary@nba.org.nz; internet www.nba.org.nz; f. 1913; 400 mems; Pres. JANE LORIMER; Sec. PAM EDWARDS.

New Zealand Animal By-Products Exporters' Association: 11 Longhurst Terrace, POB 12-222, Christchurch; tel. (3) 332-2895; fax (3) 332-2825; 25 mems; Sec. J. L. NAYSMITH.

New Zealand Council of Wool Exporters Inc: POB 2857, Christchurch; tel. (3) 353-1049; fax (3) 374-6925; e-mail cwe@woolexport.net; internet www.woolexport.net; f. 1893; Exec. Man. R. H. F. NICHOLSON; Pres. JOHN HENDERSON.

The New Zealand Forest Owners' Association: POB 1208, Wellington; tel. (4) 473-4769; fax (4) 499-8893; e-mail nzfoa@nzfoa.org.nz; internet www.nzfoa.org.nz; Pres. PETER BERG.

New Zealand Fruit Wine and Cider Makers Inc: POB 912, New Plymouth, Taranaki; tel. and fax (6) 757-8049; fax (6) 757-5523; e-mail admin@fruitwines.co.nz; internet www.fruitwines.co.nz; f. 1987; 30 mems; Chair. MARK ATKIN; Exec. Officer CHRISTINE GARNHAM.

New Zealand Meat Board: Level 13, Price Waterhouse Coopers Tower, 113–119 The Terrace, Wellington; tel. (4) 473-9150; fax (4) 474-0800; e-mail info@nzmeatboard.org; internet www.nzmeatboard.org; f. 1922; Chair. MIKE PETERSEN; Sec. A. DOMETAKIS; 10 mems.

New Zealand Pork Industry Board: POB 4048, Wellington; tel. (4) 917-4750; fax (4) 385-8522; e-mail info@pork.co.nz; internet www.pork.co.nz; f. 1937; Chair. C. TRENGROVE; CEO S. McIVOR.

New Zealand Retailers' Association Inc: Willbank House, 8th Floor, 57 Willis St, Wellington; tel. (4) 472-3733; fax (4) 472-1071; e-mail bhellberg@retail.org.nz; internet www.retail.org.nz; direct membership 5,000; Pres. PHILLIP RICHARDS; CEO JOHN ALBERTSON.

New Zealand Seafood Industry Council: Private Bag 24-901, Wellington; tel. (4) 385-4005; fax (4) 384-2727; e-mail info@seafood.co.nz; internet www.seafood.co.nz; CEO OWEN SYMMANS; Chair. DAVID SHARP.

Directory

New Zealand Timber Industry Federation: 2–8 Maginnity St, POB 308, Wellington; tel. (4) 473-5200; fax (4) 473-6536; internet www.nztif.co.uk; 350 mems; Exec. Dir W. S. COFFEY.

Registered Master Builders' Federation (Inc): 234 Wakefield St, Level 6, POB 1796, Wellington; tel. (4) 385-8999; fax (4) 385-8995; internet www.masterbuilder.org.nz; Chief Exec. C. PRESTON.

EMPLOYERS' ORGANIZATION

Business New Zealand: Lumley House, Level 6, 3–11 Hunter St, Wellington; tel. (4) 496-6555; fax (4) 496-6550; e-mail admin@businessnz.org.nz; internet www.businessnz.org.nz; f. 2001; Chief Exec. PHIL O'REILLY.

UTILITIES

Energy Efficiency and Conservation Authority (EECA): Vector Bldg, Level 1, 44 The Terrace, Wellington; tel. (4) 470-2200; fax (4) 499-5330; e-mail info@eeca.govt.nz; internet www.eeca.govt.nz; f. 2000; Chair. MARK FORD; Chief Exec. MIKE UNDERHILL.

Electricity

Electricity Commission: Level 7, ASB Bank Tower, 2 Hunter St, POB 10041, Wellington; tel. (4) 460-8860; fax (4) 460-8879; e-mail info@electricitycommission.govt.nz; internet www.electricitycommission.govt.nz; f. 2003; independent; regulatory body supervising electricity sector; Gen. Man. MERVYN ENGLISH.

Bay of Plenty Electricity Ltd: 52 Commerce St, POB 404, Whakatane 3080; tel. (7) 922-2700; fax (7) 307-0922; e-mail bopelec@bopelec.co.nz; internet www.bopelec.co.nz; f. 1995; generation, purchase and supply of electricity and natural gas; Commercial Man. CHRIS POWER; CEO DAVID BULLEY.

Contact Energy Ltd: Harbour City Tower, Level 1, 29 Brandon St, Wellington; tel. (4) 449-4001; fax (4) 499-4003; e-mail help@contact-energy.co.nz; internet www.contactenergy.co.nz; f. 1996; generation of electricity, wholesale and retail of energy; transferred to the private sector in 1999; Chair. GRANT KING; CEO DAVID BALDWIN.

Genesis Energy Ltd: 602 Great South Rd, POB 17-188, Greenlane, Auckland; tel. (9) 580-2094; fax (9) 580-4891; internet www.genesisenergy.co.nz; f. 1999; state-owned; generation and retail of electricity and gas; Chair. BRIAN CORBAN; Chief Exec. MURRAY JACKSON.

The Marketplace Co Ltd (M-CO): Level 2, 10 Brandon St, POB 5422, Wellington; tel. (4) 473-5240; fax (4) 473-5247; e-mail info@nz.m-co.com; internet www.nz.m-co.com; administers wholesale electricity market; Chief Exec. CHRIS RUSSELL.

Meridian Energy Ltd: POB 2128, Christchurch; tel. (3) 353-9500; fax (3) 353-9501; internet www.meridianenergy.co.nz; state-owned; generation and retail of electricity; Chair. Dr FRANCIS SMALL; Chief Exec. Dr KEITH TURNER.

Mighty River Power Ltd: Level 19, 1 Queen St, POB 90-399, Auckland; tel. (9) 308-8200; fax (9) 308-8209; e-mail enquiries@mightyriver.co.nz; internet www.mightyriverpower.co.nz; f. 1999; electricity generation and retail; cos include Mercury Energy; Chair. CAROLE DURBIN; Chief Exec. DOUG HEFFERMAN.

Todd Energy Ltd: POB 3141, Wellington; tel. (4) 471-6555; fax (4) 472-2474; e-mail energy@toddenergy.co.nz; internet www.toddenergy.co.nz; Man. Dir and CEO RICHARD TWEEDIE.

Transpower New Zealand Ltd: Unisys House, 56 The Terrace, POB 1021, Wellington; tel. (4) 495-7000; fax (4) 495-7100; internet www.transpower.co.nz; manages national grid; Chair. Sir WAYNE BROWN; Chief Exec. PATRICK STRANGE.

TrustPower Ltd: Private Bag 12-023, Tauranga Mail Centre, Tauranga 3143, Auckland; tel. (7) 574-4754; fax (7) 574-4803; e-mail trustpower@trustpower.co.nz; internet www.trustpower.co.nz; f. 1920 as Tauranga Electric Power Board; independent generator; Chair. HAROLD TITTER.

Vector Electricity Ltd: POB 99-882, Newmarket, Auckland; tel. (9) 978-7788; fax (9) 978-7799; internet www.vectorelectricity.co.nz; fmrly Mercury Energy Ltd; operates power networks in Auckland, Manukau and Papakura; CEO MARK FRANKLIN.

Gas

Bay of Plenty Electricity Ltd: see Electricity, above.

E-gas Ltd: Level 13, Forsyth Barr House, cnr Lambton Quay and Johnston St, POB 2577, Wellington; tel. (4) 499-4964; fax (4) 499-4965; e-mail info@e-gas.co.nz; internet www.e-gas.co.nz; supplier of natural gas.

Genesis Energy Ltd: see Electricity, above.

NGC Holdings Ltd: Level 8, NGC Bldg, 44 The Terrace, Private Bag 39-980, Wellington Mail Centre, Wellington; tel. (4) 462-8700; fax (4) 462-8600; internet www.ngc.co.nz; f. 1992; fmrly Natural Gas Corpn

NEW ZEALAND

Holdings Ltd; name changed as above 2002; purchase, processing and transport of natural gas; wholesale and retail sales; Chair. MICHAEL STIASSNY; Chief Exec. BRYAN CRAWFORD.

Nova Gas Ltd: 11th Floor, Todd Bldg, 95 Customhouse Quay, POB 10-141, Wellington; tel. (4) 472-6263; fax (4) 472-6264; e-mail info@novagas.co.nz; internet www.novagas.co.nz; Group Gas Man. HAMISH TWEEDIE.

Vector Gas Ltd: 101 Carlton Gore Rd, Newmarket, Auckland; tel. (9) 978-7788; fax (9) 978-7799; e-mail info@vectorgas.co.nz; internet www.vectorgas.co.nz; distribution of natural gas in Auckland.

Wanganui Gas Ltd: 179 Hill St, POB 32, Wanganui; tel. (6) 349-0909; fax (6) 345-4931; e-mail enquiries@wanganuigas.co.nz; internet www.wanganuigas.co.nz; f. 1879; supplier of gas on North Island; Chair. CHARLES POYNTER; Chief Exec. TREVOR GOODWIN.

Water

Waste Management NZ Ltd: 86 Lunn Ave, Mt Wellington, Auckland; tel. (9) 527-1300; fax (9) 570-5595; internet www.wastemanagement.co.nz; f. 1985; waste collection, recovery and disposal; liquid waste collection and processing; recycling; Man. Dir GREGG CAMPBELL; Regional Man. KEVIN BONNIFACE.

Watercare Services Ltd: Private Bag 92-521, Wellesley St, Auckland 1036; tel. (9) 379-4440; fax (9) 302-8013; e-mail info@water.co.nz; internet www.watercare.co.nz; f. 1993; provides water and waste water services in the Auckland area; Chair. GRAEME HAWKINS; Chief Exec. MARK FORD.

TRADE UNIONS

In December 2000 a total of 134 unions were in operation; 318,519 workers belonged to a union.

New Zealand Council of Trade Unions: Education House, West Block, 178–182 Willis St, POB 6645, Wellington 1; tel. (4) 385-1334; fax (4) 385-6051; internet www.union.org.nz; f. 1937; present name since 1987; affiliated to ITUC; 39 affiliated unions with 250,000 mems; Pres. ROSS WILSON; Sec. CAROL BEAUMONT.

Principal Affiliated Unions

Association of Staff in Tertiary Education (ASTE)/Te Hau Takitini o Aotearoa: POB 27141, Wellington; tel. (4) 801-5098; fax (4) 385-8826; e-mail enquiry@aste.ac.nz; 3,500 mems; Nat. Sec. SHARN RIGGS.

Association of University Staff (AUS): POB 11-767, Wellington; tel. (4) 803-3999; fax (4) 801-4799; e-mail national.office@aus.ac.nz; internet www.aus.ac.nz; 6,000 mems; Nat. Pres. MAUREEN MONTGOMERY.

Central Amalgamated Workers Union (AWUNZ): POB 27-291, 307 Willis St, Wellington; tel. (4) 384-4049; fax (4) 801-7306; e-mail centralawunz@xtra.co.nz; Sec. JACKSON SMITH.

FinSec Finance and Information Workers Union: POB 27-355, Wellington; tel. (4) 385-7723; fax (4) 385-2214; e-mail union@finsec.org.nz; internet www.finsec.org.nz; Pres. SUE BORASTON; Sec. ANDREW CASIDY.

Maritime Union of New Zealand: POB 27004, Wellington; tel. (4) 385-0792; fax (4) 384-8766; e-mail trevor.hanson@muno.org.nz; 2,800 mems; Sec. TREVOR HANSON.

Meat and Related Trades Workers Union of Aotearoa: POB 17056, Greenlane, Auckland; tel. (9) 520-0034; fax (9) 523-1286; e-mail meat.union@xtra.co.nz; Sec. GRAHAM COOKE.

New Zealand Dairy Workers Union, Inc: POB 9046, Hamilton; tel. (7) 839-0239; fax (7) 838-0398; e-mail nzdwu@nzdwu.org.nz; internet www.nzdwu.org.nz; f. 1992; 6,800 mems; Sec. JAMES RITCHIE; Pres. SINCLAIR WATSON.

New Zealand Educational Institute (NZEI) (Te Riu Roa): POB 466, Wellington; tel. (4) 384-9689; fax (4) 385-1772; e-mail nzei@nzei.org.nz; internet www.nzei.org.nz; f. 1883; Pres. IRENE COOPER; Sec. LYNNE BRUCE.

New Zealand Engineering, Printing & Manufacturing Union (EPMU): POB 31-546, Lower Hutt; tel. (4) 568-0086; fax (4) 576-1173; e-mail andrew.little@epmu.org.nz; internet www.epmu.org.nz; Sec. ANDREW LITTLE.

New Zealand Meat Workers and Related Trades Union: POB 13-048, Armagh, Christchurch; tel. (3) 366-5105; fax (3) 379-7763; e-mail nzmeatworkersunion@clear.net.nz; 13,788 mems; Pres. M. NAHU; Gen. Sec. D. W. EASTLAKE.

New Zealand Nurses' Organisation: POB 2128, Wellington; tel. (4) 499-9533; fax (4) 382-9993; e-mail nurses@nzno.org.nz; internet www.nzno.org.nz; 38,000 mems; CEO GEOFF ANNALS.

New Zealand Post Primary Teachers' Association: POB 2119, Wellington; tel. (4) 384-9964; fax (4) 382-8763; e-mail gensec@ppta.org.nz; internet www.ppta.org.nz; Pres. ROBIN DUFF; Gen. Sec. KEVIN BUNKER.

NZ PSA (New Zealand Public Service Association): PSA House, 11 Aurora Terrace, POB 3817, Wellington 1; tel. (4) 917-0333; fax (4) 917-2051; e-mail enquiries@psa.org.nz; internet www.psa.org.nz; 47,000 mems; Pres. KEITH GUTSELL.

Rail & Maritime Transport Union Inc: POB 1103, Wellington; tel. (4) 499-2066; fax (4) 471-0896; e-mail admin@rmtunion.org.nz; internet rmtunion.org.nz; 4,100 mems; Pres. J. KELLY; Sec. W. BUTSON.

Service and Food Workers' Union: Private Bag 68-914, Newton, Auckland; tel. (9) 375-2680; fax (9) 375-2681; internet www.sfwu.org.nz; 23,000 mems; Pres. DAELE O'CONNOR; Sec. DARIEN FENTON.

Other Unions

Manufacturing & Construction Workers Union: Manners St, POB 6287, Wellington; tel. (4) 385-8264; fax (4) 384-8007; e-mail M.C.Union@TradesHall.org.nz; Gen. Sec. GRAEME CLARKE.

National Distribution Union (NDU): 120 Church St, Private Bag 92-904, Onehunga, Auckland; tel. (9) 622-8355; fax (9) 622-8353; e-mail ndu@nduunion.org.nz; internet www.nduunion.org.nz; 18,500 mems; Pres. BILL ANDERSEN; Sec. MIKE JACKSON; Vice Pres. DENNIS DAWSON.

New Zealand Building Trades Union: Manners St, POB 11-356, Wellington; tel. (4) 385-1178; fax (4) 385-1177; Pres. P. REIDY; Sec. ASHLEY RUSS.

New Zealand Seafarers' Union: Marion Square, POB 9288, Wellington; tel. (4) 385-9288; fax (4) 384-9288; e-mail admin@seafarers.org.nz; f. 1993; Pres. DAVE MORGAN.

Transport

RAILWAYS

There were 3,898 km of railways in New Zealand in 2003, of which more than 500 km were electrified.

Toll Rail Ltd: Smales Farm, cnr Northcote Rd and Taharoto Drive, Takapuna, Auckland; tel. (4) 498-3000; fax (4) 498-3259; e-mail freight@tollnz.co.nz; internet www.tollrail.co.nz; acquired Tranz Rail Ltd 2003; 3,898 km of railway; Gen. Man. GARY TAYLOR.

ROADS

In June 2003 there were a total of 92,494 km of maintained roads in New Zealand, including 10,791 km of state highways and motorways.

Land Transport New Zealand: Level 4, NZ Post House, 7 Waterloo Quay, POB 2840, Wellington; tel. (4) 931-8700; fax (4) 931-8701; internet www.landtransport.govt.nz; f. 2003; Crown entity charged with contributing to an integrated, safe, responsive and sustainable land transport system; Chair. PAUL FITZHARRIS (acting); Chief Exec. WAYNE DONNELLY.

Transit New Zealand: 20–26 Ballance St, POB 5084, Wellington; tel. (4) 499-6600; fax (4) 496-6666; internet www.transit.govt.nz; Crown agency responsible for management and development of the state highway network; Chair. BRYAN JACKSON (acting); CEO RICK VAN BARNEVELD.

SHIPPING

There are 13 main seaports, of which the most important are Auckland, Tauranga, Wellington, Lyttleton (the port of Christchurch) and Port Chalmers (Dunedin). In December 2006 the New Zealand merchant fleet comprised 171 vessels, with a total displacement of 206,573 grt.

Principal Companies

P & O Nedlloyd Ltd: Level 4, Panasonic House, 40 Taranaki St, POB 1699, Wellington; tel. (4) 803-5000; fax (4) 803-5055; internet www.ponl.com; world-wide shipping services; Man. Dir TONY GIBSON.

Sofrana Unilines NZ Ltd: 396–404 Queen St, POB 3614, Auckland; tel. (9) 356-1400; fax (9) 356-1407; e-mail info@sofrana.co.nz; internet www.sofrana.co.nz; Chair DIDIER LEROUX; Man. Dir BENOIT MARCENAC.

Other major shipping companies operating services to New Zealand include Blue Star Line (NZ) Ltd and Columbus Line, which link New Zealand with Australia, the Pacific Islands, South-East Asia and the USA.

CIVIL AVIATION

There are international airports at Auckland, Christchurch and Wellington.

Civil Aviation Authority of New Zealand: Aviation House, 10 Hutt Rd, Petone, POB 31-441, Lower Hutt; tel. (4) 560-9400; fax (4)

569-2024; e-mail info@caa.govt.nz; internet www.caa.govt.nz; Dir of Civil Aviation STEVE DOUGLAS.

Principal Airlines

Air Nelson: Private Bag 32, Nelson 7030; tel. (3) 547-8700; fax (3) 547-8788; internet www.airnewzealand.com; f. 1979; owned by Air New Zealand; changed to present name 1986; operates services throughout New Zealand; Gen. Man. JOHN HAMBLETON.

Air New Zealand: Quay Tower, 29 Customs St West, Private Bag 92007, Auckland 1; tel. (9) 366-2400; fax (9) 366-2401; e-mail investor@airnz.co.nz; internet www.airnz.co.nz; f. 1942; privatized in 1989, recapitalized by govt 2001; 80% govt-owned; services to Australia, the Pacific Islands, Asia, Europe and North America, as well as regular daily services to 25 cities and towns in New Zealand; Chair. JOHN PALMER; CEO ROB FYFE.

Freedom Air: Quay Tower, 29 Customs St West, Private Bag 92007, Auckland; tel. (9) 366-2400; fax (9) 366-2401; internet www.freedomair.co.nz; f. 1995; subsidiary of Air New Zealand; operates regional services; Man. Dir STEPHEN JONES.

Pacific Blue Airlines (NZ) Ltd: internet www.flypacificblue.com; f. 2004; wholly-owned subsidiary of Australian Virgin Blue; services to Pacific Islands; CEO TONY MARKS.

Tourism

New Zealand's principal tourist attractions are its high mountains, lakes, forests, volcanoes, hot springs and beaches. The sector makes a substantial contribution to the country's economy, and receipts from tourism totalled an estimated $NZ6,377m. in 2006. In 2007 New Zealand received more than 2.4m. international visitors. The majority of visitors are from Australia, the United Kingdom and the USA.

Tourism New Zealand: POB 95, Wellington; tel. (4) 917-5400; fax (4) 915-3817; e-mail reception@tnz.govt.nz; internet www.newzealand.com; f. 1901; responsible for marketing of New Zealand as a tourism destination; offices in Auckland, Wellington and Christchurch; 13 offices overseas; Chair. WALLY STONE; Chief Exec. GEORGE HICKTON.

NEW ZEALAND'S DEPENDENT TERRITORIES

New Zealand's two Dependent Territories are the Ross Dependency, which is situated in Antarctica, and Tokelau, located in the Pacific Ocean.

ROSS DEPENDENCY

The Ross Dependency comprises the sector of Antarctica between 160°E and 150°W (moving eastward) and the islands lying between those degrees of longitude and south of latitude 60°S. It has been administered by New Zealand since 1923 and has a total area of 750,310 sq km (289,700 sq miles), comprising a land area of 413,540 sq km and an ice shelf of 336,770 sq km. The Territory rises to a height of 3,794 m above sea-level at the peak of the volcano, Mount Erebus.

Scott Base was established in 1957 on Ross Island, and in the following year the Ross Dependency Research Committee was formed to supervise New Zealand activity on the Territory. In 1968 a new scientific station was set up at Lake Vanda, about 130 km (80 miles) west of Scott Base. In 1986 traces of petroleum were discovered in the Territory, more than 600 m below the sea-bed. The Ross Dependency Research Committee was disbanded in 1995.

Legislation approved in the mid-1990s consolidated measures aimed at conserving the region's flora and fauna (which includes 18 species of penguin, six species of seal and several rare species of whale) included in the Antarctic Treaty (see p. 575), and reinforced the Convention for the Conservation of Antarctic Marine Living Resources. Since 1997 New Zealand has conducted exploratory fishing for toothfish in the Ross Sea. In April 2006 it was announced that an Estonian summer-only research station was to be built at Edmonson Point South, 350 km north-west of Scott Base, to provide facilities for six personnel. Following a visit by the New Zealand Minister of Research, Science and Technology in November 2006, new proposals, including emphasis on the provision of renewable energy resources and the encouragement of greater investment in scientific projects in the territory, were announced.

TOKELAU

Introductory Survey

Location, Climate, Language, Religion, Flag, Capital

Tokelau consists of three atolls (Atafu, Nukunonu and Fakaofo), which lie about 480 km (300 miles) north of Samoa, in the Pacific Ocean. The annual average temperature is 28°C (82°F), July being the coolest month and May the warmest; rainfall is heavy but inconsistent. The principal language is Tokelauan (a Polynesian language), although English is also widely spoken. The population is almost entirely Christian, with 67% adhering to the Congregational Christian Church of Samoa (a Protestant denomination) and 30% to the Roman Catholic Church. The New Zealand flag (see p. 3320) is used in the Territory. Tokelau has no capital, each atoll having its own administrative centre. However, the seat of government, the Office of the Tokelau Council for Ongoing Government (formerly the Council of Faipule) is recognized as 'the capital' and is rotated on a yearly basis among the three atolls.

Recent History

The Tokelau (formerly Union) Islands became a British protectorate in 1877. At the request of the inhabitants, the United Kingdom annexed the islands in 1916 and included them within the Gilbert and Ellice Islands Colony (now Kiribati and Tuvalu). The British Government transferred administrative control of the islands to New Zealand by legislation enacted in 1925, effective from February 1926. The group was officially designated the Tokelau Islands in 1946, and sovereignty was transferred to New Zealand by legislation of 1948, effective from January 1949. From 1962 until the end of 1971 the High Commissioner for New Zealand in Western Samoa (now Samoa) was also the Administrator of the Tokelau Islands. In November 1974 the administration of the Tokelau Islands was transferred to the Ministry of Foreign Affairs in New Zealand. In 1976 the Tokelau Islands were officially redesignated Tokelau.

New Zealand has undertaken to assist Tokelau towards increased self-government and economic self-sufficiency. The Territory was visited by the UN Special Committee on Decolonization in 1976 and 1981, but on both occasions the mission reported that the people of Tokelau did not wish to change the nature of the existing relationship between Tokelau and New Zealand. This opinion was reiterated by an emissary of the General Fono, the Territory's highest advisory body, in 1987, and by the Official Secretary in 1992. In June 1987, however, in a statement to the UN Special Committee, Tokelau had expressed a desire to achieve a greater degree of political autonomy, while maintaining its relationship with New Zealand. A report by the UN Special Committee in 2002 listed Tokelau as one of 16 dependent territories it was seeking to encourage towards independence. However, a UN decolonization mission which visited the islands in September of that year was told that the majority of Tokelauans wanted to remain part of New Zealand and that the Territory was far too dependent on that country to change its status.

In December 1980 New Zealand and the USA signed a treaty whereby a US claim to Tokelau, dating from 1856, was relinquished. At the same time New Zealand abandoned a claim, on behalf of Tokelau, to Swains Island, which had been administered by the USA since 1925 as part of American Samoa. The treaty was ratified in August 1983, although there was some dissent in Tokelau.

In 1989 Tokelau supported efforts by the South Pacific Forum to impose a regional ban on drift-net fishing (which was believed to have resulted in a serious depletion in tuna stocks). In November New Zealand prohibited drift-net fishing within Tokelau's exclusive economic zone (which extends to 200 nautical miles (370 km) from the islands' coastline). At the annual meeting of the Pacific Islands Forum (formerly the South Pacific Forum) in August 2002 New Zealand endorsed Tokelau's membership of the Forum Fisheries Agency.

In 1989 a UN report on the 'greenhouse effect' (the heating of the earth's atmosphere as a result of pollution) listed Tokelau as one of the island groups that would completely disappear beneath the sea in the 21st century, unless drastic action were taken.

A programme of constitutional change, agreed in 1992 and formalized in January 1994, provided for a more defined role for Tokelau's political institutions, as well as for their expansion. A process of relocating the Tokelau Public Service (hitherto based in Apia, Western Samoa, now Samoa) to the Territory began in 1994, and by 1995 all government departments, except Transport and Communications and part of the Administration and Finance Department, had been transferred to Tokelauan soil. However, the Tokelau Apia Liaison Office (formerly the Office for Tokelau Affairs) was to remain in Western Samoa, owing to that country's more developed communications facilities.

The development of Tokelau's institutions at a national level prompted renewed interest in the islands' prospects for greater internal autonomy. In June 1994 the General Fono adopted a National Strategic Plan, which gave details of Tokelau's progression (over the next five to 10 years) towards increased self-determination and, possibly, free association with New Zealand. The executive and administrative powers of the Administrator were formally transferred, in that year, to the General Fono and, when the Fono was not in session, to the Council of Faipule (cabinet). A draft Constitution was subsequently drawn up. In May 1996 the New Zealand House of Representatives approved the Tokelau Amendment Bill, granting the General Fono the power to enact legislation, to impose taxes and to declare public holidays, effective from 1 August 1996 (although New Zealand was to retain the right to legislate for Tokelau). A visit to the islands by the Prime Minister of Tuvalu in mid-1996, for the signing of a mutual co-operation agreement (covering shipping, trade and fisheries), was widely interpreted as an indication of Tokelau's increased autonomy. A further co-operation agreement was established in March 2003, following a five-day visit to the islands by the Prime Minister of Samoa. Tokelau's traditional leaders agreed a framework for annual meetings with the Samoan Government to discuss issues of concern and mutual benefit in what was regarded as a sign of the growing relationship between the two parties.

Following electoral reforms introduced in the latter half of the 1990s, delegates were, for the first time, elected to the General Fono for a three-year term in January 1999; they had previously been nominated by each Taupulega (Island Council or Council of Elders). As part of the same reform process, the number of delegates to the General Fono was reduced from 27 to 18. At the elections two of the Territory's Faipule (political leaders) were re-elected, while the remaining Faipule and three Pulenuku (village mayor) posts were secured by new candidates. At elections in January 2002 all three incumbent Faipule and one Pulenuku were re-elected to office; two new Pulenuku were elected. In January 2005 the three Faipule were again re-elected, along with one of the Pulenuku; two new Pulenuku were chosen.

Mounting fears among islanders that, despite their wishes, New Zealand was seeking to loosen its ties with Tokelau, led the New Zealand Minister of Foreign Affairs and Trade to state in April 2000 that his country would not impose independence on the Territory and that any change in its political status would only occur with the consent of Tokelauans. In early 2001 the head of the Tokelau Public Service Commission, Aleki Silau, reiterated the islanders' reluctance to renounce New Zealand citizenship, and emphasized that both sides had until 2010 to reach a decision. A mission from the UN Special Committee on Decolonization visited the islands in September 2002 (see above). Under legislation approved in 1999, management of the islands' public service was formally transferred to Tokelau in July 2001. In July 2003 responsibility for the islands' budget was transferred to the General Fono. In October of that year a number of constitutional changes were instituted. The Council of Faipule was renamed the Tokelau Council for Ongoing Government, henceforth to comprise the three Faipule and the three Pulenuku. In the following month New Zealand's Governor-General, Dame Sylvia Cartwright, made an official visit to Tokelau to sign the Principles of Partnership agreement. The document was described by New Zealand's Minister of Foreign Affairs, Phil Goff, as a step closer to decolonization for the islands. Goff reiterated that the final decision on Tokelau's future would be made by its inhabitants, although he also confirmed that he expected the islands to adopt a system of self-government in free association with New Zealand, similar to that existing in Niue and the Cook Islands. In March 2004 it was announced that new powers were to be granted to the three atolls' Taupulega, giving them greater control over local affairs. In May a senior government member reiterated the view that, despite the ambition of New Zealand and the UN for Tokelau to achieve self-determination, the islanders themselves were extremely reluctant to change their status. In June the Administrator's powers were formally transferred from the General Fono to the three Taupulega, as part of the Modern House of Tokelau Project.

In mid-August 2004 New Zealand's Prime Minister, Helen Clark, made an official visit to Tokelau (the first such visit in more than 20 years). During the visit Clark announced the provision of a grant worth some US $0.3m. towards improvements for boat access to the islands and a review of the islands' communications infrastructure. The Prime Minister also expressed her confidence that the islanders would vote in favour of free association with New Zealand when the issue was finally put to a referendum. In early November leaders from Tokelau travelled to New Zealand for a series of meetings with the latter's Minister of Foreign Affairs, Phil Goff, following which certain elements to be included in a treaty of free association with New Zealand were agreed upon. However, contrary to the New Zealand Government's expectations, at a referendum on the issue of the future status of Tokelau held between 11 and 15 February 2006 the requisite two-thirds' majority in favour of the proposed change to free association with New Zealand was not received: 349 votes were cast in favour of greater self-government, while 232 voters wanted Tokelau to remain a Dependent Territory. The referendum was observed by several international organizations, including representatives of the UN. The result was regarded as a major set-back for the New Zealand Government. However, in June 2006 it was announced that the General Fono had agreed to the holding of another referendum on the issue of Tokelau's status. In November regional inter-governmental groups, led by the Secretariat of the Pacific Community (see p. 377), began a fact-finding operation in Tokelau. The mission aimed to identify the islands' particular needs and priorities and to formulate a three-year strategy. In February 2007, following similar visits to the Tokelauan communities in Hawaii, American Samoa and New Zealand, an official delegation from Tokelau travelled to Samoa in order to discuss with expatriate Tokelauans the various issues relating to the next referendum. It was emphasized that if they wished to participate in the second referendum, Tokelauans resident overseas would be required to return to the islands three months prior to the poll. In March the Faipule of Fakaofo, Kolouei O'Brien, declared that if the requisite majority in favour of greater autonomy were to be secured at the next referendum then Tokelau would wish to enter immediate negotiations with the USA regarding the return of Swains Island, which had remained part of American Samoa (see above).

In October 2006 David Payton replaced Neil Walter as Tokelau's Administrator. The decision to appoint a New Zealand diplomat to the position gave rise to some controversy, and it was suggested that the appointment indicated a lack of confidence in the people of Tokelau and their ability to manage their own affairs.

At the second referendum on Tokelau's status, conducted in October 2007, the level of participation was reported to be almost 100%; UN officials were again present as observers. However, support for self-government was not sufficient to produce the requisite two-thirds' majority, with 246 out of 692 voters rejecting the proposal. There was speculation about the influence of Tokelauans living in New Zealand, although expatriates were not permitted to cast a vote. Prime Minister Clark pledged her Government's 'ongoing friendship and support'. Elections to the General Fono were held on 18–19 January 2008, when 20 delegates were elected. In the same month one new Faipule was elected to office and two incumbent Faipule were re-elected, while three new Pulenuku were also chosen.

In February 2005, meanwhile, all three atolls were struck by Cyclone Percy, which caused widespread damage to infrastructure, homes and crops. Nukunonu was subjected to severe flooding as a result of the storm. The New Zealand Government approved some $NZ0.5m. in emergency aid in the form of food supplies and temporary shelter (to be shipped from Samoa) and the restoration of essential services.

New Zealand is responsible for the external relations of Tokelau. Strong links are maintained with Samoa, to the people of which the Tokelauans are closely related. There is considerable co-operation in health and education matters.

Government

The administration of Tokelau is the responsibility of the Minister of Foreign Affairs and Trade of New Zealand, who is empowered to appoint an Administrator to the Territory. In practice, most of the Administrator's powers are delegated to the Official Secretary, who heads the Tokelau Apia Liaison Office, as well as to the General Fono and the Tokelau Council for Ongoing Government (formerly the Council of Faipule). Each atoll has its own Taupulega (Island Council or Council of Elders), which comprises the heads of family groups together with two elected members, the Faipule and the Pulenuku. The Faipule represents the atoll in its dealings with the administering power and the public service, and presides over the Council and the court. The Pulenuku is responsible for the administration of village affairs. The Faipule and the Pulenuku are democratically elected by universal adult suffrage every three years. The three Faipule, who hold ministerial portfolios and along with the three Pulenuku form the six-member Tokelau Council for Ongoing Government, choose one of their number to hold the title Ulu-O-Tokelau (Head of Tokelau) for a term of one year. The Ulu-O-Tokelau chairs sessions of the territorial assembly, the General Fono. The General Fono is a meeting of 20 delegates, who are elected by universal adult suffrage for a three-year term (including the three Faipule and the three Pulenuku) and who represent the entire Territory. There are two or three meetings of the General Fono each year, which may take place on any of the atolls.

Economic Affairs

According to estimates by the UN Development Programme (UNDP), in 1982 Tokelau's gross national product (GNP) was US $1.2m., equivalent to US $760 per head. Gross domestic product (GDP) was estimated at US $1.5m. in 1993. During 1996–2004 the population increased at an average rate of 0.8% per year.

Agriculture (including fishing) is, excluding copra production, of a basic subsistence nature. Coconuts (the source of copra) are the only cash crop, for which there is an increasingly limited market. Pulaka, breadfruit, papayas, the screw-pine (*Pandanus*) and bananas are cultivated as food crops. Livestock comprises pigs, ducks and other poultry. Ocean and lagoon fish and shellfish are staple constituents of the islanders' diet. In early 2004 the Secretariat of the Pacific Community produced a fisheries management plan for Tokelau. The plan, which was to be implemented in mid-2004, focused on community-based activities and included the increased exploitation of the islands' giant-clam resources. A five-year development plan for the fisheries sector was drafted for 2006–10. Meanwhile, the sale to foreign fleets of fishing licences permitting them to operate in Tokelau's exclusive economic zone (EEZ) provides an important, albeit fluctuating, source of income (see below).

The industrial sector has been constrained by a lack of resources. Manufacturing comprises mainly the production of handicrafts, notably woven items such as mats. However, the opening on Atafu, in 1990, of a factory processing highly priced yellowfin tuna provided another important source of income. The principal markets for the product were New Zealand and Japan.

Energy is provided by diesel-powered generators, the fuel for which is imported via Samoa. With funding from New Zealand, a major power project was initiated in 2002. The implementation of this scheme, which was ultimately to supply all three atolls with a more reliable source of electricity, was scheduled for completion in 2006. In the longer term, greater emphasis was to be given to renewable forms of energy, particularly solar power. In conjunction with the Governments of New Zealand and France, UNDP and the United Nations Educational, Scientific and Cultural Organization (UNESCO), in 2003 Tokelau embarked on a programme aimed at utilizing the territory's solar energy potential for grid-connected power generation.

The tourism sector is limited, having remained undeveloped owing to the lack of air services and the difficulty of access. There is just one recognized hotel, on the central atoll of Nukunonu. Fewer than 30 tourists visited the islands in 2001. Since 1982 the General Fono has levied a tax on the salaries of public servants who are unavailable for the community service labour levy. Public salaries and employment account for the single largest item of government expenditure (about one-third in the early 1990s). Following the purchase by a Dutch entrepreneur of the islands' internet domain address '.tk' in 2001, more than 1.6m. names had been registered to the facility by 2007. Although the Government's precise earnings from this source were not disclosed, the services of this joint venture with Teletok, the islands' communications company, were reported to be proving highly lucrative. Furthermore, the attendant upgrading of Tokelau's communications infrastructure, including a broadband connection via satellite, greatly enhanced the islanders' own information technology facilities.

Imports to the value of $NZ1.7m. were purchased in 2002. The principal imports in that year were food and live animals (which cost 55.2% of total imports), mineral fuels (11.6%) and miscellaneous manufactured goods (11.0%).

In 1999/2000 there was a budgetary deficit of $NZ0.9m. Tokelau's budget for 2001/02 was to include at least $NZ4.2m. from New Zealand and an estimated $NZ1.7m. to be obtained from local revenues such as fisheries licensing, duty, taxes, philatelic sales, freight charges and interest earned. Local revenue was estimated to have reached about $NZ2m. in 2005. Receipts from EEZ fees rose from $NZ286,000 in 2004 to an estimated $NZ569,000 in 2005. Fees from shipping, radio excises and customs duties have provided another source of revenue; local receipts from such duties increased from $NZ372,000 in 2004 to an estimated $NZ388,000 in 2005. The sale of postage stamps and souvenir coins (which are legal tender, although New Zealand currency is in general use) also makes a significant contribution to the Territory's income. Receipts from this source increased from $NZ54,000 in 2004 to an estimated $NZ70,000 in 2005. Some revenue is provided by remittances from Tokelauans working abroad, mainly in New Zealand. Since mid-2003 most of New Zealand's bilateral assistance has been transferred directly to the Territory's budget, thereby enabling Tokelau to finance its recurrent expenditure on services such as transport, education and health. Official development assistance from New Zealand was projected to reach $NZ13.0m. in 2007/08. In addition to its links to New Zealand, Tokelau maintains a bilateral development assistance plan with Australia, centred upon human resource development. Australia provides scholarships for Tokelauan students to study in Australia or at regional academic institutions.

Tokelau is a member of the Pacific Community (see p. 377), and, as a Dependent Territory of New Zealand, has been represented by that country in the Pacific Islands Forum (see p. 380) and other international organizations. In October 2005 Tokelau was granted observer status at the Pacific Islands Forum.

Tokelau's agricultural development has been constrained by the lack of suitable cultivable soil and by the adverse effects of inclement weather. In February 2005 Cyclone Percy caused serious destruction on the islands, coinciding with 'king tides' that flooded the Territory resulting in widespread damage. Moreover, the Territory's small size, remote location, lack of land-based resources and the population's continuing migration to New Zealand have severely hindered economic development. In September 2002 renewed proposals were announced for the construction of wharves and improved access for shipping to facilitate the export of fish, and of an airport to encourage tourism. It was hoped that Tokelau would derive greater benefits from its fisheries resources as a result of a plan initiated by the Secretariat of the Pacific Community in 2004 (see above). In 2004 Tokelau signed a three-year agreement relating to New Zealand's budgetary support, along with arrangements for reporting and monitoring, which were to remain in place until 2006/07. In 2001 the sum of $NZ0.68m. derived from the income from fisheries licensing was used to found the Tokelau Trust Fund. The fund was established with assistance from New Zealand and with the aim of enhancing the Territory's long-term self-reliance. By early 2006 the assets of the fund had exceeded $NZ25m. It was hoped that eventually the fund would attract international contributions. A three-year Economic Support Arrangement was to be implemented under the direction of the New Zealand Government during 2007–10, with a projected total budget of $NZ43m. Areas targeted for development included transport, communications, education and health. Under the Administrative Assistance scheme (part of the Principles of Partnership agreement—see Recent History), the limited capacity of the Tokelau Public Service is supplemented by the resources of various New Zealand government departments. The establishment of Dot TK in 2001 (see above) was believed to have increased annual government revenue by about 10%.

Education

Education is provided free of charge, and is compulsory between the ages of five and 14 years. The provision of an additional year for 15-year-olds is rotated among the Territory's three schools every five years. Government expenditure on education in 1998/99 totalled $NZ0.8m. (equivalent to 18% of total budgetary expenditure). The New Zealand Department of Education provides advisory services and some educational equipment. Scholarships are awarded for secondary and tertiary education and vocational training in Samoa, Fiji, Niue, Tonga and New Zealand. In 2004 a total of 53 Tokelauans over the age of 15 years were studying overseas under the Tokelau Sponsorship Scheme (34 in Samoa, 12 in New Zealand and seven in Fiji). In 2003 there were some 176 Tokelauan pupils enrolled at the Samoa Secondary School. Australia also provides scholarships. There were a total of 358 pupils enrolled in primary and secondary education and 54 teachers on the islands in 2003.

Public Holidays

2008: 1 January (New Year's Day), 6 February (Waitangi Day, anniversary of 1840 treaty), 21–24 March (Easter), 25 April (ANZAC Day, anniversary of 1915 landing at Gallipoli), 2 June (Queen's Official Birthday), 27 October (Labour Day), 25 December (Christmas Day), 26 December (Boxing Day).

2009: 1 January (New Year's Day), 6 February (Waitangi Day, anniversary of 1840 treaty), 10–13 April (Easter), 25 April (ANZAC Day, anniversary of 1915 landing at Gallipoli), 1 June (Queen's Official Birthday), 26 October (Labour Day), 25 December (Christmas Day), 26 December (Boxing Day).

Weights and Measures

The metric system is in force.

Statistical Survey

Source (unless otherwise indicated): Tokelau Apia Liaison Office, POB 805, Apia, Samoa; tel. 20822; fax 21761; e-mail f.aukuso@clear.net.nz.

AREA AND POPULATION

Area: Atafu 3.5 sq km; Nukunonu 4.7 sq km; Fakaofo 4.0 sq km; Total 12.2 sq km (4.7 sq miles).

Population: 1,537 (males 761, females 776) at census of 11 October 2001; 1,466 (males 736, females 730) at census of 19 October 2006. *By Atoll* (2006 census): Atafu 524; Nukunonu 426; Fakaofo 483; Total 1,466 (incl. 33 usually resident on Samoa).

Density (2006 census): 120.2 per sq km.

Births and Deaths (1996): Birth rate 33.1 per 1,000; Death rate 8.2 per 1,000. *2003:* Live births 24.

Expectation of Life (years at birth, 1996, official estimates): Males 68; Females 70. Source: Ministry of Foreign Affairs and Trade, Wellington.

Economically Active Population (2001 census, persons aged 15 years and over): Construction 78; Retail trade 12; Hotels and restaurants 4; Transport 7; Communications 20; Village services 182; Public administration 59; Education 53; Medical 23; Total 438. *2006 census:* Total in paid employment 375.

HEALTH AND WELFARE
Key Indicators

Access to Water (% of households, 2004): 88.

Access to Sanitation (% of households, 2004): 78.

For sources and definitions, see explanatory note on p. vi.

AGRICULTURE, ETC.

Crop Production (metric tons, 2005, FAO estimates): Coconuts 3,083; Copra 45; Roots and tubers 300; Bananas 15; Other tropical fruits 46. Note: Data for 2006 were not available.

Livestock (year ending September 2004, FAO estimates): Pigs 1,000; Chickens 5,000. Note: Data for 2005 and 2006 were not available.

Livestock Products (metric tons, 2005, FAO estimates): Pig meat 19; Chicken meat 5; Hen eggs 8. Note: Data for 2006 were not available.

Fishing (metric tons, live weight, 2005, FAO estimates): Total catch 200.

Source: FAO.

INDUSTRY

Production (1990, estimate): Electric energy 300,000 kWh.

FINANCE

Currency and Exchange Rates: New Zealand currency is legal tender. Tokelau souvenir coins have also been issued. New Zealand currency: 100 cents = 1 New Zealand dollar ($NZ); *Sterling, US Dollar and Euro Equivalents* (31 December 2007): £1 sterling = $NZ2.5884; US $1 = $NZ1.2920; €1 = $NZ1.9019; $NZ100 = £38.63 = US $77.40 = €52.58. *Average Exchange Rate* ($NZ per US $): 1.4203 in 2005; 1.5421 in 2006; 1.3607 in 2007.

Budget ($NZ, year ending 30 June 1998): *Revenue:* Local 734,950; New Zealand subsidy 4,600,000; Total 5,334,950. *Expenditure:* Total 5,208,449.

Overseas Aid (projection, $NZ '000, 2002/03): Official development assistance from New Zealand 8,100 (of which Budget support 4,750, Projects and training 2,650). *2007/08* (projection) Total development assistance from New Zealand $NZ13.7m. Source: Ministry of Foreign Affairs and Trade, Wellington.

EXTERNAL TRADE

Principal Commodities ($NZ, 2002): *Imports:* Food and live animals 923,766; Mineral fuels, lubricants, etc. 194,779; Animal and vegetable oils, fats and waxes 50,012; Chemicals and related products 45,429; Manufactured goods 183,488; Total (incl. others) 1,673,389.

COMMUNICATIONS MEDIA

Radio Receivers (1997, estimate): 1,000 in use.

EDUCATION

Schools (1999): 3 (one school for all levels on each atoll).

Teachers (2003): Primary 31; Secondary 23.

Pupils (2003): Primary 182; General secondary 176.

Students Overseas (1999): Secondary 22; Tertiary 20.

Directory

The Constitution

Tokelau is administered under the authority of the Tokelau Islands Act 1948 and subsequent amendments and regulations. The Act declared Tokelau (then known as the Tokelau Islands) to be within the territorial boundaries of New Zealand. The Administrator is the representative of the Crown and is responsible to the Minister of Foreign Affairs and Trade in the New Zealand Government. The office of Administrator is normally held conjointly with that of New Zealand's Secretary of Foreign Affairs and Trade, but provision is made for the offices to be held separately. Most of the powers of the Administrator are delegated to the Tokelau Apia Liaison Office, the General Fono and the Tokelau Council for Ongoing Government (formerly the Council of Faipule). The chief representative of the Administrator (and the Crown) on each atoll is the highest elected official, the Faipule, who exercises executive, political and judicial powers. The three Faipule, who hold ministerial portfolios and along with the three Pulenuku (Village Mayors) form the six-member Tokelau Council of Faipule, act as the representatives of the Territory in dealings with the administration and at international meetings, and choose one of their number to hold the title Ulu-O-Tokelau (Head of Tokelau) for a term of one year. The Ulu-O-Tokelau chairs sessions of the territorial assembly, the General Fono. The General Fono is a meeting of 20 delegates (including the Faipule and the Pulenuku from each atoll), representing the entire Territory. There are three or four meetings each year, which take place on the atoll of the Ulu-O-Tokelau. The General Fono is the highest advisory body and the administration must consult it about all policy affecting the Territory. The assembly has responsibility for the territorial budget and has the power to enact legislation, to impose taxes and to declare public holidays. There are a number of specialist committees, such as the Budget Committee and the Law Committee.

Tokelau is an association of three autonomous atoll communities. Local government consists of the Faipule, the Pulenuku and the Taupulega (Island Council or Council of Elders). The Faipule, the Pulenuku and delegates to the General Fono are elected every three years on the basis of universal adult suffrage (the age of majority being 21). The Faipule represents the atoll community, liaises with the administration and the Tokelau Public Service, acts as a judicial commissioner and presides over meetings of the Taupulega. The Pulenuku is responsible for the administration of village affairs, including the maintenance of water supplies and the inspection of plantations, and, in some instances, the resolution of land disputes (practically all land is held by customary title, by the head of a family group, and may not be alienated to non-Tokelauans). The Taupulega is the principal organ of local government. The Taupulega also appoints the Failautuhi (Island Clerk), to record its meetings and transactions. The Taupulega in Atafu consists of the Faipule, the Pulenuku and the head of every family group; in Nukunonu it consists of the Faipule, the Pulenuku, the elders of the community and the nominated heads of extended families; in Fakaofo it consists of the Faipule, the Pulenuku and the elders (meetings of all the heads of family groups take place only infrequently).

The Government

(April 2008)

Administrator: DAVID PAYTON (took office October 2006).

FAIPULE

The title of Ulu-O-Tokelau (Head of Tokelau) is held on a one-year rotational basis by each Faipule in turn. At elections in January 2008, one new Faipule was elected to office and two incumbent Faipule were re-elected.

Faipule of Fakaofo: FOUA TOLOA.

Faipule of Nukunonu: PIO TUIA.

Faipule of Atafu: KURESA NASAU.

PULENUKU

At elections in January 2008, three new Pulenuku were elected to office.

Pulenuku of Fakaofo: TINIELI TUMULI.

Pulenuku of Nukunonu: LINO ISAIA.

Pulenuku of Atafu: NOUATA TUFOUA.

GOVERNMENT OFFICES

Tokelau Apia Liaison Office/Ofiha o Fehokotakiga Tokelau Ma Apia: POB 865, Apia, Samoa; tel. 32325; fax 32328; e-mail f.aukuso@clear.net.nz; responsible for transport, accounting and consular functions; Gen. Man. FALANI AUKUSO.

The Tokelau Public Service has seven departments, divided among the three atolls, with a supervising administrative official located in each village. Two departments are established on each atoll, while the seventh department, the Office of the Tokelau Council for Ongoing Government (formerly the Council of Faipule), rotates on a yearly basis in conjunction with the position of Ulu-O-Tokelau. Management of the Tokelau Public Service was formally transferred to Tokelau in July 2001.

Legislature

GENERAL FONO

The General Fono, or territorial assembly, is a meeting of delegates representing the Territory, and includes the Faipule and Pulenuku; it is the highest advisory body and must be consulted by the administration about all policy affecting the Territory. The General Fono has responsibility for the territorial budget and has the power to enact legislation, impose taxes and declare public holidays. The assembly is elected by universal suffrage and, since the legislative elections of 2002, the number of representatives from each atoll has been determined by its proportion of the total population. Members of the General Fono elect a Chairman, and hold between three and four sessions a year on the Ulu-O-Tokelau's atoll. At the elections held on 18–19 January 2008, 20 delegates were elected.

Judicial System

Tokelau's legislative and judicial systems are based on the Tokelau Islands Act 1948 and subsequent amendments and regulations. The Act provided for a variety of British regulations to continue in force and, where no other legislation applies, the law of England and Wales in 1840 (the year in which British sovereignty over New Zealand was established) was to be applicable. New Zealand statute law applies in Tokelau only if specifically extended there. In 1986 legislation formalized the transfer of High Court civil and criminal jurisdiction from Niue to New Zealand. Most cases are judged by the Commissioner established on each atoll, who has limited jurisdiction in civil and criminal matters. Commissioners are appointed by the New Zealand Governor-General, after consultation with the elders of the atoll.

Commissioner of Fakaofo: PENEHE TULAFONO.
Commissioner of Nukunonu: IOANE TUMUA.
Commissioner of Atafu: SALASOPA SEMU IUPATI.

Religion

On Atafu almost all inhabitants are members of the Tokelau Congregational Christian Church, on Nukunonu all are Roman Catholic, while both denominations are represented on Fakaofo. In the late 1990s some 70% of the total population adhered to the Congregational Christian Church, and 30% to the Roman Catholic Church.

CHRISTIANITY

Roman Catholic Church

The Church is represented in Tokelau by a Mission, established in 1992. There were an estimated 500 adherents at 31 December 2005.
Superior: Mgr PATRICK EDWARD O'CONNOR, Catholic Mission, Nukunonu, Tokelau (via Apia, Samoa); tel. 4160; fax 3146; e-mail dr.tovite@clear.net.n3.

Broadcasting and Communications

Each atoll has a radio station to broadcast shipping and weather reports. Radio-telephone provided the main communications link with other areas until the late 1990s. A new telecommunications system established at a cost of US $2.76m. (US $1m. of which was provided by New Zealand) and operating through an earth station, linked to a communications satellite, on each atoll, became operational in 1997. A new weekly radio programme, called Vakai, broadcast by Samoa Broadcasting Service to Tokelau's three atolls, began in October 2004.

TELECOMMUNICATIONS

Telecommunications Tokelau Corporation (TeleTok): Fenuafala, Fakaofo; tel. 3100; fax 3108; e-mail apvitale@clear.net.nz; f. 1996; govt-owned; Gen. Man. AUKUSITINO VITALE.

Finance

In 1977 a savings bank was established on each atoll; commercial and other banking facilities are available in Apia, Samoa.

Trade and Industry

A village co-operative store was established on each atoll in 1977. Local industries include copra production, woodwork and plaited craft goods, and the processing of tuna. Electricity is provided by diesel generators based in the village on each atoll.

Transport

There are no roads or motor vehicles. Unscheduled inter-atoll voyages, by sea, are forbidden because the risk of missing landfall is too great. Passengers and cargo are transported by vessels that anchor off shore, as there are no harbour facilities. A scheme to provide wharves (primarily to facilitate the export of fish) was proposed in September 2002. Most shipping links are with Samoa, but a monthly service from Fiji was introduced in 1986. The vessel *Forum Tokelau*, operated by Pacific Forum Line, began a monthly service between Tokelau and Apia, Samoa, in mid-1997. A New Zealand-funded inter-atoll vessel commenced service in 1991, providing the first regular link between the atolls for 40 years. Plans to construct an airstrip on each atoll were postponed in 1987 in favour of the development of shipping links. In late 2002, however, proposals for the construction of an airport were again under consideration.

NEW ZEALAND'S ASSOCIATED STATES

New Zealand's two Associated States are the self-governing Cook Islands and Niue, both of which are situated in the Pacific Ocean.

THE COOK ISLANDS

Introductory Survey

Location, Climate, Language, Religion, Flag, Capital

The 13 inhabited and two uninhabited islands of the Cook Islands are located in the southern Pacific Ocean and lie between American Samoa, to the west, and French Polynesia, to the east. The islands extend over about 2m. sq km (more than 750,000 sq miles) of ocean, and form two groups: the Northern Cooks, which are all atolls and include Pukapuka, Rakahanga and Manihiki, and the Southern Cooks, including Aitutaki, Mangaia and Rarotonga, which are all volcanic islands. From December to March the climate is warm and humid, with the possibility of severe storms; from April to November the climate is mild and equable. The average annual rainfall on Rarotonga is 2,012 mm (79 ins). The official languages are English and Cook Islands Maori. The principal religion is Christianity, with about 70% of the population adhering to the Cook Islands Congregational Christian Church. The islands' flag (proportions 1 by 2) displays 15 five-pointed white stars (representing the islands of the group) on a royal blue field, with the United Kingdom's Union Flag as a canton in the upper hoist. The capital is Avarua, on Rarotonga.

Recent History

The first Europeans to visit the islands were members of a British expedition, led by Capt. James Cook (after whom the islands are named), in 1773. The Cook Islands were proclaimed a British protectorate in 1888, and a part of New Zealand in 1901.

On 4 August 1965 the Cook Islands became a self-governing Territory in free association with New Zealand. The people are New Zealand citizens. Sir Albert Henry, leader of the Cook Islands Party (CIP), was elected Premier in 1965 and re-elected in 1971, 1974 and March 1978. However, in July 1978, following an inquiry into alleged electoral malpractice, the Chief Justice disallowed votes cast in the elections to the Legislative Assembly (later renamed Parliament) by Cook Islands expatriates who had been flown from New Zealand, with their fares paid from public funds. The amended ballot gave a majority to the Democratic Party (DP), and its leader, Dr (later Sir) Thomas Davis, was sworn in as Premier by the Chief Justice. In August 1979 Sir Albert Henry was convicted of conspiracy to defraud, and was formally stripped of his knighthood.

In May 1981 the Cook Islands' Constitution was amended to increase the membership of Parliament from 22 to 24, and to extend the parliamentary term from four to five years. In March 1983 Sir Thomas Davis lost power to the CIP, under Geoffrey (later Sir Geoffrey) Henry, cousin of the former Premier. However, with one seat already subject to re-election, Henry's majority of three was reduced by the death of one CIP member of Parliament and the transfer of allegiance to the DP by another. Henry resigned in August, and a general election in November returned the DP to power under Davis. In August 1984 Davis announced wide-ranging government changes, with three of the seven posts going to members of the CIP, to form a coalition Government, with Henry as Deputy Prime Minister. In mid-1985, however, Davis dismissed Henry, who had endorsed an unsuccessful motion expressing no confidence in the Government, and Henry's supporters withdrew from the coalition. Henry's successor as Deputy Prime Minister was Dr (later Sir) Terepai Maoate, one of four CIP members who continued to support the Davis Government, in defiance of the CIP central committee.

Davis was forced to resign as Prime Minister in July 1987, after a parliamentary motion expressing no confidence in his administration was approved. He was succeeded by Dr Pupuke Robati, a member of the Cabinet and a leading figure in the DP. Geoffrey Henry again became Prime Minister following a general election victory for the CIP in January 1989. The defection in mid-1990 of a member of Parliament from the DP to the CIP provided the latter with 15 seats in Parliament and thus the minimum two-thirds' majority support necessary to amend the Constitution. In August 1991 a constitutional amendment was approved to increase the number of members of Parliament to 25 and, at an election to the newly created seat, a CIP candidate was successful. The amendment also provided for an increase in the number of cabinet members from seven to nine (including the Prime Minister).

At a general election in March 1994 the CIP increased its majority, winning 20 seats in Parliament; the DP secured three seats and the Alliance Party (established in 1992 by Norman George, the former DP parliamentary whip, who had been expelled from the party following a dispute over spending) two. Davis, who failed to win a seat, subsequently resigned as leader of the DP. A referendum held simultaneously revealed that a majority of the electorate favoured retaining the current name (69.8% of voters) and national anthem (80.2%), while 48.5% favoured the retention of the flag of the Cook Islands. (At subsequent by-elections the CIP lost two seats and the DP and Alliance Party each gained one seat.)

A financial scandal was narrowly averted following reports that during 1994 the Government had issued loan guarantees for foreign companies worth more than $NZ1,200m. (the island's total revenue for 1994/95 was estimated at $NZ50m.). An investigation into the affair by the New Zealand Reserve Bank found that the Government had not been guilty of fraud, but rather had been coerced into the activity by unscrupulous foreign business interests. However, the affair led many investors to remove their funds from the islands, provoking a financial crisis that resulted in Henry's decision in mid-1995 to withdraw the Cook Islands dollar from circulation, and to implement a programme of retrenchment measures. The crisis deepened during 1995 as new allegations emerged, and Henry's Government was severely criticized by New Zealand for failing to co-operate with an official inquiry into accusations of fraud and tax evasion involving several New Zealand companies. Henry maintained that the islands' bank secrecy laws prevented the disclosure of information relating to financial transactions. The situation deteriorated further when it was revealed that the Government had defaulted on a debt of some US $100m. to an Italian bank. In response to pressure from New Zealand, and in an attempt to restore a degree of financial stability to the islands, Henry (whose management of the crisis had been questioned both by his own party and by the opposition) announced a severe restructuring programme in April 1996. The measures included a 50% reduction in the pay of public sector workers, the closure of almost all diplomatic missions overseas, a 60% reduction in the number of government departments and ministries, and the privatization of the majority of government-owned authorities. A marked increase in 1995/96 in the emigration rate and a decline in the number of Cook Islanders returning to the islands following a period of residency overseas was attributed to the austere economic conditions created by the financial crisis.

In August 1997 Parliament approved the Outer Islands Local Government Act, providing for a new budgetary system to allocate funds for projects in the outer islands and for increased powers for local authorities, with the aim of reducing significantly central government administration of the outer islands. As part of the plan, three new government bodies were elected in April 1998.

Henry's administration continued to attract controversy, with the announcement in December 1997 of the closure of the Ministry of Public Works, Survey, Housing, Water Supply and Environment Services for exceeding its budget. The minister responsible, Tihina Tom Marsters, resigned in protest at the closure, which resulted in the loss of more than 100 public servants' jobs, problems with the supply of utilities (particularly water) and the suspension of several development projects.

At legislative elections in June 1999 the CIP won 11 of the 25 seats in Parliament, the Democratic Alliance Party (DAP, a grouping that included the Democratic Party) 10 seats and the New Alliance Party (NAP, formerly the Alliance Party) four seats. Sir Geoffrey Henry of the CIP was reappointed Prime Minister and formed a new Cabinet, following the establishment of a political coalition with the NAP; the leader of the NAP, Norman George, became Deputy Prime Minister. However, three members of the CIP subsequently left the party to form a coalition with the DAP, in protest at the alliance with the NAP, and at the end of July Henry resigned and was replaced by a 'rebel' CIP member, Dr Joe Williams. Williams was confirmed as the new Prime Minister by 13 votes to 12 in a vote of confidence by the Parliament. Williams' appointment provoked a public protest in Rarotonga, exacerbated by general discontent at the nomination of a Prime Minister whose parliamentary constituency was outside the Cook Islands (having been elected to the seat reserved for non-resident voters). Electors also voted in a referendum on whether the parliamentary term should be reduced from five years to four. The shorter term was favoured by 63% of voters, and thus narrowly failed to receive the support of the two-thirds' majority required to amend the Constitution. The result of the contest for the Pukapuka seat, which had been won by former Prime Minister Inatio Akaruru by just one vote, was challenged by the DAP. The matter was taken to the Court of Appeal, which subsequently declared the result invalid, stripping the Government of its one-seat majority. A by-election was held in late September 1999 to decide the Pukapuka seat; however, the result was again said to be invalid and a further by-election was scheduled. The Government became a minority administration in mid-October when the Prime Minister dismissed his deputy, Norman George, along with the Minister of Education, following their defection to the opposition. Despite the appointment of three new ministers, Williams failed to regain a majority in Parliament. In November Williams resigned, shortly before a vote of no confidence was to be tabled against him by Dr Terepai Maoate, now the leader of the opposition DAP. Maoate won the vote by 14 votes to 11 and was appointed Prime Minister, forming a new coalition Government with the NAP. He subsequently reappointed Norman George to the post of Deputy Prime Minister.

Maoate dismissed Norman George in July 2001 on the grounds that he was attempting to undermine him; this was the second time that George had lost the position of Deputy Prime Minister. He was replaced by Dr Robert Woonton. However, Woonton strongly criticized Maoate's leadership in the same month. In late 2001 the rift between the Prime Minister and his Cabinet widened. Woonton announced his resignation, which Maoate refused to accept. This led to a motion of no confidence in the Prime Minister, which he only narrowly survived. In February 2002 Maoate's leadership was again challenged: 15 of the 25 members of Parliament voted against him in a second motion of no confidence. He was therefore replaced by Robert Woonton. In an extensive ministerial reorganization Sir Geoffrey Henry returned to the Cabinet as Deputy Prime Minister. Woonton declared his priorities to be the encouragement of emigrant workers to return to the islands through income tax incentives and an ambitious redevelopment plan for the capital, Avarua.

The Government's decision not to name a senior civil servant in the Prime Minister's office who had been arrested and charged with fraud in August 2002 led to accusations of secrecy by the opposition. Criticism of the Government's position increased in the following month with the introduction of new media laws (which many observers believed would serve to suppress opposition to government policy), particularly when a government official stated his desire for 'Zimbabwe-style legislation to stop inaccurate reporting'.

In November 2002 Parliament approved a constitutional amendment abolishing the requirement for electoral candidates to reside in the islands for a qualifying period of three months. This action was widely interpreted as a way of retaining the overseas voters' parliamentary seat for the CIP leader, Dr Joe Williams, who lived permanently in New Zealand. In the same month the CIP and the DP formed a coalition government (the fifth such coalition since the previous election) which left Norman George, who had been recently dismissed from his position in the Cabinet, as the sole opposition member of Parliament. The Government's action prompted a demonstration outside the parliament building by some 150 people, organized by a recently formed organization, the Group for Political Change. The protesters claimed that the virtual absence of an opposition constituted an erosion of democracy and appealed to the Prime Minister to commit to an early general election. However, in late January 2003 the CIP was ousted from the coalition. The continued political manoeuvring was widely denounced, particularly among the business community, for creating a climate of instability in the islands. Public dissatisfaction with the situation resulted in the presentation of a petition to Government in March signed by a significant percentage of the population. The petition called for a number of political reforms including a reduction in the number of members of Parliament, the introduction of a shorter parliamentary term and the abolition of the overseas seat. Moreover, businessman Teariki Heather announced the formation of a new political party, the Cook Islands National, in the same month. In September 2003 legislation was approved providing for the abolition of the overseas seat and for a referendum (to be held concurrently with the next general election) on a proposal to shorten the parliamentary term from five years to four.

In November 2003 Terepai Maoate, who had been appointed Deputy Prime Minister earlier in the year, and the Minister of Justice, Tangata Vavia, resigned following an unsuccessful attempt by Maoate to propose a motion of no confidence in the Government. The Government was the focus of further criticism in December when about 200 people marched through Avarua to protest at the granting of a residency permit to New Zealander Mark Lyon. The protesters claimed that Lyon, a wealthy businessman with recent convictions for weapons possession and a reputation for behaviour deemed disrespectful to island traditions, was not a suitable candidate for residency in the islands. Moreover, the demonstrators demanded the resignation of the Prime Minister and his chief adviser, Norman George, over the matter, stating that the islands should not be obliged to host undesirable characters, regardless of their ability to finance important business projects.

The reputation of the public service suffered a reversal in November 2003 when the former Chief of Staff in the Office of the Prime Minister, Edward Drollet, was convicted of seven charges of receiving secret commissions and one of forgery and was sentenced to more than two years' imprisonment.

At a general election in September 2004 the DP won 14 of the 24 seats, the CIP secured nine and an independent candidate won the remaining seat. Prime Minister Robert Woonton regained his seat by only four votes, amid accusations that he had secured the support of some voters through bribery. In a referendum held concurrently, 82.3% of participating voters indicated their support for the shortening of the parliamentary term from five years to four. The period immediately after the election was characterized by political manoeuvring and the initiation of several legal cases challenging the outcome in a number of constituencies. In mid-November Woonton announced that his party was to form a coalition government with the CIP. This decision was widely opposed within the DP, whose leadership questioned its legality, and prompted the resignation of the Deputy Prime Minister, Aunty Mau Munokoa. Further controversy was caused by the appointment of the defeated former MP, Norman George, to the position of Speaker. In mid-December, with the DP effectively divided over Woonton's actions, Jim Marurai, of the minority Democratic Tumu Party, was elected Prime Minister and a governing coalition was formed between his party and the CIP. It was understood that Marurai would serve as Prime Minister for the first two years of the parliamentary term and would then be replaced by Sir Geoffrey Henry of the CIP. However, in August 2005 Henry was dismissed and replaced by DP leader Dr Terepai Maoate. In September two further CIP cabinet ministers were dismissed and replaced by DP members. Marurai declared that the coalition had been dissolved, claiming that the action followed threats to his leadership.

The islands suffered considerable damage in February and March 2005 when five cyclones struck in just over four weeks. The resultant damage to housing, infrastructure and crops was estimated at $NZ25m. A rehabilitation programme was implemented, and in October 2005 discussions took place between Jim Marurai and the Prime Minister of New Zealand, Helen Clark, regarding the progress made. The islands' economic situation was also discussed.

In October 2005 Peri Vaevae Pare, the Minister of Health and Internal Affairs, whose other portfolios included social services, was suspended from office pending police investigations into allegations of fraud. In November he was convicted on three charges of intent to defraud and gain pecuniary advantage, each conviction carrying a maximum sentence of five years' imprisonment. In early 2006 the Prime Minister requested the formal resignation of the suspended Minister, who was subsequently replaced. Dr Terepai Maoate continued as Deputy Prime Minister, retaining responsibility for the finance portfolio, while Wilkie Rasmussen remained responsible for foreign affairs. In March Robert Woonton, who had previously been appointed as the islands' High Commissioner to New Zealand, was dismissed from that post, following allegations that he had been involved in an attempt to oust the islands' Government. In July a by-election victory for the opposition CIP gave it a parliamentary majority, prompting the Queen's Representative, Sir Frederick Goodwin, to dissolve the legislature and to call an early election. Votes on a motion of no confidence in Prime Minister Marurai and a motion in favour of his replacement by Sir Geoffrey Henry, submitted at a parliamentary session following the decision, were invalidated by the dissolution of Parliament. Marurai retained the role of Prime Minister in an interim capacity pending the election, which was scheduled for September. Henry announced his retirement as leader of the CIP in August.

Provisional results of the election, held on 26 September 2006, indicated that the DP had secured 15 of the 24 parliamentary seats and the CIP seven, with one seat being taken by an independent candidate. Henry Puna, who had succeeded Sir Geoffrey Henry as leader of the CIP, failed to retain his seat. A by-election to resolve the tied result in the remaining constituency resulted in victory for the CIP candidate in November. In the following month it was announced that a by-election would also be held in Titikaveka after the eligibility of the winning candidate, Robert Wigmore of the DP, was called into question. Wigmore won the Titikaveka by-election in February 2007, thus taking the final result of the 2006 election to 15 seats for the DP and eight for the CIP, along with one independent. Jim Marurai, who had returned to the DP, thus retained the position of Prime Minister, although Maoate continued as leader of the DP. In August 2007 Wilkie Rasmussen, the cabinet member responsible for foreign affairs, among other portfolios, was elected deputy leader of the DP, having left the CIP prior to the 2006 election.

In April 2007 a proposal for legislation to regulate the media, presented by Deputy Prime Minister Maoate, provoked a public debate about the freedom of the press; the subsequent formation of a monitoring body by the industry itself was reportedly linked to the indefinite postponement of the legislation. Meanwhile, in July a report by the Fiji-based Pacific Institute of Advanced Studies in Development and Governance on seven Pacific island nations gave the Cook Islands the highest rating in the area of good governance. Preparations for the 2009 South Pacific Mini Games, which were to be hosted by the islands, attracted considerable media attention in 2007–08, with the Ministry of Finance and Economic Management warning against the acceptance of a grant from China to finance the construction of a sports complex, maintaining that it would neither be cost-effective nor serve the long-term economic interests of the islands. In February 2008 the Government took a loan of US $10.2m. from China, the bulk of which was to fund preparations for the Mini Games; the decision resulted in threats of legal action from the local Chamber of Commerce. In early 2008 Norman George warned of the possibility of a vote of no confidence against the Government in the following parliamentary session, scheduled for April. Meanwhile, Brian Donnelly was appointed to replace John Bryan as New Zealand's High Commissioner to the Cook Islands, taking office in February.

The rate of emigration, meanwhile, continued to increase. In late 2000 it was announced that some 1,400 residents had left the islands during that year (compared with 641 in the previous year). This resulted in a reduction in the population of the islands to its lowest level in more than 50 years, the majority of the loss being from the outer islands, and prompted the Government to campaign in Australia and New Zealand to encourage former citizens to return to the Cook Islands. Private-sector businesses, many of which had experienced difficulties in recruiting workers in sufficient numbers, were also involved in the campaign. At the census of 2001 the resident population was recorded at only 14,990. In August 2002 the Government announced that it would allocate US $23,350 for the campaign.

In early 2000 the islands of Penrhyn, Pukapuka, Rakahanga and Manihiki expressed their desire to become fully devolved and to take sole control over areas such as administration, public expenditure and justice. In response, the Government pledged gradually to phase out the Ministry of Outer Islands Development, as well as the post of Government Representative in the outer islands. In December of that year an additional US $2m. in funding under the Cotonou agreement was designated for projects on the outer islands.

A reported increase in the number of Russian nationals opening accounts in the Cook Islands led to allegations in early 1999 that the islands' offshore financial centre was being used extensively by criminal organizations for 'laundering' the proceeds of their activities. The claims were vigorously denied by officials in the sector. However, in June 2000 the naming of the islands by the Paris-based Financial Action Task Force (FATF, see p. 416) as one of a number of countries and territories that had failed to co-operate in regional efforts to combat money-laundering, along with the islands' identification by the Organisation for Economic Co-operation and Development (OECD, see p. 347) as a tax 'haven' that lacked financial transparency, led to increased international pressure on the Government to implement stricter controls over its offshore financial centre. Consequently, legislation was approved in August of that year providing for the creation of the Money Laundering Authority and the introduction of new regulations aimed at reducing criminal activity in the sector. In February 2005 the Cook Islands were finally removed from the FATF list of non-co-operative countries and territories.

In August 1985 eight members of the South Pacific Forum (subsequently restyled the Pacific Islands Forum, see p. 380), including the Cook Islands, signed a treaty on Rarotonga, designating a 'nuclear-free' zone in the South Pacific. The treaty imposed a ban on the manufacture, testing, storage and use of nuclear weapons, and the dumping of nuclear waste, in the region.

In January 1986, following the rift between New Zealand and the USA in respect of the ANZUS (see p. 422) security arrangements, Sir Thomas Davis declared the Cook Islands a neutral country, because he considered that New Zealand (which has control over the islands' defence and foreign policy) was no longer in a position to defend the islands. The proclamation of neutrality meant that the Cook Islands would not enter into a military relationship with any foreign power, and, in particular, would prohibit visits by US warships. Visits by US naval vessels were allowed to resume by Henry's Government. In November 2007 the Cook Islands and the USA signed agreements on maritime surveillance and anti-trafficking measures. In October 1991 the Cook Islands signed a treaty of friendship and co-operation with France, covering economic development, trade and surveillance of the islands' exclusive economic zone (EEZ). The establishment of closer relations with France was widely regarded as an expression of the Cook Islands' Government's dissatisfaction with existing arrangements with New Zealand. However, relations deteriorated considerably when the French Government resumed its programme of nuclear-weapons testing at Mururoa Atoll in September 1995. Henry was fiercely critical of the decision and dispatched a *vaka* (traditional voyaging canoe) with a crew of Cook Islands' traditional warriors to protest near the test site. The tests were concluded in January 1996. Full diplomatic relations with France were established in early 2000. Meanwhile, the islands established diplomatic relations at ambassadorial level with the People's Republic of China in July 1997. In November 1998 Henry made an official visit to China, during which the two countries signed a bilateral trade agreement and each conferred the status of 'most favoured nation' on the other. Henry stated that the move constituted a further attempt by his Government to reduce the islands' dependence on New Zealand. During her visit to the islands in June 2001, Helen Clark, the New Zealand Prime Minister, stated that if the Cook Islands desired complete independence, and membership of international organizations, the process would not be obstructed by New Zealand. Cook Islanders, however, would then be obliged to renounce their New Zealand citizenship.

Government

The Cook Islands is an internally self-governing state in free association with New Zealand, which is responsible for the Cook Islands' external affairs and defence (although the Territory has progressively assumed control over much of its foreign policy). Executive authority is vested in the British monarch, who is Head of State, and is exercised through her official representative; a representative of the New Zealand Government (redesignated High Commissioner in 1994) resides on Rarotonga. Executive government is carried out by the Cabinet, consisting of the Prime Minister and between five and seven other ministers. The Cabinet is collectively responsible to the Parliament, which is formed of 24 members (decreased from 25 in 2004, following the abolition of the seat for a member chosen by non-resident voters) who are elected by universal adult suffrage every four years (reduced from five years by a referendum in 2004). The House of Ariki, which comprises up to 15 members who are hereditary chiefs, can advise the Government, but has no legislative powers. The Koutu Nui is a similar body, comprising sub-chiefs. Each of the main islands, except Rarotonga, has an elected island council, and a government representative who is appointed by the Prime Minister.

Economic Affairs

In 2006, according to official sources, the Cook Islands' gross domestic product (GDP), measured at current prices, totalled an estimated $NZ280.3m. GDP, measured at average 2000 prices, increased, in real terms, at an average annual rate of 3.4% in 1996–2006. In 2005 GDP per head was estimated at $NZ12,878, compared with $NZ 12,730 in the previous year. During 1995–2006, it was estimated, the population increased at an average annual rate of almost 1.0%. According to the Asian Development Bank (ADB), compared with the previous year overall GDP rose by 1.4% in 2006 and by 3.0% in 2007.

According to provisional estimates by the ADB, agriculture (including forestry and fishing) contributed 11.2% of GDP in 2006. In 2005 the sector engaged 28.6% of the economically active population, according to FAO estimates. The real GDP of the agricultural sector increased by an average of 6.4% per year in 1996–2006. Compared with the previous year, the sector's GDP declined by 3.7% in 2005 and by an estimated 4.5% in 2006. Cash crops include coconuts and tropical fruits such as mangoes, pineapples, bananas and papayas. Cassava, sweet potatoes and vegetables are cultivated as food crops. Pigs and poultry are the main livestock kept. The sale of fishing licences to foreign fleets provides an important source of income. Revenue from the export of fresh and chilled fish reached $NZ3.1m. in 2007, providing 45.2% of export earnings. Pearl oyster farming is also an important industry. Receipts from pearl exports totalled $NZ2.1m. (equivalent to 30.3% of total export earnings) in 2007.

Industry (comprising mining and quarrying, manufacturing, construction and utilities) provided 8.5% of GDP in 2006, according to provisional figures. The sector engaged 13.3% of employees in 2001. Industrial GDP increased, in real terms, at an average rate of 6.9% per year during 1996–2006. Compared with the previous year, the industrial sector's GDP decreased by 10.0% in 2005 and (according to official estimates) by just under 0.1% in 2006.

Manufacturing contributed 4.1% of GDP in 1995. The sector engaged 6.0% of employees in 2001. The manufacturing and mining sectors together accounted for an estimated 3.2% of GDP in 2006. The real GDP of manufacturing and mining increased at an average rate of 6.9% per year during 1996–2006. Compared with the previous year the two sectors' GDP decreased by 0.3% in 2005 and by an estimated 8.4% in 2006. Industrial activities include fruit-processing, brewing, the manufacture of garments and handicrafts. Construction contributed an estimated 3.4% of GDP in 2006 and engaged 5.9% of the employed labour force in 2001.

The islands depend on imports for their energy requirements. Mineral fuels and lubricants accounted for 22.6% of total imports in 2007. In 1997 the Government signed an agreement with a consortium of Norwegian companies to mine cobalt, nickel, manganese and copper by extracting mineral-rich nodules found in the islands' exclusive economic zone (EEZ) between Aitutaki and Penrhyn.

Service industries contributed an estimated 80.3% to GDP in 2006. The sector engaged 79.5% of the employed labour force in 2001. The

GDP of the services sector increased, in real terms, at an average annual rate of 2.5% in 1996–2006. Compared with the previous year, the GDP of the sector rose by 2.3% in 2005 and by an estimated 2.5% in 2006. Tourism expanded considerably from the late 1980s, and generated revenue of an estimated $NZ108.5m. in 2004/05. Visitor arrivals rose from 88,405 in 2005 to 92,351 in 2006 and to an estimated 97,019 in 2007. The restaurants and hotels sector contributed an estimated 15.6% of GDP in 2006, while this sector (together with wholesale and retail trade) engaged 32.6% of the employed labour force in 2001. Offshore banking, introduced to the islands in 1982, expanded rapidly, with more than 2,000 international companies registered by 1987. In 1992 the islands were established as an alternative domicile for companies listed on the Hong Kong Stock Exchange. The financial and business services sector provided an estimated 6.9% of GDP in 2006 and engaged 5.4% of the employed labour force (including persons occupied in the real estate sector) in 2001. Significant revenue is provided by remittances from emigrants from the islands (who outnumber the residents of the islands).

In 2007 the cost of imports rose to $NZ237.1m., while export revenue reached only $NZ7.0m., thus resulting in a trade deficit of $NZ230.2m. According to the ADB, there was a surplus on the current account of the balance of payments of US $26m, equivalent to 14.1% of GDP, in 2006, but in 2007 there was a deficit of US $14m. (6.4% of GDP). The principal exports in 2007 were fresh and chilled fish and pearls. The principal imports in that year were machinery and transport equipment (accounting for 26.5% of total import costs), mineral fuels and lubricants (22.6%), food and live animals (19.0%), and basic manufactures (11.3%). The principal source of imports in 2007 was New Zealand (66.4% of the total). In the same year, Japan and New Zealand were the principal markets for exports (30.1% and 15.5% respectively).

In the financial year ending June 2006 the overall budgetary deficit was estimated at $NZ2.7m. Development assistance is provided mainly by New Zealand and Australia. In mid-2004 New Zealand and Australia agreed to combine their programmes of aid to the Cook Islands in order to improve their effectiveness. In 2006/07 aid from Australia was projected at $A3.2m. In 2007/08 New Zealand allocated aid of $NZ10.0m. to the Cook Islands. The islands were also to receive $NZ1m. per year between 2003 and 2008 (to be spent on education, health and outer islands development) under the Cotonou Agreement with the European Union. It was estimated by the ADB that the islands' external debt at the end of 2001 amounted to some US $53m. The cost of debt-servicing in that year was equivalent to 3.5% of the value of exports of goods and services. By 2004 the total debt stood at an estimated US $66m. The annual rate of inflation in Rarotonga averaged 2.2% in 1995–2006. Consumer prices rose by an average of 2.4% in 2007. The ADB estimated the unemployment rate to be 13.1% of the labour force in 2001.

The Cook Islands is a member of the Pacific Community (see p. 377) and the Pacific Islands Forum (see p. 380) and an associate member of the UN Economic and Social Commission for Asia and the Pacific (ESCAP, see p. 35). In 1999 the Cook Islands were granted observer status at the Lomé Conventions with the European Union (subsequently superseded by the Cotonou Agreement, see p. 301).

From the 1990s development plans sought to expand the economy of the Cook Islands by stimulating investment in the private sector, developing the infrastructure and promoting the offshore financial sector. However, the high rate of emigration from the islands remained a serious concern, and the Government has conducted various campaigns to encourage islanders resident abroad to return. Another major challenge for the Government in the early 21st century was that of delivering basic services to the outer islands. The principal focus of the joint aid programme being financed by New Zealand and Australia, therefore, was the improvement of the outer islands' infrastructure. Under the Development Partnership Agreement signed in September 2005, a total of $NZ7m. was to be allocated over the next three years to development projects in the outer islands. In an attempt to encourage the development of the private sector, import levies were removed in mid-2006. The removal of these levies also mitigated the impact of the sharp increase in international petroleum prices in 2007. Protective tariffs remained in place on locally produced items, with those levied on food products being of particular relevance to the costs of the islands' tourism sector. The dramatic increase in tourist arrivals led to concerns that the islands, and Rarotonga in particular, were unable to sustain such rapid development. Reports indicated that waste disposal and energy provision were inadequate in relation to the demands of the large numbers of visitors and that pollution was increasing; fears for the islands' traditional culture were also expressed. The National Sustainable Development Plan and the Infrastructure Master Plan, the latter to encompass a 20-year period, were announced in 2007. These long-term programmes envisaged substantial capital expenditure. Nevertheless, economic growth remained largely dependent on tourism and, in an effort to maintain numbers of incoming tourists from the USA, in March 2007 the Government began subsidizing Air New Zealand flights on the Los Angeles–Rarotonga route. The increase in the trade deficit was largely offset by the continued expansion of the tourist industry in 2007. The ADB projected GDP growth of 3.5% in 2008.

Education

Free secular education is compulsory for a period of 10 years between six and 15 years of age. Primary education, from the age of five, lasts for six years. Secondary education, beginning at 11 years of age, comprises two cycles, each of three years. In 1998 there were 28 primary schools and 23 secondary schools, with a total of 144 primary school teachers and 129 teachers at secondary level. In 2000 enrolment at primary school level included 77.4% of pupils in the relevant age-group, while enrolment at secondary level included 57.2% of pupils. In 2007 there were 463 pupils enrolled in pre-primary education, 1,968 in primary education and 1,915 in secondary education. Tertiary education is provided at a teacher-training college, a nursing school and through an apprenticeship scheme. Under the New Zealand Training Scheme, the New Zealand Government offers overseas scholarships in New Zealand, Fiji, Papua New Guinea, Australia and Samoa for secondary and tertiary education, career-training and short-term in-service training. There is an extension centre of the University of the South Pacific (based in Fiji) in the Cook Islands.

Public Holidays

2008: 1 January (New Year's Day), 2 January (Second day of New Year), 21–24 March (Easter), 25 April (ANZAC Day, anniversary of 1915 landing at Gallipoli), 11 May (Mothers' Day), 2 June (Queen's Official Birthday), 4 August (Constitution Day), 26 October (Cook Islands Gospel Day), 25 December (Christmas Day), 26 December (Boxing Day).

2009: 1 January (New Year's Day), 2 January (Second day of New Year), 10–13 April (Easter), 25 April (ANZAC Day, anniversary of 1915 landing at Gallipoli), 10 May (Mothers' Day), 1 June (Queen's Official Birthday), 4 August (Constitution Day), 26 October (Cook Islands Gospel Day), 25 December (Christmas Day), 26 December (Boxing Day).

Weights and Measures

The metric system is in force.

Statistical Survey

Sources (unless otherwise stated): Ministry of Finance and Economic Management, POB 41, Rarotonga; tel. 29511; fax 21511; e-mail info@stats.gov.ck; internet www.spc.int/prism/country/ck/stats; Prime Minister's Department, Government of the Cook Islands, Avarua, Rarotonga; tel. 29300; fax 22856.

AREA AND POPULATION

Area: 236.7 sq km (91.4 sq miles).

Population: 18,027 (males 9,303, females 8,724) at census of 1 December 2001; 19,569 (males 9,932, females 9,637) at census of 1 December 2006 (preliminary). *Resident Population:* 14,990 (males 7,738, females 7,252) at 2001 census. *By Island* (2006 census, preliminary): Rarotonga (including the capital, Avarua) 14,153; Aitutaki 2,194; Atiu 572; Mangaia 654; Manihiki 351; Mauke 393; Mitiaro 219; Nassau 71; Palmerston (Avarua) 63; Penrhyn (Tongareva) 251; Pukapuka 507; Rakahanga 141. *Cook Island Maoris Resident in New Zealand* (census of 6 March 2001): 52,569.

Density (2006 census): 82.7 per sq km.

Principal Town (UN population estimate at mid-2003, incl. suburbs): Avarua (capital) 12,507. Source: UN, *World Urbanization Prospects: The 2003 Revision.*

Births, Marriages and Deaths (2007): Registered live births 287 (birth rate 13.6 per 1,000); Registered marriages 786 (marriage rate 37.3 per 1,000); Registered deaths 82 (death rate 3.9 per 1,000).

Expectation of Life (years at birth, WHO estimates): 72.4 (males 70.2; females 74.7) in 2005. Source: WHO, *World Health Statistics.*

Economically Active Population (resident population aged 15 years and over, 2001 census): Agriculture, hunting, forestry and fishing 427; Mining and quarrying 3; Manufacturing 357; Electricity, gas and water 79; Construction 347; Trade, restaurants and hotels 1,938; Transport, storage and communications 587; Financing, insurance, real estate and business services 323; Community, social and personal services 1,867; *Total employed* 5,928 (males 3,386, females 2,542); Unemployed 892 (males 449, females 443); *Total labour force* 6,820 (males 3,835, females 2,985).

HEALTH AND WELFARE
Key Indicators

Total Fertility Rate (children per woman, 2005): 2.6.
Under-5 Mortality Rate (per 1,000 live births, 2005): 20.
Physicians (per 1,000 head, 2001): 0.78.
Hospital Beds (per 1,000 head, 2004): 4.0.
Health Expenditure (2004): US $ per head (PPP): 435.1.
Health Expenditure (2004): % of GDP: 3.5.
Health Expenditure (2004): public (% of total): 87.4.
Access to Water (% of persons, 2004): 94.

For sources and definitions, see explanatory note on p. vi.

AGRICULTURE, ETC.

Principal Crops (metric tons, 2005, FAO estimates, unless otherwise indicated): Cassava 1,309; Sweet potatoes 628; Coconuts 1,850 (unofficial figure); Tomatoes 385; Watermelons 168; Guavas, mangosteens and mangoes 948; Papayas 965; Bananas 40; Oranges 80. *Aggregate Production* (metric tons, may include official, semi-official or estimated data): Roots and tubers 3,937; Vegetables (incl. melons) 1,554; Fruits (excl. melons) 2,439. *2006:* Figures for aggregate production assumed to be unchanged from 2005 (FAO estimates).

Livestock (head, year ending September 2005, FAO estimates): Cattle 120; Pigs 32,000; Goats 1,000; Poultry 15,000; Horses 300. Note: Data for 2006 were not available.

Livestock Products (metric tons, 2005, FAO estimates): Hen eggs 25; Pig meat 688; Chicken meat 54. Note: Data for 2006 were not available.

Forestry ('000 cu m, 2006, FAO estimate): Roundwood removals (excl. bark) 5.

Fishing (metric tons, live weight, 2005): Albacore 2,309; Yellowfin tuna 413; Bigeye tuna 208; Total catch (incl. others) 3,737.

Source: FAO.

INDUSTRY

Electric Energy (million kWh): 30 in 2005; 32 in 2006; 33 in 2007.

FINANCE

Currency and Exchange Rates: New Zealand currency is legal tender. In mid-1995 it was announced that the Cook Islands dollar (formerly the local currency, at par with the New Zealand dollar) was to be withdrawn from circulation. New Zealand currency: 100 cents = 1 New Zealand dollar ($NZ); for details of exchange rates, see Tokelau.

Budget ($NZ '000, year ending 30 June 2006): *Revenue:* Total revenue 79,056 (Tax 67,649, Other current 6,336, Capital 5,071). (Note: Revenue excludes grants of 21,714). *Expenditure:* Total expenditure 98,068 (Current 83,971, Capital 14,097). Source: Asian Development Bank, *Key Indicators of Developing Asian and Pacific Countries*.

Overseas Aid ($NZ '000): Official development assistance from New Zealand 6,240 in 2003/04; 8,870 in 2004/05; 8,000 in 2006/07. Source: Ministry of Foreign Affairs and Trade, Wellington.

Cost of Living (Consumer Price Index for Rarotonga, average of quarterly figures; base: December 2006 = 100): All items 96.57 in 2005; 99.82 in 2006; 102.23 in 2007.

Gross Domestic Product ($NZ '000 at constant 2000 prices): 215,910 in 2004; 216,407 in 2005; 219,419 in 2006.

Gross Domestic Product by Economic Activity ($NZ '000 in current prices, 2006, provisional): Agriculture, forestry and fishing 32,026; Mining, quarrying and manufacturing 9,145; Electricity, gas and water 5,589; Construction 9,622; Wholesale and retail trade 67,302; Restaurants and hotels 44,697; Transport and communications 39,978; Finance and business services 19,682; Ownership of dwellings 17,831; Public administration 34,716; Other community, social and personal services 5,895; *Sub-total* 286,482; *Less* Imputed bank service charge 6,212; *GDP in purchasers' values* 280,270.

EXTERNAL TRADE

Principal Commodities ($NZ '000, 2007): *Imports c.i.f.:* Food and live animals 44,980; Mineral fuels, lubricants, etc. 53,521; Chemicals 10,538; Basic manufactures 26,766; Machinery and transport equipment 62,789; Miscellaneous manufactured articles 22,686; Total (incl. others) 237,124. *Exports f.o.b.:* Fish, fresh or chilled 3,141; Pearls 2,109; Total (incl. others) 6,951.

Principal Trading Partners ($NZ '000, 2007): *Imports:* Australia 14,803; Fiji 42,663; Japan 5,212; New Zealand 157,554; USA 12,049; Total (incl. others) 237,124. *Exports:* Australia 258; Japan 2,094; New Zealand 1,080; USA 582; Total (incl. others) 6,951.

TRANSPORT

Road Traffic (registered vehicles, April 1983): 6,555. *New Motor Vehicles Registered* (Rarotonga, 2007): Motorcycles 1,047; Cars and jeeps 355; Vans and pick-ups 163; Trucks and buses 65; Others 18; *Total* 1,648.

Shipping: *Merchant Fleet* (registered at 31 December 2006): 81 vessels, displacement 131,347 grt (Source: Lloyd's Register-Fairplay, *World Fleet Statistics*); *International Sea-borne Freight Traffic* (estimates, '000 metric tons): Goods unloaded 32.6 (2001); Goods loaded 9; Goods unloaded 32 (1990) (Source: UN, *Monthly Bulletin of Statistics*).

Civil Aviation (2006): *Aircraft Movements:* 844 departures. *Freight Traffic* (metric tons): Goods loaded 159; Goods unloaded 1,270.

TOURISM

Foreign Tourist Arrivals: 88,405 in 2005; 92,351 in 2006; 97,019 in 2007 (provisional).

Tourist Arrivals by Place of Residence (2007, provisional): Australia 12,481; Canada 2,723; Europe 15,162; New Zealand 58,946; USA 4,351; Total (incl. others) 97,019.

Tourism Revenue (US $ million, incl. passenger transport): 69 in 2003; 72 in 2004; 92 in 2005 (provisional). Source: World Tourism Organization.

COMMUNICATIONS MEDIA

Radio Receivers (1997): 14,000 in use*.
Television Receivers (1997): 4,000 in use*.
Telephones (main lines, 2002): 6,000 in use†.
Mobile Cellular Telephones (2002): 1,499 subscribers†.
Facsimile Machines (1990): 230 in use‡.
Internet Users (2002): 3,600.
Daily Newspaper (1996): 1; circulation 2,000*.
Non-daily Newspaper (1996): 1; circulation 1,000*.
* Source: UNESCO, *Statistical Yearbook*.
† Source: International Telecommunication Union.
‡ Source: UN, *Statistical Yearbook*.

EDUCATION

Pre-primary (2007, unless otherwise indicated): 26 schools (1998); 31 teachers (2000); 463 pupils.

Primary (2007, unless otherwise indicated): 28 schools (1998); 144 teachers (2000); 1,968 pupils.

Secondary* (1998, unless otherwise indicated): 23 schools; 129 teachers; 1,915 pupils (2007).

Higher (1980): 41 teachers; 360 pupils†.
* Includes high school education.
† Source: UNESCO, *Statistical Yearbook*.

Directory

The Constitution

On 4 August 1965 a new Constitution was proclaimed, whereby the people of the Cook Islands have complete control over their own affairs in free association with New Zealand, but they can at any time move into full independence by a unilateral act if they so wish.

Executive authority is vested in the British monarch, who is Head of State, and exercised through an official representative. The New Zealand Government also appoints a representative (from 1994 redesignated High Commissioner), resident on Rarotonga.

Executive powers are exercised by a Cabinet consisting of the Prime Minister and between five and seven other ministers including a Deputy Prime Minister. The Cabinet is collectively responsible to Parliament.

Legislation approved in September 2003 resulted in the abolition of the seat for one member elected by voters living overseas and consequently Parliament consists of 24 members elected by universal suffrage and presided over by the Speaker. Moreover, as a result of a referendum held concurrently with the general election of September 2004, the parliamentary term was shortened from five years to four. The House of Ariki comprises up to 15 members who are hereditary chiefs; it can advise the Government, particularly on matters relat-

NEW ZEALAND'S ASSOCIATED STATES

ing to land and indigenous people, but has no legislative powers. The Koutu Nui is a similar body composed of sub-chiefs, which was established by an amendment in 1972 of the 1966 House of Ariki Act.

Each of the main islands, except Rarotonga (which is divided into three tribal districts or *vaka*), has an elected mayor and a government representative who is appointed by the Prime Minister. In January 2000 it was announced that the post of Government Representative in the outer islands was to be phased out over two years.

The Government

Queen's Representative: Sir FREDERICK GOODWIN.
New Zealand High Commissioner: BRIAN DONNELLY.

CABINET
(April 2008)

Prime Minister, Minister of Information and Technology, Education, National Human Resources, Office of the Head of State, and Police: JIM MARURAI.

Deputy Prime Minister and Minister of Finance and Economic Development, Financial Intelligence Unit, Public Expenditure and Review Committee, Health, Ombudsman, Development Investment Board, Small Business Enterprise Centre, Attorney-General, Commerce Commission, National Superannuation, Parliamentary Services and Broadcasting: Sir TEREPAI MAOATE.

Minister of Foreign Affairs and Immigration, Tourism, Cultural Development and Marine Resources: WILKIE RASMUSSEN.

Minister of Agriculture, Internal Affairs, Youth and Sport, Punanganui Market, Non-Government Organizations and Works: NGAMAU ('AUNTY MAU') MUNOKOA.

Minister of Transport, Justice, Public Service Commission, Cook Islands Investment Corporation and Energy: TANGATA VAVIA.

Minister of Outer Islands Administration and National Environment Services: KETE IOANE.

GOVERNMENT OFFICES

Office of the Queen's Representative: POB 134, Titikaveka, Rarotonga; tel. 29311.

Office of the Prime Minister: Government of the Cook Islands, Private Bag, Avarua, Rarotonga; tel. 25494; fax 20856; e-mail coso@pmoffice.gov.ck.

Office of the Public Service Commissioner: POB 24, Rarotonga; tel. 29421; fax 21321; e-mail epati@psc.gov.ck.

New Zealand High Commission: 1st Floor, Philatelic Bureau Bldg, Takuvaine Rd, POB 21, Avarua, Rarotonga; tel. 22201; fax 21241; e-mail nzhraro@oyster.net.ck.

Ministries

Ministry of Agriculture: POB 96, Rarotonga; tel. 28711; fax 21881; e-mail cimoa@oyster.net.ck.

Ministry of Cultural Development: POB 8, Rarotonga; tel. 20725; fax 23725; e-mail culture1@oyster.net.ck; internet www.culture.gov.ck.

Ministry of Education: Tereora, Nikao, Rarotonga; tel. 29357; fax 28357; e-mail cieducat@oyster.net.ck; internet www.education.gov.ck.

Ministry of Energy: POB 72, Rarotonga; tel. 24484; fax 24483; e-mail punanga@energy.gov.ck.

Ministry of Finance and Economic Management: POB 120, Rarotonga; tel. 22878; fax 23877; e-mail cifinsec@mfem.gov.ck; internet www.mfem.gov.ck.

Ministry of Foreign Affairs and Immigration: POB 105, Rarotonga; tel. 29347; fax 21247; e-mail secfa@mfai.gov.ck.

Ministry of Health: POB 109, Rarotonga; tel. 22664; fax 22670; e-mail soh1@health.gov.ck; internet www.health.gov.ck.

Ministry of Internal Affairs: POB 98, Rarotonga; tel. 29370; fax 23608; e-mail secintaff@intaff.gov.ck.

Ministry of Justice: POB 111, Rarotonga; tel. 29410; fax 29610; e-mail offices@justice.gov.ck.

Ministry of Marine Resources: POB 85, Rarotonga; tel. 28721; fax 29721; e-mail I.Bertram@mmr.gov.ck.

Ministry of Outer Islands' Administration: POB 383, Rarotonga; tel. 20321; fax 24321; e-mail secmoid@moid.gov.ck.

Ministry of Transport: POB 61, Rarotonga; tel. 28810; fax 28816; e-mail transport@oyster.net.ck.

Ministry of Works: POB 102, Rarotonga; tel. 20034; fax 21134; internet www.mow.gov.ck.

National Environment Service: POB 371, Rarotonga; tel. 21256; fax 22256; e-mail resources@environment.org.ck; internet www.environment.org.ck.

Advisory Chambers

House of Ariki: POB 13, Rarotonga; tel. 26500; fax 21260; Pres. ADA RONGOMATENE ARIKI.

Koutu Nui: POB 13, Rarotonga; tel. 29317; fax 21260; e-mail nvaloa@parliament.gov.ck; Pres. TETIKA MATAIAPO DORICE REID.

Legislature

PARLIAMENT

Parliamentary Service
POB 13, Rarotonga; tel. 26500; fax 21260; e-mail nvaloa@parliament.gov.ck.

Speaker: MAPU TAIA.
Clerk of Parliament: NGA VALOA.

General Election, 26 September 2006*

Party	Seats
Democratic Party (DP)	15
Cook Islands Party (CIP)	8
Independent	1
Total	**24**

* A by-election held on 28 November 2006 in the constituency of Akaoa, where the seat had been tied at the poll of 26 September, was won by the Cook Islands Party. A second by-election was held in Titikaveka on 7 February 2007, following a court ruling that the winning Democratic Party candidate had been ineligible to contest the election; the Democratic Party candidate was re-elected.

Political Organizations

Cook Islands Labour Party: Rarotonga; f. 1988; anti-nuclear; Leader RENA ARIKI JONASSEN.

Cook Islands National: Rarotonga; f. 2003; Leader TEARIKI HEATHER.

Cook Islands Party (CIP): Rarotonga; f. 1965; Leader HENRY PUNA; Deputy Leader TUPOU FAIREKA.

Democratic Party (DP): POB 73, Rarotonga; tel. 21224; e-mail demo1@oyster.net.ck; f. 1972; Pres. MAKIUTI TONGIA; Leader Sir TEREPAI MAOATE; Deputy Leader WILKIE RASMUSSEN.

Judicial System

High Court
Avarua, Rarotonga; e-mail offices@justice.gov.ck.

The judiciary comprises the Privy Council, the Court of Appeal and the High Court.

The High Court exercises jurisdiction in respect of civil, criminal and land titles cases on all the islands, except for Mangaia, Pukapuka and Mitiaro, where disputes over land titles are settled according to custom. The Court of Appeal hears appeals against decisions of the High Court. The Privy Council, sitting in the United Kingdom, is the final appellate tribunal for the country in civil, criminal and land matters.

Attorney-General: Sir TEREPAI MAOATE.
Solicitor-General: TINGIKA ELIKANA (acting).
Chief Justice of the High Court: DAVID ARTHUR RHODES WILLIAMS.
Judges of the High Court: GLENDYN CARTER, COLIN NICHOLSON, HETA HINGSTON, CHRISTINE GRICE.

Religion

CHRISTIANITY

The principal denomination is the Cook Islands (Congregational) Christian Church, to which about 58% of the islands' population belong, according to figures recorded in the census conducted in 1996.

Religious Advisory Council of the Cook Islands: POB 147, Rarotonga; tel. 20817; fax 29817; e-mail sbish@oyster.net.ck; f. 1972; six mem. churches; Pres. Bishop S. O'CONNELL.

The Roman Catholic Church

The Cook Islands form the diocese of Rarotonga, suffragan to the archdiocese of Suva (Fiji). At 31 December 2005 the diocese contained an estimated 2,690 adherents. The Bishop participates in the Catholic Bishops' Conference of the Pacific, based in Suva.

Bishop of Rarotonga: Rt Rev. STUART FRANCE O'CONNELL, Catholic Diocese, POB 147, Avarua, Rarotonga; tel. 20817; fax 29817; e-mail sbish@oyster.net.ck.

The Anglican Communion

The Cook Islands are within the diocese of Polynesia, part of the Church of the Province of New Zealand. The Bishop of Polynesia is resident in Fiji.

Protestant Churches

Cook Islands Christian Church: Takamoa, POB 93, Rarotonga; tel. 26452; 11,193 mems (1986); Pres. Rev. TANGIMETUA TANGATA-TUTA; Gen. Sec. WILLIE JOHN.

Seventh-day Adventists: POB 31, Rarotonga; tel. 22851; fax 22852; e-mail umakatu@oyster.net.ck; 732 mems (1998); Pres. UMA KATU.

Other churches active in the islands include the Assembly of God, the Church of Latter-day Saints (Mormons), the Apostolic Church, the Jehovah's Witnesses and the Baptist Church.

BAHÁ'Í FAITH

Administrative Committee of the Bahá'ís of Cook Islands: POB 1, Rarotonga; tel. 20658; e-mail nsacooks@bahai.org.ck; mems resident in six localities; Sec. DIANE SCOTT.

The Press

Cook Islands Herald: POB 126, Tutakimoa, Rarotonga; e-mail bestread@ciherald.co.ck; internet www.ciherald.co.ck; weekly; Publr GEORGE PITT.

Cook Islands News: POB 15, Avarua, Rarotonga; tel. 22999; fax 25303; e-mail editor@cookislandsnews.com; internet www.cookislandsnews.com; f. 1954; est. by Govt; transferred to private ownership in 1989; daily; mainly English; Editor JOHN WOODS; circ. 2,100.

Cook Islands Star: POB 798, Rarotonga; tel. 29965; e-mail jason@oyster.net.ck; fortnightly; Chief Reporter JASON BROWN.

Cook Islands Sun: POB 753, Snowbird Laundry, Arorangi, Rarotonga; f. 1988; tourist newspaper; twice a year; Editor WARREN ATKINSON.

Broadcasting and Communications

TELECOMMUNICATIONS

Telecom Cook Islands Ltd: POB 106, Avarua, Rarotonga; tel. 29680; fax 26174; e-mail sales@telecom.co.ck; internet www.telecom.co.ck; CEO STUART DAVIES.

BROADCASTING

Radio

Cook Islands Broadcasting Corpn (CIBC): POB 126, Avarua, Rarotonga; tel. 29460; fax 21907; f. 1989; est. to operate new television service, and radio service of former Broadcasting and Newspaper Corpn; state-owned; Gen. Man. EMILE KAIRUA.

Radio Cook Islands: tel. 20100; e-mail tunein@radio.co.ck; internet www.radio.co.ck; broadcasts in English and Maori 18 hours daily.

KC Radio: POB 521, Avarua, Rarotonga; tel. 23203; f. 1979; est. as Radio Ikurangi; commercial; operates station ZK1ZD; broadcasts 18 hours daily on FM; Man. Dir and Gen. Man. DAVID SCHMIDT.

Television

Cook Islands Broadcasting Corpn (CIBC): see Radio

Cook Islands TV (CITV): POB 126, Rarotonga; tel. 20101; fax 21907; f. 1989; operated by Elijah Communications; broadcasts nightly, in English and Maori, from 5 p.m. to 10.15 p.m; 10 hours of local programmes per week; remainder provided by Television New Zealand.

Finance

(cap. = capital; dep. = deposits; m. = million; brs = branches)

Financial Supervisory Commission: POB 594, Avarua, Rarotonga; tel. 20798; fax 21798; e-mail Inquire@fsc.gov.ck; internet www.fsc.gov.ck; f. 1981 as Cook Islands Monetary Board, name changed as above in 2003; supervises banks and insurance companies; licences trustee companies; registers international companies, trusts, financial institutions, etc.; Commissioner LORRAINE ALLAN; Chair. TREVOR CLARKE.

Trustee Companies Association (TCA): Rarotonga; controlling body for the 'offshore' financial sector; Sec. LOU COLVEY.

BANKING

Development Bank

Bank of Cook Islands (BCI): POB 113, Avarua, Rarotonga; tel. 29341; fax 29343; e-mail bci@oyster.net.ck; f. July 2001 when Cook Islands Development Bank merged with Cook Islands Savings Bank; finances development projects in all areas of the economy and helps islanders establish small businesses and industries by providing loans and management advisory assistance; Gen. Man. UNAKEA KAUVAI; brs on Rarotonga and Aitutaki.

Commercial Banks

Australia and New Zealand (ANZ) Banking Corpn: 1st Floor, Development Bank Bldg, POB 907, Avarua, Rarotonga; tel. 21750; fax 21760; e-mail lancaster@gatepoly.co.ck; Gen. Man. GAYLE STAPLETON.

Banktec Cook Islands Ltd: POB 822, Level 2, Asiaciti Trust Pacific Ltd, BCI House, Rarotonga; tel. 23387; e-mail info@banktecgroup.com; internet www.banktecgroup.com; f. 1993 as First Trading Bank Ltd; named changed as above in 2005; 70% owned by Financial Community Partnership Inc, Panamá City, 15% owned by L. F. Vareas, 15% owned by J. L. Bado; cap. US $10.0m., dep. US $5.2m. (Dec. 2006); Dirs J. L. NAVARRO, L. F. VARGAS, J. L. BADO; Gen. Man. FACUNDO SEIGAL.

Westpac Banking Corpn (Australia): Main Rd, POB 42, Avarua, Rarotonga; tel. 22014; fax 20802; e-mail bank@westpac.co.ck; Man. TERRY SMITH.

WSBC Bank Ltd: POB 3012, Parekura House, Avarua, Rarotonga; tel. 23445; fax 23446; e-mail info@wsbcbank.com; internet www.wsbcbank.com; f. 1992; 100% owned by Natar Holdings Co Ltd; fmrly known as The Wall Street Banking Corpn Ltd; name changed as above 2007; cap. US $15m., dep. US $86m. (Sept. 2005); Chair. M. L. T. FERNANDEZ; CEO and Dir KUMUD RANJAN MOHANTY.

Legislation was adopted in 1981 to facilitate the establishment of offshore banking operations.

INSURANCE

Cook Islands Insurance: POB 44, Rarotonga.

Trade and Industry

GOVERNMENT AGENCIES

Cook Islands Development Investment Board: Private Bag, Avarua, Rarotonga; tel. 24296; fax 24298; e-mail markshort@cidib.gov.ck; f. 1996; est. as replacement for Development Investment Council; promotes, monitors and regulates foreign investment, promotes international trade, advises the private sector and Government and provides training in business skills; CEO MARK SHORT.

Cook Islands Investment Corporation: Rarotonga; tel. 29391; fax 29381; e-mail ciic@oyster.net.ck; f. 1998; manages government assets and shareholding interests; Chair. JOHN SHORT; CEO JOHN TINI.

Cook Islands Public Service Commission: POB 24, Rarotonga; tel. 29421; fax 21321; e-mail epati@psc.gov.ck; Commissioner NAVY EPATI; CEO RUSSELL THOMAS.

Cook Islands Trading Corporation: Private Bag 1, Avarua, Rarotonga; tel. 22000; fax 20857; e-mail shop@citc.co.ck.

CHAMBER OF COMMERCE

Chamber of Commerce: POB 242, Rarotonga; tel. 20925; fax 20969; f. 1956; Pres. TERESA MANARANGI-TROTT.

INDUSTRIAL AND TRADE ASSOCIATION

Pearl Guild of the Cook Islands: Rarotonga; e-mail trevon@oyster.net.ck; f. 1994; monitors standards of quality within the pearl industry and develops marketing strategies; Pres. TREVON BERGMAN.

UTILITIES

Electricity

Te Aponga Uira O Tumutevarovaro (TAUOT) (Rarotonga Electricity Authority): POB 112, Rarotonga; tel. 20054; fax 21944; Chair. TAMARII TUTANGATA.

Water

Water Supply Department: POB 102, Arorangi, Rarotonga; tel. 20034; fax 21134.

TRADE UNIONS

Airport Workers' Association: Rarotonga Int. Airport, POB 90, Rarotonga; tel. 25890; fax 21890; f. 1985; Pres. NGA JESSIE; Gen. Sec. (vacant).

Cook Islands Industrial Union of Waterside Workers: Avarua, Rarotonga.

Cook Islands Workers' Association (CIWA): POB 403, Avarua, Rarotonga; tel. 24422; fax 24423; largest union in the Cook Islands; Pres. MIRIAMA PIERRE; Gen. Sec. NGAMETUA ARAKUA.

Transport

ROADS

On Rarotonga a 33-km sealed road encircles the island's coastline. A partly sealed inland road, parallel to the coastal road and known as the Ara Metua, is also suitable for vehicles. In February 2006 it was announced that construction of a cyclone-proof road, which would encompass the flood-prone area west of Rarotonga airport, was to be initiated with aid from the People's Republic of China. Roads on the other islands are mainly unsealed.

SHIPPING

The main ports are on Rarotonga (Avatiu), Penrhyn, Mangaia and Aitutaki. The Cook Islands National Line operates a three-weekly cargo service between the Cook Islands, Tonga, Samoa and American Samoa. In August 2002 the Government approved proposals to enlarge Avatiu Harbour. The project received additional funding from the Ports Authority and from New Zealand.

Apex Maritime: POB 378, Rarotonga; tel. 27651; fax 21138.

Cook Islands National Line: POB 264, Rarotonga; tel. 20374; fax 20855; 30% govt-owned; operates three fleet cargo services between the Cook Islands, Niue, Samoa, Norfolk Island, Tonga and New Zealand; Dirs CHRIS VAILE, GEORGE ELLIS.

Cook Islands Shipping Ltd: POB 2001, Arorangi, Rarotonga; tel. 24905; fax 24906.

Ports Authority: POB 84, Rarotonga and Aitutaki; tel. 21921; fax 21191; Chair. DON BEER.

Reef Shipping Company: Rarotonga; operates services between Rarotonga and Aitutaki.

Taio Shipping Ltd: Teremoana Taio, POB 2001, Rarotonga; tel. 24905; fax 24906.

Triad Maritime (1988) Ltd: Rarotonga; fax 20855.

CIVIL AVIATION

An international airport was opened on Rarotonga in 1974. Air New Zealand is among the airlines operating services between Rarotonga and other airports in the region. Air Pacific (Fiji) began a twice-weekly service between Nadi and Rarotonga in June 2000, and in August of that year Air New Zealand began a direct service from Rarotonga to Los Angeles, USA.

Airport Authority: POB 90, Rarotonga; CEO JOE NGAMATA.

Air Rarotonga: POB 79, Rarotonga; tel. 22888; fax 23288; e-mail admin@airraro.co.ck; internet www.airraro.com; f. 1978; privately owned; operates internal passenger and cargo services and charter services to Niue and French Polynesia; Man. Dir EWAN F. SMITH.

Tourism

Tourism is the most important industry in the Cook Islands and, according to provisional estimates, there were 97,019 foreign tourist arrivals in 2007, compared with 25,615 in 1984. Of total foreign visitors in 2007, an estimated 60.8% came from New Zealand, 12.9% from Australia and 15.6% from Europe. There were 1,874 beds available at hotels and similar establishments in the islands in 1999. Most of the tourist facilities are to be found on Rarotonga and Aitutaki, but the outer islands also offer attractive scenery. Revenue from tourism was estimated at some US $92m. in 2005.

Cook Islands Tourism Corporation: POB 14, Rarotonga; tel. 29435; fax 21435; e-mail lydia@cookislands.gov.ck; internet www.cookislands.travel; Chair. DES EGGELTON; CEO JOHN DEAN.

NIUE

Introductory Survey

Location, Climate, Language, Religion, Flag, Capital

Niue is a coral island, located in the Pacific Ocean, about 480 km (300 miles) east of Tonga and 930 km (580 miles) west of the southern Cook Islands. Rainfall occurs predominantly during the hottest months, from December to March, when the average temperature is 27°C (81°F). Average annual rainfall is 7,715mm (298 ins). Niuean, a Polynesian language, and English are spoken. The population is predominantly Christian, with 66% belonging to the Ekalesia Niue, a Protestant church, in 1991. Niue's flag (proportions 1 by 2) is yellow, bearing, in the upper hoist corner, the United Kingdom's Union Flag with a yellow five-pointed star on each arm of the cross of St George and a slightly larger yellow five-pointed star on a blue disc in the centre of the cross. Some 30% of the population resides in Alofi, which is the capital and administrative centre of Niue. Plans to relocate the capital to Fonuakula on the upper plateau of the island were announced following the widespread devastation caused by Cyclone Heta in January 2004.

Recent History

The first Europeans to discover Niue were members of a British expedition, led by Capt. James Cook, in 1774. Missionaries visited the island throughout the 19th century, and in 1900 Niue was declared a British protectorate. In 1901 Niue was formally annexed to New Zealand as part of the Cook Islands, but in 1904 it was granted a separate administration.

In October 1974 Niue attained 'self-government in free association with New Zealand'. Niueans retain New Zealand citizenship, and a sizeable resident Niuean community exists in New Zealand. The 1991 population census revealed an 11.5% decrease since 1986, and many more Niueans live in New Zealand than on Niue. Robert (from 1982, Sir Robert) Rex, who had been the island's political leader since the early 1950s, was Niue's Premier when it became self-governing, and retained the post at three-yearly general elections in 1975–90.

The migration of Niueans to New Zealand has been a cause of concern, and in October 1985 the Government of New Zealand announced its intention to review its constitutional relationship with Niue, with the express aim of preventing further depopulation of the island. In 1987 a six-member committee, comprising four New Zealanders and two Niueans, was formed to examine Niue's economic and social conditions, and to consider the possibility of the island's reversion to the status of a New Zealand-administered territory.

At the 1987 general election all except three of the 20 members of the Niue Assembly were re-elected. The newly founded Niue People's Action Party (NPAP) secured one seat. The NPAP, Niue's only political party, criticized the Government's economic policy, and in particular its apparent inability to account for a substantial amount of the budgetary aid received from New Zealand. A declared aim of the party was to persuade Niueans residing in New Zealand to invest in projects on Niue.

In April 1989 the New Zealand Auditor-General issued a report which was highly critical of the Niuean Government's use of aid money from New Zealand, in particular Rex's preferential treatment of public servants in the allocation of grants. In June Young Vivian, leader of the unofficial NPAP opposition in the Niue Assembly, proposed a motion expressing no confidence in the Government, which was defeated by 13 votes to seven. In November proposed legislation which included the replacement of New Zealand's Governor-General by a Niuean citizen was rejected by the Niue Assembly, owing to the implications for relations with New Zealand.

At the 1990 general election candidates of the NPAP and its sympathizers won 12 of the 20 seats. Earlier disagreements in the NPAP leadership, however, allowed Rex to secure the support of four members previously opposed to his Government. Rex therefore remained Premier.

The announcement in mid-1991 by the New Zealand Government that it was to reduce its aid payments to Niue by about $NZ1m. (a decrease of some 10% on the average annual allocation) caused considerable concern on the island. More than one-quarter of the paid labour force on Niue were employed by the Niue Government, and, following the reduction in aid in July, about 150 (some 25%) lost their jobs. Members of the Government subsequently travelled to New Zealand to appeal against the decision and to request the provision of redundancy payments for the dismissed employees. Their attempts failed, however, with the New Zealand Government reiterating its claim that aid had been inefficiently used in the past.

In December 1992 Sir Robert Rex died, and Young Vivian (who had been serving as acting Premier at the time of Rex's death) was unanimously elected Premier by the Government. Legislative elections took place in February 1993, and in the following month the Niue Assembly elected Frank Lui, a former cabinet minister, as Premier. Lui, who defeated Young Vivian by 11 votes to nine, announced a new Cabinet following the election; among the new Premier's stated objectives were the development of tourism and further plans to encourage Niueans resident in New Zealand to return to the island.

In March 1994 Vivian proposed an unsuccessful motion of no confidence in the Government, and a further attempt by the opposition to introduce a similar motion was invalidated in the High Court in October on a procedural matter. However, during the ensuing debate, the Minister of National Planning and Economic Development, Sani Lakatani, resigned in order to join the opposition as its deputy leader, thus leaving the Government with only 10 official supporters in the Assembly. Subsequent opposition demands for the intervention of the Governor-General of New Zealand in dissolving the legislature, in preparation for a fresh general election, were rejected, and, despite Lui's assurance that an early election would take place in order to end the atmosphere of increasing political uncertainty, polls were not held until February 1996. The Premier and his three cabinet ministers were re-elected to their seats, although support among the electorate for candidates of the Niue People's Party (NPP, as the NPAP had been renamed in 1995) and independents appeared fairly equally divided; in one village the result was decided by the toss of a coin when both candidates received an equal number of votes. Frank Lui was re-elected by the Niue Assembly as Premier, defeating Robert Rex, Jr (son of Niue's first Premier) by 11 votes to nine.

The issue of Niue's declining population continued to cause concern, particularly when provisional census figures, published in late 1997, revealed that the island's population was at its lowest recorded level. The Government expressed disappointment that its policy of encouraging Niueans resident in New Zealand to return to the island had failed and announced its intention to consider introducing more lenient immigration laws in an attempt to increase the population.

At a general election on 19 March 1999 Lui lost his seat and subsequently announced his retirement from politics. The Minister of Finance, Aukuso Pavihi, also failed to be re-elected. On 29 March Sani Lakatani, leader of the NPP, was elected Premier by the new Assembly, defeating O'Love Jacobsen by 14 votes to six. Lakatani's stated priority as Premier was to increase Niue's population to at least 3,000; he claimed that the sharp decline in the number of residents constituted a threat to the island's self-governing status.

It was reported in May 1999 that New Zealand was to phase out aid to Niue by 2003; New Zealand's aid programme to the island had been reduced by $NZ250,000 annually over the previous five years. However, doubts were expressed over the legality of the New Zealand Government's action, and it was suggested that New Zealand was required by law to provide financial assistance under the 1974 act that established Niue as a self-governing state.

In December 1999 a motion of no confidence in Lakatani was proposed by a number of opposition ministers, in protest at the Government's plans to fund a new national airline (Coral Air Niue). The result of the vote was inconclusive, with an equal number of votes cast for and against the motion. The proposed airline did not materialize, and the Government lost $NZ400,000 of its initial investment in the project. The New Zealand Government subsequently criticized officials in Niue for failing to secure a business plan or feasibility study for the proposed airline.

In late 1999 allegations made by a foreign news agency that Niue was being used by criminal organizations for 'laundering' the proceeds of their illegal activities were strongly denied by Lakatani. However, the naming of the island in a report by the Financial Action Task Force (FATF, see p. 416) in June 2000 as one of a number of countries and territories that had failed to co-operate in regional efforts to combat money-laundering led the Government to suspend the issue of any further offshore banking licences until stricter regulations governing the financial sector had been introduced. In early 2001 the USA imposed sanctions on Niue (including a ban on transactions with US banks), claiming that the island had not implemented all the recommendations of the report. Lakatani appealed directly to President George W. Bush to end the embargo, which he said was having a devastating effect on Niue's economy. The Government stressed its commitment to meeting international requirements in its financial sector but claimed that it was having difficulty doing so, given its limited legal resources. Moreover, the Premier expressed strong disapproval that a nation as powerful as the USA should choose to inflict such hardship on a small, economically-vulnerable island, and urged other Pacific islands targeted by the report to unite in protest against such impositions. In June 2001 the Government engaged a US law firm in an effort to persuade two banks, Chase Manhattan and Bank of New York, to remove their bans on the transfer of some $NZ1m. to Niue via the business registry in Panama that the Government used for its offshore tax activity.

Having failed to meet an FATF deadline in August 2001, in February 2002 Niue pledged to repeal its offshore banking legislation. Premier Sani Lakatani was also considering closing down international business registrations based in Niue. The FATF announced in April 2002 that, in view of the island's commitment to improving the transparency of its tax and regulatory systems, the organization was to remove Niue from its list of non-co-operative territories; the decision was duly implemented in October. The bank-licensing legislation was repealed in June.

In December 2001 the Alliance of Independents, a new political party led by Frank Lui, was formed to contest the forthcoming general election. The party's spokesperson, O'Love Jacobsen, announced that the Alliance would campaign for a direct air link to New Zealand and for increased spending on public health.

At the general election, held on 20 April 2002, all 20 incumbent members were returned to the Niue Assembly. Independent candidate Toke Talagi polled the highest number of votes (445), but overall the NPP was victorious. However, despite having polled the second-highest number of votes (428), Sani Lakatani did not command the general support of his party, and faced a leadership challenge from his deputy, Young Vivian. Following several days of lobbying within the NPP, Vivian was chosen as Premier. Vivian announced that the party had the support of 10 elected members, having formed a coalition with several independents associated with Toke Talagi. Lakatani was appointed Deputy Premier, however, later that year and following a period of ill health, the former Premier indicated that he might withdraw from politics.

In July 2003 Niue's only formal political party, the Niue People's Party, was dissolved as a result of ongoing disagreement among its membership and the failure of several projects (the most prominent of which was the attempted establishment of Coral Air Niue, see above). Opposition member Terry Coe expressed satisfaction with the news, stating that he hoped that party politics would cease henceforth in Niue. Observers also commented that Robert Rex (Niue's widely respected first Premier) had strongly opposed party politics, believing it to cause rifts in families and communities.

In September 2003 the opposition expressed concern that too many government members were travelling overseas on business, and that a significant amount of public money was being used to fund these trips. At the time of the statement seven of the Niue Assembly's 20 members (including two cabinet ministers) were absent on engagements overseas. In the same month it was announced that Niue was to receive US $90,000 from the People's Republic of China in order to build new accommodation for the 300 delegates and visitors who were expected to visit the island for the Pacific Islands Forum summit meeting in 2004. The meeting was relocated, however, following the widespread devastation of the island by a cyclone in early 2004 (see below).

In October 2003 Niue's Premier issued a statement inviting the residents of Tuvalu (whose continued existence on those islands was increasingly threatened by rising sea levels) to migrate to Niue. The Government of Tuvalu subsequently requested that Niue produce a memorandum of understanding giving formal details of this invitation and of the rights that Tuvaluans would enjoy on Niue. Further discussions between officials from the two Governments took place in June 2005.

In early January 2004 Niue was devastated by Cyclone Heta. Damage caused by the storm, which was described as the worst in the island's recent history, included the destruction of many buildings, the loss of most food crops, the death of two people and serious injury of several others and extensive damage to Niue's infrastructure, communications and coral reef. Relief supplies were sent from New Zealand as part of an initial aid programme worth some US $3.5m. It was estimated that US $23m. would be needed for a rebuilding programme to be carried out over a five-year period. The destruction of Alofi was so severe that the Government announced plans to relocate the island's capital to Fonuakula on the upper plateau. However, fears for the continued feasibility of the island were expressed by some observers, who suggested that many Niueans might exercise their right to take up residency in New Zealand, leaving the community on Niue unviable. As work began to repair or rebuild some 300 homes under the Government's New Niue or Niue Foou recovery plan, it was announced that renewed efforts would be made to attract expatriate Niueans back to the island. A fish-processing plant, due to open later in the year, as well as a number of new agricultural projects, were expected to provide some employment opportunities. In October New Zealand's Prime Minister Helen Clark made an official visit to Niue to celebrate the 30-year anniversary of the island's attainment of self-governing status. She used the visit to urge expatriate Niueans to return to the island and support efforts to regenerate its infrastructure and economy. Moreover, she announced a programme to introduce the Niuean language into the education curriculum from pre-school level onwards by 2006, as part of Taoga Niue, an initiative aimed at preserving traditional customs and cultural practices on the island. In addition, Clark confirmed that $NZ6m. was to be made available to rebuild the hospital destroyed by Cyclone Heta. The new hospital, located at Kaimiti, opened in March 2006. In April New Zealand and France agreed jointly to finance the construction of a government administration building on Niue.

In March 2000, meanwhile, a Niue-New Zealand joint consultative committee met, for the first time, in Alofi to consider the two sides' future constitutional relationship. Later that year the committee proposed to conduct a survey of islanders' views and to consider all options, from reintegration with New Zealand to full independence. A meeting of the joint committee took place in March 2001 in Wellington at which the issues of New Zealand aid and reciprocal immigration laws were discussed, as well as options for Niue's future constitutional status. In early 2001 Hima Takelesi was appointed Niue's first High Commissioner to New Zealand. New Zealand remained committed to annual assistance of $NZ6.3m. in the years 2001–03. At New Zealand's 2001 census, a total of 20,148 Niueans were recorded as resident in New Zealand. Discussions took place in Wellington in March 2003 between the New Zealand Prime Minister, Helen Clark, and Niue's Premier, Young Vivian. Topics debated included budgetary assistance, a review of the island's development plan and the continued migration of islanders from the territory to New Zealand.

The Government conducted a survey in September 2004 to assess the current population of the island. However, its apparent reluctance to release the information prompted speculation that more people had left Niue than official reports had previously indicated. When its findings were made public in October some observers disputed the figure of 1,550 (which many believed was higher than the reality, in order to attract more favourable levels of economic assistance). A local newspaper conducted a similar survey and estimated a resident population of some 1,300. In July 2005 the Premier announced that efforts to attract Niueans back to the island, notably by promoting the farming and fisheries sectors, were to be increased. The people of Niue were also to be granted better access to health care following an agreement concluded in November 2005 between the Niue Ministry for Health and the Counties Manukau District Health Board of New Zealand. The agreement was expected to facilitate the referral of Niuean patients to New Zealand.

In November 2004 Niue's High Commissioner to New Zealand, Hima Takelesi, announced his intention to return to the island to stand for parliament in the forthcoming elections. His stated motivation was a desire to form a stronger partnership with the 20,000 Niueans resident in New Zealand, in an attempt to ensure that Niue retained its current status and did not become incorporated into New Zealand. At the election, held on 30 April 2005, candidates in two constituencies (one of whom was the Minister of Finance) received equal numbers of votes. The allocation of the seat was eventually determined by the procedure of drawing names out of a hat. Young Vivian was re-elected Premier several days later, defeating O'Love Jacobsen by 17 votes to three. Vivian's stated priorities for the new Legislative Assembly included ongoing efforts to increase Niue's population (see above), the clearing of some 350 derelict homes and continued efforts to increase economic prospects for the island. Moreover, in June Vivian announced his intention to propose political reforms to the Legislative Assembly, including an increase in the parliamentary term from three years to five years and an increase in the number of cabinet ministers from four to six members.

In February 2006 Anton Ojala replaced Kurt Meyer as New Zealand High Commissioner to Niue; Ojala was in turn replaced by Brian Smythe in January 2008. In February 2007, in an attempt to ease its financial difficulties, the Government announced a 10% decrease in public servants' salaries, along with a reduction in working hours for certain employees and decreases in local grants. In the following month a parliamentary motion of no confidence submitted by the opposition against Premier Vivian, in protest at the Government's alleged financial mismanagement, failed to garner enough votes to succeed. Niue's financial problems were again highlighted in late 2007, when a member of the opposition reported that the island's financial secretary had admitted the Government's bankruptcy. The next general election was scheduled for June 2008.

Following almost 10 years of technical and political consultations, Niue and the USA signed a maritime boundary treaty in May 1997, delineating the precise boundary between the territorial waters of Niue and American Samoa. In October 2006 Niue agreed to join the Regional Assistance Mission to Solomon Islands (RAMSI), with the deployment of two Niuean police officers to Solomon Islands. Niue was scheduled to host the Pacific Islands Forum Leaders' summit meeting in 2009.

Government

Niue enjoys self-government in free association with New Zealand. The New Zealand Government, however, remains responsible for the island's defence and external affairs. Executive government is carried out by the Premier and three other ministers. Legislation is the responsibility of the Niue Assembly, which has 20 members (14 village representatives and six elected on a common roll), but New Zealand, if called upon to do so by the Assembly, will also legislate for the island. There is a New Zealand representative in Niue, whose status was upgraded to that of High Commissioner in 1993.

Economic Affairs

Niue's gross domestic product (GDP) was estimated at $NZ17.3m. in 2003, when GDP per head was estimated at $NZ10,048. The population decreased at an average annual rate of 2.3% in 1991–2001.

Agriculture, forestry and fishing contributed 23.3% of GDP in 2003. According to the census of 2001, the sector engaged 9.5% of the employed labour force. A majority of households, however, practise subsistence gardening. The principal crops are coconuts, taro, yams, cassava and sweet potatoes. A taro export scheme was successfully introduced in the early 1990s, and production of the crop increased by more than 500% in 1993. Exports of taro, principally to New Zealand, contributed nearly 93% of total export earnings in 2003, being facilitated by a new regular shipping service. Plans to increase the production of vanilla as an export crop were discussed in 2003, but the promising crop was destroyed by the cyclone of early 2004. The reintroduction of vanilla cultivation, as well as that of organic nonu (or noni, a fruit renowned for its medicinal properties), for export was initiated during 2004 as part of the Government's post-cyclone recovery programme. Honey is also produced for export. Pigs, poultry, goats and beef cattle are raised, mainly for local consumption. An island development plan for 2003 included proposals to develop Niue's fishing industry by employing a fleet of used Korean fishing vessels. A fish-processing factory at Amanau opened in October 2004. It was estimated that the new plant could raise some $NZ9m. annually in revenue. However, a series of problems resulted in the plant remaining unable to begin operations in mid-2005, despite the issuing of five fishing licences to New Zealand vessels and four to Samoan vessels.

Industry (including mining, manufacturing, construction and utilities) contributed only 2.8% of GDP in 2003 but engaged 21.3% of the labour force in 2001. The manufacturing sector has been very limited, accounting for only 1.5% of GDP in 2003. However, in addition to the fish-processing plant (see above), a noni juice factory also opened in October 2004. Exploration for deposits of uranium continued on the island in 2005, but in November it was announced that no commercially viable resources had been identified. The extensive damage caused by Cyclone Heta led to much activity in the construction sector from early 2004, as rebuilding programmes commenced.

The island remains dependent upon imported diesel fuel for its energy requirements. In collaboration with the international environmentalist group Greenpeace, however, in December 2005 Niue confirmed its commitment to the development of wind power, hoping to become one of the first locations in the world to be completely reliant on renewable energy sources. A major fire at the island's main electricity-generating plant in May 2006 seriously disrupted power supplies.

The services sector contributed 73.9% of GDP in 2003. The sector engaged 64.8% of the labour force in 2001. The Government is the most important employer, engaging 512 members of the paid labour force in December 2004, when an estimated 269 people were employed in the private sector. Tourism has begun to make a significant contribution to the economy. In 2004 tourist arrivals by air reached a total of 2,550, increasing to 2,793 in 2005 and to 3,008 in 2006. Receipts from tourism amounted to US $1.2m. in 2005. In October 2005 it was announced that Air New Zealand was to begin a weekly service between Auckland and Niue. Meanwhile, the New Zealand Government was providing support to Niue in its attempts to rebuild tourist facilities damaged by the cyclone of January 2004.

Niue records an annual trade deficit, with imports generally far exceeding exports. The principal exports in 1993 were root crops (which provided 87.1% of total export earnings), coconuts (1.9%), honey and handicrafts. The principal imports were foodstuffs (which constituted 28.0% of the total cost of imports), electrical goods (11.8%), motor vehicles (10.6%) and machinery (5.4%). Niue's most significant exports normally include taro, coconuts, honey and vanilla. New Zealand is the island's main trading partner. The value of New Zealand's exports to Niue totalled an estimated $NZ11.6m. in 2004, while that country's imports from Niue were worth less than $NZ0.3m.

Record budgetary expenditure was projected for 2004/05 as part of ongoing efforts to regenerate Niue's economy after Cyclone Heta. In that year New Zealand provided budgetary support of $NZ5.75m., while an additional $1m. was redirected from project assistance. The fiscal balance was further improved by modest reductions, totalling $NZ0.35m., in government expenditure. As a result, the budget was almost balanced in 2004/05, thus reversing the trend of the previous three years during which substantial deficits had been recorded. However, the fiscal account returned to deficit in 2005/06, when a budget shortfall of $NZ0.35m. was reported. To reflect an increase in budgetary support, total development assistance from New Zealand was raised to $NZ14.21m. in 2007/08. In addition, an aid programme totalling $NZ20m. over five years was announced in late 2004 and a trust fund was established with $NZ10m. from New Zealand and Australia. By mid-2005 the trust fund's assets stood at $NZ12m. In May 2006 it was announced that, in response to a request from the Premier of Niue, New Zealand had agreed to provide advance funding equivalent to almost US $190,000 in budgetary support. The annual rate of inflation averaged 2.6% in 1996–2006. Compared with the previous year, consumer prices increased by 2.3% in 2006. The unemployment rate was estimated at 13.8% of the labour force in 2001.

Niue is a member of the Pacific Community (see p. 377) and the Pacific Islands Forum (see p. 380), and an associate member of the UN Economic and Social Commission for Asia and the Pacific (ESCAP, see p. 35). In 2000 Niue became a signatory of the Cotonou Agreement (see p. 301) with the European Union (EU).

Niue's economic development has been adversely affected by inclement weather, the inadequacy of transport services and the high level of emigration, mainly to New Zealand. Two-thirds of the land surface is uncultivable, and marine resources fluctuate. Various attempts to secure new sources of revenue in Niue have included the leasing of the island's telecommunications facilities to foreign companies for use in specialist telephone services. However, this enterprise (which earned the island an estimated $NZ1.5m. per year) caused considerable controversy when it was revealed that Niue's telephone code had been made available to companies offering personal services considered indecent by the majority of islanders. In addition, the island earned some US $0.5m. between 1997 and 2000 from the sale of its internet domain name '.nu', although similar controversy ensued when a report published in July 2004 claimed that the island was hosting some 3m. pages of pornographic material via its .nu domain. An offshore financial centre was established in the mid-1990s. Following the imposition of harsh economic sanctions by the US Government in 2001, however, amid accusations that Niue had allowed criminal organizations to 'launder' their funds, in February 2005 the virtual closure of the offshore centre was announced, with the expected cessation of the international business registry in 2006. Niue's entire economy was severely affected by Cyclone Heta, which struck the island in January 2004 causing extensive damage to housing, crops and infrastructure. The subsequent recovery programme, known as New Niue or Niue Foou, emphasized rebuilding works and included the fish-processing plant at Amanau and the establishment of an industrial park at Fonuakula, at a cost of $NZ0.4m., upon which work began in mid-2005. During 2005 the New Zealand Government continued to assist Niue's post-cyclone recovery programme. Major priorities were the completion of the new hospital, which reopened in early 2006, and investment in the heavy equipment required for other major construction projects, which included the development of wharf and airport facilities. New Zealand was also providing funding in areas such as government housing. In April 2007 the Niue Development Bank signed an agreement with the European Investment Bank, which was to allocate €2m. to the improvement of the island's infrastructure, including projects in the areas of agriculture, fisheries, mining, commerce, tourism and energy.

Education

Education is provided free of charge, and is compulsory for 10 years between five and 16 years of age. The school-leaving age was raised from 14 to 16 in 1998. Primary education, from the age of five, lasts for six years, and is followed by six years of secondary education. In 2004/05 estimated enrolment at primary school level was equivalent to 86% of pupils of the relevant age-group, while enrolment at secondary level was equivalent to 99% of pupils. In 2005 a total of 190 children were enrolled in pre-primary and primary schools. A total of 206 pupils were enrolled in secondary education in the same year. A number of school-leavers take up tertiary education, mainly in the Pacific region and, to a lesser extent, in New Zealand. There is an extension centre of the University of the South Pacific in Niue. An estimated 50 students were engaged in tertiary education in 1991. A private medical school opened in 2000 but subsequently closed. A private university offering online information technology and business management courses opened in late 2003. In 2002 10.2% of total government expenditure was allocated to education. A long-term programme between Niue and the Dunedin College of Education, funded by New Zealand, concluded at the end of 2005.

Public Holidays

2008: 1 January (New Year's Day), 2 January (Commission Day), 6 February (Waitangi Day, anniversary of 1840 treaty), 21–24 March (Easter), 25 April (ANZAC Day, anniversary of 1915 landing at Gallipoli), 2 June (Queen's Official Birthday), 16 October (Constitution Day celebrations), 27 October (Peniamina's Day), 25 December (Christmas Day), 26 December (Boxing Day).

2009: 1 January (New Year's Day), 2 January (Commission Day), 6 February (Waitangi Day, anniversary of 1840 treaty), 10–13 April (Easter), 25 April (ANZAC Day, anniversary of 1915 landing at Gallipoli), 1 June (Queen's Official Birthday), 16 October (Constitution Day celebrations), 26 October (Peniamina's Day), 25 December (Christmas Day), 26 December (Boxing Day).

Weights and Measures

The metric system is in force.

Statistical Survey

Source (unless otherwise indicated): Statistics Unit, Economics, Planning, Development Office, Government of Niue, POB 95, Alofi; tel. and fax 4219; fax 4148; e-mail statsniue@mail.gov.nu; internet www.spc.int/prism/country/nu/stats/.

AREA AND POPULATION

Area: 261.5 sq km (100.9 sq miles).

Population: 1,788 at census of 7 September 2001; 1,625 (males 802, females 823) at census of September 2006. An estimated 20,145 Niueans lived in New Zealand at the time of the 2001 census.

Density (at September 2006): 6.2 per sq km.

Ethnic Groups (2001 census, declared ethnicity): Niueans 1,399; Caucasian 81; Pacific Islander 182; Niuean/Caucasian 28; Niuean/Pacific Islander 42; Asian 4.

Principal Villages (estimated population at 31 March 2006): Alofi (capital) 578; Hakupu 203; Avatele 173 (Source: Thomas Brinkhoff, *City Population*—internet www.citypopulation.de).

Births, Marriages and Deaths (2001 census): Crude birth rate 18.5 per 1,000; Death rate 7.8 per 1,000. *2003:* Live births 9; Marriages 3; Deaths 9. *2004* (including Niueans temporarily resident in New Zealand): Live births 18; Marriages 14; Deaths 18.

Expectation of Life (years at birth, WHO estimates): 70.6 (males 67.7; females 74.2) in 2005. Source: WHO, *World Health Statistics*.

Immigration and Emigration (2006): Arrivals 4,538; Departures 4,472.

Economically Active Population (2001 census, persons aged 15 years and over): Agriculture, forestry and fishing 60; Mining 17; Manufacturing 19; Electricity, gas and water 27; Construction 72; Trade 48; Restaurants and hotels 29; Transport 64; Finance 35; Real estate, etc. 3; Public administration 96; Education 63; Health, etc. 72; *Total employed* (incl. others) 633; Unemployed 21; *Total labour force* 654. Note: Figures exclude 63 subsistence workers. *Paid Employment* (December 2004): Government sector 512 (males 294, females 218); Private sector (estimates) 269 (males 143, females 126).

HEALTH AND WELFARE

Key Indicators

Total Fertility Rate (children per woman, 2005): 2.8.

Under-5 Mortality Rate (per 1,000 live births, 2005): 38.

Physicians (per 1,000 head, 1996): 1.50.

Hospital Beds (per 1,000 head, 2003): 7.3.

Health Expenditure (2004): US $ per head (PPP): 245.3.

Health Expenditure (2004): % of GDP: 15.1.

Health Expenditure (2004): public (% of total): 98.8.

For sources and definitions, see explanatory note on p. vi.

AGRICULTURE, ETC.

Principal Crops (metric tons, 2005, FAO estimates): Taro 3,200; Sweet potatoes 253; Yams 120; Coconuts 2,884; Bananas 70; Lemons and limes 110. *Aggregate Production* ('000 metric tons, may include official, semi-official or estimated data): Vegetables (incl. melons) 580; Fruits (excl. melons) 100. *2006:* Figures for aggregate production assumed to be unchanged from 2005 (FAO estimates).

Livestock (year ending September 2005, FAO estimates): Cattle 112; Pigs 2,000; Chickens 15,000. Note: data for 2006 were not available.

Livestock Products (metric tons, 2005, FAO estimates): Pig meat 60; Chicken meat 18; Cows' milk 50; Hen eggs 12; Honey 6. Note: Data for 2006 were not available.

Forestry (cu m, 1985): Roundwood removals 613; Sawnwood production 201.

Fishing (metric tons, live weight, 2005, FAO estimates): Total catch 200.

Source: FAO.

NEW ZEALAND'S ASSOCIATED STATES

Niue

INDUSTRY

Production (2004): Electric energy 3 million kWh. Source: UN, *Industrial Commodity Statistics Yearbook*.

FINANCE

Currency and Exchange Rates: 100 cents = 1 New Zealand dollar ($NZ). For details, see Tokelau.

Budget ($NZ '000, year ending 30 June 2006, provisional): Internal revenue 14,206; New Zealand budgetary support 6,953; *Total revenue* 21,159; Recurrent expenditure 21,417; Capital 90; *Total expenditure* 21,507. 2006/07 ($NZ '000, forecasts): Internal revenue 16,499; New Zealand budgetary support 6,915; *Total revenue* 23,414; Recurrent expenditure 23,364; Capital projects 50; *Total expenditure* 23,414.

Overseas Aid ($NZ '000, 2006/07): Official development assistance from New Zealand 8,700. Source: Ministry of Foreign Affairs and Trade, Wellington.

Cost of Living (Consumer Price Index, average of quarterly figures; base: July–Sept. 2003 = 100): All items: 103.6 in 2004 (average of three quarters); 104.0 in 2005; 106.4 in 2006.

Gross Domestic Product ($NZ '000 in current prices): 16,711 in 2001; 16,245 in 2002; 17,252 in 2003.

GDP by Economic Activity ($NZ '000 in current prices, 2003): Agriculture, forestry and fishing 4,062; Mining and quarrying –12; Manufacturing 268; Electricity, gas and water 201; Construction 36; Trade 2,181; Restaurants and hotels 566; Transport, storage and communications 1,395; Financial and business services, real estate, etc. 1,434; Public administration 6,800; Other community, social and personal services 519; *Sub-total* 17,450; *Less* Imputed bank service charge 215; *GDP at factor cost* 17,235; Indirect taxes 970; *Less* Subsidies 953; *GDP in purchasers' values* 17,252.

EXTERNAL TRADE

Principal Commodities (Trade with New Zealand only, $NZ '000, 2004): *Imports c.i.f.*: Animals and animal products 523; Prepared foodstuffs 1,196; Mineral products 1,842; Chemical products 560; Plastics and rubber 399; Wood and wood products 717; Base metals and articles thereof 1,714; Machinery, mechanical appliances and electrical equipment 2,100; Miscellaneous manufactured articles 1,528; Total (incl. others) 11,574. *Exports f.o.b.*: Prepared foodstuffs 39; Machinery, mechanical appliances and electrical equipment 153; Optical, photographic and medical instruments, etc. 50; Total (incl. others) 264.

Principal Trading Partners ($NZ '000, 2004): *Imports c.i.f.*: New Zealand 11,574; Total (incl. others) 11,859. *Exports f.o.b.*: New Zealand 264.

TRANSPORT

Road Traffic (2001 census): Passenger cars 323; Motorcycles 134; Vans 170; Trucks 74; Pick-ups 76; Buses 11.

International Shipping: *Ship Arrivals* (1989): Yachts 20; Merchant vessels 22; Total 42. *Freight Traffic* (metric tons, 1989, official estimates): Unloaded 3,410; Loaded 10.

Civil Aviation: *Passengers* (1992): Arrivals 3,500; Departures 3,345. *Freight Traffic* (metric tons, 1992): Unloaded 41.6; Loaded 15.7.

TOURISM

Foreign Tourist Arrivals (by air): 2,550 in 2004; 2,793 in 2005; 3,008 in 2006.

Tourist Arrivals by Country of Residence (2006): Australia 343; New Zealand 2,030; United Kingdom 99; USA 129; Total (incl. others) 3,008.

Tourism Receipts (US $ million, incl. passenger transport): 1.2 in 2005. Source: World Tourism Organization.

COMMUNICATIONS MEDIA

Telephones (2002): 1,000 main lines in use.

Mobile Cellular Telephones (2001 census): 225 units in use*.

Radio Receivers (2001 census): 605 in use†.

Television Receivers (2001 census): 451 in use.

Personal Computers (2001 census): 77 in use.

Internet Users (2002): 900.

Non-daily Newspaper (2004,): 1†.

* Source: International Telecommunication Union.
† Source: UNESCO.

EDUCATION

Pre-primary and Primary (2005): 1 school; 190 pupils; 24 teachers.

Secondary (2005): 1 school; 206 pupils; 31 teachers.

Source: Department of Education, Niue.

Directory

The Constitution

In October 1974 Niue gained self-government in free association with New Zealand. The latter, however, remains responsible for Niue's defence and external affairs and will continue economic and administrative assistance. Executive authority in Niue is vested in the British monarch as sovereign of New Zealand but exercised through the government of the Premier, assisted by three ministers. Legislative power is vested in the Niue Assembly or Fono Ekepule, which comprises 20 members (14 village representatives and six elected on a common roll), but New Zealand, if requested to do so by the Assembly, will also legislate for the island. There is a New Zealand representative in Niue, the High Commissioner, who is charged with liaising between the Governments of Niue and New Zealand.

The Government

New Zealand High Commissioner: BRIAN SMYTHE.
Secretary to Government: CROSSLEY TATUI.

CABINET
(April 2008)

Premier and Minister responsible for the Legislative Assembly, Premier's Department and Cabinet, Civil Aviation, Crown Law Office, Economic Planning, Development and Statistics, External Affairs and Niueans Abroad, Niue Public Service Commission, Niue Broadcasting Corporation, Finance, Customs and Revenue, Police, Prison and National Security, Environment, Niue Tourism and Public Works (Civil and Quarry, Outside Services and Heavy Plant): YOUNG VIVIAN.

Minister of Agriculture, Forestry and Fisheries, Niue Development Bank, Shipping, Investment and Trade, Post and Telecommunications, Business Sector, Private Sector, Immigration and Public Works (including Housing, Water Supply and Building): BILL VAKAAFI MOTUFOOU.

Minister of Education, Women's Affairs, Taoga Niue and Culture, Justice, Lands and Survey: VA'AIGA PAOTAMA TUKUI-TONGA.

Minister of Health, Community Affairs, Village Councils, Religious Affairs, Youth and Sports, Meteorological Services and Climate Change, Non-Government Organisations, Niue Power and Energy, Bulk Fuel, Disaster Management and Administration, NTDC and ISO: FISA IGILISI PIHIGIA.

GOVERNMENT OFFICES

All ministries are in Alofi.

Office of the New Zealand High Commissioner: POB 78, Tapeu, Alofi; tel. 4022; fax 4173.

Office of the Secretary to Government: POB 40, Alofi; tel. 4200; fax 4232; e-mail secgov.premier@mail.gov.nu.

Legislature

ASSEMBLY

The Niue Assembly or Fono Ekepule has 20 members (14 village representatives and six members elected on a common roll). The most recent general election was held on 30 April 2005.

Speaker: ATAPANA SIAKIMOTU.

Political Organization

Alliance of Independents: Alofi; f. 2001; Leader FRANK LUI; Spokesperson O'LOVE JACOBSEN.

Judicial System

The Chief Justice of the High Court and the Land Court Judge visit Niue quarterly. In addition, lay justices are locally appointed and exercise limited criminal and civil jurisdiction. Appeals against High Court judgments are heard in the Court of Appeal of Niue (created in 1992).

The High Court: exercises civil and criminal jurisdiction.

The Land Court: is concerned with litigation over land and titles.

Land Appellate Court

Hears appeals over decisions of the Land Court.

Chief Justice: HETA HINGSTON.

Religion

About 63% of the population belong to the Ekalesia Niue, a Protestant organization, which had 1,093 adherents at the time of the 2001 census. Within the Roman Catholic Church, which had 128 adherents (equivalent to 7.4% of the population) in 2001, Niue forms part of the diocese of Tonga. The Church of Jesus Christ of Latter-day Saints (Mormon—which had 158 adherents in 2001), the Seventh-day Adventists, the Jehovah's Witnesses and the Church of God of Jerusalem are also represented.

Ekalesia Niue: Head Office, POB 25, Alofi; tel. 4195; fax 4352/4010; e-mail ekalesia.niue@niue.nu; f. 1846; est. by London Missionary Society, became Ekalesia Niue in 1966; Pres. Rev. MATAGI VILITAMA; Gen. Sec. Rev. ARTHUR PIHIGIA.

The Press

Niue Economic review: POB 91, Alofi; tel. 4235; monthly.

Niue Star: POB 151, Alofi; tel. 4207; weekly; Niuean and English; publ. by Jackson's Photography and Video; circ. 600.

Broadcasting and Communications

TELECOMMUNICATIONS

In 2003 Niue became the first location in the world to have a national wireless internet system allowing access from anywhere on the island by means of solar-powered aerials attached to coconut palms.

Director of Posts and Telecommunications: Alofi; tel. 4002.

Telecom Niue: Alofi; tel. 4000; Man. RICHARD HIPA.

BROADCASTING

Radio

Broadcasting Corporation of Niue: POB 68, Alofi; tel. 4026; fax 4217; operates television service and radio service; govt-owned; Chair. NEAL MORRISSEY; CEO TREVOR TIAKIA; Gen. Man. PATRICK LINO.

Radio Sunshine: broadcasts in English and Niuean between 6 a.m. and 10 p.m. Mon.–Sat.

Television

Broadcasting Corporation of Niue: see Radio.

Television Niue broadcasts in English and Niuean six days a week from 5 p.m. to 11 p.m.

Finance

DEVELOPMENT BANK

Niue Development Bank: POB 34, Alofi; tel. 4335; fax 4290; e-mail devbank@niue.nu; f. 1993; govt-owned; began operations July 1994; Gen. Man. ANGELA TUHIPA.

COMMERCIAL BANK

Bank of South Pacific Ltd: Main St, Alofi; tel. 4221; fax 4043; acquired from Westpac Banking Corpn in Sept. 2004; Man. R. J. COX.

Trade and Industry

GOVERNMENT AGENCIES

Business Advisory Service: Alofi; tel. 4228.

Office of Economic Affairs, Planning and Development, Statistics and Trade and Investment: POB 42, Alofi; tel. 4148; e-mail business.epdsu@mail.gov.nu; responsible for planning and financing activities in the agricultural, tourism, industrial sectors, business advisory and trade and investment.

UTILITIES

Niue Power Corporation: POB 198, Alofi; tel. 4119; fax 4385; e-mail gm.npc.@mail.gov.nu; Gen. Man. SPEEDO HETUTU.

TRADE UNION

Public Service Association: Alofi.

Transport

ROADS

There are 123 km of all-weather roads and 106 km of access and plantation roads. A total of 788 motor vehicles were registered in 2001. The road network was extensively damaged by Cyclone Heta in January 2004. In mid-2004 it was estimated that some 48 km of sealed roads were clear and in good condition.

SHIPPING

The best anchorage is an open roadstead at Alofi, the largest of Niue's 14 villages. Work to extend a small wharf at Alofi began in mid-1998 with US assistance. The New Zealand Shipping Corporation operates a monthly service between New Zealand, Nauru and Niue. Fuel supplies are delivered by a tanker (the *Pacific Explorer*) from Fiji. In December 2002 the Government signed an agreement with Reef Shipping Ltd to provide a service to New Zealand every three to four weeks.

CIVIL AVIATION

Hanan International Airport has a total sealed runway of 2,350 m, following the completion of a 700 m extension in 1995, with New Zealand assistance. In October 2005 it was announced that Air New Zealand was to begin a weekly service between Auckland and Niue.

Niue Airways Ltd (NAL): Hanan International Airport; f. 1990; registered in New Zealand; Dir RAY YOUNG.

Tourism

Niue has a small but significant tourism industry (specializing in holidays based on activities such as diving, rock-climbing, caving and game fishing), which was enhanced by an increase in the frequency of flights between the island and New Zealand in the early 1990s. The industry earned about US $1m. in 1998. The prospects for the island's tourist industry were severely hampered by the extensive damage caused by Cyclone Heta in January 2004. Experts believed that it would be several years before a recovery could be achieved. However, the island's Matavai resort was operating in mid-2004 and offering 33 rooms for visitors. A total of 3,008 people arrived by air to visit Niue in 2006. In 2005 some 55% of visitors were from New Zealand.

Niue Tourism Office: POB 42, Alofi; tel. 4224; fax 4225; e-mail niuetourism@mail.gov.nu; internet www.niueisland.com; Dir of Tourism IDA TALAGI-HEKESI.

NICARAGUA

Introductory Survey

Location, Climate, Language, Religion, Flag, Capital

The Republic of Nicaragua lies in the Central American isthmus, bounded by the Pacific Ocean to the west and by the Caribbean Sea to the east. Its neighbours are Honduras, to the north, and Costa Rica, to the south. The climate is tropical, with an average annual temperature of 25.5°C (78°F). The rainy season extends from May to October. The national language is Spanish, although English is also spoken on the Caribbean coast. Almost all of the inhabitants profess Christianity, and the great majority are Roman Catholics. The national flag (proportions 3 by 5) has three equal horizontal stripes, of blue, white and blue, with the state emblem (a triangle enclosing a dark blue sea from which rise five volcanoes, in green, surmounted by a Phrygian cap from which extend white rays and, at the top, a rainbow, all encircled by the words, in gold capitals, 'República de Nicaragua' and 'América Central') in the centre of the white stripe; the same flag without the state emblem is an alternative version of the civil flag. The capital is Managua.

Recent History

Nicaragua was under Spanish rule from the 16th century until 1821. It then became part of the Central American Federation until 1838. From 1927 US troops were based in Nicaragua at the request of the Government, which was opposed by a guerrilla group, led by Augusto César Sandino. In 1933, following the establishment of the National Guard (commanded by Gen. Anastasio Somoza García), the US troops left Nicaragua. Sandino was assassinated in 1934, but some of his followers ('Sandinistas') continued actively to oppose the new regime. Somoza seized power in a coup in 1935 and took office as President in 1936. Apart from a brief interlude in the late 1940s, Somoza remained as President until September 1956, when he was assassinated. However, the Somoza family continued to dominate Nicaraguan politics until 1979.

In 1962 the left-wing Frente Sandinista de Liberación Nacional (FSLN, the Sandinista National Liberation Front) was formed with the object of overthrowing the Somozas by revolution. Gen. Anastasio Somoza Debayle, son of the former dictator, became President in May 1967, holding office until April 1972. The Congreso Nacional (National Congress) was dissolved, and a triumvirate ruled until Gen. Somoza was re-elected President in September 1974. In January 1978 the murder of Pedro Joaquín Chamorro Cardenal, the leader of the opposition coalition and the editor of La Prensa (the country's only independent newspaper), provoked violent demonstrations against the Government.

In June 1979 the FSLN announced the formation of a provisional Junta of National Reconstruction. With the FSLN in command of many towns and preparing for the final onslaught on Managua, President Somoza resigned and left the country on 17 July 1979. (He was assassinated in Paraguay in September 1980.) After the Sandinistas had gained control of the capital, the Junta and its Provisional Governing Council took power on 20 July as the Government of National Reconstruction. The 1974 Constitution was abrogated, and the bicameral Congreso Nacional dissolved. The National Guard was disbanded and replaced by the Ejército Popular Sandinista (EPS—Sandinista People's Army), officially established in August. In that month the Junta issued a 'Statute on Rights and Guarantees for the Citizens of Nicaragua', providing for basic personal freedoms and restoring freedom of the press and broadcasting. Civil rights were restored in January 1980.

On taking office, the Junta had issued a Basic Statute, providing for the creation of an appointed Council of State to act as an interim legislature. In March 1981 Commdr Daniel Ortega Saavedra was appointed Co-ordinator of the Junta and of its new consultative body, the Council of Government.

By 1981 discontent at the postponement of elections and the increasing hegemony of the Sandinistas had led to the creation of counter-revolutionary forces ('Contras'), who were mostly members of the former National Guard and operated from camps in Honduras. Meanwhile, relations between the US and Nicaraguan Governments had seriously deteriorated, culminating in the suspension of US economic aid in April. In the same year the US Government donated US $10m. in support of the Contras, while covert operations by the US Central Intelligence Agency (CIA) attempted to destabilize the Sandinista regime. In March 1982 the Sandinista Government declared a state of emergency. However, the intensity of attacks by the Fuerzas Democráticas Nicaragüenses (FDN), anti-Sandinista guerrillas based in Honduras, increased. A Contra group, the Alianza Revolucionaria Democrática (ARDE), was also established in Costa Rica, led by Edén Pastora Gómez, a prominent figure in the revolution who had become disillusioned with the Sandinistas. In December the Sandinistas reaffirmed their support for the initiatives of the 'Contadora group' (Colombia, Mexico, Panama and Venezuela), which was attempting to find peaceful solutions to the disputes involving Central America, and adopted a more conciliatory approach towards the opposition.

In June 1984 talks commenced between the Nicaraguan and US Governments in order to foster the peace negotiations proposed by the Contadora group. However, although the Sandinistas agreed in September to sign a peace agreement, the USA rejected the agreement on the grounds that the forthcoming Nicaraguan elections would not be fairly conducted. In June 1985 the US Congress voted to allocate US $27m. in non-military aid to the Contras. None the less, the Nicaraguan Government reaffirmed its desire to resume negotiations with the USA. Concurrently, however, the civil conflict escalated, and clashes along Nicaragua's borders with Costa Rica and Honduras became increasingly frequent. In July thousands of Miskito Indians, who had allied themselves with the Contras in the early 1980s, began to return to their ancestral homelands in northern Nicaragua, following talks with the Government concerning autonomy for the region.

A presidential election and elections to a constituent assembly were held on 4 November 1984. The assembly was to draw up a constitution within two years of taking office. In August the Government had restored the majority of the civil rights that had been suspended in September 1982, in order to permit parties to campaign without restrictions. In the presidential ballot the FSLN candidate, Ortega, received 67% of the votes cast, and the party won 61 of the 96 seats in the National Constituent Assembly, which replaced the Council of State. Ortega's new Government and the National Constituent Assembly were inaugurated in January 1985.

In August 1986 the US Congress approved assistance for the Contras worth US $100m. In November the US Government disclosed that funds accruing from its clandestine sales of military equipment to Iran had been used to support the Contras.

In January 1987 a new Constitution was promulgated; on the same day, however, civil liberties, guaranteed in the Constitution, were again suspended by the renewal of the five-year-old state of emergency.

In February 1987 the Governments of Costa Rica, El Salvador, Guatemala and Honduras approved a peace plan for Nicaragua, largely based on earlier Contadora proposals, but placing greater emphasis on democratization, including the ending of the state of emergency. Following some modification, in August the peace plan was signed by the Presidents of the five nations, in Guatemala. In accordance with the plan's requirements, a four-member National Commission for Reconciliation was created in Nicaragua in August: it was chaired by Cardinal Miguel Obando y Bravo, the Archbishop of Managua, a leading critic of the Government. In January 1988 the Government ended the state of emergency, and consented to participate directly in negotiations with the Contras. In March negotiations between representatives of the Government and the Contras resulted in agreement on a 60-day cease-fire (with effect from 1 April), as a prelude to detailed peace negotiations (this was later unilaterally extended by the Government until November 1989). The Government agreed to the gradual release of political prisoners and to the participation of the Contras in domestic political dialogue and, eventually, in elections. In August 1988 the US Senate approved the provision of US $27m. in humanitarian aid for the Contras. As the hope of further military aid diminished, the Contras retreated into Honduras.

In February 1989 the five Central American Presidents met in El Salvador to discuss the reactivation of the regional peace plan. At the meeting it was agreed that, in return for the dismantling of Contra bases in Honduras, there would be moves towards greater democracy in Nicaragua. These included a pledge to hold a general election, open to opposition parties, by February 1990. A number of electoral reforms were introduced: Contra rebels were to be permitted to return to vote, on condition that they relinquished their armed struggle under a proposed demobilization plan. In June 1989 the Unión Nacional Opositora (UNO) was formed by 14 opposition parties of varying political views: the UNO was to present a joint presidential candidate and a single programme in the forthcoming elections.

In August 1989 the five Central American Presidents met in Tela, Honduras, where they signed an agreement providing for the voluntary demobilization, repatriation or relocation of the Contra forces within a 90-day period. To facilitate this process, an International Commission of Support and Verification (CIAV) was established by the UN and the Organization of American States (OAS, see p. 360). Following mediation (conducted by former US President Jimmy Carter), the Government concluded an agreement with the leaders of the Miskito Indians of the Caribbean coast. The rebels agreed to renounce their armed struggle and to join the political process. Meanwhile, the UNO designated Violeta Barrios de Chamorro (the owner and director of *La Prensa* since the assassination of her husband, Pedro Chamorro, in 1978) as its presidential candidate in the forthcoming election. Daniel Ortega was nominated as the candidate of the FSLN.

In November 1989 President Ortega declared the ending of the cease-fire with the Contras, on the grounds that the rebels had made insufficient progress in implementing the Tela agreement and disbanding their forces stationed in Honduras. In response, the UN Security Council established the UN Observer Group in Central America (ONUCA) to monitor compliance with the Tela agreement, to prevent cross-border incursions by rebels and to assist in supervising the forthcoming Nicaraguan elections.

The elections proceeded on 25 February 1990, resulting in an unexpected victory for Chamorro, who obtained some 55% of votes in the presidential election, while Ortega received 41%. Foreign observers confirmed the conduct of the polls to have been free and fair. After the elections, the Sandinista Government decreed an immediate cease-fire. The President-elect pledged to 'depoliticize' the military and security forces, and urged the Contra rebels to disband and return to civilian life. However, the UNO had not secured a sufficient majority of seats in the Asamblea Nacional to make amendments to the Constitution. In the interim period before the transfer of power on 25 April 1990, Ortega introduced a number of reforms. A General Amnesty and National Reconciliation Law was adopted: this was designed to pre-empt retaliatory measures against outgoing officials and to quash legal proceedings against those who had committed politically motivated crimes against the State since 1979.

On 19 April 1990 a cease-fire was agreed by the Contras and the Sandinista armed forces. The Contras agreed to surrender their weapons by 10 June, and to assemble in 'security zones' supervised by UN troops. A transitional agreement between the outgoing Sandinista Government and the newly elected UNO coalition provided for a reduction in the strength of the security forces and their subordination to civilian authority. Upon taking office President Chamorro assumed the post of Minister of National Defence, but allowed the previous minister, Gen. Humberto Ortega Saavedra, temporarily to retain the post of Chief of the EPS: this provoked considerable controversy within the UNO and the Contra leadership. However, in return for a commitment from the Contras to sign the demobilization accords, the Government agreed to the establishment of a special police force, composed of former Contra rebels, in order to guarantee security within the demobilization zones. Demobilization of the Contra rebels was officially concluded on 27 June, signifying the end of 11 years of civil war in Nicaragua.

On assuming office, the UNO Government immediately attempted to reverse much Sandinista policy. The suspension of the civil service law in May 1990 provoked a public sector strike, which paralysed the country. Chamorro was forced to concede wage increases of 100% and the establishment of a joint commission of trade union and government representatives to revise the civil service law. In July another general strike, involving 100,000 workers, was held in support of demands for wage increases and also in protest at the implementation of legislation allowing the restoration to private ownership of land that had been nationalized and redistributed under the Sandinista regime. Once again the Government made concessions, including a wage increase and the suspension of the programme to privatize land. The agreement was condemned by the Vice-President, Virgilio Godoy Reyes, who accused Chamorro of capitulating too readily to the demands of the FSLN. In October the Government announced the formation of a National Agrarian Commission to study problems of land distribution and illegal land seizures. The commission was to include members of the trade unions and former Contras. In mid-1991, however, the emergence of groups of rearmed Contra rebels (known as Recontras) became apparent with the reported occupation of several cities in the northern province of Jinotega. The Recontras' stated aim was to publicize the grievances of thousands of demobilized Contras in the north of the country who had not received land and aid promised them under the terms of the Government's resettlement plan.

In August 1991 a National Security Commission was established to disarm civilians. In the same month the FSLN-operated Radio Sandino acknowledged the existence of groups of rearmed Sandinistas (Re-compas), claiming that these had been formed to counter the military operations of the Re-contras. The phased disarmament of the Re-contras and the Re-compas began in January 1992. However, in April groups of the former combatants began joining forces to form the Revueltos, demanding land and credit promised to them prior to demobilization. In May the Government allocated 800 plots of land outside the capital to the Revueltos, as a gesture of its intention to address the groups' grievances. However, rebel activity continued in 1992–94, despite successive government ultimatums requiring the rebels to disarm or face military intervention. In February 1994, following the mediation of Cardinal Obando y Bravo and the OAS, a peace agreement was signed that provided for the demobilization of a prominent Re-contra group, the Frente Norte 3-80, by mid-April, in return for which the rebels were granted an amnesty and the right to be incorporated into the national police force. Nevertheless, violent incidents involving further groups of Re-contras continued in northern and central Nicaragua. In response the Government deployed security forces to combat the rebels' activities, which, it asserted, were criminal and not related to legitimate demands for land.

In June 1991 the FSLN withdrew indefinitely its 39 deputies from the Asamblea Nacional, in protest against the introduction by conservative deputies of a draft bill revoking two laws concerning redistribution of property. The so-called *piñata* laws had been introduced by the FSLN in March 1990, immediately prior to the transfer of power to the Chamorro administration. They guaranteed the property rights of the thousands of people who had benefited from the land expropriation that had been conducted by the Sandinistas. In August 1991 the legislature approved the abrogation of the *piñata* laws, but in the following month President Chamorro vetoed parts of the bill that she deemed to be unconstitutional. In response, right-wing supporters of Vice-President Godoy accused Chamorro of yielding to pressure exerted by the Sandinistas. Disagreement over the property issue had by now led to the alienation by Chamorro of the majority of UNO deputies, and the legislature only narrowly failed to overturn the veto in December. In July, meanwhile, the first congress of the FSLN appointed Daniel Ortega to the newly created post of General Secretary.

In April 1992 an announcement by Antonio Lacayo Oyanguren (son-in-law of Violeta Chamorro and widely considered to be the principal architect of government policy) that the Government was seeking 'fundamental agreements' with the FSLN served to fuel the anger of right-wing and liberal members of the UNO, who accused both Lacayo and Chamorro of being in league with the Sandinistas. In May the US Congress suspended the release of US $116m. in aid to Nicaragua, on the grounds that the Nicaraguan Government had failed to compensate US citizens for land expropriated under the Sandinista regime. In September Chamorro signed decrees establishing a property ombudsman's office and other provisions to expedite the processing of property claims. In addition, the President signed an agreement specifying that all unjustly confiscated property would be returned (or the rightful owners compensated).

A serious legislative crisis arose in September 1992, when the President of the Asamblea Nacional, Alfredo César, convened the legislature in the absence of the deputies of the FSLN and the

Grupo de Centro (GC—a group of eight dissident UNO deputies who had maintained their allegiance to the Government, thus depriving the UNO of its parliamentary majority), recruiting substitute deputies in order to elect new legislative authorities. Chamorro subsequently announced that no laws approved by the legislature would be promulgated until the assembly recognized a Supreme Court decision ruling César's actions to be unconstitutional and declaring all subsequent rulings by the legislature null and void. In late December Chamorro ordered the army to occupy the assembly building and appointed a provisional administration to manage parliamentary affairs pending the election of new legislative authorities. In January 1993 Chamorro announced a cabinet reorganization. Excluded from the new Government, the UNO declared itself an opposition party, as the Alianza Política Opositora (APO), expelling four member parties for their involvement with the GC. The APO continued to boycott the Asamblea Nacional and to demand the expulsion of Sandinistas from the Government.

In October 1993 unprecedented discussions between the APO and the FSLN resulted in a joint demand for a complete restructuring of the Government's economic policy. In addition, it was agreed that Humberto Ortega should resign as Chief of the EPS as soon as a new law regulating the armed forces was enacted. Constitutional issues were also discussed, with the APO proposing the election of a constituent assembly, while the FSLN favoured the implementation of partial constitutional reform by the incumbent legislature. In late October the APO and the FSLN signed an agreement providing for the implementation of partial constitutional reforms, on condition that a consensus was reached on the substance of the reforms by the end of November (subsequently extended to mid-December). The APO stipulated that it would support the reforms only on condition that its parliamentary majority be restored (through the dismissal of the GC deputies and their replacement by APO members) and that it gain control of the legislative authorities. However, divisions within the APO resulted in the Unión Demócrata Cristiana (UDC), the Movimiento Democrático Nicaragüense (MDN) and the Alianza Popular Conservadora (APC) breaking away from the alliance. The Asamblea Nacional reconvened in January 1994, and a new working alliance, including the FSLN, the GC, the UDC, the MDN and the APC, elected new legislative authorities. The APO subsequently abandoned its boycott of the legislature.

In February 1994 a widening division within the FSLN became apparent when Daniel Ortega founded the Izquierda Democrática Sandinista, an internal faction comprising what were termed 'orthodox revolutionaries' and intended to maintain the party's role as a revolutionary force; the faction declared support for 'all forms of struggle', aims not shared by the party's 'renewalist' faction, led by Sergio Ramírez Mercado. In May, following internal elections, the orthodox faction of the party secured control of the party's national directorate and of the party assembly, the Asamblea Sandinista, which subsequently approved a policy of opposition to the Government.

In November 1994 the Asamblea Nacional approved amendments to some 67 of the Constitution's 202 articles, which adjusted the balance of authority in favour of the legislature. In particular, the Government would be required to seek legislative approval for external loans, debt negotiations and international trade agreements. A further amendment, prohibiting close relatives of a serving President from contesting the presidential election, was widely considered to be intended specifically to prevent Lacayo, Chamorro's son-in-law and Minister of the Presidency, from securing presidential office at the next election, due in 1996. Other reforms included a reduction in the presidential and legislative terms, from six to five years, and the withdrawal of the absolute ban on presidential re-election, although consecutive terms remained prohibited. The amendments were deemed illegal by the FSLN leadership but won the support of 32 of the 39 deputies in the FSLN bloc, reflecting the seemingly irreconcilable division within the party. Amendments were also introduced enshrining civilian authority over the depoliticized security forces. The armed forces, which under the Constitution had previously been entitled the Ejército Popular Sandinista, were thenceforth referred to as the Ejército de Nicaragua (Nicaraguan Army).

In January 1995 the disunity within the FSLN finally resulted in members of the renewalist faction forming a separate political party, the Movimiento Renovador Sandinista (MRS). In the following month the constitutional amendments were signed and submitted to Chamorro for approval within 15 days. However, following Chamorro's refusal to promulgate the reforms, on 24 February the Asamblea Nacional released the amendments for publication, thereby enacting them. Chamorro condemned the decision as unconstitutional. In June a resolution to the dispute was achieved by the signing of a political accord between the Government and the legislature. Under the terms of the agreement, many of the amendments intended to reduce presidential authority were to be moderated. Legislation defining the interpretation and implementation of the amendments was approved by the Asamblea Nacional in July, and was subsequently promulgated by Chamorro.

Presidential and legislative elections were held on 20 October 1996. Arnoldo Alemán Lacayo of the Partido Liberal Constitucionalista (PLC), the presidential candidate of the Alianza Liberal (an electoral alliance comprising mainly liberal parties), secured 51% of the votes, while Ortega won 38%. However, although international observers declared the ballot to have been generally free and fair, the FSLN and several other parties disputed the result as fraudulent. Many of the provisional results were subsequently revised and, while the Consejo Supremo Electoral (CSE—Supreme Electoral Tribunal) acknowledged the existence of serious anomalies, it maintained that these had been insufficient to affect the overall outcome of the poll. The Alianza Liberal also won the largest number of seats (42) in the Asamblea Nacional, although it failed to gain a majority. The FSLN obtained 35 seats. The day before Alemán took office, in January 1997, the FSLN boycotted the newly inaugurated Asamblea Nacional in protest at the decision of the CSE to conduct an open ballot (rather than a secret vote) to elect the legislative authorities.

In November 1999 the Comptroller-General, Agustín Jarquín, was arrested on charges of committing fraud against the State. Jarquín, a vigorous critic of corruption in the Government, had launched numerous investigations into corrupt practices by members of the Alemán administration, the most notable of which had resulted in the publication of a report revealing that Alemán had increased his personal wealth by 900% during his terms of office as Mayor of Managua and as President, and that he had failed to declare these assets to the Office of the Comptroller-General, as required by law. Following his detention, Jarquín supporters alleged that the accusations made against him were politically motivated. Representatives of donor nations and multilateral organizations expressed concern over the case, and both Germany and Sweden suspended funding for various projects as a result of Jarquín's detention. In December Jarquín was acquitted of the charges against him, and formally renewed the corruption charges against Alemán.

In June 1999 the Government and the FSLN reached an agreement to begin negotiations on constitutional and electoral reform. This co-operation prompted the formation of an anti-Ortega faction within the FSLN. In July these dissident Sandinistas, in alliance with former Contras and various minor right-wing and centre-right parties, protested in Managua against the pact. In January 2000 a series of constitutional reforms came into force. The principal amendments included a reduction in the proportion of votes necessary for a President to be elected outright from 45% to 35%, thus increasing the likelihood of an FSLN victory. In return, Alemán was guaranteed a seat in the Asamblea Nacional after leaving office, thus making him virtually immune from prosecution. Other reforms included the restructuring of the judiciary, electoral authorities and the Office of the Comptroller-General—which was to be headed by a five-member board, thereby effectively removing the threat to the Alemán administration of Jarquín.

In January 2001 the Vice-President, Enrique Bolaños Geyer, resigned his position and announced his presidential candidacy, representing the PLC. If elected, Bolaños pledged to investigate legislative corruption and to reduce civil service salaries. Ortega, who was the FSLN nominee, sought to reassure the electorate that he had renounced the more militaristic policies of his past, pledging to demilitarize the border with Costa Rica and to return property belonging to US citizens confiscated by his Government during the 1980s. Nevertheless, Ortega proved to be a controversial choice of candidate. From 1998 his step-daughter, Zoilamérica Narváez Murillo, had made accusations of sexual abuse against him, and Bolaños, his main opponent, made much of the FSLN's links with the Cuban regime of Fidel Castro Ruz and with the Libyan leader, Col Muammar al-Qaddafi.

Presidential and legislative elections took place on 4 November 2001, amid tight security. The final results of the presidential poll gave Bolaños 56% of votes cast, while Ortega secured 42%.

The PLC also won a majority of votes (53%) in the elections to the Asamblea Nacional, securing 47 seats; the FSLN won 43 seats and the PCN the remaining two. In the weeks following the election the FSLN made allegations of electoral irregularities. Three FSLN magistrates on the seven-member electoral council objected to the party's allocation of seats in the Asamblea Nacional and resigned their positions in protest. However, the complaint was rejected by the Supreme Constitutional Court.

Bolaños took office on 10 January 2002. Almost immediately he encountered opposition from within his own party, when members of the PLC rejected his preferred candidate for President of the Asamblea Nacional, Jaime Cuadra, and voted with the majority in favour of former President Alemán. In March the Attorney-General announced that former President Alemán was to face charges of fraud and embezzlement relating to the state television company, Sistema Nacional de Televisión Canal 6 (SNTV Canal 6). In the months that followed President Bolaños made several attempts to remove Alemán's congressional immunity. However, internal divisions within the PLC (which had divided into pro-Alemán and pro-Bolaños factions) meant that the President lacked the votes necessary to have the motion approved. As President of the Asamblea Nacional, Alemán obstructed approval of the budget and several reforms to the tax system which the Government needed to introduce in order to negotiate credit from the IMF. In August thousands of protesters marched through Managua to demand an end to the former head of state's immunity.

In September 2002 several of Alemán's relatives and former members of his Government were convicted of 'laundering' some US $100m. from state communications, infrastructure, insurance and petroleum enterprises. One week later Alemán, who faced the same charges, suspended a parliamentary session at which the removal of his congressional immunity was to be discussed. The following day FSLN members joined the Bolaños faction of the PLC to vote in favour of Alemán's dismissal. Cuadra was installed as President of the Asamblea and a new legislative commission, comprising supporters of Bolaños, was formed to determine whether Alemán's immunity should be revoked. The former President's financial assets in Panama and those of his family in the USA were frozen while investigations into the charges were made. The USA also suspended Alemán's right to enter its territory; several members of his family and former administration had already fled the country. In December the Asamblea Nacional approved a motion revoking Alemán's congressional immunity by a narrow majority; the former President was immediately put under house arrest.

In October 2002 Bolaños himself became the subject of allegations of fraud. In response to charges filed with the Supreme Court, that he and his Vice-President, José Rizo Castellón, had used an illegal fund controlled by Alemán to finance his 2001 electoral campaign, Bolaños promised to renounce his presidential immunity at a date named by his prosecutors. In November Bolaños and Rizo were formally charged with embezzling US $4.1m. from public funds.

Alemán's arrest further deepened divisions within the PLC. In January 2003 Bolaños's veto of parts of the budget, in order to comply with conditions stipulated by the IMF for Nicaragua to qualify for financial assistance and debt relief, was opposed by both the pro-Alemán faction of the PLC and the FSLN (the Sandinistas had supported the President in his attempts to remove Alemán). In March the pro-Alemán faction of the PLC officially announced that it was in opposition to the Government, in protest at the Government's alliance with the FSLN. The departure of the deputies left Bolaños with the unconditional support of only nine PLC members in the Asamblea (although six members of the Alemán faction later declared their allegiance to the President).

In June 2003 the pro-Alemán faction of the PLC formed an alliance with the FSLN in order successfully to approve in the legislature the appointment of nine Supreme Court judges with FSLN or pro-Alemán sympathies. The PLC faction believed that the appointments would increase the likelihood that Alemán would be acquitted of the charges against him. Nevertheless, in August an FSLN-appointed Supreme Court judge ruled that the cost of keeping Alemán under house arrest was too great, and the former President was incarcerated. However, in November Alemán was returned to house arrest, allegedly following an agreement between the pro-Alemán faction of the PLC and the FSLN. In return for the support of the FSLN in the release of Alemán, the PLC agreed to support FSLN attempts to postpone municipal elections to 2006, and to replace the country's presidential system with a parliamentary one. The Supreme Court ruling was strongly opposed by many traditionalist members of the FSLN and damaged Ortega's standing within the party. The move provoked a strong reaction from the international community, particularly the USA, which declared Ortega and Alemán to be discredited figures who ought to have no further role in Nicaraguan politics. Concern was also expressed at opposition efforts to impeach President Bolaños on charges of electoral fraud. The USA suspended US $4.9m. in aid for judicial reform, and threatened to obstruct Nicaragua's access to the IMF debt-reduction programme.

In December 2003 Alemán was found guilty of charges of money-laundering, fraud and theft of state funds and was sentenced to 20 years' imprisonment. He was also fined US $17m. Owing to ill health, however, he was to serve his prison term under house arrest. The trial was considered to be a test of Nicaragua's judiciary and the outcome was welcomed by the international community. In the same month the alliance between the FSLN and the dissident PLC members collapsed, following the latter's insistence that the release of Alemán was essential if the pact were to continue. One week later the pro-Alemán PLC deputies joined with the pro-Bolaños faction of the party to approve the budget for 2004, essential to gain IMF funding. In January 2004 the two factions of the ruling party attempted a fragile truce in order to select a new directorate of the Asamblea. The new legislative President, Carlos Noguera Pastora, was an Alemán supporter, while the six remaining seats were divided evenly between the two factions of the party. In December a court of appeal acquitted Alemán of the charge of appropriating some US $1.5m. from SNTV Canal 6. However, he continued to serve his sentence for money-laundering under house arrest.

In March 2004 the Asamblea began to debate a series of measures proposed by President Bolaños. The proposed reforms included the introduction of an independently appointed judiciary, adoption of a five-year national budget and reform of the electoral system. The proposed judicial reform prompted protests in the Asamblea from judges. Bolaños declared he was willing to engage in all-party dialogue on his proposals. Throughout most of 2004 the PLC- and FSLN-dominated Asamblea blocked the reform proposals, although in October the creation of an independent judicial council to appoint judges did receive legislative approval.

Also in March 2004 President Bolaños, Vice-President Rizo and 31 other senior members of the PLC were accused of illegal campaign-financing during the previous presidential election. Seven PLC members were arrested, including party president Jorge Castillo Quant. In October the Comptroller-General, Juan Gutiérrez, requested that President Bolaños be removed from power and fined two months' salary for withholding information regarding the financing of his 2001 election campaign. Supporters of the President claimed the request was politically motivated, as the office of the Comptroller-General was controlled by the FSLN and the anti-Bolaños faction of the PLC. At the invitation of Bolaños, a delegation arrived from the OAS to investigate the Comptroller-General's findings. Following a meeting with the OAS representatives, Ortega agreed to withdraw FSLN support for the initiation of impeachment proceedings against the President until after the November municipal elections.

The FSLN won a decisive victory in the local elections of 7 November 2004, securing control of 84 of the 151 municipalities, including Managua. The following day a two-thirds' majority in the Asamblea Nacional voted in support of constitutional reform legislation limiting presidential powers. The reforms would require the President to seek legislative ratification for key appointments such as ministers, ambassadors, the chief prosecutor and banking superintendent, and would enable the Asamblea to remove officials deemed to be incompetent. A further reform provided for the transfer of control of the state energy, water and telecommunications services from the President to one regulatory body, the Superintendencia de Servicios Públicos (Sisep). In December President Bolaños appealed to the Supreme Court of Justice, contending that the reforms, supported by the FSLN and the PLC, would engender irreconcilable tension between the Government and the legislature. Furthermore, Bolaños asserted that the legislation was unconstitutional and that such an attempt to redefine the powers of the executive and legislative branches of government exceeded the remit of the Asamblea Nacional. In January 2005 the Central American Court of Justice (CCJ) ruled that ratification of the controversial constitutional amendments should be suspended. None the less, one week later the Asamblea approved the legislation. In mid-January, two days before the legislation was due to come into effect, the Presidents of El Salvador, Guatemala and Honduras issued a joint statement of support for President Bolaños. Following further negotiations between factions supporting Bolaños, Ortega and Alemán, the President agreed to promulgate the controversial reforms in return for an opposition pledge that it would work towards a consensus with the executive on such matters as the budget and social security reform. Nevertheless, in March the CCJ declared the constitutional reforms to be illegal, ruling that they could only be approved by a specially convened constituent assembly. On the same day the Supreme Court declared the reforms valid.

In July 2005 Alemán was released on probation for the remainder of his sentence, allegedly for health reasons. The Court of Appeal overruled the decision three days later, ordering that he return to house arrest. However, Alemán's probation was upheld in August by the Supreme Court of Justice, thereby permitting the former President to travel within the province of Managua and to participate in political activities. The Supreme Court of Justice also ratified the constitutional amendment to restrict presidential powers, which had been approved by the Asamblea Nacional in January. Ernesto Leal, the Secretary to the Presidency, criticized the ruling, asserting that the executive would adhere to the CCJ ruling that declared the reforms to be illegal.

Meanwhile, accusations against Bolaños and his associates of illegal campaign-financing during the 2001 elections persisted. In early September 2005 seven Central American heads of state gathered in Managua to demonstrate their support for Bolaños. None the less, later that month the Asamblea Nacional removed the immunity from prosecution of three ministers and three deputy ministers.

Dissension over the proposed constitutional reforms impeded the Government's legislative agenda, including efforts to gain approval for the proposed Dominican Republic-Central American Free Trade Agreement (DR-CAFTA, comprising Nicaragua, Costa Rica, the Dominican Republic, El Salvador, Guatemala, Honduras and the USA). In early October 2005 the US Assistant Secretary of State publicly criticized the PLC-FSLN legislative pact and proposed the implementation of DR-CAFTA without Nicaragua. This intervention, combined with ongoing mediation by the OAS, was widely seen as instrumental in resolving the political crisis: in October the FSLN withdrew its opposition to DR-CAFTA and the following day the proposed free trade agreement was approved by the Asamblea Nacional. In addition, Ortega and Bolaños reached an agreement to delay the implementation of the constitutional reforms until the end of Bolaños' mandate in January 2007; legislation providing for this postponement was subsequently adopted. In late October the Asamblea Nacional rejected a proposal to remove Bolaños' immunity from prosecution, and the charges against the ministers whose immunity had been lifted in September were dismissed in December.

In preparation for presidential and legislative elections due to be held in November 2006, in August 2005 a centre-left alliance of the MRS and the Alternativa Cristiana (AC), both former FSLN factions, nominated Herty Lewites, a popular former mayor of Managua who had been expelled from the FSLN the previous year, as its presidential candidate. (The AC withdrew from the alliance in March 2006, however, and later selected Edén Pastora Gómez as its nominee.) Also in August 2005 the former PLC Secretary to the Presidency, Eduardo Montealegre Rivas, presented his candidacy on behalf of the Alianza Liberal Nicaragüense (ALN), a recently founded party composed primarily of dissident former PLC members opposed to Alemán, in alliance with the PC. In late March 2006 former Vice-President Rizo, a close ally of Alemán, secured the presidential candidature of the PLC. By mid-2006 Ortega had overtaken his main rivals in most polls, and the sudden death of Lewites from a heart attack in July was considered most likely to benefit the FSLN, if the party could regain the support of dissident Sandinistas. Edmundo Jarquín, an economist and hitherto Lewites' running mate, became the new candidate of the MRS. Meanwhile, efforts by the US ambassador to unite the PLC and the ALN-PC behind a single candidate not linked to Alemán led to accusations of foreign interference in Nicaragua's electoral process, as did Venezuelan backing for Ortega and the FSLN. With neither Rizo nor Montealegre, the candidate favoured by the USA, willing to stand aside for the other, the right wing remained divided ahead of the polls.

During the electoral campaign Ortega focused on socio-economic issues, pledging to co-operate with the IMF, to support the implementation of DR-CAFTA and to introduce measures aimed at reducing poverty. Having been defeated by a liberal in the 1990 election and having failed in two subsequent attempts to regain power, he sought to distance himself from the more extreme Sandinista policies of the 1980s, insisting that, if elected, he would respect free enterprise, protect private property and encourage investment.

The presidential and legislative elections took place, as scheduled, on 5 November 2006. Ortega was elected to the presidency with 38.0% of the votes cast, while Montealegre secured 28.3% and Rizo 27.1%. Under the electoral reforms that took effect in January 2000 (reducing the proportion of votes necessary for a President to be elected outright from 45% to 35%), a second round of voting was not required. The poor performance of Jarquín, who, with 6.3%, obtained a substantially lower share of the vote than most polls had predicted, suggested that Ortega's moderate tone prior to the elections had succeeded in persuading dissident Sandinistas to return to the FSLN. The FSLN also became the largest party in the Asamblea Nacional, winning 38 seats; the PLC took 25 seats (compared with 47 in the 2001 elections), the ALN 22 and the MRS the remaining five elected seats. Montealegre and Bolaños were both awarded supplementary legislative seats, in accordance with electoral rules. An estimated 16,000 domestic and international observers monitored the elections, with the OAS mission concluding that the process had generally been conducted peacefully and transparently. An estimated 69% of the electorate participated in the poll.

Ortega took office on 10 January 2007. His new Cabinet included Samuel Santos López, mayor of Managua during Ortega's previous period in office, as Minister of Foreign Affairs, Ana Isabel Morales Mazún as Minister of the Interior and Alberto Guevara Obregón as Minister of Finance and Public Credit. Ortega's wife, Rosario Murillo Zambrana, was appointed to the newly created cabinet position of Co-ordinator of the Communication and Citizenship Council, in which role she was to be responsible for all governmental publicity. Later that month the President issued a decree more than halving his own salary and substantially lowering those of government ministers and other senior officials. In late January the Asamblea Nacional adopted amendments to legislation on the organization and duties of the executive. Proposed by Ortega, and supported by the PLC, these 'urgent' reforms gave the President greater control over the police force and the military (consequently reducing the powers of the Ministers of the Interior and of National Defence) and allowed the President to create 'Citizen Power Councils' by decree. Amid concerns regarding the potential power of these Councils, which were intended to encourage direct democracy by co-ordinating the work of non-governmental organizations and public institutions on a regional and local level, opposition parties insisted that they should be purely consultative and not assume any of the functions of government ministries.

Also in late January 2007 the legislature approved the further postponement, for one year, of the constitutional amendments limiting presidential powers that had been due to take effect that month. A special commission, comprising seven deputies, was designated by the four parties represented in the legislature in mid-February to draft new constitutional reform legislation. The ALN advocated a reduction in the number of deputies and an increase in the percentage of the vote required to secure an outright win in a presidential election, while the FSLN was in favour of allowing a President to serve two consecutive terms. Further discussion of possible constitutional reform continued during 2007, although by early 2008 no firm proposals had been presented. In January 2008 the Supreme Court annulled the law postponing the implementation of the constitutional reforms, although it also declared invalid the majority of the reforms themselves, including the transfer of control of utilities to Sisep. However, it did not annul the law requiring the President to seek legislative approval of key appointments, with the result that this reform duly entered into force.

There were several changes to Ortega's Cabinet in his first few months of office. In early February 2007 Ortega dismissed the Minister of the Family, Glenda Ramírez Noguera, later appointing Rosa Adilia Vizcaya to the post; no official reason was given for Ramírez's departure. In April Amanda Lorío Aranda was dismissed as Minister of the Environment and Natural

Resources, ostensibly because she had illegally allowed a private medical consultant to offer services to ministry employees at a minimal cost; she was replaced by Juana Argeñal Sandovál. The Minister of Development, Industry and Trade, Dr Horacio Brenes Icabalceta, was dismissed along with his deputy in late May due to 'internal conflicts', and was substituted by Orlando Solorzano Delgadillo.

Meanwhile, at the end of January 2007 Ortega announced the creation of a National Commission for Reconciliation and Peace, which was to lead efforts to resolve issues arising from the civil war. The commission, subsequently renamed the Commission for Verification, Reconciliation, Peace and Justice, was formally constituted in May under the chairmanship of Cardinal Obando y Bravo (who had retired as Archbishop of Managua in 2005). Its stated remit was to continue the work of the commission established following the peace accords of 1987, ensuring that former combatants and victims of the war had received land and compensation as stipulated in the accords.

The national prison service granted Alemán complete freedom of movement within Nicaragua in mid-March 2007. Montealegre claimed that the decision to ease the restrictions on the former President (who had been released on probation in July 2005, but hitherto confined to Managua—see above) had been made on the orders of Ortega, in a joint attempt by the FSLN and the PLC to ensure that the country's liberal factions remained divided. Alemán's status continued to be exploited by the Government throughout 2007 to ensure PLC support for its programme. In December the Managua Appeals Court ordered that Alemán should return to house arrest, but the order was overturned in March 2008, ensuring that he would remain at liberty.

In mid-September 2007 the Asamblea Nacional approved a law to prevent the proposed Citizen Power Councils from forming any part of the executive branch of government, ensuring that they would perform a purely consultative role and would not receive any state funding. (The law was approved by all the opposition parties in the legislature, including the PLC, which had hitherto supported the majority of the Ortega Government's proposals.) The Councils' inauguration had been scheduled for July but had been postponed until November, following the legislative vote. In mid-November the Asamblea Nacional approved a further law rejecting the presidential veto; however, following a judicial appeal the FSLN President of the Asamblea, René Núñez Téllez, refused to allow the law to be published in the official gazette, thereby rendering it invalid. The Citizen Power Councils were created by presidential decree on 29 November, and inaugurated in a public ceremony in Managua on the following day. The legality of the presidential veto was subsequently confirmed by the Supreme Court in early December. Opposition parties continued to voice strong criticism of the Councils, which they claimed would serve to consolidate the power and influence of the FSLN in local affairs.

Full military relations between Nicaragua and the USA, suspended since 1980, were re-established in May 2001. In 2003 the Government resisted pressure from the USA to destroy its stockpile of surface-to-air missiles, claiming that a certain number were necessary for defence against terrorism. However, in March 2004 it was reported that the Government had agreed to destroy one-half of the 2,000 weapons. In November President Bolaños announced that about one-half of the remaining surface-to-air missiles (an estimated 1,334) would be destroyed within 18 months. However, in the following month the opposition-controlled Asamblea approved legislation granting it authority to decide on the acquisition and disposal of armaments. The measure formed part of the controversial reforms intended to curtail President Bolaños' powers (see above). Although Bolaños vetoed the legislation, this was overridden in February 2005 by the PLC-FSLN parliamentary bloc. The issue gathered momentum in the previous month following reports in a US newspaper that Nicaraguan missiles were being sold to would-be terrorists. The outgoing Commander-in-Chief of the Armed Forces, Gen. Javier Carrión, rejected the reports; however, on 18 February two men were convicted of selling a surface-to-air missile on the 'black' (parallel, illegal) market. As a result, the Government pledged to destroy 79% of the remaining stockpile of missiles. However, dissatisfaction with a lack of progress on the issue prompted the US Administration to suspend military aid to Nicaragua in April–October. In July 2007 President Ortega—who had hitherto favoured the retention of all 1,051 missiles unless other Central American countries also agreed to reduce the size of their armed forces—proposed the destruction of 651 missiles, leaving 400 for the purposes of national defence, in exchange for military helicopters and medical equipment from the USA. Talks between the two countries concerning the destruction of the missiles took place in late 2007.

In June 1995, prompted by frequent disputes concerning fishing rights in the Gulf of Fonseca, Nicaragua signed an accord with Honduras providing for the visible demarcation of each country's territorial waters. Despite this agreement, in December the Honduran Government issued an official protest to Nicaragua at what it claimed to be the illegal seizure of Honduran fishing vessels by a Nicaraguan naval patrol in Honduran waters. In May 1997 a further incident, in which Nicaraguan and Honduran naval patrols exchanged fire following the seizure by the Nicaraguan navy of Honduran fishing boats, gave renewed impetus to the demarcation issue. However, the demarcation process did not begin until May 1998. In December 1999, following further confrontations, Nicaragua initiated proceedings at the International Court of Justice (ICJ, see p. 20) in The Hague, Netherlands, to determine the maritime delimitation in the Gulf of Fonseca. In that month a dispute arose prompting Nicaragua to sever commercial ties with, and impose import taxes on, Honduras, in direct contravention of Central American free trade undertakings (Nicaragua also imposed similar tariffs on Colombia, thereby violating commitments entered into with the World Trade Organization). Following mediation by the OAS, in January 2000 Nicaragua ended its trade sanctions against Honduras, and in March both countries signed an accord committing them to observe a maritime exclusion zone in the Caribbean and to reduce troop numbers on their common border. In addition, both countries agreed to submit all issues pertaining to maritime space in the Caribbean Sea to the ruling of the ICJ. An agreement was also made to mount co-ordinated naval patrols in the Gulf of Fonseca. However, shortly after conflict again ensued over a small islet in the disputed territory, which Nicaragua claimed had been occupied by the Honduran armed forces. Furthermore, in February 2001 the Minister of Defence, José Adán Guerra, accused Honduras of violating the March 2000 accords by carrying out military exercises in the area and, in the following month, Nicaragua submitted documentation to the ICJ contesting the treaty. Nicaragua also refused to participate in the joint patrol of the Gulf of Fonseca. In March 2001 delegates from both Governments attended OAS-sponsored discussions in Washington, DC, USA. In June Nicaragua and Honduras concluded a confidence-building agreement, which provided for OAS observers to monitor the actions of army and navy forces on both sides of the common border. None the less, in August the Nicaraguan Government claimed that Honduras was planning to launch an attack on its border. In July 2002 the situation further deteriorated when the Nicaraguan Government announced plans to sell oil-drilling rights in the disputed area. In November 2006, however, during a visit to Honduras, President-elect Ortega surprised the Honduran President, Manuel Zelaya, and the Nicaraguan Government by proposing the joint development of the disputed area. The Nicaraguan Minister of National Defence, Avil Ramírez, warned Ortega against making remarks that might jeopardize Nicaragua's claims before the ICJ. The ICJ conducted public hearings on the dispute in March 2007 and in October ruled on a revised maritime border approximately mid-way between the two countries. Both the Nicaraguan and Honduran Governments declared themselves satisfied with the ruling.

In 1997 relations with Costa Rica became strained when, following a change in that country's immigration policy, it began deporting Nicaraguans who were residing illegally in the country. Remittances from Nicaraguans in Costa Rica represented a significant contribution to the Nicaraguan economy, averaging US $240m.–$300m. per year. In February 1999 Costa Rica offered one-year renewable residence permits to registering illegal Nicaraguan immigrants. Further antagonism had developed between the two countries in July 1998 when Nicaragua prohibited Costa Rican civil guards from carrying arms while navigating the San Juan river, which forms the border between the two countries. According to a long-standing treaty, the river, which is Nicaraguan territory, was only to be used by Costa Rica for commercial purposes. Following protests by Costa Rica, agreement was reached allowing for that country's civil guard to carry arms on the river while under escort by the Nicaraguan authorities. In August, however, following concerted pressure by opposition parties, the media and the Roman Catholic Church in Nicaragua, which accused the Government of surrendering part of the nation's sovereignty, Nicaragua annulled the accord. In June 2000 both Governments agreed a procedure that would allow armed Costa Rican police officers to patrol the river. In October 2001 President Alemán further announced that Costa Rican guards could patrol the river, providing they had first obtained permission from his Government, but rejected Costa Rica's submission of the dispute to the ICJ. In September 2002 the two countries appeared to have made some progress towards resolving the dispute when Nicaragua agreed to discontinue the fees charged to Costa Ricans crossing the river in exchange for the abolition of charges levied on visas and tourist permits required by Nicaraguans to enter Costa Rica. Costa Rica also announced that it would relinquish plans to refer the matter to the ICJ. In October bilateral discussions began on the Nicaraguan Government's plans to sell oil-exploration rights in an area of the Caribbean Sea and Pacific Ocean claimed by Costa Rica. Failure to agree on the issue within the stipulated three years prompted Costa Rica, in September 2005, to refer the matter to the ICJ. In response, President Bolaños recalled the Nicaraguan ambassador to Costa Rica, ordered the troops patrolling the border area to prohibit the passage of armed Costa Rican police officers, and imposed a 35% tariff on Costa Rican imports. Furthermore, in November the Nicaraguan Government declared an interest in reclaiming the province of Guanacaste, annexed by Costa Rica in 1825. Bilateral relations deteriorated further in February 2006 when Nicaragua brought a case before the Inter-American Commission on Human Rights accusing the Costa Rican authorities of tolerating xenophobia and discrimination against immigrants, citing the violent deaths of two Nicaraguan immigrants in late 2005 as evidence of this. The Commission dismissed the case in March 2007.

In November 2001 a dispute with Colombia arose after a Nicaraguan fishing vessel was captured allegedly in Colombian waters. The Colombian authorities charged the crew with violating its sovereignty and misappropriating its natural resources. It was the third time in that year that a Nicaraguan vessel had been apprehended in Colombian waters. In the following month, Nicaragua presented a request to the ICJ that its claim over territorial waters in the Caribbean Sea and around the islands of San Andrés and Providencia be recognized. In July 2003 the Colombian Minister of Foreign Affairs formally objected to the ICJ's involvement in the case. The ICJ dismissed Nicaragua's claim to the San Andrés archipelago in December 2007, although it had yet to rule on jurisdiction of the other disputed waters. In early March 2008 Nicaragua briefly suspended diplomatic relations with Colombia in protest at that country's recent military incursion into Ecuador, during which a senior member of the Fuerzas Armadas Revolucionarias de Colombia—Ejército del Pueblo (FARC) was killed; however, relations were restored shortly afterwards.

Developing strong regional relations appeared to be a priority for Ortega following his election as President: he toured four other Central American countries in late November 2006, before visiting the leaders of Cuba and Venezuela, with whom he already had close links. At the same time, Ortega adopted a conciliatory approach towards the USA, stating that he would seek to foster a 'respectful' bilateral relationship, and in late November the US Assistant Secretary of State for Western Hemisphere Affairs, Thomas Shannon, held talks with the President-elect in Managua. None the less, on taking office Ortega sought to strengthen relations with other left-wing administrations in Latin America. His close ties to the Presidents of Bolivia and Venezuela were evident at his inauguration, on 10 January 2007, and on the following day he confirmed Nicaragua's participation in the Bolivarian Alternative for the Americas (Alternativa Bolivariana para América Latina y el Caribe—ALBA), which had been devised by Venezuela as an alternative model to the US-promoted Free Trade Area of the Americas and was also supported by Bolivia and Cuba. Furthermore, Ortega signed a number of economic agreements with the Venezuelan President, Lt-Col (retd) Hugo Rafael Chávez Frías, who pledged substantial financial assistance to Nicaragua, including the construction of a petroleum refinery, capable of processing 100,000–150,000 barrels of oil per day, and the provision of low-interest loans for impoverished Nicaraguans living in rural areas. A few days later Ortega met the Iranian President, Mahmoud Ahmadinejad, who visited Nicaragua during a tour of Latin America. The two leaders announced plans to open embassies in their respective countries and signed a co-operation agreement, which provided for Iranian investment in various projects aimed at improving the Nicaraguan economy and reducing poverty. Ortega dismissed suggestions that such alliances would damage Nicaragua's relations with the USA. In early March a joint Nicaraguan-Venezuelan committee was formed to advance plans for bilateral co-operation, particularly in the energy sector. Venezuela was to supply Nicaragua with 10,000 barrels of petroleum per day at preferential rates and 32 electricity generators to alleviate severe energy shortages. Speaking at the launch of the joint committee in Managua, Ortega compared ALBA favourably with DR-CAFTA, praising the former's focus on the principles of social justice. In June Ortega met President Ahmadinejad in Iran, as part of a tour that also included Cuba, Algeria and Libya, and in August Ortega and the Iranian Minister of Energy signed a further series of accords in Managua, under the terms of which Iran would invest in a number of infrastructure projects in Nicaragua in exchange for the establishment of trade links.

Government

Executive power is vested in the President, who is elected by popular vote for a five-year term. The President is assisted by a Vice-President and an appointed Cabinet. Legislative power is held by the Asamblea Nacional (National Assembly), elected by universal adult suffrage, under a system of proportional representation, for a five-year term.

Defence

As assessed at November 2007, the armed forces were estimated to total 14,000 (army 12,000, navy 800, air force 1,200). Compulsory military service was abolished in April 1990. In 1995 the armed forces were renamed the Ejército de Nicaragua, following a constitutional amendment removing their Sandinista affiliation. The defence budget for 2007 totalled 675m. gold córdobas.

Economic Affairs

In 2006, according to estimates by the World Bank, Nicaragua's gross national income (GNI), measured at average 2004–06 prices, was US $5,227.1m., equivalent to $1,000 per head (or $4,010 per head on an international purchasing-power parity basis). During 1996–2006 the population increased at an average annual rate of 1.4%, while gross domestic product (GDP) per head increased, in real terms, by an average of 2.3% per year. Nicaragua's GDP increased, in real terms, by an average of 3.8% per year in 1996–2006; GDP increased by an estimated 3.7% in 2006.

Agriculture (including forestry and fishing) contributed an estimated 18.7% of GDP in 2006 and engaged 34.1% of the employed work-force in 2005. The principal cash crops are coffee (which accounted for 14.5% of export earnings in 2005), groundnuts, sugar cane and beans. Maize, rice and beans are the principal food crops. Production of shellfish became increasingly important in the 1990s, and by 2000 shrimps and lobsters accounted for some 17.4% of export earnings, although this decreased to 8.3% by 2006. Meat and meat products accounted for 14.3% of export earnings in 2006. According to the World Bank, agricultural GDP increased at an average annual rate of 3.1% during 1996–2005; the sector's GDP increased by 2.7% in 2006.

Industry (including mining, manufacturing, construction and power) engaged 18.3% of the employed labour force in 2005 and provided an estimated 28.0% of GDP in 2006. According to the World Bank, industrial GDP increased by an average of 4.4% per year during 1996–2006; it increased by 3.2% in 2006.

Mining contributed an estimated 1.2% of GDP in 2006 and engaged an estimated 0.3% of the employed labour force in 2005. Nicaragua has workable deposits of gold, silver, copper, lead, antimony, zinc and iron; its non-metallic minerals include limestone, gypsum, bentonite and marble. In 2005 gold accounted for an estimated 5.0% of export earnings. The GDP of the mining sector increased at an average annual rate of 11.4% in 1990–2001; the sector's GDP decreased by about 20% in 2000, but grew by an estimated 2.5% in 2001.

Manufacturing contributed some 17.5% of GDP in 2006 and engaged 12.4% of the employed labour force in 2005. The principal branches of manufacturing were food products, beverages and tobacco (about 67% of the total), machinery and metal products and petroleum derivatives and rubber products. The *maquila*, or assembly, sector expanded rapidly in the early 1990s, although growth slowed in the early 2000s. The principal products were clothing, footwear, aluminium frames and jewellery. Manufacturing GDP increased, according to the World Bank, by an average of 4.5% per year in 1996–2006; the sector's GDP grew by 3.2% in 2006.

Energy is derived principally from imported petroleum, although two hydroelectric plants in the department of Jinotega account for one-tenth of the electrical energy generated in the country. Imports of mineral fuels and lubricants comprised an estimated 10.4% of the total value of imports in 2006. In 2007 Nicaragua produced an estimated 2,863.7 GWh of electrical energy.

The services sector contributed an estimated 53.4% of GDP in 2006 and engaged 47.6% of the employed labour force in 2005. The tourism sector expanded throughout the 1990s; in 2004 annual income totalled US $191m., with arrivals put at 614,782, a 16.9% increase on the previous year's figures. According to the World Bank, the GDP of the services sector increased by an average of 3.7% per year in 1996–2006; the sector grew by 3.9% in 2005 before declining by 2.1% in 2006.

In 2006 Nicaragua recorded a visible trade deficit of approximately US $3,421.9m., and there was a deficit of $854.4m. on the current account of the balance of payments. In 2006 the principal source of imports (an estimated 20.7%) was the USA; other major suppliers were Nicaragua's partners in the Central American Common Market (CACM—Costa Rica, El Salvador, Guatemala and Honduras, see p. 201), as well as Venezuela and Mexico. The USA was also the principal market for exports (an estimated 32.4%) in 2006; other notable purchasers were the countries of the CACM, Mexico and Canada. The principal exports in 2006 were coffee, meat and gold. The principal imports were non-durable consumer goods, primary materials and intermediate goods for industry and crude petroleum.

In 2007 Nicaragua recorded a budgetary surplus of an estimated 3,621m. gold córdobas, according to central bank figures. At the end of 2005 Nicaragua's total external debt was US $5,144m., of which $4,113m. was long-term public debt. The cost of servicing external debt in that year was equivalent to 6.9% of the value of goods and services. In 1999–2007 the average annual rate of increase in consumer prices was 7.5%. Consumer prices increased by an annual average of 11.1% in 2007. An estimated 6.5% of the labour force was unemployed in 2004.

Nicaragua is a member of the CACM (see p. 201), which aims eventually to liberalize intra-regional trade, and of the Inter-American Development Bank (IDB, see p. 308). Negotiations towards a free trade agreement, to be known as the Central American Free Trade Agreement, were concluded between El Salvador, Guatemala, Honduras, Nicaragua and the USA in December 2003. The agreement entailed the gradual elimination of tariffs on most industrial and agricultural products over the next 10 and 20 years, respectively. Ratification of the Dominican Republic-Central American Free Trade Agreement (DR-CAFTA, as the agreement was restyled in 2004) was finally approved by the Nicaraguan legislature on 10 October 2005. DR-CAFTA was inaugurated in April 2006.

The implementation of a comprehensive economic reform programme, supported by the IMF, following the end of the civil war in 1990 succeeded in bringing inflation under control, increasing foreign reserves and reducing the fiscal deficit. Nevertheless, Nicaragua was dependent on international aid in the early 2000s. The country qualified for debt relief of some US $4,500m. under the World Bank's heavily indebted poor countries (HIPC) initiative in 2000 and in the following year the IDB approved a debt-relief programme of $386m. for Nicaragua, to be implemented annually until 2019. The 'Paris Club' of official creditors also agreed to cancel $405m. of public external debt and to reschedule remaining payments. Nicaragua qualified for a gradual debt reduction under the HIPC initiative of up to 73% of the nation's total external debt in 2003, although this relief remained dependent on the Government meeting targets set by the IMF and the World Bank. In early 2004 Nicaragua qualified for an estimated $4,500m. in loans, under the enhanced HIPC initiative. In June 2005 Nicaragua was among 18 countries to be granted 100% debt relief on multilateral debt incurred prior to 2005 agreed by the Group of Eight (G-8) leading industrialized nations, subject to the approval of the lenders. This cancellation was approved by the IMF in December, under the Multilateral Debt Relief Initiative, and totalled some $201m. ($132m., excluding the remaining HIPC funding). Although the Bolaños Government succeeded in meeting IMF criteria for inclusion in the HIPC initiative, the fiscal and trade deficits remained high, and considerable social deprivation continued. The legislative impasse in 2003–05 (see Recent History) also meant that the Government was unable to implement reform. Nevertheless, the DR-CAFTA did receive legislative approval in 2005, and although not without its critics, was expected to add impetus to the economy from 2006. There were concerns internationally that the incoming Sandinista Goverment of Daniel Ortega would damage relations with the USA and mark a move away from macroeconomic orthodoxy. However, on taking office in January 2007 the new President was keen to promote continued fiscal prudency and ongoing reconciliation with the USA, despite the development of relations with Venezuela and Iran. While the new Government was expected to implement a substantive poverty alleviation programme (part-funded, it hoped, by an IMF loan of some $110m.), it did not plan to finance development through taxation on foreign investment. In early 2008 the Government agreed to buy back US $1,300m. of external commercial debt, accounting for some 94% of the total. It was expected that the policy would aid relationships with global capital markets, rather than boost short-term economic performance. Real GDP growth was estimated to have fallen to 2.9% in 2007, from 3.7% in 2006. This decline was accompanied by rising inflation, with original estimates of 11% anticipated to be nearer 17% due to increasing prices for energy and food late in the year. While growth was forecast to increase to 3.1% during 2008, inflation was expected to decline to 9.5%, although continued high prices for oil and agricultural costs were expected to have a detrimental impact. In light of inflationary pressures, the Central Bank was expected to abandon an exchange rate adjustment in 2008.

Education

Primary and secondary education have been provided free of charge since 1979. Primary education, which is officially compulsory, begins at seven years of age and lasts for six years. Secondary education, beginning at the age of 13, lasts for up to five years, comprising a first cycle of three years and a second of two years. In 2005 enrolment at primary schools included 87.2% of the relevant age-group. Secondary enrolment in that year included 42.7% of children in the relevant age-group. There are many commercial schools and eight universities. In 2003 a total of 103,577 students attended universities and other higher education institutes. In that year public expenditure on education accounted for 15.0% of total government expenditure.

Public Holidays

2008: 1 January (New Year's Day), 20 March (Maundy Thursday), 21 March (Good Friday), 1 May (Labour Day), 30 May (Mothers' Day, afternoon only), 19 July (Liberation Day), 1 and 10 August (Managua local holidays), 14 September (Battle of San Jacinto), 15 September (Independence Day), 2 November (All Souls' Day, afternoon only), 8 December (Immaculate Conception), 25 December (Christmas Day).

2009: 1 January (New Year's Day), 9 April (Maundy Thursday), 10 April (Good Friday), 1 May (Labour Day), 30 May (Mothers' Day, afternoon only), 19 July (Liberation Day), 1 and 10 August (Managua local holidays), 14 September (Battle of San Jacinto), 15 September (Independence Day), 2 November (All Souls' Day, afternoon only), 8 December (Immaculate Conception), 25 December (Christmas Day).

Various local holidays are also observed.

Weights and Measures

The metric system is officially used, although some Spanish and local units are also in general use.

NICARAGUA

Statistical Survey

Sources (unless otherwise stated): Banco Central de Nicaragua, Carretera Sur, Km 7, Apdos 2252/3, Zona 5, Managua; tel. 265-0500; fax 265-2272; e-mail bcn@cabcn.gob.ni; internet www.bcn.gob.ni; Instituto Nacional de Estadísticas y Censos (INEC), Las Brisas, Frente Hospital Fonseca, Managua; tel. 266-2031; internet www.inec.gob.ni.

Area and Population

AREA, POPULATION AND DENSITY

Area (sq km)	
Land	120,340
Inland water	10,034
Total	130,373*
Population (census results)	
25 April 1995	4,357,099
28 May–11 June 2005	
Males	2,534,491
Females	2,607,607
Total	5,142,098
Population (preliminary official estimate at mid-year)	
2006	5,529,800
Density (per sq km) at mid-2006	42.4

* 50,337 sq miles.

ADMINISTRATIVE DIVISIONS
(land area only, at 2005 census)

	Area (sq km)	Population	Density (per sq km)	Capital
Departments:				
Chinandega	4,822.4	378,970	78.6	Chinandega
León	5,138.0	355,779	69.2	León
Managua	3,465.1	1,262,978	364.5	Managua
Masaya	610.8	289,988	474.8	Masaya
Carazo	1,081.4	166,073	153.6	Jinotepe
Granada	1,039.7	168,186	161.8	Granada
Rivas	2,161.8	156,283	72.3	Rivas
Estelí	2,229.7	201,548	90.4	Estelí
Madriz	1,708.2	132,459	77.5	Somoto
Nueva Segovia	3,491.3	208,523	59.7	Ocotal
Jinotega	9,222.4	331,335	35.9	Jinotega
Matagalpa	6,803.9	469,172	69.0	Matagalpa
Boaco	4,176.7	150,636	36.1	Boaco
Chontales	6,481.3	153,932	23.8	Juigalpa
Río San Juan	7,540.9	95,596	12.7	San Carlos
Autonomous Regions:				
Atlántico Norte (RAAN)	32,819.7	314,130	9.5	Bilwi
Atlántico Sur (RAAS)	27,546.3	306,510	11.2	Bluefields
Total	120,339.5	5,142,098	42.7	—

PRINCIPAL TOWNS
(population at 2005 census)

Managua (capital)	937,489	Chinandega	121,793
León	174,051	Estelí	112,084
Masaya	139,582	Granada	105,171
Matagalpa	133,416	Tipitaga	101,685

BIRTHS AND DEATHS
(annual averages, UN estimates)

	1990–95	1995–2000	2000–05
Birth rate (per 1,000)	35.5	30.2	26.3
Death rate (per 1,000)	6.5	5.5	5.0

Source: UN, *World Population Prospects: The 2006 Revision*.

2001: Registered births 103,593 (19.9 per 1,000); Registered deaths 10,071 (1.9 per 1,000).
2002: Registered births 103,643 (19.4 per 1,000); Registered deaths 10,830 (2.0 per 1,000).
2003 (estimates): Live births 102,676; Deaths 14,630 (Source: UN, *Demographic Yearbook*).
Expectation of life (years at birth, WHO estimates): 70.2 (males 67.5; females 72.9) in 2005 (Source: WHO, *World Health Statistics*).

EMPLOYMENT
(population aged 10 years and over, 2005 census)

	Male	Female	Total
Agriculture, forestry and fishing	537,209	33,611	570,820
Mining and quarrying	5,005	503	5,508
Manufacturing	118,919	89,074	207,993
Electricity, gas and water	3,830	954	4,784
Construction	86,574	2,182	88,756
Trade, restaurants and hotels	166,863	150,580	317,443
Transport and communications	60,346	5,338	65,684
Financial services	7,104	7,320	14,424
Government services	150,992	232,220	383,212
Other activities	9,817	7,109	16,926
Total employed	1,146,659	528,891	1,675,550

Health and Welfare

KEY INDICATORS

Total fertility rate (children per woman, 2005)	3.1
Under-5 mortality rate (per 1,000 live births, 2005)	37
HIV/AIDS (% of persons aged 15–49, 2005)	0.2
Physicians (per 1,000 head, 2003)	0.37
Hospital beds (per 1,000 head, 2004)	0.9
Health expenditure (2004): US $ per head (PPP)	231.3
Health expenditure (2004): % of GDP	8.2
Health expenditure (2004): public (% of total)	47.1
Access to water (% of persons, 2004)	79
Access to sanitation (% of persons, 2004)	47
Human Development Index (2005): ranking	110
Human Development Index (2005): value	0.710

For sources and definitions, see explanatory note on p. vi.

Agriculture

PRINCIPAL CROPS
('000 metric tons)

	2004	2005	2006
Rice (paddy)	232.6	316.7	312.1
Maize	443.7	555.6	504.1
Sorghum	96.6	91.3	71.8
Cassava (Manioc)	87.4	119.4	105.0*
Sugar cane	4,027.0	3,816.6	4,682.5
Dry beans	173.2	211.9	197.1
Groundnuts (in shell)	104.4	121.5	104.4
Oil palm fruit*	56.0	60.0	60.0
Bananas	52.3	49.9	42.6
Plantains*	38.5	42.0	42.0
Oranges*	69.0	72.0	72.0
Pineapples*	47.0	49.0	49.0
Coffee (green)	57.5	95.5	54.5

* FAO estimate(s).

Aggregate production ('000 metric tons, may include official, semi-official or estimated data): Total cereals 773 in 2004; 964 in 2005, 888 in 2006; Total roots and tubers 123 in 2004, 157 in 2005, 144 in 2006; Total vegetables (incl. melons) 33 in 2004, 35 in 2005, 35 in 2006; Total fruits (excl. melons) 220 in 2004, 226 in 2005, 219 in 2006.

Source: FAO.

NICARAGUA

LIVESTOCK
('000 head, year ending September)

	2003	2004	2005*
Cattle	3,500	3,400†	3,500
Pigs*	121	122	123
Goats*	7	7	7
Horses*	260	265	268
Asses, mules or hinnies*	56	57	57
Poultry	16,000	16,500	18,000

* FAO estimates.
† Unofficial figure.

2006: Figures assumed to be unchanged from 2005 (FAO estimates).

Source: FAO.

LIVESTOCK PRODUCTS
('000 metric tons)

	2004	2005	2006
Cattle meat	74.8	76.0	84.3
Pig meat	6.5	6.6	6.8
Horse meat*	2.0	2.1	2.1
Chicken meat	66.8	70.6	83.6
Cows' milk	584.0	612.9	633.7
Hen eggs	22.2	20.4	21.1

* FAO estimates.

Source: FAO.

Forestry

ROUNDWOOD REMOVALS
('000 cubic metres, excl. bark, FAO estimates)

	2004	2005	2006
Sawlogs, veneer logs and logs for sleepers	93	93	93
Fuel wood	5,906	5,948	5,975
Total	5,999	6,041	6,068

Source: FAO.

SAWNWOOD PRODUCTION
('000 cubic metres, incl. railway sleepers, FAO estimates)

	2004	2005	2006
Coniferous	24.0	19.5	19.5
Broadleaved	42.8	34.6	34.6
Total	66.8	54.1	54.1

Source: FAO.

Fishing

('000 metric tons, live weight)

	2003	2004	2005
Capture	15.3	19.3	30.9
Snooks	1.5	1.1	1.3
Snappers	2.2	2.4	4.6
Yellowfin tuna	n.a.	3.9	7.3
Common dolphinfish	0.7	0.4	0.4
Caribbean spiny lobsters	3.9	4.3	3.8
Penaeus shrimp	3.6	3.0	4.5
Aquaculture	7.0	7.9	10.0
Whiteleg shrimp	6.9	7.9	9.6
Total catch	22.3	27.2	40.9

Source: FAO.

Mining
(estimates)

	2003	2004	2005
Gold (kg)	3,096	4,064	4,000
Silver (kg)	2,040	2,000	2,000
Sand and gravel ('000 cubic metres)	636	600	600
Limestone (metric tons)	789,000	780,000	780,000
Gypsum and anhydrite (metric tons)	30,642	30,000	30,000

Source: US Geological Survey.

Industry

SELECTED PRODUCTS
('000 barrels, unless otherwise indicated)

	2001	2002*	2003
Raw sugar ('000 metric tons)	354	363	346
Liquid gas	219	194	238
Motor spirit	905	872	860
Kerosene	451	383	368
Diesel	1,578	1,485	1,439
Fuel oil	3,174	2,726	2,674
Bitumen (asphalt)	57	35	78
Cement ('000 metric tons)	595	549	577†
Cardboad boxes ('000 sq m)	9,879	8,212	4,673†
Electric energy (million kWh)	2,614	2,620.0	2,773.7
Soap (kgs)	10,000	10,200	n.a.
Rum ('000 litres)	8,595	7,216	8,345†

* Preliminary figures.
† Estimate.

Liquid gas ('000 barrels): 188.8 in 2004; 166.9 in 2005; 178.0 in 2006; 184.7 in 2007.

Motor spirit ('000 barrels): 886.3 in 2004; 766.9 in 2005; 773.7 in 2006; 721.0 in 2007.

Kerosene ('000 barrels): 267.2 in 2004; 246.5 in 2005; 210.8 in 2006; 239.4 in 2007.

Diesel ('000 barrels): 1,525.0 in 2004; 1,329.0 in 2005; 1,485.6 in 2006; 1,515.1 in 2007.

Fuel oil ('000 barrels): 2,858.8 in 2004; 2,533.8 in 2005; 2,691.4 in 2006; 2,632.7 in 2007.

Bitumen (asphalt) ('000 barrels): 84.0 in 2004; 125.8 in 2005; 72.8 in 2006; 91.7 in 2007.

Electric energy (million kWh): 2,915.3 in 2004; 3,052.3 in 2005; 2,897.5 in 2006; 2,863.7 in 2007.

Cement ('000 metric tons, estimates): 820 in 2004; 820 in 2005 (Source: US Geological Survey).

NICARAGUA

Finance

CURRENCY AND EXCHANGE RATES

Monetary Units
100 centavos = 1 córdoba oro (gold córdoba).

Sterling, Dollar and Euro Equivalents (31 December 2007)
£1 sterling = 37.870 gold córdobas;
US $1 = 18.903 gold córdobas;
€1 = 27.827 gold córdobas;
1,000 gold córdobas = £26.41 = $52.90 = €35.94.

Average Exchange Rate (gold córdobas per US dollar)
2005   16.7333
2006   17.5700
2007   18.4485

Note: In February 1988 a new córdoba, equivalent to 1,000 of the former units, was introduced, and a uniform exchange rate of US $1 = 10 new córdobas was established. Subsequently, the exchange rate was frequently adjusted. A new currency, the córdoba oro (gold córdoba), was introduced as a unit of account in May 1990 and began to be circulated in August. The value of the gold córdoba was initially fixed at par with the US dollar, but in March 1991 the exchange rate was revised to $1 = 25,000,000 new córdobas (or 5 gold córdobas). On 30 April 1991 the gold córdoba became the sole legal tender.

BUDGET
(million gold córdobas)

Revenue*	2003	2004	2005†
Taxation	9,422.4	11,252.5	13,645.5
Income tax	2,447.9	3,176.0	3,902.3
Value-added tax	3,812.9	4,575.1	5,598.7
Taxes on petroleum products	1,566.4	1,618.4	1,756.1
Taxes on imports	628.2	684.4	898.5
Other revenue	728.6	978.3	1,062.6
Total	10,151.0	12,230.8	14,708.1

Expenditure‡	2003	2004	2005†
Compensation of employees	3,834.4	4,178.0	4,998.9
Goods and services	1,246.3	1,468.3	1,796.3
Interest payments	1,918.9	1,478.1	1,561.4
Current transfers	3,050.1	4,202.1	5,109.3
Social security contributions	223.2	227.4	278.9
Other expenditure	300.5	377.8	765.4
Total	10,573.5	11,931.6	14,510.3

* Excluding grants received (million gold córdobas): 2,079.0 in 2003; 2,373.6 in 2004; 2,723.1 in 2005 (preliminary).
† Preliminary figures.
‡ Excluding net acquisition of non-financial assets (million gold córdobas): 3,420.2 in 2003; 4,252.6 in 2004; 4,415.0 in 2005 (preliminary).

2006 (million gold córdobas): Total revenue 25,458.0; Total expenditure 24,118.7.

2007 (million gold córdobas): Total revenue 22,327.8; Total expenditure 18,706.8.

INTERNATIONAL RESERVES
(excluding gold, US $ million at 31 December)

	2004	2005	2006
IMF special drawing rights	0.50	0.31	0.39
Foreign exchange	667.70	727.50	921.50
Total	668.20	727.81	921.89

Source: IMF, *International Financial Statistics*.

MONEY SUPPLY
(million gold córdobas at 31 December)

	2004	2005	2006
Currency outside banks	3,103.3	3,808.0	4,401.3
Demand deposits at commercial banks	1,702.3	1,973.8	2,231.8
Total money (incl. others)	4,806.7	5,784.7	6,634.9

Source: IMF, *International Financial Statistics*.

COST OF LIVING
(Consumer Price Index; base: 1999 = 100)

	2004	2005	2006
Food	133.6	149.0	162.5
Clothing	114.6	117.8	122.3
Rent, fuel and light	144.8	156.0	175.0
All items (incl. others)	134.5	147.4	160.9

Source: ILO.

All items (base: 1999 = 100): 178.8 in 2007.

NATIONAL ACCOUNTS
(million gold córdobas at current prices)

Expenditure on the Gross Domestic Product

	2004	2005*	2006†
Government final consumption expenditure	8,010.0	9,101.1	11,071.9
Private final consumption expenditure	62,678.8	72,199.0	82,548.9
Increase in stocks	1,040.0	928.9	1,402.6
Gross fixed capital formation	18,897.9	23,128.5	25,962.2
Total domestic expenditure	90,626.7	105,357.5	120,985.6
Exports of goods and services	19,492.5	23,612.5	28,978.2
Less Imports of goods and services	38,963.7	47,736.9	56,828.9
GDP in purchasers' values	71,155.6	81,233.1	93,134.9
GDP at constant 1994 prices	30,252.2	31,643.0	32,810.9

* Preliminary figures.
† Estimates.

Gross Domestic Product by Economic Activity

	2004	2005*	2006†
Agriculture, hunting, forestry and fishing	11,824.3	13,623.5	16,063.0
Mining and quarrying	902.8	888.8	1,059.4
Manufacturing	12,070.0	13,381.2	15,089.6
Electricity, gas and water	2,027.9	2,261.0	2,692.6
Construction	3,893.2	4,861.4	5,249.6
Wholesale and retail trade	9,530.9	10,853.2	12,118.5
Transport and communications	4,168.5	4,677.5	5,364.6
Finance, insurance and business services	3,323.1	3,697.4	4,408.3
Real estate	5,718.2	6,214.8	6,829.9
Other private services	5,280.5	5,809.7	6,450.6
Government services	7,672.0	8,869.6	10,761.4
Sub-total	66,411.4	75,138.1	86,087.5
Net taxes on products	8,056.8	9,777.4	11,525.8
Less Imputed bank service charge	3,312.7	3,682.5	4,478.5
GDP in purchasers' values	71,155.6	81,233.1	93,134.9

* Preliminary figures.
† Estimates.

NICARAGUA

Statistical Survey

BALANCE OF PAYMENTS
(US $ million)

	2004	2005	2006
Exports of goods f.o.b.	1,369.2	1,654.2	1,977.5
Imports of goods f.o.b.	−2,457.5	−2,956.3	−3,421.9
Trade balance	**−1,088.3**	**−1,302.1**	**−1,444.4**
Exports of services	285.8	308.3	341.7
Imports of services	−409.3	−448.4	−483.1
Balance on goods and services	**−1,211.8**	**−1,442.2**	**−1,585.8**
Other income received	9.3	22.3	41.2
Other income paid	−209.8	−149.6	−165.3
Balance on goods, services and income	**−1,412.3**	**−1,569.5**	**−1,709.9**
Current transfers (net)	755.0	823.8	855.5
Current balance	**−657.3**	**−745.7**	**−854.4**
Capital (net)	306.9	289.2	282.3
Direct investment from abroad	250.0	241.4	282.3
Portfolio investment	−1.2	−7.7	−9.5
Other investment assets	278.4	−124.4	20.2
Other investment liabilities	−163.0	145.0	135.4
Net errors and omissions	−418.2	−39.1	210.8
Overall balance	**−404.4**	**−241.2**	**67.2**

Source: IMF, *International Financial Statistics*.

External Trade

PRINCIPAL COMMODITIES
(US $ million)

Imports c.i.f.	2004	2005	2006*
Consumer goods	742.4	823.9	952.4
Non-durable consumer goods	572.7	639.5	734.5
Durable consumer goods	169.7	184.4	217.9
Petroleum, mineral fuels and lubricants	401.9	541.5	676.3
Crude petroleum	225.2	284.9	366.0
Mineral fuels and lubricants	175.8	254.1	310.3
Intermediate goods	651.4	745.7	805.1
Primary materials and intermediate goods for agriculture and fishing	67.9	98.7	96.9
Primary materials and intermediate goods for industry	453.9	483.8	543.6
Construction materials	129.6	163.2	164.5
Capital goods	411.5	509.2	549.6
For agriculture and fishing	17.7	30.2	30.6
For industry	257.0	287.3	307.1
For transport	136.9	191.8	212.0
Miscellaneous	1.9	2.9	4.9
Total	**2,209.6**	**2,623.2**	**2,988.4**

* Preliminary figures.

Exports f.o.b.	2004	2005	2006*
Coffee	126.8	125.9	200.7
Groundnuts	39.7	43.6	42.5
Cattle on hoof	35.9	43.5	39.1
Beans	18.8	28.0	36.7
Bananas	10.7	11.6	9.6
Lobster	44.2	33.6	38.2
Fresh fish	7.5	11.4	13.1
Shrimp	38.3	52.2	47.5
Tobacco (leaf)	7.3	7.1	7.9
Gold	47.7	42.5	55.3
Meat and meat products	110.4	119.1	147.0
Refined sugars, etc.	36.8	60.3	58.4
Cheese	22.2	23.9	33.5
Wood products	14.1	16.2	7.2
Chemical products	27.0	36.3	30.5
Refined petroleum	8.0	12.4	13.4
Porcelain products	11.3	10.9	11.3
Total (incl. others)	**759.8**	**866.0**	**1,027.4**

* Preliminary figures.

PRINCIPAL TRADING PARTNERS
(US $ million)

Imports c.i.f.	2004	2005	2006*
Canada	22.2	21.9	23.7
Costa Rica	190.2	237.2	255.3
Ecuador	51.5	110.0	84.2
El Salvador	109.6	135.7	157.2
Germany	42.4	37.3	43.4
Guatemala	158.0	182.8	195.7
Honduras	51.6	61.2	72.6
Japan	96.9	118.0	111.0
Mexico	178.9	216.9	403.6
Panama	16.3	17.1	15.4
Spain	29.3	43.7	35.9
Sweden	6.5	18.0	10.3
Taiwan	16.2	16.2	16.3
USA	494.5	524.4	618.7
Venezuela	280.1	307.2	227.4
Total (incl. others)	**2,209.6**	**2,623.2**	**2,988.4**

* Preliminary figures.

Exports f.o.b.	2004	2005	2006*
Belgium	11.7	8.8	30.6
Canada	36.0	32.5	45.2
Costa Rica	50.9	53.6	58.0
El Salvador	109.5	122.8	147.0
France	11.5	13.1	16.5
Germany	14.1	15.4	30.2
Guatemala	32.3	44.4	47.0
Honduras	56.6	68.1	97.3
Italy	6.2	5.0	22.0
Mexico	39.9	44.0	47.0
Spain	21.7	34.0	35.1
USA	273.6	289.3	333.0
Total (incl. others)	**759.8**	**866.0**	**1,027.4**

* Preliminary figures.

Transport

RAILWAYS
(traffic)

	1990	1991	1992
Passenger-km (million)	3	3	6

Freight ton-km (million): 4 in 1985.
Source: UN, *Statistical Yearbook*.

ROAD TRAFFIC
(motor vehicles in use)

	2002	2003	2004
Cars	83,168	86,020	94,998
Buses and coaches	6,947	13,782	16,139
Lorries and vans	111,797	120,408	136,674
Motorcycles and mopeds	28,973	42,153	47,547

Source: IRF, *World Road Statistics*.

SHIPPING
Merchant fleet
(registered at 31 December)

	2004	2005	2006
Number of vessels	27	28	28
Total displacement ('000 grt)	5.0	5.7	5.7

Source: Lloyd's Register-Fairplay, *World Fleet Statistics*.

NICARAGUA

International Sea-Borne Freight Traffic
('000 metric tons)

	1997	1998	1999
Imports	1,272.7	1,964.7	1,180.7
Exports	329.3	204.5	183.6

Total freight traffic ('000 metric tons): 2,215.9 in 2000; 2,363.0 in 2001; 2,093.8 in 2002.

CIVIL AVIATION
(traffic on scheduled services)

	1998	1999	2000
Kilometres flown (million)	1.2	0.8	0.8
Passengers carried ('000)	52	59	61
Passenger-km (million)	93	67	72
Freight ton-km (million)	n.a.	0.5	0.5

Source: UN Economic Commission for Latin America and the Caribbean.

Tourism

TOURIST ARRIVALS BY COUNTRY OF ORIGIN

	2003	2004	2005
Canada	13,124	15,586	18,068
Costa Rica	76,659	99,674	99,674
El Salvador	73,806	88,103	88,103
Guatemala	40,132	48,990	58,019
Honduras	107,365	126,916	139,134
Panama	11,988	13,563	17,591
USA	117,156	131,865	147,331
Total (incl. others)	525,775	614,782	712,444

Tourism receipts (US $ million, incl. passenger transport): 164 in 2003; 196 in 2004; 211 in 2005.

Sources: World Tourism Organization.

Communications Media

	2004	2005	2006
Telephones ('000 main lines in use)	214.5	220.9	247.9
Mobile cellular telephones ('000 subscribers)	738.6	1,119.4	1,830.2
Personal computers ('000 in use)	200	220	n.a.
Internet users ('000)	125.0	140.0	155.0
Broadband subscribers ('000)	5.0	10.5	19.0

Radio receivers ('000 in use): 1,240 in 1997.
Television receivers ('000 in use): 350 in 2000.
Daily newspapers: 4 in 1996 (average circulation 135,000 copies).

Sources: UNESCO, *Statistical Yearbook*; International Telecommunication Union.

Education

(2004/05, unless otherwise indicated)

	Institutions*	Teachers	Males	Females	Total
Pre-primary	5,980	8,435	108,025	105,647	213,672
Primary	8,251	28,163	487,511	457,578	945,089
Secondary: general	1,249	12,019	197,078	218,195	415,273
Tertiary: university level	35	3,630†	47,683‡	51,222‡	98,905‡
Tertiary: other higher	73	210†	1,902‡	2,770‡	4,672‡

* 2002/03 figures.
† 2001/02 figure.
‡ 2003/04 figure.

Sources: UNESCO, *Statistical Yearbook*; Ministry of Education, Culture and Sports.

Adult literacy rate (UNESCO estimates): 76.7% (males 76.8%; females 76.6%) in 2001 (Source: UNESCO Institute for Statistics).

Directory

The Constitution

Shortly after taking office on 20 July 1979, the Government of National Reconstruction abrogated the 1974 Constitution. On 22 August 1979 the revolutionary junta issued a 'Statute on Rights and Guarantees for the Citizens of Nicaragua', providing for the basic freedoms of the individual, religious freedom and freedom of the press and abolishing the death penalty. The intention of the Statute was formally to re-establish rights which had been violated under the deposed Somoza regime. A fundamental Statute took effect from 20 July 1980 and remained in force until the Council of State drafted a political constitution and proposed an electoral law. A new Constitution was approved by the National Constituent Assembly on 19 November 1986 and promulgated on 9 January 1987. Amendments to the Constitution were approved by the Asamblea Nacional (National Assembly) in July 1995 and January 2000. The following are some of the main points of the Constitution.

Nicaragua is an independent, free, sovereign and indivisible state. All Nicaraguans who have reached 16 years of age are full citizens.

POLITICAL RIGHTS

There shall be absolute equality between men and women. It is the obligation of the State to remove obstacles that impede effective participation of Nicaraguans in the political, economic and social life of the country. Citizens have the right to vote and to be elected at elections and to offer themselves for public office. Citizens may organize or affiliate with political parties, with the objective of participating in, exercising or vying for power. The supremacy of civilian authority is enshrined in the Constitution.

SOCIAL RIGHTS

The Nicaraguan people have the right to work, to education and to culture. They have the right to decent, comfortable and safe housing, and to seek accurate information. This right comprises the freedom to seek, receive and disseminate information and ideas, both spoken and written, in graphic or any other form. The mass media are at the service of national interests. No Nicaraguan citizen may disobey the law or prevent others from exercising their rights and fulfilling their duties by invoking religious beliefs or inclinations.

LABOUR RIGHTS

All have a right to work, and to participate in the management of their enterprises. Equal pay shall be given for equal work. The State shall strive for full and productive employment under conditions that guarantee the fundamental rights of the individual. There shall be an eight-hour working day, weekly rest, vacations, remuneration for national holidays and a bonus payment equivalent to one month's salary, in conformity with the law.

EDUCATION

Education is an obligatory function of the State. Planning, direction and organization of the secular education system is the responsibility of the State. All Nicaraguans have free and equal access to education. Private education centres may function at all levels.

LEGISLATIVE POWER

The Asamblea Nacional exercises Legislative Power through representative popular mandate. The Asamblea Nacional is composed of 90 representatives elected by direct secret vote by means of a system of proportional representation, of which 70 are elected at regional

NICARAGUA

level and 20 at national level. The number of representatives may be increased in accordance with the general census of the population, in conformity with the law. Representatives shall be elected for a period of five years. The functions of the Asamblea Nacional are to draft and approve laws and decrees; to decree amnesties and pardons; to consider, discuss and approve the General Budget of the Republic; to elect judges to the Supreme Court of Justice and the Supreme Electoral Council; to fill permanent vacancies for the Presidency or Vice-Presidency; and to determine the political and administrative division of the country.

EXECUTIVE POWER

The Executive Power is exercised by the President of the Republic (assisted by the Vice-President), who is the Head of State, Head of Government and Commander-in-Chief of the Defence and Security Forces of the Nation. The election of the President (and Vice-President) is by equal, direct and free universal suffrage in secret ballot. Should a single candidate in a presidential election fail to secure the necessary 35% of the vote to win outright in the first round, a second ballot shall be held. Close relatives of a serving President are prohibited from contesting a presidential election. The President shall serve for a period of five years and may not serve for two consecutive terms. All outgoing Presidents are granted a seat in the Asamblea Nacional.

JUDICIAL POWER

The Judiciary consists of the Supreme Court of Justice, Courts of Appeal and other courts of the Republic. The Supreme Court is composed of at least seven judges, elected by the Asamblea Nacional, who shall serve for a term of six years. The functions of the Supreme Court are to organize and direct the administration of justice. There are 12 Supreme Court justices, appointed for a period of seven years.

LOCAL ADMINISTRATION

The country is divided into regions, departments and municipalities for administrative purposes. The municipal governments shall be elected by universal suffrage in secret ballot and will serve a six-year term. The communities of the Atlantic Coast have the right to live and develop in accordance with a social organization which corresponds to their historical and cultural traditions. The State shall implement, by legal means, autonomous governments in the regions inhabited by the communities of the Atlantic Coast, in order that the communities may exercise their rights.

The Government

HEAD OF STATE

President: José Daniel Ortega Saavedra (took office 10 January 2007).

Vice-President: Jaime René Morales Carazo.

CABINET
(March 2008)

Minister of Foreign Affairs: Samuel Santos López.

Minister of the Interior: Ana Isabel Morales Mazún.

Secretary-General of Defence with Ministerial Rank: Ruth Esperanza Tapia Roa.

Minister of Finance and Public Credit: Alberto José Guevara Obregón.

Minister of Development, Industry and Trade: Dr Orlando Solórzano Delgadillo.

Minister of Labour: Jeannette Chávez Gómez.

Minister of the Environment and Natural Resources: Juana Argeñal.

Minister of Transport and Infrastructure: Pablo Fernando Martínez Espinoza.

Minister of Agriculture and Forestry: Ariel Bucardo Rocha.

Minister of Health: Dr Juana Maritza Cuan Machado.

Minister of Education, Culture and Sports: Dr Miguel de Castilla Urbina.

Minister of the Family: Rosa Adilia Vizcaya Briones.

Secretary to the Presidency: Salvador Vanegas Guido.

Co-ordinator of the Communication and Citizenship Council: Rosario Murillo Zambrana.

MINISTRIES

Office of the President: Casa Presidencial, Managua; e-mail daniel@presidencia.gob.ni; internet www.presidencia.gob.ni.

Ministry of Agriculture and Forestry: Km 8½, Carretera a Masaya, Managua; tel. 276-0200; e-mail prensa@magfor.gob.ni; internet www.magfor.gob.ni.

Ministry of Defence: De los semáforos el Redentor, 4 c. arriba, donde fue la casa 'Ricardo Morales Aviles', Managua; tel. 222-2201; fax 222-5439; internet www.midef.gob.ni.

Ministry of Development, Industry and Trade: Edif. Central, Km 6, Carretera a Masaya, Apdo 8, Managua; tel. 278-8702; fax 270-095; internet www.mific.gob.ni.

Ministry of Education, Culture and Sports: Complejo Cívico Camilo Ortega Saavedra, Managua; tel. 265-1451; e-mail rivash@mecd.gob.ni; internet www.mined.gob.ni.

Ministry of the Environment and Natural Resources: Km 12½, Carretera Norte, Apdo 5123, Managua; tel. 233-1111; fax 263-1274; e-mail jargenal@marena.gob.ni; internet www.marena.gob.ni.

Ministry of the Family: Managua; tel. 278-1620; e-mail webmaster@mifamilia.gob.ni; internet www.mifamilia.gob.ni.

Ministry of Finance and Public Credit: Frente a la Asamblea Nacional, Apdo 2170, Managua; tel. 222-6530; fax 222-6430; e-mail webmaster@mhcp.gob.ni; internet www.hacienda.gob.ni.

Ministry of Foreign Affairs: Del Cine González al Sur sobre Avda Bolivar, Managua; tel. 244-8000; fax 228-5102; e-mail despacho.ministro@cancilleria.gob.ni; internet www.cancilleria.gob.ni.

Ministry of Health: Complejo Nacional de Salud 'Dra Concepción Palacios', costado oeste Colonia Primero de Mayo, Apdo 107, Managua; tel. 289-7164; e-mail secretaria@minsa.gob.ni; internet www.minsa.gob.ni.

Ministry of the Interior: Apdo 68, Managua; tel. 228-2284; fax 222-2789; e-mail webmaster@migob.gob.ni; internet www.migob.gob.ni.

Ministry of Labour: Estadio Nacional, 400 m al norte, Apdo 487, Managua; tel. 228-2028; fax 228-2103; e-mail info@mitrab.gob.ni; internet www.mitrab.gob.ni.

Ministry of Transport and Infrastructure: Frente al Estadio Nacional, Apdo 26, Managua; tel. 228-2061; fax 222-5111; e-mail webmaster@mti.gob.ni; internet www.mti.gob.ni.

President and Legislature

PRESIDENT

Election, 5 November 2006

Candidate	Votes	% of total
José Daniel Ortega Saavedra (FSLN)	930,862	37.99
Eduardo Montealegre Rivas (ALN)	693,391	28.30
José Rizo Castellón (PLC)	664,225	27.11
Edmundo Jarquín Calderón (MRS)	154,224	6.29
Edén Pastora Gómez (AC)	7,200	0.29
Total	**2,449,902**	**100.00**

ASAMBLEA NACIONAL
(National Assembly)

Asamblea Nacional

Avda Bolívar, Contiguo a la Presidencia de la República, Managua; e-mail webmaster@correo.asamblea.gob.ni; internet www.asamblea.gob.ni.

President: René Núñez Téllez.

First Vice-President: Luis Roberto Callejas.

Second Vice-President: Oscar Moncada Reyes.

Third Vice-President: Juan Ramón Jiménez.

Election, 5 November 2006, preliminary results

Party	Votes	% of total	Seats
Frente Sandinista de Liberación Nacional (FSLN)	840,851	37.59	38
Partido Liberal Constitucionalista (PLC)	592,118	26.47	25
Alianza Liberal Nicaragüense (ALN)	597,709	26.72	22
Movimiento Renovador Sandinista (MRS)	194,416	8.69	5
Alternativa por el Cambio (AC)	12,053	0.54	—
Total	**2,237,147**	**100.00**	**90***

* In addition to the 90 elected members, supplementary seats in the Asamblea Nacional are awarded to the unsuccessful candidates at the presidential election who were not nominated for the legislature

but who received, in the presidential poll, a number of votes at least equal to the average required for one of the 70 legislative seats decided at a regional level. On this basis, the ALN obtained one additional seat in the Asamblea Nacional. A legislative seat is also awarded to the outgoing President, bringing the total number of seats in the Asamblea Nacional to 92.

Election Commission

Consejo Supremo Electoral (CSE): Iglesia Las Palmas, 1 c. al sur, Apdo 2241, Managua; tel. 268-7948; e-mail info@cse.gob.ni; internet www.cse.gob.ni; Pres. ROBERTO RIVAS REYES.

Political Organizations

Alianza Liberal Nicaragüense (ALN): Managua; fmrly Movimiento de Salvación Liberal; adopted current name in 2006; formed alliance with Partido Conservador (q.v.) ahead of 2006 elections; Pres. ELISEO NÚÑEZ HERNÁNDEZ.

Alianza por la República (APRE): Casa 211, Col. Los Robles, Funeraria Monte de los Olivos 1.5 c. al norte, Managua; f. 2004 by supporters of President Enrique Bolaños Geyer; Pres. MIGUEL LÓPEZ BALDIZÓN.

> **Movimiento Democrático Nicaragüense (MDN):** Casa L-39, Ciudad Jardín Bnd, 50 m al sur, Managua; tel. 243-898; f. 1978; Leader ROBERTO SEQUEIRA GÓMEZ.

> **Partido Social Cristiano (PSC):** Ciudad Jardín, Pizza María, 1 c. al lago, Managua; tel. 222-026; f. 1957; 42,000 mems; Pres. ABEL REYES.

Alternativa por el Cambio (AC): Managua; f. as Alternativa Cristiana; fmr faction of Frente Sandinista de Liberación Nacional (q.v.); name changed as above in 2006; Pres. Dr ORLANDO J. TARDENCILLA ESPINOZA.

Camino Cristiano Nicaragüense (CCN): Managua; Pres. GUILLERMO ANTONIO OSORNO MOLINA.

Frente Sandinista de Liberación Nacional (FSLN) (Sandinista National Liberation Front): Costado Oeste Parque El Carmen, Managua; tel. and fax 266-8173; internet www.fsln.org.ni; f. 1960; led by a 15-mem. directorate; embraces Izquierda Democrática Sandinista 'orthodox revolutionary' faction, led by Daniel Ortega Saavedra; leads Nicaragua Triunfa electoral alliance; 120,000 mems; Gen. Sec. JOSÉ DANIEL ORTEGA SAAVEDRA.

Movimiento Renovador Sandinista (MRS): Tienda Katty 1 c. abajo, Apdo 24, Managua; tel. 278-0279; fax 278-0268; f. 1995; fmr faction of Frente Sandinista de Liberación Nacional (q.v.); Pres. ENRIQUE SÁENZ.

Movimiento de Unidad Cristiana (MUC): Managua; mem. of Convergencia Nacional alliance; Pres. Pastor DANIEL ORTEGA REYES.

Partido Conservador (PC): Colegio Centroamérica, 500 m al sur, Managua; tel. 267-0484; e-mail contactenos@partidoconservador.org.ni; f. 1992 following merger between Partido Conservador Demócrata and Partido Socialconservadurismo; formed alliance with Alianza Liberal Nicaragüense (q.v.) ahead of 2006 elections; Pres. AZALIA AVILÉS.

Partido Indígena Multiétnico (PIM): Residencial Los Robles, de Farmacentro 1 c. al este, 80 varas al sur, Managua; Pres. CARLA WHITE HODGSON.

Partido Liberal Constitucionalista (PLC): Semáforos Country Club 100 m al este, Apdo 4569, Managua; tel. 278-8705; fax 278-1800; f. 1967; Pres. JORGE CASTILLO QUANT; Nat. Sec. Dr NOEL RAMÍREZ SÁNCHEZ.

Partido Liberal Independiente (PLI): Ciudad Jardín, H-4, Calle Principal, Managua; tel. 244-3556; fax 248-0012; f. 1944; Leader VIRGILIO GODOY REYES.

Partido Liberal Nacionalista (PLN): Managua; f. 1913; Pres. CONSTANTINO VELÁSQUEZ ZEPEDA.

Partido Movimiento de Unidad Costeña (PAMUC): Bilwi Puerto Cabeza; Pres. KENNETH SERAPIO HUNTER.

Partido Neo-Liberal (Pali): Cine Dorado, 2 c. al sur, 50 m arriba, Managua; tel. 266-5166; f. 1986; Pres. Dr RICARDO VEGA GARCÍA.

Partido Resistencia Nicaragüense (PRN): Edif. VINSA, frente a Autonica, Carretera Sur, Managua; tel. and fax 270-6508; e-mail salvata@ibw.com.ni; f. 1993; nationalist party; Pres. SALVADOR TALAVERA ALANIZ.

Partido Socialista (PS): Hospital Militar, 100 m al norte, 100 m al oeste, 100 m al sur, Managua; tel. 266-2321; fax 266-2936; f. 1944; social democratic party; Sec.-Gen. Dr GUSTAVO TABLADA ZELAYA.

Partido Unionista Centroamericano (PUCA): Cine Cabrera, 1 c. al este, 20 m al norte, Managua; tel. 227-472; f. 1904; Pres. BLANCA ROJAS ECHAVERRY.

Unión Demócrata Cristiana (UDC): De Iglesia Santa Ana, 2 c. abajo, Barrio Santa Ana, Apdo 3089, Managua; tel. 266-2576; f. 1976 as Partido Popular Social Cristiano; name officially changed as above in Dec. 1993; mem. of Convergencia Nacional alliance; Pres. AGUSTÍN JARQUÍN ANAYA.

Yatama (Yapti Tasba Masraka Nanih Aslatakanka): Of. de Odacan, Busto José Martí, 1 c. al este y ½ c. al norte, Managua; tel. 228-1494; Atlantic coast Miskito org.; mem. of FSLN-led electoral alliance, Nicaragua Triunfa; Leader BROOKLYN RIVERA BRYAN.

Diplomatic Representation

EMBASSIES IN NICARAGUA

Argentina: Semáforos de Villa Fontana, 2 c. abajo, 1 al sur, 1 abajo, 75 varas oeste, Casa 133, Apdo 703, Managua; tel. 283-7066; fax 270-2343; e-mail embargentina@cablenet.com.ni; Chargé d'affaires a.i. NICOLÁS SERGIO REBOK.

Brazil: Km 7¾, Carretera Sur, Quinta los Pinos, Apdo 264, Managua; tel. 265-0035; fax 265-2206; e-mail ebrasil@ibw.com.ni; Ambassador VICTORIA ALICE CLEAVER.

Chile: Entrada principal los Robles, 1 c. abajo, 1 c. al sur, Apdo 1289, Managua; tel. 278-0619; fax 270-4073; e-mail echileni@cablenet.com.ni; internet www.embachileni.com; Ambassador NATACHA MOLINA GARCÍA.

China (Taiwan): Optica Matamoros, 2 c. abajo, ½ c. al lago, Carretera a Masaya, Planes de Altamira, Apdo 4653, Managua; tel. 277-1333; fax 267-4025; e-mail nic@mofa.gov.tw; internet www.roc-taiwan.org.ni; Ambassador WU CHIN-MU.

Colombia: 2da Entrada a las Colinas, 1 c. arriba, ½ c. al lago, Casa 97, Apdo 1062, Managua; tel. 276-2149; fax 276-0644; e-mail emanagua@cancilleria.gov.co; Ambassador ANTONIO GONZÁLEZ CASTAÑO.

Costa Rica: Reparto las Colinas, Prado Ecuestre 304, 1°, Managua; tel. 276-1352; fax 276-0115; e-mail infembcr@cablenet.com.ni; Ambassador ANTONIO TACSAN LAM.

Cuba: Carretera a Masaya, 3a Entrada a las Colinas, 400 varas arriba, 75 al sur, Managua; tel. 276-0742; fax 276-0166; e-mail embacuba@embacuba.net.ni; internet embacu.cubaminrex.cu/nicaragua; Ambassador LUIS HERNÁNDEZ OJEDA.

Denmark: De la Plaza España, 1 c. abajo, 2 c. al lago, ½ c. abajo, Apdo 4942, Managua; tel. 268-0250; fax 266-8095; e-mail mgaambu@um.dk; internet www.ambmanagua.um.dk; Ambassador SØREN VØHTZ.

Dominican Republic: Reparto Las Colinas, Prado Ecuestre 100, con Curva de los Gallos, Apdo 614, Managua; tel. 276-2029; fax 276-0654; e-mail embdom@alfanumeric.com.ni; Ambassador PEDRO BLANDINO.

Ecuador: De los Pipitos 1½ c. abajo, Apdo C-33, Managua; tel. 268-1098; fax 266-8081; e-mail ecuador@ibw.com.ni; Ambassador GONZALO ANDRADE RIVERA.

El Salvador: Reparto Las Colinas, Avda del Campo y Pasaje Los Cerros 142, Apdo 149, Managua; tel. 276-0712; fax 276-0711; e-mail embelsa@cablenet.com.ni; internet www.embelsanica.org.ni; Ambassador ALFREDO FRANCISCO UNGO RIVAS LAGUARDIA.

Finland: Sucursal Jorge Navarro, Apdo 2219, Managua; tel. 266-3415; fax 266-3416; e-mail sanomat.mgu@formin.fi; internet www.finlandia.org.ni; Ambassador MARJA LUOTO.

France: Iglesia el Carmen 1½ c. abajo, Apdo 1227, Managua; tel. 222-6210; fax 268-5630; e-mail info@ambafrance-ni.org; internet www.ambafrance-ni.org; Ambassador THIERRY PIERRE FRAYSSÉ.

Germany: Bolonia, de la Rotonda El Güegüense, 1½ c. al lago, contiguo a Optica Nicaragüense, Apdo 29, Managua; tel. 266-3917; fax 266-7667; e-mail alemania@cablenet.com.ni; internet www.managua.diplo.de; Ambassador GREGOR KOEBEL.

Guatemala: Km 11½, Carretera a Masaya, Apdo E-1, Managua; tel. 279-9609; fax 279-9610; e-mail embnic@minex.gob.gt; Ambassador JORGE ROLANDO ECHEVERRÍA ROLDÁN.

Holy See: Apostolic Nunciature, Km 10.8, Carretera Sur, Apdo 506, Managua; tel. 265-8657; fax 265-7416; e-mail nuntius@cablenet.com.ni; Apostolic Nuncio Most Rev. HENRYK JÓZEF NOWACKI (Titular Archbishop of Blera).

Honduras: Reparto Las Colinas, Prado Ecuestre 298, frente a Residencia de la Embajada de China (Taiwán), Apdo 321, Managua; tel. 276-2406; fax 276-1998; e-mail embhonduras@cablenet.com.ni; Ambassador JORGE ALBERTO MILLA REYES.

Iran: Managua; Ambassador AKBAR ESMAEIL POUR.

NICARAGUA

Italy: Rotonda El Güegüense, 1 c. al norte, Apdo 2092, ½ c. abajo, Managua 4; tel. 266-2961; fax 266-3987; e-mail embitaliasegr@cablenet.com.ni; internet www.ambmanagua.esteri.it; Ambassador Dr ALBERTO BONIVER.

Japan: Plaza España, 1 c. abajo y 1 c. al lago, Bolonia, Apdo 1789, Managua; tel. 266-8668; fax 266-8566; e-mail embjpnic@cablenet.com.ni; internet www.ni.emb-japan.go.jp; Ambassador SHINICHI SAITO.

Korea, Republic: De la Plaza España, 3 c. abajo, 500 m al sur, casa A-45, Managua; tel. 254-8107; fax 254-8131; e-mail hrlee92@mofat.go.kr; Ambassador LEE SANG-PAL.

Libya: Mansión Teodolinda, 1 c. al sur, ½ c. abajo, Managua; tel. (2) 66-8540; fax (2) 66-8542; e-mail ofilibia@ibw.com.ni; Sec. of the People's Bureau ABDULLAH MUHAMMAD MATOUG.

Mexico: Contiguo a Optica Matamoros, Km 4½, Carretera a Masaya, Apdo 834, Managua; tel. 278-1859; fax 278-2886; e-mail embamex@turbonett.com.ni; Ambassador RAÚL LÓPEZ-LIRA NAVA.

Netherlands: Calle Erasmus de Rotterdam, Carretera a Masaya km 5, del Colegio Teresiano 1 c. al sur, 1 c. abajo, Apdo 3688, Managua; tel. 276-8630; fax 276-0399; e-mail mng@minbuza.nl; internet www.embajadaholanda-nic.com; Ambassador LAMBERTUS CHRISTIAAN GRIJNS.

Norway: Plaza España, Apdo 2090, Correo Central, Managua; tel. 266-4199; fax 266-3303; e-mail emb.managua@mfa.no; internet www.noruega.org.ni; Ambassador KRISTEN CHRISTENSEN.

Panama: Casa 93, Reparto Mántica, del Cuartel General de Bomberos 1 c. abajo, Apdo 1, Managua; tel. 266-2224; fax 266-8633; e-mail embdpma@ibw.com.ni; Ambassador MIGUEL LECARO BÁRCENAS.

Peru: Las Cumbres, Casa D-13, contiguo a la Residencia del diputado Wilfredo Navarro Moreira, Apdo 211, Managua; tel. 266-8677; fax 266-1408; e-mail peru1@cablenet.com.ni; Ambassador HARRY GERARDO MORRIS ABARCO.

Russia: Reparto Las Colinas, Calle Vista Alegre 214, Entre Avda Central y Paseo del Club, Apdo 249, Managua; tel. 276-0374; fax 276-0179; e-mail rossia@ibw.com.ni; Ambassador IGOR SERGEEVICH KONDRASHEV.

Spain: Avda Central 13, Las Colinas, Apdo 284, Managua; tel. 276-0966; fax 276-0937; e-mail embespni@correo.mae.es; internet www.mae.es/Embajadas/Managua; Ambassador JAIME LACADENA HIGUERA.

Sweden: Plaza España, 1 c. abajo, 2 c. al lago y ½ c. al oeste, Apdo 2307, Managua; tel. 255-8400; fax 266-6778; e-mail ambassaden.managua@foreign.ministry.se; internet www.swedenabroad.se/managua; scheduled to close in August 2008; Ambassador EVA ZETTERBERG.

USA: Km 5½, Carretera Sur, Apdo 327, Managua; tel. 252-7100; fax 252-7300; e-mail consularmanagua@state.gov; internet managua.usembassy.gov; Ambassador ROBERT CALLAHAN (designate).

Venezuela: Costado norte de la Iglesia Santo Domingo, Las Sierritas, Casa 27, Apdo 406, Managua; tel. (2) 72-0267; fax (2) 72-2265; e-mail embaveznica@cablenet.com.ni; Chargé d'affaires a.i. PEDRO LUIS PENSO SÁNCHEZ.

Judicial System

The Supreme Court

Km 7½, Carretera Norte, Managua; tel. 233-0083; fax 233-0581; e-mail webmaster@csj.gob.ni; internet www.popderjudicial.gob.ni.

Deals with both civil and criminal cases, acts as a Court of Cassation, appoints Judges of First Instance, and generally supervises the legal administration of the country.

President: Dr JOSÉ MANUEL MARTÍNEZ SEVILLA.
Vice-President: Dr RAFAEL SOLÍS CERDA.
Attorney-General: Dr HERNÁN ESTRADA SANTAMARÍA.

Religion

All religions are tolerated. Almost all of Nicaragua's inhabitants profess Christianity, and the great majority belong to the Roman Catholic Church. The Moravian Church predominates on the Caribbean coast.

CHRISTIANITY

The Roman Catholic Church

Nicaragua comprises one archdiocese, six dioceses and the Apostolic Vicariate of Bluefields. At 31 December 2005 there were an estimated 5,449,789 adherents, representing about 82% of the total population.

Bishops' Conference

Conferencia Episcopal de Nicaragua, Ferretería Lang 1 c. al norte, 1 c. al este, Zona 3, Las Piedrecitas, Apdo 2407, Managua; tel. 266-6292; fax 266-8069; e-mail cen@tmx.com.ni.

f. 1975; statute approved 1987; Pres. LEOPOLDO JOSÉ BRENES SOLÓRZANO (Archbishop of Managua).

Archbishop of Managua: LEOPOLDO JOSÉ BRENES SOLÓRZANO, Arzobispado, Apdo 2008, Managua; tel. 276-0129; fax 276-0130; e-mail mob@unica.edu.ni.

The Anglican Communion

Nicaragua comprises one of the five dioceses of the Iglesia Anglicana de la Región Central de América.

Bishop of Nicaragua: Rt Rev. STURDIE W. DOWNS, Apdo 1207, Managua; tel. 222-5174; fax 222-6701; e-mail episcnic@tmx.com.ni.

Protestant Churches

Baptist Convention of Nicaragua: Apdo 2593, Managua; tel. 225-785; fax 224-131; e-mail cbn@ibw.com.ni; f. 1917; 135 churches, 20,000 mems (2006); Pres. ABEL MENDOZA; Sec. DALIA NAVARRETE.

The Moravian Church in Nicaragua: Iglesia Morava, Bilwi; tel. and fax 282-2222; 199 churches, 83,000 mems; Leader Rt Rev. JOHN WILSON.

The Nicaraguan Lutheran Church of Faith and Hope: Apdo 151, Managua; tel. 266-4467; fax 266-4609; e-mail luterana@turbonett.com.ni; f. 1994; 7,000 mems (2007); Pres. Rev. VICTORIA CORTEZ RODRÍGUEZ.

The Press

NEWSPAPERS AND PERIODICALS

Bolsa de Noticias: Col. Centroamérica 852, Apdo VF-90, Managua; tel. 270-0546; fax 277-4931; e-mail prensa@bolsadenoticias.com.ni; internet www.grupoese.com.ni/BolsadeNoticias; f. 1974; daily; Dir MARÍA ELSA SUÁREZ GARCÍA.

Confidencial: De la Iglesia El Carmen 1 c. al lago, ½ c. abajo, Managua; tel. 268-0129; fax 268-4650; e-mail revista@confidencial.com.ni; internet www.confidencial.com.ni; weekly; political analysis; Editor CARLOS F. CHAMORRO.

La Gaceta, Diario Oficial: Semáforos de Plaza Inter, 1 c. arriba, 1½ c. al lago, Managua; tel. 228-3791; e-mail lagaceta@ibw.com.ni; f. 1912; morning; official.

Novedades: Pista P. Joaquín Chamorro, Km 4, Carretera Norte, Apdo 576, Managua; daily; evening.

Nuevo Diario: Pista P. Joaquín Chamorro, Km 4, Carretera Norte, Apdo 4591, Managua; tel. 249-1190; fax 249-0700; e-mail info@elnuevodiario.com.ni; internet www.elnuevodiario.com.ni; f. 1980; morning; daily; independent; Editor XAVIER CHAMORRO CARDENAL; Dir DANILO AGUIRRE SOLÍS; circ. 45,000.

El Observador Económico: Antiguo Hospital el Retiro, 2 c. al lago, Apdo 2074, Managua; tel. 266-8708; fax 266-8711; e-mail amc@elobservadoreconomico.com; internet www.elobservadoreconomico.com; Dir-Gen. ALEJANDRO MARTÍNEZ CUENCA.

La Prensa: Km 4½, Carretera Norte, Apdo 192, Managua; tel. 249-8405; fax 249-6926; e-mail info@laprensa.com.ni; internet www.laprensa.com.ni; f. 1926; morning; daily; independent; Pres. JAIME CHAMORRO CARDENAL; Editor EDUARDO ENRÍQUEZ; circ. 30,000.

Prensa Proletaria: Managua; tel. 222-594; fortnightly; official publ. of the Movimiento de Acción Popular Marxista-Leninista.

Revista Envío: Edif. Nitlapán, 2°, Campus Universidad Centroamericana, Managua; tel. 278-2557; fax 278-1402; e-mail envio@ns.uca.edu.ni; internet www.envio.org.ni; f. 1981; 11 a year; political analysis; edns in Spanish, English and Italian; Dir JUAN RAMIRO JIMÉNEZ; Chief Editor MARÍA LÓPEZ VIGIL.

Revista Encuentro: Universidad Centroamericana, Apdo 69, Managua; tel. 278-3923; fax 267-0106; e-mail dirinv@ns.uca.edu.ni; internet www.uca.edu.ni/publicaciones; f. 1968; termly; academic publ. of the Universidad Centroamericana.

Revista 7 Días: Altamira de lo Vicky, 5½ al lago, Managua; e-mail 7dias@ibw.com.ni; internet www.7dias.com.ni.

La Semana Cómica: Centro Comercial Bello Horizonte, Módulos 7 y 9, Apdo SV-3, Managua; tel. 244-909; e-mail bmejia@lasemanacomica.com; internet www.lasemanacomica.com; f. 1980; weekly; Dir RÓGER SÁNCHEZ; circ. 45,000.

Tiempos del Mundo: Apdo 3525, Managua; tel. 270-3418; fax 270-3419; e-mail tiempos@tdm.com.ni; f. 1996; weekly; Gen. Man. TAKUYA ISHII; circ. 5,000.

NICARAGUA

La Tribuna: Detrás del Banco Mercantil, Plaza España, Apdo 1469, Managua; tel. 266-9282; fax 266-5167; e-mail tribuna@latribuna.com.ni; f. 1993; morning; daily; Dir HAROLDO J. MONTEALEGRE; Gen. Man. MARIO GONZÁLEZ.

Trinchera de la Noticia: Managua; tel. 240-0114; e-mail info@trinchera.com.ni; internet www.trinchera.com.ni; daily; Dir EMILIO NÚÑEZ.

Visión Sandinista: Costado Este, Parque El Carmen, Managua; tel. and fax 268-1565; internet www.vsandinista.com; f. 1980; weekly; official publ. of the Frente Sandinista de Liberación Nacional; Dir MAYRA REYES SANDOVAL.

Association

Unión de Periodistas de Nicaragua (UPN): Apdo 4006, Managua; Pres. CARLOS SALGADO.

Publishers

Academia Nicaragüense de la Lengua: Calle Central, Reparto Las Colinas, Apdo 2711, Managua; f. 1928; languages; Dir PABLO ANTONIO CUADRA; Sec. JULIO YCAZA TIGERINO.

Editora de Arte SA: 53 Reparto Los Robles III, Managua; tel. 278-5854.

Editorial Nueva Nicaragua: Paseo Salvador Allende, Km $3\frac{1}{2}$, Carretera Sur, Apdo 073, Managua; fax 266-6520; f. 1981; Pres. Dr SERGIO RAMÍREZ MERCADO; Dir-Gen. ROBERTO DÍAZ CASTILLO.

Editorial Unión: Avda Central Norte, Managua; travel.

Librería Hispanoamericana (HISPAMER): Costado Este de la UCA, Apdo A-221, Managua; e-mail hispamer@hispamer.com.ni; internet www.hispamer.com.ni; f. 1991.

UCA Publicaciónes: Rectoría de la Universidad Centroamericana, Apdo 69, Managua; tel. 278-3923; e-mail ucapubli@ns.uca.edu.ni; internet www.uca.edu.ni/publicaciones; academic publishing dept of the Universidad Centroamericana.

Universidad Nacional Agraria: Km $12\frac{1}{2}$ Carretera Norte, Apdo 453, Managua; tel. 233-1950; e-mail info@una.edu.ni; internet www.una.edu.ni; sciences.

Broadcasting and Communications

TELECOMMUNICATIONS

Regulatory Bodies

Instituto Nicaragüense de Telecomunicaciones y Correos (Telcor): Edif. Telcor, Avda Bolivar diagonal a Cancillería, Apdo 2264, Managua; tel. 222-7350; fax 222-7554; e-mail webmaster@telcor.gob.ni; internet www.telcor.gob.ni; Dir-Gen. FOAD HASSAN LANZAS.

Major Service Providers

Claro: Villafontana 2°, Apdo 232, Managua; tel. 277-3057; fax 270-2128; internet www.claro.com.ni; f. 2006 by merger of ALO PCS (f. 2002) and Empresa Nicaragüense de Telecomunicaciones (Enitel, f. 1925); subsidiary of América Móvil, SA de CV (Mexico); Chair. PATRICIO SLIM DOMIT; CEO DANIEL HAJJ ABOUMRAD.

Telefónica Móviles Nicaragua: Km $6\frac{1}{2}$, Carretera a Masaya, Managua; tel. 277-0731; internet www.movistar.com.ni; fmrly BellSouth; owned by Grupo Telefónica Móviles (Spain); mobile cellular telephone provider; Vice-Pres. HUMBERTO PATO-VINUESA; Gen. Man. MARÍA JOSEFINA PERALTA.

BROADCASTING

Radio

La Nueva Radio Ya: Pista de la Resistencia, Frente a la Universidad Centroamericana, Managua; tel. 278-8336; fax 278-8334; e-mail info@nuevaya.com.ni; internet www.nuevaya.com.ni; f. 1990 as Radio Ya; restyled as above in 1999; operated by Entretenimiento Digital, SA; Dir-Gen. DENNIS SCHWARTZ.

Radio Católica: Altamira D'Este 621, 3°, Apdo 2183, Managua; tel. 278-0836; fax 278-2544; e-mail catolica@ibw.com.ni; internet www.radiocatolica.org; f. 1961; controlled by Conferencia Episcopal de Nicaragua; Dir Fr ROLANDO ÁLVAREZ; Gen. Man. ALBERTO CARBALLO MADRIGAL.

Radio Corporación, Gadea y Cía: Ciudad Jardín Q-20, Apdo 24242, Managua; tel. 249-1619; fax 244-3824; e-mail rc540@radio-corporacion.com; internet www.radio-corporacion.com;

Directory

f. 1995; Gen. Man. FABIO GADEA MANTILLA; Asst Man. CARLOS GADEA MANTILLA.

Radio Estrella: Sierritas de Santo Domingo, Frente al Cementerio, Apdo UNICA 104, Managua; tel. 276-0241; fax 276-0062; e-mail radiosm@radioestrelladelmar.com; internet www.radioestrelladelmar.com.

Radio Mundial: 36 Avda Oeste, Reparto Loma Verde, Apdo 3170, Managua; tel. 266-6767; fax 266-4630; commercial; Pres. MANUEL ARANA VALLE; Dir-Gen. ALMA ROSA ARANA HARTIG.

Radio Nicaragua: Villa Fontana, Contiguo a Enitel, Apdo 4665, Managua; tel. 227-2330-1; fax 267-1448; e-mail director@radionicaragua.com.ni; internet www.radionicaragua.com.ni; f. 1960; govt station; Dir-Gen. ALBERTO CARBALLO MADRIGAL.

Radio Ondas de Luz: Costado Sur del Hospital Bautista, Apdo 607, Managua; tel. and fax 249-7058; f. 1959; religious and cultural station; Pres. GUILLERMO OSORNO MOLINA; Dir EDUARDO GUTIÉRREZ NARVÁEZ.

Radio Sandino: Paseo Tiscapa Este, Contiguo al Restaurante Mirador, Apdo 4776, Managua; tel. 228-1330; fax 262-4052; f. 1977; station controlled by the Frente Sandinista de Liberación Nacional; Pres. RAFAEL ORTEGA MURILLO.

Radio Segovia: Ocotal, Nueva Segovia; internet www.radiosegovia.net; f. 1980; commercial.

Radio Tiempo: Reparto Pancasan 217, 7°, Apdo 2735, Managua; tel. 278-2540; f. 1976; Dir DANILO LACAYO LANZAS.

Radio Universidad: Avda Card, 3 c. abajo, Apdo 2883, Managua; tel. 278-4743; fax 277-5057; f. 1984; Dir LUIS LÓPEZ RUIZ.

There are some 50 other radio stations.

Television

Nicavisión, Canal 12: Bolonia Dual Card, 1 c. abajo, $\frac{1}{2}$ c. al sur, Apdo 2766, Managua; tel. 266-0691; fax 266-1424; e-mail info@tv12-nic.com; f. 1993; Dir MARIANO VALLE PETERS.

Canal 4: Montoya, 1 c. al sur, 2 c. arriba, Managua; tel. 228-1310; fax 222-4067; Pres. DIONISIO MARENCO.

Sistema Nacional de Televisión Canal 6 (SNTV Canal 6): Km $3\frac{1}{2}$, Carretera Sur, Contiguo a Shell, Las Palmas, Apdo 1505, Managua; tel. 266-4958; fax 266-1520; state-owned; Dir WALTER RENÉ PÉREZ.

Televicentro de Nicaragua, SA, Canal 2: Casa del Obrero, $6\frac{1}{2}$ c. al Sur, Apdo 688, Managua; tel. 268-2222; fax 266-3688; e-mail canal2@canal2.com.ni; internet www.canal2.com.ni; f. 1965; Pres. OCTAVIO SACASA RASKOSKY; Gen. Man. ALEJANDRO SACASA PASOS.

Televisora Nicaragüense, SA (Telenica 8): De la Mansión Teodolinda, 1 c. al sur, $\frac{1}{2}$ c. abajo, Bolonia, Apdo 3611, Managua; tel. 266-5021; fax 266-5024; e-mail cbriceno@nicanet.com.ni; internet www.telenica.com.ni; f. 1989; Pres. CARLOS A. BRICEÑO LOVO.

Televisión Internacional, Canal 23: Casa L-852, Col. Centroamérica, Managua; tel. 268-7466; fax 266-0625; e-mail canal23@ibw.com.ni; f. 1993; Pres. CÉSAR RIGUERO.

Ultravisión de Nicaragua, SA: Casa 567, Rotonda los Cocos, Altamira, Managua; tel. 277-3524; Pres. CRISEYDA OLIVAS VEGA.

Finance

(cap. = capital; res = reserves; dep. = deposits; m. = million; amounts in gold córdobas)

BANKING

All Nicaraguan banks were nationalized in July 1979. Foreign banks operating in the country are no longer permitted to secure local deposits. All foreign exchange transactions must be made through the Banco Central or its agencies. Under a decree issued in May 1985, the establishment of private exchange houses was permitted. In 1990 legislation allowing for the establishment of private banks was enacted.

Supervisory Authority

Superintendencia de Bancos y de Otras Instituciones Financieras: Edif. SBOIF, Km 7, Carretera Sur, Apdo 788, Managua; tel. 265-1555; fax 265-0965; e-mail correo@sibiof.gob.ni; internet www.superintendencia.gob.ni; f. 1991; Supt Dr VICTOR M. URCUYO VIDAURRE.

Central Bank

Banco Central de Nicaragua: Carretera Sur, Km 7, Apdos 2252/3, Zona 5, Managua; tel. 255-7171; fax 265-0561; e-mail bcn@bcn.gob.ni; internet www.bcn.gob.ni; f. 1961; bank of issue and govt fiscal

NICARAGUA

agent; cap. and res 293.8m., dep. 40,436.3m. (Dec. 2006); Pres. Dr ANTENOR ROSALES BOLAÑOS; Gen. Man. JOSÉ DE JESÚS ROJAS RODRÍGUEZ.

Private Banks

Banco de América Central (BAC): Pista Sub-Urbana, Frente a Lotería Popular, Managua; tel. 67-0220; fax 267-0224; e-mail info@bancodeamericacentral.com; internet www.bancodeamericacentral.com; f. 1991; total assets 10,516m. (1999); Pres. CARLOS PELLAS CHAMORRO; Gen. Man. CARLOS MATUS TAPIA.

Banco de Crédito Centroamericano (BANCENTRO): Edif. BANCENTRO, Km 4½ Carretera a Masaya, Managua; tel. 278-2777; fax 278-6001; e-mail info@bancentro.com.ni; internet www.bancentro.com.ni; f. 1991; total assets 282m. (2005); Pres. ROBERTO J. ZAMORA LLANES; Gen. Man. CARLOS A. BRICEÑO RÍOS.

Banco Uno, SA: Plaza España, Rotonda el Güegüense 20 m al oeste, Managua; tel. 278-7171; fax 277-3154; e-mail info@bancouno.com.ni; internet www.bancouno.com.ni; dep. 2,372m. (Dec. 2002); fmrly Banco de la Exportación (BANEXPO), present name adopted in Nov. 2002; Dir ADOLFO ARGÜELLO LACAYO.

STOCK EXCHANGE

Bolsa de Valores de Nicaragua: Edif. Oscar Pérez Cassar, Centro BANIC, Km 5½, Carretera Masaya, Apdo 121, Managua; tel. 278-3830; fax 278-3836; e-mail info@bolsanic.com; internet bolsanic.com; f. 1993; Pres. Dr RAÚL LACAYO SOLÓRZANO; Gen. Man. GERARDO ARGÜELLO LEIVA.

INSURANCE

State Company

Instituto Nicaragüense de Seguros y Reaseguros (INISER): Centro Comercial Camino de Oriente, Km 6, Carretera a Masaya, Apdo 1147, Managua; tel. (2) 66-6772; fax (2) 66-5636; e-mail iniser@iniser.com.ni; internet www.iniser.com.ni; f. 1979 to assume the activities of all the pre-revolution national private insurance cos; Exec. Pres. EDUARDO HALLESLEVENS; Vice-Pres GUILLERMO JIMÉNEZ, JUAN JOSÉ UBEDA.

Private Companies

Compañía de Seguros del Pacífico, SA: Edif. Telefónica, 3°, Km 6½ Carretera a Masaya, Managua; tel. 268-2454; fax 270-8443; e-mail segurosp@segurospacifico.com.ni; internet www.segurospacifico.com.ni; f. 1997; Gen. Man. MARIANGELES MORALES BARCENAS.

Metropolitana Compañía de Seguros, SA: Reparto Serrano Plaza El Sol, 400 m al norte, Managua; tel. 278-8538; fax 278-2621; e-mail luciaramirez@metroseg.com; Pres. Dr LEONEL ARGÜELLO RAMÍREZ; Sec. LUCÍA RAMÍREZ SÁNCHEZ.

Seguros América, SA: Centro BAC, Km 5½ Carretera a Masaya, Apdo 6114, Managua; tel. 274-4200; fax 274-4202; e-mail sergioulvert@segamerica.com.ni; f. 1996; Pres. CARLOS F. PELLAS CHAMORRO; Man. SERGIO ULVERT SÁNCHEZ.

Seguros Lafise, SA: Centro Financiero Lafise, Km 5½ Carretera a Masaya, Managua; tel. 270-3505; fax 270-3558; e-mail seguros@seguroslafise.com.ni; internet www.seguroslafise.com.ni; fmrly Seguros Centroamericanos (Segurossa); Pres. ROBERTO ZAMORA LLANES; Gen. Man. CLAUDIO TABOADA RODRÍGUEZ.

Trade and Industry

GOVERNMENT AGENCIES

Empresa Nicaragüense de Alimentos Básicos (ENABAS): Salida a Carretera Norte, Apdo 1041, Managua; f. 1979; controls trading in basic foodstuffs; Dir ROGER ALÍ ROMERO.

Instituto de Desarrollo Rural (IDR) (Institute of Rural Development): B3, Camino de Oriente, Apdo 3593, Managua; tel. 278-4940; e-mail divulgacion@idr.gob.ni; internet www.idr.gob.ni; f. 1995; Dir JOSÉ RAMÓN KONTOROVSKY.

Instituto Nicaragüense de Apoyo a la Pequeña y Mediana Empresa (INPYME): De la Shell Plaza el Sol, 1 c. al sur, 300 m abajo, Apdo 449, Managua; tel. 277-0599; fax 277-0598; internet www.inpyme.gob.ni; supports small and medium-sized enterprises; Exec. Dir HAROLD ANTONIO ROCHA SOLÍS.

Instituto Nicaragüense de Tecnología Agropecuaria (INTA): Managua; tel. 278-0469; fax 278-1259; internet www.inta.gob.ni; f. 1993; Dir-Gen. Dr NOEL PALLAIS CHECA.

Instituto de la Vivienda Urbana y Rural: Managua; e-mail evigil@invur.gob.ni; internet www.invur.gob.ni; housing devt; Pres. EDUARDO VIGIL.

DEVELOPMENT ORGANIZATIONS

Asociación de Productores y Exportadores de Nicaragua (APEN): Del Hotel Intercontinental, 2 c. al sur y 2 c. abajo, Bolonia, Managua; tel. 266-5038; fax 266-5039; internet www.apen.org.ni; Pres. DOUGLAS REYES; Gen. Man. JORGE BRENES.

Cámara de Industrias de Nicaragua: Rotonda el Güegüense, 300 m al sur, Apdo 1436, Managua; tel. 266-8847; fax 266-1891; e-mail cadin@cadin.org.ni; internet www.cadin.org.ni; Pres. MARIO AMADOR RIVAS; Exec. Dir ANA CECILIA VEGA JACKSON.

Cámara Nacional de la Mediana y Pequeña Industria (CONAPI): Plaza 19 de Julio, Frente a la UCA, Apdo 153, Managua; tel. 278-4892; fax 267-0192; e-mail conapi@nicarao.org.ni; Pres. FLORA VARGAS LOAISIGA; Gen. Man. URIEL ARGEÑAL C.

Cámara Nicaragüense de la Construcción (CNC): Bolonia de Aval Card, 2 c. abajo, 50 varas al Sur, Managua; tel. 226-3363; fax 266-3327; e-mail camara@construccion.org.ni; internet www.construccion.org.ni; f. 1961; construction industry; Pres. ROBERTO LACAYO GABUARDI; Gen. Man. BRUNO VIDAURRE GALEANO.

Instituto Nicaragüense de Fomento Municipal (INIFOM): Edif. Central, Carretera a la Refinería, entrada principal residencial Los Arcos, Apdo 3097, Managua; tel. and fax 266-6050; internet www.inifom.gob.ni; Pres. EDUARDO CUADRA FAJARDO.

CHAMBERS OF COMMERCE

Cámara de Comercio de Nicaragua (CACONIC): Rotonda El Güegüense 300 m al sur, 20 m al oeste; tel. 268-3505; fax 268-3600; e-mail comercio@ibw.com.ni; internet www.caconic.org.ni; f. 1892; 530 mems; Pres. JOSÉ ADÁN AGUERRI CHAMORRO; Exec. Dir EDUARDO FONSECA.

Cámara de Comercio Americana de Nicaragua: Semáforos ENEL Central, 500 m al sur, Apdo 2720, Managua; tel. 267-3099; fax 267-3098; e-mail amcham@ns.tmx.com.ni; internet www.amchamnic.org.ni; f. 1974; Pres. RENÉ GONZÁLEZ CASTILLO.

Cámara Oficial Española de Comercio de Nicaragua: Restaurante la Marseilleisa, ½ c. arriba, Los Robles, Apdo 4103, Managua; tel. 278-9047; fax 278-9088; e-mail camacoesnic@cablenet.com.ni; internet www.camacoesnic.com.ni; Pres. JOSÉ ESCALANTE ALVARADO; Sec.-Gen. AUXILIADORA MIRANDA DE GUERRERO.

EMPLOYERS' ORGANIZATIONS

Asociación de Café Especiales de Nicaragua (ACEN): Managua; coffee producers and exporters; Pres. ROBERTO BENDAÑA; Gen. Man. CLAUDIA CASTELLÓN.

Consejo Superior de la Empresa Privada (COSEP): De Telcor Zacarías Guerra, 1 c. abajo, Apdo 5430, Managua; tel. 228-2030; fax 228-2041; e-mail cosep@cablenet.com.ni; internet www.cosep.org.ni; f. 1972; private businesses; consists of Cámara de Industrias de Nicaragua (CADIN), Unión de Productores Agropecuarios de Nicaragua (UPANIC), Cámara de Comercio, Cámara de la Construcción, Confederación Nacional de Profesionales (CONAPRO), Instituto Nicaragüense de Desarrollo (INDE); mem. of Coordinadora Democrática Nicaragüense; Pres. Dr ERWIN KRÜGER; Sec. Dr ORESTES ROMERO ROJAS.

Instituto Nicaragüense de Desarrollo (INDE): Camas Lunes 1 c. al oeste, Calle 27 de Mayo, Apdo 2598, Managua; tel. 268-1901; fax 268-1900; e-mail inde@inde.org.ni; internet www.inde.org.ni; f. 1963; private business org.; 650 mems; Pres. ALEJANDRO MALESPÍN SILVA.

Unión Nacional de Agricultores y Ganaderos (UNAG): Managua; Pres. ALVARO FIALLOS.

Unión de Productores Agropecuarios de Nicaragua (UPANIC): Reparto San Juan No 300, detrás del Gimnasio Hércules, Managua; tel. 278-3382; fax 278-3291; e-mail upanic@ibw.com.ni; private agriculturalists' assocn; Pres. OSCAR ALEMÁN; Exec. Sec. ALEJANDRO RASKOSKY.

UTILITIES

Regulatory Bodies

Comisión Nacional de Energía: Del Hospital Bautista 1 c. abajo, 120 varas al lago, Apdo CJ-159, Managua; tel. 222-5576; internet www.cne.gob.ni; Exec. Pres. ERNESTO ESPINOZA MARADIAGA.

Instituto Nicaragüense de Acueductos y Alcantarillados (INAA): De la Mansión Teodolinda, 3 c. al sur, Bolonia, Apdo 1084, Managua; tel. 266-7882; fax 266-7917; e-mail inaa@inaa.gob.ni; internet www.inaa.gob.ni; f. 1979; water regulator; Exec. Pres. CARLOS SCHUTZE SUGRAÑES.

NICARAGUA

Instituto Nicaragüense de Energía (INE): Edif. Petronic, 4°, Managua; tel. 228-1142; fax 228-2049; internet www.ine.gob.ni; Pres. DAVID CASTILLO.

Electricity

Empresa Nicaragüense de Electricidad (ENEL): Ofs Centrales, Pista Juan Pablo II y Avda Bolívar, Managua; tel. 267-4159; fax 267-2686; e-mail relapub@ibw.com.ni; Pres. FRANK JOHN KELLY; responsible for planning, organization, management, administration, research and development of energy resources; split into a transmission co, 2 distribution businesses and 4 generation cos in 1999

Empresa Nacional de Transmisión Eléctrica, SA (ENTRESA): Intersección Bolívar y Pista Juan Pablo II, Managua; tel. 277-4159; internet www.entresa.com.ni; operates the electricity transmission network; Gen. Man. HUMBERTO SALVO LABREAU.

GECSA: electricity generation co; 79 MW capacity thermal plant; almost obsolete and therefore difficult to privatize, GECSA was likely to be retained for emergency purposes.

GEOSA: electricity generation co; 112 MW capacity thermal plant; sold to Coastal Power International (USA) in Jan. 2002.

HIDROGESA: electricity generation co; 94 MW capacity hydroelectric plant; privatized in 2002; however, sale annulled in July 2003 owing to alleged irregularities.

ORMAT Momotombo Power Co: Momotombo; internet www.ormat.com; f. 1999 on acquisition of 15-year concession to rehabilitate and operate Momotombo power plant; subsidiary of ORMAT International, Inc; CEO LUCIEN Y. BRONICKI; 30 MW capacity geothermal plant.

Unión Fenosa DISSUR y DISNORTE: Managua; electricity distribution co; privatized in 2000; distributes some 1460 GWh (DISSUR 658 GWh, DISNORTE 802 GWh); Dir JOSÉ LEY LAU.

Water

Empresa Nicaragüense de Acueductos y Alcantarillados Sanitarios (ENACAL): 5 Km Carretera Sur 505, Asososca; tel. 266-7863; internet www.enacal.com.ni; Exec. Pres. RUTH SELMA HERRERA.

TRADE UNIONS

Asociación Nacional de Educadores de Nicaragua (ANDEN): Managua; e-mail anden@guegue.com.ni; Sec.-Gen. JOSÉ ANTONIO ZEPEDA; 19 affiliates, 15,000 mems.

Asociación de Trabajadores del Campo (ATC) (Association of Rural Workers): Apdo A-244, Managua; tel. 223-2221; e-mail atcnic@ibw.com.ni; f. 1977; Gen. Sec. EDGARDO GARCÍA; 52,000 mems.

Central Sandinista de Trabajadores (CST): Iglesia del Carmen, 1 c. al oeste, ½ c. al sur, Managua; tel. 265-1096; fax 240-1285; e-mail cts/cor@alfanumeric.com.ni; Sec.-Gen. ROBERTO GONZÁLEZ GAITÁN.

Central de Trabajadores de Nicaragua (CTN) (Nicaraguan Workers' Congress): De la Iglesia del Carmen, 1 c. al sur, ½ c. arriba y 75 varas al sur, Managua; tel. 268-3061; fax 265-2056; e-mail ctn@alfanumeric.com.ni; f. 1962; mem. of Coordinadora Democrática Nicaragüense; Sec.-Gen. CARLOS HUEMBES.

Confederación de Acción y Unidad Sindical (CAUS) (Confederation for Trade Union Action and Unity): Semáforos de Rubenia, 2 c. abajo y 2 c. al lago, Barrio Venezuela, Managua; tel. and fax 244-2587; f. 1973; trade-union wing of Partido Comunista de Nicaragua; Sec.-Gen. EMILIO MÁRQUEZ.

Confederación General de Trabajadores Independientes (CGT(I)) (Independent General Confederation of Labour): Centro Comercial Nejapa, 1 c. arriba y 3 c. al lago, Managua; tel. 222-5195; fax 228-7505; f. 1953; Sec.-Gen. NILO M. SALAZAR; 4,843 mems (est.) from six federations with 40 local unions, and six non-federated local unions.

Confederación de Unificación Sindical (CUS) (Confederation of United Trade Unions): Casa Q3, del Colegio la Tenderi 2½ c. arriba, Ciudad Jardín, Managua; tel. 248-3681; fax 240-1330; e-mail sindicatocus@yahoo.com; f. 1972; affiliated to the Inter-American Regional Organization of Workers, etc.; mem. of Coordinadora Democrática Nicaragüense; Sec.-Gen. JOSÉ ESPINOZA.

Federation Enrique Schmidt (FESC): Managua; e-mail fschmidt@tmx.com.ni; communications and postal workers' union.

Federación de Trabajadores Nicaragüenses (FTN): workers' federation; Leader DOMINGO PÉREZ.

Federación de Trabajadores de la Salud (FETSALUD) (Federation of Health Workers): Optica Nicaragüense, 2 c. arriba ½ c. al sur, Apdo 1402, Managua; tel. and fax 266-3065; e-mail fntsid@ibw.com.ni; Dir DAVE GODSON; 25,000 mems.

Federación de Transportadores Unidos Nicaragüense (FTUN) (United Transport Workers' Federation of Nicaragua): De donde fue el Vocacional, esq. este, 30 m al sur, Apdo 945, Managua; f. 1952; Pres. MANUEL SABALLOS; 2,880 mems (est.) from 21 affiliated asscns.

Frente Nacional de los Trabajadores (FNT) (National Workers' Front): Residencial Bolonia, de la Optica Nicaragüense, 2 c. arriba, 30 varas al sur, Managua; tel. and fax 266-3065; e-mail fnt@ibw.com.ni; f. 1979; affiliated to Frente Sandinista de Liberación Nacional; Leader Dr GUSTAVO PORRAS CORTÉS; Sec.-Gen. JOSÉ A. BERMÚDEZ.

Unión Nacional de Agricultores y Ganaderos (UNAG) (National Union of Agricultural and Livestock Workers): Contiguo Edif. Julia Pasos, Reparto Las Palmas, 3½ km Carretera Sur, Managua; tel. 266-1675; fax 266-2135; e-mail unag@unag.org.ni; internet www.unag.org.ni; f. 1981; Pres. ALVARO FIALLOS OYANGUREN.

Unión Nacional de Caficultores de Nicaragua (UNCAFENIC) (National Union of Coffee Growers of Nicaragua): Reparto San Juan, Casa 300, Apdo 3447, Managua; tel. 278-2586; fax 278-2587; Pres. FREDDY TORRES.

Unión Nacional de Empleados (UNE): Managua; e-mail cocentrafemenino@xerox.com.ni; f. 1978; public sector workers' union; Sec.-Gen. DOMINGO PÉREZ; 18,000 mems.

Unión de Productores Agropecuarios de Nicaragua (UPANIC) (Union of Agricultural Producers of Nicaragua): Reparto San Juan, Casa 300, Apdo 2351, Managua; tel. 278-3382; fax 278-2587; Vice-Pres. MANUEL ALVAREZ.

Transport

RAILWAYS

There are no functioning railways. The state-owned rail operator, Ferrocarril de Nicaragua, which formerly operated a network of 287 km, ceased operations in 1994, and the only remaining private line closed in 2001.

ROADS

In 2004 there were an estimated 18,669 km of roads, of which 5,117 km were highways and 6,123 km were secondary roads. Of the total, only some 9,000–10,000 km were accessible throughout the entire year. Some 8,000 km of roads were damaged by 'Hurricane Mitch', which struck in late 1998. The Pan-American Highway runs for 384 km in Nicaragua and links Managua with the Honduran and Costa Rican frontiers and the Atlantic and Pacific Highways connecting Managua with the coastal regions.

SHIPPING

Corinto, Puerto Sandino and San Juan del Sur, on the Pacific, and Puerto Cabezas, El Bluff and El Rama, on the Caribbean, are the principal ports. Corinto deals with about 60% of trade. In 2001 the US-based company Delasa was given a 25-year concession to develop and modernize Puerto Cabezas port. It was to invest some US $200m.

Empresa Portuaria Nacional (EPN): Residencial Bolonia, de la Optica Nicaragüense ½ c. al norte, 1 c.al oeste, Managua; tel. 222-3827; fax 266-3488; e-mail epn_puertos@epn.com.ni; internet www.epn.com.ni; Pres. VIRGILIO SILVA MUNGÚIA.

CIVIL AVIATION

The principal airport is the Augusto Sandino International Airport, in Managua. There are some 185 additional airports in Nicaragua.

Empresa Administradora de Aeropuertos Internacionales (EAAI): POB 5179, 11 Km Carretera Norte, Managua; tel. 233-1624; fax 263-1072; e-mail webm@eaai.com.ni; internet www.eaai.com.ni; autonomous govt entity; operates Managua International Airport and three national airports: Bluefields, Puerto Cabezas and Corn Island; Pres. DANILO LACAYO RAPPACIOLI; Gen. Man. ALFREDO CHAMORRO.

Atlantic Airlines: Estatua José Martí, 150 m este, Managua; tel. 222-3037; fax 228-5614; e-mail reservaciones@atlanticairlines.com.ni; internet www.atlanticairlines.com.ni; scheduled domestic services, charters, cargo transportation and courier services; Gen. Man. LUIS ARÉVALO.

La Costeña: Managua International Airport, Managua; tel. 263-2142; fax 263-1281; e-mail info@flycostena.com.ni; internet www.tacaregional.com/costena; Gen. Man. ALFREDO CABALLERO.

NICARAGUA

Tourism

In 2005 tourist arrivals totalled 712,444, and receipts from tourism totalled US $211m.

Instituto Nicaragüense de Turismo (INTUR): Del Hotel Crowne Plaza, 1 c. al sur, 1 c. al oeste, Apdo 5088, Managua; tel. 254-5191; fax 222-6610; e-mail promocion@intur.gob.ni; internet www.intur.gob.ni; f. 1998; Pres. María Nelly Rivas Blanco; Sec.-Gen. Ian Coronel.

Asociación Nicaragüense de Agencias de Viajes y Turismo (ANAVYT): Edif. Policlínica Nicaragüense, Reparto Bolonia, Apdo 1045, Managua; tel. 266-9742; fax 266-4474; e-mail aeromund@cablenet.com.ni; f. 1966; Pres. Ana María Rocha C.

Cámara Nacional de Turismo (CANATUR): Contiguo al Ministerio de Turismo, Apdo 2105, Managua; tel. and fax 266-5071; e-mail canatur@munditel.com.ni; f. 1976.

NIGER

Introductory Survey

Location, Climate, Language, Religion, Flag, Capital

The Republic of Niger is a land-locked country in western Africa, with Algeria and Libya to the north, Nigeria and Benin to the south, Mali and Burkina Faso to the west, and Chad to the east. The climate is hot and dry, with an average temperature of 29°C (84°F). The official language is French, but numerous indigenous languages, including Hausa (spoken by about one-half of the population), Tuareg, Djerma and Fulani, are also used (the 1991 sovereign National Conference identified 10 'national' languages). Some 95% of the population are Muslims, the most influential Islamic groups being the Tijaniyya, the Senoussi and the Hamallists. Most of the remainder of the population follow traditional beliefs, and there is a small Christian minority. The national flag (proportions 6 by 7) has three equal horizontal stripes, of orange, white and green, with an orange disc in the centre of the white stripe. The capital is Niamey.

Recent History

Formerly a part of French West Africa, Niger became a self-governing member of the French Community in December 1958 and was granted independence on 3 August 1960. Hamani Diori, leader of the Parti progressiste nigérien (the local section of the Ivorian-dominated Rassemblement démocratique africain) and Prime Minister since December 1958, became Head of State. Diori was elected President in November 1960, and re-elected in 1965 and 1970. Close links were maintained with France.

The Sahelian drought of 1968–74 was particularly damaging to the Nigerien economy and was a major factor in precipitating a military coup in April 1974. Diori was arrested, and Lt-Col (later Maj.-Gen.) Seyni Kountché, the armed forces Chief of Staff, became President. The new administration, headed by a Conseil militaire suprême (CMS), suspended the Constitution; the legislature was replaced by a consultative Conseil national de développement (CND), and political activity was banned. Kountché obtained the withdrawal of French troops and reduced French influence over the exploitation of Niger's deposits of uranium (which France had initiated in 1968).

From 1977 the proportion of army officers in the Government was progressively reduced. Senior members of Diori's administration and other political prisoners were released in 1978, and in 1980 Diori was released from prison, although he was kept under house arrest. In January 1983 a civilian, Oumarou Mamane, was appointed to the newly created post of Prime Minister. In November Mamane, who in August had been appointed President of the CND, was replaced as premier by Hamid Algabid.

A draft 'national charter' was approved by a reported 99.6% of voters in a referendum in June 1987. In November Kountché died while undergoing medical treatment in France, and Col (later Brig.) Ali Saïbou, the army Chief of Staff, was inaugurated as Chairman of the CMS and Head of State. Diori was released from house arrest, and an appeal was made to exiled Nigeriens to return to the country. (Diori died in Morocco in 1989.) In December 1987 an amnesty was proclaimed for all political prisoners. In July 1988 Mamane (who had been replaced as President of the CND in September 1987) was reinstated as Prime Minister, and the CND was given the task of drafting a new constitution. In August 1988 Brig. Saïbou formed a new ruling party, the Mouvement national pour la société de développement (MNSD).

In May 1989 an MNSD congress elected a Conseil supérieur d'orientation nationale (CSON) to succeed the CMS. The draft Constitution was endorsed by a reported 99.3% of voters in a referendum in September. At elections in December Saïbou (as President of the CSON and the sole candidate) was confirmed as President of the Republic, for a seven-year term, by 99.6% of those who voted, while 99.5% of voters endorsed a single list of CSON-approved deputies to a new, 93-member Assemblée nationale. In March 1990 a prominent industrialist, Aliou Mahamidou, was appointed Prime Minister in an extensive government reorganization. In June the CSON announced that the Constitution was to be amended to facilitate a transition to political pluralism. In November Saïbou announced that a multi-party political system would be established. A national conference on political reform was to be convened in mid-1991, and multi-party national elections would take place in 1992.

In March 1991 the armed forces Chief of Staff announced that the armed forces were to distance themselves from the MNSD—Nassara (as the MNSD had been restyled) with immediate effect. In July Saïbou resigned as Chairman of the MNSD—Nassara, in preparation for the National Conference, which was convened in Niamey later that month and attended by about 1,200 delegates, including representatives of the organs of state, 24 political organizations, the military and civil society. It declared itself sovereign, voting to suspend the Constitution and dissolve the legislature. Saïbou would remain in office as Head of State on an interim basis, but the Conference would supervise the exercise of his (now largely ceremonial) powers. The Government was dissolved in September, and in October the Conference appointed Cheiffou Amadou to head a transitional Council of Ministers, which was intended to hold office until the inauguration of democratically elected institutions, now scheduled for early 1993. Prior to the conclusion of the Conference, in November 1991, its President, André Salifou, was designated Chairman of a 15-member interim legislative body, the Haut conseil de la République (HCR), which was, *inter alia*, to supervise the drafting of a new constitution.

The new Constitution was approved by 89.8% of those who voted in a referendum held on 26 December 1992. The MNSD—Nassara won the greatest number of seats (29) at elections to the 83-member Assemblée nationale, held on 14 February 1993 and contested by 12 political parties, but was prevented from resuming power by the rapid formation, following the elections, of the Alliance des forces de changement (AFC) by six parties with a total of 50 seats in the legislature. Principal members of the AFC were the Convention démocratique et sociale—Rahama (CDS), the Parti nigérien pour la démocratie et le socialisme—Tarayya (PNDS), and the Alliance nigérienne pour la démocratie et le progrès social—Zaman Lahiya (ANDP). At the first round of the presidential election, held on 27 February and contested by eight candidates, Col (retd) Mamadou Tandja, Saïbou's successor as leader of the MNSD—Nassara, won the greatest proportion of votes cast (34.2%). He and his nearest rival, Mahamane Ousmane (the leader of the CDS, with 26.6%), proceeded to a second round on 27 March, at which Ousmane was elected President by 55.4% of voters; his inauguration took place on 16 April. Ousmane appointed Mahamadou Issoufou of the PNDS as Prime Minister. Despite an attempt by the MNSD—Nassara to block the appointment, in May Moumouni Adamou Djermakoye of the ANDP became President of the Assemblée nationale.

The new regime's efforts to curb public expenditure, combined with the effects of the 50% devaluation of the CFA franc in January 1994, provoked considerable disquiet among workers and students. In September the PNDS withdrew from the AFC, and Issoufou resigned the premiership, in protest at the perceived transfer of certain prime ministerial powers to the President. A new minority Government, led by Souley Abdoulaye of the CDS, failed to withstand a parliamentary motion of 'no confidence' proposed by the MNSD—Nassara and the PNDS in October. Ousmane therefore dissolved the Assemblée nationale.

At legislative elections held in mid-January 1995 the MNSD—Nassara won 29 seats and subsequently led a 43-strong majority group in the Assemblée nationale. Although the CDS increased its representation to 24 seats, the AFC secured only 40 seats. Ousmane declined to accept the new majority's nominee to the premiership, Hama Amadou (the Secretary-General of the MNSD—Nassara), instead appointing another member of that party, Amadou Aboubacar Cissé, a former official of the World Bank. The MNSD—Nassara and its allies announced that they would not co-operate with his administration, and Cissé was expelled from the party. Meanwhile, Issoufou was elected President of the Assemblée nationale. In February the legislature approved a motion of censure against Cissé, and Ousmane accepted the nomination of Amadou as Prime Minister. This political 'cohabitation' encountered serious difficulties, as the President and Prime Minister disputed their respective competencies, in particular with regard to a proposed programme for the reorganization and privatization of state enterprises, which Ousmane opposed. Following several months of industrial unrest, Ousmane's rejection of the Government's draft budget, in January 1996, resulted in a new impasse in relations.

On 27 January 1996 the elected organs of state were overthrown by the military. The coup leaders, who formed a Conseil de salut national (CSN), chaired by Col (later Brig.-Gen.) Ibrahim Baré Maïnassara, armed forces Chief of Staff since March 1995 and a former aide-de-camp to Kountché, asserted that their seizure of power had been necessitated by Niger's descent into political chaos. The CSN annulled the Constitution and dissolved the Assemblée nationale, while political parties were suspended. A national forum was to be convened to consider the revision of the Constitution and the electoral code, and to determine a timetable for a return to civilian rule. The CSN appointed Boukary Adji, the Deputy Governor of the Banque centrale des états de l'Afrique de l'ouest as Prime Minister. Adji's transitional Government, named in February 1996, was composed entirely of civilians although military officers were appointed to regional governorships. In that month Ousmane, Amadou and Issoufou signed a joint text which effectively endorsed the legitimacy of the CSN.

Two consultative bodies were established to prepare for the restoration of civilian government, the advisory Conseil des sages and the co-ordinating committee of the national forum. The National Forum for Democratic Renewal, which was convened in April 1996, adopted revisions to the Constitution that aimed to guarantee greater institutional stability, essentially by conferring executive power solely on the President. In April Ousmane, Amadou and Issoufou accompanied Maïnassara to northern Niger to celebrate National Concord Day, on the first anniversary of the signing of the peace agreement with the Tuareg movement (see below).

The revised Constitution was approved by some 92.3% of the votes cast at a referendum on 12 May 1996 (about 35% of the electorate participated). The ban on political activity was lifted shortly afterwards. Voting in the presidential election commenced, as scheduled, on 7 July 1996, but was quickly halted in several areas where preparations were incomplete: polling took place in these areas on 8 July. Shortly before the end of voting the authorities announced the dissolution of the Commission électorale nationale indépendante (CENI), citing its alleged obstruction of the electoral process. A new commission was appointed to collate the election results. According to provisional results, announced by the new commission, Maïnassara won the election, with some 52.2% of the votes cast, Ousmane secured 19.8%, and Tandja 15.7%. The Supreme Court validated the election results on 21 July and Maïnassara was installed as President on 7 August. A new Government, with Adji as Prime Minister, also included Abdoulaye and Cissé. Members of the CDS, the MNSD—Nassara and the PNDS who had accepted government posts were subsequently expelled from these parties.

In August 1996 the legislative elections, which had been scheduled for September, were postponed until 10 November. The Conseil des sages recommended a further delay, pending the resolution of difficulties, including the threatened boycott by the main opposition parties, now grouped in a Front pour la restauration et la défense de la démocratie (FRDD). At Maïnassara's instigation, the Government undertook inter-party negotiations, mediated by the Conseil des sages. The Government agreed to permit opposition access to the state media and to rescind the ban (in force since the presidential election) on public meetings and demonstrations, and in October announced the further postponement of the legislative elections, to 23 November, and the restoration of the CENI, with the same composition as that which had overseen the 1995 election. The commission's prerogatives were, however, amended, and the FRDD responded that it would not participate in the forthcoming poll unless the CENI was reinstated with its original powers and the presidential election annulled.

The legislative elections proceeded on 23 November 1996, contested by 11 parties and movements. According to official results, the pro-Maïnassara Union nationale des indépendants pour le renouveau démocratique (UNIRD) won 52 of the Assemblée nationale's 83 seats. International observers pronounced themselves satisfied with the organization and conduct of the election. (The Supreme Court later annulled the results in three constituencies won by the UNIRD, on the grounds of fraud.) A new Government was formed, with Cissé as Prime Minister. The FRDD rejected an invitation to participate in the Government, and the deputy leader of the CDS, Sanoussi Jackou, was expelled from the party after accepting a ministerial post.

In January 1997 an unauthorized opposition demonstration in Niamey degenerated into clashes with the security forces. Some 62 people were arrested, among them Ousmane, Tandja and Issoufou, who were to be tried by the recently restored State Security Court. In response to opposition claims that neither the Constitution nor the penal code made provision for the Court (which had been in existence under the Kountché regime), the Government cited constitutional provisions that ensured the continued validity of laws in force at the time of the promulgation of the Constitution, unless specifically repealed. Nine days later, following clashes in Zinder and a further protest in Niamey, the opposition leaders were released, reportedly on Maïnassara's direct order. The FRDD rejected an invitation by the President to participate in a government of national unity, demanding the dissolution of the Assemblée nationale and the holding of free and fair elections.

In November 1997 Maïnassara dismissed the entire Government: a resumption of hostilities in the north had been compounded by poor harvests and by further labour unrest. Maïnassara appointed Ibrahim Hassane Maiyaki, hitherto Minister of Foreign Affairs and Co-operation, as Prime Minister and named a new Council of Ministers in December.

In January 1998 it was announced that members of a commando unit had been arrested and charged with attempting to overthrow Maïnassara and other senior officials. Four of the accused made a televised confession, stating that they had been operating on the direct orders of former Prime Minister Amadou, who was himself arrested. Amadou was released on bail shortly afterwards, charged with forming a militia, criminal conspiracy and illegal possession of weapons.

In February 1998 three parties of the presidential group, including the ANDP, formed the Alliance des forces démocratiques et sociales (AFDS). However, the AFDS subsequently protested against its perceived marginalization in the political process and in the state media, observing that the alliance was increasingly associated with the opposition. Clashes in Tahoua in April between the security forces and FRDD activists, who were demanding Maïnassara's resignation, were followed by violent protests by the FRDD in Maradi and in Zinder. In July the Government and the FRDD and the AFDS signed an agreement that was intended to facilitate opposition participation in the local elections. Revisions to electoral procedures and institutions were outlined, while the equal access of all political groups to the state media and the freedom to demonstrate were to be guaranteed. However, following a dispute over the President of the CENI, in October the CENI postponed voting until February 1999.

Voting in the regional, district and municipal elections took place on 7 February 1999. Following the discovery of overt irregularities, the CENI emphasized that it favoured by-elections in affected areas. Full results, which were not released by the Supreme Court until 7 April, gave the 11 opposition parties a slim overall majority of seats in those municipal, district and regional assemblies where the elections were deemed valid. Voting was to be rerun at some 4,000 polling stations nationwide. The FRDD and AFDS denounced Maïnassara as personally responsible for the disruption to voting and demanded the President's resignation.

On 9 April 1999 Maiyaki made a broadcast to the nation, announcing the death of Maïnassara in an 'unfortunate accident' at a military airbase in Niamey. The Prime Minister stated that the defence and security forces would continue to be the guarantors of republican order and national unity, and announced the dissolution of the Assemblée nationale, as well as the temporary suspension of all party political activity. Despite the official explanation for his death, it was generally perceived that members of the presidential guard had assassinated Maïnassara in a *coup d'état*. Although members of the Assemblée nationale initially rejected its dissolution, on 11 April the Constitution was suspended, and its institutions dissolved. The February local elections were annulled. A military Conseil de réconciliation nationale (CRN), under the chairmanship of Maj. Daouda Mallam Wanké (hitherto head of the presidential guard), was to exercise executive and legislative authority during a nine-month transitional period, prior to the restoration of elected civilian institutions. Wanké immediately signed an ordinance on interim political authority, which was to function as a constitutional document during the transitional period.

Maiyaki was reappointed as Prime Minister of the transitional Government on 12 April; a new Council of Ministers was named shortly afterwards. Moussa Moumouni Djermakoye, who had been succeeded as armed forces Chief of Staff by Lt-Col Soumara Zanguina, became Minister of National Defence. In July, in a minor reshuffle, the Minister of the Interior and Territorial Administration, Lt-Col Moumouni Boureima, was appointed armed forces Chief of Staff, while Zanguina became an adviser to the Head of State.

The new draft Constitution was submitted to referendum on 18 July 1999, when it was approved by 89.6% of those who voted (about one-third of the registered electorate). The Constitution envisaged a balance of powers between the President, the Government and the legislature, but, none the less, vested strong powers in the Head of State, who was to be politically liable only in the case of high treason. The Government, under a Prime Minister appointed by the President, was to be responsible to the Assemblée nationale, which would be competent to remove the Prime Minister by vote of censure. A clause in the Constitution guaranteeing all those involved in the military take-overs of 1996 and 1999 immunity from prosecution provoked controversy and was condemned by Amnesty International, in a report in September, as undermining the rule of law. The report was regarded as particularly significant in that it published the testimony of a witness who alleged that Maïnassara had been killed by the presidential guard under Wanké's command. The Wanké regime continued to assert that Maïnassara's death had been accidental, and that a commission of inquiry into the death had been ordered in response to a complaint lodged by the late President's family.

Voting at the presidential election, which was contested by seven candidates, took place on 17 October 1999, and was considered both by the CENI and by independent observers to have been largely transparent and peaceful. Mamadou Tandja, of the MNSD—Nassara, won 32.3% of the votes cast, followed by Issoufou, of the PNDS, with 22.8%, and Ousmane, of the CDS, with 22.5%. The rate of participation by voters was 43.7%. Tandja and Issoufou proceeded to a second round on 24 November. Having secured the support of Ousmane, Tandja was elected President, with 59.9% of the votes cast. About 39% of the registered electorate voted. The MNSD—Nassara was similarly successful in the concurrent elections to the Assemblée nationale, winning 38 of the 83 seats; the CDS took 17, the PNDS 16, the pro-Maïnassara Rassemblement pour la démocratie et le progrès—Djamaa (RDP) eight and the ANDP four. Tandja, who had served in the CMS under Kountché and was Minister of the Interior in the early 1990s, was inaugurated as President on 22 December. Hama Amadou was subsequently appointed Prime Minister, and a new Council of Ministers was named in January 2000.

In January 2000 the Assemblée nationale adopted draft amnesty legislation, as provided for in the Constitution. The amnesty was opposed by the RDP, and many activists of the party joined a demonstration in February to denounce the legislation and to demand an international inquiry into the death of Maïnassara. In March 12 opposition parties, led by the PNDS, formed a coalition, the Coordination des forces démocratiques (CFD). Similarly, 17 parties loyal to the President, most notably the MNSD—Nassara and the CDS, formed the Alliance des forces démocratiques (AFD). In May Col Bourahima Moumouni was appointed armed forces Chief of Staff. None the less, rumours persisted of dissent within the army.

In September 2001 President Tandja reshuffled the Council of Ministers, retaining Prime Minister Amadou and 10 of his ministers, although there were some 13 new appointments. In October opposition parties tabled a further censure motion against the Government in the Assemblée nationale, although the motion was withdrawn before voting could proceed, in response to concerns that it would negatively affect the Government's ongoing negotiations with the World Bank and the European Union (EU, see p. 244).

In July 2002 the ANDP withdrew from the opposition CFD alliance and joined the AFD, thereby increasing the Government's parliamentary majority by four seats. Explaining his party's shift in allegiances, the leader of the ANDP, Moumouni Adamou Djermakoye, accused the CFD of intolerance and of failing to ease social tensions.

In late July 2002 a mutiny broke out at a barracks in Diffa. The mutineers arrested several officers, and the mayor of Diffa and the regional governor, and took control of a radio station to broadcast their demands for improved pay and conditions, including the payment of wage arrears. The Government declared a state of emergency in Diffa and dispatched troops to bring the rebellion, which continued for 10 days, to a halt. A further uprising, at a barracks to the east of Diffa, was also rapidly quashed. In early August, meanwhile, a military uprising broke out in Niamey, although government forces quickly restored order in the capital. By mid-September special security measures in the Diffa region had been relaxed. Amadou claimed that the rebellion in Diffa had been intended to serve as a distraction, while a *coup d'état* was being prepared in Niamey.

Tandja implemented a major government reorganization in November 2002, as a result of which the position of allies of Prime Minister Amadou was reportedly strengthened. Among the 13 new ministerial appointments was Moumouni Adamou Djermakoye as Minister of State, responsible for African Integration and the NEPAD (New Partnership for Africa's Development, see p. 169) Programmes, while seven ministers left the Government. Although several principal positions remained unchanged, new appointments were made to the Ministries of National Defence and of the Interior and Decentralization. At the end of December the Assemblée nationale approved legislation providing for the creation of a special military tribunal to try those accused of involvement in the rebellion earlier in the year (a total of 268 arrests were reported); elements within the opposition alleged that the legislation violated several articles of the Constitution. However, many soldiers were reportedly released during 2003, owing to a lack of evidence, and the three highest-ranking officers arrested were provisionally freed in February 2004. (Six of the mutineers were awarded custodial sentences at a military tribunal in early 2006.)

In mid-October 2003 the Council of Ministers announced proposals to increase the number of deputies in the Assemblée nationale from 83 to 113, in order to reflect the growth in the population recorded between the national censuses of 1988 and 2001. A minor government reshuffle was effected later in October 2003. Also in that month the Council of Ministers approved the abolition of the State Security Court.

In early February 2004 it was announced that municipal elections, initially scheduled to be held on 28 March, had been postponed until 29 May, owing to logistical difficulties experienced by several political parties. In mid-February Rhissa Ag Boula, a former Tuareg rebel leader (see below), was dismissed as Minister of Tourism and Crafts, following allegations that he was implicated in the murder of an MNSD—Nassara activist earlier in the year; he was subsequently arrested and charged with complicity in the murder. Meanwhile, another former Tuareg rebel leader, Mohamed Anako, was appointed as Minister-delegate at the Ministry of the Economy and Finance, responsible for the Taxation of Local Communities and the Informal Sector.

In mid-May 2004 the CDS announced that the party's Chairman, former President Ousmane, would be its candidate in the presidential election due to be held in December. Later that month several trade unions organized a series of strikes in support of demands for improved working and living conditions for public-sector workers following the failure of negotiations with the authorities. The municipal elections, which had been further postponed in May, were held on 24 July. According to provisional results, pro-presidential parties won a total of 2,335 of the 3,747 seats in the country's 265 communes (the MNSD—Nassara 1,388, the CDS 748 and the ANDP 199), while, of the opposition parties, the PNDS secured 821 seats, coming second overall, and the RDP 217. The non-aligned Rassemblement social-démocratique—Gaskiya (RSD), which had been formed following a split in the CDS, also unexpectedly won 217 seats; the turn-out was 43.6%.

In the first round of the presidential election, held on 16 November 2004, Tandja won 40.67% of votes cast, followed by Issoufou, who received 24.60% and both therefore proceeded to a second round of voting, while the four eliminated candidates (representing the CDS, the RSD, the ANDP and the RDP) all urged their supporters to transfer their allegiance to Tandja. In the second round of voting, held on 4 December, Tandja was victorious, receiving 65.53% of votes cast. (Turn-out in the first round was reported to be 48.5% of registered voters, declining slightly, to 45.0%, in the second round.) At elections to the newly enlarged 113-seat Assemblée nationale, held concurrently with the second round of voting in the presidential election, the MNSD—Nassara won the largest number of seats, obtaining 47, while allied pro-presidential parties secured a further 41 seats. An opposition coalition formed around the PNDS, which also comprised the Parti nigérien pour l'autogestion (PNA), the Parti progressiste nigérien pour le rassemblement démocratique africain (PPN-RDA), the Union pour la démocratie et la République (UDR) and the Union nigérienne des indépendants (UNI), won a total of 25 seats. Ousmane was subsequently re-elected as President of the Assemblée nationale, 13 seats in which, in accordance with legislation adopted in 2001, were reserved for women. Later in December President Tandja announced the formation of a new Government, in which Amadou remained as Prime Minister. During the course of 2005 several observers noted an increasing degree of political consensus in Niger between the Government and the opposition; in particular, it was reported that Issoufou was involved in regular consultations with the authorities.

In mid-March 2005 up to 20,000 people were reported to have participated in demonstrations in Niamey against the recent introduction of a 19% value-added tax on basic commodities. The demonstration was organized by an alliance of some 30 groups, including trade unions, human rights organizations and consumer movements known as the Coalition contre la vie chère (CCVC). In the following week, after the Government refused to authorize a second protest march, the CCVC staged a one-day strike, which halted most activity in the capital. The authorities subsequently agreed to hold talks with the CCVC, although they emphasized that the tax would not be withdrawn. However, before the proposed meeting, five leaders of the Coalition were arrested and accused of establishing an unauthorized association and plotting against state security. The radio station Alternative FM, which had broadcast interviews with prominent supporters of the CCVC, was also closed by police, prompting protests from international press freedom groups. (The director of the station, Moussa Tchangari, was among those arrested.) During a further one-day strike, held a few days later, protesters erected barricades and burned tyres in Maradi and Tahoua, leading to more arrests. A third strike was suspended by the Coalition in early April in the hope that a compromise could be reached with the Government. The five leaders of the CCVC were subsequently released and, following negotiations between the Government and the leadership of the CCVC, agreement was reached on numerous concessions; notably flour and milk were to be exempted from the tax, and special arrangements were to be made to limit the effect of the tax on the cost of water and electricity.

None the less, public discontent with the Government arose again in mid-2005 over severe food shortages, which had largely resulted from a poor harvest in 2004, when low rainfall had been combined with an invasion of locusts. According to the Ministry of Agricultural Development, there was a shortfall of more than 223,000 metric tons of grain, representing the country's largest deficit for more than 20 years. In early June up to 2,000 people marched through Niamey in protest at the Government's failure to respond adequately to the crisis and in support of opposition-backed demands for the distribution of free food. The Government, which had been supplying cereals at subsidized prices in the most stricken areas, appealed for international assistance (the response to a UN appeal for Niger, launched in late 2004, had been extremely limited), but insisted that it did not have the resources to distribute free food and instead announced plans to 'loan' grain to farmers most at risk until they could reimburse the Government after the harvest later in the year. As people reportedly began fleeing to Nigeria, government ministers and officials contributed financially to efforts to alleviate the crisis. In mid-July the UN World Food Programme appealed for further international aid for Niger.

In June 2006 it was revealed that some 1,118,000m. francs CFA were missing from government accounts and two cabinet ministers suspected of the embezzlement of EU funds targeted at the education sector were dismissed: Hamani Harouna, the Minister of Basic Education and Literacy, was replaced by Dr Ousmane Samba Mamadou, while Mahamane Kabaou assumed responsibility for the public health portfolio in place of Ari Ibrahim. In September more than 30 people were arrested on suspicion of fraud and corruption involving education sector funding, and in October Harouna was charged with corruption and the misappropriation of funds.

President Tandja effected a major government reorganization in March 2007, in which the number of ministers was increased from 26 to 31. Although the key portfolios remained largely unchanged, both the Minister for Agricultural Development, Labo Moussa, and the Minister for Secondary and Higher Education, Research and Technology, Ousmane Galadima, were removed from office. Two new ministerial posts were created, to assume responsibility for education and the fight against desertification, and for relations with institutions of the Republic. In May the Government was dissolved following a vote of 'no confidence' in the Assemblée nationale, supported by 62 of the 113 deputies. The administration denied any involvement in corruption and the embezzlement of public funds. The following month President Tandja named Seyni Oumarou as Prime Minister, an appointment which drew considerable criticism from opposition members. Oumarou was nevertheless sworn in and he later announced a new Council of Ministers in which many key portfolios remained unchanged, although Jidda Hamadou assumed the national defence portfolio while Dagra Mahamadou was appointed Minister of Justice, Attorney-General.

Ethnic unrest followed the return to northern Niger, during the late 1980s, of large numbers of Tuareg nomads who had migrated to Libya and Algeria in the early 1980s to escape the Sahelian drought. It was widely believed that the perceived failure of the Saïbou administration to assist in the rehabilitation of returnees was a significant factor contributing to the subsequent Tuareg uprising. In January 1992 the transitional authorities intensified security measures in the north and, for the first time, formally acknowledged that there was a rebellion in the country. Rhissa Ag Boula, the leader of the rebel Front de libération de l'Aïr et l'Azaouad (FLAA), subsequently stated that the Tuareg rebels were seeking to achieve the establishment of a federal system of governance. Although the Government and the FLAA concluded a truce agreement in May, violence swiftly resumed. In August the security forces launched a major offensive against rebel Tuareg groups. Military authority was reinforced in October by the appointment of senior members of the security forces to northern administrative posts. In November, none the less, a commission that had been appointed by the transitional Government recommended a far-reaching programme of decentralization, according legal status and financial authority to local communities. In December the Government announced the release from custody of 57 Tuaregs.

In January 1993 five people were killed in a Tuareg attack on a meeting of the MNSD—Nassara attended by Mamadou Tandja (who was Minister of the Interior at the time of the suppression of the Tchin-Tabaraden raid) in the northern town of Abala. Later in January 81 Tuaregs were released from detention, and a Minister of State for National Reconciliation, whose main responsibility would be to seek a solution to the Tuareg issue, was appointed to the Government. In March, following Algerian mediation, Ag Boula (who was based in Algeria) agreed that the FLAA would observe a truce for the duration of the campaign for the second round of the presidential election. Shortly afterwards Tuareg representatives in Niamey signed a similar (French-brokered) agreement. In April the outgoing transitional Government and the FLAA agreed to extend the truce indefinitely; the remaining Tuareg prisoners were subsequently released from detention, and the rebels released their hostages.

In mid-1993 a three-month truce agreement between representatives of the Government and the Tuaregs, which provided for the demilitarization of the north, and envisaged negotiations on the Tuaregs' political demands, was signed in Paris, France. However, a new group, the Armée révolutionnaire de libération du nord-Niger (ARLN), emerged to denounce the truce, and supporters of the truce (led by Mano Dayak, the Tuareg signatory to the agreement) broke away from the FLAA to form the Front de libération de Tamoust (FLT): Ag Boula and the remainder of the FLAA stated that they could not support any agreement that contained no specific commitment to discussion of federalism. In September the FLT and the Government agreed to extend the truce for a further three months. Although the FLAA and the ARLN refused to sign the accord, in October they joined with the FLT in a Coordination de la résistance armée (CRA), with the aim of presenting a cohesive programme in future negotiations.

Despite an escalation of violence during May 1994 negotiations took place in Paris in June. Tentative agreement was reached on the creation of ethnically based autonomous regions, each of which was to have its own elected assembly and governor to function in parallel with the organs of central government. Despite renewed unrest, in September the CRA presented Nigerien government negotiators with a plan for the restoration of peace. Formal negotiations resumed, with mediation by the Burkinabè President, Blaise Compaoré, as well as representatives of France and Algeria, in Ouagadougou (Burkina Faso) in October. A new peace accord resulted, emphasizing that Niger was 'unitary and indivisible', while proposing the establishment of elected assemblies or councils for territorial communities, which would be responsible for the implementation of economic, social and cultural policies. A renewable three-month truce was to take immediate effect, to be monitored by French and Burkinabè military units. By the time of the conclusion of the Ouagadougou agreement the number of deaths since the escalation of the Tuareg rebellion in late 1991 was officially put at 150. A commission was established in January 1995 to consider the administrative reorganization of the country.

Ag Boula, who had withdrawn from the CRA, and refused to participate in the decentralization committee, in protest at alleged delays in the implementation of the provisions of the October 1994 agreement, emerged as the leader of the Tuareg delegation (now renamed the Organisation de la résistance armée—ORA) at negotiations in Ouagadougou in March 1995. In April it was announced that a lasting peace agreement had been reached. Demobilized rebels were to be integrated into the Nigerien military and public sector; particular emphasis was to be placed on the economic, social and cultural development of the north, and the Government undertook to support the decentralization process. There was to be a general amnesty for all parties involved in the Tuareg rebellion and its suppression, and a day of national reconciliation was to be instituted in memory of the victims of the conflict. The peace agreement was formally signed by Ag Boula and a representative of the Nigerien Government on 24 April 1995, one day before the cease-fire took effect.

Meanwhile, there was increasing ethnic unrest in the Lake Chad region of south-east Niger, where several thousand (mainly Toubou) Chadian refugees had settled since the overthrow of President Hissène Habré in late 1990. The Front démocratique du renouveau (FDR) emerged in October 1994 to demand increased autonomy for the Toubou population of the south-east. In November, in compliance with a request by the UN, Niger established a committee whose stated aim was to disarm militias and to combat arms-trafficking, which was reportedly well-established in the Agadez and Lake Chad regions. A Comité spécial de la paix (CSP) was inaugurated in May 1995, and a military observer group, comprising representatives of Burkina and France, was deployed in the north in July. The Prime Minister approved an amnesty in that month, and all Tuareg prisoners were reported to have been released shortly afterwards. The peace process was undermined, however, by evidence that Dayak and other Tuareg groups in a revived CRA were making common cause with the FDR in demanding autonomy for their respective regions. In October clashes in the northeast involving rebel Tuaregs and the armed forces were attributed to elements of the CRA. In the same month bilateral and international donors pledged some 18,700m. francs CFA in support of a two-year emergency programme for the development of the north. In December Dayak was one of three leading CRA members to be killed in an air crash. In January 1996 the new leader of the FLT (and acting leader of the CRA), Mohamed Akotai, indicated that his movement favoured inter-Tuareg reconciliation and a dialogue with the Government.

Following the coup d'état of January 1996, the CSN expressed its continued commitment to the peace process. The new administration, the ORA and the CRA all expressed the view that direct contacts between the military and the Tuareg movements would expedite the peace process. In March the Nigerien authorities, the office of the UN High Commissioner for Refugees (UNHCR) and the Governments of Algeria and Burkina signed agreements on refugee repatriation. Shortly afterwards the CRA, including the FDR, affirmed its recognition of the April 1995 agreement, and announced that it would observe a unilateral truce for one month, while negotiations continued. In April 1996 the Government and the CRA signed an agreement formalizing the latter's adherence to the peace process. The following month the ORA and the CRA agreed to establish a joint committee to co-ordinate their activities and to represent their interests in negotiations. In July the CSP and the resistance movements recommended measures aimed at curbing ongoing insecurity in northern areas. In September joint peace-keeping patrols of the Nigerien armed forces and former rebels were inaugurated in the north.

In late September 1996 Ag Boula announced that the ORA no longer considered itself bound by the peace treaty. The authorities asserted that this abandonment of the 1995 accord was linked primarily to the arrest of ORA members in connection with the diversion, some months previously, of a large consignment of cigarettes bound for the north. In an apparent gesture of reconciliation, the detainees were released at the end of October 1996, and the ORA surrendered the consignment to the authorities. In November it was reported that a new group had emerged from among the ORA and the CRA; led by Mohamed Anako, the Union des forces de la résistance armée (UFRA) affirmed its commitment to the peace accord. Following a meeting between Maïnassara and Ag Boula in January 1997, and assurances regarding the implementation of provisions of the 1995 accord, the ORA declared its renewed support; it was announced, moreover, that the FLAA and FLT would establish a joint patrol aimed at combating insecurity and banditry, and other measures intended to facilitate the reintegration of former rebels proceeded.

Insecurity persisted, none the less, particularly in the east. Violent clashes were reported in March 1997, involving several hundred soldiers and Toubou rebels: the FDR protested that the operation was endangering the peace accord. In July, however, the FDR announced its withdrawal from the peace process, stating that Nigerien and Chadian military units had attacked one of its bases; the FDR reported that 17 members of the armed forces had been killed in clashes with its fighters. The Nigerien authorities denied that any engagement had taken place. The conclusion of the disarmament process was officially celebrated in Tchin-Tabaraden in late October. The armed forces subsequently undertook an offensive against positions held by rebel groups. In November a peace accord, known as the Algiers addendum protocol, providing for an immediate cease-fire, was signed in Algeria between the Nigerien Government, the UFRA and the Forces armées révolutionnaires du Sahara (FARS), which comprised both Toubou and Arab elements. In March 1998 the ORA and CRA surrendered their weapons stocks at Agadez. Meanwhile, Ag Boula was appointed as Minister-delegate responsible for Tourism in December 1997.

In June 1998 it was reported that the last units of the UFRA had disarmed at a ceremony near Agadez. A peace agreement was signed with the FDR in August. Following the death of President Maïnassara, in April 1999, the military CRN gave assurances that the peace process would be continued. Ag Boula was promoted to the rank of minister in the transitional Government, while Anako was appointed as special adviser to Wanké. Ag Boula retained his ministerial post in the new Government of Hama Amadou, formed in January 2000. In June the final groups of fighters from the UFRA and other movements participating in the peace process were disarmed near Agadez, prior to their intended integration into the national forces. Concerns remained, however, that progress still had to be made in the implementation of moves towards greater administrative decentralization, as well as regarding the delayed fulfilment of quotas for Tuaregs in military formations. In late September more than 1,200 guns, surrendered by the disarmed factions, were ceremoniously burned in Agadez, in the presence of President Mamadou Tandja, leaders of other West African nations and UN representatives. At the ceremony, Anako announced the dissolution of several of the rebel groups and militias. In September 2001 Chahayi Barkaye, the leader of the FARS, the principal rebel group to have refused disarmament, was killed in heavy fighting with Nigerien soldiers near the Libyan border.

In February 2004 Ag Boula was dismissed from his ministerial post and detained on a charge of complicity in the murder of an MNSD—Nassara activist (in order to maintain Tuareg representation in the Government, Anako was appointed as a Minister-delegate at the Ministry of the Economy and Finance). The Government subsequently denied rumours that elements of FLAA had resumed insurgent activities in the north; however, following a clash with government forces in October, in which five people were reported to have died, Ag Boula's brother, Mohammed Ag Boula, claimed responsibility for the attack during an interview with French radio broadcaster Radio France Internationale, citing the failure of the Government to implement the 1995 peace agreements, and the continuing detention of certain former insurgents, as motivation for the attack. Also in late 2004 four government soldiers were taken hostage in northern Niger; once more, Mohammed Ag Boula declared responsibility for the action, as the leader of a revived FLAA. Following mediation by the Libyan authorities, the hostages were released, after some five months in captivity, in February 2005; Rhissa Ag Boula was released from prison one month later where he had been awaiting trial. The authorities reportedly denied Ag Boula's release was linked to that of the hostages, although Mohamed Ag Boula had previously refused to free the kidnapped soldiers while his brother remained in detention.

In February 2007 a lesser known Tuareg rebel group, styling itself the Mouvement des Nigeriens pour la justice, claimed responsibility for an attack on a military base north of Niamey, prompting concerns that ethnic unrest was once again increasing. Further attacks were reported throughout mid-2007, including an assault on a military post in which some 15 government soldiers were believed to have been killed. Despite repeated demands from the rebel group for fairer distribution of revenue generated by mining the uranium resources of the northern region, the Government refused to enter into negotiations, insisting that the attacks were not considered to be a rebellion. However, by August the situation had worsened with the number of Tuareg attacks increasing, and in that month President Tandja declared a three-month state of emergency in the region and granted additional powers of arrest to the security forces. Meanwhile, residents fled the towns of northern Niger as the rebel group used landmines to block roads and prevent the delivery of food supplies.

In foreign affairs, there was a notable deterioration in relations with the USA in the immediate aftermath of the 1996 presidential election in Niger. The assumption of power by the CRN in April 1999, following the death of Maïnassara, was condemned by the USA, France and Niger's other Western creditors. Relations with the USA improved following the re-installation of an elected Government; in February 2000 Niger's Minister of Foreign Affairs, Co-operation and African Integration visited Washington, DC, and in March the USA announced an end to the sanctions imposed after Maïnassara's death. In August President Tandja met President Bill Clinton and other US representatives in Abuja, Nigeria, where the USA announced increased support for Niger in areas including food security, the promotion of democracy, education and health care.

Countries of the region with which Maïnassara had forged close relations also condemned the military take-over of April 1999: Libya notably denounced the new regime, although relations between the CRN and the Libyan Government had normalized by the end of the year. In December the two countries signed an agreement envisaging the establishment of a joint company to distribute oil and liquefied natural gas; it was also agreed to expedite the establishment of a joint company for petroleum exploration and production. On a visit to Agadez in early July, Libyan leader Col Muammar al-Qaddafi pledged support for the Tuareg peace process. In November Libya pledged to grant financial support for several construction and development projects in Niger. Meanwhile, some 1,000 Nigerien citizens were repatriated from Libya in October, following instances of inter-ethnic violence between Libyan Arabs and black Africans in that country. On 24 April 2006, the 11th anniversary of the signing of the peace agreement, President Tandja announced that a rehabilitation programme was to be launched to assist more than 3,000 former Tuareg rebels. On surrendering their weapons in 1995 the rebels were forced onto barren land in the north of the country, but, with funds from the project amounting to 850m. francs CFA, it was hoped that the Tuaregs would develop prosperous farming and agricultural communities.

The EU suspended all assistance to Niger in the aftermath of the military take-over in April 1999 and made its resumption dependent on a full investigation into Maïnassara's death; the CRN subsequently stated that its report had been lodged with organizations including the EU, and EU aid recommenced in June 2000. France also suspended military and civilian co-operation with Niger in April 1999. Following a visit to France by Mamadou Tandja in January 2000, when the newly installed Nigerien President met President Jacques Chirac and Prime Minister Lionel Jospin, the resumption of French co-operation was formalized, with the announcement of exceptional assistance principally to allow payment of outstanding salaries in the public sector. Chirac visited Niger in October 2003, when he praised 'the return of democratic life' to the country.

In May 2000 a long-term dispute between Niger and Benin regarding the ownership of a number of small islands along their common border at the Niger river escalated, reportedly following the sabotage of a Beninois administrative building on the island of Lété, apparently by Nigerien soldiers. A meeting between representatives of the two Governments failed to resolve the dispute, which was subsequently referred to the Organization of African Unity (OAU, now the African Union, see p. 164) for arbitration. Further clashes between rival groups of farmers were reported on Lété in late August. In April 2002 the two Governments officially ratified an agreement (signed in 2001) to refer the issue of ownership of the islands to the International Court of Justice (ICJ) in The Hague, Netherlands, for arbitration. Benin and Niger filed confidential written arguments with the Court, and in November 2003 a five-member chamber formed to consider the case held its first public sitting. Both countries subsequently submitted counter-arguments, and a third written pleading was submitted by both parties in December of that year. The public hearings in the case took place before the Chamber of the ICJ in March 2005. Meanwhile, in late 2004 Nigerien traders and haulage contractors boycotted Cotonou port in Benin in reaction to the shooting of two Nigerien citizens by Beninois gendarmes in the city in September. The boycott was ended in January 2005 following a visit to Niamey by the Beninois Minister of Foreign Affairs and African Integration, Rogatien Biaou, during which he announced that the Beninois Government would compensate the victims' families. In July 2005 the ICJ issued a final ruling to the effect that 16 of the 25 disputed islands, including Lété, belonged to Niger; the Governments of both countries announced their acceptance of the ruling.

In June 2001 Niger and Nigeria announced that joint border patrols of their common frontier would be instigated, in order to combat increasing cross-border crime and smuggling in the region. It was reported that the introduction of *Shari'a* law in several northern Nigerian states, from 2000, had been instrumental in encouraging Nigerian criminal gangs to operate from within Niger. Further concerns regarding regional security were raised in early 2004, when Islamic militants belonging to the Algerian-based Groupe salafiste pour la prédication et le combat (GSPC) reportedly attacked a group of tourists in northern Niger. In March clashes between the militants and Chadian and Nigerien troops reportedly resulted in the deaths of some 43 GSPC fighters in northern Niger. It was reported in that month that the Governments of Algeria, Chad, Mali and Niger were to reinforce security co-operation in the regions of their common borders. In January 2005 President Tandja was elected Chairman of the Economic Community of West African States (see p. 232); paramount among the organization's concerns during the first months of his chairmanship were common agricultural policy and the political crises in Côte d'Ivoire and Togo. In June Niger, Algeria, Chad, Mali and Nigeria were among nine North and West African countries that participated in US-led military exercises aimed at increasing co-operation in combating cross-border banditry and militancy in the region.

In October 2006 the Government announced that it was to forcibly remove some 150,000 Mahamid Arabs from eastern Niger and return them to their native Chad. Several thousand Chadians had crossed the border into Niger during the 1970s to escape widespread drought, which had caused outbreaks of violence in their homeland. During the 1980s thousands more fled to Niger when conflict escalated into civil war in Chad. Mahamid communities continued to establish themselves in the Diffa region, but there followed complaints of deteriorating relations between the Mahamids and the local population, and it was feared that the Chadians' presence posed a serious threat to national security. UNHCR responded with claims that the Mahamid communities did not hold refugee status and stipulated that it be ensured that those forced to leave would not become victims of discrimination on their return to Chad. The Niger authorities then reversed the earlier decision, stating instead that the Mahamids would be asked to move to land better suited to their agricultural needs. In late October several thousand Nigeriens protested against that ruling, threatening that they would be forced to take action to protect their land and property if the Mahamids were not returned to Chad. The Nigerien Government subsequently announced that only those who did not have the required documents would be sent back; according to the census of 2001, the majority of the Arab community held identity cards issued by the local authorities.

Government

Following the death of President Ibrahim Baré Maïnassara, in April 1999, a military Conseil de réconciliation nationale (CRN) was established, under the chairmanship of Maj. Daouda Mallam Wanké, to exercise executive and legislative authority during a nine-month transitional period prior to the restoration of elected organs of government. A new constitution was approved in a national referendum in July 1999. The Constitution of the Fifth Republic, promulgated on 9 August, envisages a balance of powers between the President, Government and legislative Assemblée nationale. The President, who is elected by universal adult suffrage, is Head of State, and is accorded 'broad ordinary and arbitral powers'. The Government, under a Prime Minister appointed by the President, is responsible to the

Assemblée nationale, which is competent to remove the Prime Minister by vote of censure. The Assemblée nationale is similarly elected by direct adult suffrage. The new President and legislature were inaugurated in December 1999.

For the purposes of local administration, Niger comprises seven regions and the municipality of Niamey. A reorganization of Niger's administrative structures, with the aim of devolving increased autonomy to local and regional authorities, was undertaken in the second half of the 1990s.

Defence

As assessed at November 2007, Niger's armed forces totalled 5,300 men (army 5,200; air force 100). Paramilitary forces numbered 5,400 men, comprising the gendarmerie (1,400), the republican guard (2,500) and the national police force (1,500). Conscription to the armed forces is selective and lasts for two years. Budgetary expenditure on defence in 2007 was estimated at 22,000m. francs CFA.

Economic Affairs

In 2006, according to estimates by the World Bank, Niger's gross national income (GNI), measured at average 2004–06 prices, was US $3,697m., equivalent to $260 per head (or $830 on an international purchasing-power parity basis). During 1996–2006, it was estimated, the population increased at an average annual rate of 3.5%, while gross domestic product (GDP) per head decreased, in real terms, by an average of 0.1% per year. Overall GDP increased, in real terms, at an average annual rate of 3.5% in 1996–2006; growth was 3.4% in 2006.

Agriculture (including hunting, forestry and fishing) contributed 45.4% of GDP in 2005. About 86.5% of the labour force were employed in the sector in 2005. The principal cash crops are cowpeas, onions, groundnuts and cotton. The principal subsistence crops are millet and sorghum. Niger is able to achieve self-sufficiency in basic foodstuffs in non-drought years. Agricultural production in northern Niger in 2004/05 was severely affected by drought and by the swarms of locusts that invaded the Sahel region from mid-2004, resulting in a grain deficit of 223,487 tons for that agricultural year. However, by 2006 a surplus had been re-established. The effects of drought and locust invasion were also thought to have caused significant damage to pasture land: livestock-rearing in Niger is especially important among the nomadic population, and live animals intended chiefly for food accounted for 18.0% of total export earnings in 2003, constituting the second most important source of export revenue, after uranium. Major anti-desertification and reafforestation programmes are in progress. According to the World Bank, agricultural GDP increased by an average of 4.1% per year in 1996–2003. Agricultural GDP increased by 6.0% in 2003.

Industry (including mining, manufacturing, construction and power) contributed 11.9% of GDP in 2005. Only 4.2% of the labour force were employed in industrial activities in 2002. According to the World Bank, industrial GDP increased by an average of 2.8% per year in 1996–2003; growth was 4.0% in 2003.

Mining contributed 1.9% of GDP in 2005, but employed only 0.3% of the labour force in 2002. Niger is among the world's foremost producers of uranium (the third largest, after Canada and Australia, in 2002), although the contribution of uranium-mining to the domestic economy has declined, as production costs have exceeded world prices for the mineral. In 2003 exports of uranium accounted for 54.0% of total export earnings. In addition, gypsum, coal, salt and cassiterite are also extracted, and commercial exploitation of gold (previously mined on a small scale) at the Samira Hill mine began in 2004, with total production of 120,000 ounces of gold forecast for 2005. In 2007 the Government awarded the US firm Caracal Gold Burkina two permits for gold exploration in western Niger. According to the IMF, the GDP of the mining sector increased at an average annual rate of 2.3% in 1998–2005; mining GDP increased by an estimated 3.8% in 2005.

Manufacturing contributed 6.2% of GDP in 2005, and employed 3.2% of the labour force in 2002. The processing of agricultural products (groundnuts, cereals, cotton and rice) constitutes the principal activity. Some light industries, including a textiles plant, a brewery and a cement works, supply the internal market. According to the World Bank, manufacturing GDP increased by an average of 4.0% per year in 1995–2003. Manufacturing GDP increased by 5.1% in 2003.

The domestic generation of electricity (almost entirely thermal) provides a little less than one-half of Niger's electrical energy requirements, much of the remainder being imported from Nigeria. Construction of a hydroelectric installation at Kandadji, on the Niger, is planned. Imports of mineral fuels accounted for 16.9% of the value of merchandise imports in 2003.

The services sector contributed 42.7% of GDP in 2005, and employed 16.2% of the labour force in 2002. The GDP of the sector increased by an average of 3.5% per year in 1996–2003, according to the World Bank; growth was 3.1% in 2003.

In 2005 Niger recorded a visible trade deficit of an estimated 94,800m. francs CFA, while there was a deficit of 124,100m. francs CFA on the current account of the balance of payments. France was Niger's principal source of imports in 2003, supplying 14.6%; other major suppliers were Côte d'Ivoire, the People's Republic of China, the USA and Nigeria. The principal markets for exports in that year were France (36.5%), Nigeria and Japan. The principal exports in 2003 were uranium (most of which is purchased by France), live animals and vegetables (principally cow-peas and onions). The principal imports in that year were food and live animals (22.2% of total imports, of which around one-half was accounted for by cereals and cereal preparations), machinery and transport equipment, refined petroleum products and fixed vegetable oils and fats (notably palm oil).

Niger's overall budget deficit for 2006 was estimated at 768.8m. francs CFA (equivalent to 22.6% of GDP). Niger's total external debt was US $1,972m. at the end of 2005, of which $1,771m. was long-term public debt. Consumer prices increased by an annual average of 2.1% during 1996–2006. Consumer prices increased by 7.9% in 2005 but remained constant in 2006. Some 64,987 people were registered as unemployed in 2001.

Niger is a member of numerous regional organizations, including the Economic Community of West African States (see p. 232), the West African organs of the Franc Zone (see p. 307), the Conseil de l'Entente (see p. 412), the Lake Chad Basin Commission (see p. 413), the Liptako–Gourma Integrated Development Authority (see p. 413), the Niger Basin Authority (see p. 413) and the Permanent Inter-State Committee on Drought Control in the Sahel (see p. 414).

Niger is one of the world's poorest countries, and has consistently been among the lowest ranking countries in the United Nations Development Programme's Human Development Report, while literacy levels are also among the lowest in the world. Niger's narrow export base, which is dominated by uranium, and political instability have adversely affected economic performance, and most major creditors withdrew support after the military take-over that followed the death of President Maïnassara in 1999. Following the restoration of civilian rule, France resumed aid and debt relief to Niger in early 2000, and in December the IMF and the World Bank announced that Niger would receive US $890m. in debt-service relief under the enhanced framework of the initiative for heavily indebted poor countries. Also in December the IMF announced the approval of a three-year loan, worth $76m., for Niger under the Poverty Reduction and Growth Facility (PRGF); in November 2003 the IMF extended this arrangement until the end of June 2004, and in January 2005 an additional PRGF arrangement, worth $10m. over three years, was concluded. The IMF completed a fifth review of this arrangement in November 2007, enabling the release of a further $1.5m. in aid. (The Fund also extended the existing PGRF, which was thereby scheduled to reach completion in May 2008.) Also in November 2007 the Government of Niger signed an agreement with the People's Republic of China securing around $5.3m. for use in rural development and the rehabilitation of infrastructure. Meanwhile, in July 2005 Niger was among 18 countries to be granted 100% debt relief on multilateral debt agreed by the Group of Eight leading industrialized nations (G-8), subject to the approval of the lender. A Poverty Reduction Strategy Paper (PRSP), approved in 2007, and covering the period 2008–11, was expected to inform the content of the next PRGF (due in May 2008). In a mission statement published March 2008, the IMF commended the authorities for its adherence to fiscal targets, particularly with regards to revenue collection, which had been augmented by the implementation of a 19% value-added tax in 2005, and by widespread allocation of mining concessions in 2007. However, the Fund advised that expenditure needed to be increased in most areas and, moreover, that a larger budgetary outlay be allocated to security. Real GDP growth of 3.2% was estimated by the IMF for 2007, with slightly increased levels of growth anticipated in both 2008 and 2009.

Education

Education is available free of charge, and is officially compulsory for eight years between the ages of seven and 15 years. Primary education begins at the age of seven and lasts for six

NIGER

years. Secondary education begins at the age of 13 years, and comprises a four-year cycle followed by a three-year cycle. According to UNESCO estimates, primary enrolment in 2003/04 included 39% of children in the appropriate age-group (boys 46%; girls 32%). Secondary enrolment in that year included only 7% of the relevant age-group (boys 8%; girls 5%). The Abdou Moumouni University (formerly the University of Niamey) was inaugurated in 1973, and the Islamic University of Niger, at Say (to the south of the capital), was opened in 1987. Some 7,300 students were enrolled at those institutions in 2004/05. In December 2001 the Assemblée nationale approved legislation providing for the introduction of teaching in all local languages, with the aim of improving the literacy rate. Expenditure on education in 2000 was 32,500m. francs CFA, representing 15.5% of total spending.

Public Holidays

2008: 1 January (New Year's Day), 10 January*† (Islamic New Year), 20 March* (Mouloud, Birth of the Prophet), 24 March (Easter Monday), 24 April (National Concord Day), 1 May (Labour Day), 3 August (Independence Day), 1 October* (Id al-Fitr, end of Ramadan), 9 December* (Tabaski, Feast of the Sacrifice), 18 December (Republic Day), 29 December*† (Islamic New Year).

2009: 1 January (New Year's Day), 9 March* (Mouloud, Birth of the Prophet), 13 April (Easter Monday), 24 April (National Concord Day), 1 May (Labour Day), 3 August (Independence Day), 20 September* (Id al-Fitr, end of Ramadan), 27 November* (Tabaski, Feast of the Sacrifice), 18 December (Republic Day), 18 December* (Islamic New Year).

* These holidays are dependent on the Islamic lunar calendar and may vary by one or two days from the dates given.

† This festival occurs twice (marking the start of the Islamic years AH 1429 and 1430) within the same Gregorian year.

Weights and Measures

The metric system is in force.

Statistical Survey

Source (unless otherwise stated): Institut national de la Statistique, Immeuble sis à la Rue Sirba, derrière la Présidence de la république, BP 720, Niamey; tel. 20-72-35-60; fax 20-72-21-74; e-mail insniger@ins.ne; internet www.stat-niger.org.

Area and Population

AREA, POPULATION AND DENSITY

Area (sq km)	1,267,000*
Population (census results)	
20 May 1988	7,248,100
20 May 2001	
Males	5,516,588
Females	5,543,703
Total	11,060,291
Population (official estimates at mid-year)	
2004	12,224,822
2005	12,628,241
2006	13,044,973
Density (per sq km) at mid-2006	10.3

* 489,191 sq miles.

ETHNIC GROUPS
(2001 census, Nigerien citizens only)

	Population	%
Hausa	6,069,731	55.36
Djerma-Sonraï	2,300,874	20.99
Tuareg	1,016,883	9.27
Peulh	935,517	8.53
Kanouri-Manga	513,116	4.68
Toubou	42,172	0.38
Arab	40,085	0.37
Gourmantché	39,797	0.36
Others	5,951	0.05
Total	**10,964,126**	**100.00**

ADMINISTRATIVE DIVISIONS
(mid-year estimates, 2006)

Agadez	379,355	Niamey (city)	834,987
Diffa	408,789	Tahoua	2,326,720
Dosso	1,776,079	Tillabéri	2,228,574
Maradi	2,636,935	Zinder	2,453,534

PRINCIPAL TOWNS
(population at 2001 census)

Niamey (capital)	707,951	Agadez	78,289
Zinder	170,575	Tahoua	73,002
Maradi	148,017	Arlit	69,435

Mid-2007 (incl. suburbs, UN estimate): Niamey 915,000 (Source: UN, *World Urbanization Prospects: The 2007 Revision*).

BIRTHS AND DEATHS
(annual averages, UN estimates)

	1990–95	1995–2000	2000–05
Birth rate (per 1,000)	55.4	53.8	51.2
Death rate (per 1,000)	21.1	18.3	15.6

Source: UN, *World Population Prospects: The 2006 Revision*.

Expectation of life (years at birth, WHO estimates): 41.7 (males 42.2; females 41.2) in 2005 (Source: WHO, *World Health Statistics*).

EMPLOYMENT
('000 persons aged 10 years and over, 2002, official estimates)

	Males	Females	Total
Agriculture, hunting, forestry and fishing	2,366	401	2,767
Mining and quarrying	8	2	10
Manufacturing	48	64	112
Electricity, gas and water	3	0	3
Construction	20	0	20
Trade, restaurants and hotels	149	197	346
Transport, storage and communications	21	0	21
Financing, insurance, real estate and business services	2	0	2
Community, social and personal services	149	46	195
Total	**2,766**	**710**	**3,476**

2001 census (persons aged 10 years and over): Total employed 4,015,951 (males 2,706,910, females 1,309,041), Unemployed 64,987 (males 49,437, females 15,550); Economically active population 4,080,938 (males 2,756,347, females 1,324,591).

Mid-2005 (estimates in '000): Agriculture, etc. 5,635; Total labour force 6,515 (Source: FAO).

NIGER

Health and Welfare

KEY INDICATORS

Total fertility rate (children per woman, 2005)	7.7
Under-5 mortality rate (per 1,000 live births, 2005)	256
HIV/AIDS (% of persons aged 15–49, 2005)	1.1
Physicians (per 1,000 head, 2004)	0.03
Hospital beds (per 1,000 head, 1998)	0.12
Health expenditure (2004): US $ per head (PPP)	25.9
Health expenditure (2004): % of GDP	4.2
Health expenditure (2004): public (% of total)	52.5
Access to water (% of persons, 2004)	47
Access to sanitation (% of persons, 2004)	13
Human Development Index (2005): ranking	174
Human Development Index (2005): value	0.374

For sources and definitions, see explanatory note on p. vi.

Agriculture

PRINCIPAL CROPS
('000 metric tons)

	2004	2005	2006
Wheat	9.0*	9.0*	7.8
Rice (paddy)	80.0	60.0	65.7
Maize	4	1	1†
Millet	2,038	2,652	3,200*
Sorghum	600	944	800*
Potatoes†	7.1	8.6	8.6
Sweet potatoes†	43	43	43
Cassava (Manioc)†	125	127	127
Sugar cane†	220	220	220
Dry cow-peas	339.5	586.1	690.6
Groundnuts (in shell)	159.0	139.1	139.3
Sesame seed	35†	40†	44
Cottonseed†	5	5	5
Cabbages†	145	159	159
Lettuce and chicory†	48	52	52
Tomatoes†	122	124	124
Chillies and green peppers†	21	23	23
Dry onions	304	322	322†
Garlic†	9	10	10
Green beans†	23	23	23
Carrots†	20	22	22
Dates†	7.8	7.9	7.9
Tobacco (leaves)	0.9*	1.0†	1.0†

* Unofficial figure.
† FAO estimate(s).

Aggregate production ('000 metric tons, may include official, semi-official or estimated data): Total cereals 2,732 in 2004, 3,669 in 2005, 4,077 in 2006; Total roots and tubers 175 in 2004, 179 in 2005, 179 in 2006; Total vegetables (incl. melons) 741 in 2004, 786 in 2005, 786 in 2006; Total pulses 362 in 2004, 609 in 2005, 713 in 2006.

Source: FAO.

LIVESTOCK
('000 head, year ending September, FAO estimates)

	2001	2002	2003
Cattle	2,260	2,260	2,260
Sheep	4,500	4,500	4,500
Goats	6,900	6,900	6,900
Pigs	39	40	40
Horses	105	105	106
Asses	580	580	580
Camels	415	415	420
Chickens	24,000	24,500	25,000

2004–05: Figures assumed to be unchanged from 2003 (FAO estimates).
2006: Cattle 2,430; Sheep 4,900; Goats 7,700; Pigs 40; Horses 106; Asses 580; Camels 439; Chickens 25,000.
Source: FAO.

Statistical Survey

LIVESTOCK PRODUCTS
('000 metric tons, FAO estimates)

	2002	2003	2004
Game meat	15	15	15
Horse meat	0.6	0.7	0.7
Other equine meat	1.6	1.8	1.8
Chicken meat	28.4	29.0	29.0
Hen eggs	10.6	10.6	10.6

2005–06: Figures assumed to be unchanged from 2004 (FAO estimates), apart from chicken meat, with estimated production of 30,200 metric tons in both years.

Source: FAO.

Forestry

ROUNDWOOD REMOVALS
('000 cubic metres, excl. bark, FAO estimates)

	2004	2005	2006
Industrial wood	411	411	411
Fuel wood	8,596	8,806	9,010
Total	9,007	9,217	9,421

Source: FAO.

SAWNWOOD PRODUCTION
('000 cubic metres, incl. railway sleepers, FAO estimates)

	1991	1992	1993
Total (all broadleaved)	0	1	4

1994–2006: Figures assumed to be unchanged from 1993 (FAO estimates).
Source: FAO.

Fishing

(metric tons, live weight)

	2003	2004	2005
Capture (freshwater fishes)	55,860	51,466	50,018
Aquaculture	40	40	40
Total catch	55,900	51,506	50,058

Source: FAO.

Mining

('000 metric tons, unless otherwise indicated)

	2003	2004	2005
Hard coal	188.9	200.4	182.1
Tin (metric tons)*†	5	4	14
Uranium (metric tons)*	3,143	3,273	3,093
Gold (kg)	34.0†	1,531.3	4,922
Gypsum	17.8†	34.9	17.4

* Data refer to the metal content of ore.
† Artisanal production only.

NIGER

Statistical Survey

Industry

SELECTED PRODUCTS
('000 metric tons, unless otherwise indicated)

	2003	2004	2005
Raw sugar ('000 metric tons)*	22.0	n.a.	n.a.
Cement	63.7	59.2	83.4
Soap	10.4	10.2	9.4
Textile fabrics (million metres)	5.6	4.0	2.0
Beer ('000 bottles)	116.5	103.5	94.9
Electric energy (million kWh)	45.8	n.a.	n.a.

* FAO estimates.

Source: mostly IMF, *Niger: Selected Issues and Statistical Appendix* (January 2007).

Finance

CURRENCY AND EXCHANGE RATES

Monetary Units
100 centimes = 1 franc de la Communauté financière africaine (CFA).

Sterling, Dollar and Euro Equivalents (31 December 2007)
£1 sterling = 892.702 francs CFA;
US $1 = 445.593 francs CFA;
€1 = 655.957 francs CFA;
10,000 francs CFA = £11.20 = $22.44 = €15.24.

Average Exchange Rate (francs CFA per US $)
2005   527.468
2006   522.890
2007   479.267

Note: An exchange rate of 1 French franc = 50 francs CFA, established in 1948, remained in force until January 1994, when the CFA franc was devalued by 50%, with the exchange rate adjusted to 1 French franc = 100 francs CFA. This relationship to French currency remained in effect with the introduction of the euro on 1 January 1999. From that date, accordingly, a fixed exchange rate of €1 = 655.957 francs CFA has been in operation.

BUDGET
('000 million francs CFA, estimates)

Revenue*	2004	2005	2006
Tax revenue	167.6	181.3	203.8
Non-tax revenue	1.4	4.9	38.5
Annexed budgets and special accounts	3.9	2.8	4.9
Statistical discrepancy	1.1	—	—
Total	173.8	189.0	247.2

Expenditure†	2004	2005	2006
Current expenditure	172.7	165.3	174.2
Wages and salaries	59.2	63.0	68.0
Materials and supplies	50.3	43.6	47.4
Subsidies and transfers	38.2	31.9	43.5
Interest	8.1	10.1	4.9
Capital expenditure	144.0	193.3	182.6
Total	316.7	358.6	356.8

* Excluding grants received ('000 million francs CFA, estimates): 89.2 in 2004; 134.1 in 2005; 878.4 in 2006.

† Excluding net lending ('000 million francs CFA): 0.9 in 2004; −0.2 in 2005; 0.0 in 2006.

Source: IMF, *Niger: Fourth Review Under the Three-Year Arrangement Under the Poverty Reduction and Growth Facility, and Request for Waiver and Modification of Performance Criteria - Staff Report; Staff Statement and Supplements; Press Release on the Executive Board Discussion; and Statement by the Executive Director for Niger* (July 2007).

INTERNATIONAL RESERVES
(US $ million at 31 December, excl. gold)

	2004	2005	2006
IMF special drawing rights	0.9	0.3	0.1
Reserve position in IMF	13.3	12.3	13.0
Foreign exchange	243.7	236.9	357.8
Total	258.0	249.5	370.9

Source: IMF, *International Financial Statistics*.

MONEY SUPPLY
('000 million francs CFA at 31 December)

	2004	2005	2006
Currency outside banks	96.8	108.1	133.1
Demand deposits at deposit money banks*	81.8	81.4	90.0
Checking deposits at post office	3.2	2.5	1.8
Total money (incl. others)*	181.9	192.2	225.4

* Excluding the deposits of public enterprises of an administrative or social nature.

Source: IMF, *International Financial Statistics*.

COST OF LIVING
(Consumer Price Index for Niamey, annual averages; base: 2000 = 100)

	2004	2005	2006
Food	105.1	120.7	118.4
Clothing	99.4	102.6	100.0
Rent	105.3	106.2	107.5
All items (incl. others)	105.2	113.5	113.6

Source: ILO.

NATIONAL ACCOUNTS

Expenditure on the Gross Domestic Product
(US $ million at current prices)

	2004	2005	2006
Government final consumption expenditure	498.41	485.50	521.33
Household final consumption expenditure	2,193.04	2,507.15	2,656.68
Gross capital formation	409.95	608.80	592.03
Total domestic expenditure	3,101.40	3,601.45	3,770.04
Exports of goods and services	530.11	672.84	684.79
Less Imports of goods and services	851.96	1,047.65	1,051.23
GDP in market prices	2,779.55	3,226.64	3,403.60

Source: African Development Bank.

Gross Domestic Product by Economic Activity
('000 million francs CFA at current prices)

	2003	2004	2005
Agriculture, hunting, forestry and fishing	614.6	553.8	718.6
Mining and quarrying	29.7	31.4	30.6
Manufacturing	90.8	94.1	97.4
Electricity, gas and water supply	19.2	18.0	18.9
Construction	36.3	39.3	41.6
Wholesale and retail trade Repair of motor vehicles, motorcycles and personal and household goods	172.9 / 31.8	182.1 / 34.3	200.6 / 35.6
Hotels and restaurants	20.9	23.1	24.3
Transport, storage and communication	78.1	88.1	90.2
Posts and telecommunications	15.8	18.4	24.3

NIGER

Statistical Survey

—continued	2003	2004	2005
Financial activities	13.5	17.9	20.9
Real estate and renting	52.2	55.6	57.4
Public administration and defence; compulsory social security	149.0	145.3	151.0
Other services	59.4	64.5	70.3
Sub-total	1,384.2	1,365.9	1,581.7
Less Financial intermediation services indirectly measured	10.4	12.7	14.2
Gross value added in basic prices	1,374.0	1,352.3	1,567.4
Taxes, *less* subsidies, on products	97.7	115.8	134.5
GDP at market prices	1,471.7	1,468.1	1,702.0
GDP at constant 1987 prices	1,042.0	1,031.9	1,103.7

BALANCE OF PAYMENTS
('000 million francs CFA)

	2003	2004	2005
Exports of goods f.o.b.	204.5	230.7	304.1
Imports of goods f.o.b.	−283.9	−311.5	−398.9
Trade balance	−79.4	−80.8	−94.8
Services (net)	−75.1	−89.2	−102.9
Balance on goods and services	−154.5	−170.0	−197.7
Income (net)	−15.2	−6.8	−7.6
Balance on goods, services and income	−169.7	−176.8	−205.3
Private unrequited transfers (net)	9.7	16.2	18.0
Public unrequited transfers (net)	32.9	38.6	63.2
Current balance	−127.1	−122.0	−124.1
Capital account (net)	46.3	203.1	71.8
Direct investment (net)	6.7	7.0	7.8
Portfolio investment (net)	1.5	2.5	14.5
Other investment (net)	38.2	−91.3	50.5
Net errors and omissions	69.5	−9.6	−9.0
Overall balance	42.5	−10.3	11.5

Source: Banque centrale des états de l'Afrique de l'ouest.

External Trade

PRINCIPAL COMMODITIES
(distribution by SITC, US $ million)

Imports c.i.f.	2001	2002	2003
Food and live animals	105.8	113.7	123.9
Dairy products and birds' eggs	11.2	11.9	13.2
Milk and cream	10.8	11.6	12.8
Milk and cream, preserved, concentrated or sweetened	10.6	11.4	12.5
Cereals and cereal preparations	60.4	66.8	59.1
Rice, semi-milled or wholly milled	39.4	47.5	37.7
Rice, semi-milled or milled (unbroken)	38.2	47.5	36.5
Meal of flour of wheat or of meslin	11.2	12.7	13.0
Flour of wheat or of meslin	11.2	12.7	10.9
Sugar, sugar preparations and honey	14.1	11.3	24.8
Refined sugar, etc.	13.5	10.5	23.6
Beverages and tobacco	15.2	20.6	22.0
Cigarettes	13.3	19.2	19.5
Crude materials (inedible) except fuel	9.8	18.2	30.9
Textile fibres (not wool tops) and their wastes (not in yarn)	2.2	10.6	21.4
Bulk textile waste, old clothing, traded in bulk or in bales	1.9	10.4	20.8
Mineral fuels, lubricants, etc., (incl. electric current)	40.7	59.2	94.5
Petroleum, petroleum products, etc.	32.7	48.6	80.9
Petroleum products, refined	32.5	46.4	76.3

Imports c.i.f.—continued	2001	2002	2003
Animal and vegetable oils, fats and waxes	22.3	29.4	41.1
Fixed vegetable oils and fats	21.2	27.8	38.1
Palm oil	16.4	23.0	32.6
Chemicals and related products	29.5	36.9	45.2
Medicinal and pharmaceutical products	9.3	12.0	16.7
Basic manufactures	34.5	56.8	67.1
Textile yarn, fabrics, made-up articles, etc.	6.6	19.7	21.2
Cotton fabrics, woven (not incl. narrow or special fabrics)	3.1	15.0	16.5
Machinery and transport equipment	48.7	76.1	109.6
Telecommunications, sound recording and reproducing equipment	3.6	15.3	22.9
Other telecommunications equipment, parts and accessories, etc.	2.8	14.6	21.8
Electrical line telephonic and telegraphic apparatus	1.1	13.1	18.3
Road vehicles	20.9	25.1	38.0
Passenger motor vehicles (excl. buses)	12.7	13.5	17.7
Miscellaneous manufactured articles	18.0	20.1	24.1
Total (incl. others)	324.5	430.9	558.4

Exports f.o.b.	2001	2002	2003
Food and live animals	61.3	71.6	58.9
Live animals chiefly for food	43.8	39.0	40.8
Animals of the bovine species (incl. buffaloes), live	16.0	13.5	16.7
Sheep and goats, live	22.4	19.0	18.5
Fish, crustaceans and molluscs, and preparations thereof	4.3	6.3	4.1
Vegetables and fruit	12.2	24.7	12.3
Vegetables, fresh or simply preserved; roots and tubers	11.4	23.8	11.8
Other fresh or chilled vegetables	8.4	21.2	9.3
Alliaceous vegetables, fresh or chilled	5.8	18.0	7.7
Beverages and tobacco	0.1	9.8	5.2
Cigarettes	—	9.7	4.8
Crude materials (inedible) except fuels	88.2	98.8	124.0
Textile fibres (not wool tops) and their wastes (not in yarn)	0.3	6.8	7.3
Ores and concentrates of uranium and thorium	86.2	90.2	113.0
Basic manufactures	1.3	12.3	12.6
Fabrics, woven, 85% plus of cotton, bleached, dyed, etc., or otherwise finished	0.5	11.4	11.8
Total (incl. others)	154.0	200.9	209.1

Source: UN, *International Trade Statistics Yearbook*.

PRINCIPAL TRADING PARTNERS
(US $ million)

Imports c.i.f.	2001	2002	2003
Bahrain	2.9	10.7	7.2
Belgium	3.6	5.9	8.1
Benin	6.3	9.8	14.7
Brazil	2.5	8.3	17.1
Burkina Faso	7.7	4.8	11.1
China, People's Republic	20.9	39.2	52.4
Côte d'Ivoire	47.3	64.2	74.6
France	62.2	67.2	81.6
Germany	4.3	5.8	10.2
Ghana	6.4	8.1	8.1
India	1.7	17.5	18.0

Imports c.i.f.—continued	2001	2002	2003
Italy	4.7	7.3	6.5
Japan	15.6	20.5	25.1
Netherlands	5.3	12.2	12.2
Nigeria	33.3	30.5	40.3
South Africa	1.8	2.5	25.4
Spain	2.6	4.6	8.1
Togo	8.7	13.5	15.2
Tunisia	4.0	7.8	9.5
United Kingdom	7.1	11.5	17.5
USA	18.9	36.1	46.0
Total (incl. others)	324.5	430.9	558.4

Exports f.o.b.	2001	2002	2003
Algeria	0.3	0.6	0.5
Benin	1.7	5.1	2.2
Burkina Faso	0.8	1.0	1.5
Chad	0.6	0.1	0.1
China, People's Republic	—	0.2	0.1
Côte d'Ivoire	2.3	7.0	5.5
France (incl. Monaco)	56.2	65.1	76.3
Germany	0.1	0.1	0.2
Ghana	1.9	9.0	3.9
Japan	25.4	23.4	31.1
Libya	0.2	0.7	1.3
Mali	0.2	0.2	0.2
Netherlands	—	1.1	3.9
Nigeria	57.1	64.4	57.5
South Africa	—	—	0.7
Spain	5.8	6.1	8.4
Switzerland-Liechtenstein	0.2	0.1	0.1
Togo	0.1	1.1	0.3
United Arab Emirates	—	—	0.7
United Kingdom	—	1.5	2.6
USA	0.5	13.1	9.5
Venezuela	—	0.6	—
Total (incl. others)	154.0	200.9	209.1

Source: UN, *International Trade Statistics Yearbook*.

Transport

ROAD TRAFFIC
(estimates, motor vehicles in use)

	1994	1995	1996
Passenger cars	38,610	37,620	38,220
Lorries and vans	13,160	14,100	15,200

Source: IRF, *World Road Statistics*.

CIVIL AVIATION
(traffic on scheduled services)*

	1999	2000	2001
Kilometres flown (million)	3	3	1
Passengers carried ('000)	84	77	46
Passenger-km (million)	235	216	130
Total ton-km (million)	36	32	19

* Including an apportionment of the traffic of Air Afrique.

Source: UN, *Statistical Yearbook*.

Tourism

FOREIGN TOURIST ARRIVALS BY ORIGIN*

	2004†	2005	2006
Africa	38,000	37,926	36,199
America	2,500	3,150	4,223
Asia	1,500	2,835	3,017
Europe	14,500	17,649	16,893
France	12,000	14,588	13,971
Total (incl. others)	57,000	63,451	60,332

* Figures refer to arrivals at national borders.
† Rounded figures.

Receipts from tourism (US $ million, excl. passenger transport): 28 in 2003; 31 in 2004; 34 in 2005.

Source: World Tourism Organization.

Communications Media

	2003	2004	2005
Telephones ('000 main lines in use)	23.0	24.1	24.0
Mobile cellular telephones ('000 subscribers)	59.3	148.3	299.9
Personal computers ('000 in use)*	8	9	10
Internet users ('000)*	19.0	24.0	24.0
Broadband subscribers	—	100	200

* Estimates.

2006: Internet users ('000) 40.0.

Television receivers ('000 in use): 395 in 2000.

Radio receivers ('000 in use): 680 in 1997.

Facsimile machines (number in use): 327 in 1995.

Daily newspapers: 1 (average circulation 2,000 copies) in 1996; 1 (average circulation 2,000 copies) in 1997; 1 (average circulation 2,000 copies) in 1998.

Non-daily newspapers: 5 (average circulation 14,000 copies) in 1996.

Books published (first editions): titles 5; copies ('000) 11 in 1991.

Sources: UNESCO, *Statistical Yearbook*; UNESCO Institute for Statistics; UN, *Statistical Yearbook*; International Telecommunication Union.

Education

(2005/06, unless otherwise indicated)

	Institutions	Teachers	Students
Pre-primary	347	914	24,287
Primary	8,301*	28,163	1,126,075
Secondary	367	4,130	210,626
Tertiary*	7	278	4,953
University	1	284	8,710

* 2004/05 figure(s).

Adult literacy rate (UNESCO estimates): 28.7% (males 42.9%; females 15.1%) in 2005 (Source: UNESCO Institute for Statistics).

Directory

The Constitution

Following the death of President Ibrahim Baré Maïnassara, on 9 April 1999, a military Conseil de réconciliation nationale (CRN) was formed to exercise executive and legislative authority during a transitional period prior to the restoration of elected organs of government. A new Constitution, of what was to be designated the Fifth Republic, was approved by national referendum on 18 July 1999. The Constitution of the Fifth Republic, promulgated on 9 August, envisages a balance of powers between the President, Government and legislative Assemblée nationale. The President, who is elected by universal adult suffrage, is Head of State, and is accorded 'broad ordinary and arbitral powers'. The Government, under a Prime Minister appointed by the President, is responsible to the Assemblée nationale, which is competent to remove the Prime Minister by vote of censure. The Assemblée nationale is similarly elected by direct adult suffrage. The new President and legislature were inaugurated in December 1999.

Enshrined in the Constitution is a clause granting immunity from prosecution for all those involved in the *coups d'état* of January 1996 and April 1999. Legislation to this effect was adopted by the Assemblée nationale in January 2000.

Among regulatory bodies provided for in the Constitution are the Conseil supérieur de la communication, responsible for the broadcasting and communications sector, and the Conseil supérieur de la défense nationale, which advises the Head of State on defence matters.

The Government

HEAD OF STATE

President: Col (retd) MAMADOU TANDJA (inaugurated 22 December 1999, re-elected 4 December 2004).

COUNCIL OF MINISTERS
(March 2008)

Prime Minister: SEYNI OUMAROU.
Minister of State, Minister of the Interior: ALBADÉ ABOUBA.
Minister of Foreign Affairs, Co-operation and African Integration: AÏCHATOU MINDAOUDOU.
Minister of the Economy and Finance: ALI MAHAMANE LAMINE ZEINE.
Minister of Agricultural Development: MAHAMAN MOUSSA.
Minister of Youth and Sports: MOUSSA ABDOURAHAMANE SEYDOU.
Minister of Town Planning, Living Conditions and the Land Register: AÏSSA DIALLO ABDOULAYE.
Minister of Mines and Energy: MOHAMED ABDOULAHI.
Minister of Secondary and Higher Education, Research and Technology: Prof. SIDIKOU OUMAROU.
Minister of Communication, Spokesperson for the Government: MOHAMED BEN OMAR.
Minister of the Civil Service and Labour: KANDA SIPTEY.
Minister of Culture, the Arts and Leisure, responsible for the Promotion of Entrepreneurship in the Arts: OUMAROU HADARY.
Minister of Population and Social Reform: BOUKARI ZILA MAHAMADOU.
Minister of National Education: Dr OUSMANE SAMBA MAMADOU.
Minister responsible for Relations with State Institutions: SALIFOU MADOU KELZOU.
Minister of the Environment and Anti-desertification: MOHAMED AKOTEY.
Minister of National Competitiveness and the Reduction of the High Cost of Living: ABDOU DAOUDA.
Minister responsible for Religious Affairs and Humanitarian Action: LABO ISSAKA.
Minister of Infrastructure: LAMIDO MOUMOUNI HAROUNA.
Minister of Trade, Industry and Normalization: HALIDOU BADJE.
Minister of National Defence: JIDDA HAMADOU.
Minister of Justice, Attorney-General: DAGRA MAHAMADOU.
Minister of Transport: KINDO HAMANI.
Minister of Tourism and Crafts: AMADOU AISSA SIDDO.
Minister of Land Management and Community Development: SADÉ SOULEY.
Minister of Public Health: ISSA LAMINE.
Minister of Animal Resources: ISSIAH KATO.
Minister for the Promotion of Young Entrepreneurs and the Reform of Public Enterprises: SALOU GOBI.
Minister of Vocational and Technical Training: MAIZAMA HADIZA.
Minister for the Promotion of Women and the Protection of Children: BARRY BIBATA NIANDOU.
Minister of African Integration and Nationals Living Abroad: SEYDOU HACHIMOU.
Minister of Water Resources: AMINOU TASSIOU.

MINISTRIES

Office of the President: BP 550, Niamey; tel. 20-72-23-80; fax 20-72-33-96; internet www.delgi.ne/presidence.
Office of the Prime Minister: BP 893, Niamey; tel. 20-72-26-99; fax 20-73-58-59.
Ministry of Agricultural Development: BP 12091, Niamey; tel. 20-73-35-41; fax 20-73-20-08.
Ministry of Animal Resources: BP 12091, Niamey; tel. 20-73-79-59; fax 20-73-31-86.
Ministry of Basic Education and Literacy: BP 557, Niamey; tel. 20-72-28-33; fax 20-72-21-05; e-mail scdameb@intnet.ne.
Ministry of Capital Works: BP 403, Niamey; tel. 20-73-53-57; fax 20-72-21-71.
Ministry of the Civil Service and Labour: BP 11107, Niamey; tel. 20-73-22-31; fax 20-73-61-69; e-mail sani.yakouba@caramail.com.
Ministry of Culture, the Arts and Communication: BP 452, Niamey; tel. 20-72-28-74; fax 20-73-36-85.
Ministry of the Economy and Finance: BP 389, Niamey; tel. 20-72-23-74; fax 20-73-59-34.
Ministry of Foreign Affairs, Co-operation and African Integration: BP 396, Niamey; tel. 20-72-29-07; fax 20-73-52-31.
Ministry of the Interior and Decentralization: BP 622, Niamey; tel. 20-72-32-62; fax 20-72-21-76.
Ministry of Justice: BP 466, Niamey; tel. 20-72-31-31; fax 20-72-37-77.
Ministry of Land Management and Community Development: BP 403, Niamey; tel. 20-73-53-57; fax 20-72-21-71.
Ministry of Mines and Energy: BP 11700, Niamey; tel. 20-73-45-82; fax 20-73-28-12.
Ministry of National Defence: BP 626, Niamey; tel. 20-72-20-76; fax 20-72-40-78.
Ministry of Population and Social Reform: BP 11286, Niamey; tel. 20-72-23-30; fax 20-73-61-65.
Ministry of Privatization and the Restructuring of Enterprises: Immeuble CCCP, BP 862, Niamey; tel. 20-73-27-50; fax 20-73-59-91; e-mail ccpp@intnet.ne.
Ministry of Professional and Technical Training: BP 628, Niamey; tel. 20-72-26-20; fax 20-72-40-40.
Ministry for the Promotion of Women and the Protection of Children: BP 11286, Niamey; tel. 20-72-23-30; fax 20-73-61-65.
Ministry of Public Health and the Fight against Epidemics: BP 623, Niamey; tel. 20-72-28-08; fax 20-73-35-70.
Ministry of Secondary and Higher Education, Research and Technology: BP 628, Niamey; tel. 20-72-26-20; fax 20-72-40-40; e-mail mesnt@intnet.ne.
Ministry of Tourism and Crafts: BP 480, Niamey; tel. 20-73-65-22; fax 20-72-23-87.
Ministry of Town Planning, Living Conditions and the Land Register: BP 403, Niamey; tel. 20-73-53-57; fax 20-72-21-71.
Ministry of Trade, Industry and the Promotion of the Private Sector: BP 480, Niamey; tel. 20-73-29-74; fax 20-73-21-50; e-mail nicom@intnet.ne.
Ministry of Transport: BP 12130, Niamey; tel. 20-72-28-21; fax 20-73-36-85.
Ministry of Water Resources, the Environment and Anti-desertification: BP 257, Niamey; tel. 20-73-47-22; fax 20-72-40-15.
Ministry of Youth, Sports and the Games of La Francophonie: BP 215, Niamey; tel. 20-72-32-35; fax 20-72-23-36.

President and Legislature

PRESIDENT

Presidential Election, First Round, 16 November 2004

Candidate	Votes	% of votes
Mamadou Tandja (MNSD—Nassara)	991,764	40.67
Mahamadou Issoufou (PNDS)	599,792	24.60
Mahamane Ousmane (CDS)	425,052	17.43
Cheiffou Amadou (RSD)	154,732	6.34
Moumouni Adamou Djermakoye (ANDP)	147,957	6.07
Hamid Algabid (RDP)	119,153	4.89
Total	**2,438,450**	**100.00**

NIGER

Directory

Second Round, 4 December 2004

Candidate	Votes	% of votes
Mamadou Tandja (MNSD—Nassara)	1,509,905	65.53
Mahamadou Issoufou (PNDS)	794,397	34.47
Total	2,304,302	100.00

LEGISLATURE

Assemblée nationale

pl. de la Concertation, BP 12234, Niamey; tel. 20-72-27-38; fax 20-72-43-08; e-mail an@assemblee.ne; internet www.assemblee.ne.

President: El Hadj MAHAMANE OUSMANE.

General Election, 4 December 2004

Party	Seats
Mouvement national pour la société de développement—Nassara (MNSD—Nassara)	47
Parti nigérien pour la démocratie et le socialisme—Tarayya (PNDS)	25*
Convention démocratique et social—Rahama (CDS)	22
Rassemblement social-démocratique—Gaskiya (RSD)	7
Rassemblement pour la démocratie et le progrès—Jama'a (RDP)	6
Alliance nigérienne pour la démocratie et le progrès social—Zaman Lahiya (ANDP)	5
Parti Social Démocrate du Niger—Alheri	1
Total	113

* Including eight seats won by parties running in coalition with the PNDS, namely the Parti nigérien pour l'autogestion (PNA), the Parti progressiste nigérien pour le rassemblement démocratique africain (PPN—RDA), the Union pour la démocratie et la République (UDR) and the Union nigérienne des indépendants (UNI).

Election Commission

Commission électorale nationale indépendante (CENI): Niamey; Chair. HAMIDOU SALIFOU KANE.

Political Organizations

In mid-2007 there were some 24 political parties registered in Niger, of which the following were among the most prominent:

Alliance nigérienne pour la démocratie et le progrès social—Zaman Lahiya (ANDP): Quartier Abidjan, Niamey; tel. 20-74-07-50; fmrly mem. of opposition Coordination des forces démocratiques (CFD); joined pro-Govt Alliance des forces démocratiques (AFD) in 2002; Leader Col (retd) MOUMOUNI ADAMOU DJERMAKOYE.

Alliance pour la démocratie et le progrès—Zumunci (ADP): Niamey; tel. 20-73-67-57; e-mail adp@zumunci.com; internet www.adpzumunci.com; f. 1992; Chair. ISSOUFOU BACHAR.

Convention démocratique et social—Rahama (CDS): BP 11973, Niamey; tel. 20-74-19-85; f. 1991; supports Govt of Hama Amadou; mem. of Alliance des forces démocratiques (AFD); Pres. MAHAMANE OUSMANE.

Mouvement national pour la société de développement—Nassara (MNSD—Nassara): rue Issa Beri 30, cnr blvd de Zarmaganda, porte 72, BP 881, Niamey; tel. 20-73-39-07; fax 20-72-41-74; e-mail presi@mnsd-nassara.org; internet www.mnsd.ne; f. 1988; sole party 1988–90; restyled as MNSD—Nassara in 1991; Chair. Col (retd) MAMADOU TANDJA; Pres. HAMA AMADOU.

Parti nigérien pour l'autogestion—al Umat (PNA): Quartier Zabarkian, Niamey; tel. 20-72-33-05; f. 1997; contested legislative elections in Dec. 2004 in coalition with the PNDS; Leader SANOUSSI JACKOU.

Parti nigérien pour la démocratie et le socialisme—Tarayya (PNDS): pl. Toumo, Niamey; tel. 20-74-48-78; f. 1990; mem. of Coordination des forces démocratiques (CFD); Sec.-Gen. MAHAMADOU ISSOUFOU.

Parti progressiste nigérien—Rassemblement démocratique africain (PPN—RDA): Quartier Sonni, Niamey; tel. 20-74-16-70; associated with the late Pres. Diori; mem. of Coordination des forces démocratiques (CFD); contested legislative elections in Dec. 2004 in coalition with the PNDS; Chair. ABDOULAYE DIORI.

Parti social-démocrate nigérien—Alheri (PSDN): tel. 20-72-28-52; Pres. LABO ISSAKA.

Rassemblement pour la démocratie et le progrès—Djamaa (RDP): pl. Toumo, Niamey; tel. 20-74-23-82; party of late Pres. Maïnassara; Chair. HAMID ALGABID; Sec.-Gen. MAHAMANE SOULEY LABI.

Rassemblement social-démocratique—Gaskiya (RSD): Quartier Poudrière, Niamey; tel. 20-74-00-90; f. 2004 following split in the CDS; Pres. CHEIFFOU AMADOU.

Rassemblement pour un Sahel vert—Ni'ima (RSV): BP 12515, Niamey; tel. and fax 20-74-11-25; e-mail agarba_99@yahoo.com; f. 1991; Pres. ADAMOU GARBA.

Union pour la démocratie et le progrès—Amici (UDP): supports Govt of Hama Amadou; mem. of Alliance des forces démocratiques (AFD); Leader ABDOULAYE TONDI.

Union pour la démocratie et le progrès social—Amana (UDPS): represents interests of Tuaregs; mem. of Coordination des forces démocratiques (CFD); Chair. RHISSA AG BOULA.

Union pour la démocratie et la République—Tabbat (UDR): Quartier Plateau, Niamey; f. 2002; contested legislative elections in Dec. 2004 in coalition with the PNDS; Pres. AMADOU BOUABACAR CISSÉ.

Union des forces populaires pour la démocratie et le progrès—Sawaba (UFPDP): Niamey; tel. 20-73-51-38; Leader IBRAHIM BAOUA SOULEY.

Union des Nigeriens indépendants (UNI): Quartier Zabarkan, Niamey; tel. 20-74-23-81; contested legislative elections in Dec. 2004 in coalition with the PNDS; Leader AMADOU DJIBO.

Union des patriotes démocratiques et progressistes—Shamuwa (UPDP): Niamey; tel. 20-74-12-59; Chair. Prof. ANDRÉ SALIFOU.

Union des socialistes nigériens—Talaka (USN): f. 2001 by mems of the UFPDP; Leader ISSOUFOU ASSOUMANE.

In March 2001 12 opposition parties, led by the PNDS, formed the **Coordination des forces démocratiques (CFD)** (Zabarkan, rue du SNEN, BP 5005, Niamey; tel. 20-74-05-69), while 17 parties loyal to Prime Minister Hama Amadou, headed by the MNSD, formed the **Alliance des forces démocratiques (AFD)**. In July 2002 the ANDP withdrew from the CFD and joined the AFD.

Diplomatic Representation

EMBASSIES IN NIGER

Algeria: route des Ambassades-Goudel, BP 142, Niamey; tel. 20-72-35-83; fax 20-72-35-93; Ambassador HAMID BOUKRIF.

Benin: BP 11544, Niamey; tel. 20-72-28-60; Ambassador TAÏROU MAMADOU DJAOUGA.

Chad: POB 12820, Niamey; tel. 20-75-34-64; fax 20-72-43-61; Ambassador YOUSSOUF MBODOU MBAMI.

China, People's Republic: BP 873, Niamey; tel. 20-72-32-83; fax 20-72-32-85; e-mail embchina@intnet.ne; Ambassador CHEN GONGLAI.

Cuba: rue Tillaberi, angle rue de la Cure Salée, face lycée Franco-Arabe, Plateau, BP 13886, Niamey; tel. 20-72-46-00; fax 20-72-39-32; e-mail embacuba@niger.cubaminrex.cu; Ambassador SERAFIN GIL RODRÍGUEZ VALDÉS.

Egypt: Terminus Rond-Point Grand Hôtel, BP 254, Niamey; tel. 20-73-33-55; fax 20-73-38-91; Ambassador MOHAMED MAHMOUD MOUSTAFA EL-ASHMAWI.

France: route de Tondibia, Quartier Yantala, BP 10660, Niamey; tel. 20-72-24-32; fax 20-72-25-18; e-mail webmestre@mail.com; internet www.ambafrance-ne.org; Ambassador FRANÇOIS PONGE.

Germany: 71 ave du Général de Gaulle, BP 629, Niamey; tel. 20-72-35-10; fax 20-72-39-85; e-mail amballny@intnet.ne; Ambassador HEIKE THIELE.

Iran: 11 rue de la Présidence, BP 10543, Niamey; tel. 20-72-21-98; fax 20-72-28-10; Ambassador MOHAMMAD AMIN NEJAD.

Korea, Democratic People's Republic: Niamey; Ambassador PAK SONG IL.

Libya: route de Goudel, BP 683, Niamey; tel. 20-72-40-19; fax 20-72-40-97; e-mail boukhari@intnet.ne; Ambassador BOUKHARI SALEM HODA.

Morocco: ave du Président Lubke, face Clinique Kaba, BP 12403, Niamey; tel. 20-73-40-84; fax 20-73-80-27; e-mail ambmang@intnet.ne; Ambassador MOHAMED JABER.

Nigeria: rue Goudel, BP 11130, Niamey; tel. 20-73-24-10; fax 20-73-35-00; e-mail embnig@intnet.ne; Ambassador Dr YAKUBU KWARI.

Pakistan: 90 rue YN 001, ave des Zarmakoye, Yantala Plateau, BP 10426, Niamey; tel. 20-75-32-57; fax 20-75-32-55; e-mail parepniamey@yahoo.com; internet www.brain.net.pk/~farata; Ambassador (vacant).

NIGER
Directory

Saudi Arabia: route de Tillabery, BP 339, Niamey; tel. 20-75-32-15; fax 20-75-24-42; e-mail neemb@mofa.gov.sa; Ambassador ABDUL KAREEM MOHAMMAD AL MALIKI.

USA: rue des Ambassades, BP 11201, Niamey; tel. 20-73-31-69; fax 20-73-55-60; e-mail NiameyPASN@state.gov; internet niamey.usembassy.gov; Ambassador BERNADETTE MARY ALLEN.

Judicial System

The Supreme Court was dissolved following the death of President Ibrahim Baré Maïnassara in April 1999, but was re-established following the return to constitutional order later in that year. In accordance with the Constitution of the Fifth Republic, promulgated in August 1999, a Constitutional Court was established to replace the former Constitutional Chamber of the Supreme Court.

High Court of Justice: Niamey; internet www.assemblee.ne/organes/hjc.htm; competent to indict the President of the Republic and all other state officials (past and present) in relation to all matters of state, including high treason; comprises seven perm. mems and three rotating mems; Pres. OUMAROU CISSE.

Supreme Court: Niamey; tel. 20-74-26-36; comprises three chambers; in 2002 the Government announced proposals to replace the Supreme Court with three separate courts: a Court of Cassation, a Council of State and an Audit Court; Pres. MAMADOU MALLAM AOUMI; Vice-Pres. SALIFOU FATIMATA BAZEYE; Pres. of the Administrative Chamber DILLE RABO; Pres. of the Judicial Chamber (vacant); Pres. of the Chamber of Audit and Budgetary Discipline SIKKOSO MORY OUSMANE; Prosecutor-Gen. MAHAMANE BOUKARY.

Constitutional Court: BP 10779, Niamey; tel. 20-72-30-81; fax 20-72-35-40; e-mail cconstit@intnet.ne; f. 1999; comprises a President, a Vice-President and five Councillors; Pres. SANI KOUTOUBI; Vice-Pres. ABDOU HASSAN.

Courts of First Instance: located at Niamey (with sub-divisions at Dosso and Tillabéri), Maradi, Tahoua (sub-divisions at Agadez, Arlit and Birni N'Konni) and Diffa (sub-division at Diffa).

Labour Courts: function at each Court of the First Instance and sub-division thereof.

Religion

It is estimated that some 95% of the population are Muslims, 0.5% are Christians and the remainder follow traditional beliefs.

ISLAM

The most influential Islamic groups in Niger are the Tijaniyya, the Senoussi and the Hamallists.

Association Islamique du Niger: Niamey; Dir CHEIKH OUMAROU ISMAEL.

CHRISTIANITY

The Roman Catholic Church

Niger comprises two dioceses, directly responsible to the Holy See. The Bishops participate in the Bishops' Conference of Burkina Faso and Niger (based in Ouagadougou, Burkina Faso). At 31 December 2005 there were an estimated 16,642 adherents in Niger.

Bishop of Maradi: Rt Rev. AMBROISE OUÉDRAOGO, Evêché, BP 447, Maradi; tel. and fax 20-41-03-30; fax 20-41-13-86; e-mail evechemi@intnet.ne.

Bishop of Niamey: Rt Rev. MICHEL CHRISTIAN CARTATÈGUY, Evêché, BP 10270, Niamey; tel. 20-73-32-59; fax 20-73-80-01; e-mail cartateguymi@voila.fr; internet www.multimania.com/cathoniger.

The Press

The published press expanded considerably in Niger after 1993, when the requirement to obtain prior authorization for each edition was lifted, although legislation continued to require that a copy of each publication be deposited at the office of the Procurator of the Republic. For the most part, however, economic difficulties have ensured that few publications have maintained a regular, sustained appearance. The following were among those newspapers and periodicals believed to be appearing regularly in early 2005:

L'Action: Quartier Yantala, Niamey; tel. 96-96-92-22; e-mail action_ne@yahoo.fr; internet www.tamtaminfo.com/action.pdf; f. 2003; fortnightly; popular newspaper intended for youth audience; Dir of Publication BOUSSADA BEN ALI; circ. 2,000 (2003).

L'Alternative: BP 10948, Niamey; tel. 20-74-24-39; fax 20-74-24-82; e-mail alter@intnet.ne; internet www.alternative.ne; f. 1994; weekly; in French and Hausa; Dir MOUSSA TCHANGARI; Editor-in-Chief ABDRAMANE OUSMANE.

Anfani: Immeuble DMK, rue du Damagaram, BP 2096, Niamey; tel. 20-74-08-80; fax 20-74-00-52; e-mail anfani@intnet.ne; f. 1992; 2 a month; Editor-in-Chief IBBO DADDY ABDOULAYE; circ. 3,000.

As-Salam: BP 451, Niamey; tel. 20-74-29-12; e-mail assa_lam@yahoo.fr; monthly; Dir IBBO DADDY ABDOULAYE.

Le Canard Déchaîné: BP 383, Niamey; tel. 93-92-66-64; satirical; weekly; Dir of Publication ABDOULAYE TIÉMOGO; Editor-in-Chief IBRAHIM MANZO.

Le Canard Libéré: BP 11631, Niamey; tel. 20-75-43-52; fax 20-75-39-89; e-mail canardlibere@caramail.com; satirical; weekly; Dir of Publication TRAORÉ DAOUDA AMADOU; Editorial Dir OUMAROU NALAN MOUSSA.

Le Démocrate: 21 rue 067, NB Terminus, BP 11064, Niamey; tel. 20-73-24-25; e-mail le_democrate@caramail.com; internet www.tamtaminfo.com/democrate.pdf; weekly; independent; f. 1992; Dir of Publication ALBERT CHAÏBOU; Editor-in-Chief OUSSEINI ISSA.

Les Echos du Sahel: Villa 4012, 105 Logements, BP 12750, Niamey; tel. and fax 20-74-32-17; e-mail ecosahel@intnet.ne; f. 1999; rural issues and devt; quarterly; Dir IBBO DADDY ABDOULAYE.

L'Enquêteur: BP 172, Niamey; tel. 93-90-18-74; e-mail lenqueteur@yahoo.fr; fortnightly; Publr TAHIROU GOURO; Editor IBRAHIM SOULEY.

Haské: BP 297, Niamey; tel. 20-74-18-44; fax 20-73-20-06; e-mail webmaster@planetafrique.com; internet www.haske.uni.cc; f. 1990; weekly; also Haské Magazine, quarterly; Dir CHEIKH IBRAHIM DIOP.

La Jeune Académie: BP 11989, Niamey; tel. 20-73-38-71; e-mail jeune.academie@caramail.com; monthly; Dir ABDOULAYE HASSOUMI GARBA.

Journal Officiel de la République du Niger: BP 116, Niamey; tel. 20-72-39-30; fax 20-72-39-43; f. 1960; fortnightly; govt bulletin; Man. Editor BONKOULA AMINATOU MAYAKI; circ. 800.

Libération: BP 10483, Niamey; tel. 96-97-96-22; f. 1995; weekly; Dir BOUBACAR DIALLO; circ. 1,000 (2003).

Matinfo: BP 11631, Niamey; tel. 20-75-43-52; fax 20-75-39-89; e-mail matinfo@caramail.com; daily; independent; Dir DAOUDA AMADOU TRAORÉ.

Nigerama: BP 11158, Niamey; tel. 20-74-08-09; e-mail anpniger@intnet.ne; quarterly; publ. by the Agence Nigérienne de Presse.

L'Opinion: BP 11116, Niamey; tel. 20-74-09-84; e-mail lopinion@dounia.ne; Dir ALZOUMA ZAKARI.

Le Regard: Niamey; tel. 20-73-84-07; e-mail le_regard@usa.net; Dir MAHAMADOU TOURÉ.

Le Républicain: Nouvelle Imprimerie du Niger, place du Petit Marché, BP 12015, Niamey; tel. 20-73-47-98; fax 20-73-41-42; e-mail webmasters@republicain-niger.com; internet www.republicain-niger.com; f. 1991; weekly; independent; Dir of Publication MAMANE ABOU; circ. 2,500.

La Roue de l'Histoire: Zabarkan, rue du SNEN, BP 5005, Niamey; tel. 20-74-05-69; internet www.tamtaminfo.com/roue.pdf; weekly; Propr SANOUSSI JACKOU; Dir ABARAD MOUDOUR ZAKARA.

Le Sahel Quotidien: BP 13182, ONEP, Niamey; tel. 20-73-34-87; fax 20-73-30-90; f. 1960; publ. by Office National d'Edition et de Presse; daily; Dir IBRAHIM MAMANE TANTAN; Editor-in-Chief ALASSANE ASOKOFARE; circ. 5,000; also Sahel-Dimanche, Sundays; circ. 3,000.

Sauyi: BP 10948, Niamey; tel. 20-74-24-39; fax 20-74-24-82; e-mail sarji@alternative.ne; fortnightly; Hausa; publ. by Groupe Alternative; Hausa; rural interest; Dir SAÏDOU ARJI.

Stadium: BP 10948, Niamey; tel. 20-74-08-80; e-mail kiabba@yahoo.fr; sports; 2 a month; Dir ABDOU TIKIRÉ.

Le Témoin: BP 10483, Niamey; tel. 96-96-58-51; e-mail istemoin@yahoo.fr; internet www.tamtaminfo.com/temoin.pdf; 2 a month; Dir of Publication IBRAHIM SOUMANA GAOH; Editors AMADOU TIÉMOGO, MOUSSA DAN TCHOUKOU, I. S. GAOH; circ. 1,000 (2005).

Ténéré Express: BP 13600, Niamey; tel. 20-73-35-76; fax 20-73-77-75; e-mail tenerefm@intnet.ne; daily; independent; current affairs; Dir ABDOULAYE MOUSSA MASSALATCHI.

La Tribune du Peuple: Niamey; tel. 20-73-34-28; e-mail tribune@intnet.ne; f. 1993; weekly; Man. Editor IBRAHIM HAMIDOU.

Le Trophée: BP 2000, Niamey; tel. 20-74-12-79; e-mail strophee@caramail.com; sports; 2 a month; Dir ISSA HAMIDOU MAYAKI.

NEWS AGENCIES

Agence Nigérienne de Presse (ANP): BP 11158, Niamey; tel. 20-74-08-09; e-mail anpniger@intnet.ne; f. 1987; state-owned; Dir YAYE HASSANE.

Sahel—Office National d'Edition et de Presse (ONEP): BP 13182, Niamey; tel. 20-73-34-86; f. 1989; Dir ALI OUSSEÏNI.

Publishers

La Nouvelle Imprimerie du Niger (NIN): pl. du Petit Marché, BP 61, Niamey; tel. 20-73-47-98; fax 20-73-41-42; e-mail imprim@intnet.ne; f. 1962 as Imprimerie Nationale du Niger; govt publishing house; brs in Agadez and Maradi; Dir Maman Abou.

Réseau Sahélien de Recherche et de Publication: Niamey; tel. 20-73-36-90; fax 20-73-39-43; e-mail resadep@ilimi.uam.ne; press of the Université Abdou Moumouni; Co-ordinator Boureima Diadie.

Broadcasting and Communications

REGULATORY AUTHORITY

Conseil Supérieur de la Communication (CSC): Plateau, Niamey; tel. 20-72-23-56; comprises 15 mems; Pres. Mariama Keïta.

TELECOMMUNICATIONS

Celtel Niger: Route de l'Aéroport, BP 11922, Niamey; tel. 20-73-23-46; fax 20-73-23-85; e-mail b-sghir@intnet.ne; internet www.ne.celtel.com; f. 2001 to operate mobile cellular telecommunications network in Niamey and Maradi; 70% owned by Celtel International (United Kingdom), 30% owned by Caren Assurance; Dir-Gen. Jean-Léon Bonnechère.

Société Nigérienne des Télécommunications (SONITEL): BP 208, Niamey; tel. 20-72-29-98; fax 20-72-24-78; e-mail sonitel@intnet.ne; internet www.intnet.ne; f. 1998; 51% jtly owned by ZTE Corpn (People's Republic of China) and Laaico (Libya), 46% state-owned; Dir-Gen. Moussa Boubacar.

Sahel Com: BP 208, Niamey; f. 2002; mobile cellular telecommunications in Niamey.

Telecel Niger: Niamey; tel. 20-74-44-44; e-mail telecel@telecelniger.com; internet www.telecelniger.com; f. 2001 to operate mobile cellular telecommunications network, initially in Niamey and western regions, expanding to cover Maradi and Zinder by 2003, and Tahoua and Agadez by 2004; 68% owned by Orascom Telecom (Egypt); Dir Hima Souley.

BROADCASTING

Radio

Independent radio stations have been permitted to operate since 1994, although the majority are concentrated in the capital, Niamey. In 2000 the first of a network of rural stations, RURANET, which were to broadcast mainly programmes concerned with development issues, mostly in national languages, was established. Several local radio stations, funded by the Agence intergouvernementale de la francophonie, were expected to commence operations in the early 2000s.

Anfani FM: blvd Nali-Béro, BP 2096, Wadata, Niamey; tel. 20-74-08-80; fax 20-74-00-52; e-mail anfani@intnet.ne; private radio station, broadcasting to Niamey, Zinder, Maradi and Diffa; Dir Ismaël Moutari.

Office de Radiodiffusion-Télévision du Niger (ORTN): BP 309, Niamey; tel. 20-72-31-63; fax 20-72-35-48; internet www.ortn.ne; f. 1967; state broadcasting authority; Dir-Gen. Yayé Harouna.

La Voix du Sahel: BP 361, Niamey; tel. 20-72-22-02; fax 72-35-48; e-mail ortny@intnet.ne; f. 1958; govt-controlled radio service; programmes in French, Hausa, Djerma, Kanuri, Fulfuldé, Tamajak, Toubou, Gourmantché, Boudouma and Arabic; Dir Ibro Na-Allah Amadou.

Ténéré FM: BP 13600, Niamey; tel. 20-73-65-76; fax 20-73-46-94; e-mail tenerefm@intnet.ne; f. 1998; Dir Abibou Garba; Editor-in-Chief Souleymane Issa Maïga.

Ruranet: Niamey; internet membres.lycos.fr/nigeradio; f. 2000; network of rural radio stations, broadcasting 80% in national languages, with 80% of programmes concerned with devt issues; 31 stations operative in April 2002.

La Voix de l'Hémicycle: BP 12234, Niamey; f. 2002 as the radio station of the Assemblée nationale; broadcasts parliamentary debates and analysis for 15 hours daily in French and national languages to Niamey and environs.

Sudan FM: Dosso; auth. 2000; private radio station; Dir Hima Adamou.

Television

Office de Radiodiffusion-Télévision du Niger (ORTN): see Radio

Tal TV: BP 309, Niamey; f. 2001; broadcasts 72 hours of programmes each week.

Télé-Sahel: BP 309, Niamey; tel. 20-72-31-55; fax 20-72-35-48; govt-controlled television service; broadcasts daily from 13 transmission posts and six retransmission posts, covering most of Niger; Dir-Gen. Abdou Souley.

Télévision Ténéré (TTV): BP 13600, Niamey; tel. 20-73-65-76; fax 20-73-77-75; e-mail tenerefm@intnet.ne; f. 2000; independent broadcaster in Niamey; Dir Abibou Garba.

The independent operator, Télé Star, broadcasts several international or foreign channels in Niamey and environs, including TV5 Monde, Canal Horizon, CFI, RTL9, CNN and Euro News.

Finance

(cap. = capital; res = reserves; dep. = deposits; m. = million; brs = branches; amounts in francs CFA)

BANKING

Central Bank

Banque centrale des états de l'Afrique de l'ouest (BCEAO): BP 487, Niamey; tel. 20-72-24-91; fax 20-73-47-43; HQ in Dakar, Senegal; f. 1962; bank of issue for the mem. states of the Union économique et monétaire ouest-africaine (UEMOA, comprising Benin, Burkina Faso, Côte d'Ivoire, Guinea-Bissau, Mali, Niger, Senegal and Togo); cap. and res 859,313m., total assets 5,671,675m. (Dec. 2002); Gov. Damo Justin Baro (acting); Dir in Niger Abdoulaye Soumana; brs at Maradi and Zinder.

Commercial Banks

Bank of Africa—Niger (BOA-Niger): Immeuble BOA, rue du Gaureye, BP 10973, Niamey; tel. 20-73-36-20; fax 20-73-38-18; e-mail information@boaniger.com; internet www.bank-of-africa.net; f. 1994 to acquire assets of Nigeria International Bank Niamey; 42.6% owned by African Financial Holding; cap. 1,500m., res 1,097m., total assets 39,755m. (Dec. 2005); Pres. Paul Derreumaux; Dir-Gen. Mamadou Séné; 2 brs.

Banque Commerciale du Niger (BCN): rue du Combattant, BP 11363, Niamey; tel. 20-73-39-15; fax 20-73-21-63; e-mail info@bcn.ne; internet www.bcn-niger.com; f. 1978; 83.15% owned by Libyan Arab Foreign Bank, 16.85% state-owned; cap. and res 1,477m., total assets 14,618m. (Dec. 2003); Administrator Ibrahim Majdoub Naji (acting).

Banque Internationale pour l'Afrique au Niger (BIA—Niger): ave de la Mairie, BP 10350, Niamey; tel. 20-73-31-01; fax 20-73-35-95; e-mail bia@intnet.ne; internet www.bianiger.com; f. 1980; 35% owned by Groupe Belgolaise (Belgium); cap. 2,800m., res 1,905m., dep. 58,108m. (Dec. 2005); Pres. Amadou Hima Souley; Dir-Gen. Daniel Hasser; 11 brs.

Banque Islamique du Niger pour le Commerce et l'Investissement (BINCI): Immeuble El Nasr, BP 12754, Niamey; tel. 20-73-27-30; fax 20-73-47-35; e-mail binci@intnet.ne; f. 1983; fmrly Banque Masraf Faisal Islami; 33% owned by Dar al-Maal al-Islami (Switzerland), 33% by Islamic Development Bank (Saudi Arabia); cap. 1,810m., total assets 7,453m. (Dec. 2003); Pres. Abderraouf Benessaïah; Dir-Gen. Aissani Omar.

Ecobank Niger: blvd de la Liberté, angle rue des Bâtisseurs, BP 13804, Niamey; tel. 20-73-71-81; fax 20-73-72-04; internet www.ecobank.com; f. 1999; 59.4% owned by Ecobank Transnational Inc. (Togo, operating under the auspices of the Economic Community of West African States), 28.6% by Ecobank Benin, 11.9% by Ecobank Togo; total assets 38,256m. (Dec. 2005); Chair. Mahamadou Ouhoumoudou; Dir-Gen. Felix Bikpo.

Société Nigérienne de Banque (SONIBANK): ave de la Mairie, BP 891, Niamey; tel. 20-73-45-69; fax 20-73-46-93; e-mail sonibank@intnet.ne; f. 1990; 25% owned by Société Tunisienne de Banque; cap. 2,000m., res 5,124m., dep. 43,216m. (Dec. 2005); Pres. Illa Kané; 6 brs.

Development Banks

Caisse de Prêts aux Collectivités Territoriales (CPCT): route Torodi, BP 730, Niamey; tel. 20-72-34-12; fax 20-72-30-80; f. 1970; 100% state-owned (94% by organs of local govt); cap. and res 744m., total assets 2,541m. (Dec. 2003); Administrator Abdou Djibo (acting).

Crédit du Niger (CDN): 11 blvd de la République, BP 213, Niger; tel. 20-72-27-01; fax 20-72-23-90; e-mail cdb-nig@intnet.ne; f. 1958; 54% state-owned, 20% owned by Caisse Nationale de Sécurité Sociale; transfer to full private ownership pending; cap. and res 1,058m., total assets 3,602m. (Dec. 2003); Administrator Abdou Djibo (acting).

Fonds d'Intervention en Faveur des Petites et Moyennes Entreprises Nigériennes (FIPMEN): Immeuble Sonara II, BP 252, Niamey; tel. 20-73-20-98; f. 1990; state-owned; cap. and res

124m. (Dec. 1991); Chair. AMADOU SALLA HASSANE; Man. Dir IBRAHIM BEIDARI.

Savings Bank

Office National de la Poste et de l'Epargne: BP 11778, Niamey; tel. 20-73-24-98; fax 20-73-35-69; fmrly Caisse Nationale d'Epargne; Chair. Mme PALFI; Man. Dir HASSOUME MATA.

STOCK EXCHANGE

Bourse Régionale des Valeurs Mobilières (BRVM): c/o Chambre de Commerce et d'Industrie du Niger, Place de la Concertation, BP 13299, Niamey; tel. 20-73-66-92; fax 20-73-69-47; e-mail imagagi@brvm.org; internet www.brvm.org; f. 1998; national branch of BRVM (regional stock exchange based in Abidjan, Côte d'Ivoire, serving the member states of UEMOA); Man. IDRISSA S. MAGAGI.

INSURANCE

Agence d'Assurance du Sahel: BP 10661, Niamey; tel. 20-74-05-47.

Agence Nigérienne d'Assurances (ANA): pl. de la Mairie, BP 423, Niamey; tel. 20-72-20-71; f. 1959; cap. 1.5m.; owned by L'Union des Assurances de Paris; Dir JEAN LASCAUD.

Caren Assurance: BP 733, Niamey; tel. 20-73-34-70; fax 20-73-24-93; e-mail carenas@intnet.ne; insurance and reinsurance; Dir-Gen. IBRAHIM IDI ANGO.

Leyma—Société Nigérienne d'Assurances et de Réassurances (SNAR—Leyma): BP 426, Niamey; tel. 20-73-57-72; fax 20-73-40-44; f. 1973; restructured 2001; Pres. AMADOU HIMA SOULEY; Dir-Gen. GARBA ABDOURAHAMANE.

La Nigérienne d'Assurance et de Réassurance: BP 13300, Niamey; tel. 20-73-63-36; fax 20-73-73-37.

Union Générale des Assurances du Niger (UGAN): rue de Kalley, BP 11935, Niamey; tel. 20-73-54-06; fax 20-73-41-85; f. 1985; cap. 500m.; Pres. PATHÉ DIONE; Dir-Gen. MAMADOU TALATA; 7 brs.

Trade and Industry

GOVERNMENT AGENCIES

Cellule de Coordination de la Programme de Privatisation: Immeuble Sonibanque, BP 862, Niamey; tel. 20-73-29-10; fax 20-73-29-58; responsible for co-ordination of privatization programme; Co-ordinator IDÉ ISSOUFOU.

Office des Eaux du Sous-Sol (OFEDES): BP 734, Niamey; tel. 20-74-01-19; fax 20-74-16-68; govt agency for the maintenance and devt of wells and boreholes; Pres. DJIBO HAMANI.

Office du Lait du Niger (OLANI): BP 404, Niamey; tel. 20-73-23-69; fax 20-73-36-74; f. 1971; devt and marketing of milk products; transferred to majority private ownership in 1998; Dir-Gen. M. DIENG.

Office National de l'Energie Solaire (ONERSOL): BP 621, Niamey; tel. 20-73-45-05; govt agency for research and devt, commercial production and exploitation of solar devices; Dir ALBERT WRIGHT.

Office National des Ressources Minières du Niger (ONAREM): Rond-Point Kennedy, BP 12716, Niamey; tel. 20-73-59-28; fax 20-73-28-12; f. 1976; govt agency for exploration, exploitation and marketing of all minerals; Pres. MOUDY MOHAMED; Dir-Gen. A. A. ASKIA.

Office des Produits Vivriers du Niger (OPVN): pl. du petit Marché, BP 474, Niamey; tel. 20-73-44-43; fax 20-73-24-68; e-mail opvn@opvn.net; internet www.opvn.net; govt agency for developing agricultural and food production; Dir-Gen. ADAMOU CHAIFOU.

Riz du Niger (RINI): BP 476, Niamey; tel. 20-71-13-29; fax 20-73-42-04; f. 1967; cap. 825m. francs CFA; 30% state-owned; transfer to 100% private ownership proposed; production and marketing of rice; Pres. YAYA MADOUGOU; Dir-Gen. M. HAROUNA.

DEVELOPMENT ORGANIZATIONS

Agence Française de Développement (AFD): 203 ave du Gountou-Yéna, BP 212, Niamey; tel. 20-72-33-93; fax 20-72-26-05; e-mail afdniamey@groupe-afd.org; internet www.afd.fr; Country Dir FRANÇOIS GIOVALUCCHI.

Mission Française de Coopération et d'Action Culturelle: BP 494, Niamey; tel. 20-72-20-66; administers bilateral aid from France; Dir JEAN BOULOGNE.

SNV (Société Néerlandais de Développement): ave des Zarmakoye, BP 10110, Niamey; tel. 20-75-36-33; fax 20-75-35-06; e-mail snvniger@snv.ne; internet www.snv.ne; present in Niger since 1978; projects concerning food security, agriculture, the environment, savings and credit, marketing, water and communications; operations in Tillabéri, Zinder and Tahoua provinces.

CHAMBERS OF COMMERCE

Chambre de Commerce d'Agriculture, d'Industrie et d'Artisanat du Niger: BP 209, Niamey; tel. 20-73-22-10; fax 20-73-46-68; e-mail cham209n@intnet.ne; internet www.ccaian.org; BP 201, Agadez; tel. 20-44-01-61; BP 91, Diffa; tel. 20-54-03-92; BP 79, Maradi; tel. 20-41-03-76; BP 172, Tahoua; tel. 20-61-03-84; BP 83, Zinder; tel. 20-51-00-78; f. 1954; comprises 80 full mems and 40 dep. mems; Pres. IBRAHIM IDI ANGO; Sec.-Gen. SADOU AISSATA.

INDUSTRIAL AND TRADE ORGANIZATIONS

Centre Nigérien du Commerce Extérieur (CNCE): pl. de la Concertation, BP 12480, Niamey; tel. 20-73-22-88; fax 20-73-46-68; f. 1984; promotes and co-ordinates all aspects of foreign trade; Dir AÏSSA DIALLO.

Société Nationale de Commerce et de Production du Niger (COPRO-Niger): Niamey; tel. 20-73-28-41; fax 20-73-57-71; f. 1962; monopoly importer of foodstuffs; cap. 1,000m. francs CFA; 47% state-owned; Man. Dir DJIBRILLA HIMA.

EMPLOYERS' ORGANIZATIONS

Syndicat des Commerçants Importateurs et Exportateurs du Niger (SCIMPEXNI): Chambre de Commerce, d'Agriculture, d'Industrie et d'Artisanat du Niger, Niamey; tel. 20-73-33-17; Pres. M. SILVA; Sec.-Gen. INOUSSA MAÏGA.

Syndicat National des Petites et Moyennes Entreprises et Industries Nigériennes (SYNAPEMEIN): Chambre de Commerce, d'Agriculture, d'Industrie et d'Artisanat du Niger, Niamey; tel. 20-73-50-97; Pres. ALZOUMA SALEY; Sec.-Gen. HASSANE LAWAL KADER.

Syndicat Patronal des Entreprises et Industries du Niger (SPEIN): BP 415, Niamey; tel. 20-73-24-01; fax 20-73-47-07; f. 1994; Pres. AMADOU OUSMANE; Sec.-Gen. NOUHOU TARI.

UTILITIES

Electricity

Société Nigérienne d'Electricité (NIGELEC): 46 ave du Gen. de Gaulle, BP 11202, Niamey; tel. 20-72-26-92; fax 20-72-32-88; e-mail nigelec@intnet.ne; f. 1968; 95% state-owned; 51% transfer to private ownership proposed; production and distribution of electricity; Dir-Gen. IBRAHIM FOUKORI.

Water

Société d'Exploitation des Eaux du Niger (SEEN): blvd Zarmaganda, BP 12209, Niamey; tel. 20-72-25-00; fax 20-73-46-40; fmrly Société Nationale des Eaux; 51% owned by Veolia Environnement (France); production and distribution of drinking water; Pres. ABARY DAN BOUZOUA SOULEYMENE; Dir-Gen. SEYNI SALOU.

TRADE UNION FEDERATIONS

Confédération des Travailleurs du Niger (CTN): Niamey; Sec.-Gen. ISSOUFOU SEYBOU.

Entente des Travailleurs du Niger (ETN): Bourse du Travail, BP 388, Niamey; tel. and fax 20-73-52-56; f. 2005 by merger of Confédération Nigérienne du Travail, Union Generale des Travailleurs du Niger and Union des Syndicats des Travailleurs du Niger.

Transport

ROADS

Niger is crossed by highways running from east to west and from north to south, giving access to neighbouring countries. A road is under construction to Lomé, Togo, via Burkina Faso, and the 428-km Zinder–Agadez road, scheduled to form part of the Trans-Sahara Highway, has been upgraded. Niger and Algeria appealed jointly in mid-1998 for international aid to fund construction of the Trans-Sahara Highway, development of which was suspended in the mid-1990s because of the conflict in northern Niger. In 2004 there were 14,565 km of classified roads, of which 3,641 km were paved.

Société Nationale des Transports Nigériens (SNTN): BP 135, Niamey; tel. 20-72-24-55; fax 20-74-47-07; e-mail stratech@intnet.ne; f. 1963; operates passenger and freight road-transport services; 49% state-owned; Chair. MOHAMED ABDOULAHI; Man. Dir BARKE M. MOUSTAPHA.

RAILWAYS

There are as yet no railways in Niger.

NIGER

Organisation Commune Bénin-Niger des Chemins de Fer et des Transports (OCBN): BP 38, Niamey; tel. 20-73-27-90; f. 1959; 50% owned by Govt of Niger, 50% by Govt of Benin; manages the Benin-Niger railway project (begun in 1978); also operates more than 500 km within Benin (q.v.); extension to Niger proposed; transfer to private ownership proposed; Dir-Gen. FLAVIEN BALOGOUN.

INLAND WATERWAYS

The River Niger is navigable for 300 km within the country. Access to the sea is available by a river route from Gaya, in south-western Niger, to the coast at Port Harcourt, Nigeria, between September and March. Port facilities at Lomé, Togo, are used as a commercial outlet for land-locked Niger.

Niger-Transit (NITRA): Zone Industrielle, BP 560, Niamey; tel. 20-73-22-53; fax 20-73-26-38; f. 1974; 48% owned by SNTN; customs agent, freight-handling, warehousing, etc.; manages Nigerien port facilities at Lomé, Togo; Pres. OUMAROU ALI BEÏOLI; Man. Dir SADE FATIMATA.

Société Nigérienne des Transports Fluviaux et Maritimes (SNTFM): Niamey; tel. 20-73-39-69; river and sea transport; cap. 64.6m. francs CFA; 99% state-owned; Man. Dir BERTRAND DEJEAN.

CIVIL AVIATION

There are international airports at Niamey (Hamani Diori), Agadez (Mano Dayak) and Zinder, and major domestic airports at Diffa, Maradi and Tahoua.

Air Continental: Niamey; f. 2003 to replace Air Niger International (f. 2002); 60% owned by private Nigerian interests, 20% by private Nigerien interests, 5% by Govt of Niger; regional and international services.

Air Inter Afrique: Niamey; tel. 20-73-85-85; fax 20-73-69-73; f. 2001; operates services within West Africa; CEO CHEIKH OUSMANE DIALLO.

Air Inter Niger: Agadez; f. 1997 to operate services to Tamanrasset (Algeria).

Niger Air Continental: Niamey; e-mail info@nigeraircontinental.com; f. 2003.

Nigeravia: BP 10454, Niamey; tel. 20-73-30-64; fax 20-74-18-42; e-mail nigavia@intnet.ne; internet www.nigeravia.com; f. 1991; operates domestic, regional and international services; Pres. and Dir-Gen. JEAN SYLVESTRE.

Société Nigérienne des Transports Aériens (SONITA): Niamey; f. 1991; owned by private Nigerien (81%) and Cypriot (19%) interests; operates domestic and regional services; Man. Dir ABDOULAYE MAIGA GOUDOUBABA.

Tourism

The Aïr and Ténéré Nature Reserve, covering an area of 77,000 sq km, was established in 1988. Tourism was hampered by insecurity in the north and east during the 1990s. However, the number of foreign arrivals at hotels and similar establishments increased from 39,190 in 1997 to 42,433 in 1999, when tourism receipts amounted to US $24m. In 2005 some 63,451 tourists entered Niger, while receipts from tourism totalled $34m. in 2003.

Centre Nigerien de Promotion Touristique (CNPT): ave de Président H. Luebke, BP 612, Niamey; tel. 20-73-24-47; fax 20-73-28-07; e-mail CNPT2@yahoo.fr; internet www.maisontourism-niger.com; Dirs BOULOU AKANO, IBRAHIM HALIDOU, KIEPIW TOYÉ FANTA.

NIGERIA

Introductory Survey

Location, Climate, Language, Religion, Flag, Capital

The Federal Republic of Nigeria is a West African coastal state on the shores of the Gulf of Guinea, with Benin to the west, Niger to the north, Chad to the north-east, and Cameroon to the east and south-east. The climate is tropical in the southern coastal areas, with an average annual temperature of 32°C (90°F) and high humidity. It is drier and semi-tropical in the north. Average annual rainfall is more than 2,500 mm (98 ins) in parts of the south-east, but in certain areas of the north is as low as 600 mm (24 ins). In 1963 the most widely spoken languages were Hausa (20.9%), Yoruba (20.3%), Ibo (16.6%) and Fulani (8.6%). English is the country's official language. In 1963 the principal religious groups were Muslims (47.2%) and Christians (34.5%), while 18% of the total population followed animist beliefs. The national flag (proportions 1 by 2) has three equal vertical stripes, of green, white and green. The capital is Abuja, to which the Federal Government was formally transferred in December 1991; however, many non-government institutions remained in the former capital, Lagos.

Recent History

The territory of present-day Nigeria, except for the section of former German-controlled Cameroon (see below), was conquered by the United Kingdom, in several stages, during the second half of the 19th century and the first decade of the 20th century. The British dependencies of Northern and Southern Nigeria were merged into a single territory in 1914, administered largely by traditional native rulers, under the supervision of the colonial authorities. In 1947 the United Kingdom introduced a new Nigerian Constitution, establishing a federal system of government, based on three regions: Northern, Western and Eastern. The federal arrangement was an attempt to reconcile religious and regional tensions, and to accommodate Nigeria's diverse ethnic groups, notably the Ibo (in the east), the Yoruba (in the west) and the Hausa and Fulani (in the north). The Northern Region, which was predominantly Muslim, contained about one-half of Nigeria's total population.

In 1954 the federation became self-governing, and the first federal Prime Minister, Alhaji Abubakar Tafawa Balewa (a Muslim northerner), was appointed in August 1957. A constitutional conference, convened in 1958, agreed that Nigeria should become independent in 1960, and elections to an enlarged federal legislature took place in December 1959. The Northern People's Congress (NPC), which was politically dominant in the north, became the single largest party in the new legislature, although lacking an overall majority. Tafawa Balewa (a prominent member of the NPC) continued to head a coalition government of the NPC and the National Council for Nigeria and the Cameroons (NCNC), which attracted most support in the Eastern Region.

On 1 October 1960, as scheduled, the Federation of Nigeria achieved independence, initially as a constitutional monarchy. In June 1961 the northern part of the UN Trust Territory of British Cameroons was incorporated into Nigeria's Northern Region as the province of Sardauna, and in August 1963 a fourth region, the Mid-Western Region, was created by dividing the existing Western Region. On 1 October a revised Constitution was adopted, and the country was renamed the Federal Republic of Nigeria, although it remained a member of the Commonwealth. Dr Nnamdi Azikiwe of the NCNC took office as Nigeria's first President (then a non-executive post).

The first national election after independence, to the federal House of Representatives, took place in December 1964. Widespread violence was reported during the election campaign, prompting a boycott of the poll by the main opposition grouping, the United Progressive Grand Alliance (UPGA), a coalition of four parties, dominated by the NCNC (previously renamed the National Convention of Nigerian Citizens). The election resulted in a large majority for the Nigerian National Alliance, a seven-party coalition, which was dominated by the NPC.

In January 1966 Tafawa Balewa's civilian Government was overthrown by junior army officers (mainly Ibos from the Eastern Region). The Commander-in-Chief of the Armed Forces, Maj.-Gen. Johnson Aguiyi-Aronsi (an Ibo), formed a Supreme Military Council, suspended the Constitution and imposed emergency rule. In July Aguiyi-Aronsi was killed in a further coup, staged by northern troops, and power was transferred to the Chief of Army Staff, Lt-Col (later Gen.) Yakubu Gowon, a Christian northerner. Gowon subsequently reintroduced the federal system, which had been suppressed after the January coup.

In early 1967 there was a rapid deterioration in relations between the Federal Government and the military Governor of the Eastern Region, Lt-Col Chukwuemeka Odumegwu Ojukwu, following a dispute between the federal and regional authorities concerning the distribution of petroleum revenues. The increasing tensions in Nigeria's federal structure prompted Gowon to propose the replacement of the four existing regions by 12 states. On 30 May Ojukwu announced the secession of the Eastern Region from the Federation, and proclaimed its independence as the Republic of Biafra. Fighting between the forces of Biafra and the Federal Government began in July; federal forces eventually suppressed the rebellion in December 1969, following Ojukwu's departure into exile, and Biafran forces formally surrendered in January 1970. Meanwhile, the proposed 12-state structure replaced the four federal regions in April 1968.

In October 1974 Gowon postponed the restoration of civilian rule indefinitely. However, increasing opposition to his regime culminated in his overthrow by other senior officers in a bloodless coup on 29 July 1975. Gowon was replaced as Head of State by Brig. (later Gen.) Murtala Ramat Muhammed, hitherto Federal Commissioner for Communications, who, in October, announced a detailed timetable for a transition to civilian rule. In February 1976, however, Muhammed was assassinated during an unsuccessful coup attempt. Power was immediately assumed by Lt-Gen. (later Gen.) Olusegun Obasanjo, the Chief of Army Staff, who promised to fulfil his predecessor's programme for the restoration of civilian rule.

In March 1976 the number of states was increased from 12 to 19, and it was announced that a new federal capital was to be constructed near Abuja, in central Nigeria. In September 1978 a new Constitution was promulgated, and the state of emergency, in force since 1966, was ended. At the same time the 12-year ban on political activity was revoked. Elections took place in July 1979 to a new bicameral National Assembly (comprising a Senate and a House of Representatives), and for State Assemblies and State Governors. The National Party of Nigeria (NPN), which included many prominent members of the former NPC, received the most widespread support in all the elections. The NPN's presidential candidate, Alhaji Shehu Shagari (who had served as an NPC federal minister prior to 1966 and as a federal commissioner in 1970–75), was elected to the new post of executive President in August 1979. He took office on 1 October, whereupon the military regime transferred power to the newly elected civilian authorities and the new Constitution came into effect.

In August–September 1983 local government, state and federal elections took place. In the presidential election Shagari was returned for a second term of office. The NPN won 13 of the 19 state governorships, and achieved substantial majorities in the Senate and the House of Representatives. On 31 December, however, the civilian Government was deposed in a bloodless military coup, led by Maj.-Gen. Muhammadu Buhari, who had been Federal Commissioner for Petroleum in 1976–78. The Government was replaced by a Supreme Military Council (SMC), headed by Buhari; the National Assembly was dissolved, and all political parties were banned. Hundreds of politicians, including former President Shagari, were arrested on charges of corruption, and legislation that severely restricted the freedom of the press was introduced.

On 27 August 1985 Buhari's administration was deposed in a bloodless coup, led by Maj.-Gen. (later Gen.) Ibrahim Babangida, the Chief of Army Staff and a member of the SMC. A new military administration, the Armed Forces Ruling Council (AFRC), was established, with Babangida as President. The decree on press censorship was revoked, and a number of journalists and other political detainees were released. (Shagari and 17 other former government officials were released in July 1986, having been acquitted of corruption charges.) In December 1985 the AFRC suppressed a coup attempt by disaffected army officers; 10 of the alleged conspirators were later executed.

In February 1986 Babangida's announcement that Nigeria had been accepted as a full member of the Organization of the Islamic Conference (OIC, see p. 369) prompted concern in the non-Muslim sector of the population at increasing 'Islamization' in Nigeria. In July 1987 Babangida announced details of a programme to transfer power to a civilian government on 1 October 1992. The ban on party politics was to be revoked in 1989, and a maximum of two associations were to be approved to contest elections. In August 1987 the Government established a National Electoral Commission (NEC); in September the number of states was increased to 21. The local government elections contested by some 15,000 non-party candidates took place in December. In May 1988 a Constituent Assembly, comprising 450 members elected by local government and 117 members nominated by the AFRC, commenced preparation of a draft constitution. The progress of the Constituent Assembly was impeded, however, by controversy over the proposed inclusion of Islamic (*Shari'a*) courts in the new document.

In April 1989 the Constituent Assembly presented a draft Constitution to Babangida. In May Babangida announced the end of the prohibition on political parties, and the new Constitution (which was scheduled to take effect on 1 October 1992) was promulgated. Only 13 of the existing parties managed to fulfil the requirements for registration by the stipulated date in July 1989. In September the NEC submitted six political associations to the AFRC; in October, however, it was decided to dissolve all the newly formed political parties, on the grounds that they were too closely associated with discredited former parties. In their place, the AFRC created two new organizations, the Social Democratic Party (SDP) and the National Republican Convention (NRC), provoking widespread criticism.

Following the completion of registration for membership of the SDP and the NRC, party executives were elected for each state in July 1990, replacing government-appointed administrators. Later in August Babangida replaced nine government ministers, and the position of Chief of General Staff, held by Vice-Adm. (later Adm.) Augustus Aikhomu, was replaced by the office of Vice-President (to which Aikhomu was immediately appointed). Babangida subsequently announced plans to reduce substantially the size of the armed forces. In September, in an attempt to restrict military influence within the Government, three ministers were obliged to retire from the armed forces. Local government elections (postponed from the previous year) took place in early December, with only an estimated 20% of registered voters participating.

In October 1990 the Movement for the Survival of the Ogoni People (MOSOP) was formed to co-ordinate opposition to the exploitation of petroleum reserves in territory of the Ogoni ethnic group (Ogoniland), in the south-central Rivers State, by the Shell Petroleum Development Co of Nigeria. Following a demonstration, organized by MOSOP in protest at environmental damage resulting from petroleum production, it was reported that security forces had killed some 80 Ogonis.

In September 1991, in an apparent attempt to relieve ethnic tensions prior to the elections, nine new states were created, increasing the size of the federation to 30 states. On 12 December the Federal Government was formally transferred from Lagos to Abuja, the new federal capital. In the gubernatorial and state assembly elections, which took place on 14 December, the NRC secured a majority in 14 State Assemblies, while the SDP won control of 16 State Assemblies; candidates representing the NRC were elected as State Governors in 16 states. Both the SDP and the NRC disputed the election results in a number of states, on the grounds of malpractice.

In January 1992 Babangida formed a new Council of Ministers, in which several portfolios were restructured. In the same month the Government announced that elections to a bicameral National Assembly, comprising a 593-member House of Representatives and a 91-member Senate, would take place on 7 November, and would be followed by a presidential election on 5 December. The formal installation of a civilian government (and the implementation of the new Constitution) was consequently scheduled for 2 January 1993, rather than, as previously planned, on 1 October 1992.

In May 1992 some 300 people were reported to have been killed in renewed violence between the Hausa ethnic group (which was predominantly Muslim) and the Kataf (predominantly Christian) in Kaduna. Shortly afterwards the Government announced that all organizations with religious or ethnic interests were to be prohibited. Later in May further rioting occurred in Lagos, following the arrest of the Chairman of the Campaign for Democracy (CD—an informal alliance of Nigerian human rights organizations, which had been established in late 1991), Dr Beko Ransome-Kuti, who had accused the Government of deliberately provoking unrest in order to delay the transition to civilian rule. In June several human rights activists, including Ransome-Kuti, were released, pending their trial (which was later deferred) on charges of conspiring to incite the previous month's riots.

At elections to the bicameral National Assembly, which had been brought forward to 4 July 1992, the SDP secured a majority in both chambers, with 52 seats in the Senate and 314 seats in the House of Representatives, while the NRC won 37 seats in the Senate and 275 seats in the House of Representatives. The formal inauguration of the National Assembly, due to take place on 27 July, was, however, postponed until 5 December, the stipulated date for the presidential election, prompting concern at the AFRC's apparent reluctance to relinquish legislative power.

Voting in primary elections for presidential candidates took place in September 1992. In October, however, shortly before a final round of voting was due to take place, Babangida suspended the primary elections, pending the outcome of an investigation by the NEC into alleged incidents of electoral malpractice. Later that month, following a report by the NEC that confirmed malpractice, Babangida announced that the leaders of the NRC and the SDP were to be removed from office.

In November 1992 Babangida postponed the presidential election until 12 June 1993. On 2 January 1993 Babangida announced that the 23 prospective presidential candidates who had contested the discredited primary elections were to be prohibited from political activity during the transitional period: new candidates were to be nominated at a series of party congresses, to be conducted at ward, local government, state and national level.

On 5 December 1992 Babangida inaugurated the National Assembly. On 2 January 1993 the AFRC and the Council of Ministers were dissolved, and a civilian Transitional Council and the National Defence and Security Council (which comprised the President, Vice-President, the heads of the armed forces and senior members of the Transitional Council) were formally installed. The Chairman of the Transitional Council, Chief Ernest Adegunle Shonekan, was officially designated Head of Government (although supreme power was vested in the NDSC and the President), while Aikhomu retained the post of Vice-President. In accordance with the new programme for the transition to civilian rule, party congresses to select presidential candidates were conducted in February–March; the NRC elected Alhaji Bashir Othman Tofa and the SDP Chief Moshood Kastumawo Olawale Abiola to contest the presidential election.

In June 1993 the Association for a Better Nigeria (ABN), a newly formed pro-Babangida pressure group, obtained an interim injunction in the Abuja High Court prohibiting the NEC from conducting the presidential election, pending an appeal by the ABN for the extension of military rule until 1997. The NEC, however, announced that the injunction was invalid, and that the election would take place as scheduled. Owing, in part, to confusion caused by the court action, only about 30% of the registered electorate voted in the presidential election, which took place on 12 June. Initial results indicated that Abiola had secured the majority of votes in 11 of 15 states. Shortly afterwards, however, the ABN obtained a further injunction suspending the promulgation of the election results. The court ruling prompted widespread demands that the results be released, and several applications were lodged in an attempt to reverse the injunction. Later in June the CD released election results (which it claimed to be official) indicating that Abiola had secured the majority of votes in 19 states, and Tofa in 11; Abiola subsequently proclaimed himself President. Amid increasing tension, the Abuja High Court declared the election results to be invalid, on the grounds that the NEC had failed to comply with the ruling that had cancelled the poll.

On 23 June 1993, in what it claimed was an effort to uphold the judicial system, the NDSC annulled the results of the presidential election, suspended the NEC and halted all proceedings pertaining to the election. Babangida subsequently announced that the poll had been marred by widespread irregularities (despite reports by international observers that voting had been conducted fairly), but insisted that he remained committed to the transition to civilian rule on 27 August. The SDP and the NRC were to select two new presidential candidates, under the supervision of a reconstituted NEC. The annulment of the election attracted international criticism, particularly from the USA and the United Kingdom, which announced the imposition of military sanctions against Nigeria. In July the NDSC announced that a new presidential election was to take place on 14 August. Legal proceedings initiated by Abiola in the Lagos Supreme Court, in an attempt to uphold his claim to the presidency, were abandoned after Babangida introduced legislation that prohibited any legal challenges to the annulment of the election.

At the end of July 1993 Babangida announced that an Interim National Government (ING) was to be established, on the grounds that there was insufficient time to permit the scheduled transition to civilian rule on 27 August. In August the CD continued its campaign of civil disobedience in protest at the annulment of the election, appealing for a three-day general strike (which was widely observed in the south-west of the country, where Abiola received most popular support). Later in August Babangida resigned; on 27 August a 32-member interim Federal Executive Council (FEC), headed by Shonekan, was installed, while the transitional period for the return to civilian rule was extended to 31 March 1994. Supporters of democracy criticized the inclusion in the ING of several members of the now-dissolved NDSC, including Gen. Sani Abacha, who was appointed to the new post of Vice-President.

At the end of August 1993 the CD staged a further three-day strike, while the Nigerian Labour Congress (NLC) and the National Union of Petroleum and Natural Gas Workers (NUPENG) also announced industrial action in support of the installation of a civilian administration, headed by Abiola. The combined strike action resulted in a severe fuel shortage and the suspension of most economic activity. Following the establishment of the ING, Shonekan pledged his commitment to the democratic process and, in an effort to restore order, initiated negotiations with the NLC and effected the release of several journalists and prominent members of the CD.

In September 1993 a series of military appointments, which included the nomination of Lt-Gen. Oladipo Diya to the office of Chief of Defence Staff, effectively removed supporters of Babangida from significant posts within the armed forces, thereby strengthening Abacha's position. Later in September the NRC and SDP agreed to a new timetable whereby local government elections and a presidential election would take place concurrently in February 1994. The CD subsequently announced the resumption of strike action in support of demands for the installation of Abiola as President, and Ransome-Kuti and other prominent members were again arrested.

In November 1993 the President of the Senate, a strong supporter of Abiola, was removed from office. Shortly afterwards the Lagos High Court ruled in favour of an application by Abiola, declaring the establishment of the ING to be invalid under the terms of the 1979 Constitution (whereby the President of the Senate was to act as interim Head of State). In the same month the ING dissolved the government councils, prior to local elections, and withdrew state subsidies on petroleum products. The resultant dramatic increase in the price of fuel prompted widespread anti-Government demonstrations, and the NLC announced the resumption of strike action. Meanwhile, the scheduled revision of the electoral register ended in failure, owing to a boycott by supporters of the SDP, and it became apparent that the new schedule for the transition to civilian rule was unviable.

On 17 November 1993, following a meeting with senior military officials, Shonekan resigned as Head of State and immediately transferred power to Abacha (confirming widespread speculation that the latter had effectively assumed control of the Government following Babangida's resignation). On the following day Abacha dissolved all state institutions that had been established under the transitional process, replaced the State Governors with military administrators, prohibited political activity (thereby proscribing the NRC and the SDP), and announced the formation of a Provisional Ruling Council (PRC), which was to comprise senior military officials and principal members of a new FEC. He insisted, however, that he intended to relinquish power to a civilian government, and pledged to convene a conference with a mandate to determine the constitutional future of the country. Restrictions on the media were revoked. On 21 November Abacha introduced legislation that formally restored the 1979 Constitution and provided for the establishment of the new government organs. In an apparent attempt to counter domestic and international criticism, several prominent supporters of Abiola, including Kingibe, and four former members of the ING were appointed to the PRC and FEC, which were installed on 24 November. Abacha subsequently removed 17 senior military officers who were believed to be loyal to Babangida. In the same month the NLC agreed to abandon strike action after the Government acted to limit the increase in the price of petroleum products.

In December 1993 the United Kingdom announced that member nations of the European Union (EU, see p. 244) were to impose further sanctions against Nigeria, including restrictions on the export of armaments. In April 1994 the Government announced a programme for the establishment of a National Constitutional Conference (NCC): some 273 delegates were to be elected in May, while 96 delegates were to be nominated by the Government from a list of eligible citizens submitted by each state. The NCC was to be convened at the end of June, and was to submit recommendations, including proposals for a new draft constitution, to the PRC in October. The ban on political activity was to end in January 1995. In May 1994 a new pro-democracy organization, comprising former politicians, retired military officers and human rights activists, the National Democratic Coalition (NADECO), demanded that Abacha relinquish power by the end of that month and urged a boycott of the NCC. In the same month the leader of MOSOP, Ken Saro-Wiwa, was arrested in connection with the deaths, during political violence, of four Ogoni traditional leaders. Saro-Wiwa was alleged to have incited his supporters to commit the murders.

In June 1994 a number of prominent opposition members, including Ransome-Kuti, were also arrested after the CD urged a campaign of civil disobedience, supported by NADECO. Following a public gathering, at which Abiola declared himself Head of State and President of a parallel government, a warrant was issued for his arrest on charges of treason; the authorities claimed that he intended to organize an uprising to force the military administration to relinquish power. Later in June he was arrested by security forces. At the initial session of the NCC, which was convened as scheduled, Abacha pledged to relinquish power at a date that would be determined by the conference.

In July 1994 Abiola was arraigned before a special High Court in Abuja and charged with treason. NUPENG initiated strike action in support of demands for Abiola's release and installation as President, and an improvement in government investment in the petroleum industry. By mid-July several affiliated unions had joined the strike action, resulting in an effective suspension of economic activity in Lagos and other regions in the south-west of the country. In September the union leaders announced the suspension of strike action, in view of the ensuing widespread hardship. Later in September Abacha enlarged the PRC from 11 to 25 members, all senior military officials.

Meanwhile, Abiola's trial was repeatedly adjourned, following his legal action, in August 1994, challenging the jurisdiction of the special High Court in Abuja with regard to an offence that had been allegedly committed in Lagos. Despite reports that he was suffering from a medical condition necessitating immediate treatment, Abiola had refused to accept the stipulated conditions for bail, requiring him to refrain from political activity.

In January 1995 the NCC, which had been scheduled to complete the preparations for a draft constitution in October 1994, adjourned until March 1995, prompting increasing concern that its protracted deliberations served to prolong the tenure of the military administration. The trial of Saro-Wiwa and a further 14 Ogoni campaigners, on charges of complicity in the murder of the four Ogoni traditional leaders, commenced in mid-January; the defendants were to challenge the legitimacy of the government-appointed Special Military Tribunal, at Port Harcourt. In February the Federal Court of Appeal dismissed Abiola's legal action challenging the jurisdiction of the High Court in Abuja.

In February 1995 Abacha dissolved the FEC, after a number of ministers announced their intention of engaging in political activity in the forthcoming transitional period. In March some 150 military officials were arrested, and the authorities subsequently confirmed reports of a conspiracy to overthrow the Government. The arrest of the former Head of State, Olusegun Obasanjo, and his former deputy, Maj.-Gen. (retd) Shehu Musa Yar'Adua, together with other prominent critics of the Government, prompted international protests. In mid-March Abacha appointed a new, 36-member FEC. In May more than 40 people, including Obasanjo, Yar'Adua and Ransome-Kuti, were arraigned before a Special Military Tribunal in Lagos, in connection with the alleged coup attempt in March.

In late June 1995 the NCC submitted a draft Constitution to Abacha, who rescinded the ban on political activity; a programme for transition to civilian rule was to be announced on 1 October. (A number of political organizations subsequently emerged, in response to the removal of the ban.) At the end of June it was reported that Yar'Adua and a further 13 military officers had been sentenced to death for conspiring to overthrow the Government, while several other defendants, including Obasanjo and Ransome-Kuti, received custodial terms. The Government subsequently confirmed that a total of 43 had been convicted in connection with the coup attempt, prompting protests and appeals for clemency from the international community. On 1 October, however, Abacha officially commuted the death sentences to terms of imprisonment and reduced the custodial sentences (although he did not withdraw the capital charges against Abiola). At the same time he announced the approval of the new Constitution (which was due to be formally endorsed later that year) and the adoption of a three-year programme for transition to civilian rule, whereby a new President was to be inaugurated on 1 October 1998, following elections at local, state and national level. (The duration of the transitional period was received with disapproval by the international community.)

At the end of October 1995 Saro-Wiwa and a further eight Ogoni activists were sentenced to death by the Special Military Tribunal in Port Harcourt, having been convicted of involvement in the murder of the four Ogoni leaders in May 1994; six defendants were acquitted. Although the defendants were not implicated directly in the incident, the nine convictions were based on the premise that the MOSOP activists had effectively incited the killings. An international campaign against the convictions and numerous appeals for clemency ensued. However, on 10 November the nine convicted Ogonis were executed, prompting immediate condemnation by the international community. Nigeria was suspended from the Commonwealth, and threatened with expulsion if the Government failed to restore democracy within a period of two years. Later that month the EU reaffirmed its commitment to existing sanctions that had been imposed in 1993 (notably an embargo on the export of armaments and military equipment to Nigeria), and extended visa restrictions to civilian members of the administration. The Governments of the USA, South Africa and the EU member nations recalled their diplomatic representatives from Nigeria in protest at the executions. The Nigerian Government condemned the imposition of sanctions and, in turn, withdrew its diplomatic representatives from the USA, South Africa and the EU member countries. Additional security forces were dispatched to Ogoniland to deter any protests against the executions.

In December 1995 Abacha approved the establishment of a number of committees, including the National Electoral Commission of Nigeria (NECON), to implement the transitional programme. NECON subsequently divided the country into seven regions (rather than six, as originally envisaged), prior to local government elections in early 1996. Later in December the Commonwealth Ministerial Action Group (CMAG—comprising the ministers with responsibility for foreign affairs of eight member countries), which had been established at the summit meeting in November, met to discuss further measures to be taken if the Nigerian Government failed to restore democracy, and announced that five of the ministers were to visit Nigeria to initiate negotiations with the military administration. In January 1996 the Government refused the Commonwealth delegation permission to visit Nigeria, and demanded that the decision to suspend Nigeria be reviewed. At the end of January the Government announced that the new Constitution would be formally adopted in 1998, upon the completion of the transitional period (rather than in late 1995).

In March 1996 local government elections were contested, on a non-party basis, as part of the transitional programme; although opposition leaders had urged a boycott, NECON claimed that a high level of voter participation had been recorded. In April a UN mission visited Ogoniland to investigate the trial and execution of the nine Ogoni activists in 1995; it was reported that Ogoni and other opposition representatives were prevented from meeting the delegation. Later that month, following the Government's continued refusal to enter into negotiations with CMAG regarding human rights issues and the restoration of democracy, the Commonwealth proposed to adopt a number of sanctions against Nigeria.

In June 1996 Nigerian officials met CMAG in an attempt to avert the threatened imposition of sanctions against Nigeria; the Nigerian delegation demanded that Nigeria be readmitted to the Commonwealth in exchange for the Government's adoption of the programme for transition to civilian rule by October 1998. The Commonwealth dismissed the programme as unsatisfactory, but remained divided regarding the adoption of consequent measures. It was finally agreed that the Commonwealth would suspend the adoption of sanctions, but that the situation would subsequently be reviewed. Canada, however, announced its opposition to this decision and unilaterally imposed a number of sanctions (similar to those already adopted by the EU). In September 1996 CMAG agreed that the Commonwealth delegation would visit Nigeria, despite conditions imposed by the military authorities, which insisted that it would not be permitted access to opposition activists or political prisoners.

In June 1996 legislation governing the formation of political parties was promulgated. Five of 15 political organizations that applied for registration were granted legal status in September. NADECO condemned the disqualification of the remaining 10 parties, which were subsequently dissolved by decree; it was widely believed that the associations that had been granted registration were largely sympathetic towards the military administration. In October Abacha announced the creation of a further six states, increasing the total size of the federation to 36 states.

In early 1997 escalating tension between the Ijaw and Itsekiri ethnic groups in the town of Warri, in south-western Nigeria, severely disrupted operations in the region of the Niger Delta by the Shell Petroleum Development Company of Nigeria. In March a demonstration by members of the Ijaw ethnic group in Warri precipitated violent clashes. Protesters seized Shell installations and took about 100 employees hostage, in an attempt to force the Government to accede to their demands. The disruption in petroleum production resulted in a national fuel shortage, effectively suspending the transportation system in much of the country. Further attacks on Shell installations were reported in May. Later that month the authorities established a commission of inquiry to investigate the cause of the unrest and submit recommendations for restoring order in the region.

In May 1997 some 22 pro-democracy and human rights organizations, including MOSOP and the CD, formed a loose alliance, the United Action for Democracy (UAD), with the aim of campaigning for the restoration of democracy in Nigeria.

At a summit meeting of the Commonwealth Heads of Government, which took place in Edinburgh, United Kingdom, in October 1997, Nigeria's suspension from the organization was extended for an additional year; it was further indicated that the country would be expelled from the Commonwealth if Abacha reneged on his pledge to restore democratic rule by 1 October 1998. The Government had announced a new electoral timetable: elections to the State Assemblies were to take place in December 1997, followed by elections to the National Assembly on 25 April 1998, and presidential and gubernatorial elections on 1 August of that year (although it was maintained that the new elected organs of government would be installed by 1 October 1998). Elections to the state legislatures, which were contested by the five registered parties, took place accordingly on 6 December 1997; the United Nigeria Congress Party (UNCP) won 637 of the 970 contested seats, securing a majority in 29 of the 36 State Assemblies. The other four parties (the Congress for National Consensus, the Democratic Party of Nigeria, the Grassroots Democratic Movement and the National Centre Party of Nigeria) subsequently attributed the electoral success of the UNCP to malpractice on the part of the authorities, and threatened to withdraw from the remainder of the electoral process. In mid-December Abacha nominated a new FEC, in which most of the ministers who had served in the previous administration were replaced. Later that month, following reports of a bomb attack at the presidential wing of the airport at Abuja, the Government announced that an attempted coup had been thwarted. About 100 people, notably several prominent military officials (including Lt-Gen. Diya), were subsequently detained. However, there was widespread speculation that government claims of a coup attempt were a pretext for the removal of a number of army officers who were perceived to be a threat to Abacha. The incident also served to divert attention from the death in detention of Yar'Adua earlier that month. In February 1998, following the report of a special board of investigation, 26 people, including Diya and two ministers who had served in the previous FEC, were charged with conspiring to overthrow the Government.

In March 1998 a number of associations that supported Abacha conducted rallies in favour of his re-election in August. The UAD organized counter-demonstrations (which resulted in the arrest of a number of protesters by the security forces), and announced that it was to initiate a campaign of civil disobedience to oppose Abacha's candidacy in the presidential election. In April all five registered parties voted separately to nominate Abacha as the sole presidential candidate; Abacha was therefore to contest the presidential election in August unopposed.

On 8 June 1998 Abacha died unexpectedly from heart failure. The PRC designated the Chief of Defence Staff, Maj.-Gen. Abdulsalami Abubakar, as Abacha's successor, and on 9 June he was inaugurated as Head of State (having been promoted to the rank of General). Abubakar pledged to continue the Abacha Government's scheduled transition to civilian rule. The UAD, however, urged continued protests against the military administration. In mid-June Abubakar ordered the release of about 26 political prisoners, including Obasanjo (ostensibly on grounds of ill health). In July, following discussions with UN officials, the authorities agreed to release Abiola from detention. Shortly after his release, however, Abiola collapsed and subsequently died. Violent rioting ensued, amid widespread speculation that the authorities were responsible for Abiola's death. Although an autopsy confirmed that he had died of heart failure, it was indicated that his period in detention had contributed to his poor health. Later in July Abubakar announced that the transition to civilian rule would be completed on 29 May 1999 (rather than 1 October 1998). The Government annulled the results of the elections that had previously been conducted, and dissolved the five authorized political parties, NECON and other electoral bodies. In August a new, 31-member FEC, which included a number of civilians, was appointed to remain in office pending the formal transition to civilian rule; an Independent National Electoral Commission (INEC) was also established. Later that month the INEC announced that local government elections would take place on 5 December 1998 and state legislative elections on 9 January 1999, followed by elections to a bicameral national legislature on 20 February and a presidential election on 27 February. On 7 September 1998 the Government published the draft Constitution that had been submitted by the NCC in June 1995. Abubakar announced that all charges against Nigerian exiles abroad had been abandoned.

Some 25 new political organizations submitted applications for registration to the INEC. The commission provisionally approved nine political associations, notably the People's Democratic Party (PDP), which principally comprised former opponents of the Abacha administration. In October 1998 CMAG recommended that Commonwealth member states end sanctions against Nigeria, in preparation for the country's readmission to the Commonwealth. At the end of that month, in response to the democratization measures undertaken by the Government, the EU ended a number of sanctions against Nigeria (while maintaining the embargo on the export of armaments).

In November 1998 Obasanjo (who had joined the PDP in October) announced that he intended to seek nomination as the party's presidential candidate. At elections to Nigeria's 768 local municipal councils, which took place, as scheduled, on 5 December, the PDP secured about 60% of the votes cast. The INEC subsequently declared that the PDP, the All Nigeria People's Party (ANPP) and the Alliance for Democracy (AD) were the only political organizations to qualify for final registration, having achieved the requisite minimum of 5% of the votes cast in 24 seats. The state legislative elections took place on 9 January 1999. The PDP, with about 50% of votes cast, secured 20 state governorships, while the ANPP obtained nine. Elections in Bayelsa State were postponed, owing to clashes between the security forces and Ijaw activists (whose continued attacks against petroleum installations resulted in the imposition of a state of emergency at the end of December 1998).

In January 1999 several prominent members of former administrations announced that they intended to seek nomination to contest the forthcoming presidential election. In early February the ANPP and AD, which, despite the stated opposition of the INEC, had established an electoral alliance, nominated a joint candidate, Samuel Oluyemisi Falae (a former Minister of Finance in the Babangida administration). Later that month Obasanjo was elected as the presidential candidate of the PDP, defeating a former civilian Vice-President, Alex Ekwueme. At the elections to the bicameral legislature, which took place on 20 February, the PDP secured 215 seats in the 360-member House of Representatives and 66 seats in the 109-member Senate. (Voting in the Niger Delta region was postponed, owing to continued unrest, and a further by-election for the vacant seat to the National Assembly took place in March.)

On 27 February 1999 Obasanjo was elected to the presidency with 62.8% of votes cast. Voting irregularities were reported, and Falae submitted a legal challenge to the electoral results at the Court of Appeal on the grounds of malpractice. In March the Government ordered the release of some 95 prisoners, including Diya, who had been detained in connection with the alleged coup attempt in December 1997. In April 1999 the Court of Appeal dismissed Falae's challenge to the declaration of Obasanjo as President-elect, and a further legal appeal at the Supreme Court was also rejected. The Constitution was promulgated on 5 May. Obasanjo was formally inaugurated as President on 29 May; on the same day Nigeria was readmitted as a full member of the Commonwealth. On 3 June the inaugural session of the National Assembly took place. Obasanjo nominated a new Cabinet, principally comprising members of the PDP, which was approved by the Senate later that month. He also undertook a reorganization of the armed forces, removing more than 150 military officers who had served under the Abacha Government.

The Christian Association of Nigeria threatened to initiate a legal challenge to the introduction of Islamic *Shari'a* law, announced in Kano and Zamfara States in December 1999 and January 2000, respectively, on the grounds that it contravened the principle of secularity enshrined in the Constitution. In February a demonstration by Christians in the northern town of Kaduna in protest at the proposed imposition of *Shari'a* in Kaduna State precipitated violent hostilities between Muslims and Christians, in which more than 300 people were killed; government troops eventually suppressed the unrest, and a curfew was imposed in the town. However, more than 50 people were killed in further clashes between Christians and Muslims in the south-eastern towns of Aba and Umuahia, which ensued in reprisal for the violence in the north. By the end of the month thousands of Christians had fled the north of the country, fearing possible retaliatory massacres. At an emergency meeting at the end of February, chaired by Obasanjo, the Governors of the 18 northern states agreed, in the interests of peace, to withdraw the new legislation introducing *Shari'a* law, and to revert to the provisions for *Shari'a* in the existing penal code, in accordance with the federal Constitution. However, the Governors of a number of the states subsequently announced that they would not comply with the federal government order, but would proceed with the implementation of *Shari'a* law. In March religious rioting in Niger State (where the adoption of the *Shari'a* law had been declared) was reported. In May some 150 people were killed in further clashes between Christians and Muslims in Kaduna; government troops were again deployed in the town to restore order. In early June Obasanjo reorganized the Cabinet, following media criticism of a number of ministers.

In August 2000, following persistent dissension between the executive and the legislature over the issue of government corruption, the President of the Senate was removed from office and charged with misusing public funds. In the same month *Shari'a* law was formally adopted in the northern states of Katsina, Jigawa and Yobe (to enter into effect later that year). In September the Governor of Borno State also announced the adoption of *Shari'a*. Although the Governors of most of these states had declared that Christians would be exempt from the provisions of *Shari'a*, social segregation of men and women and the application of punishments stipulated under Islamic law had been widely implemented in Zamfara and Kano States. In view of the violence in Kaduna State, the Governor announced that the form of *Shari'a* to be introduced in the state was to be modified to allow Islamic courts to exist in conjunction with special courts upholding secular laws.

At the end of January 2001 Obasanjo replaced 10 members of the Cabinet in an extensive reorganization, following widespread criticism of the Government's failure to resolve economic and social difficulties. In late March the Governors of Nigeria's 17 southern states, meeting in Benin City, urged that the Constitution be amended to provide for greater government decentralization, including the right for the states to establish separate security forces. In April Obasanjo replaced the heads of the three branches of the armed forces.

In mid-June 2001 religious and ethnic unrest in northern and central Nigeria intensified; some 1,000 people were killed in fighting between Christians and Muslims in Bauchi (which had become the 10th northern state to adopt *Shari'a* law). In early 2002 the death sentence imposed on a woman in northern Sokoto

State, who had been convicted in October 2001 under *Shari'a* law on charges of adultery, attracted increasing international attention. Following pressure from the international community, in March the Minister of Justice urged the 12 State Governors who had adopted *Shari'a* law to discontinue its strict enforcement, on the grounds that it contravened the Constitution for reasons of discrimination (applying only to Muslims). A Court of Appeal subsequently overturned the sentence against the convicted woman, ruling that there was insufficient evidence to justify the death penalty. However, the Governors of several northern states insisted that they would continue to implement *Shari'a*.

In April 2002 the Federal Government reached an agreement with Abacha's relatives and business associates, whereby Swiss banks were to return state funds appropriated by the former President, and the Nigerian authorities were to abandon legal proceedings against several members of Abacha's family. Also in April Obasanjo announced that he intended to seek a second term in office, while the former Head of State, Muhammadu Buhari, stated that he planned to contest the forthcoming presidential election on behalf of the ANPP. In June the INEC announced that, of 24 political parties that had applied for official registration, only three had been recognized (increasing the total number of legal associations to six). In June, after a long-standing dispute between Obasanjo and the Senate over control of public finances, the President survived an impeachment attempt by the upper chamber. In August the House of Representatives adopted by an overwhelming majority a resolution demanding that Obasanjo resign from office or face impeachment, on charges of mismanagement and abuse of power. Obasanjo refused to comply with the resolution, and at the end of that month the PDP voted in favour of drafting a list of charges against the President.

In August 2002 the *Shari'a* Court of Appeal in Katsina State upheld a sentence of death by stoning imposed in March against a woman, Amina Lawal, who had been convicted for having extramarital sexual intercourse. The case attracted international outrage, and the Minister of Justice announced that the Federal Government was opposed to the death sentence. (A further appeal against the sentence was submitted at federal level.) In the same month a *Shari'a* court in Jigawa State imposed a death sentence against a man who had been convicted for rape of a minor. In October the Federal Government announced that it would not permit executions under *Shari'a* law.

In December 2002 the INEC granted registration to a further 24 political associations, after the Supreme Court upheld an appeal by five opposition parties against their exclusion, and ordered less restrictive regulations for legalization. Later that month the Commission announced that legislative elections were to be conducted on 12 April 2003, followed by a presidential election on 19 April, and elections to regional Houses of Assembly on 3 May. In January Obasanjo was formally elected as the presidential candidate of the PDP. A further 18 political leaders subsequently announced their intention to contest the presidential election. In March further clashes between members of the Ijaw and Itsekiri ethnic group near Warri forced the suspension of the operations of a number of international petroleum companies; government troops were dispatched to the region to suppress the violence.

Incidences of violence and malpractice were reported during the federal legislative elections on 12 April 2003. The PDP emerged with an overwhelming majority in both legislative chambers (213 seats in the House of Representatives and 73 in the Senate), while the ANPP was the only other party to secure significant representation (95 seats in the House of Representatives and 28 in the Senate). At the presidential election on 19 April (the first to be organized by civilian authorities for 19 years), Obasanjo was elected for a second term by 61.9% of the valid votes cast, while Buhari received 32.2% of votes. Opposition leaders, notably Buhari, contested the results, claiming that widespread electoral malpractice had been perpetrated, and indicated that violent protests might ensue. International monitors, although generally satisfied with the organization of the elections, declared that irregularities had taken place, particularly in the region of the Niger Delta. At gubernatorial elections, which also took place on 19 April, the PDP gained eight state governorships from the ANPP and AD, losing only one (that of Kano). Later that month Obasanjo criticized a statement by EU monitors, who claimed that they had obtained evidence of electoral malpractice perpetrated in 13 states. Meanwhile, at the end of April four offshore petroleum rigs, operated by a US enterprise, Transocean, in the Niger Delta were seized by protesting Nigerian employees, who took hostage 97 foreign national workers. Military naval forces were dispatched to the region. Following negotiations between officials of NUPENG, the NLC and Transocean, all hostages were airlifted from the rigs.

Obasanjo officially dissolved the Federal Government on 21 May 2003. He was sworn in on 29 May (after a legal challenge against his inauguration by Buhari was rejected by the federal Court of Appeal), and in early June began to nominate ministers to his new administration. In mid-July Obasanjo finally inaugurated the new, 40-member Federal Government, which included the hitherto Vice-President of the World Bank, Dr Ngozi Okonjo-Iweala, as the Minister of Finance and the Economy (an appointment that reflected the authorities' stated intention to eliminate corruption and implement economic reforms).

In September 2003 the *Shari'a* Court of Appeal in Katsina State overturned the sentence of death by stoning imposed on Amina Lawal, on the grounds that procedural irregularities had discredited the previous judgment. The case had attracted international protests on Lawal's behalf. Meanwhile, legislation to repeal the death penalty was under debate at the National Assembly; the proposed abrogation was strongly opposed by the Muslim community, which perceived it as an infringement of *Shari'a* law. In January 2004 a newly established group of Islamist fundamentalist militants, known as the Taliban (styled on the Afghanistan movement of that name), attacked police stations in the capital of Yobe State, Damaturu, reportedly killing a police officer. Government troops dispatched to Yobe State restored order, killing many members of the organization, which was believed to be connected to extremist student supporters of the establishment of an Islamic state. Local government elections, conducted at the end of March, were marred by violent incidents; some 20 people were killed in ethnic clashes in central Plateau State on the day prior to the ballot. Initial results indicated that the PDP had secured about two-thirds of the contested seats, but widespread malpractice was also reported.

In early April 2004 the Government announced that some 20 army officials had been arrested, following the discovery of a conspiracy to seize power, believed to have been instigated by a former head of security in the Abacha administration, Maj. Hama al-Mustapha. (In October three senior military officers, including al-Mustapha, were charged with planning to overthrow the Government with an attack on the presidential helicopter.) Later in April reports emerged of severe clashes between Christian and Muslim tribes in farming villages on the border of Plateau State, reportedly as a result of land ownership disputes; by early May it was estimated that a total of 650 people, mainly Muslims, had been killed in the fighting. Muslims subsequently rioted in Kano in reprisal for the deaths; the Christian Association of Nigeria announced that 600 Christians had been killed and that a further 30,000 had fled from the region. Later in May Obasanjo dispatched security forces to restore order and imposed emergency powers in Plateau State, replacing the Governor with a former military officer and dissolving its legislature. (In November Obasanjo ended the state of emergency imposed in Plateau State, and reinstated the elected Governor, who, however, had been detained in London, on suspicion of financial malpractice.)

In June 2004 the NLC organized a national strike, which was widely observed, in protest at a further increase in the price of fuel. In September renewed hostilities between the Ijaw and Ijekiri in the Niger Delta prompted further concern on the part of the authorities, particularly after an Ijaw militia, the Niger Delta People's Volunteer Force, threatened a campaign to disrupt petroleum supplies by attacking installations. Consequently, the Government announced a further substantial increase in the price of fuel in that month, prompting the NLC to organize a general strike in early October. Further planned strike action by the NLC and allied organizations was suspended in mid-November, after the Government agreed to a reduction in the price. Following a peace accord between the Government and the activists, reached in October, fighting in the region declined significantly. However, Ijaw militia had failed to disarm by the scheduled date at the end of December, and a campaign of peaceful protests was threatened, on the grounds that the Government had not complied with the terms of the agreement.

In late February 2005 a three-month national conference, comprising 400 government appointed delegates, was convened to decide on political reform, including possible constitutional amendments, prior to the elections in 2007; however, the conference was boycotted by the opposition and was refused funding by the legislature. At the end of March the Government introduced new legislation permitting the establishment of unions independent of the NLC and prohibiting strikes in essential service sectors, with the aim of restricting the influence of the Congress.

In March 2005 the Minister of Education, Fabian Osuji, was dismissed for offering financial incentives to parliamentary deputies, including the Speaker of the Senate (who was subsequently also removed), with the intention of securing a substantial increase in the education budget for 2005. Osuji denied the charges, and submitted a legal appeal against his dismissal, which had been announced by Obasanjo through the national media. In early April Obasanjo dismissed the minister responsible for housing, who was accused of the clandestine sale of state property to government members. In May the trial of Osuji, together with six former senators (including the dismissed Speaker), on corruption charges commenced in Abuja. In August Vice-President Alhaji Atiku Abubakar (who was expected to contest the presidential election in 2007) became the subject of controversy, after it emerged that he was under investigation by Federal Bureau of Investigation agents in the USA for allegedly receiving payments from a member of the US Congress.

In September 2005 tension increased in the Niger Delta region, following the arrest of the leader of a prominent militant movement, the Niger Delta People Volunteer Force; Mujahid Dokubo-Asari had threatened to continue hostilities unless his demands that the Ijaw people of the region be granted self-determination were met. Petroleum installations, which had temporarily closed, resumed operations after Dokubo-Asari urged his supporters to maintain civil order. In early October he was officially charged with treason before the Abuja Federal High Court. Later that month the leader of the Movement for the Actualization of the Sovereign State of Biafra (MASSOB), Chief Ralph Uwazurike, was arrested and subsequently charged with treason (on the grounds that he had attempted to overthrow the Federal Government). In December Obasanjo placed defence and security personnel in the region on alert, following a petroleum pipeline explosion, in which several people were killed. Protests by members of MASSOB against the arrest of their leader ended in clashes, in which some 20 people were killed.

In January 2006 four foreign nationals employed by companies subcontracted by the Shell Petroleum Development Co were seized by militants in Bayelsa State; a hitherto unknown organization, the Movement for the Emancipation of the Niger Delta (MEND), claimed responsibility for taking the hostages. Following the explosion of a further petroleum pipeline, Shell suspended production from that offshore field (equivalent to one-tenth of the country's total output). MEND demanded that the Shell Petroleum Development Co pay US $1,500m. in compensation for environmental damage, and the release from custody of Dokubo-Asari and the Governor of Bayelsa State, Diepreye Alamaieyeseigha, who had been arrested in the United Kingdom and charged with financial malpractice. (Dokubo-Asari was released in June 2007; Alamaieyeseigha was given a two-year custodial sentence in August but released several days later.) At the end of January 2006 MEND announced the release of the hostages on humanitarian grounds, but maintained that it would continue attacks in the Niger Delta region and seized a further nine foreign nationals employed by a subcontracted US enterprise, Willbros. Six of the hostages were released one week later, while the remaining three (two US and one British national) were released in late March. Also in February a High Court in Port Harcourt ruled that the Shell Petroleum Development Co pay $1,500m. in compensation to the Ijaw population in the Niger Delta for environmental damage, in compliance with a decision by the National Assembly in 2000.

The situation worsened during mid-2006 and in June five Nigerian soldiers were killed in a raid by MEND on a petroleum installation. In mid-August Obasanjo ordered the establishment of a joint operation between the armed forces and the police to patrol the Niger Delta region and respond to reports of kidnapping; at least 12 oil workers had been taken hostage during that month. Shortly after the operation commenced it was reported that the security forces had opened fire in the region, forcing civilians to flee from the area. Concerns were raised that the order from the President would aggravate an already volatile situation; in October the number of kidnappings multiplied and the disturbances led to the reduction of petroleum production by some 25%.

In early 2006 the Nigerian Constitutional Committee conducted a series of public debates on proposed amendments to the Constitution, which would allow Obasanjo to seek a third term in office. In early April hostility worsened between Obasanjo and Abubakar (who protested at the proposals to end the constitutional restriction on two presidential terms). In May the National Assembly rejected the proposals, thus preventing Obasanjo from contesting the 2007 presidential election.

Prior to the 2007 presidential and legislative elections, scheduled to be held on 14 and 21 April, the security forces commenced the procurement of firearms to arm up to 50,000 new police officers. A task force was also to be established, mandated with the disarmament of criminal gangs, in an attempt to avoid the levels of violence that marred the 2003 elections.

In the months leading up to the elections several government reorganizations were effected. In June 2006 Obasanjo reassigned Okonja-Iwealato to the foreign affairs portfolio amid concerns over the durability of the Government's financial management and economic reforms, while the hitherto Minister of Solid Mineral Development, Obiageli Ezekwesili, assumed responsibility for education. Okonja-Iwealato resigned from the new position in August, having been dismissed from her role as head of the economic reform team; Prof. Joy Ogwu replaced her at the Ministry of Foreign Affairs. In October the Spritual Head of the Muslim community, Alhaji Mohamed Maccido, was killed when an aircraft carrying him crashed shortly after leaving Abuja. Several months prior to the incident Obasanjo had implemented a series of safety reforms in the civil aviation sector. In early November Prof. Babalola Borishade was dismissed as Minister of Aviation and replaced by Femi Fani-Kayode, hitherto the Minister of Culture and Tourism. Further changes to the Government were carried out in mid-January 2007 when almost one-third of the ministries were dissolved or merged to simplify the administration's structure and improve its efficiency ahead of the forthcoming elections. Three new appointments were made during the reorganization, including that of Thomas I. Aguiyi-Ironsi to the defence portfolio.

With Obasanjo prohibited from contesting the presidential election, Abubakar emerged as the primary presidential candidate. However, his relationship with the President had become increasingly strained since the 2003 elections, when he challenged Obasanjo's campaign for a second term, and Obasanjo strongly opposed Abubakar's candidacy. In September 2006 Obasanjo submitted a report to the Senate containing allegations of fraudulent activity involving Abubakar, who was subsequently indicted by the Economic and Financial Crimes Commission (EFCC), which had been established by Obasanjo in 2004. As Vice-President, Abubakar held immunity against prosecution unless impeached. Later in September 2006 he was suspended from the PDP for three months; although he retained his position as Vice-President, the suspension prevented him from seeking nomination from the PDP to stand as its presidential candidate. Abubakar continually denied the allegations against him, and it later emerged that he would represent the Action Congress (AC), a new party formed in September by the merger of several minor political parties, in the presidential election. Abubakar was disqualified from contesting the election by the INEC in mid-March 2007, owing to his indictment for corruption, but following a number of legal challenges, his candidature was confirmed by a Supreme Court ruling on 16 April.

The presidential election was expected to be a historical landmark for Nigeria; for the first time in the country's history power was to be transferred between democratically elected civilian leaders. However, polling was marred by violent incidents that followed gubernatorial and state assembly elections, which were held on 14 April 2007. According to provisional results of the state elections, the PDP secured control of 28 states, the ANPP five, while the AC and the Progressive People's Alliance each took the largest number of votes in one state. The results in the remaining two states were declared void, owing to voter irregularities.

Provisional results of the presidential election, which was held concurrently with those to the National Assembly as scheduled on 21 April 2007, released by the INEC indicated that the PDP candidate, Alhaji Umaru Musa Yar'Adua (the younger brother of the late Maj.-Gen. (retd) Shehu Musa Yar'Adua, former Vice-President in Obasanjo's military Government during the 1960s), had secured a decisive victory, receiving 70.00% of the votes cast. Buhari, who contested the election as the candidate of the ANPP, was his closest rival with 18.65% of the ballots, while Abubakar secured 7.25%. Yar'Adua was sworn in as President on 29 May. Despite claims by the INEC that the elections had been successfully held, international observers cast doubt on the credibility of the polls as reports emerged that no voting took place in some states due to delays in the distribution of ballot papers. Provisional results of elections to the National Assembly indicated that the PDP had increased its majority in both the House of Representatives and the Senate, winning 258 seats and 78 seats, respectively. The ANPP secured 64 seats in the lower house and 22 seats in the upper chamber.

Opposition parties challenged the outcome of the presidential election, calling for the results to be annulled and for an interim Government to be established. However, members of the Senate insisted that to cancel the election results would be unconstitutional. Meanwhile, shortly after the presidential election Ezekwesili announced her resignation as Minister of Education, to take effect on 27 April 2007. Ezekwesili assumed a new role at the World Bank as Regional Vice-President responsible for Africa and was replaced by Dr Sayyadi Abba Ruma, hitherto the Minister of State for Education. In June the House of Representatives elected for the first time a woman, Patricia Etteh, to the position of Speaker. However, following allegations regarding the misappropriation of funds, Etteh resigned in November, and was replaced by Dimeji Bankole.

President Yar'Adua named a new Cabinet in August 2007, which included Mahmud Yayale Ahmed as Minister of Defence, Ojo Maduekwe as Minister of Foreign Affairs and Shamsudeen Usman as Minister of Finance; in October four more ministers were sworn in, having received approval from the Senate. Yar'Adua assumed responsibility for the petroleum resources portfolio, as Obasanjo had before him, and pledged to continue with reforms to the energy sector that had commenced under the previous administration. Furthermore the new President ordered investigations, which commenced in August, into the award of numerous petroleum and gas contracts. (Yar'Adua also established a 22-member electoral reform panel to address issues that led to the violence triggered by the April elections.)

Following the election of Yar'Adua in April 2007, Buhari and Abubakar had instigated legal proceedings to have the results of the ballot annulled. However, at a final hearing in Abuja in February 2008 five judges dismissed the case, citing insufficient grounds for overruling the result. The two defeated candidates announced their intention to appeal against the decision in the Supreme Court. By this time eight State Governors had had their appointments nullified by the Court of Appeal and in April the elections of the Governors of Bayelsa and Sokoto States were also ruled invalid.

Unrest continued in the Niger Delta region throughout 2007 with numerous kidnappings and abductions reported, and in the months preceding the elections there had also been an escalation of attacks on oil installations and several car bombings in Port Harcourt; by mid-February some 52 hostages had been taken, the majority of whom had links to the petroleum sector. President Yar'Adua had indicated that his administration would give special priority to the problems of the Niger Delta and intensive discussions commenced with the newly elected Governors from the region. However, in August a cease-fire negotiated by the Nigerian Government and MEND in May broke down and further abductions and disruptions to petroleum production were reported during late 2007 and early 2008.

Nigeria has taken a leading role in African affairs and is a prominent member of the Economic Community of West African States (ECOWAS, see p. 232) and other regional organizations. The Nigerian Government has contributed a significant number of troops to the ECOWAS Monitoring Group (ECOMOG, see p. 235), which was deployed in Liberia from August 1990 in response to the conflict between government forces and rebels in that country (see the chapter on Liberia). In 1993 Nigerian troops were dispatched to Sierra Leone, in response to a formal request by the Sierra Leonean Government for military assistance to repulse attacks by rebels in that country. Following the completion of the transition to civilian rule in Nigeria in May 1999, a phased withdrawal of Nigerian troops from Sierra Leone commenced. By the end of April 2000 all Nigerian troops belonging to ECOMOG had left Sierra Leone; however, Nigeria continued to contribute troops to the UN Mission in Sierra Leone (UNAMSIL). In September an official visit to Nigeria by the US President, Bill Clinton, the first by a US Head of State since 1978, provided for a number of new trade and development initiatives. After further full-scale conflict in Liberia in mid-2003 (see the chapter on Liberia), the Liberian President, Charles Taylor, finally accepted an offer of asylum from Obasanjo, following pressure from the international community, and took up residence in Calabar, in south-eastern Nigeria, in early August. Some 1,500 Nigerian troops, which were deployed in the country, under an ECOWAS mandate, at the end of August, were instrumental in restoring peace and were incorporated into the replacement contingent, the UN Mission in Liberia (UNMIL, see p. 83), on 1 October. In October the Nigerian Government strongly protested at the US authorities' approval of a reward of some US $2m. for the arrest of Taylor (who had been indicted by the Special Court established in Sierra Leone to try war crime suspects). In March 2006 Nigeria announced that it had received a formal request from the new Liberian Government (see chapter on Liberia) to extradite Taylor to the Special Court. Obasanjo agreed to return him to the Liberian authorities, but failed to comply with demands by the Chief Prosecutor of the Special Court and the USA to take him into custody. Taylor fled from his residence in Calabar, but was apprehended two days later in Borno State, near the border with Cameroon, and dispatched to Liberia, from where he was immediately extradited by UNMIL peace-keepers to the Special Court.

In 1991 the Nigerian Government claimed that Cameroonian security forces had annexed several Nigerian fishing settlements in Cross River State (in south-eastern Nigeria), following a long-standing border dispute, based on a 1913 agreement between Germany and the United Kingdom that ceded the Bakassi peninsula in the Gulf of Guinea (a region with significant petroleum reserves) to Cameroon. Subsequent negotiations between Nigerian and Cameroonian officials in an effort to resolve the dispute achieved little progress. In December 1993 some 500 Nigerian troops were dispatched to the region, in response to a number of incidents in which Nigerian nationals had been killed by Cameroonian security forces. Later that month the two nations agreed to establish a joint patrol at the disputed area, and to investigate the cause of the incidents. In February 1994, however, the Nigerian Government increased the number of troops deployed in the region. Later in February the Cameroonian Government announced that it was to submit the dispute for adjudication by the UN, the Organization of African Unity (OAU, now the African Union, see p. 164) and the International Court of Justice (ICJ), and requested military assistance from France. Subsequent reports of clashes between Cameroonian and Nigerian forces in the region prompted fears of a full-scale conflict between the two nations.

In February 1996 renewed hostilities between Nigerian and Cameroonian forces in the Bakassi region resulted in several casualties. Later that month, however, Nigeria and Cameroon agreed to refrain from further military action, and delegations from the two countries resumed discussions, with mediation by President Gnassingbe Eyadéma of Togo, in an attempt to resolve the dispute. In March the ICJ ruled that Cameroon had failed to provide sufficient evidence to support its contention that Nigeria had instigated the border dispute, and ordered both nations to cease military operations in this respect, to withdraw troops to former positions, and to co-operate with a UN investigative mission that was to be dispatched to the region. In April, however, clashes continued, with each Government accusing the other of initiating the attacks. Although tension in the region remained high, diplomatic efforts to avoid further conflict increased in May; in that month a Cameroonian delegation visited Nigeria, while Abacha accepted an invitation to attend an OAU summit meeting, which was to be convened in Yaoundé in July. The UN investigative mission visited the Bakassi region in September. In May 1997 the Cameroonian Government denied further allegations by Nigeria that it had initiated hostilities; the UN requested that the Togolese President continue mediation efforts. Further clashes between Nigerian and Cameroonian forces were reported in December 1997 and February 1998. In March the Nigerian Government contested the jurisdiction of the ICJ to rule on the Bakassi issue, on the grounds that the two countries had agreed to settle the dispute through bilateral negotiations. In June, however, the Court pronounced that it had the necessary jurisdiction.

In October 2002 the ICJ finally ruled that the disputed Bakassi region was part of Cameroon, under the terms of the 1913 agreement. Obasanjo criticized the decision, in support of strong opposition expressed by the Nigerian majority inhabitants of the peninsula, although he subsequently pledged to abide by the ruling. In August 2003, following UN mediation, Nigeria and Cameroon finally adopted a framework agreement for the implementation of the ICJ's judgment; all military and administrative personnel were to be withdrawn from the Bakassi region, and a commission, comprising Nigerian, Cameroonian and UN officials, was to resolve outstanding issues for the redemarcation of boundaries between the two countries, in a process that was expected to continue for up to three years. In December the Nigerian Government ceded control of some 33 villages on its north-eastern border to Cameroon, but sovereignty over the disputed territory with petroleum resources remained under discussion by the commission. However, the Nigerian Government announced that the transfer of authority in the peninsula, scheduled for September 2004, had been postponed, citing technical difficulties in the final redemarcation of the joint border. Following a meeting in May 2005 between Obasanjo and the Head of State of Cameroon, conducted in Geneva, Switzerland, under the aegis of the UN Secretary-General, it was announced that the two sides had agreed to draft a new programme for Nigeria's withdrawal from the Bakassi peninsula. On 12 June 2006 an accord was signed, according to which Nigeria agreed to withdraw troops from the peninsula within 60 days, and on 14 August Nigerian troops left the peninsula. Although the peninsula would remain under Nigerian control during the interim period, a full transfer of the Bakassi peninsula was to be completed by June 2008. The situation remained calm during October 2006 as steady progress was made in the demarcation of the border between the countries and agreement was reached on the relocation of 13 villages. However, in November 2007 21 Cameroonian soldiers were reported to have been killed by Nigerian troops, raising concerns that the security of the region was under threat. The Nigerian authorities denied involvement in the attack and local sources blamed a faction of MEND; however a group styling itself the Liberators of the Southern Cameroons later claimed responsibility, claiming that the soldiers had been implicated in illegal arms trading with Nigerian forces. Meanwhile, that same month the Nigerian Senate approved a motion to declare the handover of the Bakassi peninsula to be illegal and that no Nigerian territory could be ceded without amendments to the Constitution.

In mid-February 2007, following a meeting in Abuja, Nigeria signed a pact with Benin and Togo aimed at promoting peace and stability between the three countries and which provided for the establishment of a body to be known as the Nigeria–Benin–Togo Co-prosperity Zone. The three countries also announced the implementation of the ECOWAS Protocol on Free Movement of Persons and the Right of Residence and Establishment, and an early warning system for conflict prevention.

Government

Under the terms of the Constitution of the Federal Republic of Nigeria, which entered into effect on 31 May 1999, executive power is vested in the President, who is the Head of State. The President, who is elected for a term of four years (and is restricted to two mandates), nominates a Vice-President and a Cabinet, subject to confirmation by the Senate. Legislative power is vested in the bicameral National Assembly, comprising a 360-member House of Representatives and a 109-member Senate, which is elected by universal suffrage for a four-year term. Nigeria is a federation of 36 states, comprising 774 local government areas. The executive power of a state is vested in the Governor of that state, who is elected for a four-year term, and the legislative power in the House of Assembly of that state.

Defence

As assessed at November 2007, Nigeria's total armed forces numbered 80,000 (army 62,000, navy 8,000 and air force 10,000). There was also a paramilitary force of 82,000. Military service is voluntary. Expenditure on defence by the Federal Government in 2007 was budgeted at ₦122,000m.

Economic Affairs

In 2006, according to estimates by the World Bank, Nigeria's gross national income (GNI), measured at average 2004–06 prices, was US $92,358m., equivalent to $640 per head (or $1,050 per head on an international purchasing-power parity basis). During 1996–2006, it was estimated, the population increased, in real terms, at an average annual rate of 2.6%, while gross domestic product (GDP) per head rose by 1.8%. Overall GDP increased, in real terms, at an average annual rate of 4.4% in 1996–2006; growth was 5.9% in 2006.

Agriculture (including hunting, forestry and fishing) contributed an estimated 31.1% of GDP in 2006. An estimated 29.8% of the labour force were employed in the sector in 2005. The principal cash crops are cocoa (which accounted for only 0.3% of total merchandise exports in 2006), rubber and oil palm. Staple food crops include rice, maize, taro, yams, cassava, sorghum and millet. Timber production, the raising of livestock (principally goats, sheep, cattle and poultry), and artisanal fisheries are also important. According to the World Bank, agricultural GDP increased at an average annual rate of 5.2% in 1996–2006. Growth in agricultural GDP was 7.0% in 2006.

Industry (including mining, manufacturing, construction and power) engaged an estimated 3.8% of the employed labour force in 2005, and contributed an estimated 43.5% of GDP in 2006. According to the World Bank, industrial GDP increased at an average annual rate of 3.2% in 1996–2006. It increased by 5.1% in 2006.

Mining contributed 38.8% of GDP in 2006, although the sector engaged just 0.1% of the employed labour force in 2005. The principal mineral is petroleum, of which Nigeria is Africa's leading producer (providing an estimated 97.7% of total export earnings in 2006). In addition, Nigeria possesses substantial deposits of natural gas and coal. In late 1999 the Nigerian Government commenced exports of liquefied natural gas, and by 2004 natural gas accounted for 8.8% of earnings. A 678-km pipeline, which would transport natural gas from the Escravos field, in Delta State, to Benin, Togo and Ghana, commenced operations in April 2007. Tin and iron ore are also mined, while there are plans to exploit deposits of uranium. The GDP of the mining sector was estimated by the IMF to have declined by an average of 0.1% per year in 1997–2001; mining GDP increased by 0.6% in 2001.

Manufacturing contributed 3.0% of GDP in 2006, and engaged about 1.8% of the employed labour force in 2005. The principal sectors are food-processing, brewing, petroleum-refining, iron and steel, motor vehicles (using imported components), textiles, cigarettes, footwear, pharmaceuticals, pulp and paper, and cement. According to the World Bank, manufacturing GDP increased at an average annual rate of 5.0% in 1996–2006. Manufacturing GDP increased by 7.0% in 2006.

Energy is derived principally from natural gas, which provided some 62.7% of electricity in 2004, and hydroelectric power (34.2%); petroleum provided 3.1%. Mineral fuels comprised an estimated 16% of the value of merchandise imports in 2003.

The services sector contributed an estimated 24.4% of GDP in 2006, and engaged 38.0% of the employed labour force in 2005. According to World Bank estimates, the GDP of the services sector increased at an average annual rate of 5.2% in 1996–2006. The GDP of the services sector increased by 6.3% in 2006.

In 2005 Nigeria recorded an estimated trade surplus of US $30,781m., and there was a surplus of $24,202m. on the current account of the balance of payments. In 2003 the principal source of imports (15.6%) was the USA; other major suppliers were the United Kingdom, Germany and the People's Republic of China. The USA was the principal market for exports (38.3%) in that year; other significant purchasers were India, Brazil, Spain and France. The main exports in 2004 were petroleum and natural gas. The principal imports in 2003 were machinery and transport equipment (particularly road vehicles), chemicals, manufactured goods, and food and live animals.

Nigeria's overall budget surplus for 2005 was ₦3,512,962m., equivalent to 23.6% of GDP. The country's external debt totalled US $22,178m. at the end of 2005, of which $20,342m. was long-term public debt. In that year the cost of debt-servicing was equivalent to 15.8% of the value of exports of goods and services. The annual rate of inflation averaged 13.1% in 2003–07; consumer prices increased by 5.3% in 2007. An estimated 4.5% of the labour force were unemployed at the end of 1997.

Nigeria is a member of the African Development Bank (see p. 162), of the Economic Community of West African States (see p. 232), which aims to promote trade and co-operation in West Africa, and of the Organization of the Petroleum Exporting Countries (see p. 373).

Nigeria is one of Africa's most powerful economies, but despite considerable agricultural and mineral resources, political instability has severely impeded economic reform, and it is classified as a low-income country by the World Bank. In 2004 the civilian Government of Olesegun Obasanjo promulgated a new reform policy, the National Economic Empowerment and Development Strategy (NEEDS), which was to continue for a period of three years, and comprised the main objectives of accelerated privatization and deregulation, administrative reform, greater state accountability, and improved conditions for private investment. In October 2005 the IMF endorsed the Nigerian Government's economic reform strategy detailed in

NIGERIA

NEEDS, with the approval of a two-year Policy Support Instrument (PSI) arrangement (as an alternative to a full IMF programme). Later that month the 'Paris Club' formally signed an agreement providing for the cancellation of US $18,000m. of a total $31,000m. owed to foreign Governments; Nigeria was to pay all arrears, receive the partial cancellation of debt and buy the remainder of debt with petroleum revenue generated by the higher international price. By early 2007 it was estimated that Nigeria's external debt had been reduced to just 3.0% of GDP. Meanwhile, from 2006 an escalation of unrest in the Niger Delta region, with a series of attacks against petroleum pipelines and seizures of foreign nationals as hostages, threatened national stability. Militant groups in the region continued to demand the withdrawal of all foreign enterprises exploiting the country's resources, and the violence resulted in the temporary closure of an offshore field and a 25% reduction in oil production (valued at some ₦70,000m.) in 2006. Moreover, the downturn in production further exacerbated the country's energy shortage, and many regions were subject to frequent blackouts. A number of refineries were scheduled to commence production in 2008, and in the long-term, the Government envisaged processing 50% of the economy's energy needs in Nigeria, thus reducing the reliance on imports. Meanwhile, the West African Gas Pipeline became operational in April 2007, delivering 16.4m. cu m of gas per day to Benin, Ghana and Togo. The IMF noted that strong growth had occurred in 2007, despite a decline in petroleum production in the Niger Delta, highlighting expansion in the non-oil sector, especially agriculture. GDP growth was forecast to amount to 9.1% in 2008. However, corruption remained a serious concern, and a general strike in mid-2007 caused widespread disruption to the petroleum industry, upon which Nigeria's economy was heavily reliant.

Education

Education is partly the responsibility of the state governments, although the Federal Government has played an increasingly important role since 1970. Primary education begins at six years of age and lasts for six years. Secondary education begins at 12 years of age and lasts for a further six years, comprising two three-year cycles. Education to junior secondary level (from six to 15 years of age) is free and compulsory. According to UNESCO estimates, in 2003/04 60% of children in the relevant age-group (males 64%; females 57%) were enrolled in primary education, while the comparable ratio for secondary enrolment in 1998/99 was 19% (males 19%; females 20%). In 2005 724,856 students were enrolled at Nigerian universities. Expenditure on education by the Federal Government in 2005 was ₦82,797m., equivalent to 5.0% of total expenditure in the federal budget.

Public Holidays

2008: 1 January (New Year's Day), 20 March* (Mouloud, Birth of the Prophet), 21–24 March (Easter), 1 October (National Day), 1 October* (Id al-Fitr, end of Ramadan), 9 December* (Id al-Kabir, Feast of the Sacrifice), 25–26 December (Christmas).

2009: 1 January (New Year's Day), 9 March* (Mouloud, Birth of the Prophet), 10–13 April (Easter), 1 October (National Day), 20 September* (Id al-Fitr, end of Ramadan), 27 November* (Id al-Kabir, Feast of the Sacrifice), 25–26 December (Christmas).

* These holidays are dependent on the Islamic lunar calendar, and may vary by one or two days from the dates given.

Weights and Measures

The metric system is in force.

Statistical Survey

Sources (unless otherwise stated): National Bureau of Statistics, Plot 762, Independence Avenue, Central Business District, PMB 127, Garki, Abuja; tel. (9) 2731085; fax (9) 2731084; internet www.nigerianstat.gov.ng; Central Bank of Nigeria, Central Business District, PMB 187, Garki, Abuja; tel. (9) 61639701; fax (9) 61636012; e-mail info@cenbank.org; internet www.cenbank.org.

Area and Population

AREA, POPULATION AND DENSITY

Area (sq km)	909,890*
Population (census results)	
28–30 November 1991†	88,992,220
21–27 March 2006 (provisional)	
Males	71,709,859
Females	68,293,683
Total	140,003,542
Density (per sq km) at March 2006	157.2

* 351,310 sq miles.
† Revised 15 September 2001.

STATES
(2006 census, provisional)

	Area (sq km)	Population	Density (per sq km)	Capital
Abia	4,900	2,833,999	578	Umuahia
Adamawa	38,700	3,168,101	82	Yola
Akwa Ibom	6,900	3,920,208	568	Uyo
Anambra	4,865	4,182,032	860	Awka
Bauchi	49,119	4,676,465	95	Bauchi
Bayelsa	9,059	1,703,358	188	Yenogoa
Benue	30,800	4,219,244	137	Makurdi
Borno	72,609	4,151,193	57	Maiduguri
Cross River	21,787	2,888,966	133	Calabar
Delta	17,108	4,098,391	240	Asaba
Ebonyi	6,400	2,173,501	340	Abakaliki
Edo	19,187	3,218,332	168	Benin City
Ekiti	5,435	2,384,212	439	Ado-Ekiti
Enugu	7,534	3,257,298	432	Enugu
Gombe	17,100	2,353,879	138	Gombe
Imo	5,288	3,934,899	744	Owerri
Jigawa	23,287	4,348,649	187	Dutse
Kaduna	42,481	6,066,562	143	Kaduna
Kano	20,280	9,383,682	463	Kano
Katsina	23,561	5,792,578	246	Katsina
Kebbi	36,985	3,238,628	88	Birnin Kebbi
Kogi	27,747	3,278,487	118	Lokoja
Kwara	35,705	2,371,089	66	Ilorin
Lagos	3,671	9,013,534	2,455	Ikeja
Nassarawa	28,735	1,863,275	65	Lafia
Niger	68,925	3,950,249	57	Minna
Ogun	16,400	3,728,098	227	Abeokuta
Ondo	15,820	3,441,024	218	Akure
Osun	9,026	3,423,535	379	Oshogbo
Oyo	26,500	5,591,589	211	Ibadan
Plateau	27,147	3,178,712	117	Jos
Rivers	10,575	5,185,400	490	Port Harcourt
Sokoto	27,825	6,696,999	241	Sokoto
Taraba	56,282	2,300,736	41	Jalingo
Yobe	46,609	2,321,591	50	Damaturu
Zamfara	37,931	3,259,846	86	Gusau
Federal Capital Territory (Abuja)	7,607	1,405,201	185	Abuja
Total	**909,890**	**140,003,542**	**157**	—

NIGERIA

PRINCIPAL TOWNS
(unrevised census of November 1991)

Town	Population	Town	Population
Lagos (federal capital)*	5,195,247	Enugu	407,756
Kano	2,166,554	Oyo	369,894
Ibadan	1,835,300	Warri	363,382
Kaduna	933,642	Abeokuta	352,735
Benin City	762,719	Onitsha	350,280
Port Harcourt	703,421	Sokoto	329,639
Maiduguri	618,278	Okene	312,775
Zaria	612,257	Calabar	310,839
Ilorin	532,089	Katsina	259,315
Jos	510,300	Oshogbo	250,951
Aba	500,183	Akure	239,124
Ogbomosho	433,030	Bauchi	206,537

* Federal capital moved to Abuja (population 107,069) in December 1991.

Mid-2007 ('000 incl. suburbs, UN estimates): Lagos 9,466; Kano 3,140; Ibadan 2,628; Kaduna 1,442; Benin City 1,190; Port Harcourt 1,020; Ogbomosho 951; Maiduguri 896; Zaria 889 (Source: UN, *World Urbanization Prospects: The 2007 Revision*).

BIRTHS AND DEATHS
(annual averages, UN estimates)

	1990–95	1995–2000	2000–05
Birth rate (per 1,000)	46.6	44.5	42.7
Death rate (per 1,000)	17.8	17.4	17.5

Source: UN, *World Population Prospects: The 2006 Revision*.

Expectation of life (years at birth, WHO estimates): 47.6 (males 47.0; females 48.2) in 2005 (Source: WHO, *World Health Statistics*).

EMPLOYMENT
('000 persons aged 14 years and over)

	2003	2004	2005
Agriculture, hunting, forestry and fishing	27,840	28,439	37,487
Mining and quarrying	66	67	89
Manufacturing	820	836	1,173
Electricity, gas and water	410	422	551
Construction	260	267	353
Wholesale and retail trade; repairs of motor vehicles and motorcycles and personal and household articles	93	97	134
Hotels and restaurants	87	89	125
Transport, storage and communications	400	411	537
Financial intermediation	270	275	363
Real estate, renting and business activities	59	60	78
Public administration, defence and compulsory social security	4,900	5,039	6,547
Education	8,430	8,760	12,239
Health and social welfare	280	291	383
Other community, social and personal service activities	2,885	2,942	3,874
Total employed	**46,800**	**47,993**	**63,932**

Health and Welfare

KEY INDICATORS

Total fertility rate (children per woman, 2005)	5.6
Under-5 mortality rate (per 1,000 live births, 2005)	194
HIV/AIDS (% of persons aged 15–49, 2005)	3.9
Physicians (per 1,000 head, 2003)	0.28
Hospital beds (per 1,000 head, 2000)	1.20
Health expenditure (2004): US $ per head (PPP)	52.7
Health expenditure (2004): % of GDP	4.6
Health expenditure (2004): public (% of total)	30.4
Access to water (% of persons, 2004)	48
Access to sanitation (% of persons, 2004)	44
Human Development Index (2005): ranking	158
Human Development Index (2005): value	0.470

For sources and definitions, see explanatory note on p. vi.

Agriculture

PRINCIPAL CROPS
('000 metric tons)

	2004	2005	2006*
Wheat	62	66	71
Rice (paddy)	3,334	3,567	3,924
Maize	5,567	5,957	6,404
Millet	6,699	7,168	7,705
Sorghum	8,578	9,178	9,866
Potatoes	726	776	838
Sweet potatoes	2,996	3,205	3,462
Cassava	38,845	41,565	45,721
Taro (Coco yam)	4,736	5,068	5,473
Yams	31,776	34,000	36,720
Sugar cane	854	914	987
Dry cow peas	2,631	2,815	3,040
Cashew nuts	555	594	636
Kolanuts*	85	n.a.	86
Soybeans	528	565	605
Groundnuts (in shell)	3,250	3,478	3,825
Coconuts	195	209	225
Oil palm fruit*	8,700	9,005	8,300
Sesame seed†	78	100	100
Melonseed	422	451	483
Cottonseed*	258	264	270
Tomatoes*	992	1,057	896
Green chillies and peppers*	730	738	722
Green onions and shallots*	220	n.a.	221
Dry onions*	615	n.a.	616
Carrots and turnips*	248	257	240
Okra*	730	n.a.	731
Green corn (maize)*	576	n.a.	577
Plantains	2,421	2,591	2,785
Citrus fruits*	3,436	3,546	3,300
Guavas, mangoes and mangosteens*	782	812	732
Pineapples*	905	917	895
Papayas*	804	834	759
Cocoa beans	412	441	485
Ginger	117	125	134
Cotton (lint)*	140	140	152
Tobacco (leaves)*	15	15	14
Natural rubber (dry weight)	142	n.a.	143

* FAO estimates.
† Unofficial figures.

Aggregate production ('000 metric tons, may include official, semi-official or estimated data): Total cereals 24,321 in 2004, 26,031 in 2005, 28,070 in 2006; Total roots and tubers 79,079 in 2004, 84,614 in 2005, 92,214 in 2006; Total vegetables (incl. melons) 8,957 in 2004, 9,380 in 2005, 9,654 in 2006; Total fruits (excl. melons) 9,748 in 2004, 10,101 in 2005, 9,874 in 2006.

Source: FAO.

LIVESTOCK
('000 head, year ending September)

	2003	2004	2005
Horses*	205	206	206
Asses, mules or hinnies*	1,000	1,050	n.a.
Cattle	15,164	15,700	15,875
Camels*	18	18	n.a.
Pigs	6,356	6,611*	6,650*
Sheep*	22,500	23,000	23,000
Goats*	27,000	28,000	28,000
Chickens	137,680	143,500	150,700

* FAO estimate(s).

2006: Figures assumed to be unchanged from previous year (FAO estimates).

Source: FAO.

NIGERIA

LIVESTOCK PRODUCTS
('000 metric tons, FAO estimates)

	2004	2005	2006
Cattle meat	280.0	280.0	284.1
Sheep meat	100.7	100.7	103.4
Goat meat	147.1	147.1	147.4
Pig meat	201.2	205.6	209.5
Chicken meat	191.5	189.9	221.8
Game meat	120	n.a.	120
Cows' milk	432	n.a.	463
Hen eggs	n.a.	n.a.	526

Source: FAO.

Forestry

ROUNDWOOD REMOVALS
('000 cubic metres, excluding bark, FAO estimates)

	2004	2005	2006
Sawlogs, veneer logs and logs for sleepers	7,100	7,100	7,100
Pulpwood	39	39	39
Other industrial wood	2,279	2,279	2,279
Fuel wood	60,852	61,274	61,629
Total	70,270	70,692	71,047

Source: FAO.

SAWNWOOD PRODUCTION
('000 cubic metres, including railway sleepers)

	1995	1996	1997
Broadleaved (hardwood)	2,356	2,178	2,000

1998–2006: Broadleaved (hardwood) production as in 1997.

Source: FAO.

Fishing

('000 metric tons, live weight)

	2003	2004	2005
Capture	475.2	465.3	523.2
Tilapias	31.2	22.9	31.8
Elephant snout fishes	15.4	19.5	18.6
Torpedo-shaped catfishes	15.7	9.6	16.2
Sea catfishes	18.3	20.5	21.2
West African croakers	13.5	14.1	10.7
Sardinellas	67.4	71.4	65.8
Bonga shad	21.6	14.7	19.8
Southern pink shrimp	13.2	11.4	12.4
Other shrimps and prawns	15.0	11.5	16.2
Aquaculture	30.7	44.0	56.4
Total catch	505.8	509.2	579.5

Source: FAO.

Mining

(metric tons, unless otherwise indicated)

	2004	2005	2006
Coal, bituminous	—	—	10,000
Kaolin*	58,000	93,000	100,000
Gypsum*	160,000	150,000	160,000
Crude petroleum ('000 barrels)	900,400	923,500	813,950
Natural gas (million cu m)	57,747	57,369	57,754
Tin concentrates*†	1,000	1,300	1,400

* Estimates.
† Metal content.

Source: US Geological Survey.

Industry

SELECTED PRODUCTS
('000 metric tons, unless otherwise indicated)

	2001	2002	2003
Palm oil*	903	908	915
Raw sugar*†	40	40	40
Wheat flour*†	1,564	1,730	1,598
Beer of barley*†	956	1,171	1,170
Beer of sorghum*†	698	760	794
Plywood ('000 cubic metres)*†	55	55	55
Wood pulp*†	23	23	23
Paper and paperboard*†	19	19	19
Liquefied petroleum gas ('000 barrels)†	1,000	2,300	2,000
Motor spirit—petrol ('000 barrels)†	24,400	22,400	20,000
Kerosene ('000 barrels)†	12,500	11,800	12,000
Gas-diesel (distillate fuel) oil ('000 barrels)†	18,900	18,800	19,000
Residual fuel oils ('000 barrels)†	21,500	17,200	17,000
Cement†	2,400	2,100	2,100
Tin metal—unwrought (metric tons)†	25	25	25
Electric energy (million kWh)‡	15,453	21,544	20,183

* Source: FAO.
† Estimates.
‡ Source: UN, *Industrial Commodity Statistics Yearbook*.

2004 (million kWh): 20,224 (Source: UN, *Industrial Commodity Statistics Yearbook*).

Source (unless otherwise indicated): US Geological Survey.

2004 ('000 barrels, estimates): Motor spirit–petrol 4,600; Kerosene 4,900; Gas-diesel (distillate fuel) oil 8,800; Residual fuel oils 12,400 (Source: US Geological Survey).

2005 ('000 barrels, estimates): Motor spirit–petrol 14,800; Kerosene 10,100; Gas-diesel (distillate fuel) oil 15,800; Residual fuel oils 19,200 (Source: US Geological Survey).

2006 ('000 barrels, estimates): Motor spirit–petrol 8,500; Kerosene 6,100; Gas-diesel (distillate fuel) oil 9,400; Residual fuel oils 14,400 (Source: US Geological Survey).

Finance

CURRENCY AND EXCHANGE RATES

Monetary Units
100 kobo = 1 naira (₦).

Sterling, Dollar and Euro Equivalents (28 September 2007)
£1 sterling = 225.220 naira;
US $1 = 125.644 naira;
€1 = 178.151 naira;
1,000 naira = £3.92 = $7.96 = €5.61.

Average Exchange Rate (naira per US $)
2004   132.888
2005   131.274
2006   128.652

NIGERIA

Statistical Survey

FEDERAL BUDGET
(₦ million)

Revenue	2003	2004	2005
Tax revenue	1,130,200	1,690,200	1,706,726
Income and profit	798,300	1,313,600	n.a.
Import duties	195,469	217,100	n.a.
Other duties	136,431	159,500	n.a.
Non-tax revenue	1,444,896	2,211,200	3,454,386
Total	2,575,096	3,901,400	5,161,112

Expenditure	2003	2004	2005
Recurrent expenditure	984,268	954,741	1,128,640
Administration	307,849	306,843	434,672
General	166,056	101,337	248,730
Defence	51,044	76,324	71,672
Internal security	68,352	97,800	81,950
Economic services	96,032	58,782	64,309
Social and community services	102,566	134,391	151,647
Education	64,756	76,528	82,797
Transfers	363,363	382,525	393,963
Pensions and gratuities	34,150	72,201	84,050
Other	80,309	—	—
Capital expenditure	241,689	351,260	519,510
General administration	66,706	108,964	132,610
Roads and construction	17,459	40,671	89,057
Total	1,225,957	1,306,001	1,648,150

INTERNATIONAL RESERVES
(US $ million at 31 December)

	2004	2005	2006
Total*	16,956	28,280	42,299

* Almost exclusively foreign exchange, and excluding gold reserves (687,000 troy ounces each year).

Source: IMF, *International Financial Statistics*.

MONEY SUPPLY
(₦ million at 31 December)

	2003	2004	2005
Currency outside banks	412,155	458,587	563,220
Demand deposits at commercial banks	577,664	728,552	946,640
Total money (incl. others)	1,225,559	1,330,658	1,541,650

2006 (₦ million at 31 December): Demand deposits at commercial banks 1,112,362.

Source: IMF, *International Financial Statistics*.

COST OF LIVING
(Consumer Price Index; base: May 2003 = 100)

	2005	2006	2007
Food (excl. beverages)	144.2	152.2	155.0
Alcoholic beverages, tobacco and kola	122.3	138.7	158.5
Clothing (incl. footwear)	119.1	129.4	140.5
Rent, fuel and light	158.0	184.7	203.2
Household goods and maintenance	125.7	133.0	145.3
Medical care and health	126.0	141.4	142.5
Transport	125.4	142.8	170.2
Education	144.6	151.0	173.0
All items (incl. others)	143.6	155.5	163.8

NATIONAL ACCOUNTS
(₦ '000 million at current prices)

Expenditure on the Gross Domestic Product

	2004	2005	2006*
Government final consumption expenditure	785.8	1,003.1	1,283.4
Private final consumption expenditure	8,111.1	10,258.6	12,254.3
Increase in stocks / Gross fixed capital formation	1,390.6	1,781.2	2,272.8
Total domestic expenditure	10,287.5	13,042.9	15,810.5
Exports of goods and services	3,520.9	4,664.8	6,184.6
Less Imports of goods and services	2,134.8	2,813.2	3,772.3
GDP in purchasers' values	11,673.6	14,894.5	18,222.8
GDP in constant 1990 prices	541.5	560.2	602.4

* Provisional.

Gross Domestic Product by Economic Activity

	2004	2005	2006*
Agriculture, hunting, forestry and fishing	3,903.8	4,773.2	5,794.3
Mining and quarrying	4,260.8	5,682.2	7,006.6
Crude petroleum	4,247.7	5,664.9	6,982.9
Manufacturing	349.3	412.7	548.4
Electricity, gas and water	26.8	29.4	31.6
Construction	166.1	215.8	271.5
Wholesale and retail trade	1,484.4	1,868.3	2,495.8
Hotels and restaurants	35.3	46.1	56.8
Transport, storage and communications	388.8	426.7	557.8
Finance, insurance, real estate and business services	566.2	843.6	976.7
Government services	129.9	148.1	168.8
Other community, social and personal services	99.8	126.3	159.7
Sub-total	11,411.1	14,572.2	18,067.8
Taxes, less subsidies, on products†	262.5	322.3	155.0
GDP in purchasers' values	11,673.6	14,894.5	18,222.8

* Provisional.
† Data obtained as residuals.

BALANCE OF PAYMENTS
(US $ million)

	2003	2004	2005
Exports of goods f.o.b.	23,976	34,766	48,069
Imports of goods f.o.b.	−16,152	−15,009	−17,288
Trade balance	7,824	19,757	30,781
Exports of services	3,473	3,336	4,164
Imports of services	−5,715	−5,973	−7,321
Balance on goods and services	5,582	17,120	27,624
Other income received	82	157	705
Other income paid	−3,325	−2,689	−7,437
Balance on goods, services and income	2,339	14,588	20,892
Current transfers received	1,063	2,273	3,329
Current transfers paid	−12	−21	−18
Current balance	3,391	16,840	24,202
Capital account (net)	20	36	23
Direct investment from abroad	2,005	1,874	2,013
Portfolio investment assets	183	178	2,869
Other investment assets	−5,845	−7,301	−15,786
Other investment liabilities	−6,628	−7,812	−12,682
Net errors and omissions	5,614	4,676	9,758
Overall balance	−1,260	8,491	10,397

Source: IMF, *International Financial Statistics*.

NIGERIA

Statistical Survey

External Trade

PRINCIPAL COMMODITIES
(US $ million)

Imports c.i.f.	2001	2002	2003
Food and live animals	1,628.5	1,566.1	2,090.9
Milk and cream	168.9	171.6	197.9
Fish and fish preparations*	429.6	339.5	452.6
Cereals and cereal preparations	599.4	610.5	684.0
Wheat and meslin, unmilled	330.8	346.6	388.3
Rice	205.7	234.8	231.2
Sugar and honey	221.1	270.5	178.0
Chemicals and related products	1,393.2	1,489.3	1,531.7
Organic chemicals	198.9	221.5	257.6
Manufactured fertilizers	191.3	105.5	68.6
Basic manufactures	1,534.7	1,677.4	2,377.9
Paper and paperboard	207.5	201.2	229.9
Cement	238.8	256.3	312.0
Iron and steel	501.0	483.7	802.4
Machinery and transport equipment	2,495.4	3,232.8	5,662.8
Power-generating machinery and equipment	262.3	254.3	306.8
Machinery specialized for particular industries	529.7	513.7	523.5
General industrial machinery and parts	326.6	482.7	1,682.4
Electric machinery, apparatus and parts	203.3	405.7	550.1
Road vehicles	879.6	664.7	893.0
Passenger motor vehicles (excl. buses)	435.3	257.6	331.8
Miscellaneous manufactured articles	366.4	390.8	451.0
Total (incl. others)	7,958.0	8,758.3	14,892.5

* Including crustacea and molluscs.

Exports f.o.b.	2001	2002	2003
Crude petroleum	17,732.2	16,598.0	23,211.2
Total (incl. others)	18,046.1	18,607.1	24,078.3

Source: UN, *International Trade Statistics Yearbook*.

2004 (₦ '000 million): *Imports:* Petroleum 318.1; Non-petroleum 1,668.9 (Chemicals 451.6; Manufactured goods 584.6; Machinery and transport equipment 458.9); Total 1,987.0. *Exports:* Petroleum 4,489.5; Non-petroleum 113.3; Total 4,602.8.

2005 (₦ '000 million): *Imports:* Petroleum 182.8; Non-petroleum 2,296.6 (Chemicals 599.5; Manufactured goods 795.9; Machinery and transport equipment 543.9); Total 2,479.3. *Exports:* Petroleum 6,266.1; Non-petroleum 106.0 (Cocoa beans 13.2; Processed skins 21.7); Total 6,372.1.

2006 (₦ '000 million, provisional): *Imports:* Petroleum 221.1; Non-petroleum 2,307.0 (Chemicals 608.4; Manufactured goods 816.7; Machinery and transport equipment 552.6); Total 2,528.1. *Exports:* Petroleum 5,619.2; Non-petroleum 133.6 (Cocoa beans 18.6; Processed skins 35.5); Total 5,752.7.

PRINCIPAL TRADING PARTNERS
(US $ million)*

Imports c.i.f.	2001	2002	2003
Belgium	438.2	519.3	533.6
Brazil	174.6	519.3	533.6
China, People's Repub.	526.8	740.6	1,068.0
France (incl. Monaco)	371.7	363.8	480.0
Germany	780.7	532.1	1,088.6
Greece	43.6	32.0	45.6
Hong Kong	96.4	108.7	152.7
India	315.7	310.1	377.7
Indonesia	107.8	108.0	122.4
Italy	200.7	259.7	636.5
Japan	360.2	432.4	364.2
Korea, Repub.	216.1	300.0	415.9
Netherlands	391.7	278.1	320.4
Russia	115.7	91.0	145.6
Singapore	103.7	499.4	78.9
South Africa	231.4	189.0	290.9
Spain	108.3	84.2	142.3
Switzerland-Liechtenstein	96.5	92.9	124.8
Thailand	115.6	174.8	138.7
United Kingdom	1,069.7	1,097.0	1,420.8
USA	822.8	1,123.4	2,320.8
Total (incl. others)	7,958.0	8,758.3	14,892.5

Exports f.o.b.	2001	2002	2003
Brazil	1,051.3	1,540.9	1,636.8
Cameroon	125.0	112.7	313.1
Canada	357.3	229.7	753.7
Chile	110.2	141.2	86.1
China, People's Repub.	127.0	73.2	123.5
Côte d'Ivoire	341.5	270.1	360.3
France (incl. Monaco)	1,142.3	998.8	1,359.5
Germany	243.6	365.5	505.5
Ghana	271.2	380.2	454.8
India	2,083.3	2,160.9	2,393.4
Indonesia	537.2	963.3	770.5
Italy	854.0	722.9	688.0
Korea, Repub.	49.7	41.3	99.6
Netherlands	364.8	288.7	535.4
Portugal	461.4	491.9	589.5
Senegal	174.8	118.8	254.2
South Africa	197.7	389.0	589.8
Spain	1,175.6	1,020.7	1,484.4
USA	7,320.9	5,830.0	9,211.3
Total (incl. others)	18,046.1	18,607.1	24,078.3

* Imports by country of consignment; exports by country of destination.

Source: UN, *International Trade Statistics Yearbook*.

2004 (₦ '000 million): *Non-Petroleum imports only:* Brazil 85.4; People's Republic of China 174.9; France 156.6; Germany 104.3; India 88.7; Italy 104.2; Japan 60.1; Republic of Korea 67.1; Netherlands 124.1; Russia 74.1; South Africa 81.0; United Kingdom 131.5; USA 241.5; Total (incl. others) 1,668.9. *Petroleum exports only:* Brazil 449.8; Canada 138.1; Côte d'Ivoire 122.2; France 132.0; India 469.9; Indonesia 130.9; Italy 104.1; Japan 158.5; Spain 209.7; USA 1,940.8; Total (incl. others) 4,430.2.

2005 (₦ '000 million): *Non-Petroleum imports only:* Brazil 91.9; People's Republic of China 275.6; France 114.8; Germany 80.4; India 137.8; Italy 68.9; Japan 390.4; Republic of Korea 80.4; Netherlands 103.3; Russia 68.9; South Africa 117.1; United Kingdom 91.9; USA 459.3; Total (incl. others) 2,296.6. *Petroleum exports only:* Brazil 214.7; Canada 272.1; Côte d'Ivoire 195.2; France 226.1; India 689.2; Indonesia 118.5; Italy 166.6; Japan 112.6; Netherlands 151.5; Spain 307.2; USA 2,603.6; Total (incl. others) 6,206.1.

2006 (₦ '000 million, provisional): *Non-Petroleum imports only:* Brazil 78.4; People's Republic of China 221.5; France 176.3; Germany 100.2; India 177.6; Italy 53.5; Japan 428.1; Republic of Korea 90.0; Netherlands 47.3; Russia 64.6; South Africa 71.5; United Kingdom 43.8; USA 512.0; Total (incl. others) 2,307.0. *Petroleum exports only:* Brazil 204.2; Canada 253.8; Côte d'Ivoire 160.0; France 231.7; India 651.1; Indonesia 126.9; Italy 160.0; Japan 110.4; Netherlands 137.9; Spain 298.0; USA 2,527.1; Total (incl. others) 5,517.7.

Transport

RAILWAYS
(traffic)

	1995	1996	1997
Passenger-km (million)	161	170	179
Freight ton-km (million)	108	114	120

Source: UN, *Statistical Yearbook*.

ROAD TRAFFIC
(estimates, motor vehicles in use)

	1995	1996
Passenger cars	820,069	885,080
Buses and coaches	1,284,251	903,449
Lorries and vans	673,425	912,579
Motorcycles and mopeds	481,345	441,651

Source: IRF, *World Road Statistics*.

1997 ('000 vehicles): Passenger cars 52.3; Commercial vehicles 13.5 (Source: UN *Statistical Yearbook*).

SHIPPING

Merchant Fleet
(registered at 31 December)

	2004	2005	2006
Number of vessels	330	339	350
Displacement ('000 grt)	429.0	358.1	363.3

Source: Lloyd's Register-Fairplay, *World Fleet Statistics*.

International Sea-borne Freight Traffic
(estimates, '000 metric tons)

	1991	1992	1993
Goods loaded	82,768	84,797	86,993
Goods unloaded	10,960	11,143	11,346

Source: UN Economic Commission for Africa, *African Statistical Yearbook*.

CIVIL AVIATION
(traffic on scheduled services)

	2001	2002	2003
Kilometres flown (million)	4	6	12
Passengers carried ('000)	529	512	520
Passenger-km (million)	402	522	638
Total ton-km (million)	37	57	61

Source: UN, *Statistical Yearbook*.

Tourism

ARRIVALS BY NATIONALITY*

Country	2003	2004	2005
Benin	318,716	374,491	393,215
Cameroon	86,815	102,008	107,108
Chad	68,958	81,026	85,077
France	50,149	58,925	61,871
Germany	48,915	57,475	60,348
Ghana	16,767	19,701	20,686
Italy	53,166	62,470	65,593
Liberia	87,053	102,287	107,401
Niger	503,066	591,103	620,658
Sudan	51,101	60,044	63,046
Total (incl. others)	2,253,115	2,646,411	2,778,365

* Figures refer to arrival at frontiers of visitors from abroad, including same-day visitors (excursionists).

Tourism receipts (US $ million, incl. passenger transport): 58 in 2003; 49 in 2004; 46 in 2005.

Source: World Tourism Organization.

Communications Media

	2004	2005	2006
Telephones ('000 main lines in use)	1,027.5	1,223.3	1,688.0
Mobile cellular telephones ('000 in use)	9,147.2	18,587.0	32,322.2
Personal computers ('000 in use)	867	867	n.a.
Internet users ('000)	1,770	5,000	8,000
Broadband subscribers	—	500	500

Radio receivers ('000 in use): 23,500 in 1997.

Television receivers ('000 in use): 12,000 in 2001.

Book production (titles, including pamphlets): 1,314 in 1995.

Daily newspapers: 25 (estimated average circulation 2,760,000 copies) in 1998.

Sources: International Telecommunication Union; UNESCO Institute for Statistics.

Education

(2005)

	Institutions	Teachers	Students Males	Females	Total
Primary	50,741	594,192	11,712,479	9,239,339	20,951,818
Secondary	11,010	156,635	3,079,832	2,342,779	5,422,611
Poly/Monotechnic	178	16,499	n.a.	n.a.	237,708
University	80	23,535	n.a.	n.a.	724,856

Adult literacy rate (official estimates, any language): 64.2% (males 73.0%; females 55.4%) in 2006.

Directory

The Constitution

The Constitution of the Federal Republic of Nigeria was promulgated on 5 May 1999, and entered into force on 31 May. The main provisions are summarized below:

PROVISIONS

Nigeria is one indivisible sovereign state, to be known as the Federal Republic of Nigeria. Nigeria is a Federation, comprising 36 States and a Federal Capital Territory. The Constitution includes provisions for the creation of new States and for boundary adjustments of existing States. The Government of the Federation or of a State is prohibited from adopting any religion as a state religion.

LEGISLATURE

The legislative powers of the Federation are vested in the National Assembly, comprising a Senate and a House of Representatives. The 109-member Senate consists of three Senators from each State and

NIGERIA

one from the Federal Capital Territory, who are elected for a term of four years. The House of Representatives comprises 360 members, representing constituencies of nearly equal population as far as possible, who are elected for a four-year term. The Senate and House of Representatives each have a Speaker and Deputy Speaker, who are elected by the members of the House from among themselves. Legislation may originate in either the Senate or the House of Representatives, and, having been approved by the House in which it originated by a two-thirds majority, will be submitted to the other House for approval, and subsequently presented to the President for assent. Should the President withhold his assent, and the bill be returned to the National Assembly and again approved by each House by a two-thirds majority, the bill will become law. The legislative powers of a State of the Federation will be vested in the House of Assembly of the State. The House of Assembly of a State will consist of three or four times the number of seats that the State holds in the House of Representatives (comprising not less than 24 and not more than 40 members).

EXECUTIVE

The executive powers of the Federation are vested in the President, who is the Head of State, the Chief Executive of the Federation and the Commander-in-Chief of the Armed Forces of the Federation. The President is elected for a term of four years and must receive not less than one-quarter of the votes cast at the election in at least two-thirds of the States in the Federation and the Federal Capital Territory. The President nominates a candidate as his associate from the same political party to occupy the office of Vice-President. The Ministers of the Government of the Federation are nominated by the President, subject to confirmation by the Senate. Federal executive bodies include the Council of State, which advises the President in the exercise of his powers. The executive powers of a State are vested in the Governor of that State, who is elected for a four-year term and must receive not less than one-quarter of votes cast in at least two-thirds of all local government areas in the State.

JUDICIARY

The judicial powers of the Federation are vested in the courts established for the Federation, and the judicial powers of a State in the courts established for the State. The Federation has a Supreme Court, a Court of Appeal and a Federal High Court. Each State has a High Court, a *Shari'a* Court of Appeal and a Customary Court of Appeal. Chief Judges are nominated on the recommendation of a National Judicial Council.

LOCAL GOVERNMENT

The States are divided into 768 local government areas. The system of local government by democratically elected local government councils is guaranteed, and the Government of each State will ensure their existence. Each local government council within the State will participate in the economic planning and development of the area over which it exercises authority.

Federal Government

HEAD OF STATE

President, Commander-in-Chief of the Armed Forces and Minister responsible for Petroleum Resources: Alhaji UMARU MUSA YAR'ADUA (inaugurated 29 May 2007).

Vice-President: Dr GOODLUCK EBELE JONATHAN.

CABINET
(March 2008)

Attorney-General and Minister of Justice: MICHAEL KAASE AONDOAKAA.
Minister of Agriculture and Water Resources: ABBA SAYYADI RUMA.
Minister of Commerce and Industry: CHARLES UGWU.
Minister of Culture and Tourism: ADETOKUNBO KAYODE.
Minister of Defence: MAHMUD YAYALE AHMED.
Minister of Education: IGWE AJA-NWACHUKWU.
Minister of the Environment and Housing: HALIMA TAYO ALAO.
Minister of the Federal Capital Territory: ALIYU MODIBBO UMAR.
Minister of Finance: SHAMSUDEEN USMAN.
Minister of Foreign Affairs: OJO MADUEKWE.
Minister of Health: (vacant).
Minister of Information and Communications: JOHN OGAR ODEY.
Minister of the Interior: Maj. Gen. (retd) GODWIN ABBE.
Minister of Labour: HASSAN MUHAMMAD LAWAL.
Minister of Mines and Steel Development: SARAFA TUNJI ISOLA.
Minister of Transportation: DIEZANI ALISON-MADUEKE.
Minister of Science and Technology: GRACE EKPIWHRE.
Minister of Youth Development: AKINLABI OLASUNKANMI.
Minister of Women's Affairs: SAUDATU USMAN BUNGUDU.
Minister, Chairman of the National Planning Commission: MUHAMMED SANUSI DAGGASH.
Minister, Chairman of the National Sports Commission: ABDULRAHMAN HASSAN GIMBA.

There were, in addition, 18 Deputy Ministers.

MINISTRIES

Office of the Head of State: New Federal Secretariat Complex, Shehu Shagari Way, Central Area District, Abuja; tel. (9) 5233536.

Ministry of Agriculture and Water Resources: Area 11, Secretariat Complex, Garki, PMB 135, Abuja; tel. (9) 3141931; e-mail aruma@nigeria.gov.ng.

Ministry of Commerce and Industry: Area 1, Secretariat Complex, Garki, PMB 88, Abuja; e-mail fmi@fmind.gov.ng; tel. (9) 2341662.

Ministry of Culture and Tourism: Phase II Federal Secretariat, Block A, 1st Floor, Shehu Shagari Way, Abuja; tel. (9) 2348311; fax (9) 23408297; e-mail akayode@nigeria.gov.ng; internet www.visit-nigeria.gov.ng.

Ministry of Defence: Ship House, Central Area, Abuja; tel. (9) 2340534; fax (9) 2340714; e-mail mamed@nigeria.gov.ng.

Ministry of Education: New Federal Secretariat Complex, Shehu Shagari Way, Central Area District, PMB 146, Abuja; tel. (9) 5237838; e-mail enquires@fme.gov.ng; internet www.fme.gov.ng.

Ministry of Energy: Annex 3, Federal Secretariat Complex, Shehu Shagari Way, Central Area, PMB 278, Garki, Abuja; tel. (9) 5239462; fax (9) 5236652; e-mail info@mpr.gov.ng.

Ministry of the Environment and Housing: Federal Secretariat Towers, Shehu Shagari Way, Central Area, PMB 468, Garki, Abuja; tel. (9) 5234014; fax (9) 5211847; e-mail haloa@nigeria.gov.ng; internet www.environmentnigeria.org.

Ministry of the Federal Capital Territory: Kapital St, off Obafemi Awolowo St, Garki Area 11, PMB 25, Garki, Abuja; tel. (9) 2341525; fax (9) 3143859; e-mail presunit@fct.gov.ng; internet www.fct.gov.ng.

Ministry of Finance: Ahmadu Bello Way, Central Area, PMB 14, Garki, Abuja; tel. (9) 2346290; e-mail susman@nigeria.gov.ng; internet www.fmf.gov.ng.

Ministry of Foreign Affairs: Maputo St, Zone 3, Wuse District, PMB 130, Abuja; tel. (9) 5230570; e-mail omaduekwe@nigeria.gov.ng; internet www.mfa.gov.ng.

Ministry of Health: New Federal Secretariat Complex, Ahmadu Bello Way, Central Business District, PMB 083, Garki, Abuja; tel. (9) 5238362; e-mail agrange@nigeria.gov.ng.

Ministry of Information and Communications: New Federal Secretariat Complex, Shehu Shagari Way, Central Area District, PMB 1278, Abuja; tel. (9) 5237183; e-mail jodey@nigeria.gov.ng.

Ministry of the Interior: Area 1, Secretariat Complex, Garki, PMB 16, Abuja; tel. (9) 2341934; fax (9) 2342426; e-mail gabbe@nigeria.gov.ng; internet www.fmia.gov.ng.

Ministry of Justice: New Federal Secretariat Complex, Shehu Shagari Way, Central Area, PMB 192, Garki, Abuja; tel. (9) 5235208; fax (9) 5235194.

Ministry of Labour: New Federal Secretariat Complex, Shehu Shagari Way, Central Area, PMB 04, Garki, Abuja; tel. (9) 5235980; e-mail hlawal@nigeria.gov.ng.

Ministry of Mines and Steel Development: New Federal Secretariat Complex, Shehu Shagari Way, Central Area, PMB 107, Garki, Abuja; tel. (9) 5235830; fax (9) 5235831.

Ministry of Science and Technology: New Federal Secretariat Complex, Shehu Shagari Way, Central Area, PMB 331, Garki, Abuja; tel. (9) 5233397; fax (9) 5235204.

Ministry of Transportation: Dipcharima House, Central Business District, off 3rd Ave, PMB 0336, Garki, Abuja; tel. (9) 2347451; fax (9) 2347453; e-mail info@fmt.gov.ng; internet www.fmt.gov.ng.

Ministry of Women's Affairs: New Federal Secretariat Complex, Shehu Shagari Way, Central Area, PMB 229, Garki, Abuja; tel. (9) 5237112; fax (9) 5233644; e-mail sbungudu@nigeria.gov.ng; internet www.fmwa.gov.ng.

Ministry of Youth Development: Federal Secretariat, Phase II, Shehu Shagari Way, PMB 229, Abuja; tel. (9) 5237112; fax (9) 5233644; e-mail aolasunkanmi@nigeria.gov.ng.

NIGERIA

National Planning Commission: Old Central Bank Bldg, 4th Floor, Garki, PMB 234, Abuja; e-mail info@nigerianeconomy.com; internet www.npc.gov.ng.

National Sports Commission: New Federal Secretariat Complex, Shehu Shagari Way, Maitama, Abuja; tel. (9) 5235905; fax (9) 5235901; e-mail agimba@nigeria.gov.ng.

President and Legislature

PRESIDENT

Election, 21 April 2007*

Candidate	Votes	% of votes
Umaru Musa Yar'Adua (People's Democratic Party)	24,784,227	70.00
Muhammadu Buhari (All Nigeria People's Party)	6,607,419	18.65
Atiku Abubakar (Action Congress)	2,567,798	7.25
Orji Uzor Kalu (Progressive People's Alliance)	608,833	1.72
Attahiru Dalhatu Bafarawa (Democratic People's Party)	289,324	0.82
Dim Chukwuemeka Odumegwu-Ojukwu (All Progressive Grand Alliance)	155,947	0.44
Christopher Pere Ajuwa (Alliance for Democracy)	89,511	0.25
Chris O. Okotie (Fresh Democratic Party)	74,049	0.21
Others†	248,100	0.70
Total	**35,425,208**	**100.00**

* Provisional results released by the Independent National Election Commission.
† There were 16 other candidates.

NATIONAL ASSEMBLY

House of Representatives

Speaker of the House of Representatives: DIMEJI BANKOLE.
Election, 14 April 2007

Party	Seats
People's Democratic Party	258
All Nigeria People's Party	64
Action Congress	32
Progressive People's Alliance	3
Alliance for Democracy	1
Others	1
Total	**359***

* One seat remained vacant.

Senate

Speaker of the Senate: DAVID MARK.
Election, 14 April 2007

Party	Seats
People's Democratic Party	78
All Nigeria People's Party	22
Action Congress	6
All Nigeria People's Party	1
Alliance for Democracy	1
Others	1
Total	**109**

Election Commission

Independent National Electoral Commission (INEC): Plot 436 Zambezi Cres., Maitama District, PMB 0184, Garki, Abuja; tel. (9) 2224632; e-mail contact@inecnigeria.org; internet www.inecnigeria.org; f. 1998; Chair. MAURICE IWU.

Political Organizations

Following the death of the military Head of State in June 1998, the existing authorized political parties were dissolved. The Government established a new Independent National Electoral Commission (INEC), which officially approved three political parties to contest elections in February 1999. Prior to legislative and presidential elections in April 2003, three political associations were granted registration in June 2002, as were a further 24 in December. According to INEC, by mid-2007 51 parties were registered.

Action Congress (AC): Plot 779 Ona Cres., Maitama, Abuja; tel. (9) 4139999; f. 2006 by a merger of the Alliance for Democracy, the Justice Party, the Advanced Congress of Democrats and several minor parties; Chair. Alhadji HASSAN M. ZURMI.

Alliance for Democracy (AD): Plot 2096, Bumbona Close, Zone 1, Wuse, Abuja; tel. (9) 5239357; e-mail info@alliancefordemocracy.org; f. 1998; Chair. MOJISOLUWA AKINFEWA.

Justice Party (JP): 2nd Ave, Gwarimpa, Abuja; tel. 8057764363; Chair. RALPH OBIOHA.

Advanced Congress of Democrats (ACD): Plot 882, Emeka Ampoku St, Area 11, Garki, Abuja; tel. 8044107989; Chair. ALEXIS ANIELO.

All Nigeria People's Party (ANPP): Bassan Plaza, Plot 759, Central Business Area, Abuja; tel. (9) 2347556; f. 1998; Chair. Alhaji Dr MODU SHERIF.

All Progressive Grand Alliance (APGA): 41b Libreville Cres., Wuse 11, Abuja; tel. 8035903910; regd June 2002; Chair. VICTOR C. UMEH.

Democratic People's Party (DPP): 1st Floor, Labour House, Central Business District, Abuja; tel. (9) 2343345; Chair. DAN NWANYANWU.

Fresh Democratic Party: 4 Park Close, Aguyi Ironsi St, Maitma, Abuja; Chair. Rev. CHRIS OKOTIE.

Movement for the Actualization of the Sovereign State of Biafra (MASSOB): Okwe, Imo; f. 1999; Leader Chief RALPH UWAZURIKE.

Movement for the Emancipation of the Niger Delta (MEND): f. 2005; main Ijaw militant group operating in the Niger Delta; Leader Maj.-Gen. GODSWILL TAMUNO.

Movement for the Survival of the Ogoni People (MOSOP): 27 Odu St, Ogbunabali, Port Harcourt; tel. (84) 230250; f. 1990 to organize opposition to petroleum production in Ogoni territory; Pres. LEDUM MITEE.

National Conscience Party (NCP): 18 Phase 1 Low Cost Housing Estate, Lake City Ave, Gwagwalada, Abuja; tel. (9) 4937279; e-mail info@nigeriancp.net; internet www.nigeriancp.net; Leader GANI FAWEHINMI; Chair. OSAGIE OBAYUWANA.

National Democratic Party (NDP): POB 8196, Abuja; tel. (9) 6703366; e-mail info@ndpnigeria.com; internet www.ndpnigeria.com; regd June 2002; Chair. Alhaji ALIYU HABU FARI.

Niger Delta People's Volunteer Force (NDPVF): prominent Ijaw militant group operating in the Niger Delta; Leader Alhaji MUJAHID DOKUBO-ASARI.

People's Democratic Party (PDP): Wadata Plaza, Michael Okpara Way, Zone 5, Wuse, Abuja; tel. (9) 5232589; f. 1998 by fmr opponents of the Govt of Gen. Sani Abacha; supports greater federalism; ruling party; Chair. Col Dr VINCENT OGBULAFOR.

People's Redemption Party (PRP): City Plaza, Area 11, Garki, Abuja; tel. 8033495403; regd Dec. 2002; Chair. Alhaji ABDULKADIR B. MUSA.

People's Salvation Party (PSP): 441 Oron St, Wuse Zone 1, Abuja; tel. (9) 5235359; regd Dec. 2002; Chair. Alhaji LAWAL MAITURARE.

Progressive People's Alliance (PPA): 52, Libreville St, Wuse 11, Abuja; Chair. Alhadji SULEIMAN AHMED.

United Nigeria People's Party (UNPP): Plot 1467, Safana Close, Garki 11, Abuja; tel. (9) 2340091; regd June 2002; Chair. MALLAM SALEH JAMBO.

Diplomatic Representation

EMBASSIES AND HIGH COMMISSIONS IN NIGERIA

Algeria: Plot 203, Etim Inyang Cres., POB 55238, Falomo, Lagos; tel. (1) 612092; fax (1) 2624017; Ambassador EL-MIHOUB MIHOUBI.

Angola: 5 Kasumu Ekomode St, Victoria Island, POB 50437, Falomo Ikoyi, Lagos; tel. (9) 4135121; fax (9) 4134082; Ambassador EVARISTO DOMINGOS KIMBA.

Argentina: 2 Abubakar Koko Cres., Asokoro District, Abuja; tel. (9) 3148680; fax (9) 3148683; e-mail enige@mrecic.gov.ar; Chargé d'affaires a.i. RICARDO JORGE MONTICELLI.

Australia: 5th Floor, Oakland Centre, 48 Aguyi Ironsi St, Maitama, Abuja; PMB 5152, Abuja; tel. (9) 4135226; fax (9) 4135227; e-mail ahc.abuja@dfat.gov.au; internet www.nigeria.embassy.gov.au; High Commissioner JEFF HART.

NIGERIA

Austria: Plot 9, Usuma St, Maitama, Abuja; tel. (9) 4130772; fax (9) 4612715; e-mail abuja-ob@bmeia.gv.at; Ambassador Dr PETER CHRISTIAN FELLNER.
Belgium: 9 Usuma St, Maitama, Abuja; tel. (9) 4131859; fax (9) 4132015; e-mail abuja@diplobel.org; internet www.belgiumvisas.org; Ambassador DIRK VAN EECKHOUT.
Benin: 4 Abudu Smith St, Victoria Island, POB 5705, Lagos; tel. (1) 2614411; fax (1) 2612385; Ambassador PATRICE HOUNGAVOU.
Brazil: Plot 324, Diplomatic Dr., Zone Central, Area District, Abuja; tel. (9) 4618688; fax (9) 4618687; Ambassador ALBERTO FERREIRA GUIMARAES.
Bulgaria: 10 Euphrates St, cnr Aminu Kano Cres., Maitama, Abuja; tel. (9) 4130034; fax (9) 4132741; e-mail bulgarian@nigtel.com; Ambassador (vacant).
Burkina Faso: 15 Norman Williams St, Ikoyi, Lagos; tel. (1) 617985; e-mail ebfn@nova.net.ng; Ambassador DRAMANE YAMÉOGO.
Cameroon: 5 Elsie Femi Pearse St, Victoria Island, PMB 2476, Lagos; tel. (1) 2612226; fax (1) 7747510; High Commissioner ANDRÉ E. KENDECK MANDENG.
Canada: 15 Bobo St, Maitama, POB 5144, Abuja; tel. (9) 4139910; fax (9) 4139932; e-mail abuja@international.gc.ca; internet nigeria.gc.ca; High Commissioner CAROLINE CHRÉTIEN.
Chad: 2 Goriola St, Victoria Island, PMB 70662, Lagos; tel. (1) 2622590; fax (1) 2618314; Ambassador MAHAMAT HABIB DOUTOUM.
China, People's Republic: Plot 302–303, Central Area, Abuja; tel. (9) 4618661; fax (9) 4618660; e-mail chinaemb_ng@mfa.gov.cn; internet ng.china-embassy.org; Ambassador XU JIANGUO.
Côte d'Ivoire: 3 Abudu Smith St, Victoria Island, POB 7786, Lagos; tel. (1) 610936; fax (1) 2613822; e-mail cotedivoire@micro.com.ng; Ambassador AIKO ZIKE MARC.
Cuba: Plot 935, Idejo St, Victoria Island, POB 328, Victoria Island, Lagos; tel. (1) 2614836; fax (1) 2617036; Ambassador ELIO SAVÓN OLIVA.
Czech Republic: Plot 1223, Gnassingbé Eyadéma St, Asokoro District, POB 4628, Abuja; tel. (9) 3141245; fax (9) 3141248; e-mail abuja@embassy.mzv.cz; internet www.mzv.cz/abuja; Ambassador ALEXANDR KARYCH.
Egypt: Plot 3319, Barada Close, Abuja; tel. (9) 4136091; fax (9) 4132602; Ambassador MOHAMED ASHRAF HARBY SALAMA.
Equatorial Guinea: 7 Bank Rd, Ikoyi, POB 4162, Lagos; tel. (1) 2683717; Ambassador A. S. DOUGAN MALABO.
Ethiopia: 19 Ona Cres., Maitama, POB 2488, Abuja; tel. (9) 4131691; fax (1) 4131692; e-mail etabuja@primair.net; Ambassador YOHANESS GENDA.
Finland: Maputo St Wuse, Zone 3, PMB 5140, Abuja; tel. (9) 3147256; fax (9) 3147252; e-mail sanomat.aba@formin.fi; Ambassador ANNA-LIISA KORHONEN.
France: 37 Udi Hills St, Abuja; tel. (9) 5231055; fax (9) 5235482; e-mail ambafrance.abj@micro.com.ng; internet www.ambafrance-ng.org; Ambassador YVES GAUDEUL.
Gabon: 8 Norman Williams St, SW Ikoyi, POB 5989, Lagos; tel. (1) 2684673; fax (1) 2690692; Ambassador E. AGUEMINYA.
The Gambia: 162 Awolowo Rd, SW Ikoyi, POB 873, Lagos; tel. (1) 682192; High Commissioner ANGELA COLLEY.
Germany: 9 Lake Maracaibo Close, off Amazon St, Maitama, Abuja; tel. (9) 4130962; fax (9) 4130949; e-mail info@abuja.diplo.de; internet www.abuja.diplo.de; Ambassador JOACHIM CHRISTOPH SCHMILLEN.
Ghana: 21–25 King George V Rd, POB 889, Lagos; tel. (1) 2630015; fax (1) 2630338; High Commissioner Lt-Gen. JOSHUA HAMIDU.
Greece: No 6, Takum Close, Wuse II, Abuja; tel. (9) 4139433; fax (9) 4139435; e-mail grembabuja@mfa.gr; internet grembnigeria.mfa.gr; Ambassador HARALAMBOS DAFARANOS.
Guinea: 8 Abudu Smith St, Victoria Island, POB 2826, Lagos; tel. (1) 2616961; Ambassador KOMO BEAVOGUI.
Holy See: Pope John Paul II Cres., Maitama, PMB 541, Garki, Abuja; tel. (9) 4138381; fax (9) 4136653; e-mail nuntiusabj@hotmail.com; Apostolic Nuncio Most Rev. RENZO FRATINI (Titular Archbishop of Botriana).
Hungary: Plot 1685, Jose Marti Cres., Asokoro, Abuja; tel. (1) 3141180; fax (1) 3141177; e-mail huemblgs@nova.net.ng; internet www.mfa.gov.hu/emb/abuja; Ambassador Dr FERENC KATÓ.
India: 15 Rio Negro Close, off Yedseram St, Maitama, Abuja; tel. (9) 4132323; fax (9) 4132324; e-mail hoc.abuja@mea.gov.in; internet www.hicomindlagos.com; High Commissioner HARIHARA SUBRAMANIAM VISWANATHAN.
Indonesia: 5 Anifowoshe St, Victoria Island, POB 3473, Marina, Lagos; tel. (1) 2614601; fax (1) 2613301; e-mail indlgs@infoweb.abs.net; Ambassador SUSANTO ISMODIRDJO.
Iran: 2 Udi St, Maitama, Abuja; tel. (1) 5238048; fax (1) 5237785; e-mail irembassy_abuja@yahoo.com; Ambassador JAWAD TORKABADI.
Ireland: Plot 415, Negro Cres., Maitama District, Abuja; tel. (9) 4131751; fax (9) 4131805; e-mail abujaembassy@dfa.ie; internet www.irishembassy-nigeria.net; Ambassador LIAM CANNIFFE.
Israel: Plot 12, Mary Slessor St, Asokoro, POB 10924, Abuja; tel. (9) 3143170; fax (9) 3143177; e-mail info@abuja.mfa.gov.il; internet abuja.mfa.gov.il; Ambassador NOAM KATZ.
Italy: 21st Cres., off Constitution Ave, Central Business District, Abuja; tel. (9) 5244036; fax (9) 5244034; e-mail ambasciata.abuja@esteri.it; internet www.ambabuja.esteri.it; Ambassador MASSIMO BAISTROCCHI.
Jamaica: Plot 77, Samuel Adedoyin Ave, Victoria Island, POB 75368, Lagos; tel. (1) 2611085; fax (1) 2610047; High Commissioner ROBERT MILLER (acting).
Japan: Plot 585 Bobo St, Maitama, PMB 5070, Abuja; tel. (9) 4138898; fax (9) 4137667; Ambassador AKIO TANAKA.
Kenya: 18 Yedseram St, Maitama, PMB 5160, Abuja; tel. (9) 4139155; fax (9) 4139157; e-mail abuja@mfa.go.ke; High Commissioner DANIEL MEPUKORI KOIKAI.
Korea, Democratic People's Republic: 31 Akin Adesola St, Victoria Island, Lagos; tel. (1) 2610108; Ambassador KIM PYONG GI.
Korea, Republic: Plot 934, Idejo St, Victoria Island, POB 4668, Lagos; tel. (1) 2615353; Ambassador KIE DONG-LEE.
Liberia: 3 Idejo St, Plot 162, off Adeola Odeku St, Victoria Island, POB 70841, Lagos; tel. (1) 2618899; Ambassador Prof. JAMES TAPEH.
Libya: 46 Raymond Njoku Rd, SW Ikoyi, Lagos; tel. (1) 2680880; Chargé d'affaires a.i. IBRAHIM AL-BASHAR.
Malaysia: 2 Pechora Close, Maitama PMB 5217, Abuja; tel. (9) 4133918; fax (9) 413 3922; e-mail malabuja@kln.gov.my; Chargé d'affairs a.i MELVIN CASTELINO.
Morocco: 5 Mary Slessor St, Asokoro, Abuja; tel. (9) 3141961; fax (9) 3141959; e-mail mcherkaoui45@yahoo.fr; Ambassador MUSTAPHA CHERQAOUI.
Namibia: Plot 1738 T. Y., Danyuma St, Cadasdral Zone, Asokoro, Abuja; tel. (9) 3142740; fax (9) 3142743; e-mail namibiahighcomabuja@yahoo.com; Ambassador DAVID SMITH.
Netherlands: 21st Cres., Central Business District, Abuja; tel. (9) 5244024; fax (9) 5244030; Ambassador ARIE VAN DER WIEL.
Niger: 15 Adeola Odeku St, Victoria Island, PMB 2736, Lagos; tel. (1) 2612300; Ambassador MOUSSA ELHADJI IBRAHIM.
Norway: 3 Anifowoshe St, Victoria Island, PMB 2431, Lagos; tel. (1) 2618467; fax (1) 2618469; Ambassador TORE NEDREBO.
Pakistan: 4 Molade Okoya-Thomas St, Victoria Island, POB 2450, Lagos; tel. (1) 613909; fax (1) 614822; Ambassador KHALID DURRANI.
Philippines: 16 Lake Chad Cres., cnr Kainji St, Maitama, Abuja; tel. (9) 4133649; fax (9) 4137650; Ambassador MASARANGA R. UMPA.
Poland: 16 Ona Cres., Maitama, Abuja; tel. (9) 4138280; fax (9) 4138281; e-mail poembabu@linkserve.com; internet www.abuja.polemb.net; Ambassador GRZEGORZ WALINSKI.
Portugal: 27B Gana St, Maitama, Abuja; tel. (9) 4137211; fax (9) 4137214; e-mail portemb@rosecom.net; Ambassador MARIA DE FÁTIMA DE PINA PERESTRELLO.
Romania: Plot 498, Nelson Mandela St, Zone A4, Asokoro, POB 10376, Abuja; tel. (9) 3142304; fax (9) 3142306; e-mail romnig@gmail.com; Ambassador MARIAN PARJOL.
Russia: 5 Walter Carrington Cres., Victoria Island, POB 2723, Lagos; tel. (1) 2613359; fax (1) 4619994; Ambassador GENNADY V. ILYITEHEV.
Saudi Arabia: Plot 347H, off Adetokunbo Ademola Cres., Wuse 2, Abuja; tel. (9) 4131880; fax (9) 4134906; Ambassador ANWAR A. ABD-RABBUH.
Senegal: 14 Kofo Abayomi Rd, Victoria Island, PMB 2197, Lagos; tel. (1) 2611722; Ambassador AMADOU THIALAW DIOP.
Serbia: 11, Rio Negro Close, off Yedseram St, Cadastral Zone A6, Maitama District, Abuja; tel. (9) 4139492; fax (9) 4130078; e-mail mail@ambnig.com; Ambassador DRAGAN MRAOVIĆ.
Sierra Leone: 31 Waziri Ibrahim St, Victoria Island, POB 2821, Lagos; tel. (1) 2614666; High Commissioner JOSEPH BLELL.
Slovakia: POB 1290, Lagos; tel. (1) 2621585; fax (1) 2612103; e-mail obeo.sk@micro.com.ng; Ambassador VASIL HUDÁK.
Somalia: Plot 1270, off Adeola Odeka St, POB 6355, Lagos; tel. (1) 2611283; Ambassador M. S. HASSAN.
South Africa: 71 Usuma St, Maitama, Abuja; tel. (9) 4133862; fax (9) 4133829; e-mail sahcniga@rosecom.net; High Commissioner B. SIFINGO.
Spain: Plot 611, 8 Bobo Close, Maitama, PMB 5120, Abuja; tel. (9) 4137091; fax (9) 4137095; e-mail embespng@mail.mae.es; Ambassador ÁNGEL LOSADA FERNÁNDEZ.
Sudan: 2B Kofo Abayomi St, Victoria Island, POB 2428, Lagos; tel. (1) 2615889; Ambassador AHMED ALTIGANI SALEH.

Sweden: PMB 569, Garki, Abuja; tel. (9) 3143399; fax (9) 3143398; e-mail ambassaden.abuja@foreign.ministry.se; internet www.swedenabroad.com/abuja; Ambassador LARS-OWE PERSSON.

Switzerland: 157 Adetokumbo Ademola Cres., Wuse II, Abuja; tel. (9) 4131081; fax (9) 4131089; e-mail abu.vertretung@eda.admin.ch; internet www.eda.admin.ch/abuja; Ambassador PIERRE HELG.

Syria: 25 Kofo Abayomi St, Victoria Island, Lagos; tel. (1) 2615860; Chargé d'affaires a.i. MUSTAFA HAJ-ALI.

Tanzania: 15 Yedseram St, Maitama, PMB 5125, Wuse, Abuja; tel. (9) 4132313; fax (9) 4132314; e-mail tanabuja@lytos.com; High Commissioner CISCO MTIRO (acting).

Thailand: Plot 766, Panama St, Cadastral Zone A6, Maitama, Abuja; e-mail thaiabj@mfa.go.th; Ambassador N. SATHAPORN.

Togo: 96 Awolowo Rd, SW Ikoyi, POB 1435, Lagos; tel. (1) 2617449; Ambassador FOLI-AGBENOZAN TETTEKPOE.

Trinidad and Tobago: 3A Tiamiyu Savage St, Victoria Island, POB 6392, Marina, Lagos; tel. (1) 2612087; fax (1) 612732; High Commissioner Dr HAROLD ROBERTSON.

Turkey: 3 Okunola Martins Close, Ikoyi, POB 56252, Lagos; tel. (1) 2691140; fax (1) 2693040; e-mail turkemb@infoweb.abs.net; Ambassador ÖMER SAHINKAYA.

Ukraine: Plot 1273, Parakou Cres., off Nairobi St, Wuse II, Abuja; tel. (9) 5239577; fax (9) 5239578; e-mail emb_ng@mfa.gov.ua; internet www.mfa.gov.ua/nigeria; Ambassador OLEH M. SKOROPAD.

United Kingdom: 19 Torren Close, off Mississippi St, Shehu Shagari Way, Maitama, Abuja; tel. (9) 4132010; fax (9) 4133552; e-mail information.abuja@fco.gov.uk; internet www.ukinnigeria.com; High Commissioner ROBERT DEWAR.

USA: 7 Plot 1075, Diplomatic Dr., Central District Area, Abuja; tel. (9) 4614000; fax (9) 4614036; e-mail ircabuja@state.gov; internet abuja.usembassy.gov; Ambassador ROBIN RENEE SANDERS.

Venezuela: 35B Adetokunbo Ademola St, Victoria Island, POB 3727, Lagos; tel. (1) 2611590; fax (1) 2617350; e-mail embavenez.nig@net.ng; Ambassador ALFREDO ENRIQUE VARGAS.

Zambia: 11 Keffi St, SW Ikoyi, PMB 6119, Lagos; High Commissioner B. N. NKUNIKA (acting).

Zimbabwe: Abuja; tel. (9) 4611322; fax (9) 4611327; Ambassador Dr JOHN SHUMBA MVUNDURA.

Judicial System

Supreme Court

Three Arms Complex, Central District, PMB 308, Abuja; tel. (9) 2346594.

Consists of a Chief Justice and up to 15 Justices, appointed by the President, on the recommendation of the National Judicial Council (subject to the approval of the Senate); has original jurisdiction in any dispute between the Federation and a State, or between States, and hears appeals from the Federal Court of Appeal.

Chief Justice: SALIHU MODIBBO ALPHA BELGORE.

Court of Appeal: consists of a President and at least 35 Justices, of whom three must be experts in Islamic (*Shari'a*) law and three experts in Customary law.

Federal High Court: consists of a Chief Judge and a number of other judges.

Each State has a **High Court**, consisting of a Chief Judge and a number of judges, appointed by the Governor of the State on the recommendation of the National Judicial Council (subject to the approval of the House of Assembly of the State). If required, a state may have a **Shari'a Court of Appeal** (dealing with Islamic civil law) and a **Customary Court of Appeal**. **Special Military Tribunals** have been established to try offenders accused of crimes such as corruption, drugs-trafficking and armed robbery; appeals against rulings of the Special Military Tribunals are referred to a **Special Appeals Tribunal**, which comprises retired judges.

Religion

ISLAM

According to the 1963 census, there were more than 26m. Muslims (47.2% of the total population) in Nigeria.

Spiritual Head: Col MUHAMMADU SA'AD ABUBAKAR (the Sultan of Sokoto).

CHRISTIANITY

The 1963 census enumerated more than 19m. Christians (34.5% of the total population).

Christian Council of Nigeria: 139 Ogunlana Dr., Surulere, POB 2838, Lagos; tel. (1) 7923495; f. 1929; 15 full mems and six assoc. mems; Pres. Rt Rev. ROGERS O. UWADI; Gen. Sec. Rev. IKECNUKWU OKORIE.

The Anglican Communion

Anglicans are adherents of the Church of the Province of Nigeria, comprising 61 dioceses. Nigeria, formerly part of the Province of West Africa, became a separate Province in 1979; in 1997 it was divided into three separate provinces. The Church had an estimated 10m. members in 1990.

Archbishop of Province I and Bishop of Lagos: Most Rev. EPHRAIM A. ADEMOW, Archbishop's Palace, 29 Marina, POB 13, Lagos; tel. (1) 2635681; fax (1) 2631264.

Archbishop of Province II and Bishop of Awka: Most Rev. MAXWELL ANIKWENWA, Bishopscourt, Ifite Rd, POB 130, Awka.

Archbishop of Province III and Bishop of Abuja: Most Rev. PETER JASPER AKINOLA, Archbishop's Palace, POB 212, ADCP, Abuja; fax (9) 5230986; e-mail abuja@anglican.skannet.com.ng.

General Secretary: Ven. SAMUEL B. AKINOLA, 29 Marina, POB 78, Lagos; tel. (1) 2635681; fax (1) 2631264.

The Roman Catholic Church

Nigeria comprises nine archdioceses, 40 dioceses and two Apostolic Vicariates. At 31 December 2005 the total number of adherents represented an estimated 15.5% of the population.

Catholic Bishops' Conference of Nigeria
6 Force Rd, POB 951, Lagos; tel. (1) 2635849; fax (1) 2636680; e-mail cathsec1@infoweb.abs.net.

f. 1976; Pres. Most Rev. FELIX ALABA ADEOSIN JOB (Archbishop of Ibadan); Sec.-Gen. of Secretariat Rev. Fr MATTHEW HASSAN KUKAH.

Archbishop of Abuja: Most Rev. JOHN O. ONAIYEKAN, Archdiocesan Secretariat, POB 286, Garki, Abuja; tel. (9) 2349049; fax (9) 2340662; e-mail onaiyekan7@hotmail.com.

Archbishop of Benin City: Most Rev. PATRICK E. EKPU, Archdiocesan Secretariat, POB 35, Benin City, Edo; tel. (52) 253787; fax (52) 255763; e-mail cadobc@infoweb.abs.net.

Archbishop of Calabar: Most Rev. JOSEPH EDRA UKPO, Catholic Secretariat, PMB 1044, 1 Bishop Moynagh Ave, Calabar, Cross River; tel. (87) 231666; fax (87) 239177.

Archbishop of Ibadan: Most Rev. FELIX ALABA JOB, Archbishop's House, PMB 5057, 8 Bale Latosa Rd, Onireke, Ibadan, Oyo; tel. (22) 2413544; fax (22) 2414855; e-mail archdiocese.ibadan@skannet.com.

Archbishop of Jos: Most Rev. IGNATIUS AYAU KAIGAMA, Archdiocesan Secretariat, 20 Joseph Gomwalk Rd, POB 494, Jos, Plateau; tel. (73) 452878; fax (73) 451547; e-mail josarch@hisen.org.

Archbishop of Kaduna: Most Rev. PETER YARIYOK JATAU, Archbishop's House, 71 Tafawa Balewa Way, POB 248, Kaduna; tel. (62) 246076; fax (62) 240026; e-mail catholickad@email.com.

Archbishop of Lagos: Cardinal ANTHONY OLUBUNMI OKOGIE, Archdiocesan Secretariat, 19 Catholic Mission St, POB 8, Lagos; tel. (1) 2635729; fax (1) 2633841; e-mail arclagos@yahoo.com.

Archbishop of Onitsha: Most Rev. VALERIAN OKEKE, Archdiocesan Secretariat, POB 401, Onitsha, Anambra; tel. (46) 413298; fax (46) 413913; e-mail secretariat@onitsha-archdiocese.org.

Archbishop of Owerri: Most Rev. ANTHONY JOHN VALENTINE OBINNA, Villa Assumpta, POB 85, Owerri, Imo; tel. (83) 230115; fax (83) 300206; e-mail owcathsec@owerriarcidiocese.org.

Other Christian Churches

Brethren Church of Nigeria: c/o Kulp Bible School, POB 1, Mubi, Adamawa; f. 1923; 100,000 mems; Gen. Sec. Rev. ABRAHAM WUTA TIZHE.

Church of the Lord (Aladura): Anthony Village, Ikorodu Rd, POB 308, Ikeja, Lagos; tel. (1) 4964749; f. 1930; 1.1m. mems; Primate Dr E. O. A. ADEJOBI.

Lutheran Church of Christ in Nigeria: POB 21, Numan, Adamawa; 575,000 mems; Pres. Rt Rev. Dr DAVID L. WINDIBIZIRI.

Lutheran Church of Nigeria: Obot Idim Ibesikpo, Uyo, Akwa Ibom; tel. and fax (85) 201848; f. 1936; 370,000 mems; Pres. Rev. S. J. UDOFIA.

Methodist Church Nigeria: Wesley House, 21–22 Marina, POB 2011, Lagos; tel. (1) 2702563; fax (1) 2702710; 483,500 mems; Patriarch Rev. Dr SUNDAY OLA KAKINDE.

Nigerian Baptist Convention: Baptist Bldg, PMB 5113, Ibadan; tel. (2) 2412267; fax (2) 2413561; e-mail baptconv@skannet.com; 2.5m. mems; Pres. Rev. EMMANUEL O. BOLARINWA; Gen. Sec. Dr ADEMOLA ISHOLA.

The Presbyterian Church of Nigeria: 26–29 Ehere Rd, Ogbor Hill, POB 2635, Aba, Imo; tel. (82) 222551; f. 1846; 1m. mems;

NIGERIA

Moderator Rt Rev. Dr Ubon B. Usung; Synod Clerk Rev. Dr Benebo F. Fubara-Manuel.

The Redeemed Church of Christ, the Church of the Foursquare Gospel, the Qua Iboe Church and the Salvation Army are prominent among numerous other Christian churches active in Nigeria.

AFRICAN RELIGIONS

The beliefs, rites and practices of the people of Nigeria are very diverse, varying between ethnic groups and between families in the same group.

The Press

DAILIES

Abuja Times: Daily Times of Nigeria Ltd, 2 Hasper Cres., Wuse Zone 7, PMB 115 Gaski, Abuja; tel. (1) 4900850; f. 1992; Editor Clement Iloba.

Daily Champion: Isolo Industrial Estate, Oshodi-Apapa, Lagos; fax (1) 4526011; e-mail letters@champion-newspapers.com; internet www.champion-newspapers.com; Editor Augsten Adamu.

Daily Express: Commercial Amalgamated Printers, 30 Glover St, Lagos; f. 1938; Editor Alhaji Ahmed Alao (acting); circ. 20,000.

Daily Sketch: Sketch Publishing Co Ltd, Oba Adebimpe Rd, PMB 5067, Ibadan; tel. (2) 414851; f. 1964; govt-owned; Chair. Ronke Okusanya; Editor Ademola Idowu; circ. 64,000.

Daily Star: 9 Works Rd, PMB 1139, Enugu; tel. (42) 253561; Editor Josef Bel-Molokwu.

Daily Times: Daily Times of Nigeria Ltd, Lateef Jakande Rd, Agidingbi, PMB 21340, Ikeja, Lagos; tel. and fax (1) 8510385; internet www.dailytimes-nigeria.com; f. 1925; 60% govt-owned; Editor Ogbuagu Anikwe; circ. 400,000.

The Democrat: 9 Ahmed Talib Ave, POB 4457, Kaduna South; tel. (62) 231907; f. 1983; Editor Abdulhamid Babatunde; circ. 100,000.

Evening Times: Daily Times of Nigeria Ltd, Lateef Jakande Rd, Agidingbi, PMB 21340, Ikeja, Lagos; tel. and fax (1) 8510385; Man. Dir Dr Onuka Adinoyi-Ojo; Editor Clement Iloba; circ. 20,000.

The Guardian: Rutam House, Isolo Expressway, Isolo, PMB 1217, Oshodi, Lagos; tel. (1) 524111; internet www.ngrguardiannews.com; f. 1983; independent; Publr Alex Ibru; Editor Emeka Izeze; circ. 80,000.

National Concord: Concord House, 42 Concord Way, POB 4483, Ikeja, Lagos; f. 1980; Editor Nsikak Essien; circ. 200,000.

New Nigerian: Ahmadu Bello Way, POB 254, Kaduna; tel. (62) 245220; fax (62) 245221; e-mail webmaster@newnigerian1.com; internet www.newnigeriannews.com; f. 1965; govt-owned; Chair. Prof. Tekena Tamuno; Editor Malam Tukur Abdulrahman; circ. 80,000.

Nigerian Chronicle: Cross River State Newspaper Corpn, 17–19 Barracks Rd, POB 1074, Calabar; tel. (87) 224976; fax (87) 224979; f. 1970; Editor Unimke Nawa; circ. 50,000.

Nigerian Herald: Kwara State Printing and Publishing Corpn, Offa Rd, PMB 1369, Ilorin; tel. and fax (31) 220506; f. 1973; sponsored by Kwara State Govt; Editor Razak el-Alawa; circ. 25,000.

Nigerian Observer: The Bendel Newspaper Corpn, 18 Airport Rd, POB 1143, Benin City; tel. (52) 240050; internet www.nigeriaobserver.com; f. 1968; Editor Tony Ikeakanam; circ. 150,000.

Nigerian Standard: 5 Joseph Gomwalk Rd, POB 2112, Jos; f. 1972; govt-owned; Editor Sale Iliya; circ. 100,000.

Nigerian Statesman: Imo Newspapers Ltd, Owerri-Egbu Rd, POB 1095, Owerri; tel. (83) 230099; f. 1978; sponsored by Imo State Govt; Editor Edube Wadibia.

Nigerian Tide: Rivers State Newspaper Corpn, 4 Ikwerre Rd, POB 5072, Port Harcourt; internet www.thetidenews.com; f. 1971; Editor Augustine Njoagwuani; circ. 30,000.

Nigerian Tribune: African Newspapers of Nigeria Ltd, Imalefalafi St, Oke-Ado, POB 78, Ibadan; tel. (2) 2313410; fax (2) 2317573; e-mail correspondence@nigerian-tribune.com; internet www.nigerian-tribune.com; f. 1949; Editor Folu Olamiti; circ. 109,000.

Post Express: 7 Warehouse Rd, PMB 1186, Apapa, Lagos; tel. (1) 5453351; fax (1) 5453436; e-mail postexpress@nova.net.ng; internet www.postexpresswired.com; Publr Chief S. Oduwu; Man. Dir Dr Stanley Macebuh.

The Punch: Skyway Press, Kudeti St, PMB 21204, Onipetsi, Ikeja; tel. (1) 4963580; internet www.punchng.com; f. 1976; Editor Gbmeiga Ogunleye; circ. 150,000.

This Day: 35 Creek Rd, Apapa, Lagos; tel. (1) 5871432; fax (1) 5871436; e-mail thisday@nova.net.ng; internet www.thisdayonline.com.

Vanguard: Kirikiri Canal, PMB 1007, Apapa; e-mail vanguard@linkserve.com.ng; internet www.vanguardngr.com; f. 1984; Editor Frank Aigbogun.

SUNDAY NEWSPAPERS

Sunday Chronicle: Cross River State Newspaper Corpn, PMB 1074, Calabar; f. 1977; Editor-in-Chief Etim Anim; circ. 163,000.

Sunday Concord: Concord House, 42 Concord Way, POB 4483, Ikeja, Lagos; f. 1980; Editor Dele Alake.

Sunday Herald: Kwara State Printing and Publishing Corpn, PMB 1369, Ilorin; tel. (31) 220976; f. 1981; Editor Charles Osagie (acting).

Sunday New Nigerian: Ahmadu Bello Way, POB 254, Kaduna; tel. (62) 245220; fax (62) 213778; e-mail audson@newnigerian.com; internet www.newnigerian.com; f. 1981; weekly; Editor Tawey Zakka; circ. 120,000.

Sunday Observer: PMB 1334, Bendel Newspapers Corpn, 18 Airport Rd, Benin City; f. 1968; Editor T. O. Borha; circ. 60,000.

Sunday Punch: Kudeti St, PMB 21204, Ikeja, Lagos; tel. (1) 4964691; fax (1) 4960715; f. 1973; Editor Dayo Wright; circ. 150,000.

Sunday Sketch: Sketch Publishing Co Ltd, PMB 5067, Ibadan; tel. (2) 414851; f. 1964; govt-owned; Editor Obafemi Oredein; circ. 125,000.

Sunday Standard: Plateau Publishing Co Ltd, Owerri-Egbu Rd, PMB 1095, Owerri; tel. (83) 230099; f. 1978; sponsored by Imo State Govt; Editor Edube Wadibia.

Sunday Sun: PMB 1025, Okoro House, Factory Lane, off Upper Mission Rd, New Benin.

Sunday Tide: 4 Ikwerre Rd, POB 5072, Port Harcourt; f. 1971; Editor Augustine Njoagwuani.

Sunday Times: Daily Times of Nigeria Ltd, New Isheri Rd, Agidingbi, PMB 21340, Ikeja, Lagos; tel. (1) 4900850; f. 1953; 60% govt-owned; Editor Dupe Ajayi; circ. 100,000.

Sunday Tribune: Imalefalafi St, POB 78, Oke-Ado, Ibadan; tel. (2) 2310886; Editor Wale Ojo.

Sunday Vanguard: Kirikiri Canal, PMB 1007, Apapa; Editor Dupe Ajayi.

WEEKLIES

Albishir: Triumph Publishing Co Ltd, Gidan Sa'adu Zungur, PMB 3155, Kano; tel. (64) 260273; f. 1981; Hausa; Editor Aliyu Umar (acting); circ. 15,000.

Business Times: Daily Times of Nigeria Ltd, New Isheri Rd, Agidingbi, PMB 21340, Ikeja, Lagos; tel. (1) 4900850; f. 1925; 60% govt-owned; Editor Godfrey Bamawo; circ. 22,000.

Gboungboun: Sketch Publishing Co Ltd, New Court Rd, PMB 5067, Ibadan; tel. (2) 414851; govt-owned; Yoruba; Editor A. O. Adebanjo; circ. 80,000.

The Independent: Bodija Rd, PMB 5109, Ibadan; f. 1960; English; Roman Catholic; Editor Rev. F. B. Cronin-Coltsman; circ. 13,000.

Irohin Imole: 15 Bamgbose St, POB 1495, Lagos; f. 1957; Yoruba; Editor Tunji Adeosun.

Irohin Yoruba: 212 Broad St, PMB 2416, Lagos; tel. (1) 410886; f. 1945; Yoruba; Editor S. A. Ajibade; circ. 85,000.

Lagos Life: Guardian Newspapers Ltd, Rutam House, Isolo Expressway, Isolo, PMB 1217, Oshodi, Lagos; f. 1985; Editor Bisi Ogunbadejo; circ. 100,000.

Lagos Weekend: Daily Times of Nigeria Ltd, New Isheri Rd, Agidingbi, PMB 21340, Ikeja, Lagos; tel. (1) 4900850; f. 1965; 60% govt-owned; news and pictures; Editor Sam Ogwa; circ. 85,000.

The News: Lagos; independent; Editor-in-Chief Jenkins Alumona.

Newswatch: 3 Billingsway Rd, Oregun, Lagos; tel. (1) 4935654; fax (1) 4960950; e-mail newswatchngr@aol.com; f. 1985; English; CEO Ray Ekpu; Editor-in-Chief Dan Agbese.

Nigerian Radio/TV Times: Nigerian Broadcasting Corpn, POB 12504, Ikoyi.

Sporting Records: Daily Times of Nigeria Ltd, New Isheri Rd, Agidingbi, PMB 21340, Ikeja, Lagos; tel. (1) 4900850; f. 1961; 60% govt-owned; Editor Cyril Kappo; circ. 10,000.

Tempo: 26 Ijaiye Rd, PMB 21531, Ogba, Ikeja, Lagos; tel. (1) 920975; fax (1) 4924998; e-mail ijc@linkserve.com.ng; news magazine.

Times International: Daily Times of Nigeria Ltd, 3–7 Kakawa St, POB 139, Lagos; f. 1974; Editor Dr Hezy Idowu; circ. 50,000.

Truth (The Muslim Weekly): 45 Idumagbo Ave, POB 418, Lagos; tel. (1) 2668455; f. 1951; Editor S. O. Lawal.

ENGLISH-LANGUAGE PERIODICALS

Afriscope: 29 Salami Saibu St, PMB 1119, Yaba; monthly; African current affairs.

NIGERIA

The Ambassador: PMB 2011, 1 peru-Remo, Ogun; tel. (39) 620115; quarterly; Roman Catholic; circ. 20,000.

Benin Review: Ethiope Publishing Corpn, PMB 1332, Benin City; f. 1974; African art and culture; 2 a year; circ. 50,000.

Headlines: Daily Times of Nigeria Ltd, New Isheri Rd, Agindingbi, PMB 21340, Ikeja, Lagos; f. 1973; monthly; Editor ADAMS ALIU; circ. 500,000.

Home Studies: Daily Times Publications, 3–7 Kakawa St, Lagos; f. 1964; 2 a month; Editor Dr ELIZABETH E. IKEM; circ. 40,000.

Insight: 3 Kakawa St, POB 139, Lagos; quarterly; contemporary issues; Editor SAM AMUKA; circ. 5,000.

Journal of the Nigerian Medical Association: 3–7 Kakawa St, POB 139, Apapa; quarterly; Editor Prof. A. O. ADESOLA.

Lagos Education Review: Faculty of Education, University of Lagos Akoka, Lagos; tel. (1) 5820396; fax (1) 4932669; e-mail dajeyalemi@unilag.edu.ng; f. 1978; 2 a year; African education; Editor Prof. DURO AJEYALEMI.

The Leader: 19A Assumpta Press Ave, Industrial Layout, PMB 1017, Owerri, Imo; tel. (83) 230932; fortnightly; Roman Catholic; Editor Rev. KEVIN C. AKAGHA.

Management in Nigeria: Plot 22, Idowu Taylor St, Victoria Island, POB 2557, Lagos; tel. (1) 2615105; fax (1) 614116; e-mail nim@rcl.nig.com; quarterly; journal of Nigerian Inst. of Management; Editor Rev. DEJI OLOKESUSI; circ. 25,000.

Marketing in Nigeria: Alpha Publications, Surulere, POB 1163, Lagos; f. 1977; monthly; Editor B. O. K. NWELIH; circ. 30,000.

Modern Woman: 47–49 Salami Saibu St, Marina, POB 2583, Lagos; f. 1964; monthly; Man. Editor TOUN ONABANJO.

The New Nation: 52 Iwaya Rd, Onike, Yaba, Surulere, POB 896, Lagos; tel. (1) 5863629; monthly; news magazine.

Nigeria Magazine: Federal Dept of Culture, PMB 12524, Lagos; tel. (1) 5802060; f. 1927; quarterly; travel, cultural, historical and general; Editor B. D. LEMCHI; circ. 5,000.

Nigerian Businessman's Magazine: 39 Mabo St, Surulere, Lagos; monthly; Nigerian and overseas commerce.

Nigerian Journal of Economic and Social Studies: Nigerian Economic Society, c/o Dept of Economics, University of Ibadan; tel. (2) 8700395; e-mail banayochukwu@yahoo.co.uk; internet www.nigerianeconomicsociety.org; f. 1957; 3 a year; Editor Prof. BEN AIGBOKHAN.

Nigerian Journal of Science: University of Ibadan, POB 4039, Ibadan; e-mail iyifawole@yahoo.com; publ. of the Science Asscn of Nigeria; f. 1966; 2 a year; Editor Prof. I. FAWOLE; circ. 1,000.

Nigerian Worker: United Labour Congress, 97 Herbert Macaulay St, Lagos; Editor LAWRENCE BORHA.

The President: New Breed Organization Ltd, Plot 14 Western Ave, 1 Rafiu Shitty St, Alaka Estate, Surulere, POB 385, Lagos; tel. (1) 5802690; fax (1) 5831175; fortnightly; management; Chief Editor CHRIS OKOLIE.

Quality: Ultimate Publications Ltd, Oregun Rd, Lagos; f. 1987; monthly; Editor BALA DAN MUSA.

Radio-Vision Times: Western Nigerian Radio-Vision Service, Television House, POB 1460, Ibadan; monthly; Editor ALTON A. ADEDEJI.

Savanna: Ahmadu Bello University Press Ltd, PMB 1094, Zaria; tel. (69) 550054; e-mail abupl@wwlkad.com; f. 1972; 2 a year; Editor Prof. J. A. ARIYO; circ. 1,000.

Spear: Daily Times of Nigeria Ltd, New Isheri Rd, Agindingbi, PMB 21340, Ikeja, Lagos; tel. (1) 4900850; f. 1962; monthly; family magazine; Editor COKER ONITA; circ. 10,000.

Technical and Commercial Message: Surulere, POB 1163, Lagos; f. 1980; 6 a year; Editor B. O. K. NWELIH; circ. 12,500.

Today's Challenge: PMB 2010, Jos; tel. (73) 52230; f. 1951; 6 a year; religious and educational; Editor JACOB SHAIBY TSADO; circ. 15,000.

Woman's World: Daily Times of Nigeria Ltd, New Isheri Rd, Agindingbi, PMB 21340, Ikeja, Lagos; monthly; Editor TOYIN JOHNSON; circ. 12,000.

VERNACULAR PERIODICALS

Abokiyar Hira: Albah International Publishers, POB 6177, Bompai, Kano; f. 1987; monthly; Hausa; cultural; Editor BASHARI F. FOUKBAH; circ. 35,000.

Gaskiya ta fi Kwabo: Ahmadu Bello Way, POB 254, Kaduna; tel. (62) 201420; f. 1939; 3 a week; Hausa; Editor ABDUL-HASSAN IBRAHIM.

NEWS AGENCIES

Independent Media Centre (IMC): POB 894, Benin City; e-mail nigeriaimc@yahoo.com; internet www.nigeria.indymedia.org.

News Agency of Nigeria (NAN): Independence Avenue, Central Business Area, PMB 7006, Garki, Abuja; tel. (9) 2349732; fax (9) 2349735; e-mail nanabujaq@rd.nig.com; internet www.newsagencyofnigeria.org; f. 1978; Man. Dir AKIN OSUNTOKUN; Editor-in-Chief SHEHU ABUI.

Publishers

Africana First Publishers Ltd: Book House Trust, 1 Africana-First Dr., PMB 1639, Onitsha; tel. (46) 485031; f. 1973; study guides, general science, textbooks; Chair. RALPH O. EKPEH; Man. Dir J. C. ODIKE.

Ahmadu Bello University Press: PMB 1094, Zaria; tel. (69) 550054; f. 1972; history, Africana, social sciences, education, literature and arts; Man. Dir SA'IDU HASSAN ADAMU.

Albah International Publishers: 100 Kurawa, Bompai-Kano, POB 6177, Kano City; f. 1978; Africana, Islamic, educational and general, in Hausa; Chair. BASHARI F. ROUKBAH.

Alliance West African Publishers: Orindingbin Estate, New Aketan Layout, PMB 1039, Oyo; tel. (85) 230798; f. 1971; educational and general; Man. Dir Chief M. O. OGUNMOLA.

Aromolaran Publishing Co Ltd: POB 1800, Ibadan; tel. (2) 715980; f. 1968; educational and general; Man. Dir Dr ADEKUNLE AROMOLARAN.

Cross Continent Press Ltd: 25 Egbeyemi Rd, Ilupeju, POB 282, Yaba, Lagos; tel. and fax (1) 7746348; e-mail crosscontinent@yahoo.com; f. 1974; general, educational and academic; Man. Dir Dr T. C. NWOSU.

Daar Communications PLC: Daar Communications Centre, Kpaduma Hills, off Gen. T. Y. Danjuma St, Asokoro, Abuja; tel. (9) 3144802; fax (9) 3300512; broadcasting and information services; Man. Dir. LADI LAWAL.

Daystar Press: Daystar House, POB 1261, Ibadan; tel. (2) 8102670; f. 1962; religious and educational; Man. PHILLIP ADELAKUN LADOKUN.

ECWA Productions Ltd: PMB 2010, Jos; tel. (73) 52230; f. 1973; religious and educational; Gen. Man. Rev. J. K. BOLARIN.

Ethiope Publishing Corpn: Ring Rd, PMB 1332, Benin City; tel. (52) 243036; f. 1970; general fiction and non-fiction, textbooks, reference, science, arts and history; Man. Dir SUNDAY N. OLAYE.

Evans Brothers (Nigeria Publishers) Ltd: Jericho Rd, PMB 5164, Ibadan; tel. (2) 2414394; fax (2) 2410757; f. 1966; general and educational; Chair. Dr ADEKUNLE OJORA; Man. Dir GBENRO ADEGBOLE.

Fourth Dimension Publishing Co Ltd: 16 Fifth Ave, City Layout, PMB 01164, Enugu; tel. (42) 459969; fax (42) 456904; e-mail nwankwov@infoweb.abs.net; internet www.fdpbooks.com; f. 1977; periodicals, fiction, verse, educational and children's; Chair. ARTHUR NWANKWO; Man. Dir V. U. NWANKWO.

Gbabeks Publishers Ltd: POB 37252, Ibadan; tel. (62) 2315705; e-mail gbabeks@hotmail.com; f. 1982; educational and technical; Man. Dir TAYO OGUNBEKUN.

HEBN Publishers PLC: 1 Ighodaro Rd, Jericho, PMB 5205, Ibadan; tel. (2) 2412268; fax (2) 2411089; e-mail info@hebnpublishers.com; internet www.hebnpublishers.com; f. 1962; educational, law, medical and general; Chair. AIGBOJE HIGO; Man. Dir AYO OJENIYI.

Heritage Books: The Poet's Cottage, Artistes Village, Ilogbo-Eremi, Badagry Expressway, POB 610, Apapa, Lagos; tel. (1) 5871333; e-mail theendofknowledge@yahoo; internet www.theendofknowledge.com; f. 1971; general; Chair. NAIWU OSAHON.

Ibadan University Press: Publishing House, University of Ibadan, PMB 16, IU Post Office, Ibadan; tel. (2) 400550; e-mail iup-unibadan@yahoo.com; f. 1951; scholarly, science, law, general and educational; Dir F. A. ADESANOYE.

Ilesanmi Press Ltd: Akure Rd, POB 204, Ilesha; tel. 2062; f. 1955; general and educational; Man. Dir G. E. ILESANMI.

John West Publications Ltd: Plot 2, Block A, Acme Rd, Ogba Industrial Estate, PMB 21001, Ikeja, Lagos; tel. (1) 4925459; f. 1964; general; Man. Dir Alhaji L. K. JAKAUDE.

Kolasanya Publishing Enterprise: 2 Epe Rd, Oke-Owa, PMB 2099, Ijebu-Ode; general and educational; Man. Dir Chief K. OSUNSANYA.

Literamed Publications Ltd (Lantern Books): Plot 45, Alausa Bus-stop, Oregun Industrial Estate, Ikeja, PMB 21068, Lagos; tel. (1) 3450751; fax (1) 4935258; e-mail information@lantern-books.com; internet www.lantern-books.com; f. 1969; children's, medical and scientific; Chair. O. M. LAWAL-SOLARIN.

Longman Nigeria Ltd: 52 Oba Akran Ave, PMB 21036, Ikeja, Lagos; tel. (1) 4978925; fax (1) 4964370; e-mail longman@linkserve.com; f. 1961; general and educational; Man. Dir J. A. OLOWONIYI.

Macmillan Nigeria Publishers Ltd: Ilupeju Industrial Estate, 4 Industrial Ave, POB 264, Yaba, Lagos; tel. (1) 4962185; e-mail

NIGERIA	Directory

macmillan@hotmail.com; internet www.macmillan.nigeria.com; f. 1965; educational and general; Exec. Chair. J. O. EMANUEL; Man. Dir Dr A. I. ADELEKAN.

Minaj Systems Ltd: Ivie House, 4–6 Ajose Adeogun St, POB 70811, Victoria Island, Lagos; tel. (1) 2621168; fax (1) 2621167; e-mail minaj@minaj.com; broadcasting, printing and publishing; Chair. Chief MIKE NNANYE I. AJEGBO.

Nelson Publishers Ltd: 8 Ilupeju By-Pass, Ikeja, PMB 21303, Lagos; tel. (1) 4961452; general and educational; Chair. Prof. C. O. TAIWO; Man. Dir R. O. OGUNBO.

Northern Nigerian Publishing Co Ltd: Gaskiya Bldg, POB 412, Zaria; tel. (69) 332087; f. 1966; general, educational and vernacular texts; Gen. Man. JA'AFAR D. MOHAMMED.

NPS Educational Publishers Ltd: Trusthouse, Ring Rd, off Akinyemi Way, POB 62, Ibadan; tel. (2) 316006; f. 1969; academic, scholarly and educational; CEO T. D. OTESANYA.

Nwamife Publishers: 10 Ibiam St, Uwani, POB 430, Enugu; tel. (42) 338254; f. 1971; general and educational; Chair. FELIX C. ADI.

Obafemi Awolowo University Press Ltd: Obafemi Awolowo University, Ile-Ife; tel. (36) 230284; f. 1968; educational, scholarly and periodicals; Man. Dir AKIN FATOKUN.

Obobo Books: The Poet's Cottage, Artistes Village, Ilogbo-Eremi, Badagry Expressway, POB 610, Apapa, Lagos; tel. and fax (1) 5871333; e-mail theendofknowledge@yahoo.com; internet www.theendofknowledge.com; f. 1981; children's books; Editorial Dir BAKIN KUNAMA.

Ogunsanya Press Publishers and Bookstores Ltd: SW9/1133 Orita Challenge, Idiroko, POB 95, Ibadan; tel. (2) 310924; f. 1970; educational; Man. Dir Chief LUCAS JUSTUS POPO-OLA OGUNSANYA.

Onibonoje Press and Book Industries (Nigeria) Ltd: Felele Layout, Challenge, POB 3109, Ibadan; tel. (2) 313956; f. 1958; educational and general; Chair. G. ONIBONOJE; Man. Dir J. O. ONIBONOJE.

Pilgrim Books Ltd: New Oluyole Industrial Estate, Ibadan/Lagos Expressway, PMB 5617, Ibadan; tel. (2) 317218; educational and general; Man. Dir JOHN E. LEIGH.

Spectrum Books Ltd: Spectrum House, Ring Rd, PMB 5612, Ibadan; tel. (2) 2310058; fax (2) 2318502; e-mail admin1@spectrumbooksonline.com; internet www.spectrumbooksonline.com; f. 1978; educational and fiction; Chair. JOOP BERKHOUT; Man. Dir SINA OKEOWO.

University of Lagos Press: University of Lagos, POB 132, Akoka, Yaba, Lagos; tel. (1) 825048; e-mail library@rcl.nig.com; university textbooks, monographs, lectures and journals; Man. Dir S. BODUNDE BANKOLE.

University Press Ltd: Three Crowns Bldg, Eleyele Rd, Jericho, PMB 5095, Ibadan; tel. (2) 2411356; fax (2) 2412056; e-mail unipress@skannet.com.ng; f. 1978; associated with Oxford University Press; educational; Man. Dir WAHEED O. OLAJIDE.

University Publishing Co: 11 Central School Rd, POB 386, Onitsha; tel. (46) 210013; f. 1959; primary, secondary and university textbooks; Chair. E. O. UGWUEGBULEM.

Vanguard Media Ltd: Vanguard Ave, off Mile 2/Apapa Expressway, Kirikiri Canal; tel. (1) 5871200; fax (1) 5872662; e-mail vanguard@linkserve.com.ng; Publr SAM AMUKA.

Vista Books Ltd: 59 Awolowo Rd, S. W. Ikoyi, POB 282, Yaba, Lagos; tel. (1) 7746348; e-mail vista-books@yahoo.com; f. 1991; general fiction and non-fiction, arts, children's and educational; Man. Dir Dr T. C. NWOSU.

West African Book Publishers Ltd: Ilupeju Industrial Estate, 28–32 Industrial Ave, POB 3445, Lagos; tel. (1) 4702757; fax (1) 5556854; e-mail w_bookafricapubl@hotmail.com; internet www.wabp.com; f. 1967; textbooks, children's, periodicals and general; Chair. B. A. IDRIS-ANIMASHAUN; Man. Dir FOLASHADE B. OMO-EBOH.

PUBLISHERS' ASSOCIATION

Nigerian Publishers Association: Book House, NPA Permanent Secretariat, Jericho G.R.A., POB 2541, Ibadan; tel. (2) 2413396; f. 1965; Pres. S. B. BANKOLE.

Broadcasting and Communications

TELECOMMUNICATIONS

Nigerian Communications Commission (NCC): Plot 423, Aguiyi Ironsi St, Maitama, Abuja; tel. (9) 4617000; fax (9) 4617514; e-mail ncc@ncc.gov.ng; internet www.ncc.gov.ng; f. 1932 as an independent regulatory body for the supply of telecommunications services and facilities; Chair. Alhaji AHMED JODA; CEO ERNEST C. A. NDUKWE.

Celtel Nigeria: Plot 1678 Olakunle Bakare Close, off Sanusi Fafunwa St, Victoria Island, Lagos; tel. 8021900000; fax (1) 3200477; e-mail customercare@ng.celtel.com; internet www.ng.celtel.com; f. 2000; CEO ADEBAYO WASIU LIGALI.

Globacom Nigeria Ltd: Abuja; e-mail customercare@gloworld.com; internet www.gloworld.com; f. 2003; Chair. Dr MIKE ADENUGA, Jr; 9m. subscribers (2007).

Intercellular Nigeria Ltd: UBA House, 57, Marina, PMB 80078, Victoria Island, Lagos; tel. (1) 4703010; fax (1) 2643014; internet www.intercellular-ng.com; f. 1993; internet and international telephone services; agreed to sell 70% stake to Sudatel (Sudan) in Jan. 2008; CEO ARVID KNUTSEN.

Motophone Ltd: C. & C. Towers, Plot 1684, Sanusi Fafumwa St, Victoria Island, Lagos; tel. (1) 2624168; fax (1) 2620079; e-mail motophone@hyperia.com; internet www.motophone.com; f. 1990; Man. Dir ERIC CHAMCHOUM.

MTN Nigeria Communications Ltd: Churchgate Towers, 5th Floor, Plot 30, Africabank St, Victoria Island, Lagos; tel. 8032005638; fax 8039029636; e-mail info@mtnnigeria.net; internet www.mtnonline.com; f. 2001; CEO AHMAD FARROUKH.

Multi-Links Telecommunication Ltd: 231 Adeola Odeku St, Victoria Island, POB 3453, Marina, Lagos; tel. (1) 7740000; fax (1) 7912345; internet www.multilinks.com; f. 1994; CEO and Man. Dir D. J. RAMAIYA.

Nigerian Mobile Telecommunications Ltd (M-TEL): 2 Bissau St, off Herbert Macaulay Way, Wuse Zone 6, Abuja; tel. (9) 5233031; internet www.mtelnigeria.com; f. 1996; Chair. OLULADE ADEGBOYEGA.

Nigerian Telecommunications (NITEL): 2 Bissau St, off Herbert Macaulay Way, Wuse Zone 6, Abuja; tel. (9) 5233021; Chair. Dr MARTINS IGBOKWE.

Telnet (Nigeria) Ltd: Plot 242, Kofo Abayomi St, Victoria Island, POB 53656, Falomi Ikoyi, Lagos; tel. (1) 2611729; fax (1) 2619945; e-mail contact@iteco.com; internet www.telnetng.com; f. 1985; telecommunications engineering and consultancy services; Man. Dir Dr NADU DENLOYE.

BROADCASTING
Regulatory Authority

National Broadcasting Commission: Plot 807, Ibrahim Taiwo Rd, Asokoro District, POB 5747, Garki, Abuja; tel. (9) 3147525; fax (9) 3147522; e-mail info@nbc-ng.org; internet www.nbc-ng.org; Chair. OBONG O. R. AKPAN.

Radio

Federal Radio Corpn of Nigeria (FRCN): Area 11, Garki, PMB 55, Abuja; tel. (9) 2345915; fax (9) 2345914; f. 1976; controlled by the Fed. Govt and divided into five zones: Lagos (English); Enugu (English, Igbo, Izon, Efik and Tiv); Ibadan (English, Yoruba, Edo, Urhobo and Igala); Kaduna (English, Hausa, Kanuri, Fulfulde and Nupe); Abuja (English, Hausa, Igbo and Yoruba); Chair. Y. ALABI.

Imo Broadcasting Corpn: 14 Savage Cres., Enugu, Imo; tel. (42) 250327; operates one radio station in Imo State.

Voice of Nigeria (VON): Radio House, Herbert Macaulay Way, Area 10, Garki, Abuja; tel. (9) 2344017; fax (9) 2346970; e-mail dgovon@nigol.net.ng; internet www.voiceofnigeria.org; f. 1990; controlled by the Fed. Govt; external services in English, French, Arabic, Ki-Swahili, Hausa and Fulfulde; Dir-Gen. TAIWO ALIMI.

Menage Holding's Broadcasting System Ltd: Umuahia, Imo; commenced broadcasting Jan. 1996; commercial.

Ray Power 100 Drive: Abeokuta Express Way, Ilapo, Alagbado, Lagos; tel. (1) 2644814; fax (1) 2644817; commenced broadcasting Sept. 1994; commercial; Chair. Chief RAYMOND DOKPESI.

Television

Nigerian Television Authority (NTA): Television House, Ahmadu Bello Way, Victoria Island, PMB 12036, Lagos; tel. (1) 2615949; internet www.nta.com.ng; f. 1976; controlled by the Fed. Govt; operates a network of 31 terrestrial broadcasters, which share national programming but also broadcast local programmes; also operates c. 70 regional channels; Chair. YAKUBULL HUSSAINI; Dir-Gen. Alhaji MOHAMMED IBRAHIM.

Africa Independent Television (AIT): Lagos; internet www.aittv.com; f. 1994; 100% owned by DAAR Communications Ltd; Exec. Chair. Dr ALEOGHO DOKPESI.

Minaj Broadcast International (MBI): Minaj Media Group, 130/132, Ladipo St, Matori, Mushin, POB 70811, Victoria Island, Lagos; tel. (01) 4529203; fax (01) 4528500; e-mail info@minajmedia.com; internet www.minajmedia.com; provides free-to-air services.

Murhi International Television (MITV): MITV Plaza, Ikeja Central Business District, Obafemi Awolowo Way, Alausa, Lagos;

NIGERIA

tel. (1) 4931271; fax (1) 4931272; e-mail mitv@murhi-international.com.

Finance

(cap. = capital; res = reserves; dep. = deposits; m. = million; brs = branches; amounts in naira)

BANKING

At the end of 2003 the Nigerian banking system included a total of 89 deposit banks (with 3,300 branches); of these, 11 were estimated by the Central Bank to be insolvent and 24 marginally solvent.

Central Bank

Central Bank of Nigeria: Central Business District, Cadastral Zone, PMB 0187, Garki, Abuja; tel. and fax (9) 6163012; e-mail info@cenbank.org; internet www.cenbank.org; f. 1958; bank of issue; cap. 3,000m., res 141,780m., dep. 2,097,234m. (Dec. 2004); Gov. Prof. CHARLES C. SOLUDO; 18 brs.

Commercial Banks

Afribank Nigeria Ltd: 51–55 Broad St, PMB 12021, Lagos; tel. (1) 2641566; fax (1) 2664890; e-mail info@afribank.com; internet www.afribank.net; f. 1969 as International Bank for West Africa Ltd; cap. 2,354.2m., res 19,032.8m., dep. 61,600.6m. (March 2005); Chair. Alhaji KOLA BELGORE; Man. Dir Chief Alhaji KASHIM M. NJIDDA; 137 brs.

Allstates Trust Bank PLC: Allstates Centre, Plot 1675, Oyin Jolayemi St, POB 73018, Victoria Island, Lagos; tel. (1) 4618445; fax (1) 2612206; e-mail enquiry@allstatesbankng.com; internet www.allstatesbankng.com; cap. 2,476.8m. (Sept. 2001); Man. Dir DUATE PATMORE IYABI.

Citizens' International Bank Ltd: 243 Ahmadu Bello Way, Victoria Island, Lagos; tel. (1) 2601030; fax (1) 2615138; e-mail info@citizensbankng.com; internet www.citizensbankng.com; f. 1990; cap. 619.8m., res 1,809.6m., dep. 31,496.3m. (March 2002); Chair. Chief JOYCE D. U. IFEGWU.

Ecobank Nigeria Ltd: 2 Ajose Adeogun St, Victoria Island, POB 72688, Lagos; tel. (1) 2626638; fax (1) 2616568; e-mail ecobank@linkserve.com.ng; internet www.ecobank.com; cap. 1,522.9m., res 1,996.0m., dep. 19,979.0m. (Dec. 2003); Chair. OMO-OBA ODIMAYO; Man. Dir FUNKE OSIBODU; 26 brs.

First Bank of Nigeria PLC: Samuel Asabia House, 35 Marina, POB 5216, Lagos; tel. (1) 2665900; fax (1) 2665934; e-mail suggestions@firstbanknigeria.com; internet www.firstbanknigeria.com; f. 1894 as Bank of British West Africa; total assets 377,496.0m. (March 2005); Chair. UMAR ABDUL MUTALLAB; CEO and Man. Dir JACOBS M. AJEKIGBE; 302 brs.

Intercontinental Bank Ltd: Danmole St, Plot 999C, Adela Odeku, Victoria Island, Lagos; tel. (1) 2622940; fax (1) 2622981; e-mail info@intercontinentalbankplc.com; internet www.intercontinentalbankplc.com; cap. and res 10,181.4m., total assets 96,857.9m. (Dec. 2003); Chair. RAYMOND C. OBIERI; 42 brs.

IBTC Chartered Bank PLC (IBTC): I.B.T.C. Place, Walter Carrington Cres., POB 71707, Victoria Island, Lagos; tel. (1) 2626520; fax (1) 2626541; internet www.ibtc-lagos.com; f. 1989 as Investment Banking & Trust Co Ltd; name changed 2005; cap. 2,000.0m., res 3,794.4m., dep. 10,543.65m. (March 2004); Chair. Chief OLUDOLAPO IBUKUN AKINKUGBE; Man. Dir ATEDO A. PETERSIDE.

Nigeria International Bank Ltd: Commerce House, 11 Idowu Taylor St, Victoria Island, POB 6391, Lagos; tel. (1) 2622000; fax (1) 2618916; internet www.citibanknigeria.com; f. 1984; cap. 1,000.0m., res 6,791.2m., dep. 37,821.8m. (Dec. 2002); Chair. Chief CHARLES S. SANKEY; 13 brs.

Omegabank (Nigeria) PLC: 1 Engineering Close, PMB 80134, off Idowu Taylor, Victoria Island, Lagos; tel. (1) 2622580; fax (1) 2620761; e-mail omegabank@omegabankplc.com; internet www.omegabankplc.com; f. 1982 as Owena Bank plc; name changed 2001; 30% owned by Ondo State Govt; cap. 2,896.4m., res 208.0m., dep. 11,676.8m. (Dec. 2001); Chair. Chief ANTHONY ADENIYI; CEO Rev. Dr SEGUN AGBETUYI.

Sterling Bank: 20 Marina, Lagos; tel. (1) 2709550; internet www.sterlingbank.com; f. 2005 following merger of Indo-Nigerian Bank Ltd, Magnum Trust Bank, NAL Bank PLC, NBM Bank and Trust Bank of Africa Ltd; Chair. Alhaji SULAIMAN BAFFA; Man. Dir TUNDE DABIRI.

Union Bank of Nigeria Ltd: 36 Marina, PMB 2027, Lagos; tel. (1) 2665439; fax (1) 2669873; e-mail askubn@ng.com; internet www.unionbankng.com; f. 1969; as Barclays Bank of Nigeria Ltd; cap. 2,237m., res 36,892m., dep. 200,511m. (March 2005); Chair. Prof. MUSA G. YAKUBU; CEO G. A. T. OBOH; 235 brs.

United Bank for Africa (Nigeria) Ltd: UBA House, 57 Marina, PMB 12002, Lagos; tel. (1) 2644651; fax (1) 2642287; e-mail info@ubaplc.com; internet www.ubaplc.com; f. 1961; cap. 1,275m., res 16,784m., dep. 151,929m. (March 2005); Chair. HAKEEM BELO-OSAGIE; Man. Dir Mallam ABBA KYARI; 213 brs.

Wema Bank Ltd: Wema Towers, PMB 12862, 27 Nnamdi Akkzikwe St, Lagos; tel. (1) 2668043; fax (1) 2669236; e-mail info@wemabank.com; internet www.wemabank.com; f. 1945; cap. 4,451.6m., res 19,807.2m., dep. 61,284.5m. (March 2005); Chair. Alhaji OLAPADE MOHAMMED; Man. Dir and CEO Alhaji I. A. DOSUNMU; 75 brs.

Merchant Banks

FBN (Merchant Bankers) Ltd: 9/11 Macarthy St, Onikan, POB 12715, Lagos; tel. (1) 2600880; fax (1) 2633600; e-mail bisioni@fbnmb.com; internet www.fbnmb.com; cap. 1,000m. (2003); Chair. JACOBS MOYO AJEKIGBE.

Fidelity Bank PLC: Savannah House, 62-66 Broad St, Lagos; tel. (1) 2610408; fax (1) 2610414; e-mail service.excellence@fidelitybankplc.com; internet www.fidelitybankplc.com; f. 1988; cap. and res 1,189.2m., res 1,326.2m., dep. 16,888.1m. (June 2003); Chair. Chief EMMANUEL A. OKECHUKWU; CEO KENNETH O. AIGBINODE.

First City Monument Bank Ltd: Primrose Tower, 17A Tinubu St, POB 9117, Lagos; tel. (1) 2665944; fax (1) 2665126; e-mail fcmb@fcmb-ltd.com; internet www.fcmb-ltd.com; internet www.fcmb-ltd.com; f. 1983; cap. 2,226.3m., res 4,989.9m., dep. 27,123.1m. (April 2005); Chair. and CEO OTUNBA M. O. BALOGUN.

Stanbic Bank Nigeria Ltd: Plot 688, Amodu Tijani Close, off Sanusi Fafunwa St, Victoria Island, POB 54746, Lagos; tel. (1) 2709660; fax (1) 2709677; e-mail info@stanbic.com.ng; internet www.stanbic.com.ng; f. 1983 as Grindlays Merchant Bank of Nigeria; cap. 1,000.0m., res 532.9m., dep. 6,815.4m. (Dec. 2004); Chair. Dr MATTHEW TAWO MBU; Man. Dir M. A. WEEKS.

Development Banks

Bank of Industry (BOI) Ltd: BOI House, 63/71 Broad St, Lagos; tel. (1) 2663470; fax (1) 2667074; e-mail info@boi-ng.com; internet www.boi-ng.com; f. 1964 as the Nigerian Industrial Development Bank Ltd to provide medium and long-term finance to industry, manufacturing, non-petroleum mining and tourism; name changed as above Oct. 2001; cap. 400m. (Dec. 2001); Man. Dir Dr LAWRENCE OSS-AFIANA; 6 brs.

Guaranty Trust Bank PLC: The Plural House, Plot 1669, Oyin Jolayemi St, PMB 75455, Victoria Island, Lagos; tel. (1) 2622650; fax (1) 2622698; e-mail corpaff@gtbplc.com; internet www.gtbplc.com; f. 1990; cap. 2,873.2m., res 28,021.7m., dep. 95,563.6m. (Feb. 2005); Chair. Prof. MOSOBALAJE O. OYAWOYE.

Nigerian Agricultural, Co-operative and Rural Development Bank Ltd (NACB): Yakubu Gowoh, PMB 2155, Kaduna; tel. (62) 243590; fax (62) 245012; e-mail nacb@infoweb.abs.net; f. 1973 for funds to farmers and co-operatives to improve production techniques; name changed as above Oct. 2000, following merger with People's Bank of Nigeria; cap. 1,000m. (2002); Chair. Alhaji ISA TATA YUSUF; Man. Dir Alhaji UMAR BABALE GIREI; 200 brs.

Bankers' Association

Chartered Institute of Bankers of Nigeria: PC 19 Adeola Hopewell St, POB 72273, Victoria Island, Lagos; tel. (1) 2617924; fax (1) 4618930; e-mail cibn@cibnnigeria.org; internet www.cibnnigeria.org; Chair. JOHNSON O. EKUNDAYO; CEO Dr UJU M. OGUBUNKA.

STOCK EXCHANGE

Securities and Exchange Commission (SEC): Mandilas House, 96–102 Broad St, PMB 12638, Lagos; f. 1979 as govt agency to regulate and develop capital market and to supervise stock exchange operations; Dir-Gen. MUSA AL-FAKI.

Nigerian Stock Exchange: Stock Exchange House, 2–4 Customs St, POB 2457, Lagos; tel. (1) 2660287; fax (1) 2668724; e-mail nse@nigerianstockexchange.com; internet www.nigerianstockexchange.com; f. 1960; Pres. Dr OBA OTUDEKO; Dir-Gen. Dr NDI OKEREKE-ONYIUKE; 6 brs.

INSURANCE

In early 2005 more than 450 registered insurance companies were operating in Nigeria. Since 1978 they have been required to reinsure 20% of the sum insured with the Nigeria Reinsurance Corpn.

Insurance Companies

African Alliance Insurance Co Ltd: 112 Broad St, POB 2276, Lagos; tel. (1) 2664398; fax (1) 2660943; e-mail alliance@infoweb.abs.net; f. 1960; life assurance and pensions; Man. Dir OPE OREDUGBA; 30 brs.

NIGERIA

Aiico International Insurance (AIICO): AIICO Plaza, Plot PC 12, Afribank St, Victoria Island, POB 2577, Lagos; tel. (1) 2610651; fax (1) 2617433; e-mail info@aiicoplc.com; internet www.aiicoplc.com; CEO M. E. HANSEN.

Ark Insurance Group: Glass House, 11A Karimu Kotun St, Victoria Island, POB 3771, Marina, Lagos; tel. (1) 2615826; fax (1) 2615850; e-mail ark@nova.net.ng; internet www.nigeriaweb.com/ark; Chair. F. O. AWOGBORO.

Continental Reinsurance Co Ltd: Reinsurance House, 11th Floor, 46 Marina, POB 2401, Lagos; tel. (1) 2665350; fax (1) 2665370; CEO ADEYEMO ADEJUMO.

Cornerstone Insurance Co PLC: POB 75370, Victoria Island, Lagos; tel. (1) 2631832; fax (1) 2633079; e-mail marketing@cornerstone.com.ng; internet www.cornerstone.com; f. 1991; Chair. CLEMENT O. BAIYE.

Equity Indemnity Insurance Co Ltd: POB 1514, Lagos; tel. (1) 2637802; fax (1) 2637479; e-mail equity@infoweb.abs.net; f. 1991; Chair. Prof. O. A. SERIKI.

Great Nigeria Insurance Co Ltd: 8 Omo-Osaghie St, off Obafemi Awolono Rd, Ikoyi S/W, Ikoyi, Lagos; tel. (1) 2695805; fax (1) 2693483; e-mail info@greatinsure-ng.com; internet www.greatinsure-ng.com; f. 1960; all classes; Man. Dir M. A. SIYANBOLA.

Guinea Insurance Co Ltd: Guinea Insurance House, 21 Nnandi Azikiwe St, POB 1136, Lagos; tel. (1) 2665201; f. 1958; all classes; CEO AYO BAMMEKE.

Industrial and General Insurance Co Ltd: Plot 741, Adeola Hopewell St, POB 52592, Falomo, Lagos; tel. (1) 2625437; fax (1) 2621146; Chair. Y. GOWON.

Kapital Insurance Co Ltd: 116 Hadejia Rd, POB 2044, Kano; tel. (64) 645666; fax (64) 636962; CEO MOHAMMED GAMBO UMAR.

Law Union and Rock Insurance Co of Nigeria Ltd: 88–92 Broad St, POB 944, Lagos; tel. (1) 2663526; fax (1) 2664659; fire, accident and marine; 6 brs; CEO S. O. AKINYEMI.

Leadway Assurance Co Ltd: NN 28–29 Constitution Rd, POB 458, Kaduna; tel. (62) 200660; fax (62) 236838; f. 1970; all classes; Man. Dir OYEKANMI ABIODUN HASSAN-ODUKALE.

Lion of Africa Insurance Co Ltd: St Peter's House, 3 Ajele St, POB 2055, Lagos; tel. (1) 2600950; fax (1) 2636111; f. 1952; all classes; Man. Dir G. A. ALEGIEUNO.

National Insurance Corpn of Nigeria (NICON): 5 Customs St, POB 1100, Lagos; tel. (1) 2640230; fax (1) 2666556; f. 1969; all classes; cap. 200m.; Chair. JOHN IRIATA ABUHME; 28 brs.

N.E.M. Insurance Co (Nigeria) Ltd: 22A Borno Way, Ebute, POB 654, Lagos; tel. (1) 5861920; all classes; Chair. Alhaji Dr ALIYU MOHAMMED; Man. Dir J. E. UMUKORO.

Niger Insurance Co Ltd: 47 Marina, POB 2718, Lagos; tel. (1) 2664452; fax (1) 2662196; all classes; Chair. P. M. G. SOARES; 6 brs.

Nigeria Reinsurance Corpn: 46 Marina, PMB 12766, Lagos; tel. (1) 2667049; fax (1) 2668041; e-mail info@nigeriare.com; internet www.nigre.com; all classes of reinsurance; Man. Dir T. T. MIRILLA.

Nigerian General Insurance Co Ltd: 1 Nnamdi Azikiwe St, Tirubu Square, POB 2210, Lagos; tel. (1) 2662552; e-mail odua@odua.com; f. 1951; all classes; Chair. O. O. OKEYODE; Man. Dir J. A. OLANIHUN; 15 brs.

Phoenix of Nigeria Assurance Co Ltd: Mandilas House, 96–102 Broad St, POB 12798, Lagos; tel. (1) 2661160; fax (1) 2662883; e-mail phoenixassce@alpha.linkserve.com; f. 1964; all classes; cap. 10m.; Chair. A. A. OJORA; Man. Dir A. A. AKINTUNDE; 5 brs.

Prestige Assurance Co (Nigeria) Ltd: 19 Ligali Ayorinde St, Victoria Island, POB 650, Lagos; tel. (1) 3204681; fax (1) 3204684; e-mail prestigeassurance@yahoo.co.uk; f. 1952; all classes except life; Chair. Chief C. S. SANKEY; Man. Dir N. S. R. CHANDRAPRASAD.

Royal Exchange Assurance (Nigeria) Group: New Africa House, 31 Marina, POB 112, Lagos; tel. (1) 2663120; fax (1) 2664431; all classes; Chair. Alhaji MUHTAR BELLO YOLA; Man. Dir JONAH U. IKHIDERO; 6 brs.

Sun Insurance Office (Nigeria) Ltd: Unity House, 37 Marina, POB 2694, Lagos; tel. (1) 2661318; all classes except life; Man. Dir A. T. ADENIJI; 6 brs.

United Nigeria Insurance Co Ltd (UNIC): 53 Marina, POB 588, Lagos; tel. (1) 2663201; fax (1) 2664282; f. 1965; all classes except life; CEO E. O. A. ADETUNJI; 17 brs.

Unity Life and Fire Insurance Co Ltd: 25 Nnamdi Azikiwe St, POB 3681, Lagos; tel. (1) 2662517; fax (1) 2662599; all classes; Man. Dir R. A. ODINIGWE.

West African Provincial Insurance Co: WAPIC House, 119 Awolowo Rd, POB 55508, Falomo-Ikoyi, Lagos; tel. (1) 2672770; fax (1) 2693838; e-mail wapic@alpha.linkserve.com; Man. Dir D. O. AMUSAN.

Insurance Association

Nigerian Insurance Association: Nicon House, 1st Floor, 5 Customs St, POB 9551, Lagos; tel. (1) 2640825; f. 1971; Chair. J. U. IKHIDERO.

Trade and Industry

GOVERNMENT AGENCIES

Bureau of Public Enterprises: Secretariat of the National Council on Privatization, 1 Osun Cres., off Ibib Way, Maitama District, PMB 442, Garki, Abuja; tel. (9) 4134636; fax (9) 4134657; e-mail bpe@bpeng.org; internet www.bpeng.org; Dir-Gen. Mallam NASIR AHMAD EL-RUFAI.

Corporate Affairs Commission: Area 11, Garki, Abuja; tel. (9) 2342917; fax (9) 2342669; e-mail info@cac.gov.ng; internet www.cac.gov.ng; Sec. HENRIEITA O. M. TALABI.

National Council on Privatisation: Bureau of Public Enterprises, NDIC Bldg, Constitution Ave, Central Business District, PMB 442, Garki, Abuja; tel. (9) 5237405; fax (9) 5237396; e-mail bpegen@micro.com.ng; internet www.bpe.gov.ng.

Nigeria Export Processing Zones Authority: Radio House, Fourth Floor, Herbert Macaulay Way, PMB 037, Garki, Abuja; tel. (9) 2343059; fax (9) 2343061; e-mail info@nepza.com; internet www.nepza.com; Gen. Man. SINA A. AGBOLUAJE.

DEVELOPMENT ORGANIZATIONS

Benin–Owena River Basin Development Authority: 24 Benin-Sapele Rd, PMB 1381, Obayantor, Benin City; tel. (52) 254415; f. 1976 to conduct irrigation; Gen. Man. Dr G. E. OTEZE.

Chad Basin Development Authority: Dikwa Rd, PMB 1130, Maiduguri; tel. (76) 232015; f. 1973; irrigation and agriculture-allied industries; Chair. MOHAMMED ABALI; Gen. Man. Alhaji BUNU S. MUSA.

Cross River Basin Development Authority: 32 Target Rd, PMB 1249, Calabar; tel. (87) 223163; f. 1977; Gen. Man. SIXTUS ABETIANBE.

Federal Institute of Industrial Research, Oshodi (FIIRO): Murtala Muhammed Airport, Bilnd Centre St, Oshodi, Ikeja, PMB 21023, Lagos; tel. (1) 900121; fax (1) 4525880; f. 1956; plans and directs industrial research and provides tech. assistance and information to industry; specializes in foods, minerals, textiles, natural products and industrial intermediates; Dir. Prof. S. A. ODUNFA.

Industrial Training Fund: Miango Rd, PMB 2199, Jos, Plateau; tel. and fax (73) 461887; e-mail dp@itf-nigeria.com; internet www.itf-nigeria.com; f. 1971 to promote and encourage skilled workers in trade and industry; Dir-Gen. Prof. OLU E. AKEREJOLA.

Kaduna Industrial and Finance Co Ltd: Investment House, 27 Ali Akilu Rd, PMB 2230, Kaduna; tel. (62) 240751; fax (62) 240754; e-mail kadunainvestment@yahoo.com; f. 1989; provides devt finance; Chair. HARUNA ZEGO AZIZ; Man. Dir and CEO DAHIRU MOHAMMED.

Kwara State Investment Corpn: 109–112 Fate Rd, PMB 1344, Ilorin, Kwara; tel. (31) 220510.

Lagos State Development and Property Corpn: 1 Town Planning Way, Ilupeju, Lagos; tel. (1) 4972243; e-mail isdpc@isdpc.com; internet www.isdpc.com; f. 1972; planning and devt of Lagos; Gen. Man. O. R. ASHAFA.

New Nigerian Development Co Ltd: 18/19 Ahmadu Bello Way, Ahmed Talib House, PMB 2120, Kaduna; tel. (62) 249355; fax (62) 245482; e-mail nndc@skannet.com.ng; f. 1949; owned by the Govts of 19 northern States; investment finance; 8 subsidiaries, 83 assoc. cos; Chair. Prof. HALIDU IBRAHIM ABUBAKAR.

Niger Delta Development Commission: 6 Olumeni St, Port Harcourt; internet www.nddconline.org; f. 1976; Man. Dir GODWIN OMENE.

Nigerian Enterprises Promotion Board: 15–19 Keffi St, S.W. Ikoyi, Lagos; tel. (1) 2680929; f. 1972 to promote indigenization; Chair. MINSO GADZAMA.

Northern Nigeria Investments Ltd: 4 Waff Rd, POB 138, Kaduna; tel. (62) 239654; fax (62) 230770; f. 1959 to identify and invest in industrial and agricultural projects in 16 northern States; cap. p.u. 20m.; Chair. Alhaji ABUBAKAR G. ADAMU; Man. Dir GIMBA H. IBRAHIM.

Odu'a Investment Co Ltd: Cocoa House, PMB 5435, Ibadan; tel. (2) 417710; fax (2) 413000; f. 1976; jtly owned by Ogun, Ondo and Oyo States; Man. Dir Alhaji R. S. ARUNA.

Plateau State Water Resources Development Board: Jos; incorporates the fmr Plateau River Basin Devt Authority and Plateau State Water Resources Devt Board.

Projects Development Institute: Emene Industrial Layout, Proda Rd, POB 01609, Enugu; tel. (42) 451593; fax (42) 457691;

NIGERIA

e-mail proda@rmrdc.nig.com; f. 1977; promotes the establishment of new industries and develops industrial projects utilizing local raw materials; Dir BASIL K. C. UGWA.

Raw Materials Research Development Council: Plot 427, Aguiyi, Ironsi St, Maitama, Abuja; tel. (9) 5237417.

Rubber Research Institute of Nigeria: PMB 1049, Benin City; tel. 8033197241; e-mail rubberresearchnig@yahoo.com; f. 1961; conducts research into the production of rubber and other latex products; Exec. Dir Mrs M.U.B. MOKWUNYE.

Trans Investments Co Ltd: Bale Oyewole Rd, PMB 5085, Ibadan; tel. (2) 416000; f. 1986; initiates and finances industrial and agricultural schemes; Gen. Man. M. A. ADESIYUN.

CHAMBERS OF COMMERCE

Nigerian Association of Chambers of Commerce, Industry, Mines and Agriculture: 15A Ikorodu Rd, Maryland, PMB 12816, Lagos; tel. (1) 4964727; fax (1) 4964737; e-mail naccima@supernet300.com; Pres. CLEMENT OBINEZE MADUAKO; Dir-Gen. L. O. ADEKUNLE.

Aba Chamber of Commerce and Industry: UBA Bldg, Ikot Expene Rd/Georges St, POB 1596, Aba; tel. (82) 352084; fax (82) 352067; f. 1971; Pres. IDE J. C. UDEAGBALA.

Abeokuta Chamber of Commerce and Industry: 29 Kuto Rd, Ishabo, POB 937, Abeokuta; tel. (39) 241230; Pres. Chief S. O. AKINREMI.

Abuja Chamber of Commerce, Industry, Mines & Agriculture: International Trade Fair Complex, KM8, Airport Road, PMB 86, Garki, Abuja; tel. (9) 6707428; fax (9) 2348808; e-mail abuccima@hotmail.com; Pres. Sir PETER OKOLO.

Adamawa Chamber of Commerce and Industry: c/o Palace Hotel, POB 8, Jimeta, Yola; tel. (75) 255136; Pres. Alhaji ISA HAMMANYERO.

Akure Chamber of Commerce and Industry: 57 Oyemekun Rd, POB 866, Akure; tel. (34) 242540; f. 1984; Pres. ADEDEJI OMISAMI.

Awka Chamber of Commerce and Industry: 220 Enugu Rd, POB 780, Awka; tel. (45) 550105; Pres. Lt-Col (retd) D. ORUGBU.

Bauchi Chamber of Commerce and Industry: 96 Maiduguri Rd, POB 911, Bauchi; tel. (77) 42620; f. 1976; Pres. Alhaji MAGAJI MU'AZU.

Benin Chamber of Commerce, Industry, Mines and Agriculture: 10 Murtala Muhammed Way, POB 2087, Benin City; tel. (52) 255761; Pres. C. O. EWEKA.

Benue Chamber of Commerce, Industry, Mines and Agriculture: 71 Ankpa Qr Rd, PMB 102344, Makurdi; tel. (44) 32573; Chair. Col (retd) R. V. I. ASAM.

Borno Chamber of Commerce and Industry: Grand Stand, Ramat Sq., off Central Bank, PMB 1636, Maiduguri; tel. (76) 232832; e-mail bsumar@hotmail.com; f. 1973; Pres. Alhaji MOHAMMED RIJYA; Sec.-Gen. BABA SHEHU BUKAR.

Calabar Chamber of Commerce and Industry: Desan House Bldg, 38 Ndidem Iso Rd, POB 76, Calabar, Cross River; tel. (87) 221558; 92 mems; Pres. Chief TAM OFORIOKUMA.

Enugu Chamber of Commerce, Industry and Mines: International Trade Fair Complex, Abakaliki Rd, POB 734, Enugu; tel. (42) 250575; fax (42) 252186; e-mail eccima@infoweb.abs.net; internet www.enuguchamber.com; f. 1963; Dir EMEKA OKEREKE.

Franco-Nigerian Chamber of Commerce: Big Leaf House, 7 Oyin Jolayemi St, POB 70001, Victoria Island, Lagos; tel. (1) 2621423; fax (1) 2621422; e-mail fncci@ccife.org; internet www.ccife.org/nigeria; f. 1985; Chair. S. JEGEDE; Pres. AKIN AKINBOLA.

Gongola Chamber of Commerce and Industry: Palace Hotel, POB 8, Jimeta-Yola; tel. (75) 255136; Pres. Alhaji ALIYU IBRAHIM.

Ibadan Chamber of Commerce and Industry: Commerce House, Ring Rd, Challenge, PMB 5168, Ibadan; tel. (2) 317223; Pres. JIDE ABIMBOLA.

Ijebu Chamber of Commerce and Industry: 51 Ibadan Rd, POB 604, Ijebu Ode; tel. (37) 432880; Pres. DOYIN DEGUN.

Ikot Ekpene Chamber of Commerce and Industry: 47 Aba Rd, POB 50, Ikot Ekpene; tel. (85) 400153; Pres. G. U. EKANEM.

Kaduna Chamber of Commerce, Industry and Agriculture: 24 Waff Rd, POB 728, Kaduna; tel. (62) 211216; fax (62) 214149; Pres. Alhaji MOHAMMED SANI AMINU.

Kano Chamber of Commerce, Industry, Mines and Agriculture: Zoo Rd, POB 10, Kano City, Kano; tel. (64) 666936; fax (64) 667138; Pres. MALLAM U. J. KIRU.

Katsina Chamber of Commerce and Industry: 1 Nagogo Rd, POB 92, Katsina; tel. (65) 31014; Pres. ABBA ALI.

Kwara Chamber of Commerce, Industry, Mines and Agriculture: Kwara Hotel Premises, Ahmadu Bello Ave, POB 1634, Ilorin; tel. (31) 223069; fax (31) 224131; e-mail kwaccima@yahoo.com; internet www.kwaccima.com; Pres. Alhaji JANI IBRAHIM; Dir-Gen. ABDULSALAAM A. JIMOH.

Lagos Chamber of Commerce and Industry: Commerce House, 1 Idowu Taylor St, Victoria Island, POB 109, Lagos; tel. (1) 2705386; fax (1) 2701009; e-mail inform@micro.com.ng; f. 1888; 1,267 mems; Pres. Chief OLUSOLA FALEYE.

Niger Chamber of Commerce and Industry: Trade Fair Site, POB 370, Minna; tel. (66) 223153; Pres. Alhaji U. S. NDANUSA.

Nnewi Chamber of Commerce, Industry, Mines and Agriculture: 31A Nnobi Rd, POB 1471, Nnewi, Anambra State; tel. (70) 35187662; f. 1987; Pres. PRINCE EMEKA AYABAZU.

Osogbo Chamber of Commerce and Industry: Obafemi Awolowo Way, Ajegunle, POB 870, Osogbo, Osun; tel. (35) 231098; Pres. Prince VICTOR ADEMLE.

Owerri Chamber of Commerce and Industry: OCCIMA Secretariat, 123 Okigwe Rd, POB 1439, Owerri; tel. (83) 234849; Pres. Chief OKEY IKORO.

Oyo Chamber of Commerce and Industry: POB 67, Oyo; Pres. Chief C. A. OGUNNIYI.

Plateau State Chambers of Commerce, Industry, Mines and Agriculture: POB 74, 21A Nassarawa Rd, Jos; tel. (73) 453918; f. 1976; Pres. Chief M. E. JACDOMI.

Port Harcourt Chamber of Commerce, Industry, Mines and Agriculture: Alesa Eleme, POB 585, Port Harcourt; tel. (84) 239536; f. 1952; Pres. Chief S. I. ALETE.

Remo Chamber of Commerce and Industry: 7 Sho Manager Way, POB 1172, Shagamu; tel. (37) 640962; Pres. Chief S. O. ADEKOYA.

Sapele Chamber of Commerce and Industry: 144 New Ogorode Rd, POB 154, Sapele; tel. (54) 42323; Pres. P. O. FUFUYIN.

Sokoto Chamber of Commerce and Industry: 12 Racecourse Rd, POB 2234, Sokoto; tel. (60) 231805; Pres. Alhaji ALIYU WAZIRI BODINGA.

Umahia Chamber of Commerce: 44 Azikiwe Rd, Umahia; tel. (88) 223373; fax (88) 222299; Pres. GEORGE AKOMAS.

Uyo Chamber of Commerce and Industry: 141 Abak Rd, POB 2960, Uyo, Akwa Ibom; Pres. Chief DANIEL ITA-EKPOTT.

Warri Chamber of Commerce and Industry: Block 1, Edewor Shopping Centre, Warri/Sapele Rd, POB 302, Warri; tel. (53) 233731; Pres. MOSES F. OROGUN.

INDUSTRIAL AND TRADE ASSOCIATIONS

Nigerian Export Promotion Council: Zone 2, Block 312, Wuse, PMB 133, Abuja; tel. (9) 5230930; fax (9) 5230931; f. 1976; Chair. Alhaji ISIAKA ADELEKE.

Nigerian Investment Promotion Commission (NIPC): Plot 1181, Agyuiyi-Ironsi St, Maitama District, Abuja; tel. (9) 4138026; fax (9) 4138021; e-mail nipc@nipc-nigeria.org; internet www.nipc-nigeria.org; Chair. FELIX O. A. OHIWEREI; Exec. Sec. Alhaji MUSTAFA BELLO.

EMPLOYERS' ORGANIZATIONS

Association of Advertising Practitioners of Nigeria: 3 William St, off Sylvia Cres., POB 50648, Anthony Village, Lagos; tel. (1) 4970842.

Chartered Institute of Bankers: Plot PC 19, Adeola Hopewell St, POB 72273, Victoria Island, Lagos.

Institute of Chartered Accountants of Nigeria: Plot 16, Professional Layout Centre, Idowu Taylor St, Victoria Island, POB 1580, Lagos; tel. (1) 2622394; fax (1) 4627048; e-mail info.ican@ican.org.ng; internet www.ican-ngr.org; f. 1965; CEO and Registrar OLUTOYIN ADEPATE.

Nigeria Employers' Consultative Association: Commercial House, 1–11 Commercial Ave, POB 2231, Yaba, Lagos; tel. (1) 800360; fax (1) 860309; f. 1957; Pres. Chief R. F. GIWA.

Nigerian Institute of Architects: 2 Idowu Taylor St, Victoria Island, POB 178, Lagos; tel. (1) 2617940; fax (1) 2617947; f. 1960; Pres. Chief O. C. MAJOROH.

Nigerian Institute of Building: 45 Opebi Rd, Ikeja, POB 3191, Marina, Lagos; tel. (1) 4930411; f. 1970; Pres. Dr SANI HABU GUMEL.

Nigerian Institution of Estate Surveyors and Valuers: Flat 2B, Dolphin Scheme, Ikoyi, POB 2325, Lagos; tel. (1) 2673131; fax (1) 2694314; e-mail niesv@nova.net.ng; Pres. NWEKE UMEZURUIKE.

Nigerian Society of Engineers: National Engineering Centre, off National Mosque-Labour Rd, Central Business Area, Abuja; tel. (9) 6735096; e-mail nsehqr@linkserve.com; internet www.nse.org.ng; Pres. KASHIM A. ALI.

UTILITIES

Electricity

Power Holding Company of Nigeria (PHCN): Plot 1071, Area 3, Garki, Abuja; tel. (1) 5231938; f. 1972 as National Electric Power Authority, by merger of the Electricity Corpn of Nigeria and the Niger Dams Authority; renamed as above April 2005; assets were to be diverted to six generating companies and 11 distribution companies, prior to privatization; Man. Dir JOSEPH MAKOJU.

Gas

Nigeria Liquefied Natural Gas Co Ltd (NLNG): C. & C. Towers, Plot 1684, Sanusi Fafunwa St, Victoria Island, PMB 12774, Marina, Lagos; tel. (1) 2624190; fax (1) 2616976; internet www.nigerialng.com; Man. Dir Dr CHRIS HAYNES.

TRADE UNIONS

Federation

Nigerian Labour Congress (NLC): 29 Olajuwon St, off Ojuelegba Rd, Yaba, POB 620, Lagos; tel. (1) 5835582; f. 1978; comprised 29 affiliated industrial unions in 1999; Pres. ABDULLAH-WAHID IBRAHIM OMAR.

Principal Unions

Amalgamated Union of Public Corpns, Civil Service, and Technical and Recreational Services Employees: 9 Aje St, PMB 1064, Yaba, Lagos; tel. (1) 5863722; Sec.-Gen. SYLVESTER EJIOFOR.

National Union of Journalists: Lagos; Pres. LANRE OGUNDIPE; Sec. MOHAMMED KHALID.

National Union of Petroleum Workers and Natural Gas (NUPENG): Lagos; Sec.-Gen. FRANK KOKORI.

Nigerian Union of Civil Engineering, Construction, Furniture and Woodworkers: 51 Kano St, Ebute Metta, PMB 1064, Lagos; tel. (1) 5800263.

Nigerian Union of Mine Workers: 95 Enugu St, POB 763, Jos; tel. (73) 52401.

Petroleum and Gas Senior Staff Association of Nigeria (PENGASSAN): Lagos; Sec.-Gen. KENNETH NAREBOR.

Transport

RAILWAYS

There are about 3,505 km of mainly narrow-gauge railways. The two principal lines connect Lagos with Nguru and Port Harcourt with Maiduguri.

Nigerian Railway Corpn: Plot 739, Zone A6, Panama St, off IBB Way, Maitama, Abuja; tel. (9) 5231912; f. 1955; restructured in 1993 into three separate units: Nigerian Railway Track Authority; Nigerian Railways; and Nigerian Railway Engineering Ltd; Chair. Alhaji WAZIRI MOHAMMED.

ROADS

In 2004 the Nigerian road network totalled 193,200 km, including 15,688 km of highways and 18,719 km of secondary roads; some 9,660 km were paved.

Nigerian Road Federation: Ministry of Transport, National Maritime Agency Bldg, Central Area, Abuja; tel. (9) 5237053.

INLAND WATERWAYS

Inland Waterways Department: Ministry of Transport, National Maritime Agency Bldg, Central Area, Abuja; tel. (9) 5237053; responsible for all navigable waterways; Chair. Alhaji SULE ONABIYI.

SHIPPING

The principal ports are the Delta Port complex (including Warri, Koko, Burutu and Sapele ports), Port Harcourt and Calabar; other significant ports are situated at Apapa and Tin Can Island, near Lagos. The main petroleum ports are Bonny and Burutu.

Nigerian Maritime Administration and Safety Agency (NIMASA): f. 2007 following merger of National Maritime Authority and Joint Maritime Labour Industrial Council; Dir-Gen. Dr ADE DOSUNMU.

Nigerian Ports Authority: Olusegun Obasanjo Way, Plot 126, Central Business District, Garki, Abuja; tel. (9) 2347920; fax (9) 2347930; e-mail telnpo@infoweb.abs.net; internet www.nigeria-ports.com; f. 1955; CEO Chief ADEBAYO SARUMI.

Nigerian Green Lines Ltd: Yinka Folawiyo Plaza, 38 Yinka Folawiyo Ave (fmrly Warehouse Rd), Apapa; tel. (1) 5450436; fax (1) 5450204; f. 1972; Yinka Folawiyo Group; 2 vessels totalling 30,751 grt; Chair. Alhaji W. I. FOLAWIYO.

Nigeria Unity Line: Maritime Complex, 34 Creek Rd, PMB 1175, Apapa, Lagos; tel. (1) 5804808; fax (1) 5804807; e-mail nul@hyperia.com; f. 1995 following the dissolution of the Nigerian National Shipping Line; govt-owned; Chair. Chief A. R. DIKIBO.

Association

Nigerian Shippers Council: 4 Park Lane, Apapa, Lagos; tel. (1) 5452307; e-mail info@shipperscouncil.com; internet www.shipperscouncil.com; Chair. Capt. A. A. BIU.

CIVIL AVIATION

The principal international airports are at Lagos (Murtala Mohammed Airport), Kano, Port Harcourt and Abuja. There are also 14 airports for domestic flights.

Federal Airport Authority of Nigeria: Murtala Mohammed Airport, PMB 21607, Ikeja, Lagos; tel. (1) 4900800; Chair. SARGEANT AWUSE.

Principal Airlines

Virgin Nigeria: 3rd Floor Ark Towers Plot 17, Ligali Ayorinde St Victoria Island Extension, Ikeja, Lagos; tel. (1) 4600505; e-mail commercial@virginnigeria.com; internet www.virginnigeria.com; f. Sept. 2004; private flag carrier; 51% owned by Nigerian institutional investors and 49% by Virgin Atlantic; scheduled domestic regional and international services; CEO CONRAD CLIFFORD.

Tourism

Potential attractions for tourists include fine coastal scenery, dense forests, and the rich diversity of Nigeria's arts. A total of 2,778,365 tourists visited Nigeria in 2005. Receipts from tourism amounted to US $46m. in 2005.

Nigerian Tourism Development Corpn: Old Federal Secretariat, Area 1, Garki, PMB 167, Abuja; tel. (9) 2342764; fax (9) 2342775; e-mail ntdc@metrong.com; internet www.nigeria.tourism.com; Chair. Prince ADESUYI HAASTRUP; CEO OMOTAYO OMOTOSHO.

NORWAY

Introductory Survey

Location, Climate, Language, Religion, Flag, Capital

The Kingdom of Norway forms the western part of Scandinavia, in northern Europe. It is bordered to the east by Sweden and, within the Arctic Circle, by Finland and Russia. A long, indented coast faces the Atlantic Ocean. Norway exercises sovereignty over the Svalbard archipelago, Jan Mayen island and the uninhabited dependencies of Bouvetøya and Peter I Øy. Dronning Maud Land, in Antarctica, is also a Norwegian dependency. Norway's climate is temperate on the west coast but colder inland. Average temperatures range from −2°C (28°F) to 8°C (46°F). There are two forms of the Norwegian language, which are officially recognized as equal. About 80% of children in schools use the older form, Bokmål, as their principal language, whereas only 20% use the newer form, Nynorsk (Neo-Norwegian). Lappish is also spoken by the Sámi population, in northern Norway. Almost all of the inhabitants profess Christianity: the Evangelical Lutheran Church is the established religion, with about 86% of the population professing adherence in 2003. The civil flag (proportions 8 by 11) has a dark blue cross, bordered with white, on a red background, the upright of the cross being to the left of centre; the state flag (16 by 27) displays the same cross, but forms a triple swallow-tail at the fly. The capital is Oslo.

Recent History

Norway, formerly linked to the Swedish crown, declared its independence in 1905. The union with Sweden was peacefully dissolved and the Norwegians elected their own monarch, Prince Karl of Denmark, who took the title of King Håkon VII. He reigned until his death in 1957, and was succeeded by his son, Olav V. Olav's son, Crown Prince Harald (who had acted as regent since his father suffered a stroke in May 1990), became King Harald V upon Olav's death in January 1991.

During the Second World War Norway was occupied by German forces between 1940 and 1945. Norway abandoned its traditional policy of neutrality after the war, joining the North Atlantic Treaty Organization (NATO, see p. 340) in 1949. Norway was also a founder member of the Nordic Council (see p. 424) in 1952 and of the European Free Trade Association (EFTA, see p. 412) in 1960.

Det norske Arbeiderparti (DnA—Norwegian Labour Party) governed from 1935 to 1965, except for the period of German occupation, when a pro-Nazi 'puppet' regime was administered by Vidkun Quisling, and an interlude of one month in 1963. Norway applied for membership of the European Community (EC, now European Union—EU, see p. 244) in 1962, and again in 1967. A general election to the Storting (parliament) in September 1965 resulted in a defeat for the DnA Government of Einar Gerhardsen, who had been Prime Minister almost continuously since 1955. His administration was replaced in October 1965 by a non-socialist coalition under Per Borten, leader of the Senterpartiet (Sp—Centre Party). However, in March 1971 Borten resigned, following revelations that he had deliberately disclosed confidential details of Norway's negotiations with the EC. He was succeeded by a minority DnA Government, led by Trygve Bratteli. The terms of Norway's entry into the EC were agreed in December 1971, and a preliminary Treaty of Accession was signed in January 1972. In September, however, a consultative referendum on the agreed terms produced a 53.3% majority against entering the EC. The application was withdrawn, and Bratteli resigned in October. A coalition of Venstre (Liberals), the Sp and the Kristelig Folkeparti (KrF—Christian Democrats' Party) formed a new minority Government, with Lars Korvald of the KrF as Prime Minister.

Following the general election of September 1973, Bratteli formed another minority DnA Government, dependent on the support of a socialist alliance known from 1975 as the Socialistisk Venstreparti (SV—Socialist Left Party). In January 1976 Bratteli was succeeded as Prime Minister by Odvar Nordli. Nordli resigned in February 1981, for reasons of ill health, and was succeeded by Gro Harlem Brundtland, Norway's first female Prime Minister. At the general election in September the DnA lost support to centre-right groups. In October a minority administration, led by Kåre Willoch, became Norway's first Høyre (Conservative) Government since 1928. In June 1983 a coalition of Høyre with the Sp and the KrF was formed, with 79 of the 165 parliamentary seats. Willoch's Government was returned to power, although lacking an overall majority in the Storting, following the general election in September 1985. In May 1986 Willoch resigned when the Storting narrowly rejected a proposal to increase taxation on petrol. The Norwegian Constitution did not permit a general election before the expiry of the Storting's term (due in 1989). Brundtland accepted an invitation by the King to form a minority DnA administration. The new Government devalued the krone by 12%, and a revised budget was approved by the Storting in June 1986.

At the general election in September 1989 both the DnA and Høyre lost support to more radical parties. The SV gained nine seats, to achieve a total of 17 seats. The Fremskrittspartiet (FrP—Progress Party) increased its representation from two to 22 seats, despite attracting allegations of racism during the election campaign. Brundtland's Government resigned in October, following an agreement made by Høyre, the Sp and the KrF to form a coalition. The new Government, led by Jan Syse (Høyre leader since January 1988), controlled only 62 seats in the Storting and was dependent upon the support of the FrP. Also in September 1989 the Sámi (Lapps) of northern Norway elected 39 representatives for a new Sameting (Consultative Assembly), to be based in Karasjok. This followed an amendment to the Constitution the previous year, which recognized the Sámi as an indigenous people and an ethnic minority. There was considerable support among the Sámi for a degree of autonomy, in order to protect their traditional way of life. The Sámi had officially ceased to exist by 1900, with their culture and language being declared illegal, but by 2000 they had formed a joint council comprising Sámi populations in Norway, Sweden, Finland and Russia, and received a parliament building, opened in November by King Harald V. The issue of land rights, however, remained unresolved. This was aggravated by the discovery, in 2001, of substantial platinum deposits in Finnmark, an area to which the Sámi laid claim.

While Høyre had supported EC membership since 1988, the Sp remained strongly opposed to it. In October 1990 the Government announced that the Norwegian krone was to be linked to the European Currency Unit (ECU). Later in that month the coalition collapsed, following disagreement between Høyre and the Sp regarding Norwegian demands in the negotiations between EFTA and the EC on the creation of a joint European Economic Area (EEA). In November the DnA formed another minority Government, led by Brundtland.

In October 1991 agreement was finally reached on the terms of the EEA treaty, including arrangements whereby EC countries were to be allowed to take extra quotas of fish from Norwegian waters, while Norwegian fish products were to have increased access to EC markets. Many Norwegians remained opposed to membership of the EC, fearing, in particular, that government subsidies that had allowed the survival of remote rural and coastal communities would no longer be permitted. The EEA treaty was ratified by the Storting in October 1992. (The treaty entered into effect on 1 January 1994, following ratification by all of the countries concerned.) A proposal by Brundtland to apply for EC membership was endorsed by the Storting in November 1992, and an application was duly submitted.

In November 1992 Brundtland resigned from the leadership of the DnA, and was replaced by the party's Secretary-General, Thorbjørn Jagland. At the September 1993 general election the DnA increased its representation in the Storting, from 63 to 67 seats. The Sp (which opposed EC membership) increased its total from 11 to 32 seats, thereby becoming the second largest party in the Storting, while Høyre won only 28 seats, compared with 37 at the previous election.

Negotiations on Norway's entry to the EU, as the EC had been restyled, were concluded in March 1994. However, at a national referendum held on 27–28 November (shortly after Sweden and Finland had voted to join the Union), 52.4% of voters rejected EU membership. The success of the campaign opposing Norway's entry to the EU was attributed to several factors: in particular, farmers feared the impact of an influx of cheaper agricultural goods from the EU, and fisheries workers feared that fish stocks would be severely depleted if EU boats were granted increased access to Norwegian waters. There was also widespread concern that national sovereignty would be compromised by the transfer to the EU of certain executive responsibilities.

At local elections held in September 1995, the DnA received 31% of the votes cast (compared with 37% at the 1993 general election), Høyre obtained 20% and the Sp 12%. The right-wing FrP, which had campaigned for more stringent policies on law and order, also won 12% of the vote, compared with 6% at the general election.

In October 1996 Brundtland resigned as Prime Minister and was succeeded by Jagland, who pledged to continue the previous Government's cautious fiscal policy. By the end of the year, however, the Government's credibility had been seriously undermined, after Terje Röd-Larsen, the newly appointed Minister of National Planning, and Grete Faremo, the Minister of Petroleum and Energy, were forced to resign, following, respectively, allegations of financial irregularities and abuse of power.

A general election was conducted on 16 September 1997, at which the DnA attracted the largest level of support, winning 35.0% of the votes cast (65 seats), ahead of the FrP with 15.3% (25 seats), Høyre 14.3% (23 seats) and the KrF 13.7% (25 seats). In October Jagland resigned, honouring a pre-election pledge to stand down should the DnA fail to secure at least the 36.9% of popular support that it attracted at the 1993 poll. Kjell Magne Bondevik, the parliamentary leader of the KrF, had organized an alliance of the KrF, the Sp and Venstre (with representation totalling 42 seats), and was invited to form a coalition government on that basis. The new Council of State was dominated by the KrF. There was some uncertainty regarding the durability of the Government after the Prime Minister took more than three weeks' leave from his post from the end of August 1998, owing to depression. Bondevik was reported to have been under intense pressure as a result of recent economic instability, largely attributable to the sharp decline in international prices for petroleum; this had notably necessitated the postponement of the introduction of a scheme, promoted by Bondevik, to give financial support to parents choosing to look after children aged between one and two years at home. In November, furthermore, the Government was obliged to abandon proposed tax increases in order to secure the support of the FrP (and thus parliamentary approval) for the 1999 budget. Electoral support for the DnA declined further in the local elections held in September, when it received 28.2% of the votes cast; support also declined for the three coalition partners, while the most significant gains were made by the FrP, which campaigned on an anti-immigration platform and received the third largest share of the vote.

On 9 March 2000 Bondevik resigned following his defeat in a confidence motion in the Storting by 81 votes to 71. The vote was called to resolve a dispute between the majority in the Storting and the minority Government on whether to postpone the construction of gas-fired power plants pending the introduction of new technology to render them pollution-free. Bondevik favoured postponement as he opposed amending the country's strict anti-pollution laws to allow increased carbon dioxide emissions. Bondevik recommended that Jens Stoltenberg, who had replaced Jagland as leader of the DnA in February, be approached to form a single-party minority government. Stoltenberg duly took office as Prime Minister on 17 March. The new Council of State included Jagland as Minister of Foreign Affairs. The new Government pledged to reform the public sector, resume the country's privatization programme, forge stronger links with Europe and continue Norway's role as a mediator in international peace negotiations.

In March 1999 the Storting approved compensation valued at US $57.5m. for the country's Holocaust victims and their descendants. The programme was to include compensation for plundered property, as well as funding for contemporary Jewish community projects. In October 2001 a lawsuit was brought against the Norwegian Government by surviving victims of the Nazi *Lebensborn* (Source of Life) project. The survivors, children of German soldiers and Norwegian women, were conceived during the Nazi occupation of Norway in the Second World War as part of a scheme to create a 'master race'. They alleged that, following the liberation of Norway, they and their mothers were subjected to systematic abuse and discrimination, and that the Government not only allowed this abuse to occur, but also attempted to conceal it. The lawsuit was rejected on the grounds that the alleged offences occurred too long ago to be brought to court. However, in late 2002 the Storting's Justice Committee recommended that the Government 'make amends'. In March 2007 the European Court of Human Rights commenced deliberations over the admissibility of a lawsuit against the Norwegian Government brought by a group of 159 *Lebensborn* survivors.

At a general election conducted on 10 September 2001, the DnA received only 24.3% of the valid votes cast (its poorest electoral performance since 1909), attaining 43 seats. Høyre secured 21.2% of the votes cast (38 seats), the FrP 14.7% (26 seats), the SV 12.5% (23 seats) and the KrF 12.4% (22 seats). The DnA formed a minority Government, but was unable to attract enough political support to hold a majority in the Storting. Stoltenberg consequently resigned on 17 October, and the DnA was replaced in government by a minority centre-right coalition comprising Høyre, the KrF and Venstre, with Bondevik as Prime Minister. The coalition gained a majority in the Storting with the informal support of the FrP.

In February 2003 the Government announced its decision to expel Mullah Krekar, the leader of the Kurdish guerrilla organization Ansar al-Islam, who was suspected by both the USA and the UN of having links to terrorism, and possibly to the Islamist al-Qa'ida (Base) organization. However, Krekar, who had stated that he would not leave Norway voluntarily, was not taken into custody or otherwise compelled to leave the country. The following month the Government announced that the case merited further investigation, and that the launch of the US-led military action in Iraq that month posed difficulties for his repatriation, effectively granting Krekar the right to remain in the country for a further two months. A request from Jordan for him to be extradited for drugs offences was also to be investigated. Krekar was eventually detained following an appearance on Dutch television during which he stated that Ansar al-Islam had suicide bombers ready to attack US citizens, but did not remain in custody for long. Krekar was arrested again in December and charged with plotting the murder of his political rivals in Iraq in 2000–01, and was imprisoned in January 2004 while prosecutors investigated the charges against him. Despite the prosecutors' efforts to keep Krekar in custody, he was freed by the Lagmannsrett (Court of Appeal) in February. The charges against Krekar were withdrawn in June owing to insufficient evidence. In 2005 Krekar's expulsion was further delayed pending a guarantee from the Iraqi authorities that he would not face the death penalty. (Norwegian law forbids extradition to countries with the death penalty.) In November 2007 the Høyesterett (Supreme Court) upheld the decision to expel Krekar. However, in April 2008 it was reported that the Government had failed to reach an agreement with the Iraqi authorities over his extradition and that Krekar was to be allowed to remain in Norway indefinitely.

In December 2003 the Storting adopted legislation introducing a minimum quota of 40% for female board members for all publicly owned enterprises and public limited-liability companies in the private sector. The rules applying to publicly owned companies took effect in January 2004, but private companies were given until July 2005 to achieve the desired gender representation voluntarily before the legislation would be enforced. In December 2005 the Government concluded that the gender representation requirements would not be reached on a voluntary basis and approved the entry into force of the legislation as regards public limited-liability companies in the private sector from January 2006. Companies were initially given until the end of 2007 to meet the requirements set by the legislation, but this was subsequently extended to late February 2008. By January 2008 more than 80% of companies had complied with the legislation, giving Norway the highest proportion of female directors in the world, at 36%. Informal gender quotas have operated in Norway since 1981, since when some 40% of government posts have been held by women.

In 2004 Norway introduced transitional rules aimed at limiting (for an initial period of two years) the entry of migrant workers from the eight central and east European countries that joined the EU on 1 May. While Norway was not itself a member of the EU, it nevertheless had commitments arising from its membership of the EEA and the EU's Schengen Agreement. The Government had originally planned to allow unrestricted access to Norway's labour markets, but felt compelled to change its position following the introduction of similar prohibitory legislation by neighbouring countries.

Local elections were held on 15 September 2003, at which the participation rate was the lowest since the Second World War.

The DnA remained the party with the largest share of the vote, while the KrF performed particularly poorly, receiving just one-half as much support as it had done at the 2001 general election. The biggest gains were made by the SV and the FrP, which achieved its best result in 30 years. In January 2004 Valgerd Svarstad Haugland resigned as Chairperson of the KrF; however, she retained her post as the Minister of Culture and Church Affairs. The Minister of Health, Dagfinn Høybråten, was unanimously elected to replace her as leader of the KrF. In February Jan Petersen announced his decision to step down as Chairman of Høyre after 10 years in this post, while remaining Minister of Foreign Affairs. Erna Solberg replaced him as leader of Høyre in May.

On 1 June 2004 legislation, originally approved by the Storting in April 2003, came into force, outlawing smoking in restaurants, cafés, bars and nightclubs in order to protect employees and patrons from the effects of passive smoking. Norway was the second country in the world to adopt such legislation, after Ireland.

A general election was held on 12 September 2005, at which the DnA received 32.7% of the votes cast and won 61 of the 169 seats in the enlarged Storting, thus retaining its position as the largest parliamentary party. The DnA contested the election at the head of a centre-left alliance also comprising the SV (which secured 15 seats, with 8.8% of the votes cast) and the Sp (11 seats, with 6.5%). The FrP won 22.1% of the votes cast (38 seats), while Høyre secured 14.1% (23 seats), the KrF 6.8% (11 seats) and Venstre 5.9% (10 seats). Some 77.1% of the electorate participated in the election. The DnA, the SV and the Sp subsequently formed the first majority Government since 1985, led by Stoltenberg, which was sworn into office in mid-October. The new coalition Government's programme included proposals to increase welfare spending, raise taxes and eradicate social inequality.

In January 2006 the Government announced that the State Pension Fund would henceforth no longer invest in companies whose activities 'violate fundamental humanitarian principles', including those involved in the production of nuclear weapons. Also in January, a tax was introduced on milk and juice cartons in an attempt to persuade producers and consumers to recycle more of their refuse. The tax was to be removed once recycling levels reached 95%.

The FrP elected its parliamentary leader, Siv Jensen, as party Chairperson in May 2006, replacing Carl Hagen, who had held the post for 28 years. During late 2006 Jensen commenced informal discussions with Høyre regarding co-operation between the two parties prior to the next general election, which was due in 2009, and the possible formation of a right-wing coalition government thereafter.

In late September 2006 the Minister of Trade and Industry, Odd Eriksen, of the DnA, resigned from the Government and was replaced by Dag Terje Andersen, also of the DnA. At a DnA party conference held in April 2007, Stoltenberg announced that the Government intended to reduce Norway's emissions of carbon dioxide by 30% (from 1990 levels) by 2020 and to achieve a reduction in emissions world-wide equivalent to 100% of Norwegian emissions by 2050, mainly through a system of trading in emissions with other countries. In January 2008 this date was brought forward to 2030 after the Government reached an agreement with three opposition parties to set a more ambitious target.

In September 2007 Odd Roger Enoksen resigned as Minister of Petroleum and Energy. The appointment of his successor, the leader of the Sp, Aslaug Marie Haga, created Norway's first female-majority government; with 10 of the 19 ministerial positions occupied by women. A minor government reorganization took place in October and included new appointments by the SV, following significant losses for the party in nation-wide local elections in September, which were widely attributed to popular disenchantment with the SV members of the Cabinet. Helen Bjørnøy and Øystein Djupedal, responsible for the environment and education portfolios, respectively, were removed from the Cabinet. In the same reshuffle, Manuela Ramin-Osmundsen, who had previously led the Norwegian Directorate of Immigration, was appointed Minister of Children and Equality. In February 2008, however, Ramin-Osmundsen left the Cabinet, following media allegations of favouritism over her decision to appoint a government lawyer, Ida Hjort Kraby, as children's ombudsman. Stoltenberg, who initially offered his support to Ramin-Osmundsen, announced her dismissal from the Cabinet after it emerged that she had withheld information from the Prime Minister. Ramin-Osmundsen had acknowledged that she knew Hjort Kraby, but denied that they were close friends. However, the media subsequently documented professional and social links between the two women dating back 20 years. She was succeeded later that month by a former leader of the DnA's youth organization, Anniken Huitfeldt. Hjort Kraby resigned from the post of children's ombudsman.

During 1993 the Norwegian Government was instrumental in conducting secret negotiations between the Israeli Government and the Palestine Liberation Organization (PLO), which led to agreement on Palestinian self-rule in certain areas occupied by Israel. Norway won international acclaim for its role in furthering peace in the Middle East through these negotiations, and continued to be involved in the advancement of the peace process in the late 1990s and first half of the 2000s.

In February 2000 Norway extended its role as an international mediator, agreeing to broker negotiations between the Sri Lankan Government and Tamil separatists in an attempt to end the 17-year conflict. A cease-fire agreement was signed by the two parties in February 2002, supervised by the Norwegian-led Sri-Lankan Monitoring Mission (SLMM). In May 2007 a Sri Lankan government defence spokesman, Keheliya Rambukwella, recommended that Norway should review the cease-fire because it was being consistently breached by rebels. The SLMM's activities were terminated in mid-January 2008, following an escalation of violence in the country and the Government's withdrawal from the cease-fire agreement.

In April 2001 Norway agreed to host peace negotiations between the Philippine Government and the Philippine dissident communist alliance, the National Democratic Front. These formal negotiations stalled in 2004 and 2005 and had not resumed by early 2008, although Norway continued to act as a mediator between the two parties.

Norway declared an exclusive economic zone extending to 200 nautical miles (370 km) from its coastline in 1977, and also unilaterally established a fisheries protection zone around its territory of Svalbard. The declaration of an economic zone around Jan Mayen island in 1980 led to agreements with Iceland, in 1980 and 1981, over conflicting claims to fishing and mineral rights. A similar dispute with Denmark, acting for Greenland, was not resolved, and in 1988 Denmark requested arbitration by the International Court of Justice, in The Hague, Netherlands, which gave its judgment on the delimitation of the disputed zones in June 1993 (see under Jan Mayen). During 1994 incidents were reported between vessels of the Norwegian coast-guard and Icelandic fishing boats, within the economic zone surrounding the Norwegian island of Spitsbergen (see under Svalbard). In October 2005 Norway detained two Russian vessels that were illegally transferring fish within the same zone.

Following a moratorium on commercial whaling, adopted by the International Whaling Commission (IWC, see p. 404) with effect from 1985, Norway continued to hunt small numbers of whales ostensibly for purposes of scientific research, and in 1992 the Norwegian Government declared that it would allow the resumption of commercial hunting of minke whales in 1993, claiming that (according to the findings of the IWC's scientific commission) this species was plentiful enough to allow whaling on a sustainable basis: the Government argued that many Norwegian coastal communities depended on whaling for their existence. A moratorium on the hunting of seal pups, imposed in 1989, was ended by the Norwegian Government in 1995, although it was emphasized that the killing of seals would be strictly for scientific purposes. None the less, opponents of sealing expressed concern that Norway might seek to resume commercial hunting. Norway continued to campaign against the moratorium on commercial whaling, and made some progress in its attempts to exempt the minke whale from the ban on exports of whale products imposed under the Convention on International Trade in Endangered Species (CITES). In July 1999 journalists revealed that 500 metric tons of blubber had been stockpiled by the Norwegians in anticipation of a resumption of legal trading. In January 2001 the Government announced that it would resume exports of whale meat and products without waiting for the next CITES conference, scheduled for 2004. The announcement attracted criticism from environmental groups; however, many observers (including a number within the IWC) admitted that a return to controlled commercial whaling was becoming inevitable. In March 2002 Norway declared that it was to resume exports of whale meat to Japan. In December 2005 the Norwegian Government announced an increase in its quota for minke whales from 797 in 2005 to 1,052 in 2006, the highest quota since 1993. The narrow approval, at an IWC meeting in June 2006, of a Norwegian-backed resolution for an eventual resumption of commercial whaling provoked strong protests from countries opposed to whaling. Although the vote was not binding, it was considered to represent a further step towards a return for the IWC to a role of setting limits for the capture of whales, rather than one of protection. At the annual meeting of the IWC in May 2007, Denmark lent its support to the Norwegian position of arguing for a return to commercial whaling. However, the proposal was again subject to strong criticism from several other member countries and the proceedings ended in discord.

In January 2002, following the US-led military campaign against the Taliban and al-Qa'ida militants in Afghanistan in 2001, Norway contributed 180 troops to the International Security Assistance Force (ISAF), deployed in the Afghan capital, Kabul, and at Bagram airbase to help maintain security in the area. In January 2004, at the request of the Loya Jirga (the Afghan Grand Assembly) the Norwegian troops extended their mission in Afghanistan until August of that year. Norway also contributed special forces troops from its Naval Ranger Command and the Norwegian Army's Ranger Command to the US-led operation 'Enduring Freedom', the main aim of which was to combat al-Qa'ida's terrorist network in Afghanistan. In August 2004 the mandate of Norway's ISAF troops in northern Afghanistan was extended indefinitely. In January 2006 Norway withdrew almost all its remaining troops from 'Enduring Freedom' and instead increased its commitment to the ISAF. However, in late 2006 the Norwegian Government was criticized by some of its NATO counterparts, following its refusal to contribute additional troops to the ISAF for deployment in more intensive counter-insurgency operations in southern Afghanistan; at that time 518 Norwegian troops were based in the north of the country. In February 2007 Norway announced that it would send 150 special forces troops to Kabul, and a further 200 troops were committed in February 2008.

In January 2008 the Minister of Foreign Affairs, Jonas Gahr Støre, visited Kabul as part of a Norwegian delegation. During the trip, Taliban militants attacked the hotel in which the delegation was staying, killing six people, including Carsten Thomassen, a reporter with the Oslo daily newspaper *Dagbladet*. Norway subsequently closed its embassy in Kabul; it remained closed in April.

In July 2003 Norway sent 150 soldiers from the Telemark Engineer Squadron to Iraq to help British troops south of Basra repair roads and bridges and to clear land mines, following the success of the US-led military action in removing the regime of Saddam Hussain earlier in the year. Norway had not supported the war, and insisted that its troops were in Iraq as part of a humanitarian 'stabilizing force' mandated by the UN Security Council Resolution 1483, and that they would remain separate from peace-keeping forces dispatched by the USA, the United Kingdom, Denmark and Poland. In December the Storting voted to extend the troops' presence in Iraq by at least six months. Norway withdrew its troops from Iraq in mid-2004. However, a small number of staff officers, who were attached to a Polish brigade, remained until late December 2005.

From 1999 Norway contributed 520 troops to the KFOR peace-keeping mission in Kosovo, consisting of a mechanized infantry battalion and a smaller rapid reaction force that was specially trained in riot control. In 2004 Norway increased its contribution to KFOR, sending four helicopters and support personnel. In November 2006 Norway also had troops in peace-keeping missions in Bosnia and Herzegovina, Lebanon and Sudan. The Norwegian contingent in Lebanon ended its deployment in April 2007.

Government

Norway is a constitutional monarchy. Legislative power is held by the Storting (parliament), with 165 members elected for four years by universal adult suffrage, on the basis of proportional representation. For the consideration of legislative proposals, the Storting divides itself into two chambers by choosing one-quarter of its members to form the Lagting (upper house), the remainder forming the Odelsting (lower house). Executive power is nominally held by the monarch, but is, in effect, exercised by the Statsråd (Council of State), led by the Prime Minister. The Council is appointed by the monarch in accordance with the will of the Storting, to which the Council is responsible. Norway comprises 19 counties (fylker) and 431 municipalities (kommuner).

Defence

Norway is a member of the North Atlantic Treaty Organization (NATO, see p. 340), and became an associate member of Western European Union (WEU, see p. 426) in 1992. Every male is liable for 12 months' national service at the age of 19. Periodical refresher programmes are also compulsory until the age of 44. As assessed at November 2007, the total strength of the armed forces was 15,800 (including 9,100 conscripts): army 6,700 (3,500 conscripts), navy 4,100, and air force 5,000 (3,200 conscripts). There is also a mobilization reserve of about 180,300 (army 83,000, navy 22,000, air force 25,000 and Home Guard 50,300), a coastguard of 270 and a coastal defence force of 160. The Home Guard comprises a land mobilization reserve of 73,000, a naval reserve of 4,900 and an air force reserve of 2,500. The defence budget for 2007 was projected at 31,200m. kroner.

In November 2004 the European Union (EU, see p. 244) ministers responsible for defence agreed to create 13 'battlegroups' (each numbering about 1,500 men), which could be deployed at short notice to crisis areas around the world. The EU battlegroups, two of which were to be ready for deployment at any one time, following a rotational schedule, reached full operational capacity from 1 January 2007. In December 2004 the Storting gave qualified approval for Norway's participation, with Finland and Sweden, in a joint Nordic battlegroup, which was subsequently joined by Estonia and Ireland. Norway was expected to provide an estimated 150 troops of a total of 2,400.

Economic Affairs

In 2006, according to estimates by the World Bank, Norway's gross national income (GNI), measured at average 2004–06 prices, was US $308,948m., equivalent to $66,530 per head (or $43,820 per head on an international purchasing-power parity basis). During 1996–2006, it was estimated, the population increased by an average of 0.6% per year, while gross domestic product (GDP) per head increased, in real terms, by an average of 2.0% per year. Norway's overall GDP increased, in real terms, at an average annual rate of 2.6% in 1996–2006. Real GDP increased by 3.5% in 2007, according to provisional figures.

The contribution of agriculture (including hunting, forestry and fishing) to GDP in 2007 was estimated at 1.4%. In that year the agricultural sector engaged 2.9% of the employed labour force. Around 3.4% of the land surface is cultivated, and the most important branch of the sector is livestock-rearing. Fish-farming has been intensively developed by the Government since the early 1970s. The fishing industry provided an estimated 4.4% of total export revenue in 2007. A temporary emergency ban on cod fishing in parts of the North Sea, agreed between the European Union (EU, see p. 244) and Norway, was announced in January 2001 in an attempt to prevent the collapse of fish stocks through over-fishing. In February 2004 the Government appealed against proposals by the United Kingdom to block salmon imports to the EU from non-EU countries. In 2005 Norway produced some 582,000 metric tons of farmed salmon. Agricultural GDP increased at an average annual rate of 0.7% during 1996–2005. Agricultural GDP increased by 10.8% in 2007.

Industry (including mining, manufacturing, construction, power and public utilities) contributed an estimated 43.5% of GDP in 2007, and engaged 21.0% of the employed labour force in the same year. During 1996–2005 industrial GDP increased, in real terms, at an average annual rate of 1.0%. Industrial GDP increased by 0.4% in 2005.

Mining (including gas and petroleum extraction) provided an estimated 26.1% of GDP in 2007, and engaged 1.5% of the employed labour force in 2004. Extraction of petroleum and natural gas dominates the sector, accounting for 25.9% of GDP in 2007 and 1.4% of employment in the same year. Norway possesses substantial reserves of petroleum and natural gas (exports of petroleum and petroleum products accounted for 43.6% of total export earnings in 2007). Most of the reserves are located off shore. During 1995–2005 the production of crude petroleum from fields on the Norwegian continental shelf decreased at an average annual rate of 0.6%, while output of natural gas grew at an average rate of 11.8% per year, according to the Norwegian Petroleum Directorate. Norway's other mineral reserves include iron ore, iron pyrites, copper, lead and zinc. Substantial deposits of platinum were discovered in the northern county of Finnmark in November 2001—the area was also believed to contain deposits of gold and diamonds. In October 2003 Norway signed a deal to export natural gas from the Ormen Lange gas field to the United Kingdom; it was envisaged that 20,000m. cu m of natural gas per year would be exported from the field. A large terminal to pump gas via a 1,200-km pipeline to the United Kingdom was completed in Aukra, on the island of Gossa, in 2007. In December 2003 the Government announced that it was to open the hitherto unexplored Barents Sea for petroleum and gas extraction; three exploratory wells were drilled in 2004–05. In March 2006 the Government announced that it was to allow further prospecting in the Barents Sea, but that drilling was to be prohibited until 2010 in a 50-km coastal zone (including the Lofoten Islands) in order to protect the environment and fish stocks.

Manufacturing contributed an estimated 9.9% of GDP in 2007, and employed 11.5% of the working population in the same year. In 2006 the most important branches of manufacturing were food products, transport equipment (including ships and oil platforms), metals and metal products, electrical and optical equipment, chemicals and chemical products and pulp and paper products. During 1996–2003 manufacturing GDP increased, in real terms, by an average of 0.7% per year. Manufacturing GDP increased by 3.0% in 2003.

In 2005, according to provisional figures, some 98.9% of Norway's installed capacity of electric energy was produced by hydroelectric power schemes; domestic energy demands are easily supplied, and Norway has exported hydroelectricity since 1993. Norway's extensive reserves of petroleum and natural gas are mainly exploited for sale to foreign markets, since the domestic market is limited.

The services sector contributed an estimated 55.1% of GDP in 2007, and engaged 76.1% of the employed labour force in the same year. The GDP of the services sector increased, in real terms, by an average of 3.6% per year during 1996–2005; it grew by 3.4% in 2005.

Although shipbuilding has declined since the early 1970s, Norway remains a leading shipping nation. The establishment of the Norwegian International Ship Register in 1987 allowed an expansion of the merchant fleet by more than 300%, in terms of gross tonnage. At 31 December 2006 the combined displacement of the merchant fleet totalled 18.2m. grt, of which the Norwegian International Ship Register accounted for 14.8m. grt.

In 2006, according to IMF figures, Norway recorded a visible trade surplus of US $59,721m., and there was a surplus of $55,213m. on the current account of the balance of payments. In 2007 the EU provided 68.7% of imports and took 81.1% of exports; fellow members of the European Free Trade Association (EFTA, see p. 412) accounted for 1.3% of Norway's imports and 0.9% of exports in the same year. The principal source of imports in 2007 was Sweden (providing 14.6% of the total), followed by Germany (13.6%), the United Kingdom (6.8%) and Denmark (6.4%); the principal market for exports was the United Kingdom (taking 26.0%), followed by Germany (12.7%), the Netherlands (10.2%) and France (8.5%). In 2007 the principal exports were petroleum and petroleum products (accounting for 43.6% of total exports), natural gas (21.0%), basic manufactures (12.0%, notably aluminium), and machinery and transport equipment (9.1%); the principal imports were machinery and transport equipment (39.8%), basic manufactures (17.0%), miscellaneous manufactured articles (14.3%), and chemicals and related products (8.8%).

In 2007 Norway recorded an overall surplus of 396,045m. kroner in the general budget (equivalent to some 17.3% of GDP in purchasers' values). At the end of 2007 Norway's gross external debt was estimated at 2,918,000m. kroner. General government debt was equivalent to 43.8% of GDP in 2005. During 1996–2006 the average annual rate of inflation was 2.1%; consumer prices increased by 0.8% in 2007. The average rate of unemployment was 2.1% in December 2007, according to official sources.

In addition to its membership of EFTA, Norway is a member of the European Economic Area (EEA), the Nordic Council (see p. 424) and the Nordic Council of Ministers (see p. 424). Although Norway is not a member of the EU, it joined the EU's Schengen Agreement (see p. 277) on the abolition of border controls in May 1999 (Denmark, Finland and Sweden—all EU members—had already joined in 1996) by virtue of its membership in the Nordic passport union.

The Norwegian economy, which is highly dependent on its hydrocarbons sector (Norway is the world's second largest petroleum exporter), experienced a sustained expansion during the 1990s, leading to virtually full employment, as well as rises in real incomes. Norway maintained a stable exchange rate during this period and a prudent fiscal position, and reinvested a substantial proportion of petroleum revenues abroad through the State Petroleum Fund, partly in preparation for future increased demands on pensions and also to offer limited protection to the economy against fluctuations in the petroleum sector. In the first years of the 21st century a strong policy framework underpinned enviable prosperity and a high degree of social equity in Norway. Norway's traditionally high social cohesiveness and solidarity ensured that the use of the petroleum wealth benefited people at all levels of society, and would continue to benefit future generations well after the petroleum itself was depleted. After a period of weak growth in 2001–03, reflecting economic weakness in Norway's trading partners, Norway's economy recovered in 2004–07, driven by increased investment within the petroleum industry. Moreover, low interest rates and high real income growth stimulated domestic demand, and growth in private consumption and housing investment was strong. This upturn was broadly based, with exports and business investment increasing. Norway has benefited from the globalization of the economy, exporting petroleum at high prices and importing inexpensive consumer goods from low-cost countries. Continued productivity growth and significant levels of inward migration, notably from Poland and the Baltic states, contributed to low inflation, although rapid employment growth, leading to an increasingly tight labour market, resulted in higher wage growth in 2007. The rate of economic growth was expected to remain high in 2008 but to slow in comparison with the 3.5% real GDP growth achieved in 2007.

Education

Compulsory education begins at six years of age and lasts for 10 years. Elementary education is divided into a four-year lower stage (barnetrinnet), for children aged six to 10 years, a three-year intermediate stage (mellomtrinnet), for children aged 10 to 13 years, and a three-year upper stage (ungdomstrinnet), from the age of 13. A pupil may then transfer to an upper-secondary school for a course lasting three years. Primary enrolment in 2006 included 98% of children (males 98%; females 98%) in the relevant age-group, while the comparable ratio for secondary enrolment was 97% (males 96%; females 97%). From the second half of 2002 adults who had not completed compulsory education, or who wished to refresh their competence, were given a statutory right to lower-secondary education. This also applied to special education. With effect from the 2000/01 academic year, everyone had the right to upper-secondary education. Upon completion of a three-year course in general and technical areas of study at an upper-secondary school, a pupil may seek admission to one of Norway's four universities or other colleges. From 2000 persons from the age of 25 had the right to be assessed for admittance to higher education based on non-formal learning. A broader system of higher professional education has been organized on a regional basis, including colleges of education and technology. At 1 October 2003 130,148 students were enrolled at colleges of higher education, with a further 79,611 enrolled at universities and their equivalent. Expenditure on education by all levels of government in 2006 was 113,546m. kroner (equivalent to 13.8% of total government expenditure).

Public Holidays

2008: 1 January (New Year's Day), 20 March (Maundy Thursday), 21 March (Good Friday), 24 March (Easter Monday), 1 May (Labour Day and Ascension Day), 12 May (Whit Monday), 17 May (Constitution Day), 24 December (Christmas Eve)*, 25–26 December (Christmas), 31 December (New Year's Eve)*.

2009: 1 January (New Year's Day), 9 April (Maundy Thursday), 10 April (Good Friday), 13 April (Easter Monday), 1 May (Labour Day), 17 May (Constitution Day), 21 May (Ascension Day), 1 June (Whit Monday), 24 December (Christmas Eve)*, 25–26 December (Christmas), 31 December (New Year's Eve)*.

* Half day from 12 noon.

Weights and Measures

The metric system is in force.

NORWAY

Statistical Survey

Sources (unless otherwise stated): Statistics Norway, Kongensgt. 6, Oslo; tel. 21-09-00-00; fax 21-09-49-73; e-mail biblioteket@ssb.no; internet www.ssb.no; Nordic Statistical Secretariat (Copenhagen), *Yearbook of Nordic Statistics*.

Area and Population

AREA, POPULATION AND DENSITY

Area (sq km)	
Land	304,280
Inland water	19,522
Total	323,802*
Population (census results)	
3 November 1990	4,247,546
3 November 2001	
Males	2,240,281
Females	2,280,666
Total	4,520,947
Population (official estimates at 1 January)	
2006	4,640,219
2007	4,681,134
2008	4,737,171
Density (per sq km) at 1 January 2008†	15.6

* 125,020 sq miles.
† Excluding inland water.

COUNTIES
(1 January 2008)

	Land area (sq km)*	Population†	Density (per sq km)
Østfold	3,887	265,458	68.3
Akershus	4,579	518,567	113.2
Oslo	426	560,484	1,315.7
Hedmark	26,082	189,289	7.3
Oppland	23,787	183,637	7.7
Buskerud	13,797	251,220	18.2
Vestfold	2,147	226,433	105.5
Telemark	13,854	166,731	12.0
Aust-Agder	8,312	106,130	12.8
Vest-Agder	6,677	165,944	24.9
Rogaland	8,590	412,687	48.0
Hordaland	14,551	462,674	31.8
Sogn og Fjordane	17,680	106,259	6.0
Møre og Romsdal‡	14,590	245,385	16.8
Sør-Trøndelag	17,830	282,993	15.9
Nord-Trøndelag	20,777	129,856	6.2
Nordland	36,074	234,996	6.5
Troms	24,884	154,642	6.2
Finnmark	45,757	72,399	1.6
Total	304,280	4,737,171	15.6

* Excluding inland waters, totalling 19,522 sq km.
† Estimates.
‡ 2007 figures; as a result the total is not equal to the sum of the components.

PRINCIPAL TOWNS
(estimated population of urban settlements at 1 January 2008)

Oslo (capital)	560,484	Bodø	46,049
Bergen	247,746	Sandefjord	42,333
Stavanger/Sandnes*	181,623	Ålesund	41,833
Trondheim	165,191	Larvik	41,723
Fredrikstad/ Sarpsborg*	123,029	Arendal	40,701
Porsgrunn/Skien*	85,050	Tønsberg	38,393
Kristiansand	78,919	Haugesund	32,956
Tromsø	65,286	Moss	29,073
Drammen	60,145	Hamar	27,976

* From 1 January 1999 continuous urban settlements are merged to one settlement.

BIRTHS, MARRIAGES AND DEATHS

	Registered live births		Registered marriages*		Registered deaths†	
	Number	Rate (per 1,000)	Number	Rate (per 1,000)	Number	Rate (per 1,000)
2000	59,234	13.2	25,356	5.6	44,002	9.8
2001	56,696	12.6	22,967	5.1	43,981	9.7
2002	55,434	12.3	24,069	5.3	44,465	9.8
2003	56,458	12.4	22,361	4.9	42,478	9.3
2004	56,951	12.4	22,354	4.9	41,200	9.0
2005	56,756	12.3	22,392	4.9	41,232	8.9
2006	58,545	12.6	21,721	4.7	41,253	8.9
2007	58,459	12.5	23,471	5.0	41,954	9.0

* Where bridegroom is resident in Norway.
† Including deaths of residents temporarily abroad.

Expectation of life (years at birth, WHO estimates): 80.0 (males 77.5; females 82.4) in 2005 (Source: WHO, *World Health Statistics*).

IMMIGRATION AND EMIGRATION

	2005	2006	2007
Immigrants	40,148	45,776	61,774
Emigrants	21,709	22,053	22,122

ECONOMICALLY ACTIVE POPULATION
('000 persons aged 16 to 74 years)*

	2005	2006	2007
Agriculture, fishing and forestry	75	75	70
Oil and gas extraction, etc.	32	31	35
Manufacturing and other mining	268	273	282
Electricity, gas and water	16	16	17
Construction	159	167	180
Trade, restaurants and hotels	421	419	425
Transport and communications	152	156	158
Financing, insurance, real estate and business services	282	311	324
Public administration and defence	138	142	154
Education	190	193	215
Health and social work	458	469	476
Other services	97	100	108
Total employed	2,289	2,354	2,443
Unemployed	111	85	63
Total labour force	2,400	2,439	2,506
Males	1,272	1,292	1,323
Females	1,127	1,147	1,183

* Figures are annual averages, based on quarterly sample surveys.

Health and Welfare

KEY INDICATORS

Total fertility rate (children per woman, 2005)	1.8
Under-5 mortality rate (per 1,000 live births, 2005)	4
HIV/AIDS (% of persons aged 15–49, 2005)	0.1
Physicians (per 1,000 head, 2004)	3.13
Hospital beds (per 1,000 head, 2005)	4.2
Health expenditure (2004): US $ per head (PPP)	4,079.9
Health expenditure (2004): % of GDP	9.7
Health expenditure (2004): public (% of total)	83.5
Human Development Index (2005): ranking	2
Human Development Index (2005): value	0.968

For sources and definitions, see explanatory note on p. vi.

NORWAY

Statistical Survey

Agriculture

PRINCIPAL CROPS
('000 metric tons)*

	2004	2005	2006
Wheat	406.8	395.4	389.7
Barley	630.5	589.3	552.4
Rye	40.6	34.8	28.4
Oats	366.7	279.0	258.4
Potatoes	396.4	316.6	376.0
Rapeseed	12.3	11.2	10.7
Cabbages	33.1	33.5	31.9
Tomatoes	11.8	13.3	11.7
Cucumbers and gherkins	14.3	13.3	13.7
Green onions and shallots	21.1	19.1	19.1
Carrots	40.4	44.7	40.9
Apples	16.1	10.9	15.0

* Figures refer to holdings with at least 0.5 ha of agricultural area in use.

Aggregate production ('000 metric tons, may include official, semi-official or estimated data): Total cereals 1,445 in 2004, 1,298 in 2005, 1,229 in 2006; Total roots and tubers 396 in 2004, 317 in 2005, 376 in 2006; Total vegetables (incl. melons) 177 in 2004, 184 in 2005, 167 in 2006; Total fruits (excl. melons) 34 in 2004, 26 in 2005, 33 in 2006.

Source: FAO.

LIVESTOCK
('000 head)*

	2004	2005	2006
Horses	29.0	30.0	31.0
Cattle	943.2	933.7	920.4
Sheep	2,467.0	2,423.0	2,356.2
Goats	71.8	73.1	72.5
Pigs	825.5	824.2	827.5
Chickens	3,529	3,415	3,316

* Figures refer to holdings with at least 0.5 ha of agricultural area in use.

Source: FAO.

LIVESTOCK PRODUCTS
('000 metric tons)

	2004	2005	2006
Cattle meat	86.6	87.4	87.6
Sheep meat	26.1	26.0	25.2
Pig meat	113.5	112.8	116.3
Chicken meat	47.3	49.9	55.3
Cows' milk	1,574.0	1,565.7	1,553.5
Goats' milk	21.7	22.5	21.2
Hen eggs	52.4	50.7	50.5
Honey	1.3	1.5	1.3
Wool: greasy	5.2	5.1	4.9

Source: FAO.

Forestry

ROUNDWOOD REMOVALS
('000 cubic metres, excl. bark)

	2004	2005	2006
Sawlogs, veneer logs and logs for sleepers	4,057	4,850	4,005
Pulpwood	3,266	3,615	3,386
Other industrial wood	30	25	25
Fuel wood	1,429	1,177	1,177
Total	8,782	9,667	8,593

Source: FAO.

SAWNWOOD PRODUCTION
('000 cubic metres, incl. railway sleepers)

	2004	2005	2006
Coniferous (softwood)	2,203	2,300	2,361
Broadleaved (hardwood)	27	26	28
Total	2,230	2,326	2,389

Source: FAO.

Fishing

('000 metric tons, live weight)

	2003	2004	2005
Capture	2,548.8*	2,524.5	2,392.9
Atlantic cod	217.5	230.7	226.0
Saithe (Pollock)	212.2	211.3	230.7
Blue whiting (Poutassou)	851.4	958.8	738.6
Sandeels (Sandlances)	29.6	48.7	17.3
Capelin	249.5	49.1	67.3
Atlantic herring	563.1	616.2	748.1
Atlantic mackerel	163.5	157.4	119.7
Aquaculture	584.4	636.8	656.6
Atlantic salmon	509.5	563.8	582.0
Total catch	3,133.2*	3,161.3	3,049.6

* FAO estimate.

Note: Figures exclude aquatic plants ('000 metric tons, wet weight, capture): 153.2 in 2003; 148.3 in 2004; 153.9 in 2005. Also excluded are aquatic mammals, recorded by number rather than by weight. The number of minke whales caught was: 647 in 2003; 544 in 2004; 639 in 2005. The number of harp seals caught was: 7,575 in 2003; 9,895 in 2004; 17,771 in 2005. The number of hooded seals caught was: 5,295 in 2003; 4,851 in 2004; 3,826 in 2005.

Source: FAO.

Mining

('000 metric tons, unless otherwise indicated, estimates)

	2003	2004	2005
Coal (all grades)	300	300	300
Crude petroleum (million barrels)	1,041	1,024	964
Iron ore*	340	408	420†
Natural gas (million cu m)‡	73,124	78,465	84,964

* Metal content of ore.
† Estimate.
‡ Marketed natural gas reported as total methane sales.

Source: US Geological Survey.

Industry

SELECTED PRODUCTS
('000 metric tons, unless otherwise indicated)

	2003	2004	2005
Mechanical wood pulp (dry weight)*	1,666	1,783	1,684
Chemical wood pulp (dry weight)*	548	563	597
Particle board ('000 cu m)*	358	383	366
Paper and paperboard*	2,186	2,294	2,223
Kerosene ('000 barrels)	9,000	4,774	5,771
Naphthas ('000 barrels)	2,700	8,741	10,017
Gas-diesel (distillate fuel) oil ('000 barrels)	47,000	45,765	50,121
Residual fuel oil ('000 barrels)	12,000	13,823	11,806
Cement	1,860	1,870	1,900
Ferro-silicon (75% basis)	350	300	270
Other ferro-alloys	15	15	15
Crude steel	698	695	690†
Nickel (refined): primary	77.2	71.4	84.9
Copper (refined): primary and secondary	36	36	39
Aluminium (refined): primary	1,192.4	1,321.7	1,376.5
Aluminium (refined): secondary	256.8	348.7	362.4
Zinc (refined): primary	143.5	140.9	133.3

*Source: FAO.
†Estimated or unofficial figure.

Margarine: ('000 metric tons) 50,000 in 2002.

Woven woollen fabrics: ('000 metric tons) 649,000 in 2001.

Electric energy (million kWh): 128,646 in 2001.

Source (unless otherwise indicated): US Geological Survey.

Finance

CURRENCY AND EXCHANGE RATES

Monetary Units
100 øre = 1 Norwegian krone (plural: kroner).

Sterling, Dollar and Euro Equivalents (31 December 2007)
£1 sterling = 10.840 kroner;
US $1 = 5.4110 kroner;
€1 = 7.9655 kroner;
100 Norwegian kroner = £9.22 = $18.48 = €12.55.

Average Exchange Rate (kroner per US $)
2005 6.4425
2006 6.4133
2007 5.8614

GENERAL BUDGET
(million kroner)

Revenue	2005	2006	2007
Taxation*	845,680	948,622	982,570
Taxes on income, profits and wealth*	433,589	493,950	492,636
Social security contributions	173,846	189,223	206,032
Value-added tax and investment levy	153,138	172,066	187,203
Property income	204,650	261,453	271,835
Interest	61,296	80,185	95,564
Other current transfers	8,315	8,553	9,644
Other transfers	6,904	6,866	7,821
Operating surplus	1,068	696	892
Capital transfers*	1,768	2,063	2,576
Total	1,061,482	1,221,386	1,267,516

Expenditure†	2005	2006	2007
General public services	77,903	90,805	93,116
Defence	28,720	32,665	34,940
Public order and safety	15,069	16,165	17,203
Economic affairs	68,044	70,455	73,935
Environmental protection	3,610	3,956	4,149
Housing and community amenities	3,887	4,646	4,983
Health	132,897	140,618	151,904
Recreation, culture and religion	19,076	20,195	22,626
Education	107,306	113,546	120,180
Social protection	311,426	329,425	348,435
Total	767,938	822,476	871,471
Current	748,302	798,029	843,376
Capital	19,636	24,448	28,095

* Inheritance and gift taxes are excluded from tax revenue and are treated as capital transfers.
† Excluding lending minus repayments.

INTERNATIONAL RESERVES
(excluding gold, US $ million at 31 December)

	2004	2005	2006
IMF special drawing rights	360.8	307.1	453.2
Reserve position in IMF	868.5	301.5	207.0
Foreign exchange	43,078.2	46,377.4	56,181.4
Total	44,307.5	46,986.0	56,841.6

Source: IMF, *International Financial Statistics*.

MONEY SUPPLY
(million kroner at 31 December)

	2001	2002	2003
Currency outside banks	42,100	40,410	41,687
Demand deposits at commercial and savings banks	616,023	671,850	706,246
Total money (incl. others)	658,123	712,260	747,933

Demand deposits at commercial and savings banks (million kroner at 31 December): 700,074 in 2004; 791,120 in 2005; 923,210 in 2006.

Source: IMF, *International Financial Statistics*.

COST OF LIVING
(Consumer Price Index; base: 1998 = 100)

	2004	2005	2006
Food	106.4	108.0	109.6
Alcoholic beverages and tobacco	123.6	126.7	129.1
Housing, fuel and power	130.0	132.2	140.2
Clothing and footwear	74.1	70.7	68.2
Furnishings and household equipment	100.4	100.0	98.5
Health	126.3	129.8	134.4
Transport	115.8	120.8	124.8
Communications	82.8	82.2	83.3
Recreation and culture	105.7	106.5	107.0
Education	141.5	143.4	146.6
Restaurants and hotels	122.3	124.3	128.3
Other goods and services	119.9	122.1	120.9
All items (incl. others)	113.3	115.1	117.7

2007: All items 118.6.

NORWAY

Statistical Survey

NATIONAL ACCOUNTS
(million kroner at current prices)

National Income and Product

	2005	2006*	2007*
Compensation of employees	810,715	882,807	972,634
Operating surplus	705,199	803,718	800,702
Domestic factor incomes	1,515,914	1,686,525	1,773,336
Consumption of fixed capital	247,889	269,502	293,045
Gross domestic product (GDP) at factor cost	1,763,803	1,956,027	2,066,381
Indirect taxes	213,768	238,196	254,167
Less Subsidies	31,855	32,494	31,855
GDP in purchasers' values	1,945,716	2,161,729	2,288,693
Net factor income from abroad	13,450	−5,447	9,851
Gross national product (GNP)	1,959,166	2,156,282	2,298,544
Less Consumption of fixed capital	247,889	269,502	293,045
National income in market prices	1,711,277	1,886,780	2,005,499
Other current transfers abroad (net)	−17,157	−14,541	−14,948
National disposable income	1,694,121	1,872,239	1,990,551

*Provisional.

Expenditure on the Gross Domestic Product

	2005	2006*	2007*
Government final consumption expenditure	387,186	415,377	447,067
Private final consumption expenditure	826,215	883,221	946,374
Increase in stocks	46,461	60,650	43,727
Gross fixed capital formation	365,564	409,130	474,289
Total domestic expenditure	1,625,426	1,768,378	1,911,457
Exports of goods and services	868,352	1,005,483	1,062,715
Less Imports of goods and services	548,062	612,133	685,479
GDP in purchasers' values	1,945,716	2,161,728	2,288,693
GDP at constant 2005 prices	1,945,716	1,994,924	2,065,062

*Provisional.

Gross Domestic Product by Economic Activity

	2005	2006*	2007*
Agriculture, hunting and forestry	13,961	13,518	15,332
Fishing and fish farming	12,593	15,053	13,265
Petroleum and gas extraction	447,660	537,050	527,109
Other mining and quarrying	3,720	3,850	4,752
Manufacturing	169,563	186,009	200,942
Electricity, gas and water	44,685	52,972	48,631
Construction	76,802	87,767	104,020
Wholesale and retail trade; repair of motor vehicles	140,952	148,673	163,901
Hotels and restaurants	22,262	24,108	27,871
Transport, storage and communications†	133,524	139,017	146,690
Financing, insurance, real estate and business services	235,861	259,923	294,793
Private services in households	74,284	76,781	75,409
Public administration and defence	76,051	82,346	89,502
Education	76,456	80,183	84,996
Health and social work	149,122	159,994	176,099
Other social and personal services	54,452	58,970	63,241
Sub-total	1,731,948	1,926,212	2,036,555
Value-added tax and investment levy	153,138	172,065	187,203
Other taxes on products (net)	60,630	66,131	66,964
Statistical discrepancy	—	−2,681	−2,029
GDP in purchasers' values	1,945,716	2,161,728	2,288,693

*Figures are provisional.
†Including transportation of petroleum and gas by pipeline.

BALANCE OF PAYMENTS
(US $ million)

	2004	2005	2006
Exports of goods f.o.b.	83,164	104,179	122,709
Imports of goods f.o.b.	−49,035	−54,490	−62,988
Trade balance	34,129	49,689	59,721
Exports of services	25,263	29,305	32,944
Imports of services	−24,304	−29,548	−31,506
Balance on goods and services	35,088	49,446	61,159
Other income received	17,117	18,764	26,985
Other income paid	−16,570	−18,819	−29,559
Balance on goods, services and income	35,635	49,391	58,585
Current transfers received	2,553	2,983	2,967
Current transfers paid	−5,188	−5,814	−6,339
Current balance	33,000	46,560	55,213
Capital account (net)	−154	−290	−146
Direct investment abroad	−5,250	−20,421	−12,218
Direct investment from abroad	2,544	8,621	1,799
Portfolio investment assets	−38,031	−39,535	−115,364
Portfolio investment liabilities	9,353	32,432	38,287
Financial derivatives assets	−636	—	n.a.
Financial derivatives liabilities	780	—	n.a.
Other investment assets	−16,517	−37,756	−31,040
Other investment liabilities	25,458	21,206	79,782
Net errors and omissions	−5,319	−6,306	−10,838
Overall balance	5,227	4,511	5,475

Source: IMF, *International Financial Statistics*.

OFFICIAL ASSISTANCE TO DEVELOPING COUNTRIES
(million kroner)

	2001	2002	2003
Bilateral assistance	7,901	8,493	9,646
Technical assistance	1,140	1,551	1,878
Investments	532	412	378
Sector-related project and programme aid	3,510	3,496	3,310
Non-sector related project and programme aid	2,357	3,132	3,983
Associated financing	9	69	—
Loan assistance	—	—	—
Norfund	61	57	96
Multilateral assistance	3,374	4,400	4,107
Contributions to multilateral organizations	273	—	—
Humanitarian relief work	273	—	—
Administration	595	652	704
Total official development assistance	11,870	13,545	14,457

2004 (million kroner): Bilateral assistance 6,939; Multilateral-bilateral assistance 2,622; Multilateral assistance 4,463; Administration 793; Total official development assistance 14,817.

NORWAY

Statistical Survey

External Trade

(Note: Figures include all ships bought and sold but exclude trade in military supplies under defence agreements.)

PRINCIPAL COMMODITIES
(distribution by SITC, million kroner)

Imports c.i.f.*	2005	2006	2007
Food and live animals	18,292	20,811	24,280
Crude materials (inedible) except fuels	27,178	31,208	42,582
Metalliferous ores and metal scrap	17,544	21,952	31,837
Mineral fuels, lubricants, etc. (incl. electric current)	15,441	19,203	20,301
Petroleum, petroleum products, etc.	12,960	14,110	17,061
Chemicals and related products	34,497	38,466	41,463
Basic manufactures	61,372	70,084	79,728
Metal manufactures	13,741	17,562	20,195
Machinery and transport equipment	141,206	165,130	186,650
Machinery specialized for particular industries	13,814	18,203	19,762
General industrial machinery, equipment and parts	20,762	21,372	24,890
Office machines and automatic data-processing equipment	15,926	16,734	16,420
Telecommunications and sound equipment	14,119	16,771	18,956
Other electrical machinery, apparatus, etc.	17,548	20,897	24,226
Road vehicles and parts†	37,061	41,845	47,998
Other transport equipment†	13,877	18,564	22,583
Miscellaneous manufactured articles	54,355	61,035	67,120
Clothing and accessories (excl. footwear)	11,900	12,662	13,358
Total (incl. others)	357,656	411,684	468,633

* Equipment imported directly to the Norwegian sector of the continental shelf is excluded.
† Excluding tyres, engines and electrical parts.

Exports f.o.b.	2005	2006	2007
Food and live animals	33,903	37,470	38,697
Fish and fish preparations*	31,257	34,667	35,919
Mineral fuels, lubricants, etc. (incl. electric current)	453,643	531,930	531,237
Petroleum, petroleum products, etc.	331,950	362,976	355,131
Gas (natural and manufactured)	117,117	164,401	171,182
Chemicals and related products	31,747	35,282	39,925
Basic manufactures	68,271	83,365	97,963
Non-ferrous metals	36,876	51,949	61,858
Machinery and transport equipment	55,571	66,291	74,028
Miscellaneous manufactured articles	15,369	17,230	19,611
Total (incl. others)	668,760	782,950	813,600

* Including crustaceans and molluscs.

PRINCIPAL TRADING PARTNERS
(million kroner)

Imports c.i.f.	2005	2006	2007
Belgium	9,155.6	9,523.6	9,670.0
Canada	9,088.1	11,074.7	20,433.5
China, People's Repub.	20,040.1	23,467.2	28,313.2
Denmark	26,166.7	28,378.9	30,020.5
Finland	11,254.1	13,171.6	17,203.5
France	14,192.6	16,202.3	17,007.7
Germany	48,040.3	55,368.2	63,571.2
Ireland	5,721.1	5,740.1	5,559.5
Italy	11,743.8	13,981.9	15,424.7
Japan	11,325.4	11,076.5	10,342.3
Korea, Republic	3,670.7	6,045.1	4,334.6
Netherlands	14,124.6	16,788.4	17,409.5
Poland	6,175.1	8,134.1	9,751.9
Russia	8,298.9	9,992.2	11,459.5
Spain	8,120.1	9,282.6	10,121.3
Sweden	51,546.8	61,707.0	68,572.2
Switzerland	3,676.9	4,486.8	4,963.9
Taiwan	3,390.8	3,806.8	4,242.8
United Kingdom	25,991.8	26,357.3	32,075.9
USA	17,983.2	21,878.1	22,374.2
Total (incl. others)	357,656.5	411,683.6	468,663.4

Exports f.o.b.	2005	2006	2007
Belgium	16,465.2	19,639.3	20,328.7
Canada	25,256.9	24,256.2	23,279.6
China, People's Repub.	5,854.2	10,948.9	9,492.6
Denmark	23,715.2	27,481.4	25,578.0
Finland	8,470.3	12,182.2	9,948.4
France	62,091.3	64,609.1	69,248.0
Germany	84,301.6	96,385.4	103,401.4
Ireland	11,938.2	13,830.0	12,835.3
Italy	19,086.8	24,682.2	23,796.0
Japan	6,555.7	7,650.3	7,703.2
Korea, Republic	5,084.9	4,740.8	7,132.6
Netherlands	66,446.1	80,383.9	83,052.4
Spain	16,152.1	16,941.2	18,607.1
Sweden	43,575.4	50,292.6	51,954.1
United Kingdom	167,490.7	209,483.1	211,504.4
USA	43,806.7	44,750.3	49,686.5
Total (incl. others)	668,759.5	782,949.9	813,600.1

Transport

STATE RAILWAYS
(traffic)

	1999	2000	2001
Passengers carried ('000)	50,019	50,773	49,396
Goods carried ('000 metric tons)	8,229	7,959	8,190
Passenger-kilometres (million)	2,668	2,635	2,536
Freight ton-kilometres (million)	2,456	2,399	2,451

2002: Passenger-kilometres (million) 2,543; Net ton-kilometres (million) 3,019 (Source: UN, *Statistical Yearbook*).

2003: Passenger-kilometres (million) 2,474; Net ton-kilometres (million) 2,627 (Source: UN, *Statistical Yearbook*).

2004: Passenger-kilometres (million) 2,657; Net ton-kilometres (million) 2,804 (Source: UN, *Statistical Yearbook*).

NORWAY

ROAD TRAFFIC
(motor vehicles registered at 31 December)

	2004	2005	2006
Passenger cars (incl. station wagons and ambulances)	1,977,922	2,028,909	2,084,193
Buses	30,592	28,783	26,954
Vans	284,029	302,956	331,052
Combined vehicles	85,149	79,705	73,904
Goods vehicles, etc.	80,623	82,778	83,609
Tractors	229,265	231,630	234,243
Special purpose vehicles	8,547	8,361	8,255
Motorcycles	103,716	109,338	116,875
Snow scooters	54,362	55,776	58,327
Mopeds	144,855	148,161	151,670

SHIPPING

Merchant Fleet
(registered at 31 December)

	2004	2005	2006
Number of vessels	2,173	2,068	2,078
Total displacement ('000 grt)	18,936.2	17,531.9	18,222.3

Note: Figures include vessels on the Norwegian International Ship Register.
Source: Lloyd's Register-Fairplay, *World Fleet Statistics*.

International Sea-borne Freight Traffic*
('000 metric tons)

	1998	1999	2000
Goods loaded	154,116	151,116	160,080
Goods unloaded	27,264	25,788	23,400

* Figures exclude transit traffic (other than Swedish iron ore), packing and re-export.

Source: UN, *Monthly Bulletin of Statistics*.

CIVIL AVIATION
(traffic on scheduled services)*

	2001	2002	2003
Kilometres flown (million)	149	129	127
Passengers carried ('000)	14,556	13,699	12,806
Passenger-kilometres (million)	10,461	10,546	10,506
Total ton-kilometres (million)	1,224	1,231	1,211

* Including an apportionment (2/7) of the international services of Scandinavian Airlines System (SAS), operated jointly with Denmark and Sweden.

Source: UN, *Statistical Yearbook*.

Tourism

VISITOR ARRIVALS BY COUNTRY OF ORIGIN*

	2003	2004	2005
Denmark	617,141	640,198	619,111
Finland	60,315	60,602	62,168
France	220,013	216,437	210,224
Germany	773,724	738,372	810,092
Italy	142,275	146,398	141,938
Japan	112,559	123,364	124,710
Netherlands	283,355	291,182	296,252
Spain	180,476	177,292	197,514
Sweden	475,234	503,087	531,157
United Kingdom	516,355	577,751	602,449
USA	298,081	320,953	316,340
Total (incl. others)	4,374,657	4,596,218	4,761,074

* Non-resident staying in all types of accommodation establishments.

Tourism receipts (US $ million, incl. passenger transport): 2,989 in 2003; 3,455 in 2004; 3,884 in 2005.

Source: World Tourism Organization.

Communications Media

	2004	2005	2006
Telephones ('000 main lines in use)	2,151	2,129	2,055
Mobile cellular telephones ('000 subscribers)	4,716.1	4,754.5	5,040.6
Personal computers ('000 in use)	2,630	2,630	n.a.
Internet users ('000)	1,792	2,702	4,074
Broadband subscribers ('000)	671.7	991.3	1,278.3

Source: International Telecommunication Union.

Television receivers (2000): 3,000,000 in use.

Radio receivers (1997): 4,030,000 in use*.

Books published (1999): 4,985 titles†.

Daily newspapers (2002): 61; net circulation ('000 copies) 2,201‡.

* Source: UNESCO, *Statistical Yearbook*.
† Source: UN, *Statistical Yearbook*.
‡ Issued at least six times a week.

Education

(incl. Svalbard, 1 October 2003)

	Institutions	Teachers*	Students
Pre-primary	5,924	58,422†	205,172
Primary and lower secondary	3,209	65,376	617,577
Upper secondary	462	26,618	218,089
Colleges of higher education	59	6,313	130,148
Universities and their equivalent	11	9,553	79,611

* Full-time.
† Of the total, 19,422 were trained as pre-school teachers.

Directory

The Constitution

The Constitution was promulgated on 17 May 1814.

According to the Constitution, Norway is a 'free, independent, indivisible, inalienable Realm'; its form of government a 'limited and hereditary monarchy'. (In May 1990 the law of succession, which stipulated that a male heir should have precedence in succeeding to the throne, was amended to permit men and women an equal right to the throne. The previous law would still apply to those born before 1990.) The Evangelical Lutheran Church is the established religion of the State.

Executive power is vested in the monarch, legislative power in the Storting (parliament), and judicial power in the Judicature.

EXECUTIVE POWER

The monarch exercises power through the Statsråd (Council of State). The Statsråd is composed of a Prime Minister and not fewer than seven other Councillors of State, more than one-half of whom must profess the established religion. The business to be dealt with in the Statsråd is prepared by the various executive Ministries, each with a Councillor of State at its head. These executive departments conduct the administrative work of the country.

The Government submits the budget estimates and introduces bills in the Storting.

Formally, the monarch appoints the Government, but since the introduction of the parliamentary system in 1884 it is the practice for the monarch to act in accordance with the will of the Storting.

LEGISLATIVE POWER

The Storting is elected quadrennially by universal suffrage. All Norwegian citizens aged 18 years and over are eligible to vote and every qualified voter who has resided in Norway for at least 10 years is eligible to stand for election. In 2005 the Storting was expanded from 165 seats to 169, 150 of which are elected directly, with the remaining 19 (one for each constituency) being allocated by proportional representation among parties receiving a minimum of 4% of the votes cast. The members of the Storting elect one-quarter of their own body to constitute the Lagting (upper house); the other three-quarters compose the Odelsting (lower house). All bills must first be introduced in the Odelsting, either by the Government through a Councillor of State or by a member of the Odelsting. Should the bill be approved by the Odelsting, it is sent to the Lagting, which may adopt it or return it with amendments. If a bill is approved twice by the Odelsting and rejected on both occasions by the Lagting, it is submitted to the entire Storting and decided by a two-thirds' majority. When a bill has thus been approved, it must receive royal assent in the Statsråd.

Bills for the revision of the Constitution must be introduced in the first, second or third session after a new election. However, only the Storting, after the next election, has the power to decide whether the proposed alteration should be adopted. Bills relating to the Constitution are dealt with only by the united Storting. For the adoption of a bill of this nature, a two-thirds' majority is required, and the measure becomes law without royal assent.

The Storting votes all state expenditure and determines state revenue, taxes, customs tariffs and other duties; the Odelsting exercises control over government administration, government appointments and so forth.

The Storting prepares its business through its committees and settles such business, with the exception of bills, in plenum. The Councillors of State may attend the Storting, having the right of speech, but not of voting.

The Storting determines the duration of each session. It is opened and prorogued by the monarch each year. The Storting cannot be dissolved either by the monarch or by its own resolution until the expiry of the quadrennial period for which it has been elected.

Note: In September 1989 the Sámi (Lapps) of northern Norway elected 39 representatives to a new Sameting (Consultative Assembly). The Sameting is elected quadrennially and is based in the town of Karasjok, in Finnmark.

The Government

HEAD OF STATE

Sovereign: HM King HARALD V (succeeded to the throne 17 January 1991; sworn in 21 January 1991).

COUNCIL OF STATE
(Statsråd)
(April 2008)

A majority Government, comprising Det norske Arbeiderparti (DnA), the Sosialistisk Venstreparti (SV) and the Senterpartiet (Sp).

Prime Minister: JENS STOLTENBERG (DnA).
Minister of Finance: KRISTIN HALVORSEN (SV).
Minister of Petroleum and Energy: ÅSLAUG MARIE HAGA (Sp).
Minister of Foreign Affairs: JONAS GAHR STØRE (DnA).
Minister of Defence: ANNE-GRETE STRØM-ERICHSEN (DnA).
Minister of the Environment and Development Co-operation: ERIK SOLHEIM (SV).
Minister of Local Government and Regional Development: MAGNHILD MELTVEIT KLEPPA (Sp).
Minister of Research and Higher Education: TORA AASLAND (SV).
Minister of Trade and Industry: DAG TERJE ANDERSEN (DnA).
Minister of Transport and Communications: LIV SIGNE NAVARSETE (Sp).
Minister of Education: BÅRD VEGAR SOLHJELL (SV).
Minister of Labour and Social Inclusion: BJARNE HÅKON HANSSEN (DnA).
Minister of Justice and the Police: KNUT STORBERGET (DnA).
Minister of Children and Equality: ANNIKEN HUITFELDT (DnA).
Minister of Culture and Church Affairs: TROND GISKE (DnA).
Minister of Health and Care Services: SYLVIA KRISTIN BRUSTAD (DnA).
Minister of Government Administration and Reform: HEIDI GRANDE RØYS (SV).
Minister of Agriculture and Food: TERJE RIIS-JOHANSEN (Sp).
Minister of Fisheries and Coastal Affairs: HELGA PEDERSEN (DnA).

MINISTRIES

Office of the Prime Minister: Akersgt. 42, POB 8001 Dep., 0030 Oslo; tel. 22-24-90-90; fax 22-24-95-00; e-mail postmottak@smk.dep.no; internet www.regjeringen.no/smk.

Ministry of Agriculture and Food: Akersgt. 59 (R5), POB 8007 Dep., 0030 Oslo; tel. 22-24-90-90; fax 22-24-95-55; e-mail postmottak@lmd.dep.no; internet www.regjeringen.no/lmd.

Ministry of Children and Equality: Akersgt. 59, POB 8036 Dep., 0030 Oslo; tel. 22-24-90-90; fax 22-24-95-15; e-mail postmottak@bld.dep.no; internet www.regjeringen.no/bld.

Ministry of Culture and Church Affairs: Akersgt. 59, POB 8030 Dep., 0030 Oslo; tel. 22-24-78-39; fax 22-24-90-10; e-mail postmottak@kkd.dep.no; internet www.regjeringen.no/kkd.

Ministry of Defence: Glacisgt. 1, POB 8126 Dep., 0032 Oslo; tel. 23-09-80-00; fax 23-09-60-75; e-mail postmottak@fd.dep.no; internet www.regjeringen.no/fd.

Ministry of Education and Research: Akersgt. 44, POB 8119 Dep., 0032 Oslo; tel. 22-24-90-90; fax 22-24-95-40; e-mail postmottak@kd.dep.no; internet www.regjeringen.no/kd.

Ministry of the Environment: Myntgt. 2, POB 8013 Dep., 0030 Oslo; tel. 22-24-90-90; fax 22-24-95-60; e-mail postmottak@md.dep.no; internet www.regjeringen.no/md.

Ministry of Finance: Akersgt. 40, POB 8008 Dep., 0030 Oslo; tel. 22-24-90-90; fax 22-24-95-10; e-mail postmottak@fin.dep.no; internet www.regjeringen.no/fin.

Ministry of Fisheries and Coastal Affairs: Grubbegt. 1, POB 8118 Dep., 0032 Oslo; tel. 22-24-90-90; fax 22-24-95-85; e-mail postmottak@fkd.dep.no; internet www.regjeringen.no/fkd.

Ministry of Foreign Affairs: 7 juni pl. 1, POB 8114 Dep., 0032 Oslo; tel. 22-24-36-00; fax 22-24-95-80; e-mail post@mfa.no; internet www.regjeringen.no/ud; also incl. Ministry of International Development.

Ministry of Government Administration and Reform: Akersgt. 59, POB 8004 Dep., 0030 Oslo; tel. 22-24-90-90; fax 22-24-95-16; e-mail postmottak@fad.dep.no; internet www.regjeringen.no/fad.

Ministry of Health and Care Services: Einar Gerhardsens pl. 3, POB 8011 Dep., 0030 Oslo; tel. 22-24-90-90; e-mail postmottak@hod.dep.no; internet www.regjeringen.no/hod.

Ministry of Justice and the Police: Akersgt. 42, POB 8005 Dep., 0030 Oslo; tel. 22-24-90-90; e-mail postmottak@jd.dep.no; internet www.regjeringen.no/jd.

Ministry of Labour and Social Inclusion: Einar Gerhardsens pl. 3, POB 8019 Dep., 0030 Oslo; tel. 22-24-90-90; fax 22-24-87-11; e-mail postmottak@aid.dep.no; internet www.regjeringen.no/aid.

Ministry of Local Government and Regional Development: Akersgt. 59, POB 8112 Dep., 0032 Oslo; tel. 22-24-90-90; e-mail postmottak@krd.dep.no; internet www.regjeringen.no/krd.

Ministry of Petroleum and Energy: Einar Gerhardsens pl. 1, POB 8148 Dep., 0033 Oslo; tel. 22-24-90-90; fax 22-24-95-65; e-mail postmottak@oed.dep.no; internet www.regjeringen.no/oed.

Ministry of Trade and Industry: Einar Gerhardsens pl. 1, POB 8014 Dep., 0030 Oslo; tel. 22-24-90-90; fax 22-24-95-65; e-mail postmottak@nhd.dep.no; internet www.regjeringen.no/nhd.

Ministry of Transport and Communications: Akersgt. 59 (R5), POB 8010 Dep., 0030 Oslo; tel. 22-24-90-90; fax 22-24-95-71; e-mail postmottak@sd.dep.no; internet www.regjeringen.no/sd.

Legislature

STORTING

Stortinget
Karl Johansgt. 22, 0026 Oslo; tel. 23-31-30-50; fax 23-31-38-50; e-mail stortinget.postmottak@stortinget.no; internet www.stortinget.no.

President: THORBJØRN JAGLAND (DnA).
Vice-President: CARL I. HAGEN (FrP).

NORWAY

The Storting has 169 members, one-quarter of whom sit as the upper house, the Lagting, and the rest as the lower house, the Odelsting.

President of the Lagting: INGE LØNNING (H).
Vice-President: OLA T. LÅNKE (KrF).
President of the Odelsting: BERIT BRØRBY (DnA).
Vice-President: OLAV GUNNAR BALLO (SV).

General Election, 12 September 2005

Party	Votes	% of votes	Seats
Det norske Arbeiderparti (DnA)	862,671	32.69	61
Fremskrittspartiet (FrP)	582,014	22.05	38
Høyre (H)	372,046	14.10	23
Sosialistisk Venstreparti (SV)	233,049	8.83	15
Kristelig Folkeparti (KrF)	179,109	6.79	11
Senterpartiet (Sp)	171,036	6.48	11
Venstre (V)	156,101	5.92	10
Rød Valgallianse (RV)	32,364	1.23	—
Kystpartiet (KP)	21,947	0.83	—
Pensjonistpartiet (Pp)	13,568	0.51	—
Others	15,039	0.57	—
Total	**2,638,944**	**100.00**	**169**

Political Organizations

Fremskrittspartiet (FrP) (Progress Party): Karl Johans gt. 25, 0159 Oslo; tel. 23-13-54-00; fax 23-13-54-01; e-mail frp@frp.no; internet www.frp.no; f. 1973 as Anders Langes Parti; present name adopted 1977; anti-tax; favours privatization, the diminution of the welfare state and less immigration; Chair. SIV JENSEN; Sec.-Gen. GEIR MO.

Høyre (H) (Conservative): Stortingsgt. 20, POB 1536 Vika, 0117 Oslo; tel. 22-82-90-00; fax 22-82-90-80; e-mail hoyre@hoyre.no; internet www.hoyre.no; f. 1884; aims to promote economic growth and sound state finances, achieve a property-owning democracy, and to uphold democratic govt, social security, private property, private initiative and personal liberty; 43,000 mems; Leader ERNA SOLBERG; Sec.-Gen. TROND REIDAR HOLE.

Kristelig Folkeparti (KrF) (Christian Democratic Party): Øvre Slottsgt. 18–20, POB 478 Sentrum, 0105 Oslo; tel. 23-10-28-00; fax 23-10-28-10; e-mail krf@krf.no; internet www.krf.no; f. 1933; aims to promote a democratic policy based on Christian values; Chair. DAGFINN HØYBRÅTEN; Sec. INGER HELENE VENÅS.

Kystpartiet (Coastal Party): Kanalveien 107, 5068 Bergen; tel. 55-29-25-70; e-mail post@kystpartiet.no; internet www.kystpartiet.no; nationalist; Leader KJELL IVAR VESTÅ; Sec. STIG-HAROLD FALCH PEDERSEN.

Miljøpartiet De Grønne (Green Party of Norway): POB 2169, 7412 Trondheim; tel. 73-53-09-11; fax 73-53-05-15; e-mail gronne@gronne.no; internet www.gronne.no; f. 1988; Principal Speakers BIRTE SIMONSEN, JAN BOJER VINDHEIM.

Norges Kommunistiske Parti (Communist Party of Norway): Helgesensgt. 21, POB 9288 Grønland, 0134 Oslo; tel. 22-71-60-44; fax 22-71-79-07; e-mail nkp@nkp.no; internet www.nkp.no; f. 1923; Chair. ZAFER GÖZET; Secs FRANK NÆSS, KNUT HARTMANN OLSEN.

Det norske Arbeiderparti (DnA) (Norwegian Labour Party): Youngstorget 2A, 5th floor, POB 8743, 0028 Oslo; tel. 24-14-40-00; fax 24-14-40-01; e-mail dna@dna.no; internet www.dna.no; f. 1887; social democratic; 51,576 mems (2005); Leader JENS STOLTENBERG; Gen. Sec. MARTIN KOLBERG.

Pensjonistpartiet (Pensioners' Party): Møllergt. 6, 0179 Oslo; tel. 45-28-90-10; fax 22-42-77-00; e-mail post@pensjonistpartiet.no; internet www.pensjonistpartiet.no; Leader RAGNAR DAHL; Sec. GUNNVOR TELEBOND.

Rødt: Osterhausgt. 27, 0183 Oslo; tel. 22-98-90-50; fax 22-98-90-55; e-mail raudt@raudt.no; internet roedt.no; f. 1973 as Rød Valgallianse (Red Electoral Alliance); merged with Arbeidernes Kommunistparti in March 2007; adopted current name in Oct. 2007; left-wing group; Leader TORSTEIN DAHLE; Sec. BETH HARTMANN.

Senterpartiet (Sp) (Centre Party): Akersgt. 35, 3rd Floor, POB 1191 Sentrum, 0107 Oslo; tel. 23-69-01-00; fax 23-69-01-01; e-mail epost@senterpartiet.no; internet www.senterpartiet.no; f. 1920 as the Bondepartiet (Agrarian Party), name changed 1959; advocates a decentralized society that will secure employment and diversified settlements in all parts of the country; opposes Norwegian membership of the EU; encourages the devt of an ecologically balanced society; Leader ÅSLAUG MARIE HAGA; Sec.-Gen. IVAR EGEBERG.

Sosialistisk Venstreparti (SV) (Socialist Left Party): Akersgt. 35, 0158 Oslo; tel. 21-93-33-00; fax 21-93-33-01; e-mail post@sv.no; internet www.sv.no; f. 1975 as a fusion of the Socialist People's Party, the Democratic Socialists and other socialist forces united previously in the Socialist Electoral League; advocates non-alignment and socialism independent of international centres, based on workers' control, decentralized powers, gender equality and ecological principles; Chair. KRISTIN HALVORSEN; Sec. EDLE DAASVAND.

Venstre (V) (Liberal): Møllergt. 16, 0179 Oslo; tel. 22-40-43-50; fax 22-40-43-51; e-mail venstre@venstre.no; internet www.venstre.no; f. 1884; in 1988 reunited with Det Liberale Folkepartiet (Liberal Democratic Party, f. 1972); advocates the promotion of national and democratic progress on the basis of the present system by gradual economic, social and cultural reforms; Leader LARS SPONHEIM; Sec.-Gen. TERJE BREIVIK.

Diplomatic Representation

EMBASSIES IN NORWAY

Afghanistan: Kronprinsensgt. 17, 0251 Oslo; tel. 22-83-84-10; fax 22-83-84-11; e-mail info@afghanemb.com; internet www.afghanistanembassy.no; Ambassador JAVID LODIN.

Argentina: Drammensvn 39, 0244 Oslo; tel. 22-55-24-49; fax 22-44-16-41; e-mail enoru@online.no; internet argentour.com/embajada; Ambassador JUAN MANUEL ORTIZ DE ROSAS.

Austria: Thomas Heftyesgt. 19–21, 0244 Oslo; tel. 22-54-02-00; fax 22-55-43-61; e-mail oslo-ob@bmeia.gv.at; Ambassador Dr ANTON KOZUSNIK.

Belgium: Drammensvn 103D, 0244 Oslo; tel. 23-13-32-20; fax 23-13-32-32; e-mail oslo@diplobel.org; internet www.diplomatie.be/oslo; Ambassador FRANK RECKER.

Bosnia and Herzegovina: Bygdøy allé 10, POB 2407 Solli, 0201 Oslo; tel. 22-54-09-63; fax 22-55-27-50; e-mail ambasadagkbih@gkbih.com; internet www.gkbih.com; Ambassador FAIK UZONOVIĆ.

Brazil: Sigurd Syrsgt. 4, 0244 Oslo; tel. 22-54-07-30; fax 22-44-39-64; e-mail consular@brasil.no; internet www.brasil.no; Ambassador SÉRGIO EDUARDO MOREIRA LIMA.

Bulgaria: Tidemandsgt. 11, 0244 Oslo; tel. 22-55-40-40; fax 22-55-40-24; e-mail bulgemb@online.no; Ambassador NIKOLAS IVANOV KARADIMOV.

Canada: Wergelandsvn 7, 0244 Oslo; tel. 22-99-53-00; fax 22-99-53-01; e-mail oslo@international.gc.ca; internet www.canada.no; Ambassador JILLIAN STIRK.

Chile: Meltzersgt. 5, 0244 Oslo; tel. 22-44-89-55; fax 22-44-24-21; e-mail embassy@chile.no; internet www.chile.no; Ambassador ROBERTO EDUARDO ALONSO BUDGE.

China, People's Republic: Tuengen allé 2B, Vinderen, 0244 Oslo; tel. 22-49-20-52; fax 22-92-19-78; e-mail webmaster@chinese-embassy.no; internet www.chinese-embassy.no; Ambassador GAO JIAN.

Costa Rica: Skippergt. 33, 8th Floor, 0154 Oslo; tel. 22-42-58-23; fax 22-33-04-08; e-mail embassy@costarica.no; internet www.costarica.no; Ambassador Dr CLAUDIO BOGANTES ZAMORA.

Croatia: Drammensvn 82, 0244 Oslo; tel. 23-01-40-50; fax 23-01-40-60; e-mail croemb.oslo@mvpei.hr; Ambassador DOBROSLAV SILOBRČIĆ.

Czech Republic: Fritznersgt. 14, 0244 Oslo; tel. 22-12-10-31; fax 22-55-33-95; e-mail oslo@embassy.mzv.cz; internet www.mzv.cz/oslo; Ambassador LUBOŠ NOVÝ.

Denmark: Olav Kyrresgt. 7, 0244 Oslo; tel. 22-54-08-00; fax 22-55-46-34; e-mail oslamb@um.dk; internet www.amboslo.um.dk; Ambassador THEIS TRUELSEN.

Egypt: Drammensvn 90A, 0244 Oslo; tel. 23-08-42-00; fax 22-56-22-68; e-mail information@egypt-embassy.no; internet www.egypt-embassy.no; Ambassador WAGUIH SAID HANAFI.

Estonia: Parkvn 51A, 0244 Oslo; tel. 22-54-00-70; fax 22-54-00-71; e-mail Embassy.Oslo@mfa.ee; internet www.estemb.no; Ambassador JUHAN HARAVEE.

Finland: Thomas Heftyesgt. 1, 0244 Oslo; tel. 22-12-49-00; fax 22-12-49-49; e-mail sanomat.osl@formin.fi; internet www.finland.no; Ambassador PETER STENLUND.

France: Drammensvn 69, 0244 Oslo; tel. 23-28-46-00; fax 23-28-46-70; e-mail ambafrance.oslo@diplomatie.gouv.fr; internet www.ambafrance-no.org; Ambassador CHANTAL POIRET.

Germany: Oscarsgt. 45, 0244 Oslo; tel. 23-27-54-00; fax 22-44-76-72; e-mail info@oslo.diplo.de; internet www.oslo.diplo.de; Ambassador ROLAND MAUCH.

Greece: Nobelsgt. 45, 0244 Oslo; tel. 22-44-27-28; fax 22-56-00-72; e-mail gremb@online.no; Ambassador JEAN BOUCAOURIS.

NORWAY

Guatemala: Oscarsgt. 59, 0258 Oslo; tel. 22-55-60-04; fax 22-55-60-47; e-mail guatemala@embajada.no; Ambassador LUIS RAÚL ESTÉVEZ LÓPEZ.

Hungary: Sophus Liesgt. 3, 0244 Oslo; tel. 22-55-24-18; fax 22-44-76-93; e-mail huembosl@online.no; Ambassador LAJOS BOZI.

Iceland: Stortingsgt. 30, 0244 Oslo; tel. 23-23-75-30; fax 22-83-07-04; e-mail emb.oslo@mfa.is; internet www.island.no; Ambassador STEFÁN SKJALDARSON.

India: Niels Juelsgt. 30, 0244 Oslo; tel. 24-11-59-10; fax 24-11-59-12; e-mail amb.oslo@mea.gov.in; internet www.indemb.no; Ambassador MAHESH KUMAR SACHDEV.

Indonesia: Fritznersgt. 12, 0244 Oslo; tel. 22-12-51-30; fax 22-12-51-31; e-mail kbrioslo@online.no; internet www.indonesia-oslo.no; Ambassador RETNO L. P. MARSUDI.

Iran: Drammensvn 88E, 0244 Oslo; tel. 23-27-29-60; fax 22-55-49-19; e-mail iremb@iran-embassy-oslo.no; internet www.iran-embassy-oslo.no; Ambassador ABDUL REZA FARAJI RAD.

Ireland: Haakon VIIs gt. 1, 0244 Oslo; tel. 22-01-72-00; fax 22-01-72-01; e-mail osloembassy@dfa.ie; Ambassador THELMA MARIA DORAN.

Israel: Parkvn 35, POB 534 Skøyen, 0214 Oslo; tel. 21-01-95-00; fax 21-01-95-30; e-mail israel@oslo.mfa.gov.il; internet oslo.mfa.gov.il; Ambassador MIRYAM SHOMRAT.

Italy: Inkognitogt. 7, 0244 Oslo; tel. 22-55-22-33; fax 22-44-34-36; e-mail ambasciata.oslo@esteri.it; internet www.amboslo.esteri.it; Ambassador ROSA ANNA CONIGLIO PAPALIA.

Japan: Wergelandsveien 15, 0244 Oslo; tel. 22-99-16-00; fax 22-44-25-05; e-mail info@japan-embassy.no; internet www.no.emb-japan.go.jp; Ambassador HISAO YAMAGUCHI.

Korea, Republic: Inkognitogt. 3, 0244, Oslo; tel. 22-54-70-90; fax 22-56-14-11; e-mail kornor@mofat.go.kr; internet nor.mofat.go.kr; Ambassador BYUNG-KOO CHOI.

Latvia: Bygdøy allé 76, POB 3163 Elisenberg, 0208 Oslo; tel. 22-54-22-80; fax 22-54-64-26; e-mail embassy.norway@mfa.gov.lv; Ambassador MĀRIS KLIŠĀNS.

Lithuania: Henrik Ibsensgt. 100, 0244 Oslo; tel. 22-12-92-00; fax 22-12-92-01; e-mail amb.no@urm.lt; internet no.mfa.lt; Ambassador ALFONTAS EIDINTAS.

Morocco: Holtegt. 28, 0355 Oslo; tel. 23-19-71-50; fax 23-19-71-51; e-mail sifamoslo@c2i.net; Ambassador BOUCHAÂB YAHDIH.

Netherlands: Oscarsgt. 29, 0244 Oslo; tel. 23-33-36-00; fax 23-33-36-01; e-mail nlgovosl@online.no; internet www.netherlands-embassy.no; Ambassador RONALD VAN ROEDEN.

Pakistan: Eckersbergsgt. 20, 0244 Oslo; tel. 23-16-60-80; fax 22-55-50-97; e-mail info@pakistanembassy.no; internet www.pakistanembassy.no; Ambassador RAB NAWAZ KHAN.

Poland: Olav Kyrres pl. 1, 0244 Oslo; tel. 24-11-08-50; fax 22-44-48-39; e-mail ambpol@online.no; internet www.oslo.polemb.net; Ambassador WOJCIECH LUDWIK KOLAŃCZYK.

Portugal: Josefinesgt. 37, 0244 Oslo; tel. 23-33-28-50; fax 22-56-43-55; e-mail portemb@frisurf.no; Ambassador JOÃO DE LIMA PIMENTEL.

Romania: Oscarsgt. 51, 0244 Oslo; tel. 22-44-15-12; fax 22-43-16-74; e-mail embassy@romanianembassy.no; internet oslo.mae.ro; Ambassador Dr CRISTIAN ISTRATE.

Russia: Drammensvn 74, 0244 Oslo; tel. 22-55-32-78; fax 22-55-00-70; e-mail rembassy@online.no; internet www.norway.mid.ru; Ambassador SERGEI V. ANDREEV.

Serbia: Drammensvn 105, 0244 Oslo; tel. 23-08-68-58; fax 22-55-29-92; e-mail ambasada@serbianembassy.no; internet www.serbianembassy.no; Ambassador VLADISLAV MLADENOVIĆ.

Slovakia: Thomas Heftyesgt. 24, 0244 Oslo; tel. 22-04-94-70; fax 22-04-94-74; e-mail slovakr@online.no; internet www.oslo.mfa.sk; Ambassador DUŠAN ROZBORA.

South Africa: Drammensvn 88C, POB 2822 Solli, 0204 Oslo; tel. 23-27-32-20; fax 22-44-39-75; e-mail info@saemboslo.no; internet www.saemboslo.no; Ambassador ISMAIL COOVADIA.

Spain: Oscarsgt. 35, 0244 Oslo; tel. 22-92-66-90; fax 22-55-98-22; e-mail embespno@mail.mae.es; internet www.mae.es/embajadas/oslo; Ambassador FERNANDO ALVARGONZÁLEZ SAN MARTÍN.

Sri Lanka: Nedre Vollgt. 3, 0158 Oslo; tel. 23-31-70-80; fax 23-31-70-90; e-mail embakont@online.no; internet www.srilanka.no; Ambassador ESALA RUWAN WEERAKOON.

Sudan: Holtegt. 28, 0355 Oslo; tel. 22-60-33-55; fax 22-69-83-44; e-mail embassy@sudanoslo.com; Ambassador MOHAMED ALI ELTOM.

Sweden: Nobelsgt. 16, 0244 Oslo; tel. 24-11-42-00; fax 22-55-15-96; e-mail ambassaden.oslo@foreign.ministry.se; internet www.swedenabroad.com/oslo; Ambassador MICHAEL SAHLIN.

Switzerland: Bygdøy allé 78, 0244 Oslo; tel. 22-43-05-90; fax 22-44-63-50; e-mail osl.vertretung@eda.admin.ch; internet www.eda.admin.ch/oslo; Ambassador KURT HÖCHNER.

Thailand: Eilert Sundtsgt. 4, 0244 Oslo; tel. 22-12-86-60; fax 22-04-99-69; e-mail thaioslo@online.no; internet www.thaiembassy.no; Ambassador JULLAPONG NONSRICHAI.

Tunisia: Haakon VIIs gt. 5B, 0161 Oslo; tel. 22-83-19-17; fax 22-83-24-12; e-mail at.oslo@online.no; Chargé d'affaires a.i. NEHROU AL-ARBI.

Turkey: Halvdan Svartesgt. 5, 0244 Oslo; tel. 22-12-87-50; fax 22-55-62-63; e-mail postmaster@oslo-turkish-embassy.com; Ambassador MEHMET KAZIM GÖRKAY.

Ukraine: Arbinsgt. 4, 0253 Oslo; tel. 22-83-55-60; fax 22-83-55-57; e-mail embassy@ukremb.no; internet www.mfa.gov.ua/norway; Ambassador IHOR M. SAGACH.

United Kingdom: Thomas Heftyesgt. 8, 0264 Oslo; tel. 23-13-27-00; fax 23-13-27-41; e-mail britemb@online.no; internet www.britain.no; Ambassador DAVID POWELL.

USA: Henrik Ibsensgate 48, 0244 Oslo; tel. 22-44-85-50; fax 22-43-07-77; e-mail oslo@usa.no; internet www.usa.no; Ambassador BENSON K. WHITNEY.

Venezuela: Drammensvn 82, POB 2820 Solli, 0204 Oslo; tel. 22-43-06-60; fax 22-43-14-70; e-mail embajada@venezuela.no; Ambassador FRANCISCO VÉLEZ-VALERY.

Judicial System

The judicial system in Norway is organized on three levels. The courts of first instance are the District (Herredsrett) and City (Byrett) Courts. The country is divided into 93 judicial areas, most of which are served by one professional judge and one or two deputies (in the major cities the number of judges ranges from three to 52). The Court of Appeal (Lagmannsrett) consists of six jurisdictions, each with between 10 and 52 judges, and two divisions (Appeals and Criminal Divisions). The Supreme Court (Høyesterett) sits in Oslo and decides cases in the last instance. The Court, which is served by 19 judges appointed by the Crown and presided over by a Chief Justice, is competent to try all factual and legal aspects of cases in civil and criminal cause. In criminal cases, however, the competence of the Court is limited to questions concerning the application of the law, the nature of the penalty, and procedural errors of the lower courts. Appeals to the Supreme Court may not be based on errors in the assessment of evidence in connection with the question of guilt.

SUPREME COURT

Høyesterett

Høyesteretts pl., POB 8016 Dep., 0030 Oslo; tel. 22-03-59-00; fax 22-33-23-55; e-mail post@hoyesterett.no; internet www.hoyesterett.no. f. 1815; pronounces judgment in the final instance; hears both civil and criminal cases, and has jurisdiction in all areas of law; composed of 18 ordinary justices of the Supreme Court and one Chief Justice; individual cases are heard by five justices—in some instances cases are heard by all of the justices sitting in plenary session; works in two parallel and equal divisions; Supreme Court justices also sit on the Appeals Selection Committee of the Supreme Court, which is classed as a separate court; cases brought before the Appeals Selection Committee are heard by three justices; any matter brought before the Supreme Court must initially be considered by the Appeals Selection Committee; justices sit in both divisions of the Supreme Court and on the Appeals Selection Committee in accordance with a rota system.

Chief Justice of the Supreme Court: TORE SCHEI.

Justices of the Supreme Court: LIV GJØLSTAD, KETIL LUND, KARENANNE GUSSGARD, STEINAR TJOMSLAND, KIRSTI COWARD, EILERT STANG LUND, LARS OFTEDAL BROCH, HANS FLOCK, MAGNUS MATNINGSDAL, GEORGE FREDRIK RIEBER-MOHN, KARIN MARIA BRUZELIUS, JENS EDVIN A. SKOGHØY, KARL ARNE UTGÅRD, INGER-ELSE STABEL, OLE BJØRN STØLE, TORIL MARIE ØIE, BÅRD TØNDER, CLEMENT ENDRESEN, HILDE INDREBERG.

COURTS OF APPEAL

Agder Lagmannsrett (Court of Appeal in Skien): Statens hus, Gjerpensgt. 16, 3708 Skien; tel. 35-54-05-00; fax 35-52-10-09; e-mail agder.lagmannsrett@domstol.no; internet www.domstol.no; Presiding Judge ARNE CHRISTIANSEN.

Borgarting Lagmannsrett (Court of Appeal in Oslo): Keysersgt. 13, POB 8017 Dep., 0030 Oslo; tel. 21-55-80-00; e-mail borgadm@domstol.no; internet www.domstol.no/borgarting; Presiding Judge NILS ERIK LIE.

Eidsivating Lagmannsrett (Court of Appeal in Hamar): Hamar tinghus, Østregt. 41, 2326 Hamar; tel. 62-55-06-00; fax 62-55-06-20; e-mail elag@domstol.no; internet www.domstol.no/elag; Presiding Judge ODD JARL PEDERSEN.

NORWAY

Frostating Lagmannsrett (Court of Appeal in Trondheim): Trondheim tinghus, Munkegt. 20, 7004 Trondheim; tel. 73-54-24-60; fax 73-54-24-84; e-mail frostating.lagmannsrett@domstol.no; internet www.frostating.no; Presiding Judge KJELL BUER.

Gulating Lagmannsrett (Court of Appeal in Bergen): Bergen tinghus, Tårnpl. 2, POB 7414, 5020 Bergen; tel. 55-23-71-20; fax 55-23-07-24; e-mail gulating@domstol.no; internet www.domstol.no/gulating; Presiding Judge RUNE FJELD.

Hålogaland Lagmannsrett (Court of Appeal in Tromsø): Fr. Nansens pl. 17, POB 2511, 9271 Tromsø; tel. 77-66-00-35; fax 77-66-00-60; e-mail halogaland.lagmannsrett@domstol.no; internet www.domstol.no; Presiding Judge ARILD O. EIDESEN.

CIVIL COURTS

In each municipality there is a Conciliation Board (Forliksråd) consisting of three lay members elected by the municipal council for four years. With a few exceptions, no case may be taken to a court of justice without a prior attempt at mediation by a Conciliation Court. In addition to mediation, the Conciliation Court has a judicial capacity and is intended to settle minor cases in a simple manner without great expense to the parties involved.

The ordinary lower courts are the District and City Courts, which decide all cases not adjudicated upon by the Conciliation Court, and they also act as courts of appeal from judgments given in the Conciliation Court. During the main hearing, the court is generally convened with only one professional judge, but each of the parties may request that the court be convened with two lay judges, in addition to the professional judge. When the court finds it advisable, it may also summon lay judges on its own initiative.

Judgments delivered in the District and City Courts may be taken, on appeal, to the Court of Appeal or to the Supreme Court. In the Court of Appeal cases are judged by three professional judges, but, if requested by one of the parties, lay judges may be summoned.

CRIMINAL COURTS

The criminal courts are: the Court of Examination and Summary Jurisdiction (Forhørsretten), the District and City Courts, the Court of Appeal and the Supreme Court. In the Court of Examination and Summary Jurisdiction the professional judge presides alone, but in the District and City Courts two lay judges also sit. Following the implementation of a major reform in 1995, all criminal cases now begin in a District or City Court. The gravest offences were previously tried directly before a jury in the Court of Appeal and the possibilities for appeal were thus limited. Now, however, the issue of guilt can be appealed to the Court of Appeal in all cases. (Such cases are tried either by three professional judges, and four lay judges with equal votes, or by three professional judges and a jury of 10 members. For a guilty verdict to be upheld in the latter case, at least seven members of the jury must support the original decision of the lower court. In other cases appeal is directly to the Supreme Court.) The maximum penalty permissible under Norwegian law is 21 years of imprisonment.

OMBUDSMAN

The office of Parliamentary Ombudsman was established in 1962. An Ombudsman is elected by the Storting after every general election for a four-year term (with the possibility of re-election). The Ombudsman is accessible to all citizens, and attempts to ensure against the public administration committing any injustice to the individual citizen. The Ombudsman does not cover private legal affairs, and does not have the right to reverse an official decision, but his pronouncements are normally complied with.

Sivilombudsmannen—Stortingets ombudsmann for forvaltningen (Parliamentary Ombudsman for Public Administration): Akersgt. 8, 6th Floor, POB 3 Sentrum, 0101 Oslo; tel. 22-82-85-00; fax 22-82-85-11; e-mail arkiv@sivilombudsmannen.no; internet www.sivilombudsmannen.no; Ombudsman ARNE FLIFLET.

Religion

CHRISTIANITY

Citizens are considered to be members of the National Church unless they explicitly associate themselves with another denomination; 82.7% of the population (approximately 3,871,006 persons) nominally belonged to the Church at the end of 2006. However, actual church attendance is considered to be rather low. Other Protestant Christian denominations accounted for some 4.5% of the population. There are a very small number of Orthodox Christians in Norway.

The National Church

Church of Norway

The Church Synod, POB 799 Sentrum, 0106 Oslo; tel. 23-08-12-00; fax 23-08-12-01; e-mail post.kirkeradet@kirken.no; internet www.kirken.no.

The Evangelical Lutheran Church, constituted as the State Church; there are 11 dioceses, 103 archdeaconries, 620 clerical districts and 1,298 parishes. The highest representative body of the Church is the Synod, summoned for the first time in 1984. At the end of 2006 3,871,006 persons (82.7% of the population) belonged to the State Church.

Bishop of Oslo: OLE CHRISTIAN MÆLEN KVARME.
Bishop of Borg: HELGA HAUGLAND BYFUGLIEN.
Bishop of Hamar: SOLVEIG FISKE.
Bishop of Tunsberg: LAILA RIKSAASEN DAHL.
Bishop of Agder: OLAV SKJEVESLAND.
Bishop of Stavanger: ERNST ODDVAR BAASLAND.
Bishop of Bjørgvin: OLE D. HAGESÆTHER.
Bishop of Møre: ODD BONDEVIK.
Bishop of Nidaros: FINN WAGLE.
Bishop of Sør-Hålogaland: TOR BERGER JØRGENSEN.
Bishop of Nord-Hålogaland: PER OSKAR KJØLAAS.

The Roman Catholic Church

For ecclesiastical purposes, Norway comprises the diocese of Oslo and the territorial prelatures of Tromsø and Trondheim. The diocese and the prelatures are directly responsible to the Holy See. At 31 December 2005 there were an estimated 53,817 adherents in Norway, equivalent to about 1.2% of the population. The Bishop of Oslo participates in the Scandinavian Episcopal Conference (based in Västra Frölunda, Sweden).

Bishop of Oslo: Rt Rev. BERNT IVAR (MARKUS) EIDSVIG, Oslo Katolske Bispedømme, Akersvn 5, POB 8270, 0177 Oslo; tel. 23-21-95-00; fax 23-21-95-01; e-mail okb@katolsk.no; internet www.katolsk.no.

Other Churches

Church of England: St Edmund's Anglican Church, Møllergt. 30, Oslo; tel. 22-69-22-14; fax 22-69-21-63; e-mail j-heil@online.no; internet www.osloanglicans.net; 1,800 mems (2007); also in Stavanger, Bergen and Trondheim; part of the Diocese of Gibraltar in Europe; Chaplain Rev. Canon JANET HEIL.

Evangelical Lutheran Free Church of Norway: POB 23, Bekkelagshøgda, 1109 Oslo; tel. 22-74-86-00; fax 22-74-86-01; e-mail post@frikirken.no; internet www.frikirken.no; f. 1877; c. 19,308 mems (2006); Chair. of Synod ARNFINN LØYNING.

Norwegian Baptist Union: Micheletsvei 62c, 1368 Stabekk; tel. 67-10-35-60; fax 67-10-35-69; e-mail post@baptist.no; f. 1860; 8,748 mems (2006); Gen. Sec. MAGNAR MAELAND.

Pinse Bevegelsen i Norge (Pentecostal Movement): POB 6717, St Olavs pl., 0130 Oslo; tel. 22-11-43-00; fax 22-11-43-43; e-mail jeppestol@pinsebevegelsen.no; internet www.pinsebevegelsen.no; 39,492 mems (2006).

United Methodist Church: POB 2744 St Hanshaugen, 0131 Oslo; tel. 23-33-27-00; fax 23-33-27-01; e-mail post@metodistkirken.no; internet www.metodistkirken.no; f. 1856; 12,000 mems (2007); Council Dir GUNNAR BRADLEY.

In 2007 there were 14,756 Jehovah's Witnesses in Norway and 5,281 Seventh-day Adventists.

OTHER RELIGIONS

In 2007 there were 79,068 Muslims, 10,753 Buddhists, 4,098 Hindus, 2,440 Sikhs and 868 Jews in Norway. The Human-Etisk Forbund (Norwegian Humanist Association)—the only national organization for those who do not formally practise any religion, including atheists—had 78,900 registered members in 2007.

The Press

The principle of press freedom is safeguarded in the Norwegian Constitution. There is no law specifically dealing with the Press. Editors bear wide responsibility in law for the content of their papers, especially regarding such matters as libel. Although a journalist is legally entitled to conceal his source he may be required to disclose this information under penalty of imprisonment, but such instances are rare. A three-member Council of Conduct gives judgments in cases of complaint against a paper or of disputes between papers. It has no powers of enforcement but its judgments are highly respected.

NORWAY

The Press Association has a Code of Ethics aimed at maintaining the standards and reputation of the profession.

The Eastern region dominates press activity. Oslo dailies are especially influential throughout this area, and four of these—*Aftenposten, Verdens Gang, Dagbladet* and *Dagsavisen*—have a national readership. Nevertheless, in Norway's other chief cities the large local dailies easily lead in their own districts. In 2002 Norway had 61 daily newspapers, with a combined circulation averaging 2,201,000 copies per issue. A few very large papers are responsible for the bulk of this circulation. In 1996 the most popular newspapers were *Verdens Gang* (Oslo), *Aftenposten* (Oslo), *Dagbladet* (Oslo), *Bergens Tidende* (Bergen) and *Adresseavisen* (Trondheim), with a combined circulation of almost 1m. At the beginning of 1994 the principal media holding company was Schibsted A/S, which owned *Aftenposten* and *Verdens Gang* and had substantial holdings in *Adresseavisen* (33.4%), *Stavanger Aftenblad* (30.5%) and several other newspapers. Orkla Media A/S had holdings of 90% or more in eight regional newspapers (and a 50% share in the major magazine publisher Hjemmet Mortensen—see below). The trade-union-owned Norsk Arbeiderpresse is the principal owner of the left-wing press.

PRINCIPAL NEWSPAPERS

Ålesund

Sunnmørsposten: POB 123, 6001 Ålesund; tel. 70-12-00-00; fax 70-12-46-42; e-mail redaksjon@smp.no; internet www.smp.no; f. 1882; Liberal; Editor HARALD KJØLÅS; circ. 33,712.

Arendal

Agderposten: POB 8, 4801 Arendal; tel. 37-00-37-00; fax 37-00-38-38; e-mail agderposten@agderposten.no; internet www.agderposten.no; f. 1874; independent; Editor STEIN GAUSLAA; circ. 23,746.

Bergen

Bergens Tidende: Krinkelkroken 1, POB 7240, 5020 Bergen; tel. 55-21-45-02; fax 55-21-48-48; e-mail webmaster@bt.no; internet www.bergens-tidende.no; f. 1868; Editor HANS ERIK MATRE; circ. 87,668.

Bergensavisen: Chr. Michelsensgt. 4, POB 824 Sentrum, 5807 Bergen; tel. 55-23-50-00; fax 55-31-00-30; e-mail nyhet@ba.no; internet www.ba.no; f. 1927; independent, social democratic; Editor-in-Chief OLAV BERGO; circ. 29,311.

Dagen: POB 76/77, 5002 Bergen; tel. 55-31-17-55; fax 55-31-71-06; f. 1919; religious daily; Editor FINN JARLE SÆLE; circ. 9.033.

Billingstad

Budstikka: POB 133, 1376 Billingstad; tel. 66-77-00-00; fax 66-77-00-60; e-mail redaksjonen@budstikka.no; internet www.budstikka.no; f. 1898; 6 a week; fmrly *Asker og Baerums Budstikke*; Conservative; Editor ANDREAS GJØLME; circ. 29,660.

Bodø

Avisa Nordland: Storgt. 38, 8002 Bodø; tel. 75-50-50-00; fax 75-50-50-60; e-mail kundeservice@an.no; internet www.an.no; f. 1910; Labour; Editor JAN-ELRIK HANSSEN; circ. 23,959.

Drammen

Drammens Tidende: POB 7033, 3007 Drammen; tel. 32-20-40-00; fax 32-20-40-61; e-mail redaksjonen@dt.no; internet www.dt.no; f. 1832 and 1883; Conservative daily; Dir FINN GRUNDT; Editor HANS ARNE ODDE; circ. 40,954.

Fredrikstad

Fredrikstad Blad: POB 143, 1606 Fredrikstad; tel. 46-80-77-77; e-mail tips@f-b.no; internet www.f-b.no; f. 1889; Conservative; Editor ERLING OMVIK; circ. 23,442.

Gjøvik

Oppland Arbeiderblad: POB 24, 2801 Gjøvik; tel. 61-18-93-00; fax 61-17-98-56; e-mail redaksjonen@oa.no; internet www.oa.no; f. 1924; daily; Labour; Editor-in-Chief JENS OLAI JENSSEN; circ. 27,173.

Hamar

Hamar Arbeiderblad: Torggt. 51, POB 333, 2301 Hamar; tel. 62-51-96-99; fax 62-51-96-18; e-mail post@ha-nett.no; internet www.ha-nett.no; f. 1925; daily; Labour; Editor ROLV AMDAL; circ. 27,363.

Harstad

Harstad Tidende: Storgt. 11, POB 85, 9481 Harstad; tel. 77-01-80-00; fax 77-01-80-05; e-mail redaksjonen@ht.no; internet www.ht.no; f. 1887; Conservative; Editor BÅRD MICHALSEN; circ. 13,503.

Haugesund

Haugesunds Avis: POB 2024, 5504 Haugesund; tel. 52-72-00-00; fax 52-72-04-44; e-mail redaksjonen@haugesunds-avis.no; internet www.h-avis.no; f. 1895; independent; Editor-in-Chief TONNY NUNDAL; circ. 33,013.

Hønefoss

Ringerikes Blad: POB 68, 3502 Hønefoss; tel. 32-17-95-00; fax 32-17-95-01; e-mail redaksjonen@ringblad.no; internet www.ringblad.no; f. 1845; independent; Editor TORE ROLAND; circ. 12,694.

Kongsvinger

Glåmdalen: POB 757, 2204 Kongsvinger; tel. 62-88-25-00; fax 62-88-25-01; e-mail redaksjon@glomdalen.no; internet www.glomdalen.no; f. 1926; daily; Labour; Editor ROLF NORDBERG; circ. 19,848.

Kristiansand

Fædrelandsvennen: POB 369, 4664 Kristiansand; tel. 38-11-30-00; fax 38-11-30-01; e-mail fep@fvn.no; internet www.fvn.no; f. 1875; daily; Liberal independent; Editor FINN HOLMER-HOVEN; circ. 41,326.

Lillehammer

Gudbrandsdølen Dagningen: POB 954, 2604 Lillehammer; tel. 61-22-10-00; fax 61-26-09-60; e-mail redaksjonen@gd.no; internet www.gd.no; f. 1841 and 1894; independent; Editor-in-Chief KRISTIAN SKULLERUD; circ. 26,723.

Lillestrøm

Romerikes Blad: POB 235, 2001 Lillestrøm; tel. 63-80-50-50; fax 63-80-50-60; e-mail redaksjonen@rb.no; internet www.rb.no; f. 1913; Labour; Editor-in-Chief THOR WOJE; circ. 43,238.

Molde

Romsdals Budstikke: POB 2100, 6402 Molde; tel. 71-25-00-00; fax 71-25-00-11; e-mail redaksjon@r-b.no; internet www.rbnett.no; f. 1843; Conservative independent; Editor NILS-KRISTIAN MYHRE; circ. 18,205.

Moss

Moss Avis: POB 248/250, 1530 Moss; tel. 69-20-50-00; fax 69-20-50-02; e-mail jan.tollefsen@moss-avis.no; internet www.moss-avis.no; f. 1876; Liberal/Conservative independent; Editor JAN TOLLEFSEN; circ. 15,304.

Oslo

Aftenposten: POB 1 Sentrum, 0051 Oslo; tel. 22-86-30-00; fax 22-42-63-25; e-mail aftenposten@aftenposten.no; internet www.aftenposten.no; f. 1860; Conservative independent; Editor-in-Chief HANS ERIK MATRE; circ. morning 250,179, evening 131,089.

Akers Avis/Groruddalen Budstikke: POB 100 Grorud, 0905 Oslo; tel. 22-91-88-20; e-mail redaksjonen@groruddalen.no; internet www.groruddalen.no; fax 22-16-01-05; f. 1928; 2 a week; non-political; Editor HJALMAR KIELLAND; circ. 15,171.

Dagbladet: POB 1184 Sentrum, 0107 Oslo; tel. 22-31-06-00; fax 22-31-05-10; e-mail annb@dagbladet.no; internet www.dagbladet.no; f. 1869; daily; Editor-in-Chief ANNE AASHEIM; circ. 135,611.

Dagens Næringsliv: POB 1182 Sentrum, 0107 Oslo; tel. 22-00-11-90; fax 22-00-10-70; e-mail redaksjonen@dn.no; internet www.dn.no; Editor SVEIN-THORE GRAN; circ. 81,391.

Dagsavisen: POB 1183 Sentrum, 0107 Oslo; tel. 22-72-60-00; fax 22-64-92-82; e-mail abonnement@dagsavisen.no; internet www.dagsavisen.no; f. 1884; Labour; Editor-in-Chief ARVID JACOBSEN; circ. 31,403.

Nationen: POB 9390 Grønland, 0135 Oslo; tel. 21-31-00-00; fax 21-31-00-90; e-mail hans.eldegard@nationen.no; internet www.nationen.no; f. 1918; daily; Centre; Editor-in-Chief TOVE LIE; circ. 15,871.

Verdens Gang (VG): Akersgt. 55, POB 1185 Sentrum, 0107 Oslo; tel. 22-00-00-00; fax 22-42-68-70; e-mail redaksjonen@vg.no; internet www.vg.no; f. 1945; independent; Editor-in-Chief TORRY PEDERSEN; circ. 309,610.

Vårt Land: POB 1180 Sentrum, 0107 Oslo; tel. 22-31-03-10; fax 22-31-03-05; e-mail sentral@vl.no; internet www.vl.no; f. 1945; independent, religious daily; Editor HELGE SIMONNES; circ. 27,146.

Sandefjord

Sandefjords Blad: POB 143, 3201 Sandefjord; tel. 33-42-00-00; fax 33-46-29-91; e-mail redaksjonen@sb.no; internet www.sb.no; f. 1861; Conservative; Editor LEIF MAGNE FLEMMEN; circ. 14,260.

Sarpsborg

Sarpsborg Arbeiderblad: POB 83, 1701 Sarpsborg; tel. 69-11-11-11; fax 69-11-11-00; e-mail redaksjonen@sa.no; internet www.sa.no; f. 1929; independent; Editor EIRIK MOE; circ. 15,016.

Skien

Telemarksavisa AS: POB 2833, Kjørbekk, 3702 Skien; tel. 35-58-55-00; fax 35-52-82-09; e-mail redaksjonen@ta.no; internet www.ta.no; f. 1921; independent; Editor OVE MELLINGEN; circ. 22,346.

Varden: POB 2873 Kjørbekk, 3702 Skien; tel. 35-54-30-00; fax 35-52-83-23; e-mail info@varden.no; internet www.varden.no; f. 1874; Conservative; Editor MAJ-LIS STORDAL; circ. 27,341.

Stavanger

Stavanger Aftenblad: POB 229, 4001 Stavanger; tel. 05150; fax 51-89-30-05; e-mail redaksjonen@aftenbladet.no; internet www.aftenbladet.no; independent; f. 1893; Editor-in-Chief TOM HETLAND; circ. 68,010.

Steinkjer

Trønder-Avisa: Hamnegt., 7738 Steinkjer; tel. 74-12-12-00; fax 74-12-13-13; e-mail redaksjonen@t-a.no; internet www.t-a.no; Centre/Liberal; Editor ARVE LØBERG; circ. 23,268.

Tønsberg

Tønsbergs Blad: POB 2003, Postterminalen, 3103 Tønsberg; tel. 33-37-00-00; fax 33-37-30-10; e-mail redaksjonen@tb.no; internet www.tb.no; f. 1870; Conservative; Editor-in-Chief HÅKON BORUD; circ. 30,354.

Tromsø

Nordlys: Rådhusgt. 3, POB 2515, 9272 Tromsø; tel. 77-62-35-00; fax 77-62-35-01; e-mail firmapost@nordlys.no; internet www.nordlys.no; f. 1902; Labour; Editor HANS KRISTIAN AMUNDSEN; circ. 27,647.

Trondheim

Adresseavisen: 7003 Trondheim; tel. 07200; fax 72-50-15-16; e-mail redaksjon@adresseavisen.no; internet www.adressa.no; f. 1767; Editor ROLF DYRNES SVENDSEN; circ. 79,789.

POPULAR PERIODICALS

Allers: Stenersgt. 2, 0107 Oslo; tel. 21-30-10-00; fax 21-30-12-04; e-mail allersredaktion@afj.no; family weekly; Editor-in-Chief ORY BJØRHOVDE; circ. 123,578.

Bedre Helse: 0441 Oslo; tel. 22-58-53-37; fax 22-58-58-79; e-mail ann.brendshoi@hm-media.no; internet www.bedrehelse.com; health; Editor INGVILD HAGEN; circ. 33,219 (2000).

Bonytt: 0441 Oslo; tel. 22-58-56-90; fax 22-58-05-85; e-mail bonytt@hm-media.no; internet www.klikk.no/bonytt; home and furnishing; 14 a year; Editor ANNA KOLBERG; circ. 68,000 (2003).

Byavisa: Munkegt. 66E, 7011 Trondheim; tel. 73-95-49-00; fax 73-99-05-60; e-mail redaksjon@byavisa.no; internet www.byavisa.no; f. 1996; weekly; Editor-in-Chief PAUL JOSTEIN AUNE; circ. 82,000.

Familien: 0441 Oslo; tel. 22-58-57-00; fax 22-58-07-64; e-mail abo-familien@hm-media.no; internet www.familien.no; family fortnightly; Editor-in-Chief IVAR MOE; circ. 151,303 (2002).

Foreldre & Barn: 0441 Oslo; tel. 22-58-50-50; fax 22-58-05-80; e-mail foreldreogbarn@hm-media.no; internet www.foreldreogbarn.no; 11 a year; for parents of young children; Editor EDDA ESPELAND; circ. 59,210 (2000).

Foreldremagasinet: Gullhaugvn 1, 0483 Oslo; POB 5001 Majorstuen, 0301 Oslo; tel. 22-58-55-39; e-mail vibeke.ostelie@hm-media.no; for parents; circ. 20,470 (2000).

Henne: POB 1169 Sentrum, 0107 Oslo; tel. 21-30-10-00; e-mail nettredaksjonen@henne.no; internet www.henne.no; women's; Editor-in-Chief ELLEN ARNSTAD; circ. 45,586.

Hjemmepc: Sandakervn 114B, 0483 Oslo; POB 5001 Majorstuen, 0301 Oslo; tel. 22-58-55-14; e-mail hjemmepc@hm-media.no; internet www.hjemmepc.no; home computers; Editor-in-Chief HALLVARD LUNDE; circ. 28,963 (2003).

Hjemmet: 0441 Oslo; tel. 22-58-50-00; fax 22-58-05-70; e-mail hjemmet@hm-media.no; internet www.hm-media.no; family weekly; Editor-in-Chief LISE HANSEN; circ. 228,313 (2004).

Hytteliv: 0441 Oslo; tel. 22-58-50-00; fax 22-58-58-59; e-mail hytteliv@hm-media.no; internet www.klikk.no/produkthjemmesider/hytteliv; f. 1972; 9 a year; for second-home owners; Editor TURID RØSTE; circ. 55,000 (2002).

I form: Trim.no AS, 6789 Loen; tel. 22-37-30-50; fax 91-38-59-26; e-mail redaksjonen@trim.no; internet www.iform.no; monthly; health and fitness; Editor-in-Chief JENS HENNEBERG; circ. 46,551.

Jærbladet: POB 23, 4349 Bryne; tel. 51-77-99-00; fax 51-48-37-40; internet redaksjon@jbl.no; internet www.jbl.no; 3 days a week; independent; Editor IVAR RUSDAL; circ. 12,477.

KK (Kvinner og Klær): POB 1169 Sentrum, 0107 Oslo; Stenersgt. 2, Oslo; tel. 21-30-10-00; fax 22-63-61-02; e-mail leserservice@kk.no; internet www.kk.no; women's weekly; Editor-in-Chief JUNE TRØNNES HANSSEN; circ. 88,158.

Mann: 0441 Oslo; tel. 22-58-50-00; fax 22-58-05-69; e-mail post@mann.no; internet www.mann.no; men's magazine; Editor-in-Chief ROGER GROENDALEN; circ. 20,000.

Mat & Drikke: Sandakerveien 24D, 0473 Oslo; tel. 90-04-64-40; e-mail olav@matogdrikke.no; internet www.matogdrikke.no; 7 a year; food and wine; Editor-in-Chief LINDAN SANNUM; circ. 23,032.

Norsk Ukeblad: Gullhaugvn 1, 0441 Oslo; tel. 22-58-53-00; fax 22-58-05-69; e-mail nu-tips@hm-media.no; internet www.norskukeblad.no; family weekly; Editor-in-Chief MAJ-LIS STORDAL; circ. 178,119 (2000).

Det Nye: 0441 Oslo; tel. 22-58-50-00; fax 22-58-58-09; e-mail detnye@hm-media.no; internet www.detnye.com; for young women; 14 a year; Editor-in-Chief KRISTIN MA BERG; circ. 72,000.

Programbladet: POB 1151 Sentrum, 0107 Oslo; tel. 22-31-03-10; fax 22-31-04-55; e-mail elins@programbladet.no; internet www.programbladet.no; f. 1946; radio and television weekly; Editor TORGEIR SOLLIEN; circ. 65,000.

Se og Hør: POB 1164 Sentrum, 0128 Oslo; tel. 22-41-51-80; fax 22-41-51-70; f. 1978; news weekly (radio and TV); Editors-in-Chief KNUT HÅVIK, ODD J. NELVIK; circ. 366,887.

Shape-Up: Sørkedalsvn 10A, 0301 Oslo; tel. 22-96-15-00; fax 22-96-13-52; 11 a year; health and beauty; Editor EVA SUNDENE LYNGAAS; circ. 30,986 (2000).

TOPP: POB 481 Sentrum, 0107 Oslo; tel. 21-30-12-28; e-mail vilvite@topp.no; internet www.topp.no; monthly; for young people aged between 10 and 17 years; Editors ODD J. NELVIK, KNUT HÅVIK; circ. 48,011.

Vi Menn: 0441 Oslo; tel. 22-58-50-00; fax 22-58-05-71; e-mail vimenn@hm-media.no; internet www.vimenn.com; f. 1951; men's weekly; Editor-in-Chief AXEL I. WALOE; circ. 92,000.

SPECIALIST PERIODICALS

Alt om Fiske: Gullhaugvn 1, 0483 Olso; POB 5001 Majorstuen, 0301 Oslo; tel. 22-58-55-13; fax 22-58-06-66; e-mail aud.haugvik@hm-media.no; angling; circ. 22,906 (2005).

Barnemagasinet BAM: 0441 Oslo; Gullhaugvn 1, 0483 Oslo; tel. 23-00-81-80; fax 23-00-81-89; e-mail postmaster@bam.no; internet www.bam.no; for expectant and new parents; three additional titles, *BAM Gravid*, *BAM Nyfødt* and *BAM Spedbarn*; circ. 80,000 (2000).

Batmagasinet: POB 1169 Sentrum, 0107 Oslo; tel. 21-30-10-00; fax 21-30-12-59; e-mail hans.due@afj.no; internet www.batmagasinet.no; f. 1985; owned by Aller Familie-journal AS; 12 a year; boating, powerboats; Editor HANS DUE; circ. 28,555.

Bil: POB 9247 Vaterland, 0134 Oslo; tel. 23-03-66-00; fax 23-03-66-40; e-mail bil@bilforlaget.no; internet www.bilnorge.no; 10 a year; motoring; Editor KJELL-MAGNE AALBERGSJØ; circ. 51,388.

Bondebladet: POB 9367 Grønland, 0135 Oslo; tel. 21-31-44-00; fax 21-31-44-01; e-mail post@bondebladet.no; internet www.bondebladet.no; f. 1974; weekly; farming; Editor JON LAURITZEN; circ. 85,593.

Familiens Grønne Gleder: 0441 Oslo; Gullhaugvn 1, 0483 Oslo; tel. 22-58-55-13; fax 22-58-05-06; e-mail aud.haugvik@hm-media.no; gardening; circ. 55,000 (2004).

Fjell og Vidde: Den Norske Turistforening, Youngstorget 1, 0181 Oslo; tel. 40-00-18-68; fax 22-42-64-27; e-mail redaksjonen@turistforeningen.no; internet www.turistforeningen.no; f. 1967; 6 a year; organ of The Norwegian Mountain Touring Assen; Editor HELLE ANDRESEN; circ. 131,000.

Fotball: Sørkedalsvn 10A, 0301 Oslo; tel. 22-96-15-00; fax 22-96-13-52; 8 a year; for football players and spectators; Editor ØYVIND STEEN JENSEN; circ. 98,655.

Gravid: Gullhaugvn 1, 0483 Oslo; POB 5001 Majorstuen, 0301 Oslo; tel. 22-58-55-00; fax 22-58-05-80; e-mail gravid@hm-media.no; internet www.gravid.no; for pregnant women; circ. 15,301 (2000).

Hagen for alle: Nalum., 3294 Stavern; tel. 33-19-56-06; e-mail red-hfa@online.no; internet www.altomtradgard.se/hagen-for-alle; monthly; gardening; Editor HELENE B. ØKSENHOLT; circ. 30,000.

Hundesport: POB 160 Bryn, 0611 Oslo; tel. 21-60-09-00; fax 21-60-09-01; e-mail hundesport@nkk.no; internet www.nkk.no; monthly; for dog-owners; circ. 50,000.

IngeniørNytt AS: POB 164, 1332 Østerås; Nils Lassons vei 5, 1359 Eiksmarka; tel. 67-16-34-99; fax 67-16-34-55; e-mail post@ingeniornytt.no; internet www.ingeniornytt.no; every 2 weeks; engineering, architecture; circ. 65,000.

NORWAY

Jakt & Fiske: POB 94, 1378 Nesbru; tel. 66-79-22-00; fax 66-90-15-87; e-mail jaktogfiske@njff.no; internet www.jaktogfiske.info; monthly; hunting and angling; Editor VIGGO KRISTIANSEN; circ. 76,710.

Jakt, Hund & Våpen: Gullhaugvn 1, 0483 Oslo; POB 5001 Majorstuen, 0301 Oslo; tel. 22-58-55-34; e-mail inger.storodegard@hm-media.no; hunting; circ. 25,908 (2000).

Kampanje: Sandakerv. 116, 0483 Oslo; tel. 22-58-50-00; fax 22-15-40-86; e-mail redaksjon@kampanje.com; internet www.kampanje.com; marketing and media; Editor-in-Chief GLENN Ø. STØLDAL; circ. 11,340 (2000).

Kapital: POB 444 Vinderen 0319 Oslo; tel. 23-29-65-50; fax 23-29-65-51; e-mail wenchew@kapital.no; internet www.hegnar.no; fortnightly; business, management; Editor-in-Chief FINN ØYSTEIN BERGH; circ. 40,000.

Kommuniké: POB 9202, 0134 Oslo; tel. 21-03-36-00; fax 21-03-36-50; f. 1936; 9 a year; organ of Norwegian Confederation of Municipal Employees; Editor AUDUN HOPLAND; circ. 54,000.

Kontor & Finans: POB 14 Røa, 0701 Oslo; tel. 22-52-44-60; fax 22-52-24-80; e-mail ergjerts@sn.no; f. 1977; quarterly; business; Editor THOR O. SANDBERG; circ. 100,000.

LINUXmagasinet: POB 7183 Majorstuen, 0307 Oslo; tel. 23-36-82-00; fax 23-36-82-01; e-mail redaksjonen@linmag.no; internet www.linmag.no; Linux operating system, open-source software; 5 a year; Editor-in-Chief SVEIN ERIK TOSTERUD; circ. 8,000.

Motor: POB 494 Sentrum, 0105 Oslo; tel. 22-34-15-55; fax 22-34-14-90; e-mail redaksjonen@motor.no; internet www.motor.no; monthly; motoring, travel and leisure; Editor SVEIN OLA HOPE; circ. 400,000.

NETTUERK: Lilleiorget 1, 0184 Oslo; tel. 23-06-33-74; fax 23-06-33-66; e-mail harald@lo-media.no; monthly; electricity and electronics; Editor HAROLD OLAU MOEN; circ. 43,500.

Norsk Hagetidend: POB 53 Manglerud, 0612 Oslo; tel. 23-03-16-00; fax 23-03-16-01; e-mail postkasse@hageselskapet.no; internet www.hageselskapet.no; f. 1885; monthly; gardening; Editor BERGLJOT GUNDERSEN; circ. 41,878.

Norsk Landbruk: POB 9303 Grønland, 0135 Oslo; tel. 21-31-44-00; fax 21-31-44-92; e-mail norsk.landbruk@tunmedia.no; internet www.norsklandbruk.no; f. 1882; 22 a year; agriculture, horticulture and forestry; Editor-in-Chief MARIANNE RØHME; circ. 16,172.

Okonomisk Rapport: POB 290 Skøyen, 0213 Oslo; tel. 22-40-41-00; fax 22-40-41-01; e-mail rapport@orapp.no; internet www.orapp.no; business; circ. 24,946 (2000).

PCPro: Sandakervn 114B, 0441 Oslo; POB 5001 Majorstuen, 0301 Oslo; tel. 22-58-59-34; e-mail pcpro@hm-media.no; internet www.pcpro.no; f. 2000; 8 a year; computing; circ. 25,000; Editor-in-Chief KJETIL ENSTAD.

Seilmagasinet: POB 253, 1379 Nesbru; tel. 66-77-40-60; fax 66-77-40-61; e-mail morten.jensen@seilmagasinet.no; internet www.seilmagasinet.no; f. 1975; publ. by MediaNavigering A/S; 10 a year; sailing; Editor MORTEN JENSEN; circ. 14,000.

SKOGeieren: POB 1438 Vika, 0115 Oslo; tel. 22-01-05-50; fax 22-83-40-47; e-mail anders.hals@skog.no; f. 1914; 12 a year; forestry; Editor ANDERS HALS; circ. 46,100.

Snø og Ski: Kongevn 5, 0787 Oslo; tel. 22-92-32-00; fax 22-92-32-50; quarterly; winter and summer sports; Editor KRISTIN MOE KROHN; circ. 42,000.

Teknisk Ukeblad (Technology Review Weekly): POB 5844 Majorstuen, 0308 Oslo; tel. 23-19-93-00; fax 23-19-93-01; e-mail redaksjonen@tu.no; internet www.tu.no; f. 1854; technology, industry, management, marketing and economics journal; Editor-in-Chief TOMMY RUDIHAGEN; circ. 93,542.

Tidsskriftet Sykepleien: POB 456 Sentrum, 0104 Oslo; tel. 22-04-33-04; fax 22-04-33-756; internet www.sykepleien.no; f. 1912; 21 a year; health personnel, nursing; Editor-in-Chief BARTH THOLENS; circ. 69,000.

Tips: Gullhaugvn 1, 0483 Oslo; POB 5001 Majorstuen, 0301 Oslo; tel. 22-58-50-00; fax 22-58-59-19; e-mail firmapost@tips.as; internet www.tips.as; football and betting; circ. 20,000 weekdays, 18,000 weekend (2000).

Utdanning: POB 9191 Grønland, 0134 Oslo; tel. 24-14-20-00; fax 24-14-22-85; e-mail redaksjonen@utdanning.ws; internet www.utdanning.ws; f. 1934; fmrly *Norsk Skoleblad*; weekly; teaching; Editor KNUT HOVLAND; circ. 129,423.

Utsyn: Sinsenvn 25, 0572 Oslo; tel. 22-00-72-00; fax 22-00-72-02; e-mail utsyn@nlm.no; internet www.utsyn.no; 25 a year; organ of Norsk Luthersk Misjonssamband (Norwegian Lutheran Mission); circ. 17,000.

Vi Menn Båt: 0441 Oslo; Gullhaugvn 1, 0483 Oslo; tel. 22-58-50-00; fax 22-58-05-66; e-mail inger.storodegord@hm-media.no; internet www.vimenn.no; f. 1992; 7 a year; boats; Editor MORTEN MUNCH ERICHSEN; circ. 77,000 (2004).

Vi Menn Bil: 0441 Oslo; Gullhaugvn 1, 0483 Oslo; tel. 22-58-50-00; fax 22-58-05-66; e-mail elin.hoslemo@hm-media.no; internet www.vimenn.no; f. 1996; 10 a year; cars; Editor MORTEN MUNCH ERICHSEN; circ. 105,000 (2004).

Vi Menn Fotball: Gullhaugvn 1, 0483 Oslo; POB 5001 Majorstuen, 0301 Oslo; tel. 22-58-55-15; e-mail erika-o.asker@hm-media.no; internet www.vimenn.no; football; circ. 30,000 (2000).

Villmarksliv: 0441 Oslo; tel. 22-58-50-00; fax 22-58-59-59; e-mail knut.brevik@hm-media.no; internet www.villmarksliv.no; f. 1972; monthly; angling, hunting, photography; Editor-in-Chief KNUT BREVIK; circ. 45,600 (2006).

NEWS AGENCIES

Bulls Pressetjeneste A/S: Ebbellsgt. 3, 0179 Oslo; tel. 22-98-26-60; fax 22-20-49-78; e-mail info@bulls.no; internet www.bulls.no; Man. PAUL E. VATNE.

A/S Norsk Telegrambyrå (NTB) (Norwegian News Agency): Akersgt. 55, POB 6817 St Olavs pl., 0130 Oslo; tel. 22-03-44-00; fax 22-20-12-29; e-mail ntb@ntb.no; internet www.ntb.no; f. 1867; Editor-in-Chief PÅL BJERKETVEDT.

PRESS ASSOCIATIONS

Den Norske Fagpresses Forening (Specialized Press Asscn): Akersgt. 41, 0158 Oslo; tel. 24-14-61-00; fax 24-14-61-10.

Mediebedriftenes Landsforening (Norwegian Media Businesses' Asscn): Tollbugt. 27, 0157 Oslo; tel. 22-86-12-00; fax 22-42-26-11; e-mail info@mediebedriftene.no; internet www.mediebedriftene.no; Man. Dir ARVID SAND.

Norsk Journalistlag (Norwegian Union of Journalists): Torggt. 5, 5th Floor, POB 8793 Youngstorget, 0028 Oslo; tel. 22-05-39-50; fax 22-41-33-70; e-mail nj@nj.no; internet www.nj.no; f. 1946; Sec.-Gen. JAHN-ARNE OLSEN; 8,770 mems (2004).

Norsk Presseforbund (Norwegian Press Asscn): Rådhusgt. 17, POB 46 Sentrum, 0101 Oslo; tel. 22-40-50-40; fax 22-40-50-55; e-mail np@presse.no; internet www.presse.no; f. 1910; asscn of newspapermen, editors and journalists; Pres. KJETIL HAANES; Sec.-Gen. PER EDGAR KOKKVOLD.

Publishers

Andresen & Butenschøn A/S: POB 1153 Sentrum, 0107 Oslo; tel. 23-13-92-40; fax 22-33-58-05; e-mail abforlag@abforlag.no.

Antropos Forlag: Josefinesgt. 12, 0351 Oslo; tel. 22-46-03-74; e-mail forlag@antropos.no; internet www.antropos.no.

H. Aschehoug & Co (W. Nygaard): Sehestedsgt. 3, POB 363 Sentrum, 0102 Oslo; tel. 22-40-04-00; fax 22-20-63-95; e-mail epost@aschehoug.no; internet www.aschehoug.no; f. 1872; general non-fiction, fiction, reference, children's, educational, textbooks; Man. Dir WILLIAM NYGÅRD.

Bladkompaniet A/S: Staælfjœra 5, POB 148 Kalbakken, 0902 Oslo; tel. 22-90-24-00; fax 22-90-24-01; e-mail bladkompaniet@bladkompaniet.no; internet www.bladkompaniet.no; f. 1915; general fiction, non-fiction, paperbacks, comics, magazines; Publr CLAUS HUITFELDT; Editorial Dir FINN ARNESEN.

Boksenteret Erik Pettersen & Co A/S: Krusesgt. 11, POB 3125 Elisenberg, 0207 Oslo; tel. 22-54-07-00; fax 22-54-07-07; e-mail bs@boksenteret.no; internet www.boksenteret.no; f. 1999; illustrated, non-fiction, craft, DIY; Man. Dir ERIK PETTERSEN.

Bokvennen Forlag: POB 9017, 0133 Oslo; tel. 22-19-14-25; fax 22-19-14-26; e-mail post@bokvennen.no; internet www.vidarforlaget.no; f. 1989; fiction, essays, biographies; Mans MORTEN CLAUSSEN, JAN M. CLAUSSEN.

F. Bruns Bokhandel og Forlag A/S: Kongensgt. 10–14, 7005 Trondheim; tel. 73-51-00-22; fax 73-50-93-20; f. 1873; local history, technology; Publr FRIDTHJOV BRUN.

Cappelen Akademisk Forlag: POB 350 Sentrum, 0101 Oslo; tel. 21-61-65-00; fax 21-61-72-83; e-mail cafinfo@cappelen.no; internet www.cappelendamm.no; f. 1946; textbooks for universities and colleges, social sciences, law, economics, medicine, health and nursing, educational science, psychology; Publr ESTER MOEN.

Cappelen Damm AS: Mariboesgt. 13, POB 350 Sentrum, 0101 Oslo; tel. 21-61-65-00; fax 22-36-50-40; e-mail web@cappelen.no; internet www.cappelendamm.no; f. 1829; general, educational, popular science, fiction, maps, children's, encyclopaedias; Man. Dir PIP HALLÉN.

Eide Forlag A/S: POB 6050 Postterminalen, 5892 Bergen; tel. 55-38-88-00; fax 55-38-88-01; e-mail post@eideforlag.no; internet www.eideforlag.no; f. 1945; general, children's, textbooks, fiction, non-fiction; Publr TRINE KOLDERUP FLATEN; Man. Dir ROALD FLATEN.

NORWAY

Forlaget Fag og Kultur A/S: St Olavsgt. 12, 0165 Oslo; tel. 23-30-24-00; fax 23-30-24-04; e-mail firmapost@fagogkultur.no; internet www.fagogkultur.no; f. 1987; reference; Man. Dir MARI ETTRE OLSEN.

Fagbokforlaget: Huitfeldtsgt. 15, POB 6050 Postterminalen, 5892 Bergen; tel. 55-38-88-00; fax 55-38-88-01; e-mail fagbokforlaget@fagbokforlaget.no; internet www.fagbokforlaget.no; f. 1992; general and scientific; Publrs ARNO VIGMOSTAD, ARNSTEIN BJØRKE.

Falken Forlag: Helgesens gt. 21, 0553 Oslo; tel. 22-35-54-00; e-mail falkenforlag@falkenforlag.no; internet www.falkenforlag.no; f. 1946; fiction, non-fiction; Publr KIRSTI KRISTIANSEN.

Fonna Forlag: POB 6912 St Olavs pl., 0130 Oslo; tel. 22-20-13-03; fax 22-20-12-01; e-mail fonna@fonna.no; internet www.fonna.no; f. 1934; limited co; general, fiction; Man. Dir ARNT ÅRNES.

Fono Forlag AS: Billingstadsletta 30, POB 169, 1376 Billingstad; tel. 66-84-64-90; fax 66-84-75-07; e-mail mail@fonoforlag.no; internet www.fonoforlag.no; f. 1991; audio books; Gen. Man. HALVOR HANEBORG.

Frifant Forlag A/S: Leinvn 10, 1453 Bjørnemyr; tel. 66-91-29-40; fax 66-91-29-41; e-mail frifor@online.no; internet www.frifant.no; f. 1997.

Genesis Forlag: POB 83, 2027 Kjeller; tel. 63-80-30-99; fax 63-81-69-22; e-mail genesis@genesis.no; internet www.genesis.no; f. 1996; Dir SVEIN ANDERSEN.

John Grieg Forlag A/S: Spelhaugen 20, 5147 Bergen; tel. 55-16-13-44; fax 66-16-13-44; e-mail post@grieg1721.no; internet www.grieg1721.no; f. 1721; children's, art, education, aquaculture; Publr SVEIN SKOTHEIM.

Gyldendal Akademisk: Kristian IVs gt. 13, POB 6730 St Olavs pl., 0130 Oslo; tel. 22-03-43-00; fax 22-03-43-05; e-mail akademisk@gyldendal.no; internet www.gyldendal.no/akademisk; f. 1992; university textbooks; Man. Dir FREDRIK NISSEN.

Gyldendal Norsk Forlag A/S: Sehestedsgt. 4, POB 6860 St Olavs pl., 0130 Oslo; tel. 22-03-41-00; fax 22-03-41-05; internet www.gyldendal.no; f. 1925; general, non-fiction, fiction, biography, religion, cookery, school and university textbooks, children's, manuals; Man. Dir BJØRGUN HYSING.

Hjemmet Mortensen A/S: 0441 Oslo; tel. 22-58-50-00; fax 22-58-50-68; e-mail firmapost@hm-media.no; internet www.hm-media.no; f. 1941; fiction, non-fiction, children's; Man. Dir ANNE BRITT BERENSTEN.

Imprintforlaget A/S: POB 2336 Solli, 0201 Oslo; tel. 23-13-69-30; fax 23-13-69-39; e-mail imprint@imprint.no; internet www.imprint.no; imprints: Omnipax, Pegasus, Unipax; Publr BJØRN SMITH-SIMONSEN.

InfoMediaHuset A/S: POB 382 Sentrum, 0250 Oslo; tel. 21-03-70-01; fax 21-03-70-01; e-mail post@infomediahuset.com; internet infomediahuset.com; f. 1844 as Elanders Forlag; present name adopted 2003; legislation, catalogues; Publr AINA THORSTENSEN.

Kolibri Forlag A/S: POB 44 Øvre Ullern, 0311 Oslo; tel. 92-45-25-29; e-mail post@kolibriforlag.no; internet www.kolibriforlag.no; f. 1982; fantasy, non-fiction, cookery, children's, humour, leisure; Publr ELSE LILL BJØNNES.

Kolon Forlag: Sehestedsgt. 4, POB 6860 St Olavs pl., 0130 Oslo; tel. 22-03-42-02; fax 22-03-41-05; e-mail kolon@gyldendal.no; internet www.kolonforlag.no; f. 1995; modern Norwegian poetry and fiction; Publr TORLEIV GRUE.

Kunnskapsforlaget: Gullhaug Torg 1, POB 4432 Nydalen, 0403 Oslo; tel. 22-02-22-00; fax 22-02-22-99; e-mail resepsjonen@kunnskapsforlaget.no; internet www.kunnskapsforlaget.no; f. 1975; reference books, encyclopaedias, dictionaries, atlases, electronic reference titles; Man. Dir KRISTENN EINARSSON.

Libretto Forlag: Kristian 4 gt. 15, 0164 Oslo; tel. 22-20-42-80; fax 22-20-42-81; e-mail post@librettoforlag.no; internet www.librettoforlag.no; f. 1990; children's, giftbooks and handbooks; Publr TOM THORSTEINSEN.

Lunde Forlag A/S: Sinsenvn 25, 0572 Oslo; tel. 22-00-73-50; fax 22-00-73-73; e-mail post@lundeforlag.no; internet www.lundeforlag.no; f. 1905; religious, general, fiction, children's; Dir INGEBORG EIDSVÅG FREDWALL.

Luther Forlag: Grensen 3, 0159 Oslo; tel. 22-00-87-80; fax 22-00-87-81; e-mail postkasse@lutherforlag.no; internet www.lutherforlag.no; religious, fiction, general; Dir ASLE DINGSTAD.

Lydbokforlaget A/S: Søreggen 2, 7224 Melhus; tel. 72-85-60-70; fax 72-85-60-90; e-mail info@lydbokforlaget.no; internet www.lydbokforlaget.no; f. 1987; owned by H. Aschehoug & Co (33%), Gyldendal Norsk Forlag (33%) and Stiftergruppen (34%).

Messel Forlag: Øvre Vollgate 15, 0158 Oslo; tel. 22-42-14-20; e-mail info@messelforlag.no; internet www.messelforlag.no; f. 1992; Pub. Dir ANNE-GRETHE MESSEL.

NKI Forlaget: Hans Burumsvn 30, POB 111, 1319 Bekkestua; tel. 67-58-88-00; fax 67-58-19-02; f. 1972; textbooks for secondary and technical schools and colleges; Publr JAN B. THOMSEN.

Norsk Bokreidinglag: POB 6045, 5892 Bergen; tel. 55-30-18-99; fax 55-32-03-56; e-mail post@bodonihus.no; internet www.bokreidingslaget.no; f. 1939; fiction, folklore, linguistics, cultural history; Man. FROYDIS LEHMANN.

Det Norske Samlaget: Jens Bjelkesgt. 12, POB 4672 Sofienberg, 0506 Oslo; tel. 22-70-78-00; fax 22-68-75-02; e-mail det.norske@samlaget.no; internet www.samlaget.no; f. 1868; general literature, fiction, poetry, children's, textbooks; Man. Dir NINA REFSETH.

Forlaget Oktober A/S: Kr. Augustsgt. 11, POB 6848 St Olavs pl., 0130 Oslo; tel. 23-35-46-20; fax 23-35-46-21; e-mail oktober@oktober.no; internet www.oktober.no; f. 1970; fiction, politics, social and cultural books; Publr GEIR BERDAHL.

Orion Forlag: Skippergt 33, 0154 Oslo; tel. 24-15-50-90; fax 24-15-50-99; e-mail orion@orionforlag.no; internet www.orionforlag.no; f. 1994; Man. Dir GUNN ELIN SCHMIDT.

Pantagruel Forlag A/S: POB 2370 Solli, 0201 Oslo; tel. 23-27-28-10; e-mail alle@pantagruel.no; internet www.pantagruel.no; Pub. Dir ALEXANDER ELGURÉN.

Pax Forlag A/S: Huitfeldtgt. 15, POB 2336 Solli, 0201 Oslo; tel. 23-13-69-00; fax 23-13-69-19; e-mail pax@pax.no; internet www.pax.no; f. 1964; fiction, non-fiction, feminism, social sciences; Man. Dir BJØRN SMITH-SIMONSEN.

Sambåndet Forlag AS: Vetrlidsalm. 1, 5014 Bergen; tel. 55-31-79-63; fax 55-31-09-44; e-mail vestlandskes.bokhandel@vestbok.no; f. 1945; religion, children's, poetry; Dir TARALD UELAND.

Schibsted Forlagene AS: POB 6974 St Olavs pl., 0130 Oslo; tel. 24-14-68-00; fax 24-14-68-01; e-mail schibstedforlag@schibstedforlag.no; internet www.schibstedforlag.no; f. 2004 by merger of Chr. Schibsteds Forlagene A/S (f. 1839) and other units within Schibsted Group; reference, biographies, handbooks, children's, food and drink, sports, foreign language, guides, fiction, comics; Publishing Dir TOR ERIK SOLBERG.

Skolebokforlaget A/S: Stortingsgt. 30, 0161, Oslo; tel. 22-83-77-05; fax 22-83-38-32; f. 1979; educational; Man. Dir HANS B. BUTENSCHØN; Editor SVERRE MØRKHAGEN.

Snøfugl Forlag: POB 95, 7221 Melhus; tel. 72-87-24-11; fax 72-87-10-13; e-mail snoefugl@online.no; internet www.snoefugl.no; f. 1972; fiction, general; Man. ÅSMUND SNØFUGL.

Solum Forlag A/S: Hoffsvn 18, POB 140 Skøyen, 0212 Oslo; tel. 22-50-04-00; fax 22-50-14-53; e-mail info@solumforlag.no; internet www.solumforlag.no; f. 1973; fiction, human sciences, general; Man. Dir KNUT ENDRE SOLUM.

Spartacus Forlag A/S: POB 2587 Solli, 0203 Oslo; tel. 22-44-56-70; fax 22-44-46-50; e-mail post@spartacus.no; internet www.spartacus.no; f. 1989.

Spektrum Forlag AS: Rosencrantzgt. 22, 0160 Oslo; tel. 22-00-82-60; fax 85-03-64-78; e-mail post@spektrum-forlag.no; internet www.spektrum-forlag.no; f. 1992; Pub. Dir CYRUS BRANTENBERG.

Stabenfeldt A/S: Sothammargeilen 3, 4029 Stavanger; tel. 51-84-54-00; fax 51-84-54-90; f. 1920; general fiction, adventure, reference; Man. Dir JENS OTTO HANSEN.

Tell Forlag A/S: Nilsemarka 5C, 1390 Vollen; tel. 66-78-09-18; fax 66-90-05-72; e-mail tell@tell.no; internet www.tell.no; f. 1987; textbooks and educational books; Man. TELL-CHR. WAGLE.

Tiden Norsk Forlag: Sehestedsgt. 4, POB 6704 St Olavs pl., 0130 Oslo; tel. 23-32-76-60; fax 23-32-76-97; e-mail tiden@tiden.no; internet www.tiden.no; f. 1933; literary fiction, crime, thrillers, fantasy, non-fiction; Pub. Dir RICHARD AARØ.

Tun Forlag A/S: Schweigaardsgt. 34A POB 9303 Grønland, 0135 Oslo; tel. 21-31-44-00; fax 21-31-44-92; e-mail post@tunforlag.no; internet www.boktunet.no; f. 2005; agriculture, hunting, fishing, outdoor, handicrafts, culture, horses, dogs; Editorial Man. HEIDI JANNICKE ANDERSEN.

Universitetsforlaget AS: Sehestedsgt. 3, POB 508 Sentrum, 0105 Oslo; tel. 24-14-75-00; fax 24-14-75-01; e-mail post@universitetsforlaget.no; internet www.universitetsforlaget.no; f. 1950; publishers to the Universities of Oslo, Bergen, Trondheim and Tromsø and various learned societies; school books, university textbooks, specialized journals; Man. Dir SVEIN SKARHEIM.

Verbum Forlag: Bernhard Getzgt. 3, POB 6624 St Olavs pl., 0129 Oslo; tel. 22-93-27-21; fax 22-93-27-27; e-mail verbumforlag@verbumforlag.no; internet www.verbumforlag.no; f. 1820; Christian literature; Man. TURID BARTH PETTERSEN.

Forlaget Vett & Viten AS: Nye Vakås Vn. 56, POB 203, 1379 Nesbru; tel. 66-84-90-40; fax 66-98-39-99; e-mail vv@vettviten.no; internet www.vettviten.no; f. 1987; medical, technical and engineering textbooks; Publr JAN LIEN.

NORWAY

Wigestrand Forlag A/S: POB 621, 4003 Stavanger; tel. 51-51-76-10; fax 51-51-76-40; e-mail forlag@wigestrand.no; internet www.wigestrand.no; Publr ØYVIND WIGESTRAND.

PUBLISHERS' ASSOCIATION

Den norske Forleggerforening (Norwegian Publishers' Asscn): Øvre Vollgt. 15, 0158 Oslo; tel. 22-00-75-80; fax 22-33-38-30; e-mail dnf@forleggerforeningen.no; internet www.forleggerforeningen.no; f. 1895; Chair. GEIR BERDAHL; Man. Dir PER CHRISTIAN OPSAHL; 52 mem. firms.

Broadcasting and Communications

TELECOMMUNICATIONS

Post- og Teletilsynet (Norwegian Post and Telecommunications Authority): Nygård 1, POB 93, 4791 Lillesand; tel. 22-82-46-00; fax 22-82-46-40; e-mail firmapost@npt.no; internet www.npt.no; f. 1987; issues and supervises regulations, concessions and licences; expanded to incorporate postal matters in 1997; Dir-Gen. WILLY JENSEN.

Norkring AS: Telenor Broadcast, 1331 Fornebu; tel. 67-89-20-00; fax 67-89-36-11; internet www.norkring.no; f. 1996; owned by Telenor Broadcast Holding A/S; Dir TORBJOERN TEIGEN.

Telenor ASA: Snarøyvn 30, 1331 Fornebu; tel. 67-89-00-00; e-mail infomaster@telenor.no; internet www.telenor.no; state-owned; Pres. and CEO TORMOD HERMANSEN.

BROADCASTING

Radio

Norsk Rikskringkasting (NRK) (Norwegian Broadcasting Corpn): Bj. Bjørnsons pl. 1, 0340 Oslo; tel. 23-04-70-00; fax 23-04-78-80; e-mail info@nrk.no; internet www.nrk.no; autonomous public corpn; operates three national services (including a youth programme), 18 regional services (including one in the language of the Sámi—Lappish) and an international service, Radio Norway International; Chair. of Govs ANNE CARINE TANUM; Dir-Gen. JOHN G. BERNANDER; CEO (Broadcasting) HANS-TORE BJERKAAS.

P4—Radio Hele Norge ASA: Serviceboks, 2626 Lillehammer; tel. 61-24-84-44; fax 61-24-84-45; e-mail p4@p4.no; internet www.p4.no; f. 1993; private commercial station; Man. Dir KALLE LISBERG.

Television

Norsk Rikskringkasting (NRK) (Norwegian Broadcasting Corpn): Dir of Television HANS-TORE BJERKAAS.

TV-2: Nøstegaten 72, POB 7222, 5020 Bergen; tel. 02255; fax 21-00-60-03; e-mail 02255@tv2.no; internet www.tv2.no; f. 1992; private commercial station; Man. Dir ALF HILDRUM; Dir of Programmes NILS KETIL ANDRESEN.

TV Norge: POB 11, Sentrum, 0101 Oslo; tel. 21-02-20-00; fax 22-05-10-00; e-mail nyheter@tvnorge.no; internet www.tvnorge.no; private satellite television service; Dir-Gen. MORTEN AASS.

Finance

In 2006 there were 15 commercial banks (comprising the major banks, some large regional banks and a number of smaller regional and local banks) and 123 savings banks. There were also 10 publicly financed government banks.

Kredittilsynet (Financial Supervisory Authority of Norway): Østensjøvn 43, POB 100 Bryn, 0611 Oslo; tel. 22-93-98-00; fax 22-63-02-26; e-mail post@kredittilsynet.no; internet www.kredittilsynet.no; f. 1986; finance inspectorate; Dir-Gen. BJØRN SKOGSTAD AAMO.

BANKING

(cap. = capital; res = reserves; dep. = deposits; m. = million; brs = branches; amounts in kroner)

Central Bank

Norges Bank: Bankplassen 2, POB 1179 Sentrum, 0107 Oslo; tel. 22-31-60-00; fax 22-41-31-05; e-mail central.bank@norges-bank.no; internet www.norges-bank.no; f. 1816; holds the exclusive right of note issue; cap. and res 74,124m., dep. 2,065,283m. (Dec. 2006); Chair. of Supervisory Bd MARY KVIDAL; Gov. SVEIN GJEDREM; 12 brs.

Principal Commercial Banks

Bank 1 Oslo AS: Hammersborggt. 2, POB 778 Sentrum, 0106 Oslo; tel. 21-02-50-50; fax 21-02-50-51; e-mail bank1@sparebank1.no; internet www.oslo.sparebank1.no; f. 1898; present name adopted 2000; cap. 291m., res 671m., dep. 15,647m. (Dec. 2006); CEO TORBJØRN VIK; Chair. ELDAR MATHISEN; 10 brs.

DnB NOR Bank ASA (Gjensidige NOR Sparebank ASA): Aker Brygge, Stranden 21, 0021 Oslo; tel. 91-50-30-00; fax 22-48-18-70; internet www.dnbnor.no; f. 2004 by merger of Den norske Bank ASA and Union Bank of Norway; cap. 17,214m., res 28,143m., dep. 892,311m. (Dec. 2006); Chair. OLAV HYTTA; Pres. and CEO SVEIN AASER; 187 brs.

Fokus Bank ASA: Vestre Rosten 77, 7466 Trondheim; tel. 72-88-20-11; fax 72-88-20-61; e-mail fokus@fokus.no; internet www.fokus.no; f. 1987 by merger of Böndernes Bank A/S, Buskerudbanken A/S, Forretningsbanken A/S and Vestlandsbanken; present name adopted 1996; 100% owned by Danske Bank A/S; cap. 2,220m., dep. 88,995m. (Dec. 2005); Chair. SØREN MØLLER NIELSEN; Man. Dir THOMAS BORGEN; 70 brs.

Nordea Bank Norge ASA: Middelthunsgt. 17, POB 1166 Sentrum, 0107 Oslo; tel. 22-48-50-00; fax 22-48-47-49; internet www.nordea.com; fmrly Christiania Bank og Kreditkasse ASA; present name adopted 2001; part of Nordea Bank Group (Sweden); cap. 2,594m., dep. 158,740m. (Dec. 2006); Group Pres. and CEO LARS G. NORDSTRÖM; Man. TOM RUUD.

Nordlandsbanken ASA: Molov. 16, 8002 Bodø; tel. 91-50-89-00; fax 75-55-85-10; e-mail post@nordlandsbanken.no; internet www.nordlandsbanken.no; f. 1893; 100% owned by DnB NOR Bank ASA; cap. 625m., res 780m., dep. 19,639m. (Dec. 2006); Chair. NIKOLAI STEFANOVIC; CEO MORTEN STØVER; 17 brs.

Principal Savings Banks

SpareBank 1 SR-Bank: Bjergsted Terrasse 1, 4001 Stavanger; tel. 91-50-20-02; fax 51-53-54-67; e-mail sr-kundeservice@sr-bank.no; internet www.sr-bank.no; f. 1839 as Egersund Sparebank; merged with 22 savings banks in 1976; present name adopted 2007; cap. 1,131m., res 2,667m., dep. 72,269m. (Dec. 2006); CEO TERJE VAREBERG; 52 brs.

Sparebanken Hedmark: Strandgt. 15, 2302 Hamar; tel. 62-51-20-00; fax 62-53-29-75; e-mail konsern@sparebanken-hedmark.no; internet www.sparebanken-hedmark.no; f. 1845; cap. 3,587m., dep. 30,566m. (Dec. 2006); Chair. RICHARD H. HEIBERG; Man. Dir HARRY KONTERUD; 30 brs.

Sparebanken Midt-Norge: Sondregt. 4, 7467 Trondheim; tel. 73-58-51-11; fax 73-58-64-50; e-mail smn@smn.no; internet www.smn.no; f. 1823 as Trondhjems Sparebank; present name adopted 1985; cap. 1,262m., res 2,225m., dep. 54,963m. (Dec. 2006); Chair. PER AXEL KOCHE; Man. Dir FINN HAUGAN; 75 brs.

Sparebanken Møre: Keiser Wilhelmsgt. 29–33, POB 121, 6002 Alesund; tel. 70-11-30-00; fax 70-12-99-12; e-mail sparebanken.more@sbm.no; internet www.sbm.no; f. 1985; cap. 627m., res 1,417m., dep. 19.800m. (Dec. 2006); Pres. and CEO OLAV-ARNE FISKERSTRAND; 55 brs.

Sparebanken Nord-Norge: Storgt. 65, POB 6800, 9298 Tromsø; tel. 91-50-22-44; fax 77-62-25-71; e-mail snow@snn.no; internet www.snn.no; f. 1989 by merger of Sparebanken Nord and Tromsø Sparebank; cap. 800m., dep. 48,579m. (Dec. 2006); CEO HANS OLAV KARDE; Deputy CEO ODDMUND ÅSEN; 85 brs.

Sparebanken Pluss: Rådhusgt. 7–9, POB 200, 4662 Kristiansand; tel. 38-17-35-00; fax 38-17-35-04; e-mail firmapost@sparebankenpluss.no; internet www.sparebankenpluss.no; f. 1824; merged with four savings banks in 1987; dep. 19,254m., total assets 21,542m. (Dec. 2006); Chair. JENS FREUCHEN; Man. Dir STEIN HANNEVIK.

Sparebanken Sør: Vestervn. 1, POB 602, 4800 Arendal; tel. 37-02-50-00; fax 37-02-41-50; e-mail international@sor.no; internet www.sor.no; f. 1825; cap. and res 2,039m., dep. 23,400m. (Dec. 2006); Chair. ALICIA JERVELL; Man. Dir MORTEN KRAFT; 35 brs.

Sparebanken Vest: Kaigt. 4, 5016 Bergen; tel. 81-52-20-02; fax 55-21-74-10; e-mail sparebanken.vest@spv.no; internet www.spv.no; f. 1823 as Bergens Sparebank; merger 1982 of 25 savings banks; cap. 250m., res 3,230m., dep. 53,519m. (Dec. 2006); Man. Dir STEIN KLAKEGG; 59 brs.

Bankers' Associations

Finansnaeringens Hovedorganisasjon (FNH) (Norwegian Financial Services Asscn): Hansteensgt. 2, POB 2473 Solli, 0202 Oslo; tel. 23-28-42-00; fax 23-28-42-01; e-mail fnh@fnh.no; internet www.fnh.no; f. 2000 by merger of Den norske Bankforening (Nowegian Bankers' Asscn) and Norges Forsikringsforbond (Norwegian Insurance Asscn); 53 mems; Chair. IDAR KREUTZER; Man. Dir ARNE SKAUGE.

Sparebankforeningen i Norge (Savings Banks Asscn): Universitetsgt. 8, St Olavs pl., POB 6772, 0130 Oslo; tel. 22-11-00-75; fax 22-36-25-33; e-mail firmapost@sparebankforeningen.no; internet www.sparebankforeningen.no; f. 1914; Pres. TERJE VAREBERG (Sparebanken Rogaland); Man. Dir ARNE HYTTNES; 123 mems.

NORWAY   *Directory*

STOCK EXCHANGE

Oslo Børs: Tollbugt. 2, POB 460 Sentrum, 0105 Oslo; tel. 22-34-17-00; fax 22-34-19-25; e-mail info@oslobors.no; internet www.oslobors.no; f. 1819; 10% owned by NASDAQ OMX; part of an alliance (Nordic Exchanges—NOREX) with the Copenhagen (Denmark), Reykjavík (Iceland), Helsinki (Finland) and Stockholm (Sweden) Stock Exchanges, launched 1999; Pres. and CEO BENTE A. LANDSNES.

INSURANCE

Assuranceforeningen Skuld: POB 1376 Vika, 0114 Oslo; tel. 22-00-22-00; fax 22-42-42-22; e-mail osl@skuld.com; internet www.skuld.com; f. 1897; mutual, shipowners' protection and indemnity; Chair. ERIK GLØERSEN; Pres. and CEO DOUGLAS JACOBSOHN.

Gjensidige NOR Forsikring: Drammensvn 228, POB 276, 1326 Lysaker; tel. 22-96-80-00; fax 22-96-92-00; e-mail epost@gjensidigenor.no; internet www.gjensidigenor.no; f. 1847; merged with Forenede Norge Forsikring and Forenede Skadeforsikring in 1993; Pres. HELGE KVAMME; CEO LARS AUSTIN.

Nordea Liv AS: POB 7078, 5020 Bergen; tel. 22-48-50-00; fax 55-17-33-80; internet www.nordealink.no; f. by merger of Norske Liv AS and Vesta Liv AS; life insurance; Dir JØRUND VANDVIK.

Uni Storebrand: Håkon VIIs gt. 10, POB 1380 Vika, 0114 Oslo; tel. 22-31-50-50; e-mail international@storebrand.no; internet www.storebrand.no; f. 1991 by merger of Storebrand (f. 1947) and Uni Forsikring (f. 1984); group includes life, non-life and international reinsurance operations; taken over by govt administrators in 1992 and new holding co (Uni Storebrand New) formed, following suspension of payments to creditors; CEO IDAR KREUTZER.

TrygVesta: Folke Bernadottesvei 50, 5020 Bergen; tel. 89-56-35-21; internet www.trygvesta.com; f. 1884; f. as Vesta; bought by Tryg-Baltica in 1999; current name adopted 2002; includes Skadeforsikringsselskapet Vesta A/S (general insurance), Vesta Liv A/S (life insurance), Vesta Finans A/S (financial services); Chair. MIKAEL OLUFSEN; CEO STINE BOSS.

Vital Insurance: Folke Bernadottesvei 40, 5020 Bergen; tel. 55-17-70-00; fax 55-17-86-99; e-mail kundesenter@vital.no; internet www.vital.no; f. 1990 by a merger between NKP Forsikring and Hygea; life and pension insurance; Dir-Gen. TOM RATHKE.

Insurance Association

Finansnaeringens Hovedorganisasjon (Norwegian Financial Services Asscn): (see Bankers' Associations, above).

Trade and Industry

GOVERNMENT AGENCY

Innovasjon Norge (Innovation Norway): Akersgt. 13, POB 448 Sentrum, 0104 Oslo; tel. 22-00-25-00; fax 22-00-25-01; e-mail post@invanor.no; internet www.invanor.no; f. 2004 to replace Norges Turistråd (Norwegian Tourist Board), Norges Eksportråd (Norwegian Trade Council), Statens nærings- og distriktsutviklingsfond (SND-Regional Development Fund) and Statens Veiledningskontor for Oppfinnere (SVO-Government Consultative Office for Inventors); state-owned; operates in all Norwegian counties and more than 30 countries world-wide; Pres. STEINAR OLSEN.

CHAMBERS OF COMMERCE

Bergen Chamber of Commerce and Industry: POB 843, Sentrum, 5807 Bergen; tel. 55-55-39-00; fax 55-55-39-01; e-mail firmapost@bergen-chamber.no; internet www.bergen-chamber.no; f. 1915; Pres. EGIL HERMAN SJURSEN; Man. Dir MARIT WARNCKE.

Oslo Chamber of Commerce: Drammensvn 30, POB 2874 Solli, 0230 Oslo; tel. 22-12-94-00; fax 22-12-94-01; e-mail mail@chamber.no; internet www.chamber.no; Man. Dir LARS-KÅRE LEGERNES.

INDUSTRIAL AND TRADE ASSOCIATION

Norges Skogeierforbund (Norwegian Forest Owners): Roald Amundsensgt. 6, POB 1438 Vika, 0115 Oslo; tel. 23-00-07-50; fax 22-42-16-90; e-mail nsf@skog.no; internet www.skog.no; f. 1913; aims to promote the economic and technical interests of the forest owners, a general forest policy in the interests of private ownership and co-operation between the affiliated asscns; Man. Dir GUDBRAND KVAAL; 38,000 mems.

EMPLOYERS' ASSOCIATIONS

Næringslivets Hovedorganisasjon (Confederation of Norwegian Business and Industry): Middelthunsgt. 27, POB 5250 Majorstua, 0303 Oslo; tel. 23-08-80-00; fax 23-08-80-01; e-mail firmapost@nho.no; internet www.nho.no; f. 1989; rep. org. for industry, crafts and service industries; Pres. JENS ULLTVEIT-MOE; Dir-Gen. FINN BERG-SEN, Jr; c. 18,500 mems who must also belong to one of the 21 affiliated national asscns, chief among which are the following:

Bensinforhandlernes Bransjeforening (BBF) (Petrol Retailers' Organization): POB 5488, Majorstua, 0305 Oslo; tel. 23-08-87-50; fax 23-08-87-51; e-mail bbf@nho.no; internet www.bensinforhandlerne.no; Man. Dir JAN CARHO; 700 mems.

Energibedriftenes Landsforening (EBL) (Electricity Industry Asscn): Sørkedalsveien 6, POB 7184 Majorstua, 0307 Oslo; tel. 23-08-89-00; fax 23-08-89-01; e-mail ebl@ebl.no; internet www.ebl.no; Dir-Gen. STEINAR BYSVEEN.

Fiskeri—og Havbruksnæringens Landsforening (FHL) (Fish and Aquaculture Industries): POB 5471 Majorstua, 0305 Oslo; tel. 23-08-87-30; fax 23-08-87-31; e-mail firmapost@fhl.no; internet www.fhl.no; Dir-Gen. GEIR ANDREASSEN.

NHO Grafisk (Fed. of Graphic Arts Enterprises): Tollbugt. 27, 0369, POB 5495, Majorstua, 0305 Oslo; tel. and fax 23-08-78-70; e-mail hh@nhografisk.no; internet www.nhografisk.no; f. 1906; fmrly Visuell Kommunikasjon Norge; Man. Dir PÅL STEPHENSEN; 240 mems.

NHO Håndverk (Fed. of Craft Industries): POB 5250, Majorstua, 0303 Oslo; tel. 23-08-87-60; fax 23-08-87-63; e-mail handverk@nho.no; internet www.hbl.no; Man. Dir HARRY BJERKENG.

NHO Luftfart (Norwegian Aviation Industry): POB 5474 Majorstua, 0305 Oslo; tel. 23-08-85-70; fax 23-08-85-71; e-mail nholuftfart@nho.no; internet www.nholuftfart.no; Dir TORBJØRN LOTHE.

NHO Mat og Drikke (Fed. of Norwegian Food and Drink Industry): POB 5472 Majorstua, 0305 Oslo; tel. 23-08-87-00; fax 23-08-87-20; e-mail firmapost@nhomd.no; internet www.nhomatodrikke.no; Dir-Gen. KNUT MARONI.

NHO Reiseliv (Norwegian Hospitality Asscn): POB 5465 Majorstua, Essendropsgt. 6, 0305 Oslo; tel. 23-08-86-20; fax 23-08-86-21; e-mail firmapost@nhoreiseliv.no; internet www.nhoreiseliv.no; f. 1997 as Reiselivsbedriftenes Landsforening; present name adopted 2006; Dir-Gen. KNUT ALMQUIST.

NHO Service (Fed. of Service Industries): POB 5473, Majorstua, 0305 Oslo; tel. 23-08-86-50; fax 23-08-86-59; e-mail firmapost@sbl.no; internet www.nhoservice.no; Admin. Dir PETTER FURULUND.

Norges Bilbransjeforbund (NBF) (Asscn of Norwegian Motor Car Dealers and Services): Drammensvn 97, POB 2804 Solli, 0204 Oslo; tel. 22-54-21-00; fax 22-44-10-56; e-mail firmapost@nbf.no; internet www.nbf.no; f. 1962; Admin. Dir SYVER LEIVESTAD.

Norsk Industri (Fed. of Norwegian Industries): POB 7072 Majorstuen, 0306 Oslo; Oscars gt. 20, 0352 Oslo; tel. 22-59-00-00; fax 22-59-00-01; e-mail post@norskindustri.no; internet www.norskindustri.no; f. 2005 by merger of Teknologibedriftenes Landsforening (Fed. of Norwegian Manufacturing Industries) and Prosessindustriens Landsforening (Fed. of Norwegian Process Industries); Chair. RASMUS SUNDE; Man. Dir STEIN LIER-HANSEN; c. 2,000 mems.

Skogbrukets Landsforening (SL) (Forestry Asscn): Roald Amundsensgt. 6, 0161 Oslo; POB 5496, Majorstuen 0305 Oslo; tel. 22-01-05-90; fax 22-83-40-47; e-mail firmapost@skogbruk.no; internet www.skogbruk.no; f. 1928; Man. Dir KNUT BERG.

Transportbedriftenes Landsforening (TL) (Fed. of Norwegian Transport Cos): POB 5477 Majorstua, 0305 Oslo; tel. 23-08-86-00; fax 23-08-86-01; tel. tl@transport.no; internet www.transport.no; Dir-Gen. CHRISTIAN AUBERT.

Bryggeri- og Drikkevareforeningen (Norwegian Breweries and Soft Drink Producers): POB 7087 Majorstua, 0306 Oslo; tel. 23-08-86-96; fax 22-60-30-04; e-mail info@bryggeriforeningen.no; internet www.bryggeri-ogdrikkevareforeningen.no; f. 1901; Man. Dir HALFDAN KVERNELAND OLAFSSON; 21 mems.

Entreprenørforeningen—Bygg og Anlegg (General Contractors): POB 5485 Majorstua, 0305 Oslo; tel. 23-08-75-00; fax 23-08-75-30; e-mail firmapost@ebanett.no; internet www.ebanett.no; Admin. Dir ØIVIND SERERGREN; 220 mems.

Handels- og Servicenæringens Hovedorganisasjon (HSH) (Federation of Commercial and Service Enterprises): Henrik Ibsensgt. 90, POB 2900 Solli, 0230 Oslo; tel. 22-54-17-00; fax 22-06-09-30; e-mail info@hsh-org.no; internet www.hsh-org.no; f. 1990 by merger; 10,400 mem. cos; Pres. CARL OTTO LØVENSKIOLD.

not s/oOljeindustriens Landsforening (OLF) (Oil Industry): Vassbotnen 1, POB 8065, 4068 Stavanger; tel. 51-84-65-00; fax 51-84-65-01; e-mail firmapost@olf.no; internet www.olf.no; Admin. Dir PER TERJE VOLD.

TBL Møbel- og Innredning (Asscn of Norwegian Furnishing Industries): POB 7072 Majorstuen, 0306 Oslo; tel. 22-59-00-00; fax 22-59-00-01; e-mail tbl@tbl.no; Exec. Man. EGIL SUNDET.

Treforedlingsindustriens Bransjeforening (TFB) (Pulp and Paper): Oscarsgt. 20, POB 7772 Majorstuen, 0306 Oslo; tel. 22-59-

NORWAY

00-51; fax 23-08-78-99; e-mail mb@norskindustri.no; internet www.pulp-and-paper.no; Chair. PER A. SOERLIE; 23 mems.

UTILITIES

Electricity

Hafslund ASA: Drammensvn 144, 0277 Oslo; tel. 22-43-50-00; internet www.hafslund.no; f. 1898; electrical generation (nine hydroelectric plants), sales, distribution, safety, installation, security and network infrastructure; Pres. and CEO CHRISTIAN BERG; Chair. CHRISTIAN BRINCH.

Haugaland Kraft: Haukelivegen 25, POB 2015, 5504 Haugesund; tel. 52-70-72-00; fax 52-70-70-10; e-mail kundeservice@haugaland-kraft.no; internet www.haugaland-kraft.no; f. 1998 by merger of Haugesund Energi and Karmsund Kraftlag; Dir OLAV LINGA.

Nedre Eiker Energi: Evjegata 13, POB 153, 3051 Mjøndalen; tel. 32-23-28-70; fax 32-87-72-10.

Nordmøre Energiverk AS: Industrivn 1, POB 2260, 6503 Kristiansund; tel. 71-56-55-00; fax 71-58-15-21; e-mail neas@neas.mr.no; internet www.neas.mr.no; Dir KNUT J. HANSEN.

Nord-Salten Kraftlag AL: POB 70, 8276 Ulvsvåg; tel. 75-77-10-00; fax 75-77-10-01; e-mail firmapost@nordsalten-kraft.no; internet www.nordsalten-kraft.no; f. 1946; Man. Dir ASBJØRN HANSEN.

Nord-Trøndelag Elektrisitetsverk: Sjøfartsgt. 3, 7736 Steinkjer; tel. 75-15-05-70; fax 74-15-04-00; e-mail nte@nte.no; internet www.nte.no; 70,343 customers.

Statkraft AS: POB 200 Lilleaker, 0216 Oslo; tel. 24-06-70-00; fax 24-06-70-01; e-mail info@statkraft.no; internet www.statkraft.no; Pres. and CEO BÅRD MIKKELSEN.

Statnett SF: Husebybakken 28B, POB 5192 Majorstua, 0302 Oslo; tel. 22-52-70-00; fax 22-52-70-01; e-mail firmapost@statnett.no; internet www.statnett.no; national power grid co; supervises and co-ordinates the operation of the entire Norwegian power system, also operates own transmission lines and submarine cables, as well as sub-stations and switching stations; state-owned co under the jurisdiction of the Ministry of Petroleum and Energy; Pres. and CEO ODD HÅKON HOELSÆTER.

Statnett Entreprenør AS: ; fax 22-52-71-80; subsidiary specializing in overseas sales.

Other major production and distribution companies include Akershus Energiverk, Aktieselskapet Tysselfaldene, Aust-Agder kraftverk, Bærum Energi AS, Bergen Lysverker, Elkem AS, Fredrikstad Energiverk AS, Hamar-regionen Energiverk, Hedmark Energi AS, Helgelund Kraftlag A/L, Hydro Energi, Kraftlaget Opplandskraft, Kristiansand Energiverk, Lyse Kraft, Østfold Energiverk, I/S Øvre Otta, Sira-Kvina Kraftselskap, Skiensfjorden komm. kraftselskap, Stavanger Energi, Svelvik Everk, Trønder Energi, Trondheim Energiverk, Troms Kraftforsyning and Vest-Agder Energiverk.

TRADE UNIONS

Landsorganisasjonen i Norge (LO) (Norwegian Confederation of Trade Unions): Folkets Hus, Youngstorget 11, 0181 Oslo; tel. 23-06-10-50; fax 23-06-17-43; e-mail lo@lo.no; internet www.lo.no; f. 1899; Pres. ROAR THEODORSEN; Int. Sec. KARIN BEATE FLÅTHEN; 835,000 mems in 22 affiliated unions (2007).

Member unions include:

Arbeiderbevegelsen Presseforbund (Labour Press Union): POB 8732, Youngstorget, 0028 Oslo; tel. 91-66-39-99; fax 22-41-33-70; f. 1909; Pres. EVA GRØNSETH; 800 mems.

EL & IT Forbundet (Electricians and Information Technology Workers): Youngsgt. 11, 0181 Oslo; tel. 23-06-34-00; fax 23-06-34-01; e-mail firmapost@elogit.no; internet www.elogit.no; f. 1999 by merger of Tele- og Dataforbundet (TD) and Norsk Elektriker- og Kraftstasjonsforbundet (NEKF); Pres. HANS OLAV FELIX; 37,000 mems.

Fagforbundet (Norwegian Union of Municipal and General Employees): POB 7003, St Olavs pl., 0130 Oslo; tel. 23-06-40-00; fax 23-06-40-01; e-mail post@fagforbundet.no; internet www.fagforbundet.no; f. 2003; Pres. JAN DAVIDSEN; 295,000 mems.

Fellesforbundet (The Norwegian United Federation of Trade Unions): Lilletorget 1, 0184 Oslo; tel. 23-06-31-00; fax 23-06-31-01; e-mail fellesforbundet@fellesforbundet.no; internet www.fellesforbundet.no; f. 1988; Pres. KJELL BJØRNDALEN; 160,000 mems.

Fellesorganisasjonen for barnevernpedagoger, sosionomer og vernepleiere (Social Educators and Social Workers): POB 4693 Sofienberg, 0506 Oslo; tel. 23-06-11-70; fax 23-06-11-14; e-mail kontor@fobsv.no; internet www.fobsv.no; f. 1992; Pres. RANDI REESE; Gen. Sec. HANS CHRISTIAN LILLEHAGEN; 23,000 mems.

Forbundet for Ledelse og Teknikk (Engineers and Managers): POB 8906 Youngstorget 11, 0028 Oslo; tel. 23-06-10-29; fax 23-06-10-

17; e-mail postkasse@flt.no; internet www.fltpo.flt.no; f. 1951; Pres. JARLE MOLDE; 18,000 mems.

Handel og Kontor i Norge (Commercial and Office Employees): Youngstorget 11, 0181 Oslo; tel. 22-03-11-80; fax 22-03-12-06; internet www.handelogkontor.no; f. 1908; Pres. STURE ARNTZEN; 61,000 mems.

Industri Energi (IE): Youngstorget 11, 0181 Oslo; tel. 23-06-13-40; fax 22-03-13-60; e-mail oslopost@industrienergi.no; internet www.industrienergi.no; f. 2006; Pres. LEIF SANDE.

Musikernes Fellesorganisasjon (Norwegian Musicians' Union): POB 8806 Youngstorget, 0028 Oslo; tel. 23-06-21-50; fax 23-06-21-51; e-mail mfo@musikerorg.no; internet www.musikerorg.no; f. 2001; Pres. ANNETT KLEM; 6,900 mems.

Norges Offiserforbund (Norwegian Military Officers): Møllergt. 10, 0179 Oslo; tel. 22-03-15-72; fax 22-03-15-77; f. 1978; Pres. PETER ANDRE MOE; 4,527 mems.

Norsk Arbeidsmandsforbund (Norwegian General Workers): POB 8704, Youngstorget, 0028 Oslo; tel. 23-06-10-50; fax 23-06-10-92; e-mail norsk@arb-mand.no; internet www.arbeidsmandsforbundet.no; f. 1895; Pres. ERNA C. DYNGE; 31,000 mems.

Norsk Fengsels-og-Friomsorgsforbund (Norwegian Prison and Probation Officers): Møllergt. 10, 0179 Oslo; tel. 23-06-15-65; fax 22-42-46-48; e-mail nff@loit.no; internet www.fengselogfriomsorg.no; f. 1918; Pres. GEIR BJØRKLI; 3,000 mems.

Norsk Jernbaneforbund (Norwegian Railway Workers): Møllergt. 10, 0179 Oslo; tel. 23-06-10-50; fax 23-06-13-85; e-mail njf@njf.no; internet www.njf.no; f. 1892; Pres. KJELL BRUNBORG; 19,920 mems.

Norsk Lokomotivmannsforbund (National Union of Norwegian Locomotive Workers): Svingen 2, 0196 Oslo; tel. 23-30-21-10; fax 23-30-21-11; e-mail nlf@lokmann.no; internet www.lokmann.no; f. 1893; Pres. ØYSTEIN ASLAKSEN; 1,215 mems.

Norsk Næring- og Nytelsesmiddelforbund (Norwegian Food and Allied Workers): POB 8719 Youngstorget, 0028 Oslo; tel. 23-10-29-60; fax 23-10-29-61; e-mail firmapost@nnn.no; internet www.nnn.no; f. 1923; Pres. JAN-EGIL PEDERSEN; 30,262 mems.

Norsk Post- og Kommunikasjonsforbund (Norwegian Union of Postal and Communications Workers): Møllergt. 10, 0179 Oslo; tel. 23-06-22-90; fax 22-42-74-86; e-mail postkom@postkom.no; internet www.postkom.org; f. 2000; Pres. ODD-CHRISTIAN ØVERLAND; 22,000 mems.

Norsk Sjømannsforbund (Norwegian Seamen): POB 2000, Vika, 0125 Oslo; tel. 22-82-58-00; fax 22-33-66-18; e-mail firmapost@sjomannsunion.no; internet www.sjomannsforbundet.no; f. 1910; Pres. JACQUELINE SMITH; 11,500 mems.

Norsk Tjenestemannslag (Norwegian Civil Service Union): Møllergt. 10, 0179 Oslo; tel. 23-06-15-99; fax 23-06-15-55; e-mail post@ntl.no; internet www.ntl.no; f. 1947; Pres. TURID LILLEHEIE; 47,000 mems.

Norsk Transportarbeiderforbund (Norwegian Transport Workers): Hammersborg Torg 3, 0179 Oslo; tel. 23-06-27-40; fax 23-06-27-41; e-mail ntf@transportabeider.no; internet www.transportabeider.no; f. 1896; Pres. ANNE RØNNINGSBAKK; 19,000 mems.

Norsk Treindustriarbeiderforbund (Norwegian Wood Workers): Youngstorget 11, 0181 Oslo; tel. 23-06-13-90; fax 23-06-13-95; e-mail ntafpost@ntaf.no; internet www.ntaf.no; f. 1904; Pres. OLE-KRISTIAN PAULSEN; 4,241 mems.

Skolenes Landsforbund (School Employees): POB 8783, Youngstforgt, 0028 Oslo; tel. 23-06-13-62; fax 23-06-13-83; e-mail skolenes@skolenes.no; internet www.skoleneslandforbund.no; f. 1982; Pres. STEIN GRØTTING; 3,466 mems.

Statstjenestemannskartellet (Government Employees): Møllergt. 10, 0179 Oslo; tel. 23-06-10-53; fax 22-42-00-75; e-mail lostat@lostat.no; internet www.lostat.no; f. 1939; Pres. MORTEN ØYE; 105,867 mems.

Yrkesorganisasjonenes Sentralforbund (YS) (Confed. of Vocational Unions): Brugt. 19, 0134 Grønland; tel. 21-01-36-00; fax 21-01-37-20; e-mail post@ys.no; internet www.ys.no; f. 1977; Pres. TORE EUGEN KVALHEIM; 242,000 mems in 19 affiliated unions.

Transport

RAILWAYS

At 31 December 2005 there were 4,087 km of state railways (standard gauge), of which 2,528 km were electrified.

Jernbaneverket (JBV) (Norwegian National Rail Administration): Stortovet 7, POB 4350, 2308 Hamar; tel. 22-45-50-00; fax 22-45-54-99; e-mail dsft@jbv.no; internet www.jernbaneverket.no;

f. 1996; manages railway infrastructure; Dir-Gen. SVEIN HORRISLAND.

Norges Statsbaner AS (NSB) (Norwegian State Railways): Prinsensgt. 7–9, 0048 Oslo; tel. 23-15-00-00; fax 23-15-33-00; internet www.nsb.no; f. 1854 as private line; govt-owned; Chair. INGEBORG MOEN BORGERUD; CEO EINAR ENGER.

ROADS
In 2006 there were 92,863 km of public roads in Norway, of which 717 km were motorways and 27,274 km were national main roads. In 2005 a new bridge linking Norway and Sweden was opened in Svinesund.

Vegdirektoratet: Brynsengfaret 6A, POB 8142 Dep., 0033 Oslo; tel. 22-07-35-00; fax 22-07-37-68; e-mail firmapost@vegvesen.no; internet www.vegvesen.no; f. 1864; Dir TERJE MOE GUSTAVSEN.

SHIPPING
At 31 December 2006 the Norwegian merchant fleet numbered 2,078 vessels, with a combined displacement of 18.2m. grt. The total includes vessels on the Norwegian International Ship Register (established in 1987), which numbered 617 vessels at 31 December 2006, with a combined displacement of 14.8m. grt. The Norwegian-controlled fleet represents some 5% of the world's total fleet.

Port Authorities

Ålesund: Ålesund Havn KF, Skansekaia, 6002 Ålesund; tel. 70-16-34-00; fax 70-16-34-01; e-mail post@alesund.havn.no; internet www.alesund.havn.no.

Bergen: Bergen & Omland Havnevesen, Slottsgt. 1, 5003 Bergen; tel. 55-56-89-50; fax 55-56-89-86; e-mail bergen.havn@bergen-kommune.telemax.no; internet www.bergenhavn.no; Harbour Master GUNVALD ISAKSEN.

Bodø: Bodø Havnevesen, POB 138, 8001 Bodø; tel. 75-58-15-80; fax 75-58-39-90; e-mail firmapost@bodo-havnevesen.no; Harbour Master TERJE DOKSRØD.

Borg Harbour: Borg Havnevesen, Oravn 27, POB 1205 Gamle, 1631 Fredrikstad; tel. 69-35-89-00; fax 69-35-89-20; e-mail borghavnevesen@borghavn.of.no; Port Capt. SVEN-JAN JOHANSEN.

Flekkefjord: Flekkefjord Havnevesen, Eschebrygga, 4400 Flekkefjord; tel. 38-32-89-90; fax 38-32-89-91; e-mail post@flekkefjord.kommune.no; internet flekkefjord.kommune.no; Harbour Master HELGE NILSEN.

Flora Hamn og Næring KF: POB 17, 6901 Florø; tel. 57-75-67-40; fax 57-74-09-16; e-mail hamn@flora.kommune.no; internet www.flora.kommune.no; Harbour Master NILS ARILD HOVLAND.

Grenland: Grenland Havnevesen, POB 20, 3951 Brevik; tel. 35-93-10-00; fax 35-93-10-11; e-mail ghv@grenland-havn.no; internet www.port.of.grenland.com; Port Capt. TORJUS JOHNSEN.

Halden: Halden Havnevesen, Wiels Pass 4, 1771 Halden; tel. 69-17-48-30; fax 69-17-46-83; e-mail post@haldenhavn.no; internet www.haldenhavn.no; Harbour Master ØYVIND JOHANNESSEN.

Hammerfest: Hammerfest Havnevesen, POB 123, 9615 Hammerfest; tel. 78-40-74-00; fax 78-40-74-01; e-mail harbour@hammerfest.havn.no; internet www.hammerfest.havn.no; f. 1828; Harbour Master ROLL STIANSEN.

Haugesund: Karmsund Interkommunale Havnevesen, Garpaskjaerskaien, POB 186, 55001 Haugesund; tel. 52-70-37-50; fax 52-70-37-69; e-mail post@karmsund-havn.no; internet www.karmsund-havn.no.

Horten: Borre Havnevesen, POB 167, 3192 Horten; tel. 33-03-17-17; fax 33-04-47-27; tel. horten.havnevesen@horten.kommune.no; internet www.hortenhavn.no; Harbour Master HANS CHRISTIAN GUNNENG.

Kirkenes: Municipality of Sør-Varanger, Rådhusplassen, POB 406, 9915 Kirkenes; tel. 78-97-74-99; fax 78-97-75-89; e-mail post@kirkenes-havn.no; internet www.kirkenes-havn.no.

Kopervik: Karmsund Havnevesen, POB 134, 4291 Kopervik; tel. 52-84-43-00; fax 52-84-43-10; e-mail postmattak@karmsund-havn.no; internet www.karmsund-havn.no; Harbour Master O. E. MAELAND.

Kragerø: Board of Harbour Commissioners, POB 158, 3791 Kragerø; tel. 35-98-17-50; fax 35-99-13-34; e-mail post@kragero-havnevesen.no; Harbour Master Capt. BORGAR F. THORSEN.

Kristiansand: Kristiansand Havn KF, Gravane 4, 4661 Kristiansand; tel. 38-00-60-00; fax 38-02-70-99; e-mail post@kristiansand-havn.no; internet www.kristiansand-havn.no; Port Dir STEIN E. HAARTVEIT.

Kristiansund: Kristiansund og Nordmøre Havn IKS, Kaibakken 1, 6509 Kristiansund; tel. 40-00-65-04; fax 71-67-14-83; e-mail info@knhavn.no; internet www.knhavn.no; Harbour Master JAN OLAV BJERKESTRAND.

Larvik: Larvik Havn KF, POB 246 Sentrum, Havnegt. 5, 3251 Larvik; tel. 33-16-57-50; fax 33-16-57-59; e-mail post@larvik.havn.no; internet www.larvik.havn.no; Port Dir JAN FREDRIK JONAS.

Malm: Fosdalens Bergverks Aktie, 7720 Malm; tel. 74-15-71-00; fax 74-15-78-76; Agent OLAV VAARDAL.

Mandal Port of Agder: Mandal Havnevesen KF, POB 905, 4509 Mandal; tel. 40-00-51-52; fax 38-26-34-76; e-mail mandalhavn@mandal.kommune.no; internet www.mandal-kommune.no/mandalhavn; Harbour Master JONNY O. HANSEN.

Mongstad: Statoil Mongstad, 5954 Mongstad; tel. 56-34-40-00; fax 56-34-47-29; e-mail jja@statoil.com; internet www.statoil.com/mongstad; Port Capt. JON M. JAKOBSEN.

Mosjøen: Mosjøen Havnevesen, Mosjøen 8663; tel. 75-10-18-70; fax 75-10-18-71; e-mail torbjorn.jorgensen@vefsn.kommune.no; Port Man. GUNNAR JOHANSEN.

Moss: Moss Havnevesen, Moss Maritime Centre, POB 118, 1501 Moss; tel. 69-20-87-00; fax 69-20-87-01; e-mail firmapost@moss-havn.no; internet www.moss-havn.no; Harbour Master REIDAR MAGNUS HANSEN.

Narvik: Narvik Havn KF, POB 627, 8508 Narvik; tel. 76-95-03-70; fax 76-95-03-84; e-mail post@narvikhavn.no; internet www.portofnarvik.com; Port Man. RUNE J. ARNØY.

Odda: Odda Havnevesen, Opheimsgt 31, 5750 Odda; tel. 53-64-84-00; fax 53-64-12-92; e-mail svenn.berglie@odda.kommune.no; Harbour Master OLAV BJØERKE.

Orkanger: Orkanger Havnevesen, 7300 Orkanger; tel. 72-48-00-09; fax 72-48-10-03; e-mail tom.hamborg@orkdal.kommune.no; Port Man. TOM HAMBORG.

Oslo: Oslo Havnevesen, POB 230 Sentrum, 0103 Oslo 1; tel. 81-50-06-06; fax 23-49-26-01; e-mail postmottak@havnevesenet.oslo.kommune.no; internet www.ohv.oslo.no; Port Dir ANNE SIGRID HAMRAN.

Risør: Risør Havnekontor, 4950 Risør; tel. 37-15-05-00; fax 37-15-00-58; Agent KJELL SKARHEIM.

Sandefjord: Sandefjord Havnevesen, Tollbugt. 5, 3200 Sandefjord; tel. 33-45-60-38; fax 33-46-26-13; e-mail info@visitsandefjord.com; internet www.cruisesandefjord.com; Harbour Master LEIF ALLUM.

Sauda: Sauda Havnekontor, 4200 Sauda; tel. 52-78-62-72; fax 52-78-15-65; Harbour Master OEYSTEIN TVEIT.

Stavanger: Stavanger Interkommunale Havn IKS, Nedre Strandgt. 51, 4005 Stavanger; tel. 51-50-12-00; fax 51-50-12-22; e-mail info@stavanger.havn.no; internet www.stavanger.havn.no; Port Dir BJØRN HELGOY.

Tønsberg: Tønsberg Havnevesen, Nedre Langgate 36, 3126 Tønsberg; tel. 33-35-45-00; fax 33-33-26-75; e-mail tonsberg.havn@tonsberg.havn.no; internet www.tonsberghavn.no; Harbour Master PER SVENNAR.

Tromsø Havn KF: Tromsø Havnevesen, POB 392, 9254 Tromsø; tel. 77-66-18-50; fax 77-66-18-51; e-mail adm@tromso.havn.no; internet www.tromso.havn.no; f. 1827; Port Capt. HALVAR PETTERSEN.

Trondheim: Trondheim Havn, Pirsenteret, 7462 Trondheim; tel. 73-99-17-00; fax 73-99-17-17; fax firmapost@trondheim.havn.no; internet www.trondheim.havn.no; Port Capt. SIGURD KLEIVEN.

Vardø: Vardø Havn KF, POB 50, 9951 Vardø; tel. 78-98-72-76; fax 78-98-78-28; tel. vardhavn@online.no; internet www.vardoport.no; Harbour Master INGOLF ERIKSEN.

Shipping Organizations

Nordisk Skibsrederforening (Nordisk Defence Club): Kristinelundvn 22, POB 3033 Elisenberg, 0207 Oslo; tel. 22-13-56-00; fax 22-43-00-35; e-mail post@nordisk.no; internet www.nordisk.no; f. 1889; Pres. MORTEN WERRING; Man. Dir GEORG SCHEEL.

Norges Rederiforbund (Norwegian Shipowners' Asscn): POB 1452 Vika, 0116 Oslo; tel. 22-40-15-00; fax 22-40-15-15; e-mail post@rederi.no; internet www.rederi.no; f. 1909; Dir-Gen. MARIANNE LIE.

Norsk Skipsmeglerforbund (Norwegian Shipbrokers' Asscn): Fr. Nansens pl. 9, 0160 Oslo; tel. 22-20-14-85; fax 22-42-74-13; e-mail mail@shipbroker.no; internet www.shipbroker.no; f. 1919; Pres. HARALD B. SANDER; Gen. Man. GRETE C. NOER; 150 mems.

Det Norske Veritas (DNV): Veritasvn 1, POB 300, 1322 Høvik; tel. 67-57-99-00; f. 1864; global provider of services for managing risk; acts on behalf of 130 national maritime authorities; CEO HENRIK O. MADSEN.

Rederienes Landsforening (Federation of Norwegian Coastal Shipping): Essendropsgt. 6, POB 5201 Majorstua, 0302 Oslo; tel. 23-08-85-60; fax 23-08-85-61; e-mail rlf@rlf.no; internet www.rlf.no; Admin. Dir HARALD THOMASSEN.

NORWAY

Principal Companies

Actinor Shipping ASA: Rådhusgt. 27, 0158 Oslo; tel. 22-42-78-30; fax 22-42-72-04; Pres. ALF OLSEN.

Bergshav Management AS: POB 8, 4891 Grimstad; tel. 37-25-63-00; fax 37-25-63-01; e-mail mgmt@bergshav.com; internet www.bergshav.com; Chair. ATLE BERGSHAVEN.

Bona Shipping AS: Rådhusgt. 27, POB 470 Sentrum, 0105 Oslo; tel. 22-31-00-00; fax 22-31-00-01; internet www.bona.no; Pres. RAGNAR BELCK-OLSEN.

BW Gas ASA: Drammensvn 106, POB 2800 Solli, 0204 Oslo; tel. 22-12-05-05; fax 22-12-05-00; e-mail bwgas@bwgas.com; internet www.bwgas.com; f. 1935; fmrly Bergesen d.y. ASA; Chair. MORTEN SIG. BERGESEN; Man. Dir SVEIN ERIK AMUNDSEN.

Grieg Shipping A/S: POB 781, 5804 Bergen; tel. 55-57-66-00; fax 55-57-68-55; internet www.grieg.no; Chair. ELISABETH GRIEG.

Leif Høegh & Co ASA: Wergelandsvn 7, POB 2596 Solli, 0203 Oslo; tel. 22-86-97-00; fax 22-20-14-08; e-mail ihc@hoegh.no; internet www.hoegh.no; f. 1927; vessels for the transport of liquefied gas, ores and other bulk materials, car and ro-ro ships and reefers; world-wide services; Chair. WESTYE HØEGH; Pres. THOR J. GUTTORMSEN.

Jahre-Wallem AS: Strandpromenaden 9, POB 271, 3201 Sandefjord; tel. 33-48-44-44; fax 33-48-44-43; e-mail jawa@jawa.no; Dir HENRIK LIAN.

Jebsens Management A/S: POB 4145 Dreggen, 5015 Bergen; tel. 55-31-03-20; fax 55-31-72-70; f. 1929; services in Scandinavia, and to Europe, Far East, Australia, the Americas; Owner ATLE JEBSEN.

Torvald Klaveness & Co AS: Harbitzalleen 2A, POB 182 Skøyen, 0212 Oslo; tel. 22-52-60-00; fax 22-50-67-31; e-mail management@klaveness.com; internet www.klaveness.com; Chair. TOM ERIK KLAVENESS; Man. Dir TROND HARALD KLAVENESS.

Knutsen OAS Shipping A/S: Smedasundet 40, POB 2017, 5504 Haugesund; tel. 52-70-40-00; fax 52-70-40-40; e-mail firmapost@knutsenoas.com; internet www.knutsenoas.com; Man. JENS ULLTVEIT MOE.

A/S J. Ludwig Mowinckels Rederi: Bradbenken 1, POB 4070 Dreggen, 5835 Bergen; tel. 55-21-63-00; fax 55-21-63-05; e-mail mailbox@jlmr.no; internet www.jlmr.no; f. 1898; tankers and cargo services; Man. Dir BØRGE ROSENBERG.

Norbroker Shipping & Trading A/S: POB 34, 4401 Flekkefjord; Strandgt. 36, 4400 Flekkefjord; tel. 38-32-61-00; fax 38-32-61-01; e-mail drycargo@norbroker.no; internet www.norbroker.no; Man. Dir ARNT IVAR BJOERNELI.

Odfjell ASA: Conrad Mohrsveg 29, 5892 Bergen; POB 6101 Postterminalen, 5892 Bergen; tel. 55-27-00-00; fax 55-28-47-41; e-mail bgo.mail@odfjell.com; internet www.odfjell.no; f. 1916; transportation and storage of liquid chemicals; Chair. BERNT DANIEL ODFJELL.

Fred. Olsen Marine Services AS: Prinsensgt. 2B, POB 374 Sentrum, 0101 Oslo; tel. 22-34-11-00; fax 22-42-13-14; e-mail foms@foms.no; internet www.fredolsen-marine.com; Man. Dir LEIF LAURITZEN.

OSM Ship Management AS (frmly Rasmussen Maritime Services AS): POB 69, 4661 Kristiansand; tel. 38-04-12-00; fax 38-04-12-01; e-mail osm.krs@osm.no; internet www.osm.no; part of OSM Group; Man. Dir OIVIND STAERK.

Det Stavangerske Dampskibsselskab: POB 848, 4004 Stavanger; tel. 51-84-56-00; fax 51-84-56-01; e-mail mail@dsd-shipping.no; tel. www.dsd-shipping.no; Chair. HENRIK AGER-HANSSEN.

Uglands Rederi A/S: POB 128, 4891 Grimstad; tel. 37-29-26-00; fax 37-04-47-22; e-mail jjuc@jjuc.no; internet www.jjuc.no; f. 1930; part of J. J. Ugland Cos (f. 1996; group of cos with shipping interests; tankers, bulk carriers, crane vessel, barges).

Anders Wilhelmsen & Co AS: Beddingen 8, Aker Brygge, POB 1583 Vika, 0118 Oslo; tel. 22-01-42-00; fax 22-01-43-72; e-mail thagen@awilco.no; Chair. ARNE WILHELMSEN; Man. Dir ENDRE ORDING SUND.

Wilh. Wilhelmsen ASA: Strandvn 20, POB 33, 1324 Lysaker; tel. 67-58-40-00; fax 67-58-40-80; e-mail ww@wilhelmsen.com; internet www.wilhelmsen.com; f. 1861; regular fast freight services worldwide; Chair. WILHELM WILHELMSEN; Man. Dir INGAR SKAUG.

CIVIL AVIATION

In 2007 there were 46 scheduled airports in Norway, the principal international airport being Gardermoen Airport, 47 km north of Oslo. The airport at Gardermoen opened in October 1998, replacing the previous principal international airport, Fornebu Airport, which ceased operations in the same month.

Avinor AS: POB 150, 2061 Gardermoen; Christian Fredrikspl. 6, 0154 Oslo; tel. 81-53-05-50; fax 67-03-00-01; e-mail post@avinor.no; internet www.avinor.no; f. 2003; state-owned; owns and operates 46 airports in Norway and responsible for air traffic control services; Chair. INGE K. HANSEN; Dir-Gen. SVERRE QUALE.

Luftfartstilsynet (Civil Aviation Authority): POB 243, 8001 Bodø; tel. 75-58-50-00; fax 75-58-50-05; e-mail postmottak@caa.no; internet www.caa.no; f. 2000; independent administrative body under the Ministry of Transport and Communications; Dir-Gen. HEINE RICHARDSEN.

Principal Airlines

SAS Norge ASA (SAS Norway): 0800 Oslo; tel. 64-81-77-00; fax 67-58-78-77; internet www.sas.no; f. 2004; wholly-owned subsidiary of the Scandinavian Airlines System (SAS) Group; Chair. HARALD NORVIK; Gen. Man. JOERGEN LINDEGAARD.

Braathens SAFE (Braathens South-American & Far East Airtransport) ASA: Oksenøyvn 3, POB 55 Lufthavn-Fornebu, 1330 Oslo Airport; tel. 67-59-70-00; fax 67-59-13-09; internet www.braathens.no; f. 1946; scheduled airline and charter co; domestic routes: all main cities in Norway and Longyearbyen, Svalbard; international routes within Europe; Pres. ERIK G. BRAATHEN; Chair. LARS A. CHRISTENSEN.

Norwegian Air Shuttle: Oksenøyvn 10, POB 115 Oslo Lufthavn, 1331 Oslo; tel. 67-59-30-00; fax 67-59-30-01; e-mail post@norwegian.no; internet www.norwegian.no; f. 1966; present name since 1993; charter and contract flights; CEO BJØRN KJOS.

Scandinavian Airlines System (SAS): Head Office: Snarøyvn 57, 0080 Oslo; tel. 64-81-60-50; e-mail cr@sas.no; internet www.sas.no; f. 1946; the national carrier of Denmark, Norway and Sweden; consortium owned two-sevenths by SAS Danmark A/S, two-sevenths by SAS Norge ASA and three-sevenths by SAS Sverige AB; parent org. 50% owned by the Govt and 50% by private shareholders; SAS group includes the consortium and the subsidiaries in which the consortium has a majority or otherwise controlling interest; the Board consists of two members from each of the parent cos and the chairmanship rotates among the three national chairmen on an annual basis; strategic alliance with Lufthansa (Germany) formed in 1995; Chair. FRITZ H. SCHUR; Pres. and CEO MATS JANSSON.

Widerøe's Flyveselskap AS: Langstranda 6, POB 257, 8001 Bodø; tel. 75-51-35-00; fax 75-51-35-81; e-mail kundservice@wideroe.no; internet www.wideroe.no; f. 1934; scheduled domestic service; Pres. PER ARNE WATLE.

Widerøe Norsk Air: POB 2047, 3202 Sandefjord; tel. 33-46-98-80; fax 33-47-03-25; f. 1961; acquired by Widerøe in 1989; regional services in Scandinavia; Technical Dir JAN RUNE NORDGARD.

Tourism

Norway is a popular resort for tourists who prefer holidays in rugged, peaceful surroundings. It is also a centre for winter sports. In 2005 receipts from tourism amounted to US $3,844m., compared with $3,455m. in the previous year. In 2005 visitor arrivals totalled 4.8m.

Innovasjon Norge (Innovation Norway): Akersgt 13, POB 448 Sentrum, 0104 Oslo; tel. 22-00-25-00; fax 22-00-25-01; e-mail post@invanor.no; internet www.visitnorway.com; f. 2004 to replace Norges Turistråd (Norwegian Tourist Board), Norges Eksportråd (Norwegian Trade Council), Statens nærings- og distriktsutviklingsfond (SND-Regional Development Fund) and Statens Veiledningskontor for Oppfinnere (SVO-Government Consultative Office for Inventors); state-owned; operates in all Norwegian counties and more than 30 countries world-wide; Pres. STEINAR OLSEN.

NORWEGIAN EXTERNAL TERRITORIES
SVALBARD

Introductory Survey

Location and Climate

The Svalbard archipelago is the northernmost part of the Kingdom of Norway. It lies in the Arctic Sea, 657 km north of mainland Norway, between latitudes 74°N and 81°N and longitudes 10°E and 35°E, comprising a total area of 61,022 sq km (23,561 sq miles). The group consists of nine principal islands, Spitsbergen (formerly Vestspitsbergen), the main island, Kvitøya, Edgeøya, Barentsøya, Nordaustlandet, Prins Karls Forland, Kong Karls Land, Hopen and Bjørnøya (Bear Island), some 204 km to the south of the main island, together with numerous small islands. Mild Atlantic winds lessen the severity of the Arctic climate, but almost 60% of the land area is covered with glaciers. Average temperatures range from −16°C (3°F) to 6°C (43°F), and precipitation in the lowlands averages some 200 mm per year.

History and Government

The existence of Svalbard has probably been known since Viking exploration in the 12th century. There were conflicting claims to sovereignty by Britain, the Netherlands and Denmark-Norway in the 17th century, when the area was an important centre for whale hunting, but interest subsequently lapsed until the early years of the 20th century, when coal deposits were discovered. On 9 February 1920 14 nations signed a treaty recognizing Norwegian sovereignty over Svalbard. International rights of access and economic exploitation were agreed, but the use of the islands for bellicose purposes and the construction of fortifications were expressly forbidden.

Svalbard has been part of the Kingdom of Norway since it was formally incorporated in 1925. The territory is administered by a Sysselmann (Governor), resident at Longyearbyen, on Spitsbergen, which is the administrative centre of the archipelago. The Sysselmann is responsible to the Polar Department of the Ministry of Justice and the Police. The Norwegian Polar Institute acts in an advisory capacity to the administration. Svalbard lies within the same judicial jurisdiction as the city of Tromsø.

In accordance with the Svalbard Treaty of 1920, the Norwegian Government prescribed a mining code in 1925, regulating all mineral prospecting and exploitation in the islands and their territorial waters extending to 4 nautical miles (7.4 km). The Mining Code is administered by a Commissioner of Mines.

In 1941 the population was evacuated by Allied forces for the duration of the war, and three years later the USSR, to which Svalbard was of considerable strategic interest, unsuccessfully sought Norway's agreement to a revision of the 1920 treaty whereby part of the archipelago would become a Soviet-Norwegian condominium. Russia currently maintains a helicopter station and a mobile radar station adjoining its coal-mining settlement at Barentsburg on Spitsbergen. Russia (and, before it, the USSR) has refused to recognize Norway's unilateral declaration of a fisheries protection zone around Svalbard from 1977.

In June 1994 vessels of the Norwegian coastguard severed the nets of Icelandic fishing boats that were alleged to be fishing within the fisheries protection zone. The Icelandic Government subsequently withdrew its boats from the zone; in August, however, Norway claimed that an Icelandic boat had opened fire on a Norwegian coastguard vessel.

Particularly since a Royal Decree of 1971, the Norwegian administration has endeavoured to protect the flora, fauna and environment of Svalbard. The protected areas, which total 39,815 sq km of land, or 64% of the land area, and 76,293 km of sea, include seven national parks, the most recently created (September 2005) being at Indre Wijdefjorden in northern Spitsbergen. From April 2007 visitors to Svalbard were required to pay an 'environment fee', the income from which was to be added to the territory's environmental protection fund.

Apart from a small permanent research station established by Poland, only Norway and Russia maintain permanent settlements on Svalbard. In order to continue Norwegian occupation of Svalbard, thus ensuring its future as a Norwegian territory and protecting it from potential, rival claims for sovereignty, notably from Russia, in 2000 the Svalbard administration proposed the opening of a new coal mine on Spitsbergen to exploit newly discovered reserves. Svalbard has also been promoted as a centre for scientific research; at the end of 2000 there were more than 20 scientific stations from foreign countries on the islands. In January 2004 representatives of the Norwegian Ministry of Foreign Affairs met with Russia's Deputy Minister of Foreign Affairs to discuss possible bilateral co-operation in Svalbard, in the areas of energy, fisheries and environmental protection. In February 2008 the Svalbard Global Seed Vault was inaugurated by the Norwegian Prime Minister, Jens Stoltenberg. Established at a depth of 130 m in the permafrost of a mountain at Longyearbyen, the vault was designed to store up to 4.5m. seed samples from around the world, in order to preserve biological diversity for future generations.

In November 2001 Norwegians resident on Spitsbergen conducted, for the first time, an election for a local council. The new Longyearbyen Council (Longyearbyen Lokalstyre) replaced the incumbent Svalbard Council, which had been partly appointed by the state-owned mining company, Store Norske Spitsbergen Kulkompani. The new 15-seat Council was to exercise only limited power in issues relating to health, education and the Church, which would all continue to be controlled by the state. The rate of participation in the local election was only 51.5% of the electorate; a multi-party grouping received 47.8% of the total votes cast, obtaining eight seats on the Council, while Det norske Arbeiderparti (DnA—Norwegian Labour Party) won 37.9% and secured six seats; Høyre (Conservative) took the remaining seat, with 10.1% of the votes cast. The Kristelig Folkeparti (KrF—Christian Democrats' Party) won 4.2% of the votes cast, but did not gain representation on the Council.

Elections to the Longyearbyen Council were held in October 2003. The DnA secured 44.6% of the votes cast and six seats on the Council, while the multi-party grouping won five seats, with 31.0% of the votes cast. The Fremskrittspartiet (FrP—Progress Party) and Høyre each won two seats, respectively receiving 12.3% and 12.1% of the votes cast. The Council's mandate was increased from two to four years.

At elections to the Council held in October 2007 the DnA won 44.4% of the votes cast and seven seats on the Council. The multi-party grouping won 26.9% of the votes cast and four seats, while Høyre received 17.7% of the votes and three seats. The Fremskrittspartiet failed to secure any seats. The rate of voter participation was recorded at just 40.3% of the electorate.

Social and Economic Affairs

The total population in January 2006 was 2,226, of whom 1,721 were resident in Norwegian settlements, 535 in Russian settlements and 10 in Polish settlements. There are limited recreational, transport, financial and educational facilities on Svalbard. There are hospitals in the capital, Longyearbyen (which had a population of 2,075 in March 2007), and in Barentsburg.

Coal is the islands' main product. In 2004 2,991,166 metric tons were shipped from mines on Svalbard (2,859,089 tons from Norwegian mines). The Norwegian state-owned coal company Store Norske Spitsbergen Grubekompani (SNSG) directly employs some 230 people. Until 1989 Store Norske Spitsbergen Kulkompani (SNSG's parent company) operated many local services and provided most of the infrastructure, but in that year these functions were assumed by the state company Svalbard Samfunnsdrift, which employed 140 people in 1998. By 1998 the number of people employed in the Norwegian mines had declined to 201 (from 358 in 1991), but the number increased again, to 265, in 2004. SNSG's most productive mine, at Svea Nord, about 60 km from Longyearbyen, was opened in 2001 to exploit significant newly discovered reserves of coal. The coal was of high calorific value (1,200 kilocalories per kilo more than usual) and therefore burnt more cleanly than normal coal. Svea is extremely well-placed for exporting coal to Europe, as it is located only 10 km from the port; the mine is linked to the port by road, and in 2004 a conveyor belt was constructed to transport the coal directly to the ships. A second Norwegian coal-mining camp, Gruve 7, some 15 km from Longyearbyen, is used largely to supply a coal-burning power station, which provides electricity for Longyearbyen. Russia had only one camp on Svalbard in early 2008, at Barentsburg, where around 160,000 tons of coal were produced annually and shipped to Russia. Barentsburg, located about 40 km south-west of Longyearbyen, with a population of almost 500 in March 2007, has its own coal-fired power station. Mining activity at a second Russian settlement, Pyramiden, was largely discontinued in 1998, and the town was subsequently abandoned.

Deep drillings for petroleum have been carried out by Norwegian and other companies, but no commercial results have been reported. Svalbard's other mineral resources include reserves of phosphate, asbestos, iron ore, anhydrite, limestone and various sulphides.

Tourism has been encouraged on Svalbard; cruise ships make stops at the islands and there is also a small industry in skiing and trekking across the wilderness. In 2006 visitors spent a total of 83,049 nights in Svalbard. The services sector has grown substantially in recent years, particularly in the areas of education and research. Many jobs are connected to Norwegian government organizations, such as Statsbygg, the state-owned building agency, and Longyearbyen Elementary and High School.

For 2005 the Svalbard budget was 195.2m. kroner, of which 135.9m. kroner was a direct subsidy from the Norwegian state budget. Svalbard raises some revenue from the sale of hunting and fishing licences.

Statistical Survey

Source: Statistics Norway, Kongensgt. 6, Oslo; tel. 21-09-00-00; fax 21-09-49-73; e-mail biblioteket@ssb.no; internet www.ssb.no.

AREA AND POPULATION

Area: 61,022 sq km (23,561 sq miles).

Population (1 January 2006): 2,266 (Norwegian 1,721, Russian 535, Polish 10).

Density (1 January 2006): 0.04 per sq km.

Economically Active Population (2003): Mining and quarrying 233; Manufacturing 8; Construction 194; Wholesale and retail trade 107; Hotels and restaurants 100; Transport and storage 177; Supporting and auxiliary transport activities 120; Public administration 147; Education, health and social work 133; Other community, social and personal service activities 15; *Total* 1,234.

MINING

Coal Shipments ('000 metric tons): 2,363.2 (Norwegian mines 2,131.7) in 2002; 3,173.5 (Norwegian mines 2,809.2) in 2003; 2,991.2 (Norwegian mines 2,859.1) in 2004.

FINANCE

(Norwegian currency is used; 100 øre = 1 Norwegian krone)

Budget (million kroner, 2005): Estimated revenue 195.2 (incl. direct grant of 135.9 from central Govt); Budgeted expenditure 195.2.

TRANSPORT

Road Traffic (vehicles registered at 31 December 2004): Passenger cars 930; Buses 41; Goods vehicles 394; Mopeds and motorcycles 130; Snow scooters 1,468.

Civil Aviation (2004, metric tons unless otherwise specified): Passengers (number) 86,232; Goods received 641; Goods sent 42; Mail received 412; Mail sent 54.

TOURISM

Overnight Stays (Longyearbyen): 77,926 in 2004; 76,570 in 2005; 83,049 in 2006.

EDUCATION

(2004)

Pre-primary: Schools 3; Teachers 33; Pupils 103.

Primary and Lower Secondary: Schools 1; Pupils 144.

Upper Secondary: Schools 1; Pupils 55.

Directory

The Government

(April 2008)

ADMINISTRATION

Governor (Sysselmann): Per Sefland.
Commissioner of Mines: Per Zakken Brekke.

OFFICES

Office of the Governor: Kontoret til Sysselmannen på Svalbard, POB 633, 9171 Longyearbyen, Svalbard; tel. 79-02-43-00; fax 79-02-11-66; e-mail firmapost@sysselmannen.no; internet www.sysselmannen.no.

Ministry of Justice and the Police (Polar Affairs Department): Akersgt. 42, POB 8005 Dep., 0030 Oslo; tel. 22-24-56-01; fax 22-24-95-30; e-mail postmottak@jd.dep.no; responsible for the administration of Svalbard and Jan Mayen, and for the Norwegian Antarctic dependencies.

Norsk Polarinstitutt på Svalbard (Norwegian Polar Institute in Svalbard): Næringsbygget, POB 505, 9171 Longyearbyen, Svalbard; tel. 79-02-26-00; fax 79-02-26-04; e-mail post@npolar.no; internet npweb.npolar.no; f. 1928 as Norges Svalbard- og Ishavs-undersøkelser; adopted present name and expanded functions in 1948; branch of Norwegian Polar Institute, Tromsø; mapping and research institute; responsible for advising Govt on matters concerning Svalbard, Jan Mayen and the Antarctic dependencies; monitors and investigates environment of the territories; organizes regular Antarctic research expeditions; establishes and maintains aids to navigation in Svalbard waters; Dir Jan-Gunnar Winther.

Norsk Polarinstitutts Forskningsstasjon (Norwegian Polar Institute Research Station): Sverdrupstasjonen, 9173 Ny-Ålesund, Svalbard; tel. 79-02-74-00; fax 79-02-70-02; permanent research base in Svalbard.

Longyearbyen Lokalstyre (Longyearbyen Council): POB 350, 9171 Longyearbyen, Svalbard; tel. 79-02-21-50; fax 79-02-21-51; e-mail postmottak@lokalstyre.no; internet www.lokalstyre.no; f. 2002; first locally elected body in Svalbard; replaced Svalbard Council; Leader Kjell Mork.

Svalbard, as an integral part of the Kingdom of Norway, has provision for its Norwegian inhabitants to participate in the national elections. For judicial matters Svalbard lies in the jurisdiction of Tromsø. The state Evangelical Lutheran Church provides religious services.

Press

There is only one newspaper published in the Svalbard archipelago.

Svalbardposten: POB 503, 9171 Longyearbyen, Svalbard; tel. 79-02-47-00; fax 79-02-47-01; e-mail post@svalbardposten.no; internet www.svalbardposten.no; f. 1948; weekly; Editor-in-Chief Birger Amundsen; circ. 3,300.

Finance

Norwegian currency is used. Most banking facilities are available.

Sparebank 1 Nord-Norge: POB 518, 9171 Longyearbyen, Svalbard; tel. 79-02-29-10; fax 79-02-29-11; e-mail kundesenter@snn.no; internet www.snn.no; savings bank.

Trade and Industry

Store Norske Spitsbergen Kulkompani A/S (SNSK): 9171 Longyearbyen, Svalbard; tel. 79-02-52-00; fax 79-02-18-41; e-mail firmapost@snsk.no; internet www.snsk.no; state-owned; develops the Store Norske group's proprietary and coal mining rights on Svalbard, with the exception of the Svea area; 230 employees; Chair. Bård Mikkelsen; CEO Robert Hermansen.

Store Norske Spitsbergen Grubekompani A/S (SNSG): f. 2002; manages all assets, rights, contractual obligations and liabilities in connection with the Svea Nord mine, responsible for coal production and sales in Longyearbyen and Svea, and for exploration at both its own and SNSK's claims; 230 employees.

Store Norske Boliger A/S: f. 2002; manages the group's accommodation in Longyearbyen and some of the accommodation in Svea.

Svalbard Næringsutvikling A/S: 9170 Longyearbyen, Svalbard; tel. 79-02-21-00; fax 79-02-10-19; state-owned; encourages devt of industry and trade; Admin. Dir Endre Hoflandsdal.

Svalbard Samfunnsdrift A/S: POB 475, 9171 Longyearbyen, Svalbard; tel. 79-02-23-00; fax 79-02-23-01; e-mail firmapost@ssd.no; internet www.ssd.no; state-owned; operates most local services, undertakes infrastructure devt; 140 employees (1998); Admin. Dir Endre Hoflandsdal.

Transport

Shipping links operate from June to August, with weekly sailings from Honningsvåg to Longyearbyen and Ny-Ålesund and back via Tromsø. In 1975 an airport was opened near Longyearbyen. SAS and Braathens SAFE operate services to Tromsø up to five times per week. There are air strips at Ny-Ålesund and Svea, and a Russian helicopter facility at Barentsburg. Apart from helicopters, and a fixed-wing service between Longyearbyen and Ny-Ålesund, internal traffic is little developed.

AIRPORT

Svalbard Lufthavn: POB 550, 9170 Longyearbyen, Svalbard; tel. 79-02-38-00; fax 79-02-38-01; e-mail ole.m.rambech@avinor.no; internet www.avinor.no/lufthavn/svalbard; f. 1975; owned by Avinor; Man. Ole M. Rambech.

Tourism

Svalbard Reiseliv AS: 9171 Longyearbyen, Svalbard; tel. 79-02-55-50; fax 79-02-55-51; e-mail info@svalbard.net; internet www.svalbard.net; f. 2001; represents and promotes tourism-related enterprises in Svalbard; produces brochures for tourists and collates statistics.

JAN MAYEN

The lofty volcanic island of Jan Mayen is located in the Arctic Ocean, some 910 km west-north-west of Bodø on the Norwegian mainland, 610 km north-north-east of Iceland and 480 km east of Greenland (Denmark). The island is 53 km in length and has a total area of 377 sq km (145 sq miles). The highest point is the summit of Mt Beerenberg (2,277 m above sea-level). The climate is severe, cold and usually misty.

The sea north and west of Jan Mayen (which was frequented by various whalers and hunters for a brief period in the 17th century) has been an important area for sealing by Norwegians since the mid-19th century. Partly to assist their navigation, the Norwegian Meteorological Institute instigated activities on the island in the early 20th century. In 1922 Jan Mayen was declared annexed by the Institute, and on 8 May 1929 Norwegian sovereignty was proclaimed by Royal Decree. The island was made an integral part of the Kingdom of Norway by the Jan Mayen Act of 1930. Jan Mayen is not included in the Svalbard Treaty.

The island has no known exploitable mineral resources and is largely barren. Fishing in the surrounding waters is intermittently productive, and it was once considered that a base for fishing fleets could be established. This is now believed to be unlikely, particularly because of the high cost of building a harbour. In September 1970 there was a violent volcanic eruption on the island, the first since the early 19th century. In the course of the first few days of the eruption a huge glacier melted and millions of cubic metres of ice disappeared as steam. Lava poured into the sea and formed about 3.5 sq km of new land. The island's main use remains as a meteorological, navigational and radio station.

During the Second World War Jan Mayen remained the only part of Norway under Norwegian rule, following the German invasion of the mainland. Despite some conflict, the Norwegian Government and its allies maintained the strategic meteorological station and established a radio-locating station on the island during the war.

In 1946 a new base was established at Nordlaguna, both as a meteorological and a coastal radio station. As a result of a North Atlantic defence co-operation exercise in 1959–60, a long-range navigation (LORAN) network was established, with one base on Jan Mayen. At the same time, it was decided to build an airstrip near the new LORAN C base, and in 1962 the personnel of the weather and coastal radio services also moved to the same area.

After negotiations with Iceland in 1980, the Norwegian Government declared an economic zone extending for 200 nautical miles (370 km) around the coast of Jan Mayen. In 1981 a further agreement was made with Iceland, regarding mineral and fishing rights. A dispute with Denmark, acting on behalf of Greenland, concerning the delimitation of maritime economic zones between Greenland and Jan Mayen was referred by Denmark to the International Court of Justice (based in The Hague, Netherlands) in 1988. The Court delivered its judgment in June 1993, deciding that 57% of the disputed area belonged to Norway. A subsequent accord on maritime delimitation, agreed between the Governments of Norway, Greenland and Iceland in November 1997, established the boundaries of a 1,934-sq km area of Arctic sea that had been excluded from the terms of the 1993 settlement.

The commanding officer in charge of the LORAN C base is the chief administrative official of the island. The officer is responsible for the 15–25 inhabitants (who usually remain on the island for only one year at a time), and is accountable to the Chief of Police in Bodø, and the Ministry of Justice and the Police (as in Svalbard). The LORAN C commander may grant permission for visits of not more than 24 hours. For longer visits, the Bodø Chief of Police or the Ministry must approve the application. Visits are normally allowed only for scientific purposes and only if private provision has been made for transport. There is no public transport or accommodation on Jan Mayen.

Station Commander: ÅGE-LEIF GODØ, LORAN C Base, 8099 Jan Mayen; tel. 32-17-79-00; fax 32-17-79-01; e-mail janmayen@www.jan-mayen.no; internet www.jan-mayen.no.

Chief of Police (Bodø): Kongensgt. 81, POB 1023, 8006 Bodø; e-mail politiet@bodo.politiet.no.

For the Ministry of Justice and the Police and the Norsk Polarinstitutt (Norwegian Polar Institute), see under Svalbard.

NORWEGIAN DEPENDENCIES

Norway's so-called 'Antarctic' dependencies are all uninhabited and were acquired as a result of Norwegian whaling interests in the region since the 1890s. The three territories are dependencies of the Kingdom of Norway, and are administered by the Polar Department of the Ministry of Justice and the Police, with the advice of the Norsk Polarinstitutt (Norwegian Polar Institute: for details, see under Svalbard) and the assistance of the Ministry of the Environment.

Bouvetøya

Bouvetøya (Bouvet Island) is a volcanic island in the South Atlantic Ocean, some 2,400 km south-west of the Cape of Good Hope (South Africa) and 1,600 km north of Antarctica. The island lies north of the Antarctic Circle (it is not, therefore, encompassed by the terms of the Antarctic Treaty). Bouvetøya has an area of 49 sq km, but about 93% of the surface is covered by ice. The climate is maritime antarctic, with a mean annual temperature of −1°C and a persistent heavy fog.

Regular landings on the island occurred only as part of Norwegian Antarctic expeditions in the 1920s and 1930s. Bouvetøya was claimed for Norway in 1927, placed under its sovereignty in 1928, and declared a Norwegian dependency in 1930. A Royal Decree of 1971 declared the entire island to be a nature reserve. An automatic weather station was established in 1977, and the island is regularly visited by Norwegian scientific expeditions.

Dronning Maud Land

Dronning Maud Land (Queen Maud Land) is that sector of the Antarctic continent lying between the longitudes of 20°W (adjoining the British Antarctic Territory to the west) and 45°E (neighbouring the Australian Antarctic Territory). The territory is, in area, several times the size of Norway, and 98% of its surface is covered by ice. The climate is severe, the usual temperature always being below 0°C and, in the winter months of mid-year, falling to −60°C on the coast and −88°C inland. The territory's coast is divided into five named sectors (the exact delimitations of which, and of the territory as a whole, have varied at different periods): Kronprinsesse Märtha Kyst (Crown Princess Märtha Coast), Prinsesse Astrid Kyst, Prinsesse Ragnhild Kyst, Prins Harald Kyst and Kronprins Olav Kyst.

The first Norwegian territorial claims in Antarctica were made in 1929, following many years of Norwegian involvement in the exploration and survey of the continent. Further claims were made in 1931 and 1936–37. These claims were formalized by the Norwegian authorities, and the land placed under their sovereignty, only in 1939. The extent of Dronning Maud Land then received its current limits, between the British and Australian claims. Norway now follows a policy which upholds its claim to sovereignty but supports the pattern of international co-operation, particularly that established under the terms of the Antarctic Treaty (see p. 575) (signed in 1959), to which the Kingdom of Norway is an original signatory. There are six wintering stations, staffed by personnel of various nationalities, in Dronning Maud Land.

Peter I Øy

Peter I Øy (Peter I Island) is located in the Bellingshausen Sea, some 450 km north of Antarctica and more than 1,800 km south-west of Chile, the nearest inhabited territory. It covers an area of some 156 sq km, 95% of which is covered by ice. The island lies within the Antarctic Circle and the area covered by the terms of the Antarctic Treaty. The first recorded landing on the island was not made until 1929, by a Norwegian expedition, which then claimed the island. A Royal Proclamation placed Peter I Øy under Norwegian sovereignty in 1931, and the island was declared a dependency in 1933. Few landings have been made since, but in 1987 the Norsk Polarinstitutt (Norwegian Polar Institute) conducted a relatively long survey and established an automatic weather station on the island.

OMAN

Introductory Survey

Location, Climate, Language, Religion, Flag, Capital

The Sultanate of Oman occupies the extreme east and south-east of the Arabian peninsula. It is bordered to the west by the United Arab Emirates (UAE), Saudi Arabia and Yemen. A detached portion of Oman, separated from the rest of the country by UAE territory, lies at the tip of the Musandam peninsula, on the southern shore of the Strait of Hormuz. Oman has a coastline of more than 1,600 km (1,000 miles) on the Indian Ocean, and is separated from Iran by the Gulf of Oman. In Muscat average annual rainfall is 100 mm and the average temperature varies between 21°C (70°F) and 35°C (95°F). Rainfall is heavier on the hills of the interior, and the south-western province of Dhofar is the only part of Arabia to benefit from the summer monsoon. The official language is Arabic. Islam is the official religion. The majority of the population are Ibadi Muslims; there are also Sunni Muslim, Hindu and Christian minorities. The national flag (proportions 1 by 2) has three equal horizontal stripes, of white, red and green, with a vertical red stripe at the hoist. In the upper hoist is a representation, in white, of the state emblem, two crossed swords and a dagger (*khanjar*), surmounted by a belt. The capital is Muscat.

Recent History

Officially known as Muscat and Oman until 1970, the Sultanate has had a special relationship with the United Kingdom since the 19th century. Full independence was confirmed by a treaty of friendship with the United Kingdom on 20 December 1951, although the armed forces and police retain some British officers on loan service. Sultan Said bin Taimur succeeded his father in 1932 and maintained a strictly conservative and isolationist rule until July 1970, when he was overthrown by his son in a bloodless palace coup. The new Sultan, Qaboos bin Said as-Said, then began a liberalization of the regime, and spending on development was increased.

A Consultative Assembly (comprising representatives of the Government, the private sector and the regions, appointed by the Sultan) was created in 1981, in order to advise Sultan Qaboos on economic and social development. In November 1990 it was announced that the Assembly was to be replaced by a Consultative Council (Majlis ash-Shoura), comprising regional representatives, which was intended to extend participation by Omani citizens in national affairs. A selection process was duly announced whereby representatives of each of the country's 59 districts (*wilayat*—increased to 61 in 2006) would nominate three candidates; the nominations would then be submitted to the Deputy Prime Minister for Legal Affairs, who, with the Sultan's approval, would choose one representative for each district to join the new Majlis. No government official or civil servant would be eligible for election to the new body. The President of the Consultative Council would be appointed by royal decree; other executive officers and committee members would be designated by, and from among, the local delegates. Although the role of the Majlis was strictly advisory, government ministers were to be obliged to submit reports to the assembly and to answer any questions addressed to them. The Majlis was formally established by royal decree in November 1991 and was convened in January 1992, when its members were sworn in for a three-year term. In 1994 membership of the Majlis was increased from 59 to 80, to include an additional member for any district with 30,000 or more inhabitants. For the first time women were nominated as candidates in six regions in and around the capital; two women were subsequently appointed to the enlarged Majlis.

In mid-1994 the Government was reported to be employing stringent measures to curb an apparent rise in Islamist militancy in Oman. In August the security forces arrested more than 200 members of an allegedly foreign-sponsored Islamist organization, including two junior ministers, university lecturers, students and soldiers. Most were later released, but in November several of those against whom charges had been brought were sentenced to death, having been found guilty of conspiracy to foment sedition; the Sultan subsequently commuted the death sentences to terms of imprisonment. In November 1995 139 prisoners were released, under a general amnesty granted by Sultan Qaboos.

In November 1996 Sultan Qaboos issued a decree promulgating a Basic Statute of the State, a constitutional document defining for the first time the organs and guiding principles of the state. The Statute provided for a Council of Oman, to be composed of the Majlis ash-Shoura and a new Council of State (Majlis ad-Dawlah). The latter was to be appointed from among prominent Omanis, and would liaise between the Government and the people of Oman. It was subsequently reported that 23 senior government ministers had resigned as directors of public joint-stock companies, in accordance with a stipulation in the Basic Statute that ministers should not abuse their official position for personal gain. In December a Defence Council was established by royal decree, comprising the Minister of the Royal Court, the heads of the armed and police forces, and the chief of internal security. The Basic Statute defined a process of succession to the Sultan, requiring that the ruling family determine a successor within three days of the throne's falling vacant, failing which the Defence Council would confirm the appointment of a successor predetermined by the Sultan.

Voting was organized in October 1997 to select candidates for appointment to the Majlis ash-Shoura. Women from all regions were permitted to seek nomination. Of a total of 736 candidates, 164 were chosen, from whom the Sultan selected the 82 members of the newly expanded Majlis in November. The two female members of the outgoing Majlis were returned to office. In December Sultan Qaboos issued a decree appointing the 41 members of the Majlis ad-Dawlah, which was reportedly dominated by former politicians, business leaders and academics. A further decree established the Council of Oman, which was formally inaugurated by the Sultan on 27 December.

The elections to the Majlis ash-Shoura held on 14 September 2000 were the first in which members were directly elected rather than appointed by the Sultan. However, voting rights were restricted to prominent business leaders, intellectuals, professionals and tribal chiefs. Of a total of 541 candidates, 21 of whom were women, 83 (including two women) were elected to the (again expanded) Majlis. The number of eligible voters had tripled, to some 150,000, since the previous election; according to official figures, an estimated 90% of the electorate participated in the poll. A new Majlis ad-Dawlah was appointed in October, and the Council of Oman convened for its second term on 4 November.

From late 2000 the Government intensified measures aimed at reducing the number of expatriates in Oman's labour force, a process termed 'Omanization'. In April 2001 more than 100 suspected illegal immigrants were detained by the Omani authorities, who announced that all foreign nationals employed illegally in the country and who had not supplied the correct documentation within a period of two months would be liable to deportation. About 130 alleged illegal immigrants were reportedly arrested in September.

In March 2003 Sultan Qaboos issued a decree establishing a Public Authority for Craft Industries. The President of the Authority, Sheikha Aisha bint Khalfan bin Jumiel as-Siyabiah, was given the rank of Minister, and thus became the first female to be appointed to that level of government. Elections to the Majlis ash-Shoura were held on 4 October, for which voting rights were granted to all Omani citizens over 21 years of age—some 820,000 people. Few changes to the composition of the Majlis resulted from the elections. A total of 506 candidates, 15 of them women, stood for election to the 83-seat assembly. While the electoral process was described by observers as fair and open, the turn-out was a disappointing 32% of the electorate. Critics of the elections claimed that tribal loyalties had guided the decision-making of most voters, resulting in a predictable set of results—a situation that was exacerbated by the lack of legislative power wielded by council members. Only two female candidates secured election to the Majlis, both of whom were already serving members. A royal decree issued in October extended the term of office for members of both the Majlis ash-Shoura and the Majlis ad-Dawlah from three to four years. In November a new Council of State was appointed, with an expanded membership of 57 (including eight women); membership of the Council was subsequently increased to 59 (nine of whom were women) and then again, to 70 (see below).

Sultan Qaboos announced a limited reorganization of the Council of Ministers in February 2004. A further decree signed in March appointed Dr Rawya bint Saud bin Ahmad al-Busaidiyah as Minister of Higher Education (the first female member of the Council of Ministers) and Sheikh Yahya bin Mahfoudh al-Mantheri as President of the Council of State. Following further cabinet changes implemented in May, in June the Sultan created by royal decree a Ministry of Tourism; another woman, Rajha bint Abd al-Amir bin Ali, was appointed as the new minister. A third woman was appointed to the Council of Ministers as part of a limited reorganization in October, when Dr Sharifah bint Khalfan bin Nasser al-Yahiyaia was given the role of Minister of Social Development.

In May 2005 30 suspected Islamist militants were sentenced to prison terms ranging from one to 20 years for allegedly planning a series of attacks on a cultural and trade festival in Muscat, with the supposed aim of overthrowing the regime. However, in the following month Sultan Qaboos pardoned all those convicted. Although Oman has remained free from acts of terrorism, the convictions raised concerns that militant Islamism was flourishing in the country. In October 31 Omanis were sentenced to prison terms on charges including bribery and forgery, thus apparently signalling that the Government was keen to combat administrative corruption. Several high-ranking government officials were reportedly among those convicted. Meanwhile, as permitted by the approval of a press and broadcasting law in 2004, the country's first private radio stations received licences in 2005. (The law also allowed the establishment of private television stations.) Although Omanis can, against the wishes of the state, receive private broadcasts from foreign broadcasters, this represented a significant concession to reformist elements in society. Nevertheless, despite such reforms, two writers were imprisoned for criticizing the Government in 2005 (one of whom had not received a trial).

'Cyclone Gonu' struck the eastern coast of Oman in early June 2007, causing the deaths of some 50 people and widespread destruction to the region's infrastructure. Much of the country, including Muscat, suffered severe flooding, and some hydrocarbon installations were damaged by the storm, which was said to have been the worst in the Arabian peninsula's history. The estimated cost of the damage in Oman was reported to be around US $3,900m.

In early September 2007 Sultan Qaboos carried out a further reorganization of the Council of Ministers, which included the creation of new Ministries of Fisheries and of Environment and Climate Affairs. A Public Authority for Electricity and Water was also established to plan and supervise the development of Oman's utilities. The same female ministers remained in charge of the higher education, tourism and social development portfolios after the reshuffle. Sheikh Ahmad bin Muhammad al-Issai was appointed as President of the Majlis ash-Shoura, elections to which were held on 27 October. Membership of the Majlis was increased from 83 to 84. The polls were contested by 632 candidates, 21 of them women; however, none of the contested seats were secured by women. The majority of elected members of the new Majlis ash-Shoura were reported to be tribal leaders or businessmen. The conduct of the ballot was assessed by independent observers to have been free and fair, and turn-out of some 62.7% was recorded. A new Majlis ad-Dawlah, comprising 70 members, was appointed on 5 November.

An agreement on the demarcation of Oman's border with Yemen, which had been the subject of a lengthy dispute with the former People's Democratic Republic of Yemen, was signed in October 1992 and ratified in December; demarcation was completed in June 1995. In July 1996 Oman withdrew an estimated 15,000 troops from the last of the disputed territories on the Yemeni border, in accordance with the 1992 agreement, and in May 1997 the border demarcation maps were signed in Muscat. Several bilateral economic co-operation accords were announced in September 1998, as were plans for the establishment of a free trade zone. Oman and Yemen agreed in October 2001 to extend co-operation between their hydrocarbon industries. In April 2005 talks were held in Muscat over the enhancement of joint security arrangements.

In response to the invasion of Kuwait by Iraq in August 1990, Oman, together with the other members of the Co-operation Council for the Arab States of the Gulf (Gulf Co-operation Council—GCC, see p. 219), gave its support to the deployment of a US-led defensive force in Saudi Arabia. The Omani Government expressed the view that the imposition of international economic sanctions would compel Iraq to withdraw from Kuwait. In November there was evidence that Oman was attempting to mediate in the crisis when the Iraqi Minister of Foreign Affairs, Tareq Aziz, visited Oman. By the mid-1990s Oman's stance regarding the continuation of economic sanctions against Iraq appeared ambivalent: Oman and Qatar were, notably, absent from talks held in March 1995 between the US Secretary of State, Warren Christopher, and other GCC members to discuss the issue. In November 1997 and again in early 1998 Oman stated its opposition to possible military action to force Iraq to submit to inspections of its weapons capabilities by the UN Special Commission (UNSCOM, see the chapter on Iraq), maintaining that the UN should remove the economic sanctions against Iraq once UNSCOM had been permitted to complete its task.

Although the Omani Government was swift to condemn the September 2001 suicide attacks in New York and Washington, DC, it expressed concern that the US-led military campaign in Afghanistan against the al-Qa'ida (Base) network of Osama bin Laden (held by the USA to be principally responsible for the attacks) and the Taliban regime should not be extended to target any Arab state, notably Iraq. Street demonstrations were held in October by Omani students protesting against the war in Afghanistan. During an official visit to Oman by the US Secretary of Defense, Donald Rumsfeld, in that month, it was reported that the USA was to supply Oman with 12 F-16 fighter aircraft and other advanced weaponry, at a cost of some US $1,120m. From 2002 Oman opposed attempts led by the USA, as part of its 'war on terror', to garner international support for a military offensive against the Iraqi regime of Saddam Hussain, and advocated a diplomatic solution to the escalating crisis. In March 2003, as the US-led force began assaults on targets in Iraq, Sultan Qaboos appealed for a swift curtailment of the conflict, which he described as 'unjustified' and 'illegitimate'. Frequent anti-war protests were held in Oman during March and April.

In April 1994 the Israeli Deputy Minister of Foreign Affairs, Yossi Beilin, participated in talks in Oman. This constituted the first official visit by an Israeli government member to an Arab Gulf state since Israel's declaration of independence in 1948. In September 1994, moreover, Oman and the other GCC member states announced the partial ending of their economic boycott of Israel. In December the Israeli Prime Minister, Itzhak Rabin, made an official visit to Oman to discuss the Middle East peace process, and in February 1995 it was announced that low-level diplomatic relations were to be established between Oman and Israel. An Omani trade office was opened in Tel-Aviv in August 1996, despite concerns that bilateral relations would be undermined by the uncompromising stance adopted by the new Israeli Government of Binyamin Netanyahu. In March 1997 ministers responsible for foreign affairs of the countries of the League of Arab States (the Arab League, see p. 332) recommended, in condemnation of Israeli settlement policy, the suspension of involvement in multilateral negotiations with Israel, a reassertion of the primary economic boycott and the ending, by means of closing representative offices in Tel-Aviv, of efforts to normalize bilateral relations. In April Oman prohibited Israeli participation at a Muscat trade fair. Oman attended the Middle East and North Africa economic conference in Doha, Qatar, in November, despite a boycott by most Arab League and GCC members in response to the perceived failure of Israel (which was represented at the conference) to comply with its obligations under the Middle East peace process. In October 2000, in view of the deepening crisis in Israeli–Palestinian relations, Oman closed both its trade office in Tel-Aviv and the Israeli trade office in Muscat. Oman hosted the annual summit meeting of GCC heads of state in December 2001, at the close of which a statement was issued blaming Israel for the collapse of the peace process and expressing support for the Palestinian leadership. Demonstrations have subsequently taken place in Muscat to demand an end to Israeli military incursions into Palestinian territory. Nevertheless, the Israeli Vice-Prime Minister and Minister of Foreign Affairs, Tzipi Livni, held discussions with Oman's Minister Responsible for Foreign Affairs, Yousuf bin al-Alawi bin Abdullah, during a visit to Qatar in April 2008.

In July 2004 Oman signed a Trade and Investment Framework Agreement with the USA, regarded as a preliminary step on the path towards a bilateral free trade agreement (FTA). Negotiations between Oman and the USA concerning the FTA duly took place in March–October 2005 and the deal was signed following their conclusion. Ratification of the legislation by both

Omani and US institutions was confirmed in late 2006, but implementation of the FTA was still pending in December 2007. The FTA followed similar agreements between the USA and Bahrain, Israel, Jordan and Morocco, with a view to establishing a wider free trade area across the Middle East. The development of US-Omani relations was expected to displease the Saudi Government, which had previously argued that the GCC should negotiate a trade deal as a single body and in 2004 claimed that the FTA with Bahrain contravened the GCC's external tariff agreement. Meanwhile, Oman's close ties with Iran are a potential source of disagreement with the USA, since Oman supports the right of the Iranian regime to pursue the peaceful development of nuclear energy and opposes any use of military force against Iran—a proposal that apparently remained under consideration by the US Administration in early 2008.

Government

The Basic Statute of the State, which was promulgated by Royal Decree on 6 November 1996, defines Oman's organs of government. The Sultan, who is Head of State, is empowered to promulgate and ratify legislation. He is assisted in formulating and implementing the general policy of the state by a Council of Ministers. Members of the Council of Ministers are appointed by the Sultan, who presides, or may appoint a Prime Minister to preside, over the Council. There is no legislature. However, a Majlis ash-Shoura (Consultative Council) is now elected for four years at national polls. Voters were previously nominated within the country's *wilayat*, or districts, with the franchise effectively limited to prominent business leaders, intellectuals, professionals and tribal chiefs; with effect from elections held in October 2003, however, voting rights were granted to all Omani citizens over 21 years of age. The Majlis is composed of one representative from each *wilaya* with fewer than 30,000 inhabitants, and two from each *wilaya* with 30,000 or more inhabitants. The Majlis ash-Shoura elected in October 2007 comprised 84 members. A Majlis ad-Dawlah (Council of State) is appointed by the Sultan from among prominent Omanis; currently it comprises 70 members, who also serve a four-year term of office. The two Councils together comprise the Council of Oman.

Oman comprises four governorates and five regions, which are subdivided into 61 *wilayat*; each *wilaya* has its own governor (*wali*).

Defence

As assessed in November 2007, the Omani armed forces numbered 42,600 (including about 2,000 expatriate personnel): army 25,000; navy 4,200; air force 5,000; royal household 6,400. Paramilitary forces numbered 4,400: tribal home guard (*firqat*) 4,000; police coastguard 400. Military service is voluntary. Government expenditure on defence was budgeted at RO 1,230m. in 2007.

Economic Affairs

In 2004, according to estimates by the World Bank, Oman's gross national income (GNI), measured at average 2002–04 prices, was US $22,994m., equivalent to $9,070 per head (or $14,570 per head on an international purchasing-power parity basis). During 1996–2006, it was estimated, the population increased at an average annual rate of 1.6%, while real gross domestic product (GDP) per head increased, in real terms, by an average of 1.8% per year during 1996–2004. Overall GDP increased, in real terms, at an average annual rate of 3.4% in 1996–2004; growth was 7.2% in 2006, according to provisional official figures.

Agriculture (including fishing) contributed 1.4% of GDP in 2006, according to provisional official figures, and engaged 32.4% of the labour force in 2005, according to FAO. The major crops are dates, tomatoes, bananas, watermelons and other fruits. The production of frankincense, formerly an important export commodity, has been revived. Livestock and fishing are also important. The real GDP of the agricultural sector increased by an average of 2.5% annually in 1996–2004, according to the World Bank. Real agricultural GDP decreased by some 0.5% in 2005, according to official figures, but remained broadly unchanged in 2006.

Industry (including mining and quarrying, manufacturing, construction and power) provided 61.1% of GDP in 2006, according to provisional official figures, and employed 27.9% of the working population in 2003. According to the World Bank, real industrial GDP increased by an average of 1.6% annually in 1996–2004. The sector's real GDP decreased by 1.0% in 2004.

The mining sector contributed 47.3% of GDP in 2006, according to provisional official figures, and engaged 2.8% of the employed labour force in 2003. The principal mineral reserves are petroleum and natural gas, which together provided around 47.1% of GDP in 2006. There were proven petroleum reserves of 5,600m. barrels at the end of 2006. Production in that year averaged an estimated 743,000 barrels per day (b/d). Petroleum reserves were estimated to be sufficient to sustain production at that level until 2026. Exports of Omani crude petroleum provided 66.6% of total export earnings in 2006. Natural gas is also an important mineral resource; there were proven reserves of some 980,000m. cu m at the end of 2006, sustainable for about 39 years at 2006 production levels (output in that year totalled 25,100m. cu m—an increase of some 27% compared with 2005). Budgetary revenue from petroleum and natural gas contributed some 77.1% of the total in 2006. Chromite, gold, silver, salt, marble, gypsum and limestone are also mined, and the exploitation of coal deposits is planned. The GDP of the mining sector increased at an average annual rate of 3.5% in 1990–2000; mining GDP (including petroleum activities) expanded by an estimated 0.4% in 2006.

Manufacturing contributed 10.2% of GDP in 2006, according to provisional official figures, and engaged 8.2% of the employed labour force in 2003. The most important branches of the sector are petroleum-refining, construction materials, cement production and copper-smelting. Assembly industries, light engineering and food-processing are being encouraged at industrial estates in Muscat, Sohar and Salalah. Completion in 2000 of a US $9,000m. liquefied natural gas plant at Sur reduced domestic demand for petroleum and also produced a surplus for export. The GDP of the manufacturing sector increased, in real terms, at an average rate of 9.7% annually in 1995–2004. The sector's real GDP increased by an estimated 14.7% in 2006, according to official figures.

Energy is derived almost exclusively from domestic supplies of natural gas (which accounted for 82.0% of electricity produced in 2004) and petroleum. Imports of fuel products comprised just 3.3% of total imports in 2006.

Services provided 37.5% of GDP in 2006, according to provisional official figures, and engaged 64.0% of the employed population in 2003. With the Government seeking to diversify Oman's petroleum-dependent economy, the construction of several large-scale tourism projects have been initiated in recent years. Pre-eminent among these was Al-Madina az-Zarqa (Blue City) resort, the plans for which were announced in June 2005, and which was expected to cost US $15,000m. and to take some 15 years to complete. The Government intends to increase the contribution of tourism to GDP to 5% by 2020. The GDP of the services sector increased, in real terms, at an average rate of 4.9% per year during 1996–2004. Real services GDP increased by an estimated 9.3% in 2006, according to official figures.

In 2006 Oman recorded a visible trade surplus of US $11,691m., and there was a surplus of $4,377m. on the current account of the balance of payments. In 2006 the principal sources of imports were the UAE and Japan (which supplied, respectively, 25.9% and 17.3% of Oman's imports). India, the USA and Germany were also important suppliers. The most important market for non-petroleum exports in 2006 was the UAE (taking 47.7%). India, Saudi Arabia and Iran were also important markets for non-petroleum exports. Petroleum and natural gas is, by far, the principal export category, comprising 81.0% of the total in 2006. Live animals and animal products made the most notable contribution to export revenue of all non-oil exports of Omani origin in the same year. The principal imports in 2006 were machinery and transport equipment, basic manufactures, food and live animals, and chemicals.

Oman recorded an estimated overall budgetary surplus of RO 44m. in 2006 (equivalent to some 0.3% of GDP in that year). At the end of 2005 Oman's total external debt was US $3,472m., of which $842m. was long-term public debt. The cost of debt-servicing in that year was equivalent to 7.5% of the total value of exports of goods and services. Annual inflation increased by an average of 0.2% in 1997–2006, and consumer prices grew by an average of 3.2% in 2006. Although Oman has traditionally relied on a high level of immigrant labour (non-Omanis accounted for 57.6% of the employed labour force in 2003), employment opportunities for young Omanis declined in the early 1990s and, according to census results, unemployment among Omanis stood at 11.9% in 1993; the figure was estimated at 12%–15% in 2006, although unemployment in rural areas was assumed to be far greater.

Oman is a member of the Arab Fund for Economic and Social Development (see p. 174), the Islamic Development Bank (see

p. 329) and the Arab Monetary Fund (see p. 175). It was a founder member of the Co-operation Council for the Arab States of the Gulf (the Gulf Co-operation Council—GCC, see p. 219), and of the Indian Ocean Rim Association for Regional Co-operation (see p. 413). Oman is not a member of the Organization of the Petroleum Exporting Countries (OPEC, see p. 373) nor of the Organization of Arab Petroleum Exporting Countries (OAPEC, see p. 366), but it generally respects OPEC's policies regarding levels of petroleum production and pricing. Oman was admitted to the World Trade Organization (see p. 396) in November 2000. In preparation for admittance to the WTO, the Government abolished import fees, raised the limit on foreign ownership of local industries from 49% to 70% (effective from 1 January 2001) and authorized 100% foreign ownership in banking, insurance and brokerage firms (from 1 January 2003). The GCC's six members established a unified regional customs tariff in January 2003, and the organization has undertaken to establish a single market and currency no later than January 2010. The economic convergence criteria for the proposed monetary union were agreed at a GCC summit in Abu Dhabi, the UAE, in December 2005. However, it was announced in February 2007 that the Omani authorities had decided to withdraw their participation from the project, owing to concerns regarding the convergence criteria. In January 2008 the GCC launched its common market.

Oman's limited petroleum reserves and fluctuations in the price of petroleum have necessitated a series of five-year development plans to diversify the country's economic base, in particular through the expansion of the private sector. Nevertheless, a number of foreign oil companies have been brought in to explore Oman's territorial waters, in the hope of increasing oil and gas reserves. According to the Ministry of Oil and Gas in early 2007, petroleum production was expected to reach 1m. b/d by 2012. The state-owned Petroleum Development Oman (PDO) announced in early 2008 that, in anticipation of a rapid increase in demand for energy (which was forecast to rise by as much as 170% by 2016), it planned to make significant improvements to its existing infrastructure. Massive investment in nascent oil projects was also expected to ensue, with 50 new oilfields being targeted for development. Owing to constraints on gas supplies in the Sultanate, PDO was also considering the development of the region's first coal-fired plant. Meanwhile, under the seventh Development Plan (2006–10), emphasis was to be placed on the development of the non-petroleum sector (with gas-based industry and tourism being notable targets), and the expansion of the privatization programme (begun in 1994). Under the Plan, the Government aimed to achieve annual GDP growth of at least 3% and to maintain low annual rates of inflation. The previous Plan (2001–05) had sought, in particular, to create more jobs for Omani nationals, to increase state funding for their education and training, and to limit the employment of expatriates in certain fields, under the so-called 'Omanization' policy. Omanis were now reported to constitute at least 90% of employees in banking and finance. Plans for the establishment of a free trade zone at Salalah, which was expected to create new employment opportunities for Omani nationals and also to encourage foreign investment, were again in progress in 2006; a major investor had departed from the venture in 2002, alluding to the political instability in the region as a reason for its withdrawal. The development of the non-petroleum sector was also in progress, while the relatively new tourism industry was experiencing a construction-led transformation in 2004–08; the largest projects to date were The Wave and Al-Madina az-Zarqa (Blue City) resorts, which were launched in 2004 and 2005, respectively. To co-ordinate the nascent industry, the Government established a Ministry of Tourism in June 2004; Oman joined the World Tourism Organization in July of that year. In 2007 the budget deficit was forecast to decrease by 38% compared with the previous year, as a result of continuing high international petroleum prices and the Government's prudent fiscal policies. World oil prices remained extremely high during 2007 and early 2008, engendering an expected 20% increase in state revenues in 2008. Consequently, the Government's 2008 fiscal programme provided for a 19% rise in budgetary expenditure. Substantial outlays were allocated to the tourism sector and infrastructure projects; however, there remained concerns that increased spending would exacerbate inflation, which was reported to have reached almost 7% by the end of 2007.

Education

In 1970 there were only three schools, with a total of 909 pupils. By 2004/05 there were 1,038 schools at the primary, preparatory and secondary levels, as well as 143 private kindergartens and schools regulated by the Ministry of Education; in total, 572,864 students were in state education (at the primary–secondary level) and 25,472 in private education in that year. According to the Basic Statute, the state endeavours to make education available to all; it provides public education and encourages the establishment of private educational institutions. However, education is still not compulsory. Primary education begins at six years of age and lasts for six years. The next level of education, divided into two equal stages, lasts for a further six years. In 1998/99 a new system, comprising 10 years of basic education and two extra years of secondary education, dependent on attainment, was introduced in 17 schools; it was to be implemented gradually throughout the country. Primary enrolment in 2005/06 included 73.3% of children in the relevant age-group, while secondary enrolment included 76.8% of children in the relevant age-group. In 2004/05 there were six teacher-training colleges, five technical colleges, 16 institutes of health and four vocational institutes, together with the College of *Shari'a* and Law, the Academy of Tourism and Catering and the College of Banking and Financial Studies. There were seven Islamic colleges in 1995/96. Oman's first national university, named after Sultan Qaboos, was opened in late 1986, and had 12,855 students in 2004. There are four private universities and several private technical colleges. In the 2006 budget, RO 525m. (12.4%) of current and investment expenditure was allocated to education by the central Government.

Public Holidays

2008: 10 January*† (Muharram, Islamic New Year), 20 March* (Mouloud, Birth of the Prophet), 30 July* (Leilat al-Meiraj, Ascension of the Prophet), 2 September* (Ramadan begins), 1 October* (Id al-Fitr, end of Ramadan), 18 November (National Day), 19 November (Birthday of Sultan Qaboos), 9 December* (Id al-Adha, Feast of the Sacrifice), 29 December*† (Muharram, Islamic New Year).

2009: 9 March* (Mouloud, Birth of the Prophet), 19 July* (Leilat al-Meiraj, Ascension of the Prophet), 22 August* (Ramadan begins), 20 September* (Id al-Fitr, end of Ramadan), 18 November (National Day), 19 November (Birthday of Sultan Qaboos), 27 November* (Id al-Adha, Feast of the Sacrifice).

* These holidays are dependent on the Islamic lunar calendar and may vary by one or two days from the dates given.

† This festival occurs twice (marking the start of the Islamic years AH 1429 and 1430) within the same Gregorian year.

Weights and Measures

The imperial, metric and local systems are all used, although the metric system was officially adopted in 1974.

OMAN   Statistical Survey

Statistical Survey

Sources (unless otherwise stated): Information and Publication Centre, Ministry of National Economy, POB 506, Muscat 113; tel. 24604285; fax 24698467; e-mail mone@omantel.net.om; internet www.moneoman.gov.om; Central Bank of Oman, POB 1161, 44 Mutrah Commercial Centre, Ruwi 112; tel. 24702222; fax 24788995; e-mail cboccr@omantel.net.om; internet www.cbo-oman.org.

Area and Population

AREA, POPULATION AND DENSITY

Area (sq km)	309,500*
Population (census results)	
1 December 1993	2,018,074†
1 December 2003	
Males	1,313,239
Females	1,027,576
Total	2,340,815‡
Population (UN estimates at mid-year)§	
2005	2,507,000
2006	2,546,000
2007	2,595,000
Density (per sq km) at mid-2007	8.4

* 119,500 sq miles.
† Comprising 1,483,226 Omani nationals and 534,848 non-Omanis.
‡ Comprising 1,781,558 Omani nationals and 559,257 non-Omanis.
§ Source: UN, *World Population Prospects: The 2006 Revision*.

ADMINISTRATIVE DIVISIONS
(2003 census)

	Area (sq km)	Population	Density (per sq km)
Muscat Governorate	3,900	632,073	162.1
Al-Batinah Region	12,500	653,505	52.3
Musandam Governorate	1,800	28,378	15.8
Adh-Dhahira Region	44,000	207,015	4.7
Ad-Dakhliya Region	31,900	267,140	8.4
Ash-Sharqiya Region	36,400	313,761	8.6
Al-Wosta Region	79,700	22,983	0.3
Dhofar Governorate	99,300	215,960	2.2
Total	309,500	2,340,815	7.6

PRINCIPAL TOWNS
(population at 2003 census)

Salalah	156,530	Nizwa	68,785
Suhar	104,312	Al-Buraymi	67,963
Ibri	97,429	Sur	66,785
Ar-Rustaq	74,224	Muscat (capital)	24,893

Source: Thomas Brinkhoff, *City Population* (internet www.citypopulation.de).

BIRTHS AND DEATHS
(Omani nationals only, official estimates)

	2004	2005	2006
Birth rate (per 1,000)	24.0	24.8	24.2
Death rate (per 1,000)	2.6	2.5	n.a.

Expectation of life (years at birth, provisional): 74.29 (males 73.18; females 75.43) in 2006.

EMPLOYMENT
(persons aged 15 years and over, 2003 census)

	Omanis	Non-Omanis	Total
Agriculture and fishing	14,210	43,904	58,114
Mining and quarrying	11,998	8,117	20,115
Manufacturing	13,831	45,661	59,492
Electricity, gas and water	1,826	2,219	4,045
Construction	10,128	108,129	118,257
Trade, hotels and restaurants	24,999	84,158	109,157
Transport, storage and communications	17,202	10,472	27,674
Finance, insurance and real estate	12,657	12,543	25,200
Public administration and defence	144,699	18,043	162,742
Other community, social and personal services	54,923	83,299	138,222
Activities not adequately defined	5,973	7,633	13,606
Total employed	312,446	424,178	736,624
Males	258,655	364,337	622,992
Females	53,791	59,841	113,632

Mid-2005 (estimates in '000): Agriculture, etc. 317; Total labour force 977 (Source: FAO).

Health and Welfare

KEY INDICATORS

Total fertility rate (children per woman, 2005)	3.4
Under-5 mortality rate (per 1,000 live births, 2005)	12
HIV/AIDS (% of persons aged 15–49, 2003)	0.1
Physicians (per 1,000 head, 2005)	1.67
Hospital beds (per 1,000 head, 2005)	2.1
Health expenditure (2004): US $ per head (PPP)	418.9
Health expenditure (2004): % of GDP	3.0
Health expenditure (2004): public (% of total)	81.4
Access to water (% of persons, 2002)	79
Access to sanitation (% of persons, 2002)	89
Human Development Index (2005): ranking	58
Human Development Index (2005): value	0.814

For sources and definitions, see explanatory note on p. vi.

Agriculture

PRINCIPAL CROPS
('000 metric tons)

	2004	2005	2006
Sorghum	1.3	9.5	8.8
Potatoes	15.5*	5.9	5.4
Tomatoes	44.5	39.4	40.4
Dry onions	17.6	5.4	4.2
Watermelons	27.0	27.0	n.a.
Bananas	34.0	26.7	26.0
Lemons and limes	5.9	6.2	5.9
Mangoes, mangosteens and guavas	8.7	7.7	6.9
Dates	231.0	247.3	258.7
Papayas	2.9	1.4	1.4

* FAO estimate.

Aggregate production ('000 metric tons, may include official, semi-official or estimated data): Total cereals 7.6 in 2004, 15.1 in 2005, 14.1 in 2006; Total roots and tubers 15.5 in 2004, 5.9 in 2005, 5.4 in 2006; Total vegetables (incl. melons) 238.5 in 2004, 206.1 in 2005, 204.9 in 2006; Total fruits (excl. melons) 288.7 in 2004, 298.4 in 2005, 308.4 in 2006.

Source: FAO.

OMAN

LIVESTOCK
('000 head, year ending September)

	2004	2005	2006
Asses, mules or hinnies*	29	29	n.a.
Cattle	333	302	308
Camels	116	117	120
Sheep	377	351	358
Goats	1,059	1,557	1,598
Chickens*	4,000	4,200	n.a.

* FAO estimates.

Source: FAO.

LIVESTOCK PRODUCTS
('000 metric tons, FAO estimates, unless otherwise indicated)

	2003	2004	2005
Cattle meat	4.1	4.2	4.2
Camel meat	6.5	6.6	6.6
Sheep meat	12.0	10.8	10.8
Goat meat*	22.5	15.0	22.5
Chicken meat	5.8	5.7	5.7
Cows' milk	18.5	45.0*	46.0*
Sheep's milk	4.0	4.0	4.0
Goats' milk	83.6	84.2	84.7
Hen eggs	8.2*	8.6	8.6

* Official figure(s).

2006: Cows' milk 47.0 (official figure).

Source: FAO.

Fishing

('000 metric tons, live weight)

	2003	2004	2005
Capture	138.5	165.1	150.6
Groupers	4.2	5.9	4.2
Emperors (Scavengers)	8.0	10.3	8.0
Porgies and seabreams	5.9	8.2	6.3
Hairtails and cutlassfishes	8.8	3.5	4.8
Demersal percomorphs	5.9	6.5	8.0
Indian oil sardine	32.0	34.9	40.2
Longtail tuna	8.0	7.8	7.5
Yellowfin tuna	10.2	24.3	15.9
Indian mackerel	4.1	5.8	5.2
Carangids	2.6	3.2	2.5
Sharks, rays, skates, etc.	5.9	5.6	5.1
Cuttlefish and bobtail squids	11.4	11.8	9.8
Aquaculture	0.4	0.5	0.2
Total catch	138.8	165.5	150.7

Source: FAO.

Mining

('000 metric tons, unless otherwise indicated, estimates)

	2004	2005	2006
Crude petroleum (million barrels)	285.4	282.6	269.2*
Natural gas (dry, million cu m)	17,000	17,390	21,754
Chromium	18.6	34.0	67.0*
Gold (kg)	211	384	144*
Marble	163.8	220.9	220.0*
Salt	12.4	10.9	11.0*
Gypsum	103.0	133.1	130.0*

* Provisional.

Source: US Geological Survey.

Industry

SELECTED PRODUCTS
('000 barrels, unless otherwise indicated, estimates)

	2004	2005	2006
Jet fuel and kerosene	1,407	1,770	2,339
Motor spirit (petrol)	5,215	5,436	5,078
Gas-diesel (distillate fuel) oils	6,442	7,089	6,750
Residual fuel oils	14,247	15,445	14,947
Electric energy (million kWh)	11,499	12,648	13,585

Source: mainly US Geological Survey.

Finance

CURRENCY AND EXCHANGE RATES

Monetary Units
1,000 baiza = 1 rial Omani (RO).

Sterling, Dollar and Euro Equivalents (31 December 2007)
£1 sterling = 770.3 baiza;
US $1 = 384.5 baiza;
€1 = 566.0 baiza;
10 rials Omani = £12.98 = $26.01 = €17.67.

Exchange Rate: Since January 1986 the official exchange rate has been fixed at US $1 = 384.5 baiza (1 rial Omani = $2.6008).

BUDGET
(RO million)

Revenue	2004	2005	2006*
Petroleum revenue (net)	2,904.9	3,161.9	3,225.9
Gas revenues	250.9	393.6	613.5
Other current revenue	850.0	888.3	1,073.4
Taxes and fees	217.4	289.6	305.5
Income tax on enterprises	65.3	79.0	85.4
Customs duties	71.0	88.5	114.6
Non-tax revenue	632.6	598.7	767.9
Electricity	116.1	14.0	—
Surplus from public authorities	15.0	7.6	5.4
Income from government investments	319.8	302.0	369.6
Capital revenue	16.6	35.0	49.0
Capital repayments	17.8	31.8	18.1
Total	**4,040.2**	**4,510.5**	**4,979.9**

Expenditure	2004	2005	2006*
Current expenditure	2,661.2	3,179.4	3,531.0
Defence and national security	1,143.6	1,404.2	1,549.6
Civil ministries	1,304.4	1,531.9	1,735.0
Investment expenditure	1,003.8	966.5	1,199.5
Share of PDO expenditure†	257.4	249.5	322.5
Participation and subsidies	113.9	61.7	205.6
Total	**3,778.9**	**4,207.6**	**4,936.1**

* Preliminary figures.
† Referring to the Government's share of current and capital expenditure by Petroleum Development Oman.

INTERNATIONAL RESERVES
(US $ million at 31 December)

	2004	2005	2006
Gold (national valuation)	0.3	0.3	0.3
IMF special drawing rights	13.9	14.8	16.7
Reserve position in IMF	98.9	34.6	27.2
Foreign exchange	3,484.5	4,308.7	4,970.2
Total	**3,597.6**	**4,358.4**	**5,014.4**

Source: IMF, *International Financial Statistics*.

OMAN

MONEY SUPPLY
(RO million at 31 December)

	2004	2005	2006
Currency outside banks	329.0	383.2	470.9
Demand deposits at commercial banks	582.7	750.4	756.9
Total money	911.7	1,133.6	1,227.8

Source: IMF, *International Financial Statistics*.

COST OF LIVING
(Consumer Price Index for Muscat; base: 2000 = 100)

	2004	2005	2006
Food, beverages and tobacco	100.1	102.7	108.7
Textiles, clothing and footwear	98.3	99.2	98.8
Rent, electricity, water and fuel	96.9	97.4	98.6
All items (incl. others)	99.1	100.2	103.4

NATIONAL ACCOUNTS
(RO million in current prices)

Expenditure on the Gross Domestic Product

	2004	2005	2006*
Government final consumption expenditure	2,031.8	2,289.0	2,457.2
Private final consumption expenditure	4,198.0	4,258.6	5,326.8
Gross fixed capital formation	1,958.1	2,130.2	2,545.7
Total domestic expenditure	8,187.9	8,677.8	10,329.7
Exports of goods and services	5,424.0	7,472.0	8,651.0
Less Imports of goods and services	4,087.0	4,260.0	5,243.0
GDP in purchasers' values	9,524.9	11,889.8	13,737.7
GDP at constant 1988 prices	6,694.7	7,095.8	7,609.2

Gross Domestic Product by Economic Activity

	2004	2005	2006*
Agriculture and fishing	176.5	184.7	195.9
Mining and quarrying	4,040.0	5,809.0	6,595.2
Crude petroleum	3,771.0	5,362.8	6,082.1
Natural gas	247.9	421.8	489.4
Non-petroleum	21.1	24.4	23.7
Manufacturing	802.2	983.1	1,421.7
Electricity and water	122.5	143.6	151.3
Construction	272.8	292.1	349.5
Wholesale and retail trade	1,145.9	1,240.9	1,478.9
Hotels and restaurants	73.3	86.7	103.2
Transport, storage and communications	661.5	684.0	847.1
Financial intermediation	333.3	374.8	451.6
Real estate and business activities	467.1	489.0	517.9
Public administration and defence	848.2	926.1	922.8
Education	449.0	525.7	573.4
Health	152.0	172.2	183.4
Other community and personal services	113.7	125.6	131.1
Private household with employed persons	16.5	16.5	16.6
Sub-total	9,674.5	12,054.0	13,939.6
Less Financial intermediation services indirectly measured	220.6	252.7	316.4
Gross value added in basic prices	9,453.9	11,801.3	13,623.1
Taxes on imports	71.0	88.5	114.6
GDP in purchasers' values	9,524.9	11,889.8	13,737.7

*Provisional.

BALANCE OF PAYMENTS
(US $ million)

	2004	2005	2006
Exports of goods f.o.b.	13,381	18,692	21,586
Imports of goods f.o.b.	−7,873	−8,029	−9,896
Trade balance	5,508	10,663	11,691
Exports of services	726	741	913
Imports of services	−2,756	−3,052	−3,740
Balance on goods and services	3,478	8,353	8,864
Other income received	658	676	1,202
Other income paid	−1,508	−2,596	−2,900
Balance on goods, services and income	2,627	6,433	7,165
Current transfers paid	−1,826	−2,257	−2,788
Current account	802	4,176	4,377
Capital account (net)	21	−16	−96
Direct investment from abroad (net)	−21	786	705
Portfolio investments (net)	93	47	471
Other investment assets	−830	−2,528	−5,532
Other investment liabilities	1,769	947	3,352
Net errors and omissions	−987	−666	−1,077
Overall balance	847	2,746	2,200

Source: IMF, *International Financial Statistics*.

External Trade

PRINCIPAL COMMODITIES
(RO million)

Imports c.i.f. (distribution by SITC)*	2004	2005	2006
Food and live animals	369.1	340.2	382.0
Beverages and tobacco	43.5	31.2	32.8
Crude materials (inedible) except fuels	104.5	88.6	122.9
Metalliferous ores and metal scrap	68.6	54.4	80.5
Minerals, fuels, lubricants, etc.	83.8	141.0	139.2
Petroleum and related products	83.2	140.3	138.5
Chemicals and related products	246.2	284.7	280.7
Basic manufactures	587.3	568.9	587.3
Machinery and transport equipment	1,564.6	1,637.3	2,084.9
Machinery specialized for particular industries	254.5	187.6	285.7
General industrial machinery, equipment and parts	209.0	153.7	290.0
Road vehicles	671.2	795.4	1,063.1
Passenger motor cars	445.7	524.3	696.3
Motor vehicles for transport of goods	101.6	100.2	167.6
Miscellaneous manufactured articles	183.2	198.3	239.3
Commodities not elsewhere classified by SITC	104.5	78.8	80.2
Total (incl. others)	3,312.6	3,394.0	4,189.8

Exports f.o.b.	2004	2005	2006
Petroleum and natural gas	4,186.4	6,047.8	6,720.3
Crude petroleum	3,490.9	5,071.1	5,528.3
Refined petroleum	61.5	88.3	47.4
Natural gas	634.0	888.4	1,144.6
Non-oil and -gas exports	958.5	1,139.1	1,579.2
Live animals and animal products	102.5	95.0	87.0
Base metals and articles thereof	77.9	106.5	135.0
Total†	5,144.9	7,186.9	8,299.5

* Excluding unrecorded imports (RO million): 96.2 in 2004; 55.3 in 2005; 54.3 in 2006.

† Including re-exports (RO million): 538.2 in 2004; 583.8 in 2005; 766.7 in 2006.

OMAN

Statistical Survey

PRINCIPAL TRADING PARTNERS
(RO million)

Imports c.i.f.	2004	2005	2006
Australia	72.5	70.0	83.2
Bahrain	31.8	59.2	34.6
Belgium	37.5	38.3	54.1
China, People's Republic	57.5	81.8	141.7
France	131.4	71.4	73.6
Germany	163.2	232.9	212.0
India	121.3	153.3	222.2
Italy	195.2	67.7	86.8
Japan	464.0	534.0	724.0
Korea, Republic	74.9	109.0	147.7
Netherlands	82.0	59.4	83.7
Saudi Arabia	46.5	97.5	144.8
Singapore	37.6	32.9	49.2
United Arab Emirates	1,072.3	898.3	1,083.7
United Kingdom	164.0	147.8	142.1
USA	163.1	208.8	219.3
Total (incl. others)	3,312.7	3,394.0	4,190.1

Exports f.o.b.*	2004	2005	2006
Belgium	14.6	6.0	16.8
China, People's Republic	15.2	14.7	16.2
Germany	10.3	9.8	9.7
Hong Kong	21.5	18.1	23.5
India	14.0	78.2	134.6
Iran	87.8	52.0	83.0
Iraq	20.1	15.4	15.5
Jordan	27.2	24.3	6.0
Kenya	0.9	1.3	1.3
Kuwait	15.8	15.6	16.9
Libya	10.8	11.9	17.1
Pakistan	11.1	9.6	18.0
Qatar	17.0	27.0	43.2
Saudi Arabia	85.8	99.5	85.7
Singapore	15.0	11.3	12.7
Syria	12.6	14.4	7.9
Tanzania	4.6	3.8	3.1
United Arab Emirates	357.0	510.9	752.6
United Kingdom	26.2	27.1	37.0
USA	34.1	22.2	20.7
Yemen	27.6	28.7	29.2
Total (incl. others)	958.5	1,139.1	1,579.2

* Excluding petroleum exports.

Transport

ROAD TRAFFIC
(registered vehicles at 31 December)

	2001	2002	2003
Private cars	309,217	335,771	284,902
Taxis	20,901	23,639	23,761
Commercial	132,920	140,270	109,118
Government	27,788	29,175	14,861
Motorcycles	5,195	5,436	3,977
Diplomatic	1,274	1,386	561
Other	23,631	24,625	7,320
Total	520,926	560,302	444,500

SHIPPING
Merchant Fleet
(registered at 31 December)

	2004	2005	2006
Number of vessels	26	31	33
Total displacement ('000 grt)	17.1	18.7	20.3

Source: Lloyd's Register-Fairplay, *World Fleet Statistics*.

International Sea-borne Freight Traffic
('000 metric tons, unless otherwise specified)

	2004	2005	2006
Port Sultan Qaboos:			
Goods loaded onto vessels ('000 US shipping tons)	1,180	1,226	1,298
Goods unloaded from vessels ('000 US shipping tons)	5,415	5,748	6,967
Goods loaded onto launches	154	346	9,065
Goods unloaded from launches	63,535	40,997	36,263
Port Salalah:			
Goods loaded	1,070	1,185	1,691
Goods unloaded	464	603	617
Mina Al-Fahal Coastal Area			
Petroleum loaded	36,889	36,759	31,993
Petroleum products unloaded	328	417	1,231

CIVIL AVIATION
(aircraft movements, passengers and cargo handled at Seeb International Airport)

	2004	2005	2006
International flights:			
flights (number)	35,803	44,408	42,087
passengers ('000)	3,187	3,778	4,460
goods handled (metric tons)	65,917	75,332	96,493
Domestic flights:			
flights (number)	7,819	8,373	7,814
passengers ('000)	274	292	318
goods handled (metric tons)	1,234	1,231	1,415

Tourism

FOREIGN TOURIST ARRIVALS*

Country of nationality	2003	2004	2005
Bahrain	29,881	26,536	31,539
Egypt	16,886	20,276	15,922
France	14,803	23,495	21,289
Germany	31,133	78,129	92,481
India	83,065	106,456	104,778
Kuwait	11,218	15,564	10,226
Netherlands	9,052	11,408	8,605
Pakistan	12,017	16,506	17,125
Saudi Arabia	22,163	31,066	25,233
Switzerland	9,735	17,203	23,463
Tanzania	6,202	7,828	4,520
United Arab Emirates	87,407	103,317	75,292
United Kingdom	60,532	92,887	118,411
USA	24,620	26,910	22,708
Total (incl. others)	629,525	908,466	1,114,498

* Figures refer to international arrivals at hotels and similar establishments.

Tourism receipts (US $ million, incl. passenger transport): 546 in 2003; 604 in 2004; 679 in 2005.

Source: World Tourism Organization.

OMAN

Communications Media

	2004	2005	2006
Telephones ('000 main lines in use)	240.3	265.2	278.3
Mobile cellular telephones ('000 subscribers)	805.0	1,333.2	1,818.0
Personal computers ('000 in use)	118	118	n.a.
Internet users ('000)	245	285	319
Broadband subscribers ('000)	0.7	8.3	15.2

Daily newspapers (number): 6 in 2004.

Non-daily newspapers and other periodicals (number): 23 in 2004.

Television receivers (number in use): 1,430,000 in 2000.

Radio receivers (number in use): 1,400,000 in 1997.

Facsimile machines (number in use): 6,356 in 1997.

Book production (number of titles): 7 in 1996; 136 in 1998; 12 in 1999.

Sources: mainly UNESCO, *Statistical Yearbook*, and International Telecommunication Union.

Education

(state schools, 2005/06 unless otherwise indicated)

	Institutions	Teachers	Males	Females	Total
Pre-primary	5	529	4,973	4,456	9,429
Basic*		22,862	117,199	111,411	228,610
General*:					
Grades 1–6	1,038†	4,416	50,115	48,399	98,514
Grades 7–9		5,922	63,311	56,736	120,047
Grades 10–12		39,750	72,614	67,043	139,657
Higher‡§	34	1,608	12,282	11,004	23,286
University§	1	955	6,416	6,439	12,855

* The Basic education system began to replace the General education system from 1998/99.
† 2001/02.
‡ Comprising six teacher-training colleges, the College of *Shari'a* and Law, five technical colleges, the Academy of Tourism and Catering, the College of Banking and Financial Studies, 16 institutes of health and four vocational-training centres.
§ 2004/05.

Adult literacy rate (UNESCO estimates): 81.4% (males 86.8%; females 73.5%) in 2003 (Source: UNESCO Institute for Statistics).

Directory

The Constitution

The Basic Statute of the State was promulgated by royal decree on 6 November 1996, as Oman's first document defining the organs and guiding principles of the State.

Chapter 1 defines the State and the system of government. Oman is defined as an Arab, Islamic and independent state with full sovereignty. Islamic law (*Shari'a*) is the basis for legislation. The official language is Arabic. The system of government is defined as Sultani (Royal), hereditary in the male descendants of Sayyid Turki bin Said bin Sultan. Article 6 determines the procedure whereby the Sultan is designated.

Chapter 2 defines the political, economic, social, cultural and security principles of the State. Article 11 (economic principles) includes the stipulation that 'All natural resources and revenues therefrom shall be the property of the State which will preserve and utilize them in the best manner taking into consideration the requirements of the State's security and the interests of the national economy'. The constructive and fruitful co-operation between public and private activity is stated to be the essence of the national economy. Public property is inviolable, and private ownership is safeguarded. Article 14 (security principles) provides for a Defence Council to preserve the safety and defence of the Sultanate.

Chapter 3 defines public rights and duties. Individual and collective freedoms are guaranteed within the limits of the law.

Chapter 4 concerns the Head of State, the Council of Ministers, Specialized Councils and financial affairs of the State. Article 41 defines the Sultan as Head of State and Supreme Commander of the Armed Forces. The article states that 'His person is inviolable. Respect for him is a duty and his command must be obeyed. He is the symbol of national unity and the guardian of its preservation and protection'. The Sultan presides over the Council of Ministers, or may appoint a person (Prime Minister) to preside on his behalf. Deputy Prime Ministers and other Ministers are appointed by the Sultan. The Council of Ministers and Specialized Councils assist the Sultan in implementing the general policy of the State.

Chapter 5 comprises a single Article (58). This states that the Council of Oman shall consist of the Majlis ash-Shura (Consultative Council) and the Majlis ad-Dawlah (State Council). The jurisdiction, terms, sessions, rules of procedure, membership and regulation of each shall be determined by the law.

Chapter 6 concerns the judiciary. Articles 59 and 60 state that the supremacy of the law shall be the basis of governance, and enshrine the dignity, integrity, impartiality and independence of the judiciary. Article 66 provides for a Supreme Council of the judiciary.

Chapter 7 defines the general provisions pertaining to the application of the Basic Statute.

The Government

HEAD OF STATE

Sultan: Qaboos bin Said as-Said (assumed power on 23 July 1970, after deposing his father).

COUNCIL OF MINISTERS
(April 2008)

Prime Minister and Minister of Foreign Affairs, Defence and Finance: Sultan Qaboos bin Said as-Said.

Deputy Prime Minister for the Council of Ministers: Sayyid Fahd bin Mahmoud as-Said.

Personal Representative of the Sultan: Sayyid Thuwaini bin Shihab as-Said.

Minister of National Economy, Supervisor of the Finance Ministry and Deputy Chairman of the Financial Affairs and Energy Resources Council: Ahmad bin Abd an-Nabi Macki.

Minister Responsible for Defence Affairs: Sayyid Badr bin Saud bin Hareb al-Busaidi.

Minister of Legal Affairs: Muhammad bin Ali bin Nasir al-Alawi.

Minister of Oil and Gas: Dr Muhammad bin Hamad bin Saif ar-Rumhi.

Minister of Justice: Sheikh Muhammad bin Abdullah bin Zahir al-Hinai.

Minister of Awqaf (Religious Endowments) and Religious Affairs: Sheikh Abdullah bin Muhammad bin Abdullah as-Salimi.

Minister Responsible for Foreign Affairs: Yousuf bin al-Alawi bin Abdullah.

Minister of Information: Hamad bin Muhammad bin Muhsin ar-Rashdi.

Minister of Housing: Sheikh Saif bin Muhammad ash-Shabaibi.

Minister of Education: Yahya bin Saud bin Mansoor as-Sulaimi.

Minister of Higher Education: Dr Rawya bint Saud bin Ahmad al-Busaidiyah.

Minister of Heritage and Culture: Sayyid Haitham bin Tariq as-Said.

Minister of Tourism: Dr Rajha bint Abd al-Amir bin Ali.

Minister of Social Development: Dr Sharifah bint Khalfan bin Nasser al-Yahiyaia.

Minister of Manpower: Juma bin Ali bin Juma.

Minister of Sports Affairs: Eng. Ali bin Massoud bin Ali as-Sinaidi.

OMAN

Minister of Transport and Communications: Dr KHAMIS BIN MUBARAK BIN ISA AL-ALAWI.
Minister of the Interior: Sayyid SAUD BIN IBRAHIM BIN SAUD AL-BUSAIDI.
Minister of Commerce and Industry: MAQBOOL BIN ALI BIN SULTAN.
Minister of Agriculture: Sheikh SALIM BIN HILAL AL-KHALILI.
Minister of Fisheries: Sheikh MUHAMMAD BIN ALI AL-QATABI.
Minister of Environment and Climate Affairs: Sayyid HAMOUD BIN FAISAL AL-BUSAIDI.
Minister of Health: Dr ALI BIN MUHAMMAD BIN MOUSA AR-RAISI.
Minister of Regional Municipalities and Water Resources: Sheikh ABDULLAH BIN SALEM BIN AMER AR-RAWAS.
Minister of the Civil Service: Sheikh MUHAMMAD BIN ABDULLAH AL-HARTHI.
Minister of State and Governor of Muscat: Sayyid AL-MUTASSIM BIN HAMOUD AL-BUSAIDI.
Minister of State and Governor of Dhofar: Sheikh MUHAMMAD BIN MARHOUD AL-MAMARI.
Minister of the Diwan of the Royal Court: Sayyid ALI BIN HAMOUD BIN ALI AL-BUSAIDI.
Minister of the Palace Office and Head of the Office of the Supreme Commander of the Armed Forces: Maj.-Gen. ALI BIN MAJID AL-MA'AMARI.

MINISTRIES

Diwan of the Royal Court: POB 632, Muscat 113; tel. 24738711; fax 24739427.
Ministry of Agriculture: POB 3738, Ruwi 112; tel. 24700896; fax 24707939; e-mail info@maf.gov.om; internet www.maf.gov.om.
Ministry of Awqaf (Religious Endowments) and Religious Affairs: POB 3232, Ruwi 112; tel. 24696870; e-mail info@mara.gov.om; internet www.maraoman.net.
Ministry of the Civil Service: POB 3994, Ruwi 112; tel. 24696000; fax 24601365.
Ministry of Commerce and Industry: POB 550, Muscat 113; tel. 24774290; fax 24817238; e-mail info@mocioman.gov.om; internet www.mocioman.gov.om.
Ministry of Defence: POB 113, Muscat 113; tel. 24312605; fax 24702521.
Ministry of Education: POB 3, Muscat 113; tel. 24775334; fax 24704465; e-mail moe@moe.gov.om; internet www.moe.gov.om.
Ministry of Environment and Climate Affairs: Muscat.
Ministry of Finance: POB 506, Muscat 113; tel. 24738201; fax 24737028; e-mail info@mof.gov.om; internet www.mof.gov.om.
Ministry of Fisheries: Muscat.
Ministry of Foreign Affairs: POB 252, Muscat 113; tel. 24699500; fax 24699589; internet www.mofa.gov.om.
Ministry of Health: POB 393, Muscat 113; tel. 24602177; fax 24601430; e-mail moh@moh.gov.om; internet www.moh.gov.om.
Ministry of Heritage and Culture: POB 668, Muscat 113; tel. 24641300; fax 24641331; e-mail info@mhc.gov.om; internet www.mhc.gov.om.
Ministry of Higher Education: POB 82, Ruwi 112; tel. 24755999; internet www.mohe.gov.om.
Ministry of Housing: POB 1491, Ruwi 112; tel. 24603906; fax 24699180; internet www.mhew.gov.om.
Ministry of Information: POB 600, Muscat 113; tel. 24603222; fax 24693770; e-mail informus@omantel.net.om; internet www.omanet.om.
Ministry of the Interior: POB 127, Ruwi 112; tel. 24602244; fax 24696660.
Ministry of Justice: POB 354, Ruwi 112; tel. 24697699; internet www.moj.gov.om.
Ministry of Legal Affairs: POB 578, Ruwi 112; tel. 24605802; fax 24605697; internet www.mola.gov.om.
Ministry of Manpower: POB 413, Ruwi 112; tel. 24794175; internet www.manpower.gov.om.
Ministry of National Economy: POB 881, Muscat 100; tel. 24698900; fax 24698467; e-mail mone@omantel.net.om; internet www.moneoman.gov.om.
Ministry of Oil and Gas: POB 551, Muscat 113; tel. 24603333; fax 24696972.
Ministry of the Palace Office: POB 2227, Ruwi 112; tel. 24600841.
Ministry of Regional Municipalities and Water Resources: POB 323, Muscat 113; tel. 24692550; fax 24694015; e-mail aid@mrmewr.gov.om; internet www.mrmewr.gov.om.

Ministry of Sports Affairs: POB 211, Muscat 113; tel. 24755240; fax 24704558; e-mail feedback@sportsoman.com; internet www.sportsoman.com.
Ministry of Tourism: Madinat Al-Sultan Qaboos, POB 200, Muscat 115; tel. 24588700; fax 24588819; e-mail info@omantourism.gov.om; internet www.omantourism.gov.om.
Ministry of Transport and Communications: POB 338, Ruwi 112; tel. 24697870; fax 24696817; e-mail pttdiwan@omantel.net.om; internet www.comm.gov.om.

MAJLIS OMAN
(Council of Oman)

Majlis ash-Shoura
(Consultative Council)

President: Sheikh AHMAD BIN MUHAMMAD AL-ISSAI.

The Majlis ash-Shoura was established by royal decree in November 1991. Initially, members of the Majlis were appointed by the Sultan from among nominees selected at national polls, but from the September 2000 elections, members were directly elected. Two representatives are appointed from four candidates in each *wilaya* (province) of more than 30,000 inhabitants, and one from two candidates in each *wilaya* of fewer than 30,000 inhabitants. Members of the Majlis are appointed for a single four-year term of office. The Majlis elected in October 2007 comprised 84 members. The Majlis is an advisory body, the duties of which include the review of all social and economic draft laws prior to their enactment; public-service ministries are required to submit reports and answer questions regarding their performance, plans and achievements. The President of the Majlis ash-Shoura is appointed by royal decree.

Majlis ad-Dawlah
(State Council)

President: Sheikh YAHYA BIN MAHFOUDH AL-MANTHERI.

The Majlis ad-Dawlah was established in December 1997, in accordance with the terms of the Basic Statute of the State. Like the Majlis ash-Shoura, it is an advisory body, whose function is to serve as a liaison between the Government and the people of Oman. Its members are appointed by the Sultan for a four-year term. A new Majlis, comprising 70 members, was appointed in November 2007.

Political Organizations

There are no political organizations in Oman.

Diplomatic Representation

EMBASSIES IN OMAN

Algeria: POB 216, Muscat 115; tel. 24601698; fax 24694419; e-mail algeria@omantel.net.om; Ambassador TAYEB SAÂDI.
Austria: Moosa Complex Bldg, No. 477, 2nd Floor, Way No. 3109, POB 2070, Ruwi 112; tel. 24793135; fax 24793669; e-mail maskat-ob@bmaa.gv.at; Ambassador Dr ANDREAS KARABACZEK.
Bahrain: POB 66, Madinat Qaboos, Al-Khuwair; tel. 24605912; fax 24605072; Ambassador ISMAIL SALIM ALI.
Bangladesh: POB 3959, Ruwi 112, St 664, Bldg 5903, Muscat; tel. 24707462; fax 24708495; e-mail bangla@omantel.net.om; Ambassador GOLAM AKBAR KHANDAKAR.
Brunei: POB 91, Ruwi 112, Shati al-Qurum, St 3050, Villa 4062, Muscat; tel. 24603533; fax 24605910; e-mail kbopuni@omantel.net.om; Ambassador Dato SERI SETIA Haji ADAM BIN Haji AHMAD.
China, People's Republic: Al-Ansherah St, Way No. 1507, House No. 465, Madinat Alalam, POB 315, Muscat 112; tel. 24696698; fax 24602322; e-mail chinaemb_om@mfa.gov.cn; Ambassador PAN WEI-FANG.
Egypt: Jamiat ad-Dowal al-Arabiya St, Diplomatic City, Al-Khuwair, POB 2252, Ruwi 112; tel. 24600411; fax 24603626; e-mail egyembmuscat@hotmail.com; Ambassador IZZADIN FAHMY MAHMOUD.
France: Diplomatic City, Al-Khuwair, POB 208, Madinat Qaboos 115; tel. 24681800; fax 24681843; e-mail diplofr1@omantel.net.om; internet www.ambafrance-om.org; Ambassador MARC BARETY.
Germany: POB 128, Ruwi 112, Muscat; tel. 24832482; fax 24835690; e-mail info@maskat.diplo.de; internet www.maskat.diplo.de; Ambassador KLAUS GEYER.
India: POB 1727, Ruwi 112; tel. 24813838; fax 24811607; e-mail indiamct@omantel.net.om; internet www.indemb-oman.org; Ambassador ANIL WADHWA.

OMAN

Iran: Diplomatic Area, Jamiat ad-Dowal al-Arabiya St, POB 3155, Ruwi 112; tel. 24696944; fax 24696888; e-mail iranembassy@hotmail.com; internet www.iranembassy.gov.om; Ambassador MORTEZA RAHIMI.

Iraq: POB 262, Way 1737, House No. 2803, Ruwi 112; tel. 604178; fax 602026; e-mail musemb@iraqmofamail.net; Ambassador ABD AR-RASOUL KADHIM ALOUSH.

Italy: Shati al-Qurum, Way No. 3034, House No. 2697, POB 3727, Ruwi 112; tel. 24693727; fax 24695161; e-mail ambasciata.mascate@esteri.it; internet www.ambmascate.esteri.it; Ambassador CESARE CAPITANI.

Japan: Shati al-Qurum, Villa No. 760, Way No. 3011, Jamiat ad-Dowal al-Arabiya St, POB 3511, Ruwi 112; tel. 24601028; fax 24698720; internet www.oman.emb-japan.go.jp; Ambassador KEIJI OMORI.

Jordan: Diplomatic City, Arab League St, POB 70, Al-Adhaiba 130; tel. 24692760; fax 24692762; e-mail embhkjom@omantel.net.om; Ambassador MAZIN MIDHAT JUMAH.

Korea, Republic: POB 377, Madinat Qaboos 115; tel. 24691490; fax 24691495; e-mail emboman@mofat.go.kr; Ambassador CHO SUNG-HWAN.

Kuwait: Al-Khuwair Diplomatic Area, Arab League St, Block No. 13, Bldg No. 58, POB 1798, Ruwi 112; tel. 24699626; fax 24604732; Ambassador SHAMLAN AR-ROUMI.

Lebanon: Shati al-Qurum, Way No. 3019, Villa No. 1613, POB 67, Al-Harthy Complex, Muscat 118; tel. 24695844; fax 24695633; e-mail lebanon1@omantel.net.om; Ambassador AFIF AYYUB.

Malaysia: Shati al-Qurum, Villa No. 1611, Way No. 3019, POB 3939, Ruwi 112; tel. 24698329; fax 24605031; e-mail mwmuscat@omantel.net.om; internet www.kln.gov.my/perwakilan/muscat; Ambassador Dato MUHAMMAD ZAMRI MUHAMMAD KASSIM.

Morocco: Shati al-Qurum, Villa No. 2443, Way No. 3030, POB 3125, Ruwi 112; tel. 24696152; fax 24601114; e-mail sifamamu@omantel.net.om; Ambassador Dr NOUREDDINE BENOMAR.

Netherlands: Shati al-Qurum, Way No. 3017, Villa No. 1366, POB 3302, Ruwi 112; tel. 24603706; fax 24603778; e-mail mus@minbuza.nl; internet www.mfa.nl/mus; Ambassador ANNELIES BOOGAERDT.

Pakistan: POB 1302, Ruwi 112; tel. 24603439; fax 24697462; e-mail parepmuscat@gmail.com; Ambassador SOHAIL AMIN.

Philippines: POB 420, Madinat Qaboos 115; tel. 24605140; fax 24605176; e-mail muscatpe@omantel.net.om; Ambassador ACMAD D. OMAR.

Qatar: Diplomatic City, Jamiat ad-Dowal al-Arabiya St, Al-Khuwair, POB 802, Muscat 113; tel. 24691152; fax 24691156; Ambassador ABDULLAH BIN MUHAMMAD BIN KHALID AL-KHATIR.

Russia: Shati al-Qurum, Way No. 3032, Surfait Compound, POB 80, Ruwi 112; tel. 24602894; fax 24604189; e-mail rusoman@omantel.net.om; Ambassador Dr SERGEI E. EVANOV.

Saudi Arabia: Diplomatic City, Jamiat ad-Dowal al-Arabiya St, POB 1411, Ruwi 112; tel. 24601744; fax 24603540; e-mail omemb@mofa.gov.sa; Ambassador ABDULLAH BIN ABD AR-RAHMAN ALIM.

Somalia: Mumtaz Street, Villa Hassan Jumaa Baker, POB 1767, Ruwi 112; tel. 24564412; fax 24564965; Ambassador Gen. ISMA'IL QASIM NAJI.

South Africa: Al-Harthy Complex, POB 231, Muscat 118; tel. 24694791; fax 24694792; e-mail southae@omantel.net.om; internet www.saembassymuscat.gov.om; Ambassador YACOOB ABBA OMAR.

Sri Lanka: POB 95, Madinat Qaboos 115; tel. 24697841; fax 24697336; e-mail lankaemb@omantel.net.om; Ambassador MAHROOF MEERASAHIB.

Spain: Shati al-Qurum, Way No. 2834, House No. 2573, POB 3492, Ruwi 112; tel. 24691101; fax 24698969; e-mail emb.mascate@mae.es; Ambassador TOMÁS RODRÍGUEZ-PANTOJA MÁRQUEZ.

Sudan: Diplomatic City, Al-Khuwair, POB 3971, Ruwi 112; tel. 24697875; fax 24699065; e-mail suanimt@gto.net.om; Ambassador ABD AR-RAHMAN MUHAMMAD BUKHEIT.

Syria: Madinat Qaboos, Al-Ensharah Street, Villa No. 201, POB 85, Muscat 115; tel. 24697904; fax 24603895; e-mail syria@omantel.net.om; internet www.syrianembassy.gov.om; Ambassador FAROUK MAHMOUD QADDOUR.

Thailand: Shati al-Qurum, Villa No. 1339, Way No. 3017, POB 60, Ruwi 115; tel. 24602683; fax 24605714; e-mail thaimct@omantel.net.om; Ambassador THINAKORN KANASUTA.

Tunisia: Al-Ensharah Street, Way No. 1507, POB 220, Muscat 115; tel. 24603486; fax 24697778; Ambassador HAMMOUDA RIHANI.

Turkey: Bldg No. 3270, Street No. 3042, Shati al-Qurum, POB 47, Mutrah 115; tel. 24697050; fax 24697053; e-mail turemmus@omantel.net.om; Ambassador ENGIN TÜRKER.

United Arab Emirates: Diplomatic City, Al-Khuwair, POB 551, Muscat 111; tel. 24600302; fax 24604182; Ambassador MUHAMMAD ALI ABD AR-RAHMAN AL-OSAIMI.

United Kingdom: POB 185, Mina al-Fahal 116; tel. 24609000; fax 24609010; e-mail enquiries.muscat@fco.gov.uk; internet www.britishembassy.gov.uk/oman; Ambassador Dr NOEL GUCKIAN.

USA: Jamiat ad-Dowal al-Arabiya St, Madinat Qaboos, POB 202, Muscat 115; tel. 24643400; fax 24699771; e-mail webmastermuscat@state.gov; internet oman.usembassy.gov; Ambassador GARY A. GRAPPO.

Yemen: Shati al-Qurum, Area 258, Way No. 2840, Bldg No. 2981, POB 105, Madinat Qaboos 115; tel. 24600815; fax 24605008; Ambassador ABD AR-RAHMAN KHAMIS UBAID.

Judicial System

Oman's Basic Statute guarantees the independence of the judiciary. The foundation for the legal system is *Shari'a* (Islamic law), which is the basis for family law, dealing with matters such as inheritance and divorce. Separate courts have been established to deal with commercial disputes and other matters to which *Shari'a* does not apply.

Courts of the First Instance are competent to try cases of criminal misdemeanour; serious crimes are tried by the Criminal Courts; the Court of Appeal is in Muscat. There are district courts throughout the country. Special courts deal with military crimes committed by members of the armed and security forces.

The Basic Statute provides for a Supreme Council to supervise the proper functioning of the courts.

An Administrative Court, to review the decisions of government bodies, was instituted in April 2001.

The office of Public Prosecutor was established in 1999 and the first such appointment was made in June 2001.

Religion

ISLAM

The majority of the population (estimated at 89.2% in 2001) are Muslims, of whom approximately three-quarters are of the Ibadi sect and about one-quarter are Sunni Muslims.

HINDUISM

According to 2001 estimates, 6.0% of the population are Hindus.

CHRISTIANITY

According to 2001 estimates, 2.9% of the population are Christians.

Protestantism

The Protestant Church in Oman: POB 1982, Ruwi 112; tel. 24702372; fax 24789943; e-mail pcomct@omantel.net.om; internet protestantchurchinoman.blogspot.com; joint chaplaincy of the Anglican Church and the Reformed Church of America; four inter-denominational churches in Oman, at Ruwi and Ghala in Muscat, at Sohar and at Salalah; Senior Pastor Rev. BENJAMIN CHASE (acting).

The Roman Catholic Church

A small number of adherents, mainly expatriates, form part of the Apostolic Vicariate of Arabia. The Vicar Apostolic is resident in the United Arab Emirates.

The Press

Article 31 of Oman's Basic Statute guarantees the freedom of the press, printing and publishing, according to the terms and conditions specified by the law. Published matter 'leading to discord, harming the State's security or abusing human dignity or rights' is prohibited.

NEWSPAPERS

Oman: POB 3002, Ruwi 112; tel. 24699689; fax 24697443; e-mail editor@omandaily.com; internet www.omandaily.com; daily; Arabic; publ. by Oman Establishment for Press, News, Publication and Advertising; Editor-in-Chief ABDULLAH BIN NASSER AR-RAHBI; circ. 15,560.

Ash-Shabiba (Youth): POB 2998, Ruwi 112; tel. 24814373; fax 24811722; e-mail editor@shabiba.com; internet www.shabiba.com; f. 1993; daily; Arabic; culture, leisure and sports; publ. by Muscat Press and Publishing House SAOC; Editor-in-Chief AHMAD BIN ESSA AZ-ZEDJALI.

Al-Watan (The Nation): POB 463, Muscat 113; tel. 24491919; fax 24491280; e-mail alwatan@omantel.net.om; internet www.alwatan

OMAN

.com; f. 1971; daily; Arabic; Editor-in-Chief MUHAMMAD BIN SULAYMAN AT-TAI; circ. 40,000.

English Language

Oman Daily Observer: POB 3002, Ruwi 112; tel. 24699647; fax 24600362; e-mail editor@omanobserver.com; internet www.omanobserver.com; f. 1981; daily; publ. by Oman Establishment for Press, News, Publication and Advertising; Chair. ABDULLAH BIN NASSER AR-RAHBI; Editor IBRAHIM BIN SAIF AL-HAMDANI; circ. 22,000.

Oman Tribune: POB 463, Muscat 113; tel. 24491919; fax 24498444; e-mail eomantribune@omantribune.com; internet www.omantribune.com; f. 2004; Founder and Chair. MUHAMMAD BIN SULAYMAN AT-TAI; Editor-in-Chief ABD AL-HAMID BIN SULAYMAN AT-TAI.

Times of Oman: POB 770, Ruwi 112; tel. 24811953; fax 24813153; e-mail online@timesofoman.com; internet www.timesofoman.com; f. 1975; daily; publ. by Muscat Press and Publishing House SAOC; Founder, Chair. and Editor-in-Chief ESSA BIN MUHAMMAD AZ-ZEDJALI; Man. Dir ANIS BIN ESSA AZ-ZEDJALI; circ. 34,000.

TheWeek: POB 2616, Ruwi 112, Muscat; tel. 24799388; fax 24793316; e-mail theweek@apexstuff.com; internet www.theweek.co.om; f. 2003; weekly; free; publ. by Apex Press and Publishing; Man. Editor MOHANA PRABHAKAR; circ. 50,254 (copies per week).

PERIODICALS

Alam al-Iqtisad Wa al-A'mal (World of Economy and Business): POB 3305, Ruwi 112; tel. 24700896; fax 24707939; f. 2007; monthly; Arabic; business magazine; publ. by United Press and Publishing LLC.

Al-'Aqida (The Faith): POB 1001, Ruwi 112; tel. 24701000; fax 24709917; weekly illustrated magazine; Arabic; political; Editor SAID AS-SAMHAN AL-KATHIRI; circ. 10,000.

Al-Ayn as-Sahira (The Vigilant Eye): Royal Oman Police, POB 302, Mina' al-Fahl 116; tel. 24569270; fax 24567161; quarterly magazine of Royal Oman Police.

Business Today: POB 2616, Ruwi 112; tel. 24799388; fax 24793316; e-mail editorial@apexstuff.com; internet www.apexstuff.com; monthly; publ. by Apex Press and Publishing; Man. Editor MOHANA PRABHAKAR.

The Commercial: POB 2002, Ruwi 112; tel. 24704022; fax 24795885; e-mail omanad@omantel.net.om; f. 1978; monthly; Arabic and English; business news; Man. MUHAMMAD AYOOB; Chief Editor ALI BIN ABDULLAH AL-KASBI; circ. 10,000.

Al-Ghorfa (The Chamber): POB 1400, Ruwi 112; tel. 24703082; fax 24708497; e-mail alghorfa@chamberoman.com; internet www.chamberoman.com; f. 1978; bi-monthly; English and Arabic; business; publ. by Oman Chamber of Commerce and Industry; Editor HAMOOD HAMAD AL-MAHROUQ; circ. 10,500.

Al-Jarida ar-Rasmiya (Official Gazette): POB 578, Ruwi 112; tel. 24605802; fax 24605697; f. 1972; fortnightly; publ. by Ministry of Legal Affairs.

Jund Oman (Soldiers of Oman): Ministry of Defence, POB 113, Muscat 113; tel. 24613615; fax 24613369; f. 1974; monthly; Arabic; illustrated magazine of the Ministry of Defence; Supervisor Chief of Staff of the Sultan's Armed Forces.

Al-Mar'a (Woman): United Media Services, POB 3305, Ruwi 112; tel. 24700896; fax 24707939; e-mail almara@umsoman.com; internet www.almaraonline.com; monthly; Arabic and English; women's interest; publ. by United Press and Publishing LLC.

Al-Markazi (The Central): POB 1161, Ruwi 112; tel. 24702222; fax 24707913; e-mail cboccr@omantel.net.om; f. 1975; bi-monthly economic magazine; Arabic and English; publ. by Central Bank of Oman; Editor-in-Chief HAIDER BIN ABD AR-REDHA AL-LAWATI.

An-Nahda (The Renaissance): POB 979, Muscat 113; tel. 24563104; fax 24563106; weekly illustrated magazine; Arabic; political and social; Editor TALEB SAID AL-MEAWALY; circ. 10,000.

Nizwa: POB 855, 117 Wadi Kabir; tel. 24601608; fax 24694254; e-mail nizwa99@omantel.net.om; internet www.nizwa.com; f. 1994; quarterly; Arabic; literary and cultural; publ. by Oman Establishment for Press, News, Publication and Advertising; Editor-in-Chief SAIF AR-RAHBI.

Oman Economic Review: POB 3305, Ruwi 112; tel. 24700896; fax 24707939; e-mail editor@oeronline.com; internet www.oeronline.com; f. 1998; monthly; English; business news; publ. by United Press and Publishing LLC; Editor-in-Chief Sayyid TARIK BIN SHABIB.

Oman Today: POB 2616, Ruwi 112; tel. 24799388; fax 24793316; e-mail editorial@apexstuff.com; internet www.apexstuff.com; f. 1981; monthly; English; leisure and sports; publ. by Apex Press and Publishing; Man. Editor MOHANA PRABHAKAR; circ. 20,000.

Al-Omaniya (Omani Woman): POB 3303, Ruwi 112; tel. 24792700; fax 24707765; f. 1982; monthly; Arabic; Editor AIDA BINT SALIM AL-HUJRI; circ. 10,500.

Risalat al-Masjid (The Mosque Message): POB 6066, Muscat; tel. 24561178; fax 24560607; issued by Diwan of the Royal Court Protocol Dept (Schools and Mosques Section); Editor JOUMA BIN MUHAMMAD BIN SALEM AL-WAHAIBI.

Al-Usra (The Family): POB 440, Mutrah 114; tel. 24794922; fax 24795348; e-mail admeds@omantel.net.om; f. 1974; fortnightly; Arabic; socio-economic illustrated magazine; Chief Editor SADEK ABDOWANI; circ. 15,000.

NEWS AGENCY

Oman News Agency: Ministry of Information, POB 3659, Ruwi 112; tel. 24698891; fax 24699657; e-mail onaoman@omantel.net.om; internet www.omannews.com; f. 1986; Dir-Gen. and Editor-in-Chief MAJID BIN MUHAMMAD BIN FARAJ AR-ROWAS.

Publishers

Apex Press and Publishing: POB 2616, Ruwi 112, Muscat; tel. 24799388; fax 24793316; internet www.apexstuff.com; f. 1980; art, history, trade directories, maps, leisure and business magazines, and guidebooks; Pres. SALEH M. TALIB AZ-ZAKWANI; Man. Editor MOHANA PRABHAKAR.

Dar al-Usra: POB 440, Mutrah 114; tel. 24794922; fax 24795348; e-mail alusra@omantel.net.om.

Muscat Press and Publishing House SAOC: POB 770, Ruwi 112; tel. 24811953; fax 24813153; Chair. ESSA MUHAMMAD AZ-ZEDJALI; CEO AHMAD BIN ESSA AZ-ZEDJALI.

National Publishing and Advertising LLC: POB 3112, Ruwi 112; tel. 24793098; fax 24708445; e-mail npanet@usa.net; f. 1987; Man. ASHOK SUVARNA.

Oman Establishment for Press, News, Publication and Advertising (OEPNPA): Information City, Al-Qurum, Muscat; f. 1996 as Oman Newspaper House; Chair. ABDULLAH BIN NASSER AR-RAHBI.

Oman Establishment for Printing and Publishing: POB 463, Muscat 113; tel. 24591919; fax 24591280; Editor-in-Chief SAID BIN KHALFAN AL-HARTHY.

Ash-Shahmi Publishers and Advertisers: POB 6112, Ruwi; tel. 24703416.

United Press and Publishing LLC (UPP): POB 3305, Ruwi 112; tel. 24700896; fax 24707939; internet www.renaissanceoman.com; f. 1995; part of Renaissance Services SAOG; publishes Alam al-Iqtisad (Arabic monthly) and Oman Economic Review (English monthly); Gen. Man. SANDEEP SEHGAL.

Broadcasting and Communications

TELECOMMUNICATIONS

Regulatory Authority

Telecommunications Regulatory Authority: POB 579, Ruwi 112; tel. 24574300; fax 24565464; e-mail traoman@tra.gov.om; internet www.tra.gov.om; f. 2002 to oversee the privatization of Omantel (see below) and to set tariffs and regulate the sale of operating licences; Chair. MUHAMMAD BIN NASSER AL-KHUSAIBI.

Service Providers

Oman Telecommunications Company SAOC (Omantel): POB 789, Ruwi 112; tel. 24631417; fax 24697066; e-mail info@omantel.net.om; internet www.omantel.net.om; f. 1999 as successor to the General Telecommunications Organization; state-owned, but undergoing privatization; Chair. Eng. SULTAN BIN HAMDOUN AL-HARTHI; Exec. Pres. Eng. MUHAMMAD BIN ALI AL-WAHAIBI.

Oman Mobile Telecommunications Company LLC (Oman Mobile): POB 694, Al-Azaiba 130; tel. 24474000; e-mail enquiry@omanmobile.om; internet www.omanmobile.om; subsidiary of Omantel; Chair. Eng. SULTAN BIN HAMDOUN AL-HARTHI.

Nawras: POB 874, Muscat 111; tel. 95011500; fax 95011555; e-mail customerservice@nawras.om; internet www.nawras.om; f. 2004; mobile telephone operator; Chair. Sheikh SAIF BIN HASHIL AL-MASKERY; CEO ROSS CORMACK.

BROADCASTING

Broadcast media in Oman is currently operated by the Government. However, legislation enacted in 2004 allowed the establishment of private broadcasters; the first two licences to private radio operators were issued in 2005.

Radio

Radio Sultanate of Oman: Ministry of Information, POB 600, Muscat 113; tel. 24602058; fax 24601393; e-mail feedback@oman-radio.gov.om; internet www.oman-tv.gov.om/rdeng; f. 1970; transmits in Arabic 20 hours daily, English on FM (Oman FM) 15 hours daily; Dir-Gen. NASSER SULAYMAN AS-SAIBANI.

Radio Salalah: f. 1970; transmits daily programmes in Arabic and the Dhofari languages; Dir MUHAMMAD BIN AHMAD AR-ROWAS.

The British Broadcasting Corpn (BBC) has built a powerful medium-wave relay station on Masirah island. It is used to expand and improve the reception of the BBC's Arabic, Farsi, Hindi, Pashtu and Urdu services.

Television

Sultanate of Oman Television: Ministry of Information, POB 600, Muscat 113; tel. 24603222; fax 24605032; internet www.oman-tv.gov.om; began broadcasting in 1974; programmes broadcast via Arabsat and Nilesat satellite networks.

Finance

(cap. = capital; res = reserves; dep. = deposits; m. = million; brs = branches; amounts in rials Omani)

BANKING

At the end of December 2006 there were 14 commercial banks (five local and nine foreign) and three specialized banks, with a total network of 366 domestic branch offices operating throughout Oman. Legislation introduced in January 2001 increased the minimum capital requirement for Omani commercial banks from RO 10m. to RO 20m., and set a minimum capital requirement of RO 3m. for foreign banks established in Oman.

Central Bank

Central Bank of Oman: POB 1161, 44 Mutrah Commercial Centre, Ruwi 112; tel. 24702222; fax 24788995; e-mail cboccr@omantel.om; internet www.cbo-oman.org; f. 1974; cap. 300.0m., res 523.2m., dep. 620.2m. (Dec. 2006); 100% state-owned; Exec. Pres. HAMOUD SANGOUR AZ-ZADJALI; 2 brs.

Commercial Banks

Bank Dhofar SAOG: POB 1507, Ruwi 112; tel. 24790466; fax 24797246; e-mail info@bankdhofar.com; internet www.bankdhofar.com; f. 1990 as Bank Dhofar al-Omani al-Fransi SAOG; renamed as above in 2004 after merger with Majan International Bank SAOC; cap. 46.2m., res 23.4m., dep. 568.0m. (Dec. 2006); Chair. Eng. ABD AL-HAFIDH SALIM RAJAB AL-AUJAILI; CEO AHMAD BIN ALI ASH-SHANFARI; 47 brs.

BankMuscat SAOG: POB 134, Ruwi 112; tel. 24768888; fax 24785572; e-mail banking@bkmuscat.com; internet www.bankmuscat.com; f. 1993 by merger as Bank Muscat Al-Ahli Al-Omani; renamed Bank Muscat International in 1998, and as above in 1999; merged with Commercial Bank of Oman Ltd SAOG in 2000 and with Industrial Bank of Oman in 2002; 88.8% owned by Omani shareholders; cap. 83.2m., res 165.8m., dep. 2,371.7m. (Dec. 2006); Chair. Sheikh ABD AL-MALEK BIN ABDULLAH AL-KHALILI; CEO ABD AR-RAZAK ALI ISSA; 95 brs.

National Bank of Oman SAOG (NBO): POB 751, Ruwi 112; tel. 24778000; fax 24778585; e-mail ask@nbo.co.om; internet www.nbo.co.om; f. 1973; 100% Omani-owned; cap. 80.0m., res 101.2m., dep. 833.9m. (Dec. 2006); Chair. Sheikh SUHAIL BIN SALIM BAHWAN; CEO ANDREW MCGREGOR DUFF; 52 brs.

Oman Arab Bank SAOC: POB 2010, Ruwi 112; tel. 24706265; fax 24797736; e-mail mktoab@omantel.net.om; internet www.omanab.com; f. 1984; purchased Omani European Bank SAOG in 1994; 51% Omani-owned, 49% by Arab Bank PLC (Jordan); cap. 38.0m., res 26.2m., dep. 438.7m. (Dec. 2006); Chair. RASHAD MUHAMMAD AZ-ZUBAIR; CEO ABD AL-QADER ASKALAN; 39 brs.

Oman International Bank SAOG: POB 1727, Muscat 111; tel. 24682500; fax 24682800; e-mail oibgm@omantel.net.om; internet www.oiboman.com; f. 1984; 100% Omani-owned; cap. 75.5m., res 25.9m., dep. 782.3m. (Dec. 2006); Chair. REEM BINT OMAR AZ-ZAWAWI; Gen. Man. DOUGLAS EMMETT; 82 brs.

Development Banks

Alliance Housing Bank: POB 545, Mina al-Fahal 116; tel. 24568845; fax 24568003; e-mail info@alliance-housing.com; internet www.alliance-housing.com; f. 1997; privately owned; cap. 21.0m. (Dec. 2004), total assets 163.6m. (March 2006); Chair. Sayyid KHALID HAMAD HAMOOD AL-BUSAIDI; Gen. Man. KEITH SCOTT; 7 brs.

Oman Development Bank SAOG: POB 3077, Ruwi 112; tel. 24814348; fax 24813621; e-mail odebe@omantel.net.om; f. 1977; absorbed Oman Bank for Agriculture and Fisheries in 1997; short-, medium- and long-term finance for devt projects in industry, agriculture and fishing; state-owned; cap. 20.0m., res 3.0m., dep. 0.3m. (Dec. 2005); Chair. Sheikh YAQOOB BIN HAMAD AL-HARTHY; Gen. Man. MURTADHA BIN MUHAMMAD FADHIL; 9 brs.

Oman Housing Bank SAOC: POB 2555, Ruwi 112; tel. 24704444; fax 24704071; e-mail ohb@ohb.co.om; internet www.ohb.co.om; f. 1977; long-term finance for housing devt; 100% state-owned; cap. 30.0m., total assets 162.6m. (Dec. 2005); Chair. DARWISH ISMAIL ALI AL-BULUSHI; Gen. Man. ADNAN HAIDAR DARWISH AZ-ZA'ABI; 9 brs.

STOCK EXCHANGE

Muscat Securities Market (MSM): POB 3265, Muscat 112; tel. 24823600; fax 24815776; e-mail msm.info.news@msm.gov.om; internet www.msm.gov.om; 155 cos listed (March 2008); f. 1989; Chair. ABDULLAH BIN SALEM AS-SALMI; Dir-Gen. AHMAD SALEH AL-MARHOON.

Supervisory Body

Capital Markets Authority (CMA): POB 3359, Ruwi 112; tel. 24823258; fax 24817471; e-mail info@cma-oman.gov.om; internet www.omancma.org; f. 2000 to regulate stock exchange; Chair. MAQBOOL BIN ALI BIN SULTAN (Minister of Commerce and Industry); Exec. Pres. YAHYA BIN SAID ABDULLAH AL-JABRI.

INSURANCE

In 2006 there were 17 licensed insurance companies operating in Oman. Of these, 10 were local firms and the remainder were branches of non-resident companies.

Al-Ahlia Insurance Co SAOG: POB 1463, Ruwi 112; tel. 24709441; fax 24797151; e-mail aaic@alahliaoman.com; internet www.alahliaoman.com; f. 1985; cap. 5.0m., total assets 57.3m. (Sept. 2007); Chair. Sayyid KHALID HAMAD HAMOOD AL-BUSAIDI; Gen. Man. A. R. SRINIVASAN.

Dhofar Insurance Co SAOG: POB 1002, Ruwi 112; tel. 24793640; fax 24793641; e-mail dhofar@dhofarinsurance.com; internet www.dhofarinsurance.com; f. 1989; cap. 20.0m. (Dec. 2007); Chair. Sheikh SALIM BIN MUBARAK ASH-SHANFARI.

Falcon Insurance Co SAOG: POB 2279, Ruwi 112; tel. 24660900; fax 24565323; e-mail ficins@omantel.net.om; f. 1977 as Al-Ittihad al-Watani; cap. 5.4m.; Gen. Man. MICHAEL JAN WRIGHT.

Muscat Insurance Co SAOG: POB 72, Ruwi 112; tel. 24695897; fax 24695847; e-mail mic@omzest.com; Gen. Man. MALCOLM A. JACK.

National Life and General Insurance Co SAOC: POB 798, Wadi Kabir 117; tel. 24793666; fax 24795222; e-mail natlife@nlicgulf.com; internet www.nlicgulf.com; f. 1983; Gen. Man. S. VENKATACHALAM.

Oman National Insurance Co SAOC (ONIC): POB 2254, Ruwi 112; tel. 24795020; fax 24790372; f. 1978; cap. 2m., total assets 51.2m. (2004); Chair. SALIM BIN HASSAN MACKI; Gen. Man. MICHAEL J. WRIGHT.

Oman United Insurance Co SAOG: POB 1522, Ruwi 112; tel. 24477300; fax 24477334; e-mail admin@ouic.com.om; internet www.ouic-oman.com; f. 1985; cap. 10.0m., total assets 58.2m. (Sept. 2007); Chair. SAID SALIM BIN NASSIR AL-BUSAIDI; Gen. Man. KHALID MANSOUR HAMED.

Trade and Industry

GOVERNMENT AGENCY

Omani Centre for Investment Promotion and Export Development (OCIPED): POB 25, Al-Wadi Kabir 117, Muscat; tel. 24812344; fax 24810890; e-mail info@ociped.com; internet www.ociped.com; f. 1996; promotes investment to Oman and the devt of non-oil Omani exports; Chair. MAQBOOL BIN ALI BIN SULTAN; Exec. Pres. SALEM BIN NASSER AL-ISMAILY.

CHAMBER OF COMMERCE

Oman Chamber of Commerce and Industry: POB 1400, Ruwi 112; tel. 24707684; fax 24708497; e-mail occi@chamberoman.com; internet www.chamberoman.com; f. 1973; Chair. KHALIL BIN ABDULLAH BIN MUHAMMAD AL-KHONJI; 119,281 mems (Dec. 2004).

STATE HYDROCARBONS COMPANIES

National Gas Co SAOG: POB 95, Rusayl 124; tel. 24446073; fax 24446307; e-mail natgas@omantel.net.om; f. 1979; bottling of liquefied petroleum gas; Chair. Sheikh KHALID AHMAD SULTAN AL-HOSNI; Gen. Man. PRADYOT KUMAR BAGCHI; 158 employees.

OMAN — Directory

Oman Gas Co SOAC (OGC): POB 799, al-Khuwair 133; tel. 24681600; fax 24681678; e-mail info@oman-gas.com.om; internet www.oman-gas.com.om; f. 1999; govt-owned (80% Ministry of Oil and Gas; 20% Oman Oil Co); operates gas network and builds pipelines to supply power plants and other industries in Oman; Chair. Dr MUHAMMAD BIN HAMAD BIN SAIF AR-RUMHI (Minister of Oil and Gas); CEO YOUSUF BIN MUHAMMAD AL-OJAILI.

Oman LNG LLC: POB 560, Mina al-Fahal 116; tel. 24609999; fax 24609900; e-mail info@omanlng.co.om; internet www.omanlng.com; f. 1992; 51% state-owned; Royal Dutch Shell 30%; manages 6.6m. metric-tons-per-year liquefied natural gas plant at Qalhat; manufacturing, shipping and marketing; Chair. NASSER BIN KHAMIS AL-JASHMI; CEO and Gen. Man. Dr BRIAN BUCKLEY; 225 employees.

Oman Oil Co SAOC (OOC): POB 261, al-Harthy Complex, Ruwi 118; tel. 24567392; fax 24567386; e-mail oman-oil@oman-oil.com; internet www.oman-oil.com; f. late 1980s to invest in foreign commercial enterprises and oil trading operations; 100% state-owned; Chair. MAQBOOL BIN ALI BIN SULTAN; CEO AHMAD AL-WAHAIBI.

Oman Refinery Co LLC: POB 3568, Ruwi 112; tel. 24561200; fax 24561384; e-mail info@refinery.co.om; internet www.orc.co.om; f. 1982; production of light petroleum products; production averaged 85,000 b/d (2005); Chair. NASSER BIN KHAMIS AL-JASHMI; CEO Dr ADIL BIN ABD-AL AZIZ AL-KINDY; 355 employees.

Petroleum Development Oman LLC (PDO): POB 81, Muscat 113; tel. 24678111; fax 24677106; e-mail external-affairs@pdo.co.om; internet www.pdo.co.om; incorporated in Sultanate of Oman since 1980 by royal decree as limited liability co; 60% owned by Oman Govt, 34% by Royal Dutch Shell; crude oil production (2005) averaged 631,000 b/d from some 106 fields, linked by a pipeline system to terminal at Mina al-Fahal, near Muscat; gas production (2005) totalled 43.1m. cu m/d; Chair. Dr MUHAMMAD BIN HAMAD BIN SAIF AR-RUMHI (Minister of Oil and Gas); Man. Dir JOHN MALCOLM; 5,000 employees.

UTILITIES

As part of its privatization programme, the Omani Government is divesting the utilities on a project-by-project basis. Private investors have already been found for several municipal waste water projects, desalination plants and regional electricity providers. Listed below are the state agencies currently responsible for each utility.

A new Public Authority for Electricity and Water, established in September 2007, plans and supervises the development of the utilities in Oman.

Electricity

Oman National Engineering and Investment Co SAOG (ONEIC): POB 1393, Ruwi 112; tel. 24700369; fax 24797394; e-mail oneic@oneic.com.om; internet www.onec.org; f. 1978 as Oman National Electric Co SAOG; Chair. Sheikh AIMAN BIN AHMAD BIN SULTAN AL-HOSNI; Man. Dir Eng. MUHAMMAD AMIN BIN MOUSTAFA AS-SALIH.

Water

Ministry of Regional Municipalities and Water Resources: (see The Government); assesses, manages, develops and conserves water resources.

Transport

ROADS

A network of adequate graded roads links all the main centres of population and only a few mountain villages are inaccessible by off-road vehicles. In 2006 there were 41,634 km of roads, of which 982 km were dual carriageways and a further 16,551 km were asphalted roads. Several large-scale road-building projects were under way in 2007–08, including the construction of a 56-km partial ring-road around Muscat, at a cost of some US $342m.

Directorate-General of Roads: POB 7027, Mutrah; tel. 24701577; Dir-Gen. of Roads Sheikh MUHAMMAD BIN HILAL AL-KHALILI.

Oman National Transport Co SAOG (ONTC): POB 620, Muscat 113; tel. 24590046; fax 24590152; e-mail info@ontcoman.com; internet www.ontcoman.com; f. 1972; re-established in 1984; operates local, regional and long-distance bus services from Muscat; Chair. MAJID SAID SALIM AR-RUWAHI; Man. Dir SULAYMAN BIN MUHANA AL-ADAWI.

SHIPPING

Port Sultan Qaboos (Mina Sultan Qaboos), at the entrance to the Persian (Arabian) Gulf, was built in 1974 to provide nine deep-water berths varying in length from 250 ft to 750 ft (76 m to 228 m), with draughts of up to 43 ft (13 m), and three berths for shallow-draught vessels drawing 12 ft to 16 ft (3.7 m to 4.9 m) of water. A total of 12 new berths have been opened and two of the existing berths have been upgraded to a container terminal capable of handling 60 containers per hour. The port also has a 3,000-metric-ton-capacity cold store which belongs to the Oman Fisheries Co. In the 1990s Port Sultan Qaboos underwent a further upgrade and expansion. In 2006 1,698 ships visited the port and 2.6m. tons of cargo were handled.

The oil terminal at Mina al-Fahal can also accommodate the largest super-tankers on offshore loading buoys. Similar facilities for the import of refined petroleum products exist at Mina al-Fahal. Mina Raysut, near Salalah (now known as Salalah port), has been developed into an all-weather port, and, in addition to container facilities, has four deep-water berths and two shallow berths. The port is currently undergoing transformation into a free trade zone. During 2006 739 ships called at Salalah. In 2002 the port handled a reported 2m. 20-ft equivalent units (TEU). The construction of two further deep-water berths was due to be completed in 2008, increasing the port's capacity to some 3m. TEUs per year. Loading facilities for smaller craft exist at Sohar and Khasab (both of which are being expanded), Khaboura, Sur, Marbet, Ras Al Hadd, Al-Biaa, Masirah and Salalah. A US $479m. contract to construct a new port at Duqm, on the Gulf of Masirah, was awarded in mid-2007; the project was to include two docks capable of accommodating large tankers. A dry dock complex was also planned.

Directorate-General of Ports and Maritime Affairs: POB 684, Ruwi 113; tel. 24700986; fax 24702044; e-mail dgpma@omantel.net.om; Dir-Gen. Eng. JAMAL T. AZIZ.

Port Services Corpn SAOG (PSC): POB 133, Muscat 113; tel. 24714000; fax 24714007; e-mail mktg@pscoman.com; internet www.pscoman.com; f. 1976; cap. RO 7.2m. (2004); jointly owned by the Govt of Oman and private shareholders; Exec. Pres. SAUD BIN AHMAD AN-NAHARI.

Salalah Port Services Co SAOG (SPS): POB 105, Muscat 118; tel. 24600586; fax 24600736; e-mail info@salalahport.com; internet www.salalahport.com; port authority for Salalah port; CEO and Gen. Man. TIEMEN MEESTER.

CIVIL AVIATION

Domestic and international flights operate from Seeb International Airport. In 2006 4.8m. passengers passed through the airport; however, it was planned to increase annual passenger capacity to 12.5m. over a 25-year period. Seeb International Airport and Oman's second international airport, at Salalah (completed in 1978), were both effectively privatized in October 2001. Responsibility for the management and refurbishment of the airports passed to Oman Airports Management Company (OAMC); however, following the failure of the Government successfully to agree financial terms for the privatization and ongoing development of the airports with OAMC, the 25-year contract was cancelled in October 2004 and Seeb and Salalah airports were returned to state control. Plans for substantial development and expansion of both international airports to provide additional terminals and increase passenger handling capacity were announced as part of the Government's seventh Development Plan in 2006. There are also airports at Sur, Masirah, Khasab and Diba, with three further airports planned for Sohar, Duqum and Ras Al Hadd; most other sizeable towns have airstrips.

Directorate-General of Civil Aviation and Meteorology: POB 1, CPO Seeb Airport, Muscat 111; tel. 24519356; fax 24519880; internet www.met.gov.om; Dir-Gen. Eng. AHMAD BIN SAID BIN SALIM AR-RAWAHY.

Oman Aviation Services Co SAOG (Oman Air): POB 58, Seeb International Airport 111; tel. 24519953; fax 24521075; internet www.omanair.aero/wy; f. 1981; cap. RO 11m.; 100% owned by Govt since 2007; air-charter, maintenance, handling and catering; operators of Oman's domestic airline (Oman Air); international services to Bangladesh, India, Kenya, Kuwait, Lebanon, Pakistan, Qatar, Saudi Arabia, Sri Lanka, Tanzania and the UAE; Chair. AHMAD BIN ABD AN-NABI MACKI; CEO ZIAD KARIM AL-HAREMI.

Tourism

Tourism, introduced in 1985, is strictly controlled. Oman's attractions, apart from the capital itself, include Nizwa, ancient capital of the interior, Dhofar and the forts of Nakhl, Rustaq and Al-Hazm. The country also possesses an attractive and clean environment, including around 1,700 km of sandy beaches. The Government promotes, in a limited capacity, high-quality adventure, cultural and marine tourism. In 2005 there were 1,114,498 visitor arrivals in Oman and tourism receipts totalled US $679m.

Directorate-General of Tourism: Madinat Al-Sultan Qaboos, POB 200, Muscat 115; tel. 24588700; fax 24588819; e-mail info@omantourism.gov.om; internet www.omantourism.gov.om; Dir-Gen. MUHAMMAD ALI SAID.

PAKISTAN

Introductory Survey

Location, Climate, Language, Religion, Flag, Capital

The Islamic Republic of Pakistan lies in southern Asia, bordered by India to the east and by Afghanistan and Iran to the west. It has a short frontier with the People's Republic of China in the far north-east. The climate is dry and generally hot, with an annual average temperature of 27°C (80°F), except in the mountains, which have very cold winters. Temperatures in Karachi are generally between 13°C (55°F) and 34°C (93°F), with negligible rainfall. The principal languages are Punjabi (the language usually spoken in 44.2% of households in 1998), Pushto (Pashtu) (15.4%), Sindhi (14.1%) and Saraiki (10.5%). Urdu (7.6%) is the national language, and English is extensively used. The state religion is Islam, embracing about 97% of the population, the remainder being mainly Hindus or Christians. The national flag (proportions 2 by 3) has a vertical white stripe at the hoist, while the remainder is dark green, with a white crescent moon and a five-pointed star in the centre. The capital is Islamabad.

Recent History

Pakistan was created in August 1947 by the partition of the United Kingdom's former Indian Empire into the independent states of India and Pakistan, in response to demands by elements of the Muslim population in the subcontinent for the establishment of a specifically Islamic state. Pakistan originally comprised two distinct regions: East Pakistan and West Pakistan, separated by some 1,600 km (1,000 miles) of Indian territory, and united only by a common religion. Although the majority of the population lived in the smaller part, East Pakistan, political and military power was concentrated in the west, where the Muslim League was the dominant political movement. The leader of the Muslim League, Muhammad Ali Jinnah, popularly known as Quaid-i-Azam ('Great Leader'), became the first Governor-General of Pakistan but died in 1948. The country, formerly a dominion with the British monarch as Head of State, became a republic on 23 March 1956, when Pakistan's first Constitution was promulgated. At the same time Maj.-Gen. Iskander Mirza became Pakistan's first President.

Pakistan came under military rule in early October 1958, when President Mirza abrogated the Constitution, declared martial law, dismissed the national and provincial governments and dissolved all political parties. In late October, however, Gen. (later Field Marshal) Muhammad Ayub Khan, the Martial Law Administrator appointed by Mirza, removed Mirza from office and became President himself. Ayub Khan's autocratic but modernizing regime lasted until March 1969, when he was forced to resign following widespread unrest. Gen. Agha Muhammad Yahya Khan, the Commander-in-Chief of the Army, replaced him, and martial law was reimposed.

In December 1970 the country's first general election was held for a national assembly. Sheikh Mujibur Rahman's Awami League, which advocated autonomy for East Pakistan, won almost all the seats in the east (thus gaining an absolute majority in the National Assembly), while the Pakistan People's Party (PPP), led by Zulfikar Ali Bhutto, won a majority of seats in the west. Following the failure of negotiations to achieve a coalition government of the two parties, on 23 March 1971 East Pakistan declared its independence as the People's Republic of Bangladesh. Civil war immediately broke out, as Pakistani troops clashed with Bengali irregular forces. In December the Indian army intervened in the conflict to support the Bengalis, and the Pakistani army was forced to withdraw, thus permitting Bangladesh to establish firmly its independence. In the truncated Pakistan that remained in the west, Yahya Khan resigned, military rule was ended, and Bhutto became the new President.

A new Constitution, which came into effect in August 1973, provided for a parliamentary system of government. Bhutto became executive Prime Minister, while Fazal Elahi Chaudry, hitherto Speaker of the National Assembly, became constitutional President. The PPP won an overwhelming majority of seats in elections to the National Assembly in March 1977. However, the opposition Pakistan National Alliance (PNA) accused the PPP of widespread electoral malpractice and launched a nation-wide campaign of civil disobedience. An estimated 1,000 people died in subsequent clashes between troops and demonstrators, and some 40,000 people were arrested. In July the armed forces intervened in the crisis: Bhutto was deposed in a bloodless military coup and a martial law regime was instituted, with Gen. Mohammad Zia ul-Haq, the Army Chief of Staff, as Chief Martial Law Administrator. President Chaudry remained in office as Head of State. Bhutto was subsequently charged with instigating the murder of a PPP dissident and a member of the dissident's family in 1974. He was sentenced to death in March 1978 and executed in April 1979.

In September 1978 President Chaudry resigned and Gen. Zia became President. General elections were postponed several times by the military administration, and in October 1979 Gen. Zia announced an indefinite postponement of the polls. Opposition to the military regime was severely suppressed, particularly after new martial law orders were adopted in May 1980. In March 1981 nine political parties formed an opposition alliance, the Movement for the Restoration of Democracy (MRD), which advocated an end to military rule and a return to a parliamentary system of government. Several opposition politicians were subsequently interned or placed under house arrest. In August 1983 the MRD, led by the PPP, launched a civil disobedience campaign to press for the restoration of parliamentary democracy on the basis of the 1973 Constitution. The campaign enjoyed considerable support in Sindh province, where anti-Government protests resulted in numerous deaths. However, there was limited popular support elsewhere in the country, and the campaign ended in December 1983. Many political leaders and activists, including Benazir Bhutto (daughter of the former President and herself a leading PPP activist), were subsequently imprisoned or went into exile.

Gen. Zia's regime zealously pursued a policy of 'Islamization' of the country's institutions, including the enforcement of Islamic penal codes, and the introduction of Islamic economic principles, such as interest-free banking. In December 1984 a referendum was held, which sought affirmation of the Islamization process and, indirectly, endorsement of a further five-year term for Gen. Zia. The referendum was boycotted by the MRD, but, according to official figures, 98% of those participating supported the proposal. There were, however, widespread allegations of electoral malpractice.

In February 1985 a general election was held for a national assembly, followed shortly afterwards by elections to four provincial assemblies. The elections were held on a non-party basis, but widespread dissatisfaction with the regime was indicated by the defeat of several of Zia's cabinet ministers and close supporters. The largest two groupings in the new National Assembly were formed by a faction of the Pakistan Muslim League (PML, the successor to the Muslim League), known as the Pagara Group, and former members of the PPP. In late March Gen. Zia appointed Muhammad Khan Junejo, a member of the PML (Pagara Group), as Prime Minister, and an almost entirely civilian Cabinet was formed.

In October 1985 the National Assembly approved changes to the Constitution (the 'Eighth Amendment'), proposed by Gen. Zia, which introduced a powerful executive presidency and indemnified all actions of the military regime during the previous eight years. On 30 December Gen. Zia announced the repeal of martial law and the restoration of the Constitution (as amended in October). The military courts were dissolved, and military personnel were removed from civilian posts, with the exception of Gen. Zia, who remained as President and head of the armed forces. Junejo retained the post of Prime Minister in a new Cabinet. However, the MRD continued to demand the restoration of the unamended 1973 Constitution. In April 1986 its cause was strengthened by the return from exile of Benazir Bhutto, who travelled throughout the country holding political rallies which attracted thousands of supporters. She demanded the resignation of President Zia and the holding of a free general election, open to all political parties. In May Benazir Bhutto and her mother, Nusrat Bhutto, were elected as Co-Chairwomen of the PPP. In August the Government adopted a less tolerant approach towards the MRD by banning all rallies scheduled for

Independence Day and by detaining hundreds of opposition members, including Benazir Bhutto. The arrests provoked violent anti-Government demonstrations in a number of cities.

In late 1986 violent clashes occurred in Karachi, Quetta and Hyderabad as a result of disputes between rival ethnic groups (primarily between the Pathans, originally from the North-West Frontier Province—NWFP—and Afghanistan, and the Urdu-speaking Mohajirs, who migrated from India when the subcontinent was partitioned in 1947). The violence was most severe in Karachi, where some 170 people were killed in December. The rise of ethnic communalism in Pakistan was reflected in the results of local elections held throughout the country in November 1987. The party of the Mohajirs, the Mohajir Qaumi Movement (MQM), won the majority of seats in Karachi and was also successful in other urban areas of Sindh province. Nationwide, the government-supported PML received the majority of votes, while the PPP won less than 20% of total seats.

In May 1988, in accordance with the authority vested in him through the Eighth Amendment, President Zia dismissed the Prime Minister and his Cabinet, and dissolved the National Assembly and the four provincial assemblies. Zia became head of an interim administration, which was to govern until a general election was held. In July Zia announced that the elections to the National Assembly and the provincial assemblies would be held in November. On 17 August 1988, however, President Zia was killed in an air crash in eastern Pakistan. Subsequent speculation that the cause of the crash was sabotage was not officially confirmed. The Chairman of the Senate, Ghulam Ishaq Khan, was appointed acting President, and an emergency National Council (composed of senior military officers, the four provincial governors and four federal ministers) was appointed to take charge of government.

Despite the imposition of a state of emergency after the death of Zia, the general election took place, as scheduled, in November 1988. In the elections to the National Assembly the PPP won 93 of the 207 directly elected seats, and was the only party to secure seats in each of Pakistan's four provinces. The Islamic Democratic Alliance (IDA), a grouping of nine Islamic and right-wing parties (including the PML), gained 54 seats, with the remaining seats going to independents and candidates representing seven smaller parties. The PPP did not achieve such a high level of support, however, in the elections to the provincial assemblies, held three days later. The PPP was able to form coalition governments in Sindh and the NWFP, but the IDA took power in Punjab, the most populous province. At the federal level, a coalition Government was formed by the PPP and the MQM, which together had a working majority in the National Assembly (the MQM had 14 seats). Benazir Bhutto, the leader of the PPP, was appointed Prime Minister on 1 December, thus becoming the first female leader of a Muslim country. The state of emergency was repealed on the same day. A new Cabinet was formed, and later in December an electoral college (comprising the Senate, the National Assembly and the four provincial assemblies) elected Ghulam Ishaq Khan as President.

Benazir Bhutto's attempts, in early 1989, to repeal the Eighth Amendment to the Constitution, which severely constrained her powers as Prime Minister, were unsuccessful. Moreover, the fragile coalitions that the PPP had formed in the provincial assemblies soon came under pressure. In April the coalition Government formed by the PPP and the Awami National Party (ANP) in the NWFP collapsed. In May the coalition with the MQM in Sindh province also failed, following renewed ethnic conflict in the region. In the same month the opposition was strengthened by the formation of an informal parliamentary grouping, the Combined Opposition Party (COP), comprising the IDA, the ANP, Jamiat-e-Ulema-e-Islam (JUI) and the Pakistan Awami Ittehad. In October the Government suffered a serious reversal when the MQM withdrew its parliamentary support for the PPP and transferred it to the opposition, claiming that the PPP had failed to honour any of the promises made in the original co-operation agreement between the two parties. In November a parliamentary motion of 'no confidence', proposed by the COP against the Government, was narrowly defeated. In January 1990 the COP organized a campaign to undermine the Government, accusing it of corruption, political bribery and mismanagement. Rallies and demonstrations in Sindh province culminated in violence between supporters of the PPP and the MQM; in May about 100 people were killed during violent clashes between police and demonstrators in the region. Calm was temporarily restored by the deployment of army units.

By mid-1990 the initial popularity of the PPP Government appeared to have declined considerably: the maintenance of law and order had worsened; no significant new legislation had been introduced; the economic situation was deteriorating; and there were widespread allegations of corruption against high-ranking officials. On 6 August the President, in accordance with his constitutional powers, dissolved the National Assembly, dismissed the Prime Minister and her Cabinet and declared a state of emergency. He also announced that a general election would take place in late October. The President alleged that the ousted Government had violated the Constitution, accusing it of corruption, nepotism and incompetence. Ghulam Mustafa Jatoi, the leader of the COP in the National Assembly, was appointed acting Prime Minister in an interim Government. The four provincial assemblies were also dissolved, and 'caretaker' Chief Ministers appointed. Benazir Bhutto claimed that the dissolution of her administration was illegal and strongly denied the various charges made against her Government. At the end of August several of Benazir Bhutto's former ministers were arrested, and in the following month she herself was indicted on more than 10 charges of corruption and abuse of power. In early October Benazir Bhutto's husband, Asif Ali Zardari, was arrested on charges of extortion, kidnapping and financial irregularities (he was later acquitted on all counts).

At the general election, which took place, as scheduled, on 24 October 1990, the IDA doubled its representation in the National Assembly, leaving it only four seats short of an absolute majority, while the People's Democratic Alliance (PDA, an electoral alliance comprising the PPP and three smaller parties) suffered a heavy defeat. Support for the PPP also declined in the provincial elections, where it unexpectedly lost control of its traditional stronghold in Sindh and fared badly elsewhere. Regional and ethnic parties continued to expand their influence, notably the MQM in urban areas of Sindh, and the ANP in the NWFP. On 6 November Mohammad Nawaz Sharif, the leader of the IDA and the former Chief Minister of Punjab, was elected as the new Prime Minister. He officially ended the three-month-long state of emergency, and appointed a new Cabinet, which included several ministers who had served under President Zia. Nawaz Sharif promised that one of the Government's major priorities was to establish lasting peace in Sindh, where ethnic conflict and general lawlessness continued to prevail. It was alleged, however, that the Government's subsequent campaign of suppression in the province, in response to numerous local murders and kidnappings, was aimed primarily at supporters of the PPP, hundreds of whom were arrested. In January 1991 the IDA won 19 of the 25 by-elections for seats in the National Assembly and the provincial assemblies, and in March won a decisive majority in elections to 42 seats in the Senate.

In May 1991 the National Assembly adopted legislation imposing the incorporation of *Shari'a*, the Islamic legal code, in Pakistan's legal system. The Assembly also adopted legislation providing for the Islamization of the educational, economic and judicial systems. Benazir Bhutto criticized the legislation as being extreme and fundamentalist, while the right-wing JUI claimed that the new law's provisions were not stringent enough.

The fundamentalist Jamaat-e-Islami Pakistan (JIP) left the IDA in May 1992, in protest at the Government's decision to support the new moderate *mujahidin* Government in Kabul, Afghanistan. The JIP accused the Government of abandoning the extremist Afghan guerrilla leader, Gulbuddin Hekmatyar, and also of failing to effect the full Islamization of Pakistan.

In response to continuing violence in Sindh, the Government launched 'Operation Clean-up' in May 1992, whereby the army was to apprehend criminals and terrorists, and seize unauthorized weapons. A violent clash between two factions of the MQM (the majority Altaf faction and the small breakaway Haqiqi faction) in Karachi in June provided the armed forces with the opportunity to suppress the extremist elements within the MQM. More than 500 people were arrested; caches of arms were located and seized; and 'torture cells', allegedly operated by the MQM, were discovered. The leader of the MQM (A), Altaf Hussain, accused the Government of attempting to crush the MQM through the military operation. In protest, 12 of the 15 MQM members in the National Assembly and 24 of the 27 members in the Sindh assembly resigned their seats. The Government, however, repeatedly gave assurances that the operations were against criminals, and not specifically against the MQM.

In mid-November 1992 the PDA intensified its campaign of political agitation and was now supported by the majority of the components of the newly formed opposition National Democratic Alliance (NDA), including the National People's Party (NPP—which had been expelled from the IDA in March). The large-scale demonstrations and marches organized by Benazir Bhutto were, however, ruthlessly suppressed by the Government. By mid-December tensions between the Government and opposition had eased considerably, and in January 1993, in an apparently conciliatory move on the part of Nawaz Sharif's administration, Benazir Bhutto was elected Chairperson of the National Assembly's Standing Committee on Foreign Affairs. Shortly after Benazir Bhutto had accepted the nomination, her husband was released on bail.

In March 1993 a growing rift between the Prime Minister and the President became evident when the Government initiated discussions regarding proposed modifications to the provisions of the Eighth Constitutional Amendment, which afforded the President the power to dismiss the Government and dissolve assemblies, and to appoint judicial and military chiefs. In late March three cabinet ministers resigned in protest at Nawaz Sharif's nomination as President of the PML (Junejo Group), to succeed Muhammad Khan Junejo (who had died earlier that month), and voiced their support for Ghulam Ishaq Khan in his political struggle with the Prime Minister. In a seemingly final attempt at reconciliation, the Cabinet unanimously decided, in early April, to nominate Ghulam Ishaq Khan as the PML's candidate for the forthcoming presidential election. By mid-April, however, a total of eight ministers had resigned from the Cabinet in protest at Nawaz Sharif's continued tenure of the premiership. On 18 April the President dissolved the National Assembly and dismissed the Prime Minister and his Cabinet, accusing Nawaz Sharif of 'maladministration, nepotism and corruption'. The provincial assemblies and governments, however, remained in power, despite demands by the PDA and the NDA for their dissolution. A member of the dissolved National Assembly, Mir Balakh Sher Mazari, was sworn in as acting Prime Minister. It was announced that elections to the National Assembly would be held on 14 July. In late April a broadly-based interim Cabinet, including Benazir Bhutto's husband, was sworn in. In early May the PML (Junejo Group) split into two factions: one led by Nawaz Sharif, the other by Hamid Nasir Chattha (with the support of the President).

On 26 May 1993, in an historic and unexpected judgment, the Supreme Court ordered that the National Assembly, the Prime Minister and the Cabinet (dismissed in April) should be restored to power immediately, stating that President Khan's order had been unconstitutional. The President agreed to honour the Court's ruling, and the National Assembly and Nawaz Sharif's Government were reinstated with immediate effect. On the following day Nawaz Sharif's return to power was consolidated when he won a vote of confidence in the National Assembly. A few days later, however, there was renewed political turmoil following the dissolution, through the machinations of supporters of the President, of the provincial assemblies in Punjab and the NWFP. Lacking effective authority in each of the four provinces, Nawaz Sharif resorted to the imposition of federal government's rule on Punjab through a resolution passed by the National Assembly in late June. However, the Punjab provincial government refused to obey the federal Government's orders, claiming that they subverted provincial autonomy, prompting the Government to threaten the imposition of a military administration. Meanwhile, an All Parties Conference (APC), including, amongst others, Benazir Bhutto and the Chief Ministers of Punjab and the NWFP, convened in Lahore to pass a resolution, urging the President to dissolve the legislature, dismiss Nawaz Sharif's Government and hold fresh elections. In early July the Chief of Army Staff, following an emergency meeting of senior army officers, acted as an intermediary in talks between the President and Prime Minister in an attempt to resolve the political crisis. Benazir Bhutto, supported by her APC collaborators, announced a 'long march' on 16 July, with the intention of laying siege to the federal capital and forcing Nawaz Sharif to resign. Fearing the outbreak of serious violence, the army persuaded Benazir Bhutto to postpone the march, reportedly assuring her that both the President and the Prime Minister would resign and that a general election would be held under a neutral administration. On 18 July, in accordance with an agreement reached under the auspices of the army, both Khan and Nawaz Sharif resigned from their posts, the Federal Legislature and the provincial assemblies were dissolved, the holding of a general election in October was announced, and neutral administrations were established, at both federal and provincial level. As specified in the Constitution, Khan was succeeded by the Chairman of the Senate, Wasim Sajjad Jan, who was to hold the presidency for the remaining tenure of the deposed President. A small, apolitical Cabinet was sworn in, headed by Moeenuddin Ahmad Qureshi, a former Executive Vice-President of the World Bank, as interim Prime Minister.

The general election, held in early October 1993 under military supervision, was widely considered to have been fair, although the turn-out, which some officials estimated to be less than 50%, was disappointing. The polling was closely contested between the PML faction led by Nawaz Sharif—PML (Nawaz—N)—and the PPP (the MQM boycotted the elections to the National Assembly, claiming systematic intimidation by the army, but took part in the provincial assembly elections a few days later). However, neither of the two leading parties won an outright majority in the federal elections, and in the provincial elections an outright majority was only achieved by the PPP in Sindh. Following intensive negotiations with smaller parties and independents in the National Assembly, on 19 October Benazir Bhutto was elected to head a coalition Government. On the following day a PPP-led coalition assumed control of the provincial administration in Punjab (traditionally a PML stronghold). The provincial governments in the NWFP and in Balochistan were, however, headed by alliances led by the PML (N).

In November 1993 the PPP's candidate, the newly appointed Minister of Foreign Affairs, Sardar Farooq Ahmad Khan Leghari, was elected President, having secured 274 votes (62% of the total) in the electoral college. The incumbent acting President, Wasim Sajjad Jan, who stood as the candidate of the PML (N), obtained 168 votes (38%). On assuming office, Leghari stated that he intended to end his political ties with the PPP and that he hoped for the early repeal or modification of the controversial Eighth Constitutional Amendment.

In February 1994 the President dismissed the Chief Minister and government of the NWFP, suspended the provincial legislature and imposed governor's rule, following the thwarted introduction of a vote of no confidence against the PML (N)-led coalition by the PPP. The PPP consolidated its hold on federal power in March by winning the majority of the contested seats in elections to the Senate. In April a PPP member was elected as Chief Minister of the newly revived provincial government in the NWFP; the opposition alliance boycotted the proceedings.

September 1994 witnessed an upsurge in political unrest when Nawaz Sharif organized a nation-wide general strike; in response, the Government arrested hundreds of PML supporters. In November the Government was confronted with a series of uprisings staged by heavily-armed tribesmen in the mountainous regions of Malakand and Swat demanding the enforcement of *Shari'a*. The fundamentalist revolt was suppressed by paramilitary forces (but only after the deaths of several hundred people), and the *Shari'a* measures were implemented in the tribal areas. By the end of the year, however, the police and paramilitary forces appeared to be losing control of Karachi, which was riven by rapidly escalating ethnic and criminal violence; nearly 170 people were killed in the city in December alone, following the lengthy 'Operation Clean-up' and the withdrawal of the army in the previous month. Much of the violence stemmed from the bloody rivalry between the opposing factions of the MQM, whilst other killings were linked to drugs mafias and to sectarian disputes between Sunni and Shi'a Muslims.

In early 1995, despite the arrest of large numbers of suspected Islamist militants, there was an upsurge in religious violence between Sunni and Shi'a Muslims in Karachi. In March the murder of two US consular officials by unidentified gunmen in the troubled Sindh capital provoked international condemnation. There was no respite from the violence in the following months, and by June the security forces had lost control of large areas of Karachi to MQM activists. Negotiations between representatives of the MQM (A) and government officials in mid-1995 proved fruitless and, although there was a temporary abatement in urban violence in the latter half of the year, the city's problems were far from resolved. It was estimated that during 1995 almost 2,000 people (including about 250 members of the security forces) were killed as a result of the political and ethnic violence in Karachi. In September of that year the growing political instability in Pakistan was underlined by the arrest of nearly 40 army officers on suspicion of plotting to overthrow the Government and to establish an Islamist fundamentalist state. In November 18 people were killed when a car bomb exploded at the Egyptian embassy in Islamabad; within hours of the attack three militant Islamist groups in Egypt had claimed responsibility for the bombing. During the previous year the Pakistani Government had been co-operating with Egypt in attempts to apprehend and extradite members of illegal Islamist militant organizations operating in the NWFP or across the border in Afghanistan. (In 1993–95 the Pakistan authorities, concerned at the country's growing reputation as a refuge for Islamist extremists, expelled more than 2,000 Arabs, the majority of whom were reported to have been involved in the civil war in Afghanistan.) Acts of violence and terrorism in Pakistan continued throughout late 1995 and early 1996.

A new political force emerged in Pakistan in early 1996, when the popular former international cricketer Imran Khan (of late a prominent benefactor of charitable causes) established a political reform movement known as the Tehrik-e-Insaf (Movement for Justice), to oppose Benazir Bhutto's administration.

In March 1996 the Supreme Court in Karachi ruled that the Government no longer had the exclusive mandate to appoint judges to the higher courts; these appointments would, in future, be required to have the consent of the Chief Justices of the High Courts and the Chief Justice of Pakistan. This ruling aroused considerable controversy since it deprived the executive of substantial authority within the national judicial system.

The Government's popularity was undermined by the necessary introduction of an austere budget, including the introduction of new taxes, in mid-June 1996, in an attempt to reduce the budget deficit. The volatile political situation was intensified by a bomb explosion at Lahore airport in late July, a series of debilitating public-sector strikes and by a resurgence of violence in Karachi. In addition, the appointment of the Prime Minister's unpopular husband, Asif Ali Zardari, as Minister of Investment as part of a cabinet expansion in July aroused much controversy and criticism. At the end of that month the Government's position appeared even less secure when about 16 opposition parties, including the PML (N), the MQM and the JIP, established an informal alliance with a one-point agenda: to oust Prime Minister Bhutto and her Government. Pakistan was thrown into further political turmoil in mid-September following the fatal shooting of Benazir Bhutto's estranged brother, Mir Murtaza Bhutto, in a gun battle with police in Karachi. A number of opposition politicians accused the Prime Minister and her husband of complicity in the killing, while Benazir Bhutto implied in a number of public statements that she believed that the President and the army were to blame. In 1995 Mir Murtaza Bhutto had established a rival faction of the PPP, known as the PPP (Shaheed Bhutto Group), charging his sister's Government with corruption and misrule; the breakaway faction, however, attracted no substantial support and posed little threat to the Prime Minister. Meanwhile, growing discord between Benazir Bhutto and President Leghari became more apparent.

Amid mounting public discontent, President Leghari dismissed Prime Minister Benazir Bhutto and her Government and dissolved the National Assembly on 5 November 1996 (the state assemblies were dissolved over the following week), citing the deteriorating law and order situation, severe economic problems, widespread corruption, disregard for judicial authority and the violation of various constitutional provisions as justification for his action. A former Speaker of the National Assembly, Malik Meraj Khaled, who claimed no affiliation to any political party, was named as acting Prime Minister and an interim Cabinet was appointed. Following the dismissal of her Government, it was reported that several leading members of Benazir Bhutto's PPP, including her husband, had been arrested. In mid-November the President promulgated a decree providing for a five-year disqualification from public office of politicians (with the exception of the President and members of the judiciary and armed forces) involved in corruption and abuses of power. At the end of December the JIP announced its intention to boycott the forthcoming general election, accusing the 'caretaker' Government of failing in its much-vaunted anti-corruption drive. Sectarian violence between Sunni and Shi'a Muslims escalated in January 1997, culminating in a bomb blast outside a district court in Lahore, which killed the leader of the Sunni extremist group Sipah-e-Sahaba Pakistan, and 25 others. Meanwhile, in early January the President instituted an official advisory role for the military, with the formation of a 10-member Council of Defence and National Security (CDNS), which was to advise the Government on a broad range of issues from national security to the economy. The President chaired the new body, which comprised the Prime Minister, four senior cabinet ministers, the Chairman of the Joint Chiefs of Staff and the three armed services chiefs, and could refer any matter to it without previously consulting the Prime Minister. In response to this unexpected development, many political parties, including the PPP, but with the notable exception of the PML (N), accused the President of an unconstitutional usurpation of authority. The Government insisted, however, that the role of the CDNS would be purely advisory.

The general election, which was held on 3 February 1997, was marred by an extremely low turn-out (an estimated 30%–40%). The PML (N) won a decisive victory, obtaining 134 of the 204 directly elective seats in the National Assembly (voting in three seats was deferred until a later date), while the PPP was routed, both at federal and state level, winning only 18 seats. The MQM emerged as the country's third political force (obtaining 12 seats), while Imran Khan's Tehrik-e-Insaf failed to win a single seat. Nawaz Sharif was sworn in as Prime Minister on 17 February and a small Cabinet was appointed the following week. In March the PML (N) and its allies secured a two-thirds' majority in the 87-seat Senate following elections for about one-half of the seats.

Nawaz Sharif's political authority was strengthened considerably in April 1997, when both the National Assembly and the Senate voted unanimously to repeal the major components of the 1985 Eighth Constitutional Amendment, thereby divesting the President of the power to appoint and dismiss the Prime Minister and Cabinet, to dissolve the legislature, to order a national referendum on any national issue, and to appoint provincial Governors, the Chairman of the Joint Chiefs of Staff and the three armed forces chiefs (these functions and appointments were, in future, to be carried out subject to mandatory advice from the Prime Minister). The President thus became a largely ceremonial figure whose main executive role was the appointment of judges. President Leghari was reported to have 'willingly agreed' to the constitutional changes.

In July 1997 Asif Ali Zardari was formally charged with ordering the killing of Mir Murtaza Bhutto; 21 other former officials were simultaneously charged with murder and conspiracy in the death. In September the Swiss police ordered four banks in Geneva to 'freeze' the accounts of Benazir Bhutto and her family after Pakistan's Accountability Commission alleged that up to US $80m. had been illegally transferred to them. In January 1998 the British authorities, at the request of the Pakistani Government, ordered the seizure of documents relating to assets and bank accounts of Benazir Bhutto in the United Kingdom. In March the Sindh High Court issued an arrest warrant for the leader of the PPP on a charge of misuse of power during her final term in office as Prime Minister. In April the High Court in Lahore ordered that all assets belonging to Benazir Bhutto, her husband and her mother be 'frozen' as the government investigation into allegations of corruption continued.

Meanwhile, in the latter half of 1997 a serious rift developed between Nawaz Sharif and the Chief Justice of the Supreme Court, Sajjad Ali Shah, over the appointment of new judges to the Court. In early November, however, a compromise was reached between the Supreme Court and the Government, allowing the former to appoint five new judges while confirming the right of the legislature to determine the total number of judges. Yet, despite this outcome, the crisis was not over and later that month the Supreme Court charged Nawaz Sharif and five other officials with contempt for slandering the Court and defying its orders in the previous month. The Prime Minister, who, if found guilty, was liable to be disqualified from office, denied the charges. The Chief Justice was forced to adjourn Nawaz Sharif's trial in late November, however, when thousands of the Prime Minister's supporters stormed the Supreme Court in Islamabad. The constitutional crisis came to a dramatic end on 2 December when the Chief Justice was suspended from office by rebel members of the Supreme Court; on the same day President Leghari also stood down from office. The Chairman of the Senate, Wasim Sajjad Jan, assumed the position of acting President. It was widely speculated that the army, in tacitly supporting the Prime Minister, had exerted considerable influence in resolving the constitutional impasse. Nawaz Sharif strengthened his hold on power on 31 December when his nominee and fellow Punjabi, Mohammad Rafiq Tarar (a personal acquaintance of the Prime Minister and a former Supreme Court judge), won the presidential election by a record margin (winning more than 80% of the total votes cast by the electoral college).

In January 1998 sectarian violence erupted again in Lahore when at least 24 Shi'a Muslims were massacred by a clandestine Sunni group. In response, the Government approved measures to control illicit weapons in an attempt to curb terrorism. (A controversial anti-terrorist law had been passed in August 1997, giving the security forces extensive powers of arrest and enabling the Government to ban any group or association without parliamentary approval.) In late February, however, two Iranian engineers were murdered by unidentified terrorists in Karachi, and in the following month more than 20 people were killed in two bomb explosions on passenger trains in Lahore.

Despite the temporary public euphoria and heightened popularity of the Prime Minister arising from the conduct of the controversial nuclear tests in May 1998 (see below), the repercussions (particularly the international sanctions) left Pakistan in dire financial straits. In late August the Prime Minister introduced the Fifteenth Constitutional Amendment Bill to the National Assembly, seeking to replace Pakistan's legal code with *Shari'a*. Nawaz Sharif attempted to allay fears of a move towards Islamist extremism by promising to uphold women's rights and to safeguard minorities. The Bill was passed in the National Assembly in October; it was denounced by human rights activists as 'regressive'.

The Government suffered a severe reverse in late October 1998 when the Muttahida Qaumi Movement—MQM (A)—(formerly known as the Mohajir Qaumi Movement) withdrew its support for the PML (N)-led provincial administration in Sindh. On 30 October the provincial legislature was suspended and the troubled province was placed under governor's rule in an effort to curb the violence. In November the Prime Minister announced the establishment of anti-terrorist military courts in Karachi (which were designed to dispense rapid and punitive justice), and the suspension of civil rights in Sindh.

In April 1999 the Lahore High Court found Benazir Bhutto (now in self-imposed exile abroad) and her husband guilty of corruption; they were each sentenced to five years' imprisonment, their property was confiscated and they were jointly fined US $8.6m. The verdict automatically removed the former Prime Minister and Asif Ali Zardari (who was already in prison serving a separate sentence) from their seats in the National Assembly and Senate, respectively.

Meanwhile, in early January 1999 the Prime Minister escaped an apparent assassination attempt when a bomb exploded near his country residence in Punjab, killing four people. The following day there was an upsurge in sectarian violence in the province when unidentified gunmen murdered 17 worshippers in a Shi'a mosque near Multan. Sindh became the focus of political attention later in the month when the Supreme Court declared unlawful the central Government's decision (made in November 1998) to remove the powers of the Speaker and Deputy Speaker of the suspended Sindh assembly. In mid-February 1999 the Supreme Court ruled that military trials could not be used for cases against civilians, thus sparing 14 people from death sentences imposed in the military tribunals in Sindh and effectively barring the establishment of military courts throughout the country (as the Government had proposed). The Supreme Court ordered the transfer of the cases to civilian anti-terrorist courts.

A dangerous escalation in the Kashmir crisis between Pakistan and India in mid-1999 (see below) and the former's effective defeat in the face of almost universal condemnation and diplomatic isolation appeared to represent a major turning point in the fortunes of the PML Government. Although Nawaz Sharif attempted to ensure that any blame attached to the episode would be diverted to the army, many of his opponents in Pakistan declared that his seeming haste to concede defeat and to agree to a Pakistani withdrawal in the face of US pressure constituted a national 'betrayal'. In mid-September Nawaz Sharif's position looked increasingly precarious following the formation of a Grand Democratic Alliance by 19 conservative and centrist opposition parties, including the PPP, the MQM (A) and the ANP, which demanded the Prime Minister's immediate resignation. The various Islamist parties, including the JIP, also stepped up their anti-Government protests and rallies throughout the country. The opposition was weakened to some extent, however, by the fact that Benazir Bhutto was unwilling to return to Pakistan for fear of being arrested.

Events took a dramatic turn on 12 October 1999, when, shortly after Nawaz Sharif's announcement of a decision to dismiss the Chief of Army Staff and Chairman of the Joint Chiefs of Staff Committee, Gen. Pervez Musharraf, the army chief flew back from an official tour in Sri Lanka and promptly organized a bloodless military coup in Islamabad. Nawaz Sharif and his Government were overthrown, and the deposed Prime Minister was placed under house arrest. On 15 October Gen. Musharraf assumed the position of Chief Executive, declared a nation-wide state of emergency and suspended the Constitution, the National Assembly, the Senate, the four provincial legislatures and all political officials, with the exception of the President and judiciary. He also ensured, by means of a Provisional Constitution Order, that his actions could not be challenged by any court of law, thus imposing virtual martial law. On 18 October the Commonwealth Ministerial Action Group (CMAG) condemned the coup and demanded a time-frame for the restoration of democracy; Pakistan was suspended from participation in meetings of the Commonwealth with immediate effect (it was re-admitted to full membership in May 2004). Meanwhile, on 22 October Gen. Musharraf appointed four new provincial governors, and on 26 October he installed a three-member Cabinet (which was later expanded) and named the members of a National Security Council (NSC), which was expected to be the supreme executive body of the country.

Following his seizure of power, Gen. Musharraf attempted to win over international opinion by portraying himself as a moderate, liberal leader. He was aided, in this respect, by the fact that the majority of the Pakistani people appeared to support the army's coup (it was a widely-held opinion that the military had no provincial bias and represented all levels of society—rather than purely the landed élite). Although expressing regret at Pakistan's effective suspension from the Commonwealth, the military regime was more concerned with the reaction of the USA and international financial organizations to the coup. The US Government's initial relations with the new administration in Pakistan appeared cautious but conciliatory. Gen. Musharraf promised an eventual return to civilian rule and announced wide-ranging measures to tackle corruption, loan defaulters, tax evasion, regional instability and religious extremism. The new regime's major priority was the revival of the almost bankrupt economy.

In November 1999 Nawaz Sharif and six other senior officials (including Mohammad Shahbaz Sharif, the brother of the ousted Prime Minister and the former Chief Minister of Punjab) were arrested on charges of criminal conspiracy, hijacking (a charge that carried the maximum penalty of the death sentence), kidnapping and attempted murder in relation to the alleged refusal of landing rights to the commercial aircraft carrying Gen. Musharraf from Sri Lanka to Karachi on 12 October; the aircraft ran precariously low on fuel before troops loyal to the army chief seized control of the airport and permission to land was finally granted (although the aircraft was rerouted to Nawabshah). The military authorities also charged Nawaz Sharif and his brother in November with corruption and non-repayment of bank loans. Later that month a new law was enacted barring politicians from holding public office for 21 years if found guilty of corruption or of defaulting on loans. The bill also allowed for the establishment of special courts to conduct trials within 30 days and gave the newly formed National Accountability Bureau far-reaching powers of investigation.

In early April 2000 Nawaz Sharif was sentenced to life imprisonment on charges of terrorism and hijacking, despite the prosecution having demanded the maximum penalty of the death sentence; in addition to the life sentence, all of the former Prime Minister's property in Pakistan was to be confiscated by the State. The six other defendants were acquitted. In May Nawaz Sharif's trial on charges of corruption opened; two months later the deposed Prime Minister was convicted and sentenced to 14 years' imprisonment, and barred from holding public office for 21 years. In August the Chief Executive issued a decree disqualifying those convicted of criminal offences and of terrorist acts from holding public office. The decision was viewed by many as a ban on convicted political leaders, notably former Prime Ministers Benazir Bhutto and Nawaz Sharif. In October the Karachi High Court upheld Nawaz Sharif's conviction and sentence for hijacking, but sustained the deposed Prime Minister's appeal against a conviction for terrorism.

Meanwhile, in late January 2000 Gen. Musharraf was accused of undemocratic conduct and of attempting to erode the independence of the judiciary when he dismissed the country's Chief Justice, Saiduzzaman Siddiqui, together with five other judges of the Supreme Court, following their refusal to swear allegiance to the military regime under a new oath. In May Gen. Musharraf's regime was strengthened by a unanimous decision by the pro-military Supreme Court to validate the October 1999 coup as having been necessary to spare the country from chaos and bankruptcy. At the same time, the Court announced that the Chief Executive should name a date not later than 90 days before the expiry of the three-year period from 12 October 1999 for the holding of elections to the National Assembly, the provincial assemblies and the Senate. Gen. Musharraf stated that he would comply with the Supreme Court ruling regarding the restoration of democracy.

In July 2000 Gen. Musharraf issued a decree to revive the Islamic provisions of the suspended Constitution and to incorporate them in the Provisional Constitution Order, thereby supporting a ban on the passing of any law that conflicted with Islamic principles. In mid-August the NSC was reconstituted and redefined as the supreme executive body, comprising the three chiefs of staff and the Ministers of Foreign Affairs, of Interior, of Finance and of Commerce.

In late 2000 former leaders Nawaz Sharif and Benazir Bhutto, with 16 other smaller political parties, agreed to form the Alliance for the Restoration of Democracy (ARD), in an effort to end military rule and accelerate a return to democracy. The new alliance superseded the PPP-led Grand Democratic Alliance. On 10 December Nawaz Sharif was unexpectedly released from prison and sent into exile in Saudi Arabia, with his wife and 17 other members of his family. The Government announced that the deposed Prime Minister had been granted a 'presidential pardon' and had been permitted to leave the country to seek medical treatment. In return, Nawaz Sharif relinquished his personal and business assets worth approximately Rs 500m., promised not to return to Pakistan for 10 years, and agreed not to take part in Pakistani politics for 21 years. The deal, reportedly negotiated by a member of the Saudi Arabian royal family, weakened Nawaz Sharif's prospects as a serious opponent to the Chief Executive, and adversely affected the credibility of Gen. Musharraf's campaign against political corruption.

In early April 2001 the Supreme Court ordered that Benazir Bhutto's conviction for corruption be set aside and a retrial held. Later that month the court concluded that the verdict had been politically motivated. Meanwhile, Bhutto and her husband faced further charges of corruption. In May a warrant was issued for Bhutto's arrest on her return to Pakistan. However, owing to her continued exile in Dubai (United Arab Emirates), in June she was sentenced, *in absentia,* to three years' imprisonment for failing to appear in court to answer these latest corruption allegations; this criminal conviction effectively disqualified Bhutto from holding further public office in Pakistan.

In late December 2000 the first phase of local elections was held. According to the Government, the turn-out reached 43.5%. The opposition PPP, however, claimed that less than 20% of the electorate had participated, attributing the low turn-out to the ban on political parties. Of a total of 20,076 seats, 33% were reserved for female candidates, but few women were able or willing to participate. The next three phases of local elections took place in March, May and July 2001. Although the elections were conducted on a non-party basis, it was believed that the majority of candidates were sponsored by either the PML (N) or the PPP. Elections to the 40-member legislative assembly for Azad Kashmir also took place in early July. Meanwhile, Musharraf insisted that a ban on party political activity in public would be maintained until after the forthcoming parliamentary elections, and opposition attempts at organizing pro-democracy rallies in March and May were suppressed by the authorities, who detained thousands of ARD supporters prior to the planned demonstrations.

On 20 June 2001 Gen. Musharraf unexpectedly assumed the presidency, having dismissed Mohammad Rafiq Tarar (who had reportedly refused to resign from the post). Musharraf immediately issued a formal dissolution of both houses of the Federal Legislature (which had been suspended since October 1999) in preparation for the elections. In an Independence Day address to the nation in August, Musharraf confirmed that elections to the four provincial legislatures and to the bicameral federal parliament would be conducted between 1 and 11 October 2002, thereby providing for the full restoration of democratic institutions by 12 October (the deadline established by the Supreme Court). Musharraf also announced that certain 'checks and balances' would be contained in constitutional amendments to be promulgated before June 2002; these were expected to include enhanced presidential powers and an advisory executive role for the military.

In response to a continuing escalation in sectarian and ethnically motivated violence, in June 2001 the Government approved new legislation to tackle terrorist activity. Earlier in the month Musharraf had complained that Pakistan's growing reputation as a centre for militant religious intolerance and fundamentalism was having a detrimental effect on the country's international standing and on its economic prospects. In his Independence Day address to the nation in August, Musharraf appealed for greater tolerance and understanding and announced an immediate ban on the activities of two militant Islamist groups: the Sunni Lashkar-e-Jhangvi and the Shi'a Sipah-e-Mohammad.

As one of only three states to have recognized the legitimacy of the Taliban administration in Afghanistan, and as the most significant trading partner and political associate of the regime, Pakistan's support was crucial to the efforts of the US-led anti-terrorism coalition in the aftermath of the 11 September 2001 terrorist attacks on the US mainland, and Musharraf was left in little doubt that his refusal to co-operate with the campaign to apprehend those members of the al-Qa'ida (Base) organization held responsible for the attacks would result in Pakistan's increased economic and political isolation. Therefore, Musharraf's political opponents in the PML and PPP appeared to accept his declaration of co-operation with US requests for shared intelligence and use of air space with resignation. However, large-scale popular opposition to the President's decision was inevitable, particularly in the NWFP bordering Afghanistan, which was home to large numbers of Pakhtoon (Pashtun) Pakistanis who were fiercely opposed to any assault on the Pashtun-dominated Taliban. Despite Musharraf's insistence that the US-led activities in the region did not represent an attack on Islam, protests against the action spread throughout the country, and on 21 September a grouping of more than 30 Pakistani militant Islamist organizations known as the Afghan Defence Council (ADC) organized an opposition campaign of demonstrations and industrial action nation-wide. There was further opposition to Pakistan's support for the intervention in Afghanistan from within the armed forces and the Inter-Services Intelligence (ISI) agency, both having enjoyed particularly close links with the Taliban. In early October, having extended indefinitely his term of office as Chief of Army Staff, Musharraf implemented a radical reorganization of the military high command and the intelligence service, replacing a number of senior personnel with known sympathies for the country's militant Islamist cause, including Lt-Gen. Mahmood Ahmed, head of the ISI. However, popular protests against co-operation with the US-led coalition continued. None the less, Musharraf's resolve remained firm (strengthened, in part, by the promise of financial recognition of his political support from the USA and the European Union—EU), and despite the uncompromising response of the security forces to sporadic rioting, an attempt to capture the Jacobabad airbase in Sindh province (which was providing logistical support to US forces) by some 5,000 demonstrators and an opposition rally attended by around 20,000 protesters in Karachi, there were surprisingly few casualties. In early November the leaders of the JUI and the JIP were detained following allegations that they were continuing to promote anti-Government activities and demonstrations. Earlier in the month a Qatar-based Arab satellite television channel, Al-Jazeera, had broadcast details of a new communication from Osama bin Laden, the Saudi-born leader of the al-Qa'ida organization, in which he issued a renewed call to *jihad* against non-Muslims and urged Pakistanis to rise up and overthrow Musharraf's administration for its part in the US-led campaign. Bin Laden's exhortations were particularly resonant in the border regions of the NWFP and Balochistan, where reports were emerging of large numbers of armed local tribesmen crossing the border as willing recruits for the Taliban. By mid-November there were believed to be significant numbers of Pakistanis fighting in Afghanistan (and reports that supply lines were being maintained into north-western Pakistan), rekindling long-standing animosity with the forces of the United National Islamic Front for the Salvation of Afghanistan (commonly known as the United Front or Northern Alliance), whose impressive territorial gains in Afghanistan (with the support of the US-led coalition) in early November alarmed Musharraf sufficiently for him to request a suspension of all bombing in Afghanistan during the Muslim holy month of Ramadan and to seek assurances that the United Front would not be allowed to occupy Kabul (the Afghan capital) unilaterally, during an official visit to Europe and the USA in the second week of November. However,

Musharraf's concerns were overtaken by events, and by mid-November the United Front had taken Kabul, leaving Musharraf to concentrate his efforts in attempting to convince the international community of the need for plural (including Pashtun, perhaps even moderate Taliban) representation in any interim administration in Afghanistan. As the rout of Taliban forces in Afghanistan continued in December and the USA intensified its bombardment of suspected al-Qa'ida positions in the Tora Bora region of southern Afghanistan, Pakistan reinforced security personnel along its north-western border (believed to number some 125,000 by the end of 2001) in order to intercept fleeing combatants. Many ethnic Pashtuns (both Pakistani and Afghan) were believed to have evaded capture on the border and escaped into north-western Pakistan. Violent exchanges between Pakistani security forces and intercepted (mostly Arab) al-Qa'ida fighters in the border regions resulted in a number of casualties on both sides.

Meanwhile, relations with India had become openly hostile as a result of the deteriorating security situation in Kashmir and the increasingly violent activities of Pakistan's militant Islamist groups in India (see below). Following intense international pressure (particularly from the USA) to address the continuing security risk presented by these groups, in December 2001 the security forces began to detain some of their most prominent members, and financial assets were 'frozen' and offices closed down. Moreover, in January 2002 Musharraf announced an indefinite ban on the activities of five predominantly separatist groups (Tehrik-e-Nifaz-e-Shariat-e-Mohammadi, Sipah-e-Sahaba Pakistan, Jaish-e-Mohammed, Tehrik-e-Jafria and Lashkar-e-Taiba) and plans to reform the country's system of *madrassa* religious schools, many of which were accused of promoting extremism and theocracy. Musharraf's counter-terrorism initiative and new moderate vision drew plaudits from the international community, but the murder of US journalist Daniel Pearl (see below) and several subsequent sectarian attacks, mainly on Shi'a Muslims, appeared to undermine the success of Musharraf's rhetoric. Nevertheless, in mid-June it was announced that the Government had approved an ordinance for the registration of *madrassas*, according to which only *madrassas* that were registered by the Madrassa Education Board within the next six months would be allowed to operate.

During early 2002 Musharraf reiterated his commitment to returning the country to democracy, beginning with the parliamentary elections scheduled for October. In early April the Government approved a plan to hold a national referendum seeking endorsement for Musharraf's term of office as President to be extended by five years and approval of the Government's political and economic programme. Opposition parties and the independent Human Rights Commission of Pakistan condemned the decision as unconstitutional and illegal and resolved to boycott the vote; however, on 27 April the Supreme Court ruled that the referendum was legitimate, allowing the poll to take place three days later. According to official figures, 98% of those participating supported the proposal. There were, however, widespread allegations of gross irregularities and fraud. The Government claimed that the turn-out was 70%, but opposition parties and independent monitors estimated that it was only about 5%. In late June Musharraf dismissed the head of the political wing of the ISI and chief organizer of the presidential referendum, Maj.-Gen. Ehtesam Zamir, after being forced to admit that his referendum victory had been fraudulent. In an attempt to reduce the political influence wielded by feudal landowning families, on 24 June the President issued a Chief Executive's Order stipulating that all candidates for future elections to federal and provincial legislatures should hold a university degree. Several days later Musharraf publicly announced a set of radical proposals for constitutional reform. The reforms were strongly criticized by political parties, constitutional experts and human rights groups for attempting to remodel Pakistan's prime ministerial system into a presidential one and to undermine the authority of any elected government. Among the changes, Musharraf proposed to reduce the parliamentary term from five years to four; to lower the voting age from 21 years to 18 years; to restrict the number of terms premiers or provincial chief ministers could hold in office to two; and to disqualify those members of the legislature who had criminal convictions, had defaulted on loans or had absconded. The last two amendments were widely considered to be aimed at preventing former Prime Ministers Benazir Bhutto and Nawaz Sharif from returning to office. Furthermore, in early July Musharraf issued a decree barring former premiers and chief ministers from seeking a third term in office. Several days later Musharraf announced that elections to the federal and provincial legislatures would be held on 10 October.

Instead of presenting the constitutional amendments before the next legislature, on 21 August 2002 President Musharraf unilaterally enacted the Legal Framework Order (LFO), which introduced 29 amendments to the Constitution and validated all the military decrees approved since the coup in 1999. The amendments would take effect from 12 October. As a result, the President's powers were enlarged and the military was ensured influence in decision-making beyond the parliamentary elections in October. The above proposals were endorsed. One of the most significant amendments, the permanent establishment of an NSC, which would include Musharraf in his capacity as President and Chief of Army Staff, as well as the three other armed forces chiefs, the Prime Minister, the provincial chief ministers, the leader of the parliamentary opposition and Speakers of both houses of the Federal Legislature, was also authorized. The NSC would provide consultation to the elected government on strategic issues. The President was also restored the right to dissolve the National Assembly, and to dismiss the Prime Minister and Cabinet; furthermore, he was given the authority to override parliamentary majorities and provincial assemblies in order to appoint a Prime Minister and provincial governors himself if necessary. The amendments allowed the President to appoint Supreme Court judges and to extend his term in office. The changes were heavily criticized by the PML (N) and PPP. Musharraf, however, insisted that a formal role for the military in governing the country was necessary to ensure a stable transition to democracy and to forestall a potential military coup. According to the LFO, the size of the National Assembly would be increased to 342 members, with 60 seats reserved for women and 10 seats reserved for non-Muslims. The Senate would consist of 100 members. The PML (N) and Pakistan People's Party Parliamentarians (PPPP—see below) were permitted to take part in the elections.

Meanwhile, in late July 2002 Benazir Bhutto was re-elected as leader of the PPP. However, the decree barring parties from contesting an election if any of its office-holders have a criminal conviction prompted the PPP in early August to create the PPPP under new leadership to contest the forthcoming general elections. At the same time Shahbaz Sharif was elected leader of the pro-Nawaz PML. Bhutto's plans to return to the political arena were thwarted in late August when election officials in Sindh province rejected her candidacy in the National Assembly elections, owing to her criminal conviction. In response, Nawaz Sharif withdrew his nomination papers (although they had been accepted by the Election Commission), reportedly in solidarity with Bhutto. In mid-September Shahbaz Sharif was disqualified from entering the general election, for defaulting on a bank loan. Meanwhile, a pro-Musharraf faction of the PML, the Quaid-e-Azam group, was reportedly receiving covert support from the Government.

On 9 October 2002 Musharraf declared that he was relinquishing the title of Chief Executive. The following day elections for the National Assembly and provincial assemblies took place. In elections to the National Assembly the PML (Quaid-e-Azam—Q) won 77 of the 272 directly elective seats (25.7% of the vote). The PPPP won 25.8% of the vote, but only 63 seats. A surprising outcome was the success of the Muttahida Majlis-e-Amal (MMA), an alliance of six Islamist parties, in securing 45 seats (11.3% of the vote). The PML (N) won only 14 seats (9.4% of the vote). According to the Election Commission, the turn-out at the election was 41.8%; voting to five seats was deferred to a later date. The PML (Q)'s strong performance had been expected, since Musharraf had publicly voiced his support for the party during the election campaign. Opposition parties, independent analysts and the Human Rights Commission of Pakistan claimed that the army had provided financial and other support to the PML (Q), while hampering other parties' campaign efforts. Meanwhile, Benazir Bhutto claimed that the election had been rigged. EU election monitors reported that the poll was 'seriously flawed'. The emergence of the MMA as a third political force suggested that a significant proportion of the population objected to Musharraf's support for the US-led military action against the Taliban and al-Qa'ida in Afghanistan, and the ongoing campaign against al-Qa'ida in Pakistan. PPPP and PML (N) leaders considered the religious alliance's success to be a result of the military Government's attempts to prevent their parties from achieving power. However, many observers held the opinion that the army and ISI sponsored the MMA in an attempt to convince the West that continued military rule was necessary to contain the religious parties, to gain further concessions from the USA, and to ensure support from the new Government for aggressive policies towards India, particularly over the Kashmir issue. On 31 October the 60 seats reserved for women and 10 for non-Muslims were allocated by the Election Commission. The three leading parties entered intensive and protracted negotiations on forming a governing coalition: the PML (Q) and PPPP each attempted to gain the support of the MMA. However, the parties failed to reach common ground; neither the PML (Q) or PPPP was able to persuade the MMA to withdraw its candidate for prime minister. By mid-November the parties had yet to reach a compromise; nevertheless, the National Assembly convened and elected a Speaker and Deputy Speaker. Shortly beforehand, the President revived the 1973 Constitution, which had been in abeyance since he assumed power in 1999—it was believed that the Constitution incorporated the controversial LFO—and took an oath to begin his new five-year term as President. On 21 November the PML (Q) candidate, Zafarullah Khan Jamali, was elected Prime Minister by the National Assembly. Jamali's victory ensured a PML (Q)-led, pro-army Government with a slim majority, which was sworn in two days later. Meanwhile, Musharraf agreed to transfer power to the elected Government, but emphasized that he would continue to carry out his 'important role'.

The MMA won a majority in the provincial elections in the NWFP in October 2002 and formed a provincial government in late November, with Muhammad Akram Durrani elected Chief Minister. The MMA and PML (Q) announced a coalition government in the province of Balochistan in late November, led by a PML (Q) Chief Minister. The PML (Q) assumed power in Punjab at the same time. The PPPP emerged as the single largest party in the Sindh assembly, but failed to form a coalition government despite support from the MMA. Eventually, in mid-December the PML (Q), MMA and several smaller parties agreed to a power-sharing arrangement with Ali Mohammad Maher, a PML (Q) representative, as Chief Minister. The delay in forming new federal and provincial governments meant that the Senate elections were finally held on 25–27 February 2003. Some 88 of the 100 seats in the Senate were elected by the four provincial assemblies. The remaining 12 seats were chosen by the National Assembly from a list of candidates provided by the Federally Administered Tribal Areas and the federal capital. The PML (Q) secured 34 seats, making it the largest single party in the Senate. The Senate convened on 12 March. The PML (Q) candidate, Mian Mohammad Soomro, was elected unopposed as Chairman of the Senate after the eight opposition parties boycotted the vote in protest at the President's LFO and the alleged military interference in the Senate elections.

At the end of April 2003 the National Assembly suspended its session, following a month of disruption caused by opposition parties. The MMA, PPPP and other opposition parties had refused to allow Musharraf to address the legislature (a constitutional requirement before it could begin to legislate) and repeatedly demanded that the President submit the LFO to approval by the National Assembly; however, the President, mindful of the fact that the amendments would not secure the two-thirds' majority required for constitutional change, refused to accede to this demand. A joint committee formed by the Government and opposition to discuss the LFO failed to reach an agreement and the consultations collapsed. In June the opposition presented a motion of no confidence in the Speaker of the National Assembly, Chaudhry Amin Hussain, following his ruling that Musharraf's constitutional amendments were valid and that the legislature should function according to them. The opposition argued that Hussain had contravened the 1973 Constitution (which it regarded as the only legitimate Constitution) by ruling in favour of the LFO, and, as a result, the Speaker no longer had the right to the confidence of the Assembly. However, when the Deputy Speaker ruled that the vote would be by secret ballot, the opposition refused to vote and the motion collapsed. The opposition's campaign of boycott and agitation of parliamentary proceedings continued, however. Tensions between the MMA and Musharraf increased after an election tribunal barred an MMA legislator from office on educational grounds. Members of the Islamist coalition who did not hold a degree were eventually permitted by Musharraf to stand as candidates. The tribunal, however, ruled against the exemption, prompting further protests by the MMA. The National Assembly reconvened on 20 August 2003, after having being forced to suspend its session for more than two months.

Meanwhile, in early June 2003 the legislative assembly in the NWFP unanimously voted in favour of legislation to implement *Shari'a* throughout the province (the NWFP Government had already issued a directive requiring civil servants to pray twice a day and introduced legislation forbidding male doctors to examine women). In response to the bill, which gave Islamic law precedence over secular provincial law, Musharraf dismissed two senior NWFP officials—the chief secretary and police chief—for failing to secure law and order in the provincial capital of Peshawar against attacks by militant Islamists. During a visit to the NWFP later that month Musharraf warned against the adoption of Taliban-style Islam, promoting instead the practice of 'tolerant, progressive and civilized' Islam. In July, however, a journalist was sentenced to life imprisonment for blasphemy in Peshawar.

In September 2003 the Cabinet unanimously endorsed a modified version of the LFO. Although the PML (N) and PPPP appeared to be willing to compromise regarding their opposition to the measures, the MMA remained dissatisfied and negotiations between the Government and opposition continued. Finally, in December Musharraf announced seven further concessions to the LFO, including his commitment to resign as Chief of Army Staff by December 2004. On 29 December 2003 the National Assembly passed the Constitution (Seventeenth Amendment) Bill, which comprised the seven modifications. The opposition ARD had boycotted the parliamentary proceedings, dismissing the concessions as 'cosmetic'; none the less, the amendments received the necessary two-thirds' majority in the National Assembly vote. According to the Bill, which became law on 31 December following the Senate's approval, the existing NSC, which had been inactive since its creation one year previously, disbanded. A new NSC was to be established by an act of parliament, rather than be incorporated into the Constitution by the LFO. Furthermore, while the President would have the right to dismiss the National Assembly, he would be obliged to refer the matter to the Supreme Court within 15 days. Despite the concessions, Musharraf retained most of the special powers that he had awarded himself in 2002. In early January 2004 the federal and provincial legislatures passed votes of confidence in Musharraf, allowing him to complete his five-year term as President (which was due to expire in 2007). In April 2004 the National Assembly passed an item of legislation on the establishment of the NSC amid strong protest by opposition members. The Council was to comprise the President, the Prime Minister, the Chairman of the Senate, the Speaker of the National Assembly, the leader of the parliamentary opposition, the provincial chief ministers and the three other chiefs of armed forces. The new Chief of Army Staff (who was to be appointed in late 2004 following Musharraf's resignation from the position) would also be a member. The NSC law, approved by the Senate several days later, gave the armed forces a formal, albeit supervisory, role in civilian politics for the first time in Pakistan's history.

In the mean time, in late September 2003 the leader of the ARD, Nawabzada Nasrullah Khan, died; he was replaced by Makhdoom Javed Hashmi, the acting President of the PML (N), in early October. In late October, however, Hashmi was arrested on charges of inciting mutiny after circulating a letter at a press conference criticizing the military's involvement in politics that he claimed was written by junior army officers. The authorities asserted that the letter, which was also critical of President Musharraf and his alliance with the USA, was a forgery. Hashmi was convicted of inciting mutiny in the army, forgery and defamation in mid-April 2004 and was sentenced to up to seven years' imprisonment. The PML (N) condemned the verdict, claiming that it proved that the judiciary was under the control of Musharraf. Meanwhile, in December 2003 the President of the MMA and leader of Jamiat-e-Ulema-e-Pakistan, Maulana Shah Ahmed Noorani Siddiqui, died. Amir Qazi Hussain Ahmad was appointed President of the MMA in an acting capacity. In the same month, in a landmark judgment, the Supreme Court ruled that all adult Muslim women were able to marry anyone of their own free will, with or without the consent of their father or guardian (*wali*). The ruling supported a similar judgment declared by the Federal Shari'a Court in 1981 and overturned 1997 rulings by the Lahore High Court that a marriage without the consent of the *wali* was invalid.

In mid-August 2003 Asif Ali Zardari was acquitted of all charges relating to the 1998 murder of Sajjad Hussain, the former Chairman of Pakistan Steel Mills. Earlier that month, however, Zardari and Benazir Bhutto were convicted by a Swiss investigative judge in Geneva of money-laundering and receiving bribes from two Swiss companies in 1995. Bhutto and her husband each received a suspended six-month prison sentence and a fine of US $50,000. They were also ordered to repay the Pakistani Government $11.9m. (The Lahore High Court had convicted Bhutto and Zardari in the same case in 1999, but the Supreme Court overturned the verdict two years later, concluding that it had been politically motivated, and ordered a retrial by a state accountability court.) In early November 2003, however, a court in Geneva quashed the prison sentences and fines following an appeal by Benazir Bhutto and her husband. At the same time, opposition parties in Pakistan held widespread protests on the seventh anniversary of Zardari's arrest to demand his release from prison. Zardari, now largely considered a political prisoner, was implicated in 14 pending criminal cases, but had been convicted on only one corruption charge (in September 2002). Meanwhile, Bhutto faced further corruption cases in Pakistan, Switzerland, the United Kingdom and the USA. In June 2004 Bhutto was indicted by a Geneva court on a new, more serious charge of 'money-laundering by profession', relating to alleged commissions and bribes that she had received from Swiss companies in the 1990s. In September the Lahore High Court overturned Zardari's corruption conviction following an appeal. However, Zardari remained in custody owing to another pending case against him. In November the Supreme Court ordered that Zardari be released on bail, following eight years of imprisonment. His freedom initially appeared to be short-lived, as he was rearrested the following month upon his arrival in Islamabad; a judge in Karachi had cancelled bail as Zardari had allegedly failed to attend a hearing into a 1996 murder case in which he was accused of involvement. However, later in that month the decision was overturned and Zardari's bail was restored. In June 2005 Zardari suffered a major heart attack and was admitted to a hospital in Dubai. In September an arrest warrant was issued for him, after he failed to attend a court hearing in Rawalpindi related to ongoing corruption allegations against him. In the same month Bhutto testified at a Geneva court in relation to the money-laundering charges against her and her husband. In November the former Prime Minister was acquitted by a court in Karachi of corruption charges against her. Later in that month Bhutto claimed that President Musharraf had offered to abandon all remaining charges against her, on the condition that she declined to contest elections scheduled for 2007; she asserted that she was unable to accept the condition.

Attacks by suspected militant Islamists on Western targets, meanwhile, continued to take place in 2003. Although Musharraf decided not to support the USA in its attempt to gain UN endorsement of the planned military campaign to remove the regime of Saddam Hussain in Iraq in March, the President was condemned by some sectors of the Pakistani community for not opposing the war in stronger terms. In November Musharraf proscribed six militant Islamist groups under the 1997 Anti-Terrorist Act. Three of the organizations—Islami Tehrik-e-Pakistan (formerly Tehrik-e-Jafria-e-Pakistan), Millat-e-Islamia Pakistan (formerly Sipah-e-Sahaba) and Khudam ul-Islam (formerly Jaish-e-Mohammed)—had disregarded an earlier ban by changing their names, thus bringing into question the President's commitment to curbing militant activity. The activities of Jamiat ul-Furqan, Jamiat ul-Ansar (formerly Harakat ul-Mujahideen) and Hizb-ut-Tahrir were also proscribed. Jamaat-ud-Dawa (considered by some to be the new identity for the banned Lashkar-e-Taiba movement) was placed under surveillance. Some commentators doubted the effectiveness of Musharraf's approach to militant Islamism, claiming that the groups would continue to receive covert support from the army and judiciary. Indeed, in December the President narrowly escaped two assassination attempts by suspected Islamist militants near his residence in Rawalpindi. No one was hurt in the first suicide bomb attack, but the second killed at least 17 people and injured about 50 others. (In August 2005 five men, including one soldier, were sentenced to death, having been found guilty of involvement in one of the assassination attempts. In October four junior members of the air force were convicted of involvement in the other attempted assassination and sentenced to death.) Islamist militants had reportedly been greatly angered by the Government's agreement to enter negotiations with India (see below), and by Musharraf's decision to allow the UN International Atomic Energy Agency (IAEA, see p. 107) to investigate the sale of Pakistani nuclear technology to Iran, the Democratic People's Republic of Korea (North Korea) and Libya (see below). It was suggested that al-Qa'ida, which in September had issued a death threat to Musharraf, blaming him for the arrest of hundreds of its members, was responsible for organizing the attacks. There was also speculation that the extremists had infiltrated Musharraf's security apparatus in order to gain secret information on his travel plans.

From mid-2003 the frequency and scale of sectarian attacks increased. In June gunmen shot dead 11 Shi'a Muslims and wounded nine others in Quetta; 18 members of Millat-e-Islamia Pakistan were arrested on suspicion of involvement in the attacks. In the following month a suicide bomb attack took place in a Shi'a mosque also in Quetta, killing at least 50 worshippers and injuring more than 60; the Sunni militant organization Lashkar-e-Jhangvi claimed responsibility for the attack. In early October seven Shi'a Muslims were killed in a gun attack in Karachi by Sunni militants. The Government held a group called 313, a newly formed alliance of Lashkar-e-Jhangvi, Harakat ul-Mujahideen and Harakat ul-Jihad al-Islami, responsible for the attack, claiming that its motives were sectarian and anti-Government. On 6 October the legislator and leader of Millat-e-Islamia Pakistan, Maulana Azam Tariq, was assassinated in Islamabad; a previously unknown Shi'a group, Fedayim Imam Mahdi, claimed responsibility for the attack. The shooting provoked riots in Islamabad and the city of Jhang: Sunni militants, vowing revenge, burnt down a Shi'a shrine and cinema in the capital and a Shi'a mosque in Tariq's home city, Jhang. The leader of the Shi'a extremist Islami Tehrik-e-Pakistan, Allama Sajid Ali Naqvi, was arrested in mid-November, in connection with Tariq's murder. Sectarian strife continued to afflict Quetta: in March 2004 more than 40 Shi'a Muslims were killed and more than 150 injured after Sunni extremists attacked a Shi'a procession during a religious ceremony to commemorate the holy day of Ashoura.

In December 2003 the Minister of Information and Media Development, Sheikh Rashid Ahmad, admitted that the authorities were investigating allegations that Pakistan had transferred nuclear technology to other countries, and that Dr Abdul Qadeer Khan, the founder of Pakistan's nuclear weapons programme, and two other nuclear scientists were being questioned. The Government was under tremendous pressure from the USA and IAEA, which had recently concluded that Iran had been supplied with designs for nuclear equipment that originated from Pakistan, to investigate the accusations. The authorities, however, were quick to deny any official involvement, suggesting that 'rogue' individuals motivated by personal greed were to blame. Khan was reportedly placed under house arrest and in late January 2004 was removed from his post as scientific adviser to the Prime Minister. On 4 February, in a dramatic development, Khan confessed on television that during the past 15 years he had provided Iran, North Korea and Libya with designs and technology to develop nuclear weapons (he had already signed a detailed confession). He apologized, asked for forgiveness, and took full responsibility for his actions; he also denied any government involvement and absolved the military and his fellow scientists. Dr Khan's plea for clemency was granted two days later by Musharraf. The President announced that he and the Cabinet had taken into account the nuclear scientist's services to the country before coming to their decision and that Khan would remain under strict surveillance. Musharraf also refused to allow independent investigators to continue their inspection, provoking speculation that the authorities were trying to protect the Pakistani military. It was widely acknowledged that prosecuting Dr Khan would have led to unrest throughout the country (he had been long revered as the 'father' of Pakistan's nuclear bomb and had the status of a national hero) and political problems (there were fears that if put on trial the scientist would provide evidence that incriminated Pakistani leaders and generals). Musharraf countered allegations that he might have been involved in the sale of weapons, claiming that he tried to curb the proliferation after becoming suspicious three years ago by forcing Khan's retirement from his post as head of the Khan Research Laboratories, and that he delayed holding an investigation into the matter owing to the scientist's popularity and privileged position. He also stated that he was only able to take action once the USA had provided him with enough information in October 2003. Musharraf attempted to evade allegations that Khan was ideologically motivated by attributing the scientist's activities to personal gain. Military analysts, however, continued to doubt that Khan was solely responsible, declaring that it was unlikely that the transfer of nuclear materials could have been conducted without the knowledge and involvement of at least parts of the military. Meanwhile, two former chiefs of army staff, retired Gen. Mirza Aslam Beg and retired Gen. Jehangir Karamat, were questioned and exonerated of any wrongdoing. Musharraf stated that Pakistan would continue to co-operate with the IAEA but would not allow IAEA inspectors to monitor its nuclear programmes. In November 2004 the Supreme Court rejected a petition that Khan be released from house arrest on the grounds of ill health. In February 2005 the Government denied a report in the US magazine *Time* that Khan had also sold nuclear technology to Saudi Arabia and Egypt.

In the first half of 2004 violence between Sunni and Shi'a Muslims in Karachi escalated. In early May the Shi'a Hyderi mosque was attacked by a suicide bomber, resulting in the deaths of 16 people. Later that month a senior Sunni cleric and known Taliban supporter, Mufti Nizamuddin Shamzai, was assassinated. In an apparent revenge attack, another Shi'a mosque in the centre of the city was bombed, killing 16 people and prompting an outbreak of rioting in the city. In June the Chief Minister of Sindh, Sardar Ali Mohammed Maher, was forced to resign as a result of Karachi's deteriorating law and order situation; he was replaced by Dr Arbab Ghulam Rahim. In the same month at least 10 people were killed following an attack on the motorcade of the commander of the Karachi army corps, Lt-Gen. Ahsan Saleem Hayat. Shortly afterwards it was announced that 10 suspected members of al-Qa'ida had been apprehended in the city; they allegedly confessed to having participated in Lt-Gen. Hayat's attempted assassination. The men were charged with terrorist offences in September. Meanwhile, in August several more explosions occurred in Karachi.

In the mean time, in June 2004 Prime Minister Jamali tendered his resignation, having been placed under considerable pressure to do so by President Musharraf. Musharraf was reportedly frustrated at the weakness of Jamali's Government and, in particular, its apparent inability to curb sectarian violence in Pakistan. Later in the same month Musharraf's nominee, Chaudhry Shujaat Hussain, President of the newly formed PML (which had been created following the merger of several factions of the PML and the Sindh Democratic Alliance in the previous month), was elected to serve as interim Prime Minister. It was reported that Minister of Finance Shaukat Aziz was Musharraf's choice to serve in the post permanently, but, as Aziz was a Senator, he would first need to be elected to the House of Representatives. In July Hussain announced five new appointments to his Cabinet, including that of Babar Khan Gauri as Minister of Communications. In the same month Shaukat Aziz survived an assassination attempt by an alleged suicide bomber in the town of Attock in Punjab, one of the two constituencies that he was contesting in forthcoming by-elections (the other being that of Tharparkar in Sindh). In late August, following victories in both constituencies, Aziz was elected as Prime Minister and leader of the house by the National Assembly and, on the following day, was formally sworn in to his new office. In the following month a new Cabinet was appointed, which included the 20 members of Chaudhry Shujaat Hussain's interim Government and incorporated an additional 13 members. Aziz retained the finance portfolio, while Aftab Ahmad Khan Sherpao became Minister of the Interior and Rao Sikander Iqbal continued as Minister of Defence.

In October 2004 the National Assembly approved legislation enabling Musharraf to retain his dual role as President and Chief of Army Staff, contrary to his December 2003 pledge that he would resign from his military position by the end of 2004. The opposition protested that the bill was unconstitutional and condemned it strongly, although the Speaker curtailed debate on the issue. The Government claimed that the ongoing terrorist threat necessitated Musharraf's retention of both roles, a claim supported by the state assemblies of Punjab and Sindh, both of which passed motions requesting that Musharraf stay on as army chief. In November, having been approved by the Senate, the bill was signed into law by its Chairman, Mian Mohammad Soomro, who was acting President while Musharraf was out of the country. In December Musharraf formally confirmed that he intended to retain his military position until the end of his presidential term, in 2007. In March 2005 the MMA orchestrated protest marches in Karachi, Quetta, Peshawar and Lahore to protest against Musharraf's actions; its supporters also observed a series of nation-wide strikes, culminating in a general strike in early April. However, this received only limited support. Later that month the Supreme Court dismissed all petitions challenging Musharraf's dual role as unconstitutional. In May it was announced that Musharraf would definitely seek re-election as President following the expiry of his term of office in 2007; the opposition denounced his decision.

Meanwhile, in late 2004 and early 2005 outbreaks of sectarian violence intensified in frequency. In October in Multan two bombs exploded at a Sunni Muslim rally, held to commemorate the first anniversary of the assassination of Maulana Azam Tariq, killing at least 40 people. Minister of the Interior Sherpao subsequently announced that he would order provincial governments to ban all religious gatherings apart from prayers at mosques. There was speculation that the bombing was revenge for a suicide attack on a Shi'a mosque in Sialkot in Punjab earlier in that month, in which an estimated 30 people lost their lives. Meanwhile, in Karachi another prominent Sunni religious leader, Mufti Muhammad Jamil, was assassinated and, on the following day, a suicide bomber attacked a Shi'a mosque in Lahore. In December at least 11 people died when a bomb exploded next to an army vehicle at a market in Quetta; the separatist Balochistan National Army claimed responsibility for the attack, but denied that it had intended to kill civilians, declaring that members of the armed forces were its target. In March 2005 a bomb explosion at a Sufi Muslim shrine, sacred to both Sunni and Shi'a Muslims, in the town of Fatehpur resulted in the deaths of at least 50 pilgrims. Four suspects, believed to be members of the banned Sunni Millat-e-Islamia Pakistan group, were subsequently arrested in connection with the attack. In May a suicide bombing at a Sufi shrine in Islamabad killed at least 20 people. Later in the same month an attack on a Shi'a mosque in Karachi resulted in five deaths.

In January 2005 claims that military personnel had raped and assaulted a female doctor employed by Pakistan Petroleum Ltd in Balochistan precipitated an outbreak of violence in the province, which had become increasingly lawless throughout late 2004. Bugti tribesmen clashed with security forces at the Sui gas processing plant, causing severe damage to the plant and to three gas pipelines and affecting gas supplies throughout the country (the Sui gas field accounted for some 45% of total gas production in Pakistan). In response to an appeal by the provincial government, the federal Government sent army and paramilitary troops to protect the gas field, resulting in a temporary cessation of the unrest in Sui. However, later in the month three bombs exploded in the provincial capital, Quetta. The violence in the province was seen to some extent to be indicative of local resentment at the federal Government's exploitation of its mineral wealth. It was feared that further clashes between the army and local rebels would encourage Balochi nationalist sentiment. In February a spate of bomb attacks took place in various different areas of Balochistan as the violence continued. Responsibility for several of the attacks was claimed by the Balochistan Liberation Army (BLA), an insurgent group operating in the province. In March more than 60 civilians died during clashes between security forces and tribesmen in the area as the conflict intensified. Following an attack on a military convoy, a stand-off ensued between the two sides, with tribal leader and President of the Jamhuri Watan Party, Nawab Akbar Bugti, refusing to compromise in the tribesmen's struggle to secure political autonomy and a greater share of revenue from Balochistan's gas reserves. Following talks between Bugti and a government delegation that included former Prime Minister Chaudhry Shujaat Hussain, an agreement was reached to defuse the crisis. The process of implementing the agreement, which included the withdrawal of troops by both sides, began in April. Meanwhile, later in March a bomb exploded at a Muslim shrine in the town of Usa Mohammad, killing 35 people. Sporadic unrest continued throughout 2005, intensifying again during a visit by President Musharraf to the province in December of that year. The violence continued into 2006: in August Bugti was killed in clashes between government forces and tribesmen, triggering a spate of strikes and civil unrest. Preliminary talks were initiated between the Government and Baluch nationalists in December. However, in July 2007 the spokesman of the Balochistan provincial government was shot dead, and in November it was reported that Mir Balaach Marri, who was alleged to be the leader of the BLA, had been killed.

In the mean time, the issue of religious extremism continued to resonate in Pakistani society. In July 2005, following the discovery that at least two of the four British Muslim suicide bombers who had attacked the transport network in London, United Kingdom, in that month had previously visited Pakistan and had allegedly received instruction at one of the country's many *madrassas*, President Musharraf announced the implementation of a more stringent policy to prevent the spread of Islamic extremism. Hundreds of suspected Islamist militants were arrested and several *madrassas* suspected of being involved in extremism were raided. Musharraf stressed, however, that he did not believe that the British bombers had been radicalized in Pakistan. In August the National Assembly gave its assent to legislation requiring all *madrassas* to register with the Government and to submit annual reports. They were also barred from encouraging militancy and propagating religious hatred. Furthermore, all foreign students studying at *madrassas* in Pakistan were to be expelled. Meanwhile, President Musharraf filed a petition with the Supreme Court objecting to certain sections of legislation passed in the previous month by the provincial assembly of the NWFP. The new laws made provision for 'morality police' in the province, who would enforce prayer attendance, discourage singing and dancing and practise strict media censorship. The legislation had been proposed by the conservative religious alliance the MMA, which dominated the province's assembly. The Supreme Court subsequently ruled that sections of the law relating to the powers of an Islamic *Mohtasib* (moral guardian), which had been established by the bill, were unconstitutional. The increasing dominance of the MMA and its implementation of guidelines to govern social behaviour, in line with Islamic values, provided an indication of the increasing 'Talibanization' of some sections of Pakistani society.

During August to October 2005 local government elections took place over several stages. Although political parties were theoretically prohibited from participating in the elections, the political allegiances of most candidates were widely known. The polls were marred by violence and intimidation in many areas; in particular, the exercise of the franchise by women and the candidature of some for office attracted controversy, with re-polling ordered in several areas as a result of complaints that women had been prevented from voting. Overall, the results indicated a decline in support for religious parties, with more moderate parties reported to have won a majority of seats in Punjab and Sindh. Meanwhile, in the NWFP and Balochistan support for the MMA had apparently decreased significantly. However, the results of the polls were called into question by widespread allegations of malpractice and corruption.

Meanwhile, in October 2005 a huge earthquake, the epicentre of which was in the town of Balakot, in the NWFP, devastated Azad Kashmir and much of the NWFP, resulting in the deaths of more than 81,000 people and leaving many thousands homeless. The response of the Government and armed forces to the tragedy attracted criticism for its tardiness and lack of co-ordination, although the logistical challenge of delivering relief to many of the remote areas affected was considerable. Furthermore, the aid committed by international donors in the aftermath of the disaster was reportedly criticized as inadequate by President Musharraf. At a meeting of donors held in November in Islamabad, a total of US $5,800m. was pledged by the international community for the relief and reconstruction effort, exceeding the Government's target. Most of the aid donated was intended for the long-term effort, however, and funds for immediate humanitarian relief remained slow to arrive. Although relief efforts focused on reconstruction in 2006, it was estimated by the Government that only 17% of the 400,000 homes affected by the earthquake had been rebuilt, and in October Musharraf appealed for further aid from foreign donors.

In February 2006 widespread protests occurred in towns and cities across Pakistan, as demonstrators gathered to condemn the publication of cartoons of the Prophet Mohammed in a Danish newspaper in September 2005. Although the demonstrations began peacefully and on a relatively small scale, they became increasingly violent in some areas, resulting in several deaths. The MMA exploited the protests to increase public opposition to President Musharraf, whose Government had condemned the cartoons but who was widely perceived to be allied with the West. The protests culminated in the withdrawal of the Danish ambassador from the country.

In March 2006 elections took place for one-half of the seats in the Senate; Mohammad Mian Soomro was subsequently re-elected as Chairman. Legislative decisions were the subject of much public debate in 2006 and the first half of 2007. In November 2006 the federal legislature passed the Women's Protection Bill, which amended the *Hudood* ordinance, giving civil courts jurisdiction in rape cases and revoking the death penalty for extra-marital sexual intercourse. Religious groups voiced their opposition to the bill, arguing that it was 'un-Islamic', while others called for the abolition of the *Hudood* ordinance in its entirety. Further reform was anticipated in February 2007 when it was reported that the Prevention of Anti-Women Practices Bill, regarding women's property and inheritance rights, had been tabled at the National Assembly. Meanwhile, in December 2006 the Supreme Court issued a delaying order against the *Hasba* (Accountability) Bill, which had been approved by the NWFP provincial assembly in July 2005 to regulate the application of Islamic values, on the grounds that it breached human rights. There was also much conjecture about the forthcoming presidential election, which was scheduled to be held in September–October 2007, before the expiry of the incumbent National Assembly's term of office. In March 2007 Musharraf suspended the Chief Justice of the Supreme Court, Iftikhar Mohammad Chaudhry—who was widely recognized for his independent stance on controversial issues and for his investigations into human rights violations—on charges of abuse of office. This controversial action provoked the holding of large-scale, violent demonstrations by the legal community and the resignation of several senior judicial officials. The authorities' decision to dispatch riot police to contain the protests precipitated further unrest and strengthened the protesters' cause in the eyes of ordinary citizens. The escalation in anti-Government sentiment amongst the general public led many observers to question the solidity of Musharraf's power base. In mid-May Chaudhry arrived in Karachi to address a political rally organized by his supporters, but was unable to leave the airport because the roads into the city were blocked. Demonstrations in Karachi subsequently escalated into violent clashes between supporters of the Government and the opposition, resulting in some 41 fatalities. The campaign to reinstate Chaudhry appeared to have succeeded when the Supreme Court voted to restore him to the position of Chief Justice in July.

Sectarian violence and terrorist attacks continued to pose a threat to internal security and stability in 2006 and 2007. In April 2006 a suicide bombing at a religious gathering of approximately 10,000 Sunni Muslims in Karachi resulted in the deaths of at least 58 people. In January 2007 a bomb explosion in Peshawar, immediately prior to the commencement of a Shi'a religious procession, killed at least 14 people, including several police officers. The incident followed a suicide attack at a hotel in Islamabad the previous day, when the bomber and a security officer were killed and several people were wounded. In the following month the provincial Minister for Social Welfare for Punjab and PML member, Zill-e-Huma, was assassinated in Gujranwala; her attacker, who was arrested at the scene of the crime, objected to women's involvement in politics on the grounds that it was 'un-Islamic'. In April a suicide bombing at a public meeting in Charsadda, NWFP, resulted in at least 22 fatalities; the federal Minister of the Interior, Aftab Ahmad Khan Sherpao, who appeared to have been the target of the attack, sustained injuries. A bomb explosion at a hotel in Peshawar in mid-May killed some 24 people and injured several more.

In 2007 the growing prominence of religious leaders of the Lal Masjid (Red Mosque) in central Islamabad posed a further threat to the Government's attempts to stabilize the security situation. Members of the Lal Masjid and its two *madrassas*, who called for the imposition of *shari'a* law, had been involved in increasingly overt challenges to authority, issuing a *fatwa* (Islamic edict) against Minister of Tourism Nilofar Bakhtyar and even abducting security officers and alleged prostitutes. The religious extremism advocated by the mosque was rejected by protesters who took part in demonstrations in major cities in April. Matters came to a head in July with violent clashes between paramilitary forces and occupants of the large Lal Masjid compound; although some 1,500 students reportedly surrendered and the imam was taken into custody, the imam's brother and a contingent of students remained until negotiations collapsed and security forces invaded the compound. It was later estimated that some 100 people, many of them Lal Masjid followers, had been killed, but some estimates put the death toll much higher. The siege aggravated anti-Government sentiment in certain quarters, and resulted in a spate of retaliatory attacks in Islamabad, the NWFP and elsewhere, exacerbating an already deteriorating security situation. The rise of another radical cleric in the Swat valley, NWFP, in late 2007 opened up a new front in the Government's struggles against militancy.

Meanwhile, conjecture about the possible return to Pakistan of two former prime ministers, Benazir Bhutto and Nawaz Sharif, intensified. In August 2007 the Supreme Court decided that, regardless of the terms of his exile agreement, Sharif was entitled to return to the country; however, upon his arrival in Islamabad in the following month, Sharif was sent back to Saudi Arabia, prompting a legal challenge to the deportation. There were reports of negotiations between Musharraf and Bhutto about the latter's re-entry into domestic politics as the former apparently searched for an alternative power base. Bhutto's conditions for working with Musharraf were said to include Musharraf's resignation from the army and the withdrawal of corruption charges against herself and others. In early October Musharraf passed the 'national reconciliation' ordinance, giving Bhutto and other politicians immunity from prosecution under charges brought during 1986–99. Despite the absence of a conclusive agreement, Bhutto entered Pakistan later that month. She was greeted by hundreds of thousands of supporters in Karachi, but fears for her safety were confirmed when a bomb attack on her procession resulted in approximately 139 fatalities. Bhutto herself was unharmed.

On 6 October 2007 Musharraf was re-elected as President by the incumbent national and provincial legislatures, securing 671 votes against the eight received by Wajihuddin Ahmed. Members of the MMA, the PML (N) and other parties of the All Parties Democratic Movement opposition grouping had resigned in protest prior to the ballot, while the PPP abstained from the vote. Just before the vote, the Supreme Court had ruled that the victor could not be declared until the legality of the election had been confirmed pending legal challenges from the opposition, a decision that was not expected until later in the month. The Supreme Court was also expected to rule on the legality of the national reconciliation ordinance. In early November the presiding judge estimated that a decision would not be made before the middle of the month. On 3 November Musharraf declared a state of emergency and suspended the Constitution, citing, among other contributing factors, the deteriorating law and order situation and the judiciary's interference in government affairs. Immediate measures included the dismissal of Chief Justice Chaudhry and the swearing in of Abdul Hameed Dogar as his replacement. Members of the judiciary were reportedly among those detained, together with lawyers, opposition figures and human rights activists who had taken part in demonstrations to protest against the declaration. Meanwhile, the police force was accorded special powers, and the broadcasting of private and international television channels was suspended. The National Assembly was dissolved on 15 November, and the Chairman of the Senate, Mohammad Mian Soomro, was sworn in to lead an interim government the following day. The Punjab, Balochistan and Sindh provincial legislatures were subsequently dissolved, the provincial assembly of NWFP having been dissolved in early October. On 20 November the Chief Election Commissioner confirmed that parliamentary and provincial assembly elections would be held on 8 January 2008. Gen. Musharraf resigned as Chief of Army Staff on 28 November 2007, following the Supreme Court's dismissal, on 22 November, of the final legal challenge to Musharraf's re-election as President, thus facilitating Musharraf's inauguration as civilian head of state (which duly took place on 29 November). Meanwhile, also on 22 November, the Commonwealth Ministerial Action Group on the Harare Declaration suspended Pakistan from the Councils of the Commonwealth. Musharraf revoked the state of emergency on 15 December.

A power-sharing agreement between Musharraf and Bhutto had appeared increasingly unlikely as Bhutto called for Musharraf's resignation as Chief of Army Staff in the aftermath of his declaration of a state of emergency. PPP supporters joined the ranks of opposition members detained under the emergency measures, and Bhutto herself was placed under temporary house arrest to prevent her participation in political rallies. In mid-November 2007 Bhutto had announced an end to the negotiations, demanded Musharraf's resignation from the post of President as well as the head of the military, and indicated a willingness to consider the formation of a coalition government with other opposition parties. Nawaz Sharif was allowed to return to Pakistan at the end of November, following the reported intervention of the King of Saudi Arabia. As the country prepared for elections, in late December Bhutto was killed in an attack on a PPP rally in Rawalpindi. The cause of death was initially unclear, with conflicting reports from different quarters: some claimed she had been shot, while others asserted that she had died as a result of the suicide bombing, which killed some 20 others (in February British detectives corroborated the results of a domestic investigation, which concluded that Bhutto had died from a head injury caused by the force of the explosion). The Government, which declared three days of mourning, was criticized for not arranging adequate security measures, and some voiced suspicion about the perpetrators' possible links to sections of the Government or the intelligence establishment, a claim that Musharraf vehemently denied. According to officials, Baitullah Mehsud, an extremist in the Federally Administered Tribal Areas (FATA), and al-Qa'ida were involved in the attack. News of the assassination provoked rioting in several cities, resulting in more than 45 deaths. On 30 December Bilawal Bhutto Zardari was named to succeed his mother as leader of the PPP following the completion of his university studies, with Asif Ali Zardari assuming the role in an interim capacity. In January 2008 the Election Commission of Pakistan announced that legislative elections, hitherto scheduled for 8 January, would be postponed until February.

At the legislative elections, which were held on 18 February 2008, the PPPP—established by the PPP in 2002 in order to meet electoral requirements—secured a total of 121 general and reserved seats in the National Assembly. The PML (N) won 91 seats, while the PML, which supported Musharraf, took just 54 seats. Turn-out was estimated at some 45% of the electorate. The PML was also defeated in all of the provincial assemblies except Balochistan. On 9 March 2008 the PPP and the PML (N) announced a coalition agreement, the terms of which reportedly included the reinstatement of judges dismissed in November 2007 and the entry of the latter party into the new cabinet. A coalition Government was consequently sworn in on 31 March, under the premiership of Yousaf Raza Gillani of the PPP, who had formally assumed the post of Prime Minister on 24 March. The new Cabinet included 11 members of the PPP, nine from the PML (N), two from the ANP, one from a faction of the JUI and one independent member of the National Assembly from the FATA. Among the new holders of the most important government positions, Chaudhry Ahmed Mukhtar of the PPP was appointed Minister of Defence, Shah Mehmud Qureshi of the PPP became Minister of Foreign Affairs, while Muhammad Ishaq Dar of the PML (N) took the finance portfolio. Shortly after assuming office, Gillani ordered the release of several judges arrested in November 2007. With popular and political support for President Musharraf severely diminished, there was much speculation about his future role. Following the reinstallation of a democratically elected government, the Commonwealth readmitted Pakistan as a full member in May 2008.

In foreign relations Pakistan has traditionally pursued a policy of maintaining close links with Islamic states in the Middle East and Africa and with the People's Republic of China, while continuing to seek aid and assistance from the USA. Pakistan's controversial nuclear programme prompted the USA to terminate development aid in April 1979, but, as a result of the Soviet invasion of Afghanistan in December of that year, military and economic assistance was renewed in 1981. However, increased concern about Pakistan's ability to develop nuclear weapons and its refusal to sign the Treaty on the Non-Proliferation of Nuclear Weapons led to the suspension of military and economic aid by the US Government again in 1990 (under the Pressler Amendment). In February 1992 the Pakistani Government admitted for the first time that Pakistan had nuclear-weapons capability, but added that it had 'frozen' its nuclear programme at the level of October 1989, when its capabilities were insufficient to produce a nuclear device. In September 1995 the US Senate voted in favour of the Brown Amendment, which allowed a limited resumption of defence supplies to Pakistan. The Brown Amendment (which was ratified by the US President, Bill Clinton, in January 1996) also deleted the Pressler Amendment requirements for economic sanctions, thus paving the way for the resumption of US economic aid to Pakistan. In August 1996 the first consignment of US military equipment released by the US Government after a six-year delay arrived in Pakistan. In December 1998 Prime Minister Nawaz Sharif held talks with President Clinton in the US capital in an attempt to gain support for Pakistan's ailing economy and to persuade the US leader further to ease sanctions imposed on Pakistan following nuclear tests carried out by the latter in May (see below). During 1998–99 the USA lifted some of the sanctions imposed on Pakistan and India, whilst reiterating requests that the two countries sign the Comprehensive Test Ban Treaty (CTBT) and exercise restraint in their respective missile development programmes to ensure peace in South Asia. During 2000 US foreign policy appeared to favour closer co-operation with India at the expense of improved relations with

Pakistan. However, Pakistan's strategic importance to US efforts to dismantle the Taliban regime in Afghanistan and thus apprehend members of the al-Qa'ida terrorist organization held responsible for the devastating attacks on New York and Washington, DC, USA, in September 2001 resulted in attempts by the USA to promote Pakistan's political rehabilitation in the Western international community. Although in September the US Government withdrew sanctions imposed on Pakistan in May 1998, and Gen. Musharraf was warmly received on official visits to the USA in November 2001 and February 2002, a 1990 suspension order on the delivery to Pakistan of 28 US F-16 fighter aircraft was not lifted, to the evident disappointment of the Pakistani President.

Despite the international acclaim that greeted Musharraf's public declaration of his commitment to the eradication of militant religious extremism in January 2002, US concerns about the proliferation of armed fundamentalist groups in Pakistan's border regions, and the possibility of their assisting scattered al-Qa'ida units to regroup in these areas, persisted. A US journalist, Daniel Pearl, was abducted in Karachi in January by a previously unknown group called the National Movement for the Restoration of Pakistani Sovereignty; the group made a number of demands in exchange for his safe return, including the release of all Pakistani nationals captured by US forces in Afghanistan and transported (together with other suspected al-Qa'ida members) to a detention centre at the US military base in Guantánamo Bay, Cuba. Despite the prompt arrest by the Pakistani authorities of a British-born militant Islamist, Ahmed Omar Saeed Sheikh, who was believed to have organized the kidnapping, it soon emerged that Pearl had been murdered by his abductors. Confounding speculation that suspects in the case would be extradited for trial in the USA, in March Saeed Sheikh and three alleged accomplices appeared in a specially instituted anti-terrorism court in Karachi on charges of kidnapping, murder and terrorism. The men were convicted of the charges in mid-July; Saeed Sheikh was sentenced to death and his co-defendants were each sentenced to life imprisonment. Following an anti-US grenade attack on the Protestant International Church in Islamabad in March, in which five people (including the wife and daughter of a US diplomat) were killed, Musharraf dismissed five senior police officers for what he considered a serious lapse in security. It was widely believed that intelligence proceeding from Pakistani investigations to discover the identities of the assailants was a crucial factor in the arrest of Abu Zubaydah, one of al-Qa'ida's most senior commanders, by officers of the US Federal Bureau of Investigation (FBI) in Faisalabad at the end of March. However, it was reported that several prominent Islamic clerics and at least 1,300 of their supporters who had been detained in late 2001 were released in early April 2002. In early May a suicide bomber killed 14 people, the majority of whom were French engineers, in Karachi. (Three men were convicted on charges of conspiracy relating to the suicide bombing and sentenced to death in June 2003; two of the men were reportedly members of the banned Islamist Harakat ul-Jihad-al-Islami and Harakat ul-Mujahideen.) Another attack occurred in mid-June 2002 outside the US consulate in Karachi, killing 12 people. One month later two Pakistani members of the al-Alami faction of Harakat ul-Mujahideen claimed responsibility for the attack on the US consulate as well as other attacks on Western targets. (In April 2003 four men were convicted of organizing the attack on the consulate; two were sentenced to death. The same two were also convicted in October of attempting to assassinate Musharraf in April 2002, along with one other member of Harakat ul-Jihad-al-Islami, and sentenced to 10 years' imprisonment.) In September 2002 Pakistani security forces arrested 12 alleged members of al-Qa'ida in Karachi, including the Yemeni-born Ramzi Binalshibh, a principal suspect in the attacks on the USA on 11 September 2001. The USA took custody of Binalshibh and four other al-Qa'ida suspects. In December 2002 Pakistani authorities arrested Dr Ahmed Javed Khawaja, a US citizen, and his brother, for allegedly sheltering and medically treating al-Qa'ida members and their families. The two suspects were charged a month later, prompting criticisms from human rights activists.

In an apparent breakthrough in the campaign against religious extremism, the alleged operations chief of the al-Qa'ida network, Khalid Sheikh Mohammed, who was suspected of having planned the attacks on the USA in September 2001, was arrested in Rawalpindi in March 2003. It was hoped that the suspect, who was promptly taken into US custody, would provide information on the identity and whereabouts of al-Qa'ida cells in Pakistan and elsewhere in the world. Two other suspected Islamist militants were also arrested. The ISI's involvement in the arrest of the alleged militants suggested that the intelligence agency was genuinely attempting to curb militant activity. Furthermore, in early March the ISI declared that since 11 September 2001 Pakistan had arrested 442 suspected foreign militants, of whom 346 had been handed over to US custody. However, the discovery of Mohammed in a house owned by an army officer's brother raised questions about links between al-Qa'ida and the Pakistani military. Furthermore, the proprietor's prominent role in the Jamaat-e-Islami generated speculation about that political party's connections with al-Qa'ida. The arrests temporarily eased US pressures to support a UN Security Council resolution authorizing the removal of the regime of Saddam Hussain in Iraq. Later that month Pakistan, influenced by widespread large-scale protest marches against military action in Iraq, stated that it would not support the USA in this action. In the same month the USA removed all remaining sanctions imposed on Pakistan after the 1999 military coup. In late April 2003 security forces arrested 10 allegedly senior members of the terrorist network and seized a large quantity of weapons in Peshawar. In early April the USA agreed to waive a total of US $1,000m. in debt, in recognition of Pakistan's efforts in the 'war on terror'. During Musharraf's visit to the USA in June, the Pakistani President hoped to secure further pledges of co-operation, economic aid and possibly military sales in return for his support. Indeed, the US President, George W. Bush, offered an aid package of $3,000m. in financial and military assistance over the next five years. The Bush Administration, however, declined to cancel a further $1,800m. debt, owing to reservations over whether enough was being done to curb militant activity and to prevent the infiltration of separatist militants into Indian-controlled Kashmir. There were also concerns expressed with regard to Islamist fundamentalism in Pakistani politics, the country's incomplete return to democratic rule and Pakistan's nuclear weapons programme (the USA had already placed a symbolic two-year ban on trade with Khan Research Laboratories following allegations that the latter had assisted North Korea in supplying nuclear designs).

In early October 2003 Pakistani forces arrested 18 suspected militants in South Waziristan, one of the Federally Administered Tribal Areas. The offensive followed reports of increased militant activity in the region, particularly in conservative Pashtun areas where Taliban members were known to enjoy support. At least eight Taliban and al-Qa'ida suspects were killed during the operation; it was later reported that the majority of the dead were of foreign origin. Later that month the armed forces arrested a further 40 people, including tribal elders who were accused of sheltering al-Qa'ida suspects. However, despite the apparent attempts to combat Taliban activity in the tribal areas, there were claims that Pakistani troops continued to allow Taliban movement across the Afghan–Pakistani border and that senior Taliban members were openly living in Quetta, a city close to Waziristan. In January 2004 Musharraf, during a speech to the Pakistani legislature, attempted to reassure the USA and the rest of the world that Pakistan was committed to defeating militant Islamism. While an army operation in South Waziristan earlier that month largely failed, by the end of January seven al-Qa'ida suspects and the Taliban former governor of Baghis province in Afghanistan, had been arrested. The search for suspected militants remained focused on South Waziristan, where the USA believed bin Laden and other al-Qa'ida leaders were receiving shelter. Several thousands of Pakistani troops were deployed to force al-Qa'ida fugitives across the border into Afghanistan, where US soldiers were active (US troops were not allowed to operate from Pakistani soil). In late February, following the expiry of a deadline for tribal leaders to hand over Islamist fugitives, the army launched another attack, this time arresting 58 suspects. Pakistan's recent efforts were largely in response to the USA's restraint over the nuclear proliferation scandal (see above). However, the reluctance by Pakistani troops to attack Afghanistan's former rulers threatened to affect Musharraf's relations with the US Government. Nevertheless, the USA remained anxious not to destabilize the Pakistani President, who was facing growing domestic opposition owing to his support for the 'war on terror'.

Meanwhile, fighting between Pakistani troops and militants in March 2004 resulted in the deaths of more than 100 people, including the al-Qa'ida intelligence chief, Abdullah. Many other militants were believed to have evaded capture and escaped. The army subsequently offered a temporary amnesty to both the militants and those tribesmen sheltering them. However, by the 30 April deadline only five tribesmen had surrendered. Meanwhile, during a visit to Pakistan in March, the US Secretary of State announced that, in recognition of the close military relations between the two countries, the USA had decided to designate Pakistan a 'major non-North Atlantic Treaty Organization (NATO) ally'. Shortly afterwards President Bush announced that all remaining US sanctions against Pakistan would be lifted. However, concerns continued to be expressed by the USA that more progress was not being made in the campaign against al-Qa'ida. Renewed fighting in June, after a period of calm in Waziristan, resulted in the deaths of 72 people, including the popular Waziri tribal leader and former Taliban commander Nek Mohammed. In the following month it was announced that several suspected al-Qa'ida members, including the Tanzanian Ahmed Khalfan Ghailani, who was wanted in connection with the 1998 bombing of US embassies in Kenya and Tanzania, had been arrested in the town of Gujrat in Punjab. Ghailani was later placed in the custody of the USA. In August 2004 the Government announced that it had thwarted a plan to carry out several attacks in Islamabad, and had subsequently arrested at least 12 al-Qa'ida suspects. Meanwhile, the authorities in the United Arab Emirates had arrested Qari Saifullah Akhtar, who was believed to be one of bin Laden's chief advisers and the leader of Harakat ul-Jihad-al-Islami, and extradited him to Pakistan. Akhtar was suspected of having been involved in the December 2003 plot to assassinate President Musharraf.

In the mean time military operations continued in Waziristan, although it was believed that the death of Nek Mohammed had strengthened local resistance to the army campaign. The fighting escalated in September 2004 and military officials claimed that, as a result of intensified military pressure, al-Qa'ida fighters were being driven out of the area, possibly leaving for Iraq. In the same month it was announced that police had killed a prominent al-Qa'ida figure, Amjad Hussain Farooq, during a gun battle in Nawabshah, north of Karachi. Farooq was believed to have planned the failed assassination attempts on Musharraf in December 2003 and to have been involved in both the murder of Daniel Pearl and in several bombings in Karachi in 2002. In February 2005 the army announced that it had concluded a peace agreement with five tribal leaders in South Waziristan under which, in exchange for an amnesty, the leaders had promised that they would not fight the Pakistani army or support Taliban and al-Qa'ida fighters in the area. In the same month, in a move indicative of the improved relations between the two countries, the USA revived the deal that it had suspended in 1990 to supply Pakistan with F-16 fighter aircraft. The agreement constituted part of a US $3,000m., five-year assistance programme. Following the devastating earthquake of October, however, the purchase of the aircraft was postponed, in order that the funds could be allocated instead to the reconstruction effort. Meanwhile, in May it was announced that Abu Faraj al-Libbi, reported to be the operational head of al-Qa'ida in Pakistan, had been captured in the city of Mardan in the NWFP. A further 20 suspected al-Qa'ida operatives were arrested in the following weeks. Al-Libbi was subsequently transferred into US custody for interrogation. In December five militants were reported to have been killed following a missile strike on a house in the town of Mir Ali in North Waziristan.

In January 2006 several civilians were killed in a US air-strike on a house in a village near the border with Afghanistan that intelligence sources claimed was being visited by Ayman al-Zawahiri, a leading al-Qa'ida figure. Al-Zawahiri was, however, not present at the house. In March US President Bush visited Pakistan, although his one-night stay was overshadowed somewhat by a visit that he had made to India several days previously, in which a landmark nuclear co-operation agreement had been announced. Shortly before his arrival in Pakistan, a suicide bomb attack on the US consulate in Karachi resulted in the deaths of three people, including a US diplomat.

In April 2006 President Musharraf was reported to have acknowledged the increase of extremism in Waziristan and other border areas. In September the signing of a peace accord by the Government and tribal leaders in North Waziristan prompted criticism from international observers for what was seen as a strategy of appeasement: under the terms of the agreement the Government was to downgrade its military presence in the area in exchange for a cessation of rebel offensives against the army and across the border with Afghanistan. In October some 80 people were killed in an army attack on a *madrassa* in the Bajaur region of the FATA bordering Afghanistan; the army's contention that the victims were militants who were using the school as a training facility conflicted with accounts by some locals, who claimed that they were innocent students. In an apparent act of retaliation, at least 42 army troops were killed in a suicide bombing at an army base in Dargai, NWFP, in November. In March 2007, however, the Government signed a peace agreement with tribal elders in Bajaur under which the latter confirmed that they would not provide refuge to foreign militants, while the Government, for its part, was obliged to consult tribal elders before launching operations in the region. In late March fighting broke out between Uzbek militants in the area and local tribesmen; by the beginning of April it was estimated that the violence had resulted in approximately 200 fatalities. In July 2007 Baitullah Mehsud (a militant later accused of involvement in Benazir Bhutto's assassination in December, see above), along with a group of tribal leaders, declared an end to the cease-fire in North Waziristan. Clashes between militants and security forces resulted in many deaths in North and South Waziristan in 2007.

Relations with Afghanistan were strained during the 1980s and early 1990s, as rebel Afghan tribesmen (*mujahidin*) used areas inside Pakistan (notably the city of Peshawar) as bases for their activities. In early 1988 there were an estimated 3.2m. Afghan refugees in Pakistan, most of them in the NWFP. The presence of the refugees prompted cross-border attacks against *mujahidin* bases by Soviet and Afghan government troops. In 1988 Pakistan signed the Geneva Accords on the withdrawal of Soviet troops from Afghanistan, which included agreements on the voluntary repatriation of Afghan refugees from Pakistan. Following the withdrawal of Soviet troops from Afghanistan in 1989, Pakistan maintained its support for the guerrillas' cause, while denying accusations by the Afghan Government that it was taking an active military part in the conflict, or that it was acting as a conduit for arms supplies to the *mujahidin*. The Pakistani Government welcomed the overthrow of the Afghan regime by the guerrillas in April 1992 and supported the interim coalition Government that was formed to administer Afghanistan until the holding of free elections. Relations between Pakistan and Afghanistan deteriorated, however, in 1994. The turbulence and increasing anti-Pakistan feeling in Afghanistan threatened not only to result in an extension of the violence into the Pakhtoon (Pashtun) areas of the NWFP, but also obstructed the trade route from the Central Asian republics of the former USSR to the Arabian Sea at Karachi. The situation worsened in September 1995 when the Pakistani embassy in Kabul was ransacked and burned down by a mob of about 5,000 Afghans protesting at Pakistan's alleged active support for the Islamist Taliban militia. In the following month the Afghan ambassador to Pakistan was expelled from the country. Following the capture of Kabul by Taliban troops in late September 1996 and their assumption of power, the Pakistani Government issued a statement in which it recognized the Taliban militia as the new Afghan Government.

In December 1999 there were signs of distinct changes in Pakistan's policy towards Afghanistan. Following the imposition of UN-mandated sanctions on Afghanistan the previous month for refusing to hand over the terrorist suspect bin Laden, Pakistan appeared to be exerting pressure on the Taliban to accede to Western demands by closing down a number of Afghan banking operations in Pakistan. The Pakistani Government continued to offer financial and diplomatic support to the Taliban, although Gen. Musharraf repeatedly and strongly denied giving military assistance. Allegations regarding the involvement of Pakistan's special forces in the Taliban campaign grew, however, following the latter's successful offensive in August–September 2000. The Pakistani Government agreed to implement the UN sanctions imposed on Afghanistan in January 2001, but announced that it would attempt to mitigate the effect of the restrictions, warning of a steep increase in refugee numbers and a worsening of the civil war. The failure of (somewhat unconvincing) attempts by senior Pakistani military officers to persuade the Taliban administration to comply with US demands that bin Laden and members of his al-Qa'ida terrorist organization thought to be resident in Afghanistan should be handed over to the US authorities to answer charges of responsibility for the September 2001 terrorist attacks on the US mainland ultimately resulted in a US-led military campaign to remove the Taliban from power. Despite considerable opposition from ethnic Pashtuns (who comprised the majority of the Taliban administration) in north-western Pakistan and from elements of the armed forces who had spent years consolidating relations with the Taliban regime, Musharraf was forced to co-operate with the US-led coalition to avoid potentially devastating economic and political isolation. Long-standing enmity between the Pakistani Government and the tribes of the United Front, arising from Pakistani sponsorship of the Taliban regime, was exacerbated by the participation of Pakistani nationals in the armed resistance to the United Front's renewed military campaign (supported by the international coalition) to recapture Afghanistan (see above). As the United Front continued to make impressive territorial gains in Afghanistan, culminating in the capture of the capital, Kabul, in mid-November, the Pakistani Government announced the closure of all Taliban consular offices in Pakistan, including the embassy in Islamabad. It was hoped that the broad-based ethnicity of the Afghan Interim Administration (which included Pashtun representatives) installed in December would help to foster improved relations between the Pakistani authorities and the tribes of the United Front.

Publicly, Musharraf supported Hamid Karzai and the new Afghan Transitional Administration. However, Afghan officials were convinced that the Pakistani ISI was giving sanctuary to senior Taliban members and other anti-Afghan Government military commanders, such as Gulbuddin Hekmatyar. In mid-February 2003 the Pakistani and Afghan military intelligence services held talks in Rome, Italy, in an attempt to resolve deep-rooted differences. Some two months later, during an official visit to Pakistan, President Karzai urged the Pakistani Government to assist in curbing the cross-border attacks by militant Islamists. Relations were strained when Pakistan delivered a formal protest to Afghanistan in June over the dumping of the bodies of some 21 Taliban fighters on its territory; the Afghan authorities were forced to recover the bodies after Pakistani border guards discovered that the dead were, in fact, not Pakistani, but Afghan citizens. One month later, in a seemingly well-planned operation, the Pakistani embassy in Afghanistan was stormed and raided by hundreds of Afghans in protest against alleged incursions by Pakistani border troops into Afghan territory. The crowds were dispersed by Afghan police; Karzai apologized for the incident to the Pakistani President and promised to pay compensation. The embassy was reopened almost two weeks later. In January 2004 the Pakistani Prime Minister paid his first ever official visit to Afghanistan; the two countries agreed to work together to combat cross-border infiltration. In August Karzai visited Islamabad, where he held talks with Musharraf, who insisted that Taliban and al-Qa'ida militants operating in the NWFP and Balochistan would not be permitted to use the areas as bases from which to disrupt the Afghan presidential election, which was scheduled to take place in October. In March 2005, during a visit by Karzai, who had secured victory in the presidential election, the improvement in bilateral relations was illustrated when the two countries agreed to establish bus services linking Peshawar with the Afghan city of Jalalabad and Quetta with the Afghan city of Qandahar. However, in mid-2005 relations became strained again, when Afghan police apprehended three Pakistani men thought to have been plotting to kill the outgoing US ambassador to Afghanistan. The Afghan Government accused Pakistan of failing to prevent Taliban insurgents hiding in the border regions from perpetrating an increasing number of attacks in its southern and eastern provinces. In response, Musharraf assured Karzai of his continued co-operation in the battle against terrorism. However, questions continued as to the extent of Pakistan's commitment to preventing the resurgence of the Taliban.

In September 2005 additional Pakistani troops were deployed along the border with Afghanistan in order to prevent disruption of the Afghan legislative elections that were to take place in that month. Bilateral relations deteriorated further in 2006 when Karzai gave Musharraf a list of militants believed to be hiding in Pakistan; Musharraf responded by claiming that the Afghan Government's intelligence on the militants was out of date and accused Karzai of being unaware of security issues in his own country. In late 2006 the announcement of Pakistan's plans to lay landmines and construct a series of fences along sections of the Afghan–Pakistani border to prevent insurgents based in Pakistan from launching cross-border raids, while also reducing drugs-smuggling from Afghanistan, elicited a negative response from Karzai, who complained that the strategy (which had originally been proposed by Musharraf in 2005) was divisive. Preparatory work on the fence carried out by Pakistani officials in March 2007 raised further protests from the Afghan Government, which argued that the demarcation of the border was in dispute, but construction continued. Meanwhile, following talks held in Kabul between Karzai and the Pakistani Prime Minister, Shaukat Aziz, in January 2007, the latter announced that the two countries were to establish a *Jirga* Commission, which would be headed by the Pakistani Minister of the Interior and would work towards combating cross-border terrorism (the Commission met for the first time in March). The two leaders also agreed to accelerate the repatriation process for the Afghan refugees remaining in Pakistan.

Drought conditions in the region contributed to a new influx of Afghan refugees in early 2001 (there were estimated to be more than 2m. refugees in Pakistan in March), placing renewed strain on limited resources and threatening to exacerbate the country's deteriorating economy and security situation. Military operations by the US-led anti-terrorism coalition in Afghanistan in October resulted in a fresh exodus of refugees. Although Pakistan had officially closed its border with Afghanistan in late September, it was estimated that as many as 80,000 refugees had illegally crossed into Pakistan before the Government approved plans at the end of October to reopen the border to allow the inflow of up to 300,000 of the most vulnerable refugees; the measure constituted part of an agreement with the office of the UN High Commissioner for Refugees (UNHCR) that was to include the establishment of 15 new camps. (In February 2002 it was announced that thousands of refugees had been transferred from the notorious Jalozai camp in northern Pakistan—which was subsequently closed—to a new UNHCR-supervised camp near Peshawar.) According to UNHCR, by April 2002 (following the decisive defeat of Taliban forces in most of Afghanistan) repatriation offices in Pakistan were processing the return of as many as 50,000 Afghan refugees each week. At the end of 2002 UNHCR announced that more than 1.5m. Afghan refugees in Pakistan had returned to their homeland, surpassing all expectations; a further 400,000 returned in 2003 and approximately 384,000 in 2004. In early 2005 the Pakistani Government and UNHCR launched a census intended to determine how many Afghan refugees remained in Pakistan, in order to aid the development of policies to assist them. According to reports, between early 2002 and April 2007 more than 3m. refugees had returned to Afghanistan from Pakistan.

Relations with India have dominated Pakistan's foreign policy since the creation of the two states in 1947. Relations deteriorated during the late 1970s and early 1980s, owing to Pakistan's programme to develop nuclear weapons, and as a result of major US weapons deliveries to Pakistan. The other major contentious issue between the two states was the disputed region of Kashmir, where, since 1949, a cease-fire line, known as the Line of Control (LoC), has separated Indian-controlled Kashmir (the state of Jammu and Kashmir) and Pakistani Kashmir, which comprises Azad (Free) Kashmir and the Northern Areas. While Pakistan demanded that the sovereignty of the region be decided in accordance with earlier UN resolutions (which advocated a plebiscite in both parts of the region), India argued that a solution should be reached through bilateral negotiations.

Relations between Pakistan and India reached a crisis in late 1989, when the outlawed Jammu and Kashmir Liberation Front (JKLF) and several other Muslim groups in Indian-controlled Kashmir intensified their campaigns of terrorism, strikes and civil unrest, in support of demands for an independent Kashmir or unification with Pakistan. In response, the Indian Government dispatched troops to Jammu and Kashmir. By early February 1990 it was officially estimated that about 80 people (mostly civilians) had been killed in resulting clashes between troops and protesters. The opposition parties in Pakistan organized nation-wide strikes, to express their sympathy for the Muslims in Jammu and Kashmir, and urged the Government to adopt more active measures regarding the crisis.

In December 1990 discussions were held between the Ministers of External Affairs of Pakistan and India, at which an agreement not to attack each other's nuclear facilities was finalized, but no solution was found to the Kashmiri problem. Further high-level talks held between the two countries during the first half of the 1990s made no progress in resolving the crisis, and skirmishes between Pakistani and Indian troops along the border in Kashmir continued. In December 1994 Pakistan was successful in securing the passage of a resolution condemning reported human rights abuses by Indian security forces in Kashmir at the summit meeting of the Organization of the Islamic Conference held in Casablanca, Morocco. (In the same month Pakistan's decision to close down its consulate in Mumbai (Bombay), amid claims of Indian support for acts of terrorism in Karachi, provided a further indication of the growing rift between the two countries.) In February 1995 (and again in

February 1996) Benazir Bhutto's Government organized a nation-wide general strike to express solidarity with the independence movement in Jammu and Kashmir and to protest against alleged atrocities carried out by the Indian forces. In January 1996 relations between the two countries deteriorated when the Pakistani Government accused the Indian forces of having launched a rocket attack on a mosque in Azad Kashmir, which killed 20 people. The Indian authorities claimed that the deaths had been caused by Pakistani rockets that had been misfired. Tensions between Pakistan and India were also exacerbated in early 1996 by allegations that each side was on the verge of conducting nuclear tests. Later that year, India's decision to hold state assembly elections in Jammu and Kashmir (described as 'farcical' by Benazir Bhutto) and its refusal to sign the CTBT did nothing to encourage an improvement in relations between Islamabad and New Delhi. In March 1997, however, talks (which had been suspended since 1994) were resumed, both at official and at ministerial level. Of most significance were the negotiations between India and Pakistan's foreign secretaries, which took place in Islamabad in June. These talks resulted in an agreement to establish a series of distinct working parties to consider groups of issues. One such group of issues specifically related to Jammu and Kashmir. Little progress was made, however, in improving bilateral relations during a further round of high-level talks held in New Delhi in September and tension increased at the end of the month.

In April 1998 Pakistan provoked stern condemnation from the recently elected right-wing Government in India following its successful test-firing of a new intermediate-range missile (capable of reaching deep into Indian territory). The arms race escalated dramatically and to potentially dangerous proportions in the following month when India conducted five underground nuclear test explosions. The test programme was condemned world-wide, and the USA imposed economic sanctions against India. The US President, Bill Clinton, and the UN Security Council urged Pakistan to show restraint in not carrying out its own retaliatory test explosions. However, at the end of May Pakistan carried out six underground atomic test explosions. In early June the Pakistani Government ordered a 50% reduction in public expenditure in an attempt to mitigate the effects of the resultant economic sanctions imposed by various foreign countries, including the USA. Immediately after the nuclear tests, India and Pakistan announced self-imposed moratoriums on further testing and engaged themselves in intense diplomatic activity. In September, however, the Pakistani Minister of Foreign Affairs categorically stated that Pakistan would not sign the CTBT until all of the sanctions were lifted and other legitimate concerns addressed.

Indo-Pakistani talks at foreign secretary level regarding Kashmir and other issues were resumed in Islamabad in October 1998. In February 1999 relations appeared to improve considerably when the Indian Prime Minister, Atal Bihari Vajpayee, made an historic journey (inaugurating the first passenger bus service between India and Pakistan) over the border to Lahore. Following his welcome by the Pakistani Prime Minister, the two leaders held a summit meeting (the first to be conducted in Pakistan for 10 years), at the end of which they signed the Lahore Declaration, which, with its pledges regarding peace and nuclear security, seemed designed to allay world-wide fears of a nuclear 'flashpoint' in South Asia. The contentious subject of Jammu and Kashmir was, however, largely avoided. Concern over the escalating arms race in South Asia again deepened in April, following a series of ballistic missile tests carried out first by India and then by Pakistan (both countries, however, appeared to have adhered to the procedures incorporated in the Lahore Declaration, by informing each other of their test plans well in advance).

In May 1999 the Kashmir conflict intensified to reach what was termed a 'near-war situation' following the reported infiltration of 600–900 well-armed Islamist militants, reinforced by regular Pakistani troops, across the LoC into the area around Kargil in the Indian-held sector of Kashmir. It was widely believed that the incursion of the guerrillas had been planned months in advance by the Pakistani army and intelligence agents; the Pakistani Government, however, claimed that it had no direct involvement whatsoever with the Islamist insurgents. In response, the Indian troops launched a series of airstrikes against the militants at the end of the month, a move that represented a serious provocation to Pakistan since it constituted the first peacetime use of air power in Kashmir. Within days tensions were heightened when a militant Kashmiri group claimed responsibility for shooting down an Indian helicopter gunship and Pakistani troops destroyed two Indian fighter aircraft, which had reportedly strayed into Pakistani airspace. Artillery exchanges increased along the LoC (with both sides suffering heavy casualties) and reports of the massing of troops and evacuation of villages along the international border aroused considerable concern. In early July, however, Indian military dominance combined with US diplomatic pressure prompted Nawaz Sharif's precipitate visit to Washington, DC, in the USA for talks with President Clinton. The resultant Washington Declaration prepared the ground for an end to the Kargil crisis through the Pakistan leader's agreement to the withdrawal of all 'intruders' from Indian-controlled Kashmir. In August there was renewed tension between Pakistan and India when India shot down a Pakistani naval reconnaissance aircraft near Pakistan's border with Gujarat, killing all 16 personnel on board; Pakistan retaliated the following day by opening fire on Indian military aircraft in the same area.

In October–November 1999 there was a notable increase in terrorist incidents in Kashmir, and Indian and Pakistani forces were reported to have resumed skirmishes across the LoC. Relations between the two countries worsened in early November after the success of Vajpayee in promoting an official condemnation of the new Pakistani military regime by the Commonwealth heads of government, following the military coup in Pakistan in mid-October. In December the Indian Government stated that it would not resume dialogue with Pakistan until the latter halted 'cross-border terrorism'.

In late December 1999 the Kashmir conflict came to international attention when five Islamist fundamentalists hijacked an Indian Airlines aircraft and held its passengers captive at Qandahar airport in southern Afghanistan for one week. Among the hijackers' demands was the release from Indian prisons of 36 Muslim militants who supported the Kashmiri separatist movement. Under increasing domestic pressure to prioritize the safety of the hostages, the Indian Government agreed to release three of the prisoners in exchange for the safe return of the captive passengers and crew. Despite Indian accusations of complicity, the Pakistani Government denied any links with the hijackers. In late March 2000 the US President's recent visit to the region appeared to have failed to bring Pakistan and India any closer together when Gen. Musharraf's offer of peace talks regarding Kashmir was firmly rejected by the Indian Government (which still seemed deeply suspicious of the Pakistani Chief Executive). India continued to demand that Pakistan cease 'cross-border terrorism' as a precondition for negotiations, while Pakistan repeatedly denied arming and funding militants.

In mid-August 2000 Pakistan renewed its offer to resume negotiations, despite claims of increased violence on the part of the Indian army against separatists. The impasse in relations, however, remained unchanged and there was an escalation of violent incidents in the region. In November the Indian Government declared the suspension of combat operations against Kashmiri militants during the Muslim holy month of Ramadan. The unilateral cease-fire began at the end of November (and was subsequently extended, at intervals, until the end of May); Indian security forces were, however, authorized to retaliate if fired upon. The majority of national parties and foreign governments supported the cessation of hostilities, although the Pakistani authorities described the cease-fire as 'meaningless' without simultaneous constructive dialogue. The moderate All-Party Hurriyat Conference in Indian-administered Kashmir welcomed the development and offered to enter negotiations with Pakistani authorities in order to prepare for tripartite discussions. The Hizbul Mujahideen and other militant groups, however, rejected the offer and continued their campaign of violence, extending their activities as far as the Red Fort in Old Delhi, where three people were shot dead in December. In the same month Pakistan extended an invitation to the All-Party Hurriyat Conference to participate in joint preparations for the establishment of tripartite negotiations. At the end of December India agreed to issue passports to a delegation of All-Party Hurriyat Conference leaders to allow them to visit Pakistan; however, processing of the applications was subsequently stalled. In mid-January 2001 the Indian High Commissioner to Pakistan visited Gen. Musharraf. This meeting signified the first high-level contact since the military coup in Pakistan in 1999. The two officials urged an early resumption of negotiations on the Kashmir question.

Relations with India appeared to improve following the earthquake in Gujarat in January 2001, when Pakistan offered humanitarian relief to India and the leaders of the two countries thus established contact. In May Prime Minister Vajpayee issued an unexpected invitation to Gen. Musharraf to attend bilateral negotiations in Agra in July. However, hopes for a significant breakthrough on the issue of Kashmir were frustrated by the failure of the two leaders to agree to a joint declaration at the conclusion of the dialogue; the divergent views of the two sides on the priority issue in the dispute (cross-border terrorism according to India, and Kashmiri self-determination in the opinion of Pakistan) appeared to be more firmly entrenched than ever. Tension with India was heightened considerably following a guerrilla-style attack on the state assembly building in Srinagar on 1 October. An estimated 38 people (including two of the four assailants) were killed and around 70 were wounded in the attack and in the subsequent confrontation with security forces. The Indian Government attributed responsibility for the attack to the Pakistan-based Jaish-e-Mohammed and Lashkar-e-Taiba groups. Tensions were exacerbated later in the month when Gen. Musharraf rejected official Indian requests to ban the activities of the organizations in Pakistan, although he did publicly condemn the attack.

On 13 December 2001 five armed assailants gained access to the grounds of the Indian union Parliament in New Delhi and attempted to launch an apparent suicide attack on the parliament building. Although no parliamentary deputies were hurt in the attack, nine people were killed and some 25 were injured in the botched assault; the five assailants were also killed in the attack. The Indian authorities again attributed responsibility for the attack to the Jaish-e-Mohammed and Lashkar-e-Taiba groups, and suggested that the assailants appeared to be of Pakistani origin. Pakistan, which had been among the many countries to express immediate condemnation of the attack (which was popularly described as an assault on democracy), now demanded to see concrete proof to support the allegations made by the Indian Government, while the US Government urged the Indian authorities to exercise restraint in their response. Tensions between India and Pakistan continued to mount when Mohammed Afzal, a member of Jaish-e-Mohammed arrested in Kashmir on suspicion of complicity in the incident, admitted his involvement and alleged publicly that Pakistani security and intelligence agencies had provided support to those directly responsible for the attack. India recalled its High Commissioner from Islamabad and announced that overground transport services between the two countries would be suspended from 1 January 2002. As positions were reinforced with troops and weapons (including missiles) on both sides of the LoC, there was considerable international concern that such brinkmanship might propel the two countries (each with nuclear capabilities) into renewed armed conflict. Mindful of the potential detriment to security at Pakistan's border with Afghanistan that could result from escalated conflict in Kashmir, the USA applied increased pressure on the beleaguered Pakistani Government (already facing vociferous domestic opposition to its accommodation of US activities in Afghanistan) to adopt a more conciliatory attitude towards India's security concerns, and in late December the Pakistani authorities followed the US Government's lead in 'freezing' the assets of the two groups held responsible for the attack by India. The leaders of the two groups were later detained by the Pakistani authorities (who arrested some 80 suspected militants in the last week of December), but, despite an evident satisfaction at this development, the Indian Government continued to dismiss much of the Pakistani response as superficial and demanded that the two leaders be extradited (together with 20 other named Pakistan-based militants) to stand trial in India.

It had been hoped that tensions between the two countries might be defused by renewed dialogue between Vajpayee and Musharraf at a summit meeting of the South Asian Association for Regional Co-operation (SAARC) convened in Nepal in the first week of January 2002, but contacts between the two men were minimal, and troops on both sides of the LoC continued to exchange gunfire in the days following the conference. However, on 12 January Musharraf yielded to relentless international pressure by publicly condemning the activities of militant extremists based in Pakistan and announcing the introduction of a broad range of measures to combat terrorist activity and religious zealotry, including the proscription of five extremist organizations (among them Jaish-e-Mohammed and Lashkar-e-Taiba). It was hoped that reports published in late January, which indicated that the number of terrorist incidents in Jammu and Kashmir had halved since the introduction of the counter-insurgency measures, would help foster a more substantial improvement in future relations between the two countries. However, in March India and (subsequently) Pakistan expelled a number of each other's diplomats for alleged improprieties, and, in a somewhat belligerent interview published in April, Musharraf stated that he was prepared to use nuclear weapons in the event of war. In mid-May suspected Islamist militants attacked an Indian army camp in Jammu and Kashmir, killing more than 30 people. In response, India expelled Pakistan's High Commissioner from New Delhi. Indo-Pakistani relations deteriorated further following the assassination of Abdul Ghani Lone, the leader of the moderate All-Party Hurriyat Conference on 21 May, by suspected Islamist militants. India accused the Pakistani Government of supporting the Islamist extremists. Despite US attempts to calm tensions, artillery fire was exchanged along the LoC. More than 1m. soldiers were mobilized on both sides of the border as the two countries appeared once more to be on the brink of war. Pakistan would not rule out first use of nuclear weapons, and India declared that it would be prepared to go to war after the monsoon season ended (in September) if its neighbour refused to halt 'cross-border terrorism'. Musharraf, however, denied that Pakistan was aiding incursions into Jammu and Kashmir, and ordered several 'routine' tests of its ballistic-missile arsenal at the end of May. An attempt to broker peace at a security summit held in Kazakhstan in early June failed after the Indian Prime Minister refused to meet Musharraf. Following intense diplomatic efforts by British and US officials, the threat of war appeared to diminish. On 10 June India lifted its ban on Pakistani commercial aircraft flying over its territory and prepared to appoint a new High Commissioner to Pakistan, in response to Pakistani pledges to halt cross-border infiltration. India's campaign against 'cross-border terrorism' gained impetus as a result of the US Secretary of Defense Donald Rumsfeld's declaration in mid-June that there were strong indications that al-Qa'ida was operating near the LoC. In late June Rumsfeld announced that Pakistan had significantly reduced cross-border infiltration. However, an attack on Hindus by suspected Islamist militants in Jammu and Kashmir in mid-July disrupted attempts to restore diplomatic relations between India and Pakistan, and the Indian Government decided to delay the appointment of a new High Commissioner to Pakistan. Both countries conducted 'routine' ballistic-missile tests in early October. In mid-October the Indian Minister of Defence stated that India would withdraw a large number of troops from the international border with Pakistan; the number of troops along the LoC would remain unchanged, however. Pakistan reciprocated the announcement shortly afterwards. India's gradual removal of troops began in late October; Pakistan responded by withdrawing a portion of its troops in November. President Musharraf dismissed elections in Jammu and Kashmir in September–October as a 'sham' and 'farcical'.

Relations with India deteriorated in early 2003. Tensions were exacerbated by India's latest set of 'routine' ballistic-missile tests, the violence in Kashmir and India's new military agreement with Russia. In late January India ordered four officials at Pakistan's High Commission in New Delhi to leave the country within 48 hours for 'indulging in activities incompatible with their official status', regarded by some as a euphemism for spying. Pakistan reacted by expelling four officials at the Indian High Commission in Islamabad. In early February India expelled Pakistan's acting High Commissioner, accusing him of funding Kashmiri separatist groups. Four other Pakistani officials were charged with spying and expelled. Pakistan retaliated by giving India's acting High Commissioner and four colleagues 48 hours to leave for alleged spying. Tensions between India and Pakistan increased after Pakistan responded to India's decision to conduct 'routine' missile tests without advance warning by carrying out a set of its own tests. Nevertheless, in mid-April, during a visit to Jammu and Kashmir, Vajpayee offered to enter dialogue with Pakistan; the Pakistani Prime Minister, Zafarullah Khan Jamali, welcomed the decision and formally invited Vajpayee to visit Pakistan. Commentators initially attributed Vajpayee's change in tone to diplomatic pressure from the United Kingdom and USA to begin peace negotiations with Pakistan. However, it soon transpired that the USA had not been notified in advance of the Indian Prime Minister's initiative; indeed, Vajpayee had hardly consulted his Council of Ministers. In early May the two neighbours agreed to restore diplomatic relations and civil aviation links. Two months later the bus service between Lahore and New Delhi was restored. India, however, continued to insist on a complete cessation of cross-border infiltration as a precondition for peace talks.

In mid-August 2003 President Musharraf proposed a cease-fire along the LoC, but wanted India to reciprocate by reducing its armed personnel in the Srinagar valley and by ending the alleged atrocities committed by the Indian armed forces. India refused Musharraf's offer and continued to hold Pakistan-based militants responsible for the recent rise in attacks in Jammu and Kashmir. Two months later, however, the Indian Minister of External Affairs, Yashwant Sinha, announced 12 confidence-building measures to improve and normalize relations with Pakistan, including offers to enter another round of talks to restore civil aviation links, to introduce more transport links (including a bus service between the capitals of the disputed region across the LoC), to resume full sporting contacts, and to enter dialogue with separatist politicians in Kashmir. Sinha emphasized, however, that no direct talks on Kashmir between India and Pakistan would take place until the latter put a stop to cross-border infiltration by militant Islamists. Pakistan issued a cautious welcome to most of the proposals, while declaring that bus travellers in Kashmir would need UN travel documents, but expressed disappointment that there was no offer of a meeting. On 23 November Pakistani Prime Minister Jamali announced a unilateral cease-fire along the LoC, which was to begin at midnight two days later (on the Muslim festival of Id). Jamali also responded to Vajpayee's offer to discuss transport links by proposing an additional bus service between Lahore and the Indian city of Amritsar. India reciprocated the gesture (but reserved the right to fire at so-called 'infiltrators') and offered to extend the cease-fire across the Actual Ground Position Line in Siachen as well as across the international border. Pakistan agreed to the proposal and at midnight on 25–26 November a cease-fire came into effect. In mid-December the chances of a peace agreement between India and Pakistan improved after Musharraf declared that Pakistan was prepared to cede a long-standing demand for a UN-sponsored plebiscite for the Kashmiri people; India welcomed the initiative. At the same time, Indian and Pakistani officials signed a three-year agreement on the restoration from mid-January 2004 of a passenger and freight train service between New Delhi and Lahore. Direct aviation links were resumed on 1 January 2004. In late December 2003 it was reported that, since the implementation of the cease-fire, separatist-related violence in Jammu and Kashmir had declined. Meanwhile, in November President Musharraf banned six Islamist militant groups (three of which had been banned in 2002 but had re-emerged under different names—see above), closed down their offices and 'froze' their bank accounts.

At the ground-breaking SAARC summit meeting in Islamabad in early January 2004, Musharraf assured Vajpayee that he would not permit any territory under Pakistan's control to be used to support terrorism; in return Vajpayee agreed to begin negotiations on all bilateral issues, including Kashmir, in February. Meanwhile, however, Islamist militants who were unhappy with what they perceived as a betrayal by Musharraf continued their violent campaign. Indian and Pakistani senior officials opened discussions in Islamabad in mid-February; a timetable for future dialogue was established. In June several rounds of discussions took place between Indian and Pakistani officials in New Delhi. In a joint statement issued at the end of the month, both sides stressed their renewed commitment to reaching a negotiated final settlement on the Kashmir issue and agreed to restore their diplomatic missions to full strength and, in principle, to reopen their respective consulates in Mumbai and Karachi. An agreement was also reached that each country would, in future, notify the other of any forthcoming missile tests. In September Pakistan and India held their first, official, ministerial-level talks in more than three years in New Delhi. As a result, the two sides again agreed to implement a series of confidence-building measures, including the restoration of bilateral transport links.

In November 2004 Pakistan welcomed a move by India to reduce the number of Indian troops deployed in Jammu and Kashmir. Later in that month Indian Prime Minister Manmohan Singh met with his Pakistani counterpart, Shaukat Aziz, in New Delhi. In the following month further high-level talks on the Kashmir issue were held in Islamabad, but with no tangible progress. Tensions resurfaced in early 2005 when each side accused the other of violating the ongoing cease-fire along the LoC. However, in February, following talks between the Indian and Pakistani ministers responsible for foreign affairs, the two countries agreed to open a bus service across the LoC, linking Srinagar with Muzaffarabad. Despite militant threats of disruption, and several attacks on the proposed route, the service opened in early April. Plans were also announced to reopen the consulates in Mumbai and Karachi. In March, in a gesture of goodwill, Musharraf ordered the early release of 700 Indian prisoners, most of them fishermen, who had been imprisoned in Pakistan. Meanwhile, in the same month India made clear its disapproval of the US decision to supply Pakistan with F-16 fighter aircraft, stating its concerns that the deal would exacerbate security tensions in the region. In mid-April Musharraf travelled to India for the first time since 2001 and met with Manmohan Singh in Delhi for further peace talks; the two leaders subsequently issued a statement referring to the peace process as 'irreversible' and agreeing to improve trade and transport links over the LoC.

In October 2005 the devastating consequences of the massive earthquake centred in Azad Kashmir had significant implications for the ongoing peace process. In the aftermath of the disaster, Pakistan accepted an Indian offer of aid. Following a series of negotiations, the two countries subsequently agreed to open a number of crossing points on the LoC, in order to permit the reunification of divided families. The crossing points were finally opened in November. However, continued fears on the part of both countries that the other would take advantage of the situation to conduct military surveillance hampered prospects for more extensive co-operation. Despite speculation that many militants operating in the area had been killed by the earthquake, sporadic separatist violence continued. None the less, there was an indication of the extent to which bilateral relations had improved; while a bomb attack on New Delhi, India, in late October was believed to have been perpetrated by Pakistani militants, Indian Prime Minister Manmohan Singh refrained from blaming Pakistan directly for the attacks. He stressed instead that he expected Pakistan to take responsibility for the prevention of terrorism directed against India. However, in January 2006 a suggestion by Musharraf in a televised interview that India demilitarize three cities in the Kashmir valley in order to advance the peace process was rejected by the Indian Government. In February a second rail link was opened between the two countries, linking the town of Khokrapar in Sindh with the Indian town of Munabao in Rajasthan.

In March 2006 the peace process advanced further when Manmohan Singh proposed, during the launch of a new bus service linking the two countries, that they sign a treaty of friendship, peace and security, a suggestion welcomed by the Pakistani Government. However, the proposal was criticized for separating the resolution of the Kashmir dispute from other issues affecting the bilateral relationship. It was subsequently agreed that trade links would be further developed, as part of efforts to restore normal relations through the improvement of economic and commercial ties. Relations became temporarily strained in the aftermath of the Mumbai train bombings in July, when, despite Musharraf's condemnation of the atrocities, Singh suggested the perpetrators had links to Pakistan. Bilateral peace talks were postponed but the two leaders agreed to resume negotiations in September. In November, during foreign secretary-level talks, the two countries agreed to form an intelligence-sharing panel to combat terrorism; the panel's first meeting took place in Islamabad in March 2007. The Indian Minister of External Affairs, Pranab Mukherjee, travelled to Pakistan in January amid relative optimism about the resolution of outstanding issues such as Kashmir; further rounds of talks on the issue were scheduled to be held later that year. The explosions on the Delhi–Lahore Samjhauta Express train in February 2007, which claimed 68 lives, were widely believed to have been a deliberate attempt to sabotage negotiations between Pakistan and India.

Relations with Bangladesh deteriorated in September 2000 when, at the UN Millennium Summit meeting in the USA, the Bangladeshi Prime Minister condemned the Pakistani military leadership, ostensibly as part of a general request for the UN to take action against undemocratic changes of government. Gen. Musharraf subsequently cancelled forthcoming meetings with the Prime Minister of Bangladesh. Later, the Bangladeshi leader demanded that Pakistan apologize for the atrocities committed by its army during the Bangladesh war of liberation and that those involved be brought to justice. In late November Pakistan withdrew its Deputy High Commissioner to Bangladesh, following his insistence that the ruling Bangladesh Awami League, rather than the Pakistani army, was responsible for the bloodshed. The Bangladesh Government declared the diplomat *persona non grata* in mid-December and demanded his immediate departure. During his visit to Bangladesh in late July 2002, President Musharraf apologized unreservedly for the atrocities committed by Pakistani troops during Bangladesh's war of liberation.

Pakistan withdrew from the Commonwealth in January 1972, in protest at the United Kingdom's role in the East Pakistan crisis. Pakistan recognized Bangladesh in February 1974, but attempts to rejoin the Commonwealth in the late 1970s and early 1980s were thwarted by India. In January 1989, however, India announced that it would no longer oppose Pakistan's application to rejoin the organization, and in July, during an official visit to the United Kingdom by Benazir Bhutto, Pakistan was formally invited to rejoin the Commonwealth, which it did on 1 October 1989. In October 1999, however, Pakistan was suspended from participation in meetings of the Commonwealth. In September 2003 the CMAG agreed to maintain Pakistan's suspension from participation in meetings, as it was not convinced that democracy had been completely restored in the country. However, in May 2004 the CMAG agreed to restore fully Pakistan's Commonwealth membership, stating that it had decided that the country had consolidated the progress made towards democracy following the October 2002 general election, owing to President Musharraf's statement that he would step down as Chief of Army Staff by the end of 2004 and the subsequent legislative vote of confidence in his leadership. However, Commonwealth Secretary-General Don McKinnon stated that the Commonwealth would continue to monitor Pakistan and, in particular, progress towards the fulfilment of Musharraf's pledge to become a civilian president. Despite this statement, following the passage of legislation later in that year enabling Musharraf to retain his military role, McKinnon commented that it might be acceptable for Musharraf to keep his dual role as he would do so with parliamentary approval. In February 2005 the CMAG criticized Musharraf for reneging on his pledge and insisted that he must relinquish his military role by 2007. Following Musharraf's imposition of a state of emergency and suspension of the Constitution in November 2007, the CMAG once again suspended Pakistan from participation in meetings. Full membership was restored, however, in May 2008 as a result of the restoration of democratic government in February.

In early 1992 the Economic Co-operation Organization (ECO, see p. 238), comprising Pakistan, Iran and Turkey, was reactivated, and by the end of the year had been expanded to include Afghanistan, Azerbaijan and the five Central Asian, mainly Muslim, republics of the former USSR; the 'Turkish Republic of Northern Cyprus' joined ECO in 1993. Trade delegations from Turkey and the new republics visited Pakistan, and an agreement for the restoration and construction of highways in Afghanistan, to link Pakistan with these republics, was signed. In 1995 Pakistan, the People's Republic of China, Kazakhstan and Kyrgyzstan signed a transit trade agreement, restoring Pakistan's overland trade route with Central Asia, through China. During a commemorative visit to Pakistan by the Chinese Premier, organized in May 2001 to celebrate 50 years of bilateral relations, the two countries concluded a number of agreements on technical and economic co-operation. Bilateral relations were consolidated and further co-operation agreements were signed during an official visit to China made by Gen. Musharraf in December. Meanwhile, in March Pakistan's Chasma Nuclear Power Plant in Punjab province, which had been built in the 1990s with substantial assistance from the Chinese National Nuclear Corporation, was opened. In early January 2002 it was reported that China had supplied several dozen fighter aircraft and air defence missiles to Pakistan. The two countries were also co-operating to develop a new fighter aircraft. Musharraf visited China again in August 2002 and reaffirmed the close relations between the two countries. In November President Musharraf made another visit during which various Sino-Pakistani agreements were concluded, including a US $500m. loan to Pakistan, a trade agreement and an extradition treaty. In May 2004 the two countries signed an agreement to construct a second nuclear power plant at Chasma. Further accords on the construction of the plant were signed during a visit to Pakistan by Chinese Premier Wen Jiabao in April 2005. In November 2006 the Chinese President, Hu Jintao, paid a visit to Pakistan, signing trade and defence agreements and pledging to increase bilateral military, economic, trade and anti-terrorism co-operation. In February 2003, meanwhile, President Musharraf visited Moscow, the first official visit by a Pakistani head of state to the Russian capital in 33 years.

Government

The President is a constitutional Head of State, who is normally elected for five years by an electoral college, comprising the Federal Legislature and the four provincial assemblies. The former consists of a lower and upper house.

Pakistan comprises four provinces (each with an appointed Governor and provincial government), the federal capital of Islamabad and the Federally Administered Tribal Areas.

According to the 2002 Legal Framework Order and the 2003 Seventeenth Constitutional Amendment Act, the number of seats in the lower house of the Federal Legislature, called the National Assembly, was increased from 217 to 342, with 272 members directly elected (on the basis of adult suffrage), 60 seats reserved for women and 10 for non-Muslims. The term of the National Assembly was reduced to four years. The size of the upper house, called the Senate, was increased to 100 seats (from 87). The provincial assemblies directly elected 88 members (of which 16 had to be women and a further 16 technocrats), and the remaining 12 members were chosen by the National Assembly from a list of candidates provided by the Federally Administered Tribal Areas and federal capital. The term of the Senate is six years, with one-half of the membership being renewed every three years. The Prime Minister is elected by the National Assembly and he/she and the other ministers in the Cabinet are responsible to it. The powers of the President were greatly enhanced by the constitutional amendments (see The Constitution).

The establishment of a National Security Council (NSC) was endorsed in 2004, giving the armed forces a formal, albeit supervisory, role in civilian politics for the first time in Pakistan's history. The NSC was to comprise the President, the Prime Minister, the Chairman of the Senate, the Speaker of the National Assembly, the leader of the parliamentary opposition, the provincial chief ministers and the four armed forces chiefs. The new body was to provide consultation to the elected government on strategic issues.

Defence

As assessed at November 2007, the armed forces totalled 619,000: 550,000 in the army, 24,000 in the navy and 45,000 in the air force. Active paramilitary forces numbered up to 3042,000 (including a National Guard of 185,000 men). The projected defence budget for 2007 was Rs 275,000m. at the federal level. Military service is voluntary.

Economic Affairs

In 2006, according to estimates by the World Bank, Pakistan's gross national income (GNI), measured at average 2004–06 prices, was US $122,295m., equivalent to $770 per head (or $2,500 per head on an international purchasing-power parity basis). During 1996–2006, it was estimated, the population increased at an average annual rate of 2.4%, while gross domestic product (GDP) per head increased, in real terms, by an average of 1.8% per year. Overall GDP increased, in real terms, at an average annual rate of 4.2% in 1996–2006. According to official figures, growth reached 6.6% in 2005/06 and 7.0% in 2006/07.

Agriculture (including forestry and fishing) contributed an estimated 19.6% of GDP in the year ending 30 June 2007. An estimated 43.4% of the employed labour force was engaged in the sector at 30 June 2006. The principal cash crops are cotton (which accounted for around 21.6% of export earnings in 2005/06) and rice; sugar cane, wheat and maize are also major crops. Fishing and leather production provide significant export revenues. In 2004/05 the cotton and wheat harvests reached record levels. During 1996–2006 agricultural GDP increased at an average annual rate of 2.6%; it rose by 1.6% in 2005/06 and by an estimated 5.0% in 2006/07.

Industry (including mining, manufacturing, power and construction) engaged an estimated 20.7% of the employed labour force in June 2007, and provided an estimated 26.8% of GDP in 2006/07. During 1996–2006 industrial GDP increased by an average of 5.6% per year. According to official sources, industrial GDP grew by 5.0% in 2005/06 and by an estimated 6.8% in 2006/07.

Mining and quarrying contributed an estimated 3.1% of GDP in 2006/07, and, according to the ILO, engaged 0.09% of the employed labour force at 30 June 2006. Petroleum and petroleum products are the major mineral exports. Limestone, rock salt, gypsum, silica sand, natural gas and coal are also mined. In addition, Pakistan has reserves of graphite, copper and manganese. The GDP of the mining sector increased at an average annual rate of 7.6% during 1999/2000–2006/07; mining GDP grew by 4.6% in 2005/06 and by an estimated 5.6% in 2006/07.

Manufacturing contributed an estimated 19.4% of GDP in 2006/07, and engaged about 13.8% of the employed labour force at 30 June 2006. The most important sectors include the manufacture of textiles, food products, automobiles and electrical goods and also petroleum refineries. During 1996–200 manufacturing GDP increased at an average annual rate of 6.7%; according to official figures, manufacturing GDP rose by 10.0% in 2005/06 and by an estimated 8.4% in 2006/07.

Energy is derived principally from natural gas (providing 50.7% of the total electrical energy supply in 2004), hydroelectric power (30.0%) and petroleum (15.9%). Imports of petroleum and petroleum products comprised about 23.4% of the cost of total imports in 2005/06.

Services engaged 35.9% of the employed labour force at 30 June 2006, and provided an estimated 53.7% of GDP in 2006/07. The combined GDP of the service sectors increased at an average rate of 5.0% per year in 1996–2006. According to official figures, the GDP of services expanded by 9.6% in 2005/06 and by an estimated 8.0% in 2006/07.

In 2006 Pakistan recorded a visible trade deficit of US $9,647m., and there was a deficit of $6,750m. on the current account of the balance of payments. Remittances from Pakistanis working abroad declined substantially during the 1990s, and by 2000/01 had levelled off to about $1,087m. The flow of remittances recovered significantly, however, during the 2000s and increased from $4,168.8m. in 2004/05 to $4,600m. in 2005/06 and to $5,490m. in 2006/07. The principal source of imports in 2005/06 was Saudi Arabia (which provided 10.5% of the total), and the principal market for exports was the USA (25.5%). Other major trading partners were the United Arab Emirates, the People's Republic of China, Germany, Japan, Kuwait, and the United Kingdom. The principal exports in 2005/06 were textiles and textile articles (particularly cotton), and vegetable products. The principal imports were machinery and transport equipment, mineral products and chemicals and related products.

For the financial year ending 30 June 2006 there was a budgetary deficit of Rs 173,661m. (equivalent to approximately 2.4% of GDP). For 2006/07 there was an estimated deficit of Rs 170,846m. Pakistan's total external debt was US $35,687m. at the end of 2004, of which $31,029m. was long-term public debt. The cost of debt-servicing in that year was equivalent to 21.2% of earnings from exports of goods and services. During 1996–2006 the average annual rate of inflation was 6.0%; according to official figures, consumer prices rose by 9.3% in 2004/05 and by 7.9% in 2005/06. About 6.2% of the labour force was estimated to be unemployed in June 2006.

Pakistan is a member of the South Asian Association for Regional Co-operation (SAARC, see p. 384), of the Asian Development Bank (ADB), of the UN Economic and Social Commission for Asia and the Pacific (ESCAP, see p. 35) and of the Colombo Plan (see p. 411). Pakistan is also a founder member of the Islamic Financial Services Board.

During the 1990s economic growth was constrained by poor investment in manufacturing and inadequate agricultural production, while widespread corruption and inefficient revenue management (particularly in the collection and administration of taxes) undermined attempts to address worsening levels of poverty and deteriorating infrastructure and social services. However, the Musharraf administration that took office in 1999 demonstrated renewed commitment to radical economic reform. In December of that year the International Monetary Fund (IMF) agreed to extend a US $1,320m. Poverty Reduction and Growth Facility (PRGF) to Pakistan, in support of a three-year social and economic reform programme, which was implemented during October 2001–September 2004. Despite the economic repercussions of the terrorist attacks on the USA in September 2001, the prolonged drought, and regional and domestic security problems, Pakistan made substantial progress in implementing the programme's crucial objectives, which were: increased potential for economic growth; improved social provisions; and reduced vulnerability to external factors. The economy experienced steady growth, while foreign-exchange reserves increased sharply, owing to an improved trade balance, increased remittances from Pakistanis working abroad and a current-account surplus. Encouraged by the IMF's extension of the PRGF, in December 2001 the 'Paris Club' of creditor governments agreed to reschedule Pakistan's entire bilateral debt stock of $12,500m. In 2003 Pakistan's privatization programme was accelerated. In 2003/04 the Government pledged to use 90% of the proceeds from privatization to pay off some of its foreign debt; the remaining 10% would help to alleviate poverty. In 2005 the Government's privatization programme accelerated significantly, the most significant divestment being the sale of a controlling 26% stake in Pakistan Telecommunications (Pvt) Ltd (PTCL) in June to Dubai-based Emirates Telecommunications (the finalization of the sale was delayed, however, until March 2006). In mid-2006 the Pakistani Supreme Court blocked the sale of Pakistan Steel Mills Corporation Ltd, the country's largest steel producer, to a Russian-led consortium. The Government promised, however, that this decision would have no impact on future privatization plans and it remained focused on concluding the sale of the state-owned Oil and Gas Development Corporation Ltd. Despite expectations of a slight economic deceleration, in 2004/05 GDP expanded by 8.4%, its fastest rate of expansion for 20 years. This growth, which was driven by the manufacturing, financial and agricultural sectors, also led to a decelerating rate of inflation. In addition, with the recent improvement in its relations with India, Pakistan was now importing greater quantities of machinery, chemicals and surgical items from its neighbour. There were fears, however, that the political strife, domestic and regional security concerns, bureaucratic obstacles, corruption and inadequate infrastructure would continue to deter potential investors. Nevertheless, foreign investment improved, and in late 2006 it was announced that the Standard Chartered Bank had acquired a majority shareholding in the Union Bank of Pakistan and a few months later the Pakistani mobile telephone operator Paktel Ltd was bought by China Mobile. In early 2007, however, foreign debt reached US $38,420m., mainly owing to the inflow of international loans following the 2005 earthquake. In mid-2008 negotiations on the proposed Iran-Pakistan-India (IPI) gas pipeline were nearing completion; the project was expected to provide much-needed energy in the region, particularly in Pakistan, where an energy crisis was imminent. Meanwhile, the trade gap continued to widen in 2007/08; the current-account deficit was projected to reach 6.2% of GDP by 30 June 2008, a significant increase on the Government's target of 4.8%. The economy revealed other signs of weakening in 2007–08, particularly amid the political strife and violence following the assassination of Benazir Bhutto in December 2007. Increases in food prices, continuing energy shortages and poor export figures for textiles and rice—especially significant considering the ongoing global rice shortages—negatively affected GDP growth, which for the year ending 30 June 2008 was projected to reach 6.6%, compared with the 7.0% estimated for the previous year. Foreign direct investment was also forecast to decline in 2007/08, to some $4,000m., compared with around $5,100m. in 2006/07.

Education

Universal free primary education is a constitutional right, but education is not compulsory. Primary education begins at five years of age and lasts for five years. Secondary education, beginning at the age of 10, is divided into two stages, of three and four years respectively. In 2004/05 enrolment at primary schools included 67% of children in the relevant age-group (76% of boys; 58% of girls), while enrolment at secondary level included an estimated 20% of pupils of the relevant age (23% of boys; 17% of girls). In 2003/04 it was estimated that there were 19,794,000 children enrolled at pre-primary and primary schools (including mosque schools), and 6,119,000 at middle and secondary schools. All institutions, except missions and an increasing number of private schools, are nationalized. From 1976 agrotechnical subjects were introduced into the school curriculum, and 25 trade schools were established in that year. There are 51 universities and degree-awarding institutions. Development expenditure on science and technology and education and training in 2001/02 was projected at Rs 4,343.3m. (only 3.3% of the Government's total development spending).

Public Holidays

2008: 10 January*† (Muharram, Islamic New Year), 19 January* (Ashoura), 20 March* (Eid-i-Milad-un-Nabi, Birth of the Pro-

PAKISTAN

phet), 23 March (Pakistan Day, proclamation of republic in 1956), 1 May (Labour Day), 14 August (Independence Day), 2 September* (Ramadan begins), 6 September (Defence of Pakistan Day), 11 September (Anniversary of Death of Quaid-i-Azam), 1 October* (Id al-Fitr, end of Ramadan), 9 November (Allama Iqbal Day), 8 December* (Id al-Adha, Feast of the Sacrifice), 25 December (Birthday of Quaid-i-Azam), 29 December*† (Muharram, Islamic New Year).

2009: 19 January*‡ (Ashoura), 9 March* (Eid-i-Milad-un-Nabi, Birth of the Prophet), 23 March (Pakistan Day, proclamation of republic in 1956), 1 May (Labour Day), 14 August (Independence Day), 22 August* (Ramadan begins), 6 September (Defence of Pakistan Day), 11 September (Anniversary of Death of Quaid-i-Azam), 20 September* (Id al-Fitr, end of Ramadan), 9 November (Allama Iqbal Day), 27 November* (Id al-Adha, Feast of the Sacrifice), 18 December* (Muharram, Islamic New Year), 25 December (Birthday of Quaid-i-Azam), 27 December*‡ (Ashoura).

* These holidays are dependent on the Islamic lunar calendar and may vary by one or two days from the dates given.

† This festival occurs twice (marking the start of the Islamic years AH 1429 and AH 1430) within the same Gregorian year.

‡ This festival occurs twice (in the Islamic years AH 1430 and AH 1431) within the same Gregorian year.

Weights and Measures

The metric system has been officially introduced. Also in use are imperial and local weights, including:

1 maund = 82.28 lb (37.32 kg).
1 seer = 2.057 lb (933 grams).
1 tola = 180 grains (11.66 grams).

Statistical Survey

Sources (unless otherwise stated): Federal Bureau of Statistics, 5-SLIC Building, F-6/4, Blue Area, Islamabad; fax (51) 9203233; e-mail statpak@isb.paknet.com.pk; internet www.statpak.gov.pk/depts/index.html; State Bank of Pakistan, Karachi; internet www.sbp.org.pk.

Area and Population

AREA, POPULATION AND DENSITY*

Area (sq km)	796,095†
Population (census results)	
1 March 1981	84,253,644
2 March 1998	
Males	68,873,686
Females	63,478,593
Total	132,352,279
Population (official estimates at 1 January)	
2005	151,550,000
2006	155,360,000
2007	158,700,000
Density (per sq km) at 1 January 2007	199.3

* Excluding data for the disputed territory of Jammu and Kashmir. The Pakistani-held parts of this region are known as Azad ('Free') Kashmir, with an area of 11,639 sq km (4,494 sq miles) and a population of 1,980,000 in 1981, and Northern Areas (including Gilgit and Baltistan), with an area of 72,520 sq km (28,000 sq miles) and a population of 562,000 in 1981. Also excluded are Junagardh and Manavadar. The population figures exclude refugees from Afghanistan (estimated to number 1.0m. in early 2007).

† 307,374 sq miles.

ADMINISTRATIVE DIVISIONS
(population at 1998 census)

	Area (sq km)	Population	Density (per sq km)
Provinces:			
Balochistan	347,188	6,565,885	18.9
North-West Frontier Province	74,522	17,743,645	238.1
Punjab	205,345	73,621,290	358.5
Sindh	140,913	30,439,893	216.0
Federally Administered Tribal Areas	27,221	3,176,331	116.7
Federal Capital Territory:			
Islamabad	906	805,235	888.8
Total	796,095	132,352,279	166.3

PRINCIPAL TOWNS
(population at 1998 census)

Karachi	9,339,023	Bahawalpur	408,395
Lahore	5,143,495	Sukkur	335,551
Faisalabad (Lyallpur)	2,008,861	Jhang Maghiana (Jhang Sadar)	293,366
Rawalpindi	1,409,768	Shekhupura	280,263
Multan	1,197,384	Larkana	270,283
Hyderabad	1,166,894	Gujrat	251,792
Gujranwala	1,132,509	Mardan	245,926
Peshawar	982,816	Kasur	245,321
Quetta	565,137	Rahimyar Khan	233,537
Islamabad (capital)	529,180	Sahiwal	208,778
Sargodha	458,440	Okara	201,815
Sialkot	421,502		

Mid-2007 ('000, incl. suburbs, UN estimates): Karachi 12,130; Lahore 6,577; Faisalabad (Lyallpur) 2,617; Rawalpindi 1,858; Multan 1,522; Gujranwala 1,513; Hyderabad 1,459; Peshawar 1,303; Islamabad 780; Quetta 768 (Source: UN, *World Urbanization Prospects: The 2007 Revision*).

BIRTHS AND DEATHS
(annual averages, UN estimates)

	1990–95	1995–2000	2000–05
Birth rate (per 1,000)	38.7	33.3	27.5
Death rate (per 1,000)	9.8	8.8	7.7

Source: UN, *World Population Prospects: The 2006 Revision*.

2006 (preliminary): Crude birth rate 26.1 per 1,000; crude death rate 7.1 per 1,000 (Source: Ministry of Finance, *Economic Survey, 2006/07*).

Expectation of life (years at birth, WHO estimates): 61.5 (males 60.9; females 62.1) in 2005 (Source: WHO, *World Health Statistics*).

PAKISTAN

ECONOMICALLY ACTIVE POPULATION
('000 persons aged 10 years and over, excl. armed forces, at 30 June)

	2004	2005	2006
Agriculture, hunting, forestry and fishing	18,084	18,431	20,364
Mining and quarrying	28	29	43
Manufacturing	5,770	5,881	6,499
Electricity, gas and water	282	287	308
Construction	2,449	2,496	2,880
Wholesale and retail trade, and restaurants and hotels	6,216	6,336	6,886
Transport, storage and communication	2,409	2,455	2,697
Financing, insurance, real estate and business services	444	453	518
Community, social and personal services	6,306	6,427	6,739
Activities not adequately defined	21	21	18
Total employed	42,009	42,816	46,952
Unemployed	3,499	3,566	3,103
Total labour force	45,508	46,382	50,055
Males	37,364	38,081	39,974
Females	8,144	8,301	10,081

Source: ILO.

Health and Welfare

KEY INDICATORS

Total fertility rate (children per woman, 2005)	4.0
Under-5 mortality rate (per 1,000 live births, 2005)	100
HIV/AIDS (% of persons aged 15–49, 2005)	0.1
Physicians (per 1,000 head, 2004)	0.74
Hospital beds (per 1,000 head, 2003)	0.68
Health expenditure (2004): US $ per head (PPP)	47.7
Health expenditure (2004): % of GDP	2.2
Health expenditure (2004): public (% of total)	19.6
Access to water (% of persons, 2004)	91
Access to sanitation (% of persons, 2004)	59
Human Development Index (2005): ranking	136
Human Development Index (2005): value	0.551

For sources and definitions, see explanatory note on p. vi.

Agriculture

PRINCIPAL CROPS
('000 metric tons)

	2004	2005	2006
Wheat	19,500	21,612	21,277
Rice (paddy)	7,537	8,321	8,137
Barley	98	92	88
Maize	2,797	3,110	2,971
Millet	193	221	212
Sorghum	186	153	155
Potatoes	1,938	2,025	1,568
Sugar cane	53,419	47,244	44,666
Sugar beet	250	121	93
Dry beans	148	130	154
Chick-peas	611	868	480
Groundnuts (in shell)	76	69	59
Sunflower seed	359	328	348
Rapeseed	401	347	350
Cottonseed	4,853	4,123	4,065
Tomatoes	413	432	468
Cauliflower and broccoli	205	206	209
Pumpkins, squash and gourds	244	247	254
Dry onions	1,449	1,765	2,056
Carrots and turnips	232	242	244
Okra	107	109	112
Watermelons	386	353	393
Cantaloupes and other melons	258	236	263
Bananas	148	164	155
Oranges	1,232	1,361	1,721

—continued	2004	2005	2006
Tangerines, mandarins, clementines and satsumas	458	505	639
Lemons and limes	78	78	98
Apples	352	351	350
Apricots	215	197	190
Peaches and nectarines	70	70	72
Plums and sloes	61	60	61
Guavas, mangoes and mangosteens	1,566	1,606	2,243
Dates	622	497	507
Pimento and allspice	90	123	62
Cotton (lint)	2,427	2,214	2,187
Tobacco (leaves)	86	101	113

Aggregate production ('000 metric tons, may include official, semi-official or estimated data): Total cereals 30,311 in 2004, 33,508 in 2005, 32,839 in 2006; Total roots and tubers 2,403 in 2004, 2,493 in 2005, 2,048 in 2006; Total vegetables (incl. melons) 4,751 in 2004, 5,032 in 2005, 5,449 in 2006; Total fruits (excl. melons) 5,161 in 2004, 5,236 in 2005, 6,379 in 2006.

Source: FAO.

LIVESTOCK
('000 head, year ending September)

	2004	2005	2006
Cattle	23,800	24,200	25,500
Buffaloes	25,500	26,300	28,400
Sheep	24,700	24,900	25,400
Goats	54,700	56,700	61,900
Horses	315	313	339
Asses, mules or hinnies	4,353	4,450	4,580
Camels	743	736	738
Chickens*	n.a.	n.a.	162,000
Ducks*	3,500	n.a.	3,500

* FAO estimates.

Source: FAO.

LIVESTOCK PRODUCTS
('000 metric tons)

	2004	2005	2006
Cattle meat	455	465	486
Buffalo meat	524	540	571
Sheep meat	161	162	172
Goat meat	357	370	392
Chicken meat	378	384	463
Cows' milk	8,840	9,082	9,404
Buffaloes' milk	19,240	19,884	21,136
Sheep's milk	32	31	31
Goats' milk	675	675	676
Ghee*	560.8	n.a.	n.a.
Hen eggs	381.0†	400.0†	425.7*
Other poultry eggs*	7.2	7.2	7.2
Wool: greasy	40.0	40.7	41.0

* FAO estimate(s).
† Unofficial figure.

Source: FAO.

Forestry

ROUNDWOOD REMOVALS
('000 cubic metres, excl. bark, FAO estimates)

	2004	2005	2006
Sawlogs, veneer logs and logs for sleepers	1,900	1,950	1,961
Other industrial wood	780	820	859
Fuel wood	26,000	26,500	26,124
Total	28,680	29,270	28,944

Source: FAO.

PAKISTAN

SAWNWOOD PRODUCTION
('000 cubic metres, incl. railway sleepers)

	2004	2005	2006
Coniferous (softwood)	420	432	432
Broadleaved (hardwood)	840	856	881
Total	1,260	1,288	1,313

Source: FAO.

Fishing

('000 metric tons, live weight)

	2003	2004	2005
Capture	491.8	480.3	434.9
Freshwater fishes	92.8	93.7	94.6
Sea catfishes	30.3	30.4	26.3
Croakers and drums	19.7	16.9	15.9
Largehead hairtail	25.7	25.6	23.2
Indian oil sardine	32.9	34.3	31.5
Other clupeoids	25.8	21.7	17.7
Jacks and crevalles	31.1	6.0	3.3
Requiem sharks	18.7	15.5	12.3
Skates, rays and mantas	13.7	11.1	9.9
Aquaculture	73.0	76.7	80.6
Total catch	564.9	557.0	515.5

Source: FAO.

Mining

('000 metric tons, unless otherwise indicated)

	2004	2005	2006
Barite (metric tons)	44,207	42,087	49,221
Chromite (metric tons)	29,230	46,359	52,572
Limestone	13,150	14,857	18,391
Gypsum	467	552	601
Fireclay (metric tons)	192,728	253,501	332,528
Rock salt	1,640	1,648	1,859
Coal	3,325	3,367	3,854
Crude petroleum ('000 barrels)*	22,625	24,119	23,935
Natural gas (million cu ft)*	1,202,752	1,344,953	1,400,043

* Estimated production.

Industry

SELECTED PRODUCTS
('000 metric tons, unless otherwise indicated, year ending 30 June)

	2003/04	2004/05	2005/06*
Cotton cloth (million sq m)	683.4	899.0	728.0
Cotton yarn	1,929.1	2,111.1	212.3
Jute goods	102*	n.a.	n.a.
Refined sugar	4,020.8	3,112.8	2,247.0
Vegetable ghee	888.0	104.8	105.4
Cement	12,862	15,448	15,150
Urea	4,431.6	4,212.3	4,388.8
Superphosphate	167.7	149.8	151.0
Sulphuric acid	64.7	91.3	87.6
Soda ash	286.5	297.3	221.5
Caustic soda	187.5	206.7	199.4
Chlorine gas	17.2	19.1	16.9
Cigarettes ('000 million)	55.4	61.1	59.4
Beverages (million bottles)	2,691	3,424	4,000

—continued	2003/04	2004/05	2005/06*
Ammonium nitrate	350.4	302.5	297.5
Nitrophosphate	363.5	314.5	326.9
Pig-iron	1,180.0	1,137.2	698.3
Paper	156.8	163.7	15.4
Paperboard	247.9	236.5	260.0
Tractors ('000)	36.1	43.7	44.3
Bicycles ('000)	664.1	587.9	552.5
Motor tyres and tubes ('000)	1,889	11,559	11,665
Bicycle tyres and tubes ('000)	13,038	14,512	13,854
Electric energy (million kWh)	78,290	85,629	94,030

* Provisional figure(s).

Finance

CURRENCY AND EXCHANGE RATES

Monetary Units
100 paisa = 1 Pakistani rupee.

Sterling, Dollar and Euro Equivalents (31 December 2007)
£1 sterling = 122.65 rupees;
US $1 = 61.22 rupees;
€1 = 90.12 rupees;
1,000 Pakistani rupees = £8.15 = $16.33 = €11.10.

Average Exchange Rate (Pakistani rupees per US $)
2005   59.515
2006   60.271
2007   60.739

CENTRAL GOVERNMENT BUDGET
(million rupees, year ending 30 June)

Revenue	2004/05	2005/06*	2006/07†
Tax revenue	590,000	715,712	840,923
Income and corporate taxes‡	175,400	215,500	257,800
Other direct taxes	7,300	19,239	14,113
Excise duty	54,400	56,500	68,100
Sales tax‡	239,000	286,500	341,600
Taxes on international trade	113,900	126,000	157,100
Non-tax revenue	249,017	264,499	223,817
Surcharges‡	36,289	42,493	18,071
Total	875,306	1,022,704	1,082,811

Expenditure	2004/05	2005/06*	2006/07†
Current expenditure	784,680	918,793	879,780
General public service	468,974	563,675	504,290
Debt-servicing	274,717	304,794	295,843
Defence‡	216,258	241,062	250,182
Economic affairs	62,172	67,572	74,663
Development expenditure	82,091	153,432	236,054
Capital expenditure	119,672	124,140	137,823
Total	986,443	1,196,365	1,253,657

* Revised estimates.
† Budget estimates.
‡ Exclusively federal.

PLANNED DEVELOPMENT EXPENDITURE
(million rupees, year ending 30 June)

	1999/2000*	2000/01†	2001/02†
Sectoral programme:			
Agriculture (incl. subsidy for fertilizers)	329.1	329.2	665.2
Water	11,298.9	10,077.9	} 8,957.7
Power	2,963.0	2,682.5	
Industry	260.1	692.3	364.0
Fuels	1,170.0	2,238.7	—
Minerals	38.0	8.1	
Transport and communication	3,188.2	4,057.1	754.3
Physical planning and housing	13,274.7	1,748.5	221.4
Science and technology and education and training	7,129.2	4,064.6	4,343.3

PAKISTAN

Statistical Survey

—continued

	1999/2000*	2000/01†	2001/02†
Social welfare, culture, tourism, sport and manpower and employment	457.8	263.6	381.5
Health	2,566.4	2,841.4	2,547.5
Population planning	2,200.0	2,200.0	1,800.0
Rural development	117.2	2,419.8	—
Mass media	126.0	126.9	207.3
Special programmes	3,500.0	—	20,170.0
Corporation	—	—	26,678.3
Provincial Development Programme	—	—	30,000.0
Provincial Social Action Programme Tied Allocation	—	—	11,000.0
Total planned development expenditure (incl. others)	116,296.6	120,432.5	130,000.0

* Revised estimates.
† Provisional figures.

Source: Ministry of Finance.

INTERNATIONAL RESERVES
(US $ million, last Thursday of the year)

	2005	2006	2007
Gold*	915	1,273	1,645
IMF special drawing rights	216	216	215
Foreign exchange	9,817	11,328	13,829
Total	10,948	12,817	15,689

* Revalued annually, in June, on the basis of London market prices.

Source: IMF, *International Financial Statistics*.

MONEY SUPPLY
(million rupees, last Thursday of the year)

	2005	2006	2007
Currency outside banks	732,011	874,597	1,008,186
Demand deposits at scheduled banks	1,571,500	1,821,017	2,216,451
Total money*	2,306,838	2,700,412	3,229,783

* Including also private-sector deposits at the State Bank.

Source: IMF, *International Financial Statistics*.

COST OF LIVING
(Consumer Price Index; base: 2000/01 = 100; year ending 30 June)

	2003/04	2004/05	2005/06
Food, beverages and tobacco	111.7	125.7	134.4
Clothing and footwear	109.7	113.0	117.6
Rent	108.2	120.4	132.4
Fuel and lighting	120.3	128.5	147.2
All items (incl. others)	111.6	122.0	131.6

Source: Ministry of Finance, *Economic Survey 2006/07*.

NATIONAL ACCOUNTS
(million rupees at current prices, year ending 30 June)

Expenditure on the Gross Domestic Product

	2004/05	2005/06	2006/07*
Government final consumption expenditure	509,864	824,300	902,603
Private final consumption expenditure	5,001,499	5,732,321	6,527,372
Increase in stocks	105,298	116,465	134,196
Gross fixed capital formation	1,134,942	1,529,897	1,864,180
Total domestic expenditure	6,751,603	8,202,983	9,428,351
Exports of goods and services	1,019,783	1,161,257	1,214,051
Less Imports of goods and services	1,271,604	1,770,386	1,935,485
Gross domestic product (GDP) in market prices	6,499,782	7,593,854	8,706,917
GDP at constant 1999/2000 prices	4,881,796	5,219,631	5,552,708

* Provisional figures.

Gross Domestic Product by Economic Activity

	2004/05	2005/06	2006/07*
Agriculture, forestry and fishing	1,314,234	1,382,660	1,608,522
Mining and quarrying	182,051	219,590	256,068
Manufacturing	1,136,634	1,387,708	1,597,525
Electricity and gas distribution	187,267	159,368	143,534
Construction	153,333	172,494	206,363
Wholesale and retail trade	1,093,114	1,314,010	1,519,008
Transport, storage and communications	759,711	933,184	1,056,555
Banking and insurance	236,254	338,997	431,754
Ownership of dwellings	165,441	184,812	205,109
Public administration and defence	343,348	404,228	466,398
Community, social and personal services	551,181	632,125	735,683
GDP at factor cost	6,122,568	7,129,176	8,226,519
Indirect taxes	468,573	569,077	631,808
Less Subsidies	91,359	104,399	151,410
GDP in market prices	6,499,782	7,593,854	8,706,917

* Provisional figures.

Source: Ministry of Finance, *Economic Survey 2006/07*.

BALANCE OF PAYMENTS
(US $ million)

	2004	2005	2006
Exports of goods f.o.b.	13,297	15,432	17,049
Imports of goods f.o.b.	−16,693	−21,773	−26,696
Trade balance	−3,396	−6,341	−9,647
Exports of services	2,749	3,678	3,506
Imports of services	−5,333	−7,508	−8,418
Balance on goods and services	−5,980	−10,171	−14,559
Other income received	221	658	864
Other income paid	−2,584	−3,172	−3,995
Balance on goods, services and income	−8,343	−12,685	−17,691
Current transfers received	7,666	9,169	11,030
Current transfers paid	−140	−90	−89
Current balance	−817	−3,606	−6,750
Capital account (net)	591	202	345
Direct investment abroad	−56	−44	−109
Direct investment from abroad	1,118	2,201	4,273
Portfolio investment assets	9	19	−4
Portfolio investment liabilities	392	906	1,973
Other investment assets	−1,339	126	−242
Other investment liabilities	−1,934	871	1,545
Net errors and omissions	685	−200	520
Overall balance	−1,351	475	1,551

Source: IMF, *International Financial Statistics*.

OFFICIAL DEVELOPMENT ASSISTANCE
(US $ million)

	1998	1999	2000
Bilateral donors	531.0	435.9	476.0
Multilateral donors	522.0	297.2	226.8
Total	1,053.0	733.1	702.8
Grants	294.1	296.9	206.5
Loans	758.9	436.2	496.3
Per caput assistance (US $)	7.9	5.4	5.0

Source: UN, *Statistical Yearbook for Asia and the Pacific*.

External Trade

Note: Data exclude trade in military goods.

PRINCIPAL COMMODITIES
(million rupees, year ending 30 June)

Imports c.i.f. (excl. re-imports)	2003/04	2004/05	2005/06
Food and live animals	29,486.3	64,540.2	103,890.2
Mineral fuels, lubricants, etc.	191,640.0	255,009.8	414,113.7
Animal and vegetable oils, fats and waxes	45,518.5	51,009.7	50,332.0
Chemicals and related products	161,118.4	213,948.9	250,349.8
Basic manufactures	91,508.8	134,011.6	200,619.4
Machinery and transport equipment	243,143.1	351,553.7	498,388.5
Total (incl. others)	897,824.6	1,223,080.0	1,711,158.4

Exports f.o.b. (excl. re-exports)	2003/04	2004/05	2005/06
Rice	36,534.0	55,392.3	69,325.1
Raw cotton	2,741.5	6,549.3	4,079.7
Leather, leather manufactures and dressed furskins	14,491.4	18,013.0	17,504.5
Carpets and rugs	13,324.2	16,499.1	15,398.3
Cotton fabrics, cotton yarn and thread	163,410.3	173,384.4	209,008.2
Petroleum and related products	16,958.0	28,281.0	49,438.4
Garments and hosiery	141,220.8	161,492.9	183,251.8
Synthetic textiles	27,113.6	17,812.2	11,990.6
Sports goods	18,699.8	18,236.1	20,560.1
Total (incl. others)	709,036.1	854,087.7	984,840.6

PRINCIPAL TRADING PARTNERS
(million rupees, year ending 30 June)

Imports c.i.f. (excl. re-imports)	2003/04	2004/05	2005/06
Australia	17,699.9	33,269.7	14,611.0
Belgium	15,078.7	10,511.4	21,136.9
Canada	11,824.0	11,671.8	19,242.1
China, People's Republic	66,423.1	109,390.7	161,990.7
France	9,245.2	12,324.3	20,380.4
Germany	18,002.2	53,266.5	70,423.9
Hong Kong	8,416.2	5,618.9	9,799.6
India	22,003.8	32,487.7	48,071.6
Indonesia	20,592.9	34,131.1	45,379.1
Iran	16,349.1	14,374.7	26,942.1
Italy	35,227.3	21,597.6	31,353.2
Japan	53,913.0	86,045.9	110,175.4
Korea, Republic	21,909.5	32,935.2	36,914.6
Kuwait	57,061.9	55,810.4	101,934.9
Malaysia	34,697.0	40,265.7	42,405.4
Netherlands	12,686.0	8,717.6	14,939.5
Saudi Arabia	102,437.0	147,166.5	179,258.4
Singapore	28,291.6	22,172.0	27,735.4
Switzerland	19,013.1	25,123.4	28,230.6
Thailand	15,498.6	24,578.7	38,924.1
Turkey	4,481.5	6,108.5	11,302.2
United Arab Emirates	98,391.8	101,053.7	n.a.
United Kingdom	25,228.4	31,601.7	48,194.1
USA	76,513.2	92,813.5	99,219.8
Total (incl. others)	897,824.6	1,223,079.1	1,711,158.4

Exports f.o.b. (excl. re-exports)	2002/03	2003/04	2004/05
Afghanistan	18,380.1	28,393.5	44,320.9
Australia	7,033.9	7,494.1	6,600.3
Bangladesh	6,675.9	11,225.8	12,226.3
Belgium	14,018.5	15,108.7	18,566.8
Canada	12,047.1	10,459.5	11,494.1
China, People's Republic	14,306.5	16,588.3	20,975.6
France	17,028.1	19,502.0	21,794.1
Germany	33,866.7	34,927.4	40,798.7
Hong Kong	30,216.4	33,511.1	33,120.6
Italy	19,919.9	26,147.0	34,835.7

—continued	2002/03	2003/04	2004/05
Japan	8,311.7	7,758.9	9,742.7
Korea, Republic	12,831.9	11,625.2	10,965.6
Netherlands	16,768.2	19,296.0	20,053.8
Saudi Arabia	27,844.8	20,071.5	20,782.5
Spain	13,365.9	17,355.6	20,196.3
Turkey	8,538.0	12,598.2	15,321.8
United Arab Emirates	60,647.1	54,308.8	65,054.0
United Kingdom	46,074.5	54,173.6	52,992.9
USA	153,061.3	169,512.0	204,214.4
Total (incl. others)	652,293.8	709,036.1	854,087.7

2005/06 (selected trading partners): Belgium 19,265.8; Canada 12,510.4; France 20,155.4; Germany 41,141.6; Italy 35,045.2; Netherlands 23,889.4; Spain 24,875.6; United Kingdom 53,529.8; USA 250,989.8; Total (incl. others) 984,840.6.

Transport

RAILWAYS
(year ending 30 June)

	2003/04	2004/05	2005/06
Passenger journeys ('000)	75,700	78,180	81,430
Passenger-km (million)	23,045	24,238	25,621
Freight ('000 metric tons)	6,140	6,410	6,030
Net freight ton-km (million)	5,336	5,532	5,916

Source: Ministry of Finance, *Economic Survey, 2006/07*.

ROAD TRAFFIC
('000 vehicles in use, year ending 30 June)

	2003/04	2004/05	2005/06
Motorcycles and scooters	2,882.5	3,063.0	3,791.0
Passenger cars	1,193.1	1,264.7	1,999.2
Jeeps	47.8	51.8	65.7
Station wagons	132.4	140.5	140.8
Road tractors	722.7	778.1	822.3
Buses	100.4	102.4	103.6
Taxicabs	112.6	120.3	122.1
Rickshaws	81.0	81.3	77.8
Delivery vans and pick-ups	205.7	209.5	236.8
Trucks and tankers	157.7	160.4	160.4

Source: Ministry of Finance, *Economic Survey, 2006/07*.

SHIPPING

Merchant Fleet
(displacement at 31 December)

	2004	2005	2006
Number of vessels	49	53	53
Total displacement ('000 grt)	300.7	397.6	414.6

Source: Lloyd's Register-Fairplay, *World Fleet Statistics*.

International Sea-borne Shipping
(port of Karachi, year ending 30 June)

	2003/04	2004/05	2005/06
Goods ('000 long tons):			
loaded	6,081	6,515	6,697
unloaded	21,732	22,100	25,573

Source: Ministry of Finance, *Economic Survey, 2006/07*.

PAKISTAN

CIVIL AVIATION

(PIA only, domestic and international flights, '000, year ending 30 June)

	2002/03	2003/04	2004/05
Kilometres flown	63,863	58,146	80,699
Passengers carried	4,391	4,796	5,132
Passenger-km ('000)	11,276	12,769	13,634

Source: Ministry of Finance, *Economic Survey, 2005/06*.

Tourism

FOREIGN TOURIST ARRIVALS
('000)

Country of nationality	2004	2005	2006
Afghanistan	117.6	77.6	84.9
Canada	15.0	23.0	30.8
China, People's Republic	17.2	29.6	36.4
Germany	18.9	24.7	27.3
India	119.7	59.6	70.2
Japan	13.4	14.1	14.4
United Kingdom	196.3	248.6	275.1
USA	87.3	121.6	126.2
Total (incl. others)	648.0	798.3	850.6

Receipts from tourism (US $ million, incl. passenger transport): 620 in 2003; 765 in 2004; 827 in 2005.

Source: partly World Tourism Organization.

Communications Media

	2004	2005	2006
Television receivers (number in use)*	3,833,237	7,047,308	7,971,882
Telephones ('000 main lines in use)	4,502.2	5,227.8	5,240.0
Mobile cellular telephones ('000 subscribers)	5,022.9	12,771.2	34,506.6
Internet users ('000)	10,000	10,500	12,000
Broadband subscribers ('000)	22.3	44.6	56.6
Daily newspapers:			
number	291	438	370
average circulation	7,817,958	7,889,639	8,208,874
Other newspapers and periodicals:			
number	988	1,559	1,094
average circulation	2,166,062	2,196,295	2,438,008

Radio receivers ('000 in use): 13,500 in 1997.

Facsimile machines ('000 in use): 268 in 1998.

* Estimates as at 30 June; includes Azad Kashmir and Northern Areas.

Sources: partly UNESCO, *Statistical Yearbook*; International Telecommunication Union.

Education

(2005/06)

	Institutions	Teachers	Students
Primary*	157,600	444,000	25,226,000
Middle	39,400	310,800	5,318,000
Secondary	22,900	362,200	2,181,000
of which secondary vocational institutes	643	8,264	181,000
Higher:			
arts and science colleges	1,208	32,502	1,047
professional	431	10,773	207,290
universities/degree-awarding institutes	61	13,316	221,541

* Including mosque schools.

Source: Ministry of Finance, *Economic Survey 2005/06*.

Adult literacy rate (UNESCO estimates): 49.9% (males 64.1%; females 35.4%) in 2005 (Source: UNESCO Institute for Statistics).

Directory

The Constitution

The Constitution was promulgated on 10 April 1973, and amended on a number of subsequent occasions (see Amendments, below). Several provisions were suspended following the imposition of martial law in 1977. The (amended) Constitution was restored on 30 December 1985. The Constitution was placed in abeyance on 15 October 1999 following the overthrow of the Government in a military coup. The Constitution, incorporating a Legal Framework Order, was revived on 15 November 2002.

GENERAL PROVISIONS

The Preamble upholds the principles of democracy, freedom, equality, tolerance and social justice as enunciated by Islam. The rights of religious and other minorities are guaranteed.

The Islamic Republic of Pakistan consists of four provinces—Balochistan, North-West Frontier Province, Punjab and Sindh—and the tribal areas under federal administration. The provinces are autonomous units.

Fundamental rights are guaranteed and include equality of status (women have equal rights with men), freedom of thought, speech, worship and the press and freedom of assembly and association. No law providing for preventive detention shall be made except to deal with persons acting against the integrity, security or defence of Pakistan. No such law shall authorize the detention of a person for more than one month.

PRESIDENT

The President is Head of State and acts on the advice of the Prime Minister. He is elected by an electoral college, comprising the two chambers of the Federal Legislature and the four Provincial Assemblies, to serve for a term of five years. He must be a Muslim. The President may be impeached for violating the Constitution or gross misconduct.

FEDERAL LEGISLATURE

The Federal Legislature consists of the President, a lower and an upper house. The lower house, called the National Assembly, has 272 members elected directly for a term of five years, on the basis of universal suffrage (for adults over the age of 21 years), plus 60 female members and 10 members representing minorities. The upper house, called the Senate, has 87 members who serve for six years, with one-half retiring every three years. Each Provincial Assembly is to elect 19 Senators. The tribal areas are to return eight members and the remaining three are to be elected from the Federal Capital Territory by members of the Provincial Assemblies.

There shall be two sessions of the National Assembly and Senate each year, with not more than 120 days between the last sitting of a session and the first sitting of the next session.

The role of the Senate in an overwhelming majority of the subjects shall be merely advisory. Disagreeing with any legislation of the National Assembly, it shall have the right to send it back only once for reconsideration. In case of disagreement in other subjects, the Senate and National Assembly shall sit in a joint session to decide the matter by a simple majority.

GOVERNMENT

The Constitution provides that bills may originate in either house, except money bills. The latter must originate in the National Assembly and cannot go to the Senate. A bill must be passed by both houses and then approved by the President, who may return the bill and suggest amendments. In this case, after the bill has been reconsidered and passed, with or without amendment, the President must give his assent to it.

PROVINCIAL GOVERNMENT

In the matter of relations between Federation and Provinces, the Federal Legislature shall have the power to make laws, including laws bearing on extra-territorial affairs, for the whole or any part of Pakistan, while a Provincial Assembly shall be empowered to make laws for that Province or any part of it. Matters in the Federal Legislative List shall be subject to the exclusive authority of the Federal Legislature, while the Federal Legislature and a Provincial Assembly shall have power to legislate with regard to matters referred to in the Concurrent Legislative List. Any matter not referred to in either list may be subject to laws made by a Provincial Assembly alone, and not by the Federal Legislature, although the latter shall have exclusive power to legislate with regard to matters not referred to in either list for those areas in the Federation not included in any Province.

Four provisions seek to ensure the stability of the parliamentary system. First, the Prime Minister shall be elected by the National Assembly and he and the other Ministers shall be responsible to it. Secondly, any resolution calling for the removal of a Prime Minister shall have to name his successor in the same resolution, which shall be adopted by not less than two-thirds of the total number of members of the lower house. The requirement of a two-thirds' majority is to remain in force for 15 years or three electoral terms, whichever is more. Thirdly, the Prime Minister shall have the right to seek dissolution of the legislature at any time even during the pendency of a no-confidence motion. Fourthly, if a no-confidence motion is defeated, such a motion shall not come up before the house for the next six months.

All these provisions for stability shall apply *mutatis mutandis* to the Provincial Assemblies also.

A National Economic Council, to include the Prime Minister and a representative from each province, shall advise the Provincial and Federal Governments.

There shall be a Governor for each Province, appointed by the President, and a Council of Ministers to aid and advise him, with a Chief Minister appointed by the Governor. Each Province has a provincial legislature consisting of the Governor and Provincial Assembly.

The executive authorities of every Province shall be required to ensure that their actions are in compliance with the Federal laws which apply in that Province. The Federation shall be required to consider the interests of each Province in the exercise of its authority in that Province. The Federation shall further be required to afford every Province protection from external aggression and internal disturbance, and to ensure that every Province is governed in accordance with the provisions of the Constitution.

To further safeguard the rights of the smaller provinces, a Council of Common Interests has been created. Comprising the Chief Ministers of the four provinces and four Central Ministers to decide upon specified matters of common interest, the Council is responsible to the Federal Legislature. The constitutional formula gives the net proceeds of excise duty and royalty on gas to the province concerned. The profits on hydroelectric power generated in each province shall go to that province.

OTHER PROVISIONS

Other provisions include the procedure for elections, the setting up of an Advisory Council of Islamic Ideology and an Islamic Research Institute, and the administration of tribal areas.

AMENDMENTS

Amendments to the Constitution shall require a two-thirds' majority in the National Assembly and the Senate.

In 1975 the Constitution (Third Amendment) Bill abolished the provision that a State of Emergency may not be extended beyond six months without the approval of the National Assembly and empowered the Government to detain a person for three months instead of one month.

In July 1977, following the imposition of martial law, several provisions, including all fundamental rights provided for in the Constitution, were suspended.

An amendment of September 1978 provided for separate electoral registers to be drawn up for Muslims and non-Muslims.

In October 1979 a martial law order inserted a clause in the Constitution establishing the supremacy of military courts in trying all offences, criminal and otherwise.

On 26 May 1980 the President issued a Constitution Amendment Order, which amended Article 199, debarring High Courts from making any order relating to the validity of effect of any judgment or sentence passed by a military court or tribunal granting an injunction; from making an order or entering any proceedings in respect of matters under the jurisdiction or cognizance of a military court or tribunal, and from initiating proceedings against the Chief Martial Law Administrator or a Martial Law Administrator.

By another amendment of the Constitution, the Federal Shari'a Court was to replace the Shari'a Benches of the High Courts. The Shari'a Court, on the petition of a citizen or the Government, may decide whether any law or provision of law is contrary to the injunction of Islam as laid down in the Holy Koran and the Sunnah of the Holy Prophet.

In March 1981 the Government promulgated Provisional Constitution Order 1981, whereby provision is made for the appointment of one or more Vice-Presidents, to be appointed by the Chief Martial Law Administrator, and a Federal Advisory Council (*Majlis-i-Shura*) consisting of persons nominated by the President. All political parties not registered with the Election Commission on 13 September 1979 were to be dissolved and their properties made forfeit to the Federal Council. Any party working against the ideology, sovereignty or security of Pakistan may be dissolved by the President.

The proclamation of July 1977, imposing martial law, and subsequent orders amending the Constitution and further martial law regulations shall not be questioned by any court on any grounds.

All Chief Justices and Judges shall take a new oath of office. New High Court benches for the interior of the provinces shall be set up and retired judges are debarred from holding office in Pakistan for two years. The powers of the High Courts shall be limited for suspending the operation of an order for the detention of any person under any law providing for preventative detention, or release of any person on bail, arrested under the same law.

The Advisory Council of Islamic Ideology, which was asked by the Government to suggest procedures for the election and further Islamization of the Constitution, recommended non-party elections, separate electorates, Islamic qualifications for candidates and a federal structure with greater devolution of power by changing the present divisions into provinces.

Under the Wafaqi Mohtasib Order 1982, the President appointed a Wafaqi Mohtasib (Federal Ombudsman) to redress injustice committed by any government agency.

In March 1985 the President, Gen. Zia ul-Haq, promulgated the Revival of the 1973 Constitution Order, which increased the power of the President by amendments such as those establishing a National Security Council, powers to dismiss the Prime Minister, the Cabinet and provincial Chief Ministers, to appoint judicial and military chiefs, and to call elections, and indemnity clauses to ensure the power of the President. The Constitution was then revived with the exception of 28 key provisions relating to treason, subversion, fundamental rights and jurisdiction of the Supreme Court. In October 1985 the Constitution (Eighth Amendment) Bill became law, incorporating most of the provisions of the Revival of the 1973 Constitution Order and indemnifying all actions of the military regime. In December the enactment of the Political Parties (Amendment) Bill allowed political parties to function under stringent conditions (these conditions were eased in 1988). In December Gen. Zia lifted martial law and restored the remainder of the Constitution.

In March 1987 the Constitution (Tenth Amendment) Bill reduced the minimum number of working days of the National Assembly from 160 days to 130 days.

In April 1997 the Constitution (Thirteenth Amendment) Bill repealed the main components of the Eighth Constitutional Amendment, thus divesting the President of the power to appoint and dismiss the Prime Minister and Cabinet, to dissolve the legislature, to order a national referendum, and to appoint provincial Governors, the Chairman of the Joint Chiefs of Staff and the three armed forces chiefs (these functions and appointments were, in future, to be carried out subject to a mandatory advice from the Prime Minister).

In October 1998 the Constitution (Fifteenth Amendment) Bill replaced the country's existing legal code with full *Shari'a*; the bill remained to be ratified by the Senate.

Following the overthrow of the Government in a military coup on 12 October 1999, the Constitution was placed in abeyance on 15 October. On the same day a Provisional Constitution Order was promulgated, according to which executive power was transferred to a National Security Council, under the leadership of a Chief Executive. A federal Cabinet, which was to aid and advise the Chief Executive in the exercise of his functions, was to be appointed by the President on the advice of the Chief Executive. The President was to act on, and in accordance with, the advice of the Chief Executive. The National Assembly, Senate and the Provincial Assemblies were suspended and the Chairman and Deputy Chairman of the Senate ceased to hold office.

In July 2000 the Chief Executive issued a decree to revive the Islamic principles of the suspended Constitution and to incorporate them in the Provisional Constitution Order.

On 20 June 2001 the Proclamation of Emergency (Amendment) Order 2001 was promulgated, according to which the Chief Executive assumed the office of President of Pakistan. The National Assembly, Senate and Provincial Assemblies were dissolved with immediate effect. The Speaker and Deputy Speaker of the National Assembly and Provincial Assemblies ceased to hold office with immediate effect. The President later announced that elections to federal and provincial legislatures would be held on 10 October 2002 (see Recent History).

On 21 August 2002 the Legal Framework Order 2002 was promulgated, which sanctioned the President's 29 amendments to the Constitution, including the restoration of Article 58 (2-B), which authorized the President to dissolve the National Assembly (the article was also amended to allow the President to appoint provincial governors in consultation with the Prime Minister), the restoration of Article 243, which gave the President power to appoint the Chairman of the Joint Chiefs of Staff Committee and the three armed forces chiefs and the power to establish the National Security Council to provide consultation to the elected government on strategic matters. Other amendments included the extension of the President's term in office and role as Chief of Army Staff for five years from the date of the election (10 October 2002). The terms of the National Assembly and Senate were to be decreased to four and five years, respectively, and the number of seats in each house to be increased to 342 and 100, respectively. Part III of the Legal Framework Order sanctioned an amendment to Article 71: a Mediation Committee would be established in instances where the Senate disagrees with legislation of the National Assembly, or vice versa. The Mediation Committee would formulate an agreed item of legislation and place it separately before each house for consideration. According to the amendments, the Prime Minister would continue to have the right to seek dissolution of the legislature at any time, but not during the pendency of a no-confidence motion. Ten Orders endorsed by Musharraf since the establishment of military rule were placed in 'Schedule Six', and therefore could not be altered, repealed or amended without the approval of the President. Constitutional protection was thereby awarded to the offices of the National Accountability Bureau and the Governor of the State Bank of Pakistan. Other provisions granted constitutional protection included the lowering of the voting age from 21 to 18 years, the Political Parties' Order, the Local Government Ordinances and the autonomy of the Election Commission. The 1973 Constitution, incorporating the Legal Framework Order, was revived on 15 November 2002.

In late December 2003 the legislature passed the Constitution (Seventeenth Amendment) Bill, comprising several amendments to the 2002 Legal Framework Order (in passing this Bill the legislature also endorsed for the first time the validity of the Legal Framework Order). The Bill allowed the President to remain as Chief of Army Staff until 31 December 2004, when he would have to relinquish his military role. The President also retained the right to dissolve the legislature (on the recommendation of the Prime Minister); the matter would then have to be referred to the Supreme Court within 15 days. The Bill endorsed the lowering of the minimum national voting age to 18 years, and accepted the revised composition of the Senate, National Assembly and provincial assemblies, and clauses relating to political parties.

In April 2004 the legislature approved the National Security Council Bill. This enabled the formation, under the protection of the Constitution, of the National Security Council, a 13-member council chaired by the President and composed of nine civilian politicians and four members of the military. The Council was to serve as a forum for consultation with the Government on matters of national security. Critics protested that the Bill institutionalized the role of the military in national government.

The Government

HEAD OF STATE

President: Gen. (retd) PERVEZ MUSHARRAF (sworn in 20 June 2001).

CABINET
(April 2008)

Following the general election held on 18 February 2008, a coalition Government was formed, comprising members of the Pakistan People's Party (PPP), the Pakistan Muslim League—Nawaz (PML—N), the Awami National Party (ANP) and the Jamiat-e-Ulema-e-Islam—Fazl (JUI—F), along with one independent member of the National Assembly from the Federally Administered Tribal Areas.

Prime Minister: YOUSAF RAZA GILLANI.

Senior Minister of Communications and Inter-Provincial Co-ordination, with additional charge of Food, Agriculture and Livestock: CHAUDHRY NISAR ALI KHAN (PML—N).

Minister of Commerce, Trade and Industry: SHAHID KHAQAN ABBASI (PML—N).

Minister of Culture, with additional charge of Youth Affairs: KHAWAJA SAAD RAFIQUE (PML—N).

Minister of Defence: CHAUDHRY AHMED MUKHTAR (PPP).

Minister of Defence Production: RANA TANVEER HUSSAIN (PML—N).

Minister of Education, with additional charge of Minorities: AHSAN IQBAL (PML—N).

Minister of the Environment: HAMEEDULLAH JAN AFRIDI.

Minister of Finance, Revenue, Economic Affairs and Statistics: MUHAMMAD ISHAQ DAR (PML—N).

Minister of Foreign Affairs: SHAH MEHMUD QURESHI (PPP).

Minister of Housing and Works: REHMATULLAH KAKAR (JUI—F).

Minister of Information and Broadcasting, with additional charge of Health: SHERRY REHMAN (PPP).

Minister of the Interior: (vacant).

Minister of Kashmir Affairs and Northern Areas (KANA) and of Information Technology: QAMAR ZAMAN KAIRA (PPP).

Minister of Labour, Manpower and Overseas Pakistanis and of Religious Affairs, Zakat and Ushr: SYED KHURSHEED AHMED SHAH (PPP).

Minister of Law and Justice, with additional charge of Parliamentary Affairs and Human Rights: FAROOQ H. NAIK (PPP).

Minister of Local Government and Rural Development: Haji GHULAM AHMAD BILOUR (ANP).

Minister of Narcotics Control: NAZAR MUHAMMAD GONDAL (PPP).

Minister of Petroleum and Natural Resources, with additional charge of Sports: KHAWAJA MUHAMMAD ASIF (PML—N).

Minister of Population Welfare: HUMAYUN AZIZ KURD (PPP).

Minister of Ports and Shipping, with additional charge of Privatisation and Investment, and of Industries and Production: SYED NAVEED QAMAR (PPP).

Minister of Railways: Sardar MEHTAB AHMED KHAN (PML—N).

Minister of Science and Technology: TEHMINA DAULTANA (PML—N).

Minister of Social Welfare and Special Education: Nawabzada KHAWAJA MUHAMMAD KHAN HOTI (ANP).

Minister of States and Frontier Regions: NAJMUDDIN KHAN (PPP).

Minister of Water and Power, with additional charge of Tourism: RAJA PERVAIZ ASHRAF (PPP).

Minister of Women Development: (vacant).

MINISTRIES

Office of the President: Aiwan-e-Sadr, Islamabad; tel. (51) 9206060; fax (51) 9208046; internet www.presidentofpakistan.gov.pk.

Office of the Prime Minister's Secretariat: Cabinet Secretariat, Cabinet Division, Islamabad; tel. (51) 925190512; e-mail contact@cabinet.gov.pk; internet www.cabinet.gov.pk.

Ministry of Commerce: Block A, Pakistan Secretariat, Islamabad; tel. (51) 9201816; fax (51) 9205241; e-mail naveed@commerce.gov.pk; internet www.commerce.gov.pk.

Ministry of Culture, Minorities, Sports and Youth Affairs: NFCH, 12th Floor, Green Tower, Blue Area, F-6/3, Islamabad; tel. (51) 9206127; fax (51) 9224697; internet www.heritage.gov.pk.

Ministry of Defence: Pakistan Secretariat, No. II, Rawalpindi 46000; tel. (51) 9271107; fax (51) 9271113; e-mail tahir@mod.gov.pk.

Ministry of Education: Block D, Pakistan Secretariat, Islamabad; tel. (51) 9212020; fax (51) 9202851; e-mail pak@yahoo.com; internet www.moe.gov.pk.

Ministry of Environment, Local Government and Rural Development: Block 4, Old Naval Headquarters, Civic Centre, G-6, Melody, Islamabad; tel. (51) 9224291; fax (51) 9202211; e-mail minister@moenv.gov.pk; internet www.moenv.gov.pk.

Ministry of Finance: Block Q, Pakistan Secretariat, Islamabad; tel. (51) 9201941; fax (51) 9202640; e-mail webmaster@finance.gov.pk; internet www.finance.gov.pk.

PAKISTAN

Ministry of Food, Agriculture and Livestock: Block B, Pakistan Secretariat, Islamabad; tel. (51) 9203307; fax (51) 9210616.

Ministry of Foreign Affairs: Constitution Ave, Islamabad; tel. (51) 9210335; fax (51) 9207600; e-mail sadiq@mofa.gov.pk; internet www.mofa.gov.pk.

Ministry of Health: Block C, Pakistan Secretariat, Islamabad; tel. (51) 9213933; fax (51) 9203944; e-mail minister@health.gov.pk; internet www.health.gov.pk.

Ministry of Housing and Works: Block B, Pakistan Secretariat, Islamabad; tel. (51) 9214121; fax (51) 9209125; e-mail minister@housing.gov.pk; internet www.pha.gov.pk.

Ministry of Industries, Production and Special Initiatives: Block A, Pakistan Secretariat, Islamabad; tel. (51) 9212164; fax (51) 9205130; e-mail info@moip.gov.pk; internet www.moip.gov.pk.

Ministry of Information and Broadcasting: Cyber Wing, 4th Floor, Cabinet Block, Pakistan Secretariat, Islamabad; tel. (51) 9206176; fax (51) 9201350; e-mail webmaster@infopak.gov.pk; internet www.infopak.gov.pk.

Ministry of Information Technology and Telecommunications: 4th Floor, Evacuee Trust Bldg, Aga Khan Rd, F-5/1, Islamabad; tel. (51) 9201990; fax (51) 9205233; e-mail minister@moitt.gov.pk; internet www.moitt.gov.pk.

Ministry of the Interior: Block R, Room 404, Pakistan Secretariat, Islamabad; tel. (51) 9212026; fax (51) 9202624; e-mail info@interior.gov.pk; internet www.interior.gov.pk.

Ministry of Kashmir Affairs, Northern Areas and States and Frontier Regions (SAFRON): Block R, Pakistan Secretariat, Islamabad; tel. (51) 9208442; fax (51) 9207084; e-mail minister@moka.gov.pk; internet www.moka.gov.pk.

Ministry of Labour, Manpower and Overseas Pakistanis: Block B, Pakistan Secretariat, Islamabad; tel. (51) 9210077; fax (51) 9203462.

Ministry of Law, Justice and Human Rights: Block R, Pakistan Secretariat, Islamabad; tel. and fax (51) 9211278.

Ministry of Local Government and Rural Development: Pakistan Secretariat, Islamabad; tel. (51) 9202080; fax (51) 9201165; e-mail minister@lgrd.gov.pk; internet www.lgrd.gov.pk.

Ministry of Petroleum and Natural Resources: 3rd Floor, Block A, Pakistan Secretariat, Islamabad; tel. (51) 9210220; fax (51) 9213180; e-mail minister@mpnr.gov.pk; internet www.mpnr.gov.pk.

Ministry of Planning and Development: Block P, Pakistan Secretariat, Islamabad; tel. (51) 9204926; fax (51) 9202704; internet www.mopd.gov.pk.

Ministry of Population Welfare: Jamil Mohsin Mansion, Civic Centre, G-6, Islamabad 44000; tel. (51) 9207383; fax (51) 9201408; e-mail minister@mopw.gov.pk; internet www.mopw.gov.pk.

Ministry of Privatisation and Investment: 5-A, EAC Bldg, Constitution Ave, Islamabad 44000; tel. (51) 9205146; fax (51) 9203076; e-mail info@privatisation.gov.pk; internet www.privatisation.gov.pk.

Ministry of Railways: Block D, Pakistan Secretariat, Islamabad; tel. (51) 9218515; fax (51) 9210247; e-mail minister@railways.gov.pk; internet www.railways.gov.pk.

Ministry of Religious Affairs, Zakat and Ushr: G-6, Civic Centre, Islamabad; tel. (51) 9214856; fax (51) 9205833; e-mail minister@mra.gov.pk; internet www.mra.gov.pk.

Ministry of Scientific and Technological Research: 4th Floor, Evacuee Trust Complex, Aga Khan Rd, F-5/1, Islamabad; tel. (51) 9208026; fax (51) 9204541; e-mail minister@most.gov.pk; internet www.most.gov.pk.

Ministry of the Textiles Industry: 2nd Floor, FBC Bldg, Attaturk Ave, G-5/2, Islamabad; tel. (51) 9212799; fax (51) 9214015; e-mail minister@textile.gov.pk; internet www.textile.gov.pk.

Ministry of Tourism: Green Trust Towers, 7th Floor, Jinnah Ave, Blue Area, Islamabad 44000; tel. (51) 9203772; fax (51) 9207427; e-mail secretary@tourism.gov.pk; internet www.tourism.gov.pk.

Ministry of Water and Power: Block A, 15th Floor, Shaheed-e-Millat, Pakistan Secretariat, Islamabad; tel. (51) 9212442; fax (51) 9224825; e-mail fminister@mowp.gov.pk; internet www.mowp.gov.pk.

Ministry of Women's Development, Social Welfare and Special Education: State Life Bldg, 1st Floor, No. 5, Blue Area, China Chowk, F-6/4, Islamabad; tel. (51) 9206328; fax (51) 9201083; e-mail secretary@moya.gov.pk.

Federal Legislature

SENATE

The Legal Framework Order, promulgated by the President in August 2002, increased the number of seats in the Senate from 87 to 100. Eighty-eight of the members are elected by the four provincial legislatures; eight are chosen by representatives of the Federally Administered Tribal Areas; and four by the federal capital. Its term of office is six years, but one-half of the membership is renewed after three years. The most recent election was held on 6 March 2006.

Chairman: MOHAMMAD MIAN SOOMRO.

Deputy Chairman: JAN MOHAMMAD KHAN JAMALI.

Distribution of Seats, March 2006

	Seats
Pakistan Muslim League (Quaid-e-Azam Group)	38
Muttahida Majlis-e-Amal*	17
Pakistan People's Party Parliamentarians	9
Muttahida Qaumi Movement	6
Pakistan Muslim League (Nawaz Group)	4
Pakistan People's Party (Sherpao Group)	3
Pakhtoonkhwa Milli Awami Party	3
Awami National Party	2
Balochistan National Party (Awami)	1
Balochistan National Party (Maingal)	1
Jamhuri Watan Party	1
Jamiat-e-Ulema-e-Islam (F)	1
National Alliance†	1
Pakistan Muslim League (Functional Pir Pagara Group)	1
Independents	12
Total	**100**

* Coalition comprising Jamaat-e-Islami Pakistan, Jamiat-e-Ulema-e-Pakistan, Jamiat-e-Ulema-e-Islam (S), Jamiat-e-Ulema-e-Islam (F), Islami Tehreek Pakistan and Jamiat Ahl-e-Hadith.
† Coalition comprising the National People's Party, the Millat Party, the Sindh National Front, the Sindh Democratic Alliance and the National Awami Party.

NATIONAL ASSEMBLY

In accordance with the Legal Framework Order (LFO), which was promulgated by the President in August 2002, the number of seats in the National Assembly increased from 217 to 342, with 60 seats reserved for women and 10 for non-Muslims. Also incorporated in the LFO was a reduction in the National Assembly's term of office by one year to four.

Speaker: Dr FEHMIDA MIRZA.

Deputy Speaker: FAISAL KARIM KUNDI.

General Election, 18 February 2008

	Seats
Pakistan People's Party Parliamentarians	87
Pakistan Muslim League (Nawaz Group)	67
Pakistan Muslim League	42
Muttahida Qaumi Movement	19
Awami National Party	10
Muttahida Majlis-e-Amal	5
Pakistan Muslim League (Functional Group)	4
Balochistan National Party (Awami)	1
National People's Party	1
Pakistan People's Party (Sherpao Group)	1
Independents and others	29
Reserved	70
Vacant	6
Total	**342**

Provincial Governments

(May 2008)

Pakistan comprises the four provinces of Sindh, Balochistan, Punjab and the North-West Frontier Province, plus the federal capital and Federally Administered Tribal Areas.

BALOCHISTAN
(Capital—Quetta)

Governor: ZULFIQAR ALI MAGSI.

Chief Minister: Nawab ASLAM RAISANI.

Legislative Assembly: 65 seats (Pakistan Muslim League—Quaid-e-Azam Group 20, Pakistan People's Party Parliamentarians 11, Muttahida Majlis-e-Amal 10, Balochistan National Party—Awami 7, Awami National Party 4, National Party 1, independents 10, vacant 2).

NORTH-WEST FRONTIER PROVINCE
(Capital—Peshawar)

Governor: OWAIS AHMED GHANI.
Chief Minister: AMIR HAIDER KHAN HOTI.
Legislative Assembly: 124 seats (Awami National Party 46, Pakistan People's Party Parliamentarians 30, Muttahida Majlis-e-Amal 14, Pakistan Muslim League—Nawaz 9, Pakistan People's Party—Sherpao 7, Pakistan Muslim League—Quaid-e-Azam Group 6, independents 9, vacant 3).

PUNJAB
(Capital—Lahore)

Governor: SALMAAN TASEER.
Chief Minister: Sardar DOST MUHAMMAD KHOSA.
Legislative Assembly: 371 seats (Pakistan Muslim League—Nawaz 165, Pakistan People's Party Parliamentarians 106, Pakistan Muslim League—Quaid-e-Azam Group 86, Pakistan Muslim League—Functional 4, Muttahida Majlis-e-Amal 2, independents 2, vacant or withheld 6).

SINDH
(Capital—Karachi)

Governor: Dr ISHRATUL EBAD KHAN.
Chief Minister: SYED QAIM ALI SHAH.
Legislative Assembly: 168 seats (Pakistan People's Party Parliamentarians 90, Muttahida Qaumi Movement 51, Pakistan Muslim League—Quaid-e-Azam Group 10, Pakistan Muslim League—Functional 9, Awami National Party 2, National People's Party 2, vacant, withheld and others 4).

Election Commission

Election Commission of Pakistan: Secretariat, Election House, Constitution Ave, G-5/2, Islamabad; e-mail info@ecp.gov.pk; internet www.ecp.gov.pk; independent; Chief Election Commr Justice (retd) Qazi MUHAMMAD FAROOQ.

Political Organizations

Some 49 parties, issued with election symbols by the Election Commission, contested the general election on 18 February 2008.

All Jammu and Kashmir Muslim Conference: f. 1948; advocates the holding of a free plebiscite in the whole of Kashmir; Leader Sardar ATTIQ AHMED KHAN.

Awami National Party (ANP) (People's National Party): Bacha Khan Markaz, Pajagi Rd, Peshawar; tel. (91) 2246851-3; fax (91) 2252406; e-mail info@awaminationalparty.org; internet www.awaminationalparty.org; f. 1986 by the merger of the National Democratic Party, the Awami Tehrik (People's Movement) and the Mazdoor Kissan (Labourers' and Peasants' Party); federalist and nationalist; the Pakhtoonkhawa Qaumi Party merged with the ANP in February 2006, followed by the National Awami Party Pakistan in June of the same year; Leader ABDUL LATIF AFRIDI; Pres. ASFANDYAR WALI KHAN.

Awami Qiyadat Party (People's Leadership Party): 88 Race Course Rd, St 3, Rawalpindi Cantt; f. 1995; Chair. Gen. (retd) MIRZA ASLAM BEG.

Balochistan National Party (BNP)—Awami: Quetta; Leader SYED EHSAN SHAH; Pres. ISRARULLAH ZEHRI.

Balochistan National Party (BNP)—Maingal: Quetta; e-mail bnpwebadmin@balochistan.net; Leader Sardar MOHAMMAD AKHTAR MAINGAL.

Jamaat-e-Islami Pakistan (JIP): Mansoorah, Multan Rd, Lahore 54570; tel. (42) 5419520; fax (42) 5419505; e-mail uroubah@gmail.com; internet www.jamaat.org; f. 1941; seeks the establishment of Islamic order through adherence to teaching of Maulana MAUDUDI, founder of the party; revivalist; right-wing; mem. of Muttahida Majlise Amal (United Action Front); Chair. Amir QAZI HUSSAIN AHMAD; Sec.-Gen. SYED MUNAWAR HASAN; c. 5m. mems (2005).

Jamhuri Watan Party (Bugti) Balochistan: Bugti House, Dera Bugti; Pres. Nawab TALAL AKBAR KHAN BUGTI.

Jamiat-e-Ulema-e-Islam (JUI): Jamia al-Maarf, al-Sharia, Dera Ismail Khan; f. 1950; mem. Muttahida Majlis-e-Amal alliance; advocates adoption of a constitution in accordance with (Sunni) Islamic teachings; split into factions led by Maulana Fazlur Rehman (JUI—F) and Sami ul-Haq (JUI—S).

Jamiat-e-Ulema-e-Pakistan (JUP): Burns Rd, Karachi; f. 1948; mem. Muttahida Majlis-e-Amal alliance; advocates progressive (Sunni) Islamic principles and enforcement of Islamic laws in Pakistan; Pres. Dr ABUL KHAIR MOHAMMAD ZUBAIR (acting); Gen. Sec. QARI ZAWWAR BAHADUR.

Millat Party: 21-E/3, Gulberg III, Lahore; tel. (42) 5757805; fax (42) 5756718; e-mail millat@lhr.comsats.net.pk; advocates 'true federalism'; Chair. FAROOQ AHMAD KHAN LAGHARI.

Muttahida Qaumi Movement (MQM): 494/8 Azizabad, Federal Area B, Karachi; tel. (21) 6313690; fax (21) 6329955; e-mail mqm@mqm.org; internet www.mqm.org; f. 1984 as Mohajir Qaumi Movement; name changed to Muttahida Qaumi Movement in 1997; associated with the All Pakistan Muttahida Students' Organization (f. 1978 as the All Pakistan Mohajir Students' Organization; name changed July 2006); represents the interests of Muslim, Urdu-speaking immigrants (from India) in Pakistan; seeks the designation of Mohajir as fifth nationality (after Sindhi, Punjabi, Pathan and Balochi); aims to abolish the prevailing feudal political system and to establish democracy; Founder and Leader ALTAF HUSSAIN; Pres. AFTAB SHEIKH.

National Party: Faiz Arbab Saryab Rd, Quetta; f. 2003 following merger of Balochistan National Movement and Balochistan National Democratic Party; Chair. Dr ABDUL HAYAI BALOCH.

National People's Party (NPP): 18 Khayaban-e-Shamsheer, Defence Housing Authority, Phase V, Karachi; tel. (21) 5854522; fax (21) 5873753; f. 1986; centre left-wing party advocating a just, democratic welfare state for Pakistan; breakaway faction from PPP; Chair. GHULAM MUSTAFA JATOI; Parl. Leader Dr IBRAHIM KHAN.

Pakhtoonkhwa Milli Awami Party: Leader MEHMOOD KHAN ACHAKZAI.

Pakistan Awami Tehreek (PAT): 365-M Model Town, Lahore; tel. (42) 5169111; fax (42) 5169114; e-mail info@pat.com.pk; internet www.pat.com.pk; Pres. SAHIBZADA MISKEEN FAIZ UR REHMAN KHAN DURANI; Sec.-Gen. Dr ANWAAR AKHTAR.

Pakistan Democratic Party (PDP): f. 1969; advocates democratic and Islamic values; Pres. NAWABZADA MANSOOR AHMED KHAN.

Pakistan Muslim League (PML): PML House, F-7/3, Islamabad; internet www.pakistanmuslimleague.info; f. 2004 following merger of PML Quaid-e-Azam Group, PML (Junejo), PML (Functional), PML (Zia-ul-Haq Shaheed), PML (Jinnah) and the Sindh Democratic Alliance; PML (Functional) subsequently split from party; Pres. CHAUDHRY SHUJAAT HUSSAIN; Sec.-Gen. Sen. MUSHAHID HUSSAIN SYED.

Pakistan Muslim League—Functional (PML—F): Islamabad; merged with PML Quaid-e-Azam Group, PML (Junejo), PML (Zia-ul-Haq Shaheed), PML (Jinnah) and the Sindh Democratic Alliance in 2004 but subsequently split from party; Leader PIR PAGARA.

Pakistan Muslim League—Nawaz (PML—N): House No. 20-H, St 10, F-8/3, Islamabad; tel. (51) 2852662; e-mail pmlisb@hotmail.com; internet www.pmln.org.pk; f. 1993 as faction of Pakistan Muslim League (Junejo); Leader NAWAZ SHARIF; Pres. SHAHBAZ SHARIF; Chair RAJA ZAFARUL HAQ.

Pakistan People's Party (PPP): 8, St 19, F-8/2, Islamabad; tel. (51) 2255264; fax (51) 2282741; e-mail ppp@comsats.net.pk; internet www.ppp.org.pk; formed Pakistan People's Party Parliamentarians (PPPP) 2002 in order to meet electoral requirements; advocates Islamic socialism, democracy and a non-aligned foreign policy; Leaders BILAWAL BHUTTO ZARDARI, ASIF ALI ZARDARI.

Pakistan People's Party (Shaheed Bhutto Group): 71 Clifton, Karachi; f. 1995 as a breakaway faction of the PPP; Chair. GHINWA BHUTTO; Sec.-Gen. Dr MUBASHIR HASAN.

Punjabi Pakhtoon Ittehad (PPI): f. 1987 to represent the interests of Punjabis and Pakhtoons in Karachi; Pres. MALIK MIR HAZAR KHAN.

Sindh National Front (SNF): Pres. MUMTAZ BHUTTO.

Sindh Taraqi Passand Party (STPP): Leader Dr QADIR MAGSI.

Tehreek-e-Insaf (Movement for Justice): Central Secretariat, H-07, Parliament Lodges, Islamabad; tel. (51) 2270744; fax (51) 2873893; e-mail info@insaf.org.pk; internet www.insaf.org.pk; f. 1996; Leader IMRAN KHAN; Sec.-Gen. A. M. SHAHID ZULFIQAR.

PAKISTAN   *Directory*

Diplomatic Representation

EMBASSIES AND HIGH COMMISSIONS IN PAKISTAN

Afghanistan: 8, St 90, G-6/3, Islamabad 44000; tel. (51) 2824505; fax (51) 2824504; e-mail afghanem@yahoo.com; Ambassador MAJNOON GHULAB.

Algeria: 107, St 9, E-7, POB 1038, Islamabad; tel. (51) 2653793; fax (51) 2820912; Ambassador NADIR LARBAOUI.

Argentina: 20, Hill Rd, Shalimar F-6/3, POB 1015, Islamabad; tel. (51) 2821242; fax (51) 2825564; e-mail epaki@mrecic.gov.ar; Ambassador RODOLFO MARTIN SARAVIA.

Australia: Diplomatic Enclave 1, Constitution Ave and Isphani Rd, G-5/4, POB 1046, Islamabad; tel. (51) 2824345; fax (51) 2820112; e-mail consular.islm@dfat.gov.au; internet www.pakistan.embassy.gov.au; High Commissioner ZORICA MCCARTHY.

Austria: 13, St 1, F-6/3, POB 1018, Islamabad 44000; tel. (51) 2209710; fax (51) 2828306; e-mail islamabad-ob@bmeia.gv.at; Ambassador Dr MICHAEL STIGELBAUER.

Azerbaijan: House 14, St 87, G-6/3, Atatürk Ave, Islamabad; tel. (51) 2829345; fax (51) 2820898; e-mail azeremb@isb.paknet.com.pk; internet www.azembassy.com.pk; Ambassador Dr EYNULLA YADALLA OGLU MADATLI.

Bahrain: House 5, St 83, G-6/4, Islamabad; tel. (51) 2831114; fax (51) 2206732; Ambassador MOHAMMED EBRAHIM MOHAMMED ABD AL-QADIR.

Bangladesh: 1, St 5, F-6/3, Islamabad; tel. (51) 2279267; fax (51) 2279266; e-mail bdhcisb@sat.net.pk; High Commissioner YASMEEN MURSHED.

Belgium: 14, St 17, F-7/2, Islamabad; tel. (51) 2652635; fax (51) 2652631; e-mail islamabad@diplobel.org; internet www.diplomatie.be/islamabad; Ambassador MICHEL GOFFIN.

Bosnia and Herzegovina: House No. 1, Kaghan Rd, F-8/3, Islamabad; tel. (51) 2261003; fax (51) 2261004; e-mail ambassador@bosnianembassypakistan.org; internet www.bosnianembassypakistan.org; Ambassador DAMIR DZANKO.

Brazil: 50, Atatürk Ave, G-6/3, POB 1053, Islamabad; tel. (51) 2279690; fax (51) 2823034; e-mail brasembp@isb.compol.com; Ambassador CARLOS EDUARDO SETTE CAMARA DA FONSECA COSTA.

Brunei: House 5, St 6, F-6/3, Islamabad; tel. (51) 2879636; fax (51) 2823688; High Commissioner Pehin Dato' Haji Panglima Col (retd) Haji ABDUL JALIL BIN Haji AHMAD.

Bulgaria: Plot No. 6-11, Diplomatic Enclave, Ramna 5, POB 1483, Islamabad; tel. (51) 2279196; fax (51) 2279195; e-mail bul@isb.compol.com; Ambassador GEORGI GRANCHAROV.

Canada: Diplomatic Enclave, Sector G-5, POB 1042, Islamabad; tel. (51) 2086000; fax (51) 2279188; e-mail isbad@international.gc.ca; High Commissioner DAVID B. COLLINS.

China, People's Republic: Ramna 4, Diplomatic Enclave, Islamabad; tel. (51) 2877279; fax (51) 2279600; e-mail chinaemb_pk@mfa.gov.cn; internet pk.china-embassy.org; Ambassador LUO ZHAOHUI.

Cuba: House 37, School Rd, F-6/2, Islamabad; tel. (51) 2824077; fax (51) 2824076; e-mail embacubapakistan@yahoo.com; Ambassador GUSTAVO MACHÍN GÓMEZ.

Czech Republic: 49, St 27, Shalimar F-6/2, POB 1335, Islamabad; tel. (51) 2274304; fax (51) 2825327; e-mail islamabad@embassy.mzv.cz; internet www.mzv.cz/islamabad; Ambassador ALEXANDR LANGER.

Denmark: House No. 16, Street 21, F-6/2, POB 1118, Islamabad; tel. (51) 2824078; fax (51) 2824076; e-mail isbamb@um.dk; internet www.ambislamabad.um.dk; Ambassador BENT WIGOTSKI.

Egypt: 38–51, UN Blvd, Diplomatic Enclave, Ramna 5/4, POB 2088, Islamabad; tel. (51) 2209072; fax (51) 2279552; Ambassador HUSSEIN KAMEL HARIDY.

Finland: House No. 24, St 89, G-6/3, Islamabad; tel. (51) 2828426; fax (51) 2828427; e-mail finnemb@isd.wol.net.pk; Ambassador PIRJO IRMELI MUSTONEN.

France: Constitution Ave, G-5, Diplomatic Enclave 1, POB 1068, Islamabad; tel. (51) 2278730; fax (51) 2823236; e-mail Ambafrance.ISLAMABAD@diplomatie.gouv.fr; Ambassador RÉGIS DE BELENET.

Germany: Ramna 5, Diplomatic Enclave, POB 1027, Islamabad 44000; tel. (51) 2007100; fax (51) 2279436; e-mail info@isla.diplo.de; internet www.islamabad.diplo.de; Ambassador Dr GÜNTER MULACK.

Greece: 22, Margalla Rd, F-6/3, Islamabad; tel. (51) 2822558; fax (51) 2825161; e-mail greece@isb.paknet.com.pk; internet www.greekembassy.org.pk; Ambassador ATHANASIOS VALASIDIS.

Holy See: Apostolic Nunciature, St 5, G-5, Diplomatic Enclave 1, POB 1106, Islamabad 44000; tel. (51) 2278218; fax (51) 2820847; e-mail vatipak@dsl.net.pk; Apostolic Nuncio Most Rev. ADOLFO TITO YLLANA (Titular Archbishop of Montecorvino).

Hungary: 12, Margalla Rd, F-6/3, POB 1103, Islamabad; tel. (51) 2823352; fax (51) 2825256; e-mail hungemb@comsats.net.pk; Ambassador BELA FAZEKAS.

India: G-5, Diplomatic Enclave, Islamabad; tel. (51) 2206950; fax (51) 2823102; e-mail hicomind@isb.compol.com; High Commissioner SATYABRATA PAL.

Indonesia: St 5, G-5/4, Diplomatic Enclave 1, POB 1019, Islamabad; tel. (51) 2832017; fax (51) 2832013; e-mail unitkom@kbri-islamabad.go.id; internet www.kbri-islamabad.go.id; Ambassador ANWAR SANTOSO.

Iran: Plot No. 222, 238, St 2, F-5/1, Islamabad; tel. (51) 2276270; fax (51) 2824839; Ambassador MASHALLAH SHAKERI.

Iraq: 57, St 48, F-8/4, Islamabad; tel. (51) 2253734; fax (51) 2253688; e-mail iraqiya@sat.net.pk; Ambassador KAIS SUBHI AL-YACOUBI.

Italy: 54 Margalla Rd, F-6/3, POB 1008, Islamabad; tel. (51) 2828982; fax (51) 2829026; e-mail segreteria.ambislamabad@esteri.it; internet www.italian-embassy.org.ae/Ambasciata_Islamabad; Ambassador VINCENZO PRATI.

Japan: Plot No. 53-70, Ramna 5/4, Diplomatic Enclave 1, Islamabad 44000; tel. (51) 2279320; fax (51) 2279340; e-mail japanemb@comsats.net.pk; internet www.pk.emb-japan.go.jp; Ambassador SEIJI KOJIMA.

Jordan: 99, Main Double Rd, F-10/1, Islamabad; tel. (51) 2297383; fax (51) 2211630; e-mail jordanem@isb.paknet.com.pk; Ambassador SALEH JAWARNEH.

Kazakhstan: House 11, St 45, F-8/1, Islamabad; tel. (51) 2262926; fax (51) 2262806; e-mail embkaz@isb.comsats.net.pk; Ambassador VAKYTBEK S. SHABARBAYEV.

Kenya: 8A, Embassy Rd, F-6/4, POB 2097, Islamabad; tel. (51) 2876024; fax (51) 2876027; e-mail kenreppk@apollo.net.pk; High Commissioner MISHI MASIKA MWATSAHU.

Korea, Democratic People's Republic: House 16 A-B, Park Rd, F-B/2, Islamabad; tel. and fax (51) 2252756; Ambassador RI YONG HWAN.

Korea, Republic: Block 13, St 29, G-5/4, Diplomatic Enclave 2, POB 1087, Islamabad; tel. (51) 2279380; fax (51) 2279391; e-mail emb-pk@mofat.go.kr; Ambassador KIM JOO-SEOK.

Kuwait: Plot Nos 1, 2 and 24, University Rd, G-5, Diplomatic Enclave, POB 1030, Islamabad; tel. (51) 229413; fax (51) 2829487; Ambassador FAISAL ABDULAZIZ AL-MULAIFI.

Kyrgyzstan: House 163, Street 36, F-10/1, Islamabad; tel. (51) 2212196; fax (51) 2212169; e-mail kyrgyzembassy@dsl.net.pk; Ambassador NURLAN T. AITMURZAYEV.

Lebanon: House 6, Street 27, F-6/2, Islamabad; tel. (51) 2278338; fax (51) 2826410; e-mail lebemb@comsats.net.pk; internet www.lebanonembassy.pak.4t.com; Ambassador WAFIC MUHAMMAD REHAIME.

Libya: House 736, Margalla Rd, F-10/2, Islamabad; tel. (51) 2214378; fax (51) 2290093; Ambassador MOHAMMAD ALI WARSHFANI.

Malaysia: House 34, St 56, F-7/4, Islamabad; tel. (51) 2279570; fax (51) 2824761; e-mail malislamb@kln.gov.my; internet www.kln.gov.my/perwakilan/islamabad; High Commissioner AHMAD SHAHIZAN ABD SAMAD.

Mauritius: House 13, St 26, F-6/2, POB 1084, Islamabad; tel. (51) 2824657; fax (51) 2824656; e-mail mauripak@dsl.net.pk; High Commissioner ABDOOL RASCHID MEERUN.

Morocco: 6, Gomal Rd, E-7, POB 1179, Islamabad; tel. (51) 2829656; fax (51) 2822745; e-mail sifamapak@morocco-embassy.com.pk; internet www.morocco-embassy.com.pk; Ambassador MOHAMMAD RIDA EL FASSI.

Myanmar: 43, St 26, F-6/2, Islamabad; tel. (51) 2879612; fax (51) 2879616; e-mail embassy_myanmar@yahoo.com; Ambassador U MAUNG NYO.

Nepal: 2, St 8, F-8/3, Islamabad; tel. (51) 2854696; fax (51) 2854722; e-mail nepem@isb.comsats.net.pk; Ambassador BAL BAHADUR KUNWAR.

Netherlands: House No. 28, Margalla Rd, F-7/3, POB 1065, Islamabad; tel. (51) 2004444; fax (51) 2279512; e-mail isl@minbuza.nl; internet www.mfa.nl/isl-en; Ambassador CORNELIS WILHELMUS ANDREAE.

Nigeria: 132–135, Diplomatic Enclave 1, Isphani Rd, G-5/4, POB 1075, Islamabad; tel. (51) 2823542; fax (51) 2824104; e-mail nigeria@isb.comsats.net.pk; High Commissioner UMAR EL-GASH MAINA.

Norway: 25, St 19, F-6/2, Islamabad; tel. (51) 2279720; fax (51) 2279729; e-mail emb.islamabad@mfa.no; internet www.norway.org.pk; Ambassador AUD MARIT WIIG.

Oman: 53, St 48, F-8/4, POB 1194, Islamabad; tel. (51) 2254869; fax (51) 2255074; Ambassador MOHAAMAD BIN SAID BIN MOHAMMAD AL-LAWATI.

PAKISTAN

Philippines: House 20C, College Rd, F-7/2, Islamabad; tel. (51) 2824933; fax (51) 2653665; e-mail isdpe@isb.comsats.net.pk; Ambassador JAIME J. YAMBAO.

Poland: St 24, G-5/4, Diplomatic Enclave 2, POB 1032, Islamabad; tel. (51) 2279491; fax (51) 2825442; e-mail polemb@isb.comsats.net.pk; Ambassador WIESLAW KUCHAREK.

Portugal: 66, Main Margalla Rd, F-7/2, Islamabad; tel. (51) 2652491; fax (51) 2652492; e-mail portugal@isb.paknet.com.pk; Ambassador Dr ANTONIO JOSÉ DA CAMARARA ROMALHO ORTIGÃO.

Qatar: 20, University Rd, Diplomatic Enclave, G-5/4, Islamabad; tel. (51) 2270833; fax (51) 2270207; e-mail islamabad@mofa.gov.qa; Ambassador HAMAD ALI AL-HENZAB.

Romania: 13, St 88, G-6/3, Islamabad; tel. (51) 2826514; fax (51) 2826515; e-mail romania@isb.comsats.net.pk; Ambassador MIREEA HURMUZ.

Russia: Khayaban-e-Suhrawardy, Diplomatic Enclave, Ramna 4, Islamabad; tel. (51) 2278670; fax (51) 2826552; e-mail russia2@comsats.net.pk; internet www.pakistan.mid.ru; Ambassador SERGEY N. PESKOV.

Saudi Arabia: 14, Hill Rd, F-6/3, Islamabad; tel. (51) 2820156; fax (51) 2278816; Ambassador ALI S. AWADH ASSERI.

Somalia: 17, St 60, F-8/4, Islamabad; tel. (51) 2854733; fax (51) 2854733; Ambassador ABDISALAAM Haji AHMAD LIBAN.

South Africa: House No. 48, Margalla Rd, Khayaban-e-Iqbal, F-8/2, Islamabad; tel. (51) 2262354; fax (51) 2250114; e-mail xhosa@isb.comsats.net.pk; internet www.southafrica.org.pk; High Commissioner DANIEL JABULANI MAVIMBELA.

Spain: St 6, G-5, Diplomatic Enclave 1, POB 1144, Islamabad; tel. (51) 2088777; fax (51) 2088774; e-mail embspain@dsl.net.pk; Ambassador JOSÉ MARÍA ROBLES FRAGA.

Sri Lanka: 2C, St 55, F-6/4, Islamabad; tel. (51) 2828723; fax (51) 2828751; e-mail srilanka@isb.comsats.net.pk; High Commissioner WIJERATNE BANDARA DORAKUMBURKA.

Sudan: 1A, St 32, F-8/1, Islamabad; tel. (51) 2263926; fax (51) 2264404; e-mail sudanipk@isb.compol.com; Ambassador DAFAA ALLAH EL-HAJ ALI.

Sweden: 4, St 5, F-6/3, Islamabad; tel. (51) 2828712; fax (51) 2825284; e-mail ambassaden.islamabad@foreign.ministry.se; internet www.swedenabroad.se/Start____28997.aspx; Ambassador ANNA KARIN ENESTRÖM.

Switzerland: St 6, G-5/4, Diplomatic Enclave, POB 1073, Islamabad; tel. (51) 2272991; fax (51) 2279286; e-mail vertretung@isl.rep.admin.ch; Ambassador MARKUS PETER.

Syria: 30 Hill Rd, F-6/3, Islamabad; tel. (51) 2279470; fax (51) 2279472; Ambassador Dr RIAD ISMAT.

Tajikistan: House 90, Main Double Rd, F-10/1, Islamabad; tel. (51) 2293462; fax (51) 2299710; e-mail tajemb_islamabad@inbox.ru; Ambassador SAIDBEK B. SIADOV.

Thailand: 23, St 25, F-8/2, Islamabad; tel. (51) 5838245; fax (51) 5837422; e-mail thaiemb@dslplus.net.pk; internet www.mfa.go.th/web/1330.php?depid=231; Ambassador SUKHO PIROMNAM.

Tunisia: 221, St 21, E-7, Islamabad; tel. (51) 2652781; fax (51) 2653564; Ambassador SOUHIER DHAOUDI.

Turkey: St 1, Diplomatic Enclave 1, Islamabad; tel. (51) 8319800; fax (51) 2278752; e-mail turkemb@dsl.net.pk; internet www.turkishembassy.org.pk; Ambassador RAUF ENGIN SOYSAL.

Turkmenistan: House 22A, Nazim-Ud-Din Rd, F-7/1, Islamabad; tel. (51) 2274913; fax (51) 2278790; e-mail turkmen@isb.comsats.net.pk; Ambassador SAPOR BERDINIYAZOV.

Ukraine: 20, St 18, F-6/2, Islamabad; tel. (51) 2274732; fax (51) 2274643; e-mail ukremb@isb.compol.com; Ambassador Dr IGOR SERGIYOVYEH.

United Arab Emirates: Plot No. 1-22, Quaid-e-Azam University Rd, Diplomatic Enclave, POB 1111, Islamabad; tel. (51) 2279052; fax (51) 2279063; e-mail uaeempk@isb.paknet.pk; Ambassador ALI MOHAMMED ASH-SHAMSI.

United Kingdom: Diplomatic Enclave, Ramna 5, POB 1122, Islamabad; tel. (51) 2012000; fax (51) 2823439; e-mail bhcmedia@isb.comsats.net.pk; internet www.britainonline.org.pk; High Commissioner ROBERT BRINKLEY.

USA: Diplomatic Enclave, Ramna 5, POB 1048, Islamabad; tel. (51) 2080000; fax (51) 2276427; e-mail webmasterisb@state.gov; internet islamabad.usembassy.gov; Ambassador ANNE WOODS PATTERSON.

Uzbekistan: 2, St 21, F-8/3, Kohistan Rd, Islamabad; tel. (51) 2264746; fax (51) 2261739; e-mail uzbekemb@isb.comsats.net.pk; Ambassador OYBEK A. USMANOV.

Vietnam: House 10A, Street 31, F-6/1, Islamabad; tel. (51) 2850581; fax (51) 2850582; Chargé d'affaires a.i. NGUYEN QUANG THUC.

Yemen: 220, St 21, E-7, POB 1523, Islamabad 44000; tel. (51) 2653612; fax (51) 2653615; e-mail yemen22@isb.apollo.net.pk; Ambassador ABDUL ELAH MOHAMED HAJAR.

Judicial System

A constitutional amendment bill was passed in the National Assembly in October 1998 replacing the country's existing legal code with full Islamic *Shari'a*. The bill remained to be approved, however, by the Senate.

SUPREME COURT

Chief Justice: ABDUL HAMEED DOGAR.
Attorney-General: MALIK MUHAMMAD QAYYUM.

Federal Shari'a Court

Chief Justice: HAZIQ UL-KHAIRI.
Federal Ombudsman: Justice JAVED SADIQ MALIK.
Federal Tax Ombudsman: Justice MUNIR A. SHEIKH.

Religion

ISLAM

Islam is the state religion. The majority of the population are Sunni Muslims, while estimates of the Shi'a sect vary between 5% and 20% of the population. Only about 0.001% are of the Ahmadi sect.

CHRISTIANITY

About 3% of the population are Christians.

National Council of Churches in Pakistan: 32-B, Shahrah-e-Fatima Jinnah, POB 357, Lahore 54000; tel. (42) 7592167; fax (42) 7569782; e-mail nccp@lhr.comsats.net.pk; internet nccpakistan.org; f. 1949; four mem. bodies, 14 assoc. mems; Gen. Sec. VICTOR AZARIAH.

The Roman Catholic Church

For ecclesiastical purposes, Pakistan comprises two archdioceses, four dioceses and one apostolic prefecture. At 31 December 2005 there were an estimated 1,013,224 adherents in the country.

Bishops' Conference: Pakistan Catholic Bishops' ConferenceSt 55, F-8/4, Kaghan Rd, Islamabad 44000; tel. (42) 6366137; fax (42) 6368336; e-mail cbcp2000@isb.comsats.net.pk; internet www.pcbcsite.org; f. 1976; Pres. Most Rev. LAWRENCE J. SALDANHA (Archbishop of Lahore); Sec.-Gen. Rt Rev. ANTHONY LOBO (Bishop of Islamabad-Rawalpindi).

Archbishop of Karachi: Most Rev. EVARIST PINTO, St Patrick's Cathedral, Shahrah-e-Iraq, Karachi 74400; tel. (21) 7781533; fax (21) 7781532.

Archbishop of Lahore: Most Rev. LAWRENCE J. SALDANHA, Sacred Heart Cathedral, 1 Mian Mohammad Shafi Rd, POB 909, Lahore 54000; tel. (42) 6366137; fax (42) 6368336; e-mail abishop@lhr.comsats.net.pk; internet www.rcarchdioceselahore.org.pk.

Protestant Churches

Church of Pakistan: Moderator Rt Rev. Dr ALEXANDER JOHN MALIK (Bishop of Lahore), Bishopsbourne, Cathedral Close, The Mall, Lahore 54000; tel. (42) 7233560; fax (42) 7221270; e-mail bishop_lahore@hotmail.com; f. 1970 by union of the fmr Anglican Church in Pakistan, the United Methodist Church in Pakistan, the United Church in Pakistan (Scots Presbyterians) and the Pakistani Lutheran Church; eight dioceses; c. 700,000 mems (1993); Gen. Sec. HUMPHREY PETERS.

Presbyterian Church of Pakistan: Gujranwala Theological Seminary, Civil Lines, POB 13, Gujranwala; tel. (431) 259512; fax (431) 258314; e-mail kamil65@gjr.paknet.com.pk; f. 1961; c. 340,000 mems (1989); Moderator Rev. Dr ARTHUR JAMES; Sec. Rev. Dr MAGSOOD KAMIL.

Other denominations active in the country include the Associated Reformed Presbyterian Church and the Pakistan Salvation Army.

HINDUISM

Hindus comprise about 1.8% of the population.

BAHÁ'Í FAITH

National Spiritual Assembly: 56, H-8/4, Islamabad; tel. (51) 4444699; fax (51) 4444691; e-mail nsapakistan@cyber.net.pk; internet www.bahai.org; f. 1956; Gen. Sec. Prof. MEHRDAD YOSUF.

PAKISTAN
Directory

The Press

The Urdu press comprises almost 800 newspapers, with *Daily Jang, Daily Khabrain, Nawa-i-Waqt* and *Jasarat* among the most influential. The daily newspaper with the largest circulation is *Daily Jang*. Although the English-language press reaches only a small percentage of the population, it is influential in political, academic and professional circles. The four main press groups in Pakistan are Jang Publications (the *Daily Jang, The News*, the *Daily News* and the weekly *Akhbar-e-Jehan*), the Dawn or Herald Group (the *Dawn*, and the monthly *Herald* and *Spider*), the Khabrain Group (the *Daily Khabrain* and the English language daily *The Post*) and the Nawa-i-Waqt Group (the *Nawa-i-Waqt, The Nation* and the weekly *Family*).

PRINCIPAL DAILIES

Islamabad

Al-Akhbar: Al-Akhbar House, Markaz, G-8, Islamabad; tel. (51) 852023; fax (51) 256522; Urdu; also publ. in Muzaffarabad; Editor GHULAM AKBAR.

Daily Khabrain: 12 Lawrence Rd, Lahore; tel. (42) 111-55-88-55; fax (42) 6314658; e-mail editor1@khabrain.com; internet www.khabrain.com; Urdu; Editor and Proprietor ZIA SHAHID.

The Nation: Nawa-i-Waqt House, Zero Point, Islamabad; tel. (51) 277631; fax (51) 278353; e-mail editor@nation.com.pk; internet www.nation.com.pk; English; Editor ARIF NIZAMI; circ. 15,000.

Pakistan Observer: Al-Akhbar House, Markaz, G-8, Islamabad 44870; tel. (51) 2852027; fax (51) 2262258; e-mail observer@comsats.net.pk; internet www.pakobserver.net; f. 1988; English; independent; Editor-in-Chief ZAHID MALIK.

Karachi

Aghaz: 11 Japan Mansion, Preedy St, Sadar, Karachi 74400; tel. (21) 2720228; fax (21) 2722125; e-mail ex101@hotmail.com; internet www.aghaz.com; f. 1962; evening; Urdu; Chief Editor MOHAMMAD ANWAR FAROOQI; circ. 65,000.

Amn: Amn House, Maulana Deen Muhammad Wafai Rd, opposite NED City Campus, nr Pakistan Chowk, Karachi; tel. (21) 2634451; fax (21) 2634454; e-mail amn@cyber.net.pk; Urdu; Editor AJMAL DEHLVI.

Awami Awaz: 2nd Floor, New Central Block No. 2, Hockey Stadium, Liaquat Barracks, off Shahrah-e-Faisal, Karachi; tel. (21) 5672949; fax (21) 5672946; e-mail awamiawaz@hotmail.com; Man. Editor Dr KHAIR MUHAMMAD JUNO.

Barsat: 246/D-6, PECHS, Karachi; tel. (21) 4535228; fax (21) 4535227; Editor MUHAMMAD SALEEM DAUDPOTA.

Beopar: 205 Alfalah Court, I. I. Chundrigar Rd, Karachi; tel. (21) 2636442; fax (21) 2630784; e-mail beopar@yahoo.com.

Business Recorder: Recorder House, 53 Business Recorder Rd, Karachi 74550; tel. (21) 2250071; fax (21) 2222866; e-mail ed.khi@br-mail.com; internet www.brecorder.com; f. 1965; English; Editor WAMIQ A. ZUBERI; Editor-in-Chief M. A. ZUBERI.

Daily Awam: HQ Printing House, I. I. Chundrigar Rd, POB 52, Karachi; tel. (21) 2637111; fax (21) 2636066; f. 1994; evening; Urdu; Editor-in-Chief Mir SHAKIL-UR-RAHMAN.

Daily Beopar: 205 Alfalah Court, I. I. Chundrigar Rd, Karachi; tel. (21) 2636442; fax (21) 2630784; Urdu; Man. Editor YOUNUS RIAZ.

Daily Express: 5 Expressway, off Korangi Rd, Karachi; tel. (21) 5800051-6; fax (21) 58000510; Urdu; Editor TAHIR NAJMI.

Daily Intekhab: Liaison Office, 3rd Floor, Mashhoor Mahal Bldg, Kucha Haji Usman, off I. I. Chundrigar Rd, Karachi; tel. (21) 2634518; fax (21) 2631092; e-mail intekhab@comsats.net.pk; internet www.dailyintekhab.com; Urdu; also publ. from Hub (Balochistan) and Quetta; Man. Editor NARGIS BALOCH; Publr and Exec. Editor ANWAR SAJIDI.

Daily Jang: HQ Printing House, I. I. Chundrigar Rd, POB 52, Karachi; tel. (21) 2637111; fax (21) 2634395; e-mail jangkarachi@janggroup.com.pk; internet www.jang.com.pk; f. 1940; morning; Urdu; also publ. in Quetta, Rawalpindi, Lahore and London; Editor-in-Chief Mir SHAKIL-UR-RAHMAN; combined circ. 750,000.

Daily Khabar: A-8 Sheraton Centre, F. B. Area, Karachi; tel. (21) 210059; Urdu; Exec. Editor FAROOQ PARACHA; Editor and Publr SAEED ALI HAMEED.

Daily Mohasaba: Imperial Hotel, M. T. Khan Rd, Karachi; tel. (21) 519448; Urdu; Editor TALIB TURABI.

Daily Naya Akhbar: Zia Shahid Printer and Publisher, Muzammil Press, 1301, Mehmoodabad No. 6, Masjid-e-Awais Qarni, Block 7, Karachi; tel. (21) 111-55-88-55; fax (21) 5382271; CEO ZIA SHAHID; Editor AMTNAN SHAHID.

Daily News: Al-Rahman Bldg, I. I. Chundrigar Rd, Karachi; tel. (21) 2637111; fax (21) 2634395; f. 1962; evening; English; Editor S. M. FAZIL; circ. 50,000.

Daily Public: Falak Printing Press, 191 Altaf Hussain Rd, New Challi, Karachi; tel. (21) 5687522; Man. Editor INQUILAB MATRI; Editor ANWAR SANROY.

Daily Sindh Sujag: Suite 414, 6th Floor, Amber Medical Centre, M. A. Jinnah Rd, Karachi; tel. (21) 2700252; fax (21) 2700249; e-mail sindhsujag786@yahoo.com; Sindhi; political; Editor NASIR DAD BALOCH.

Daily Special: Ahbab Printers, Beauty House, nr Regal Chowk, Abdullah Haroon Rd, Sadar, Karachi; tel. (21) 7771655; fax (21) 7722776; Urdu; Editor MOHAMMAD AT-TAYYAB.

Daily Times: Plot No. SR 5/12/1, 2nd Floor, Nelson Chamber, I. I. Chundrigar Rd, Karachi; tel. (21) 2213822; fax (21) 2213874; e-mail sarfaraz@dailytimes.com.pk; internet www.dailytimes.com.pk; Editor NAJAM SETHI.

Dawn: Haroon House, Dr Ziauddin Ahmed Rd, POB 3740, Karachi 74200; tel. (21) 111444777; fax (21) 5683801; e-mail editor@dawn.com; internet www.dawn.com; f. 1947; English; also publ. from Islamabad, Rawalpindi and Lahore; Chief Exec. HAMEED HAROON; Editor ABBAS NASIR; circ. 110,000 (weekdays), 125,000 (Sundays).

Deyanet: 4th Floor, Al Warid Centre, off I. I. Chundrigar Rd, Karachi; tel. (21) 2631556; fax (21) 2631888; Urdu; also publ. in Sukkur and Islamabad; Editor NAJMUDDIN SHAIKH.

The Finance: 903–905 Uni Towers, I. I. Chundrigar Rd, Karachi; tel. (21) 2411665; fax (21) 2422560; e-mail tfinance@super.net.pk; English; Chief Editor S. H. SHAH.

Financial Post: Bldg No. 106/C, 11 Commercial St, Phase II, Extension, Defence Housing Authority, Karachi; tel. (21) 5381626; fax (21) 5802760; e-mail fpost@gerrys.net; internet www.dailyfpost.com; f. 1994; English; Chief Editor and CEO QUDSIA K. KHAN; Publr WAJID JAWAD.

Hilal-e-Pakistan: Court View Bldg, 2nd Floor, M. A. Jinnah Rd, POB 3737, Karachi 74200; tel. (21) 2624997; fax (21) 2624996; Sindhi; Editor MOHAMMAD IQBAL DAL.

Jago: Karachi; tel. (21) 2635544; fax (21) 2628137; f. 1990; Sindhi; political; Editor AGHA SALEEM.

Janbaz: 9th Floor, Uni Tower, I. I. Chundrigar Rd, Karachi; tel. (21) 2411665; fax (21) 2422560; Editor ALI AKHBAR RIZVI.

Jasarat: 3rd Floor, Syed House, I. I. Chundrigar Rd, Karachi 74200; tel. (21) 2630391; fax (21) 2629344; e-mail jasarat@cyber.net.pk; f. 1970; Urdu; Editor ATHAR HASHMI; circ. 50,000.

Jurat: Jurat House, off I. I. Chundrigar Rd, Karachi; tel. (21) 2637641-4; fax (21) 2637640; Editor MUKHTAR AAQIL.

The Leader: Block 5, 609, Clifton Centre, Clifton, Karachi 75600; tel. (21) 5820801; fax (21) 5872206; e-mail info@theleader.com.pk; f. 1958; English; independent; Man. Editor MUNIR M. LADHA; circ. 7,000.

Mazdur: Spencer Bldg, I. I. Chundrigar Rd, Karachi 2; f. 1984; Urdu; Editor MOHAMMAD ANWAR BIN ABBAS.

Millat: 3rd Floor, Saify Market, Shahrah-e-Liaquat, New Challi, Karachi; tel. (21) 2219022; fax (21) 2211764; internet www.millat.com; f. 1946; Gujarati; independent; Editor INQUILAB MATRI; circ. 22,550.

Mohasib: Karachi; fax (21) 2632763; Urdu; also publ. from Abbotabad; Chief Editor ZAFAR MAJAZI; Editor NAEEM AHMAD.

The Nation: Block-I, Hockey Stadium, off Khayaban-e-Shamsher, Phase V, Defence Housing Authority, Karachi; tel. (21) 5846622; fax (21) 5848892; e-mail editor@nation.com.pk; internet www.nation.com.pk; English; Editor ARIF NIZAMI.

The News International: Al-Rahman Bldg, I. I. Chundrigar Rd, POB 52, Karachi; tel. (21) 2630611; fax (21) 2636976; f. 1990; English; also publ. from Lahore and Rawalpindi/Islamabad; Editor-in-Chief Mir SHAKIL-UR-RAHMAN; Sr Editor HUSUNIA AHMAD.

Qaum (Nation): Karachi; Urdu; Editor and Publr MUSHTAQUE SOHAIL; Man. Editor MAMNOONUR REHMAN.

Qaumi Akhbar: 14 Ramzan Mansion, Dr Bilmoria St, off I. I. Chundrigar Rd, Karachi; tel. (21) 2633381; fax (21) 2635774; f. 1988; Urdu; offices in Islamabad; Editor ILYAS SHAKIR.

Roznama Special: Falak Printing Press, 191 Altaf Hussain Rd, Karachi; tel. (21) 5687522; fax (21) 5687579; Publr and Man. Editor INQUILAB MATRI; Editor ANWAR SEN ROY.

Savera: 108 Adam Arcade, Shaheed-e-Millat Rd, Karachi; tel. (21) 419616; Urdu; Editor RUKHSANA SAHAM MIRZA.

Sindh Tribune: No. 246-D/6, PECHS, Karachi; tel. (21) 4535227; fax (21) 4332680; English; political; Editor YOUSUF SHAHEEN.

The Times of Karachi: Al-Falah Chambers, 9th Floor, Abdullah Haroon Rd, Karachi; tel. (21) 7727740; e-mail iqbalmir@yahoo.com; evening; English; independent; city news; Editor Mir IQBAL AZIZ.

Ummat: Room Nos 1–3, VIP Block IV, Hockey Club of Pakistan Stadium, Liaquat Barracks, Karachi; tel. (21) 5655270; fax (21) 5655275; Editor NASEER HASHMI.

PAKISTAN

Lahore

Daily Asas: 15/26, Davis Rd, Lahore; tel. (42) 6302823; fax (42) 6317096; e-mail info@dailyasas.com.pk; internet www.dailyasas.com.pk.

Daily Pakistan: 41 Jail Rd, Lahore; tel. (42) 7576301; fax (42) 7586251; internet www.daily-pakistan.com; f. 1990; Urdu; Chief Editor MUJIBUR RAHMAN SHAMI.

Daily Times: Media Times (Pvt) Ltd, 41-N, Industrial Area, Gulberg II, Lahore; tel. (42) 5878614; fax (42) 5878620; e-mail editor@dailytimes.com.pk; Editor NAJAM SETHI.

Daily Wifaq: 6A Warris Rd, Lahore; tel. (42) 6367467; e-mail dailywiqaf@hotmail.com; Urdu; also publ. in Rawalpindi, Sargodha and Rahimyar Khan; Editor MAZHAR WAQAR; circ. 20,000.

Mahgribi Pakistan: Lahore; tel. (42) 53490; Urdu; also publ. in Bahawalpur and Sukkur; Editor M. SHAFAAT.

The Nation: NIPCO House, 4 Sharah-e-Fatima Jinnah, POB 1815, Lahore 54000; tel. (42) 6367580; fax (42) 6367005; e-mail editor@nation.com.pk; internet www.nation.com.pk; f. 1986; English; Chair. MAJEED NIZAMI; Editor ARIF NIZAMI; circ. 52,000.

Nawa-i-Waqt (Voice of the Time): 4 Sharah-e-Fatima Jinnah, Lahore 54000; tel. (42) 6367551; fax (42) 6367583; internet www.nawaiwaqt.com.pk; f. 1940; English, Urdu; also publ. edns in Karachi, Islamabad and Multan; Editor MAJID NIZAMI; combined circ. 560,000.

The Sun International: 15-L, Gulberg III, Ferozepur Rd, Lahore; tel. (42) 5883540; fax (42) 5839951; Editor MAHMOOD SADIQ.

Tijarat: 14 Abbot Rd, opp. Nishat Cinema, Lahore; Urdu; Editor JAMIL ATHAR.

Rawalpindi

Daily Jang: Murree Rd, Rawalpindi; internet www.jang.com.pk; f. 1940; also publ. in Quetta, Karachi, Lahore and London; Urdu; independent; Editor Mir JAVED REHMAN; circ. (Rawalpindi) 65,000.

Daily Wifaq: Mohallah Waris Khan 604, Murree Rd, Rawalpindi; tel. (51) 553979; e-mail dailywifaq@hotmail.com; f. 1959; also publ. in Lahore, Sargodha and Rahimyar Khan; Urdu; Editor MUSTAFA SADIQ.

The News: Al-Rehman Bldg, Murree Rd, Rawalpindi; tel. (51) 5962444; fax (51) 5962269; e-mail thenews@isb.comsats.net.pk; internet www.jang-group.com; f. 1991; also publ. in Lahore and Karachi; English; independent; Chief Editor Mir SHAKIL-UR-RAHMAN.

Other Towns

Aftab: Opposite WASA Office, Bagh Langay Khan Rd, Multan; tel. (61) 4546080; fax (61) 4786083; e-mail aftabmultan@aftabdaily.com; Sindhi; Editor ASAD MUMTAZ SEYAL.

Al Falah: Al Falah House, Al Falah Bazar, nr State Life Bldg, Mall Rd, Peshawar; tel. (91) 5853694; f. 1939; Urdu and Pashtu; Editor SYED BADRUDDIN SHAH.

Al-Jamiat-e-Sarhad: Kocha Gilania Chakagali, Karimpura Bazar, Peshawar; tel. (91) 2567757; e-mail sagha@brain.net.pk; f. 1941; Urdu and Pashtu; Propr and Chief Editor S. M. HASSAN GILANI.

Balochistan Times: Jinnah Rd, Quetta; Editor SYED FASIH IQBAL.

Basharat: Peshawar; Urdu; general; also publ. in Islamabad; Chief Editor ANWAR-UL-HAQ; Editor KHALID ATHER.

Daily Awaz: Peshawar; political; Man. Editor ALI RAZA MALIK.

Daily Business Report: Railway Rd, Faisalabad; tel. (41) 2642131; fax (41) 2621207; f. 1948; Editor ABDUL RASHID GHAZI; circ. 26,000.

Daily Hewad: 32 Stadium Rd, Peshawar; tel. (521) 270501; Pashtu; Editor-in-Chief REHMAN SHAH AFRIDI.

Daily Ibrat Hyderabad: Ibrat Building, Gadi Khata, Hyderabad; e-mail ibrat@yahoo.com; internet www.dailyibrat.com; Sindhi; Man. Editor Qazi ASAD ABID.

Daily Khadim-e-Waten: B-2, Civil Lines, Hyderabad; Editor MUSHATAQ AHMAD.

Daily Rehber: 17-B East Trust Colony, Bahawalpur; tel. (621) 884664; fax (621) 874032; e-mail rehberbwp@yahoo.co.uk; f. 1951; Urdu; Chief Editor AKHTER HUSSAIN ANJUM; circ. 250,000.

Daily Sarwan: 11-EGOR Colony, Hyderabad; tel. (221) 781382; Sindhi; Chief Editor GHULAM HUSSAIN.

Daily Shabaz: Peshawar; tel. (521) 220188; fax (521) 216483; Urdu; organ of the Awami National Party; Chief Editor Begum NASEEM WALI KHAN.

Frontier Post: 32 Stadium Rd, Peshawar; tel. (521) 79174; fax (521) 76575; e-mail editor@frontierpost.com.pk; internet www.frontierpost.com.pk; f. 1985; English; left-wing; also publ. in Lahore; closed down temporarily in January 2001, reopened in June; Editor-in-Chief REHMAT SHAH AFRIDI; Editor MUZAFFAR SHAH AFRIDI.

Jihad: 15A Islamia Club Bldg, Khyber Bazar, Peshawar; tel. (521) 210522; e-mail jehad@pes.comsats.net.pk; also publ. in Karachi, Rawalpindi, Islamabad and Lahore; Editor SHARIF FAROOQ.

Kaleem: Shahi Bazar Thalla, POB 88, Sukkur; tel. (71) 22086; fax (71) 22087; Urdu; Editor SHAHID MEHR SHAMSI.

Kavish: Sindh Printing and Publishing House, Civil Lines, POB 43, Hyderabad; Chief Editor MUHAMMAD AYUB QAZI; Publr/Editor ASLAM A. QAZI.

Mashriq: Quetta; Chief Editor AZIZ MAZHAR.

Nawai Asma'n: Mubarak Ali Shah Rd, Hyderabad; tel. and fax (221) 21925; Urdu, Sindhi and Pashtu; Chief Editor DOST MUHAMMAD.

The News: Qaumi Printing Press, Peshawar; English; Editor KHURSHID AHMAD.

Punjab News: Iftikhar Heights, Aminpur Bazar, POB 419, Faisalabad; tel. (41) 633102; fax (41) 615731; e-mail imranlateef1@hotmail.com; internet www.punjabnews.com.pk; f. 1968; Chief Editor and Publr Sheikh Sultan MAHMOOD; circ. 10,000.

Sarhad: New Gate, Peshawar.

Sindh Guardian: Tulsi Das Rd, POB 300, Hyderabad; tel. and fax (221) 21926; English; Chief Editor DOST MUHAMMAD.

Sindh News: Garikhata, Hyderabad; tel. (221) 20793; fax (221) 781867; Editor Kazi SAEED AKBER.

Sindh Observer: POB 43, Garikhata, Hyderabad; tel. (221) 27302; English; Editor ASLAM AKBER KAZI.

Sindhu: Popular Printers, Ibrat Bldg, Garhhi Khata, Hyderabad; tel. (221) 783571; fax (221) 783570; Sindhi; political.

Watan: 10 Nazar Bagh Flat, Peshawar.

Zamana: Jinnah Rd, Quetta; tel. (81) 71217; Urdu; Editor SYED FASIH IQBAL; circ. 5,000.

SELECTED WEEKLIES

Akhbar-e-Jehan: Printing House, off I. I. Chundrigar Rd, Karachi; tel. (21) 2634368; fax (21) 2635693; e-mail editor-in-chief@akhbar-e-jehan.com; internet www.akhbar-e-jehan.com; f. 1967; Urdu; independent; illustrated family magazine; Editor-in-Chief Mir JAVED RAHMAN; circ. 285,000.

Amal: Shah Qabool Colony, POB 185, Peshawar; tel. (91) 5704673; e-mail maab_kaifi@hotmail.com; f. 1958; Urdu, Pashtu and English; Chief Editor F. M. ZAFAR KAIFI; Publr MUNAZIMA MAAB KAIFI.

Badban: Nai Zindagi Publications, Rana Chambers, Old Anarkali, Lahore; Editor MUJIBUR REHMAN SHAMI.

Chatan: Chatan Bldg, 88 McLeod Rd, Lahore; tel. (42) 6311336; fax (42) 6374690; f. 1948; Urdu; Editor MASUD SHORISH.

Family Magazine: 4 Shara-i-Fatima Jinnah, Lahore 54000; tel. (42) 6367551; fax (42) 6367583; circ. 100,000.

The Friday Times: 72-F. C. C. Gulberg IV, Lahore; tel. (42) 5673510; fax (42) 5751025; e-mail tft@lhr.comsats.net.pk; internet www.thefridaytimes.com; independent; Editor/Owner NAJAM SETHI.

Hilal: Hilal Rd, Rawalpindi 46000; tel. (51) 56134605; fax (51) 565017; f. 1951; Friday; Urdu; illustrated armed forces; Editor MUMTAZ IQBAL MALIK; circ. 90,000.

Insaf: P/929, Banni, Rawalpindi 46000; tel. and fax (51) 5550903; e-mail insafrwp@isb.paknet.com.pk; f. 1955; Editor Mir WAQAR AZIZ.

Lahore: Galaxy Law Chambers, 1st Floor, Room 1, Turner Rd, Lahore 5; f. 1952; Editor SAQIB ZEERVI; circ. 8,500.

Mahwar: D23, Block H, North Nazimabad, Karachi; Editor SHAHIDA NAFIS SIDDIQI.

Memaar-i-Nao: 39 KMC Bldg, Leamarket, Karachi; Urdu; labour magazine; Editor M. M. MUBASIR.

The Muslim World: 49-B, Block 8, Gulshan-e-Iqbal, Karachi 75300; POB 5030, Karachi 74000; tel. (21) 4960738; fax (21) 466878; English; current affairs.

Nairang Khayal: 8 Mohammadi Market, Rawalpindi; f. 1924; Urdu; Chief Editor Sultan RASHK.

Nida-i-Millat: 4 Sharah-e-Fatima Jinnah, Lahore 54000.

Noor Jehan Weekly: 32A National Auto Plaza, POB 8833, Karachi 74400; tel. and fax (21) 7723946; f. 1948; Urdu; film journal; Editor KHALID CHAWLA.

Pak Kashmir: Pak Kashmir Office, Soikarno Chowk, Liaquat Rd, Rawalpindi; tel. (51) 74845; f. 1951; Urdu; Editor MUHAMMED FAYYAZ ABBAZI.

Pakistan and Gulf Economist: 1st Floor, 20-C, Sunset Lane 9, Phase 2 Extension, D. H. A., Karachi 75500; tel. (21) 5883967; fax (21) 5883295; e-mail information@pakistaneconomist.com; internet www.pakistaneconomist.com; f. 1960; English; Editor ALI HAIDER GOKAL; circ. 30,000.

Parsi Sansar and Loke Sevak: 8 Mehrabad, 5 McNeil Rd, Karachi 75530; tel. and fax (21) 5656217; e-mail organ@cyber.net.pk; f. 1909; English and Gujarati; Editor MEHERJI P. DASTUR.

PAKISTAN

Parwaz: Madina Office, Bahawalpur; Urdu; Editor MUSTAQ AHMED.

Qallandar: Peshawar; f. 1950; Urdu; Editor M. A. K. SHERWANI.

Quetta Times: Albert Press, Jinnah Rd, Quetta; f. 1924; English; Editor S. RUSTOMJI; circ. 4,000.

Shahab-e-Saqib: Shahab Saqib Rd, Maulana St, Peshawar; f. 1950; Urdu; Editor S. M. RIZVI.

Takbeer: A-1, 3rd Floor, 'Namco Centre', Campbell St, Karachi 74200; tel. (21) 2626613; fax (21) 2627742; e-mail irfanfaruqi@usa.com; f. 1984; Urdu; Sr. Exec. IRFAN KALIM FAROOQ; circ. 70,000.

Tarjaman-i-Sarhad: Peshawar; Urdu and Pashtu; Editor MOHAMMAD SHAFI SABIR.

Times of Kashmir: P/929, Banni, Rawalpindi 46000; tel. (51) 5550903; fax (51) 4411348; e-mail insafrwp@isb.paknet.com.pk; f. 1982; English; Editor Mir IQBAL AZIZ.

Ufaq: 44H, Block No. 2, PECHS, Karachi; tel. (21) 437992; f. 1978; Editor WAHAJUDDIN CHISHTI; circ. 2,000.

SELECTED PERIODICALS

Aadab Arz: 190 N. Ghazali Rd, Saman Abad, Lahore 54500; tel. (42) 7582449; monthly; Editor KHALID BIN HAMID.

Aalami Digest: B-1, Momin Sq., Rashid Minhas Rd, Gulshan-e-Iqbal, Karachi; monthly; Urdu; Editor ZAHEDA HINA.

Akhbar-e-Watan: 68-C, 13th Commercial St, Phase-II, Extension Defence, Karachi; tel. (21) 5886071; fax (21) 5890179; e-mail akhbarewatan@hotmail.com; f. 1977; monthly; Urdu; cricket; Man. Editor MUNIR HUSSAIN; circ. 63,000.

Albalagh Darul Uloom: Korangi Rd, Karachi; monthly; Editor MOHAMMED TAQI USMANI.

Al-Ma'arif: Institute of Islamic Culture, Club Rd, Lahore 54000; tel. (42) 6363127; f. 1950; quarterly; Urdu; Dir and Editor-in-Chief Dr RASHID AHMAD JALLANDHRI.

Anchal: 24 Saeed Mansion, I. I. Chundrigar Rd, Karachi; monthly.

Archi Times: Ghafoor Chambers, 7th Floor, Abdullah Haroon Rd, Karachi; tel. (21) 7772397; fax (21) 7772417; e-mail archtime@cyberaccess.com.pk; f. 1986; monthly; English; architecture; Editor MUJTABA HUSSAIN.

Architecture and Interiors: B-34, Block 15, Gulshan-e-Iqbal, Karachi; tel. (21) 4977652; fax (21) 4967656; e-mail aplusi@cyberaccess.com.pk; internet www.archpresspk.com; f. 2001; quarterly; English; Editor MUTJUBA HUSSAIN; Man. Editor MURTUZA SHIKOH.

Asia Travel News: 101 Muhammadi House, I. I. Chundrigar Rd, Karachi 74000; tel. (21) 2424837; fax (21) 2420797; fortnightly; travel trade, tourism and hospitality industry; Editor JAVED MUSHTAQ.

Auto Times: 5 S. J. Kayani Shaheed Rd, off Garden Rd, Karachi; tel. (21) 713595; fortnightly; English; Editor MUHAMMAD SHAHZAD.

Bachoon Ka Risala: 108–110 Adam Arcade, Shaheed-e-Millat Rd, Karachi; tel. (21) 419616; monthly; Urdu; Editor RUKHSANA SEHAM MIRZA.

Bagh: 777/18 Federal B Area, POB 485, Karachi; tel. (21) 449662; monthly; Urdu; Editor RAHIL IQBAL.

Bayyenat: Jamia Uloom-e-Islamia, Binnori Town, Karachi 74800; tel. (21) 4927233; f. 1962; monthly; Urdu; religious and social issues.

Beauty: Plot No. 4-C, 14th Commercial St, Defence Housing Authority, Phase II Extension, Karachi; tel. (21) 5805391; fax (21) 5896269; e-mail rmansuri@fascom.com; f. 2000; bi-monthly; English; Chief Editor RIAZ AHMED MANSURI.

Beemakar (Insurer): 58 Press Chambers, I. I. Chundrigar Rd, Karachi; e-mail tahakn@cyber.net.pk; f. 1990; monthly; Urdu; Man. Editor SHAMSHAD AHMAD; Editor AYAZ KHAN.

Chand: 190 N. Ghazali Rd, Saman Abad, Lahore 54500; tel. (42) 7582449; monthly; Editor MASOOD HAMID.

The Cricketer: Plot No. 4-C, 14th Commercial St, Defence Housing Authority, Phase II Extension, Karachi; tel. (21) 5805391; fax (21) 5896269; e-mail rmansuri@fascom.com; f. 1972; monthly; English/Urdu; Chief Editor RIAZ AHMED MANSURI.

Dastarkhuan: Plot No. 4-C, 14th Commercial St, Defence Housing Authority, Phase II Extension, Karachi; tel. (21) 5805391; fax (21) 5896269; e-mail rmansuri@fascom.com; f. 1998; bi-monthly; Urdu; Chief Editor RIAZ AHMED MANSURI.

Defence Journal: 16B, 7th Central St, Defence Housing Authority, POB 12234, Karachi 75500; tel. (21) 5894074; fax (21) 571710; f. 1975; monthly; English; Editor-in-Chief IKRAM SEHGAL; circ. 10,000.

Dentist: 70/7, Nazimabad No. 3, Karachi 18; f. 1984; monthly; English and Urdu; Editor NAEEMULLAH HUSAIN.

Dosheeza: 108–110 Adam Arcade, Shaheed-e-Millat Rd, Karachi; tel. (21) 4930470; fax (21) 4934369; monthly; Urdu; Editor RUKHSANA SEHAM MIRZA.

Duniya-e-Tibb: Eveready Chambers, 2nd Floor, Mohd Bin Qasim Rd, off I. I. Chundrigar Rd, POB 1385, Karachi 1; tel. (21) 2630985; fax (21) 2637624; e-mail mcm@digicom.net.pk; f. 1986; monthly; Urdu; modern and Asian medicine; Editor QUTUBUDDIN; circ. 12,000.

Economic Review: Al-Masiha, 3rd Floor, 47 Abdullah Haroon Rd, POB 7843, Karachi 74400; tel. (21) 7728963; fax (21) 7728957; f. 1969; monthly; economic, industrial and investment research; Editor AHMAD MUHAMMAD KHAN.

Engineering Horizons: 13-J, Markaz F-7, Islamabad 44000; tel. (51) 2650174; fax (51) 2650943; e-mail asad@imtiaz-faiz.com; internet www.engghorizons.com; f. 1988; monthly; English; Chief Editor IMTIAZ SHEIKH.

Engineering Review: 305 Spotlit Chambers, Dr Billimoria St, off I. I. Chundrigar Rd, POB 807, Karachi 74200; tel. (21) 2632567; fax (21) 2639378; e-mail engineeringreview@yahoo.com; internet www.engineeringreview.com.pk; f. 1975; fortnightly; English; circ. 5,000.

Film Asia: 68-C, 13th Commercial St, Phase-II, Extension Defence, Karachi; tel. (21) 5886071; fax (21) 5890179; e-mail akhbarewatan@hotmail.com; f. 1973; monthly; film, television, fashion, art and culture; Man. Editor MUNIR HUSSAIN; circ. 38,000.

Good Food: Plot No. 4-C, 14th Commercial St, Defence Housing Authority, Phase II Extension, Karachi; tel. (21) 5805391; fax (21) 5896269; e-mail rmansuri@fascom.com; f. 1997; bi-monthly; English; Chief Editor RIAZ AHMED MANSURI.

Hamdard-i-Sehat: Institute of Health and Tibbi Research, Hamdard Foundation Pakistan, Nazimabad, Karachi 74600; tel. (21) 6616001; fax (21) 6611755; e-mail hamdardfoundation@hamdard.com.pk; f. 1933; monthly; Urdu; Editor-in-Chief SADIA RASHID; circ. 13,000.

Hamdard Islamicus: Hamdard Foundation Pakistan, Nazimabad, Karachi 74600; tel. (21) 6620949-54; fax (21) 6611755; e-mail hamdardfoundation@hamdard.com.pk; internet hamdardfoundation.org; f. 1978; quarterly; English; Editor-in-Chief SADIA RASHID; Dir-Gen. FURQAN AHMAD SHAMSI; circ. 750.

Hamdard Medicus: Hamdard Foundation Pakistan, Nazimabad, Karachi 74600; tel. (21) 6620949-54; fax (21) 6611755; e-mail hamdardfoundation@hamdard.com.pk; internet hamdardfoundation.org; f. 1957; quarterly; English; Editor-in-Chief SADIA RASHID; Dir-Gen. FURQAN AHMAD SHAMSI; circ. 1,000.

Hamdard Naunehal: Hamdard Foundation Pakistan, Nazimabad, Karachi 74600; tel. (21) 6620949-54; fax (21) 6611755; e-mail hamdardfoundation@hamdard.com.pk; internet hamdardfoundation.org; f. 1952; monthly; Urdu; Editor MASOOD AHMAD BARAKATI; Dir-Gen. FURQAN AHMAD SHAMSI; circ. 34,000.

The Herald: Haroon House, Dr Ziauddin Ahmed Rd, Karachi 74200; tel. (21) 5670001; fax (21) 5687221; e-mail saquib.herald@dawn.com; f. 1970; monthly; English; Editor SAQUIB HANIF; circ. 38,000.

Hikayat: 26 Patiala Ground, Link McLeod Rd, Lahore; monthly; Editor SHAHID JAMIL; circ. 25,000.

Honhar-e-Pakistan: 56 Aurangzeb Market, Karachi; monthly; Editor MAZHAR YUSAFZAI.

Hoor: Hoor St, Lahore; monthly; Editor KHULA RABIA.

Islami Jumhuria: Laj Rd, Old Anarkali, Lahore; monthly; Editor NAZIR TARIQ.

Islamic Studies: Islamic Research Institute, Faisal Masjid Campus, POB 1035, Islamabad 44000; tel. (51) 850751; fax (51) 250821; e-mail amzia555@apollo.net.pk; f. 1962; quarterly; English, Urdu (Fikro-Nazar) and Arabic (Al Dirasat al-Islamiyyah) edns; Islamic literature, religion, history, geography, language and the arts; Editor Dr ZAFAR ISHAQ ANSARI (acting); circ. 3,000.

Jamal: Institute of Islamic Culture, 2 Club Rd, Lahore 54000; tel. (42) 6363127; f. 1950; annual; English; Dir and Editor-in-Chief Dr JULUNDHRI RASHEED.

Journal of the Pakistan Historical Society: c/o Hamdard Foundation, Nazimabad, Karachi 74600; tel. (21) 6616001; fax (21) 6611755; e-mail hamdard@khi.paknet.com.pk; f. 1953; quarterly; English; Editor Dr ANSAR ZAHID KHAN; circ. 700.

Khel-Ke-Duniya: 6/13 Alyusaf Chamber, POB 340, Karachi; tel. (21) 216888.

Khwateen Digest: Urdu Bazar, M. A. Jinnah Rd, Karachi; monthly; Urdu; Editor MAHMUD RIAZ.

Kiran: 37 Urdu Bazar, M. A. Jinnah Rd, Karachi; tel. (21) 216606; Editor MAHMUD BABAR FAISAL.

Leather News: Iftikhar Chambers, opp. UNI Plaza, Altaf Hussain Rd, POB 4323, Karachi 74000; fax (21) 2631545; f. 1989; Editor ABDUL RAFAY SIDDIQI.

Medical Variety: 108–110 Adam Arcade, Shaheed-e-Millat Rd, Karachi; tel. (21) 419616; monthly; English; Editor RUKHSANA SEHAM MIRZA.

PAKISTAN

Muslim World Business: 20 Sasi Arcade, 4th Floor, Main Clifton Rd, POB 10417, Karachi 6; tel. (21) 534870; f. 1989; monthly; English; political and business; Editor-in-Chief MUZAFFAR HASSAN.

Naey-Ufaq: 24 Saeed Mansion, I. I. Chundrigar Rd, Karachi; fortnightly.

NGM Communication: POB 3540, Post Mall, Gulberg, Lahore 54660; tel. (42) 5879524; e-mail ghufran6@yahoo.com; internet www.geocities.com/anjeeam; f. 1980; owned by Nizam Nizami; English; lists newly released Pakistani publications on the internet; updated weekly; Editor GHUFRAN NIZAMI.

Pakistan Journal of Applied Economics: Applied Economics Research Centre, University of Karachi, POB 8403, Karachi 75270; tel. (21) 9243168; fax (21) 4829730; e-mail pjae@aerc.edu.pk; internet www.aerc.edu.pk; twice a year; Editor Prof. Dr SHAHIDA WIZARAT.

Pakistan Journal of Scientific and Industrial Research: Pakistan Council of Scientific and Industrial Research, Scientific Information Centre, PCSIR Laboratories Campus, off University Rd, Karachi 75280; tel. (21) 4651740; fax (21) 4651738; e-mail pcsir@cyber.net.pk; f. 1958; bi-monthly; English; Exec. Editor Dr KANIZ FIZZA AZHAR; circ. 1,000.

Pakistan Management Review: Pakistan Institute of Management, Management House, Shahrah Iran, Clifton, Karachi 75600; tel. (21) 9251711; e-mail pimkhi@pim.com.pk; internet www.pim.com.pk; f. 1960; quarterly; English; Editor IQBAL A. QAZI.

Pasban: Faiz Modh Rd, Quetta; fortnightly; Urdu; Editor MOLVI MOHD ABDULLAH.

Phool: 4 Sharah-e-Fatima Jinnah, Lahore 54000; tel. (42) 6314099; fax (42) 6367616; e-mail editor@phool.com.pk; internet www.phool.com.pk; f. 1989; monthly; children's; Chief Editor MAJID NIZAMI; Editor MUHAMMAD SHOAIB MIRZA; circ. 50,000.

Progress: 4th Floor, PIDC House, Dr Ziauddin Ahmed Rd, Karachi 75530; tel. (21) 111-568-568; fax (21) 5680005; e-mail n_nusrat@ppl.com.pk; f. 1956; monthly; publ. by Pakistan Petroleum Ltd; Editor and Publr NUSRAT NASARULLAH; Chief Exec./Man. Dir S. MUNSIF RAZA.

Qaumi Digest: 50 Lower Mall, Lahore; tel. (42) 7225143; fax (42) 7233261; monthly; Editor MUJIBUR REHMAN SHAMI.

Sabrang Digest: 47–48 Press Chambers, I. I. Chundrigar Rd, Karachi 1; tel. (21) 211961; f. 1970; monthly; Urdu; Editor SHAKEEL ADIL ZADAH; circ. 150,000.

Sach-Chee Kahaniyan: 108–110 Adam Arcade, Shaheed-e-Millat Rd, Karachi; tel. (21) 4930470; fax (21) 4934369; monthly; Urdu; Editor RUKHSANA SEHAM MIRZA.

Sayyarah: Aiwan-e-Adab, Urdu Bazar, Lahore 54000; tel. (42) 7321842; f. 1962; monthly; Urdu; literary; Man. Editor HAFEEZ-UR-RAHMAN AHSAN.

Sayyarah Digest: 244, Main Market Riwaz Garden, Lahore 54000; tel. (42) 7245412; fax (42) 7325080; e-mail sayyaradigest@brain.com.pk; f. 1963; monthly; Urdu; Chief Editor AMJAD RAUF KHAN; Editor KAMRAN AMJAD KHAN; circ. 40,000.

Science Magazine: Science Book Foundation, Haji Bldg, Hassan Ali Efendi Rd, Karachi; tel. (21) 2625647; monthly; Urdu; Editor QASIM MAHMOOD.

Seep: Alam Market, Block No. 16, Federal B Area, Karachi; quarterly; Editor NASIM DURRANI.

Show Business: 108–110 Adam Arcade, Shaheed-e-Millat Rd, POB 12540, Karachi; tel. (21) 419616; monthly; Urdu; Editor RUKHSANA SEHAM MIRZA.

Sindh Quarterly: 36D Karachi Administrative Co-operative Housing Society, off Shaheed-e-Millat Rd, Karachi 75350; tel. (21) 4531988; f. 1973; Editor SAYID GHULAM MUSTAFA SHAH.

Smash: Plot No. 4-C, 14th Commercial St, Defence Housing Authority, Phase II Extension, Karachi; tel. (21) 5805391; fax (21) 5896269; e-mail mansuri@fascom.com; f. 2000; monthly; English; Chief Editor RIAZ AHMED MANSURI.

Spider: Haroon House, Dr Ziauddin Ahmed Rd, Karachi 74200; tel. (21) 111-444-777; fax (21) 5681544; e-mail spider@spider.tm; internet www.spider.tm; f. 1998; internet monthly; Editor ALI AHSAN HALAI; CEO HAMEED HAROON.

Sports International: Arshi Market, Firdaus Colony, Nazimabad, Karachi 74600; tel. (21) 6602171; fax (21) 6683768; e-mail ibp-khi@cyber.net.pk; f. 1972; fortnightly; Urdu and English; Chief Editor KANWAR ABDUL MAJEED; Editor RAHEEL MAJEED.

Taj: Jamia Tajia, St 13, Sector 14/B, Buffer Zone, Karachi 75850; monthly; Editor BABA M. ATIF SHAH ANWARI ZAHEENI TAJI.

Talimo Tarbiat: Ferozsons (Pvt) Ltd, 60 Shahrah-e-Quaid-e-Azam, Lahore 54000; tel. (42) 6301196; fax (42) 6369204; f. 1941; children's monthly; Urdu; Chief Editor A. SALAM; circ. 50,000.

Textile Times: Arshi Market, Firdaus Colony, Nazimabad, Karachi 74600; tel. (21) 6683768; e-mail ibp-khi@cyber.net.pk; f. 1993; monthly; English; Chief Editor KANWAR ABDUL MAJEED; Exec. Editor RAHEEL MAJEED KHAN.

Trade Chronicle: Iftikhar Chambers, Altaf Hussain Rd, POB 5257, Karachi 74000; tel. (21) 2631587; fax (21) 2635007; e-mail arsidiqi@fascom.com; f. 1953; monthly; English; trade, politics, finance and economics; Editor ABDUL RAB SIDDIQI; circ. 6,000.

Trade Link International: Zahoor Mansion, Tariq Rd, Karachi; monthly; English; Man. Editor M. IMRAN BAIG; Editor IKRAMULLAH QUREISHI.

TV Times: Plot No. 4-C, 14th Commercial St, Defence Housing Authority, Phase II Extension, Karachi; tel. (21) 5805391; fax (21) 5896269; e-mail rmansuri@fascom.com; f. 1987; monthly; English; Chief Editor RIAZ AHMED MANSURI.

UNESCO Payami: 30 UNESCO House, Sector H-8/1, Islamabad; tel. (51) 434196; fax (51) 431815; monthly; Urdu; publ. by Pakistan National Commission for UNESCO; Editor Dr MUNIR A. ABRO.

The Universal Message: D-35, Block 5, Federal 'B' Area, Karachi 75950; tel. (21) 6349840; fax (21) 6361040; f. 1979; journal of the Islamic Research Acad; monthly; English; literature, politics, economics, religion; Editor ASADULLAH KHAN.

Urdu Digest: 21-Acre Scheme, Samanabad, Lahore 54500; tel. (42) 7589957; fax (42) 7563646; e-mail urdudigest42@hotmail.com; monthly; Urdu; Editor ALTAF HASAN QURESHEE.

Voice of Islam: Jamiatul Falah Bldg, Akbar Rd, Saddar, POB 7141, Karachi 74400; tel. (21) 7721394; f. 1952; monthly; Islamic Cultural Centre magazine; English; Editor Prof. ABDUL QADEER SALEEM; Man. Editor Prof. WAQAR ZUBAIRI.

Wings: 101 Muhammadi House, I. I. Chundrigar Rd, Karachi 74000; tel. (21) 2412591; fax (21) 2420797; monthly; aviation and defence; English; Editor and Publr JAVED MUSHTAQ.

Women's Own: Plot No. 4-C, 14th Commercial St, Defence Housing Authority, Phase II Extension, Karachi; tel. (21) 5805391; fax (21) 5896269; e-mail rmansuri@fascom.com; f. 1987; monthly; English; Chief Editor RIAZ AHMED MANSURI.

Yaqeen International: Darut Tasnif (Pvt) Ltd, Main Hub River Rd, Mujahidabad, Karachi 75760; tel. (21) 2814432; fax (21) 2811304; e-mail daruttasnif@yaqeendtl.com; internet www.yaqeendtl.com; f. 1952; English and Arabic; Islamic organ; Editor Dr HAFIZ MUHAMMAD ADIL.

Yaran-e-Watan: Overseas Pakistanis Foundation, Shahrah-e-Jamhuriate, G-5/2, POB 1470, Islamabad 44000; tel. (51) 9210175; fax (51) 9224518; e-mail opf@comsats.net.pk; f. 1982; monthly; Urdu; publ. by the Overseas Pakistanis Foundation; Editor HAROON RASHID.

Youth World International: 104/C Central C/A, Tariq Rd, Karachi; tel. (21) 442211; f. 1987; monthly; English; Editor SYED ADIL EBRAHIM.

NEWS AGENCIES

Associated Press of Pakistan (APP): 18 Mauve Area, Zero Point, G-7/1, POB 1258, Islamabad; tel. (51) 2203073; fax (51) 2203074; e-mail news@app.com.pk; internet app.com.pk; f. 1948; Man. Dir RAI RIAZ HUSSAIN.

National News Agency (NNA): 491-C, Margalla Town, Islamabad 45510; tel. (51) 2840896; fax (51) 2841746; e-mail nnaisb@yahoo.com; f. 1990; Chief Editor SUHAIL ILYAS.

News Network International: 2nd Floor, Redco Plaza, Islamabad 44000; tel. (51) 2874344; fax (51) 2826289; e-mail nni2005@isb.paknet.com.pk; internet www.nni-news.com; f. 1992; independent international news agency; news in Arabic, Urdu and English; provides services to 435 newspapers and radio and television channels in South Asia, Europe, the Middle East, the Far East and the USA; Editor-in-Chief QAISAR JAVED; Editor MUHAMMAD TAHIR KHAN.

Pakistan—International Press Agency (PPA): 6, St 39, G-6/2, Islamabad 44000; tel. (51) 2279830; fax (51) 2272405; e-mail ppapublications@gawab.com; f. 1991; Urdu; Chief Editor KHALID ATHAR.

Pakistan Press International (PPI): Press Centre, Shahrah Kamal Atatürk, POB 541, Karachi; tel. (21) 2623215; fax (21) 2217069; e-mail ppi@ppinewsagency.com; f. 1956; pvt ltd co; Chair. OWAIS ASLAM ALI.

United Press of Pakistan (Pvt) Ltd (UPP): 1 Victoria Chambers, Haji Abdullah Haroon Rd, Karachi 74400; tel. (21) 2822738; fax (21) 5682694; e-mail pnrupp2000@yahoo.com; f. 1949; Man. Editor MAHMUDUL AZIZ; 5 brs.

PRESS ASSOCIATIONS

All Pakistan Newspaper Employees Confederation: Karachi Press Club, M. R. Kayani Rd, Karachi; f. 1976; confed. of all press

PAKISTAN

industry trade unions; Pres. MAZHAR ABBAS; Sec.-Gen. PERVAIZ SHAUKAT.

All Pakistan Newspapers Society: 32 Farid Chambers, Abdullah Haroon Rd, POB 74400, Karachi 3; tel. (21) 5671256; fax (21) 5671310; e-mail theapns@gmail.com; internet www.apns.com.pk; f. 1949; Pres. HAMEED HAROON; Sec.-Gen. MUHAMMAD ASLAM KAZI.

Council of Pakistan Newspaper Editors: c/o United Press of Pakistan, 1 Victoria Chambers, Haji Abdullah Haroon Rd, Karachi 74400; tel. and fax (21) 5682694; Pres. SYED FASEIH IQBAL; Sec.-Gen. WAMIQ A. ZUBERI.

Pakistan Press Foundation: Press Centre, Shahrah Kamal Ataturk, Karachi 74200; tel. (21) 2633215; fax (21) 2217069; e-mail ppf@pakistanpressfoundation.org; internet www.pakistanpressfoundation.org; f. 1967; independent media research and training centre for promotion of press freedom; Sec.-Gen. OWAIS ASLAM ALI.

Publishers

Alhamra Publishing: Al-Babar Centre, Office 6, 1st Floor, F-8 Markaz, Islamabad 44000; tel. (51) 2818033; fax (51) 2818076; e-mail contact@alhamra.com; internet www.alhamra.com; f. 2000; publs broad range of subjects incl. fiction, literary criticism, languages, history, education and religion in Urdu and English translations; Man. Dir SHAFIQ NAZ.

Anjuman Taraqq-e-Urdu Pakistan: D-159, Block 7, Gulshan-e-Iqbal, Karachi 75300; tel. (21) 461406; f. 1903; literature, religion, textbooks, Urdu dictionaries, literary and critical texts; Pres. AFTAB AHMED KHAN; Hon. Sec. JAMIL UDDIN AALI.

Camran Publishers: Jalaluddin Hospital Bldg, Circular Rd, Lahore; f. 1964; general, technical, textbooks; Propr ABDUL HAMID.

Chronicle Publications: Iftikhar Chambers, Altaf Hussain Rd, POB 5257, Karachi 74000; tel. (21) 2631587; fax (21) 2635007; e-mail arsidiqi@fascom.com; f. 1953; reference, directories, religious books; Dir ABDUL RAUF SIDDIQI.

Dasnavi Book House: Book St, G-6, Mazang Rd, Lahore; tel. (42) 2231518; e-mail bookhome@hotmail.com.

Economic and Industrial Publications: Al-Masiha, 3rd Floor, 47 Abdullah Haroon Rd, POB 7843, Karachi 74400; tel. (21) 7728963; fax (21) 7728434; f. 1965; industrial, economic and investment research.

Elite Publishers Ltd: D-118, SITE, Karachi 75700; tel. (21) 2573435; fax (21) 2564720; e-mail elite@elite.com.pk; internet www.elite.com.pk; f. 1951; general commercial printing and packaging; Chair. AHMED MIRZA JAMIL; Chief Exec. KHALID JAMIL.

Ferozsons (Pvt) Ltd: 60 Shahrah-e-Quaid-e-Azam, Lahore; tel. (42) 111-626-262; fax (42) 6369204; e-mail support@ferozsons.com.pk; internet www.ferozsons.com.pk; f. 1894; general books, school books, periodicals, maps, atlases, stationery products; Man. Dir ZAHEER SALAM; Dir (Business Development) MUQEET SALAM.

Fiction House: 18, Mozang House, Lahore; publs quarterly social science journal Tareekh.

Frontier Publishing Co: 22 Urdu Bazar, Lahore; tel. (42) 7355262; fax (42) 7247323; e-mail fpc@wol.net.pk; internet www.brain.net.pk/~masim; f. 1951; academic and general; Execs MUHAMMAD ARIF, MUHAMMAD ASIM.

Sh. Ghulam Ali and Sons (Pvt) Ltd: 199 Circular Rd, Lahore 54000; tel. (42) 7352908; fax (42) 6315478; e-mail niazasad@hotmail.com; internet www.ghulamali.com.pk; f. 1887; general, religion, technical, textbooks; Dirs NIAZ AHMAD, ASAD NIAZ.

Harf Academy: G/307, Amena Plaza, Peshawar Rd, Rawalpindi.

Idara Taraqqi-i-Urdu: S-1/363 Saudabad, Karachi 27; f. 1949; general literature, technical and professional books and magazines; Propr IKRAM AHMED.

Ilmi Kitab Khana: Kabeer St, Urdu Bazar, Lahore; tel. (42) 62833; f. 1948; technical, professional, historical and law; Propr Haji SARDAR MOHAMMAD.

INAYAT Sons: YMCA Bldg, 16 The Mall, Lahore 54000; tel. (42) 8401335; fax (42) 7231896; e-mail general@inayatsons.com; internet www.inayatsons.com; f. 1971; Propr S. PERVEZ.

Indus Publications: 25 Fared Chambers, Abdullah Haroon Rd, Karachi; tel. (21) 5660242; e-mail muzaffar_indus@hotmail.com; f. 1959; printers, publishers and importers of books; Dir AATIF SAFDAR.

Islamic Book Centre: 25B Masson Rd, POB 1625, Lahore 54000; tel. (42) 6361803; fax (42) 6360955; e-mail lsaeed@paknetl.ptc.pk; religion in Arabic, Urdu and English; Islamic history, textbooks, dictionaries and reprints; Propr and Man. Dir SUMBLEYNA SAJID SAEED.

Islamic Publications (Pvt) Ltd: 3 Court St, Lower Mall, Lahore 54000; tel. (42) 7248676; fax (42) 7214974; e-mail islamicpak@hotmail.com; internet www.islamicpak.com.pk; f. 1959; Islamic literature in Urdu and English; Man. Dir Prof. MUHAMMAD AMIN JAVED; Gen. Man. AMANAT ALI.

Jamiatul Falah Publications: Jamiatul Falah Bldg, Akbar Rd, Saddar, POB 7141, Karachi 74400; tel. (21) 7721394; f. 1952; Islamic history and culture; Pres. MUZAFFAR AHMED HASHMI; Sec. Prof. SHAHZADUL HASAN CHISHTI.

Kazi Publications: 121 Zulqarnain Chambers, Ganpat Rd, POB 1845, Lahore; tel. (42) 7311359; fax (42) 7350805; e-mail kazipublications@hotmail.com; internet www.brain.net.pk/~kazip; f. 1978; Islamic literature, religion, law, biographies; Propr/Man. MUHAMMAD IKRAM SIDDIQI; Chief Editor MUHAMMAD ASIM BILAL.

Lark Publishers: Urdu Bazar, Karachi 1; f. 1955; general literature, magazines; Propr MAHMOOD RIAZ.

Liberty Books (Pvt) Ltd: 3 Rafiq Plaza, M. R. Kayani Rd, Saddar, Karachi; tel. (21) 5683026; fax (21) 5684319; e-mail libooks@cyber.net.pk; internet www.libertybooks.com; f. 1980.

Lion Art Press (Pvt) Ltd: 112 Shahrah-e-Quaid-e-Azam, Lahore 54000; tel. (42) 6304444; fax (42) 6367728; e-mail lionart786@hotmail.com; f. 1919; general publs in English and Urdu; Chief Exec. KHALID A. SHEIKH; Dir ASMA KHALID.

Maktaba Darut Tasnif: Main Hub River Rd, Mujahidabad, Karachi 75760; tel. (21) 2814432; fax (21) 2811307; e-mail daruttasnif@yaqeendtl.com; internet www.yaqeendtl.com; f. 1951; Koran Majeed and Islamic literature; Dir ABDUL BAQI FAROOQI.

Malik Sirajuddin & Sons: 48/C, Lower Mall, POB 2250, Lahore 54000; tel. (42) 7657527; fax (42) 7657490; e-mail sirajco@brain.net.pk; f. 1905; general, religion, law, textbooks; Man. MALIK ABDUL ROUF.

Malik Sons: Karkhana Bazar, Faisalabad.

Medina Publishing Co: M. A. Jinnah Rd, Karachi 1; f. 1960; general literature, textbooks; Propr HAKIM MOHAMMAD TAQI.

Mehtab Co: Ghazni St, Urdu Bazar, Lahore; tel. (42) 7120071; fax (42) 7353489; e-mail shashraf@brain.net.pk; f. 1978; Islamic literature; Propr SHAHZAD RIAZ SHEIKH.

Mohammad Hussain and Sons: 17 Urdu Bazar, Lahore 2; tel. (42) 7244114; f. 1941; religion, textbooks; Partners MOHAMMAD HUSSAIN, AZHAR ALI SHEIKH, PERVEZ ALI SHEIKH.

Sh. Muhammad Ashraf: 7 Aibak Rd, New Anarkali, Lahore 7; tel. (42) 7353171; fax (42) 7353489; e-mail shashraf@brain.net.pk; f. 1923; books in English on all aspects of Islam; Man. Dir SHAHZAD RIAZ SHEIKH.

National Book Service: 22 Urdu Bazar, Lahore; tel. (42) 7247310; fax (42) 7247323; e-mail fpc@wol.net.pk; internet www.brain.net.pk/~masim; f. 1950; academic and primary, secondary and ELT school books; Execs MUHAMMAD ARIF, MUHAMMAD AMIR, MUHAMMAD ASIM.

Oxford University Press: Plot No. 38, Sector 15, Korangi Industrial Area, Karachi; tel. (21) 111-693-673; fax (21) 5055071; e-mail oup.pk@oup.com; internet www.oup.com.pk; academic, educational and general; Man. Dir AMEENA SAIYID.

Pakistan Law House: Pakistan Chowk, POB 90, Karachi 1; tel. (21) 2212455; fax (21) 2627549; e-mail plh_law_house@hotmail.com; f. 1950; importers and exporters of legal books and reference books; Man. K. NOORANI.

Pakistan Publishing House: Victoria Chambers 2, A. Haroon Rd, Karachi 75400; tel. (21) 5681457; fax (21) 5682036; e-mail danyalbooks@hotmail.com; f. 1959; Propr HOORI NOORANI; Gen. Man. AAMIR HUSSEIN.

Paramount Books: 152/0, Block 2, PECHS, Karachi 75400; tel. (21) 4310030; e-mail paramount@cyber.net.pk.

Pioneer Book House: 1 Avan Lodge, Bunder Rd, POB 37, Karachi; periodicals, gazettes, maps and reference works in English, Urdu and other regional languages.

Premier Bookhouse: Shahin Market, Room 2, Anarkali, POB 1888, Lahore; tel. (42) 7321174; Islamic and law.

Publishers United (Pvt) Ltd: c/o Gulam Ali Medicine Market, Chowk Lohari Gate, POB 1689, Lahore 54000; tel. (42) 6361306; fax (42) 6316015; e-mail smalipub2@hotmail.com; f. 1950; Islamic studies, history, art, archaeology, literature, Oriental studies, genealogy, scientific, medical, humanities and social sciences; Man. Dir ASAD NIAZ.

Punjab Religious Books Society: Anarkali, Lahore 2; tel. (42) 54416; educational, religious, law and general; Gen. Man. A. R. IRSHAD; Sec. NAEEM SHAKIR.

Reprints Ltd: 16 Bahadur Shah Market, M. A. Jinnah Rd, Karachi; f. 1983; Pakistani edns of foreign works; Chair. A. D. KHALID; Man. Dir AZIZ KHALID.

Royal Book Co: BG-5, Rex Centre, Basement, Fatima Jinnah Rd, Karachi 75530; tel. (21) 5653418; e-mail royalbook@hotmail.com.

PAKISTAN

Sang-e-Meel Publications: 25 Lower Mall, Lahore 54000; tel. (42) 7220100; fax (42) 7245101; e-mail smp@sang-e-meel.com; internet www.sang-e-meel.com; f. 1962; Marketing and Sales Exec. ALI KAMRAN.

Say Publishing (Pvt) Ltd: SAI-3, Shahnawaz Arcade, Shahid-e-Millat Rd, Karachi; tel. (21) 4129552; e-mail saybooks@gerry.net.

Sindhi Adabi Board (Sindhi Literary and Publishing Organization): Hyderabad; tel. (221) 771276; e-mail sindhiab@yahoo.com; f. 1951; history, literature, culture of Sindh; in Sindhi, Urdu, English, Persian and Arabic; translations into Sindhi, especially of literature and history; chaired by Minister of Education and Literacy, Sindh; Sec. INAM SHEIKH.

Taj Co Ltd: Manghopir Rd, POB 530, Karachi; tel. (21) 294221; f. 1929; religious books; Man. Dir A. H. KHOKHAR.

The Times Press (Pvt) Ltd: C-18, Al-Hilal Society, off University Rd, Karachi 74800; tel. (21) 4932931; fax (21) 4935602; e-mail timekhi@cyber.net.pk; internet www.timespress.8m.com; f. 1948; printers, publishers and stationery manufacturers, incl. security printing (postal stationery and stamps); registered publishers of Koran, school textbooks, etc.; Dir S. M. MINHAJUDDIN.

Tooba Publishers: 85 Sikandar Block, Allama Iqbal Town, Lahore; tel. (42) 5410185; e-mail haroonkallem@hotmail.com; f. 1983; poetry; Man. HAROON KALEEM USMANI.

Urdu Academy Sind: Main Urdu Bazar, M. A. Jinnah Rd, Karachi; tel. (21) 2628655; fax (21) 2625992; e-mail urduacademy@cyber.net.pk; f. 1947; brs in Hyderabad and Lahore; academic, reference, general and textbooks; Man. Dir AZIZ KHALID.

Vanguard Books (Pvt) Ltd: 72-FCC, Gulberg IV, Lahore; tel. (42) 5763510; fax (42) 5751025; e-mail vbl@brain.net.pk; Chief Exec. NAJAM SETHI.

West-Pak Publishing Co (Pvt) Ltd: 17 Urdu Bazar, Lahore; tel. (42) 7230555; fax (42) 7120077; e-mail pakcompany@hotmail.com; f. 1932; textbooks and religious books; Chief Exec. SYED AHSAN MAHMUD.

GOVERNMENT PUBLISHING HOUSE

Government Publications: Office of the Deputy Controller, Stationery and Forms, nr Old Sabzi Mandi, University Rd, Karachi 74800; tel. (21) 9231989; publ. Gazette of Pakistan; Dep. Controller MUHAMMAD AMIN BUTT.

PUBLISHERS' ASSOCIATION

Pakistan Publishers' and Booksellers' Association: YMCA Bldg, Shahrah-e-Quaid-e-Azam, Lahore; Chair. SYED AHSAN MAHMUD; Sec. ZUBAIR SAEED.

Broadcasting and Communications

TELECOMMUNICATIONS

Since 2000 the mobile cellular telephone industry has made significant progress in Pakistan. In January 2004 the Government approved legislation providing for enhanced competition in the industry. In 2006 there were 34.5m. mobile cellular telephone subscribers nation-wide.

Pakistan Telecommunication Authority (PTA): F-5/1, Islamabad 44000; tel. (51) 2878143; fax (51) 2878155; e-mail administration@pta.gov.pk; internet www.pta.gov.pk; f. 1997; regulatory authority; Chair. Maj.-Gen. SHAHZADA ALAM MALIK; Dir-Gen. CH. MOHAMMAD DIN.

Burraq Telecom (Pvt) Ltd: Plot 94A, St 7, Sector I-10/3, Islamabad; tel. (51) 111-287-727; fax (51) 2112380; e-mail info@burraqtel.com.pk; internet www.burraqtel.com.pk; f. 2004; jt venture between three telecommunications cos; CEO SADIQ YOUSAF YALMAZ.

Carrier Telephone Industries (Pvt) Ltd: 1-9/2 Industrial Area, POB 1098, Islamabad 44000; tel. (51) 4434981; fax (51) 4449581; e-mail snmctipv@isb.comsats.net.pk; internet www.ctipak.com.pk; f. 1969; Man. Dir MALIK MOHAMMAD AMIN.

Callmate Telips Telecom Ltd: 99-CF, 1/5 Clifton, Karachi; tel. (21) 5867696; fax (21) 5833006; e-mail info@cttelecom.net; internet www.cttelecom.net; f. 2003; telecommunications services.

CMPak Ltd fmrly Paktel Ltd: 68E, Jinnah Ave, Blue Area, Islamabad 44000; tel. (51) 2271105; fax (51) 2271111; private mobile telephone co; acquired from Millicom, Luxembourg, by China Mobile Communications Corpn in Feb. 2007; co name changed from Paktel Ltd to CMPak Ltd in May 2007; CEO GUO YONG HONG.

Instaphone: 75 East, Fazal-ul-Haq Rd, Blue Area, POB 1681, Islamabad; tel. (51) 2277400; fax (51) 111-501501; internet www.instaphone.com; private mobile telephone co; CEO SHAHID FEROZ.

Megatech Communications (Pvt) Ltd: 47 Banglore Town, off Tipu Sultan Rd, Karachi 75350; tel. (21) 4528954; fax (21) 4533768;

Directory

e-mail info@megatech.com.pk; internet www.megatech.com.pk; f. 1992; supplier of new digital telephone systems integrated with ISDN/BRI.

Mobilink: 42 Kulsum Plaza, 1st Floor, Blue Area, Islamabad; tel. (21) 2273984-9; fax (21) 2826999; e-mail customercare@mobilink.net; internet www.mobilinkgsm.com; private mobile telephone co; Pres. and CEO ZOUHAIR ABDUL KHALIQ.

National Telecommunication Corporation: NTC Building, F-5/1, Islamabad; tel. (51) 9206450; e-mail infolhr@ntc.net.pk; internet www.ntc.net.pk; f. 1996 by government; Chair. NOOR-UD-DIN BAQAI.

Pakistan Telecommunications (Pvt) Ltd (PTCL): G-8/4, Islamabad 44000; tel. (51) 4844463; fax (51) 4843991; e-mail gmpr@ptcl.com.pk; internet www.ptcl.com.pk; f. 1990; 74% state-owned; 26% owned by Etisalat (United Arab Emirates); Chair. WASHID IRSHAD.

TeleCard Ltd: 7th Floor, World Trade Centre, 10 Khayaban-e-Roomi, Block 5, Clifton, Karachi 75600; tel. (21) 111-222-124; e-mail customerservices@telecard.com.pk; internet www.telecard.com.pk; Chief Exec. SHAHID FIROZ.

Telenor: 13-K, Moaiz Centre, F-7 Markaz, Islamabad; tel. (51) 111-345-700; fax (51) 2651923; internet www.telenor.com.pk; f. 2004; private mobile telephone co; Pres. and CEO TORE JOHNSEN.

Ufone: 13-B, F-7 Markaz, Jinnah Super Market, Islamabad; fax (51) 111-333-100; e-mail customercare@ufonegsm.net; internet www.ufone.com; f. 2001; subsidiary of Pakistan Telecommunications (Pvt) Ltd; private mobile telephone co; Pres. and Chief Exec. ABDUL AZIZ.

Warid Telecom (Pvt) Ltd: 9th Floor, EFU Bldg, Jail Rd, Lahore; e-mail customerservice@waridtel.com; internet www.waridtel.com; owned by Abu Dhabi Group; CEO MARWAN ZAWAYDEH.

Wateen Telecom (Pvt) Ltd: Business Avenue Bldg, 10th Floor, Shahrah-e-Faisal, Karachi; fax (21) 4324096; e-mail info@wateen.com; internet www.wateen.com; subsidiary of the Abu Dhabi Group, UAE; mobile and fixed line telephone services; internet, television and multimedia provider; CEO TARIQ MALIK; Gen. Man. of Operations JAHANGIR AHMAD.

Other telecommunications companies operating in Pakistan include Telephone Industries of Pakistan and Alcatel Pakistan Ltd.

RADIO

Pakistan Broadcasting Corporation: National Broadcasting House, Constitution Ave, Islamabad 4400; tel. (51) 9208306; fax (51) 9223827; e-mail info@radio.gov.pk; internet www.radio.gov.pk; f. 1947 as Radio Pakistan; national broadcasting network of 33 stations; home service 24 hrs daily in 17 languages and dialects; external services 11 hrs daily in 15 languages; world service 11.49 hrs daily in two languages; 80 news bulletins daily; Dir-Gen. ASHFAQ GONDAL; Programme Dir NAYYAR MEHMOOD.

Pakistan Broadcasting Foundation: Planning and Development, Headquarters, Constitution Ave, Islamabad; tel. (51) 9216942; fax (51) 9204363.

Azad Kashmir Radio: Muzaffarabad; state-owned; Station Dir MASUD KASHFI; Dep. Controller (Eng.) SYED AHMED.

Capital FM: Islamabad; f. 1995; privately owned; broadcasts music and audience participation shows 24 hrs daily.

CityFM89: Penthouse, Anum Empire, Block 7 & 8, KCHS, Karachi; tel. (21) 4390155; fax (21) 4390160; e-mail info@cityFM89.com; internet cityfm89.com; f. 2004; owned by Kohinoor Airwaves (Pvt) Ltd; broadcasts in Karachi, Lahore, Islamabad and Faisalabad; Chief Operating Officer NERMEEN CHINOY.

FM-100: Karachi; tel. (21) 2630611; fax (21) 2629311; music station; broadcasts in Karachi, Lahore and Islamabad.

TELEVISION

Geo TV: I. I. Chundrigar Rd, Jang Building, Karachi; tel. (21) 2628614; fax (21) 2636937; e-mail distribution@geo.tv; internet www.geo.tv; f. 2003; Pakistan's first private broadcasting network; broadcasts in Urdu; operates four channels; Pres. IMRAN ASLAM.

Indus TV Network: 2nd Floor, Shafi Court, Civil Lines, Mereweather Rd, Karachi; tel. (21) 5693801; fax (21) 5693813; internet www.indus.tv; f. 2000; Pakistan's first independent satellite channel; CEO GHAZANFAR ALI.

I-Plus TV: 2nd Floor, Shafi Court, Mereweather Rd, Karachi; tel. (21) 5652283; fax (21) 5652285; e-mail im@industvnetwork.com.

Pakistan Television Corpn Ltd: Federal TV Complex, Constitution Ave, POB 1221, Islamabad; tel. (51) 9208651; fax (51) 9211184; e-mail md@ptv.com.pk; internet ptv.com.pk; f. 1964; transmits 24 hrs daily; four channels; Chair. SYED ANWAR MEHMOOD; Man. Dir MUHAMMAD ASHRAF AZIM.

Shalimar Television Network (Shalimar Recording and Broadcasting Co Ltd): 36, Sector H-9, POB 1246, Islamabad; tel. (51) 9257396; fax (51) 4434830; e-mail contact@stn.com.pk; internet www

PAKISTAN

.stn.com.pk; f. 1989 as People's Television Network; 92.81% state-owned, 7.19% privately owned; 20 terrestrial stations throughout Pakistan; Man. Dir and CEO Rashid Choudhry; Gen. Man. Tariq Mahmood.

Tele Biz: Techno City, Altaf Hussain Rd, Karachi 74000; tel. (51) 2273886; fax (51) 2278795; e-mail telebiz@cyber.net.pk; Bureau Chief Zafar Siddiqi.

WAQT Television: 4 Sharah Fatimah Jinnah, Lahore; tel. (42) 6278981; fax (42) 6278980.

Finance

(cap. = capital; auth. = authorized; p.u. = paid up; res = reserves; dep. = deposits; m. = million; brs = branches; amounts in rupees unless otherwise stated)

BANKING

In January 1974 all domestic banks were nationalized. In December 1990 the Government announced that it intended to transfer the five state-owned commercial banks to private ownership. By late 1991 the majority of shares in the Muslim Commercial Bank Ltd and the Allied Bank of Pakistan Ltd had been transferred to private ownership. In 1991 the Government granted 10 new private commercial bank licences, the first since banks were nationalized in 1974. In June 2002 the Supreme Court reversed its 1999 ruling that ordered the Government to abolish charging interest. Interest charges, known as 'riba', are forbidden under Islamic law. The ruling would have required all financial institutions to adopt the Islamic style of banking. In late 2002 the State Bank of Pakistan gave banks three options for the launching of Islamic banking: to establish an independent Islamic bank; to open subsidiaries of existing commercial banks; and to establish new branches to carry out Islamic banking operations. By mid-2007 only four banks were operating as Islamic banking institutions (Meezan Bank Ltd, Bank Islami Ltd, Dubai Islamic Bank, and Emirates Global Islamic Bank).

Central Bank

State Bank of Pakistan: Central Directorate, I. I. Chundrigar Rd, POB 4456, Karachi 2; tel. (21) 9212400; fax (21) 9217234; e-mail info@sbp.org.pk; internet www.sbp.org.pk; f. 1948; bank of issue; controls and regulates currency and foreign exchange; cap. 100m., res 76,067m., dep. 392,506m. (June 2005); Gov. Dr Shamshad Akhtar; 17 brs.

Commercial Banks

ABN AMRO Bank Pakistan Ltd: 16 Abdullah Haroon Rd, Karachi; tel. (21) 5683097; fax (21) 5683432; e-mail info@abnamro.com.pk; internet www.abnamro.com.pk/Pakistan; CEO Naved A. Khan.

Allied Bank Ltd: Central Office, Main Clifton Rd, Bath Island, Karachi; tel. (21) 5370499; fax (21) 5370500; e-mail aftab.manzoor@abl.com.pk; internet www.abl.com.pk; f. 1942 as Australasia Bank Ltd; name changed as above 2005; cap. 4,404.6m., res 5,336.2m., dep. 161,907.5m. (Dec. 2005); 49% state-owned; Pres. and Chief Exec. Mohammad Aftab Manzoor; Exec. Vice-Pres. Rashid Maqsood Hamidi; 741 brs in Pakistan.

Arif Habib Bank Ltd: 2A, R. Y. 16, Old Queens Rd, Karachi; tel. (21) 111–124–725; fax (21) 2463553; e-mail kamalkhan@arifhabibbank.com; internet www.arifhabibbank.com; f. 2006; President and CEO Kamal Uddin Khan.

Askari Bank Ltd: AWT Plaza, The Mall, POB 1084, Rawalpindi; tel. (51) 9272289; fax (51) 9273180; e-mail president@askaribank.com.pk; internet www.askaribank.com.pk; f. 1992; cap. 1,507.0m., res 5,862.1m., dep. 118,794.7m. (Dec. 2005); Chair. Lt-Gen. Waseem Ahmed Ashraf; Pres. and Chief Exec. Shaharyar Ahmad; 98 brs.

Atlas Bank Ltd: 3rd Floor, Federation House, Abdullah Shah Ghazi Rd, Clifton, Karachi; tel. (21) 111–333–225; fax (21) 5877197; e-mail info@atlasbank.com.pk; internet www.atlasbank.com.pk; President and CEO Abdul Aziz Rajkotwala.

Bank Al Habib Ltd: Mackinnons Bldg, I. I. Chundrigar Rd, Karachi; tel. (21) 2412421; fax (21) 2419752; e-mail info@bankalhabib.com; internet www.bankalhabib.com; f. 1991; cap. 2,191.1m., res 2,668.0m., dep. 75,795.9m. (Dec. 2005); Chief Exec. and Man. Dir Abbas D. Habib; 103 brs.

Bank Alfalah Ltd: BA Bldg, I. I. Chundrigar Rd, POB 6773, Karachi; tel. (21) 2416811; fax (21) 2424901; e-mail figroup@bankalfalah.com; internet www.bankalfalah.com; f. 1992 as Habib Credit and Exchange Ltd; name changed as above 1998; cap. 5,000.0m., res 2,749.5m., dep. 239,509.3m. (Dec. 2006); 61.66% owned by Abu Dhabi Consortium, 20% public, 12.60% non-residents, 5.19% employees and execs, 0.55% dirs; CEO Sirajuddin Aziz; 231 brs.

The Bank of Khyber: 24 The Mall, Peshawar; tel. (521) 111-959-595; fax (915) 278146; e-mail bokforex@psh.paknet.com.pk; internet www.bok.com.pk; f. 1991; cap. 1,231.0m., res 1,288.9m., dep. 17,452.2m. (Dec. 2005); 51% state-owned; 49% public shareholders; the main branch in Peshawar began Islamic banking operations in June 2003; Man. Dir Syed Ahmad Iqbal Ashraf; 29 brs.

The Bank of Punjab: 7 Egerton Rd, POB 2254, Lahore 54000; tel. (42) 9200421; fax (42) 9200297; e-mail bop@lhr.comsats.net.pk; internet www.bop.com.pk; f. 1989; cap. 2,349.7m., res 11,150.6m., dep. 95,256.1m. (Dec. 2005); 51.6% owned by provincial govt; Chair. Shahzad Ali Malik; Pres. Hamesh Khan; 266 brs.

Crescent Commercial Bank Ltd: 5th Floor, Sidco Avenue Centre, Maulana Deen Mohammad Wafai Rd, Karachi 74000; tel. (21) 111-999-333; internet www.cresbank.com; f. 2002; Pres. and CEO Shehzad Naqvi; Chair. Zaki Abdulmohsen al-Mousa; 18 brs.

Faysal Bank Ltd: Faysal House, 4th Floor, ST-02 FIG, Main Shahrah-e-Faisal, Karachi; tel. (21) 2795306; fax (21) 2793131; e-mail fbl@faysalbank.com.pk; internet www.faysalbank.com.pk; f. 1995; merged with Al-Faysal Investment Bank Ltd 2002; cap. 3,684.5m., res 8,664.7m., dep. 90,032.4m. (Dec. 2005); Pres. and CEO Khalid S. Timizey; 50 brs.

Habib Bank Ltd: 22 Habib Bank Plaza, I. I. Chundrigar Rd, Karachi 75650; tel. (21) 2411530; fax (21) 2411556; e-mail zmahmood@hblpk.com; internet www.habibbankltd.com; f. 1941; cap. 6,900m., res 16,817m., dep. 439,724m. (Dec. 2006); transferred to private sector Feb. 2004; 51% owned by Agha Khan Fund for Economic Development (United Kingdom), 41% by State Bank of Pakistan and 8% by Government and National Bank of Pakistan; Pres. Zakir Mahmood; 1,437 brs in Pakistan; 39 foreign brs.

Habib Metropolitan Bank Ltd: Mezzanine Floor, Spencer's Bldg, I. I. Chundrigar Rd, POB 1289, Karachi; tel. (21) 2638080; fax (21) 2630404; e-mail info@hmb.com.pk; internet www.hmb.com.pk; f. 1992; fmrly Metropolitan Bank; merged with Habib Bank AG Zurich in 2006; cap. 3,005.0m., equity 10,665.0m., dep. 102,493.0m. (Dec. 2006); Pres. and Chief Exec. Kassim Parekh; Exec. Dir Mohamadali R. Habib; 82 brs.

JS Bank Ltd: 1st Floor, Shaheen Commercial Complex, Dr Ziauddin Ahmed Rd, Karachi 74200; tel. (21) 2635208; fax (21) 2631803; e-mail info@jsbl.com; internet www.jsbl.com; Pres. Naveed Qazi.

KASB Bank Ltd: Business and Finance Centre, I. I. Chundrigar Rd, Karachi 74000; tel. (21) 2446800; fax (21) 9217588; e-mail international@kasb.com; internet www.kasbbank.com; f. 1995 as Platinum Commercial Bank Ltd; name changed as above 2003; cap. 2,292.7m., res 84.3m., dep. 15,409.7m. (March 2006); Pres. and CEO Muneer Kamal; 35 brs.

Khushhali Bank: 94 West, 4th Floor, Jinnah Ave, Blue Area, POB 3111, Islamabad; fax (51) 9206080; cap. 1,705.0m., res 15,023.4m. (Dec. 2004); Chair. and Man. Dir Ghalib Nishtar.

MCB Bank Ltd: MCB Tower, I. I. Chundrigar Rd, POB 4976, Karachi 74000; tel. (21) 2270075; fax (21) 2270076; e-mail atif.bajwa@mcb.com.pk; internet www.mcb.com.pk; f. 1947; cap. 4,265.3m., res 18,831.8m., dep. 229,345.2m. (Dec. 2005); Chair. Mian Muhammad Mansha; Pres. and CEO Atif Aslam Bajwa; 1,057 brs in Pakistan, 4 brs abroad.

Mybank Ltd: 10th Floor, Business & Finance Centre, I. I. Chundrigar Rd, Karachi; tel. (21) 2440100; fax (21) 2471951; e-mail president@mybankltd.com; internet www.mybankltd.com; f. 1991; fmrly Bolan Bank Ltd; cap. 1,523.8m., res 101.2m., dep. 11,397.4m. (Dec. 2004); Chair. Iqbal Alimohamed; Pres. and CEO Muhammad Bilal Sheikh; 50 brs.

National Bank of Pakistan (NBP): NBP Bldg, I. I. Chundrigar Rd, POB 4937, Karachi 2; tel. (21) 9212208; fax (21) 9212774; e-mail nbp@nbp.com.pk; internet www.nbp.com.pk; f. 1949; cap. 4,924.1m., res 28,798.8m., dep. 476,656.5m. (Dec. 2004); 100% state-owned; Pres. Syed Ali Raza; 1,491 brs in Pakistan and 22 brs abroad.

NIB Bank Ltd: Muhammadi House, I. I. Chundrigar Rd, Karachi; tel. (21) 2420333; fax (21) 2472258; e-mail info@nibpk.com; internet www.nibpk.com; f. 2003; Pres. and CEO Khawaja Iqbal Hassan; 27 brs.

PICIC Commercial Bank Ltd: Spencer Bldg, I. I. Chundrigar Rd, POB 572, Karachi 74200; tel. (21) 2638817; fax (21) 2639760; e-mail info@picicbank.com.pk; internet www.picicbank.com.pk; f. 1994 as Schön Bank Ltd; name changed to Gulf Commercial Bank Ltd in 1998; 60% shares and full management of bank acquired by PICIC in February 2001, name changed to above in June 2001; controlling 63.36% stake acquired by NIB Bank (subsidiary of Tamasek Holdings, Singapore) in June 2007 in preparation for proposed full merger with NIB later that year; cap. 2,734.9m., res 867.5m., dep. 59,148.3m. (Dec. 2005); Chair. Frances A. Rozario; Pres. and CEO Khawaja Iqbal Hassan; 129 brs.

Prime Commercial Bank Ltd: 77-Y, Phase III, Defence Housing Authority, Lahore 54792; tel. (42) 5728282; fax (42) 5728181; e-mail primebank@primebank.com.pk; internet www.primebank.com.pk;

f. 1991; cap. 2,321.5m., res 1,116.5m., dep. 38,876.1m. (Dec. 2005); Pres. SAEED I. CHAUDHRY; Chair. ABDUL ELAH A. MUKRED; 62 brs.

Saudi Pak Commercial Bank Ltd: Saudi Pak Bldg, I. I. Chundrigar Rd, Karachi; tel. (21) 2460475; e-mail president@spcb.com.pk; internet www.saudipakbank.com; f. 1994 as Prudential Commercial Bank, acquired by Saudi Pak Industrial and Agricultural Investment Co (Pvt) Ltd in 2001; cap. 3,847.5m., res 819.2m., dep. 42,617.3m. (Dec. 2005); Chair. MUHAMMAD RASHID ZAHIR; Pres. and CEO MANSOOR MASOOD KHAN; 38 brs.

Soneri Bank Ltd: 87 Shahrah-e-Quaid-e-Azam, POB 49, Lahore; tel. (42) 6368142; fax (42) 6368138; e-mail main.lahore@soneribank.com; internet www.soneribank.com; f. 1991; cap. 1,653.5m., res 2,563.3m., dep. 55,848.5m. (Dec. 2005); Chair. ALAUDDIN FEERASTA; Pres. and CEO SAFAR ALI K. LAKHANI; 69 brs.

Standard Chartered Bank (Pakistan) Ltd: 3rd Floor, Main Br., POB 5556, I. I. Chundrigar Rd, Karachi; tel. (21) 2450288; fax (21) 2414914; e-mail badar.kazmi@pk.standardchartered.com; internet www.standardchartered.com/pk; Pres. and CEO BADAR KAZMI; 144 brs.

Union Bank Ltd: New Jubilee Insurance House, I. I. Chundrigar Rd, Karachi 74200; tel. (21) 2412520; fax (21) 2400842; e-mail ubrokhi@digicom.net.pk; internet www.unionbankpk.com; f. 1991; negotiations towards proposed acquisition by Standard Chartered Bank (India) were well advanced by August 2007; cap. 2,819.8m., res 1,599.9m., dep. 105,918.0m. (Dec. 2005); Chair. ABDULLAH M. A. BASODAN; Pres. and Group CEO SHAUKAT TARIN; 27 brs.

United Bank Ltd: State Life Bldg, No. 1, I. I. Chundrigar Rd, POB 4306, Karachi 74000; tel. (21) 2417021; fax (21) 2413492; e-mail president@ubl.com.pk; internet www.ubl.com.pk; f. 1959; cap. 5,180.0m., res 9,137.5m., dep. 311,016.8m. (Dec. 2005); privatized in 2002; Pres. and CEO ATIF BOKHARI; 1,040 brs in Pakistan and 15 brs abroad.

Leasing Banks (*Modarabas*)

The number of leasing banks (*modarabas*), which conform to the strictures placed upon the banking system by *Shari'a* (the Islamic legal code), rose from four in 1988 to about 45 in 2002. The following are among the most important *modarabas* in Pakistan.

Asian Leasing Corporation Ltd: 85-B Jail Rd, Gulberg, POB 3176, Lahore; tel. (42) 484417; fax (42) 484418.

Atlas Lease Ltd: Ground Floor, Federation House, Shahrah-e-Firdousi, Main Clifton, Karachi 75600; tel. (21) 5866817; fax (21) 5870543; e-mail all@atlasgrouppk.com; Chair. YUSUF H. SHIRAZI.

B. R. R. International Modaraba: 3rd Floor, Dean Arcade, Block 8, Kehkeshan, Clifton, Karachi 75600; tel. (21) 5835026; fax (21) 5870324; e-mail brr@cyber.net.pk.

Dadabhoy Leasing Co Ltd: 5th Floor, Maqbool Commercial Complex, JCHS Block, Main Shahrah-e-Faisal, Karachi; tel. (21) 4548171; fax (21) 4547301; Man. (Finance) MOHAMMAD AYUB.

English Leasing Ltd: M. K. Arcade, Ground Floor, 32 Davis Rd, Lahore; tel. (42) 6303855; fax (41) 6304251; e-mail englease@hotmail.com; Chair. JAVAID MAHMOOD; CEO MANZOOR ELAHI.

First Habib Bank Modaraba: 18 Habib Bank Plaza, I. I. Chundrigar Rd, Karachi 75650; tel. (21) 2412294; fax (21) 2411860; e-mail sukhan@hblpk.com; internet www.habibbankltd.com/html/first_habib_modaraba.htm; f. 1991; wholly owned subsidiary of Habib Bank Ltd; Chair. R. ZAKIR MAHMOOD; CEO SAEED UDDIN KHAN.

Orix Leasing Pakistan Ltd: Overseas Investors Chamber of Commerce Bldg, Talpur Rd, Karachi 74000; tel. (21) 2425896; fax (21) 2425897; e-mail olp@orixpakistan.com; internet www.orixpakistan.com; f. 1986; cap. US $10m. (June 2004) Chief Exec. HUMAYUN MURAD.

Pakistan Industrial and Commercial Leasing Ltd: 504 Park Ave, 24-A, Block 6, PECHS, Shahrah-e-Faisal, Karachi 75210; tel. (21) 4551045; fax (21) 4520655; e-mail picl@super.net.pk; f. 1987; Chief Exec. MINHAJ-UL-HAQ SIDDIQI.

Standard Chartered Modaraba: Standard Services of Pakistan (Pvt) Ltd, Standard Bank Bldg, I. I. Chundrigar Rd, POB 5556, Karachi 74000; tel. (21) 223917; fax (21) 2417197; fmrly First Grindlays Modaraba; Man. Dir SHARIQ SALEEM.

Islamic Banks

BankIslami Pakistan Ltd: 11th Floor, Executive Tower One, Dolmen City, Marine Dr., Block 4, Clifton, Karachi; tel. (21) 111-247-111; fax (21) 5378373; e-mail info@bankislami.com.pk; internet www.bankislami.com.pk; CEO HASSAN BILGRAMI.

Dawood Islamic Bank Ltd: Trade Centre, I. I. Chundrigar Rd, Karachi; tel. (21) 2272440; fax (21) 2272465; e-mail nicholaus.schwarz@dawoodislamic.com; internet www.dawoodislamic.com; Pres. and CEO NICOLAUS SCHWARZ.

Dubai Islamic Bank Pakistan Ltd: Hassan Chambers, Plot DC-7, Block 7, Clifton, Karachi; tel. (21) 5368556; fax (21) 5821071; e-mail saad.zaman@dib.ae; internet www.dibpak.com; CEO SAAD ZAMAN.

Emirates Global Islamic Bank Ltd: Shopping Arcade, Karachi Sheraton Hotel and Towers, Club Rd, Karachi; tel. (21) 5633418; fax (21) 5633427; e-mail feedback@egibl.com; internet www.egibl.com; sponsored by Emirates Investment Group LLC, UAE, and Saudi Arabian investors; Pres. and CEO SYED TARIQ HUSSAIN.

Meezan Bank Ltd: 2nd Floor, PNSC Bldg, Moulvi Tamizuddin Khan Rd, Karachi 74000; tel. (21) 5610582; fax (21) 5610375; e-mail info@meezanbank.com; internet www.meezanbank.com; f. 1997 as Al-Meezan Investment Bank; became commercial bank 2002 and name changed as above; cap. 2,036.6m., res 988.0m., dep. 26,011.7m. (Dec. 2005); Pres. and CEO IRFAN SIDDIQUI; Gen. Man. NAJMUL HASAN; 37 brs.

Co-operative Banks

In 1976 all existing co-operative banks were dissolved and given the option of becoming a branch of the appropriate Provincial Co-operative Bank, or of reverting to the status of a credit society.

Federal Bank for Co-operatives: State Bank Bldg, G-5/2, POB 1218, Islamabad; tel. (51) 9204518; fax (51) 9204534; f. 1976; owned jtly by the fed. Govt, the prov. govts and the State Bank of Pakistan; provides credit facilities to each of six prov. co-operative banks and regulates their operations; they in turn provide credit facilities through co-operative socs; supervises policy of prov. co-operative banks and of multi-unit co-operative socs; assists fed. and prov. govts in formulating schemes for development and revitalization of co-operative movement; carries out research on rural credit, etc.; Man. Dir M. AFZAL HUSSAIN; four regional offices.

Investment Banks

Asset Investment Bank Ltd: Rm 1-B, 1st Floor, Ali Plaza, Khayaban-e-Quaid-e-Azam, Blue Area, Islamabad; tel. (51) 2270625; fax (51) 2272506; Chief Exec. SYED NAVEED ZAIDI.

Atlas Investment Bank Ltd: 3rd Floor, Federation House, Shaheen-e-Firdousi, Main Clifton, Karachi; tel. (21) 5866817; fax (21) 5870543; e-mail info@atlasbank.com.pk; internet www.atlasbank.com.pk; 15% owned by Bank of Tokyo-Mitsubishi UFJ Ltd; Man. Dir NAEEM KHAN; Pres. and CEO FRAHIM ALI KHAN.

Crescent Standard Investment Bank Ltd: 4th Floor, Crescent Standard Tower, 10-B, Block E-2, Gulberg III, Lahore; tel. (42) 5763306; fax (42) 5870359; e-mail csibl@csibl.com; internet www.csibl.com; f. 1990 as Al-Towfeek Investment Bank Ltd; became First Standard Investment Bank Ltd 2002; name changed as above 2004; cap. 737.7m., res 212.1m., dep. 2,219.4m. (Dec. 2003); Chair. MANZUR UL HAQ; Chief Exec. MAHMOOD AHMED.

Escorts Investment Bank Ltd: Escorts House, 26 Davis Rd, Lahore; tel. (42) 6371931; fax (42) 6375950; e-mail mailmanager@escortsbank.net; internet escortsbank.net; Pres. and CEO RASHID MANSUR.

ICI Investment Bank Ltd: 7th Floor, The Forum, Suite 701–703, 4-20, Block 9, Khayaban-e-Jami, Clifton, Karachi; tel. (21) 111-234-234; fax (21) 111-567-567; e-mail fiibl.khi@interbank.com.pk; Man. Dir and CEO SAMIR AHMED.

Orix Investment Bank Pakistan Ltd: 2nd Floor, Islamic Chamber of Commerce Bldg, St 2/A, Block 9, Clifton, Karachi 75600; tel. (21) 5861266; fax (21) 5868862; e-mail ihalvi@orixbank.com; internet www.orixbank.com; f. 1995; Chair. KUNWAR IDREES; Gen. Man. INTISAR H. ALVI.

Development Finance Organizations

Bankers' Skill Development Centre: Hamilton Court, 1st Floor, Suite 206/A, G-1, Main Clifton Rd, Block 7, Karachi 75600; tel. (21) 5306244; fax (21) 5306245; e-mail bsdcvalad@hotmail.com; Pres. and CEO Dr AHSAN H. KHAN.

First MicroFinanceBank Ltd: President's Secretariat, 62-C, 25th Commercial St, Tauheed Commercial Area, DHA Phase V, Karachi; tel. (21) 5822432; fax (21) 5822434; Pres. and CEO HUSSAIN TEJANY.

First Women Bank Ltd: S.T.S.M. Foundation Bldg, CL-10/20/2 Beaumont Rd, Civil Lines, Karachi 75530; tel. (21) 111-676-767; fax (21) 5657755; e-mail president@cyber.net.pk; internet www.fwbl.com.pk; f. 1989; cap. and res 590m., dep. 8,690m. (Dec. 2004); Pres. ZARINE AZIZ; 38 brs.

House Building Finance Corpn: Finance and Trade Centre, 3rd Floor, Shahrah-e-Faisal, Karachi 74400; tel. (21) 9202314; fax (21) 9202360; e-mail info@hbfc.com.pk; internet www.hbfc.com.pk; provides loans for the construction and purchase of housing units; Man. Dir ZAIGHAM MEHMOOD RIZVI.

Industrial Development Bank of Pakistan: State Life Bldg No. 2, Wallace Rd, off I. I. Chundrigar Rd, POB 5082, Karachi 74000; tel. (21) 9213601-10; fax (21) 9213644; e-mail idbp@idbp.com.pk;

internet www.idbp.com.pk; f. 1961; provides credit facilities for small and medium-sized industrial enterprises in the private sector; 100% state-owned; Chair. and Man. Dir NAEEM IQBAL; 19 brs.

Investment Corpn of Pakistan: NBP Bldg, 5th Floor, I. I. Chundrigar Rd, POB 5410, Karachi 74400; tel. (21) 9212360; fax (21) 9212388; e-mail icp@paknet3.ptc.pk; f. 1966 by the Govt to encourage and broaden the base of investments and to develop the capital market; Man. Dir ISTIQBAL MEHDI; 10 brs.

Khushhali Bank: 94W, 4th Floor, Jinnah Ave, Blue Area, Islamabad 44000; tel. (51) 111092-092; internet www.khushhalibank.com.pk; f. 2000 by the Govt under the Asian Development Bank's microfinance sector development programme; provides micro-loans to the poor and finances reforms in the micro-finance sector; cap. 1,705m. (Aug. 2000); Pres. GHALIB NISHTAR.

National Investment (Unit Trust) Ltd: NBP Bldg, 6th Floor, I. I. Chundrigar Rd, POB 5671, Karachi; tel. (21) 2419061; fax (21) 2430623; e-mail info@nit.com.pk; internet www.nit.com.pk; f. 1962; an open-ended mutual fund, mobilizes domestic savings to meet the requirements of growing economic development and enables investors to share in the industrial and economic prosperity of the country; 67,000 Unit holders (1999/2000); Man. Dir ISTIQBAL MEHDI.

Network Microfinance Bank Ltd: 202 Azayam Plaza, opp. FTC Bldg, SMCHS, Shahrah-e-Faisal, Karachi; fax (21) 4311722; e-mail nmb@networkmicrobank.com; internet www.networkmicrobank.com; Pres. and CEO M. MOAZZAM KHAN.

Pak Oman Microfinance Bank Ltd: 2nd Floor, Tower C, Finance and Trade Centre, Shahrah-e-Faisal, Karachi; tel. (21) 5630941; fax (21) 5630999; e-mail info@pomicro.com; internet www.pomicro.com; Pres. and CEO OZAIR A. HANAFI.

Pakistan Industrial Credit and Investment Corpn Ltd (PICIC): State Life Bldg No. 1, I. I. Chundrigar Rd, POB 5080, Karachi 74000; tel. (21) 2414220; fax (21) 2419100; internet www.picic.com; f. 1957 as an industrial development bank to provide financial assistance in both local and foreign currencies, for the establishment of new industries in the private sector and balancing modernization, replacement and expansion of existing industries; merchant banking and foreign exchange activities; total assets 33,949m., cap. 2,736m., res 4,188m. (June 2005); held 97.9% and 2.1% by local and foreign investors respectively; Man. Dir MOHAMMAD ALI KHOJA; Chair. ALTAF M. SALEEM; 19 brs.

Pakistan Kuwait Investment Co (Pvt) Ltd: Tower 'C', 4th Floor, Finance and Trade Centre, Shahrah-e-Faisal, POB 901, Karachi 74200; tel. (21) 5660750; fax (21) 5683669; jt venture between the Govt and Kuwait to promote investment in industrial and agro-based enterprises; Man. Dir ISTIQBAL MEHDI.

Pak-Libya Holding Co (Pvt) Ltd: Finance and Trade Centre, 5th Floor, Tower 'C', Shahrah-e-Faisal, POB 10425, Karachi 74400; tel. (21) 111-111-115; fax (21) 5682389; e-mail paklibya@paklibya.com.pk; jt venture between the Govts of Pakistan and Libya to promote industrial investment in Pakistan; Man. Dir KHALID SHARWANI.

Regional Development Finance Corpn: Ghausia Plaza, 20 Blue Area, POB 1893, Islamabad; tel. (51) 2825131; fax (51) 2201179; promotes industrial investment in the less developed areas of Pakistan; CEO MIRZA GHAGANFAR BAIG; 13 brs.

Saudi Pak Industrial and Agricultural Investment Co (Pvt) Ltd: Saudi Pak Tower, 61-A Jinnah Ave, Islamabad; tel. (51) 2273514; fax (51) 2273508; e-mail saudipak@saudipak.com; internet www.saudipak.com; f. 1981 jtly by Saudi Arabia and Pakistan to finance industrial and agro-based projects and undertake investment-related activities in Pakistan; cap. 2,000m., res 732m., dep. 5,900m. (March 2001); CEO MUHAMMAD RASHID ZAHIR; Exec. Vice-Pres. ABDUL JALEEL SHAIKH; 1 br.

SME Bank Ltd: Jang Plaza, 2nd Floor, 40 Fazal-ul-Haq Rd, Blue Area, POB 1587, Islamabad; tel. (51) 9217000; fax (51) 9217001; e-mail info@smebank.org; internet www.smebank.org; formed through merger of Regional Development Finance Corpn (RDFC) and Small Business Finance Corpn (SBFC); provides loans for small businesses; Pres. and CEO MANSUR KHAN.

Youth Investment and Promotion Society: PIA Bldg, 3rd Floor, Blue Area, Islamabad; tel. (51) 815581; Man. Dir ASHRAF M. KHAN.

Zarai Taraqiati Bank Ltd (ZTBL): 1 Faisal Ave, POB 1400, Islamabad; tel. (51) 9252727; fax (51) 9252737; e-mail info@ztbl.com.pk; internet www.ztbl.com.pk; f. 1961; provides credit facilities to agriculturists (particularly small-scale farmers) and cottage industrialists in the rural areas and for allied projects; 100% state-owned; Pres. MANSUR KHAN; 24 zonal offices and 342 brs.

Banking Associations

Investment Banks Association of Pakistan: 7th Floor, Shaheen Commercial Complex, Dr Ziauddin Ahmed Rd, POB 1345, Karachi; tel. (21) 2631396; fax (21) 2630678.

Modaraba Association of Pakistan: Chair. WAQAR AJMAL CHAUDHRY.

Pakistan Banks' Association: National Bank of Pakistan, Head Office Bldg, 2nd Floor, I. I. Chundrigar Rd, POB 4937, Karachi 2; tel. and fax (21) 2416686; e-mail pba@cyber.net.pk; Chair. M. YOUNAS KHAN; Sec. A. GHAFFAR K. HAFIZ.

Banking Organizations

Banking Mohtasib Pakistan: Secretariat, 5th Floor, Shaheen Complex, POB 604, M. R. Kiyani Rd, Karachi; tel. (21) 9217334; fax (21) 9217375; e-mail info@bankingmohtasib.gov.pk; internet www.bankingmohtasib.gov.pk; resolves public grievances against banks and disputes between banking institutions; offices in Quetta, Lahore, Rawalpindi and Peshawar; Banking Ombudsman AZHAR HAMID.

Pakistan Banking Council: Habib Bank Plaza, I. I. Chundrigar Rd, Karachi; tel. (21) 227121; fax (21) 222232; f. 1973; acts as a co-ordinating body between the nationalized banks and the Ministry of Finance and Revenue; Chair. MUHAMMAD ZAKI; Sec. Mir WASIF ALI.

Pakistan Development Banking Institute: 4th Floor, Sidco Ave Centre, Stratchen Rd, Karachi; tel. (21) 5688049; fax (21) 5688460.

STOCK EXCHANGES

Securities and Exchange Commission of Pakistan: NIC Bldg, 63 Jinnah Ave, Blue Area, Islamabad 44000; tel. (51) 9207091; fax (51) 9204915; e-mail enquiries@secp.gov.pk; internet www.secp.gov.pk; oversees and co-ordinates operations of exchanges and registration of companies; registration offices in Faisalabad (356-A, 1st Floor, Al-Jamil Plaza, People's Colony, Small D Ground, Faisalabad; tel. (41) 713841), Karachi (No. 2, 4th Floor, State Life Building, North Wing, Karachi; tel. (21) 2415855), Lahore (3rd and 4th Floors, Associated House, 7 Egerton Rd, Lahore; tel. (42) 9202044), Multan (61 Abdali Rd, Multan; tel. (61) 542609), Peshawar (Hussain Commercial Bldg, 3 Arbab Rd, Peshawar), Quetta (382/3, IDBP House, Shahrah-e-Faisal, Quetta; tel. (81) 844138) and Sukkur (B-30, Sindhi Muslim Housing Society, Airport Rd, Sukkur; tel. (71) 30517); Chair. RAZI-UR-RAHMAN KHAN.

Islamabad Stock Exchange (Guarantee) Ltd: 4th Floor, Stock Exchange Bldg, 101E Faz-ul-haq Rd, Blue Area, Islamabad; tel. (51) 2275045; fax (51) 2275044; e-mail ise@ise.com.pk; internet www.ise.com.pk; f. 1991; 103 mems; Chair. SHAHARYAR AHMAD; Sec. YOUSUF H. MAKHDOOMI.

Karachi Stock Exchange (Guarantee) Ltd: Stock Exchange Bldg, Stock Exchange Rd, Karachi 74000; tel. (21) 111-001-122; fax (21) 2410825; e-mail info@kse.com.pk; internet www.kse.com.pk; f. 1947; 200 mems, 654 listed cos (Jan. 2007); Chair. SHAUKAT TARIN; Man. Dir MOHAMMAD YACOUB MEMON (acting).

Lahore Stock Exchange (Guarantee) Ltd: Lahore Stock Exchange Bldg, 19 Khayaban-e-Aiwan-e-Iqbal, POB 1315, Lahore 54000; tel. (42) 6368000; fax (42) 6368484; e-mail info@lahorestock.com; internet www.lahorestock.com; f. 1970; 576 listed cos, 151 mems; Pres. IBRAR MUMTAZ; Man. Dir HAMID M. IMTIAZI.

National Commodity Exchange Ltd: 9th Floor, PIC Towers, 32-A Lalazar Drive, M. T. Khan Rd, Karachi; tel. (21) 111-623-623; fax (21) 5611263; e-mail info@ncel.com.pk; internet www.ncel.com.pk; f. 2002; online commodity futures exchange; regulated by Securities and Exchange Commission of Pakistan; Chair. SHAUKAT TARIN; Man. Dir ASSIM JANG.

Central Depository Co: CDC House, 99-B, Block B, S. M. C. H. Society, Main Shahrah-e-Faisal, Karachi 74400; tel. (21) 2416774; fax (21) 4326016; e-mail info@cdcpak.com; internet www.cdcpakistan.com; f. 1993 to manage and operate Central Depository System of the financial services industry; CEO HANIF JAKHURA.

INSURANCE

In 1995 legislation came into effect allowing foreign insurance companies to operate in Pakistan.

Insurance Division: Securities and Exchange Commission, 4th Floor, NIC Bldg, Jinnah Ave, Islamabad; tel. (51) 9208887; fax (51) 9208955; internet www.secp.gov.pk; under the Ministry of Finance and Revenue; Commissioner of Insurance SHARIF EJAZ GHAURI; Exec. Dir SHAFAAT AHMED.

Life Insurance

American Life Insurance Co (Pakistan) Ltd: 13th Floor (Level 16), Block 4, Scheme 5, Clifton, Karachi 75600; tel. (21) 111-111-711; fax (21) 5290042; e-mail alico@cyber.net.pk; internet www.alico.com.pk; Chair. and CEO ARIF SULTAN MUFTI.

EFU Life Assurance Ltd: 37-K, Block 6, PECHS, Karachi; tel. (21) 111-338-111; e-mail info@efulife.com; internet www.efulife.com; f. 1932; Chair. SAIFUDDIN N. ZOOMKAWALA; Man. Dir and CEO TAHER G. SACHAK.

PAKISTAN

Metropolitan Life Assurance Co of Pakistan Ltd: 310 EFU House, M. A. Jinnah Rd, Karachi 74000; tel. (21) 2311662; fax (21) 2311667; e-mail clientservices@metropolitanlifeassurance.com; internet www.metropolitanlifeassurance.com; f. 1992; Chief Exec. and Man. Dir MAHEEN YUNUS.

Postal Life Insurance Organization: 2nd and 3rd Floors, Karachi GPO Bldg, I. I. Chundrigar Rd, Karachi; tel. (21) 9211102; e-mail gmplikar@paknet.pk.com; f. 1884; life and group insurance; Gen. Man. SHAHAR YARUDDIN.

State Life Insurance Corpn of Pakistan: State Life Bldg No. 9, Dr Ziauddin Ahmed Rd, POB 5725, Karachi 75530; tel. (21) 111-111-888; fax (21) 9202868; e-mail dhasp@statelife.com.pk; internet www.statelife.com.pk; f. 1972; life and group insurance and pension schemes; Chair. KAMAL ASFAR.

General Insurance

ACE Insurance Ltd: 6th Floor, NIC Bldg, Abbasi Shaheed Rd, off Shahrah-e-Faisal, Karachi; tel. (21) 5681320; fax (21) 5683935; e-mail zehra.naqvi@ace-ina.com; internet www.ace-ina.com; f. 1853; Chief Exec. ZEHRA NAQVI.

Adamjee Insurance Co Ltd: Adamjee House, 6th Floor, I. I. Chundrigar Rd, POB 4850, Karachi 74000; tel. (21) 2410145; fax (21) 2412627; e-mail info@adamjeeinsurance.com; internet www.adamjeeinsurance.com; f. 1960; Man. Dir and CEO ARIF IJAZ.

Agro General Insurance Co Ltd: Room No. 416–418, 4th Floor, Continental Trade Centre, Block 8, Main Clifton Rd, Karachi; tel. (21) 5302902-06; fax (21) 5302913; e-mail agiho@cyber.net.pk; f. 1987; Man. Dir and CEO M. JALILULLAH.

AIG Pakistan New Hampshire Insurance Co: 7th Floor, Dawood Centre, M. T. Khan Rd, Karachi 75530; tel. (21) 111-111-244; fax (21) 5634022; e-mail info-pakistan@aig.com; internet www.aigpakistan.com; f. 1869; Country Man. GOKTUG GUR.

Alpha Insurance Co Ltd: State Life Bldg No. 1B–1C, 2nd Floor, off I. I. Chundrigar Rd, POB 4359, Karachi 74000; tel. (21) 2412609; fax (21) 2419968; f. 1952; Chair. IQBAL M. QURESHI; Man. Dir V. C. GONSALVES; 9 brs.

Amicus Insurance Co Ltd: F-50, Block 7, Feroze Nana Rd, Bath Island, POB 3971, Karachi; tel. (21) 5831082; fax (21) 5870220; f. 1991; Chair. M. IRSHAD UDDIN.

Asia Insurance Co Ltd: 19C and 19D, Block L, Gulberg III, Ferozepur Rd, Lahore; tel. (42) 5858532; fax (42) 5865579; e-mail asiains@nexlinx.net.pk; f. 1979; Chief Exec. ZAFAR IQBAL SHEIKH.

Askari General Insurance Co Ltd: 4th Floor, AWT Plaza, The Mall, POB 843, Rawalpindi; tel. (51) 9272425; fax (51) 9272424; e-mail agicoho@agico.com.pk; internet www.agico.com.pk; f. 1995; Pres. and Chief Exec. M. JAMALUDDIN.

Business and Industrial Insurance Co Ltd: 65 East Pak Pavilions, 1st Floor, Fazal-e-Haq Rd, Blue Area, Islamabad; tel. (51) 2278757; fax (51) 2271914; e-mail biic.ltd@yahoo.com; f. 1995; Chair. and Chief Exec. Mian MUMTAZ ABDULLAH.

Capital Insurance Co Ltd: Muradia Rd, Model Town, Sialkot; tel. (52) 3563771; fax (52) 3552958; e-mail info@capital-insurance.net; internet www.capital-insurance.net; f. 1998; CEO NAVID IQBAL SHEIKH; Sec. M. I. BUTT.

Central Insurance Co Ltd: Dawood Centre, 5th Floor, M. T. Khan Rd, POB 3988, Karachi 75530; tel. (21) 5684019; fax (21) 5680218; e-mail cicl@khi.wol.net.pk; internet www.coninsure.com; f. 1960; Chief Exec. VIQUAR SIDDIQI.

Century Insurance Co Ltd: 11th Floor, Lakson Square Bldg No. 3, Sarwar Sheheed Rd, POB 4895, Karachi 74200; tel. (21) 5657445; fax (21) 5671665; e-mail cic@cyber.net.pk; f. 1988; Chair. and Chief Exec. IQBALALI LAKHANI; Dir Mir NADIR ALI.

CGU Inter Insurance PLC: 74/1-A, Lalazar, M. T. Khan Rd, POB 4895, Karachi 74000; tel. (21) 5611802; fax (21) 5611456; f. 1861; general and life insurance; Gen. Man. ABDUR RAHIM; 3 brs.

Commerce Insurance Co Ltd: 11 Shahrah-e-Quaid-e-Azam, POB 1132, Lahore 54000; tel. (42) 7325330; fax (42) 7230828; f. 1992; Chief Exec. SYED MOIN-UD-DIN.

Co-operative Insurance Society of Pakistan Ltd: Co-operative Insurance Bldg, Shahrah-e-Quaid-e-Azam, POB 147, Lahore; tel. (42) 7352306; fax (42) 7352794; f. 1949; Chief Exec. and Gen. Man. CH. AKHTAR MAHMOOD.

Credit Insurance Co Ltd: Asmat Chambers, 68 Mazang Rd, Lahore; tel. (42) 6316774; fax (42) 6368868; f. 1995; Chief Exec. MUHAMMAD IKHLAQ BUTT.

Crescent Star Insurance Co Ltd: Nadir House, I. I. Chundrigar Rd, POB 4616, Karachi 74000; tel. (21) 2415521; fax (21) 2415474; e-mail crescent_star_ins@hotmail.com; f. 1957; Man. Dir MUNIR I. MILLWALA.

Dadabhoy Insurance Co Ltd: Maqbool Commercial Complex, JCHS Block, Main Shahrah-e-Faisal, Karachi; tel. (21) 4545704; fax (21) 4548625; f. 1983; Chief Exec. USMAN DADABHOY.

Delta Insurance Co Ltd: 101 Baghpatee Bldg, Altaf Hussain Rd, New Challi, Karachi; tel. (21) 2632297; fax (21) 2422942; f. 1991; Man. Dir SYED ASIF ALI.

East West Insurance Co Ltd: 410, EFU House, M. A. Jinnah Rd, POB 6693, Karachi 74000; tel. (21) 2313304; fax (21) 2310821; e-mail info@eastwestins.com; f. 1983; Chair. and Chief Exec. NAVED YUNUS.

EFU General Insurance Ltd: EFU House, M. A. Jinnah Rd, Karachi 74000; tel. (21) 2313471; fax (21) 2310450; e-mail info@efuinsurance.com; internet www.efuinsurance.com; f. 1932; Man. Dir and Chief Exec. SAIFUDDIN N. ZOOMKAWALA.

Excel Insurance Co Ltd: 38/C-1, Block 6, PECH Society, Shahrah-e-Faisal, Karachi 75400; tel. (21) 111-777-666; fax (21) 4548076; e-mail eicl@cyber.net.pk; f. 1991; Man. Dir GHULAM H. ALI MOHAMMAD.

Gulf Insurance Co Ltd: Gulf House, 1-A Link McLeod Rd, Patiala Grounds, Lahore; tel. (42) 7312028; fax (42) 7234987; f. 1988; Chief Exec. S. ARIF SALAM.

Habib Insurance Co Ltd: Insurance House, 6 Habib Sq., M. A. Jinnah Rd, POB 5217, Karachi 74000; tel. (21) 2424038; fax (21) 2421600; e-mail hic@cyber.net.pk; f. 1942; Chair. HAMID D. HABIB; Man. Dir and Chief Exec. ALI RAZA D. HABIB.

IGI Insurance Ltd: 7th Floor, The Forum, Suite 701–713m G-20, Block 9, Khayaban-e-Jami, Clifton, Karachi; tel. (21) 5301726-8; fax (21) 5301729; e-mail skhalid@gi.com.pk; internet www.igi.com.pk; Chief Operating Officer S. KHALID YUSUF.

International General Insurance Co of Pakistan Ltd: Finlay House, 1st Floor, I. I. Chundrigar Rd, POB 4576, Karachi 74000; tel. (21) 2424976; fax (21) 2416710; e-mail igikhi@cubexs.net.pk; internet www.igi.com.pk; f. 1953; Gen. Man. AHMED SALAHUDDIN.

Ittefaq General Insurance Co Ltd: H-16 Murree Rd, Rawalpindi; tel. (51) 5771333; f. 1982; Chief Exec. and Man. Dir Dr SYED ISHTIAQ HUSSAIN SHAH.

Jupiter Insurance Co Ltd: 4th Floor, Finlay House, I. I. Chundrigar Rd, POB 4655, Karachi 74000; tel. (21) 2426070; fax (21) 2427660; e-mail jicl20@cyber.net.pk; f. 1994; Chief Exec. MAHMUD HASAN.

Muslim Insurance Co Ltd: 3 Bank Sq., Shahrah-e-Quaid-e-Azam, POB 1219, Lahore; tel. (42) 7320542; fax (42) 7234742; e-mail fariq.rohilla@mickhi.atlasgrouppk.com; f. 1935; Chief Exec. S. C. SUBJALLY.

National General Insurance Co Ltd: 401-B, Satellite Town, nr Commercial Market, Rawalpindi; tel. (51) 4427818; fax (51) 4427361; f. 1969; Gen. Man. F. A. JAFFERY.

National Insurance Corpn: NIC Bldg, Abbasi Shaheed Rd, Karachi 74400; tel. (21) 9202741; fax (21) 9202779; e-mail info@nicl.com.pk; internet www.niclpk.com; govt-owned; sole govt insurance co; Man. Dir ABID JAVED AKBAR.

New Jubilee Insurance Co Ltd: 2nd Floor, Jubilee Insurance House, I. I. Chundrigar Rd, POB 4795, Karachi 74000; tel. (21) 2416022; fax (21) 2416728; e-mail nji@cyber.net.pk; internet www.nji.com.pk; f. 1953; Man. Dir TAHIR AHMED.

North Star Insurance Co Ltd: 37–38 Basement, Sadiq Plaza, 69 The Mall, Lahore 54000; tel. (42) 6314308; fax (42) 6375366; e-mail northstarins@hotmail.com; f. 1995; Chief Exec./Man. Dir M. RAFIQ CHAUDHRY.

Orient Insurance Co Ltd: 2nd Floor, Dean Arcade, Block No. 8, Kahkeshan, Clifton, Karachi; tel. (21) 5865327; fax (21) 5865724; f. 1987; Man. Dir FAZAL REHMAN.

Pak Equity Insurance Co Ltd: M. K. Arcade, 32 Davis Rd, Lahore; tel. (42) 6361536; fax (42) 6365959; f. 1984; Chief Exec. CH. ATHAR ZAHOOR.

Pakistan General Insurance Co Ltd: 3 Bank Sq., Shahrah-e-Quaid-e-Azam, POB 1364, Lahore; tel. (42) 7323569; fax (42) 7230634; f. 1948; Chair. CH. AZFAR MANZOOR; Pres. and CEO CH. ZAHOOR AHMAD.

Pakistan Guarantee Insurance Co Ltd: Al-Falah Court, 3rd and 5th Floors, I. I. Chundrigar Rd, POB 5436, Karachi 74000; tel. (21) 2636111; fax (21) 2638740; f. 1965; Chief Exec. SHAKIL RAZA SYED.

Pakistan Reinsurance Co Ltd: PRC Towers, 32A Lalazar Dr., M. T. Khan Rd, POB 4777, Karachi 74000; tel. (21) 9202908; fax (21) 9202921; e-mail pic1@pk.netsolir.com; internet www.pakre.org.pk; Chair. RUKHSANA SALEEM.

PICIC Insurance Ltd: 8th Floor, Shaheen Complex, M. R. Kiyani Rd, Karachi; tel. (21) 2219550; fax (21) 2219561; e-mail info@picicinsurance.com; internet www.picicinsurance.com; Man. Dir and CEO AHMED SALAHUDDIN.

Premier Insurance Co of Pakistan Ltd: 2-A State Life Bldg, 5th Floor, Wallace Rd, off I. I. Chundrigar Rd, POB 4140, Karachi 74000;

tel. (21) 2416331; fax (21) 2416572; f. 1952; Chair. ZAHID BASHIR; CEO FAKHIR A. RAHMAN.

Prime Insurance Co Ltd: 505–507, Japan Plaza, M. A. Jinnah Rd, POB 1390, Karachi; tel. (21) 7770801; fax (21) 7725427; f. 1989; Chief Exec. ABDUL MAJEED.

Progressive Insurance Co Ltd: 2nd Floor, Sasi Arcade, Block 7, Main Clifton Rd, Clifton, Karachi; tel. (21) 5823560; fax (21) 5823561; f. 1989; Man. Dir and CEO ABDUL MAJEED.

Raja Insurance Co Ltd: Panorama Centre, 5th Floor, 256 Fatimah Jinnah Rd, POB 10422, Karachi 4; tel. (21) 5670619; fax (21) 5681501; f. 1981; Chair. RAJA ABDUL RAHMAN; Man. Dir Sheikh HUMAYUN SAYEED.

Reliance Insurance Co Ltd: Reliance Insurance House, 181-A, Sindhi Muslim Co-operative Housing Society, POB 13356, Karachi 74400; tel. (21) 4539415; fax (21) 4539412; e-mail reli-ins@cyber.net.pk; Chief Exec. and Man. Dir ABDUL RAZAK AHMED.

Royal & SunAlliance Insurance: 8th Floor, Shaheen Complex, POB 4930, M. R. Kayani Rd, Karachi 74000; tel. (21) 2635141; fax (21) 2631369; e-mail rsa@cyber.net.pk; internet www.royalsunalliance.com; f. 1989; Chief Exec. and Man. Dir Dr MUMTAZ A. HASHMI.

Royal Exchange Assurance: P&O Plaza, I. I. Chundrigar Rd, POB 315, Karachi 74000; tel. (21) 2635141; fax (21) 2631369; Man. (Pakistan) Dr MUMTAZ A. HASHMI.

Saudi Pak Insurance Co Ltd: 2nd Floor, State Life Bldg, No. 2A, Wallace Rd, Karachi; tel. (21) 2418430; fax (21) 2417885; e-mail info@saudipakinsurance.com.pk; Man. Dir and CEO Capt. AZHAR EHTESHAM AHMED.

Seafield Insurance Co Ltd: 86-Q, Block 2, Allama Iqbal Rd, PECHS, Karachi; tel. (21) 4527592; fax (21) 4527593; e-mail sifcpk89@hotmail.com; f. 1989; Man. Dir ADNAN HAFEEZ.

Security General Insurance Co Ltd: Nishat House, 53A Lawrence Rd, Lahore; tel. (42) 6279192; fax (42) 6303466; e-mail sgicl@hotmail.com; f. 1996; Man. Dir SYED JAWAD GILLANI.

Shaheen Insurance Co Ltd: 10th Floor, Shaheen Complex, M. R. Kayani Rd, Karachi 74200; tel. (21) 2626870; fax (21) 2626674; e-mail sihifc@cyber.net.pk; internet www.shaheeninsurance.com.pk; f. 1996; Chief Exec. SHEHRAYAR AKBAR RAJA.

Silver Star Insurance Co Ltd: Silver Star House, 2nd Floor, 5 Bank Sq., POB 2533, Lahore 54000; tel. (42) 7324488; fax (42) 7229966; e-mail info@silverstarinsurance.com; internet www.silverstarinsurance.com; f. 1984; Man. Dir and Chief Exec. ZAHIR MUHAMMAD SADIQ; Chair. CHAUDHRY MUHAMMAD SADIQ.

Trakker Direct Insurance Ltd: 172-B, 2nd Floor, Najeeb Centre, Block 2, P.E.C.H.S., Karachi; tel. (21) 4322555; fax (21) 4322515; e-mail insurance@trakkerdirect.com; internet www.trakkerdirect.com; CEO ALI JAMEEL.

UBL Insurers Ltd: 8th Floor, State Life Bldg, No. 2, Wallace Rd, off I. I. Chundrigar Rd, Karachi; tel. (21) 111–845–111; fax (21) 2463117; e-mail khalid.hamid@ublinsurers.com; internet www.ublinsurers.com; CEO and Man. Dir KHALID HAMID.

Union Insurance Co of Pakistan Ltd: Adamjee House, 9th Floor, I. I. Chundrigar Rd, Karachi; tel. (21) 2416171; fax (21) 2420174; e-mail unionins@cyber.net.pk; Pres. NISHAT RAFFIQ.

United Insurance Co of Pakistan Ltd: Nizam Chambers, 5th Floor, Shahrah-e-Fatima Jinnah, POB 532, Lahore; tel. (42) 6361471; fax (42) 6375036; f. 1959; Man. Dir and CEO M. A. SHAHID.

Universal Insurance Co Ltd: Universal Insurance House, 63 Shahrah-e-Quaid-e-Azam, POB 539, Lahore; tel. (42) 7353458; fax (42) 7230326; e-mail tuic@nexlinx.net.pk; internet www.uic.com.pk; f. 1958; Chief Exec. Begum ZEB GAUHAR AYUB KHAN; Man. Dir SARDAR KHAN.

Insurance Associations

Insurance Association of Pakistan: Jamshed Katrak Chamber, G. Allana Rd, POB 4932, Karachi 74000; tel. (21) 2311784; fax (21) 2310798; e-mail iapho@cyber.net.pk; internet www.iap.net.pk; f. 1948; mems comprise 30 cos (Pakistani and foreign) transacting general insurance business; issues tariffs and establishes rules for insurance in the country; regional office in Lahore; Chair. SAIFUDDIN N. ZOOMKAWALA; Sec. N. A. USMANI.

Pakistan Insurance Institute: Shafi Court, 2nd Floor, Mereweather Rd, Karachi 4; f. 1951 to encourage insurance education; Chair. MOHAMMAD CHOUDHRY.

Trade and Industry

GOVERNMENT AGENCIES

Alternative Energy Development Board (AEDB): 344-B, Prime Minister's Secretariat, Constitution Ave, Islamabad; tel. (51) 9223427; fax (51) 9205790; e-mail support@aedb.org; internet www.aedb.org; f. 2003; mandate incl. development of national plans and policies, undertaking promotion and dissemination of activities in field of renewable energy technologies, facilitation of power generation projects using alternative or renewable energy resources; Chair. Air Marshal (retd) SHAHID HAMID.

Board of Investment (BOI): Government of Pakistan, Atatürk Ave, Sector G-5/1, Islamabad; tel. (51) 9204339; fax (51) 9215554; e-mail secretary@pakboi.gov.pk; internet www.pakboi.gov.pk; operates under the chairmanship of the Prime Minister of Pakistan and viceroy of the Minister for Privatisation and Investment; Exec. Dir-Gen. TALAT RASHEED RASHAD MIYAN; Sec. MUSHTAQ MALIK.

Central Board of Revenue: Constitution Ave, G-5, Islamabad; tel. (51) 9207545; fax (51) 9207540; e-mail helpline@cbr.gov.pk; internet www.cbr.gov.pk; tax authority; Chair. M. ABDULLAH YUSUF.

Corporate and Industrial Restructuring Corpn: 13-C-II, M. M. Alam Rd, Gulberg III, Lahore; tel. (42) 5871532; fax (42) 5761650; e-mail info@circ-gov.com.

Earthquake Reconstruction and Rehabilitation Authority (ERRA): Prime Minister's Secretariat (Public), Constitution Ave, Islamabad; tel. (51) 9201254; fax (51) 9209525; e-mail chairman@erra.gov.pk; internet www.erra.gov.pk; f. 2005; Chair. ALTAF SALEEM.

Electronic Government Directorate: 10-D, 3rd Floor, Taimur Chambers, Blue Area West, Islamabad; tel. (51) 9205992; fax (51) 9205981; e-mail contact@e-government.gov.pk; internet www.pakistan.gov.pk/e-government-directorate; f. 2002; fmrly the Information Technology Commission; subsidiary department of the Ministry of Information Technology and Communications; Dir-Gen. of Projects SYED RAZA ABBAS SHAH.

Engineering Development Board: 5-A, Constitution Ave, SEDC Bldg (STP), Sector F-5/1, Islamabad 44000; tel. (51) 9205595; fax (51) 9203584; e-mail ceo@edb.gov.pk; internet www.engineeringpakistan.com; CEO IMTIAZ A. RASTGAR.

Environmental Protection Agency: Govt of Sindh, EPA Complex, ST-2/1, Sector 23, Korangi Industrial Area, Karachi; tel. (21) 5065950; fax (21) 5065940.

Export Processing Zones Authority (EPZA): Landhi Industrial Area Extension, Mehran Highway, Landhi, Karachi 75150; tel. (21) 5082008; fax (21) 5082009; e-mail info@epza.gov.pk; internet www.epza.gov.pk; Chair. KAMRAN MIRZA.

Family Planning Association of Pakistan (Rahnuma—FPAP): 3-A Temple Rd, Lahore 54000; tel. (42) 111-223-366; fax (42) 6368692; e-mail info@fpapak.org; internet www.fpapak.org; f. 1953; executes diversified community uplift programmes and activities; Pres. Begum SURAYYA JABEEN; CEO SYED KAMAL SHAH.

Geological Survey of Pakistan: Sariab Rd, POB 15, Quetta; tel. (81) 9211032; fax (81) 9211018; e-mail qta@gsp.gov.pk; internet www.gsp.gov.pk; Dir-Gen. MIRZA TALIB HASAN; Asst Dir MOHSIN ANWAR KAZIM.

Gwadar Port Authority: GPA Complex, Fish Harbour Rd, Gwadar 92100; tel. (864) 210073; fax (864) 210075; e-mail gwadarport@hotmail.com; internet www.gwadarport.gov.pk.

Higher Education Commission: H-9, Islamabad; tel. (51) 9040305; fax (51) 9290120; e-mail info@hec.gov.pk; internet www.hec.gov.pk; Exec. Dir Dr S. SOHAIL H. NAQVI.

Intellectual Property Organization of Pakistan (IPO-PAKISTAN): House 23, St 87, Ataturk Ave (West), G-6/3, Islamabad; tel. (51) 9208146; fax (51) 9208157; e-mail info@ipo.gov.pk; internet www.ipo.gov.pk; f. 2005; Dir-Gen. YASIN TAHIR.

Karachi Export Processing Zone (KEPZ): Landhi Industrial Area Extension, Mehran Highway, POB 17011, Karachi 75150; tel. (21) 5082010; fax (21) 5082009; e-mail info@epza.gov.pk; internet www.epza.gov.pk.

National Accountability Bureau: Atatürk Ave, G-5/2, Islamabad; tel. (51) 111-622-622; fax (51) 9214502; e-mail infonab@nab.gov.pk; internet www.nab.gov.pk.

National Aliens Registration Authority (NARA): C-82, Block 2, Clifton, Karachi; tel. (21) 9251083; f. 2001; registers all foreign nationals who wish to work in Pakistan.

National Commission for Human Development: 14th Floor, Shaheed-e-Millat Secretariat, Jinnah Ave, Islamabad; tel. (51) 9216200; fax (51) 9216164; e-mail info@nchd.org.pk; internet www.nchd.org.pk; f. 2002.

National Database and Registration Authority (NADRA): State Bank of Pakistan Bldg, Shahrah-e-Jamhuriat, G-5/2, Islamabad; tel. (51) 9201120; e-mail info@nadra.gov.pk; internet www.nadra.gov.pk.

National Economic Council: supreme economic body; the governors and chief ministers of the four provinces and fed. ministers in charge of economic ministries are its mems; sr fed. and provincial officials in the economic field are also associated; Chair. Prime Minister.

National Electric Power Regulatory Authority (NEPRA): (see Utilities).

National Energy Conservation Centre (ENERCON): ENERCON Bldg, G-5/2, Islamabad; tel. (51) 9206005; fax (51) 9206004; e-mail ferts@enercon.gov.pk; internet www.enercon.gov.pk; Man. Dir Dr FERVAIZ TAHIR.

National Highway Authority (NHA): (see Transport: Roads).

National Housing Authority: Prime Minister's Office, Islamabad; tel. (51) 9202279; fax (51) 9217813; Dir-Gen. SALIM IQBAL QURESHI.

National Tariff Commission: State Life Bldg, No. 5, Blue Area, Jinnah Ave, POB 1689, Islamabad 44000; tel. (51) 9208790; fax (51) 9221205; e-mail ntc@ntc.gov.pk; internet www.ntc.gov.pk; f. 1990; Chair. Dr FAIZULLAH KHILJI.

National Testing Service (NTS): 10–11, Plaza 2000, 1st Floor, Plot 43, Markaz I-8, Islamabad; tel. (51) 9258478; fax (51) 9258480; e-mail support@nts.org.pk; internet www.nts.org.pk; conducts assessment programs for students at all educational levels; facilitates employment and career development through subject testing.

Oil and Gas Regulatory Authority: Tariq Chambers, Civic Centre, G-6, Islamabad; tel. (51) 9221715; fax (51) 9221714; e-mail secretary@ogra.org.pk; internet www.ogra.org.pk; regulates oil and gas sector; Chair. MUNIR AHMAD.

Pakistan Electronic Media Regulatory Authority: Islamabad; tel. (51) 9202174; fax (51) 9219634; e-mail info@pemra.gov.pk; internet www.pemra.gov.pk; f. 2002; Chair. IFTIKHAR RASHID; Dir-Gen. RANA ALTAF MAJID.

Pakistan National Accreditation Council (PNAC): Ministry of Scientific and Technological Research, 4th Floor, Evacuee Trust Complex, Aga Khan Rd, F-5/1, Islamabad; tel. (51) 9222310; fax (51) 9222312; e-mail ismailgulkhatak@yahoo.com; f. 1998; Dir-Gen. ABDUL RASHID KHAN.

Pakistan Software Export Board (Guarantee) Ltd: 2nd Floor, Evacuee Trust Complex, F-5/1, Aga Khan Rd, Islamabad; tel. (51) 9204074; fax (51) 9204075; e-mail info@pseb.org.pk; internet www.pseb.org.pk; Man. Dir YUSUF HUSSAIN.

Pakistan Standards and Quality Control Authority (PSQCA): Pakistan Secretariat, Block 77, Karachi 74400; tel. and fax (21) 9206260; fax (21) 9206263; e-mail psqcadg@super.net.pk; internet www.psqca.com.pk; f. 1996; regulates standards in industry; Dir-Gen. ABDUL GHAFFAR SOOMRO.

Pakistan Stone Development Co: I. C. C. I. Bldg, 2nd Floor, Mauve Area, G-8/A, Islamabad; tel. (51) 9263465; fax (51) 9263464; f. 2006; promotes devt of marble and granite sector; Chair. IHSANULLAH KHAN.

Pakistan Telecommunication Authority: (see Telecommunications).

Pakistan Tobacco Board: 46-B Office Enclave, Phase-V, Hayatabad, POB 188, Peshawar; tel. (91) 9217151; fax (91) 9217149; e-mail mail@ptb.gov.pk; internet www.ptb.gov.pk; f. 1968; regulates, controls and promotes the export of tobacco and related products, and fixes grading standards; Chair. Maj. SAHIBZADA MUHAMMAD KHALID; Research and Devt Dir MUHAMMAD TARIQ.

Privatisation Commission: Experts Advisory Cell Bldg, 5A Constitution Ave, Islamabad 44000; tel. (51) 9205146; fax (51) 9203076; e-mail info@privatisation.gov.pk; internet www.privatisation.gov.pk; supervised by Ministry of Privatisation and Investment.

Sindh Katchi Abadis Authority (SKAA): Maulana Din Muhammad Wafai Rd, Karachi 74200; tel. (21) 9211278; fax (21) 9211272; e-mail skaa@khi.compol.com; internet www.lgdsindh.com.pk/skaa.htm; f. 1987; govt agency established to regulate and improve slums in Pakistan's southern province; Dir-Gen. MIR NASIR ABBAS.

Sindh Privatisation Commission: Sindh Secretariat, 4-A, Block 15, Court Rd, Karachi; tel. (21) 9202077; fax (21) 9202071; e-mail spcsecretary@yahoo.com; Sec. SYED ZULFIQAR ALI SHAH.

Sustainable Development Policy Institute: St 3, UN Blvd, Diplomatic Enclave 1, Islamabad; tel. (51) 2278134; fax (51) 2278135; e-mail msf@sdpi.org; internet www.sdpi.org; f. 1992; Co-ordinator MOHAMMAD SHAH FARRUKH.

Trade Development Authority of Pakistan (TDAP): Finance and Trade Centre, Block A, 5th Floor, POB 1203, Shahrah-e-Faisal, Karachi 75200; tel. (21) 1114441; fax (21) 9206487; e-mail tdap@tdap.gov.pk; internet www.tdap.gov.pk; f. 1963 as Export Promotion Bureau (EPB) affiliated to the Ministry of Commerce; Trade Development Authority was established in Nov. 2006 by an Ordinance of President Musharraf to assume all functions fmrly dispatched by the EPB; Chair. TARIQ IKRAM; Sec. ZAFAR MAHMOOD.

Trading Corporation of Pakistan: 4th and 5th Floors, Finance and Trade Centre, Main Shahrah-e-Faisal, Karachi 75530; tel. (21) 9202947-9; fax (21) 9202722; e-mail tcp@tcp.gov.pk; internet www.tcp.gov.pk; f. 1967; Chair. ABDUL MALIK.

Utility Stores Corporation of Pakistan: Plot No. 2039, G-7/F-7, POB 1339, Jinnah Ave, Blue Area, Islamabad; tel. (51) 9210976; fax (51) 9210982; e-mail usc_ho@yahoo.com; internet www.usc.com.pk; f. 1971; Man. Dir Brig. (retd) HAFEEZ AHMED.

DEVELOPMENT ORGANIZATIONS

Balochistan Development Authority: Civil Secretariat, Block 7, Quetta; tel. (81) 9202491; created for economic devt of Balochistan; exploration and exploitation of mineral resources; development of infrastructure, water resources, etc.

Capital Development Authority: Islamabad; tel. (51) 9201016; fax (51) 9219413; internet www.cda.gov.pk; Chair. KAMRAN LASHARI.

Center for International Private Enterprise (Pakistan) (CIPE): Glass Tower, Suite 214–15, 2 Ft 3, adjacent to PSO House, Main Clifton Rd, Karachi 75530; tel. (21) 5656993; e-mail pakistan@cipe.org; internet www.cipe.org; international org.; affiliate of US Chamber of Commerce and key member of National Endowment for Democracy; US Agency for international Development supports programs of CIPE; Country Dir M. MOIN FUDDA.

Council for Works and Housing Research (CWHR): F-40, SITE Hub River Rd, Karachi 75730; tel. (21) 2577236; fax (21) 2577235; e-mail cwhr@khi.comsats.net.pk; internet www.cwhr.gov.pk; f. 1964.

Faisalabad Industrial Estate Development & Management Co (FIEDMC): Faisalabad; tel. (41) 8523106; fax (41) 8522884; e-mail fiedmc@fiedmc.com.pk; internet www.fiedmc.com.pk; established by the Punjab state government under the Public Private Partnership system to promote devt of industrial estates; Chair. Mian MUHAMMAD LATIF; CEO KHURRAM IFTIKHAR.

Gwadar Development Authority: Governor House Rd, Gwadar; tel. and fax (86) 4211775; e-mail info@gda.gov.pk; internet www.gda.gov.pk; Dir-Gen. AHMAD BAKSH LEHRI.

Lahore Development Authority (LDA): LDA Plaza, 9th Floor, Egerton Rd, Lahore; tel. (42) 9201510; internet www.lda.gop.pk; f. 1975; Dir of Admin. ABDUL HAMEED CHAUDHRY.

Lasbella Industrial Estate Development Authority (LIEDA): Hub Industrial Trading Estate, Lasbella, Balochistan; tel. (853) 303361; fax (853) 302470; e-mail lieda@lieda.gov.pk; est. under section 3 of Government of Balochistan Ordinance IX (1989); promotes devt of industrial concerns over 1,000 acre coastal Highway region; Man. Dir Col (retd) BASHIR AHMED NADIM.

Malir Development Authority: Main Northern By-Pass, Scheme No. 45, Taisar Town, Karachi; Dir-Gen. AMEERZADA KOHATI; Chair. SYED MUSTAFA KAMAL.

National Commission for Human Development: Shaheed-e-Millat Secretariat, 14th Floor, Jinnah Ave, Islamabad; tel. (51) 9216200; fax (51) 9216164; e-mail info@nchd.org.pk; internet www.nchd.org.pk; f. 2001 by presidential decree; facilitates programs towards achievement of the UNDP Millennium Development Goals; Chair. Dr NASIM ASHRAF.

Pakistan Engineering Council: Ataturk Ave (East), G-5/2, Islamabad; tel. (51) 9206974; fax (51) 2276224; e-mail info@pec.org.pk; internet www.pec.org.pk; f. 1976; Chair. M. AKRAM SHEIKH.

Pakistan Gems & Jewellery Development Co (PGJDC): Regent Plaza Hotel and Convention Centre, M-3 Mezzanine Floor, Shahra-e-Faisal, Karachi; tel. (21) 5631394; fax (21) 5631398; e-mail info@pgjdc.org; internet www.pgjdc.org; f. 2006; est. as non-profit org under Ministry of Industries, Production and Special Initiatives; subsidiary of Pakistan Industrial Devt Corpn; promotes devt of Pakistan's gem and jewellery industry; CEO FAWAD KHAN.

Pakistan Industrial Technical Assistance Centre (PITAC): 234 Maulana Jalaluddin Roomi Rd (old Ferozepur Rd), Lahore 54600; tel. (42) 9230699; fax (42) 9230589; e-mail info@pitac.gov.pk; internet www.pitac.gov.pk; f. 1962 by the Govt to provide prototype tooling facilities and spare parts to manufacturing industries and advanced training to industrial personnel in the fields of metal trades and tool engineering design and related fields; under Ministry of Industries, Production and Special Initiatives; provides human resource devt programmes; Chair. MANZAR SHAMIM; Gen. Man. Lt-Col (retd) KHAN M. NAZIR.

Pakistan Poverty Alleviation Fund: House No. 1, St 20, F-7/2, Islamabad; tel. (51) 111-000-102; fax (51) 2652246; e-mail info@ppaf.org.pk; internet www.ppaf.org.pk; f. 1997 by the Government; funded by the World Bank; works with non-governmental organizations and private-sector institutions to alleviate poverty; 68 partner orgs nationwide; Chief Exec. and Man. Dir KAMAL HAYAT.

Quetta Development Authority: Sarai Rd, Quetta; tel. (81) 9211069.

Sarhad Development Authority (SDA): PIA Bldg, Arbab Rd, POB 172, Peshawar; tel. (91) 9211608; fax (91) 9211605; e-mail sdap@psh.paknet.com.pk; internet www.sda.org.pk; f. 1972; pro-

PAKISTAN

motes industrial (particularly mining) and commercial devt in the North-West Frontier Province; Chair. KHALID AZIZ.

Small and Medium Enterprises Development Authority (SMEDA): 6th Floor, LDA Plaza, Egerton Rd, Lahore; tel. (42) 111-111-456; fax (42) 6304926; e-mail helpdesk@smeda.org.pk; internet www.smeda.org.pk; f. 1998; four brs; 18 regional business centres; CEO SHAHAB KHAWAJA.

CHAMBERS OF COMMERCE

The Federation of Pakistan Chambers of Commerce and Industry: Federation House, Main Clifton, POB 13875, Karachi 75600; tel. (21) 5873691; fax (21) 5874332; e-mail fpcci@cyber.net.pk; internet www.fpcci.com.pk; f. 1950; 163 mem. bodies; Pres. TANVIR AHMED SHAIKH; Sec.-Gen. and CEO ZAHID HUSSAIN.

Islamic Chamber of Commerce and Industry: St 2/A, Block 9, KDA Scheme No. 5, Clifton, POB 3831, Karachi 75600; tel. (21) 5874756; fax (21) 5870765; e-mail icci@icci-oic.org; internet www.icci-oic.org; f. 1979; Pres. Sheikh SALEH BIN ABDULLAH KAMEL; Sec.-Gen. AQEEL AHMAD AL-JASSEM.

Overseas Investors' Chamber of Commerce and Industry: Chamber of Commerce Bldg, Talpur Rd, POB 4833, Karachi 74000; tel. (21) 2426076; fax (21) 2427315; e-mail info@oicci.org; internet www.oicci.org; f. 1860 as the Karachi Chamber of Commerce, name changed to above in 1968; 169 mem. bodies; Pres. SALMAN BURNEY; Sec.-Gen. ADNAN AFRIDI.

Principal Affiliated Chambers

Azad Jammu and Kashmir Chamber of Commerce and Industry: 9, Sector G/1, Haul Rd, POB 12, Mirpur 10250; tel. (58610) 34760; fax (58610) 34761; e-mail ajkcci@hotmail.com; internet www.ajkcci.com; f. 1980; Sec. CHAUDHRY MUHAMMAD SHAFIQ.

Bahawalpur Chamber of Commerce and Industry: 28 C/A, Abbasi Rd, off Shahrah-e-Azia Bhatti Shaheed, Model Town A, Bahawalpur; tel. and fax (621) 883192; e-mail chamber@pakview.com; Pres. Khawaja MOHAMMAD ILYAS.

Balochistan Chamber of Commerce and Industry: Zarghoon Rd, POB 117, Quetta 87300; tel. (81) 2835717; fax (81) 2821948; e-mail qcci@hotmail.com; f. 1984; Pres. Sheikh ABDUL AZIZ; Sec. MUHAMMAD AHMAD.

Chaman Chamber of Commerce and Industry: Commerce House, Chaman; tel. (826) 613308.

Dadu Chamber of Commerce and Industry: 816, 8th Floor, Progressive Plaza, Beaumont Rd, Karachi; tel. (21) 5219026; fax (21) 5650006; e-mail daduchamber@hotmail.com.

Dera Ghazi Khan Chamber of Commerce and Industry: Block 34, Khakwani House, Dera Ghazi Khan, Punjab; tel. (641) 62338; fax (641) 64938; Pres. Khawaja MOHAMMAD YUNUS; Sec. MOHAMMAD MUJAHID.

Dera Ismail Khan Chamber of Commerce and Industry: Circular Rd, POB 5, D. I. Khan; tel. (961) 811334; fax (961) 811334; e-mail sjbdn@epistemics.net.

Faisalabad Chamber of Commerce and Industry: 2nd Floor, National Bank Bldg, Jail Rd, Faisalabad; tel. (41) 616045; fax (41) 615085; e-mail fcci@fsd.paknet.com.pk; Pres. Mian AFTAB AHMAD; Sec. SYED RIAZ HUSSAIN RIZVI.

Gwadar Chamber of Commerce and Industry: Main Clifton Rd, Gwadar; tel. (21) 5375071; fax (21) 5876336; e-mail info@gawadarchamber.com; internet gawadarchamber.com; Pres. ASGHAR AZIZ SANJARANI.

Gujranwala Chamber of Commerce and Industry: Aiwan-e-Tijarat Rd, Gujranwala; tel. (55) 3256701; fax (55) 3254440; internet www.gcci.org.pk; f. 1978; Pres. RANA SHAHZAD HAFEEZ; Sec. SYED MUJAHID MUMTAZ.

Gujrat Chamber of Commerce and Industry: 26-A, G. T. Rd, S.I.E. POB 169, Gujrat; tel. (4331) 523012; fax (4331) 523011; Pres. CH. IFTIKHAR AHMED.

Haripur Chamber of Commerce and Industry: Chamber House, GPO Rd, Haripur; tel. (995) 613364; fax (995) 614664; e-mail haripur-chamber@yahoo.com; internet www.hcci.org.pk; Pres. Haji FAKHAR-E-ALAM; Sec.-Gen. FAQIR MUHAMMAD KHAN.

Hyderabad Chamber of Commerce and Industry: Aiwan-e-Tijarat Rd, Saddar, POB 99, Hyderabad 71000; tel. (22) 2784972; fax (22) 2784977; e-mail hcci@muchomail.com; internet www.hyderabadchamber.com; f. 1961; Pres. MEHMOOD AHMAD; Sec. BASHIR ALI NOORANI.

Islamabad Chamber of Commerce and Industry: Aiwan-e-Sana't-o-Tijarat Rd, Mauve Area, Sector G-8/1, Islamabad; tel. (51) 2250526; fax (51) 2252950; e-mail icci@brain.net.pk; internet www.icci.com.pk; f. 1984; Pres. MUHAMMED IJAZ ABBASI; Sec. MAJID SHABBIR.

Jhelum Chamber of Commerce and Industry: Rani Nagar, G. T. Rd, Jhelum; tel. (541) 646532; fax (541) 646533; Pres. RAJA TARIQ REHMAN; Sec. Capt. (retd) MUHAMMAD ZAMAN.

Karachi Chamber of Commerce and Industry: Aiwan-e-Tijarat Rd, off Shahrah-e-Liaquat, POB 4158, Karachi 74000; tel. (21) 5873691; fax (21) 5874332; e-mail info@karachichamber.com; internet www.karachichamber.com; f. 1960; 11,705 mems; Pres. HAROON FARUQI; Sec. M. NAZIR ALI.

Khairpur Chamber of Commerce and Industry: Shop 8, Sachal Shopping Centre, Khairpur; tel. (792) 51505.

Lahore Chamber of Commerce and Industry: 11 Shahrah-e-Aiwan-e-Tijarat, POB 597, Lahore; tel. (42) 6305538; fax (42) 6368854; e-mail sect@lcci.org.pk; internet www.lcci.org.pk; f. 1923; 8,000 mems; Pres. SHAHID HUSSAIN SHAIKH; Sec. M. LATIF CHAUDHRY.

Larkana Chamber of Commerce and Industry: 21–23 Kenedy Market, POB 78, Larkana, Sindh; tel. (741) 457136; fax (741) 440709; e-mail president@larkanachamber.com; internet www.larkanachamber.com; Pres. MOHAMMAD ASLAM SHEIKH.

Mirpurkhas Chamber of Commerce and Industry: Khan Chamber, New Town, POB 162, Mirpurkhas, Sindh; tel. (233) 872175; fax (233) 872195; Pres. ABDUL KHALIQUE KHAN; Sec. MOHAMMAD BASIT-ULLAH BAIG.

Multan Chamber of Commerce and Industry: Shahrah-e-Aiwan-e-Tijarat-o-Sanat, Multan; tel. (61) 4517087; fax (61) 4570463; e-mail mccimultan@hotmail.com; Pres. Mian MUGHIS A. SHEIKH; Sec. G. A. BHATTI.

Quetta Chamber of Commerce and Industry: Zarghoon Rd, POB 117, Quetta 87300; tel. (81) 2821943; fax (81) 2821948; e-mail qcci@hotmail.com; Pres. MOHAMMAD SIDDIQUE KAKAR; Sec. MUHAMMAD AHMED.

Rawalpindi Chamber of Commerce and Industry: 39 Mayo Rd, Civil Lines, Rawalpindi; tel. (51) 5110514; fax (51) 5111055; e-mail rcci@isd.wol.net.pk; f. 1952; Pres. HUSSAIN AHMED OZGAN; Sec. MUHAMMAD IFTIKHAR-UD-DIN.

SAARC Chamber of Commerce and Industry: House No. 397, St No. 64, I-8/3, Islamabad; tel. (51) 2281396; fax (51) 2281390; e-mail eaqav.ahmad@saarcchamber.com; internet www.saarcchamber.com; f. 1993; Dir WAQAV AHMAD.

Sargodha Chamber of Commerce and Industry: 80/2-A, Satellite Town, Sargodha 40100; tel. (48) 9230662; fax (48) 9230663; e-mail sgdacci@hotmail.com; f. 1986; Pres. ABID RAFIQUE KHAWAJA; Sec.-Gen. KASHIF MUKHTAR SHEIKH.

Sarhad Chamber of Commerce and Industry: Sarhad Chamber House, Chacha Younis Park, G. T. Rd, Peshawar; tel. (91) 9213314; fax (91) 9213316; e-mail sccip@brain.net.pk; internet www.scci.org.pk; f. 1958; 2,735 mems; Pres. LIAQAT AHMED KHAN; Sec. FAQIR MUHAMMAD.

Sialkot Chamber of Commerce and Industry: Shahrah-e-Aiwan-e-Sanat-o-Tijarat, POB 1870, Sialkot 51310; tel. (52) 4261881; fax (52) 4268835; e-mail directorrnd@scci.com.pk; internet www.scci.com.pk; f. 1982; 7,500 mems; Pres. Sheikh ABDUL WAHEED SANDAL; Sec. NAWAZ AHMED TOOR.

Sukkur Chamber of Commerce and Industry: Sukkur Chamber House, 1st Floor, opp. Mehran View Plaza, Bunder Rd, Sukkur; tel. (71) 23938; fax (71) 23059; Pres. SHAKEEL AHMED MUKHTAR; Sec. MIRZA IQBAL BEG.

Thatta Chamber of Commerce and Industry: PO Shaffiabad, Gharo, Thatta; tel. (14) 7726243; fax (14) 7725122; e-mail malodhi@lodhico.khi2.erum.com.pk.

INDUSTRIAL AND TRADE ASSOCIATIONS

Air Cargo Agents' Association of Pakistan: Suite 305, 3rd Floor, Fortune Centre, 45-A, Block 6, PECHS, Shahrah-e-Faisal, Karachi 75400; tel. (21) 4383501; e-mail acaap@pk.netsolier.com; Sec.-Gen. S. MOHAMMAD ABBAS.

All Pakistan Cement Manufacturers' Association: 5th Floor, Maqbool Commercial Comp., J.C.H.S., Shahrah-e-Faisal, Karachi; tel. (21) 5758360.

All Pakistan Cloth Exporters' Association: 30/7, Civil Lines, Faisalabad; tel. (41) 644750; fax (41) 617985; e-mail apcea@fsd.paknet.com.pk; Chair. AHMAD KAMAL; Sec. AFTAB AHMAD.

All Pakistan Cloth Merchants' Association: 4th Floor, Hasan Ali Centre, Hussaini Cloth Market, nr Mereweather Tower, M. A. Jinnah Rd, Karachi; tel. (21) 2444274; fax (21) 2401423; e-mail pcma@cyber.net.pk; Chair. AHMED CHINOY; Sec.-Gen. RAFIQ KHAN.

All Pakistan Cotton Powerlooms' Association: P-79/3, Montgomery Bazaar, Faisalabad; tel. (411) 612929; fax (411) 28171; Chair. CHAUDRY JAVAID SADIQ.

All Pakistan Furniture Exporters' Association: Karachi; tel. (21) 5861963; Chair. TURHAN BAIG MOHAMMAD.

PAKISTAN

All Pakistan Textile Mills' Association (APTMA): APTMA House, 44A Lalazar, off Moulvi Tamizuddin Khan Rd, POB 5446, Karachi 74000; tel. (21) 111-700-000; fax (21) 5611305; e-mail aptma@cyber.net.pk; internet www.aptma.org.pk; f. 1959; COO MUHAMMAD AZAM; Chair. SHAFQAT ELLAHI SHEIKH.

Association of Builders and Developers of Pakistan: Abed House, St 1-1/10, Block 16, Gulistan-e-Jauhar, Karachi 75290; tel. (21) 8136456; fax (21) 8113648.

Cigarette Manufacturers' Association of Pakistan: Caesars Towers (opp. Aisha Bawany Academy), Rm 102, 1st Floor, Main Shahrah-e-Faisal, Karachi 75400; tel. and fax (21) 2789555; e-mail cmaofpak@cyber.net.pk; Sec. TARIQ FAROOQ.

Cotton Board: Dr Abbasi Clinic Bldg, 76 Strachan Rd, Karachi 74200; tel. (21) 215669; fax (21) 5680422; f. 1950; Dep. Sec. Dr MUHAMMAD USMAN.

Federal 'B' Area Association of Trade and Industry: ST-7, Block 22, Federal 'B' Area, Karachi 75950; tel. (21) 6340362; fax (21) 6360203; e-mail info@fbati.com; internet www.fbati.com; Chair. MASROOR AHMAD ALVI.

Karachi Cotton Association: The Cotton Exchange, I. I. Chundrigar Rd, Karachi; tel. (21) 2410336; fax (21) 2413035; e-mail kcapak@cyber.net.pk; internet www.kcapak.org; Chair. A. SHAKOOR DADA; Sec. S. A. JAWED.

Korangi Association of Trade and Industry: ST-4/2, 1st Floor, Aiwan-e-Sanat, Sector 23, Korangi Industrial Area, Karachi 74900; tel. (21) 5061211; fax (21) 5061215; e-mail kati@cyber.net.pk; Chair. MASOOD NAQI; Sec. NIHAL AKHTAR.

Management Association of Pakistan: 36-A/4, Lalazar, opp. Beach Luxury Hotel, Karachi 74000; tel. (21) 5610903; fax (21) 5611683; e-mail info@mappk.org; internet www.mappk.org; f. 1964; Pres. SOHAIL WAJAHAT H. SIDDIQUI; Exec. Dir FAROOQ HASSAN.

Pakistan Advertising Association: Rm 318, 3rd Floor, Hotel Metropole, Club Rd, Karachi; tel. (21) 5671567; fax (21) 5671571; e-mail paa1@cyber.net.pk; internet www.paa.com.pk; Sec. S. NAJMUL HASSAN.

Pakistan Agricultural Machinery and Implements Manufacturers' Association: Samundari Rd, Faisalabad; tel. (41) 714517; fax (41) 722721; e-mail iqra@fsd.comsats.net.pk.

Pakistan Arms and Ammunition Merchants' and Manufacturers' Association: Metropole Cinema Bldg, Rm 7, Abbot Rd, Lahore; tel. (42) 7239973; fax (42) 7230170; e-mail ssalimali@hotmail.com.

Pakistan Art Silk Fabrics and Garments Exporters' Association: 60, The Mall, Lahore; tel. (42) 6360919; fax (42) 6361291; e-mail pasfgea@hotmail.com; internet www.pasfgea.org; Chair. JAMIL MEHBOOB MAGOON; Sec.-Gen. IFTIKHAR AHMED KHAN.

Pakistan Association of Automotive Parts and Accessories Manufacturers: 894 Circular Rd, nr Nigar Cinema, Lahore; tel. (42) 7312452; fax (42) 7237613; e-mail secypaapam@hotmail.com.

Pakistan Association of Builders and Developers: Abad House, St 1/D, Block 16, Gulistan-e-Jauhar, Karachi; tel. (21) 8113645; fax (21) 8113648; e-mail abadhouse@yahoo.com.

Pakistan Association of Printing and Graphic Arts: 214, Mashriq Centre, 2nd Floor, Staduim Rd, Karachi; tel. (21) 4920175; fax (21) 4926625; e-mail info@papgai.com.pk; internet www.papgai.com.pk; f. 1959; affiliated with the federation of Pakistan Chambers of Commerce and Industry; promotion and devt of the printing and graphic arts industry; Chair. GHAS AHMED PIRZADA.

Pakistan Automotive Manufacturers' Association: 11 Ilaco House, Abdullah Haroon Rd, Karachi; tel. (21) 5662493; fax (21) 5687247; e-mail pamauto@cyber.net.pk.

Pakistan Bedwear Exporters' Association: 245-1-V, Block 6, PECHS, Karachi; tel. (21) 4541149; fax (21) 4541192; e-mail bedwear@fascom.com; Chair. SHABIR AHMED; Sec. S. IFTIKHAR HUSSAIN.

Pakistan Beverage Manufacturers' Association: C, 1st Floor, Kiran Centre, M-28, Model Town Extension, Lahore; tel. (42) 5167306; fax (42) 5167316.

Pakistan Canvas and Tents Manufacturers' and Exporters' Association: 15/63, Shadman Commercial Market, Afridi Mansion, Lahore 3; tel. (42) 7578836; fax (42) 7577572; e-mail pctmea@wol.net.pk; Chair. ABDUL RAZAK CHHAPRA; Sec. IJAZ HUSSAIN.

Pakistan Carpet Manufacturers' and Exporters' Association: 401-A, 4th Floor, Panorama Center, Fatima Jinnah Rd, Saddar, Karachi 75530; tel. (21) 5212189; fax (21) 5679649; e-mail pcmeaho@gerrys.net; internet www.pakistanrug.com.pk; Chair. ABDUL GHAFOOR SAJID; Sec. A. S. HASHMI.

Pakistan Chemicals and Dyes Merchants' Association: Chemical and Dye House, Jodia Bazar, Rambharti St, Karachi 74000; tel. (21) 2432752; fax (21) 2430117; Chair. MOHAMMAD SABIR CHIPPA.

Pakistan Commercial Exporters of Towels Association: PCETA House, 7-H, Block 6, PECHS, Karachi; tel. (21) 4535757; fax (21) 4522372; e-mail pceta@cyber.net.pk; Chair. JAMIL MAHBOOB MAGOON.

Pakistan Cotton Fashion Apparel Manufacturers' and Exporters' Association: Rm 5, Amber Court, 2nd Floor, Shahrah-e-Faisal, Shaheed-e-Millat Rd, Karachi 75350; tel. (21) 4533936; fax (21) 4546711; e-mail pcfa@cyber.net.pk; f. 1982; 650 mems; Chair. Dr SHAHZAD ARSHAD.

Pakistan Cotton Ginners' Association: 1119–1120, 11th Floor, Uni-Plaza, I. I. Chundrigar Rd, Karachi; tel. (21) 2411406; fax (21) 2423181; e-mail pcga@pgca.org; Pres. MOHAMMAD SAEED; Sec. AIJAZUDDIN GHAURI.

Pakistan Dairy Association: 11/19-B, Link Shami Rd, Lahore; tel. (42) 6680041; fax (42) 6682042; e-mail pakdairy@yahoo.com.

Pakistan Electronic Manufacturers' Association: 1st Floor, Rizvi Chambers, Akbar Rd, Karachi; tel. (21) 7766912; fax (21) 5874546.

Pakistan Engineering Council: Atatürk Ave (East), Sector G-5/2, Islamabad; tel. (51) 2276625; fax (51) 2276224; e-mail info@pec.org.pk; internet www.pec.org.pk; f. 1976.

Pakistan Film Producers' Association: Regal Cinema Bldg, Shahrah-e-Quaid-e-Azam, Lahore; tel. (42) 7322904; fax (42) 7241264; Chair. Mian AMJAD FARZEND; Sec. SAMI DEHLVI.

Pakistan Flour Mills' Association: Taj Complex, Block C-3, 1st Floor, Line Development Area, M. A. Jinnah Rd, Karachi; tel. (21) 5010556; fax (21) 7780137.

Pakistan Footwear Manufacturers' Association: 6-F, Rehman Business Centre, 32-B-III, Gulberg III, Lahore 54660; tel. (42) 5750051; fax (42) 5780276; e-mail pfma@pakfootwear.org; internet www.pakfootwear.org; f. 1984; Chair. NASIR ANWAR; Sec. Col (retd) ARSHAD AYYAZ.

Pakistan Gloves Manufacturers' and Exporters' Association: PGMEA Bldg, Kashmir Rd, POB 1330, Sialkot; tel. (52) 4272959; fax (52) 4274860; e-mail pgmea@brain.net.pk; internet www.brain.net.pk/~pgmea; f. 1978; Chair. SOHAIL MASOOD; Sec. MUHAMMAD TAYYAB SHAIKH.

Pakistan Hardware Merchants' Association: Mandviwala Bldg, Serai Rd, Karachi 74000; tel. (21) 2420610; fax (21) 2432878; e-mail phmasbcircle@hotmail.com; f. 1961; more than 1,500 mems; Chair. BASIT ALAVI; Sec. SYED ZAFRUN NABI.

Pakistan Hosiery Manufacturers' Association: Karachi; tel. (21) 4522769; fax (21) 4543774; Chair. IMRAN ALI; Sec. YUNUS BIN AIYOOB.

Pakistan Iron and Steel Merchants' Association: Corner House, 2nd Floor, Preedy St, Saddar, Karachi; tel. (21) 5660270; fax (21) 5682724; Pres. MALIK AHMAD HUSSAIN; Gen. Sec. S. S. REHMAN.

Pakistan Jute Mills' Association: 8 Sasi Town Houses, Abdullah Haroon Rd, Civil Lines, Karachi 75530; tel. (21) 5676986; fax (21) 5676463; e-mail pjma@cyber.net.pk; Chair. HUMAYUN MAZHAR; Sec. S. A. H. RIZVI.

Pakistan Knitwear and Sweaters Exporters' Association: Rms Nos 1014–1016, 10th Floor, Park Ave, Block 6, PECHS, Shahrah-e-Faisal, Karachi 95350; tel. (21) 4522604; fax (21) 4525747; Chair. NASIR HUSSAIN.

Pakistan Leather Garments Manufacturers' and Exporters' Association: 92-C, Khayaban-e-Ittehad, DHA Phase II (Extension), Karachi; tel. (21) 5387356; fax (21) 5388799; e-mail info@plgmea.org; internet www.plgmea.org; f. 2002; Chair. AHMAD ZULFIQAR HAYAT.

Pakistan Paint Manufacturers' Association: St 6/A, Block 14, Federal 'B' Area, Karachi 38; tel. (21) 6321103; fax (21) 2560468; f. 1953; Chair. WASSIM A. KHAN; Sec. SYED AZHAR ALI.

Pakistan Petroleum Exploration and Production Companies' Association: 1 St 49, Sector F-6/4, Islamabad; tel. (51) 2823928; fax (51) 2276084; e-mail ppepca@isb.comsats.net.pk; internet www.ppepca.org; f. 1995; Chair. PHILIP BYRNE.

Pakistan Pharmaceutical Manufacturers' Association: 130–131, Hotel Metropole, Karachi; tel. (21) 5211773; fax (21) 5675608.

Pakistan Plastic Manufacturers' Association: 410 Mashrique Shopping Centre, St 6/A, Block No. 14, Gulshan-e-Iqbal, Karachi; tel. (21) 4942336; fax (21) 4944222; e-mail pakppma@pk.netsolir.com; Sec. FAYYAZ A. CHAUDHRY; Pres. ZAKARIA USMAN.

Pakistan Polypropylene Woven Sacks Manufacturers' Association: Karachi; Chair. SHOUKAT AHMED.

Pakistan Poultry Association: 219 Mashriq Centre, Block 14, Sir Shah Muhammad Suleman Rd, Gulshan-e-Iqbal, Karachi; tel. (21) 4940362; fax (21) 4940364; e-mail ppasee@cyber.net.pk.

Pakistan Pulp, Paper and Board Mills' Association: 402 Burhani Chambers, Abdullah Haroon Rd, Karachi 74400; tel. (21) 7726150; Chair. KAMRAN KHAN.

Pakistan Readymade Garments Manufacturers' and Exporters' Association: Shaheen View Bldg, Mezzanine Floor, Plot No. 18A, Block 6, PECHS, Shahrah-e-Faisal, Karachi; tel. (21) 4547912; fax (21) 4539669; e-mail info@prgmea.org; internet www.prgmea.org; Chair. BILAL MULLA.

Pakistan Seafood Industries' Association: A-2, Fish Harbour, West Wharf, Karachi; tel. (21) 2311117; fax (21) 2310939; e-mail psiapk@hotmail.com.

Pakistan Ship Breakers' Association: 608, S. S. Chamber, Siemens Chowrangi, S.I.T.E., Karachi; tel. (21) 293958; fax (21) 256533.

Pakistan Silk and Rayon Mills' Association: Rms Nos 44–48, Textile Plaza, 5th Floor, M. A. Jinnah Rd, Karachi 2; tel. (21) 2410288; fax (21) 2415261; e-mail ctech@edu.pk; f. 1974; Chair. M. ASHRAF SHEIKH; Sec. M. H. K. BURNEY.

Pakistan Small Units Powerlooms' Association: 2nd Floor, Waqas Plaza, Aminpura Bazar, POB 8647, Faisalabad; tel. (411) 627992; fax (411) 633567.

Pakistan Soap Manufacturers' Association: 148 Sunny Plaza, Hasrat Mohani Rd, Karachi 74200; tel. (21) 2634648; fax (21) 2563828; e-mail pakistansma@yahoo.com; Chair. YAQOOB KARIM.

Pakistan Software Houses Association (PASHA): D-30, Block 9, Clifton, Karachi 75600; tel. (21) 5866595; fax (21) 5869991; e-mail karachi@pasha.org.pk; internet www.pasha.org.pk; f. 1992; Pres. ZAIN I. SYED.

Pakistan Sports Goods Manufacturers' and Exporters' Association: Paris Rd, Sialkot 51310; tel. (432) 267962; fax (432) 261774; e-mail psga@brain.net.pk; Chair. Sheikh AHMED HUSSAIN.

Pakistan Steel Melters' Association: 30-S, Gulberg Centre, 84-D/1, Main Boulevard, Gulberg-III, Lahore; tel. (42) 5759284; fax (42) 5712028; e-mail steelmelters@angelfire.com; Chair. Mian MUHAMMAD SAEED.

Pakistan Steel Re-rolling Mills' Association: Rashid Chambers, 6-Link McLeod Rd, Lahore 54000; tel. (42) 7227136; fax (42) 7231154; e-mail steel_re_rollers@hotmail.com; Chair. Mian MANZOOR AHMAD; Sec. Lt-Col (retd) S. H. A. BUKHARI.

Pakistan Sugar Mills' Association: Mezzanine Floor, 24D Rashid Plaza, Jinnah Ave, Islamabad; tel. (51) 270525; fax (51) 274153; Chair. CHAUDHRY ZAKA ASHRAF; Sec.-Gen. K. ALI QAZILBASH.

Pakistan Tanners' Association: Plot No. 46-C, 21st Commercial St, Phase II Extension, Defence Housing Authority, Karachi 75500; tel. (21) 5880180; fax (21) 5880093; e-mail pta@fascom.com; Chair. KHAWAJA MOHAMMAD YOUSUF.

Pakistan Tea Association: Suite 307, Business Plaza, Mumtaz Hassan Rd, off I. I. Chundrigar Rd, Karachi; tel. (21) 2422161; fax (21) 2422209; e-mail pta@cyber.net.pk; Chair. HANIF JANOO.

Pakistan Vanaspati Manufacturers' Association: No. 5-B, College Rd, F-7/3, Islamabad; tel. (51) 2274358; fax (51) 2272529; Chair. Sheikh ANJAD RASHEED; Sec. Dr GHULAM M. SAMDANI.

Pakistan Wool and Hair Merchants' Association: 27 Idris Chambers, Talpur Rd, Karachi; Pres. Mian MOHAMMAD SIDDIQ KHAN; Sec. KHALID LATEEF.

Pakistan Woollen Mills' Association: 25A, Davis Rd, Lahore 54000; tel. (42) 6307691; fax (42) 6306881; e-mail pwma@brain.net.pk; internet www.lcci.org.pk; Chair. Mian MUZAFFAR ALI; Sec. MUHAMMAD RAHEEL CHOHAN.

Pakistan Yarn Merchants' Association: Rms Nos 802–803, Business Centre, 8th Floor, Dunolly Rd, Karachi 74000; tel. (21) 2410320; fax (21) 2424896; e-mail pyma@cubexs.net.pk; Pres. KHURSHID A. SHEIKH; Sec. MANZOORUL HASAN HASHMI.

Rice Exports Association of Pakistan: 4th Floor, Sadiq Plaza, The Mall, Lahore; tel. and fax (42) 6280196; e-mail reaplhr@brain.net.pk; Chair. Haji ABDUL MAJID.

Towel Manufacturers' Association of Pakistan: 77-A, Block A, Sindhi Muslim Co-operative Housing Society, Karachi 74400; tel. (21) 111-360-360; fax (21) 4551628; e-mail tma@towelassociation.com; internet www.towelassociation.com; Chair. PERVEZ AHMED.

EMPLOYERS' ORGANIZATION

Employers' Federation of Pakistan: 2nd Floor, State Life Bldg No. 2, Wallace Rd, off I. I. Chundrigar Rd, POB 4338, Karachi 74000; tel. (21) 2411049; fax (21) 2439347; e-mail efpak@cyber.net.pk; internet www.efpak.com; f. 1950; Pres. ASHRAF WALI MOHAMMAD TABANI; Sec.-Gen. Prof. M. MATIN KHAN.

UTILITIES

Water and Power Development Authority (WAPDA): WAPDA House, Shahrah-e-Quaid-e-Azam, Lahore; tel. (42) 6366911; fax (42) 9202454; internet www.wapda.gov.pk; f. 1958 for devt of irrigation, water supply and drainage, building of replacement works under the World Bank-sponsored Indo-Pakistan Indus Basin Treaty; flood-control and watershed management; reclamation of waterlogged and saline lands; inland navigation; generation, transmission and distribution of hydroelectric and thermal power; partial transfer to private ownership carried out in 1996; Chair. TARIQ HAMID.

Electricity

Kohinoor Energy Ltd: Near Tablighi Ijtima, PO Kohinoor Energy, Raiwind Bypass, Lahore; tel. (42) 5392317; fax (42) 5393415; e-mail info@kel.com.pk; internet www.kel.com.pk; f. 1994; jt venture of Saigols Group of Cos and Toyota Tsusho Corpn; Chair. M. NASEEM SAIGOL; CEO MUNEKI UDAKA.

National Electric Power Regulatory Authority (NEPRA): OPF Bldg, 2nd Floor, Shahrah-e-Jamhuriat, G-5/2, Islamabad 44000; tel. (51) 9207200; fax (51) 9210215; e-mail info@nepra.org.pk; internet www.nepra.org.pk; f. 1997; fixes the power tariff; Chair. Lt-Gen. (retd) SAEED UZ ZAFAR.

Hub Power Co Ltd (Hubco): Islamic Chamber Bldg, 3rd Floor, St 2/A, Block No. 9, Clifton, POB 13841, Karachi 75600; tel. (21) 5874677; fax (21) 5870397; e-mail info@hubpower.com; internet www.hubpower.com; f. 1991; supplies electricity; Chair. MOHAMMAD AHMED ZAINAL ALIREZA; Chief Exec. JAVED MAHMOOD.

Karachi Electric Supply Corpn Ltd (KESC): Aimai House, Abdullah Haroon Rd, POB 7197, Karachi; tel. (21) 5685492; fax (21) 5682408; internet www.kesc.com.pk; f. 1913; Chair. ABDUL AZIZ HAMEED AL-JOMAIH; CEO Lt-Gen. SYED MOHAMMAD AMJAD.

Kot Addu Power Co (KAPCO): Kot Addu Power Complex, Kot Addu, District Muzaffargarh 34060; tel. (66) 2241336; e-mail info@kapco.com.pk; fax (66) 2241817; internet www.kapco.com.pk; f. 1996; 46% owned by Pakistan Water and Power Development Authority; Chair. IMTIAZ ANJUM.

National Power Construction Corpn (Pvt) Ltd: 9 Shadman II, Lahore 54000; tel. (42) 7566019; fax (42) 7566022; e-mail npcc@wol.net.pk; internet www.npcc.com.pk; f. 1974; execution of power projects on turnkey basis, e.g. extra high voltage transmission lines, distribution networks, substations, power generation plants, industrial electrification, external lighting of housing complexes, etc.; Chair. MUHAMMAD ISMAIL QURESHI; Man. Dir MUHAMMAD AJAZ MALIK; project office in Jeddah (Saudi Arabia).

Pakistan Atomic Energy Commission (PAEC): POB 1114, Islamabad; tel. (51) 9209032; fax (51) 9204908; responsible for harnessing nuclear energy for devt of nuclear technology as part of the nuclear power programme; operates Karachi Atomic Nuclear Power Plant—KANUPP (POB 3183, nr Paradise Point, Hawksbay Rd, Karachi 75400; tel. (21) 9202222; fax (21) 7737488; e-mail knpc@khi.comsats.net.pk) and Chasma Nuclear Power Plant (CHASNUPP) at Chasma District, Mianwali (tel. (45202) 41481-5; fax (51) 9278524; email chasnupp@fsd.paknet.com.pk); building another nuclear power station at Kundian; two further facilities were under construction near Karachi in March 2007; establishing research centres, incl. Pakistan Institute of Nuclear Science and Technology (PINSTECH); promoting peaceful use of atomic energy in agriculture, medicine, industry and hydrology; searching for indigenous nuclear mineral deposits; training project personnel; Chair. SHAMIM ANWAR KHAN; Gen. Man. (KANUPP) QAMRUL HODA.

Pakistan Electric Power Co: Lahore; f. 1998; Man. Dir MUNAWAR BASEER.

Pakistan Nuclear Regulatory Authority (PNRA): POB 1912, Islamabad 44000; tel. (51) 9205917; fax (51) 9204112; e-mail officialmail@pnra.org; internet www.pnra.org; f. 2001 by presidential ordinance; Chair. JAMSHED AZIM HASHMI.

Private Power and Infrastructure Board (PPIB): 50 Nazimuddin Rd, F-7/4, Islamabad; tel. (51) 9205421; fax (51) 9217735; e-mail ppib@ppib.gov.pk; internet www.ppib.gov.pk; f. 1994; facilitates participation of private sector in national power generation; Man. Dir MOHAMMAD YOUSUF MEMON.

Quetta Electric Supply Co Ltd (QESCO): Zarghoon Rd, Quetta Cantt, Balochistan; tel. (81) 9202211; fax (81) 836554; e-mail qesco@qta.infolink.net.pk; f. 1998; CEO Eng. MUHAMMAD KHATTAK.

Gas

Hydrocarbon Development Institute of Pakistan: Plot 18, Street 6, H-9/1, POB 1308, Islamabad; tel. (51) 9258301; fax (51) 9258310; e-mail info@hdip.com.pk; internet www.hdip.com.pk; f. 1975; re-established Jan. 2006 under Ministry of Petroleum and Natural Resources; national petroleum research and devt org.; provides consultancy and laboratory services to petroleum industry; Chair. AMANULLAH KHAN JADOON; Dir-Gen. and Chief Exec. HILAL A. RAZA.

Mari Gas Co Ltd (MGCL): 21 Mauve Area, 3rd Rd, Sector G-10/4, POB 1614, Islamabad; tel. (51) 111-410-410; fax (51) 2297686; e-mail info@marigas.com.pk; internet www.marigas.com.pk; 20% govt-owned; Chair. Lt-Gen. (retd) SYED ARIF HASSAN; Resident Gen. Man. Col (retd) AMJAD JAVED.

PAKISTAN

Oil and Gas Development Corpn Ltd (OGDCL): OGDC House, Blue Area, Islamabad; tel. (51) 9209882; fax (51) 9209859; f. 1961; became a publicly limited co in 1997; 95% govt-owned; plans, promotes, organizes and implements programmes for the exploration and devt of petroleum and gas resources, and the production, refining and sale of petroleum and gas; transfer to private ownership pending; Man. Dir ARSHAD NASSAR; 11,624 employees (Aug. 2005).

Oil and Gas Regulatory Authority: Tariq Chambers, Main Civic Centre, Islamabad; tel. (51) 9204516; e-mail registrar@ogra.org.pk; internet www.ogra.org.pk; f. 2002; Chair. MUNIR AHMAD; Vice-Chair. JAWAID INAM.

Pakistan Petroleum Ltd (PPL): PIDC House, 4th Floor, Dr Ziauddin Ahmed Rd, POB 3942, Karachi 75530, Sindh; tel. (21) 111-568-568; fax (21) 5680005; e-mail info@ppl.com.pk; internet www.ppl.com.pk; 78.4% govt-owned, 15.5% owned by private Pakistani shareholders and 6.1% owned by International Finance Corpn; Pakistan's largest producer of natural gas; cap. and res Rs 18,393m., sales Rs 10,732m. (July–Dec. 2004); Chief Exec./Man. Dir S. MUNSIF RAZA; 2,520 employees (2006).

Petroleum Institute of Pakistan (PIP): Federation House, 1st Floor, Street 28, Block V, Kehkashan, Clifton, Karachi 75600; tel. (21) 5378701; fax (21) 5378704; e-mail pip@cyber.net.pk; internet www.pip.org.pk; f. 1963; represents all sectors of the petroleum industry (incl. exploration, production, refining, marketing and natural gas); promotes and co-ordinates industry activities; mem. of the International Gas Union and World Petroleum Council; 25 Industrial Collective mems, over 860 individual industry mems; Chair. S. MUNSIF RAZA.

Sui Northern Gas Pipelines Ltd: Gas House, 21 Kashmir Rd, Lahore; tel. (42) 9201451; fax (42) 9201302; e-mail info@sngpl.com.pk; internet www.sngpl.com.pk; f. 1964; 36% state-owned; transmission and distribution of natural gas in northern Pakistan; sales Rs 107,897.3m. (2005/06); Chair. ALTAF M. SALEEM; Man. Dir ABDUL RASHID LONE.

Sui Southern Gas Co Ltd: 4B Sir Shah Suleman Rd, Block 14, Gulshan-e-Iqbal, Karachi 75000; tel. (21) 9231602; fax (21) 9231604; e-mail info@ssgc.com.pk; internet www.ssgc.com.pk; f. 1988; 70% state-owned; Chief Exec. and Man. Dir MUNAWAR BASEER AHMAD.

Water

Faisalabad Development Authority (Water and Sanitation Agency): POB 229, Faisalabad; tel. (411) 767606; fax (411) 782113; e-mail fwasa@fsd.paknet.com.pk; internet www.fda.gov.pk; f. 1978; Man. Dir Lt-Col (retd) SYED GHIAS-UD-DIN.

Karachi Water and Sewerage Board: 9th Mile, Karsaz, Shahrah-e-Faisal, Karachi; tel. (21) 9231882; fax (21) 9231814; e-mail mdkwsb@yahoo.co.uk; f. 1983; Man. Dir Brig. IFTIKHAR HAIDER.

Lahore Development Authority (Water and Sanitation Agency): 4-A Gulberg V, Jail Rd, Lahore; tel. (42) 5752483; fax (42) 5752960; f. 1967; Dir-Gen. RAJA MUHAMMAD ABBAS.

TRADE UNIONS

National Trade Union Federation Pakistan: Bharocha Bldg, 2-B/6, Commercial Area, Nazimabad No. 2, Karachi 74600; tel. (21) 628339; fax (21) 6622529; e-mail ntuf@super.net.pk; f. 1999; 50 affiliated unions; covers following fields: steel, agriculture, textiles, garments, leather, automobiles, pharmaceuticals, chemicals, transport, printing, food, shipbuilding, engineering and power; Pres. MUHAMMAD RAFIQUE; Gen. Sec. SALEEM RAZA.

Pakistan Workers Federation (PWF): Bakhtiar Labour Hall, 28 Nisbet Rd, Lahore; tel. (42) 7229192; fax (42) 7239529; e-mail cpr@pwf.org.pk; internet www.pwf.org.pk; f. 2005 following the merger of the All Pakistan Federation of Trade Unions, Pakistan National Federation of Trade Unions and All Pakistan Federation of Labour; affiliated with the International Confederation of Free Trade Unions; 10 regional offices; Pres. CH. TALIB NAWAZ; Chair. MUHAMMAD AHMED; Gen. Sec. KHURSHID AHMED.

The principal affiliated federations are:

Muttahida Labour Federation: 24, Circular Bldg, Risala Rd, Hyderabad; c. 120,000 mems; Pres. KHAMASH GUL KHATTAK; Sec.-Gen. NABI AHMED.

National Labour Federation (NLF): 28, Circular Rd, Hyderabad; Pres. RANA MAHMOOD ALI KHAN.

Pakistan Central Federation of Trade Unions: 220 Al-Noor Chambers, M. A. Jinnah Rd, Karachi; tel. (21) 728891.

Pakistan Railway Employees' Union (PREM): City Railway Station, Karachi; tel. (21) 2415721; Divisional Sec. BASHIRUDDIN SIDDIQUI.

Pakistan Trade Union Federation: Khamosh Colony, Karachi; Pres. KANIZ FATIMA; Gen. Sec. SALEEM RAZA.

Pakistan Transport Workers' Federation: 110 McLeod Rd, Lahore; 17 unions; 92,512 mems; Pres. MEHBOOB-UL-HAQ; Gen. Sec. CH. UMAR DIN.

Other affiliated federations include: Pakistan Bank Employees' Federation, Pakistan Insurance Employees' Federation, Automobile, Engineering and Metal Workers' Federation, Pakistan Teachers Organizations' Council, Sarhad WAPDA Employees' Federation, and Balochistan Ittehad Trade Union Federation.

Transport

RAILWAYS

Pakistan Railways: Empress Rd, Lahore; tel. (42) 9201776; fax (42) 9201783; e-mail gmopr@pakrail.com; internet www.pakrail.com; state-owned; 11,515 km of track and 7,791 route km; seven divisions (Karachi, Lahore, Multan, Quetta, Rawalpindi, Peshawar and Sukkur); Chair. KHURSHEED AHMED KHAN; Gen. Man. SALEEMUR RAHMAN KHAN.

ROADS

The total length of roads was 254,410 km (motorways 339 km, main 6,587 km, secondary 211,846 km, other roads 35,638 km) in 1999. By June 2004 the total length of roads had increased to 258,340 km, 64.7% of which were paved, including 9,031 km of highways and motorways.

Government assistance comes from the Road Fund, financed from a share of the excise and customs duty on sales of petrol and from development loans.

National Highways Authority: 27 Mauve Area, G-9/1, Islamabad; tel. (51) 9260350; fax (51) 9261075; e-mail info@nha.gov.pk; internet www.nha.gov.pk; f. 1991; jt venture between Govt and private sector; Chair. Maj.-Gen. IMTIAZ AHMED; Dir-Gen. Brig. SOHAIL MASOOD ALVI.

Punjab Road Transport Board: Department of Transport, Pension Cell, 11A Egerton Rd, Lahore.

SHIPPING

In 1974 maritime shipping companies were placed under government control. The chief port is Karachi. A second port, Port Qasim, started partial operation in 1980. A third port, Port Gwadar, has been developed as a deep-water seaport; construction was completed in March 2005 and the port opened in March 2007. Another port, Port Pasni, which is situated on the Balochistan coast, was completed in 1988. In 1991 the Government amended the 1974 Pakistan Maritime Shipping Act to allow private companies to operate.

Mercantile Marine Dept: 70/4, Timber Pond, N. M. Reclamation, Keamari, Karachi 74000; tel. and fax (21) 2851307; f. 1930; ensures safety of life and property at sea and prevention of marine pollution through implementation of national legislation and international conventions; Chief Officer Capt. M. SALEEM BALOCH.

Ports and Shipping: Government of Pakistan, Plot No. 12, Misc. Area, Mai Kolachi Bypass, Karachi 74200; tel. (21) 9204191; e-mail contact@mops.gov.pk; internet www.mops.gov.pk; Dir-Gen. HASSAN ZAIDI.

Al-Hamd International Container Terminal (Pvt) Ltd: Plot No. 28, O & L Trans Lyari Quarters, Hawkesbay Rd, New Truck Stand, Karachi; tel. (21) 2352660; fax (21) 2351556; e-mail info@aictpk.com; internet www.aictpakistan.com; Gen. Man. JANAKA GUNAWARDENA.

Engro Vopak Terminal Ltd: 1st Floor, Bahrai Complex 1, 24 M. T. Khan Rd, POB 5736, Karachi 74000; tel. (21) 5610954; fax (21) 5611394; e-mail evtl@engro.com; internet www.engro.com.

Karachi International Container Terminal (KICT): Administration Bldg, Berths 28–30, Dockyard Rd, West Wharf, Karachi 74000; tel. (21) 2316401; fax (21) 2313816; e-mail info@kictl.com; internet www.kictl.com; f. 1996; Chief Exec. ROGER L. HAWKE.

Karachi Port Trust (KPT): Eduljee Dinshaw Rd, Karachi 74000; tel. (21) 9214312; fax (21) 9214329; e-mail chairman@kpt.gov.pk; internet www.kpt.gov.pk; Chair. Vice-Adm. AHMED HAYAT; Gen. Operations Man. Rear-Adm. AGHA DANISH; Sec. KHALID MOBIN ARSHAD.

Karachi Shipyard and Engineering Works Ltd: POB 4419, West Wharf, Dockyard Rd, Karachi 74000; tel. (21) 9214045; fax (21) 9214020; e-mail contact@karachishipyard.com.pk; internet www.karachishipyard.com.pk; f. 1953; building and repairing ships; general engineering; Man. Dir Vice-Adm. IFTIKHAR AHMED RAO.

Korangi Fisheries Harbour Authority: Ghashma Goth, Landhi, POB 15804, Karachi 75160; tel. (21) 5013315; fax (21) 5015096; e-mail kfha@sat.net.pk.

National Tanker Co (Pvt) Ltd (Pak): 15th Floor, PNSC Bldg, M. T. Khan Rd, Karachi 74000; tel. (21) 5611843; fax (21) 5610780; f. 1981 by the Pakistan National Shipping Corpn and the State Petroleum Refining and Petrochemical Corpn Ltd; aims to make

PAKISTAN

Pakistan self-reliant in the transport of crude petroleum and petroleum products; Chief Exec. Vice-Adm. A. U. KHAN; Dep. Chief Exec. TURAB ALI KHAN.

Pakistan International Container Terminal Ltd: 2nd Floor, Business Plaza, Mumtaz Hussain Rd, Karachi 74000; tel. (21) 9203974; fax (21) 2400281; e-mail info@pict.com.pk; internet www.pict.com.pk; Chair. Capt. HALEEM A. SIDDIQI; CEO SHARIQ SIDDIQI.

Pakistan National Shipping Corpn: PNSC Bldg, M. T. Khan Rd, POB 5350, Karachi 74000; tel. (21) 9203980; fax (21) 9203974; e-mail communication@pnsc.com.pk; f. 1979 by merger; state-owned; national flag carrier; undertakes global shipping operations; Chair. Vice-Adm. S. T. H. NAQVI; Sec. ZAINAB SULEMAN.

Port Qasim Authority (PQA): Bin Qasim, Karachi 75020; tel. (21) 9204211; fax (21) 4730108; e-mail webmaster@portqasim.org.pk; internet www.portqasim.org.pk; f. 1973; Chair. Rear Adm. SYED AFZAL; Sec. AFSAR DIN TALPUR.

Qasim International Container Terminal: Berths 5–7, Marginal Wharfs, POB 6425, Port Mohammad Bin Qasim, Karachi 75020; tel. (21) 4739100; fax (21) 4730021; e-mail info@qict.net; internet www.qict.net; f. 1994; CEO CHANGEZ NIAZI; Gen. Man. DARAYUS DIVECHA.

Associations

All Pakistan Shipping Association: 01-E, 1st Floor, Sattar Chambers, West Wharf Rd, Karachi; tel. (21) 2200742; fax (21) 2200743; e-mail apsa-pak@cyber.net.pk; Chair. MUHAMMAD F. QAISER.

Pakistan Ship Agents' Association: GSA House, 19 Timber Pound, Keamari, Karachi 75620; tel. (21) 2850837; fax (21) 2851528; e-mail psaa@cyber.net.pk; internet www.shipezee.com/psaa/; f. 1976; Chair. FAROUQ H. RAHIMTOOLA.

Terminal Association of Pakistan: 8th Floor, Adamjee House, I. I. Chundrigar Rd, Karachi 74000; tel. (21) 2417131; fax (21) 2416477; e-mail terasspak@cyber.net.pk; Chair. MOHAMMED KASIM HASHAM; Sec. AKHTAR SULTAN.

CIVIL AVIATION

Karachi, Lahore, Rawalpindi, Peshawar and Quetta have international airports. In April 2007 the first phase of construction for the development of a new international airport at Islamabad commenced following a series of postponements; the project was to cost an estimated Rs 35,000m. and would handle 6.5m. passengers annually upon completion.

In 1992 the Government ended the air monopoly held by the Pakistan International Airlines Corpn, and opened all domestic air routes to any Pakistan-based company.

Civil Aviation Authority: Terminal 1 Bldg, Karachi Airport, Karachi; tel. (21) 9248778; fax (21) 9248121; e-mail chr@caapakistan.com.pk; internet www.caapakistan.com.pk; controls all the civil airports; Chair. KAMRAN RASOOL; Sec. KHURSHID ANWAR.

Aero Asia International: 47-E/1, Block 6, PECHS, Karachi 75400; tel. (21) 4544951; fax (21) 4544940; e-mail info@aeroasia.com; internet www.aeroasia.com; f. 1993; operates scheduled passenger and cargo services to domestic destinations and to the neighbouring Gulf states; Chair. MOHAMMED YAQUB TABANI; Man. Dir KHURSHID ANWAR.

Air Blue Ltd: Ground Floor, Saudi Pak Bldg, Jinnah Ave, Islamabad; tel. (51) 111-247-258; e-mail writetous@airblue.com; internet www.airblue.com; f. 2004; CEO SHAHID KHAQAN ABBASI.

Pakistan International Airlines Corpn (PIA): Jinnah International Airport, Karachi 75200; tel. (21) 4572011; fax (21) 4570419; e-mail info@piac.com.pk; internet www.piac.com.pk; f. 1954; merged with Orient Airways in 1955; 57.7% govt-owned; operates domestic services to 35 destinations and international services to 40 destinations in 31 countries; reduced number of weekly flights to Europe and the USA from 42 to 24 in March 2007 in response to proscriptive new European Union safety regulations; Chair. KAMRAN RASOOL.

Shaheen Air International: 157B Clifton Rd, Clifton, Karachi 75600; tel. (21) 9251921; fax (21) 9251935; e-mail info@shaheenair.com; internet www.shaheenair.com; f. 1993; operates scheduled domestic services and international services to the Gulf region; Chair. KHALID M. SEHBAI; CEO Air Vice-Marshal (retd) AAMER ALI SHARIEFF.

Tourism

The Himalayan hill stations of Pakistan provide magnificent scenery, a fine climate and excellent opportunities for field sports, mountaineering, trekking and winter sports. The archaeological remains and historical buildings are also impressive.

In 2006 Pakistan received some 850,600 foreign visitors; receipts from tourism amounted to around US $827m. in 2005.

Pakistan Tourism Development Corpn: 22A Saeed Plaza, Jinnah Ave, Blue Area, Islamabad 44000; tel. (51) 9203772; fax (51) 9207427; e-mail info@tourism.gov.pk; internet www.tourism.gov.pk; f. 1970; Chair. HASHIM KHAN; Man. Dir SALMAN JAVED.

RELATED TERRITORIES

The status of Jammu and Kashmir has remained unresolved since the 1949 cease-fire agreement, whereby the area was divided into sectors administered by India and Pakistan separately. Pakistan administers Azad (Free) Kashmir and the Northern Areas as *de facto* dependencies, being responsible for foreign affairs, defence, coinage, currency and the implementation of UN resolutions concerning Kashmir.

AZAD KASHMIR

Area: 11,639 sq km (4,494 sq miles).

Population: 1,980,000 (1981 census).

Administration: Government is based on the Azad Jammu and Kashmir Interim Constitution Act of 1974. There are seven administrative districts: Bagh, Bhimber, Kotli, Mirpur, Muzaffarabad, Poonch and Sudhnuti.

Legislative Assembly: consists of 48 members: 40 directly elected and eight indirectly elected, including five women.

Azad Jammu and Kashmir Council: consists of the President of Pakistan as Chairman, the President of Azad Kashmir as Vice-Chairman, five members nominated by the President of Pakistan, six members by the Legislative Assembly, and, *ex officio*, the Pakistan Minister of Kashmir Affairs and Northern Areas.

President of Azad Kashmir: Raja Zulqarnain Khan.

Prime Minister: Sardar Attiq Ahmed Khan.

NORTHERN AREAS

Area: 72,520 sq km (28,000 sq miles).

Population: 562,000 (1981 census).

Administration: There are five administrative districts: Gilgit, Skardu, Diamir, Ghizer and Ghanche. The Northern Areas Council consists of 26 members (24 members are elected in a party-based election and two seats are reserved for women), headed by the federal Minister of Kashmir Affairs and Northern Areas.

PALAU

Introductory Survey

Location, Climate, Language, Religion, Flag, Capital

The Republic of Palau (also known as Belau) consists of more than 200 islands, in a chain about 650 km (400 miles) long, lying about 7,150 km (4,450 miles) south-west of Hawaii and about 1,160 km (720 miles) south of Guam. With the Federated States of Micronesia (q.v.), Palau forms the archipelago of the Caroline Islands. Palau is subject to heavy rainfall, and seasonal variations in precipitation and temperature are generally small. Palauan and English are the official languages. The principal religion is Christianity, much of the population being Roman Catholic. The flag (proportions 3 by 5) features a large golden disc (representing the moon), placed off-centre, towards the hoist, on a light blue background. The capital is Melekeok, on the island of Babeldaob.

Recent History

The Republic of Palau's independence, under the Compact of Free Association, in October 1994 marked the end of the Trust Territory of the Pacific Islands, of which Palau was the final component (for history up to 1965, see the chapter on the Marshall Islands). From 1965 there were increasing demands for local autonomy within the Trust Territory. In that year the Congress of Micronesia was formed, and in 1967 a commission was established to examine the future political status of the islands. In 1970 the commission declared Micronesians' rights to sovereignty over their own lands, self-determination, the right to their own constitution and to revoke any form of free association with the USA. In May 1977, after eight years of negotiations, US President Jimmy Carter announced that his Administration intended to adopt measures to terminate the trusteeship agreement by 1981. In the Palau District a referendum in July 1979 approved a proposed local Constitution, which came into effect on 1 January 1981, when the district became the Republic of Palau.

The USA signed the Compact of Free Association with the Republic of Palau in August 1982, and with the Marshall Islands and the Federated States of Micronesia in October. The trusteeship of the islands was due to end after the principle and terms of the Compacts had been approved by the respective peoples and legislatures of the new countries, by the US Congress and by the UN Security Council. Under the Compacts, the four countries (including the Northern Mariana Islands) would be independent of each other and would manage both their internal and foreign affairs separately, while the USA would be responsible for defence and security. In addition, the USA was to allocate some US $3,000m. in aid to the islands.

More than 60% of Palauans voted in February 1983 to support their Compact, but fewer than the required 75% approved changing the Constitution to allow the transit and storage of nuclear materials. A revised Compact, which contained no reference to nuclear issues, was approved by 66% of votes cast in a referendum in September 1984. However, the US Government had hoped for a favourable majority of 75% of the votes cast, which would have allowed the terms of the Compact to override the provisions of the Palau Constitution in the event of a conflict between the two.

In June 1985 President Haruo Remeliik of Palau was assassinated. Relatives of a rival candidate in the 1984 presidential election, Roman Tmetuchl, were convicted of the murder, but remained at liberty pending an appeal; this was upheld, on the grounds of unreliable evidence, by Palau's Supreme Court in August 1987. Lazarus Salii was elected President in September 1985.

In January 1986 representatives of the Palau and US administrations reached a preliminary agreement on a new Compact, whereby the USA consented to provide US $421m. in economic assistance to the islands. However, the proportion of votes in favour of the new Compact at a referendum in the following month was still less than that required for the constitutional ban on nuclear material to be waived. Both Salii and US President Ronald Reagan supported the terms of the Compact, arguing that a simple majority would suffice for its approval, as the USA had guaranteed that it would observe the constitutional ban on nuclear material.

In May 1986 the UN Trusteeship Council endorsed the US Administration's request for the termination of the existing trusteeship agreement with the islands. However, a writ was subsequently submitted to the Palau High Court, in which it was claimed that approval of the Compact with the USA was unconstitutional because it had failed to obtain the requisite 75% of votes. The High Court ruled in favour of the writ, but the Palau Government appealed against the ruling and in October the Compact was approved by the US Congress. At a new plebiscite in December, however, only 66% of Palauans voted in favour of the Compact. Ratification of the Compact thus remained impossible.

A fifth plebiscite on Palau's proposed Compact with the USA, in June 1987, again failed to secure the 75% endorsement required by the Constitution. Under alleged physical intimidation by pro-nuclear supporters of the Compact, the House of Delegates (the lower house of the Palau National Congress) agreed to a further referendum in August. In this referendum an amendment to the Constitution was approved, ensuring that a simple majority would henceforth be sufficient to approve the Compact. This was duly achieved in a further referendum in the same month. When a writ was entered with the Supreme Court challenging the legality of the decision to allow approval of the Compact by a simple majority, a campaign of arson and bombing followed, and one person was murdered.

In February 1988 a team from the US General Accounting Office travelled to Palau to investigate allegations of corruption and intimidation on the part of the Palau Government. Approval of the Compact by the US Congress was to be delayed until the investigators had published their findings. However, in April a ruling by Palau's Supreme Court invalidated the procedure by which the Compact had finally been approved by a simple majority in the previous August. Three government employees, including Salii's personal assistant, were imprisoned in April, after being found guilty of firing on the home of Santos Olikong, Speaker of Palau's House of Delegates. The attack was widely considered to have been prompted by Olikong's public opposition to the Compact.

In August 1988 Salii, the principal subject of the bribery allegations, apparently committed suicide. At an election in November Ngiratkel Etpison was elected President, with just over 26% of the total votes. Although Etpison advocated the proposed Compact and was supported by the pro-Compact Ta Belau Party, his closest challenger, Tmetuchl, opposed it and was supported by the anti-nuclear Coalition for Open, Honest and Just Government, which had demanded that a special prosecutor from the USA be dispatched to Palau to investigate alleged corruption and violent attacks against opponents of the Compact.

Only 60% of voters approved the proposed Compact at a seventh referendum in February 1990. In July the US Department of the Interior declared its intention to impose stricter controls on the administration of Palau, particularly in financial matters. In the following year the leader of Palau's Council of Chiefs (a presidential advisory body), Yutaka Gibbons, initiated proceedings to sue the US Government: his claim centred on demands for compensation for the extensive damage caused to Palau's infrastructure by US forces during the Second World War and the subsequent retardation of the economy, allegedly as a result of the US administration of the islands.

During 1991 the US authorities reopened investigations into the assassination of Remeliik in 1985. In March 1992 Palau's Minister of State, John Ngiraked, his wife, Emerita Kerradel, and Sulial Heinrick (already serving a prison sentence for another killing) were charged with Remeliik's murder. In March 1993 Ngiraked and Kerradel were found guilty of aiding and abetting the assassination of the President, while Heinrick was acquitted.

Legislative and presidential elections were held in November 1992. (The electoral system had been modified earlier in the year to include primary elections for the selection of two presidential candidates.) At the presidential election the incumbent Vice-President, Kuniwo Nakamura, narrowly defeated Johnson Toribiong to become President. A concurrent referendum endorsed a proposal that, in future polls, a simple majority be sufficient to approve the adoption of the Compact of Free Association. Some 62% of voters were in favour of the proposal, which was approved in 14 of Palau's 16 states. A further referendum on the proposed Compact took place in November 1993. Some 68.3% of participating voters approved the proposed Compact, giving the Government a mandate to proceed with its adoption. Nevertheless, opposition to the changes remained fierce, and in January 1994 two legal challenges were mounted that questioned the validity of the amendments and stated that the Compact's approval had been procured by coercion. The challenges failed, however, and on 1 October Palau achieved independence under the Compact of Free Association. At independence celebrations, Nakamura appealed to opponents of the Compact to support Palau's new status. He announced that his Government's principal concern was the regeneration of the country's economy, which he aimed to initiate with an economic programme financed by funds from the Compact. Palau was admitted to the UN in December 1994, and became a member of the IMF in December 1997.

A preliminary round of voting in the presidential election took place in September 1996; Nakamura secured 52.4% of total votes, Toribiong received 33.5%, and Yutaka Gibbons 14.2%. Nakamura and Toribiong were, therefore, expected to proceed to a second election due to take place in November. However, in late September a serious crisis struck Palau when the bridge linking the islands of Koror and Babeldaob collapsed, killing two people and injuring several others. The collapse of the bridge left the capital isolated from the international airport on Babeldaob, with disastrous economic repercussions for Palau, which was reliant on the route for all domestic and international communications. It was subsequently revealed that major repairs had recently been carried out on the bridge, at a cost of US $3.2m., and several reports implied that inappropriate changes made to its structure during the work were responsible for the disaster. Toribiong was harshly critical of Nakamura, who had commissioned the repair work, and demanded his resignation along with those of the public works officials involved. However, following the revelation that Toribiong's running-mate in the election for the vice-presidency was one of the officials involved in the work, Toribiong withdrew his candidacy from the second round of the presidential election. Yutaka Gibbons thus re-entered the contest by default; none the less, at the second round of the presidential poll, held concurrently with legislative elections on 5 November 1996, Nakamura was re-elected with 62.0% of total votes. Meanwhile, the Japanese Government offered to finance the construction of a new bridge linking Koror to Babeldaob; the work was completed in January 2002.

In October 1998 the Senate approved legislation providing for the establishment of an 'offshore' financial centre in Palau. The measure was strongly opposed by Nakamura, who believed that it might attract criminal organizations seeking to 'launder' the proceeds of their illegal activities. In December 1999, following discussions with US government officials, President Nakamura signed an executive order establishing a National Banking Review Commission, with the aim of maintaining a legally responsible banking environment in Palau: both the Bank of New York (of the USA) and Deutsche Bank (of Germany) had alleged that Palau's 'offshore' banks were facilitating money-laundering. The new body was given wide-ranging powers to examine banking operations in the country and to evaluate current banking regulations.

At the presidential election held on 7 November 2000, Thomas E. Remengesau, Jr, hitherto the Vice-President of Palau, was elected with 52% of the votes cast, defeating Senator Peter Sugiyama. Sandra Pierantozzi was elected as Vice-President. Remengesau was officially inaugurated on 19 January 2001. In July 2001 Remengesau introduced a formal resolution proposing the reduction of the legislature to a single chamber, to replace the existing House of Delegates and the Senate, claiming that a unicameral legislature would reduce bureaucracy. However, owing to a lack of legislative progress on the necessary constitutional changes, in early 2004 Remengesau endorsed a congressional resolution to conduct a popular referendum. The poll, which would first require the signatures of 25% of the electorate, was scheduled to take place in November. The proposals included the creation of a unicameral legislature and restrictions on legislators' terms of office; furthermore, it was proposed that Palauans resident in the USA be offered the opportunity of dual citizenship.

Despite President Remengesau's inauguration pledges to improve transparency in public office, there were several instances of fraudulent use of official funds in the early 2000s. In December 2002 the Speaker of the House of Delegates, Mario Gulibert, was arrested on charges relating to the alleged misuse of travel expenses (he was dismissed on unrelated charges in March 2004). In February 2003 the former Governor of Ngardmau state, Albert Ngirmekur, was fined and sentenced to six months' imprisonment following his impeachment for theft. In late 2003 President Remengesau was obliged to veto an attempt by legislators to eliminate the Office of the Special Prosecutor, which had conducted a number of investigations into alleged misuse of public funds. In February 2004, however, members of the National Congress under investigation for alleged misuse of expenses agreed to pay some US $250,000 on condition that the cases against them be withdrawn. In November the Senate overturned President Remengesau's veto of a bill to ease bank-licensing restrictions, although this decision was reversed in December, following the threat of international financial sanctions.

At the presidential election of 2 November 2004, President Remengesau was re-elected with 6,494 of the votes cast; his opponent, Polycarp Basilius, received 3,268 votes. Elias Camsek Chin was elected Vice-President. Following his re-election, Remengesau announced that the priorities of his new administration would include increasing government revenues, promoting economic diversification and tourism, and maintaining programmes of infrastructural development. Concurrent to the presidential election, voters also approved various amendments to the Constitution: to restrict members of the National Congress to three terms of four years, to permit dual US-Palauan citizenship, to provide for the joint election of the country's President and Vice-President as a team and to adjust congressional members' salaries. A proposal to create a unicameral legislature, however, was rejected. A plan to hold a constitutional convention was approved by 5,085 votes (some 53% of the votes cast), with 3,742 votes (some 39%) against the motion. In April 2005 16 state delegates and nine delegates-at-large were elected to the Constitutional Convention, which in mid-June ended its deliberations, following consultations with the general public and special-interest groups. The Convention concluded with 251 proposals, of which 22 were to be submitted for the electorate's consideration at a referendum to be held concurrently with the general elections scheduled for 2008.

The issue of misuse of public funds was highlighted by several political developments in 2006–08. In March 2006 the legislature of Peleliu state approved a resolution to impeach Governor Jackson Ngiraingas on charges of treason, unlawful spending of state finances and the lodging of accusations, against President Remengesau and others, purporting to be on the state's behalf. In April Ngiraingas failed to gain the support of a majority in the state legislature to revoke the impeachment and was removed from office; he subsequently filed a civil suit, claiming that the allegations against him were false and not necessarily grounds for impeachment, and that his removal from office was unconstitutional. The Supreme Court invalidated the legislature's resolution in the following month, deciding that Ngiraingas had been denied due process. Meanwhile, in March the Ngardmau state legislature adopted a resolution to impeach Governor J. Schwartz Tudong. Tudong was accused of illegally spending state funds and making payments to himself without legal authority; a trial court later decided that it did not have the jurisdiction to rule on his appeal against the impeachment, and in May Akiko C. Sugiyama was elected to succeed him. In August Augustine Mesebeluu, the Speaker of the House of Delegates, was charged on numerous counts related to personal use of public finances (Mesebeluu later entered into settlement agreements to repay costs he had incurred during trips off the island). In July 2007 Antonio Bells, who had replaced Mesebeluu as Speaker, was charged with misuse of public funds, reportedly in relation to inappropriate use of expenses. In March 2008 the Governor of Melekeok, Lazarus Kodep, was charged on numerous counts of misuse of public funds dating back to 2002–04. Meanwhile, the closure of the Pacific Savings Bank, which went into receivership in late 2006, was followed by charges against the bank's President, Timothy Taunton, and other employees in 2007.

In October 2006 the relocation of Palau's seat of government from Koror to the new capital, Melekeok, on the island of Babeldaob, was marked with official ceremonies and celebrations. In March 2007 the President of the Senate, Johnny Reklai, was killed in a fishing accident. Joshua Koshiba was subsequently elected as his successor, but, following a successful legal appeal by some members of the Senate, Surangel Whipps replaced Koshiba. A special election to fill the Senate vacancy took place in May. By February 2008 three candidates, Whipps, Koshiba and Johnson Toribiong, had announced plans to contest the forthcoming presidential election, scheduled for 4 November. Preparations for a review of the Compact with the USA, which was due to expire in 2009, were under way with the formation of the Palau Compact Review Commission; President Remengesau was reported to be eager to begin the negotiating process in order to allow Palauans the opportunity to vote on the issues in 2008. However, in 2007 the US Government reportedly indicated that aid to Palau would be terminated following the expiry of the Compact.

In mid-1999 a delegation from Solomon Islands visited Palau to discuss the possibility of allowing Solomon Islanders to work in Palau, in an attempt to resolve the latter's severe labour shortage. In August 2001, however, the Government imposed a ban on the hiring of Indian and Sri Lankan workers, citing rising tensions and disputes with local employers which the Government claimed were largely due to religious differences. The ban was to remain in place until legislation to create official recruitment agencies in Palau had been approved. In July 2002 the Senate approved a bill that would amend the islands' immigration law in order to give greater authority over immigration affairs to the President of Palau. (Non-Palauan nationals were estimated to represent about 73% of the islands' population in 2003.) In March 2003 the Government introduced a measure to extend employment permits for foreign workers, which allowed a new maximum extension of two years. In April some 200 Chinese migrant employees of a failed clothing business were stranded on Palau and placed under house arrest. However, the migrants were subsequently repatriated, following diplomatic intervention from the People's Republic of China. In December 2006 the House of Delegates approved legislation banning the employment of Bangladeshi nationals in Palau, making an exception for those Bangladeshis already contracted to work in the country, who would be allowed to complete their terms.

Diplomatic relations were established, at ambassadorial level, with Taiwan in late 1999; the first Taiwanese ambassador to Palau was formally appointed in April 2000. Reports in December 2000 that the Palau Government was considering establishing diplomatic relations with the People's Republic of China were denied, and President-elect Remengesau reaffirmed Palau's diplomatic ties with Taiwan. In early 2000, meanwhile, Palau and Taiwan signed an agreement pledging to develop bilateral projects in a number of areas, including agriculture, fisheries and tourism. In late January 2005 President Chen Shui-bian of Taiwan visited Palau to discuss economic co-operation and to strengthen bilateral political relations.

In October 2001 the Government sought to establish diplomatic relations with Malaysia and Indonesia in an attempt to facilitate the resolution of disputes about overlapping territorial boundaries, amid concern over increasing instances of illegal fishing in Palauan waters. (Palau introduced more stringent regulations to counter illegal fishing in 2002 and 2003.) Diplomatic relations with Indonesia were established in July 2007.

Palau maintains strong diplomatic links with Japan, which has been a leading source of tourist revenue since the 1980s. The Japanese Government provided US $25m. for the reconstruction of the Koror bridge (see above) and contributed to the construction of a new terminal building at Palau International Airport, which opened in May 2003. In June 2002 President Remengesau undertook his first state visit to the Republic of Korea. His itinerary incorporated visits to a number of infrastructural development projects.

Government

In October 1994 Palau, the last remaining component of the Trust Territory of the Pacific Islands (a United Nations Trusteeship administered by the USA), achieved independence under the Compact of Free Association. Administrative authority was transferred to the Government of Palau (with the USA retaining responsibility for the islands' defence—see below).

A locally drafted Constitution of the Republic of Palau entered into effect on 1 January 1981. Under the Constitution, executive authority is vested in the President, elected by direct suffrage for a four-year term. Legislative power is exercised by the Olbiil era Kelulau ('House of Whispered Decisions', or Palau National Congress), composed of the elected House of Delegates (comprising one Delegate from each of the 16 states of Palau) and the Senate (currently comprising nine Senators).

Local governmental units are the municipalities and villages. Elected Magistrates and Councils govern the municipalities. Village government is largely traditional.

Defence

The USA is responsible for the defence of Palau, according to the Compact of Free Association implemented in October 1994, and has exclusive military access to its waters, as well as the right to operate two military bases on the islands.

Economic Affairs

In 2006, according to estimates by the World Bank, Palau's gross national income (GNI), measured at average 2004–06 prices, totalled US $162m., equivalent to $7,990 per head. During 2003–06, it was estimated, the population increased at an average annual rate of 0.8%, while gross domestic product (GDP) per head increased, in real terms, by an average of 4.5% per year. In 1996–2006 overall GDP increased, in real terms, at an average annual rate of 1.1%. The Asian Development Bank (ADB) estimated real GDP growth at 5.4% in 2006 and at 5.7% in 2007.

Agriculture (including forestry and fishing) is mainly on a subsistence level, the principal crops being coconuts, root crops and bananas. Pigs and chickens are kept for domestic consumption. Eggs are produced commercially, and the introduction of cattle-ranching on Babeldaob was under consideration in the early 2000s. The agricultural sector engaged 7.8% of the employed labour force and, according to provisional figures, provided 3.2% of GDP in 2006. Fishing licences are sold to foreign fleets, including those of Taiwan, the USA, Japan and the Philippines, although revenue from the sale of these licences totalled only US $76,000 in 2000/01, compared with $230,000 in 1994/95. Fish have traditionally been a leading export, accounting for almost $8.9m. of exports in 2004. According to the ADB, the agricultural sector's GDP expanded in real terms by 6.8% in 2006 and by 8.4% in 2007.

The industrial sector (including mining and quarrying, manufacturing, construction and utilities) engaged 18.7% of the employed labour force and provided an estimated 20.0% of GDP in 2006, according to provisional figures. The only manufacturing activity of any significance is the production of garments; the sector has employed mainly non-resident workers. In 2005 manufacturing accounted for 2.3% of employment, but only 0.4% of GDP. Construction is the most important industrial activity, contributing 16.4% of GDP and engaging 14.0% of the employed labour force in 2005. Electrical energy is produced by two power plants at Aimeliik and Malakal. According to the ADB, real growth in the industrial sector's GDP was 9.9% in both 2006 and 2007.

Service industries dominate Palau's economy, providing some 76.8% of GDP in 2006, according to provisional results, and engaging 73.5% of the employed labour force in 2005. The Government is a significant employer within the sector, public administration engaging 17.7% of the total employed labour force in 2005. Tourism is an important source of foreign exchange. Expenditure by tourists totalled an estimated US $97m. in the year ending September 2004. The trade, hotels and restaurants sector engaged 17.1% of the employed labour force and provided 30.8% of GDP in 2005. In 2004 a total of 83,041 tourists (mostly from Taiwan and Japan) arrived in the islands. Visitor arrivals declined slightly in 2005 and 2006 (when tourist receipts accounted for an estimated 45% of GDP), but recovered to reach 84,566 in 2007. The real GDP of the services sector increased by 4.3% in 2006 and by 4.6% in 2007, according to the ADB.

In the year ending September 2006 the visible trade deficit was provisionally estimated at $101.7m. The deficit on the current account of the balance of payments, including grants, totalled a provisional $13.5m. in 2005/06, equivalent to 8.7% of GDP. Import costs were a provisional US $115.3m. in that year, while revenue from exports totalled a provisional $13.6m. The principal sources of imports in 2005 were the USA (which supplied 32.3% of the total), Singapore (25.3%) and Guam (13.4%). The principal imports in 2004, according to the ADB, were machinery and transport equipment (40.7% of the total), mineral fuels and lubricants (25.8%) and food and live animals (9.3%).

The islands record a persistent budget deficit, which reached US $3.9m. in the year ending 30 September 2006. Financial assistance from the USA contributes a large part of the islands' external revenue. Furthermore, upon implementation of the Compact of Free Association with the USA in 1994, Palau became eligible for an initial grant of US $142m. and for annual aid of $23m. over a period of 14 years. Palau's external debt was estimated by the ADB to have risen from $32m. in 2005 to $38m. in 2006. The cost of debt-servicing decreased to the equivalent of 1.6% of the value of exports of goods and services in 2005. The annual rate of inflation averaged 2.6% between 2001 and 2006. The inflation rate rose from 3.9% in 2005 to 4.5% in 2006, but eased to 3.2% in 2007. At the 2005 census 4.2% of the total labour force were unemployed.

Palau is a member of the Pacific Community (see p. 377) and of the Pacific Islands Forum (see p. 380); it is also an associate member of the UN Economic and Social Commission for Asia and the Pacific (ESCAP, see p. 35). In 1996 Palau joined representatives of the other countries and territories of Micronesia at a meeting in Hawaii, at which a new regional organization, the Council of Micronesian Government Executives, was established. The new body aimed to facilitate discussion of economic developments in the region. Palau was admitted to the IMF in late 1997. In December 2002 Palau requested to join the World Trade Organization (WTO, see p. 396), and in December 2003 the country became a member of the Asian Development Bank (ADB, see p. 182).

The economy of Palau has benefited greatly from the substantial aid payments from the US Government that followed the implementation of the Compact of Free Association in 1994 and from the rapid expansion of tourism in the country. Tourism is expected to remain essential to Palau's economic growth upon the cessation of compact grants, scheduled for 2008/09. Following allegations that Palau's 'offshore' banking system was being used for the purposes of international money-laundering (see Recent History), various new banking laws were enacted, and in 2002 the legislature approved proposals for the establishment of a Financial Institutions Commission (FIC). An IMF consultation in March 2006 stressed the need for the FIC to be allocated more funding and wider powers, and for the Financial Institutions Act to be amended in order to increase financial scrutiny. Financial reforms were subsequently introduced. The granting of greater rights to foreign investors, along with the liberalization of the communications sector and the implementation of legislation to counter money-laundering, was expected to lead to an improvement in business conditions. Although the Government was optimistic that it might be able to renegotiate the terms of the Compact and secure the continuation of grants after 2009 (see Recent History), the administration was nevertheless obliged to address the issue of the eventual reduction in funding. The Government therefore aimed to reduce its annual recurrent expenditure. Having accelerated in 2007, GDP growth was forecast by the ADB to decline to about 2.0% in 2008. The robust expansion recorded in 2007 was largely due to an increase in the number of tourist arrivals, aided by a weakening of the US dollar. In that year the hotels and restaurant sector grew by an estimated 15% in comparison with 2006. The construction sector (notably the building of additional, and renovation of existing, tourist facilities) also remained buoyant; however, the growth rate of this sector was expected to decline in 2008. Although the Government continued its efforts to improve investment conditions, uncertainty remained with regard to the likely outcome of Palau's renegotiations on the Compact with the USA.

Education

Education is compulsory for children between the ages of six and 14 years. In 1999/2000 enrolment at primary school level included 96.4% of pupils from the relevant age-group. In 2006/07 an estimated 2,683 pupils attended elementary school. There were 19 public elementary schools in 2006/07. After eight years of compulsory elementary education, a pupil may enrol in the government-operated high school or one of the five private (church-affiliated) high schools. In 2006/07 an estimated total of 1,309 pupils attended secondary school. The Micronesian Occupational College, based in Palau, provides two-year training programmes. Government spending on education in 1999/2000 totalled US $9.1m., equivalent to 10.7% of total budgetary expenditure.

Public Holidays

2008: 1 January (New Year's Day), 14 March (Youth Day), 5 May (Senior Citizens' Day), 2 June (Presidents' Day), 10 July (Constitution Day), 1 September (Labor Day), 1 October (Independence Day), 24 October (United Nations Day), 27 November (Thanksgiving), 25 December (Christmas).
2009: 1 January (New Year's Day), 15 March (Youth Day), 5 May (Senior Citizens' Day), 1 June (Presidents' Day), 10 July (Constitution Day), 1 September (Labor Day), 1 October (Independence Day), 23 October (United Nations Day), 26 November (Thanksgiving), 25 December (Christmas).

Weights and Measures

With certain exceptions, the imperial system is in force. One US cwt equals 100 lb; one long ton equals 2,240 lb; one short ton equals 2,000 lb. A policy of gradual voluntary conversion to the metric system is being undertaken.

Statistical Survey

Source (unless otherwise indicated): Office of Planning and Statistics, Ministry of Finance, POB 6011, Koror; tel. 767-1269; fax 767-5642; e-mail ops@palaugov.net; internet www.palaugov.net/stats/index.htm.

AREA AND POPULATION

Area: 508 sq km (196 sq miles); Babeldaob (Babeldaop, Babelthuap) island 409 sq km (158 sq miles).

Population: 19,129 at census of 15 April 2000; 19,907 (males 10,699, females 9,208) at census of 1 April 2005.

Density (2005 census): 39.2 per sq km.

Principal Towns (population at 2005 census): Koror (capital) 10,743; Meyuns 1,153. Source: Thomas Brinkhoff, *City Population* (internet www.citypopulation.de).

Births and Deaths (2005): Registered live births 279 (birth rate 14.0 per 1,000); Registered deaths 134 (death rate 6.7 per 1,000). *2006:* Registered live births 259; Registered deaths 144.

Expectation of Life (years at birth, WHO estimates): 69.7 (males 68.1; females 71.7) in 2005. Source: WHO, *World Health Statistics*.

Economically Active Population (persons aged 16 years and over, 2005 census): Agriculture 451; Forestry and fishing 310; Mining 34; Manufacturing 225; Utilities and sanitary services 208; Construction 1,365; Transport and communications 561; Trade, restaurants, etc. 1,670; Finance, insurance and real estate 132; Public administration 1,734; Professional and related services 1,466; Private households 915; Other personal services 387; Other services 319; *Total employed* 9,777 (males 5,982, females 3,795); Unemployed 426 (males 232, females 194); *Total labour force* 10,203 (males 6,214, females 3,989).

HEALTH AND WELFARE

Key Indicators

Total Fertility Rate (children per woman, 2005): 1.8.
Under-5 Mortality Rate (per 1,000 live births, 2005): 11.
Physicians (per 1,000 head, 1998): 1.11.
Hospital Beds (per 1,000 head, 1998): 4.4.
Health Expenditure (2004): US $ per head (PPP): 841.0.
Health Expenditure (2004): % of GDP: 9.7.
Health Expenditure (2004): public (% of total): 91.2.
Access to Water (% of persons, 2004): 85.
Access to Sanitation (% of persons, 2004): 80.

For sources and definitions, see explanatory note on p. vi.

AGRICULTURE, ETC.

Fishing (metric tons, live weight, 2005): Marine fishes 929; Trochus shells 499; Total catch (incl. others) 1,436. Source: FAO.

INDUSTRY

Production (2004): Electric energy 171 million kWh. Source: Asian Development Bank, *Key Indicators of Developing Asian and Pacific Countries*.

FINANCE

Currency and Exchange Rates: United States currency is used: 100 cents = 1 United States dollar (US $). *Sterling and Euro Equivalents* (31 December 2007): £1 sterling = US $2.0034; €1 = US $1.4721; US $100 = £49.92 = €67.93.

Budget (US $ '000, year ending September 2006): *Revenue:* Domestic revenue 38,724 (Tax 29,224, Other current revenues 6,580, Local trust fund 2,920); Grants 44,948; Total 83,672. *Expenditure:* Current expenditure 64,927; Capital expenditure 22,659; Total 87,586.

Cost of Living (Consumer Price Index, average of quarterly figures; base: October–December 2004 = 100): 103.3 in 2005; 107.9 in 2006; 111.4 in 2007.

Gross Domestic Product (US $ '000 at current prices): 144,665 in 2005; 157,685 in 2006 (provisional); 170,144 in 2007 (projected).

Gross Domestic Product by Economic Activity (US $ '000 at current prices, 2006, provisional): Agriculture and fishing 4,974; Mining 249; Manufacturing 553; Electricity, gas and water 4,811; Construction 25,421; Trade 33,166; Hotels and restaurants 17,628; Transport and communications 13,349; Finance 5,108; Real estate and business services 6,292; Public administration 33,077; Other services 10,588; *Sub-total* 155,216; Import duties 4,335, less imputed bank service charges 2,469; *GDP in purchasers' values* 157,685.

Balance of Payments (US $ million, year ending September 2006, provisional): Exports of goods f.o.b. 13.6; Imports of goods f.o.b. −115.3; *Trade balance* −101.7; Exports of services 91.1; Imports of services −9.7; *Balance on goods and services* −20.3; Other income (net) 1.7; *Balance on goods, services and income* −18.6; Private current transfers (net) −17.6; Official current transfers (net) 22.8; *Current balance* −13.5; Capital grants received 21.8; Loan repayments −1.1; Foreign direct investment 14.3; Net errors and omissions −23.4; *Overall balance* −1.8.

EXTERNAL TRADE

Principal Commodities (US $ '000): *Imports f.o.b.* (2004): Food and live animals 10,862; Beverages and tobacco 4,947; Mineral fuels, lubricants, etc. 30,061; Chemicals 5,772; Basic manufactures 8,597; Machinery and transport equipment 47,405; Miscellaneous manufactured articles 7,129; Total (incl. others) 116,499. *Exports* (2004/05): 13,414 (including trochus shells, tuna, copra and handicrafts). Source: Asian Development Bank, *Key Indicators of Developing Asian and Pacific Countries*.

Principal Trading Partners (US $ '000, year ending September 2004): *Imports:* Japan 8,531; Korea, Republic 5,411; Philippines 6,934; Singapore 29,885; Taiwan 5,343; USA (incl. Guam) 48,225; Total (incl. others) 107,280. *Exports:* Total 5,882.

TRANSPORT

International Shipping (1995): *Ship Arrivals:* 280. *Freight Traffic* (metric tons): Goods unloaded 64,034.

TOURISM

Tourist Arrivals: 76,180 in 2005; 78,252 in 2006; 84,566 in 2007.

Tourist Arrivals by Country of Residence (2007): Guam 1,245; Japan 28,792; Korea, Republic 14,234; Philippines 1,425; Taiwan 28,785; USA (mainland) 4,982; Total (incl. others) 84,566.

Tourism Receipts (US $ million, incl. passenger transport): 76 in 2003; 97 in 2004; 97 in 2005 (provisional).

Source: World Tourism Organization.

COMMUNICATIONS MEDIA

Radio Receivers (1997): 12,000 in use.

Television Receivers (1997): 11,000 in use.

Telephones (2006): 7,000 main lines in use.

Mobile Cellular Telephones (2006): 8,300 subscribers.

Source: partly International Telecommunication Union.

EDUCATION

Pre-Primary (public institutions only, 2006/07): 13 schools; 30 teachers; 509 pupils.

Enrolment (2006/07): *Elementary:* Total 2,683 (Public 2,135, Private 548). *Secondary:* Total 1,309 (Public 810, Private 499).

Teachers (1999/200, estimates): *Elementary:* 124. *Secondary:* 126.

Institutions (2006/07): *Elementary:* Total 21 (Public 19, Private 2). *Secondary:* Total 6 (Public 1, Private 5).

Tertiary (Palau Community College): 54 teachers (full-time and part-time, 2005/06); 545 students (at 2005 census).

Directory

The Constitution

In October 1994 Palau, the last remaining component of the Trust Territory of the Pacific Islands (a United Nations Trusteeship administered by the USA), achieved independence under the Compact of Free Association. Full responsibility for defence lies with the USA, which undertakes to provide regular economic assistance.

From 1986 the three polities of the Commonwealth of the Northern Mariana Islands, the Republic of the Marshall Islands and the Federated States of Micronesia ceased, de facto, to be part of the Trust Territory. In December 1990 the United Nations Security Council agreed formally to terminate the Trusteeship Agreement for all the territories except Palau. The agreement with Palau was finally terminated in October 1994.

The islands became known as the Republic of Palau when the locally drafted Constitution came into effect on 1 January 1981. The Constitution provides for a democratic form of government, with executive authority vested in the directly elected President and Vice-President. Presidential elections are held every four years. Legislative power is exercised by the Olbiil era Kelulau, the Palau National Congress, which is an elected body consisting of the Senate and the House of Delegates. A new capital, located at Melekeok on Babeldaob, was inaugurated in mid-2006. The Senators represent geographical districts, determined by an independent reapportionment commission every eight years, according to population. There are currently nine Senators. There are 16 Delegates, one elected to represent each of the 16 states of the Republic. The states are: Kayangel, Ngerchelong, Ngaraard, Ngardmau, Ngaremlengui, Ngiwal, Melekeok, Ngchesar, Ngatpang, Aimeliik, Airai, Koror, Peleliu, Angaur, Sonsorol and Tobi. Each state elects its own Governor and legislature.

The Government

HEAD OF STATE

President: Thomas E. Remengesau, Jr (took office 19 January 2001, re-elected 2 November 2004).

Vice-President: Elias Camsek Chin.

CABINET
(April 2008)

Minister of Health: Dr Victor Yano.

Minister of Commerce and Trade: Otoichi Besebes.

Minister of Resources and Development: Fritz Koshiba.

Minister of Education: Mario Katosang.

Minister of Justice: Elias Camsek Chin.

Minister of Community and Cultural Affairs: Alexander R. Merep.

Minister of State: Temmy L. Shmull.

Minister of Finance: Elbuchel Sadang.

COUNCIL CHIEFS

The Constitution provides for an advisory body for the President, comprising the 16 highest traditional chiefs from the 16 states. The chiefs advise on all traditional laws and customs, and on any other public matter in which their participation is required.

Chairman: Ibedul Yutaka Gibbons (Koror).

GOVERNMENT OFFICES AND MINISTRIES

Office of the President: POB 6051, Koror, PW 96940; tel. 488-2403; fax 488-1662; e-mail pres@palaunet.com.

PALAU — Directory

Department of the Interior, Office of Insular Affairs (OIA): OIA Field Office, POB 6031, Koror, PW 96946; tel. 488-2601; fax 488-2649; internet www.doi.gov/oia/Islandpages/palaupage.htm; Field Rep. J. Victor Hobson, Jr; Co-ordinator Hauro Willter.

Ministry of Commerce and Trade: POB 1471, Koror, PW 96940; tel. 488-4343; fax 488-3207; e-mail mincat@palaunet.com.

Ministry of Community and Cultural Affairs: POB 100 Koror, PW 96940; tel. 488-1126; fax 488-3354; e-mail mcca@palaunet.com; internet www.palaugov.net/mincommunity.

Ministry of Education: POB 189, Koror, PW 96940; tel. 488-1464; fax 488-1465; e-mail moe@palaumoe.net; internet www.palaumoe.net.

Ministry of Finance: POB 6011, Koror, PW 96940; tel. 767-2561; fax 767-2168; e-mail stechitong@palaugov.net.

Ministry of Health: POB 6027, Koror, PW 96940; tel. 488-2552; fax 488-1211; e-mail moh@palau-health.net; internet www.palau-health.net.

Ministry of Justice: POB 3022, Koror, PW 96940; tel. 488-2487; fax 488-4567; internet www.palaugov.net/minjustice.

Ministry of Resources and Development: POB 100, Koror, PW 96940; tel. 488-2701; fax 488-3380; e-mail mrd@palaunet.com.

All national government offices were transferred from Koror to Melekeok in October 2006. Each state has its own administrative headquarters.

President and Legislature

PRESIDENT

At the presidential election held on 2 November 2004, Thomas E. Remengesau, Jr, who won 67% of the votes cast, decisively defeated his opponent, Polycarp Basilius.

OLBIIL ERA KELULAU
(Palau National Congress)

President of the Senate: Surangel Whipps.
Vice-President of the Senate: Mlib Tmetuchl.
Speaker of the House of Delegates: Antonio Bells.
Vice-Speaker of the House of Delegates: Augustine Mesebeluu.

Election Commission

Palau Election Commission: POB 826, Koror, PW 96940; tel. 488-1554; fax 488-3327; Chair. Santos Borja.

Political Organizations
(There are currently no active political parties in Palau)

Palau Nationalist Party: c/o Olbiil era Kelulau, Koror, PW 96940; inactive; Leader Johnson Toribiong.

Ta Belau Party: c/o Olbiil era Kelulau, Koror, PW 96940; inactive; Leader Kuniwo Nakamura.

Diplomatic Representation

EMBASSIES IN PALAU

China (Taiwan): WCTC Bldg, Of. 3f, POB 9087, Koror, PW 96940; tel. 488-8150; fax 488-8151; e-mail embrocb@palaunet.com; Ambassador Matthew S. Lee.

Japan: POB 6050, Palau Pacific Resort, Arakebesang, Koror, PW 96940; tel. 488-6455; fax 488-6458; Ambassador Masashi Namekawa (resident in Fiji).

Philippines: 2nd Flr, M. Ueki Bldg, Iyebukel Hamlet, POB 1497, Koror, PW 96940; tel. 488-5077; fax 488-6310; e-mail philkor@palaunet.com; Ambassador Ramoncito Mariño.

USA: POB 6028, Koror, PW 96940; tel. 488-2920; fax 488-2911; e-mail usembassykoror@palaunet.com; internet palau.usembassy.gov; Chargé d'affaires Mark Bezner.

Judicial System

The judicial system of the Republic of Palau consists of the Supreme Court (including Trial and Appellate Divisions), presided over by the Chief Justice, the National Court (inactive), the Court of Common Pleas and the Land Court.

Supreme Court of the Republic of Palau: POB 248, Koror, PW 96940; tel. 488-2482; fax 488-1597; e-mail cjngiraklsong@palaunet.com; Chief Justice Arthur Ngiraklsong.

Office of the Attorney-General: 1365 Koror, PW 96940; tel. 488-2481; fax 488-3329; e-mail agoffice@palaunet.com; internet www.palaugov.net/minjustice/attrgeneral.html; Attorney-Gen. Jeffrey L. Beattie.

Religion

The population is predominantly Christian, mainly Roman Catholic. The Assembly of God, Baptists, Seventh-day Adventists, the Church of Jesus Christ of Latter-day Saints (Mormons), and the Bahá'í and Modignai (or Modeknai) faiths are also represented.

CHRISTIANITY

The Roman Catholic Church

Palau forms part of the diocese of the Caroline Islands, suffragan to the archdiocese of Agaña (Guam). The Bishop, who is resident in Chuuk, Eastern Caroline Islands (see the Federated States of Micronesia), participates in the Catholic Bishops' Conference of the Pacific, based in Suva, Fiji.

MODIGNAI FAITH

Modignai Church: Koror, PW 96940; an indigenous, non-Christian religion; also operates a high school.

The Press

Palau Gazette: POB 100, Koror, PW 96940; tel. 488-3257; fax 488-1662; e-mail roppresoffice@palaunet.com; newsletter publ. by Govt; monthly; Publr Roman Yano.

Palau Horizon: POB 10207, Koror, PW 96940; tel. 488-4588; fax 488-4565; e-mail hprinting@palautelecoms.com; twice weekly; f. 1998; Publr Abed E. Younis; circ. 1,500.

Rock Islander: POB 1217, Koror, PW 96940; tel. 488-1461; fax 488-1614; e-mail jerome@palaunet.com; quarterly; articles about Palau; Publr Jackson Henry.

Roureur Belau: POB 477, Koror, PW 96940; tel. 488-6365; fax 488-4810; e-mail myu@palaunet.com; weekly; Publr Clifford 'Spade' Ebas.

Tia Belau (This is Palau): POB 477, Koror, PW 96940; tel. 488-6365; fax 488-4810; e-mail tiabelau@palaunet.com; internet www.tiabelau.com; f. 1992; weekly; English and Palauan; Editor Raoul G. Briones; Publr Moses Uludong; circ 1,500.

Broadcasting and Communications

BROADCASTING

Radio

High Adventure Ministries: POB 66, Koror, PW 96940; tel. 488-2162; fax 488-2163; e-mail hamadmin@palaunet.com; f. 1992; broadcasts religious material; Engineering Man. Bentley Chan.

KRFM: Sure Save Store, Koror, PW 96940; tel. 488-1359; e-mail rudimch@palaunet.com.

Palau National Communications Corpn (PNCC): POB 99, Koror, PW 96940; tel. 587-9000; fax 587-1888; e-mail pncc@palaunet.com; internet www.palaunet.com; f. 1982; mem. of the Pacific Islands Broadcasting Asscn; operates station WSZB; broadcasts American, Japanese and Micronesian music; 18 hrs daily; Chair. Leilani Reklai; Gen. Man. Richard L. Misech.

T8AA (Eco Paradise): POB 279, Koror, PW 96940; tel. 488-2417; fax 488-1932; broadcasts news, entertainment and music; govt-owned.

WSZB Broadcasting Station: POB 279, Koror, PW 96940; tel. 488-2417; fax 488-1932; Station Man. Albert Salustiano.

WWFM: POB 1327, Koror, PW 96940; tel. 488-4848; fax 488-4420; e-mail wwfm@palaunet.com; internet www.brouhaha.net/palau/wwfm.html; Man. Alfonso Diaz.

Television

PNCC Digital Television: POB 39, Koror, PW 96940; tel. 488-1490; fax 587-1888; internet www.palaunet.com; owned by the Palau National Communications Corpn; fmrly Island Cable Television.

STV-TV Koror: POB 2000, Koror, PW 96940; tel. 488-1357; fax 488-1207; broadcasts 12 hrs daily; Man. DAVID NOLAN; Technical Man. RAY OMELEN.

Finance

(cap. = capital; res = reserves; amounts in US dollars)

BANKING

Bank of Guam: POB 338, Koror, PW 96940; tel. 488-2696; fax 488-1384; internet www.bankofguam.com; Man. KATHRINE C. LUJAN.

Bank of Hawaii (USA): POB 340, Koror, PW 96940; tel. 488-2428; fax 488-2427; internet www.boh.com.

Bank Pacific: POB 1000, Koror, PW 96940; tel. 488-5635; fax 488-4752; Man. JOSEPH KOSHIBA.

National Development Bank of Palau: POB 816, Koror, PW 96940-0816; tel. 488-2578; fax 488-2579; e-mail ndbp@palaunet.com; internet www.ndbp.com; f. 1982; cap. and res 11.5m. (Sept. 2002); 100% govt-owned; Pres. KALEB ADUI, Jr; Chair. NORIWO UBEDEI.

INSURANCE

Century Insurance Co: POB 318, Koror, PW 96940; tel. 488-8580; fax 488-8632; e-mail knakamura@palaunet.com.

Moylan's Insurance Underwriters Palau: POB 156, Koror, PW 96940; tel. 488-2761; fax 488-2744; e-mail palau@moylansinsurance.com; internet www.moylansinsurance.com; Branch Man. KENJI DENGOKL.

NECO Insurance Underwriters Ltd: POB 129, Koror, PW 96940; tel. 488-2325; fax 488-2880; e-mail necogroup@palaunet.com.

Poltalia National Insurance: POB 12, Koror, PW 96940; tel. 488-2254; fax 488-2834; e-mail psata@palaunet.com; f. 1974; Pres. and CEO EPHRAM POLYCARP.

Trade and Industry

CHAMBER OF COMMERCE

Palau Chamber of Commerce: POB 1742, Koror, PW 96940; tel. 488-3400; fax 488-3401; e-mail pcoc@palaunet.com; f. 1984; Pres. SURANGEL WHIPPS, Jr.

CO-OPERATIVES

These include the Palau Fishermen's Co-operative, Palau Boatbuilders' Asscn and the Palau Handicraft and Woodworkers' Guild. In 1990, of the 13 registered co-operatives, eight were fishermen's co-operatives, three consumers' co-operatives (only two in normal operation) and two farmers' co-operatives (one in normal operation).

DEVELOPMENT ORGANIZATION

Palau Conservation Society: POB 1811, Koror, PW 96940; tel. 488-3993; fax 488-3990; e-mail pcs@palaunet.com; internet www.palau-pcs.org; f. 1994; sustainable devt, environmental protection; Exec. Dir TIARE TURANG HOLM.

Transport

ROADS

Macadam and concrete roads are found in the more important islands. Other islands have stone and coral-surfaced roads and tracks. The Government is responsible for 36 km (22 miles) of paved roads and 25 km (15 miles) of coral- and gravel-surfaced roads. Most paved roads are located on Koror and are in a poor state of repair. A major project to construct a new 85-km (53-mile) road around Babeldaob began in 1999 and was completed in 2007. The project was funded with US $150m. from the Compact of Free Association.

SHIPPING

Most shipping in Palau is government-organized. However, the Micronesia Transport Line operates a service from Sydney (Australia) to Palau. A twice-weekly inter-island service operates between Koror and Peleliu. There is one commercial port at Malakal Harbor, which is operated by the privately owned Belau Transfer and Terminal Company.

CIVIL AVIATION

There is an international airport on Babeldaob. A new terminal building, construction of which was funded by a grant of US $16m. from Japan, opened in May 2003. Domestic airfields (former Japanese military airstrips) are located on Angaur and Peleliu. Continental Micronesia (Northern Mariana Islands and Guam) provides daily flights to Koror from Guam, and twice-weekly flights from Manila (Philippines). Cebu Pacific operates direct flights from Davao (Philippines) to Koror. A civil aviation agreement with Taiwan was signed in 1997, and direct charter flights between Taiwan and Palau began in the following year, operated by the Far Eastern Air Transport Corpn. Palau Trans Pacific also operates from Taiwan. In August 2004 Palau's first locally owned airline, Palau Micronesia Air, made its inaugural flight to Manila. Its routes were to include the Federated States of Micronesia, the Philippines and Australia. However, operations were suspended in December 2004.

Rock Island Airlines: managed by Aloha Airlines (Hawaii).

Tourism

Tourism is becoming increasingly important in Palau. The islands are particularly rich in their marine environment, and the Government has taken steps to conserve and protect these natural resources. The myriad Rock Islands, now known as the Floating Garden Islands, are a noted reserve in the lagoon to the west of the main group of islands. There were 959 hotel rooms in 2004. In 2007 Palau received 84,566 visitors, most of whom were from Taiwan and from Japan. Tourist revenue reached US $97m. (according to a provisional estimate) in 2005.

Belau Tourism Association: POB 9032, Koror, PW 96940; tel. 488-4377; fax 488-1725; e-mail bta@palaunet.com.

Palau Visitors' Authority: POB 256, Koror, PW 96940; tel. 488-2793; fax 488-1453; e-mail info@visit-palau.com; internet www.visit-palau.com; Man. Dir DARIN DE LEON.

PALESTINIAN AUTONOMOUS AREAS

Introductory Survey

Location, Climate, Language, Religion, Flag, Capital

The Palestinian Autonomous Areas are located in the West Bank and the Gaza Strip. (For a more detailed description of the location of the Palestinian territories, see Government, below.) The West Bank lies in western Asia, to the west of the Jordan river and the Dead Sea, with the State of Israel to the north, west and south. The Gaza Strip lies on the easternmost coast of the Mediterranean, with Israel to the north and east and Egypt to the south. The Interim Agreement of September 1995 (see below) provides for the creation of a corridor, or safe passage, linking the Gaza Strip with the West Bank. A 'southern' safe passage between Hebron and Gaza was opened in October 1999 (although it has been closed since October 2000). Including East Jerusalem, the West Bank covers an area of 5,655 sq km. Precipitation ranges between 600 mm and 800 mm on the Mount Hebron massif and 200 mm in the Jordan valley. Apart from the urban centres of Beit Lahm (Bethlehem) and Al-Khalil (Hebron) to the south, the majority of the Palestinian population is concentrated in the northern localities around Ram Allah (Ramallah), Nabulus (Nablus), Janin (Jenin) and Tulkarm. The Gaza Strip covers an area of 365 sq km. Annual average rainfall is 300 mm. The language of Palestinians in the West Bank and Gaza is Arabic. The majority of the Palestinian population are Muslims, with a Christian minority representing about 2% of the Palestinian population of the territories. This minority, in turn, represents about 45% of all Palestinian Christians. The national flag (proportion 1 by 2) comprises three equal horizontal stripes of black, white and green, with a red triangle with its base corresponding to the hoist. Gaza City is the main population centre and the centre of administration for the Palestinian (National) Authority (PA), appointed in May 1994. Ramallah is the PA's administrative centre in the West Bank. In November 1988 the Palestine National Council (PNC) proclaimed Jerusalem as the capital of the newly declared independent State of Palestine. Israel (q.v.) declares Jerusalem as its capital. In 1967 East Jerusalem was formally annexed by the Israeli authorities, although the annexation has never been recognized by the UN. The permanent status of Jerusalem remains subject to negotiation on so-called 'final status' issues under the Oslo accords (see Recent History).

Recent History

Until the end of the 1948 Arab–Israeli War, the West Bank formed part of the British Mandate of Palestine, before becoming part of the Hashemite Kingdom of Jordan under the Armistice Agreement of 1949. It remained under Jordanian sovereignty, despite Israeli occupation in 1967, until King Hussein of Jordan formally relinquished legal and administrative control on 31 July 1988. Under Israeli military occupation the West Bank was administered by a military government, which divided the territory into seven sub-districts. The Civil Administration, as it was later termed, did not extend its jurisdiction to the many Israeli settlements that were established under the Israeli occupation; settlements remained subject to the Israeli legal and administrative system. By October 2000 approximately 17.2% of the West Bank was under exclusive Palestinian jurisdiction and security control, although Israel retained authority over access to and from the zone; about 23.8% was under Israeli military control, with responsibility for civil administration and public order transferred to the PA; the remaining 59% was under Israeli occupation.

An administrative province under the British Mandate of Palestine, Gaza was transferred to Egypt after the 1949 armistice and remained under Egyptian administration until June 1967, when it was invaded by Israel. Following Israeli occupation the Gaza Strip, like the West Bank, became an 'administered territory'. Until the provisions of the Declaration of Principles on Palestinian Self-Rule (see below) began to take effect, the management of day-to-day affairs was the responsibility of the area's Israeli military commander. Neither Israeli laws nor governmental and public bodies—including the Supreme Court—could review or alter the orders of the military command to any great extent. In 2001 an estimated 42% of the Gaza Strip was under Israeli control, including Jewish settlements, military bases, bypass roads and a 'buffer zone' along the border with Israel. However, Israel withdrew its settlers and military personnel from Gaza in August–September 2005 (see below).

In accordance with the Declaration of Principles on Palestinian Self-Rule of 13 September 1993, and the Cairo Agreement on the Gaza Strip and Jericho of 4 May 1994, the Palestine Liberation Organization (PLO) assumed control of the Jericho area of the West Bank, and of the Gaza Strip, on 17 May 1994. In November and December 1995, under the terms of the Israeli-Palestinian Interim Agreement on the West Bank and the Gaza Strip concluded on 28 September 1995, Israeli armed forces withdrew from the West Bank towns of Nablus, Ramallah, Jenin, Tulkarm, Qalqilya and Bethlehem. (These three agreements and associated accords are referred to collectively as the 'Oslo accords', owing to the role played by Norwegian diplomacy in their negotiation.) In late December the PLO assumed responsibility in some 17 areas of civil administration in the town of Hebron, with a view to eventually assuming full responsibility for civil affairs in the 400 surrounding villages. However, despite a partial withdrawal from Hebron in January 1997, Israeli armed forces were to retain freedom of movement to act against potential hostilities there and also to provide security for some 400 Jewish settlers. Responsibility for security in the rest of Hebron (excluding access roads) passed to the Palestinian police force. Following the first phase of the redeployment and the holding, on its completion, of elections to a Palestinian Legislative Council and for a Palestinian executive president, Israel was to have completed a second redeployment from rural areas by July 1997. The Israeli occupation was to be maintained in military installations, Jewish settlements, East Jerusalem and the settlements around Jerusalem until the conclusion of 'final status' negotiations between Israel and the Palestinians, scheduled for May 1999.

Diplomatic developments within the context of the Oslo peace process led to a new timetable for Israeli redeployment which envisaged two phases, subsequent to the Hebron withdrawal, to be completed by October 1997 and August 1998. Discussions on 'final status' issues—borders, Jerusalem, Jewish settlements and Palestinian refugees—were to commence within two months of the signing of the agreement on Hebron. As guarantor of the Oslo accords, the USA undertook to obtain the release from Israeli custody of Palestinian prisoners, and to ensure that Israel continued to engage in negotiations for the establishment of a Palestinian airport in the Gaza Strip and for safe passage for Palestinians between the West Bank and Gaza. The USA also endeavoured to ensure that the Palestinians would continue to combat terrorism, complete the revision of the Palestinian National Charter (or PLO Covenant), adopted in 1964 and amended in 1968, and consider Israeli requests to extradite Palestinians suspected of involvement in attacks in Israel.

In February 1997 the Israeli Government of Binyamin Netanyahu announced the construction of a new Jewish settlement at Jabal Abu Ghunaim (Har Homa in Hebrew), near Beit Sahur, which would prejudice 'final status' negotiations concerning Jerusalem because it would effectively separate East Jerusalem from the West Bank. In response, the PA withdrew from 'final status' talks scheduled to commence in March. The start of construction work at Jabal Abu Ghunaim provoked rioting among Palestinians and a resumption of attacks by the military wing of the Islamic Resistance Movement (Hamas) on Israeli civilian targets. Israel responded by ordering a general closure of the West Bank and Gaza. Both the Jabal Abu Ghunaim construction and Israel's unilateral decision to redeploy its armed forces from only 9% of West Bank territory (announced in March) were regarded by many observers as a vitiation of both the Oslo and the subsequent post-Hebron agreements. Moreover, the Israeli newspaper Ha'aretz later reported that Israeli plans, evolved within the framework of the Oslo accords, to relinquish 90% of the West Bank had been revised to a 40% redeployment.

In June 1997 the US House of Representatives voted in favour of recognizing Jerusalem as the undivided capital of Israel and of transferring the US embassy to the city from Tel-Aviv. The vote (which was opposed by US President Bill Clinton) coincided with violent clashes between Palestinian civilians and Israeli troops in Gaza and Hebron. In July, on the eve of a scheduled visit by Dennis Ross, the US Special Co-ordinator to the Middle East, to reactivate negotiations between Israel and the PA, Hamas carried out a suicide bomb attack at a Jewish market in Jerusalem, in which 14 civilians were killed. Ross cancelled his visit and the Israeli Government immediately halted payment of tax revenues to the PA and closed the Gaza Strip and the West Bank. In the aftermath of the bombing the PA undertook a campaign to detain members of Hamas and another militant organization, Islamic Jihad. As a result of US diplomacy, Israeli and Palestinian officials agreed to resume negotiations focusing on the outstanding issues of the Oslo accords in October.

Meanwhile, the attempted assassination in Amman, Jordan, in September 1997, of Khalid Meshaal, the head of the Hamas political bureau there, provoked warnings of retaliation against Israel, even before official confirmation that agents of the Israeli security service, Mossad, had been responsible for the attack. In order to secure the release of its agents by the Jordanian authorities, Israel was obliged to free a number of Arab political prisoners, most notably Sheikh Ahmad Yassin, the founder and spiritual leader of Hamas, who had been sentenced to life imprisonment in Israel in 1989 for complicity in attacks on Israeli soldiers. The release of Sheikh Yassin into Jordanian custody was swiftly followed by his return, in October 1997, to Gaza.

It was reported in December 1997 that, under further US pressure, the Israeli Cabinet had agreed in principle to withdraw troops from an unspecified area of the West Bank. However, the Israeli Government subsequently reiterated that it would not conduct such a redeployment until the Palestinian leadership had fulfilled a series of conditions: these included the adoption of effective measures to counter terrorism, a reduction in the strength of its security forces from 40,000 to 24,000, and a revision of the Palestinian National Charter to recognize explicitly Israel's right to exist. Moreover, prior to a summit meeting in January 1998 between Clinton and Netanyahu in Washington, DC, the Israeli Cabinet issued a communiqué detailing 'vital and national interests' in the West Bank (amounting to some 60% of the entire territory) that it was not prepared to relinquish; the document asserted that Israel would, among other areas, retain control of the territory surrounding Jerusalem. In late January, however, direct contacts between Palestinian representatives and the Israeli Prime Minister collapsed.

In March 1998 it emerged that the USA planned to present new proposals regarding the withdrawal of Israeli armed forces from the West Bank at separate meetings in Europe between US Secretary of State Madeleine Albright and the PA President, Yasser Arafat, and Israeli Prime Minister Netanyahu. However, it was evident that, even if agreement could be reached on the extent of territory involved, the issue of whether a subsequent withdrawal should take place prior to the commencement of 'final status' talks remained far more contentious. The Israeli Cabinet rejected the new US initiative. Having persuaded Arafat to attend a conference in London, United Kingdom, based on the most recent US initiative, during a visit to Gaza City on behalf of the European Union (EU), in early May the British Prime Minister, Tony Blair, hosted a summit meeting attended by Netanyahu, Arafat and Albright. At its conclusion the US Secretary of State invited Netanyahu and Arafat to attend a summit meeting with Bill Clinton in Washington, DC, to discuss the apparent US proposal that Israeli and Palestinian officials could proceed to 'final status' negotiations as soon as the scope of the next Israeli withdrawal from the West Bank had been agreed. In June details of the latest US initiative were unofficially disclosed in the Israeli press: Israel would be required to agree to 'no significant expansion' of Jewish settlements and to relinquish slightly more than 13% of West Bank territory over a period of 12 weeks, in exchange for increased Palestinian co-operation on security issues. The adoption by the Israeli Cabinet later that month of a plan to extend the boundaries of Jerusalem and construct homes there for a further 1m. people prompted accusations by the PA that it amounted to a de facto annexation of territories that were officially subject to 'final status' discussions.

On 7 July 1998 the UN General Assembly overwhelmingly approved a resolution to upgrade the status of the PLO at the UN. The new provision, which the USA and Israel had opposed, allowed the PLO to participate in debates, to co-sponsor resolutions, and to raise points of order during discussions of Middle East affairs.

On 19–22 July 1998 Israeli and Palestinian delegations held direct negotiations for the first time since March 1997, in order to discuss the US peace initiative disclosed in June. In September 1998 Netanyahu and Arafat met in Washington, DC, and agreed to participate in a peace conference in the USA in the following month. The summit meeting, also attended by President Clinton, commenced at the Wye Plantation, Maryland, USA, on 15 October 1998, and culminated in the signing, on 23 October, of the Wye River Memorandum, which was intended to facilitate the implementation of the Oslo accords. Under the terms of the Wye Memorandum, to be implemented within three months of its signing, Israel was to transfer a further 13.1% of West Bank territory from exclusive Israeli control to joint Israeli-Palestinian control. An additional 14% of the West Bank was to be transferred from joint Israeli-Palestinian control to exclusive Palestinian control. The Wye Memorandum also stipulated that: negotiations with regard to a third Israeli redeployment (under the terms of the Oslo accords) should proceed concurrently with 'final status' discussions; the PA should reinforce anti-terrorism measures and arrest 30 suspected terrorists; the strength of the Palestinian police force should be reduced by 25%; Israel should carry out the phased release of 750 Palestinian prisoners (including political detainees); the Palestine National Council (PNC) should annul those clauses of the PLO Covenant deemed to be anti-Israeli; Gaza International Airport was to become operational with an Israeli security presence; and an access corridor between the West Bank and the Gaza Strip should be opened. The Memorandum was endorsed by both the Israeli Cabinet and the Knesset (parliament) by mid-November. On 20 November Israel redeployed its armed forces from about 500 sq km of the West Bank (with the PA assuming responsibilty for all civil affairs and for security affairs in some 400 sq km); released some 250 (mainly non-political) Palestinian prisoners; and signed a protocol for the opening of Gaza International Airport. Israel retained the right to decide which airlines could use the airport, which was officially inaugurated by Arafat on 24 November.

However, implementation of the Wye Memorandum did not proceed smoothly. In the weeks prior to a visit by Bill Clinton to Israel and the Gaza Strip, planned for December 1998, violent clashes erupted in the West Bank between Palestinians and Israeli security forces. One cause of the unrest was a decision by the Israeli Cabinet to suspend further releases of Palestinian prisoners under the terms of the Wye Memorandum, and its insistence that no Palestinians convicted of killing Israelis, nor members of Hamas or Islamic Jihad, would be released. On 14 December, meanwhile, in the presence of President Clinton, the PNC voted to annul articles of the Palestinian National Charter that were deemed to be anti-Israeli. However, at a summit meeting the following day between Clinton, Netanyahu and Arafat at the Erez checkpoint between Israel and the Gaza Strip, the Israeli Prime Minister reiterated Israel's stance regarding the release of Palestinian prisoners and further demanded that the Palestinians should honour their commitments by ceasing incitement to violence and formally relinquishing plans for a unilateral declaration of Palestinian statehood on 4 May 1999 (the original deadline as established by the Oslo accords). Netanyahu announced that Israel would not proceed with the second scheduled redeployment of its armed forces on 18 December 1998, and on 20 December the Israeli Cabinet voted to suspend implementation of the Wye Memorandum.

Palestinians reacted to the death of King Hussein of Jordan in February 1999 with public grief—about 65% of the Kingdom's inhabitants are believed to be of Palestinian origin—especially in the West Bank, which King Hussein ruled for 15 years until June 1967. For Arafat, the death of Hussein was a major political reverse since the King had frequently supported him when the peace process with Israel appeared to be on the verge of collapse. Arafat subsequently surprised many Jordanians by proposing the establishment of a Palestinian-Jordanian confederation. The proposal (which had been put forward as part of a peace initiative in 1985, but was rejected by King Hussein) was not welcomed in Jordan, where it was considered to be premature while the West Bank was still largely under Israeli occupation.

President Arafat came under intense international pressure to postpone a unilateral declaration of Palestinian statehood, at least until after the Israeli elections scheduled for May 1999. In late April PLO chief negotiators Mahmud Abbas (also known as Abu Mazen) and Saeb Erakat (the Minister of Local Government) visited Washington, DC, in order to secure certain assurances from the USA in return for an extension of the 4 May deadline. Following a meeting of the Palestinian Central Council (PCC), together with Hamas representatives, in Gaza, it was announced that a declaration on Palestinian statehood would be postponed until after the Israeli elections. The decision was applauded internationally, but provoked violent demonstrations among many Palestinians.

Meeting at Sharm esh-Sheikh, Egypt, on 4 September 1999, during a visit to the region by US Secretary of State Albright, Arafat and the new Israeli Prime Minister, Ehud Barak, signed the Sharm esh-Sheikh Memorandum (or Wye Two accords), outlining a revised timetable for implementation of the outstanding provisions of the original Wye agreement. Under the terms of the Memorandum, on 9 September Israel released some 200 Palestinian 'security' prisoners, and the following day Israel transferred a further 7% of the West Bank to PA control. A ceremonial opening of 'final status' negotiations between Israel and the PA was held at the Erez checkpoint on 13 September; shortly afterwards details emerged of a secret meeting between Barak and Arafat to discuss an agenda for such talks. However, in early October the Palestinians' chief negotiator and Minister of Culture and Information, Yasser Abd ar-Rabbuh, warned that the PA would boycott 'final status' talks unless Israel ended its settlement expansion programme. In mid-October Barak, also under pressure from left-wing groups in Israel, responded by dismantling 12 'settlement outposts' in the West Bank which he deemed to be illegal. Meanwhile, Israel released a further 151 Palestinian prisoners under the terms of Wye Two. The first 'safe passage' between the West Bank and Gaza was inaugurated on 25 October. Israel asserted that it would maintain almost complete control over the so-called 'southern route', which linked Hebron to the Erez checkpoint.

'Final status' negotiations between Israel and the PA commenced in Ramallah on 8 November 1999, following a summit meeting held earlier in the month in Oslo, Norway, between Arafat, Barak and Clinton. A further redeployment of Israeli armed forces from 5% of the West Bank, scheduled for 15 November, was postponed owing to disagreement over the areas to be transferred. In early December Palestinian negotiators walked out of the talks, following reports that settlement activity had intensified under Barak. Apparently in response to US pressure, the Israeli Prime Minister subsequently announced a halt to settlement construction until the close of negotiations regarding a framework agreement on 'final status'. In late December Arafat conducted talks in Ramallah with Barak, who became the first Israeli premier to hold peace discussions on Palestinian territory. At the end of the month Israel released some 26 Palestinian 'security' prisoners as a gesture of 'goodwill'. Israeli armed forces withdrew from a further 5% of the West Bank on 6–7 January 2000; however, Israel announced in mid-January that a third redeployment from 6.1% of the territory (scheduled to take place on 20 January) would be postponed until Barak had returned from revived peace talks with Syria in the USA. During a meeting with Arafat on his return from the USA (where talks on the Israeli-Syrian track had collapsed), Barak was reported to have proposed that the deadline for reaching a framework agreement be postponed for two months. The approval by the Israeli Cabinet of a withdrawal of its troops from a sparsely populated area of the West Bank led the PA to break off negotiations in early February. On 19–20 March Israel released 15 Palestinian 'security' prisoners, and the resumption of 'final status' talks was announced on 21 March. On the same day Israeli armed forces withdrew from a further 6.1% of the West Bank.

In mid-April 2000, following talks between Barak and Clinton in Washington, DC, Israel was said to have agreed to Palestinian demands for greater US involvement in future discussions. Moreover, the Israeli premier reportedly indicated that a Palestinian entity could be established in what was now PA-controlled territory—covering 60%–70% of the West Bank—although he refused to speak of a Palestinian 'state'. Later in April Arafat met with Clinton in Washington, where he sought US intervention in halting Israel's settlement expansion programme. The third round of 'final status' talks between Israel and the PA opened at the Israeli port of Eilat on 30 April, at which Palestinian negotiators denounced a recent decision by the Israeli Government to construct 174 new Jewish homes in the West Bank. At crisis talks between Arafat and Barak in Ramallah in early May, mediated by Dennis Ross, Barak reportedly proposed the transfer to full PA control of three Palestinian villages close to Jerusalem, on condition that the third West Bank redeployment (scheduled to be implemented in June) be postponed. After PA negotiators admitted that the 13 May deadline for reaching a framework agreement would not be met, 'final status' talks were suspended. Moreover, on 21 May Israel suspended 'secret' talks being conducted between Israeli and Palestinian representatives in Stockholm, Sweden, after an Israeli child was seriously wounded in continuing violence in the West Bank. (The latest unrest came after Palestinians declared 15 May—the anniversary of the declaration of the State of Israel in 1948—to be a 'day of rage' and amid growing anger over the apparent unaccountability of the PA leadership.) The Israeli Government also reversed its decision to transfer the three Arab villages to PA control, demanding that Arafat take action to curb Palestinian unrest.

Following a tour of Israel and the Palestinian areas by US Secretary of State Madeleine Albright in early June 2000, President Clinton received Arafat for discussions in Washington, DC, in an attempt to reinvigorate the Israeli-Palestinian track of the Middle East peace process. Four days later Israel released three Palestinian prisoners as a 'goodwill' gesture. On 21 June, two days prior to the scheduled date, the PA reportedly agreed to a postponement of the third redeployment of Israeli forces from the West Bank. The PCC convened on 2 July, and after two days of discussions stated that the PLO would declare a State of Palestine on or before 13 September. On 11 July Bill Clinton inaugurated a peace summit between Arafat and Barak at the US presidential retreat at Camp David, Maryland, with the aim of achieving a framework agreement on 'final status'. However, the talks ended without agreement on 25 July. Despite reported progress regarding the borders of a future Palestinian entity and the question of Palestinian refugees, disagreements over the future status of Jerusalem had been the principal obstacle to an accord. Israel was said to have offered the Palestinians municipal authority over certain parts of East Jerusalem, as well as access to the Islamic holy sites. PA officials, however, demanded full sovereignty over the holy sites (in particular the al-Aqsa Mosque and the Dome of the Rock), with East Jerusalem as the capital of a Palestinian state. Nevertheless, Israel and the PA pledged to continue peace negotiations and to avoid 'unilateral actions'—interpreted as Arafat's threat unilaterally to declare an independent Palestinian state. During a tour principally of Europe, the Middle East and Asia, intense pressure was exerted on Arafat not to announce the establishment of a Palestinian state on 13 September. The PCC convened in Gaza on 9–10 September and agreed to postpone the declaration of statehood for an indefinite period (although 15 November was reportedly designated as the new target date). Later in September negotiations between Israeli and PA officials resumed in the USA, and on 20 September an agreement was signed allowing for construction of the Gaza seaport to begin (the work failed to progress owing to the worsening security situation). On 26 September Barak and Arafat met at the Israeli premier's home for their first direct talks since the Camp David summit.

From late September 2000 the West Bank and Gaza Strip became engulfed in what became known as the al-Aqsa *intifada* (uprising—the first *intifada* began at the end of 1987 and continued for some five years), as Palestinians demonstrated their frustration at the lack of progress in the Oslo peace process and at their failure to achieve statehood. The outbreak of violence was triggered by the visit of Ariel Sharon, leader of Israel's right-wing Likud party, to Temple Mount/Haram ash-Sharif in Jerusalem—the site of the al-Aqsa Mosque and the Dome of the Rock—on 28 September. Sharon's visit to the Islamic holy sites provoked violent protests and stone-throwing by Palestinians, to which Israeli security forces responded forcefully. The clashes spread rapidly to other Palestinian towns: by the end of October at least 140 people had died—all but eight of them Palestinians—and thousands had been wounded. In early October Arafat and Barak travelled to Paris, France, for negotiations led by the US Secretary of State, but no agreement was reached on the composition of an international commission of inquiry into the causes of the violence. The Israeli authorities subsequently sealed off the borders of the West Bank and Gaza, and on 7 October the UN Security Council issued a resolution condemning the 'provocation carried out' at Temple Mount/Haram ash-Sharif and the 'excessive use of force' employed by the Israeli security forces against Palestinians. Meanwhile, Israel accused Arafat of failing to intervene to halt the violence, as members of Arafat's own Fatah movement joined Hamas and other militant groups in the quickly escalating *intifada*. In an attempt to prevent the crisis from developing into a major regional conflict, a US-sponsored summit meeting between Barak and Arafat was convened on 16–17 October at Sharm esh-Sheikh. At the close of the meeting US President Clinton announced that the Israeli and Palestinian leaders had agreed the terms of a 'truce' to halt the spiralling violence. The two sides had also reportedly agreed on the formation of a US-appointed committee to investigate the clashes. Barak, however, demanded that Arafat rearrest some 60 militant Islamists whom the PA had freed in early October. The League of Arab States (the Arab League, see p. 332) held an emergency summit meeting in the Egyptian capital on 21–22 October, and issued a strong condemnation of Israel's actions towards the Palestinians. Barak responded by announcing that Israel was calling a 'time-out' in the peace process.

At the end of October 2000 Islamic Jihad claimed responsibility for a suicide bombing on an Israeli army post in Gaza, signalling a new campaign against Israeli forces by militant Palestinian organizations opposed to the Oslo process. Israel responded by launching air-strikes on Fatah military bases, and declared a new strategy of targeting leading officials of militant Islamist groups suspected of terrorist activities. On 1 November Arafat held a crisis meeting in Gaza with the Israeli Minister for Regional Co-operation, Shimon Peres; the two sides were reported to have agreed a 'cease-fire', based on the truce brokered in Egypt in October. The following day, however, a car bomb exploded in Jerusalem, for which Islamic Jihad claimed responsibility. In early November President Clinton appointed the five-member international commission of inquiry, to be chaired by former US Senator George Mitchell. Meeting with Clinton in the USA shortly afterwards, Arafat demanded that the USA support Palestinian requests for the establishment of a UN peace-keeping force in the self-rule areas (Barak was opposed to such a force). Israel reinforced its closure of the West Bank and Gaza in mid-November, imposing an economic blockade on the territories, and launched air-strikes against PA offices in Gaza later that month, in reprisal for the deaths of two people in the bombing of a school bus for Jewish settlers. At the end of November the Palestinians rejected a partial peace plan, announced by Barak, whereby Israel would withdraw its armed forces from additional West Bank territory provided that the PA agreed to postpone any discussion of the remaining 'final status' issues. In late 2000 Palestinian militants concentrated their attacks against Jewish settlers, while in early December Israel eased some of the sanctions imposed on the Palestinian enclaves at the outbreak of the crisis. In mid-December the US-led commission of inquiry began conducting investigations into the violence.

A further round of peace talks opened in mid-December 2000, at which Clinton was reported to have proposed a peace deal that included plans for a future Palestinian state covering the Gaza Strip and some 95% of the West Bank, as well as granting the Palestinians sovereignty over the Islamic holy sites in the Old City of Jerusalem. However, the US plan also required that Palestinians renounce the right of return for 3.7m. refugees, which the PA deemed unacceptable. The negotiations broke down in late December after two Israelis died in bombings by Palestinian militants in Tel-Aviv and the Gaza Strip. In January 2001 Arafat visited Washington, DC, to seek official clarification of Clinton's proposals; meanwhile, following a car bomb explosion in northern Israel, the Israeli authorities again tightened their blockade of the West Bank and Gaza. Israel subsequently confirmed its policy of assassinating local Palestinian officials who were regarded as endangering Israeli society, which it referred to as 'targeted killings'.

The election of Ariel Sharon to the Israeli premiership in early February 2001 provoked violent demonstrations by Palestinians, who held Sharon responsible—as Israel's Minister of Defence at that time—for the Phalangist massacre of Palestinian refugees in Lebanese camps in 1982 (see the chapters on Israel and Lebanon). Immediately after Sharon's election Palestinian militants carried out a car bombing in Jerusalem, and in mid-February a Palestinian bus driver launched an attack on Israeli soldiers and civilians in Tel-Aviv, killing nine people. Israel responded by again sealing off the Palestinian territories.

At the beginning of June 2001 21 Israelis were killed in a suicide bomb attack, apparently perpetrated by Hamas, at a Tel-Aviv nightclub. The PA agreed the following day to implement the recommendations listed in the final report of the international commission of inquiry under George Mitchell (the Sharm esh-Sheikh Fact-Finding Committee, or 'Mitchell Committee'), published in late May. The Mitchell Report recommended a freeze on Israeli settlement expansion; a clear statement by the PA demanding an end to Palestinian violence; an 'immediate and unconditional' end to the conflict and the disengagement of forces by both sides; and the resumption of security co-operation. Moreover, in mid-June the PA also agreed to an extended cease-fire brokered by the US Central Intelligence Agency (CIA) Director, George Tenet, although in early July both Hamas and Islamic Jihad formally announced that the cease-fire was ended. In late July Palestinian security forces in Gaza arrested a number of militants, including members of Fatah's military wing, the *tanzim*.

In August 2001 the PA rejected a demand by Israel for the arrest of seven alleged 'terrorists', who headed a 'most wanted' list of about 100 Palestinians suspected of involvement in attacks against Israeli targets. Soon afterwards Israel ordered its armed forces to occupy several PA offices including Orient House, the PA's de facto headquarters in East Jerusalem, following a Hamas suicide bombing which killed at least 15 Israelis at a restaurant in central Jerusalem. Israeli troops entered the West Bank town of Jenin in mid-August—the first Israeli reoccupation of territory transferred to full PA control under the terms of the Oslo accords. Palestinian officials called the action a 'declaration of war'. Later in the month Abu Ali Moustafa, the leader of the Popular Front for the Liberation of Palestine (PFLP), was assassinated by Israeli forces in the West Bank.

The unprecedented scale of the suicide attacks launched against New York and Washington, DC, on 11 September 2001—for which the USA held the al-Qa'ida (Base) network led by the Saudi-born militant Islamist Osama bin Laden principally responsible—precipitated efforts by the US Administration to encourage Israel and the PA to end the violence in the Palestinian territories, as President George W. Bush (who had been elected to the presidency in November 2000) sought to garner support for an international 'war on terror'. In mid-September 2001 Yasser Arafat, who had condemned the attacks in the strongest terms, declared that he had ordered militant Palestinian groups to halt their actions against Israelis, while Israel agreed to withdraw from PA-controlled areas of the West Bank. However, Sharon stated that his Government required 48 hours without violence prior to any resumption of peace talks. Arafat and Peres finally met in the Gaza Strip in late September, in an attempt to consolidate the cease-fire arrangements outlined in the Mitchell Report. However, on the first anniversary of the al-Aqsa *intifada* five Palestinians were shot dead by Israeli forces in Gaza, and retaliatory attacks between the two sides resumed.

President Bush disclosed for the first time in early October 2001 that the USA would accept the creation of a Palestinian state, on condition that Israel's existence was not threatened. The assassination in Jerusalem of Israel's ultra-nationalist Minister of Tourism, Rechavam Ze'evi, by three members of the PFLP—apparently in revenge for the murder of the PFLP leader in August—led Israel, in late October, to order its armed forces into six major West Bank towns. Shortly after Ze'evi's death Arafat banned all military factions of Palestinian political groups, and his security forces arrested several PFLP militants; however, the PA refused Israeli demands for their extradition. At least five Palestinians reportedly died in Beit Rima, near Ramallah, in a raid by Israeli forces searching for Ze'evi's assassins. Towards the end of October Israel stated that it would carry out a phased withdrawal from the six West Bank towns; however, its 'anti-terrorist' operation continued in Jenin and Tulkarm, and Israeli tanks continued to surround Ramallah.

Hamas claimed responsibility for a series of attacks in Jerusalem and Haifa over a 24-hour period in early December 2001, in which at least 25 Israelis were killed. Palestinian security forces subsequently claimed to have arrested more than 150 militants, mostly in Jenin, and also reportedly placed the spiritual leader of Hamas, Sheikh Ahmad Yassin, under house arrest. Meanwhile, an Israeli missile strike on Arafat's official residence in Gaza destroyed two of his helicopters, while in Ramallah Israeli tanks advanced to the edge of the presidential compound, where Arafat was then residing. The Israeli Prime Minister increasingly began to draw parallels between Israel's efforts to suppress the *intifada* and the USA's 'war on terror', describing the PA as a 'terror-supporting entity'. In mid-December Israel responded to an assault on a settlers' bus in the West Bank (in which some 10 Israelis died) by declaring the PA leader to be 'irrelevant', owing to his failure to prevent such attacks, and announced that it was severing all contacts with Arafat. The

PALESTINIAN AUTONOMOUS AREAS

Israeli military launched air-raids across the West Bank and Gaza, reoccupied large areas of Ramallah and reinforced its military blockade of Arafat's headquarters; several Palestinian police officers and civilians were killed during the Israeli operations. Meanwhile, the USA again vetoed a proposed UN resolution calling for international observers to be deployed in the Palestinian areas. In a televised speech Arafat issued a strong condemnation of groups that carried out gun attacks and suicide bombings against Israelis, although Sharon insisted that Arafat would not be permitted to leave Ramallah until the PA arrested the perpetrators of Ze'evi's murder.

In January 2002 Arafat ordered an investigation into Israeli and US claims that the PA was complicit in a massive shipment of largely Iranian-produced weaponry—including *Katyusha* rockets, mortar shells and anti-tank missiles—which Israeli forces had intercepted in the Red Sea; the freighter, the *Karine A*, was apparently en route for the Gaza Strip to be used in attacks against Israeli targets. (In February Arafat finally accepted responsibility on behalf of his administration for the shipment.) Following a gun attack by members of another militant group, the Al-Aqsa Martyrs Brigades, that killed six guests at a bar mitzvah ceremony in Hadera, northern Israel, Sharon ordered tanks and armoured vehicles to tighten their blockade of Arafat's Ramallah headquarters (the President had effectively been under house arrest for several weeks), and also reoccupied Tulkarm in order to arrest known Palestinian 'terrorists'. Although the troops withdrew a day later, it was reported to be the largest military incursion since the start of the al-Aqsa *intifada*. Meanwhile, EU officials increasingly distanced themselves from the US position towards the conflict, reaffirming their support for Arafat as a crucial partner in the peace process. The EU also issued a formal complaint to Israel, listing EU-funded projects in the West Bank and Gaza that had undergone physical damage during recent military operations.

In early February 2002 Israel carried out the 'targeted killing' of at least four members of the radical Democratic Front for the Liberation of Palestine (DFLP) in the Gaza Strip. The violence came at a time of renewed efforts to restart peace negotiations. Ariel Sharon met leading PA representatives, while Shimon Peres held a series of discussions with the PLC Speaker, Ahmad Quray (also known as Abu Ala). However, Israeli officials were angered when a large number of Palestinian militants were freed during Israeli air-strikes on the PA's security headquarters in Nablus. Requests for calm by the UN and attempts by the EU to launch a new peace initiative in the second week of February—reportedly based on the convening of new elections to the PLC—failed to prevent an escalation of violence in the territories, particularly in Gaza. As Hamas appeared to be intensifying its attacks on Israelis by firing a new type of missile, the *Qassam-2*, against Jewish settlers, four Palestinian security officers died during incursions by the Israeli army into three Gazan towns. Israel also accelerated its military offensive in Hebron and Ramallah. In late February up to 30 Palestinians were reportedly killed in Israeli military operations across the West Bank and Gaza in retaliation for the shooting of six Israelis at an army checkpoint near Ramallah. The Israeli Cabinet subsequently agreed to withdraw its tanks from Arafat's compound in Ramallah but refused to allow the Palestinian leader freedom of movement beyond the town: Sharon stated that the travel ban would remain in place despite the arrest by Palestinian security forces of three militants believed to have been responsible for Ze'evi's murder. The Israeli position led PA security officials to suspend recently resumed bilateral talks.

Gun battles raged across the West Bank, despite efforts by Crown Prince Abdullah of Saudi Arabia to promote his proposals for peace in the Middle East prior to a summit meeting of the Arab League Council, due to be held in Beirut, Lebanon, in March 2002. Abdullah's proposals centred on Arab recognition of the State of Israel and the normalization of diplomatic relations, in exchange for agreement by Israel to withdraw from all Arab land occupied since 1967 and on the establishment of a Palestinian state with East Jerusalem as its capital. Arafat announced that he would not attend the Beirut conference owing to threats by Sharon to prevent his return to the West Bank and Gaza. Meanwhile, in response to a suicide bombing by a Palestinian woman at an Israeli army checkpoint, Israel for the first time sent ground troops into two refugee camps in the West Bank which it claimed were centres of Islamist militancy: the Balata camp near Nablus and the camp at Jenin. Fierce fighting ensued, and the PA announced subsequently that it was suspending all contacts with the Israeli Government. The USA, meanwhile, urged Israel to show restraint, while UN and EU officials demanded an immediate Israeli withdrawal from the camps.

PA officials categorically rejected an offer made by Ariel Sharon in early March 2002 that Yasser Arafat should agree to go into voluntary exile. At the same time Israel refused to allow senior UN and EU diplomats to visit Arafat. A number of Palestinians were killed as Israeli forces entered Ramallah, Bethlehem and Tulkarm in an attempt to find those responsible for two attacks apparently perpetrated by the Al-Aqsa Martyrs Brigades, in which 20 Israelis had died. The US Secretary of State, Gen. Colin Powell, publicly criticized Sharon's declared aim of forcing the PA to return to peace talks by defeating them militarily. On 8 March five Jewish settler students were killed by Hamas gunmen in Gaza; an estimated 40 Palestinians died during the fierce fighting that ensued. Meanwhile, Sharon declared that Arafat had met the conditions required for his release after a fifth suspect in Ze'evi's murder was arrested by Palestinian security forces in the first week of March. However, after a suicide bombing in Jerusalem, killing 11 Israelis, and a shooting in Netanya in which two died, Israel's 'inner' Security Cabinet voted to intensify its military offensive. Tanks entered Qalqilya and the Jabalia refugee camp in Gaza (where 18 Palestinians, including four Hamas members, were reported to have been killed), while Arafat's headquarters in Gaza were destroyed by Israeli helicopters and gunboats.

On 11 March 2002 Israel announced that it was lifting its travel ban on Arafat, although the Palestinian leader would still not be permitted to travel abroad. The following day some 20,000 Israeli troops began a massive ground offensive in the Palestinian territories as part of a campaign to dismantle the 'infrastructure of terror'; hundreds of Palestinian men were detained for questioning, and several civilians died during the incursions. This was reported to be the largest Israeli operation against Palestinian militants since the 1982 invasion of Lebanon. Israeli forces again took control of most of Ramallah, with tanks coming to within a short distance of Arafat's presidential compound. On 12 March 2002 the UN Security Council adopted Resolution 1397, affirming its 'vision' of both Israeli and Palestinian states 'within secure and recognized borders'; the US-drafted resolution also demanded an immediate end to 'all acts of violence' by both sides, and called upon Israel and the Palestinians to co-operate in implementation of the Mitchell Report and George Tenet's recommendations. US special envoy to the Middle East Anthony Zinni returned to the region on the following day. Under pressure to withdraw as a 'goodwill' gesture to Zinni, the Israeli army later withdrew from Ramallah, Tulkarm and Qalqilya, although they continued to surround the towns. Following discussions between Zinni and Arafat, and US-brokered talks between Israeli and PA security officials in Jerusalem, Israel also agreed to redeploy its troops from Bethlehem and Beit Jala. After the security talks ended without agreement on 21 March, the Israeli Government again ordered troops into much of the West Bank and detained several alleged militants. A further suicide attack by the Al-Aqsa Martyrs Brigades, which killed three Israelis in central Jerusalem, prompted the USA to add the group to its list of proscribed terrorist organizations.

The Arab League summit proceeded in Beirut on 27–28 March 2002, in the notable absence of both President Hosni Mubarak of Egypt and King Abdullah of Jordan (the two leaders had apparently boycotted the meeting as a gesture of support for the PA President). Palestinian officials were angered when the Lebanese hosts refused to permit Arafat to address the session via a live satellite link from Ramallah: the Lebanese authorities had stated that they feared an Israeli disruption of such a broadcast. At the close of the conference the participating Arab states unanimously endorsed the Saudi peace initiative, which also included a clause calling for a 'just solution' to the question of Palestinian refugees. Israel rejected the plan, however, stating that its terms would lead to the destruction of the Jewish state.

The Israeli–Palestinian crisis deepened at the end of March 2002, following an attack by a Hamas suicide bomber at a hotel in the Israeli town of Netanya, where Jews were celebrating the festival of Passover; 30 people died as a result of the attack and some 140 were injured. Although Arafat personally condemned the bombing, and reportedly ordered the immediate arrest of four prominent West Bank militants, Sharon blamed the PA for its failure to prevent such attacks. In response to what was swiftly called the 'Passover massacre', Israel mobilized about 20,000 army reservists and convened an emergency cabinet meeting, at which 'extensive operational activity against Palestinian terrorism' was agreed. With Arafat effectively isolated at his compound in Ramallah, on 29 March Israeli armed forces began a huge campaign of incursions into West Bank towns—code-named 'Operation Defensive Shield'—with the declared aim of dismantling the Palestinian 'terrorist infrastructure' in order to prevent future suicide bombings against Israeli citizens. During the offensive Israeli forces entered and conducted house-to-house searches for militants in Ramallah, Bethlehem, Beit Jala, Qalqilya, Tulkarm, Jenin and Nablus. On 30 March the UN Security Council met in emergency session and demanded, in Resolution 1402, an immediate Israeli withdrawal from all towns that had been transferred to the PA under the Oslo accords. At the end of the month a Hamas suicide bomber from Jenin killed 15 Israelis at a café in Haifa. Sharon declared that Israel was 'at war', and his 'inner' Security Cabinet gave the army permission to broaden its offensive in the West Bank. Israeli armed forces reoccupied Ramallah and declared it to be a 'closed military area'; many Palestinians were reported to have been killed as a result of the invasion. The US Administration expressed 'grave concern' about the situation in the Palestinian areas, and President Bush urged Arafat to take action to prevent further attacks against Israelis by Palestinian militants.

In early April 2002 Yasser Arafat again dismissed a suggestion by Sharon that the Palestinian leader should go into exile. On 2 April fighting between Israelis and Palestinians in Bethlehem escalated into a siege at the Church of the Nativity—believed to mark the site of Christ's birth. As many as 200 people—Palestinian civilians and priests as well as some 30 armed militants wanted by Israel—sought shelter from Israeli troops inside the church. On 3 April Israeli tanks entered Jenin and its refugee camp. By the following day Israel had effectively reoccupied all but two major towns (Jericho and Hebron) in the West Bank and detained more than 1,000 Palestinians; Bethlehem, like Ramallah, was declared a 'closed military area'. Israel prevented an EU delegation from holding discussions with Arafat, and George W. Bush demanded that Israel withdraw its forces immediately from Palestinian towns and implement the Tenet and Mitchell recommendations for a cease-fire. On 4 April Israeli troops reportedly withdrew from Nablus but entered Hebron. Israel also intensified its offensive in the Jenin refugee camp, the alleged base of several of the suicide bombers. According to PA reports, more than 80 Palestinians died during the first week of Israeli military operations in Jenin. The UN Security Council unanimously adopted a resolution (No. 1403) that demanded the implementation of Resolution 1402 (i.e. an Israeli withdrawal from Palestinian territories) 'without delay'. On 9 April 13 Israeli army reservists were killed in ambushes in the Jenin camp, and the following day, in response to the deaths of at least eight people in the Hamas suicide bombing of a bus near Haifa, Israel ruled out the prospect of further withdrawals from the West Bank. US Secretary of State Powell arrived in Israel on 11 April; he held talks with the besieged Palestinian leader in Ramallah three days later, but stated subsequently that a suggested conference on the Middle East crisis would not necessarily require Arafat's physical presence. The Secretary of State's mission ended on 17 April without having achieved a cease-fire.

During mid-April 2002 Palestinians made increasingly vocal allegations of an Israeli 'massacre' at the Jenin refugee camp—where many buildings had been destroyed by tanks and bulldozers—and claimed that Israeli armed forces were guilty of war crimes. Palestinian sources suggested that at least 100 Palestinians had died during the Israeli invasion; 23 Israelis were believed to have died. (In May the US-based Human Rights Watch issued a report stating that Israeli forces had been guilty of 'excessive force' and of war crimes in Jenin, but that there had been no massacre, findings echoed by a UN report released in August.) Meanwhile, although Israel's forces began to withdraw from some Palestinian-administered towns, a number of Palestinians were killed as Israeli tanks entered the Gazan town of Rafah. Also in mid-April Marwan Barghouthi, the Fatah leader in the West Bank (whom Israel also claimed was the commander of the Al-Aqsa Martyrs Brigades), was arrested by Israeli forces in Ramallah; his trial, on charges of leading Palestinian 'terrorist' groups in the West Bank and of orchestrating a number of suicide bombings against Israeli citizens, began in August. (Barghouthi claimed that the Israeli judiciary had no jurisdiction over him, as an elected member of the PLC.) Meanwhile, Sharon announced on 21 April 2002 that the first stage of Operation Defensive Shield had been completed; however, Israeli forces were to remain in Ramallah and Bethlehem. Some reports stated that more than 4,000 Palestinians were detained during the offensive, although many were subsequently released. According to the Palestine Red Crescent Society (PRCS), by the end of April at least 1,500 Palestinians had been killed, and more than 19,000 injured, since the start of the al-Aqsa *intifada* in September 2000. According to Israeli sources, more than 470 Israelis had been killed, and many more wounded, as a result of the violence.

Yasser Arafat was freed by the Israeli authorities on 1 May 2002. His release came after the USA secured an arrangement whereby Israel agreed to end its siege of Ramallah, including Arafat's headquarters, on condition that the PA leader handed over six prisoners sheltering in the presidential compound who were wanted by Israel in connection with 'terrorist' activities. In late April four of the prisoners were convicted of direct involvement in the assassination of Rechavam Ze'evi by an ad hoc Palestinian court inside the compound and variously sentenced to between one and 18 years' imprisonment. The other two detainees were the PFLP leader, Ahmad Saadat, and a militant implicated in the *Karine A* affair. In early May the six prisoners were moved from Ramallah to a gaol in Jericho, where they were to remain in 'international custody' under US and British guard. Despite Arafat's release, US President Bush declared that he was not yet willing to meet the Palestinian leader. Following protracted negotiations, the siege at the Church of the Nativity in Bethlehem finally came to an end, after more than five weeks, on 10 May, when 13 remaining militants were transferred under international guard to Cyprus pending their dispersal to permanent exile elsewhere in Europe. The agreement ending the siege envisaged that 26 other militants who were removed to the Gaza Strip should be tried by a Palestinian court there. It was reported in mid-June that Israel had begun construction of an electrified (later, partially concrete) 'security fence', which would eventually extend along the length of its border with the West Bank, in an attempt to prevent further suicide bombings. In response to a series of fatal suicide attacks against Israeli citizens by Palestinian militants in late June, Israel again ordered its armed forces into several towns in the West Bank and Gaza.

The Israeli Cabinet responded to the latest suicide bombing in Tel-Aviv in September 2002 by announcing that it would seek to 'isolate' Yasser Arafat. Sharon declared that Arafat had failed to arrest militant Islamists known to advocate violence against Israeli citizens, and Israeli forces began the systematic destruction of Arafat's compound in Ramallah while the Palestinian leader reportedly remained inside one of the office buildings. At the same time Israeli armed forces launched a series of incursions into the Gaza Strip, which increasingly became the focus of Israeli military operations. At the end of September the Israeli siege of Arafat's headquarters was brought to an end, after the UN Security Council had issued a resolution (No. 1435), demanding the immediate cessation of Israeli military actions in and around Ramallah. However, the Israeli–Palestinian violence continued in subsequent months and the number of people killed since the start of the al-Aqsa *intifada* increased dramatically.

The stalled peace process was temporarily revived by the publication of the 'roadmap' peace plan (sponsored by the Quartet group, comprising the USA, Russia, the UN and the EU) on 30 April 2003. The release of the roadmap, which had originally been agreed in December 2002, was conditional on the announcement of a new Palestinian Cabinet under Prime Minister Mahmud Abbas (see below). However, it also affirmed George W. Bush's pledge to focus attention on Israeli-Palestinian affairs following the successful US-led coalition's campaign during March–April 2003 to overthrow the regime of Saddam Hussain in Iraq. The roadmap envisaged an end to Israeli–Palestinian conflict and the establishment of a sovereign Palestinian state by 2005–06 (for further details, see the chapter on Israel). Broadly speaking, Palestinian responsibilities under the terms of the roadmap were restricted to a commitment to ending militant actions against Israeli targets and the establishment of a civilian and government infrastructure; otherwise, crucial issues concerning the Palestinian population, such as the borders of a future state, the status of refugees and Jerusalem, were to be decided during Israel's negotiations with Lebanon, Syria and other Arab states. Initially, Sharon objected to the issue of the right to return of Palestinian refugees and refused to consider the dismantling of Jewish settlements, but on 25 May 2003 the Israeli Cabinet accepted the terms of the roadmap. At the end of the month Sharon made the unprecedented acknowledgement that Israel was indeed in occupation of the Palestinian areas. In early June Sharon, Abbas and President Bush met in Aqaba, Jordan, to discuss the implementation of the roadmap, particularly the contentious issue of Jewish settlements.

Israeli troops had begun dismantling settlements in the West Bank in early June 2003, but this positive development in the peace process was overshadowed by a resumption of violence: on 10 June Israel attempted to kill the prominent Hamas leader, Abd al-Aziz ar-Rantisi, leading to a retaliatory suicide attack against a bus in Jerusalem, in which 16 people died. Subsequently, Israeli helicopter gunships attacked targets in Gaza. Twenty-six people were killed in the renewed fighting, and the USA condemned the attempted Israeli assassination of ar-Rantisi. Nevertheless, Israel continued to dismantle some Jewish settlements, to withdraw troops from certain areas of the West Bank and Gaza, and to release Palestinian prisoners. This latter development was not a condition of the roadmap, but was viewed as a 'goodwill' gesture to Mahmud Abbas, who was now apparently engaged in a power struggle with Yasser Arafat (see below). Some 400 prisoners were released in August, but excluded those members of Hamas and Islamic Jihad who had been involved in planning or executing attacks against Israeli targets. Along with Fatah, these two militant groups had declared a three-month cease-fire at the end of June. Following the cease-fire declaration, Israeli troops withdrew from key parts of northern and central Gaza and removed roadblocks from the arterial north–south highway. In July Bethlehem was handed over to Palestinian control. The successful implementation of the roadmap was threatened, however, by Israel's ongoing construction of a 'security fence' in the West Bank.

Construction of Israel's 'security fence' in the West Bank had begun in mid-2002. Ostensibly intended to act as a barrier against Palestinian militants who infiltrated Israel to carry out attacks, by mid-2003 Israel was being accused of seeking to annex Palestinian territory. However, construction of the barrier continued despite international criticism, and Israel also maintained its policy of targeting and killing Palestinian militant leaders. A senior commander of Islamic Jihad in Hebron was killed by Israeli forces on 14 August; on 19 August a suicide bomber killed 20 Israelis on a bus in Jerusalem, an attack for which both Hamas and Islamic Jihad claimed responsibility; and Israel raided militant targets in both the West Bank and Gaza Strip. The resumption of hostilities between Israel and the Palestinian militant groups effectively marked the end of the cease-fire declared in June. A prominent member of Hamas, Ismael Abu Shanab, was killed in an Israeli missile attack on 21 August; the following day Israel reimposed roadblocks on the main north–south highway in the Gaza Strip, a reversal of one of the first initiatives under the terms of the roadmap.

In September 2003 it was reported that the Israeli Cabinet had agreed in principle to the removal of Yasser Arafat as 'a total obstacle to peace'. It was not made clear whether Israel sought to eliminate Arafat or to send him into exile, and although the US Administration declared that it was opposed to either outcome, the USA vetoed a UN Security Council resolution on 16 September condemning Israel's new policy, on the grounds that the resolution did not condemn the actions of Palestinian militant groups. At the end of October Sharon denied that Israel had any intention of 'removing' Yasser Arafat from power. Earlier in the month the Israeli Cabinet had approved the next phase of the 'security fence', and although the new sections were not contiguous to those already built, they would completely enclose Jewish settlements in the West Bank.

Senior Palestinian and Israeli political figures launched a new peace plan in Geneva, Switzerland, in early December 2003. Yasser Abd ar-Rabbuh, the former Palestinian Minister of Information, and Yossi Beilin, Israel's former Minister of Justice, were the most prominent supporters of the so-called 'Geneva Accords', which did not have the official approval of either the Israeli or Palestinian administrations. The Geneva Accords outlined a two-state solution to the Israeli–Palestinian issue, including proposals that: Palestinians would receive compensation for giving up the right of return; most settlements in the West Bank and Gaza (except those neighbouring Jerusalem) would be dismantled; and Jerusalem (to become the capital of two states) would be divided administratively rather than physically.

On 19 December 2003 Israel declared that, unless the PA started disarming and disbanding Palestinian militant groups, it was prepared to initiate a 'disengagement plan', consisting of the accelerated construction of the 'security fence' in the West Bank and the physical separation of Israel from the Palestinian territories. In February 2004 Ariel Sharon announced in an interview published in Ha'aretz that a plan had been drawn up for the evacuation of all Jewish settlements in the Gaza Strip: this would reportedly affect 7,500 settlers in 17 settlements (although details of the plan were subsequently amended—see below). This news was welcomed by the recently appointed Palestinian Prime Minister, Ahmad Quray. On 14 March 10 Israelis were killed in a double suicide bombing at the southern Israeli port of Ashdod, an attack for which both Hamas and the Al-Aqsa Martyrs Brigades claimed responsibility. In retaliation for the attack Ariel Sharon and his inner 'Security Cabinet' ordered Israel's most high profile 'targeted killing'. On 22 March Israeli helicopter gunships in the Gaza Strip attacked the founder and spiritual leader of Hamas, Sheikh Ahmad Yassin, and his entourage as they left a mosque, killing the cleric and several others. Yassin's assassination prompted international condemnation, especially from Iran and from Arab countries, where mass protests took place. However, a UN Security Council resolution condemning the killing was vetoed by the USA, which criticized the absence of any reference to Hamas as a 'terrorist organization'. Immediately after Yassin's assassination, Abd al-Aziz ar-Rantisi was appointed to the leadership of Hamas in Gaza; however, ar-Rantisi himself was killed in a targeted airstrike by Israeli forces in Gaza City on 17 April. EU leaders condemned both of the 'targeted killings' as illegal and unjustified. Hamas did not disclose the identity of ar-Rantisi's successor and reportedly adopted a policy of 'collective leadership' in order to prevent future leaders of the organization from being victims of Israel's strategy. Khalid Meshaal apparently remained the head of the group's political bureau, based in Damascus, Syria. Meanwhile, details of Sharon's 'disengagement plan' were published in Israeli newspapers: it combined a complete Israeli withdrawal from the Gaza Strip, and evacuation of all Jewish settlements there, with the consolidation of six settlement blocs in the West Bank. In May the US Secretary of State, Gen. Colin Powell, urged Quray to consider an Israeli withdrawal from the Gaza Strip as a sign of progress towards Palestinian self-sufficiency, while expressing US opposition to the demolition of Palestinian houses there. In October the Israeli Knesset voted in favour of Sharon's proposal to dismantle all 21 settlements in Gaza, and four in the northern West Bank, entailing the eviction of about 9,000 Jewish settlers. The removal of settlements in Gaza was scheduled to commence in July 2005, but was later postponed until August (see below).

In May 2004 imprisoned Fatah leader Marwan Barghouthi was convicted by a Tel-Aviv court on five counts of murder and of leading a 'terrorist organization' which had launched Palestinian militant assaults on Israeli forces and settlers, although lack of evidence forced the court to acquit Barghouthi on 33 counts of resistance attacks. The court's verdict provoked strong criticism from the PA, which called the conviction 'illegal, immoral and unjust'. In early June Barghouthi was sentenced to five terms of life imprisonment and two additional 20-year terms.

Following a ruling by the Israeli Supreme Court, in June 2004 Israel altered the route of part of the 'security fence', including a 30-km section in a Palestinian village, Beit Sourik. In early July the International Court of Justice (ICJ) in the Hague, Netherlands, issued a non-binding ruling that the barrier breached international law and effectively constituted the annexation of Palestinian land. The ICJ urged Israel to remove sections of the fence and to pay compensation to affected Palestinians. Sharon rejected the court's recommendations, while the Palestinian leadership hoped that the decision would mobilize public opinion. In late July the UN General Assembly voted to demand that Israel comply with the ICJ ruling and take down the barrier (the USA voted against the resolution). Meanwhile, in August Sharon approved the construction of 1,000 new Jewish settlements in the West Bank.

In September 2004, following a double suicide bombing by Hamas in Beersheba, Israel, that killed 16 people, Israeli tanks and aircraft attacked a Hamas training camp in the centre of the Gaza Strip. In October the UN reported that 135 Palestinians had been killed and an estimated 95 homes destroyed following a 16-day Israeli military assault in northern and southern Gaza, prompted by a Hamas rocket that killed two children in Sderot, close to the border with Gaza. Following the death of Yasser Arafat in November (see below), Sharon expressed hope that the new Palestinian leadership would understand the need to end 'terrorist' attacks before relations between the two sides could be improved and outstanding issues resolved, and international leaders similarly looked forward to positive change, with US President Bush, urged by British Prime Minister Tony Blair, promising to redouble US efforts to assist in the creation of a

Palestinian state, which he considered to be possible within four years.

Israel and Egypt agreed in early December 2004 that 750 Egyptian troops would be deployed along the country's border with Gaza in advance of Israel's planned withdrawal; however, Jewish settlers in Gaza vowed to resist eviction. In mid-December Mahmud Abbas issued a call (rejected by Hamas) for an end to the continuing use of violence in resistance to Israeli occupation, while in early January 2005, during the week of the Palestinian presidential election (see below), having earlier criticized Israeli offensives in Gaza as a ploy to disrupt the poll, he demanded that Israel release all Palestinian prisoners before they reached a political agreement. Abbas later strengthened his criticism of Israel, calling it 'the Zionist enemy' when Israeli armed forces responded to Palestinian mortar attacks by firing two shells into a field in Beit Lahiya, killing seven Palestinians. However, Abbas continued to express hopes of implementing the roadmap and of achieving peace with Israel in the event of his election to the Palestinian presidency. Israel announced that it would withdraw troops from Palestinian areas prior to the election, and that its military would remain outside towns in the West Bank and Gaza Strip for 72 hours. Towards the end of December Israel released 159 Palestinian prisoners as a gesture of 'goodwill' prior to the Palestinian election.

In mid-January 2005 the deaths of six Israelis in a Palestinian militant attack at the Karni crossing prompted Sharon to sever ties with the Palestinian leadership and to order the Israeli army to raid several areas of Gaza. Following a demand by the PLO leadership that Palestinians should cease all military action against Israel, Sharon called off the offensive and announced that Israel would co-operate on security issues, although he instructed his troops to prepare for a full-scale assault on an area in the northern Gaza Strip from where rockets were being fired on Israeli targets, and in late January Palestinian security forces were deployed in the area to prevent such attacks. Despite talks being held between Hamas, Islamic Jihad and other militant groups chaired by newly elected PA President Abbas, Hamas continued to insist on its right to retaliate against Israeli attacks and demanded that Israel released more than 7,000 Palestinian prisoners and end its policy of targeting militants before it would enter into negotiations.

Security talks between Palestinian and Israeli officials began in late January 2005, and, despite attacks on Palestinian police vehicles by Jewish settlers, an agreement was reached on the deployment of Palestinian security forces in the southern Gaza Strip within 24 hours to reduce attacks on Israeli targets. (By this time 2,500 Palestinian security forces were patrolling northern Gaza, on the orders of the new Palestinian President.) Hamas and Islamic Jihad dismissed an announcement by Israelis that 'targeted killings' of militants in areas where Palestinian security forces were successfully operating would stop, and Hamas demanded that Israel cease all military action. Later in the month the former Palestinian Minister of Security, Muhammad Dahlan, and the Israeli Minister of Defence, Lt-Gen. Shaul Mofaz, agreed to the withdrawal of Israeli troops and the deployment of PA security forces in the five West Bank towns of Ramallah, Qalqilya, Tulkarm, Jericho and Bethlehem.

Abbas and Sharon finally met in early February 2005 at a summit meeting held in Sharm esh-Sheikh, with Egypt's President Mubarak and King Abdullah of Jordan also in attendance. At the summit Abbas announced a Palestinian cease-fire and Sharon declared that Israeli military operations would end if Palestinian militant attacks stopped, emphasizing that Israel would not compromise in its fight against 'terrorism'; Sharon also agreed to release 500 Palestinian prisoners as a gesture of 'goodwill'. However, although some Palestinian militant groups signed up to the cease-fire, Hamas asserted that it would not be bound by it, criticizing the fact that it had been negotiated unilaterally, and demanded that Israel cease all acts of aggression against Palestinians and release all Palestinian prisoners before agreeing to a formal cease-fire, although they apparently agreed to an informal 'truce'. Soon after the Sharm esh-Sheikh meeting, Israel permitted 56 deported Palestinians to return to the West Bank, and also transferred the bodies of 15 Palestinian bombers to the PA. The relative lull in violence was interrupted in late February by a suicide bomb attack outside a nightclub in Tel-Aviv that killed four Israelis, halting Israeli plans to withdraw from the five West Bank towns. The Israeli army entered a West Bank village and arrested Palestinians suspected of involvement in the attack, but Israeli officials announced that their response would be limited to those who had actually masterminded the bombing (believed to be members of Islamic Jihad), while urging Abbas to intensify his crackdown on Palestinian militant organizations.

In early March 2005, at an international conference in support of the PA hosted by British Prime Minister Tony Blair in London, Abbas expressed his commitment to reforms and to a crackdown on militants, advocating renewed efforts to realize the objectives of the roadmap. Shortly afterwards it was reported that Palestinian militant groups had declared their readiness to cease attacks against Israelis, although this was denied by Hamas, and Israel viewed the declaration with scepticism. In mid-March Israel officially surrendered Jericho to Palestinian security control, and also announced plans to remove all 24 outposts constructed since Sharon was elected to the premiership in February 2001, after a ministerial report condemned the illegal use of budget funds to develop the outposts. Although this development fulfilled a condition of the roadmap, it was criticized for the fact that not all of the 105 outposts, which were deemed by many to be illegal, would be dismantled. In late March 2005 Israeli forces withdrew from the West Bank town of Tulkarm.

Meanwhile, in late February 2005 Israel announced plans to alter the route of the 'security fence' so that it would cut out 7% of the territory of the West Bank instead of the 16% outlined in the original route. In mid-March the Israeli Government announced that the barrier (to be completed by the end of 2005) would divide the town of Bethlehem and also separate East Jerusalem and the settlement of Ma'aleh Edomin from the rest of the West Bank; the decision provoked protests by Palestinians, who demanded that the ICJ's recommendations be implemented and expressed concern at the unilateralism of the move and the negative impact that this could have on future peace talks with Israel.

Abbas travelled to Washington, DC, in May 2005 for his first meeting with President Bush since becoming President of the PA. Bush reportedly offered US $50m. in direct aid to the PA to develop the Gaza Strip after the Israeli withdrawal. The US President also urged Israel to dismantle illegal settlement outposts in the West Bank, to end the expansion of settlements and to ensure that Israel's 'security fence' did not become a 'political border'. Abbas later advocated the start of 'final status' negotiations with Israel after its disengagement from the Gaza Strip. Meanwhile, in accordance with the agreement reached by Abbas and Sharon in February at Sharm esh-Sheikh, the Israeli Government approved the release of 400 Palestinian prisoners. (A total of 398 prisoners were released in early June—two had chosen to remain in gaol.) Israel had released 500 prisoners shortly after the February summit meeting, but had delayed further releases, urging the PA to curb terrorism more effectively.

Following a series of Palestinian militant attacks on Israeli and Jewish targets (which the militants justified as retaliation for Israeli violations of the cease-fire, and for Israeli arrests of militants), in late June 2005 Israel carried out raids across the West Bank and detained around 50 members of Islamic Jihad. The Israeli Minister of Defence, Lt-Gen. Shaul Mofaz, asserted that the PA's incompetence had prompted Israel to carry out the raids. Israel apparently readopted its policy of 'targeted assassinations' of militants (suspended at the February summit between Abbas and Sharon), when it launched a missile strike on Gaza in a failed attempt to kill an Islamic Jihad activist. Palestinian Minister of the Interior and National Security Maj.-Gen. Nasser Yousuf declared a state of emergency in the Gaza Strip, and gave his forces permission to prevent militants from launching rocket and mortar attacks on targets in Israel. As clashes broke out between members of the Palestinian security services and Hamas militants, Israel carried out further air attacks on Hamas targets, killing seven fighters. Islamic Jihad claimed responsibility for a suicide bomb attack near a shopping mall in Netanya in mid-July that killed four Israelis. Israeli troops re-entered Tulkarm (military control and responsibility for security of which Israel had surrendered to the PA in March—see above), after it was reported that the suicide bomber had come from a nearby village. Meanwhile, Hamas launched a series of rocket attacks from Gaza, killing an Israeli woman and prompting Israel to carry out air-strikes on targets in Gaza used by the militant group. Abbas and Sharon held their second summit meeting since Abbas's election to the presidency in Jerusalem in late July, when Sharon again urged Abbas to rein in militants and suppress terrorism.

Although Israel's withdrawal from the Gaza Strip was accompanied by relatively little violence (see the chapter on Israel), in late August 2005 Israeli troops raided a refugee camp near

Tulkarm, killing five Palestinians. Israel asserted that the five were suspected of involvement in two suicide bombings and had resisted arrest. In response, the Popular Resistance Committees claimed responsibility for firing a rocket that landed near Sderot. Israel completed its withdrawal from the Gaza Strip (according to the terms of its unilateral Disengagement Plan) ahead of schedule on 12 September, when the last Israeli forces left Gaza. Thousands of Palestinians entered the evacuated settlements and started to damage buildings and demolish synagogues. Although in July Israeli and Palestinian officials had reportedly agreed in principle to establish a 'safe passage' between the West Bank and Gaza Strip following the withdrawal, the status of Gaza's southern crossing into Egypt at Rafah was still disputed. Soon after it had completed the disengagement, Israel declared that the crossing would be closed for six months. Meanwhile, in late August Israel had approved the deployment of 750 Egyptian troops along Egypt's border with the Gaza Strip, having accepted Egypt's offer to deploy the troops in December 2004 (see above). In mid-November 2005, following intervention by US Secretary of State Condoleezza Rice, Israel reached an agreement with Palestinian officials to reopen the Rafah crossing later that month. The PA, assisted by European monitors, was to manage the crossing, which Israeli, Palestinian and EU observers were to monitor remotely from a control centre via live television cameras.

In September 2005 21 people were killed when a Palestinian truck carrying rockets exploded during a Hamas parade in the Jabalia refugee camp in the Gaza Strip. Hamas accused Israel of having fired a missile at the truck from a remote-controlled drone aircraft; both Israel and the PA denied the accusation. However, Hamas responded by launching mortars into Sderot. The Israeli Government decided at an emergency meeting to permit the army to use any means necessary to suppress militants. Accordingly, the Israeli army stationed tanks and artillery batteries on Gaza's eastern and northern borders, began seizing Hamas and Islamic Jihad activists in the West Bank and readopted its policy of 'targeted killings', using air-strikes to kill militants in Gaza and to destroy a weapons store and weapons-production facilities, despite a pledge from Hamas to end attacks and return to the cease-fire. Abbas condemned the operations as unjustified aggression. Later in the month Israeli security forces killed three militants in the West Bank. Israel also killed two senior Islamic Jihad militants in Tulkarm in October, and arrested five other members of the Tulkarm cell, which it believed to be responsible for the suicide attacks in Tel-Aviv in February and in Netanya in July. Islamic Jihad avenged the 'targeted killings' by launching a suicide bomb attack on a market in Hadera, resulting in the deaths of five Israelis. Israeli Prime Minister Ariel Sharon declared a 'broad and continuous' offensive against militant Islamist groups, and hours later the Israeli army launched an air-strike on a car carrying two senior Islamic Jihad militants in Gaza: eight Palestinians, mostly civilians, died. In December Islamic Jihad launched a further suicide attack on the shopping mall in Netanya that it had targeted in July, killing another five Israelis. Israel responded by arresting Palestinians thought to be associated with the bomber, and carrying out air-strikes to target further militants.

Israel reacted to Hamas's victory in the legislative elections held in January 2006 (see below) by declaring that it would not negotiate with a Palestinian authority that included 'an armed terrorist organization' which advocated Israel's destruction. US President Bush announced that his country would also refuse to deal with Hamas until it renounced its call to destroy Israel, and stated that the USA would consider halting aid to the Palestinians. At the end of the month the Quartet group announced that financial assistance to a future Palestinian administration would depend on the extent to which Hamas fulfilled the following conditions: that it renounce violence, respect agreements approved under the Fatah regime and recognize Israel's right to exist. Egypt and Jordan also demanded that the militant organization reject violence and accept Israel's existence. The head of Hamas's political bureau, Khalid Meshaal, announced that his organization could enter into a long-term truce with Israel, under certain conditions, including the return of Israel to its pre-1967 borders. However, Meshaal asserted that violent resistance of the occupation was legal.

Israel announced in mid-February 2006 that, in order to punish the new Palestinian regime until it renounced violence and recognized Israel's right to exist, it would stop collecting customs and tax revenues on Palestinians' behalf, and would ask foreign donors to cease all payments to the PA; however, it would permit the transfer of humanitarian aid to Palestinians. President Abbas announced that the PA faced a financial crisis, while Hamas asserted that Arab and Islamic countries would compensate for a reduction in aid from Israel and the West. Later in the month the EU, which—like Israel and the USA—considered Hamas to be a terrorist organization, announced that it was to give the PA US $140m.-worth of aid to save the interim administration from financial collapse; however, the EU refused to indicate whether it would finance any future Hamas-led administration. In the event, following the installation of the new Cabinet on 28 March, both the USA and the EU announced that they were withdrawing direct aid to the PA until Hamas fulfilled the three conditions placed on it by the Quartet group.

Meanwhile, as Israel continued to kill militants in the Palestinian territories following further missile strikes, it declared that, should Hamas resume attacks on Israel, all members of the organization would be deemed to be legitimate targets for assassinations, including Prime Minister-designate Ismail Haniya and future ministers. In March 2006 Israeli forces stormed the gaol in Jericho in which the Secretary-General of the PFLP, Ahmad Saadat, was being held prisoner, detaining him and other inmates suspected of involvement in attacks against Israel. US and British monitors had left the gaol immediately prior to the raid, ostensibly to protest against poor security arrangements there. A Palestinian high court had announced in 2002 that there was no evidence that Saadat had been involved in Rechavam Ze'evi's murder, and both President Abbas and Hamas had recently announced plans to release him, as he had been elected to the PLC at the elections in January 2006. Israel, however, still wished to interrogate Saadat in connection with the murder, and therefore resolved to detain him before the Palestinian authorities released him. The raid, in which two Palestinians were killed, provoked unrest throughout the territories. Palestinians set fire to the British Council building in Jericho in protest at perceived British collusion with the Israeli authorities, and gunmen kidnapped 11 foreign workers (they were released the following day). Palestinian factions urged schools and businesses to go on strike, and the PFLP vowed to avenge Saadat's capture, which President Abbas condemned as a crime and a humiliation for Palestinians. In April the Israeli Ministry of Justice announced that a pre-trial inquiry had not produced enough evidence to try Saadat for Ze'evi's murder, but that he would be tried for other security offences. However, four other militant PFLP members detained with him were charged with the murder, among them the man accused of firing the shot.

Israel's new Government under Prime Minister Ehud Olmert, which was appointed in May 2006, was at this time pursuing plans to establish Israel's permanent borders, if necessary unilaterally, by 2010. Olmert's so-called Convergence Plan entailed the annexation of West Bank settlement blocs to Israel and the transfer of other, majority-Palestinian, sections of the West Bank to full PA control. (Israel would retain the whole of Jerusalem under the plans.) The Israeli premier affirmed that Israel was, however, seeking to secure an internationally supported peace plan with Hamas, but that such a solution required the group to reject violence and adhere to peace agreements signed by Israel and the previous Fatah administration. Khalid Meshaal dismissed the Convergence Plan as allowing Israel to: illegally retain its possession of the largest section of the West Bank and its 'security fence'; reject concessions on the status of Jerusalem; and thwart the 'right of return' of Palestinian refugees. Meanwhile, in the early part of 2006 Israeli armed forces fired missiles into northern Gaza, in response to a series of rocket attacks launched by Palestinian militants; large numbers of Palestinian fatalities were reported.

In June 2006 Palestinians claimed that the shelling of a beach in the northern Gaza Strip, in which seven members of one family were killed while they were having a picnic, had been carried out by Israeli forces firing from gunboats. (The Israeli Prime Minister later declared that a technical failure had been to blame for the deaths, and issued an apology to the Palestinian authorities.) On 25 June Hamas militants from Gaza launched a cross-border raid, which resulted in the kidnapping of an Israeli soldier, Corporal Gilad Shalit; two other Israeli soldiers were killed during the raid, as were two of the militants. The following day Palestinian militant groups issued a statement demanding that Israel release all female Palestinian prisoners and prisoners under 18 years of age in exchange for Shalit. Israel responded by launching air-strikes on Gaza and entering the southern part of the Strip. Israel's military actions (code-named 'Operation Summer Rains') to seek to secure the release of Corporal Shalit in the Gaza Strip continued despite the conflict that began between Israel and Hezbollah in July (see the chapters on Israel and Lebanon). Several bridges and official buildings were bombed by the Israeli military, while the territory's only power plant was also destroyed, leaving thousands of Gazans without electricity or water. Palestinian officials denounced Israel for what they considered to be the 'collective punishment' of the Palestinian people. (A senior Hamas representative affirmed in early April 2008 that Shalit was still alive, but reiterated that this would not remain the case unless Israel agreed to release 350 Palestinian prisoners.)

On 29 June 2006 Israeli security forces arrested 64 senior Palestinian officials, including eight Hamas ministers from the Cabinet and 20 other parliamentarians, for questioning in relation to their alleged involvement in attacks against Israeli targets. On the following day an Israeli missile destroyed the offices of the Ministry of the Interior and Civil Affairs in Gaza City. On 2 July an Israeli air-strike destroyed the office of the Palestinian Prime Minister, Hamas's Ismail Haniya. The crisis continued to escalate during July, and many Palestinians died in the ensuing violence: it was estimated that Israeli troops killed more than 160 Palestinians in the period between late June and 23 July. Israel arrested the Speaker of the PLC, Dr Aziz Duweik, on 6 August, while some of the Cabinet ministers arrested in June were released during subsequent weeks. Meanwhile, it became apparent that, following Israel's month-long conflict with Hezbollah in Lebanon and the ongoing military campaign in Gaza, Olmert had abandoned his plans for Israel to withdraw unilaterally from parts of the West Bank.

In November 2006 Israeli armed forces began a new military offensive in the town of Beit Hanoun, in northern Gaza. 'Operation Autumn Clouds' was aimed at destroying the infrastructure and weapons supplies used by Palestinian militants across the border in order to prevent the firing of rockets into Israel by the armed groups. It was reported that more than 50 Palestinians, including many civilians, were killed in the operation. A cease-fire between the sides was secured by President Abbas towards the end of the month, however, and Israel withdrew its troops from Gaza. Nevertheless, relations between Israel and the PA deteriorated once again in early 2007, after the truce was broken by militant Palestinian groups, who continued to launch large numbers of rockets against Israeli targets such as the town of Sderot. Two human rights organizations claimed that the number of Palestinians killed by Israeli security forces in the West Bank and Gaza had tripled in 2006. A report issued by the Israeli human rights organization B'Tselem in December put the death toll at 657 people (including 140 minors); of this total, B'Tselem assessed that more than 322 Palestinians were unarmed civilians. In May 2007 Amnesty International also reported that at least 650 Palestinians (including 120 minors) had been killed by Israeli troops in 2006, of whom more than 50% were civilians. The majority of fatalities had occurred in the Gaza Strip, following the intensification of Israeli bombardments of the territory from mid-2006. In mid-April 2007 Abbas and Olmert held discussions concerning a future Palestinian state and a possible prisoner exchange, in what was intended to be the first of a series of regular fortnightly meetings between the two leaders. However, in late April Hamas militants, announcing that they were ending the truce brokered in November 2006, resumed the firing of rockets into Israel from the Gaza Strip. Israel responded in May 2007 by conducting a series of air-strikes against alleged militant targets in Gaza; a number of Hamas legislators, ministers and local government officials were also detained by Israeli security forces.

Following the takeover of the Gaza Strip by militants of Hamas on 14 June 2007 and the subsequent naming of an Emergency Cabinet—consisting principally of independents and technocrats—by President Abbas in the West Bank on 17 June (see below), on 24 June the Israeli Government agreed to transfer tax revenues to the PA that it had withdrawn following Hamas's election victory of January 2006. On 25 June 2007 a summit meeting was held in Sharm esh-Sheikh between Egypt's President Mubarak, King Abdullah of Jordan, Israeli Prime Minister Ehud Olmert and President Abbas, aimed at expressing solidarity with Abbas's newly appointed Emergency Cabinet in the West Bank. Olmert declared that Israel was to free 250 Palestinian security prisoners as a gesture of 'goodwill' to the Palestinian President; a final total of 255 (mainly Fatah-affiliated) prisoners were duly released on 20 July. In that month Israel also granted an amnesty for some 180 Fatah militants who were sought by the Israeli security forces in the West Bank, provided that the men renounced violence against Israel and handed themselves over to the PA.

Abbas held discussions with Olmert in Jericho on 6 August 2007—the first meeting between Israeli and Palestinian leaders on Palestinian territory since May 2000—in preparation for the US-sponsored Middle East peace meeting scheduled for November. The Israeli premier was said to have expressed his hope that bilateral negotiations concerning the establishment of a Palestinian state could soon commence. The two leaders held further talks on 'fundamental issues' in late August and early September 2007. On 5 September Israel's Supreme Court issued a ruling that the route of a further section of the 'security fence' along Israel's boundary with the West Bank should be altered in order to improve the living conditions of Palestinians residing at the affected village of Bil'in; the villagers had been conducting regular protests against the Israeli barrier since it had separated their homes from the land they were cultivating. During 26–27 September the Israeli military took firm action against the continued launching by Palestinian militants of *Qassam* rockets against northern Israel by carrying out air raids and sending tanks into the north of the Gaza Strip; at least 12 Palestinians were reported to have died during the military campaign. Nevertheless, Israel released another 57 (mainly Fatah) Palestinian prisoners to the West Bank and 29 to the Gaza Strip on 1 and 2 October, respectively. In mid-October President Abbas for the first time outlined his specific demands with regard to the territory on which a future Palestinian state should be established: Abbas demanded that the state should cover 6,205 sq km (2,400 sq miles) of the West Bank and Gaza Strip—the exact amount of territory occupied by Israel in 1967. Towards the end of October 2007 the Israeli Government responded to the launching of missiles into northern Israel by Gazan militants by confirming a policy of reducing fuel and electricity supplies to Gaza, which it now classified as a 'hostile entity'. (An intervention by the Supreme Court prevented the authorities from phasing out electricity supplies until they could prove that this would not impede vital services such as hospitals and sanitation provision, although the fuel sanctions were permitted.)

An international peace meeting intended officially to relaunch the Middle East peace process was held in Annapolis, Maryland, USA, on 27 November 2007, with members of the Quartet group and the Arab League in attendance. Prior to the meeting the US Secretary of State, Condoleezza Rice, had stated that it must advance the prospect of Palestinians achieving statehood, and had affirmed that reaching a two-state solution between Israelis and Palestinians was one of the priorities of the Bush Administration. At the close of the Annapolis summit US President George W. Bush read a statement of 'joint understanding' between Ehud Olmert and Mahmud Abbas, who expressed their commitment to achieving a final settlement of the outstanding issues of contention between Israelis and Palestinians by the end of 2008. It was announced that: an Israeli-Palestinian steering committee would oversee 'vigorous, ongoing and continuous' negotiations between the two sides; the Israeli and Palestinian leaders would continue to meet on a fortnightly basis; and both Israel and the PA would comply with their obligations as agreed under the terms of the roadmap signed in 2003. However, on 4 December 2007 Palestinians complained that Israel had again contravened its obligations by issuing tenders for 307 new homes to be built at the Jabal Abu Ghunaim settlement in East Jerusalem; Rice warned the Israeli Government that such an expansion could jeopardize the newly restarted peace process. Moreover, Olmert appeared to indicate that Israel would not be required to conclude a peace treaty with the PA by the end of 2008 if it considered that the Palestinians had not met their security obligations; the Israeli leader was reported to have told his Cabinet that there was 'no commitment to a specific timetable' made at Annapolis. A Hamas spokesman reportedly responded to the Annapolis meeting by pledging that Palestinian 'resistance' to Israeli occupation would continue. Nevertheless, the Israeli authorities released a further 429 Palestinian prisoners (408 to the West Bank and 21 to Gaza—none of whom had been involved in attacks against Israelis) on 3 December 2007 as a further 'goodwill' gesture to President Abbas; most of those freed were Fatah members from the West Bank, with no Hamas or Islamic Jihad detainees on the list.

Meanwhile, on 2 December 2007 a court in Jerusalem sentenced a PFLP militant, Hamdi Koran, to a term of life imprisonment (and an additional 100 years in prison), after he was convicted of having assassinated the Israeli Minister of Tourism, Rechavam Ze'evi, in Jerusalem in October 2001 (see above), as well as involvement in other attacks against Israeli citizens. (Koran had been serving a sentence for the crime at a West Bank prison; however, when Western supervisors withdrew from the Jericho gaol and Israeli forces entered it in 2006, he was handed over to the Israeli legal system.) In the second week of December 2007 Israeli forces conducted a series of air-strikes against militants in the Gaza Strip, as well as sending tanks into the southern part of the Strip in an attempt to prevent the continuing rocket fire against Sderot in northern Israel; a number of Palestinian militants (mostly from Islamic Jihad) were reported to have died.

The first session of the Israeli-Palestinian steering committee established at the Annapolis peace meeting was held on 12 December 2007. However, against the backdrop of increased violence between Israeli forces and Palestinian militants in the Gaza Strip, and following the announcement of Israel's proposed settlement expansion, the talks failed to achieve significant progress. An international donors' conference was held in Paris on 17 December, with 68 states and international instititutions in attendance. At the meeting donors pledged US $7,400m. in financial assistance to the PA; the funds were to ease the budgetary crisis and to assist with proposed development projects. (This represented a larger sum than the $5,600m. sought by Abbas by 2010 in order to assist the PA with the creation of a Palestinian state.) Meanwhile, Israeli air-strikes against alleged militant targets in the Gaza Strip continued during December, with several members of Islamic Jihad again being targeted. According to B'Tselem at the end of December, 344 Palestinians had been killed as a result of inter-factional violence in 2007—the highest number since the start of the second *intifada* in 2000.

The Palestinian death toll increased rapidly in early January 2008, as Israel intensified its military campaign in Gaza following a Palestinian rocket assault on the town of Ashkelon; Israeli officials explained the high number of casualties by claiming that militants were deliberately firing on Israeli security forces from civilian areas. Several suspected militants were also detained during an Israeli incursion into Nablus. By mid-January it was estimated that at least 100 Palestinians (mostly militants) had been killed by Israeli forces in Gaza since the Annapolis peace conference in November 2007. Nevertheless, B'Tselem reported at the end of 2007 that there had been a decline in the number of fatalities in the Israeli–Palestinian conflict in that year, compared with 2006: some 373 Palestinians were killed by Israeli troops during 2007, of whom 131 were estimated to be civilians and 53 minors; 290 of the deaths occurred in the Gaza Strip. During a visit to Israel and the West Bank in the second week of January 2008, US President Bush asserted that a future Palestinian state should be contiguous territory and not a 'Swiss cheese' of separate cantons; he also urged Israel to withdraw from Arab territory that its forces had occupied in 1967. Bush reiterated his demand that the PA dismantled the territories' militias.

On 17 January 2008 Israel imposed virtually a complete blockade on the Gaza Strip, which prompted vehement international criticism: the Israeli response to Palestinian violence targeted at its citizens was widely viewed as 'collective punishment' of the people of Gaza for the actions of a minority of militants. The blockade resulted in severe disruption to Gaza's electricity supplies, although Olmert did subsequently agree to allow some essential supplies into the Strip. None the less, on 23 January hundreds of thousands of Palestinians entered Egypt from Gaza in search of food, fuel and medical supplies, after Hamas militants had breached the Rafah crossing separating the two territories. (The crossing had been almost permanently closed since Hamas's takeover of the Strip in June 2007 because the Egyptian Government, as does Israel, refuses to recognize Hamas as the legitimate administration there.) Egyptian officials responded by offering their backing to a plan proposed by President Abbas which would allow for the PA, rather than Hamas, to assume control of the Egypt–Gaza border. Although the breaches in the border were repaired by 3 February 2008, there were reports of exchanges of gunfire between Egyptian security forces and Palestinian gunmen as tensions continued. The UN estimated that 700,000 Gazans (about 50% of the territory's population) had crossed the border into Egypt. On 4 February the Al-Aqsa Martyrs Brigades reportedly claimed responsibility for the first suicide bombing in Israel for more than a year, in the southern town of Dimona (in which an Israeli woman died), although a Hamas representative apparently alleged that militants from its Hebron branch had in fact carried out the attack. The Israeli Government implied that the perpetrator of the bombing, whom it believed to be Gazan, must have entered Israel via Egypt as a direct result of the border having been breached. As Israeli officials threatened a full-scale invasion of the Gaza Strip and also pledged to restart its policy of 'targeted killings' of Hamas and other militants, Olmert declared that he considered the status of Jerusalem to be the final 'core issue' to be negotiated by the two parties—a proposal that was rejected strongly by many Palestinians. According to the PRCS, by the end of February 2008 some 4,895 Palestinians had been killed, and 32,213 injured, since the start of the al-Aqsa *intifada* in September 2000.

In early March 2008 a militant Palestinian, believed to be a resident of East Jerusalem, entered a Jewish religious college in West Jerusalem and shot dead eight students. As with the Dimona bombing, the issue of whether ultimate responsibility for the shooting could be attributed to Hamas was unclear: a spokesman for the militant group appeared to claim, and later deny, its involvement in the crime. Although the Israeli Government affirmed that it would not break off peace negotiations with the PA, the likelihood of a swift breakthrough in the peace process was again impeded when, shortly after the Jerusalem shooting, Olmert approved a plan to construct a further 330 homes for Jewish settlers in the West Bank. Later in the month officials from Israel and Hamas denied that the two sides were conducting talks with a view to securing a cessation of hostilities. At the end of April 12 Palestinian militant factions, meeting in Cairo under the auspices of the Egyptian Government, reportedly agreed to new proposals for a cease-fire to be reached with Israel; under the proposals, a cessation of violence was to be implemented gradually, beginning in the Gaza Strip and then being undertaken in the West Bank.

Legislative elections took place on 20 January 1996, with the participation of some 79% of the estimated 1m. eligible Palestinian voters, selecting 88 deputies to the 89-seat PLC. (One seat was reserved for the president of the Council's executive body—the Palestinian President.) At the concurrent election for a Palestinian Executive President, Yasser Arafat defeated his only rival, Samiha Khalil, winning 88.1% of the votes cast, and took office as President on 12 February. Deputies returned to the PLC automatically became members of the PNC, the existing 483 members of which were subsequently permitted to return from exile by the Israeli authorities. The PLC held its first session in Gaza City on 7 March, electing Ahmad Quray as its Speaker. At the 21st session of the PNC, held in Gaza City on 22–24 April, the PNC voted to amend the Palestinian National Charter (or PLO Covenant) by annulling those clauses that sought the destruction of the State of Israel and those that were inconsistent with the agreement of mutual recognition concluded by Israel and the PLO in September 1993. At the close of its session the PNC elected a new Executive Committee, and in May 1996 President Arafat appointed a Palestinian Cabinet. The appointments were approved by the PLC in July.

In April 1997 Arafat's audit office disclosed evidence of the misappropriation by PA ministers of some US $326m. of public funds. The PA General Prosecutor, Khalid al-Qidram, resigned in response to the findings, and was reportedly placed under house arrest in June. In August the findings of a parliamentary committee appointed by Arafat to investigate the affair led to the resignation of the Cabinet; however, the ministers remained in office until new appointments were made in early 1998. The Cabinet resigned in June, apparently in order to obstruct a second vote of no confidence in Arafat's leadership, in protest partly at alleged corruption within the PA. A new Cabinet was appointed by Arafat in August, but soon attracted criticism from officials of the principal international organizations granting funds to the PA. In November donors pledged aid worth more than $3,000m., to be disbursed over the next five years. In October 1998 the PA was again accused of financial mismanagement, after customs revenues amounting to some $70m. allegedly failed to be deposited at the PA treasury.

US officials reportedly confirmed in March 1998 that the CIA was assisting the Palestinian security forces in the spheres of espionage, information-gathering and interrogation, in an attempt to reassure the Israeli Government of the PA's ability to take effective action against groups involved in attacks on Israeli targets. (Under the terms of the Wye Memorandum—see above—the CIA was to monitor the PA's compliance with the security provisions of the accord.) In October the PA detained 11 journalists who had attempted to obtain an interview with the spiritual leader of Hamas, Sheikh Ahmad Yassin (who was subsequently placed under house arrest). In subsequent weeks several radio and television stations, as well as press offices, were closed down by the PA, and numerous journalists were imprisoned. There was also a marked increase in self-censorship in the state-controlled and pro-Government media. In May 2000 the chief news editor at the Voice of Palestine radio station, Fathi Barqawi, was arrested after publicly criticizing the PA's 'secret' talks with Israel in Sweden.

In January 1999 the PLC approved a motion urging an end to political detentions and the release of all those imprisoned on exclusively political charges; the motion further demanded the formation of a special committee to assess the case of every political prisoner in the Palestinian territories and to recommend prisoner releases. The committee was duly appointed in February, under the chairmanship of the Minister of Justice. Despite the release of 37 political prisoners by the PA, however, in late January Hamas and Islamic Jihad activists began a hunger strike in Jericho and Nablus, in protest at their continued detention without trial. In February some 3,000 protesters marched to the headquarters of the PA, whom they accused of 'subservience to Israel and the CIA'. In March a security agent and former member of Hamas's military wing was sentenced to death for the killing of a Palestinian intelligence officer in Rafah. The verdict provoked serious clashes between Palestinian police and protesters in the Gaza Strip, and Arafat was forced to curtail an official visit to Jordan to address the domestic security crisis. In November 20 leading Palestinian intellectuals (including members of the PLC) issued a joint statement in which they criticized alleged corruption, mismanagement and abuse of power within the PA, and accused Palestinian officials of ineffectiveness in the peace talks with Israel. An official crackdown on Arafat's critics was subsequently instigated, during which several of the document's signatories were detained or placed under house arrest (they were later released on bail). The establishment, announced in January 2000, of a Higher Council for Development under Arafat's chairmanship was welcomed by foreign donors as a major step towards ending corruption and mismanagement within the Palestinian administration.

In August 1999 a Palestinian national dialogue conference was held in Cairo, Egypt, between representatives of Fatah and the PFLP. Later in August Arafat and the Secretary-General of the DFLP, Nayef Hawatmeh, met, also in Cairo, for the first time since 1993. At the end of the month representatives of nine Palestinian political factions, meeting in Ramallah, agreed on an agenda for a comprehensive national dialogue; Hamas and Islamic Jihad, however, refused to participate. In September the PFLP's deputy leader, Abu Ali Moustafa, was permitted by the Israeli Government to return to the West Bank from exile in Jordan, in order to participate in reconciliation talks with Arafat. George Habash stepped down as leader of the PFLP in April 2000, and Abu Ali Moustafa was elected to lead the organization in July. (Following Moustafa's assassination in August 2001, Ahmad Saadat assumed the party leadership.)

The start of the al-Aqsa *intifada* by Palestinians in September 2000 (see above) moved some analysts to suggest that Arafat's influence over Palestinians might be waning, as other Fatah leaders began to pursue their own agendas and to speak out against the President: Marwan Barghouthi, in particular, was said to be attracting considerable support among Palestinians in the West Bank, where he was the regional leader of Fatah. In December a court in Nablus sentenced to death a Palestinian who had been convicted of collaborating with Israeli secret services in the assassination of a Hamas commander. The harsh sentence apparently signalled a change in policy by the PA, which in January 2001 carried out the executions, by firing squad, of two alleged collaborators. The Al-Aqsa Martyrs Brigades claimed responsibility for the assassination in mid-January of Hisham Mekki, the Chairman of Palestinian Satellite Television, director of the state broadcasting corporation and a close associate of Arafat. In August a group of Palestinians were sentenced to death, and at least 100 others arrested, on charges of having collaborated with Israeli security services in recent attacks against Hamas officials. In October three Palestinians were killed by security forces in Gaza during violent protests in support of Osama bin Laden. Although the al-Qa'ida leader claimed to have launched the previous month's suicide attacks against the USA partly in protest against Israel's occupation of Palestinian territory, the PA sought to distance itself from the atrocities.

A report published by Human Rights Watch in November 2001 accused the PA of systematic abuses of human rights since the start of the al-Aqsa *intifada*, citing incidences of arbitrary arrests and of detention without trial and torture of prisoners. When Sheikh Ahmad Yassin was placed under house arrest in December, hundreds of Hamas supporters demanded his release, resulting in clashes between Hamas gunmen and security forces. Fierce protests by militants also ensued in January 2002 when Palestinian security services in Ramallah arrested the PFLP leader, Ahmad Saadat. There were also an increasing number of 'vigilante killings': in February a crowd led by members of the security services entered a military court in Jenin and killed three defendants, two of whom had just been sentenced to death for the murder of a security official; and during one day in April 11 suspected collaborators were reportedly murdered by Palestinians in Tulkarm, Qalqilya and Bethlehem.

At an emergency meeting of the PA leadership held following Arafat's release from Israeli house arrest in May 2002, the Minister of Parliamentary Affairs, Nabil Amr, tendered his resignation, reportedly after the President had rejected his proposals for a reorganization of the Cabinet. Arafat implemented major government changes in early June: membership of the Cabinet was reduced from 31 ministers to 21, with several ministries being either merged or abolished. Maj.-Gen. Abd ar-Razzaq al-Yahya was appointed Minister of the Interior—a position previously held by Arafat. Dr Salam Fayyad was named as the new Minister of Finance. The new Government was described as an interim administration, its main task to be the preparation and supervision of far-reaching reforms, including the organization of municipal elections towards the end of 2002 and of presidential and legislative elections by early 2003. The planned reforms would also include the streamlining of the Palestinian security services. Perhaps most importantly, draft legislation was prepared in order to create a new post of Prime Minister, to be responsible for the day-to-day administration of the PA. President Bush emphasized in late June 2002 that the USA would give its support to the creation of a 'provisional Palestinian state' if the PA undertook constitutional and judicial reforms. In September the entire Palestinian Cabinet resigned in order to prevent a vote of no confidence being brought in the legislature; a new administration was announced in the following month. Meanwhile, the PA President set 20 January 2003 as the day on which legislative and presidential elections were to be held. However, in December 2002 Arafat announced a postponement of the polls, claiming that it would be untenable to hold elections while Israel continued to occupy PA-controlled population centres in the West Bank and Gaza.

Palestinian representatives participated in a conference on reform of the Palestinian administration, held in London in January 2003, via a video link, after the Israeli Government refused to allow the delegates to attend the talks following a double suicide bombing in Tel-Aviv in which more than 20 Israelis died. At the conference, which was also attended by officials of the Quartet group and representatives from Jordan, Egypt and Saudi Arabia, it was agreed that a new draft Palestinian constitution would be presented within two weeks. In March the PLC endorsed a bill defining the role to be played by a future Palestinian Prime Minister, after having rejected amendments to the legislation proposed by Arafat according to which the President would retain authority over the appointment of Cabinet ministers. In the proposed power-sharing arrangement, the President was reportedly to control security and foreign affairs and would also have the authority to appoint and dismiss a premier, while the Prime Minister would nominate ministers and retain responsibility for domestic affairs. Mahmud Abbas, the Secretary-General of the PLO Executive Committee, formally accepted the post of Prime Minister on 19 March; on 29 April the Palestinian legislature endorsed his appointment. A newly expanded Palestinian Cabinet was announced on that day, comprising 25 ministers under the premiership of Mahmud Abbas (who also became Minister of the Interior). Muhammad Dahlan was confirmed as the Minister of State for Security Affairs, while Dr Nabil Shaath was named as the Minister of External Affairs and Saeb Erakat as the Minister of Negotiation Affairs. The announcement of the new PA Cabinet prompted the publication of the Quartet-sponsored 'roadmap' peace plan (see above).

Ongoing tensions between Arafat and Abbas appeared to be the principal reason for the resignation of Saeb Erakat in May 2003. Erakat was regarded as an Arafat ally and had traditionally been at the forefront of Palestinian negotiations with Israel; however, his resignation was interpreted as a protest against his omission from the Palestinian delegation, which included Abbas, Muhammad Dahlan and the Speaker of the PLC, Ahmad Quray, scheduled to hold talks with Ariel Sharon and leading Israeli officials. Immediately following the Aqaba summit (see above), Abbas had engaged in a round of discussions with Hamas and Islamic Jihad to effect a cease-fire in attacks by those groups against Israeli targets; despite an early walk-out by Hamas, a truce was duly brought into effect at the end of June, with the support of Fatah. Abbas and Arafat continued to clash on the issue of security: after a meeting of the Fatah Central Committee in July, Abbas offered to resign, having been criticized for making too many concessions to Israel. In early August Palestinian security forces arrested 20 militants, mostly believed to belong to the Al-Aqsa Martyrs Brigades, who were sheltering in Arafat's Ramallah compound. Arafat's appointment of a new National Security Adviser, Brig.-Gen. Jibril Rajoub (who had been dismissed as commander of the Preventive Security Force in the West Bank in 2002), in late August, was interpreted as a snub to Abbas and Muhammad Dahlan: as head of the Palestinian National Security Council (PNSC), Rajoub would be de facto commander in the field of the Palestinian security forces. (Rajoub was reported to have resigned from the post in January 2005.)

Mahmud Abbas resigned as Prime Minister in September 2003, seemingly representing the culmination of his power struggle with Arafat over control of the Palestinian security apparatus. Arafat nominated PLC Speaker Quray to replace Abbas. Meanwhile, Saeb Erakat was reinstated as Minister of Negotiation Affairs, and it appeared that Arafat had effectively regained control of the PA. However, in October Yasser Arafat declared a state of emergency in the Palestinian territories, following Israel's continuing construction of the 'security fence' (see above) and the arrest of a key member of Islamic Jihad; he also announced the establishment of an eight-member Emergency Cabinet. Shortly after the formation of the Emergency Cabinet, Quray reportedly offered his resignation. In early November the PLC approved Ahmad Quray's first full Cabinet. Ministers who retained their portfolios from the previous administration under Mahmud Abbas included Dr Nabil Shaath as Minister of Foreign Affairs and Dr Salam Fayyad as Minister of Finance; notable new appointments included Hakam Balawi as Minister of the Interior and Nahid ar-Rayyis as Minister of Justice. Rafiq an-Natsheh was elected Speaker of the PLC (but was replaced by Rawhi Fattouh in March 2004).

In late November 2003 the EU initiated an investigation into claims that EU funding for the PA had been channelled to the Al-Aqsa Martyrs Brigades. An audit of the PA's finances carried out by the IMF in 2003 had estimated that in the period 1995–2000 nearly US $900m. had been diverted into accounts controlled by Yasser Arafat. Moreover, documents seized by Israeli forces during the reoccupation of Palestinian areas in 2001 reportedly revealed that some EU funds had been used by the Al-Aqsa Martyrs Brigades. In February 2004 Israeli soldiers raided banks in Ramallah in an operation to seize funds reputedly belonging to Palestinian militant groups. The Arab Bank and the Cairo-Amman Bank were among those raided, and it was later reported that nearly $9m. had been confiscated.

In December 2003 Quray held talks in Cairo with the principal militant organizations, including Fatah, Hamas, Islamic Jihad and the PFLP, in order to achieve a full cessation of attacks against Israeli targets. Several of the Palestinian groups rejected a total cease-fire, and a joint statement by all parties at the conclusion of the talks stated that while attacks against civilian targets inside Israel would cease, attacks would continue against Israeli military targets and Jewish settlements in the Palestinian areas. In February 2004 more than 300 members of Fatah resigned from the group in protest at alleged corruption and the failure to instigate reform, particularly with regard to elections to the organization's leadership, which had last been held in 1989.

Arafat's authority was further threatened in July 2004 by mass disorder in the Gaza Strip, in protest against PA corruption and incompetence, as well as a threat by Prime Minister Quray to bring about the collapse of the administration if his powers were not increased. In mid-July Arafat took measures against the growing anarchy in Gaza, discharging two senior security commanders, declaring a state of emergency and sending loyal troops to protect official buildings in Gaza. He also replaced the national police chief and the commander of general security forces in Gaza (the latter with his cousin, Musa Arafat), and amalgamated eight rival security forces into three, following internal pressure on Arafat to combat corruption and to reform the PA and its security services. However, Fatah members demanding reforms rejected those introduced by the President as 'superficial and unconvincing', and pressure on Arafat (especially from the Al-Aqsa Martyrs Brigades) apparently forced him to reverse his decision to appoint his cousin as head of security. In late July Quray reportedly announced his resignation (which was rejected by Arafat) after chaos erupted in Gaza following the kidnapping of the Palestinian police commander, a colonel in the PA security forces and four French aid workers. However, Quray later announced his intention to stay in office as caretaker Prime Minister, having, according to one of his ministers, urged Arafat to forgo some of his powers to prevent the PA from collapsing further. Yet Quray did little to combat the widespread poverty in the Palestinian territories—a principal cause of popular anger—nor to address the power struggle within the Fatah movement, and in August the Minister of Justice, Nahid ar-Rayyis, resigned, citing the ongoing disorder in Gaza.

It was announced on 11 November 2004 that Yasser Arafat, who had been undergoing treatment at a military hospital in France, had died. In accordance with Palestinian law, the Speaker of the PLC, Rawhi Fattouh, was sworn in as acting President, pending elections due to take place in the territories within 60 days. Mahmud Abbas assumed the chairmanship of the PLO, and Quray was chosen to head the PNSC in addition to taking charge of the administration of the PA. Farouk Kaddoumi was appointed leader of Fatah. In late November Abbas was nominated to contest the elections as Fatah's only candidate. Although the Al-Aqsa Martyrs Brigades supported Abbas, concern was expressed at the possibility of inciting militants' anger, and further fighting within the group, if Abbas conceded too much to the Israelis. In early December Hamas declared that it would not be fielding a candidate for the forthcoming election, which they urged voters to boycott, while Marwan Barghouthi registered as a candidate. Islamic Jihad also announced a boycott of the ballot. Palestinian election officials declared that a total of 10 candidates had qualified for registration, including a human rights activist, Mustafa Barghouthi, who was to stand as an independent. Marwan Barghouthi later withdrew from the campaign, following pressure on him to give Abbas the best chance of securing the presidency; it had been feared that, had Barghouthi won the ballot, Israel would have refused to negotiate with him due to his imprisonment.

The first municipal elections to be held in the West Bank since 1976 began on 23 December 2004, at which Hamas, participating in an election in the Palestinian territories for the first time, won 16 councils and Fatah secured nine, with the two movements to share the control of one municipality. At the local elections held in the Gaza Strip in late January 2005 Hamas secured control of seven of the 10 councils. The lack of support for Fatah was attributed to its association with corruption, while voters were encouraged by Hamas's provision of welfare and educational services and by its opposition to Israel.

The election to appoint a successor to Yasser Arafat was held in the West Bank, Gaza Strip and East Jerusalem on 9 January 2005. The Palestinian Central Elections Commission (CEC) asserted that the presence of Israeli forces in Jerusalem interfered with the voting process, forcing international observers to intervene. Moreover, polling centres remained open for an extra two hours because some citizens had difficulty locating them, and owing to problems with voter registration. Nevertheless, international observers considered the overall conduct of the election to have been free and fair. Final results showed that, from the seven candidates, Abbas had received 62.5% of votes cast and Mustafa Barghouthi 19.5%. The other candidates had all secured less than 4% of the votes. Abbas was sworn in as Executive President of the PA on 15 January.

In early February 2005 a Hamas militant attack on Israeli army outposts and settlements in the Gaza strip prompted Abbas to dismiss senior security commanders. Later in the month the PLC voted to approve a new Cabinet under Prime Minister Ahmad Quray. Dr Nabil Shaath was appointed Deputy Prime Minister and Minister of Information; Shaath's previous role as Minister of Foreign Affairs was assumed by Dr Nasser al-Kidwa, hitherto the Palestinian representative to the UN. Maj.-Gen. Nasr Yousuf became Minister of the Interior and National Security. Quray pledged the new administration's determination to heighten security and combat poverty. In March, after militants from the Fatah-affiliated Al-Aqsa Martyrs Brigades reportedly shot at the presidential compound in Ramallah,

President Abbas removed the military chief in the West Bank and the Ramallah district commander, explaining that the security apparatus had failed and needed to be reorganized. In an effort to consolidate various (often rival) factions into a unified command, in the following month Abbas nominated four new heads of security forces in the West Bank and Gaza Strip, and ordered 10 senior officers to resign.

A reported 82% of eligible voters took part in a second round of municipal elections in the West Bank and Gaza Strip on 5 May 2005. According to official results, 45 of the 84 municipal districts contested were to be governed by councils with a majority of Fatah representatives (which took 56% of votes). Hamas, which had not participated in the presidential elections, took 23 councils (33% of votes), and left-wing and independent lists secured 16 councils. Later in the month the CEC declared that elections to the PLC, scheduled for July, would be delayed while the PLC ratified a new elections law, intended to replace the system of simple majority by which the 1996 general elections had been held, with a 'mixed' electoral system (see President and Legislature). The PLC ratified the new law in June 2005. In August Abbas issued a decree setting 25 January 2006 as the date for the legislative elections. A third round of municipal elections was held in 82 towns and villages in the West Bank on 29 September 2005. Fatah won a reported 54% of the votes, and Hamas took 26%. At local elections in some of the largest cities in the West Bank conducted on 15 December, Fatah secured 35% of the 414 contested seats, while Hamas won 26%. However, although Fatah retained control of Ramallah, Hamas notably gained control of Nablus and Jenin.

In accordance with Palestinian elections law (which stipulates that officials intending to contest seats in elections to the PLC must resign their posts two months in advance of the ballot), various ministers were reported to have submitted their resignations in November 2005, including the Minister of Finance, Dr Salam Fayyad. Prime Minister Ahmad Quray also resigned in mid-December in order to be eligible to participate in the elections. Deputy Prime Minister and Minister of Information Dr Nabil Shaath was appointed to replace him; however, later in the month Quray declared that he would not take part in the poll, and returned to his former post.

Israel announced in late December 2005 that it would not allow Arabs in East Jerusalem to vote if Hamas participated in the forthcoming legislative elections. After PA officials threatened to postpone the elections, and amid international pressure, in mid-January 2006 Israel declared that it would allow a small number of Arabs in East Jerusalem to vote on 25 January, and that candidates from groups other than Hamas could campaign there. In the event, Hamas, competing as the Change and Reform list in order to avoid a ban on its direct participation, secured 74 of the 132 seats, and Fatah only 45. A large part of Change and Reform's election campaign had focused on the movement's social welfare programme and its strong stance against official corruption. Other groups, including the PFLP (contesting the poll as Martyr Abu Ali Moustafa) and independents, also achieved representation. Quray announced the resignation of his administration on 26 January.

The new PLC was inaugurated on 18 February 2006. Dr Aziz Duweik was appointed to replace Rawhi Fattouh as Speaker, and President Abbas called on Hamas to establish a new administration. Hamas subsequently held discussions with Abbas and other factions, including Fatah, concerning the possibility of forming a coalition administration of national unity, and nominated Ismail Haniya as Prime Minister. Haniya, who had led the organization's national list for the elections, had held senior positions within Hamas; imprisoned in Israeli gaols in 1987–89 for his participation in the first *intifada* and leading one of Hamas's security apparatuses, Haniya had survived an Israeli assassination attempt in 2003, five years after assuming control of Sheikh Ahmad Yassin's office. Hamas began to assert its authority at a PLC session in early March 2006 when it reversed legislation that the Fatah-led parliament had approved immediately prior to its dissolution. Fatah deputies walked out of the session, asserting that Hamas had no right to reverse their decisions. The new laws had given President Abbas further powers, apparently in an attempt to increase his authority and curb that of parliament, in anticipation of Hamas's domination of the legislature. One of the rulings had provided for the establishment of a constitutional court and granted Abbas the right to elect its members.

Hamas leaders continued their attempts to persuade Fatah to enter into an administration of national unity. However, in late March 2006, after weeks of discussions between the two factions, Fatah rejected Hamas's offer, and the Islamist organization decided to form a cabinet alone. One of the most important matters of dispute had been Hamas's rejection of bilateral Israeli-Palestinian agreements approved by the former legislature: Hamas considered that by recognizing these accords it would be accepting Israeli occupation of Palestinian territory. The PLC approved Hamas's proposed Cabinet on 28 March, and President Abbas inaugurated the new administration on the following day. Notable appointees included Nasser ash-Shaer as Deputy Prime Minister and Minister of Education and Higher Education, Mahmud az-Zahhar as Minister of Foreign Affairs and Said Siyam as Minister of the Interior and Civil Affairs.

In the weeks following the elections to the PLC, there were sporadic violent clashes between rival militias and security forces of Hamas and Fatah. The increased tensions in the Palestinian territories were aggravated by the decision by the USA and the EU to withdraw all direct aid to the PA until Hamas fulfilled the three conditions that the Quartet group had placed on it (see above). Nevertheless, in June 2006 Hamas and Fatah reportedly agreed to a joint political platform which contained implicit recognition of Israel's existence. The representatives approved a document drawn up in May by a group of Palestinian political prisoners in Israeli gaols, led by Marwan Barghouthi and fellow prisoner Sheikh Abd al-Khaliq an-Natsheh of Hamas, which detailed 18 points for a return to negotiations with Israel. The so-called 'prisoners' document' called for the formation of an administration of national unity in which all political parties that accepted the terms of the document would be represented, as well as the establishment of a 'unified resistance front' against Israeli occupation. Shortly afterwards Hamas endorsed the prisoners' document and agreed in principle to share power with Fatah in an administration committed to a two-state settlement and negotiations with Israel on the basis of an independent Palestinian state on territories occupied in 1967. (The group had been under intense pressure from President Abbas to accept the proposals or face a referendum.) However, the agreement was rejected by Hamas's military wing and the organization's political leaders in exile. Moreover, it failed to achieve the immediate resumption of foreign aid to the PA, which was urgently required in order to allow the authorities to begin paying workers' salaries.

Officials of the Hamas and Fatah movements pursued difficult negotiations with a view to forming an administration of national unity during September 2006. In that month a general strike was organized by public sector workers in protest against unpaid wages. In early November Arab ministers responsible for foreign relations, meeting in Cairo, pledged to increase levels of financial assistance given to the PA; Iran also gave funds to the Hamas-led administration in the following month. In mid-November it was announced that Fatah and Hamas had agreed to nominate Muhammad Shbeir, a former head of the Islamic University in Gaza, as Prime Minister in a coalition administration. However, despite lengthy discussions, it proved impossible for Shbeir to form a cabinet. On 8 February 2007 Fatah and Hamas—represented by President Abbas and Khalid Meshaal, respectively—signed an agreement to form a national unity administration; the accord followed two days of discussions in Mecca, Saudi Arabia, held at the invitation of King Abdullah. Although Hamas continued to reject an acceptance of Israel's right to exist, it was reported that the organization had agreed, for the first time, to 'respect and work to implement' the 'land-for-peace' proposal adopted at the Beirut summit in 2002 (see above).

Finally, on 17 March 2007 the PLC approved the composition of a new Cabinet, which replaced the former Hamas-dominated administration with a coalition of ministers from Hamas and Fatah, together with independents and representatives from the DFLP and the Palestinian People's Party. Hamas's Ismail Haniya retained the post of Prime Minister, while Azzam al-Ahmad, of Fatah, became Deputy Prime Minister. Three prominent ministries were allocated to independents: Hani Talab al-Qawasmeh was appointed Minister of the Interior, Dr Ziad Abu Amr Minister of Foreign Affairs and Dr Salam Fayyad Minister of Finance. At the end of March EU ministers responsible for foreign affairs, meeting in Germany, declared their support for the peace initiative revived in Saudi Arabia a few days previously, and announced that they would be willing to have contacts with non-Hamas members of the new Palestinian Cabinet. Israel declared that it would continue its boycott of the PA, however, until the new administration met the conditions demanded by the Quartet group. Having initially tendered

PALESTINIAN AUTONOMOUS AREAS

his resignation in April, when it was rejected by President Abbas, in mid-May al-Qawasmeh formally resigned as Minister of the Interior. His departure from the Cabinet appeared to demonstrate the divisions within the administration with regard to the difficult security issues facing the West Bank and Gaza. Prime Minister Haniya assumed the interior portfolio in an acting capacity.

Abbas announced in mid-March 2007 that he had appointed Muhammad Dahlan as Secretary of the newly re-established PNSC, which in theory meant that he became general commander of the Palestinian security forces; Dahlan, however, was profoundly disliked by Hamas. Following several unsuccessful attempts to achieve a lasting cease-fire between the rival militias in the Palestinian territories, a new security plan to restore order in Gaza was announced by the Cabinet in early May. Yet the factional fighting between gunmen from Hamas and Fatah continued, leading Abbas, speaking in early June, on the anniversary of 40 years of Israeli occupation, to warn of the threat of a Palestinian civil war. In mid-2007 scores of Palestinians were killed in the violence, some of which even occurred within hospital buildings. On 12 June gun battles between Hamas and Fatah fighters intensified across the Gaza Strip. As Hamas began to demonstrate its military superiority, it seized control of the headquarters of security forces in the north and south of the Strip, before taking over Gaza City itself. At the same time Fatah militias in the West Bank stormed Hamas-controlled institutions, seeking revenge for the Islamist movement's takeover of the Strip. On 14 June Abbas dissolved the national unity Cabinet under Haniya's premiership, declared a state of emergency and appointed the independent Minister of Finance, Dr Salam Fayyad, as Prime Minister. As a respected economist and former employee of the World Bank and the IMF, Fayyad had wide support in Israel, the USA and the EU. Meanwhile, Haniya sought to consolidate his power over Gaza by naming a new chief of security in the territory, Maj.-Gen. Said Fanouna.

An Emergency Cabinet, consisting principally of independents and technocrats, as well as one Fatah representative, was sworn in by President Abbas in Ramallah on 17 June 2007. Besides assuming the premiership, Fayyad was also to head the foreign affairs and finance portfolios (although Riyad al-Maliki was later to assume the former portfolio). Fatah's Abd ar-Razzaq al-Yahya became Minister of the Interior and of Civil Affairs. The hope was that this administration would restore law and order throughout the Palestinian territories, but it became apparent that divisions between the Fatah-controlled West Bank and Hamas-administered Gaza Strip were widening. Abbas refused to enter into a dialogue with Hamas until it withdrew its militias from former Fatah positions in Gaza. Moreover, the President granted himself the power to take decisions without the endorsement of the PLC, where Hamas held a majority of the seats. Abbas also declared that he was outlawing Hamas's paramilitary wing and other militias associated with the Islamist group. On 18 June the USA and the EU, in a demonstration of support for President Abbas and his formation of an administration that excluded Hamas ministers, lifted their 15-month economic and political boycott of the PA. The Bush Administration additionally pledged assistance valued at some US $190m. to the Ramallah-based Cabinet.

Upon the expiry of the 30-day state of emergency, on 13 July 2007 President Abbas accepted the resignation of the Emergency Cabinet and appointed three new ministers to a reshuffled Cabinet, which was to function as a caretaker administration until either the PLC convened or new legislative elections were called. (Hamas was unwilling for a vote to be held in the PLC as, with so many of its legislators in Israeli detention, it would lose its parliamentary majority.) Hamas leaders again refused to recognize the legitimacy of this interim administration. On 4 July, three days after Israel began transferring $117m. of withheld Palestinian taxes to the Fayyad administration, thousands of Palestinian civil servants began receiving their first full salaries since March 2006. However, the West Bank administration continued to withhold the salaries of thousands of civil servants in the Gaza Strip. On 19 July 2007, at the first meeting of the international Quartet group since the appointment of former British Prime Minister Tony Blair as its representative, members of the Quartet affirmed their joint refusal to deal with Hamas. Muhammad Dahlan resigned as National Security Adviser on 26 July, citing ill health; however, some reports alleged that Dahlan had been asked to resign after his security forces in Gaza had allowed Hamas militants to oust Fatah from power in Gaza (when Dahlan was undergoing medical treatment

Introductory Survey

abroad). Nevertheless, the resignation was essentially a formality since President Abbas had dissolved the PNSC following Hamas's takeover of Gaza. In mid-August Fayyad issued a statement outlining the conditions required for inter-Palestinian dialogue to begin: Hamas should renounce any claims to be the legal authority governing Gaza (although Fayyad did not insist on an annulment of the 2006 election results) and disband all armed militias. This demand apparently included the Hamas Executive Force, which was responsible for maintaining law and order in Gaza.

In mid-October 2007 Haniya appeared to demonstrate a move towards reconciliation with Fatah, when he described Hamas's administration of the Gaza Strip as 'temporary'. In early November President Abbas hosted Hamas representatives for discussions at his Ramallah headquarters; it was hoped that there would soon be a resumption of complete negotiations with Abbas's faction, with a view to restoring Palestinian unity. However, Abbas's administration in the West Bank launched a major clampdown on the activities of Hamas-affiliated clerics in the territories, with a number of preachers being dismissed or arrested on charges of fomenting political unrest. Moreover, the third anniversary of the death of Yasser Arafat in November provoked a further outbreak of factional violence; more than seven Palestinians were reported to have died, and many more were wounded, in clashes between rival Fatah and Hamas supporters in Gaza City. Abbas subsequently declared that the PA must bring an end to Hamas's control of Gaza.

In early March 2008 international aid organizations stated that the humanitarian crisis afflicting the Gazan population was the worst in the territory since 1967; in that month both the USA and the EU released to the PA the first instalments of the funds pledged at the donors' conference held in Paris in December 2007 (see Economic Affairs). In late March 2008 Hamas and Fatah signed a reconciliation agreement brokered by the Yemeni President, Ali Abdullah Saleh, and thus termed the San'a Declaration, which included a pledge to resume direct discussions between the feuding parties and affirmed the 'unity of the Palestinian people, territory and authority'. However, doubts were immediately expressed as to exactly what preconditions had been agreed for a resumption of dialogue, with President Abbas's principal negotiator, Saeb Erakat, insisting that Hamas must surrender its control of the Gaza Strip prior to the resumption of talks.

Government

In accordance with the Declaration of Principles on Palestinian Self-Rule and the Cairo Agreement on the Gaza Strip and Jericho (see Recent History), the PLO assumed control of the Jericho area of the West Bank and of the Gaza Strip on 17 May 1994. In November and December 1995, under the terms of the Israeli-Palestinian Interim Agreement on the West Bank and the Gaza Strip concluded in September 1995, Israeli armed forces withdrew from the West Bank towns of Nablus, Ramallah, Jenin, Tulkarm, Qalqilya and Bethlehem. In late December the PLO assumed responsibility in some 17 areas of civil administration in the town of Hebron. The Interim Agreement divided the West Bank into three zones: Areas A, B and C. As of July 1998, the PA had sole jurisdiction and security control in Area A (2% of the West Bank), but Israel retained authority over movement into and out of the area. In Area B (26% of the West Bank) the PA had some limited authority while Israel remained in control of security. Area C, the remaining 72% of the West Bank, was under Israeli military occupation. In accordance with the Wye Memorandum of October 1998 (see Recent History), Israel effected a further redeployment of its armed forces from approximately 500 sq km of West Bank territory in November. Of this, about 400 sq km became Area A territory and the remainder Area B territory. The Sharm esh-Sheikh Memorandum of September 1999 was intended to facilitate completion of outstanding commitments under agreements previously signed, as well as to enable the resumption of 'final status' negotiations with Israel. By October 2000 approximately 17.2% of the West Bank (Area A) was under sole Palestinian jurisdiction and security control, although Israel retained authority over access to and from the zone; about 23.8% (Area B) was under Israeli military control, with the PA responsible for civil administration and public order; the remaining 59% (Area C) remained under Israeli military occupation. Israel implemented its unilateral Disengagement Plan, according to which it dismantled Israeli military installations and settlements in the Gaza Strip, and withdrew from four settlements in the West Bank, in August–September 2005 (see Recent History). The total area of the territory over which the PA

PALESTINIAN AUTONOMOUS AREAS

Introductory Survey

will eventually assume control, and the extent of its jurisdiction there, remain subject to 'final status' talks.

Defence

As assessed at November 2007, paramilitary forces in the Gaza Strip and in the areas of the West Bank where the PA has assumed responsibility for security totalled an estimated 56,000; however, figures for personnel strength in the various forces were impossible to confirm, owing to the uncertain situation in the Palestinian territories at that time. There is, *inter alia*, a Presidential Security Force, a Preventative Security Force, a Civil Defence Force and a Police Force. Units of the Palestine National Liberation Army (PNLA) have been garrisoned in various countries in the Middle East and North Africa; however, much of the PNLA's personnel strength has now been incorporated into the PA's various security forces. The public security and order budget of the Palestinian Autonomous Areas was estimated at US $433.9m. in 2004.

Economic Affairs

In 2005, according to estimates by the World Bank, the gross national income (GNI) of the West Bank and the Gaza Strip, measured at average 2003–05 prices, was US $4,452m., equivalent to $1,230 per head. During 1996–2006, it was estimated, the population increased at an average annual rate of 4.0%, while in 1996–2004 gross domestic product (GDP) per head decreased, in real terms, by an average of 6.9% per year. Overall GDP increased, in real terms, at an average annual rate of an estimated 1.9% in 1996–2006; GDP growth of 1.4% was recorded in 2006.

Agriculture and fishing contributed 10.7% of the GDP of the West Bank and Gaza Strip in 2004, according to official figures. In 2006 agriculture (including hunting, forestry and fishing) engaged 16.1% of the employed Palestinian labour force. Citrus fruits are the principal export crop, and horticulture also makes a significant contribution to trade. Other important crops are tomatoes, cucumbers, olives and grapes. The livestock sector is also significant. According to the World Bank, agricultural GDP decreased at an average annual rate of 4.0% during 1995–2003. The GDP of the sector declined by 2.6% in 2003.

Industry (including mining, manufacturing, electricity and water supply, and construction) contributed 20.6% of Palestinian GDP in 2004. The industrial sector engaged 23.9% of the employed labour force of the West Bank and Gaza in 2006. Construction alone accounted for 5.0% of GDP in 2004 and employed 11.1% of the working population in 2006. During 1995–2003 industrial GDP decreased at an average rate of 9.7% annually. The sector's GDP contracted by 10.0% in 2003.

Mining and quarrying contributed 0.7% of the GDP of the Palestinian territories in 1998, and engaged 0.3% of the employed labour force in 2006. Two significant gasfields were discovered off the Gazan coast in 1999; however, the exploration and supply of this offshore gas is dependent upon agreement being reached with Israel, which is likely to be the principal purchaser.

Manufacturing contributed 9.8% of the GDP of the West Bank and Gaza Strip in 2003, according to the World Bank. In 2006 12.1% of the employed labour force were engaged in the sector. Palestinian manufacturing is characterized by small-scale enterprises, which typically engage in food-processing and the production of textiles and footwear. The frequent closure of the West Bank and Gaza by the Israeli authorities has prompted the development of free trade industrial zones on the Palestinian side of the boundaries separating Israel from the territories: Israeli and Palestinian enterprises can continue to take advantage of low-cost Palestinian labour at times of closure, and the zones also benefit from tax exemptions and export incentives. Manufacturing GDP contracted at an average annual rate of 5.1% during 1995–2003. The GDP of the sector decreased by 8.3% in 2003.

The energy sector (comprising electricity and water supply) accounted for an estimated 2.0% of Palestinian GDP in 1998. Electricity, gas and water utilities together employed 0.4% of the labour force of the West Bank and Gaza in 2006. In the West Bank, the Jerusalem District Electric Company supplies electric power to Jerusalem, Bethlehem, Jericho, Ramallah and Al-Birah, while the National Electric Company operates in the northern West Bank. The Israel Electric Corporation (IEC) was the only source of electricity to municipalities in the Gaza Strip prior to the establishment of the Palestine Electric Company in 1999, and Palestinian utility firms remain reliant on the purchase of electricity from the IEC.

In 2004 the services sector contributed 68.7% of Palestinian GDP. Services engaged 60.1% of the employed labour force in 2006. Although tourism previously contributed more than 10% of the GDP of the West Bank and Gaza, it has been all but halted by the ongoing violence in the territories. The GDP of the services sector decreased at an average rate of 0.1% per year during 1995–2003. Services GDP declined by 3.4% in 2003.

In 2005, according to preliminary estimates, the West Bank and Gaza Strip recorded a visible trade deficit of US $2,638m. and a deficit of $1,707m. on the current account of the balance of payments. In the absence of seaport facilities and of an airport (Gaza International Airport was opened in November 1998 but has frequently been closed by the Israeli authorities), foreign trade (in terms of value) has been conducted almost exclusively with Israel since occupation. Most Palestinian exports are of agricultural or horticultural products. One notable feature of this trade is that Palestinian goods have often been exported to Israel, and subsequently re-exported as originating in Israel. In 2003 imports (c.i.f.) from Israel alone were valued at $1,800.4m. and exports (f.o.b.) to Israel and elsewhere totalled $276.4m.

In 2004, according to official revised estimates, the PA recorded an overall budget deficit of US $790.1m. The annual rate of inflation in the West Bank and Gaza averaged 4.1% in 1996–2007; consumer prices increased by an average of 2.7% in 2007. According to official estimates, some 23.6% of the labour force in the Palestinian territories (18.6% in the West Bank; 34.8% in Gaza) were unemployed in 2006.

The prospects for an improvement in economic conditions in the Palestinian Autonomous Areas, which remain highly dependent on Israel, are inextricably linked to the full implementation of the Oslo accords (see Recent History) and the outcome of 'final status' negotiations between the PA and Israel. Examples of this economic dependency are the large number of Palestinian workers employed in Israel, and the reliance of the trade sector on Israel as a market for exports and source of imports. The underdevelopment of Palestinian agriculture and industry is a consequence of the Israeli occupation, when investment became orientated towards residential construction at the expense of these sectors. Agriculture remains focused mainly on meeting local demand, although the sector supplies the bulk of Palestinian exports and there is proven demand for Palestinian products beyond the Israeli market. The expansion of Palestinian agriculture is also limited by problems with irrigation: access to water supplies is subject to 'final status' discussions. Economic conditions in the West Bank and Gaza have deteriorated markedly since 1993, largely as a result of frequent border closures enforced by the Israeli authorities in reprisal for terrorist attacks by militant Islamist groups. Such closures lead to an immediate rise in the rate of unemployment among Palestinians, increase transportation costs for Palestinian goods and, at times, halt trade entirely. The Oslo accords provide for the development of seaport facilities and for the opening of Gaza International Airport and of a safe passage linking the Gaza Strip with the West Bank. However, by early 2008 the provision for a seaport at Gaza had still not been implemented, while the airport and safe passage were both closed by the Israeli authorities.

In the context of the second Palestinian *intifada* from September 2000, in November Israel imposed a complete economic blockade on the West Bank and Gaza, and halted the payment of tax transfers to the PA. The closure quickly reversed any recent economic successes, and by the beginning of 2003 economic losses resulting from the blockade were estimated at US $2,240m. With the economy in a state of paralysis, the PA was effectively bankrupt; for this reason, donor support has arguably become its key source of funding. As the Palestinian economy continued to suffer from a deep recession, in 2004 the World Bank cited closures by the Israeli authorities as a principal factor in the stagnation. Shortly after the militant Islamic Resistance Movement (Hamas) secured the highest number of seats at the legislative elections of January 2006, Israel again halted payments of tax and customs duties to the PA. Following the installation of the Hamas-led administration in March, the USA and the EU declared that they were withdrawing direct aid to the PA. Every year since the creation of the PA in 1994, the EU had donated an estimated $600m., and the USA some $400m. However, the USA pledged to increase by over 50% the amount of humanitarian aid it donated to the Palestinians via agencies not linked to the administration, to $245m. The EU asserted that its direct humanitarian aid to Palestinians, which included annual donations from individual states of some $262m., would not be affected by its decision to withdraw direct aid to the PA. At an international donors' conference in Stockholm, Sweden, in September 2006, donors pledged funds of $500m. to assist non-governmental bodies operating in the PA-controlled territories. As GDP per caput fell in 2006, up to 83% of Palestinians were estimated to be living in poverty, while unemployment in the territories averaged 23.6% (the figure for Gaza being considerably higher). Economic prospects in the West Bank and Gaza appeared improved following the formation, in March 2007, of a national unity administration; however, the takeover of Gaza by Hamas militants in June resulted in a de facto separation between an internationally approved emergency administration appointed by Fatah's President Abbas in the West Bank and a Hamas-led cabinet in the Gaza Strip. Abbas's establishment of a Cabinet that excluded ministers from Hamas did, however, result in the international embargo imposed on the West Bank in 2006 being lifted. At a further conference held in Paris in December 2007, international donors pledged some $7,500m. to the PA for humanitarian aid and to assist with the creation of a Palestinian state, following the Middle Eastern peace meeting held in the USA in November (see Recent History); among the largest donors, Saudi Arabia pledged $750m., the EU $640m. and the USA $550m. However, concerns remained in early 2008 that this finance would not be realized unless a political settlement was reached with Israel. The PA's Prime Minister in the West Bank, Dr Salam Fayyad, had launched a three-year Palestinian Reform and Development Plan in late 2007, which was intended to stimulate the economy and to encourage private sector development. Moreover, the Middle East's envoy for the international Quartet group, Tony Blair, announced a series of economic projects in an effort to rejuvenate the Palestinian economy and provide thousands of jobs; these included a sewage treatment plant in Gaza, industrial parks in Hebron and Jericho, and measures to encourage tourists to visit Bethlehem. Israel's economic blockade of Gaza (which was tightened in January 2008) has effectively led to the collapse of the Gazan economy. The Association of Palestinian Businessmen assessed in late 2007 that Gazan industry had suffered cumulative losses worth some $23m. since Hamas's seizure of power in mid-2007. Moreover, the Strip's vital fishing industry had been severely affected by the Israeli siege and fuel supplies also reduced (see Recent History). Yet, although many sectors of the Palestinian economy have been weakened by restrictions on the movement of people and goods, the IT sector has proved resilient, with growth experienced in recent years; should these restrictions be lifted, the sector has the potential to make a significant contribution to future economic growth. Meanwhile, the Palestinian Monetary Authority made progress towards becoming a central bank in 2007; it was anticipated that it might be in a position to issue its own currency by 2010–12, thereby replacing the range of currencies currently accepted in the West Bank and Gaza.

Education

In the West Bank the Jordanian education system is in operation. Services are provided by the Israeli Civil Administration, the UN Relief and Works Agency for Palestine Refugees in the Near East (UNRWA) and private, voluntary organizations, which provide all university and most community college education. There are 20 community and teacher training colleges in the West Bank, and six universities (including an open university). The Egyptian system of education operates in the Gaza Strip, where there are three universities and one teacher training college. Palestinian education has been severely disrupted since 1987, and more recently as a result of the al-Aqsa *intifada*, which began in late 2000. Since May 1994 the PA has assumed responsibility for education in Gaza and parts of the West Bank. According to UNESCO estimates, enrolment at primary schools in 2004/05 included 80.0% of pupils in the relevant age group, while 94.8% of children in the appropriate age group were enrolled at secondary schools. In 2005/06, according to the Palestinian Central Bureau of Statistics, 77,142 pupils attended 935 pre-primary schools, 944,713 pupils attended 1,537 primary schools and 122,776 students were enrolled at 740 secondary institutions. In 2004/05 138,139 students attended universities or equivalent third-level institutions.

Since 1950 UNRWA has provided education services to all Palestinian refugees, numbering 745,776 in the West Bank and 1,048,125 in the Gaza Strip in December 2007. The focus of UNRWA's education programme is basic primary and junior secondary schooling, offered free of charge to all refugee children and youth in accordance with local systems. In 2006/07 UNRWA operated 92 schools in the West Bank and 214 in the Gaza Strip, providing education to 57,818 pupils in the West Bank and to 196,008 pupils in Gaza. In addition, UNRWA operated five vocational training centres. In 2007 UNRWA budgeted some US $146.3m. for expenditure on education in the Palestinian territories.

Public Holidays

2008: 1 January (Fatah Day), 20 March* (Mouloud/Yum an-Nabi, Birth of Muhammad), 30 July* (Leilat al-Meiraj, Ascension of Muhammad), 1 October* (Id al-Fitr, end of Ramadan), 15 November (Independence Day), 9 December* (Id al-Adha, Feast of the Sacrifice).

2009: 1 January (Fatah Day), 9 March* (Mouloud/Yum an-Nabi, Birth of Muhammad), 19 July* (Leilat al-Meiraj, Ascension of Muhammad), 20 September* (Id al-Fitr, end of Ramadan), 15 November (Independence Day), 27 November* (Id al-Adha, Feast of the Sacrifice).

*These holidays are dependent on the Islamic lunar calendar and may vary by one or two days from the dates given.

Christian holidays are observed by the Christian Arab community.

Weights and Measures

The metric system is in force, although local weights and measures are also used.

Statistical Survey

Source (unless otherwise indicated): Palestinian Central Bureau of Statistics (PCBS), POB 1647, Ramallah; tel. (2) 2406340; fax (2) 2406343; e-mail diwan@pcbs.gov.ps; internet www.pcbs.gov.ps.

Note: Unless otherwise indicated, data include East Jerusalem, annexed by Israel in 1967.

Area and Population

AREA, POPULATION AND DENSITY

Area (sq km)	6,020*
Population (census of 9 December 1997)†	2,895,683
Population (census of 1 December 2007, preliminary figures)	
Males	1,908,432
Females	1,853,214
Total	3,761,646
Density (per sq km) at 1 December 2007	624.9

* 2,324 sq miles. The total comprises: West Bank 5,655 sq km (2,183 sq miles); Gaza Strip 365 sq km (141 sq miles).

† Figures include an estimate of 210,209 for East Jerusalem and an adjustment of 83,805 for estimated underenumeration. The total comprises 1,873,476 (males 951,693, females 921,783) in the West Bank (including East Jerusalem) and 1,022,207 (males 518,813, females 503,394) in the Gaza Strip. The data exclude Jewish settlers. According to official Israeli estimates, the population of Israelis residing in Jewish localities in the West Bank (excluding East Jerusalem) and Gaza Strip was 243,900 at 31 December 2004 (West Bank 235,700, Gaza Strip 8,200). The withdrawal of Israeli settlers residing in Jewish localities in the Gaza Strip was completed in September 2005 (see Recent History).

Note: Official projected estimates of a total world-wide Palestinian population of 10,094,565 at 31 December 2006 included 1,134,293 Palestinians resident in Israel and 2,799,440 resident in Jordan.

GOVERNORATES
(census of 1 December 2007, preliminary results)

	Area (sq km)	Population*	Density (per sq km)
West Bank			
Janin (Jenin)	583	256,212	439.5
Tubas	402	48,771	121.3
Tulkarm	246	158,213	643.1
Qalqilya	166	91,046	548.5
Salfeet	204	59,464	291.5
Nabulus (Nablus)	605	321,493	531.4
Ram Allah (Ramallah) and Al-Birah	855	278,018	325.2
Al-Quds (Jerusalem)†	345	362,521	1,050.8
Ariha (Jericho) and Al-Aghwar	593	41,724	70.4
Beit Lahm (Bethlehem)	659	176,515	267.9
Al-Khalil (Hebron)	997	551,130	552.8
Gaza Strip			
North Gaza	61	270,245	4,430.2
Gaza	74	496,410	6,708.2
Deir al-Balah	58	205,534	3,543.7
Khan Yunus (Khan Yunis)	108	270,979	2,509.1
Rafah	64	173,371	2,708.9
Total	6,020	3,761,646	624.9

* Figures exclude Jewish settlers.
† Figures refer only to the eastern sector of the city.

PRINCIPAL LOCALITIES
(estimated population at mid-2002, excluding Jewish settlers)

West Bank			
Al-Quds (Jerusalem)	242,081*	Adh-Dhahiriya	25,348
Al-Khalil (Hebron)	147,291	Ar-Ram and Dahiyat al-Bareed	23,038
Nabulus (Nablus)	121,344		
Tulkarm	41,109	Ram Allah (Ramallah)	22,493
Qalqilya	39,580	Halhul	19,345
Yattah (Yatta)	38,023	Dura	19,124
Al-Birah	34,920	Ariha (Jericho)	18,239
Janin (Jenin)	32,300	Qabatiya	17,788
Beit Lahm (Bethlehem)	26,847		

Gaza Strip			
Ghazzah (Gaza)	361,651	Beit Lahya	50,576
Khan Yunus (Khan Yunis)	110,677	Deir al-Balah	43,593
		Bani Suhaylah	28,761
Jabalyah (Jabalia)	104,620	Beit Hanun	27,341
Rafah	62,452	Tel as-Sultan Camp	21,477
An-Nuseirat	56,449	Al-Maghazi Camp	21,278

* The figure refers only to the eastern sector of the city.

BIRTHS AND DEATHS
(official estimates)*

	2002	2003	2004
Live births:			
West Bank	58,954	58,090	57,680
Gaza Strip	43,507	43,981	46,781
Deaths:			
West Bank	5,908	5,719	5,392
Gaza Strip	4,254	4,299	4,241

* Excluding Jewish settlers.

Birth rate (official estimates per 1,000): 39.6 in 2002; 38.8 in 2003; 38.1 in 2004.

Death rate (official estimates per 1,000): 4.3 in 2002; 4.2 in 2003; 4.1 in 2004.

2006: Birth rate 36.7 per 1,000; Death rate 3.9 per 1,000.

MARRIAGES
(number registered)

	2004	2005	2006
West Bank	15,551	16,706	16,380
Gaza Strip	12,083	12,170	11,853

Marriage rate (rates per 1,000, official estimates): West Bank: 6.8 in 2004; 7.0 in 2005; 6.8 in 2006. Gaza Strip: 9.0 in 2004; 8.8 in 2005; 8.2 in 2006.

ECONOMICALLY ACTIVE POPULATION
(persons aged 15 years and over)

	2004	2005	2006
Agriculture, hunting, forestry and fishing	92,078	92,310	107,024
Mining and quarrying	1,717	1,377	2,237
Manufacturing	71,535	80,874	80,543
Electricity and gas	2,067	2,366	2,500
Construction	67,436	81,644	73,905
Wholesale and retail trade	102,340	110,110	114,662
Hotels and restaurants	10,508	12,813	13,492
Transport, storage and communications	31,252	36,134	38,242
Financial intermediation	4,492	3,513	4,503
Real estate, renting and business activities	9,413	10,492	11,217
Public administration and defence	78,038	92,977	98,922
Education	60,850	60,743	67,704
Health and social work	23,711	22,804	24,400
Services	15,390	17,462	19,426
Others	7,613	7,319	7,599
Total employed	578,439	632,939	666,375
Males	473,755	527,806	546,000
Females	104,683	105,132	120,375
Unemployed	212,157	194,458	206,150
Total labour force	790,596	827,397	872,525

Source: ILO.

Health and Welfare

KEY INDICATORS

Total fertility rate (children per woman, 2005)	5.6
Under-5 mortality rate (per 1,000 live births, 2004)	24
Physicians (per 1,000 head, 2005, official estimate)	1.62
Hospital beds (per 1,000 head, 2006, official estimate)	1.4
Access to water (% of persons, 2004)	92
Access to sanitation (% of persons, 2004)	73
Human Development Index (2005): ranking	106
Human Development Index (2005): value	0.731

For other sources and definitions, see explanatory note on p. vi.

Agriculture

PRINCIPAL CROPS
('000 metric tons)

	2003	2004	2005
Wheat	44.9	46.3	44.7
Barley	21.4	14.7	22.2
Potatoes	56.6	41.1	54.8
Sweet potatoes	4.9	5.0	5.0
Olives	141.4	141.4	85.8
Cabbages	17.9	18.1	18.3
Tomatoes	197.9	205.8	212.1
Cauliflower	19.7	21.2	20.9
Cucumbers and gherkins	152.8	141.6	132.1
Aubergines (Eggplants)	41.2	48.7	56.0
Dry onions	18.7	26.1	36.2
Watermelons	11.3	12.4	16.5
Grapes	57.1	56.3	66.2
Plums	7.9	9.8	6.5
Oranges	46.8	41.2	37.7
Tangerines, mandarins, clementines and satsumas	8.4	7.3	7.2
Lemons and limes	14.6	13.5	12.9
Grapefruit and pomelos	2.1	1.9	1.6
Bananas	7.8	9.1	9.8
Strawberries	5.7	7.6	6.0

Aggregate production ('000 metric tons, may include official, semi-official or estimated data): Total cereals 68.1 in 2003, 62.4 in 2004, 68.2 in 2005; Total roots and tubers 63.9 in 2003, 49.0 in 2004, 62.3 in 2005; Total vegetables (incl. melons) 580.1 in 2003, 608.3 in 2004, 619.3 in 2005; Total fruits (excl. melons) 185.5 in 2003, 188.4 in 2004, 183.7 in 2005.

Note: Data for 2006 were not available.

Source: FAO.

LIVESTOCK
('000 head)

	2003	2004	2005
Cattle	33.2	32.4	33.7
Sheep	828.7	811.9	803.2
Goats	392.1	398.8	371.2
Chickens*	10.0	9.0	11.0

* FAO estimates.

Note: Data for 2006 were not available.

Source: FAO.

Fishing

GAZA STRIP
(metric tons, live weight)

	2003	2004	2005
Bogue	33	29	27
Jack and horse mackerels	75	82	88
Sardinellas	620	2,080	928
Chub mackerel	124	113	82
Cuttlefish and bobtail squids	80	66	73
Total catch (incl. others)	1,508	2,951	1,805

Source: FAO.

Finance

CURRENCY AND EXCHANGE RATES

Monetary Units

At present there is no domestic Palestinian currency in use. The Israeli shekel, the Jordanian dinar and the US dollar all circulate within the West Bank and the Gaza Strip.

BUDGET OF THE PALESTINIAN AUTHORITY
(US $ million, estimates)

Revenue	2002	2003*	2004†
Domestic revenue	185	259	298
Revenue clearances‡	150	442	508
Total	335	701	806

Expenditure	2002	2003*	2004†
Central administration	141.8	128.0	109.2
Public security and order	310.4	392.1	433.9
Financial affairs	292.5	352.2	410.7
Foreign affairs	13.8	17.2	25.6
Economic development	35.8	39.8	43.1
Social services	340.5	432.9	526.6
Cultural and information services	25.4	29.2	32.8
Transport and communication services	10.4	12.1	14.2
Total	1,170.6	1,403.5	1,596.1

* Revised estimates.
† Provisional figures.
‡ Figures refer to an apportionment of an agreed pool of selected tax revenues arising as a result of the de facto customs union between Israel and the Palestinian territories. Israel is the collecting agent for these receipts and periodically makes transfers to the Palestinian Authority.

Source: Ministry of Finance, Ramallah.

COST OF LIVING
(Consumer Price Index; base: 1996 = 100)

	2004	2005	2006
Food	132.3	137.3	144.0
Beverages and tobacco	154.1	162.7	168.1
Textiles, clothing and footwear	127.4	129.5	130.3
Housing	152.0	158.4	163.0
All items (incl. others)	141.9	146.8	152.3

2007: All items 156.4.

PALESTINIAN AUTONOMOUS AREAS

NATIONAL ACCOUNTS
(US $ million at current prices, preliminary figures)

Expenditure on the Gross Domestic Product

	2001	2002	2003
Final consumption expenditure	5,697.9	5,507.7	5,376.3
Households	4,222.3	4,140.4	4,131.7
Non-profit institutions serving households	149.5	144.3	116.4
General government	1,326.1	1,223.0	1,128.2
Gross capital formation	1,186.2	727.2	1,127.2
Gross fixed capital formation	1,160.2	698.6	1,118.3
Changes in inventories	26.0	28.6	8.9
Statistical discrepancy*	−8.1	−15.5	—
Total domestic expenditure	6,876.0	6,219.4	6,503.5
Net exports and imports of goods and services	−2,550.3	−2,050.2	−2,338.2
GDP in purchasers' values	4,325.7	4,169.3	4,165.3

* Referring to the difference between the sum of the expenditure components and official estimates of GDP, compiled from the production approach.

Gross Domestic Product by Economic Activity

	2002	2003	2004
Agriculture and fishing	387.1	422.1	403.0
Mining, manufacturing, electricity and water	636.1	489.7	586.0
Construction	111.7	145.2	188.8
Wholesale and retail trade	460.6	378.6	401.1
Transport, storage and communications	454.7	378.5	315.9
Financial intermediation	146.5	139.6	139.5
Public administration and defence	523.9	647.6	653.9
Domestic services of households	8.6	8.7	7.6
Public-owned enterprises	142.9	83.7	—*
Other services	1,005.3	975.5	1,071.5
Sub-total	3,877.4	3,669.2	3,767.3
Financial intermediation services indirectly measured	−109.6	−118.9	−115.6
Customs duties	184.2	144.9	216.7
VAT on imports (net)	217.2	470.3	262.8
GDP in purchasers' values	4,169.3	4,165.3	4,131.2

* Value added by public-owned enterprises in 2004 was distributed by contribution to each activity.

BALANCE OF PAYMENTS
(US $ million, preliminary estimates)

	2003	2004	2005
Exports of goods f.o.b.	326.6	404.4	411.6
Imports of goods f.o.b.	−1,825.8	−2,769.9	−3,049.5
Trade balance	−1,499.3	−2,365.5	−2,638.0
Exports of services	77.9	181.4	265.3
Imports of services	−676.1	−489.8	−487.4
Balance on goods and services	−2,097.5	−2,674.0	−2,860.1
Other income received (net)	481.4	426.1	573.3
Balance on goods, services and income	−1,616.1	−2,247.9	−2,286.8
Current transfers (net)	1,417.8	764.6	1,179.8
Current balance	−198.3	−1,483.3	−1,107.1
Capital account (net)	413.7	670.3	422.2
Direct investment abroad (net)	−367.8	99.7	37.8
Portfolio investment (net)	−177.3	61.9	2.4
Other investment (net)	874.6	587.0	616.5
Net errors and omissions	−402.1	91.7	2.6
Overall balance	142.7	27.4	−25.7

External Trade

PRINCIPAL COMMODITIES
(US $ million)

Imports c.i.f.*	2003	2004	2005
Food and live animals	305.2	470.3	452.1
Beverages and tobacco	90.6	108.7	102.4
Crude materials (inedible) except fuels	62.7	47.9	62.0
Mineral fuels, lubricants, etc.	425.7	660.1	718.3
Animal and vegetable oils and fats	37.9	20.8	20.3
Chemicals and related products	182.4	201.8	222.9
Basic manufactures	353.1	449.6	490.4
Machinery and transport equipment	211.9	281.6	358.6
Miscellaneous manufactured articles	124.4	132.4	147.5
Commodities not classified elsewhere	6.4	0.3	92.4
Total	1,800.3	2,373.2	2,666.8

Exports f.o.b.	2003	2004	2005
Food and live animals	34.2	35.9	36.2
Beverages and tobacco	13.0	17.2	14.3
Crude materials (inedible) except fuels	13.4	11.1	13.2
Mineral fuels, lubricants, etc.	3.9	10.5	12.2
Animal and vegetable oils and fats	7.2	9.9	12.3
Chemicals and related products	26.0	29.4	28.9
Basic manufactures	110.5	122.7	129.8
Machinery and transport equipment	14.8	14.8	18.5
Miscellaneous manufactured articles	51.0	61.1	64.6
Other commodities and transactions	5.7	0.3	5.5
Total	279.7	312.7	335.4

* Figures refer to imports from Israel only.

Transport

ROAD TRAFFIC
(registered motor vehicles holding Palestinian licence, 2006)

	West Bank	Gaza Strip
Private cars	36,323	42,372
Taxis	7,432	3,392
Buses	950	219
Trucks and commercial cars	12,013	10,788
Motorcycles and mopeds	29	219
Tractors	615	1,416

Tourism

ARRIVALS OF VISITORS AT HOTELS*

	2004	2005	2006
Total	100,184	131,908	151,801†

* Including Palestinians.
† Preliminary.

2005: Total guest nights in hotels 350,220 (Palestinians 98,862; European Union members 109,347; Israelis 30,400; Asians 49,179).

2006: Total guest nights in hotels 383,603 (Palestinians 52,309; European Union members 142,980; Israelis 44,602; Asians 47,421).

PALESTINIAN AUTONOMOUS AREAS

Communications Media

	2004	2005	2006
Telephones ('000 main lines in use)	357.3	349.0	341.3
Mobile cellular telephones ('000 subscribers)	974.3	1,094.6	821.8
Personal computers ('000 in use)	169	169	n.a.
Internet users ('000)	160	243	266
Broadband subscribers ('000)	—	7.7	28.8

Source: International Telecommunication Union.

Book production (1996): 114 titles; 571,000 copies (Source: UNESCO, *Statistical Yearbook*).

Daily newspapers (titles): 2 in 2004.

Non-daily newspapers (titles): 11 in 2004.

Education

(2005/06, unless otherwise indicated)

	Institutions	Teachers	Students
Pre-primary	935	2,967	77,142
Primary	1,537	40,957	944,713
Secondary	740		122,776
Higher:[*]			
universities, etc.	16	3,731	129,137
other	22	459	9,002

[*] 2004/05.

Adult literacy rate (official estimates): 92.4% (males 96.7%; females 88.0%) in 2004.

Directory

Administration

PALESTINIAN NATIONAL AUTHORITY

Appointed in May 1994, the Palestinian National Authority (PNA), generally known internationally as the Palestinian Authority (PA), has assumed some of the civil responsibilities formerly exercised by the Israeli Civil Administration in the Gaza Strip and parts of the West Bank.

Executive President: MAHMUD ABBAS (assumed office 15 January 2005).

CABINET
(April 2008)

Following the seizure of control by militants of the Islamic Resistance Movement (Hamas) in the Gaza Strip, on 14 June 2007 President Mahmud Abbas dissolved the national unity administration under the premiership of Ismail Haniya of Hamas and appointed Dr Salam Fayyad, an independent, as Prime Minister. An Emergency Cabinet, consisting principally of independents (Ind.), as well as one representative of the Fatah movement, was sworn in on 17 June. Upon the expiry of the 30-day state of emergency, on 13 July President Abbas appointed three new ministers to the Cabinet, which was to function as a caretaker administration under Fayyad's premiership. Hamas refused to recognize the legitimacy of this interim administration, as it had the Emergency Cabinet.

Prime Minister and Minister of Finance: Dr SALAM KHALED ABDULLAH FAYYAD (Ind.).

Minister of the Interior and of Civil Affairs: ABD AR-RAZZAQ AL-YAHYA (Fatah).

Minister of Foreign Affairs and of Information: RIYAD NAJIB AL-MALIKI (Ind.).

Minister of Local Government: ZIAD ABDULLAH AL-BANDAK (Ind.).

Minister of Tourism and Antiquities, and of Women's Affairs: KHOULOUD IHADEB DEIBAS (Ind.).

Minister of National Economy, of Public Works and Housing, and of Telecommunications and Information Technology: MUHAMMAD KAMAL IBRAHIM HASSOUNEH (Ind.).

Minister of Education and Higher Education, and of Culture: LAMIS AL-ALAMI (Ind.).

Minister of Planning and of Labour: Dr SAMIR ABDULLAH (Ind.).

Minister of Health: Dr FATHI ABDULLAH ABU MUGHLI (Ind.).

Minister of Awqaf (Religious Endowments) and of Social Affairs: Sheikh JAMAL MUHAMMAD AHMAD BAWATINA (Ind.).

Minister of Transport: MASHHUR MUHAMMAD ABU DAQQA (Ind.).

Minister of Prisoners' Affairs: ASHRAF EID AL-AJRAMI (Ind.).

Minister of Agriculture: MAHMUD SIDQI AL-HABBASH (Ind.).

Minister of Justice: ALI AHMAD SALIM KHASHAN (Ind.).

Minister of Youth and Sports: TAHANI SULAYMAN MAHMUD ABU DAQQA (Ind.).

MINISTRIES

Office of the President: Ramallah.

Ministry of Agriculture: POB 197, Ramallah; tel. (2) 2961080; fax (2) 2961212; e-mail moa@planet.edu.

Ministry of Awqaf (Religious Endowments): POB 17412, Jerusalem; tel. (2) 6282085; fax (2) 2986401.

Ministry of Civil Affairs: Ramallah; tel. (2) 2987336; fax (2) 2987335.

Ministry of Culture: POB 147, Ramallah; tel. (2) 2986205; fax (2) 2986204.

Ministry of Education and Higher Education: POB 576, Al-Masioun, Ramallah; POB 5285, Al-Wihda St, Gaza; tel. (2) 2983200; fax (2) 2983222; e-mail irp@mohe.gov.ps; tel. (8) 2865200; fax (8) 2865909; e-mail moehe@gov.ps; internet www.moe.gov.ps.

Ministry of Environmental Affairs: POB 3841, Ramallah; Ath-Thawra St, Gaza; tel. (2) 2403495; fax (2) 2403494; e-mail menawb@gov.ps; tel. (7) 2822000; fax (7) 2847198; e-mail environment@gov.ps; internet www.mena.gov.ps.

Ministry of Finance: POB 795, Sateh Marhaba, Al-Birah/Ramallah; POB 4007, Gaza; tel. (2) 2400650; fax (2) 2400595; tel. (8) 2826188; fax (8) 2820696; e-mail cbomof@palnet.com; internet www.mof.gov.ps.

Ministry of Foreign Affairs: POB 1336, Ramallah; POB 4017, Gaza; tel. (2) 2405040; fax (2) 2403772; tel. (8) 2829260; fax (8) 2868971; e-mail info@mofa.gov.ps; internet www.mofa.gov.ps.

Ministry of Health: POB 14, al-Mukhtar St, Nablus; POB 1035, Abu Khadra Center, Gaza; tel. (9) 2384772; fax (9) 2384777; e-mail moh@gov.ps; tel. (8) 2829173; fax (8) 2826295; internet www.moh.gov.ps.

Ministry of Industry: POB 2073, Ramallah; POB 4053, Gaza; tel. (2) 2987641; fax (2) 2987640; tel. (8) 2826463; fax (8) 2824884; e-mail industry_wb@gov.ps.

Ministry of Information: Al-Masyoun Area, Ramallah; tel. (2) 2954042; fax (2)2954043; e-mail minfo@minfo.gov.ps; internet www.minfo.gov.ps.

Ministry of the Interior: Gaza; tel. (8) 2829185; fax (8) 2862500.

Ministry of Jerusalem Affairs: POB 20479, Jerusalem; tel. (2) 6273330; fax (2) 6286820.

Ministry of Justice: POB 267, Ramallah; POB 1012, Gaza; tel. (2) 2987661; fax (2) 2974491; e-mail info@moj.gov.ps; internet www.moj.gov.ps.

Ministry of Labour: POB 350, Al-Irsal St, Ramallah; tel. (2) 2900375; fax (2) 2900607; e-mail info@mol.pna.org; internet www.mol.gov.ps.

Ministry of Local Government: POB 731, Albaloo, Al-Birah/Ramallah; Gaza; tel. (2) 2401092; fax (2) 2401091; tel. (8) 2820272; fax (8) 2828474; e-mail info@molg.gov.ps; internet www.molg.gov.ps.

Ministry of National Economy: Umm ash-Sharayet, Ramallah; Maqqusi Bldg, An-Nasser St, Gaza; tel. (2) 2981218; fax (2) 2981207; tel. (8) 2874146; fax (8) 2874145; e-mail info@met.gov.ps; internet www.met.gov.ps.

Ministry of Planning: POB 4557, Al-Birah/Ramallah; POB 4017, Gaza; tel. (2) 2973010; fax (2) 2973012; tel. (8) 2828825; fax (8) 2830509; e-mail mop@gov.ps; internet www.mop.gov.ps.

Ministry of Public Works and Housing: Gaza; tel. (8) 2829232; fax (8) 2823653; e-mail mopgaza@palnet.com.

Ministry of Social Affairs: POB 3525, Ramallah; tel. (2) 2986181; fax (2) 2985239; e-mail Msa@hally.net; internet www.mosa.gov.ps.

Ministry of Supply: Gaza; tel. (8) 2824324; fax (8) 2826430.

PALESTINIAN AUTONOMOUS AREAS

Ministry of Telecommunications and Information Technology: Ramallah; Gaza; tel. (2) 2409354; fax (2) 2409352; tel. (8) 2829171; fax (8) 2824555; e-mail mdiwan@mtit.gov.ps; internet www.mtit.gov.ps.

Ministry of Tourism and Antiquities: POB 534, Manger St, Bethlehem; tel. (2) 2741581; fax (2) 2743753; e-mail mota@visit-palestine.com; internet www.visit-palestine.com.

Ministry of Transport: POB 399, Ramallah; tel. (2) 2986945; fax (2) 2986943.

Ministry of Women's Affairs: Al-Birah/Ramallah; tel. (2) 2403315; e-mail contactus@mowa.ps; internet www.mowa.gov.ps.

Ministry of Youth and Sports: POB 52, Irsal St, Ramallah; POB 1416, Rimal Izz ed-Din Qassam St, Gaza; tel. (2) 2985983; fax (2) 2985991; tel. (8) 2826668; fax (8) 2822736; e-mail youth@p-ol.com; internet www.mys.gov.ps.

President and Legislature

PRESIDENT

Election, 9 January 2005

Candidates	Votes	%
Mahmud Abbas (Fatah)	501,448	62.52
Mustafa Barghouthi (Ind.)	156,227	19.48
Tayseer Khalid (DFLP)	26,848	3.35
Abd al-Halim al-Ashqar (Ind.)	22,171	2.76
Bassam es-Salhi (PPP)	21,429	2.67
As-Said Baraka (Ind.)	10,406	1.30
Abd al-Karim Shbeir (Ind.)	5,717	0.71
Invalid votes	57,831	7.21
Total	**802,077**	**100.00**

PALESTINIAN LEGISLATIVE COUNCIL

Speaker: Dr AZIZ DUWEIK.

General Election, 25 January 2006

Parties, Lists and Coalitions	Majority system	Proportional system	Total
Change and Reform*	29	45	74
Fatah	28	17	45
Martyr Abu Ali Moustafa†	3	0	3
The Third Way	2	0	2
The Alternative‡	2	0	2
Independent Palestine§	2	0	2
Independents	0	4	4
Total	**66**	**66**	**132**

* The Islamic Resistance Movement (Hamas) contested the elections as Change and Reform.
† The Popular Front for the Liberation of Palestine contested the elections as Martyr Abu Ali Moustafa.
‡ Electoral list comprising the Palestinian Democratic Union, the Coalition of the Democratic Front (representing the Democratic Front for the Liberation of Palestine) and the Palestinian People's Party.
§ Coalition comprising independents and representatives of the Palestinian National Initiative.

On 18 June 2005 the Palestinian Legislative Council (PLC) had approved a new election law, adopting a 'mixed' electoral system for forthcoming legislative polls: the system combined a 'majority system' and a system of proportional representation. Under the majority system, according to which candidates were elected to 66 of the PLC's 132 seats, the Palestinian territories were divided into 16 electoral districts (11 in the West Bank and five in the Gaza Strip), and candidates contested seats allocated to their district in proportion to the size of its population. The remaining 66 deputies were elected to the PLC by the system of proportional representation, under which the Palestinian enclaves were treated as one electoral district, and voters chose between nation-wide lists of political organizations and coalitions ('party lists'). Six of the seats were reserved for Christians. All deputies elected to the PLC automatically became members of the Palestine National Council (see the Palestinian Liberation Organization).

Election Commission

Central Elections Commission (CEC): POB 2319, Qasr al-Murjan Bldg, Al-Balou, nr Jawwal Circle, Ramallah; tel. (2) 2969700; fax (2) 2969712; e-mail info@elections.ps; internet www.elections.ps; f. 2002; independent; comprises nine mems, appointed by the Exec. Pres. of the PA; Chair. Dr HANNA NASIR; Sec.-Gen. Dr RAMI HAMDALLAH.

Political Organizations

Alliance of Palestinian Forces: f. 1994; 10 members representing the PFLP, the DFLP, the PLF, the PPSF, the Palestine Revolutionary Communist Party and the PFLP—GC; opposes the Declaration of Principles on Palestinian Self-Rule signed by Israel and the PLO in September 1993, and subsequent agreements concluded within its framework (the 'Oslo accords'). The PFLP and DFLP left the Alliance in 1996. The **Fatah Revolutionary Council**, headed by Sabri Khalil al-Banna, alias 'Abu Nidal', split from Fatah in 1973. Its headquarters were formerly in Baghdad, Iraq, but the office was closed down and its staff expelled from the country by the Iraqi authorities in November 1983; a new base was established in Damascus, Syria, in December. Al-Banna was readmitted to Iraq in 1984, having fled Syria. With 'Abu Musa' (whose rebel Fatah group is called **Al-Intifada** or 'Uprising'), 'Abu Nidal' formed a joint rebel Fatah command in February 1985, and both had offices in Damascus until June 1987, when those of 'Abu Nidal' were closed by the Syrian Government. Forces loyal to 'Abu Nidal' surrendered to Fatah forces at the Rashidiyeh Palestinian refugee camp near Tyre, northern Lebanon, in 1990. 'Abu Nidal' was reportedly found dead in Baghdad in August 2002.

Arab Liberation Front (ALF): Ramallah; f. 1969; fmrly supported by Iraq's Arab Baath Socialist Party under the leadership of former President Saddam Hussain; member of the PLO; opposes Oslo accords; Sec.-Gen. RAKAD SALIM (imprisoned in 2002).

Democratic Front for the Liberation of Palestine (DFLP) (Al-Jabha ad-Dimuqratiyya li-Tahrir Filastin): Damascus, Syria; tel. (11) 4448993; fax (11) 4442380; Ramallah; tel. (2) 2954438; fax (2) 2980401; e-mail dflp-palestine@dflp-palestine.org; internet www.dflp-palestine.org; f. 1969 following split with PFLP; Marxist-Leninist; contested Jan. 2006 legislative elections on The Alternative electoral list as the Coalition of the Democratic Front; Sec.-Gen. NAIF HAWATMEH (Damascus).

Fatah (Harakat at-Tahrir al-Watani al-Filasini—Palestine National Liberation Movement): e-mail fateh@fateh.net; internet www.fateh.net; f. 1957; militant group which became the single largest Palestinian organization and strongest faction in both the administration and Palestinian Legislative Council until the legislative elections of Jan. 2006; leadership is nominally shared by the members of the Central Committee, who were elected at Fatah's Fifth General Conference on 8 August 1989; however, some of those elected to the Central Committee have since died; Chair. of Central Cttee FAROUK KADDOUMI (Tunis, Tunisia).

Islamic Jihad (Al-Jihad al-Islami): Damascus, Syria; f. 1979–80 by Palestinian students in Egypt; militant Islamist; opposed to the Oslo accords; Sec.-Gen. RAMADAN ABDULLAH SHALLAH.

Islamic Resistance Movement (Hamas—Harakat al-Muqawama al-Islamiyya): Gaza; Damascus, Syria; f. 1987; originally welfare organization Mujama (f. 1973) led by the late Sheikh AHMAD YASSIN (killed by Israeli forces in March 2004); militant Islamist; opposes the Oslo accords and does not recognize the PA as the sole national authority in the Palestinian territories; following the killing by Israeli forces of Hamas's leader in the Gaza Strip, Abd al-Aziz ar-Rantisi, in April 2004, the group announced that it was adopting a policy of 'collective leadership'; contested Jan. 2006 legislative elections as Change and Reform; Head of Political Bureau KHALID MESHAAL (Damascus); Gen. Commdr of military wing, Izz ad-Din al-Qassam Brigades, MUHAMMAD DEIF (in hiding from the Israeli authorities since 1992, though presumed to be in Gaza).

Palestine Liberation Front (PLF): f. 1977 following split with PFLP—GC; the PLF split into three factions in the early 1980s, all of which retained the name PLF; one faction (Leader MUHAMMAD 'ABU' ABBAS) was based in Tunis, Tunisia, and Baghdad, Iraq, and remained nominally loyal to Yasser Arafat; the second faction (Leader TALAAT YAQOUB) belonged to the anti-Arafat National Salvation Front and opened offices in Damascus, Syria, and Libya; a third group derived from the PLF was reportedly formed by its Central Cttee Secretary, ABD AL-FATTAH GHANIM, in June 1986; the factions of Yaqoub and Ghanim were reconciled in early 1985; at the 18th session of the PNC a programme for the unification of the PLF was announced, with Yaqoub (died November 1988) named as Secretary-General and 'Abu Abbas' appointed to the PLO Executive Committee, while unification talks were held. The merging of the two factions was announced in June 1987, with Abu Abbas becoming Deputy Secretary-General. Abu Abbas was apprehended by US-led coalition forces in Iraq in April 2003, and reportedly died of natural causes in March 2004 while still in US custody; Sec.-Gen. ABU NIDAL AL-ASHQAR.

Palestine Liberation Organization (PLO) (Munazzimat at-Tahrir al-Filastiniyya): Negotiations Affairs Dept, POB 4120, Ramallah; tel. (2) 2963741; fax (2) 2963740; internet www.nad-plo.org; f. 1964; the supreme organ of the PLO is the Palestine National Council (PNC; Pres. SALIM AZ-ZA'NUN), while the PLO Executive Committee (Chair. MAHMUD ABBAS; Sec.-Gen. FAROUK KADDOUMI) deals with day-to-day business. Fatah (the Palestine National Liberation Movement) joined the PNC in 1968, and all the guerrilla organizations joined the Council in 1969. In 1973 the Palestinian Central Council (PCC; Chair. SALIM AZ-ZA'NUN) was established to act as an intermediary between the PNC and the Executive Committee. The Council meets when the PNC is not in session and approves major policy decisions on its behalf; Chair. MAHMUD ABBAS.

Palestine Revolutionary Communist Party (PRCP) (Al-Hizb ash-Shuyu'i ath-Thawri al-Filastini): principally based in Lebanon; promotes armed struggle in order to achieve its aims; Sec.-Gen. ARABI AWAD.

Palestinian Democratic Union (FIDA): POB 247, Ramallah; fax (2) 2954071; e-mail fida@palnet.com; internet www.fida.ps; f. 1990 following split from the DFLP; contested Jan. 2006 legislative elections on The Alternative electoral list; Leader YASSER ABD AR-RABBUH; Sec.-Gen. SALEH RA'FAT.

Palestinian National Initiative (Al-Mubadara): Ramallah; tel. (5) 9293006; e-mail almubadara@almubadara.org; internet www.almubadara.org; f. 2002; seeks peaceful resolution of conflict with Israel through establishment of an independent, viable and democratic Palestinian state, with East Jerusalem as its capital; advocates reform of internal political structures, and aims to fight corruption and injustice, and to uphold citizens' rights; contested Jan. 2006 legislative elections as part of the Independent Palestine coalition; Gen. Sec. Dr MUSTAFA BARGHOUTHI.

Palestinian People's Party (PPP) (Hezb ash-Sha'ab): Ramallah; tel. (2) 2963593; fax (2) 2963592; e-mail shaab@palpeople.org; internet www.palpeople.org; f. 1921 as Palestine Communist Party; adopted current name in 1991; admitted to the PNC at its 18th session in 1987; contested Jan. 2006 legislative elections on The Alternative electoral list; Sec.-Gen. BASSAM ES-SALHI.

Palestinian Popular Struggle Front (PPSF) (Jabhat an-Nidal ash-Sha'biyya al-Filastiniyya): f. 1967; has reportedly split into two factions which either support or oppose the PA; the pro-PA faction (Leader SAMIR GHOSHEH) is based in the West Bank; the anti-PA faction (Leader KHALID ABD AL-MAJID) is based in Damascus, Syria.

Popular Front for the Liberation of Palestine (PFLP) (Al-Jabha ash-Sha'biyya li-Tahrir Filastin): Damascus, Syria; internet www.pflp.ps; f. 1967; Marxist-Leninist; publ. Democratic Palestine (English; monthly); contested Jan. 2006 legislative elections as Martyr Abu Ali Moustafa; Sec.-Gen. AHMAD SAADAT (imprisoned in 2002).

Popular Front for the Liberation of Palestine—General Command (PFLP—GC): Damascus, Syria; f. 1968 following split from the PFLP; pro-Syrian; Leader AHMAD JIBRIL.

Popular Front for the Liberation of Palestine—National General Command: Amman, Jordan; split from the PFLP—GC in 1999; aims to co-operate with the PA; Leader ATIF YUNUS.

As-Saiqa (Thunderbolt, or Vanguard of the Popular Liberation War): f. 1968; Syrian-backed; pan-Arab; opposed to the Oslo accords; Sec.-Gen. ISSAM AL-QADI.

The formation of the **Right Movement for Championing the Palestinian People's Sons** by former members of Hamas was announced in April 1995. The movement, based in Gaza City, was reported to support the PA. The **Al-Aqsa Martyrs Brigades** (internet www.kataebaqsa.org), consisting of a number of Fatah-affiliated activists, emerged soon after the start of the al-Aqsa intifada in September 2000, and have carried out attacks against Israeli targets in Israel, the West Bank and Gaza Strip.

Diplomatic Representation

Countries with which the PLO maintains diplomatic relations include:

Afghanistan, Albania, Algeria, Angola, Austria, Bahrain, Bangladesh, Benin, Bhutan, Botswana, Brunei, Bulgaria, Burkina Faso, Burundi, Cambodia, Cameroon, Cape Verde, Central African Republic, Chad, China (People's Rep.), Comoros, Congo (Dem. Rep.), Congo (Rep.), Costa Rica, Cuba, Cyprus, Czech Republic, Djibouti, Egypt, Equatorial Guinea, Ethiopia, Gabon, Gambia, Ghana, Guinea, Guinea-Bissau, Hungary, India, Indonesia, Iran, Iraq, Jordan, Korea (Dem. People's Rep.), Kuwait, Laos, Lebanon, Libya, Madagascar, Malaysia, Maldives, Mali, Malta, Mauritania, Mauritius, Mongolia, Morocco, Mozambique, Nepal, Nicaragua, Niger, Nigeria, Norway, Oman, Pakistan, Philippines, Poland, Qatar, Romania, Russia, Rwanda, São Tomé and Príncipe, Saudi Arabia, Senegal, Serbia, Seychelles, Sierra Leone, Somalia, Sri Lanka, Sudan, Swaziland, Sweden, Tanzania, Togo, Tunisia, Turkey, Uganda, the United Arab Emirates (UAE), Uzbekistan, Vanuatu, the Vatican City, Viet Nam, Yemen, Zambia and Zimbabwe.

The following states, while they do not recognize the State of Palestine, allow the PLO to maintain a regional office: Belgium, Brazil, France, Germany, Greece, Italy, Japan, the Netherlands, Portugal, Spain, Switzerland and the United Kingdom.

A Palestinian passport has been available for residents of the Gaza Strip and the Jericho area only since April 1995. In September of that year the passport was recognized by 29 states, including: Algeria, Bahrain, Bulgaria, China (People's Rep.), Cyprus, Egypt, France, Germany, Greece, India, Israel, Jordan, Malta, Morocco, the Netherlands, Pakistan, Qatar, Romania, Saudi Arabia, South Africa, Spain, Sweden, Switzerland, Tunisia, Turkey, the UAE, the United Kingdom and the USA.

Judicial System

In the Gaza Strip, the West Bank towns of Jericho, Nablus, Ramallah, Jenin, Tulkarm, Qalqilya, Bethlehem and Hebron, and in other, smaller population centres in the West Bank, the PA has assumed limited jurisdiction with regard to civil affairs. However, the situation is confused owing to the various and sometimes conflicting legal systems which have operated in the territories occupied by Israel in 1967: Israeli military and civilian law; Jordanian law; and acts, orders-in-council and ordinances that remain from the period of the British Mandate in Palestine. Religious and military courts have been established under the auspices of the PA. In February 1995 the PA established a Higher State Security Court in Gaza to decide on security crimes both inside and outside the PA's area of jurisdiction; and to implement all valid Palestinian laws, regulations, rules and orders in accordance with Article 69 of the Constitutional Law of the Gaza Strip of 5 March 1962.

General Prosecutor of the PA: AHMAD AL-MOGHANI.

Religion

The vast majority of Palestinians in the West Bank and Gaza are Muslims, while a small (and declining) minority are Christians of the Greek Orthodox and Roman Catholic rites.

ISLAM

The PA-appointed Grand Mufti of Jerusalem and the Palestinian Lands is the most senior Muslim cleric in the Palestinian territories.

Mufti of Jerusalem: Sheikh MUHAMMAD AHMAD HUSSEIN.

CHRISTIANITY

The Roman Catholic Church

Latin Rite

The Patriarchate of Jerusalem covers Israel and the Occupied Territories, the Palestinian Autonomous Areas, Jordan and Cyprus. At 31 December 2005 there were an estimated 78,215 adherents.

Patriarchate of Jerusalem: Patriarcat Latin, POB 14152, Jerusalem 91141; tel. (2) 6282323; fax (2) 6271652; e-mail chancellery@latinpat.org; internet www.lpj.org; Patriarch His Beatitude MICHEL SABBAH; Archbishop Coadjutor FOUAD TWAL; Vicar-General for Jerusalem KAMAL HANNA BATHISH (Titular Bishop of Jericho); Vicar-General for Israel GIACINTO-BOULOS MARCUZZO (Titular Bishop of Emmaus Nicopolis); Coadjutor Of the Patriarch FOUAD TWAL.

Melkite Rite

The Greek-Melkite Patriarch of Antioch and all the East, of Alexandria and of Jerusalem (GRÉGOIRE III LAHAM) is resident in Damascus, Syria.

Patriarchal Vicariate of Jerusalem: Patriarcat Grec-Melkite Catholique, POB 14130, Porte de Jaffa, Jerusalem 91141; tel. (2) 6282023; fax (2) 6289606; e-mail gcpjer@p-ol.com; about 3,300 adherents (31 December 2005); Protosyncellus Archim. Archbishop GEORGES MICHEL BAKAR.

The Greek Orthodox Church

The Patriarchate of Jerusalem contains an estimated 260,000 adherents in Israel and the Occupied Territories, the Palestinian Autonomous Areas, Jordan, Kuwait, the UAE and Saudi Arabia.

PALESTINIAN AUTONOMOUS AREAS   *Directory*

Patriarchate of Jerusalem: POB 19632-633, Greek Orthodox Patriarchate St, Old City, Jerusalem; tel. (2) 6274941; fax (2) 6282048; internet www.jerusalem-patriarchate.info; Patriarch THEOPHILOS III.

The Press

NEWSPAPERS

Al-Ayyam: POB 1987, Al-Ayyam St Commercial Area, Ramallah; tel. (2) 2987341; fax (2) 2987342; e-mail info@al-ayyam.com; internet www.al-ayyam.com; f. 1995; weekly; Arabic; Editor-in-Chief AKRAM HANIYAH.

Al-Ayyam al-Arabi: Ramallah; f. 1999; daily newspaper publ. by the PA; Arabic; Editor-in-Chief SALIM SALAMAH.

Filastin ath-Thawra (Palestine of the Revolution): fmrly publ. in Beirut, but resumed publication from Cyprus in November 1982; weekly newspaper of the PLO; Arabic.

Al-Hadaf (The Target): e-mail alhadaf@alhadafmagazine.com; internet www.alhadafmagazine.com; f. 1969 in Beirut, Lebanon; weekly; Arabic; organ of the Popular Front for the Liberation of Palestine.

Al-Hayat al-Jadidah: POB 1822, Ramallah; tel. (2) 2407251; fax (2) 2407250; e-mail info1@alhayat-j.com; internet www.alhayat-j.com; f. 1994; weekly; Arabic; Editor NADIL AMR.

Al-Hourriah (Liberation): e-mail info@alhourriah.org; internet www.alhourriah.org; Arabic; organ of the Democratic Front for the Liberation of Palestine; publ. in Beirut, Lebanon and Damascus, Syria; Editor-in-Chief HAMADEH MU'TASIM.

Al-Istiqlal (Independence): Ath-Thawra St, Gaza City; e-mail alesteqlal@p-i-s.com; weekly; Arabic; organ of Islamic Jihad; Sec. TAWFIQ AS-SAYYID SALIM.

Palestine Times: POB 4195, Al-Birah, Ramallah; tel. (2) 599399033; fax (2) 22972277; e-mail palestimes@ptimes.org; internet www.ptimes.org; f. 2006; monthly; English; privately owned; independent; Editor-in-Chief AHMAD KARMAWI; circ. 5,000; temporary closure in May 2007.

Al-Quds (Jerusalem): POB 19788, Jerusalem; tel. (2) 5833501; fax (2) 5856937; e-mail info@alquds.com; internet www.alquds.com; Arabic; independent; pro-PA; supports peace negotiations; reportedly has largest circulation of all Palestinian newspapers; daily; Editor MAHER AL-ALAMI.

Ar-Risala (Letter): Gaza City; weekly; Arabic; affiliated with the Islamic Resistance Movement (Hamas); Editor-in-Chief GHAZI HAMAD.

Al-Watan: Gaza City; weekly; Arabic; supports Hamas.

PERIODICALS

Filastin (Palestine): Gaza City; e-mail adel@falasteen.com; internet www.falasteen.com; f. 1994; weekly; Arabic.

The Jerusalem Times: POB 51169, 19 Nablus Road, Jerusalem; tel. (2) 6264883; fax (2) 6287893; e-mail webmaster@jerusalem-times.net; internet www.jerusalem-times.net; f. 1994; weekly; English; independent; Chair. of Bd SHUKRI BISHARA; Publr HANNA SINIORA; Man. Editor SAMI KAMAL.

Al-Karmel Magazine: POB 1887 Ramallah; tel. (2) 2965934; fax (2) 2987374; e-mail editor@alkarmel.org; internet www.alkarmel.org; f. 1981 in Beirut, Lebanon; literature; Editor-in-Chief MAHMOUD DARWISH.

Madar: Madar—al-Markaz al-Filastini lil-Dirasat al-Israiliyah, Ramallah; publ. by Madar—The Palestinian Centre for Israeli Studies; political; Editor SALMAN NATOUR.

Palestine Report: Jerusalem Media and Communications Centre, POB 25047, 7 Nablus Rd, Jerusalem; tel. (2) 5819777; fax (2) 5829534; e-mail palreport@palestinereport.org; internet www.jmcc.org; f. 1990; weekly; English; current affairs; publ. by the Jerusalem Media and Communications Centre; Man. Dir OMAR KARMI; Editor-in-Chief JOHARAH BAKER.

Youth Times: POB 50465, Flat 12, 4th Floor, Julani Bldg, Ar-Ram, Jerusalem; tel. (2) 2343428; fax (2) 2343430; e-mail pyalara@pyalara.org; internet www.pyalara.org; f. 1998; monthly; Arabic and English; publ. by the Palestinian Youth Association for Leadership and Rights Activation; Editor-in-Chief HANIYA BITAR.

NEWS AGENCY

Wikalat Anbaa' Filastiniya (WAFA, Palestine News Agency): POB 5300, Gaza City; tel. (8) 2824036; fax (8) 2824046; e-mail edit@wafa.ps; internet www.wafa.ps; official PLO news agency; Editor ZIAD ABD AL-FATTAH.

Publishers

Al-Ayyam Press, Printing, Publishing and Distribution Co: POB 1987, Ramallah; tel. (2) 2987341; fax (2) 2987342; e-mail info@al-ayyam.com; internet www.al-ayyam.com; f. 1995; publishes Al-Ayyam newspaper, books and magazines.

Beit Al-Maqdes for Publishing and Distribution: Ramallah; history, politics, fiction, children's.

Centre for Palestine Research and Studies (CPRS): POB 132, Nablus; tel. (9) 2380383; fax (9) 2380384; f. 1993; history, politics, strategic studies and economics; Dir SAID KANAAN.

Ogarit Centre for Publishing and Distribution: Ramallah; non-fiction, children's.

Broadcasting and Communications

TELECOMMUNICATIONS

Palestine Telecommunications Co PLC (PalTel): POB 1570, Nablus; tel. (9) 2376225; fax (9) 2376227; e-mail paltel@palnet.net; internet www.paltel.ps/index.php; f. 1995; privately owned monopoly; launched cellular telephone service (Palcel, now Jawwal) in 1999; Chair. SABIH T. MASRI; Vice-Chair. and CEO Dr ABD AL-MALEK JABER.

Palestine Cellular Co (Jawwal): POB 3999, Al-Birah; tel. (2) 2402440; fax (2) 2968636; e-mail atyourservice@jawwal.ps; internet www.jawwal.ps/index.php; f. 1999; 100% owned by PalTel; 700,000 subscribers (May 2006), representing some 55% of the Palestinian mobile (cellular) telecommunications market; CEO AMMAR AKER.

BROADCASTING

Palestinian Broadcasting Co (PBC): POB 984, Al-Birah/Ramallah; tel. (2) 2959894; fax (2) 2959893; e-mail pbcinfo@pbc.gov.ps; internet www.pbc.gov.ps; f. 1994; state-controlled; Chair. BASEM ABU SUMAYA.

Sawt Filastin (Voice of Palestine): c/o Police HQ, Jericho; tel. (2) 921220; f. 1994; official radio station of the PA; broadcasts in Arabic from Jericho and Ramallah; Dir RADWAN ABU AYYASH.

Palestine Television: f. 1994; broadcasts from Ramallah and Gaza City; Dir RADWAN ABU AYYASH.

Finance

(cap. = capital; res = reserves; dep. = deposits; brs = branches; m. = million)

BANKING

The Palestine Monetary Authority (PMA) is the financial regulatory body in the Palestinian Autonomous Areas, and is expected to evolve into the Central Bank of Palestine. Three currencies circulate in the Palestinian economy—the Jordanian dinar, the Israeli shekel and the US dollar—and the PMA currently has no right of issue. According to the PMA, there were 22 banks with a total of 137 branches operating in the West Bank and Gaza in mid-2005.

Palestine Monetary Authority (PMA): Nablus Rd, Ramallah; tel. (2) 2409920; fax (2) 2409922; e-mail info@pma.gov.ps; internet www.pma-palestine.org; f. 1994; began licensing, inspection and supervision of the Palestinian and foreign commercial banks operating in the Gaza Strip and the Jericho enclave in the West Bank in July 1995; assumed responsibility for 13 banks in the Palestinian territories over which the Central Bank of Israel had hitherto exercised control in Dec. 1995; Gov. Dr JIHAD AL-WAZIR.

National Banks

Bank of Palestine PLC: POB 50, Omar al-Mukhtar St, Gaza City; tel. (8) 2823272; fax (8) 2865667; e-mail info@bankofpalestine.com; internet www.bankofpalestine.com; f. 1960; cap. US $36.3m., res $9.5m., dep. $527.2m., total assets $602.6m. (Dec. 2006); Chair. and Gen. Man. Dr HANI HASHEM SHAWA; 30 brs and sub-brs in West Bank and Gaza.

Commercial Bank of Palestine PLC: POB 1799, Michael Tanous Bldg, Alawda St, Ramallah; tel. (2) 2954141; fax (2) 2953888; e-mail cbp@cbpal.palnet.com; internet www.cbpal.com; f. 1992; total assets US $73m.; Gen. Man. Dr ANIS AL-HAJJEH; 5 brs.

Palestine International Bank: Al-Birah/Ramallah; tel. (2) 2983300; fax (2) 2983344; e-mail issam@ias.intranets.com; internet www.pibank.net; f. 1997; cap. US $20m.; Chair. OSAMA MUHAMMAD KHADIR; 4 brs.

Investment Banks

Arab Palestinian Investment Bank: POB 1260, Al-Harji Bldg, Ramallah; tel. (2) 2987151; fax (2) 2987125; e-mail apibank@palnet.com; f. 1996; Arab Bank of Jordan has a 51% share; cap. US $15m.; Dir ABD AL-MAJID SHOMAN; Gen. Man. BESHARA DABBAH.

Palestine Investment Bank PLC: POB 3675, Al-Helal St, Al-Birah/Ramallah; tel. (2) 2407880; fax (2) 2407887; e-mail info@pinvbank.com; f. 1995 by the PA; some shareholders based in Jordan and the Gulf states; cap. US $60m.; provides full commercial and investment banking services throughout the West Bank and Gaza; Chair. ABD AL-QADER AHMAD QADI; Man. ZAKARIA GHAWANMEH; 9 brs and 2 rep. offices.

Al-Quds Bank for Development and Investment: POB 2471, Ramallah; tel. (2) 2961750; fax (2) 2961754; e-mail quds@alqudsbank.ps; internet www.alqudsbank.ps; f. 1995; merchant bank; cap. p.u. US $50m.; Gen. Man. AZZAM A. SHAWWA; Dep. Gen. Man. GHAZI A. MUSLEH; 8 brs and 12 offices.

Islamic Banks

Arab Islamic Bank: POB 631, Nablus St, Al-Birah/Ramallah; tel. (2) 2407060; fax (2) 2407065; e-mail aib@aibnk.com; internet www.aibnk.com; f. 1995; cap. US $21.0m., res $2.7m., dep. $156.9m., total assets $187.0m. (Dec. 2005); Chair. WALID T. FAKHOURI; Gen. Man. ATIYEH A. SHANANIER; 8 brs.

Palestine Islamic Bank: POB 1244, Omar al-Mukhtar St, Gaza City; tel. (8) 2827360; fax (8) 2825269; e-mail info@islamicbank.ps; internet www.islamicbank.ps; f. 1996; Chair. and Gen. Man. ABDULLAH HASSAN HUSRI.

STOCK EXCHANGE

Palestine Securities Exchange (PSE): POB 128, 3rd Floor, Al-Qaser Bldg, Nablus; tel. (9) 2345555; fax (9) 2341341; e-mail habulibdeh@p-s-e.com; internet www.p-s-e.com; f. 1997; Chair. and CEO Dr HASSAN ABU LIBDEH.

INSURANCE

A very small insurance industry exists in the West Bank and Gaza.

Ahleia Insurance Group Ltd (AIG): POB 1214, Al-Jalaa Tower, Remal, Gaza; tel. (8) 2824035; fax (8) 2824015; e-mail info@aig.ps; internet www.aig.ps; f. 1994; Chair. and CEO Dr MUHAMMAD AS-SABAWI; 11 brs.

Arab Insurance Establishment Co Ltd (AIE): POB 166, Al-Qasr St, Nablus; tel. (9) 2384040; fax (9) 2384033; e-mail info@aie.com.ps; internet aie.com.ps; f. 1975; Chair. WALID ALOUL.

National Insurance Co: POB 1819, 34 Municipality St, Al-Birah/Ramallah; tel. (2) 2983800; fax (2) 2407460; e-mail nic@nic-pal.com; internet www.nic-pal.com; f. 1992; Chair. MUHAMMAD MAHMOUD MASROUJI; Gen. Man. AZIZ MAHMOUD ABD AL-JAWAD; 8 brs.

DEVELOPMENT FINANCE ORGANIZATIONS

Arab Palestinian Investment Co Ltd: POB 2396, Kharaz Center, Yafa St, Industrial Zone, Ramallah; tel. (2) 2981060; fax (2) 2981065; e-mail apic@apic.com.jo; internet www.apic-pal.com; f. 1995; headquarters in Amman, Jordan; Chair. and CEO TAREK OMAR AGGAD.

Jerusalem Real Estate Investment Co: POB 1876, Ramallah; tel. (2) 2965215; fax (2) 2965217; e-mail jrei@palnet.com; f. 1996; Man. Dir WALID AL-AHMAD.

Palestine Development & Investment Co (PADICO): POB 316, Nablus; tel. (9) 2384480; fax (9) 2384355; e-mail padico@padico.com; internet www.padico.com; f. 1993; 12 subsidiary and affiliate cos; Chair. MUNIB R. AL-MASRI; CEO Dr FAROUK A. ZOUAITER.

Palestine Real Estate Investment Co (Aqaria): POB 4049, Gaza; tel. (8) 2824815; fax (8) 2824845; e-mail aqaria@rannet.com; internet www.aqaria.com; f. 1994; Chair. NABIL SARRAF; Man. MUHAMMAD ISMAEL.

Palestinian Economic Council for Development and Reconstruction (PECDAR): POB 54910, Dahiyat al-Barid, Jerusalem; tel. (2) 2974300; fax (2) 2974331; e-mail info@pecdar.pna.net; internet www.pecdar.org; privately owned; Dir-Gen. Dr MUHAMMAD SHTAYYEH.

Trade and Industry

CHAMBERS OF COMMERCE

Federation of Chambers of Commerce, Industry and Agriculture: tel. (2) 2344923; fax (2) 2344924; e-mail fpccia@palnet.com; internet www.pal-chambers.org; f. 1989; 14 chambers, 32,000 mems.

Bethlehem Chamber of Commerce and Industry: POB 59, Bethlehem; tel. (2) 2742742; fax (2) 2764402; e-mail bcham@palnet.com; internet www.pal-chambers.org/chambers/bethlehem.html; f. 1952; 2,500 mems; Chair. of Bd SAMIR HAZBOUN.

Gaza Chamber of Commerce, Industry and Agriculture: POB 33, Sabra Quarter, Gaza; tel. and fax (8) 2864588; e-mail gazacham@palnet.com; internet www.gazacham.ps; f. 1954; Chair. MUHAMMAD QUDWAH; Man. Dir BASSAM MORTAJA; 14,000 mems.

Hebron Chamber of Commerce and Industry: POB 272, Hebron; tel. (2) 2228218; fax (2) 2227490; e-mail info@hebroncci.org; internet www.hebroncci.org; f. 1954; Chair. HASHEM NATSHEH; 7,350 mems.

Jenin Chamber of Commerce, Industry and Agriculture: Jenin; tel. (4) 2501107; fax (4) 2503388; e-mail jencham@hally.net; internet www.pal-chambers.org/chambers/jenin.html; f. 1953; 3,800 mems.

Jericho Chamber of Commerce, Industry and Agriculture: POB 91, Jericho 00970; tel. (2) 2323313; fax (2) 2322394; e-mail jericho@pal-chambers.org; internet www.pal-chambers.org/chambers/jericho.html; f. 1953; 400 mems; Chair. HAJ MANSOUR SALAYMEH.

Jerusalem Arab Chamber of Commerce and Industry: POB 19151, Jerusalem 91191; tel. (2) 2344923; fax (2) 2344914; e-mail chamber@jerusalemchamber.org; internet www.jerusalemchamber.org; f. 1936; 2,050 mems; Chair. AHMAD HASHEM ZUGHAYAR; Dir AZZAM ABU SAUD.

Nablus Chamber of Commerce and Industry: POB 35, Nablus; tel. (9) 2380335; fax (9) 2377605; e-mail nabluschamber@gmail.com; internet www.pal-chambers.org/chambers/nablus.html; f. 1941; Pres. MA'AZ NABULSI; Dir TAJ ED-DIN BITAR; 7,000 mems.

Palestinian-European Chamber of Commerce: Jerusalem; tel. (2) 894883; Chair. HANNA SINIORA.

Qalqilya Chamber of Commerce, Industry and Agriculture: POB 13, Qalqilya; tel. (9) 2941473; fax (9) 2940164; e-mail chamberq@hally.net; internet www.pal-chambers.org/chambers/qalqilya.html; f. 1972; 1,068 mems.

Ramallah Chamber of Commerce and Industry: POB 256, Al-Birah/Ramallah; tel. (2) 2955052; fax (2) 2984691; e-mail info@ramallahcci.org; internet www.ramallahcci.org; f. 1950; Chair. MUHAMMAD AHMAD AMIN; Vice-Chair. YOUSUF ASH-SHARIF; 4,100 mems.

Salfeet Chamber of Commerce, Industry and Agriculture: Salfit; tel. and fax (9) 2515970; e-mail salfeetchamber@hotmail.com; internet www.salfeetchamber.org; f. 1997; Chair. FOUAD AWAD.

Tulkarm Chamber of Commerce, Industry and Agriculture: POB 51, Tulkarm; tel. (9) 2671010; fax (9) 2675623; e-mail tulkarem@palnet.com; internet www.tulkrmchamber.org; f. 1945; 2,000 mems; Chair. SHUKRI AHMAD JALLAD.

TRADE AND INDUSTRIAL ORGANIZATIONS

Palestinian General Federation of Trade Unions (PGFTU): POB 102, Nablus; tel. (9) 2385136; fax (9) 2384374; e-mail pgftu@pgftu.org; internet www.pgftu.org; f. 1965; Sec.-Gen. SHAHER SAED.

Union of Industrialists: POB 1296, Gaza; tel. (8) 2866222; fax (8) 2862013; Chair. MUHAMMAD YAZIJI.

UTILITIES

Electricity

Palestinian Energy Authority (PEA): POB 3591, Nablus St, Al-Birah/Ramallah; POB 3041, Gaza; tel. (2) 2986190; fax (2) 2986191; tel. (8) 2821702; fax (8) 2824849; e-mail pea@palnet.com; internet pea-pal.tripod.com; f. 1994; Chair. Dr ABD AR-RAHMAN T. HAMAD.

Jerusalem District Electricity Co (JDECO): POB 19118, 15 Salah ed-Din St, Jerusalem; tel. (2) 6283335; fax (2) 6282441; e-mail info@jdeco.net; internet www.jdeco.net.

National Electric Co (NEC): West Bank; f. 2000.

Palestine Electric Co (PEC): Gaza; f. 1999; 33% state-owned; Chair. SAID KHOURY; Man. Dir SAMIR SHAWWA.

Water

Palestinian Water Authority (PWA): POB 1438, Gaza; tel. (8) 2827520; fax (8) 2822697; e-mail pwa@pwa-gaza.org; internet www.pwa-gaza.org; f. 1995; Dir Eng. NABIL ASH-SHARIF.

Transport

CIVIL AVIATION

Palestinian Civil Aviation Authority (PCAA): Yasser Arafat International Airport, POB 8007, Rafah, Gaza; tel. and fax (8)

2827844; e-mail abuhalib@gaza-airport.org; internet www.gaza-airport.org; f. 1994; Gaza International Airport (renamed as above after Arafat's death in Nov. 2004) was formally inaugurated in November 1998 to operate services by Palestinian Airlines (its subsidiary), Egypt Air and Royal Jordanian Airline; Royal Air Maroc began to operate services to Amman, Abu Dhabi, Cairo, Doha, Dubai, Jeddah, Istanbul and Larnaca, and intends to expand its network to Europe; the airport was closed by the Israeli authorities in February 2001 and the runway seriously damaged by Israeli air-strikes in late 2001 and early 2002; Dir-Gen. SALMAN ABU HALIB; Admin. Man. JAMAL AL-MASHHARAWI.

Palestinian Airlines: POB 4043, Gaza; tel. (8) 2822800; fax (8) 2821309; e-mail commercial@palairlines.com; internet www.palairlines.com; f. 1994; state-owned; Dir-Gen. Capt. MANSOUR IBRAHIM; Exec. Dir YASSER IRQAYEQ.

Tourism

Although the tourism industry in the West Bank was virtually destroyed as a result of the 1967 Arab–Israeli War, by the late 1990s the sector was expanding significantly, with a number of hotels being opened or under construction. Much of the tourism in the West Bank centres around the historical and biblical sites of Jerusalem and Bethlehem. However, the renewed outbreak of Israeli–Palestinian conflict in the West Bank and Gaza Strip from late 2000, as well as the recent increase in inter-Palestinian violence, has generally prevented the recovery of the tourism industry.

Ministry of Tourism and Antiquities: See Administration.

NET—Near East Tourist Agency: POB 19015, 30 Mount of Olives Rd, Jerusalem 91190; tel. (2) 5328720; fax (2) 5328701; e-mail jerusalem@netours.com; internet www.netours.com; f. 1964; CEO SAMI ABU DAYYEH; Man. STEVE USTIN.

PANAMA

Introductory Survey

Location, Climate, Language, Religion, Flag, Capital

The Republic of Panama is a narrow country situated at the southern end of the isthmus separating North and South America. It is bounded to the west by Costa Rica and to the east by Colombia in South America. The Caribbean Sea is to the north, and the Pacific Ocean to the south. Panama has a tropical maritime climate (warm, humid days and cool nights). There is little seasonal variation in temperatures, which average 23°C–27°C (73°F–81°F) in coastal areas. The rainy season is from April until December. Spanish is the official language. Almost all of the inhabitants profess Christianity, and some 84% are Roman Catholics. The national flag (proportions 2 by 3) is composed of four equal rectangles: on the top row the quarter at the hoist is white, with a five-pointed blue star in the centre, while the quarter in the fly is red; on the bottom row the quarter at the hoist is blue, and the quarter in the fly is white, with a five-pointed red star in the centre. The capital is Panamá (Panama City).

Recent History

Panama was subject to Spanish rule from the 16th century until 1821, when it became independent as part of Gran Colombia. Panama remained part of Colombia until 1903, when it declared its separate independence with the support of the USA. In that year the USA purchased the concession for construction of the Panama Canal, which was opened in 1914. The 82-km Canal links the Atlantic and Pacific Oceans, and is a major international sea route. Under the terms of the 1903 treaty between Panama and the USA concerning the construction and administration of the Canal, the USA was granted ('in perpetuity') control of a strip of Panamanian territory, known as the Canal Zone, extending for 8 km on either side of the Canal route. The treaty also established Panama as a protectorate of the USA. In exchange for transferring the Canal Zone, Panama was to receive an annuity from the USA. The terms of this treaty and its successors have dominated relations between Panama and the USA since 1903.

In 1939 a revised treaty with the USA ended Panama's protectorate status. A new Constitution for Panama was adopted in 1946. Following a period of rapidly changing governments, the 1952 presidential election was won by Col José Antonio Remón, formerly Chief of Police. During his term of office, President Remón negotiated a more favourable treaty with the USA, whereby the annuity payable to Panama was increased. In January 1955, however, before the treaty came into force, Remón was assassinated. He was succeeded by José Ramón Guizado, hitherto the First Vice-President, but, less than two weeks after assuming power, the new President was implicated in the plot to assassinate Remón. Guizado was removed from office and later imprisoned. Remón's Second Vice-President, Ricardo Arias Espinosa, then completed the presidential term, which expired in 1956, when Ernesto de la Guardia was elected President. The next presidential election was won by Roberto Chiari, who held office in 1960–64, and his successor was Marco Aurelio Robles (1964–68). During this period there were frequent public demands for the transfer to Panama of sovereignty over the Canal Zone.

The presidential election of May 1968 was won by Dr Arnulfo Arias Madrid, the candidate supported by the coalition Unión Nacional (which included his own Partido Panameñista). Dr Arias had been President in 1940–41 and 1949–51, but both terms had ended in his forcible removal from power. He took office for a third term in October 1968 but, after only 11 days, he was deposed by the National Guard (Panama's only military body), led by Col (later Brig.-Gen.) Omar Torrijos Herrera, who accused him of planning to establish a dictatorship. The Asamblea Nacional (National Assembly) was dissolved, and political activity suspended. Political parties were banned in February 1969.

In August 1972 elections were held to a new legislative body, the 505-member Asamblea Nacional de Corregidores (National Assembly of Community Representatives). In October the Asamblea conferred extraordinary powers on Gen. Torrijos as Chief of Government for six years.

In February 1974 representatives of Panama and the USA concluded an agreement on principles for a new treaty whereby the USA would surrender its jurisdiction over the Canal Zone. Discontent arising from the Government's handling of subsequent protracted negotiations, combined with deteriorating living standards, culminated in student riots in 1976. Intensified talks in 1977 resulted in two new Canal treaties, which were approved by voters at a referendum in October. The treaties became effective from October 1979. Panama assumed control of the former Canal Zone, which was abolished. Administration of the Canal was placed under the control of a joint Panama Canal Commission until the end of 1999. US military forces in Panama were to remain until 2000, and the USA was to be entitled to defend the Canal's neutrality thereafter.

In August 1978 elections were held to the Asamblea Nacional de Corregidores; in October the new representatives elected Dr Arístides Royo Sánchez to be President for a six-year term. Gen. Torrijos resigned as Chief of Government, but continued in the post of Commander of the National Guard, and effectively retained power until his death in an air crash in July 1981. President Royo failed to gain the support of the National Guard, and in July 1982 he was forced to resign by Col Rubén Darío Paredes, who had ousted Col Florencio Flores as Commander-in-Chief in March. The Vice-President, Ricardo de la Espriella, was installed as President, and, under the direction of Col Paredes, promoted business interests and pursued a foreign policy more favourable to the USA.

In April 1983 a series of amendments to the Constitution were approved by referendum. However, in spite of new constitutional measures to limit the power of the National Guard, de facto power remained with the armed forces, whose position was strengthened by a decision in September to unite all security forces within one organization (subsequently known as the National Defence Forces). In June Paredes was succeeded as Commander-in-Chief by Brig. (later Gen.) Manuel Antonio Noriega Morena. In February 1984 Dr Jorge Illueca, hitherto the Vice-President, became Head of State after the sudden resignation of President de la Espriella, who was believed to have been ousted from power by the National Defence Forces.

Elections to the presidency and the legislature (the new 67-member Asamblea Legislativa—Legislative Assembly) took place in May 1984. Despite allegations of extensive electoral fraud, Dr Nicolás Ardito Barletta, the candidate of the Partido Revolucionario Democrático (PRD) who received the electoral support of the armed forces, was eventually declared President-elect, narrowly defeating Arias Madrid, standing as candidate of the Partido Panameñista Auténtico (PPA). However, as a result of protracted opposition to his economic policies, President Ardito was unable to secure a political base to support his administration, and in September 1985 he resigned. Ardito claimed that his resignation had been prompted by the deterioration in his relations with the legislature and with the National Defence Forces, although there was considerable speculation that he had been forced to resign by Gen. Noriega, to prevent a public scandal over the alleged involvement of the National Defence Forces in the murder of Dr Hugo Spadafora, a former deputy minister under Torrijos and a leading critic of Noriega. Ardito was succeeded as President in September by Eric Arturo Delvalle, formerly First Vice-President.

In June 1986 US sources alleged that Noriega was involved in the trafficking of illegal drugs and weapons and in the transfer of proceeds from these activities through Panamanian banks. In addition, Noriega was implicated in the sale of US national security information and restricted technology to Cuba. There were also renewed allegations of his involvement in the murder of Dr Spadafora and in electoral fraud during the 1984 presidential election. Strikes and demonstrations in support of demands for Noriega's dismissal resulted in violent clashes with the National Defence Forces. Following this outbreak of violence, the US Senate approved a resolution urging the establishment of democracy in Panama, the suspension of Noriega and the holding of an independent investigation into the allegations against him. The Panamanian Government responded by accusing the USA of interfering in Panamanian affairs, and a wave of anti-US sentiment was unleashed, including an attack on the US embassy building by protesters in July 1987. The USA subsequently suspended economic and military aid to Panama and downgraded its official links with the country. Protests against Noriega continued, in an atmosphere of mounting political and economic insecurity.

In February 1988 Noriega was indicted by two US Grand Juries on charges of drugs-smuggling and racketeering. President Delvalle subsequently dismissed Noriega from his post, following his refusal to resign voluntarily. However, leading members of the ruling coalition and the National Defence Forces united in support of their Commander-in-Chief, and on the following day the Asamblea Legislativa voted to remove President Delvalle from office because of his 'failure to abide by the Constitution'. The Minister of Education, Manuel Solís Palma, was appointed acting President. Delvalle refused to accept his dismissal, and the US Administration affirmed its support for the ousted President by declining to recognize the new leadership. Delvalle, who went into hiding, became the figurehead of the USA's attempts to oust Noriega, and at the end of the month, following Delvalle's demand that the US Government impose an economic boycott on Panama, US courts authorized a 'freeze' on some US $50m. of Panamanian assets held in US banks. This move, coupled with a general strike organized by the Cruzada Civilista Nacional (a broadly based opposition grouping led by the business sector) after Delvalle's dismissal, brought economic chaos to Panama, prompting the closure of all banks for more than two months.

In March 1988 a coup attempt by the chief of police, Col Leónidas Macías, was thwarted by members of the National Defence Forces loyal to Noriega. The attempted coup represented the first indication of opposition to Noriega from within the security forces. The Government announced a state of emergency (which was revoked in April) and the suspension of civil rights. Negotiations between Noriega and a representative of the US Administration, during which the USA was reported to have proposed the withdrawal of charges against Noriega in exchange for his retirement and departure into exile before the elections scheduled for 1989, ended acrimoniously in late March. The US Administration subsequently reinforced economic sanctions against Panamanian interests.

Presidential, legislative and municipal elections were held on 7 May 1989. The presidential candidate of the pro-Government electoral alliance, the Coalición de Liberación Nacional (COLINA), was Carlos Duque Jaén, the leader of the PRD and a close associate of Noriega. Guillermo Endara Galimany of the PPA was the presidential candidate of the opposition alliance, the Alianza Democrática de Oposición Civilista (ADOC). The election campaign was dominated by accusations of electoral malpractice, and, following the voting, both ADOC and COLINA claimed victory, despite indications from exit polls and unofficial sources that ADOC had received between 50% and 75% of votes cast. A group of international observers declared that the election had been conducted fraudulently. A delay in announcing the results was interpreted by the opposition as an attempt by the Government to falsify the outcome. Endara declared himself President-elect; in subsequent demonstrations crowds clashed with the National Defence Forces, and many members of the opposition, including Endara and other leaders, were severely beaten. On 10 May the election results were annulled by the Electoral Tribunal, which cited US interference.

On 31 August 1989, following intervention by the Organization of American States (OAS, see p. 360), Panama's General State Council announced the appointment of a provisional Government and a 41-member Legislative Commission to preserve 'institutional order'. The holding of elections was to be considered within six months, but this was to be largely dependent upon the cessation of US 'hostilities' and the withdrawal of US economic sanctions. On 1 September Francisco Rodríguez, a known associate of Noriega, was inaugurated as President, and Carlos Ozores Typaldos as Vice-President. The USA immediately severed diplomatic relations with Panama. In October an attempted coup, led by middle-ranking officers seeking to replace Noriega at the head of the de facto military dictatorship, was suppressed by forces loyal to Noriega.

In November 1989 the Asamblea Nacional de Corregidores was provisionally restored. This body, now numbering 510 members, was intended to fulfil a consultative and (limited) legislative function. Noriega was elected as its 'national co-ordinator'. In December the Asamblea adopted a resolution declaring Noriega to be Head of State and 'leader of the struggle for national liberation', and announced that a state of war existed with the USA. On 20 December a US military offensive ('Operation Just Cause'), involving some 24,000 troops, was launched against Noriega and the headquarters of the National Defence Forces from US bases within Panama. The objects of the assault were swiftly brought under US control, although sporadic attacks on US bases by loyalist forces continued for several days, and Noriega eluded capture long enough to take refuge in the residence of the Papal Nuncio in Panama. On 21 December Endara, who had been installed as Head of State in a ceremony attended by a Panamanian judge at the Fort Clayton US military base only hours before the invasion, was officially inaugurated as President. President Endara declared that the Panamanian judicial system was inadequate to try Noriega. Following his surrender to US forces in January 1990, Noriega was immediately transported to the USA and arraigned on several charges of involvement in drugs-trafficking and money-laundering operations. (Noriega, who claimed the status of a prisoner of war, refused to recognize the right of jurisdiction of a US court.) In April 1992 Noriega was found guilty on eight charges of conspiracy to manufacture and distribute cocaine; he was sentenced to 40 years' imprisonment.

International criticism of the USA's military operation was widespread, although the Administration cited the right to self-defence, under Article 51 of the UN Charter, as a legal justification for armed intervention, and US President George Bush asserted that military action was necessary for the protection of US citizens, the protection of the Panama Canal, support for Panama's 'democratically elected' officials and the pursuit of an indicted criminal. According to the US Government, 'Operation Just Cause' resulted in about 500 Panamanian casualties, but a total of at least 1,000 Panamanian deaths was estimated by the Roman Catholic Church and other unofficial sources; 26 US troops were killed, and more than 300 wounded, during the invasion.

Following the appointment of a new Cabinet (comprising members of the ADOC alliance) in December 1989, the Endara administration declared itself to be a 'democratic Government of reconstruction and national reconciliation'. Shortly afterwards the Electoral Tribunal revoked its annulment of the May elections and announced that ADOC had obtained 62% of the votes cast in the presidential election, according to copies of incomplete results (covering 64% of total votes) that had been held in safe keeping by the Bishops' Conference of the Roman Catholic Church. In February 1990 the composition of the Asamblea Legislativa was announced, based on the same documentation, with 51 seats awarded to ADOC and six to COLINA; fresh elections were to be held for nine seats that could not be reliably allocated. The National Defence Forces were officially disbanded, and a new, 'non-political' Public Force was created.

Although the overthrow of Noriega immediately released US $375m. in assets that had previously been withheld by the US Government, the new administration inherited serious economic difficulties. The cost of 'Operation Just Cause', in terms of damage and lost revenues alone, was estimated to be at least $2,000m. Although the Bush Administration agreed to provide aid amounting to more than $1,000m., the US Congress was slow to approve the appropriation of funds. In April 1990 the USA revoked the economic restrictions that had been imposed two years previously, and in May Congress approved financial assistance to Panama totalling $420m. Disbursement of a substantial tranche was to be dependent upon the successful negotiation of a Mutual Legal Assistance Treaty (MLAT) between the two countries, whereby the US authorities sought to gain greater access to information amassed by Panama City's 'offshore' international finance centre, in order to combat the illegal laundering of money.

Accusations from public and political opponents that the security forces had not been adequately purged following the ousting of Noriega were seemingly justified by a succession of coup attempts during the early 1990s. Meanwhile, growing public concern at the Government's failure to restore civil and economic order was reflected in the results of elections held in January 1991 for the nine seats in the Asamblea Legislativa that had not been awarded by the Electoral Tribunal following the elections of May 1989 (see above). Member parties of the former electoral alliance COLINA, which had supported the previous regime, secured five of the contested seats, while parties represented in the governing alliance secured only four seats. President Endara's recently formed Partido Arnulfista

(PA, formerly a faction of the PPA) failed to secure a single seat. Serious concern had been expressed at the increasing level of influence exerted by the US Government over the President, particularly when it became known that in July 1990 the Government had accepted US funds to establish, by decree, a 100-strong Council for Public Security, which would maintain close links with the US Central Intelligence Agency.

Long-standing political differences within the Government reached a crisis in March 1991, when the PDC initiated proceedings to impeach Endara for involving the US armed forces in suppressing an uprising in December 1990 (a technical violation of the 1977 Panama Canal Treaty). Although the proposal was dismissed by the Asamblea Legislativa, Endara and his supporters strongly criticized leaders of the PDC and dismissed the five PDC members of his Cabinet.

In July 1991 the Asamblea Legislativa approved the terms of the MLAT, following indications in US intelligence documents that drugs-related activities in Panama (and money-laundering in particular) had returned to the levels that had prevailed prior to the removal of Gen. Noriega. The Panamanian Government's urgent need of direct financial aid (the disbursement of which the USA had made dependent on the MLAT) prompted it to sign the treaty with only minor modifications to the terms of the agreement.

In October 1991 and February 1992 two further alleged coup attempts were immediately suppressed, and resulted in the detention of several more members of the former National Defence Forces, and the creation, in March 1992, of a presidential police force to be directly responsible to the Head of State. In November, however, the President suffered a serious political reverse, when proposals for more than 50 reforms (including the constitutional abolition of the armed forces and the creation of the post of ombudsman to protect the rights of Panamanian citizens) were rejected by 64% of voters in a referendum.

The acquittal, in September 1993, of seven former soldiers tried for involvement in the 1985 assassination of Dr Spadafora provoked widespread public outrage. Noriega was tried in connection with the affair *in absentia* and, in October 1993, was found guilty and sentenced to 20 years' imprisonment for ordering his murder. In March 1994 Noriega was also convicted *in absentia* for the 1989 murder of an army major who had led an unsuccessful military coup against him; he was sentenced to a further 20 years' imprisonment. Furthermore, in August 2001 he was sentenced to a further eight years' imprisonment after being convicted, again *in absentia*, of corruption charges. In September 2007 the French authorities sought the extradition of Noriega from the USA to France where he had been convicted *in absentia* on money-laundering charges in 1999.

A presidential election was held on 8 May 1994. Ernesto Pérez Balladares, the candidate of the Pueblo Unido alliance (that included the PRD), won a narrow victory, winning 33% of the votes cast, ahead of Mireya Moscoso de Gruber (the widow of former President Arias Madrid), who attracted 30%. Moscoso was the nominee of the Alianza Democrática, a grouping of the PA with the Partido Liberal (PL), the Partido Liberal Auténtico (PLA), the Unión Democrática Independiente and the Partido Nacionalista Popular (PNP). The failure of the Pueblo Unido alliance to secure a majority in the legislature was reflected in the broad political base of Pérez Balladares' proposed Cabinet, announced in May. Post-electoral political manoeuvring resulted in the creation of the Alianza Pueblo Unido y Solidaridad, Pérez Balladares' electoral alliance having secured the additional support of the Partido Solidaridad in the Asamblea. Pérez Balladares assumed the presidency on 1 September 1994. A new Cabinet, installed on the same day, included former members of the PA and the PDC who had been obliged to resign their party membership in order to take up their cabinet posts.

In May 1996 the credibility of the Government was damaged by the discovery that a private Panamanian bank (Banaico, which had collapsed earlier in the year), in whose activities senior PRD members were implicated, had been a centre for money-laundering. In June, moreover, the position of President Pérez Balladares was undermined by reports that an alleged drugs-trafficker had contributed some US $51,000 to his 1994 presidential campaign. Pérez Balladares was forced to admit that his campaign fund had 'unwittingly' received the payment; the Procurator-General subsequently announced a thorough investigation into the origin of the 1994 campaign funds.

At a presidential election conducted on 2 May 1999, Mireya Moscoso de Gruber, the candidate of the Unión por Panamá alliance (comprising the PA, Movimiento Liberal Republicano Nacionalista—MOLIRENA, Movimiento de Renovación Nacional and Cambio Democrático), was elected with 45% of the votes, ahead of Martín Torrijos Espino, son of former dictator Omar Torrijos, the candidate of the Nueva Nación alliance (comprising the PRD, the Partido Solidaridad, the Partido Liberal Nacional—PLN—and the Movimiento Papa Egoró—MPE), who secured 38%. However, the Unión por Panamá failed to secure a majority in the concurrent legislative election, obtaining 24 of the 71 contested seats in the Asamblea Legislativa, while Nueva Nación secured 41 seats and Acción Opositora won six seats. Moscoso assumed the presidency on 1 September. A new Cabinet, installed on the same day, included members of the Partido Solidaridad, the PLN, the PDC and the PRC, each of which had abandoned their respective electoral alliances in order to form a 'Government of national unity', thereby giving Moscoso a narrow majority in the legislature.

In July 1999 the Commander-in-Chief of the US Southern Command, Gen. Charles Wilhelm, caused considerable unease in Panama when he indicated that the USA had contingency plans for defending the Panama Canal, following US withdrawal at the end of 1999, should violence spread from Colombia into Panama: according to the 1977 Canal treaties, the USA was entitled unilaterally to intervene if it had reason to suppose that the security of the Canal was threatened. In November the USA completed its withdrawal from Howard airbase, and the last of the US military bases, Fort Clayton, was ceded to Panama. In December the Panamanian Government announced that a national security plan was under negotiation to ensure the security of the Canal and to combat border incursions, drugs-trafficking and international crime. On 31 December the USA officially relinquished ownership of the Canal to Panama. In early 2000 a five-year canal-modernization project was initiated. In February the Government negotiated a counter-narcotics agreement with the USA.

In August 2000 the governing coalition lost its narrow legislative majority after the PRD and the PDC formed an alliance. The effective legislative impasse was ended in February 2002 following the defection of three opposition deputies.

Following the discovery of human remains in a former military barracks in Tocumen, in December 2000 President Moscoso announced the establishment of a Truth Commission, headed by Alberto Santiago Almanza Henríquez, to investigate 'disappearances' during the military dictatorships of 1968–89. Following excavations in 12 separate areas, the Commission reported in October 2001 that 72 of the 189 people believed to have 'disappeared' had been killed or tortured by state forces. In March 2004 the Asamblea approved the establishment of a Special Prosecutor's Office to investigate crimes committed during the military dictatorships; in February 2006 the Special Prosecutor announced that four officers who served in the military regimes were prepared to offer anonymous testimonies against former colleagues.

President Moscoso's administration encountered problems in the wake of an agreement signed in February 2002, which provided for US authorities to join the Panamanian National Maritime Service in patrolling its territorial waters, in an attempt to control the illegal trade in narcotics. The agreement was strongly criticized by opposition members. However, in September a number of defections from the opposition to the governing coalition gave Moscoso a working majority in the Asamblea for the first time since taking office. An additional accord, which provided the USA with increased powers to inspect Panama's financial and tax records as part of its campaign against money-laundering, provoked protests from opposition parties. In April 2002 Panama was removed from the Organisation for Economic Co-operation and Development's (OECD) list of 'un-co-operative tax havens' after the Government committed to making its financial sector more transparent. In January 2004 the country's bank auditors, the Unidad de Análisis Financiero, identified 392 bank accounts that it suspected were being used for money-laundering purposes. They included 40 accounts associated with the former President of Nicaragua, Arnoldo Alemán Lacayo, and a further 14 connected to the former Guatemalan President, Alfonso Portillo Cabrera.

In September 2003 President Moscoso dismissed Juan Jované as Director of the social security fund, the Caja de Seguro Social (CSS), after he had refused to agree on a balanced budget with the other members of the CSS board. The CSS had been running at a loss for years, and, according to the Government, would go bankrupt without reform. In a subsequent television appearance, however, Jované alleged that he had been removed to allow for the privatization of the CSS. Furthermore, he claimed that the Government was intending to compel the CSS to purchase US $500m. of government debt, in order to finance the PA's re-election campaign. In mid-September CSS employees, trade union members and students marched through the capital to protest at Jované's dismissal. Moscoso subsequently signed a declaration pledging not to sell off the CSS. Nevertheless, a second march took place and in late September an umbrella trade union organization, known as the Frente Nacional por la Defensa de la Seguridad Social (FRENADESSO), held a widely observed 24-hour general strike (although only 40% of government workers were estimated to have participated following a threat of dismissal).

Presidential and legislative elections took place on 2 May 2004, in which 76.9% of the electorate participated. Martín Torrijos Espino, the candidate of the PRD (which contested the elections as part of the Patria Nueva electoral alliance with the Partido Popular) won the presidential ballot, winning 47.4% of the votes cast. Former President Endara, representing the Partido Solidaridad, came second with 30.9% of the ballot. The PA's presidential candidate, former Minister of Foreign Affairs José Miguel Alemán (officially the representative of the Visión de País electoral alliance, comprising the PA, MOLIRENA and the PLN) attracted only 16.4% of the votes cast. The Patria Nueva also performed well in the concurrently held elections to the enlarged, 78-seat Asamblea Legislativa: the party won 43.9% of the votes cast and secured a total of 43 seats, 42 of which were won by the PRD. The PA obtained 19.3% of the ballot and 16 seats, while the Partido Solidaridad received 15.7% of the votes cast and nine seats. Torrijos assumed office on 1 September.

In August 2004, just prior to the end of her mandate, President Moscoso pardoned and released four prisoners sought by the authorities in Cuba for allegedly plotting to assassinate the Cuban leader Fidel Castro Ruz in 2000. The men had been found guilty by a Panamanian court in April of illegal possession of weapons and sentenced to varying terms of imprisonment. The Venezuelan Government also had been attempting to extradite one of the men in connection with the bombing of a Cuban aeroplane in 1976.

Even before he assumed the presidency, Torrijos was successful in bringing about several constitutional amendments. In July 2004 his proposed reform of the Asamblea Legislativa received legislative approval. The number of parliamentary seats was to be reduced to 71 (from 78) from 2009. Furthermore, deputies voted to end parliamentary immunity from prosecution and to transfer the authority to ratify constitutional amendments from the legislature to a constituent assembly. President Torrijos also pledged to address the problem of official corruption. One week after Torrijos' Government took office, Panama's ambassador to Cuba, Abraham Bárcenas, who had been recalled at the end of the previous month, was arrested as part of an investigation into the alleged sale of Panamanian visas to Cuban citizens. Bárcenas' predecessor, Oscar Alarcón, was also under investigation for alleged corruption. Then, in November the Government announced that corruption charges had been filed against former Minister of Finance and the Treasury Norberto Delgado. His successor, Ricaurte Vázquez Morales, criticized the former administration's fiscal management, and stated that the fiscal deficit was an estimated 5.4% of gross domestic product, rather than the 2.7% announced by his predecessor. Fiscal reform legislation was submitted to the Asamblea Nacional in January 2005 that proposed, *inter alia*, to reduce the public sector workforce by 12% over five years and to revise methods of corporate taxation. Despite opposition from business associations and trade unions, the legislation was approved at the end of the month.

In October 2004 some 5,000 people participated in a protest march organized by the FRENADESSO, the social organization established to resist privatization of the CSS. The new Government denied it intended fully to privatize the CSS, but emphasized the need for reform in light of the institution's estimated deficit of between US $2,500m.–$3,000m. Proposed social security reforms included an increase in the retirement age, a reduction in retirement benefits and the transfer of some pensions into private funds. Despite further protests and industrial action co-ordinated by FRENADESSO in May 2005, the pension reforms were approved by the Asamblea Nacional in early June. However, they included a number of concessions, including proportional pensions for those who failed to make sufficient contributions, and the reduction in the proposed pensionable retirement age for women from 62 years of age to 60 (hitherto 57).

None the less, industrial unrest continued and one week later medical workers joined the ongoing strike. In late June the Government partially suspended implementation of the new law and a revised series of measures (which maintained the retirement age for women at 57 years of age and increased the minimum qualifying number of monthly pension contributions from 180 to just 240—rather than 300 as initially suggested), was voted into law in December.

On 10 January 2006, the day before the commencement of the ninth round of negotiations towards a free trade agreement with the USA (see below), the Minister of Agricultural Development, Laurentino Cortizo, submitted his resignation. Cortizo reportedly stood down in protest at US pressure to adopt that country's plant and livestock regulations, which he claimed could compromise Panama's food health standards. He was replaced by Guillermo Augusto Salazar Nicolau.

In April 2006 the Autoridad del Canal de Panamá (ACP) announced plans to expand the Canal's capacity to allow the passage of larger commercial container vessels through the construction of a third set of locks at either end of the waterway. The projected cost of US $5,250m. to build the wider locks was to be funded by toll revenues and loans totalling an estimated $2,270m. President Torrijos pledged to hold a national debate and an eventual referendum on the ACP's proposals. While widely considered to be vital to the future of the Canal and therefore the country's commercial sector, concerns were raised relating to the environmental consequences of the expansion and the possible relocation of farmers in communities bordering the Canal. Environmental groups criticized the high volume of water that would be required. However, the ACP countered that an estimated 60% of the water was to be recycled, using a system of overspill reservoirs. At the end of the month Héctor Alemán and Vázquez Morales, previously Ministers of the Interior and Justice and of the Economy and Finance, respectively, were appointed co-ordinators of the national debate. (In mid-April 2007 Vázquez Morales also stood down as Chairman of the ACP. He was subsequently replaced by Dani Kuzniecky.) Responsibility for the interior and justice was subsequently assumed by Olga Gólcher, while the economy and finance portfolio was transferred to Carlos Vallarino, hitherto Minister of Public Works. Vallarino was succeeded at the public works ministry by Benjamín Colamarco. In mid-July 2006, in the second of three scheduled debates, the Asamblea Nacional overwhelmingly approved the ACP's plan to expand the canal. At the referendum duly conducted on 22 October, the project was approved by a clear majority of 78.3% of those voting. However, voter participation was much lower than expected, at just 43.3% of the electorate. A ceremony to launch the project took place in September 2007. It was anticipated that work on enlarging the canal, which would not disrupt normal operations, would begin in 2008 and last for seven years.

Allegations of corruption in public institutions continued to be a problem for the Government in 2006. In mid-July the head of the counter-terrorism and counter-narcotics police unit, Franklin Brewster, died from poisoning. Following an investigation by the Public Prosecutor's office, in collaboration with the US Federal Bureau of Investigations, in November three police officers were arrested on suspicion of contaminating Brewster's food with pesticide. Shortly prior to his assassination Brewster had launched an investigation into possible links between drugs-traffickers and the police force.

A number of deaths from poisoning by CSS-manufactured medicines in late 2006 led to demands for the resignation of the Minister of Public Health, Camilo Alleyne, together with the other members of the CSS board of directors. In mid-October the Government announced that a poisonous industrial alcohol had been detected in four remedies manufactured by the CSS. According to official figures, 51 people died from ingesting the contaminated medicine, although the unofficial death toll was much higher, at 250. In November President Torrijos announced that an independent standards agency was to be established to oversee the manufacture of prescription drugs. In mid-January 2007 the Government announced that compensation was to be paid to the families of 113 confirmed and suspected victims. Despite calls by human rights activists and members of the opposition for Alleyne and the other CSS directors to stand down, they remained in office in April 2007. A major cabinet reorganization, which included new appointments to the public health and interior ministries, carried out in September, was thought to have been prompted by public concern over the scandal.

In July 1997, in the light of the increasing number of incursions by Colombian guerrillas and paramilitary groups into Panamanian territory, the Government deployed more than 1,200 members of the security forces to Darién Province to secure the border with Colombia. In previous months Colombian paramilitary members were reported to have forcibly occupied several settlements in the area while in pursuit of guerrillas who had taken refuge over the border. Following discussions between Pérez Balladares and his Colombian counterpart, Andrés Pastrana Arango, an agreement on improved co-operation concerning border security was reached. In June 1999, following further incursions by Colombian guerrillas into Darién Province, Panama and Colombia reached agreement on the strengthening of military patrols on both sides of the countries' joint border. However, in October 2000 one person was killed and 12 people were injured when Colombian paramilitaries attacked the town of Nazaret.

In October 1993 President Endara signed a protocol to establish Panama's membership of the Central American Parliament (Parlacen), a regional political forum with its headquarters in Guatemala. Later in the month Endara, together with the five Presidents of the member nations of the Central American Common Market (CACM, see p. 201), signed a protocol to the 1960 General Treaty on Central American Integration, committing Panama to fuller economic integration in the region. However, at a meeting of Central American Presidents, convened in Costa Rica in August 1994, Pérez Balladares (attending as an observer) stated that his administration considered further regional economic integration to be disadvantageous to Panama, owing to the differences between Panama's services-based economy and the reliance on the agricultural sector of the other Central American states. Negotiations on a free trade agreement with El Salvador were concluded in March 2002. Although Panama was excluded from the negotiations towards a Dominican Republic-Central American Free Trade Agreement (DR-CAFTA) with the USA, discussions regarding a bilateral free trade agreement with the USA were finally concluded in December 2006 and signed in June 2007. However, the accord had still to be ratified by both legislatures, and further negotiations on labour laws were also to be held. Panama has observer status within the Andean Community of Nations (see p. 170).

In November 2006 the Government agreed to become the consensus candidate to represent the Latin American and Caribbean Group (Grulac) on the UN Security Council during 2007-08. Panama's candidacy was proposed following the failure of either of the hitherto main contenders, Guatemala and Venezuela, to garner the support of two-thirds of the 33 members of Grulac during 47 rounds of voting. In early November Panama's bid was unanimously approved by Grulac and subsequently by the UN General Assembly. Panama's tenure commenced in January 2007.

Government

Legislative power is vested in the unicameral Asamblea Nacional (National Assembly), which was known as the Asamblea Legislativa (Legislative Assembly) until 2004 and which replaced the Asamblea Nacional de Corregidores (National Assembly of Community Representatives) in 1984 (except for its brief reintroduction in late 1989), with a total of 78 members elected for five years by universal adult suffrage. Executive power is held by the President, also directly elected for a term of five years, assisted by two elected Vice-Presidents and an appointed Cabinet. Panama is divided into nine provinces and three autonomous Indian Reservations. Each province has a governor, appointed by the President.

Defence

In 1990, following the overthrow of Gen. Manuel Noriega, the National Defence Forces were disbanded and a new Public Force was created. This numbered 12,000 men, as assessed at November 2007, comprising the National Police (11,000 men), the National Air Service (400 men) and the National Maritime Service (an estimated 600 men). Budgeted security expenditure for 2007 was estimated at US $200m.

Economic Affairs

In 2006, according to estimates by the World Bank, Panama's gross national income (GNI), measured at average 2004–06 prices, was US $16,067m., equivalent to $4,890 per head (or $7,680 on an international purchasing-power parity basis). During 1996–2006, it was estimated, the population increased at an average annual rate of 1.9%, while gross domestic product (GDP) per head increased, in real terms, by an average of 3.0% per year. Overall GDP increased, in real terms, at an average annual rate of 5.0% in 1996–2006; according to official estimates, growth was 11.2% in 2007.

Agriculture (including hunting, forestry and fishing) contributed an estimated 6.5% of GDP and engaged some 15.9% of the employed labour force in 2006. Rice, maize and beans are cultivated as subsistence crops, while the principal cash crops are bananas (which accounted for an estimated 9.6% of total export earnings in 2005), melons, sugar cane and coffee. Cattle-raising, tropical timber and fisheries (particularly shrimps and yellowfin tuna for export) are also important. The banana sector was adversely affected by industrial action and poor weather conditions in the early 2000s. The end of the European Union's (EU, see p. 244) quota system on banana imports from 2006 was predicted to boost the sector; however, Panama was expected to appeal against the EU's introduction of a tariff on Latin American bananas of €176 per metric ton. In the 1990s, in an attempt to diversify the agricultural sector, new crops such as oil palm, cocoa, coconuts, various winter vegetables and tropical fruits were introduced. Fish exports increased steadily from the 1990s. In 2006 exports of yellowfin tuna and fish fillet accounted for an estimated 22.6% of export revenue. Agricultural GDP increased by an average of 4.7% annually during 1996–2006; the sector increased by an estimated 2.1% in 2007.

Industry (including mining, manufacturing, construction and power) contributed an estimated 16.3% of GDP and engaged 18.1% of the employed labour force in 2006. According to World Bank figures, industrial GDP increased at an average annual rate of 2.9% during 1996–2007; the sector's GDP increased by an estimated 10.5% in 2007.

Mining contributed an estimated 1.2% of GDP and engaged 0.2% of the employed labour force in 2006. Panama has significant deposits of copper and coal. The GDP of the mining sector increased by an estimated average of 12.3% per year in 2003–07; the sector expanded by an estimated 19.6% in 2007.

Manufacturing contributed an estimated 7.0% of GDP and engaged an estimated 8.7% of the employed labour force in 2006. The most important sectors, measured by output in producers' prices, were refined petroleum products, food-processing, beverages, and cement, lime and plaster. Manufacturing GDP decreased by an average of 0.4% annually during 1996–2006; however, the sector increased by an estimated 5.7% in 2007.

The country's topography and climate make it ideal for hydroelectric power, and in 2004 approximately 71.2% of Panama's total output of electricity was water-generated. Petroleum accounted for the remainder (28.8%) of the country's generating capacity. In 2006 imports of fuels and lubricants accounted for an estimated 17.5% of the value of merchandise imports.

Panama's economy is dependent upon the services sector, which contributed an estimated 77.3% of GDP and engaged 66.0% of the employed labour force in 2006. The Panama Canal contributed an estimated 6.3% of the country's GDP in that year. Panama is an important 'offshore' financial centre, and in 2006 financial, property and business services contributed an estimated 26.4% of GDP. Important contributions to the economy are also made by trade in the Colón Free Zone (CFZ—in which some 1,800 companies were situated in 2005, and which contributed an estimated 8.4% of GDP the following year), and by the registration of merchant ships under a 'flag of convenience' in Panama. The tourism sector also increased steadily from the last decade of the 20th century. In 2005 income from tourism totalled US $1,108m., compared with $903m. in the previous year. According to the World Bank, the GDP of the services sector increased by an average of 5.6% per year in 1996–2006; the sector grew by an estimated 13.4% in 2007.

In 2006 Panama recorded a visible trade deficit of US $1,725.6m., and there was a deficit of $552.0m. on the current account of the balance of payments. In 2007 the principal source of imports (30.2%) was the USA, which was also the principal market for exports (34.9%). Other major trading partners are Costa Rica, Japan, Mexico and Spain. The principal exports in 2006 were yellowfin tuna and fish fillet, bananas and melons. The principal imports in that year were primary materials and products for industry, non-durable consumer goods, and transport and telecommunications equipment.

In 2006 there was an estimated overall budgetary surplus of 296.3m. balboas (equivalent to 1.7% of GDP). Panama's external debt at the end of 2005 was US $9,765m., of which $7,514m. was long-term public debt. In that year the cost of debt-servicing was equivalent to 17.5% of the value of exports of goods and services.

Annual inflation averaged 1.1% in 1998–2003; consumer prices increased by 0.4% in 2004 and by 2.9% in 2005. Some 9.1% of the labour force were unemployed in August 2006.

Panama is a member of the Inter-American Development Bank (IDB, see p. 308). In September 1997 Panama joined the World Trade Organization (WTO, see p. 396). In March 2002 Panama concluded a free trade agreement with El Salvador. In August 2003 a free trade accord between Panama and Taiwan was concluded. In December 2006 negotiations towards a free trade agreement with the USA were finally concluded. Once ratified by both countries' legislatures, the accord would remove 90% of tariffs on Panamanian–US trade, with the remaining 10% to be eliminated over the next 10 years.

Following the cession to Panamanian control of the Panama Canal at the end of 1999, the waterway was operated as a profit-making venture, providing the Government with a considerable source of funds. (Toll revenues from the Canal totalled US $848m. in 2005.) Nevertheless, the administration of President Martín Torrijos Espino, which took office in September 2004, faced the problems of high unemployment and widespread poverty (affecting an estimated 40% of the population). In October 2006 plans to expand the Canal (at a cost of $5,250m.) were approved. The upgrade would create some 7,000 jobs and lead to a considerable expansion in the construction sector. Once finished, the Canal was expected to increase GDP growth by 1%–2% per year until 2025. In February 2005 the Asamblea Nacional approved a fiscal adjustment programme designed to reduce the deficit to 1% of GDP by 2009: this was to be achieved by increasing the tax yield, rationalizing public spending and reducing expenditure on salaries. Tax revenue was particularly low, having declined from the equivalent of 11.4% of GDP in 1995 to an estimated 8.7% of GDP in 2005. The Government intended to reduce business tax evasion and to increase the penalties for non-compliance. The cost of services to businesses in the CFZ was also increased. It was hoped that implementation of the much-needed reforms would help the Torrijos Government secure financing, on favourable terms, for the planned Canal expansion. It was also hoped that ratification of the free trade agreement with the USA in 2007 would lead to increased foreign investment. Strong growth in 2006–07 was driven primarily by foreign investment and rising Canal traffic. Increased revenues allowed the Government to turn a fiscal deficit into a surplus in 2007. However, foreign debt remains a problem, as does the deficit on their current account and rising inflation. Growth was forecast to reach 7.2% in 2008.

Education

The education system is divided into elementary, secondary and university schooling, each of six years' duration. Education is free up to university level, and is officially compulsory for six years between six and 15 years of age. In 2005 some 55.2% of children aged 4–5 years were enrolled at pre-primary schools (males 54.9%; females 55.5%). Primary education begins at the age of six, and secondary education, which comprises two three-year cycles, at the age of 12. The enrolment at primary schools of children in the relevant age-group was 98.5% (males 98.8%; females 98.1%) in 2005, and secondary enrolment was 63.8% (males 61.0%; females 66.7%) in the same year. There are four public universities, with regional centres in the provinces, and 11 private ones, including one specializing in distance learning. Budgetary expenditure on education by the central Government in 2004 totalled 637m. balboas (equivalent to 24.6% of total expenditure).

Public Holidays

2008: 1 January (New Year's Day), 9 January (National Martyrs' Day), 4–5 February (Carnival), 6 February (Ash Wednesday), 20 March (Maundy Thursday), 21 March (Good Friday), 1 May (Labour Day), 14 August (Foundation of Panama City, Panama City only)*, 11 October (Revolution Day), 1 November (National Anthem Day)*, 2 November (Day of the Dead), 3 November (Independence from Colombia), 4 November (Flag Day)*, 5 November (Independence Day, Colón only), 10 November (First Call for Independence), 28 November (Independence from Spain), 8 December (Immaculate Conception, Mothers' Day), 25 December (Christmas).

2009: 1 January (New Year's Day), 9 January (National Martyrs' Day), 23–24 February (Carnival), 25 February (Ash Wednesday), 9 April (Maundy Thursday), 10 April (Good Friday), 1 May (Labour Day), 15 August (Foundation of Panama City, Panama City only)*, 11 October (Revolution Day), 1 November (National Anthem Day)*, 2 November (Day of the Dead), 3 November (Independence from Colombia), 4 November (Flag Day)*, 5 November (Independence Day, Colón only), 10 November (First Call for Independence), 28 November (Independence from Spain), 8 December (Immaculate Conception, Mothers' Day), 25 December (Christmas).

* Official holiday: banks and government offices closed.

Weights and Measures

Both the metric and the imperial systems of weights and measures are in use.

Statistical Survey

Sources (unless otherwise stated): Dirección de Estadística y Censo, Contraloría General de la República, Avda Balboa y Federico Boyd, Apdo 5213, Panamá 5; tel. 210-4800; fax 210-4801; e-mail cgrdec@contraloria.gob.pa; internet www.contraloria.gob.pa; Ministry of the Economy and Finance, Edif. Ogawa, Vía España, Apdo 5245, Panamá 5; e-mail webmaster@mef.gob.pa; internet www.mef.gob.pa.

Note: The former Canal Zone was incorporated into Panama on 1 October 1979.

Area and Population

AREA, POPULATION AND DENSITY

Area (sq km)	75,517*
Population (census results)	
13 May 1990	2,329,329
14 May 2000	
Males	1,432,566
Females	1,406,611
Total	2,839,177
Population (official estimates at mid-year)	
2005	3,228,186
2006	3,283,959
2007	3,339,781
Density (per sq km) at mid-2007	44.2

* 29,157 sq miles.

ADMINISTRATIVE DIVISIONS
(official estimates at mid-2007)

Province	Population	Capital (and population)*
Bocas del Toro	110,585	Bocas del Toro (12,653)
Chiriquí	414,048	David (9,602)
Coclé	229,816	Penonomé (81,823)
Colón	239,206	Colón (205,557)
Comarca Emberá	9,397	—
Comarca Kuna Yala	37,031	—
Comarca Ngöbe-Buglé	139,509	—
Darién	44,953	Chepigana (30,839)
Herrera	111,144	Chitré (48,142)
Los Santos	89,849	Las Tablas (26,709)
Panamá	1,689,304	Panamá (845,684)
Veraguas	224,939	Santiago (83,094)
Total	**3,339,781**	—

* Population of district in which capital is located.

Note: Population figures include the former Canal Zone.

PANAMA

PRINCIPAL TOWNS
(population at 2000 census)

Panamá (Panama City, capital)	463,093	Pacora		57,232
San Miguelito	291,769	Santiago		55,146
Tocumen	81,250	La Chorrera		54,823
David	76,481	Colón		52,286
Nuevo Arraiján	63,753	Changuinola		45,063
Puerto Armuelles	60,102	Pedregal		45,033

Mid-2007 ('000, incl. suburbs, UN estimate): Panama City 1,281 (Source: UN, *World Urbanization Prospects: The 2007 Revision*).

BIRTHS, MARRIAGES AND DEATHS

	Registered live births		Registered marriages*		Registered deaths	
	Number	Rate (per 1,000)†	Number	Rate (per 1,000)†	Number	Rate (per 1,000)†
1998	62,351	22.6	10,415	4.1	11,824	4.3
1999	64,248	22.9	10,388	3.9	11,938	4.2
2000	64,839	22.7	10,430	3.9	11,841	4.1
2001	63,900	21.3	9,687	3.6	12,442	4.1
2002	61,671	20.2	9,558	3.1	12,428	4.1
2003	61,753	19.8	10,310	3.3	13,248	4.3
2004	62,743	19.8	10,290	3.2	13,475	4.2
2005	63,645	19.7	10,512	3.3	14,180	4.4

* Excludes tribal Indian population.
† Based on official mid-year population estimates.

2006: Live births 65,764 (birth rate 20.0 per 1,000); Deaths 14,358 (estimate) (Source: UN, *Population and Vital Statistics Report*).

Expectation of life (years at birth, WHO estimates): 75.9 (males 73.7; females 78.3) in 2005 (Source: WHO, *World Health Statistics*).

ECONOMICALLY ACTIVE POPULATION
('000 persons aged 15 years and over, August of each year)

	2004	2005	2006
Agriculture, hunting and forestry	172.3	176.8	183.1
Fishing	9.4	9.5	9.9
Mining and quarrying	0.7	1.0	2.3
Manufacturing	100.4	104.3	105.2
Electricity, gas and water supply	8.4	7.7	8.4
Construction	90.6	91.1	102.8
Wholesale and retail trade; repair of motor vehicles, motorcycles and personal and household goods	207.2	226.9	229.6
Hotels and restaurants	61.1	69.6	64.5
Transport, storage and communications	89.4	91.3	90.8
Financial intermediation	25.0	24.3	26.4
Real estate, renting and business activities	54.1	61.7	62.6
Public administration and defence; compulsory social service	73.7	69.4	70.3
Education	66.8	64.9	62.7
Health and social work	43.2	47.6	48.3
Other community, social and personal service activities	62.2	71.6	68.0
Private households with employed persons	69.4	70.0	74.9
Extra-territorial organizations and bodies	0.7	0.6	0.8
Total employed	1,134.7	1,188.3	1,210.7
Unemployed	159.9	136.8	121.4
Total labour force	1,294.6	1,325.1	1,332.1

Source: ILO.

Health and Welfare

KEY INDICATORS

Total fertility rate (children per woman, 2005)	2.6
Under-5 mortality rate (per 1,000 live births, 2005)	24
HIV/AIDS (% of persons aged 15–49, 2005)	0.9
Physicians (per 1,000 head, 2000)	1.50
Hospital beds (per 1,000 head, 2004)	2.4
Health expenditure (2004): US $ per head (PPP)	631.6
Health expenditure (2004): % of GDP	7.7
Health expenditure (2004): public (% of total)	66.9
Access to water (% of persons, 2004)	90
Access to sanitation (% of persons, 2004)	73
Human Development Index (2005): ranking	62
Human Development Index (2005): value	0.812

For sources and definitions, see explanatory note on p. vi.

Agriculture

PRINCIPAL CROPS
('000 metric tons)

	2004	2005	2006*
Rice (paddy)	243.4	235.2	280.0
Maize	90.5	89.1	70.0
Sugar cane	1,749.5	1,766.1	1,766.1
Watermelons	44.5	71.9	71.9
Cantaloupes and other melons	69.0	102.9	102.9
Bananas	497.1	439.2	439.2
Plantains	109.5	95.2	95.2
Oranges	40.6	41.9	41.9
Coffee (green)	12.8	13.2†	13.2
Tobacco (leaves)*	2.3	2.4	2.4

* FAO estimates.
† Unofficial figure.

Aggregate production ('000 metric tons, may include official, semi-official or estimated data): Total cereals 341.1 in 2004, 334.3 in 2005, 360.0 in 2006; Total roots and tubers 87.3 in 2004, 89.5 in 2005, 89.5 in 2006; Total vegetables (incl. melons) 181.2 in 2004, 247.8 in 2005, 245.1 in 2006; Total fruits (excl. melons) 734.0 in 2004, 659.3 in 2005, 659.3 in 2006.

Source: FAO.

LIVESTOCK
('000 head, year ending September)

	2003	2004	2005
Horses*	175	178	180
Asses, mules or hinnies*	4	4	4
Cattle	1,498	1,550*	1,600*
Pigs*	265	270	272
Goats*	6	6	6
Chickens	13,143	13,500*	14,000*
Ducks*	220	225	225
Turkeys*	33	35	35

* FAO estimate(s).

2006: Figures assumed to be unchanged from 2005 (FAO estimates).
Source: FAO.

LIVESTOCK PRODUCTS
('000 metric tons)

	2003	2004	2005*
Cattle meat	60.5	63.6	57.0
Pig meat	20.3	20.9	20.6
Chicken meat	82.8	87.4	85.1
Cows' milk	179.7	175.8	187.0
Hen eggs	19.9	20.0*	21.0

* FAO estimate(s).

2006: Figures assumed to be unchanged from 2005 (FAO estimates).
Source: FAO.

PANAMA
Statistical Survey

Forestry

ROUNDWOOD REMOVALS
('000 cubic metres, excluding bark)

	2004	2005	2006
Sawlogs, veneer logs and logs for sleepers	2	64	69
Other industrial wood	1	1	1
Fuel wood*	1,219	1,205	1,189
Pulp wood	90†	90*	90*
Total	**1,312†**	**1,360***	**1,349***

* FAO estimate(s).
† Unofficial figure.
Source: FAO.

SAWNWOOD PRODUCTION
('000 cubic metres, incl. railway sleepers)

	2003	2004	2005*
Total (all broadleaved)	27	30	30

* FAO estimate.
2006: Production assumed to be unchanged from 2005 (FAO estimate).
Source: FAO.

Fishing

('000 metric tons, live weight)

	2003	2004	2005
Capture	215.4	203.2	214.7
Snappers and jobfishes	13.1	5.0	11.0
Pacific thread herring	50.9	45.5	32.0
Pacific anchoveta	76.5	47.0	59.5
Skipjack tuna	11.5	18.5	39.2
Yellowfin tuna	28.7	33.6	36.1
Bigeye tuna	3.9	10.4	11.4
Marine fishes	12.8	25.9	10.9
Aquaculture	6.2	7.0	8.0
Whiteleg shrimp	6.1	6.5	7.1
Total catch	**221.6**	**210.3**	**222.8**

Note: Figures exclude crocodiles. The number of spectacled caimans caught was: 13,298 in 2003; 14,694 in 2004; 9,648 in 2005.
Source: FAO.

Industry

SELECTED PRODUCTS
('000 metric tons, unless otherwise indicated)

	2002	2003	2004
Salt	16	13	19
Sugar	152	147	157
Beer (million litres)	135	149	164
Wines and spirits (million litres)	13	13	14
Non-alcoholic, carbonated beverages (million litres)	163	—	—
Evaporated, condensed and powdered milk	28	23	20
Fish oil	10	8	5
Footwear ('000 pairs)	78	73	30
Electricity (million kWh, net)	4,996	5,281	5,475

2005 ('000 metric tons, unless otherwise indicated): Sugar 157; Beer (million litres) 167; Wine and spirits (million litres) 13.
2006 ('000 metric tons, unless otherwise indicated): Sugar 168; Beer (million litres) 180; Wines and spirits (million litres) 12.

Finance

CURRENCY AND EXCHANGE RATES
Monetary Units
100 centésimos = 1 balboa (B).

Sterling, Dollar and Euro Equivalents (31 December 2007)
£1 sterling = 2.003 balboas;
US $1 = 1.000 balboas;
€1 = 1.472 balboas;
100 balboas = £49.92 = $100.00 = €67.93.

Exchange Rate: The balboa's value is fixed at par with that of the US dollar.

BUDGET
(consolidated general government budget, '000 balboas)

Revenue	2004	2005	2006*
Central government revenue	3,221,129	3,438,186	3,783,081
Current revenue	1,998,857	2,328,211	3,158,010
Tax revenue	1,245,801	1,378,673	1,813,549
Direct taxes	603,011	708,181	1,020,263
Income tax	488,956	583,901	878,407
Taxes property and inheritance	77,168	88,037	91,715
Educational insurance	36,887	36,243	50,141
Indirect taxes	642,790	670,492	793,286
Non-tax revenue	675,666	866,506	1,281,780
Panama Canal	183,709	200,000	334,181
Transfers from balance of public sector	2,084	2,626	2,523
Other current revenue	77,390	83,032	62,681
Surplus on cash account	9,839	22,265	12,564
Capital revenue	1,212,433	1,087,710	612,507
Decentralized institutional revenue	1,916,000	1,796,600	1,971,100
Department of social security	1,511,600	1,388,900	1,494,300
University of Panama	107,700	114,800	116,900
State enterprises	2,464,300	1,412,000	1,683,800
Non-financial	465,500	532,300	568,200
Financial	1,998,800	879,700	1,115,600
Municipalities	93,300	101,400	—
Total revenue	**7,694,700**	**6,748,200**	**7,437,900**

Expenditure	2004	2005	2006*
Central government expenditure	3,209,110	3,408,186	3,772,692
Current expenditure	2,706,179	3,020,194	3,041,525
National Assembly	42,461	45,245	50,722
State treasury	34,162	34,122	38,106
Ministry of the Presidency	44,909	41,299	51,863
Ministry of the Interior and Justice	212,075	210,398	224,806
Ministry of Foreign Affairs	33,100	30,807	33,498
Ministry of Social Development	15,214	15,507	16,774
Ministry of the Economy and Finance	149,433	154,515	138,825
Ministry of Education	500,037	533,327	594,516
Ministry of Commerce and Industry	17,110	37,067	33,050
Ministry of Public Works	19,184	22,454	36,003
Ministry of Agricultural Development	32,817	33,755	39,280
Ministry of Public Health	431,333	358,734	473,234
Ministry of Labour and Social Welfare	8,003	8,719	7,197
Ministry of Housing	9,896	11,177	12,147
Judiciary	36,142	36,553	40,474
Ombudsman	45,136	42,244	45,581

PANAMA

Statistical Survey

Expenditure—continued	2004	2005	2006*
Electoral tribunal	39,335	23,237	32,247
Other expenditures of administration	10,538	11,148	11,314
Debt servicing	993,912	1,333,411	1,115,816
Education fund	31,382	36,475	46,072
Ministerial development expenditure	502,931	387,992	731,167
Decentralized institutional expenditure	1,874,200	1,617,900	1,745,100
Department of social security	1,502,900	1,261,100	1,312,600
State enterprises	2,382,800	1,316,400	1,623,800
Municipalities	90,400	94,000	—
Total	7,556,500	6,436,500	7,141,600

* Preliminary figures.

Note: Totals may not be equal to the sum of component parts, owing to rounding.

INTERNATIONAL RESERVES
(US $ million at 31 December*)

	2004	2005	2006
IMF special drawing rights	0.9	1.1	1.3
Reserve position in IMF	18.4	17.0	17.8
Foreign exchange	611.4	1,192.5	1,315.9
Total	630.6	1,210.5	1,335.0

* Excludes gold, valued at US $476,000 in 1991–93.

Note: US treasury notes and coins form the bulk of the currency in circulation in Panama.

Source: IMF, *International Financial Statistics*.

COST OF LIVING
(Consumer Price Index, base: 2000 = 100)

	2004	2005	2006
Food (incl. beverages)	101.3	105.6	107.0
Rent, fuel and light	99.8	104.0	109.3
Clothing (incl. footwear)	97.1	97.1	96.3
All items (incl. others)	100.4	103.3	105.9

Source: ILO.

NATIONAL ACCOUNTS
(million balboas at current prices)

National Income and Product

	2004	2005	2006*
Compensation of employees	4,919.0	5,122.5	5,582.3
Operating surplus	5,293.7	6,006.0	6,532.2
Net mixed income	1,824.7	1,996.2	2,249.7
Domestic factor incomes	12,037.4	13,124.7	14,364.2
Consumption of fixed capital	1,039.6	1,060.4	1,161.1
Gross domestic product (GDP) at factor cost	13,077.0	14,185.1	15,525.3
Indirect taxes	1,186.8	1,366.3	1,770.5
Less Subsidies	84.5	86.7	162.0
GDP in purchasers' values	14,179.3	15,464.7	17,133.8
Less Net factor income paid to the rest of the world	1,268.9	1,436.5	1,576.4
Gross national product	12,910.4	14,028.2	15,557.4
Less Consumption of fixed capital	1,039.6	1,060.4	1,161.1
National income in market prices	11,870.8	12,967.8	14,396.3
Other current transfers from abroad (net)	151.0	165.6	159.1
National disposable income	12,021.8	13,133.4	14,555.4

* Provisional figures.

Expenditure on the Gross Domestic Product

	2004	2005	2006*
Government final consumption expenditure	1,929.7	2,033.8	2,116.3
Private final consumption expenditure	9,072.9	9,597.2	10,333.0
Increase in stocks	300.9	237.7	200.0
Gross fixed capital formation	2,351.0	2,601.3	3,134.9
Total domestic expenditure	13,654.5	14,470.0	15,784.2
Exports of goods and services	9,586.5	11,674.2	13,269.6
Less Imports of goods and services	9,061.7	10,679.5	11,920.0
GDP in purchasers' values	14,179.3	15,464.7	17,133.8
GDP at constant 1996 prices	13,099.2	14,041.2	15,256.1

* Provisional figures.

Gross Domestic Product by Economic Activity

	2004	2005	2006*
Agriculture, hunting, forestry and fishing	987.8	1,006.6	1,066.1
Mining and quarrying	142.7	151.1	190.4
Manufacturing	1,023.4	1,072.4	1,156.5
Electricity, gas and water	422.6	504.5	498.6
Construction	677.1	692.2	845.8
Wholesale and retail trade, repair of vehicles, motorcycles and other household goods	1,911.1	2,201.7	2,510.5
Colón Free Zone	960.0	1,209.1	1,383.5
Hotels and restaurants	324.1	364.5	426.4
Transport, storage and communications	2,165.5	2,409.9	2,944.1
Financial intermediation	1,193.4	1,343.5	1,426.9
Renting, real estate and business services	2,507.9	2,709.9	2,941.8
Public administration	645.4	637.9	695.1
Education	588.4	603.5	639.1
Social services and health	511.2	539.2	535.9
Other community, social and personal services	456.2	479.3	508.2
Other services	123.1	128.9	139.3
Sub-total	13,679.9	14,845.1	16,524.7
Less Financial intermediation services indirectly measured	404.0	422.2	441.4
Gross value added in basic prices	13,275.9	14,422.9	16,083.3
Import duties and other taxes, less subsidies	903.4	1,041.8	1,050.5
GDP in market prices	14,179.3	15,464.7	17,133.8

* Provisional figures.

BALANCE OF PAYMENTS
(US $ million)*

	2004	2005	2006
Exports of goods f.o.b.	6,078.3	7,591.2	8,475.6
Imports of goods f.o.b.	−7,616.6	−8,907.2	−10,201.2
Trade balance	−1,538.3	−1,316.0	−1,725.6
Exports of services	2,788.3	3,217.2	3,939.8
Imports of services	−1,457.2	−1,780.9	−1,726.4
Balance on goods and services	−207.2	120.3	487.8
Other income received	787.0	1,056.1	1,421.6
Other income paid	−1,811.3	−2,181.0	−2,719.3
Balance on goods, services and income	−1,231.5	−1,004.6	−809.9
Current transfers received	300.1	341.8	393.8
Current transfers paid	−80.5	−96.5	−135.9
Current balance	−1,011.9	−759.3	−552.0
Direct investment from abroad	1,019.1	962.1	2,574.2
Portfolio investment assets	−650.8	−1,103.3	−676.1
Portfolio investment liabilities	775.9	545.7	254.9
Other investment assets	−1,542.8	−358.9	−3,645.2
Other investment liabilities	895.4	1,943.6	2,163.5
Net errors and omissions	118.9	−553.7	56.4
Overall balance	−396.1	676.2	175.7

* Including the transactions of enterprises operating in the Colón Free Zone.

Source: IMF, *International Financial Statistics*.

PANAMA

External Trade

PRINCIPAL COMMODITIES
(US $ million, excl. Colón Free Zone)

Imports c.i.f.	2004*	2005	2006†
Consumer goods	1,574.2	1,793.0	2,060.5
Non-durable	596.1	580.1	664.2
Semi-durable	303.5	325.8	373.5
Domestic utensils	131.2	150.6	177.0
Fuels, lubricants and related products	516.4	736.6	845.9
Intermediate goods	1,119.2	1,266.0	1,492.2
Primary materials and products for agriculture	88.5	113.2	113.4
Primary materials and products for industry	735.9	767.7	831.6
Construction materials	254.9	354.3	502.4
Other	39.3	30.8	44.9
Capital goods	925.8	1,093.9	1,278.2
Agricultural	25.2	24.6	28.8
For industry, construction and electricity	277.8	214.0	275.1
Transport and telecommunications equipment	525.1	375.5	416.5
Other	97.8	479.8	557.8
Total (incl. others)	3,592.2	4,152.8	4,830.9

* Preliminary figures.

Exports f.o.b.*	2004†	2005	2006†
Products derived from petroleum	4.9	7.1	7.7
Sugar	10.4	23.7	n.a.
Bananas	108.2	96.5	109.1
Melons	70.9	117.0	n.a.
Coffee	10.9	13.5	13.1
Shrimps	53.8	57.8	50.2
Fresh and frozen fish and fillets (incl. yellowfin tuna)	281.8	264.8	230.8
Clothing	8.8	10.3	9.9
Meat from cattle	14.4	12.4	12.2
Standing cattle	13.2	21.2	n.a.
Total (incl. others)	939.0	963.2	1,021.9

* Including re-exports.
† Preliminary figures.

PRINCIPAL TRADING PARTNERS
(US $ '000)

Imports c.i.f.	2002	2003	2005*
Canada	20,035	20,192	n.a.
Colombia†	179,627	123,191	143,638
Costa Rica	127,822	151,133	194,623
Ecuador	99,116	7,003	n.a.
Germany	45,747	49,211	52,774
Guatemala	62,953	71,097	83,664
Japan	164,610	193,231	188,157
Korea, Republic	63,536	63,803	102,877
Mexico	112,440	119,155	154,058
Netherlands Antilles‡	52,013	89,613	475,190
Spain	41,617	48,693	63,151
Trinidad and Tobago	38,551	19,550	43,823
United Kingdom	18,590	31,815	n.a.
USA	1,016,191	1,066,132	1,130,661
Venezuela	127,675	84,877	44,789
Total (incl. others)	3,035,737	3,124,885	4,155,293

Exports f.o.b.	2003	2004	2005
Belgium-Luxembourg	24,340	29,684	24,907
China, People's Republic	n.a.	10,817	20,046
Colombia†	8,574	11,892	15,465
Costa Rica	33,466	36,772	38,748
Dominican Republic	8,264	9,744	16,441
Ecuador	3,883	5,696	5,302
El Salvador	9,403	10,591	9,335
Guatemala	13,254	11,612	24,907
Honduras	13,362	15,403	15,620
Hong Kong	5,122	7,656	6,595

Exports f.o.b.—continued	2003	2004	2005
India	n.a.	18,125	6,552
Italy	9,517	12,525	15,153
Mexico	12,060	13,916	17,112
Netherlands	n.a.	38,784	47,056
Nicaragua	24,815	18,227	21,380
Portugal	27,469	23,240	12,645
Puerto Rico	12,954	11,894	13,121
Spain	45,593	44,999	85,626
Sweden	48,262	57,994	54,332
Taiwan	6,618	11,390	20,046
United Kingdom	n.a.	6,565	18,430
USA	402,604	433,004	419,412
Total (incl. others)	798,747	891,105	963,764

* Figures for 2004 not available.
† Excluding San Andrés island.
‡ Curaçao only.

2006 ('000 balboas, preliminary results): *Imports:* Colombia 170,009; Costa Rica 247,634; Germany 56,873; Guatemala 86,510; Japan 229,232; Korea, Republic 165,558; Mexico 173,017; Spain 73,912; Trinidad and Tobago 32,316; United Kingdom 35,784; USA 1,294,298; Venezuela 53,133; Total (incl. others) 4,830,904. *Exports:* Belgium-Luxembourg 38,647; China, People's Republic 14,679; Colombia 18,564; Costa Rica 45,725; Dominican Republic 15,955; El Salvador 9,232; Guatemala 33,018; Honduras 17,974; Hong Kong 4,982; India 6,119; Italy 26,397; Mexico 10,366; Netherlands 68,309; Nicaragua 17,582; Portugal 11,731; Puerto Rico 13,872; Spain 83,190; Sweden 56,933; Taiwan 23,698; USA 392,881; Total (incl. others) 1,021,941.

2007 ('000 balboas, preliminary results): *Imports:* Colombia 192,280; Costa Rica 326,850; Germany 87,516; Guatemala 108,702; Japan 328,958; Korea, Republic 267,671; Mexico 211,967; Spain 107,107; USA 2,078,151; Venezuela 55,403; Total (incl. others) 6,874,686. *Exports:* Belgium-Luxembourg 42,310; China, People's Republic 62,904; Colombia 19,075; Costa Rica 57,003; Dominican Republic 13,574; El Salvador 8,051; Guatemala 16,651; Honduras 20,380; Hong Kong 5,250; India 7,800; Italy 18,291; Mexico 9,084; Netherlands 114,820; Nicaragua 12,874; Portugal 12,925; Puerto Rico 9,023; Spain 55,983; Sweden 62,150; Taiwan 39,513; USA 391,173; Total (incl. others) 1,120,471.

Transport

RAILWAYS
(traffic)

	2002*	2003	2004
Passenger-km (million)	35,693	52,324	53,377
Freight ton-km (million)	20,665	41,863	52,946

* Panama Railway only.

Source: UN, *Statistical Yearbook*.

ROAD TRAFFIC
(motor vehicles in use)

	2000	2001	2002
Cars	223,433	219,372	224,504
Buses and coaches	16,865	15,558	16,371
Lorries and vans	75,454	73,139	74,247

Source: IRF, *World Road Statistics*.

SHIPPING

Merchant Fleet
(registered at 31 December)

	2003	2004	2005
Number of vessels	6,302	6,477	6,838
Total displacement ('000 grt)	125,721.7	131,451.7	141,821.7

Source: Lloyd's Register-Fairplay, *World Fleet Statistics*.

PANAMA

International Sea-borne Freight Traffic
('000 metric tons)

	2001	2002	2003
Goods loaded	108,456	110,556	99,516
Goods unloaded	84,864	99,288	76,152

Panama Canal Traffic

	2003	2004	2005
Transits	13,154	14,035	14,011
Cargo (million long tons)	188.3	200.2	193.8

Source: Panama Canal Authority.

CIVIL AVIATION
(traffic on scheduled services)

	2003	2004	2005
Kilometres flown (million)	42	46	55
Passengers carried ('000)	1,264	n.a.	n.a.
Passengers-km (million)	3,408	4,101	5,206
Total ton-km (million)	20	35	37

Source: UN Economic Commission for Latin America and the Caribbean, *Statistical Yearbook*.

Tourism

VISITOR ARRIVALS BY COUNTRY OF ORIGIN
(arrivals at Tocumen International Airport)

	2003	2004	2005
Argentina	8,950	10,108	11,629
Canada	14,297	16,911	19,660
Chile	6,946	7,406	8,150
Colombia	90,697	93,510	108,628
Costa Rica	20,378	21,459	25,455
Dominican Republic	6,110	5,923	7,396
Ecuador	20,252	22,391	25,903
El Salvador	7,624	9,031	9,279
France	6,766	6,881	7,289
Germany	4,091	4,222	4,745
Guatemala	12,121	12,400	14,349
Honduras	5,470	6,027	6,584
Italy	4,945	5,198	6,617
Jamaica	4,575	4,629	5,593
Mexico	23,765	24,532	29,280
Nicaragua	5,341	5,304	6,056
Peru	10,514	11,508	12,592
Puerto Rico	7,526	8,129	8,625
Spain	9,196	9,569	10,838
USA	128,897	140,062	160,288
Venezuela	14,607	16,249	18,892
Total (incl. others)	468,686	498,415	576,050

Tourism receipts (US $ million, incl. passenger transport): 804 in 2003; 903 in 2004; 1,108 in 2005.

Source: World Tourism Organization.

Communications Media

	2003	2004	2005
Telephones ('000 main lines in use)	381.4	410.2	468.8
Mobile cellular telephones ('000 subscribers)	692.4	1,259.9	1,693.5
Personal computers ('000 in use)	120	130	147
Internet users ('000)	173.1	196.5	206.2
Broadband subscribers ('000)	15.0	16.7	17.6

Telephones ('000 main lines in use): 432.9 in 2006.
Internet users ('000): 220.0 in 2006.
Radio receivers ('000 in use): 815 in 1997.
Television receivers ('000 in use): 550 in 2000.
Daily newspapers: 8 in 2004.

Sources: UNESCO, *Statistical Yearbook*; UN, *Statistical Yearbook*; International Telecommunication Union.

Education

(provisional, 2004/05, unless otherwise indicated)

	Institutions*	Teachers	Pupils
Pre-primary	1,662	4,227	74,857
Primary	3,116	17,751	430,152
Secondary	442	16,392	256,224
Tertiary	24	11,431†	126,242

* 2001/02 figures.
† 2000/01 figure.

Sources: Ministry of Education; UNESCO, *Statistical Yearbook*.

Adult literacy rate (UNESCO estimates): 91.9% (males 92.5%; females 91.2%) in 2000 (Source: UNESCO Institute for Statistics).

Directory

The Constitution

Under the terms of the amendments to the Constitution, implemented by the adoption of Reform Acts No. 1 and No. 2 in October 1978, and by the approval by referendum of the Constitutional Act in April 1983, the 67 (later 78) members of the unicameral Asamblea Legislativa (Legislative Assembly) are elected by popular vote every five years. Executive power is exercised by the President of the Republic, who is also elected by popular vote for a term of five years. Two Vice-Presidents are elected by popular vote to assist the President. The President appoints the Cabinet. The armed forces are barred from participating in elections. In July 2004 further amendments to the Constitution were adopted, including a reduction (to 71) in the number of members of the Asamblea from 2009, the abolition of parliamentary immunity from prosecution, and the creation of a constitutional assembly to consider future changes to the Constitution.

The Government

HEAD OF STATE

President: MARTÍN TORRIJOS ESPINO (took office 1 September 2004).
First Vice-President: SAMUEL LEWIS NAVARRO.

PANAMA

THE CABINET
(April 2008)

Minister of the Interior and Justice: DANIEL DELGADO DIAMANTE.
Minister of Foreign Affairs: SAMUEL LEWIS NAVARRO.
Minister of Public Works: BENJAMÍN COLAMARCO.
Minister of the Economy and Finance: HÉCTOR ALEXANDER.
Minister of Agricultural Development: GUILLERMO AUGUSTO SALAZAR NICOLAU.
Minister of Commerce and Industry: ALEJANDRO FERRER.
Minister of Health: Dr ROSARIO TURNER.
Minister of Labour and Social Welfare: EDWIN ANTONIO SALAMIN JAÉN.
Minister of Education: BELGIS CASTRO JAÉN.
Minister of Housing: BALBINA HERRERA ARAÚZ.
Minister of the Presidency: RUBÉN AROSEMENA VALDÉS.
Minister of Social Development: MARÍA DEL CARMEN ROQUEBERT LEÓN.

MINISTRIES

Office of the President: Palacio Presidencial, Valija 50, Panamá 1; tel. 227-4062; fax 227-0076; internet www.presidencia.gob.pa.

Ministry of Agricultural Development: Edif. 576, Calle Manuel E. Melo, Altos de Curundú, Apdo 5390, Panamá 5; tel. 507-0600; e-mail infomida@mida.gob.pa; internet www.mida.gob.pa.

Ministry of Commerce and Industry: El Paical, 3°, Avda Ricardo J. Alfaro, Plaza Edison, Apdo 9658, Panamá 4; tel. 560-0600; fax 560-0663; e-mail uti@mici.gob.pa; internet www.mici.gob.pa.

Ministry of the Economy and Finance: Edif. Ogawa, Vía España, Apdo 5245, Panamá 5; tel. 507-7008; e-mail webmaster@mef.gob.pa; internet www.mef.gob.pa.

Ministry of Education: Edif. Poli y Los Rios, Avda Justo Arosemena, Calles 26 y 27, Apdo 0816-04049, Panamá 3; tel. 511-4400; fax 262-9087; e-mail meduca@meduca.gob.pa; internet www.meduca.gob.pa.

Ministry of Foreign Affairs: Altos de Ancón, Complejo Narciso Garay, Panamá 4; tel. 511-4100; e-mail prensa@mire.gob.pa; internet www.mire.gob.pa.

Ministry of Health: Apdo 2048, Panamá 1; tel. and fax 512-9202; e-mail saludaldia@minsa.gob.pa; internet www.minsa.gob.pa.

Ministry of Housing: Avda Ricardo J. Alfaro, Edif. Plaza Edison, 4°, Apdo 5228, Panamá 5; tel. 579-9200; e-mail webmaster@mivi.gob.pa; internet www.mivi.gob.pa.

Ministry of the Interior and Justice: Avda Central, entre calle 2 y 3, San Felipe, Apdo 1628, Panamá 1; tel. 512-2000; fax 512-2126; e-mail informa@gobiernoyjusticia.gob.pa; internet www.gobiernoyjusticia.gob.pa.

Ministry of Labour and Social Welfare: Avda Ricardo J. Alfaro, Plaza Edison, 5°, Apdo 2441, Panamá 3; tel. 560-1100; e-mail mitrabs2@sinfo.net; internet www.mitradel.gob.pa.

Ministry of the Presidency: Palacio de Las Garzas, Corregimiento de San Felipe, Apdo 2189, Panamá 1; tel. 527-9600; e-mail ofasin@presidencia.gob.pa; internet www.presidencia.gob.pa.

Ministry of Public Works: Edif. 1019, Curundú, Zona 1, Apdo 1632, Panamá 1; tel. 507-9600; e-mail info@mop.gob.pa; internet www.mop.gob.pa.

Ministry of Social Development: Avda Ricardo J. Alfaro, 4°, Plaza Edison, Apdo 680-50, El Dorado, Panamá; tel. 500-6000; e-mail mides@mides.gob.pa; internet www.mides.gob.pa.

President and Legislature

PRESIDENT
Election, 2 May 2004

Candidate	Votes	% of votes
Martín Torrijos Espino (Patria Nueva*)	711,447	47.44
Guillermo Endara Galimany (Partido Solidaridad)	462,766	30.86
José Miguel Alemán (Visión de País†)	245,845	16.39
Ricardo A. Martinelli Berrocal (Cambio Democrático)	79,595	5.31
Total	1,499,653	100.00

* Electoral alliance comprising the Partido Revolucionario Democrático and the Partido Popular.

† Electoral alliance comprising the Partido Arnulfista (now the Partido Panameñista), the Movimiento Liberal Republicano Nacionalista and the Partido Liberal Nacional.

ASAMBLEA LEGISLATIVA
(Legislative Assembly)

President: PEDRO MIGUEL GONZÁLEZ PINZÓN.

General Election, 2 May 2004

Affiliation/Party	% of votes	Seats
Patria Nueva		
Partido Revolucionario Democrático (PRD)	37.9	42
Partido Popular (PP)	6.0	1
Visión de País		
Partido Arnulfista (PA)	19.3	16
Movimiento Liberal Republicano Nacionalista (MOLIRENA)	8.6	4
Partido Liberal Nacional (PLN)*	5.2	3
Partido Solidaridad*	15.7	9
Cambio Democrático (CD)	7.4	3
Total	100.0	78

* The Partido Liberal Nacional and the Partido Solidaridad merged in 2007 to form the Unión Patriótica.

Election Commission

Tribunal Electoral: Avda Ecuador y Justo Arosemena, Edif. Dirección Superior, Apdo 5281, Panamá 5; tel. 207-8000; e-mail secretaria-general@tribunal-electoral.gob.pa; internet www.tribunal-electoral.gob.pa; f. 1956; independent; Pres. ERASMO PINILLA CASTILLERO.

Political Organizations

Cambio Democrático (CD): Parque Lefevre, Plaza Carolina, arriba de la Juguetería del Super 99, Panamá; tel. 217-2643; fax 217-2645; e-mail cambio.democratico@hotmail.com; formally registered 1998; Pres. RICARDO A. MARTINELLI BERROCAL; Sec.-Gen. GIACOMO TAMBURELLI.

Movimiento Liberal Republicano Nacionalista (MOLIRENA): Calle Venezuela, Casa No 5, entre Vía España y Calle 50, Panamá; tel. 213-5928; fax 265-6004; formally registered 1982; conservative; contested the 2004 elections as part of the Visión de País electoral alliance; Pres. SERGIO GONZÁLEZ RUIZ.

Partido Panameñista (PP): Avda Perú y Calle 38E, No 37–41, al lado de Casa la Esperanza, Apdo 9610, Panamá 4; tel. 227-1267; f. 1990 by Arnulfista faction of the Partido Panameñista Auténtico as Partido Arnulfista (PA); contested the 2004 elections as part of the Visión de País electoral alliance; name changed as above in Jan. 2005; Pres. JUAN CARLOS VARELA.

Partido Popular: Avda Perú, frente al Parque Porras, Apdo 6322, Panamá 5; tel. 227-3204; fax 227-3944; e-mail pdc@cwpanama.net; f. 1960 as Partido Demócrata Cristiano; name changed as above in 2001; contested the 2004 elections as part of the Patria Nueva electoral alliance; Pres. CAMILO BRENES.

Partido Revolucionario Democrático (PRD): Calle 42 Bella Vista, entre Avda Perú y Avda Cuba, bajando por el teatro Bella Vista, Panamá 9; tel. 225-1050; e-mail prdpanama@yahoo.com; f. 1979; supports policies of late Gen. Omar Torrijos Herrera; combination of Marxists, Christian Democrats and some business interests; contested the 2004 elections as part of the Patria Nueva electoral alliance; Pres. BALBINA HERRERA; Sec.-Gen. MARTÍN TORRIJOS ESPINO.

Unión Patriótica (UP): Panamá; f. 2007 following merger of Partido Liberal Nacional and Partido Solidaridad; Pres. GUILLERMO FORD.

Vanguardia Moral de la Patria (VMP): Vía España, esq. con Vía Porras, Panamá; tel. 212-7300; f. 2004; Pres. GUILLERMO ENDARA; Gen. Sec. Dr JOHN HOGER CASTRELLÓN.

Diplomatic Representation

EMBASSIES IN PANAMA

Argentina: Edif. del Banco de Iberoamérica, 7°, Avda 50 y Calle 53, Apdo 1271, Panamá 1; tel. 264-6561; fax 269-5331; e-mail embargen@c-com.net.pa; Ambassador JORGE ALBERTO ARGUINDEGUI.

Belize: Villa de la Fuente 1, F-32, Calle 22, POB 0819-12255, Panamá; tel. 236-3762; fax 236-4132; e-mail nmusag@cwpanama.net; Ambassador ALMA MUSA.

Bolivia: Calle Eric Arturo del Valle, Bella Vista 1, Panamá; tel. 269-0274; fax 264-3868; e-mail emb_bol_pan@cwpanama.net; Ambassador EDGAR SOLIZ MORALES.

Brazil: Edif. El Dorado, 1°, Calle Elvira Méndez y Avda Ricardo Arango, Urb. Campo Alegre, Apdo 4287, Panamá 5; tel. 263-5322; fax 269-6316; e-mail embrasil@embrasil.org.pa; Ambassador LUÍZ TUPY CALDAS DE MOURA.

Canada: Edif. World Trade Center, Galería Comercial, 1°, Urb. Marbella, Apdo 0832-2446, Panamá; tel. 264-7115; fax 263-8083; e-mail panam@international.gc.ca; internet www.dfait-maeci.gc.ca/panama; Ambassador JOSÉ HERRÁN LIMA.

Chile: Edif. Banco de Boston, 11°, Calle Elvira Méndez y Vía España, Apdo 7341, Panamá 5; tel. 223-9748; fax 263-5530; e-mail echilepa@cw.panama.net; internet www.embachilepanama.com; Ambassador CARLOS KLAMMER BORGOÑO.

China (Taiwan): Edif. Torre Hong Kong Bank, 10°, Avda Samuel Lewis, Panamá; tel. 223-3424; fax 269-8757; e-mail embchina@cableonda.net; Ambassador TOMAS PING-FU HOU.

Colombia: Edif. World Trade Center, Of. 1802, Calle 53, Urb. Marbella, Panamá; tel. 264-9644; fax 223-1134; e-mail epanama@minrelext.gov.co; Ambassador GINA BENEDETTI DE VÉLEZ.

Costa Rica: Edif. Plaza Omega, 3°, Calle Samuel Lewis, Apdo 8963, Panamá; tel. 264-2980; fax 264-4057; e-mail embarica@cwp.net.pa; Ambassador EKHART PETERS SEVEERS.

Cuba: Avda Cuba y Ecuador 33, Apdo 6-2291, Bellavista, Panamá; tel. 227-5277; fax 225-6681; e-mail embacuba@cableonda.net; Ambassador CARLOS ELOY GARCÍA TRÁPAGA.

Dominican Republic: Casa 40A, Calle 75, Apdo 6250, Panamá 5; tel. 270-3884; fax 270-3886; e-mail embajdom@sinfo.net; Ambassador VIRGILIO AUGUSTO ALVAREZ BONILLA.

Ecuador: Edif. Torre 2000, 6°, Calle 50, Marbella, Bellavista, Panamá; e-mail eecuador@cwpanama.net; tel. 264-2654; fax 223-0159; Ambassador ELSA BEATRIZ VILLACÍS ROCA.

Egypt: Calle 55, No 15, El Cangrejo, Apdo 7080, Panamá 5; tel. 263-5020; fax 264-8406; Chargé d'affaires a.i. TAREK SIRAG.

El Salvador: Edif. Metropolis, 4°, Avda Manuel Espinosa Batista, Panamá; tel. 223-3020; fax 264-1433; e-mail embasalva@cwpanama.net; Ambassador GERARDO SOL MIXCO.

France: Plaza de Francia 1, Las Bovedas, San Felipe, Apdo 869, Panamá 1; tel. 211-6200; fax 211-6201; e-mail pierre_henri.guignard@diplomatie.gouv.fr; internet www.ambafrance-pa.org; Ambassador PIERRE HENRI GUIGNARD.

Germany: Edif. World Trade Center, 20°, Calle 53E, Marbella, Apdo 0832-0536, Panamá 5; tel. 263-7733; fax 223-6664; e-mail germpanama@cwp.net.pa; internet www.panama.diplo.de; Ambassador BORUSSO VON BLÜCHER.

Guatemala: Edif. Altamira, Of. 925, Vía Argentina, El Cangrejo, Corregimiento de Bella Vista, Panamá 9; tel. 269-3475; fax 223-1922; Ambassador LIONEL VALENTÍN MAZA LUNA.

Haiti: Edif. Dora Luz, 2°, Calle 1, El Cangrejo, Apdo 442, Panamá 9; tel. 269-3443; fax 223-1767; Chargé d'affaires a.i. BOCCHIT EDMOND.

Holy See: Punta Paitilla, Avda Balboa y Vía Italia, Apdo 4251, Panamá 5 (Apostolic Nunciature); tel. 269-2102; fax 264-2116; e-mail nuncio@cableonda.net; Apostolic Nuncio Most Rev. GIAMBATTISTA DIQUATTRO (Titular Archbishop of Giru Mons).

Honduras: Edif. Bay Mall, 1°, Avda Balboa 112, Apdo 8704, Panamá 5; tel. 264-5513; fax 224-5513; e-mail ehpan@cableonda.net; Ambassador JUAN ALFARO POSADAS.

India: Avda Federico Boyd y Calle 51, Bella Vista, Apdo 8400, Panamá 7; tel. 264-3043; fax 264-2855; e-mail indempan@c-com.net.pa; internet www.indempan.org; Ambassador ASHOK TOMAR.

Israel: Panamá; tel. 208-4700; fax 208-4755; Ambassador MENASHE BAR-ON.

Italy: Torre Banco Exterior, 25°, Avda Balboa, Apdo 2369, Panamá 9; tel. 225-8950; fax 227-4906; e-mail ambpana.mail@esteri.it; internet www.ambpanama.esteri.it; Ambassador PLACIDO VIGO.

Japan: Calle 50 y 60E, Obarrio, Apdo 1411, Panamá 1; tel. 263-6155; fax 263-6019; e-mail taiship2@cwpanama.net; internet www.panama.emb-japan.go.jp; Ambassador SHUJI SHIMOKOJI.

Korea, Republic: Edif. Plaza, planta baja, Calle Ricardo Arias y Calle 51E, Campo Alegre, Apdo 8096, Panamá 7; tel. 264-8203; fax 264-8825; e-mail panama@mofat.go.kr; Ambassador GWANG-KEUN KIM.

Libya: Avda Balboa y Calle 32 (frente al Edif. Atalaya), Apdo 6-894 El Dorado, Panamá; tel. 227-3342; fax 227-3886; Chargé d'affaires a.i. ABDULMAJID MILUD SHAHIN.

Mexico: Edif. Torre ADR, 10°, Avda Samuel Lewis y Calle 58, Urb. Obarrio, Corregimiento de Bella Vista, Panamá; tel. 263-4900; fax 263-5446; e-mail embamexpan@cwpanama.net; internet www.sre.gob.mx/panama; Ambassador YANERIT CRISTINA MORGAN SOTOMAYOR.

Nicaragua: Quarry Heights, 16°, Ancón, Apdo 772, Zona 1, Panamá; tel. 211-2113; fax 211-2116; e-mail embapana@sinfo.net; Ambassador ANTENOR ALBERTO FERREY PERNUDI.

Peru: Edif. World Trade Center, 12°, Calle 53, Urb. Marbella, Apdo 4516, Panamá 5; tel. 223-1112; fax 269-6809; e-mail embaperu@pananet.com; Ambassador JOSÉ BARBA CABALLERO.

Russia: Torre IBC, 10°, Avda Manuel Espinosa Batista, Apdo 6-4697, El Dorado, Panamá; tel. 264-1408; fax 264-1588; e-mail emruspan@sinfo.net; Ambassador EVGENY ROSTISLAVOVICH VORONIN.

Spain: Calle 53 y Avda Perú (frente a la Plaza Porras), Apdo 1857, Panamá 1; tel. 227-5122; fax 227-6284; e-mail embesppa@correo.mae.es; Ambassador JOSÉ MANUEL LÓPEZ-BARRÓN DE LABRA.

United Kingdom: MMG Tower, 4°, Calle 53, Urb. Marbella, Apdo 0816-07946, Panamá 1; tel. 269-0866; fax 263-5138; e-mail britemb@cwpanama.net; internet www.britishembassy.gov.uk/panama; Ambassador RICHARD AUSTEN.

USA: Avda Balboa y Calle 38, Apdo 6959, Panamá 5; tel. 207-7000; fax 227-1964; e-mail panamaweb@state.gov; internet panama.usembassy.gov; Ambassador WILLIAM ALAN EATON, BARBARA J. STEPHENSON (designate).

Uruguay: Edif. Los Delfines, Of. 8, Avda Balboa, Calle 50E Este, Apdo 8898, Panamá 5; tel. 264-2838; fax 264-8908; e-mail urupanam@cwpanama.net; Ambassador DOMINGO FRANCISCO SCHIPANI BRIAN.

Venezuela: Torre Hong Kong Bank, 5°, Avda Samuel Lewis, Apdo 661, Panamá 1; tel. 269-1014; fax 269-1916; e-mail embvenp@c-com.net.pa; Chargé d'affaires a.i. JOSÉ ALFREDO GUERRERO SOSA.

Viet Nam: 52 José Gabriel Duque, La Cresta, Apdo 12434-6A, El Dorado, Panamá; tel. 264-2551; fax 265-6056; e-mail embavinapa@cwpanama.net; Ambassador NGHIEM XUAN LUONG.

Judicial System

The judiciary in Panama comprises the following courts and judges: Corte Suprema de Justicia (Supreme Court of Justice), with nine judges appointed for a 10-year term; 10 Tribunales Superiores de Distrito Judicial (High Courts) with 36 magistrates; 54 Jueces de Circuito (Circuit Judges) and 89 Jueces Municipales (Municipal Judges).

Panama is divided into four judicial districts and has seven High Courts of Appeal. The first judicial district covers the provinces of Panamá, Colón, Darién and the region of Kuna Yala and contains two High Courts of Appeal, one dealing with criminal cases, the other dealing with civil cases. The second judicial district covers the provinces of Coclé and Veraguas and contains the third High Court of Appeal, located in Penonomé. The third judicial district covers the provinces of Chiriquí and Bocas del Toro and contains the fourth High Court of Appeal, located in David. The fourth judicial district covers the provinces of Herrera and Los Santos and contains the fifth High Court of Appeal, located in Las Tablas. Each of these courts deals with civil and criminal cases in their respective provinces. There are two additional special High Courts of Appeal. The first hears maritime, labour, family and infancy cases; the second deals with antitrust cases and consumer affairs.

Corte Suprema de Justicia
Edif. 236, Calle Culebra, Ancón, Apdo 1770, Panamá 1; tel. 262-9833; e-mail prensa@organojudicial.gob.pa; internet www.organojudicial.gob.pa.

President of the Supreme Court of Justice: HARLEY JAMES MITCHELL DALE.

Procurator-General: ANA MATILDE GÓMEZ DE RUILOBA.

Religion

The Constitution recognizes freedom of worship and the Roman Catholic Church as the religion of the majority of the population.

CHRISTIANITY

The Roman Catholic Church

For ecclesiastical purposes, Panama comprises one archdiocese, five dioceses, the territorial prelature of Bocas del Toro and the Apostolic Vicariate of Darién. At 31 December 2005 Roman Catholics represented some 84% of the population.

PANAMA   *Directory*

Bishops' Conference
Conferencia Episcopal de Panamá, Secretariado General, Apdo 870933, Panamá 7; tel. 223-0075; fax 223-0042; internet www.iglesia.org.pa.
f. 1958; statutes approved 1986; Pres. Mgr José Luis Lacunza Maestrojuan (Bishop of David).
Archbishop of Panamá: Most Rev. José Dimas Cedeño Delgado, Arzobispado Metropolitano, Calle 1a Sur Carrasquilla, Apdo 6386, Panamá 5; tel. 261-0002; fax 261-0820; e-mail asccn4@keops.utp.ac.pa.

The Baptist Church
The Baptist Convention of Panama (Convención Bautista de Panamá): Apdo 0816-01761, Panamá 5; tel. and fax 259-5485; e-mail convencionbautistadepanama@hotmail.com; f. 1959; Pres. Francisco Medina; Sec. Esmeralda de Tuy; 7,573 mems.

The Anglican Communion
Panama comprises one of the five dioceses of the Iglesia Anglicana de la Región Central de América.
Bishop of Panama: Rt Rev. Julio Murray, Edif. 331A, Calle Culebra, Apdo R, Balboa; tel. 212-0062; fax 262-2097; e-mail anglipan@sinfo.net; internet www.episcopalpanama.org.

BAHÁ'Í FAITH
National Spiritual Assembly of the Bahá'ís: Apdo 815-0143, Panamá 15; tel. 231-1191; fax 231-6909; e-mail panbahai@cwpanama.net; internet www.pa.bahai.org; mems resident in 529 localities; Nat. Sec. Emelina Rodríguez.

The Press
DAILIES
Crítica Libre: Vía Fernández de Córdoba, Apdo B-4, Panamá 9A; tel. 261-0575; fax 230-0132; e-mail esotop@epasa.com; internet www.critica.com.pa; f. 1925; morning; Pres. Rosario Arias de Galindo; Dir Juan Pritsiolas; circ. 40,000.
DIA a DIA: Vía Ricardo J. Alfaro, al lado de la USMA, Apdo B-4, Panamá 9A; tel. 230-7777; fax 230-2279; e-mail editor.diaadia@epasa.com; internet www.diaadia.com.pa; Pres. Francisco Arias V.; Gen. Man. Ramón R. Vallarino A.
La Estrella de Panamá: Calle Alejandro Duque, Vía Transistmica y Frangipani, Panamá; tel. 227-0555; fax 227-1026; e-mail laestre@estrelladepanama.com; internet www.estrelladepanama.com; f. 1853; morning; Pres. Ebrahim Asvat; Editor Gerardo Berroa; circ. 10,000.
El Panamá América: Vía Ricardo J. Alfaro, al lado de la USMA, Apdo 0834-02787, Panamá 9A; tel. 230-7777; fax 230-7773; e-mail director@epasa.com; internet pa-digital.com.pa; f. 1925; morning; independent; affiliated to Interamerican Press Asscn; Pres. Francisco Arias V.; Dir Guido Rodríguez Lugari; circ. 25,000.
La Prensa: Avda 12 de Octubre y Calle C, Hato Pintado, Pueblo Nuevo, Apdo 0819-05620, Panamá; tel. 222-1222; fax 221-7328; e-mail editor@prensa.com; internet www.prensa.com; f. 1980; morning; independent; Pres. Ricardo Alberto Arias; Editor Fernando Berguido; circ. 38,000.
El Siglo: Calle 58 Obarrio, Panama; tel. 264-3921; fax 269-6954; e-mail redaccion@elsiglo.com; internet www.elsiglo.com; f. 1985; morning; acquired by Geo-Media, SA, in 2001; Pres. Dr Nivia Rossana Castrellón; Editor Octavio Cogley; circ. 30,000.

PERIODICALS
Dirección de Estadística y Censo: Avda Balboa y Federico Boyd, Apdo 0816-01521, Panamá 5; tel. 210-4800; fax 210-4801; e-mail cie_dec@contraloria.gob.pa; internet www.contraloria.gob.pa/dec; f. 1941; published by the Contraloría General de la República; statistical survey in series according to subjects; Controller-Gen. Carlos A. Vallarino R.; Dir of Statistics and Census Dimas Quiel.
FOB Colón Free Zone: Apdo 0819-06908, El Dorado, Panamá; tel. 225-6638; fax 225-0466; e-mail focusint@sinfo.net; internet www.colonfreezone.com; annual; bilingual trade directory; publ. by Focus Publications (Int.), SA; Editor Israel Arguedas; circ. 60,000.
Focus Panama: Apdo 6-3287, Panamá; tel. 225-6638; fax 225-0466; e-mail focusint@sinfo.net; internet www.focuspublicationsint.com; f. 1970; 2 a year; publ. by Focus Publications; visitors' guide; separate English and Spanish editions; Dir Kenneth J. Jones; circ. 100,000.
Informativo Industrial: Apdo 6-4798, El Dorado, Panamá 1; tel. 230-0482; fax 230-0805; monthly; organ of the Sindicato de Industriales de Panamá; Pres. Gaspar García de Paredes.

Mi Diario, La Voz de Panamá: Avda 12 de Octubre y Calle C, Hato Pintado, Pueblo Nuevo, Apdo 0819-05620, Panamá; tel. 222-9000; fax 222-9090; e-mail midiario@midiario.com; internet www.midiario.com; f. 2003 by La Prensa (q.v.); Dir Lorenzo Abrego.
Revista SIETE: Vía Ricardo J. Alfaro, al lado de la USMA, Apdo B-4, Panamá 9A; tel. 230-7777; fax 230-1033; e-mail revista.siete@epasa.com; internet www.epasa.com/siete; weekly; Editor Nayla G. Montenegro.

PRESS ASSOCIATION
Sindicato de Periodistas de Panamá: Avda Gorgas 287, Panamá; tel. 214-0163; fax 214-0164; e-mail sindiperpana@yahoo.com; f. 1949; Sec.-Gen. Jaime Beitia.

Publishers
Editora Panamá América (EPASA): Vía Ricardo J. Alfaro, al lado de la USMA, Apdo B-4, Panamá 9A; tel. 230-7777; fax 230-0136; e-mail gerente.general@epasa.com; internet www.epasa.com; Pres. Francisco Arias V.; Gen. Man. Ramón R. Vallarino A.
Editora Sibauste, SA: Panamá; tel. 229-4577; fax 229-4582; e-mail esibauste@cwpanama.net; Dir Enrique Sibauste Barría.
Editorial Universitaria: Vía José de Fábrega, Panamá; tel. 264-2087; f. 1969; history, geography, law, sciences, literature.
Focus Publications: Apdo 6-3287, El Dorado, Panamá; tel. 225-6638; fax 225-0466; e-mail focusint@sinfo.net; internet www.focuspublicationsint.com; f. 1970; guides, trade directories, yearbooks and maps; Gen. Man. Kenneth J. Jones.
Ruth Casa Editorial: Edif. Los Cristales, Of. No 6, Calle 38 y Avda Cuba, Apdo 2235, Zona 9A, Panamá; e-mail webmaster@forumdesalternatives.org; internet www.forumdesalternatives.org/Ruth_editorial.htm; Pres. François Houtart.

GOVERNMENT PUBLISHING HOUSE
Editorial Mariano Arosemena: Instituto Nacional de Cultura, Apdo 662, Panamá 1; tel. 211-4000; fax 211-4016; e-mail comunicacion@inac.gob.pa; internet www.inac.gob.pa; f. 1974; division of National Institute of Culture; literature, history, social sciences, archaeology; Dir Leslie Mock.

Broadcasting and Communications
REGULATORY AUTHORITY
Autoridad Nacional de los Servicios Públicos: Vía España, Edif. Office Park, Apdo 4931, Panamá 5; tel. 278-4500; fax 278-4600; e-mail webmaster@ersp.gob.pa; internet www.enteregulador.gob.pa; f. 1996 as Ente Regulador de los Servicios Públicos; name changed as above in 2006; state regulator with responsibility for television, radio, telecommunications, water and electricity; Deputy Dir Horacio Hoquee.

TELECOMMUNICATIONS
Dirección Nacional de Medios de Comunicación Social: Avda 7A Central y Calle 3A, Apdo 1628, Panamá 1; tel. 262-3197; fax 262-9495.

Major Service Providers
Cable & Wireless Panama: Box 0834-00659, Panamá; e-mail cwp@cwpanama.com; internet www.cwpanama.com.pa; 49% govt-owned, 49% owned by Cable & Wireless; major telecommunications provider; Pres. Jorge Nicolau.
Movistar: Edif. Magna, Area Bancaria, Calle 51 Este y Manuel M. Icaza, Panamá; tel. 265-0955; internet www.movistar.com.pa; f. 1996 as BellSouth Panamá SA; acquired by Telefónica Móviles, SA (Spain) in Oct. 2004; name changed as above in April 2005; mobile telephone services; Gen. Man. Claudio Hidalgo.
Optynex Telecom SA: Edif. Aliado, 2°, Calle 50 y 56, Urb. Obarrio, Apdo 0832-2650, Panamá; tel. 380-0000; fax 380-0099; e-mail info@optynex.com; internet www.optynex.com; f. 2002; Gen. Man. Eric Meyer.

BROADCASTING
Radio
Asociación Panameña de Radiodifusión: Apdo 7387, Estafeta de Paitilla, Panamá; tel. 263-5252; fax 226-4396; Pres. Alessio Gronchi; Vice-Pres. Ricardo A. Bustamante.

In 2004 there were 109 AM (Medium Wave) and 181 FM stations registered in Panama. Most stations are commercial.

La Mega 98.3 FM: Casa 35, Calle 50 y 77 San Francisco, Panamá; tel. 270-3242; fax 226-1021; e-mail ventas@lamegapanama.com; internet www.lamegapanama.com; f. 2000.

Omega Stereo: Calle G, El Cangrejo 3, Panamá; e-mail omegaste@omegastereo.com; internet www.omegastereo.com; f. 1981; Pres. Guillermo Antonio Adames.

RPC Radio: Calle 50, Urb. Obarrio 6, Panamá; e-mail rpcradio@medcom.com.pa; internet www.rpcradio.com; f. 1949; broadcasts news, sports and commentary; Man. Luís Eduardo Quirós.

SuperQ: Calle 45 Este, Bella Vista, Panamá; tel. 227-0366; e-mail exitosa@psi.net.pa; internet www.superqpanama.com; f. 1984; Pres. G. Aris De Icaza.

WAO 97.5: Edif. Plaza 50, 2°, Calle 50 y Vía Brasil, Panamá; tel. 223-8348; fax 223-8351; internet www.wao975.com; Gen. Man. Rogelio Campos.

Television

Fundación para la Educación en la Televisión—FETV (Canal 5): Vía Ricardo J. Alfaro, Apdo 0819-02874, Panamá; tel. 230-8000; fax 230-1955; e-mail comentarios@fetv.org; internet www.fetv.org; f. 1992; Pres. José Dimas Cedeño Delgado; Dir Manuel Santiago Blanquèr i Planells; Gen. Man. Teresa Wong de Fong.

Medcom: Avda 12 de Octubre, Hato Pintado, Apdo 0827-00116, Panamá 8; tel. 390-6802; fax 390-6895; e-mail murrutia@medcom.com.pa; internet www.rpctv.com; f. 1998 by merger of RPC Televisión (Canal 4) and Telemetro (Canal 13); commercial; also owns Cable Onda 90, and RPC radio; Pres. Fernando Eleta; CEO Nicolás González-Revilla.

RTVE_Panama (Canal 11): Curundu, Area Revertida, Avda Omar Torrijos, al lado del MOP, Panamá; tel. 232-8558; fax 223-2921; f. 1978; educational and cultural; Dir-Gen. Carlos Aguilar Navarro.

Televisora Nacional—TVN (Canal 2): Vía Bolívar, Apdo 6-3092, El Dorado, Panamá; tel. 236-2222; fax 236-2987; e-mail tvn@tvn-2.com; internet www.tvn-2.com; f. 1962; Dir Jaime Alberto Arias.

In 2005 there were 133 authorized television channels broadcasting in Panama.

Finance

(cap. = capital; res = reserves; dep. = deposits; m. = million; br(s) = branch(es); amounts in balboas, unless otherwise stated)

BANKING

Superintendencia de Bancos (Banking Superintendency): Torre HSBC, 18°, Apdo 2397, Panamá 1; tel. 206-7800; fax 264-9422; internet www.superbancos.gob.pa; f. 1970 as Comisión Bancaria Nacional (National Banking Commission); licenses and controls banking activities within and from Panamanian territory; Comisión Bancaria Nacional superseded by Superintendencia de Bancos in June 1998 with enhanced powers to supervise banking activity; Supt Olegario Barrelier Chiari.

National Bank

Banco Nacional de Panamá: Torre BNP, Vía España, Apdo 5220, Panamá 5; tel. 263-5151; fax 269-0091; e-mail bnpvalores@cwp.net.pa; internet www.banconal.com.pa; f. 1904; govt-owned; cap. 500.0m., dep. 2,996.1m., res 19.0m. (Dec. 2005); Chair. Arturo Melo Sarasqueta; Gen. Man. Juan Ricardo De Dianuos; 53 brs.

Savings Bank

Caja de Ahorros: Vía España y Calle Thays de Pons, Apdo 1740, Panamá 1; tel. 205-1000; fax 269-3674; e-mail atencionalcliente@cajadeahorros.com.pa; internet www.cajadeahorros.com.pa; f. 1934; govt-owned; cap. 150.7m., res 47.9m., dep. 170.9m. (Dec. 2006); Pres. Rogelio Alemán; Gen. Man. Sergio Altamiranda; 37 brs.

Domestic Private Banks

Banco Alemán Platina, SA: Edif. Banco Continental, Entrepiso, Calle 50 esq. Avda Aquilino de la Guardia, Apdo 0816-01679, Panamá; tel. 303-7002; fax 269-0910; e-mail bapservices@bcontinental.com; internet www.bancoalemanplatina.com; f. 1965 as Banco Alemán-Panameño; current name adopted in 1993; cap. US $42.0m., res $10.3m., dep. $244.6m. (Aug. 2001); owned by Banco Continental de Panamá, SA (q.v.); Gen. Man. Ramón Chiari.

Banco Continental de Panamá, SA: Calle 50 y Avda Aquilino de la Guardia, Apdo 135, Panamá 9A; tel. 215-7000; fax 215-7134; e-mail bcp@bcocontinental.com; internet www.bbvabancocontinental.com; f. 1972; merged with Banco Internacional de Panamá in 2002; took over Banco Atlántico (Panamá), SA in 2006; cap. 126.7m., res 29.0m., dep. 3,079.8m. (Dec. 2006); Chair. Stanley A. Motta C.; Gen. Man. Osvaldo F. Mouynes G.; 36 brs.

Banco Cuscatlán-Panabank: Edif. Panabank, Casa Matriz, Calle 50, Apdo 1828, Panamá 1; tel. 208-8300; fax 269-1537; e-mail gerencia@panabank.com; internet www.bancocuscatlan.com/panama; f. 1983; acquired Banco Panamericano (Panabank) in 2004; Chair. Mauricio Samayoa; Gen. Man. Guido J. Martinelli, Jr.

Banco General, SA: Calle Aquilino de la Guardia, Apdo 4592, Panamá 5; tel. 227-3200; fax 265-0210; e-mail info@bgeneral.com; internet www.bgeneral.com; f. 1955; purchased Banco Comercial de Panamá (BANCOMER) in 2000; cap. 300.0m., res 14.8m., dep. 2,504.6m. (Dec. 2006); Chair. and CEO Federico Humbert; Exec. Vice-Pres. and Gen. Man. Raúl Alemán Z.; 36 brs.

Banco Panameño de la Vivienda (BANVIVIENDA): Casa Matriz-Bella Vista, Avda Chile y Calle 41, Apdo 8639, Panamá 5; tel. 227-4020; fax 227-5433; e-mail bpvger@pty.com; internet www.banvivienda.com; f. 1981; cap. 12.4m., dep. 128.0m., total assets 150.3m. (2004); Pres. Orlando Sánchez Aviles; Dir Frank Morrice Jiménez; 3 brs.

Banco Pichincha Panamá: Torre Banco General Marbella, 23°, Calle Aquilino de la Guardia, Panamá; tel. 264-6323; fax 269-1537; e-mail banco@pichinchapanama.com; internet wwwp2.pichinchapanama.com; f. 2006; Gen. Man. Francisco Javier Lejarraga López de Arroyabe.

Banco Universal: Edif. Miguel A. Brenes, Calle B Norte y Avda 1ra, Apdo 0426-00564, David, Chiriquí; tel. 775-4394; fax 775-2308; e-mail cosorio@bancouniversal.com; internet www.bancouniversal.com; f. 1970 as Asociación Chiricana de Ahorros y Préstamos para la Vivienda, present name adopted 1994; Pres. José Isaac Virzi López; Gen. Man. Lorenzo D. Escudé Saab.

Global Bank Corporation: Torre Global Bank, Calle 50, Apdo 55-1843, Paitilla, Panamá; tel. 206-2000; fax 263-3518; e-mail global@pan.gbm.net; internet www.globalbank.com.pa; f. 1994; Pres. and Gen. Man Jorge Vallarino S.

Multibank: Edif. Prosperidad, planta baja, Vía España 127, Apdo 8210, Panamá 7; tel. 269-0188; fax 264-4014; e-mail banco@grupomulticredit.com; internet www.multibank.com.pa; f. 1990 as Multi Credit Bank, current name adopted 2008; total assets 536.1m. (Dec. 2005); Pres. Alberto S. Btesh; Gen. Man. Rafael Sánchez Garrós.

Primer Banco del Istmo, SA: Edif. Banco del Istmo, Calle 77 Este y 50, San Francisco, Panamá; tel. 270-0015; fax 270-1952; internet www.banistmo.com; f. 1984 as Banco del Istmo; current name adopted in 2000 following merger of Primer Grupo Nacional and Banco del Istmo; merged with Banco de Latinoamerica in 2002; acquired by HSBC in July 2006; cap. US $692.2m., dep. $4,343.7m. (Dec. 2006); Chair. Samuel Lewis Galindo; CEO Alberto Vallarino Clément.

Towerbank International Inc: Edif. Tower Plaza, Calle 50 y Beatriz M. de Cabal, Apdo 6-6039, Panamá; tel. 269-6900; fax 269-6800; e-mail towerbank@towerbank.com; internet www.towerbank.com; f. 1971; cap. 34.8m., res –90.8m., dep. 371.1m. (Dec. 2006); Pres. Fred Kardonski; Gen. Man. José Campa.

Foreign Banks

Principal Foreign Banks with General Licence

BAC International Bank (Panamá), Inc (USA): Edif. BAC Credomatic, Calle Aquilino de la Guardia, Apdo 6-3654, Panamá; tel. 213-0822; fax 269-3879; e-mail rcucalon@bacbank.com; internet www.bac.net/panama; f. 1995; Chair. Carlos Pellas; Gen. Man. Rodolfo Tabash.

BANCAFE (Panamá), SA (Colombia): Avda Manuel María Icaza y Calle 52E, No 18, Apdo 384, Panamá 9A; tel. 264-6066; fax 263-6115; e-mail bancafe@bancafe-panama.com; internet www.bancafe-pa.com; f. 1966 as Banco Cafetero; current name adopted in 1995; Pres. Jorge Castellanos Rueda; Gen. Man. Jaime de Gamboa Gamboa; 2 brs.

Banco Aliado, SA: Calle 50 y 56, Urb. Obarrio, 0831-2109 Paitilla, Panamá; tel. 302-1555; fax 302-1556; internet www.bancoaliado.com; f. 1992; Gen. Man. Alexis A. Arjona.

Banco Bilbao Vizcaya Argentaria (Panama), SA (Spain): Torre BBVA, Avda Balboa, Apdo 8673, Panamá 5; tel. 227-0973; fax 227-3663; e-mail fperezp@bbvapanama.com; internet www.bbvapanama.com; f. 1982; cap. 28.7m., res 56.6m., dep. 907.8m. (Dec. 2006); Chair. Manuel Zubiría Pastor; Gen. Man. Felix Perez Parra; 15 brs.

Banco Delta, SA (BMF): Edif. Torre Delta, planta baja, Vía España 122 y Calle Elvira Méndez, Apdo 0816-00548, Panamá; tel. 340-0000; fax 340-0076; internet www.bandelta.com; f. 2006; Gen. Man. Ariel Antonio Sanmartín Méndez.

Banco Internacional de Costa Rica, SA: Casa Matriz, Calle Manuel M. Icaza 25, Apdo 0816-07810, Panamá 1; tel. 208-9500;

fax 208-9581; e-mail informacion@bicaspan.net; internet www.bicsa.com; f. 1976; Gen. Man. FEDERICO CARRILLO ZURCHER.

Banco Latinoamericano de Exportaciones (BLADEX) (Multinational): Casa Matriz, Calles 50 y Aquilino de la Guardia, Apdo 6-1497, El Dorado, Panamá; tel. 210-8500; fax 269-6333; e-mail infobla@blx.com; internet www.blx.com; f. 1979; groups together 254 Latin American commercial and central banks, 22 international banks and some 3,000 New York Stock Exchange shareholders; cap. US $280.0m., res $97.8m., dep. $3,265.6m. (Dec. 2006); CEO JAIME RIVERA; Chair. GONZALO MENÉNDEZ DUQUE.

Citibank Panamá (USA): Plaza Panama Bldg, Calle 50, Apdo 555, Panamá 9A; tel. 210-5900; fax 210-5901; internet www.citibank.com.pa; f. 1904; Gen. Man. FRANCISCO CONTO; 4 brs.

Credicorp Bank, SA: Plaza Credicorp Bank, Nicanor de Obarrio, Calle 50, Apdo 833-0125, Panamá; tel. 210-1111; fax 210-0412; internet www.credicorpbank.com; f. 1992; cap. 24.1m., res –0.5m., dep. 340.3m. (Dec. 2006); Pres. RAYMOND HARARI; Gen. Man. CARLOS E. GUEVARA.

HSBC Bank (Panama), SA: Plaza HSBC, Calle Aquilino de La Guardia, Urb. Marbella, Panamá; tel. 263-5855; fax 263-6009; e-mail hsbcpnm@sinfo.net; internet www.pa.hsbc.com; dep. 477m. (1999); in 2000 it acquired the 11 br. operations of the Chase Manhattan Bank, with assets of US $752m. (2000); Gen. Man. JOSEPH L. SALTERIO; 3 brs.

Stanford Bank (Panamá), SA: Torre Generali, 19°, Avda Samuel Lewis y Calle 54, Urb. Obarrio, Panamá; tel. 208-7300; fax 263-4165; e-mail sbpanama@stanfordeagle.com; internet www.stanfordbankpanama.com; f. 2003; Pres. and Gen. Man. JUAN FERNANDO POSADA CORPAS.

Principal Foreign Banks with International Licence

Austrobank Overseas (Panamá), SA: Torre Morgan y Morgan, planta baja, Calle 53, Este Marbella, Apdo 6-3197, El Dorado, Panamá; tel. 223-4455; fax 264-6918; internet www.austrobank.com; f. 1995; Gen. Man. GUILLERMO WILLIS.

Banco Agrícola (Panamá), SA: Edif. Global Bank, 17°, Local E y F, Calle 50, Apdo 6-2637, Panamá; tel. 263-5762; fax 263-5626; internet www.bancoagricolapanama.com; f. 2002; Gen. Man. RUTH BARNES DE ARAÚZ.

Banco de la Nación Argentina: Edif. World Trade Center 501, Calle 53, Urb. Marbella, Panamá; tel. 269-4666; fax 269-6719; e-mail bnapanama@bna.com.pa; internet www.bna.com.ar; f. 1977; Gen. Man. OLGA DOMÍNGUEZ.

Banco de Occidente (Panama), SA: Edif. American International, Calle 50 y Aquilino de la Guardia, Apdo 6-7430, El Dorado, Panamá; tel. 263-8144; fax 269-3261; internet www.bancoccidente.com.pa; f. 1982; cap. US $6.3m., res $6.0m., dep. $199.0m. (Dec. 2002); Gen. Man. OSCAR LUNA GORDILLO.

Banco del Pacífico (Panama), SA: Calle Aquilino de la Guardia y Calle 52, Apdo 6-3100, El Dorado, Panamá; tel. 263-5833; fax 263-7481; e-mail bpacificopanama@pacifico.fin.ec; internet www.bancodelpacifico.com.pa; f. 1980; Pres. ANA ESCOBAR.

Bancolombia (Panama), SA: Plaza Marbella, Calle Aquilino de la Guardia y Calle 47, Apdo 0816-03320, Panamá; tel. 263-6955; fax 269-1138; e-mail mdebetan.bicpma@mail.bic.com.co; internet www.bancolombiapanama.com; f. 1973; current name adopted in 1999; cap. US $14.0m., res $3.8m., dep. $1,171.9m. (Dec. 2006); Gen. Man. MARÍA ISABEL URIBE RAMÍREZ.

FPB International Bank Inc: Ofs. A y C, 16°, Calle 50 y Aquilino de la Guardia, Panamá; tel. 210-6600; fax 263-0919; f. 2005; Gen. Man. JOSÉ APARECIDO PAULUCCI.

GNB Sudameris Bank, SA: Area Bancaria, Calle Manuel María Icaza 19, Panamá; tel. 206-6900; fax 206-6901; internet www.gnbsudameris.com; f. 1970; Gen. Man. ANGELMIRO CASTILLO H.

Popular Bank Ltd Inc: Apdo 0816-00265, Panamá; tel. 269-4166; fax 269-1309; e-mail gversari@bpt.com.pa; internet www.popularbank.com.pa; f. 1983 as Banco Popular Dominicano (Panama), SA; current name adopted in 2003; cap. 24.4m., res 11.3m., dep. 372.3m. (Dec. 2006); Pres. RAFAEL A. RODRÍGUEZ; Gen. Man. GIANNI VERSARI.

Banking Association

Asociación Bancaria de Panamá (ABP): Torre Hong Kong Bank, 15°, Avda Samuel Lewis, Apdo 4554, Panamá 5; tel. 263-7044; fax 223-5800; e-mail abp@orbi.net; internet www.asociacionbancaria.com; f. 1962; 79 mems; Pres. ALEXIS A. ARJONA.

STOCK EXCHANGE

Bolsa de Valores de Panamá: Edif. Vallarino, planta baja, Calles Elvira Méndez y 52, Apdo 87-0878, Panamá; tel. 269-1966; fax 269-2457; e-mail bvp@pty.com; internet www.panabolsa.com; f. 1960; Pres. RICARDO ARANGO; Gen. Man. ROBERTO BRENES PÉREZ.

INSURANCE

Arca Internacional de Reaseguros, SA: Edif. Bolsa de Valores, 1°, Avda Federico Boyd, Frente al Restaurante Rinos, Panamá; tel. 300-2858; fax 300-2859; f. 1996; Gen. Man. CARLOS G. DE LA LASTRA.

Aseguradora Ancón, SA: Avda Samuel Lewis y Calle 54, Urb. Obarrio, Panamá; tel. 210-8700; fax 210-8790; e-mail info@asegurancon.com; internet www.asegurancon.com; f. 1992; Pres. TOBIAS CARRERO NACAR; Gen. Man. CARLOS G. CHAMORRO.

Aseguradora Mundial, SA: Edif. Aseguradora Mundial, Avda Balboa y Calle 41, Apdo 8911, Panamá 5; tel. 207-6600; fax 207-8787; e-mail info@mundial.com; internet www.amundial.com; f. 1937; general; Pres. ORLANDO EDMUNDO SÁNCHEZ ÁVILES.

ASSA Cía de Seguros, SA: Edif. ASSA, Avda Nicanor de Obarrio (Calle 50), Apdo 0816-01622, Panamá 5; tel. 300-2772; fax 300-2729; e-mail assamercadeo@assanet.com; internet www.assanet.com; f. 1973; Pres. STANLEY MOTTA.

Assicurazioni Generali, Spa: Torre Generali, Avda Samuel Lewis y Calle 54, Urb. Obarrio, Apdo 0816-02206, 507 Panamá; tel. 206-9100; fax 206-9101; e-mail mercadeo@generali.com.pa; internet www.generali.com.pa; f. 1977; Gen. Man. GABRIEL R. DE OBARRIO, III.

Cía Interoceánica de Seguros, SA: Plaza Margella, Frente Banco HSBC, Calle Alquilino de la Guardia, Panamá; tel. 205-0700; fax 264-7668; e-mail info@interoceanica.com; internet www.interoceanica.com; f. 1978; Gen. Man. SALVADOR MORALES BACA.

Empresa General de Seguros, SA: Edif. Bancomer, Enre Piso, Calles 50 y 53, Panamá; tel. 269-1896; fax 264-1107; internet www.asecomer.com; f. 1987; Gen. Man. LUIS E. BANDERA.

HSBC Seguros (Panamá), SA (CONASE): Edif. HSBC, No 62, Calle 50, Apdo 5303, Panamá 5; tel. 205-0300; fax 223-1146; e-mail ines.m.arosemena@hsbc.com.pa; internet www.conase.com; f. 1957 as Cía Nacional de Seguros, SA; current name adopted July 2007; Pres. JOSEPH SALTERIO.

Internacional de Seguros, SA: Avda Cuba y Calles 35 y 36, Apdo 1036, Panamá 1; tel. 227-4000; e-mail conase@conase.net; internet www.iseguros.com; f. 1910; Pres. RICHARD A. FORD.

Mitsui Sumitomo Insurance Co Ltd: Of. 701, 7°, Plaza Credicorp Bank Panamá, Panamá; tel. 210-0133; fax 210-0122; f. 1979; Gen. Man. TA KASHI MORIMOTO.

Provincial Re Panamá, SA: Edif. Alexandra, Of. 3A, Avda Octavio de Icaza, Panamá; tel. 260-5078; fax 260-5055; f. 1984; Gen. Man. FRANK CASTAGNET.

QBE del Istmo Cía de Reaseguros, Inc: Costa del Este, Avda Paseo del Mar y Calle Vista del Pacífico, Apdo 51, Panamá; tel. 301-0610; fax 223-0479; f. 1979; Gen. Man. RAMÓN FERNÁNDEZ.

La Seguridad de Panamá, Cía de Seguros, SA: Edif. American International, Calle 50, esq. Aquilino de la Guardia, Apdo 5306, Panamá 5; tel. 263-6700; f. 1986; Gen. Man. MARIELA OSORIO.

Trade and Industry

Colón Free Zone (CFZ): Avda Roosevelt, Apdo 1118, Colón; tel. 445-1033; fax 445-2165; e-mail zonalibre@zolicol.org; internet www.zonalibredecolon.com.pa; f. 1948 to manufacture, import, handle and re-export all types of merchandise; some 1,800 companies were established in 2005; well-known international banks operate in the CFZ, where there are also customs, postal and telegraph services; the main exporters to the CFZ are Japan, the USA, Hong Kong, Taiwan, the Republic of Korea, Colombia, France, Italy and the United Kingdom; the main importers from the CFZ are Brazil, Venezuela, Mexico, Ecuador, the Netherlands Dependencies, Bolivia, the USA, Chile, Argentina and Colombia; the total area of the CFZ was 485.3 ha; Gen. Man. NILDA IRIS QUIJANO.

CHAMBERS OF COMMERCE

American Chamber of Commerce and Industry of Panama: POB 0843-00152, Panamá; tel. 301-3881; fax 301-3882; e-mail amcham@panamcham.com; internet www.panamcham.com; Pres. CARLOS M. URRIOLA; Exec. Dir DAVID HUNT.

Cámara Oficial Española de Comercio: Calle 33E, Apdo 1857, Panamá 1; tel. 225-1487; fax 225-0626; internet www.caespan.com.pa; Pres. NOEL RIANDE; Sec.-Gen. MARCO ANTONIO SAAVEDRA.

Cámara de Comercio, Industrias y Agricultura de Panamá: Avda Cuba y Ecuador 33A, Apdo 74, Panamá 1; tel. 227-1233; fax 227-4186; e-mail infocciap@panacamara.com; internet www.panacamara.com; f. 1915; Pres. DIEGO ELETA Q.; Exec. Dir JOSÉ RAMÓN VARELA C.; 1,300 mems.

INDUSTRIAL AND TRADE ASSOCIATIONS

Asociación Panameña de Exportadores (APEX): Apdo 6-6527, El Dorado, Panamá; tel. 230-0169; e-mail apex@cableonda.net; internet www.industriales.org; f. 1971; export asscn; Pres. Máximo Gallardo.

Cámara Panameña de la Construcción: Calle Aquilino de la Guardia No 19, Apdo 0816-02350, Panamá 5; tel. 265-2500; fax 265-2571; e-mail informacion@capac.org; internet www.capac.org; represents interests of construction sector; Pres. Manuel R. Vallarino.

Corporación Azucarera La Victoria: Transístmica, San Miguelito; tel. 229-4794; state sugar corpn; scheduled for transfer to private ownership; Dir Prof. Alejandro Vernaza.

Corporación para el Desarrollo Integral del Bayano: Avda Balboa, al lado de la estación del tren, Estafeta El Dorado, Panamá 2; tel. 232-6160; f. 1978; state agriculture, forestry and cattle-breeding corpn.

Dirección General de Industrias: Edif. Plaza Edison, 3°, Apdo 9658, Panamá 4; tel. 360-0720; govt body which undertakes feasibility studies, analyses and promotion; Dir-Gen. Lucía Fuentes de Ferguson; Nat. Dir of Business Devt Francisco de la Barrera.

Sindicato de Industriales de Panamá: Vía Ricardo J. Alfaro, Entrada Urb. Sara Sotillo, Apdo 6-4798, Estafeta El Dorado, Panamá; tel. 230-0169; fax 230-0805; e-mail sip@cableonda.net; internet www.industriales.org; f. 1945; represents and promotes activities of industrial sector; Pres. Gaspar García de Paredes.

EMPLOYERS' ORGANIZATIONS

Asociación Panameña de Ejecutivos de Empresas (APEDE): Edif. APEDE, Calle 42, Bella Vista y Avda Balboa, Apdo 1331, Panamá 1; tel. 227-3511; fax 227-1872; e-mail apede@sinfo.net; internet www.apede.org; Pres. Antonio Fletcher.

Consejo Nacional de la Empresa Privada (CONEP): Avda Morgan, Balboa, Ancón, Casa 302, Apdo 1276, Panamá 1; tel. 211-2672; fax 211-2964; e-mail conep1@cwpanama.net; internet www.conep.org.pa; Pres. Severo Sousa.

UTILITIES

Regulatory Authority

Ente Regulador de los Servicios Públicos: see Broadcasting and Communications—Regulatory Authority.

Electricity

The partial divestment of generation and distribution services was completed in December 1998. The restructuring of the state-owned Instituto de Recursos Hidráulicos y Electrificación (IRHE) resulted in the sale of four generation and three distribution companies. However, transmission operations remained under state control.

AES Panama: Panamá; internet www.aes.com; f. 1998 upon acquisition by AES Corpn of 49% interest in Empresa de Generación Electrica Bayano and Empresa de Generación Electrica Chiriqui; operates three hydroelectric facilities in Bayano (248 MW), Estí (120 MW) and Chiriqui (90 MW) and one 43 MW thermal facility; Pres. Paul Hanrahan; Gen. Man. David J. Sundstrom.

Elektra Noreste, SA: Edif. Hatillo, Torre A, entre Avda Cuba y Justo Arosemena, Apdo 0833-0202, Plaza Panamá; tel. 323-7100; internet www.elektra.com.pa; electricity distribution; Gen. Man. Javier Pariente.

Empresa de Transmisión Eléctrica, SA (ETESA): Plaza Sun Tower, 3°, Avda Ricardo J. Alfaro, Panamá; tel. 501-3800; fax 501-3506; e-mail info@etesa.com.pa; internet www.etesa.com.pa; f. 1998; state-owned transmission co; Pres. Ricaurte Vázquez; Gen. Man. Isaac Castillo.

Unión FENOSA—EDEMET EDECHI: Albrook, Panamá; internet www.ufpanama.com; f. 1998 by acquisition from IRHE of Empresa de Distribución Eléctrica Metro Oeste (EDEMET) and Empresa de Distribución Eléctrica Chiriquí (EDECHI) by Unión FENOSA, Spain; Pres. Ricardo Barranco.

Water

Instituto de Acueductos y Alcantarillados Nacionales (IDAAN) (National Waterworks and Sewage Systems Institute): Apdo 5234, Panamá; tel. 523-8570; e-mail consultas@idaan.gob.pa; internet www.idaan.gob.pa; Exec. Dir Javier Cardoze.

TRADE UNIONS

Central General Autónoma de Trabajadores de Panamá (CGTP): Casa 15, Calle 3a Perejil, Vía España, Panamá; tel. 269-9741; fax 223-5287; e-mail cgtpan@cwpanama.net; fmrly Central Istmeña de Trabajadores; Sec.-Gen. Mariano E. Mena.

Confederación Nacional de Unidad Sindical Independiente (CONUSI): 0421B Calle Venado, Ancón, Apdo 830344, Zona 3, Panamá; tel. 212-3865; fax 212-2565; e-mail conusipanama@hotmail.com; Sec.-Gen. Gabriel E. Castillo C.

Confederación de Trabajadores de la República de Panamá (CTRP) (Confederation of Workers of the Republic of Panama): Calle 31, entre Avdas México y Justo Arosemena 3-50, Apdo 0816-03647, Panamá 5; tel. 225-0293; fax 225-0259; e-mail ctrp@cableonda.net; f. 1956; admitted to ITUC/ORIT; Sec.-Gen. Guillermo Puga; 62,000 mems from 13 affiliated groups.

Consejo Nacional de Trabajadores Organizados (CONATO) (National Council of Organized Labour): Edif. 777, 2°, Balboa-Ancón, Panamá; tel. and fax 228-0224; e-mail conato@cwpanama.net; Coordinator José Pedroza; 150,000 mems.

Convergencia Sindical: Casa 2490, Balboa-Ancón, Calle Bomparte Wise, Apdo 0815-00863, Panamá 4; tel. and fax 314-1615; e-mail conversind@cwpanama.net; f. 1995; Sec.-Gen. Victor Manuel Torres.

Federación Nacional de Asociaciones de Empleados y Servidores Públicos (FENASEP) (National Federation of Associations of Public Employees): Galerías Alvear, 2°, Of. 301, Vía Argentina, Apdo 66-48, Zona 5, Panamá; tel. and fax 269-1316; e-mail fenasep@sinfo.net; f. 1984; Sec.-Gen. Leandro Avila.

A number of unions exist without affiliation to a national centre.

Transport

RAILWAYS

In 1998 there were an estimated 485 km of track in Panama. In 2000 a US $75m. project to modernize the line between the ports at either end of the Panama Canal began. In July 2001 the 83-km transisthmian railway, originally founded in 1855, reopened.

Ferrocarril Nacional de Chiriquí: Apdo 12B, David City, Chiriquí; tel. 775-4241; fax 775-4105; 126 km linking Puerto Armuelles and David.

Panama Canal Railway Company: Edif. T-376, Corozal Oeste, Apdo 0843-02448, Balboa Ancón, Panamá; tel. 317-6070; fax 317-6061; e-mail info@panarail.com; internet www.panarail.com; private investment under 50-year govt concession; 83 km linking Panama City and Colón, running parallel to Panama Canal; operation on concession by Kansas City Southern (KS, USA) and Mi-Jack Products (IL, USA); modernization programme completed in 2001; operates daily passenger and cargo service; Marketing Dir Thomas Kenna.

ROADS

In 2004 there were an estimated 11,985 km of roads, of which some 4,387 km were paved. The two most important highways are the Pan-American Highway and the Boyd-Roosevelt or Trans-Isthmian, linking Panama City and Colón. The Pan-American Highway to Mexico City runs for 545 km in Panama and was being extended towards Colombia. There is also a highway to San José, Costa Rica.

SHIPPING

The Panama Canal opened in 1914. In 1984 more than 4% of all the world's seaborne trade passed through the waterway. It is 82 km long, and ships take an average of eight hours to complete a transit. In 2007 some 13,223 transits were recorded. The Canal can accommodate ships with a maximum draught of 12 m, beams of up to approximately 32.3 m (106 ft) and lengths of up to about 290 m (950 ft), roughly equivalent to ships with a maximum capacity of 65,000–70,000 dwt. In 2000 a five-year modernization project was begun. The project included: a general improvement of facilities; the implementation of a satellite traffic-management system; the construction of a bridge; and the widening of the narrowest section of the Canal, the Culebra Cut (which was completed in 2001). Plans were also announced to construct a 203-ha international cargo-handling platform at the Atlantic end of the Canal, including terminals, a railway and an international airport. Terminal ports are Balboa, on the Pacific Ocean, and Cristóbal, on the Caribbean Sea.

Autoridad del Canal de Panamá (ACP): Administration Bldg, Balboa, Ancon, Panamá; tel. 272-7602; fax 272-7693; e-mail info@pancanal.com; internet www.pancanal.com; f. 1997; manages, operates and maintains the Panama Canal; succeeded the Panama Canal Commission, a US govt agency, on 31 December 1999, when the waterway was ceded to the Govt of Panama; the ACP is the autonomous agency of the Govt of Panama; there is a Board of 11 mems; Chair. Dani Kuzniecky; Administrator Alberto Alemán Zubieta; Dep. Administrator José Barrios Ng.

Autoridad Marítima de Panamá: Edif. 5534, Diablo Heights, Ancón, Apdo 8062, Panama 7; tel. 232-5528; fax 232-5527; e-mail ampadmin@amp.gob.pa; internet www.amp.gob.pa; f. 1998 to unite and optimize the function of all state institutions with involvement in maritime sector; Administrator Fernando Solorzano.

Panama City Port Authority and Foreign Trade Zone 65: Apdo 15095, Panamá; FL 32406, USA; tel. 767-3220; e-mail wstubbs@portpanamacityusa.com; internet www.portpanamacityusa.com; Chair. JOSEPH K. TANNEHILL; Exec. Dir WAYNES STUBBS.

There are deep-water ports at Balboa and Cristóbal (including general cargo ships, containers, shipyards, industrial facilities); Coco Solo (general cargo and containers); Bahía Las Minas (general bulk and containers); Vacamonte (main port for fishing industry); Puerto Armuelles and Almirante (bananas); Aguadulce and Pedregal (export of crude sugar and molasses, transport of fertilizers and chemical products); and Charco Azul and Chiriquí Grande (crude oil).

The Panamanian merchant fleet was the largest in the world in December 2006, numbering 7,183 vessels with total displacement of 155.0m. gross registered tons. In November 2000 construction was completed on the largest container terminal in Latin America, in Balboa.

CIVIL AVIATION

Tocumen (formerly Omar Torrijos) International Airport, situated 19 km (12 miles) outside Panamá (Panama City), is the country's principal airport and is served by many international airlines. A project to expand the airport's facilities, at a cost of US $20m., was completed in 2006. The France Airport in Colón and the Rio Hato Airport in Coclé province have both been declared international airports. There are also 11 smaller airports in the country.

Aerolíneas Pacífico Atlántico, SA (Aeroperlas): Apdo 6-3596, El Dorado, Panamá; tel. 315-7500; fax 315-0331; e-mail info@aeroperlas.com; internet www.aeroperlas.com; f. 1970; fmrly state-owned, transferred to private ownership in 1987; operates scheduled regional and domestic flights to 16 destinations; initiated international flights in 2000; Pres. GEORGE F. NOVEY; Gen. Man. EDUARDO STAGG.

Compañía Panameña de Aviación, SA (COPA): Avda Justo Arosemena 230 y Calle 39, Apdo 1572, Panamá 1; tel. 227-2522; fax 227-1952; e-mail proquebert@mail.copa.com.pa; internet www.copaair.com; f. 1947; scheduled passenger and cargo services from Panamá (Panama City) to Central America, South America, the Caribbean and the USA; Chair. ALBERTO MOTTA; CEO PEDRO O. HEILBRON.

Tourism

Panama's attractions include Panamá (Panama City), the ruins of Portobelo and 800 sandy tropical islands, including the resort of Contadora, one of the Pearl Islands in the Gulf of Panama, and the San Blas Islands, lying off the Atlantic coast. In 2005 the number of visitor arrivals at Tocumen International Airport stood at 576,050. Income from tourism was some US $1,108m. in 2005. In 2003 there were some 16,766 hotel rooms in Panama.

Instituto Panameño de Turismo (IPAT): Centro de Convenciones ATLAPA, Vía Israel, Apdo 4421, Panamá 5; tel. 226-7000; fax 226-3483; e-mail ggral@ns.ipat.gob.pa; internet www.ipat.gob.pa; f. 1960; Dir-Gen. RUBÉN BLADES.

Asociación Panameña de Agencias de Viajes y Turismo (APAVIT): Bella Vista Local 24, Calle 51, Apdo 55-1000 Paitilla, Panamá 3; tel. 264-3526; fax 264-5355; e-mail apavit@cableonda.net; internet www.apavitpanama.org; f. 1957; Pres. AIDA QUIJANO JIMÉNEZ; Vice-Pres. ERICK GOLDONI.

PAPUA NEW GUINEA

Introductory Survey

Location, Climate, Language, Religion, Flag, Capital

The Independent State of Papua New Guinea lies east of Indonesia and north of the north-eastern extremity of Australia. It comprises the eastern section of the island of New Guinea (the western section being Papua (West Papua), formerly Irian Jaya, which forms part of Indonesia) and about 600 smaller islands, including the Bismarck Archipelago (mainly New Britain, New Ireland and Manus) and the northern part of the Solomon Islands (mainly Bougainville and Buka). The climate is hot and humid throughout the year, with an average maximum temperature of 33°C (91°F) and an average minimum of 22°C (72°F). Rainfall is heavy on the coast but lower inland: the annual average varies from about 1,000 mm (40 ins) to 6,350 mm (250 ins). There are more than 800 native languages, but Pidgin and, to a lesser extent, standard English are also spoken, and, together with Motu, are the official languages in Parliament. More than 90% of the population profess Christianity. The national flag (proportions 3 by 4) is divided diagonally from the upper hoist to the lower fly: the upper portion displays a golden bird of paradise in silhouette on a red ground, while the lower portion has five white five-pointed stars, in the form of the Southern Cross constellation, on a black ground. The capital is Port Moresby.

Recent History

Papua New Guinea was formed by the merger of the Territory of Papua, under Australian rule from 1906, with the Trust Territory of New Guinea, a former German possession which Australia administered from 1914, first under a military Government, then under a League of Nations mandate, established in 1921, and later under a trusteeship agreement with the UN. During the Second World War, parts of both territories were occupied by Japanese forces from 1942 to 1945.

A joint administration for the two territories was established by Australia in July 1949. The union was named the Territory of Papua and New Guinea. A Legislative Council was established in November 1951 and was replaced by a House of Assembly, with an elected indigenous majority, in June 1964. The territory was renamed Papua New Guinea in July 1971. It achieved internal self-government in December 1973 and full independence on 16 September 1975, when the House of Assembly became the National Parliament.

Michael Somare, who from 1972 served as Chief Minister in an interim coalition Government, became Prime Minister on independence. He remained in office until 1980, despite widespread allegations of inefficiency in government ministries and of discrimination against the Highland provinces. The first elections since independence were held in mid-1977, following which Somare's Pangu (Papua New Guinea Unity) Pati formed a governing coalition, first with the People's Progress Party (PPP) and later with the United Party (UP).

In March 1980 the Government lost a vote of confidence, the fourth in 15 months, and Sir Julius Chan, the leader of the PPP and a former Deputy Prime Minister, succeeded to the premiership. Somare became Prime Minister again following a general election in June 1982. In 1983 the Somare Government effected a constitutional change to provide the central authorities with greater control of the provincial governments as a means of preventing abuse of their powers. As a result, between 1983 and 1991 a total of nine provincial governments were suspended by the central Government for alleged maladministration.

In March 1985 a motion expressing no confidence in Somare's Government was introduced in Parliament by Chan, who nominated Paias Wingti (hitherto Deputy Prime Minister and a member of the Pangu Pati) as alternative Prime Minister. Somare quickly formed a coalition, comprising the ruling Pangu Pati, the National Party (NP) and the Melanesian Alliance (MA), and the no confidence motion was defeated. Fourteen Members of Parliament (MPs) who had supported the motion were expelled from the Pangu Pati, and subsequently formed a new political party, the People's Democratic Movement (PDM), under the leadership of Wingti.

In August 1985 the NP withdrew from Somare's coalition Government, and in November Chan presented another motion of no confidence, criticizing Somare's handling of the economy. Somare was defeated and Wingti took office as Prime Minister of a new five-party coalition Government (comprising the PDM, the PPP, the NP, the UP and the MA), with Chan as Deputy Prime Minister.

At the mid-1987 election to the National Parliament Somare's Pangu Pati won 26 of the 109 elective seats, while Wingti's PDM obtained 18. However, by forming a coalition with minor parties, Wingti succeeded in securing a parliamentary majority and was re-elected Prime Minister. In July 1988 Wingti was defeated in a no confidence motion, proposed by Rabbie Namaliu, who had replaced Somare as leader of the Pangu Pati. As a result, Namaliu took office as Prime Minister and announced a new coalition Government, comprising members of the Pangu Pati and five minor parties: the People's Action Party (PAP), the MA, the NP, the League for National Advancement (LNA) and the Papua Party. In August Ted Diro, the leader of the PAP, was acquitted on a charge of perjury by the Supreme Court (having been accused of illegally appropriating funds for his party). An amendment to the Constitution, whereby a motion expressing no confidence in the Prime Minister could not be proposed until the premier had completed 18 months in office, was approved by Parliament in August 1990 and incorporated into the Constitution in July 1991.

In September 1991 a leadership tribunal found Ted Diro, the leader of the PAP, guilty of 81 charges of misconduct in government office. However, the Governor-General, Sir Serei Eri, refused to ratify the tribunal's decision and reinstated Diro as Deputy Prime Minister, despite recommendations that he be dismissed. A constitutional crisis subsequently arose, during which a government envoy was sent to the United Kingdom to request that the monarch dismiss Eri, but in early October the resignation of the Governor-General was announced; this was followed shortly afterwards by that of Diro.

In 1992 the Government continued to be troubled by allegations of corruption and misconduct (notably bribery and misuse of public funds). Campaigning for the 1992 general election began amid serious fighting among the various political factions, which led to rioting, in April, by some 10,000 supporters of rival candidates. At the election in June a total of 59 members of the legislature (including 15 ministers) lost their seats. The final result gave the Pangu Pati 22 of the 109 elective seats, while the PDM secured 15. Independent candidates won a total of 31 seats. Paias Wingti of the PDM was subsequently elected Prime Minister by the National Parliament, defeating Rabbie Namaliu of the Pangu Pati by a single vote. Wingti formed a coalition Government, comprising PDM, PPP and LNA members, as well as several independents. As part of the new administration's anti-corruption policy, Wingti suspended six provincial governments for financial mismanagement in October, and threatened to abolish the entire local government system.

In early 1993 a resurgence of tribal violence, mainly in the Enga Province, resulted in the deaths of more than 100 people. This development, together with a continued increase in violent crime throughout the country (despite the implementation in 1991 of severe measures to combat crime, including the introduction of the death penalty and the tattooing of the foreheads of convicted criminals) prompted the National Parliament to approve a new internal security act in May 1993. The measures, which included an amendment of the legal system that required defendants accused of serious crimes to prove their innocence, rather than be proven guilty, were criticized by the opposition as oppressive. In May 1994 the Supreme Court nullified six of the 26 sections of the act (most of which concerned the extension of police powers), denouncing them as unconstitutional.

In September 1993 Prime Minister Wingti announced his resignation to Parliament. The Speaker immediately requested nominations for the premiership, and Wingti was re-elected unopposed with 59 of the 109 votes. According to the Constitution (as amended in 1991), a motion of no confidence in the Prime Minister could not be presented for at least 18 months, and

Wingti claimed that his action had been necessary in order to secure a period of political stability for the country. However, opposition members described the events as an abuse of the democratic process, and several thousand demonstrators gathered in the capital to demand Wingti's resignation. In December the National Court rejected a constitutional challenge from the opposition to Wingti's re-election, but in August 1994 the Supreme Court declared Wingti's re-election in September 1993 invalid. Wingti did not contest the ensuing parliamentary vote for a new Prime Minister, in which Sir Julius Chan of the PPP defeated the Speaker, Bill Skate, by 66 votes to 32; Chris Haiveta, the leader of the Pangu Pati, was appointed Deputy Prime Minister.

The abolition of the directly elected provincial government system, as proposed by Wingti, was rejected by Chan's Government, although there was still considerable support among members of the opposition for the planned changes and, as a result, it was decided that Parliament would vote on a series of motions to amend the Constitution accordingly; the first of these was approved in March 1995. However, in June the Pangu Pati withdrew its support for the reforms, and considerable opposition to the proposals was expressed by the provincial governments. Nevertheless, the controversial legislation was approved later that month on condition that Chan lent his support to several opposition amendments to be considered later in the year. Chan subsequently dismissed six ministers for failing to vote for the legislation and effected a major reorganization of portfolios. The new regional authorities, comprising national politicians and selected local councillors and led by appointed governors, were appointed in that month. Wingti resigned as parliamentary leader of the opposition in order to assume the post of Governor in the Western Highlands Province, and was replaced by another PDM member, Roy Yaki.

The involvement of mercenaries to counter the secessionist movement on the island of Bougainville in early 1997 (see below) led to a period of extreme instability throughout the country, culminating in Chan's temporary resignation and the appointment of John Giheno as acting Prime Minister for about two months. The atmosphere of political uncertainty was exacerbated by serious outbreaks of violence in the weeks preceding the legislative election (which had been set for mid-June). The Government imposed a dusk-to-dawn curfew and a nationwide ban on the sale of alcohol. Many senior politicians, including Giheno and Wingti, failed to secure re-election at the polls. Outbreaks of violence were reported in several Highlands constituencies as the results were declared. A period of intense political manoeuvring followed the election, as various members sought to form coalitions and groupings in an attempt to achieve a majority in Parliament. In July Bill Skate of the People's National Congress (PNC), who was the former Speaker and Governor of the National Capital District, was elected Prime Minister, defeating Sir Michael Somare (who had established a new party—the National Alliance—in 1996) by 71 votes to 35. Skate was supported by a coalition of the PNC, PDM, PPP, Pangu Pati and independent members. A new Government was appointed in late July 1997, and extensive changes in the functional responsibilities of ministries were announced.

In September 1997 the Government declared a national disaster following a prolonged period of drought. By December more than 1,000 people had died. Several countries and organizations that had provided relief funds during the disaster were highly critical of the Government's management of the aid it received. The Minister for Finance, Roy Yaki, was dismissed, in part for his role in the affair, and responsibility for the administration of relief funds was subsequently transferred from the Department of Finance to the Department of Provincial Affairs. In March 1998 (when the drought was deemed to have ended following heavy rainfall) it was revealed that less than one-half of the relief aid received had been deployed to help the victims of the disaster.

In mid-November 1997 Silas (later Sir Silas) Atopare was appointed Governor-General, defeating Sir Getake Gam, head of the Evangelical Lutheran Church, by 54 votes to 44 in the legislature. A serious political scandal erupted in late November, following allegations of corruption against the Prime Minister. The accusations centred on a videotape broadcast on Australian television, which appeared to show Skate arranging bribes and boasting of his strong connections with criminal elements in Port Moresby. The Prime Minister dismissed his recorded comments (and the resultant allegations) stating that he had been drunk at the time of filming. Several senior politicians, including Somare, demanded his resignation over the affair. Meanwhile, Skate dismissed the leaders of the Pangu Pati and the PPP (Chris Haiveta and Andrew Baing, respectively), his coalition partners, accusing them of conspiring against him. The situation intensified with the resignation of seven Pangu Pati members from the Government in early December, and the announcement that the Pangu Pati and the PPP would join the opposition. However, the PPP rejoined the Government shortly afterwards, having voted to replace Baing as leader of the party with Michael Nali. Similarly, four Pangu Pati ministers rejoined the Government, thereby restoring Skate's majority in the National Parliament. A major ministerial reorganization was subsequently announced, in which Nali was appointed Deputy Prime Minister.

In April 1998 the Prime Minister announced the formation of a new political grouping, the Papua New Guinea First Party (which absorbed the PNC, the Christian Country Party and several other minor parties); Skate also effected a ministerial reorganization. However, the Government's majority was subsequently undermined, following a series of decisions by the Court of Disputed Returns during mid-1998, which declared the election in 1997 of seven government MPs to be null and void. Furthermore, in June 1998 the Pangu Pati officially joined the opposition, thereby reducing the Government's representation to 61 members in the National Parliament. Rumours of a forthcoming motion of no confidence in the Prime Minister prompted the establishment of a new pro-Skate coalition in the National Parliament in late July 1998. In the same month Skate announced a number of major reforms in the structure of the Government and an extensive ministerial reorganization. In October the PPP left the governing coalition and, in a subsequent ministerial reorganization, the party's leader, Nali, was replaced as Deputy Prime Minister by Iairo Lasaro.

In late 1998 there was a series of scandals relating to the various serious misdemeanours of a number of provincial governors. Moreover, outbreaks of tribal fighting continued to cause problems (particularly in the Highlands) in 1998–99. A serious conflict in the Eastern Highlands in early 1999 involved villagers using rocket launchers and grenades, and resulted in numerous deaths. In mid-1999 a state of emergency was declared in the Southern Highlands, following serious disturbances provoked by the death of a former provincial Governor, Dick Mune, in a road accident.

The establishment of a new political party, the PNG Liberal Party, in May 1999 by the Speaker, John Pundari (relaunched in June as the Advance PNG Party—APP), encouraged rumours of a forthcoming vote of no confidence against the Prime Minister. In early June, as part of a government reorganization, Skate dismissed the PDM leader, Sir Mekere Morauta, and three other PDM ministers, replacing them with four Pangu Pati members, including Haiveta. Later that month both the PDM and the United Resource Party (URP) announced their decision to withdraw completely from the coalition Government, following the resignation of nine government ministers. Both parties were expected to support the APP, in an attempt to subject the Prime Minister to a vote of no confidence. In early July, however, Skate unexpectedly resigned, but declared that he would remain in power in an acting capacity, pending the appointment of a new Prime Minister. The opposition alliance announced Morauta as their candidate for the premiership. Skate claimed that the APP had pledged support for the Government, thereby ensuring that it would have a sufficient majority to defeat any motion of no confidence. At the opening session of the National Parliament in mid-July, Lasaro, the incumbent Prime Minister's nominee, defeated the opposition candidate, Bernard Narokobi of the PDM, by 57 votes to 45, to become Speaker. However, on the next day Morauta was elected Prime Minister by an overwhelming majority, following his nomination by Pundari, who had transferred his allegiance from Skate, having refused to accept the latter's nomination of himself as candidate for the premiership. Lasaro immediately resigned as Speaker, and Narokobi was elected unopposed to the position. Morauta subsequently appointed a new coalition Government, with Pundari as Deputy Prime Minister.

In early August 1999 Sir Mekere Morauta, a former Governor of the central bank, presented a 'mini-budget', in an attempt to combat various economic problems which, he claimed, were a consequence of the previous Government's mismanagement. In October legislation was drafted to prevent ministers transferring political allegiances. In early December the Prime Minister expelled the APP from the coalition Government and dismissed Pundari from his post as Deputy Prime Minister, claiming that this constituted a further move towards the restoration of political stability. (Pundari was rumoured to have conspired with the opposition leader, Skate, to oust the Prime Minister.) Pundari was replaced by the former Minister of Works and deputy leader of the PDM, Mao Zeming. Following Pundari's sudden dismissal, four small political parties within the governing coalition—the National Alliance, the People's National Party, the Melanesian Alliance and the Movement for Greater Autonomy—joined to form the People's National Alliance. Also in that month, Skate (who was faced with a charge of attempted fraud during his term in office as Governor of the National Capital District Commission), announced that his party, the PNC, which had 10 MPs, was to join the coalition Government; in May he assumed leadership of the party. Later in December, the resignation of the Minister of Agriculture and Livestock, Ted Diro, prompted Morauta to carry out a government reorganization.

Morauta dismissed three ministers in March 2000, on the grounds that they had allegedly conspired to introduce a parliamentary motion of no confidence in the Prime Minister. The parliamentary strength of the ruling coalition was increased to 76 MPs in April, following the readmission of the APP to government, including the appointment of Pundari to the post of Minister of Lands and Physical Planning. In an attempt to increase government stability, Morauta proposed legislation in August that would restrict the ability of MPs to change their party allegiance within a parliamentary session. Moreover, Morauta also announced the adjournment of Parliament between January and July 2001, the only period during which votes of no confidence could be tabled. (The Constitution forbade such votes in the 18 months following the election of a Prime Minister, and in the 12 months prior to a general election.) In November, however, a revolt by 25 government MPs (including six cabinet ministers) prevented a vote on the so-called Political Parties Integrity Bill. The rebellion prompted a major cabinet reorganization, in which all of the ministers involved in the revolt, including the Deputy Prime Minister, Mao Zeming, were dismissed. Further changes to the composition of the cabinet were made in December, notably the dismissal of Michael Somare, the Minister for Foreign Affairs and Trade, following which Morauta secured the parliamentary approval of the bill. The Prime Minister claimed that the introduction of the new legislation represented the most important constitutional change in Papua New Guinea since independence and would greatly enhance the political stability of the country, as it required MPs who wished to change party allegiance to stand down and contest a by-election.

Allegations of corruption and mismanagement resulted in the suspension of four provincial governments (Western Province, Southern Highlands, Enga and the National Capital District—NCD) in late 2000 and early 2001. The central Government claimed that a failure to deliver services had resulted from the misuse of public funds. Moreover, in January 2001 the Minister for Provincial and Local Government, Iairo Lasaro, was arrested for the alleged misappropriation of public funds, and in mid-March Bill Skate was charged with the same crime, having been acquitted earlier in the month of conspiring to defraud an insurance company (the trial was to be abandoned in December 2001 owing to lack of evidence).

A Commonwealth report into the Papua New Guinea Defence Force, published in January 2001, recommended reducing the number of army personnel by one-third. Subsequent plans by the Government to make more than 2,000 soldiers redundant (equivalent to some 50% of the entire Defence Force) resulted in a revolt at the Port Moresby barracks in March. It was believed that senior officers had helped to distribute weapons to the rebels, who demanded the resignation of the Prime Minister and the transfer of power to an interim administration. The rebellion ended two weeks later with an amnesty for the soldiers involved, during which hundreds of looted weapons were surrendered. In March 2002 another rebellion by soldiers protesting against the proposed reductions in defence personnel took place at the Moem barracks on the northern coast. The leader of the rebellion, Nebare Dege, was sentenced to 15 years' imprisonment in December.

In April 2001 the Advance PNG Party, led by John Pundari, was dissolved and merged with the PDM, led by the Prime Minister. In May, following a minor ministerial reorganization in March, Morauta expelled the National Alliance from the ruling coalition and dismissed the party's ministers (including Bart Philemon, Minister for Foreign Affairs) from the National Executive Council, accusing Somare, the party's leader, of attempting to destabilize the Government. In late June, following several days of protests against the Government's economic reforms, police used tear gas to disperse hundreds of demonstrators outside the Prime Minister's office in Port Moresby. In a separate incident, four students were killed and several injured when riot police allegedly entered the premises of the University of Papua New Guinea and opened fire. A temporary curfew was imposed, and a Commission of Inquiry was established; in December relatives of one of the dead students began legal action against the police force.

In October 2001 the Prime Minister effected another reallocation of ministerial portfolios. At the end of the month, furthermore, the Minister for Foreign Affairs, John Pundari, was dismissed. His removal from office followed his criticism of the Government's participation in Australia's 'Pacific Solution', whereby 216 refugees, who had attempted to enter Australia illegally, were being housed in a former military prison on Manus Island. In December negotiations with Australia were under way to accommodate a further 1,000 asylum-seekers, and Australia had requested the Government to hold the refugees for an additional six months, although no formal agreement was made. In January 2002 the Government decided to accept 784 additional asylum-seekers. It was understood that they were to remain only until their asylum claims were processed. The agreement with Australia to accommodate the asylum-seekers on Manus Island was extended for a further 12 months in October 2002 and was to provide for the housing of an additional 1,000 people. The camp remained open, despite the Australian Government's announcement in August 2003 that it intended to close the facility. In early 2004 it was revealed that the sole occupant of the camp was a Palestinian refugee who had been held in solitary confinement for almost seven months at a cost of more than US $3m.

A legislative election was held in mid-2002. Voting commenced on 15 June and was to extend over a two-week period. However, many polling stations failed to open as scheduled, amid reports of the theft of ballot papers and subsequent strike action by electoral staff. Some 25 people were killed and dozens injured in election-related violence, much of which occurred in the Highlands provinces as a result of disputes between clan-based candidates. A Commonwealth inquiry was subsequently planned to investigate the events surrounding the election, which was described as the worst in the country's history. In the final results, announced in August, six seats in the Highlands provinces remained vacant where voting had been unable to proceed (elections for these seats were held in April and May 2003). Of the 103 seats determined, Somare's National Alliance won 19 and Morauta's PDM secured 12. Independent candidates won 17 seats, with the remainder divided among a large number of minor parties, many of which had been formed specifically to contest the election.

On 5 August 2002 Sir Michael Somare was elected unopposed as Prime Minister, receiving 88 parliamentary votes. Bill Skate, who had played an important part in Somare's campaign, was elected Speaker. After appointing a 28-member Cabinet (which was dominated by 19 newly elected MPs), Somare began his third term as Prime Minister, pledging to restore stability, halt the privatization programme and reduce expenditure. Instability within the parliamentary opposition in late 2002 resulted in the dismissal of Morauta as leader of the opposition in December.

In June 2003 the Government submitted proposals for a number of changes to the political system, including a mandatory general election following the approval of a no confidence motion and stricter rules governing the switching of party allegiances among members of the National Parliament. In late 2003 the Government proposed legislation that would extend the period during which a new government should be exempt from votes of no confidence, from 18 months to three years. Both attempts to introduce these constitutional changes were unsuccessful, despite government inducements of some US $25,000 for members of the National Parliament to support the proposals.

In mid-September 2003 Sir Albert Kipalan defeated Sir Paulias Matane by a single vote in the final poll to elect a new Governor-General. Kipalan was expected to take up the position in mid-November, when the term of the incumbent, Sir Silas Atopare, expired. However, questions concerning possible irregularities in the procedure arose in the following week, casting doubt on the validity of the election, and the Supreme Court subsequently declared it to be defective and invalid. Speaker Bill Skate was appointed acting Governor-General until a new election could be arranged. At the poll, which was duly held in early December, Sir Pato Kakaraya was the successful candidate. However, Kipalan, who had also contested the election, challenged the result and was granted a legal injunction against Kakaraya's inauguration, which had been due to take place in late January 2004. In March the Supreme Court declared the election of Sir Pato Kakaraya to be null and void. Somare consequently ordered the recall of the National Parliament in order that a new election to the post could be organized. Following four rounds of voting Sir Paulias Matane, a former Minister of Foreign Affairs, was narrowly elected Governor-General in late May and, when the Supreme Court had dismissed an injunction against his appointment by Kakaraya, was duly sworn in in the following month.

In May 2004 Somare dismissed Deputy Prime Minister Moses Maladina, together with all the PNC members of the Cabinet who had refused to support proposed government legislation and who were believed to be planning a vote of no confidence in the Government. Meanwhile, ongoing fears about increasing gun ownership were highlighted in early August, when the National Parliament was adjourned for a period of three months after both the Government and the opposition expressed concern over the number of legislators who were reported to be bringing firearms into the National Parliament building. In early 2005 Somare announced a reorganization of cabinet portfolios which included the appointment of his son, Arthur, to the role of Minister for National Planning and Monitoring. In February 2006, however, Arthur Somare resigned from his cabinet position following allegations of misappropriation of public funds; he was referred to the Public Prosecutor for failing to submit annual statements on time and to account for the application of local grants. The Minister for Forestry, Patrick Pruaitch, was appointed to the post in an acting capacity. In a reallocation of portfolios in early April, Pruaitch also assumed responsibility for the finance portfolio, which was removed from Bart Philemon, who nevertheless remained as Minister for Treasury. Mark Maipakai, hitherto Minister of Justice, was appointed Minister for Housing and Urban Resettlement, being replaced in the former position by Bire Kimisopa. Kimisopa had previously served as Minister for Internal Security, a post to which Alphonse Willie was appointed. A major reorganization of the National Executive Council was carried out in July; five cabinet ministers, including the Minister for Treasury, Bart Philemon, and the Minister for Defence, Mathew Gubag, were dismissed. Sir Michael Somare himself took the foreign affairs portfolio from Rabbie Namaliu, who became Minister for Treasury, while Arthur Somare, whose case with the Public Prosecutor was still pending, was reappointed to the cabinet as Minister for State Enterprise, Communication and Information. In November Prime Minister Somare assigned the foreign affairs portfolio to Paul Tiensten.

In early 2007 the Prime Minister announced further cabinet changes, including the appointment of Michael Nali as Minister for Commerce and Industry and Nick Kuman as Minister for Culture and Tourism. In late February Martin Aini, the Minister for Defence, was dismissed by Somare, reportedly for reasons related to the Julian Moti affair (see below).

Meanwhile, in April 2006 it was reported that the Public Prosecutor had found enough evidence to justify the establishment of a leadership tribunal to investigate alleged misconduct on the part of Puka Temu, the Minister for Lands and Physical Planning, and Andrew Baing, the Deputy Leader of the Opposition. In February 2007 a tribunal was formed to examine allegations of misconduct against Melchior Pep, who had previously served as Minister for Correctional and Administrative Services. In May 2007 a leadership tribunal recommended the dismissal of Sir Moi Avei, the former Deputy Prime Minister who had subsequently held the cabinet portfolio of petroleum and energy, over charges of financial misconduct; however, a final decision was postponed pending his appeal.

In June 2007 the Minister for Commerce and Industry, Michael Nali, and the Minister for Culture and Tourism, Nick Kuman, resigned in order to contest the next legislative election as PNC candidates. Polling took place, under a new 'limited preferential voting' system, in relatively peaceful circumstances between 30 June and 15 July, although there were some fatalities. The National Alliance ultimately secured 27 of the 109 seats, with its nearest rival, the PNG Party, winning only eight. Following coalition negotiations with several smaller parties including the PAP, the Pangu Pati and the URP, along with additional support from independents, Sir Michael Somare was re-elected as Prime Minister in mid-August; Sir Mekere Morauta became leader of the opposition soon after. In late August the composition of the new National Executive Council was announced. The National Alliance, from which a total of 13 ministers were taken, was allocated important portfolios: Puka Temu was appointed Deputy Prime Minister and Minister for Lands, Physical Planning and Mining, while Patrick Pruaitch assumed responsibility for the finance and treasury portfolio, and a new appointee to the cabinet, Sam Abal, became Minister for Foreign Affairs and Trade. Bob Dadae of the UP was appointed Minister for Defence, and Allan Marat of the Melanesian Labour Party (MLP) received the justice portfolio. Other parties represented included the PAP and the PNC. Somare announced his intention to expand the National Executive Council from 28 ministers to 35, in order fully to represent the composition of the governing coalition; the cost of the additional ministers was reported to have been estimated at US $1m. In early 2008 Somare's proposals for the creation of five new ministries were criticized by the opposition.

Controversy surrounding the role of foreign interests in the exploitation of the country's natural resources re-emerged in early 2005 when a group representing landowners near the Porgera gold mine protested at the mysterious deaths of villagers while panning for alluvial gold near the mine. The group claimed that several local people had been shot dead by Porgera security personnel and their bodies removed and that others had been seriously assaulted. Mine officials denied the allegations, stating that most of the deaths had been caused by falling rocks or other accidents, and that any shootings by their security guards had been carried out in self-defence. The opposition leader, Peter O'Neill, demanded an official inquiry into the deaths, which by early May had reached 29, with many others having been seriously assaulted.

Tribal conflicts, principally between the Ujimap and Wagia tribes, broke out near Mendi, the capital of Southern Highlands Province, in December 2001. It was alleged that national and local politicians, along with tribal leaders, had made little effort to end the fighting, which had originated in a dispute over the governorship of the province in 1997; furthermore, many were dissatisfied at the election of Tom Tomiape as Governor, in late November 2001, and at the widespread political corruption and deteriorating public services in the province. Tomiape's election was ruled invalid by the Supreme Court in December, and Wambi Nondi was appointed acting Governor. A brief ceasefire was brokered in early January 2002 and an independent peace commission was established in February, headed by Francis Awesa, a local businessman. By early 2002 more than 120 people had been killed since the onset of the fighting.

Ethnic and tribal violence continued in several regions of the country during 2003. Eight people were killed in fighting near Port Moresby in May, and 17 died during inter-clan violence involving more than 1,000 people in Enga Province in July. Further killings led to rioting in the following month and to an appeal by the Governor of the province for those responsible to be hanged. In early 2004 eight villagers were killed in Enga Province in further tribal conflicts, and by mid-2004 ethnic violence in Morobe, Chimbu and East Highlands Provinces had resulted in many more deaths, including those of several children. Concerns regarding the conduct of the national police force in tackling such conflicts intensified following an incident in August when a confrontation between security personnel and a group of youths in Enga Province resulted in police setting fire to an entire village, shooting dead a villager and injuring several others, and killing domestic animals. Earlier in the year the former Commander-in-Chief of the Defence Force, Jerry Singirok, stated his belief that the marked increase in ownership of illegal firearms, particularly in the Highlands region, was the single most significant problem in Papua New Guinea. Ethnic violence continued in 2005 with at least 10 people being killed in February in an incident in Enga Province prompted by the incorrect allocation of a village magistrate's allowance. Some 5,000 villagers were left homeless following fighting in Chimbu Province in April. Further violence during the year, particularly in the Highlands provinces, resulted in many more deaths. In one outbreak of fighting in July, resulting from a land dispute, an estimated 7,000 guns were believed to have been used and police officers declined to intervene as they were considerably less well-armed. In another incident fuel shortages prevented police from attending a serious tribal conflict in which many people were killed. A report published in July 2005 claimed that the majority of illegal firearms in circulation in the country originated from Papua New Guinea Defence Force or police stocks. Another report released in early 2006 confirmed that many of the weapons used in these inter-tribal conflicts had been bought or stolen from the security forces, who appeared to be unable or unwilling to intervene in such incidents, while home-made shotguns were increasingly being replaced by more sophisticated weaponry.

In early August 2006 a state of emergency was declared in Southern Highlands Province in response to allegations of financial mismanagement and corruption within the regional administration; the provincial Government was later suspended. In February 2007 the central Government extended the state of emergency for a further nine months, but in the following month the Supreme Court annulled the Government's decision, maintaining that conditions in the Southern Highlands Province did not warrant such extreme measures.

From the late 1980s the status of the province of Bougainville was increasingly questioned, becoming an issue that developed into civil unrest and a long-term national crisis. In April 1988 landowners on the island of Bougainville submitted claims for financial compensation for land that had been mined by the Australian-owned Bougainville Copper Ltd since 1972. When no payment was forthcoming, acts of sabotage were perpetrated in late 1988 by the Bougainville Revolutionary Army (BRA), led by Francis Ona, a former mine surveyor and landowner, and the mine was obliged to suspend operations. However, when repairs had been completed, the mine's owners refused to resume operations for fear of further attack, and members of the national security forces were deployed in the area. Production at the mine recommenced in December, but, after further violence in January 1989, a curfew was imposed. In early 1989 it was announced that, in an attempt to appease landowners, their share of mining royalties was to be increased from 5% to 20%.

The BRA's demands increasingly favoured secession from Papua New Guinea for Bougainville (and for North Solomons Province as a whole), together with the closure of the mine until their demands for compensation and secession had been met. In May 1989, as the violent campaign on the island intensified, the mine was forced once more to suspend production, and in June the Papua New Guinea Government declared a state of emergency on Bougainville, sending 2,000 security personnel to the island. In September a minister in the Bougainville provincial government, who had been negotiating an agreement with Bougainville landowners to provide them with financial compensation, was shot dead. The signing of the accord, due to take place the following day, was postponed indefinitely. Diro, who had been reinstated in the Government in May, as Minister of State with responsibility for overseeing the Bougainville crisis, responded by offering a reward for the capture or killing of Ona and seven of his deputies, including the BRA's military commander, Sam Kauona. In January 1990 the owners of the Bougainville mine made redundant 2,000 of the remaining 2,300 staff.

The escalation of violence on Bougainville led the Australian Government to announce plans to send in military forces to evacuate its nationals trapped on the island, and to withdraw the remaining 300 personnel of Bougainville Copper Ltd. Criticism of the Government's failure to resolve the dispute, the rising death toll among the security forces, rebels and civilians and a worsening economic crisis, which was aggravated by the conflict, led the Government to negotiate a cease-fire with the BRA, with effect from the beginning of March 1990. The Government undertook to withdraw its security forces and to release 80 detainees. Bougainville came under the control of the BRA in mid-March, after the sudden departure of the security forces. The premature withdrawal of the troops was seen as an attempt by Paul Tohian, the police commissioner who had been in charge of the state of emergency on Bougainville, to disrupt the peace process, and was followed by an apparent abortive coup attempt, allegedly led by Tohian, who was summarily dismissed from his post.

In late March 1990 the Government imposed an economic blockade on Bougainville; this was intensified in May, when banking, telecommunications and public services on the island were suspended. In May the BRA, apparently in response to the Government's implementation of economic sanctions, proclaimed Bougainville's independence, renaming the island the Republic of Bougainville. The unilateral declaration of independence, made by Ona, who also proclaimed himself interim President, was immediately dismissed by the central Government as unconstitutional and invalid. In July negotiations between the BRA and the Government finally began on board a New Zealand naval vessel, *Endeavour*. In the resulting 'Endeavour Accord', the BRA representatives agreed to defer implementation of the May declaration of independence and to hold further discussions on the political status of the island. The Government agreed to end the blockade, and to restore essential services to the island. However, despite assurances from Prime Minister Namaliu that troops would not be sent to the island, the first two ships that left for Bougainville with supplies were found to be carrying 100 security personnel, intending to disembark on the island of Buka, north of Bougainville. The BRA accused the Government of violating the accord, and a week later the security forces and the two ships, together with the supplies, withdrew. In mid-September the Government sent armed troops to take control of Buka, stating that this was in response to a petition for help from Buka islanders. Violent clashes ensued between the BRA and the armed forces on Buka, in which many people were reported to have been killed.

In January 1991 further negotiations took place between representatives of the Papua New Guinea Government and of Bougainville in Honiara, the capital of Solomon Islands, which resulted in the 'Honiara Accord'. The agreement stated that the Papua New Guinea Government would not station its security forces on Bougainville if the islanders agreed to disband the BRA and to surrender all prisoners and weapons to a multinational peace-keeping force. The Bougainville secessionists were guaranteed immunity from prosecution. However, the agreement made no provision for any change in the political status of Bougainville, and by early March it appeared to have failed. Government troops launched a further attack on Bougainville in April 1991. In June Col Leo Nuia was dismissed from his post as Commander of the Papua New Guinea Defence Force, after admitting that his troops had committed atrocities during fighting on Bougainville in early 1990. Further allegations of human rights abuses and summary executions of BRA members and sympathizers by government troops prompted Namaliu to announce plans for an independent inquiry into the claims.

Fighting continued throughout 1991 and the situation deteriorated further in early 1992 when, in an attempt to force the Government to end its economic blockade of the island, the BRA intercepted and set fire to a supply ship, and held its crew hostage. As a result, all shipping and air services to Bougainville were suspended. In October government troops began a major offensive against rebel-held areas of Bougainville and, later in the month, announced that they had taken control of the main town, Arawa. However, the BRA denied the claim and began a campaign of arson against government offices and public buildings in Arawa. Violence on the island intensified in early 1993, and allegations of atrocities and violations of human rights by both sides were widely reported.

Talks between government representatives and Bougainville secessionists in Honiara during 1994 led to the signing of a cease-fire agreement in September. Under the terms of the agreement, a regional peace-keeping force, composed of troops from Fiji, Vanuatu and Tonga, was deployed in October (with the Governments of Australia and New Zealand in a supervisory role) and the economic blockade of Bougainville was lifted. In the following month Prime Minister Chan and a group of non-BRA Bougainville leaders signed the Charter of Mirigini, which provided for the establishment of a transitional Bougainville government. The BRA declared its opposition to the proposed authority, reiterating its goal of outright secession.

In April 1995, following the suspension of the Bougainville provincial government, 27 members of the 32-member transitional administration were sworn in at a ceremony on Buka Island, attended by the Prime Minister and several foreign dignitaries. Theodore Miriong, a former legal adviser to Ona, was elected Premier of the authority. However, the three seats reserved for the BRA leaders, Ona, Kauona and Joseph Kabui (a former Premier of North Solomons Province), remained vacant, as the rebels urged their supporters to reject the new administration. An amnesty, declared in May by the transitional administration and the Government, for all who had committed crimes during the conflict, was rejected by the BRA, which during July and August conducted a campaign of arson against public buildings. Meanwhile, the Government denied any involvement in a series of attacks on BRA leaders, including an assassination attempt on Kabui. The murder of several more members of the security forces in March 1996 led the Government to abandon all talks with the secessionists and to reimpose a military blockade on Bougainville. An escalation of violence in mid-1996 culminated in a major military offensive against rebel-held areas in

June. Civilians on the island were encouraged to seek refuge in government 'care centres', and by August it was estimated that some 67,000 Bougainvilleans were being accommodated in 59 such centres. In the same month defence forces arrested Miriong, accusing him of incitement regarding the killing of 13 government soldiers at an army camp. The incident, in which Miriong was removed from Bougainville and kept under surveillance on Buka, caused the Government considerable embarrassment, particularly as it followed a number of similar cases in which the security forces had chosen to act independently of government policy. In October Miriong was assassinated at his home in south-west Bougainville by unidentified gunmen. In the following month an official inquiry concluded that a group of government soldiers was responsible for the killing, assisted by pro-Government civilians (known as 'resistance fighters'). Meanwhile, Gerard Sinato was elected as the new Premier of the Bougainville Transitional Government.

An apparent deterioration in the situation on Bougainville in late 1996 was characterized by an increase in BRA attacks against civilian targets and a similar escalation in violence by government troops and 'resistance fighters'. The Red Cross temporarily suspended its operations on the island following an attack on one of its vehicles, and human rights organizations repeated demands that observers be allowed to monitor incidents on the island, following a series of attacks on civilians (for which both sides denied reponsibility). A report commissioned by the Government and published in late 1996 recommended a thorough reorganization of the country's armed forces. The report identified a number of problems that had contributed to a lack of discipline among troops, with many soldiers refusing to serve in Bougainville.

In February 1997 unofficial reports suggested that the Government was planning to engage the services of a group of mercenaries on Bougainville. The Prime Minister reacted angrily to the reports, which Chan claimed were inaccurate; however, he confirmed that a company based in the United Kingdom, Sandline International (a subsidiary of Executive Outcomes, a supplier of private armed forces in Africa), had been commissioned to provide military advice and training for soldiers on Bougainville. Subsequent reports of mercenary activity on the island and of the large-scale purchase of military equipment and weapons provoked expressions of condemnation from numerous interests in the region. The situation developed into a major crisis in mid-March when the Commander of the Defence Force, Brig.-Gen. (later Maj.-Gen.) Jerry Singirok, announced that the country's armed forces were refusing to co-operate with the mercenary programme and demanded the immediate resignation of Chan. He explained that the mercenaries (most of whom were from South Africa) had been captured by the armed forces and were being detained while arrangements were made for their deportation. Singirok denied that his actions constituted a coup attempt. On the following day the Prime Minister dismissed Singirok, replacing him with Col Alfred Aikung. However, the armed forces rejected the new leadership, remaining loyal to Singirok. Popular support for the army's stance became increasingly vocal, as several thousand demonstrators rampaged through the streets of the capital, looting and clashing with security forces. The contract with Sandline International was suspended, pending an inquiry into the affair, and the remaining mercenaries left the country. Aikung was replaced as Commander of the Defence Force by Col Jack Tuat. However, demands for the Prime Minister's resignation intensified; military, political and religious leaders, as well as the Governor-General, urged Chan to leave office. Moreover, four government ministers resigned from their posts in an attempt to increase the pressure on Chan to do likewise. Following the defeat of a motion of no confidence in the Prime Minister, protesters laid siege to the parliament building, effectively imprisoning more than 100 legislators. An estimated 15,000 demonstrators marched on Parliament from across the capital. Chan therefore announced his resignation, along with that of the Deputy Prime Minister and the Minister for Defence. John Giheno, the erstwhile Minister for Mining and Petroleum, was subsequently elected acting Prime Minister.

In April 1997 an inquiry was initiated into the mercenary affair. The chief executive of Sandline International, Col (retd) Tim Spicer, was questioned over his alleged acceptance of bribes and in connection with various firearms offences. It was revealed that the company had requested part-ownership of the Panguna copper mine as payment for its military services. Criminal charges against Spicer were withdrawn within several days.

The inquiry concluded in early June that Chan had not been guilty of misconduct in relation to the mercenary affair, and, as a result (despite Giheno's stated intention to continue as acting Prime Minister until a general election had taken place), Chan announced his immediate resumption of his former position. Shortly after resuming office, Chan again provoked controversy by appointing Col Leo Nuia to the position of Commander of the Defence Force. (Nuia had been dismissed from the post in 1991, after an admission that his troops had committed atrocities during fighting on Bougainville.)

Following the election of a new Government, it was announced in August 1997 that a second inquiry into the mercenary affair, based on broader criteria, would be conducted. Meanwhile, government soldiers reacted angrily to the prosecution of military leaders involved in the operation to oust Sandline mercenaries from Bougainville in March. Nuia was imprisoned in his barracks by members of the Defence Force, while Maj. Walter Enuma, who was being held while awaiting trial on charges of 'raising an illegal force', was freed by rebel soldiers. The second inquiry concluded in September 1998 that Chris Haiveta (the former Deputy Prime Minister) had been the beneficiary of corrupt payments from Sandline, and upheld the first inquiry's finding that Chan had not been guilty of any wrongdoing in the affair. In the same month an international tribunal ruled that the Government owed $A28m. to Sandline in outstanding payments under the mercenary contract.

In July 1997 talks were held in New Zealand (at the Burnham army base) between secessionists and representatives of the Bougainville Transitional Government. As a result of the negotiations, Sinato and Kabui signed the 'Burnham Declaration', which recommended the withdrawal of government troops from Bougainville and the deployment of a neutral peace-keeping force. Hopes of a significant improvement in the Bougainville situation were encouraged by an official visit by the new Prime Minister, Bill Skate, in August (the first such visit since 1994) and by the resumption of talks in New Zealand in the following month. Negotiations concluded in October 1997 with the signing of the 'Burnham Truce', in which representatives from both sides agreed to a series of interim measures, which included refraining from acts of armed confrontation pending a formal meeting of government and secessionist leaders in early 1998. Ona (who appeared to be becoming increasingly marginalized within the BRA) refused to be a party to the truce, however, claiming that similar agreements had not been honoured by government troops and 'resistance fighters' in the past. The Prime Ministers of both Papua New Guinea and Solomon Islands made an extended visit to Bougainville in December 1997 to demonstrate their united support for the truce. Further talks held at Lincoln University in Christchurch, New Zealand, in January 1998 resulted in the 'Lincoln Agreement', providing for an extension to the truce, the initiation of a disarmament process and the phased withdrawal of government troops from the island. The Prime Minister also issued a public apology for the mistakes of successive administrations during the conflict, which was estimated to have resulted in the deaths of some 20,000 people.

A permanent cease-fire agreement was signed in Arawa on 30 April 1998. The occasion was attended by senior government members from Australia, New Zealand, Solomon Islands and Vanuatu, as well as Papua New Guinea government representatives and secessionist leaders. Ona declined to take part in the ceremony, reiterating his opposition to the peace agreement. In June government troops were withdrawn from Arawa, and reconstruction projects on Bougainville, financed by funds from various sources, including New Zealand, were initiated.

In August 1998 more than 2,000 representatives from different groups in Bougainville met in Buin (in the south of the island) to discuss their response to the 'Burnham Truce'. The resultant 'Buin Declaration' stated that the islanders were united in their aspiration for independence through peaceful negotiation. In October the National Parliament voted to amend the Constitution to allow the Bougainville Reconciliation Government to replace the Bougainville Transitional Government. The new authority came into existence on 1 January 1999, following the renewed suspension of the Bougainville provincial government, and at its first sitting elected Sinato and Kabui as its co-leaders. In April an agreement signed by Bougainville and Papua New Guinea government representatives (although not acknowledged by the BRA), known as the Matakana and Okataina Understanding, reaffirmed both sides' commitment to the cease-fire, while undertaking to discuss options for the political future of the island. Elections to the Bougainville People's

Congress (BPC, formerly the Bougainville Reconciliation Government) were held in early May 1999, and were reported to have proceeded smoothly. At the first session of the BPC, Kabui was elected President by an overwhelming majority, securing 77 of the 87 votes, thus defeating his former co-leader, Sinato, who received only 10 votes. Kabui subsequently appointed 29 members to the Congressional Executive Council. Ona refused Kabui's offer to join the BPC. At a subsequent session of the Council, Kabui announced his intention to campaign for independence for Bougainville. In response, Prime Minister Bill Skate stated that, although there was no possibility of independence (as this was not provided for in the Constitution), Parliament would consider terms for greater autonomy for the island. In August the suspension of the Bougainville provincial government was extended for a further six months in an attempt to find a peaceful resolution to the autonomy issue. Following a visit to the province, the Minister for Bougainville Affairs and for Foreign Affairs, Sir Michael Somare (as he had become), stated that the Government was willing to grant the island a greater degree of autonomy. Somare proposed that Bougainville be self-governing in all matters except foreign affairs, defence and policing, all of which would remain the responsibility of the central Government. The proposal was welcomed by members of the BPC, although they also announced their intention not to surrender their weapons until the Government had agreed to the holding of a referendum on independence.

In October 1999 a Supreme Court ruling declared the suspension of the Bougainville provincial government illegal on technical grounds. On 9 December the provincial government was formally recognized, in theory, despite protests by members of the BPC and concerns that this development would hinder the peace process. In effect, however, the provincial government comprised only four members—the Bougainville Regional Member of Parliament, John Momis, who thus became Governor-elect (although he agreed not to exercise his powers for the time being) and the three other Bougainville parliamentarians. Following talks in mid-December between Somare and members of the BPC, the BRA and elders of the island, Somare agreed to consider the possibility of a referendum on independence for Bougainville. The agreement, known as the Hutjena Record, stated that the highest possible degree of autonomy should be accorded to the island. Further talks regarding the future status of Bougainville commenced in early March 2000. However, following the rejection of an initial proposal on the island's autonomy by secessionist leaders, the talks were suspended. Negotiations resumed in mid-March, and an agreement was subsequently signed: known as the Loloata Understanding, this allowed for the eventual holding of a referendum on independence, once full autonomy had been implemented, and the formal establishment of the Bougainville Interim Provincial Government (BIPG), composed of an Executive Council and a 25-member Provincial Assembly (including the four original members).

At the end of March 2000 the Provincial Assembly and the Executive Council were sworn in by the Governor-General. Six seats were left vacant in the Provincial Assembly for other Bougainville officials such as Kabui and Ona; however, Kabui stated that, rather than joining the BIPG, he would await the establishment of a fully autonomous government (which he hoped would be in place by early 2001). In May 2000 the Office of Bougainville Affairs was renamed the Office of Peace and Reconstruction. In July Somare approved an allocation of K200,000, as part of a scheme co-ordinated by the United Nations Development Programme (UNDP), to facilitate the collection and disposal of weapons held by dissident groups. Uncertainties regarding the proposed date of a referendum continued to delay the progress of negotiations; Somare's statement in May that the referendum would be held 15 years hence contradicted a previously-stated deadline of December 2000. Concerns about renewed Australian funding of the Papua New Guinea Defence Force troops stationed on Bougainville, and the failure of the BRA to begin disarmament before the implementation of political autonomy, further impeded progress. In October the BRA's commander, Ishmael Toroama, threatened to abandon the organization's cease-fire. Following a further round of peace talks in November, Kabui confirmed that he had secured an agreement from Somare that a future referendum would include a legally-binding option of independence, although disagreement over how soon the vote should be held persisted. In the following month Somare was abruptly dismissed from his ministerial position and replaced by Bart Philemon; Morauta believed Somare was impeding the progress of the Political Parties Integrity Bill.

In February 2001 agreement on the terms of the referendum was finally reached following the intervention of the Australian Minister for Foreign Affairs. The agreement stated that the referendum would be held in 10–15 years' time and would contain the option of independence. In the interim the provincial government was to be granted increased autonomy and the BRA would be expected to disarm. Despite a temporary breakdown in negotiations, in early May commanders of the BRA and the Bougainville Resistance Force (BRF, a militia that was allied to the Government during the civil conflict on Bougainville) signed an agreement to surrender their weapons. In late June Moi Avei, who had replaced Philemon as Minister for Bougainville Affairs in May, announced that negotiations had resulted in a comprehensive agreement on autonomy for the island, with the Government ceding to demands that Bougainville be accorded its own system of criminal law and an autonomous police force. It was also agreed that the Papua New Guinea Defence Force's jurisdiction on the island would be strictly limited. On 30 August the Government and island leaders signed the Bougainville peace agreement in Arawa. Although he signed the accord, which was still to be approved by the National Parliament, Toroama stated that the BRA would campaign for the referendum to be held in three–five years' time and would continue to seek full independence. (Francis Ona did not attend the signing ceremony; he died in July 2005.)

The weapons disposal process was threatened in late November 2001 when Henry Kiumo, a former commander of the pro-Government BRF militia, was murdered. However, weapons disposal by the BRA and BRF began in early December, and the UN Observer Mission on Bougainville (UNOMB) formally acknowledged the Bougainville Peace Agreement later in that month. In January 2002 the National Parliament unanimously endorsed the Organic Law enacting the Bougainville peace agreement, along with a bill containing the requisite constitutional amendment. A second vote, held in late March, ratified the legislation, and the Papua New Guinea Defence Force began its withdrawal from Bougainville. The withdrawal of troops was completed in late December.

In January 2003 it was announced that the BIPG and the BPC would be merged to form the Bougainville Constituent Assembly (BCA). The new body, which was expected to be composed of some 90 members, would debate and approve a proposed constitution for the island and complete the weapons disposal process. In late June an Australian-led group of regional representatives, who had been monitoring the truce on Bougainville since its signing in 1997, officially left the island. Joseph Kabui used the opportunity of their departure to appeal to ex-combatants not to endanger the peace process. Meanwhile, members of a rebel group calling itself the Me'ekamui Fighters reiterated their disillusionment with the peace process and stated that they were fighting for independence rather than autonomy. Regional concern for the future of the island was highlighted in August 2003 when the Pacific Islands Forum (see p. 380) urged the UN Security Council to remain involved in the peace process on Bougainville. In the same month the Government of Papua New Guinea formally announced its plan for autonomy in Bougainville, allowing provincial authorities to proceed with the establishment of a constitution and the eventual organization of elections for an autonomous government leader and local assembly. In March 2004 the BIPG approved legislation providing for the establishment of the BCA, which was finally convened later that month to consider the third and final draft of the proposed constitution. In June the UN agreed to extend the term of its Observer Mission on the island by six months, but stressed that there would be no further extensions and urged the BCA to organize elections by the end of 2004. In the following month 50 newly trained officers began duty in their role as Bougainville's first police force. They were to be supported by a small team of police officers from Australia under the terms of that country's ECP with Papua New Guinea (see above). In mid-December the Government of Papua New Guinea finally approved Bougainville's Constitution. Elections for the President of the new Autonomous Bougainville Government (ABG) and for the 39 members of the first local assembly began on 20 May 2005 and continued for two weeks to allow islanders, some of whom had to travel for several days on foot or by canoe, sufficient time to reach the polling stations. Despite some attempts by armed rebels to disrupt the election process, it was deemed to have been largely successful. Joseph Kabui was declared to be Bougainville's first

President, with 37,928 votes, defeating several other candidates (the closest of whom, former Governor John Momis, received 23,861 votes). The inauguration of the autonomous assembly took place on 14 June and was attended by most members of the Cabinet, as well as by several foreign dignitaries. Kabui appointed his 10-member cabinet several days later.

In December 2004 the UN agreed to extend its Observer Mission to the island by another six months to cover the period of the election. The leader of the Observer Mission left Papua New Guinea at the beginning of August 2005. Also in August the Government announced its commitment to ensuring that a referendum on the independence of Bougainville be carried out by 2020. In March 2006 the ABG requested that the UN assist in the ongoing efforts to resolve peacefully the issue of the continued presence of five former Fijian soldiers in Bougainville. It had been reported that the former soldiers had been recruited by an alleged fraudster, Noah Musingku, and in the south-west of the island were training a militia group in the use of powerful weaponry. Musingku, the self-proclaimed 'King of Me'ekamui', was accused of misappropriating large sums of money from investors through U-Vistract, a financial scheme which he claimed was still functional. In May clashes in Buin and Siwai between police and activists reportedly linked to Musingku caused fires in three police buildings, raising fears of a renewed civil conflict. It was reported that a Me'ekamui rebel faction had joined Musingku, who had retreated to Tonu in Siwai and erected a roadblock in the area. The ABG subsequently authorized the use of force to suppress the rebels, to the dismay of local Me'ekamui leaders. President Kabui later gave assurances that, for the time being, a resolution would be sought without recourse to the use of force. In June the Bougainville police affirmed that negotiations between Musingku's supporters and the authorities were ongoing. In the following month the Fijian High Commission in Papua New Guinea confirmed its participation in discussions to repatriate the Fijian fugitives, who remained at Musingku's camp but had allegedly requested safe passage out. In mid-July a police officer in Buka revealed that the ABG had imposed a ban on Fijian nationals travelling to Bougainville amid concerns that large numbers were en route to the region. In what appeared to be an important advance, in September the Chief Administrator of Bougainville, Peter Tsiamalili, headed a delegation of ABG and local officials in a visit to Tonu to discuss with Musingku the provision of government services to the area. Tsiamalili later returned for further discussions with Musingku and local chiefs after they submitted to the ABG proposals for local development. At the end of October Musingku declared his willingness to begin containing his group's weapons, expressing concern at the escalation of violence and crime in the area and citing threats to his own group by alternative Me'ekamui factions. At the beginning of November, however, the Bougainville Freedom Fighters (BFF), a group of former combatants from Buin and Siwai aligned with the ABG, conveyed its dissatisfaction with the negotiation process and emphasized that immediate disarmament was the only solution to the lawlessness perpetuated by Musingku's group, without which it intended to act. It was this group that, later in November, reportedly carried out an offensive against Musingku's base, resulting in the deaths of four of his bodyguards and injuring Musingku, who apparently escaped to Siwai with the Fijian fugitives. According to the Minister for Bougainville Affairs, the Papua New Guinea Government was reluctant to become involved in the fighting, as it feared an escalation of the conflict. It later emerged that the Bougainville police had formed part of the offensive, but Tsiamalili refuted suggestions that the ABG had been involved. The Fijian members of Musingku's group were, according to the latter, refusing to leave the area without the millions of dollars in salaries promised to them by Musingku, and did not surrender until February 2007, when they were charged with 'raising illegal force' at a Buka court. In February 2008 four of the Fijian members of Musingku's group were released by the National Court in Buka, owing to lack of evidence; two others reportedly remained with Musingku. Meanwhile, the 'Me'ekamui Government of Unity' organization was said to have entered into an agreement with the ABG in August 2007, signalling a new phase of co-operation.

In September 2000 a group of landowners from Bougainville initiated legal action in a US court against Rio Tinto, the operator of the Panguna copper mine between 1972 and 1988. The group was reported to be suing the company for the environmental and social damage caused by its activities, including health problems experienced by workers and islanders living near the mine. Moreover, their case alleged that the company had effectively transformed the Papua New Guinea Defence Force into its own private army and was therefore responsible for the deaths of some 15,000 civilians in military action and a further 10,000 as a result of the economic blockade on the island. A committee was established by the provincial Government in late 2005 to work on reopening the mine following an overwhelming vote in favour of the proposal.

In 1984 more than 9,000 refugees crossed into Papua New Guinea from the Indonesian province of Irian Jaya (officially known as Papua from January 2002), as a consequence of operations by the Indonesian army against Melanesian rebels of the pro-independence Organisasi Papua Merdeka (Free Papua Movement—OPM). For many years relations between Papua New Guinea and Indonesia had been strained by the conflict in Irian Jaya, not least because the independence movement drew sympathy from many among the largely Melanesian population of Papua New Guinea. A new border treaty was signed in October 1984, and attempts were made to repatriate the refugees, based on assurances by the Indonesian Government that there would be no reprisals against those who returned. In October 1985 representatives of the Papua New Guinea and Indonesian Governments signed a treaty providing for the settlement of disputes by consultation, arbitration and 'other peaceful means'. However, the treaty provoked strong criticism among opposition politicians in Papua New Guinea, who claimed that it effectively precluded the censure of any violation of human rights in Irian Jaya. In 1988 the Government condemned the incursions by Indonesian soldiers into Papua New Guinea, in search of OPM members, and the resultant violence and killings as a breach of bilateral accords, and affirmed that Papua New Guinea would not support Indonesia in its attempt to suppress the OPM. In late 1995 the Indonesian consulate in the border town of Vanimo was attacked by OPM rebels and a subsequent increase in Indonesian troops along the border was reported. Violent confrontations resulted in the killing of several rebels and security personnel and the kidnapping by OPM activists of some 200 villagers. Australia urged the Papua New Guinea Government to accept several thousand refugees living in camps along the border, and in May 1996 the Government announced that 3,500 Irian Jayans would be allowed to remain in Papua New Guinea on condition that they were not involved in OPM activities. In mid-1998, on an official visit to Indonesia, Prime Minister Bill Skate signed a memorandum of understanding on bilateral relations, which was expected to provide the basis for closer co-operation in political, economic and defence matters. Under the terms of the agreement, troop numbers along the border were increased in March 1999. In May of that year 11 Javanese people were taken hostage and three people were reported to have been killed by OPM rebels in the West Sepik Province of Papua New Guinea. The hostages were later released as a result of the intervention of Papua New Guinea security forces. The OPM subsequently demanded an inquiry into the operation leading to the release of the hostages, after its communications director was allegedly shot dead at a border post. During 2000 hundreds of refugees were voluntarily repatriated to Indonesia (including more than 600 in a major operation in early September), although approximately 7,000 were believed to remain in Papua New Guinea in September. In late 2000 it was reported that Indonesian security forces had made some 400 incursions into Papua New Guinea in the previous two months while pursuing separatists. In December the border with Irian Jaya was officially closed.

In January 2003 the Papua New Guinea Government denied a number of security breaches, which were reported to have occurred along its border with Indonesia. Concerns grew following a dramatic increase in the numbers of Indonesian troops along the border, from some 150 in late 2002 to a reported 1,500 in early 2003. In late January the Government of Papua New Guinea ordered its security forces to arrest OPM rebels believed to be staying in refugee camps along the border, following complaints from the Indonesian authorities that rebels based there were carrying out operations in the province of Papua. The Government also confirmed in April that it had been unable to persuade more than 400 Papuans living in a camp near the border town of Vanimo to return to Indonesia, despite assurances that their safety would not be at risk. In July 2004 it was announced that Vanuatu would host a series of negotiations between the Indonesian authorities and Papuan separatists.

In regional affairs, relations with Australia have been affected by various developments. In December 2003, following the apparent success of the intervention in Solomon Islands earlier in the year, Australia announced the deployment of some 250 of its security personnel to different regions of Papua New Guinea, as part of plans for a five-year operation costing US $325m., aimed at restoring order to troubled areas of the country. Moreover, the Australian Government was to send up to 70 officials to Papua New Guinea to take up senior public roles in the spheres of finance, justice, public sector management, immigration, border security and transport safety. The agreement, known as the Enhanced Co-operation Program (ECP), was officially concluded in June 2004 and incorporated a total aid 'package' worth US $690m. Prime Minister Somare had initially been reluctant to accept Australia's expanded role in the country, fearing that it would erode national sovereignty, but had been obliged to reconsider when the Australian Prime Minister, John Howard, implied that aid payments to Papua New Guinea were dependent on the country's co-operation. A report by the Australian Strategic Policy Institute, published in December 2004, claimed that Papua New Guinea was facing economic and social collapse. It urged the Australian Government to intervene further in the country by radically increasing the amount of aid it provided and by taking control of some aspects of government, particularly immigration. Research by the organization indicated that government and state institutions had become too weak to prevent drugs and weapons smuggling, human trafficking and money-laundering activities, operated by international criminal groups, which had relocated to Papua New Guinea from South-East Asia in recent years. Furthermore, an investigation carried out by Australian journalists, the results of which were published in early 2005, alleged that Chinese mafia groups had infiltrated the highest levels of Papua New Guinea's police force. According to the report, the corruption of the country's authorities was facilitating serious criminal activities that posed a threat to the national security of Australia. It was also believed that the criminals had been recruiting Port Moresby's notorious 'raskol' gangs (groups of heavily armed, disaffected young men responsible for much of the violent crime in the capital) to commit armed robberies, assaults and other crimes in support of their activities.

The ECP suffered a serious reversal in May 2005 when Papua New Guinea's Supreme Court ruled that the deployment of Australian security personnel in the country was unconstitutional (principally because they had been given immunity from prosecution). Personnel began to return to Australia shortly after the ruling. Relations between the two countries had deteriorated in March when Prime Minister Sir Michael Somare had been subjected to a security search at Brisbane airport. A demonstration by more than 7,000 people in Lae, demanding an apology from Australia for the incident and accusing that country's authorities of showing contempt and disrespect for Papua New Guinea, took place in the following month. In October, following revisions to the ECP, it was announced that Australia was to commit as many as 40 police officers to assist the local forces in a renewed attempt to curb the increasing levels of violence and crime in the country. The dispatch of the new police component was part of the revised ECP. In February 2006 an internal police investigation that had begun in 2003 revealed that as many as 66 police officers had been implicated in corrupt activities, such as receiving funds from Asian crime syndicates.

Relations between the two countries became increasingly strained towards the end of 2006 over the extradition of the newly appointed Solomon Islands Attorney-General, Julian Moti, who was wanted by the authorities in Australia on a child molestation charge (see the chapter on Australia). Moti had been arrested in Port Moresby in September, but escaped to Solomon Islands at the beginning of October, reportedly on an aircraft of the Papua New Guinea Defence Force. Prime Minister Somare denied any knowledge of the flight, which he described as setting a 'dangerous precedent'. Australia subsequently imposed a ban on ministerial exchanges with Papua New Guinea and ministerial-level travel to Australia. At the end of the month the Papua New Guinea Government recalled its High Commissioner to Australia, Charles Lepani, for consultations, amid fears that the dispute would intensify. In November it was reported that the Papua New Guinea Chief Secretary, the Commander of the Defence Force and the acting Police Commissioner had been suspended, ostensibly owing to the Moti affair. Meanwhile, Prime Minister Somare indicated that, according to the findings of an investigation into the incident, Moti's arrest might not have followed correct procedures; both Papua New Guinean and Australian officials were implicated. The newly appointed Minister for Foreign Affairs, Paul Tiensten, declared his aim of restoring normal relations with Australia. The progress of a Papua New Guinea Defence Force inquiry was closely scrutinized by both countries in early 2007. In February, following a testimony that Somare had given instructions to fly Moti out to Solomon Islands, the inquiry issued a summons to the Prime Minister, prompting him to criticize it for exceeding its jurisdiction. Somare's dismissal of the Minister for Defence, Martin Aini, who had established the board of inquiry and admitted that the Prime Minister had exerted pressure on him to disband it, prompted further speculation over Somare's involvement. In September 2007 the National Court overruled Somare's attempt to dismiss the inquiry's conclusions. According to media sources, the report alleged that Somare had given the order to fly Moti out of the country and was therefore liable to prosecution. In October the new Minister for Defence, Bob Dadae, rejected the findings of the report on the basis that the 'composition of the board was not legally constituted'. Relations between Papua New Guinea and Australia appeared to improve when the latter removed its ban on contact between ministers of the two countries in September. The new Australian Prime Minister, Kevin Rudd, paid a three-day visit to Papua New Guinea in March 2008.

From 1990 relations with Solomon Islands were overshadowed by the conflict on Bougainville. Solomon Islands (the inhabitants of which are culturally and ethnically very similar to Bougainville islanders) protested against repeated incursions by Papua New Guinea defence forces into Solomon Islands' territorial waters, while the Papua New Guinea Government consistently accused Solomon Islands of harbouring members of the BRA and providing them with supplies. Despite several attempts during the 1990s to improve the situation between the two countries (including an agreement by Solomon Islands in 1993 to close the BRA office in the capital, Honiara), relations remained tense. In April 1997 the Solomon Islands Government announced that it was considering the initiation of proceedings against the Papua New Guinea Government concerning the latter's attempted use of mercenaries on Bougainville. In June of that year Papua New Guinea and Solomon Islands concluded a maritime border agreement, following several years of negotiations. The purpose of the agreement (which took effect in January 1998) was not only to delineate the sea boundary between the two countries but also to provide a framework for co-operation in matters of security, natural disaster, customs, quarantine, immigration and conservation. In March 2000 relations between Papua New Guinea and Solomon Islands were further strengthened following the opening of a Solomon Islands High Commission in Port Moresby. In March 2004 the two countries signed a number of treaties and agreements relating to the management of their common border area.

Concerns were expressed in mid-2003 that the rebel Solomon Islands leader Harold Keke (alleged to be responsible for a campaign of terror in Solomon Islands) was recruiting new members for his Guadalcanal Liberation Force in Bougainville and strengthening his links with the BRA. These fears were exacerbated by sightings of Keke in Buka and Bougainville and attacks against journalists who had reported on the activities of Keke's supporters (including the stockpiling of weapons) along the border between Papua New Guinea and Solomon Islands. However, in August the Governor of Bougainville, John Momis, officially stated that he did not believe that any link existed between Keke and the BRA. In that month Keke surrendered and was arrested by the regional peace-keeping force in Solomon Islands.

In February 2004 Prime Minister Sir Michael Somare led a delegation of 80 officials (the largest such group Papua New Guinea had ever sent on a state visit) to the People's Republic of China. Almost one-half of the delegates were representatives from the mining sector, who were hoping to secure agreements with Chinese interests relating to petroleum, gas and other mineral developments in Papua New Guinea.

In March 1988 Papua New Guinea signed an agreement with Vanuatu and Solomon Islands to form the Melanesian Spearhead Group, which was subsequently joined by Fiji. The grouping was dedicated to the preservation of Melanesian cultural traditions and to achieving independence for the French Overseas Territory of New Caledonia. In March 2007 the members of the Melanesian Spearhead Group signed a constitution. In 1989 Papua New Guinea increased its links with South-East Asia, signing a Treaty of Amity and Co-operation with the Association of South East Asian Nations (ASEAN, see p. 185).

By the early 21st century environmental concerns were increasingly being expressed. Fears that rising sea-levels might have very serious consequences for Pacific islanders intensified in May 2003 when an emergency operation was undertaken to save the inhabitants of Carteret and Mortlock islands, near Bougainville. Food supplies were sent to the islands, the 2,000 inhabitants of which were reported to be suffering from starvation and health problems related to poor diet, since the failure of their crops, which had been flooded by sea water. However, the islanders were reluctant to accept a government proposal to relocate them to Bougainville, fearing the loss of their distinct Polynesian culture and way of life. In November 2005 it was reported that the proposed relocation of families was finally to commence. The country was beset by a series of severe floods in late 2003 and early 2004 which affected some 5,000 people in Morobe Province and more than 10,000 in West Highlands Province.

The growing exploitation of Papua New Guinea's natural resources led to considerable anxiety about the impact of the activities of numerous foreign business interests on the environment. Activity in the forestry sector increased dramatically in the early 1990s, and an official report published in 1994 indicated that the current rate of logging was three times the sustainable yield of the country's forests. However, attempts to introduce new regulations to govern the industry were strongly opposed by several Malaysian logging companies with operations in the country. In early 2000, however, environmentalists welcomed a commitment by the Papua New Guinea Government to impose a moratorium on all new forestry licences and to review all existing licences. Concern continued among conservation organizations as the Government failed to enforce laws promoting sustainable forestry activity, which if upheld were deemed sufficient to ensure the long-term survival of the forestry sector. Conservationists hoped that pressure from consumers in the destination countries might lead to a reduction in illegal logging.

The exploitation of Papua New Guinea's extensive mineral resources has also resulted in considerable environmental damage. In 1989 the Government gave Ok Tedi Mining Ltd (OTML), the owners of a gold and copper mine, permission to discharge 150,000 metric tons of toxic waste per day into the Fly River. In 1994 6,000 people living in the region began a compensation claim against the Australian company operating the mine for damage caused by the resultant pollution. A settlement worth some $A110m. was reached in an Australian court in 1995 (and a further settlement worth $A400m. for the establishment of a containment system was concluded in mid-1996), despite opposition from the Papua New Guinea Government, which feared that such action might adversely affect the country's prospects of attracting foreign investment in the future. Similar claims were initiated by people living near the Australian-controlled Porgera gold-mine in early 1996 for pollution of the Strickland River system, as well as by landowners near the Kutubu oilfield. The results of an independent study into the effects of mining activities by OTML, published in mid-1999, showed that damage to the environment might be greater than originally believed. The results of an independent review, carried out by the World Bank and published in March 2000, recommended the closure of the mine on environmental grounds, but also emphasized the potentially damaging impact of the mine's early closure on both the local economy and world copper markets. In October 2001 BHP Billiton, the Australian operator, announced its withdrawal from the OTML venture and in early 2002 it transferred its 52% stake in the company to a development fund called the PNG Sustainable Development Programme Ltd. In early 2006 the managing director of OTML acknowledged that mining operations had caused major damage to the Ok Tedi and Fly River systems, resulting in flooding and forest die-back. Furthermore, the toxic effects of this waste were now believed to be threatening supplies of ground and drinking water.

Government

Executive power is vested in the British monarch (the Head of State), represented locally by the Governor-General, who is appointed on the proposal of the National Executive Council (the Cabinet) in accordance with the decision of the National Parliament by simple majority vote. The Governor-General acts on the advice of the National Executive Council, which is led by the Prime Minister. The Prime Minister is appointed and dismissed by the Head of State on the proposal of the National Parliament. Legislative power is vested in the unicameral National Parliament, with 109 members elected by universal adult suffrage for a term of five years. The National Executive Council is responsible to the National Parliament. The local government system underwent extensive reform in 1995, when the 19 directly-elected provincial governments were replaced by new regional authorities, composed of members of the National Parliament and local councillors, and led by an appointed Governor. The National Capital District (NCD) has its own governing body.

In January 2005 the National Government approved the final draft of the proposed Constitution for the province of Bougainville, and elections for the President of the new autonomous Government and for the 39 members of the House of Representatives commenced in May (see Recent History). In mid-June the new President was duly sworn in and the House of Representatives was inaugurated.

Defence

As assessed at November 2007 Papua New Guinea's national Defence Force numbered an estimated 3,100, comprising an army of 2,500, a navy of 400 and an air force of 200. In addition, 38 troops from Australia were stationed in the country for training purposes. Military service is voluntary. Budget estimates for 2007 allocated K94m. to defence.

Economic Affairs

In 2006, according to estimates by the World Bank, Papua New Guinea's gross national income (GNI), measured at average 2004–06 prices, was US $4,637m., equivalent to $770 per head (or $2,410 per head on an international purchasing-power parity basis). During 1996–2006, it was estimated, the population increased at an average annual rate of 2.2%, while gross domestic product (GDP) per head decreased, in real terms, by an average of 1.2% per year. Overall GDP increased, in real terms, at an average annual rate of 1.0% in 1996–2006. According to the Asian Development Bank (ADB), real GDP increased by 2.6% in 2006 and by 6.2% in 2007.

Agriculture (including hunting, forestry and fishing) contributed 34.6% of GDP in 2006, according to the ADB. In mid-2005, according to FAO, the sector engaged an estimated 71.4% of the labour force. The principal cash crops are palm oil (accounting for 3.5% of export earnings in 2006) and coffee (coffee beans accounting for 2.8% of export earnings in 2006). Other significant crops are cocoa and coconuts (for the production of copra and coconut oil), rubber, tea and vanilla. Roots and tubers, vegetables, bananas and melons are grown as food crops. Forestry is an important activity, and Papua New Guinea is one of the world's largest exporters of unprocessed tropical timber. Exports of forest products accounted for 4.3% of total export earnings in 2006, when revenue reached US $520m., compared with $476m. in the previous year. However, there is serious concern about the environmental damage caused by extensive logging activity in the country. The sale of fishing licences to foreign fleets has provided a substantial source of revenue. Most of the tuna caught by foreign operators is shipped directly overseas. During 1996–2003, according to figures from the World Bank, agricultural GDP increased by an average annual rate of 0.7%. According to the ADB, the GDP of the agricultural sector expanded by 0.7% in 2006 and by 3.7% in 2007.

Industry (including mining, manufacturing, construction and power) contributed an estimated 45.6% of GDP in 2006. During 1996–2003 industrial GDP decreased by an average of 2.4% per year, according to figures from the World Bank. The ADB estimated that industrial GDP increased by 3.2% in 2006 and by 7.7% in 2007.

Mining and quarrying provided an estimated 29.5% of GDP and 74.7% of total export earnings in 2003. Copper (which accounted for an estimated 35.6% of the country's total export revenue in 2006), gold (25.2%) and crude petroleum (24.4%) are the sector's major exports. Papua New Guinea also has substantial reserves of natural gas, and deposits of silver, chromite, cobalt, nickel and quartz. The country's largest petroleum refinery, at Napa Napa, which has a capacity of 32,500 barrels per day, began production in 2004. From the 1980s large gold deposits were discovered at several sites (including the largest known deposit outside South Africa at Lihir, which began operations in 1997). In early 2006 the opening of two new gold mines was announced by Ok Tedi Mining Ltd. The development of the important Ramu cobalt-nickel project, one of the world's largest unexploited deposits of these minerals, continued. However, according to figures from the ADB, the GDP of the mining sector decreased at an average annual rate of 4.8% during 1995–2002. Excluding oil and gas, the sector was reported to have contracted by 4.9% in 2006.

Manufacturing contributed an estimated 5.9% of GDP in 2006. The sector employed 1.1% of the working population in 2000. The principal branches of manufacturing are food products, beverages, tobacco, wood products, metal products, machinery and transport equipment. Several fish canneries were established in the 1990s and exports of canned tuna were expected to increase significantly, following the signing of a new quota agreement with the European Union (EU) in March 2003. A major tuna-loining plant in Wewak, processing 110 metric tons of fish per day and providing direct employment for 1,900 people, was scheduled to extend its activities to include canning in mid-2007. According to the World Bank, during 1996–2003 manufacturing GDP decreased by an average of 0.4% per year. Compared with the previous year, the sector's GDP expanded by 5.5% in 2003.

Energy is derived principally from hydroelectric power, which in 2000 accounted for more than 50% of electricity supplies. Plans to build a new hydroelectric power station at the Yonki Dam on the Ramu River were announced in 2006. At a cost of some K60m., the station was to be constructed alongside the existing dam wall and was expected to provide an output of at least 16 MW. In 2003 fuel imports accounted for 13.3% of the value of total merchandise imports.

The services sector contributed an estimated 19.9% of GDP in 2006, according to the ADB. Tourism is an expanding industry, although political instability and reports of widespread violent crime have had a detrimental effect on the sector. Total foreign visitor arrivals were reported to have increased from 77,731 in 2006 to 104,122 in 2007. Tourism receipts were worth an estimated US $168m. in 2005. The GDP of the services sector declined at an average annual rate of 1.1% in 1996–2003, according to figures from the World Bank. The sector's GDP expanded by 4.5% in 2006 and by 8.3% in 2007, according to the ADB.

In 2006 Papua New Guinea recorded a visible trade surplus of K6,668m., and a surplus of K1,255m. on the current account of the balance of payments. In 2006 the principal source of imports (51.7%) was Australia; other major suppliers were Singapore (13.3%), Japan, New Zealand, the People's Republic of China and the USA. In that year Australia was also the principal market for exports (30.4%), followed by Japan (8.9%), China and Germany. The principal exports were copper, gold, crude petroleum, forestry products, palm oil, coffee beans and cocoa. The principal imports included machinery and transport equipment, basic manufactures, food and live animals, miscellaneous manufactured articles, chemicals and mineral fuels.

In contrast to the original forecast of a deficit, the budget outcome for 2006 resulted in a surplus of K421.8m. (equivalent to 2.4% of the GDP). A deficit of K43.0m. was forecast for 2007. Papua New Guinea receives grants for budgetary aid from Australia. In 2007/08 official development assistance from Australia was projected at $A355.9m., while New Zealand's allocation of aid totalled $NZ21.5m. According to the ADB, Papua New Guinea's external debt totalled US $1,128m. at the end of 2007. In that year the cost of debt-servicing was equivalent to 3.5% of the value of exports of goods and services, compared with 1.3% in the previous year. At the census of 2000, 2.8% of the registered labour force were reported to be unemployed. In urban areas, however, the unemployment rate was estimated at some 70%. In the rural areas underemployment remained a serious problem. The annual rate of inflation averaged 8.6% in 1997–2007. Consumer prices increased by 0.9% in 2007.

Papua New Guinea is a member of Asia-Pacific Economic Co-operation (APEC, see p. 176), the Asian Development Bank (ADB, see p. 182), the Colombo Plan (see p. 411), the Pacific Community (see p. 377), the Pacific Islands Forum (see p. 380), the UN Economic and Social Commission for Asia and the Pacific (ESCAP, see p. 35), the International Cocoa Organization (see p. 408) and the International Coffee Organization (see p. 408). Papua New Guinea is also a member of the Melanesian Spearhead Group, which among other benefits provides for free trade among members.

Papua New Guinea has remained dependent on international aid. Foreign investment has been discouraged by the country's high levels of crime and ethnic unrest, as well as by the problems of corruption (see Recent History). The country's difficult terrain, vulnerability to extreme climatic conditions, lack of infrastructure and the limitations of the domestic market have also impeded progress. Only one in 10 of the total labour force was estimated to be in paid employment in 2006. Furthermore, the economy remains highly susceptible to fluctuations in world commodity prices. From 2006, however, the strength of prices for gold, copper, petroleum and timber was very advantageous to Papua New Guinea, while the Government also benefited from an increase in revenue from taxes on the mining sector. However, global coffee prices weakened in 2006, and in the following year adverse weather conditions resulted in a poor harvest. The Government's Medium Term Development Strategy for 2005–10 focused on improvements to the transport network. The plan also stressed the importance of wider opportunities for the generation of income within the agricultural sector, and the improvement of the country's basic education and health services, with emphasis on the prevention of HIV/AIDS. In May 2007 it was announced that the EU was to allocate US $159m. to various development projects in Papua New Guinea, over a six-year period commencing in 2008. The strong GDP growth of 2007 was largely due to high international prices for the country's export commodities. In particular, in terms of kina, prices for palm oil and copra rose by more than 50% over the year, which subsequently enabled an increase in government expenditure. The strength of commodity prices also raised rural incomes and levels of household spending. The ADB anticipated that economic expansion would continue, with GDP growth of 6.6% being forecast for 2008. The inflation rate remained stable in 2007 despite the high growth in GDP, although the likely impact on the economy of higher fuel prices, concomitant with increased public expenditure, led to projections of a much higher rate of inflation in 2008.

Education

Education is not compulsory. Primary education, available at community schools, begins at seven years of age and lasts for six years. Secondary education, beginning at the age of 13, lasts for up to six years (comprising two cycles, the first of four years, the second two). Originally, schooling was free; fees and charges for equipment were introduced, although the 2002 budget provided for the reinstatement of free education. In 2002/03 enrolment at pre-primary schools was equivalent to 59% of pupils in the relevant age-group (males 61%; females 57%). In the same year enrolment at primary schools was equivalent to 75.4% of children in the relevant age-group (80% of boys; 70% of girls) and secondary enrolment was equivalent to 25.8% of children in the relevant age-group (boys 29%; girls 23%). Tertiary education is provided by the University of Papua New Guinea and the University of Technology. There are also teacher-training colleges and higher institutions, which cater for specific professional training, such as a medical school, which had a total enrolment of 656 students in early 2005. Budget allocations for 2006 granted K43m. to the education sector. In February 2006 it was announced that the European Union was to grant a total of K156m. over the next six years in support of education and training in Papua New Guinea. The Government hoped that this would enable it to provide universal primary education by 2015 and to eliminate gender disparities.

Public Holidays

2008: 1 January (New Year's Day), 21–24 March (Easter), 9 June (Queen's Official Birthday), 23 July (Remembrance Day), 16 September (Independence Day and Constitution Day), 25 December (Christmas Day), 26 December (Boxing Day).

2009: 1 January (New Year's Day), 10–13 April (Easter), 8 June (Queen's Official Birthday), 23 July (Remembrance Day), 16 September (Independence Day and Constitution Day), 25 December (Christmas Day), 26 December (Boxing Day).

Weights and Measures

The metric system is in force.

PAPUA NEW GUINEA   Statistical Survey

Statistical Survey

Source (unless otherwise stated): Papua New Guinea National Statistical Office, POB 337, Waigani, NCD; tel. 3011200; fax 3251869; e-mail pmaime@nso.gov.pg; internet www.nso.gov.pg.

Area and Population

AREA, POPULATION AND DENSITY

Area (sq km)	462,840*
Population (census results)	
11 July 1990†	3,607,954
9 July 2000	
Males	2,691,744
Females	2,499,042
Total	5,190,786
Population (UN estimates at mid-year)‡	
2005	6,070,000
2006	6,202,000
2007	6,331,000
Density (per sq km) at mid-2007	13.7

* 178,704 sq miles.
† Excluding North Solomons Province (estimated population 154,000).
‡ Source: UN, *World Population Prospects: The 2006 Revision*.

PRINCIPAL TOWNS
(census of 9 July 2000, provisional)

Port Moresby (capital)	254,158	Mount Hagen	27,782
Lae	78,038	Madang	27,394
Arawa	36,443	Kokopo/Vunamami	20,262

Source: Thomas Brinkhoff, *City Population* (internet www.citypopulation.de).

Mid-2007 (incl. suburbs, UN estimate): Port Moresby 299,000 (Source: UN, *World Urbanization Prospects: The 2007 Revision*).

BIRTHS AND DEATHS
(2003)

Registered live births 192,817; Registered deaths 7,054. Registration is incomplete (Source: UN, *Population and Vital Statistics Report*).

Birth rate (per 1,000): 36.7 in 1990–95; 36.9 in 1995–2000; 34.0 in 2000–05.
Death rate (per 1,000): 10.6 in 1990–95; 10.2 in 1995–2000; 9.9 in 2000–05 (Source: UN, *World Population Prospects: The 2006 Revision*).

Expectation of life (years at birth, WHO estimates): 60.8 (males 59.4; females 62.6) in 2005 (Source: WHO, *World Health Statistics*).

ECONOMICALLY ACTIVE POPULATION
(2000 census, persons aged 10 years and over)

Agriculture, hunting and forestry	1,666,247
Fishing	30,024
Mining and quarrying	9,282
Manufacturing	25,557
Electricity, gas and water	2,208
Construction	48,312
Wholesale and retail trade; repair of motor vehicles, motorcycles and personal and household goods	353,186
Hotels and restaurants	4,395
Transport, storage and communications	24,513
Financial intermediation	3,670
Real estate, renting and business activities	27,459
Public administration and defence; compulsory social security	32,043
Education	27,118
Health and social work	12,341
Other community, social and personal service activities	31,409
Private households with employed persons	15,523
Extra-territorial organizations and bodies	163
Activities not adequately defined	31,284
Total employed	2,344,734
Unemployed	68,623
Total labour force	2,413,357
Males	1,256,887
Females	1,156,470

Source: ILO.

Mid-2005 (estimates in '000): Agriculture, etc. 2,032; Total labour force 2,844 (Source: FAO).

Health and Welfare

KEY INDICATORS

Total fertility rate (children per woman, 2005)	3.8
Under-5 mortality rate (per 1,000 live births, 2005)	74
HIV/AIDS (% of persons aged 15–49, 2005)	1.8
Physicians (per 1,000 head, 2000)	0.05
Hospital beds (per 1,000 head, 1990)	4.02
Health expenditure (2004): US $ per head (PPP)	146.7
Health expenditure (2004): % of GDP	3.6
Health expenditure (2004): public (% of total)	84.3
Access to water (% of persons, 2004)	39
Access to sanitation (% of persons, 2004)	44
Human Development Index (2005): ranking	145
Human Development Index (2005): value	0.530

For sources and definitions, see explanatory note on p. vi.

Agriculture

PRINCIPAL CROPS
('000 metric tons)

	2003	2004	2005
Sweet potatoes*	500.0	492.9	492.2
Cassava (Manioc)*	125	120	125
Yams*	290	280	290
Taro (Coco yam)*	255	256	260
Sugar cane*	445	442	450
Coconuts*	630.0	745.1	795.1
Oil palm fruit*	1,200	1,250	1,300
Pineapples*	18	18	20
Bananas*	870.0	897.4	919.8
Coffee (green)	69.3	59.8	76.1
Cocoa beans†	42.5	42.5	42.5
Tea (made)	6.4†	9.0*	9.0*
Natural rubber (dry weight)	4.4†	4.0†	4.0*

* FAO estimate(s).
† Unofficial figure(s).

Aggregate production ('000 metric tons, may include official, semi-official or estimated data): Total cereals 10.3 in 2003, 10.8 in 2004, 12.8 in 2005; Total oilcrops 1,999 in 2003, 2,174 in 2004, 2,279 in 2005; Total vegetables (incl. melons) 495 in 2003, 500 in 2004, 501 in 2005; Total fruits (excl. melons) 1,792 in 2003, 1,820 in 2004, 1,855 in 2005.

Note: No data were available for 2006.

Source: FAO.

LIVESTOCK
('000 head, year ending September)

	2003	2004*	2005*
Horses	2.2*	2.2	2.2
Cattle	90.0*	91.0	91.5
Pigs	1,800†	1,700	1,750
Sheep	7.0*	7.0	7.5
Goats	2.5*	2.6	2.7
Chickens	3,900†	3,900	4,000

* FAO estimate(s).
† Unofficial figure.

Note: No data were available for 2006.

Source: FAO.

PAPUA NEW GUINEA

LIVESTOCK PRODUCTS
('000 metric tons, FAO estimates)

	2003	2004	2005
Cattle meat	3.2	3.2	3.3
Pig meat	68	64	66
Chicken meat	5.7	5.6	5.7
Game meat	310	320	330
Hen eggs	4.8	4.8	4.8

Note: No data were available for 2006.

Source: FAO.

Forestry

ROUNDWOOD REMOVALS
('000 cubic metres, excluding bark)

	2000	2001	2002*
Sawlogs, veneer logs and logs for sleepers	2,064	1,611	1,611
Pulpwood	120	97	97
Fuel wood*	5,533	5,533	5,533
Total	7,717	7,241	7,241

* FAO estimates.

2003–06: Annual production assumed to be unchanged from 2002 (FAO estimates).

Source: FAO.

SAWNWOOD PRODUCTION
('000 cubic metres, including railway sleepers)

	2001	2002	2003
Coniferous (softwood)	—	10	10*
Broadleaved (hardwood)	40	60	50†
Total	40	70	60*

* FAO estimate.
† Unofficial figure.

2004-06: Production assumed to be unchanged from 2003 (FAO estimates).

Source: FAO.

Fishing

('000 metric tons, live weight of capture)

	2003	2004	2005
Mozambique tilapia*	2.3	2.3	2.3
Other freshwater fishes*	8.5	8.5	8.5
Sea catfishes*	1.9	1.9	1.9
Skipjack tuna	118.7	172.4	166.3
Yellowfin tuna	37.4	24.4	44.9
Total catch (incl. others)*	186.7	229.7	250.3

* FAO estimates.

Note: Figures exclude crocodiles, recorded by number rather than weight. The number of estuarine crocodiles caught was: 8,000 in 2003; 11,043 in 2004; 10,475 in 2005. The number of New Guinea crocodiles caught was: 18,482 in 2003; 40,358 in 2004; 19,129 in 2005. Figures also exclude shells (0.3 metric tons in each year, FAO estimates).

Source: FAO.

Mining

	2004	2005	2006
Petroleum, crude ('000 barrels)	15,495	17,113	17,300*
Copper ('000 metric tons)†	173.4	193.0	194.4
Silver (metric tons)†	55.6	51.1	50.0*
Gold (metric tons)†	73.7	68.5	50.0*

* Estimate.
† Figures refer to metal content of ore.

Source: US Geological Survey.

Industry

SELECTED PRODUCTS
('000 metric tons)

	2003	2004	2005
Beer of barley	40*	39*	45†
Palm oil ('000 metric tons)	326*	345*	350†
Raw sugar ('000 metric tons)*	51	46	46

* Unofficial figure(s).
† FAO estimate.

Electric energy (million kWh): 1,398 in 2003; 1,399 in 2004.

Wood products ('000 cu m, excl. furniture): 1,611 in 2003.

Sources: FAO; UN, *Industrial Commodity Statistics Yearbook*; Asian Development Bank, *Key Indicators of Developing Asian and Pacific Countries*.

Finance

CURRENCY AND EXCHANGE RATES

Monetary Units
100 toea = 1 kina (K).

Sterling, Dollar and Euro Equivalents (31 December 2007)
£1 sterling = 5.683 kina;
US $1 = 2.837 kina;
€1 = 4.176 kina;
100 kina = £17.60 = $35.25 = €23.95.

Average Exchange Rate (kina per US $)
2005   3.1020
2006   3.0567
2007   2.9654

Note: The foregoing information refers to the mid-point exchange rate of the central bank. In October 1994 it was announced that the kina would be allowed to 'float' on foreign exchange markets.

BUDGET
(million kina)

Revenue*	2005	2006†	2007†
Taxation	3,766.9	4,944.7	4,129.9
Personal tax	841.0	907.0	890.3
Company tax	1,593.3	2,497.1	1,804.5
Other direct tax	359.6	419.3	376.8
Import duties	101.9	90.4	96.9
Excise duties	334.5	408.1	395.2
Export tax	136.3	162.6	118.0
Goods and services tax	326.2	401.1	420.0
Other indirect tax	74.1	59.1	28.2
Non-tax revenue	263.2	452.1	412.6
Dividends	165.1	339.3	242.8
Interest revenue/fees	0.5	0.6	2.6
Other internal revenue	97.6	112.2	167.2
Total	4,030.1	5,396.8	4,542.5

PAPUA NEW GUINEA

Statistical Survey

Expenditure‡	2005	2006†	2007†
Recurrent expenditure	3,419.6	3,700.8	3,374.0
National departmental	2,223.6	2,347.8	1,929.2
Provincial governments	656.5	811.7	747.3
Interest payments	332.8	307.0	475.9
Foreign	116.7	119.9	117.1
Domestic	216.1	187.1	358.8
Other grants and expenditure	206.7	234.3	221.6
Development expenditure	1,849.4	1,559.6	1,636.6
National projects	1,632.4	1,247.7	1,309.3
Provincial projects	217.0	311.9	327.3
Additional priority expenditure	—	625.0	450.0
Total	5,269.0	5,885.4	5,460.6

* Excluding grants received from abroad (million kina): 1,283.1 in 2005; 914.6 in 2006 (forecast); 879.1 in 2007 (forecast).
† Forecasts.
‡ Excluding net lending (million kina): −2.7 in 2005; −4.2 in 2006 (forecast); −4.0 in 2007 (forecast).

Source: Bank of Papua New Guinea, Port Moresby.

INTERNATIONAL RESERVES
(US $ million at 31 December)

	2004	2005	2006
Gold (national valuation)	27.55	30.65	26.76
IMF special drawing rights	0.73	0.03	0.06
Reserve position in IMF	0.66	0.63	0.66
Foreign exchange	631.17	717.45	1,399.96
Total	660.11	748.76	1,427.44

Source: IMF, *International Financial Statistics*.

MONEY SUPPLY
(million kina at 31 December)

	2004	2005	2006
Currency outside banks	399.54	445.47	519.82
Demand deposits at deposit money banks	1,780.95	2,512.70	3,222.51
Total money (incl. others)	2,188.19	2,966.14	3,745.15

Source: IMF, *International Financial Statistics*.

COST OF LIVING
(Consumer Price Index; base: 1977 = 100)

	2005	2006	2007
Food	784.1	826.0	831.3
Clothing and footwear	480.5	480.8	514.1
Rent, fuel and power	328.6	361.8	374.2
All items (incl. others)	795.9	814.7	822.2

Source: Bank of Papua New Guinea, Port Moresby.

NATIONAL ACCOUNTS

National Income and Product
(million kina at current prices)

	2000	2001	2002
Compensation of employees	1,927.3	2,063.5	2,259.7
Operating surplus	6,374.8	6,770.4	7,617.1
Domestic factor incomes	8,302.1	8,833.9	9,876.8
Consumption of fixed capital	549.0	642.2	690.2
Gross domestic product (GDP) at factor cost	8,851.1	9,476.1	10,567.1
Indirect taxes / *Less* Subsidies	884.7	920.2	1,001.4
GDP in purchasers' values	9,735.8	10,396.3	11,568.6
Net factor income from abroad	−391.3	−408.1	−405.3
Gross national product	9,344.5	9,988.2	11,163.3
Less Consumption of fixed capital	549.0	642.2	690.2
National income in market prices	8,795.5	9,346.0	10,473.1

Source: Bank of Papua New Guinea, Port Moresby.

Expenditure on the Gross Domestic Product
(million kina at current prices)

	2002	2003	2004
Government final consumption expenditure	1,788	1,917	1,938
Private final consumption expenditure	7,060	6,515	6,891
Increase in stocks	206	222	236
Gross fixed capital formation	2,264	2,281	2,294
Total domestic expenditure	11,318	10,935	11,359
Exports of goods and services	7,100	8,724	9,130
Less Imports of goods and services	6,761	6,790	7,455
Statistical discrepancy	—	−80	827
GDP in purchasers' values	11,657	12,949	13,861
GDP at constant 1998 prices	7,728	7,953	8,183

Source: IMF, *International Financial Statistics*.

Gross Domestic Product by Economic Activity
(million kina at current prices, unofficial estimates)

	2004	2005	2006
Agriculture, hunting, forestry and fishing	4,550.8	5,683.2	5,819.5
Mining and quarrying	2,391.1	3,631.9	4,961.8
Manufacturing	848.8	942.5	999.5
Electricity, gas and water	263.7	284.4	301.7
Construction	1,177.0	1,245.8	1,411.5
Wholesale and retail trade	890.5	944.8	1,011.7
Transport, storage and communications	304.7	317.0	326.2
Finance, insurance, real estate and business services*	415.2	449.0	490.3
Community, social and personal services (incl. defence)	1,395.0	1,427.2	1,514.0
Sub-total	12,236.8	14,925.8	16,836.2
Import duties, *less* subsidies	415.3	413.4	433.0
GDP in purchasers' values	12,652.1	15,339.2	17,269.2

* Including services of owner-occupied dwellings.

Source: Asian Development Bank, *Key Indicators of Developing Asian and Pacific Countries*.

PAPUA NEW GUINEA

BALANCE OF PAYMENTS
(million kina)

	2004	2005	2006
Exports of goods f.o.b.	8,233	10,168	12,752
Imports of goods f.o.b.	−4,703	−4,732	−6,084
Trade balance	3,530	5,436	6,668
Exports of services	656	938	965
Imports of services	−3,217	−3,621	−4,519
Balance on goods and services	969	2,753	3,114
Other income received	64	81	215
Other income paid	−1,470	−1,751	−2,677
Balance on goods, services and income	−437	1,083	652
Current transfers received	1,080	1,093	999
Current transfers paid	−250	−290	−396
Current balance	393	1,887	1,255
Capital account (net)	—	101	135
Direct investment abroad	0	−20	−3
Direct investment from abroad	83	104	−21
Portfolio investment assets	−336	82	382
Portfolio investment liabilities	−2	−6	7
Financial derivatives assets	−32	−6	−35
Other investment assets	110	−1,984	867
Other investment liabilities	97	139	−613
Net errors and omissions	17	−1	−16
Overall balance	329	296	1,957

Source: Bank of Papua New Guinea, Port Moresby.

External Trade

PRINCIPAL COMMODITIES
(US $ million)

Imports f.o.b.*	2001	2002	2003
Food and live animals	180.9	176.8	192.4
Meat and meat preparations	38.9	32.9	34.8
Fresh, chilled or frozen meat	36.4	30.2	32.7
Cereals and cereal preparations	82.5	81.4	94.6
Rice	53.0	53.2	61.5
Milled or semi-milled rice	40.1	23.5	20.5
Mineral fuels, lubricants and related materials	294.7	153.9	173.2
Petroleum and petroleum products	291.5	150.0	169.9
Chemicals and related products	98.5	90.6	109.6
Basic manufactures	200.7	239.2	233.6
Iron and steel	37.2	35.5	39.2
Manufactures of other metals	68.1	100.1	82.0
Machinery and transport equipment	415.5	399.9	454.3
Power-generating machinery and equipment	38.0	36.1	51.2
Machinery specialized for particular industries	83.1	89.5	90.6
General industrial machinery and equipment	68.2	84.3	92.4
Electrical machinery, apparatus and appliances, etc.	38.2	40.3	46.7
Road vehicles and parts†	107.6	63.2	68.1
Motor vehicles for goods transport	41.3	24.0	24.2
Other transport equipment and parts†	38.9	27.9	46.4
Miscellaneous manufactured articles	82.8	90.3	100.7
Total (incl. others)	1,309.4	1,186.0	1,302.4

Exports f.o.b.	2001	2002	2003
Food and live animals	99.8	206.3	285.1
Coffee, tea, cocoa and spices, etc.	7.9	127.9	193.2
Crude materials, inedible, except fuels	582.2	588.8	1,107.2
Cork and wood	79.6	96.4	54.3
Metalliferous ores and metal scrap	488.3	478.9	1,043.4
Ores and concentrates of precious metals	228.9	263.2	645.0
Mineral fuels, lubricants and related materials	561.1	367.8	459.3
Crude petroleum and oils obtained from bituminous materials	561.1	367.7	458.1
Animal and vegetable oils, fats and waxes	90.2	107.0	146.5
Palm oil	73.7	86.0	122.8
Gold, non-monetary, unwrought or semi-manufactured	392.1	278.7	143.9
Total (incl. others)	1,804.7	1,625.1	2,260.2

* Figures include migrants' and travellers' dutiable effects, but exclude military equipment and some parcel post.
† Data on parts exclude tyres, engines and electrical parts.

Source: UN, *International Trade Statistics Yearbook*.

2004 (million kina): *Imports c.i.f.*: Total 5,660. *Exports f.o.b.*: Gold 2,780; Crude petroleum 1,652; Copper 1,544; Forestry products 460; Coffee beans 284; Palm oil 439; Cocoa 218; Total (incl. others) 8,233 (Source: Asian Development Bank, *Key Indicators of Developing Asian and Pacific Countries*).

2005 (million kina): *Imports c.i.f.*: Total 5,677. *Exports f.o.b.*: Gold 2,834; Crude petroleum 2,283; Copper 2,498; Forestry products 476; Coffee beans 471; Palm oil 391; Cocoa 199; Total (incl. others) 10,168 (Source: Asian Development Bank, *Key Indicators of Developing Asian and Pacific Countries*).

2006 (million kina): *Imports c.i.f.*: Total 7,146. *Exports f.o.b.*: Gold 3,069; Crude petroleum 2,967; Copper 4,330; Forestry products 520; Coffee beans 337; Palm oil 428; Cocoa 204; Total (incl. others) 12,167 (Source: Asian Development Bank, *Key Indicators of Developing Asian and Pacific Countries*).

PRINCIPAL TRADING PARTNERS
(US $ million)

Imports c.i.f.	2004	2005	2006
Australia	745.2	1,103.2	1,155.1
China, People's Republic	55.5	73.1	139.0
Indonesia	39.9	54.0	67.9
Japan	69.6	87.6	99.6
Korea, Republic	15.4	18.6	21.8
Malaysia	45.2	84.4	85.9
New Zealand	67.2	79.2	80.1
Singapore	347.1	271.0	296.7
Thailand	25.7	38.8	57.0
USA	46.9	60.8	48.2
Total (incl. others)	1,603.8	2,017.9	2,232.4

Exports f.o.b.	2004	2005	2006
Australia	1,198.3	1,506.6	1,865.1
China, People's Republic	194.7	281.3	356.1
Germany	201.4	207.1	242.4
Indonesia	84.9	45.4	56.1
Japan	247.6	449.9	543.6
Korea, Republic	35.3	65.4	76.7
Philippines	60.3	104.5	115.3
Thailand	29.6	45.4	35.6
United Kingdom	101.7	98.2	67.6
USA	52.2	56.6	60.1
Total (incl. others)	4,265.2	5,236.0	6,130.8

Source: Asian Development Bank, *Key Indicators of Developing Asian and Pacific Countries*.

PAPUA NEW GUINEA

Archbishop of Mount Hagen: Most Rev. MICHAEL MEIER, Archbishop's Office, POB 54, Mount Hagen, Western Highlands Province 281; tel. 5421285; fax 5422128; e-mail archdios@online.net.pg.

Archbishop of Port Moresby: Most Rev. Sir BRIAN BARNES, Archbishop's House, POB 1032, Boroko, NCD 111; tel. 3251192; fax 3256731; e-mail archpom@daltron.com.pg.

Archbishop of Rabaul: Most Rev. KARL HESSE, Archbishop's House, POB 357, Kokopo 613, East New Britain Province; tel. 9829384; fax 9828404; e-mail abkhesse@online.net.pg.

Other Christian Churches

Baptist Union of Papua New Guinea Inc: POB 705, Mount Hagen, Western Highlands Province; tel. 5522364; fax 5522402; e-mail bupng@global.net.pg; f. 1976; Gen. Sec. JOHN KAENKI; 48,000 mems.

Evangelical Lutheran Church of Papua New Guinea: Bishop Rt Rev. WESLEY KIGASUNG, POB 80, Lae, Morobe Province; tel. 4723711; fax 4721056; e-mail bishop.admin@global.net.pg; f. 1956; Sec. ISAAC TEO; 900,000 mems.

Gutnius Lutheran Church of Papua New Guinea: Bishop Rev. DAVID P. PISO, POB 111, 291 Wabag, Enga Province; tel. 5471280; fax 5471235; e-mail dpisoglc@online.net.pg; f. 1948; Gen. Sec. RICHARD R. MOSES; 138,000 mems.

Papua New Guinea Union Mission of the Seventh-day Adventist Church: POB 86, Lae, Morobe Province 411; tel. 4721488; fax 4721873; Pres. Pastor WILSON STEPHEN; Sec. Pastor BRADLEY RICHARD KEMP; 200,000 adherents.

The United Church in Papua New Guinea: POB 1401, Port Moresby; tel. 3211744; fax 3214930; e-mail ucpng@daltron.com.pg; f. 1968; formed by union of the Methodist Church in Melanesia, the Papua Ekalesia and United Church, Port Moresby; Moderator Rev. SAMSON LOWA; 600,000 mems; Gen. Sec. Rev. SIULANGI KAVORA.

BAHÁ'Í FAITH

National Spiritual Assembly: Private Mail Bag, Boroko, NCD; tel. 3250286; fax 3236474; e-mail nsapng@datec.net.pg.

ISLAM

In 2000 the Muslim community in Papua New Guinea numbered about 1,500, of whom approximately two-thirds were believed to be expatriates. The religion was introduced to the island in the 1970s. The first mosque there was opened in late 2000 at Poreporena Highway, Hohola, Port Moresby; Imam KHALID ARAI (acting).

The Press

There are numerous newspapers and magazines published by government departments, statutory organizations, missions, sporting organizations, local government councils and regional authorities. They are variously in English, Tok Pisin (Pidgin), Motu and vernacular languages.

Ailans Nius: POB 1239, Rabaul, East New Britain Province; weekly.

Foreign Affairs Review: Dept of Foreign Affairs, Central Government Offices, Kumul Ave, Post Office, Wards Strip, Waigani, NCD; tel. 3271401; fax 3254886.

Hailans Nius: Mount Hagen, Western Highlands Province; weekly.

Lae Nius: POB 759, Lae, Morobe Province; 2 a week.

The National: POB 6817, Boroko, NCD; tel. 3246888; fax 3246868; e-mail national@thenational.com.pg; internet www.thenational.com.pg; f. 1993; daily; Editor BRIAN GOMEZ; circ. 20,000.

Papua and New Guinea Education Gazette: Dept of Education, PSA Haus, POB 446, Waigani, NCD; tel. 3272413; fax 3254648; monthly; Editor J. OBERLENTER; circ. 8,000.

Papua New Guinea Post-Courier: POB 85, Port Moresby; tel. 3091000; fax 3212721; e-mail postcourier@ssp.com.pg; internet www.postcourier.com.pg; f. 1969; daily; English; published by News Corpn; Gen. Man. TONY YIANNI; Editor OSEAH PHILEMON; circ. 25,044.

Sunkamap Times: POB 322, Buka, Bougainville, North Solomons Province; e-mail info@viscom.co.nz; internet www.viscom.co.nz/SunkamapTimes; monthly; f. 2004; community newsletter.

Wantok (Friend) Niuspepa: POB 1982, Boroko, NCD; tel. 3252500; fax 3252579; e-mail word@global.net.pg; f. 1970; weekly in New Guinea Pidgin; mainly rural readership; Publr ANNA SOLOMON; Editor NEVILLE CHOI; circ. 10,000.

Directory

Publishers

Gordon and Gotch (PNG) Pty Ltd: POB 107, Boroko, NCD; tel. 3254855; fax 3250950; e-mail ggpng@online.net.pg; f. 1970; books, magazines and stationery; Gen. Man. PETER G. PORTER.

Scripture Union of Papua New Guinea: POB 280, University, Boroko, NCD; tel. and fax 3253987; f. 1966; religious; Chair. RAVA TAVIRI.

Word Publishing Co Pty Ltd: POB 1982, Boroko, NCD; tel. 3252500; fax 3252579; e-mail word@global.net.pg; f. 1982; 60% owned by the Roman Catholic Church, 20% by Evangelical Lutheran, 10% by Anglican and 10% by United Churches; Gen. Man. JEREMY BURGESS.

Broadcasting and Communications

TELECOMMUNICATIONS

Office of Information and Communication: POB 639, Waigani; tel. 3250148; fax 3250412; e-mail hiduhu@datec.com.pg; internet www.communication.gov.pg; Dir-Gen. HENAO IDUHU.

Digicel (PNG) Ltd: POB 1618, Port Moresby, NCD; e-mail customercarepng@digicelgroup.com; internet www.digicelpng.com; GSM services; CEO KEVIN O'SULLIVAN.

Pacific Mobile Communications Company Ltd: POB 785, Waigani, NCD; tel. 3236336; fax 3258916; e-mail pmc@tiare.net.pg; internet www.pacificmobile.com.pg; Chair. FLORIAN GUBON.

Papua New Guinea Telecommunication Authority (Pangtel): POB 8444, Boroko, NCD; tel. 3258633; fax 3256868; e-mail uoome@pangtel.gov.pg; internet www.pangtel.gov.pg; f. 1997; CEO CHARLES PUNAHA.

Telikom PNG Pty Ltd: POB 736, Port Moresby, NCD; tel. 3004688; fax 3004689; e-mail webadmin@telikompng.com.pg; internet www.telikompng.com.pg; Chair. GEREA AOPI; CEO DAVID WATERHOUSE.

In 2006 Green Communications (GreenCom), an Indonesian company, acquired a licence to expand into Papua New Guinea. The new venture was reportedly due to become operational in early 2009.

BROADCASTING

Radio

National Broadcasting Corporation of Papua New Guinea: POB 1359, Boroko, NCD; tel. 3257175; fax 3256296; e-mail md.nbc@global.net.pg; internet www.nbc.com.pg; f. 1973; commercial and free govt radio programmes services; broadcasting in English, Melanesian, Pidgin, Motu and 30 vernacular languages; Chair. CHRIS RANGATIN; Man. Dir Dr KRISTOFFA NINKAMA.

Kalang Service (FM): POB 1359, Boroko, NCD; tel. 3255233; commercial radio co established by National Broadcasting Commission; Chair. CAROLUS KETSIMUR.

Nau FM/Yumi FM: POB 774, Port Moresby; tel. 3201996; fax 3201995; internet www.naufm.com.pg; f. 1994; Gen. Mans MARK ROGERS, JUSTIN KILI.

Television

EM TV: POB 443, Boroko, NCD; tel. 3257322; fax 3254450; e-mail emtv@emtv.com.pg; internet www.emtv.com.pg; f. 1988; operated by Media Niugini Pty Ltd; Gen. Man. GLENN ARMSTRONG.

Media Niugini Pty Ltd: POB 443, Boroko, NCD; tel. 3257322; fax 3254450; e-mail emtv@emtv.com.pg; internet www.emtv.com.pg; f. 1987; owned by Nine Network Australia; Gen. Man. GLENN ARMSTRONG.

Finance

(cap. = capital; res = reserves; dep. = deposits; m. = million; brs = branches; amounts in kina unless otherwise stated)

BANKING

Central Bank

Bank of Papua New Guinea: Douglas St, POB 121, Port Moresby; tel. 3227200; fax 3211617; internet www.bankpng.gov.pg; f. 1973; bank of issue since 1975; sold to Bank of South Pacific in 2002; cap. 74.0m., res 582.7m., dep. 1,599.6m. (Dec. 2004); Gov. WILSON KAMIT; Deputy Gov. BENNY POPOITAI.

Commercial Banks

Australia and New Zealand Banking Group (PNG) Limited: Defens Haus, 3rd Floor, cnr of Champion Parade and Hunter St, POB

PAPUA NEW GUINEA

1152, Port Moresby; tel. 3223203; fax 3223302; f. 1976; Chair. R. G. Lyon; Man. Dir Allan Marlin; 8 brs.

Bank of South Pacific Ltd: POB 78, Allotment 12–13, Section 5, Cnr Douglas and Musgrave Sts, Granville, Port Moresby; tel. 3211999; fax 3211954; internet www.bsp.com.pg; f. 1974; acquired from National Australia Bank Ltd by Papua New Guinea consortium (National Investment Holdings, now BSP Holdings Ltd) in 1993; merged with Papua New Guinea Banking Corpn in 2002; cap. 191.1m., res 19.8m., dep. 1,876.3m. (Dec. 2004); Chair. Noreo Beangke; Man. Dir Garth McIlwain; 8 brs and 2 sub-brs.

Maybank (PNG) Ltd: Waigani, NCD; f. 1995.

MBf Finance (PNG) Ltd: Elsa Beach Towers, Ground Floor, cnr of Musgrave St, POB 329, Port Moresby; tel. 3213555; fax 3213480; f. 1989.

Westpac Bank—PNG—Ltd: Deloitte Tower, 9th Floor, Douglas St, POB 706, Port Moresby; tel. 3220888; fax 3220997; e-mail westpacpng@westpac.com.au; internet www.westpac.com.pg; f. 1910; est. as Bank of New South Wales, present name since 1982; 90% owned by Westpac Banking Corpn, Australia; cap. 5.8m., res 6.1m., dep. 554.7m. (Sept. 1999); Chair. Alan Walter; Man. Dir Ross Hammond; 15 brs.

Development Bank

Rural Development Bank of Papua New Guinea: Somare Crescent, POB 686, Waigani, NCD; tel. 3247500; fax 3259817; f. 1967; est. as Agriculture Bank of Papua New Guinea; name changed as above in 1994; statutory govt agency; Chair. Rupa Mulina; Man. Dir Andrew Nagari; 10 brs.

Savings and Loan Societies

Registry of Savings and Loan Societies: Bank of Papua New Guinea, Financial System Supervision Dept, POB 121, Port Moresby; tel. 3227200; fax 3214548; 21 savings and loan societies; 205,205 mems (2007); total funds 631.2m., loans outstanding 27.2m., investments 359m. (Dec. 2007); Man. Elizabeth Gima.

STOCK EXCHANGE

Port Moresby Stock Exchange (POMSoX) Ltd: Level 4, Defens Haus, POB 1531, Port Moresby; tel. 3201980; fax 3201981; e-mail pomsox@pomsox.com.pg; internet www.pomsox.com.pg; f. 1999; Chair. Gerea Aopi; Gen. Man. Vincent Ivosa.

INSURANCE

Capital Life Insurance Co: POB 1972, Port Moresby, NCD; tel. 3234036; fax 3232533; e-mail cilc@daltron.com.pg; f. 1993; fmrly Pan Asia Pacific Assurance (PNG).

Kwila Insurance Corpn: POB 1457, Boroko, NCD; tel. 3258811; fax 3112867; internet www.kwilainsurance.com.pg; f. 1977; Gen. Man. Jason R. McIlvena.

Pacific MMI Insurance Ltd: POB 331, Port Moresby, NCD; tel. 3214077; fax 3214837; e-mail enquiries@pacificmmi.com; internet www.pacificmmi.com; f. 1998; fmrly Niugini Insurance Corpn Ltd; jt venture; general and life insurance; financial services; Chair. Dr John Mua; Man. Dir Wayne Dorgan.

There are branches of several Australian and United Kingdom insurance companies in Port Moresby, Rabaul, Lae and Kieta.

Trade and Industry

GOVERNMENT AGENCIES

Investment Promotion Authority (IPA): POB 5053, Boroko, NCD 111; tel. 3217311; fax 3212819; e-mail biepd@ipa.gov.pg; internet www.ipa.gov.pg; f. 1992; est. following reorganization of National Investment and Development Authority; a statutory body responsible for the promotion of foreign investment; the first contact point for foreign investors for advice on project proposals and approvals of applications for registration to conduct business in the country; contributes to planning for investment and recommends priority areas for investment to the Govt; also co-ordinates investment proposals; Man. Dir Ivan Pomaleu.

Privatization Commission: POB 45, Konedobu, NCD; tel. 3212977; fax 3213134; internet www.ipbc.com.pg; f. 1999; to oversee transfer of state-owned enterprises to private ownership; Exec. Chair. Ben Micah.

DEVELOPMENT ORGANIZATIONS

CDC Capital Partners Ltd: CDC Haus, 2nd Floor, POB 907, Port Moresby; tel. 3212944; fax 3212867; e-mail png@cdc.com.pg; internet www.cdcgroup.com; fmrly Commonwealth Development Corpn; Man. Dir Ashley Emberson-Bain.

Industrial Centres Development Corporation: POB 1571, Boroko, NCD; tel. 3232913; fax 3231109; promotes foreign investment in non-mining sectors through establishment of manufacturing facilities.

CHAMBERS OF COMMERCE

Lae Chamber of Commerce Inc: POB 265, Lae, Morobe Province; tel. 4722340; fax 4726038; e-mail lcci@global.net.pg; internet www.lcci.org.pg; Pres. Alan McLay.

Papua New Guinea Chamber of Commerce and Industry: POB 1621, Port Moresby; tel. 3213057; fax 3210566; e-mail pngcci@global.net.pg; internet www.pngcci.org.pg; Pres. Michael Mayberry; CEO (vacant).

Papua New Guinea Chamber of Mines and Petroleum: POB 1032, Port Moresby; tel. 3212988; fax 3217107; e-mail ga@pngchamberminpet.com.pg; internet www.pngchamberminpet.com.pg; Exec. Dir Greg Anderson; Pres. Peter Botten.

Port Moresby Chamber of Commerce and Industry: POB 1764, Port Moresby; tel. 3213077; fax 3214203; Pres. David Conn.

INDUSTRIAL AND TRADE ASSOCIATIONS

Cocoa Board of Papua New Guinea: POB 532, Rabaul, East New Britain Province; tel. 9829083; fax 9828712; e-mail l.tautea@global.net.pg; f. 1974; Chair. Jimmy Simitab; CEO Lauatu Tautea.

Coffee Industry Corpn Ltd: POB 137, Goroka, Eastern Highlands Province; tel. 7321266; fax 7321431; e-mail cicgka@daltron.com.pg; internet www.coffeecorp.org.pg; CEO Ricky Mittio.

Fishing Industry Association (PNG) Inc: POB 5860, Boroko, NCD; tel. 3258222; fax 3258994; e-mail netshop1@daltron.com.pg; Chair. Maurice Brownjohn.

Forest Industries Association: POB 229, Waigani, NCD; internet www.fiapng.com; Pres. Stanis Bai; CEO Robert Tate.

Higaturu Oil Palms Pty Ltd: POB 28, Popondetta, Oro Province; tel. 3297177; fax 3297137; f. 1976; jtly owned by the Commonwealth Development Corpn (UK) and the Papua New Guinea Govt; major producer of palm oil and cocoa; Gen. Man. Richard Caskie.

Kokonas Indasti Korporesen (KIK): POB 81, Port Moresby; tel. 3211133; fax 3214257; e-mail infor@kik.com.pg; regulates and markets all copra and coconut products in Papua New Guinea; consists of a chair. and mems representing producers; fmrly known as the Copra Marketing Board of Papua New Guinea (f. 1950s); name changed as above 2002; govt-owned; Chair. David Nipuega; Man. Dir Tore Ovasuru.

Manufacturers' Council of Papua New Guinea: POB 598, Port Moresby; tel. 3259512; fax 3230199; e-mail pngmade@global.com.pg; internet www.pngmade.org.pg; Chair. Wayne Golding; CEO Bruce Reville.

Mineral Resources Development Corporation: POB 1076, Port Moresby; tel. 3255822; fax 3252633; Man. Dir Francis Kaupa.

Morobe Produce Marketing Ltd: POB 3434, Lae 411, Morobe Province; tel. 4724144; fax 4725186; f. 1982; owned by Gerard Kananimara; handles distribution of fruit and vegetables throughout the country.

National Fisheries Authority: POB 2016, Port Moresby; tel. 3212643; fax 3202061; e-mail nfa@fisheries.gov.pg; internet www.fisheries.gov.pg; Man. Dir Tony Lewis; Dep. Man. Dir Michael Batty.

National Housing Corpn (NHC): POB 1550, Boroko, NCD; tel. 3247000; fax 3254363; Man. Dir Gabriel Tovo.

New Britain Palm Oil Ltd: POB 389, Kimbe, West New Britain; tel. 9852177; fax 9852003; e-mail nbpol@nbpol.com.pg; internet www.nbpol.com.pg; f. 1967; 80% owned by Kulim (Malaysia), 20% owned by Govt, employees and local producers; major producer of palm oil, coffee trader and exporter, supplier of high quality oil palm seed; Man. Dir Nick Thompson; Sec. Himson Waninara.

Palm Oil Producers Association: Port Moresby; Exec. Sec. Allan Maino.

Papua New Guinea Contractor Association: POB 2289, Boroko, NCD; tel. 3202239; formed by construction cos for the promotion of education, training and professional conduct in the construction industry; Pres. Roy Thorpe.

Papua New Guinea Forest Authority: POB 5055, Boroko, NCD; tel. 3277800; fax 3254433; Man. Dir Thomas Nen; Chair. Valentine Kambori.

Papua New Guinea Growers Association: POB 14, Kokopo, East New Britain Province 613; tel. 9829123; fax 9829264; e-mail growers@global.net.pg; Pres. Paul Arnold; Exec. Dir David Loh.

Papua New Guinea Holdings Corpn: POB 131, Port Moresby; fax 3217545; f. 1992; responsible for managing govt privatization programme; Chair. Michael Mel; Man. Dir Peter Steele.

Papua New Guinea Log Carriers Association: f. 1993.

Pita Lus National Silk Institute: Kagamuga, Mount Hagen, Western Highlands Province; f. 1978; govt silk-producing project.

Rural Industries Council: Chair. PETER COLTON.

UTILITIES

Electricity

PNG Electricity Commission (Elcom): POB 1105, Boroko, NCD; tel. 3243200; fax 3214051; plans to privatize the organization were announced in 1999; Chair. PAUL AISA; Chief Exec. SEV MASO.

Water

Eda Ranu (Our Water): POB 1084, Waigani, NCD; tel. 3122100; fax 3122190; internet www.edaranu.com.pg; fmrly Port Moresby Water Supply Company; Gen. Man. BILLY IMAR.

PNG Waterboard: POB 2779, Boroko, NCD; tel. 3235700; fax 3236317; e-mail pamini@pngwater.com.pg; f. 1986; govt-owned; operates 12 water supply systems throughout the country; Man. Dir PATRICK AMINI.

TRADE UNIONS

The Industrial Organizations Ordinance requires all industrial organizations that consist of no fewer than 20 employees or four employers to register. In 1977 there were 56 registered industrial organizations, including a general employee group registered as a workers' association in each province and also unions covering a specific industry or profession.

Papua New Guinea Trade Unions Congress (PNGTUC): POB 4279, Boroko, NCD; tel. 3257642; fax 3257890; e-mail tucl@daltron.com.pg; Pres. GASPER LAPAN; Gen. Sec. JOHN PASKA; 52 affiliates, 76,000 mems.

The following are among the major trade unions:

Bougainville Mining Workers' Union: POB 777, Panguna, North Solomons Province; tel. 9958272; Pres. MATHEW TUKAN; Gen. Sec. ALFRED ELISHA TAGORNOM.

Central Province Building and Construction Industry Workers' Union: POB 265, Port Moresby.

Central Province Transport Drivers' and Workers' Union: POB 265, Port Moresby.

Employers' Federation of Papua New Guinea: POB 490, Port Moresby; tel. 3214772; fax 3214070; f. 1963; Pres. G. J. DUNLOP; Exec. Dir TAU NANA; 170 mems.

National Federation of Timber Workers: Madang; f. 1993; Gen. Sec. MATHIAS KENUANGI (acting).

Papua New Guinea Communication Workers' Union: Pres. BOB MAGARU; Gen. Sec. EMMANUEL KAIRU.

Papua New Guinea National Doctors' Association: Pres. Dr BOB DANAYA; 225 mems.

Papua New Guinea Teachers' Association: POB 1027, Waigani, NCD; tel. 3262588; fax 321514; f. 1971; Pres. TOMMY HECKO; Gen. Sec. MURRAY PAIVA; 20,049 mems.

Papua New Guinea Waterside Workers' and Seamen's Union: POB 76, Kimbe 621; tel. 9835603; f. 1979; an amalgamation of four unions; Sec. DOUGLAS GADEBO.

Police Association of Papua New Guinea: tel. 3214172; f. 1964; Pres. ROBERT ALI; 4,596 mems.

Port Moresby Council of Trade Unions: POB 265, Boroko, NCD; Gen. Sec. JOHN KOSI.

Port Moresby Miscellaneous Workers' Union: POB 265, Boroko, NCD.

Printing and Kindred Industries Union: Port Moresby.

Public Employees' Association: POB 965, Boroko, NCD; tel. 3252955; fax 3252186; f. 1974; Pres. NAPOLEON LIOSI; Gen. Sec. JACK N. KUTAL; 28,000 mems.

Transport

There are no railways in Papua New Guinea. The capital city, Port Moresby, is not connected by road to other major population centres. Therefore, air and sea travel are of particular importance.

ROADS

In 1999 there were an estimated 19,600 km of roads in Papua New Guinea, of which 3.5% were paved. Japan offered a grant-in-aid in 1998 of 940m. yen for the reconstruction of a bridge on the Highlands Highway. In October 2000 it was announced that this highway was to be upgraded over six years at a cost of K26.3m., financed through a loan negotiated with the Asian Development Bank (ADB). In October 2005 the ADB agreed to provide US $18m. for road improvements during 2006–07, in addition to the $42m. loan already arranged for the same two-year period.

National Roads Authority: Lae, Morobe Province; f. 2004; statutory authority established to maintain the road network, particularly the Highlands Highway; Chair. ALLAN MCLAY; Deputy Chair. ALPHONSE NIGGINS.

SHIPPING

Papua New Guinea has 16 major ports and a coastal fleet of about 300 vessels. In early 1999 a feasibility study was commissioned to investigate the possible relocation of port facilities in Port Moresby. In February 2006 it was announced that facilities at the port of Lae were to be upgraded. The Asian Development Bank was expected to provide assistance.

Papua New Guinea Harbours Board: POB 671, Port Moresby; tel. 3211400; fax 3211546; Chair. TIMOTHY BONGA.

PNG Ports Corporation Ltd: POB 273, Madang; tel. 8523381; fax 8523097; e-mail Casper.Petrus@pngharbours.com.pg; internet www.pngports.com.pg; CEO BRIAN RICHES.

Port Authority of Kieta: POB 149, Kieta, North Solomons Province; tel. 9956066; fax 9956255; Port Man. SAKEUS GEM.

Port Authority of Lae: POB 563, Lae, Morobe Province; tel. 4422477; fax 4422543; Port Man. JOSHUA TARUNA.

Port Authority of Port Moresby: POB 671, Port Moresby; tel. 211400; fax 3211546; Gen. Man. T. AMAO.

Port Authority of Rabaul: POB 592, Rabaul, East New Britain Province; tel. 9821533; fax 9821535.

Shipping Companies

Coastal Shipping Co Ltd: Sulphur Creek Rd, POB 423, Rabaul, East New Britain Province; tel. 9821746; fax 9821734; e-mail coastco@global.net.pg; f. 1967; Man. Dir HENRY CHOW.

Lutheran Shipping: POB 789, Madang; tel. 8522577; fax 8522180; e-mail finance.luship@global.net.pg.

Morehead Shipping Pty Ltd: POB 1908, Lae, Morobe Province; tel. 4423602.

New Guinea Australia Line Pty Ltd: POB 145, Port Moresby; tel. 3212377; fax 3214879; e-mail ngal@daltron.com.pg; f. 1970; operates regular container services between Australia, Papua New Guinea, Singapore, Indonesia, Vanuatu, Tuvalu and Solomon Islands; Chair. (vacant); Gen. Man. GEOFFREY CUNDLE.

P & O PNG Ltd (trading as Western Tug and Barge): MMI House, 3rd Floor, Champion Parade, POB 1403, Port Moresby; tel. 3229200; fax 3229251; e-mail jhulse@popng.com.pg; owned by P & O (Australia); Country Man. JOHN HULSE.

Papua New Guinea Shipping Corporation Pty Ltd: POB 634, Port Moresby; tel. 3220290; fax 3212815; e-mail shipping@steamships.com.pg; f. 1977; owned by Steamships Trading Co Ltd; provides a container/break-bulk service to Australia and the Pacific islands; Chair. CHRISTOPHER PRATT; Man. Dir JOHN DUNLOP.

South Sea Lines Proprietary Ltd: POB 5, Lae, Morobe Province; tel. 4423455; fax 4424884; Man. Dir R. CUNNINGHAM.

Western Tug & Barge Co P/L: POB 1403, Port Moresby; tel. 3229290; fax 3229251; shipowning division of P & O PNG; operates 24 vessels.

CIVIL AVIATION

There is an international airport at Port Moresby, Jackson's Airport, and there are more than 400 other airports and airstrips throughout the country. International services from Lae and Mount Hagen airports began in March 1999. A programme to upgrade eight regional airports over three years, with finance of $A30m. from the Australian Government, was initiated in mid-1997. New domestic and international terminal buildings were opened at Jackson's Airport in 1998, following a 13-year project financed with K120m. from the Japanese Government. A project to redevelop Tari airport was announced in late 1999. It was expected that, following redevelopment, the airport would receive international flights.

Air Niugini: POB 7186, Boroko, NCD; tel. 3259000; fax 3273482; e-mail airniugini@airniugini.com.pg; internet www.airniugini.com.pg; f. 1973; govt-owned national airline (plans to privatize the airline were announced in 1999); operates scheduled domestic cargo and passenger services within Papua New Guinea and international services to Australia, Fiji, Solomon Islands, Philippines, Hong Kong, Singapore and Japan; Chair. JIM TJOENG; CEO WASANTHA KUMARASIRI.

Airlines PNG: Jacksons Airport, Port Moresby; tel. 3252011; fax 3252219; e-mail apng@apng.com; internet www.apng.com; f. 1984 as Milne Bay Air (MBA); operates domestic scheduled and charter services; Chair. JOHN R. WILD; Gen. Man. SIMON D. WILD.

National Aviation Services: Boroko, NCD; f. 2005; provides services between all small airstrips in Central, Oro, Gulf and Western provinces, primarily for the transport of agricultural products from producers to markets; Operations Man. GILBERT YENBARI; Propr and CEO TED DIRO.

Tourism

Despite Papua New Guinea's spectacular scenery and abundant wildlife, tourism makes only a small contribution to the economy. Visitor arrivals rose from an estimated 77,731 in 2006 to 104,122 in 2007. The industry earned an estimated US $3.7m. in 2005.

PNG Tourism Promotion Authority: POB 1291, Port Moresby; tel. 3200211; fax 3200223; e-mail info@pngtourism.org.pg; internet www.pngtourism.org.pg; CEO PETER VINCENT.

Tour Operators Association (TOAPNG): tel. 3200211; fax 3200223; e-mail lflynn@pngtourism.org.pg; f. 2006; Pres. MICHAEL BULEAU (acting); Sec.-Treas. JANET SIOS (acting).

PARAGUAY

Introductory Survey

Location, Climate, Language, Religion, Flag, Capital

The Republic of Paraguay is a land-locked country in central South America. It is bordered by Bolivia to the north, by Brazil to the east, and by Argentina to the south and west. The climate is sub-tropical. Temperatures range from an average maximum of 34.3°C (93.7°F) in January to an average minimum of 14°C (51°F) in June. The official languages are Spanish and Guaraní, the latter, an indigenous Indian language, being spoken by the majority of the population. Almost all of the inhabitants profess Christianity, and some 92% adhere to the Roman Catholic Church, the country's established religion. There is a small Protestant minority. The national flag (proportions 3 by 5) has three equal horizontal stripes, of red, white and blue. It is the only national flag with a different design on each side, having a varying emblem in the centre of the white stripe: the obverse side bears the state emblem (a white disc with a red ring bearing the words 'República del Paraguay', in yellow capitals, framing a blue disc with the five-pointed 'May Star', in yellow, surrounded by a wreath, in green), while the reverse side carries the seal of the Treasury (a white disc with a red ribbon bearing the words 'Paz y Justicia' in yellow capitals above a lion supporting a staff, surmounted by the red 'Cap of Liberty'). The capital is Asunción.

Recent History

Paraguay, ruled by Spain from the 16th century, achieved independence in 1811. In 1865 Paraguay was involved in a disastrous war against Brazil, Argentina and Uruguay (the Triple Alliance), resulting in the loss of more than one-half of its population. Paraguay also suffered heavy losses in the Chaco Wars of 1928–30 and 1932–35 against Bolivia, but won a large part of the disputed territory when the boundary was fixed in 1938. Gen. Higinio Morínigo established an authoritarian regime in 1940, but the return of a number of political exiles in 1947 precipitated a civil war in which supporters of the right-wing Asociación Nacional Republicana (Partido Colorado) defeated the Liberals and the Partido Revolucionario Febrerista, leading to the overthrow of Gen. Morínigo in June 1948. A period of great instability ensued. In May 1954 Gen. Alfredo Stroessner Mattiauda, the Army Commander-in-Chief, assumed power in a military coup. He nominated himself for the presidency, as the Colorado candidate, and was elected unopposed in July to complete the term of office of his predecessor, Federico Chávez. In 1955 Stroessner assumed extensive powers, and established a state of siege. Regular purges of the Partido Colorado membership, together with the mutual co-operation of the ruling party, the armed forces and the business community, enabled Stroessner to become the longest-serving dictator in Latin America: he was re-elected President, by large majorities, at five-yearly elections in 1958–88.

In February 1978 President Stroessner revoked the state of siege in all areas except Asunción. The assassination of the former Nicaraguan dictator, Gen. Anastasio Somoza Debayle, in Asunción in September 1980, however, caused President Stroessner to doubt the security of his own position, and the state of siege was reimposed throughout the country; harassment of leaders of the political opposition and of peasant and labour groups continued. The leader of the Partido Demócrata Cristiano, Luis Alfonso Resck, was expelled from the country in June 1981, and Domingo Laíno, leader of the Partido Liberal Radical Auténtico (PLRA), was deported in December 1982. After Ronald Reagan took office as President of the USA in 1981, Paraguay encountered less pressure from the US Administration to curb abuses of human rights, and the use of torture against detainees reportedly became widespread once more. It was estimated at this time that more than 60% of all Paraguayans resided outside the country.

The majority of opposition parties boycotted the presidential and legislative elections of February 1983, enabling Stroessner to obtain more than 90% of the votes cast in the presidential poll, and in August he formally took office for a further five-year term. In May 1983 the Government instigated a campaign of repression against students and trade unionists. In February 1984 opposition parties organized demonstrations in Asunción for the first time in 30 years.

Divisions over Stroessner's continuance in office led to factionalism within the Partido Colorado in the mid-1980s. In April 1987 Stroessner announced that the state of siege was to be ended, since extraordinary security powers were no longer necessary to maintain peace. (Later in the month Laíno was finally allowed to return to Paraguay.) However, the suppression of civil liberties and of political activity continued under the new penal code that replaced the state of siege. The level of participation in the 1988 presidential election (which took place simultaneously with legislative elections) was reported to be 93% of eligible voters, and it was announced that Stroessner had received 89% of the votes cast. However, opposition leaders (who had urged voters to boycott the elections) complained of electoral malpractice, and denounced Stroessner's re-election as fraudulent.

On 3 February 1989 Gen. Stroessner was overthrown in a coup led by Gen. Andrés Rodríguez, the second-in-command of the armed forces. Stroessner was allowed to leave for exile in Brazil, as Gen. Rodríguez assumed the presidency (in a provisional capacity) and appointed a new Council of Ministers. The interim President pledged to respect human rights and to strengthen links with neighbouring countries. At the presidential election in May Rodríguez, the candidate of the Partido Colorado, was confirmed as President, receiving 74% of the votes cast; his closest rival, Laíno, secured 20% of the votes. The Partido Colorado, having won 73% of the votes in the concurrent congressional election, automatically took two-thirds of the seats in both the Cámara de Diputados (Chamber of Deputies) and the Senado (Senate—48 and 24, respectively). The most successful opposition party was the PLRA, which obtained 19 seats in the Cámara and 10 in the Senado. Despite widespread allegations of electoral fraud, all parties agreed to respect the results.

In July 1989 the Cámara ratified the San José Pact on Human Rights, adopted by the Organization of American States (OAS, see p. 360) in 1978. In August 1989 the Congreso Nacional (National Congress—comprising the Cámara de Diputados and the Senado) initiated judicial proceedings against former government officials for violations of human rights. Following the repeal, in August 1989, of laws that had provided a basis for political repression under the Stroessner regime, the PCP was formally legalized. In November 1990, however, Rodríguez vetoed congressional proposals for the establishment of a legislative commission to investigate alleged violations of human rights.

Divisions within the Partido Colorado became evident at its annual convention in December 1989, when the 'Tradicionalistas' attempted to elect new party officials drawn exclusively from their own membership. The newly emerged Coloradismo Democrático faction, led by Blas Riquelme (a vice-president of the party at that time), succeeded in obtaining a judicial annulment of all decisions of the convention. The political crisis led to the resignation of the entire Council of Ministers. However, Rodríguez subsequently reappointed all but one of the outgoing ministers to their former posts. In February 1990 a new electoral code was adopted; this banned party affiliation for serving members of the armed forces and the police, and reformed procedures for the election of party officials.

Paraguay's first direct municipal elections took place in May 1991. Although the Partido Colorado secured control of a majority of municipalities, the important post of mayor of Asunción was won by a relatively unknown candidate, Carlos Filizzola, the representative of a new centre-left coalition, Asunción Para Todos (APT). Defeat in the capital precipitated mutual recriminations within the increasingly fragmented Partido Colorado.

In August 1991 the Congreso Nacional approved proposals for a complete revision of the 1967 Constitution. In anticipation of the elections to a National Constituent Assembly, President Rodríguez and military leaders made concerted efforts to forge unity within the Partido Colorado, with the result that the party's three main factions, the 'Renovadores', the 'Democráticos' and the 'Autónomos' were persuaded to present a single list of candidates, under the title 'Tradicionalistas'. In the December elections the Partido Colorado won 55% of the votes cast, thus securing an overwhelming majority of the Assembly's 198 seats. The PLRA won 27% of the votes, while Constitución Para Todos, formed as a result of APT's success in the municipal elections, won 11% of the votes. The new body was convened in January 1992.

In November 1991 new legislation, drafted by President Rodríguez in co-operation with military leaders, was approved by the Congreso Nacional. The law appeared to guarantee the autonomy of the armed forces, and the definition of the role of the military was expanded to include responsibility, at the request of the Head of State, for civil defence and internal order. Apparently in contradiction of the 1990 electoral code, no restrictions were placed on political activities by serving members of the armed forces. Provision was made for the President to delegate the functions of Commander-in-Chief of the Armed Forces to a senior military officer (with the Head of State retaining only ceremonial powers as the military commander). Opposition parties protested that, should the new legislation be entrenched in the new Constitution, the armed forces would remain a 'parallel' political force, following the transition to civilian rule.

On 20 June 1992 the new Constitution was promulgated before the Constituent Assembly. Under the new Constitution, the President and the Vice-President (a new post) were to be elected by a simple majority of votes. The Constituent Assembly had ostensibly disregarded the November 1991 military legislation by confirming the President as Commander-in-Chief of the Armed Forces and excluding officers on active duty from participating directly in politics. Other significant changes in the Constitution included the abolition of the death penalty and the granting of the right to unionize and to strike to public sector employees (excluding the armed forces and police).

In August 1992, following the party's first direct internal elections, Riquelme was appointed President of the Partido Colorado. However, serious divisions within the party persisted. An internal election, conducted in December, to select the party's presidential candidate was declared to have been won by Luis María Argaña (who had resigned the position in 1992), the candidate of the far-right. However, the candidate believed to be favoured by Rodríguez, Juan Carlos Wasmosy, refused to recognize the result, claiming that the vote had been fraudulent. An electoral tribunal failed to resolve the issue, and, following intense pressure and alleged death threats by both factions, several members of the tribunal resigned. Party leaders organized an extraordinary national convention in February 1993, at which a new electoral tribunal was to be chosen. Wasmosy was eventually confirmed as the presidential candidate of the Partido Colorado. The decision was denounced by Argaña, whose supporters threatened to resign *en masse* from the party.

At the general election of May 1993 Wasmosy was elected President with 40% of the votes cast, ahead of Laíno (32%) and Guillermo Caballero Vargas of Encuentro Nacional (EN) (23%). However, the Partido Colorado failed to gain a majority in either the Cámara or the Senado. Moreover, the faction of the Partido Colorado led by Argaña, the Movimiento de Reconciliación Colorada (MCR), negotiated with the PLRA and the EN to exclude supporters of the President-elect from appointment to important posts in the Congreso Nacional (with the support of the MCR, the overall opposition strength stood at 35 of a total of 45 seats in the Senado and 64 of the 80 seats in the Cámara, sufficient to approve legislation affecting the Constitution).

Wasmosy was inaugurated as President on 15 August 1993. The opposition expressed some concern over the composition of his first Council of Ministers, many of whom had served in the administrations of Rodríguez and Stroessner. Despite Wasmosy's apparent desire to restrict the influence of the military (he notably appointed a civilian to the post of Minister of National Defence), the designation of Gen. Lino César Oviedo Silva as Commander of the Army provoked further criticism, since, prior to the elections, Oviedo had publicly stated that the army would not accept an opposition victory.

A preliminary agreement on a 'governability pact' between the Government and the opposition, initiated in an attempt to facilitate the implementation of a coherent economic and legislative programme, was signed in October 1993, and this, in turn, facilitated an agreement between the Government and the legislature towards resolving the controversial question of judicial reform. Under the latter agreement, the two were to appoint members of the Supreme Court and the Supreme Electoral Tribunal by consensus. (The new members of the Supreme Court, enlarged from five to nine justices in accordance with the 1992 Constitution, were eventually elected in April 1995). In January 1994 Riquelme resigned as President of the Partido Colorado, following disagreements with Wasmosy. By early 1995 speculation concerning unrest in the armed forces, prompted by Wasmosy's recent uncompromising manipulation of the ranks of the military high command, and by a reported clash of interests between the President and Gen. Oviedo, had reached such a level that Wasmosy was forced to issue a public statement discounting the possibility of a military coup. In February Wasmosy announced a further reorganization of the military high command, thus consolidating his position of authority.

In May 1995 an investigation into corruption at the Central Bank revealed the existence of an illegal 'parallel' financial system involving a network of institutions, including the Central Bank. The investigation precipitated the collapse of the system and a severe liquidity crisis. In December the Government issued an emergency decree extending the powers of intervention of the Central Bank, with the aim of resolving the financial crisis and restoring confidence in the banking sector. By late December the Central Bank had disbursed almost US $400m. of reserves in order to contain the liquidity crisis, which had resulted in the closure of several financial institutions.

In April 1996 a serious confrontation arose between President Wasmosy and Gen. Oviedo, with the result that a military coup was only narrowly averted. Following an attempt by Oviedo to postpone the internal elections of the Partido Colorado, Wasmosy accused Oviedo of contravening the ban on political activity by serving members of the military, and, on 22 April, demanded his resignation as Commander of the Army. When Oviedo refused to resign, Wasmosy promptly announced his dismissal, naming Gen. Oscar Rodrigo Díaz Delmas as his successor. Oviedo rejected the decision, and installed himself at the army headquarters in Asunción, from where he issued demands for Wasmosy's resignation and threatened, with the support of the army, violently to overthrow the Government. Wasmosy took refuge in the US embassy building. The following day, in a demonstration of popular support for Wasmosy, thousands rallied outside the presidential palace. Declarations of support were also issued by the Commanders of the Navy and the Air Force, and by the Congreso Nacional. External pressure for Wasmosy to resist the overthrow of democratic rule came from the USA, which immediately suspended military aid, and from neighbouring South American countries, and was sufficient to prompt Wasmosy to seek a compromise: in return for his retirement from military service, Oviedo was given the position of Minister of Defence. However, the measure was condemned by the legislature, which threatened to initiate impeachment proceedings against Wasmosy should Oviedo be appointed. Public opinion was also strongly opposed to the appointment, and on 25 April, following Oviedo's retirement from military service and his replacement by Gen. Díaz, Wasmosy withdrew the offer of the defence portfolio. Despite fears of an outright coup, Oviedo accepted the final outcome of the dispute and announced that, as a private citizen, he would now dedicate himself to the political campaign of the Partido Colorado.

In late April 1996 the internal elections of the Partido Colorado resulted in victory for Luis María Argaña, the leader of the MRC faction, who was appointed President of the party. In May Oviedo announced the creation of a new faction of the Partido Colorado, the Unión Nacional de Colorados Eticos (UNACE). In that month, in an effort to purge the armed forces of officers sympathetic to Oviedo, Wasmosy announced the retirement of some 20 high-ranking officers, including the Commander of the First Army Corps and the Chief of Staff of the Army. In June Oviedo was placed under house arrest on charges of insurrection and insubordination with respect to the events of April. In July Oviedo's assets were seized and the order for his detention was revised from house arrest to preventative imprisonment. This development provoked protest by Oviedo's supporters, who rallied outside the Congreso Nacional to demand his release. Wasmosy continued to reorganize the military hierarchy, replacing several senior officers. In August an appeal court acquitted Oviedo of the charge of insurrection, ruling that there was insufficient evidence to suggest that he had made military preparations to overturn the constitutional order. In December 1996 Oviedo was acquitted of the lesser charge of insubordination.

In August 1997 Juan Carlos Galaverna, a Colorado senator and prominent supporter of Argaña, presented a motion to the Senado seeking the impeachment of President Wasmosy on the grounds that he had contravened the Constitution by attempting to influence the outcome of the forthcoming Partido Colorado primary election; Wasmosy denied the allegations. Although the impeachment motion was unsuccessful, it illustrated the extent of division between rival factions of the Partido Colorado in advance of the forthcoming general election. In September Gen. Oviedo succeeded in securing the Partido Colorado's presidential nomination, defeating Wasmosy's preferred candidate, Carlos Facetti Masulli, and Argaña himself, in the party's primary. However, Argaña's faction, which effectively controlled the party's executive board, refused to accept the outcome of the ballot, claiming that it had been fraudulent, and presented a legal challenge to the result.

In early October 1997 Wasmosy issued an executive order for the 'disciplinary arrest', for a period of 30 days, of Gen. Oviedo; the grounds for the detention was contempt of the President and Commander-in-Chief of the Armed Forces, after Oviedo had publicly accused Wasmosy of corruption. An appeal court subsequently issued an injunction suspending the arrest order, prompting Wasmosy to file a petition requesting that the Supreme Court uphold his order. Oviedo, meanwhile, had gone into hiding. In December, following a ruling by the Supreme Court endorsing the arrest order issued by Wasmosy in October, Oviedo surrendered to the military authorities in order to serve the 30-day period of confinement. Later that month the Supreme Electoral Tribunal rejected the petition by Argaña's MRC faction to have the results of the party's primary election annulled, and in early January 1998 it registered Oviedo as the official presidential candidate of the Partido Colorado, without the endorsement of the party's executive board. Oviedo completed his period of confinement on 11 January; however, a special military tribunal, established by Wasmosy to investigate the events of the coup attempt led by Oviedo in April 1996, ordered that he be detained indefinitely pending the results of the investigation. In March the special military tribunal found Oviedo guilty of crimes committed against the order and security of the armed forces, and also of sedition, and sentenced him to 10 years' imprisonment. In the following month the Supreme Court ratified the military tribunal's decision and the Supreme Electoral Tribunal consequently annulled Oviedo's presidential candidacy. In accordance with the law, the candidacy of the Partido Colorado was assumed by Raúl Cubas Grau, hitherto the vice-presidential nominee; Argaña was to be the new candidate for the vice-presidency.

The presidential election of 10 May 1998 resulted in victory for Cubas Grau, who secured some 55% of the votes cast, ahead of the candidate of the Alianza Democrática (an electoral alliance comprising the PLRA and the EN), Domingo Laíno, who received 44% of the votes. Colorado candidates were also most successful at legislative elections and at elections for provincial administrators held concurrently. Cubas Grau's election campaign had emphasized his support for his long-time political ally, Oviedo. Prior to the inauguration of the new administration, in July Vice-President-elect Argaña (a staunch opponent of Oviedo) concluded an informal political pact involving his faction of the Partido Colorado and the opposition PLRA and EN, effectively depriving Cubas Grau of a congressional majority, while in early August President Wasmosy implemented a comprehensive reorganization of the military high command, which promoted the interests of many of Oviedo's military opponents.

Cubas Grau duly took office on 15 August 1998, and a new Council of Ministers, largely composed of supporters of Gen. Oviedo, was sworn in on the same day. On 18 August, deliberately circumventing the new law restricting presidential pardons, Cubas Grau issued a decree commuting Oviedo's prison sentence to time already served. On the following day the Congreso Nacional voted to condemn the decree and to initiate proceedings to impeach the President for unconstitutional procedure. (A successful impeachment would have resulted in the elevation of Oviedo's severest critic, Vice-President Argaña, to the presidency.) The new President's confrontational stance (and the release of Oviedo) also provoked dissent among his own supporters and associates; Cubas Grau's brother, Carlos, resigned the industry and commerce portfolio in the new Council of Ministers later that month. On 5 December the Argaña faction-controlled central apparatus of the Partido Colorado expelled Oviedo from the party. While the Congreso Nacional was unable to muster the two-thirds' majority support necessary to impeach President Cubas Grau, the country remained in effective political deadlock, prompting serious concerns in the business community that the country's mounting economic difficulties would not be addressed.

In March 1999, however, the political impasse ended dramatically. On 23 March Vice-President Argaña was assassinated, prompting nation-wide speculation that Oviedo was behind the attack, and galvanizing the Congreso Nacional sufficiently to secure the support of the two-thirds' majority needed to initiate Cubas Grau's impeachment. Increasing tensions were exacerbated three days later by the killing of seven protesters who were demonstrating in Asunción in support of demands for the resignation of the President, in the light of Argaña's assassination. On 28 March Cubas Grau resigned the presidency and sought refuge in Brazil, while Oviedo crossed the border to Argentina. (In February 2002 Cubas Grau surrendered to the Paraguayan authorities to face trial for the killings of the protesters and was placed under house arrest until June 2003, when he was released without the charges against him having been dismissed.) In early April the judicial authorities ordered the arrest of Oviedo for involvement in the death of Argaña, after three of his close collaborators were identified as the assassins. (In October 2000 Maj.-Gen. Reinaldo Servin, Constantino Rodas and Pablo Vera Esteche were sentenced to long prison terms for their roles in the assassination.) However, the Argentine Government rejected Paraguay's request for extradition, resulting in a rapid deterioration in the relationship between the two countries. Oviedo left Argentina in early December in order to avoid being extradited by the new Argentine Government of Fernando de la Rúa.

Meanwhile, in accordance with the terms of the Constitution, in the absence of the elected President and Vice-President, the President of the Congreso Nacional, the pro-Argaña Colorado senator Luis González Macchi was swiftly installed as Head of State. He announced the composition of a multi-party Government of National Unity at the end of March 1999. In late April, following careful scrutiny of the articles of the Constitution, the Supreme Court ruled that González Macchi should serve the remainder of Cubas Grau's presidential term (scheduled to expire in 2003). The Court also ruled that an election to select a new Vice-President should be conducted. Hoping to consolidate the new Government, González Macchi announced that his own party would not present a vice-presidential candidate. However, prominent figures within the Partido Colorado decided to contest the election none the less, precipitating tension with the PLRA, which had effectively been promised the post. Meanwhile, factionalism within the PLRA placed increasing strains on the Government of National Unity. Events culminated in February 2000 when PLRA members voted to withdraw from the ruling coalition, depriving the Government of a legislative majority. The Partido Colorado's remaining coalition partner, the EN, was, furthermore, divided over its continuing participation in the Government.

In late May 1999 González Macchi forcibly retired more than 100 army officers, including several high-ranking supporters of Gen. Oviedo. By mid-November another 45 senior commanders, who were thought to be supporters of Oviedo, had been replaced. However, the reorganization did not prevent a coup attempt, in mid-May 2000, by rebellious soldiers thought to be sympathetic to Oviedo. It was swiftly defeated by the Government (most army brigades and the air force remained loyal to the President), which declared a 30-day nation-wide state of emergency, assuming extraordinary powers that resulted in the arrest of more than 70 people, mostly members of the security forces. Oviedo denied any involvement with the coup, but in mid-June he was arrested by Brazilian police in Foz do Iguaçu, near the Brazilian border with Paraguay. In March 2001 the Brazilian Chief Prosecutor ruled that Oviedo could be extradited, but in December the Supreme Court rejected the ruling, stating that Oviedo was a victim of political persecution, and released him from imprisonment.

The initial popularity of the Government of National Unity collapsed as thousands of peasants, assembled by rural organizations, mobilized on several occasions during 1999 to protest against the Government's lack of action on rural issues. In response to the protests, in November the Government offered a US $168m. rescue package for the agricultural and livestock sector, mostly for debt-refinancing schemes. In March 2000 the Government announced a scheme to assist 250,000 small farmers. However, by the end of the month there were an estimated 10,000 smallholders camped outside the Congreso building. (The protest continued until March 2001, when government concessions were eventually secured.) Strikes were undertaken by power and telecommunications workers and by public sector workers during March and June 2000, respectively. However, the Government insisted it would continue with its 'state restructuring' programme. In mid-November the Congreso Nacional approved legislation allowing for the sale of the state railway, water and telecommunications companies.

In April 2000 the Partido Colorado nominated Félix Argaña, son of the late Vice-President, to be its candidate in the forthcoming vice-presidential ballot. However, at the election, which was finally held on 13 August, the 53-year Colorado monopoly on power was ended when Argaña was narrowly defeated (by less than 1% of the votes cast) by the PLRA candidate, Julio César Franco. The election of Franco, whose candidacy was endorsed by Oviedo, increased the divisions within the Partido Colorado and resulted in the resignation of the Minister of National Defence, Nelson Argaña, another son of the late Vice-President.

A corruption scandal in early May 2001 forced the President of the Central Bank, Washington Ashwell, to resign over his alleged involvement in the fraudulent transfer of US $16m. to a US bank account. An opposition attempt to impeach the President over his alleged involvement in the fraud was defeated by the Cámara de Diputados in August. In September several thousand protesters marched in Asunción to demand the resignation of González Macchi. In April 2002 González Macchi was formally charged with involvement in the corruption scandal.

In late January 2002 the credibility of the Government was further undermined after two leaders of the left-wing party Movimiento Patria Libre (MPL) alleged that they had been illegally detained for 13 days and tortured by the police, with the knowledge of government ministers, as part of an investigation into a kidnapping case. In response to the allegations, in early February the head of the national police force and his deputy, as well as the head of the judicial investigations department, were dismissed. Following sustained public and political pressure the Minister of the Interior and the Minister of Justice and Labour resigned soon afterwards, although both protested their innocence. In addition, the national intelligence agency, the Secretaría Nacional de Informaciones, was disbanded. The Cámara de Diputados issued a statement assigning some responsibility for the detention of the MPL leaders to the President and the Attorney-General, and describing the event as 'state terrorism'. In April former President Wasmosy was convicted of misuse of public funds and sentenced to four years' imprisonment. (His conviction was quashed, however, in September 2004.)

Throughout 2002 an alliance of farmers, trade unions and left-wing organizations staged mass protests throughout the country to call for an end to the Government's free-market policies and to protest at widely perceived government corruption. In response to the mounting opposition, in June the Government suspended its planned privatization of the state telecommunications company, Corporación Paraguaya de Comunicaciones (COPACO). Nevertheless, the protests continued as the economic situation worsened, prompting González Macchi to declare a state of emergency in July, which was lifted two days later after clashes between anti-Government protesters and security forces resulted in two fatalities.

In August 2002 the IMF approved, subject to conditions, a US $200m. stand-by loan to Paraguay. However, in November the Congreso failed to approve the financial reforms necessary to fulfil the Fund's conditions. The congressional impasse prompted the resignation of the Minister of Finance. In early December the lower house of the Congreso voted in favour of the impeachment of President González Macchi on five charges of corruption. In an attempt to avoid the charges, González Macchi offered to resign early from office, immediately following the presidential election that was scheduled to be held in April 2003 (his term of office officially ended in August of that year). However, in February 2003 the Senado voted narrowly against impeachment. Proceedings began against González Macchi in mid-2004 on charges relating to the May 2001 embezzlement scandal; in February 2005 further charges were brought against him for misuse of public funds and irregularities connected to the sale of two state-owned banks. He was found guilty on charges of embezzlement and false testimony and, despite appealing against the verdict, was sentenced to eight years' imprisonment in December 2006.

Legislative and presidential elections were held on 27 April 2003. The Partido Colorado extended its unbroken 56-year hold on power as its candidate, Oscar Nicanor Duarte Frutos, won 37% of the votes cast in the presidential ballot, compared with the 24% attracted by the PLRA candidate and former Vice-President, Julio César Franco, who had resigned in October 2002 in order to contest the election. A businessman, Pedro Nicolás Fadul Niella, of the Patria Querida movement, came third with 21.3% of the votes, while Guillermo Sánchez Guffanti of UNACE (which had disassociated itself from the Partido Colorado and been renamed the Unión Nacional de Ciudadanos Eticos) attracted 13% of the ballot. However, the Partido Colorado secured only 37 of the 80 seats in the Cámara de Diputados, thus losing its majority in the chamber. The Partido Colorado performed better in the upper-house election, winning 16 of the 45 seats in the Senado, followed by the PLRA with 12 seats. At his inauguration on 15 August 2003, President Duarte reiterated his election pledges to reduce corruption, improve the public finances and restore the country's international credibility. A number of well-regarded technocrats were appointed to the Council of Ministers, notably including the new Minister of Finance, Dionisio Borda. On taking office, Duarte announced his intention to effect wide-ranging judicial reform; to this effect, in October the Congreso reached consensus on impeachment proceedings against six Supreme Court judges suspected of corruption. Four of the judges resigned during the impeachment process, which finally resulted in the indictment of the remaining two judges in December. However, despite hopes that political influence in the selection of new judges might be avoided, two of the six new Supreme Court judges appointed in March 2004 were Colorado supporters.

In June 2004 Oviedo returned voluntarily from Brazil. On arrival, he was taken to military prison to serve a 10-year sentence for organizing the attempted coup in 1996 against the Government of President Wasmosy. Oviedo was also to be tried on other charges still pending against him. In October, however, Oviedo was provisionally acquitted of having organized the failed coup attempt of May 2000, and in January 2005 charges against him relating to a discovered arms cache were dismissed. In March the Supreme Court ruled that Oviedo would nevertheless have to serve out his prison sentence. Throughout the rest of 2005 demonstrations against his detention were staged by his supporters.

In October 2004 the kidnap and murder of an 11-year-old child provoked a vociferous public outcry against the perceived deterioration of security in Paraguay. In response, President Duarte dismissed the Minister of the Interior, Orlando Fiorotto Sánchez (who was replaced by Attorney-General Nelson Mora), and the head of the national police, Umberto Núñez. In February 2005 Mora was himself dismissed—in addition to some 50 senior members of the police force—following the discovery on 16 February of the body of Cecilia Cubas under a house in a suburb of Asunción. Cubas, the daughter of former President Raúl Cubas Grau, had been kidnapped in the previous September. In advance of the police inquiry, President Duarte held the MPL responsible for the killing and subsequently supported claims made by the Colombian President, Alvaro Uribe Vélez, that the MPL had been assisted by the Fuerzas Armadas Revolucionarias de Colombia—Ejército del Pueblo (FARC). Twelve of the 15 people charged with involvement in the kidnap and murder of Cecilia Cubas, all of whom were members or sympathizers of the MPL, were found guilty in November 2006.

In November 2005 President Duarte announced plans to reform the Constitution in order to allow for presidential re-election. At that time, Duarte was also seeking re-election to the leadership of the Partido Colorado, which he had ceded on taking office as President. However, opposition groups argued that it was unconstitutional for the President to hold any additional public office, and, in mid-December, a motion to impeach President Duarte was proposed in the Cámara de Diputados by the opposition Patria Querida. However, the proposal was defeated, receiving only 39 votes in favour (a minimum two-thirds' majority, or 53 votes, was required to pass an impeachment motion). In January 2006 the Electoral Court rejected criminal charges against President Duarte, brought by the leader of the Frente Colorado faction, Luis Talavera, for attempting to hold two public offices, although the Court ruled that it would be unconstitutional for Duarte to hold another office concurrently with the presidency of the Republic.

In February 2006, nevertheless, Duarte won a convincing victory in the Partido Colorado leadership election, defeating his rival Osvaldo Domínguez Dibb, who represented the pro-Stroessner ('Stronista') faction of the party. In March the Supreme Court overturned the Electoral Court's earlier ruling that forbade the President of the Republic from holding an additional office; as a result, Duarte assumed the leadership of his party. He simultaneously announced a proposed referendum on whether to amend the Consitution to allow presidential re-election. In response to the Supreme Court's ruling, opposition

PARAGUAY

groups again initiated impeachment proceedings against Duarte, as well as against the five judges of the Court's Constitutional Panel. Faced with such resistance, the following day Duarte resigned from the party presidency (José Alderete Rodríguez, hitherto Minister of Public Works and Communications, assumed the post in an acting capacity).

In February 2007 a group of more than 30 social and labour organizations joined the principal opposition parties in signing an accord to form the Concertación Nacional (CN). The new coalition announced its intention to present a single candidate in the presidential election in 2008 in the hope of providing an effective challenge to the Partido Colorado. In July six of the eight political parties in the CN, including the PLRA and the EN, announced their support for Fernando Armindo Lugo Méndez, a popular former Roman Catholic bishop known for his frequent pronouncements on social justice and his work with deprived communities, who had retired from the priesthood in late 2006 in order to become more actively involved in politics. However, Patria Querida and UNACE rejected the nomination of Lugo, arguing that it contravened the February accord's requirement to hold a primary election to select the opposition candidate, and both parties subsequently withdrew from the CN. As a result, in September Lugo founded the Alianza Patriótica para el Cambio (APC) to support his candidacy. Earlier in September Oviedo, who had previously declared his intention to stand in the election, was granted conditional release from gaol by a military tribunal. In the following month the Supreme Court acquitted Oviedo of involvement in the 1996 coup attempt, thereby making him eligible to stand for the presidency, and he was declared the UNACE candidate in January 2008. There was speculation that Oviedo's release and acquittal had been orchestrated by the Government in order to divide the opposition.

Meanwhile, a primary election held by the Partido Colorado in December 2007 to determine its presidential candidate resulted in a very narrow victory for President Duarte's nominee, former Minister of Education and Culture Blanca Ovelar. However, the result was contested by the defeated candidate, former Vice-President Luis Castiglioni (who had resigned the vice-presidency in October in order to contest the election), amid allegations of malpractice, causing damaging divisions within the party. Ovelar was not declared the winner of the primary contest until late January 2008. In February an outbreak of yellow fever, which had been absent from Paraguay for 34 years, resulted in a severe shortage of vaccines, further damaging the ruling party's reputation.

At the presidential election, held on 20 April 2008, Lugo won a comfortable victory, securing 40.8% of votes cast according to partial, provisional results, against 30.7% for Ovelar. Oviedo won 22.0% of votes, while Pedro Fadul, again representing Patria Querida, obtained just 2.4%. Lugo's election campaign had concentrated on agricultural reform and the renegotiation of the Itaipú and Yacyretá hydroelectric projects jointly operated with Brazil and Argentina, respectively (almost all electricity generated by the projects being exported to the neighbouring countries at well below the market rates). However, according to provisional results of the concurrent legislative elections, the Partido Colorado narrowly retained its status as the largest party in both chambers of the Congreso Nacional, securing 29 of the 80 seats in the Cámara de Diputados and 15 out of 45 seats in the Senado. The PLRA obtained 29 seats in the lower house and 14 in the upper, while UNACE won 15 and 9 seats, respectively. Following the elections, President-elect Lugo, who was scheduled to take office in mid-August, announced a number of appointments to his future cabinet. Notably, Dionisio Borda, who had served as Minister of Finance under Duarte from 2003–06, was to be reappointed to the post.

Throughout 2003 and 2004 strikes, roadblocks, marches and illegal land occupations were organized by farmers and indigenous groups in protest at a range of government policies, including agrarian reform and privatizations. In response to the continuing civil unrest, in September 2004 the Government signed an agreement to distribute some 13,000 ha of land in six western departments to landless peasants; the main peasant grouping, the Federación Nacional Campesina de Paraguay, however, maintained its demand for the redistribution of some 100,000 ha of land. In October President Duarte submitted to the Congreso a proposal for a new tax on landowners that would raise an estimated US $100m.–$125m. in government revenues (intended for poverty reduction rather than agrarian reform). Illegal land occupations and other protests continued in late 2004 and 2005, none the less, resulting in the arrest of hundreds of protesters and several fatalities. In February 2005 Duarte announced the creation of a three-year security plan, which included a greater role of the armed forces in policing rural areas. The plan was publicly opposed in Asunción by some 5,000 rural activists in March. In the same month, following discussions in the Colombian capital with President Uribe, Duarte announced that the Paraguayan and Colombian security services would strengthen bilateral co-operation.

In March 1991 the Presidents and Ministers of Foreign Affairs of Argentina, Brazil, Uruguay and Paraguay signed a formal agreement in Asunción creating a common market of the 'Southern Cone' countries, the Mercado Común del Sur (Mercosur, see p. 391). The agreement allowed for the dismantling of trade barriers between the four countries, and entered into full operation in 1995. In mid-2006 President Duarte announced that his Government was to seek engagement for Paraguay in other free trade agreements aside from Mercosur.

Paraguay's relations with the USA were strained in late 2006 when the Government of Paraguay announced that US military personnel operating in that country would no longer enjoy immunity from prosecution. Unlike other Mercosur countries, Paraguay had signed an agreement with the USA in 2005 protecting US soldiers from extradition to the International Criminal Court. The decision by Paraguay not to renew this agreement prompted the USA to announce the withdrawal of humanitarian and medical services that it had been providing to people living in remote, rural areas of Paraguay.

In late 2006 the US Government reported that it intended to encourage greater co-operation between Paraguay, Argentina and Brazil in monitoring terrorist activity in the so-called tri-border area. The Paraguayan border town of Ciudad del Este was believed to generate some 30% of the country's entire tax revenue from customs, much of which was known to come from illegal trade in arms, drugs and counterfeit goods. There was evidence that proceeds from illegal dealings, such as these, were funding the activities of terrorist groups in the area.

Government

Under the 1992 Constitution, legislative power is held by the bicameral Congreso Nacional (National Congress), whose members serve for five years. The Senado (Senate) has 45 members, and the Cámara de Diputados (Chamber of Deputies) 80 members. Elections to the legislature are by universal adult suffrage. Executive power is held by the President, directly elected for a single term of five years at the same time as the legislature. The President of the Republic governs with the assistance of a Vice-President and an appointed Council of Ministers. Paraguay is divided into 17 departments, each administered by an elected governor.

Defence

As assessed at November 2007, the armed forces totalled 10,650 men (including 2,550 conscripts). There was an army of 7,600 men and an air force of 1,100. The navy, which is largely river-based, had 1,950 men, including 900 marines and a naval air force of 100. There is also a 14,800-strong paramilitary police force, including 4,000 conscripts. Military service, which is compulsory, lasts for 12 months in the army and for two years in the navy. The defence budget for 2007 totalled an estimated 500,000m. guaraníes.

Economic Affairs

In 2006, according to estimates by the World Bank, Paraguay's gross national income (GNI), measured at average 2004–06 prices, was US $8,396m., equivalent to $1,400 per head (or $5,070 per head on an international purchasing-power parity basis). During 1996–2006, it was estimated, the population increased at an average annual rate of 2.1%, while gross domestic product (GDP) per head decreased, in real terms, by an average of 0.5% per year. Overall GDP increased, in real terms, at an average annual rate of 1.5% in 1996–2006; GDP increased by an estimated 3.9% in 2006.

According to preliminary figures, agriculture (including forestry, hunting and fishing) contributed an estimated 22.2% of GDP in 2006. In November–February 2006/07 31.2% of the economically active population were employed in the sector. The principal cash crop is soya bean seeds, which accounted for an estimated 23.0% of total export revenue in 2006. Other significant crops are sugar cane, cassava, sunflowers, cotton, wheat and maize. Timber and wood manufactures provided an estimated 5.2% of export revenues in 2006. The raising of livestock (particularly cattle and pigs) is also important. Meat accounted for an estimated 22.3% of export earnings in 2006. Agricultural GDP increased at an average annual rate of 3.3% in 1996–2006; real agricultural GDP increased by 0.1% in 2005 and by 3.5% in 2006.

According to provisional figures, industry (including mining, manufacturing, construction and power) contributed an estimated 22.4% of GDP in 2006 and employed 17.2% of the working population in November–February 2006/07. Industrial GDP increased by an average of 0.5% per year in 1996–2006; the sector increased by 3.5% in 2006.

Paraguay has almost no commercially exploited mineral resources, and the mining sector employed only 0.1% of the labour force in 2004 and contributed a provisional 0.1% of GDP in 2006. Production is confined to gypsum, kaolin and limestone. However, foreign companies have been involved in exploration for gold and petroleum deposits, and deposits of natural gas were discovered in 1994.

Manufacturing contributed a provisional 15.1% of GDP in 2006, and, including the mining sector, employed 10.7% of the working population in November–February 2006/07. The main branch of manufacturing (in terms of value added) was production of food and beverages. The other principal sectors were wood and wood products, handicrafts, paper, printing and publishing, hides and furs, and non-metallic mineral products. Manufacturing GDP increased at an average annual rate of 0.6% in 1996–2006. Manufacturing GDP increased by 3.5% in 2006.

Energy is derived almost completely from hydroelectric power. Imports of mineral fuels comprised an estimated 13.2% of the value of total merchandise imports in 2006. Ethyl alcohol (ethanol), derived from sugar cane, is widely used as a component of vehicle fuel.

The services sector contributed a provisional 55.3% of GDP in 2006, and engaged 51.5% of the working population in November–February 2006/07. Paraguay traditionally serves as an entrepôt for regional trade. The GDP of the services sector increased by an average of 1.2% per year in 1996–2006; the sector increased by 4.3% in 2006.

In 2006 Paraguay recorded a visible trade deficit of US $934.6m., and there was a deficit of $217.4m. on the current account of the balance of payments. According to preliminary figures, in 2006 the principal source of registered imports was the People's Republic of China (27.0%); other major suppliers in this year were Brazil, Argentina and Japan. Uruguay was the principal market for registered exports in that year (a preliminary 22.0% of total exports); other notable purchasers were Brazil and Russia. The principal exports in 2006 were, according to preliminary estimates, soya bean seeds and meat products. The principal imports were motors, general industrial machinery equipment and parts, mineral fuels, machinery and transport equipment, and chemicals and related products.

In 2005 there was, according to revised projections, an overall general budget deficit of 71m. guaraníes (equivalent to 0.3% of GDP). Paraguay's total external debt was US $3,120m. at the end of 2005, of which $2,264m. was long-term public debt. In that year the cost of debt-servicing was equivalent to 11.4% of the total value of exports of goods and services. Annual inflation averaged 8.7% in 1996–2006; consumer prices increased by an average of 10.6% in 2006. An estimated 6.7% of the labour force were unemployed in November–February 2006/07.

Paraguay is a member of the Inter-American Development Bank (IDB, see p. 308), of the Latin American Integration Association (ALADI, see p. 331), of the Latin American Economic System (SELA, see p. 413) and of the Mercado Común del Sur (Mercosur, see p. 391). In December 2004 Paraguay was one of 12 countries that were signatories to the agreement, signed in Cusco, Peru, creating the South American Community of Nations (Comunidad Sudamericana de Naciones), intended to promote greater regional economic integration. It had been anticipated that the new entity, to be styled after the EU, would become operational by 2007; however, by April 2008 implementation of the necessary legal frameworks, to achieve the integrated structure envisaged, remained incomplete. A treaty for the community—referred to as the Union of South American Nations (Unasur) since its reinvention at the first South American Energy Summit of 16 April 2007—was expected to be initialled in June 2008, with full functionality of economic union tentatively scheduled for 2019.

The Government was paralysed by a lack of resources until 1999, when Taiwan agreed to underwrite a US $400m. bond issue and when the Government agreed on a long-term structural reform strategy with the IMF and World Bank. However, in 2002 the Government was again forced to postpone the planned sale of state assets owing to political instability. An IMF stand-by loan of $200m., approved in August, was conditional on the Government implementing a controversial fiscal reform programme, known as the 'economic transition law' or 'el impuestazo' (the 'tax shock'), but the proposed legislation was rejected by the legislature in November. A series of financial scandals relating to state-owned enterprises in 2003, as well as the collapse of the private bank Multibanco in June of that year, further undermined investor confidence. However, the economic policies set out by the new administration of President Oscar Nicanor Duarte Frutos, which took office in August, resulted in the agreement of a $73m. IMF stand-by loan in December, again on condition of structural reform. Some $44m. was disbursed immediately, and the Fund approved the reviews of its programme in April and December 2004. In March 2005 the IMF gave a broadly positive assessment of the Government's economic management, while encouraging further reform. In November the IMF released a further $71.2m. in funding. Government revenues increased significantly in both 2005 and 2006, owing to improved tax collection and a widening of the tax base. While in 2006 the IMF renewed its praise of Paraguay's continued fiscal prudence, the allocation of additional subsidies to the country's ailing cotton industry, as well as government plans to increase spending on health, education and social security ahead of the expected presidential and legislative elections in 2008, threatened to increase the budget deficit in 2007. The 2008 budget, passed by the Senado in late 2007, also increased expenditure, particularly current expenditure, including a 20% wage increase for government employees. Capital expenditure, however, was budgeted to increase by just 1.6% in 2008. None the less, the budget deficit was forecast at only 0.2% of GDP for that year. Meanwhile, the Banco Central de Paraguay's capacity to regulate government expenditure weakened following the resignation of three of its five directors in 2006 (the Bank's President, Mónica Pérez, later also resigned). More positively, Paraguay successfully reduced its debt burden by some $6,200m. after Argentina agreed to forgive one-half of the debt owed on the Yacyretá power plant. The development of relations with Venezuela was expected to yield further debt relief in 2007. GDP was estimated to have increased by 6.4% in 2007, the highest in over 25 years. Growth was driven by increased soy production, high soy prices and greater export demand for the crop, the latter in spite of a strongly performing currency against the US dollar. According to the Banco Central de Paraguay, total exports increased by 77% in 2007, compared with 24% for imports. However, the current account deficit remained high at 26% of GDP for that year, while inflationary pressures continued to cause concern. In March 2008 year-on-year inflation stood at 12.3% up from just 6.0% at the end of 2007. GDP growth of 4.2% was forecast for 2008.

Education

Education is, where possible, compulsory for six years, to be undertaken between six and 12 years of age, but there are insufficient schools, particularly in the remote parts of the country. Primary education begins at the age of six and lasts for six years. Secondary education, beginning at 12 years of age, lasts for a further six years, comprising two cycles of three years each. In 2003 enrolment at primary and secondary schools was equivalent to 85.3% of the total school-age population. There is one state and one Roman Catholic university in Asunción. Expenditure by the Ministry of Education in 1996 amounted to 777,652m. guaraníes, equivalent to some 18.6% of total government spending.

Public Holidays

2008: 1 January (New Year's Day), 1 March (Heroes' Day), 20 March (Maundy Thursday), 21 March (Good Friday), 1 May (Labour Day), 15 May (Independence Day), 12 June (Peace of Chaco), 15 August (Founding of Asunción), 29 September (Battle of Boquerón), 8 December (Immaculate Conception), 25 December (Christmas Day).

2009: 1 January (New Year's Day), 2 March (for Heroes' Day), 20 March (Maundy Thursday), 21 March (Good Friday), 1 May (Labour Day), 15 May (Independence Day), 12 June (Peace of Chaco), 17 August (for Founding of Asunción), 29 September (Battle of Boquerón), 8 December (Immaculate Conception), 25 December (Christmas Day).

Weights and Measures

The metric system is in force.

PARAGUAY

Statistical Survey

Finance

CURRENCY AND EXCHANGE RATES

Monetary Units
100 céntimos = 1 guaraní (G).

Sterling, Dollar and Euro Equivalents (31 December 2007)
£1 sterling = 9,716.5 guaraníes;
US $1 = 4,850.0 guaraníes;
€1 = 7,139.7 guaraníes;
100,000 guaraníes = £10.29 = $20.62 = €14.01.

Average Exchange Rate (guaraníes per US dollar)
2005   6,178.0
2006   5,635.5
2007   5,030.3

BUDGET
('000 million guaraníes)

Revenue	2003	2004	2005*
Taxation	3,676	4,929	5,283
Non-tax revenue and grants	2,318	2,696	2,810
Capital revenues	7	12	3
Total	6,001	7,637	8,096

Expenditure	2003	2004	2005*
Current expenditure	4,981	5,363	6,275
Goods and services	408	447	555
Wages and salaries	2,724	2,984	3,321
Interest payments	489	483	568
Transfers	1,334	1,431	1,807
Pensions and benefits	943	940	1,172
Other	26	18	23
Capital expenditure and net lending	1,165	1,625	1,895
Net lending	−88	−29	−17
Statistical discrepancy	−29	151	0
Total	6,117	7,139	8,170

* Revised projections.

Source: IMF, *Paraguay: Sixth Review Under the Stand-By Arrangement—Staff Report; and Press Release on the Executive Board Discussion* (March 2006).

INTERNATIONAL RESERVES
(excl. gold, US $ million at 31 December)

	2005	2006	2007
IMF special drawing rights	126.08	137.82	43.65
Reserve position in IMF	30.69	32.31	33.94
Foreign exchange	1,140.32	1,531.52	2,385.45
Total	1,297.09	1,701.65	2,463.04

Source: IMF, *International Financial Statistics*.

MONEY SUPPLY
('000 million guaraníes at 31 December)

	2005	2006	2007
Currency outside banks	2,540.94	2,987.15	3,804.17
Demand deposits at commercial banks	3,196.75	3,579.42	5,495.71
Total money (incl. others)	5,751.40	6,703.92	9,473.95

Source: IMF, *International Financial Statistics*.

COST OF LIVING
(Consumer Price Index for Asunción; base: 2000 = 100)

	2004	2005	2006
Food (incl. beverages)	149.7	156.2	182.5
Housing (incl. fuel and light)	139.8	145.5	155.7
Clothing (incl. footwear)	122.5	128.6	137.1
All items (incl. others)	141.3	149.5	165.4

Source: ILO.

NATIONAL ACCOUNTS
('000 million guaraníes at current prices)

Expenditure on the Gross Domestic Product

	2004	2005*	2006*
Final consumption expenditure	34,275.8	39,079.8	46,430.8
Households†	30,185.5	34,069.8	40,569.7
General government	4,090.3	5,010.0	5,861.1
Gross capital formation	7,983.9	9,128.7	10,269.6
Total domestic expenditure	42,259.7	48,208.5	56,700.4
Exports of goods and services	19,605.5	23,636.1	30,475.9
Less Imports of goods and services	20,343.4	25,675.2	34,906.2
GDP in purchasers' values	41,521.9	46,169.3	52,270.1
GDP at constant 1994 prices	15,230.9	15,666.3	16,346.3

* Preliminary figures.
† Including non-profit institutions serving households.

Gross Domestic Product by Economic Activity

	2004	2005*	2006*
Agriculture, hunting, forestry and fishing	9,010.1	9,756.2	10,560.0
Mining and quarrying	45.9	55.5	65.7
Manufacturing	5,898.7	6,414.8	7,141.2
Construction	1,941.5	2,132.6	2,457.5
Electricity and water	915.1	940.9	1,024.7
Trade	8,230.6	9,093.4	10,859.9
Transport and communications	2,829.1	3,547.6	3,959.2
Financial intermediation	895.5	1,095.5	1,352.7
Government services	3,446.0	4,186.8	4,827.2
Real estate, renting and business activities	1,511.4	1,647.1	1,868.6
Hotels and restaurants	469.3	492.7	563.5
Other services	2,534.7	2,721.5	2,903.9
Gross value added in basic prices	37,728.1	42,084.4	47,584.0
Net taxes on products	3,793.8	4,084.9	4,686.0
GDP in market prices	41,521.9	46,169.3	52,270.1

* Preliminary figures.

BALANCE OF PAYMENTS
(US $ million)

	2004	2005	2006
Exports of goods f.o.b.	2,861.2	3,351.8	4,837.6
Imports of goods f.o.b.	−3,105.3	−3,814.3	−5,772.2
Trade balance	−244.1	−462.5	−934.6
Exports of services	627.6	692.8	807.0
Imports of services	−301.0	−343.5	−424.5
Balance on goods and services	82.5	−113.2	−552.1
Other income received	165.4	192.7	258.1
Other income paid	−299.1	−266.4	−309.3
Balance on goods, services and income	−51.2	−186.9	−603.4
Current transfers received	195.7	225.3	390.0
Current transfers paid	−1.5	−1.5	−4.0
Current balance	143.0	36.9	−217.4
Capital account (net)	16.0	20.0	30.0
Direct investment abroad	−6.0	−6.4	−4.0
Direct investment from abroad	37.7	73.9	188.9
Portfolio investment liabilities	−0.1	—	—
Other investment assets	−39.1	385.7	125.1
Other investment liabilities	26.5	−139.0	48.5
Net errors and omissions	95.2	−207.9	211.6
Overall balance	273.2	163.2	382.7

Source: IMF, *International Financial Statistics*.

PARAGUAY

External Trade
(excl. border trade)

PRINCIPAL COMMODITIES
(US $ million)

Imports f.o.b.	2004	2005*	2006*
Food and live animals	133.1	173.6	192.7
Beverages and tobacco	119.5	110.0	129.9
Mineral fuels	437.4	501.2	691.1
Chemical products	293.2	286.8	328.7
Road vehicles	80.8	97.5	240.3
Transport equipment and accessories	169.0	212.7	365.1
Electrical appliances	54.7	106.4	187.9
Motors, general industrial machinery equipment and parts	433.7	701.5	1,743.1
Total (incl. others)	2,657.7	3,251.4	5,254.3

Exports f.o.b.	2004	2005*	2006*
Meat and derivatives	161.7	253.8	424.3
Cereals	74.5	121.6	216.5
Oleaginous seeds	578.7	566.2	439.1
Vegetable oils	132.3	106.6	117.6
Feeding stuff for animals	180.1	141.8	142.3
Wood and wooden products	74.9	79.5	99.5
Cotton fibres	110.1	40.3	34.3
Total (incl. others)	1,626.6	1,687.8	1,906.4

* Preliminary figures.

PRINCIPAL TRADING PARTNERS
(US $ '000)

Imports c.i.f.	2004	2005	2006*
Argentina	619,344	639,188	715,757
Brazil	821,008	883,944	1,052,630
Chile	35,592	38,208	73,063
China, People's Republic	439,401	667,440	1,416,641
France	35,523	38,137	39,431
Germany	44,832	50,683	125,406
Japan	86,710	93,401	435,161
Korea, Republic	26,918	35,453	86,575
Malaysia	10,779	30,539	65,134
Switzerland-Liechtenstein	64,621	136,981	176,183
Taiwan	33,898	53,711	64,613
USA	108,055	169,299	331,904
Uruguay	61,272	52,987	59,095
Venezuela	6,075	5,697	139,922
Total (incl. others)	2,657,707	3,251,429	5,254,271

Exports f.o.b.	2004	2005	2006*
Argentina	101,844	107,304	168,498
Brazil	312,498	325,528	327,983
Cayman Islands	173,736	169,329	180,228
Chile	29,567	64,787	130,835
Germany	14,202	13,865	19,438
Italy	24,565	16,335	21,198
Japan	18,144	18,479	24,699
Netherlands	33,148	47,194	41,661
Peru	19,807	19,606	27,841
Russia	41,216	101,084	227,802
Switzerland-Liechtenstein	66,661	14,565	34,127
USA	52,211	51,561	62,376
Uruguay	451,211	479,290	420,243
Total (incl. others)	1,626,584	1,687,823	1,906,367

* Preliminary figures.

Transport

RAILWAYS
(traffic)

	1988	1989	1990
Passengers carried	178,159	196,019	125,685
Freight (metric tons)	200,213	164,980	289,099

Source: UN, *Statistical Yearbook*.

Passenger-kilometres: 3.0 million per year in 1994–96.
Freight ton-kilometres: 5.5 million in 1994.

Source: UN Economic Commission for Latin America and the Caribbean.

ROAD TRAFFIC
(vehicles in use)

	1999	2000
Cars	267,587	274,186
Buses	8,991	9,467
Lorries	41,329	42,992
Vans and jeeps	134,144	138,656
Motorcycles	6,872	8,825

Source: Organización Paraguaya de Cooperación Intermunicipal.

SHIPPING

Merchant Fleet
(registered at 31 December)

	2004	2005	2006
Number of vessels	44	43	43
Total displacement ('000 grt)	44.3	44.3	44.1

Source: Lloyd's Register-Fairplay, *World Fleet Statistics*.

CIVIL AVIATION
(traffic on scheduled services)

	2003	2004	2005
Kilometres flown (million)	5.8	6.9	7.3
Passengers carried ('000)	313.0	n.a.	n.a.
Passenger-km (million)	320.4	433.4	500.6

Source: UN Economic Commission for Latin America and the Caribbean, *Statistical Yearbook*.

Tourism

ARRIVALS BY NATIONALITY

	2003	2004	2005
Argentina	177,741	197,563	209,130
Brazil	40,651	48,985	56,036
Chile	6,262	7,282	9,941
Germany	4,826	6,336	7,622
Uruguay	5,775	6,692	9,287
USA	9,210	12,012	13,044
Total (incl. others)	268,175	309,287	340,845

Tourism receipts (US $ million, incl. passenger transport): 81 in 2003; 87 in 2004; 96 in 2005.

Source: World Tourism Organization.

Communications Media

	2004	2005	2006
Telephones ('000 main lines in use)	303.4	320.3	331.1
Mobile cellular telephones ('000 subscribers)	1,749.0	1,887.0	3,232.8
Personal computers ('000 in use)	356	460	n.a.
Internet users ('000)	200	200	260
Broadband subscribers ('000)	3.1	5.6	16.0

Television receivers ('000 in use): 1,200 in 1997.

Radio receivers ('000 in use): 925 in 1997.

Facsimile machines (number in use): 1,691 in 1992.

Daily newspapers: 5* in 1996 (average circulation 213,000* copies).

Non-daily newspapers: 2 in 1988 (average circulation 16,000* copies).

Book production: 152 titles (incl. 23 pamphlets) in 1993.
* Estimate.

Sources: UNESCO, *Statistical Yearbook*; UN, *Statistical Yearbook*; International Telecommunication Union.

Education

(2003/04, unless otherwise indicated)

	Institutions*	Teachers	Students
Pre-primary schools	4,071	5,671	128,625
Primary	7,456	33,434	935,722†
Secondary	2,149	44,440	526,001
Tertiary: university level	111	1,844‡	149,120§

* 1999.
† 2002/03.
‡ 1999/2000.
§ Estimate.
Source: partly UNESCO Institute for Statistics.

Adult literacy rate (UNESCO estimates): 93.5% (males 94.3%; females 92.7%) in 2004 (Source: UNESCO Institute for Statistics).

Directory

The Constitution

A new Constitution for the Republic of Paraguay came into force on 22 June 1992, replacing the Constitution of 25 August 1967.

FUNDAMENTAL RIGHTS, DUTIES AND FREEDOMS

Paraguay is an independent republic whose form of government is representative democracy. The powers accorded to the legislature, executive and judiciary are exercised in a system of independence, equilibrium, co-ordination and reciprocal control. Sovereignty resides in the people, who exercise it through universal, free, direct, equal and secret vote. All citizens over 18 years of age and resident in the national territory are entitled to vote.

All citizens are equal before the law and have freedom of conscience, travel, residence, expression, and the right to privacy. The freedom of the press is guaranteed. The freedom of religion and ideology is guaranteed. Relations between the State and the Catholic Church are based on independence, co-operation and autonomy. All citizens have the right to assemble and demonstrate peacefully. All public- and private-sector workers, with the exception of the Armed Forces and the police, have the right to form a trade union and to strike. All citizens have the right to associate freely in political parties or movements.

The rights of the indigenous peoples to preserve and develop their ethnic identity in their respective habitat are guaranteed.

LEGISLATURE

The legislature (Congreso Nacional—National Congress) comprises the Senado (Senate) and the Cámara de Diputados (Chamber of Deputies). The Senado is composed of 45 members, the Cámara of 80 members, elected directly by the people. Legislation concerning national defence and international agreements may be initiated in the Senado. Departmental and municipal legislation may be initiated in the Cámara. Both chambers of the Congreso are elected for a period of five years.

GOVERNMENT

Executive power is exercised by the President of the Republic. The President and the Vice-President are elected jointly and directly by the people, by a simple majority of votes, for a period of five years. They may not be elected for a second term. The President and the Vice-President govern with the assistance of an appointed Council of Ministers. The President participates in the formulation of legislation and enacts it. The President is empowered to veto legislation sanctioned by the Congreso, to nominate or remove ministers, to direct the foreign relations of the Republic, and to convene extraordinary sessions of the Congreso. The President is Commander-in-Chief of the Armed Forces.

JUDICIARY

Judicial power is exercised by the Supreme Court of Justice and by the tribunals. The Supreme Court is composed of nine members who are appointed on the proposal of the Consejo de la Magistratura, and has the power to declare legislation unconstitutional.

The Government

HEAD OF STATE

President: Oscar Nicanor Duarte Frutos (took office 15 August 2003).
Vice-President: Francisco Oviedo Britez.
President-elect: Fernando Armindo Lugo Méndez (scheduled to take office 15 August 2008).

COUNCIL OF MINISTERS
(April 2008)

Minister of the Interior: Libio Wilfredo Florentín Bogado.
Minister of Foreign Affairs: Rubén Ramírez Lezcano.
Minister of Finance: Miguel Angel Gómez (acting).
Minister of Industry and Commerce: Juan Ramón Ibarra Del Prado.
Minister of Public Works and Communications: Roberto Eudez González Segovia.
Minister of National Defence: Nelson Alcides Mora Rodas.
Minister of Public Health and Social Welfare: Dr Oscar Martínez Doldán.
Minister of Justice and Labour: Derlis Ariel Alejandro Osorio Nunes.
Minister of Agriculture and Livestock: Alfredo Silvio Molinas Maldonado.
Minister of Education and Culture: María Ester Jiménez.

MINISTRIES

Ministry of Agriculture and Livestock: Presidente Franco 472, Asunción; tel. (21) 44-9614; fax (21) 49-7965.
Ministry of Education and Culture: Chile, Humaitá y Piribebuy, Asunción; tel. (21) 44-3078; fax (21) 44-3919; internet www.paraguaygobierno.gov.py/mec.
Ministry of Finance: Chile 128, esq. Palmas, Asunción; tel. (21) 44-0010; e-mail info@hacienda.gov.py; internet www.hacienda.gov.py.
Ministry of Foreign Affairs: Juan E. O'Leary y Presidente Franco, Asunción; tel. (21) 49-4593; fax (21) 49-3910; internet www.mre.gov.py.
Ministry of Industry and Commerce: Avda España 323, Asunción; tel. (21) 20-4638; fax (21) 21-3529; e-mail msalcedo@mic.gov.py; internet www.mic.gov.py.
Ministry of the Interior: Estrella y Montevideo, Asunción; tel. (21) 49-3661; fax (21) 44-6448; internet www.ministeriodelinterior.gov.py.

PARAGUAY

Ministry of Justice and Labour: G. R. de Francia y Estados Unidos, Asunción; tel. (21) 49-3515; fax (21) 20-8469; e-mail mjt@conexion.com.py.

Ministry of National Defence: Avda Mariscal López y Vice-Presidente Sánchez, Asunción; tel. (21) 20-4771; fax (21) 21-1583; e-mail ministro@mdn.gov.py; internet www.mdn.gov.py.

Ministry of Public Health and Social Welfare: Avda Pettirossi y Brasil, Asunción; tel. (21) 20-7328; fax (21) 20-6700; internet www.mspbs.gov.py.

Ministry of Public Works and Communications: Oliva y Alberdi, Asunción; tel. (21) 44-4411; fax (21) 44-4421; internet www.mopc.gov.py.

President and Legislature

PRESIDENT

Election, 20 April 2008, provisional results

Candidate	votes	% of votes
Fernando Armindo Lugo Méndez (APC)	704,966	40.8
Blanca Ovelar de Duarte (Partido Colorado)	530,552	30.7
Lino César Oviedo Silva (UNACE)	379,571	22.0
Pedro Nicolás Fadul Niella (Patria Querida)	41,004	2.4
Others	10,928	0.6
Total	1,726,906*	100.0

* Including 34,588 blank and 25,297 invalid ballots.

CONGRESO NACIONAL
(National Congress)

President of the Senado and the Congreso Nacional: MIGUEL ABDÓN SAGUIER CARMONA.

President of the Cámara de Diputados: OSCAR RUBÉN SALOMÓN.

General Election, 20 April 2008, provisional results

Party	Cámara de Diputados	Senado
Partido Colorado	30	15
Partido Liberal Radical Auténtico	29	14
Unión Nacional de Ciudadanos Eticos	15	9
Patria Querida	4	4
Others	2	3
Total	80	45

Election Commission

Tribunal Superior de Justicia Electoral (TSJE): Eusebio Ayala y Santa Cruz de la Sierra, Asunción; tel. (21) 61-8011; e-mail protocolo@tsje.gov.py; internet www.tsje.gov.py; f. 1995; Pres. Dr JUAN MANUEL MORALES SOLER.

Political Organizations

Alianza Patriótica para el Cambio: República Argentina, esq. Fernando de la Mora, Asunción; tel. (21) 55-9400; internet fernandolugo.blogspot.com; f. 2007 to support the presidential campaign of Fernando Armindo Lugo Méndez; alliance of parties and other orgs; mems incl. PLRA, EN and PRF.

Asociación Nacional Republicana—Partido Colorado (National Republican Association—Colorado Party): Casa de los Colorados, 25 de Mayo 842, Asunción; tel. (21) 44-4137; fax (21) 49-7857; internet www.anr.org.py; f. 19th century; principal factions include: Paz y Progreso (the 'Stronista' faction), led by ALFREDO (GOLI) STROESSNER; Movimiento de Reconciliación Colorada; Pres. JOSÉ ALBERTO ALDERETE RODRÍGUEZ (acting).

Encuentro Nacional (EN): 370 Avda Senador Long, Asunción; tel. (21) 60-3935; fax (21) 61-0699; e-mail parenac@pla.net.py; internet www.quanta.net.py/ifes/partidos/pen.htm; f. 1991; coalition comprising factions of PRF, PDC, Asunción Para Todos and a dissident faction of the Partido Colorado; formed to contest presidential and legislative elections of May 1993; Pres. LUIS TORALES KENNEDY; Vice-Pres. Dr SECUNDINO NÚÑEZ.

Movimiento Patria Libre (MPL): 15 de Agosto 1939, Asunción; tel. (21) 37-2384; left-wing; Asst. Sec.-Gen. ANUNCIO MARTI MÉNDEZ.

Movimiento Popular Tekojoja: Asunción; e-mail joaquinbonett@gmail.com; internet www.tekojoja.org; f. 2006 to support the electoral campaign of Fernando Lugo; left-wing, mainly comprising social and indigenous groups; Leader FERNANDO LUGO.

Partido Blanco: Asunción; tel. (21) 55-4068; Pres. GREGORIO SEGOVIA SILVERA; Vice-Pres. EDGAR A. ORTIGOZA CARDOZO.

Partido Comunista Paraguayo (PCP): Asunción; internet www.pcparaguay.org; f. 1928; banned 1928–46, 1947–89; Sec.-Gen. ANANÍAS MAIDANA.

Partido Demócrata Cristiano (PDC): Colón 871, Casilla 1318, Asunción; internet www.pdc.org.py; f. 1960; 20,500 mems; Pres. Dr LUIS M. ANDRADA NOGUÉS; Vice-Pres. Dr JOSÉ V. ALTAMIRANO.

Partido Frente Amplio Paraguayo: Antequera 764, esq. Fulgencio R. Moreno, Asunción; tel. (21) 44-1389; Sec.-Gen. VÍCTOR BAREIRO ROA.

Partido Humanista Paraguayo: Fulgencio R. Moreno 584, esq. Paraguari, Asunción; tel. (21) 44-2625; f. 1985; recognized by the Tribunal Superior de Justicia Electoral in March 1989; campaigns for the protection of human rights and environmental issues; Gen. Sec. NICOLÁS SERVÍN.

Partido Liberal Radical Auténtico (PLRA): Iturbe 936, casi Manuel Domínguez, Asunción; tel. (21) 49-8442; e-mail plra-prensa@mmail.com.py; internet www.plra.org.py; f. 1978; centre party; 806,000 mems; Pres. LUIS FEDERICO FRANCO GÓMEZ.

Partido País Solidario: Avda 5, esq. Méjico, Asunción; tel. (21) 39-1271; Pres. Dr CARLOS FILIZZOLA; Vice-Pres. JORGE GIUCICH.

Partido Revolucionario Febrerista (PRF): Casa del Pueblo, Mandurira 552, Asunción; tel. (21) 49-4041; e-mail partyce@mixmail.com; f. 1951; social democratic party; affiliated to the Socialist International; Pres. NILS CANDIA GINI.

Partido de los Trabajadores (PT): Asunción; f. 1989; Socialist.

Patria Querida: 469 Padre Cardozo, Asunción; tel. 21-3300; e-mail info@patriaquerida.org; internet www.patriaquerida.org; f. 2002; recognized by the Tribunal Superior de Justicia Electoral in March 2004; Leader PEDRO NICOLÁS FADUL NIELLA.

Unidad Popular: Azara 2843, esq. Rodó, Asunción; tel. (21) 21-5059; recognized by the Tribunal Superior de Justicia Electoral in March 2004; Pres. JUAN DE DIOS ACOSTA MENA.

Unión Nacional de Ciudadanos Eticos (UNACE): Eusebio Ayala 4135, esq. Corrales, Asunción; e-mail loviedo@unace.org.py; internet www.unace.org.py; f. 1996 as Unión Nacional de Colorados Eticos, a faction of the Partido Colorado; f. as political party under current name in 2002; left-wing; Pres. Gen. (retd) LINO CÉSAR OVIEDO SILVA.

OTHER ORGANIZATIONS

Federación Nacional Campesina de Paraguay (FNC): Nangariry 1196, esq. Cacique Cará Cará, Asunción; tel. (21) 51-2384; grouping of militant peasants' orgs; Sec.-Gen. ODILÓN ESPÍNOLA; Asst Sec.-Gen. MARCIAL GÓMEZ.

Frente en Defensa de los Bienes Públicos y el Patrimonio Nacional: Asunción; left-wing grouping of orgs opposed to privatization; Co-ordinator GABRIEL ESPÍNOLA.

Frente Nacional de Lucha por la Soberanía y la Vida: Asunción; left-wing grouping of orgs campaigning for agrarian reform and opposed to privatization; Co-ordinator LUIS AGUAYO.

Diplomatic Representation

EMBASSIES IN PARAGUAY

Argentina: Avda España, esq. Avda Perú, Casilla 757, Asunción; tel. (21) 21-2320; fax (21) 21-1029; e-mail embarpy@supernet.com.py; internet www.embajada-argentina.org.py; Ambassador RAFAEL EDGARDO ROMÁ.

Bolivia: Calle Campos Cervera 6421, Asunción; tel. (21) 61-4984; fax (21) 60-1999; e-mail embolivia.asuncion@personaldata.net.py; Ambassador MARCO ANTONIO VIDAURRE NORIEGA.

Brazil: Col Irrazábal, esq. Eligio Ayala, Casilla 22, Asunción; tel. (21) 21-4466; fax (21) 21-2693; e-mail acesar@embajadabrasil.org.py; internet www.embajadabrasil.org.py; Ambassador WALTER PECLY MOREIRA.

Chile: Capital Emilio Nudelman 351, Asunción; tel. (21) 61-3855; fax (21) 66-2755; e-mail echilepy@conexion.com.py; Ambassador FABIO VIO UGARTE.

China (Taiwan): Avda Mariscal López 1143 y Mayor Bullo, Casilla 503, Asunción; tel. (21) 21-3362; fax (21) 21-2373; e-mail embroc01@highway.com.py; Ambassador DAVID C. Y. HU.

Colombia: Calle Coronel Brizuela, esq. Ciudad del Vaticano, Asunción; tel. (21) 22-9888; fax (21) 22-9703; e-mail easuncio@cancilleria.gov.co; Ambassador MAURICIO GONZÁLEZ LÓPEZ.

PARAGUAY

Costa Rica: Shopping del Sol 13104, Avda Antonio Mena Porta, casi Dr Manuel Peña, Asunción; tel. and fax (21) 29-7158; e-mail embarica@tigo.com.py; Ambassador ESTEBAN ARIAS MONGE.

Cuba: Luis Morales 757, esq. Luis León y Luis Granado, Barrio Jara, Asunción; tel. (21) 22-2763; fax (21) 21-3879; e-mail embacuba@cmm.com.py; internet www.embacuba.org.py; Ambassador IRMA GONZÁLEZ CRUZ.

Ecuador: Justo Román y Julio C. Escobar, esq. Barrio Manorá, Casilla 13162, Asunción; tel. (21) 61-4814; fax (21) 61-4813; e-mail mecuapy@conexion.com.py; Ambassador JULIO CÉSAR PRADO ESPINOSA.

France: Avda España 893, Calle Pucheu, Casilla 97, Asunción; tel. (21) 21-2449; fax (21) 21-1690; e-mail chancellerie@ambafran.gov.py; internet www.ambafran.gov.py; Ambassador GILLES BIENVENUE.

Germany: Avda Venezuela 241, Casilla 471, Asunción; tel. (21) 21-4009; fax (21) 21-2863; e-mail aaasun@pla.net.py; internet www.pla.net.py/embalem; Ambassador DIETMAR BLAAS.

Holy See: Calle Ciudad del Vaticano 350, casi con 25 de Mayo, Casilla 83, Asunción (Apostolic Nunciature); tel. (21) 21-5139; fax (21) 21-2590; e-mail nunapos@conexion.com.py; Apostolic Nuncio Most Rev. ORLANDO ANTONINI (Titular Archbishop of Formia).

Italy: Quesada 5871 con Bélgica, Asunción; tel. (21) 61-5620; fax (21) 61-5622; e-mail ambitalia@cmm.com.py; internet www.embajadadeitalia.org.py; Ambassador GIOVANNI MAROCCO.

Japan: Avda Mariscal López 2364, Casilla 1957, Asunción; tel. (21) 60-4616; fax (21) 60-6901; e-mail japoncul@rieder.net.py; internet www.py.emb-japan.go.jp; Ambassador KENRO IINO.

Korea, Republic: Avda Rep. Argentina Norte 678, esq. Pacheco, Casilla 1303, Asunción; tel. (21) 60-5606; fax (21) 60-1376; e-mail paraguay@mofat.go.kr; internet pry.mofat.go.kr; Ambassador JOO TECK KIM.

Lebanon: San Francisco 629, esq. República Siria y Juan de Salazar, Asunción; tel. 22-9375; fax 23-2012; e-mail embajadadelibano@tigo.com.py; Ambassador FARAS EID.

Mexico: Avda España 1428, casi San Rafael, Casilla 1184, Asunción; tel. (21) 618-2000; fax (21) 618-2500; e-mail evamx@embamex.com.py; internet www.embamex.com.py; Ambassador ERNESTO CAMPOS TENORIO.

Panama: Carmen Soler 3912 y Radio Operadores del Chaco, Asunción; tel. and fax (21) 21-1091; e-mail embapana@conexion.com.py; Ambassador GONZALO MONCADA LUNA.

Peru: Feliciano Marecos 441, casi Agustín Barrios y España, Manorá, Casilla 433, Asunción; tel. (21) 60-0226; fax (21) 60-7327; e-mail embperu@embperu.com.py; Ambassador ENRIQUE PALACIOS REYES.

Spain: Edif. S. Rafael, 5° y 6°, Yegros 437, Asunción; tel. (21) 49-0686; fax (21) 44-5394; e-mail embesppy@correo.mae.es; Chargé d'affaires a.i. MARTA DE BLAS MAYORDOMO.

USA: Avda Mariscal López 1776, Casilla 402, Asunción; tel. (21) 21-3715; fax (21) 21-3728; e-mail paraguayusembassy@state.gov; internet asuncion.usembassy.gov; Ambassador JAMES CALDWELL CASON.

Uruguay: Guido Boggiani 5832, 3°, Asunción; tel. (21) 66-4244; fax (21) 60-1335; e-mail embauru@telesurf.com.py; internet www.embajadauruguay.com.py; Ambassador CARLOS ERNESTO ORLANDO BONET.

Venezuela: Mariscal Estigarribia 1023 con Estados Unidos, Asunción; tel. (21) 66-4682; fax (21) 66-4683; e-mail bolivar@pla.net.py; internet www.embaven.org.py; Ambassador NORA MARGARITA URIBE TRUJILLO.

Judicial System

The Corte Suprema de Justicia (Supreme Court of Justice) is composed of nine judges appointed on the recommendation of the Consejo de la Magistratura (Council of the Magistracy).

Corte Suprema de Justicia: Palacio de Justicia, Asunción; internet www.pj.gov.py; Members Dr VÍCTOR MANUEL NÚÑEZ (President), Dr SINDULFO BLANCO (First Vice-President), Dr JOSÉ RAÚL TORRES KIRMSER (Second Vice-President), Dra ALICIA BEATRIZ PUCHETA DE CORREA, Dr MIGUEL O. BAJAC, Dr ANTONIO FRETES, Dr JOSÉ V. ALTAMIRANO AQUINO, Dr CÉSAR ANTONIO GARAY ZUCCOLILLO; one vacancy.

Consejo de la Magistratura

Escuela Judicial del Paraguay, Asunción; Members CRISTÓBAL R. SÁNCHEZ DÍAZ (President), Dr RAÚL BATTILANA NIGRA (Vice-President), MARIO W. SOTO ESTIGARRIBIA, EUSEBIO RAMÓN AYALA, Dr RODOLFO ENRIQUE BACCHETTA CHIRIANI, JOSÉ MARÍA CABRAL, AMPARO SAMANIEGO DE PACIELLO, EDMUNDO MANUEL ROLLÓN, VÍCTOR MANUEL NÚÑEZ.

Attorney-General: RUBÉN CANDIA AMARILLA.

Under the Supreme Court are the Courts of Appeal, the Tribunal of Jurors and Judges of First Instance, the Judges of Arbitration, the Magistrates (Jueces de Instrucción), and the Justices of the Peace.

Religion

The Roman Catholic Church is the established religion, although all sects are tolerated.

CHRISTIANITY

The Roman Catholic Church

For ecclesiastical purposes, Paraguay comprises one archdiocese, 11 dioceses and two Apostolic Vicariates. At 31 December 2005 there were an estimated 5,898,651 adherents in the country, representing about 84% of the total population.

Bishops' Conference

Conferencia Episcopal Paraguaya, Calle Alberdi 782, Casilla 1436, 1209 Asunción; tel. (21) 49-0920; fax (21) 49-5115; e-mail cep@infonet.com.py; internet www.episcopal.org.py.

f. 1977, statutes approved 2000; Pres. Rt Rev. IGNACIO GOGORZA IZAGUIRRE (Bishop of Encarnación).

Archbishop of Asunción: Most Rev. EUSTAQUIO PASTOR CUQUEJO VERGA, Arzobispado, Avda Mariscal López 130 esq. Independencia Nacional, Casilla 654, Asunción; tel. (21) 44-5551; fax (21) 44-4150; e-mail asa@pla.net.py.

The Anglican Communion

Paraguay constitutes a single diocese of the Iglesia Anglicana del Cono Sur de América (Anglican Church of the Southern Cone of America). The Presiding Bishop of the Church is the Bishop of Northern Argentina.

Bishop of Paraguay: Rt Rev. JOHN ELLISON, Iglesia Anglicana, Avda España casi Santos, Casilla 1124, Asunción; tel. (21) 20-0933; fax (21) 21-4328; e-mail iapar@sce.cnc.una.py; internet www.anglicanos.net/paraguay.htm.

The Baptist Church

Baptist Evangelical Convention of Paraguay: Casilla 1194, Asunción; tel. (21) 22-7110; fax (21) 21-0588; e-mail cebp@sce.cnc.una.py; internet www.ublaonline.org/paises/paraguay.htm; Exec. Sec. AUGUSTO VEGA.

BAHÁ'Í FAITH

National Spiritual Assembly of the Bahá'ís of Paraguay: Eligio Ayala 1456, Apdo 742, Asunción; tel. (21) 22-5747; e-mail bahai@highway.com.py; internet www.bahai.org.py; Sec. MIRNA LLAMOSAS DE RIQUELME.

The Press

DAILIES

ABC Color: Yegros 745, Apdo 1421, Asunción; tel. (21) 49-1160; fax (21) 415-1310; e-mail azeta@abc.com.py; internet www.abc.com.py; f. 1967; independent; Propr ALDO ZUCCOLILLO; circ. 45,000.

El Día: Avda Mariscal López 2948, Asunción; tel. (21) 60-3401; fax (21) 66-0385; e-mail eldia@infonet.com.py; internet www.infonet.com.py/eldia; Dir HUGO OSCAR ARANDA; circ. 12,000.

La Nación: Avda Zavala Cué entre 2da y 3ra, Fernando de la Mora, Asunción; tel. (21) 51-2520; fax (21) 51-2535; e-mail redaccion@lanacion.com.py; internet www.lanacion.com.py; f. 1995; Dir-Gen. OSVALDO DOMÍNGUEZ DIBB; circ. 10,000.

Noticias: Avda Artigas y Avda Brasilia, Casilla 3017, Asunción; tel. (21) 29-2721; fax (21) 29-2716; e-mail alebluth@diarionoticias.com; internet www.diarionoticias.com.py; f. 1985; independent; Dir ALEJANDRO BLUTH; circ. 20,000.

Popular: Avda Mariscal López 2948, Asunción; tel. (21) 60-3401; fax (21) 60-3400; e-mail popular@mm.com.py; internet www.diariopopular.com.py; Dir JAVIER PIROVANO PEÑA; circ. 28,000.

Ultima Hora: Benjamín Constant 658, Asunción; tel. (21) 49-6261; fax (21) 44-7071; e-mail ultimahora@uhora.com.py; internet www.ultimahora.com; f. 1973; independent; Dir DEMETRIO ROJAS; circ. 30,000.

PERIODICALS

Acción: Casilla 1072, Asunción; tel. (21) 37-0753; e-mail cepag@uninet.com.py; internet www.uninet.com.py/accion; monthly; Dir JOSÉ MARÍA BLANCH.

La Opinión: Boggiani, esq. Luis Alberto de Herrera, Asunción; tel. (21) 50-7501; fax (21) 50-2297; weekly; Dir FRANCISCO LAWS; Editor BERNARDO NERI.

TeVeo: Santa Margarita de Youville 250, Santa María, Asunción; tel. (21) 67-2079; fax (21) 21-1236; e-mail sugerencias@teveo.com.py; internet www.teveo.com.py; weekly; society.

Tiempo 14: Mariscal Estigarribia 4187, Asunción; tel. (21) 60-4308; fax (21) 60-9394; weekly; Dir HUMBERTO RUBÍN; Editor ALBERTO PERALTA.

NEWS AGENCY

Jaku'éke Paraguay—Agencia Nacional de Noticias: Itapúa y Río Monday, Asunción; tel. (21) 29-7806; fax (21) 28-1950; internet www.jakueke.com; f. 2002; independent.

Publishers

La Colmena, SA: Asunción; tel. (21) 20-0428; Dir DAUMAS LADOUCE.

Dervish SA, Editorial: Avda Mariscal López 1735, CP 1584, Asunción; tel. (21) 21-1729; fax (21) 22-2580; e-mail dervish@dervish.com.py; f. 1989; Co-ordinator JORGELINA MIGLIORISI; Vice-Pres. and Dir JANINE GIANI PATTERSON.

Ediciones Diálogo: Calle Brasil 1391, Asunción; tel. (21) 20-0428; f. 1957; fine arts, literature, poetry, criticism; Man. MIGUEL ANGEL FERNÁNDEZ.

Ediciones Nizza: Eligio Ayala 1073, Casilla 2596, Asunción; tel. (21) 44-7160; medicine; Pres. Dr JOSÉ FERREIRA MARTÍNEZ.

Editorial Comuneros: Cerro Corá 289, Casilla 930, Asunción; tel. (21) 44-6176; fax (21) 44-4667; e-mail rolon@conexion.com.py; f. 1963; social history, poetry, literature, law; Man. OSCAR R. ROLÓN.

Librería Intercontinental: Caballero 270, Calle Mariscal, Estigarribia, Asunción; tel. (21) 49-6991; fax (21) 44-8721; e-mail agatti@libreriaintercontinental.com.py; internet www.libreriaintercontinental.com.py; political science, law, literature, poetry; Dir ALEJANDRO GATTI VAN HUMBEECK.

R. P. Ediciones: Eduardo Víctor Haedo 427, Asunción; tel. (21) 49-8040; Man. RAFAEL PERONI.

ASSOCIATION

Cámara Paraguaya del Libro: Nuestra Señora de la Asunción 697, esq. Eduardo Víctor Haedo, Asunción; tel. (21) 44-4104; fax (21) 44-7053; Pres. PABLO LEÓN BURIAN; Sec. EMA DE VIEDMA.

Broadcasting and Communications

TELECOMMUNICATIONS

Comisión Nacional de Telecomunicaciones (CONATEL): Edif. San Rafael, 2°, Yegros 437 y 25 de Mayo, Asunción; tel. (21) 44-0020; fax (21) 49-8982; e-mail presidencia@conatel.gov.py; internet www.conatel.gov.py; Pres. (vacant).

COPACO, SA (Corporación Paraguaya de Comunicaciones, SA): Edif. Morotí, 1°–2°, esq. Gen. Bruguéz y Teodoro S. Mongelos, Casilla 2042, Asunción; tel. (21) 20-3800; fax (21) 20-3888; e-mail infoweb@copaco.com.py; internet www.copaco.com.py; fmrly Administración Nacional de Telecomunicaciones (ANTELCO); changed name as above in Dec. 2001 as part of the privatization process; privatization suspended in June 2002; Gen. Man. EDGAR PINEDA.

CTI Móvil: Asunción; internet www.cti.com.py; bought by América Móvil, SA de CV (Mexico) in July 2005; mobile cellular telephone services.

BROADCASTING

Radio

Radio Arapysandú: Avda Mariscal López y Capitán del Puerto San Ignacio, Misiones; tel. (82) 2374; fax (82) 2206; f. 1982; AM; Dir HECTOR BOTTINO.

Radio Asunción: Avda Artígas y Capitán Lombardo 174, Asunción; tel. and fax (21) 28-2662; e-mail radioasuncion@cmm.com.py; internet www.radioasuncion.com.py; AM; Dir MIGUEL G. FERNÁNDEZ.

Radio Cáritas: Kubitschek y 25 de Mayo, Asunción; tel. (21) 21-3570; fax (21) 20-4161; f. 1936; station of the Franciscan order; AM; Pres. Most Rev. EUSTAQUIO PASTOR CUQUEJO VERGA (Archbishop of Asunción); Dir MARIO VELÁZQUEZ.

Radio Cardinal: Río Paraguay 1334 y Guarinies, Casilla 2532, Lambaré, Asunción; tel. (21) 31-0555; fax (21) 31-0557; f. 1991; AM and FM; Pres. NÉSTOR LÓPEZ MOREIRA.

Radio City: Edif. Líder III, Antequera 652, 9°, Asunción; tel. (21) 44-3324; fax (21) 44-4367; f. 1950; FM; licence until 2014; Dir GREGORIO RAMAN MORALES.

Radio Concepción: Coronel Panchito López 241, entre Schreiber y Profesor Guillermo A. Cabral, Casilla 78, Concepción; tel. (31) 42318; fax (31) 42254; f. 1963; AM; Dir SERGIO E. DACAK.

Radio Emisoras del Paraguay, SRL: Teniente Martínez Ramella 1355, Calle Avda Eusebio Ayala, Asunción; tel. (21) 22-0132; e-mail administracion@emisorasparaguay.com.py; FM; licence until 2014; Dir FRANCISCO JAVIER BOSCARINO BÁEZ.

Radio Guairá: Presidente Franco 788 y Alejo García, Villarica; tel. (541) 42130; fax (541) 42385; f. 1950; AM and FM; Dir LÍDICE RODRÍGUEZ DE TRAVERSI.

Radio Itapirú SRL: Avda San Blás esq. Coronel Julián Sánchez, Ciudad del Este, Alto Paraná; tel. (61) 57-2206; fax (61) 57-2210; f. 1969; AM and FM; Gen. Man. ANTONIO ARANDA ENCINA.

Radio La Voz de Amambay: 14 de Mayo y Cerro León, Pedro Juan Caballero, Amambay; tel. (36) 72537; f. 1959; AM and FM; Gen. Man. DANIEL ROLÓN DANTAS P.

Radio Nacional del Paraguay: Blas Garay 241 y Iturbe, Asunción; tel. (21) 39-0374; fax (21) 39-0376; f. 1957; AM and FM; Dir TEODOSO FERMÍN ESPINOSA.

Radio Ñandutí: Choferes del Chaco y Carmen Soler, Asunción; tel. (21) 60-4308; fax (21) 60-6074; internet www.infonet.com.py/holding/nanduam; f. 1962; FM; Dir HUMBERTO LEÓN RUBÍN.

Radio Nuevo Mundo: Coronel Romero 1181 y Flórida, San Lorenzo, Asunción; tel. (21) 58-6258; fax (21) 58-2424; f. 1972; AM; Dir JULIO CÉSAR PEREIRA BOBADILLA.

Radio Primero de Marzo: Avda General Perón y Concepción, Casilla 1456, Asunción; tel. (21) 31-1564; fax (21) 33-3427; AM and FM; Dir-Gen. ANGEL R. GUERREÑOS.

Radio Santa Mónica FM: Avda Boggiani y Herrera, 3°, Asunción; tel. (21) 50-7501; fax (21) 50-9494; f. 1973; FM; Dir RICARDO FACCETTI.

Radio Uno: Avda Mariscal López 2948, Asunción; tel. (21) 61-2151; f. 1968; as Radio Chaco Boreal; AM; Dir JAVIER MARÍA PIROVANO SILVA.

Radio Venus: Avda República Argentina y Souza, Asunción; tel. (21) 61-0151; fax (21) 60-6484; e-mail 105.1@venus.com.py; internet www.venus.com.py; f. 1987; FM; Dir ANGEL AGUILERA.

Radio Ysapy: Independencia Nacional 1260, 1°, Asunción; tel. (21) 44-4037; FM; Dir JOSÉ TOMÁS CABRIZA SALVIONI.

Television

Teledifusora Paraguaya—Canal 13: Comendador Nicolás Bó y Guarinies, Lambaré, Asunción; tel. (21) 33-2823; fax (21) 33-1695; e-mail prensa@rpc.com.py; internet www.rpc.com.py; f. 1980; Dir-Gen. JORGE LÓPEZ MOREIRA.

Sistema Nacional de Televisión Cerro Corá—Canal 9: Avda Carlos A. López 572, Asunción; tel. (21) 42-4222; fax (21) 48-0230; e-mail snt@snt.com.py; internet www.snt.com.py; f. 1965; commercial; Dir Gen. ISMAEL HADID.

Televisora del Este: San Pedro, Calle Pilar, Area 5, Ciudad del Este; tel. (61) 8859; subsidiary of Sistema Nacional de Televisión; commercial.

Televisión Itapúa—Canal 7: Encarnación; tel. (71) 20-4450; subsidiary of Sistema Nacional de Televisión; commercial.

Finance

(cap. = capital; res = reserves; dep. = deposits; m. = million; brs = branches; amounts in guaraníes, unless otherwise indicated)

BANKING

Superintendencia de Bancos: Edif. Banco Central del Paraguay, Avda Federación Rusa y Avda Marecos, Barrio Santo Domingo, Asunción; tel. (21) 60-8011; fax (21) 60-8149; e-mail eleguiza@bcp.gov.py; internet www.bcp.gov.py/supban/principal.htm; Supt EDGAR ANDRÉS LEGUIZAMON CARMONA.

Central Bank

Banco Central del Paraguay: Avda Federación Rusa y Cabo 1° Marecos, Casilla 861, Barrio Santo Domingo, Asunción; tel. (21) 61-0088; fax (21) 60-8149; e-mail webmaster@bcp.gov.py; internet www.bcp.gov.py; f. 1952; cap. 828,145m., res 454,695m., dep. 4,605,137m. (Dec. 2005); Pres. ANGEL GABRIEL GONZÁLEZ CÁCERES; Gen. Man. GILBERTO RODRÍGUEZ GARCETE.

PARAGUAY

Development Banks

Banco Nacional de Fomento: Independencia Nacional y 25 de Mayo, Asunción; tel. (21) 44-4440; fax (21) 44-6056; e-mail correo@bnf.gov.py; internet www.bnf.gov.py; f. 1961 to take over the deposit and private banking activities of the Banco del Paraguay; Pres. Lic. GERMÁN HUGO ROJAS IRIGOYEN; Sec.-Gen. CÉSAR LEONARDO FURIASSE ROLÓN; 52 brs.

Crédito Agrícola de Habilitación: Caríos 362 y Willam Richardson, Asunción; tel. (21) 56-9010; fax (21) 55-4956; e-mail cah@quanta.com.py; f. 1943; Pres. Ing. WALBERTO FERREIRA.

Fondo Ganadero: Avda Mariscal López 1669 esq. República Dominicana, Asunción; tel. (21) 29-4361; fax (21) 44-6922; internet www.fondogan.gov.py; f. 1969; govt-owned; Pres. GUILLERMO SERRATTI G.

Commercial Banks

Banco Amambay, SA: Avda Aviadores del Chaco, entre San Martín y Pablo Alborno, Asunción; tel. (21) 60-8831; fax (21) 60-8813; e-mail bcoama@bcoamabancoamambay.com.py; internet www.bancoamambay.com.py; f. 1992; Pres. GUIOMAR DE GÁSPERI; Gen. Man. HUGO PORTILLO SOSA.

Banco Bilbao Vizcaya Argentaria Paraguaya, SA (Spain): Yegros 435 y 25 de Mayo, Casilla 824, Asunción; tel. (21) 49-2072; fax (21) 44-8103; e-mail bbva.paraguay@bbva.com.py; f. 1961 as Banco Exterior de España, SA; renamed Argentaria Banco Exterior in 1999, present name adopted in 2000; Pres. and Gen. Man. ANGEL SORIA TABUENCA; 5 brs.

Banco Continental, SAECA: Estrella 621, Casilla 2260, Asunción; tel. (21) 44-2002; fax (21) 44-2001; e-mail contil@conexion.com.py; f. 1980; cap. US $4.2m., res $2.5m., dep. $44.6m. (Dec. 2001); Chair. GUILLERMO GROSS BROWN; First Vice-Pres. JAVIER GONZÁLEZ PÉREZ.

Banco Finamérica SA: Chile y Oliva, Casilla 1321, Asunción; tel. (21) 49-1021; fax (21) 44-5199; f. 1988; Pres. Dr GUILLERMO HEISECKE VELÁZQUEZ; Gen. Man. ENRIQUE FERNÁNDEZ ROMAY.

Interbanco, SA: Oliva 349, esq. Chile y Alberdi, Asunción; tel. (21) 49-4992; fax (21) 41-71372; e-mail interban@conexion.com.py; internet www.interbanco.com.py; f. 1978; owned by Unibanco (Brazil); cap. 21,739m., res 176,386m., dep. 2,234,925m. (Dec. 2006); Pres. CLAUDIO YAMAGUTI; 17 brs.

Sudameris Bank, SAECA: Independencia Nacional y Cerro Corá, Casilla 1433, Asunción; tel. (21) 44-8670; fax (21) 44-4024; e-mail gerencia@sudameris.com.py; internet www.sudamerisbank.com.py; f. 1961; savings and commercial bank; cap. 142,991m., surplus and res 20,824m., dep. 837,319m. (Dec. 2006); Chair. CONOR MCENROY; Vice-Chair. and Gen. Man. JUAN LUIS KOSTNER; 8 brs.

Banking Associations

Asociación de Bancos del Paraguay: Jorge Berges 229, esq. EEUU, Asunción; tel. (21) 21-4951; fax (21) 20-5050; e-mail abp.par@pla.net.py; mems: Paraguayan banks and foreign banks with brs in Asunción; Pres. CELIO TUNHOLI.

Cámara de Bancos Paraguayos: 25 de Mayo, esq. 22 de Setiembre, Asunción; tel. (21) 22-2373; fax (21) 20-5050; Pres. MIGUEL ANGEL LARREINEGABE.

STOCK EXCHANGE

Bolsa de Valores y Productos de Asunción SA: Estrella 540, Asunción; tel. (21) 44-2445; fax (21) 44-2446; internet www.bvpasa.com.py; f. 1977; Pres. JORGE DANIEL PECCI MILTOS; Gen. Man. HUGO EUGENIO SALINAS VALDÉS.

INSURANCE

Supervisory Authority

Superintendencia de Seguros: Edif. Banco Central del Paraguay, 1°, Federación Rusa y Sargento Marecos, Asunción; tel. (21) 619-2605; fax (21) 619-2637; e-mail gbenitez@bcp.gov.py; internet www.bcp.gov.py/supseg/default.html; Supt MÁXIMO GUSTAVO BENÍTEZ GIMÉNEZ.

Principal Companies

La Agrícola SA de Seguros Generales: Mariscal López 5377 y Consejal Vargas, Asunción; tel. (21) 60-9509; fax (21) 60-9606; e-mail laagricola@rieder.net.py; f. 1982; general; Pres. Dr VICENTE OSVALDO BERGUES; Gen. Man. CARLOS ALBERTO LEVI SOSA.

ALFA SA de Seguros y Reaseguros: Yegros 944, Asunción; tel. (21) 44-9992; fax (21) 44-9991; e-mail alfa.seg@conexion.com.py; Pres. NICOLAS SARUBBI ZAYAS.

América SA de Seguros y Reaseguros: Alberdi 980 esq. Manduvirá, 1°, Asunción; tel. (21) 49-1713; fax (21) 44-8036; e-mail amea@telesurf.com.py; Pres. EDUARDO NICOLÁS BO PEÑA.

Aseguradora del Este SA de Seguros: Edif. Castilla Center, 3°, Carlos A. López esq. Paí Pérez, Ciudad del Este; tel. (61) 51-2941; fax (61) 50-4843; e-mail dcespedes@aesaseguros.com.py; Pres. VÍCTOR ANDRÉS RIBEIRO ESPÍNOLA.

Aseguradora Paraguaya, SA: Israel 309 esq. Rio de Janeiro, Casilla 277, Asunción; tel. (21) 21-5086; fax (21) 22-2217; e-mail asepasa@asepasa.com.py; f. 1976; life and risk; Pres. GERARDO TORCIDA CONEJERO.

Aseguradora Yacyretá SA de Seguros y Reaseguros: Oliva 685, esq. Juan E. O'Leary y 15 de Agosto, Asunción; tel. (21) 45-2374; fax (21) 44-5070; e-mail spalomar@yacyreta.com.py; f. 1980; Pres. OSCAR HARRISON JACQUET; Vice-Pres. NORMAN HARRISON PALEARI; Gen. Man. EDUARDO BARRIOS PERINI; 5 brs.

Atalaya SA de Seguros Generales: Independencia Nacional 565, 1°, esq. Azara y Cerro Corá, Asunción; tel. (21) 49-2811; fax (21) 49-6966; e-mail ataseg@telesurf.com.py; f. 1964; general; Pres. KARIN M. DOLL.

Cenit de Seguros, SA: Ayolas 1082, esq. Ibáñez del Campo, Asunción; tel. (21) 49-4972; fax (21) 44-9502; e-mail cenitsa@rieder.net.py; Pres. Dr FELIPE OSCAR ARMELE BONZI.

Central SA de Seguros: Edif. Betón I, 1° y 2°, Eduardo Víctor Haedo 179, Independencia Nacional, Casilla 1802, Asunción; tel. (21) 49-4654; fax (21) 49-4655; e-mail censeg@conexion.com.py; f. 1977; general; Pres. MIGUEL JACOBO VILLASANTI; Gen. Man. Dr FÉLIX AVEIRO.

El Comercio Paraguayo SA Cía de Seguros Generales: Alberdi 453 y Oliva, Asunción; tel. (21) 49-2324; fax (21) 49-3562; f. 1947; life and risk; Dir Dr BRAULIO OSCAR ELIZECHE.

La Consolidada SA de Seguros y Reaseguros: Chile 719 y Eduardo Víctor Haedo, Casilla 1182, Asunción; tel. (21) 49-5174; fax (21) 44-5795; e-mail info@laconsolidada.com.py; f. 1961; life and risk; Pres. JUAN CARLOS DELGADILLO ECHAGÜE.

Fénix SA de Seguros y Reaseguros: Iturbe 823 y Fulgencio R. Moreno, Asunción; tel. (21) 49-5549; fax (21) 44-5643; e-mail fenix@pla.net.py; Pres. VÍCTOR MARTÍNEZ YARYES.

Garantía SA de Seguros y Reaseguros: 25 de Mayo 640, Asunción; tel. (21) 44-3748; fax (21) 44-0678; e-mail garantia@rieder.net.py; Pres. GERALDO CRISTALDO JURE.

Grupo General de Seguros y Reaseguros, SA: Edif. Grupo General, Jejuí 324 y Chile, 2°, Asunción; tel. (21) 49-7897; fax (21) 44-9259; e-mail general_de_seguros@ggeneral.com.py; Pres. JORGE OBELAR LAMAS.

La Independencia de Seguros y Reaseguros, SA: Edif. Parapatí, 1°, Juan E. O'Leary 409, esq. Estrella, Casilla 980, Asunción; tel. (21) 44-7021; fax (21) 44-8996; e-mail la_independencia@par.net.py; f. 1965; general; Pres. REGINO MOSCARDA; Gen. Man. JUAN FRANCISCO FRANCO LÓPEZ.

Intercontinental SA de Seguros y Reaseguros: Iturbe 1047 con Teniente Fariña, Altos, Asunción; tel. (21) 49-2348; fax (21) 49-1227; e-mail mvmodica@yahoo.com; f. 1978; Pres. Dr JUAN MÓDICA LUCENTE; Gen. Man. LUIS SANTACRUZ.

Mapfre Paraguay, SA: Avda Mariscal López 910 y General Aquino, Asunción; tel. (21) 44-1983; fax (21) 49-7441; e-mail sac@mapfre.com.py; Pres. LUIS MARÍA ZUBIZARRETA.

La Meridional Paraguaya SA de Seguros: Iturbe 1046, Teniente Fariña, Asunción; tel. (21) 49-8827; fax (21) 49-8826; e-mail meridian@conexion.com.py; Pres. TITO LIVIO MUJICA VARELA.

Mundo SA de Seguros: Estrella 917 y Montevideo, Asunción; tel. (21) 49-2787; fax (21) 44-5486; e-mail mundosa@par.net.py; f. 1970; risk; Pres. JUAN MARTÍN VILLALBA DE LOS RÍOS; Gen. Man. BLÁS MARCIAL CABRAL BARRIOS.

La Paraguaya SA de Seguros: Estrella 675, 7°, Asunción; tel. (21) 49-1367; fax (21) 44-8235; e-mail lps@conexion.com.py; f. 1905; life and risk; Pres. JUAN BOSCH BEYNEN.

Patria SA de Seguros y Reaseguros: General Santos 715 esq. Siria, Asunción; tel. (21) 22-5250; fax (21) 21-4001; e-mail patria@conexion.com.py; f. 1968; general; Pres. Dr MARCOS PERERA R.

El Productor SA de Seguros y Reaseguros: Ind. Nacional 811 esq. Fulgencio R. Moreno, 8°, Asunción; tel. (21) 49-1577; fax (21) 49-1599; e-mail ncabanas@elproductor.com.py; Pres. REINALDO PAVÍA MALDONADO.

Real Paraguaya de Seguros, SA: Edif. Banco Real, 1°, Estrella esq. Alberdi, Casilla 1442, Asunción; tel. (21) 49-2221; fax (21) 49-8129; e-mail realseg@pla.net.py; f. 1974; general; Pres. EUCLIDES HUMBERTO VARNIERI RIBEIRO.

Regional SA de Seguros y Reaseguros: Roque González 390 y Dr Hassler, Asunción; tel. (21) 61-0692; fax (21) 22-4447; e-mail regisesa@itacom.com.py; Pres. JUAN A. DIAZ DE VIVAR PRIETO.

Rumbos SA de Seguros: Estrella 851, Ayolas, Casilla 1017, Asunción; tel. (21) 44-9488; fax (21) 44-9492; e-mail rumbos@conexion.com.py; f. 1960; general; Pres. MIGUEL A. LARREINEGAVE LESME; Man. Dir ROBERTO GÓMEZ VERLANGIERI.

La Rural SA de Seguros: Avda Mariscal López 1082, esq. Mayor Bullo, Casilla 21, Asunción; tel. (21) 49-1917; fax (21) 44-1592; e-mail larural@larural.com.py; f. 1920; general; Pres. JUAN CARLOS MANEGLIA; Gen. Man. EDUARDO BARRIOS PERINI.

Seguros Chaco SA de Seguros y Reaseguros: Mariscal Estigarribia 982, Casilla 3248, Asunción; tel. (21) 44-7118; fax (21) 44-9551; e-mail segucha@conexion.com.py; f. 1977; general; Pres. EMILIO VELILLA LACONICH; Exec. Dir ALBERTO R. ZARZA TABOADA.

Seguros Generales, SA (SEGESA): Edif. SEGESA, 1°, Oliva 393 esq. Alberdi, Casilla 802, Asunción; tel. (21) 49-1362; fax (21) 49-1360; e-mail segesa@conexion.com.py; f. 1956; life and risk; Pres. CÉSAR AVALOS.

El Sol del Paraguay, Cía de Seguros y Reaseguros, SA: Cerro Corá 1031, Asunción; tel. (21) 49-1110; fax (21) 21-0604; e-mail elsol@elsol.com.py; internet www.elsol.com.py; f. 1978; Pres. MIGUEL ANGEL BERNI CENTURIÓN; Vice-Pres. CAROLINA VEGA DE ONETTO.

Universo de Seguros y Reaseguros, SA: Edif. de la Encarnación, 9°, 14 de Mayo esq. General Díaz, Casilla 788, Asunción; tel. (21) 44-8530; fax (21) 44-7278; f. 1979; Pres. ZENÓN AGÜERO MIRANDA.

Insurance Association

Asociación Paraguaya de Cías de Seguros: 15 de Agosto, esq. Lugano, Casilla 1435, Asunción; tel. (21) 44-6474; fax (21) 44-4343; e-mail apcs@activenet.com.py; f. 1963; Pres. Dr EMILIO VELILLA LACONICH; Gen. Man. RUBÉN RAPPENECKER COSCIA.

Trade and Industry

GOVERNMENT AGENCIES

Consejo Nacional para las Exportaciones: Asunción; f. 1986; founded to eradicate irregular trading practices; Dir JOSÉ MARÍA IBÁÑEZ (Minister of Industry and Commerce).

Consejo de Privatización: Edif. Ybaga, 10°, Presidente Franco 173, Asunción; fax (21) 44-9157; responsible for the privatization of state-owned enterprises; Exec. Dir RUBÉN MORALES PAOLI.

Instituto Nacional de Tecnología y Normalización (INTN) (National Institute of Technology and Standardization): Avda General Artigas 3973 y General Roa, Casilla 967, Asunción; tel. (21) 29-0160; fax (21) 29-0266; e-mail intn@intn.gov.py; internet www.intn.gov.py; national standards institute; Dir-Gen. LILIAN MARTÍNEZ DE ALONSO.

Instituto de Previsión Social: Constitución y Luis Alberto de Herrera, Casilla 437, Asunción; tel. (21) 22-5719; fax (21) 22-3654; f. 1943; responsible for employees' welfare and health insurance scheme; Pres. PEDRO FERREIRA ESTIGARRIBIA.

DEVELOPMENT ORGANIZATIONS

Secretaría Técnica de Planificación del Desarrollo Económico y Social: Edif. AYFRA, 3°, Presidente Franco y Ayolas, Asunción; tel. (21) 45-0422; fax (21) 49-6510; e-mail webmarketing@stp.gov.py; govt body responsible for overall economic and social planning; Exec. Sec. CARLOS LUIS FILIPPI SANABRÍA; Sec.-Gen. Lic. OSVALDO MARTÍNEZ ORTEGA.

Acuerdo Ciudadano (Articulación de la Sociedad Civil): República de Siria 35, Asunción; tel. (21) 20-7757; fax (21) 20-2918; e-mail info@acuerdociudadano.org.py; internet www.acuerdociudadano.org.py; f. 2001; grouping of social devt orgs; Gen. Co-ordinator PASCUAL RUBIANI YANHO.

AFS: Azara 2242 con 22 de Setiembre, Asunción; tel. (21) 44-2369; fax (21) 49-3277; e-mail info-paraguay@afs.org; internet www.afs.org.py; educational and social devt; Exec. Dir VICTORIA VILLALBA.

Alter Vida (Centro de Estudios y Formación para el Ecodesarrollo): Itapúa 1372, esq. Primer Presidente y Río Monday, Barrio Trinidad, Asunción; tel. (21) 29-8842; fax (21) 29-8845; e-mail info@altervida.org.py; internet www.altervida.org.py; f. 1985; ecological devt; Exec. Dir JORGE ABBATE CORDAZZO.

Asociación Rural del Paraguay (ARP): Ruta Transchaco, Km. 14, Asunción; tel. (21) 75-4412; e-mail ania@arp.org.py; internet www.arp.org.py; grouping of agricultural cos and farmers; Dir ALBERTO SOLJANCIC.

Centro de Información y Recursos para el Desarrollo (CIRD): Asunción; tel. (21) 22-6071; fax (21) 21-2540; e-mail cird@cird.org.py; internet www.cird.org.py; f. 1988; information and resources for devt orgs; Exec. Pres. AGUSTÍN CARRIZOSA.

Consejo Nacional de Coordinación Económica: Presidencia de la República, Paraguayo Independiente y Juan E. O'Leary, Asunción; responsible for overall economic policy; Sec. FULVIO MONGES OCAMPOS.

Cooperación Empresarial y Desarrollo Industrial (CEDIAL): Edif. UIP, 2°, Cerro Corá 1038, esq. Estados Unidos y Brasil, Asunción; tel. and fax (21) 23-0047; e-mail cedial@cedial.org.py; internet www.cedial.org.py; f. 1991; promotes commerce and industrial devt; Gen. Man. HERNÁN RAMÍREZ.

Instituto Nacional de Desarrollo Rural y de la Tierra (INDERT): Tacuary 276, Asunción; tel. (21) 44-0578; fax (21) 44-6534; internet www.indert.gov.py; f. 1963 as Instituto de Bienestar Rural; name changed as above in 2004; responsible for rural welfare and colonization; Pres. ERICO IBÁÑEZ.

Instituto Paraguayo del Indígena (INDI): Don Bosco 745, Casilla 1575, Asunción; tel. (21) 49-3737; fax (21) 44-7154; f. 1981; responsible for welfare of Indian population; Pres. OLGA ROJAS DE BAEZ.

Red de Inversiones y Exportaciones (REDIEX): Avda Mariscal López 3333, Asunción; tel. and fax (21) 66-5112; e-mail info@rediex.gov.py; internet www.rediex.gov.py; replaced ProParaguay in 2007; responsible for promoting investment in Paraguay and the export of national products; Dir VICTOR VARELA.

Red Rural de Organizaciones Privadas de Desarrollo: Manuel Domínguez 1045, Asunción; tel. (21) 22-9740; e-mail redrural@telesurf.com.py; internet www.redrural.org.py; f. 1989; co-ordinating body for rural devt orgs; Gen. Co-ordinator IDALINA GÓMEZ; Sec. HEBE GONZÁLEZ.

CHAMBERS OF COMMERCE

Cámara Nacional de Comercio y Servicios de Paraguay: Estrella 540–550, Asunción; tel. (21) 49-3321; fax (21) 44-0817; e-mail info@ccparaguay.com.py; internet www.ccparaguay.com.py; f. 1898; fmrly Cámara y Bolsa de Comercio; name changed 2002; Pres. MARTÍN HEISECKE; Gen. Man. Lic. MIGUEL RIQUELME OLAZAR.

Cámara de Comercio Paraguayo-Americano (Paraguayan-American Chamber of Commerce): Edif. El Faro Internacional, 4°, Of. 1, General Díaz 521, Asunción; tel. and fax (21) 44-2135; e-mail pamcham@pamcham.com.py; internet www.pamcham.com.py; f. 1981; c. 120 mem. cos.

Cámara de Comercio Paraguayo-Arabe: Próceres de Mayo 296, esq. Ana Díaz, Asunción; tel. 22-7197; fax 21-3240; Pres. MOHAMED RAHAL.

Cámara de Comercio Paraguayo-Británico: Avda Boggiani 5848, Asunción; tel. 61-2611; fax 60-5007; e-mail britcham@conexion.com.py; Pres. RONALD BURNETT.

Cámara de Comercio Paraguayo-Chileno: Guido Spano 1687, Asunción; tel. and fax 66-3085; e-mail ccpch@quanta.com.py; Pres. GUSTAVO OLMEDO SISUL.

Cámara de Comercio Paraguayo-Francesa (CCPF): Yegros 837, 1°, Of. 12, CP 3009, Asunción; tel. 49-7852; fax 44-6324; e-mail info@ccpf.com.py; internet www.ccpf.com.py; Pres. HUMBERT SOLENTE; Man. IRIS FELIU DE FLEITAS.

EMPLOYERS' ORGANIZATIONS

Asociación de Empresas Financieras del Paraguay (ADEFI): Edif. Ahorros Paraguayos, Torre II, 6°, Of. 05, General Díaz 471, Asunción; tel. (21) 44-8298; fax (21) 49-8071; e-mail adefi@conexion.com.py; internet www.adefi.org.py; f. 1975; grouping of financial cos; Pres. BELTRÁN MACCHI SALÍN.

Asociación Paraguaya de la Calidad: Luis Alberto de Herrera 195, 19°, Asunción; tel. (21) 44-7348; fax (21) 45-0705; e-mail apc@apc.org.py; internet www.apc.org.py; f. 1988; grouping of cos to promote quality of goods and services; Pres. MIGUEL ANGEL CASTILLO.

Federación de la Producción, Industria y Comercio (FEPRINCO): Edif. Union Club, Palma 751, 3°, esq. O'Leary y Ayolas, Asunción; tel. (21) 44-6634; fax (21) 44-6638; e-mail feprinco@quanta.com.py; org. of private-sector business execs; Pres. MIGUEL ANGEL CARRIZOSA GALLIANO.

Unión Industrial Paraguaya (UIP): Cerro Corá 1038, entre Estados Unidos y Brasil, Casilla 782, Asunción; tel. (21) 21-2556; fax (21) 21-3360; e-mail uip@uip.org.py; internet www.uip.org.py; f. 1936; org. of business entrepreneurs; Pres. Ing. GUILLERMO STANLEY.

UTILITIES

Electricity

Administración Nacional de Electricidad (ANDE): Avda España 1268, Asunción; tel. (21) 21-1001; fax (21) 21-2371; e-mail ande@ande.gov.py; internet www.ande.gov.py; f. 1949; national electricity board, privatization plans cancelled in June 2002; Pres. MARTÍN GONZÁLEZ GUGGIARI; Sec.-Gen. MIRNA E. CHAMORRO.

Entidad Binacional Yacyretá: see Argentina—Utilities.

PARAGUAY

Itaipú Binacional: Centro Administrativo, Ruta Internacional Km 3.5, Avda Señor Rodríguez 150, Ciudad del Este; tel. (61) 57-2600; e-mail itaipu@itaipu.gov.br; internet www.itaipu.gov.br; f. 1974; jtly owned by Paraguay and Brazil; hydroelectric power-station on Brazilian-Paraguayan border; 1.3m. GWh of electricity produced in 2004; Dir-Gen. (Paraguay) Dr Víctor Bernal Garay.

Water

Empresa de Servicios Sanitarios del Paraguay Sociedad Anónima (ESSAP, SA): José Berges 516, entre Brasil y San José, Asunción; tel. (21) 21-0330; fax (21) 21-2624; e-mail secretaria@essap.com.py; fmrly Corporación de Obras Sanitarias (CORPOSANA); responsible for public water supply, sewage disposal and drainage; privatization plans suspended in 2002; Pres. Marcial Manuel López Cano.

TRADE UNIONS

Central Nacional de Trabajadores (CNT): Piribebuy 1078, Asunción; tel. (21) 44-4084; fax (21) 49-2154; e-mail cnt@telesurf.com.py; Sec.-Gen. Eduardo Ojeda; 80,000 mems.

Central de Sindicatos de Trabajadores del Estado Paraguayo (Cesitep): Asunción; Pres. Reinaldo Barreto Medina.

Central Unitaria de Trabajadores (CUT): San Carlos 836, Asunción; tel. (21) 44-3936; fax (21) 44-8482; f. 1989; Pres. Alan Flores; Sec.-Gen. Jorge Alvarenga.

Confederación Paraguaya de Trabajadores (CPT) (Confederation of Paraguayan Workers): Yegros 1309–33 y Simón Bolívar, Asunción; tel. (21) 44-4921; fax (21) 20-5070; e-mail sixto10@telesurf.com.py; f. 1951; Pres. Sixto Alonso Mendoza; Sec.-Gen. Patrocinio Carmona; 43,500 mems from 189 affiliated groups.

Coordinadora Agrícola de Paraguay (CAP): Asunción; farmers' org.; Pres. Héctor Cristaldo.

Organización de Trabajadores de Educación del Paraguay (OTEP): Avda del Pueblo 845 con Ybyra Pyta, Barrio Santa Lucía, Lambaré; tel. and fax (21) 55-5525; e-mail otepsn@highway.com.py.

Transport

RAILWAYS

Ferrocarriles del Paraguay: México 145, Casilla 453, Asunción; tel. (21) 44-3273; fax (21) 44-2733; e-mail ferroca@rieder.net.py; internet www.ferrocarriles.com.py; f. 1854; state-owned since 1961; 376 km of track; scheduled for privatization; Pres. Lauro Manuel Ramírez López.

ROADS

In 1999 there were an estimated 29,500 km of roads, of which 14,986 km were paved. The Pan-American Highway runs for over 700 km in Paraguay and the Trans-Chaco Highway extends from Asunción to Bolivia.

SHIPPING

Administración Nacional de Navegación y Puertos (ANNP) (National Shipping and Ports Administration): Cólon y El Paraguayo Independiente, Asunción; tel. (21) 49-5086; fax (21) 49-7485; e-mail annp@mail.pla.net.py; internet www.annp.gov.py; f. 1965; responsible for ports services and maintaining navigable channels in rivers and for improving navigation on the Rivers Paraguay and Paraná; Pres. (vacant).

Inland Waterways

Flota Mercante Paraguaya SA (FLOMEPASA): Estrella 672-686, Casilla 454, Asunción; tel. (21) 44-7409; fax (21) 44-6010; boats and barges up to 1,000 tons displacement on Paraguay and Paraná rivers; cold storage ships for use Asunción–Buenos Aires–Montevideo; Pres. Capt. Aníbal Gino Pertile R.; Commercial Dir Dr Emigdio Duarte Sostoa.

Ocean Shipping

Compañía Paraguaya de Navegación de Ultramar, SA: Presidente Franco 625, 2°, Casilla 77, Asunción; tel. (21) 49-2137; fax (21) 44-5013; f. 1963 to operate between Asunción, US and European ports; 10 vessels; Exec. Pres. Juan Bosch B.

Navemar S.R.L.: B. Constant 536, 1°, Casilla 273, Asunción; tel. (21) 49-3122; 5 vessels.

Transporte Fluvial Paraguayo S.A.C.I.: Edif. de la Encarnación, 13°, 14 de Mayo 563, Asunción; tel. (21) 49-3411; fax (21) 49-8218; e-mail tfpsaci@tm.com.py; Admin. Man. Daniella Charbonnier; 1 vessel.

CIVIL AVIATION

The major international airport, Aeropuerto Internacional Silvio Pettirossi, is situated 15 km from Asunción. A second international airport, Aeropuerto Internacional Guaraní, 30 km from Ciudad del Este, was inaugurated in 1996.

National Airlines

Transportes Aéreos del Mercosur (TAM Mercosur): Aeropuerto Internacional Silvio Pettirossi, Hangar TAM/ARPA, Luque, Asunción; tel. (21) 49-1039; fax (21) 64-5146; e-mail tammercosur@uninet.com.py; internet www.tam.com.py; f. 1963 as Líneas Aéreas Paraguayas (LAP); name changed as above in 1997; services to destinations within South America; 80% owned by TAM Linhas Aéreas (Brazil); Pres. Miguel Candia.

Aerolíneas Paraguayas (ARPA): Terminal ARPA, Aeropuerto Internacional Silvio Pettirossi, Asunción; tel. (21) 21-5072; fax (21) 21-5111; f. 1994; domestic service; wholly owned by Transportes Aéreos del Mercosur (TAM Mercosur).

Tourism

Tourism is undeveloped, but, with recent improvements in infrastructure, efforts were being made to promote the sector. Tourist arrivals in Paraguay in 2005 totalled 340,845 (of whom some 61% came from Brazil). In that year tourism receipts were US $96m.

Secretaría Nacional de Turismo: Palma 468, Asunción; tel. (21) 49-4110; fax (21) 49-1230; e-mail ministra@senatur.gov.py; internet www.senatur.gov.py; f. 1998; Exec. Sec. Liz Rosanna Crámer Campos.

PERU

Introductory Survey

Location, Climate, Language, Religion, Flag, Capital

The Republic of Peru lies in western South America, bordered by Ecuador and Colombia to the north, by Brazil and Bolivia to the east, and by Chile to the south. Peru has a coastline of more than 2,300 km (1,400 miles) on the Pacific Ocean. The climate varies with altitude, average temperatures being about 11°C (20°F) lower in the Andes mountains than in the coastal plain. The rainy season is between October and April, with heavy rainfall in the tropical forests. Temperatures in Lima are usually between 13°C (55°F) and 28°C (82°F). The three official languages are Spanish, Quechua and Aymará. Almost all of the inhabitants profess Christianity, and the great majority are adherents of the Roman Catholic Church. The civil flag (proportions 2 by 3) has three equal vertical stripes, of red, white and red. The state flag additionally has the national coat of arms (a shield divided into three unequal segments: red, with a golden cornucopia spilling coins of yellow and white at the base, blue, with a yellow vicuña in the dexter chief, and white, with a green tree in the sinister chief; all surmounted by a green wreath, and framed by branches of palm and laurel, tied at the bottom with a red and white ribbon) in the centre of the white stripe. The capital is Lima.

Recent History

Since independence from Spain, declared in 1821 and finally achieved in 1824, Peruvian politics have been characterized by alternating periods of civilian administration and military dictatorship. In the early 1920s opposition to the dictatorial regime of President Augusto Bernardino Leguía resulted in the creation of the Alianza Popular Revolucionaria Americana (APRA), Peru's oldest political party to command mass support. The party, founded as a nationalist revolutionary movement, was formally established in Peru as the Partido Aprista Peruano (PAP) in 1930, when Leguía was deposed and the party's founder (and its leader for more than 50 years), Dr Víctor Raúl Haya de la Torre, returned from enforced exile in Mexico. A long-standing tradition of hostility developed between the Apristas and the armed forces, and the party was banned in 1931–45, and again in 1948–56.

During 1945–63 political power shifted regularly between the armed forces and elected government. In 1948 Dr José Luis Bustamante y Rivera was deposed by Gen. Manuel Odría, following a right-wing military rebellion. Odría established a military junta which governed until 1950, when the General was elected unopposed to the presidency, and subsequently appointed a cabinet composed of military officers and civilians. In 1956 Odría was succeeded by Dr Manuel Prado y Ugartache (who had been President in 1939–45). An inconclusive presidential election in 1962 precipitated military intervention, and power was assumed by Gen. Ricardo Pérez Godoy, at the head of a military junta. In March 1963, however, Pérez was supplanted by his second-in-command, Gen. Nicolás Lindley López.

Fernando Belaúnde Terry, the joint candidate of his own Acción Popular (AP) party and the Partido Demócrata Cristiano, was elected President in June 1963. An increase in internal disturbances in predominantly Indian areas resulted in the temporary suspension of constitutional guarantees in 1965–66 and an intensive military campaign of counter-insurgency. Lack of congressional support for the Government contributed to a succession of ministerial crises which, together with continuing internal unrest, prompted renewed military intervention in October 1968, when Gen. Juan Velasco Alvarado assumed the presidency, dissolved Congress and appointed a military cabinet.

Despite the re-emergence of internal disturbances and dissension within the armed forces, Velasco retained power until August 1975, when he was overthrown and replaced by Gen. Francisco Morales Bermúdez. In July 1977 President Morales announced plans for the restoration of civilian rule. Accordingly, a national election was conducted in June 1978 to select the members of a constituent assembly, which was to draft a new constitution in preparation for presidential and congressional elections. In the election, PAP emerged as the largest party, and in July the assembly elected the 83-year-old Dr Haya de la Torre to be its President. The new Constitution, adopted in July 1979, provided for elections by universal adult suffrage, and extended the franchise to the sizeable illiterate population.

The presidential contest of May 1980 was won decisively by Belaúnde. At the same time, the AP won an outright majority in the Cámara de Diputados (Chamber of Deputies) and also secured the greatest representation in the Senado (Senate). The new organs of state were inaugurated in July, when the new Constitution became fully effective. While Belaúnde sought to liberalize the economy and to reverse many of the agrarian and industrial reforms implemented under Velasco, much of his term of office was dominated by the increasing threat to internal stability posed by the emergence, in the early 1980s, of the Maoist terrorist group, the Sendero Luminoso (SL—Shining Path). The situation deteriorated following the uncompromising response of the armed forces to terrorist activity in a designated emergency zone, which extended to 13 provinces (primarily in the departments of Ayacucho, Huancavelica and Apurímac) by mid-1984, and a dramatic increase in violent deaths and violations of human rights was reported.

At elections in April 1985 Alan Gabriel Ludwig García Pérez (the candidate for PAP) received 46% of the total votes in the presidential poll, while PAP secured a majority in both houses (the Cámara and the Senado) of the Congreso (legislature). García's victory was ensured in May, prior to a second round of voting, when his closest opponent, Dr Alfonso Barrantes Lingán (of the left-wing Izquierda Unida coalition), withdrew his candidature. At his inauguration in July, García announced that his Government's priorities would be to arrest Peru's severe economic decline and to eradicate internal terrorism.

Despite PAP successes at municipal elections in 1986, widespread opposition to the Government's economic programme was manifested in a succession of well-supported general strikes in 1987 and 1988. Government plans in 1987 for the nationalization of Peru's banks and private financial and insurance institutions encountered considerable opposition from the financial sector, and prompted the creation of Libertad, a 'freedom movement' expressing opposition to the plans (which were subsequently modified), which was established under the leadership of a well-known writer, Mario Vargas Llosa. The authority of the García administration was further undermined by persistent rumours of military unrest, allegations of links between members of the Government and the right-wing paramilitary 'death squad', the Comando Rodrigo Franco, and by the continuing terrorist activities of the SL and a resurgence of activity by the Movimiento Revolucionario Tupac Amarú (MRTA) guerrilla group, in northeast Peru. In addition, the Government was criticized by international human rights organizations for its methods of combating political violence.

General elections took place on 8 April 1990, despite the attempts of the SL to disrupt the elections with another 'armed strike' and a campaign of bombing and looting. In the presidential poll Vargas Llosa, the candidate of the centre-right FREDEMO alliance (established in 1988 by the AP, Libertad and the Partido Popular Cristiano), obtained the largest percentage of the total votes cast, followed by a hitherto little-known agronomist, Alberto Fujimori, the candidate of the Cambio 90 group of independents. In a second round of voting, conducted on 10 June, Fujimori emerged as the successful candidate, having attracted late support from left-wing parties and from PAP. Following his inauguration in July, Fujimori announced the composition of a new centre-left Council of Ministers, with Juan Carlos Hurtado Miller, a member of the AP, as Prime Minister and Minister of Economy and Finance.

Proposals for economic readjustment announced in August 1990 abolished subsidies for consumers, thereby increasing prices by more than 3,000% for petrol and by as much as 600% for basic foods. Although these economic reforms secured Peru's rehabilitation within the international financial community, they provoked widespread opposition and industrial unrest (as well as the resignation of Hurtado). In November 1991, despite public and congressional dissent, Fujimori took advantage of a 150-day period of emergency legislative powers (granted to him in June in order that the country's potentially destabilizing economic and security problems might be addressed) to issue a series of economic decrees that represented a continuation of policies which concerned the elimination of state monopolies of telecommunications, postal networks and railways, the opening to private investment of the power sector, the privatization of schools and a reform of the health and social security services.

On 5 April 1992 Fujimori announced the immediate suspension of the 1979 Constitution and the dissolution of the Congreso, pending a comprehensive restructuring of the legislature. The President maintained that the reform of the Congreso was essential in order to eradicate 'corruption and inefficiency', to enable him to implement a programme of 'pacification' of the nation by combating terrorism and drugs-trafficking, and also fully to implement free-market economic policies. In the interim an Emergency and National Reconstruction Government would govern the country, and legislative power would be exercised by the President, with the approval of the Council of Ministers. Fujimori also announced a reform of the judiciary. The constitutional coup (or 'autogolpe') was implemented with the full co-operation and support of the armed forces. On the following day the Prime Minister, Alfonso de los Heros Pérez Albela, resigned in protest, and was replaced by Oscar de la Puente; most government ministers, however, elected to remain in office. Members of the dissolved parliament declared Fujimori to be incapable of continuing in office, although an attempt to establish Máximo San Román, the First Vice-President, as the head of an alternative 'constitutional government' was undermined by a lack of domestic and international support. Moreover, while Fujimori's actions prompted outrage from politicians, the judiciary and the media, popular reaction to the 'autogolpe' was less hostile. Bolstered by demonstrations of public support for his actions, Fujimori dismissed 13 of Peru's 28 Supreme Court judges, whom he accused of corruption, and detained several prominent opposition party figures. The President of the Central Bank was also removed from office, as were 134 judges. The Organization of American States (OAS, see p. 360) deplored Fujimori's actions, and dispatched a mission to attempt to effect a reconciliation between the legislature and the executive. Later in April Fujimori announced that congressional elections would be conducted in February 1993.

The threat posed to Fujimori's programme of radical reform by economic constraints resulting from the suspension of international financial aid to Peru prompted the revision of the timetable for a return to democracy, and in June 1992 Fujimori confirmed that national elections would be conducted in October to a unicameral constituent congress, which would then draft a new constitution. The President also announced that, pending approval of a new document, the 1979 Constitution would be reinstated without certain articles that might 'impede the progress of the Government'.

A 'National Dialogue for Peace and Development', comprising a series of discussions with representatives of the political opposition and with the public, sought to identify important issues for future consideration by the new Congreso Constituyente Democrático (CCD). Elections to the CCD, conducted on 22 November 1992 and attended by OAS observers, were a qualified success for pro-Government parties. An electoral coalition of Cambio 90 and the Nueva Mayoría (a new independent party supported by many former cabinet ministers), headed by Fujimori's former Minister of Energy and Mines, Jaime Yoshiyama Tanaka (who was subsequently elected President of the CCD), secured 44 of the 80 congressional seats. The only significant opposition party not to boycott the elections, the Partido Popular Cristiano, took eight seats. In December, at the inaugural meeting of the CCD, Yoshiyama identified its immediate aims as the restoration of the autonomy of the judiciary, the eradication of terrorism, the generation of employment and of favourable conditions for foreign investment, and the projection of an enhanced national image abroad. In January 1993, having formally reinstated the 1979 Constitution, the CCD confirmed Fujimori as constitutional Head of State. Following the resignation of de la Puente's Government in July, Alfonso Bustamente y Bustamente was appointed Prime Minister in August.

The final text of the draft Constitution, which enhanced presidential powers and provided for the establishment of a unicameral legislature, was approved by the CCD in September 1993. Among the text's most controversial articles were the introduction of the death penalty for convicted terrorists and a provision permitting a President of the Republic to be re-elected for a successive five-year term of office. At a national referendum held on 31 October—the first occasion on which such popular consultation had been sought in Peru—the Constitution was narrowly approved, by an overall 52% of the votes cast. The Constitution was promulgated on 29 December, at a ceremony boycotted by opposition members of the CCD.

In a presidential election conducted on 9 April 1995, Fujimori secured an unexpected outright victory over his closest opponent, Javier Pérez de Cuéllar de la Guerra (the former UN Secretary-General and the candidate of the Unión por el Perú—UPP), obtaining 64% of the total votes. In concurrent legislative elections, Fujimori's coalition movement, Cambio 90-Nueva Mayoría, also secured an absolute majority in the unicameral Congreso. The composition of the new Government, installed following Fujimori's inauguration in July, was largely unaltered. Efraín Goldenberg, who had succeeded Bustamante as Prime Minister in February 1994, was replaced by Dante Córdova Blanco.

In June 1995 legislation was approved by the Congreso granting an amnesty to all members of the military, police and intelligence forces who had been convicted of human rights violations committed since 1980 in the internal conflict against separatist violence; ostensibly the legislation was to promote national reconciliation, although it was also widely thought to have been introduced by the President in order to consolidate his relationship with the military leadership. The legislation attracted broad criticism from opposition parties, and internationally. In August an international warrant was issued for the arrest of former President Alan García, who had been accused of receiving bribes and other corrupt practices during his term of office.

In April 1996 the sudden resignation of the Prime Minister demonstrated the extent of disunity within the Government, particularly over economic policy. Alberto Pandolfi Arbulu was appointed Prime Minister, and the Government's privatization programme was accelerated. Meanwhile, Fujimori was attempting to formulate legislation that would allow him to stand for election for a third presidential term. A congressional committee approved a new 'interpretation' of the Constitution in August (on the grounds that Fujimori was first elected under the 1979 Constitution), and the legislation was approved by the Congreso later in that month (with a boycott of the vote by the majority of opposition politicians). In January 1997 the Constitutional Court ruled the new interpretation of the Constitution to be invalid.

On 17 December 1996 MRTA activists launched an assault on the residence of the Japanese ambassador in Lima, and detained by force more than 500 people attending an evening reception. Among those taken hostage were the Peruvian Ministers of Foreign Affairs and of Agriculture, at least nine foreign ambassadors and other diplomatic personnel, leading police and security officials and representatives of the business community. The MRTA activists' demands included the release of all 458 MRTA prisoners in detention in Peru, safe passage to an area in Peru's central highlands, greater economic assistance to the country's poorest people and payment of a 'war tax'. On 27 December Fujimori declared a state of emergency in Lima. On 22 April 1997 Peruvian troops launched an unexpected assault on the ambassador's residence, ending the MRTA siege. Two soldiers and all 14 of the MRTA activists were killed in the operation, and one of the 72 remaining hostages died of heart failure. President Fujimori presented the assault as a measure of his Government's uncompromising stance against terrorism; it was later alleged that some of the MRTA members might have been killed after having surrendered to army officers.

Fujimori's immediate hopes for election to a third presidential term were encouraged in February 1998 by the Supreme Court's announcement that it could foresee no significant obstacle to Fujimori's candidature in 2000. However, a final decision on his eligibility was to be decided by the Jurado Nacional Electoral (JNE—National Electoral Board). The Government was accused of further supporting the subversion of normal judicial processes in March, when the Congreso approved a new law severely reducing the regulatory powers of the National Council of the Judiciary. The legislation prompted the resignation of all seven members of the Council, and the cancellation, by the World Bank, of a substantial loan to the Peruvian Government, intended for judicial reform projects.

There was further evidence of the President's circumvention of the traditional role of the judiciary in May 1998 when Fujimori introduced draconian anti-crime legislation by decree (subsequently approved by the Congreso) seeking to extend the extreme powers and penalties employed in the recent successful anti-terrorism initiatives (see below) to other areas of criminal activity. Among the provisions of the new law were plans to increase the powers of military tribunals to try civilians. Despite calls by international observers and opposition groups for greater judicial independence and respect for human rights, in December the Congreso voted to extend the period of judicial reorganization initiated by Fujimori's administration for a further two-year period.

Fujimori's popularity continued to wane during 1998 (the ruling party chose not to field candidates for local elections conducted in October, as a consequence), and the President's attempts to consolidate his position and reassert his authority resulted in repeated changes to the Council of Ministers. In April 1999 the entire Council of Ministers resigned, amid a rift over corruption allegations against officials at the state customs authority. Another mass cabinet resignation followed in October, in accordance with the law requiring public officials intending to stand for election to resign their posts six months before the April 2000 polls. Alberto Bustamante Belaúnde was appointed Prime Minister in a new cabinet.

Meanwhile, Fujimori's continuing efforts to secure support for a third presidential term were encouraged by the defeat in the Congreso, in September 1998, of an opposition proposal to decide the question of Fujimori's eligibility by a national referendum. Opposition to Fujimori's possible re-election was vociferously expressed when a broad range of labour unions and political parties participated in April 1999 in a one-day general strike. However, this, together with a demonstration involving some 20,000 people in October, failed to prevent the announcement in December of Fujimori's candidature on behalf of the Perú 2000 alliance (a new movement formed to support the incumbent's re-election campaign). On 1 January 2000 the JNE, which was dominated by Fujimori's supporters, ratified his registration as a candidate in response to a legal challenge issued by the political opposition. The election board's rationale was that although the Constitution did not permit a President to serve three terms, Fujimori had only served one term under the current Constitution, as amended in 1993, and therefore was eligible for re-election. The ruling precipitated further street protests. Allegations of electoral fraud and campaign misconduct were widespread. Accusations by opposition leaders included government manipulation of the media to deny them equal access, the use of state resources to promote Fujimori's campaign, and alleged falsification of more than 1m. signatures by members of Perú 2000 to register Fujimori's candidacy. Opposition plans to reach a consensus on a single candidate to challenge Fujimori did not materialize, and in January 2000 seven opposition candidates registered to stand for election to the presidency.

The general election proceeded on 9 April 2000. During the vote count opposition candidates and international observers alleged that the ballot was marred by fraud. US officials issued increasingly strong statements stressing the need for a second round of voting as the only credible proof of legitimacy. At the final count Fujimori officially received 49.9% of the votes cast and Alejandro Toledo (the first presidential candidate of Amerindian descent) 40.2%. In the congressional elections Perú 2000 won 52 of the 120 seats, while Perú Posible (PP), which supported Toledo, won 29 seats. The JNE resisted both domestic and external pressure for a postponement of the second round (scheduled for 28 May), in order to correct irregularities noted in the first round. In response, Toledo withdrew his candidature one week before the election and urged his supporters to spoil their votes in protest. Violent incidents, including the fire-bombing of the presidential palace, followed the JNE decision. The OAS and US-based Carter Center suspended monitoring of the election, citing difficulties with the computer system for tabulating votes. Amid further mass demonstrations, Fujimori contested the election effectively unopposed (although the JNE ruled that Toledo remained a candidate and refused to remove his name from the ballot papers), taking 51.2% of the total votes; Toledo received 17.7%. Excluding spoiled (29.9%) and blank (1.2%) papers, the incumbent was thus returned to office with 74.3% of the valid votes cast. The result was denounced as invalid by the political opposition and by the US Government (though it later moderated its position, describing the outcome as imperfect). Fujimori's inauguration on 28 July was accompanied by violent protests in Lima.

In September 2000 a major political scandal erupted after the disclosure of a video that allegedly showed Vladimiro Montesinos, the head of the national intelligence service and a close ally of the President, bribing an opposition member of the Congreso. In response Fujimori declared that new elections would be held, in which he would not participate. He also announced that the national intelligence service would be disbanded. At the same time, 10 Perú 2000 deputies defected to the opposition, thus depriving Fujimori of his majority in the legislature. Demonstrations, led by Toledo, demanded the immediate resignation of Fujimori and the arrest of Montesinos, who fled to Panama. On 5 October the Congreso approved OAS-mediated proposals paving the way for power to be transferred from Fujimori to his successor in mid-2001, as well as the disbandment of the Congreso to make way for a newly elected legislature. Later in the month Fujimori announced the replacement of the most senior commanders of the armed forces.

In late October 2000 the political crisis deepened, when Montesinos returned from Panama, after failing to obtain political asylum there. His apparent impunity supported the widely held view that the armed forces were protecting him. At the same time, the first Vice-President, Francisco Tudela, resigned in protest at government attempts to make new elections conditional upon an amnesty for those in the armed forces accused of human rights violations. Further OAS-sponsored negotiations between opposition groups and the Government led to the announcement that new elections would be held on 8 April 2001, without any conditions attached. An investigation into Montesinos' activities was launched, with charges ranging from corruption to torture and murder. In mid-November the Congreso voted to replace its pro-Fujimori President, Martha Hildebrandt Pérez Treviño, with Valentín Paniagua Corazao, effectively giving the opposition control of the legislature. The following day Fujimori travelled to Japan, from where, on 20 November, he resigned the presidency. The Congreso, however, refused to accept the resignation, and instead voted to dismiss Fujimori.

On 22 November 2000 Paniagua was appointed interim President. A new cabinet was sworn in three days later, which included Javier Pérez de Cuéllar as Prime Minister and Minister of Foreign Affairs. The aims of the interim Government, the mandate of which would last until 28 July 2001, included the achievement of a balanced budget and the strengthening of democracy. Several days later the new Minister of Defence, Walter Ledesma Rebaza, announced the decision to retire 13 generals who were known to be associates of Montesinos. A congressional commission, established in the same month to investigate the activities of Montesinos, uncovered hundreds of secret videotapes that seemed to compromise the integrity of judges, politicians, military officers, businessmen and bishops. In early December it was announced that the commission's investigations were to extend to Fujimori. In mid-December it was announced that Fujimori had taken up Japanese citizenship and was thus, in effect, protected from the threat of extradition from Japan. Nevertheless, in February 2001 corruption charges were formally filed against him. Furthermore, in August the Congreso voted unanimously to lift Fujimori's constitutional immunity and issued an international warrant for his arrest on the charge of dereliction of duty. Further charges of embezzlement and illicit enrichment were subsequently filed against the former President. However, the Japanese Government proved unresponsive to diplomatic pressure and stated that it had no intention of allowing Fujimori's extradition. In June 2005 the Japanese authorities rejected a further extradition request for Fujimori, citing a lack of further evidence to justify its approval. Meanwhile, in February of that year the Constitutional Court ruled that Fujimori was ineligible to stand in the presidential election scheduled for April 2006. In September 2005 the Government submitted to the Japanese authorities a third request for Fujimori's extradition. Then, in November, Fujimori was arrested on his arrival in Santiago, Chile, where he had arrived unannounced from Japan via Mexico. It was believed he had planned to conduct his election campaign from Chile. Immediately following the former President's arrest, the Peruvian authorities informally requested that Chile extradite him to Peru to face charges pending against him. An extradition petition was formally submitted to the Chilean Government in January 2006. Fujimori was released on bail in May. In November a Peruvian judge issued a new international arrest warrant for Fujimori on the charge that he ordered the killing of 20 members of the SL during a prison riot in May 1992. In September 2007, following a ruling by the Chilean Supreme Court, Fujimori was extradited to Peru on seven charges, including responsibility for the killing of 25 people in Barrios

Altos in 1991 and La Canuta in 1992 by an assassination squad known as the Colina group (see below). In December the former President went on trial in Lima accused of the Barrios Altos and La Canuta massacres and two instances of abduction.

In June 2001 Montesinos was arrested in Venezuela. He was sent back to Peru and, in July 2002, sentenced to nine years' imprisonment on charges relating to 'usurpation of power'. However, investigating judges subsequently brought a further 80 indictments against him, including murder, bribery and the illegal sale of weapons and narcotics. Following his first public trial in February 2003, Montesinos was convicted on corruption charges and sentenced to a further five years' imprisonment. In June 2004 Montesinos was found guilty of bribing newspaper editors to support Fujimori's re-election attempt in 2000, and was sentenced to a further 15 years' imprisonment. (In January 2005 eight newspaper chiefs were sentenced to five years in gaol after being convicted of receiving payments from Montesinos.) In August 2005 the trial began of Montesinos and 56 alleged members of the Colina group on charges of involvement in the disappearances of 36 people under the administration of President Fujimori. In September 2006 Montesinos received another gaol term of 20 years after being convicted of arms-trafficking.

In January 2001, only a few days after corruption charges against him were ruled to have expired under the statute of limitations, the former President, Alan García Pérez, returned to Peru to launch his campaign for the forthcoming presidential election. The first round of the election was held on 8 April, following a bitter campaign. Toledo won 37% of the votes cast, while García attracted 26% of the ballot and Lourdes Flores Nano of the Unidad Nacional alliance 24%. In concurrently held elections to the 120-seat Congreso, no party secured a majority: PP took 45 seats, PAP 27 and the Unidad Nacional 17, while the right-wing Frente Independiente Moralizador (FIM) won 12 seats. Election monitors declared the election process to have been open and fair. In the second round of the presidential election, held on 3 June, Toledo won with 53% of the vote. Toledo was inaugurated on 28 July. A broad-based 15-member cabinet was appointed, headed by lawyer Roberto Dañino and with Pedro Pablo Kuczynski as Minister of the Economy and Finance. The new Government promised to create more jobs, to reduce poverty and to put an end to the corruption of the Fujimori regime. In the previous month a congressional commission implicated 180 people in corruption scandals that took place during Fujimori's presidencies, including Gen. Walter Chacón Málaga, the recently appointed head of the armed forces.

However, the popularity of the Toledo Government declined sharply after only a few months in power, as high expectations were not matched by an increase in economic prospects. In September and October 2001 popular protests erupted throughout Peru as workers demanded more jobs and improvements to transport infrastructure and health care. Hundreds of former public sector workers protested in central Lima in January 2002 to demand their jobs back, and in February cotton producers and fishery workers staged demonstrations to demand more government aid. The protests proliferated, and in June, following a week of violent demonstrations in protest at government plans to privatize two regional electricity companies in Arequipa, the Minister of the Interior, Fernando Rospigliosi Capurro, resigned and the privatization process was suspended indefinitely. An extensive cabinet reshuffle was carried out in July, in which the Secretary-General of PP, Luis Solari, replaced Dañino as prime minister and Kuczynski was succeeded as Minister of Economy and Finance by Javier Silva Ruete. Nevertheless, popular dissatisfaction continued, and in January 2003 difficulties in the reform of the police service led to the resignation of the Minister of the Interior, Gino Costa Santolaya. He was succeeded by Alberto Sanabría Ortiz, a leading member of PP. In the same month the ruling party's congressional majority was reduced after five PP deputies resigned from the party in order to form a new movement, Perú Ahora.

In January 2003 a constitutional tribunal ruled that anti-terrorism legislation passed by the Fujimori administration had violated the Constitution. In order to alleviate the potential pressure on the judiciary, and to prevent the release of large numbers of alleged terrorists, the Congreso granted President Toledo exceptional temporary powers to legislate by decree on security issues. In February the Government announced that all military sentences passed during Fujimori's presidency were to be annulled. The courts would have 60 days to decide whether to release convicted individuals or commit them for retrial. In March anti-terrorism legislation received congressional approval.

In February 2003 coca growers staged demonstrations to demand the suspension of the Government's coca-eradication policy. The demonstrations escalated after a coca growers' federation leader, Nelson Palomino La Serna, was imprisoned on terrorism charges. At the end of the month the Government announced that some US $3,000m. was to be invested in a coca-eradication plan by 2020. Following 11 days of protests, a temporary truce was declared between the coca growers and the Government, although the Government refused to release Palomino La Serna and pledged to continue with its eradication strategy. Following 20 days of further negotiations, the Government agreed to give $11m. in direct aid to farmers affected by the eradication efforts. In April thousands of coca growers began a protest march towards Lima to demand subsidies for alternative crops and an increase in the amount of coca that could legally be grown. Following a meeting with the coca leaders, on 23 April President Toledo signed into law a decree which pledged that the eradication programme would be gradual and that the Government would discuss policy with the growers. Nevertheless, civil unrest continued; in May public sector workers began a series of demonstrations against salary levels and conditions, and farmers also continued to mount protests. Outbreaks of violence during these demonstrations prompted the President to declare a state of emergency in 12 of the country's 25 regions. In June the Government acquiesced to teachers' demands and in July the Congreso approved a series of limited fiscal measures intended to pay for the wage increases.

In 2003 and 2004 a rapid succession of government changes reflected President Toledo's deteriorating public credibility. Following the resignation of the entire cabinet in June 2003, the President appointed Beatriz Merino Lucero, previously the head of the tax inspection service, as prime minister. Merino Lucero proved popular, although she was obliged to resign in December following reports of nepotistic practices during her previous career and opposition allegations relating to her personal life. Carlos Ferrero Costa, a former President of the Congreso and a leading member of PP, was appointed to succeed her. In February 2004 Ferrero Costa effected a wide-ranging cabinet reshuffle, appointing a number of independent technocrats. A notable inclusion in the new cabinet was Pedro Pablo Kuczynski, who was reappointed Minister of the Economy and Finance. Furthermore, the reallocation of portfolios removed members of the FIM from the Government; nevertheless, the FIM pledged to continue its legislative alliance with PP.

Throughout 2004 President Toledo, his family and advisers were implicated in several major scandals. In January a purported recording was made public of his former legal adviser, César Almeyda, meeting with an associate of Vladimiro Montesinos. Almeyda was placed under house arrest at the end of January, but was cleared of any wrongdoing in June. Almeyda had been director of the national intelligence service until April 2003, when he had been forced to resign after being accused of authorizing the illegal use of surveillance technology. He was replaced by Adm. (retd) Alfonso Panizzo; however, in September Panizzo also tendered his resignation after it emerged that the intelligence agency had been spying on journalists investigating corrupt practices in public office. Panizzo's successor, Gen. (retd) Daniel Mora, held the post until March 2004, when the revelation that the agency had been compiling a dossier on Minister of the Interior Fernando Rospigliosi Capurro forced his resignation. In late March Toledo announced that the national intelligence agency was to be abolished. A government committee was immediately formed to oversee the establishment of a successor body, the Agencia de Inteligencia Estratégica. In early May Rospigliosi Capurro himself was forced to resign from the Government, having been held responsible for the authorities' inability to quell violent disturbances in the southern region of Puno, which had culminated in late April in the lynching of a local mayor. Javier Reátegui was named as the new Minister of the Interior.

In July 2004 the President's sister, Margarita Toledo, was ordered by a judge not to leave the country pending investigations into an alleged large-scale forging of signatures in 1999 in order to register PP for the 2000 legislative elections. Toledo and her husband were placed under house arrest in January 2005. A special congressional commission was established to investigate the case. Meanwhile, in July 2004 President Toledo granted investigators authority to probe bank accounts held in Peru and abroad by himself and his wife, Eliane Karp, following media accusations that they had accepted bribes. In mid-July a general strike was held in protest at, *inter alia*, the perceived corruption of the Toledo administration and its failure to fulfil electoral promises, as well as at the proposed free trade agreement with the USA and the Government's failure to act upon the findings of the Truth Commission (see below). Then, in late July, PP suffered another major set-back when its candidate for the presidency of the Congreso, Luis Solari, was defeated by Antero Flores-Aráoz of the Unidad Nacional. In early May a congressional committee concluded that Toledo and his associates had violated electoral law by forging signatures to register PP for the 2000 legislative elections. However, on 20 May the Congreso decided, by 57 to 47 votes, not to impeach President Toledo. In February 2006 the Supreme Court issued a ruling ending Margarita Toledo's house arrest; however, the charges of electoral fraud against her remained. Having left office in July, former President Toledo was charged in December in connection with the forgery case; he denied all allegations against him.

Meanwhile, on 1 January 2005 about 200 members of an ultranationalist grouping, the Movimiento Etnocacerista (allied to the Movimiento Nacionalista Peruana), forcibly occupied a police station in the southern province of Andahuaylas, taking 21 people hostage. President Toledo declared a state of emergency in the province and troops were dispatched to the region. The uprising, which resulted in the death of seven people, including four police officers, was primarily intended to force the resignation of President Toledo, whom the group accused of incompetence, corruption, acquiescence to foreign interests and the debasement of the armed forces. On 3–4 January the insurgents and their leader, Maj. (retd) Antauro Igor Humala Tasso, surrendered to the police; all were arrested on terrorism charges. In response to public dissatisfaction with the authorities' handling of events, Reátegui resigned as Minister of the Interior; he was succeeded by Félix Murazzo, the former head of the national police.

In August 2005, following the resignation of the Minister of Foreign Affairs, Manuel Rodrígues Cuadros, President Toledo appointed the outspoken FIM leader, Fernando Olivera, to succeed him. However, Olivera's appointment caused dissent within the Council of Ministers (ostensibly over Olivera's approval of the legalization of coca cultivation for traditional use in the province of Cusco), and prompted the resignation of the prime minister, Carlos Ferrero Costa. Three days after his appointment, Olivera resigned as Minister of Foreign Affairs. President Toledo was forced to effect a major cabinet reorganization. The appointment of Pedro Pablo Kuczynski, hitherto Minister of the Economy and Finance, as prime minister received broad congressional and popular approval, although Toledo's approval ratings remained low for the remainder of the year.

Presidential and legislative elections were held on 9 April 2006. According to opinion polls in the months preceding the ballot, the leading contender to secure the presidency was the candidate of the conservative Unidad Nacional, Lourdes Flores Nano. Her main rivals were former President García, representing PAP, and a left-wing nationalist candidate, Lt-Col (retd) Ollanta Moisés Humala Tasso, who was the nominee of a coalition of his own party, the Partido Nacionalista Peruano (PNP), and the UPP. However, Humala came first with 30.6% of valid votes, while García secured 24.3% and Flores 23.8%. A high turn-out, of 88.7%, was recorded. In the concurrently held legislative elections the UPP emerged as the largest party in the new Congreso, winning 45 of the 120 seats, while PAP took 36 seats, the Unidad Nacional 17 and the Alianza por el Futuro (a coalition of Cambio 90 and Nueva Mayoría) 13. At a second round of presidential voting, held on 4 June, García defeated Humala, securing 52.6% of the votes cast. By portraying himself as a moderate who had learned from past errors, García had succeeded in attracting sufficient numbers of votes from those who had supported Flores in the first round, despite concerns regarding the policies he had pursued during his previous period in office (1985–90). Moreover, fears that Humala's intention to increase state control over Peru's natural resources would damage the economy had been heightened by the controversial endorsement of his candidacy by the Venezuelan President, Lt-Col (retd) Hugo Rafael Chávez Frías, which had provoked considerable diplomatic tensions (see below).

García took office on 28 July 2006. At his inauguration the new President focused on the need to reduce poverty, announcing plans to lower administrative expenses, including his own salary and those of members of the Congreso and other officials, and to invest some US $1,600m. in rural areas to improve public infrastructure and the provision of education and health care. Nine independents were appointed to the new 16-member Council of Ministers, including Luis Carranza Ugarte, a former director of the central bank, as Minister of Economy and Finance, and Antonio García Belaúnde, a senior diplomat, as Minister of Foreign Affairs. Jorge del Castillo Gálvez, the Secretary-General of PAP and a close ally of García, was designated President of the Council of Ministers.

Although the UPP-PNP coalition had secured the largest number of seats in the legislature, divisions within the alliance became apparent soon after the elections, with the UPP favouring the adoption of a less confrontational approach towards García's administration. In late June 2006 Carlos Torres Caro and two other deputies withdrew from the coalition to form the Partido Demócrata Peruano, and in mid-August the UPP announced that it had severed ties with Humala and the PNP, leaving PAP as the largest bloc in the Congreso. Humala suffered a further set-back in late August, when he was formally charged with human rights abuses based on allegations of murder and torture by counter-insurgency troops under his command at a military base in the department of San Martín in 1992; the former army officer denied any involvement in rights violations, claiming that the charges were a form of political persecution. In late December Humala was also charged with rebellion in relation to his alleged involvement in the uprising at a police station in Andahuaylas in January 2005 (led by his imprisoned brother, Antauro—see above). Meanwhile, he formed a new alliance, the Gran Alianza Nacionalista Peruana (Gran Perú), with the aim of uniting the regional and local movements that had supported his candidacy in the presidential election.

In late August 2006 the Congreso endorsed the Government's five-year programme, which was dominated by measures to alleviate poverty. A social welfare fund was to be established to finance projects in the High Andes and the Amazon (where Humala had received strong support in the presidential election), while, under the 'Sierra Exportadora' initiative, US $102m. was to be spent over five years on cultivating 150,000 hectares of land in the Andes, with the aim of producing 730,000 metric tons of agricultural goods for export and creating 300,000 jobs. However, critics expressed doubt about the viability of the 'Sierra Exportadora' project, questioning the agricultural capacity of the area concerned. In mid-November García announced funding for 2007 of some $900m. for 11 social welfare programmes.

Non-governmental organizations (NGOs) expressed strong opposition to legislation, approved by the Congreso in early November 2006, that would force them to provide details of their funding and activities to a government agency, the Agencia Peruana de Cooperación Internacional (APCI), which would monitor their work to ensure that it was compatible with the Government's development policy. The Government relied on the support of the Unidad Nacional and the Alianza por el Futuro, as well as PAP, to secure the adoption of the controversial legislation, which it insisted was intended to promote transparency. Minor amendments to the legislation were adopted in early December, reducing the APCI's control over NGOs that received all their funding from abroad, without aid from the state.

President García suffered his first congressional defeat in January 2007, when the legislature rejected his proposal to apply the death penalty to those convicted of terrorism. Although the Constitution provided for the death penalty to be imposed in cases of treason in times of war or of terrorism, the penal code did not allow capital punishment for acts of terrorism. García declared that he would seek a referendum on the issue as, according to opinion polls, 80% of the public supported his proposal. However, other senior PAP officials considered that such a vote would contravene the Constitution, which prohibited referendums on initiatives that would suppress a fundamental right, such as the right to life.

Pilar Mazzetti, the independent Minister of the Interior, resigned in late February 2007, following accusations of corruption relating to the overpriced purchase of 469 police cars. Her replacement by Luis Alva Castro, a PAP veteran who had served as prime minister in 1985–87, prompted criticism from the PNP and the Unidad Nacional, which asserted that another unaffiliated minister should have been appointed. In May the Minister of Agriculture, Juan José Salazar García, was also forced to resign after acting against the Government's counter-narcotics policy (see below); he was replaced by Ismael Benavides Ferreyros.

The Government's reputation was damaged by widespread social unrest in several of the country's regions in July 2007. An indefinite strike, initiated in early July by teachers protesting against the introduction of a controversial education law, later escalated into a two-day general strike organized by the Confederación General de Trabajadores del Perú, during which one person was killed in Satipo. The army was mobilized to support the police in maintaining order. Later that month—following the end of the teachers' 15-day strike, as it became—the Government issued a number of decrees intended to restrict future unrest, including one prohibiting regional presidents and mayors from participating in strikes.

President García replaced six members of his cabinet in December 2007. Among other appointments, Antero Flores-Aráoz replaced Allan Wagner Tizón as Minister of Defence and Rosario Fernández Figueroa substituted María Zavala Valladares as Minister of Justice. It was announced that Wagner was to head the Peruvian delegation to the International Court of Justice (ICJ) in its maritime border dispute with Chile (see below). Further violent anti-Government demonstrations took place in February 2008, in particular by farmers striking in protest against the Government's agricultural policies. In May García created of a long-awaited Ministry of the Environment, subsequently appointing Antonio Brack Egg, a well-known ecologist, as Minister.

In the early 1990s the SL intensified its attacks against government and military targets, strategic power installations, commercial enterprises and rural defence groups. Following Fujimori's 'autogolpe' of April 1992 (effected partly in response to continuing congressional opposition to his efforts to expand the role of the armed forces), considerable concern was expressed by human rights organizations that the security forces would be permitted an increasing degree of autonomy. In September 1992 government forces succeeded in capturing the SL's founder and leader, Abimael Guzmán Reynoso, together with 20 prominent SL members. Guzmán was tried by a military court, where he was found guilty of treason and sentenced to life imprisonment. The SL, however, remained highly active, and in early 1993 was held responsible for the assassination of 20 candidates campaigning in local elections, and for attacks on rural communities that had formed self-defence militia units. The Government actively pursued its offensive against terrorist organizations in the mid-1990s, and publicized the detention of leading members of the SL, the MRTA and the dissident SL 'Sendero Rojo' faction (which advocated a continuation of the armed struggle). In 1999 Oscar Ramírez Durand (alias 'Comrade Feliciano'), the leader of Sendero Rojo, was captured and sentenced to life imprisonment.

The SL emerged again in 2001, with at least 31 deaths attributed to the terrorist organization in that year. In March 2002, three days before the US President, George W. Bush, was due to visit Peru, the first such visit by a serving US head of state, a car bomb killed 10 people and injured at least 40 more near the US embassy in Lima. The attack was attributed to a radical wing of the SL, and did not herald an immediate return to a sustained campaign of terrorism. In June 2003 the Government attributed the abduction of 60 pipeline construction workers in the Ayacucho region to the remnants of the SL; the hostages were subsequently released unharmed. In November the kidnappers' alleged leader, Jaime Zuñiga Córdova, was captured by security forces. In early November 2004 a retrial of Gúzman and 16 other SL militants began in a civilian court after the Constitutional Court ruled that their convictions by military court in 1992 were invalid. The retrial was subsequently suspended for 30 days following the resignation, at the request of the state prosecutor, of two of the three judges. President Toledo's announcement in late November 2004, in advance of the verdict, that none of the defendants would go free also contributed to the collapse of the retrial soon afterwards. In September 2005, however, the retrial of Guzmán began anew. Guzmán and his former second-in-command, Elena Iparraguirre, were both sentenced to life imprisonment in October 2006, while the 10 other defendants being retried received prison sentences ranging between 24 and 35 years. Meanwhile, in December 2005 13 police officers were killed in ambushes by SL guerrillas in rural provinces known to be centres of coca cultivation and cocaine production. It was believed the SL attacks were motivated by a desire to protect the illegal drugs trade, from which the SL allegedly derived a substantial part of its funding. In January 2006 President Toledo announced the establishment of a new police unit to combat the resurgence of the SL. Eight people, including five police officers, were killed in December in an ambush mounted against a coca-eradication operation near the town of Machente in Ayacucho. The Government dispatched some 500 commandos to the area, and eight alleged SL rebels were subsequently arrested. A month earlier the Minister of Defence had announced the deployment of 1,500 special troops to combat terrorism and drugs-trafficking in the regions of Ayacucho and Huancayo, in co-ordination with military personnel already stationed at bases in that area. An attack on a police station in Ocobamba, Apurímac, by some 50–80 armed men in early November 2007, which resulted in the death of a police officer, was blamed by the Government on SL members involved in the drugs trade. Increased military operations in the wake of the attack resulted in the killing, later that same month, of a senior SL commander, Mario Epifanio Espíritu Acosta.

The Peruvian Government attracted criticism from human rights organizations for its methods in achieving the apparent subjugation of the terrorist movements in the 1990s. In July 1999 Peru withdrew from the jurisdiction of the Inter-American Court of Human Rights (IACHR, see p. 361), a branch of the OAS, after the court ruled the previous month that new trials should be held for four Chilean MRTA activists who were serving life sentences. However, in January 2001, apparently as part of its effort to improve the country's international image, the Congreso approved Peru's return to the jurisdiction of the IACHR. In March, one week after the IACHR ruled that a military amnesty law approved in 1995 was incompatible with the American Convention on Human Rights, two former intelligence generals were arrested on charges of involvement in the early 1990s with the right-wing Colina death squad. In September 2001 the Attorney-General charged Fujimori with responsibility for two mass killings by the Colina group that took place in the early 1990s. In late November 2006 the IACHR ruled that the Peruvian state was responsible for the killings of 41 suspected members of the SL during an assault by the security forces on a prison in 1992, and ordered the current Government to pay compensation totalling some US $20m. to relatives of the deceased and to survivors who were injured during the attack. President García later declared that the Government would challenge the ruling. In a separate case, the court also held the state responsible for the abduction and subsequent summary execution by Colina of a professor and nine students from a Lima university campus, again in 1992; compensation of $1.8m. was to be paid to the victims' relatives. The opposition PNP suggested that the President's efforts to restore the death penalty in early 2007 (see above) were intended to undermine the authority of the IACHR ahead of the court's ruling on human rights cases dating from García's first term in office (1985–90).

In January 2001 a Truth Commission, composed of church leaders and civil and military representatives, was established to investigate the impact of the campaign against the guerrilla groups in the 1980s and 1990s. The Commission conducted some 17,000 interviews, and initially secured the support of the Peruvian army (although the navy refused to co-operate). In August 2003 the body presented its findings, which estimated the number of deaths during the conflict at some 69,000, twice the previous official total, with some 6,000 individuals reported as 'disappeared'. Nevertheless, despite the report's conclusion that the SL was responsible for the greater part of the killings, its conclusions were criticized by elements of the Roman Catholic Church, the military and PAP. In November President Toledo publicly apologized for the state's actions during the period and announced a US $817m. plan to improve social conditions in the regions most affected by the violence.

In February 1990, in Cartagena, Colombia, the Presidents of Peru, Colombia, Bolivia and the USA signed the Cartagena Declaration, pledging the intensification of efforts to combat the consumption, production and trafficking of illegal drugs. However, commitments to fund subsequent anti-drugs schemes in Peru were suspended by the US Administration as a result of international criticism of the Peruvian Government's record on human rights and its flouting of accepted democratic processes. In January 1996 responsibility for combating the drugs trade was transferred from the military to the national police force, following a series of allegations that army officers had themselves been involved in illegal trafficking. A new bilateral agreement to combat the drugs trade was signed with the USA in July. Following the approval of the Andean Trade Promotion and Drug Eradication Act by the US Congress in August 2002, it was announced that Peru qualified for expanded US benefits and trade preferences. In March 2003 a new US $3,000m. development strategy for the regions of Peru affected by coca cultivation was announced; the plans envisaged the reforestation of 1m. hectares of arable land judged to be capable of producing coca, and the replanting of some 500,000 ha with alternative crops. The Government also envisaged that the new initiatives would lead to the creation of some 2.5m. jobs by 2020, with the complete elimination of coca in the area under illegal cultivation (which totalled approximately 24,600 ha). However, in February 2005 it was reported that US funding to the Andean region for drugs eradication would prioritize Colombia over Bolivia and Peru, which were to receive some 16% less in 2005 (Peru's funding would total some $115m. and $97m. in 2005 and 2006, respectively). There was speculation that the reduction of funding to Peru reflected the US Administration's disappointment with the lack of progress made by the Toledo Government in coca eradication. In that same month Nils Ericsson, head of the Comisión Nacional para el Desarrollo y Vida sin Drogas (Devida—Peru's anti-narcotics agency), announced that some 17,000 ha of coca had been planted in 2004, exceeding the quantities eradicated, and that cocaine production had increased by 13% in the previous year, to 160 metric tons. In October 2005 Ericsson announced that international funding for Peru's counter-narcotics operations in 2006 would be some $10m. less than in the previous year. In September 2006 Rómulo Pizarro Tomasio, Minister of the Interior under Toledo, replaced Ericsson as head of Devida. Pizarro announced that García's new Government intended to increase the state's presence in coca-producing areas and to extend crop-replacement programmes. However, US funding for drugs eradication continued to decline, with a total of only $66m. proposed for 2007/08. In mid-March 2007, following protests in the province of Tocache by coca growers who claimed that crops destined for sale to the state coca company were being destroyed by the authorities, the Minister of Agriculture, Juan José Salazar, agreed to suspend coca eradication in the province for 10 days and provide compensation for those whose crops had been mistakenly destroyed. Salazar subsequently proposed a shift in Peru's counter-narcotics policy, to focus more on combating the production and smuggling of cocaine rather than the eradication of coca. Salazar provoked further controversy in May by signing an agreement with coca producers in the Cusco region that committed the Government to re-evaluating its membership of the Vienna Convention on Narcotic Drugs (ratified by Peru in November 1991, and which required that the authorities implement measures to control coca production). Following Salazar's resignation over the issue later that month, the new Minister of Agriculture, Ismael Benavides, signalled that his ministry would avoid involvement in coca eradication, stating that it was the sole responsibility of Devida.

Meeting in Caracas, Venezuela, in May 1991, the Presidents of the five South American nations comprising the Andean Group (now the Andean Community of Nations, see p. 170) formalized their commitment to the full implementation of an Andean free trade area by the end of 1995, to be achieved by a gradual reduction in tariffs and other trade barriers. An agreement to restructure the Group into the Andean Community, thus strengthening regional integration, was signed in March 1996 in Trujillo. In June 1997 the Peruvian Government announced plans to abolish tariffs on some 2,500 goods entering Peru from within the Community (with immediate effect), and its intention to remove tariffs on a further 3,500 goods (including more than 600 deemed 'sensitive') by 2005. Peru was admitted as an associate member of the Southern Common Market (Mercosur—Mercado Común del Sur, see p. 391) in August 2003. In August 2002 the US Andean Trade Promotion and Drug Eradication Act (ATPDEA) came into operation, which awarded Peru significant new tariff reductions on exports to the USA, including clothing and manufactures. In late February 2008 the ATPDEA was renewed for a further 10 months. Peru also concluded a free trade agreement with the USA in December 2005, in spite of vociferous opposition from left-wing and indigenous groups. The free trade agreement was ratified by the Peruvian Congreso in June 2006, and by the US House of Representatives and Senate in November and December 2007, respectively.

A long-standing border dispute with Ecuador over the Cordillera del Cóndor descended into armed conflict in January 1981. A cease-fire was declared a few days later, under the auspices of the guarantors (Argentina, Brazil, Chile and the USA) of the Rio de Janeiro Protocol of 1942, which had awarded the area, affording access to the Amazon river basin, to Peru. However, the Protocol had never been recognized by Ecuador, and, despite mutual efforts to achieve a constructive dialogue, the matter continued to be a source of tension and recurrent skirmishes between the two countries. In January 1995 serious fighting broke out. In February representatives of both countries, meeting in Brazil under the auspices of the Rio de Janeiro Protocol guarantors, approved a provisional cease-fire. Following further negotiations, on 17 February both countries signed the Itamaraty Peace Declaration. Foreign affairs ministers from both countries, meeting in Uruguay at the end of the month, signed the Montevideo Declaration, which ratified the Itamaraty agreement. The withdrawal of forces from the disputed border area was achieved by mid-May. None the less, reports of further armed clashes prompted requests from both countries for an extension of the observer mission. Agreement on the delimitation of a demilitarized zone in the disputed Cenepa river region came into effect on 1 August. In September Fujimori agreed to reopen the border with Ecuador for commercial purposes, and in November both countries agreed to pursue further confidence-building measures. In October 1996 the Ministers of Foreign Affairs of both countries, meeting in Chile under the auspices of the guarantor countries, signed the Santiago Agreement, which was to provide a framework for a settlement of the border issue.

Following further negotiations in early 1998 a number of commissions were established to examine specific aspects of a potential agreement between Peru and Ecuador, including a trade and navigation treaty and the fixing of frontier markers on the ground in the Cordillera del Cóndor. Talks culminated in the signing of an accord in Brasília, Brazil, in October by the Ministers of Foreign Affairs of Peru and Ecuador in the presence of the two countries' Presidents and of six other regional leaders. The accord confirmed Peru's claim regarding the delineation of the border, but granted Ecuador navigation and trading rights on the Amazon and its tributaries and the opportunity to establish two trading centres in Peru (although this was not to constitute sovereign access). Moreover, Ecuador was given 1 sq km of territory, as private property, at Tiwintza in Peru where many Ecuadorean soldiers, killed during the conflict in 1995, were buried. Both countries were committed to establish ecological parks along the border where military personnel would not be allowed access. Although considerable opposition to the accord was expressed in Peru, notably in the town of Iquitos, international reaction was very favourable and resulted in several offers of finance from multilateral agencies for cross-border development projects. The Presidents of Peru and Ecuador met in May 1999 at the Peru–Ecuador frontier to mark the placing of the last boundary stone on the border.

In January 1992 the Presidents of Peru and Bolivia concluded an agreement whereby Bolivia would be granted access to the Pacific Ocean via the Peruvian port of Ilo (which would be jointly developed as a free zone). In return, Bolivia agreed to help facilitate Peruvian access to the Atlantic Ocean (through Brazil) by way of the Bolivian town of Puerto Suárez. In August 2004, following negotiations on economic integration, the Presidents of Peru and Bolivia signed a declaration of intent to create a special zone in Ilo for the exportation of Bolivian gas.

The support of President Chávez for Humala in the presidential election of 2006 severely strained Peru's relations with Venezuela. In late April Chávez threatened to sever diplomatic ties with Peru if García won the election. In response, President Toledo criticized Chávez for interfering in Peru's domestic affairs and withdrew Peru's ambassador from Venezuela, prompting Chávez to recall the Venezuelan ambassador from Peru a few days later. Full diplomatic relations were restored in February 2007, with the exchange of new ambassadors, following talks between Presidents García and Chávez in the previous month. The establishment in March 2008 of a congressional committee to investigate the 'Casas del Alba'—ostensibly humanitarian organizations founded in previous months by Peruvian supporters of Chávez—threatened once again to strain relations between the two countries. Venezuela strongly denied allegations that the offices, named after Chávez's regional integration project, the Alternativa Bolivariana para América Latina y el Caribe (ALBA), were funded by the Venezuelan Government as a means of promoting 'Bolivarian' ideology in Peru.

Peru's relations with Chile, which had been strained during Toledo's presidency, improved significantly after García took office in July 2006. In August the two countries agreed to expand the scope of a bilateral economic agreement reached in 1998 by including provisions related to cross-border investment and trade in services. It was hoped that this would eventually lead to the conclusion of a free trade agreement. García also urged the Chilean Government to rejoin the Andean Community as an associate member (which it did in November 2006), and an agreement on military co-operation was reached in October. Notwithstanding these advances, an ongoing dispute over maritime boundaries was rekindled in August 2007 by the Peruvian Government's publication of an official map that restated the country's long-standing claim to some 37,900 sq km of the Pacific Ocean controlled by Chile. The move prompted the Chilean Government, which maintained that the issue had already been resolved by previous bilateral treaties, to recall its ambassador for consultations. In January 2008 Peru presented an application to the ICJ for adjudication on the disputed border.

Government

A new Constitution, drafted by the Congreso Constituyente Democrático, was approved by a national referendum on 31 October 1993, and was promulgated on 29 December. Under the terms of the Constitution, executive power is vested in the President, who is elected for a five-year term by universal adult suffrage and is eligible for re-election for a successive term of office. Two Vice-Presidents are also elected. The President governs with the assistance of an appointed Council of Ministers. Legislative power is vested in a single chamber Congreso, elected for five years by a single national list system. For administrative purposes, Peru comprises 25 regional presidencies, 278 regional authorities and 12,138 municipal authorities, following amendments to the Constitution approved in December 2002.

Defence

Military service is selective and lasts for two years. As assessed at November 2007, the armed forces numbered 80,000 men: an army of 74,000, a navy of 23,000 and an air force of 17,000. There are paramilitary police forces numbering 84,000 men. The 2007 budget allocated 3,800m. new soles for defence and domestic security.

Economic Affairs

In 2006, according to estimates by the World Bank, Peru's gross national income (GNI), measured at average 2004–06 prices, was US $82,739m., equivalent to $2,920 per head (or $6,080 per head on an international purchasing-power parity basis). During 1996–2006, it was estimated, the population increased by an average of 1.6% per year, while gross domestic product (GDP) per head increased, in real terms, at an average annual rate of 2.3%. Overall GDP increased, in real terms, at an average annual rate of 3.9% in 1996–2006; growth was 8.0% in 2006.

Agriculture (including forestry and fishing) contributed 7.2% of GDP in 2005 and the sector engaged 27.9% of the economically active population, according to the FAO. Rice, maize and potatoes are the principal food crops. The principal cash crop is coffee. Peru is the world's leading producer of coca, and the cultivation of this shrub, for the production of the illicit drug cocaine, reportedly generated revenue of US $1,500m.–$2,500m. per year. Undeclared revenue from the export of coca is believed to exceed revenue from legal exports. Fishing, particularly for the South American pilchard and the anchoveta, provides another important source of revenue, and the fishing sector contributed an estimated 0.7% of GDP in 2005. Fishing accounted for 7.0% of the total value of exports in 2007. During 1997–2007 agricultural GDP (including fishing) increased at an average annual rate of 4.2%; the sector's GDP increased by 3.4% in 2007.

Industry (including mining, manufacturing, construction and power) provided an estimated 34.8% of GDP in 2005 and the sector employed 17.9% of the working population in 2001. During 1997–2007 industrial GDP increased by an average of 4.5% per year; industrial GDP increased by 9.7% in 2007.

Mining (including hydrocarbon extraction) contributed 10.3% of GDP in 2005 and employed 0.6% of the working population in 2001. The sector's contribution to GDP increased following the start of operations of the Camisea natural gas export pipeline in August 2004 (mining contributed 6.9% of GDP in 2003). Production of natural gas rose sharply from 2005 onwards, reaching 94,485.5m. cu ft in 2007 (representing a 28.6% increase on the previous year). Copper output increased by 25.5% in 2007 and rising international prices for this commodity improved export revenues (copper accounted for 25.9% of total export earnings in that year). Zinc, gold, petroleum and its derivatives, lead and silver are also major mineral exports. During 1997–2007 the GDP of the mining and petroleum sector increased at an average annual rate of 6.3%; real GDP growth in the sector was 2.1% in 2007.

Manufacturing contributed 16.3% of GDP in 2005 and employed 12.6% of the working population in 2001. The principal branches of manufacturing, measured by gross value of output, were food products, petroleum refineries, non-ferrous metals, beverages, and textiles and clothing. During 1997–2007 manufacturing GDP increased by an average of 4.4% per year. The sector's GDP increased by 10.6% in 2007.

Energy is derived principally from domestic supplies of hydroelectric power (72.3% of total electricity production in 2004) and petroleum (15.1%). Imports of mineral fuels and lubricants comprised 19.8% of the value of merchandise imports in 2005.

The services sector contributed an estimated 58.0% of GDP in 2005 and employed 73.3% of the working population in 2001. Tourism is gradually emerging as an important source of foreign revenue (US $1,371m. in 2005). In 1997–2007 the GDP of the services sector increased by an average annual rate of 3.9%. The sector's GDP grew by 9.7% in 2007.

In 2006 Peru recorded a visible trade surplus of US $8,934m. and there was a surplus of $2,589m. on the current account of the balance of payments. In 2004 the principal source of imports (19.6%) was the USA, which was also the principal market for exports (29.0%). Other major trading partners were Colombia, the People's Republic of China and Brazil for imports, and the United Kingdom, China and Chile for exports. Trade between Peru and China increased significantly in 2004. In January 2005 Peru signed an agreement with China to increase bilateral trade as 'strategic partners'. In December of that year Peru also concluded a free trade agreement with the USA. The accord was ratified by the Peruvian legislature in June 2006 and by the US Congress in late 2007. The principal exports in 2004 were basic manufactures, crude materials (particularly copper and tin), and food and live animals. The principal imports in the same year were machinery and transport equipment, mineral fuels and lubricants, and chemicals.

In 2007 there was a preliminary general budgetary surplus of 10,256m. new soles. Peru's external debt at the end of 2005 was US $28,653m., of which $22,222m. was long-term public debt. In that year the cost of debt-servicing was equivalent to 26.0% of the value of exports of goods and services. The annual rate of inflation averaged 2.3% in 2002–07. Consumer prices increased by an average of 1.8% in 2007. An estimated 9.6% of the urban labour force were unemployed in 2005.

Peru is a member of the Andean Community of Nations (see p. 170), the Inter-American Development Bank (IDB, see p. 308) and the Latin American Integration Association (see p. 331), all of which encourage regional economic development, and of the Rio Group (formerly the Group of Eight, see p. 425), which attempts to reduce regional indebtedness. Peru became a member of the Asia-Pacific Economic Co-operation group (APEC, see p. 176) in 1998. In December 2004 Peru was one of 12 countries that were signatories to the agreement, signed in Cusco, creating the South American Community of Nations (Comunidad Sudamericana de Naciones), intended to promote greater regional economic integration, due to become operational by 2007.

The election of the left-wing Government of Alan García (who had presided over a period of economic decline during 1985–90) in June 2006 initially tempered investor confidence; however, the new President signalled that fiscal austerity would be adhered to, and measures were subsequently taken to improve private investment. The economy performed well in 2006–07, owing largely to high commodity prices, which significantly increased revenues from mineral exports. Meanwhile, infrastructure projects benefited from strong investment which, in turn, stimulated growth in the construction sector. Real GDP rose by 9.0% in 2007. However, despite widespread acclaim for the Government's efforts in providing greater economic stability, concerns remained that strong levels of growth had not led to an improvement in per caput income. Unofficial sources estimated that around one-half of the population were living on less than $1 per day and were subject to food shortages, poor sanitation and an intermittent electricity supply. Rising international prices for food were likely to exacerbate the hardships experienced by these people in 2008. The IMF forecast inflation of 4.2% for that year (compared to 1.8% in 2007). Slightly slower growth of 7.0% was projected for 2008. Despite a new free trade agreement with the USA (see above), the faltering US economy was expected to precipitate a significant decrease in external demand, which in turn was likely to have a negative impact on Peruvian exports.

Education

Reforms introduced after the 1968 revolution have instituted a three-level educational system. The first is for children up to six years of age in either nurseries or kindergartens. Basic (primary) education is free and compulsory, and is received between six and 11 years of age. Secondary education, beginning at the age of 12,

PERU

is divided into two stages, of two and three years, respectively. In 2005 enrolment at primary schools included 96.5% of pupils in the relevant age-group, while secondary enrolment included 69.7% of students in the relevant age-group. Higher education includes the pre-university and university levels. There were 78 universities in 2000. There is also provision for adult literacy programmes and bilingual education. Under the new Constitution, adopted in 1993, the principle of free university education was abolished. Total central government expenditure on education was estimated at 2.9% of GDP in 2000.

Public Holidays

2008: 1 January (New Year's Day), 20 March (Maundy Thursday), 21 March (Good Friday), 1 May (Labour Day), 24 June (Day of the Peasant, half-day only), 29 June (St Peter and St Paul), 28–29 July (Independence), 30 August (St Rose of Lima), 8 October (Battle of Angamos), 1 November (All Saints' Day), 8 December (Immaculate Conception), 25 December (Christmas Day).

2009: 1 January (New Year's Day), 9 April (Maundy Thursday), 10 April (Good Friday), 1 May (Labour Day), 24 June (Day of the Peasant, half-day only), 29 June (St Peter and St Paul), 28–29 July (Independence), 30 August (St Rose of Lima), 8 October (Battle of Angamos), 1 November (All Saints' Day), 8 December (Immaculate Conception), 25 December (Christmas Day).

Weights and Measures

The metric system is in force.

Statistical Survey

Sources (unless otherwise stated): Banco Central de Reserva del Perú, Jirón Antonio Miró Quesada 441–445, Lima 1; tel. (1) 4276250; fax (1) 4275880; e-mail webmaster@bcrp.gob.pe; internet www.bcrp.gob.pe; Instituto Nacional de Estadística e Informática, Avda General Garzón 658, Jesús María, Lima; tel. (1) 4334223; fax (1) 4333140; e-mail infoinei@inei.gob.pe; internet www.inei.gob.pe.

Area and Population

AREA, POPULATION AND DENSITY
(excluding Indian jungle population)

Area (sq km)	
Land	1,280,086
Inland water	5,130
Total	1,285,216*

Population (census results)†	
11 July 1993	22,048,356
18 July–20 August 2005	
Males	13,590,840
Females	13,628,424
Total	27,219,264

Population (official projected estimates at mid-year)	
2006	28,348,700
2007	28,750,770
Density (per sq km) at mid-2007	22.4

* 496,225 sq miles.

† Excluding adjustment for underenumeration, estimated at 2.35% in 1993, but including adjustment for an estimated 3.92% underenumeration in 2005 (when the enumerated total was 26,152,265).

REGIONS
(2005 census)

	Area (sq km)	Population (estimates)	Density (per sq km)	Capital
Amazonas	39,249	404,714	10.3	Chachapoyas
Ancash	35,915	1,079,460	30.1	Huaraz
Apurímac	20,896	435,020	20.8	Abancay
Arequipa	63,345	1,184,761	18.7	Arequipa
Ayacucho	43,815	643,199	14.7	Ayacucho
Cajamarca	33,318	1,411,381	42.4	Cajamarca
Callao*	147	841,796	5,727.3	Callao
Cusco	71,987	1,216,637	16.9	Cusco (Cuzco)
Huancavelica	22,131	464,277	21.0	Huancavelica
Huánuco	36,849	759,029	20.6	Huánuco
Ica	21,328	691,235	32.4	Ica
Junín†	44,197	1,193,125	27.0	Huancayo
La Libertad	25,500	1,599,096	62.7	Trujillo
Lambayeque	14,231	1,133,588	79.7	Chiclayo
Lima	34,802	8,120,688	233.3	Lima
Loreto	368,852	918,207	2.5	Iquitos
Madre de Dios	85,301	95,569	1.1	Puerto Maldonado
Moquegua	15,734	165,443	10.5	Moquegua
Pasco	25,320	277,041	10.9	Cerro de Pasco
Piura	35,892	1,693,600	47.2	Piura
Puno	71,999	1,293,493	18.0	Puno
San Martín	51,253	695,785	13.6	Moyabamba
Tacna	16,076	285,071	17.7	Tacna
Tumbes	4,669	199,099	42.6	Tumbes
Ucayali	102,411	417,950	4.1	Pucallpa
Total	**1,285,216**	**27,219,264**	**21.2**	—

* Province.

† Population figure includes estimate for the districts of Pagoa and Mazamari, where execution of the census was not permitted by local authorities.

PRINCIPAL TOWNS
(estimated population of towns and urban environs at 1 July 1998)

Lima (capital)	7,060,600*	Piura	308,155
Arequipa	710,103	Huancayo	305,039
Trujillo	603,657	Chimbote	298,800
Callao	515,200†	Cusco (Cuzco)	278,590
Chiclayo	469,200	Pucallpa	220,866
Iquitos	334,013	Tacna	215,683

* Metropolitan area (Gran Lima) only.

† Estimated population of town, excluding urban environs, at mid-1985.

Mid-2005 (metropolitan area, official estimate): Lima 8,187,398.

Mid-2007 (incl. suburbs, '000, UN estimates): Lima 8,012; Arequipa 815 (Source: UN, *World Population Prospects: The 2007 revision*).

BIRTHS AND DEATHS*

	Live births		Deaths	
	Number	Rate (per 1,000)	Number	Rate (per 1,000)
1996	656,435	27.1	160,045	6.6
1997	652,467	26.4	160,830	6.5
1998	648,075	25.8	161,615	6.4
1999	642,874	25.2	162,457	6.4
2000	636,064	24.5	163,263	6.3
2001	630,947	24.0	164,296	6.2
2002	626,714	23.4	165,467	6.2
2003	623,521	23.0	166,777	6.1

* Data are estimates and projections based on incomplete registration, but including an upward adjustment for under-registration.

Marriages: 78,946 in 1997 (marriage rate 3.2 per 1,000); 60,730 in 1998 (marriage rate 2.4 per 1,000) (Source: UN, *Demographic Yearbook*).

Expectation of life (years at birth, WHO estimates): 71.5 (males 69.6; females 73.6) in 2005 (Source: WHO, *World Health Statistics*).

PERU

ECONOMICALLY ACTIVE POPULATION
('000 persons aged 14 and over, urban areas, July–September)

	1999	2000	2001
Agriculture, hunting and forestry	355.0	456.4	620.7
Fishing	65.3	25.8	47.1
Mining and quarrying	31.3	52.5	45.9
Manufacturing	897.6	963.5	956.4
Electricity, gas and water	41.3	28.1	20.4
Construction	378.2	299.5	341.3
Wholesale and retail trade; repair of motor vehicles, motorcycles and personal and household goods	2,077.0	2,060.5	2,124.5
Hotels and restaurants	470.6	431.9	593.8
Transport, storage and communications	618.2	639.0	641.0
Financial intermediation	76.3	66.6	47.9
Real estate, renting and business activities	407.5	413.4	342.6
Public administration and defence; compulsory social security	349.0	346.7	298.1
Education	551.5	479.7	552.1
Health and social work	165.1	169.7	213.5
Other services	372.9	368.2	406.2
Private households	353.8	326.8	366.3
Not classifiable	—	—	1.9
Total employed	7,211.2	7,128.4	7,619.9
Unemployed	624.9	566.5	651.5
Total labour force	7,836.1	7,694.9	8,271.4

Source: ILO.

2005 (labour force survey, October–December): Males employed 7,143,675; Females employed 5,976,050; Total employed 13,119,725 (Agriculture 36.9%, Mining 0.9%, Industry—consumer goods 7.3%, Industry—raw and intermediate goods 2.1%, Construction 3.2%, Trade 17.6%, Non-personal services 19.6%, Personal services 9.1%, Households 3.5%).

Health and Welfare

KEY INDICATORS

Total fertility rate (children per woman, 2005)	2.7
Under-5 mortality rate (per 1,000 live births, 2005)	27
HIV/AIDS (% of persons aged 15–49, 2005)	0.6
Physicians (per 1,000 head, 1999)	1.17
Hospital beds (per 1,000 head, 2004)	1.10
Health expenditure (2004): US $ per head (PPP)	235.4
Health expenditure (2004): % of GDP	4.1
Health expenditure (2004): public (% of total)	46.9
Access to water (% of persons, 2004)	83
Access to sanitation (% of persons, 2004)	63
Human Development Index (2005): ranking	87
Human Development Index (2005): value	0.773

For sources and definitions, see explanatory note on p. vi.

Agriculture

PRINCIPAL CROPS
('000 metric tons)

	2004	2005	2006
Wheat	170.4	178.5	195.0*
Rice (paddy)	1,844.9	2,468.4	2,225.0†
Barley	177.2	193.1	190.0*
Maize	1,200.0	1,240.8	1,230.0*
Potatoes	3,008.2	3,289.7	3,289.7†
Sweet potatoes	184.4	184.4	184.4†
Cassava (Manioc)	971.0	1,004.5	945.0†
Sugar cane	6,945.7	6,304.1	7,600.0†
Dry beans	58.5	71.7	71.7†
Oil palm fruit	208.5	190.0*	190.0†
Cabbages	29.9	30.2	30.2†
Asparagus	192.5	206.0	206.0†
Tomatoes	183.5	159.2	159.2†
Pumpkins, squash and gourds	98.0	86.5	86.5†
Green chillies and peppers	5.9	8.1	8.1†

—continued	2004	2005	2006
Dry onions	515.5	493.3	493.3†
Garlic	49.2	54.9	54.9†
Green peas	66.5	80.4	80.4†
Dry broad beans	47.2	52.9	52.9†
Carrots	163.6	164.1	164.1†
Green corn	377.9	351.3	351.3†
Plantains	1,664.1	1,697.1	1,697.1†
Oranges	330.4	334.5	334.5†
Tangerines, mandarins clementines and satsumas	175.4	171.3	171.3†
Lemons and limes	210.7	225.8	225.8†
Apples	146.9	139.3	139.3†
Grapes	155.4	196.5	196.5†
Watermelons	54.1	55.4	55.4†
Guavas, mangoes and mangosteens	281.9	239.3	239.3†
Avocados	108.5	103.4	103.4
Pineapples	177.1	203.9	203.9†
Papayas	193.9	171.1	171.1†
Coffee (green)	224.6	175.0	175.0†

* Unofficial figure.
† FAO estimate.

Aggregate production ('000 metric tons, may include official, semi-official or estimated data): Total cereals 3,438 in 2004, 4,132 in 2005, 3,873 in 2006; Total roots and tubers 4,425 in 2004, 4,760 in 2005, 4,701 in 2006; Total vegetables (incl. melons) 2,040 in 2004, 2,020 in 2005, 2,020 in 2006; Total fruits (excl. melons) 3,808 in 2004, 3,853 in 2005, 3,853 in 2006.

Source: FAO.

LIVESTOCK
('000 head, year ending September)

	2003	2004	2005
Horses*	720	725	730
Asses, mules or hinnies*	880	895	910
Cattle	5,133	5,181	5,241
Pigs	2,992	3,004	3,005
Sheep	14,752	14,735	14,822
Goats	1,984	1,959	1,957
Poultry	92,846	98,165	99,255

* FAO estimates.

2006: Figures assumed to be unchanged from 2005 (FAO estimates).

Source: FAO.

LIVESTOCK PRODUCTS
('000 metric tons)

	2003	2004	2005
Cattle meat	138.3	146.4	153.1
Sheep meat	31.9	33.7	33.8
Pig meat	92.7	98.0	102.9
Chicken meat	690.4	668.8	732.9
Cows' milk	1,224.3	1,269.5	1,329.7
Hen eggs	181.4	175.5	182.3
Wool (greasy)	11.6	11.2	10.9

2006: Figures assumed to be unchanged from 2005 (FAO estimates).

Source: FAO.

Forestry

ROUNDWOOD REMOVALS
('000 cubic metres, excluding bark)

	2004	2005	2006
Sawlogs, veneer logs and logs for sleepers	1,306	1,438	1,657
Other industrial wood	315	304	147
Fuel wood	7,300	7,364	7,454
Total	8,921	9,106	9,258

Source: FAO.

PERU

SAWNWOOD PRODUCTION
('000 cubic metres, including railway sleepers)

	2004	2005	2006
Coniferous (softwood)	9	7	16
Broadleaved (hardwood)	662	736	840
Total	671	743	856

Source: FAO.

Fishing

('000 metric tons, live weight)

	2003	2004	2005
Capture	6,086.1	9,604.5	9,388.7
Chilean jack mackerel	217.7	187.4	80.7
Anchoveta (Peruvian anchovy)	5,347.2	8,808.5	8,655.5
Aquaculture	13.8	22.3	27.5
Total catch	6,099.8	9,626.8	9,416.1

Note: Figures exclude aquatic plants ('000 metric tons, all capture): 7.9 in 2003; 7.4 in 2004; 5.0 in 2005.

Source: FAO.

Mining

('000 metric tons, unless otherwise indicated, preliminary figures)*

	2005	2006	2007
Crude petroleum ('000 barrels)	40,622.6	42,187.2	41,562.2
Natural gas (million cubic feet)	53,567.1	62,691.1	94,485.5
Copper	790.2	818.5	1,027.5
Lead	294.0	288.4	303.0
Zinc	1,028.4	1,029.9	1,236.1
Iron ore	4,638.0	4,861.2	5,185.3
Gold (kg)	202.1	197.0	165.3
Silver (kg)	3,013.8	3,263.0	3,284.8

* Figures for metallic minerals refer to metal content only.

Industry

SELECTED PRODUCTS
('000 metric tons, unless otherwise indicated)

	2002	2003	2004
Canned fish	35.3	91.6	45.4
Wheat flour	988	986	1,003
Raw sugar	878	970	n.a.
Beer ('000 hectolitres)	6,180	6,483	6,733
Cigarettes (million)	3,766	2,707	2,168
Motor spirit (petrol, '000 barrels)*	11,593	9,202	8,848
Kerosene ('000 barrels)*	6,532	4,354	2,467
Distillate fuel oils ('000 barrels)*	15,417	14,972	15,082
Residual fuel oils ('000 barrels)*	22,894	23,134	20,462
Cement	4,115	4,203	4,602
Crude steel*	510	510	510
Lead (refined)	119.6	112.3	118.6
Zinc (refined)	203.0	223.0	225.0
Electric energy (million kWh)	21,981	22,925	22,547

* US Geological Survey estimates.

Source (unless otherwise indicated): partly UN, *Industrial Commodity Statistics Yearbook*.

Finance

CURRENCY AND EXCHANGE RATES

Monetary Units
100 céntimos = 1 nuevo sol (new sol).

Sterling, Dollar and Euro Equivalents (31 October 2007)
£1 sterling = 6.216 new soles;
US $1 = 2.998 new soles;
€1 = 4.330 new soles;
100 new soles = £16.09 = $33.36 = €23.09.

Average Exchange Rate (new soles per US $)
2004 3.4132
2005 3.2958
2006 3.2738

Note: On 1 February 1985 Peru replaced its former currency, the sol, by the inti, valued at 1,000 soles. A new currency, the nuevo sol (equivalent to 1m. intis), was introduced in July 1991.

CENTRAL GOVERNMENT BUDGET
(million new soles, preliminary figures)

Revenue	2005	2006	2007
Taxation	35,589	45,485	52,454
Taxes on income, profits, etc.	11,188	18,414	22,847
Taxes on imports (excl. VAT)	3,143	2,847	2,198
Value-added tax	18,302	21,517	25,258
Domestic	10,587	11,982	13,586
Imports	7,715	9,535	11,672
Excises	4,066	4,042	4,291
Fuel duty	2,607	2,399	2,419
Other taxes	2,980	3,369	3,848
Less Refunds	4,090	4,704	5,989
Other current revenue	5,458	7,229	8,659
Capital revenue	386	361	386
Total	41,432	53,076	61,499

Expenditure	2005	2006	2007
Current non-interest expenditure	33,577	37,252	42,613
Compensation of employees	11,593	12,553	13,020
Goods and non-labour services	8,960	10,192	10,994
Transfers	13,024	14,506	18,599
Pensions	4,012	4,027	4,077
National savings fund	2,692	2,564	2,648
Municipal compensation fund	2,032	2,410	2,806
Interest payments	4,794	5,413	5,525
Internal	657	1,117	1,279
External	4,138	4,297	4,247
Capital expenditure	4,891	6,008	7,349
Gross capital formation	4,458	4,779	6,000
Total	43,263	48,673	55,488

General Budget (million new soles, preliminary figures): *2005:* Total revenue 48,201 (current 47,815, capital 386); Total expenditure 49,453 (current non-interest 37,320, capital 7,162, interest payments 4,971). *2006:* Total revenue 60,416 (current 60,055, capital 361); Total expenditure 54,912 (current non-interest 40,833, capital 8,485, interest payments 5,593). *2007:* Total revenue 69,841 (current 69,455, capital 386); Total expenditure 59,585 (current non-interest 43,407, capital 10,244, interest payments 5,934).

INTERNATIONAL RESERVES
(US $ million at 31 December)

	2005	2006	2007
Gold	575.9	705.9	927.8
IMF special drawing rights	0.5	0.9	3.7
Foreign exchange	13,598.9	16,732.4	26,852.7
Total	14,175.3	17,439.2	27,784.2

Source: IMF, *International Financial Statistics*.

PERU

MONEY SUPPLY
(million new soles at 31 December)

	2005	2006	2007
Currency outside banks	10,116	11,796	14,985
Demand deposits at commercial and development banks	11,606	16,791	25,586
Total money (incl. others)	26,338	32,694	43,983

Source: IMF, *International Financial Statistics*.

COST OF LIVING
(Consumer Price Index, Lima metropolitan area; base: 2000 = 100)

	2004	2005	2006
Food (incl. beverages)	106.6	107.6	110.2
Rent	115.5	120.3	123.3
Electricity, gas and other fuels	121.8	129.7	132.5
Clothing (incl. footwear)	105.9	107.5	109.1
All items (incl. others)	108.3	110.1	112.3

Source: ILO.

NATIONAL ACCOUNTS
(million new soles at current prices)

Expenditure on the Gross Domestic Product

	2005	2006	2007
Government final consumption expenditure	26,298	29,144	31,155
Private final consumption expenditure	173,171	187,673	207,023
Increase in stocks	−1,024	2,200	5,178
Gross fixed capital formation	47,966	58,363	73,260
Total domestic expenditure	246,411	277,380	316,616
Exports of goods and services	65,647	87,592	99,145
Less Imports of goods and services	50,151	59,855	74,534
GDP in purchasers' values	261,907	305,117	341,227
GDP at constant 1994 prices	148,716	159,955	174,328

Gross Domestic Product by Economic Activity

	2004	2005	2006*
Agriculture, hunting and forestry	14,266	14,897	16,596
Fishing	1,571	2,041	2,099
Mining and quarrying	18,264	23,235	35,606
Manufacturing	35,452	39,425	44,993
Electricity and water	4,895	5,379	5,618
Construction	12,885	14,214	17,041
Wholesale and retail trade	30,709	32,750	37,660
Restaurants and hotels	9,164	9,811	10,520
Transport and communications	18,226	20,075	22,772
Government services	17,474	19,249	20,970
Finance, insurance, real estate, business and other services	53,756	57,492	62,679
Gross value added at basic prices	216,661	238,570	276,553
Import duties	2,744	3,143	2,847
Other taxes on products	18,610	20,195	23,150
GDP in purchasers' values	238,015	261,907	302,550

* Preliminary.

BALANCE OF PAYMENTS
(US $ million)

	2004	2005	2006
Exports of goods f.o.b.	12,809	17,368	23,800
Imports of goods f.o.b.	−9,805	−12,082	−14,866
Trade balance	3,004	5,286	8,934
Exports of services	1,993	2,289	2,451
Imports of services	−2,725	−3,123	−3,400
Balance on goods and services	2,273	4,452	7,985
Other income received	332	625	1,033
Other income paid	−4,017	−5,701	−8,614
Balance on goods, services and income	−1,413	−624	405
Current transfers received	1,439	1,781	2,194
Current transfers paid	−6	−10	−10
Current balance	19	1,148	2,589
Capital account (net)	−86	−123	−127
Direct investment from abroad	1,599	2,579	3,467
Portfolio investment assets	−425	−817	−1,829
Portfolio investment liabilities	1,244	2,579	155
Other investment assets	14	−1,084	8
Other investment liabilities	−146	−3,233	−597
Net errors and omissions	236	362	−445
Overall balance	2,456	1,411	3,221

Source: IMF, *International Financial Statistics*.

External Trade

PRINCIPAL COMMODITIES
(distribution by SITC, US $ million)

Imports c.i.f.	2002	2003	2004
Food and live animals	795.9	811.1	1,023.1
Cereals and cereal preparations	354.4	382.6	486.6
Mineral fuels, lubricants, etc.	1,033.6	1,457.4	1,886.2
Petroleum, petroleum products, etc.	915.6	1,294.3	1,673.0
Crude petroleum oils, etc.	646.4	867.3	1,098.7
Refined petroleum products	260.0	418.1	557.6
Chemicals and related products	1,275.1	1,396.4	1,689.5
Plastics in primary forms	256.1	309.7	427.3
Basic manufactures	1,288.3	1,264.4	1,448.6
Paper, paperboard and pulp	244.7	251.6	276.2
Iron and steel	383.6	307.6	338.4
Machinery and transport equipment	2,089.7	2,389.2	2,809.6
Machinery specialized for particular industries	331.0	369.7	435.5
General industrial machinery equipment and parts	351.4	422.6	456.3
Office machines and automatic data-processing equipment	229.5	266.1	323.4
Telecommunications and sound equipment	371.2	465.0	530.0
Parts and accessories for telecommunications and sound equipment	219.1	268.5	316.8
Other electrical machinery apparatus, etc.	254.8	280.3	348.8
Road vehicles and parts (excl. tyres, engines and electrical parts)	408.7	412.0	512.8
Miscellaneous manufactured articles	636.6	661.7	721.8
Total (incl. others)	7,493.0	8,414.0	10,101.0

PERU

Statistical Survey

Exports f.o.b.	2002	2003	2004
Food and live animals	1,695.1	1,715.1	2,285.0
Fish and fish preparations	172.4	205.9	278.3
Vegetables and fruit	366.0	416.7	516.9
Coffee, tea, cocoa and spices	226.3	227.5	375.6
Coffee (not roasted); husks and skins	187.8	180.7	289.9
Feeding stuff for animals (excl. unmilled cereals)	848.0	769.4	990.2
Flours and meals of meat, fish, etc. (unfit for human consumption)	820.0	740.7	958.9
Crude materials (inedible) except fuels	1,283.2	1,426.8	2,672.7
Metalliferous ores and metal scrap	1,092.8	1,219.3	2,430.9
Ores and concentrates of base metals	533.7	662.3	1,106.0
Copper ores and concentrates	425.4	422.0	1,098.7
Zinc ores and concentrates	338.4	430.2	479.4
Mineral fuels, lubricants, etc.	471.9	667.9	694.2
Petroleum, petroleum products, etc.	471.7	667.8	674.9
Refined petroleum products	308.5	401.2	506.6
Basic manufactures	1,499.7	1,652.6	2,696.3
Non-ferrous metals	1,209.7	1,339.8	2,276.0
Copper and copper alloys	829.3	910.9	1,473.4
Unwrought copper and alloys	759.9	835.6	1,344.5
Refined copper (excl. master alloys)	710.7	792.5	1,263.1
Zinc and zinc alloys	110.5	129.8	139.0
Miscellaneous manufactured articles	718.2	861.4	1,137.5
Clothing and accessories	530.1	652.8	882.9
Non-monetary gold (excl. gold ores and concentrates)	1,467.4	2,021.2	2,360.9
Total (incl. others)	7,490.4	8,749.4	12,434.9

Source: UN, *International Trade Statistics Yearbook*.

2005 (US $ million): *Imports f.o.b.*: Total 12,082 (Consumer goods 2,308, Fuels and raw materials 6,600, Capital goods 3,064, Other 110). *Exports f.o.b.*: Fishing (traditional and non-traditional) 1,626; Mining (excl. petroleum, but incl. non-traditional non-metallic minerals) 9,908; Petroleum and derivatives 1,526; Agricultural products 1,008; Textiles 1,275; Total (incl. others) 17,368.

2006 (US $ million): *Imports f.o.b.*: Total 14,866 (Consumer goods 2,611, Fuels and raw materials 7,987, Capital goods 4,145, Other 122). *Exports f.o.b.*: Fishing (traditional and non-traditional) 1,767; Mining (excl. petroleum, but incl. non-traditional non-metallic minerals) 14,842; Petroleum and derivatives 1,760; Agricultural products 1,216; Textiles 1,471; Worked metal and jewellery 829; Total (incl. others) 23,800.

2007 (US $ million): *Imports f.o.b.*: Total 19,599 (Consumer goods 3,191, Fuels and raw materials 10,416, Capital goods 5,885, Other 106). *Exports f.o.b.*: Fishing (traditional and non-traditional) 1,954; Mining (excl. petroleum, but incl. non-traditional non-metallic minerals) 17,493; Petroleum and derivatives 2,248; Agricultural products 1,503; Textiles 1,730; Worked metal and jewellery 907; Total (incl. others) 27,956.

PRINCIPAL TRADING PARTNERS
(US $ million)

Imports c.i.f.	2002	2003	2004
Argentina	593.7	525.5	560.1
Brazil	489.5	549.3	698.4
Canada	123.5	113.0	194.8
Chile	419.0	429.2	470.7
China, People's Republic	463.4	639.9	768.1
Colombia	456.5	498.6	779.4
Ecuador	436.3	650.6	667.9
France (incl. Monaco)	115.8	126.2	127.5
Germany	230.9	242.3	273.1
Italy	140.8	190.3	169.9
Japan	411.1	368.7	358.7
Korea, Republic	228.9	276.1	296.6
Mexico	275.3	278.9	283.0
Nigeria	128.8	156.1	37.4
Spain	165.2	177.7	214.8
United Kingdom	73.4	77.4	81.8
USA	1,440.4	1,565.7	1,981.4
Venezuela	245.6	313.9	692.9
Total (incl. others)	7,493.0	8,414.0	10,101.0

Exports f.o.b.	2002	2003	2004
Belgium	103.1	95.8	168.9
Bolivia	90.2	99.2	131.2
Brazil	193.5	231.2	356.1
Canada	140.2	134.9	325.5
Chile	251.3	416.0	634.5
China, People's Republic	596.9	675.3	1,235.7
Colombia	156.7	187.2	261.2
Ecuador	135.4	154.3	206.5
Germany	251.3	254.6	381.9
Italy	174.0	187.1	284.0
Japan	372.6	390.2	552.0
Korea, Republic	168.1	176.3	201.7
Mexico	128.5	108.0	229.0
Netherlands	126.7	139.7	384.4
Panama	48.5	145.4	173.2
Spain	231.4	288.8	417.2
Switzerland-Liechtenstein	563.3	672.0	282.1
Thailand	25.9	26.7	30.5
United Kingdom	864.3	1,082.4	1,126.8
USA	1,917.0	2,318.5	3,603.7
Venezuela	113.9	108.6	196.1
Total (incl. others)	7,490.4	8,749.4	12,434.9

Source: UN, *International Trade Statistics Yearbook*.

Transport

RAILWAYS
(traffic)*

	2001	2002	2003
Passenger-km (million)	124	99	103
Freight ton-km (million)	1,154	1,112	1,117

*Incl. service traffic.

Source: UN, *Statistical Yearbook*.

ROAD TRAFFIC
(motor vehicles in use)

	2002	2003	2004
Passenger cars	781,751	812,978	824,613
Buses and coaches	44,576	44,486	43,919
Lorries and vans	425,679	415,206	418,884
Motorcycles	231,148	248,395	268,125

Source: IRF, *World Road Statistics*.

SHIPPING

Merchant Fleet
(registered at 31 December)

	2004	2005	2006
Number of vessels	726	727	749
Total displacement ('000 grt)	226.8	227.2	235.3

Source: Lloyd's Register-Fairplay, *World Fleet Statistics*.

International Sea-borne Freight Traffic
('000 metric tons)

	2004*	2005*	2006
Goods loaded	6,600	6,800	6,329
Goods unloaded	10,100	8,900	9,490

*Approximate figures extrapolated from monthly averages.

Source: UN, *Monthly Bulletin of Statistics*.

CIVIL AVIATION
(traffic on scheduled services)

	2004	2005	2006
Kilometres flown (million)	50	67	66
Passenger-km (million)	3,901	5,298	5,752
Total ton-km (million)	221	139	112

Source: UN Economic Commission for Latin America and the Caribbean, *Statistical Yearbook*.

Tourism

ARRIVALS BY NATIONALITY

	2003	2004	2005
Argentina	38,039	45,434	53,834
Bolivia	59,337	63,043	71,183
Brazil	28,211	32,893	43,154
Canada	21,846	24,385	33,124
Chile	249,040	307,432	352,703
Colombia	33,782	38,216	48,611
Ecuador	81,411	111,072	88,215
France	39,736	45,753	53,749
Germany	33,123	35,033	42,400
Italy	21,679	24,460	27,247
Japan	20,299	27,767	32,991
Mexico	16,908	22,858	27,411
Spain	29,853	42,042	58,483
United Kingdom	48,410	50,867	60,452
USA	200,800	240,104	291,073
Total (incl. others)	1,069,517	1,276,610	1,486,005

Tourism receipts (US $ million, incl. passenger transport): 1,001 in 2003; 1,169 in 2004; 1,371 in 2005.

Source: World Tourism Organization.

Communications Media

	2004	2005	2006
Telephones ('000 main lines in use)	2,049.8	2,250.5	2,332.0
Mobile cellular telephones ('000 subscribers)	4,092.6	5,583.4	8,500.0
Personal computers ('000 in use)	2,689	2,800	n.a.
Internet users ('000)	3,220	4,600	6,100
Broadband subscribers ('000)	227.6	352.6	484.9

Television receivers ('000 in use): 3,800 in 2000.

Radio receivers ('000 in use): 6,650 in 1997.

Facsimile machines ('000 in use, estimate): 15 in 1995.

Book production (titles): 612 in 1996.

Daily newspapers: 73 in 2004.

Sources: UNESCO, *Statistical Yearbook*; International Telecommunication Union.

Education

(2005 unless otherwise indicated, incl. adult education)

	Institutions	Teachers	Pupils
Nursery	17,629	47,496	847,911
Primary	35,944	186,919	4,106,899
Secondary	11,856	153,140	2,630,740
Higher: universities*	78	33,177	435,637
Higher: other tertiary	1,062	27,207	384,956
Special	399	3,423	24,984
Vocational	2,000	12,571	268,458

*Figures for 2000.

Source: Ministerio de Educación del Perú.

Adult literacy rate (UNESCO estimates): 87.9% (males 93.7%; females 82.5%) in 2005 (Source: UNESCO Institute for Statistics).

Directory

The Constitution

In 1993 the Congreso Constituyente Democrático (CCD) began drafting a new constitution to replace the 1979 Constitution. The CCD approved the final document in September 1993, and the Constitution was endorsed by a popular national referendum that was conducted on 31 October. The Constitution was promulgated on 29 December 1993.

EXECUTIVE POWER

Executive power is vested in the President, who is elected for a five-year term of office by universal adult suffrage; this mandate is renewable once. The successful presidential candidate must obtain at least 50% of the votes cast, and a second round of voting is held if necessary. Two Vice-Presidents are elected in simultaneous rounds of voting. The President is competent to initiate and submit draft bills, to review laws drafted by the legislature (Congreso) and, if delegated by the Congreso, to enact laws. The President is empowered to appoint ambassadors and senior military officials without congressional ratification, and retains the right to dissolve parliament if two or more ministers have been censured or have received a vote of 'no confidence' from the Congreso. In certain circumstances the President may, in accordance with the Council of Ministers, declare a state of emergency for a period of 60 days, during which individual constitutional rights are suspended and the armed forces may assume control of civil order. The President appoints the Council of Ministers.

LEGISLATIVE POWER

Legislative power is vested in a single-chamber Congreso (removing the distinction in the 1979 Constitution of an upper and lower house) consisting of 120 members. The members of the Congreso are elected

PERU

for a five-year term by universal adult suffrage. The Congreso is responsible for approving the budget, for endorsing loans and international treaties and for drafting and approving bills. It may conduct investigations into matters of public concern, and question and censure the Council of Ministers and its individual members. Members of the Congreso elect a Standing Committee, to consist of not more than 25% of the total number of members (representation being proportional to the different political groupings in the legislature), which is empowered to make certain official appointments, approve credit loans and transfers relating to the budget during a parliamentary recess, and conduct other business as delegated by parliament.

ELECTORAL SYSTEM

All citizens aged 18 years and above, including illiterate persons, are eligible to vote. Voting in elections is compulsory for all citizens aged 18–70, and is optional thereafter.

JUDICIAL POWER

Judicial power is vested in the Supreme Court of Justice and other tribunals. The Constitution provides for the establishment of a National Council of the Judiciary, consisting of nine independently elected members, which is empowered to appoint judges to the Supreme Court. An independent Constitutional Court, comprising seven members elected by the Congreso for a five-year term, may interpret the Constitution and declare legislation and acts of government to be unconstitutional.

The death penalty may be applied by the Judiciary in cases of terrorism or of treason (the latter in times of war).

Under the Constitution, a People's Counsel is elected by the Congreso with a five-year mandate which authorizes the Counsel to defend the constitutional and fundamental rights of the individual. The Counsel may draft laws and present evidence to the legislature.

According to the Constitution, the State promotes economic and social development, particularly in the areas of employment, health, education, security, public services and infrastructure. The State recognizes a plurality of economic ownership and activity, supports free competition, and promotes the growth of small businesses. Private initiative is permitted within the framework of a social market economy. The State also guarantees the free exchange of foreign currency.

The Government

HEAD OF STATE

President: ALAN GABRIEL LUDWIG GARCÍA PÉREZ (took office 28 July 2006).

First Vice-President: LUIS GIAMPIETRI ROJAS.

Second Vice-President: LOURDES MENDOZA DEL SOLAR.

COUNCIL OF MINISTERS
(April 2008)

President of the Council of Ministers: JORGE DEL CASTILLO GÁLVEZ.

Minister of Foreign Affairs: JOSÉ ANTONIO GARCÍA BELAÚNDE.

Minister of Defence: ANTERO FLORES-ARÁOZ.

Minister of the Interior: Dr LUIS ALVA CASTRO.

Minister of Justice: ROSARIO FERNÁNDEZ FIGUEROA.

Minister of Economy and Finance: LUIS CARRANZA UGARTE.

Minister of Labour and Employment: MARIO PASCO COSMÓPOLIS.

Minister of International Trade and Tourism: MERCEDES ARÁOZ FERNÁNDEZ.

Minister of Transport and Communications: VERÓNICA ZAVALA LOMBARDI.

Minister of Housing, Construction and Sanitation: ENRIQUE JAVIER CORNEJO RAMÍREZ.

Minister of Health: HERNÁN JESÚS GARRIDO-LECCA MONTAÑEZ.

Minister of Agriculture: ISMAEL BENAVIDES FERREYROS.

Minister of Energy and Mines: JUAN GUALBERTO VALDIVIA ROMERO.

Minister of Production: RAFAEL REY REY.

Minister of Education: JOSÉ ANTONIO CHANG ESCOBEDO.

Minister for the Advancement of Women and Social Development: SUSANA ISABEL PINILLA CISNEROS.

Minister of the Environment: ANTONIO BRACK EGG.

MINISTRIES

Office of the President of the Council of Ministers: Avda 28 de Julio 878, Miraflores, Lima; tel. (1) 6109800; fax (1) 4449168; e-mail webmaster@pcm.gob.pe; internet www.pcm.gob.pe.

Ministry for the Advancement of Women and Social Development: Jirón Camaná 616, Lima 1; tel. (1) 4289800; fax (1) 4261665; e-mail postmaster@mimdes.gob.pe; internet www.mimdes.gob.pe.

Ministry of Agriculture: Avda Salaverry s/n, Jesús María, Lima 11; tel. (1) 4310424; fax (1) 4310109; e-mail postmast@minag.gob.pe; internet www.minag.gob.pe.

Ministry of Defence: Avda Arequipa 291, Lima 1; tel. (1) 4335150; fax (1) 4333636; e-mail webmaster@mindef.gob.pe; internet www.mindef.gob.pe.

Ministry of Economy and Finance: Jirón Junín 339, 4°, Circado de Lima, Lima 1; tel. (1) 4273930; fax (1) 4282509; e-mail postmaster@mef.gob.pe; internet www.mef.gob.pe.

Ministry of Education: Avda Van De Velde 160, cuadra 33 Avda Javier Prado Este, San Borja, Lima 41; tel. (1) 4353900; fax (1) 4370471; e-mail postmaster@minedu.gob.pe; internet www.minedu.gob.pe.

Ministry of Energy and Mines: Avda Las Artes Sur 260, San Borja, Apdo 2600, Lima 41; tel. (1) 4750065; fax (1) 4750689; internet www.minem.gob.pe.

Ministry of the Environment: Lima.

Ministry of Foreign Affairs: Jirón Lampa 535, Lima 1; tel. (1) 3112402; fax (1) 3112406; internet www.rree.gob.pe.

Ministry of Health: Avda Salaverry 801, Jesús María, Lima 11; tel. (1) 4310408; fax (1) 3156600; e-mail webmaster@minsa.gob.pe; internet www.minsa.gob.pe.

Ministry of Housing, Construction and Sanitation: Avda Paseo de la República 3361, San Isidro, Lima; tel. (1) 2117930; e-mail webmaster@vivienda.gob.pe; internet www.vivienda.gob.pe.

Ministry of the Interior: Plaza 30 de Agosto 150, San Isidro, Lima 27; tel. (1) 2242406; fax (1) 2242405; e-mail ofitel@mininter.gob.pe; internet www.mininter.gob.pe.

Ministry of International Trade and Tourism: Calle 1 Oeste 50, Urb. Corpac, San Isidro, Lima 27; tel. (1) 2243345; fax (1) 2243362; e-mail webmaster@mincetur.gob.pe; internet www.mincetur.gob.pe.

Ministry of Justice: Scipión Llona 350, Miraflores, Lima 18; tel. (1) 4222654; fax (1) 4223577; e-mail webmaster@minjus.gob.pe; internet www.minjus.gob.pe.

Ministry of Labour and Employment: Avda Salaverry 655, cuadra 8, Jesús María, Lima 11; tel. (1) 4332512; fax (1) 4230741; e-mail webmaster@mintra.gob.pe; internet www.mintra.gob.pe.

Ministry of the Presidency: Avda Paseo de la República 4297, Lima 1; tel. (1) 4465886; fax (1) 4470379; internet www.peru.gob.pe.

Ministry of Production: Calle 1 Oeste 60, Urb. Corpac, San Isidro, Lima 27; tel. (1) 4151111; fax (1) 2243237; e-mail portal@produce.gob.pe; internet www.produce.gob.pe.

Ministry of Transport and Communications: Avda 28 de Julio 800, Lima 1; tel. (1) 4330010; fax (1) 4339378; internet www.mtc.gob.pe.

Regional Presidents
(April 2008)

Amazonas: OSCAR RAMIRO ALTAMIRANO QUISPE.
Ancash: CÉSAR JOAQUÍN ALVAREZ AGUILAR.
Apurímac: DAVID ABRAHAM SALAZAR MOROTE.
Arequipa: JUAN MANUEL GUILLÉN BENAVIDES.
Ayacucho: ISAAC ERNESTO MOLINA CHÁVEZ.
Cajamarca: JESÚS CORONEL SALIRROSAS.
Callao: ALEXANDER MARTÍN KOURI BUMACHAR.
Cusco: HUGO EULOGIO GONZALES SAYÁN.
Huancavelica: LUIS FEDERICO SALAS GUEVARA SCHULTZ.
Huánuco: JORGE ESPINOZA EGOÁVIL.
Ica: RÓMULO TRIVEÑO PINTO.
Junín: VLADIMIRO HUAROC PORTOCARRERO.
La Libertad: JOSÉ HUMBERTO MURGIA ZANNIER.
Lambayeque: YEHUDE SIMON MUNARO.
Lima: NELSON OSWALDO CHUI MEJÍA.
Loreto: YVÁN ENRIQUE VÁSQUEZ VALERA.
Madre de Dios: SANTOS KAWAY KOMORI.
Moquegua: JAIME ALBERTO RODRÍGUEZ VILLANUEVA.

PERU

Pasco: Félix Rivera Serrano.
Piura: César Trelles Lara.
Puno: Pablo Hernán Fuentes Guzmán.
San Martín: César Villanueva Arévalo.
Tacna: Hugo Froilán Ordoñez Salazar.
Tumbes: Wilmer Florentino Dios Benites.
Ucayali: Jorge Velásquez Portocarrero.

President and Legislature

PRESIDENT
Election, 9 April and 4 June 2006

Candidate	First round % of votes	Second round % of votes
Alan Gabriel Ludwig García Pérez (PAP)	24.32	52.63
Lt-Col (retd) Ollanta Moisés Humala Tasso (UPP*)	30.62	47.38
Lourdes Flores Nano (Unidad Nacional)	23.81	—
Martha Gladys Chávez Cossío de Ocampo (Alianza por el Futuro)	7.43	—
Valentín Paniagua Corazao (Frente de Centro)	5.75	—
Humberto Lay Sun (Restauración Nacional)	4.38	—
Others	3.68	—
Total	100.00	100.00

* In coalition with the Partido Nacionalista Peruano.

CONGRESO
President: Luis Javier Gonzales Posada Eyzaguirre (PAP).
General Election, 9 April 2006

Parties	% of votes	Seats
Unión por el Perú (UPP)	21.15	45
Partido Aprista Peruano (PAP)	20.59	36
Unidad Nacional	15.33	17
Alianza por el Futuro	13.09	13
Frente de Centro	7.07	5
Perú Posible (PP)	4.11	2
Restauración Nacional	4.02	2
Others	14.64	—
Total	100.00*	120

* Excluding 1,682,768 blank votes and 2,188,789 spoiled votes.

Election Commission

Oficina Nacional de Procesos Electorales (ONPE): Jirón Washington 1894, Lima; tel. (1) 4170630; internet www.onpe.gob.pe; independent; Nat. Dir Magdalena Chú Villanueva.

Political Organizations

Acción Popular (AP): Paseo Colón 218, Lima 1; tel. and fax (1) 3321965; e-mail webmaster@accionpopular.org.pe; internet www.accionpopular.org.pe; f. 1956; 1.2m. mems; liberal; contested the presidential and legislative elections of April 2006 as part of the Frente de Centro coalition; Pres. Víctor Andrés García Belaúnde; Sec.-Gen. Luis Alberto Velarde Yañez.

Alianza por el Futuro (AF): Lima; f. 2005 as a coalition of Cambio 90 and Nueva Mayoría in order to contest the 2006 presidential and legislative elections; supporters of fmr President Fujimori.

Alianza para el Progreso: Avda de la Policía 643, Jesús María, Lima; tel. (1) 4601251; e-mail alianzaparaelprogreso2006@hotmail.com; internet www.app-peru.org.pe; f. 2001; Sec.-Gen. César Acuña Peralta.

Avanza País—Partido de Integración Social: Huaura 175, Of. 104, Rímac, Lima; tel. (1) 3813250; f. 2005.

Cambio 90 (C90): Jirón Santa Isabel 590, Urb. Colmenares, Pueblo Libre, Lima; tel. (1) 9441739; internet www.fujimori2006.com; f. 1990; part of Alianza por el Futuro coalition formed with Nueva Mayoría in order to contest the 2006 presidential and legislative elections; Pres. Andrés Reggiardo Sayán.

Coordinadora Nacional de Independientes (CNI): Domingo Elías 1450, Surquillo, Lima; tel. (1) 2411884; fax (1) 4455968; e-mail info@independientes.org.pe; internet www.independientes.org.pe; f. 2003; contested the presidential and legislative elections of April 2006 as part of the Frente de Centro coalition; Leader Drago Kisic.

Frente de Centro: Avda Paseo de la República 3920, Miraflores, Lima; f. 2005 as a coalition of Acción Popular, Somos Perú and the Coordinadora Nacional de Independientes in order to contest the presidential and legislative elections of April 2006; Presidential Candidate Valentín Paniagua Corazao.

Frente Independiente Moralizador (FIM): Pancho Fierro 133, San Isidro, Lima; tel. (1) 4220583; internet www.congreso.gob.pe/grupo_parlamentario/fim/inicio.htm; f. 1990; right-wing; Pres. Luis Fernando Olivera Vega; Sec.-Gen. Gonzalo Carriquiry Blondet.

Frente Popular Agrícola del Perú (Frepap): Avda Morro Solar 1234; Santiago de Surco, Lima; tel. (1) 2753847; f. 1989; Leader Ezequiel Ataucusi Gamonal.

Fuerza Democrática (FD): Avda La Marina 1520, Pueblo Libre, Lima; tel. (1) 4606335; e-mail editor@fuerzademocratica.net; internet www.fuerzademocratica.info; Leader Alberto Borea Odría.

Movimiento Descentralista Perú Ahora: Plaza Bolognesi 600, Breña, Lima 5; tel. (1) 3309230; e-mail partidopolitico@peruahora.org; internet www.peruahora.org; f. 1998; relaunched in 2003 by fmr mems of Perú Posible; Sec.-Gen. Luis Guerrero Figueroa.

Movimiento Nueva Izquierda (MNI): Jirón Miró Quesada 360, Lima; tel. (1) 4264640; e-mail mni_peru@yahoo.es; internet www.mni.org.pe; f. 2005; left-wing; Leader Rafael Edwin Ríos López.

Nueva Mayoría: Lima; internet www.fujimori2006.com; f. 1992; part of Alianza por el Futuro coalition formed with Cambio 90 in order to contest the presidential and legislative elections of April 2006; Pres. Martha Gladys Chávez Cossío de Ocampo; Sec.-Gen. Demetrio Patsias Mella.

Partido Aprista Peruano (PAP): Avda Alfonso Ugarte 1012, Lima 5; tel. (1) 4281736; internet www.apra.org.pe; f. in Mexico 1924, in Peru 1930; legalized 1945; democratic left-wing party; Pres. Alan Gabriel Ludwig García Pérez; Secs-Gen. Jorge del Castillo Gálvez, Mauricio Mulder Bedoya; 700,000 mems.

Partido Comunista Peruano (PCP): Plaza Ramón Castilla 67, Lima; tel. and fax (1) 3306106; e-mail unidad@ec-red.com; internet www.pcp.miarroba.com; f. 1928; Pres. Jorge del Prado.

Partido Demócrata Cristiano (PDC): Avda España 321, Lima 1; tel. (1) 4238042; f. 1956; 95,000 mems; Chair. Carlos Blancas Bustamante.

Partido Democrático Descentralista (PDD): Plaza Bolognesi 590, Breña, Lima 5; tel. (1) 3305558; e-mail pddperu@yahoogroups.com; f. 2002; left-wing; regionalist; Leader Julio Sergio Castro Gómez.

Partido Justicia Nacional: Avda Arequipa 1799, Lince, Lima; tel. (1) 4723744; e-mail info@justicianacional.com; internet www.justicianacional.com; f. 2003; Pres. Jaime Salinas López-Torres.

Partido Nacionalista Peruano: Lima; tel. (1) 2641738; e-mail pnacionalista@yahoo.com; internet www.partidonacionalista peruano.com; f. 2005 to support presidential candidacy of Lt-Col (retd) Ollanta Moisés Humala Tasso; contested the 2006 elections in coalition with the Unión por el Perú; Leader Lt-Col (retd) Ollanta Moisés Humala Tasso.

Partido Popular Cristiano (PPC): Avda Alfonso Ugarte 1484, Lima; tel. (1) 4238723; fax (1) 4238721; e-mail estflores@terra.com.pe; f. 1967; splinter group of Partido Demócrata Cristiano; 250,000 mems; Pres. Lourdes Flores Nano; Sec.-Gen. Raúl Castro Stagnaro.

Partido Socialista: Plaza Bolognesi 590, Breña, Lima 5; tel. (1) 3305558; internet www.socialista.org.pe; contested the 2006 election; Presidential Candidate Javier Diez Canseco.

Partido Verde: Avda Jorge Chávez 654, 4°, Lima 33; tel. (1) 96437268; e-mail alternativaverde@verdes.org.pe; internet www.verdes.org.pe; ecologist; Pres. Alex González.

Perú Posible (PP): Avda Faustino Sánchez Carrión, Lima; tel. (1) 4620303; e-mail sgpp@mixmail.com; internet www.peruposible.org.pe/indice.htm; f. 1994; Leader Alejandro Toledo; Sec.-Gen. Javier Reátegui Roselló.

Proyecto País: Nicolás de Piérola 917, Of. 211, Plaza San Martín, Lima; tel. (1) 3312696; fax (1) 2222785; e-mail info@proyectopais.org.pe; internet www.proyectopais.org.pe; f. 1998; Leader Marco Antonio Arrunategui Cevallos.

Renacimiento Andino: Calle Real 583, 2°, Huancayo; tel. (4) 214620; fax (4) 217480; e-mail webmaster@renacimientoandino.org.pe; internet www.renacimientoandino.org.pe; f. 2001; Leader Ciro Alfredo Gálvez Herrera.

Renovación Nacional: Jirón Tacna 3321, San Martín de Porres, Lima; tel. (1) 5673798; f. 1992; Leader Rafael Rey Rey.

Restauración Nacional: Jirón Lampa 974, Cercado de Lima; tel. (9) 7566117; internet www.restauracionnacional.org; f. 2005; evangelical Christian party; Pres. HUMBERTO LAY SUN; Sec.-Gen. JUAN DAVID PERRY.

Sí Cumple: Lima; tel. (1) 4266451; internet www.fujimorialberto .com; f. 2003; supporters of fmr President Fujimori; Sec.-Gen. LUIS DELGADO APARICIO.

Solidaridad Nacional (SN): Armando Blondet 106, San Isidro, Lima; tel. (1) 2218948; e-mail fsandoval@psn.org.pe; internet www .psn.org.pe; f. 1999; centre-left; Pres. LUIS CASTAÑEDA LOSSIO; Sec.-Gen. MARCO ANTONIO PARRA SÁNCHEZ.

Somos Perú (SP): Avda Arequipa 3990, Miraflores, Lima; tel. (1) 4219363; e-mail postmaster@somosperu.org.pe; internet www .somosperu.org.pe; f. 1998; contested the April 2006 elections as part of the Frente de Centro coalition; Leader ALBERTO ANDRADE CARMONA; Sec.-Gen. EDUARDO CARHUARICRA MEZA.

Unidad Nacional: Calle Ricardo Palma 1111, Miraflores, Lima; tel. (1) 2242773; f. 2000; centrist alliance; Leader LOURDES FLORES NANO.

Unión por el Perú (UPP): Pablo de Olavide 270, San Isidro, Lima; tel. (1) 4403227; e-mail ivega@partidoupp.org; internet www .partidoupp.org; f. 1994; ind. movt; contested 2006 elections in coalition with Partido Nacionalista Peruano, led by Lt-Col (retd) Ollanta Moisés Humala Tasso; Pres. Dr ALDO ESTRADA CHOQUE.

ARMED GROUPS

Movimiento Nacionalista Peruano (MNP) (Movimiento Etnocacerista): Pasaje Velarde 188, Of. 204, Lima; tel. (1) 3311074; e-mail movnacionalistaperuano@yahoo.es; internet mnp.tripod.com.pe; ultra-nationalist paramilitary group; Pres. Dr ISAAC HUMALA NÚÑEZ; Leader of paramilitary wing Maj. (retd) ANTAURO IGOR HUMALA TASSO (arrested Jan. 2005 following an armed uprising in Andahuaylas).

Sendero Luminoso (Shining Path): f. 1970; began armed struggle 1980; splinter group of PCP; based in Ayacucho; advocates the policies of the late Mao Zedong and his radical followers, including the 'Gang of Four' in the People's Republic of China; founder Dr ABIMAEL GUZMÁN REYNOSO (alias 'Comandante Gonzalo'—arrested Sept. 1992); current leaders MARGIE CLAVO PERALTA (arrested March 1995), PEDRO DOMINGO QUINTEROS AYLLÓN (alias 'Comrade Luis'—arrested April 1998).

Sendero Rojo (Red Path): dissident faction of Sendero Luminoso opposed to leadership of Abimael Guzmán; Leader FILOMENO CERRÓN CARDOSO (alias 'Comrade Artemio').

Diplomatic Representation

EMBASSIES IN PERU

Argentina: Arequipa 121, Lima 1; tel. (1) 4339966; fax (1) 4330769; e-mail embajada@terra.com.pe; Chargé d'affaires a.i. HÉCTOR ISAAC NIKI.

Austria: Avda Central 643, 5°, San Isidro, Lima 27; tel. (1) 4420503; fax (1) 4428851; e-mail lima-ob@bmaa.gv.at; Ambassador GEORG WOUTSAS.

Bolivia: Los Castaños 235, San Isidro, Lima 27; tel. (1) 4402095; fax (1) 4402298; e-mail jemis@emboli.attla.com.pe; Ambassador FRANZ SOLANO CHUQUIMIA.

Brazil: Avda José Pardo 850, Miraflores, Lima; tel. (1) 5120830; fax (1) 4452421; e-mail embajada@embajadabrasil.org.pe; internet www .embajadabrasil.org.pe; Ambassador JORGE D'ESCRAGNOLLE TAUNAY, Filho.

Canada: Casilla 18-1126, Correo Miraflores, Lima; tel. (1) 4444015; fax (1) 4444347; e-mail lima@dfait-maeci.gc.ca; internet www .dfait-maeci.gc.ca/peru; Ambassador GENEVIÈVE DES RIVIÈRES.

Chile: Avda Javier Prado Oeste 790, San Isidro, Lima; tel. (1) 6112211; fax (1) 6112223; e-mail embajada@embachileperu.com .pe; Ambassador CRISTIÁN BARROS MELET.

China, People's Republic: Jirón José Granda 150, San Isidro, Apdo 375, Lima 27; tel. (1) 2220841; fax (1) 4429467; e-mail chinaemb_pe@mfa.gov.cn; internet www.embajadachina.org.pe; Ambassador GAO ZHENGYUE.

Colombia: Avda J. Basadre 1580, San Isidro, Lima 27; tel. (1) 4410954; fax (1) 4419806; e-mail emperu@embajadacolombia.org .pe; Ambassador ÁLVARO PAVA CAMELO.

Costa Rica: Baltazar La Torre 828, San Isidro, Lima; tel. (1) 2642999; fax (1) 2642799; e-mail costarica.peru@hotmail.com; Ambassador SARA FAIGENZICHT WEISLEDER.

Cuba: Coronel Portillo 110, San Isidro, Lima; tel. (1) 2642053; fax (1) 2644525; e-mail embacuba@ecuperu.minrex.gov.cu; internet embacu.cubaminrex.cu/peru; Ambassador LUIS DELFÍN PÉREZ OSORIO.

Czech Republic: Baltazar La Torre 398, San Isidro, Lima 27; tel. (1) 2643374; fax (1) 2641708; e-mail lima@embassy.mzv.cz; internet www.mfa.cz/lima; Ambassador VĚRA ZEMANOVÁ.

Dominican Republic: Calle Tudela y Varela 360, San Isidro, Lima; tel. (1) 4219765; fax (1) 4219763; e-mail embdomperu@terra.com.pe; Ambassador RAFAEL JULIÁN CEDANO.

Ecuador: Las Palmeras 356 y Javier Prado Oeste, San Isidro, Lima 27; tel. (1) 2124171; fax (1) 4220711; e-mail embajada@ mecuadorperu.org.pe; internet www.mecuadorperu.org.pe; Ambassador DIEGO RIBADENEIRA ESPINOSA.

Egypt: Avda Jorge Basadre 1470, San Isidro, Lima 27; tel. (1) 4402642; fax (1) 4402547; e-mail emb-egypt@amauta.rcp.net.pe; Ambassador DESOUKY ALI FAYED.

El Salvador: Avda Javier Prado 2108, San Isidro, Lima 27; tel. (1) 4403500; fax (1) 2212561; e-mail embajadasv@terra.com.pe; Ambassador RAÚL SOTO-RAMÍREZ.

Finland: Avda Víctor Andrés Belaúnde 147, Edif. Real Tres, Of. 502, San Isidro, Lima; tel. (1) 2224466; fax (1) 2224463; e-mail sanomat .lim@formin.fi; internet www.finlandiaperu.org.pe; Ambassador PEKKA ORPANA.

France: Avda Arequipa 3415, Lima 27; tel. (1) 2158400; fax (1) 2158410; e-mail france.consulat@ambafrance-pe.org; internet www .ambafrance-pe.org; Ambassador PIERRE CHARRASSE.

Germany: Avda Arequipa 4210, Miraflores, Lima 18; tel. (1) 2125016; fax (1) 4226475; e-mail kanzlei@embajada-alemana.org .pe; internet www.embajada-alemana.org.pe; Ambassador CHRISTOPH MÜLLER.

Greece: Avda Principal 190, 6°, Urb. Santa Catalina, Lima 13; tel. (1) 4761548; fax (1) 4761329; e-mail emgrecia@terra.com.pe; Ambassador VASSILOS SIMANTIRAKIS.

Guatemala: Inca Ripac 309, Jesús María, Lima 11; tel. (1) 4602078; fax (1) 4635885; e-mail embperu@minex.gob.gt; Ambassador LUIS PEDRO QUEZADA CÓRDOVA.

Holy See: Avda Salaverry, 6a cuadra, Apdo 397, Lima 100 (Apostolic Nunciature); tel. (1) 4319436; fax (1) 4315704; e-mail nunciatura@ speedy.com.pe; Apostolic Nuncio Most Rev. RINO PASSIGATO (Titular Archbishop of Nova Caesaris).

Honduras: Avda Las Camelias 491, Of. 202, San Isidro, Lima; tel. (1) 4228111; fax (1) 2211677; internet www.embhonpe.org; Ambassador JUÁN JOSÉ CUEVA MEMBREÑO.

India: Avda Salaverry 3006, San Isidro, Lima 27; tel. (1) 4602289; fax (1) 4610374; e-mail hoc@indembassy.org.pe; internet www .indembassy.org.pe; Ambassador APPUNNI RAMESH.

Indonesia: Avda Las Flores 334, San Isidro, Lima; tel. (1) 2220308; fax (1) 2222684; e-mail kbrilima@indonesia-peru.org.pe; internet www.indonesia-peru.org.pe; Ambassador I GDE DJELANTIK.

Israel: Edif. El Pacifico, 6°, Plaza Washington, Natalio Sánchez 125, Santa Beatriz, Lima; tel. (1) 4334431; fax (1) 4338925; e-mail info@ lima.mfa.gov.il; internet lima.mfa.gov.il; Ambassador WALID MANSOUR.

Italy: Avda Gregorio Escobedo 298, Apdo 0490, Lima 11; tel. (1) 4632727; fax (1) 4635317; e-mail segretaria@italembperu.org.pe; internet www.italembperu.org.pe; Ambassador FABIO CLAUDIO DE NARDIS.

Japan: Avda San Felipe 356, Apdo 3708, Jesús María, Lima 11; tel. (1) 2181130; fax (1) 4630302; internet www.pe.emb-japan.go.jp; Ambassador SHUICHIRO MEGATA.

Korea, Democratic People's Republic: Los Nogales 227, San Isidro, Lima; tel. (1) 4411120; fax (1) 4409877; e-mail embcorea@ hotmail.com; Ambassador YU CHANG UN.

Korea, Republic: Avda Principal 190, 7°, Urb. Santa Catalina, La Victoria, Lima; tel. (1) 4760815; fax (1) 4760950; e-mail korembj-pu@ mofat.go.kr; internet per.mofat.go.kr; Ambassador HAHN YOUNG-HEE.

Malaysia: Avda Daniel Hernández 350, San Isidro, Lima 27; tel. (1) 4220297; fax (1) 2210786; e-mail mallima@kln.gov.my; internet www .kln.gov.my/perwakilan/lima; Ambassador Datuk Haji MOHAMMED NOR BIN HAJI ATAN.

Mexico: Avda Jorge Basadre 710, esq. Los Ficus, San Isidro, Lima; tel. (1) 2211100; fax (1) 4404740; e-mail info@mexico.org.pe; internet www.mexico.org.pe; Ambassador ANTONIO GUILLERMO VILLEGAS VILLALOBOS.

Morocco: Calle Manuel Ugarte y Morosco 790, San Isidro, Lima; tel. (1) 2643323; fax (1) 2640006; e-mail sifamlim@chavin.rcp.net.pe; internet www.embajadamarruecoslima.com; Ambassador ABDERRAHIM MOHANDIS.

Netherlands: Avda Principal 190, 4°, Urb. Santa Catalina, La Victoria, Lima; tel. (1) 4150660; fax (1) 4150689; e-mail info@ nlgovlim.com; internet www.nlgovlim.com; Ambassador BAREND VAN DER HEIJDEN.

PERU — Directory

Nicaragua: Avda Alvarez Calderón 738, San Isidro, Lima; tel. (1) 4223892; fax (1) 4223895; e-mail embanic@telefonica.net.pe; Ambassador Tomás Wigberto Borge Martínez.

Panama: Avda Alvarez Calderón 738, San Isidro, Lima 27; tel. (1) 4413652; fax (1) 4419323; e-mail panaemba@amauta.rcp.net.pe; Ambassador Roberto Díaz Herrera.

Paraguay: Alcanfores 1286, Miraflores, Lima; tel. (1) 4474762; fax (1) 4442391; e-mail embaparpe@terra.com.pe; Chargé d'affaires a.i. Felipe Santiado Jara Aguero.

Poland: Apdo 180174, Miraflores, Lima 18; tel. (1) 4713920; fax (1) 4714813; e-mail wojciech@amauta.rcp.net.pe; Ambassador Przemysław Marzec.

Portugal: Calle Antequera 777, 3°, San Isidro, POB 3692, Lima 100; tel. (1) 4409905; fax (1) 4429655; e-mail limaportugal@hotmail.com; Ambassador Mário Alberto Lino da Silva.

Romania: Avda Jorge Basadre 690, San Isidro, Lima; tel. (1) 4224587; fax (1) 4210609; e-mail ambrom@terra.com.pe; Ambassador Ștefan Costin.

Russia: Avda Salaverry 3424, San Isidro, Lima 27; tel. (1) 2640036; fax (1) 2640130; e-mail embrusa@amauta.rcp.net.pe; Ambassador Mijaeil Troyanski.

Serbia: Carlos Porras Osores 360, Apdo 18-0392, San Isidro, Lima 27; Apdo 0392, Lima 18; tel. (1) 4212423; fax (1) 4212427; e-mail yugoembperu@amauta.rcp.net.pe; Ambassador Goran Mesic.

South Africa: Edif. Real Tres, Avda Víctor Andres Belaúnde 147, Of. 801, Lima 27; tel. (1) 4409996; fax 4223881; e-mail saemb@amauta.rcp.net.pe; Ambassador Dr C. J. Streeter.

Spain: Jorge Basadre 498, San Isidro, Lima 27; tel. (1) 2125155; fax (1) 4410084; e-mail embesppe@correo.mae.es; internet www.mae.es/embajadas/lima; Ambassador Julio Albi de la Cuesta.

Switzerland: Avda Salaverry 3240, San Isidro, Lima 27; tel. (1) 2640305; fax (1) 2641319; e-mail lana.llosa@eda.admin.ch; internet www.eda.admin.ch/lima; Ambassador Beat Loeliger.

Ukraine: José Dellepiani 470, San Isidro, Lima; tel. (1) 2642884; fax (1) 2642892; e-mail emb_pe@mfa.gov.ua; internet www.mfa.gov.ua/peru; Chargé d'affaires a.i. Oleksii Liashenko.

United Kingdom: Torre Parque Mar, 22°, Avda José Larco 1301, Miraflores, Lima; tel. (1) 6173000; fax (1) 6173100; e-mail belima@fco.gov.uk; internet www.britemb.org.pe; Ambassador Catherine Nettleton.

USA: Avda La Encalada 17, Surco, Lima 33; tel. (1) 4343000; fax (1) 6182397; internet usembassy.state.gov/lima; Ambassador Peter Michael McKinley.

Uruguay: José D. Anchorena 84, San Isidro, Lima; tel. (1) 2640099; fax (1) 2640112; e-mail uruinca@embajada-uruguay.com; Ambassador Juan José Arteaga Sáenz de Zumarán.

Venezuela: Avda Arequipa 298, Lima; tel. (1) 4334511; fax (1) 4331191; Ambassador Vice-Adm. Armando José Laguna Laguna.

Judicial System

The Supreme Court consists of a President and 17 members. There are also Higher Courts and Courts of First Instance in provincial capitals. A comprehensive restructuring of the judiciary was implemented during the late 1990s.

SUPREME COURT

Corte Suprema
Palacio de Justicia, 2°, Avda Paseo de la República, Lima 1; tel. (1) 4284457; fax (1) 4269437; internet www.pj.gob.pe.
President: Dr Francisco Artemio Távara Córdova.
Attorney-General: Dra Flora Adelaida Bolivar Arteaga.

Religion

CHRISTIANITY

The Roman Catholic Church

For ecclesiastical purposes, Peru comprises seven archdioceses, 18 dioceses, 11 territorial prelatures and eight Apostolic Vicariates. At 31 December 2005 88% of the country's population were adherents of the Roman Catholic Church.

Bishops' Conference

Conferencia Episcopal Peruana, Jirón Estados Unidos 838, Apdo 310, Lima 100; tel. (1) 4631010; fax (1) 4636125; e-mail sgc@iglesiacatolica.org.pe.

f. 1981 statutes approved 1987, revised 1992 and 2000; Pres. Héctor Miguel Cabrejos Vidarte (Archbishop of Trujillo).

Archbishop of Arequipa: Javier Augusto Del Rio Alba, Arzobispado, Moral San Francisco 118, Apdo 149, Arequipa; tel. (54) 234094; fax (54) 242721; e-mail arzobispadoaqp@planet.com.pe.

Archbishop of Ayacucho or Huamanga: Luis Abilio Sebastiani Aguirre, Arzobispado, Jirón 28 de Julio 148, Apdo 30, Ayacucho; tel. and fax (64) 812367; e-mail arzaya@mail.udep.edu.pe.

Archbishop of Cusco: Juan Antonio Ugarte Pérez, Arzobispado, Herrajes, Hatun Rumiyoc s/n, Apdo 148, Cusco; tel. (84) 225211; fax (84) 222781; e-mail arzobisp@terra.com.pe.

Archbishop of Huancayo: Pedro Ricardo Barreto Jimeno, Arzobispado, Jirón Puno 430, Apdo 245, Huancayo; tel. (64) 234952; fax (64) 239189; e-mail arzohyo@hotmail.com.

Archbishop of Lima: Cardinal Juan Luis Cipriani Thorne, Arzobispado, Jirón Carabaya, Plaza Mayor, Apdo 1512, Lima 100; tel. (1) 4275980; fax (1) 4271967; e-mail arzolim@terra.com.pe; internet www.arzobispadodelima.org.

Archbishop of Piura: José Antonio Eguren Anselmi, Arzobispado, Libertad 1105, Apdo 197, Piura; tel. and fax (74) 327561; e-mail ocordova@upiura.edu.pe.

Archbishop of Trujillo: Héctor Miguel Cabrejos Vidarte, Arzobispado, Jirón Mariscal de Orbegozo 451, Apdo 42, Trujillo; tel. (44) 256812; fax (44) 231473; e-mail arztrujillo@terra.com.pe.

The Anglican Communion

The Iglesia Anglicana del Cono Sur de América (Anglican Church of the Southern Cone of America), formally inaugurated in April 1983, comprises seven dioceses, including Peru. The Presiding Bishop of the Church is the Bishop of Northern Argentina.

Bishop of Peru: Rt Rev. Harold William Godfrey, Apdo 18-1032, Miraflores, Lima 18; tel. and fax (1) 4229160; e-mail diocesisperu@anglicanperu.org; internet www.peru.anglican.org.

The Methodist Church

There are an estimated 4,200 adherents of the Iglesia Metodista del Perú.

President: Rev. Jorge Brazo Caballero, Baylones 186, Lima 5; Apdo 1386, Lima 100; tel. (1) 4245970; fax (1) 4318995; e-mail iglesiamp@computextos.com.pe; internet www.iglesiametodista.org.pe.

Other Protestant Churches

Among the most popular are the Asamblea de Dios, the Iglesia Evangélica del Perú, the Iglesia del Nazareno, the Alianza Cristiana y Misionera and the Iglesia de Dios del Perú.

BAHÁ'Í FAITH

National Spiritual Assembly of the Bahá'ís of Peru: Horacio Urteaga 827, Jesús María, Apdo 11-0209, Lima 11; tel. (1) 4316077; fax (1) 4333005; e-mail bahai@pol.com.pe; mems resident in 220 localities.

The Press

DAILIES

Lima

El Bocón: Jirón Jorge Salazar Araoz 171, Urb. Santa Catalina, Apdo 152, Lima 1; tel. (1) 4756355; fax (1) 4758780; internet www.elbocon.com.pe; f. 1994; football; Editorial Dir Jorge Estéves Alfaro; circ. 90,000.

El Comercio: Empresa Editora 'El Comercio', SA, Jirón Antonio Miró Quesada 300, Lima; tel. (1) 4264676; fax (1) 4260810; e-mail editorweb@comercio.com.pe; internet www.elcomercioperu.com.pe; f. 1839; morning; Editor Juan Carlos Luján; Dir-Gen. Alejandro Miró Quesada G., Francisco Miró Quesada C.; circ. 150,000 weekdays, 220,000 Sundays.

Expreso: Jirón Antonio Elizalde 753, Lima; tel. (1) 6124000; fax (1) 4447125; e-mail webmaster@expreso.com.pe; internet www.expreso.com.pe; f. 1961; morning; conservative; Pres. Manuel Ulloa; Dir Carlos Espá; circ. 100,000.

Extra: Jirón Libertad 117, Miraflores, Lima; tel. (1) 4447088; fax (1) 4447117; e-mail extra@expreso.com.pe; f. 1964; evening edition of Expreso; Dir Carlos Sánchez; circ. 80,000.

Gestión: Avda Salaverry 156, Miraflores, Lima 18; tel. (1) 4776919; fax (1) 4476569; e-mail gestion@gestion.com.pe; internet www.gestion.com.pe; f. 1990; Gen. Editor Julio Lira; Gen. Man. Oscar Romero Caro; circ. 131,200.

PERU

Ojo: Jirón Jorge Salazar Araoz 171, Urb. Santa Catalina, Apdo 152, Lima; tel. (1) 4709696; fax (1) 4761605; internet www.ojo.com.pe; f. 1968; morning; Editorial Dir AGUSTÍN FIGUEROA BENZA; circ. 100,000.

El Peruano (Diario Oficial): Avda Alfonso Ugarte 873, Lima 1; tel. (1) 3150400; fax (1) 4245023; e-mail gbarraza@editoraperu.com.pe; internet www.elperuano.com.pe; f. 1825; morning; official State Gazette; Editorial Dir GERARDO BARRAZA SOTO; circ. 27,000.

Perú 21: Jirón Miró Quesada 247, 6°, Lima; tel. (1) 3116500; fax (1) 3116391; e-mail director@peru21.com; internet www.peru21.com; independent; Editor AUGUSTO ÁLVAREZ RODRICH.

La República: Jirón Camaná 320, Lima 1; tel. (1) 4276455; fax (1) 2511029; e-mail otxoa@larepublica.com.pe; internet www.larepublica.com.pe; f. 1982; left-wing; Dirs GUSTAVO MOHME SEMINARIO, GUSTAVO GORRITI; circ. 50,000.

Arequipa

Arequipa al Día: Avda Jorge Chávez 201, IV, Centenario, Arequipa; tel. (54) 223566; fax (54) 217810; f. 1991; Editorial Dir CARLOS MENESES CORNEJO.

Correo de Arequipa: Calle Bolívar 204, Arequipa; tel. (54) 235150; e-mail diariocorreo@epensa.com.pe; internet www.correoperu.com.pe; Dir ALDO MARIÁTEGUI; circ. 70,000.

El Pueblo: Sucre 213, Apdo 35, Arequipa; tel. (54) 211500; fax (54) 213361; f. 1905; morning; independent; Editorial Dir EDUARDO LAIME VALDIVIA; circ. 70,000.

Chiclayo

La Industria: Tacna 610, Chiclayo; tel. (74) 237952; fax (74) 227678; internet www.laindustria.com.pe; f. 1952; Dir JULIO ALBERTO ORTIZ CERRO; circ. 20,000.

Cusco

El Diario del Cusco: Centro Comercial Ollanta, Avda El Sol 346, Cusco; tel. (84) 229898; fax (84) 229822; e-mail buzon@diariodelcusco.com; internet www.diariodelcusco.com; morning; independent; Exec. Pres. WASHINTON ALOSILLA PORTILLO; Gen. Man. JOSÉ FERNANDEZ NÚÑEZ.

Huacho

El Imparcial: Avda Grau 203, Huacho; tel. (34) 2392187; fax (34) 2321352; e-mail elimparcial1891@hotmail.com; f. 1891; evening; Dir ADÁN MANRIQUE ROMERO; circ. 5,000.

Huancayo

Correo de Huancayo: Jirón Cusco 337, Huancayo; tel. (64) 235792; fax (64) 233811; evening; Editorial Dir RODOLFO OROSCO.

La Opinión Popular: Huancayo; tel. (64) 231149; f. 1922; Dir MIGUEL BERNABÉ SUÁREZ OSORIO.

Ica

La Opinión: Avda Los Maestros 801, Apdo 186, Ica; tel. (56) 235571; f. 1922; evening; independent; Dir GONZALO TUEROS RAMÍREZ.

La Voz de Ica: Castrovirreyna 193, Ica; tel. and fax (56) 232112; e-mail lavozdeica1918@infonegocio.net.pe; f. 1918; Dir ATILIO NIERI BOGGIANO; Man. MARIELLA NIERI DE MACEDO; circ. 4,500.

Pacasmayo

Diario Ultimas Noticias: Ancash 691, San Pedro de Lloc, Pacasmayo; fax (44) 9651477; e-mail ultimasnoticias@pacasmayo.net; internet www.pacasmayo.net/ultimasnoticias; f. 1973; morning; independent; Editor MARÍA DEL CARMEN BALLENA RAZURI; circ. 3,000.

Piura

Correo: Zona Industrial Manzana 246, Lote 6, Piura; tel. (74) 321681; fax (74) 324881; Editorial Dir ROLANDO RODRICH ARANGO; circ. 12,000.

El Tiempo: Ayacucho 751, Piura; tel. (74) 325141; fax (74) 327478; e-mail direccion@eltiempo.com.pe; internet www.eltiempo.com.pe; f. 1916; morning; independent; Dir LUZ MARÍA HELGUERO; circ. 18,000.

Tacna

Correo: Jirón Hipólito Unanue 636, Tacna; tel. (54) 711671; fax (54) 713955; Editorial Dir RUBÉN COLLAZOS ROMERO; circ. 8,000.

Trujillo

La Industria: Gamarra 443, Trujillo; tel. (44) 234720; fax (44) 427761; e-mail industri@united.net.pe; internet www.unitru.edu.pe/eelitsa; f. 1895; morning; independent; Gen. Man. ISABEL CERRO DE BURGA; circ. 8,000.

PERIODICALS AND REVIEWS

Alerta Agrario: Avda Salaverry 818, Lima 11; tel. (1) 4336610; fax (1) 4331744; f. 1987 by Centro Peruano de Estudios Sociales; monthly review of rural problems; Dir BERTHA CONSIGLIERI; circ. 100,000.

Caretas: Jirón Huallaya 122, Portal de Botoneros, Plaza de Armas, Lima 1; Apdo 737, Lima 100; tel. (1) 4289490; fax (1) 4262524; e-mail info@caretas.com.pe; internet www.caretas.com.pe; weekly; current affairs; Editor ENRIQUE ZILERI GIBSON; circ. 90,000.

Cosas: Calle Recaveren 111, Miraflores, Lima 18; tel. (1) 2411178; fax (1) 4473776; internet www.cosasperu.com; weekly; society; Editor ELIZABETH DULANTO.

Debate: Apdo 671, Lima 100; tel. (1) 2425656; fax (1) 4455946; f. 1980; every 2 months; Editor GONZALO ZEGARRA-HUILANDVICH.

Debate Agrario: Avda Salaverry 818, Lima 11; tel. (1) 4336610; fax (1) 4331744; e-mail cepes@cepes.org.pe; f. 1987 by Centro Peruano de Estudios Sociales; every 4 months; rural issues; Dir FERNANDO EGUREN L.

Gente: Eduardo de Habich 170, Miraflores, Lima 18; tel. (1) 4465046; fax (1) 4461173; e-mail correo@genteperu.com; internet www.genteperu.com; f. 1958; weekly; circ. 25,000.

Hora del Hombre: Lima; tel. (1) 4220208; f. 1943; monthly; cultural and political journal; illustrated; Dir JORGE FALCÓN.

Industria Peruana: Los Laureles 365, San Isidro, Apdo 632, Lima 27; f. 1896; monthly publication of the Sociedad de Industrias; Editor ROLANDO CELI BURNEO.

Lima Times: Pasaje Los Pinos 156, Of. B6, Miraflores, Apdo 531, Lima 100; tel. (1) 4469120; fax (1) 4467888; e-mail perutimes@amauta.rcp.net.pe; internet www.perutimes.com; f. 1975; monthly; travel, cultural events, general news on Peru; English; Editor ELEANOR GRIFFIS DE ZÚÑIGA; circ. 10,000.

Mercado Internacional: Lima; tel. (1) 4445395; business.

Monos y Monadas: Lima; tel. (1) 4773483; f. 1981; fortnightly; satirical; Editor NICOLÁS YEROVI; circ. 17,000.

Oiga: Pedro Venturo 353, Urb. Aurora, Miraflores, Lima; tel. (1) 4475851; weekly; right-wing; Dir FRANCISCO IGARTUA; circ. 60,000.

Ollanta: e-mail ollantaprensa@yahoo.com; internet ollantaprensa.tripod.com.pe; fortnightly; published by the Movimiento Nacionalista Peruano (MNP—'Movimiento Etnocacerista'); Dir Maj. (retd) ANTAURO IGOR HUMALA TASSO (arrested Jan. 2005 following an armed uprising in Andahuaylas).

Onda: Jorge Vanderghen 299, Miraflores, Lima; tel. (1) 4227008; f. 1959; monthly cultural review; Dir JOSÉ ALEJANDRO VALENCIA-ARENAS; circ. 5,000.

Orbita: Parque Rochdale 129, Lima; tel. (1) 4610676; weekly; f. 1970; Dir LUZ CHÁVEZ MENDOZA; circ. 10,000.

Perú Económico: Apdo 671, Lima 100; tel. (1) 2425656; fax (1) 4455946; f. 1978; monthly; Editor GONZALO ZEGARRA-HUILANDVICH.

The Peruvian Times: Paseo de la República 291, Of. 702, Lima 1; tel. (1) 4284069; fax (1) 4467888; e-mail egriffis@peruviantimes.com; internet www.peruviantimes.com; f. 1912 as The Andean Report; name changed as above in 2007; weekly internet publ; general news, analysis and features; English; Publr ELEANOR GRIFFIS; circ. 1,000.

QueHacer: León de la Fuente 110, Lima 17; tel. (1) 6138300; fax (1) 6138308; e-mail qh@desco.org.pe; internet www.desco.org.pe/qh/qh-in.htm; f. 1979; 6 a year; supported by Desco research and devt agency; Editor-in-Chief MARTÍN PAREDES; Dir ABELARDO SÁNCHEZ-LEÓN; circ. 5,000.

Runa: Lima; f. 1977; monthly; review of the Instituto Nacional de Cultura; Dir MARIO RAZZETO; circ. 10,000.

Semana Económica: Apdo 671, Lima 100; tel. (1) 2425656; fax (1) 4455946; f. 1985; weekly; Editor GONZALO ZEGARRA-HUILANDVICH.

Unidad: Jirón Lampa 271, Of. 703, Lima; tel. (1) 4270355; weekly; Communist; Dir GUSTAVO ESTEVES OSTOLAZA; circ. 20,000.

Vecino: Avda Petit Thouars 1944, Of. 15, Lima 14; tel. (1) 4706787; f. 1981; fortnightly; supported by Yunta research and urban publishing institute; Dirs PATRICIA CÓRDOVA, MARIO ZOLEZZI; circ. 5,000.

NEWS AGENCY

Andina—Agencia de Noticias Peruana: Jirón Quilca 556, Lima; tel. (1) 3306341; fax (1) 4312849; e-mail bbecerra@editoraperu.com.pe; internet www.andina.com.pe; f. 1981; state-owned; Pres. MARÍA DEL PILAR TELLO LEYVA; Dir of Media DELFINA BECERRA GONZÁLEZ.

PRESS ASSOCIATIONS

Asociación Nacional de Periodistas del Perú: Jirón Huancavélica 320, Apdo 2079, Lima 1; tel. (1) 4270687; fax (1) 4278493;

e-mail anp@amauta.rcp.net.pe; internet ekeko2.rcp.net.pe/anp; f. 1928; 8,800 mems; Pres. ROBERTO MARCOS MEJÍA ALARCÓN.

Federación de Periodistas del Perú (FPP): Avda Abancay 173, Lima; tel. (1) 4284373; f. 1950; Pres. PABLO TRUEL URIBE.

Publishers

Asociación Editorial Bruño: Avda Arica 751, Breña, Lima 5; tel. (1) 4244134; fax (1) 4251248; f. 1950; educational; Man. FEDERICO DÍAZ PINEDO.

Biblioteca Nacional del Perú: Avda Abancay, 4a cuadra, Apdo 2335, Lima 1; tel. (1) 4287690; fax (1) 4277331; e-mail dn@binape.gob.pe; internet www.binape.gob.pe; f. 1821; general non-fiction, directories; Nat. Dir SINESIO LÓPEZ JIMÉNEZ.

Colección Artes y Tesoros del Perú: Calle Centenario 156, Urb. Las Laderas de Melgarejo, La Molina, Lima 12; tel. (1) 3493128; fax (1) 3490579; e-mail acarulla@bcp.com.pe; f. 1971; Dir ALVARO CARULLA.

Ediciones Médicas Peruanas, SA: Lima; f. 1965; medical; Man. ALBERTO LOZANO REYES.

Editora Normas Legales SA: La Santa María 173, San Isidro, Lima; tel. and fax (1) 2212598; e-mail enormaslegales@terra.com.pe; law textbooks; Man. JAVIER SANTA MARÍA SILVE.

Editorial Book City: Calle José R. Pizarro 1260 (espalda cuadra 11 de La Mar), Pueblo Libre, Lima; tel. (1) 2613266; general interest, juvenile, reference and literature; Man. MIRTHA YI YANG.

Editorial Colegio Militar Leoncio Prado: Avda Costanera 1541, La Perla, Callao; f. 1946; textbooks and official publications; Man. OSCAR MORALES QUINA.

Editorial Cuzco SA: Calle 5 Marzo, Jirón Lote 3, Urb. Las Magnolias, Surco, Lima; tel. (1) 4453261; e-mail ccuzco@camaralima.org.pe; law; Man. SERGIO BAZÁN CHACÓN.

Editorial D.E.S.A.: General Varela 1577, Breña, Lima; f. 1955; textbooks and official publications; Man. ENRIQUE MIRANDA.

Editorial Desarrollo, SA: Ica 242, 1°, Apdo 3824, Lima; tel. and fax (1) 4286628; f. 1965; business administration, accounting, auditing, industrial engineering, English textbooks, dictionaries, and technical reference; Dir LUIS SOSA NÚÑEZ.

Editorial Horizonte: Avda Nicolás de Piérola 995, Lima 1; tel. (1) 4279364; fax (1) 4274341; e-mail damonte@terra.com.pe; f. 1968; social sciences, literature, politics; Man. HUMBERTO DAMONTE.

Editorial Labrusa, SA: Los Frutales Avda 670-Ate, Lima; tel. (1) 4358443; fax (1) 4372925; f. 1988; literature, educational, cultural; Gen. Man. ADRIÁN REUILLA CALVO; Man. FEDERICO DÍAZ TINEO.

Editorial Milla Batres, SA: Lima; f. 1963; history, literature, art, archaeology, linguistics and encyclopaedias on Peru; Dir-Gen. CARLOS MILLA BATRES.

Editorial Navarrete SRL-Industria del Offset: Manuel Tellería 1842, Apdo 4173, Lima; tel. (1) 4319040; fax (1) 4230991; Man. LUIS NAVARRETE LECHUGA.

Editorial Océano Peruana SA: Avda Salaverry 2890, San Isidro, Lima; tel. (1) 2613999; fax (1) 4618628; e-mail ocelibros@oceano.com.pe; general interest and reference.

Editorial Peisa: Avda 2 de Mayo 1285, San Isidro, Lima; tel. (1) 4410473; fax (1) 2215988; e-mail burtech@yahoo.com; fiction and scholarly; Man. BENJAMIN URTECHO.

Editorial Salesiana: Avda Brasil 218, Apdo 0071, Lima 5; tel. (1) 4235225; f. 1918; religious and general textbooks; Man. Dir Dr FRANCESCO VACARELLO.

Editorial Santillana: Avda San Felipe 731, Jesús María, Lima; tel. (1) 4610277; fax (1) 2181014; e-mail santillana@santillana.com.pe; internet www.santillana.com; literature, scholarly and reference; Man. ANA CECILIA HALLO.

Editorial Universo, SA: Lima; f. 1967; literature, technical, educational; Pres. CLEMENTE AQUINO; Gen. Man. Ing. JOSÉ A. AQUINO BENAVIDES.

Fundación del Banco Continental para el Fomento de la Educación y la Cultura (EDUBANCO): Avda República de Panamá 3055, San Isidro, Apdo 4687, Lima 27; tel. (1) 2111000; fax (1) 2112479; f. 1973; Pres. PEDRO BRESCIA CAFFERATA; Man. FERNANDO PORTOCARRERO.

Industrial Gráfica, SA: Jirón Chavín 45, Breña, Lima 5; fax (1) 4324413; f. 1981; Pres. JAIME CAMPODONICO V.

INIDE: Van de Velde 160, Urb. San Borja, Lima; f. 1981; owned by National Research and Development Institute; educational books; Editor-in-Chief ANA AYALA.

Librerías ABC, SA: Avda Paseo de la República 3440, Local B-32, Lima 27; tel. (1) 4422900; fax (1) 4422901; f. 1956; history, Peruvian art and archaeology; Man. Dir HERBERT H. MOLL.

Librería San Pablo: Jirón Callao 198, Lima 1; tel. (1) 3795336; fax (1) 4593842; e-mail admlima@paulinas.org.pe; internet www.paulinas.org.pe; f. 1981; religious and scholastic texts; Man. Sister MARÍA GRACIA CAPALBO.

Librería Studium, SA: Lima; tel. (1) 4326278; fax (1) 4325354; f. 1936; textbooks and general culture; Man. Dir EDUARDO RIZO PATRÓN RECAVARREN.

Pablo Villanueva Ediciones: Lima; f. 1938; literature, history, law, etc.; Man. AUGUSTO VILLANUEVA PACHECO.

Pontificia Universidad Católica del Perú: Fondo Editorial, Plaza Francia 1164, Lima; tel. (1) 330710; fax (1) 3307405; e-mail feditor@pucp.edu.pe; internet www.pucp.edu.pe; Dir of Admin. AUGUSTO EGUIGUREN PRAELI.

Sociedad Bíblica Peruana, AC: Avda Petit Thouars 991, Apdo 14-0295, Lima 100; tel. (1) 4335815; fax (1) 4336389; internet www.members.tripod.com/sbpac; f. 1821; Christian literature and bibles; Gen. Sec. PEDRO ARANA-QUIROZ.

Universidad Nacional Mayor de San Marcos: Of. General de Editorial, Avda República de Chile 295, 5°, Of. 508, Lima; tel. (1) 4319689; f. 1850; textbooks, education; Man. Dir JORGE CAMPOS REY DE CASTRO.

PUBLISHING ASSOCIATION

Cámara Peruana del Libro: Avda Cuba 427, esq. Jesús María, Apdo 10253, Lima 11; tel. (1) 4729516; fax (1) 2650735; e-mail cp-libro@amauta.rep.net.pe; internet www.pl.org.pe; f. 1946; 102 mems; Pres. CARLOS A. BENVIDES AGUIJE; Exec. Dir LOYDA MORÁN BUSTAMANTE.

Broadcasting and Communications

TELECOMMUNICATIONS

Regulatory Authorities

Dirección General de Gestión de Telecomunicaciones: Ministerio de Transportes y Comunicaciones, Avda 28 de Julio 800, Lima 1; tel. (1) 4330752; fax (1) 4331450; e-mail dgtdir@mtc.gob.pe; Dir-Gen. MANUEL ANGEL CIPRIANO PIRGO.

Instituto Nacional de Investigación y Capacitación de Telecomunicaciones (INICTEL): Avda San Luis 1771, esq. Bailetti, San Borja, Lima 41; tel. (1) 3461808; fax (1) 3464354; e-mail informes@inictel.gob.pe; internet www.inictel.gob.pe; Pres. MANUEL ADRIANZEN.

Organismo Supervisor de Inversión Privada en Telecomunicaciones (OSIPTEL): Calle de la Prosa 136, San Borja, Lima 41; tel. (1) 2251313; fax (1) 4751816; e-mail sid@osiptel.gob.pe; internet www.ospitel.gob.pe; f. 1993; established by the Peruvian Telecommunications Act to oversee competition and tariffs, to monitor the quality of services and to settle disputes in the sector; Pres. Dr GUILLERMO THORNBERRY VILLARÁN.

Major Service Providers

AT&T Perú: Avda Víctor Andrés Belaúnde 147, Lima 27; internet www.att.com.pe; f. 1997; known as BellSouth Perú until Dec. 2006; 97% owned by Telefónica Móviles, SA (Spain); mobile telephone services; Pres. JUAN SACA; Exec. Vice-Pres. FABIO COELHO; 900,000 customers.

Claro Perú: Lima; internet www.claro.com.pe; f. 2005; owned by América Móvil, SA de SV (Mexico); mobile cellular telecommunications services; Gen. Dir HUMBERTO CHÁVEZ.

Telefónica MoviStar: Juan de Arona 786, San Isidro, Lima; tel. (1) 9817000; internet www.telefonicamoviles.com.pe; f. 1994; 98% bought by Telefónica Móviles, SA (Spain) in 2000; mobile telephone services; 1.8m. customers.

Telefónica del Perú, SA: Avda Arequipa 1155, Santa Beatriz, Lima 1; tel. (1) 2101013; fax (1) 4705950; e-mail mgarcia@tp.com.pe; internet www.telefonica.com.pe; Pres. ANTONIO CARLOS VALENTE.

BROADCASTING

Regulatory Authorities

Asociación de Radio y Televisión del Perú (AR&TV): Avda Roma 140, San Isidro, Lima 27; tel. (1) 4703734; Pres. HUMBERTO MALDONADO BALBÍN; Dir DANIEL LINARES BAZÁN.

Coordinadora Nacional de Radio: Santa Sabina 441, Urb. Santa Emma, Apdo 2179, Lima 100; tel. (1) 5640760; fax (1) 5640059; e-mail postmaster@cnr.org.pe; internet www.cnr.org.pe; f. 1978; Pres. HUGO RAMÍREZ HUAMÁN; Exec. Dir JORGE ACEVEDO ROJAS.

Instituto Nacional de Comunicación Social: Jirón de la Unión 264, Lima; Dir HERNÁN VALDIZÁN.

PERU

Unión de Radioemisoras de Provincias del Perú (UNRAP): Mariano Carranza 754, Santa Beatriz, Lima 1.

State Corporation

Instituto Nacional de Radio y Televisión Peruana (IRTP): Avda Paseo de la República 1110, Lima 1; tel. (1) 471-8200; internet www.irtp.com.pe; f. 1996; Exec. Pres. ALFONSO SALCEDO RUBIO; runs the following stations:

Radio Nacional del Perú: Avda Petit Thouars 447, Santa Beatriz, Lima 1; tel. (1) 4331404; fax (1) 4338952; internet www.radionacional.com.pe; state broadcaster; Man. FELIPE TOMÁS GRANADOS VÁSQUEZ.

Televisión Nacional del Perú (TV Perú): Lima; tel. (1) 6190707; internet www.tnp.gob.pe; f. 1958 as Radio y Televisión Peruana; state broadcaster; 22 stations; Commercial Man. RODOLFO RUSCA LEVANO.

Radio

Radio Agricultura del Perú, SA—La Peruanísima: Casilla 625, Lima 11; tel. (1) 4246677; e-mail radioagriculturadelperu@yahoo.com; f. 1963; Gen. Man. LUZ ISABEL DEXTRE NÚÑEZ.

Radio América: Montero Rosas 1099, Santa Beatriz, Lima 1; tel. (1) 2653841; fax (1) 2653844; e-mail kcrous@americatv.com.pe; f. 1943; Dir-Gen. KAREN CROUSILLAT.

Cadena Peruana de Noticias: Gral Salaverry 156, Miraflores, Lima; tel. (1) 4461554; fax (1) 4457770; e-mail webmastercpn@gestion.com.pe; internet www.cpnradio.com.pe; f. 1996; Pres. MANUEL ROMERO CARO; Gen. Man. OSCAR ROMERO CARO.

Radio Cutivalú, La Voz del Desierto: Jirón Ignacio de Loyola 300, Urb. Miraflores, Castilla, Piura; tel. (74) 342802; fax (74) 343370; e-mail cutivalu@cipcaorg.pe; f. 1986; Pres. FRANCISCO MUGUIRO IBARRA; Dir RODOLFO AQUINO RUIZ.

Emisoras 'Cruz del Perú': Victorino Laynes 1402, Urb. Elio, Lima 1; tel. (1) 4521028; Pres. FERNANDO CRUZ MENDOZA; Gen. Man. MARCO CRUZ MENDOZA M.

Emisoras Nacionales: León Velarde 1140, Lince, Lima 1; tel. (1) 4714948; fax (1) 4728182; Gen. Man. CÉSAR COLOMA R.

Radio Inca del Perú: Pastor Dávila 197, Lima; tel. (1) 2512596; fax (1) 2513324; e-mail corporacion@corporacionradial.com.pe; f. 1951; Gen. Man. ABRAHAM ZAVALA CHOCANO.

Radio Panamericana: Paseo Parodi 340, San Isidro, Lima 27; tel. (1) 4226787; fax (1) 4221182; e-mail mad@radiopanamericana.com; internet www.radiopanamericana.com; f. 1953; Dir RAQUEL DELGADO DE ALCÁNTARA.

Radio Programas del Perú (GRUPORPP): Avda Paseo de la República 38667, San Isidro, Lima; tel. (1) 4338720; Pres. MANUEL DELGADO PARKER; Gen. Man. HUGO DELGADO NACHTIGALL.

Radio Santa Rosa: Jirón Camaná 170, Apdo 206, Lima; tel. (1) 4277488; fax (1) 4269219; e-mail santarosa@viaexpresa.com.pe; f. 1958; Dir P. JUAN SOKOLICH ALVARADO.

Sonograbaciones Maldonado: Mariano Carranza 754, Santa Beatriz, Lima; tel. (1) 4715163; fax (1) 4727491; Pres. HUMBERTO MALDONADO B.; Gen. Man. LUIS HUMBERTO MALDONADO.

Television

América Televisión, Canal 4: Jirón Montero Rosas 1099, Santa Beatriz, Lima; tel. (1) 2657361; fax (1) 2656979; e-mail infoamerica@americatv.com.pe; internet www.americatv.com.pe; Gen. Man. MARISOL CROUSILLAT.

ATV, Canal 9: Avda Arequipa 3570, San Isidro, Lima 27; tel. (1) 2118800; fax (1) 4427636; e-mail andinatelevision@atv.com.pe; internet www.atv.com.pe; f. 1983; Gen. Man. MARCELLO CÚNEO LOBIANO.

Frecuencia Latina, Canal 2: Avda San Felipe 968, Jesús María, Lima; tel. (1) 4707272; fax (1) 4714187; internet www.frecuencialatina.com.pe; Pres. BARUCH IVCHER.

Global Televisión, Canal 13: Gen. Orbegoso 140, Breña, Lima; tel. (1) 3303040; fax (1) 4238202; f. 1989; Pres. GENARO DELGADO PARKER; Gen. Man. RAFAEL LEGUÍA.

Nor Peruana de Radiodifusión, SA: Avda Arequipa 3520, San Isidro, Lima 27; tel. (1) 403365; fax (1) 419844; f. 1991; Dir FRANCO PALERMO IBARGUENGOITIA; Gen. Man. FELIPE BERNINZÓN VALLARINO.

Panamericana Televisión SA, Canal 5: Avda Alejandro Tirado 217, Santa Beatriz, Lima; tel. (1) 4113201; fax (1) 4703001; e-mail fanchorena@pantel.com.pe; internet www.24horas.com.pe; Pres. RAFAEL RAVETTINO FLORES; Gen. Man. FREDERICO ANCHORENA VÁSQUEZ.

Cía Peruana de Radiodifusión, Canal 4 TV: Mariano Carranza y Montero Rosas 1099, Santa Beatriz, Lima; tel. (1) 4728985; fax (1) 4710099; f. 1958; Dir JOSÉ FRANCISCO CROUSILLAT CARREÑO.

RBC Televisión, Canal 11: Avda Manco Cápac 333, La Victoria, Lima; tel. (1) 4310169; fax (1) 4331237; Pres. FERNANDO GONZÁLEZ DEL CAMPO; Gen. Man. JUAN SÁENZ MARÓN.

Cía de Radiodifusión Arequipa SA, Canal 9: Centro Comercial Cayma, R2, Arequipa; tel. (54) 252525; fax (54) 254959; e-mail crasa@ibm.net; f. 1986; Dir ENRIQUE MENDOZA NÚÑEZ; Gen. Man. ENRIQUE MENDOZA DEL SOLAR.

Uranio, Canal 15: Avda Arequipa 3570, 6°, San Isidro, Lima; e-mail agamarra@atv.com.pe; internet www.uranio15.com; Gen. Man. ADELA GAMARRA VÁSQUEZ.

Finance

In April 1991 a new banking law was introduced, relaxing state control of the financial sector and reopening the sector to foreign banks (which had been excluded from the sector by a nationalization law promulgated in 1987).

BANKING

(cap. = capital; res = reserves; dep. = deposits; m. = million; brs = branches; amounts in new soles unless otherwise indicated)

Superintendencia de Banca y Seguros: Los Laureles 214, San Isidro, Lima 27; tel. (1) 2218990; fax (1) 4417760; e-mail mostos@sbs.gob.pe; internet www.sbs.gob.pe; f. 1931; Supt JUAN JOSÉ MARTHANS LEÓN; Sec.-Gen. NORMA SOLARI PRECIADO.

Central Bank

Banco Central de Reserva del Perú: Jirón Antonio Miró Quesada 441-445, Lima 1; tel. (1) 4267041; fax (1) 4273091; e-mail webmaster@bcrp.gob.pe; internet www.bcrp.gob.pe; f. 1922; refounded 1931; cap. 295.7m., res 110.3m., dep. 39,030.5m. (Dec. 2006); Chair. JULIO VELARDE FLORES; Gen. Man. RENZO ROSSINI MIÑÁN; 7 brs.

Other Government Banks

Banco de la Nación: Avda Canaval y Moreyra 150, San Isidro, Lima 1; tel. (1) 4405858; fax (1) 4223451; e-mail imagen@bn.com.pe; internet www.bn.com.pe; f. 1966; cap. 866.5m., res 336.4m., dep. 10,928.0m. (Dec. 2006); conducts all commercial banking operations of official govt agencies; Exec. Pres. ENRIQUE JAVIER CORNEJO RAMÍREZ; Gen. Man. HUMBERTO ORLANDO MENESES ARANCIBIA; 391 brs.

Corporación Financiera de Desarrollo (COFIDE): Augusto Tamayo 160, San Isidro, Lima 27; tel. (1) 6154000; fax (1) 4423374; e-mail postmaster@cofide.com.pe; internet www.cofide.com.pe; f. 1971; also owners of Banco Latino; Pres. AURELIO LORET DE MOLA BÖHME; Gen. Man. MARCO CASTILLO TORRES; 11 brs.

Commercial Banks

Banco de Comercio: Avda Paseo de la República 3705, San Isidro, Lima; tel. (1) 5136000; fax (1) 4405458; e-mail postmaster@bancomercio.com.pe; internet www.bancomercio.com; f. 1967; fmrly Banco Peruano de Comercio y Construcción; cap. 54.6m., res 0.3m., dep. 548.8m. (Dec. 2005); Chair. WILFREDO JESÚS LAFOSSE QUINTANA; Gen. Man. CARLOS ALBERTO MUJICA CASTRO; 23 brs.

Banco de Crédito del Perú: Calle Centenario 156, Urb. Las Laderas de Melgarejo, Apdo 12-067, Lima 12; tel. (1) 3132000; internet www.viabcp.com; f. 1889; cap. 1,286.5m., res 805.5m., dep. 18,969.3m., total assets 23,431.8m. (Dec. 2004); Pres. and Chair. DIONISIO ROMERO SEMINARIO; 217 brs.

Banco Interamericano de Finanzas, SA: Avda Rivera Navarrete 600, San Isidro, Lima 27; tel. (1) 2113000; fax (1) 2212489; internet www.bif.com.pe; f. 1991; total assets US $695m. (Dec. 2005); Pres. FRANCISCO ROCHE; Gen. Man. and CEO RAÚL BALTAR; 33 brs.

Banco del Trabajo: Avda Paseo de la República 3587, 4°, San Isidro, Lima; tel. (1) 4219000; fax (1) 4212521; e-mail informes@bantra.com.pe; internet www.bantra.com.pe; Chair. CARLOS ENRIQUE CARRILLO QUIÑONES; Gen. Man. MAX JULIO CHION LI; 46 brs.

BBVA Banco Continental: Avda República de Panamá 3055, San Isidro, Lima 27; tel. (1) 2111000; fax (1) 2111788; internet www.bbvabancocontinental.com; f. 1951; merged with BBVA of Spain in 1995; 92.01% owned by Holding Continental, SA; cap. 852.9m., res 225.6m., dep. 12,292.4m. (Dec. 2004); Pres. and Chair. PEDRO BESCIA CAFFERATA; Gen. Man. JOSÉ ANTONIO COLOMER GUIU; 190 brs.

INTERBANK (Banco Internacional del Perú): Carlos Villarán 140, Urb. Santa Catalina, Lima 13; tel. (1) 2192000; fax (1) 2192336; e-mail krubin@intercorp.com.pe; internet www.interbank.com.pe; f. 1897; commercial bank; cap. 406.2m., res 101.6m., dep. 6,220.4m. (Dec. 2006); Chair. and Pres. CARLOS RODRÍGUEZ-PASTOR; Gen. Man. JORGE FLORES ESPINOZA; 90 brs.

PERU *Directory*

Scotiabank Peru, SAA: Avda Dionisio Derteano 102, San Isidro, Apdo 1235, Lima; tel. (1) 2116060; fax (1) 4407945; e-mail scotiaenlinea@scotiabank.com.pe; internet www.scotiabank.com.pe; f. 2006 by merger of Banco Sudamericano (owned by Scotiabank, Canada) and Banco Wiese Sudameris; cap. 502.6m., res 1,353.6m., dep. 10,671.7m. (Dec. 2006); Chair. JIM MEEK; Vice-Pres. and CEO CARLOS GONZÁLEZ-TABOADA.

Banking Association

Asociación de Bancos del Perú: Calle 41, No 975, Urb. Córpac, San Isidro, Lima 27; tel. (1) 6123333; fax (1) 6123316; e-mail earroyo@asbanc.com.pe; internet www.asbanc.com.pe; f. 1929; refounded 1967; Pres. OSCAR JOSÉ RIVERA; Gen. Man. JULIO ENRIQUE ARROYO RIZO PATRÓN.

STOCK EXCHANGE

Bolsa de Valores de Lima: Pasaje Acuña 106, Lima 100; tel. (1) 4260714; fax (1) 4267650; internet www.bvl.com.pe; f. 1860; Exec. Pres. RAFAEL D'ANGELO SERRA.

REGULATORY AUTHORITY

Comisión Nacional Supervisora de Empresas y Valores (CONASEV): Santa Cruz 315, Miraflores, Lima; tel. (1) 4416620; fax (1) 4428401; e-mail cendoc@conasev.gob.pe; internet www.conasev.gob.pe; f. 1968; regulates the securities market; responsible to Ministry of Economy and Finance; Pres. LILLIAN ROCA CARBAJAL.

INSURANCE

Lima

Altas Cumbres Cía de Seguros de Vida, SA: Avda Paseo de la República 3587, San Isidro, Lima; tel. (1) 4428228; fax (1) 2213313; e-mail asalazar@altascumbres.com.pe; internet www.altascumbres.com.pe; f. 1999; life; Pres. CARLOS CARRILLO QUIÑONES; Gen. Man. ALFREDO SALAZAR DELGADO.

Generali Perú, Cía de Seguros y Reaseguros: Jirón Antonio Miró Quesada 191, Apdo 1751, Lima 100; tel. (1) 3111000; fax (1) 3111004; e-mail borlandini@generali-peru-com.pe; internet www.generali-peru.com.pe; f. 1896; Pres. RAFFAELE TIANO SAMBO; Gen. Man. BRUNO ORLANDINI ALVAREZ-CALDERÓN.

Interseguro Cía de Seguros de Vida, SA: Avda Pardo y Aliaga 640, 4°, San Isidro, Lima; tel. (1) 2223233; fax (1) 2223222; e-mail juan.vallejo@intercorp.com.pe; f. 1998; life; Pres. FELIPE MORRIS GUERINONI; Gen. Man. JUAN CARLOS VALLEJO BLANCO.

Invita Seguros de Vida, SA: Torre Wiese, Canaval y Moreyra 532, San Isidro, Lima; tel. (1) 2222222; fax (1) 2211683; e-mail dcosta@invita.com.pe; internet www.invita.com.pe; f. 2000; life; fmrly Wiese Aetna, SA; Pres. CARIDAD DE LA PUENTE WIESE; Gen. Man. DULIO COSTA OLIVERA.

Mapfre Perú Cía de Seguros: Avda 28 de Julio 873, Miraflores, Apdo 323, Lima 100; tel. (1) 4444515; fax (1) 4469599; e-mail fmarco@mapfreperu.com; internet www.mapfreperu.com; f. 1994; general; fmrly Seguros El Sol, SA; Pres. Dr FRANCISCO JOSÉ MARCO ORENES.

Pacífico, Cía de Seguros y Reaseguros: Avda Arequipa 660, Lima 100; tel. (1) 4333626; fax (1) 4333388; e-mail arodrigo@pps.com.pe; f. 1943; general; Pres. CALIXTO ROMERO SEMINARIO; Gen. Man. ARTURO RODRIGO SANTISTEVAN.

La Positiva Cía de Seguros y Reaseguros, SA: esq. Javier Prado Este y Francisco Masías 370, San Isidro, Lima; tel. (1) 2110000; fax (1) 2110020; e-mail jaimep@lapositiva.com.pe; internet www.lapositiva.com.pe; f. 1947; Pres. Ing. JUAN MANUEL PEÑA ROCA; Gen. Man. JAIME PÉREZ RODRÍGUEZ.

Rimac Internacional, Cía de Seguros: Las Begonias 475, 3°, San Isidro, Lima; tel. (1) 4218383; fax (1) 4210570; e-mail jortecho@rimac.com.pe; internet www.rimac.com.pe; f. 1896; acquired Seguros Fénix in 2004; Pres. Ing. PEDRO BRESCIA CAFFERATA; Gen. Man. PEDRO FLECHA ZALBA.

SECREX, Cía de Seguro de Crédito y Garantías: Avda Angamos Oeste 1234, Miraflores, Lima; Apdo 0511, Lima 18; tel. (1) 4424033; fax (1) 4423890; e-mail ciaseg@secrex.com.pe; internet www.secrex.com.pe; f. 1980; Pres. Dr RAÚL FERRERO COSTA; Gen. Man. JUAN A. GIANNONI MURGA.

Sul América Cía de Seguros, SA: Jirón Sinchi Roca 2728, Lince, Lima; tel. (1) 2150515; fax (1) 4418730; e-mail lavila@sulamerica.com.pe; internet www.sulamerica.com.pe; f. 1954; part of Sul América, SA (Brazil); Pres. RAÚL BARRIOS ORBEGOSO; Gen. Man. LUIS MIGUEL AVILA MERINO.

Insurance Association

Asociación Peruana de Empresas de Seguros (APESEG): Arias Araguez 146, Miraflores, Lima 18; tel. (1) 4442294; fax (1) 4468538; e-mail rda@apeseg.org.pe; internet www.apeseg.org.pe; f. 1904; Pres. RENZO CALDA; Gen. Man. RAÚL DE ANDREA DE LAS CARRERAS.

Trade and Industry

GOVERNMENT AGENCIES

Agencia de Promoción de la Inversión Privada (ProInversión): Avda Paseo de la República 3361, 9°, San Isidro, Lima 27; tel. (1) 6121200; fax (1) 2212942; e-mail gvillegas@proinversion.gob.pe; internet www.proinversion.gob.pe; f. 2002 to promote economic investment; Dir RENÉ CORNEJO DÍAZ; Gen. Sec. ITALO BIZERRA.

Empresa Nacional de la Coca, SA (ENACO): Avda Arequipa 4528, Miraflores, Lima; tel. (1) 4271369; fax (1) 4273071; e-mail lmarin@enaco.com.pe; internet www.enaco.com.pe; f. 1949; agency with exclusive responsibility for the purchase and resale of legally produced coca and the promotion of its derivatives; Pres. LIDA MARIN LOAYZA; Gen. Man. RAÚL CAMPANA RAMOS.

Fondo Nacional de Compensación y Desarrollo Social (FONCODES): Avda Paseo de la República 3101, San Isidro, Lima; tel. (1) 4212102; fax (1) 4218026; e-mail consultas@foncodes.gob.pe; internet www.foncodes.gob.pe; f. 1991; responsible for social devt and eradicating poverty; Exec. Dir CARLOTA CLELIA HUAROTO MUNAREZ DE PONCE.

Instituto Nacional de Recursos Forestales (INRENA): Calle Diecisiete 355, Urb. El Palomar, Lima; tel. (1) 2252113; fax (1) 2243218; e-mail gerencia.general@inrena.gob.pe; internet www.inrena.gob.pe; f. 1992; promotes sustainable devt of Amazon rainforest; Pres. ISAAC ROBERTO ANGELES LAZO; Gen. Man. MIGUEL DE LOS REYES ROSAS SILVA.

Perupetro: Luis Aldana 320, San Borja, Lima; tel. (1) 4759590; fax (1) 4757722; e-mail admweb@perupetro.com.pe; internet www.perupetro.com.pe; f. 1993; responsible for promoting investment in hydrocarbon exploration and exploitation; Chair. DANIEL SABA DE ANDREA; CEO CARLOS VIVES SUÁREZ.

DEVELOPMENT ORGANIZATIONS

ACP Inversiones y Desarrollo: Avda Domingo Orue 165, Surquillo, Lima 34; tel. (1) 2220202; fax (1) 2224166; e-mail accion@accion.org.pe; f. 1969; promotes economic, social and cultural devt through improvements in service provision.

Asociación de Exportadores (ADEX): Javier Prado Este 2875, San Borja, Lima 41; Apdo 1806, Lima 1; tel. (1) 3462530; fax (1) 3461879; e-mail prensa@adexperu.org.pe; internet www.adexperu.org.pe; f. 1973; exporters' asscn; Pres. LUIS VEGA MONTEFERRI; Gen. Man. ALVARO BARRENECHEA; 600 mems.

Asociación Kallpa para la Promoción Integral de la Salud y el Desarrollo: Jirón Rospigliosi 105, Barranco, Lima 4; tel. (1) 4455521; fax (1) 2429693; e-mail postmast@kallpa.org.pe; internet www.kallpa.org.pe; health devt for youths; Pres. ARIELA LUNA FLORES.

Asociación Nacional de Centros de Investigación, Promoción Social y Desarrollo: Pablo Bermúdez 234, Jesús María, Lima; tel. (1) 4411063; fax (1) 4411227; e-mail postmaster@anc.org.pe; internet www.anc.org.pe; umbrella grouping of devt orgs; Pres. LUIS SIRUMBAL; Exec. Dir FEDERICO ARNILLAS L.

Asociación para la Naturaleza y Desarrollo Sostenible (ANDES): Calle Ruinas 451, Cusco; tel. (8) 4245021; e-mail andes@andes.org.pe; internet www.andes.org.pe; devt org. promoting the culture, education and environment of indigenous groups.

Sociedad Nacional de Industrias (SNI) (National Industrial Association): Los Laureles 365, San Isidro, Apdo 632, Lima 27; tel. (1) 4218830; fax (1) 4422573; e-mail sni@sni.org.pe; internet www.sni.org.pe; f. 1896; comprises permanent commissions covering various aspects of industry including labour, integration, fairs and exhibitions, industrial promotion; its Small Industry Cttee groups over 2,000 small enterprises; Pres. EDUARDO FARAH; Gen. Man. FEDERICO DE APARICI; 90 dirs (reps of firms); 2,500 mems; 60 sectorial cttees.

  Centro de Desarrollo Industrial (CDI): Los Laureles 365, San Isidro, Lima; tel. (1) 2158888; fax (1) 2158877; e-mail cdi@sni.org.pe; internet www.cdi.org.pe; f. 1986; supports industrial devt and programmes to develop industrial cos; Exec. Dir LUIS TENORIO PUENTES.

CHAMBERS OF COMMERCE

Cámara de Comercio de Lima (Lima Chamber of Commerce): Avda Gregorio Escobedo 398, Jesús María, Lima 11; tel. (1) 4633434; fax (1) 2191777; e-mail secreceex@camaralima.org.pe; internet www.camaralima.org.pe; f. 1888; Pres. SAMUEL GLEISER KATZ; 5,500 mems.

Cámara Nacional de Comercio, Producción y Servicios (PERUCAMARAS): Avda Gregorio Escobedo 396, Jesús María, Lima 11;

PERU

e-mail administracion@perucam.com; internet www.perucamaras.com; national asscn of chambers of commerce; Pres. SAMUEL GLEISER KATZ; Gen. Man. JOSÉ MARTÍN TELLO.

There are also Chambers of Commerce in Arequipa, Cusco, Callao and many other cities.

EMPLOYERS' ORGANIZATIONS

Asociación Automotriz del Perú: Dos de Mayo 299, Apdo 1248, San Isidro, Lima 27; tel. (1) 4404119; fax (1) 4428865; e-mail aap@terra.com.pe; f. 1926; asscn of importers of motor cars and accessories; 360 mems; Pres. CARLOS BAMBARÉN GARCÍA-MALDONADO; Gen. Man. CÉSAR MARTÍN BARREDA.

Asociación de Ganaderos del Perú (Association of Stock Farmers of Peru): Pumacahua 877, 3°, Jesús María, Lima; f. 1915; Gen. Man. Ing. MIGUEL J. FORT.

Confederación Nacional de Instituciones Empresariales Privadas (CONFIEP): Pasaje Acuña 106, Lima; e-mail postmaster@confiep.org.pe; internet www.confiep.org.pe; f. 1984; federation of 20 employers' orgs; Pres. JAIME CÁCERES SAYAN.

Consejo Nacional del Café: Lima; reps of govt and industrial coffee growers; Pres. ENRIQUE ALDAVE.

Sociedad Nacional de Minería y Petróleo: Francisco Graña 671, Magdalena del Mar, Lima 17; tel. (1) 4601600; fax (1) 4601616; e-mail postmaster@snmpe.org.pe; internet www.snmpe.org.pe; f. 1940; Pres. YSSAC CRUZ RAMÍREZ; Sec.-Gen. DANTE LAGATTA STELLA; asscn of cos involved in mining, petroleum and energy.

Sociedad Nacional de Pesquería (SNP): Javier Prado Oeste 2442, San Isidro, Lima 27; tel. (1) 2612970; fax (1) 2617912; e-mail snpnet@snp.org.pe; internet www.snp.org.pe; f. 1952; private-sector fishing interests; Pres. RAÚL ALBERTO SÁNCHEZ SOTOMAYOR; Gen. Man. RICHARD INURRITEGUI BAZÁN.

UTILITIES
Regulatory Authority

Gerencia Adjunta de Regulación Tarifaria (GART): Avda Canadá 1470, San Borja, Lima 41; tel. (1) 2240487; fax (1) 2240491; internet www2.osinerg.gob.pe/gart.htm; autonomous agency controlling tariffs.

Electricity

Electrolima, SA: Jirón Zorritos 1301, Lima 5; tel. (1) 4324153; fax (1) 4323042; e-mail junta.directiva@electrolima.com; internet www.electrolima.com; f. 1906; produces and supplies electricity for Lima and the surrounding districts; state-owned; Gen. Man. Dr DARÍO CUERVO VILLAFAÑE.

Electroperú: Prolongación Pedro Miotta 421, San Juan de Miraflores, Lima 29; tel. (1) 2170600; fax (1) 2170621; internet www.electroperu.com; state-owned; Pres. CÉSAR BUTRÓN FERNÁNDEZ; Gen. Man. RAÚL TENGAN MATSUTAHARA.

Distriluz: Vicente de la Vega 318, Chiclayo; tel. (74) 231580; fax (74) 227751; e-mail jvelasquez@distriluz.com.pe; internet www.distriluz.com.pe; operates 4 energy distribution cos: Enosa, Ensa, Hidrandina and Electrocentro; Co-ordinator JUAN VELÁSQUEZ GONZALES.

Sociedad Eléctrica del Sur-Oeste, SA (SEAL): Consuelo 310, Arequipa; tel. (54) 212946; fax (54) 213296; e-mail seal@sealperu.com; internet www.sealperu.com; f. 1905; Pres. MAURICIO CHIRINOS CHIRINOS; Gen. Man. JOSÉ OPORTO VARGAS.

TRADE UNIONS

The right to strike was restored in the Constitution of July 1979. In 1982 the Government recognized the right of public employees to form trade unions.

Central Unica de Trabajadores Peruanos (CUTP): Lima; f. 1992; Pres. JULIO CÉSAR BAZÁN; includes:

Confederación General de Trabajadores del Perú (CGTP): Plaza 2 de Mayo 4, Lima 1; tel. (1) 4314738; e-mail cgtp@cgtp.org.pe; internet www.cgtp.org.pe; f. 1968; Pres. MARIO HUAMÁN RIVERA; Sec.-Gen. JUAN JOSÉ GORRITI VALLE.

Confederación Nacional de Trabajadores (CNT): Avda Iquitos 1198, Lima; tel. (1) 4711385; affiliated to the PPC; c. 12,000 mems; Sec.-Gen. ANTONIO GALLARDO EGOAVIL.

Confederación de Trabajadores del Perú (CTP): Jirón Ayacucho 173, CP 3616, Lima 1; tel. (1) 4261310; e-mail ctp7319@hotmail.com; affiliated to PAP; Sec.-Gen. ELÍAS GRIJALVA ALVARADO.

Confederación Intersectorial de Trabajadores Estatales (CITE) (Union of Public Sector Workers): Lima; tel. (1) 4245525; f. 1978; Sec.-Gen. ALAVARO COLE; Asst Sec. OMAR CAMPOS; 600,000 mems.

Federación de Empleados Bancarios (FEB) (Union of Bank Employees): Jirón Miró Quesada 260, 7°, Lima; tel. (1) 7249570; e-mail febperu@terra.com.pe; Sec.-Gen. HÉCTOR PÉREZ PÉREZ.

Federación Nacional de Trabajadores Mineros, Metalúrgicos y Siderúrgicos (FNTMMS) (Federation of Peruvian Mineworkers): Jirón Callao 457, Of. 311, Lima; tel. (1) 4277554; Sec.-Gen. PEDRO ESCATE SULCA; 70,000 mems.

Movimiento de Trabajadores y Obreros de Clase (MTOC): Lima.

Sindicato Unitario de los Trabajadores en la Educación del Perú (SUTEP) (Union of Peruvian Teachers): Camaná 550, Lima; tel. (1) 4276677; fax (1) 4268692; e-mail suteperu@yahoo.es; internet www.sutep.org.pe; f. 1972; Sec.-Gen. LUIS MUÑOZ.

Independent unions, representing an estimated 37% of trade unionists, include the Comité para la Coordinación Clasista y la Unificación Sindical, the Confederación de Campesinos Peruanos (CCP) and the Confederación Nacional Agraria (Pres. MIGUEL CLEMENTE ALEGRE).

Confederación Nacional de Comunidades Industriales (CONACI): Lima; co-ordinates worker participation in industrial management and profit-sharing.

The following agricultural organizations exist:

Confederación Nacional de Productores Agropecuarios de las Cuencas Cocaleras del Perú (CONPACCP): Lima; coca-growers' confederation; Sec.-Gen. NELSÓN PALOMINO.

Consejo Unitario Nacional Agrario (CUNA): f. 1983; represents 36 farmers' and peasants' orgs, including:

Confederación Campesina del Perú (CCP): radical left-wing; Pres. ANDRÉS LUNA VARGAS; Sec. HUGO BLANCO.

Organización Nacional Agraria (ONA): org. of dairy farmers and cattle-breeders.

Transport

RAILWAYS

In 2006 there were some 1,691 km of track.

Ministry of Transport and Communications: see section on The Government (Ministries).

Consorcio Ferrocarriles del Perú: in July 1999, following the privatization of the state railway company, Empresa Nacional de Ferrocarriles (ENAFER), the above consortium won a 30-year concession to operate the following lines:

Empresa Minera del Centro del Perú SA—División Ferrocarriles (Centromín-Perú SA) (fmrly Cerro de Pasco Railway): Edif. Solgas, Avda Javier Prado Este 2175, San Borja, Apdo 2412, Lima 41; tel. (1) 4761010; fax (1) 4769757; acquired by Enafer-Perú in 1997; 212.2 km; Pres. HERNÁN BARRETO; Gen. Man. GUILLERMO GUANILO.

Ferrocarril Transandino, SA (Southern Railway): Calle Alcanfores 775, Miraflores, Lima; tel. (54) 215350; fax (54) 231603; 915 km open; also operates steamship service on Lake Titicaca; Man. C. NORIEGA.

Ferrocarril Transandino SA: operates Ferrocarril del Sur y Oriente.

Ferrovías Central Andina, SA: Avda José Galvez Barrenechea 566, 5°, San Isidro, Lima; tel. (1) 2266363; e-mail ferroviasperu@fcca.com.pe; internet www.ferroviasperu.com.pe; f. 1999; operates Ferrocarril del Centro del Perú.

Tacna–Arica Ferrocarril (Tacna–Arica Railway): Avda Aldarracín 484, Tacna; 62 km open.

Ferrocarril Pimentel (Pimentel Railway): Pimentel, Chiclayo, Apdo 310; 56 km open; owned by Empresa Nacional de Puertos; cargo services only; Pres. R. MONTENEGRO; Man. LUIS DE LA PIEDRA ALVIZURI.

Private Railways

Ferrocarril Ilo–Toquepala–Cuajone: Apdo 2640, Lima; 219 km open, incl. five tunnels totalling 27 km; owned by the Southern Peru Copper Corpn for transporting copper supplies and concentrates only; CEO OSCAR GONZÁLEZ ROCHA; Gen. Dir, Operations MAURICIO PERÓ.

Ferrocarril Supe–Barranca–Alpas: Barranca; 40 km open; Dirs CARLOS GARCÍA GASTAÑETA, LUIS G. MIRANDA.

ROADS

There were an estimated 78,000 km of roads in Peru, of which approximately 30% was paved or semi-paved. The most important highways are: the Pan-American Highway (3,008 km), which runs southward from the Ecuadorean border along the coast to Lima; Camino del Inca Highway (3,193 km) from Piura to Puno; Marginal de la Selva (1,688 km) from Cajamarca to Madre de Dios; and the

Trans-Andean Highway (834 km), which runs from Lima to Pucallpa on the River Ucayali via Oroya, Cerro de Pasco and Tingo María.

SHIPPING

Most trade is through the port of Callao but there are 13 deep-water ports, mainly in northern Peru (including Salaverry, Pacasmayo and Paita) and in the south (including the iron-ore port of San Juan). There are river ports at Iquitos, Pucallpa and Yurimaguas, aimed at improving communications between Lima and Iquitos, and a further port is under construction at Puerto Maldonado.

Agencia Naviera Maynas, SA: Avda San Borja Norte 761, San Borja, Lima 41; tel. (1) 4752033; fax (1) 4759680; e-mail lima@navieramaynas.com.pe; f. 1996; Pres. R. USSEGLIO D.; Gen. Man. ROBERTO MELGAR B.

Empresa Nacional de Puertos, SA (Enapu): Avda Contralmirante Raygada 110, Callao; tel. (1) 4299210; fax (1) 4691010; e-mail enapu@inconet.net.pe; internet www.enapu.com.pe; f. 1970; govt agency administering all coastal and river ports; Gen. Man. ROBERTO COLOMBO MISCHIATTI.

Asociación Marítima del Perú: Avda Javier Prado Este 897, Of. 33, San Isidro, Apdo 3520, Lima 27; tel. and fax (1) 4221904; f. 1957; asscn of 20 int. and Peruvian shipping cos; Pres. LUIS FELIPE VILLENA GUTIÉRREZ.

Consorcio Naviero Peruano, SA: Avda Central 643, San Isidro, Apdo 18-0736, Lima 1; tel. (1) 4116500; fax (1) 4116599; e-mail cnp@cnpsa.com; internet www.cnpsa.com; f. 1959.

Naviera Humboldt, SA: Edif. Pacífico–Washington, 9°, Natalio Sánchez 125, Apdo 3639, Lima 1; tel. (1) 4334005; fax (1) 4337151; e-mail postmast@sorcomar.com.pe; internet www.humboldt.com.pe; f. 1970; cargo services; Pres. AUGUSTO BEDOYA CAMERE; Man. Dir LUIS FREIRE R.

Naviera Universal, SA: Calle 41 No 894, Urb. Corpac, San Isidro, Apdo 10307, Lima 100; tel. (1) 4757020; fax (1) 4755233; Chair. HERBERT C. BUERGER.

Petrolera Transoceánica, SA (PETRANSO): San Isidro, Lima 27; tel. (1) 5139300; fax (1) 5139322; e-mail petranso@petranso.com; internet www.petranso.com; Gen. Man. JUAN VILLARÁN.

CIVIL AVIATION

Of Peru's 294 airports and airfields, the major international airport is Jorge Chávez Airport near Lima. Other important international airports are Coronel Francisco Secada Vignetta Airport, near Iquitos, Velasco Astete Airport, near Cusco, and Rodríguez Ballón Airport, near Arequipa.

Corporación Peruana de Aeropuertos y Aviación Comercial: Aeropuerto Internacional Jorge Chávez, Callao; tel. (1) 5750912; fax (1) 5745578; internet www.corpac.gob.pe; f. 1943; Pres. LEOPOLDO PFLUCKER LLONA; Gen. Man. ROBERT MCDONALD ZAPFF.

Domestic Airlines

Aero Condor: Juan de Arona 781, San Isidro, Lima; tel. (1) 4425215; fax (1) 2215783; internet www.aerocondor.com.pe; domestic services; Pres. CARLOS PALACÍN FERNÁNDEZ.

LAN Perú, SA: Lima; tel. (1) 2138200; internet www.lan.com; f. 1999; operations temporarily suspended in Oct. 2004; Exec. Vice-Pres. ENRIQUE CUETO P.

Nuevo Continente: Avda José Pardo 605, Lima 18; tel. (1) 2414816; fax (1) 2413074; internet www.aerocontinente.com.pe; f. 1992; domestic services; fmrly Aero Continente; operations suspended in July 2004; acquired by Vuela Perú in Nov. 2004; Pres. LUPE L. Z. GONZALES.

Tourism

Tourism is centred on Lima, with its Spanish colonial architecture, and Cusco, with its pre-Inca and Inca civilization, notably the 'lost city' of Machu Picchu. Lake Titicaca, lying at an altitude of 3,850 m above sea level, and the Amazon jungle region to the north-east are also popular destinations. From the mid-1990s there was evidence of a marked recovery in the tourism sector, which had been adversely affected by health and security concerns. In 2005 Peru received 1,486,005 visitors, and receipts from tourism in that year generated US $1,371m.

Comisión de Promoción del Perú (PromPerú): Edif. Mitinci, Calle Uno Oeste, 13°, Urb. Corpac, San Isidro, Lima 27; tel. (1) 2243279; fax (1) 2243323; e-mail postmaster@promperu.gob.pe; internet www.peru.org.pe; f. 1993; Head of Tourism MARÍA DEL PILAR LAZARTE CONROY; Gen. Man. MARÍA M. SEMINARIO MARÓN.

THE PHILIPPINES

Introductory Survey

Location, Climate, Language, Religion, Flag, Capital

The Republic of the Philippines lies in the western Pacific Ocean, east of mainland South-East Asia. The island of Borneo is to the south-west, and New Guinea to the south-east. The principal islands of the Philippine archipelago are Luzon, in the north, and Mindanao, in the south. Between these two (which together account for 66% of the country's area) lie the 7,000 islands of the Visayas. The climate is maritime and tropical. It is generally hot and humid, except in the mountains. There is abundant rainfall, and the islands are frequently in the path of typhoons. At the 1995 census there were 102 languages; the most frequently used were Tagalog (by 29.3% of the population), Cebuano (21.2%), Ilocano (9.3%), Hiligaynon (Ilongo—9.1%) and Bicol (5.7%). Filipino, based on Tagalog, is the native national language. English is widely spoken, and Spanish is used in some communities. In 1991 94.2% of the population were Christians (84.1% Roman Catholics, 6.2% belonged to the Philippine Independent Church (Aglipayan) and 3.9% were Protestants). In 1990 an estimated 4.6% of the population were Muslims. The national flag (proportions 1 by 2) has two equal horizontal stripes, of blue and red, with a white triangle, enclosing a yellow 'Sun of Liberty' (with eight large and 16 small rays) and three five-pointed yellow stars (one in each corner), at the hoist. The capital is Manila, on the island of Luzon.

Recent History

The Philippines became a Spanish colony in the 16th century. During the Spanish–American War, the independence of the Philippines was declared on 12 June 1898 by Gen. Emilio Aguinaldo, leader of the revolutionary movement, with the support of the USA. Under the Treaty of Paris, signed in December 1898, Spain ceded the islands to the USA. A new Constitution, ratified by plebiscite in May 1935, gave the Philippines internal self-government and provided for independence after 10 years. During the Second World War the islands were occupied by Japanese forces from 1942, but, after Japan's surrender in 1945, US rule was restored. The Philippines became an independent republic on 4 July 1946, with Manuel Roxas as its first President. A succession of Presidents, effectively constrained by US economic interests and the Filipino land-owning class, did little to help the peasant majority or to curb disorder and political violence.

At elections in November 1965 the incumbent President, Diosdado Macapagal of the Liberal Party (LP), was defeated by Ferdinand Marcos of the Nacionalista Party (NP). Rapid development of the economy and infrastructure followed. President Marcos was re-elected in 1969. His second term was characterized by civil unrest and economic difficulties. During the early 1970s there was also an increase in guerrilla activity, by the New People's Army (NPA), the armed wing of the outlawed (Maoist) Communist Party of the Philippines (CPP), in the north of the country, and by the Moro National Liberation Front (MNLF), a Muslim separatist movement, in the south.

In September 1972, before completing the (then) maximum of two four-year terms of office, President Marcos declared martial law in order to deal with subversive activity and to introduce drastic reforms. The bicameral Congress was suspended, opposition leaders were arrested, the private armies of the landed oligarchs were disbanded, stringent press censorship was introduced, and Marcos began to rule by decree. In November a new Constitution was approved by a constitutional convention, and in January 1973 it was ratified by Marcos. It provided for a unicameral National Assembly and a Constitutional President, with executive power held by a Prime Minister, to be elected by the legislature. Transitional provisions gave the incumbent President the combined authority of the presidency (under the 1935 Constitution) and the premiership, without any fixed term of office. Under martial law, the definitive provisions of the new Constitution remained in abeyance.

A referendum in July 1973 approved Marcos's continuation in office beyond his elected term. Referendums in February 1975 and October 1976 approved the continuation of martial law and the adoption of constitutional amendments, including a provision for the formation of an interim assembly. In December 1977 a fourth referendum approved the extension of Marcos's presidential term.

Criticism of President Marcos became more widespread after November 1977, when a sentence of death was imposed by a military tribunal on the principal opposition leader, Benigno Aquino, Jr (a former senator and Secretary-General of the LP, who had been detained since 1972), for alleged murder, subversion and the possession of firearms. Marcos allowed a stay of execution, and conceded some relaxation of martial law in 1977. Elections to the interim National Assembly took place in April 1978. Opposition parties were allowed to participate, but the pro-Government Kilusang Bagong Lipunan (KBL—New Society Movement), founded in 1978 by Marcos and former members of the NP, won 151 of the Assembly's 165 elective seats. The Assembly was inaugurated in June, when Marcos was also confirmed as Prime Minister. Martial law remained in force, and Marcos retained the power to legislate by decree. Local elections held in January 1980 resulted in decisive victories for the KBL. In May Benigno Aquino was released from prison to undergo medical treatment in the USA, where he renewed his opposition to Marcos's regime.

In January 1981 martial law was ended, although Marcos retained most of his former powers. A referendum in April approved constitutional amendments that permitted Marcos to renew his presidential mandate by direct popular vote and to nominate a separate Prime Minister. In June, amid allegations of electoral malpractice, Marcos was re-elected President for a six-year term. In April 1982 the United Nationalist Democratic Organization (UNIDO), an alliance of opposition groups, formed an official coalition: it included Lakas ng Bayan (the People's Power Movement, founded by Aquino in 1978) and the Pilipino Democratic Party (PDP), which merged to form PDP-Laban in 1983.

In August 1983 Aquino, returning from exile in the USA, was shot dead on arrival at Manila airport. Rolando Galman, the alleged communist assassin, was killed immediately by military guards. A commission of inquiry, nominated by the Government, concluded that Aquino's murder had been a military conspiracy. The Supreme Court announced in December 1985, however, that the evidence submitted to the commission was inadmissible, acquitted the 26 military personnel who had been accused of conspiring to murder Aquino and upheld the Government's assertion that the assassin was Galman.

Aquino's death proved to be a turning-point in Philippine politics, uniting the opposition in its criticism of Marcos. At elections to the National Assembly in May 1984, public participation was high, and, after numerous accusations by the opposition of electoral fraud and corruption by Marcos, the opposition won 59 of the 183 elective seats, compared with 14 in 1978.

In November 1985, in response to US pressure (and after continued appeals for domestic reform), Marcos announced that a presidential election would be held in February 1986, 18 months earlier than scheduled. Corazon Aquino, the widow of Benigno Aquino, was chosen as the UNIDO presidential candidate, in spite of her lack of political experience. More than 100 people were killed in violence during the election campaign. Vote-counting was conducted by the government-controlled National Commission on Elections (Comelec) and by the independent National Citizens' Movement for Free Elections (Namfrel). Allegations of large-scale electoral fraud and irregularities, apparently perpetrated by supporters of Marcos, were substantiated by numerous international observers. The National Assembly declared Marcos the winner of the presidential election, with 10.8m. votes, compared with 9.3m. for Aquino, according to figures from Comelec. According to Namfrel figures (based on 69% of the total votes), Aquino was in the lead. Marcos immediately announced the resignation of the Cabinet, and declared his intention to establish a council of presidential advisers. Aquino rejected an offer to participate in the council, and launched a campaign of non-violent pressure on the Government.

Later in February 1986 Lt-Gen. (later Gen.) Fidel Ramos, the acting Chief of Staff of the Armed Forces, and Juan Enrile, the Minister of National Defense, along with about 300 troops, established a rebel headquarters in the Ministry of National Defense in Manila (later moving to the police headquarters), stating that they no longer accepted Marcos's authority and asserting that Aquino was the rightful President. Attempts by forces loyal to Marcos to attack the rebels were foiled by large unarmed crowds, which gathered to protect them at the instigation of the Catholic Archbishop of Manila, Cardinal Jaime Sin. Troops supporting Ramos subsequently secured control of the government broadcasting station, with little bloodshed. Rival ceremonies were held, at which both Marcos and Aquino were sworn in as President. Later the same day, however, under pressure from the USA, Marcos finally agreed to withdraw, and left the Philippines for Hawaii.

President Aquino appointed her Vice-President, Salvador Laurel (the President of UNIDO), to be Prime Minister and Minister of Foreign Affairs, while Enrile retained the post of Minister of National Defense. Ramos was appointed Chief of Staff of the Armed Forces. At the end of February 1986 Aquino ordered the controversial release of all political prisoners, including communist leaders. In March the Government announced the restoration of habeas corpus, the abolition of press censorship and the suspension of local government elections (scheduled for May). The Government also secured the resignation of all Justices of the Supreme Court, as well as the resignation of Comelec members. Aquino announced that the 1973 Constitution was to be replaced by an interim document, providing for the immediate abolition of the National Assembly and for the inauguration of a provisional government, with the President being granted emergency powers. The post of Prime Minister was temporarily abolished, and in May a commission was appointed to draft a new constitution.

In March 1986 military leaders pledged their loyalty to Aquino. The Government then began to implement a programme of military reform, in accordance with the demands of officers of the Rebolusyonaryong Alyansang Makabayan (RAM—Nationalist Revolutionary Alliance—also known as the Reform the Armed Forces Movement), who had supported the February revolution. In September the Supreme Court ordered the retrial of the members of the military who had earlier been acquitted of the murder of Benigno Aquino. In September 1990 a special court convicted 16 members of the armed forces of the murder of both Aquino and Galman.

In July 1986 an abortive coup took place in Manila, led by Arturo Tolentino, a former Minister of Foreign Affairs and Marcos's vice-presidential candidate, and a group of 300 pro-Marcos troops. One of the principal reasons for military dissatisfaction was the new Government's conciliatory attitude towards communist insurgents. In June the Government had attempted to bring guerrilla activity by the NPA (estimated to number 25,000–30,000 members at that time) to an end, announcing that formal negotiations for a cease-fire agreement would begin with representatives of the National Democratic Front (NDF—a left-wing group that included the CPP and the NPA). In October, however, increasing pressure from Enrile and the RAM prompted Aquino to threaten the insurgents with open warfare if a solution were not reached by the end of November. In late November a group of army officers attempted to gain control of several military camps and to replace Aquino with Nicanor Yniguez, a former Speaker of the National Assembly. The rebellion was quelled by Ramos and troops loyal to Aquino; Enrile was dismissed from the Cabinet. In January 1987 there was a further coup attempt by 500 disaffected soldiers; an attempt by Marcos to return to the Philippines was thwarted by US officials, and the two-day rebellion was suppressed by forces loyal to Aquino.

In February 1987 a new Constitution was approved by 76% of voters in a national plebiscite. The new Constitution gave President Aquino a mandate to rule until 30 June 1992, and established an executive presidency (see Government, below). All members of the armed forces swore an oath of allegiance to the new Constitution. An order followed disbanding all 'fraternal organizations' (such as the RAM) within the armed forces, because they 'encouraged divisiveness'. Elections to the bicameral Congress of the Philippines took place on 11 May 1987, at which more than 83% of the electorate participated. Aquino's Lakas ng Bayan coalition secured 180 of the 200 elective seats in the House of Representatives and 22 of the 24 seats in the Senate.

In August 1987 Ramos and troops loyal to Aquino averted a serious coup attempt, when rebel officers (led by Col Gregorio Honasan, an officer closely associated with Enrile) occupied the army headquarters, and captured a radio and television station. In the intense fighting that ensued in Manila and Cebu, 53 people were killed. Honasan and his supporters fled the following day, successfully evading capture until December. (However, Honasan escaped from detention in April 1988.) In December 1990 a military court sentenced 81 members of the armed forces to prison terms of up to 32 years for their part in the rebellion.

In October 1988 former President Marcos and his wife, Imelda, were indicted in the USA and charged with the illegal transfer into the country of some US $100m. that had allegedly been obtained by embezzlement and racketeering. In November thousands of civilian supporters of Marcos entered Manila and distributed leaflets demanding a military rebellion to overthrow Aquino, before being dispersed by the armed forces. In February 1989 Laurel (who had formally dissociated himself from Aquino in August) visited Marcos in hospital in Hawaii, and began to campaign for Marcos to be permitted to return to the Philippines. In May Marcos's NP was revived, with Laurel as President and Enrile as Secretary-General.

In September 1989 the Philippine Government began the first of 35 planned civil suits against Marcos *in absentia* on charges of corruption. After the former President's death in Hawaii at the end of September, the opposition exerted pressure on Aquino to allow a funeral to be conducted in the Philippines. In October the Supreme Court upheld a previous ruling prohibiting the return of Marcos's body. Imelda Marcos was acquitted of charges of fraud and of the illegal transfer of stolen funds into the USA in New York in July 1990.

In December 1989 an abortive coup was staged by members of two élite military units, in collusion with the now illicit RAM and officers loyal to Marcos. President Aquino subsequently addressed a rally of 100,000 supporters, during which she accused Laurel and Enrile (who were both included in an eight-member provisional junta named by the rebels) of involvement in the coup attempt. At the end of August 1990 Aquino expressed willingness to hold discussions with both dissident troops (who had perpetrated a series of bombings of allegedly corrupt businesses owned by US interests or associated with the Aquino Government) and communist rebels (who had unilaterally declared a cease-fire in Manila and in northern areas affected by an earthquake in July), in an effort to achieve a general reconciliation. Opposition leaders, including Enrile (who had been charged with rebellion), were also invited to attend. In early September Aquino belatedly suspended offensives against the NPA in the affected areas. Later that month, however, the NPA ended the truce and threatened to intensify the insurgency. The dissident members of the armed forces also continued their campaign to destabilize the Government, allegedly planting incendiary devices in and around Manila.

In July 1991 Ramos resigned as Secretary of National Defense in order to contest the presidential election (scheduled for 1992). Having failed to secure the nomination of the ruling party, Laban ng Demokratikong Pilipino (LDP, formed in 1988 by members of pro-Government parties), Ramos, with Aquino's endorsement, resigned from the LDP and registered a new party, EDSA-LDP, with the support of 25 former LDP members of Congress. (EDSA was the popular acronym for the Epifanio de los Santos Avenue, the main site of the February 1986 uprising.) The party, which subsequently altered its title to Lakas ng EDSA, formed an alliance with the National Union of Christian Democrats to become Lakas-NUCD. The Roman Catholic Church extended its support to the LDP's candidate, Ramon Mitra, and criticized Ramos, a Protestant, for his involvement in the Marcos regime.

In February 1992 a prominent human rights organization, Amnesty International, published a report accusing the Aquino administration of acquiescence in violations of human rights by the armed forces. The report alleged that 550 extrajudicial killings had taken place during 1988–91. The armed forces denied the report's findings. The NPA had killed 563 members of the armed forces between January and April 1991.

On 11 May 1992 elections took place to select the President, Vice-President, 12 senators, 200 members of the House of Representatives and 17,014 local officials. Fidel Ramos was elected to the presidency, winning 23.6% of the votes cast; his closest rivals were Miriam Defensor Santiago, a former Secretary of Agrarian Reform, (with 19.7%) and Eduardo Cojuangco (Aquino's estranged cousin, whose wing of the NP had been renamed the Nationalist People's Coalition—NPC) (18.2%). The success of Ramos and the high level of support for Santiago (whose electoral campaign had emphasized the need to eradicate corruption) was widely regarded as a rejection of traditional patronage party politics, since neither candidate was supported by a large-scale party organization. However, in the legislative elections the LDP (the only party that had local bases in every province) won 16 of the 24 seats in the Senate and 89 of the 200 elective seats in the House of Representatives.

Following his inauguration on 30 June 1992, President Ramos formed a new administration that included six members of the outgoing Government and many senior business executives. Despite his party's poor representation in Congress, Ramos managed to gain the support of Cojuangco's NPC, the LP and 55 defectors (now known as Laban) from the LDP, to form a 'rainbow coalition', comprising 145 of the 200 elected members of the House of Representatives. The Senate remained nominally under the control of the LDP, but Ramos ensured that he maintained good relations with individual senators.

In July 1992 Ramos formed the Presidential Anti-Crime Commission (PACC), to combat organized crime. Joseph Estrada, who was elected Vice-President, was appointed to head the Commission. A principal concern of the PACC was the increase in abduction, mainly of wealthy ethnic Chinese Filipinos, for ransom. It emerged that members of the Philippine National Police (PNP) were largely responsible for the abductions, and in August the Chief of Police resigned. In April 1993, following a review of the PNP, Ramos ordered the discharge of hundreds of personnel, including 63 of the 194 senior officers. There was also a serious decline in public respect for the judiciary, following allegations that seven Supreme Court judges were accepting bribes from drugs-dealers and other criminal syndicates. In February Congress adopted legislation (which was signed into law in December) to reinstate the death penalty, which had been banned under the 1987 Constitution.

On assuming power, Ramos undertook to give priority to the restoration of order by persuading mutinous right-wing soldiers, communist insurgents and Muslim separatists to abandon their armed struggle. In July 1992 two communist leaders were conditionally released, and Ramos submitted to Congress an amnesty proclamation for about 4,500 members of the NPA, the MNLF and renegade former members of the armed forces who had already applied for amnesty. In August the National Unification Commission (NUC) was formed to consult rebel groups and formulate a viable amnesty programme. Later that month Ramos ordered the temporary release from prison of more communist leaders, including the Commander of the NPA, Romulo Kintanar, and the NDF Spokesman, Saturnino Ocampo, and also of 16 rebel soldiers. In the same month the Government began discussions with exiled representatives of the NDF in the Netherlands.

In September 1992 Ramos repealed anti-subversion legislation, in place since 1957, that proscribed the CPP. Nevertheless, the exiled leadership of the NDF issued a statement to the effect that the CPP would continue its armed struggle, although there was a widening division within the CPP over co-operation with the NUC. Jose Maria Sison, a founder member of the CPP who had been based in the Netherlands since his release from prison in 1986, resumed the party chairmanship in April 1992. However, his election to the leadership was not recognized by all party members. In December Sison, who initiated the (largely ignored) removal from the CPP of those members who had deviated from Maoist orthodoxy, accused his opponents, including Kintanar, of collusion with the Ramos administration.

In July 1993 the CPP's influential Manila-Rizal regional committee publicly broke away from the CPP Central Committee led by Sison. This followed the attempted dissolution by Sison of the region's leading committee and its armed unit, the Alex Boncayao Brigade (ABB), accused of factionalism and military excesses. The Manila-Rizal organization, which comprised about 40% of CPP members, was subsequently joined by the CPP regional committee of the Visayas. In October four communist leaders, including Kintanar, were expelled from the CPP and the NPA for refusing to recognize the authority of Sison.

Negotiations between the Government and the NDF in 1994–96 were marred by their failure to agree terms for the granting of immunity for NDF members and the arrest and subsequent release of a number of leading members of the organization. In March 1998, despite the intensification during 1997 of both attacks by communist rebels and security operations by the Government, the Government and the NDF signed a Comprehensive Agreement on Respect for Human Rights and International Law, the first of four agreements that would complete the peace process.

In December 1992 seven military renegades, including Honasan, emerged from hiding to sign a preliminary agreement to take part in talks with the Government. Discussions between the NUC and representatives of the RAM and the Young Officers' Union (YOU—a progressive offshoot of the RAM, which was alleged to have played an important role in the December 1989 coup attempt) began in January 1993, but were subsequently suspended. In February 1994 it was announced that peace negotiations with the RAM and the YOU would remain suspended, pending the release of six military detainees. In the following month Ramos proclaimed a general amnesty for all rebels and for members of the security forces charged with offences committed during counter-insurgency operations, as recommended by the NUC; however, the amnesty did not include persons convicted of torture, arson, massacre, rape and robbery. The RAM rejected the amnesty on the grounds that it failed to address the causes of the rebellion, while Ocampo dismissed the proclamation as being biased against the communist rebels. Following agreement between the RAM and the Government during 1994 on certain government programmes and the issue of electoral reform, in 1995 formal negotiations resumed. In October the RAM and the YOU signed a peace agreement with the Government, which provided for the return of the rebels' military weapons within 90 days and the reintegration of members of the two organizations into the armed forces.

In September 1993, with the permission of President Ramos, Marcos's remains were returned to the Philippines, and a funeral service was conducted in the former President's native province of Ilocos Norte, attended by only a few thousand supporters. Later that month Imelda Marcos (who had returned to the Philippines in 1991, with Aquino's permission, to stand trial on charges of fraud and tax evasion) was convicted of corruption and sentenced to 18 years' imprisonment; she remained at liberty pending an appeal against the conviction. In February 1994 a district court in Honolulu, Hawaii, awarded US $2,000m. in punitive damages to 10,000 Filipinos tortured under President Marcos's administration, following a court ruling in October 1992 that victims of abuses of human rights under the Marcos regime could sue his estate for compensation. Imelda Marcos announced that she would appeal against the decision. Further charges of embezzlement were filed against her in April and June 1994 and in September 1995. In March 1995 she declared that she would seek election to the House of Representatives. Comelec disqualified her candidacy, ruling that she failed to fulfil residency criteria; however, she appealed to the Supreme Court to overrule the disqualification, and was allowed to contest the election pending the outcome of her appeal. Although her candidacy was successful, she was not permitted to take her seat in Congress until November, following a ruling in her favour by the Supreme Court.

On 8 May 1995 elections were held to contest 12 of the 24 seats in the Senate, the 204 elective seats in the House of Representatives, 76 provincial governorships and more than 17,000 local government positions. Prior to the elections, in which an estimated 80% of all eligible voters participated, more than 80 people were killed in campaign violence. The ruling coalition won the vast majority (about 70%) of seats in the House of Representatives and an electoral alliance between Lakas-NUCD and the LDP (Lakas-Laban) won nine of the 12 seats in the Senate. One of the three opposition seats was secured by Honasan, despite a campaign by Aquino against his candidacy.

During 1995–97 Ramos's supporters campaigned to amend the constitutional stipulation that restricted the President to a single term of office; however, the Senate opposed the proposal. In September a rally organized by Cardinal Sin (to coincide with the 25th anniversary of the declaration of martial law by Marcos), to protest against any such constitutional change, was attended by more than 500,000 demonstrators. The rally was supported by Corazon Aquino as well as opposition politicians and influential business executives, who attributed the rapid decline of the peso, in part, to the insecurity created by speculation regarding Ramos's ambitions for a second term of office. Prior to the rally Ramos finally stated categorically that he would not contest the presidential election.

The formation of an opposition grouping, the Laban ng Makabayang Masang Pilipino (LaMMP—Struggle of Nationalist Filipino Masses), to contest the elections scheduled for May 1998 was announced in June 1997. The LaMMP was composed of the Partido ng Masang Pilipino, led by Estrada, the LDP, led by

Edgardo Angara (which had withdrawn from its alliance with Lakas-NUCD in February 1996), and the NCP, led by Ernesto Maceda. In December Estrada and Angara were formally endorsed as the LaMMP's presidential and vice-presidential candidates respectively. A total of 10 candidates contested the election. The campaign was characterized by an emphasis on personalities and scandals and failed to address substantive policy issues.

Elections to the presidency, the vice-presidency, the Senate, the House of Representatives, provincial governorships and local government positions took place on 11 May 1998; an estimated 80% of the electorate participated in the polls. Although an estimated 51 people were killed in pre-election violence (mostly in the southern province of Mindanao), the elections were considered relatively orderly and free. Estrada was elected to the presidency with 39.9% of the votes cast. His closest rival was the Lakas-NUCD candidate, Jose de Venecia (who was responsible for progress in negotiations with both the Islamist separatists and the NDF), who secured 15.9% of the votes. The vice-presidency was won by Gloria Macapagal Arroyo (the daughter of former President Diosdado Macapagal), who had been second in the opinion polls as a presidential candidate before agreeing to support de Venecia's candidacy. According to Comelec, seven of the victorious senators were members of the LaMMP, while the other five were Lakas-NUCD candidates. However, Lakas-NUCD dominated the House of Representatives, winning 106 seats compared with only 66 for the LaMMP. In a development indicative of the weakness of the party system, many congressional members subsequently defected to Estrada's party, which was renamed Laban ng Masang Pilipino (Fight of the Filipino Masses).

President Estrada's election altered considerably the situation for the family and former associates of Marcos. In June 1998 the Solicitor-General, Romeo de la Cruz, recommended that the Supreme Court acquit Imelda Marcos of charges of corruption. A ruling by the Supreme Court in January had upheld her appeal against one charge of corruption but dismissed an appeal against her conviction in 1993 on a second corruption charge, which carried a sentence of between nine and 12 years' imprisonment. She remained at liberty pending the reconsideration of the verdict by the court. However, Ramos dismissed de la Cruz and his appointed successor, Silvestre Bello, and withdrew the Government's petition for acquittal. Marcos was, nevertheless, acquitted in October 1998, although numerous civil suits remained pending against her. In December Marcos announced plans to initiate a legal appeal to recover 500,000m. pesos in assets allegedly belonging to her late husband, including shares in the Philippine Long Distance Telephone Co, the San Miguel Corporation and Philippine Airlines (PAL). Marcos claimed her husband had entrusted the money to close associates who had refused to return it. The election of the Marcoses' daughter, Imee, to Congress and of their son, Ferdinand Jr, to the governorship of Ilocos Norte was indicative of the general rehabilitation of the Marcos family. Estrada favoured a negotiated settlement with the Marcos family to resolve the dispute over funds misappropriated by the former President and also gave his support to the burial of Marcos in the cemetery of National Heroes. However, popular outrage and public protests supported by Aquino and Ramos towards the end of June prompted Imelda Marcos to postpone the burial indefinitely in the national interest.

In January 1998 the Swiss Supreme Court ruled that the total sum of US $560m. of Marcos's wealth in Swiss bank accounts be released (to be disbursed by the Philippine courts). In February 1999 the Marcos family agreed to pay a total of $150m. in damages to 9,539 victims of human rights abuses. However, the court subsequently ruled against the release of funds from those sequestered by the Government from Swiss bank accounts. In March the Supreme Court upheld a 1990 decision by the Bureau of Internal Revenue assessing the unpaid inheritance tax owed by the heirs of Ferdinand Marcos at 23,500m. pesos. (In July 2003 the Supreme Court ruled that the sum of approximately $658m. that had been held by Ferdinand Marcos in several Swiss bank accounts should be released to the Philippine Government.)

Joseph Estrada was inaugurated as President at the end of June 1998. In his inaugural address he reiterated campaign pledges to eradicate poverty and corruption, but also assured the business sector that he would continue Ramos's programme of economic reform. His new Cabinet, which elicited widespread approval, comprised members from a wide political and social spectrum, including wealthy ethnic Chinese business executives, former associates of Marcos, and allies from Estrada's career as mayor and senator, as well as former activists from the communist movement and left-wing non-governmental organizations (NGOs). Five members of Lakas-NUCD were allocated portfolios and Ramos accepted a post as Senior Adviser. However, Estrada was criticized for appointing friends and relatives to lucrative and influential positions. Additional concerns about a reversion to the Marcos era of 'cronyism' were raised by the return to prominence of former Marcos associates, some of whom had made substantial financial contributions to Estrada's presidential campaign fund, while Estrada also dismissed political adversaries.

In spite of widespread apprehension regarding his leadership abilities, Estrada was credited with several successes during his first year in office. His creation in July 1998 of the Presidential Anti-Organized Crime Task Force resulted in a dramatic reduction in kidnappings for ransom. The elimination of several large organized syndicates was achieved by granting autonomy from the PNP (which had been implicated in many incidents) to the head of the Task Force, Brig.-Gen. Panfilo Lacson. (However, Lacson's appointment attracted criticism from human rights organizations, owing to his conviction with other military officers in 1993 for the illegal detention and torture of anti-Government dissidents in the 1970s.) Estrada effectively abolished 'pork barrel' funds (state funds from which congress members financed projects in their constituencies), which had led to corruption and the reinforcement of patronage politics. Subsequently, however, Estrada became the target of renewed criticism in the media, which he attributed to a conspiracy to discredit his administration. In February 1999 The Manila Times described Estrada as an 'unwitting godfather' to an allegedly improper government contract. Estrada sued the newspaper for 101m. pesos and only abandoned his legal complaint after he received an apology.

The strained relationship between President Estrada and former President Ramos deteriorated in March 1999 when the Senate Blue Ribbon Committee, which had been established to investigate anomalies in government and was led by a member of Estrada's party, Aquilino Pimentel, recommended the prosecution of Ramos and five members of his Cabinet for the misapplication of public funds to celebrate the centennial anniversary of Philippine independence in June 1998. Ramos was issued with a summons to this effect in April 1999 and was obliged to justify his actions before a newly formed Independent Citizens' Committee. Ramos claimed that the accusations were politically motivated and designed to distract attention from investigations into misconduct by Estrada's friends and relatives. The Committee's final report recommended the indictment for graft of the former Vice-President, Salvador Laurel, who had led the centennial celebration committee, and fines for Ramos and his Secretary of Finance, Salvador Enrique, for failing to prevent Laurel's abuses.

In late 1999 President Estrada's hitherto excellent popularity ratings began to decline amid increasing concern about 'cronyism' and corruption in his administration. In August Aquino and Cardinal Sin mobilized 100,000 demonstrators in a Rally for Democracy to protest particularly against government plans to amend the 1987 Constitution. Estrada's stated aim in amending the Constitution was to extend economic deregulation by altering the provisions limiting to 40% foreign ownership of land and public utilities. While in any case opposed to these proposals, critics feared the potential removal from the Constitution of the stipulation limiting the President to a single term of office. Later in August 1999 Estrada relaunched the ruling coalition, re-styling it the Lapian ng Masang Pilipino (LAMP—Party of the Filipino Masses). Estrada's popularity was also adversely affected by his failure to fulfil his pledges to alleviate poverty. Little progress had been made with regard to land redistribution or 'food security' apart from the rehousing of 25,000 poor in Manila in the year to September.

Following a report by the World Bank in November 1999 alleging that 20% of the Philippine budget was lost to corruption, President Estrada pledged to intensify investigations of officials suspected of dishonesty. (The former chief of police, Roberto Lastimoso, and the former Secretary of the Interior and Local Government, Ronaldo Puno, were indicted on charges of graft in February 2000.) In the same month, in a further attempt to dispel criticism, Estrada established the EDSA People Power Commission to promote the ideals of the 1986 uprising; its 15 members included Aquino, Ramos and Estrada. Also in November, having achieved significant reductions in kidnappings for ransom in his previous post, Lacson was appointed to head the PNP. However, all of these measures proved inadequate to reverse a trend that was compounded by the unexpected resignation of the respected Secretary of Finance, Edgardo Espiritu, in January 2000 and his subsequent accusations concerning the undue influence exerted by unelected associates of Estrada. Estrada responded to growing public dissatisfaction by announcing the reform of his administration. He dismissed his informal advisers, replacing them with a six-member Economic Co-ordinating Council to promote coherence in economic affairs, and recruited five eminent business leaders to act as an economic advisory council. The proposed constitutional reforms were suspended and replaced by plans to achieve economic liberalization through legislation. Estrada's attempts to improve his popularity were swiftly undermined by the testimony in January of the Chairman of the Securities and Exchange Commission (SEC), Perfecto Yasay, to a Senate Committee investigating possible illegal share trading. Yasay alleged that Estrada had pressed him to exonerate his close associate, Dante Tan, who was suspected of illegally manipulating the share price of BW Resources Corporation. Estrada denied the intervention, although he admitted telephoning Yasay four times in relation to the investigation. Despite frequent rumours of an impending coup attempt and a request for Estrada's resignation from Teofisto Guingona, the President of Lakas-NUCD, an attempt to mobilize anti-Estrada sentiment in a mass protest in April received very little support.

In October 2000 the Philippines was engulfed by a political crisis that arose as a result of allegations, made to an investigative committee of the Senate by the Governor of Ilocos Sur, Luis Singson, that President Estrada had accepted large sums of money as bribes from illegal gambling businesses. Despite the President's denial of these allegations, opposition parties announced their intention to begin the process of impeaching him. Earlier in the month Vice-President Gloria Arroyo had announced her resignation from the Cabinet, in which she served as Secretary of Social Welfare and Development. The fact that she did not relinquish the vice-presidency at the same time led to speculation that she was preparing to succeed Estrada in the event of his being forced out of office. Following her resignation from the Cabinet, Arroyo established an alliance of opposition parties.

In November 2000 anti-Government protests throughout the Philippines intensified. Vice-President Arroyo announced that a transitional government was prepared to assume power should the President resign. In mid-November the House of Representatives endorsed the impeachment of the President after more than one-third of its members signed a petition favouring this action. Supporters of Estrada condemned the impeachment proceedings as unconstitutional since they had not been submitted to a formal vote in the House of Representatives. (The Speaker of the House had ruled that such a vote was unnecessary because more than one-third of its members had signed the petition.) Estrada himself welcomed an impeachment trial in the Senate as an opportunity to prove his innocence, and he was formally summoned by the Senate. The legal action pursued by Estrada in order to force the Senate to dismiss the charges against him was unsuccessful, and at the beginning of December he pleaded not guilty to charges of bribery, corruption, betrayal of public trust and violation of the Constitution. The impeachment trial in the Senate was adjourned indefinitely in mid-January 2001, however, after prosecutors failed to obtain the disclosure of bank records as evidence against him. This effective acquittal of the President provoked mass demonstrations against him. Estrada had lost the support of many members of his Cabinet, the police and the armed forces, and, in response to a request by Vice-President Gloria Arroyo, the Supreme Court declared the presidency to be vacant.

Gloria Arroyo was sworn in as President on 20 January 2001, and by the end of the month most of the positions in her new Cabinet had been filled. The new administration moved quickly to prevent Estrada, members of his family and his associates from leaving the Philippines and insisted that the former President would be prosecuted for his alleged crimes. However, the manner in which Arroyo had assumed the presidency exacerbated the continued political crisis and raised fears of an impending military *coup d'état*. Estrada continued to assert that he remained the legitimate Head of State and pledged to take legal action to regain the presidency. In March, however, the Supreme Court affirmed the legitimacy of Arroyo's office. In April Estrada was formally indicted for a number of alleged offences, including one of economic plunder, which was punishable by the death penalty. Estrada was arrested for the first time in mid-April and charged with graft and perjury. At the beginning of May there was violent unrest in Manila when supporters of Estrada attempted to storm the presidential palace. Three members of the Senate were arrested for having allegedly conspired to bring down the Government, and President Arroyo declared a state of rebellion, which permitted her to deploy the armed forces to quell the unrest. Estrada, who had subsequently been rearrested, was removed to a detention centre outside Manila, having had his application for bail denied.

Legislative and local elections were held on 14 May 2001. Lakas-NUCD secured 87 seats in the House of Representatives, followed by the NPC with 62. The People Power Coalition (PPC)—a coalition of Lakas-NUCD, the LP and several smaller parties, which had been formed by President Arroyo to contest the election—won eight seats in the Senate, while allies of the Laban ng Demokratikong Pilipino-Puwersa ng Masa (LDP-PnM)—the opposition coalition formed to support Estrada—secured four. The remaining seat went to an independent candidate. President Arroyo thus succeeded in securing a majority in both chambers. As a result of violence throughout the election period, 83 people died. The elections were further marred by reports of widespread corruption.

In early October 2001 Estrada's trial on charges of perjury and plunder finally commenced; he had refused to enter a plea to any of the charges against him. Later in the month Estrada won an initial victory when the judge refused to permit the presentation of crucial evidence in the prosecution case for perjury owing to a legal technicality. In November the trial was overshadowed by a feud between two of the judges involved, presiding judge Justice Anacleto Badoy and his senior colleague, Justice Francis Garchitorena. The trial was interrupted further when the chief prosecutor, Aniano Desierto, was accused of corruption. Shortly afterwards the Supreme Court rejected a legal challenge brought by Estrada against his ongoing trial and affirmed the constitutionality of the anti-plunder law under which he was being tried. At the end of November the Supreme Court suspended Justice Garchitorena following complaints that cases under his remit, including that of Estrada, were proceeding too slowly. In December Justice Badoy was also suspended indefinitely, following defence allegations that he lacked impartiality. The trial was subsequently adjourned and resumed in January 2002 in a special anti-graft court. In February Estrada instructed his entire legal team to resign in protest at what he alleged to be a prejudiced court. In July 2004 the court ruled that Estrada was not guilty of money-laundering when he opened a bank account under a different name in 2000. A few days later the court approved Estrada's transfer from military detention to house arrest. In mid-September 2007 Estrada was convicted of plunder, having misappropriated some US $80m. during his tenure of office, and sentenced to life imprisonment; he was found not guilty of the charge of perjury. He denounced the verdict as being a 'political decision'. However, after apparently agreeing not to seek political office, Estrada was pardoned by President Arroyo in late October. The pardon, and in particular the swiftness with which it had been granted, provoked considerable controversy, prompting not only concern that it would undermine efforts to combat official corruption, but also speculation that it was politically motivated.

In October 2001 Jose Miguel Arroyo, the husband of the President, was investigated by the Senate over allegations that he had diverted funds from a state lottery in order to finance electoral campaigns for prospective senators. In the same month Imelda Marcos was rearrested on four charges of corruption, connected to the suspected plunder of the economy under the regime of her late husband, before being released on bail. In November the widow of President Marcos appeared in court and denied all the charges. She was reported to be seeking huge damages from the Government over the claims that had been made against her.

In June 2002 Senator John Osmeña defected to the opposition, depriving the PPC of its narrow majority in the Senate. Owing to the simultaneous absence abroad of another senator, proceedings in the Senate were suspended for almost two months. The Government was weakened further in July when Vice-President Teofisto Guingona announced his resignation from his concurrent position as Secretary of Foreign Affairs, owing largely to his disagreement with the Government's decision to allow the deployment of US troops in the country.

In October 2002 the Senate gave its assent to the Absentee Voting Bill, which rendered Filipino citizens living and working abroad eligible to vote in future legislative and presidential elections. The bill was enacted in February 2003. In November 2002 President Arroyo announced her intention to adopt a strict policy aimed at ending the corruption apparently endemic within the Government. In the following month the Director-General of the National Economic and Development Authority (NEDA), Dante Canlas, resigned from his post at the request of the President. Later in December the President announced that she did not intend to contest the presidential election scheduled to take place in 2004, claiming that her decision was motivated by a desire to spare the country further political division. She subsequently stated her intention to revive the Council of State, an advisory body originally established by her father, Diosdado Macapagal, during his time in power, while holding exploratory talks with leading members of the opposition with the possible aim of forming a 'government of national unity'.

In July 2003 approximately 350 disaffected members of the armed forces staged a mutiny, taking control of a shopping centre in the Manila commercial district of Makati. The rebels, who demanded the resignation of the President and the Secretary of National Defense, finally surrendered peacefully. While the Government claimed that the mutiny constituted an attempted *coup d'état*, those who had participated claimed that they were merely seeking a chance to air their grievances, which included, most notably, allegations that senior military personnel were guilty of systematic collusion with Muslim rebels in the south. Later in that month the head of military intelligence, Brig.-Gen. Victor Corpus, who had been accused of misconduct by the rebels, resigned. In the aftermath of the mutiny President Arroyo declared a nation-wide state of rebellion, which was lifted in August. In that month charges were filed against more than 1,000 people in connection with the coup attempt. Senator Gregorio Honasan was charged with involvement, along with six of his associates. Meanwhile, Secretary of National Defense Angelo Reyes resigned, while denying the allegations of corruption. President Arroyo assumed the defence portfolio on an interim basis before appointing Eduardo Ermita to the position in September. In November the criminal charges of *coup d'état* that had been filed against 290 of those who had taken part in the July mutiny were abandoned; however, it was announced that the 31 officers believed to have led the mutiny would be tried by a civilian court. In addition, all 321 soldiers were to face a court martial on separate charges related to their involvement in the mutiny. Six of the leaders of the uprising publicly apologized to the President in September 2004. In November at least 117 members of Congress signed a resolution urging the granting of amnesty to the accused. None the less, after several delays, both the trial and the court martial continued in 2005. In May 2005 the court martial sentenced 184 of the soldiers to one year's confinement with hard labour, demotion in rank and forfeiture of two-thirds of their basic salaries for three–six months; the soldiers had pleaded guilty to lesser offences in exchange for the withdrawal of a mutiny charge against them. Charges against a number of others had already been dismissed, while the court martial of a further 67 soldiers and 29 suspected leaders of the mutiny continued. In April 2007 54 soldiers, mostly junior officers, were sentenced to seven years and six months in prison for their involvement in the mutiny; their sentences were reduced to four years in June, and they were later dishonourably discharged from the armed forces, before being released in December. Charges against several other officers were dismissed. In August, having pleaded guilty, 12 of the 29 officers believed to have led the mutiny were convicted of the charge of conduct unbecoming an officer by the court martial and ordered to be discharged. A further five officers changed their plea before the court martial to guilty in April 2008. The civilian trial of the 29 officers on separate charges of mounting a coup was ongoing in early 2008. In April, having changed their plea to guilty, two of the officers were sentenced to life imprisonment, while seven received prison terms ranging from six to 12 years; the trial of the other officers continued. (In November 2007 several of the defendants had briefly attempted to stage a further coup, but soon surrendered—see below.)

In October 2003, in a reversal of her statement of December 2002, President Arroyo announced that she did intend to contest the next presidential election, scheduled to take place in May 2004. Vice-President Teofisto Guingona resigned from Lakas-NUCD (which restyled itself as Lakas-Christian Muslim Democrats—Lakas-CMD—in 2003), in advance of the announcement, citing differences of principle, but he retained his cabinet position. In the same month 80 members of the House of Representatives filed an impeachment complaint against Chief Justice Hilario G. Davide, Jr, alleging that he had misused judicial funds. However, the Supreme Court later prohibited the House of Representatives from referring the complaint to the Senate, on the grounds that it was unconstitutional, owing to a previous failed impeachment attempt earlier in that year brought by former President Joseph Estrada. In November 2003 the House of Representatives voted against continuing proceedings against Davide. Nevertheless, the attempted impeachment was widely perceived to be illustrative of increasing tensions between the legislative branch and the judiciary. Meanwhile, Secretary of Finance Jose Isidro Camacho tendered his resignation; Under-Secretary Juanita Amatong was appointed to succeed him. In the same month two armed men, one of whom was the former head of the Air Transportation Office, occupied the air traffic control tower at the Ninoy Aquino International Airport in Manila, protesting against government corruption and prompting speculation of another coup attempt. Both men were shot dead by the police.

In December 2003 Secretary of Foreign Affairs Blas Ople died unexpectedly; Under-Secretary Delia Domingo-Albert was appointed as his successor. Meanwhile, in advance of the legislative and presidential elections to be held in May 2004, Senator Edgardo Angara, President of the opposition LDP, announced that his party had merged with the PDP-Laban Party and Estrada's Puwersa ng Masang Pilipino (PMP) to form the Koalisyon ng Nagkakaisang Pilipino (KNP—Coalition of the United Filipino). The KNP subsequently announced that it had nominated the film actor Fernando Poe, Jr, as its presidential candidate. Later in the same month, however, former chief of police Gen. Panfilo Lacson stated his intention to stand as the official presidential candidate of the LDP, supported by another faction of the party, which was led by its Secretary-General, Agapito Aquino. The former Secretary of Education, Culture and Sports, Raul Roco, who had resigned in August 2002, secured the presidential nomination of Aksyon Demokratiko. The fifth presidential candidate to emerge was Eduardo Villanueva, the leader of the 'Jesus is Lord' Church, who was to represent the newly established Bangon Pilipinas (Rise Philippines). The incumbent President Arroyo formed a new coalition in support of her candidacy—the Koalisyon ng Katapatan at Karanasan sa Kinabukasan (K-4). The alliance consisted of Lakas-CMD, the LP, Reporma and Probinsya Muna Development Intiatives (PROMDI). The coalition replaced the PPC, which had effectively been disbanded following the withdrawal of its most important members.

On 10 May 2004 elections took place to select the President, Vice-President, 12 members of the Senate and 212 members of the House of Representatives, and also to choose more than 17,000 local officials. Almost 100 people were killed as a result of violence during the campaign period, despite the deployment of some 230,000 police officers and troops at polling stations throughout the country. Arroyo won a narrow victory in the presidential election, receiving 40.0% of the votes cast, compared with Poe's 36.5%. Poe refused to accept the result, alleging widespread fraud. Noli de Castro, representing Lakas-CMD, was elected to the vice-presidency. Lakas-CMD also performed well in the legislative elections, securing 93 of the 212 elective seats in the House of Representatives, while the NPC won 54 seats and the LP 34. Seven candidates of the K-4 coalition, dominated by Lakas-CMD, were elected to the Senate, with the remaining five seats taken by the KNP.

Having secured an electoral mandate for her presidency, Arroyo was sworn in for a second term of office at the end of June 2004. During her inauguration speech she pledged to curb corruption, to improve basic services and to reform the economy, notably promising to create 6m. new jobs during her six-year term. On the day before the ceremony police had dispersed several thousand supporters of Poe who were demonstrating against the Government in Manila and, in a separate incident, arrested four Muslims suspected of planning a bomb attack in the capital during the inauguration. In early July Angelo Reyes, a close ally of the President, returned to the Government as Secretary of the Interior and Local Government, following the resignation of Jose Lina from that position. Later that month Poe and his defeated vice-presidential candidate, Loren Legarda, lodged separate complaints with the Supreme Court, demanding a recount of votes cast in more than 118,000 voting precincts on the grounds of massive electoral fraud. Poe died in December after suffering a stroke. His burial, attended by thousands of supporters, was held under heightened security in Manila, amid government concerns about an alleged plot to use the funeral march to incite unrest; in the event, however, the procession was largely peaceful.

In mid-August 2004 Arroyo announced a cabinet reorganization, in which former Executive Secretary Alberto Romulo succeeded Delia Albert as Secretary of Foreign Affairs, while Eduardo Ermita, hitherto Secretary of National Defense, replaced Romulo, and Avelino Cruz, the President's former chief legal adviser, was allocated the defence portfolio. The Government launched a medium-term development plan for 2004–10 in October. As well as setting various economic targets, the plan proposed a number of political reforms, some of which would require the amendment of the Constitution. Major changes envisaged included the introduction of a federal form of government and a unicameral parliamentary system; the revision of restrictive provisions on foreign ownership; and the reform of the electoral system.

In late 2004 and early 2005 a number of military officers were charged with corruption, as the authorities demonstrated their commitment to eradicating graft in the armed forces. The most high-profile case was that of Maj.-Gen. Carlos Garcia, the former comptroller of the armed forces, who faced charges relating to 143m. pesos in unexplained wealth that he had allegedly amassed. He went on trial before both a military court and the special anti-graft court in November 2004. (Garcia was sentenced to two years' hard labour by the military court in December 2005; his trial by the anti-graft court on plunder and perjury charges was ongoing in early 2008.) Eight people were killed and more than 50 others injured in mid-November when police dispersed several thousand workers who were protesting against low wages and the failure to implement land redistribution laws on a sugar plantation in Tarlac province, owned by the family of former President Corazon Aquino. Two senior police commanders were subsequently dismissed for excessive use of force, and an investigation into the police action was ordered.

In early January 2005 the police claimed to have foiled a plot to bomb a forthcoming Roman Catholic festival in the capital, arresting 16 people. Later that month the Secretary of Finance, Juanita Amatong, and the Secretary of Energy, Vicente Perez, resigned from office. The finance portfolio was allocated to Cesar Purisima, hitherto Secretary of Trade and Industry, who was replaced by Juan Santos. Perez agreed to remain in the post until the end of March, when he was succeeded by Raphael Lotilla.

In June 2005 a major political scandal arose over the issue of a recording of a telephone conversation held between President Arroyo and an election official while votes in the 2004 presidential poll were still in the process of being counted. Arroyo acknowledged that she had made an 'error of judgement' by speaking with an election official at that time, but strenuously denied having tried to influence the outcome of the poll. Secretary of Agriculture Arthur Yap tendered his resignation from the Cabinet at the end of the month in order to focus his efforts on contesting tax evasion charges filed against him following the purchase of property in Pasig City (he was reappointed in October 2006). Further resignations from the Cabinet followed in July, in protest at what the departing ministers, who included Secretary of Finance Purisima, perceived to be the illegality of Arroyo's presidency. Later that month Arroyo announced that Purisima's position was to be assumed by Margarito Teves. In September Congress formally rejected three separate impeachment cases against Arroyo, deeming the complaints too weak to stand up to legislative scrutiny. In January 2006 the influential 120-member Catholic Bishops' Conference urged that investigations into the allegations against Arroyo be continued since previous efforts were perceived to have been undermined by 'acts of evasion and obstruction of truth'. In February the National Bureau of Investigation announced that it had concluded its own investigation into the episode, since (because the recording of the conversation had been adjudged to have been tampered with) there was no longer any sound basis for continuing with the proceedings. In the same month an estimated 20,000 people marched through the capital to demand President Arroyo's resignation as they marked the 20th anniversary of the ousting of President Ferdinand Marcos. In March it was reported that members of the opposition were compiling evidence with which to file another impeachment complaint against Arroyo, regarding not only the vote-manipulation allegations but also accusations concerning the mismanagement of a sum of 728m. pesos that had been intended to fund a fertilizer scheme, which, it was claimed, had been misappropriated by Arroyo and her allies to help fund her presidential election campaign in 2004. A fresh impeachment motion against Arroyo was defeated in the House of Representatives in August 2006. A Senate inquiry into the vote-manipulation allegations commenced in September 2007.

Meanwhile, in February 2006 President Arroyo effected a minor reorganization of the Cabinet. Notable changes included the transfer of the Secretary of the Budget and Management, Romulo Neri, to the position of Director-General of NEDA, and the appointment of Rolando Andaya, Jr, as Neri's replacement. Ronaldo Puno was appointed to the position of Secretary of the Interior and Local Government in place of Angelo Reyes, who was transferred to the Department of the Environment and Natural Resources. In the same month the Presidential Anti-Graft Commission (PGAC) signed an agreement with the NGO Volunteers Against Crime and Corruption (VACC) that was intended to bolster the Government's efforts to address the problem of corruption. The VACC submitted the names of 10 senior government officials, thought to include one minister of cabinet rank, to be investigated through the new joint initiative. In the same month a minor explosion within the presidential palace compound at Malacañang led to rumours of a potential military coup. A statement purporting to be from a rebel military faction, the Young Officers' Union-new generation (YOUng), claimed responsibility for the explosion; however, the YOUng leadership distanced itself from the statement, and, furthermore, forensic tests revealed the blast to have been the result of an inadvertent chemical reaction, rather than of terrorist activity. In late February it was reported that an attempted military coup intended to displace the Arroyo Government had been averted after 14 junior army officers had confessed to their involvement in the plot. A few days later President Arroyo issued Presidential Proclamation 1017, the declaration of a state of emergency, in response to the 'clear threat' to the nation, a decision that attracted considerable censure from the opposition, the media and civil liberties groups, which lambasted Arroyo for infringing upon public freedoms. Under the terms of martial law, the authorities were granted the right to arrest people without warrant and to detain suspects without charge for an extended period of time; public protests were also prohibited. One week after the military's announcement that the threat had been successfully countered, Arroyo removed the state of emergency. A Supreme Court hearing into the legality of Proclamation 1017 commenced in March. Only days after the start of proceedings Solicitor-General Alfredo Benipayo tendered his resignation, effective from the beginning of April, amid rumours that Arroyo was dissatisfied with his efforts. In the same month a special task force, comprising élite army units, was created in order to counter any further threats to the Government. In April a total of 49 people, including members of the legislature and the military, were charged with rebellion for their alleged involvement in the February coup plot. In May the Supreme Court ruled that President Arroyo's declaration of a state of emergency had been legal, but that several actions that had followed the declaration, including certain arrests, were unlawful. In June 2007 the Supreme Court dismissed charges of rebellion against six members of the legislature.

The Arroyo administration's campaign for constitutional amendments to transform the bicameral presidential system into a unicameral parliamentary system was the subject of intense debate during 2006. The Government chose to pursue reform through two possible channels: a people's initiative, involving the collection of signatures and the holding of a plebiscite; and the formation of a constituent assembly. In October, however, following Comelec's rejection of the people's initiative petition, the Supreme Court ruled that approach to be unconstitutional. Signalling the adoption of the alternative method of amending the Constitution, the Speaker of the House of Representatives, Jose de Venecia, announced in November that the House would adopt a resolution to alter into a constituent assembly, whereupon a new constitution would be approved by mid-December. The Speaker envisioned the postponement of elections from May 2007 to November and the completion of the transformation of the legislature after June 2010. The move encountered significant opposition from the Senate, which was effectively excluded from the reform process, the Catholic Bishops' Conference of the Philippines and large sections of the public, with plans for anti-Government demonstrations in several cities. Under considerable pressure, the reformists in the House of Representatives proposed the formation of a constitutional convention of elected delegates as an alternative means towards constitutional amendments, but, with the suspension of the original resolution and a loss of momentum, the future of the initiative was uncertain.

In June 2006 President Arroyo ratified a law that abolished the death penalty. In further changes to the Cabinet, Jesli Lapus was appointed Secretary of Education, Culture and Sports in July. Avelino Cruz resigned as Secretary of National Defense in November; Arroyo assumed personal responsibility for the portfolio in December, pending the appointment of Hermogenes Ebdane in January 2007. In February Congress approved the Human Security Act, anti-terrorism legislation giving security officials powers of detention for a period of up to three days in the absence of a warrant or charge, and allowing access to suspicious financial accounts. Critics, including human rights organizations, opposition politicians and the Roman Catholic Church, expressed concern that the Act could be used to suppress legitimate political dissent.

The increasing occurrence of extra-judicial killings and human rights violations was highlighted in 2006 and 2007 by several independent reports. In February 2007 the UN Special Rapporteur on extra-judicial, summary or arbitrary executions, Philip Alston, contended that, although the highest level of Government recognized the gravity of the situation, the army was 'in a state of almost total denial of its need to respond effectively and authentically to the significant number of killings which have been convincingly attributed to them'. Also in February, an inquiry supported by the Government and led by Jose Melo, a retired judge, found links between sections of the military and politically motivated murders. As part of efforts to address the issue, the armed forces and the national police established their own human rights offices, and in March the Chief Justice designated 99 special tribunals to try cases of political killings, with the intention of giving priority to such cases. In late November Arroyo ordered the creation of a task force against political violence, comprising representatives of eight government departments and agencies. On the following day Alston's final report was released, in which he concluded that claims by the armed forces that extra-judicial killings of leftist activists were a result of internal purges within communist groups were 'strikingly unconvincing' and observed that no one had been convicted of these killings. Other victims identified by Alston included civil society leaders, human rights activists, trade unionists and advocates of land reform. While welcoming measures initiated by the Government to combat the problem, Alston noted that they had yet to succeed.

Legislative and local elections held on 14 May 2007 were marred by numerous reports of fraud, voter intimidation and violence; some 120 people had been killed in election-related violence since the beginning of the year. Polling in 13 towns in the province of Lanao del Sur on Mindanao was postponed owing to the threat of violence, finally taking place on 26 May, amid heightened security. Meanwhile, clashes between the NPA and government forces in the central Philippines were also linked to the election campaign, with casualties being reported on both sides. Moreover, six days before the elections at least eight people were killed in a bomb attack in the city of Tacurong, on Mindanao, which the security forces attributed to the regional terrorist organization Jemaah Islamiah (JI). President Arroyo described the electoral process as 'good, relatively peaceful, free and fair'. However, opposition leaders claimed that her portrayal was dishonest, demanding that the national police force take full responsibility for the deaths.

In the elections for 12 of the 24 seats in the Senate, the pro-Arroyo TEAM (Together Everyone Achieves More) Unity coalition—including Lakas-CMD, Kabalikat ng Malayang Pilipino (KAMPI, founded in 1997 to support Arroyo) and the LDP—won three seats, while the Genuine Opposition (GO) coalition—including the LP, the PDP-Laban Party and the NP—won seven, giving a majority to opponents of President Arroyo. Notably elected for the GO was Antonio Trillanes IV, who remained in detention for his alleged role in the 2003 mutiny. The remaining two seats in the Senate were secured by independent candidates, one of whom was Gregorio Honasan, who was on bail accused of involvement in the same mutiny (the charges were dismissed in July). None the less, supporters of Arroyo retained control of the House of Representatives, with parties belonging to TEAM Unity reportedly securing 168 elective seats to the GO's 44. Voter turn-out was estimated at 68% for the upper chamber and 70% for the lower chamber. Some 17,000 provincial and municipal posts, including 81 provincial governorships, were also contested on the same day.

Addressing the newly elected Congress in late July 2007, Arroyo focused on her Government's economic achievements and pledged to allocate more resources to reducing poverty and to ending the insurgencies in the south of the country. As some 3,000 protesters participated in anti-Government demonstrations outside the legislative building, the President also urged Congress to adopt legislation aimed at curbing politically motivated killings and defended the Human Security Act, which came into force earlier that month.

In late September 2007 President Arroyo suspended a US $329m. contract signed by the Government and the Chinese ZTE Corporation in April for the provision of a national broadband telecommunications network, amid claims that Philippine officials brokering the agreement had both solicited and offered bribes. Testifying before a Senate investigation into the allegations earlier that month, the son of the Speaker of the House of Representatives, Jose de Venecia III, whose company had unsuccessfully bid for the broadband contract, and the former Director-General of NEDA, Romulo Neri, had both implicated the Chairman of Comelec, Benjamin Abalos, in the scandal. De Venecia III had also claimed that the President's husband, Jose Miguel Arroyo, had warned him not to pursue the project. Abalos and Jose Miguel Arroyo denied any wrongdoing. Meanwhile, additional troops were deployed in Manila after the Chief of Staff of the Armed Forces, Lt-Gen. Hermogenes Esperon, announced that several junior officers who were suspected of recruiting soldiers to join a plot to destabilize the Government had been suspended or reassigned. The contract with ZTE Corporation, whose bid had been substantially higher than those of rival companies, was cancelled in early October. In mid-October the House of Representatives began considering a new impeachment complaint against President Arroyo based on her alleged failure to act on the bribery accusations concerning Abalos, who had resigned earlier that month; the impeachment bid was dismissed in November owing to 'lack of substance'.

A bomb exploded outside the House of Representatives in mid-November 2007, killing four people, including Wahab Akbar, the suspected target, who represented the island of Basilan in the lower chamber. The attack was attributed to Abu Sayyaf, the Muslim secessionist group (see below) of which Akbar was allegedly a former member. Later that month several military officers walked out of a court in Manila where they were being tried on charges of staging a coup in July 2003 (see above) and occupied a nearby hotel, from where, joined by other dissident soldiers, former Vice-President Teofisto Guingona and a number of Catholic priests, among others, they appealed to the armed forces to withdraw support for President Arroyo. More than 1,000 heavily armed troops were deployed to quash the rebellion. Having failed to inspire a mass uprising, the leaders of the mutiny, Senator Antonio Trillanes IV and Brig.-Gen. Danilo Lim, surrendered to the authorities after several hours, claiming that they were doing so in order to avoid casualties. Most of the rebels were detained, although three reportedly managed to evade capture. Several journalists covering the incident were also detained, but later released, and an overnight curfew was imposed in Manila. In early December Trillanes, Lim, Guingona and 33 others were charged with rebellion and incitement to rebellion; the charges against 18 civilians, including Guingona, were dismissed later that month.

The controversy over the broadband contract with ZTE Corporation persisted in early 2008, as the Senate hearings into the affair continued, with further witnesses corroborating the bribery allegations. Jose de Venecia was removed from the position of Speaker of the House of Representatives in a vote in early February, after accusing President Arroyo and the Government of corruption. Prospero Nograles was immediately elected to replace him. Once a close alliance, de Venecia's relationship with Arroyo had recently been strained as a result of the allegations made by his son before the Senate inquiry. De Venecia resigned as President of Lakas-CMD in March; he was again succeeded in this post by Nograles. Meanwhile, in late February an estimated 10,000 people participated in a demonstration in Manila to demand the resignation of Arroyo over the corruption scandal, while more than 50 former government officials issued a joint statement also urging the President to leave office. Further protests followed, and at the end of the month former Presidents Aquino and Estrada addressed an anti-Government rally attended by some 15,000 people in the capital, while smaller demonstrations were held in other towns. Yielding to considerable pressure, notably from the Catholic Bishops' Conference, in early March Arroyo revoked a controversial executive order issued in September 2005 that prevented public officials from attending congressional hearings on alleged corruption in the Government unless permitted by the President. Meanwhile, it was announced that three alleged militants, believed to have links to Abu Sayyaf or JI, had been arrested on suspicion of plotting to bomb foreign embassies in Manila and to assassinate President Arroyo.

Meanwhile, the Philippines continued to be affected by regional instability, owing to the activities of several insurgent groups, operational particularly in the central and southern areas of the country. Despite President Estrada's inclusion of former communist activists in the Government, the leadership of the NDF-CPP-NPA condemned his administration. In July 1998 Estrada approved the human rights agreement that had been reached by the NDF and the Ramos administration, and invited the exiled leadership of the NDF to the Philippines to resume peace negotiations. In February 1999, however, Estrada suspended peace talks with the communists following the NPA's abduction of three hostages. The Government also suspended the Joint Agreement on Safety and Immunity Guarantees, exposing NDF-CPP-NPA members to the risk of arrest. A total of five hostages were released by the NPA in April, although the communists continued to reject other conditions for negotiations.

In May 1999 the NDF withdrew from peace negotiations in response to the Senate's ratification of a defence treaty with the USA (see below). Estrada subsequently adopted a position of outright hostility towards the movement. However, the NDF-CPP-NPA were recruiting increasing numbers of members, who were disillusioned with the Estrada administration. In an attempt to divide the communist movement, Estrada entered into negotiations with several breakaway factions, but failed to make substantial progress. In January 2000 the Government suspended military operations against the communists to facilitate the release of two NPA hostages. In December Estrada announced that a peace agreement had been concluded with the Revolutionary Proletarian Army (RPA)-ABB. The agreement, which applied only to the central Philippines, was accompanied by a presidential amnesty for some political prisoners whose death sentences had been upheld by the Supreme Court, and by the release of an additional 235 political detainees. In the same month the NPA rejected an offer by the Government of a truce.

In April 2001 the Government of President Arroyo held peace talks with the NDF in Oslo, Norway. The talks were reported to have made some progress, with both sides agreeing to undertake confidence-building measures, including the release of political prisoners. Further discussions were held in May 2001, but were suspended in June when the NDF was implicated in the assassination of Congressman Rodolfo Aguinaldo. In November a total of 28 people were killed on the island of Mindanao when fighting broke out between the NPA and government soldiers. However, despite the renewal of violence exiled NDF members announced shortly afterwards that they had agreed to resume peace talks with the Government in Oslo in December. In the same month President Arroyo announced a temporary cease-fire with the NDF, following its offer to suspend hostilities for one month if the Government made a reciprocal gesture. However, the arrival of US troops in the Philippines in 2002 (see below) threatened further peace negotiations, as the NDF continued to oppose any US involvement in the country. In May President Arroyo called off further peace negotiations after a number of political assassinations occurred.

In August 2002 the USA added the CPP and the NPA to its list of international terrorist organizations and requested that the Government of the Netherlands cease benefit payments to all group members resident there. In the same month government representatives met with members of the NDF in Quezon City, with the intention of resuming peace talks. However, the Chairman of the CPP, Jose Maria Sison, continued to oppose any negotiations while President Arroyo remained in power. In October the Government formally designated the NDF a terrorist organization, while emphasizing that it remained willing to continue peace negotiations. In December the NPA rejected the Government's offer of a unilateral cease-fire over the Christmas period. In January 2003 police officials announced that they intended to charge Sison with involvement in several murders, including those of Congressman Rodolfo Aguinaldo and former NPA army leader Romulo Kintanar (who was killed by unidentified gunmen in that month), and to seek his extradition to face trial in the Philippines. In June fighting broke out between government troops and NPA rebels on the island of Samar and in July, following continued hostilities by the NPA, the Government announced that it intended to launch a military offensive in order to quell the insurgency. In January 2004 NPA rebels attacked a power station near Manila, causing eight deaths.

Peace negotiations between the Government and the NDF finally recommenced in Oslo in February 2004, despite ongoing clashes between the two sides. A third round of talks took place in Oslo in June. Negotiations were scheduled to resume in August, but were suspended after the NDF claimed that the Government was failing to meet its demands, including the implementation of measures to secure the removal of the CPP and the NPA from the USA's list of international terrorist organizations. Sporadic violence continued, and at the end of 2004 the armed forces announced that a total of 182 NPA members had been killed in clashes with government troops that year and a further 910 had surrendered or been captured. In February 2005 14 NPA rebels and two government soldiers were killed in skirmishes in the town of Compostela, some 930 km south-east of Manila. Negotiations between the NDF and the Government resumed during the first half of 2005, but were abandoned by the former in August in response to the political scandal surrounding President Arroyo (see above). Discussions between the two sides resumed in September. However, hopes for a peaceable resolution to the ongoing conflict suffered a set-back in November, when at least nine soldiers were killed and approximately 20 were injured in an ambush near Calinog, in the province of Iloilo, which was alleged to have been carried out by NPA members. Furthermore, in January 2006 a group of suspected NPA members conducted a raid on a prison in Barangay Cuta, Iloilo, during which they released 14 detainees. Later that month it was reported that Philippine troops had killed at least 18 NPA rebels during fierce clashes in Santa Ignacia, north of Manila. In October President Arroyo declared that she hoped that the NPA movement would be largely defeated by the expiry of her term in 2010. In May 2007 five police officers were killed on the island of Mindoro by a landmine believed to have been planted by the NPA. In late August Sison was arrested in the Netherlands, where he remained in exile, on suspicion of ordering the assassinations of former associates Romulo Kintanar and Arturo Tabara in 2003 and 2004; he was released in mid-September owing to lack of evidence. Meanwhile, at the beginning of September the Philippines military filed charges with the Commission on Human Rights accusing Sison and 18 other members of the CPP and the NPA of the murder or attempted murder of six people. Shortly afterwards, in an effort to restart the stalled peace negotiations, Arroyo signed a proclamation offering amnesty to communist rebels who relinquished their weapons. However, the NPA continued its activities, raiding a mining project of a Swiss company in January 2008. In March at least one government soldier and seven NPA rebels were killed in fighting after the NPA attacked an army base in the province of Surigao del Sur, on Mindanao.

During 1986 the Aquino Government conducted negotiations to seek a solution to the conflict with Muslim separatists in the south. A cease-fire was established with the MNLF in September, following an announcement by the Government that it would grant legal and judicial autonomy to four predominantly Muslim provinces in Mindanao. Further talks ensued, under the auspices of the Organization of the Islamic Conference (OIC, see p. 369), and on 5 January 1987 the MNLF signed an agreement to relinquish demands for complete independence in Mindanao, and to accept autonomy. In February 1988, however, the MNLF resumed its offensive against the Government, which had attempted to prevent the MNLF from gaining membership of the OIC (which would imply that the MNLF was regarded as representing an independent state). The 1987 Constitution granted eventual autonomy to Muslim provinces in Mindanao, which had been promised by President Marcos in 1976. In November 1989 a referendum was held, in the country's 13 southern provinces and nine cities in Mindanao, on proposed legislation that envisaged the autonomy of these provinces and cities, with direct elections to a unicameral legislature in each province; this contrasted with the MNLF's demand for autonomy in 23 provinces, to be granted without a referendum. Four provinces (Lanao del Sur, Maguindanao, Tawi-Tawi and Sulu) voted in favour of the government proposal, and formed the autonomous region of Muslim Mindanao.

In February 1990 the candidate favoured by Aquino, Zacaria Candao (formerly the legal representative of the MNLF), was elected to the governorship of Muslim Mindanao. In October the autonomous regional government was granted limited executive powers. The MNLF boycotted the election, on the grounds that the provisions for autonomy were more limited than those reached with Marcos in 1976. Under Ramos's programme of reconciliation, the MNLF participated in discussions with the NUC. In October 1992 the leader of the MNLF, Nur Misuari, agreed to return to the Philippines from exile in Libya to facilitate negotiations. In January 1993 talks were suspended, and violence in Mindanao escalated prior to the impending elections for the region's Governor and Assembly. At the elections, which took place on 25 March, a former ambassador, Lininding Pangandaman, won 72% of the votes cast in the gubernatorial contest, with the unofficial support of Ramos; 81% of the electorate voted.

In April 1993 exploratory discussions in Jakarta, Indonesia, between Nur Misuari and representatives of the Philippine Government led to an agreement on the resumption of formal peace talks under the auspices of the OIC. Further exploratory talks took place in Saudi Arabia in June, prior to the first formal negotiations in October in Jakarta, where the MNLF demanded the creation of an autonomous Islamic state in the south, as agreed in 1976. In November 1993 the two sides signed a memorandum of understanding and an interim cease-fire was agreed.

The second round of formal peace negotiations between the Government and the MNLF took place in Jakarta in April. Agreement was subsequently reached on government administration in the proposed autonomous region, Islamic law, education and revenue-sharing between Manila and the autonomous zones. In August 1995 Misuari agreed for the first time to a referendum (which was required under the Constitution) prior to the establishment of an autonomous zone, but demanded the immediate establishment of a provisional MNLF government to ensure that the referendum was conducted fairly.

In June 1996 it was announced that the MNLF and the Government had finally reached agreement on a proposal by Ramos for the establishment of a transitional administrative council, to be known as the Southern Philippines Council for Peace and Development (SPCPD), which was to derive powers from the Office of the President. The five-member SPCPD, which was to be headed by Misuari, was to co-ordinate peace-keeping and development efforts in 14 provinces and 10 cities in Mindanao, with the assistance of an 81-member Consultative Assembly and a religious advisory council. After a period of three years a referendum was to be conducted in each province and city to determine whether it would join the existing Autonomous Region of Muslim Mindanao (ARMM—the MNLF had abandoned its demands for autonomy in 23 provinces in Mindanao). In July 1996 government officials announced that, under the peace agreement, Muslims were to be allocated one cabinet post, and were to be granted representation in state-owned companies and constitutional commissions. In addition, Ramos offered to support the candidacy of Misuari in the forthcoming gubernatorial election in the ARMM. In early September the Government and the MNLF signed a final draft of the peace agreement in Jakarta. In the same month elections took place peacefully in the ARMM for the region's Governor and Assembly; Misuari, who, as agreed, contested the gubernatorial election with the support of Lakas-NUCD, was elected unopposed. In October it was announced that Misuari had been officially appointed Chairman of the SPCPD. In March 1997 more than 1,000 former members of the MNLF were integrated into the armed forces under the terms of the peace accord.

In August 2001, after some delay, the referendum was finally held. As a result, the city of Marawi and the province of Basilan elected to join the ARMM. However, 10 provinces and 13 cities rejected the offer of membership and the electoral turn-out was low. In November around 600 supporters of Governor Misuari (who had been dismissed from the leadership of the MNLF in April owing to his widespread unpopularity) led an armed uprising against military and police outposts on the island of Jolo, resulting in the deaths of more than 100 people. The violence was reportedly intended to prevent an election to the governorship of the ARMM, scheduled for late November, from taking place. By instigating the rebellion Misuari had violated the terms of his five-year peace accord with the Government, although he claimed that by holding an election the Government was itself breaking the terms of the agreement. Shortly afterwards President Arroyo suspended Misuari from his post. Later in November Misuari and six of his supporters were arrested by the Malaysian authorities for attempting to gain illegal entry into the country. On 26 November polls to elect a new governor, vice-governor and 44 regional legislators for the province were conducted. The turn-out was low, a fact partly attributed to the escalating military presence in the region. The next day government forces launched air strikes on MNLF insurgents who remained in Zamboanga City, killing 25 rebels and one civilian. As they attempted to flee, the rebels took several local residents hostage. The next day the hostages were released in return for the rebels' safe passage out of the city, thus bringing an end to the confrontation. In early December the President's favoured candidate, former MNLF member Farouk Hussein, was declared Governor. He immediately urged the establishment of peace in the troubled region and stated that he would seek to open a dialogue with the remaining followers of Misuari and other radical groups in the area, including Abu Sayyaf. In January 2002 Misuari was finally deported from Malaysia to face trial in Manila on charges of inciting a rebellion. Misuari remained in custody, awaiting trial, in early 2004, having refused to enter a plea to the charges against him. Meanwhile, in January 2003 the four factions comprising the MNLF signed a declaration of unity in advance of the election of a new leadership; significantly, Misuari's name was excluded from the statement, preventing him from regaining the chairmanship of the group.

In February 2005 more than 500 MNLF rebels loyal to Misuari, led by Habier Malik, attacked government troops in several towns on the island of Jolo, in retaliation for a recent army assault, which military leaders insisted had been targeted at Abu Sayyaf (see below), rather than the MNLF; an estimated 30 soldiers and 70 MNLF fighters were killed in the ensuing clashes. At least nine MNLF rebels were killed in April 2007 during an offensive by government troops on a base commanded by Malik, who was believed to be responsible for a recent attack on an army outpost in which two soldiers and a child had died; some 8,000 people reportedly fled the violence. The OIC appealed for both sides to cease fighting and to abide by the 1996 peace agreement, but the Chief of Staff of the Armed Forces, Lt-Gen. Hermogenes Esperon, maintained that the operation was not targeted at the MNLF, but rather at Malik and his followers, who had allegedly aligned themselves with Abu Sayyaf. Misuari, who remained under house arrest near Manila but was yet to be convicted, contested the Sulu gubernatorial election in May, but was overwhelmingly defeated. In August President Arroyo insisted that efforts would be made to maintain the cease-fire with the MNLF, despite the apparent involvement of members of the group in clashes between the armed forces and Abu Sayyaf (see below). Tripartite talks between the OIC, the Philippine Government and the MNLF were held in Jeddah, Saudi Arabia, in November 2007 with the aim of addressing complaints by the MNLF that the Government had failed fully to implement the 1996 agreement; a second round of discussions was held in Istanbul, Turkey, in February 2008. Meanwhile, there was disquiet among MNLF members over the accord being negotiated between the Government and the MILF (Moro Islamic Liberation Front—see below), amid fears that it would violate the group's own peace agreement. The appointment by the MNLF Central Committee of Muslimin Sema, hitherto Secretary-General of the group, as its Chairman was rejected by Misuari loyalists in April, prompting the OIC to express concern at the internal divisions within the group.

The MILF, an Islamist fundamentalist grouping demanding secession for Mindanao, which was formed as a breakaway movement from the MNLF in 1978, was covered by the government cease-fire agreed in January 1994 but was not a party to the peace talks. The grouping was widely suspected of having taken advantage of negotiations between the MNLF and the Government to strengthen its position, both by an accumulation of arms and the recruitment of young militants disaffected with the compliance of the MNLF. During early 1996 the MILF initiated further attacks on villages and churches in Mindanao and was engaged in clashes with government troops. In April the Government and the MILF agreed to a cease-fire in North Cotabato.

In August 1996, for the first time, MILF and government officials met in Davao City for preliminary peace discussions. The MILF had rejected the peace agreement with the MNLF and continued to demand separatism for 23 provinces in Mindanao. Alternating hostilities and short-term cease-fires, together with a high incidence of abductions by the rebels, characterized relations between the Government and the MILF between late 1996 and late 1997. In November 1997 a further cease-fire agreement was signed in which so-called terrorist acts (including abduction and arson) were banned as well as public executions based on Islamic (*Shari'a*) law. However, when the leader of the MILF, Hashim Salamat, returned to the Philippines (after living in Libya for 20 years) in December, he announced that public executions would continue in defiance of the government ban. Despite further clashes between the MILF and the Government in January 1998, with mutual accusations of violations of the cease-fire agreement, peace negotiations continued in February when the MILF demanded recognition of 13 MILF camps in Mindanao as 'legitimate territories'. In March the two sides agreed to create a 'quick response team' to resolve conflicts and confrontations before they escalated into serious clashes. In October the MILF and the Government agreed to disclose the location of their forces to prevent accidental encounters. However, in January 1999, following a statement by the MILF advocating independence for Mindanao, Estrada conducted successive offensives against the MILF, causing the collapse of the 1997 cease-fire agreement. Up to 60 people were estimated to have died in the ensuing fighting and 90,000 residents were displaced. A new cease-fire was implemented at the end of January 1999 and at the beginning of February the Presidential Adviser, Robert Aventajado, was sent to Mindanao to meet Salamat inside an MILF camp. They agreed to the resumption of peace negotiations and to a meeting between Salamat and Estrada to re-establish goodwill between the two sides. However, Estrada cancelled the meeting, as a result of a dispute over its location and security considerations. In March Salamat and Nur Misuari met for the first time in 20 years in an attempt to promote the peace process.

Estrada continued to vacillate between supporting the economic development of Mindanao to eradicate insurrection and threatening to eliminate the rebels through military action. Negotiations between the Government and the MILF took place in October 1999, despite MILF protests at continued government attacks on MILF camps in Mindanao. Clashes between the Government and the MILF continued despite reports of a renewed cease-fire agreement in November. Formal peace negotiations, originally scheduled for December, finally commenced in January 2000 but failed to achieve substantial progress. In that month Estrada announced a new anti-insurgency programme, the National Peace and Development Plan, which aimed to remove the causes of insurgency in Mindanao, including poverty, injustice and disease. Peace talks resumed in March after negotiations scheduled for February were suspended owing to escalating violence, during which the Government claimed to have captured an important MILF base, Camp Omar. Several incendiary devices planted on buses in Mindanao in February, which resulted in nearly 50 civilian deaths, were attributed to the MILF, but the MILF claimed that the bombings were perpetrated by government agents in an attempt to justify the intensification of the military campaign against the MILF. At a second round of talks in March a protocol was signed with improved cease-fire provisions, whereby the Government agreed to recognize 39 MILF camps as 'safe areas' while the MILF representatives agreed to carry a government identity card during talks (which they had formerly claimed would represent a surrender of sovereignty). However, intense fighting took place between the MILF and government forces in March and April in Lanao del Norte and Maguindanao Provinces. The MILF, which captured a small town in Lanao del Norte, claimed the attacks were designed to pressure government forces into the immediate cessation of its offensive against the MILF in central Mindanao. The escalation of violence in Mindanao prompted Estrada to convene a meeting of the National Security Council in March.

In May 2000 the MILF was reported to have withdrawn from a section of the Narciso Ramos highway, a strategically significant route, which it had controlled for more than five years. The withdrawal appeared to augur well for the resumption of peace negotiations, although the Government held Islamist separatist movements responsible for bomb attacks in Manila and Mindanao in the same month. Peace negotiations between the Government and the MILF resumed later in May, and in June the MILF was reported to be assessing an improved offer of autonomy by the Government. However, the MILF subsequently rejected the extension of the deadline for its acceptance of this offer from 1 July to 15 December, owing to a stipulation that it should meanwhile abandon its pursuit of independence. In late June, following a major offensive, government forces captured the MILF's military headquarters at Abubakar. In December the MILF appeared to have resumed its armed struggle after an attack on government forces on Jolo island was attributed to the movement. Bomb explosions in Manila at the end of the month, in which 22 people died, were also blamed on the group. (In August 2004, however, two Filipino Muslim militants with alleged links to JI were arrested in connection with the bombings.)

The new Cabinet appointed by President Arroyo in January 2001 included two members who originated from Mindanao. The incoming President stated that she would seek to resume the peace negotiations with the MILF, and in February the Government's military campaign against the MILF ceased. The MILF welcomed the Government's offer to resume talks, although sporadic clashes between its forces and those of the Government continued throughout February. In late March the Government announced that it had reached an agreement with the MILF to resume peace negotiations, and appeared prepared to accept the MILF's condition that renewed talks should be held in an OIC member state. In April the MILF announced a unilateral cease-fire, declaring its intention to observe this until the conclusion of a peace agreement. In June government representatives initiated talks with the MILF in Libya, leading to the conclusion of a preliminary cease-fire agreement in July. Later in the same month a new round of peace talks commenced, and in August a further cease-fire agreement was signed. In the same month the MILF also reached an accord with the MNLF. In September sporadic fighting between the MILF and army troops on Mindanao, which led to the deaths of 15 rebels, threatened to undermine the peace process. However, in October the MILF signed a pact with the Government to safeguard the recent cease-fire agreement. In November 2001 the Pentagon Gang—formed in 2000 and mainly comprised of renegade members of the MILF—kidnapped an Italian priest, Father Giuseppe Pierantoni, in northern Manila. The leader of the faction, Akiddin Abdusalem, was shot dead as he attempted to escape from custody after being captured by government troops. In January 2002 39 separatist MILF guerrillas surrendered to government forces and relinquished a large cache of weapons. In February the MILF announced that it was to hold a new series of discussions with the Government as the situation had been complicated by the arrival of US troops on the island of Basilan (see below). In April government troops finally secured the release of Father Pierantoni after conducting intensive operations against the Pentagon Gang.

In May 2002 the Government signed several new peace agreements with the MILF in Putrajaya, Malaysia. In December the MILF denied responsibility for an ambush on Mindanao that resulted in the deaths of 12 employees of a Canadian mining company, as well as for a bomb attack that killed 17 people in the same week; the group claimed that it continued to observe the cease-fire agreed upon in 2001. Meanwhile, President Arroyo succeeded in deterring the US Government from classifying the MILF as an international terrorist organization, citing concerns that the ongoing negotiation process might be undermined by such an action. In February 2003 peace negotiations broke down when government troops assumed control of the important MILF base of Pikit, on Mindanao, in violation of the cease-fire arrangement. The Government claimed that it had ordered the military action in an attempt to capture members of the Pentagon Gang, whom it believed were being sheltered by the MILF. Although President Arroyo called for a halt to the operation several days later and proposed a peace agreement, many rebels were believed to have been killed in the fighting that had resulted. Insurgency in the area continued to intensify, as the MILF refused to negotiate unless government troops withdrew from Pikit. A number of attacks occurred, the most serious of which took place in March when a bomb exploded near Davao Airport, resulting in the deaths of 23 people. Although the MILF denied responsibility for the attack, the police subsequently filed charges against 150 of its members; four of the group's leaders were charged with murder and warrants issued for their arrest. (Five alleged members of the MILF were arrested in late 2004 in connection with the bomb attack. One of those detained reportedly claimed to have been trained by a leader of JI.) In late March 2003 the MILF sent representatives for preliminary discussions with government officials in Malaysia and, in April, the Government declared that formal peace negotiations would restart, although with the exclusion of those indicted in connection with the March attack on Davao Airport, including MILF leader Hashim Salamat. However, shortly afterwards the MILF was responsible for several further outbreaks of violence in the area and, in May, the Government abandoned peace talks and renewed its military offensive against the organization. Later in that month the MILF declared a 10-day unilateral cease-fire in order, it claimed, to prepare the way for the renewal of negotiations, but the Government rejected the offer following the perpetration of further attacks by the MILF during the cease-fire period. Nevertheless, at the request of the Malaysian Government, the MILF extended the cease-fire by a further 10 days in June and, later in that month, Salamat announced that the group had renounced terrorism, an important precondition for any peace agreement. Despite this, the Government continued to take military action against the organization. However, in July it was announced that the two sides had finally concluded a peace agreement. In August it was reported that Hashim Salamat had died as a result of a heart attack in the previous month; he was replaced as Chairman by Al Haj Murad.

Following exploratory talks in February 2004, formal peace negotiations were to take place in April, but were postponed owing to the May elections (see above). In late April the MILF protested against the arrest of four of its members on suspicion of collaborating with JI, claiming it contravened the cease-fire agreement. In July it was announced that the MILF had agreed to co-operate with the armed forces in operations against kidnapping gangs and JI elements based in Mindanao. A 60-member international monitoring team, led by Malaysia, was deployed in Mindanao in October to oversee the ongoing cease-fire between the government forces and the MILF; it was expected to remain on the island for at least one year. Further exploratory talks aimed at restarting the stalled formal peace negotiations were held in December; the two sides reportedly made progress on the contentious issue of ancestral domain. In mid-January 2005 at least six government soldiers were killed in an attack on an army outpost by MILF rebels. The Government stated that it regarded the attack, which had not been sanctioned by the MILF leadership, as an isolated incident. Exploratory talks between the two sides were conducted between February and December.

In March 2005 the Government and the MILF finally agreed to resume formal peace negotiations in Malaysia, which commenced in February 2006 at Port Dickson, near Kuala Lumpur. ARMM Governor Zaldy Puti U. Ampatuan called for the holding of a plebiscite to assist the efforts to resolve the contentious issue of ancestral domain. Both the Government and the MILF announced that they hoped to have signed an agreement on ancestral domain by the end of the following month, the first time in almost a decade that a time frame for the signing of a peace pact between the two sides had been agreed upon. In early March, however, the Malaysian Government postponed the next round of talks, scheduled for 5–7 March, owing to the state of emergency imposed upon the Philippines by President Arroyo (see above), although negotiations were resumed in late March following the removal of martial law. In the same month rumours circulated of a failed attempt to oust Murad Ebrahim from the MILF leadership, but senior MILF members denied such reports. Also in March it was reported that at least 50 suspected members of the MILF had surrendered to the army in advance of the resumption of peace talks with the Government; however, a spokesman for the organization disputed that those who had surrendered were in any way associated with the MILF, alleging that they were instead affiliated to the MNLF. In June a bomb explosion in Mindanao resulted in several fatalities and precipitated clashes between local paramilitaries and MILF rebels after the latter was accused of responsibility for the attack; in the following month, however, the two sides agreed to a cease-fire. The MILF denied perpetrating further bomb attacks in Mindanao in October, but suspicions were raised about the group's links to JI and Abu Sayyaf. Several MILF members were reported to be among at least 47 prisoners who escaped during an attack on a prison in Mindanao by a group of around 25 armed men in February 2007; the MILF denied any involvement in the incident. An Italian priest, Father Giancarlo Bossi, was kidnapped in June in his parish on Mindanao by suspected renegade members of the MILF. In July clashes between some 300 rebels and a group of marines who were searching for the priest on Basilan resulted in the deaths of 14 marines, 10 of whom were beheaded. The MILF claimed that it had ambushed the soldiers in self-defence, but denied beheading them. Father Bossi was released later that month on Mindanao. There was speculation that Abu Sayyaf members might have been involved in the kidnapping or the fighting.

In November 2007 the Government announced that the latest round of peace negotiations with the MILF in Malaysia had resulted in agreement on the demarcation of the land and maritime boundaries of a proposed new autonomous area on Mindanao, to be known as the Bangsamoro Juridical Entity (BJE). Although no details of the borders were disclosed, it was reported that the BJE would cover a larger area than the ARMM. It was hoped that an accord on ancestral domain would lead to a full peace agreement by mid-2008, although the MILF chief negotiator warned that several contentious issues remained to be resolved. Talks faltered in December 2007 over continued disagreement on ancestral domain, with the MILF opposed to the Government's position that any agreement should be implemented through the 'constitutional process' and demanding the inclusion of some 1,000 villages in the proposed BJE without conducting a plebiscite on the issue.

In early June 1994 the Government undertook a major offensive against Abu Sayyaf, which was held responsible for numerous attacks, principally on the islands of Jolo and Basilan, to the south of Mindanao. In retaliation for the capture by the armed forces of its base on Jolo, the group took a number of Christians hostage on Basilan, killing 15 of them. All but one of the remaining 21 hostages were released in mid-June, following the apparent payment of a ransom and the intercession of the MNLF. Later in June government troops captured the group's main headquarters in Basilan. In early August the group's remaining hostage was released, and the authorities announced that Abu Sayyaf had been 'eliminated'. In April 1995, however, the group was believed to be responsible for an attack on the town of Ipil, in Mindanao, in which as many as 100 people were killed. Some of the assailants were also believed to belong to a splinter group of the MNLF, the Islamic Command Council. Some 14 hostages were reportedly killed as the army pursued the rebels in their retreat from Ipil. Despite intense counter-insurgency measures by government troops, Abu Sayyaf perpetrated a further assault on the Tungawan, in which six civilians were killed. In April 1996 two bomb explosions in Zamboanga City were widely attributed to Abu Sayyaf or to other groups opposed to the peace negotiations between the Government and the MNLF. Abu Sayyaf subsequently denounced the MNLF's peace agreement with the Government. Clashes between government forces and Abu Sayyaf were reported on the island of Basilan in March 1998. In December the leader of Abu Sayyaf, Abdurajat Abubakar Janjalani, was killed in an exchange of fire with government security forces.

In April 2000 armed Abu Sayyaf troops abducted 21 people, including 10 foreign tourists, from the island resort of Sipadan in Malaysia, and held them hostage on Jolo. One month earlier members of a separate Abu Sayyaf group had seized a number of Filipino hostages on the island of Basilan where, demanding the release of convicted Islamist terrorists held in US prisons, they had at the end of April managed to evade capture by government forces by which they had been besieged. The Government's military response to the hostage crisis remained largely ineffective, and a stalemate lasting several months ensued, punctuated by both formal and informal negotiations and a partially successful intervention, involving the payment of ransoms, by Libyan mediators. While sporadic releases were secured, however, some hostages were also killed by their captors. In April 2001 President Arroyo declared 'all-out war' against Abu Sayyaf.

In May 2001 Abu Sayyaf rebels abducted 20 people, including three US tourists, from a holiday resort off the western island of Palawan. President Arroyo immediately ordered a military response, although the group threatened to kill the hostages if it was attacked. In early June the rebels succeeded in fleeing from under military siege; nine Filipino captives escaped as a result. Later in the same month the Government was forced to bring in a Malaysian mediator in order to avert the threatened execution of the three US hostages still being held. It was reported that one, Guillermo Sobero, had already been beheaded, although his body had not been found. In early July two Filipino hostages were released, but Abu Sayyaf stated that it intended to continue attacking US and European citizens until government forces had been withdrawn from the southern Philippines. Shortly afterwards Nadzmie Sabtulah, the rebel leader alleged to have planned the May abductions, was arrested, together with three other members of the group. However, the arrests failed to bring an end to Abu Sayyaf activities, and in August a group of Abu Sayyaf guerrillas raided the town of Lamitan on the island of Basilan, taking at least 36 hostages and beheading 10. The next day 11 hostages were released and soon afterwards 13 more were freed, following an armed raid by government troops. However, the military failed to capture any members of the Abu Sayyaf leadership and 21 hostages remained in captivity, leading to allegations of collusion between Abu Sayyaf and the Philippine military. Soon afterwards three Chinese nationals were abducted as they tried to negotiate the release of a Chinese engineer who had been held by the group since June 2001. Two of the Chinese hostages were later killed following a clash between the kidnappers and government forces in Sultan Kudurat province.

In October 2001 Abu Sayyaf was responsible for two explosions in Zamboanga City. Meanwhile, government soldiers were reported to have cornered the kidnappers and their hostages following two days of fighting, which had resulted in the deaths of 21 guerrillas. Shortly afterwards the group threatened to behead its two US hostages—Martin and Gracia Burnham—prior to President Arroyo's scheduled November visit to the USA unless the military halted its offensive. In late October an explosion in Zamboanga, which killed six people, was attributed to the group. In the following month a Canadian man was abducted by men claiming to be Abu Sayyaf separatists. Shortly afterwards the group released one hostage, followed one week later by a further seven. In December government troops succeeded in rescuing the Canadian man. Three hostages remained—the Burnhams and Ediborah Yap, a Filipino nurse. The military offensive against the guerrilla group was intensified by the arrival of US troops on Basilan in 2002. In April a series of bombs exploded in the southern city of General Santos, killing 15 people and prompting President Arroyo to declare a state of emergency in the area. The police later arrested five men in connection with the attacks. While the suspects were initially thought to be connected to the MILF, Abu Sayyaf claimed responsibility for the bombings. Shortly afterwards four men reported to be members of Abu Sayyaf were killed during a gun battle with police in the area. In June 2002 Gracia Burnham was rescued in a military operation, but her husband and Ediborah Yap were killed. Later in the same month it was reported that Aldam Tilao (alias Abu Sabaya), a senior member of the organization, had died during a gunfight at sea.

In July 2002 the joint US-Philippine military exercises that had been conducted on Basilan were formally concluded; President Arroyo subsequently ordered the redeployment of government forces to combat insurgency elsewhere in the country. Although it was thought that the exercises had achieved some success in defeating Abu Sayyaf, in August the group was responsible for the kidnapping of eight members of a Christian sect on Jolo; although two of the hostages were released, a further two were beheaded. Following the group's threat to perpetrate attacks in retaliation for the military offensive being conducted against it, in early October a bomb exploded in Zamboanga City, resulting in the deaths of three people, including a US soldier. Responsibility for the attack was attributed to Abu Sayyaf. Later in the same month two further explosions in Zamboanga, which led to the deaths of seven people, were also suspected to have been carried out by members of Abu Sayyaf, although there was speculation that JI members might also have been involved. The bombings followed the terrorist attack on the island of Bali, Indonesia, several days previously (see the chapter on Indonesia). Meanwhile, a bomb exploded on a bus in the capital, Manila, killing at least three people.

In January 2003 three government soldiers were killed during a battle with Abu Sayyaf rebels on the island of Jolo. In the following month further fighting broke out in advance of the resumption of counter-terrorism exercises between US and Philippine troops in the area. In late February President Arroyo imposed a 90-day deadline upon military commanders for the elimination of the threat posed by Abu Sayyaf. In May the final two members of the Christian sect captured in August 2002 were freed from captivity and, in June, the last hostage to have been taken from Sipadan in April 2000 escaped. Meanwhile, the Government announced the establishment of a commission to investigate claims by former hostage Gracia Burnham that collusion had taken place between Abu Sayyaf and Philippine military forces during her time in captivity. In December 2003 it was announced that government forces had captured Galib Andang, alias 'Commander Robot', a senior Abu Sayyaf figure, following a gun battle in Sulu. Abu Sayyaf claimed responsibility for a bomb explosion in February 2004 that caused a fire on a passenger ferry in Manila Bay in which 116 were presumed to have died. In March the Government announced that it had apprehended six members of Abu Sayyaf, thought to have connections to JI, who were believed to have been planning a bomb attack on Manila; one of those detained also allegedly confessed to planting the bomb on the ferry. In April the armed forces claimed to have killed Hamsiraji Sali, a leading member of Abu Sayyaf for whose capture the USA had offered a reward of US $1m., following a gun battle on the island of Basilan. Also in April at least eight members of Abu Sayyaf were among 53 prisoners who escaped from a prison on Basilan, using smuggled firearms; within four days 34 of the prisoners had been killed or recaptured by the security forces. In August 17 members of Abu Sayyaf were sentenced to death, having been convicted of kidnapping Ediborah Yap, two other nurses and a general hospital worker in 2001; four of the defendants were among those who had escaped in April and were sentenced *in absentia*. Sitra Tilao, the sister of Aldam, was arrested in September for her alleged participation in the kidnapping operations of Abu Sayyaf. In October President Arroyo announced that six members of Abu Sayyaf had been charged with murder and attempted murder in connection with the ferry bombing in February; Redendo Dellosa and Alhamser Limbong had been arrested in March, but the other four remained at large. A bomb exploded in a market in General Santos in mid-December, killing 16 people and injuring 52. The police arrested five men in connection with the attack, for which Abu Sayyaf was suspected of being responsible.

In late January 2005 the armed forces commenced a major offensive against Abu Sayyaf. Some 30,000 people fled the heavy fighting that ensued in the following month on the island of Jolo between government troops and Abu Sayyaf members, joined by followers of former MNLF leader Nur Misuari. Meanwhile, in mid-February Abu Sayyaf claimed responsibility for three co-ordinated bomb explosions, in Manila, General Santos and Davao City, in which 12 people were killed and some 150 injured. Amid fears of further attacks, the Government increased security at airports, seaports, bus terminals and shopping centres. In mid-March the security forces quashed an uprising at a prison near Manila, killing at least 22 detainees, including the Abu Sayyaf leaders Nadzmie Sabtulah, Galib Andang and Alhamser Limbong, after the expiry of an ultimatum for the prisoners to surrender weapons that they had seized from guards. Abu Sayyaf subsequently threatened to retaliate for the deaths of its members.

In the southern Philippines in August 2005 three explosive devices were detonated in Zamboanga City, injuring 26 people. In the same month a bomb exploded on a ferry, injuring at least 30 people. The Philippine authorities attributed the attacks to Abu Sayyaf. In October two alleged Abu Sayyaf members were sentenced to death, together with a suspected member of JI, for their part in a bomb attack on a bus in Manila's financial district, which had killed four people in February. In November at least 23 alleged Abu Sayyaf members were killed, and dozens more wounded, in violent clashes with government troops on the island of Jolo. In February 2006, in another suspected Abu Sayyaf attack, an explosion near an army base that was being used by US troops killed one person and injured an estimated 28 others. In January 2007 the campaign against Abu Sayyaf seemed to have made significant progress when it was reported that Jainal Antel Sali, or Abu Sulaiman, a senior Abu Sayyaf leader wanted for his alleged involvement in the kidnapping of several tourists in 2001 (see above) and the bombing of a ferry in 2004, had been killed by government forces on Jolo island. In the same month DNA tests confirmed earlier reports that the leader of Abu Sayyaf, Khadafi Janjalani, had been killed in September 2006. Four Filipinos later received a US $10m. reward from the US authorities for providing information that led to the two killings. None the less, Abu Sayyaf militants remained active, decapitating seven Christians who they had taken hostage on Jolo in April 2007, and sending the severed heads to military camps on the island. In June it emerged that Abu Sayyaf had chosen one of its founders, Yasser Igasan, to replace Janjalani as leader. In mid-August President Arroyo ordered the temporary transfer of the headquarters of the armed forces to Zamboanga City and announced that a major offensive had been launched against Abu Sayyaf on Jolo and Basilan, following clashes on Jolo in which 26 soldiers and an estimated 31 militants died. Rogue elements of the MNLF were also reported to be involved in the fighting, which prompted some 24,000 people to flee their homes. Later that month the armed forces claimed to have killed 42 members of Abu Sayyaf in an attack on a camp on Basilan. Clashes continued in the following months, with further casualties reported on both sides. Abu Sayyaf was also held responsible for a bomb explosion outside the House of Representatives in Manila in November, in which four people died. In early December 14 members of Abu Sayyaf were sentenced to life imprisonment for the May 2001 abduction of 20 people from a holiday resort off Palawan (see above). Later that month government troops killed Mobin Abdurajak, a senior leader of Abu Sayyaf and brother-in-law of Khadafi Janjalani, who was wanted for the April 2000 abduction of 21 people from a Malaysian resort (see above). A Catholic priest who had reportedly been receiving death threats from Abu Sayyaf was abducted and killed on the island of Tawi-Tawi in January 2008.

Meanwhile, at the end of November 1991 the US military formally transferred management of the Clark Air Base to the Philippines, in accordance with the Constitution's stipulation that foreign military bases should not be allowed in the country after 1991. In late December negotiations for an extended withdrawal period of US forces from Subic Bay naval base collapsed, owing principally to the USA's policy of refusing to confirm or deny the presence of nuclear weapons (prohibited from the Philippines under the 1987 Constitution) on board naval vessels. US personnel withdrew from Subic Naval Bay at the end of September 1992, and from the Cubi Point Naval Air Station towards the end of November.

In November 1994 the Philippine Government rejected draft proposals (presented by President Bill Clinton of the USA during a visit to the Philippines earlier in the month) intended to facilitate access for US naval vessels to ports in the Philippines. Relations between the USA and the Philippines improved, following the Chinese occupation of a reef in the Spratly Islands claimed by the Philippines (see below). A joint naval exercise between US and Philippine forces took place in July 1995 about 100 km from the Spratly Islands. In January 1998 the Philippine and US Governments signed a Visiting Forces Agreement (VFA), which provided legal status for US military visits to Philippine territory and for the holding of joint military exercises, pending ratification by the Senate. However, the powerful Catholic Church opposed the agreement and the communist guerrillas announced that they would terminate peace talks if the VFA were ratified; in September popular protests against the VFA took place. Owing to the intensification of the dispute with the People's Republic of China concerning the Spratly Islands, the Philippines signed an agreement with the USA in October to allow for the formal resumption of joint military exercises. The Senate ratified the VFA on 27 May. The first phase of joint military exercises between the USA and the Philippines, which took place in January 2000, provoked popular protests outside the US embassy against the return to the Philippines of US troops. In July Estrada visited the USA where he requested financial assistance to combat rebel movements in the Philippines.

Following the terrorist attacks on the USA in September 2001 (see the chapter on the USA) President Arroyo offered President George W. Bush her unqualified support for the US campaign against terrorism. In October the President stated that she had volunteered logistical and intelligence assistance, the use of Philippine airspace, and the former US military bases at Clark and Subic Bay to the US Government. An offer of combat troops had also been made, pending congressional approval. In November President Arroyo left for the USA to address the UN General Assembly and to hold talks with President Bush. In return for the ongoing support of the Philippines in the US anti-terrorist campaign, the US President promised the country US $100m. in military assistance and further development aid for Mindanao. The funds included $39m. to aid the Government in its continuing war against Abu Sayyaf, which had proven links to the al-Qa'ida terrorist network thought to be responsible for the attacks on the USA. President Arroyo declined an offer of direct US military involvement, limiting its role to the provision of technical and financial assistance for the offensive.

In January 2002 it was reported that the US Government had sent 660 soldiers to the southern Philippines. While they would engage in joint training exercises with Philippine troops, they would not participate in any direct combat as this would contravene the Constitution. The deployment marked the first significant extension of the US war on terrorism beyond Afghanistan. Despite some popular opposition to the deployment, President Arroyo's stance was considerably strengthened when she succeeded in winning support for the US military presence from the National Security Council, which accepted that it was authorized under the terms of the VFA. In February more than 20 people died following clashes in the city of Jolo between police and soldiers; a later bomb blast in the city killed a further five people. A second explosion in Zamboanga—serving as a temporary base for US servicemen—occurred on the same day. The incidents were attributed to opponents of the ongoing military exercises. President Arroyo also faced fierce criticism from many members of Congress over her decision to allow the deployment, with several claiming that the exercises were intended to conceal a US offensive against Abu Sayyaf. Her most outspoken critic was the Vice-President and Secretary of Foreign Affairs, Teofisto Guingona, whose stance was a decisive factor in his resignation from the foreign affairs portfolio in July of that year. In April President Arroyo sanctioned the deployment of hundreds more US troops to the region and extended the deadline for their departure, owing to the apparent success of the exercises in containing terrorist activities in the Philippines. The exercises were formally concluded at the end of July.

In late 2002 the US Government signed a five-year military agreement with the Philippines, pledging to extend co-operation between the armed forces of the two countries and to facilitate the movement of heavy equipment and logistical supplies. In January 2003 an advance deployment of US Special Forces troops arrived in Zamboanga to commence anti-terrorism training exercises. In February the USA announced that it intended to send a new deployment of soldiers to the island of Jolo, a stronghold of Abu Sayyaf; it specified, controversially, that the troops would assume a combat role for the first time. However, the Philippine Government stressed later that US forces would play an entirely non-combative role in any counter-terrorism exercises. In March the President stated that, owing to local opposition, military exercises would not be conducted on Jolo. In April a new joint exercise—'Balikatan 03-1'—was announced, to take place in north Luzon and south-west Sulu.

In May 2003 President Arroyo visited the USA. During her visit, US President George W. Bush designated the country as a Major Non-North Atlantic Treaty Organization (NATO) Ally (MNA), entitling it to increased US military co-operation and supplies of armaments. Later in that month the Government stated that it expected to receive a total of US $356m. in military assistance from the USA. In October President Bush visited the Philippines during a tour of the region and thanked the country for its continued co-operation in the US-led war on terrorism. Relations with the USA were strained in July 2004 by President Arroyo's decision to withdraw the small Philippine contingent from the US-led coalition forces in Iraq a month ahead of schedule in order to comply with the demands of militants who had taken a Filipino civilian hostage in the country. Nevertheless, joint US-Philippine military exercises continued throughout 2004, and in February 2005 officials from both countries met to plan the 28 exercises scheduled to take place in that year. In August bilateral trade discussions were held; issues discussed by the two countries included agriculture, trade and investment, intellectual property rights and telecommunications, with both the Philippines and the USA affirming that the negotiations had generated mutually beneficial results.

In May 2007 President Arroyo and the Australian Prime Minister, John Howard, signed a new security pact designed to assist the Philippines in its efforts to combat insurgents in the south of the country. Under the agreement, Australian special forces would train Philippine troops and joint counter-terrorism exercises would be organized.

Following his inauguration in mid-1992, President Ramos visited Brunei, Thailand, Malaysia, Singapore and Japan, demonstrating an increasing interest in regional relations. The Philippines' commitment to the Association of South East Asian Nations (ASEAN, see p. 185) also deepened. Relations with Malaysia were somewhat strained, owing to the Philippines' claim to the Malaysian state of Sabah, dating from 1962, before Sabah joined the Federation of Malaysia. Sabah was ruled by the Sultan of Sulu, in the southern Philippines, until 1878, when it was leased to what was to become the British North Borneo Company. The Malaysian Government continues to pay a nominal rent to the Sultan. Attempts by both Presidents Marcos and Aquino to abandon the claim were thwarted by the Senate. In August 1993 the Philippine and Malaysian ministers responsible for foreign affairs signed a memorandum creating a commission to address bilateral issues, including the Philippines' claim to Sabah. Following his inauguration in June 1998, Estrada pledged to continue Ramos's commitment to regional relations. At the ASEAN ministerial meeting in Manila in July, Domingo Siazon, Jr, whom Estrada had retained as Secretary of Foreign Affairs, joined his Thai counterpart in expressing support for 'constructive intervention' in member countries' internal affairs, in marked contrast to ASEAN's policy of non-interference hitherto. Later that year relations with Malaysia were strained by Estrada's public condemnation of the arrest and beating of the former Malaysian Deputy Prime Minister, Dato' Seri Anwar Ibrahim. Despite Malaysian opposition, Estrada held a private meeting with Anwar's wife, Wan Azizah Wan Ismail, during her visit to the Philippines in May 1999. In August 2001 President Arroyo visited Malaysia on her first overseas trip since assuming the presidency. In November, however, relations were jeopardized again when the Malaysian authorities detained rebel leader Nur Misuari for attempting to enter the country illegally. After some vacillation, Misuari was finally deported in January 2002 and relations remained cordial. However, in August the bilateral relationship deteriorated following the implementation of stringent new laws in Malaysia under which all illegal immigrants remaining in the country faced harsh penalties and deportation. Many of those affected were Filipino workers. The Philippine Government filed a formal complaint against Malaysia over its treatment of the immigrants and sent an official delegation to investigate allegations of maltreatment. Malaysia subsequently suspended implementation of the legislation.

In late November 1999 an informal summit meeting took place of the leaders of ASEAN and of China, Japan and the Republic of Korea (collectively known as ASEAN + 3), the third such meeting in three years. It was formally agreed to hold annual East Asian summit meetings of all 13 nations and to strengthen present economic co-operation with the distant aim of forming an East Asian bloc, with a common market and monetary union. At the annual ASEAN summit meeting held in Laos in November 2004, it was agreed to transform the ASEAN + 3 summit meeting into the East Asia summit, with the long-term objective of establishing an East Asian Community. In January 2007 the Philippines hosted the 12th annual ASEAN summit meeting and the second East Asia summit in Cebu. Meanwhile, in September 2006 President Arroyo and the Japanese Prime Minister, Junichiro Koizumi, signed an economic partnership agreement, which would eliminate tariffs on almost 95% of trade and provide for the entry of more Filipino workers to Japan. The agreement was approved by the Japanese legislature in December, but was still awaiting ratification by the Philippine Senate in early 2008, having provoked controversy over concerns that it would allow Japan to export toxic waste to the Philippines (a claim denied by officials) and that provisions apparently granting Japanese investors almost equal rights to Filipinos would violate constitutional restrictions on foreign ownership.

In August 2001 Indonesian President Megawati Sukarnoputri visited the Philippines on her first overseas trip since assuming power. During her brief stay she met with President Arroyo, and the two leaders promised to assist each other in overcoming the separatist violence endemic in both their countries. In March 2002 bilateral relations threatened to become strained when the Philippine police filed charges against three Indonesian men who had been arrested at Manila Airport for illegal possession of explosives. One of those arrested was believed to be a member of the Majelis Mujahidin Indonesia (MMI—Indonesian Mujahidin Council), an extremist Islamist organization, and to have links to JI. The Indonesian Government was reported to have been angered by the arrests and stated that the detentions should not be used as a pretext to portray Indonesia as a haven for Islamist extremists. However, in early 2003 it was reported that Philippine rebels were engaged in smuggling arms to militant groups in Indonesia, despite increased anti-terrorism co-operation between the two countries. In October 2003 Fathur Rohman al-Ghozi, believed to be a senior Indonesian member of JI, was shot dead by government forces three months after his escape from a prison in Manila, where he had been detained following his conviction for illegal possession of explosives.

The Philippines contributed 1,000 troops to a UN multinational force to restore peace and security in East Timor (which became Timor-Leste upon its accession to independence in May 2002), following the violence that erupted after the East Timorese voted in a referendum for independence from Indonesia; the International Force for East Timor (Interfet) was deployed in the territory in September 1999. The transfer of military command from Interfet to the newly established UN Transitional Administration in East Timor (UNTAET) took place in February 2000; the military component of UNTAET was commanded by a Filipino, Gen. Jaime de los Santos. The two East Timorese independence leaders, José Alexandre (Xanana) Gusmão and José Ramos Horta, visited the Philippines in that month and held a meeting with President Estrada.

Diplomatic relations were established with the People's Republic of China in 1975, at which time the Philippine Government recognized Taiwan as an 'inalienable' part of the People's Republic. However, conflicting claims to the Spratly Islands, in the South China Sea, were a source of tension between the Philippines and China. (Viet Nam, Brunei, Malaysia and Taiwan also claimed sovereignty over some or all of the islands.) In February 1989 Chinese and Philippine warships exchanged gunfire in the vicinity of the Spratly Islands, although it was later declared that the incident occurred as a result of 'confusion over rules of engagement'. Indonesia hosted six rounds of negotiations over the sovereignty of the Spratly Islands between January 1990 and October 1995; all parties agreed to reach a settlement by peaceful means and to develop jointly the area's natural resources. In December 1993 the Philippines and Malaysia agreed to co-operate on fishing rights for the disputed Spratly Islands in the area not claimed by the other four countries. Following a visit to Viet Nam (the first official visit by a Philippine Head of State to that country) in March 1994, Ramos appealed for the six countries with claims to the Spratly Islands to remove all armed forces from the area.

In May 1994 China made an official protest after the Philippine Government granted a permit to a US company to explore for petroleum off Palawan, in an area including part of the disputed territory of the Spratly Islands. In February 1995 the Philippine Government formally protested when it was revealed that Chinese armed forces had occupied a reef, Mischief Reef, which lay within the Philippines' 200-mile exclusive economic zone established by a UN Convention on the Law of the Sea. Tensions in the disputed region were exacerbated during March by the arrest, by the Philippine naval forces, of more than 60 Chinese fishermen, as well as the seizure of vessels and the destruction of territorial markers allegedly deployed China. (Most of the fishermen were released in October and the remainder in January 1996.) Following two days of consultations in August 1995, however, the Chinese Government agreed for the first time to settle disputes in the South China Sea according to international law, rather than insisting that historical claims should take precedence. The Chinese and Philippine Governments issued a joint statement agreeing on a code of conduct to reduce the possibility of a military confrontation in the area. A similar agreement was signed with Viet Nam in November 1995. In March 1996 the Philippines and China agreed to co-operate in combating piracy, which was also a source of tension between the two countries as pirate vessels in the area often sailed under Chinese flags. Despite these agreements, sporadic tension continued during 1996–98.

In August 1998 the Philippines rejected an offer from China for the joint use of the Chinese structures on Mischief Reef. In the same month Philippine and US warships staged military exercises in the South China Seas. The Philippines lodged a diplomatic protest against China in November, claiming that China was extending its structures on Mischief Reef, in contravention of the mutually agreed code of conduct. China insisted that it was only reinforcing existing structures. Estrada ordered increased naval and air patrols around the Spratly Islands to block entry and exit to the reef. A further 20 Chinese fishermen were arrested by the Philippine navy in November for violating Philippine waters. In January 1999 the National Security Council was convened for the first time in three years to discuss the Spratly Islands and Muslim unrest in Mindanao. The Philippines favoured a multilateral solution to the problems, whereas China opposed any external intervention. China rebuffed the Philippines' attempts to involve the UN through a meeting with the Secretary-General, Kofi Annan, in the USA and threatened to leave the Asia-Europe meeting in Berlin, Germany, if the Spratly issue were discussed. A meeting in Manila achieved little progress, with the Chinese dismissing a Philippine proposal for joint use of the facility, owing to the allegedly aggressive behaviour of the Philippine armed forces. ASEAN, which had failed to condemn China strongly at its summit meeting in December 1998, supported the proposal by the Philippines to draft a regional code of conduct in the South China Sea to prevent the escalation of conflict in the area. In April 1999 the Philippines and Viet Nam agreed to joint operations and leisure activities to reduce the risk of military confrontation. In October, however, the Philippines lodged a protest at the Vietnamese embassy, following an incident in which Vietnamese forces had fired on a Philippine aircraft patrolling in the area of the Spratly Islands.

In November 1999 ASEAN officials agreed on a regional code of conduct drafted by the Philippines to prevent conflicts in the Spratlys. In the same month the Chinese Premier, Zhu Rongji, visited the Philippines, and he and Estrada agreed to strengthen co-operation between the two countries. However, China rejected the proposed regional code of conduct although it agreed to participate in further discussions on the draft. In early 2000 China proposed a new draft code omitting previous references to a ban on construction on islands or atolls and excluded the Paracel Islands, which China had seized from Viet Nam in 1974. However, China did meet with all the ASEAN representatives to discuss the draft, a departure from its previously exclusively bilateral approach. In May 2000 Estrada made a visit to China where he met President Jiang Zemin and signed a joint statement on the framework for co-operation between China and the Philippines.

In mid-2002 relations with China were jeopardized when the Secretary of Justice, Hernando Perez, demanded that the Chinese ambassador be expelled from the country. His request marked the culmination of a dispute regarding the fate of more than 100 Chinese fishermen, who had been arrested over the preceding months and accused of fishing illegally in Philippine waters. Perez accused the ambassador of reneging on an agreement whereby the fishermen would be freed on condition that they entered guilty pleas and paid fines; he claimed that the ambassador had attempted to coerce the Philippine Government into releasing the fishermen without penalty. Perez subsequently withdrew his expulsion demand and, shortly afterwards, the Chinese Minister of Defence, Chi Haotian, paid a goodwill visit to the country. In November 2002 the improvement in bilateral relations was demonstrated when a high-level delegation from the Chinese Communist Party arrived in the Philippines. Also in that month a 'declaration on the conduct of parties in the South China Sea' was signed by the ministers responsible for foreign affairs of China and the ASEAN member states. In September 2004, during a three-day state visit by President Arroyo to China, her first foreign trip since her election, the two countries signed five bilateral agreements, including one to conduct joint marine research in the South China Sea. It was also agreed to explore the possibility of defence co-operation. In March 2005 the national oil companies of the Philippines, China and Viet Nam signed a three-year agreement on undertaking joint research into petroleum resources in the South China Sea. In March 2006 the Chinese Government granted the Philippine administration US $3m. with which to establish a Chinese-language military training programme, in return for the Philippines' continued adherence to the 'One China' policy, which recognized Taiwan as an integral part of the People's Republic of China. The Chinese Government also donated engineering equipment and invited the Philippines to participate in joint naval exercises. In January 2007 the Chinese Premier, Wen Jiabao, spent two days in Manila, after attending the 10th ASEAN-China summit and other ASEAN-related meetings in Cebu. During his visit several bilateral accords were signed, most notably a framework agreement on expanding economic and trade co-operation. President Arroyo visited China in October, shortly after suspending a telecommunications contract with China's ZTE corporation, following allegations of bribery in the bidding process (see above). In talks with the Chinese President, Hu Jintao, Arroyo sought to ensure that the cancellation of the contract did not adversely affect bilateral relations. However, Arroyo's administration was subsequently forced to defend the propriety of other economic agreements with China, amid criticism from Philippine opposition parties.

Relations between the Philippines and Taiwan deteriorated in October 1999, following Estrada's termination of all flights between Taipei and Manila after a failure to settle a dispute over passenger quotas. The Philippine authorities demanded that two Taiwanese airlines reduce passengers from the previously agreed 9,600 per week to 3,000 per week, in order to protect PAL's share of the market. Following negotiations it was agreed in January 2000 that flights would resume in February. However, a disagreement over the interpretation of the new arrangement arose: the Taiwanese authorities claimed that the new quota of 4,800 passengers per week applied only to the Manila–Taipei flights, whereas the Philippines sought to include the route between Manila and Kaohsiung route. The Philippines again severed air links after only six weeks, despite Taiwanese threats of an investment boycott and curbs on Filipino workers in Taiwan. The dispute was finally resolved in September 2000 when the Philippines and Taiwan agreed to reinstate a bilateral accord concluded in 1996. The Philippines had reportedly accepted that Taiwanese airlines should be allowed to fly passengers on to other destinations after arrival in the Philippines.

Government

The Constitution, which was approved by a national referendum on 2 February 1987, provided for a bicameral Congress, comprising a Senate, with 24 members directly elected by universal suffrage (for a six-year term, with one-half of the membership being elected every three years), and a House of Representatives (with a three-year mandate), with a maximum of 250 members, one being directly elected from each legislative district: in addition, one-fifth of the total number of representatives was to be elected under a party list system from lists of nominees proposed by minority groups. The number of members in the House of Representatives was increased to 275 at the 2007 election.

The President is Head of State, Chief Executive of the Republic and Commander-in-Chief of the Armed Forces. The President is elected by the people for a six-year term, and is not eligible for re-election. The President cannot prevent the enactment of legislative proposals if they are approved by a two-thirds' majority vote in Congress. The President may declare martial law in times of national emergency, but Congress is empowered to revoke such actions at any time by a majority vote of its members. The President appoints a Cabinet and other officials, with the approval of the Commission on Appointments (drawn from members of both chambers of Congress).

Local government is by Barangays (citizens' assemblies), and autonomy is granted to any region where its introduction is endorsed in a referendum. The Autonomous Region of Muslim Mindanao (ARMM), granted autonomy in November 1989, has its own 24-seat Regional Legislative Assembly (RLA).

Defence

The total strength of the active armed forces as assessed at November 2007 was an estimated 106,000, comprising an army of 66,000, a navy of approximately 24,000 and an air force of 16,000. There were also reserve forces of 131,000. Paramilitary forces included the Citizens Armed Forces Geographical Units, which comprised about 40,000 men. The 2006 budget allocated an estimated 46,100m. pesos to defence.

Economic Affairs

In 2006, according to estimates by the World Bank, the Philippines' gross national income (GNI), measured at average 2004–06 prices, was US $120,166m., equivalent to $1,420 per head (or $5,980 per head on an international purchasing-power parity basis). During 1996–2006, it was estimated, the population increased at an average annual rate of 1.9%, while gross domestic product (GDP) per head increased, in real terms, by an average of 2.2% per year. According to figures from the World Bank, overall GDP increased, in real terms, at an average annual rate of 4.1% in 1996–2006. According to the Asian Development Bank (ADB), GDP increased by 5.4% in 2006 and by 7.3% in 2007.

Agriculture (including hunting, forestry and fishing) contributed 14.2% of GDP in 2006 and engaged 35.6% of the employed labour force in July of that year. Rice, maize and cassava are the main subsistence crops. The principal crops cultivated for export are coconuts, sugar cane, bananas and pineapples. Livestock (mainly pigs, buffaloes, goats and poultry) and fisheries are important. According to the World Bank, agricultural GDP increased at an average annual rate of 2.9% during 1996–2006. According to the ADB, agricultural GDP increased by 5.1% in 2007.

Industry (including mining, manufacturing, construction and power) contributed 31.6% of GDP in 2006 and engaged 15.1% of the employed labour force in July of that year. According to the World Bank, industrial GDP increased at an average annual rate of 3.4% in 1996–2006. According to the ADB, industrial GDP increased by 6.6% in 2007.

Mining contributed 1.3% of GDP in 2006 and engaged less than 0.4% of the employed labour force in July of that year. Copper is the Philippines' leading mineral product; gold, silver, chromium, nickel and coal are also extracted and there are plans to resuscitate the iron ore industry. Commercial production of crude petroleum began in 1979. Production from a substantial natural gas field and petroleum reservoir, off the island of Palawan, commenced in 2001. According to figures from the ADB, mining GDP increased by an annual average of 9.7% in 2000–06. The GDP of the mining sector increased by 9.3% in 2005, but contracted by 6.0% in 2006.

Manufacturing contributed 22.9% of GDP in 2006, and engaged 9.2% of the employed labour force in July of that year. The most important branches of manufacturing include food products and beverages, electronic products and components (mainly telecommunications equipment), petroleum refineries and chemicals. According to the World Bank, the GDP of the manufacturing sector increased by an annual average of 3.7% in 1996–2006. Manufacturing GDP increased by 5.2% in 2006.

The energy sector's reliance on imported petroleum has decreased significantly, as new sources of power have become available. In 2004 coal accounted for 28.9% of the total amount of electrical energy produced, natural gas for 22.1%, hydroelectric power for 15.4% and petroleum for 15.2%. In 2005 fuel imports accounted for 13.9% of the value of total merchandise imports. The transfer to private ownership of various government holdings in the power sector continued in 2007.

The services sector contributed 54.2% of GDP in 2006, and engaged 49.3% of the employed labour force in July of that year. Remittances from Filipino workers abroad constitute the Government's principal source of foreign exchange. Such remittances continued to increase in 2007, when they reached an estimated US $14,500m. Although periodically affected by political unrest, tourism remains a significant sector of the economy, with receipts reaching $2,620m. in 2005. Arrivals rose from 1.9m. in 2003 to almost 2.6m. in 2005. In the early 2000s the provision of business process outsourcing and attendant call-centre services was of increasing significance to the economy. Revenue from these activities was estimated to have increased by 48% between 2004 and 2006 alone. According to the World Bank, the GDP of the services sector increased at an average annual rate of 5.3% in 1996–2006. According to the ADB, the GDP of the services sector increased by 8.7% in 2007.

In 2006 the Philippines recorded a visible trade deficit of US $6,817m., while there was a surplus of $5,897m. on the current account of the balance of payments. In 2006 the principal source of imports was the USA (accounting for 16.3% of the total); other significant suppliers were Japan (13.6%) Singapore, Taiwan, the People's Republic of China, Hong Kong and the Republic of Korea. The principal market for exports in that year was the USA (18.3%); other major purchasers were Japan (16.5%), the Netherlands, China, Hong Kong and Singapore. The principal imports in 2005 were machinery and transport equipment (34.0%), mineral fuels, basic manufactures, chemical products and food and live animals. The principal exports in that year were machinery and transport equipment, which accounted for 41.2% of total exports.

The budgetary deficit for 2006 was recorded at 64,800m. pesos (compared with 149,118m. pesos in the previous year), equivalent to 1.1% of GDP. According to the ADB, the Philippines' external debt totalled US $54,427m. at the end of 2007; in that year the cost of servicing the debt was equivalent to 9.9% of the value of exports of goods and services. The annual rate of inflation averaged 6.0% in 1996–2006. According to the ADB, consumer prices increased by 2.8% in 2007. In 2007, according to the ADB, 7.3% of the labour force were unemployed (compared with 11.8% in 2004).

The Philippines is a member of the UN Economic and Social Commission for Asia and the Pacific (ESCAP, see p. 35), the Asian Development Bank (ADB, see p. 182), the Association of South East Asian Nations (ASEAN, see p. 185), the Asia-Pacific Economic Co-operation forum (APEC, see p. 176) and the Colombo Plan (see p. 411). In January 1993 the establishment of an ASEAN Free Trade Area (AFTA) commenced; a reduction in tariffs to a maximum of 5% was originally to be implemented over 15 years but this was later advanced to 2003 before being formally initiated on 1 January 2002. In November 1999 the target date for zero tariffs in ASEAN was brought forward from 2015 to 2010.

The inauguration of President Gloria Arroyo in January 2001 and the inception of a programme of economic liberalization restored a degree of stability to the Philippines. The Medium-Term Philippine Development Plan (MTPDP) for 2004–10 accorded priority to the creation of new jobs and reforms in the power sector. Privatization was an important aim of the Arroyo administration. Although the level of underemployment remained high, being estimated at about 20% of the labour force in 2007, there was a notable improvement in the employment situation in that year, partly due to the expansion of opportunities in the construction and services sectors, which sustained much of the strong economic performance in 2007. At 7.3%, GDP growth reached it highest level for three decades in 2007. Foreign direct investment rose from US $2,921m. in 2006 to an estimated $2,928m. in 2007. Alongside strong growth in consumption, increases in net exports and higher levels of investment, the services sector continued to record very robust rates of growth. Particularly strong performance was evident in areas such as business outsourcing, mobile phone services, retail trading and financial services. Furthermore, in 2007 the rate of inflation declined to its lowest level for 21 years. However, the incidence of poverty was reported to have increased in the mid-2000s, reaching 27% of families in 2006. The large fiscal deficit also remained a concern in 2007. More than 8m. Filipinos work overseas, with many employed in the oil industry and as nurses in the USA and the United Kingdom. By 2006 remittances from these emigrant workers were estimated to account for 11% of GDP. While overseas remittances remained an important part of the economy in 2007, a substantial decrease in their rate of growth was anticipated in 2008, owing to the deceleration in the global economy. Nevertheless, the Philippines' GDP growth rate was forecast to remain high, at 6.0%, in 2008, although inflation was expected to rise substantially as a result of sharp increases in international prices for essential commodities.

Education

Elementary education, beginning at seven years of age and lasting for six years, is officially compulsory, and is provided free of charge at public (government-administered) schools. In 2004/05 enrolment at pre-primary level included 40% of pupils from the relevant age-group (males 39%; females 41%). In 2004/05 enrolment at primary level included 93.0% of pupils in the relevant age-group (males 92%; females 94%). Secondary education begins at the age of 13 and lasts for five years: there is a common general curriculum for all students in the first two years, and more varied curricula in the third and fourth years, leading to either college or technical vocational courses. In 2004/05 enrolment at secondary level included 60% of pupils from the relevant age-group (males 55%; females 66%). Instruction is in both English and Filipino. In the same year enrolment at tertiary level included 28% of students from the relevant age-group (males 25%, females 31%). According to the UN Development Programme, in 2002 the annual expenditure per pupil was just 7,590 pesos (US $138). The Government's budget for 2005 allocated 135,470m. pesos (15.1% of total national expenditure) to education, culture and training.

Public Holidays

2008: 1 January (New Year's Day), 25 February (EDSA Revolution Day), 20 March (Maundy Thursday), 21 March (Good Friday), 9 April (Bataan Day, Araw ng Kagitingan), 1 May (Labour Day), 12 June (Independence Day, anniversary of 1898 declaration), 24 June (Araw ng Maynila)*, 19 August (Quezon Day)†, 31 August (National Heroes' Day), 1 November (All Saints' Day), 1 December (Bonifacio Day), 25 December (Christmas Day), 30 December (Rizal Day), 31 December (Last Day of the Year).

2009: 1 January (New Year's Day), 25 February (EDSA Revolution Day), 9 April (Maundy Thursday), (Bataan Day, Araw ng Kagitingan), 10 April (Good Friday), 1 May (Labour Day), 12 June (Independence Day, anniversary of 1898 declaration), 24 June (Araw ng Maynila)*, 19 August (Quezon Day)†, 31 August (National Heroes' Day), 1 November (All Saints' Day), 30 November (Bonifacio Day), 25 December (Christmas Day), 30 December (Rizal Day), 31 December (Last Day of the Year).

* Observed only in Metro Manila.

† Observed only in Quezon City.

Weights and Measures

The metric system is in force.

THE PHILIPPINES

Statistical Survey

Source (unless otherwise stated): National Statistics Office, Solicarel 1, R. Magsaysay Blvd, Sta. Mesa, 1008 Metro Manila; tel. (2) 7160807; fax (2) 7137073; internet www.census.gov.ph.

Area and Population

AREA, POPULATION AND DENSITY

Area (sq km)	300,000*
Population (census results)	
1 May 2000	
Males	38,524,267
Females	37,979,810
Total	76,504,077
1 August 2007	88,574,614
Density (per sq km) at census of 1 August 2007	295.2

* 115,831 sq miles.

REGIONS
(population at 2007 census)

	Population
National Capital Region	11,553,427
Ilocos (Region I)	4,545,906
Cagayan Valley (Region II)	3,051,487
Central Luzon (Region III)	9,720,982
CALABARZON (Region IV-A)*	11,743,110
MIMAROPA (Region IV-B)*	2,559,791
Bicol (Region V)	5,109,798
Western Visayas (Region VI)	6,843,643
Central Visayas (Region VII)	6,398,628
Eastern Visayas (Region VIII)	3,912,936
Zamboanga Peninsula (Region IX)†	3,091,208
Northern Mindanao (Region X)†	2,747,585
Davao (Region XI)‡	5,189,335
SOCCSKSARGEN (Region XII)§	2,598,210
Cordillera Administrative Region	1,365,412
Autonomous Region of Muslim Mindanao	2,412,159
Caraga	2,095,367
Total	76,504,077‖

* Southern Tagalog region prior to September 2001.
† Western Mindanao region prior to September 2001.
‡ Southern Mindanao region prior to September 2001.
§ Including area designated Central Mindanao region prior to September 2001.
‖ Total includes Filipinos in Philippine embassies, consulates and missions abroad (2,279 persons) and populations of areas of dispute between the National Capital Region and the province of Rizal (24,789 persons) and between the province of Davao Oriental and Surigao del Sur (4,555 persons).

PRINCIPAL TOWNS
(population at 2000 census)

Manila (capital)*	1,581,082		Gen. Santos City	411,822
Quezon City*	2,173,831		Marikina City	391,170
Caloocan City*	1,177,604		Muntinlupa City*	379,310
Davao City	1,147,116		Iloilo City	365,820
Cebu City	718,821		Pasay City*	354,908
Zamboanga City	601,794		Iligan City	285,061
Pasig City*	505,058		Mandaluyong City*	278,474
Valenzuela City	485,433		Butuan City	267,279
Las Piñas City	472,780		Angeles City	263,971
Cagayan de Oro City	461,877		Mandaue City	259,728
Parañaque City	449,811		Baguio City	252,386
Makati City*	444,867		Olongapo City	194,260
Bacolod City	429,076		Cotabato City	163,849

* Part of Metropolitan Manila.

Mid-2005 ('000, incl. suburbs, UN estimates): Metropolitan Manila 10,686; Davao City 1,327; Cebu 799 (Source: UN, *World Urbanization Prospects: The 2005 Revision*).

BIRTHS, MARRIAGES AND DEATHS*

	Registered live births		Registered marriages		Registered deaths	
	Number	Rate (per 1,000)	Number	Rate (per 1,000)	Number	Rate (per 1,000)
1996	1,608,468	23.0	525,555	7.5	344,363	4.9
1997	1,653,236	23.1	562,808	7.9	339,400	4.7
1998	1,632,859	22.3	549,265	7.5	352,992	4.8
1999	1,613,335	21.6	551,445	7.4	347,989	4.7
2000	1,766,440	23.1	577,387	7.5	366,931	4.8
2001	1,714,093	22.0	559,162	7.2	381,834	4.9
2002	1,666,773	21.0	583,167	7.3	396,297	5.0
2003	1,669,442	20.6	593,553	7.3	396,331	4.9
2004	1,710,994	20.7	582,281	7.0	403,191	4.9

* Registration is incomplete. According to UN estimates, the average annual rates per 1,000 were: births 31.7 in 1990–95, 29.1 in 1995–2000, 28.1 in 2000–05; deaths 6.3 in 1990–95, 5.5 in 1995–2000, 5.1 in 2000–05 (Source: UN, *World Population Prospects: The 2006 Revision*).

Expectation of life (years at birth, WHO estimates): 67.1 (males 64.0; females 70.6) in 2005 (Source: WHO, *World Health Statistics*).

ECONOMICALLY ACTIVE POPULATION*
('000 persons aged 15 years and over, July)

	2004	2005	2006†
Agriculture, hunting and forestry	10,082	10,595	10,415
Fishing	1,368	1,395	1,426
Mining and quarrying	114	111	134
Manufacturing	3,056	3,068	3,070
Electricity, gas and water	110	111	114
Construction	1,653	1,709	1,691
Wholesale and retail trade; repair of motor vehicles, motorcycles and personal and household goods	5,901	6,064	6,397
Hotels and restaurants	805	859	873
Transport, storage and communications	2,465	2,419	2,470
Financial intermediation	348	358	347
Real estate, renting and business activities	691	715	806
Public administration and defence; compulsory social security	1,414	1,497	1,552
Education	976	1,005	994
Health and social work	375	380	367
Other community, social and personal services	782	714	824
Private households with employed persons	1,491	1,521	1,776
Extra-territorial organizations and bodies	2	2	1
Total employed	31,632	32,522	33,257
Unemployed	n.a.	2,715	2,908
Total labour force	n.a.	35,237	36,165

* Figures refer to civilians only and are based on quarterly household surveys (excluding institutional households).
† Preliminary figures.

THE PHILIPPINES

Health and Welfare

KEY INDICATORS

Total fertility rate (children per woman, 2005)	3.0
Under-5 mortality rate (per 1,000 live births, 2005)	33
HIV/AIDS (% of persons aged 15–49, 2005)	<0.1
Physicians (per 1,000 head, 2004)	0.58
Hospital beds (per 1,000 head, 2002)	1.20
Health expenditure (2004): US $ per head (PPP)	202.8
Health expenditure (2004): % of GDP	3.4
Health expenditure (2004): public (% of total)	39.8
Access to water (% of persons, 2004)	85
Access to sanitation (% of persons, 2004)	72
Human Development Index (2005): ranking	90
Human Development Index (2005): value	0.771

For sources and definitions, see explanatory note on p. vi.

Agriculture

PRINCIPAL CROPS
('000 metric tons)

	2004	2005	2006
Rice (paddy)	14,497	14,603	15,327
Maize	5,413	5,253	6,082
Potatoes	69	70	69
Sweet potatoes	545	575	567
Cassava (Manioc)	1,641	1,678	1,757
Taro	102	110	112
Yams	29	29	30
Sugar cane	25,579	22,917	24,345
Dry beans	26	27	26
Groundnuts (in shell)	27	28	29
Coconuts	14,366	14,825	14,958
Oil palm fruit	356	355	373
Cabbages	93	91	91
Tomatoes	172	174	176
Pumpkins, squash and gourds	397	393	371
Aubergines (Eggplants)	183	188	192
Dry onions	87	82	76
Watermelons	107	115	117
Bananas	5,631	6,298	6,795
Grapefruit and pomelos	41	41	39
Mangoes	987	1,003	937
Avocados	31	38	26
Pineapples	1,760	1,788	1,834
Papayas	134	147	157
Coffee (green)	103	106	104
Ginger	24	25	227
Tobacco (leaves)	48	45	38
Natural rubber	311	316	352

Aggregate production ('000 metric tons, may include official, semi-official or estimated data): Total cereals 19,910 in 2004, 19,856 in 2005, 21,409 in 2006; Total roots and tubers 2,457 in 2004, 2,532 in 2005, 2,606 in 2006; Total vegetables (incl. melons) 5,849 in 2004, 5,756 in 2005, 5,733 in 2006; Total fruits (excl. melons) 12,458 in 2004, 13,110 in 2005, 13,582 in 2006.

Source: FAO.

LIVESTOCK
('000 head, year ending 30 June)

	2004	2005	2006
Cattle	2,593	2,489	2,525
Pigs	12,562	12,140	13,430
Buffaloes	3,270	3,327	3,358
Horses*	230	230	230
Goats	3,358	3,535	3,736
Sheep*	30	30	30
Chickens	122,010	136,001	134,300
Ducks	10,211	10,439	11,147

* FAO estimates.
Source: FAO.

LIVESTOCK PRODUCTS
('000 metric tons)

	2004	2005	2006
Cattle meat	179.2	172.8	166.8
Buffalo meat	79.7	77.1	70.0
Pig meat	1,365.6	1,415.0	1,466.8
Chicken meat	658.1	649.5	643.1
Cows' milk	11.6	13.0*	12.0
Hen eggs†	n.a.	n.a.	530
Other poultry eggs†	72.0	72.0	72.0

* Unofficial figure.
† FAO estimates.
Source: FAO.

Forestry

ROUNDWOOD REMOVALS
('000 cubic metres, excl. bark)

	2004	2005	2006
Sawlogs, veneer logs and logs for sleepers	410	345	396
Pulpwood	355	489	236
Other industrial wood*	2,295	2,295	2,295
Fuel wood*	13,070	12,950	12,821
Total	16,130	16,079	15,748

* FAO estimates.
Source: FAO.

SAWNWOOD PRODUCTION
('000 cubic metres, incl. railway sleepers)

	2004	2005	2006
Total (all broadleaved)	339	288	468

Source: FAO.

Fishing

('000 metric tons, live weight)

	2003	2004	2005
Capture	2,166.3	2,216.0	2,246.4
Scads (Decapterus)	436.3	418.5	392.9
Sardinellas	243.0	270.2	336.3
Frigate and bullet tunas	179.1	208.1	174.0
Skipjack tuna	138.3	143.1	143.1
Yellowfin tuna	117.7	124.1	95.6
Indian mackerel	79.1	77.3	85.6
Aquaculture	459.6	512.2	557.3
Nile tilapia	111.3	118.1	126.6
Milkfish	246.5	273.6	289.2
Total catch	2,625.9	2,728.3	2,803.6

Note: Figures exclude aquatic plants ('000 metric tons): 989.4 (capture 0.5, aquaculture 988.9) in 2003; 1,205.2 (capture 0.4, aquaculture 1,204.8) in 2004; 1,338.9 (capture 0.3, aquaculture 1,338.6) in 2005.

Source: FAO.

THE PHILIPPINES

Mining

('000 metric tons, unless otherwise indicated)

	2003	2004	2005
Coal	2,029	2,727	3,165
Crude petroleum ('000 barrels)	2,000*	139	208
Chromium ore (gross weight)	33.8	42.1	36.1
Copper ore†	20.4	16.0	16.3
Salt (unrefined)	429.2	427.6	421.0
Nickel ore†	19.5	17.0	22.6
Gold (metric tons)†	37.8	35.5	37.5
Silver (metric tons)†	9.6	9.3	19.2
Dolomite	750.0*	1,408.9	874.4
Limestone‡	16,432	20,959	21,236

* Estimate.
† Figures refer to the metal content of ores and concentrates.
‡ Excludes limestone for road construction.

Source: US Geological Survey.

Industry

SELECTED PRODUCTS
('000 metric tons, unless otherwise indicated)

	2003	2004	2005
Plywood ('000 cubic metres)	351	386	233
Mechanical wood pulp*	37	38	38
Chemical wood pulp*	147	147	147
Paper and paperboard*	1,091	1,097	1,097
Jet fuels ('000 barrels)	29,400*	45,800	46,000*
Motor spirit—petrol ('000 barrels)	79,800	127,600	128,000
Kerosene ('000 barrels)	21,000*	17,700	18,000*
Distillate fuel oils ('000 barrels)	168,000*	170,000	170,000*
Residual fuel oils ('000 barrels)	215,000*	234,200	234,000*
Liquefied petroleum gas	25,200*	30,600	31,000*
Cement	13,067	13,346	15,494
Smelter (unrefined) copper	112	120	170
Electric energy (million kWh)	52,941	55,957	56,568

* Estimate(s).

2002 ('000 metric tons): Raw Sugar 1,956; Nitrogenous fertilizers (nitrogen content) 201; Phosphorous fertilizers (phosphoric acid content) 192.

2006: Electric energy (million kWh) 56,770.

Sources: FAO; US Geological Survey; Asian Development Bank.

Finance

CURRENCY AND EXCHANGE RATES

Monetary Units
100 centavos = 1 Philippine peso.

Sterling, Dollar and Euro Equivalents (31 December 2007)
£1 sterling = 82.94 pesos;
US $1 = 41.40 pesos;
€1 = 60.95 pesos;
1,000 Philippine pesos = £12.06 = $24.15 = €16.41.

Average Exchange Rate (pesos per US $)
2005   55.086
2006   51.314
2007   46.148

GENERAL BUDGET
(million pesos)

Revenue*	2003	2004	2005†
Tax revenue	537,684	596,408	677,707
Taxes on net income and profits	243,735	278,848	319,102
Taxes on property	712	798	914
Taxes on domestic goods and services	186,784	203,779	225,041
General sales tax	82,444	93,727	109,094
Excises on goods	56,865	51,433	50,699
Taxes on international trade	106,453	112,983	132,650
Non-tax revenue	87,748	79,491	80,239
Bureau of the Treasury income	56,657	40,735	45,369
Fees and charges	29,375	22,993	24,643
Privatization	1,716	1,000	500
Other non-tax revenue	—	14,763	9,726
Total	**625,432**	**675,898**	**757,945**

Expenditure‡	2003	2004	2005†
Economic services	169,881	155,585	159,158
Agriculture	32,932	25,262	25,941
Natural resources and the environment	6,752	6,776	6,803
Trade and industry	2,722	2,833	3,020
Tourism	1,182	1,200	1,412
Power and energy	1,099	1,999	1,512
Water resources, development and flood control	7,007	6,180	6,471
Transport and communications	67,149	54,908	54,949
Other economic services	1,688	7,077	5,982
Allotment to local government units	49,350	49,350	53,068
Social services	237,532	247,888	254,297
Education, culture and training	128,995	133,321	135,470
Health	12,400	12,880	12,927
Social security, welfare and employment	39,096	38,381	40,080
Housing and community development	3,019	2,577	1,739
Land distribution	907	4,284	4,422
Other social services	945	4,275	3,558
Allotment to local government units	52,170	52,170	56,101
Defence	44,439	43,847	44,193
General public services	141,233	137,278	140,650
General administration	43,442	42,254	40,143
Public order and safety	52,565	53,213	54,290
Other general public services	5,746	2,331	3,763
Allotment to local government units	39,480	39,480	42,454
Interest payments	226,408	271,531	301,692
Total	**819,493**	**856,129**	**899,990**

* Excluding grants received (million pesos): 1,198 in 2003; 511 in 2004; 527 in 2005 (forecast).
† Forecasts.
‡ Excluding net lending (million pesos): 5,620 in 2003; 5,500 in 2004; 7,600 in 2005 (forecast).

2006 ('000 million pesos): Total revenue 979.6; Total expenditure 1,044.4 (Source: IMF, *International Financial Statistics*).

INTERNATIONAL RESERVES
(US $ million at 31 December)

	2005	2006	2007
Gold*	2,568	2,941	3,541
IMF special drawing rights	1	2	1
Reserve position in IMF	125	132	138
Foreign exchange	15,800	19,891	30,071
Total	**18,494**	**22,966**	**33,751**

* Valued at market-related prices.

Source: IMF, *International Financial Statistics*.

THE PHILIPPINES

MONEY SUPPLY
(million pesos at 31 December)

	2004	2005	2006
Currency outside banks	259,572	273,672	312,019
Demand deposits at commercial banks	300,959	336,409	446,348
Total money (incl. others)	567,737	620,220	772,296

Source: IMF, *International Financial Statistics*.

COST OF LIVING
(Consumer Price Index; base: 2000 = 100)

	2003	2004	2005
Food (incl. beverages and tobacco)	109.5	116.3	123.8
Fuel, light and water	123.2	132.3	156.2
Clothing (incl. footwear)	111.4	114.4	118.4
Housing and repairs	117.0	121.4	126.9
Services	121.6	132.8	148.5
Miscellaneous	111.1	113.5	117.1
All items	113.8	120.6	129.8

All items (Consumer Price Index; base: 2000 = 100): 137.9 in 2006; 141.8 in 2007 (Source: IMF, *International Financial Statistics*).

NATIONAL ACCOUNTS
('000 million pesos at current prices)

Expenditure on the Gross Domestic Product

	2004	2005	2006
Government final consumption expenditure	492.1	521.6	587.5
Private final consumption expenditure	3,346.7	3,773.0	4,226.1
Increase in stocks	31.9	10.6	30.1
Gross fixed capital formation	784.1	783.4	834.4
Statistical discrepancy	394.8	575.7	430.1
Total domestic expenditure	5,049.6	5,664.4	6,108.2
Exports of goods and services	2,481.0	2,589.7	2,798.0
Less Imports of goods and services	2,659.0	2,816.2	2,873.6
GDP in purchasers' values	4,871.6	5,437.9	6,032.6
GDP at constant 1985 prices	1,154.3	1,210.5	1,276.4

Gross Domestic Product by Economic Activity

	2004	2005	2006
Agriculture, hunting, forestry and fishing	734.1	780.1	855.5
Mining and quarrying	52.9	63.6	75.6
Manufacturing	1,122.9	1,264.7	1,381.2
Electricity, gas and water	155.8	196.7	216.1
Construction	212.8	210.2	235.2
Wholesale and retail trade, restaurants and hotels	681.7	776.9	877.5
Transport, storage and communications	367.4	413.9	446.2
Financial intermediation	215.7	263.7	312.0
Real estate, renting and business activities	292.2	320.4	350.7
Public administration	382.7	405.8	452.6
Other services	653.3	742.0	830.2
GDP in purchasers' values	4,871.6	5,437.9	6,032.6

Source: Central Bank of the Philippines, Manila.

BALANCE OF PAYMENTS
(US $ million)

	2004	2005	2006
Exports of goods f.o.b.	38,794	40,263	46,526
Imports of goods f.o.b.	−44,478	−48,036	−53,343
Trade balance	−5,684	−7,773	−6,817
Exports of services	4,043	4,525	6,453
Imports of services	−5,815	−5,865	−6,120
Balance on goods and services	−7,456	−9,113	−6,484
Other income received	3,725	3,937	4,390
Other income paid	−3,796	−4,231	−5,189
Balance on goods, services and income	−7,527	−9,407	−7,283
Current transfers received	9,420	11,711	13,511
Current transfers paid	−260	−320	−331
Current balance	1,633	1,984	5,897
Capital account (net)	17	40	138
Direct investment abroad	−579	−189	−103
Direct investment from abroad	688	1,854	2,086
Portfolio investment assets	−862	−145	−1,567
Portfolio investment liabilities	288	3,446	4,885
Financial derivatives assets	58	98	159
Financial derivatives liabilities	−85	−141	−297
Other investment assets	−907	−4,791	−3,512
Other investment liabilities	−272	1,309	−2,314
Net errors and omissions	−282	−1,803	−657
Overall balance	−303	1,662	4,715

Source: IMF, *International Financial Statistics*.

External Trade

PRINCIPAL COMMODITIES
(distribution by SITC, US $ million)

Imports c.i.f.	2002	2003	2004
Food and live animals	2,277.6	2,317.4	2,293.1
Mineral fuels, lubricants, etc.	3,282.5	3,990.2	4,684.8
Petroleum, petroleum products, etc.	2,993.7	3,593.9	4,276.2
Crude petroleum oils, etc.	2,262.8	2,632.1	2,519.8
Chemicals and related products	2,654.0	3,192.6	3,293.2
Basic manufactures	3,481.2	3,881.9	4,544.3
Textile yarn, fabrics, etc.	1,093.3	1,070.0	1,037.6
Machinery and transport equipment	21,379.2	23,028.6	26,233.5
Office machines and automatic data-processing equipment	3,905.1	4,276.4	3,355.7
Parts and accessories for office machines, etc.	3,750.1	4,022.2	3,157.5
Telecommunications and sound equipment	1,321.5	1,304.4	1,139.0
Other electrical machinery, apparatus, etc.	13,099.9	13,840.4	18,585.0
Thermionic valves, tubes, etc.	11,325.0	11,712.7	16,908.2
Electronic microcircuits	1,861.5	2,032.4	1,951.3
Parts for electronic microcircuits	9,128.7	9,185.1	13,434.8
Road vehicles and parts (excl. tyres, engines and electrical parts)	1,069.1	1,258.5	1,076.6
Miscellaneous manufactured articles	1,134.9	1,7137	1,257.0
Total (incl. others)	35,426.5	39,543.5	44,039.2

THE PHILIPPINES

Exports f.o.b.	2002	2003	2004
Food and live animals	1,390.6	1,530.1	1,539.6
Basic manufactures	1,136.7	1,258.1	1,575.5
Machinery and transport equipment	26,806.2	27,103.7	17,664.3
Office machines and automatic data-processing equipment	7,354.0	6,943.1	6,365.9
Automatic data-processing machines and units	4,686.4	4,108.4	3,971.7
Complete digital central processing units	2,053.6	1,429.5	1,489.0
Digital central storage units, separately consigned	2,218.0	2,259.5	2,070.3
Parts and accessories for data-processing machines	2,583.0	2,773.2	2,363.2
Telecommunications and sound equipment	1,113.0	933.1	1,324.3
Other electrical machinery, apparatus, etc.	16,872.9	17,349.8	7,922.1
Thermionic valves, tubes, etc.	14,895.8	15,899.7	6,589.5
Diodes, transistors, etc.	995.9	1,595.4	1,463.4
Electronic microcircuits	13,123.5	13,370.6	4,565.6
Road vehicles and parts (excl. tyres, engines and electrical parts)	849.6	1,166.0	1,389.0
Miscellaneous manufactured articles	4,152.0	4,125.5	2,416.4
Clothing and accessories (excl. footwear)	2,374.5	2,250.0	1,310.8
Unclassified transactions and commodities	88.8	127.5	14,069.6
Total (incl. others)	35,208.2	36,231.2	39,680.5

Source: UN, *International Trade Statistics Yearbook*.

2005 (US $ million): *Imports:* Food and live animals 2,945; Mineral fuels, lubricants, etc. 6,524; Chemicals and related products 3,519; Basic manufactures 4,065; Machinery and transport equipment 16,847; Miscellaneous manufactured articles 1,200; Unclassified transactions and commodities 12,920; Total (incl. others) 49,487. *Exports:* Food and live animals 1,612; Basic manufactures 1,505; Machinery and transport equipment 17,016; Miscellaneous manufactured articles 2,528; Unclassified transactions and commodities 15,892; Total (incl. others) 41,255 (Source: Asian Development Bank, *Key Indicators of Developing Asian and Pacific Countries*).

2006 (US $ million): *Imports:* Food and live animals 3,182; Mineral fuels, lubricants, etc. 8,403; Chemicals and related products 3,862; Basic manufactures 4,183; Machinery and transport equipment 18,015; Miscellaneous manufactured articles 1,325; Unclassified transactions and commodities 13,292; Total (incl. others) 53,721. *Exports:* Food and live animals 1,785; Basic manufactures 3,036; Machinery and transport equipment 19,556; Miscellaneous manufactured articles 3,005; Unclassified transactions and commodities 16,284; Total (incl. others) 39,681 (Source: Asian Development Bank, *Key Indicators of Developing Asian and Pacific Countries*).

PRINCIPAL TRADING PARTNERS
(US $ million)

Imports f.o.b.	2004	2005	2006
Australia	579	531	627
China, People's Republic	2,659	2,973	3,672
Germany	1,196	1,131	1,374
Hong Kong	1,739	1,929	2,065
Indonesia	936	1,003	990
Iran	847	1,004	1,689
Japan	7,674	8,071	7,004
Korea, Republic	2,740	2,294	3,218
Malaysia	1,981	1,779	2,100
Saudi Arabia	1,274	2,182	2,981
Singapore	3,421	3,727	4,356
Taiwan	3,214	3,549	4,145
Thailand	1,572	1,583	2,089
United Kingdom	449	393	354
USA	8,270	9,096	8,394
Total (incl. others)	44,039	47,418	51,522

Exports f.o.b.	2004	2005	2006
China, People's Republic	2,653	4,077	4,617
Germany	1,436	1,349	1,775
Hong Kong	3,146	3,341	3,700
Japan	7,981	7,205	7,764
Korea, Republic	1,113	1,391	1,406
Malaysia	2,070	2,459	2,615
Netherlands	3,583	4,033	4,753
Singapore	2,631	2,707	3,449
Taiwan	2,228	1,888	2,006
Thailand	1,064	1,169	1,325
United Kingdom	555	437	482
USA	7,088	7,418	8,606
Total (incl. others)	39,681	41,255	47,027

Transport

RAILWAYS
(traffic)

	2002	2003	2004
Passenger-km (million)	93	83	84
Freight ton-km ('000)	63	69	76

Source: UN, *Statistical Yearbook*.

ROAD TRAFFIC
(registered motor vehicles)

	2004	2005	2006
Passenger cars	798,160	788,408	792,373
Utility vehicles	1,647,524	1,633,856	1,618,101
Sports utility vehicles (SUVs)	141,447	157,938	172,794
Buses	35,003	30,977	29,144
Trucks	267,977	266,915	285,901
Motorcycles and mopeds*	1,847,361	2,157,737	2,409,363
Trailers	23,121	23,922	23,898

* Including tricycles.

Source: Land Transportation Office, Manila.

SHIPPING

Merchant Fleet
(registered at 31 December)

	2004	2005	2006
Number of vessels	1,730	1,866	1,840
Total displacement (grt)	5,137,000	5,199,088	5,072,004

Source: Lloyd's Register-Fairplay, *World Fleet Statistics*.

International Sea-borne Shipping
(freight traffic)

	1994	1995	1996
Vessels ('000 net registered tons):			
entered	53,453	61,298	n.a.
cleared	53,841	61,313	n.a.
Goods ('000 metric tons):			
loaded	14,581	16,658	15,687
unloaded	38,222	42,418	51,830

THE PHILIPPINES

CIVIL AVIATION
(traffic on scheduled services)

	2001	2002	2003
Kilometres flown (million)	69	79	75
Passengers carried ('000)	5,652	6,449	6,435
Passenger-km (million)	13,454	14,216	13,904
Total ton-km (million)	1,666	1,755	1,729

Source: UN, *Statistical Yearbook*.

Tourism

FOREIGN TOURIST ARRIVALS

Country of residence	2003	2004	2005
Australia	69,846	89,175	96,465
Canada	53,601	64,537	72,853
China, People's Republic	32,039	39,581	107,456
Germany	38,684	45,092	50,411
Hong Kong	139,753	162,381	107,195
Japan	322,896	382,307	415,456
Korea, Republic	303,867	378,602	489,465
Singapore	51,257	60,253	69,435
Taiwan	92,740	115,182	122,946
United Kingdom	47,447	56,770	63,002
USA	387,879	478,091	528,493
Total (incl. others)*	1,907,226	2,291,352	2,623,084

* Including Philippines nationals residing abroad.

Tourism receipts (US $ million, incl. passenger transport): 1,821 in 2003; 2,390 in 2004; 2,620 in 2005.

Source: World Tourism Organization.

Communications Media

	2004	2005	2006
Telephones ('000 main lines in use)	3,437.5	3,367.3	3,633.2
Mobile cellular telephones ('000 subscribers)	32,936	34,779	42,869
Personal computers ('000 in use)	3,684	3,684	n.a.
Internet users ('000)	4,400	4,615	4,615
Broadband subscribers ('000)	89	123	123

Radio receivers ('000 in use): 11,500 in 1997.

Television receivers ('000 in use): 13,500 in 2001.

Facsimile machines (estimated number in use): 50,000 in 1995.

Book production (titles, excluding pamphlets): 1,380 in 1999.

Daily newspapers: 42 (with average circulation of 4,712,000 copies) in 1997.

Non-daily newspapers: 47 (with average circulation of 199,000 copies) in 1997.

Sources: International Telecommunication Union; UN, *Statistical Yearbook*; UNESCO, *Statistical Yearbook*.

Education

(2005/06, estimates, unless otherwise stated)

	Institutions	Teachers	Pupils
Pre-primary	41,949	341,789*	911,899
Primary schools			12,913,845
Secondary schools	8,287	126,141*	6,267,015
University and other tertiary education†	1,538	113,716	2,420,856

* Excluding private education.
† 2003/04 figures.

Sources: Department of Education, Culture and Sports; Commission on Higher Education.

Adult literacy rate (UNESCO estimates): 92.6% (males 92.5%; females 92.7%) in 2003 (Source: UNESCO Institute for Statistics).

Directory

The Constitution

A new Constitution for the Republic of the Philippines was ratified by national referendum on 2 February 1987. Its principal provisions are summarized below:

BASIC PRINCIPLES

Sovereignty resides in the people, and all government authority emanates from them; war is renounced as an instrument of national policy; civilian authority is supreme over military authority.

The State undertakes to pursue an independent foreign policy, governed by considerations of the national interest; the Republic of the Philippines adopts and pursues a policy of freedom from nuclear weapons in its territory.

Other provisions guarantee social justice and full respect for human rights; honesty and integrity in the public service; the autonomy of local governments; and the protection of the family unit. Education, the arts, sport, private enterprise, and agrarian and urban reforms are also promoted. The rights of workers, women, youth, the urban poor and minority indigenous communities are emphasized.

BILL OF RIGHTS

The individual is guaranteed the right to life, liberty and property under the law; freedom of abode and travel, freedom of worship, freedom of speech, of the press and of petition to the Government are guaranteed, as well as the right of access to official information on matters of public concern, the right to form trade unions, the right to assemble in public gatherings, and free access to the courts.

The Constitution upholds the right of habeas corpus and prohibits the intimidation, detention, torture or secret confinement of apprehended persons.

SUFFRAGE

Suffrage is granted to all citizens over 18 years of age, who have resided for at least one year previously in the Republic of the Philippines, and for at least six months in their voting district. Voting is by secret ballot.

LEGISLATURE

Legislative power is vested in the bicameral Congress of the Philippines, consisting of the Senate and the House of Representatives, with a maximum of 274 members (subsequently increased to 299). All members shall make a disclosure of their financial and business interests upon assumption of office, and no member may hold any other office. Provision is made for voters to propose laws, or reject any act or law passed by Congress, through referendums.

The Senate shall be composed of 24 members; Senators are directly elected for six years by national vote, and must be natural-born citizens, at least 35 years of age, literate and registered voters in their district. They must be resident in the Philippines for at least two years prior to election, and no Senator shall serve for more than two consecutive terms. One-half of the membership of the Senate shall be elected every three years. No treaty or international agreement may be considered valid without the approval, by voting, of at least two-thirds of members.

A maximum of 250 Representatives (increased to 275 at the 2007 election) may sit in the House of Representatives. Its members may serve no more than three consecutive three-year terms. Representatives must be natural-born citizens, literate, and at least 25 years of age. Each legislative district may elect one representative; the number of legislative districts shall be determined according to population and shall be reapportioned following each census. Representatives must be registered voters in their district, and resident there for at least one year prior to election. In addition, one-fifth of the total number of representatives shall be elected under a party list system from lists of nominees proposed by indigenous, but non-religious, minority groups (such as the urban poor, peasantry, women and youth).

The Senate and the House of Representatives shall each have an Electoral Tribunal which shall be the sole judge of contests relating to the election of members of Congress. Each Tribunal shall have nine members, three of whom must be Justices of the Supreme Court, appointed by the Chief Justice. The remaining six members shall be members of the Senate or of the House of Representatives, as appropriate, and shall be selected from the political parties represented therein, on a proportional basis.

THE COMMISSION ON APPOINTMENTS

The President must submit nominations of heads of executive departments, ambassadors and senior officers in the armed forces to the Commission on Appointments, which shall decide on the appointment by majority vote of its members. The President of the Senate shall act as ex-officio Chairman; the Commission shall consist of 12 Senators and 12 members of the House of Representatives, elected from the political parties represented therein, on the basis of proportional representation.

THE EXECUTIVE

Executive power is vested in the President of the Philippines. Presidents are limited to one six-year term of office, and Vice-Presidents to two successive six-year terms. Candidates for both posts are elected by direct universal suffrage. They must be natural-born citizens, literate, at least 40 years of age, registered voters and resident in the Philippines for at least 10 years prior to election.

The President is Head of State and Chief Executive of the Republic. Bills (legislative proposals) that have been approved by Congress shall be signed by the President; if the President vetoes the bill, it may become law when two-thirds of members in Congress approve it.

The President shall nominate and, with the consent of the Commission on Appointments, appoint ambassadors, officers of the armed forces and heads of executive departments.

The President is Commander-in-Chief of the armed forces and may suspend the writ of habeas corpus or place the Republic under martial law for a period not exceeding 60 days when, in the President's opinion, public safety demands it. Congress may revoke either action by a majority vote.

The Vice-President may be a member of the Cabinet; in the event of the death or resignation of the President, the Vice-President shall become President and serve the unexpired term of the previous President.

THE JUDICIARY

The Supreme Court is composed of a Chief Justice and 14 Associate Justices, and may sit *en banc* or in divisions comprising three, five or seven members. Justices of the Supreme Court are appointed by the President, with the consent of the Commission on Appointments, for a term of four years. They must be citizens of the Republic, at least 40 years of age, of proven integrity, and must have been judges of the lower courts, or engaged in the practice of law in the Philippines, for at least 15 years.

The Supreme Court, sitting *en banc*, is the sole judge of disputes relating to presidential and vice-presidential elections.

THE CONSTITUTIONAL COMMISSIONS

These are the Civil Service Commission and the Commission on Audit, each of which has a Chairman and two other Commissioners, appointed by the President (with the approval of the Commission on Appointments) to a seven-year term; and the Commission on Elections, which enforces and administers all laws pertaining to elections and political parties. The Commission on Elections has seven members, appointed by the President (and approved by the Commission on Appointments) for a seven-year term. The Commission on Elections may sit *en banc* or in two divisions.

LOCAL GOVERNMENT

The Republic of the Philippines shall be divided into provinces, cities, municipalities and barangays. The Congress of the Philippines shall enact a local government code providing for decentralization. A region may become autonomous, subject to approval by a majority vote of the electorate of that region, in a referendum. Defence and security in such areas will remain the responsibility of the national Government.

ACCOUNTABILITY OF PUBLIC OFFICERS

All public officers, including the President, Vice-President and members of Congress and the Constitutional Commissions, may be removed from office if impeached for, or convicted of, violation of the Constitution, corruption, treason, bribery or betrayal of public trust.

Cases of impeachment must be initiated solely by the House of Representatives, and tried solely by the Senate. A person shall be convicted by a vote of at least two-thirds of the Senate, and will then be dismissed from office and dealt with according to the law.

SOCIAL JUSTICE AND HUMAN RIGHTS

The Congress of the Philippines shall give priority to considerations of human dignity, the equality of the people and an equitable distribution of wealth. The Commission on Human Rights shall investigate allegations of violations of human rights, shall protect human rights through legal measures, and shall monitor the Government's compliance with international treaty obligations. It may advise Congress on measures to promote human rights.

AMENDMENTS OR REVISIONS

Proposals for amendment or revision of the Constitution may be made by:
  i) Congress (upon a vote of three-quarters of members);
  ii) A Constitutional Convention (convened by a vote of two-thirds of members of Congress);
  iii) The people, through petitions (signed by at least 12% of the total number of registered voters).

The proposed amendments or revisions shall then be submitted to a national plebiscite, and shall be valid when ratified by a majority of the votes cast.

MILITARY BASES

Foreign military bases, troops or facilities shall not be allowed in the Republic of the Philippines following the expiry, in 1991, of the Agreement between the Republic and the USA, except under the provisions of a treaty approved by the Senate, and, when required by Congress, ratified by the voters in a national referendum.

The Government

HEAD OF STATE

President: GLORIA MACAPAGAL ARROYO (assumed office 20 January 2001; inaugurated for second term 30 June 2004).
Vice-President: NOLI DE CASTRO.

THE CABINET
(April 2008)

Executive Secretary: EDUARDO ERMITA.
Secretary of Agrarian Reform: NASSER C. PANGANDAMAN.
Secretary of Agriculture: ARTHUR C. YAP.
Secretary of the Budget and Management: ROLANDO G. ANDAYA.
Secretary of Education: JESLI A. LAPUS.
Secretary of Energy: ANGELO REYES.
Secretary of the Environment and Natural Resources: JOSE LIVIOKO ATIENZA, Jr.
Secretary of Finance: MARGARITO B. TEVES.
Secretary of Foreign Affairs: ALBERTO G. ROMULO.
Secretary of Health: FRANCISCO T. DUQUE III.
Secretary of the Interior and Local Government: RONALDO V. PUNO.
Secretary of Justice: RAUL M. GONZALES.
Secretary of Labor and Employment: ARTURO D. BRION.
Secretary of National Defense: GILBERTO C. TEODORO, Jr.
Secretary of Public Works and Highways: HERMOGENES E. EBDANE, Jr.
Secretary of Science and Technology: ESTRELLA F. ALABASTRO.
Secretary of Social Welfare and Development: ESPERANZA CABRAL.
Secretary of Tourism: JOSEPH 'ACE' DURANO.
Secretary of Trade and Industry: PETER B. FAVILA.
Secretary of Transportation and Communications: LEANDRO R. MENDOZA.
Director-General of the National Economic and Development Authority: AUGUSTO B. SANTOS.
Presidential Spokesman and Press Secretary: IGNACIO BUNYE.
Presidential Chief of Staff: (vacant).

There are a further 16 officials of cabinet rank.

MINISTRIES

Office of the President: New Executive Bldg, Malacañang Palace Compound, J. P. Laurel St, San Miguel, Metro Manila; tel. (2) 7356201; fax (2) 9293968; e-mail opnet@ops.gov.ph; internet www.opnet.ops.gov.ph.

Office of the Vice-President: PNB Financial Center, 7th Floor, President Diosdado Macapagal Blvd, Pasay City, Metro Manila; tel. (2) 8333311; fax (2) 8312618; e-mail vp@ovp.gov.ph; internet www.ovp.gov.ph.

Department of Agrarian Reform: DAR Bldg, Elliptical Rd, Diliman, Quezon City, Metro Manila; tel. (2) 9287031; fax (2) 9292527; e-mail info@dar.gov.ph; internet www.dar.gov.ph.

Department of Agriculture: DA Bldg, 4th Floor, Elliptical Rd, Diliman, Quezon City, Metro Manila; tel. (2) 9288741; fax (2) 9277152; e-mail admin@da.gov.ph; internet www.da.gov.ph.

Department of the Budget and Management: DBM Bldg, Gen. Solano St, San Miguel, Metro Manila; tel. (2) 7354807; fax (2) 7357814; e-mail dbmtis@dbm.gov.ph; internet www.dbm.gov.ph.

Department of Education, Culture and Sports: DepED Complex, Meralco Ave, Pasig City, 1600 Metro Manila; tel. (2) 6321361; fax (2) 6388634; internet www.deped.gov.ph.

Department of Energy: Energy Center, Merritt Rd, Fort Bonifacio, Taguig, Metro Manila; tel. (2) 8441021; fax (2) 8442495; e-mail v_perez@doe.gov.ph; internet www.doe.gov.ph.

Department of the Environment and Natural Resources: DENR Bldg, Visayas Ave, Diliman, Quezon City, 1100 Metro Manila; tel. (2) 9296626; fax (2) 9204352; e-mail web@denr.gov.ph; internet www.denr.gov.ph.

Department of Finance: DOF Bldg, Roxas Blvd, cnr Pablo Ocampo St, 1004 Metro Manila; tel. (2) 4041774; fax (2) 5219495; e-mail hotline@dof.gov.ph; internet www.dof.gov.ph.

Department of Foreign Affairs: DFA Bldg, 2330 Roxas Blvd, Pasay City, 1330 Metro Manila; tel. (2) 8344000; fax (2) 8321597; e-mail webmaster@dfa.gov.ph; internet www.dfa.gov.ph.

Department of Health: San Lazaro Compound, Rizal Ave, Santa Cruz, 1003 Metro Manila; tel. (2) 7438301; fax (2) 7431829; e-mail info@doh.gov.ph; internet www.doh.gov.ph.

Department of the Interior and Local Government: A. Francisco Gold Condominium II, Epifanio de los Santos Ave, cnr Mapagmahal St, Diliman, Quezon City, 1100 Metro Manila; tel. (2) 9250349; fax (2) 9250386; e-mail dilgmail@dilg.gov.ph; internet www.dilg.gov.ph.

Department of Justice: Padre Faura St, Ermita, Metro Manila; tel. (2) 5216264; fax (2) 5211614; e-mail sechbp@info.com.ph; internet www.doj.gov.ph.

Department of Labor and Employment: DOLE Executive Bldg, 7th Floor, Muralla Wing, Muralla St, Intramuros, 1002 Metro Manila; tel. (2) 5273000; fax (2) 5272121; e-mail osec@dole.gov.ph; internet www.dole.gov.ph.

Department of National Defense: DND Bldg, 3rd Floor, Camp Aguinaldo, Quezon City, 1100 Metro Manila; tel. (2) 9113300; fax (2) 9116213; e-mail webmaster@dnd.gov.ph; internet www.dnd.gov.ph.

Department of Public Works and Highways: DPWH Bldg, Bonifacio Drive, Port Area, Metro Manila; tel. (2) 3043000; fax (2) 5275635; e-mail pid@dpwh.gov.ph; internet www.dpwh.gov.ph.

Department of Science and Technology: DOST Compound, Gen. Santos Ave, Bicutan, Taguig, 1631 Metro Manila; tel. (2) 8372071; fax (2) 8373161; e-mail efa@dost.gov.ph; internet www.dost.gov.ph.

Department of Social Welfare and Development: Batasang Pambansa, Constitution Hills, Quezon City, Metro Manila; tel. (2) 9318101; fax (2) 9318191; e-mail eicabral@dswd.gov.ph; internet www.dswd.gov.ph; f. 1951.

Department of Tourism: Rm 317, DOT Bldg, T. M. Kalaw St, 1000 Metro Manila; tel. (2) 5251805; fax (2) 5256538; e-mail ejarquejr@tourism.gov.ph; internet www.wowphilippines.com.ph.

Department of Trade and Industry: Industry and Investments Bldg, 385 Sen. Gil J. Puyat Ave, Buendia, Makati City, 1200 Metro Manila; tel. (2) 8953611; fax (2) 8956487; e-mail mis@dti.dti.gov.ph; internet www.dti.gov.ph.

Department of Transportation and Communications: Columbia Tower, 17th Floor, Ortigas Ave, Mandaluyong City, 1555 Metro Manila; tel. and fax (2) 7238235; e-mail aksyonagad@dotc.gov.ph; internet www.dotc.gov.ph.

National Economic and Development Authority (NEDA—Department of Socio-Economic Planning): NEDA-sa-Pasig Bldg, 12 St Josemaria Escriva St, Pasig City, 1605 Metro Manila; tel. (2) 6313747; fax (2) 6313282; e-mail info@neda.gov.ph; internet www.neda.gov.ph.

Philippine Information Agency (Office of the Press Secretary): PIA Bldg, Visayas Ave, Diliman, Quezon City, Metro Manila; tel. (2) 9204339; fax (2) 9815025; e-mail pia@ops.gov.ph; internet www.pia.gov.ph.

President and Legislature

PRESIDENT

Election, 10 May 2004

Candidate	Votes	% of votes
Gloria Macapagal Arroyo (Lakas-CMD)	12,905,808	39.99
Fernando Poe, Jr (KNP)	11,782,232	36.51
Panfilo Lacson (LDP)	3,510,080	10.88
Raul S. Roco (Aksyon Demokratiko)	2,082,762	6.45
Eduardo Villanueva (Bangon Pilipinas)	1,988,218	6.16
Total*	32,269,100	100.00

*Total may not be equal to sum of components, owing to rounding.

THE CONGRESS OF THE PHILIPPINES

Senate

President of the Senate: MANNY VILLAR.

Elections for 12 of the 24 seats were held on 14 May 2007. The TEAM Unity coalition won three seats and the Genuine Opposition (GO) coalition won seven, giving a majority to opponents of President Arroyo. Two seats were secured by independent candidates.

House of Representatives

Speaker of the House: PROSPERO NOGRALES.

General Election, 14 May 2007

	Seats
Lakas ng EDSA-Christian Muslim Democrats (Lakas-CMD)	70
Kabalikat ng Malayang Pilipino (KAMPI)	47
Nationalist People's Coalition (NPC)	26
Liberal Party (LP)	16
Nacionalista Party (NP)	6
PDP-Laban Party	4
Others	106
Total	275

Note: The distribution of seats in the House of Representatives was yet to be completed and confirmed. The total includes members of minority and cause-orientated groups allocated seats under the party list elections, which also took place on 14 May 2007.

Autonomous Region

MUSLIM MINDANAO

The Autonomous Region of Muslim Mindanao (ARMM) originally comprised the provinces of Lanao del Sur, Maguindanao, Tawi-Tawi and Sulu. The Region was granted autonomy in November 1989. Elections took place in February 1990, and the formal transfer of limited executive powers took place in October of that year. In August 2001 a plebiscite was conducted in 11 provinces and 14 cities in Mindanao to determine whether or not they would become members of the ARMM. The city of Marawi and the province of Basilan subsequently joined the Region. Elections for the 21 seats of the Regional Legislative Assembly (RLA) were held on 26 November 2001. Elections for the expanded 24-seat RLA took place on 8 August 2005. A total of six candidates contested the concurrent gubernatorial election; Zaldy Puti U. Ampatuan, the candidate of Lakas ng EDSA-Christian Muslim Democrats (Lakas-CMD), won an estimated 63.7% of the votes cast, defeating Mahid Mutilan of the Ompia Party, a Muslim grouping, and Ibrahim Paglas of the Liberal Party, who received 24.3% and 11.8% of the votes respectively.

Governor: Datu ZALDY PUTI U. AMPATUAN (took office 30 September 2005).

Vice-Governor: ANSARUDDIN-ABDULMALIK A. ADIONG.

Election Commission

Commission on Elections (COMELEC): Postigo St, Intramuros, 1002 Metro Manila; tel. (2) 527-5581; e-mail asd@comelec.gov.ph; internet www.comelec.gov.ph; f. 1940; Chair. JOSE MELO.

Political Organizations

Akbayan (Citizens' Action Party): 101 Matahimik St, Teacher's Village West, Quezon City, 1101 Metro Manila; tel. (2) 4336933; fax (2) 9252936; e-mail secretariat@akbayan.org; internet www.akbayan.org; f. 1998; left-wing party list; Pres. RONALD LLAMAS; Sec.-Gen. ARLENE SANTOS.

Aksyon Demokratiko (Democratic Action Party): 16th Floor, Strata 2000 Bldg, Emerald Ave, Ortigas Center, Pasig City, 1600 Metro Manila; tel. (2) 6385381; fax (2) 6319530; e-mail senator@raulroco.com; internet 203.115.161.138/library/raulroco/aksyond/aksyond.htm; f. 1997; est. to support presidential candidacy of RAUL ROCO; joined Alyansa ng Pag-asa in 2003 to contest 2004 elections; Chair. SULPICIO ROCO; Pres. HERMINIO AQUINO.

Bangon Pilipinas (Rise Philippines): 8th Floor, Dominion Bldg, 833 Arnaiz Ave, Legaspi Village, Makati City, 1200 Metro Manila; tel. (2) 8113355; fax (2) 8111110; e-mail feedback@bangonpilipinas.org; internet www.broeddie.com; Pres. EDUARDO VILLANUEVA.

Bayan Muna (People First): 153 Scout Rallos St, Kamuning, Quezon City, 1103 Metro Manila; tel. (2) 4251045; fax (2) 9213473; e-mail information@bayanmuna.net; internet www.bayanmuna.net; f. 1999; Pres. SATUR OCAMPO; Chair. Dr REYNALDO LESACA, Jr.

Genuine Opposition (GO): internet genuineopposition.com; fmrly known as the United Opposition Coalition; alliance of parties incl. the Genuine Opposition party, the Liberal Party (LP), PDP-Laban Party and Nacionalista Party (NP).

Kabalikat ng Malayang Pilipino (KAMPI): 7th Floor, LTA Bldg, 118 Perea St, Legaspi St, Makati City, Metro Manila; tel. (2) 8171316; fax (2) 8121138; internet kampi.ph; f. 1997; Chair. MARGARITA TINGTING COJUANGCO; Pres. RONALDO PUNO.

Kilusan para sa Pambansang Pagpapanibago (BAGO): Metro Manila; f. 1997; est. to support presidential candidacy of SANTIAGO F. DUMLAO, Jr; Chair. EDUARDO D. BONDOC.

Kilusang Bagong Lipunan (KBL) (New Society Movement): Metro Manila; f. 1978 by Pres. MARCOS and fmr mems of the Nacionalista Party; Chair. FERDINAND 'BONG BONG' MARCOS, Jr.

Laban ng Demokratikong Pilipino (LDP) (Fight of Democratic Filipinos): c/o House of Representatives, Metro Manila; f. 1987; reorg. 1988 as an alliance of Lakas ng Bansa and a conservative faction of the PDP-Laban Party; mem. of Lapian ng Masang Pilipino (LAMP) until Jan. 2001; split into two factions, led by EDGARDO ANGARA and AGAPITO AQUINO, to contest 2004 elections; Angara faction joined Koalisyon ng Nagkakaisang Pilipino (KNP) in Dec. 2003 to support presidential candidacy of FERNANDO POE, Jr; Aquino faction supported presidential candidacy of PANFILO LACSON; Pres. EDGARDO ANGARA.

Lakas ng EDSA (Power of EDSA)-Christian Muslim Democrats (Lakas-CMD): c/o House of Representatives, Metro Manila; f. 1992; est. as alliance to support the presidential candidacy of Gen. FIDEL V. RAMOS; formed alliance with UMDP to contest 1998 and 2001 elections; fmrly Lakas-National Union of Christian Democrats (Lakas-NUCD); name changed as above in 2003; joined Koalisyon ng Katapatan at Karanasan sa Kinabukasan (K-4) in 2003; Pres. PROSPERO NOGRALES; Sec.-Gen. HEHERSON ALVAREZ.

Liberal Party (LP): 2nd Floor, Matrinco Bldg, Chino Roces Ave, Makati City, 1231 Metro Manila; tel. (2) 8937483; fax (2) 8930218; e-mail admin@liberalparty.ph; internet www.liberalparty.ph; f. 1946; represents centre-liberal opinion of the fmr Nacionalista Party, which split in 1946; joined Koalisyon ng Katapatan at Karanasan sa Kinabukasan (K-4) in Jan. 2004 to contest 2004 elections; Chair. FRANKLIN M. DRILON; Pres. MANUEL ROXAS II.

Nacionalista Party (NP): Metro Manila; tel. (2) 854418; fax (2) 865602; internet www.nacionalistaparty.com; Pres. MANUEL VILLAR.

Nationalist People's Coalition (NPC): 8 Bouganvilla St, cnr Balete Dr., Mariana, 1112, Quezon City, Metro Manila; tel. (2) 7227882; fax (2) 7227568; e-mail npcsecretariat@npcparty.org; internet npcparty.org; f. 1991; breakaway faction of the Nacionalista Party; mem. of Lapian ng Masang Pilipino (LAMP) from 1997 until Jan. 2001; Chair. FAUSTINO DY, Jr; Pres. FRISCO SAN JUAN.

Partido Demokratiko Sosyalista ng Pilipinas (PDSP) (Philippine Democratic Socialist Party): 4A Maalindog St, UP Village, Diliman, Quezon City, Metro Manila; tel. and fax (2) 9288692; fax 9286225; e-mail pinoysocdem@yahoo.com; internet pdsp.net/site1; f. 1981; formed by mems of the Batasang Pambansa allied to the Nacionalista (Roy faction), Pusyon Visaya and Mindanao Alliance parties; joined People Power Coalition (PPC) in Feb. 2001; Leader NORBERTO GONZALES.

Partido ng Bayan (New People's Alliance): f. May 1986; formed by JOSE MARIA SISON (imprisoned in 1977–86), the head of the Communist Party of the Philippines (CPP); militant left-wing nationalist group.

Partido ng Manggagawang Pilipino (PMP) (Filipino Workers' Party): e-mail pinoy_bolshevik@yahoo.com; internet manggagawangpilipino.tripod.com; f. 2002; est. by fmr supporters of the CPP (see below).

Partido para sa Demokratikong Reporma-Lapiang Manggagawa Coalition (Reporma): c/o House of Representatives, Metro Manila; joined People Power Coalition (PPC) in Feb. 2001; Leader RENATO DE VILLA.

PDP-Laban Party: c/o House of Representatives, Metro Manila; f. Feb. 1983; est. following merger of Pilipino Democratic Party (f. 1982 by fmr mems of the Mindanao Alliance) and Laban (Lakas ng Bayan—People's Power Movement, f. 1978 and led by BENIGNO S. AQUINO, Jr, until his assassination in Aug. 1983); centrist; formally dissolved in Sept. 1988, following the formation of the LDP, but a faction continued to function as a political movement; Pres. JEJOMAR BINAY; Chair. AQUILINO PIMENTEL.

People's Reform Party (PRP): c/o House of Representatives, Metro Manila; f. 1991; formed by MIRIAM DEFENSOR SANTIAGO to support her candidacy in the 1992 presidential election; joined Koalisyon ng Katapatan at Karanasan sa Kinabukasan (K-4) to contest 2004 elections to Senate; Pres. MIRIAM DEFENSOR SANTIAGO.

Probinsya Muna Development Initiatives (PROMDI): 7 Pasteur St, Lahug, Cebu City; tel. (32) 2326692; fax (32) 2313609; e-mail emro@cebu.pw.net.ph; f. 1997; joined People Power Coalition (PPC) to contest 2001 elections; Leader EMILIO ('LITO') OSMEÑA.

Puwersa ng Masang Pilipino (PMP): Metro Manila; mem. of Lapian ng Masan Pilipino (LAMP) from 1997 until Jan. 2001; joined Koalisyon ng Nagkakaisang Pilipino (KNP) to contest 2004 elections; Leader JOSEPH EJERCITO ESTRADA; Pres. HORACIO MORALES, Jr.

Sandigan ng Lakas at Demokrasya ng Sambayanan (SANLAKAS) (Upholder of People's Power and Democracy): 150K 6th St, Barangay East Kamias, Quezon City, Metro Manila; tel. (2) 4338377; fax (2) 4262422; e-mail sanlakas1@yahoo.com; internet www.geocities.com/sanlakasonline; leftist multi-sectoral; Pres. and Chair. WILSON FORTALEZA.

TEAM Unity: coalition of parties incl. supporters of Pres. Gloria Arroyo; mems include Kabalikat ng Malayang Pilipino (KAMPI), Laban ng Demokratikong Pilipino (LDP), Lakas ng EDSA (Power of EDSA)-Christian Muslim Democrats (Lakas-CMD) and Partido Demokratiko Sosyalista ng Pilipinas (PDSP).

United Muslim Democratic Party (UMDP): Mindanao; moderate Islamic party; formed an electoral alliance with Lakas-NUCD for the election to the House of Representatives in May 2001.

United Negros Alliance (UNA): Negros Occidental.

The following organizations are, or have been, in conflict with the Government:

Abu Sayyaf (Bearer of the Sword): Mindanao; radical Islamic group seeking the establishment of an Islamic state in Mindanao; breakaway grouping of the MILF; est. strength 1,500 (2000); Leader YASSER IGASAN.

Alex Boncayao Brigade (ABB): communist urban guerrilla group, fmrly linked to CPP, formed alliance with Revolutionary Proletarian Party in 1997; est. strength 500 (April 2001); Leader NILO DE LA CRUZ.

Islamic Command Council (ICC): Mindanao; splinter group of MNLF; Leader MELHAM ALAM.

Maranao Islamic Statehood Movement: Mindanao; f. 1998; armed grouping seeking the establishment of an Islamic state in Mindanao.

Mindanao Independence Movement (MIM): Mindanao; claims a membership of 1m; Leader REUBEN CANOY.

Moro Islamic Liberation Front (MILF): Camp Abubakar, Lanao del Sur, Mindanao; aims to establish an Islamic state in Mindanao; comprises a faction that broke away from the MNLF in 1978; its armed wing, the Bangsa Moro Islamic Armed Forces, est. 12,500 armed regulars; Chair. Al-Haj MURAD EBRAHIM.

Moro Islamic Reform Group: Mindanao; breakaway faction from MNLF; est. strength of 200 in 2000.

Moro National Liberation Front (MNLF): internet www.mnlf.org; seeks autonomy for Muslim communities in Mindanao; signed a peace agreement with the Govt in Sept. 1996; its armed wing, the Bangsa Moro Army, comprised an est. 10,000 mems in 2000; Chair. and Pres. of Cen. Cttee MUSLIMIN SEMA.

Moro National Liberation Front—Islamic Command Council (MNLF—ICC): Basak, Lanao del Sur; f. 2000; Islamist separatist movement committed to urban guerrilla warfare; breakaway faction from MNLF.

National Democratic Front (NDF): a left-wing alliance of 14 mem. groups; Chair. MARIANA OROSA; Spokesman GREGORIO ROSAL.

The NDF includes:

Communist Party of the Philippines (CPP): f. 1968; a breakaway faction of the PKP; legalized Sept. 1992; in July 1993 the Metro Manila-Rizal and Visayas regional committees, controlling 40% of total CPP membership (est. 15,000 in 1994), split from the

THE PHILIPPINES   *Directory*

Central Committee; Chair. JOSE MARIA SISON; Gen. Sec. BENITO TIAMZON.

New People's Army (NPA): f. 1969 as the military wing of the CPP; based in central Luzon, but operates throughout the Philippines; est. strength 9,500; Leader JOVENCIO BALWEG; Spokesman GREGORIO ROSAL.

Revolutionary Proletarian Party: Metro Manila; f. 1996; comprises mems of the Metro Manila-Rizal and Visayas regional committees, which broke away from the CPP in 1993; has a front organization called the Bukluran ng Manggagawang Pilipino (Association of Filipino Workers); Leader ARTURO TABARA.

Rajah Solaiman Movement (RSM): Mindanao; f. 2002; radical Islamic group seeking to establish an Islamic state in the Philippines; predominantly composed of converts to Islam.

Diplomatic Representation

EMBASSIES IN THE PHILIPPINES

Argentina: 8th Floor, Liberty Center, 104 H. V. de la Costa St, Salcedo Village, Makati City, 1227 Metro Manila; tel. (2) 8453218; fax (2) 8453220; e-mail embarfil@eastern.com.ph; Ambassador ISMAEL MARIO SCHUFF.

Australia: 23rd Floor, Tower II, RCBC Plaza, 6819 Ayala Ave, Makati City, 1200 Metro Manila; tel. (2) 7578100; fax (2) 7578268; e-mail public-affairs-MNLA@dfat.gov.au; internet www.australia.com.ph; Ambassador ROD SMITH (designate).

Austria: Prince Bldg, 4th Floor, 117 Rada St, Legaspi Village, Makati City, 1200 Metro Manila; tel. (2) 8179191; fax (2) 8134238; e-mail manila-ob@bmaa.gv.at; Ambassador HERBERT JÄGER.

Bangladesh: Universal-Re Bldg, 2nd Floor, 106 Paseo de Roxas, Legaspi Village, Makati City, Metro Manila; tel. (2) 8175001; fax (2) 8164941; Ambassador (vacant).

Belgium: Multinational Bancorporation Center, 9th Floor, 6805 Ayala Ave, Makati City, Metro Manila; tel. (2) 8451869; fax (2) 8452076; e-mail manila@diplobel.org; internet www.diplomatie.be/manila; Ambassador GRÉGOIRE VARDAKIS.

Brazil: 16th Floor, Liberty Center, 104 H. V. de la Costa St, Salcedo Village, Makati City, 1227 Metro Manila; tel. (2) 8453651; fax (2) 8453676; e-mail brascom@info.com.ph; internet www.brasemb.org.ph; Ambassador ALCIDES G. R. PRATES.

Brunei: Bank of the Philippine Islands Bldg, 11th Floor, Ayala Ave, cnr Paseo de Roxas, Makati City, 1227 Metro Manila; tel. (2) 8162836; fax (2) 8916646; Ambassador EMALEEN ABDUL RAHMAN TEO.

Cambodia: Unit 7A, 7th Floor, Country Space One Bldg, Sen. Gil J. Puyat Ave, Makati City, Metro Manila; tel. (2) 8189981; fax (2) 8189983; e-mail cam.emb.ma@netasia.net; Ambassador IN MAY.

Canada: Floors 6–8, Tower 2, RCBC Plaza, 6819 Ayala Ave, Makati City, 1200 Metro Manila; tel. (2) 8579000; fax (2) 8431082; e-mail manil@dfait-maeci.gc.ca; internet www.dfait-maeci.gc.ca/manila; Ambassador ROBERT DESJARDINS.

Chile: 17th Floor, Liberty Center, 104 H. V. de la Costa St, cnr Leviste St, Salcedo Village, Makati City, 1227 Metro Manila; tel. (2) 8433461; fax (2) 8431976; e-mail echileph@meridiantelekoms.net; internet www.embachileph.com; Ambassador (vacant).

China, People's Republic: 4896 Pasay Rd, Dasmariñas Village, Makati City, Metro Manila; tel. (2) 8443148; fax (2) 8452465; e-mail chinaemb_ph@mfa.gov.cn; internet ph.chineseembassy.org; Ambassador SONG TAO.

Cuba: 101 Aguirre St, cnr Trasierra St, Cacho-Gonzales Bldg Penthouse, Legaspi Village, Makati City, Metro Manila; tel. (2) 8171192; fax (2) 8164094; Ambassador RAMÓN ALONSO MEDINA.

Czech Republic: 30th Floor, Rufino Pacific Tower, 6784 Ayala Ave, 1200 Makati City, Metro Manila; tel. (2) 8111155; fax (2) 8111020; e-mail manila@embassy.mzv.cz; internet www.mzv.cz/manila; Ambassador JAROSLAV LUDVA.

Egypt: 2229 Paraiso St, cnr Banyan St, Dasmariñas Village, Makati City, Metro Manila; tel. (2) 8439232; fax (2) 8439239; Ambassador SALWA MOUFID KAMEL MAGARIOUS.

Finland: 21st Floor, BPI Buendia Center, Sen. Gil J. Puyat Ave, Makati City, Metro Manila; tel. (2) 8915011; fax (2) 8914106; e-mail sanomat.mni@formin.fi; internet www.finland.ph; Ambassador RITTA RESCH.

France: Pacific Star Bldg, 16th Floor, Makati Ave, cnr Sen. Gil J. Puyat Ave, 1200 Makati City, Metro Manila; tel. (2) 8576900; fax (2) 8576951; e-mail consulat@ambafrance-ph.org; internet www.ambafrance-ph.org; Ambassador GÉRARD CHESNEL.

Germany: 25th Floor, Tower 2, RCBC Plaza, 6819 Ayala Ave, Makati City, Metro Manila; tel. (2) 7023000; fax (2) 7023015; e-mail deboma@pldtdsl.net; internet www.manila.diplo.de; Ambassador CHRISTIAN-LUDWIG WEBER-LORTSCH.

Holy See: 2140 Taft Ave, POB 3364, 1099 Metro Manila (Apostolic Nunciature); tel. (2) 5210306; fax (2) 5211235; e-mail nuntiusp@info.com.ph; Apostolic Nuncio Most Rev. FERNANDO FILONI (Titular Archbishop of Volturnum).

India: 2190 Paraiso St, Dasmariñas Village, POB 2123, Makati City, Metro Manila; tel. (2) 8430101; fax (2) 8158151; e-mail amb@embindia.org.ph; internet www.embindia.org.ph; Ambassador Shri RAJEET MITTER.

Indonesia: 185 Salcedo St, Legaspi Village, Makati City, Metro Manila; tel. (2) 8925061; fax (2) 8925878; e-mail bidpen_manila@yahoo.com; internet www.kbrimanila.org.ph; Ambassador Dr IRZAN TANJUNG.

Iran: 2224 Paraiso St, cnr Pasay Rd, Dasmariñas Village, Makati City, Metro Manila; tel. (2) 8884757; fax (2) 8884777; Ambassador ALI MOJTABA ROUZBEHANI.

Israel: Trafalgar Plaza, 23rd Floor, 105 H. V. de la Costa St, Salcedo Village, Makati City, 1227 Metro Manila; tel. (2) 8925330; fax (2) 8941027; e-mail info@manila.mfa.gov.il; internet manila.mfa.gov.il; Ambassador ZVI VAPNI.

Italy: Zeta II Bldg, 6th Floor, 191 Salcedo St, Legaspi Village, Makati City, Metro Manila; tel. (2) 8924531; fax (2) 8171436; e-mail informazioni.manila@esteri.it; internet www.ambmanila.esteri.it; Ambassador RUBENS ANNA FEDELE.

Japan: 2627 Roxas Blvd, Pasay City, 1300 Metro Manila; tel. (2) 5515710; fax (2) 5515780; e-mail jicc-mnl@japanembassy.ph; internet www.ph.emb-japan.go.jp; Ambassador MAKOTO KATSURA.

Korea, Republic: Pacific Star Bldg, 10th Floor, Sen. Gil J. Puyat Ave, cnr Makati Ave, Makati City, 1226 Metro Manila; tel. (2) 8116139; fax (2) 8116148; internet phl.mofat.go.kr; Ambassador HONG JONG-KI.

Kuwait: 1230 Acacia Rd, Dasmariñas Village, Makati City, Metro Manila; tel. (2) 8876880; fax (2) 8876666; Ambassador BADER NASSER AL-HOUTI.

Laos: 34 Lapu-Lapu St, Magallanes Village, Makati City, Metro Manila; tel. and fax (2) 8525759; Ambassador LEUANE SOMBOUNKHAN.

Libya: 1644 Dasmarinas St, cnr Mabolo St, Dasmariñas Village, Makati City, Metro Manila; tel. (2) 8177331; fax (2) 8177337; e-mail lpbmanila@skynet.net; Chargé d'affaires a.i. SADEK A. A. OMAN.

Malaysia: 107 Tordesillas St, Salcedo Village, Makati City, 1200 Metro Manila; tel. (2) 8174581; fax (2) 8163158; e-mail mwmanila@indanet.com; internet www.kln.gov.my/perwakilan/manila; Ambassador AHMAD RASIDI HAZIZI.

Mexico: 2157 Paraiso St, Dasmariñas Village, Makati City, Metro Manila; tel. (2) 8122211; fax (2) 8929824; e-mail ebmexfil@info.com.ph; internet portal.sre.gob.mx/filipinaseng/; Ambassador ERENDIRA ARACELI PAZ CAMPOS.

Myanmar: Xanland Center, 4th Floor, 152 Amorsolo St, Legaspi Village, Makati City, Metro Manila; tel. (2) 8931944; fax (2) 8928866; e-mail embmyanmnl@mindgate.net; Ambassador U HIN TUN.

Netherlands: Equitable PCI Bank Tower, 26th Floor, 8751 Paseo de Roxas, Makati City, Metro Manila; tel. (2) 7866666; fax (2) 7866600; e-mail man@minbuza.nl; internet www.netherlandsembassy.ph; Ambassador ROBERT BRINKS.

New Zealand: BPI Buendia Center, 23rd Floor, Sen. Gil J. Puyat Ave, POB 3228, MCPO, Makati City, Metro Manila; tel. (2) 8915358; fax (2) 8915353; e-mail nzmanila@nxdsl.com.ph; internet www.nzembassy.com/philippines; Ambassador DAVID PINE.

Nigeria: 2211 Paraiso St, Dasmariñas Village, Makati City, 1221 Metro Manila; POB 3174, MCPO, Makati City, 1271 Metro Manila; tel. (2) 8439866; fax (2) 8439867; e-mail embassy@nigeriamanila.org; internet www.nigeriamanila.org; Chargé d'affaires a.i. NDUBUISI V. AMAKU.

Norway: Petron Mega Plaza Bldg, 21st Floor, 358 Sen. Gil J. Puyat Ave, Makati City, 1209 Metro Manila; tel. (2) 8863245; fax (2) 8863384; e-mail emb.manila@mfa.no; internet www.norway.ph; Ambassador STÅLE TORSTEIN RISA.

Pakistan: Alexander House, 6th Floor, 132 Amorsolo St, Legaspi Village, Makati City, Metro Manila; tel. (2) 8172776; fax (2) 8400229; e-mail pakrepmanila@yahoo.com; internet www.cpsctech.org/~pkembphil; Ambassador MUHAMMAD NAEEM KHAN.

Palau: Marbella Condominium II, Unit 101, Ground Floor, 2071 Roxas Blvd, Malate, Manila; tel. (2) 5221982; fax (2) 5210402; e-mail rop_piembassy@yahoo.com; Ambassador RAMON RECHEBEI.

Panama: 10th Floor, MARC 2000 Tower, 1973 Taft Ave and San Andres St, cnr Quirino Ave, Malate, 1004 Metro Manila; tel. (2) 5212790; fax (2) 5215755; e-mail panaembassy@i-manila.com.ph; Ambassador JUAN FELIPE PITTY.

Papua New Guinea: 3rd Floor, Corinthian Plaza Condominium Bldg, cnr Paseo de Roxas and Gamboa St, Makati City, Metro Manila; tel. (2) 8113465; fax (2) 8113466; e-mail kundumnl@pngembmnl.com.ph; Ambassador DAMIEN DOMINIC GAMIANDU.

THE PHILIPPINES

Portugal: 17th Floor, Units C and D, Trafalgar Plaza, 105 H. V. de la Costa St, Salcedo Village, Makati City, Metro Manila; tel. (2) 8483789; fax (2) 8483791; Chargé d'affaires a.i. LUÍS BRITO CAMARA.

Qatar: 1398 Cabellero St, cnr Lumbang St, Dasmariñas Village, Makati City, Metro Manila; tel. (2) 8874944; fax (2) 8876406; e-mail gemanila2000@yahoo.com; Ambassador ABDULLAH AHMED YOUSIF AL-MUTAWA.

Romania: 1216 Acacia Rd, Dasmariñas Village, Makati City, Metro Manila; tel. (2) 8439014; fax (2) 8439063; e-mail amaron@zpdee.net; Ambassador VALERIU GHEORGHE.

Russia: 1245 Acacia Rd, Dasmariñas Village, Makati City, Metro Manila; tel. (2) 8930190; fax (2) 8109614; e-mail RusEmb@i-manila.com.ph; Ambassador VITALIY VOROBIEV.

Saudi Arabia: Saudi Embassy Bldg, 389 Sen. Gil J. Puyat Ave Ext., Makati City, Metro Manila; tel. (2) 8909735; fax (2) 8953493; e-mail phemb@mofa.gov.sa; Ambassador MOHAMMAD AMEEN WALI.

Singapore: Enterprise Center, Tower I, 35th Floor, 6766 Ayala Ave, cnr Paseo de Roxas, Makati City, Metro Manila; tel. (2) 7512345; fax (2) 7512346; e-mail singemb_mnl@sgmfa.gov.sg; internet www.mfa.gov.sg/manila; Ambassador LIM KHENG HUA.

Spain: ACT Tower, 5th Floor, 135 Sen. Gil J. Puyat Ave, Makati City, 1200 Metro Manila; tel. (2) 8183561; fax (2) 8102885; e-mail embesphh@mail.mae.es; Ambassador LUIS ARIAS ROMERO.

Sri Lanka: 2260 Avocado Ave, Dasmariñas Village, Makati City, Metro Manila; tel. and fax (2) 8439813; e-mail srilanka@bronline.com; Ambassador (vacant).

Switzerland: Equitable Bank Tower, 24th Floor, 8751 Paseo de Roxas, Makati City, 1226 Metro Manila; tel. (2) 7579000; fax (2) 7573718; e-mail man.vertretung@eda.admin.ch; internet www.eda.admin.ch/manila; Ambassador PETER SUTTER.

Thailand: 107 Rada St, Legaspi Village, Makati City, 1229 Metro Manila; tel. (2) 8154220; fax (2) 8157873; e-mail thaimnl@pacific.net.ph; Ambassador KULKUMUT SINGHARA NA AYUDHYA.

Turkey: 2268 Paraiso St, Dasmariñas Village, Makati City, Metro Manila; tel. (2) 8439705; fax (2) 8439702; Ambassador ADNAN BASAGA.

United Arab Emirates: Renaissance Bldg, 2nd Floor, 215 Sakedo St, Legaspi Village, Makati City, Metro Manila; tel. (2) 8173906; fax (2) 8183577; Ambassador MOHAMMED EBRAHIM ABDULLAH AL-JOWAID.

United Kingdom: Locsin Bldg, 15th–17th Floors, 6752 Ayala Ave, cnr Makati Ave, Makati City, 1226 Metro Manila; tel. (2) 5808700; fax (2) 8197206; e-mail uk@info.com.ph; internet www.britishembassy.gov.uk/philippines; Ambassador PETER BECKINGHAM.

USA: 1201 Roxas Blvd, 1000 Metro Manila; tel. (2) 5286300; fax (2) 5223242; e-mail manila1@pd.state.gov; internet manila.usembassy.gov; Ambassador KRISTIE A. KENNEY.

Venezuela: Unit 17A, Multinational Bancorporation Center, 6805 Ayala Ave, Makati City, Metro Manila 1226; tel. (2) 8452841; fax (2) 8452866; e-mail venezemb@info.com.ph; Chargé d'affaires a.i. MANUEL VICENTE PÉREZ ITURBE.

Viet Nam: 670 Pablo Ocampo St, Malate, Metro Manila; tel. (2) 5216843; fax (2) 5260472; e-mail vnembph@yahoo.com; internet www.vietnamembassy-philippines.org; Ambassador VU XUAN TRUONG.

Judicial System

The February 1987 Constitution provides for the establishment of a Supreme Court comprising a Chief Justice and 14 Associate Justices; the Court may sit *en banc* or in divisions of three, five or seven members. Justices of the Supreme Court are appointed by the President from a list of a minimum of three nominees prepared by a Judicial and Bar Council. Other courts comprise the Court of Appeals, Regional Trial Courts, Metropolitan Trial Courts, Municipal Courts in Cities, Municipal Courts and Municipal Circuit Trial Courts. There is also a special court for trying cases of corruption (the Sandiganbayan). The Office of the Ombudsman (Tanodbayan) investigates complaints concerning the actions of public officials.

SUPREME COURT
Taft Ave, cnr Padre Faura St, Ermita, 1000 Metro Manila; tel. (2) 5268123; e-mail infos@supremecourt.gov.ph; internet www.supremecourt.gov.ph.

Chief Justice: REYNATO S. PUNO.

COURT OF APPEALS
Consists of a Presiding Justice and 68 Associate Justices.

Presiding Justice: CONRADO M. VASQUEZ, Jr.

Directory

Islamic *Shari'a* courts were established in the southern Philippines in July 1985 under a presidential decree of February 1977. They are presided over by three district magistrates and six circuit judges.

Religion

According to the results of the 2000 census, 81.1% of the population were Roman Catholics and 11.6% belonged to other Christian denominations. The Islamic community constituted 5% of the population, Buddhists accounted for 0.1%, while indigenous and other religious traditions comprised a further 1.7%. Atheists and persons who did not state a religious preference accounted for 0.5%.

CHRISTIANITY

Sangguniang Pambansa ng mga Simbahan sa Pilipinas (National Council of Churches in the Philippines): 879 Epifanio de los Santos Ave, West Triangle, Quezon City 1104, Metro Manila; tel. (2) 9293745; fax (2) 9267076; e-mail library@nccphilippines.org; internet www.nccphilippines.org; f. 1963; 10 mem. churches, 10 assoc. mems; Gen. Sec. REX R. B. REYES, Jr.

The Roman Catholic Church

For ecclesiastical purposes, the Philippines comprises 16 archdioceses, 55 dioceses, six territorial prelatures and seven apostolic vicariates. At 31 December 2005 approximately 80.7% of the population were adherents.

Catholic Bishops' Conference of the Philippines (CBCP) 470 General Luna St, Intramuros, 1076 Metro Manila; tel. (2) 5274054; fax (2) 5279634; e-mail cbcp@info.com.ph; internet www.cbcponline.org.

f. 1945; statutes approved 1952; Pres. Most Rev. ANGEL N. LAGDAMEO (Archbishop of Jaro).

Archbishop of Caceres: Most Rev. LEONARDO Z. LEGASPI, Archbishop's House, Elias Angeles St, POB 6085, 4400 Naga City; tel. (54) 4738483; fax (54) 4732800.

Archbishop of Cagayan de Oro: Most Rev. JESUS B. TUQUIB, Archbishop's Residence, POB 113, 9000 Misamis Oriental, Cagayan de Oro City; tel. (8822) 8571357; fax (8822) 726304; e-mail orochan@cdo.weblinq.com.

Archbishop of Capiz: Most Rev. ONESIMO C. GORDONCILLO, Chancery Office, POB 44, 5800 Roxas City; tel. (36) 6215595; fax (36) 6211053.

Archbishop of Cebu: Cardinal RICARDO J. VIDAL, Archbishop's Residence, cnr P. Gomez St and P. Burgos St, POB 52, 6000 Cebu City; tel. (32) 2541861; fax (32) 2530123; e-mail adelito@skynet.net.

Archbishop of Cotabato: Most Rev. ORLANDO B. QUEVEDO, Archbishop's Residence, 154 Sinsuat Ave, POB 186, 9600 Cotabato City; tel. (64) 4212918; fax (64) 4211446.

Archbishop of Davao: Most Rev. FERNANDO R. CAPALLA, Archbishop's Residence, 247 Florentino Torres St, POB 80418, 8000 Davao City; tel. (82) 2275992; fax (82) 2279771; e-mail bishop-davao68@yahoo.com.

Archbishop of Jaro: Most Rev. ANGEL N. LAGDAMEO, Archbishop's Residence, Jaro, 5000 Iloilo City; tel. (33) 3294442; fax (33) 3293197; e-mail abpjaro@skyinet.net.

Archbishop of Lingayen-Dagupan: Most Rev. OSCAR V. CRUZ, Archbishop's House, 2400 Pangasinan, Dagupan City; tel. (75) 5235357; fax (75) 5221878; e-mail oscar@rezcom.com.

Archbishop of Lipa: Most Rev. RAMON C. ARGÜELLES, Archbishop's House, St Lorenzo Ruiz Rd, Lipa City, 4217 Batangas; tel. (43) 7562572; fax (43) 7560005; e-mail chancery@batangas.net.ph.

Archbishop of Manila: Most Rev. GAUDENCIO B. ROSALES, Arzobispado, 121 Arzobispo St, Intramuros, POB 132, 1099 Metro Manila; tel. (2) 5273956; fax (2) 5276159; e-mail chancery@pldtdsl.net; internet www.rcam.org.

Archbishop of Nueva Segovia: Most Rev. EDMUNDO M. ABAYA, Archbishop's House, Vigan, 2700 Ilocos Sur; tel. (77) 7222018; fax (77) 7221591.

Archbishop of Ozamis: Most Rev. JESUS A. DOSADO, Archbishop's House, POB 2760, Rizal Ave, Banadero, 7200 Ozamis City; tel. (65) 5212771; fax (65) 5211574.

Archbishop of Palo: Most Rev. PEDRO R. DEAN, Archdiocesan Chancery, Bukid Tabor, Palo, 6501 Leyte; POB 173, Tacloban City, 6500 Leyte; tel. (53) 3232213; fax (53) 3235607; e-mail rcap@mozcom.com.

Archbishop of San Fernando (Pampanga): Most Rev. PACIANO B. ANICETO, Chancery Office, San José, San Fernando, 2000 Pampanga; tel. (45) 9612819; fax (45) 9616772; e-mail rca@pamp.pworld.net.ph.

THE PHILIPPINES

Archbishop of Tuguegarao: Most Rev. Diosdado A. Talamayan, Archbishop's House, Rizal St, Tuguegarao, 3500 Cagayan; tel. (78) 8441663; fax (78) 8462822; e-mail dtalamayan-32@yahoo.com.

Archbishop of Zamboanga: Most Rev. Carmelo Dominador F. Morelos, Sacred Heart Center, POB 1, Justice R. T. Lim Blvd, 7000 Zamboanga City; tel. (62) 9927668; fax (62) 9932808; e-mail aofzam@yahoo.com.ph.

Other Christian Churches

Convention of Philippine Baptist Churches: POB 263, 5000 Iloilo City; tel. (33) 3290621; fax (33) 3290618; e-mail gensec@iloilo.net; f. 1935; Gen. Sec. Rev. Dr Nathaniel M. Fabula; Pres. Donato Enabe.

Episcopal Church in the Philippines: 275 E. Rodriguez Sr Ave, Quezon City, 1102 Metro Manila; POB 10321, Broadway Centrum, Quezon City, 1102 Metro Manila; tel. (2) 7228481; fax (2) 7211923; e-mail sitedeacon@episcopalphilippines.net; internet www.episcopalphilippines.net; f. 1901; six dioceses; Prime Bishop Most Rev. Ignacio C. Soliba.

Iglesia Evangélica Metodista en las Islas Filipinas (Evangelical Methodist Church in the Philippines): Beulah Land, Iemelif Center, Greenfields 1, Subdivision, Marytown Circle, Novaliches, Quezon City, 1123 Metro Manila; tel. (2) 9356519; fax (2) 4185017; e-mail admin@iemelif.org; internet www.iemelif.org; f. 1909; 40,000 mems (2003); Gen. Supt Bishop Nathanael P. Lazaro.

Iglesia Filipina Independiente (Philippine Independent Church): 1500 Taft Ave, Ermita, 1000 Metro Manila; tel. (2) 5237242; fax (2) 5213932; e-mail gensec@ifi.ph; internet ifi.ph; f. 1902; 34 dioceses; 6.0m. mems; Obispo Maximo (Supreme Bishop) Most Rev. Tomas Millamena.

Iglesia ni Cristo: 1 Central Ave, New Era, Quezon City, 1107 Metro Manila; tel. (2) 9814311; fax (2) 9811111; f. 1914; 2m. mems; Exec. Minister Brother Eraño G. Manalo.

Lutheran Church in the Philippines: 4461 Old Santa Mesa, 1008 Metro Manila; POB 507, 1099 Metro Manila; tel. (2) 7157084; fax (2) 7142395; f. 1946; Pres. Rev. Eduardo Ladlad.

Union Church of Manila: cnr Legaspi St and Rada St, Legaspi Village, Makati City, Metro Manila; tel. (2) 8126062; fax (2) 8172386; e-mail ucmweb@unionchurch.ph; internet www.unionchurch.ph; Senior Pastor Rev. David Ginter.

United Church of Christ in the Philippines: 877 Epifanio de los Santos Ave, West Triangle, Quezon City, Metro Manila; POB 718, MCPO, Ermita, 1099 Metro Manila; tel. (2) 9240215; fax (2) 9240207; e-mail uccpnaof@manila-online.net; f. 1948; 900,000 mems (1996); Gen. Sec. Rev. Elmer M. Bolocon (Bishop).

Among other denominations active in the Philippines are the Iglesia Evangélica Unida de Cristo and the United Methodist Church.

ISLAM

Some 14 different ethnic groups profess the Islamic faith in the Philippines. Mindanao and the Sulu and Tawi-Tawi archipelago, in the southern Philippines, are predominantly Muslim provinces, but there are 10 other such provinces, each with its own Imam, or Muslim religious leader. More than 500,000 Muslims live in the north of the country (mostly in, or near to, Manila).

Confederation of Muslim Organizations of the Philippines (CMOP): Metro Manila; Nat. Chair. Jamil Dianalan.

BAHÁ'Í FAITH

National Spiritual Assembly: 1070 A. Roxas St, cnr Bautista St, Singalong Subdiv., Malate, 1004 Metro Manila; POB 4323, 1099 Metro Manila; tel. (2) 5240404; fax (2) 5245918; e-mail nsaphil@skyinet.net; mems resident in 129,949 localities; Chair. Gil Marvel Tabucanon; Sec.-Gen. Virginia S. Toledo.

The Press

The Office of the President implements government policies on information and the media. Freedom of the press and freedom of speech are guaranteed under the Constitution.

METRO MANILA

Dailies

Abante: 167 Liberty Bldg, Roberto S. Oca St, Port Area, Manila; tel. (2) 5276722; fax (2) 5280147; e-mail abante@abante-tonite.com; internet www.abante.com.ph; morning; Filipino and English; Editor Nicolas Quijano, Jr; circ. 417,000.

Abante Tonite: 301 BF Condominium, cnr of Solana and A. Soriano Sts, Intramuros, 1002 Metro Manila; tel. (2) 5276722; fax (2) 5280147; e-mail tonite@abante-tonite.com; internet www.abante-tonite.com; afternoon; Filipino and English; Man. Editor Nicolas Quijano, Jr; circ. 277,000.

Ang Pilipino Ngayon: 202 Railroad St, cnr 13th St, Port Area, Metro Manila; tel. (2) 401871; fax (2) 5224998; Filipino; Publr and Editor Jose M. Buhain; circ. 286,452.

Balita: Liwayway Publishing Inc, 2249 China Roces Ave, Makati City, Metro Manila; tel. (2) 8193101; fax (2) 8175167; internet www.balita.org; f. 1972; morning; Filipino; Editor Marcelo S. Lagmay; circ. 151,000.

Daily Tribune: Penthouse Suites, GLC Bldg, T. M. Kalaw St, cnr A. Mabini St, Ermita, Metro Manila; tel. (2) 5215511; fax (2) 5215522; e-mail nco@tribune.net.ph; internet www.tribune.net.ph; f. 2000; English; Publr and Editor-in-Chief Ninez Cacho-Olivares.

Malaya: 371 Bonifacio Drive, Port Area, 1018 Metro Manila; tel. (2) 5277651; fax (2) 5271839; e-mail apm_malaya@yahoo.com; internet www.malaya.com.ph; f. 1983; English; Editor Joy C. de los Reyes; circ. 175,000.

Manila Bulletin: Bulletin Publishing Corpn, cnr Muralla and Recoletos Sts, Intramuros, POB 769, Metro Manila; tel. (2) 5271519; fax (2) 5277534; e-mail bulletin@mb.com.ph; internet www.mb.com.ph; f. 1900; English; Publr Hermogenes P. Pobre; Editor-in-Chief Chris J. Icban, Jr; circ. 265,000.

Manila Standard Today: Leyland Bldg, 21st St, cnr Railroad St, Port Area, Metro Manila; tel. (2) 5278351; fax (2) 5246649; e-mail mst@manilastandardtoday.com; internet www.manilastandardtoday.com; f. 1987; morning; English; Editor-in-Chief Jojo Robles; circ. 96,000.

Manila Times: 371a Bonifacio Drive, Port Area, Metro Manila; tel. (2) 5245664; fax (2) 5216897; e-mail newsboy1@manilatimes.net; internet www.manilatimes.net; f. 1945; morning; English; Publr and Editor-in-Chief Fred dela Rosa.

People's Tonight: 6th Floor, Universal-Re Bldg, 106 Paseo de Roxas, cnr Perea and Gallardo Sts, Legaspi Village, Makati City, Metro Manila; tel. (2) 5278421; fax (2) 5274627; internet www.journal.com.ph; f. 1978; English and Filipino; Editor Ferdie Ramos; circ. 500,000.

People's Journal: 6th Floor, Universal-Re Bldg, 106 Paseo de Roxas, cnr Perea and Gallardo Sts, Legaspi Village, Makati City, Metro Manila; tel. (2) 5278421; fax (2) 5274627; English and Filipino; Editor August B. Villanueva; circ. 219,000.

People's Taliba: 6th Floor, Universal-Re Bldg, 106 Paseo de Roxas, cnr Perea and Gallardo Sts, Legaspi Village, Makati City, Metro Manila; tel. (2) 5278121; fax (2) 5274627; Filipino; Editor Benjamin Defensor; circ. 229,000.

Philippine Daily Inquirer: Philippine Daily Inquirer Bldg, Chico Roces Ave, cnr Mascardo St and Yague St, Pasong Tamo, Makati City, 1220 Metro Manila; tel. (2) 8978808; fax (2) 8974793; e-mail feedback@inquirer.com.ph; internet www.inquirer.com.ph; f. 1985; English; Chair. Marixi R. Prieto; Editor-in-Chief Letty Jimenez-Magsanoc; circ. 250,000.

Philippine Herald-Tribune: V. Esguerra II Bldg, 140 Amorsolo St, Legaspi Village, Makati City, Metro Manila; tel. (2) 853711; f. 1987; Christian-orientated; Pres. Amada Valino.

Philippine Star: 13th and Railroad Sts, Port Area, Metro Manila; tel. (2) 5277901; fax (2) 5276851; e-mail philippinestar@hotmail.com; internet www.philstar.com; f. 1986; Editor Bobby de la Cruz; circ. 275,000.

Tempo: Bulletin Publishing Corpn, Recoletos St, cnr Muralla St, Intramuros, Metro Manila; tel. (2) 5278121; fax (2) 5277534; internet www.tempo.com.ph; f. 1982; English and Filipino; Editor Ben Rodriguez; circ. 230,000.

Today: Independent Daily News, 55 Paseo de Roxas, Makati City, 1225 Metro Manila; tel. (2) 8940644; fax (2) 8131417; e-mail today@impactnet.com; f. 1993; Editor-in-Chief Teodoro L. Locsin, Jr; Man. Editor Lourdes Molina-Fernandez; circ. 106,000.

United Daily News: 812 and 818 Benavides St, Binondo, Metro Manila; tel. (2) 2447171; f. 1973; Chinese; Editor-in-Chief Chua Kee; circ. 85,000.

Selected Periodicals

Weeklies

Bannawag: Liwayway Bldg, 2249 Pasong Tamo, Makati City, Metro Manila; tel. (2) 8193101; fax (2) 8175167; f. 1934; Ilocano; Editor Dionisio S. Bulong; circ. 42,900.

Bisaya: Liwayway Bldg, 2249 Pasong Tamo, Makati City, Metro Manila; tel. (2) 8193101; fax (2) 8175167; f. 1934; Cebu-Visayan; Editor Edgar S. Godin; circ. 90,000.

Liwayway: Liwayway Bldg, 2249 Pasong Tamo, Makati City, Metro Manila; tel. (2) 8193101; fax (2) 8175167; f. 1922; Filipino; Editor Rodolfo Salandanan; circ. 102,400.

THE PHILIPPINES

Panorama: Manila Bulletin Publishing Corpn, POB 769, cnr Muralla and Recoletos Sts, Intramuros, Metro Manila; tel. and fax (2) 5277509; e-mail panorama@mb.com.ph; internet www.mb.com.ph; f. 1968; English; Editor RANDY V. URLANDA; circ. 239,600.

Philippine Starweek: 13th St, cnr Railroad St, Port Area, Metro Manila; tel. (2) 5277901; fax (2) 5275819; e-mail starweek@pacific.net.ph; internet www.philstar.com; English; Editor JOSEPH NACINO; circ. 268,000.

SELECTED PROVINCIAL PUBLICATIONS

The Aklan Reporter: 1227 Rizal St, Kalibo, Panay, Aklan; tel. (33) 3181; f. 1971; weekly; English and Aklanon; Editor ROMAN A. DE LA CRUZ; circ. 3,500.

Baguio Midland Courier: 16 Kisad Rd, POB 50, Baguio City; tel. (74) 4422444; fax (74) 4439485; e-mail admin@baguiomidlandcourier.com.ph; internet www.baguiomidlandcourier.com.ph; English and Ilocano; Editor CECILE C. AFABLE; circ. 6,000.

Bayanihan Weekly News: Bayanihan Publishing Co, P. Guevarra Ave, Santa Cruz, Laguna; tel. (645) 1001; f. 1966; Mon.; Filipino and English; Editor ARTHUR A. VALENOVA; circ. 1,000.

Bohol Chronicle: 56 B. Inting St, Tagbilaran City, 6300 Bohol; tel. and fax (32) 4113100; e-mail bohol-rd@mozcom.com; internet www.boholchronicle.com; f. 1954; 2 a week; English and Cebuano; Editor and Publr ZOILO DEJARESCO; circ. 5,500.

The Bohol Times: 100 Gallares St, Tagbilaran City, 6300 Bohol; tel. (38) 4112961; fax (38) 4112656; e-mail boholtimes@yahoo.com; Publr Dr LILIA A. BALITE; Editor-in-Chief SALVADOR D. DIPUTADO.

The Kapawa News: L. V. Moles and Jose Abad Santos Sts, Tangub, POB 365, 6100 Bacolod City; tel. and fax (34) 4441941; e-mail LM-Kapawa@eudoramail.com; f. 1966; weekly; Sat.; Hiligaynon and English; Publr HENRY G. DOBLE; circ. 2,000.

Mindanao Star: 44 Kolambagohan-Capistrano St, Cagayan de Oro City; weekly; Editor ROMULFO SABAMAL; circ. 3,500.

Mindanao Times: UMBN Bldg, Ponciano Reyes St, Davao City, Mindanao; tel. 2273252; e-mail timesmen@mozcom.com; internet www.mindanaotimes.com.ph; daily; Publr JOSEFINA SAN PEDRO; Editor-in-Chief AMALIA CABUSAO; circ. 5,000.

Pagadian Times: 0519 Alano St, Pagadian City, 7016; tel. (62) 2151504; fax (62) 2141721; e-mail pedelu@lasialink.com; internet pagtimes.com; f. 1969; weekly; English; Publr PEDE G. LU; Editor REMAI ALEJADS; circ. 7,000.

Sorsogon Today: 2903 Burgos St, East District, 4700 Sorsogon; tel. and fax (56) 4215306; fax (56) 2111340; e-mail sortoday@yahoo.com; f. 1977; weekly; Publr and CEO MARCOS E. PARAS, Jr; circ. 2,250.

Sun Star Cebu: Sun Star Bldg, 3rd Floor, cnr of P. del Rosario St and P. Cui St, Cebu City; tel. (32) 2546100; fax (32) 2537256; e-mail sunnex@sunstar.com.ph; internet www.sunstar.com.ph/cebu; f. 1982; daily; English; Editor-in-Chief PACHICO A. SEARES; Gen. Man. ORLANDO P. CARVAJAL.

The Tribune: Maharlika Highway, 2301 Cabanatuan City, Luzon; f. 1960; weekly; English and Filipino; Editor and Publr ORLANDO M. JARLEGO; circ. 8,000.

The Valley Times: Daang Maharlika, San Felipe, Ilagan, Isabela; f. 1962; weekly; English; Editor AUREA A. DE LA CRUZ; circ. 4,500.

The Visayan Tribune: 1973 Mezzanine Floor, Masonic Temple Bldg, Plaza Libertad 5000, Iloilo City; f. 1959; weekly; Tue.; English; Editor HERBERT L. VEGO; circ. 5,000.

The Voice of Islam: Davao City; tel. (82) 81368; f. 1973; monthly; English and Arabic; official Islamic news journal; Editor and Publr NASHIR MUHAMMAD AL'RASHID AL HAJJ.

The Weekly Negros Gazette: Broce St, San Carlos City, 6033 Negros Occidental; f. 1956; weekly; Editor NESTORIO L. LAYUMAS, Sr; circ. 5,000.

NEWS AGENCY

Philippines News Agency: PIA Bldg, 2nd Floor, Visayas Ave, Diliman, Quezon City, Metro Manila; tel. (2) 9206551; fax (2) 9206566; e-mail bert.panganiban@gmail.com; internet www.pna.gov.ph; f. 1973; Gen. Man. VITTORIO V. VITUG; Exec. Editor RUBEN B. CAL.

PRESS ASSOCIATION

National Press Club of the Philippines: National Press Club Bldg, Magallanes Drive, Intramuros, 1002 Metro Manila; tel. (2) 3010521; fax (2) 3010522; e-mail ad-nationalpressclub@yahoo.com; f. 1952; Pres. ANTONIO ANTONIO; Vice-Pres. ALICE H. REYES; 1,405 mems.

Directory

Publishers

Abiva Publishing House Inc: Abiva Bldg, 851 Gregorio Araneta Ave, Quezon City, 1113 Metro Manila; tel. (2) 7120245; fax (2) 7320308; e-mail mmrabiva@i-manila.com.ph; internet www.abiva.com.ph; f. 1937; reference and textbooks; Pres. LUIS Q. ABIVA, Jr.

Ateneo de Manila University Press: Bellarmine Hall, Ateneo de Manila University, Katipunan Ave, Loyola Heights, Quezon City, Metro Manila; tel. (2) 4265984; fax (2) 4265909; e-mail unipress@admu.edu.ph; internet www.ateneopress.org; f. 1972; literary, textbooks, humanities, social sciences, reference books on the Philippines; Dir MARICOR E. BAYTION.

Bookman, Inc: 373 Quezon Ave, Quezon City, 1114 Metro Manila; tel. (2) 7124818; fax (2) 7124843; e-mail bookman@info.com.ph; f. 1945; textbooks, reference, educational; Pres. LINA PICACHE-ENRIQUEZ; Exec. Vice-Pres. MARIETTA PICACHE-MARTINEZ.

Capitol Publishing House, Inc: 13 Team Pacific Bldg, Jose C. Cruz St, cnr F. Legaspi St, Barrio Ugong, Pasig City, Metro Manila; tel. (2) 6712662; fax (2) 6712664; e-mail cacho@mozcom.com; f. 1947; Gen. Man. MANUEL L. ATIENZA.

Heritage Publishing House: 33 4th Ave, cnr Main Ave, Cubao, Quezon City, POB 3667, Metro Manila; tel. (2) 7216218; fax (2) 7220468; e-mail heritage@skydsl.com.ph; art, anthropology, history, political science; Pres. MARIO R. ALCANTARA; Man. Dir GEORGE B. ALCANTARA.

The Lawyers' Co-operative Publishing Co Inc: 1071 Del Pan St, Makati City, 1206 Metro Manila; tel. (2) 5634073; fax (2) 5642021; e-mail lawbooks@info.com.ph; f. 1908; law, educational; Pres. ELSA K. ELMA.

Liwayway Publishing Inc: 2249 Chino Roces Ave, Makati City, Metro Manila; tel. (2) 8193101; fax (2) 8175167; magazines and newspapers; Pres. RENE G. ESPINA; Chair. DIONISIO S. BULONG.

Mutual Books Inc: 429 Shaw Blvd, Mandaluyong City, Metro Manila; tel. (2) 7257538; fax (2) 7213056; f. 1959; textbooks on accounting, management and economics, computers and mathematics; Pres. ALFREDO S. NICDAO, Jr.

Reyes Publishing Inc: Mariwasa Bldg, 4th Floor, 717 Aurora Blvd, Quezon City, 1112 Metro Manila; tel. (2) 7221827; fax (2) 7218782; e-mail reyespub@skyinet.net; f. 1964; art, history and culture; Pres. LOUIE REYES.

SIBS Publishing House Inc: Phoenix Bldg, 927 Quezon Ave, Quezon City, Metro Manila; tel. (2) 3764041; fax (2) 3764034; e-mail sibsbook@sibs.com.ph; internet www.sibs.com.ph; f. 1996; science, language, religion, literature and history textbooks; Pres. CARMEN MIMETTE M. SIBAL.

Sinag-Tala Publishers Inc: GMA Lou-Bel Plaza, 6th Floor, Chino Roces Ave, cnr Bagtikan St, San Antonio Village, Makati City, 1203 Metro Manila; tel. (2) 8971162; fax (2) 8969626; e-mail stpi@info.com.ph; internet www.sinagtala.com; f. 1972; educational textbooks; business, professional and religious books; Man. Dir LUIS A. USON.

University of the Philippines Press: Epifanio de los Santos St, U. P. Campus, Diliman, Quezon City, 1101 Metro Manila; tel. (2) 9252930; fax (2) 9282558; e-mail mricana@eee.upd.edu.ph; internet www.upd.edu.ph/~uppress; f. 1965; literature, history, political science, sociology, cultural studies, economics, anthropology, mathematics; Dir MARIA LUISA T. CAMAGAY.

Vibal Publishing House Inc: 1253 G. Araneta Ave, cnr Maria Clara St, Talayan, Quezon City, Metro Manila; tel. (2) 7122722; fax (2) 7118852; e-mail inquire@vibalpublishing.com; internet www.vibalpublishing.com; f. 1955; linguistics, social sciences, mathematics, religion; Pres. and Publr ESTHER A. VIBAL.

PUBLISHERS' ASSOCIATIONS

Philippine Educational Publishers' Assen: 84 P. Florentino St, Quezon City, 1104 Metro Manila; tel. (2) 7402698; fax (2) 7115702; e-mail dbuhain@pldtdsl.net; Pres. DOMINADOR D. BUHAIN.

Publishers' Association of the Philippines Inc: 4th Floor, Dominga Bldg, 2113 Pasong Tamo, cnr de la Rosa St, Makati City, Metro Manila; tel. (2) 8191215; fax (2) 8931690; f. 1974; mems comprise all newspaper, magazine and book publrs in the Philippines; Pres. KERIMA P. TUVERA; Exec. Dir ROBERTO M. MENDOZA.

Broadcasting and Communications

TELECOMMUNICATIONS

National Telecommunications Commission (NTC): NTC Bldg, BIR Rd, East Triangle, Diliman, Quezon City, 1104 Metro Manila; tel. (2) 9244042; fax (2) 9217128; e-mail ntc@ntc.gov.ph; internet www.ntc.gov.ph; f. 1979; supervises and controls all private and public telecommunications services; Commr RUEL V. CANOBAS.

THE PHILIPPINES

BayanTel: BayanTel Corporate Center, Maginhawa St, cnr Malingap St, Teacher's Village East, Quezon City, 1101 Metro Manila; tel. (2) 4493000; fax (2) 4492174; e-mail bayanserve@bayantel.com.ph; internet www.bayantel.com.ph; 359,000 fixed lines (1999); Chair. OSCAR M. LOPEZ; Pres. and CEO EUGENIO L. LOPEZ III.

Bell Telecommunications Philippines (BellTel): Pacific Star Bldg, 3rd and 4th Floors, Sen. Gil J. Puyat Ave, cnr Makati Ave, Makati City, Metro Manila; tel. (2) 8400808; fax (2) 8915618; e-mail info@belltel.ph; internet www.belltel.ph; f. 1997; Pres. EDRAGDO REYES.

Capitol Wireless Inc: Dolmar Gold Tower, 6th Floor, 107 Carlos Palanca, Jr, St, Legaspi Village, Makati City, Metro Manila; tel. (2) 8159961; fax (2) 8941141; Pres. EPITACIO R. MARQUEZ.

Digital Telecommunications Philippines Inc (DIGITEL): 110 Eulogio Rodriguez, Jr, Ave, Bagumbayan, Quezon City, 1110 Metro Manila; tel. and fax (2) 6330000; e-mail support@digitelone.com; internet www.digitelone.com; provision of fixed line telecommunications services; 484,036 fixed lines (1998); Chief Exec. RICARDO J. ROMULO; Pres. JOHN GOKONGWEI.

Domestic Satellite Philippines Inc (DOMSAT): Solid House Bldg, 4th Floor, 2285 Pasong Tamo Ext., Makati City, 1231 Metro Manila; tel. (2) 8105917; fax (2) 8671677; Pres. SIEGFRED MISON.

Globe Telecom (GMCR) Inc: Globe Telecom Plaza, 57th Floor, Pioneer St, cnr Madison St, 1552 Mandaluyong City, Metro Manila; tel. (2) 7302701; fax (2) 7302586; e-mail custhelp@globetel.com.ph; internet www.globe.com.ph; 700,000 fixed and mobile telephone subscribers (1999); Pres. and CEO GERARDO C. ABLAZA, Jr.

Philippine Communications Satellite Corpn (PhilcomSat): 12th Floor, Telecoms Plaza, 316 Sen. Gil J. Puyat Ave, Makati City, Metro Manila; tel. (2) 8158406; fax (2) 8159287; Pres. MANUEL H. NIETO.

Philippine Global Communications, Inc (PhilCom): 8755 Paseo de Roxas, Makati City, 1259 Metro Manila; tel. (2) 8451101; fax (2) 8189720; e-mail helpdesk@philcom.com; internet www.philcom.com; Chair. WILLY N. OCIER; CEO SALVADOR M. CASTILLO.

Philippine Long Distance Telephone Co: Ramon Cojuangco Bldg, Makati Ave, POB 2148, Makati City, Metro Manila; tel. (2) 8168883; fax (2) 8446654; e-mail media@pldt.com.ph; internet www.pldt.com.ph; f. 1928; monopoly on overseas telephone service until 1989; transferred to private sector in 2007; Chair. MANUEL V. PANGILINAN; Pres. and CEO NAPOLEON L. NAZARENO.

Smart Communications, Inc (SCI): SMART Tower, 6799 Ayala Ave, Makati City, 1226 Metro Manila; tel. (2) 8881111; fax (2) 8488830; e-mail customercare@smart.com.ph; internet www.smart.com.ph; 20.8m. subscribers (2005); Pres. and CEO NAPOLEON L. NAZARENO.

Pilipino Telephone Corpn (Piltel): SMART Tower, 25th Floor, 6799 Ayala Ave, Makati City, 1200 Metro Manila; tel. (2) 8913888; fax (2) 8171121; subsidiary of Smart Communications, Inc; major cellular telephone provider; 400,000 subscribers (1999); Chair. MANUEL V. PANGILINAN; Pres. and CEO NAPOLEON L. NAZARENO.

BROADCASTING

Radio

Banahaw Broadcasting Corpn: Broadcast City, Capitol Hills, Diliman, Quezon City, 3005 Metro Manila; tel. (2) 9329949; fax (2) 9318751; 14 stations; Station Man. BETTY LIVIOCO.

Bureau of Broadcast Services (BBS) (Philippine Broadcasting Service): Office of the Press Sec., Philippine Information Agency Bldg, 4th Floor, Visayas Ave, Diliman, Quezon City, 1100 Metro Manila; tel. (2) 9203931; fax (2) 9200461; e-mail mpangilinan@pbs.ops.gov.ph; internet www.pbs.gov.ph; f. 1952 as Philippine Broadcasting Service; govt-operated; 32 radio stations; Dir JOHN S. MANALILI.

Cebu Broadcasting Co: c/o Manila Broadcasting Co, Philippine Information Agency Bldg, 4th Floor, Visayas Ave, Quezon City, 1100 Metro Manila; tel. (2) 9203931; fax (2) 9242745; Chair. HADRIAN ARROYO.

Far East Broadcasting Co Inc: POB 1, Valenzuela, 0560 Metro Manila; 62 Karuhatan Rd, Karuhatan, Valenzuela City, 1441 Metro Manila; tel. (2) 2921152; fax (2) 2925790; e-mail info@febc.org.ph; internet www.febc.org.ph; f. 1948; 18 stations; operates a classical music station, eight domestic stations and an overseas service in 64 languages throughout Asia; Pres. CARLOS L. PEÑA.

Filipinas Broadcasting Network: Legaspi Towers 200, Room 306, Paseo de Roxas, Makati City, Metro Manila; tel. (2) 8176133; fax (2) 8177135; Gen. Man. DIANA C. GOZUM.

GMA Network Inc: GMA Network Center, EDSA cnr Timog Ave, Diliman, Quezon City, 1103 Metro Manila; tel. and fax (2) 9287021; e-mail yourgmafamily@gmanetwork.com; internet www.igma.tv; f. 1950; fmrly Republic Broadcasting System Inc; transmits

Directory

nation-wide through 44 television stations; Chair., Pres. and CEO FELIPE L. GOZON; Exec. Vice-Pres. GILBERTO R. DUAVIT, Jr.

Manila Broadcasting Co: Philippine Information Agency Bldg, 4th Floor, Visayas Ave, Quezon City, 1100 Metro Manila; tel. (2) 9203931; fax (2) 9242745; internet www.dagupan.com/dwidfm/mbc.htm; f. 1946; affiliate of Philippine Broadcasting Service; 10 stations; Pres. RUPERTO NICDAO, Jr; Gen. Man. EDUARDO L. MONTILLA.

Nation Broadcasting Corpn: NBC Tower, Epifanio de los Santos Ave, Guadelupe, Makati City, 1200 Metro Manila; tel. (2) 8195673; fax (2) 8197234; e-mail radio@philexport.com; internet philexport.org/philradio/network/nbchome.htm; f. 1963; 31 stations; Pres. FRANCIS LUMEN.

Newsounds Broadcasting Network Inc: Florete Bldg, Ground Floor, 2406 Nobel, cnr Edison St, Makati City, 3117 Metro Manila; tel. (2) 8430116; fax (2) 8173631; 10 stations; Gen. Man. E. BILLONES; Office Man. HERMAN BASBANO.

Pacific Broadcasting System: c/o Manila Broadcasting Co, Philippine Information Agency Bldg, 4th Floor, Visayas Ave, Quezon City, 1100 Metro Manila; tel. (2) 9203931; fax (2) 9242745; Pres. RUPERTO NICDAO, Jr; Vice-Pres. RODOLFO ARCE.

PBN Broadcasting Network: Ersan Bldg, 3rd Floor, 32 Quezon Ave, Quezon City, Metro Manila; tel. (2) 7120190; fax (2) 7438162; e-mail pbnbroadcasting@yahoo.com; f. 1958; Pres. JORGE D. BAYONA.

Philippine Federation of Catholic Broadcasters: 2307 Pedro Gil, Santa Ana, POB 3169, Metro Manila; tel. (2) 5644518; fax (2) 5637316; e-mail nomm.xh@gmail.com; f. 1965; all 48 radio stations are united by the Dream Satellite; Pres. Rev. FRANCIS LUCAS.

Radio Philippines Network, Inc: Broadcast City, Capitol Hills, Diliman, Quezon City, Metro Manila; tel. (2) 9318627; fax (2) 984322; f. 1969; seven TV stations, 14 radio stations; Pres. EDGAR SAN LUIS; Gen. Man. FELIPE G. MEDINA.

Radio Veritas Asia: Buick St, Fairview Park, POB 2642, Quezon City, Metro Manila; tel. (2) 9390011; fax (2) 9381940; e-mail rveritas-asia@rveritas-asia.org; internet www.rveritas-asia.org; f. 1969; Catholic short-wave station, broadcasts in 17 languages; Pres. and Chair. Archbishop GAUDENCIO B. ROSALES; Gen. Man. Fr ROBERTO M. EBISA (SVD).

UM Broadcasting Network: cnr P Reyes and Palma Gil Sts, Davao City; tel. (82) 2279535; fax (82) 2217824; e-mail umbndvo@mozcom.com; internet www.radyoukay.com.ph; Exec. Vice-Pres. WILLY TORRES.

Vanguard Radio Network: J & T Bldg, Room 208, Santa Mesa, Metro Manila; tel. (2) 7161233; fax (2) 7160899; Pres. MANUEL GALVEZ.

Television

In July 1991 there were seven originating television stations and 105 replay and relay stations. The seven originating stations were ABS-CBN (Channel 2), PTV4 (Channel 4), ABC (Channel 5), GMA (Channel 7), RPN (Channel 9), IBC (Channel 13) and SBN (Channel 21). The following are the principal operating television networks:

ABC Development Corpn: APMC Bldg, 136 Amorsolo St, cnr Gamboa St, Legaspi Village, Makati City, Metro Manila; tel. (2) 8923801; fax (2) 8128840; CEO EDWARD U. TAN.

ABS-CBN Broadcasting Corpn: ABS-CBN Broadcasting Center, Sgt E. Esguerra Ave, cnr Mother Ignacia Ave, Quezon City, 1103 Metro Manila; tel. (2) 9244101; fax (2) 9215888; e-mail feedback_web@abs-cbn.com; internet www.abs-cbn.com; Chair. EUGENIO LOPEZ III; Gen. Man. FEDERICO M. GARCIA.

AMCARA Broadcasting Network: ABS-CBN Broadcasting Centre, Mother Ignacia St, cnr Sgt Esguerra Ave, Quezon City, 1103 Metro Manila; tel. (2) 4152272; fax (2) 4121259; e-mail studio23@abs.pinoycentral.com; internet www.studio23.tv; Man. Dir LEONARDO P. KATIGBAK.

Banahaw Broadcasting Corpn: Broadcast City, Capitol Hills, Quezon City, 3005 Metro Manila; tel. (2) 9329949; fax (2) 9318751; Station Man. BETTY LIVIOCO.

Channel V Philippines: Sagittarius Bldg, 6th Floor, H. V. de la Costa St, Salcedo Village, Makati City, Metro Manila; tel. (2) 8173747; fax (2) 8184192; e-mail channelv@i-next.net; Pres. JOEL JIMENEZ; Gen. Man. MON ALCARAZ.

GMA Network, Inc: GMA Network Center, Timog Ave, cnr Epifanio de los Santos Ave, Diliman, Quezon City, 1103 Metro Manila; tel. and fax (2) 9287021; internet www.igma.tv; f. 1950; transmits nation-wide through 45 VHF and 2 affiliate stations and in Asia, Australia and Hawaii through Measat-2 satellite; Chair., Pres. and CEO FELIPE L. GOZON; Exec. Vice-Pres. GILBERTO R. DUAVIT, Jr.

Intercontinental Broadcasting Corpn: Broadcast City Complex, Capitol Hills, Diliman, Quezon City, Metro Manila; tel. (2) 9318781; fax (2) 9318743; 19 stations; Pres. and Chair. BOOTS ANSON-ROA.

People's Television Network Inc (PTV4): Broadcast Complex, Visayas Ave, Quezon City, Metro Manila; tel. (2) 9206514; fax (2)

9204342; f. 1992; public television network; Chair. LOURDES I. ILLUSTRE.

Radio Mindanao Network: State Condominium, 4th Floor, 1 Salcedo St, Legaspi Village, Makati City, Metro Manila; tel. (2) 8120530; fax (2) 8163680; e-mail sales@rmn.com.ph; internet www.rmn.com.ph; f. 1952; owns and operates 50 radio and television stations; Chair. HENRY CANOY; Pres. ERIC S. CANOY.

Radio Philippines Network, Inc: Broadcast City, Capitol Hills, Diliman, Quezon City, Metro Manila; tel. (2) 9315080; fax (2) 9318627; 7 primary TV stations, 14 relay stations; Pres. EDGAR SAN LUIS; Gen. Man. FELIPE G. MEDINA.

Rajah Broadcasting Network, Inc (RJ TV 29): Save a Lot Bldg, 3rd Floor, 2284 Pasong Tamo Ext., Makati City, Metro Manila; tel. (2) 8932360; fax (2) 8933404; e-mail rjofc@compass.com; f. 1993; Gen. Man. BEA J. COLAMONICI.

Southern Broadcasting Network, Inc: Suite 2901, Jollibee Plaza, Ortigas Center, Emerald Ave, Pasig City, Metro Manila; tel. (2) 6363286; fax (2) 6363288; e-mail genceo@sbnphilippines.net; Pres. and CEO TEOFILO A. HENSON; Vice-Pres. LINNIE MAYORALGO.

United Broadcasting Network: FEMS Tower 1, 11th Floor, 1289 Zobel Roxas, cnr South Superhighway, Malate; tel. (2) 5216138; fax (2) 5221226; Gen. Man. JOSEPH HODREAL.

Broadcasting Association

Kapisanan ng mga Brodkaster sa Pilipinas (KBP) (Association of Broadcasters in the Philippines): LTA Bldg, 6th Floor, 118 Perea St, Legaspi Village, Makati City, 1226 Metro Manila; tel. (2) 8151990; fax (2) 8151989; e-mail kbp@pacific.net.ph; internet www.kbp.org.ph; f. 1973 in order to regulate the broadcasting industry, elevate standards, disseminate govt information and strengthen relations with advertising industry; Chair. RUPERTO S. NICDAO, Jr; Pres. BUTCH S. CANOY.

Finance

(cap. = capital; res = reserves; dep. = deposits; m. = million; brs = branches; amounts in pesos, unless otherwise stated)

BANKING

Legislation enacted in 1993 provided for the establishment of a new monetary authority, the Bangko Sentral ng Pilipinas, to replace the Central Bank of the Philippines. In 1994 legislation providing for the establishment in the Philippines of additional foreign bank branches was enacted. By the end of 2002 the number of foreign banks had increased to 13; at that time some 44 principal commercial banks were operating in the Philippines.

Central Bank

Bangko Sentral ng Pilipinas (Central Bank of the Philippines): A. Mabini St, cnr Pablo Ocampo St, Malate, 1004 Metro Manila; tel. (2) 5247011; fax (2) 5231252; e-mail bspmail@bsp.gov.ph; internet www.bsp.gov.ph; f. 1993; cap. 10,000m., surplus and res 238,139.9m., dep. 429,017.0m. (Dec. 2005); Gov. AMANDO M. TETANGCO, Jr; 19 brs.

Principal Commercial Banks

Allied Banking Corpn: 6754 Allied Bank Centre, Ayala Ave, cnr Legaspi St, Makati City, 1200 Metro Manila; tel. (2) 8187961; fax (2) 8160921; e-mail info@alliedbank.com.ph; internet www.alliedbank.com.ph; f. 1977; cap. 495.3m., res 2,894.4m., dep. 122,348.6m. (Dec. 2005); Chair. PANFILO O. DOMINGO; Pres. REYNALDO A. MACLANG; 285 brs.

Banco de Oro–EPCI Inc: 12 ADB Ave, Mandaluyong City, 1550 Metro Manila; tel. (2) 6366060; fax (2) 6317810; e-mail investor-relations@bdo.com.ph; internet www.bancodeoro.com.ph; f. 1996; fmrly known as Banco de Oro Universal Bank; name changed as above following merger with Equitable PCI Bank in 2007; acquired 1st e-Bank June 2003; Chair. TERESITA T. SY; Pres. NESTOR V. TAN; 185 brs.

Bank of Commerce: Phil First Bldg, 6764 Ayala Ave, Makati City, 1226 Metro Manila; tel. (2) 8120000; fax (2) 8300437; e-mail mscallangan@bankcom.com.ph; internet www.bankcom.com.ph; f. 1983; fmrly Boston Bank of the Philippines; merged with Traders Royal Bank 2001; cap. 4,017m., dep. 41,040m. (Aug. 2005); Chair. ANTONIO COJUANGCO; Pres. and CEO RAUL B. DE MESA; 38 brs.

Bank of the Philippine Islands: BPI Bldg, Ayala Ave, cnr Paseo de Roxas, POB 1827, MCC, Makati City, 0720 Metro Manila; tel. (2) 8910000; fax (2) 8910170; e-mail expressonline@bpi.com.ph; internet www.bpiexpressonline.com; f. 1851; merged with Far East Bank and Trust Co in April 2000; merged with DBS Bank Philippines, Inc, 2001; cap. 22,479m., res 2,327m., dep. 434,455m. (Dec. 2005); Pres. and Dir AURELIO R. MONTINOLA III; Chair. JAIME ZOBEL DE AYALA; 339 local brs; 1 overseas br.

China Banking Corpn: CBC Bldg, 8745 Paseo de Roxas, cnr Villar St, Makati City, 1226 Metro Manila; tel. (2) 8855555; fax (2) 8920220; e-mail online@chinabank.com.ph; internet www.chinabank.com.ph; f. 1920; cap. 6,166.4m., res 3,950.6m., dep. 125,491.4m. (Dec. 2006); Chair. GILBERT U. DEE; Pres. and CEO PETER S. DEE; 141 brs.

Development Bank of the Philippines: DBP Bldg, Makati Ave, cnr Sen. Gil J. Puyat Ave, Makati City, 1200 Metro Manila; tel. (2) 8189511; fax (2) 8128089; e-mail info@devbankphil.com.ph; internet www.devbankphil.com.ph; f. 1947 as the Rehabilitation Finance Corpn; govt-owned; provides medium- and long-term loans for strategic devt projects; cap. 30,871m., dep. 71,091m. (Dec. 2006); Chair. PATRICIA A. SANTO TOMAS, Jr; Pres. and CEO REYNALDO G. DAVID; 77 brs.

East West Banking Corpn: 20th Floor, PBCOM Tower, 6795 Ayala Ave, cnr Herrera St, Salcedo Village, Makati City, 1226 Metro Manila; tel. (2) 8150233; fax (2) 3250412; e-mail service@eastwestbanker.com; internet www.eastwestbanker.com; f. 1994; Chair. JONATHAN T. GOTIANUN; Pres. and CEO ANTONIO C. MONCUPA, Jnr; 20 brs.

Export and Industry Bank, Inc (Exportbank): Exportbank Plaza, Chino Roces Ave, cnr Sen. Gil J. Puyat Ave, Makati City, 1200 Metro Manila; tel. (2) 8789100; fax (2) 8780000; e-mail expertinfo@exportbank.com.ph; internet www.exportbank.com.ph; merged with Urban Bank, Inc, 2002; cap. 4,787m., dep. 12,479m. (June 2007); Chair. JAIME GONZALEZ; Pres. NILO PACHECHO, Jr.

Land Bank of the Philippines: LandBank Plaza, 1598 M. H. del Pilar St, cnr J. Quintos St, Malate, 1004 Metro Manila; tel. (2) 5220000; fax (2) 5288580; e-mail landbank@mail.landbank.com; internet www.landbank.com; f. 1963; specialized govt bank with universal banking licence; cap. 11,471m., res 12,170m., dep. 244,697m. (Dec. 2005); Chair. GARY B. TEVES; Pres. and CEO GILDA E. PICO (acting); 323 brs.

Manila Banking Corpn: Manila Bank Bldg, 6772 Ayala Ave, Makati City, 1226 Metro Manila; tel. (2) 7516000; fax (2) 8645016; internet www.manilabank.com; f. 1999; cap. 573m., res 2,333m., dep. 4,547m. (Dec. 2005); Pres. BENJAMIN J. YAMBAO; Chair. LUIS B. PUYAT.

Maybank Philippines Inc: Legaspi Towers 300, Pablo Ocampo St, cnr Roxas Blvd, Malate, 1100 Metro Manila; tel. (2) 5237777; fax (2) 5218514; e-mail mayphil@maybank.com.ph; internet www.maybank2u.com.my/philippines/index.shtml; f. 1961; cap. 3,679m., res –925m., dep. 6,202m. (Dec. 2004); Chair. Tan Sri MOHAMED BASIR BIN AHMAD; Pres. and CEO LIM HONG TAT; 45 brs.

Metropolitan Bank and Trust Co (Metrobank): Metrobank Plaza, Sen. Gil J. Puyat Ave, Makati City, 1200 Metro Manila; tel. (2) 8988000; fax (2) 8176248; e-mail metrobank@metrobank.com.ph; internet www.metrobank.com.ph; f. 1962; acquired Global Business Bank (Globalbank) 2002; cap. 36,145.4m., res 22,262.5m., dep. 531,640.8m. (Dec. 2006); Chair. GEORGE S. K. TY; Pres. ANTONIO S. ABACAN, Jr; 344 local brs, 6 overseas brs.

Philippine Bank of Communications: PBCOM Tower, 6795 Ayala Ave, cnr V. A. Rufino St, 1226 Makati City; tel. (2) 8307000; fax (2) 8182598; e-mail info@pbcom.com.ph; internet www.pbcom.com.ph; f. 1939; merged with AsianBank Corpn in 1999; cap. 5,259.9m., res 3,909.6m., dep. 41,674.3m. (Dec. 2005); Chair. LUY KIM GUAN; Pres. and CEO ISIDRO C. ALCANTARA; 64 brs.

Philippine National Bank (PNB): PNB Financial Center, President Diosdado Macapagal Blvd, Pasay City, 1300 Metro Manila; tel. (2) 8916040; fax (2) 8331245; e-mail cmcd@pnb.com.ph; internet www.pnb.com.ph; f. 1916; partially transferred to the private sector in 1996 and 2000; 10.93% govt-owned; cap. 22,930m., res 3,545m., dep. 168,484m. (Dec. 2005); Chair. FLORENCIA G. TARRIELA; Pres. and CEO OMAR BYRON T. MIER; 324 local brs, 5 overseas brs.

Philippine Veterans Bank: PVB Bldg, 101 V. A. Rufino St, cnr de la Rosa St, Legaspi Village, Makati City, Metro Manila; tel. (2) 7515000; fax (2) 7518577; e-mail corpcomm@veteransbank.com.ph; internet www.veteransbank.com.ph; cap. 4,200m., assets 29,600m. (Dec. 2006); Chair. EMMANUEL V. DE OCAMPO; Pres. and CEO RICARDO A. BALBIDO, Jr; 45 brs.

Philtrust Bank (Philippine Trust Co): Philtrust Bank Bldg, United Nations Ave, cnr San Marcelino St, Ermita, 1045 Metro Manila; tel. (2) 5249061; fax (2) 5217309; e-mail ptc@bancnet.net; f. 1916; cap. 3,683m., res 1,870m., dep. 36,870m. (Dec. 2005); Pres. ANTONIO H. OZAETA; Chair. EMILIO T. YAP; 38 brs.

Rizal Commercial Banking Corpn: Yuchengco Tower, RCBC Plaza, 6819 Alaya Ave, Makati City, 0727 Metro Manila; tel. (2) 8949000; fax (2) 8949958; e-mail customercontact@rcbc.com; internet www.rcbc.com; f. 1960; cap. 7,384.6m., res 10,841.2m., dep. 185,269.2m. (Dec. 2006); Chair. HELEN Y. DEE; Pres. and Dir FRANCISCO S. MAGSAIO, Jr; 287 brs.

Security Bank Corpn: 6776 Ayala Ave, Makati City, 0719 Metro Manila; tel. (2) 8676788; fax (2) 8911079; e-mail herrera@

THE PHILIPPINES

securitybank.com.ph; internet www.securitybank.com; f. 1951; fmrly Security Bank and Trust Co; cap. 3,293.5m., res 5,250.4m., dep. 99,127.3m. (Dec. 2006); Pres. and CEO ALBERTO S. VILLAROSA; Chair. FREDERICK Y. DY; 114 brs.

Union Bank of the Philippines: SSS Makati Bldg, Ayala Ave, cnr V. A. Rufino St, Makati City, 1200 Metro Manila; tel. (2) 8920011; fax (2) 8938593; e-mail online@unionbankph.com; internet www.unionbankph.com; f. 1982; cap. 19,895m. (Dec. 2006), res 6,442m. (Dec. 2002), dep. 115,982m. (Dec. 2006); Chair. and CEO JUSTO A. ORTIZ; Pres. VICTOR B. VALDEPEÑAS; 111 brs.

United Coconut Planters' Bank: UCPB Bldg, 7907 Makati Ave, Makati City, 0728 Metro Manila; tel. (2) 8119000; fax (2) 8119706; e-mail crc@ucpb.com; internet www.ucpb.com; f. 1963; cap. 1,484.8m., res 9,135.5m., dep. 79,974.2m. (Dec. 2005); Chair. ARMAND V. FABELLA; Pres. and CEO JOSE L. QUERUBIN; 178 brs.

United Overseas Bank Philippines: 17th Floor, Pacific Star Bldg, Sen. Gil J. Puyat Ave, cnr Makati Ave, Makati City, Metro Manila; tel. (2) 8788686; fax (2) 8115917; e-mail crd@uob.com.ph; internet www.uob.com.ph; f. 1999; cap. 5,000m., res −3,904m., dep. 10,382m. (Dec. 2007); Pres. and CEO WANG LIAN KHEE (acting); 67 brs.

Rural Banks

Small private banks have been established with the assistance of the Government in order to promote the rural economy. Their principal objectives are to provide credit facilities on reasonable terms and, in co-operation with other agencies of the Government, to give advice on management.

Thrift Banks

Thrift banks mobilize small savings and provide loans to lower income groups. The thrift banking system comprises savings and mortgage banks, stock savings and loan associations and private development banks.

Development Bank

Pampanga Development Bank: MacArthur Highway, Dolores San Fernando, Pampanga, Luzon; tel. (45) 9612786; fax (45) 9633931; e-mail pdb@ag.triasia.net; originally Agribusiness Development Bank; name changed as above 1995; cap. 75.0m., res 2.5m., dep. 78.7m. (Dec. 2004); Pres. JOSE ERIBERTO H. SUAREZ.

Islamic Bank

Al-Amanah Islamic Investment Bank of the Philippines: 10th Floor, Telecoms Plaza Bldg, 316 Sen. Gil Puyat Ave, Makati City, Metro Manila; tel. (2) 8164258; fax (2) 8195249; e-mail al-amanah@pldtdsl.net; internet www.islamicbank.com.ph; f. 1989; Chair. and CEO ALI B. SANGKI.

Banking Associations

Bankers Association of the Philippines: Sagittarius Cond. Bldg, 11th Floor, H. V. de la Costa St, Salcedo Village, Makati City, Metro Manila; tel. (2) 8103858; fax (2) 8103860; internet www.bap.org.ph; Pres. CESAR E. A. VIRATA; Exec. Dir LEONILO G. CORONEL.

Bankers Institute of the Philippines, Inc (BAIPhil): TRB Tower, Paseo de Roxas, Makati City, Metro Manila; tel. (2) 8325890; e-mail secretariat@baiphil.org; internet www.baiphil.org; f. 1941 under the National Asscn of Auditors and Comptrollers; name changed to Bank Administration Institute in 1968, and as above in 2001; Pres. GRACE DELA CRUZ.

Chamber of Thrift Banks: Cityland 10 Condominium Tower 1, Unit 614, H. V. de la Costa St, Salcedo Village, Makati City, Metro Manila; tel. (2) 8126974; fax (2) 8127203; Pres. DIONISIO C. ONG.

Offshore Bankers' Association of the Philippines, Inc: MCPO 3088, Makati City, 1229 Metro Manila; tel. (2) 8103554; Chair. TERESITA MALABANAN.

Rural Bankers' Association of the Philippines: RBAP Bldg, A. Soriano, Jr, Ave, cnr Arzobispo St, Intramuros, Manila; tel. (2) 5272968; fax (2) 5272980; e-mail info@rbap.org; internet www.rbap.org; Pres. WILLIAM K. HOTCHKISS III.

STOCK EXCHANGES

Securities and Exchange Commission: SEC Bldg, Epifanio de los Santos Ave, Greenhills, Mandaluyong City, Metro Manila; tel. (2) 7260931; fax (2) 7255293; e-mail mis@sec.gov.ph; internet www.sec.gov.ph; f. 1936; Chair. FE B. BARIN.

Philippine Stock Exchange: Philippine Stock Exchange Center, Exchange Rd, Ortigas Center, Pasig City, 1605 Metro Manila; tel. (2) 6887600; fax (2) 6345113; e-mail piac@pse.com.ph; internet www.pse.com.ph; f. 1994 following the merger of the Manila and Makati Stock Exchanges; 237 listed cos (Dec. 2005); Chair. JOSE C. VITUG; Pres. FRANCISCO ED. LIM.

INSURANCE

At the end of 2000 a total of 156 insurance companies were authorized by the Insurance Commission to transact in the Philippines. Foreign companies were also permitted to operate in the country.

Principal Domestic Companies

Ayala Life Assurance Inc: Ayala Life Bldg, 6786 Ayala Ave, Makati City, Metro Manila; tel. (2) 8885433; fax (2) 8180171; e-mail customer.service@ayalalife.com.ph; internet www.ayalalife.com.ph; Pres. AURELIO R. MONTINOLA III.

BPI/MS Insurance Corpn: Ayala Life-FGU Center, 11th Floor, 6811 Ayala Ave, Makati City, 1226 Metro Manila; tel. (2) 8409000; fax (2) 8409099; e-mail insure@bpims.com; internet www.bpims.com; f. 2002 as result of merger of FGU Insurance Corpn and FEB Mitsui Marine Insurance Corpn; jt venture of Bank of the Philippine Islands and Sumitomo Insurance Co (Japan); cap. 731m. (2006), sales 2,140m.; Chair. AURELIO R. MONTINOLA III; Pres. NORIAKI HAMANAKA.

Central Surety & Insurance Co: UniversalRe Bldg, 2nd Floor, 106 Paseo de Roxas, Legaspi Village, Makati City, 1200 Metro Manila; tel. (2) 8174931; fax (2) 8170006; f. 1945; bonds, fire, marine, casualty, motor car; Pres. FERMIN T. CASTAÑEDA.

Commonwealth Insurance Co: 10th Floor, 1st e-Bank Tower, 8737 Paseo de Roxas, Makati City, Metro Manila; tel. (2) 8187626; fax (2) 8138575; internet www.cic.com.ph; f. 1935; Pres. MARIO NOCHE.

Co-operative Insurance System of the Philippines: CISP Bldg, 80 Malakas St, Diliman, Quezon City, Metro Manila; tel. (2) 9240388; fax (2) 9240471; Chair. LEONIDA V. CHAVEZ; Pres. AMBROSIO M. RODRIGUEZ.

Domestic Insurance Co of the Philippines: 5th Floor, Champ Bldg, Anda Circle, Bonifacio Drive, Port Area, Manila; tel. (2) 5278181; fax (2) 5273052; e-mail gdicp@skyinet.net; f. 1946; cap. 10m.; Pres. and Chair. MAR S. LOPEZ.

Empire Insurance Co: Prudential Life Bldg, 2nd Floor, 843 Arnaiz Ave, Legaspi Village, Makati City, 1229 Metro Manila; tel. (2) 8159561; fax (2) 8152599; e-mail empire_ins_co@yahoo.com; f. 1949; fire, bonds, marine, accident, motor car, extraneous perils; Pres. and CEO JOSE MA G. SANTOS.

Equitable Insurance Corpn: Equitable Bank Bldg, 4th Floor, 262 Juan Luna St, Binondo, POB 1103, Metro Manila; tel. (2) 2430291; fax (2) 2415768; e-mail info@equitableinsurance.com.ph; internet www.equitableinsurance.com.ph; f. 1950; fire, marine, casualty, motor car, bonds; Pres. NORA T. GO; Exec. Vice-Pres. ANTONIO C. OCAMPO.

Insular Life Assurance Co Ltd: Insular Life Corporate Center, Insular Life Drive, Filinvest Corporate City, Alabang, 1781 Muntinlupa City; tel. (2) 7711818; fax (2) 7711717; e-mail inquiry@insular.com.ph; internet www.insularlife.com.ph; f. 1910; members' equity 7,251m. (Dec. 2002); Chair. and CEO VICENTE R. AYLLÓN.

Makati Insurance Co Inc: BPI Buendia Center, 19th Floor, Sen. Gil J. Puyat Ave, Makati City, 1200 Metro Manila; tel. (2) 8459576; fax (2) 8915229; f. 1965; non-life; Pres. and Gen. Man. JAIME L. DARANTINAO; Chair. OCTAVIO V. ESPIRITU.

Malayan Insurance Co Inc: Yuchengco Tower, 4th Floor, 484 Quintin Paredes St, Binondo, 1099 Metro Manila; tel. (2) 2428888; fax (2) 2412188; e-mail malayan@malayan.com; internet www.malayan.com; f. 1949; cap. 100m. (1998); insurance and bonds; Pres. YVONNE S. YUCHENGCO; Chair. ADELITA VERGEL DE DIOS.

Manila Surety & Fidelity Co Inc: 66 P. Florentino St, Quezon City, Metro Manila; tel. (2) 7122251; fax (2) 7124129; f. 1945; cap. p.u. 50m., members' equity 85m. (Dec. 2003); Pres. MARIA LOURDES V. PEÑA; Vice-Pres. MARIA EDITHA PEÑA-LIM; 4 brs.

Metropolitan Insurance Co: Ateneum Bldg, 3rd Floor, Leviste St, Salcedo Village, Makati City, Metro Manila; tel. (2) 8108151; fax (2) 8162294; f. 1933; non-life; Pres. JOSE M. PERIQUET, Jr; Exec. Vice-Pres. ROBERTO ABAD.

National Life Insurance Co of the Philippines: National Life Insurance Bldg, 6762 Ayala Ave, Makati City, Metro Manila; tel. (2) 8100251; fax (2) 8178718; f. 1933; Pres. BENJAMIN L. DE LEON; Sr Vice-Pres. DOUGLAS MCLAREN.

National Reinsurance Corpn of the Philippines: AXA Life Center, 18th Floor, Sen. Gil J. Puyat Ave, cnr Tindalo St, Makati City, 1200 Metro Manila; tel. (2) 7595801; fax (2) 7595886; e-mail nrcp@nrcp.com.ph; internet www.nrcp.com.ph; f. 1978; Chair. WINSTON F. GARCIA; Pres. and CEO WILFRIDO C. BANTAYAN.

Paramount Life and General Insurance Corpn: Sage House, 14th and 15th Floors, 110 V. A. Rufino St, Legaspi Village, Makati City, 1229 Metro Manila; tel. (2) 8127956; fax (2) 8131140; e-mail insure@paramount.com.ph; internet www.paramount.com.ph; f. 1950; fmrly Paramount General Insurance Corpn; name changed to Paramount Union Insurance Corpn in 2001; name changed as above in 2002; fire, marine, casualty, motor car; Chair. PATRICK L. GO; Pres. GEORGE T. TIU.

Philippine American Life and General Insurance Co (Philamlife): Philamlife Bldg, United Nations Ave, Metro Manila; POB 2167, 0990 Metro Manila; tel. (2) 5269258; fax (2) 5269253; e-mail philamwebmaster@aig.com; internet www.philamlife.com.ph; Pres. JOSE CUISIA.

Pioneer Insurance and Surety Corpn: Pioneer House Makati, 108 Paseo de Roxas, Legaspi Village, Makati City, 1229 Metro Manila; tel. (2) 812777; fax (2) 8171461; e-mail info@pioneer.com.ph; internet www.pioneer.com.ph; f. 1954; cap. 3,300m. (2007); Pres. and CEO DAVID C. COYUKIAT.

Rizal Surety and Insurance Co: Prudential Life Bldg, 3rd Floor, 843 Arnaiz Ave, Legaspi Village, Makati City, Metro Manila; tel. (2) 8159561; fax (2) 8152599; e-mail rizalsic@mkt.weblinq.com; f. 1939; fire, bond, marine, motor car, accident, extraneous perils; Chair. and Pres. S. CORPUS.

Standard Insurance Co Inc: Standard Insurance Tower, 999 Pedro Gil St, cnr F. Agoncillo St, Metro Manila; tel. (2) 5223230; fax (2) 5261479; f. 1958; Chair. LOURDES T. ECHAUZ; Pres. ERNESTO ECHAUZ.

Sterling Insurance Co: Zeta II Annex Bldg, 6th Floor, 191 Salcedo St, Legaspi Village, Makati City, Metro Manila; tel. (2) 8925787; fax (2) 8183630; f. 1960; fmrly Dominion Insurance Corpn; name changed as above Nov. 2001; fire, marine, motor car, accident, engineering, bonds; Pres. RAFAEL GALLAGA.

Tico Insurance Co Inc: Trafalgar Plaza, 7th Floor, 105 H. V. de la Costa St, Salcedo Village, Makati City, 1227 Metro Manila; tel. (2) 8140143; fax (2) 8140150; f. 1937; fmrly Tabacalera Insurance Co Inc; Chair. and Pres. CARLOS CATHOLICO.

UCPB General Insurance Co Inc: 25th Floor, LKG Tower, 6801 Ayala Ave, Makati City, Metro Manila; tel. (2) 8841234; fax (2) 8841264; e-mail ucpbgen@ucpbgen.com; internet www.ucpbgen.com; f. 1963; non-life; Pres. ISABELO P. AFRICA; Chair. SERGIO ANTONIO F. APOSTOL.

Universal Reinsurance Corpn: Ayala Life Bldg, 9th Floor, 6786 Ayala Ave, Makati City, Metro Manila; tel. (2) 7514977; fax (2) 8173745; f. 1949; life and non-life; Chair. JAIME AUGUSTO ZOBEL DE AYALA II; Pres. HERMINIA S. JACINTO.

Regulatory Body

Insurance Commission: 1071 United Nations Ave, Metro Manila; tel. (2) 4041758; fax (2) 5238461; e-mail pubassist_ic@yahoo.com.ph; internet www.insurance.gov.ph; regulates the private insurance industry by, among other things, issuing certificates of authority to insurance companies and intermediaries and monitoring their financial solvency; Commr EVANGELINE CRISOSTOMO-ESCOBILLO.

Trade and Industry

GOVERNMENT AGENCIES

Board of Investments: 385 Sen. Gil J. Puyat Ave, Makati City, 1200 Metro Manila; tel. (2) 8901332; fax (2) 8953512; e-mail OSAC@boi.gov.ph; internet www.boi.gov.ph; Chair. PETER B. FAVILA.

Bureau of Domestic Trade (BDT): Trade and Industry Bldg, 2nd Floor, 361 Sen. Gil J. Puyat Ave, Makati City, Metro Manila; tel. (2) 8904877; fax (2) 8904858; e-mail morbeta@yahoo.com; Dir MEYNARD R. ORBETA.

Cagayan Economic Zone Authority: Westar Bldg, 7th Floor, 611 Shaw Blvd, Pasig City, 1603 Metro Manila; tel. (2) 6365776; fax (2) 6313997; e-mail info@ceza.gov.ph; internet www.ceza.gov.ph; CEO JOSÉ MARI PONCE.

Clark Development Corpn: Bldg 2122, C. P. Garcia St, cnr E. Quirino St, Clark Field, Pampanga; tel. (2) 5999000; fax (2) 5994602; e-mail info@clark.com.ph; internet www.clark.com.ph; Pres. and CEO LIBERATO P. LAUS.

Industrial Technology Development Institute: DOST Compound, Gen. Santos Ave, Bicutan, Taguig, 1631 Metro Manila; tel. (2) 8372071; fax (2) 8373167; e-mail adiv@dost.gov.ph; internet mis.dost.gov.ph/itdi; Dir Dr NUNA E. ALMANZOR.

Maritime Industry Authority (MARINA): PPL Bldg, 1000 United Nations Ave, cnr San Marcelino St, Ermita, Metro Manila; tel. (2) 5238651; fax (2) 5242746; e-mail feedback@marina.gov.ph; internet www.marina.gov.ph; f. 1974; development of inter-island shipping, overseas shipping, shipbuilding and repair, and maritime power; Administrator VICENTE T. SUAZO, Jr.

National Tobacco Administration: NTA Bldg, Scout Reyes St, cnr Panay Ave, Quezon City, Metro Manila; tel. (2) 3743987; fax (2) 3742505; e-mail ntamis@ph.inter.net; internet www.geocities.com/miscsdnta; f. 1987; Administrator CARLITOS S. ENCARNACION.

Philippine Coconut Authority (PCA): PCA R & D Bldg, Elliptical Rd, Diliman, Quezon City, 1104 Metro Manila; tel. (2) 9278116; fax (2) 9216173; e-mail pca_cpo@yahoo.com.ph; internet www.pca.da.gov.ph; f. 1972; Chair. DOMINGO F. PANGANIBAN; Administrator OSCAR G. GARIN.

Philippine Council for Advanced Science and Technology Research and Development (PCASTRD): DOST Main Bldg, Gen. Santos Ave, Bicutan, Taguig, 1631 Metro Manila; tel. (2) 8377522; fax (2) 8373168; e-mail pcastrd@dost.gov.ph; internet www.pcastrd.dost.gov.ph; f. 1987; Exec. Dir Dr REYNALDO V. EBORA.

Philippine Economic Zone Authority: Roxas Blvd, cnr San Luis St, Pasay City, Metro Manila; tel. (2) 5513454; fax (2) 8916380; e-mail info@peza.gov.ph; internet www.peza.gov.ph; Dir-Gen. LILIA B. DE LIMA.

Privatization and Management Office: Department of Finance, 104 Gamboa St, Legaspi Village, Makati City, 1229 Metro Manila; tel. (2) 8932383; fax (2) 8933453; e-mail pmo@eastern.com.ph; f. 2002; formed to handle the privatization of govt assets; succeeded Asset Privatization Trust; Chief Exec. RENATO V. VALDECANTOS.

Subic Bay Metropolitan Authority: SBMA Center, Bldg 229, Waterfront Rd, Subic Bay Freeport Zone, 2222 Zambales; tel. (47) 2524000; fax (47) 2524216; e-mail webteam@sbma.com; internet www.sbma.com; Chair. FELICIANO G. SALONGA; CEO and Admin. ARMAND C. ARREZA.

DEVELOPMENT ORGANIZATIONS

Bases Conversion Development Authority: 2nd Floor, Bonifacio Technology Center, 31st St, Crescent Park West, Bonifacio Global City, Taguig, 1634 Metro Manila; tel. (2) 8166666; fax (2) 8160996; e-mail bcda@bcda.gov.ph; internet www.bcda.gov.ph; f. 1992; est. to facilitate the conversion, privatization and development of fmr military bases; Chair. ALOYSIUS R. SANTOS; Pres. and CEO NARCISO L. ABAYA.

Bureau of Land Development: DAR Bldg, Elliptical Rd, Diliman, Quezon City, Metro Manila; tel. (2) 9287031; fax (2) 9260971; Dir EUGENIO B. BERNARDO.

Bureau of Small and Medium Business Development: Oppen Bldg, 3rd Floor, 349 Sen. Gil J. Puyat Ave, Makati City, Metro Manila; tel. and fax (2) 8967916; e-mail bsmbd@mnl.sequel.net; initiates and implements programmes and projects addressing the specific needs of SMEs in areas concerning entrepreneurship, institutional development, productivity improvement, organization, financing and marketing; Dir MEYNARDO R. ORBETA.

Capital Market Development Council (CMDC): Unit 310, Atrium Bldg, Makati Ave, Makati City, POB 1125, Metro Manila; tel. (2) 8114185; e-mail cmdc_phil@yahoo.com; internet cmdc-phil.net; Chair. DAVID L. BALANGUE.

Co-operatives Development Authority: 5th Floor, Benlor Bldg, 1184 Quezon Ave, Quezon City, Metro Manila; tel. (2) 3736894; fax (2) 3712077; e-mail cda.oed@gmail.com; internet www.cda.gov.ph; Chair. LECIRA V. JUAREZ; Exec. Dir NIEL A. SANTILLAN.

National Development Co (NDC): NDC Bldg, 8th Floor, 116 Tordesillas St, Salcedo Village, Makati City, Metro Manila; tel. (2) 8404898; fax (2) 8404862; e-mail info@ndc.gov.ph; internet www.ndc.gov.ph; f. 1919; govt-owned corpn engaged in the organization, financing and management of subsidiaries and corpns incl. commercial, industrial, mining, agricultural and other enterprises assisting national economic development, incl. jt industrial ventures with other ASEAN countries; Chair. MANUEL A. ROXAS; Gen. Man. OFELIA V. BULAONG.

Philippine National Oil Co (PNOC): Energy Complex, Bldg 6, 6th Floor, Merritt Rd, Fort Bonifacio, Makati City, Metro Manila; tel. (2) 5550254; fax (2) 8442983; internet www.pnoc.com.ph; f. 1973; state-owned energy development agency mandated to ensure stable and sufficient supply of oil products and to develop domestic energy resources; Chair. ANGELO T. REYES; Pres. and CEO ANTONIO M. CAILAO.

Southern Philippines Development Authority: Basic Petroleum Bldg, 104 Carlos Palanca, Jr, St, Legaspi Village, Makati City, Metro Manila; tel. (2) 8183893; fax (2) 8183907; Chair. ROBERTO AVENTAJADO; Manila Rep. GERUDIO 'KHALIQ' MADUENO.

CHAMBERS OF COMMERCE AND INDUSTRY

Cebu Chamber of Commerce and Industry: CCCI Center, cnr 11th and 13th Ave, North Reclamation Area, Cebu City 6000; tel. (32) 2321421; fax (32) 2321422; e-mail m@cebuchamber.com.ph; internet www.cebubusinesswebportal.com; f. 1921; Pres. FRANCIS O. MONERA.

Federation of Filipino-Chinese Chambers of Commerce and Industry Inc: Federation Center, 6th Floor, Muelle de Binondo St, POB 23, Metro Manila; tel. (2) 2419201; fax (2) 2422361; e-mail ffcccii@yahoo.com; internet www.ffcccii.com.ph; Pres. JOHN K. TAN.

THE PHILIPPINES
Directory

Philippine Chamber of Coal Mines (Philcoal): Rm 1007, Princeville Condominium, S. Laurel St, cnr Shaw Blvd, 1552 Mandaluyong City; tel. (2) 5330518; fax (2) 5315513; f. 1980; Exec. Dir BERTRAND GONZALES.

Philippine Chamber of Commerce and Industry: 3rd Floor, ECC Bldg, 355 Senator Gil Puyat Ave, Makati City, Metro Manila; tel. (2) 8964549; fax (2) 8991727; e-mail pcci@philippinechamber .com; internet www.philippinechamber.com; f. 1977; Chair. MIGUEL B. VARELA; Pres. SAMIE LIM.

Philippine Chamber of Mines: Rm 809, Ortigas Bldg, Ortigas Ave, Pasig City, 1605 Metro Manila; tel. (2) 6354123; fax (2) 6354160; e-mail comp@pldtdsl.net; f. 1975; Chair. ARTEMIO F. DISINI; Pres. BENJAMIN PHILIP G. ROMUALDEZ.

FOREIGN TRADE ORGANIZATIONS

Bureau of Export Trade Promotion: New Solid Bldg, 5th–8th Floors, 357 Sen. Gil J. Puyat Ave, Makati City, 1200 Metro Manila; tel. (2) 8990133; fax (2) 8904707; e-mail betpod@dti.gov.ph; internet tradelinephil.dti.gov.ph; Dir FERNANDO P. CALA, II.

Bureau of Import Services: Oppen Bldg, 3rd Floor, 349 Sen. Gil J. Puyat Ave, Makati City, Metro Manila; tel. (2) 8905418; fax (2) 8957466; e-mail bis@dti.gov.ph; Exec. Dir ALEXANDER B. ARCILLA.

Garments and Textile Export Board (GTEB): New Solid Bldg, 2nd and 3rd Floors, 357 Sen. Gil J. Puyat Ave, Makati City, Metro Manila; tel. (2) 8904810; fax (2) 8904653; e-mail gtebebs@dti.gov.ph; manages and supervises the garment textile quota system; Exec. Dir FELICITAS R. AGONCILLO REYES.

Philippine International Trading Corpn (PITC): National Development Company, 5th Floor, 116 Tordesillas St, Salcedo Village, 1227 Metro Manila; tel. (2) 8920425; fax (2) 8920782; e-mail pitc@info.com.ph; internet pitc.gov.ph; f. 1973; state trading company to conduct international marketing of general merchandise, industrial and construction goods, raw materials, semi-finished and finished goods, and bulk trade of agri-based products; also provides financing, bonded warehousing, shipping, cargo and customs services; Chair. FRANCISCO P. DUQUE III; Pres. and CEO JORGE MENDOZA JUDAN.

INDUSTRIAL AND TRADE ASSOCIATIONS

Beverage Industry Association of the Philippines: SMPC Bldg, 23rd Floor, St Francis St, Mandaluyong City, Metro Manila; tel. (2) 6346840; fax (2) 6318672; e-mail rbkmlo@mnl.sequel.net; Pres. HECTOR GUBALLA.

Chamber of Automotive Manufacturers of the Philippines (CAMPI): Suite 1206, 12th Floor, Jollibee Plaza, San Miguel Ave, Ortigas Center, Pasig City, Metro Manila; tel. (2) 6329733; fax (2) 6315313; e-mail campi@pacific.net.ph; Pres. ELIZABETH LEE.

Construction Industry Authority of the Philippines (CIAP): Jupiter I Bldg, 4th Floor, Jupiter St, Makati City, Metro Manila; tel. (2) 8979336; e-mail pocb@skynet.net; Officer-in-Charge KATHERINE T. DELA CRUZ.

Cotton Development Administration (CODA): Agricultural Training Institute, 1st Floor, Elliptical Rd, Diliman, Quezon City, 1100 Metro Manila; tel. (2) 9208878; fax (2) 9209238; e-mail coda@da .gov.ph; internet www.coda.da.gov.ph; Administrator Dr EUGENIO D. ORPIA, Jr.

Federation of Philippine Industries (FPI): Suite 701, Atlanta Center, Annapolis St, Greenhills, San Juan, Metro Manila; tel. (2) 7223409; fax (2) 7229737; e-mail fpi@philonline.com; internet www .fpi.ph; f. 1991; Chair. MENELEO J. CARLOS, Jr; Pres. JESUS L. ARRANZA.

Fiber Industry Development Authority: Asiatrust Bank Annex Bldg, 1424 Quezon Ave, Quezon City, Metro Manila; tel. (2) 3737489; fax (2) 3737494; e-mail fibernetwk@yahoo.com; internet fida.da.gov .ph; Administrator CECILIA GLORIA J. SORIANO.

Philippine Association of Electrical Industries: Banks of the Philippines Bldg, Suite 702, Plaza Cervantes, Binondo, Metro Manila; tel. and fax (2) 2421144; Pres. RICARDO SY.

Philippine Fisheries Development Authority: 2nd Floor, PCA Annex Bldg, 1 Elliptical Rd, Diliman, Quezon City, 1109 Metro Manila; tel. (2) 9258472; fax (2) 9256138; e-mail oagm@pfda.gov.ph; internet pfda.da.gov.ph; f. 1976; Gen. Man. PETRONILO B. BUENDIA.

Philippine Liquefied Petroleum Gas Association: 218 San Vicente St, Binondo, Metro Manila; tel. (2) 2412668; fax (2) 6337781; f. 1966; Pres. JOSELITO ASENTERO.

Semiconductor and Electronic Industries in the Philippines (SEIPI): Unit 902, RCBC Plaza, Tower 2, Sen. Gil J. Puyat Ave, Makati City, Metro Manila; tel. (2) 8449028; fax (2) 8449037; e-mail philippine.electronics@seipi.org.ph; internet www.seipi.org.ph; Exec. Dir ERNESTO B. SANTIAGO.

EMPLOYERS' ORGANIZATIONS

Employers' Confederation of the Philippines (ECOP): ECC Bldg, 2nd Floor, 355 Sen. Gil J. Puyat Ave, Makati City, Metro Manila; tel. (2) 8904845; fax (2) 8958623; e-mail ecop@webquest.com; internet www.ecop.org.ph; f. 1975; Chair. MIGUEL B. VARELA; Pres. SERGIO ORTIZ-LUIS, Jr.

Filipino Shipowners' Association: Victoria Bldg, Room 503, 429 United Nations Ave, Ermita, 1000 Metro Manila; tel. (2) 5227318; fax (2) 5243164; e-mail filiship@info.com.ph; internet www .filipinoshipowners.com.ph; f. 1950; 24 mems, including 6 assoc. mems; Chair. CARLOS C. SALINAS; Exec. Sec. AUGUSTO Y. ARREZA, Jr.

Philippine Cement Manufacturers Corporation (PHILCEMCOR): Corporal Cruz, cnr E. Rodriguez Jr Ave, Bagong Ilog, Pasig City, Metro Manila; tel. (2) 6717585; fax (2) 6717588; e-mail alfiler@ info.com.ph; Pres. FELIX ENRICO R. ALFILER.

Philippine Coconut Producers' Federation, Inc: Wardley Bldg, 2nd Floor, 1991 Taft Ave, cnr San Juan St, Pasay City, 1300 Metro Manila; tel. (2) 5230918; fax (2) 5211333; e-mail cocofed@pworld.net .ph; Pres. MARIA CLARA L. LOBREGAT.

Philippine Retailers' Association: Unit 2610, Jollibee Plaza, Emerald Ave, Ortigas Center, Pasig City; tel. (2) 6874180; fax (2) 6360825; e-mail pra@philretailers.com; internet www.philretailers .com; f. 1976; Pres. BIENVENIDO V. TANTOCO, III.

Philippine Sugar Millers' Association Inc: 1402 Security Bank Centre, 6776 Ayala Ave, Makati City, 1226 Metro Manila; tel. (2) 8911138; fax (2) 8911144; e-mail psma@psma.com.ph; internet www .psma.com.ph; f. 1922; Chair. JULIO O. SY; Pres. PEDRO E. ROXAS.

Textile Mills Association of the Philippines, Inc (TMAP): Ground Floor, Alexander House, 132 Amorsolo St, Legaspi Village, Makati City, 1229 Metro Manila; tel. (2) 8186601; fax (2) 8183107; e-mail tmap@pacific.net.ph; f. 1956; 11 mems; Pres. HERMENEGILDO C. ZAYCO; Chair. JAMES L. GO.

Textile Producers' Association of the Philippines, Inc: Downtown Center Bldg, Room 513, 516 Quintin Paredes St, Binondo, Metro Manila; tel. (2) 2411144; fax (2) 2411162; Pres. GO CUN UY; Exec. Sec. ROBERT L. TAN.

UTILITIES

Energy Regulatory Commission: Pacific Center Bldg, San Miguel Ave, Ortigas Center, Pasig City, 1600 Metro Manila; tel. (2) 9145000; fax (2) 6315818; e-mail info@erc.gov.ph; internet www .erc.gov.ph; Chair. and CEO RODOLFO B. ALBANO, Jr; Exec. Dir FRANCIS SATURNINO C. JUAN.

Electricity

Davao Light and Power Co: 163–5 C. Bangoy, Sr, St, Davao City 8000; tel. (82) 2212191; fax (82) 2212105; e-mail davaolight@ davao-online.com; internet www.davaolight.com; the country's third largest electric utility with a peak demand of 175 MW in 2000.

Manila Electric Co (Meralco): Lopez Bldg, 2nd Floor, Meralco Center, Ortigas Ave, Pasig City, 0300 Metro Manila; tel. (2) 6312222; fax (2) 6315591; e-mail finplan.inv.relations@meralco.com.ph; internet www.meralco.com.ph; f. 1903; supplies electric power to Manila and seven provinces in Luzon; largest electricity distributor, supplying 54% of total consumption in 2000; privatized in 1991, 34% govt-owned; cap. and res 54,382m., sales 85,946m. (1998); Chair. and CEO MANUEL M. LOPEZ; Pres. JESUS P. FRANCISCO.

National Power Corpn (NAPOCOR): Quezon Ave, cnr BIR Rd, Quezon City, Metro Manila; tel. (2) 9213541; fax (2) 9212468; e-mail webmaster@napocor.gov.ph; internet www.napocor.gov.ph; f. 1936; state-owned corpn supplying electric and hydroelectric power throughout the country; scheduled for privatization; installed capacity in 1998, 11,810 MW; sales 86,611m. pesos (Dec. 1998); 12,043 employees; chaired by the Secretary of Finance; Pres. CYRIL C. DEL CALLAR.

Gas

First Gen Corpn: Benpres Bldg, 3rd Floor, Exchange Rd, cnr Meralco Ave, Pasig City, Metro Manila; tel. (2) 6343428; fax (2) 6352737; e-mail info@firstgen.com.ph; internet www.firstgen.com .ph; major interests in power generation and distribution; Chair. OSCAR M. LOPEZ; Pres. FEDERICO R. LOPEZ.

Water

Regulatory Authority

Metropolitan Waterworks and Sewerage System: 4th Floor, Administration Bldg, MWSS Complex, 489 Katipunan Rd, Balara, Quezon City, 1105 Metro Manila; tel. (2) 9223757; fax (2) 9212887; e-mail info@mwss.gov.ph; internet www.mwss.gov.ph; govt regulator for water supply, treatment and distribution within Metro Manila; Administrator LORENZO H. JAMORA.

Distribution Companies

Davao City Water District: Km 5, Jose P. Laurel Ave, Bajada, 8000 Davao City; tel. (82) 2219400; fax (82) 2264885; e-mail dcwd@davao-water.gov.ph; internet www.davao-water.gov.ph; f. 1973; public utility responsible for the water supply of Davao City; Chair. EDUARDO A. BANGAYAN; Gen. Man. Eng. RODORA N. GAMBOA.

Manila Water: Administration Bldg, 2nd Floor, MWSS Compound, 489 Katipunan Rd, Balara, Quezon City, 1105 Metro Manila; tel. (2) 9281223; fax (2) 9223761; e-mail info@manilawateronline.com; internet www.manilawater.com; f. 1997 following the privatization of Metro Manila's water services; responsible for water supply to Manila East until 2023; Pres. ANTONINO T. AQUINO.

Maynilad Water: MWSS Compound, Katipunan Rd, Balara, Quezon City, Metro Manila; tel. (2) 4353583; fax (2) 9223759; internet www.mayniladwater.com.ph; f. 1998 following the privatization of Metro Manila's water services; responsible for water supply, sewage and sanitation services for Manila West until 2021; Pres. FIORELLO R. ESTUAR.

Metropolitan Cebu Water District: Magallanes St, cnr Lapulapu St, 6000 Cebu City; tel. (32) 2560413; fax (32) 2545391; e-mail mcwd@cvis.net.ph; internet www.mcwd.gov.ph; f. 1974; public utility responsible for water supply and sewerage of Cebu City and surrounding towns and cities; Chair. JUAN SAUL F. MONTECILLO; Gen. Man. ARMANDO H. PAREDES.

TRADE UNION FEDERATIONS

In 1986 the Government established the Labor Advisory Consultation Committee (LACC) to facilitate communication between the Government and the powerful labour movement in the Philippines. The LACC granted unions direct recognition and access to the Government, which, under the Marcos regime, had been available only to the Trade Union Congress of the Philippines (KMP-TUCP). The KMP-TUCP refused to join the Committee.

In May 1994 a new trade union alliance, the Caucus for Labor Unity, was established; its members included the KMP-TUCP and three groups that had dissociated themselves from Kilusang Mayo Uno (see Independent Labour Federations).

Katipunang Manggagawang Pilipino (KMP-TUCP) (Trade Union Congress of the Philippines): TUCP Training Center Bldg, TUCP-PGEA Compound, Masaya St, cnr Maharlika St, Diliman, Quezon City, 1101 Metro Manila; tel. (2) 9247551; fax (2) 9219758; e-mail secrtucp@tucp.org.ph; internet www.tucp.org.ph; f. 1975; 1.2m. mems; Pres. DEMOCRITO T. MENDOZA; Gen. Sec. ERNESTO F. HERRERA; 39 affiliates, incl.:

Associated Labor Union for Metalworkers (ALU—METAL): TUCP-PGEA Compound, Diliman, Quezon City, 1101 Metro Manila; tel. (2) 9222575; fax (2) 9247553; e-mail alumla@info.com.ph; 29,700 mems; Pres. DEMOCRITO T. MENDOZA.

Associated Labor Union for Textile Workers (ALU—TEXTILE): TUCP-PGEA Compound, Elliptical Rd, Diliman, Quezon City, 1101 Metro Manila; tel. (2) 9222575; fax (2) 9247553; e-mail alumla@info.com.ph; 41,400 mems; Pres. DEMOCRITO T. MENDOZA.

Associated Labor Unions (ALU—TRANSPORT): 1763 Tomas Claudio St, Baclaran, Parañaque, Metro Manila; tel. (2) 8320634; fax (2) 8322392; 49,500 mems; Pres. ALEXANDER O. BARRIENTOS.

Associated Labor Unions—Visayas Mindanao Confederation of Trade Unions (ALU—VIMCONTU): ALU Bldg, Quezon Blvd, Port Area, Elliptical Rd, cnr Maharlika St, Diliman, Quezon City, 1101 Metro Manila; tel. (2) 9222185; fax (2) 9247553; e-mail alumla@info.com.ph; f. 1954; 350,000 mems; Pres. DEMOCRITO T. MENDOZA.

Associated Professional, Supervisory, Office and Technical Employees Union (APSOTEU): TUCP-PGEA Compound, Elliptical Rd, Diliman, Quezon City, 1101 Metro Manila; tel. (2) 9222575; fax (2) 9247553; e-mail alumla@info.com.ph; Pres. CECILIO T. SENO.

Association of Independent Unions of the Philippines: Vila Bldg, Mezzanine Floor, Epifanio de los Santos Ave, Cubao, Quezon City, Metro Manila; tel. (2) 9224652; Pres. EMMANUEL S. DURANTE.

Association of Trade Unions (ATU): Antwel Bldg, Room 1, 2nd Floor, Santa Ana, Port Area, Davao City; tel. (82) 2272394; 2,997 mems; Pres. JORGE ALEGARBES.

Confederation of Labor and Allied Social Services (CLASS): Doña Santiago Bldg, TUCP Suite 404, 1344 Taft Ave, Ermita, Metro Manila; tel. (2) 5240415; fax (2) 5266011; f. 1979; 4,579 mems; Pres. LEONARDO F. AGTING.

Federation of Agrarian and Industrial Toiling Hands (FAITH): Kalayaan Ave, cnr Masigla St, Diliman, Quezon City, Metro Manila; tel. (2) 9225244; 220,000 mems; Pres. RAYMUNDO YUMUL.

Federation of Consumers' Co-operatives in Negros Oriental (FEDCON): Bandera Bldg, Cervantes St, Dumaguete City; tel. (32) 2048; Chair. MEDARDO VILLALON.

Federation of Unions of Rizal (FUR): Suite 307, Buenavista Bldg, 3rd Floor, 82 Quirino Ave, cnr Rivera St, Parañaque City, Metro Manila; tel. and fax (2) 8320110; 10,853 mems; Officer-in-Charge EDUARDO ASUNCION.

Lakas sa Industriya ng Kapatirang Haligi ng Alyansa (LIKHA): 32 Kabayanihan Rd Phase IIA, Karangalan Village, Pasig City, Metro Manila; tel. and fax (2) 6463234; e-mail jbvlikha@yahoo.com; Pres. JESUS B. VILLAMOR.

National Association of Free Trade Unions (NAFTU): Rm 404, San Luis Terrace, T. M. Kalaw St, Ermita, Metro Manila; tel. (2) 598705; 7,385 mems; Pres. JAIME RINCAL.

National Congress of Unions in the Sugar Industry of the Philippines (NACUSIP): 7431 A Yakal St, Barangay San Antonio, Makati City, Metro Manila; tel. and fax (2) 8437284; e-mail nacusip@compass.com.ph; 32 affiliated unions and 57,424 mems; Nat. Pres. ZOILO V. DELA CRUZ, Jr.

National Mines and Allied Workers' Union (NAMAWU): Unit 201, A. Dunville Condominium, 1 Castilla St, cnr Valencio St, Quezon City, Metro Manila; tel. (2) 7265070; fax (2) 4155582; 13,233 mems; Pres. ROBERTO A. PADILLA.

Pambansang Kilusan ng Paggawa (KILUSAN): TUCP-PGEA Compound, Elliptical Rd, Diliman, Quezon City, 1101 Metro Manila; tel. (2) 9284651; 13,093 mems; Pres. AVELINO V. VALERIO; Sec.-Gen. IGMIDIO T. GANAGANA.

Philippine Agricultural, Commercial and Industrial Workers' Union (PACIWU): 5 7th St, Lacson, Bacolod City; fax (2) 7097967; Pres. ZOILO V. DELA CRUZ, Jr.

Philippine Federation of Labor (PFL): FEMII Bldg, Suite 528, Aduana St, Intramuros, Metro Manila; tel. (2) 5271686; fax (2) 5272838; 8,869 mems; Pres. ALEJANDRO C. VILLAVIZA.

Philippine Federation of Teachers' Organizations (PFTO): BSP Bldg, Room 112, Concepcion St, Ermita, Metro Manila; tel. (2) 5275106; Pres. FEDERICO D. RICAFORT.

Philippine Government Employees' Association (PGEA): TUCP-PGEA Compound, Elliptical Rd, Diliman, Quezon City, Metro Manila; tel. (2) 6383541; fax (2) 6375764; e-mail eso_pgea@hotmail.com; f. 1945; 65,000 mems; Pres. ESPERANZA S. OCAMPO.

Philippine Integrated Industries Labor Union (PIILU): Mendoza Bldg, Room 319, 3rd Floor, Pilar St, Zamboanga City; tel. (992) 2299; f. 1973; Pres. JOSE J. SUAN.

Philippine Labor Federation (PLF): ALU Bldg, Quezon Blvd, Port Area, Cebu City; tel. (32) 71219; fax (32) 97544; 15,462 mems; Pres. CRISPIN B. GASTARDO.

Philippine Seafarers' Union (PSU): TUCP-PGEA Compound, Elliptical Rd, Diliman, Quezon City, 1101 Metro Manila; tel. (2) 9222575; fax (2) 9247553; e-mail psumla@info.com.ph; f. 1984; 10,000 mems; Pres. DEMOCRITO T. MENDOZA; Gen. Sec. ERNESTO F. HERRERA.

Philippine Transport and General Workers' Organization (PTGWO–D): Cecilleville Bldg, 3rd Floor, Quezon Ave, Quezon City, Metro Manila; tel. (2) 4115811; fax (2) 4115812; f. 1953; 33,400 mems; Pres. VICTORINO F. BALAIS.

Port and General Workers' Federation (PGWF): Capilitan Engineering Corpn Bldg, 206 Zaragoza St, Tondo, Manila; tel. 208959; Pres. FRANKLIN D. BUTCON.

Public Services Labor Independent Confederation (PSLINK): 15 Clarion Lily St, Congressional Ave, Quezon City, 1100 Metro Manila; tel. (2) 9244710; fax (2) 9281090; e-mail annie.geron@pslink.org; internet www.pslink.org; f. 1987 as Public Sector Labor Integrative Center; 35,108 mems; Pres. JARAH HAMJAH; Gen. Sec. ANNIE ENRIQUEZ-GERON.

United Sugar Farmers' Organization (USFO): SPCMA Annex Bldg, 3rd Floor, 1 Luzuriaga St, Bacolod City; Pres. BERNARDO M. REMO.

Workers' Alliance Trade Unions (WATU): Delta Bldg, Room 300, Quezon Ave, cnr West Ave, Quezon City, Metro Manila; tel. (2) 9225093; fax (2) 975918; f. 1978; 25,000 mems; Pres. TEMISTOCLES S. DEJON, Sr.

INDEPENDENT LABOUR FEDERATIONS

The following organizations are not affiliated to the KMP-TUCP:

Associated Marine Officers and Seamen's Union of the Philippines (AMOSUP): Seaman's Centre, cnr Cabildo and Sta Potenciana Sts, Intramuros, Metro Manila; tel. (2) 5278491; fax (2) 5273534; e-mail s_center@amosup.org; internet www.amosup.org; f. 1960; 23 affiliated unions with 55,000 mems; Pres. GREGORIO S. OCA.

THE PHILIPPINES

Federation of Free Workers (FFW): FFW Bldg, 1943 Taft Ave, Malate, Metro Manila; tel. (2) 5219435; fax (2) 4006656; internet www.ffw.org.ph; f. 1950; affiliated to International Trade Union Confederation (ITUC); 300 affiliated local unions and 400,000 mems; Pres. ALLAN S. MONTANO.

Kilusang Mayo Uno (KMU): 63 Narra St, Barangay Claro, Quezon City, 1102 Metro Manila; tel. (2) 4210986; fax (2) 4210768; e-mail obrero@kilusangmayouno.org; internet www.kilusangmayouno.org; f. 1980; Chair. ELMER LABOG; Sec.-Gen. JOEL MAGLUNSOD.

Lakas ng Manggagawa Labor Center: Rm 401, Femii Bldg Annex, A. Soriano St, Intramuros, Metro Manila; tel. and fax (2) 5280482; a grouping of 'independent' local unions; Chair. OSCAR M. ACERSON.

Manggagawa ng Komunikasyon sa Pilipinas (MKP): 22 Libertad St, Mandaluyong City, Metro Manila; tel. (2) 5313701; fax (2) 5312109; f. 1951; Pres. PETE PINLAC.

National Confederation of Labor: Suite 402, Carmen Bldg, Ronquillo St, cnr Evangelista St, Quiapo, Metro Manila; tel. and fax (2) 7334474; f. 1994 by fmr mems of Kilusang Mayo Uno; Pres. ANTONIO DIAZ.

Philippine Social Security Labor Union (PSSLU): Carmen Bldg, Suite 309, Ronquillo St, Quiapo, Metro Manila; f. 1954; Nat. Pres. ANTONIO B. DIAZ; Nat. Sec. OFELIA C. ALAVERA.

Samahang Manggagawang Pilipino (SMP) (National Alliance of Teachers and Office Workers): Fersal Condominium II, Room 33, 130 Kalayaan Ave, Quezon City, 1104 Metro Manila; tel. and fax (2) 9242299; Pres. ADELISA RAYMUNDO.

Solidarity Trade Conference for Progress: Rizal Ave, Dipolog City; tel. and fax (65) 2124303; Pres. NICOLAS E. SABANDAL.

Trade Unions of the Philippines and Allied Services (TUPAS): Med-dis Bldg, Suites 203–204, Solana St, cnr Real St, Intramuros, Metro Manila; tel. (2) 493449; affiliated to the World Fed. of Trade Unions; 280 affiliated unions and 75,000 mems; Nat. Pres. DIOSCORO O. NUÑEZ; Sec.-Gen. VLADIMIR R. TUPAZ.

Transport

RAILWAYS

The railway network is confined mainly to the island of Luzon.

Light Rail Transit Authority (Metrorail): Adm. Bldg, LRTA Compound, Aurora Blvd, Pasay City, Metro Manila; tel. (2) 8530041; fax (2) 8316449; e-mail lrtamain@lrta.gov.ph; internet www.lrta.gov.ph; managed and operated by Light Rail Transit Authority (LRTA); electrically driven mass transit system; Line 1 (15 km, Baclaran to Monumento) began commercial operations in Dec. 1984; Line 2 (13.8 km, Santolan to Recto) became fully operational in Oct. 2004; in 2006 the Government was working with advisers to conduct an open-market invitation to tender for the proposed Line 1 South Extension (12 km, Baclaran to Bacoot); Administrator MELQUIADES A. ROBLES.

Philippine National Railways: PNR Management Center, Torres Bugallon St, Kalookan City, 1408 Metro Manila; tel. (2) 3654716; fax (2) 3620824; e-mail info@pnr.gov.ph; internet www.pnr.gov.ph; f. 1887; govt-owned; northern line services run from Manila to Caloocan, 6 km (although the track extends to San Fernando, La Union) and southern line services run from Manila to Legaspi, Albay, 479 km; Chair. MANUEL D. ANDAL; Gen. Man. JOSÉ M. SARASOLA II.

ROADS

In 2000 there were 201,994 km of roads in the Philippines, of which 30,013 km were highways and 49,992 km were secondary roads; an estimated 42,419 km of the network were paved. Bus services provided the most widely used form of inland transport.

Department of Public Works and Highways: Bonifacio Drive, Port Area, Metro Manila; tel. (2) 5274111; fax (2) 5275635; e-mail soriquez.florante@dpwh.gov.ph; internet www.dpwh.gov.ph; responsible for the construction and maintenance of roads and bridges; Sec. HERMOGENES E. EBDANE, Jr.

Land Transportation Franchising and Regulatory Board: East Ave, Diliman, Quezon City, Metro Manila; tel. (2) 4262505; fax (2) 4262515; internet www.ltfrb.gov.ph; f. 1987; Chair. THOMPSON C. LANTION.

Land Transportation Office (LTO): East Ave, Quezon City, 1100 Metro Manila; tel. (2) 9219072; fax (2) 9219071; e-mail ltombox@lto.gov.ph; internet www.lto.gov.ph; f. 1987; plans, formulates and implements land transport rules and regulations, safety measures; registration of motor vehicles; issues licences; Exec. Dir BELLA G. BERMUNDO; Asst Sec. ANNELI R. LONTOC.

SHIPPING

In 2000 there were 102 national and municipal ports, 20 baseports, 58 terminal ports and 270 private ports. The eight major ports are Manila, Cebu, Iloilo, Cagayan de Oro, Zamboanga, General Santos, Polloc and Davao.

Pangasiwaan ng Daungan ng Pilipinas (Philippine Ports Authority): Bonifacio Dr., South Harbour, Port Area, 1018 Metro Manila; tel. (2) 5274856; fax (2) 5274853; e-mail info@ppa.com.ph; internet www.ppa.com.ph; f. 1977; supervises all ports within the Philippine Ports Authority port system; Gen. Man. OSCAR M. SEVILLA.

Philippine Shippers' Bureau (PSB): Trade and Industry Bldg, 5th Floor, 361 Sen. Gil J. Puyat Ave, Makatic City, Metro Manila; tel. and fax (2) 8904880; e-mail psb@dti.gov.ph; shipping facilitator for international and domestic trade; promotes and protects the interests of shippers, exporters, importers and domestic traders; Dir PEDRO VICENTE C. MENDOZA.

Domestic Lines

Aboitiz Transport System Inc: 12th Floor, Times Plaza Bldg, United Nations Ave, cnr Taft Ave, Ermita, Metro Manila; tel. (2) 5287171; internet www.atsc.com; f. 1996 following the merger of William Lines, Aboitiz Shipping and Carlos A. Gothong Lines; fmrly WG & A Philippines; passenger and cargo inter-island services; Chair. JON RAMON ABOITIZ; Pres. ENRIQUE M. ABOITIZ.

Albar Shipping and Trading Corpn: 2649 Molave St cnr East Service Road, United Hills Village, Parañaque, 1713 Metro Manila; tel. (2) 8232391; fax (2) 8233046; e-mail info@albargroup.com.ph; internet www.albargroup.com.ph; f. 1974; manning agency (maritime), trading, ship husbanding; Chair. AKIRA S. KATO; Pres. JOSE ALBAR G. KATO.

Candano Shipping Lines, Inc: Victoria Bldg, 6th Floor, 429 United Nations Ave, Ermita, 2802 Metro Manila; tel. (2) 5238051; fax (2) 5211309; f. 1953; inter-island and Far East chartering, cargo shipping; Pres. and Gen. Man. JOSE CANDANO.

Delsan Transport Lines Inc: Magsaysay Center Bldg, 520 T. M. Kalaw St, Ermita, Metro Manila; tel. (2) 5219172; fax (2) 2889331; Pres. VICENTE A. SANDOVAL; Gen. Man. CARLOS A. BUENAFE.

Eastern Shipping Lines, Inc: ESL Bldg, 54 Anda Circle, Port Area, POB 4253, 2803 Metro Manila; tel. (2) 5277841; fax (2) 5273006; e-mail eastship@skyinet.net; f. 1957; services to Japan; Pres. ERWIN L. CHIONGBIAN; Exec. Vice-Pres. ROY L. CHIONGBIAN.

Loadstar Shipping Co Inc: Loadstar Bldg, 1294 Romualdez St, Paco, 1007 Metro Manila; tel. (2) 5238381; fax (2) 5218061; Pres. and Gen. Man. TEODORO G. BERNARDINO.

Lorenzo Shipping Corpn: 20th Floor, Times Plaza Bldg, United Nations Ave, cnr Taft Ave, Ermita, Metro Manila; tel. (2) 5672180; fax (2) 5672030; internet www.lorenzoshipping.com; Pres. Capt. ROMEO L. MALIG.

Luzteveco (Luzon Stevedoring Corpn): Magsaysay Bldg, 520 T.M. Kalaw St, Ermita, Metro Manila; f. 1909; two brs; freight-forwarding, air cargo, world-wide shipping, broking, stevedoring, salvage, chartering and oil drilling support services; Pres. JOVINO G. LORENZO; Vice-Pres. RODOLFO B. SANTIAGO.

National Shipping Corpn of the Philippines: Knights of Rizal Bldg, Bonifacio Drive, Port Area, Metro Manila; tel. (2) 473631; fax (2) 5300169; services to Hong Kong, Taiwan, Korea, USA; Pres. TONY CHOW.

Negros Navigation Co Inc: Pier 2, North Harbor, Metro Manila; tel. and fax (2) 2454395; e-mail gcabalo@negrosnavigation.ph; internet www.negrosnavigation.ph; Chair. and CEO SULFICIO O. TAGUD.

Philippine Pacific Ocean Lines Inc: Delgado Bldg, Bonifacio Drive, Port Area, POB 184, Metro Manila; tel. (2) 478541; Vice-Pres. C. P. CARANDANG.

Philippine President Lines, Inc: PPL Bldg, 1000–1046 United Nations Ave, POB 4248, Metro Manila; tel. (2) 5249011; fax (2) 5251308; trading world-wide; Chair. EMILIO T. YAP, Jr; Pres. ENRIQUE C. YAP.

Sulpicio Lines, Inc: Don Sulpicio Go Bldg, Sulpicio Go St, Reclamation Area, POB 137, Cebu City 6000; tel. (32) 2325361; fax (32) 2321216; internet www.sulpiciolines.com; Chair. ENRIQUE S. GO; Man. Dir CARLOS S. GO.

Sweet Lines Inc: Pier 6, North Harbor, Metro Manila; tel. (2) 201791; fax (2) 205534; f. 1937; Pres. EDUARDO R. LOPINGCO; Exec. Vice-Pres. SONNY R. LOPINGCO.

Transocean Transport Corpn: Magsaysay Bldg, 8th Floor, 520 T. M. Kalaw St, Ermita, POB 21, Metro Manila; tel. (2) 506611; Pres. and Gen. Man. MIGUEL A. MAGSAYSAY; Vice-Pres. EDUARDO U. MANESE.

United Philippine Lines, Inc: UPL Bldg, Santa Clara St, Intramuros, POB 127, Metro Manila; tel. (2) 5277491; fax (2) 5271603; e-mail mailadmin@uplines.net; internet www.uplines.net; services world-wide; Pres. FERNANDO V. LISING.

THE PHILIPPINES

CIVIL AVIATION

In addition to the international airports in Metro Manila (Ninoy Aquino International Airport), Cebu (Mactan International Airport), Angeles City (Clark International Airport) and Olongapo City (Subic Bay International Airport), there are five alternative international airports: Laoag City, Ilocos Norte; Davao City; Zamboanga City; Gen. Santos (Tambler) City; and Puerto Princesa City, Palawan. There are also numerous domestic and private airports. By late 2006 the development of new airports in Silay City, Iloilo City and Bohol was under way.

Civil Aviation Authority: MIA Rd, Pasay City, Metro Manila; tel. (2) 8799104; fax (2) 8340143; e-mail director_gen@ato.gov.ph; internet www.ato.gov.ph; implements govt policies for the development and operation of a safe and efficient aviation network; Dir-Gen. NILO C. JATICO.

Civil Aeronautics Board: Airport Rd, Pasay City, Metro Manila; tel. (2) 8337266; fax (2) 8336911; e-mail tmanalac@cab.gov.ph; internet www.cab.gov.ph; exercises general supervision and regulation of, and jurisdiction and control over, air carriers, their equipment facilities and franchise; Exec. Dir TOMAS T. MAÑALAC.

Manila International Airport Authority (MIAA): NAIA Complex, Pasay City, Metro Manila; tel. (2) 8322938; fax (2) 8331180; e-mail gm@miaa.gov.ph; internet www.miaa.gov.ph; Gen. Man. ALFONSO G. CUSI.

Air Philippines: R1 Hangar, APC Gate 1, Andrews Ave, Nichols, Pasay City, Metro Manila; tel. (2) 8517601; fax (2) 8517922; e-mail info@airphilippines.com.ph; internet www.airphils.com; f. 1995; domestic and regional services; Chair. and Pres. WILLIAM GATCHALIAN.

Asian Spirit: G & A Bldg, 3rd Floor, 2303 Don Chino Roces Ave, Makati City, Metro Manila; tel. (2) 8403811; fax (2) 8130183; e-mail info@asianspirit.com; internet www.asianspirit.com; Man. ANTONIO BUENDIA.

Cebu Pacific Air: Robinsons Equitable Tower, 16th Floor, ADB Ave, Cnr Poveda Rd, Ortigas Center, Pasig City, Metro Manila; tel. (2) 7020888; fax (2) 6379170; e-mail customerservice@cebupacificair.com; internet www.cebupacificair.com; f. 1995; domestic and international services; Chair. RICARDO J. ROMULO; Pres. and CEO LANCE Y. GOKONGWEI.

Grand Air: Mercure Hotel, Philippines Village Airport Compound, 8th Floor, Pasay City, 1300 Metro Manila; tel. (2) 8313001; fax (2) 8917682; f. 1994; Pres. REBECCA PANLILI.

Philippine Airlines Inc (PAL): PAL Corporate Communications Dept, PAL Center, Ground Floor, Legaspi St, Legaspi Village, Makati City, 0750 Metro Manila; tel. (2) 8171234; fax (2) 8136715; e-mail webmgr@pal.com.ph; internet www.philippineairlines.com; f. 1941; in Jan. 1992 67% of PAL was transferred to the private sector; operates domestic, regional and international services to destinations in the Far East, Australasia, the Middle East, the USA and Canada; Chair. and CEO LUCIO TAN; Pres. and COO JAIME J. BAUTISTA.

Tourism

Tourism, although adversely affected from time to time by political unrest, remains an important sector of the economy. In 2005 arrivals totalled 2,623,084, compared with 2,291,352 in the previous year. Tourist receipts, including passenger transport, totalled US $2,620m. in 2005.

Philippine Convention and Visitors' Corpn: Legaspi Towers, 4th Floor, 300 Roxas Blvd, 1004 Metro Manila; tel. (2) 5259318; fax (2) 5253314; e-mail pcvcnet@dotpcvc.gov.ph; internet www.dotpcvc.gov.ph; Chair. JOSEPH H. DURANO; Exec. Dir DANIEL G. CORPUZ.

Philippine Tourism Authority: Department of Tourism Bldg, T. M. Kalaw St, Teodoro F. Valencia Circle, Ermita, 1000 Metro Manila; tel. (2) 5247141; fax (2) 5218113; e-mail info@philtourism.gov.ph; internet www.philtourism.com; Gen. Man. and CEO ROBERT DEAN BARBERS.

POLAND

Introductory Survey

Location, Climate, Language, Religion, Flag, Capital

The Republic of Poland is situated in eastern Europe, bounded to the north by the Baltic Sea and an exclave of the Russian Federation (Kaliningrad Oblast), to the north-east by Lithuania, to the east by Belarus, to the south-east by Ukraine, to the west by Germany, and to the south by the Czech Republic and Slovakia. The climate is temperate in the west but continental in the east. Poland has short summers and cold, snowy winters. Temperatures in Warsaw are generally between −6°C (21°F) and 24°C (75°F). Most of the inhabitants profess Christianity: more than 95% are adherents of the Roman Catholic Church, but there are numerous other denominations. The official language is Polish, spoken by almost all of the population, and there is a small German-speaking community. The national flag (proportions 5 by 8) has two equal horizontal stripes of white and red. The capital is Warsaw (Warszawa).

Recent History

Poland, partitioned since the 18th century, was declared an independent republic on 11 November 1918, at the end of the First World War. The country was ruled by a military regime from 1926 until 1939, when Poland was invaded by both Germany and the USSR and partitioned between the two powers. After Germany declared war on the USSR in June 1941, its forces occupied the whole of Poland until they were expelled by Soviet troops in March 1945.

At the end of the Second World War a pro-communist 'Polish Committee of National Liberation', established under Soviet auspices in July 1944, was transformed into a Provisional Government. Under the Potsdam Agreement, signed by the major Allied powers in 1945, the former German territories lying east of the rivers Oder and Neisse (which now comprise one-third of Poland's total area) came under Polish sovereignty, while Poland's frontier with the USSR was shifted westward. These border changes were accompanied by a major resettlement of the population in the affected areas.

Non-communist political groups suffered severe intimidation during national elections in January 1947, in which the communist-led 'democratic bloc' claimed victory. A People's Republic was established in February, with the Polish Workers' Party (PPR), led by Władysław Gomułka, as the dominant group. Gomułka's reluctance to implement certain aspects of Soviet economic policies, notably the collectivization of agriculture, led to his dismissal as First Secretary of the PPR in 1948. In December of that year the PPR merged with the Polish Socialist Party to form the Polish United Workers' Party (PZPR). Two other parties, the United Peasants' Party (ZSL) and the Democratic Party (SD), were permitted to remain in existence, but were closely controlled by the PZPR, and Poland effectively became a one-party state.

In 1956 mass demonstrations, provoked by food shortages, were suppressed by security forces. In the ensuing political crisis, Gomułka was returned to office, despite Soviet opposition. In 1964–70 limited economic reforms were implemented. In December 1970 a sharp rise in food prices led to strikes and demonstrations in the Baltic port of Gdańsk and in other cities. Many demonstrators were killed or injured in clashes with the police and army, and Gomułka was forced to resign as First Secretary of the PZPR; he was succeeded by Edward Gierek.

In July 1980 an increase in meat prices prompted widespread labour unrest, and shipyard employees in the Baltic ports, notably at Gdańsk, demanded the right to form free trade unions. Following negotiations, the Government finally granted permission to establish several self-governing trade unions, under the guidance of Solidarity, the organization involved in the Gdańsk strike, which was led by a local worker, Lech Wałęsa. In September, as labour unrest continued, Gierek was replaced as First Secretary of the PZPR by Stanisław Kania. Under the growing influence of Solidarity (which claimed an estimated 10m. members in 1981), strikes continued throughout the country, and in February Józef Pińkowski resigned as Chairman of the Council of Ministers. He was succeeded by Gen. Wojciech Jaruzelski, Minister of Defence (a post he retained) since 1968. Despite further concessions to Solidarity, the crisis persisted, forcing Kania's resignation in October; he was succeeded by Jaruzelski, who thus held the leading posts in both the PZPR and the Government.

On 13 December 1981 martial law was imposed throughout Poland. A governing Military Council of National Salvation, led by Jaruzelski, was established; all trade union activity was suspended, and Wałęsa and other Solidarity leaders were detained. Violent clashes between workers and security forces ensued, and thousands of protesters were arrested. Sporadic disturbances continued in 1982, particularly in response to legislation abolishing all trade unions. Wałęsa was released in November, and in December martial law was suspended and some other prisoners were freed. (During 1982 about 10,000 prisoners had been detained, and at least 15 demonstrators killed.) In July 1983 martial law was formally ended; the Military Council of National Salvation was dissolved, and an amnesty was declared for most political prisoners and activists. In October Wałęsa was awarded the Nobel Peace Prize.

In July 1984, to mark the 40th anniversary of the Polish communist regime, some 35,000 detainees were granted amnesty. In August US sanctions (imposed following the declaration of martial law) were relaxed. However, the murder, in October, of Fr Jerzy Popiełuszko, a well-known pro-Solidarity Roman Catholic priest, provoked renewed unrest. In February 1985 four officers from the Ministry of Internal Affairs were found guilty of the murder, and received lengthy prison sentences. (The case was subsequently reopened; two generals, accused of directing the murder, were acquitted in August 1994, but the verdict was overturned in March 1996.)

Legislative elections took place in October 1985. New regulations gave voters a choice of two candidates for 410 of the 460 seats in the Sejm (Assembly), the remaining 50 deputies being elected unopposed on a national list. Solidarity appealed to voters to boycott the poll, and subsequently disputed the Government's claim that 79% of the electorate had participated. In November Jaruzelski resigned as Chairman of the Council of Ministers, in order to become President of the Council of State (Head of State). He was succeeded by Prof. Zbigniew Messner, hitherto a Deputy Chairman of the Council of Ministers.

In December 1986, in an effort to increase support for the regime, Jaruzelski established a 56-member Consultative Council, which was attached to the Council of State and comprised mainly non-PZPR members. Nevertheless, public discontent intensified in 1987. Solidarity activists attempted to disrupt the official May Day celebrations in several cities, and in June there were violent clashes between police and protesters during a visit by Pope John Paul II to his native country. Significant price rises were imposed in early 1988, prompting widespread protests, and the May Day celebrations were again disrupted. In August a strike by coal workers rapidly spread to other sectors, leading to the most serious industrial unrest since 1981.

The Messner Government resigned in September 1988. Dr Mieczysław Rakowski, Deputy Chairman in 1981–85, was appointed Chairman of a new Council of Ministers, which included several non-PZPR members and younger, reformist politicians. However, the Government's announcement that the Lenin Shipyard in Gdańsk was to be closed provoked further strike action. By April 1989 agreement had been reached on the restoration of legal status to Solidarity, as well as on the holding of elections to a new, bicameral legislature, the Zgromadzenie Narodowe (National Assembly). Solidarity and other non-communist groups were to be permitted to contest all the seats in a new upper chamber, the Senat (Senate), which would have a limited right of veto over the lower chamber, the Sejm. Just 35% of the seats in the Sejm were to be subject to free elections, with the remainder open only to candidates of the PZPR and its associate organizations. A new post of executive President was also to be introduced. The necessary amendments to the Constitution were duly approved by the Sejm. In May the Roman Catholic Church was accorded legal status.

Elections to the new legislature took place on 4 and 8 July 1989, with 62% of eligible voters participating in the first round, but only 25% in the second. In the elections to the Senat, the Solidarity Citizens' Committee, the electoral wing of the trade union movement, secured all but one of the 100 seats. In the elections to the 460-member Sejm, Solidarity secured all the 161 seats that it was permitted to contest, and the other 299 seats were divided between the PZPR (173 seats), its allied parties—the ZSL (76) and the SD (27)—and members of Roman Catholic organizations (23).

The new legislature narrowly elected Jaruzelski, unopposed, to the post of executive President. He was replaced as First Secretary of the PZPR by Rakowski. Jaruzelski accepted Wałęsa's proposal of a coalition of Solidarity, the SD and the ZSL. The appointment of Tadeusz Mazowiecki, a newspaper editor and moderate member of Solidarity, as Chairman of the Council of Ministers, was approved by the Sejm on 24 August 1989, thus ending almost 45 years of exclusive communist rule in Poland. A Solidarity-dominated administration was formed in September.

The new Government's programme of radical political and economic reforms emphasized the creation of democratic institutions and the introduction of a market economy. In December 1989 the legislature voted to rename the country the Republic of Poland, and the national symbols of pre-communist Poland were reintroduced. In January 1990 the PZPR was dissolved to allow the establishment of a new left-wing party, Social Democracy of the Republic of Poland (SdRP). Local elections held in May were the first entirely free elections in Poland for more than 50 years. Candidates of the Solidarity Citizens' Committee won more than 41% of the seats, while nominally independent candidates secured 38%. By mid-1990 tension had developed between Wałęsa, who advocated an acceleration of economic reform and privatization, and the more cautious Mazowiecki.

In September 1990 Jaruzelski agreed to resign, to permit a direct presidential election to take place. In the first round, held on 25 November, Mazowiecki was placed third. Wałęsa and an émigré business executive, Stanisław Tymiński, proceeded to a second round of voting on 9 December, at which Wałęsa won 74.3% of the votes cast. Wałęsa resigned the chairmanship of Solidarity (he was replaced in February 1991 by Marian Krzaklewski), and in December 1990 was inaugurated as President for a five-year term. Jan Krzysztof Bielecki, a reformist economist, became Prime Minister. The new regime rapidly encountered challenges to its reform programme. In May 1991 Solidarity organized a nation-wide day of strikes and demonstrations, in protest at the Government's economic policies.

Legislative elections took place on 27 October 1991, with the participation of 43.2% of the electorate. Some 29 parties won representation in the Sejm. The party with the largest number of deputies (62) was Mazowiecki's Democratic Union (UD). The Democratic Left Alliance (SLD), an electoral coalition of the SdRP and the All Poland Trade Unions' Alliance, won 60 seats. The UD was also the largest single party in the Senat, with 21 seats, while Solidarity returned 11 senators. After Bronisław Geremek of the UD failed to form a government, Wałęsa nominated Jan Olszewski of the Centre Alliance (PC) as Prime Minister. Criticism of his economic programme by the President and the withdrawal of two parties from the coalition negotiations caused Olszewski to submit his resignation. However, this was rejected by the Sejm, which proceeded, in December, to approve a new centre-right Council of Ministers, incorporating members of the PC, the Peasant Alliance and the Christian-National Union (ZChN).

In June 1992, following controversy regarding government attempts to expose alleged communist conspirators, the Sejm approved a motion of no confidence in the Olszewski Government. After the failure of Waldemar Pawlak, the leader of the Polish People's Party (PSL), to form a government, the appointment of Hanna Suchocka of the UD was approved by the Sejm. Her new Government, a seven-party coalition dominated by the UD and the ZChN, was immediately challenged by a month-long strike by 40,000 workers at a copper plant in Legnica, supported by several transport and power workers' unions. In December an interim 'Small Constitution' entered into effect, pending a comprehensive revision of the 1952 Constitution. A motion of no confidence in the Suchocka administration, proposed by the Solidarity group after the failure of negotiations between the Government and striking teachers and health workers, was narrowly approved by the Sejm in May 1993. Wałęsa refused to accept Suchocka's resignation; instead, he dissolved the Sejm, scheduling new elections to both houses of parliament for September. The electoral code was amended, in order to achieve greater political stability, with a new stipulation that a party (with the exception of organizations representing national minorities) must secure at least 5% of the total votes cast (8% in the case of an electoral alliance) in order to achieve parliamentary representation.

The general election held on 19 September 1993 resulted in victory for parties of the left, as voters demonstrated their dissatisfaction with the recent economic reforms. The SLD and the PSL, both dominated by former communists and their allies, won, respectively, 171 and 132 seats in the Sejm, and 37 and 36 seats in the Senat. The two parties, which together won 35.8% of the total votes in the elections to the Sejm, benefited from the new law to secure more than 65% of the seats in the lower chamber. The UD took 74 seats in the Sejm (with 10.6% of the votes cast) and four in the Senat, while Solidarity won 10 seats in the Senat (although none in the Sejm). Wałęsa's Non-Party Bloc for Reform, established in June, won 16 seats in the Sejm and two seats in the Senat. Almost 35% of the votes cast in elections to the Sejm were for parties that received fewer than 5% of the total votes, notably the PC and the ZChN, and therefore secured no representation; the rate of participation by voters was 52.1%.

In October 1993 Pawlak formed a coalition Government, dominated by members of his PSL and the SLD. The new Prime Minister expressed his commitment to a continuation of market-orientated reforms, but pledged new measures to alleviate their adverse social effects. In early 1994 the Deputy Prime Minister and Minister of Finance, Marek Borowski (of the SLD), resigned. In February at least 20,000 people took part in a Solidarity-led demonstration in Warsaw, to demand increased government investment in the public sector and improved measures to combat unemployment. Solidarity began a nation-wide programme of strike action in March.

In January 1995 Wałęsa refused to endorse legislation to increase rates of personal income tax; however, he was obliged to approve the legislation after his actions were ruled to be unconstitutional. Relations between the Government and the President deteriorated sharply in February, when Wałęsa threatened to dissolve parliament if the Prime Minister did not resign. Further conflict was averted by Pawlak's departure, and in March Józef Oleksy, a member of the SLD and hitherto Marshal (Speaker) of the Sejm, took office as Prime Minister.

The first round of the 1995 presidential election took place on 5 November. The two leading candidates, Aleksander Kwaśniewski, the Chairman of the SdRP (and formerly a leading member of the PZPR), and Wałęsa proceeded to a second round on 19 November, when Kwaśniewski achieved a narrow victory, with 51.7% of the votes cast. On taking office on 23 December, Kwaśniewski asserted his commitment to the further integration of Poland into Western institutions and to the continuation of policies of economic liberalization. Following Kwaśniewski's election, the ministers responsible for foreign affairs, the interior and national defence (all effectively presidential appointees) submitted their resignations. The outgoing Minister of Internal Affairs, Andrzej Milczanowski, claimed that Oleksy had acted on behalf of Soviet (and subsequently Russian) espionage agents since the 1980s; although Oleksy vehemently denied the charges, he resigned as Prime Minister in January 1996 (he was fully exonerated in an official report published in October). He was subsequently elected Chairman of the SdRP, replacing Kwaśniewski, who had resigned his party membership following his election as President. Włodzimierz Cimoszewicz (the deputy leader of the SLD and hitherto deputy Marshal of the Sejm) was appointed as Prime Minister in February.

In June 1996 the Government's decision to file for bankruptcy for the loss-making Gdańsk shipyard prompted Solidarity-led demonstrations. Also in June some 25 centre-right political parties, including Solidarity, the PC and the ZChN, established Solidarity Electoral Action (AWS) to contest the 1997 parliamentary elections. In September 1996 the Prime Minister dismissed Jacek Buchacz as Minister of Foreign Economic Relations, prompting his party, the PSL, to withdraw from government negotiations on proposed administrative reforms. Talks resumed at the end of September, after Cimoszewicz conceded that he had reneged on the coalition accord. Agreement was subsequently reached on the distribution of ministerial portfolios, whereby the PSL was accorded responsibility for the new Ministry of the Treasury, while the SLD secured the Ministry of Internal Affairs and Administration and the new Ministry of the Economy.

On 2 April 1997 the legislature adopted a new Constitution, which was approved by 52.7% of the votes cast by some 42.9% of the electorate in a national referendum on 25 May. Right-wing parties, notably AWS and the Movement for the Reconstruction of Poland (ROP), had opposed the Constitution, which slightly reduced presidential powers and committed Poland to a social market economy based on the freedom of economic activity and private ownership. The new Constitution came into force on 17 October.

In the general election of 21 September 1997, AWS secured 201 seats in the Sejm (with 33.8% of the valid votes cast) and 51 in the Senat, while the SLD won 164 seats in the Sejm (with 27.1% of the votes) and 28 in the Senat. The PSL retained only 27 seats in the Sejm and three in the Senat. The rate of voter participation was 48%. Krzaklewski, the leader of AWS, subsequently initiated coalition talks with the economically liberal Freedom Union (UW) and the ROP, which had won, respectively, 60 and six seats in the Sejm, and eight and five in the Senat. Jerzy Buzek (a member of Solidarity since its formation in 1980) was nominated as Prime Minister in mid-October. Following lengthy negotiations, AWS and the UW signed a coalition agreement later that month, despite some opposition from the ZChN and the PC (both members of AWS). A new Council of Ministers was subsequently appointed, which included Leszek Balcerowicz, leader of the UW, as Deputy Prime Minister, Minister of Finance and Chairman of the Economic Committee. In November the Sejm approved the new Government's programme, which prioritized rapid integration with the North Atlantic Treaty Organization (NATO, see p. 340) and the European Union (EU, see p. 244), and accelerated privatization and government reform. Shortly afterwards, the Social Movement of Solidarity Electoral Action, which was to replace Solidarity within AWS, applied for registration as a new political party. In December Wałęsa officially formed the Christian Democratic Party of the Third Republic.

In July 1998 a new structure of local and regional government was approved, which reduced the number of voivodships (provinces) from 48 to 16. Local elections were held in the 16 new voivodships in October. In nine voivodships, the opposition SLD was returned as the largest party, although the governing AWS-UW coalition won the largest number of seats overall, and secured control of the seven remaining voivodships. Meanwhile, the Government's programme of industrial restructuring continued to provoke public unrest, as well as discord among the governing parties. Railway workers took industrial action in June, and in July around 10,000 farmers attended a demonstration in Warsaw, to demand increased government protection for the agricultural sector. There was further unrest by farmers in August and December 1998, and in February 1999, when it was announced that the leader of the Self-Defence Trade Union (which had organized the protests), Andrzej Lepper, was to stand trial for having organized illegal road blocks. Meanwhile, the approval, in July 1998, of the divestment of the Gdańsk shipyard (which was completed in September), had prompted six AWS deputies to withdraw their support for the Government. (In preceding weeks nine other deputies had also left the ruling coalition.) In December a strike by coal miners over imminent changes to the pensions system spread to more than 50 mines, and resulted in government concessions; industrial unrest also affected the steel, armaments and railway sectors.

In June 1998 the Sejm adopted a resolution condemning the communist regime imposed on post-war Poland by the USSR; the resolution, which was opposed by the SLD, held the PZPR responsible for offences committed during the communist period. In late September the Sejm approved legislation granting access for Polish citizens to files compiled on them by the security services during the communist era.

During March 1999 the Prime Minister undertook a major government reorganization, in preparation for a significant reform of state administration, which took effect in April. The Secretary-General of the UW resigned in protest at the appointment of two ministers. In September a new political organization, the Alliance of Polish Christian Democrats (PPChD), was officially founded; members included the PC—a member of the governing AWS—and the Party of Christian Democrats (PChD).

During May 1999 farmers resumed their protests against agricultural policy. In June a protest in Warsaw by workers from a weapons factory in the central town of Radom resulted in violent clashes between the police and demonstrators. In August farmers joined demonstrations against the low price of grain; an estimated 80 people were injured when violence erupted between police and farmers in northern Poland. Protests against the economic slowdown and the implementation of government reforms in education, health and pensions provision culminated, in September 1999, in a march through Warsaw by some 35,000 agricultural and industrial workers (as well as leaders from the opposition SLD and PSL parties).

During September 1999 Buzek came under growing criticism from leading members of his governing coalition, who accused him of weak leadership. At the beginning of the month the Deputy Prime Minister and Minister of Internal Affairs and Administration, Janusz Tomaszewski, announced his resignation. A minor government reorganization took place in early October, and AWS and the UW renewed their coalition agreement for a further two years. In late October the Government reached a compromise with miners' representatives from Solidarity regarding the restructuring of the industry, following protests in the capital. It was announced in December that Solidarity was to withdraw from political activities and become an 'organization of employees'; the movement's voting rights within AWS were transferred to the Social Movement of Solidarity Electoral Action. In January 2000 Lepper announced the formation of the Self-Defence Party of the Republic of Poland (SRP), an anti-Government party incorporating elements of several farmers' organizations and trade unions, under his leadership.

In mid-May 2000 the ruling coalition entered a serious crisis, when the Prime Minister suspended the Government of Warsaw's central commune (a coalition of the UW and the SLD) and replaced it with an AWS-affiliated commissioner. At the end of May the UW announced its withdrawal from the coalition, in protest at the blocking of Balcerowicz's proposals for economic reform by AWS deputies. Negotiations aimed at maintaining the coalition collapsed in early June, and Buzek subsequently formed a minority AWS Government. In August the treasury minister, Emil Wąsacz, was dismissed, following controversy surrounding his privatization policies.

In the presidential election, held on 8 October 2000, Kwaśniewski was re-elected, with 53.9% of the valid votes cast. The second-placed candidate, an independent former foreign minister, Andrzej Olechowski, secured 17.3% of the votes; Krzaklewski obtained 15.6%, Lepper 3.1% and Wałęsa just 1.0%. The rate of participation by the electorate was 61.1%. Wałęsa subsequently announced that he was to retire from politics. Krzaklewski resigned as leader of AWS in January 2001, and was succeeded by Prime Minister Buzek. (Krzaklewski remained Chairman of Solidarity until September 2002.) Meanwhile, Balcerowicz resigned the leadership of the UW, and became President of the central bank in December 2000.

In January 2001 Olechowski, together with the Marshal of the Sejm, Maciej Plazyński of AWS, and a Vice-Marshal of the Senat, Donald Tusk of the UW, founded a new political movement, the Civic Platform (PO). Kwaśniewski signed a new electoral law at the end of April, introducing a new method for the calculation of voting under the system of proportional representation. Following the enactment of the law, legislative elections were scheduled for 23 September. Thereafter, significant political realignment took place, and in May AWS was restructured as Solidarity Electoral Action of the Right (AWSP), in alliance with the ROP. At the end of May the traditionalist Roman Catholic, nationalist League of Polish Families (LPR), which opposed Polish membership of the EU, was registered as a party. In August the legislature rejected an austerity plan proposed by the Minister of Finance, Jarosław Bauc, in an attempt to address the predicted deficit in the budget for 2002, and in late August Buzek announced Bauc's dismissal.

The legislative elections took place as scheduled, on 23 September 2001, with a rate of voter participation of 46.3%. Neither AWSP nor the UW received the requisite 8% of the votes to obtain seats in the Sejm, although both parties contested the elections to the Senat as part of the Blok Senat 2001 (also comprising the PO, Law and Justice—PiS and the ROP), which won 15 of the 100 seats. Right-wing support was, instead, divided between PiS, which obtained 44 seats in the Sejm, and the LPR, which secured 38 seats in the Sejm and two seats in the Senat. Another party elected to the Sejm for the first time was the SRP, which took 53 seats in the Sejm (with 10.2% of the votes) and two seats in the Senat, and which also opposed accession to the EU. An electoral coalition of the SLD and the Union of Labour (UP) won 216 seats in the Sejm (with 41.0% of the votes) and 75 seats in the Senat, but failed to achieve an overall majority. The PO, which received 65 seats in the Sejm (with 12.7% of the votes), rejected an initial proposal to form a coalition with the SLD-UP. Instead, on 9 October the SLD and the UP signed a coalition agreement with the PSL, which had obtained 42 seats in the elections to the Sejm (with 9.0% of the votes) and four seats in the Senate. The leader of the SLD, Leszek Miller, was sworn in as Prime Minister and Chairman of the European Integration Committee on 19 October; the PSL's leader, Jarosław Kalinowski, and the leader of the UP, Marek Pol, were appointed as Deputy Prime Ministers. Miller pledged to revive economic progress and announced that a referendum on entry to the EU would be held in mid-2003.

In May 2001 Andrzej Lepper was sentenced to 16 months' imprisonment, after being found guilty of charges associated with the farmers' blockades of 1998–99. In November 2001 Lepper was dismissed as a Vice-Marshal of the Sejm, and in January 2002 he was fined for having insulted the President. In the following month he was charged with seven counts of slander. In March, on appeal, Lepper's prison sentence was reduced to a suspended one-year term. Government changes in July included the resignation of Marek Belka as Minister of Finance; Grzegorz Kołodko subsequently assumed the post (which he had previously held in 1994–97), and in December survived a vote of no confidence in the Sejm.

Meanwhile, on 27 October 2002 local elections were held, in which the ruling SLD-UP coalition won 33.7% of the votes cast; the SRP won 18.0% of the votes and the LPR secured 16.4%. A second round of voting took place on 10 November. In January 2003 the Prime Minister reorganized the Government, consolidating the Ministries of the Economy and of Labour into a new Ministry of the Economy, Labour and Social Policy, under Jerzy Hausner. On 1 March Miller expelled the junior coalition partner, the PSL, from the Government, after it voted with opposition deputies against new tax legislation in the Sejm. In mid-March the Sejm rejected a motion, proposed by the LPR, to dissolve parliament. The following day the SLD-UD coalition formed a parliamentary alliance with the Peasant Democratic Party (PLD), although it remained 13 seats short of a majority. Meanwhile, public dissatisfaction at the state of the economy and the high rate of unemployment was expressed by frequently violent demonstrations led by the Solidarity trade union.

In June 2003 Miller transferred responsibility for economic policy from the Ministry of Finance to Hausner's Ministry of the Economy, Labour and Social Policy, prompting the resignation of the Deputy Prime Minister and Minister of Finance, Kołodko. Hausner was then appointed a Deputy Prime Minister (retaining his previous portfolio), and Andrzej Raczko became Minister of Finance. The Government subsequently won a vote of confidence in the Sejm. On 20 January 2004 Miller appointed Deputy Chairman of the SLD and former premier Józef Oleksy as Deputy Prime Minister and Minister of Internal Affairs and Administration, in an apparent attempt to reduce tensions within the party. The following day Miller dismissed Piotr Czyżewski as Minister of the Treasury, reportedly owing to his failure to implement the privatization of state-owned companies; he was replaced by Zbigniew Kaniewski.

In late January 2004 the PLD withdrew its support for the ruling coalition, thereby reducing the Government's majority in parliament. Following increasing divisions within the SLD, in mid-February Miller announced that he was to resign as Chairman of the party, but retain the premiership, to enable him to focus on Poland's planned accession to the EU on 1 May (see below). At a party congress on 6 March Krzysztof Janik was elected as the new party Chairman. None the less, in late March more than 20 deputies, led by Marek Borowski, announced that they were to defect from the SLD in order to establish a new party, Polish Social Democracy (SDPL); Borowski subsequently resigned as Marshal of the Sejm. On 26 March Miller acknowledged the loss of support for his leadership and announced that he would resign as Prime Minister on 2 May. Three days later President Kwaśniewski nominated former Minister of Finance Belka (latterly Director of Economic Policy in the US-led Coalition Provisional Authority in Iraq) to head a new government; Belka announced that he intended to retain key ministers, including Hausner, who had devised a controversial economic austerity programme for 2004–07, which some observers believed had contributed to Miller's loss of popular support. The lengthy investigation into a media bribery scandal that had emerged in late 2002 had also eroded the credibility of Miller's Government. In early April 2004 Miller, who had consistently denied the charges, was exonerated by a parliamentary investigative commission. In late April Oleksy (who had been widely regarded as a potential candidate for the premiership) was elected as the new Marshal of the Sejm.

Miller resigned on 2 May 2004, as planned, and Belka's Government, principally composed of SLD members and independents, took office, pending approval by the Sejm. Isabela Jaruga-Nowacka, who had been elected one week earlier to replace Marek Pol as the leader of the UP, was appointed as a Deputy Prime Minister. In mid-May, however, the Sejm rejected Belka's nomination, forcing the resignation of the new Government. The Sejm failed to propose a new candidate for the premiership within the requisite two weeks, and Kwaśniewski duly renominated Belka. In late June the Sejm approved Belka's appointment by 236 votes to 215, thus averting early elections. In order to secure the support of the SDPL, Belka agreed to hold a further confidence vote in October to confirm his mandate to govern.

In July 2004 the Minister of Finance, Andrzej Raczko, resigned to become Poland's representative at the IMF; he was succeeded by Mirosław Gronicki. In August the Government abandoned some elements of its economic austerity programme in order to secure political support for the majority of its proposals. In September the Minister of Justice, Marek Sadowski, resigned, after media reports suggested that he had abused his position as a judge and later as a government minister (both of which granted him immunity from prosecution) to avoid investigation into a road accident that he had been involved in in 1995.

In mid-October 2004 Belka narrowly won the scheduled vote of confidence in the Sejm, by 234 votes to 218. Ahead of the vote Belka had announced to the lower chamber that Poland would begin reducing its 2,500-strong military contingent in Iraq (see below) from early 2005. Krzysztof Pater resigned as Minister of Social Policy in November, after the Sejm rejected austerity measures on corporate social insurance and pensions. Deputy Prime Minister Jaruga-Nowacka subsequently assumed additional responsibility for social policy.

In December 2004, at a congress of the SLD, Oleksy was elected Chairman of the party, defeating Krzysztof Janik in a second round of voting. The election increased tension within the SLD, which was suffering a decline in popularity, and Janik and his allies announced plans to form an opposition faction within the party. A few days later, following several years of investigations, the Vetting Court ruled that Oleksy had concealed his collaboration with the communist-era military intelligence services; Oleksy, who strongly refuted the charges against him, announced that he would appeal against the Court's verdict. In response to mounting pressure, Oleksy resigned as Marshal of the Sejm, and in early January 2005 Włodzimierz Cimoszewicz, hitherto Minister of Foreign Affairs, was elected as his replacement. Adam Rotfeld assumed the foreign affairs portfolio.

In early February 2005 Hausner resigned from the SLD, after the party's national council voted against holding early legislative elections in June, but announced his intention to retain his ministerial positions. In early March, however, in response to increasing pressure, particularly from the SLD, Hausner tendered his resignation as Deputy Prime Minister and Minister of the Economy and Labour. Jacek Piechota was appointed to the position of Minister of the Economy and Labour. In late February Hausner and Władysław Frasyniuk, the leader of the UW, announced plans to create a new centrist political organization: the Democratic Party (PD) held its founding congress in May. Amid speculation that he was to join the new party, in March Belka urged the Sejm to dissolve itself to allow early elections to take place, as the minority Government lacked sufficient support in the Sejm to approve proposed budget reforms. In early May, however, the Sejm voted to reject three motions submitted by opposition parties for its dissolution, and President Kwaśniewski rejected Belka's resignation, tendered on 6 May, stating that the Government should remain in office until the forthcoming legislative elections. Meanwhile, Jaruga-Nowacka resigned from the leadership of the UP. In late May Wojciech Olejniczak was elected as Chairman of the SLD, succeeding Józef Oleksy. Olejniczak was replaced as Minister of Agriculture and Rural Development by Jerzy Pilarczyk. A new Minister of the Environment was appointed in the same month. In June Belka made public his police file, in response to allegations that he had collaborated with the communist security services.

In the legislative elections, which took place on 25 September 2005, with a rate of participation of 40.5% of the electorate, the conservative PiS obtained the largest number of seats in both the Sejm (taking 155 of the 460 seats, with 27.0% of the votes) and the Senat (with 49 of the 100 available). The centre-right PO won 133 seats in the Sejm (with 24.1% of the votes) and 34 seats in the Senat, whereas the incumbent SLD received just 55 seats in the

Sejm (with 11.3% of the votes cast). Two days later the leader of PiS, Jarosław Kaczyński, announced that he did not intend to lead the new government, and instead proposed Kazimierz Marcinkiewicz for the premiership, while Kaczyński's twin brother, Lech, the PiS Mayor of Warsaw, was to contest the forthcoming presidential election.

After a first round of voting in the presidential election, conducted on 9 October 2005, PO leader Donald Tusk (who obtained 36.3% of the votes) and Lech Kaczyński (33.1%) progressed to a second round on 23 October. Kaczyński emerged as the winner in the 'run-off' poll, with 54.0% of the votes. The rate of participation by the electorate was 49.7% in the first round and 51.0% in the second. Kaczyński was inaugurated as President on 23 December.

Although, as the two principal parties of the centre-right, PiS and the more economically liberal PO had been widely expected to negotiate a coalition government, the two parties were unable to agree on the distribution of senior positions, and on 31 October 2005 Marcinkiewicz was appointed as Prime Minister of a minority Government, comprising nine members of PiS and eight independents. Stefan Meller, a career diplomat, became Minister of Foreign Affairs, and non-partisan ministers were also appointed to the treasury, finance and economy portfolios, apparently in an attempt to reassure international investors. Bogdan Borusewicz, an independent, was appointed Marshal of the Senat, and Marek Jurek, of PiS, became Marshal of the Sejm. On 10 November the Government won a motion of confidence in the Sejm, by 272 to 187 votes, with the support of smaller rightist parties (the SRP, the LPR and the PSL).

In January 2006 the Minister of the Treasury, Andrzej Mikosz, resigned, following media allegations that his wife had been involved in financial misdemeanours in 2002; he was replaced by Wojciech Jasinski in mid-February 2006. Also in January Teresa Lubinska was removed from her position as Minister of Finance; she was succeeded by Zyta Gilowska, an independent (formerly aligned with the PO), who also became Deputy Prime Minister. In mid-February President Kaczyński confirmed that he would not schedule early legislative elections, despite the failure of the Senat to approve the budget by the constitutional deadline of 31 January (it was adopted by the Senat on 1 February). In late April PiS signed a coalition agreement with the SRP and the LPR. Stefan Meller subsequently resigned as Minister of Foreign Affairs, in protest at the Government's decision to co-operate with the SRP. Several new ministers were appointed to the Government on 5 May, giving the Government a majority in the Sejm for the first time. The leaders of both the SRP and LPR were awarded with deputy prime ministerial positions, with Lepper additionally gaining responsibility for agriculture and rural development, while the leader of the LPR, Roman Giertych, also became the Minister of National Education.

In June 2006 Gilowska resigned from the Council of Ministers following the opening of an investigation into claims, which she denied, that she had lied about collaborating with the secret services during the communist era. (Former members of the Soviet-backed secret services were eligible to hold public office, but falsely denying such links was considered a serious offence.) Gilowska was initially replaced as Minister of Finance by Pawel Wojciechowski, an economic adviser to Prime Minister Marcinkiewicz. In early July, however, Marcinkiewicz tendered his resignation, reportedly owing to disagreements with Jarosław Kaczyński over economic policy, as a result of which the entire Government was constitutionally obliged to resign. Shortly afterwards President Kaczyński nominated his twin brother as Marcinkiewicz's replacement; this appointment was subsequently approved by the Sejm, and Jarosław Kaczyński was formally sworn into office on 14 July, together with his new Council of Ministers, to which only one change had been made—the replacement of Wojciechowski with Stanisław Kluza, hitherto Deputy Minister of Finance. However, Kluza remained in the position only until September, when Gilowska was reappointed as Deputy Prime Minister and Minister of Finance, having been cleared of the accusations levied against her. Also in September President Kaczyński removed Lepper from the Government, following several policy disagreements. In response, the SRP withdrew from the ruling coalition, thereby ending its parliamentary majority. However, in October, a few days prior to a planned parliamentary vote on an opposition-initiated motion for the legislature to dissolve itself and force elections three years earlier than anticipated, Lepper's dismissal was retracted and the alliance between PiS and the SRP revived.

Also in October 2006 both pro- and anti-Government rallies were held in Warsaw, following the broadcast in late September of a video purporting to show an aide of Prime Minister Kaczyński attempting to buy the support of a member of the opposition. There were numerous demands for the Prime Minister to resign over the furore, a source of embarrassment for PiS, which had secured election, at least partially, on the strength of its pledge to combat corruption. The Prime Minister refuted any claim of wrongdoing, insisting that his aide had been engaged in legitimate political bargaining. In local elections held in the following month, PiS performed well overall, but crucially lost the mayoralty of Warsaw, which was secured by the PO's Hanna Gronkiewicz-Waltz, a former Governor of the central bank, who defeated Marcinkiewicz.

In January 2007 Stanisław Wielgus, the newly appointed Archbishop of Warsaw, succumbed to widespread pressure on him to resign, shortly before he was to be formally inaugurated. Wielgus's decision followed rumours that he had co-operated with the secret services in the 1970s, allegations that Wielgus had initially denied but which, in a highly damaging reversal, he had subsequently conceded to be true. In March new legislation entered into effect, dramatically expanding the remit of existing procedures intended to prevent those who had formerly collaborated with the communist-era secret services from acceding to positions of power. Previously, only those holding public office (approximately 30,000 people) had been required to declare whether or not they had co-operated with the secret services; henceforth, this was also to include, *inter alia*, teachers, journalists and state company executives, increasing the number to whom the law applied to as many as 700,000 people, who were given until 15 May to submit their declarations; furthermore, those found not to have divulged any past collaboration would be liable to a ban on practising their profession for up to 10 years, and even those who openly admitted to having assisted the secret services could be dismissed. The so-called lustration law deeply divided opinion among the Polish population. In May the Constitutional Tribunal ruled that the legislation was unconstitutional.

In February 2007 the Minister of National Defence, Radosław Sikorski, tendered his resignation, following policy differences with Prime Minister Kaczyński; he was replaced by a former head of the presidential chancellery, Aleksander Szczygło. In the same month Ludwik Dorn resigned the internal affairs portfolio (while initially retaining the post of Deputy Prime Minister), owing to disagreement with the Prime Minister. A former Prosecutor-General, Janusz Kaczmarek, became the new Minister of Internal Affairs and Administration. Andrzej Krawczyk, foreign policy adviser to the President, was dismissed in March, owing to his alleged collaboration with the communist-era secret services in 1982. (Although Krawczyk denied the accusation and was exonerated by a court in the same month, the President refused to rescind the dismissal.) In April Dorn was elected Marshal of the Sejm, replacing Marek Jurek who had recently resigned after the chamber's failure to adopt a constitutional amendment enforcing stricter legislation on abortion. Jurek also resigned from PiS to form a new party, the Right of the Republic (PR), which was to emphasize pro-life and other traditionalist Christian policies. In May Przemysław Gosiewski was appointed as a Deputy Prime Minister. In early July Prime Minister Kaczyński again removed Lepper from his government post, on the grounds that he was under investigation for corrupt practice in the designation of agricultural land. The Minister of Sports was also dismissed, after allegations of corruption. Lepper announced that his SRP would provisionally remain in the Government, after deputies threatened to divide the party. However, on 13 August President Kaczyński dismissed the remaining SRP representatives and the LPR members from the Government, thereby ending the ruling coalition; they were replaced by PiS representatives on an interim basis, and it was announced that early legislative elections were to be organized. Proposals that received widespread publicity at this time, for the merger of the LPR and the SRP, failed to come to fruition.

On 7 September 2007 the Sejm voted to dissolve itself and elections to both parliamentary chambers were officially scheduled for 21 October. Prime Minister Kaczyński dismissed all 15 government ministers to prevent a motion of no confidence planned by the PO; they were subsequently reappointed on an interim basis. At the elections to the Sejm, conducted on 21 October, the PO obtained 209 seats, receiving 41.5% of the votes cast, with PiS receiving 166 seats (32.1% of the votes); an SLD-led coalition, known as Left and Democrats (LiD), secured 53 seats

(13.2% of the votes), and the PSL 31 seats (8.9% of the votes). The rate of participation was recorded at 53.8% of the electorate. Later in October Giertych resigned from the leadership of the LPR (which had contested the elections in a coalition with the PR), after it failed to secure parliamentary representation. On 5 November Prime Minister Kaczyński submitted the resignation of his minority Government. On 9 November President Kaczyński nominated Tusk, as leader of PO, as Prime Minister. Tusk reached a coalition agreement with the PSL; together, the PO and the PSL held 240 seats in the 460-member Sejm (and thus required the support of the LiD for the approval of motions that required a two-thirds' majority). The new PO-PSL Government was approved by 238 of the votes cast in the Sejm. Also in November, Lepper was formally charged with sexual misconduct against female employees. Although Jarosław Kaczyński won a vote of confidence in his leadership of PiS at a party congress in December, increasing divisions within the party were demonstrated by the defection of three deputies from the PiS faction in the Sejm.

After 1991 close relations were retained with the Czech Republic, Hungary and Slovakia through the structures of the Visegrad Group and the Central European Free Trade Agreement, and also with other countries of the Baltic region. In 1991–92 Poland established diplomatic relations with the former republics of the USSR, developing particularly strong links with Ukraine. In May 1997 the Polish and Ukrainian Presidents signed a declaration of reconciliation, which included the condemnation of the killing of tens of thousands of Poles by Ukrainian nationalists in 1942–43, and of the 'Wisła Operation' of 1947, in which more than 100,000 Ukrainians were forcibly deported from their homes in south-east Poland. During 1998 and early 1999 Poland sought to reassure Ukraine (as well as Russia) that good relations and mutual co-operation between their two countries would continue following Poland's entry into NATO in March 1999 and its eventual membership of the EU. In November and December 2004 President Kwaśniewski mediated in negotiations in Ukraine (q.v.) aimed at resolving a political crisis that had resulted from a disputed presidential election in that country. Following a new election in December, Kwaśniewski attended the inauguration of the new President of Ukraine, Viktor Yushchenko, in January 2005. The Polish Government later welcomed the new Ukrainian Government's pro-European stance, pledging to assist with Ukraine's efforts to join the EU.

All former Soviet combat troops had been withdrawn from Poland by November 1992, and the last remaining (non-combat) Russian military presence was withdrawn in September 1994. Relations between Poland and Russia deteriorated after Poland acceded to NATO in 1999. However, tensions eased in July 2000, when President Kwaśniewski became the first Polish head of state to pay an official visit to Moscow since the collapse of communist rule, and relations improved further in January 2002, when Russian President Vladimir Putin made an official visit to Poland. However, the Polish Government continued to oppose Russia's plans to construct a natural gas pipeline to Slovakia via Poland, bypassing Ukraine, as it feared that the project threatened adversely to affect Polish-Ukrainian relations. Relations were also perceived to have deteriorated following President Kwaśniewski's mediation in Ukraine in late 2004 (see above). In 2005 Poland expressed concern at plans to construct a North European Natural Gas Pipeline between Russia and Germany, under the Baltic Sea, effectively bypassing Poland. Relations suffered a marked deterioration in late 2005, when Russia imposed a ban on imports of meat and other agricultural products from Poland, ostensibly owing to health and sanitation concerns, but which Poland claimed was a politically motivated decision intended to punish a former satellite state. Following Russia's continued refusal to lift the ban, in November 2006 the Polish Government vetoed the commencement of EU negotiations on a new strategic partnership agreement with Russia. In April 2007 Prime Minister Kaczyński announced that Poland would retract its veto only when Russia had removed the import restrictions. Kaczyński attracted the support of the President of the European Commission, José Manuel Durão Barroso, who urged the Russian Government to comply with the request, following an inspection of Polish meat-processing plants by a team of EU and Russian experts, which had indicated that Russian health concerns were unfounded. Shortly after his installation as premier in November (see above), Donald Tusk announced that Poland was to end its objections to the initiation of negotiations on Russia's entry to the Organisation for Economic Co-operation and Development (OECD), which was required for membership of the World Trade Organization (WTO). In December the Russian Government announced its decision to end the embargo on meat imports from Poland. In January 2008 the Polish Minister of Defence announced that US officials had agreed to hold discussions on a possible US commitment to support Polish air defences in exchange for the proposed deployment in Poland (and in the Czech Republic) of US anti-missile interceptors as part of the US national missile defence system. It was reported that the Polish Minister of Foreign Affairs, Radosław Sikorski, when meeting his Russian counterpart, Sergei Lavrov, in Moscow later that month, had agreed that his Government would consult the Russian leadership regarding the installation of the interceptor units. However, Sikorski, during a visit to Washington, DC, at the end of January, accused Russia of threatening to aim nuclear missiles at Poland in the event that it agreed to host the units. In March Poland announced that it was prepared to accept Russian inspections of any future US anti-missile installations on its territory. At a NATO summit meeting, which took place in Bucharest, Romania, in early April, member states endorsed the US plans to position missile defence bases in the Czech Republic and Poland.

On 1 October 2003 the Polish Government introduced visa requirements for Belarusian, Moldovan, Russian and Ukrainian citizens, in accordance with EU policy, although simplified visa arrangements had been agreed for residents of the Russian exclave of Kaliningrad. In July 2005 the offices of the Union of Poles in Belarus were seized by the Belarusian authorities, and the newly elected leadership replaced, apparently owing to fears that the organization might participate in the eventual overthrow of the regime of Belarusian President Alyaksandr Lukashenka. Meanwhile, Polish journalists in Belarus were compelled to pay large fines, after protesting at the suppression by the authorities of the country's main Polish-language newspaper. In late July Poland recalled its ambassador to Belarus, and appealed to the EU for assistance in protecting the Polish minority there. The Polish ambassador returned to Belarus in October. Tensions arose again prior to the presidential election held in Belarus in March 2006. Polish journalists and a number of Polish parliamentarians were refused entry to Belarus, and a former Polish ambassador to Belarus was imprisoned for 15 days after participating in an unauthorized protest demonstration; in late March Belarus briefly recalled its ambassador to Poland.

In November 1990 Poland and Germany signed a border treaty confirming their post-1945 borders, and in June 1991 the two countries signed a treaty of 'good neighbourliness and friendly co-operation'. Poland welcomed the announcement made by the German Government in February 1999 of the establishment of a compensation fund for over 2m. Poles who were employed as forced labour in German companies during the Second World War. Following a campaign by Polish veteran groups, in May Polish and German representatives began complex negotiations regarding the payment of compensation by several leading German firms. In mid-December a compensation agreement was signed, whereby DM 10,000m. was to be paid by German companies into a compensation fund; however, payments were subject to delays. The German Chancellor, Gerhard Schröder, attended a ceremony in Warsaw in August 2004 to mark the 60th anniversary of the city's failed uprising against the Nazi occupation, becoming the first German leader to participate in such an event. In September, however, a resolution adopted by the Sejm urging Germany to pay reparations for the Nazi invasion of Poland in 1939 threatened to strain relations between the two countries. Both the German and Polish Governments rejected the resolution, which was regarded as a response to demands from groups of Germans for the restitution of ancestral property lost when Poland's borders shifted westward at the end of the Second World War. In November 2004, at a joint press conference following talks in Kraków, Belka and Schröder announced that a joint commission had concluded that there was no legal basis for compensation claims to be filed. The two leaders each appointed a special adviser to co-ordinate bilateral relations. In January 2005 the German President, Horst Köhler, attended a ceremony in Poland to commemorate the 60th anniversary of the liberation of the Nazi concentration camp at Oświęcim (Auschwitz). In August an exhibition devoted to the expulsion of Germans from Eastern Europe in the aftermath of the Second World War provoked outrage in Poland, the Government of which argued that it sought to rewrite history by portraying Germany as the victim of the war; the acting Mayor of Warsaw, former Prime

Minister Marcinkiewicz, cancelled a planned visit to Berlin in protest.

Andrzej Byrt, the Polish ambassador to Germany, was dismissed following his public criticism of President Kaczyński for the latter's angry response to satirical comments published about him and his brother in a German newspaper in July 2006. President Kaczyński failed to attend a tripartite summit with German Federal Chancellor Angela Merkel and French President Jacques Chirac, ostensibly owing to ill health, but his withdrawal was widely interpreted as an implicit rebuff to his German counterpart, who had ignored his demands that action be taken against the German newspaper in question. In March 2007 Merkel met President Kaczyński during an official visit to Poland. In December the new Prime Minister, Donald Tusk, met Merkel in Berlin in an effort to improve bilateral relations; issues discussed included the proposed construction of the North European Natural Gas Pipeline between Russia and Germany (see above).

Poland joined the Council of Europe (see p. 225) in November 1991. In December Poland signed an association agreement with the European Community (now EU), and in April 1994 Poland made a formal application for membership of the EU; accession negotiations began in March 1998. In December 2002 Poland, and nine other countries, were formally invited to join the EU from May 2004. In February 2003 the Government reached agreement with the EU on farm subsidies. A national referendum on EU membership took place in June 2003, at which some 77% of the votes cast by 58.9% of the electorate were in favour of accession. Poland became a full member of the EU on 1 May 2004, as scheduled. On 13 June the first elections to the European Parliament to be held in Poland were marked by a very low rate of voter participation, of 20.9%. The PO secured 15 of the 54 seats available, while the LPR won 10 seats, PiS seven seats and the SRP six seats. The ruling SLD-UP coalition took only five seats. In December 2007, following the approval of legislation in the Sejm in August, Poland, together with eight other nations, implemented the EU's Schengen Agreement on freedom of travel, effectively removing border controls between those states subject to the Agreement.

Poland, in common with other central and eastern European countries, regarded membership of NATO as a priority in guaranteeing regional security. In January 1994 Poland announced that it was to join that organization's 'Partnership for Peace' programme, and a defence co-operation agreement was duly signed with NATO in March. In May Poland was granted associate partnership status in Western European Union (see p. 426). In July 1997 Poland, together with the Czech Republic and Hungary, was officially invited to commence negotiations on potential membership of NATO. A protocol providing for the accession of the three states was signed in December, and Poland, the Czech Republic and Hungary secured full membership of NATO on 12 March 1999. The Polish Government strongly supported the US-led military campaign to remove from power the regime of the Iraqi President, Saddam Hussain, in early 2003, and Poland was subsequently offered the opportunity to manage one of three reconstruction zones in Iraq, under overall US command. In September the USA transferred responsibility for security in an area of central Iraq to a 9,500-strong multinational force led by Poland, which contributed some 2,500 troops. In early 2005 Poland reduced its military contingent in Iraq to 1,700 troops, following elections there. Although the Polish Minister of Defence announced in April that the country's troops would be withdrawn from Iraq by the end of that year, the new Government elected in September retracted this decision. In September 2007 President Kaczyński ordered that the deployment of 1,100 Polish troops in Afghanistan, which had been due to end in the following month, be extended until the end of October 2008. Following his installation as Prime Minister in November 2007, Donald Tusk announced his decision to withdraw the 900 Polish troops in Iraq, despite the continued opposition of President Kaczyński; in early 2008 it was announced that they would leave the country by October.

Government

Under the Constitution, which came into force in October 1997, legislative power is vested in the bicameral Zgromadzenie Narodowe (National Assembly), which is elected for a four-year term and comprises the 100-member Senat (Senate, upper chamber) and the 460-member Sejm (Assembly, lower chamber). The Senat reviews the laws adopted by the Sejm and may propose their rejection. Senators and deputies are elected by universal, direct suffrage. In the Sejm, deputies are elected under a system of proportional representation. Executive power is vested in the President of the Republic, who is directly elected (a second ballot being held if necessary) for a five-year term and may be re-elected only once, and in the appointed Council of Ministers, led by the Prime Minister. The Council of Ministers is responsible for its activities to the Sejm. On 1 January 1999 new legislation on local government came into effect, as a result of which Poland is divided into 16 voivodships (provinces) and 308 powiats (districts).

Defence

As assessed at November 2007, the strength of Poland's active armed forces was estimated to be 127,266 (including an estimated 39,000 conscripts and 8,200 centrally controlled staff): army 79,000, air force 28,466 and navy 11,600. Paramilitary forces of some 21,400 comprised border guards (14,100) and interior ministry units (7,300). Reserves totalled 234,000. In 1988 legislation was enacted permitting conscientious objectors to perform an alternative community service, and from January 2005 compulsory military service was reduced from one year to nine months. State budget expenditure on defence in 2007 was projected at 20,150m. new złotys. In 1994 Poland joined the North Atlantic Treaty Organization's (NATO, see p. 340) 'Partnership for Peace' programme of military co-operation, and it became a full member of the Alliance in March 1999.

Economic Affairs

In 2006, according to the World Bank, Poland's gross national income (GNI), measured at average 2004–06 prices, was US $312,198m., equivalent to $8,190 per head (or $14,830 per head on an international purchasing-power parity basis). During 1996–2006 the population decreased by 0.1%, while gross domestic product (GDP) per head increased, in real terms, at an average annual rate of 4.3%. Overall GDP increased, in real terms, at an average annual rate of 4.2% in 1996–2006; growth was 5.8% in 2006.

Agriculture contributed 4.8% of GDP in 2005, and engaged 15.8% of the employed labour force in 2006. The principal crops are potatoes, sugar beet, wheat, rye and barley. Livestock production is important to the domestic food supply. During 1996–2006 the average annual GDP of the agricultural sector increased, in real terms, by 2.0%; real agricultural GDP decreased by 2.3% in 2005, before increasing by 6.7% in 2006.

Industry (including mining, manufacturing, power and construction) accounted for 30.7% of GDP in 2005, and engaged 30.0% of the employed labour force in 2006. During 1996–2006 industrial GDP increased, in real terms, by an average of 4.6% per year; real industrial GDP increased by 9.1% in 2006.

Mining and quarrying contributed 2.6% of GDP in 2005, and engaged 1.6% of the employed labour force in 2006. Poland is a significant producer of copper, silver and sulphur, and there are also considerable reserves of natural gas. During 1992–96 mining GDP declined at an average annual rate of 1.5%; the sector's GDP declined by an estimated 4.6% in 1998.

The manufacturing sector contributed 18.6% of GDP in 2005, and engaged 20.3% of the employed labour force in 2006. In 1996–2006 manufacturing GDP increased, in real terms, at an average annual rate of 6.7%. Manufacturing GDP increased by 9.1% in 2006.

Energy is derived principally from coal, which satisfied 94.1% of the country's total energy requirements in 2004. In 1998 the Government announced plans to reduce Poland's dependence on coal: it was projected that by 2010 some 15% of power generation would be fuelled by imported natural gas. Mineral fuels and lubricants accounted for 11.4% of the value of merchandise imports in 2005; some 6.5% of electricity generated was exported in 2000.

The services sector contributed 64.5% of GDP in 2005. The sector engaged 54.2% of the employed labour force in 2006. Services expanded rapidly from the early 1990s, with considerable growth in financial services, retailing, tourism and leisure. The GDP of the services sector increased, in real terms, by an average of 3.9% per year in 1996–2006. Real services GDP increased by 4.2% in 2006.

In 2006 Poland recorded a visible trade deficit of US $4,953m., and there was a deficit of $7,925m. on the current account of the balance of payments. In 2006, according to preliminary figures, the principal source of imports was Germany (accounting for 23.9%); other major suppliers were Russia (9.7%), Italy (6.7%) and France (5.5%). Germany was also the principal market for exports (27.2%); other significant purchasers were Italy (6.4%), France (6.3%) and the United Kingdom (5.7%). The principal exports in 2005 were machinery and transport equipment, basic manufactures, miscellaneous manufactured articles, food and live animals, chemicals and related products, and mineral fuels and lubricants. The principal imports in that year were machinery and transport equipment, basic manufactures, chemicals and related products, mineral fuels and lubricants, miscellaneous manufactured articles, and food and live animals.

According to government figures, Poland's overall budgetary deficit for 2006 was 22,420m. new złotys (equivalent to some 2.1% of GDP). Poland's external debt totalled US $98,821m. at the end of 2005, of which $35,094m. was long-term public debt. In that year the cost of debt-servicing was equivalent to 28.8% of the value of exports of goods and services. The annual rate of inflation averaged 3.5% in 1999–2006. Consumer prices increased by 1.0% in 2006. In 2006 13.8% of the labour force were registered as unemployed.

Poland is a member, as a 'Country of Operations', of the European Bank for Reconstruction and Development (EBRD, see p. 239). Poland joined the WTO in 1995 and the OECD in 1996. In May 2004 Poland became a full member of the European Union (EU, see p. 244).

In the 1990s Poland undertook an ambitious, market-orientated programme of economic reform. Poland's economic performance was adversely affected by the Russian financial crisis in August 1998. However, economic recovery was evident in 2002, and was further sustained by Poland's accession to the EU in 2004, with a concomitant increase in exports to other member nations. Following Poland's accession to the EU, unemployment declined, as a result of increasing numbers of Poles moving abroad to find work, notably to the United Kingdom and Ireland. It was estimated that some 1.95m. Poles, equating to over 10% of the work-force, had emigrated by the end of 2006. Despite these figures, unemployment in Poland remained high, at 11.5% in February 2008. Meanwhile, in March 2006 the EU initiated legal proceedings against Poland, which it accused of protectionism, after the Government continued to obstruct attempts by an Italian company to merge two majority foreign-owned banks in Poland, thereby challenging the influence of the leading state-owned Polish bank. According to the central bank, foreign direct investment in Poland increased by 46.6% in 2006, totalling US $15,190m. in that year. The Government of Prime Minister Donald Tusk that took office in late 2007 favoured a strategy of liberalizing the labour market in order to improve productivity, privatizing state enterprises and reducing bureaucracy. The need to reduce the budgetary deficit to less than 3% of GDP remained the most challenging element of the EU's financial criteria for the adoption of the common European currency, the euro. The new central bank Governor appointed in January 2007 advocated far greater caution towards the adoption of the currency than had his predecessor, and by 2008 it appeared unlikely that Poland would adopt the currency before 2012. Meanwhile, although Poland has remained reliant on imported energy, the Minister of the Economy advocated utilizing domestic energy resources or risking imported inflation, owing to increasing international fuel prices. The IMF anticipated that the rate of inflation would rise to 4.1% during 2008, while GDP growth of 4.9% was forecast.

Education

Education is free and compulsory for eight years, between the ages of seven and 14 years. Before the age of seven, children may attend crèches (żłobki) and kindergartens (przedszkola). In 1998/99 49.6% of children between the ages of three and six years attended kindergarten, and in 2001/02 99.7% of six-year-olds attended pre-school educational establishments. A reform of primary and secondary education was undertaken in 1999–2004. Basic schooling begins at seven years of age with primary school (szkoła podstawowa), for which there is a common curriculum throughout the country. Primary education lasts for six years, divided into two equal cycles. Lower secondary education (at the gimnazjum) is compulsory for three years. In 2003/04 net enrolment at primary schools included 97.3% of children in the relevant age-group and enrolment in lower secondary schools included 90.0% of children in the relevant age-group. Three years of education at general secondary schools (liceum ogólnokształcące) commence at the age of 16 years, for pupils who successfully complete the entrance examination; in 2000/01 enrolment at secondary schools was equivalent to 90.1% of children in the appropriate age-group. At this level, there are general secondary schools (accounting for 34%), vocational technical schools (technika zawodowe—56%) and basic vocational schools (zasadnicze szkoły—20%). The last provide courses consisting of three days' theoretical and three days' practical training per week, and in addition some general education is given. New post-secondary schools (szkoła policealna) were introduced in 1999 to prepare students from technical and vocational schools for skilled jobs. Curricula are standardized throughout Poland. In 2003/04 there were 400 higher education establishments in Poland, including 17 universities and 22 technical universities. In 2003 state budgetary expenditure on basic education amounted to 1,498m. new złotys (0.8% of total expenditure), while 7,071m. złotys (3.7%) were allocated to higher education.

Public Holidays

2008: 1 January (New Year's Day), 24 March (Easter Monday), 1 May (Labour Day), 3 May (Polish National Day, Proclamation of 1791 Constitution), 22 May (Corpus Christi), 15 August (Assumption), 1 November (All Saints' Day), 11 November (Independence Day), 25–26 December (Christmas).

2009: 1 January (New Year's Day), 13 April (Easter Monday), 1 May (Labour Day), 3 May (Polish National Day, Proclamation of 1791 Constitution), 11 June (Corpus Christi), 15 August (Assumption), 1 November (All Saints' Day), 11 November (Independence Day), 25–26 December (Christmas).

Weights and Measures

The metric system is in force.

Statistical Survey

Source (unless otherwise indicated): Główny Urząd Statystyczny (Central Statistical Office), 00-925 Warsaw, Al. Niepodległości 208; tel. (22) 6083161; fax (22) 6083869; internet www.stat.gov.pl.

Area and Population

AREA, POPULATION AND DENSITY

Area (sq km)	
Land	304,465
Inland water	8,220
Total	312,685*
Population (census results)†	
7 December 1988	37,879,105
20 May 2002	
Males	18,516,403
Females	19,713,677
Total	38,230,080
Population (official estimates at 31 December)†	
2005	38,157,055
2006	38,125,479
Density (per sq km) at 31 December 2006	121.9

* 120,728 sq miles.
† Figures exclude civilian aliens within the country and include civilian nationals temporarily outside the country.

VOIVODSHIPS
(official estimates at 31 December 2006)

	Area (sq km)	Population ('000)	Density*	Principal city
Dolnośląskie	19,948	2,882.3	144.5	Wrocław
Kujawsko-Pomorskie	17,970	2,066.4	115.0	Bydgoszcz
Lubelskie	25,114	2,172.8	86.5	Lublin
Lubuskie	13,984	1,008.5	72.1	Gorzów Wlkp†
Łódzkie	18,219	2,566.2	140.9	Łódź
Malopolskie	15,144	3,271.2	216.0	Kraków
Mazowieckie	35,597	5,171.7	145.3	Warsaw
Opolskie	9,412	1,041.9	110.7	Opole
Podkarpackie	17,926	2,097.6	117.0	Rzeszów
Podlaskie	20,180	1,196.1	59.3	Białystok
Pomorskie	18,293	2,203.6	120.5	Gdańsk
Śląskie	12,294	4,669.1	379.8	Katowice
Świętokrzyskie	11,672	1,279.8	109.6	Kielce
Warmińsko-Mazurskie	24,203	1,426.9	59.0	Olsztyn
Wielkopolskie	29,826	3,378.5	113.3	Poznań
Zachodniopomorskie	22,902	1,692.8	73.9	Szczecin
Total	**312,685**	**38,125.5**	**121.9**	—

* Per sq km.
† Gorzów Wielkopolski.

PRINCIPAL TOWNS
(official estimates at 31 December 2005)

Warszawa (Warsaw, the capital)	1,697,596	Bielsko-Biała	176,684
Łódź	767,628	Olsztyn	174,473
Kraków	756,629	Rzeszów	158,539
Wrocław	635,932	Ruda Śląska	146,582
Poznań	567,882	Rybnik	141,580
Gdańsk	458,053	Tychy	131,153
Szczecin	411,119	Dąbrowa Górnicza	130,128
Bydgoszcz	366,074	Opole	128,268
Lublin	354,967	Płock	127,461
Katowice	317,220	Elbląg	127,275
Białystok	291,823	Wałbrzych	126,465
Gdynia	252,791	Gorzów Wielkopolski	125,467
Częstochowa	246,890	Włocławek	119,939
Radom	227,018	Zielona Góra	118,221
Sosnowiec	226,034	Tarnów	117,560
Kielce	208,193	Chorzów	114,686
Toruń	208,007	Kalisz	108,841
Gliwice	199,451	Koszalin	107,886
Zabrze	191,247	Legnica	105,750
Bytom	187,943		

BIRTHS, MARRIAGES AND DEATHS

	Registered live births Number	Rate (per 1,000)	Registered marriages Number	Rate (per 1,000)	Registered deaths Number	Rate (per 1,000)
1999	382,002	9.9	219,398	5.7	381,415	9.9
2000	378,348	9.8	211,150	5.5	368,028	9.5
2001	368,205	9.5	195,122	5.0	363,220	9.4
2002	353,765	9.3	191,935	5.0	359,486	9.4
2003	351,072	9.2	195,446	5.1	365,230	9.6
2004	356,131	9.3	191,824	5.0	363,522	9.5
2005	366,095	9.6	206,916	5.4	368,300*	9.7
2006	374,244	9.8	226,181	5.9	369,686	9.7

* Figure is rounded.

Expectation of life (years at birth, WHO estimates): 75.0 (males 70.8; females 79.3) in 2005 (Source: WHO, *World Health Statistics*).

IMMIGRATION AND EMIGRATION
('000)*

	2004	2005	2006
Immigrants	9.5	9.3	10.8
Emigrants	18.9	22.2	46.9

* Figures refer to immigrants arriving for permanent residence in Poland and emigrants leaving for permanent residence abroad.

ECONOMICALLY ACTIVE POPULATION*
('000 persons aged 15 years and over)

	2004	2005	2006
Agriculture, hunting and forestry	2,472	2,439	2,294
Fishing	12	13	10
Mining and quarrying	227	225	237
Manufacturing	2,740	2,831	2,988
Electricity, gas and water supply	222	228	223
Construction	789	843	925
Wholesale and retail trade; repair of motor vehicles, motorcycles, and personal and household goods	1,997	2,020	2,060
Hotels and restaurants	236	247	272
Transport, storage and communications	832	862	942
Financial intermediation	271	294	329

POLAND

—continued	2004	2005	2006
Real estate, renting and business activities	799	822	836
Public administration and defence; compulsory social security	865	892	917
Education	1,060	1,103	1,140
Health and social work	824	820	871
Other community, social and personal service activities	436	459	534
Private households with employed persons	15	12	11
Activities not adequately defined	—	5	—
Total employed	13,795	14,116	14,594
Unemployed	3,230	3,045	2,344
Total labour force	17,025	17,161	16,938

* Excluding regular military personnel living in barracks, and conscripts.

Note: Totals may not be equal to the sum of component parts, owing to rounding.

Source: ILO.

Health and Welfare

KEY INDICATORS

Total fertility rate (children per woman, 2005)	1.2
Under-5 mortality rate (per 1,000 live births, 2005)	8
HIV/AIDS (% of persons aged 15–49, 2005)	0.1
Physicians (per 1,000 head, 2004)	2.47
Hospital beds (per 1,000 head, 2004)	5.3
Health expenditure (2004): US $ per head (PPP)	814.1
Health expenditure (2004): % of GDP	6.2
Health expenditure (2004): public (% of total)	68.6
Human Development Index (2005): ranking	37
Human Development Index (2005): value	0.870

For sources and definitions, see explanatory note on p. vi.

Agriculture

PRINCIPAL CROPS
('000 metric tons)

	2004	2005	2006
Wheat	9,892.5	8,771.0	7,059.7
Barley	3,570.8	3,582.0	3,161.0
Maize	2,344.0	1,945.4	1,260.7
Rye	4,280.7	3,404.0	2,621.6
Oats	1,430.5	1,324.0	1,034.7
Triticale (wheat-rye hybrid)	3,723.3	3,903.0	3,197.0
Mixed grain	4,321.9	3,916.4	3,379.0
Potatoes	13,998.6	10,369.0	8,982.0
Sugar beet	12,730.4	11,731.0	11,474.8
Rapeseed	1,632.9	1,449.8	1,651.5
Cabbages	1,371.0	1,381.6	1,249.1
Tomatoes	212.7	600.7	651.6
Cauliflowers	205.7	238.8	250.4
Cucumbers and gherkins	255.9	468.5	491.9
Dry onions	865.7	714.1	590.2
Carrots	927.9	929.0	833.2
Mushrooms*	130.0	135.0	135.0
Apples	2,521.5	2,075.0	2,304.9
Pears	87.3	59.3	59.3
Sour (Morello) cherries	201.7	37.5	38.4
Plums and sloes	132.6	91.4	93.6
Strawberries	185.6	184.6	193.7
Currants	194.5	186.8	194.5

* FAO estimates.

Aggregate production ('000 metric tons, may include official, semi-official or estimated data): Total cereals 29,635 in 2004, 26,928 in 2005, 21,776 in 2006; Total roots and tubers 14,021 in 2004, 10,378 in 2005, 8,981 in 2006; Total vegetables (incl. melons) 5,746 in 2004, 5,621 in 2005, 5,282 in 2006; Total fruits (excl. melons) 3,520 in 2004, 2,920 in 2005, 3,212 in 2006.

Source: FAO.

LIVESTOCK
('000 head year ending September)

	2004	2005	2006
Horses	330	312	307
Cattle	5,353	5,483	5,606
Pigs	16,988	18,112	18,881
Sheep	318	316	301
Chickens	147,981	134,424	124,870
Geese and guinea fowls	4,899	4,418	3,943
Turkeys	8,660	7,658	8,099
Ducks	6,082	6,299	4,895

Source: FAO.

LIVESTOCK PRODUCTS
('000 metric tons)

	2004	2005	2006
Cattle meat	310.5	309.5	367.5
Pig meat	1,956.0	1,955.5	2,092.4
Horse meat	7.5	10.0	9.6
Game meat*	6.0	6.0	6.0
Chicken meat*	876.0	980.0	960.0
Duck meat*	18.1	18.2	16.0
Turkey meat*	23.0	25.0	25.0
Cows' milk	11,822.0	11,933.0	11,982.4
Hen eggs	514.3	539.8	537.2
Honey	12.0	10.0	13.5

* FAO estimates.

Source: FAO.

Forestry

ROUNDWOOD REMOVALS
('000 cubic metres, excl. bark)

	2004	2005	2006
Sawlogs, veneer logs and logs for sleepers	13,076	12,715	13,142
Pulpwood	13,960	13,640	13,570
Other industrial wood	2,301	2,176	2,055
Fuel wood	3,396	3,413	3,617
Total	32,733	31,944	32,384

Source: FAO.

SAWNWOOD PRODUCTION
('000 cubic metres, incl. railway sleepers)

	2004	2005	2006
Coniferous (softwood)	3,102	2,813	3,018
Broadleaved (hardwood)	641	547	589
Total	3,743	3,360	3,607

Source: FAO.

POLAND

Fishing

('000 metric tons, live weight)

	2003	2004	2005
Capture	180.3	192.1	156.2
Freshwater fishes	22.8	23.5	23.1
European flounder	—	8.7	11.1
Flatfishes	7.3	—	—
Atlantic cod	17.3	16.5	13.8
Atlantic herring	30.7	27.9	22.9
European sprat	84.1	95.8	74.3
Antarctic krill	8.9	9.0	4.3
Aquaculture	34.5	35.3	36.6
Common carp	20.5	18.3	18.6
Rainbow trout	11.7	14.6	15.7
Total catch	**214.8**	**227.4**	**192.9**

Source: FAO.

Mining

('000 metric tons, unless otherwise indicated)

	2002	2003*	2004
Hard coal	103,546	103,016	101,230
Brown coal (incl. lignite)	58,210	60,919	61,197
Crude petroleum	721	765	886
Salt (unrefined)	3,558	4,660	5,142
Native sulphur	760	762	821
Copper ore (metric tons)†	568,000	570,000	590,000
Lead ore (metric tons)†	73,500	55,000	51,000
Magnesite ore—crude	24,000	24,000	24,000*
Silver (metric tons)†	1,222	1,237	1,344
Zinc ore (metric tons)†	171,200	174,700	175,000
Natural gas (million cu metres)	5,259	5,315	5,400*

* Estimate(s).
† Figures refer to the metal content of ores.

Source: US Geological Survey.

2005: Hard coal ('000 metric tons) 98,275; Lignite ('000 metric tons) 61,589; Natural gas (million cu metres) 5,703.

Industry

SELECTED PRODUCTS

('000 metric tons, unless otherwise indicated)

	2004	2005	2006
Sausages and smoked meat	856	756	822
Refined sugar	2,222	2,258	1,755
Margarine	355	348	345
Beer ('000 hl)	30,108	31,572	34,084
Wine, mead and other fermented beverages ('000 hl)	3,236	2,765	2,680
Cigarettes (million)	86,597	102,355	110,976
Leather footwear ('000 pairs)	16,825	14,904	14,642
Mechanical wood pulp	82,000	86,200	64,500
Chemical wood pulp	791,000	802,000	824,600
Newsprint	217	221	191
Rubber tyres ('000)[1]	50,039	47,056	43,003
Sulphuric acid—100%	1,811	1,807	1,907
Caustic soda—96%	97	84	90
Soda ash—98%	1,120	1,136	1,119
Nitrogenous fertilizers (a)[2]	4,662	4,908	4,850
Phosphate fertilizers (b)[2]	453	410	359
Motor spirit—Petrol[3]	3,784	4,178	4,257
Distillate fuel oils	5,323	6,140	n.a.
Residual fuel oils	4,523	3,362	n.a.
Coke-oven coke	7,752	5,610	7,458
Cement	12,566	12,646	14,688
Pig-iron[4]	6,427	4,481	5,333
Crude steel	10,578	8,336	9,992
Rolled steel products	7,507	6,188	n.a.
Aluminium—unwrought[5]	45.8	42.7	38.7
Refined copper—unwrought	547	556	556

Statistical Survey

—continued	2004	2005	2006
Refined lead—unwrought	73.7	75.1	58.5
Zinc—unwrought[5]	131	114	110
Radio receivers ('000)	35	15	18
Television receivers ('000)	7,012	6,732	9,427
Merchant ships launched (gross reg. tons)	582	722	692
Passenger motor cars ('000)	522	540	632
Lorries and tractors (number)	59,002	67,683	76,412
Domestic washing machines ('000)	1,206	1,481	1,637
Domestic refrigerators and freezers ('000)	1,280	1,674	1,976
Electric energy (million kWh)	154,132	156,935	161,489

* Source: FAO.
[1] Tyres for passenger motor cars and commercial vehicles, including inner tubes and tyres for animal-drawn road vehicles, and tyres for non-agricultural machines and equipment.
[2] Fertilizer production is measured in terms of (a) nitrogen or (b) phosphoric acid. Phosphate fertilizers include ground rock phosphate.
[3] Including synthetic products.
[4] Including blast furnace ferro-alloys.
[5] Figures refer to both primary and secondary metal. Zinc production includes zinc dust and remelted zinc.

Finance

CURRENCY AND EXCHANGE RATES

Monetary Units

100 groszy (singular: grosz) = 1 new złoty.

Sterling, Dollar and Euro Equivalents (31 December 2007)
£1 sterling = 4.878 new złotys;
US $1 = 2.435 new złotys;
€1 = 3.585 new złotys;
100 new złotys = £20.50 = $41.07 = €27.90.

Average Exchange Rate (new złotys per US dollar)
2005 3.2355
2006 3.1032
2007 2.7680

Note: On 1 January 1995 Poland introduced a new złoty, equivalent to 10,000 of the former units.

GOVERNMENT FINANCE

(general government transactions, non-cash basis, '000 million new zlotys)

Summary of Balances

	2004	2005	2006
Revenue	347.17	379.39	413.27
Less Expense	389.88	409.24	435.69
Net operating balance	**−42.71**	**−29.85**	**−22.42**
Less Net acquisition of non-financial assets	8.95	12.49	17.09
Net lending/borrowing	**−51.67**	**−42.34**	**−39.51**

Revenue

	2004	2005	2006
Taxes	181.68	203.67	228.04
Taxes on income, profits and capital gains	54.24	63.10	74.04
Taxes on goods and services	109.73	122.57	134.49
Social contributions	113.75	120.84	128.89
Grants	5.57	6.83	6.85
Other revenue	46.18	48.05	49.49
Total	**347.17**	**379.39**	**413.27**

POLAND

Statistical Survey

Expense/Outlays

Expense by economic type	2004	2005	2006
Compensation of employees	94.21	98.87	104.35
Use of goods and services	53.40	55.61	60.86
Consumption of fixed capital	18.83	19.71	20.76
Interest	25.74	27.52	25.89
Subsidies	5.26	5.09	7.33
Grants	2.37	10.12	10.06
Social benefits	169.52	170.95	183.47
Other expense	20.55	21.38	22.99
Total	**389.88**	**409.24**	**435.69**

Outlays by functions of government*	2004	2005	2006
General public services	53.99	60.40	60.03
Defence	11.75	12.31	14.61
Public order and safety	17.14	19.04	20.23
Economic affairs	29.46	35.37	43.68
Environmental protection	6.04	6.05	6.20
Housing and community amenities	12.37	10.74	10.23
Health	40.63	41.36	46.63
Recreation, culture and religion	7.61	8.05	9.65
Education	50.85	54.75	58.48
Social protection	168.99	173.67	183.04
Total	**398.84**	**421.73**	**452.78**

* Including net acquisition of non-financial assets.

Source: IMF, *Government Finance Statistics Yearbook*.

INTERNATIONAL RESERVES
(US $ million at 31 December)

	2004	2005	2006
Gold (national valuation)	1,448.8	1,697.2	2,103.1
IMF special drawing rights	70.1	77.8	89.1
Reserve position in IMF	700.9	299.0	174.9
Foreign exchange	34,552.8	40,486.9	46,107.0
Total	**36,772.6**	**42,560.9**	**48,474.1**

Source: IMF, *International Financial Statistics*.

MONEY SUPPLY
(million new złotys at 31 December)

	2003	2004	2005
Currency outside banks	49,417	50,776	57,155
Demand deposits at commercial banks	84,142	95,278	117,575
Total money (incl. others)	**133,576**	**146,098**	**174,834**

Source: IMF, *International Financial Statistics*.

COST OF LIVING
(Consumer Price Index; base: 2000 = 100)

	2004	2005	2006
Food (incl. alcoholic beverages)	108.6	110.6	110.6
Electricity, gas and other fuels	124.7	129.5	138.1
Clothing (incl. footwear)	94.6	89.5	83.3
Rent	133.4	138.2	142.0
All items (incl. others)	**112.2**	**114.6**	**115.8**

Source: ILO.

NATIONAL ACCOUNTS
(million new złotys at current prices)

Composition of the Gross National Product

	1998	1999	2000
Compensation of employees	250,314.0	276,363.0	297,820.6
Operating surplus / Consumption of fixed capital	227,649.6	250,783.0	293,518.2
Gross domestic product (GDP) at factor cost	**477,963.6**	**527,146.0**	**591,338.8**
Indirect taxes	82,681.1	94,680.5	100,153.3
Less Subsidies	6,763.1	6,711.2	6,566.0
GDP in purchasers' values	**553,881.6**	**615,115.3**	**684,926.1**
Factor income received from abroad / *Less* Factor income paid abroad	−4,115.6	−4,007.2	−6,350.1
Gross national product	**549,766.0**	**611,108.1**	**678,576.0**

Expenditure on the Gross Domestic Product

	2004	2005	2006
Final consumption expenditure	756,034	795,365	844,924
Households / Non-profit institutions serving households	592,375	616,336	656,658
General government	163,659	179,029	188,266
Gross capital formation	185,542	188,656	213,094
Gross fixed capital formation	167,158	178,391	210,496
Changes in inventories / Acquisitions, less disposals, of valuables	18,384	10,265	2,598
Total domestic expenditure	**941,576**	**984,021**	**1,058,018**
Exports of goods and services	346,631	364,658	427,098
Less Imports of goods and services	364,959	368,013	434,197
GDP in purchasers' values	**923,248**	**980,666**	**1,050,919**

Source: IMF, *International Financial Statistics*.

Gross Domestic Product by Economic Activity

	2003	2004	2005
Agriculture, hunting, forestry and fishing	20,875	41,749	41,160
Construction	40,432	44,583	49,812
Other industry	173,907	207,299	214,619
Mining and quarrying	n.a.	20,683	22,300
Manufacturing	136,721	156,687	159,945
Electricity, gas and water	n.a.	29,929	32,374
Market services	357,893	523,481	555,348
Non-market services	116,059		
Gross value added in basic prices*	**709,166**	**817,112**	**860,939**
Taxes, *less* subsidies, on products	106,915	106,136	119,945
GDP in market prices	**816,081**	**923,248**	**980,884**

* Financial intermediation services indirectly measured (FISIM) is distributed to uses.

BALANCE OF PAYMENTS
(US $ million)

	2004	2005	2006
Exports of goods f.o.b.	81,862	96,395	117,294
Imports of goods f.o.b.	−87,484	−99,161	−122,247
Trade balance	**−5,622**	**−2,766**	**−4,953**
Exports of services	13,471	16,227	20,559
Imports of services	−12,457	−14,315	−18,327
Balance on goods and services	**−4,608**	**−854**	**−2,721**
Other income received	2,017	2,513	3,473
Other income paid	−13,536	−13,699	−16,905
Balance on goods, services and income	**−16,127**	**−12,040**	**−16,153**
Current transfers received	8,101	11,036	12,794
Current transfers paid	−2,650	−4,101	−4,566
Current balance	**−10,676**	**−5,105**	**−7,925**

POLAND

Statistical Survey

—continued	2004	2005	2006
Capital account (net)	1,180	995	2,122
Direct investment abroad	−793	−3,024	−4,266
Direct investment from abroad	12,890	9,602	13,922
Portfolio investment assets	−1,331	−2,485	−4,535
Portfolio investment liabilities	10,612	15,139	1,776
Financial derivatives liabilities	200	253	−1,000
Other investment assets	−11,809	−2,856	−3,161
Other investment liabilities	−1,351	−2,105	8,659
Net errors and omissions	1,879	−2,268	−3,102
Overall balance	801	8,146	2,490

Source: IMF, *International Financial Statistics*.

External Trade

PRINCIPAL COMMODITIES
(distribution by SITC, million new złotys)

Imports c.i.f.	2003	2004	2005
Food and live animals	12,269.6	15,556.2	17,226.9
Crude materials (inedible) except fuels	7,948.3	11,005.1	9,873.3
Mineral fuels, lubricants, etc.	24,133.2	29,806.2	37,571.6
Chemicals and related products	39,106.7	46,138.1	46,583.4
Basic manufactures	55,739.6	67,624.5	67,666.4
Machinery and transport equipment	100,858.4	125,965.7	116,797.0
Miscellaneous manufactured articles	23,011.2	26,805.1	27,488.4
Total (incl. others)	265,133.5	325,596.3	326,110.3

Exports f.o.b.	2003	2004	2005
Food and live animals	15,882.0	21,008.8	25,008.4
Mineral fuels, lubricants, etc.	9,008.6	14,857.3	15,555.9
Chemicals and related products	13,619.1	17,499.6	19,604.2
Basic manufactures	49,584.6	63,620.4	65,023.4
Machinery and transport equipment	78,951.6	105,538.2	112,890.8
Miscellaneous manufactured articles	35,710.0	41,036.5	41,870.8
Total (incl. others)	208,944.3	272,102.4	288,682.3

PRINCIPAL TRADING PARTNERS
(million new złotys)*

Imports c.i.f.	2001	2002	2003
Austria	4,032.1	4,309	5,147
Belgium	5,611.0	6,242	6,949
China, People's Republic	6,649.5	8,473	11,273
Czech Republic	7,132.4	7,296	9,089
Denmark	3,607.2	3,896	3,916
Finland	3,475.0	3,492	3,994
France	14,033.7	15,663	18,730
Germany	49,448.0	54,692	64,669
Hungary	3,262.9	3,785	4,750
Italy	17,013.0	18,812	22,570
Japan	4,044.9	4,237	4,948
Korea, Republic	2,135.8	2,357	n.a.
Netherlands	7,323.3	7,891	8,978
Norway	2,008.7	2,737	4,691
Russia	18,201.3	17,978	20,292
Slovakia	3,102.1	3,310	4,073
Spain	5,255.0	5,948	6,911
Sweden	5,547.2	5,942	6,934
Switzerland	2,691.3	2,946	3,050
Turkey	1,633.7	2,569	3,405
Ukraine	1,840.9	2,003	2,902
United Kingdom	8,574.8	8,746	9,879
USA	6,924.7	7,321	6,877
Total (incl. others)	206,252.8	224,816	265,133

Exports f.o.b.	2001	2002	2003
Austria	3,003.2	3,070	3,552
Belgium	4,567.8	5,425	6,742
Czech Republic	5,878.2	6,692	8,470
Denmark	3,827.3	4,622	4,939
France	8,017.0	10,090	12,730
Germany	50,944.5	54,071	67,416
Hungary	3,102.1	3,783	5,047
Italy	7,975.2	9,195	11,992
Netherlands	7,003.4	7,510	9,384
Norway	1,676.8	2,977	4,423
Russia	4,346.3	5,437	5,900
Slovakia	2,119.2	2,337	3,405
Spain	2,381.3	2,953	4,433
Sweden	4,048.3	5,411	7,548
Ukraine	4,114.9	4,817	6,084
United Kingdom	7,376.9	8,683	10,522
USA	3,493.3	4,490	4,662
Total (incl. others)	148,114.5	167,338	208,944

* Imports by country of purchase; exports by country of sale.

2004 (million złotys, preliminary data): *Imports:* China, People's Republic 15,004.6; Czech Republic 11,738.6; France 21,827.5; Germany 78,651.4; Italy 25,541.5; Netherlands 11,252.4; Russia 23,586.2; Spain 8,527.9; Sweden 8,794.4; United Kingdom 10,740.0; Total (incl. others) 324,663.1. *Exports:* Belgium 8,597.9; Czech Republic 11,714.3; France 16,475.6; Germany 81,632.3; Italy 16,398.3; Netherlands 11,648.1; Russia 10,443.9; Sweden 9,572.9; Ukraine 7,483.0; United Kingdom 14,881.3; Total (incl. others) 272,105.9.

2006 (million złotys, preliminary data): *Imports:* Czech Republic 13,595.5; France 21,357.9; Germany 93,293.0; Italy 26,283.3; Netherlands 12,412.6; Russia 38,062.4; United Kingdom 11,136.0; Total (incl. others) 390,955.5. *Exports:* Czech Republic 18,956.7; France 21,460.3; Germany 92,973.5; Italy 21,864.3; Netherlands 13,104.7; Russia 14,684.4; Sweden 10,975.8; Ukraine 12,372.1; Hungary 10,420.0; United Kingdom 19,592.1; Total (incl. others) 342,300.0.

Transport

POLISH STATE RAILWAYS
(traffic)

	2002	2003	2004
Paying passengers ('000 journeys)	304,144	283,390	272,162
Passenger-kilometres (million)	20,809	19,653	18,690*
Freight carried ('000 metric tons)	222,908	241,629	282,919
Freight ton-kilometres (million)	47,756	49,584	52,332*

* Source: UN, *Statistical Yearbook*.

ROAD TRAFFIC
('000 motor vehicles registered at 31 December)

	2001	2002	2003
Passenger cars	10,503	11,029	11,244
Lorries and vans (incl. road tractors)	1,979	2,163	2,313
Buses and coaches	82	83	83
Motorcycles*	803	869	845

* Figures for 2001 and 2002 also include scooters.

INLAND WATERWAYS
(traffic, including coastal transport)

	2001	2002	2003
Passengers carried ('000)	1,637	1,648	1,795
Passenger-kilometres (million)	42	37	34
Freight carried ('000 metric tons)	10,255	7,729	7,976
Freight ton-kilometres (million)	1,264	1,126	872

2004: Freight carried 8,748,000 metric tons.

POLAND

SHIPPING

Merchant Fleet
(registered at 31 December)

	2004	2005	2006
Number of vessels	378	359	355
Displacement ('000 gross registered tons)	162.7	190.1	193.4

Source: Lloyd's Register-Fairplay, *World Fleet Statistics*.

Sea Transport
(by owned or leased ships)

	2001	2002	2003
Passengers carried ('000)	582	559	526
Passenger-kilometres (million)	154	150	137
Freight carried ('000 metric tons)	22,426	25,222	25,435
Freight ton-kilometres (million)	108,517	104,190	100,455

International Sea-borne Shipping at Polish Ports

	2001	2002	2003
Vessels entered ('000 net reg. tons)	39,594	41,563	50,794
Vessels entered (number)	32,299	30,212	29,771
Passengers ('000): arrivals	2,220	1,718	1,617
Passengers ('000): departures	2,197	1,587	1,572
Cargo ('000 metric tons): loaded*	31,526	33,168	35,848
Cargo ('000 metric tons): unloaded*	14,684	14,943	15,171

* Including ships' bunkers and transshipments.

Source: Centre of Maritime Statistics.

CIVIL AVIATION
(scheduled and non-scheduled flights)

	2001	2002	2003
Passengers carried ('000)	3,436	3,667	3,976
Passenger-kilometres (million)	6,412	6,672	6,870
Cargo ('000 metric tons)	27	28	31
Cargo ton-kilometres (million)	79	80	86

Tourism

FOREIGN TOURIST ARRIVALS
('000, including visitors in transit)

Country of residence	2003	2004	2005
Belarus	3,830	3,523	3,651
Czech Republic	8,827	9,286	7,855
Germany	25,457	34,122	37,436
Lithuania	1,366	1,336	1,344
Russia	1,534	1,420	1,599
Slovakia	2,896	4,048	3,378
Ukraine	4,830	4,523	5,279
Total (incl. others)	52,130	61,918	64,606

Receipts from tourism (US $ million): 4,070 in 2003; 5,785 in 2004; 6,230 in 2005.

Source: Institute of Tourism.

Communications Media

	2001	2002	2003
Radio subscribers ('000)*	9,219	n.a.	n.a.
Television subscribers ('000 in use)*	8,969	n.a.	n.a.
Telephones ('000 main lines in use)†	11,400.0	11,859.5	12,292.5
Mobile cellular telephones ('000 subscribers)†	10,004.7	13,898.5	17,401.2
Personal computers ('000 in use)†	3,300	4,079	5,480
Internet users ('000)†	3,800	8,880	8,970
Book production: titles‡	19,189	19,246	20,686
Book production: copies (million)‡	74.4	67.6	81.5
Daily and non-daily newspapers: number	66	67	54
average circulation ('000 copies)	4,438	4,191	4,335
Other periodicals: number	5,771	6,122	5,627
Other periodicals: average circulation ('000 copies)	74,043	71,903	69,409

* At 31 December.
† Source: International Telecommunication Union.
‡ Including pamphlets.

2004: Telephones ('000 main lines in use) 12,292.5; Mobile cellular telephones ('000 subscribers) 23,096.1; Personal computers ('000 in use) 7,362; Internet users ('000) 9,000 (Source: International Telecommunication Union).

2005: Telephones ('000 main lines in use) 11,803.1; Mobile cellular telephones ('000 subscribers) 29,260.0; Internet users ('000) 10,000; Broadband subscribers ('000) 945.2 (Source: International Telecommunication Union).

2006: Telephones ('000 main lines in use) 11,474.6; Mobile cellular telephones ('000 subscribers) 36,745.5; Internet users ('000) 11,000; Broadband subscribers ('000) 2,640.0 (Source: International Telecommunication Union).

Facsimile machines (estimate, 1995): 55,000 in use (Source: UN, *Statistical Yearbook*).

Education

(2004/05, unless otherwise indicated)

	Institutions	Teachers*	Males	Females	Total
Pre-primary	17,337†	47,220	415.5	396.2	811.7
Primary	15,344‡	235,950	1,400.4	1,323.3	2,723.7
Secondary	17,825‡	271,100	813.6	2,631.3	3,444.9
Tertiary	400‡	95,143	900.0	1,218.1	2,118.1

Students ('000)*

* Data from UNESCO Institute for Statistics.
† 2001 figure.
‡ 2004/05 figure.

Directory

The Constitution

The Constitution of the Republic of Poland was adopted by the National Assembly on 2 April 1997 and endorsed by popular referendum on 25 May of that year. The following is a summary of the main provisions of the Constitution, which came into force on 17 October 1997:

THE REPUBLIC

The Republic of Poland shall be a unitary, democratic state, ruled by law, and implementing the principles of social justice. The Republic shall safeguard the independence and integrity of its territory, ensure the freedom and rights of persons and citizens, and safeguard the national heritage. The Constitution shall be the supreme law of the Republic, which shall respect international law binding upon it. Legislative power shall be vested in the Sejm (Assembly) and the Senat (Senate), executive power shall be vested in the President and the Council of Ministers, and judicial power shall be vested in the courts and tribunals.

The Republic shall ensure freedom for the creation and functioning of political parties, trade unions and other voluntary associations. The financing of political parties shall be open to public inspection.

Political parties and other organizations whose programmes are based upon totalitarian methods and the modes of activity of nazism, fascism and communism, as well as those whose programmes or activities sanction racial or national hatred, or the application of violence for the purpose of obtaining power or to influence the State's policy, or provide for the secrecy of their own structure or membership, shall be forbidden. The Republic shall ensure freedom of the press and other means of social communication.

A social market economy, based on the freedom of economic activity, private ownership, and solidarity, dialogue and co-operation between social partners, shall be the basis of the economic system of Poland.

Churches and other religious organizations shall have equal rights. Public authorities shall be impartial in matters of personal conviction, and shall ensure their freedom of expression within public life. The Armed Forces shall observe neutrality regarding political matters and shall be subject to civil and democratic control.

THE FREEDOMS, RIGHTS AND OBLIGATIONS OF PERSONS AND CITIZENS

All persons shall be equal before the law. Polish citizens belonging to national or ethnic minorities shall be guaranteed the freedom to maintain and develop their own language, to maintain customs and traditions, and to develop their own culture.

The Republic shall ensure the legal protection of the life of every human being; the inviolability of the person and of the home; freedom of movement; freedom of faith and religion; and the freedom to express opinions. The freedom of peaceful assembly and association shall be guaranteed. At the age of 18 every citizen shall have the right to participate in referendums, and to vote in presidential, legislative and local elections. Everyone shall have the right to own property; the freedom to choose and pursue his occupation; the right to health protection; and the right to education.

THE SEJM AND THE SENAT

The Sejm shall be composed of 460 Deputies. Elections to the Sejm shall be universal, equal, direct, proportional and conducted by secret ballot. The Senat shall be composed of 100 Senators. Elections to the Senat shall be universal, direct and conducted by secret ballot. The Sejm and the Senat shall be elected for a four-year term of office. At the ages of 21 and 30, respectively, every citizen having the right to vote shall be eligible for election to the Sejm and the Senat.

The Sejm shall elect from among its members a Marshal and Vice-Marshals. The Sejm adopts laws; may adopt a resolution on a state of war; may order a nation-wide referendum; and may appoint investigative committees to examine particular matters.

The Senat reviews laws adopted by the Sejm; it may adopt amendments or resolve upon complete rejection. The Senat can be overriden by the Sejm by an absolute majority vote in the presence of at least one-half of the statutory number of Deputies.

In instances specified in the Constitution, the Sejm and the Senat, sitting in joint session, shall act as the National Assembly (Zgromadzenie Narodowe). The right to introduce legislation shall belong to Deputies, to the Senat, to the President of the Republic, to the Council of Ministers, and to a group of at least 100,000 citizens having the right to vote in elections to the Sejm.

THE PRESIDENT OF THE REPUBLIC

The President of the Republic of Poland shall be the supreme representative of the Polish State and the guarantor of the continuity of state authority. The President shall ensure observance of the Constitution, safeguard the sovereignty and security of the State, as well as the inviolability and integrity of its territory. The President shall be elected in universal, equal and direct elections by secret ballot. The President shall be elected for a five-year term, and may be re-elected only once. Only a Polish citizen aged over 35 years, with full electoral rights in elections to the Sejm, may be elected President. Any such candidature shall be supported by the signatures of at least 100,000 citizens having the right to vote in elections to the Sejm. If the President of the Republic is unable to discharge the duties of his office, the Marshal of the Sejm shall temporarily assume presidential duties.

The President's duties include the calling of elections to the Sejm and the Senat; heading the Armed Forces; nominating and appointing the Prime Minister; appointing senior public officials; and representing the State in foreign affairs.

Bringing an indictment against the President shall be done by resolution of the National Assembly, passed by a majority of at least two-thirds of the statutory number of members, on the motion of at least 140 members.

THE COUNCIL OF MINISTERS AND GOVERNMENT ADMINISTRATION

The Council of Ministers shall conduct the internal affairs and foreign policy of the Republic, and shall manage the government administration. The President shall nominate a Prime Minister who shall propose the composition of a Council of Ministers. The Prime Minister shall, within 14 days following his appointment, submit a programme of activity of the Council of Ministers to the Sejm, together with a motion requiring a vote of confidence.

The members of the Council of Ministers shall be responsible to the Sejm, both collectively and individually. The Sejm may pass a vote of no confidence in the Council of Ministers by a majority of votes of the statutory number of Deputies, on a motion of at least 46 Deputies, specifying the name of a candidate for Prime Minister.

LOCAL SELF-GOVERNMENT

The commune (gmina) shall be the basic unit of local self-government. Other units of regional and/or local self-government shall be specified by statute. Public duties aimed at satisfying the needs of a self-governing community shall be the direct responsibility of such units. Units of local self-government shall perform their duties through constitutive and executive organs. Units of local self-government shall be assured public funds for the performance of the duties assigned to them.

COURTS AND TRIBUNALS

The courts and tribunals shall constitute a separate and independent power. The administration of justice in Poland shall be implemented by the Supreme Court, the common courts, administrative courts and military courts. Judges, within the exercise of their office, shall be independent and subject only to the Constitution and statutes. The Supreme Court shall exercise supervision over common and military courts.

The Constitutional Tribunal

The Constitutional Tribunal shall adjudicate on the conformity of statutes and other normative acts issued by central state organs to the Constitution. Its judgments shall be universally binding and final. Judges of the Tribunal shall be independent and subject only to the Constitution.

The Tribunal of State

Persons holding high state positions (as specified in the Constitution) shall be accountable to the Tribunal of State for violations of the Constitution or statutes. The First President of the Supreme Court shall be Chairman of the Tribunal. Its members shall be independent and subject only to the Constitution and statutes.

ORGANS OF STATE CONTROL FOR THE DEFENCE OF RIGHTS

The Supreme Chamber of Control shall be the chief organ of state order, and shall be subordinate to the Sejm. It shall audit the activity of the organs of government administration, the National Bank of Poland, state legal persons and other state organizational units. The Commissioner for Citizens' Rights shall safeguard the freedoms and rights of persons and citizens as specified in the Constitution and other normative acts. The National Council of Radio and Television Broadcasting shall safeguard freedom of speech and the right to information, as well as the public interest regarding radio and television broadcasting.

EXTRAORDINARY MEASURES

In situations of particular danger, if ordinary constitutional measures are inadequate, any of the following appropriate extraordinary measures may be introduced in a part or upon the whole territory of the State: martial law, a state of emergency or a state of natural disaster.

The Government

HEAD OF STATE

President: LECH KACZYŃSKI (inaugurated 23 December 2005).

COUNCIL OF MINISTERS
(April 2008)

A coalition comprising the Civic Platform (PO) and the Polish People's Party (PSL).

Prime Minister: DONALD TUSK (PO).
Deputy Prime Minister and Minister of the Economy: WALDEMAR PAWLAK (PSL).
Deputy Prime Minister and Minister of Internal Affairs and Administration: GRZEGORZ SCHETYNA (PO).
Minister of Foreign Affairs: RADOSŁAW SIKORSKI (PO).
Minister of National Defence: BOGDAN KLICH (PO).
Minister of the State Treasury: ALEKSANDER GRAD (PO).

POLAND

Minister of Justice: ZBIGNIEW ĆWIĄKALSKI (PO).
Minister of Science and Higher Education: BARBARA KUDRYCKA (PO).
Minister of Labour and Social Policy: JOLANTA FEDAK (PSL).
Minister of National Education: KATARZYNA HALL (PO).
Minister of Agriculture and Rural Development: MAREK SAWICKI (PSL).
Minister of Regional Development: ELŻBIETA BIEŃKOWSKA (Independent).
Minister of Culture and National Heritage: BOGDAN ZDROJEWSKI (PO).
Minister of Health: EWA KOPACZ (PO).
Minister of the Environment: MACIEJ NOWICKI (PO).
Minister of Finance: JACEK ROSTOWSKI (Independent).
Minister of Sport and Tourism: MIROSŁAW DRZEWIECKI.
Minister of Infrastructure: CEZARY GRABARCZYK (PO).
Minister without Portfolio: ZBIGNIEW DERDZIUK (PO).

MINISTRIES

Chancellery of the President: 00-902 Warsaw, ul. Wiejska 10; tel. (22) 6952900; fax (22) 6952238; e-mail listy@prezydent.pl; internet www.prezydent.pl.

Chancellery of the Prime Minister: 00-583 Warsaw, Al. Ujazdowskie 1/3; tel. (22) 8413832; fax (22) 6284821; e-mail cirinfo@kprm.gov.pl; internet www.kprm.gov.pl.

Ministry of Agriculture and Rural Development: 00-930 Warsaw, ul. Wspólna 30; tel. (22) 6231000; fax (22) 6231782; e-mail kanceleria@minrol.gov.pl; internet www.minrol.gov.pl.

Ministry of Culture and National Heritage: 00-071 Warsaw, ul. Krakowskie Przedmieście 15/17; tel. (22) 4210100; fax (22) 8260726; e-mail rzecznik@mkidn.gov.pl; internet www.mkidn.gov.pl.

Ministry of the Economy: 00-507 Warsaw, pl. Trzech Krzyży 3/5; tel. (22) 6935000; fax (22) 6934048; e-mail bpi@mg.gov.pl; internet www.mg.gov.pl.

Ministry of the Environment: 00-922 Warsaw, ul. Wawelska 52/54; tel. (22) 5792900; fax (22) 5792511; e-mail info@mos.gov.pl; internet www.mos.gov.pl.

Ministry of Finance: 00-916 Warsaw, ul. Świętokrzyska 12; tel. (22) 6945555; fax (22) 8272722; e-mail kancelaria@mf.gov.pl; internet www.mf.gov.pl.

Ministry of Foreign Affairs: 00-580 Warsaw, Al. Szucha 23; tel. (22) 5239000; fax (22) 6290287; e-mail dsi@msz.gov.pl; internet www.msz.gov.pl.

Ministry of Health: 00-952 Warsaw, ul. Miodowa 15; tel. (22) 6349600; fax (22) 6349213; e-mail kancelaria@mz.gov.pl; internet www.mz.gov.pl.

Ministry of Infrastructure: 00-928 Warszawa, ul. Chałubińskiego 4/6; tel. (22) 6301000; fax (22) 6301116; e-mail info@mi.gov.pl; internet www.mi.gov.pl.

Ministry of Internal Affairs and Administration: 02-591 Warsaw, ul. Stefana Batorego 5; tel. (22) 6014427; fax (22) 6227973; e-mail wp@mswia.gov.pl; internet www.mswia.gov.pl.

Ministry of Justice: 00-950 Warsaw, Al. Ujazdowskie 11; tel. (22) 5212888; fax (22) 6215540; e-mail nagorska@ms.gov.pl; internet www.ms.gov.pl.

Ministry of Labour and Social Policy: 00-513 Warsaw, ul. Nowogrodzka 1/3/5; tel. (22) 6610100; fax (22) 6610709; internet www.mps.gov.pl.

Ministry of National Defence: 00-909 Warsaw, ul. Klonowa 1; tel. (22) 6280031; fax (22) 8455378; e-mail bpimon@wp.mil.pl; internet www.wp.mil.pl.

Ministry of National Education: 00-918 Warsaw, Al. Szucha 25; tel. (22) 3474100; fax (22) 5224100; e-mail informacja@men.gov.pl; internet www.men.gov.pl.

Ministry of Regional Development: 00-926 Warsaw, ul. Wspólna 2/4; tel. (22) 4613000; fax (22) 4613000; internet www.mrr.gov.pl.

Ministry of Science and Higher Education: 00-529 Warsaw, ul. Wspólna 1/3; tel. (22) 5292718; fax (22) 6280922; e-mail dip@mnii.gov.pl; internet www.nauka.gov.pl.

Ministry of Sport and Tourism: 00-921 Warsaw, ul. Senatorska 14; tel. (22) 2443142; fax (22) 2443255; e-mail rzecznik@msport.gov.pl; internet www.msport.gov.pl.

Ministry of the State Treasury: 00-522 Warsaw, ul. Krucza 36; tel. (22) 6958000; fax (22) 6280872; e-mail minister@msp.gov.pl; internet www.msp.gov.pl.

President

Presidential Election, First Ballot, 9 October 2005

Candidates	Votes	%
Donald Tusk	5,429,666	36.33
Lech Kaczyński	4,947,927	33.10
Andrzej Lepper	2,259,094	15.11
Marek Borowski	1,544,642	10.33
Others	765,360	5.12
Total	**14,946,689**	**100.00**

Second Ballot, 23 October 2005

Candidates	Votes	%
Lech Kaczyński	8,257,468	54.04
Donald Tusk	7,022,319	45.96
Total	**15,279,787**	**100.00**

Legislature

The Zgromadzenie Narodowe (National Assembly) is bicameral, comprising the Sejm (Assembly), the lower chamber, and the Senat (Senate), the upper chamber.

Sejm (Assembly)

00-902 Warsaw, ul. Wiejska 4/6; tel. (22) 285927; e-mail zjablon@sejm.gov.pl; internet www.sejm.gov.pl.

Marshal: BRONISŁAW KOMOROWSKI.

Election, 21 October 2007

Parties and alliances	Votes	% of votes	Seats
Civic Platform (PO)	6,701,010	41.51	209
Law and Justice (PiS)	5,183,477	32.11	166
Left and Democrats (LiD)*	2,122,981	13.15	53
Polish People's Party (PSL)	1,437,638	8.91	31
German Minority (MN)	32,462	0.20	1
Self-Defence Party of the Republic of Poland (SRP)	247,335	1.53	—
League of Polish Families (LPR)	209,171	1.30	—
Others	208,128	1.29	—
Total	**16,142,202**	**100.00**	**460**

* A coalition of the Democratic Left Alliance (SLD), Polish Social Democracy (SDPL), the Democratic Party and the Union of Labour (UP).

Senat (Senate)

00-902 Warsaw, ul. Wiejska 6; tel. (22) 6949265; fax (22) 6949428; internet www.senat.gov.pl.

Marshal: BOGDAN BORUSEWICZ.

Election, 21 October 2007

Parties and alliances	Seats
Civic Platform	60
Law and Justice	39
Independent	1
Total	**100**

Election Commission

Państwowa Komisja Wyborcza (PKW) (State Election Commission): 00-902 Warsaw, ul. Wiejska 10; tel. (22) 6250617; fax (22) 6293959; internet www.pkw.gov.pl; Pres. FERDYNAND RYMARZ.

Political Organizations

Centre Party (Partia Centrum): 00-057 Warsaw, pl. Dąbrowskiego 5; tel. (22) 8278442; fax (22) 8278441; e-mail centrum@centrum.org.pl; f. 2004; Hon. Chair. ZBIGNIEW RELIGA; Leader JANUSZ STEINHOFF.

Civic Platform (PO) (Platforma Obywatelska): 00-159 Warsaw, ul. Andersa 21; tel. (22) 6357879; fax (22) 6357641; e-mail poczta@platforma.org; internet www.platforma.org; f. 2001 by independent presidential candidate and factions of the Freedom Union (UW) and Solidarity Electoral Action (AWS); conservative-liberal; Leader DONALD TUSK.

Democratic Left Alliance (SLD) (Sojusz Lewicy Demokratycznej): 00-419 Warsaw, ul. Rozbrat 44 A; tel. (22) 6210341; fax (2) 6216069; e-mail rk@sld.org.pl; internet www.sld.org.pl; f. 1999; contested 2007 legislative elections as mem. of Left and Democrats coalition; Chair. WOJCIECH OLEJNICZAK; Gen. Sec. GRZEGORZ NAPIERALSKI.

Democratic Party (PD) (Partia Demokratyczna): 00-683 Warsaw, ul. Marszałkowska 77/79; tel. (22) 3355800; fax (22) 3355817; e-mail sekretariat@demokraci.pl; internet www.demokraci.pl; f. 2005 to replace Freedom Union (UW); contested 2007 legislative elections as mem. of Left and Democrats coalition; Leader JANUSZ ONYSZKIEWICZ.

German Minority (Mniejszość Niemiecka—MN): 45-004 Opole, ul. M. Konopnickiej 6; tel. (77) 4021070; fax (77) 4230262; Leader HENRYK KRÓL.

Law and Justice (PiS) (Prawo i Sprawiedliwość): 02-018 Warsaw, ul. Nowogrodzka 84/86; tel. (22) 6215035; fax (22) 6216767; e-mail biuro@pis.org.pl; internet www.pis.org.pl; f. 2001; conservative; Leader JAROSŁAW KACZYŃSKI.

League of Polish Families (LPR) (Liga Polskich Rodzin): 00-528 Warsaw, ul. Hoża 9; tel. (22) 6223648; fax (22) 6223138; e-mail biuro@lpr.pl; internet www.lpr.pl; f. 2001 as alliance comprising the National Party, All-Poland Youth, the Polish Accord Party, the Catholic National movement and the Peasant National Bloc; Roman Catholic, nationalist, anti-EU; Leader SYLWESTER CHRUSZCZ.

Polish Labour Party (Polska Partia Pracy—PPP): 00-570 Warsaw, al. Wyzwolenia 18; tel. (22) 6293095; e-mail sekretariat@partiapracy.pl; internet www.partiapracy.pl; Chair. BOGUSŁAW ZIĘTEK.

Polish People's Party (PSL) (Polskie Stronnictwo Ludowe): 00-131 Warsaw, ul. Grzybowska 4; tel. (22) 6206020; fax (22) 6543583; e-mail biuronkw@psl.org.pl; internet www.psl.pl; f. 1990 on basis of United Peasant Party (f. 1949) and Polish Peasant Party—Rebirth (f. 1989); centrist, stresses development of agriculture and social market economy; Chair. WALDEMAR PAWLAK.

Polish Social Democracy (SDPL) (Socjaldemokracja Polski): 00-560 Warsaw, ul. Mokotowska 29A; tel. (22) 6213640; fax (22) 6215342; e-mail sdpl@sdpl.pl; internet www.sdpl.pl; f. 2004; contested 2007 legislative elections as mem. of Left and Democrats coalition; Leader MAREK BOROWSKI.

Right of the Republic (PR) (Prawica Rzeczypospolitej): 02-819 Warsaw, ul. Puławska 294; tel. (69) 1491864; e-mail biuro@prawicarzeczypospolitej.org; internet www.prawicarzeczypospolitej.org; f. 2007; opposed to abortion, euthanasia, and supportive of traditional Roman Catholic values; Leader MAREK JUREK.

Self-Defence Party of the Republic of Poland (SRP) (Partia Samoobrona Rzeczypospolitej Polskiej): 00-024 Warsaw, Al. Jerozolimskie 30; tel. (22) 6250472; fax (22) 6250477; e-mail samoobrona@samoobrona.org.pl; internet www.samoobrona.pl; agrarian, populist, anti-EU; Leader ANDRZEJ LEPPER.

Union of Labour (UP) (Unia Pracy): 00-513 Warsaw, ul. Nowogrodzka 4; tel. (22) 6285859; fax (22) 6256776; e-mail biuro@uniapracy.pl; internet www.uniapracy.org.pl; f. 1992; contested 2007 legislative elections as mem. of Left and Democrats coalition; Chair. WALDEMAR WITKOWSKI.

Women's Party (Partia Kobiet—PK): Warsaw; tel. (22) 4440022; e-mail info@polskajestkobieta.org; internet www.polskajestkobieta.org; f. 2007; Chair. ANNA KORNACKA.

Diplomatic Representation

EMBASSIES IN POLAND

Afghanistan: 02-954 Warsaw, ul. Goplańska 1; tel. (22) 8855410; fax (22) 8856500; e-mail warsaw@afghanembassy.com.pl; internet www.afghanembassy.com.pl; Ambassador ZIAUDDIN MOJADEDI.

Albania: 02-386 Warsaw, ul. Altowa 1; tel. (22) 8241427; fax (22) 8241426; e-mail embassy.warsaw@mfa.gov.al; Ambassador FLORENT ÇELIKU.

Algeria: 03-932 Warsaw, ul. Dąbrowiecka 21; tel. (22) 6175855; fax (22) 6160081; e-mail ambalgva@zigzag.pl; Ambassador ABDELAZIZ LAHIOUEL.

Angola: 02-635 Warsaw, ul. Balonowa 20; tel. (22) 6463529; fax (22) 8447452; e-mail embaixada@emb-angola.pl; Ambassador LIZETH NAWANGA SATUMBO PENA.

Argentina: 03-973 Warsaw, ul. Brukselska 9; tel. (22) 6176028; fax (22) 6177162; e-mail epolo@home.pl; Ambassador CARLOS ALBERTO PASSALACQUA.

Armenia: 02-908 Warsaw, ul. Woziwody 15; tel. (22) 8408130; fax (22) 6420643; e-mail main@embarmenia.it.pl; Ambassador ASHOT GALOYAN.

Australia: 00-513 Warsaw, ul. Nowogrodzka 11, Nautilus Bldg, 3rd Floor; tel. (22) 5213444; fax (22) 6273500; e-mail ambasada.australia@dfat.gov.au; internet www.poland.embassy.gov.au; Ambassador IAN K. FORSYTH.

Austria: 00-748 Warsaw, ul. Gagarina 34; tel. (22) 8410081; fax (22) 8410085; e-mail warschau-ob@bmaa.gv.at; internet www.ambasadaaustrii.pl; Ambassador ALFRED LÄNGLE.

Azerbaijan: 03-941 Warsaw, ul. Zwycięców 12; tel. (22) 6162188; fax (22) 6161949; e-mail info@azer-embassy.pl; internet www.azer-embassy.pl; Ambassador VILAYAT GULIYEV.

Belarus: 02-952 Warsaw, ul. Wiertnicza 58; tel. (22) 7420990; fax (22) 7420980; e-mail poland@belembassy.org; internet www.belembassy.org/poland; Ambassador PAVEL P. LATUSHKA.

Belgium: 00-095 Warsaw, ul. Senatorska 34; tel. (22) 5512800; fax (22) 8285711; e-mail warsaw@diplobel.org; internet www.diplomatie.be/warsawfr; Ambassador JAN LUYKX.

Bosnia and Herzegovina: 00-789 Warsaw, ul. Humanska 10; tel. (22) 8569935; fax (22) 8481521; Ambassador ZORAN SKENDERIJA.

Brazil: 03-931 Warsaw, ul. Poselska 11, Saska Kepa; tel. (22) 6174800; fax (22) 6178689; e-mail brasil@brasil.org.pl; internet www.brasil.org.pl; Ambassador MARCELO ANDRADE DE MORAES JARDIM.

Bulgaria: 00-540 Warsaw, Al. Ujazdowskie 33/35; tel. (22) 6294071; fax (22) 6282271; e-mail office@bgemb.com.pl; Ambassador IVAN A. NAYDENOV.

Cambodia: 03-969 Warsaw, ul. Drezdeńska 3; tel. (22) 6165231; fax (22) 6161836; e-mail royalembassyofcambodia@neostrada.pl; Ambassador CHAN KY SIM.

Canada: 00-481 Warsaw, ul. Matejki 1/5; tel. (22) 5843100; fax (22) 5843190; e-mail wsaw@international.gc.ca; internet www.canada.pl; Ambassador DAVID PRESTON.

Chile: 02-925 Warsaw, ul. Okrężna 62; tel. (22) 8582330; fax (22) 8582329; e-mail embachile@onet.pl; internet www.embachile.pl; Ambassador JOSÉ MANUEL OVALLE BRAVO.

China, People's Republic: 00-203 Warsaw, ul. Bonifraterska 1; tel. (22) 8313836; fax (22) 6354211; e-mail ambchina@pol.pl; internet www.chinaembassy.org.pl; Ambassador SUN RONGMIN.

Colombia: 03-936 Warsaw, ul. Zwycięców 29; tel. (22) 6170973; fax (22) 6176684; e-mail embcol@medianet.pl; Ambassador JORGE ALBERTO BARRANTES ULLOA.

Congo, Democratic Republic: 02-637 Warsaw, ul. Miączyńska 50; tel. (22) 8496999; fax (22) 8485215; e-mail ambardcvarsovie@yahoo.fr; Ambassador ISIDORE MAVAMBU MATUMONA.

Costa Rica: 02-954 Warsaw, ul. Kubickiego 9/5; tel. (22) 8589112; fax (22) 6427832; e-mail emcoripol@neostrada.pl; Chargé d'affaires a.i. HILDA MARÍA SANTIESTEBAN MONTERO.

Croatia: 02-611 Warsaw, ul. Ignacego Krasickiego 25; tel. (22) 8442393; fax (22) 8444808; e-mail croemb.warszawa@mvpei.hr; internet pl.mvp.hr; Ambassador NEBOJŠA KOHAROVIĆ.

Cuba: 02-516 Warsaw, ul. Rejtana 15/8; tel. (22) 8481715; fax (22) 8482231; e-mail embacuba@medianet.pl; internet emba.cubaminrex.cu/polonia; Ambassador ROSARIO CRISTINA NAVAS MORATA.

Cyprus: 02-629 Warsaw, ul. Pilicka 4; tel. (22) 8444577; fax (22) 8442558; e-mail embassyofcyprus@neostrada.pl; Ambassador KALLIOPI AVRAAM.

Czech Republic: 00-555 Warsaw, ul. Koszykowa 18; tel. (22) 5251850; fax (22) 5251898; e-mail warsaw@embassy.mzv.cz; internet www.mfa.cz/warsaw; Ambassador (vacant).

Denmark: 02-517 Warsaw, ul. Rakowiecka 19; tel. and fax (22) 5652900; e-mail wawamb@um.dk; internet www.ambwarszawa.um.dk; Ambassador HANS MICHAEL KOFOED-HANSEN.

Ecuador: 02-516 Warsaw, ul. Rejtana 15/15; tel. (22) 8487230; fax (22) 8488196; e-mail eccupolonia@mmrree.gov.ec; Ambassador FERNANDO FLORES MACÍAS.

Egypt: 03-972 Warsaw, ul. Alzacka 18; tel. (22) 6176973; fax (22) 6179058; e-mail embassyofegypt@neostrada.pl; Ambassador FAHMY AHMED FAYED SALAMA.

Estonia: 02-639 Warsaw, ul. Karwińska 1; tel. (22) 8811810; fax (22) 8811812; e-mail embassy@estemb.pl; internet www.estemb.pl; Ambassador ANTS FROSCH.

Finland: 00-559 Warsaw, ul. Chopina 4/8; tel. (22) 5989500; fax (22) 6213442; e-mail sanomat.var@formin.fi; internet www.finland.pl; Ambassador JAN STORE.

POLAND

France: 00-477 Warsaw, ul. Piękna 1; tel. (22) 5293000; fax (22) 5293001; e-mail presse@ambafrance-pl.org; internet www.ambafrance-pl.org; Ambassador BARRY DELONGCHAMPS.

Georgia: 03-934 Warsaw, ul. Wąchocka 1s; tel. (22) 6166221; fax (22) 6166226; e-mail warsaw.emb@mfa.gov.ge; Ambassador KONSTANTIN KAVTARADZE.

Germany: 00-467 Warsaw, ul. Jazdów 12; tel. (22) 5841700; fax (22) 5841739; e-mail warszawa@wars.diplo.de; internet www.ambasadaniemiec.pl; Ambassador Dr MICHAEL H. GERDTS.

Greece: 00-432 Warsaw, ul. Górnośląska 35; tel. (22) 6229460; fax (22) 6229464; e-mail gremb.war@mfa.gr; internet www.greece.pl; Ambassador PANTELIS CARCABASSIS.

Holy See: 00-582 Warsaw, Al. J. Ch. Szucha 12, POB 163; tel. (22) 6288488; fax (22) 6284556; e-mail nuncjatura@episkopat.pl; Apostolic Nuncio Most Rev. JÓZEF KOWALCZYK (Titular Archbishop of Heraclea).

Hungary: 00-559 Warsaw, ul. Chopina 2; tel. (22) 6284451; fax (22) 6218561; e-mail mission.vao@kum.hu; internet www.mfa.gov.hu/emb/warsaw; Ambassador RÓBERT KISS.

India: 02-516 Warsaw, ul. Rejtana 15, m. 2–7; tel. (22) 8495800; fax (22) 8496705; e-mail hoc.warsaw@mea.gov.in; internet www.indianembassy.pl; Ambassador CHANDRA MOHAN BHANDARI.

Indonesia: 03-903 Warsaw, ul. Estońska 3, POB 33; tel. (22) 6175179; fax (22) 6178451; e-mail info@indonesianembassy.pl; internet www.indonesianembassy.pl; Ambassador HAZAIRIN POHAN.

Iran: 03-928 Warsaw, ul. Królowej Aldony 22; tel. (22) 6171585; fax (22) 6178452; e-mail iranemb@iranemb.warsaw.pl; internet www.iranemb.warsaw.pl; Ambassador HADI FARAJVAND.

Iraq: 03-932 Warsaw, ul. Dąbrowiecka 9A; tel. (22) 6175773; fax (22) 6177065; e-mail iraqembassy@ambasadairaku.pl; Ambassador Dr WALID HAMID SHILTAGH.

Ireland: 00-496 Warsaw, ul. Mysia 5; tel. (22) 8496633; fax (22) 8498431; e-mail warsawembassy@dfa.ie; internet www.irlandia.pl; Ambassador DECLAN O'DONOVAN.

Israel: 02-078 Warsaw, ul. Krzywickiego 24; tel. (22) 5970500; fax (22) 8251607; e-mail publicaffairs@warsaw.mfa.gov.il; internet www.israel.pl; Ambassador DAVID ABRAHAM AKIVA PELEG.

Italy: 00-055 Warsaw, pl. Dąbrowskiego 6; tel. (22) 8263471; fax (22) 8278507; e-mail ambasciata.varsavia@esteri.it; internet www.ambvarsavia.esteri.it; Ambassador ANNA BLEFARI MELAZZI.

Japan: 00-464 Warsaw, ul. Szwoleżerów 8; tel. (22) 6965000; fax (22) 6965001; e-mail info-cul@emb-japan.pl; internet www.pl.emb-japan.go.jp; Ambassador RYUICHI TANABE.

Kazakhstan: 02-954 Warsaw, ul. Królowej Marysieńki 14; tel. (22) 6425388; fax (22) 6423427; e-mail kazdipmis@hot.pl; internet www.kazakhstan.pl; Ambassador ALEKSEI VOLKOV.

Korea, Democratic People's Republic: 00-728 Warsaw, ul. Bobrowiecka 1A; tel. (22) 8405813; fax (22) 8405710; e-mail korembpl@yahoo.com; Ambassador KIM PYONG IL.

Korea, Republic: 00-464 Warsaw, ul. Szwoleżerów 6; tel. (22) 5592906; fax (22) 5592905; e-mail koremb_waw@mofat.go.kr; Ambassador SI-HYUNG LEE.

Kuwait: 00-486 Warsaw, ul. Franciszka Nullo 13; tel. (22) 6222860; fax (22) 6274314; e-mail embassy@kue.com.pl; Ambassador KHALED MOHAMMED ASH-SHAIBANI.

Laos: 02-516 Warsaw, ul. Rejtana 15/26; tel. (22) 8484786; fax (22) 8497122; e-mail sotholaw@yahoo.com; Chargé d'affaires a.i. SENGPHET HOUNGBOUNGNUANG.

Latvia: 03-928 Warsaw, ul. Królowej Aldony 19; tel. (22) 6174389; fax (22) 6174289; e-mail embassy.poland@mfa.gov.lv; internet www.latvia.pl; Ambassador ALBERTS SARKANIS.

Lebanon: 02-516 Warsaw, ul. Starościńska 1B/10–11; tel. (22) 8445065; fax (22) 6460030; e-mail embassy@lebanon.com.pl; internet www.lebanon.com.pl; Chargé d'affaires a.i. KABALAN FRANGIEH.

Lithuania: 00-478 Warsaw, Al. Ujazdowskie 14; tel. (22) 6253368; fax (22) 6253440; e-mail ambasada@lietuva.pl; internet www.lietuva.pl; Ambassador EGIDIJUS MEILŪNAS.

Luxembourg: 00-789 Warsaw, ul. Słoneczna 15; tel. (22) 5078650; fax (22) 5078661; e-mail varsovie.amb@mae.etat.lu; Ambassador RONALD DOFING.

Macedonia, former Yugoslav republic: 02-954 Warsaw, ul. Królowej Marysieńki 40; tel. (22) 6517291; fax (22) 6517292; e-mail ambrmwar@zigzag.pl; internet www.ambasadarm.zigzag.pl; Ambassador DIMKO KOKAROVSKI.

Malaysia: 03-902 Warsaw, Saska-Kepa, ul. Gruzińska 3; tel. (22) 6174413; fax (22) 6176256; e-mail mwwarsaw@poczta.neostrada.pl; Ambassador ROSMIDAH BINTE ZAHID.

Mexico: 02-516 Warsaw, ul. Starościńska 1B/4–5; tel. (22) 6468800; fax (22) 6464222; e-mail embamex@ikp.pl; Ambassador RAPHAEL STEGER CATAÑO.

Moldova: 02-710 Warsaw, ul. Imielińska 1; tel. (22) 6462099; e-mail embassy@moldova.pl; internet www.moldova.pl; Ambassador BORIS GAMURARI.

Mongolia: 02-516 Warsaw, ul. Rejtana 15/16; tel. (22) 8482063; fax (22) 8499391; e-mail mongamb@ikp.atm.com.pl; internet www.ambmong.net7.pl; Chargé d'affaires a.i. BARKHAS DORJ.

Morocco: 02-516 Warsaw, ul. Starościńska 1/11–12; tel. (22) 8496341; fax (22) 8481840; e-mail info@moroccoembassy.org.pl; internet www.moroccoembassy.org.pl; Ambassador ABDESSELAM ALEM.

Netherlands: 00-468 Warsaw, ul. Kawalerii 10; tel. (22) 5591200; fax (22) 8402638; e-mail war@minbuza.nl; internet www.nlembassy.pl; Ambassador MARNIX KROP.

New Zealand: 00-536 Warsaw, Al. Ujazdowskie 51; tel. (22) 5210500; fax (22) 5210510; e-mail nzwsw@nzembassy.pl; Ambassador PHILIP WALLACE GRIFFITHS.

Nigeria: 02-952 Warsaw, ul. Wiertnicza 94; tel. (22) 8486944; fax (22) 8485379; e-mail info@nigeriaembassy.pl; internet www.nigeriaembassy.pl; Chargé d'affaires a.i. AYODEJI OLUKAYODE ROBERTS.

Norway: 00-559 Warsaw, ul. Chopina 2A; tel. (22) 6964030; fax (22) 6280938; e-mail emb.warsaw@mfa.no; internet www.amb-norwegia.pl; Ambassador KNUT HAUGE.

Pakistan: 02-516 Warsaw, ul. Starościńska 1/1–2; tel. (22) 8494808; fax (22) 8491160; e-mail parepwarsaw@wp.pl; Ambassador SEEMA ILAHI BALOCH.

Panama: 02-946 Warsaw, ul. Biedronki 13A; tel. (22) 6422143; fax (22) 6517616; e-mail panamaembassy@neostrada.pl; Ambassador ROKO IVAN SETKA SAGEL.

Peru: 02-516 Warsaw, ul. Starościńska 1/3; tel. (22) 6468806; fax (22) 6468617; e-mail embperpl@atomnet.pl; internet www.perupol.pl; Ambassador JORGE DANTE FEDERICO CHÁVEZ SOTO.

Portugal: 03-905 Warsaw, ul. Francuska 37; tel. (22) 5111010; fax (22) 5111013; e-mail embaixada@embport.internetdsl.pl; internet www.ambasadaportugalii.pl; Ambassador JOSÉ SEQUEIRA E SERPA.

Romania: 00-559 Warsaw, ul. Chopina 10; tel. (22) 6283156; fax (22) 6285264; e-mail embassy@roembassy.com.pl; internet varsovia.mae.ro; Ambassador GABRIEL CONSTANTIN BĂRTAŞ.

Russia: 00-761 Warsaw, ul. Belwederska 49; tel. (22) 6213453; fax (22) 6253016; e-mail rusemb_poland@mail.ru; internet www.poland.mid.ru; Ambassador VLADIMIR M. GRININ.

Saudi Arabia: 00-739 Warsaw, ul. Stępińska 55; tel. (22) 8400000; fax (22) 8405636; e-mail info@saudiembassy.pl; internet www.saudiembassy.pl; Ambassador NASSER BIN AHMED ALBRAIK.

Serbia: 00-540 Warsaw, Al. Ujazdowskie 23/25; tel. (22) 6285161; fax (22) 6297173; e-mail yuabapl@zigzag.pl; Chargé d'affaires a.i. (vacant).

Slovakia: 00-581 Warsaw, ul. Litewska 6; tel. (22) 5258110; fax (22) 5258122; e-mail embassy@varsava.mfa.sk; internet www.ambasada-slowacji.pl; Ambassador FRANTIŠEK RUŽIČKA.

Slovenia: 02-516 Warsaw, ul. Starościńska 1/23–24; tel. (22) 8498282; fax (22) 8484090; e-mail vvr@gov.si; Ambassador JOŻEF DROFENIK.

South Africa: 00-675 Warsaw, ul. Koszykowa 54, IPC Business Centre, 6th floor; tel. (22) 6256228; fax (22) 6256270; e-mail warsaw.political@foreign.gov.za; internet www.southafrica.pl; Ambassador FÉBÉ CHARLENE POTGIETER-GQUBULE.

Spain: 00-459 Warsaw, ul. Myśliwiecka 4; tel. (22) 5834000; fax (22) 6225408; e-mail embesppl@mail.mae.es; Ambassador RAFAEL MENDÍVIL PEYDRO.

Sri Lanka: 02-665 Warsaw, Al. Wilanowska 313A; tel. (22) 8535648; fax (22) 8435348; e-mail lankaemb@medianet.pl; internet www.srilankaembassy.pl; Ambassador CLARENCE FELICIAN CHINNIAH.

Sweden: 00-585 Warsaw, ul. Bagatela 3; tel. (22) 6408900; fax (22) 6408983; e-mail ambassaden.warszawa@foreign.ministry.se; internet www.swedishembassy.pl; Ambassador TOMAS BERTELMAN.

Switzerland: 00-540 Warsaw, Al. Ujazdowskie 27; tel. (22) 6280481; fax (22) 6210548; e-mail var.vertretung@eda.admin.ch; internet www.eda.admin.ch/warsaw; Ambassador HANS BÉNÉDICT DE CERJAT.

Syria: 02-610 Warsaw, ul. Goszczyńskiego 30; tel. (22) 8484809; fax (22) 8491847; e-mail embsyria@palmyra.neostrada.pl; internet www.syrian-embassy.com; Chargé d'affaires a.i. WISSAL ISSA.

Thailand: 00-790 Warsaw, ul. Willowa 7; tel. (22) 8492655; fax (22) 8492630; e-mail thaiemb@thaiemb.internetdsl.pl; Ambassador THAKUR PHANIT.

POLAND

Tunisia: 00-459 Warsaw, ul. Myśliwiecka 14; tel. (22) 6286330; fax (22) 6216298; e-mail at.varsovie@it.com.pl; Ambassador BÉCHIR CHEBAANE.

Turkey: 02-622 Warsaw, ul. Malczewskiego 32; tel. (22) 6464323; fax (22) 6463757; e-mail turkemb@zigzag.pl; Ambassador (vacant).

Ukraine: 00-580 Warsaw, Al. J. Ch. Szucha 7; tel. (22) 6250127; fax (22) 6298103; e-mail emb_pl@mfa.gov.ua; internet www.mfa.gov.ua/poland; Ambassador OLEKSANDR F. MOTSYK.

United Kingdom: 00-556 Warsaw, Al. Róż 1; tel. (22) 3110000; fax (22) 3110311; e-mail info@britishembassy.pl; internet www.britishembassy.pl; Ambassador DAMIAN RODERIC (RIC) TODD.

USA: 00-540 Warsaw, Al. Ujazdowskie 29/31; tel. (22) 6283041; fax (22) 6288298; internet poland.usembassy.gov; Ambassador VICTOR HENDERSON ASHE.

Uruguay: 02-516 Warsaw, ul. Rejtana 15/12; tel. (22) 8495040; fax (22) 6466887; e-mail urupol@urupol.ikp.pl; Ambassador (vacant).

Uzbekistan: 02-804 Warsaw, ul. Kraski 21; tel. (22) 8946230; fax (22) 8946231; e-mail info@uzbekistan.pl; internet www.uzbekistan.pl; Chargé d'affaires a.i. TIMUR RAHMANOV.

Venezuela: 02-516 Warsaw, ul. Rejtana 15/10–11; tel. (22) 6461846; fax (22) 6468761; e-mail embavenez.pl@qdnet.pl; Chargé d'affaires a.i. ANA MARGARITA PINO PASQUIER.

Viet Nam: 02-956 Warsaw, ul. Resorowa 36; tel. (22) 6516098; fax (22) 6516095; e-mail office@ambasadawietnamu.org; internet www.vietnamembassy-poland.org; Ambassador NGUYEN VAN XUONG.

Yemen: 03-941 Warsaw, ul. Zwycięzców 18; tel. (22) 6176025; fax (22) 6176022; e-mail biuro@ambasada-jemenu.pl; internet www.ambasada-jemenu.pl; Ambassador SHAIF BADR ABDULLAH QAID.

Judicial System

Supreme Court (Sąd Najwyższy Rzeczpospolitej Polskiej): 00-951 Warsaw, pl. Krasińskich 2/4/6; tel. (22) 5308000; fax (22) 5309100; e-mail pp@sn.pl; internet www.sn.pl; the highest judicial organ; exercises supervision over the decision-making of all other courts; justices are appointed by the President of the Republic on motions of the National Council of Judiciary and serve until the age of retirement. The First President of the Supreme Court is appointed from among the Supreme Court Justices by the President of the Republic, and serves a six-year term. The First President is also the Chairman of the Tribunal of State (Trybunał Stanu), before which certain, constitutionally determined, high state positions are accountable to the Tribunal of State for violations of the Constitution or statutes; First Pres. Prof. LECH GARDOCKI.

Supreme Administrative Court (Naczelny Sąd Administracyjny): 00-013 Warsaw, ul. Jasna 6; tel. (22) 5516000; fax (22) 8267531; e-mail informacje@nsa.gov.pl; internet www.nsa.gov.pl; f. 1980; examines complaints concerning the legality of administrative decisions; 11 regional brs; Pres. JANUSZ TRZCIŃSKI.

Constitutional Tribunal (Trybunał Konstytucyjny): 00-918 Warsaw, Al. J. Ch. Szucha 12A; tel. and fax (22) 6295526; e-mail prasainfo@trybunal.gov.pl; internet www.trybunal.gov.pl; comprises 15 judges, each appointed by the Sejm for a nine-year term; supervises compliance of legislation with the Constitution; Pres. JERZY STĘPIEŃ.

Religion

CHRISTIANITY

The Roman Catholic Church

The Roman Catholic Church was granted full legal status in May 1989, when legislation guaranteeing freedom of worship was approved. The Church was also permitted to administer its own affairs, and to operate schools, hospitals and other charitable organizations. A Concordat, agreed by the Polish Government and the Holy See in 1993, was ratified in January 1998.

For ecclesiastical purposes, Poland comprises 15 archdioceses (including one for the Catholics of the Byzantine-Ukrainian rite) and 28 dioceses (including one for the Catholics of the Byzantine-Ukrainian Rite), an Ordinariate for the faithful of the Oriental Rite, and a Military Ordinariate. At 31 December 2005 there were some 34.3m. adherents in Poland (96.1% of the population).

Bishops' Conference: 01-015 Warsaw, Skwer Kardynała Stefana Wyszyńskiego 6; tel. (22) 5304800; fax (22) 8380967; Pres. Most Rev. JÓZEF MICHALIK (Latin Rite Archbishop of Przemyśl).

Primate of Poland: Cardinal JÓZEF GLEMP (Archbishop Emeritus of Warsaw).

Latin Rite

Archbishop of Białystok: Most Rev. EDWARD OZOROWSKI, 15-087 Białystok, Pl. Jana Pawła II 1; tel. (85) 7416473; fax (85) 7322213; e-mail sekretariat@bialystok.opoka.org.pl.

Archbishop of Częstochowa: Most Rev. STANISŁAW NOWAK, 42-200 Częstochowa, Al. Najśw. Maryi Panny 54; tel. (34) 3241044; fax (34) 3651182; e-mail kuria@czestochowa.opoka.org.pl.

Archbishop of Gdańsk: Most Rev. TADEUSZ GOCŁOWSKI, 80-330 Gdańsk-Oliwa, ul. Biskupa Edmunda Nowickiego 1; tel. (58) 5520051; fax (58) 5522775; e-mail kuria@diecezja.gda.pl.

Archbishop of Gniezno: Most Rev. HENRYK MUSZYŃSKI, 62-200 Gniezno, ul. Kanclerza Jana Łaskiego 7; tel. (61) 4262102; fax (61) 4262105; e-mail kuriagni@gniezno.opoka.org.pl.

Archbishop of Katowice: Most Rev. DAMIAN ZIMOŃ, 40-043 Katowice, ul. Jordana 39; tel. (32) 2512160; fax (32) 2514830; e-mail kancelaria@kuria.katowice.pl.

Archbishop of Kraków: Cardinal STANISŁAW DZIWISZ, 31-004 Kraków, ul. Franciszkańska 3; tel. (12) 6288100; fax (12) 4294617; e-mail kuria@diecezja.krakow.pl.

Archbishop of Łódź: Most Rev. WŁADYSŁAW ZIÓŁEK, 90-458 Łódź, ul. Ks Ignacego Skorupki 1; tel. (42) 6648700; fax (42) 6648796; e-mail kuria@archidiecezja.lodz.pl.

Archbishop of Lublin: Most Rev. JÓZEF MIROSŁAW ŻYCIŃSKI, 20-950 Lublin, ul. Ks Prymasa Stefana Wyszyńskiego 2; tel. (81) 5321058; fax (81) 5346141; e-mail kanclerz@kuria.lublin.pl.

Archbishop of Poznań: Most Rev. STANISŁAW GĄDECKI, 61-109 Poznań, ul. Ostrów Tumski 2; tel. (61) 8512800; fax (61) 8512814; e-mail kuria@archpoznan.org.pl.

Archbishop of Przemyśl (Latin Rite): Most Rev. JÓZEF MICHALIK, 37-700 Przemyśl, pl. Katedralny 4A; tel. (16) 6786694; fax (16) 6782674; e-mail kuria@przemysl.opoka.org.pl.

Archbishop of Szczecin-Kamień: Most Rev. ZYGMUNT KAMIŃSKI, 71-459 Szczecin, ul. Papieża Pawła VI 4; tel. (91) 4542292; fax (91) 4536908; e-mail kuria@szczecin.opoka.org.pl.

Archbishop of Warmia: Most Rev. WOJCIECH ZIEMBA, 10-006 Olsztyn, ul. Pieniężnego 22; tel. (89) 5272280; fax (89) 5355172; e-mail kuria@olsztyn.opoka.org.pl.

Archbishop of Warsaw: Most Rev KAZIMIERZ NYCZ, 00-246 Warsaw, ul. Miodowa 17/19; tel. (22) 5317200; fax (22) 6354324; e-mail kanclerz@mkw.pl; internet www.spp.episkopat.pl.

Archbishop of Wrocław: Most Rev. MARIAN GOŁĘBIEWSKI, 50-328 Wrocław, ul. Katedralna 13; tel. (71) 3271111; fax (71) 3228269; e-mail kuria@archidiecezja.wroc.pl.

Byzantine-Ukrainian Rite

Archbishop of Przemyśl-Warsaw: Most Rev. IVAN MARTYNIAK, 37-700 Przemyśl, ul. Basztowa 13; tel. and fax (16) 6787868; e-mail kuria@przemyslgr.opoka.pl.

The Orthodox Church

Polish Autocephalous Orthodox Church (Polski Autokefaliczny Kościół Prawosławny): 03-402 Warsaw, Al. Solidarności 52; tel. (22) 6190886; internet www.orthodox.pl; comprises five archbishoprics and five bishoprics; 509,500 mems (2001); Archbishop of Warsaw and Metropolitan of All Poland Sawa (MICHAŁ HRYCUNIAK).

Protestant Churches

In 1999 there were an estimated 148,738 Protestants in Poland.

Evangelical Augsburg (Lutheran) Church in Poland (Kościół Ewangelicko-Augsburski czyli Luterański w Polsce): 00-246 Warsaw, ul. Miodowa 21; tel. (22) 8870200; fax (22) 8870218; e-mail luteranie@luteranie.pl; internet www.luteranie.pl; 75,000 mems, 134 parishes (2007); Bishop and Pres. of Consistory JANUSZ JAGUCKI.

Pentecostal Church in Poland (Kościół Zielonoświątkowy w Polsce): 00-825 Warsaw, ul. Sienna 68/70; tel. and fax (22) 5951820; e-mail sekretariat@kz.pl; internet www.kz.pl; f. 1910; 20,000 mems (2000); Chief Presbyter Bishop MIECZYSŁAW CZAJKO.

There are also several other small Protestant churches, including the Church of Christ, the Church of Evangelical Christians, the Evangelical Christian Church, the Jehovah's Witnesses, the Pentecostal Church, the Seventh-day Adventist Church and the United Methodist Church.

ISLAM

In 1999 there were about 5,125 Muslims, principally of Tatar origin, in Białystok Voivodship (Prefecture), in eastern Poland, and smaller communities in Warsaw, Gdańsk and elsewhere.

Religious Union of Muslims in Poland (Muzułmański Związek Religijny): 15-426 Białystok, Rynek Kosciuszki 26, m. 2; tel. (85) 414970; Chair. STEFAN MUCHARSKI.

JUDAISM

The overwhelming majority of the Jewish population of Poland were killed during the occupation by Nazi Germany in the Second World War (1939–45). In the mid–2000s there were believed to be between 10,000 and 20,000 Jews in Poland.

Union of Jewish Communities in Poland (Związek Gmin Wyznaniowych Żydowskich w Rzeczypospolitej Polskiej): 00-950 Warsaw, ul. Twarda 6; tel. (22) 6204324; fax (22) 6201037; e-mail union@jewish.org.pl; 14 synagogues and about 2,500 registered mems; Pres. Piotr Kadlčik.

The Press

In 2003 there were 54 newspapers in Poland, with a total circulation of 4,335,000. In that year there were 5,627 periodicals, with a combined circulation of 69.4m. copies.

Axel Springer Polska Sp. z o.o.: 02-672 Warsaw, ul. Domaniewska 52; tel. (22) 2320000; e-mail asp@axelspringer.pl; internet axelspringer.pl; subsidiary of Axel Springer AG (Germany); publishes two major dailies, *Dziennik* and *Fakt*, and is the country's second largest magazine publisher, printing women's, fiction, computer, food, economics, news and motoring magazines; Chair. of Management Bd Florian Fels.

PRINCIPAL DAILIES

Białystok

Gazeta Współczesna: 15-419 Białystok, POB 193, ul. Św. Mikołaja 1; tel. (85) 7487474; fax (85) 7487473; e-mail online@wspolczesna.pl; internet www.wspolczesna.pl; f. 1951; Editor Konrad Kruszewski; circ. 35,000.

Bydgoszcz

Gazeta Pomorska: 85-063 Bydgoszcz, ul. Zamoyskiego 2; tel. (52) 3263100; fax (52) 3221542; internet www.pomorska.pl; f. 1948; independent; Editor Maciej Kamiński; circ. 100,000 (weekdays), 300,000 (weekends).

Gdańsk

Dziennik Bałtycki (Baltic Newspaper): 80-894 Gdańsk, Targ Drzewny 9/11; tel. (58) 3003180; fax (58) 3003303; e-mail opinie@prasabalt.gda.pl; internet www.dziennikbaltycki.pl; f. 1945; non-party; Chief Editor Maciej Wośko; circ. 180,000.

Katowice

Dziennik Zachodni (Western Daily): 40-954 Katowice, ul. Młyńska 1; tel. (32) 3582100; fax (32) 1538196; e-mail redakcja@dz.com.pl; internet www.dz.com.pl; f. 1945; non-party; Chief Editor Marek Chyliński; circ. 510,000.

Trybuna Śląska (Silesian Tribune): 40-092 Katowice, ul. Młyńska 1; tel. (32) 2537822; fax (32) 2537997; f. 1945; independent; Editor Romuald Orzet; circ. 180,000 (weekdays), 800,000 (weekends).

Kielce

Echo Dnia (Echo of the Day): 25-520 Kielce, ul. Targowa 18; tel. (41) 3495353; fax (41) 3682218; e-mail redakcja@echodnia.eu; internet www.echondnia.eu; f. 1971; Chief Editor Stanisław Wróbel.

Kraków

Dziennik Polski (Polish Daily): 31-072 Kraków, ul. Wielopole 1; tel. (12) 6199200; fax (12) 6199276; e-mail redakcja@dziennik.krakow.pl; internet www.dziennik.krakow.pl; Editor Piotr Aleksandrowicz.

Gazeta Krakowska (Kraków Gazette): 31-548 Kraków, Al. Pokoju 3; tel. (12) 6888000; fax (12) 6888109; e-mail sekretariat@gk.pl; internet www.gk.pl; f. 1949; Editor-in-Chief Marek Zalejski; circ. 60,000 (weekdays), 150,000 (weekends).

Łódź

Dziennik Łódzki (Łódz Daily): 90-532 Łódź, ul. Ks. Skorupki 17/19; tel. (42) 6303565; fax (42) 6377364; e-mail dziennik@dziennik.lodz.pl; internet www.dziennik.lodz.pl; f. 1945; non-party; Editor Julian Beck; circ. 50,000 (weekdays), 110,000 (weekends).

Lublin

Dziennik Wschodni (Eastern Daily): 20-081 Lublin, ul. Staszica 20; tel. (81) 4626800; fax (81) 4626801; e-mail redakcja@dziennikwschodni.pl; internet www.dziennikwschodni.pl; Chief Editor Krzysztof Wiejak.

Kurier Lubelski (Lublin Courier): 20-950 Lublin, POB 176; tel. (81) 5326634; fax (81) 5326835; e-mail redakcja@kurierlubelski.pl; internet www.kurier.lublin.pl; f. 1830; independent; evening; Editor Małgorzata Ilka; circ. 40,000 (weekdays), 100,000 (weekends).

Olsztyn

Gazeta Olsztyńska (Olsztyn Gazette): 10-364 Olsztyn, ul. Tracka 5; tel. (89) 5397520; e-mail internet@gazetaolsztynska.pl; internet gazetaolsztynska.wm.pl; f. 1886; Editor-in-Chief Tomasz Śrutkowski; circ. 45,000 (weekdays), 90,000 (weekends).

Opole

Nowa Trybuna Opolska (New Opole Tribune): 45-086 Opole, ul. Powstańców Śląskich 9; tel. (77) 4432500; fax (77) 4432515; e-mail nto@nto.pl; internet www.nto.pl; f. 1952; independent; Editor Wojciech Potocki; circ. 80,000.

Poznań

Głos Wielkopolski (Voice of Wielkopolska): 60-782 Poznań, ul. Grunwaldzka 19; tel. (61) 8694100; fax (61) 8659672; e-mail glosmar@sylaba.poznan.pl; internet www.glos.com; f. 1945; independent; Editor-in-Chief Marek Przybylski; circ. 110,000 (weekdays), 160,000 (weekends).

Rzeszów

Noviny (News): 35-016 Rzeszów, ul. Kraszewskiego 2; tel. (17) 8672200; fax (17) 8672201; e-mail nowiny@gcnowiny.pl; internet www.gcnowiny.pl; f. 1949; evening; Editor-in-Chief Janusz Pawlak; circ. 100,000.

Słupsk

Głos Pomorza (Voice of Pomerania): 76-200 Słupsk, ul. Pobożnego 19; tel. (59) 8488100; fax (59) 8488104; e-mail online@gp24.pl; internet www.gp24.pl; f. 1952; Chief Editor Krzysztof Nałęcz; circ. 60,000 (weekdays), 130,000 (weekends).

Szczecin

Głos Szczeciński (Szczecin Voice): 70-550 Szczecin, ul. Nowy Rynek 3; tel. (91) 4813300; fax (91) 4334864; e-mail online@gs24.pl; internet www.gs24.pl; f. 1947; Chief Editor Krzysztof Nałęcz; circ. 30,000 (weekdays), 100,000 (weekends).

Kurier Szczeciński (Szczecin Courier): 70-550 Szczecin, pl. Hołdu Pruskiego 8; tel. and fax (91) 4345741; e-mail redakcja@kurier.szczecin.pl; internet www.kurier.szczecin.pl; Editor Andrzej Łapciewicz.

Warsaw

Dziennik (Daily): 02-672 Warsaw, ul. Domaniewska 52; fax (22) 2325550; internet www.dziennik.pl; f. 2006; Mon.–Sat.; published by Axel Springer Polska; Editor-in-Chief Robert Krasowski; circ. 259,039 (2006).

Fakt (Fact): 02-672 Warsaw, Ul. Domaniewska 52; tel. (22) 6085554; fax (22) 6085508; e-mail redakcja@efakt.pl; internet www.efakt.pl; f. 2003; owned by Axel Springer Polska Sp. z o.o.; Editor Katarzyna Sielicka; circ. 520,000.

Gazeta Wyborcza: 00-732 Warsaw, ul. Czerska 8/10; tel. (22) 5556000; fax (22) 5554780; e-mail listy@agora.pl; internet wyborcza.gazeta.pl; f. 1989; non-party; national edn and 20 local edns; weekend edn: *Gazeta Świateczna*; special supplements; Editor-in-Chief Adam Michnik; circ. 516,000 (weekdays), 86,000 (weekends).

Nasz Dziennik (Our Daily): 04-476 Warsaw, ul. Żeligowskiego 16/20; tel. (22) 5157777; fax (22) 5157778; e-mail redakcja@naszdziennik.pl; internet www.naszdziennik.pl; national; Editor Ewa Sołowiej; circ. 250,000.

Polska Zbrojna (Military Poland): 00-909 Warsaw, Al. Jerozolimskie 97; tel. (22) 6845365; fax (22) 6845503; e-mail sekretariat@redakcjawojskowa.pl; internet www.polska-zbrojna.pl; f. 1943; Editor Jerzy Śląski; circ. 50,000.

Przegląd Sportowy (Sports Review): 02-017 Warsaw, Al. Jerozolimskie 125/127, POB 181; tel. (22) 6289116; fax (22) 218697; internet www.sports.pl; f. 1921; Editor Maciej Polkowski; circ. 110,000.

Rzeczpospolita (The Republic): 02-015 Warsaw, pl. Starynkiewicza 7; tel. (22) 6283401; fax (22) 6280588; e-mail p.aleksandrowicz@rzeczpospolita.pl; internet www.rp.pl; f. 1982; 51% owned by Orkla (Norway); Editor-in-Chief Grzegorz Gauden; circ. 275,000.

Super Express: 00-939 Warsaw, ul. Jubilerska 10; tel. (22) 5159000; fax (22) 5159100; e-mail listy@superexpress.com.pl; internet www.se.com.pl; f. 1991; popular; Editor-in-Chief Sławomir Jastrzębowski; circ. 371,106.

POLAND

Trybuna (Tribune): 00-835 Warsaw, ul. Miedziana 11; tel. (22) 3898831; fax (22) 6204100; e-mail redakcja@trybuna.com.pl; f. 1990; organ of Polish Social Democracy; Editor-in-Chief WIESŁAW DĘBSKI; circ. 110,000 (weekdays), 150,000 (weekends).

Wprost (To The Point): 02-017 Warsaw, Al. Jerozolimskie 123, Reform Plaza; tel. (22) 5291100; fax (22) 8529016; e-mail redakcja@wprost.pl; internet www.wprost.pl; f. 1982; Editor MAREK KRÓL.

Życie Warszawy (Warsaw Life): 00-175 Warsaw, Al. Jana Pawła II 80; tel. (22) 3348855; fax (22) 3348863; e-mail zycie@zw.com.pl; internet www.zw.com.pl; f. 1944; independent; Editor-in-Chief ANDRZEJ ZAŁUCKI; circ. 250,000 (weekdays), 460,000 (weekends).

Wrocław

Gazeta Robotnicza (Workers' Gazette): 50-010 Wrocław, ul. Podwale 62; tel. and fax (71) 335756; f. 1948; Editor ANDRZEJ BUŁAT; circ. 30,000 (weekdays), 315,000 (weekends).

Gazeta Wrocławska (Wrocław Gazette): 53-611 Wrocław, ul. Strzegomska 42A; tel. (71) 3748151; fax (71) 3748175; e-mail redakcja@gazeta.wroc.pl; internet gazeta.naszemiasto.pl; Editor-in-Chief MAREK TWARÓG.

Zielona Góra

Gazeta Lubuska: 65-042 Zielona Góra, Al. Niepodległości 25, POB 120; tel. (68) 3248811; fax (68) 3248815; e-mail redakcja@gazetalubuska.pl; internet www.gazetalubuska.pl; f. 1952; independent; Chief Editor IWONA ZIELIŃSKA; circ. 60,000 (weekdays), 150,000 (weekends).

PERIODICALS

Computerworld Polska: 04-204 Warsaw, ul. Jordanowska 12, POB 73; tel. (22) 3217810; fax (22) 3217888; e-mail Krzysztof_Frydrychowicz@idg.com.pl; internet www.computerworld.pl; weekly; Editor-in-Chief KRZYSZTOF FRYDRYCHOWICZ.

Dobre Rady (Good Advice): 54-432 Wrocław, ul. Strzegornska 236A; tel. (71) 3517758; fax (71) 3737288; e-mail a.sokolowska@burda.pl; f. 2002; published by Burda Polska.

Dom i Wnętrze (Home and Interior): 00-480 Warsaw, ul. Wiejska 19; tel. (22) 5842200; fax (22) 5842318; internet www.domiwnetrze.pl; f. 1991; illustrated monthly; Editor-in-Chief EWA MIERZEJEWSKA.

Dziecko (Child): 00-732 Warsaw, ul. Czerska 8/10; tel. (22) 5556882; fax (22) 5556669; e-mail dziecko@agora.pl; internet www.edziecko.pl; f. 1995; monthly; women's magazine concerning children's affairs; Editor JUSTYNA DĄBROWSKA; circ. 95,000.

Dziewczyna (Girl): 02-222 Warsaw, Al. Jerozolimskie 181, Axel Springer Polska; tel. (22) 6363681; fax (22) 6365281; e-mail redakcja@dziewczyna.pl; internet www.dziewczyna.pl; f. 1990; monthly; lifestyle magazine for young women; Editor DONATA CIESLIK; circ. 420,000.

Les Echos de Pologne: 02-536 Warsaw, ul. Narbutta 15A/6; tel. (22) 6464212; fax (22) 6462369; e-mail echos@echos.pl; internet www.echos.pl; f. 2003; fortnightly; in French; Editor-in-Chief SYLWIA KAMIŃSKA.

Gazeta Bankowa (Banking Gazette): 00-140 Warsaw, Al. Solidarności 117; tel. (22) 6525914; fax (22) 6525910; e-mail redakcja@wtrendy.pl; internet www.gazetabankowa.pl; f. 1988; weekly; business and finance; Editor-in-Chief ANDRZEJ S. NARTOWSKI.

Głos Nauczycielski (Teachers' Voice): 00-389 Warsaw, ul. J. Smulikowskiego 6/8; tel. (22) 8263420; fax (22) 8281355; e-mail glos@glos.pl; internet www.glos.pl; f. 1917; weekly; organ of the Polish Teachers' Union; Chief Editor JAKUB RZEKANOWKSI (acting); circ. 40,000.

Lubie Gotować (I Love Cooking): 00-732 Warsaw, ul. Czerska 8/10; tel. (22) 5556606; fax (22) 5556668; e-mail czasopisma@agora.pl; internet www.lubiegotowac.pl; f. 1997; monthly; cookery; Editor-in-Chief JOANNA NOWICKA.

Nie (No): 00-789 Warsaw, ul. Słoneczna 25; tel. (22) 6286794; fax (22) 6220731; e-mail nie@redakija.nie.com.pl; internet www.nie.com.pl; f. 1990; satirical; weekly; Editor JERZY URBAN; circ. 500,000.

Nowa Fantastyka (New Fantasy): 02-651 Warsaw, ul. Garażowa 7; tel. (22) 6077790; fax (22) 8482266; e-mail nowafantastyka@fantastyka.pl; internet www.fantastyka.pl; f. 1982; monthly; science fiction and fantasy; Editor-in-Chief PAWEŁ MATUSZEK; circ. 57,000.

Nowe Życie Gospodarcze (New Economic Life): 00-549 Warsaw, ul. Piękna 24/26; tel. (22) 6280628; fax (22) 6288392; e-mail nzg@nzg.pl; internet www.nzg.pl; f. 1945 as Życie Gospodarcze (Economic Life); weekly; economic; Chair. and Editor-in-Chief ADAM CYMER; circ. 35,700.

Państwo i Prawo (State and Law): 00-330 Warsaw, ul. Nowy Świat 72; tel. (22) 6288296; e-mail panstwoiprawo@pwp.pl; internet www.panstwoiprawo.pl; f. 1946; monthly organ of the Polish Academy of Sciences; publ. by Wolters Kluwer Polska; Chief Editor Dr LESZEK KUBICKI; circ. 3,000.

Polityka (Politics): 02-309 Warsaw, ul. Słupecka 6, POB 13; tel. (22) 4516133; fax (22) 4516135; e-mail polityka@polityka.com.pl; internet polityka.onet.pl; f. 1957; weekly; political, economic, cultural; Editor JERZY BACZYŃSKI; circ. 340,000.

Poradnik Gospodarski (Farmers' Guide): 60-163 Poznań, ul. Sieradzka 29; tel. and fax (61) 8685492; e-mail poradnik@wodr.poznan.pl; internet www.poradnik.wodr.poznan.pl; f. 1889; monthly; agriculture; Editor-in-Chief TADEUSZ SZALCZYK; circ. 10,000.

Przekrój (Review): 00-480 Warsaw, ul. Wiejska 19; tel. (22) 2842533; fax (22) 5842521; e-mail redakcja@przekroj.pl; internet www.przekroj.pl; f. 1945; weekly; illustrated; cultural; Chief Editor JACEK KOWALCZYK; circ. 77,500.

Przyjaciółka (Girlfriend): 00-480 Warsaw, ul. Wiejska 19; tel. (22) 5842438; fax (22) 5842436; e-mail info@przyjaciolka.pl; internet www.przyjaciolka.pl; f. 1948; weekly; women's magazine; Editor-in-Chief AGNIESZKA SWIECKA-PILASZEK; circ. 720,000.

Res Publica Nowa (The New Republic): 02-309 Warsaw 1, ul. Słupecka 6, POB 856; tel. (22) 4516180; fax (22) 4516109; e-mail respublica@pro.onet.pl; internet respublica.onet.pl; f. 1987; monthly; political and cultural; Editor MARCIN KRÓL; circ. 5,000.

Sprawy Międzynarodowe (International Affairs): 02-630 Warsaw, ul. Tyniecka 15/17; tel. (22) 5239086; fax (22) 5239027; e-mail sprawy@pism.pl; internet www.sprawymiedzynarodowe.pl; f. 1948; quarterly; published by the Polish Institute of International Affairs; Editor HENRYK SZLAJFER; circ. 800.

Swiat Nauki (World of Science): 02-651 Warsaw, ul. Garażowa 7; tel. (22) 6077815; fax (22) 8482266; e-mail swiatnauki@proszynskimedia.pl; internet www.swiatnauki.pl; f. 1991; monthly; Polish edn of Scientific American; Editor-in-Chief JOANNA ZIMAKOWSKA; circ. 45,000.

Szpilki (Needles): Warsaw; tel. (22) 6280429; f. 1935; weekly; illustrated satirical; Editor JACEK JANCZARSKI; circ. 100,000.

Tygodnik Solidarność (Solidarity Weekly): 02-390 Warsaw, ul. Grójecka 186, POB 613; tel. and fax (22) 8822796; e-mail tygodniksolidarnosc.com; internet www.tygodniksolidarnosc.com; f. 1981; reactivated 1989; weekly; Editor-in-Chief JERZY KŁOSIŃSKI; circ. 60,000.

The Warsaw Voice: 01-452 Warsaw, ul. Księcia Janusza 64; tel. (22) 3359700; fax (22) 3359720; e-mail voice@warsawvoice.pl; internet www.warsawvoice.pl; f. 1988; weekly; political, social, cultural and economic; in English; Editor ANDRZEJ JONAS; circ. 10,500.

Wiedza i Życie (Knowledge and Life): 02-651 Warsaw, ul. Garażowa 7; tel. (22) 6077630; fax (22) 6077645; e-mail wiedza@proszynski.com.pl; internet www.proszynski.com.pl/wiedzaizycie; f. 1926; monthly; popular science; Editor ANDRZEJ GORZYM; circ. 112,000.

Żołnierz Polski (Polish Soldier): 00-909 Warsaw, Al. Jerozolimskie 97; tel. (22) 6845365; fax (22) 6845503; e-mail sekretariat@redakcjawojskowa.pl; internet www.zolnierz-polski.pl; f. 1945; monthly; illustrated magazine primarily about the armed forces; Editor IRENEUSZ CZYŻEWSKI; circ. 40,000.

NEWS AGENCY

Polska Agencja Prasowa (PAP) (Polish Press Agency): 00-502 Warsaw, ul. Bracka 6/8; tel. (22) 6280001; fax (22) 6286407; e-mail webmaster@pap.com.pl; internet www.pap.com.pl; f. 1944; brs in 28 Polish towns and 22 foreign capitals; 274 journalist and photojournalist mems; Pres. PIOTR SKWIECINSKI.

PRESS ASSOCIATION

Stowarzyszenie Dziennikarzy Polskich (SDP) (Polish Journalists' Association): 00-366 Warsaw, ul. Foksal 3/5; tel. and fax (22) 8278720; e-mail sdp@sdp.pl; internet www.sdp.pl; f. 1951; dissolved 1982, legal status restored 1989; 2,320 mems; Pres. KRYSTYNA MOKROSIŃSKA; Gen. Sec. STEFAN TRUSZCZYŃSKI.

Publishers

Bertelsmann Media Sp. z o.o.: 02-786 Warsaw, ul. Rosoła 10; tel. (22) 6458200; fax (22) 6484732; e-mail poczta@swiatksiazki.com.pl; internet www.swiatksiazki.com.pl; f. 1994 as Bertelsmann Publishing Świat Książki Sp. z o.o.; belles-lettres, science-fiction, popular science, albums, books for children and teenagers; Pres. ANDRZEJ KOSTARCZYK; Editor-in-Chief BOGUSŁAW DĄBROWSKI.

Dom Wydawniczy ABC Sp. z o.o.: 01-231 Warsaw, ul. Płocka 5A; tel. (22) 5358000; fax (22) 5358001; e-mail info@abc.com.pl; internet www.abc.com.pl; f. 1989; legal, business and financial books; part of Polskie Wydawnictwa Profesjonalne Sp. z o.o; owned by Wolters

POLAND

Kluwer (Netherlands); Owners WŁODZIMIERZ ALBIN, KRZYSZTOF BRZESKI.

Dom Wydawniczy Bellona: 00-844 Warsaw, ul. Grzybowska 77; tel. (22) 6204291; fax (22) 6522695; e-mail bellona@bellona.pl; internet www.bellona.pl; f. 1947; fiction, history and military; Pres. Col JÓZEF SKRZYPIEC; Dir ZBIGNIEW CZERWIŃSKI.

Dom Wydawniczy Rebis Sp. z o.o.: 60-171 Poznań, ul. Żmigrodzka 41/49; tel. (61) 8678140; fax (61) 8673774; e-mail rebis@rebis.com.pl; internet www.rebis.com.pl; f. 1990; psychology, self-help books and parental guides; Pres. and Man. Dir TOMASZ SZPONDER.

Drukarnia i Księgarnia św. Wojciecha (St Adalbert—Wojciech Printing and Publishing Co): 60-967 Poznań, pl. Wolności 1; tel. (61) 8529186; fax (61) 8523746; e-mail wydawnictwo@ksw.com.pl; internet www.ksw.com.pl; f. 1895; textbooks and Catholic publications; Dir Rev. BOGDAN REFORMAT; Editor-in-Chief BOŻYSŁAW WALCZAK.

Egmont Sp. z o.o.: 01-029 Warsaw, ul. Dzielna 60; tel. (22) 8384100; fax (22) 8384200; e-mail kluby@egmont.pl; internet www.egmont.pl; f. 1990; books and comics for children and teenagers; Man. Dir JACEK BEŁDOWSKI; Editor-in-Chief HANNA BALTYN.

Instytut Wydawniczy Pax (Pax Publishing Institute): 00-390 Warsaw, ul. Wybrzeże Kościuszkowskie 21A; tel. (22) 6253398; fax (22) 6251378; e-mail iwpax@iwpax.com.pl; internet sklep.iwpax.com.pl; f. 1949; theology, philosophy, religion, history, literature; Dir KRZYSZTOF PRZESTRZELSKI; Editor-in-Chief ZBIGNIEW BOROWIK.

Ludowa Spółdzielnia Wydawnicza (People's Publishing Co-operative): 00-131 Warsaw, ul. Grzybowska 4/8; tel. (22) 6205718; fax (22) 6207277; f. 1949; fiction, poetry and popular science; Chair. and Editor-in-Chief JAN RODZIM.

Muchomor Publishers: 01-552 Warsaw, pl. Inwalidów 10/29; tel. and fax (22) 8394968; e-mail muchomor@muchomor.pl; internet www.muchomor.pl; f. 2002; illustrated books for children; Editorial Dir MARIA DESKUR.

Muza SA: 00-590 Warsaw, ul. Marszałkowska 8; tel. (22) 6211776; fax (22) 6292349; e-mail muza@muza.com.pl; internet www.muza.com.pl; f. 1991; albums, encyclopedias, lexicons, handbooks, dictionaries, belles-lettres, books for children and youth; Man. Dir MARCIN GARLINSKI.

Niezależna Oficyna Wydawnicza NOWA (Independent Publishing House NOWA): 00-251 Warsaw, ul. Miodowa 10; tel. and fax (22) 6359994; f. 1972; belles-lettres, memoirs, essays, recent history, politics; Pres. GRZEGORZ BOGUTA; Editor-in-Chief MIROSŁAW KOWALSKI.

Oficyna Literacka: 31-436 Kraków, ul. A. Sokołowskiego 19; tel. (12) 4117365; fax (12) 4127599; f. 1982 clandestinely, 1990 officially; belles-lettres, poetry, essays; Editor-in-Chief HENRYK KARKOSZA.

Oficyna Wydawnicza Volumen: 00-354 Warsaw, ul. Dynasy 2A; tel. and fax (22) 8260501; f. 1984 (working clandestinely as WERS), 1989 officially; science, popular history, anthropology and socio-political sciences; Dir MIROSLAWA LATKOWSKA.

Pallottinum—Wydawnictwo Stowarzyszenia Apostolstwa Katolickiego: 60-959 Poznań, Al. Przybyszewskiego 30, POB 23; tel. (61) 8675233; fax (61) 8675238; e-mail pallottinum@pallottinum.pl; internet www.pallottinum.pl; f. 1947; religious and philosophical books; Dir STEFAN DUSZA.

Państwowe Wydawnictwo Rolnicze i Leśne (State Agricultural and Forestry Publishers): 02-272 Warsaw, ul. Malownicza 14; tel. and fax (22) 8684529; e-mail pwril@pwril.com; internet www.pwril.com; f. 1947; professional publications on agriculture, forestry, health and veterinary science; Dir and Editor-in-Chief JOLANTA KUCZYŃSKA.

Państwowy Instytut Wydawniczy (State Publishing Institute): 00-372 Warsaw, ul. Foksal 17; tel. (22) 8260201; fax (22) 8261536; e-mail piw@piw.pl; internet www.piw.pl; f. 1946; Polish and foreign classical and contemporary literature, fiction, literary criticism, biographies, performing arts, culture, history, popular science, and fine arts; Dir and Editor-in-Chief RAFAŁ SKĄPSKI.

Pierwszy wybór profesjonalisty: 01-231 Warsaw, ul. Płocka 5A; tel. (22) 5358000; fax (22) 5358001; e-mail obsluga.klienta@wolterskluwer.pl; internet www.pwp.pl; country's largest legal publisher; Pres. ALBIN WŁODZIMIERZ.

Polskie Przedsiębiorstwo Wydawnictw Kartograficznych im. E. Romera (E. Romer Polish Cartographical Publishing House): 00-410 Warsaw, ul. Solec 18; tel. (22) 5851800; fax (22) 5851801; e-mail ppwk@ppwk.com.pl; internet www.ppwk.com.pl; f. 1951; maps, atlases, travel guides, books on geodesy and cartography; Man. Dir JACEK BŁASCZYŃSKI.

Polskie Wydawnictwo Muzyczne (Polish Publishing House for Music): 31-111 Kraków, Al. Krasińskiego 11A; tel. (12) 4227044; fax (12) 4220174; e-mail pwm@pwm.com.pl; internet www.pwm.com.pl; f. 1945; music and books on music; Chair. and Man. Dir Dr SŁAWOMIR J. TABKOWSKI; Editor-in-Chief ANDRZEJ KOSOWSKI.

Prószyński i S-ka Publishing House: 02-651 Warsaw, ul. Garazowa 7; tel. (22) 6077700; fax (22) 6077704; e-mail wydawnictwo@proszynski.pl; internet www.proszynski.pl; f. 1990; poetry, fiction, non-fiction, educational text and reference books, popular science, etc.; Pres. MIECZYSŁAW PRÓSZYŃSKI; 110 employees.

Spółdzielnia Wydawnicza Czytelnik (Reader Co-operative Publishing House): 00-490 Warsaw, ul. Wiejska 12A; tel. (22) 6281441; fax (22) 6283178; e-mail sekretariat@czytelnik.pl; internet www.czytelnik.pl; f. 1944; general, especially fiction and contemporary Polish literature; Pres. MAREK ZAKOWSKI; Editor-in-Chief JANUSZ DRZEWUCKI.

Spółdzielnia Wydawniczo-Handlowa 'Książka i Wiedza' ('Books and Knowledge' Trade Co-operative Publishing House): 00-375 Warsaw, ul. Smolna 13; tel. (22) 8275401; fax (22) 8279423; e-mail publisher@kiw.com.pl; internet www.kiw.com.pl; f. 1948; philosophy, religion, linguistics, literature and history; Chair. WŁODZIMIERZ GAŁĄSKA; Editor-in-Chief ELŻBIETA KONECKA.

Wydawnictwa Naukowo-Techniczne (Scientific-Technical Publishers): 00-048 Warsaw, ul. Mazowiecka 2/4, POB 359; tel. (22) 8267271; fax (22) 8268293; e-mail wnt@pol.pl; internet www.wnt.com.pl; f. 1949; scientific and technical books on mathematics, physics, chemistry, foodstuffs industry, electrical and electronic engineering, computer science, automation, mechanical engineering, light industry, technological encyclopedias and dictionaries; Man. Dir and Editor Dr ANIELA TOPULOS.

Wydawnictwa Normalizacyjne Alfa-Wero (Alfa-Wero Standardization Publishing House): 00-820 Warsaw, ul. Sienna 63; tel. (22) 6204500; fax (22) 6207131; e-mail ckn@alfawero.pl; internet www.normy.pl; f. 1956; standards, catalogues and reference books on standardization, periodicals, political and historical literature, science fiction, general; Man. Dir ANDRZEJ SWIĘCICKI.

Wydawnictwa Polskiej Agencji Ekologicznej (Polish Ecological Publishing House): 02-078 Warsaw, ul. Krzywickiego 34; tel. (22) 3130400; fax (22) 3130446; e-mail ekologia@pae.com.pl; internet www.pae.com.pl; f. 1953; geology; Dir JERZY CHODKOWSKI.

Wydawnictwa Szkolne i Pedagogiczne (WSiP) (School and Pedagogical Publishers): 00-965 Warsaw, Al. Jerozolimskie 136, p. 9; tel. (22) 5762510; fax (22) 5762509; e-mail wsip@wsip.pl; internet www.wsip.pl; f. 1945; school textbooks and popular science books, scientific literature for teachers, visual teaching aids, periodicals for teachers and youth; Chair. (vacant).

Wydawnictwo Amber Sp. z o.o.: 00-060 Warsaw, ul. Królewska 27; tel. (22) 6204061; fax (22) 6201393; e-mail media@amber.sm.pl; internet www.amber.sm.pl; reference books, fiction, biography and autobiography; Dir ZBIGNIEW FONIOK; Editor MAŁGORZATA CEBO-FONIOK.

Wydawnictwo Arkady: 00-344 Warsaw, ul. Dobra 28, POB 137; tel. (22) 8269316; fax (22) 8274194; e-mail arkady@arkady.com.pl; internet www.arkady.com.pl; f. 1957; publications on building, town planning, architecture and art; Dir and Pres. JANINA KRYSIAK.

Wydawnictwo C. H. Beck.: 01-518 Warsaw, ul. Gen. Zajączka 9; tel. (22) 3377600; fax (22) 3377601; e-mail redakcja@beck.pl; internet www.beck.pl; f. 1993; law and economics; Man. Dir PAWEŁ ESSE.

Wydawnictwo Dolnośląskie Sp. z o.o.: 50-010 Wrocław, ul. Podwale 62; tel. (71) 7859040; fax (71) 7859066; e-mail sekretariat@wd.wroc.pl; internet www.wd.wroc.pl; f. 1986; belles-lettres, essays, memoirs, translations, general non-fiction; Pres. of Bd ANDRZEJ ADAMUS.

Wydawnictwo Infor: 01-042 Warsaw, ul. Okopowa 58/72; tel. (22) 5304050; fax (22) 5304054; e-mail sekretariat.dg@infor.pl; internet www.infor.pl; f. 1987; law, economics, marketing, management; Pres. RYSZARD PIEŃKOWSKI.

Wydawnictwo Iskry (Sparks Publishing House Ltd): 00-375 Warsaw, ul. Smolna 11; tel. and fax (22) 8279415; e-mail iskry@iskry.com.pl; internet www.iskry.com.pl; f. 1952; travel, Polish and foreign fiction, science fiction, essays, popular science, history, memoirs; Chair. Dr WIESŁAW UCHAŃSKI; Editor-in-Chief MAGDALENA SŁYSZ.

Wydawnictwo Kurpisz: 01-341 Poznań, ul. Przemysława 46; tel. (61) 8331517; fax (61) 8351294; e-mail kurpisz@kurpisz.pl; internet www.kurpisz.pl; f. 1991; belles-lettres, reprints, dictionaries, encyclopedias, periodicals; Dir KAZIMIERZ GRZESIAK.

Wydawnictwo Lekarskie PZWL (PZWL Medical Publishers): 00-251 Warsaw, ul. Miodowa 10; tel. and fax (22) 6954497; e-mail promocja@pzwl.pl; internet www.pzwl.pl; f. 1945; medical literature and manuals, lexicons, encyclopedias; Pres. KRYSTYNA REGULSKA.

Wydawnictwo Literackie (Literary Publishing House): 31-147 Kraków, ul. Długa 1; tel. (12) 4232254; fax (12) 4225423; e-mail redakcja@wl.net.pl; internet www.wl.net.pl; f. 1953; works of literature and belles-lettres; Dir BARBARA DRWOTA; Editor-in-Chief MAŁGORZATA NYCZ.

Wydawnictwo Nasza Księgarnia (Our Booksellers' Publishing House): 02-868 Warsaw, ul. Sarabandy 24c; tel. (22) 6439389; fax (22) 6437028; e-mail naszaksiegarnia@nk.com.pl; internet www.nk.com

POLAND

.pl/nasza; f. 1921; books and periodicals for children and young readers; educational publications; Pres. AGNIESZKA TOKARCZYK; Editor JOLANTA SZTUCZYŃSKA.

Wydawnictwo Naukowe PWN (PWN Scientific Publishers): 00-251 Warsaw, ul. Miodowa 10; tel. (22) 6954180; fax (22) 6954288; e-mail international@pwn.com.pl; internet www.pwn.pl; f. 1951; prominent Central European publisher of works of reference, academic publications, multimedia; Pres. BARBARA JOZWIAK.

Wydawnictwo Nowa Era: 02-305 Warsaw, Al. Jerozolimskie 146D; tel. (22) 5702580; fax (22) 5702581; e-mail nowaera@nowaera.com.pl; internet www.nowaera.com.pl; school textbooks; Chair. MARIUSZ KOPER.

Wydawnictwo Ossolineum (Ossolineum Publishing House): 50-062 Wrocław, pl. Solny 14A; tel. (71) 3436961; fax (71) 3448103; e-mail wydawnictwo@ossolineum.pl; internet www.ossolineum.pl; f. 1817; publishing house of the Polish Academy of Sciences; academic publications in humanities and sciences; Man. Dir WOJCIECH KARWACKI; Editor-in-Chief STANISŁAW ROŚCICKI.

Wydawnictwo Prawnicze LexisNexis—LexPolonia (LexPolonia—LexisNexis Legal Publishing House): 02-520 Warsaw, ul. Gen. K. Sosnkowskiego 1; tel. (22) 5729500; fax (22) 5729508; e-mail biuro@lexisnexis.pl; internet www.lexisnexis.pl; f. 1952; present name adopted 2003; Exec. Dir OLGA DYMKOWSKA-PULCHNY.

Wydawnictwo Publicat: 61-003 Poznań, ul. Chlebowa 24; tel. (61) 8679546; fax (61) 6529200; internet www.najlepszyprezent.pl; f. 1990 as Wydawnictwo Podsiedlik-Raniowski Sp. z o.o.; popular and children's literature, poetry, prose, classical works, educational books; Pres. MICHAŁ KAIK.

Wydawnictwo RTW (RTW Publishers): 01-780 Warsaw, ul. Broniewskiego 9A; tel. (22) 6337010; fax (22) 6637474; f. 1992; education, geography, geology, history, science, atlases, dictionaries, encyclopedias and audio books.

Wydawnictwo Śląsk Sp. z o.o. (Silesia Publishing House Ltd): 40-161 Katowice, Al. W. Korfantego 51; tel. (32) 580756; fax (32) 583229; e-mail biuro@slaskwn.com.pl; internet www.slaskwn.com.pl; f. 1952; social, popular science, technical, and regional literature; Chair. and Editor-in-Chief Dr TADEUSZ SIERNY.

Wydawnictwo W.A.B. (WAB Publishers): 02-502 Warsaw, ul. Łowicka 31; tel. (22) 6460510; fax (22) 6460511; e-mail wab@wab.com.pl; internet www.wab.com.pl; f. 1991; contemporary Polish fiction, historical and cultural essays, and literature for children; Editor ANGELIKA SASIN.

Wydawnictwo Wam (For You Publishers): 31-501 Kraków, ul. Kopernika 26; tel. (12) 6293200; fax (12) 4295003; e-mail wam@wydawnictwowam.pl; internet www.wydawnictwowam.pl; f. 1872; Roman Catholic textbooks, encyclopedias, non-fiction, fiction and children's books; Dir HENRYK PIETRAS.

Wydawnictwo Wiedza Powszechna (General Knowledge Publishers): 00-054 Warsaw, ul. Jasna 26; tel. and fax (22) 8270799; e-mail info@wiedza.pl; internet www.wiedza.pl; f. 1952; popular science books, Polish and foreign language dictionaries, foreign language textbooks, encyclopedias and lexicons; Dir TERESA KORSAK.

Wydawnictwo Wilga (Yellow Thrush Publishers): 00-389 Warsaw, ul. Smulikowskiego 1/3; tel. (22) 8260882; fax (22) 8260643; e-mail wilga@wilga.com.pl; internet www.wilga.com.pl; f. 1993; education and fiction; Pres. JAN WOJNITKO.

Wydawnictwo Zysk i S-ka (Zysk Publishers): 61-744 Poznań, ul. Wielka 10; tel. (61) 8532767; fax (61) 8526326; e-mail sekretariat@zysk.com.pl; internet www.zysk.com.pl; f. 1994; belles-lettres, popular, scientific and religious literature; Pres. TADEUSZ ZYSK.

Znak Społeczny Instytut Wydawniczy (Znak Social Publishing Institute): 30-105 Kraków, ul. Kościuszki 37; tel. (12) 6199500; fax (12) 6199502; internet www.znak.com.pl; f. 1959; religion, philosophy, belles-lettres, essays, history; Chief Exec. HENRYK WOŹNIAKOWSKI; Editor-in-Chief JERZY ILLG.

PUBLISHERS' ASSOCIATION

Polskie Towarzystwo Wydawców Książek (Polish Society of Book Editors): 00-048 Warsaw, ul. Mazowiecka 2/4; tel. and fax (22) 8260735; internet www.wydawca.com.pl; f. 1921; Pres. JANUSZ FOGLER; 500 mems.

Broadcasting and Communications

TELECOMMUNICATIONS

Regulatory Authority

Office of Electronic Communications (Urząd Komunikacji Elektronicznej—UKE): 01-211 Warsaw, ul. Kasprzaka 18/20; tel. (22) 5349190; fax (22) 5349162; e-mail uke@uke.gov.pl; internet www.uke.gov.pl; f. 2001; formerly the Office of Telecommunications and Post Regulation (URTIP); reorganized Jan. 2006; Chair. ANNA STREŻYŃSKA.

Service Providers

Polkomtel: 02-676 Warsaw, ul. Postępu 3; tel. (22) 6071000; fax (22) 4260103; internet www.polkomtel.com.pl; f. 1996; provides mobile cellular telecommunications services under the brand names Plus GSM, SimplusTeam and mixPlus; 3G network commenced operations Sept. 2004; Pres. WŁADYŁSAW BARTOSZEWICZ.

Polska Telefonia Cyfrowa (PTC) (Polish Digital Telephone): 02-222 Al. Jerozolimskie 181, Warsaw; tel. (22) 4136000; fax (22) 4134949; e-mail biznes@era.pl; internet www.era.pl; f. 1996; provides mobile cellular telecommunications under the brand names Era, Heyah and Blue Connect; 70.5% owned by T-Mobile Deutschland GmbH; 22.5% owned by T-Mobile Poland Holding B.V.; Chair. Dr KLAUS HARTMANN.

PTK Centertel (Polish Cellular Telecommunications Co 'Centertel'): 01-230 Warsaw, ul. Skierniewicka 10A; tel. (22) 6342882; fax (22) 5887883; e-mail info@idea.pl; internet www.orange.pl; f. 1998; provides mobile cellular telecommunications services under the brand name Orange; 66% owned by TP, 34% by France Telecom (France).

TP—Telekomunikacja Polska (Polish Telecommunications): 00-105 Warsaw, ul. Twarda 18; tel. (22) 5270000; internet www.tp.pl; f. 1992; mem. of France Telecom group (France); Chair. MACIEJ WITUCKI.

BROADCASTING

Regulatory Authority

National Broadcasting Council (Krajowa Rada Radiofonii i Telewizji—KRRiTV): 00-015 Warsaw, Skwer Kardinala Wyszyńskiego, Prymasa Polski 9; tel. (22) 5973001; fax (22) 5973054; internet www.krrit.gov.pl; f. 1993; Chair. ELŻBIETA KRUK.

Radio

Polskie Radio (Polish Radio): 00-977 Warsaw, Al. Niepodległości 77/85; tel. (22) 6459259; fax (22) 6455924; internet www.polskieradio.pl; Home Service: four national channels, continual broadcasting; Foreign Service: broadcasting programmes in Polish, English, German, Russian, Belarusian, Ukrainian and Hebrew; Pres. KRZYSZTOF CZABAŃSKI.

Radio Maryja: 87-100 Toruń, ul. Żwirki i Wigury 80; tel. (56) 6552361; fax (56) 6552362; e-mail radio@radiomaryja.pl; internet www.radiomaryja.pl; traditionalist Catholic; Dir TADEUSZ RYDZYK.

Radio Musyka Fakty (RMF FM): 30-204 Kraków, Al. Waszyngtona 1, Kopiec Kosciuszki; tel. (12) 4219696; fax (12) 4217895; e-mail redakcja@rmf.pl; internet www.rmf.pl; Pres. STANISŁAW TYCZYNSKI; Dir JOLANTA WIŚNIEWSKA.

Radio Zet: 00-503 Warsaw, ul. Żurawia 8; tel. (22) 5833382; fax (22) 5833356; e-mail radiozet@radiozet.com.pl; internet www.radiozet.com.pl; f. 1990; independent; 24 hours; national broadcasts commenced 1994; wholly owned by the Eurozet media group; Pres. and Editor-in-Chief ROBERT KOZYRA.

Television

Telewizja Polska (Polish Television): 00-999 Warsaw, ul. J. P. Woronicza 17, POB 211; tel. (22) 5474450; fax (22) 5477719; e-mail pr@tvp.pl; internet www.tvp.pl; f. 1952; Chair. BRONISŁAW WILDSTEIN.

PolSat: 04-028 Warsaw, Al. Stanów Zjednoczonyck 53; tel. (22) 104001; fax (22) 134295; internet www.polsat.com.pl; f. 1992; satellite broadcasts; Propr ZYGMUNT SOLORZ.

TVN: 02-952 Warsaw, ul. Wiertnicza 166; tel. (22) 8566060; fax (22) 8566666; e-mail widzowie@tvn.pl; internet www.tvn.pl; f. 1997; Pres. PIOTR WALTER.

Finance

(cap. = capital; res = reserves; dep. = deposits; m. = million; amounts in new złotys unless otherwise indicated; brs = branches)

BANKING

Foreign banks were permitted to operate freely in the country from 1997. At the end of 2006 there were 51 domestic commercial banks, 584 co-operative banks and 12 branches of credit institutions operating in Poland.

Supervisory Authority

Polish Financial Supervision Authority (PFSA) (Komisja Nadzoru Finansowego): 00-950 Warsaw, Plac Powstańców Warszawy 1; tel. (22) 3326600; fax (22) 3326602; internet www.knf.gov.pl; f. 1 Jan.

POLAND

2008, succeeding the Financial Supervision Commission; Chair. Stanisław Kluza.

National Bank

Narodowy Bank Polski—NBP (National Bank of Poland): 00-919 Warsaw, ul. Świętokrzyska 11/21, POB 1011; tel. (22) 6531000; fax (22) 6208518; e-mail nbp@nbp.pl; internet www.nbp.pl; f. 1945; state central bank; cap. 1,500.0m., res 883.7m., dep. 66,283.3m. (Dec. 2005); Pres. Sławomir Skzypek; 16 brs.

Other Banks

Bank BPH SA: 31-548 Kraków, Al. Pokoju 1; tel. (12) 6186888; fax (12) 6186863; e-mail bank@bphpbk.pl; internet www.bph.pl; f. 1989; fmrly Bank Przemysłowo-Handlowy PBK SA; present name adopted 2004; 52.1% owned by Bank Austria Creditanstalt AG (HVB Group, Austria); cap. and res 6,360.9m., dep. 49,675.3m. (Dec. 2005); Chair. of Sup. Bd Alicja Kornasiewicz; Pres. Józef Wancer; 483 brs.

Bank Gospodarki Żywnościowej—BGZ (BGZ) (Bank of Food Economy): 01-211 Warsaw, ul. Kasprzaka 10/16; tel. (22) 8604000; fax (22) 8605000; e-mail info@bgz.pl; internet www.bgz.pl; f. 1919; present name adopted 1994; universal commercial bank; finances agriculture, forestry and food-processing; 37.3% state-owned; 44.5% owned by Rabobank (Netherlands); cap. 37.0m., res 1,386.1m., dep. 16,038.7m. (Dec. 2006); Exec. Pres. Jacek Bartkiewicz; 256 brs.

Bank Gospodarstwa Krajowego—BGK (National Economy Bank): 00-955 Warsaw, Al. Jerozolimskie 7, POB 41; tel. (22) 5229127; fax (22) 6270378; e-mail bgk@bgk.com.pl; internet www.bgk.com.pl; f. 1924; 100% state-owned; cap. 958.4m., res 4,544.4m., dep. 12,298.4m. (Dec. 2005); Pres. of Bd Ireneusz Fafara; 20 brs.

Bank Inicjatiw Społeczno-Economiczynich (Bank for Socio-Economic Initiatives—BISE): 00-184 Warsaw, ul. Dubois 5A; tel. (22) 8601100; fax (22) 8601103; e-mail info@bise.pl; internet www.bise.pl; f. 1990; cap. 93.8m., res 45.1m., dep. 2,404.4m. (Dec. 2006); Pres. Jarosław Dabrowski; 49 brs.

Bank Millennium: 02-017 Warsaw, Al. Jerozolimskie 123A; tel. (22) 5981565; fax (22) 5981563; e-mail wojciech.kaczorowski@bankmillennium.pl; internet www.bankmillennium.pl; f. 1989 as Bank Inicjatyw Gospodarczych (BIG); present name adopted 2003; 50.0% owned by Banco Comercial Português SA (Portugal); cap. 849.2m., res 1,366.1m., dep. 21,427.0m. (Dec. 2006); Chair. of Bd Bogusław Kott; 354 brs.

Bank Ochrony Środowiska—BOS (Environmental Protection Bank): 00-950 Warsaw 1, Al. Jana Pawła II 12, POB 150; tel. (22) 8508735; fax (22) 8508891; e-mail bos@bosbank.pl; internet www.bosbank.pl; f. 1991; 47.0% owned by SEB Group (Sweden), 44.7% by Polish National Fund for the Protection of the Environment and Water; cap. 132.0m., res 500.8m., dep. 7,296.6m. (Dec. 2006); Pres. of Exec. Bd Jerzy Witold Pietrwicz; 48 brs.

Bank Polska Kasa Opieki—Bank Pekao: 00-950 Warsaw, ul. Grzybowska 53/57; tel. (22) 6560000; fax (22) 6560004; e-mail info@pekao.com.pl; internet www.pekao.com.pl; f. 1929; universal bank; 52.9% owned by UniCredito Italiano SpA (Italy); cap. 166.8m., res 7,028.1m., dep. 56,564.4m. (Dec. 2006); Chair. Jerzy Woznicki; Pres. Jan Krzysztof Bielecki; 720 brs and sub-brs.

Bank Polskiej Spóldzielczości: 01-231 Warsaw, ul. Plocka 9/11B; tel. (22) 5396224; fax (22) 5395133; e-mail sekretariat.bps@bankbps.pl; internet www.bankbps.pl; f. 1992; present name adopted 2002; cap. 133.2m., res 160.6m., dep. 7,979.8m. (Dec. 2006); Pres. Mirosław Potulski.

Bank Zachodni WBK (Western Bank): 50-950 Wrocław, Dolnośląskie Rynek 9/11; tel. (71) 3701000; fax (71) 3702771; e-mail dorota.bernatowicz@bzwbk.pl; internet www.bzwbk.pl; f. 1989; present name adopted 2001; 70.5% owned by AIB European Investments Ltd (Ireland); cap. 729.6m., res 2,290.8m., dep. 26,847.3m. (Dec. 2006); Pres. Jacek Kseń; 433 brs.

BNP Paribas, Poland: 00-078 Warsaw, Pl. Pilsudskiego 1; tel. (22) 6972308; fax (22) 6972309; e-mail warsaw.office@bnpparibas.com; internet www.bnpparibas.pl; f. 1994; 100% owned by BNP Paribas (France); present name adopted 2006; commercial and investment bank; cap. 193.4m., res 151.9m., dep. 3,043.2m. (Dec. 2005); Gen. Man. Jean-Claude Chaval.

BRE Bank: 00-950 Warsaw, ul. Senatorska 18, POB 728; tel. (22) 8290000; fax (22) 8290033; e-mail info@brebank.pl; internet www.brebank.com.pl; f. 1987 as Bank Rozwoju Eksportu; 70.3% owned by Commerzbank AG (Germany); present name adopted 1999; specializes in corporate banking; cap. 118.1m., res 1,910.8m., dep. 32,425.0m. (Dec. 2006); Pres. and CEO Sławomir Lachowski; 172 brs.

Citibank Handlowy: 00-923 Warsaw, ul. Senatorska 16; tel. (22) 6904000; fax (22) 6925023; e-mail listybh@citicorp.com; internet www.citihandlowy.pl; f. 1870; trade and finance bank; specializes in corporate and investment banking; fmrly Bank Handlowy w Warszawie (Trade Bank in Warsaw); 89.3% owned by Citibank Overseas Investment Corpn (USA); cap. 522.6m., res 4,160.3m., dep. 29,096.4m. (Dec. 2006); Pres. Sławomir Sikora; Chair. Stanisław Sołtysiński; 149 brs.

Deutsche Bank PBC: 00–609 Warsaw, Al. Armii Ludowej; tel. (22) 5799800; fax (22) 5799801; e-mail info@db-pbc.pl; internet www.deutsche-bank-pbc.pl; f. 1991; fmrly Bank Wspolpracy Regionalnej SA w Krakowie; present name adopted 2003; 95.6% owned by Deutsche Bank Privat- und Geschäftskunden Aktiengesellschaft (Germany); cap. 396.7m., res 110.5m., dep. 4,393.2m. (Dec. 2006); Chair. of Supervisory Bd Ulrich Kissing; Pres. Marek Kulczycki.

Deutsche Bank Polska: 00-609 Warsaw, Al. Armii Ludowej 26; tel. (22) 5799000; fax (22) 5799001; e-mail public.relations@db.com; internet www.db-polska.pl; f. 1995; 100% owned by Deutsche Bank AG (Germany); corporate banking; cap. 230.0m., res 195.0m., dep. 4,609.7m. (Dec. 2006); Pres. Krzysztof Kalicki; Chair. Tessen von Heydebreck.

DZ Bank Polska: 00-078 Warsaw, Pl. Piłsudskiego 3; tel. (22) 5057000; fax (22) 5057430; e-mail info@dzbank.pl; internet www.dzbank.pl; f. 1989; fmrly Bank Amerykański w Polsce SA—AmerBank; 99.75% owned by Deutsche Zentral-Genossenschaftsbank (Germany); commercial bank; cap. 123.0m., res 97.3m., dep. 1,892.2m. (Dec. 2006); Chair. of Bd Dr Thomas Duhnkrack; 3 brs.

Fortis Bank Polska: 02-676 Warsaw, ul. Suwak 3; tel. (22) 5669000; fax (22) 5669010; e-mail info@fortisbank.com.pl; internet www.fortisbank.com.pl; f. 1990; present name adopted 2000; 99.1% owned by Fortis Bank (Belgium); cap. 452.3m., res 237.9m., dep. 9,107.0m. (Dec. 2006); Pres. Jan Bujak; Chair. Jos Clijsters.

Getin Bank: POB 593, 40-479 Katowice, ul. Pszczyńska 10; tel. (32) 2008500; fax (32) 2008685; e-mail marketing@getinbank.pl; internet www.getinbank.pl; f. 1990; fmrly Górnośląski Bank Gospodarczy; present name adopted 2004; cap. 241.9m., res 534.0m., dep. 9,858.5m. (Dec. 2006); Pres. Jarosław Dowbaj; Chair. Piotr Stepniak; 60 brs.

Gospodarczy Bank Wielkopolski: 61-725 Poznań, ul. Mielzyńskiego 22; tel. (61) 8562434; fax (61) 8517981; internet www.sgb.pl; f. 1990; 97.7% owned by Banki Spółdzielcze (Co-operative Banks); cap. 58.5m., res 159.5m., dep. 4,398.2m. (Dec. 2006); Pres. and Gen. Man. Andrzej Chmielecki.

ING Bank Śląski: 40-086 Katowice, ul. Sokolska 34; tel. (32) 3577000; e-mail info@ing.pl; internet www.ing.pl; f. 1989; 75% owned by ING Bank NV (Netherlands); cap. 130.1m., res 1,077.0m., dep. 43,833.9m. (Dec. 2006); Chair. Anna Fornalczyk; Pres. Brunon Bartkiewicz; 350 brs and sub-brs.

Kredyt Bank: 01-211 Warsaw, ul. Kasprzaka 2/8, POB 93; tel. (22) 6345400; fax (22) 6345335; internet www.kredytbank.com.pl; f. 1997; 85.5% owned by KBC Bank NV (Belgium); cap. 1,358.3m., res 244.0m., dep. 19,131.8m. (Dec. 2006); Chair. Andrzej Witkowski; Pres. Ronnie Richardson; 75 brs.

Nordea Bank Polska: 81-303 Gdynia, ul. Kielecka 2, POB 11; tel. (58) 6691111; fax (58) 6691110; e-mail nordea@nordea.com; internet www.nordeabank.pl; f. 1991; 98.9% owned by Nordea Bank AB (Sweden); cap. 168.1m., res 349.0m., dep. 6,198.1m. (Dec. 2006); Pres. Wlodzimierz Kicinski; Chair. Wojciech Rybowski.

PKO Bank Polski—Powszechna Kasa Oszczędności Bank Państwowy—PKO (State Savings Bank): 00-975 Warsaw, ul. Pulawska 15, POB 183; tel. (22) 5356565; fax (22) 5218862; internet www.pkobp.pl; f. 1919; 51.5% state-owned; cap. 1,000.0m., res 6,988.3m., dep. 86,487.6m. (Dec. 2006); Pres. of Management Bd Rafał Juszczak; Chair. of Supervisory Bd Marek Głuchowski; 1,153 brs and sub-brs.

Rabobank Polska: 00-958 Warsaw 66, Aleja Jana Pawla II 27; tel. (22) 6535000; fax (22) 6535004; e-mail ewa.biedka@rabobank.com; internet www.rabobank.pl; f. 1993; present name adopted 1998; 100% owned by Rabobank Nederland (Netherlands); cap. 82.0m., res 58.1m., dep. 4,879.0m. (Dec. 2006); Pres. Dariusz Władysław Ledworowski.

Raiffeisen Bank Polska: 00-549 Warsaw, ul. Piekna 20, POB 53; tel. (22) 5852000; fax (22) 5852585; internet www.raiffeisen.pl; f. 1991; present name adopted 2000; 100% owned by Raiffeisen International Bank Holding AG (Austria); cap. 573.0m., res 474.6m., dep. 13,407.4m. (Dec. 2006); Pres. Piotr Czarnecki; Chair. Herbert Stepic; 37 brs.

WestLB Bank Polska: 02-781 Warsaw, ul. Pileckiego 65; tel. (22) 6530500; fax (22) 6530501; e-mail westlb@westlb.pl; internet www.westlb.pl; f. 1995; present name adopted 2005; 100% owned by WestLB AG (Germany); cap. 183.6m., res 60.4m., dep. 2,086.1m. (Dec. 2006); Chair. and Gen. Man. Maciej Stanczuk.

STOCK EXCHANGE

The Warsaw Stock Exchange was re-established in April 1991. In March 1999 it had 37 member companies and listed shares in 205 firms, in addition to 43 issues of treasury bonds. In January 1998 a derivatives market was launched.

Warsaw Stock Exchange: 00-498 Warsaw, ul. Książęca 4; tel. (22) 6283232; fax (22) 6281754; e-mail gielda@wse.com.pl; internet www.wse.com.pl; opened for trading in 1991; Pres. and Chief Exec. Dr LUDWIK SOBOLEWSKI.

INSURANCE

In early 2005 there were 32 insurance companies operating in Poland. The largest companies were Polish National Insurance (Powszechny Zakład Ubezpieczeń—PZU), which dominated the property insurance market, and Warta Insurance and Reinsurance, which specialized in vehicle insurance and foreign business. PZU's subsidiary, PZU Life, was the largest life insurance company.

Commercial Union Polska—Towarzystwo Ubezpieczeń na Życie: 00-838 Warsaw, ul, Prosta 70; tel. (22) 5574050; fax (22) 5574075; e-mail bok@cu.com.pl; internet www.cu.com.pl; f. 1991; owned by Aviva Group (United Kingdom); pensions, life insurance; Pres. ZBIGNIEW ANDRZEJEWSKI.

Grupa Powszechnly Zakład Ubezpieczeń (PZU) (Polish National Insurance Group): 00-133 Warsaw, Al. Jana Pawła II 24; tel. (22) 5823400; fax (22) 5823401; internet ww.pzu.pl; f. 1803; insurance group comprising two principal companies dealing in various areas of insurance (PZU SA—property insurance, and PZU Życie SA—life insurance), and six support companies; 55% state-owned; further privatization scheduled; Pres. CEZARY STYPUŁKOWSKI; 400 brs; 14,000 employees.

Warta—Towarzystwo Ubezpieczeń i Reasekuracji Warta (Warta Insurance and Reinsurance Co): 00-805 Warsaw, ul. Chmielna 85/87; tel. (22) 5810100; fax (22) 5811374; e-mail info@warta.pl; internet www.warta.pl; f. 1920; marine, air, motor, fire, luggage and credit; Pres. AGENOR JAN GAWRZYAL; 25 brs.

Trade and Industry

GOVERNMENT AGENCIES

Agency for the Restructuring and Modernization of Agriculture (Agencja Restrukturyzacji i Modernizacji Rolnictwa): 00-175 Warsaw, Al. Jana Pawła II 70; fax (22) 3185330; e-mail info@arimr.gov.pl; internet www.arimr.gov.pl; f. 1994; Pres. Prof. GRZEGORZ SPYCHALSKI.

Agricultural Market Agency (Agencja Rynku Rolnego): 00-400 Warsaw, ul. Nowy Świat 6/12; tel. (22) 6617272; fax (22) 6289353; e-mail tpi@arr.gov.pl; internet www.eng.arr.gov.pl; f. 1991; implements selected schemes under the Common Agricultural Policy (CAP) of the European Union; Pres. STANISŁAW GRZEGORZ KAMIŃSKI.

Polish Agency for Enterprise Development (PARP) (Polska Agencja Rozwoju Przedsiębiorczości): 00-834 Warsaw, ul. Pańska 81/83; tel. (22) 4328080; fax (22) 4328620; e-mail biuro@parp.gov.pl; internet www.parp.gov.pl; f. 2000; government agency; manages funds assigned from the state budget and the European Union for the support of entrepreneurship and the development of human resources, giving particular consideration to the needs of small and medium-sized enterprises; Chief Exec. DANUTA JABŁOŃSKA.

Polish Information and Foreign Investment Agency (Polska Agencja Informacji i Inwestycji Zagranicznych): 00-585 Warsaw, ul. Bagatela 12; tel. (22) 3349800; fax (22) 3349999; e-mail post@paiz.gov.pl; internet www.paiz.gov.pl; f. 2003; Pres. ANDRZEJ KANTHAK.

DEVELOPMENT AGENCY

Industrial Development Agency (Agencja Rozwoju Przemysłu): 02-675 Warsaw, ul. Woloska 7, Budynek Mars, Klatka A; tel. (22) 4603636; fax (22) 4603637; e-mail lucyna.stepien@arp.com.pl; internet www.arp.com.pl; Pres. PAWEŁ BRZEZICKI.

CHAMBERS OF COMMERCE

Polish Chamber of Commerce (National Economic Chamber—Krajowa Izba Gospodarcza): 00-074 Warsaw, ul. Trębacka 4, POB 361; tel. (22) 6309600; fax (22) 8274673; e-mail kig@kig.pl; internet www.kig.pl; f. 1990; Pres. ANDRZEJ ARENDARSKI; Chair. WOJCIECH KRUK; 145 mems.

Foreign Investors' Chamber of Industry and Trade in Poland (Izba Przemysłowo-Handlowa Inwestorów Zagranicznych—IPHIZ): 00-834 Warsaw, ul. Pańska 73; tel. (22) 3147575; fax (22) 3147576; e-mail biuro@iphiz.com.pl; internet www.iphiz.com.pl; f. 1989; Pres. ZDZISŁAW JAGODZIŃSKI.

UTILITIES

Energy Regulatory Authority (Urząd Regulacji Energetyki): 00-872 Warsaw, ul. Chłodna 64; tel. (22) 6616107; fax (22) 6616152; e-mail ure@ure.gov.pl; internet www.ure.gov.pl; Pres. Dr LESZEK JUCHNIEWICZ.

Electricity

The electricity sector has been reorganized into separate generation, transmission and distribution entities.

Koncern Energetyczny ENERGA: 80-557 Gdańsk, ul. Marynarki Polskiej 130; tel. (58) 3473013; fax (58) 3010152; internet www.energa.pl; f. 2004; renamed as above 2005; group of eight regional electricity distributors in central and northern Poland, known as G8; holds 16% share of electricity-distribution market; partial privatization suspended in 2004; Chief Exec. WALDEMAR BARTELIK; 7,500 employees.

Polish Power Grid Company JSC (Polskie Sieci Elektroenergetyczne SA—PSE): 00-496 Warsaw, ul. Mysia 2; tel. (22) 6931580; fax (22) 6285964; internet www.pse.pl; f. 1990; national transmission-system operator; state-owned; Pres. Prof. Dr hab. STANISŁAW DOBRZAŃSKI.

National Atomic Energy Agency (Państwowa Agencja Atomistyki): 00-522 Warsaw, ul. Krucza 36; tel. (22) 6282722; fax (22) 6290164; e-mail niewodniczanski@paa.gov.pl; internet www.paa.gov.pl; f. 1982; central govt organ concerned with issues of nuclear safety and radiological protection; Pres. Prof. JERZY NIEWODNICZAŃSKI.

STOEN Stołeczny Zakład Energetyczny (STOEN Capital-City Power Distribution Co): 00-347 Warsaw, Wybrzeże Kopciuszkowskie 41; tel. (22) 8214646; fax (22) 8214647; e-mail stoen@stoen.pl; internet www.stoen.pl; f. 1993; transmits and distributes electric energy; privatized in 2002; 85% owned by RWE Energie AG (Germany); 15% state-owned; Chief Exec. HARRY SCHUR; Chair. of Supervisory Bd Dr ANDREAS RADMACHER.

Gas

EuRoPol GAZ: 04-028 Warsaw, Al. Stanów Zjednoczonych 61; tel. (22) 5174000; fax (22) 5174040; e-mail konto@europolgaz.com.pl; internet www.europolgaz.com.pl; f. 1993; jt venture between PGNiG and Gazprom (Russia); Pres. KAZIMIERZ ADAMCZYK.

Polish Oil and Gas Co (Polskie Górnictwo Naftowe i Gazownictwo—PGNiG): 00-537 Warsaw, ul. Krucza 6/14; tel. (22) 5835000; fax (22) 5835856; e-mail pr@pgnig.pl; internet www.pgnig.pl; f. 1982; divided into 6 regional distribution subsidiaries in 2003; state-owned natural gas producer and supplier; scheduled for partial privatization; Pres. of Bd KRZYSZTOF GŁOGOWSKI; 47,300 employees.

TRADE UNIONS

All Poland Trade Unions' Alliance (Ogólnopolskie Porozumienie Związków Zawodowych—OPZZ): 00-924 Warsaw, ul. Kopernika 36/40; tel. (22) 8267106; fax (22) 8265102; e-mail opzz@opzz.org.pl; internet www.opzz.org.pl; f. 1984; Chair. JAN GUZ.

Independent Self-governing Trade Union—Solidarity (NSZZ Solidarność): 80-855 Gdańsk, ul. Wały Piastowskie 24; tel. (58) 3016737; fax (58) 3010143; e-mail zagr@solidarnosc.org.pl; internet www.solidarnosc.org.pl; f. 1980; outlawed 1981–89; Chair. JANUSZ SNIADEK.

Transport

RAILWAYS

At the end of 2002 there were 21,073 km of railway lines making up the state network, of which 12,207 km were electrified.

Offfice for Railway Transport (Urząd Transportu Kolejowego): 00-928 Warsaw, ul. Chałubinskiego 4/6; tel. (22) 6301950; fax (22) 6301892; e-mail utk@utk.gov.pl; internet www.utk.gov.pl; reorganized in July 2003; fmrly the General Railway Inspectorate; Pres. WIESŁAW JAROSIEWICZ; Dir-Gen. LIDIA OSTROWSKA.

Polish State Railways (Polskie Koleje Państwowe—PKP): 00-973 Warsaw, ul. Szczęśliwicka 62; tel. (22) 4749000; fax (22) 4749102; e-mail biuro.zarzadu@pkp.pl; internet www.pkp.pl; f. 1926; freight and passenger transport; PKP Group comprises 12 cos; from January 2004 Regional Services (WKD), a principal subsidiary, has been operated by local governments; Polskie Koleje Państwowe Polskie Linie Kolejowe (PKP PLK) operates the railway network; Pres. ANDRZEJ WACH; Gen. Dir MACIEJ MECLĘWSKI; 125,000 employees.

ROADS

In 2003 there were 423,997 km of roads, of which 484 km were motorways; 69.7% of the road network was paved. Poland launched a road construction scheme in mid-2002, partly funded by the European Union (EU), which aimed to enhance the country's position as a major transit route between western and eastern Europe. The EU was, additionally, to provide funding of €19,000m. for road construction in Poland in 2007–13.

General Directorate of Public Roads and Motorways (Generalna Dyrekcja Dróg Krajowych i Autostrad): 00-848 Warsaw, ul. Żelazna 59; tel. (22) 3758888; fax (22) 3758763; e-mail kancelaria@gddkia.gov.pl; internet www.gddkia.gov.pl; Dir ZBIGNIEW KOTLAREK.

INLAND WATERWAYS

Poland has 6,850 km of waterways, of which 3,640 km were navigable in 2002. The main rivers are the Wisła (Vistula), Odra (Oder), Bug, Warta and San. There are some 5,000 lakes. In addition, there is a network of canals.

About 1,795,000 passengers and 8.0m. metric tons of freight were carried on inland water transport in 2003. In 2004 the quantity of freight transported increased to 8.7m. tons.

SHIPPING

Poland has three large harbours on the Baltic Sea: Gdynia, Gdańsk and Szczecin. At 31 December 2006 the Polish merchant fleet comprised 355 vessels, with a total displacement of 193,400 grt.

Authority of Szczecin and Świnoujście Authority Co: 70-603 Szczecin, ul. Bytomska 7; tel. (91) 4308240; fax (91) 4624842; e-mail info@port.szczecin.pl; internet www.port.szczecin.pl; f. 1950; Pres. and Man. Dir JANUSZ CATEWICZ.

Port of Gdańsk Authority Co: 80-955 Gdańsk, ul. Zamknięta 18; tel. (58) 7379100; fax (58) 7379485; e-mail info@portgdansk.pl; internet www.portgdansk.pl; f. 1997; management of land and port infrastructure; Pres. of Bd STANISLAW CORA.

Port of Gdynia Authority Co: 81-337 Gdynia, ul. Rotterdamska 9; tel. (58) 6274002; fax (58) 6203191; e-mail marketing@port.gdynia.pl; internet www.port.gdynia.pl; f. 1922; Pres. PRZEMYSLAW MARCHLEWICZ.

Principal Shipping Companies

Polska Żegluga Bałtycka—Polferries (Polish Baltic Shipping Co—POLFERRIES): 78-100 Kołobrzeg, ul. Portowa 41; tel. (94) 3552102; fax (94) 3552208; internet www.polferries.pl; f. 1976; operates three ferries on four routes between Denmark and Sweden; also serves as travel agency and tour operator.

Polska Żegluga Morska (PZM) (Polish Steamship Co—Polsteam): 70-419 Szczecin, Pl. Rodła 8; tel. (91) 3594333; fax (91) 3594288; e-mail pzmmanagement@polsteam.com.pl; internet www.polsteam.com.pl; f. 1951; state-owned; world-wide tramping; operates 75 vessels totalling 2m. dwt, incl. four liquid sulphur carriers; largest dry bulk carrier in Europe; operates ferry service between Poland and Sweden (Unity Line); Gen. Dir PAWEŁ SZYNKARUK; 2,800 employees.

Polskie Linie Oceaniczne (PLO) (Polish Ocean Lines): 81-364 Gdynia, ul. 10 Lutego 24; tel. (58) 6900670; fax (58) 6900672; e-mail pol@pol.com.pl; internet www.pol.com.pl; f. 1951; holding co for six shipping cos operating within PLO group; tonnage operated by the POL-Levant Shipping Lines; Pres. of Bd ANDRZEJ OSIECIMSKI.

CIVIL AVIATION

Fryderyka Chopin—Okęcie international airport is situated near Warsaw. In addition, international flights serve a number of other airports, including those at Bydgoszcz, Gdańsk, Katowice, Kraków, Łódź, Poznań, Rzeszów, Szczecin, and Wrocław.

Civil Aviation Office (Urząd Lotnictwa Cywilnego): 00-848 Warsaw, ul. Żelazna 59; tel. (22) 5207200; fax (22) 5207300; e-mail kancelaria@ulc.gov.pl; internet www.ulc.gov.pl; Pres. GRZEGORZ KRUSZYŃSKI.

Centralwings: 90-312 Łódź, Pl. Zwyciestwa 2; e-mail comments@centralwings.com; internet www.centralwings.com; f. 2004; 'low-cost' subsidiary of LOT (q.v.), in association with Germanwings, a subsidiary of Lufthansa (Germany); operates flights to 11 European destinations from Warsaw, Katowice and Kraków; Pres. PIOTR KOCIOŁEK.

LOT—Polskie Linie Lotnicze (Polish Airlines): 00-906 Warsaw, ul. 17 Stycznia 39; tel. (22) 6066111; fax (22) 8460909; e-mail lot@lot.com; internet www.lot.com; f. 1929; 67.97% state-owned; 90 air routes, domestic services and international services to the Middle East, Africa, Asia, Canada, USA, and throughout Europe; operates low-cost subsidiary Eurolot (f. 1996) and is a parent co of Centralwings (q.v.); Pres. and Chief Exec. TOMASZ DEMBSKI (acting).

Tourism

Poland is rich in historic cities, such as Gdańsk, Wrocław, Kraków, Poznań and Warsaw. There are 30 health and climatic resorts, while the mountains, forests and rivers provide splendid scenery and excellent facilities for touring and sporting holidays. In 2005 Poland was visited by some 64.6m. foreign tourists, 57.9% of whom were from Germany. Receipts from tourism amounted to US $6,230m. in that year.

Polish Tourist Organization (Polska Organizacja Turystyczna—POT): 00-613 Warsaw, ul. Chałubskińego 8, XIX piętro; tel. (22) 5367070; fax (22) 5367004; e-mail pot@pot.gov.pl; internet www.pot.gov.pl; Pres. TOMASZ WILCZAK.

PORTUGAL

Introductory Survey

Location, Climate, Language, Religion, Flag, Capital

The mainland portion of the Portuguese Republic lies in western Europe, on the Atlantic side of the Iberian peninsula, bordered by Spain to the north and east. The country also includes two archipelagos in the Atlantic Ocean, the Azores and the Madeira Islands. The climate is mild and temperate, with an annual average temperature of 16°C (61°F). In the interior the weather is drier and hotter. Almost all of the inhabitants speak Portuguese and are Christians of the Roman Catholic Church. The national flag (proportions 2 by 3) has two vertical stripes, of green and red, the green occupying two-fifths of the total area; superimposed on the stripes (half on the green, half on the red) is the state coat of arms: a white shield, containing five small blue shields (each bearing five white roundels) in the form of an upright cross, with a red border containing seven yellow castles, all superimposed on a yellow armillary sphere. The capital is Lisbon (Lisboa).

Recent History

The monarchy that had ruled Portugal from the 11th century was overthrown in 1910, when the King was deposed in a bloodless revolution, and a republic was proclaimed. A period of great instability ensued until a military coup installed the regime of the Estado Novo (New State) in 1926. Dr António de Oliveira Salazar became Minister of Finance in 1928 and Prime Minister in 1932, establishing a right-wing dictatorial regime, influenced by Italian Fascism. A new Constitution, establishing a corporate state, was adopted in 1933. Only one political party was authorized, and suffrage was limited. Portugal remained neutral during the Second World War. The Government strove to achieve international acceptance, but Portugal was not admitted to the UN until 1955. Unlike the other European colonial powers, Portugal insisted on maintaining its overseas possessions, regarding them as 'inalienable'. In 1961 Portuguese enclaves in India were successfully invaded by Indian forces, and in the same year a rebellion against Portuguese rule began in Angola. Similar rebellions followed, in Portuguese Guinea (1963) and Mozambique (1964), and protracted guerrilla warfare ensued in the three African provinces. Salazar remained in power until illness forced his retirement in September 1968. He was succeeded by Dr Marcello Caetano, who had been Deputy Prime Minister in 1955–58. Caetano pursued slightly more liberal policies. Opposition parties were legalized for elections to the Assembléia Nacional in October 1969, but the União Nacional, the government party, won all 130 seats. Immediately after the elections, the opposition groups were outlawed again. The government party, renamed Acção Nacional Popular in February 1970, also won every seat at the next elections to the Assembléia, in October 1973, following the withdrawal of all opposition candidates.

The drain on Portugal's economy by the long wars against nationalist forces in the overseas provinces contributed to the overthrow of Caetano in a bloodless coup on 25 April 1974, initiated by the Movimento das Forças Armadas (MFA), a group of young army officers. Gen. António Ribeiro de Spínola, head of the Junta da Salvação Nacional (Junta of National Salvation) that assumed power, became President in May and promised liberal reforms. The new Government recognized the right of Portugal's overseas territories to self-determination. The independence of Guinea-Bissau (formerly Portuguese Guinea), proclaimed in September 1973, was recognized by Portugal in September 1974. The remaining African territories were all granted independence in 1975. Portugal also withdrew from Portuguese Timor (Timor-Leste) in that year.

Following a split between the Junta's right and left wings, President Spínola resigned in September 1974 and was replaced by Gen. Francisco da Costa Gomes. An abortive counter-coup by senior officers in March 1975 resulted in a move to the left. All existing organs of the MFA were dissolved, a Supreme Revolutionary Council (SRC) was created, and six of the country's political parties agreed that the SRC would stay in power for five years. On 25 April a general election was held for a Constituent Assembly. Of the 12 parties contesting the election, the Partido Socialista (PS) obtained the largest share of the votes cast and won 116 of the Assembly's 250 seats. However, disputes between Socialists and Communists provoked withdrawals from the new coalition Government, and the Prime Minister, Gen. Vasco Gonçalves, was dismissed. Adm. José Pinheiro de Azevedo became Prime Minister in August. In September a new Government of 'united action' was formed, including members of the armed forces, the PS, the Partido Popular Democrático (PPD) and the Partido Comunista Português (PCP). In November the Government suspended its activities, owing to a lack of support from the armed forces. An abortive leftist military coup resulted from the political turmoil. Changes took place within the SRC, and in December the armed forces announced a plan to reduce their political power.

A new Constitution, committing Portugal to make a transition to socialism, took effect on 25 April 1976. The SRC was renamed the Council of the Revolution, becoming a consultative body, headed by the President, with powers to delay legislation and the right of veto in military matters. At the general election for the new Assembléia da República (Assembly of the Republic), the PS won 107 of the Assembléia's 263 seats. In June the Army Chief of Staff, Gen. António Ramalho Eanes, a non-party candidate supported by the PS, the PPD and the Centro Democrático Social (CDS), was elected President. He took office in July, when a minority Socialist Government was formed under Dr Mário Lopes Soares, who had been Minister of Foreign Affairs in 1974–75. The Government resigned in December 1977, but the President again invited Soares to take office as Prime Minister. A new PS-CDS coalition was established in January 1978, but it collapsed after only six months. A new Government was formed in November under Prof. Carlos Mota Pinto, but he resigned in July 1979.

President Eanes appointed Dr Maria de Lourdes Pintasilgo to head a provisional Government. The centre-right alliance, Aliança Democrática (AD), which included the Partido Social Democrata (PSD, formerly the PPD) and the CDS, won 128 of the 250 seats in the Assembléia da República in an early general election held in December 1979. Dr Francisco Sá Carneiro, the leader of the PSD, was appointed Prime Minister. At the general election held in October 1980, the AD increased its parliamentary majority. In December Sá Carneiro and his Minister of Defence, Adelino Amaro da Costa, were killed in an apparent air accident. (In 2004 tests revealed that a bomb had exploded on board the aircraft, and the eighth commission of inquiry into the crash cited Amaro da Costa's attempt to stop the illegal sale of arms to Iran as a possible motive for the bombing.) The presidential election took place as planned, however, and Eanes won a clear victory, receiving 56.4% of the valid votes cast. Dr Francisco Pinto Balsemão, co-founder of the PSD, was appointed Prime Minister. In March 1981 the offices of the President of the Republic and the Chief of Staff of the Armed Forces were formally separated.

In August 1982 the Assembléia da República approved the final draft of the new Constitution, which completed the transition to full civilian government. Following divisions within the PSD, and losses at local elections in December, Balsemão resigned as Prime Minister. In addition, the Deputy Prime Minister and leader of the CDS, Prof. Diogo Freitas do Amaral, resigned from all party and political posts. In February 1983 Mota Pinto became leader of the PSD. At an early general election, held in April, the PS, led by former Prime Minister Soares, won 101 seats. Soares formed a coalition Government with the PSD (the AD having been dissolved).

In February 1985 Mota Pinto resigned as leader of the PSD, and subsequently as Deputy Prime Minister and Minister of Defence, and was replaced by Rui Machete, the Minister of Justice. In May Machete was replaced as leader of the PSD by Prof. Aníbal Cavaco Silva, a former Minister of Finance. In June, on the day after Portugal signed its treaty of accession to the European Community (EC, now European Union—EU, see p. 244), the PS-PSD coalition disintegrated. Eanes called a general election for October, at which the PSD won 88 seats, while the PS won 57 seats and the Partido Renovador Democrático (PRD, a new party founded in early 1985 by supporters of President Eanes) won 45 seats. Cavaco Silva was able to form a minority PSD-led Government.

During the mid-1980s terrorist attacks were perpetrated by the radical left-wing group Forças Populares de 25 Abril (FP-25) and other groups, targets including both Portuguese and foreign business interests, installations of the North Atlantic Treaty Organization (NATO) and the US embassy in Lisbon. In July 1985 the trial opened of more than 70 alleged members of FP-25—including Lt-Col Otelo Saraiva de Carvalho, the former revolutionary commander—but was adjourned owing to the fatal shooting of a key prosecution witness. The trial later resumed and, in May 1987, Saraiva de Carvalho was found guilty of subversion and sentenced to 15 years' imprisonment (subsequently increased to 18 years). In March 1996, following a personal initiative by President Soares, the Assembléia da República approved a pardon for Saraiva de Carvalho and other members of FP-25. However, in December 1999 Saraiva de Carvalho was placed on trial on renewed charges of terrorism relating to his alleged leadership of FP-25. More than 60 other defendants also faced charges. Saraiva de Carvalho was acquitted in 2001.

Four candidates contested the January 1986 presidential election. As no candidate achieved the requisite 50% majority, a second round of voting was held in February: Mário Soares narrowly defeated Freitas do Amaral, former leader of the CDS, to become Portugal's first civilian President for 60 years, taking office in March.

Cavaco Silva's minority Government encountered difficulties in securing the adoption of reformist legislation. In April 1987 Cavaco Silva resigned, following his defeat in a motion of censure. President Soares dissolved the Assembléia da República, prior to the holding of an early general election in July. The PSD secured 148 of the 250 seats in the Assembléia, becoming the first party since 1974 to win an absolute majority. The PS won 60 seats, and the Coligação Democrático Unitária (CDU, a new left-wing coalition comprising mainly the PCP) won 31 seats.

Cavaco Silva was reappointed as Prime Minister and announced a programme of radical economic reform. The gradual partial privatization of state industries was to continue, and fundamental changes in the sectors of agriculture, education and the media were proposed. The most controversial aspect of the programme, however, was the Government's renewed attempt to reform the restrictive labour laws. In March 1988 an estimated 1.5m. workers took part in a 24-hour general strike to protest against the Government's proposed legislation. Nevertheless, in April the labour laws were approved by the Assembléia da República; the following month, however, the Constitutional Court ruled that the new legislation violated the Constitution. The legislation was approved by President Soares in February 1989, although labour unrest persisted.

Having gained the approval of the Assembléia da República and the agreement of President Soares, amendments removing Marxist elements from the Constitution entered into force in August 1989. At municipal elections, held in December, the PS, supported by the PCP and the Greens, took control of Lisbon; Jorge Sampaio, the new Secretary-General of the PS, became Mayor of the capital. The PSD also lost other major cities.

Supported by both the PS and the PSD, Soares was re-elected President at an election held in January 1991, defeating three other candidates to secure an outright victory with more than 70% of the votes cast. At legislative elections held in October the PSD renewed its absolute majority, winning 135 of the 230 seats (reduced from 250) in the Assembléia da República. The PS secured 72 seats, the CDU 17 and the CDS five. A new Government was appointed in late October. In February 1992 Sampaio was replaced as Secretary-General of the PS by António Guterres. During 1992 tension between President Soares and Cavaco Silva became more evident, owing to the President's increasingly frequent use of his power of veto in order to obstruct the passage of legislation.

In January 1995 Cavaco Silva announced his intention to resign as leader of the PSD. At the party congress in the following month the Minister of Defence, Joaquim Fernando Nogueira, narrowly defeated his principal rival, the Minister of Foreign Affairs, José Manuel Durão Barroso, in the contest for the leadership. In March Fernando Nogueira resigned as Minister of Defence, following the President's veto of his proposed appointment as Deputy Prime Minister. At legislative elections held in October the PS won 112 of the 230 seats in the Assembléia da República. The PSD won 88 seats, the Centro Democrático Social-Partido Popular (CDS-PP—formerly the CDS) 15 and the CDU also 15. António Guterres was appointed Prime Minister, heading a minority administration that incorporated several non-party ministers.

In November 1995 Jorge Sampaio resigned as Mayor of Lisbon and declared his candidacy for the forthcoming presidential election. At the election, held in January 1996, Sampaio secured 53.9% of the votes cast, defeating Cavaco Silva. President Sampaio took office in March. Following the presidential election, Fernando Nogueira resigned from the leadership of the PSD and was replaced by Marcelo Rebelo de Sousa.

In August 1996 the Prime Minister announced proposals for radical reform of the country's political system. The opening of electoral lists to independent citizens (thus ending the monopoly of the major parties) and provision for the holding of referendums on issues of national interest were among the changes envisaged. In early 1997 the ruling PS and the opposition PSD reached a broad consensus on these proposals, also agreeing upon the gradual establishment of a professional army and a reduction in compulsory military service. In September the Assembléia da República gave its approval to the various constitutional reforms.

In February 1997, in a free vote, the Assembléia da República narrowly rejected proposals to liberalize the country's abortion law. The issue aroused bitter controversy, and created a deep division within the PS. The Prime Minister expressed his strong opposition, while certain PS veterans supported the proposed change in the legislation. In February 1998 the legislature voted by a narrow margin to relax the law on abortion. A referendum on the issue was held in June. Although 51% of those casting a vote favoured the liberalization of the law, only 31% (compared with the requisite minimum of 50%) of the electorate participated in the country's first referendum, thereby rendering the result null and void.

At local elections in December 1997 the PS consolidated its position, receiving more than 38% of the votes cast and retaining control of Lisbon and Oporto. The PSD obtained 33% of the votes, while the PCP lost considerable support.

In October 1998 the Prime Minister announced the establishment of an anti-corruption unit and various other measures, in response to repeated accusations that political parties and public officials had been in receipt of illicit payments in return for the awarding of public-works contracts.

The Prime Minister suffered a setback in November 1998 when a referendum on the question of regional devolution resulted in an overwhelming rejection (by 63.6% of participants) of the Government's proposals to divide mainland Portugal into eight administrative regions, each with a proposed elected local assembly and regional president. However, owing to the high abstention rate (over 50%), the referendum result was declared invalid.

In March 1999 Rebelo de Sousa announced his resignation as leader of the opposition PSD and the termination of the party's recently established electoral alliance with the CDS-PP, citing disloyalty on the part of the President of the CDS-PP, Paulo Portas.

The general election conducted on 10 October 1999 was partially overshadowed by the crisis in the former Portuguese colony of Timor-Leste (see below). Nevertheless, the PS secured 115 of the 230 seats in the Assembléia da República, while the PSD won 81 seats, and the left-wing CDU 17 seats (including two seats allocated to the ecologist Partido Ecologista 'Os Verdes'—PEV). The recently established Bloco de Esquerda (BE), a militant left-wing grouping, unexpectedly obtained two seats. Thus, one seat short of an absolute majority, Guterres was returned to office and a new Council of Ministers was appointed. In November the incoming Government announced a programme of reforms aimed at narrowing the disparity between Portugal and the more developed member countries of the EU.

At a presidential election held on 14 January 2001 Sampaio was re-elected for a second term, obtaining 55.8% of the votes cast and defeating four other candidates. His nearest rival, the PSD candidate Joaquim Ferreira do Amaral, secured 34.5% of the votes. In October 2001 the Assembléia da República ratified the Treaty of Nice, which aimed to reform the institutions of the EU in anticipation of its forthcoming enlargement. The PS, the PSD and the CDS-PP voted in favour of the ratification, while the BE and the PCP rejected the Treaty.

The PS was overwhelmingly defeated at municipal elections held in December 2001, at which the party lost control of Lisbon and Oporto to the PSD. In response, Guterres resigned as Prime

Minister and relinquished the leadership of the PS. The poor electoral results were widely attributed to a decline in the economy, as well as to discontent with public services, which had been adversely affected by reductions in government expenditure. President Sampaio announced that legislative elections would be held in early 2002. Guterres was replaced as Secretary-General of the PS in January by Eduardo Ferro Rodrigues. At the elections, held on 17 March, the PSD, whose campaign had featured reductions in corporate taxation and public expenditure and the privatization of state services, emerged victorious, winning 105 seats in the Assembléia da República, although without an overall majority. The PS secured 96 seats, the CDS-PP 14 seats, the PCP-PEV alliance 12 seats and the BE three seats. The leader of the PSD, José Manuel Durão Barroso, was appointed Prime Minister and formed a centre-right coalition Government with the CDS-PP.

Durão Barroso's Government expressed its intention to introduce austerity measures to counter the large public deficit, which contravened the country's obligations under the regulations for the European single currency (see Economic Affairs). In July 2002 the Government proposed a new labour code designed to combat low productivity by increasing the ease of recruitment and dismissal of staff and limiting the power of the unions. In November and December two public sector one-day general strikes, involving up to 500,000 workers, were organized to protest against the introduction of the labour legislation and other recent austerity measures. In November many public sector workers observed a one-day strike to demand higher wages and in protest at government proposals to reform the public sector. Following the extension for a second consecutive year of a freeze on certain public sector salaries, in January 2004 the public sector unions organized a further one-day strike.

In early 2003 a number of establishment figures, including a former ambassador, Jorge Ritto, and a television presenter, Carlos Cruz, were arrested in connection with a child abuse scandal surrounding the Casa Pia children's home in Lisbon. In May Paolo Pedroso, the deputy leader and parliamentary spokesman of the PS, was also arrested. Throughout his custody he maintained that the allegations against him were part of a PSD plot to discredit him and requested that his parliamentary immunity be lifted to enable him to be questioned. Pedroso was released in October and permitted to resume his former role. However, he was charged in December (with nine other prominent figures) on 23 counts of sexual abuse, although the charges against him were later dropped. The investigation was concluded in May 2004, and seven people, including Cruz and Ritto, went on trial in late November; proceedings were ongoing in early 2008. Meanwhile, the Government established a tribunal to consider compensation claims brought by victims of abuse at Casa Pia, which in March 2006 awarded a total of more than €50m. to 44 claimants.

At elections to the European Parliament on 13 June 2004 the ruling coalition performed poorly, winning only 33.3% of the votes cast, compared with the 48.9% it had achieved in the 2002 legislative elections. The PS made significant gains, winning 44.5% of the votes cast, compared with 37.8% in the previous legislative elections. Unexpectedly, Durão Barroso was invited in late June to take over the role of President of the European Commission in October. In order to accept this appointment, Durão Barroso resigned as leader of the PSD, and subsequently as Prime Minister on 5 July; the populist Mayor of Lisbon and Secretary-General of the PSD, Pedro Santana Lopes, was elected leader of the PSD. President Sampaio invited Santana Lopes to form a new Government, which was inaugurated on 17 July. Eduardo Ferro Rodrigues subsequently resigned as Secretary-General of the PS, claiming that the left-wing Sampaio had betrayed the party's interests by not holding early legislative elections. José Sócrates, a moderate and a former Minister of the Environment, was elected Secretary-General of the PS in September.

Santana Lopes's Government was beset by problems, including claims that it was trying to control the media. In November 2004 directors and a prominent newscaster resigned from the state broadcasting company, Radiotelevisão Portuguesa (RTP), in protest at pressure from the Government, and the state media authority criticized the Government for attempting to limit RTP's freedom. A series of cabinet reorganizations took place, culminating in the resignation of Henrique Chaves, formerly a close associate of the Prime Minister, as Minister for Youth and Sport. Chaves, who had been moved from the position of Minister in Assistance to the Prime Minister days earlier, cited Santana Lopes's disloyalty. At the end of November President Sampaio informed Santana Lopes of his decision to dissolve parliament and call legislative elections. Prior to the dissolution, the President permitted time for the adoption of the 2005 budget. However, the expansionary budget, which was approved by the Assembléia da República in early December, proved controversial as it contained tax reductions and increases in the state pension that were likely to cause Portugal to breach the budget deficit limit (equivalent to 3% of gross domestic product—GDP) specified in the EU's Stability and Growth Pact. Sampaio formally dissolved the legislature on 10 December, citing a loss of confidence in the Government, and announced that legislative elections would be held on 20 February 2005.

In December 2004 Santana Lopes was chosen as the PSD's prime ministerial candidate. It was subsequently announced that the PSD and the CDS-PP would not be jointly contesting the elections. The PSD's electoral agenda included pledges not to increase taxes and to reduce public expenditure. In the elections, which took place as scheduled on 20 February 2005, the PS, which during the campaign had advocated institutional reform and policies to increase economic growth, achieved an overwhelming victory, winning an outright majority; voter participation was 64.3%. The PS won 121 of the 230 seats in the Assembléia da República, with 45.0% of the votes cast; the PCP-PEV coalition and the BE also performed well at the expense of the right. The PSD won 75 seats, with 28.8% of the votes cast, while its junior partner in the previous Government, the CDS-PP, won 12 seats (7.2%). Santana Lopes and Paulo Portas, the leader of the CDS-PP, subsequently resigned their party positions. In April Luís Marques Mendes was elected leader of the PSD, while José Ribeiro e Castro became President of the CDS-PP.

A new 16-member Council of Ministers, headed by Sócrates, took office in March 2005. It included an equal number of members of the PS and independents, most notably former CDS leader Diogo Freitas do Amaral, who had been an outspoken critic of the US-led invasion of Iraq in 2003, as Minister of Foreign Affairs. Another independent, and former deputy governor of the Banco de Portugal, Luís Campos e Cunha, was allocated the finance portfolio.

On taking office the new Government adopted a policy of strict economic austerity in an effort to reduce the budget deficit, which was forecast to be considerably higher than the EU limit of 3% of GDP. Disagreements arose between Campos e Cunha and Sócrates, however, and the Minister of Finance resigned in July 2005; he was replaced by Fernando Teixeira dos Santos of the PS. Plans to increase value-added tax and reduce government expenditure, notably on social security, led to a series of protests and strikes by public sector employees. A one-day strike in July, observed by an estimated 500,000 workers, was followed, in September and October, by protests and industrial action staged by employees in various sectors. The ruling PS performed poorly in local elections in October, with the PSD retaining control over a majority of municipalities. In November, and again in February 2006, public sector workers participated in large-scale protests against the reduction in social welfare benefits, a wage freeze and the raising of the retirement age.

In November 2005 President Sampaio announced that a presidential election would take place on 22 January 2006. Six candidates contested the election, including former President Soares and former Prime Minister Cavaco Silva. (Sampaio was not eligible to stand for a third term.) Cavaco Silva was the only candidate representing the centre-right parties, while the centre-left vote was largely split between Soares and Manuel Alegre, also a member of the PS, who was standing as an independent. Cavaco Silva narrowly won an overall majority (with 50.5% of the valid votes cast), thereby avoiding the need for a second round of voting. Alegre won 20.7% of the vote, while Soares took 14.3%. Some 62.6% of the electorate participated in the ballot. Cavaco Silva, the first centre-right President since the coup of 1974, took office on 9 March. In June Freitas do Amaral resigned as Minister of Foreign Affairs, for health reasons, and was replaced by Luís Amado, hitherto Minister of National Defence; Amado's portfolio was taken by Nuno Severiano Teixeira.

In November 2006 the 2007 draft budget was approved in the Assembléia da República with the sole support of the PS. All other parties opposed the budget, which included significant reductions in public expenditure, to be largely financed by a reform of public administration. The public sector trade unions organized a two-day strike to coincide with the passage of the legislation, in protest against cuts in wages and pensions for public sector workers. General discontent with government policies had also been manifested in a demonstration organized by one of the principal trade union federations, the Confederação Geral dos Trabalhadores Portugueses-Intersindical Nacional (CGTP—General Confederation of Portuguese Workers) in October and by industrial action by the teaching unions in the same month. In January 2007 the Government began negotiations with trade unions over the reform of labour legislation, which was to be implemented in 2008. The trade unions expressed vehement opposition to the proposals, which were likely to entail significant reductions in the number of civil servants. In March 2007 the CGTP organized a further demonstration to protest against government employment and fiscal policy, which was attended by 120,000 protesters.

In a referendum held in February 2007, 59.2% of those voting approved plans to legalize abortion for all women up to the 10th week of pregnancy; however, only 43.6% of the electorate voted, below the 50% needed to make the result legally binding. None the less, Sócrates declared that the result represented a mandate for reform. Legislation providing for decriminalization was adopted by the Assembléia da República in March and, after receiving presidential approval in April, entered into force in July. Abortion had hitherto only been permitted in restricted circumstances, including those where the pregnancy was as a result of rape or posed a danger to the mother's health.

In March 2007 the former President of the CDS-PP, Paulo Portas, challenged Ribeiro e Castro for the leadership of the party. An election was held in April at which Portas was re-elected President by 74.6% of party members. In mid-May António Costa, the Minister of Internal Administration, resigned from his post to stand as the PS candidate for Mayor of Lisbon, where a city council election had been precipitated by a corruption scandal. He was replaced by Rui Pereira, hitherto a judge of the Constitutional Court. Costa was duly elected as Mayor of Lisbon in July.

The Government's reform programme continued to provoke labour unrest in mid-2007, with a one-day general strike called by the CGTP causing significant disruption to public services in late May. In June the Government approved a new system of remuneration and career progression for civil servants, despite ongoing opposition from the CGTP. (However, elements of the new legislation, under which judges would be considered as civil servants rather than separately, as they were under the current system, were declared unconstitutional by the Constitutional Court in December.) Meanwhile, an apparent decline in support for Sócrates and his Government indicated by opinion polls was attributed to discontent with the public administration reforms and to recent controversy over the authenticity of the Prime Minister's engineering degree. In November the three principal public sector unions organized a one-day strike in protest against a 2.1% pay increase for civil servants for 2008. The unions had demanded rises of between 3.5% and 5.8%. None the less, the Government appeared to be succeeding in its efforts to reduce the budget deficit, despite the unpopularity of its reforms, and it was expected to achieve its target of reducing the deficit to below 3% of GDP by 2008 (see Economic Affairs).

In late September 2007 Luís Filipe Menezes, the Mayor of Vila Nova de Gaia, was narrowly elected leader of the PSD, defeating the incumbent, Marques Mendes, with 54.1% of the votes cast. The resignation of two ministers in late January 2008 prompted Sócrates to effect a minor government reorganization. Ana Jorge was appointed as Minister of Health, replacing António Correia de Campos, whose plans to restructure hospital emergency services had prompted a series of protests, while José António Pinto Ribeiro became Minister of Culture, succeeding Isabel Pires de Lima, who had also been criticized in recent months over her ministry's policies.

After only seven months as leader of the PSD, in mid-April 2008 Menezes resigned from the post, citing criticism of his performance by a number of senior party members and ongoing disagreements within the PSD. His successor was due to be elected at a special party conference on 31 May.

The EU Treaty establishing a Constitution for Europe was signed by the EU Heads of State and of Government in October 2004. It required ratification by all 25 EU member states, either through a referendum or by a vote in the national legislature, before it could come into force. In March 2005 the new PS administration announced its intention to hold a referendum on the EU constitutional treaty in October, at the same time as local elections, after seeking the necessary constitutional amendment. However, following the rejection of the treaty in referendums in France and the Netherlands, in June 2005 the Portuguese Government postponed its own national referendum. The constitutional treaty was subsequently abandoned and, shortly after Portugal assumed the six-month rotating Presidency of the Council of the European Union, an Intergovernmental Conference was convened in Lisbon in July 2007 to draft a replacement. The resulting Treaty of Lisbon amending the Treaty on European Union and the Treaty establishing the European Community, which retained many of the provisions of the constitutional treaty (although it amended existing treaties rather than replacing them), was signed in December by the EU Heads of State or of Government. In January 2008 Sócrates announced that Portugal's ratification of the Treaty of Lisbon would be subject to a vote in the Assembléia da República, rather than a national referendum, as had been promised for the constitutional treaty. It was speculated that the Prime Minister had come under pressure from other European leaders who feared that a referendum in Portugal might jeopardize the ratification process in their own countries. The treaty was ratified by the Assembléia da República on 23 April and received presidential approval on 9 May.

Portugal's leaders were deeply divided over the issue of the proposed US-led military campaign to remove the regime of Saddam Hussain in Iraq in early 2003. Despite domestic popular opposition to a proposed US-led military response and general support for a diplomatic solution to the Iraqi problem, Durão Barroso was a vocal supporter of the US stance on Iraq. In January Barroso announced that his Government had authorized the USA to use an airbase in the Portuguese mid-Atlantic archipelago of the Azores in the event of war. The left-wing President Sampaio was, however, resolutely opposed to any military action in Iraq without a UN mandate and clashed publicly with the Prime Minister over the issue (although under the Constitution foreign policy is the responsibility of the Government, the President is empowered to veto decisions by the Council of Ministers). In early March Durão Barroso affirmed Portuguese support for US-led military action with or without UN endorsement and subsequently hosted an emergency summit on Iraq between leaders of the USA, the United Kingdom and Spain, at which it was announced that they would launch a military strike even in the event that UN support could not be achieved. However, following the failure of the coalition to gain support for a second UN Security Council resolution endorsing military action, President Sampaio announced a compromise agreed between himself and Durão Barroso: Portuguese armed forces would not participate in the conflict, although Portugal would make transit facilities available to its allies. At the end of March all four left-wing opposition parties, reflecting public discontent with the Government's handling of the crisis, submitted censure motions against the Government for hosting the emergency summit, claiming that Durão Barroso had linked Portugal to a war and had contributed to the weakening of international institutions; the Government defeated the motions owing to its majority in the Assembléia da República. Durão Barroso announced in April that Portugal was prepared to deploy military forces in Iraq for humanitarian and peace-keeping purposes. The opposition subsequently affirmed its support for the deployment only if it took place under the auspices of the UN. In November a contingent of 120 members of the paramilitary National Republican Guard was sent to Iraq. The mission ended in February 2005, following democratic elections in Iraq. In mid-2005 Portuguese troops were deployed in Afghanistan as part of the NATO-led International Security Assistance Force (ISAF). In February 2008 132 Portuguese troops, who had been stationed in the Afghan capital, Kabul, returned to Portugal following the completion of their mission; in March some 162 Portuguese troops remained in Afghanistan as part of ISAF.

In early 1988 Portugal announced that it was to review the terms of the 1983–91 agreement permitting the continued use by the USA of the Portuguese airbase at Lajes in the Azores, in return for US economic and military aid. In February 1989 the USA agreed to increase its level of compensation for its use of the base. In June 1995 the two countries signed a five-year accord whereby the USA undertook to supply to Portugal weapons and military equipment worth US $173m. In January 2003 Portugal agreed to US use of the Azores base in the event of war against Iraq, but only if action was ratified by the UN. This was later modified and use was granted without a UN resolution.

Relations with Spain improved in the late 1970s and 1980s following the restoration of democracy in both countries, and in

May 1989 King Juan Carlos became the first Spanish monarch to address the Portuguese Assembléia da República. By the mid-1990s the principal bilateral issue had become that of the division of water supply, and in November 1998 Portugal and Spain signed an historic accord relating to the sharing of river resources. In December 2003 the two Governments reached a reciprocal agreement, to last 10 years, defining access to fishing waters.

Negotiations with the People's Republic of China on the question of the Portuguese overseas territory of Macao commenced in June 1986, and in April 1987 Portugal and China signed an agreement whereby Portugal would transfer the administration of Macao to China in December 1999. At midnight on 19 December 1999 the sovereignty of Macao was duly transferred (see chapter on Macao).

The former Portuguese territory of Timor-Leste (East Timor) was unilaterally annexed by Indonesia in 1976. UN-sponsored negotiations between Portugal and Indonesia began in 1983 but proved inconclusive. Under UN auspices, talks between Portugal and Indonesia on the Timor-Leste issue were resumed in December 1992, but again ended without agreement. In January 1995 Portugal and Indonesia agreed to the holding of discussions, under UN auspices, between the factions of Timor-Leste. In early 1996, the UN-sponsored discussions having continued, Portugal offered to re-establish a diplomatic presence in Jakarta in return for the release of the East Timorese resistance leader, Xanana Gusmão, who had been sentenced to life imprisonment in 1993. In August 1998, following President Suharto's replacement in May and the subsequent implementation of a series of Indonesian troop withdrawals from the disputed region, the UN Secretary-General announced that Portugal and Indonesia had agreed to hold discussions on the possibility of autonomy for Timor-Leste. In March 1999 it was announced that Portugal and Indonesia had reached an accord providing for the holding of a referendum in the territory on the question of either autonomy or independence. In August, following two postponements and despite continuing intimidation and violence, the referendum on the future of Timor-Leste finally proceeded, and resulted in an overwhelming endorsement of proposals for full independence for the territory. The announcement of the result, however, precipitated a rapid decline in the security situation, leading to the declaration of martial law in the territory. In mid-September a multinational peace-keeping force, led by Australia, was deployed in the territory. Following the restoration of order in Timor-Leste and the Indonesian Government's acceptance of the result of the referendum, in December 1999 Portugal and Indonesia resumed full diplomatic relations, which had been severed in 1975, and in January 2001 a new Indonesian ambassador to Portugal was appointed. Meanwhile, Portugal committed an initial 700 troops to the UN peace-keeping force that replaced the Australian-led multinational force in early 2000. The Portuguese Government also pledged an annual sum of US $75m. towards the reconstruction of Timor-Leste. Official diplomatic relations with Timor-Leste were established with the creation of an embassy in Lisbon in 2002. In June 2006 120 members of the Portuguese National Republican Guard were dispatched to Timor-Leste to assist in efforts to restore public order following an upsurge in violence in that country. Portugal also contributed police and military liaison officers to the UN Integrated Mission in Timor-Leste, which was established in August.

Portugal played a significant role in the peace process in Angola, a former Portuguese overseas possession. Several meetings between representatives of the Angolan Government and the União Nacional para a Independência Total de Angola (UNITA) rebel group were held in Lisbon, culminating in the signing of a peace accord in 1991. In June 1993, following the resumption of hostilities in January, UNITA rejected Portugal's status as an observer in the new peace process; however, in May 1994 a UNITA spokesman welcomed the possibility of further Portuguese mediation. A new peace agreement was signed in November of that year. In early 1995, however, the neutrality of the Portuguese Government was impugned by allegations that it had given technical assistance to the Angolan Government. In July 1998, following renewed hostilities in Angola, Portugal requested the intervention of the UN Secretary-General. In August UNITA severed its links with Portugal and the other observers in the peace process, accusing them of bias towards the Angolan Government. In March 2000 tensions between Angola and Portugal increased, following comments by the Angolan Minister of Social Communication, accusing the former Portuguese President, Mario Soares, and his son, João Soares, of benefiting from UNITA's illegal trade in diamonds. The allegations were strongly denied by UNITA. However, in May it was announced that military co-operation between Portugal and the government forces was to be increased. Following the cessation of hostilities in Angola in April 2002, Portugal was one of three states with representatives observing the peace process according to the Lusaka Protocol. Portugal was to continue with military support, including overseeing the integration of UNITA soldiers into new armed forces and the establishment of a military academy.

Portugal was also active in the quest for peace in Mozambique. Relations with Mozambique deteriorated in March 1989, however, when a Mozambican diplomat was expelled from Portugal, following his implication in the assassination, in April 1988, of a Mozambican resistance leader. Nevertheless, in January 1992 Portugal received a formal invitation to attend the peace talks as an observer, and in October a peace treaty was signed in Italy.

In July 1996 Portugal hosted the inaugural meeting of the Comunidade dos Países de Língua Portuguesa (CPLP, see p. 423), a grouping of lusophone countries (including Angola, Brazil, Mozambique and Guinea-Bissau), which aimed to promote closer political and economic co-operation. In late 1998, as part of a CPLP initiative, Portugal played a major role in the implementation of a peace agreement in Guinea-Bissau, ending several months of conflict between government and rebel forces in the former colony. In the aftermath of a coup in May 1999, the deposed President of Guinea-Bissau, João Vieira, was granted asylum in Portugal. Following the bloodless coup in Guinea-Bissau in September 2003, the Portuguese Government provided US $1.5m. in aid to the new Government. New Portuguese legislation on immigration, which entered into force in August 2007, was aimed, *inter alia*, at integrating foreign workers by facilitating the granting of residence permits to undocumented migrants, the majority of whom came from Brazil and lusophone African countries.

Government

A new Constitution, envisaging the construction of a socialist society in Portugal, was promulgated in 1976 and revised in 1982. Subsequent revisions included the provision in 1997 for the holding of referendums on issues of national interest. The organs of sovereignty are the President, the Assembléia da República and the Government. The President, elected by popular vote for a five-year term, appoints the Prime Minister and, on the latter's proposal, other members of the Government, principally the Council of Ministers. The Council of State (Conselho de Estado) is a consultative body. Following the election of October 1991, the unicameral Assembléia had 230 members, including four representing Portuguese citizens abroad, elected by universal adult suffrage for four years (subject to dissolution). The mainland comprises 18 administrative districts. The Azores and Madeira (integral parts of the Portuguese Republic) were granted autonomy in 1976. The overseas territory of Macao was governed by special statute until December 1999, when it reverted to Chinese sovereignty.

Defence

Compulsory military service was abolished in 2004. Portugal is a member of the North Atlantic Treaty Organization (NATO, see p. 340) and of Western European Union (see p. 426). As assessed at November 2007, the total strength of the armed forces was 42,910, comprising: army 26,700 (including 8,740 conscripts), navy 9,110 (including 1,725 marines) and air force 7,100. There were reserves of 210,900. The paramilitary National Republican Guard and the Public Security Police totalled 26,100 and 21,600, respectively. A total of 856 US troops were stationed in Portugal, mainly at the air force base at Lajes in the Azores. In November 2004 Portugal confirmed its participation (with Italy, Spain and Greece) in one of a number of European Union (EU, see p. 244) battle groups, which were ready for deployment to crisis areas by 2007. Portugal subsequently agreed to participate in a second EU battle group, led by Spain and also involving Germany and France. The 2007 state budget allocated €1,880m. to defence.

Economic Affairs

In 2006, according to estimates by the World Bank, Portugal's overall gross national income (GNI), measured at average 2004–06 prices, was US $191,624m., equivalent to $18,100 per head (or $21,580 on an international purchasing-power parity basis). During 1996–2006, it was estimated, the population increased at an average rate of 0.5% per year, while gross domestic product

(GDP) per head increased, in real terms, by an average of 1.6% per year. Overall GDP expanded, in real terms, at an average annual rate of 2.1% in 1996–2006; GDP increased by 1.3% in 2006.

Agriculture (including forestry and fishing) contributed an estimated 2.8% of GDP in 2006, while engaging 11.7% of the employed labour force, according to estimates. The principal crops are grapes, tomatoes, potatoes, maize, sugar beets, olives, wheat, apples and oranges. The production of wine, particularly port, is significant. The fishing industry is important, the sardine catch, at 67,400 metric tons in 2005, being by far the largest. Agricultural GDP decreased, in real terms, by 2.6% per year during 1996–2005, agricultural GDP declined by 8.4% in 2005, owing largely to the effects of a severe drought, but a recovery was reported in 2006.

Industry (comprising mining, manufacturing, construction and power) contributed an estimated 24.9% of GDP and engaged 30.6% of the employed labour force in 2006, according to estimates. The GDP of the industrial sector increased, in real terms, by an estimated 1.2% per year during 1996–2005; industrial GDP declined by 1.8% in 2005. The mining and quarrying industry makes a minimal contribution to GDP, employing, together with electricity, gas and water, an estimated 0.8% of the employed labour force in 2006. Limestone, granite, marble, copper pyrites, gold and uranium are the most significant products.

Manufacturing provided 15.8% of GDP in 2005, and engaged 19.0% of the employed labour force in 2006, according to estimates. Manufacturing GDP grew by an estimated annual average of 1.5% in 1996–2003. The textile industry is the most important branch of manufacturing, accounting for 21.3% of total export earnings in 2003. Other significant manufactured products include cork items, chemicals, electrical appliances, ceramics and paper pulp.

In 2004 33.1% of electricity production was derived from coal, 26.1% from natural gas, 22.0% from hydroelectric power and 12.7% from petroleum. Total electricity production was 41,346m. kWh in 2004. In 2005 imports of fuel and oil accounted for 14.4% of total import costs. Portugal's heavy dependence on petroleum was reduced in 1997 when a pipeline carrying natural gas from Algeria (via Morocco and Spain) was inaugurated. Investment in renewable energy sources has increased significantly during recent years, in accordance with the Government's aim to produce some 60% of Portugal's energy from renewable sources by 2020. (In 2007 40.7% of energy production was from renewable sources.) In January 2007 the construction of an 11-MW solar power plant was completed in Serpa, some 200 km southeast of Lisbon; in early 2008 a 62-MW plant, which was to be the largest in the world, was under construction at Moura, in the southern region of Alentejo. The use of wind power has expanded in recent years: by March 2007 wind farms with a total generating capacity of 1,874.0 MW had been connected to the national electricity grid, while additional farms with a capacity of 908.5 MW were under construction. In addition, a commercial wave-energy project was under way off the coast of northern Portugal.

Services provided 72.4% of GDP and engaged 57.7% of the employed labour force in 2006, according to estimates. The tourism industry remained a significant source of foreign exchange earnings in 2005, when receipts totalled an estimated US $9,222m. In 2006 there were 11.3m. tourist arrivals in Portugal. Emigrants' remittances are also important to the Portuguese economy, reaching €1,277m. in 2005. The GDP of the services sector increased, in real terms, by an estimated average of 2.7% per year during 1996–2005; services GDP increased by 0.9% in 2005.

In 2006 Portugal recorded a visible trade deficit of US $20,872m., and there was a deficit of $18,281m. on the current account of the balance of payments. Most of Portugal's trade is with other members of the European Union (EU, see p. 244). In 2006 Spain, Germany and France supplied 40.4%, 18.2% and 11.1%, respectively, of total imports. The principal export markets were also Spain (which purchased 35.5% of the total), Germany (17.0%) and France (16.0%). The main exports in 2003 were textiles, clothing and footwear (21.3%), machinery (19.7%), transport equipment (15.3%), and mineral products and base metals (9.9%). The principal imports were machinery, transport equipment, food and agricultural products, mineral fuels, and mineral products and base metals.

The budget deficit for 2007 was estimated at €4,257.4m., equivalent to 2.6% of GDP, compared with 3.9% in 2006 and 6.1% in 2005. In 2007 Portugal's general government debt was estimated at €103,552.0m., equivalent to 63.6% of GDP. In 1996–2006 the annual rate of inflation averaged 2.9%. The average rate of inflation was 2.5% in 2007. The unemployment rate averaged 7.7% in 2006.

Portugal became a member of the European Community (EC, now EU) in January 1986. The Treaty on European Union was ratified by the Portuguese legislature in December 1992. In April 1992 Portugal joined the Exchange Rate Mechanism of the European Monetary System (see p. 288). Portugal is also a member of the Organisation for Economic Co-operation and Development (OECD, see p. 347) and of the Comunidade dos Países de Língua Portuguesa (CPLP, see p. 423), which was established in Lisbon in 1996.

Financial transfers from the EU, of which Portugal has been a net recipient since its accession in 1986, were reduced from 2006, as a consequence of the enlargement of the EU from 15 to 25 members in May 2004. Following a period of strong growth during the late 1990s, the economy slowed considerably in the early 2000s, precipitating a sharp decline in tax revenue. In 2001 the budget deficit was equivalent to 4.1% of GDP, thus exceeding the 3% limit stipulated in the EU's Stability and Growth Pact. The Government responded with austerity measures. The deficit was reduced to 2.9% in 2002, but by the end of that year Portugal became the first country in the euro zone to enter into a recession, which continued through 2003. There was a modest recovery in 2004, when growth of 1.5% was achieved. However, growth slowed once again in 2005 to only 0.5%. A modest economic recovery took place in 2006, and exports increased by 8.0%. However, with GDP growth of 1.3% in that year, Portugal remained the slowest growing economy in the EU. The Government narrowly succeeded in maintaining the budget deficit below 3% of GDP in 2003, at 2.9%, but, by 2005, the deficit had increased to some 6.1%. The Government that took office in early 2005 announced a four-year economic programme including the promotion of private investment in infrastructure and the reversal of the previous administration's policy of tax cuts. In September EU leaders agreed to allow the Government until 2008 to reduce the budget deficit to less than 3% of GDP. The Government achieved some progress in its programme of fiscal and administrative reforms during 2005–07, most notably reducing benefit payments and raising the minimum age of retirement for public sector workers from 60 to 65 years. The budget deficit was recorded at 2.6% in 2007. A further reduction in the deficit, to 2.4%, was projected for 2008. The Banco de Portugal envisaged economic growth of 2.0% in 2008, driven by continued growth in exports. Portugal's rate of growth, however, remained among the lowest in the EU and observers expressed concerns over the slow progress of reform. During 2008, the Government was expected to introduce measures to steady the economy in the light of a global downturn. In March 2008 Prime Minister José Sócrates announced a reduction in the rate of value-added tax (VAT), from 21% to 20%, with effect from 1 July.

Education

Formal education at all levels is provided at both public and private institutions. Pre-school education, for three- to six-year olds, is not compulsory, and is available free of charge. Basic education is compulsory for nine years, between the ages of six and 15, and is provided free of charge in public schools. It is divided into three cycles: the first lasts for four years, the second for two years and the third for three years. Secondary education, which is not compulsory, lasts for three years, and comprises a single three-year cycle, with two types: general and vocational. In 2005/06 98% of children in the relevant age-group were enrolled in primary schools, while 82% of children in the relevant age-group were enrolled in secondary schools (males 78%; females 86%).

Higher education comprises two systems. Universities award the following academic degrees: the *licenciatura*, after four to six years of study, the *mestrado*, after one or two years of study and research work, and the *doutoramento*. Regional polytechnic institutes, grouping technical, management, educational and fine arts schools, offer three-year courses leading to the *bacharel* and specialized studies leading to a diploma after one to two years. New curricula were introduced in 2003/04 and 2004/05. In 2005/06 a total of 367,934 students were enrolled in higher education. Expenditure on education in 2004 was €7,132m.

Public Holidays

2008: 1 January (New Year's Day), 5 February (Carnival Day), 20 March (Maundy Thursday)*, 21 March (Good Friday), 25 April (Liberty Day), 1 May (Labour Day), 22 May (Corpus Christi), 10 June (Portugal Day), 13 June (St Anthony—Lisbon only),

PORTUGAL

24 June (St John the Baptist—Oporto only), 15 August (Assumption), 5 October (Proclamation of the Republic), 1 November (All Saints' Day), 1 December (Restoration of Independence), 8 December (Immaculate Conception), 24 December (Christmas Eve), 25 December (Christmas Day).

2009: 1 January (New Year's Day), 24 February (Carnival Day), 9 April (Maundy Thursday)*, 10 April (Good Friday), 25 April (Liberty Day), 1 May (Labour Day), 10 June (Portugal Day), 11 June (Corpus Christi), 13 June (St Anthony—Lisbon only), 24 June (St John the Baptist—Oporto only), 15 August (Assumption), 5 October (Proclamation of the Republic), 1 November (All Saints' Day), 1 December (Restoration of Independence), 8 December (Immaculate Conception), 24 December (Christmas Eve), 25 December (Christmas Day).

* Afternoon only.

Weights and Measures

The metric system is in force.

Statistical Survey

Source (unless otherwise stated): Instituto Nacional de Estatística (INE), Av. António José de Almeida 2, 1000-043 Lisbon; tel. (21) 8426100; fax (21) 8426380; e-mail ine@ine.pt; internet www.ine.pt.

Area and Population

AREA, POPULATION AND DENSITY

Area (sq km)	
Land	91,906
Inland water	439
Total	92,345*
Population (census results)	
15 April 1991	9,862,540
1 March 2001	
Males	5,000,141
Females	5,355,976
Total	10,356,117
Population (official estimates at 31 December)	
2004	10,529,255
2005	10,569,592
2006	10,599,095
Density (per sq km) at 31 December 2006	115.3

* 35,655 sq miles.

REGIONS
(2001 census)

	Area (sq km)*	Population	Density (per sq km)
Continental Portugal	88,796	9,869,343	111.1
Norte	21,278	3,687,293	173.3
Centro	23,668	2,348,397	99.2
Lisboa e Vale do Tejo	11,931	2,661,850	223.1
Alentejo	26,931	776,585	28.8
Algarve	4,988	395,218	79.2
Autonomous Regions	3,109	486,774	156.6
Os Açores (Azores)	2,330	241,763	103.8
Madeira	779	245,011	314.5
Total	91,905	10,356,117	112.7

* Excluding river estuaries (439 sq km).

PRINCIPAL TOWNS
(population at 2001 census)

Lisboa (Lisbon, the capital)	564,657	Vila Nova de Gaia	69,698
Porto (Oporto)	263,131	Guimarães	63,058
Amadora	151,486	Algueirão-Mem Martins	62,557
Braga	112,039	Parede	61,821
Coimbra	104,489	Odivelas	53,449
Funchal	103,961	Amora	50,991
Setúbal	96,776	Leiria	50,167
Agualva-Cacém	81,845		

Source: Thomas Brinkhoff, *City Population* (internet www.citypopulation.de).

BIRTHS, MARRIAGES AND DEATHS

	Registered live births		Registered marriages		Registered deaths	
	Number	Rate (per 1,000)	Number	Rate (per 1,000)	Number	Rate (per 1,000)
1999	116,002	11.4	68,710	6.8	108,268	10.6
2000	120,008	11.7	63,752	6.2	105,813	10.3
2001	112,774	11.0	58,390	5.7	105,092	10.2
2002	114,456	11.0	56,457	5.4	106,690	10.2
2003	112,589	10.8	53,735	5.1	109,148	10.4
2004	109,356	10.4	49,178	4.7	102,371	9.7
2005	109,399	10.4	48,671	4.6	107,462	10.2
2006	105,449	10.0	47,857	4.5	101,990	9.6

Expectation of life (years at birth, WHO estimates): 78.2 (males 74.9; females 81.5) in 2005. (Source: WHO, *World Health Statistics*).

ECONOMICALLY ACTIVE POPULATION
(ISIC major divisions, '000 persons aged 15 years and over)

	2004	2005	2006
Agriculture, hunting and forestry	596.7	587.5	587.7
Fishing	21.4	18.7	16.2
Mining and quarrying	14.5	19.1	17.6
Electricity, gas and water supply	31.2	24.9	26.1
Manufacturing	1,002.2	968.6	980.5
Construction	548.0	554.1	553.0
Wholesale and retail trade; repair of motor vehicles, motorcycles and personal and household goods	782.0	773.0	751.2
Hotels and restaurants	265.4	275.8	280.0
Transport, storage and communications	214.5	220.8	239.6
Financial intermediation	96.6	95.2	90.1
Real estate, renting and business activities	292.2	283.7	294.5
Public administration and defence; compulsory social security	336.3	347.5	354.3
Education	306.6	314.9	318.7
Health and social work	313.0	326.8	329.8
Other community, social and personal service activities*	157.2	158.6	164.9
Private households with employed persons	147.3	150.9	152.4
Unallocated	2.2	2.6	2.9
Total employed*	5,127.5	5,122.6	5,159.5
Unemployed	365.0	422.3	427.8
Total labour force	5,492.5	5,544.9	5,587.3

* Including regular members of the armed forces, but excluding persons on compulsory military service.

Source: ILO.

PORTUGAL

Health and Welfare

KEY INDICATORS

Total fertility rate (children per woman, 2005)	1.5
Under-5 mortality rate (per 1,000 live births, 2005)	5
HIV/AIDS (% of persons aged 15–49, 2005)	0.4
Physicians (per 1,000 head, 2003)	3.42
Hospital beds (per 1,000 head, 2004)	3.7
Health expenditure (2004): US $ per head (PPP)	1,896.9
Health expenditure (2004): % of GDP	9.8
Health expenditure (2004): public (% of total)	71.6
Human Development Index (2005): ranking	29
Human Development Index (2005): value	0.897

For sources and definitions, see explanatory note on p. vi.

Agriculture

PRINCIPAL CROPS
('000 metric tons)

	2004	2005	2006
Wheat	293	81	260
Rice (paddy)	149	121	150
Barley	26	20	94
Maize	789	513	536
Rye	27	19	25
Oats	61	21	68
Triticale (wheat-rye hybrid)	17	8	33
Potatoes	770	576	577
Sweet potatoes*	21	22	25
Sugar beets	627	605	319
Olives	312	212	276
Sunflower seeds	14	2	3
Cabbages and other brassicas*	191	185	145
Lettuce and chicory*	107	115	100
Tomatoes	1,201	1,085	922
Cauliflower and broccoli*	38	40	38
Onions (dry)*	110	110	115
Broad beans (dry)*	15	17	18
Beans (green)*	15	15	16
Carrots and turnips*	170	182	160
Carobs*	20	20	20
Chestnuts	31	22	29
Bananas*	28	26	26
Oranges	250	219	228
Tangerines, mandarins, clementines and satsumas	60	58	58
Apples	277	249	240
Pears	188	130	169
Peaches and nectarines	52	52	55
Grapes	838*	989	973
Cantaloupes and other melons*	20	20	20

* FAO estimate(s).

Aggregate production ('000 metric tons, may include official, semi-official or estimated data): Total cereals 1,363 in 2004, 785 in 2005, 1,167 in 2006; Total oilcrops 350 in 2004, 238 in 2005, 303 in 2006; Total roots and tubers 793 in 2004, 601 in 2005, 604 in 2006; Total vegetables (incl. melons) 2,520 in 2004, 2,420 in 2005, 2,210 in 2006; Total fruits (excl. melons) 1,817 in 2004, 1,845 in 2005, 1,867 in 2006.

Source: FAO.

LIVESTOCK
('000 head, year ending September)

	2004	2005	2006
Horses*	17	17	18
Asses, mules or hinnies*	165	165	166
Cattle	1,389	1,443	1,441
Pigs	2,249	2,348	2,344
Sheep	3,356	3,541	3,583
Goats	502	547	551
Chickens*	35,000	35,000	36,000
Turkeys*	7,000	7,000	7,200

* FAO estimates.
Source: FAO.

LIVESTOCK PRODUCTS
('000 metric tons)

	2004	2005	2006
Cattle meat	118	118	105
Sheep meat	22	22*	22†
Pig meat	315	327	339
Chicken meat	196	198	193
Cows' milk	1,950	1,991	1,851
Sheep's milk	99	100	100†
Goats' milk	29	29	29†
Hen eggs	132	120	121

* Unofficial figure.
† FAO estimate.
Source: FAO.

Forestry

ROUNDWOOD REMOVALS
('000 cubic metres, excluding bark)

	2004	2005	2006
Sawlogs, veneer logs and logs for sleepers	2,246	2,483	2,510
Pulpwood	7,843	7,483	7,514
Other industrial wood*	180	180	180
Fuel wood*	600	600	600
Total	10,869	10,746	10,805

* FAO estimates.
Source: FAO.

SAWNWOOD PRODUCTION
('000 cubic metres, including railway sleepers)

	2003	2004	2005
Coniferous (softwood)	910	954	909
Broadleaved (hardwood)	473	106	101
Total	1,383	1,060	1,010

2006: Production assumed to be unchanged from 2005 (FAO estimates).
Source: FAO.

Fishing

('000 metric tons, live weight)

	2003	2004	2005
Capture	212.4	221.6	212.4
Atlantic horse mackerel	14.7	16.7	15.9
European pilchard (sardine)	66.6	75.9	67.4
Black scabbardfish	6.5	7.1	6.8
Atlantic redfishes	11.7	10.7	12.1
Chub mackerel	8.9	15.2	15.6
Blue shark	5.6	5.2	8.4
Octopuses	8.6	7.8	7.9
Aquaculture	8.0	6.7	6.5
Total catch	220.5	228.3	218.9

Note: Figures exclude aquatic plants ('000 metric tons): 0.4 in 2003; 0.3 in 2004; 0.6 in 2005.
Source: FAO.

PORTUGAL

Mining

('000 metric tons, estimated production, unless otherwise indicated)

	2004	2005	2006
Iron ore: gross weight	14.0	14.0	14.0
Iron ore: metal content	10.0	10.0	10.0
Copper ore*	95.7†	89.5†	78.6
Tungsten ore (metric tons)*	746†	816†	780
Silver ore (metric tons)*	24.4†	23.8†	20.1
Marble	749†	752†	n.a.
Granite (crushed and ornamental)	30.3†	30.7	n.a.
Kaolin	152.1†	164.1†	n.a.
Salt (rock)	661.7†	597.9†	586.2
Gypsum and anhydrite	461.2†	289.2†	n.a.
Talc (metric tons)	6,231†	5,362†	5,517

* Figures refer to the metal content of ores.
† Official figure.

Source: US Geological Survey.

Industry

SELECTED PRODUCTS
('000 metric tons, unless otherwise indicated)

	2002	2003	2004
Frozen fish	39.8	37.6	42.7
Tinned fish	43.3	43.3	48.9
Wheat flour	689	692	650
Refined sugar	400	370	n.a.
Prepared animal feeds	3,747	3,942	4,315
Distilled alcoholic beverages ('000 hectolitres)	284	297	266
Wine ('000 hectolitres)	6,449	7,149	7,257
Beer ('000 hectolitres)	6,689	7,110	7,712
Cigarettes (million units)	25,581	24,950	26,415
Wool yarn (pure and mixed)	5.3	3.6	n.a.
Cotton yarn (pure and mixed)	95.9	82.9	n.a.
Woven cotton fabrics (million sq metres)	350	305	n.a.
Woven woollen fabrics (million sq metres)	9.0	5.4	n.a.
Knitted fabrics	51.6	59.4	58.6
Footwear, excl. rubber ('000 pairs)	73,191	67,272	n.a.
Wood pulp (sulphate and soda)	714	677	647
Caustic soda (Sodium hydroxide)	87	88	81
Soda ash (Sodium carbonate)*	150	150	150
Nitrogenous fertilizers	123	n.a.	n.a.
Jet fuels	511	703	779
Motor spirit (petrol)	2,518	2,732	2,551
Naphthas	1,084	1,130	1,175
Distillate fuel oils	4,827	4,955	4,703
Residual fuel oils	2,358	2,388	2,969
Liquefied petroleum gas	341	379	365
Household ware of porcelain or china (metric tons)	29,223	26,939	n.a.
Household ware of other ceramic materials (metric tons)	95,712	115,241	n.a.
Cement	9,728	8,598	8,839
Pig-iron*	100	100	100
Crude steel (ingots)*	894	722	720
Refrigerators for household use ('000)	440	452	399
Radio receivers ('000)	8,470	7,310	7,805
Electric energy (million kWh)	46,107	46,852	45,105

* Figures from US Geological Survey.

2005 ('000 metric tons, unless otherwise indicated): Wine ('000 hectolitres) 7,051.3; Soda ash (sodium carbonate) 150; Pig-iron 100 (estimate); Crude steel (ingots) 725.

2006 ('000 metric tons, estimates): Soda ash (sodium carbonate) 150; Pig-iron 100; Crude steel (ingots) 725.

Source: mainly UN, *Industrial Commodity Statistics Yearbook*.

Finance

CURRENCY AND EXCHANGE RATES

Monetary Units
100 cent = 1 euro (€).

Sterling and Dollar Equivalents (31 December 2007)
£1 sterling = 1.3609 euros;
US $1 = 0.6793 euros;
€10 = £7.35 = $14.72.

Average Exchange Rate (euros per US dollar)
2005   0.8041
2006   0.7971
2007   0.7306

Note: The national currency was formerly the Portuguese escudo. From the introduction of the euro, with Portuguese participation, on 1 January 1999, a fixed exchange rate of €1 = 200.482 escudos was in operation. Euro notes and coins were introduced on 1 January 2002. The euro and local currency circulated alongside each other until 28 February, after which the euro became the sole legal tender.

BUDGET
(€ million)*

Revenue	2004	2005	2006
Current revenue	57,024	59,796	64,033
Direct taxes	12,316	12,788	13,750
Indirect taxes	20,387	22,214	23,842
Social contributions	17,573	18,671	19,347
Sale of goods and services	3,377	3,461	3,567
Other current revenue	3,371	2,662	3,527
Capital revenue	5,124	1,955	1,568
Total	62,148	61,751	65,601

Expenditure	2004	2005	2006
Current expenditure	60,501	64,566	66,322
Wages and salaries	20,340	21,457	20,958
Social transfers	30,616	33,084	34,836
Intermediate consumption	5,725	5,997	6,174
Interest payments	3,820	4,029	4,354
Subsidies	2,170	2,407	2,144
Other current expenditure	3,008	3,427	3,625
Capital expenditure	6,439	6,237	5,333
Gross capital formation	4,487	4,196	3,563
Other	1,952	2,041	1,771
Total	66,940	70,803	71,656

* Figures refer to the consolidated accounts of the central Government, excluding assets and liabilities.

Source: Direcção-Geral do Orçamento, Ministério das Finanças.

INTERNATIONAL RESERVES
(US $ million at 31 December)*

	2005	2006	2007
Gold†	6,885	7,819	10,288
IMF special drawing rights	103	113	123
Reserve position in IMF	202	115	90
Foreign exchange	3,173	1,835	1,044
Total	10,364	9,882	11,545

* Reserves are defined in accordance with the Eurosystem's statistical definition.
† Valued at $513.0 per troy ounce in 2005, $635.7 in 2006 and $836.4 in 2007.

Source: IMF, *International Financial Statistics*.

MONEY SUPPLY
(€ million at 31 December)

	2005	2006	2007
Currency in circulation*	1,327	1,472	1,583
Demand deposits at banking institutions	56,140	57,830	56,140

* Currency put into circulation by the Banco de Portugal was €5,450m. in 2005, €4,970m. in 2006 and €3,520m. in 2007.

Source: IMF, *International Financial Statistics*.

PORTUGAL

COST OF LIVING
(Consumer Price Index; base: 2000 = 100)

	2004	2005	2006
Food	112.1	111.3	114.2
Clothing	104.3	103.1	103.9
Electricity, gas and other fuels	112.6	119.4	124.3
Rent	116.0	119.5	123.4
All items (incl. others)*	114.2	116.7	120.4

* Excluding rent.

Source: ILO.

NATIONAL ACCOUNTS
(€ million at current prices, preliminary)

Composition of the Gross National Income

	2004	2005	2006
Gross domestic product at market prices	144,222.9	148,927.8	155,215.8
Primary incomes received from abroad	8,343.2	9,868.1	11,412.8
Less Primary incomes paid abroad	11,238.9	13,843.8	17,590.2
Gross national income	141,327.2	144,952.1	149,038.4
Less Consumption of fixed capital	23,593.8	24,221.5	25,650.2
Net national income	117,733.4	120,730.6	123,388.2
Current transfers from abroad	6,177.8	6,867.7	7,179.3
Less Current transfers paid abroad	3,665.1	4,438.8	4,211.4
Net national disposable income	120,246.1	123,159.5	126,356.1

Expenditure on the Gross Domestic Product

	2004	2005	2006
Final consumption expenditure	122,134.9	128,310.4	133,133.4
Households and non-profit institutions serving households	89,486.3	93,672.6	98,014.4
General government	32,648.6	34,637.8	35,119.0
Gross capital formation	33,229.0	33,439.5	34,161.9
Total domestic expenditure	155,363.9	161,749.9	167,295.3
Exports of goods and services	41,024.9	42,501.0	48,311.1
Less Imports of goods and services	52,165.9	55,323.1	60,390.6
GDP in market prices	144,222.9	148,927.8	155,215.8
GDP at constant 2000 prices	126,424.1	127,017.0	128,683.3

Gross Domestic Product by Economic Activity

	2004	2005	2006
Agriculture, hunting, forestry and fishing	3,927.2	3,511.6	3,717.7
Electricity, gas and water	3,474.8	3,523.7	3,779.1
Industry	19,822.4	20,073.2	20,997.3
Construction	8,713.7	8,651.8	8,498.8
Trade, restaurants and hotels	21,840.2	22,745.3	23,875.8
Transport, storage and communications	8,624.0	8,622.7	8,770.1
Finance, insurance and real estate	17,948.4	18,507.7	19,789.4
Other services	41,116.3	43,097.3	44,451.1
Gross value added in basic prices	125,467.0	128,733.3	133,879.3
Taxes on products (net)	18,817.9	20,421.8	22,025.9
Statistical discrepancy	−62.0	−227.3	−689.4
GDP in market prices	144,222.9	148,927.8	155,215.8

BALANCE OF PAYMENTS
(US $ million)

	2004	2005	2006
Exports of goods f.o.b.	36,956	38,238	43,579
Imports of goods f.o.b.	−55,673	−59,073	−64,451
Trade balance	−18,716	−20,836	−20,872
Exports of services	14,701	15,193	17,809
Imports of services	−9,746	−10,463	−11,612
Balance on goods and services	−13,760	−16,106	−14,675
Other income received	8,025	9,297	12,308
Other income paid	−11,652	−14,066	−19,062
Balance on goods, services and income	−17,387	−20,875	−21,429
Current transfers received	7,297	7,226	8,039
Current transfers paid	−3,761	−4,399	−4,892
Current balance	−13,851	−18,048	−18,281
Capital account (net)	2,808	2,139	1,578
Direct investment abroad	−7,778	−2,221	−3,507
Direct investment from abroad	2,062	4,099	7,366
Portfolio investment assets	−13,598	−19,659	−8,101
Portfolio investment liabilities	13,882	18,141	12,086
Financial derivatives assets	4,135	4,865	6,679
Financial derivatives liabilities	−4,226	−5,076	−6,992
Other investment assets	1,127	−602	−18,195
Other investment liabilities	14,385	15,728	23,335
Net errors and omissions	−809	−1,106	1,675
Overall balance	−1,863	−1,741	−2,357

Source: IMF, *International Financial Statistics*.

External Trade

PRINCIPAL COMMODITIES
(€ million, preliminary)

Imports c.i.f.	2004	2005	2006
Food and beverages	4,975.9	4,863.7	5,571.3
Fuels and oils	4,956.0	6,970.5	7,912.3
Machines, other capital goods (except transport equipment) and accessories	8,610.2	8,638.7	9,729.1
Transport equipment and accessories	7,454.0	6,866.7	7,234.4
Other industrial goods	12,903.0	12,648.7	14,756.2
Other consumer goods	6,951.9	6,818.3	7,649.3
Total (incl. others)	45,860.4	49,178.2	53,098.2

Exports f.o.b.	2004	2005	2006
Food and beverages	2,121.4	2,145.3	2,548.0
Fuels and oils	745.9	1,184.9	1,756.6
Machines, other capital goods (except transport equipment) and accessories	4,186.3	3,983.4	5,390.7
Transport equipment and accessories	6,327.9	5,828.6	6,371.2
Other industrial goods	9,341.3	8,677.7	11,359.8
Other consumer goods	6,764.1	6,178.0	6,707.4
Total (incl. others)	29,573.5	30,663.0	34,509.5

PRINCIPAL TRADING PARTNERS
(€ million)

Imports c.i.f.	2004	2005	2006
Belgium	1,324.1	1,391.2	1,463.1
France	4,278.9	4,162.2	4,463.6
Germany	6,504.9	6,598.7	7,309.3
Italy	2,761.2	2,553.0	3,066.0
Netherlands	2,116.7	2,101.4	2,401.4
Spain	13,749.9	14,226.4	16,172.8
United Kingdom	2,109.0	2,068.8	2,266.8
USA	1,058.1	1,067.1	780.8
Total (incl. others)	45,861.5	49,179.1	40,070.8

PORTUGAL   *Statistical Survey*

Exports f.o.b.	2004	2005	2006
Belgium	1,242.0	1,128.8	1,085.0
France	4,083.7	3,985.1	4,267.8
Germany	3,954.5	3,574.6	4,523.4
Italy	1,280.9	1,281.1	1,415.4
Netherlands	1,194.6	991.1	1,288.0
Spain	7,541.0	7,913.7	9,459.3
United Kingdom	2,803.2	2,420.4	2,433.3
USA	1,746.5	1,648.8	2,105.3
Total (incl. others)	29,576.4	30,644.7	26,625.3

Transport

RAILWAYS
(traffic)

	2002	2003	2004
Passenger journeys (million)	161	151	153
Passenger-kilometres (million)	3,926	3,585	3,693
Freight ('000 metric tons)	10,739	8,718	11,151
Freight ton-kilometres (million)	2,583	2,073	2,589

ROAD TRAFFIC
(motor vehicles registered at 31 December)

	2001	2002	2003
Light and heavy vehicles	7,361,572	7,690,019	7,910,572
Motorcycles	371,114	390,209	402,759
Tractors	309,775	322,283	329,761
Trailers and semi-trailers	363,722	376,719	377,552

SHIPPING
Merchant Fleet
(registered at 31 December)

	2004	2005	2006
Number of vessels	456	451	460
Total displacement (grt)	1,336,480	1,239,618	1,223,616

Source: Lloyd's Register-Fairplay, *World Fleet Statistics*.

International Sea-borne Freight Traffic
(Figures exclude the Azores)

	2004	2005	2006
Vessels entered ('000 gross registered tons)	118,457	136,225	148,826
Goods loaded ('000 metric tons)	16,621	17,828	19,975
Goods unloaded ('000 metric tons)	45,202	47,473	46,886

CIVIL AVIATION
(million)

	2001	2002	2003
Passenger-kilometres	12,857	14,244	16,421
Freight ton-kilometres	218	206	217
Mail ton-kilometres	20	20	21

2004: 18,591m. passenger-kilometres.

Tourism

FOREIGN TOURIST ARRIVALS BY COUNTRY OF RESIDENCE*

Country of origin	2003	2004	2005
Belgium	125,952	121,809	127,966
Brazil	130,835	148,110	172,180
France	549,716	497,278	485,076
Germany	681,507	661,776	669,325
Ireland	129,905	118,855	122,661
Italy	315,603	318,511	311,214
Japan	79,726	117,428	98,185
Netherlands	302,194	281,388	290,755
Spain	931,575	1,039,849	1,150,492
Sweden	98,257	116,257	105,493
United Kingdom	1,029,226	1,052,806	1,110,441
USA	216,171	220,242	226,732
Total (incl. others)	5,301,778	5,514,268	5,675,805

* Arrivals at all accommodation establishments.

Receipts from tourism (US $ million, incl. passenger transport): 7,607 in 2003; 8,991 in 2004; 9,222 in 2005.

Source: World Tourism Organization.

Communications Media

	2004	2005	2006
Telephones ('000 main lines in use)	4,238.3	4,233.7	4,230.7
Mobile cellular telephones ('000 subscribers)	10,362.1	11,447.3	12,226.4
Personal computers ('000 in use)	1,402	n.a.	n.a.
Internet users ('000)	2,575.7	2,856.1	3,213.0
Broadband subscribers ('000)	838.4	1,186.8	1,460.3

Source: International Telecommunication Union.

Facsimile machines ('000 in use): 70 in 1997.

Radio receivers ('000 in use): 3,020 in 1997.

Television receivers ('000 in use): 6,319 in 2000.

Books published (titles): 2,186 in 1998.

Daily newspapers (number of titles): 28 (total distribution 1,026,000) in 2000; 27 in 2004.

Non-daily newspapers: 242 (average circulation 1,152,000) in 1999; 596 in 2004.

Sources: mainly UN, *Statistical Yearbook*; UNESCO Institute for Statistics; UNESCO, *Statistical Yearbook*.

Education

(public and private, 2005/06, unless otherwise indicated)

	Institutions	Teachers	Students
Pre-school	6,858	18,213	262,002
Basic: 1st cycle	8,234	39,396	495,628
Basic: 2nd cycle	1,140	34,754	256,252
Basic: 3rd cycle	1,489	89,048	393,354
Secondary	926		347,400
Higher*	319	36,069	366,729

* 2006/07.

Adult literacy rate (UNESCO estimates): 93.8% (males 95.8%; females 92.0%) in 2004. (Source: UNESCO Institute for Statistics).

Directory

The Constitution

The Constitution of the Portuguese Republic was promulgated on 2 April 1976, and came into force on 25 April. It was revised in 1982, when ideological elements were diminished and the Council of the Revolution was abolished; in 1989, to permit economic reforms and a greater role for the private sector; in 1992, prior to the ratification of the Treaty on European Union (the Maastricht Treaty); in 1997 when changes included provision for the holding of referendums on questions of national interest; and in 2001 to incorporate reciprocal political rights for citizens of lusophone countries, to impose a ban on strike action by police trade unions and officially to recognize the UN International Criminal Court. The following is a summary of the Constitution's main provisions:

FUNDAMENTAL PRINCIPLES

Portugal is a sovereign Republic based on the dignity of the individual and the will of the people, which strives to create a just, caring and free society and to realize economic, social and cultural democracy. It comprises the territory defined by history on the European continent and the archipelagos of the Azores and Madeira. The Azores and Madeira shall constitute autonomous regions.

The fundamental duties of the State include the following: to safeguard national independence; to guarantee fundamental rights and freedoms; to defend political democracy and to encourage citizens' participation in the solving of national problems; and to promote the welfare, quality of life and equality of the people.

FUNDAMENTAL RIGHTS AND DUTIES

All citizens are equal before the law. Rights, freedoms and safeguards are upheld by the State and include the following: the right to life; of habeas corpus; to the inviolability of the home and of correspondence; to freedom of expression and of conscience; to freedom of movement, emigration and of assembly. Freedom of the press is guaranteed.

Rights and duties of citizens include the following: the right and the duty to work; the right to vote (at 18 years of age); the right to form and participate in political associations and parties; the freedom to form trade unions and the right to strike; the right to set up co-operatives; the right to private property; the right to social security and medical services; the duty of the State and of society to protect the family and the disabled; the right to education, culture and sport; consumer rights.

ECONOMIC ORGANIZATION

The economic and social organization of Portugal shall be based on the subordination of economic power to political power, the co-existence of the public, private, co-operative and social sectors of ownership, and the public ownership of the means of production and land, in accordance with the public interest, as well as natural resources; and on the democratic planning of the economy, and democratic intervention by the workers. Enterprises nationalized after 25 April 1974 may be reprivatized. The aims of economic and social development plans include the promotion of economic growth, the harmonious development of sectors and regions, the fair individual and regional distribution of the national product and the defence of the environment and of the quality of life of the Portuguese people. The consultative Economic and Social Council participates in the formulation of development plans. It comprises representatives of the Government, workers' organizations, economic enterprises and representatives of autonomous regions and local organizations.

The aims of agrarian policy are to improve the situation of farm workers and to increase agricultural production and productivity. *Latifúndios* (large estates) will be adjusted in size, and property which has been expropriated, with compensation, shall be handed over to small farmers or co-operatives for exploitation. *Minifúndios* (small estates) will be adjusted in size, through the granting of incentives to integrate or divide. The aims of commercial policy include the development and diversification of foreign economic relations. The aims of industrial policy include an increase in production in the context of modernization and adjustment, greater competition, the support of small and medium enterprises and the support of industrial and technological innovation. The financial and fiscal system aims at encouraging savings and achieving the equal distribution of wealth and incomes. The State Budget shall be supervised by the Accounts Court and the Assembly of the Republic. Economic policy includes the stimulation of competition, the protection of consumers and the combating of speculative activities and restrictive trade practices.

POLITICAL ORGANIZATION

Political power shall lie with the people. The organs of sovereignty shall be: the President of the Republic, the Assembly of the Republic, the Government and the Courts. Direct, secret and regular elections shall be held. No-one shall hold political office for life.

PRESIDENT OF THE REPUBLIC

The President of the Republic shall represent the Republic. The President guarantees national independence, the unity of the State, and the proper working of democratic institutions. The President shall be elected by direct and secret universal adult suffrage. The candidate who obtains more than one-half of the valid votes will be elected President. The President shall hold office for five years. The President may not be re-elected for a third consecutive term of office.

The duties of the President include the following: to preside over the Council of State; to set dates for elections; to convene extraordinary sessions of the Assembly of the Republic; to dissolve the Assembly; to appoint and dismiss the Prime Minister; to appoint and dismiss the members of the Government at the proposal of the Prime Minister; to promulgate laws; to veto laws; to apply to the Constitutional Court; to nominate ambassadors, upon the proposal of the Government; to accredit diplomatic representatives; to ratify international treaties, after they have been duly approved; to dismiss the Government if and when the normal functioning of institutions is at stake.

COUNCIL OF STATE

The Council of State (Conselho de Estado) is the political consultative organ of the President of the Republic. It is presided over by the President of the Republic and comprises the President of the Assembly of the Republic, the Prime Minister, the President of the Constitutional Court, the Superintendent of Justice, the Presidents of the Regional Governments, certain former Presidents of the Republic, five citizens nominated by the President of the Republic and five citizens elected by the Assembly.

ASSEMBLY OF THE REPUBLIC

The Assembly of the Republic (Assembléia da República) represents all Portuguese citizens, and shall have a minimum of 180 and a maximum of 230 members, elected under a system of proportional representation by the electoral constituencies. The duties of the Assembly include the following: to present and approve amendments to the Constitution and to approve the political and administrative statutes of the Autonomous Regions; to enact legislation; to confer legislative authority on the Government; to approve plans and the Budget; to approve international conventions and treaties; to propose to the President of the Republic that questions of national interest be submitted to referendum; to supervise the fulfilment of the Constitution and laws. The Assembly supports the participation of Portugal in the process of building the European Union. Each legislative period shall last four years. The legislative session shall run from 15 September to 15 June each year.

GOVERNMENT

The Government formulates the general policy of the country and is the highest organ of public administration. It shall comprise the Prime Minister, Ministers, Secretaries and Under-Secretaries of State and may include one or more Deputy Prime Ministers. The Prime Minister is appointed and dismissed by the President. Other members of the Government are appointed by the President at the proposal of the Prime Minister. The Government shall be responsible to the President and the Assembly. The Government's programme shall be presented to the Assembly of the Republic for scrutiny within 10 days of the appointment of the Prime Minister.

JUDICIARY

The courts are independent organs of sovereignty with competence to administer justice. There shall be Courts of First Instance (District Courts), Courts of Second Instance (Courts of Appeal), the Supreme Administrative Court and the Supreme Court of Justice, in addition to the Constitutional Court. There shall also be military courts (when the State is at war) and an Accounts Court. There may be maritime courts and courts of arbitration.

The jury shall comprise the judges of the plenary court and the jurors. People's judges may be created. It is the duty of the Ministério Público to represent the State. Its highest organ is the Procuradoria-Geral, which is presided over by the Procurador-Geral, who is appointed and dismissed by the President of the Republic.

AUTONOMOUS REGIONS

The special political and administrative arrangements for the archipelagos of the Azores and Madeira shall be based on their geographical, economic and social conditions and on the historic aspirations of the people to autonomy. The State is represented in each of the Autonomous Regions by a Minister of the Republic.

The organs of government in the Autonomous Regions (which are subject to dissolution by the President of the Republic if a major breach of the Constitution occurs) are: the Regional Legislative Assembly, elected by direct and secret universal adult suffrage, and the Regional Government which shall be politically responsible to the Regional Legislative Assembly. Its Chairman is appointed by the Minister of the Republic. The Minister shall appoint or dismiss members of the Regional Government on the proposal of its Chairman.

LOCAL GOVERNMENT

The local authorities shall be territorial bodies corporate with representative organs serving the particular interests of the local population. The local authorities on the mainland shall be the parishes, municipal authorities and administrative regions. The Autonomous Regions of the Azores and Madeira shall comprise parishes and municipal authorities.

PUBLIC ADMINISTRATIVE AUTHORITIES

The public administrative authorities shall seek to promote the public interest whilst respecting the legal interests and rights of all citizens. Citizens shall have the right to be informed of, and to have redress against, the public administrative authorities when the matter directly concerns them.

ARMED FORCES

The President of the Republic is Supreme Commander-in-Chief of the Armed Forces, and appoints and dismisses the Chiefs of Staff. The defence forces shall safeguard national independence and territorial integrity. Military service shall be regulated by law, which shall decide the form (compulsory, or otherwise), duration and content of that service. The right to conscientious objection is recognized.

SAFEGUARDS AND REVISION OF THE CONSTITUTION

Changes in the Constitution shall be approved by a majority of two-thirds of the members of the Assembly of the Republic present, provided that the number of such members exceeds an absolute majority of the members entitled to vote. Constitutional revisions must comply with the independence, unity and secularism of the State; the rights, freedoms and safeguards of citizens; universal, direct and secret suffrage and the system of proportional representation, etc.

The Government

HEAD OF STATE

President: ANÍBAL CAVACO SILVA (took office 9 March 2006).

COUNCIL OF MINISTERS
(April 2008)

The Government comprises the Partido Socialista (PS) and independents (Ind.).

Prime Minister: JOSÉ SÓCRATES CARVALHO PINTO DE SOUSA (PS).
Minister of State and of Foreign Affairs: LUÍS FILIPE MARQUES AMADO (PS).
Minister of State and of Finance: FERNANDO TEIXEIRA DOS SANTOS (PS).
Minister of the Presidency: MANUEL PEDRO CUNHA DA SILVA PEREIRA (PS).
Minister of National Defence: NUNO SEVERIANO TEIXEIRA (PS).
Minister of Internal Administration: RUI CARLOS PEREIRA (Ind.).
Minister of Justice: ALBERTO BERNARDES COSTA (PS).
Minister of the Environment, Territorial Planning and Regional Development: FRANCISCO CARLOS DA GRAÇA NUNES CORREIA (Ind.).
Minister of the Economy and Innovation: MANUEL ANTÓNIO GOMES DE ALMEIDA DE PINHO (Ind.).
Minister of Agriculture, Rural Development and Fisheries: JAIME DE JESUS LOPES SILVA (Ind.).
Minister of Public Works, Transport and Communications: MÁRIO LINO SOARES CORREIA (PS).
Minister of Labour and Social Solidarity: JOSÉ ANTÓNIO FONSECA VIEIRA DA SILVA (PS).
Minister of Health: ANA MARIA TEODORO JORGE (PS).
Minister of Education: MARIA DE LURDES REIS RODRIGUES (Ind.).
Minister of Science, Technology and Higher Education: JOSÉ MARIANO REBELO PIRES GAGO (Ind.).
Minister of Culture: JOSÉ ANTÓNIO PINTO RIBEIRO (Ind.).
Minister of Parliamentary Affairs: AUGUSTO SANTOS SILVA (PS).

There are also 24 secretaries of state.

MINISTRIES

Office of the President: Presidência da República, Palácio de Belém, Calçada da Ajuda 11, 1349-022 Lisbon; tel. (21) 3614600; fax (21) 3614611; e-mail belem@presidencia.pt; internet www.presidencia.pt.

Office of the Prime Minister, Presidency of the Council of Ministers: Rua da Imprensa à Estrela 4, 1200-888 Lisbon; tel. (21) 3923500; fax (21) 3951616; e-mail pm@pm.gov.pt; internet www.portugal.gov.pt.

Ministry of Agriculture, Rural Development and Fisheries: Praça do Comércio, 1149-010 Lisbon; tel. (21) 3234600; fax (21) 3234601; e-mail geral@min-agricultura.pt; internet www.min-agricultura.pt.

Ministry of Culture: Palácio Nacional da Ajuda, 1349-021 Lisbon; tel. (21) 3614500; fax (21) 3649872; e-mail infocultura@min-cultura.pt; internet www.min-cultura.pt.

Ministry of the Economy and Innovation: Rua da Horta Seca 15, 1200-221 Lisbon; tel. (21) 3245400; fax (21) 3245440; e-mail gmei@mei.gov.pt; internet www.min-economia.pt.

Ministry of Education: Av. 5 de Outubro 107, 1069-018 Lisbon; tel. (21) 7811800; fax (21) 7811835; e-mail gme@me.gov.pt; internet www.min-edu.pt.

Ministry of the Environment, Territorial Planning and Regional Development: Rua de O Século 51, 1200-433 Lisbon; tel. (21) 3232500; fax (21) 3232531; e-mail gsea@maotdr.gov.pt; internet www.maotdr.gov.pt.

Ministry of Finance and Public Administration: Av. Infante D. Henrique 1, 1149-009 Lisbon; tel. (21) 8816800; fax (21) 8816819; e-mail rtamagnini@mf.gov.pt; internet www.min-financas.pt.

Ministry of Foreign Affairs: Palácio das Necessidades, Largo do Rilvas, 1399-030 Lisbon; tel. (21) 3946000; fax (21) 3946053; e-mail gii@mne.gov.pt; internet www.min-nestrangeiros.pt.

Ministry of Health: Av. João Crisóstomo 9, 1049-062 Lisbon; tel. (21) 3305000; fax (21) 3305044; e-mail info_portal@sg.min-saude.pt; internet www.min-saude.pt.

Ministry of Internal Administration: Praça do Comércio, 1149-015 Lisbon; tel. (21) 3233000; fax (21) 3468031; e-mail dirp@sg.mai.gov.pt; internet www.mai.gov.pt.

Ministry of Justice: Praça do Comércio, 1149-019 Lisbon; tel. (21) 3222300; fax (21) 3479208; e-mail gmj@mj.gov.pt; internet www.mj.gov.pt.

Ministry of Labour and Social Solidarity: Praça de Londres 2, 1049-056 Lisbon; tel. (21) 8441100; fax (21) 8424108; e-mail gmtss@mtss.gov.pt; internet www.mtss.gov.pt.

Ministry of National Defence: Av. Ilha da Madeira 1, 1400-204 Lisbon; tel. (21) 3038528; fax (21) 3020284; e-mail gcrp@sg.mdn.gov.pt; internet www.mdn.gov.pt.

Ministry of Parliamentary Affairs: Palácio de São Bento, 1249-068 Lisbon; tel. (21) 3920500; fax (21) 3920515; e-mail map@map.gov.pt.

Ministry of the Presidency: Rua Prof. Gomes Teixeira, 1399-265 Lisbon; tel. (21) 3923600; fax (21) 3927860; e-mail gab.mp@mp.gov.pt; internet www.mp.gov.pt.

Ministry of Public Works, Transport and Communications: Palácio do Conde de Penafiel, Rua de São Mamede (ao Caldas) 21, 1149-050 Lisbon; tel. (21) 8815100; fax (21) 8867622; e-mail gmoptc@moptc.gov.pt; internet www.moptc.pt.

Ministry of Science, Technology and Higher Education: Palácio de Laranjeiras, Estrada de Laranjeiras 197–205, 1649-018 Lisbon; tel. (21) 7231000; fax (21) 7271457; e-mail mctes@mctes.gov.pt; internet www.mctes.pt.

COUNCIL OF STATE

The Council of State (Conselho de Estado) is a consultative body, presided over by the President of the Republic (see The Constitution).

PORTUGAL

President

Election, 22 January 2006

Candidate	Votes	% of votes
Aníbal Cavaco Silva (PSD)	2,773,431	50.54
Manuel Alegre de Melo Duarte (Ind.)	1,138,297	20.74
Mário Lopes Soares (PS)	785,355	14.31
Jerónimo Carvalho de Sousa (PCP)	474,083	8.64
Francisco Anacleto Louçã (BE)	292,198	5.32
António Pestana Garcia Pereira (PCTP/MRPP)	23,983	0.44
Total	**5,487,347***	**100.00**

*Excluding 59,636 blank and 43,149 spoiled votes.

Legislature

Assembléia da República
(Assembly of the Republic)

Palácio de São Bento, 1249-068 Lisbon; tel. (21) 3919000; fax (21) 3917440; e-mail correio.geral@ar.parlamento.pt; internet www.parlamento.pt.

President: JAIME JOSÉ MATOS DA GAMA (PS).

General Election, 20 February 2005

Party	Votes	% of votes	Seats
Partido Socialista (PS)	2,588,312	45.03	121
Partido Social Democrata (PSD)	1,653,425	28.77	75
Partido Comunista Português (PCP)-Partido Ecologista 'Os Verdes' (PEV)	433,369	7.54	14
Centro Democrático Social-Partido Popular (CDS-PP)	416,415	7.24	12
Bloco de Esquerda (BE)	364,971	6.35	8
Total (incl. others)	**5,747,834**	**100.00**	**230**

Autonomous Regions

OS AÇORES
(The Azores)

President of the Regional Government: CARLOS MANUEL MARTINS DO VALE CÉSAR (PS).

Assembléia Legislativa da Região Autónoma dos Açores: Rua Marcelino Lima, 9901-858 Horta, Azores; tel. (292) 207600; fax (292) 293798; e-mail secgeral@alra.pt; internet www.alra.pt; Pres. FERNANDO MANUEL MACHADO MENEZES (PS).

MADEIRA

President of the Regional Government: Dr ALBERTO JOÃO JARDIM (PSD).

Assembléia Legislativa da Região Autónoma da Madeira: Av. do Mar e das Comunidades Madeirenses, 9004-506 Funchal, Madeira; tel. (291) 210500; fax (291) 232977; e-mail presidencia@alram.pt; internet www.alram.pt; Pres. JOSÉ MIGUEL JARDIM D'OLIVAL MENDONÇA (PSD).

Election Commission

Comissão Nacional de Eleições (CNE): Av. D. Carlos I 128, 7°, 1249-065 Lisbon; tel. (21) 3923800; fax (21) 3953543; e-mail cne@cne.pt; internet www.cne.pt; Pres. appointed by the judiciary, other mems by the Assembléia da República and the Govt; Pres. Dr JOÃO CARLOS DE BARROS CALDEIRA.

Political Organizations

Bloco de Esquerda (BE) (Left Bloc): Av. Almirante Reis 131, 2°, 1150-015 Lisbon; tel. (21) 3510510; fax (21) 3510519; e-mail bloco.esquerda@bloco.org; internet bloco.esquerda.net; f. 1999; union of several left-wing groups, including the following:

    Associação Política Socialista Revolucionário (APSR) (Revolutionary Socialist Politics Association): Rua da Palma 268, 1100-394 Lisbon; tel. (21) 8864643; fax (21) 8882736; internet combate.info; f. 1978 as Partido Socialista Revolucionário through merger of two Trotskyist groups; renamed as above 2005.

    O Ruptura/Frente da Esquerda Revolucionária (FER): Rua de Terreirinho 4, 2°, 1100 Lisbon; tel. (21) 8850450; e-mail info@rupturafer.org; internet www.rupturafer.org; f. 2000; revolutionary Marxist party, affiliated with Workers International League.

    União Democrática Popular (UDP) (People's Democratic Union): Rua de São Bento 698, 1°, 1250-223 Lisbon; tel. (21) 3826110; fax (21) 3885035; e-mail udp@netcabo.pt; internet www.udp.pt; f. 1974; Marxist-Leninist; comprises various political groups of the revolutionary left; Leader LUÍS FAZENDA.

Centro Democrático Social-Partido Popular (CDS-PP) (Social Democratic Centre-Popular Party): Largo Adelino Amaro da Costa 5, 1149-063 Lisbon; tel. (21) 8814700; fax (21) 8860454; e-mail cds-pp@cds.pt; internet www.cds.pt; f. 1974 as Centro Democrático Social; present name adopted 1993; centre-right; mem. of International Democrat Union; supports social market economy and reduction of public sector intervention in the economy; defended revision of 1976 Constitution; Pres. PAULO SACADURA CABRAL PORTAS.

Coligação Democrática Unitária (CDU): coalition of left-wing parties, led by PCP:

    Partido Comunista Português (PCP) (Portuguese Communist Party): Rua Soeiro Pereira Gomes 3, 1600-196 Lisbon; tel. (21) 7813800; fax (21) 7969126; e-mail pcp@pcp.pt; internet www.pcp.pt; f. 1921; legalized 1974; theoretical foundation is Marxism-Leninism; aims are the defence and consolidation of the democratic regime and the revolutionary achievements, and ultimately the building of a socialist society in Portugal; 140,000 mems (1996); Sec.-Gen. JERÓNIMO DE SOUSA.

    Partido Ecologista 'Os Verdes' (PEV) (The Greens): Rua da Boavista 83, 3°D, 1200-066 Lisbon; tel. (21) 3960291; fax (21) 3960424; e-mail osverdes@mail.telepac.pt; internet www.osverdes.pt; f. 1982; ecological party.

Novo Democracia: Rua da Trinidade 36, 1200-302 Lisbon; tel. (21) 3247020; fax (21) 3247029; internet www.pnd.pt; f. 2003 by disaffected mems of the PP; right-wing, nationalist and Eurosceptic; Pres. MANUEL MONTEIRO.

Partido Comunista dos Trabalhadores Portugueses/Movimento Revolucionário Português do Proletariado (PCTP/MRPP) (Communist Workers' Party/Proletarian Portuguese Revolutionary Movement): Rua da Palma 159, 2°D, 1100-391 Lisbon; tel. (21) 8880780; fax (21) 8884036; e-mail pctp@pctpmrpp.org; internet www.pctpmrpp.org; f. 1970 as Movimento Reorganizativo do Partido do Proletariado; present name adopted 1976; Leader ANTÓNIO PESTANA GARCIA PEREIRA.

Partido Social Democrata (PSD) (Social Democratic Party): Rua de São Caetano 9, 1249-087 Lisbon; tel. (21) 3918500; fax (21) 3976967; e-mail psd@psd.pt; internet www.psd.pt; f. 1974; fmrly Partido Popular Democrático; centre-right; aims to promote market economy, taking into account the welfare of the community; encourages European integration; 60,000 mems; Leader LUÍS FILIPE MENEZES; Sec.-Gen. JOSÉ A. RIBAU ESTEVES.

Partido Socialista (PS) (Socialist Party): Largo do Rato 2, 1269-143 Lisbon; tel. (21) 3822000; fax (21) 3822022; e-mail portal@ps.pt; internet www.ps.pt; f. 1973 from fmr Acção Socialista Portuguesa (Portuguese Socialist Action); affiliate of the Socialist International and Party of European Socialists; advocates a society of greater social justice and co-operation between public, private and co-operative sectors, while respecting public liberties and the will of the majority attained through free elections; 100,000 mems; Pres. ANTÓNIO DE ALMEIDA SANTOS; Sec.-Gen. JOSÉ SÓCRATES CARVALHO PINTO DE SOUSA.

Partido da Terra (MPT) (The Earth Party): Rua da Beneficência 111, 1°, Apartado 43050, 1601-301 Lisbon; tel. (96) 9640021; e-mail mpt@mpt.pt; internet www.mpt.pt; f. 1993; contested 2005 election in coalition with PSD; Pres. PAULO NORONHA TRANCOSO.

Diplomatic Representation

EMBASSIES IN PORTUGAL

Algeria: Rua Duarte Pacheco Pereira 58, 1400-140 Lisbon; tel. (21) 3041520; fax (21) 3010393; e-mail embaixada-argelia@clix.pt; internet www.emb-argelia.pt; Ambassador SABRI BOUKADOUM.

Andorra: Rua do Possolo 76, 2350-251 Lisbon; tel. (21) 3913740; fax (21) 3913749; Ambassador ANTONI CALVÓ ARMENGOL.

Angola: Av. da República 68, 1069-213 Lisbon; tel. (21) 7961830; fax (21) 7971238; e-mail embaixadadeangola@mail.telepac.pt; internet www.embaixadadeangola.org; Ambassador ASSUNÇÃO AFONSO SOUSA DOS ANJOS.

Argentina: Av. João Crisóstomo 8, r/c esq., 1000-178 Lisbon; tel. (21) 7977311; fax (21) 7959225; e-mail eport@mrecic.gov.ar; Ambassador JORGE MARCELO FAURIE.

PORTUGAL

Australia: Av. da Liberdade 200, 2°, 1250-147 Lisbon; tel. (21) 33101500; fax (21) 3101555; e-mail austemb.lisbon@dfat.gov.au; internet www.portugal.embassy.gov.au; Ambassador LUKE WILLIAMS.

Austria: Av. Infante Santo 43, 4°, 1399-046 Lisbon; tel. (21) 3943900; fax (21) 3958224; e-mail lissabon-ob@bmeia.gv.at; Ambassador EWALD JÄGER.

Belgium: Praça Marquês de Pombal 14, 6°, 1269-024 Lisbon; tel. (21) 3170510; fax (21) 3561556; e-mail lisbon@diplobel.org; internet www.diplomatie.be/lisbon; Ambassador RUDY HUYGELEN.

Brazil: Quinta de Mil Flores, Estrada das Laranjeiras 144, 1649-021 Lisbon; tel. (21) 7248510; fax (21) 7267623; e-mail geral@embaixadadobrasil.pt; internet www.embaixadadobrasil.pt; Ambassador CELSO MARCOS VIEIRA DE SOUZA.

Bulgaria: Rua do Sacramento à Lapa 31, 1200-792 Lisbon; tel. (21) 3976364; fax (21) 3979272; e-mail ebul@mail.telepac.pt; Ambassador MAKSIM GEORGIEV GAYTANDZHIEV.

Canada: Av. da Liberdade 196–200, 3°, 1269-121 Lisbon; tel. (21) 3164600; fax (21) 3164691; e-mail lsbon.ag@dfait-maeci.gc.ca; internet international.gc.ca/lisbon; Ambassador ANNE-MARIE BOURCIER.

Cape Verde: Av. do Restelo 33, 1449-025 Lisbon; tel. (21) 3041440; fax (21) 3041466; e-mail emb.caboverde@netcabo.pt; Ambassador ARNALDO ANDRADE RAMOS.

Chile: Av. Miguel Bombarda 5, 1°, 1000-207 Lisbon; tel. (21) 3148054; fax (21) 3150909; e-mail embachile@net.novis.pt; internet www.emb-chile.pt; Ambassador FRANCISCO PÉREZ WALKER.

China, People's Republic: Rua do Pau de Bandeira 11–13, 1200-756 Lisbon; tel. (21) 3928430; fax (21) 3975632; e-mail chinaemb_pt@mfa.gov.cn; internet pt.china-embassy.org/pot; Ambassador GAO KEXIANG.

Colombia: Palácio Sottomayor, 6°, Av. Fontes Pereira de Melo 16, 1050-021 Lisbon; tel. (21) 3188480; fax (21) 3188499; e-mail elisboa@cancilleria.gov.co; Ambassador FUAD RICARDO CHAR ABDALA.

Congo, Democratic Republic: Av. Fontes Pereira de Melo 31, 7°, 1050-117 Lisbon; tel. (21) 3522895; fax (21) 3544862; e-mail ambalisbonne@minaffecirde.cd; Chargé d'affaires LOKOSU N'KULUFA.

Croatia: Rua D. Lourenço de Almeida 24, 1400-126 Lisbon; tel. (21) 3021033; fax (21) 3021251; e-mail croemb.lisboa@mvpei.hr; Ambassador ŽELJKO VUKOSAV.

Cuba: Rua Pero da Covilhã 14 (Restelo), 1400-297 Lisbon; tel. (21) 3015317; fax (21) 3011895; e-mail embaixada.cuba@netcabo.pt; internet pwp.netcabo.pt/embaixada.cuba; Ambassador JORGE CASTRO BENÍTEZ.

Cyprus: Av. da Liberdade 229, 1°, 1250-142 Lisbon; tel. (21) 3194180; fax (21) 3194189; e-mail chipre@netcabo.pt; internet www.mfa.gov.cy/embassylisbon; Ambassador NEARCHOS PALAS.

Czech Republic: Rua Pero de Alenquer 14, 1400-294 Lisbon; tel. (21) 3010487; fax (21) 3010629; e-mail lisbon@embassy.mzv.cz; internet www.mfa.cz/lisbon; Ambassador LADISLAV SKEŘIK.

Denmark: Rua Castilho 14, 3°C, 1269-077 Lisbon; tel. (21) 3512960; fax (21) 3554615; e-mail lisamb@um.dk; internet www.amblissabon.um.dk; Ambassador Dr LARS VISSING.

Dominican Republic: Av. das Forças Armadas 133, Quinta das Mil Flores, Bloco B, Escritório 3, 1600-081 Lisbon; tel. (21) 7247030; fax (21) 7247039; e-mail embdomportugal@serex.gov.do; Ambassador MARINA ISABEL CÁCERES ESTÉVEZ.

Egypt: Av. D. Vasco da Gama 8, 1400-128 Lisbon; tel. (21) 3018301; fax (21) 3017909; e-mail gabemh@egyemb.jazznet.pt; Ambassador AMGAD MAHER ABDEL GHAFFAR.

Estonia: Rua Filipe Folque 10J, 2° esq., 1050-113 Lisbon; tel. (21) 3194150; fax (21) 3194155; e-mail embest@embest.pt; internet www.embest.pt; Ambassador MART TARMAK.

Finland: Rua do Possolo 76, 1°, 1350-251 Lisbon; tel. (21) 3933040; fax (21) 3904758; e-mail sanomat.lis@formin.fi; internet www.finlandia.org.pt; Ambassador SAULI ERIK FEODOROW.

France: Rua de Santos-o-Velho 5, 1249-079 Lisbon; tel. (21) 3939100; fax (21) 3939151; e-mail consulat.lisbonne@ambafrance-pt.org; internet www.ambafrance-pt.org; Ambassador PATRICK GAUTRAT.

Germany: Campo dos Mártires da Pátria 38, 1169-043 Lisbon; tel. (21) 8810210; fax (21) 8853846; e-mail info@lissabon.diplo.de; internet www.lissabon.diplo.de; Ambassador JOACHIM BROUDRÉ-GRÖGER.

Greece: Rua do Alto do Duque 13, 1449-026 Lisbon; tel. (21) 3031260; fax (21) 3011205; e-mail gremb.lis@mfa.gr; Ambassador SPYRIDON THEOCHAROPOULOS.

Guinea-Bissau: Rua de Alcolena 17, 1400-004 Lisbon; tel. (21) 3030440; fax (21) 3019653; Ambassador CONSTANTINO LOPES DA COSTA.

Holy See: Av. Luís Bivar 18, 1069-147 Lisbon; tel. (21) 3171130; fax (21) 3171149; e-mail nunciatura@netcabo.pt; Apostolic Nuncio Most Rev. ALFIO RAPISARDA (Titular Archbishop of Cannae).

Hungary: Calçada de Santo Amaro 85, 1349-042 Lisbon; tel. (21) 3630395; fax (21) 3632314; e-mail mission.lis@kum.hu; internet www.mfa.gov.hu/emb/lisbon; Ambassador ATTILA GECSE.

India: Rua Pêro da Covilhã 16, 1400-297 Lisbon; tel. (21) 3041090; fax (21) 3016576; e-mail main@indembassy-lisbon.org; internet www.indembassy-lisbon.org; Ambassador NILIMA MITRA.

Indonesia: Rua Miguel Lupi 12, 1°, 1249-080 Lisbon; tel. (21) 3932070; fax (21) 3932079; e-mail info@indonesianembassy-lisbon.org; internet www.indonesianembassy-lisbon.org; Ambassador FRANCISCO XAVIER LOPES DA CRUZ.

Iran: Rua do Alto do Duque 49, 1400-009 Lisbon; tel. (21) 3010871; fax (21) 3010777; e-mail iranembassy@emb-irao.pt; internet www.emb-irao.pt; Ambassador MUHAMMAD TAHERI.

Iraq: Rua do Arriaga à Lapa 9, 1200-608 Lisbon; tel. (21) 3933310; fax (21) 3977052; e-mail lisemb@iraqmofa.net; Ambassador HUSSAIN MUAALA.

Ireland: Rua da Imprensa à Estrela 1, 4°, 1200-684 Lisbon; tel. (21) 3929440; fax (21) 3977363; e-mail lisbon@dfa.ie; Ambassador JAMES BRENNAN.

Israel: Rua António Enes 16, 4°, 1050-025 Lisbon; tel. (21) 3553640; fax (21) 3553658; e-mail israemb@lisboa.mfa.gov.il; internet lisbon.mfa.gov.il; Ambassador AHARON RAM.

Italy: Largo Conde de Pombeiro 6, 1150-100 Lisbon; tel. (21) 3515320; fax (21) 3521516; e-mail ambasciata.lisbona@esteri.it; internet www.amblisbona.esteri.it; Ambassador LUCA DEL BALZO DI PRESENZANO.

Japan: Av. da Liberdade 245–6, 1269-033 Lisbon; tel. (21) 3110560; fax (21) 3534802; e-mail bunka@ip.pt; internet www.pt.emb-japan.go.jp; Ambassador SATOSHI HARA.

Korea, Republic: Edif. Presidente 7°, Av. Miguel Bombarda 36, 1051-802 Lisbon; tel. (21) 7937200; fax (21) 7977176; e-mail embpt@mofat.go.kr; internet prt.mofat.go.kr; Ambassador CHUNG EUI-MIN.

Latvia: Travessa da Palmeira 31A, 1200-315 Lisbon; tel. (21) 3407170; fax (21) 3469045; e-mail embassy.portugal@mfa.gov.lv; Ambassador ARTIS BERTULIS.

Libya: Av. das Descobertas 24, 1400-092 Lisbon; tel. (21) 3016301; fax (21) 3012378; e-mail bureau.popular.libia@clix.pt; Chargé d'affaires ALI EMDORED.

Lithuania: Av. 5 de Outubro 81, 1°, 1050-050 Lisbon; tel. (21) 7990110; fax (21) 7996363; e-mail ambasadorius@mail.telepac.pt; internet pt.mfa.lt; Ambassador ALGIMANTAS RIMKŪNAS.

Luxembourg: Rua das Janelas Verdes 43, 1200-690 Lisbon; tel. (21) 3931940; fax (21) 3901410; e-mail lisbonne.amb@mae.etat.lu; Ambassador ALAIN DE MUYSER.

Malta: Av. da Liberdade 49, 5°, 1250-139 Lisbon; tel. (21) 3405470; fax (21) 3405479; e-mail maltaembassy.lisbon@mail.telepac.pt; Ambassador SALV STELLINI.

Mexico: Estrada de Monsanto 78, 1500-462 Lisbon; tel. (21) 7621290; fax (21) 7620045; e-mail embamex.port@mail.telepac.pt; internet www.sre.gob.mx/portugal; Ambassador MAURICIO TOUSSAINT RIBOT.

Moldova: Rua Gonçalo Velho Cabral 31A, 1400-188 Lisbon; tel. (21) 3009064; fax (21) 3009067; e-mail lisabona@mfa.md; Ambassador MIHAEL CAMARZAN.

Morocco: Rua Alto do Duque 21, 1400-099 Lisbon; tel. (21) 3020842; fax (21) 3020935; e-mail sifmar@emb-marrocos.pt; internet www.emb-marrocos.pt; Ambassador SAMIR ARROUR.

Mozambique: Av. de Berna 7, 1050-036 Lisbon; tel. (21) 7961672; fax (21) 7932720; e-mail embamoc.portugal@minec.gov.mz; Ambassador MIGUEL DA COSTA MKAIMA.

Netherlands: Av. Infante Santo 43, 5°, 1399-011 Lisbon; tel. (21) 3914900; fax (21) 3966436; e-mail nlgovlis@netcabo.pt; internet www.emb-paisesbaixos.pt; Ambassador ROBERT JAN VAN HOUTUM.

Nigeria: Rue Fernão Mendes Pinto 50, Apdo 3146, 1400 Lisbon; tel. (21) 3016189; fax (21) 3018152; e-mail nigerlis@mail.telepac.pt; Ambassador AKATU A. ELLA.

Norway: Av. D. Vasco da Gama 1, 1400-127 Lisbon; tel. (21) 3015344; fax (21) 3016158; e-mail emb.lisboa@mfa.no; internet www.noruega.org.pt; Ambassador INGA MAGISTAD.

Pakistan: Rua António Saldanha 46, 1400-021 Lisbon; tel. (21) 3009070; fax (21) 3013514; e-mail parep.lisbon.1@mail.telepac.pt; Ambassador FAUSIA M. SANA.

Panama: Av. Helen Keller 15, Lote C, 4° esq., 1400-197 Lisbon; tel. (21) 3642899; fax (21) 3644589; e-mail panemblisboa@netcabo.pt; Ambassador MINERVA LARA BATISTA.

PORTUGAL

Directory

Paraguay: Av. Campo Grande 4, 7° dto, 1700-092 Lisbon; tel. (21) 7965907; fax (21) 7965905; e-mail embaparlisboa@mail.telepac.pt; Chargé d'affaires a.i. Luís Domingo Laino Guanes.

Peru: Rua Castilho 50, 4° dto, 1250-071 Lisbon; tel. (21) 3827470; fax (21) 3827479; e-mail embperuport@mail.telepac.pt; Ambassador Luzmila Zanabria Ishikawa.

Poland: Av. das Descobertas 2, 1400-092 Lisbon; tel. (21) 3012350; fax (21) 3041429; e-mail emb.polonia@mail.telepac.pt; internet www.lizbona.polemb.ne; Ambassador Katarzyna Skórzyńska.

Romania: Rua de São Caetano a Lapa 5, 1200-828 Lisbon; tel. (21) 3968812; fax (21) 3960984; e-mail ambrom@mail.telepac.pt; internet lisabona.mae.ro; Ambassador Gabriel Gafiţa.

Russia: Rua Visconde de Santarém 59, 1000-286 Lisbon; tel. (21) 8462423; fax (21) 8463008; e-mail mail@embaixadarussia.pt; internet www.portugal.mid.ru; Ambassador Pavel F. Petrovskii.

São Tomé and Príncipe: Edif. EPAC 6°, Av. Gago Coutinho 26, 1000-017 Lisbon; tel. (21) 8461917; fax (21) 8461895; e-mail embstp@mail.telepac.pt; Ambassador Alda Alves de Melo dos Santos.

Saudi Arabia: Av. do Restelo 42, 1400-315 Lisbon; tel. (21) 3041750; fax (21) 3014209; e-mail saudiembassy@netcabo.pt; Ambassador Muhammad ar-Rashid.

Serbia: Av. das Descobertas 12, 1400-092 Lisbon; tel. (21) 3015311; fax (21) 3015313; e-mail serviaemba@netcabo.pt; Ambassador Duško Lopandić.

Slovakia: Av. Fontes Pereira de Melo 19, 7° dto, 1050-116 Lisbon; tel. (21) 3583300; fax (21) 3583309; e-mail emb.lisbon@mzv.sk; Ambassador Radomír Boháč.

Slovenia: Av. da Liberdade 49, 6° esq., 1250-139 Lisbon; tel. (21) 3423301; fax (21) 3423305; e-mail vli@gov.si; Ambassador Peter Andrej Bekeš.

South Africa: Av. Luís Bivar 10, 1069-024 Lisbon; tel. (21) 3192200; fax (21) 3535713; e-mail embsa@embaixada-africadosul.pt; internet www.embaixada-africadosul.pt; Ambassador Thandiwe Profit-McLean.

Spain: Rua do Salitre 1, 1296-052 Lisbon; tel. (21) 3472381; fax (21) 3472384; e-mail emb.lis@mae.es; internet www.mae.es/embajadas/lisboa; Ambassador Enrique Panés Calpe.

Sweden: Rua Miguel Lupi 12, 2°, 1249-077 Lisbon; tel. (21) 3942260; fax (21) 3942261; e-mail ambassaden.lissabon@foreign.ministry.se; internet www.swedenabroad.com/lissabon; Ambassador Marie Gabriella Lindholm.

Switzerland: Travessa do Jardim 17, 1350-185 Lisbon; tel. (21) 3944090; fax (21) 3955945; e-mail lis.vertretung@eda.admin.ch; internet www.eda.admin.ch/lisbon; Ambassador Catherine Krieg Polejack.

Thailand: Rua de Alcolena 12, 1400-005 Lisbon; tel. (21) 3014848; fax (21) 3018181; e-mail thai.lis@mail.telepac.pt; internet www.thaiembassy.org/lisbon; Ambassador Kasivat Paruggamanont.

Timor-Leste: Av. Infante Santo 17, 6°, 1350-175 Lisbon; tel. (21) 3933730; fax (21) 3933739; e-mail embaixada.rdtl@mail.telepac.pt; Ambassador Manuel Abrantes.

Tunisia: Rua Rodrigo Rebelo 16, 1400-318 Lisbon; tel. (21) 3010330; fax (21) 3016817; e-mail at.lisbonne@netcabo.pt; Ambassador Muhammad Ridha Farhat.

Turkey: Av. das Descobertas 22, 1400-092 Lisbon; tel. (21) 3003110; fax (21) 3017934; e-mail info-turk@mail.telepac.pt; Ambassador Ömer Kaya Türkmen.

Ukraine: Av. das Descobertas 18, 1400-092 Lisbon; tel. (21) 3010043; fax (21) 3010059; e-mail emb_pt@mfaa.gov.ua; internet www.mfa.gov.ua/portugal; Ambassador Rostyslav Tronenko.

United Kingdom: Rua de São Bernardo 33, 1249-082 Lisbon; tel. (21) 3924000; fax (21) 3924021; e-mail ppa@fco.gov.uk; internet www.uk-embassy.pt; Ambassador Alexander Ellis.

USA: Av. das Forças Armadas (Sete Rios), 1600-081 Lisbon; Apdo 43033, 1601-301 Lisbon; tel. (21) 7273300; fax (21) 7269109; e-mail reflisbon@state.gov; internet lisbon.usembassy.gov; Ambassador Thomas F. Stephenson.

Uruguay: Rua Sampaio Pina 16, 2°, 1070-249 Lisbon; tel. (21) 3889265; fax (21) 3889245; e-mail urulusi@sapo.pt; Ambassador Gastón Lasarte.

Venezuela: Av. Duque de Loulé 47, 4°, 1050-086 Lisbon; tel. (21) 3573803; fax (21) 3527421; e-mail embavenez@mail.telepac.pt; internet www.embavenezuela.pt; Ambassador Lucas Enrique Rincón Romero.

Judicial System

The judicial system of the Portuguese Republic comprises several categories of courts which, according to the Constitution, are sovereign bodies. The country is divided into four judicial districts, which are, in turn, divided into 37 judicial circuits. The principle of habeas corpus is recognized. Citizens who have been unjustly convicted are entitled to a review of their sentence and to compensation. The death penalty is prohibited by the Constitution. The jury system, reintroduced for certain types of crime in 1976, operates only at the request of the Public Prosecutor or defendant.

Judges are appointed for life and are irremovable. Practising judges may not hold any other office, whether public or private, except a non-remunerated position in teaching or research in the legal field. The Conselho Superior da Magistratura controls their appointment, transfer and promotion and the exercise of disciplinary action.

PUBLIC PROSECUTION

The State is represented in the courts by the Public Prosecution, whose highest organ is the Procuradoria-Geral da República (Attorney-General's Office).

Procuradoria-Geral da República: Rua da Escola Politécnica 140, 1269-269 Lisbon; tel. (21) 3921900; fax (21) 3975255; e-mail mailpgr@pgr.pt; internet www.pgr.pt; Attorney-General Dr Fernando José Matos Pinto Monteiro.

Gabinete de Documentação e Direito Comparado (Office of Documentation and Comparative Law): Rua Vale de Pereiro 2, 1269-113 Lisbon; tel. (21) 3820300; fax (21) 3820301; e-mail mail@gddc.pt; internet www.gddc.pt; Dir Joana Gomes Ferreira.

SUPREME COURT

Supremo Tribunal de Justiça

Praça do Comércio, 1149-012 Lisbon; tel. (21) 3218900; fax (21) 3474919; e-mail correio@lisboa.stj.pt; internet www.stj.pt.

The highest organ of the judicial system; consists of 60 judges, incl. the President.

President: Luís António Noronha do Nascimento.

COURTS OF SECOND INSTANCE

There are five Courts of Second Instance (or Courts of Appeal):

Tribunal da Relação de Coímbra: Palácio da Justiça, Rua da Sofia, 3004-501 Coimbra; tel. (239) 852950; fax (239) 824310; e-mail coimbra.tr@tribunais.org.pt; internet www.trc.pt; 46 judges, incl. the President; Pres. António Joaquim Piçarra.

Tribunal da Relação de Évora: Largo das Alterações 1, 7004-501 Évora; tel. (266) 758800; fax (266) 701529; e-mail correio@evora.tr.mj.pt; internet www.tre.pt; 39 judges, incl. the President; Pres. Manuel Cipriano Nabais.

Tribunal da Relação de Guimarães: Largo João Franco 248, 4810-269 Guimarães; tel. (253) 439900; fax (253) 439999; e-mail correio@guimaraes.tr.mj.pt; internet www.trg.mj.pt; 31 judges, incl. the President; Pres. Dr Lázaro Martins de Faria.

Tribunal da Relação de Lisboa: Rua Arsenal G, 1100-048 Lisbon; tel. (21) 3222900; fax (21) 3479844; e-mail correio@lisboa.tr.mj.pt; internet www.trl.pt; 108 judges, incl. the President; Pres. Dr Luís Maria Vaz das Neves.

Tribunal da Relação do Porto: Campo Mártires de Pátria, 4099-012 Porto; tel. (22) 2008531; fax (22) 2000715; e-mail correio@porto.tr.mj.pt; internet www.trp.pt; 91 judges, incl. the President; Pres. Dr Gonçalo Xavier Silvano.

COURTS OF FIRST INSTANCE

There are 258 Courts of First Instance within Portuguese territory: 195 *comarca* courts hear cases of a general nature, while 46 labour courts hear specific matters. There are five family courts and two courts for the enforcement of sentences. Circuit Courts total 33.

CONSTITUTIONAL COURT

Tribunal Constitucional

Palácio Ratton, Rua de O Século 111, 1249-117 Lisbon; tel. (21) 3233600; fax (21) 3233649; e-mail tribunal@tribconstitucional.pt; internet www.tribunalconstitucional.pt.

Rules on matters of constitutionality according to the terms of the Constitution of the Portuguese Republic; exercises jurisdiction over all Portuguese territory; consists of 13 judges.

President: Rui Manuel Gens de Moura Ramos.

SUPREME ADMINISTRATIVE COURT

Supremo Tribunal Administrativo

Rua de S. Pedro de Alcântara 73–79, 1269-137 Lisbon; tel. (21) 3216200; fax (21) 3466129; e-mail correio@lisboa.sta.mj.pt; internet www.stadministrativo.pt.

The highest organ of the administrative system; has jurisdiction over metropolitan Portugal, the Azores and Madeira; there is also a

Supremo Tribunal Administrativo Norte and Sul; consists of 37 judges, incl. the President.
President: Manuel Fernando dos Santos Serra.

Religion

There is freedom of religion in Portugal. The dominant Christian denomination is Roman Catholicism. In the 2001 census, of the 8,699,515 respondents to the question regarding religion, 7,353,548 identified themselves as Roman Catholic, 17,443 as Orthodox Christian, 48,301 as Protestant and 122,745 as other Christian. A further 1,773 were Jewish, 12,014 were Muslim and 13,882 followed another religion.

CHRISTIANITY
The Roman Catholic Church

For ecclesiastical purposes, Portugal comprises 17 dioceses, grouped into three metropolitan sees (the patriarchate of Lisbon and the archdioceses of Braga and Évora). At 31 December 2005 some 9,392,573 Portuguese were adherents of the Roman Catholic Church, representing 88.8% of the population.

Bishops' Conference

Conferência Episcopal Portuguesa, Campo dos Mártires da Pátria 43, 1° esq., 1150-225 Lisbon; tel. (21) 8855460; fax (21) 8855461; e-mail webmaster@ecclesia.pt; internet www.ecclesia.pt.
f. 1932; Pres. Most Rev. Jorge Ferreira da Costa Ortiga (Archbishop of Braga); Sec. Carlos Azevedo.

Patriarch of Lisbon: Cardinal José da Cruz Policarpo, Casa Patriarcal, Quinta do Cabeço, 1800-076, Moscavide, Lisbon; tel. (21) 9457310; fax (21) 9457329; e-mail gab.patriarca@patriarcado-lisboa.pt; internet www.patriarcado-lisboa.pt.

Archbishop of Braga: Most Rev. Jorge Ferreira da Costa Ortiga, Paço Arquiepiscopal, Rua de Santa Margarida 181, 4710-306 Braga; tel. (253) 203189; fax (253) 203191; e-mail jorge.ortiga@diocese-braga.pt; internet www.diocese-braga.pt.

Archbishop of Évora: Most Rev. José Francisco Sanches Alves, Cúria Arquiepiscopal, Dr Alves Branco, 7000-501 Évora; tel. (266) 777300; fax (266) 777309; e-mail diocese@diocese-evora.pt; internet www.diocese-evora.pt.

Other Christian Churches and Organizations

Associação de Igrejas Baptistas Portuguesas (Asscn of Portuguese Baptist Churches): Rua da Escola 18, Maceira, 2715 Pero Pinheiro; tel. (21) 9271150; f. 1955; Pres. Rev. João S. Regueiras.

Conselho Português de Igrejas Cristãs (COPIC) (Portuguese Council of Christian Churches): Apto 392, 4430-003 Vila Nova de Gaia; tel. (22) 3754018; fax (22) 3752016; e-mail igreja@lusitana.org; f. 1971; mems include the Igreja Lusitana Católica Apostólica Evangélica, the Igreja Evangélica Metodista Portuguesa and the Igreja Evangélica Presbiteriana de Portugal; Pres. Rt Rev. Fernando Luz Soares.

Convenção Baptista Portuguesa (Portuguese Baptist Convention): Rua Luís Simões 7, 1°, Apdo 3085, 2745 Queluz; tel. (21) 4343370; fax (21) 4343379; e-mail geral@acampamentobaptista .com.pt; f. 1920; Pres. Pastor António Pires; Sec. Maria Hercília Melo; 4,338 mems (2003).

Igreja Evangélica Metodista Portuguesa (Portuguese Evangelical Methodist Church): Praça Coronel Pacheco 23, 4050-453 Porto; tel. (22) 2007410; fax (22) 2086961; e-mail sede-geral@igreja-metodista.pt; internet www.igreja-metodista.pt; Bishop Sifredo Teixeira.

Igreja Evangélica Presbiteriana de Portugal (Presbyterian Church of Portugal): Rua Tomás da Anunciação, 56, 1° dto, 1350-328 Lisbon; tel. (21) 3974959; fax (21) 3956326; e-mail office@iepp .org; internet www.iepp.org; f. 1952; Pres. José Salvador; Gen. Sec. David Valente.

Igreja Lusitana Católica Apostólica Evangélica—Comunhão Anglicana (Lusitanian Catholic Apostolic Evangelical Church—Anglican Communion): Apdo 392, 4431-905 Vila Nova de Gaia; tel. (22) 3754018; fax (22) 3752016; e-mail comunicacao@igreja-lusitana .org; internet www.igreja-lusitana.org; f. 1880; extraprovincial diocese of the Anglican Communion under the metropolitan authority of the Archbishop of Canterbury (United Kingdom) since 1980; Bishop Rt Rev. Fernando Luz Soares.

ISLAM

Comunidade Islamica de Lisboa: Mesquita Central de Lisboa, Av. José Malhoa, 1070 Lisbon; tel. (21) 3874142; fax (21) 3872230; e-mail info@comunidadeislamica.pt; internet www .comunidadeislamica.pt; Pres. Abdul Karim Vakil.

JUDAISM

There are Jewish communities in Lisbon, Oporto, Belmonte and Faro.

Comunidade Israelita de Lisboa: Rua do Monte Olivete 16, r/c, 1200-280 Lisbon; tel. (21) 3931130; fax (21) 3931139; e-mail secretaria@cilisboa.org; internet www.cilisboa.org; Pres. Dr José Oulman Carp.

The Press

In 2003 754 newspapers and 773 magazines were published. The daily newspapers had an average circulation of 727,625 per edition.

PRINCIPAL DAILIES

Aveiro

Diário de Aveiro: Av. Dr Lourenço Peixinho 15, 5°, 3800-801 Aveiro; tel. (234) 000030; fax (234) 000033; e-mail diarioaveiro@diarioaveiro.pt; internet www.diarioaveiro.pt; f. 1985; morning; Dir Adriano Callé Lucas; circ. 4,500.

Braga

Diário do Minho: Rua de Santa Margarida 4, 4710-306 Braga; tel. (253) 609460; fax (253) 609465; e-mail redaccao@diariodominho.pt; internet www.diariodominho.pt; f. 1919; morning; Dir José Miguel Pereira; circ. 5,357 (2006).

Coímbra

Diário as Beiras: Rua 25 de Abril, Apdo 44, 3040-935 Taveiro, Coímbra; tel. (239) 980280; fax (239) 983574; internet beirastexto@asbeiras.pt; internet www.asbeiras.pt; Dir António Abrantes; circ. 6,960 (2006).

Diário de Coímbra: Rua Adriano Lucas, 3020-264 Coímbra; tel. (239) 492133; fax (239) 492128; e-mail redac@diariocoimbra.pt; internet www.diariocoimbra.pt; f. 1930; morning; *Domingo* publ. on Sun. (f. 1974; circ. 8,000); Dir Adriano Mário da Cunha Lucas; circ. 9,596 (2006).

Évora

Diário do Sul: Estrada de Arraiolos, Évora; tel. (266) 730410; fax (266) 730411; internet www.diariodosul.com.pt; f. 1969; morning; Dir Manuel Madeira Piçarra; circ. 5,574 (2006).

Leiria

Diário de Leiria: Edif. Maringá, Rua S. Franciso 7, 4° esq., 2400-232 Leiria; tel. (244) 000031; fax (244) 000032; e-mail diarioleiria@diarioleiria.pt; internet www.diarioleiria.pt; f. 1987; morning; Dir Adriano Callé Lucas; circ. 3,500.

Lisboa
(Lisbon)

A Bola: Travessa da Queimada 23, 2°D r/c esq., 1294 Lisbon; tel. (21) 3463981; fax (21) 3432275; internet www.abola.pt; f. 1945; sport; Dir Victor Serpa; circ. 180,000.

Correio da Manhã: Av. João Crisóstomo 72, 1069-043 Lisbon; tel. (21) 3185200; fax (21) 3156146; e-mail geral@correiomanha.pt; internet www.correiomanha.pt; f. 1979; morning; independent; Dir Octávio Ribeiro; circ. 111,585 (2006).

Diário Económico: Rua de Oliveira ao Carmo 8, 1249-111 Lisbon; tel. (21) 3236800; fax (21) 3236775; e-mail deconomico@economicasgps.com; internet diarioeconomico.sapo.pt; Dir André Macedo; circ. 13,267 (2006).

Diário de Notícias: Av. da Liberdade 266, 1250-149 Lisbon; tel. (21) 3187500; fax (21) 3187515; e-mail webmaster@dn.pt; internet dn .sapo.pt; f. 1864; morning; Dir João Marcelino; circ. 39,987 (2006).

Público: Rua Viriato 13, 1069-315 Lisbon; tel. (21) 0111000; fax (21) 0111006; internet www.publico.pt; f. 1990; morning; Dir José Manuel Fernandes; circ. 41,706 (2006).

Record: Av. Conde Valbom 30, 4-5°, 1050-068 Lisbon; tel. (21) 0124900; fax (21) 3476279; e-mail record@record.pt; internet www .record.pt; f. 1949; sport; Dir Alexandre Pais; circ. 70,610 (2006).

24 Horas: Av. da Liberdade 266, 5°, 1250-149 Lisbon; e-mail ptadeu@24horas.com.pt; Editor Pedro Tadeu; circ. 39,830 (2006).

Porto
(Oporto)

O Jogo: Rua de Gil Vicente 129, 1°, 4000-814 Porto; tel. (22) 5071900; fax (22) 5504550; e-mail ojogo@mail.telepac.pt; internet www.ojogo.pt; sporting news; Dir MANUEL TAVARES; circ. 38,380 (2006).

Jornal de Notícias: Rua Gonçalo Cristóvão 195–219, 4049-011 Porto; tel. (22) 2096111; fax (22) 2006330; e-mail noticias@jn.pt; internet www.jn.pt; f. 1888; morning; Dir JOSÉ LEITE PEREIRA; circ. 97,122 (Dec. 2006).

O Primeiro de Janeiro: Rua Coelho Neto 65, 4000 Porto; tel. (22) 0109100; fax (22) 5103291; e-mail geral@oprimeirodejaneiro.pt; internet www.oprimeirodejaneiro.pt; f. 1868; independent; morning; Dir NASSALETE MIRANDA; circ. 20,200.

Setúbal

Correio de Setúbal: Rua Camilo Castelo Branco 163, F–H, Apdo 549, 2900 Setúbal; tel. (265) 538818; fax (265) 538819.

Viseu

Diário de Viseu: Rua Alexandre Herculano 198, 1° esq., 3510-033 Viseu; tel. (232) 000031; fax (232) 000032; e-mail diarioviseu@diarioregional.pt; internet www.diarioregional.pt; Dir ADRIANO CALLÉ LUCAS.

Notícias de Viseu: Av. do Convento 1, Apdo 3115, 3511-689 Viseu; tel. (232) 410410; fax (232) 410418; e-mail geral@noticiasdeviseu.com; internet www.noticiasdeviseu.com; f. 1974; Dir FERNANDO ABREU.

Os Açores
(The Azores)

Açoriano Oriental: Rua Dr Bruno Tavares Carreiro 36, 9500-055 Ponta Delgada; tel. (296) 202800; fax (296) 202826; e-mail pub.ao@acorianooriental.pt; internet www.acorianooriental.pt; f. 1835; morning; Dir PAOLO SIMÕES; circ. 4,253 (2006).

Correio dos Açores: Rua Dr João Francisco de Sousa 14, 9500 Ponta Delgada; tel. (296) 201060; fax (296) 286119; f. 1920; morning; Dir AMÉRICO NATALINO VIVEIROS; circ. 4,460.

Diário dos Açores: Rua Dr João Francisco de Sousa 16, 9500-187 Ponta Delgada; tel. (296) 284355; fax (296) 284840; e-mail diario@da.online.pt; internet www.da.online.pt; f. 1870; morning; Dir PAULO HUGO VIVEIROS; circ. 2,380.

Diário Insular: Av. Infante D. Henrique 1, 9700-098 Angra do Heroísmo, Terceira; tel. (295) 401050; fax (295) 214246; e-mail diarioins@mail.telepac.pt; internet www.diarioinsular.com; f. 1946; morning; Dir JOSÉ LOURENÇO; circ. 3,400.

O Telégrafo: Rua Conselheiro Medeiros 30, 9902 Horta; tel. and fax (292) 22245; f. 1893; morning; Dir RUBEN RODRIGUES; circ. 3,200.

Madeira

Diário de Notícias: Rua Dr Fernão de Ornelas 56, 3°, 9054-514 Funchal; tel. (291) 202300; fax (291) 202306; e-mail dnmad@dnoticias.pt; internet www.dnoticias.pt; f. 1876; morning; independent; Dir JOSÉ BETTENCOURT DA CÂMARA; circ. 15,087 (2006).

Jornal da Madeira: Rua Dr Fernão de Ornelas 35, 4°, 9001-905 Funchal; tel. (291) 210400; fax (291) 210401; e-mail editorial@jornaldamadeira.pt; internet www.jornaldamadeira.pt; f. 1927; morning; Catholic; Dir JOÃO AFONSO DE ALMEIDA; circ. 8,000.

PRINCIPAL PERIODICALS

Activa: Rua Calvet de Magalhães 242, Laveiras, 2770-022 Paço de Arcos; tel. (21) 4143078; fax (21) 4107050; internet pub.edimpresa.pt; f. 1991; monthly; for women; Editor ROSÁRIA BARRETO; circ. 80,279 (2006).

Africa Hoje: Rua Joaquim António de Aguiar 45, 5° esq., 1070 Lisbon; tel. (21) 557175; fax (21) 3557667; e-mail geral@lucidus.pt; f. 1985; monthly; African affairs; circ. 30,000; Dir ALBÉRICO CARDOSO.

Anglo-Portuguese News: Apdo 113, 2766-902 Estoril, Lisbon; tel. (21) 4661471; fax (21) 4660358; e-mail apn@mail.telepac.pt; f. 1937; Thurs.; English language newspaper; Publr and Editor NIGEL BATLEY; circ. 30,000.

Autosport: Edif. São Francisco de Sales, Rua Calvet de Magalhães 242, 2770-022 Paço de Arcos; tel. (21) 4698197; fax (21) 4698552; e-mail autosport@autosport.pt; internet www.autosport.pt; weekly; motoring; Dir RUI FREIRE; circ. 10,880 (2006).

Avante: Av. Almirante Gago Coutinho 121, 1700-029 Lisbon; tel. (21) 7817190; fax (21) 7817193; e-mail avante.pcp@mail.telepac.pt; internet www.avante.pt; weekly; organ of the Portuguese Communist Party; Dir JOSÉ CASANOVA.

Brotéria—Revista de Cultura: Rua Maestro António Taborda 14, 1249-094 Lisbon; tel. (21) 3961660; fax (21) 3956629; e-mail broteria@netcabo.pt; internet www.broteria.pt; f. 1902; monthly; review of culture; Dir HERMÍNIO RICO; circ. 1,400.

Casa e Decoração: Av. Duque d'Avila 26, 3°, 1049-042 Lisbon; tel. (21) 3168500; fax (21) 3168578; f. 1981; 12 a year; home and interior decoration; Dir URSULA BASTOS; circ. 35,000.

Casa & Jardim: Rua da Misericórdia 137, s/loja, 1249-037 Lisbon; tel. (21) 3472127; fax (21) 3421490; e-mail direccao@casajardim.pt; internet www.casajardim.net; f. 1978; monthly; home, interior and exterior design, fine arts, exhibitions and antique fairs; Dir EDUARDO FORTUNATO DE ALMEIDA; circ. 14,486 (2006).

Colecções Moda & Beleza: Rua Dona Filipa de Vilhena 4, 5° esq., 1000-135 Lisbon; tel. (21) 3105300; fax (21) 3105309; e-mail bdesenhada@meriberica.pt; internet www.meriberica.pt; 5 a year; fashion and beauty; Editor CRISTINA COSTA; circ. 240,000.

Colóquio/Letras: Av. de Berna 45A, 1067-001 Lisbon; tel. (21) 7823000; fax (21) 7823021; e-mail coloquioletras@gulbenkian.pt; internet www.gulbenkian.pt/educacao/revista.asp; f. 1971; 4 a year; literary; Dir Dra JOANA VARELA; circ. 3,600.

Correio da Madeira: Rua do Carmo 19, 3° dto, 9000 Funchal; tel. (291) 20738; f. 1987; weekly newspaper; Dir JOSÉ CAMPOS; circ. 5,000.

Cosmopolitan: Rua Calvet de Magalhães 242, Laveiras, 2770-022 Paço de Arcos; tel. (21) 4698861; internet pub.edimpresa.pt; f. 1992; monthly; women's magazine; Editor MARIA SERINA; circ. 53,787 (2006).

Eles e Elas: Praça Luiz de Camões 36, 2°D, 1200-243 Lisbon; tel. (21) 3224660; fax (21) 3224679; e-mail gabinete1@gabinete1.pt; internet www.gabinete1.pt; f. 1983; monthly; fashion, culture, social events; Dir MARIA DA LUZ DE BRAGANÇA.

Elle: Rua Filipe Folque 40, 4°, 1050 Lisbon; tel. (21) 3156907; fax (21) 3164205; e-mail elle@hachette.pt; f. 1988; monthly; women's magazine; Dir FÁTIMA COTTA; circ. 54,697 (2006).

Expresso: Edif. S. Francisco de Sales, Rua Calvet de Magalhães 242, 2770-022 Paço de Arcos; tel. (21) 4544000; fax (21) 4435349; e-mail director@expresso.pt; internet www.expresso.pt; weekly newspaper; Dir HENRIQUE MONTEIRO; circ. 149,554 (2006).

Gente e Viagens: Rua Joaquim António de Aguiar 45, 1099-058 Lisbon; tel. (21) 3839810; fax (21) 862746; e-mail lucidus@mail.telepac.pt; internet genteviagens.sapo.pt; f. 1980; monthly; tourism; Dir ALBÉRICO CARDOSO; circ. 30,000.

Guia—Revista Prática: Av. Almirante Gago Coutinho 113, 1749-087 Lisbon; tel. (21) 8474410; fax (21) 8474396; e-mail mpcorreia@tvguia.pt; weekly women's magazine; fashion and housekeeping; Dir MARGARIDA PINTO CORREIA; Editor-in-Chief PALMIRA SIMÕES; circ. 40,000.

JL (Jornal de Letras, Artes e Ideias): Rua Calvet de Magalhães 242, Laveiras, 2770-022 Paço de Arcos; tel. (21) 574520; e-mail jcvasconcelos@edimpresa.pt; internet pub.edimpresa.pt; fortnightly; Dir JOSÉ CARLOS DE VASCONCELOS; circ. 8,358 (2006).

Manchete: Rua das Flores 105, 1° esq., 1200-194 Lisbon; tel. (21) 3224660; fax (21) 3224679; e-mail gabinete1@gabinete1.pt; f. 1992; monthly; national and international events; Dir MARIA DA LUZ DE BRAGANÇA.

Maria: Av. Miguel Bombarda 33, 2745 Queluz; tel. 4364401; fax 4365001; internet www.impala.pt; f. 1977; weekly; women's magazine; Dir JACQUES RODRIGUES; Editor-in-Chief PAULA RODRIGUES; circ. 251,404 (2006).

Máxima: Av. João Crisóstomo 72, 3°, 1069-043 Lisbon; tel. (21) 3309400; fax (21) 3540410; e-mail lauratorres@maxima.cofina.pt; internet www.maxima.pt; f. 1989; women's magazine; Dir LAUZA LUZES TORRES; circ. 68,459 (2006).

Moda & Moda: Rua Braamcamp 12, r/c esq., 1250-050 Lisbon; tel. (21) 3886068; fax (21) 3862426; e-mail modaemoda@netcabo.pt; f. 1984; 5 a year; fashion, beauty and art; Dir MARIONELA GUSMÃO; circ. 20,000.

Mulher Moderna: Av. Miguel Bombarda 33, 2745 Queluz; tel. 4364401; fax 4365001; internet www.impala.pt; f. 1988; weekly; women's magazine; Dir JACQUES RODRIGUES; Editor-in-Chief PAULA RODRIGUES; circ. 16,512 (2006).

Nova Gente: Av. Miguel Bombarda 33, 2745 Queluz; tel. 4364388; fax 4365001; internet www.impala.pt; f. 1979; weekly; popular; Dir JACQUES RODRIGUES; Editor-in-Chief ANTÓNIO SIMÕES; circ. 200,000.

Portugal Socialista: Largo do Rato 2, 1269-143 Lisbon; tel. (21) 3822000; f. 1967; quarterly; organ of the Socialist Party; Dir AUGUSTO SANTOS SILVA; circ. 5,000.

Povo Livre: Rua S. Caetano 9, 1249-087 Lisbon; tel. (21) 3952140; fax (21) 3976967; e-mail povolivre@psd.pt; weekly; organ of the Social Democratic Party; Dir JORGE MANUEL FERRAZ DE FREITAS NETO.

Revista ACP: Rua Rosa Araújo 5, 1250-195 Lisbon; tel. (21) 3180100; fax (21) 3180170; e-mail apoio.socio@acp.pt; internet www.acp.pt; f. 1908; monthly; motoring and tourism; Propr

PORTUGAL

Automóvel Club de Portugal; Editor António Raposo de Magalhães; circ. 177,765 (2006).

Revista Exame: Rua Calvet de Magalhães 242, Laveiras, 2770-022 Paço de Arcos; tel. (21) 4698000; fax (21) 4698500; e-mail icanha@edimpresa.pt; internet www.exame.pt; monthly; finance; Dir Isabel Canha; circ. 24,468 (2006).

Segredos de Cozinha: Edif. do Grupo Impala, Ranholas, 2710-460 Sintra; tel. (21) 92398033; fax (21) 9238044; e-mail gracamorais@impala.pt; internet www.impala.pt; f. 1985; weekly; cookery; Dir Graça Morais; Editor-in-Chief Paula Rodrigues; circ. 20,736 (2006).

Selecções do Reader's Digest: Rua Joaquim António de Aguiar 43, 1092-001 Lisbon; tel. (21) 3810000; fax (21) 3859203; internet www.rd.com/international/shared/index.jhtml?countryid=pt; monthly magazine; Dir Isabel Bivar; circ. 114,762 (2006).

Semanário: Rua S. Cabral 26–30, 1495 Lisbon; tel. (21) 4198065; fax (21) 4243328; weekly newspaper; Dir Dr Alvaro Mendonça; circ. 55,000.

Semanário Económico: Rua da Oliveira ao Carmo 8, 5°, 1249-111 Lisbon; tel. (21) 3236900; fax (21) 3236901; e-mail seconomico@economicasgps.com; internet www.semanarioeconomico.com; weekly; economy, business and finance; Dir Inês Serra Lopes; circ. 11,065 (2006).

TV Guia: Av. Almirante Gago Coutinho 113, 1749-087 Lisbon; tel. (21) 8474410; fax (21) 8474395; e-mail jgobern@tvguia.pt; weekly; TV programmes and general features; Dir João Gobern; circ. 73,065 (2006).

TV 7 Dias: Av. Miguel Bombarda 33, 2745 Queluz; tel. 4364401; fax 4365001; internet www.impala.pt; f. 1985; weekly; television magazine; Dir Ventura Martins; Editor-in-Chief Frederico Valarinho; circ. 174,789 (2006).

Vida Económica: Rua Gonçalo Cristovão 111, 5°–7°, 4049-037 Porto; tel. (22) 3399400; fax (22) 2058098; e-mail redaccao@vidaeconomica.pt; internet www.vidaeconomica.pt; weekly; financial; Dir João Peixoto de Sousa; Editor-in-Chief João Luís de Sousa; circ. 14,232 (2006).

Visão: Rua Calvet de Magalhães 242, Laveiras, 2770-022 Paço de Arcos; tel. (22) 4698000; fax (22) 8347557; e-mail visao@ajc.pt; internet www.visaoonline.pt; f. 1993; weekly magazine; Dir-Gen. Pedro Camaho; circ. 92,116 (2006).

NEWS AGENCY

Lusa (Agência de Notícias de Portugal, SA): Rua Dr João Couto, Lote C, 1500 Lisbon; tel. (21) 7116500; fax (21) 7116531; e-mail dinformacao@lusa.pt; internet www.lusa.pt; f. 1987; Pres. Teresa Isabel Carvalho Costa; News Editor Luís Miguel Viana.

PRESS ASSOCIATIONS

Associação Portuguesa da Imprensa (APIMPRENSA) (Portuguese Press Association): Rua Gomes Freire 183, 4° esq., 1169-041 Lisbon; tel. (21) 3555092; fax (21) 3142191; e-mail geral@apimprensa.pt; internet www.apimprensa.pt; f. 1961; represents 600 publications, both local and national; Pres. João Palmeiro; Sec.-Gen. Joana Ramada Curto.

Associação da Imprensa Diária (Association of the Daily Press): Rua de Artilharia Um 69, 2°, 1297 Lisbon; tel. (21) 3857584; fax (21) 3873541; f. 1976; 27 mems; Pres. António Freitas Cruz; Sec. Jorge Moura.

Associação da Imprensa Estrangeira em Portugal (AIEP): Sala da Imprensa, Palácio Foz, Praça dos Restauradores, 1250-187 Lisbon; fax (21) 3464145; e-mail belenchurg@yahoo.com; internet www.aiep.eu; f. 1976; Pres. Belén Rodrigo; Exec. Sec. Jair Rattner.

Publishers

Âncora Editora: Av. Infante Santo 52, 3° esq., 1350-179 Lisbon; tel. (21) 3951223; fax (21) 3951222; e-mail ancora.editora@ancora-editora.pt; internet www.ancora-editora.pt; f. 1998; Portuguese literature and culture, factual and educational works.

Areal Editores: Rua da Torrinha 228h, 3°, 4050-610 Porto; tel. (22) 3393900; fax (22) 2005708; e-mail areal@arealeditores.pt; internet www.arealeditores.pt; educational.

Assírio & Alvim: Rua Passos Manuel 67b, 1150-258 Lisbon; tel. (21) 3583033; fax (21) 3583039; e-mail assirio@assirio.com; internet www.assirio.pt; f. 1972; poetry, fiction, essays, gastronomy, photography, art, children's literature, history, social science; Man. Vasco David.

Bertrand Editora, SA: Rua Anchieta 15, 1249-060 Lisbon; tel. (21) 3476122; fax (21) 3479728; e-mail info@bertrand.pt; internet www.bertrand.pt; literature, arts, humanities, educational; Man. Mario Correia.

Directory

Campo das Letras: Edif. Mota-Galiza, Rua Júlio Dinis 247, 6°, 4050-324 Porto; tel. (22) 6080870; fax (22) 6080880; e-mail campo.letras@mail.telepac.pt; internet www.campo-letras.pt; f. 1994; literature, juvenile, current affairs.

Casa das Letras: Rua Bento de Jesus Caraça 17, 1495-686 Cruz Quebrada; tel. (21) 0052350; fax (21) 0052340; e-mail info@casadasletras.pt; fiction, politics, religion, history, economics, management, biographies, dictionaries, memoirs.

Circulo de Leitores: Rua Prof. Jorge da Silva Horta 1, 1500-499 Lisbon; tel. (21) 7626100; fax (21) 7607149; e-mail correio@circuloleitores.pt; internet www.circuloleitores.pt; fiction and non-fiction.

Coímbra Editora, Lda: Rua do Armado, Apdo 101, 3001-951 Coímbra; tel. (239) 8526540; fax (239) 852651; e-mail info@coimbraeditora.pt; internet www.coimbraeditora.pt; f. 1920; law, education, linguistics; Man. Dr João Carlos A. Oliveira Salgado.

Edições Afrontamento, Lda: Rua de Costa Cabral 859, 4200-225 Porto; tel. (22) 5074220; fax (22) 5074229; e-mail editorial@edicoesafrontamento.pt; internet www.edicoesafrontamento.pt; f. 1963; fiction, poetry, cinema, children's books, history, sociology, philosophy, economics, politics, etc.; Dirs J. Sousa Ribeiro, A. Sousa Luís.

Edições Almedina, SA: Av. Fernão de Magalhães 584, 5°, 3000-174 Coimbra; tel. (239) 851903; e-mail editora@almedina.net; internet www.almedina.net; law, education; Dir Joaquim Machado.

Edições Asa: Estrada de Paço de Arcos 66–66A, 2735-336 Cacém; tel. (22) 6166030; fax (22) 5322831; e-mail edicoes@asa.pt; internet www.asa.pt; f. 1951; literature, arts, schoolbooks, children's books, educational equipment; Gen. Man. Américo A. Areal.

Edições Caixotim: Rua dos Clérigos 23, 4050-205 Porto; tel. (22) 3390831; fax (22) 3390833; e-mail edicoescaixotim@mail.telepac.pt; internet www.caixotim.pt; f. 2001; literature, history, criticism, essays, art, etc.; Publr and Editorial Dir Paulo Samuel.

Edições 70, Lda: Rua Luciano Cordeiro 123, 1° esq., 1069-157 Lisbon; tel. (21) 3190240; fax (21) 3190249; e-mail geral@edicoes70.pt; internet www.edicoes70.pt; f. 1970; history, linguistics, anthropology, philosophy, psychology, education, art, architecture, science, reference books; Dir Joaquim José Soares da Costa.

Editora Educação Nacional, Lda: Rua do Almada 125, 4050 Porto; tel. (22) 2005351; fax (22) 2080742; e-mail contacto@editoraeducnacional.pt; internet www.editoraeducnacional.pt; school textbooks and review, *Educação Nacional*.

Editora Livros do Brasil, SA: Estrada da Outurela 121, 2794-051 Carnaxide; tel. (21) 3462621; fax (21) 3428487; e-mail geral@livrosdobrasil.com; internet www.livrosdobrasil.com; f. 1944; literature, history, politics, science, management, health, children's books; Dir António Luis de Souza Pinto.

Editora Pergaminho, Lda: Rua de Alegria 486A, Amoreira, 2645-167 Cascais; tel. (21) 4646110; fax (21) 4674008; e-mail info@editorapergaminho.pt; internet www.editorapergaminho.pt; f. 1991; cinema, music, humour, fiction; Dir Mário Mendes de Moura.

Editora Portugalmundo, Lda: Rua Gonçalves Crespo 47, r/c, 1150-184 Lisbon; tel. (21) 3304685; fax (21) 3590420; e-mail editoraportugalmundo@gmail.com; internet www.editoraportugalmundo.com; f. 1976; children's books, poetry, biographies, law, music, fiction, theatre; Dir Maria Alexandra Santos.

Editora Replicação, Lda: Av. Infante Santo 343, r/c, 1350-277 Lisbon; fax (21) 3969808; e-mail replic@mail.telepac.pt; f. 1982; textbooks, children's books, dictionaries, language materials; Dir José Carlos Anaia Cristo.

Editorial Bizancia, Lda: Largo Luis Chaves 11–11A, 1600-487 Lisbon; tel. (21) 7550228; fax (21) 7520072; e-mail bizancio@editorial-bizancio.pt; internet www.editorial-bizancio.pt; f. 1998; general fiction and non-fiction.

Editorial Confluência: Calçada do Combro 99, 1200-112 Lisbon; tel. and fax (21) 3466917; e-mail livroshorizonte@mail.telepac.pt; f. 1945; dictionaries; Man. Rogério Mendes de Moura.

Editorial Estampa, Lda: Rua da Escola do Exército 9, r/c dto, 1169-090 Lisbon; tel. (21) 3555663; fax (21) 3141911; e-mail estampa@estampa.pt; internet www.estampa.pt; sociology, economics, occult, fiction, sport, history, art, alternative medicine, children's; Dir António Carlos Manso Pinheiro.

Editorial Futura: Rua General Morais Sarmento 9, c/v esq., 1500-310 Lisbon; tel. and fax (21) 7155848; e-mail editorialfutura@netcabo.pt; literature, comics.

Editorial Minerva: Rua da Alegria 30, 1250-007 Lisbon; tel. (21) 3224950; fax (21) 3224952; e-mail minerva_dna@netcabo.pt; internet www.editorialminerva.com; f. 1927; literature, politics, children's; Man. Narcisa Fernandes.

Editorial Nova Ática, SA: Calçada Nova de S. Francisco, 10, 1° esq., 1200-300 Lisbon; tel. (21) 3420557; fax (21) 3420305; e-mail editorialnovaatica@sapo.pt; f. 1935; poetry, literature, essays, theatre, history, philosophy; Chief Execs VASCO SILVA, JOSÉ RODRIGUES.

Editorial Presença, Lda: Estrada das Palmeiras 59, Queluz de Baixo, 2730-132 Barcarena; tel. (21) 4347000; fax (21) 4346502; e-mail info@presenca.pt; internet www.presenca.pt; f. 1960; social sciences, fiction, textbooks, computer books, business, leisure, health, children's books, etc.; Dir FRANCISCO ESPADINHA.

Editorial Verbo SA: Av. António Augusto de Aguiar 148, 2B, 1069-019 Lisbon; tel. (21) 3801100; fax (21) 3865397; e-mail comerciais@editorialverbo.pt; internet www.editorialverbo.pt; f. 1958; imprints include Editora Ulisseia; encyclopaedias, dictionaries, reference, history, general science, textbooks, education and children's books; Dir FERNANDO GUEDES.

Europress—Editores e Distribuidores de Publicações, Lda: Praceta da República, Loja A, 2620-162 Póvoa de Santo Adrião; tel. (21) 9381450; fax (21) 9381452; e-mail europress@mail.telepac.pt; internet www.europress.pt; f. 1982; academic, children's, law, poetry, health, novels, history, social sciences, medicine, etc.; Man. ANTÓNIO BENTO VINTÉM.

FCA (Editora de Informática, Lda): Rua D. Estefânia 183, 1° esq., 1000-154 Lisbon; tel. (21) 3532735; fax (21) 3577827; e-mail fca@fca.pt; internet www.fca.pt; f. 1991; computer science.

Gradiva—Publicações, Lda: Rua Almeida e Sousa 21, r/c esq., 1399-041 Lisbon; tel. (21) 3933760; fax (21) 3953471; e-mail geral@gradiva.mail.pt; internet www.gradiva.pt; f. 1981; philosophy, education, history, fiction, science, social science, children's books, cartoons; Man. Dir GUILHERME VALENTE.

Guimarães Editores Lda: Rua da Misericórdia 68–70, 1200-273 Lisbon; tel. (21) 3243120; fax (21) 3243129; e-mail geral@guimaraes-ed.pt; internet www.guimaraes-ed.pt; f. 1899; literature, philosophy, history, etc.

Impala Editores, SA: Edif. Grupo Impala, Ranholas, 2710-460 Sintra; tel. (21) 9238218; fax (21) 9238463; e-mail assinaturas@impala.pt; internet www.impala.pt; f. 1983; magazines and children's books; Dir JACQUES RODRIGUES.

Imprensa Nacional—Casa da Moeda, SA (INCM): Edif. Casa da Moeda, Av. António de José de Almeida, 1000-042 Lisbon; tel. (21) 7810700; e-mail comercial@incm.pt; internet www.incm.pt; f. 1972 as Imprensa Nacional—Casa da Moeda, EP; changed status as above in 1999; Portuguese literature, arts, philosophy, history, geography, sociology, economics, encyclopaedias, dictionaries, and the *Diário da República*; Dir Dr ALCIDES GAMA.

Lello Editores, Lda: Rua Dom João de Castro 539, 4435-674 Baguim do Monte; tel. (22) 3326084; fax (22) 3326086; e-mail joselello@lelloeditores.com; internet www.lelloeditores.com; fiction, poetry, history, reference, biography, religion; Dir-Gen. JOSÉ MANUEL BERNARDES PEREIRA LELLO.

Lidel Edições Técnicas, Lda: Rua D. Estefânia 183, r/c dto, 1049-057 Lisbon; tel. (21) 3511440; fax (21) 3577827; e-mail lidel@lidel.pt; internet www.lidel.pt; f. 1963; Portuguese as a foreign language, management, technology, computer science; Man. Dir FREDERICO CARLOS DA SILVA ANNES.

Lisboa Editora, Lda: Av. dos Estados Unidos da América 1B, 1700-163 Lisbon; tel. (21) 8430910; fax (21) 8430911; e-mail geral@lisboaeditora.pt; internet www.lisboaeditora.pt; textbooks; Editorial Dirs MARIA DE LOURDES PAIXÃO, BRIGITTE THUDICHUM.

Livraria Civilização Editora: Rua Alberto Aires de Gouveia 27, 4050-023 Porto; tel. (22) 6050917; fax (22) 6050999; e-mail info@civilizacao.pt; internet www.civilizacao.pt; f. 1920; social sciences, politics, economics, history, art, medicine, fiction, children's; Man. Dir MOURA BESSA.

Livraria Editora Figueirinhas, Lda: Rua do Freixo 643, 4300-217 Porto; tel. (22) 5309026; fax (22) 5309027; e-mail correio@liv-figueirinhas.pt; f. 1898; literature, school textbooks; Dir FRANCISCO GOMES PIMENTA.

Livraria Multinova: Av. Santa Joana Princesa 12E, 1700-357 Lisbon; tel. (21) 8421820; fax (21) 8483436; e-mail geral@multinova.pt; internet www.multinova.pt; f. 1970; schoolbooks, general, religion, Brazilian works; Dir CARLOS SANTOS.

Livraria Romano Torres: Rua João de Paiva 9A e B, 1400-225 Lisbon; tel. (21) 3014914; fax (21) 3015625; e-mail info@estudodidactico.pt; f. 1885; fiction; Dir FRANCISCO NORONHA DE ANDRADE.

Livros Cotovia: Rua Nova da Trindade 24, 1200-303 Lisbon; tel. (21) 3471447; fax (21) 3470467; e-mail geral@livroscotovia.pt; internet www.livroscotovia.pt; f. 1988; literature, drama, poetry, etc.

Livros Horizonte, Lda: Rua das Chagas 17, 1° dto, 1200-106 Lisbon; tel. (21) 3466917; fax (21) 3159259; e-mail info@livroshorizonte.pt; internet www.livroshorizonte.pt; f. 1953; art, education, history, social sciences; Dirs ROGÉRIO MENDES DE MOURA, MANUELA DUARTE.

Lusodidacta (Sociedade Portuguesa de Materia Didáctico, Lda): Rua Darío Cannas 5A, 2670-427 Loures; tel. (21) 9839840; fax (21) 9839847; e-mail loures1@lusodidacta.pt; internet www.lusodidacta.pt; f. 1976; textbooks, dictionaries, medicine.

McGraw-Hill de Portugal: Edif. Castilho 5, r/c A, Rua Barata Salgueiro, 51A, 1250-043 Lisbon; tel. (21) 3553180; fax (21) 3553189; e-mail servico_clientes@mcgraw-hill.com; internet www.mcgraw-hill.pt; scientific, technical and medical; Gen. Man. ANTÓNIO DE MARCO.

PAULUS Editora: Rua Dom Pedro de Cristo 10, 1749-092 Lisbon; tel. (21) 8437621; fax (21) 8437629; e-mail editor@paulus.pt; internet www.paulus.pt; religion, theology, psychology, etc.; Dir JOHN FREDY.

Plátano Editora, SARL: Av. de Berna 31, 2° esq., 1069-054 Lisbon; tel. (21) 7979278; fax (21) 7954019; e-mail geral@platanoeditora.pt; internet www.platanoeditora.pt; f. 1972; literature, educational, science, technical, dictionaries, etc.; Dir FRANCISCO PRATA GINJA.

Porto Editora, Lda: Rua da Restauração 365, 4099-023 Porto; tel. (22) 6088300; fax (22) 6088301; e-mail secretariado@portoeditora.pt; internet www.portoeditora.pt; f. 1944; general literature, school books, dictionaries, children's books, multimedia; Dirs VASCO TEIXEIRA, JOSÉ ANTÓNIO TEIXEIRA, ROSÁLIA TEIXEIRA.

Publicações Dom Quixote: Edif. Anas, 2°, Rua Ivan Silva 6, 1050-124 Lisbon; tel. (21) 1203010; fax (21) 1209030; e-mail editorial@dquixote.pt; internet www.dquixote.pt; f. 1965; general fiction, poetry, history, philosophy, psychology, politics, didactics and sociology; university text books; children's books.

Publicações Europa-América, Lda: Estrada Nacional 249 (Lisboa–Sintra), Km 14, Apdo 8, 2725-397 Mem Martins; tel. (21) 9267700; fax (21) 9267771; e-mail secretariado@europa-america.pt; internet www.europa-america.pt; f. 1945; imprints include Edições CETOP, Editorial Inquerito, Livros de Vida Editores, Lyon Edições and Publicações Alfa; fiction, current affairs, economics, reference, history, technical, children's; Dir TITO LYON DE CASTRO.

Quimera Editores Lda: Rua do Vale Formoso 37, 1949-013 Lisbon; tel. (21) 8455950; fax (21) 8455951; e-mail quimera@quimera-editores.com; internet www.quimera-editores.com; f. 1987; literature, art, history, photography, etc.; Dirs JOSÉ ALFARO, LUÍS VEIGA.

Rés—Editora, Lda: Praça Marquês de Pombal 78, 4000-390 Porto; tel. (22) 5024174; fax (22) 5026098; e-mail res-editora@res-editora.pt; internet www.res-editora.pt; f. 1975; economics, philosophy, law, sociology; Dir REINALDO DE CARVALHO.

Texto Editora, Lda: Estrada de Paço de Arcos 66 e 66A, 2735-336 Cacém; tel. (21) 4272200; fax (21) 4272201; e-mail info@textoeditores.com; internet pt.textoeditores.com; f. 1977; school textbooks, management, pedagogy, health, beauty, cooking, children's books, multimedia; Man. Dir MANUEL JOSÉ DO ESPÍRITO SANTO FERRÃO.

PUBLISHERS' ASSOCIATION

Associação Portuguesa de Editores e Livreiros (Portuguese Association of Publishers and Booksellers): Av. dos Estados Unidos da América 97, 6°, 1700-167 Lisbon; tel. (21) 8435180; fax (21) 8489377; e-mail apel@apel.pt; internet www.apel.pt; f. 1927; Pres. ANTÓNIO BAPTISTA LOPES; Sec.-Gen. AUGUSTO SILVA.

Broadcasting and Communications

TELECOMMUNICATIONS

Portugal Telecom, SA (PT): Av. Fontes Pereira de Melo 40, 6°, 1069-300 Lisbon; tel. (21) 5002000; fax (21) 3562624; e-mail geral@telecom.pt; internet www.telecom.pt; f. 1994; by merger of three regional telecommunications operators; state holding reduced to 25% in 1997; relinquished monopoly on fixed-line operations in Jan. 2000; Chair. HENRIQUE GRANADEIRO; CEO ZEINAL BAVA.

AR Telecom, SA: Edif. Diogo Cão, Doca de Alcântara Norte, 1350-352 Lisbon; tel. (21) 0301030; fax (21) 0301300; e-mail contacto@artelecom.pt; internet www.artelecom.pt; f. 2000 as Jazztel Portugal, SA; renamed as above in 2005; subsidiary of Grupo SGC; fixed-line operator.

Novis Telecom, SA: Edif. Sonaecom, Av. D. João II, Lote 1.06.24, 1990-095 Lisbon; tel. (21) 0100000; fax (21) 0129210; e-mail info@novis.pt; internet www.novis.pt; fixed-line operator.

Oni Communications, SA: Edif. Qualidade A1 e A2, Tagus Park, Av. Prof. Dr Cavaco Silva, 2740-269 Porto Salvo; tel. (21) 0005300; fax (21) 0007175; e-mail geral@oni.pt; internet www.oni.pt; f. 2000; fixed-line operator; CEO XAVIER RODRÍGUEZ-MARTÍN.

Optimus Telecomunicações, SA: Edif. Green Park, 13° e 14°A, Av. do Combatentes 43, 1600 Lisbon; tel. (21) 7233600; fax (21) 7546275; e-mail contacto@optimus.pt; internet www.optimus.pt; f. 1998; provides mobile telephone services.

PORTUGAL

TMN (Telecomunicações Móveis Nacionais), SA: Av. Álvaro Pais 2, 1649-041 Lisbon; tel. (21) 7914400; fax (21) 7914500; e-mail tmn.comunica@tmn.pt; internet www.tmn.pt; commenced mobile telephone services in 1989; part of Portugal Telecom; CEO ZEINAL ABEDIN MAHOMED BAVA.

UZO: Av. Álvaro Pais 2, 1649-041 Lisbon; e-mail info@uzo.pt; internet www.uzo.com.pt; f. 2005; part of Portugal Telecom; mobile operator; Exec. Dir JOÃO MENDES.

Vodafone—Comunicações Pessoais, SA: Parque das Nações, Av. D. João II, Lote 1.04.01, 1998-017 Lisbon; tel. (21) 0915252; fax (21) 0915480; e-mail ir.pt@vodafone.com; internet www.vodafone.pt; f. 1991; fmrly Telecel-Comunicações Pessoais; provides mobile and fixed-line telephone services; Chief Exec. ANTÓNIO CARRAPATOSO.

Other fixed-line operators include Cabovisão, Coltel, Refer Telecom, Telemilénio, TV Cabo and TVTEL.

Regulatory Authority

Autoridade Nacional de Comunicações (ANACOM): Av. José Malhoa 12, 1009-017 Lisbon; tel. (21) 7211000; fax (21) 7211001; internet www.anacom.pt; formerly known as the Instituto das Comunicações de Portugal (ICP); Pres. JOSÉ MANUEL AMADO DA SILVA.

BROADCASTING

In 2006 there were around 350 radio stations in operation.

Radio

State-controlled Radio

Radiodifusão Portuguesa, SA (RDP): Av. Marechal Gomes da Costa 37, Lisbon; tel. (21) 7947000; fax (21) 7947669; internet tv.rtp.pt/EPG/radio; f. 1975; part of Radiotelevisão Portuguesa (see below); Dir of Programmes RUI PÊGO.

Domestic Services:

Antena 1: tel. (21) 3820000; fax (21) 3873977; Dir JOÃO COELHO; broadcasts 24 hours daily on medium-wave and FM; news, sport, music, etc.

Antena 2: tel. (21) 3820000; fax (21) 3873986; Dir JOÃO PEREIRA BASTOS; broadcasts classical music 24 hours daily on FM.

Antena 3: tel. (21) 3820000; fax (21) 3873977; Dir JORGE ALEXANDRE LOPES; broadcasts 24 hours daily on FM; music and entertainment for young people.

Commercial and Private Radio

Cidade FM: Rua Sampaio e Pina 24, 1099-044 Lisbon; tel. (21) 3821500; fax (21) 3821589; internet cidadefm.clix.pt; one FM transmitter; broadcasts 24 hours a day; Dir-Gen. JORDI JORDÀ; Dir of Programmes NUNO GONÇALVES.

Orbital FM: Travessa do Olival 6, 2685 Sacavém; tel. (21) 9401019; fax (21) 9427757; e-mail orbital@orbital.pt; internet www.orbital.pt; one FM transmitter; broadcasts 24 hours a day in Lisbon region.

Rádio Capital: Rua Viriato 25, 4° dto, 1050-234 Lisbon; tel. (21) 0105760; fax (21) 2740781; e-mail net@radiocapital.fm; internet www.radiocapital.fm; one FM transmitter; broadcasts 24 hours a day in Lisbon and Oporto; Dir-Gen. JOSÉ AUGUSTO MADALENO.

Rádio Clube: Rua Sampaio e Pina 26, 1099-044 Lisbon; tel. (21) 3821500; fax (21) 3821559; e-mail internet@radiocomercial.pt; f. 1992; fmrly Radio Nostalgia; broadcasts music 24 hours daily on FM; Head LUÍS MONTEZ; Dir of Programmes MIGUEL CRUZ.

Rádio Comercial, SA: Rua Sampaio e Pina 24/26, 1000 Lisbon; tel. (21) 3821500; fax (21) 3821559; e-mail geral@radiocomercial.pt; internet www.radiocomercial.pt; f. 1979 as RDP-3; transferred to private ownership in 1993; broadcasts music, news and sport 24 hours daily on Rádio Comercial: (FM); and since March 1998 on Rádio Nacional on MW to central and southern Portugal, also music, news and sport; Head LUÍS MONTEZ; Dir of Programmes MIGUEL CRUZ.

Rádio Europa Lisboa: Rua Latino Coelho 50, 1°, 1050-137 Lisbon; tel. (21) 3510580; fax (21) 3510598; e-mail programas@radioeuropa.fm; internet www.radioeuropa.fm; fmrly Rádio Paris Lisboa; present name adopted 2006; one FM transmitter; broadcasts 24 hours a day; Dir ANTONIETA LOPES DA COSTA.

Rádio Juventude: Edif. Plátano, Loja A, Rua Prof. Hugo Correia Pardal, 6000-267 Castelo Branco; tel. (272) 341758; fax (272) 347660; e-mail radiojuventude@netvisao.pt; internet www.radiojuventude.com; one FM transmitter; broadcasts 24 hours a day.

Rádio Viriato: Complexo Conventurispress, Orgens, Apdo 3115, 3511-689 Viseu; tel. (232) 410416; fax (232) 410418; e-mail inforadio@viriato.fm.com; internet www.viriatofm.com; f. 1987; one FM transmitter; broadcasts 24 hours a day; Dir ANABELA ABREU.

RR (Rádio Renascença): Rua Capelo 5, 1294-108 Lisbon; tel. (21) 3239200; fax (21) 3239220; e-mail info@rr.pt; f. 1937; Roman Catholic station; broadcasts 24 hours a day on Rádio Renascença (FM, medium-wave and satellite; internet www.rr.pt), on RFM (FM and satellite; internet www.rfm.pt; Dir ANTÓNIO MENDES) and on MEGA FM (FM and satellite; internet www.mega.fm.pt; Dir NELSON RIBEIRO); Chair. FERNANDO MAGALHÃES CRESPO.

TSF—Rádio Jornal: Edif. Altejo, Sala 301, Rua 3 da Matinha, 1900-823 Lisbon; tel. (21) 8612500; fax (21) 8612510; e-mail tsf@tsf.pt; internet www.tsf.pt; broadcasts news and sport 24 hours daily on FM; Pres. JOAQUIM OLIVEIRA.

Television

State-controlled Television

Radiotelevisão Portuguesa, SA (RTP): Av. Marechal Gomes da Costa 37, 1849-030 Lisbon; tel. (21) 7947000; fax (21) 7947570; e-mail rtp@rtp.pt; internet www.rtp.pt; f. 1956; nationalized in 1975; became jt-stock co (with 100% public capital) in 1992; 12 studios incl. Lisbon, Porto, Ponta Delgada and Funchal; Pres. GUILHERME COSTA; Dir of Programmes JOSÉ FRAGOSO.

Regional Centres:

RTP/Porto: Rua Conceição Fernandes, Apdo 174, 4402 Vila Nova de Gaia; tel. (22) 7156000; fax (22) 7110963; Dir DJALME NEVES.

RTP/Açores: Rua Ernesto Canto 40, 9500 Ponta Delgada, São Miguel; tel. (296) 202700; fax (296) 202771; e-mail rtpa@rtp.pt; internet www.rtp.pt; Dir PEDRO BICUDO.

RTP/Madeira: Sítio da Madalena, Caminho Santo António 145, 9000 Funchal; tel. (291) 709100; fax (291) 741859; Dir J. LEONEL FREITAS.

RTP/Internacional (RTPi): e-mail rtpi@rtp.pt; internet rtpi.rtp.pt; commenced satellite transmissions in June 1992; broadcasts in Portuguese 24 hours a day; Dir FERNANDO BALSINHA.

RTP/Africa: commenced transmissions to lusophone countries of Africa in 1997; broadcasts 24 hours a day; Dir AFONSO RATO.

Cable, Commercial and Private Television

Bragatel—Companhia de Televisão por Cabo de Braga, SA: Av. 31 de Janeiro 177, Apdo 17, 4715-052 Braga; tel. (253) 616600; fax (253) 616998; e-mail mail@bragatel.pt; internet www.bragatel.pt; f. 1993; authorized to operate in Braga, Barceios and Espsende.

Cabo TV Açoreana: Av. Antero de Quental 9c, 1°, 9500-160 Ponta Delgada; tel. (296) 302401; fax (296) 302405; internet www.cabotva.net.

Cabo TV Madeirense: Av. Estados Unidos da América, Nazaré, 9000-090 Funchal; tel. (291) 700800; fax (291) 766132; e-mail tvcabo@cabotvm.pt; internet www.cabotvm.pt; 71% owned by TV Cabo.

Cabovisão—Sociedade de Televisão por Cabo, SA: Lugar de Poços, Vale de Touros, 2950-425 Palmela; tel. (21) 0801080; fax (21) 0801000; e-mail info@cabovisao.pt; internet www.cabovisao.pt; authorized to operate in 156 municipalities (4.5m. homes).

Pluricanal Leiria: Av. General Humberto Delgado 2, 2400 Leiria; tel. (244) 824925; fax (244) 824943.

Pluricanal Santarém: Edif. Ribatel, Estrada Nacional 3, S. Pedro, 2000 Santarém; tel. (244) 824925; fax (244) 824943.

SIC (Sociedade Independente de Comunicação, SA): Estrada da Outurela, Carnaxide, 2795 Linda-a-Velha; tel. 4173111; fax 4173118; e-mail atendimento@sic.pt; internet www.sic.pt; commenced transmissions in 1992; news and entertainment; Head FRANCISCO PINTO BALSEMÃO; Dir of Programmes EMÍDIO RANGEL.

TV Cabo: Rua Adelina Abranches Ferrão 10, 1600 Lisbon; tel. 808 200400; e-mail cliente@netcabo.pt; internet www.tvcabo.pt; offers subscription-based television services, also broadband internet access and fixed-line telecommunications; operates 17 regional companies.

TVI (Televisão Independente, SA): Rua Mário Castelhano 40, 2740-502 Barcarena; tel. (21) 4347500; fax (21) 4347654; internet www.tvi.pt; commenced transmissions in 1993; Pres. MANUEL POLANCO; Gen. Man. JOSÉ EDUARDO MONIZ.

TVTEL Comunicações, SA: Rua Delfim Ferreira 383, 4100-201 Porto; tel. (22) 0325800; fax (22) 6154949; e-mail info@tvtel.pt; internet www.tvtel.pt.

Zon Multimédia—Serviços de Telecomunicações e Multimédia, SGPS, SA: Av. 5 de Outubro 208, 1069-203, Lisbon; tel. (21) 7824725; fax (21) 7824735; e-mail ir@pt-multimedia.pt; internet www.pt-multimedia.pt; fmrly PT Multimédia; renamed as above in 2008; Chair. RODRIGO JORGE LUÍS DE ARAÚJO COSTA; 1.7m. customers.

Finance

(cap. = capital; res = reserves; dep. = deposits; m. = million; brs = branches; amounts in euros)

BANKING

Central Bank

Banco de Portugal: Rua do Ouro 27, 1100-150 Lisbon; tel. (21) 3213200; fax (21) 3464843; e-mail info@bportugal.pt; internet www.bportugal.pt; f. 1846; reorganized 1931 with the sole right to issue notes; nationalized in 1974; cap. 1.0m., res 4,033.7m., dep. 5,149.4m. (Dec. 2006); Gov. VÍTOR MANUEL RIBEIRO CONSTÂNCIO; 10 brs.

Other Banks

Banco Activobank (Portugal), SA: Rua Augusta 84, 1149-023 Lisbon; tel. (21) 4232673; fax (21) 0066883; e-mail ab7_dop@activobank7.pt; internet www.activobank7.com; f. 1969 as Sociedade Financeira Portuguesa; nationalized 1975; privatized 1991 and name changed to Banco Mello, SA; name changed to above in 2001; 100% owned by Banco Comercial Português, SA; Chair. PAULO TEIXEIRA PINTO.

Banco Bilbao Vizcaya Argentaria (Portugal), SA: Av. da Liberdade 222, 1250-148 Lisbon; tel. (21) 3117200; fax (21) 3117500; e-mail helpdesk@bbva.pt; internet www.bbva.pt; f. 1991 as Banco Bilbao Vizcaya; name changed 2000; cap. 160.0m., res 42.4m., dep. 4,382.2m. (Dec. 2005); Pres. JOSÉ VERA JARDIM; Country Man. JOSÉ MANUEL DOIZTUA; 100 brs.

Banco BPI, SA: Rua Tenente Valadim 284, 4100-476 Porto; tel. (22) 2075000; fax (22) 6002954; e-mail dirint@bpi.pt; internet www.bancobpi.pt; f. 1998 following the absorption of Banco Fonsecas e Burnay and Banco Borges e Irmão by Banco de Fomento e Exterior; cap. 760.0m., res 381.8m., dep. 29,711m. (Dec. 2006); Chair. FERNANDO ULRICH; 574 brs.

Banco Comercial dos Açores: Edif. BCA, Rua Dr José Bruno Tavares Carreiro, 9500-119 Ponta Delgada, São Miguel, Azores; tel. (296) 629070; fax (296) 629657; e-mail bca@mail.telepac.pt; internet www.bca.pt; f. 1912 as Banco Micaelense; present name adopted 1980; 100% owned by Banif Comercial SGPS, SA; cap. 51.9m., res 24.2m., dep. 1,144.1m. (Dec. 2006); Chair. HORÁCIO DA SILVA ROQUE; Pres. and CEO Dr JOAQUIM MARQUES DOS SANTOS; 43 brs.

Banco Comercial Português (Millennium BCP): Praça D. João I 28, 4000-295 Porto; tel. (22) 7502424; fax (22) 2064139; internet www.millenniumbcp.pt; f. 1985; cap. 3,611.3m., res 450.7m., dep. 69,590.6m. (Dec. 2006); Chair., Exec. Bd CARLOS JORGE RAMALHO DOS SANTOS FERREIRA; 909 brs.

Banco Efisa, SA: Av. Antonio Augusto de Aguiar 134, 4°, 1050-020 Lisbon; tel. (21) 3117800; fax (21) 3117908; e-mail dcb@bancoefisa.pt; internet www.bancoefisa.pt; f. 1994 by merger; 99.8% owned by BPN Participações Financeiras SGPS, Lisbon; cap. 18.3m., res 4.7m., dep. 265.6m. (Dec. 2005); Pres. ABDOOL MAGID ABDOOL KARIM VAKIL.

Banco Espírito Santo, SA: Av. da Liberdade 195, 1250-142 Lisbon; tel. (21) 3501000; fax (21) 3501033; e-mail info@bes.pt; internet www.bes.pt; f. 1884; nationalized in 1975; transfer to private sector completed in Feb. 1992; fmrly Banco Espírito Santo e Comercial de Lisboa; 42% owned by BESPAR SGPS Lisbon; cap. 2,500.0m., res 1,815.2m., dep. 50,441.8m. (Dec. 2006); Pres. and CEO RICARDO ESPÍRITO SANTO SILVA SALGADO; Chair., Bd of Dirs ANTÓNIO LUIS ROQUETTE RICCIARDI; 457 brs.

Banco Finantia, SA: Rua General Firmino Miguel 5, 1600-100 Lisbon; tel. (21) 7202000; fax (21) 7202030; e-mail finantia@finantia.com; internet www.finantia.com; f. 1987; investment bank; 50% owned by Finantipar SGPS, SA; cap. 115.0m., res 225.6m., dep. 4,510.0m. (Dec. 2006); Pres. ANTÓNIO MANUEL AFONSO GUERREIRO; 1 br.

Banco Itaú Europa, SA: Centro Comercial Amoreiras, Torre 3, 11°, Rua Tierno Galvan, 1099-048 Lisbon; tel. (21) 3811000; fax (21) 3887219; e-mail bie.global@itaueuropa.pt; internet www.itaueuropa.pt; f. 1994; owned by Itaúsa Portugal SGPS, Lisbon; cap. 317.9m., res 38.5m., dep. 2,540.5m. (Dec. 2006); Pres. and Chair. ROBERTO EGYDIO SETÚBAL; CEO ALMIR VIGNOTO.

Banco Popular Portugal, SA: Rua Ramalho Ortigão 51, 1099-090 Lisbon; tel. (21) 0071000; fax (21) 0071187; e-mail s.mercados@bancopopular.pt; internet www.bancopopular.pt; f. 1991 as Banco Nacional de Crédito; present name adopted 2005; cap. 176.0m., res 144.9m., dep. 6,206.1m. (Dec. 2006); Chair. JOÃO FILIPE MAIA DE LIMA MAYER; CEO RUI MANUEL MORGANHO SEMEDO; 174 brs.

Banco Privado Português, SA: Rua Mouzinho da Silveira 12, 1250-167 Lisbon; tel. (21) 3137000; fax (21) 3137092; internet www.bpp.pt; f. 1996; cap. 125.0m., res 21.5m., dep. 555.0m. (Dec. 2005); Chair. Dr JOÃO OLIVEIRA RENDEIRO; CEO Dr PAULO GUICHARD.

Banco Santander Totta: Rua do Ouro 88, 1100-063 Lisbon; tel. (21) 3262000; fax (21) 3262271; e-mail santandertotta@santandertotta.pt; internet www.santandertotta.pt; f. 2004 by merger of Banco Totta & Açores, Banco Santander Portugal and Crédito Predial Português; owned by Banco Santander (Spain); cap. 589.8m., res 425.5m., dep. 30,328.1m. (Dec. 2005); CEO NUNO MANUEL DA SILVA AMADO; 640 brs.

BANIF—Banco Internacional do Funchal SA: Rua de João Tavira 30, 9000-509 Funchal, Madeira; tel. (291) 207700; fax (291) 224822; e-mail info@banif.pt; internet www.banif.pt; f. 1988; cap. 240.0m., res 21.9m., dep. 6,057.1m. (Dec. 2006); Chair. HORÁCIO DA SILVA ROQUE; CEO Dr JOAQUIM FILIPE MARQUES DOS SANTOS; 210 brs.

BPN (Banco Português de Negócios, SA): Edif. Fronteira, Av. António Augusto de Aguiar 132, 1050-020 Lisbon; tel. (21) 3598000; fax (21) 3598669; e-mail marketing@banco.bpn.pt; internet www.bpn.pt; f. 1993; owned by BPN-SGPS SA; cap. 360.0m., res 15.1m., dep. 5,508.7m. (Dec. 2006); Chair. ABDOOL MAGID ABDOOL KARIM VAKIL; 200 brs.

Caixa-Banco de Investimento, SA (CaixaBI): Rua Barata Salgueiro 33, 1269-057 Lisbon; tel. (21) 3137300; fax (21) 3522905; e-mail caixabi@caixabi.pt; internet www.caixabi.pt; f. 1984 as Manufacturers Hanover Trust Co; present name adopted 2000; 99.7% owned by Caixa Geral de Depósitos, SA; cap. 81.3m., res 74.5m., dep. 1,291.4m. (Dec. 2006); Pres. and Chair. Dr CARLOS JORGE RAMALHO SANTOS FERREIRA; CEO JORGE HUMBERTO CORREIA TOMÉ; 3 brs.

Caixa Central de Crédito Agrícola Mútuo, CRL (Crédito Agrícola): Rua Castilho 233–233A, 1099-004 Lisbon; tel. (21) 3860006; fax (21) 3805546; e-mail dint.cccam@creditoagricola.pt; internet www.creditoagricola.com; f. 1984; co-operative bank; cap. 678.2m., res 54.5m., dep. 8,790.3m. (Dec. 2006); Chair. and Pres. ADRIANO AUGUSTO DIEGUES; CEO JOÃO ANTÓNIO MORAIS DA COSTA PINTO; 632 brs.

Caixa Económica Montepio Geral (Montepio Geral): Rua Áurea 219–241, POB 2882, 1100-062 Lisbon; tel. (21) 3248220; fax (21) 3248228; internet www.montepio.pt; f. 1844 as Caixa Económica de Lisboa; present name adopted 1991; cap. 585.0m., res 177.0m., dep. 13,885.0m. (Dec. 2006); Chair. JOSÉ DA SILVA LOPES; 55 brs.

Caixa Geral de Depósitos, SA (CGD): Av. João XXI 63, 1000-300 Lisbon; tel. (21) 7953000; fax (21) 7905050; e-mail cgd@cgd.pt; internet www.cgd.pt; f. 1876; state-owned; grants credit for agriculture, industry, building, housing, energy, trade and tourism; cap. 2,950.0m., res 636.0m., dep. 74,695.4m. (Dec. 2006); Pres. and Chair. FERNANDO MANUEL BARBOSA FARIA DE OLIVEIRA; 768 brs.

Deutsche Bank (Portugal), SA: Rua Castilho 20, 1250-069 Lisbon; tel. (21) 3111225; fax (21) 3111234; e-mail dbonline.dbp@db.com; internet www.deutsche-bank.pt; f. 1990 as Deutsche Bank de Investimento; name changed 1999; Pres. Dr HOMERO JOSÉ DE PINHO COUTINHO.

Finibanco, SA: Rua Júlio Dinis 157, 4050-323 Porto; tel. (22) 0004676; fax (22) 0004101; e-mail comunicacao@finibanco.pt; internet www.finibanco.pt; f. 1993; cap. 104.0m., res 7.7m., dep. 2,022.4m. (Dec. 2006); Pres. ALVARO DA COSTA LEITE; CEO HUMBERTO DA COSTA LEITE; 140 brs.

Banking Association

Associação Portuguesa de Bancos (APB): Av. da República 35, 5°, 1050-186 Lisbon; tel. (21) 3510070; fax (21) 3579533; e-mail apbancos@apb.pt; internet www.apb.pt; f. 1984; Pres. Dr JOÃO SALGUEIRO; Sec.-Gen. Dr JOÃO MENDES RODRIGUES; 29 mems.

STOCK EXCHANGE

Euronext Lisbon: Av. da Liberdade 196, 1250-147 Lisbon; tel. (21) 7900000; fax (21) 7952021; internet www.euronext.com; f. 1769 as Bolsa de Valores de Lisboa e Porto; merged with Euronext in 2002 and adopted current name; merged with New York Stock Exchange in 2007 to form NYSE Euronext; Chair. MIGUEL ATHAYDE MARQUES.

Regulatory Authority

Comissão do Mercado de Valores Mobiliários (CMVM): Av. da Liberdade 252, 1056-801 Lisbon; tel. (21) 3177000; fax (21) 3537077; e-mail cmvm@cmvm.pt; internet www.cmvm.pt; f. 1991; independent securities exchange commission; Pres. Dr CARLOS TAVARES.

INSURANCE

The Portuguese insurance market is developing in accordance with EU regulations and practices. At the end of 2006 there were 449 insurance companies in operation, of which 15 specialized in life insurance and 32 were foreign. Net profits in that year were estimated at €704.3m.

Supervisory Authority

Instituto de Seguros de Portugal (ISP): Av. de Berna 19, 1050-037 Lisbon; tel. (21) 7903100; fax (21) 7938568; e-mail isp@isp.pt; internet www.isp.pt; f. 1982; office in Oporto; Pres. FERNANDO DIAS NOGUEIRA.

Representative Bodies

Associação das Empresas Gestoras de Fundos de Pensões (AEGFP): Rua da Misericórdia 76, 1200-273 Lisbon; tel. (21) 3210147; fax (21) 3210264; e-mail aegfp.pensoes@mail.telepac.pt; f. 1990; pension funds; Pres. Dr Rui Pedras; Sec.-Gen. Dr Francisco J. de Medeiros Cordeiro.

Associação Nacional dos Agentes e Corretores de Seguros (ANACS): Rua da Xabregas, Lote A, Sala 138, 1900-440 Lisbon; tel. (21) 8688013; fax (21) 8688014; e-mail anacsegur@netc.pt; Pres. Manuel Gaspar da Cunha.

Associação Portuguesa de Seguradores (APS): Rua Rodrigo da Fonseca 41, 1250-190 Lisbon; tel. (21) 3848100; fax (21) 3831422; e-mail aps@apseguradores.pt; internet www.apseguradores.pt; f. 1982; Pres. Jaime d'Almeida.

Associação Portuguesa dos Produtores Profissionais de Seguros (APROSE): Edif. Infante D. Dinis, Praça da República 93, Sala 301, 4050-497 Porto; tel. (22) 2003000; fax (22) 3322519; e-mail aprose@aprose.pt; internet www.aprose.pt; f. 1976; Pres. António Vilela; Exec. Dir Paulo Corvaceira Gomes.

Principal Companies

Axa-Portugal—Companhia de Seguros, SA: Rua Gonçalo Sampaio 39, 4002-001 Porto; tel. (22) 6081100; fax (22) 6081136; e-mail contacto@axa-seguros.pt; internet www.axa.pt; non-life; net profits 27.3m. (2005); Pres. Dr João Leandro.

Axa-Portugal—Companhia de Seguros de Vida, SA: Praça Marquês de Pombal 14, Apdo 1953, 1250-162 Lisbon; tel. (21) 3506100; fax (21) 3506136; e-mail contacto@axa-seguros.pt; internet www.axa.pt; life and pension funds; Pres. Dr Carlos Pedro Brandão de Melo de Sousa e Brito.

BPI Vida—Companhia de Seguros de Vida, SA: Rua Braamcamp 11, 8°, 1250-049 Lisbon; tel. (21) 3111020; fax (21) 3111082; internet www.bpiinvestimentos.pt; life and pension funds; net profits 23.7m. (2006); Pres. Dr Fernando Maria Costa Duarte Ulrich.

Companhia de Seguros Açoreana, SA: Largo da Matriz 45–52, 9500-094 Ponta Delgada, S. Miguel, Azores; tel. (296) 201400; fax (296) 201483; e-mail info@csanet.pt; internet www.acornet.pt; f. 1892; life and non-life; net profits 17.7m. (2006); Pres. Dr Horácio da Silva Roque.

Companhia de Seguros Allianz Portugal, SA: Rua Andrade Corvo 32, 1069-014 Lisbon; tel. (21) 3165300; fax (21) 3193125; e-mail info@allianz.pt; internet www.allianz.pt; f. 1907; fmrly Allianz Portugal; life, non-life and pension funds; net profits 21.4m. (2004); CEO Iván José de la Sota Duñabeitia.

Companhia de Seguros Fidelidade–Mundial, SA: Largo do Calhariz 30, 1249-001 Lisbon; tel. (21) 3238000; fax (21) 3238001; e-mail csc@fidelidademundial.pt; internet www.fidelidademundial.pt; f. 1980 from merger of four cos; life, non-life and pension funds; net profits 95.4m. (2005); Pres. Dr Vitor Manuel Lopes Fernandes.

Companhia de Seguros Tranquilidade, SA: Av. da Liberdade 242, 1250-149 Lisbon; tel. (21) 3503500; fax (21) 8553051; e-mail infogeral@tranquilidade.pt; internet www.tranquilidade.pt; f. 1871; non-life; net profits 32.5m. (2006); 100% privatized in 1990; Pres. Pedro de Brito e Cunha.

Companhia de Seguros Tranquilidade Vida, SA (T-Vida): Av. da Liberdade 230, 1250-148 Lisbon; tel. (21) 3167500; fax (21) 3153194; e-mail correio@tranquilidade-vida.pt; internet www.tranquilidade.pt; life and pension funds; net profits 34.2m. (2005); Pres. Dr Luís Frederico Redondo Lopes.

Cosec (Companhia de Seguro de Créditos, SA): Av. da República 58, 1069-057 Lisbon; tel. (21) 7913700; fax (21) 7913720; e-mail cosec@cosec.pt; internet www.cosec.pt; f. 1969; domestic and export credit insurance; bond insurance; net profits 4.2m. (2006); Chair. José Miguel Gomes da Costa.

Crédito Agrícola Vida, SA: Rua Castilho 233A, 1050-185 Lisbon; tel. (21) 3805660; fax (21) 3859695; e-mail linhadirecta@creditoagricola.pt; internet www.credito-agricola.pt; life; net profits 3.4m. (2004); Pres. Joaquim da Silva Bernardo.

Eurovida, SA: Rua Castilho 39, 14°, 1250-068 Lisbon; tel. (21) 7924700; fax (21) 7924701; e-mail seguros@eurovida.pt; internet www.eurovida.pt; net profits 1.9m. (2004); Pres. Dr Luís Barbosa.

Global—Companhia de Seguros, SA: Av. Duque de Avila 171, 1069-031 Lisbon; tel. (21) 3137500; fax (21) 3554021; e-mail globalseguros@global-seguros.pt; internet www.global-seguros.pt; non-life; net profits 12.1m. (2006); Exec. Pres. Albertino Silva.

GroupAMA Seguros: Av. de Berna 24D, 1069-170 Lisbon; tel. (21) 7923187; fax (21) 7923232; e-mail groupama@groupama.pt; internet www.groupama.pt; life and non-life; cap. 31.0m. (2004).

Império Bonança—Companhia de Seguros, SA: Rua Alexandre Herculano 53, 1269-152 Lisbon; tel. (21) 3702000; fax (21) 3702835; internet www.imperiobonanca.pt; f. by merger of Companhia de Seguros Bonança, SA and Companhia de Seguros Império, SA; net income 29.0m. (2006); Chair. Dr Jorge Manuel Baptista Magalhães Correia.

Liberty Seguros, SA: Av. Fontes Pereira de Melo 6, 1069-001 Lisbon; tel. (21) 3124300; fax (21) 3183800; e-mail producao@libertyseguros.pt; internet www.libertyseguros.pt; f. 1922; life and non-life; fmrly Companhia Europeia de Seguros, SA; net profits 9.6m. (2006); CEO Dr José António Sousa.

Lusitânia—Companhia de Seguros, SA: Rua São Domingos à Lapa 35–41, 1249-130 Lisbon; tel. (21) 3926900; fax (21) 3973090; e-mail sede@lusitania-cs.pt; internet www.lusitania-cs.pt; non-life; net profits 2.3m. (2006); Pres. Dr José da Silva Lopes.

MAPFRE Seguros Gerais, SA: Rua Castilho 52, 1250-071 Lisbon; tel. (21) 3819700; fax (21) 3819799; e-mail martafernandes@mapfre.pt; internet www.mapfre.pt; f. 1998; non-life; net profits 5.3m., cap. 33.1m. (2006); CEO António Belo (acting).

Real Seguros, SA: Edif. Capitólio, Av. de França 316, 4050-276 Porto; tel. (22) 8330100; fax (22) 8330149; e-mail info@realseguros.pt; internet www.realseguros.pt; f. 1988; non-life; net profits 7.3m. (2006); Pres. Fernando Soares Ferreira.

Totta Seguros—Companhia de Seguros de Vida, SA: Rua da Mesquita 6, Torre A, S. S. Pedreira, Lisbon; internet www.totta.pt; life; net profits 10.9m. (2006); Pres. Pedro Aires Coruche de Castro e Almeida.

Victoria—Seguros de Vida, SA/Victoria—Seguros, SA: Edif. Victoria, Av. da Liberdade 200, 1250-147 Lisbon; tel. (21) 3134450; fax (21) 334451; e-mail victoria@victoria-seguros.pt; internet www.victoria-seguros.pt; f. 1930/1981; transferred to private sector in 1993; life and pensions; non-life; total net profits 7.0m. (2006); Pres. Michael Rosenberg.

Zurich—Companhia de Seguros, SA/Zurich—Companhia de Seguros Vida, SA: Rua Barata Salgueiro 41, 1269-058 Lisbon; tel. (21) 3133100; fax (21) 3133111; internet www.zurichportugal.com; f. 1918; fmrly Companhia de Seguros Metrópole; net profits (non-life) 25.7m., (life) 5.8m. (2006); Pres. Dr Nuno Maria Serra Soares da Fonseca; Chief Exec. José M. Coelho.

Mutual Companies

Mútua dos Armadores da Pesca do Arrasto: Av. António Augusto de Aguiar 7, 1°, 1069-145 Lisbon; tel. (21) 3561051; fax (21) 3561058; f. 1942; marine and workers' compensation, personal accident, sickness, fire, etc.; Pres. Dr António Alberto Carvalho da Cunha.

Mútua dos Pescadores—Mútua dos Seguros, C.R.L.: Av. Santos Dumont 57, 6°, 1050-202 Lisbon; tel. (21) 3936300; fax (21) 3936310; e-mail geral@mutuapescadores.pt; internet www.mutuapescadores.pt; f. 1942; co-operative; personal accident, marine, fire, workers' compensation, etc.; net profits 0.5m. (2007); Dir-Gen. Jerónimo Teixeira.

Trade and Industry

GOVERNMENT AGENCIES

AICEP Portugal Global: Av. 5 de Outubro 101, 1050-051 Lisbon; tel. (21) 7909500; fax (21) 7935028; e-mail aicep@portugalglobal.pt; internet www.portugalglobal.pt; fmrly Agência para o Investimento e Comércio Externo de Portugal; promotes internationalization of the Portuguese economy; Chair. and Chief Exec. Basílio Horta.

Autoridade de Segurança Alimentar e Económica (ASAE): Av. Conde de Valbom 98, 1050-070 Lisbon; tel. (21) 7983600; fax (21) 7983654; e-mail correio.asae@asae.pt; internet www.asae.pt; f. 2005; regulatory authority for food safety and economic activities (Ministry of the Economy and Innovation); Inspector-Gen. Dr António Nunes.

Gabinete de Estratégia e Estudos (GEE): Av. da República 79, 1050-243 Lisbon; tel. (21) 7998150; fax (21) 7998154; e-mail gee@gee.min-economia.pt; internet www.gee.min-economia.pt; advises on economic policy and strategy (Ministry of the Economy and Innovation); Dir Miguel Lebre de Freitas.

Instituto de Apoio às Pequenas e Médias Empresas e a Inovação (IAPMEI): Rua Rodrigo da Fonseca 73, 1269-158 Lisbon; tel. (21) 3836000; fax (21) 3836283; internet www.iapmei.pt; financial and technical support to small and medium-sized enterprises (Ministry of the Economy and Innovation); Pres. Jaime Serrão Andrez.

Instituto de Financiamento da Agricultura e Pescas (IFAP): Rua Castilho 45–51, 1269-163 Lisbon; tel. (21) 3846000; fax (21) 3846170; e-mail ifap@ifap.min-agricultura.pt; internet www.ifap.min-agricultura.pt; f. 2007; provides loans for agriculture and fisheries, acts as intermediary with the European Agricultural Guarantee Fund (EAGF), the European Agricultural Fund for Rural

PORTUGAL

Development (EAFRD) and the European Fisheries Fund (EFF); Pres. Dr Joaquim Mestre.

Instituto Nacional de Engenharia Tecnologia e Inovação (INETI): Estrada do Paço do Lumiar, 1649-038 Lisbon; tel. (21) 0924602; fax (21) 71619211; e-mail teresa.leao@ineti.pt; internet www.ineti.pt; f. 1977; industrial and technological research (Ministry of the Economy and Innovation); Pres. Prof. Maria Teresa Costa Pereira da Silva Ponce de Leão.

Instituto Português de Apoio ao Desenvolvimento (IPAD): Av. da Liberdade 192, 2°, 1250-147 Lisbon; tel. (21) 3176700; fax (21) 3147897; e-mail cooperacao.portuguesa@ipad.mne.gov.pt; internet www.ipad.mne.gov.pt; f. 2003; part of Ministry of Foreign Affairs; supports international devt; Pres. Augusto Manuel Correia.

Instituto Português da Qualidade (IPQ): Rua António Gião 2, 2829-513 Caparica; tel. (21) 2948100; fax (21) 2948101; e-mail ipq@mail.ipq.pt; internet www.ipq.pt; manages and develops the Portuguese Quality System (Ministry of the Economy and Innovation); Pres. José Manuel Diogo Marques dos Santos.

DEVELOPMENT ORGANIZATIONS

Centro para o Desenvolvimento e Inovação Tecnológicos (CEDINTEC): Rua de São Domingos à Lapa 117, 2° dto, 1200-834 Lisbon; tel. (21) 3955302; fax (21) 3961203; e-mail geral@cedintec.pt; internet www.cedintec.pt; f. 1982; supports the creation of technological infrastructures; Pres. Eng. João Pedro de Saldanha Verschneider Gonçalves.

Cotec Portugal: Rua de Salazares 842, 4149-002 Porto; tel. (22) 6192910; fax (22) 6192919; e-mail secretariado@cotec.pt; internet www.cotec.pt; f. 2003; co-ordinates research and innovation between public and private bodies; Pres. Dr Artur Santos Silva; Dir-Gen. Prof. Rui Campos Guimarães.

Instituto do Vinho do Douro e do Porto (IVDP): Rua dos Camilos 90, 5050 Peso da Régua; tel. (25) 4320130; fax (25) 4320149; e-mail ivdp@ivdp.pt; internet www.ivdp.pt; an official body dealing with quality control and the promotion of port and Douro wines; also gives technical advice to exporters; Pres. Eng. Jorge Nicolau da Costa Monteiro.

Sociedade de Desenvolvimento da Madeira (SDM): Rua da Mouraria 9, 1°, 9000-047 Funchal, Madeira; tel. (291) 201333; fax (291) 201399; e-mail sdm@sdm.pt; internet www.sdm.pt; concessionaire of Madeira's International Business Centre; Chair. Dr Francisco Costa.

Sociedade Nacional de Empreendimentos e Desenvolvimento Económico, SA (SNEDE): Av. Fontes Pereira de Melo 35, 19a, 1050-118 Lisbon; tel. and fax (21) 3139889; e-mail snede@mail.telepac.pt; internet www.snede.pt; f. 1976; private consultancy co in economy and management; Pres. Dr Alfredo Gonzalez Esteves Belo.

CHAMBERS OF COMMERCE AND TRADE ASSOCIATIONS

Associação Comercial e Industrial do Funchal/Câmara de Comércio e Indústria da Madeira (ACIF/CCIM): Rua dos Aranhas 24–26, 9000-044 Funchal; tel. (291) 206800; fax (291) 206868; e-mail geral@acif-ccim.pt; internet www.acif-ccim.pt; f. 1836; Pres. Francisco Miguel Azinhais Abreu dos Santos.

Associação Comercial de Lisboa/Câmara de Comércio e Indústria Portuguesa (ACL/CCIP): Palácio do Comércio, Rua das Portas de Santo Antão 89, 1169-022 Lisbon; tel. (21) 3224050; fax (21) 3224051; e-mail geral@port-chambers.com; internet www.port-chambers.com; f. 1834; Pres. Bruno Bobone; Sec.-Gen. Dr Pedro Madeira Rodrigues; 2,100 mems.

Associação Comercial do Porto/Câmara de Comércio e Indústria do Porto (ACP/CCIP): Palácio da Bolsa, Rua Ferreira Borges, 4050-253 Porto; tel. (22) 3399000; fax (22) 3399090; e-mail cciporto@mail.telepac.pt; internet www.cciporto.com; f. 1834; Pres. Dr Rui Moreira; 800 mems.

Associação Industrial Portuguesa—Confederação Empresarial (AIP-CE): Praça das Indústrias, Apdo 3200, 1300-965 Lisbon; tel. (21) 3601000; fax (21) 3641301; e-mail info@aip.pt; internet www.aip.pt; f. 1837; Chief Exec. António Manuel Vinagre Alfaiate; 4,500 mems (2008).

Câmara de Comércio e Indústria de Ponta Delgada/Associação Empresarial das Ilhas de São Miguel e Santa Maria (CCIPD): Rua Ernesto do Canto 13–15, 9504-531 Ponta Delgada, Azores; tel. (296) 305000; fax (296) 305050; e-mail ccipd@ccipd.pt; internet www.ccipd.pt; f. 1979; Dir Carlos Alberto da Costa Martins; 800 mems.

OTHER INDUSTRIAL AND TRADE ASSOCIATIONS

Associação dos Comerciantes e Industriais de Bebidas Espirituosas e Vinhos (ACIBEV): Largo do Carmo 15, 1°, 1200-095 Lisbon; tel. (21) 3462318; fax (21) 3427517; e-mail acibevmail@acibev.pt; internet www.acibev.pt; f. 1975; spirit and wine traders and manufacturers; Chair. Eng. João Calleya Serra; Pres. Dr António Soares Franco.

Associação Empresarial de Portugal: Av. da Boavista 2671, 4100-135 Porto; tel. (22) 6158500; fax (22) 6176840; e-mail aep@aeportugal.com; internet www.aeportugal.pt; f. 1849; represents industry in northern Portugal in all sectors; organizes trade fairs, exhibitions, congress, etc.; Pres. Eng. Angelo Ludgero Marques; 2,500 mems.

Associação dos Industriais e Exportadores de Cortiça (AIEC): Av. Duque de Avila 169, 2° esq., 1050-081 Lisbon; tel. (21) 3158506; fax (21) 3570878; e-mail geral@aiec.pt; internet www.aiec.pt; f. 1993; national asscn of cork manufacturers and exporters; Pres. Edmundo Pereira.

Associação Nacional de Comerciantes e Industriais de Produtos Alimentares (ANCIPA): Largo de São Sebastião da Pedreira 31, 1050-205 Lisbon; tel. (21) 3528803; fax (21) 3154665; e-mail ancipa@netcabo.pt; internet www.ancipa.pt; f. 1975; national asscn of food products manufacturers and traders; Pres. Manuel Fulgéncio Tarré Fernandes; Gen. Sec. Domitília Lopes de Almeida.

Associação Nacional das Indústrias de Vestuário e Confecção (ANIVEC/APIV): Av. da Boavista 3523, 7°, 4100-139 Porto; tel. (22) 6165470; fax (22) 6100049; e-mail geral@anivec.com; internet www.anivec.com; clothing manufacturers' asscn; Pres. Orlando Lopes da Cunha.

Associação Portuguesa da Indústria de Cerâmica (APICER): Edif. C, Rua Col Veiga Simão, 3020-053 Coimbra; tel. (239) 497600; fax (239) 497601; e-mail info@apicer.pt; internet www.apicer.pt; ceramics asscn; Pres. Duarte Manuel Palma Leal Garcia.

Associação Portuguesa de Cortiça (APCOR) (Portuguese Cork Association): Av. Comendador Henrique Amorim 580, 4536-904 Sta Maria de Lamas; tel. (22) 7474040; fax (22) 7474049; e-mail realcork@apcor.pt; internet www.corkmasters.com; www.apcor.pt; f. 1956; asscn of cork manufacturers and exporters; Pres. António Rios de Amorim.

Associação Portuguesa dos Industriais de Calçado, Componentes, e Artigos de Pele e seus Sucedâneos (APICCAPS): Rua Alves Redol 372, 4011-001 Porto; tel. (22) 5074150; fax (22) 5074179; e-mail apiccaps@mail.telepac.pt; internet www.apiccaps.pt; f. 1975; footwear and leather goods manufacturers' asscn; Pres. Fortunato Frederico.

Associação Têxtil e Vestuário de Portugal (ATP): Edif. do Citeve, Rua Fernando Mesquita 2785, 4760-034 Vila Nova de Famalicão; tel. (22) 5074250; fax (22) 5074259; e-mail atp@atp.pt; internet www.atp.pt; knitwear and ready-to-wear clothing industries; Pres. Dr Paulo Nunes de Almeida.

Confederação dos Agricultores de Portugal (CAP): Av. do Colégio Militar, Lote 1786, 1549-012 Lisbon; tel. (21) 7100000; fax (21) 7166122; e-mail cap@cap.pt; internet www.cap.pt; farmers' confederation; Pres. João Pedro Gorjão Ciryllo Machado.

Confederação do Comércio e Serviços de Portugal (CCP): Av. D. Vasco da Gama 29, 1449-032 Lisbon; tel. (21) 3031380; fax (21) 3031400; e-mail ccp@ccp.pt; internet www.ccp.pt; f. 1976; Pres. Dr José António da Silva; c. 100 mem. trade asscns.

Confederação da Indústria Portuguesa (CIP): Av. 5 de Outubro 35, 1°, 1069-193 Lisbon; tel. (21) 3164700; fax (21) 3579986; e-mail geral@cip.org.pt; internet www.cip.org.pt; f. 1974; represents employers; Pres. Francisco van Zeller; over 35,000 mems.

UTILITIES

In 2006 Spain and Portugal began operating an integrated electricity market, the Mercado Ibérico de Electricidade (MIBEL). One of the world's largest solar power plants, an 11-MW station near Serpa in Alentejo, opened in 2007.

Regulatory Authority

Entidade Reguladora dos Serviços Energéticos (ERSE): Rua Dom Cristovão da Gama 1, 1400-113 Lisbon; tel. (21) 3033200; fax (21) 3033201; e-mail erse@erse.pt; internet www.erse.pt; regulator of electricity and natural gas in Portugal; Pres. Prof. Vítor Manuel da Silva Santos.

Electricity

Rede Eléctrica Nacional, SA (REN): Av. Estados Unidos da América 55, 1749-061 Lisbon; tel. (21) 0013500; fax (21) 0013950; e-mail secretariaren@ren.pt; internet www.ren.pt; f. 1994; subsidiary of Redes Energéticas Nacionais, SGPS, SA; concessionaire of the Portuguese transmission grid and transmission system operator in mainland Portugal; Pres. José Rodrigues Pereira dos Penedos.

Energias de Portugal—EDP, SA: Praça Marquês de Pombal 12, 1250-162 Lisbon; tel. (21) 0012500; fax (21) 0021403; internet www.edp.pt; fmrly Electricidade de Portugal; production, purchase,

PORTUGAL   *Directory*

transport, distribution and sale of electrical energy in Portugal and Spain (via Hidrocantábrico); partially privatized in 2004; Pres. ANTÓNIO MEXIA.

EDP Comercial—Comercialização de Energia, SA: Rua Camilo Castelo Branco 46, 5°, 1050-045 Lisbon; tel. (21) 0015318; fax (21) 0015491; internet www.corporate.edp.pt; Pres. Eng. JORGE CRUZ MORAIS.

EDP Distribuição—Energia, SA: Rua Camilo Castelo Branco 43, 1050-044 Lisbon; tel. (21) 0021000; fax (21) 0021610; internet www.edp.pt; electricity distribution.

EDP Produção—Gestãoda Produção de Energia, SA: Av. José Malhoa, Lote A-13, 1070-157 Lisbon; tel. (21) 0012300; fax (21) 0012490; e-mail geral@edpproducao.edp.pt; internet www.edp.pt; production and sale of electrical energy; in 2005 the Govt reduced its stake from 30% to 10%; Pres. Eng. JOÃO TALONE; Vice-Pres. Eng. JORGE RIBEIRINHO MACHADO.

Gas

REN Gasodutos, SA: Av. Estados Unidos da América 55, 1749-061 Lisbon; tel. (21) 0013500; fax (21) 0013950; e-mail secretariaren@ren.pt; internet www.ren.pt; f. 2006; subsidiary of Redes Energéticas Nacionais, SGPS, SA; concessionaire of the national gas transmission network; Pres. JOSÉ RODRIGUES PEREIRA DOS PENEDOS.

Galp Energia, SGPS, SA: Edif. Galp Energia, Rua Tomás de Fonseca, 1600-209 Lisbon; tel. (21) 7242500; fax (21) 7242965; e-mail comunicacao@galpenergia.com; internet www.galpenergia.com; partially privatized in 2000; also comprises Petróleos de Portugal (Petrogal), SA, a petroleum refining co, and Gás de Portugal (GDP), SA, a gas distribution co; Chair. FRANCISCO LUÍS MURTEIRA NABO; CEO MANUEL FERREIRA DE OLIVEIRA.

Lisboagás GDL—Sociedade Distribuidora de Gás Natural de Lisboa, SA: Rua Tomás da Fonseca, Torre C, 1600-209 Lisbon; tel. (21) 7242500; fax (21) 8681161; regional natural gas distribution; there are five other regional distributors operating in Portugal: Portgás, Lusitâniagás, Setgás, Tagusgás and Beiragás; Pres. Dr JOÃO CARLOS FEVEREIRO FERREIRA DE LIMA.

Water

Aguas de Portugal, SGPS, SA (AdP): Rua Visconde de Seabra 3, 1700-421 Lisbon; tel. (21) 2469500; fax (21) 2469501; e-mail info@adp.pt; internet www.adp.pt; f. 1993; Pres. PEDRO CUNHA SERRA.

TRADE UNIONS

Confederação Geral dos Trabalhadores Portugueses-Intersindical Nacional (CGTP-IN) (General Confederation of Portuguese Workers): Rua Victor Cordon 1, 2°, 1249-102 Lisbon; tel. (21) 3236500; fax (21) 3236695; e-mail cgtp@cgtp.pt; internet www.cgtp.pt; f. 1970; reorganized 1974; 107 affiliated unions; 704,048 mems; Sec.-Gen. MANUEL CARVALHO DA SILVA.

União Geral dos Trabalhadores de Portugal (UGTP): Rua Buenos Aires 11, 1249-067 Lisbon; tel. (21) 3931200; fax (21) 3974612; e-mail ugt@mail.telepac.pt; internet www.ugt.pt; f. 1978; pro-socialist; comprises 58 unions and two feds; c. 0.9m. mems; Pres. JOÃO DIAS DA SILVA; Sec.-Gen. JOÃO PROENÇA.

Transport

RAILWAYS

In 2006 the total length of the rail track totalled 3,614.8 km, of which 1,436.2 km was electrified. In 2005 the Government announced plans to develop two high-speed rail links connecting Lisbon and Oporto with the Spanish capital, Madrid. Construction was to begin in 2008, with the Lisbon–Madrid link scheduled to open in 2013, followed by the link to Oporto in 2015.

Rede Ferroviária Nacional—REFER, E.P.: Estação de Santa Apolónia, Largo dos Caminhos de Ferro, 1100-105 Lisbon; tel. (21) 1022000; fax (21) 1022439; internet www.refer.pt; f. 1997; assumed responsibility for rail infrastructure in 1999; Pres. LUÍS FILIPE MELO E SOUSA PARDAL.

Comboios de Portugal (CP): Calçada do Duque 20, 1249-109 Lisbon; tel. (21) 1023000; fax (21) 3473093; e-mail webmaster@mail.cp.pt; internet www.cp.pt; f. 1856; nationalized in 1975 as Caminhos de Ferro Portugueses; incorporated Sociedade Estoril Caminhos de Ferro from Cais do Sodré to Cascais in 1977; renamed as above in 2004; Pres. FRANCISCO JOSÉ CARDOSO DOS REIS.

Metropolitano de Lisboa, EP (ML): Av. Fontes Pereira de Melo 28, 1069-095 Lisbon; tel. (21) 7980600; fax (21) 7980605; e-mail relacoes.publicas@metrolisboa.pt; internet www.metrolisboa.pt; opened 1959; operates the underground system, consisting of 46 stations and four lines covering 37.7 km (2007); Pres. JOAQUIM JOSÉ DE OLIVEIRA REIS.

ROADS

In 2006 there were 12,890 km of roads in continental Portugal, of which 2,545 km were motorway.

Brisa (Auto-Estradas de Portugal, SA): Edif. Brisa, Quinta da Torre da Aguilha, 2785-599 São Domingos de Rana; tel. (21) 4448500; fax (21) 4448672; e-mail ir@brisa.pt; internet www.brisa.pt; f. 1972; responsible for construction, maintenance and operation of motorways; Pres. VASCO DE MELLO.

Estradas de Portugal (EP): Praça da Portagem, 2809-013 Almada; tel. (21) 2879000; fax (21) 2951997; e-mail ep@estradasdeportugal.pt; internet www.estradasdeportugal.pt; f. 1999 as Instituto de Estradas de Portugal; merged with Instituto para a Conservação e Exploração da Rede Rodoviária (ICERR) and Instituto para a Construção Rodoviária (ICOR) in 2002; renamed as above in 2004; road infrastructure policy, construction and maintenance of the road network; Pres. ALMERINDO MARQUES.

SHIPPING

The principal Portuguese ports are Lisbon, Leixões (Oporto), Setúbal and Funchal (Madeira). The ports of Portimão (Algarve) and the Azores regularly receive international cruise liners. At December 2006 Portugal's registered merchant fleet comprised 460 vessels, totalling 1,223,616 grt.

Principal Shipping Companies

Portline (Transportes Marítimos Internacionais, SA): Av. Infante D. Henrique 332, 3°, 1849-025 Lisbon; tel. (21) 8391800; fax (21) 8376680; e-mail mail@portline.pt; internet www.portline.pt; f. 1984; marine transport; Gen. Man. MANUEL PINTO DE MAGALHÃES.

Sacor Marítima, SA: Rua do Açúcar 86, 1950-010 Lisbon; tel. (21) 3585100; fax (21) 3585195; e-mail sacor.maritima@petrogal.pt; tanker transport; Chair. LUÍS MARTINS CARNEIRO.

CIVIL AVIATION

There are international airports at Lisbon, Oporto, Faro (Algarve), Funchal (Madeira), Santa Maria (Azores) and São Miguel (Azores). Construction of a second international airport serving Lisbon was to be completed by 2017.

TAP Portugal: Aeroporto de Lisboa, CP 50194, 1704-801 Lisbon; tel. (21) 8415000; fax (21) 8415881; e-mail gcrp.com@tap.pt; internet www.flytap.com; f. 1945; due to be partially privatized in 2007–08; national airline serving destinations in Europe, Africa, North, Central and South America; scheduled, international, domestic, passenger and cargo services; joined Star Alliance in 2005; Chair. of Supervisory Board MANUEL PINTO BARBOSA; CEO FERNANDO PINTO.

Portugália Airlines (PGA): Edif. 70, Aeroporto de Lisboa, Rua C, 1749-078 Lisbon; tel. (21) 8938070; fax (21) 8938049; f. 1988; subsidiary of TAP Portugal; regional airline operating scheduled and charter, international and domestic flights from Lisbon.

SATA (Air Açores—Serviço Açoreano de Transportes Aéreos—EP): Av. Infante D. Henrique 55, 9505-528 Ponta Delgada, São Miguel, 9500 Azores; tel. (296) 209727; fax (296) 209722; e-mail pdlsd@sata.pt; internet www.sata.pt; f. 1941; owned by the regional govt of the Azores; inter-island services in the Azores archipelago; Pres. and Chief Exec. ANTÓNIO GOMES DE MENEZES.

Tourism

Portugal is popular with visitors because of its mild and clement weather. Apart from Lisbon and the Algarve on the mainland, Madeira and the Azores are much favoured as winter resorts. In 2005 the number of tourist arrivals at accommodation establishments totalled 5.7m. and revenue from tourism (including passenger transport) totalled US $9,222m.

Turismo de Portugal: Rua Ivone Silva 6, 1050-124 Lisbon; tel. (21) 7808800; fax (21) 7937537; e-mail correio@turismodeportugal.pt; internet www.turismodeportugal.pt; f. 2007 to replace the Direcção-Geral do Turismo, the Instituto de Formação Turística and the Instituto de Turismo de Portugal; an agency of the Ministry of the Economy and Innovation; Pres. LUÍS MANUEL DOS SANTOS SILVA PATRÃO.

QATAR

Introductory Survey

Location, Climate, Language, Religion, Flag, Capital

The State of Qatar occupies a peninsula, projecting northwards from the Arabian mainland, on the west coast of the Persian (Arabian) Gulf. It is bordered, to the south, by Saudi Arabia and the United Arab Emirates. The archipelago of Bahrain lies to the north-west. On the opposite side of the Gulf lies Iran. The climate is exceptionally hot in the summer, when temperatures may reach 49°C (120°F), with high humidity on the coast; conditions are relatively mild in the winter. Rainfall is negligible. The official language is Arabic. Almost all of the inhabitants are adherents of Islam, although an influx of guest workers in recent years has precipitated official recognition of Christian denominations. Native Qataris, who comprise less than one-third of the total population, belong mainly to the strictly orthodox Wahhabi sect of Sunni Muslims. The national flag (proportions 11 by 28) is maroon, with a broad vertical white stripe at the hoist, the two colours being separated by a serrated line. The capital is Doha.

Recent History

Qatar was formerly dominated by the al-Khalifa family of Bahrain. The peninsula became part of Turkey's Ottoman Empire in 1872, but Turkish forces evacuated Qatar at the beginning of the First World War (1914–18). The United Kingdom recognized Sheikh Abdullah ath-Thani as Ruler of Qatar, and in 1916 made a treaty with him, providing British protection against aggression in return for supervision of Qatar's external affairs. A 1934 treaty extended fuller British protection to Qatar.

In October 1960 Sheikh Ali ath-Thani, Ruler of Qatar since 1949, abdicated in favour of his son, Sheikh Ahmad. In 1968 the British Government announced its intention to withdraw British forces from the Persian (Arabian) Gulf area by 1971. Qatar thus attempted to associate itself with Bahrain and Trucial Oman (now the United Arab Emirates—UAE) in a proposed federation. In April 1970 Sheikh Ahmad announced a provisional Constitution, providing for a partially elected Consultative Assembly, although he retained effective power. In May the Deputy Ruler, Sheikh Khalifa ath-Thani (a cousin of Sheikh Ahmad), was appointed Prime Minister. After the failure of attempts to agree terms for union with neighbouring Gulf countries, Qatar became fully independent on 1 September 1971, whereupon the Ruler took the title of Amir. The 1916 treaty was replaced by a new treaty of friendship with the United Kingdom.

In February 1972 the Amir was deposed in a bloodless coup. Claiming support from the royal family and the armed forces, Sheikh Khalifa proclaimed himself Amir. Sheikh Khalifa, who retained the premiership, adopted a policy of wide-ranging social and economic reform, and the previous extravagance and privileges of the royal family were curbed. In accordance with the 1970 Constitution, the Amir appointed an Advisory Council in April 1972 to complement the ministerial Government. The Council was expanded from 20 to 30 members in 1975 and to 35 members in 1988. Its term was extended for four years in 1978, and for further four-year terms in 1982, 1986, 1990, 1994 and 1998.

On 27 June 1995 the Deputy Amir, Heir Apparent, Minister of Defence and Commander-in-Chief of the Armed Forces, Maj.-Gen. Sheikh Hamad bin Khalifa ath-Thani, deposed his father in a bloodless coup. Sheikh Hamad proclaimed himself Amir, claiming the support of the royal family and the Qatari people. Sheikh Khalifa, who was in Switzerland at the time of the coup, immediately denounced his son's actions, and vowed to return to Qatar. Although Sheikh Khalifa had effectively granted Sheikh Hamad control of the emirate's affairs (with the exception of the treasury) in 1992, a power struggle was reported to have emerged between the two in the months prior to the coup: Sheikh Khalifa was particularly opposed to his son's independent foreign policy (notably the strengthening of relations with both Iran and Iraq, and with Israel), and had attempted to regain influence in policy-making. Sheikh Hamad, however, reputedly enjoyed widespread support both nationally and internationally, and his domestic reforms were perceived as having contributed to Qatar's stability at a time when social unrest and Islamist extremism were emerging in the region. The United Kingdom, the USA and Saudi Arabia swiftly recognized the new Amir. In July 1995 Sheikh Hamad reorganized the Council of Ministers and appointed himself Prime Minister, while retaining the posts of Minister of Defence and Commander-in-Chief of the Armed Forces.

Meanwhile, the deposed Amir took residence in the UAE, and visited several other countries of the region in an apparent attempt to assert his legitimacy as ruler of Qatar. In January 1996 it was confirmed that Sheikh Khalifa had gained control of a substantial part of Qatar's financial reserves. In the following month security forces in Qatar were reported to have foiled an attempted coup. As many as 100 people were arrested, and a warrant was issued for the arrest of Sheikh Hamad bin Jasim bin Hamad ath-Thani, a former government minister and a cousin of the Amir. Sheikh Khalifa denied any involvement, although he was quick to imply that the alleged plot indicated popular support for his return. In July legal proceedings were initiated in Qatar, Europe and the USA in an attempt to recover some US $3,000m.–$8,000m. in overseas assets that were asserted by the new Amir to have been amassed by his father from state oil and investment revenues. In October, however, it was reported that Sheikh Hamad and Sheikh Khalifa had been reconciled and had reached an out-of-court settlement regarding the return of state funds. By early 1997 all lawsuits issued against the former Amir had been withdrawn. In November 1997, meanwhile, the trial began of 110 people (40 of whom were charged *in absentia*) accused of involvement in the attempted coup of February 1996. Hearings were immediately adjourned. A number of those being tried *in absentia* were apprehended during 1998, including Qatar's former deputy head of intelligence, who was extradited from Yemen.

In October 1996 Sheikh Hamad named the third of his four sons, Sheikh Jasim bin Hamad bin Khalifa ath-Thani, as Heir Apparent. The Amir subsequently appointed his younger brother, Sheikh Abdullah bin Khalifa ath-Thani (the Minister of the Interior), as Prime Minister. Further to the ending of media censorship earlier in the year, the post of Minister of Information and Culture was abolished. (The relevant ministry was dissolved in March 1998.) In November 1996 Sheikh Hamad announced the creation of a new Defence Council, over which he would preside. The Council, to be comprised of senior ministers and armed forces and security personnel, was expected to function in an advisory and consultative capacity. It was also reported that the Amir had appointed the Gulf region's first female member of government (as Under-Secretary of State for Education and Culture).

Elections to Qatar's new 29-member Central Municipal Council (CMC), held by universal suffrage on 8 March 1999, were the first in the country's history. Announced by Sheikh Hamad in November 1997 and provided for by law in July 1998, the CMC was to have a consultative role in the operations of the Ministry of Municipal Affairs and Agriculture. The rate of participation by voters reportedly exceeded 90% in Doha, and was estimated at 60%–70% of the registered electorate in rural areas. However, only about 22,000 voters of an eligible 40,000 actually participated in the elections.

In July 1999 a 32-member constitutional committee was established to draft a permanent constitution; this was to include provision for the creation of a new National Assembly. The committee produced a draft constitution in July 2002, which provided for a separation of the executive, the judiciary and the legislature, but which would retain executive power in the hands of the Amir and the Council of Ministers. The draft constitution also guaranteed freedom of expression, religion and association, and provided for the establishment of an independent judiciary and of a new 45-member Consultative Council (to replace the Advisory Council), comprising 30 elected and 15 appointed members. Under the proposed constitution, the Amir would be obliged to provide reasons for rejecting draft laws adopted by the Council. The Amir would be required to approve such legislation sent to him a second time by the Council with two-thirds' majority support, although he would have a discretionary right to halt implementation of laws in question on a temporary basis if he deemed this to be in the greater interests of the country. The parliament was to have a four-year mandate, and suffrage was to be extended to all citizens, including women, aged 18 years and above. In a referendum held in April 2003, an overwhelming majority (96.6%) of the 71,406 voters approved the new Constitution, and it was expected that the affirmative vote would lead to legislative elections being conducted in 2004. These were delayed, however, and in March 2005 the Amir announced that the elections would take place between June 2005 and June 2006. In December 2005 the First Deputy Prime Minister and Minister of Foreign Affairs, Sheikh Hamad bin Jasim bin Jaber ath-Thani, stated that preparations were now directed at holding the elections in early 2007. The delay was apparently related partly to the controversy over the legal status of the Murra tribe, whose Qatari citizenship had been revoked after it had been discovered that some members of the tribe also held Saudi citizenship. Dual nationality is not recognized under Qatari law and some members of the tribe were expelled to Saudi Arabia over the issue; in addition, it was alleged that severe punishments were extended to individuals who expressed sympathy for the victims. It was reported in February 2006, however, that the tribe members were expected to have their Qatari citizenship returned. In October it was announced that only 'original' Qatari nationals above the age of 30 would be eligible to register as candidates in the elections. The projected deadline of early 2007 for the staging of elections lapsed, and it was announced in February 2008 that further delays—while an appropriate legal framework was finalized and implemented—were expected, thus rendering the possibility of a ballot before the end of the year unlikely.

Meanwhile, Sheikh Hamad bin Jasim bin Hamad ath-Thani was arrested in July 1999 for his alleged role in the coup plot of 1996. The trial of those accused of involvement in the coup ended in February 2000, with the former minister and 32 co-defendants sentenced to life imprisonment; 85 others were acquitted. Appeal proceedings were subsequently lodged by all 33 who had been convicted. In May 2001 the Court of Appeal overruled the previous sentences of life imprisonment, sentencing to death 19 of the defendants (including Sheikh Hamad bin Jasim bin Hamad); the court was also reported to have sentenced 26 defendants to terms of life imprisonment, and acquitted two others.

In January 2002 it was reported that a group styling itself the General Congress of the Qatari Opposition had emerged to demand that the Amir stand down in favour of his son, Crown Prince Jasim. The group, which claimed to include former members of the armed forces, tribal chiefs, businessmen, students and officials who had served under the previous regime, accused the Amir of pursuing 'reckless' policies, of corruption and of alienating Qatar's Gulf neighbours. This last charge was interpreted as possibly referring not only to Qatar's pursuit of an increasingly independent foreign policy but also to the activities of Al-Jazeera, a satellite television station linked to the ath-Thani family with a wide audience throughout the region. Al-Jazeera's reporting style and scope of coverage had on occasions caused several governments to threaten to restrict its freedom to operate in their country: notably, in May 2002 authorities in Bahrain announced that the station was to be banned from reporting there, apparently in response to its recent unauthorized coverage of anti-US demonstrations in Bahrain, and in June the Jordanian Government ordered the closure of Al-Jazeera's Amman office after the station broadcast programmes considered unfavourable to Jordan. In January 2005 it was announced that Al-Jazeera was to be privatized; the sale was regarded as a means of distancing the Qatari Government from Al-Jazeera's more controversial broadcasts and was a further indication of the closeness of the relationship between Qatar and the US Administration, which had allegedly considered launching a military attack on the station. An English-language sister channel, Al-Jazeera English, was launched in November 2006, together with a complementary website, which served to raise the organization's international profile by securing the participation of respected media personalities and by establishing broadcast centres in Malaysia, the United Kingdom and the USA.

The second elections to the CMC were held on 7 April 2003. A turn-out of about 35% was estimated for the country as a whole, but the rate of participation was reportedly as low as 25% of the registered electorate at several polling stations, including in the largest constituency, al-Kharitaat. A female candidate was elected unopposed after the competing candidates stood aside, and thus became the first woman in the Gulf region to hold elected office, but none of the five other women who contested the elections was successful. Three further candidates were also elected unopposed, and the remaining 25 seats were contested by 85 candidates, including 18 incumbents. In May the Amir appointed Sheikha bint Ahmad al-Mahmoud as Minister of Education; she replaced Dr Ahmad bin Khalifa Busherbak al-Mansouri and became the first woman to join the Council of Ministers. Further government changes were effected in December, when Sheikh Muhammad bin Ahmad bin Jassim ath-Thani replaced Sheikh Hamad bin Faisal ath-Thani as Minister of Economy and Commerce, and in March 2004 when the Amir appointed Sultan bin Hassan adh-Dhabit ad-Dousary as Minister of Municipal Affairs and Agriculture in place of Ali bin Saad al-Kawari.

Meanwhile, in February 2004 the Government approved an anti-terrorism law, which included the provision of the death penalty for anyone who killed 'through a terror act' and for anyone 'founding, organizing or managing a group or organization to commit a terror act'. In addition, the crime of assisting a terrorist group was to be punishable by a life sentence. In May a law permitting the formation of trade unions was approved. In addition, the legislation granted workers the right to strike, banned children aged under 16 years from employment and set a maximum eight-hour working day.

In December 2004 Sheikh Hamad bin Nasser bin Jasim ath-Thani was demoted from the position of Minister of State for the Interior to that of Minister of State without Portfolio; Sheikh Abdullah bin Nasser bin Khalifa ath-Thani, whose background was in the intelligence services, was appointed to the interior ministry as his replacement in February 2005. In April the Amir removed from their posts his Chief of Staff, Abdullah bin Muhammad bin Sa'ud ath-Thani, and two recently appointed ministers—Muhammad bin Abd al-Latif bin Abd ar-Rahman al-Mana, the Minister of Awqaf (Religious Endowments) and Islamic Affairs, and Muhammad bin Isa Hamad al-Mehannadi, the Minister of State for Council of Ministers' Affairs—amid allegations that three cabinet members and several businessmen had been questioned by officials over their connections to fraudulent activities relating to the sale of the state-owned Qatar Gas Transport Co (Nakilat) in early 2005. Faisal bin Abdullah al-Mahmud was awarded the religious affairs portfolio, ad-Dousary received the position of Minister of State for Council of Ministers' Affairs in addition to his existing responsibilities and Sheikh Abd ar-Rahman bin Sa'ud ath-Thani was appointed as the new Chief of Staff.

A bomb exploded outside a theatre frequented by Western expatriates in Doha in March 2005. One British citizen was killed in the suicide attack and 12 people were injured. The bomber was reported to be an Egyptian citizen, Omar Ahmad Abdullah Ali, and Jund ash-Sham (the Army of the Levant), a previously little known militant grouping, claimed responsibility for the attack. Although the bombing was the first of its kind in Qatar, Western embassies had previously issued warnings to expatriates that the threat from terrorism in the emirate was high.

In March 2006 the Minister of Economy and Commerce, Sheikh Muhammad, was unexpectedly dismissed from the Council of Ministers. No official explanation was given for his removal; however, the decision was widely believed to have been prompted by a recent crash on the Doha Securities Market. The ministerial portfolio was added to the responsibilities of the Minister of Finance, Yousuf bin Hussain Kamal, in an acting capacity. In September the Qatar Ladies' Forum was established, the stated objective of which was to aid the empowerment of women in Qatari society and thereby to facilitate their efforts to secure positions of power within, *inter alia*, government and trade and industry. In December Qatar hosted the Asian Games, becoming the first Arab nation to do so since the Games' inception in 1951; it was hoped that the publicity garnered by staging the event would have boosted Qatar's profile on the international stage, as well as significantly increasing tourism revenues in that year.

The third elections to the CMC, contested by 118 candidates, took place on 1 April 2007. Turn-out, although relatively low, exceeded expectations, at 51.1% of the electorate, compared with an estimated 35% in the 2003 polls. One of three female candidates was elected, securing more votes than any other candidate across the country. A few days later it was announced that the Prime Minister, Sheikh Abdullah, had resigned, but no explanation was offered for his decision. Sheikh Hamad, hitherto First Deputy Prime Minister and Minister of Foreign Affairs, was sworn in as his replacement; he retained the foreign affairs portfolio.

In July 1991 Qatar instituted proceedings at the International Court of Justice (ICJ) regarding sovereignty of the Hawar islands (in 1939 a British judgment had awarded sovereignty of the islands to Bahrain), the shoals of Fasht ad-Dibal and Qit'at Jaradah (over which the British had recognized Bahrain's 'sovereign rights' in 1947), together with the delimitation of the maritime border between Qatar and Bahrain. Bahrain's insistence that the two countries seek joint recourse to the ICJ was rejected by Qatar. The matter was further confused in April 1992, when the Government of Qatar issued a decree redefining its maritime borders to include territorial waters claimed by Bahrain. Furthermore, Bahrain attempted to widen the issue to include its long-standing claim to the area around Zubarah, in mainland Qatar. In February 1994 a hearing of the ICJ opened in The Hague, Netherlands, in order to determine whether the court was competent to rule on the dispute. In July the ICJ requested that Qatar and Bahrain resubmit their dispute by 30 November, either jointly or separately. The two states failed to reach agreement on joint presentation to the court, and in November Qatar submitted a unilateral request to pursue its case through the ICJ. In February 1995, while the ICJ declared that it would have authority to adjudicate in the dispute (despite Bahrain's refusal to accept the principle of an ICJ ruling), Saudi Arabia also proposed to act as mediator between the two countries. Qatar subsequently indicated its willingness to withdraw the case from the ICJ if Saudi arbitration proved successful.

Relations with Bahrain subsequently deteriorated, and in December 1996 Bahrain boycotted the annual summit meeting of the Co-operation Council for the Arab States of the Gulf (Gulf Co-operation Council—GCC, see p. 219), which took place in Doha. The meeting none the less decided to establish a quadripartite committee, comprising those GCC countries not involved in the dispute, to mediate between Qatar and Bahrain. The committee's efforts achieved a degree of success, and meetings between senior Qatari and Bahraini representatives in London, United Kingdom, and Manama, Bahrain, in early 1997 resulted in the announcement that diplomatic relations at ambassadorial level were to be established. In September, however, Bahrain challenged the authenticity of documents presented to the ICJ by Qatar in support of its territorial claim; the ICJ subsequently directed Qatar to produce a report on the authenticity of the documents by September 1998. Following the submission of the report, in which four experts differed in their opinion of the documents, Qatar announced its decision to disregard them, to enable the case to proceed 'without further procedural complications'.

In December 1999 the Amir made his first official visit to Manama, during which it was agreed that a joint committee, headed by the Crown Princes of Bahrain and Qatar, would be established to encourage bilateral co-operation. Qatar also agreed to withdraw its petition from the ICJ in the event of the joint committee reaching a solution to the territorial disputes. A second senior-level meeting was held in January 2000, when the new Amir of Bahrain made his first visit to Qatar. The two countries agreed to expedite the opening of embassies in Manama and Doha. In February, following the first meeting of the Bahrain-Qatar Supreme Joint Committee, it was announced that the possibility of constructing a causeway to link the two states was to be investigated. In May Bahrain announced its decision to suspend the activities of the Supreme Joint Committee pending the ICJ ruling on the dispute. Hearings at the ICJ, which began later that month, ended in June. The final verdict, issued in March 2001, was virtually identical to the British judgment of 1939. Bahrain was found to have sovereignty over the Hawar islands and Qit'at Jaradah, while Qatar held sovereignty over Zubarah, Janan island and the low-tide elevation of Fasht ad-Dibal; the Court drew a single maritime boundary between the two states. Both Qatar and Bahrain accepted the ICJ ruling, and declared that their territorial dispute was ended. Later in March 2001 it was announced that meetings of the Supreme Joint Committee would resume.

In August 2002 a Danish consortium completed a feasibility study for the construction of the planned causeway linking Qatar to Bahrain (the Friendship Bridge). Both Governments had approved the US $2,000m. project by May 2004, and international companies were invited to present bids for the contract in late 2004. By this time Bahrain and Qatar were reportedly discussing co-operation on gas projects and other economic issues. Following extensive negotiations, a memorandum of understanding between the Qatar and Bahrain Causeway Foundation and a Qatari-French joint venture in respect of the Friendship Bridge project was signed in September 2007. It was anticipated at that time that construction would commence in May 2008, with completion scheduled for 2011; however, the contract for the work had yet to be awarded by March 2008.

Following the multinational military operation to liberate Kuwait from Iraq in early 1991, Qatar resumed tentative contact with Iraq in 1993. In March 1995, during the first official visit to the country by a senior Iraqi official since the Gulf War, Iraq's Minister of Foreign Affairs met with his Qatari counterpart to discuss the furtherance of bilateral relations; the Qatari Minister subsequently indicated Qatar's determination to pursue a foreign policy independent from that of its GCC neighbours when he announced his country's support for the ending of UN sanctions against Iraq. In early 1998, as the crisis deepened regarding UN weapons inspections in Iraq (see the chapter on Iraq), Qatar urged a diplomatic solution, and appealed to Iraq to comply with all pertinent UN Security Council resolutions. With Qatar continuing to advocate an end to sanctions against Iraq, in December 2001 a meeting took place in Doha between the new Iraqi Minister of Foreign Affairs, Naji Sabri, and Qatari and Omani officials. In June 2003, after the removal of Saddam Hussain's regime by the US-led coalition, Qatar Airways became the first airline for 12 years to operate commercial air services to Iraq, after the scheduling of a bi-weekly service to Basra. Meanwhile, in September the US-appointed interim Cabinet in Iraq voted to expel Al-Jazeera reporters for one month, pending a review of their broadcasts, after the station was accused of inciting violence against US and Iraqi authorities. By early 2006 negotiations had yet to take place with the new Iraqi administration regarding the cancellation of the estimated US $4,000m. worth of debt owed to Qatar by Iraq, and in April 2008 the Iraqi Prime Minister, Nuri al-Maliki, urged the Gulf Arab states to agree to further debt relief.

In September 1992 tension arose with Saudi Arabia (with which Qatar had previously enjoyed close ties) when Qatar accused Saudi forces of attacking a Qatari border post, killing two border guards and capturing a third in the process. In protest, in October Qatar suspended a 1965 border agreement with Saudi Arabia (which had never been fully ratified) and temporarily withdrew its 200-strong contingent from the Saudi-based GCC 'Peninsula Shield' force (at the time stationed in Kuwait). The Saudi Government denied the involvement of its armed forces, claiming that the incident had been caused by fighting between rival Bedouin tribes within Saudi territory. Relations between the two countries reportedly improved as a result of Kuwaiti mediation, and the Qatari hostage was released later in October 1992; Qatar nevertheless registered its disaffection by not attending meetings of GCC ministers held in Abu Dhabi (the UAE) and Kuwait in November. In December, after mediation by Egypt, Sheikh Khalifa and King Fahd of Saudi Arabia signed an agreement whereby a committee was to be established formally to demarcate the border between the two states. In November 1994, however, Qatar boycotted a GCC ministerial meeting in Saudi Arabia, in protest at what it alleged to have been armed incidents on the border with Saudi Arabia in March and October. Bilateral relations appeared to improve in August 1995, when the new Amir held talks with King Fahd in Saudi Arabia. In December, nevertheless, Qatar boycotted the closing session of the annual GCC summit, following the appointment of a Saudi national as the next GCC Secretary-General (in preference to a Qatari candidate). In March 1996 the dispute was reported to have been settled, after mediation by Oman, and in April Qatar and Saudi Arabia agreed to establish a joint committee to complete the demarcation of their mutual border. Officials from both countries met in Saudi Arabia in June 1999 to sign the border demarcation maps. In March 2001, at a ceremony in Doha, Saudi and Qatari officials signed a final agreement concerning the land and maritime demarcation of their joint border; the accord included provision for a joint Saudi-

Qatari committee, whose task was to ensure that all provisions of the 1965 accord were implemented.

In October 2002 relations between Saudi Arabia and Qatar worsened, however, when the Saudi ambassador to Qatar was recalled following the airing of a television programme via the Al-Jazeera network that was deemed to be critical of the Saudi regime. Relations had already been strained by the expansion of US military facilities in Qatar and by the relocation, in April, of the main US air operations in the Gulf region from Saudi Arabia to Doha (see the chapter on Saudi Arabia). A visit to Jeddah, Saudi Arabia, undertaken by Sheikh Hamad in September 2007 engendered optimism for an improvement in bilateral ties, with the announcement of a number of agreements arising from the Amir's dialogue with King Abdullah: Sheikh Hamad gave an assurance that Al-Jazeera would not broadcast material that could be regarded as defamatory in respect of Saudi Arabia, in return for which Al-Jazeera would be permitted to establish a presence in the kingdom. Saudi Arabia also confirmed the return of its diplomatic envoy to Qatar, and King Abdullah agreed to attend the forthcoming GCC summit in Doha (an invitation he had refused in 2002, when Qatar had last hosted a meeting of the organization). Qatar's Amir subsequently attended a summit of the Organization of the Petroleum Exporting Countries (OPEC, see p. 373) in Saudi Arabia in November. The new Saudi ambassador to Qatar acceded to his position in February 2008, and relations were further bolstered in March following an official visit to the emirate by Crown Prince Sultan, cementing gestures of renewed co-operation and promoting the objectives of the GCC. Yet evidence of continuing bilateral tensions arose in February of that year, when a proposed regional policy to restrict the nature and content of satellite broadcasting, presented to members of the League of Arab States (the Arab League, see p. 332) by Saudi Arabia and Egypt, was openly opposed by Qatar. While international human rights organizations similarly rejected the proposed legislation as representing a significant threat to press freedoms, the issue demonstrated a persistent distrust between the Arab states and, regionally, of Al-Jazeera, whose often controversial broadcasts continued to precipitate diplomatic rifts between Qatar and its neighbours in the following months.

In January 1994 Qatar was reported to have commenced discussions with Israel regarding the supply of natural gas to that country, in apparent disregard for the Arab economic boycott of Israel. Following pressure from its GCC allies, Qatar subsequently announced that the proposed sale would depend on Israel's withdrawal from all Arab territories occupied in 1967. In September 1994, however, Qatar, along with the other GCC states, revoked aspects of the economic boycott of Israel. In November 1995 Israel signed a memorandum of intent to purchase Qatari liquefied natural gas (LNG). Relations between the two countries were consolidated further in April 1996, when Shimon Peres made the first official visit to Qatar by an Israeli Prime Minister. However, in late 1996 Israel declared that the memorandum of intent had expired, although negotiations would continue, and in November Qatar stated that any deal would be dependent on progress in the peace process. The fourth Middle East and North Africa economic summit was scheduled to take place in Doha in November 1997. However, in protest at the intended presence of representatives of Israel, which was regarded by the Arab states as failing to comply with its obligations with regard to the Middle East peace process, most of Qatar's fellow members of the Arab League and the GCC refused to attend. As a result of the boycott, the summit was downgraded to a conference, and was attended by representatives of only seven Arab states; a low-level Israeli delegation attended, as did the US Secretary of State, Madeleine Albright.

In March 1998 the Qatari Government stated that it was reviewing its relations with Israel, given the severe difficulties in the Middle East peace process. Nevertheless, Qatar was criticized by other Arab states in September 2000 following a meeting in New York, USA, at the UN Millennium Summit between the Amir and the Israeli Prime Minister, Ehud Barak. Prior to the ninth conference of the Organization of the Islamic Conference (OIC, see p. 369), held in Doha in November, several Islamic states (notably Saudi Arabia and Iran) threatened to boycott the summit unless Qatar agreed to sever its low-level diplomatic relations with Israel. (Arab and Islamic states were keen to demonstrate support for the Palestinians in their renewed uprising against Israeli occupation from late September.) The Qatari leadership apparently bowed to regional pressure when, in November, it announced that the Israeli trade office in Doha was to be closed, although there were subsequent reports that the office was still functioning. An emergency session of the OIC was convened in Doha in December 2001 to demonstrate solidarity with the Palestinians as the crisis deepened still further; Sheikh Hamad proposed the establishment of a panel comprising prominent representatives of the Islamic community to lobby Western governments to support an independent Palestinian state. In March 2002 Qatar's Minister of Foreign Affairs travelled to the Palestinian territories for talks with the leader of the Palestinian (National) Authority (PA), Yasser Arafat, who at that time remained under Israeli siege in Ramallah. In late 2002 it was again reported that the Israeli trade office in Doha was still functioning; Qatar's continuing refusal to close the establishment exacerbated tensions with Saudi Arabia in particular. In October 2006 the Secretary-General of the GCC, Abd ar-Rahman al-Attiya, praised Qatar's mediation efforts between the two rival Palestinian movements Hamas and Fatah, singling out in particular the endeavours of Sheikh Hamad. In the same month the Israeli Vice-Prime Minister and Minister of Foreign Affairs, Tzipi Livni, cancelled a scheduled visit to Doha to attend an international conference upon learning that the PA was to be represented by members of Hamas, which refuses to recognize the State of Israel.

Delegations from both Israel and Qatar attended the 62nd UN General Assembly in New York in September 2007. At a meeting with Livni initiated by Sheikh Hamad, the Israeli Minister of Foreign Affairs reiterated the importance of the involvement of 'moderate' Arab states in regional discussions towards promoting political negotiations with the Palestinians, and appealed for greater solidarity with Israel against the emergence of extremist elements in the region. Despite Qatar's unprecedented, and isolated, invitation to Iran to attend the GCC's annual summit meeting, held in Doha on 3–4 December (see below), Livni maintained Israeli dialogue with Qatar and subsequently embarked on a series of diplomatic visits to the country in early 2008, including attendance at the Doha Forum on Democracy, Development and Free Trade in mid-April. While Qatar, together with other GCC members, strongly condemned Israel's renewed military offensive in the Gaza Strip in January 2008 (see the chapters on Israel and the Palestinian Autonomous Areas), in February the country pledged its willingness to facilitate a cease-fire agreement between Israel and Hamas. Qatar's accommodation of the Israeli Minister of Foreign Affairs, however, precipitated the withdrawal from the conference of several other participants, notably members of the Hezbollah-led opposition in Lebanon.

An emergency summit meeting of the OIC was convened in Doha in October 2001, in response to the previous month's suicide attacks against New York and Washington, DC, and the subsequent commencement of US-led military action against targets in Afghanistan linked to the Taliban regime and to the al-Qa'ida (Base) organization of Osama bin Laden, the Saudi-born fundamentalist Islamist held principally responsible for the attacks in the USA.

Despite Qatar's active support for an end to UN sanctions against Iraq, and its pursuit of contacts with the incumbent regime of Saddam Hussain (see above), by the time US Vice-President Dick Cheney visited Qatar in March 2002—as part of a tour of the Gulf aimed at garnering support for a potential extension of the US-led 'war on terror' to target the Iraqi regime—Qatar was apparently alone among the Gulf states in indicating that it would allow the use of its territory as a base for action against Saddam Hussain. During the decade after the Gulf War the Government had signed a number of defence agreements with the USA and there was reported to have been a significant increase in the amount of US military personnel and equipment positioned in Qatar since September 2001; some 5,000 US troops had arrived at a military base south of Doha in late 2001 for what a Qatari official had described as 'routine' exercises. Furthermore, the construction of a major air facility at the Al-Udaid military base enhanced its strategic importance within the US military network in the region; in December 2002 the US Department of Defense dispatched more than 600 personnel from the US military command centre to the base, which was to act as the main US command post in the Gulf. None the less, Qatar, concerned about the popular reaction to a US-led war in Iraq and the regional implications such a conflict might have, continued to advocate a diplomatic solution to the crisis. By the time of the commencement of hostilities in March 2003, the USA had stationed some 3,000 air force personnel and 36 tactical jets at Al-Udaid. In April, following the removal of

Saddam Hussain's regime by the US-led coalition, Qatar's Minister of Foreign Affairs, Sheikh Hamad, urged the USA to reject the possibility of pursuing its 'war on terror' to target the Syrian regime of President Bashar al-Assad. Concern was raised within the Bush Administration by the announcement in December 2006 that Qatar was to pay the salaries of teachers in the Palestinian territories; it was feared by some US officials that the funds might be misappropriated by Hamas militants. However, following a meeting between US Secretary of State Condoleezza Rice and Sheikh Hamad, the US Administration appeared content not to impose any change of policy towards Qatar, which remained one of its closest allies in the Gulf region. In January 2007 US Secretary of Defense Robert Gates visited Doha as part of a tour of the Middle East, the focus of which was the situation in Iraq. During his stay he met with the Amir to discuss the further improvement of bilateral relations. In March the Qatari Government announced that it would not allow from its soil the launch by the USA of any military action against Iran, and strongly advocated a peaceful resolution to the ongoing impasse between the US and Iranian Governments.

In October 2005 Qatar was elected to a non-permanent seat on the UN Security Council. The two-year term commenced on 1 January 2006, expiring on 31 December 2007. Qatar's decision to endorse the candidacy of Ban Ki-Moon, rather than that of the Jordanian candidate, Prince Zeid bin Hussein, for the position of UN Secretary-General prompted Jordan to recall its ambassador from Doha in October 2006. Jordanian officials insisted that the decision had been based not on specific grievances, but rather on Qatar's persistent 'negative attitude' towards Jordan. Doha hosted the annual summit of the GCC in early December 2007, when, *inter alia*, consensus was reached upon the establishment of a common market, to become effective on 1 January 2008, which would permit the free movement of both capital and citizens of GCC member countries for the purposes of travel, residency and employment, and serve to enhance regional integration and co-operation.

The assassination in mid-February 2004 of an exiled Chechen militant, Zelimkhan Yandarbiyev, apparently with the involvement of the Russian military, brought into question the emirate's security regime and disrupted its relationship with Russia. Yandarbiyev was acting President of Chechnya in 1996–97, but had been sheltered with his family by Qatar since 2000. Despite Qatar's close ties with the USA and Russia, both of which accused Yandarbiyev of being involved in international terrorism (with alleged links to al-Qa'ida), the Qatari Government had refused to extradite the Chechen. Later in February 2004 three Russians were arrested by Qatari security agents; although one of the men was subsequently released and deported following the intervention of the Russian foreign ministry, the other two were charged with involvement in Yandarbiyev's murder. The two defendants reportedly admitted, under interrogation, to being members of Russian special security forces; Russia, however, demanded their immediate release. In June a Qatari court sentenced the two Russian intelligence officers to terms of life imprisonment. An appeal against their sentences was rejected in July, but the officers were allowed to return to Russia in December.

In November 2006 Qatari-Japanese ties were bolstered by the signing of an agreement providing for the establishment of a bilateral ministerial committee, intended to improve co-operation on economic, commercial and environmental activities. Later that month it was announced that a free trade agreement between Qatar and Singapore was expected soon to be formalized; the terms of the deal, which had already been agreed upon provisionally, were reported to cover a comprehensive range of concerns, including trade in goods and services, investment, e-commerce and government procurement. During a state visit to the People's Republic of China by the Qatari Prime Minister and Minister of Foreign Affairs, Sheikh Hamad, in April 2008, economic relations were augmented through an agreement for Qatar, as the largest producer of LNG globally, to supply annual shipments of 2m. metric tons of LNG to China's largest offshore oil producer, the China National Offshore Oil Corporation. A separate contract, incorporating the purchase of 3m. tons of LNG per year from Qatargas by PetroChina over a period of 25 years, was also signed between the two companies and Shell of the United Kingdom during Sheikh Hamad's discussions with Chinese President Hu Jintao as part of enhanced Qatari-Chinese investment and co-operative initiatives.

Government

According to the provisional Constitution that took effect in 1970, Qatar is an absolute monarchy, with full powers vested in the Amir as Head of State. Executive power is exercised by the Council of Ministers, appointed by the Head of State. An Advisory Council was formed in April 1972, with 20 nominated members (expanded to 30 in 1975 and to 35 in 1988). The Advisory Council's constitutional entitlements include the power to debate legislation drafted by the Council of Ministers before ratification and promulgation. It also has the power to request ministerial statements on matters of general and specific policy, including the draft budget. In March 1999 elections took place, by universal adult suffrage, for a 29-member Central Municipal Council, which was to have a consultative role in the operations of the Ministry of Municipal Affairs and Agriculture; further elections were held in April 2003 and April 2007. The Amir formally adopted a new Constitution following its approval at a referendum held on 29 April. Under the Constitution, the Amir is to remain head of the executive, while a 45-member unicameral parliament, of which two-thirds are to be directly elected (the remainder being appointed by the Amir), is to have the powers, *inter alia*, to legislate, review the state budget and monitor government policy. It had been expected that elections to the new legislature, after which the Advisory Council was to be abolished, would take place in 2007; following a series of postponements, however, an official announcement in February 2008 indicated that the staging of such elections was not anticipated before the end of the year.

Defence

As assessed at November 2007, the armed forces comprised 11,800 men: army 8,500; navy 1,800 (including Marine Police); air force 1,500. In September 2006 Qatar became the first Arab nation to contribute personnel to the UN Interim Force in Lebanon (UNIFIL); at November 2007 the number of Qatari peace-keeping troops deployed in Lebanon stood at 203. Government expenditure on defence was budgeted at an estimated QR 8,500m. in 2006.

Economic Affairs

In 1997, according to estimates by the World Bank, Qatar's gross national income (GNI), measured at average 1995–97 prices, was US $11,627m., equivalent to $22,147 per head. According to unofficial sources, GNI totalled $17,150m. in 2001 and $17,490m. in 2002 (equivalent to some $28,300 per head). During 1996–2006, it was estimated, the population increased at an average annual rate of 4.4%, while gross domestic product (GDP) per head increased, in real terms, by an average of 5.7% per year. Non-Qataris accounted for some 80% of the total population by the beginning of the 21st century. Overall GDP was estimated to have increased, in real terms, at an average rate of 10.5% per year in 1996–2006; according to official figures, real GDP growth was 6.1% in 2005.

Agriculture (including fishing) contributed a preliminary 0.1% of GDP in 2006, and, according to census figures, employed some 2.7% of the economically active population in March 2004. All agricultural land is owned by the Government, and most farm managers are immigrants employing a largely expatriate workforce. The main crops are cereals (principally barley), vegetables and dates. Qatar is self-sufficient in winter vegetables and nearly self-sufficient in summer vegetables. Some vegetables are exported to other Gulf countries. The Government has prioritized education in agricultural techniques and experimentation with unconventional methods of cultivation (including the use of sea water and solar energy to produce sand-based crops). Livestock-rearing and fishing are also practised. The GDP of the agricultural sector was estimated to have declined at an average annual rate of 4.5% during 1993–2002, and decreased at an average annual rate of 4.3% during 2001–05. However, real agricultural GDP increased by an estimated 11.2% in 2003 and by 1.0% in 2004. The sector's contribution to GDP, in real terms, remained constant in 2005.

Industry (including mining, manufacturing, construction and power) contributed a preliminary 73.8% of GDP in 2006, and the sector employed 41.0% of the economically active population at the time of the 2004 census. Industrial GDP was estimated to have increased by an average of 9.8% per year during 1993–2002, and by 8.7% in 2001–05. According to official figures, growth in the sector's real GDP was 16.1% in 2004 and 5.2% in 2005.

The mining and quarrying sector (comprising principally the extraction and processing of petroleum and natural gas) provided a preliminary 60.2% of GDP in 2006, and employed 4.1% of the economically active population at the time of the March 2004 census. Petroleum is currently the major mineral export. Proven recoverable petroleum reserves at the end of 2006 were 15,200m. barrels, sufficient to maintain production for almost 37 years at 2006 levels—averaging some 1,133,000 barrels per day (b/d). As a member of the Organization of the Petroleum Exporting Countries (OPEC, see p. 373), Qatar is subject to production quotas agreed by the Organization's Conference. Proven gas reserves were 25,360,000m. cu m at the end of 2006 (representing 14.0% of known world reserves at that date—behind only Russia and Iran), primarily located in the North Field, the world's largest gas reserve not associated with petroleum. The real GDP of the mining and quarrying sector was estimated to have increased at an average annual rate of 11.7% in 1993–2002, and of 6.9% in 2001–05. According to official figures, growth in the sector was 18.0% in 2004, but just 0.6% in 2005.

Manufacturing contributed a preliminary 7.2% of GDP in 2006 (excluding activities related to petroleum and natural gas), and the sector employed 9.2% of the economically active population according to the 2004 census. The principal manufacturing activities are linked to the country's oil and gas resources—petroleum refining and the production of liquefied natural gas (LNG—developed as part of the North Field project), together with industrial chemicals (particularly fertilizers) and steel production. Manufacturing GDP (excluding hydrocarbons) was estimated to have increased by an average of 4.5% per year in 1993–2002, and by 9.2% in 2001–05. According to official figures, the sector's real GDP increased by 6.5% in 2004 and by 12.6% in 2005.

Electrical energy is derived almost exclusively from Qatar's natural gas resource. Solar energy is being developed in conjunction with desalination.

The services sector contributed a preliminary 26.1% of GDP in 2006, and engaged 56.2% of the employed labour force at the 2004 census. The establishment in March 2005 of the Qatar Financial Centre, which was to provide a hub for the emirate's financial services sector, had reportedly proved popular with investors by early 2006 and was expected to stimulate further activity in the sector. The GDP of the services sector was estimated to have increased by an average of 6.1% per year in 1993–2002, and by 9.5% per year in 2001–05. According to official figures, services GDP increased by 27.2% in 2004 and by 8.6% in 2005.

According to official figures for 2006, Qatar recorded a visible trade surplus of QR 70,034m., while there was a surplus of QR 34,430m. on the current account of the balance of payments. In 2006 the principal source of imports (12.0% of the total value) was Japan; other important suppliers in that year were the USA (9.9%), Germany, Italy, the United Arab Emirates (UAE) and the Republic of Korea (South Korea). In the same year Japan took 41.5% of Qatar's exports by value. The principal exports are petroleum and gas and their derivatives (mineral fuels and lubricants provided 90.2% of domestic export revenues in 2005). The principal imports in 2005 were machinery and transport equipment (road vehicles alone accounted for 7.8% of the total value of imports), basic manufactures, food and live animals, and chemicals and related products.

In the financial year ending 31 March 2008 Qatar recorded an estimated budget surplus of QR 16,891m. According to ILO, the annual rate of inflation averaged 4.0% in 1996–2006; consumer prices increased by an average of 11.8% in 2006. The Qatari economy is heavily dependent on immigrant workers, owing to a shortage of indigenous labour; 88.5% of the employed population were non-Qataris at the census of March 2004.

Other than its membership of OPEC, Qatar is a member of the Organization of Arab Petroleum Exporting Countries (OAPEC, see p. 366), the Co-operation Council for the Arab States of the Gulf (GCC, see p. 219), the Arab Fund for Economic and Social Development (AFESD, see p. 174), the Arab Monetary Fund (see p. 175) and the Islamic Development Bank (see p. 329). GCC member states created a unified regional customs tariff in January 2003, and have undertaken to establish a single market and currency no later than January 2010. The economic convergence criteria for the proposed monetary union were agreed at a heads of state meeting in Abu Dhabi, the UAE, in December 2005, and in January 2008 the GCC launched its common market.

A priority following the assumption of power by Sheikh Hamad in 1995 was the maximizing of Qatar's energy-derived wealth so as to replenish state reserves, much of which were under the control of the deposed Amir. The development of the North Field gas project has been of prime importance, with the aim that Qatar should become a major regional and international supplier of gas and associated products. One of the most notable recent generators of income has been LNG, exports of which began in 1997 and by 2004, with related products, were valued at some US $6,912m.: by 2007 Qatar had become the world's largest exporter of LNG. In the petroleum sector, meanwhile, efforts have been made to expand production capacity (which was expected to reach 1m. b/d by the end of 2009—considerably in excess of Qatar's recent OPEC production quotas). The investment of over $30,000m. in oil and gas projects during 1995–2003, which led to a succession of budgetary deficits, entailed the accumulation of an external debt equivalent to some 90% of GDP by the end of 2002. In addition, a further $80,000m. was scheduled to be invested in the sector during 2004–10. However, revenue from the gas industry (particularly sales of LNG under long-term sales contracts with companies in the Far East and Europe) ensured the prompt dispatch of debt; since the 2000/01 financial year seven successive fiscal surpluses have been recorded, and by late 2006 external debt was equivalent to less than 40% of GDP. In April 2008 Qatar signed a significant deal with the People's Republic of China to provide 5m. metric tons of LNG per year over a 25-year-period. Meanwhile, the sale of shares in a number of state-owned companies has been undertaken since the 1990s. However, despite the enactment in 2002 of legislation allowing 100% foreign ownership of companies involved in areas of agriculture, manufacturing, education, health and tourism, and the inauguration in that year of Qatar's first semi-private company in the energy sector, the state retained responsibility for some 75% of GDP. Alongside measures to increase the size of the private sector, the Government's priority for the early part of the 21st century was the development of the emirate's infrastructure. In particular, Doha's status as the venue for the 2006 Asian Games tournament entailed huge expenditure on infrastructure projects, while other non-energy sector projects included the construction of numerous hotels and of multi-purpose complexes such as the residential, commercial and leisure centre to be called 'Entertainment City'. Furthermore, following the establishment of the GCC common market in January 2008, tourism arrivals and migrant labour (from the emirate's neighbouring countries) were expected to increase. However, greater wealth—with increased revenues from LNG being a significant factor—and higher GDP growth rates have driven inflation, which at February 2008 stood at 13.7%, the highest in the region. The increased rate also jeopardized the emirate's chances of joining the GCC single currency, the criteria of which stipulate that inflation cannot be more than 2% above the GCC average. This led to speculation that Qatar would either devalue its currency or remove the dollar peg in order to reduce the rate. Bolstered by huge petroleum and gas revenues, Qatar's robust growth was expected to continue for the foreseeable future.

Education

A state education system was introduced in 1956. Education is free at all levels, although not compulsory. In 2005 there was a combined total of around 67,592 students at the primary, intermediate and secondary levels of government-funded education in Qatar; in addition, there were about 44,000 students in private schools in the 1999/2000 academic year. Primary education begins at six years of age and lasts for six years. The next level of education, beginning at the age of 12, is divided into two cycles of three years (preparatory and secondary). In 2004/05 95.9% of children in the relevant age-group were enrolled at primary schools, while the comparable ratio for secondary enrolment was 90.1%. In late 2004 12 government-funded schools were leased to private operators in an attempt to improve educational standards. There are specialized religious, industrial, commercial and technical secondary schools for boys; the technical school admitted its first students in 1999/2000, as did two scientific secondary schools (one for girls). In 2005/06 there were 7,452 undergraduate students, 165 postgraduate students and a teaching staff of 779 at the University of Qatar. The Qatar Foundation for Education, Science and Community Development, established in 1995, is involved in programmes including the development of a faculty of medicine, in association with a US university, and a technology college, in association with a Canadian educational body and an international university, as part of its Education City complex, which opened in October 2003 and was scheduled for completion in 2008. The 2005/06 budget allocated QR 4,863m. to expenditure on education.

QATAR

Public Holidays

2008: 10 January*† (Islamic New Year), 27 June (Anniversary of the Amir's Accession), 30 July* (Leilat al-Meiraj, Ascension of the Prophet), 2 September* (Ramadan begins), 3 September (National Day), 1 October* (Id al-Fitr, end of Ramadan), 9 December* (Id al-Adha, Feast of the Sacrifice), 29 December*† (Islamic New Year).

2009: 27 June (Anniversary of the Amir's Accession), 19 July* (Leilat al-Meiraj, Ascension of the Prophet), 22 August* (Ramadan begins), 3 September (National Day), 20 September* (Id al-Fitr, end of Ramadan), 27 November* (Id al-Adha, Feast of the Sacrifice), 18 December* (Islamic New Year).

* These holidays are dependent on the Islamic lunar calendar and may differ by one or two days from the dates given.

† This festival occurs twice (marking the start of the Islamic years AH 1429 and 1430) within the same Gregorian year.

Weights and Measures

The metric system has been adopted legally, but imperial measures are still used.

Statistical Survey

Sources (unless otherwise stated): Press and Publications Dept, Ministry of Education, POB 80, Doha; tel. 4333444; fax 4413886; internet www.moe.edu.qa; Dept of Economic Policies, Qatar Central Bank, POB 1234, Doha; tel. 4456456; fax 4413650; e-mail elzainys@qcb.gov.qa; internet www.qcb.gov.qa; Planning Council, POB 1855, Doha; tel. 4381222; fax 4445573; e-mail statistics@planning.gov.qa; internet www.planning.gov.qa.

AREA AND POPULATION

Area: 11,493 sq km (4,437 sq miles).

Population: 522,023 (males 342,459, females 179,564) at census of 1 March 1997; 744,029 (males 496,382, females 247,647) at census of 1 March 2004. *Mid-2006* (official estimate) 838,065.

Density (at mid-2006): 72.9 per sq km.

Principal Towns (population of municipalities, 2006 estimates): Ad-Dawhah (Doha, the capital) 370,656; Ar-Rayyan 317,227; Umm Salal 37,334; Al-Khawr (Al-Khor) 37,600; Al-Wakrah 34,716.

Births and Deaths (2005): Registered live births 13,401 (birth rate 16.8 per 1,000); Registered marriages 2,734 (marriage rate 3.4 per 1,000); Registered deaths 1,545 (death rate 1.9 per 1,000).

Expectation of Life (years at birth, WHO estimates): 77.7 (males 77.2; females 77.9) in 2005. Source: WHO, *World Health Statistics*.

Employment (persons aged 15 years and over, 2004 census): Agriculture and fishing 12,025; Mining and quarrying 17,997; Manufacturing 40,038; Electricity, gas and water 4,364; Construction 117,049; Trade, restaurants and hotels 64,718; Transport and communications 15,218; Finance, insurance and real estate 16,624; Community, social and personal services 149,528; *Total employed* 437,561 (Qatari nationals 50,282, non-Qataris 387,279).

HEALTH AND WELFARE
Key Indicators

Total Fertility Rate (children per woman, 2005): 2.9.

Under-5 Mortality Rate (per 1,000 live births, 2005): 12.

Physicians (per 1,000 head, 2001): 2.22.

Hospital Beds (per 1,000 head, 2005): 2.40.

Health Expenditure (2004): US $ per head (PPP): 687.9.

Health Expenditure (2004): % of GDP: 2.4.

Health Expenditure (2004): public (% of total): 76.5.

Human Development Index (2005): ranking: 35.

Human Development Index (2005): value: 0.875.

For sources and definitions, see explanatory note on p. vi.

AGRICULTURE, ETC.

Principal Crops ('000 metric tons, 2005, FAO estimates): Barley 4.9; Maize 0.8; Cabbages 0.9; Tomatoes 5.3; Cauliflowers and broccoli 1.1; Pumpkins, squash and gourds 1.3; Cucumbers and gherkins 0.7; Aubergines (Eggplants) 3.1; Chillies and green peppers 0.8; Dry onions 3.0; Cantaloupes and other melons 4.6; Dates 19.8. *Aggregate Production* ('000 metric tons, 2006, may include official, semi-official or estimated data): Total cereals 7; Total vegetables (incl. melons) 26; Total fruit (excl. melons) 22.

Livestock ('000 head, year ending September 2005, FAO estimates): Horses 2; Cattle 7; Camels 14; Sheep 200; Goats 112; Chickens 4,500.

Livestock Products ('000 metric tons, 2005, FAO estimates unless otherwise indicated): Camel meat 1.1; Chicken meat 4.6; Cows' milk 11.2; Camels' milk 9.9; Sheep's milk 5.1; Goats' milk 5.7; Hen eggs 4.1 (unofficial figure).

Fishing (metric tons, live weight, 2005): Groupers 2,094; Grunts and sweetlips 761; Emperors—Scavengers 4,200; King soldier bream 626; Spinefeet—Rabbitfishes 658; Narrow-barred Spanish mackerel 1,882; Carangids 381; *Total catch* (incl. others) 13,935.

Source: FAO.

MINING

Production (2006, estimates): Crude petroleum ('000 barrels) 290,000; Natural gas (gross, million cu m) 63,000. Source: US Geological Survey.

INDUSTRY

Production (2006, unless otherwise indicated, estimates): Wheat flour (including bran, '000 metric tons, 2005) 34; Ammonia (nitrogen content, '000 metric tons) 1,800; Urea (nitrogen content, '000 metric tons) 1,350; Motor spirit (petrol, '000 barrels) 16,500; Kerosene ('000 barrels) 8,000; Gas diesel (distillate fuel) oils ('000 barrels) 8,000; Residual fuel oils ('000 barrels) 2,400; Other refinery products ('000 barrels) 80,000; Liquefied natural gas ('000 barrels) 100,000; Cement ('000 metric tons) 1,400; Crude steel ('000 metric tons) 1,039; Electric energy (million kWh, 2005) 14,396. Source: mainly US Geological Survey.

FINANCE

Currency and Exchange Rates: 100 dirhams = 1 Qatar riyal (QR). *Sterling, Dollar and Euro Equivalents* (31 December 2007): £1 sterling = 7.292 riyals; US $1 = 3.640 riyals; €1 = 5.358 riyals; 100 Qatar riyals = £13.71 = $27.47 = €18.66. *Exchange Rate*: Since June 1980 the official mid-point rate has been fixed at US $1 = QR 3.64.

Budget (QR million, 2007/08, year ending 31 March, preliminary estimates): *Revenue:* Petroleum and natural gas revenue 42,095; Investment revenue 17,867; Total (incl. others) 82,603. *Expenditure:* Wages and salaries 15,627; Current expenditure 24,434; Capital expenditure 4,672; Major projects 20,979; Total 65,712.

International Reserves (US $ million at 31 December 2006): Gold 12.2; IMF special drawing rights 40.4; Reserve position in IMF 35.2; Foreign exchange 5,307.1; Total 5,394.9. Source: IMF, *International Financial Statistics*.

Money Supply (QR million at 31 December 2006): Currency outside banks 3,959; Demand deposits at commercial banks 23,924; *Total money* 27,883. Source: IMF, *International Financial Statistics*.

Cost of Living (Consumer Price Index; base: 2000 = 100): 111.1 in 2004; 120.9 in 2005; 135.2 in 2006. Source: IMF, *International Financial Statistics*.

Gross Domestic Product (QR million at constant 2001 prices): 70,781 in 2003; 85,524 in 2004; 90,780 in 2005.

Expenditure on the Gross Domestic Product (QR million at current prices, 2006, preliminary): Government final consumption expenditure 30,088; Private final consumption expenditure 36,470; Increase in stocks 4,150; Gross fixed capital formation 81,467; *Total domestic expenditure* 152,175; Exports of goods and services 111,556; *Less* Imports of goods and services 71,822; *GDP in purchasers' values* 191,909.

Gross Domestic Product by Economic Activity (QR million at current prices, 2006, preliminary): Agriculture and fishing 233; Mining and quarrying 118,707; Manufacturing 14,098; Electricity and water 2,424; Construction 10,291; Trade, restaurants and hotels 7,616; Transport and communications 5,612; Finance, insurance and financial intermediation 7,684; Real estate and business services

8,076; Government services 17,928; Other services 4,495; *Sub-total* 197,164; *Less* Imputed bank service charge 5,255; *GDP in purchasers' values* 191,909.

Balance of Payments (QR million, 2006): Exports f.o.b. 123,945; Imports f.o.b. −53,911; *Trade balance* 70,034; Exports of services 15,263; Imports of services −25,322; *Balance on goods and services* 59,975; Other income received 7,207; Other income paid −19,148; *Balance on goods, services and income* 48,034; Transfers (net) −13,604; *Current balance* 34,430; Capital account (net) −3,608; Financial account (net) −16,731; Net errors and omissions 5,709; *Overall balance* 19,800.

EXTERNAL TRADE

Principal Commodities (distribution by SITC, QR million, 2005): *Imports c.i.f.:* Food and live animals 2,106.1; Chemicals and related products 2,446.6; Basic manufactures 8,811.6; Machinery and transport equipment 17,986.7 (Road vehicles 2,844); Miscellaneous manufactured articles 3,931.5; Total (incl. others) 36,621.0. *Exports f.o.b.:* Mineral fuels and lubricants 83,222.6 (Crude petroleum 46,749; Natural and manufactured petroleum gases 28,899); Chemicals and related products 7,172.9; Basic manufactures 1,498.7; Total (incl. others) 92,233.6 (excluding re-exports valued at 1,540.2).

Principal Trading Partners (QR million, 2006): *Imports c.i.f.:* People's Republic of China 3,482.8; France 2,311.6; Germany 5,581.0; India 1,642.0; Italy 5,543.3; Japan 7,182.8; Republic of Korea 3,278.4; Saudi Arabia 3,054.9; United Arab Emirates 3,606.5; United Kingdom 2,985.0; USA 5,899.6; Total (incl. others) 59,841.1. *Exports f.o.b.:* People's Republic of China 1,449.6; India 6,035.6; Japan 51,387.5; Republic of Korea 17,198.5; Singapore 11,715.4; Spain 3,050.9; Taiwan 1,943.6; Thailand 3,389.5; United Arab Emirates 5,355; Total (incl. others) 123,945.0.

TRANSPORT

Road Traffic (registered motor vehicles, 2004): Private cars 265,609; Other private transport 114,115; Heavy equipment 11,162; Motor cycles and mopeds 4,420; Total (incl. others) 406,626.

Shipping (international sea-borne freight traffic, '000 metric tons, 1994): *Goods loaded:* 5,853; *Goods unloaded:* 2,500. *Merchant Fleet* (registered at 31 December 2006): 86 vessels; 652,280 gross registered tons (Source: Lloyd's Register-Fairplay, *World Fleet Statistics*).

Civil Aviation (scheduled services, 2003): Kilometres flown (million) 75; Passengers carried ('000) 3,184; Passenger-km (million) 8,003; Total ton-km (million) 1,003. Figures include an apportionment (one-quarter) of the traffic of Gulf Air, a multinational airline with its headquarters in Bahrain. Source: UN, *Statistical Yearbook*.

TOURISM

Tourist Arrivals: 556,965 in 2003; 732,454 in 2004; 912,997 in 2005.

Tourism Receipts (US $ million, incl. passenger transport): 369 in 2003; 498 in 2004; 760 in 2005.

Source: World Tourism Organization.

COMMUNICATIONS MEDIA

Radio Receivers ('000 in use, 1997): 256*.

Television Receivers ('000 in use, 2000): 520†.

Telephones ('000 main lines in use, 2006): 228.3†.

Facsimile Machines ('000 in use, 1996): 10.4‡.

Mobile Cellular Telephones ('000 subscribers, 2006): 919.8†.

Personal Computers ('000 in use, 2004): 133†.

Internet Users ('000, 2006): 289.9†.

Broadband Subscribers ('000, 2006): 46.8†.

Daily Newspapers: 5 (circulation 90,000 copies, 1996*) in 2001; 5 in 2004§.

Weekly Newspapers (2001): 2 (circulation 7,000 copies, 1995*).

Book Production (titles, 1996): 209*.

* Source: UNESCO, *Statistical Yearbook*.
† Source: International Telecommunication Union.
‡ Source: UN, *Statistical Yearbook*.
§ Source: UNESCO Institute for Statistics.

EDUCATION

Pre-primary (2004/05, unless otherwise indicated): 64 schools (1995/96); 826 teachers; 13,082 pupils.

Primary (2005, government schools only): 99 schools; 3,738 teachers; 33,127 pupils.

Intermediate (2005, government schools only): 51 schools; 1,656 teachers; 17,588 pupils.

Secondary (2005, government schools only): 42 schools; 1,793 teachers; 16,877 pupils.

University (2005): 1 institution; 664 teaching staff; 11,304 students (incl. 1,544 graduate students).

Source: partly UNESCO, *Statistical Yearbook*; UNESCO Institute for Statistics.

Adult Literacy Rate (UNESCO estimates): 89.0% (males 89.1%; females 88.6%) in 2004. Source: UNESCO Institute for Statistics.

Directory

The Constitution

According to the provisional Constitution adopted on 2 April 1970, executive power was vested in the Amir, as Head of State, and exercised by the Council of Ministers, appointed by the Head of State. The Amir was assisted by the appointed Advisory Council of 20 members (increased to 30 in 1975 and to 35 in 1988), whose term was extended for six years in 1975, for a further four years in 1978, and for further four-year terms in 1982, 1986, 1990, 1994 and 1998. All fundamental democratic rights were guaranteed. In 1975 the Advisory Council was granted the power to summon individual ministers to answer questions on legislation before promulgation. In March 1999 elections took place, by universal adult suffrage, for a 29-member Central Municipal Council, which was to have a consultative role in the operations of the Ministry of Municipal Affairs and Agriculture. The Amir formally adopted a new Constitution following a referendum held on 29 April 2003. Under this Constitution, the Amir was to remain head of the executive, while a 45-member unicameral parliament, of which two-thirds was to be directly elected (the remainder being appointed by the Amir), was to have the powers to legislate, review the state budget, monitor government policy and hold ministers accountable for their actions. The parliament was to have a four-year mandate. Suffrage was to be extended to all citizens, including women, aged 18 years and above. Elections to the new legislature, after which the Advisory Council was to be abolished, were initially expected to be conducted in 2004; however, owing to alleged difficulties pertaining to the electoral roll, this was subsequently deferred until 2008. The Constitution guarantees freedom of association, expression and religious affiliation, and provides for the establishment of an independent judiciary; however, it does not authorize political parties.

The Government

HEAD OF STATE

Amir: Maj.-Gen. Sheikh HAMAD BIN KHALIFA ATH-THANI (assumed power 27 June 1995).

Crown Prince and Commander-in-Chief of the Armed Forces: Sheikh TAMIM BIN HAMAD BIN KHALIFA ATH-THANI.

COUNCIL OF MINISTERS
(April 2008)

Amir and Minister of Defence: Maj.-Gen. Sheikh HAMAD BIN KHALIFA ATH-THANI.

Prime Minister and Minister of Foreign Affairs: Sheikh HAMAD BIN JASIM BIN JABER ATH-THANI.

Deputy Prime Minister and Minister of Energy and Industry: ABDULLAH BIN HAMAD AL-ATTIYA.

Minister of Finance, and Acting Minister of Economy and Commerce: YOUSUF BIN HUSSAIN KAMAL.

Minister of the Interior: Sheikh ABDULLAH BIN KHALID ATH-THANI.

Minister of Awqaf (Religious Endowments) and Islamic Affairs: FAISAL BIN ABDULLAH AL-MAHMOUD.

QATAR

Minister of Municipal Affairs and Agriculture: Sheikh ABD AR-RAHMAN BIN KHALIFA BIN ABD AL-AZIZ ATH-THANI.

Minister of Justice: HASSAN BIN ABDULLAH AL-GHANIM.

Minister of Education: Sheikha BINT AHMAD AL-MAHMOUD.

Minister of Labour and Social Affairs: Dr SULTAN BIN HASSAN ADH-DHABIT AD-DOUSARY.

Minister of State for Foreign Affairs: AHMAD BIN ABDULLAH AL-MAHMOUD.

Minister of State for the Interior: Sheikh ABDULLAH BIN NASSER BIN KHALIFA ATH-THANI.

Minister of State for Energy and Industrial Affairs: Dr MUHAMMAD SALEH AS-SADA.

Minister of State without Portfolio: Sheikh MUHAMMAD BIN KHALID ATH-THANI.

MINISTRIES

Ministry of Amiri Diwan Affairs: POB 923, Doha; tel. 4367575; fax 4361212; e-mail adf@diwan.gov.qa; internet www.diwan.gov.qa.

Ministry of Awqaf (Religious Endowments) and Islamic Affairs: POB 422, Doha; tel. 4470777; fax 4470700; e-mail awqaf@awqaf.gov.qa; internet www.islam.gov.qa.

Ministry of Defence: Qatar Armed Forces, POB 37, Doha; tel. 4614111.

Ministry of Economy and Commerce: POB 1968, Doha; tel. 4945555; fax 4932111; e-mail pru@mec.gov.qa; internet www.mec.gov.qa.

Ministry of Education: POB 80, Al-Waqf Tower, Dafna, Doha; tel. and fax 4941111; e-mail e.alhorr@moe.edu.qa; internet www.moe.edu.qa.

Ministry of Energy and Industry: Salam Plaza Bldg, West Bay, Dafna, Doha; tel. 4846444; fax 4832024; e-mail did@mei.gov.qa; internet www.mei.gov.qa.

Ministry of Finance: POB 83, Doha; tel. 4461444; fax 4431177; internet www.mof.gov.qa.

Ministry of Foreign Affairs: POB 250, Doha; tel. 4334334; fax 4324131; e-mail webmaster@mofa.gov.qa; internet www.mofa.gov.qa.

Ministry of the Interior: POB 115, Doha; tel. 4330000; fax 4449228; e-mail info@moi.gov.qa; internet www.moi.gov.qa.

Ministry of Justice: POB 917 (Dept of Legal Affairs), Doha; tel. 4842222; fax 4832875; e-mail info@moj.gov.qa; internet www.moj.gov.qa.

Ministry of Labour and Social Affairs: POB 36, Doha; tel. 4841111; fax 4841000; e-mail customerservice@mcsah.gov.qa; internet www.mlsa.gov.qa.

Ministry of Municipal Affairs and Agriculture: POB 22332, Main Bldg, Corniche St, Doha; tel. 4413331; fax 4430239; e-mail info@baladiya.gov.qa; internet www.baladiya.gov.qa.

ADVISORY COUNCIL

The Advisory or *Shura* Council was established in 1972, with 20 nominated members. It was expanded to 30 members in 1975, and to 35 members in 1988. Under the terms of the new Constitution, promulgated in 2003, the Advisory Council is to be replaced by a 45-member unicameral, elected parliament.

Speaker: MUHAMMAD BIN MUBARAK AL-KHOLAIFI.

Diplomatic Representation

EMBASSIES IN QATAR

Afghanistan: POB 22104, Isteolal St, West Bay, Doha; tel. 4930821; fax 4930819; e-mail afgembqatar@hotmail.com; Ambassador WALI MONAWAR.

Algeria: POB 2494, Doha; tel. 4831186; fax 4836452; Ambassador MUHAMMAD BOUROUBA.

Bahrain: POB 24888, Doha; tel. 4839360; fax 4831018; e-mail doha.mission@mofa.gov.bh; Ambassador KHALID MUHAMMAD JABER AL-MUSALEM.

Bangladesh: POB 3080, Doha; tel. 4671927; fax 4671190; e-mail bdootqat@qatar.net.qa; Ambassador MAROOF ZAMAN.

Belgium: POB 24418, As-Sanaa St, District 64, Doha; tel. 4931542; fax 4930151; e-mail doha@diplobel.be; Ambassador GUY DE LAUWER.

Bosnia and Herzegovina: POB 876, Doha; tel. 4670194; fax 4670595; e-mail ambasada@qatar.net.qa; internet www.bhembassyqatar.org; Ambassador AZRA KALAJDŽISALIHOVIĆ.

Brunei: POB 22772, Doha; tel. 4831956; fax 4836798; e-mail bruemb@qatar.net.qa; Chargé d'affaires Haji ALI HASSAN Haji MUHAMMAD SALLEH.

China, People's Republic: POB 17200, Doha; tel. 4934203; fax 4934201; e-mail chinashi@qatar.net.qa; internet www.mfa.gov.cn/eng/wjb/zwjg/2490/2492/t14412.htm; Ambassador YUE XIAOYONG.

Cuba: POB 12017, Saha 76, New Dafna, West Bay Lagoon, Doha; tel. 4110713; fax 4110387; e-mail embacuba@qatar.net.qa; internet www.embacubaqatar.com; Ambassador ARMANDO VERGARA BUENO.

Cyprus: POB 24482, 3 Saba Saha 12 St, District 63, West Bay, Doha; tel. 4934390; fax 4933087; e-mail kyprosdoha@qatar.net.qa; Ambassador GEORGE C. KASOULIDES.

Egypt: POB 2899, Doha; tel. 4832555; fax 4832196; e-mail info@egyptembqatar.com; Ambassador ABD AL-AZIZ DAWOUD.

Eritrea: POB 4309, D-Ring Rd 14, Doha; tel. 4667934; fax 4664139; Ambassador ALI IBRAHIM AHMED.

France: POB 2669, Doha; tel. 4832283; fax 4832254; e-mail ambadoha@qatar.net.qa; internet www.ambafrance-qa.org; Ambassador ANTOINE SIVAN.

Gambia: POB 22377, Doha; tel. 4651429; fax 4651705; Chargé d'affaires BASSIROU DRAMMEH.

Germany: POB 3064, 6 Al-Jazeera al-Arabiya St, Doha; tel. 4876959; fax 4876949; e-mail germany@qatar.net.qa; internet www.doha.diplo.de; Ambassador Dr DIRK BAUMGARTNER.

Hungary: POB 23525, Doha; tel. 4932531; fax 4932537; e-mail mission.doh@kum.hu; internet www.mfa.gov.hu/kulkepviselet/qu; Ambassador FERENC CSILLAG.

India: POB 2788, Doha; tel. 4255777; fax 4670448; e-mail indembdh@qatar.net.qa; internet www.indianembassy.gov.qa; Ambassador GEORGE JOSEPH.

Indonesia: POB 22375, Al-Maheed St, Doha; tel. 4657945; fax 4657610; e-mail inemb@qatar.net.qa; internet www.kbridoha.com; Ambassador ROZY MUNIR.

Iran: POB 1633, Doha; tel. 4835300; fax 4831665; e-mail irembsdoha@yahoo.com; internet www.iranembassy.org.qa; Ambassador MUHAMMAD TAHER RABBANI.

Iraq: POB 1526, Doha; tel. 4672237; fax 4673347; e-mail dohemb@iraqmofamail.net; Ambassador SADIQ HAMEEDI AR-RAKAWI.

Italy: POB 4188, Doha; tel. 4831828; fax 4831909; e-mail ambasciata.doha@esteri.it; internet sedi.esteri.it/doha; Ambassador GIUSEPPE BUCCINO GRIMALDI.

Japan: POB 2208, Doha West Bay, Diplomatic Area, Doha; tel. 4840888; fax 4832178; Ambassador YUKIO KITAZUME.

Jordan: POB 2366, Doha; tel. 4832202; fax 4832173; e-mail jordand@qatar.net.qa; internet www.jordanembassy.com.qa; Ambassador OMAR IBRAHIM AL-AHMAD (recalled Oct. 2006).

Kazakhstan: POB 25513, Doha; tel. and fax 4128015; e-mail kazembassyqatar@mail.ru; Ambassador AZAMAT R. BERDYBAI.

Korea, Democratic People's Republic: POB 799, Doha; tel. 4417614; fax 4424735; Ambassador HO JONG.

Korea, Republic: POB 3727, West Bay Diplomatic Area, Doha; tel. 4832238; fax 4833264; e-mail koemb_ga@mofa.go.kr; Ambassador KIM JONG YONG.

Kuwait: POB 1177, Doha; tel. 4832111; fax 4832042; e-mail kuwaitembassy@qatar.net.qa; Ambassador SULEIMAN IBRAHIM AL-MARJAN.

Lebanon: POB 2411, 63 United Nations St, Al-Haditha Area, Doha; tel. 4933330; fax 4933331; e-mail embleb@qatar.net.qa; Ambassador HASSAN SAAD.

Libya: POB 574, Doha; tel. 4429546; fax 4429548; Chargé d'affaires AL-MABROUK MUHAMMAD AL-MUADANE.

Malaysia: POB 23760, Doha; tel. 4836463; fax 4836453; e-mail maldoha@kln.gov.my; Ambassador Dato' MUHAMMAD SHAHRUL IKRAM YAAKOB.

Mauritania: POB 3132, Doha; tel. 4836003; fax 4836015; Ambassador MUHAMMAD AL-AMIN AS-SALEM OULD DADA.

Morocco: POB 3242, Doha; tel. 4831885; fax 4833416; e-mail moroccoe@qatar.net.qa; Ambassador ABDELADIM TABIR.

Nepal: POB 23002, Doha; tel. 4675681; fax 4675680; e-mail nembdoha@qatar.net.qa; internet www.rnedoha.org.qa; Ambassador SHYAMANANDA SUMAN.

Oman: POB 1525, 41 Ibn al-Qassim St, Villa 7, Doha; tel. 4931514; fax 4932278; e-mail oman_e126@hotmail.com; Ambassador RASHED BIN MUBARAK BIN RASHED AL-GHELANY.

Pakistan: POB 334, Diplomatic Area, Plot 30, West Bay, Doha; tel. 4832525; fax 4832227; e-mail parepqat@qatar.net.qa; Ambassador MUHAMMAD ASGHAR AFRIDI.

Philippines: POB 24900, Doha; tel. 4831585; fax 4831595; e-mail dohape@qatar.net.qa; Ambassador ISAIAS FLORENDO BEGONIA.

Romania: POB 22511, Doha; tel. 4934848; fax 4934747; e-mail romamb@qatar.net.qa; Ambassador ADRIAN MĂCELARU.
Russia: POB 15404, Doha; tel. 4836231; fax 4836243; e-mail rusemb@qatar.net.qa; internet www.qatar.mid.ru; Ambassador ANDREW V. ANDREEV.
Saudi Arabia: POB 1255, Doha; tel. 4832030; fax 4832720; Ambassador AHMAD BIN ALI AL-QAHTANI.
Senegal: Ibn Almoutas St, House 65, Dafna, Doha; tel. 4837644; fax 4838872; Ambassador ADAMA SARR.
Somalia: POB 1948, Doha; tel. 4832771; fax 4834568; Ambassador SHARIF MUHAMMAD OMAR.
South Africa: POB 24744, Doha; tel. 4857111; fax 4835961; e-mail saembdoha@qatar.net.qa; Ambassador Dr VINCENT TINIZA ZULU.
Sri Lanka: 4 Al-Kharja St, POB 19705, Doha; tel. 4677627; fax 4674788; e-mail lankaemb@qatar.net.qa; Ambassador S. B. ATUGODA.
Sudan: POB 2999, Doha; tel. 4831474; fax 4833031; e-mail suemdoha@yahoo.com; Ambassador IBRAHIM ABDULLAH FAKIRI.
Syria: POB 1257, Doha; tel. 4831844; fax 4832139; Ambassador DEEB ABU LATIF.
Thailand: POB 22474, Doha; tel. 4550715; fax 4550835; e-mail thaidoh@qatar.net.qa; internet www.thaiembqatar.com; Ambassador SUVAT CHIRAPANT.
Turkey: POB 1977, Doha; tel. 4951300; fax 4951320; e-mail tcdohabe@qatar.net.qa; Ambassador MITHAT RENDE.
United Arab Emirates: POB 3099, 22 al-Markhiyah St, Khalifa Northern Town, Doha; tel. 4838880; fax 4836186; e-mail emarat@qatar.net.qa; Ambassador ABD AR-REDHA ABDULLAH KHOURI.
United Kingdom: POB 3, Doha; tel. 4962000; fax 4962086; e-mail consular_qatar@fco.gov.uk; internet www.britishembassy.gov.uk/qatar; Ambassador RODERICK IAN DRUMMOND.
USA: 22nd February St, Al-Luqta district, POB 2399, Doha; tel. 4884101; fax 4884298; e-mail pasdoha@state.gov; internet qatar.usembassy.gov; Ambassador JOSEPH LEBARON (designate).
Yemen: POB 3318, Doha; tel. 4432555; fax 4429400; Ambassador ABD AL-MALIK SAID.

Judicial System

Independence of the judiciary is guaranteed by the provisional Constitution. All aspects pertaining to the civil judiciary are supervised by the Ministry of Justice, which organizes courts of law through its affiliated departments. The Shari'a judiciary hears all cases of personal status relating to Muslims, other claim cases, doctrinal provision and crimes under its jurisdiction. Legislation adopted in 1999 unified all civil and Shari'a courts in one judicial body, and determined the jurisdictions of each type of court. The law also provided for the establishment of a court of cassation; this was to be competent to decide on appeals relating to issues of contravention, misapplication and misinterpretation of the law, and on disputes between courts regarding areas of jurisdiction. In addition, the law provided for the establishment of a supreme judiciary council, to be presided over by the head of the court of cassation and comprising, *inter alia*, the heads of the Shari'a and civil courts of appeal. The establishment of a judicial inspection system was also envisaged. An amiri decree published in June 2002 sought to establish an independent public prosecution system. Further elaboration of provisions for the creation of an independent judiciary were contained in the Constitution formally adopted by the Amir in April 2003.

Chief Justice: MUBARAK BIN KHALIFA AL-ASARI.
Public Prosecutor: Dr ALI BIN FITAISE AL-MERRI.
Presidency of Shari'a Courts: POB 232, Doha; tel. 4452222; Pres. Sheikh ABD AR-RAHMAN BIN ABDULLAH AL-MAHMOUD.

Religion

The indigenous population are Muslims of the Sunni sect, most being of the strict Wahhabi persuasion. In March 2008 the first official Christian church (of the Roman Catholic branch) was consecrated in Doha; open worship among adherents of Christianity had previously been prohibited.

CHRISTIANITY

The Anglican Communion

Within the Episcopal Church in Jerusalem and the Middle East, Qatar forms part of the diocese of Cyprus and the Gulf. The Anglican congregation in Qatar is entirely expatriate. The Bishop in Cyprus and the Gulf is resident in Cyprus, while the Archdeacon in the Gulf is resident in Bahrain.

The Roman Catholic Church

An estimated 100,000 adherents in Qatar, mainly expatriates, form part of the Apostolic Vicariate of Arabia. The Vicar Apostolic is resident in the United Arab Emirates.

The Press

Al-'Arab (The Arabs): Doha; internet www.alarab.com.qa; f. 1972; ceased publication in 1996 but recommenced, following relaunch in Nov. 2007; daily; Arabic; publ. by Dar al-Ouroba Printing and Publishing; Editor-in-Chief Prof. ABD AL-AZIZ IBRAHIM AL-MAHMOUD.
Ad-Dawri (The Tournament): POB 310, Doha; tel. 4328782; fax 4447039; f. 1978; weekly; Arabic; sport; publ. by Abdullah Hamad al-Atiyah and Ptnrs; Editor-in-Chief Sheikh RASHID BIN OWAIDA ATH-THANI; circ. 6,000.
Gulf Times: POB 2888, Doha; tel. 4350478; fax 4350474; e-mail edit@gulf-times.com; internet www.gulf-times.com; f. 1978; daily and weekly edns; English; political; publ. by Gulf Publishing and Printing Co; Editor-in-Chief NEIL COOK; circ. 20,000 (daily).
Al-Jawhara (The Jewel): POB 2531, Doha; tel. 4414575; fax 4671388; f. 1977; monthly; Arabic; women's magazine; publ. by al-Ahd Establishment for Journalism, Printing and Publications Ltd; Editor-in-Chief ABDULLAH YOUSUF AL-HUSSAINI; circ. 8,000.
Nada (A Gathering): POB 4896, Doha; tel. 4445564; fax 4433778; f. 1991; weekly; social and entertainment; publ. by Akhbar al-Usbou'; Editor-in-Chief ADEL ALI BIN ALI.
Al-Ouroba (Arabism): POB 663, Doha; tel. 4325874; fax 4429424; f. 1970; weekly; Arabic; political; publ. by Dar al-Ouroba Printing and Publishing; Editor-in-Chief YOUSUF NAAMA; circ. 12,000.
The Peninsula: POB 3488, Doha; tel. 4663945; fax 4663965; e-mail penqatar@qatar.net.qa; f. 1995; daily; English; political; publ. by Dar ash-Sharq Printing, Publishing and Distribution; Editor RACHEL MORRIS; Man. Editor GEORGE ABRAHAM; circ. 8,000.
Qatar Lil Inshaa (Qatar Construction): POB 2203, Doha; tel. 4424988; fax 4432961; f. 1989; publ. by Almaha Trade and Construction Co; Gen. Man. MUHAMMAD H. AL-MIJBER; circ. 10,000.
Ar-Rayah (The Banner): POB 3464, Doha; tel. 4466555; fax 4350476; e-mail www.edit@raya.com; internet www.raya.com; f. 1979; daily and weekly edns; Arabic; political; publ. by Gulf Publishing and Printing Co; Editor NASSER AL-OTHMAN; circ. 25,000.
Saidat ash-Sharq: POB 3488, Doha; tel. 4662445; fax 4662450; f. 1993; monthly; Arabic; women's magazine; publ. by Dar ash-Sharq Printing, Publishing and Distribution; Editor NASSER AL-OTHMAN; circ. 15,000.
Ash-Sharq (The Orient): POB 3488, Doha; tel. 4662444; fax 4662450; e-mail webmaster@al-sharq.com; internet www.al-sharq.com; f. 1985; daily; Arabic; political; publ. by Dar ash-Sharq Printing, Publishing and Distribution; Editor-in-Chief ABDULLATIF AL-MAHMOUD; circ. 45,018.
At-Tarbiya (Education): POB 9865, Doha; tel. 4941709; fax 4838890; e-mail netcom@qatar.net.qa; f. 1971; quarterly; publ. by Qatar National Commission for Education, Culture and Science; Editor-in-Chief SALAH MUHAMMAD SOROUR; circ. 2,000.
This is Qatar and What's On: POB 4015, Doha; tel. 4413813; fax 4413814; f. 1978; quarterly; English; tourist information; publ. by Oryx Publishing and Advertising Co; Editor-in-Chief YOUSUF J. AD-DARWISH; circ. 10,000.
Al-Ummah: POB 893, Doha; tel. 4447300; fax 4447022; e-mail m_dirasat@islam.gov.qa; f. 1982; bi-monthly; Islamic thought and affairs, current cultural issues, book serializations.
Al-Watan: POB 22345, Doha; tel. 4652244; fax 4660440; e-mail feedback@al-watan.com; internet www.al-watan.com; f. 1995; daily; Arabic; political; publ. by Dar al-Watan Printing, Publishing and Distribution; Editor-in-Chief AHMAD ALI AL-ABDULLAH; circ. 25,000.

NEWS AGENCY

Qatar News Agency (QNA): POB 3299, Doha; tel. 4450321; fax 4438316; e-mail info@qnaol.com; internet www.qnaol.com/english/home2.php; f. 1975; affiliated to Ministry of Foreign Affairs; Dir and Editor-in-Chief AHMAD JASSIM AL-HUMAR.

Publishers

Ali bin Ali Media and Publishing: POB 75, Doha; tel. 4469888; fax 4369911; e-mail publishing@alibinali.com; internet www.alibinali.com; publrs of Qatar Telephone Directory and Yellow Pages; Chair. and Pres. ADEL ALI BIN ALI; CEO PETER D. MCELWAINE.
Dar al-Ouroba Printing and Publishing: POB 52, Doha; tel. 4423179.

Dar ash-Sharq Printing, Publishing and Distribution: POB 3488, Doha; tel. 4557866; fax 4557871; e-mail alsharq1@qatar.net.qa; Gen. Man. ABDULLATIF AL-MAHMOUD.

Gulf Publishing and Printing Co: POB 533, Doha; tel. 4466555; fax 4438571; e-mail gm@gulftimes.com; internet www.gulf-times.com; Gen. Man. MUHAMMAD ALLAM ALI.

Oryx Publishing and Advertising Co: POB 405, Doha; tel. 4672139; fax 4550982.

Qatar National Printing Press: POB 355, Doha; tel. 4448453; fax 4449550; Man. ABD AL-KARIM DEEB.

Broadcasting and Communications

TELECOMMUNICATIONS

Supreme Council for Communications and Information Technology (ICTQatar): POB 23264, Al-Mirqab Tower, Al-Corniche St, Doha; tel. 4995333; fax 4935913; e-mail info@ict.gov.qa; internet www.ict.gov.qa; f. 2005 to oversee the deregulation of the telecommunications sector; Chair. Crown Prince Sheikh TAMIM BIN HAMAD BIN KHALIFA ATH-THANI; Sec.-Gen. Dr HESSA SULTAN AL-JABER.

Qatar Telecommunications Corpn—Qatar Telecom (Q-Tel): POB 217, Doha; tel. 4830000; fax 4476231; e-mail customer.service@qtel.com.qa; internet www.qtel.com.qa; f. 1987; majority state-owned; provides telecommunications services within Qatar; Chair. Sheikh ABDULLAH BIN MUHAMMAD ATH-THANI; CEO Dr NASSER MARAFIH.

BROADCASTING

Regulatory Authority

Qatar Radio and Television Corpn (QRTC): POB 1414, Doha; tel. 4894444; fax 4882888; e-mail info@qatarradio.net; internet www.qrtc.com; f. 1997; autonomous authority reporting direct to the Council of Ministers.

Radio

Qatar Broadcasting Service (QBS): POB 3939, Doha; tel. 4894444; fax 4882888; f. 1968; govt service transmitting in Arabic, English, French and Urdu; programmes include Holy Quran Radio and Doha Music Radio; Dir MUHAMMAD A. AL-KUWARI.

Television

Al-Jazeera Satellite Network: POB 23123, Doha; tel. 4896044; fax 4873577; e-mail imr@aljazeera.net; internet www.aljazeera.net; f. 1996; 24-hr broadcasting of news and current affairs in Arabic; English-language service launched Nov. 2006; documentary channel launched Jan. 2007; Dir-Gen. WADAH KHANFAR; Chief Editor AHMED SHEIKH.

Qatar Television Service (QTV): POB 1944, Doha; tel. 4894444; fax 4874170; f. 1970; operates two channels (of which one broadcasts in English); 24-hr broadcasting; Dir AHMAD AR-RASHID; Asst Dir ABD AL-WAHAB MUHAMMAD AL-MUTAWA'A.

Finance

(cap. = capital; res = reserves; dep. = deposits; m. = million; brs = branches; amounts in Qatar riyals)

STATE FINANCIAL AUTHORITIES

In March 2005 the Government established the Qatar Financial Centre (QFC), which was intended to attract international financial institutions and multinational corporations to Qatar, 'to establish business operations in a best-in-class international environment'. The QFC comprised the QFC Authority and the QFC Regulatory Authority (see below), as well as two legal bodies—the QFC Regulatory Tribunal and the QFC Civil and Commercial Court—which were charged with upholding the rule of law and ensuring the transparency of QFC transactions. In July 2007 plans were announced for the creation of a single, integrated, fully independent financial regulatory authority, which would oversee all banking, insurance, securities, asset management and other financial services. The new body was expected to become operational in 2008.

Qatar Financial Centre Authority (QFCA): POB 23245, Doha; tel. 4967777; fax 4830928; e-mail info@qfc.com.qa; internet www.qfc.com.qa; f. 2005; charged with promoting Qatar as an attractive location for international banking, insurance and financial services; Chair. YOUSUF BIN HUSSAIN KAMAL (Minister of Finance and Acting Minister of Economy and Commerce); CEO and Dir-Gen. STUART PEARCE.

Qatar Financial Centre Regulatory Authority (QFCRA): POB 22989, Level 14, Qatar Financial Centre Tower, Doha; tel. 4956888; fax 4835031; e-mail info@qfcra.com; internet www.qfcra.com; f. 2005; charged with the regulation and supervision of a wide range of financial activities, incl. banking, insurance, asset management and financial advisory services; Chair. and CEO PHILLIP THORPE.

BANKING

Central Bank

Qatar Central Bank: POB 1234, Doha; tel. 4456456; fax 4414190; e-mail webmaster@qcb.gov.qa; internet www.qcb.gov.qa; f. 1966 as Qatar and Dubai Currency Board; became Qatar Monetary Agency in 1973; renamed Qatar Central Bank in 1993; state-owned; cap. 1,000m., res 4,508.2m., dep. 3,065.6m., currency in circulation 3,123.2m. (Dec. 2004); Gov. ABDULLAH SAUD ATH-THANI.

Commercial Banks

ahlibank QSC: POB 2309, Suhmin bin Hamad St, As-Sadd Area, Doha; tel. 4232222; fax 4232323; e-mail info@ahlibank.com.qa; internet www.ahlibank.com.qa; f. 1984 as Al-Ahli Bank of Qatar QSC; name changed as above in 2004; cap. 406.3m., res 759.6m., dep. 8,174.7m. (Dec. 2006); Chair. AHMED ABD AR-RAHMAN ABD AL-LATIF AL-MANA; CEO BASSEL GAMAL ALY; 9 brs.

Commercial Bank of Qatar QSC (CBQ): POB 3232, Grand Hamad Ave, Doha; tel. 4900000; fax 4490072; e-mail info@cbq.com.qa; internet www.cbq.com.qa; f. 1975; cap. 1,401.6m., res 4,185.5m., dep. 19,903.4m. (Dec. 2006); Chair. ABDULLAH BIN KHALIFA AL-ATTIYA; Gen. Man. ANDREW C. STEVENS; 21 brs.

Doha Bank: POB 3818, Grand Hamad Ave, Doha; tel. 4456600; fax 4410625; e-mail international@dohabank.com.qa; internet www.dohabank.com.qa; f. 1979; cap. 1,248.2m., res 1,519.8m., dep. 17,142.9m. (Dec. 2006); Chair. Sheikh FAHAD BIN MUHAMMAD BIN JABER ATH-THANI; CEO and Man. Dir Sheikh ABD AR-RAHMAN BIN MUHAMMAD BIN JABER ATH-THANI; 24 brs in Qatar, 1 abroad.

International Bank of Qatar QSC (IBQ): POB 2001, Suhaim bin Hamad St, Doha; tel. 4473700; fax 4473710; e-mail qatarenq@ibq.com.qa; internet www.ibq.com.qa; f. 2000 as Grindlays Qatar Bank QSC; previously a branch of ANZ Grindlays Bank, f. 1956; name changed as above in 2004, after National Bank of Kuwait SAK assumed management of the bank; cap. 281.3m., res 909.5m., dep. 5,262.8m. (Dec. 2006); Chair. HAMAD BIN JASIM BIN JABER ATH-THANI; Gen. Man. MICHAEL WILLIAMS.

Qatar Development Bank (QDB): POB 22789, Doha; tel. 4421600; fax 4350433; e-mail contact@qidb.com; internet www.qidb.com.qa; f. 1996 as the Qatar Industrial Development Bank; inaugurated Oct. 1997; relaunched under above name in April 2007 with expanded capital provision to facilitate private sector involvement in national economic devt; state-owned; provides long-term low-interest industrial loans; finances wide range of industrial and social projects; broadened consultancy services following relaunch; cap. 5,000m.; Chair. Sheikh ABDULLAH BIN SA'UD ATH-THANI; Gen. Man. Sheikh HAMAD NASSER ATH-THANI.

Qatar International Islamic Bank QSC (QIIB): POB 664, Grand Hamad St, Doha; tel. 4385555; fax 4444101; e-mail qiibit@qiib.com.qa; internet www.qiib.com.qa; f. 1990; cap. 203.1m., res 676.9m., dep. 5,269.2m. (Dec. 2005); Chair. KHALID BIN THANI BIN ABDULLAH ATH-THANI; Gen. Man. ABD AL-BASIT ASH-SHAIBEI; 10 brs.

Qatar Islamic Bank SAQ: POB 559, Grand Hamad St, Doha; tel. 4409409; fax 4412700; e-mail qib@qib.com.qa; internet www.qib.com.qa; f. 1983; cap. 1,193.4m., res 2,899.5m., dep. 9,933.0m. (Dec. 2006); Chair. Sheikh JASIM BIN HAMAD BIN JASIM BIN JABER ATH-THANI; Man. Dir ABD AL-LATIF BIN ABDULLAH AL-MAHMOUD; 12 brs.

Qatar National Bank SAQ: POB 1000, Doha; tel. 4407777; fax 4413753; e-mail ccsupport@qnb.com.qa; internet www.qnb.com.qa; f. 1964; owned 50% by Govt of Qatar and 50% by Qatari nationals; cap. 1,297.8m., res 6,006.2m., dep. 62,044.9m. (Dec. 2006); Chair. YOUSUF BIN HUSSAIN KAMAL (Minister of Finance and Acting Minister of Economy and Commerce); Chair. of Exec. Cttee Sheikh HAMAD BIN FAISAL ATH-THANI; 32 brs in Qatar, 3 abroad.

STOCK EXCHANGE

Doha Securities Market (DSM): POB 22114, Grand Hamad St, Doha; tel. 4333666; fax 4319233; e-mail dsm@dsm.com.qa; internet www.dsm.com.qa; f. 1997; 42 cos listed in Mar. 2008; Gen. Man. SAIF KHALIFA AL-MANSORI.

INSURANCE

Doha Insurance Co: POB 7171, Doha; tel. 4335000; fax 4657777; e-mail mohammad.qasmi@dicqatar.com; internet www.dicqatar.com; f. 1999 as public shareholding co; cap. 127.2m. (2003); Chair. Sheikh NAWAF BIN NASSER BIN KHALID ATH-THANI; Gen. Man. BASSAM HUSSAIN.

Al-Khaleej Insurance and Reinsurance Co QSC (SAQ): POB 4555, Doha; tel. 4414151; fax 4430530; e-mail alkhalej@qatar.net.qa;

internet www.alkhaleej.com; f. 1978; cap. and res 568.4m. (2007); all classes except life; Chair. ABDULLAH BIN MUHAMMAD JABER ATH-THANI; Gen. Man. KARAM AHMAD MAHMOUD.

Qatar General Insurance and Reinsurance Co SAQ: POB 4500, A Ring Road, Al-Asmakh Area, Doha; tel. 4282222; fax 4437302; e-mail qgirc-tec@qatar.net.qa; internet www.qgirco.com; f. 1979; total assets 1,729.7m. (2007); all classes; Chair. and Man. Dir Sheikh NASSER BIN ALI ATH-THANI; Gen. Man. GHAZI ABU NAHL.

Qatar Insurance Co SAQ: POB 666, Tamin St, West Bay, Doha; tel. 4962222; fax 4831569; e-mail qatarins@qic.com.qa; internet www.qatarinsurance.com; f. 1964; cap. 424.7m., total assets 4,019.4m. (Dec. 2006); all classes; the Govt has a majority share; Chair. and Man. Dir Sheikh KHALID BIN MUHAMMAD ALI ATH-THANI; Pres. and CEO KHALIFA A. AS-SUBAY'I; brs in Doha and Khalifa Town, Dubai and Abu Dhabi (UAE), Saudi Arabia, Kuwait, Oman and Malta.

Qatar Islamic Insurance Co: POB 22676, Doha; tel. 4658888; fax 4550111; e-mail qiic@qatar.net.qa; internet www.qiic.net.qa; f. 1993; cap. 150m., res 137.0m. (Dec. 2007); Chair. Sheikh THANI BIN ABDULLAH ATH-THANI; Gen. Man. IZZAT M. AR-RASHID.

Trade and Industry

DEVELOPMENT ORGANIZATIONS

Department of Industrial Development: POB 2599, Doha; tel. 4846444; fax 4832024; e-mail did@mei.gov.qa; govt-owned; conducts research, licensing, devt and supervision of new industrial projects; Dir-Gen. SAID MUBARAK AL-KUWAIRI.

Public Works Authority (Ashgal): POB 22188, Doha; tel. 4950000; fax 4950999; e-mail info@ashghal.gov.qa; internet www.ashghal.com; f. 2004; Chair. Crown Prince Sheikh TAMIM BIN HAMAD BIN KHALIFA ATH-THANI; CEO Eng. ZAYED MANSOOR AL-KHAYARIN.

CHAMBER OF COMMERCE

Qatar Chamber of Commerce and Industry: POB 402, Doha; tel. 4559111; fax 4661693; e-mail info@qcci.org; internet www.qcci.org; f. 1963; 17 elected mems; Pres. MUHAMMAD BIN KHALID AL-MANA; Chair. Sheikh KHALIFA BIN JASIM BIN MUHAMMAD ATH-THANI.

STATE HYDROCARBONS COMPANIES

Qatar Petrochemical Co (QAPCO) SAQ: POB 756, Doha; tel. 4242444; fax 4324700; e-mail information@qapco.com.qa; internet www.qapco.com; f. 1974; Industries Qatar (IQ) has an 80% share; 20% is held by Total Petrochemicals (France); total assets QR 5,090.7m. (2006); operation of petrochemical plant at Mesaieed; produced 547,494 metric tons of ethylene, 413,180 tons of low-density polyethylene, and 40,000 tons of solid sulphur in 2006; Chair. ABDULLAH BIN HAMAD AL-ATTIYA (Minister of Energy and Industry); Gen. Man. MUHAMMAD YOUSEF AL-MULLA; 879 employees (2004).

Qatar Petroleum (QP): POB 3212, Doha; tel. 4402000; fax 4831125; e-mail webmaster@qp.com.qa; internet www.qp.com.qa; f. 1974 as Qatar General Petroleum Corpn (QGPC), name changed 2001; total assets QR 105,142m. (2005); oil production 850,000 b/d (2006); the State of Qatar's interest in companies active in petroleum and related industries has passed to QP; has responsibility for all phases of oil and gas industry both on shore and off shore, including exploration, drilling, production, refining, transport and storage, distribution, sale and export of oil, natural gas and other hydrocarbons; Oryx gas to liquids (GTL) plant became operational in 2006, with capacity for 34,000 b/d of GTL products; Chair. and Man. Dir ABDULLAH BIN HAMAD AL-ATTIYA (Minister of Energy and Industry); Vice-Chair. YOUSUF HUSSAIN KAMAL; 5,500 employees.

Qatar Petroleum wholly or partly owns: Industries Qatar (IQ) and its subsidiaries, Qatar Gas Transport Co (Nakilat), Ras Laffan LNG Co Ltd (Rasgas), Gulf Helicopters Co Ltd (GHC), Qatar Vinyl Co (QVC), Qatar Chemical Co (Q-Chem), Qatar Clean Energy Co (QACENCO), Qatar Electricity and Water Co (QEWC), Qatar Shipping Co (Q-Ship), Arab Maritime Petroleum Transport Co (AMPTC), Arab Petroleum Pipelines Co (SUMED), Arab Shipbuilding and Repair Yard Co (ASRY), Arab Petroleum Services Co (APSC) and Arab Petroleum Investments Corpn (APICORP); and also the following:

Qatar Liquefied Gas Co (QATARGAS): POB 22666, Doha; tel. 4736000; fax 4736666; e-mail infos@qatargas.com.qa; internet www.qatargas.com; f. 1984 to develop the North Field of unassociated gas; cap. QR 500m.; QP has a 65% share; ExxonMobil and Total hold 10% each; the Marubeni Corpn and Mitsui & Co of Japan hold 7.5% each; expansion plans to supply 42m. metric tons of LNG to European, Asian and North American markets scheduled for completion by 2010; Chair. ABDULLAH BIN HAMAD AL-ATTIYA (Minister of Energy and Industry); Vice-Chair. and CEO FAISAL MUHAMMAD AS-SUWAIDI.

UTILITIES

Qatar General Electricity and Water Corpn (Kahramaa): POB 41, Doha; tel. 4845555; fax 4845496; e-mail pr@km.com.qa; internet www.kahramaa.com.qa; f. 2000; state authority for planning, implementation, operation and maintenance of electricity and water sectors; Chair. ABDULLAH BIN HAMAD AL-ATTIYA (Minister of Energy and Industry).

Qatar Electricity and Water Co (QEWC): POB 22046, Doha; tel. 4858585; fax 4831116; e-mail welcome@qewc.com; internet www.qewc.com; f. 1990; 57% privately owned; has responsibility for adding new generating capacity in Qatar; total assets 9,189m. (Dec. 2007); Chair. ABDULLAH BIN HAMAD AL-ATTIYA (Minister of Energy and Industry); Gen. Man. FAHAD HAMAD AL-MOHANNADI.

Transport

A Transportation Master Plan for Qatar, intended to provide a comprehensive framework for the development of the transport infrastructure over a 20-year period, was implemented in late 2007. Expanded public transport provisions under the Plan constituted an important preparatory component of Qatar's candidacy for hosting the 2016 Olympic Games in Doha. Projected government expenditure on infrastructure projects, particularly roads, amounted to US $8,400m. for the 2008/09 fiscal year, equivalent to 31.3% of total budgeted expenditure.

ROADS

In 1991 there were some 1,191 km of surfaced road linking Doha and the petroleum centres of Dukhan and Umm Said with the northern end of the peninsula. The total road network in 1999 was estimated to be 1,230 km, 90% of which was paved. A 105-km road from Doha to Salwa was completed in 1970, and joins one leading from Al-Hufuf in Saudi Arabia, giving Qatar land access to the Mediterranean. A 418-km highway, built in conjunction with Abu Dhabi, links both states with the Gulf network. A major upgrading of the national road network was planned for the first years of the 21st century. A project to construct a causeway (the Friendship Bridge) linking Qatar with Bahrain, at an estimated cost of over US $2,000m., was approved by both Governments in 2004. After protracted negotiations, it was announced in September 2007 that construction of the causeway was expected to commence in May 2008 and to be concluded by 2011; however, the contract had yet to be awarded by March 2008. In addition, plans for the construction of a 65-km causeway between Qatar and the United Arab Emirates, first mooted in 2002, remained under development in early 2008.

SHIPPING

Doha Port has nine general cargo berths of 7.5 m–9.0 m depth. The total length of the berths is 1,699 m. In addition, there is a flour mill berth, and a container terminal (with a depth of 12.0 m and a length of 600 m) with a roll-on, roll-off berth at the north end currently under construction. Cold storage facilities exist for cargo of up to 500 metric tons. At Umm Said Harbour the Northern Deep Water Wharves consist of a deep-water quay 730 m long with a dredged depth alongside of 15.5 m, and a quay 570 m long with a dredged depth alongside of 13.0 m. The General Cargo Wharves consist of a quay 400-m long with a dredged depth alongside of 10.0 m. The Southern Deep Water Wharves consist of a deep water quay 508 m long with a dredged depth alongside of 13.0 m. The North Field gas project has increased the demand for shipping facilities. A major new industrial port was completed at Ras Laffan in 1995, providing facilities for LNG and condensate carriers and roll-on, roll-off vessels. Qatar Petroleum initiated a US $1,000m. expansion of Ras Laffan port in mid-2005; work was scheduled for completion by the end of 2008. Further expansion plans at Ras Laffan, to accommodate the shipping requirements of the burgeoning LNG and associated industries, were finalized early in 2008; completion of the project would render Ras Laffan the largest man-made harbour in the world, bounded by 26 km of breakwaters. A proposal to move Doha port to a fresh site, near Doha International Airport, was approved in 2005, although significantly increased traffic in 2006 necessitated subsequent re-evaluation of both area size and budget; upon completion of the new facility, the existing port was to be decommissioned.

Customs and Ports General Authority: POB 81, Doha; tel. 4457457; fax 4413563; e-mail admin@customs.gov.qa; internet www.customs.gov.qa; Dir-Gen. Sheikh ABDULLAH BIN JASSIM ATH-THANI.

Qatar National Navigation and Transport Co Ltd (QNNTC): 60 Al-Tameen St, West Bay, POB 153, Doha; tel. 4468666; fax 4468777; e-mail navigation@qnntc.com; f. 1957; 100%-owned by Qatari nationals; shipping agents, stevedoring, chandlers, forwarding, shipowning, repair, construction, etc.; Chair. SALEH MUBARAK

AL-KHOLEILI; Vice-Chair. and Chair. of Exec. Cttee Sheikh ABDULLAH MUHAMMAD JABER ATH-THANI.

Qatar Shipping Co QSC (Q-Ship): POB 22180, Al-Muntazah St, Doha; tel. 4315500; fax 4328361; e-mail qshipops@qship.com; internet www.qship.com; f. 1992; oil and bulk cargo shipping; Chair. and Man. Dir SALEM BIN BUTTI AN-NAIMI; CEO K. K. KOTHARI.

CIVIL AVIATION

Doha International Airport is equipped to receive all types of aircraft. In 2001 some 2.7m. passengers used the airport. In 2004 Bechtel, a US engineering company, won the contract to manage the redevelopment of the airport (to be known upon completion of the project as New Doha International Airport), 4 km to the east of the existing site. Phase one of the project, which was expected to cost some QR 9,500m., was set to increase annual passenger-handling capacity to around 24m. by late 2009. Upon completion of phase three of the expansion, scheduled for 2015, passenger-handling capacity was to reach 50m.

Civil Aviation Authority: POB 3000, Doha; tel. 4557333; fax 4557105; e-mail info@caa.gov.qa; internet www.caa.gov.qa; Chair. and Man. Dir ABD AL-AZIZ MUHAMMAD AN-NOAIMI.

Doha International Airport: POB 22550, Doha; tel. 4622999; fax 4622044; e-mail diainfo@qatarairways.com.qa; internet www.dohaairport.com; CEO AKBAR AL-BAKER.

Gulf Helicopters Co Ltd (GHC): POB 811, Doha; tel. 4333888; fax 4411004; e-mail enquiries@gulfhelicopters.com; internet www.gulfhelicopters.com; f. 1974; owned by QP; Chair. ABDULLAH BIN HAMAD AL-ATTIYA (Minister of Energy and Industry).

Qatar Airways: POB 22550, Qatar Airways Tower, Airport Rd, Doha; tel. 4496000; fax 4621792; e-mail infodesk@qatarairways.com; internet www.qatarairways.com; f. 1993; services to 82 international destinations; CEO AKBAR AL-BAKER.

Tourism

Qatar's tourism industry is small, owing to the country's hitherto limited infrastructure. Since 2000, however, tourism has been actively promoted, and Qatar's reputation as a venue for international conferences and sporting events has grown. The 15th Asian Games, held in Doha in December 2006, provided a substantial impetus for increased hotel construction from 2004. Doha's status as an applicant city to host the 2016 Olympic Games promoted further extensive construction of accommodation facilities, with 22 new hotels expected to open by mid-2008; in total, 98 new hotels were due to be built by 2016. There were 912,997 tourist arrivals in 2005, and receipts from tourism totalled US $760m.

Qatar Tourism Authority (QTA): POB 24624, Doha; tel. 4997499; fax 4991919; e-mail info@qatartourism.gov.qa; internet www.qatartourism.gov.qa; f. 2000 by Amiri decree; affiliated with Council of Ministers; Chair. AKBAR AL-BAKER; CEO JAN POUL N. DE BOER (acting).

ROMANIA

Introductory Survey

Location, Climate, Language, Religion, Flag, Capital

Romania lies in south-eastern Europe, bounded to the north and east by Ukraine, to the north-east by Moldova, to the north-west by Hungary, to the south-west by Serbia and to the south by Bulgaria. The south-east coast is washed by the Black Sea. Romania has hot summers and cold winters, with moderate rainfall. The average summer temperature is 23°C (73°F) and the winter average is −3°C (27°F). The official language is Romanian, although minority groups speak Hungarian (Magyar), German and other languages. Most of the inhabitants profess Christianity, and about 87% of believers are adherents of the Romanian Orthodox Church. The national flag (proportions 3 by 5) consists of three equal vertical stripes, of blue, yellow and red. The capital is Bucharest (București).

Recent History

Formerly part of Turkey's Ottoman Empire, Romania became an independent kingdom in 1881. During the dictatorship of the Fascist 'Iron Guard' movement, Romania entered the Second World War as an ally of Nazi Germany. However, Soviet forces entered Romania in 1944, when the pro-Nazi regime was overthrown. Under Soviet pressure, King Michael (Mihail) I accepted the appointment of a communist-led coalition Government in March 1945. At elections in November 1946 a communist-dominated bloc claimed 89% of the votes cast, but the results were widely believed to have been fraudulent. In 1947 the small Romanian Communist Party (RCP) merged with the Social Democratic Party to become the Romanian Workers' Party (RWP). King Michael was forced to abdicate on 30 December 1947, when the Romanian People's Republic was proclaimed. The republic's first Constitution was adopted in 1948, and in the same year the nationalization of the main industrial and financial institutions was begun. In 1949 private landholdings were expropriated and amalgamated into state and collective farms. The implementation of Soviet-style economic policies was accompanied by the establishment of full political control by the RWP.

In 1952, following a purge of the RWP membership, a new Constitution, closer to the Soviet model, was adopted. Gheorghe Gheorghiu-Dej, the First Secretary of the RWP, became Romania's unchallenged leader and proceeded to implement large-scale plans for industrialization. Gheorghiu-Dej died in 1965; he was succeeded as First Secretary of the RWP by Nicolae Ceaușescu, a Secretary of the RWP Central Committee since 1954. In June 1965 the RWP again became the RCP, and Ceaușescu's post of First Secretary was restyled General Secretary. A new Constitution, adopted in August, changed the country's name to the Socialist Republic of Romania.

Ceaușescu continued his predecessor's relatively independent foreign policy, criticizing the invasion of Czechoslovakia by troops of the Warsaw Pact (the defence grouping of the Soviet bloc) in 1968, and establishing links with Western states and institutions. However, the use of foreign loans for investment led to severe economic problems by the early 1980s. In order to strengthen his position, Ceaușescu (who had become President of the Republic in 1974) implemented frequent changes in the RCP leadership and the Government. In March 1980 his wife, Elena, became a First Deputy Chairman of the Council of Ministers, and numerous other family members held government and party posts.

In late 1985 an energy crisis resulted in a declaration of a state of emergency in the electric power industry and the dismissal of ministers and senior officials. Shortages led to strict energy rationing in 1987, and strikes were organized in provincial factories. In November thousands of people marched through the city of Brașov and stormed the local RCP headquarters, protesting against the decline in living standards and in working conditions. Hundreds of arrests were made, and similar protests followed in other cities. In March 1988 Ceaușescu announced details of a rural urbanization programme, to entail the demolition of some 8,000 villages, and the resettlement of their residents (mostly ethnic Hungarians) in new 'agro-industrial centres'. The plan attracted much domestic and international criticism, but Ceaușescu maintained that the programme would raise living standards and ensure social equality.

In December 1989 there was unrest in the western city of Timișoara as supporters of László Tőkés, a Protestant clergyman (an ethnic Hungarian who had repeatedly criticized the Government's policies), demonstrated their opposition to his eviction from his church. A further protest was attended by thousands of local residents. Security forces opened fire on the crowd, reportedly killing several hundred people. There were reports of protests in other towns, and the country's borders were closed.

On 21 December 1989 President Ceaușescu attended a mass rally in Bucharest, intended to demonstrate popular support. Instead, his address was interrupted by hostile chanting, and anti-Government demonstrations followed later in the day, leading to clashes between protesters and members of the Securitate (the secret police force), during which many civilians were killed. The disturbances quickly spread to other parts of the country, and on the following day Ceaușescu declared a state of emergency; however, soldiers of the regular army declared their support for the protesters. Nicolae and Elena Ceaușescu escaped from the RCP Central Committee headquarters by helicopter as demonstrators stormed the building. The Ceaușescus were captured near Târgoviște and, on 25 December, after a summary trial, were executed by firing squad. Fighting continued for several days, mainly between Securitate forces and regular soldiers.

Meanwhile, a 145-member National Salvation Front (NSF) was formed, and a provisional Government was established. Ion Iliescu, a former Secretary of the RCP Central Committee, became interim President, and Petre Roman, an academic, was appointed Prime Minister. The new Government immediately decreed an end to the RCP's constitutional monopoly of power, and cancelled the rural urbanization programme. The RCP was banned, it was announced that free elections would be held in 1990, and the designation of Socialist Republic was abandoned. By early January 1990 the army had restored order, and the Securitate was abolished. According to official figures, 689 people were killed during the revolution.

Special military tribunals were established to try Ceaușescu's former associates. In February 1990 four senior RCP officials were found guilty of responsibility for the shootings in Timișoara and Bucharest and were sentenced to life imprisonment. Numerous other former government and RCP members were similarly charged. In September Ceaușescu's son, Nicu, who was found to have ordered security forces to open fire on demonstrators in Sibiu in December 1989, received a 20-year prison sentence. (He was released in 1992 on the grounds of ill health, and died in 1996.) Gen. Iulian Vlad, the former head of the Securitate, was sentenced to 12 years' imprisonment in 1991; in January 1994, however, he was released as part of a general amnesty. In December 1991 eight associates of the former President were sentenced to prison terms of up to 25 years for their part in the shootings in Timișoara.

Despite the widespread jubilation that followed the downfall of Ceaușescu, the NSF did not enjoy total public support. Many citizens believed that the Front's leadership was too closely linked with the Ceaușescu regime, and were particularly critical of the NSF's control of the media. Furthermore, the NSF's announcement, in January 1990, that it was to contest the forthcoming elections, and its reversal of the prohibition of the RCP, increased fears that members of the disgraced regime were attempting to regain power. In January the offices of two opposition parties, the National Liberal Party (NLP) and the National Peasants' Party, were attacked by NSF supporters. In February, after negotiations among representatives of 29 political parties, the NSF agreed to share power with the opposition, pending the elections, in a 180-member Provisional National Unity Council (PNUC). Each of the political parties represented in the talks was allocated three seats on the Council, and the PNUC was subsequently expanded to 253 members to permit representation by other political parties; nevertheless, NSF members and supporters occupied 111 seats in the Council. The PNUC elected an Executive Bureau, with Iliescu as its

President. Opposition to the NSF persisted, particularly in the armed forces. The Minister of National Defence was replaced in compliance with demands from within the military, but shortly afterwards thousands of anti-Government demonstrators demanded the resignation of Iliescu, and some 250 protesters forcibly entered the NSF headquarters.

As the elections approached, there were mass anti-communist demonstrations in Bucharest. The election campaign was acrimonious, and there were widespread accusations of systematic intimidation and harassment of the NSF's opponents. At the presidential and legislative elections, held on 20 May 1990, the NSF achieved an overwhelming victory. Allegations of irregularities were, however, confirmed by international observers. According to official figures, Iliescu won 85.1% of the valid votes cast in the presidential poll. In the elections to the bicameral legislature, the NSF won 65% of the votes cast, securing 263 of the 387 seats in the Camera Deputaților (Chamber of Deputies) and 91 of the 119 seats in Senatul (the Senate).

Unrest continued, and in June 1990 a protest in Bucharest was forcibly broken up by the police. The brutal treatment of the demonstrators provoked renewed clashes, in which the armed forces opened fire on rioters. Following an appeal for support by Iliescu, some 7,000 miners and other workers were transported to the capital, where they swiftly seized control of the streets. The disturbances resulted in several deaths and hundreds of injuries. Following President Iliescu's inauguration in late June, Roman was reappointed Prime Minister, and a new Council of Ministers was formed, in which nearly all the members of the interim administration were replaced. In the following months, as popular discontent at the deteriorating economic situation intensified, there was widespread strike action. In October Roman announced extensive economic reforms. In the following month price increases led to demonstrations in Bucharest, including a protest march by some 100,000 people, organized by a new opposition grouping, the Civic Alliance. Nevertheless, the Government proceeded with its (slightly modified) reform programme, resulting in further large price rises in April 1991. At the end of that month Roman allocated three government portfolios to opposition politicians.

In September 1991 miners, by this time opposed to President Iliescu, began a strike in support of demands for pay increases and the resignation of the Government. Thousands of miners travelled to Bucharest, where they attacked government offices and ransacked the parliament building. Four people were killed and hundreds injured during violent clashes with the security forces, as a result of which the Council of Ministers was obliged to resign. Theodor Stolojan, a former Minister of Finance, was appointed as Prime Minister, leading a coalition Government formed in October, comprising members of the NSF, the NLP, the Agrarian Democratic Party of Romania (ADPR) and the Romanian Ecological Movement.

A new Constitution, enshrining a multi-party system, a free-market economy and guarantees of the respect of human rights, was approved by the legislature in November 1991 and was endorsed by some 77.3% of voters in a referendum in December. The results of local elections, which took place between February and April 1992, confirmed the decline in support for the NSF. Many seats were won by the centre-right Democratic Convention of Romania (DCR), an alliance of 18 parties and organizations, including the Christian Democratic National Peasants' Party (CDNPP) and the Party of the Civic Alliance. The NSF divided into two factions, and in April the faction loyal to Iliescu, which favoured only limited reforms, was registered as the Democratic National Salvation Front (DNSF).

Against a background of renewed labour unrest, legislative and presidential elections took place on 27 September 1992. The DNSF won 117 of the 328 elective seats in the Camera Deputaților and 49 of the 143 seats in Senatul, making it the largest party in the new Parlamentul (Parliament). Its closest rival was the DCR, with 82 seats in the Camera Deputaților and 34 in Senatul. The NSF secured only 43 and 18 seats, respectively. In the presidential election, the two leading candidates, Iliescu and Emil Constantinescu, representing the DCR, proceeded to a second round of voting on 11 October, at which Iliescu won 61.4% of the votes cast. In November Nicolae Văcăroiu, an economist with no professed political party affiliation, formed a Government comprising equal numbers of DNSF members and independents.

The abolition of price subsidies for many basic commodities and services, from May 1993, precipitated renewed labour unrest. The Government's position was also undermined by successive confidence motions. Meanwhile, the DNSF had changed its name to the Party of Social Democracy of Romania (PSDR) in July and absorbed three other parties. In May, in an apparently similar attempt to distance itself from the events of 1989–90, Roman's NSF renamed itself the Democratic Party—National Salvation Front (DP–NSF). By late 1993 Văcăroiu's administration appeared increasingly unstable. In November a protest march in Bucharest, demanding rapid economic reforms, was the largest public demonstration in the country since the overthrow of the Ceaușescu regime. In February 1994 renewed industrial unrest led to a general strike. A government reshuffle in March continued the pattern of single-party (PSDR) rule supplemented by independent 'technocrats' (although later in the year two members of the Romanian National Unity Party—RNUP—were appointed to the Council of Ministers). In November 1995 Iliescu approved legislation providing for the restitution of property confiscated by the communist regime in the late 1940s and 1950s.

In May 1996 the PSDR terminated its parliamentary co-operation with the RNUP. Although the PSDR secured the largest number of mayoral and council seats at the local elections in June, the results indicated a decline in support for the party. The DCR and the Social Democratic Union (SDU), formed by the DP–NSF and the Romanian Social Democratic Party (RSDP) in January, won control of many major cities, including Bucharest. In September the RNUP ministers were dismissed from the Government: the breakdown in relations with the PSDR had been exacerbated by the RNUP's opposition to the signing of a treaty with Hungary (see below).

Legislative and presidential elections took place on 3 November 1996. The DCR won the largest number of parliamentary seats, with 122 of the 328 seats in the Camera Deputaților and 53 of the 143 seats in Senatul. The PSDR took 91 and 41 seats in the respective chambers, and the SDU 53 and 23. The DCR and the SDU subsequently reached agreement on political co-operation. In the first round of the presidential election, which was contested by 16 candidates, Iliescu won 32.3% of the valid votes cast, and Constantinescu took 28.2%. With the support of nearly all the opposition parties, Constantinescu was duly elected in a second round on 17 November, with 54.4% of the votes cast. Constantinescu pledged to combat corruption and accelerate economic reform, and had asserted his commitment to the integration of Romania into Western political, economic and defence institutions. At the end of November Victor Ciorbea of the DCR, who had been elected as Mayor of Bucharest earlier in the year, was nominated as Prime Minister, and in mid-December a new coalition Government, comprising the DCR, the SDU and the Democratic Alliance of Hungarians in Romania (DAHR), was officially sworn in.

Despite protests from opposition parties, the Government restored citizenship to former King Michael, who visited Romania in February 1997. Meanwhile, in January a National Council for Action against Corruption and Organized Crime, headed by Constantinescu, was established; a number of leading bankers were subsequently arrested, principally on charges of fraud, and several senior members of the security forces were dismissed. The arrest, in February, of Miron Cozma, the leader of the miners' demonstrations in Bucharest in June 1990 and September 1991, prompted protests from miners and their trade-union leaders. In November 1997 an estimated 40,000 people attended a rally in Bucharest to protest against increasing poverty.

Meanwhile, several prominent members of the PSDR resigned from the party in June 1997, and formed a new party, the Alliance for Romania (AFR). A government reorganization in December, which included the appointment of a number of technocrats to principal portfolios, failed to ease mounting tensions within the coalition, and the DAHR temporarily suspended its participation in the Government.

Adrian Severin, Minister of State and Minister of Foreign Affairs, and a member of the DP (as the DP–NSF had been renamed), resigned in December 1997, after a judicial investigation failed to confirm his allegations that certain political leaders and newspaper editors were working with foreign intelligence services. In January 1998 the resignation of the Minister of Transport, Traian Băsescu of the DP, owing to his criticism of Ciorbea's Government, led the DP to demand his reinstatement, and DP ministers eventually withdrew from the Government.

In March 1998, in response to increasing pressure within the coalition, Ciorbea and his Government resigned. Radu Vasile, the Secretary-General of the CDNPP and a Deputy Chairman of Senatul, was designated Prime Minister in April. A new Council of Ministers was appointed, which was endorsed by Parlamentul in mid-April. A new coalition protocol was designed to strengthen the authority of the Prime Minister and improve co-operation between government members. In June the approval of legislation by Senatul that debarred former secret police agents from holding public office led to the resignation of the Minister of Health, Francis Baranyi.

As Romania's economic situation worsened, the Minister of Finance, Daniel Dăianu, was dismissed in September 1998; he was replaced by Decebal Trăian Remes. In October Sorin Dimitriu resigned as Minister of Privatization and head of the State Ownership Fund. Meanwhile, in early September the DAHR threatened to leave the ruling coalition unless Parlamentul adopted legislation providing for the establishment of a minority-language university. At the end of the month the Government duly agreed to create an independent university in Cluj-Napoca for Hungarian and German minorities.

Protests against austerity measures, which had begun the previous month, intensified in December 1998. In January 1999 a strike by miners escalated when Vasile refused to negotiate with Cozma, who had been released from prison in mid-1998, after serving an 18-month sentence for the possession of firearms and ammunition. Encouraged by nationalist politicians (notably from the Greater Romania Party—GRP), 10,000–20,000 miners marched towards Bucharest, and in Costești, some 190 km north-west of Bucharest, violent clashes broke out with the security forces. Following emergency talks between the Prime Minister and miners' leaders, a temporary agreement was reached. The Minister of the Interior, Gavril Dejeu, resigned, amid severe criticism of the security forces' failure to halt the march; he was replaced by Constantin Dudu Ionescu. In February the Supreme Court of Justice sentenced Cozma, *in absentia*, to 18 years' imprisonment for undermining state authority. In protest, some 2,000–4,000 miners, led by Cozma, again marched towards Bucharest. The miners were stopped by the security forces some 160 km west of Bucharest, where more than 100 people were injured and one miner died during the violence that ensued; Cozma and several hundred miners were arrested. Labour unrest continued throughout the first half of 1999. (In June 2002 Cozma was sentenced to an additional 12 years' imprisonment—to be served concurrently—for his involvement in the 1999 violence; in January 2007, however, it was reported that he had been granted early release.)

In early June 1999 the Camera Deputaților approved amendments to the electoral law, increasing the threshold for parliamentary representation from 3% to 5%, with alliances required to secure a further 3% for each member party. Later that month the Camera Deputaților voted in favour of providing public access to the files of the Securitate (although many documents were believed to have been destroyed); the President promulgated the legislation in December. Also in June legislation was approved by Parlamentul, providing for minority-language education at every level of the education system. In July Gen. Victor Stănculescu and Gen. Mihai Chițac were sentenced to 15 years' imprisonment, having been found guilty of the murders of 72 people, by ordering the security forces to open fire on protesters during the Timișoara uprising in December 1989. The ruling was severely criticized by Victor Babiuc, the Minister of National Defence, whose ministry was ordered to pay damages to those wounded in the shootings and the relatives of the dead. (Babiuc resigned from the Government and from his party several months later.)

In November 1999 students undertook strike action, and some 10,000 trade union members participated in protest rallies to demand the resignation of the Government. In mid-December, as labour unrest continued, Constantinescu dismissed Vasile, after all seven CDNPP government ministers, followed by the three NLP ministers, resigned from the Government. Constantinescu nominated Mugur Isărescu, hitherto Governor of the National Bank of Romania (and without affiliation to any political party), as Prime Minister. The legislature subsequently approved the appointment of Isărescu and his Council of Ministers, which remained largely unchanged, although Roman joined the new Government as Minister of State and Minister of Foreign Affairs. Vasile was expelled from the CDNPP later that month.

In local elections, held on 4 June 2000, the PSDR won the largest proportion of the votes cast (36.7%). Băsescu left the Government, after being elected as Mayor of Bucharest. In July President Constantinescu unexpectedly announced that he would not stand for re-election at the forthcoming presidential election. In September the RSDP withdrew from the governing coalition, announcing that it was to merge with the main opposition party, the PSDR.

Legislative and presidential elections took place concurrently on 26 November 2000. The PSDR secured 155 seats in the Camera Deputaților and 65 in Senatul, while the GRP obtained 84 and 37 seats, respectively. The rate of voter participation was the lowest recorded since the collapse of communism, at 57.5%. Representatives of the PSDR and the GRP were also the principal candidates in the presidential election, in which the former President, Iliescu, obtained 36.4% of the votes cast and Corneliu Vadim Tudor of the GRP won 28.3%. As neither candidate secured an overall majority, a 'run-off' election was held on 10 December, in which Iliescu won 66.8% of the votes cast. The increased support for the extreme nationalists was thought to reflect popular disillusionment with economic hardship and high unemployment.

In December 2000 President Iliescu nominated Adrian Năstase of the PSDR as Prime Minister. Năstase subsequently signed a joint statement on priorities for the development of Romania with the leaders of the DAHR, the NLP and the DP. Although Năstase insisted that the declaration did not represent a coalition agreement, the support of those parties enabled the PSDR to form a minority Government, and ensured the isolation of the GRP. The new, expanded Council of Ministers was sworn in on 28 December. Despite their shared objective of implementing reform with a view to attaining membership of the European Union (EU, see p. 244), the new President and Prime Minister came from different ideological backgrounds.

In February 2001 President Iliescu endorsed a law, which provided for the return of some 300,000 properties nationalized during the communist era to their original owners; it superseded legislation on the restitution of property that had been approved in 1995. In mid-June the PSDR and the RSDP formally merged, creating the Social Democratic Party (SDP), under the leadership of Prime Minister Năstase. In November some 15,000 people took part in a demonstration in Bucharest against poverty and the Government's austerity programme. A further large-scale protest took place in December.

In March 2002 attempts to tackle corruption led the Government to announce the establishment, with effect from September, of a new National Anti-corruption Prosecution office. Also in March the Government sought to moderate the power of labour organizations through the signature of a 'social pact' with three of the five largest trade unions, which provided for an increased minimum wage and the creation of 10,000 jobs. In September Senatul approved a new law on political parties, which required all parties to re-register by 31 December, and to be composed of a minimum of 10,000 members from at least 21 of Romania's 41 administrative sub-divisions. On 10 November local elections took place in 21 counties, in which the SDP was the most successful party. In early 2003 a number of prominent CDNPP members were expelled from the party after participating in the foundation of the new Popular Action civic movement, led by former President Constantinescu; in February it was confirmed that the movement was to become a political party.

In June 2003 Năstase reorganized the Council of Ministers, reducing the number of portfolios from 23 to 14. In a referendum held on 18–19 October, some 90% of votes cast by 55.7% of the electorate approved 79 proposed amendments to the Constitution, which aimed to bring it into conformity with EU requirements (by, *inter alia*, guaranteeing the right to private property, strengthening legal rights for ethnic minorities and limiting the powers of the executive branch of government). The revised Constitution entered into force on 29 October.

In March 2004 Năstase announced the appointment of three new Ministers of State (effectively deputy prime ministers). Three existing ministers also assumed the additional positions of Ministers of State. In August charges of abuse of office and embezzlement were brought against 79 people, including Băsescu (in his former capacity as Minister of Transport in 1991–92 and 1997–2000), relating to the alleged illegal sale of 16 ships from the national maritime fleet in 1991–2000. Some commentators suggested that the charge was an attempt to discredit the opposition prior to national legislative and presidential elections; Băsescu had been re-elected as Mayor of Bucharest two months earlier. In local elections held on 6 and 20 June 2004 the SDP received the greatest number of mayoral mandates, closely followed by the NLP.

In September 2004 the SDP and the Humanist Party of Romania (HPR) formed an electoral alliance, known as the National Union. Meanwhile, the NLP and the DP announced their intention to contest the forthcoming legislative elections as the Justice and Truth Alliance. On 28 November presidential and legislative elections were held, as scheduled. The National Union emerged as the largest bloc in both legislative chambers, with 132 seats (of a total of 332) in the Camera Deputaților and 57 (of a total of 137) in Senatul. The Justice and Truth Alliance received 112 seats in the Camera Deputaților and 49 in Senatul. The representation of the GRP was markedly reduced in both chambers, to 48 deputies in the lower chamber, and 21 senators. In the presidential ballot no candidate secured an absolute majority of votes cast, and Năstase (with 40.9%) and Traian Băsescu (with 33.9%) proceeded to a second round of voting on 12 December. In the 'run-off' election, Băsescu achieved a narrow victory, with 51.2% of the votes cast. (As President, Băsescu was immune from prosecution.) On 18 December Băsescu resigned from the DP, in compliance with constitutional requirements, and he was inaugurated as President two days later. Năstase was elected as Chairman of the Camera Deputaților, and Văcăroiu, a Deputy Chairman of the SDP, was elected as Chairman of Senatul in a vote that was boycotted by senators of the Justice and Truth Alliance and the DAHR.

Băsescu nominated Călin Popescu-Tăriceanu to form a government, but the approval of a cabinet was dependent upon its ability to achieve a majority in Parlamentul; ultimately, the grouping that would hold the majority in the legislature was to be determined by the allegiance of the HPR (as the DAHR did not possess a sufficient number of mandates to decide the issue). The HPR was persuaded to abandon its electoral partner, the SDP, but even collectively, the coalition of the NLP, the DP, the DAHR and the HPR only amounted to one more than the requisite quorum in the bicameral legislature. On 28 December 2004 the new Council of Ministers was approved by both chambers of the legislature; it was to comprise 25 ministers: nine from the NLP, eight from the DP, four from the DAHR and three from the HPR. In February 2005 Popescu-Tăriceanu was elected as Chairman of the NLP.

The HPR was renamed the Conservative Party (CP) in May 2005. In June Iliescu reportedly became the subject of an investigation into the deaths of six people during the demonstrations by miners in 1990 (see above); however, as a member of Senatul and a former Head of State, Iliescu was immune from prosecution. In late June 2005 Emil Boc was elected President of the DP. In early July the Constitutional Court rejected a programme for judicial reform that had been proposed by the Government in order to satisfy requirements for membership of the EU, prompting Popescu-Tăriceanu to announce that he intended to submit the resignation of his administration, in an attempt to precipitate early elections. However, on 13 July an extraordinary session of Parlamentul approved amendments to the legislation on judicial reform, in conformity with the Court's objections. Meanwhile, central and eastern parts of the country were affected by severe flooding, which resulted in more than 20 deaths, and on 19 July Popescu-Tăriceanu announced that his Government would remain in place in order to respond to the emergency. In August Popescu-Tăriceanu reorganized the Council of Ministers.

In October 2005 the EU Commissioner responsible for Enlargement, Olli Rehn, warned Romania that its planned accession to the EU in 2007 could be subject to delay if measures were not taken to combat corruption and accelerate the pace of judicial reform. In early 2006 a number of political figures duly came under investigation as a result of allegations of fraud, and in January Năstase resigned from the leadership of the SDP, following concerns about the legitimacy of an inheritance received by his wife. In early February Năstase was indicted on charges of bribery, pertaining to the acquisition of land in 1998. However, Senatul rejected legislation that would have permitted officials from the National Anti-corruption Prosecution office increased powers to facilitate the investigation of senior politicians and members of the judiciary (and subsequently restricted prosecutors from searching Năstase's property). Năstase resigned as Chairman of the Camera Deputaților in mid-March, following a vote of no confidence by the SDP; he was succeeded by Bogdan Olteanu of the NLP. Meanwhile, in late February the Government survived a parliamentary motion of no confidence prompted by its proposed health care reforms, submitted by the opposition SDP and GRP.

In September 2006 the Minister of National Defence, Teodor Atanasiu of the NLP, was removed from his post by President Băsescu, following allegations of abuse of military intelligence; he was replaced in late October by Sorin Frunzăverde of the DP, who had previously held that position in 2000. In December 2006 the CP announced its withdrawal from the coalition Government, prompting the resignation of two ministers and ending the parliamentary majority commanded by Popescu-Tăriceanu.

In January 2007 Băsescu publicly accused Popescu-Tăriceanu of attempting to influence a criminal investigation against a close associate accused of financial misconduct, while the Prime Minister issued counter-accusations that Băsescu was undermining government stability. In February Mihai Ungureanu tendered his resignation as Minister of Foreign Affairs at the request of Popescu-Tăriceanu, after he had failed to inform the Government about the detention of two Romanian nationals by US forces in Iraq; Băsescu subsequently refused to endorse the Prime Minister's nomination of an NLP representative, Adrian Cioroianu, to the post. The intra-administrative tensions were further exacerbated in March, when Popescu-Tăriceanu repeated demands for the withdrawal of Romania's military contingent in Iraq, and for the replacement of three DP ministers, notably the Minister of Justice, Monica Luisa Macovei (whose efforts to reform the legal system had helped to ensure Romania's admission to the EU on 1 January). At the beginning of April Popescu-Tăriceanu accused Băsescu of provoking dissension within the Government and ended his party's coalition with the DP, thereby removing eight DP ministers. He formed a new minority Government, comprising 13 representatives of the NLP and four of the DAHR, which was approved by Parlamentul, with the support of the SDP, on 3 April (and endorsed by Băsescu on the following day). Cioroianu became Minister of Foreign Affairs, while Tudor Chiuariu of the NLP, who had hitherto headed the anti-corruption department in the Office of the Prime Minister, was appointed Minister of Justice; Teodor Meleșcanu of the NLP was appointed Minister of Defence. On 19 April a motion initiated by the SDP to suspend Băsescu from office on grounds of unconstitutional conduct (by creating political instability, pressurizing the judiciary and interfering in government affairs) was approved by Parlamentul, after receiving the support of the ruling coalition deputies. Văcăroiu, as Chairman of Senatul, was to act as interim President, and a national referendum on Băsescu's impeachment was scheduled to take place one month later, in accordance with the Constitution. A Constitutional Court ruling earlier in April on the charges against Băsescu had been in his favour, and it was widely believed that his efforts to combat corruption had antagonized former communists. At a rally of his supporters in early May Băsescu demanded the resignation of Chiuariu, who had reportedly proposed the dismissal of a prominent anti-corruption prosecutor. On 9 May, in accordance with EU requirements, Senatul approved legislation providing for the creation of a national agency to monitor the activities of civil servants, including parliamentary deputies, in an effort to prevent corruption. At the national referendum, held on 19 May, Băsescu's removal from office was opposed by about 74.5% of those who voted. Băsescu was officially reinstated as President on 23 May. In the same month he was obliged to issue an apology, following the disclosure of remarks he had made about a journalist that referred to the Roma ethnic group in a racially offensive manner.

In early October 2007 a motion of no confidence against Popescu-Tăriceanu's Government was narrowly defeated in a joint session of both parliamentary chambers. The continuation of the minority administration, and of the hostility between Popescu-Tăriceanu and Băsescu, subsequently proved an impediment to the adoption of reforms required by the EU. In the same month Decebal Trăian Remes, the Minister of Agriculture and Rural Development, resigned, after an investigation into allegations of corruption against him was initiated.

On 25 November 2007 elections (postponed since May) to 35 seats in the European Parliament (see below) were conducted. The DP won 13 seats and the SDP 10 seats, while the NLP secured six seats and its coalition partner, the DAHR, two seats; a breakaway group of the NLP, formed in late 2006 and known as the Liberal Democratic Party, won three seats, and the remaining seat was obtained by an independent. A referendum on changing the electoral system to single-mandate voting was organized on the same day; although more than 80% of voters supported the proposed amendment, the referendum was ruled to be invalid, owing to a rate of participation of only 26% of the electorate.

In early December 2007 Chiuariu resigned from his post as Minister of Justice, following the initiation of a criminal investigation into his alleged abuse of office. In January 2008 Băsescu refused to endorse Popescu-Tăriceanu's selected candidate, demanding that the new minister be a representative of a party other than the NLP. After the Constitutional Court ruled in support of Băsescu, in March Cătălin Marian Predoiu, a lawyer with no political affiliation, was appointed as the new Minister of Justice. Meanwhile, the EU continued to urge the implementation of judicial reforms and measures to address high-level corruption. In April Cioroianu resigned from his post as Minister of Foreign Affairs, following controversy over the death in January of a Romanian national imprisoned in Poland for theft, who had staged a hunger strike to protest his innocence. (The Romanian consul in Poland had been recalled, after failing to inform the Romanian Ministry of Foreign Affairs of the situation.) Later in April Băsescu approved Popescu-Tăriceanu's nomination of Lazăr Comănescu, hitherto Romania's ambassador to the EU, as Minister of Foreign Affairs.

Romania experienced frequent occurrences of ethnic unrest after the fall of Ceaușescu. In 1991 there were organized attacks on Roma (Gypsy) communities throughout Romania, resulting in the emigration of many Roma to Germany. In September 1992 Germany repatriated 43,000 Romanian refugees, more than one-half of whom were Roma, having agreed to provide financial assistance for their resettlement in Romania. The migration of Roma to the member countries of the EU strained relations with Romania throughout the remainder of the 1990s. However, in January 2002 the Council of Europe (see p. 225) published a report condemning police brutality and widespread discrimination against Roma communities in Romania, and the EU made the improvement of the treatment of the Roma minority a requirement for Romania to be declared eligible to accede to the Union. In February 2005 Romania was one of eight countries in the region to announce its adherence to a World Bank-financed 10-year plan to assist the Roma community.

Following the overthrow of Ceaușescu, ethnic Hungarians (a sizeable minority, numbering more than 7% of the total population at the 1992 census) sought to increase their cultural and linguistic autonomy in Transylvania. In March 1990 demonstrations by ethnic Hungarians demanding such rights were attacked by Romanian nationalists in Târgu Mureș. Tanks and troops were deployed to quell the unrest, in which several people were killed, and a state of emergency was declared in the town. In mid-1992 there was renewed tension when the Mayor of Cluj-Napoca, Gheorghe Funar (later head of the right-wing RNUP), ordered the removal of Hungarian-language street signs in the city, and ethnic Hungarian prefects in Covasna and Harghita were replaced by ethnic Romanians. The Government attempted to calm the situation by appointing 'parallel' prefects of ethnic Hungarian background, but further controversy was caused by the removal, in September, of the only ethnic Hungarian State Secretary in the Government. An agreement on Hungarian minority rights was signed in July 1993, which included guarantees for the training of Hungarian-speaking schoolteachers and bilingual street signs in areas with Hungarian populations of at least 30%. In August Bela Marko, the President of the DAHR, insisted that any Hungarian-Romanian state treaty should enshrine a 'special status' for ethnic Hungarians in Romania. Marko's proposals included the equal status of the Hungarian and Romanian languages in predominantly Hungarian-populated areas and greater control for the minority over educational and cultural affairs. In May Romania ratified the Framework Convention of the Council of Europe on the general protection of national minorities. In September 1996 Romania and Hungary signed a treaty of friendship, as a result of which Romania agreed to safeguard the rights of ethnic Hungarians, and Hungary relinquished any claim to territory in Transylvania. In December two DAHR leaders were appointed to the new Government. Relations between Romania and Hungary improved further in February 1997 with the signature of a defence co-operation agreement. Proposals to amend legislation on education, in favour of ethnic minorities, provoked controversy in Romania in 1997 and 1998, although the amendments were finally approved in June 1999.

In January 2001 the Camera Deputaților approved a new public administration law, which made compulsory bilingual place names and signs, and the use of a given minority's language in local administration, in towns where that minority formed at least 20% of the population. In June the Government condemned Hungary's intention to introduce a new 'status law', which was to grant education, employment and medical rights to ethnic Hungarians living in neighbouring countries (including Romania) from January 2002. In December 2001 the Prime Ministers of the two countries signed a memorandum of understanding, which extended the short-term employment rights offered to ethnic Hungarians under the terms of the status law to all Romanian citizens. Finally, in September 2003 Prime Minister Năstase and his Hungarian counterpart, Péter Medgyessy, signed a bilateral agreement on the implementation of the status law in Romania. Hungary proved to be a staunch supporter of Romania's candidacy for EU membership. In October 2005 the first joint Romanian-Hungarian inter-governmental meeting was held in Bucharest, at which a treaty was concluded on the border regime, co-operation and mutual assistance.

Diplomatic relations with the former Soviet republic of Moldova (much of which formed part of Romania in 1918–40, and where a majority of the population are ethnic Romanians) were established in August 1991, and some political groups began to advocate the unification of the two states. The Romanian leadership opposed unification, but encouraged the development of closer cultural and economic ties with Moldova. The support of the Russian military in Moldova for the secessionist movement in the self-proclaimed 'Transdnestrian Moldovan Soviet Socialist Republic' damaged relations between Romania and Russia. In March 1994 a plebiscite was held in Moldova on the question of reunification with Romania; more than 95% of those who took part in the referendum voted for an independent state, effectively signalling the demise of the pro-unification movement. In 2000, as formal negotiations on Romania's accession to the EU commenced, hundreds of Moldovans applied for Romanian citizenship, in anticipation of the eventual tightening of border regulations. Relations with Moldova deteriorated from late 2001. In October Năstase cancelled a planned visit to Moldova, after President Vladimir Voronin of Moldova accused Romania of 'expansionism'. Relations had improved by 2003, following a meeting between the respective Presidents at a conference in Beirut, Lebanon, in September 2002, and inter-ministerial co-operation was restored in April 2003; Romania confirmed that it would not require Moldovan citizens to possess entry visas until its accession to the EU. Relations improved further over the course of 2004, with the apparent reorientation of Moldovan foreign policy towards the West. Moldova was the first country to which newly elected President Traian Băsescu paid a state visit in January 2005, and Romania offered support for Moldova's objective of securing eventual membership of the EU, as its relations with Russia deteriorated in 2005–06 (see the chapter on Moldova). In March 2007, after Romania's official accession to the EU on 1 January necessitated the possession of entry visas for Moldovan citizens wishing to visit Romania, the Moldovan Government (which had strongly criticized Romania for granting Romanian citizenship to large numbers of Moldovan nationals) reversed a decision to allow Romania to open two new consulates in the country. In December Moldova expelled two Romanian diplomats, who had allegedly supplied funds to opposition newspapers, for activities 'incompatible with their status'.

A basic treaty between Romania and Ukraine, signed in early June 1997, guaranteed the inviolability of their joint border, and provided for separate treaties to be established regarding the administration of the frontier and the disputed ownership of the Black Sea continental shelf. In June 2003 President Iliescu and President Leonid Kuchma of Ukraine signed an accord confirming the mutual land border of the two countries, as it was delineated in 1961, with the exception of the continental shelf. No further progress was made in resolving the disagreement over the disputed area (known as Serpent's Island). In late 2003 Romania accused Ukraine of populating the area in an attempt to claim exclusive rights over petroleum and gas reserves, and in 2004 submitted a formal complaint over the matter to the International Court of Justice (see p. 20). A further dispute arose between the two countries in that year over the construction by Ukraine of a canal through the environmentally sensitive Danube Delta. In February 2006 President Băsescu and President Viktor Yushchenko of Ukraine announced the establishment of a bilateral commission, with responsibility, *inter alia*, for the resolution of the border dispute.

Following the overthrow of President Ceaușescu in 1989, President François Mitterrand of France visited Romania in April 1991, and in April 1992 Romania and Germany signed a treaty of friendship and co-operation. Relations with other Western European countries took longer to develop, but an association agreement with the European Community (now EU) was signed in February 1993; in June 1995 Romania formally applied for full membership of the EU. Romania applied for membership of the Council of Europe in May 1993, but was initially rejected, owing to its poor record on civil liberties. In October, however, Romania was admitted to the organization. In December 1999 Romania was one of six countries invited to begin negotiations on possible entry to the EU, and formal accession talks finally commenced in February 2000. In December the EU decided to impose conditions on Romania before granting its citizens the right to visa-free travel in Europe, partly in response to Romania's failure to combat illegal immigration. In December 2004 Romania concluded accession negotiations, but with a cautionary clause whereby the country's accession could be delayed by one year if it failed to meet its reform commitments. In April 2005 members of the European Parliament voted to approve 2007 as the anticipated accession date for Romania (despite the concerns remaining among some existing members). Formal accession agreements were signed by both Bulgaria and Romania on 25 April 2005. In mid-May both chambers of the legislature unanimously ratified the EU accession treaty.

In May 2006 the European Commission announced that a final decision on Romania's scheduled date of accession to the EU was to be postponed until October, and emphasized the need to implement further reform measures. In a report issued at the end of September, the European Commission confirmed that Romania was sufficiently prepared to meet the accession criteria by 1 January 2007, but also identified issues requiring further attention; a mechanism was to be established for co-operation and verification of progress in the areas of judicial reform and measures against corruption, money-laundering, and organized crime. In October a principal negotiator with the EU, Leonard Orban, was appointed to represent Romania in the European Commission. Romania's accession to the EU on 1 January 2007 was welcomed with mass celebrations in Bucharest.

In June 1992 Romania, together with 10 other countries (including six of the former Soviet republics), established what became known as the Organization of the Black Sea Economic Co-operation (see p. 367), which aimed to encourage regional trade and co-operation in developing transport and infrastructure.

In early 1997 Romania appealed directly to member countries of the North Atlantic Treaty Organization (NATO, see p. 340) to support its candidacy for admittance to the Alliance. Following the large-scale suicide attacks against the USA on 11 September 2001, attributed by the USA to the Saudi-born Islamist fundamentalist, Osama bin Laden (see the chapter on the USA), Romania immediately pledged full co-operation with US efforts to assemble a coalition of allied countries to combat global terrorism, and opened its airspace to US military flights to and from Afghanistan, the Taliban regime of which was harbouring militants of bin Laden's al-Qa'ida (Base) organization. The strategic importance of the Black Sea increased, and Romania made available basing facilities in the port city of Constanța, and offered the USA the use of its air bases. None the less, concerns remained about the presence in the Romanian intelligence services of former members of the communist-era Securitate, and there were doubts about Romania's economic preparedness for NATO membership. However, the intelligence services were restructured in January 2002, and Romania secured an invitation to join NATO at a summit meeting held in Prague, Czech Republic, in November, after which US President George W. Bush paid a visit to the country. Romania supported US-led military action in Iraq in early 2003 (despite some criticism from within the EU, notably France), opening its airspace and offering other resources to the coalition. Romania was officially admitted to NATO on 29 March 2004, together with six other countries. In 2005 a parliamentary commission was established to investigate allegations that Romania had permitted US aircraft (transporting possible terrorist suspects) to use one of its airbases, without due attention to international law; the Council of Europe also launched an investigation. In December 2005 the US Secretary of State signed an agreement with the Romanian Minister of Foreign Affairs, granting US troops access to military bases under the command of the Romanian army. Romania hosted a NATO summit meeting, which was convened in Bucharest on 2–4 April 2008. President Bush subsequently met President Băsescu in Constanța for consultations.

Government

Under the Constitution of 1991 (and as subsequently modified, most substantially in 2003), legislative power is vested in the bicameral Palamentul (Parliament), comprising the Camera Deputaților (Chamber of Deputies, lower house) and Senatul (the Senate, upper house). Parlamentul is elected by universal adult suffrage on the basis of proportional representation for a term of four years. Executive power is vested in the President of the Republic, who may serve a maximum of two five-year terms and who is directly elected by universal adult suffrage. The President appoints the Prime Minister, who in turn appoints the Council of Ministers.

For administrative purposes, Romania comprises 40 administrative divisions (counties) and the municipality of Bucharest.

Defence

As assessed at November 2007, active forces totalled 74,267: army 42,200, navy 8,067, air force 10,500 and a joint force of 13,500. Reserves totalled 45,000. There were also 22,900 border guards and a gendarmerie of an estimated 57,000 (under the control of the Ministry of the Interior and Administrative Reform). Conscription was officially abolished in October 2006. The defence budget for 2007 was an estimated 7,630,000m. lei. In January 1994 Romania became the first former Warsaw Pact state to join the North Atlantic Treaty Organization's (NATO) 'Partnership for Peace' (see p. 342) programme. Romania became a full member of NATO on 29 March 2004.

Economic Affairs

In 2006, according to the World Bank, Romania's gross national income (GNI), measured at average 2004–06 prices, totalled US $104,382m., equivalent to $4,850 per head (or $9,820 per head on an international purchasing-power parity basis). During 1996–2006, it was estimated, the population decreased at an average annual rate of 0.5%, while gross domestic product (GDP) per head increased, in real terms, at an average annual rate of 3.0%. Overall GDP increased, in real terms, by an average of 2.5% annually during 1996–2006. Real GDP increased by 7.7% in 2006.

Agriculture (including hunting, forestry and fishing) contributed 9.1% of GDP in 2006, when the sector employed 30.5% of the employed labour force. The principal crops are maize, wheat, potatoes, sugar beet, barley, apples and grapes. Wine production plays a significant role. Forestry, the cropping of reeds (used as a raw material in the paper and cellulose industry) and the breeding of fish are also important. By 1999, according to the IMF, some 97.2% of agricultural land was privately owned. During 1996–2006, according to the World Bank, agricultural GDP increased, in real terms, by an average of 2.1% per year. Real agricultural GDP increased by 3.0% in 2006.

Industry (including mining, manufacturing, construction, power and water) accounted for 34.9% of GDP in 2006, and employed 30.6% of the working population. According to the World Bank, industrial GDP increased, in real terms, by an average of 1.9% annually in 1996–2006. Real industrial GDP increased by 6.0% in 2006.

The mining sector employed 1.3% of the employed labour force in 2006. Lignite (brown coal), hard coal, salt, iron ore, bauxite, copper, lead and zinc are mined. Onshore production of crude petroleum began to increase in the early 1990s. At the end of 2006 Romania had proven reserves of 400m. barrels of petroleum, remaining the largest producer in central and eastern Europe, despite a dramatic decline in production. At the beginning of the 1990s seven offshore platforms were operating in the Romanian sector of the Black Sea, accounting for more than 10% of annual hydrocarbons production. Methane gas is also extracted. In April 1996 Romania launched an international invitation to tender for exploration and production rights on 15 new blocks in the Black Sea. IMF figures indicated that mining output declined by 0.3% in 2005.

Manufacturing employed 21.2% of the employed labour force in 2006 and, according to the World Bank, accounted for 25.5% of GDP. The sector is based mainly on the metallurgical, mechanical engineering, chemical and timber-processing industries. However, many industries (particularly iron and steel) have been hampered by shortages of electricity and raw materials. According to the World Bank, manufacturing GDP increased, in real terms, by an average of 0.1% annually in 1994–2001. Real sectoral GDP increased by some 8.0% in 2001.

According to the World Bank, in 2004 some 38.5% of gross electricity production was derived from coal, 29.2% from hydroelectric power and 18.5% from natural gas. The initial unit of Romania's first nuclear power station, at Cernavoda, became operational in December 1996; the second (700 MW) unit entered into operation in 2008. The construction of a further two units was scheduled to commence in 2008. In 2006 an agreement was reached with the Turkish power grid operator TEIAȘ on the construction of a 400-km undersea transmission cable, which was to be completed by 2009. A natural gas pipeline to connect the country with Hungary, and ultimately with a 'corridor' between Austria and Turkey (the Nabucco project), was also under construction. In April 2008 Romania signed an agreement with Croatia and Serbia on a project that envisaged the construction of a pipeline linking the Romanian port city of Constanța with Trieste, Italy, via Croatia, Serbia and Slovenia. According to official data, 36.1% of energy resources were imported in 2005. In that year mineral fuels accounted for 14.0% of total imports.

According to official figures, in 2006 the services sector contributed 56.0% of GDP and engaged 38.8% of the labour force. According to the World Bank, the GDP of the services sector increased, in real terms, by an average of 2.4% per year in 1996–2006; the real GDP of the sector increased by 5.0% in 2006.

In 2006 Romania recorded a visible trade deficit of US $14,836m., and there was a deficit of $12,785m. on the current account of the balance of payments. In 2005 the principal source of imports was Italy, which provided 15.5% of the total. Other major suppliers were Germany, Russia and France. The main market for exports in that year was also Italy (accounting for 19.2% of the total); other important purchasers were Germany, Turkey, France and the United Kingdom. In 2005 the principal imports were machinery and transport equipment, basic manufactures (particularly textiles), mineral fuels and lubricants, chemical products, and miscellaneous manufactured articles. The major exports in that year were miscellaneous manufactured articles, machinery and transport equipment, basic manufactures, mineral fuels, and chemical products.

The overall budget deficit for 2005 was an estimated 79,300m. new lei (equivalent to 2.3% of GDP). The budgetary deficit for 2006 was forecast at 45,100m. new lei. Romania's total external debt at the end of 2005 was US $38,694m., of which $31,199m. was long-term public debt. In that year the cost of debt-servicing was equivalent to 18.1% of revenue from exports of goods and services. The annual rate of inflation averaged 35.7% in 1996–2006; the rate of inflation was 6.6% in 2006. In 2006 some 7.3% of the labour force were unemployed.

Romania is a member (as a 'Country of Operations') of the European Bank for Reconstruction and Development (EBRD, see p. 239). In January 2007 Romania acceded to full membership of the EU.

During the 1990s Romania's progress towards the development of a market economic system was considerably slower than that of many other post-communist states of central and eastern Europe. In 2001 an extensive privatization programme encountered opposition, although in October the Government succeeded in divesting the Sidex steel works, in what was Romania's most significant privatization to date. In late October the IMF, which had been withholding further assistance pending substantive progress on reform, approved a new stand-by credit. During 2003 the process of privatization accelerated, and in October the EU stated that Romania could be considered to have achieved the status of a functioning market economy, provided it continued to consolidate the progress that it had made. In January 2005 a uniform rate of corporate and personal income tax, of 16%, was introduced, greatly diminishing budgetary revenue. Uncomfortable reforms remained to be implemented in preparation for EU membership and in conformity with a two-year IMF stand-by agreement (finalized in July 2004); the Government committed to making some 7,000 redundancies in the mining sector in 2005, as part of a national restructuring plan that also encompassed the iron, steel and railway industries. The Romanian currency (the leu) was redenominated from 1 July 2005, but was subject to strong appreciation pressures thereafter. The IMF arrangement was suspended in October owing to disagreements over the economic programme for 2006. None the less, the Romanian economy demonstrated considerable growth prior to EU accession, although large deficits remained on both the current account of the balance of payments and the budget. Romania joined the EU on 1 January 2007, as scheduled. However, the collapse of the ruling coalition and the installation of a minority Government in April, together with continuing antagonism between the President and Prime Minister (see Recent History), represented an impediment to the adoption of essential reforms required by the EU. In October, in response to the Government's failure to introduce stipulated agricultural measures, the EU threatened to withhold aid to the sector unless the system of payments to farmers was regulated. High-level corruption remained endemic in 2007, despite the establishment in May of a national agency to monitor the activities of civil servants. Although the National Bank urged fiscal restraint, the budget for 2008 established a target budgetary deficit of 2.7% of GDP and provided for substantial pay rises in the public sector. Forthcoming local and legislative elections in that year contributed to pressure on the Government to increase public sector expenditure. Economic growth remained strong, but the rate of inflation and the current account deficit rose sharply; the reduction of inflation was to be prioritized in order to meet criteria for the planned adoption of the common European currency, the euro, in 2013–14.

Education

Children under the age of six years may attend crèches (creșe), and kindergartens (grădinițe de copii). In 2002/03 76.5% of pre-school age children were attending kindergarten. Between the ages of six and 16 years, children are obliged to attend the general education school (școală de cultură generală de zece ani). The general secondary school (liceul), for which there is an entrance examination, provides a specialized education suitable for entering college or university. There are also specialized secondary schools, where the emphasis is on industrial, agricultural and teacher training, and art schools, which correspond to secondary schools, but cover several years of general education. Vocational secondary schools (școli profesionale de ucenici) train pupils for a particular career. Tuition in minority languages, particularly Hungarian and German, is available. In 2003/04 primary enrolment included 91.9% of children in the relevant age-group, while the comparable ratio for secondary education was 80.8%. Enrolment in tertiary education was equivalent to 40.7% in 2002/03. Expenditure on education by the state budget in 2003 amounted to 15,561m. lei (representing 5.5% of total expenditure).

Public Holidays

2008: 1–2 January (New Year), 6 January (Epiphany), 27–28 April (Orthodox Easter), 1 May (Labour Day), 1 December (National Day), 25–26 December (Christmas).

2009: 1–2 January (New Year), 6 January (Epiphany), 19–20 April (Orthodox Easter), 1 May (Labour Day), 1 December (National Day), 25–26 December (Christmas).

Weights and Measures

The metric system is in force.

ROMANIA

Statistical Survey

Source (unless otherwise indicated): Institutul National de Statistică (National Institute of Statistics), 050706 Bucharest, Bd. Libertăţii 16; tel. (21) 3124875; fax (21) 3124873; e-mail romstat@insse.ro; internet www.insse.ro/cms/rw/pages/index.ro.do.

Area and Population

AREA, POPULATION AND DENSITY

Area (sq km)	238,391*
Population (census results)	
7 January 1992	22,810,035
18–27 March 2002	
Males	10,568,741
Females	11,112,233
Total	21,680,974
Population (official estimates at mid-year)	
2005	21,623,849
2006	21,584,365
2007	21,537,563
Density (per sq km) at mid-2007	90.3

* 92,043 sq miles.

POPULATION BY ETHNIC GROUP
(2002 census)

	Number	% of total
Romanian	19,399,597	89.5
Hungarian	1,431,807	6.6
Gypsy (Roma)	535,140	2.5
Others and unknown	314,430	1.5
Total	21,680,974	100.0

ADMINISTRATIVE DIVISIONS
(at mid-2005)

	Area (sq km)	Population	Density (per sq km)	Administrative capital
Counties				
Alba	6,242	379,189	60.7	Alba Iulia
Arad	7,754	459,286	59.2	Arad
Argeş	6,826	646,320	94.7	Piteşti
Bacău	6,621	723,518	109.3	Bacău
Bihor	7,544	595,685	79.0	Oradea
Bistriţa-Năsăud	5,355	317,254	59.2	Bistriţa
Botoşani	4,986	459,900	92.2	Botoşani
Brăila	4,766	370,428	77.7	Brăila
Braşov	5,363	595,211	111.0	Braşov
Buzău	6,103	494,052	81.0	Buzău
Călăraşi	5,088	317,632	62.4	Călăraşi
Caraş-Severin	8,520	331,876	39.0	Reşiţa
Cluj	6,674	694,511	104.1	Cluj-Napoca
Constanţa	7,071	715,148	101.1	Constanţa
Covasna	3,710	223,886	60.3	Sfântu Gheorghe
Dâmboviţa	4,054	537,090	132.5	Târgovişte
Dolj	7,414	718,874	97.0	Craiova
Galaţi	4,466	620,500	138.9	Galaţi
Giurgiu	3,526	286,208	81.2	Giurgiu
Gorj	5,602	384,852	68.7	Târgu Jiu
Harghita	6,639	326,558	49.2	Miercurea-Ciuc
Hunedoara	7,063	480,459	68.0	Deva
Ialomiţa	4,453	292,666	65.7	Slobozia
Iaşi	5,476	813,943	148.6	Iaşi
Ilfov*	1,593	283,409	177.9	Bucharest
Maramureş	6,304	515,610	81.8	Baia Mare
Mehedinţi	4,933	303,869	61.6	Drobeta-Turnu Severin
Mureş	6,714	583,383	86.9	Târgu Mureş
Neamţ	5,896	570,682	96.8	Piatra Neamţ
Olt	5,498	483,674	88.0	Slatina
Prahova	4,716	827,512	175.5	Ploieşti
Sălaj	3,864	245,638	63.6	Zalău
Satu Mare	4,418	368,702	83.5	Satu Mare
Sibiu	5,432	422,259	77.7	Sibiu

—continued	Area (sq km)	Population	Density (per sq km)	Administrative capital
Suceava	8,553	705,752	82.5	Suceava
Teleorman	5,790	422,314	72.9	Alexandria
Timiş	8,697	658,837	75.8	Timişoara
Tulcea	8,499	252,485	29.7	Tulcea
Vâlcea	5,765	415,181	72.0	Râmnicu Vâlcea
Vaslui	5,318	460,751	86.6	Vaslui
Vrancea	4,857	393,766	81.1	Focşani
Capital City				
Bucharest*	228	1,924,959	8,442.8	Bucharest
Total	238,391	21,623,849	90.7	

* The Bucharest Municipality is a separate administrative division, but the city is also the capital of the surrounding Ilfov region. The area and population of Bucharest are included only in figures for the municipality.

PRINCIPAL TOWNS
(at mid-2005)

Bucureşti (Bucharest, the capital)	1,924,959	Arad	168,606
Cluj-Napoca	310,182	Sibiu	154,201
Iaşi	307,377	Târgu Mureş	147,112
Constanţa	306,332	Baia Mare	140,937
Timişoar	303,640	Buzău	136,624
Craiova	300,182	Botoşani	117,318
Galaţi	298,366	Satu Mare	115,197
Braşov	282,517	Râmnicu Vâlcea	111,701
Ploieşti	233,699	Piatra Neamţ	109,720
Brăila	218,744	Drobeta-Turnu Severin	109,444
Oradea	206,223	Suceava	106,732
Bacău	180,516	Focşani	101,083
Piteşti	171,071		

BIRTHS, MARRIAGES AND DEATHS

	Registered live births		Registered marriages		Registered deaths	
	Number	Rate (per 1,000)	Number	Rate (per 1,000)	Number	Rate (per 1,000)
1998	237,297	10.5	145,303	6.5	269,166	12.0
1999	234,600	10.4	140,014	6.2	265,194	11.8
2000	234,521	10.5	135,808	6.1	255,820	11.4
2001	220,368	9.8	129,930	5.8	259,603	11.6
2002	210,529	9.7	129,018	5.9	269,666	12.4
2003	212,459	9.8	133,953	6.2	266,575	12.3
2004	216,261	10.0	143,304	6.6	258,890	11.9
2005	221,020	10.2	141,832	6.6	262,101	12.1

Expectation of life (years at birth, WHO estimates): 71.9 (males 68.4; females 75.5) in 2005 (Source: WHO, *World Health Statistics*).

ROMANIA

ECONOMICALLY ACTIVE POPULATION
(labour force surveys, '000 persons aged 15 years and over)

	2004	2005	2006
Agriculture, hunting and forestry	2,892.8	2,939.3	2,840.3
Fishing	3.4	4.1*	3.1*
Mining and quarrying	134.5	119.2	119.7
Manufacturing	2,051.3	1,959.7	1,978.5
Electricity, gas and water	191.8	190.3	197.5
Construction	478.5	506.6	557.6
Wholesale and retail trade; repair of motor vehicles, motorcycles, and personal and household goods	943.4	967.7	1,049.3
Hotels and restaurants	147.9	150.7	143.0
Transport, storage and communications	454.1	450.0	491.8
Financial intermediation	86.2	85.5	92.0
Real estate, renting and business services	231.5	231.7	281.6
Public administration	538.2	520.1	507.5
Education	402.7	412.7	410.6
Health and social assistance	361.7	353.5	378.3
Other services	239.6	255.5	262.5
Total employed	9,157.6	9,146.6	9,313.3
Unemployed	799.5	704.5	728.4
Total labour force	9,957.1	9,851.0	10,041.7
Males	5,470.8	5,431.5	5,526.4
Females	4,486.3	4,419.5	4,515.3

* Figure obtained as residual.

Registered unemployed ('000 persons, at end of year): 658.9 in 2003; 557.9 in 2004; 523.0 in 2005.

Source: mainly ILO.

Health and Welfare

KEY INDICATORS

Total fertility rate (children per woman, 2005)	1.3
Under-5 mortality rate (per 1,000 live births, 2005)	19
HIV/AIDS (% of persons aged 15–49, 2005)	<0.1
Physicians (per 1,000 head, 2003)	1.90
Hospital beds (per 1,000 head, 2005)	6.6
Health expenditure (2004): US $ per head (PPP)	432.7
Health expenditure (2004): % of GDP	5.1
Health expenditure (2004): public (% of total)	66.1
Access to water (% of persons, 2004)	57
Access to sanitation (% of persons, 2002)	51
Human Development Index (2005): ranking	60
Human Development Index (2005): value	0.813

For sources and definitions, see explanatory note on p. vi.

Agriculture

PRINCIPAL CROPS
('000 metric tons)

	2004	2005	2006
Wheat	7,812.4	7,340.7	5,526.2
Barley	1,406.0	1,079.1	772.9
Maize	14,541.6	10,388.5	8,984.7
Rye	55.0	49.0	35.7
Oats	447.1	377.5	346.9
Potatoes	4,230.2	3,738.6	4,015.9
Sugar beet	672.7	729.7	1,152.2
Dry beans	53.5	41.7	34.9
Dry peas	57.0	38.8	35.7
Walnuts	15.6	47.8	38.5
Soybeans (Soya beans)	298.5	312.8	344.9
Sunflower seed	1,557.8	1,340.9	1,526.2
Rapeseed	98.7	147.6	175.1
Cabbages and other brassicas	924.7	1,011.6	1,011.6
Lettuce and chicory	3.6	1.8	4.4
Tomatoes	1,330.1	627.0	835.0
Pumpkins, squash and gourds	290.8	49.2	69.2

—continued	2004	2005	2006
Cucumbers and gherkins	199.5	142.9	156.4
Chillies and green peppers	237.2	203.8	279.1
Dry onions	332.8	363.6	390.7
Garlic	65.9	68.4	64.2
Green beans	52.2	54.3	64.2
Green peas	17.4	23.3	26.1
Watermelons	723.2	628.3	587.8
Cantaloupes and other melons	41.9	63.4	54.0
Apples	1,097.8	638.0	590.4
Pears	45.9	88.9	62.4
Cherries	51.0	117.9	104.8
Apricots	20.6	52.4	38.8
Plums and sloes	475.8	622.4	598.8
Grapes	1,230.4	505.8	912.4
Tobacco (leaves)	7.5	3.7	1.7

Aggregate production ('000 metric tons, may include official, semi-official or estimated data): Total cereals 24,401.7 in 2004, 19,350.5 in 2005, 15,759.3 in 2006; Total roots and tubers 4,230.2 in 2004, 3,738.6 in 2005, 4,015.9 in 2006; Total vegetables (incl. melons) 4,775.9 in 2004, 3,826.6 in 2005, 4,141.1 in 2006; Total fruits (excl. melons) 3,038.4 in 2004, 2,156.7 in 2005, 2,434.7 in 2006.

Source: FAO.

LIVESTOCK
('000 head, year ending September)

	2004	2005	2006
Horses	897	840	834
Cattle	2,897	2,808	2,862
Pigs	5,145	6,495	6,622
Sheep	7,447	7,425	7,611
Goats	678	661	687
Chickens	76,616	87,014	86,552

Source: FAO.

LIVESTOCK PRODUCTS
('000 metric tons)

	2004	2005	2006
Cattle meat	161.6	189.1	194.4
Sheep meat	66.8	50.0	53.9
Goat meat	6.3	3.4	5.2
Pig meat	374.0	454.5	468.1
Horse meat*	9.9	10.1	10.1
Chicken meat	302.9	315.1	265.7
Cows' milk	5,716.2	5,704.9	5,704.9*
Sheep's milk	451.9	545.4	545.4*
Hen eggs	335.1	355.4	355.4*
Other poultry eggs	34.0	10.2	10.2*
Honey	19.2	19.2	20.0*
Wool: greasy	17.5	17.6	17.6*

* FAO estimate(s).
Source: FAO.

Forestry

ROUNDWOOD REMOVALS
('000 cubic metres, excluding bark)

	2004	2005	2006
Sawlogs, veneer logs and logs for sleepers	8,198	7,847	7,798
Pulpwood	2,500	1,878	1,919
Other industrial wood	2,096	1,817	1,498
Fuel wood	3,015	2,959	2,624
Total	15,809	14,501	13,839

Source: FAO.

ROMANIA

SAWNWOOD PRODUCTION
('000 cubic metres, including railway sleepers)

	2004	2005	2006
Coniferous (softwood)	2,808	2,584	2,620
Broadleaved (hardwood)	1,780	1,737	1,850
Total	4,588	4,321	4,470

Source: FAO.

Fishing

(metric tons, live weight)

	2003	2004	2005
Capture	9,890	5,095	6,068
Freshwater bream	1,828	615	581
Goldfish	2,348	1,447	1,917
Pontic shad	651	403	518
European sprat	1,219	1,350	1,487
Aquaculture	9,042	8,137	7,284
Common carp	2,309	1,726	2,256
Goldfish	1,705	1,249	1,139
Silver carp	1,970	1,588	1,562
Bighead carp	1,400	867	921
Rainbow trout	606	964	815
Total catch	18,932	13,232	13,352

Source: FAO.

Mining

('000 metric tons, unless otherwise indicated)

	2003	2004	2005
Brown coal (incl. lignite)	33,063	31,592	31,122
Crude petroleum	5,651	5,465	5,212
Iron ore*	304	275	265
Copper concentrates†	23.4	20.4	14.9
Lead concentrates†	15.7	18.3	11.6
Zinc concentrates†	22.1	23.6	13.8
Salt (unrefined)	2,417	2,400	2,420
Natural gas (million cu metres)	13,174	13,290	12,472

* Figures refer to gross weight.
† Figures refer to the metal content of concentrates.

Source: partly US Geological Survey.

Industry

SELECTED PRODUCTS
('000 metric tons, unless otherwise indicated)

	2003	2004	2005
Meat and meat products	408	464	555
Refined sugar	460	506	539
Margarine	68.2	60.9	65.8
Wine ('000 hectolitres)	5,457	7,071	2,602
Beer ('000 hectolitres)	13,292	14,406	15,295
Tobacco products	36	35	33
Cotton yarn—pure and mixed	31	32	28
Cotton fabrics—pure and mixed (million sq metres)	177	201	112
Woollen yarn—pure and mixed	23	24	22
Woollen fabrics—pure and mixed (million sq metres)	12	12	15
Silk fabrics—pure and mixed (million sq metres)*	35	31	23
Flax and hemp yarn—pure and mixed	3	4	2
Linen, hemp and jute fabrics—pure and mixed (million sq metres)	4	2	1
Chemical filaments and fibres	22	21	16

—continued	2003	2004	2005
Footwear (million pairs)	80	75	72
Chemical wood pulp	260	237	134
Paper and paperboard	489	521	411
Synthetic rubber	12	12	12
Rubber tyres ('000)	11,242	12,408	14,208
Sulphuric acid	65	28	11
Caustic soda (sodium hydroxide)	382	414	443
Soda ash (sodium carbonate)	406	398	346
Nitrogenous fertilizers (a)†	1,207	1,104	1,580
Phosphatic fertilizers (b)†	102	86	76
Pesticides	2	3	3
Motor spirit (petrol)	3,841	4,292	4,956
Kerosene and white spirit	443	429	455
Distillate fuel oils	3,721	3,947	4,542
Residual fuel oils	1,558	1,560	1,707
Petroleum bitumen (asphalt)	204	203	157
Liquefied petroleum gas	327	366	658
Coke	1,638	1,675	1,891
Cement	5,992	6,239	7,043
Pig-iron	4,101	4,244	4,098
Crude steel	5,693	6,076	6,280
Aluminium—unwrought	205	229	258
Refined copper—unwrought	4	—	—
Television receivers ('000)	90	76	32
Merchant ships launched ('000 deadweight tons)	160	222	103
Passenger motor cars ('000)	76	99	175
Motor tractors, lorries and dump trucks (number)	257	277	171
Buses ('000)	5	2	—
Domestic refrigerators ('000)	522	700	826
Domestic washing and drying machines ('000)	35	42	25
Domestic vacuum cleaners ('000)	108	112	318
Domestic cookers ('000)	598	737	855
Electric energy (million kWh)	56,645	56,482	59,413

* Including fabrics of artificial silk.
† Production in terms of (a) nitrogen or (b) phosphoric acid.

Finance

CURRENCY AND EXCHANGE RATES

Monetary Units
100 bani (singular: ban) = 1 Romanian leu (plural: lei).

Sterling, Dollar and Euro Equivalents (31 December 2007)
£1 sterling = 4.921 lei;
US $1 = 2.456 lei;
€1 = 3.616 lei;
100 Romanian lei = £20.32 = $40.71 = €27.65.

Average Exchange Rate (lei per US $)
2005 2.9137
2006 2.8090
2007 2.4383

Note: On 1 July 2005 the leu was revalued at a rate of 10,000 old lei = 1 new leu. Some figures given in the survey are in terms of the former valuation.

STATE BUDGET
(hundred million new lei)

	2004*	2005*	2006†
Tax revenue	610.6	698.3	782.3
Value-added tax	138.1	151.0	160.2
Social security taxes	228.2	257.7	276.6
Profits tax	48.8	55.5	59.3
Income tax	73.2	86.1	98.4
Excise taxes	62.0	83.2	118.7
Customs duties	9.0	9.4	10.1
Other indirect taxes	51.3	55.4	59.0
Non-tax revenue	32.5	27.0	26.5
Capital revenue (incl. grants)	0.9	0.9	1.0
Total	644.0	726.2	809.8

ROMANIA

Statistical Survey

Expenditure	2004*	2005*	2006†
Public authorities	36.8	38.6	40.9
Defence	41.5	47.7	52.9
Public order and safety	40.4	42.2	43.9
Education	86.7	98.8	108.8
Health	78.4	82.6	83.9
Social security and welfare	216.2	235.5	249.9
Community services, public development and housing	47.5	50.3	52.6
Recreational, cultural and religious affairs	11.3	12.1	12.7
Agriculture and forestry	24.9	28.9	31.4
Industry	16.5	18.4	19.1
Transport and communications	77.1	81.9	85.2
Other economic affairs and services	14.4	16.1	18.1
National debt expenditure	48.0	40.9	42.4
Other	8.4	9.8	11.4
Loans	1.6	1.7	1.7
Total	**749.7**	**805.5**	**854.9**

* Estimates.
† Forecasts.

Source: Ministry of Public Finance, Bucharest.

INTERNATIONAL RESERVES
(US $ million at 31 December)

	2004	2005	2006
Gold (national valuation)	1,480	1,728	2,140
IMF special drawing rights	1	1	—
Foreign exchange	14,616	19,872	28,066
Total	**16,097**	**21,601**	**30,206**

Source: IMF, *International Financial Statistics*.

MONEY SUPPLY
('000 million lei at 31 December)

	2004	2005	2006
Currency outside banks	7.46	11.39	15.13
Demand deposits at deposit money banks	7.82	13.17	20.24
Total money	**15.29**	**24.55**	**35.37**

Source: IMF, *International Financial Statistics*.

COST OF LIVING
(Consumer Price Index; base: 2000 = 100)

	2004	2005	2006
Food	201.5	213.8	222.0
Fuel and light	297.8	350.9	388.2
Clothing	175.4	183.2	188.7
Rent	187.8	204.6	216.7
All items (incl. others)	**212.5**	**231.7**	**246.9**

Source: ILO.

NATIONAL ACCOUNTS

Expenditure on the Gross Domestic Product
(million new lei at current prices)

	2004	2005	2006
Government final consumption expenditure	46,540	34,758	31,996
Private final consumption expenditure	167,162	212,901	265,281
Changes in inventories	1,708	−1,170	−968
Gross fixed capital formation	53,292	66,248	84,530
Total domestic expenditure	**268,702**	**312,737**	**380,839**
Exports of goods and services	88,555	94,847	110,904
Less Imports of goods and services	110,884	124,599	152,387
Statistical discrepancy	—	—	3,018
GDP in purchasers' values	**246,372**	**282,986**	**342,374**

Source: IMF, *International Financial Statistics*.

Gross Domestic Product by Economic Activity
('000 million new lei at current prices)

	2003	2004	2005
Agriculture, hunting and forestry	22,835.2	30,565.8	24,372.4
Fishing	14.0	13.8	15.7
Construction	11,483.1	14,653.1	18,290.0
Other industry*	49,489.7	60,794.9	69,350.4
Trade	16,806.9	22,311.3	29,028.2
Hotels and restaurants	3,735.6	4,615.0	6,097.1
Transport, storage and communications	19,310.6	24,151.0	29,584.2
Financial intermediation	3,654.9	5,578.4	6,276.1
Real estate transactions, renting and service activities	24,627.8	30,548.8	36,181.5
Public administration and defence	12,816.4	12,728.0	17,690.0
Education	6,020.9	8,022.2	9,930.1
Health and social assistance	4,606.7	5,993.6	7,573.1
Gross value added in basic prices	**175,401.8**	**219,975.9**	**254,388.8**
Taxes on products	22,072.0	26,278.2	33,715.5
Import duties	1,329.7	1,632.5	2,033.4
Less Subsidies on products	1,238.7	1,417.8	2,089.9
GDP in market prices	**197,564.8**	**246,468.8**	**288,047.8**

* Comprising mining and quarrying, manufacturing, electricity, gas and water.

2006 (million new lei at current prices): Agriculture, forestry and fishing 27,524.3; Construction 24,018.5; Other industry 81,886.2; Services 169,855.0; *Gross value added in basic prices* 303,284.0; Net taxes on product 39,134.0; *GDP in market prices* 342,418.0.

BALANCE OF PAYMENTS
(US $ million)

	2004	2005	2006
Exports of goods f.o.b.	23,485	27,730	32,336
Imports of goods f.o.b.	−30,150	−37,348	−47,172
Trade balance	**−6,665**	**−9,618**	**−14,836**
Exports of services	3,614	5,083	7,032
Imports of services	−3,879	−5,518	−7,027
Balance on goods and services	**−6,930**	**−10,053**	**−14,831**
Other income received	433	1,533	2,176
Other income paid	−3,582	−4,432	−6,255
Balance on goods, services and income	**−10,079**	**−12,952**	**−18,910**
Current transfers received	4,188	4,939	6,995
Current transfers paid	−491	−607	−870
Current balance	**−6,382**	**−8,621**	**−12,785**
Capital account (net)	643	731	−34
Direct investment abroad	−70	30	−422
Direct investment from abroad	6,443	6,482	11,393
Portfolio investment assets	−559	−140	−828
Portfolio investment liabilities	28	1,089	589
Financial derivatives assets	—	36	48
Financial derivatives liabilities	—	−62	−156
Other investment assets	−212	−1,078	−1,323
Other investment liabilities	5,131	7,731	9,598
Net errors and omissions	1,167	612	521
Overall balance	**6,189**	**6,811**	**6,602**

Source: IMF, *International Financial Statistics*.

External Trade

PRINCIPAL COMMODITIES
(distribution by SITC, € million)

Imports c.i.f.	2003	2004	2005
Food and live animals	1,204	1,297	1,528
Crude materials (inedible) except fuels	631	778	903
Mineral fuels, lubricants, etc.	2,312	3,114	4,548
Petroleum, petroleum products, etc.	1,306	1,893	3,019
Gas, natural and manufactured	724	631	936
Chemicals and related products	2,186	2,727	3,324
Basic manufactures	5,942	6,908	7,955
Textiles and textile articles	2,537	2,686	2,656
Iron and steel	705	1,004	1,299
Manufactures of metals	672	860	1,160
Machinery and transport equipment	6,251	8,548	10,819
Machinery specialized for particular industries	718	883	1,034
General industrial machinery and parts	945	1,216	1,501
Telecommunications, sound recording and reproducing equipment	629	884	1,093
Electric machinery, apparatus, etc.	1,778	2,040	2,421
Road vehicles	1,058	2,108	3,058
Miscellaneous manufactured articles	2,415	2,581	3,100
Total (incl. others)	21,201	26,281	32,568

Exports f.o.b.	2003	2004	2005
Crude materials (inedible) except fuels	974	1,147	1,078
Cork and wood	424	468	451
Mineral fuels, lubricants, etc.	1,023	1,282	2,378
Petroleum, petroleum products, etc.	926	1,159	2,167
Chemicals and related products	746	1,039	1,277
Basic manufactures	3,019	4,024	4,654
Iron and steel	1,149	1,745	2,009
Non-ferrous metals	296	402	461
Machinery and transport equipment	3,356	4,491	5,663
Telecommunications, sound recording and reproducing equipment	427	440	313
Electrical machinery, apparatus, etc.	1,095	1,492	1,964
Other transport equipment	451	556	680
Miscellaneous manufactured articles	6,071	6,435	6,600
Furniture and parts	699	833	901
Clothing and accessories (excl. footwear)	3,606	3,803	3,709
Footwear	1,262	1,220	1,273
Total (incl. others)	15,614	18,935	22,255

PRINCIPAL TRADING PARTNERS
(€ million)*

Imports c.i.f.	2003	2004	2005
Austria	749	919	1,206
Belgium	313	393	467
Brazil	226	321	400
China, People's Republic	583	854	1,319
Czech Republic	433	568	748
France (incl. Monaco)	1,542	1,866	2,196
Germany	3,145	3,918	4,550
Greece	287	355	374
Hungary	766	832	1,077
Italy	4,140	4,515	5,032
Japan	265	353	469
Kazakhstan	211	471	1,063
Korea, Republic	219	287	443
Netherlands	413	488	576
Poland	491	659	940
Russia	1,751	1,792	2,690
Slovakia	213	270	355
Spain	383	578	727
Sweden	199	280	313
Switzerland-Liechtenstein	190	262	325
Turkey	815	1,098	1,583
Ukraine	487	716	418
United Kingdom	702	860	934
USA	493	752	897
Total (incl. others)	21,201	26,281	32,568

Exports f.o.b.	2003	2004	2005
Austria	502	590	692
Belgium	248	374	386
Bulgaria	254	363	593
China, People's Republic	248	158	165
France (incl. Monaco)	1,145	1,609	1,656
Germany	2,458	2,832	3,123
Greece	379	507	475
Hungary	545	724	922
Israel	88	85	n.a.
Italy	3,774	4,014	4,270
Netherlands	555	603	598
Spain	279	375	540
Turkey	798	1,324	1,762
United Kingdom	1,046	1,259	1,213
USA	551	539	906
Serbia and Montenegro	135	182	256
Total (incl. others)	15,614	18,935	22,255

* Imports by country of production; exports by country of last consignment.

Transport

RAILWAYS
(traffic)

	2003	2004	2005
Passenger journeys (million)	95	99	92
Passenger-km (million)	8,529	8,638	7,985
Freight transported (million metric tons)	71	73	69
Freight ton-km (million)	15,039	17,022	16,582

ROAD TRAFFIC
('000 motor vehicles in use at 31 December)

	2003	2004	2005
Passenger cars	3,088	3,225	3,364
Buses and coaches	42	43	39
Lorries and vans	463	482	494
Motorcycles and mopeds	236	235	197

ROMANIA

INLAND WATERWAYS
(traffic)

	2003	2004	2005
Passenger journeys ('000)	174	214	218
Passenger-km (million)	16	19	24
Freight transported (million metric tons)	13	15	17
Freight ton-km ('000 million)	4	4	5

SHIPPING

Merchant Fleet
(registered at 31 December)

	2004	2005	2006
Number of vessels	221	209	193
Total displacement ('000 grt)	426.7	336.5	272.1

Sources: Lloyd's Register-Fairplay, *World Fleet Statistics*.

International Sea-borne Freight Traffic
('000 metric tons)

	2003	2004	2005
Goods loaded	17,147	18,225	24,534
Goods unloaded	19,513	22,306	28,444

CIVIL AVIATION
(traffic)

	2003	2004	2005
Passengers carried ('000)	1,172	1,337	1,750
Passenger-km (million)	1,760	1,613	2,093
Freight transported ('000 metric tons)	6	5	n.a.
Freight ton-km (million)	9	7	7

Tourism

FOREIGN VISITOR ARRIVALS
('000)*

Country of origin	2003	2004	2005
Bulgaria	340.3	375.4	389.5
Germany	380.5	296.1	353.6
Hungary	1,537.1	2,603.5	1,522.2
Italy	258.8	230.6	270.9
Moldova	1,058.6	1,212.8	1,435.2
Poland	108.7	132.9	62.0
Serbia and Montenegro	271.3	220.3	148.0
Slovakia	84.4	88.7	47.7
Turkey	205.2	195.3	200.9
Ukraine	349.3	309.8	328.4
Total (incl. others)	5,594.8	6,600.1	5,839.4

* Figures refer to arrivals at frontiers of visitors from abroad, including same day visitors (excursionists).

Tourism receipts (US $ million, incl. passenger transport): 523 in 2003; 607 in 2004; 1,310 in 2005.

Source: World Tourism Organization.

Communications Media

	2003	2004	2005
Radio users ('000 subscribers)	6,180	5,369	5,313
Television users ('000 subscribers)	5,945	5,822	5,618
Telephones ('000 main lines in use)	4,331.6	4,389.0	4,386.3
Mobile cellular telephones ('000 subscribers)	7,039.9	10,215.4	13,354.1
Personal computers ('000 in use)	2,100	2,450	2,450
Internet users ('000)	4,000	4,500	4,773.0
Broadband subscribers ('000)	196.1	382.8	751.1
Book production (incl. pamphlets):			
titles	12,864	13,288	14,115
copies ('000)	8,350	9,288	11,746
Daily newspapers	69	84	80
Other periodicals	1,944	2,036	2,044

2006: Telephones ('000 main lines in use) 4,204.0; Mobile cellular telephones ('000 subscribers) 17,400.0; Internet users ('000) 7,000; Broadband subscribers ('000) 1,769.3.

Source: partly International Telecommunication Union.

Education

(2005/06)

	Institutions	Pupils	Teachers
Kindergartens	3,769	648,338	35,755
Primary and gymnasium schools	6,411	1,900,561	144,489
Secondary schools	1,410	767,439	61,914
Vocational schools	90	284,412	6,234
Specialized technical schools	78	43,617	1,099
Higher education	107	716,464	31,543

Adult literacy rate (UNESCO estimates): 97.3% (males 98.4%; females 96.3%) in 2002 (Source: UNESCO Institute for Statistics).

Directory

The Constitution

Following its assumption of power in December 1989, the National Salvation Front decreed radical changes to the Constitution of 1965. The name of the country was changed from the Socialist Republic of Romania to Romania. The leading role of a single political party was abolished, a democratic and pluralist system of government being established.

The combined chambers of the legislature elected in May 1990, working as a constituent assembly, drafted a new Constitution (based on the Constitution of France's Fifth Republic), which was approved in a national referendum on 8 December 1991. A plebiscite held on 18–19 October 2003 approved 79 amendments to the Constitution, bringing it into conformity with EU legislation. The amendments entered into force on 29 October.

Under the amended Constitution, political power in Romania belongs to the people and is exercised according to the principles of democracy, freedom, human dignity, and the inviolability and inalienability of basic human rights. Romania is governed on the basis of a multi-party democratic system and of the separation of the

ROMANIA

legal, executive and judicial powers. Romania's legislature, consisting of the Camera Deputaţilor (Chamber of Deputies—the lower house) and Senatul (the Senate—the upper house), and President are elected by universal, free, direct and secret vote, with the President serving a maximum of two terms. The term of office of the legislature is four years and five years for the President, with effect from the elections held in late 2004. The number of Deputies and Senators is established under the election law, in proportion to Romania's overall population. Citizens have the right to vote at the age of 18, and may be elected at the age of 21 to the Camera Deputaţilor and at the age of 30 to Senatul, with no upper age limit. Those ineligible for election include former members of the Securitate (the secret police of President Ceauşescu) and other former officials guilty of repression and abuses. Independent candidates are eligible for election to the Camera Deputaţilor and to Senatul if supported by at least 251 electors and to the Presidency if supported by 100,000 electors. Once elected, the President may not remain a member of any political party. The President appoints the Prime Minister, who in turn appoints the Council of Ministers.

The Government

HEAD OF STATE

President: TRAIAN BĂSESCU (elected 12 December 2004; inaugurated 14 December 2004).

COUNCIL OF MINISTERS
(April 2008)

A coalition, comprising members of the National Liberal Party (NLP) and the Democratic Alliance of Hungarians in Romania (DAHR).

Prime Minister: CĂLIN POPESCU-TĂRICEANU (NLP).
Minister of Foreign Affairs: LAZĂR COMĂNESCU (NLP).
Minister of Justice: CĂTĂLIN MARIAN PREDOIU (Independent).
Minister of the Interior and Administrative Reform: CRISTIAN DAVID (NLP).
Minister of the Economy and Finance: VARUJAN VOSGANIAN (NLP).
Minister of Defence: TEODOR MELEŞCANU (NLP).
Minister of Labour, the Family and Equal Opportunities: PAUL PĂCURARU (NLP).
Minister of Small and Medium-Sized Enterprises, Trade, Tourism and the Liberal Professions: OVIDIU SILAGHI (NLP).
Minister of Agriculture and Rural Development: DACIAN CIOLOŞ (NLP).
Minister of Transport: LUDOVIC ORBAN (NLP).
Minister of Education, Research and Youth: CRISTIAN ADOMNIŢEI (NLP).
Minister of Culture and Religious Affairs: ADRIAN IORGULESCU (NLP).
Minister of Public Health: EUGEN NICOLĂESCU (NLP).
Minister of Development, Public Works and Housing: LÁSZLÓ BORBÉLY (DAHR).
Minister of Communications and Information Technology: KÁROLY BORBÉLY (DAHR).
Minister of the Environment and Sustainable Development: ATTILA KORODI (DAHR).
Minister-delegate for Relations with Parliament: MIHAI ALEXANDRU VOICU (NLP).

MINISTRIES

Office of the President: 060116 Bucharest, Palatul Cotroceni, Str. Geniuliu 1–3, Sector 5; tel. (21) 4100581; fax (21) 4103858; e-mail presedinte@presidency.ro; internet www.presidency.ro.

Office of the Prime Minister: 011791 Bucharest 1, Piaţa Victoriei 1; tel. (21) 3131450; fax (21) 3139846; e-mail drp@gov.ro; internet www.cancelarie.ro.

Ministry of Agriculture and Rural Development: 020921 Bucharest 3, Bd. Carol I 24, POB 37; tel. (21) 3078500; fax (21) 3078554; e-mail comunicare@maa.ro; internet www.mapam.ro.

Ministry of Communications and Information Technology: 050706 Bucharest 5, Bd. Libertăţii 14; tel. (21) 4001190; fax (21) 3365887; e-mail office@mcti.ro; internet www.mcti.ro.

Ministry of Culture and Religious Affairs: 011374 Bucharest 1, Şos. Kiseleff 30; tel. (21) 2242510; fax (21) 2234951; e-mail cabinet.ministru@cultura.ro; internet www.cultura.ro.

Ministry of Defence: 050561 Bucharest 5, Str. Izvor 3–5, Sector 5; tel. (21) 4023400; fax (21) 3195698; internet www.mapn.ro.

Ministry of Development, Public Works and Housing: 050741 Bucharest 5, Str. Apolodor 17; tel. (21) 3011501; fax (21) 3368509; e-mail laszlo.borbely@mdlpl.ro; internet www.mdlpl.ro.

Ministry of the Economy and Finance: 050741 Bucharest 5, Str. Apolodor 17; tel. (21) 3199759; fax (21) 3122509; e-mail presamfp@mfinante.gv.ro; internet www.mfinante.ro.

Ministry of Education, Research and Youth: 010174 Bucharest, Str. Gen. Berthelot 28–30, Sector 1; tel. (21) 4056200; fax (21) 3124719; internet www.edu.ro.

Ministry of the Environment and Sustainable Development: 040129 Bucharest 5, Bd. Libertăţii 12; tel. (1) 3160215; fax (1) 3124227; e-mail mmediu@mmediu.ro; internet www.mmediu.ro.

Ministry of Foreign Affairs: 011822 Bucharest, Al. Alexandru 31; tel. (21) 3192108; fax (21) 3196862; e-mail mae@mae.ro; internet www.mae.ro.

Ministry of the Interior and Administrative Reform: 010086 Bucharest, Piaţa Revoluţiei 1A, Sector 1; tel. (21) 3037080; fax (21) 3103072; e-mail drp@mai.gov.ro; internet www.mai.gov.ro.

Ministry of Justice: 050741 Bucharest 5, Str. Apolodor 17; tel. (21) 3144400; fax (21) 3101664; e-mail relatiipublice@just.ro; internet www.just.ro.

Ministry of Labour, the Family and Equal Opportunities: 010026 Bucharest 1, Str. Demetru I. Dobrescu 2–4; tel. (21) 3156563; fax (21) 3122768; e-mail relatiicupublicul@mmssf.ro; internet www.mmssf.ro.

Ministry of Public Health: 010024 Bucharest 1, Str. Cristian Popişteanu 1–3; tel. (21) 3072500; fax (21) 3141526; e-mail presa@ms.ro; internet www.ms.ro.

Ministry of Small and Medium-sized Enterprises, Trade, Tourism and the Liberal Professions: Bucharest, Str. Poterasi 11; tel. (21) 3362820; fax (21) 3361843; e-mail publicinfo@mimmc.ro; internet www.mimmc.ro.

Ministry of Transport: 010873 Bucharest 1, Bd. Dinicu Golescu 38; tel. (21) 3199565; fax (21) 3138869; e-mail relpub@mt.ro; internet www.mt.ro.

President

Presidential Election, First Ballot, 28 November 2004

Candidates	Votes	%
Adrian Năstase (National Union*)	4,278,864	40.94
Traian Băsescu (Justice and Truth Alliance†)	3,545,236	33.92
Corneliu Vadim Tudor (Greater Romania Party)	1,313,714	12.57
Bela Marko (Democratic Alliance of Hungarians in Romania)	533,446	5.10
Others	780,945	7.47
Total	10,452,205	100.00

Second Ballot, 12 December 2004

Candidates	Votes	%
Traian Băsescu (Justice and Truth Alliance†)	5,126,794	51.23
Adrian Năstase (National Union*)	4,881,520	48.77
Total	10,008,314	100.00

* An alliance of the Social Democratic Party and the Humanist Party of Romania (renamed the Conservative Party in 2005).
† An alliance of the National Liberal Party and the Democratic Party.

Legislature

PARLAMENTUL ROMÂNIEI
(The Romanian Parliament)

The bicameral Parlamentul României comprises the 346-member lower chamber, the Camera Deputaţilor (Chamber of Deputies), and the 140-member upper chamber, Senatul (the Senate). Members of both chambers are directly elected, for a term of four years.

Camera Deputaţilor
(Chamber of Deputies)

050563 Bucharest, Palatul Parlamentului, Str. Izvor 2–4, Sector 5; tel. (21) 4021444; fax (21) 4022149; e-mail secretar.general@cdep.ro; internet www.cdep.ro.

Chairman: BOGDAN OLTEANU.

ROMANIA

General Election, 28 November 2004

Parties	Seats
National Union*	132
Justice and Truth Alliance†	112
Greater Romania Party	48
Democratic Alliance of Hungarians in Romania	22
Minority parties	18
Total	**332**

* An alliance of the Social Democratic Party and the Humanist Party of Romania (renamed the Conservative Party in 2005).
† An alliance of the National Liberal Party and the Democratic Party.

Senatul
(The Senate)

050711 Bucharest 5, Calea 13 Septembrie 1–3; tel. (21) 4021111; fax (21) 3121184; e-mail csava@senat.ro; internet www.senat.ro.

Chairman: NICOLAE VĂCĂROIU.

General Election, 28 November 2004

Parties	Seats
National Union*	57
Justice and Truth Alliance†	49
Greater Romania Party	21
Democratic Alliance of Hungarians in Romania	10
Others	—
Total	**137**

* An alliance of the Social Democratic Party and the Humanist Party of Romania (renamed the Conservative Party in 2005).
† An alliance of the National Liberal Party and the Democratic Party.

Election Commission

Central Electoral Office (Biroul Electoral Central): 030595 Bucharest 3, Str. Zborului 10; tel. (21) 3268427; fax (21) 3268430; internet www.bec2004.ro; Pres. EMIL GHERGUT.

Political Organizations

Civic Alliance (Alianţa Civică): 010343 Bucharest, Piaţa Amzei 13, etaj 2, Sector 1; tel. and fax (21) 3119142; e-mail office@aliantacivica.ro; internet www.aliantacivica.ro; f. 1990 as alliance of opposition groupings outside legislature; Pres. CHRISTIAN MITITELU.

Conservative Party (CP) (Partidul Conservator): 010093 Bucharest 1, Calea Victoriei 118, etaj 5, Sector 1; tel. (21) 3170614; fax (21) 3170613; e-mail secretariat@partidulconservator.ro; internet www.partidulconservator.ro; f. 1991 as the Humanist Party of Romania; contested legislative and presidential elections in 2004 in alliance with the SDP, as the National Alliance; renamed in May 2005; absorbed the Romanian National Unity Party in Feb. 2006; Pres. DAN VOICULESCU.

Democratic Alliance of Hungarians in Romania (DAHR) (Uniunea Democrată Maghiară din România—UDMR): 024015 Bucharest, Str. Avram Iancu 8; tel. and fax (21) 3144356; e-mail elhivbuk@rmdsz.rdsnet.ro; internet www.rmdsz.ro; f. 1990; supports the rights of Hungarians in Romania; Pres. BELA MARKO; Exec. Pres. CSABA TAKÁCS.

Democratic Force of Romania (Forţa Democrâta din România—FDR): 030627 Bucharest 3, Calea Călăraşi 76; e-mail contact@fortademocratatimis.ro; f. 2004; Chair. PETRE ROMAN.

Democratic Party (DP) (Partidul Democrat—PD): 011825 Bucharest, Al. Modrogan 1; tel. and fax (21) 2301332; e-mail office@pd.ro; internet www.pd.ro; f. 1993; fmrly Democratic Party—National Salvation Front; centre-left; social-democratic; contested legislative and presidential elections in 2004 in alliance with the NLP, as the Justice and Truth Alliance; Pres. EMIL BOC; Exec. Chair. ADRIAN VIDEANU.

Greater Romania Party (GRP) (Partidul România Mare—PRM): 010296 Bucharest, Str. G. Clemenceau 8–10; tel. (21) 3130967; fax (21) 3126182; e-mail prm@prm.org.ro; internet www.prm.org.ro; f. 1991; known as the Popular Greater Romania Party (under the chairmanship of Corneliu Ciontu) in March–June 2005; nationalist; splinter group formed under Ciontu in mid-2005 (People's Party), which subsequently merged with the New Generation—Christian Democratic Party; Chair. CORNELIU VADIM TUDOR.

Liberal Democratic Party (Partidul Liberal Democrat—PLD): Bucharest; internet www.platformaliberala.ro; f. 2006 by fmr mems of National Liberal Party; Chair. THEODOR STOLOJAN.

National Liberal Party (NLP) (Partidul Naţional Liberal—PNL): 011866 Bucharest, Bd. Aviatorilor 86; tel. (21) 2310795; fax (21) 2310796; e-mail dre@pnl.ro; internet www.pnl.ro; f. 1990 as revival of party originally founded in 1869 and banned in 1947; merged with Liberal Party in 1993, and with Party of the Civic Alliance and Liberal Party of Romania in 1998, absorbed Alliance for Romania in 2002 and the Union of Rightist Forces in 2003; supports the integration of Romania into the European Union and the North Atlantic Treaty Organizaton, advocates freedom of expression and religion, a market economy and the decentralization of state powers; contested legislative and presidential elections in 2004 in alliance with the DP, as the Justice and Truth Alliance; Pres. CĂLIN TĂRICEANU; Sec.-Gen. DAN STEFAN MOTREANU.

New Generation—Christian Democratic Party (Partidul Noua Generatie—Crestin Democrat—PNG): 030061 Bucharest 3, Str. Blănari 21–23; tel. (21) 3149360; fax (21) 3149361; e-mail contact@png.ro; internet www.png.ro; f. 2003; Chair. GHEORGHE BECALI.

Popular Action (Actiunea Populara): 050093 Bucharest 5, Splaiul Independenţei 17/101; tel. (21) 3160293; fax (21) 3160399; e-mail office@actiunea.ro; internet www.actiunea.ro; f. 2003 by mems of the Christian Democratic National Peasants' Party of Romania; merged with the Popular Christian Party in Nov. 2003; Chair. EMIL CONSTANTINESCU; Sec.-Gen. MARIUS VLADU.

Popular Christian-Democratic Party of Romania (Partidul Popular Creştin-Democrat din România—PPCD): 020922 Bucharest, Bd. Carol I 34; tel. (21) 6154533; fax (21) 6143277; internet www.pntcd.ro; f. 1989 by merger of centre-right Christian Democratic Party and traditional National Peasant Party, as revival of party originally founded in 1869 and banned in 1947; changed name as above from Christian Democratic National Peasants' Party of Romania (CDNPP) in 2005; absorbed the Union for the Reconstruction of Romania in March 2005; supports pluralist democracy and the restoration of peasant property; Chair. MARIAN MILUŢ; Sec.-Gen. ADRIAN GHIŢĂ.

Romanian Ecological Federation (REF) (Federaţia Ecologistă din România—FER): 021457 Bucharest, Str. Matei Voievod 102; tel. (21) 6352743; alliance incl. the Romanian Ecological Movement; Leader EDWARD GUGUI.

Social Democratic Party (SDP) (Partidul Social Democrat—PSD): 011346 Bucharest 2, Şos. Kiseleff 10; tel. (21) 2222958; fax (21) 2223272; internet www.psd.ro; f. 2001 by the merger of the Romanian Social Democratic Party and the Party of Social Democracy of Romania; contested legislative and presidential elections in 2004 in alliance with the Humanist Party of Romania, as the National Alliance; Pres. MIRCEA DAN GEOANĂ; Sec.-Gen. MIRON MITREA.

Diplomatic Representation

EMBASSIES IN ROMANIA

Albania: 011811 Bucharest, Str. Duiliu Zamfirescu 7, Sector 1; tel. (21) 2119829; fax (21) 2108039; Ambassador DASHNOR DERVISHI.

Algeria: 010663 Bucharest, Bd. Lascăr Catargiu 29; tel. (21) 2124185; fax (21) 2115695; e-mail ambalgerie@roumanie.eunet.ro; Ambassador ABDEL HAMID SENOUCI BEREKSI.

Argentina: 010031 Bucharest, Union Internacional Centre, Str. Ion Campineanu 11, 3rd Floor, Rm 101; tel. (21) 3122626; fax (21) 3120116; e-mail eruma@mrecic.gov.ar; Chargé d'affaires a.i. MIGUEL ANGEL SUAREZ.

Armenia: Bucharest, Str. Intr. Poiana 27, Sector 1; tel. (21) 3197604; fax (21) 3197603; e-mail armembro@starnets.ro; Ambassador YEGISHE SARKISSIAN.

Austria: 020461 Bucharest, Str. Dumbrava Roşie 7; tel. (21) 2015612; fax (21) 2100885; e-mail bukarest-ob@bmeia.gv.at; Ambassador MARTIN EICHTINGER.

Azerbaijan: 014132 Bucharest 1, Str. Grigore Gafencu 10; tel. (21) 2332484; fax (21) 2332465; e-mail azsefroman@azembassy.ro; internet www.azembassy.ro; Ambassador ELDAR HASANOV.

Belarus: Bucharest, Str. Tuberozelor 6, Sector 1; tel. (21) 2231776; fax (21) 2231763; e-mail romania@belembassy.org; Chargé d'affaires a.i. DMITRIY SHEMETOV.

Belgium: 020061 Bucharest, Bd. Dacia 58, Sector 2; tel. (21) 2102970; fax (21) 2102803; e-mail bucharest@diplobel.org; internet www.diplobel.org/romania; Ambassador PHILIPPE ROLAND.

Bosnia and Herzegovina: 011786 Bucharest 1, Str. Stockholm 12; tel. (21) 4092601; fax (21) 4092603; Ambassador BRANKO T. NEŠKOVIĆ.

ROMANIA

Brazil: Bucharest, Bd Aviatorilor 40, Sector 1; tel. (21) 2301130; fax (21) 2301599; e-mail braembuc@starnets.ro; Ambassador VITOR CANDIDO PAIM GOBATO.

Bulgaria: 011835 Bucharest, Str. Rabat 5; tel. (21) 2302150; fax (21) 2307654; e-mail bulembassy@pcnet.ro; internet www.bgembassy-romania.org; Ambassador KONSTANTIN ANDREEV.

Canada: 011411 Bucharest, Str. Tuberozelor 1–3, Sector 1; tel. (21) 3075000; fax (21) 3075010; e-mail bucst@dfait-maeci.gc.ca; internet www.dfait-maeci.gc.ca; Ambassador MARTA MOSZCZENSKA.

Chile: 010991 Bucharest, Str. Sevastopol 13–17/111; tel. (21) 3127239; fax (21) 3127246; e-mail info@chile.ro; Ambassador CARLOS PARKER.

China, People's Republic: 014103 Bucharest, Şos. Nordului 2; tel. (21) 2334188; fax (21) 2334189; e-mail chinaemb_ro@mfa.gov.cn; internet www.chinaembassy.org.ro; Ambassador LIU ZENGWEN.

Congo, Democratic Republic: 010517 Bucharest, Str. Mihai Eminescu 50–54/15/7, Sector 1; tel. (21) 2105498; e-mail ambardcbuc@yahoo.fr; Chargé d'affaires a.i. PHOBA KI KUMBU.

Congo, Republic: 021412 Bucharest 2, Bd. Pache Protopopescu 14; tel. and fax (21) 3153371; e-mail ambacobuc@yahoo.fr; Chargé d'affaires GEORGES AMBARA.

Croatia: 024031 Bucharest, Str. Dr Burghelea 1, Sector 2; tel. (21) 3130457; fax (21) 3130384; e-mail croemb.bucharest@mvp.hr; Ambassador IVICA MAŠTRUKO.

Cuba: 010516 Bucharest, Str. Mihai Eminescu 44–48, 2nd Floor, Rm 5; tel. and fax (21) 2118916; e-mail embacuba@kappa.ro; Ambassador MANUEL ISMAEL HERMIDA MEDINA.

Cyprus: 050726 Bucharest, J. W. Marriot Grand Hotel, Calea 13 Septembrie 90, Sector 5; tel. (21) 4034900; fax (21) 4034901; Ambassador SPYROS ATTAS.

Czech Republic: 030045 Bucharest, Str. Ion Ghica 11, Sector 3; tel. (21) 3039230; fax (21) 3122539; e-mail bucharest@embassy.mzv.cz; internet www.mzv.cz/bucharest; Ambassador Dr PETR DOKLÁDAL.

Denmark: 024031 Bucharest, Str. Dr Burghelea 3; tel. (21) 3000800; fax (21) 3120358; e-mail buhamb@um.dk; internet www.ambbukarest.um.dk; Ambassador ULRIK HELWEG-LARSEN.

Egypt: 010407 Bucharest 1, Bd. Dacia 67; tel. (21) 2110938; fax (21) 2100337; e-mail egyptemb@canad.ro; Ambassador MUHAMMAD AL-SAYYID GOHAR.

Finland: 011832 Bucharest, Str. Atena 2 bis; tel. (21) 2307504; fax (21) 2307505; e-mail sanomat.buk@formin.fi; internet www.finlandia.ro; Ambassador TAPIO SAARELA.

France: 010392 Bucharest, Str. Biserica Amzei 13–15; tel. (21) 3031000; fax (21) 3031090; e-mail chancellerie.bucarest-amba@diplomatie.gouv.fr; internet www.ambafrance-ro.org; Ambassador HENRI PAUL.

Georgia: 010516 Bucharest 1, Str. Mihai Eminescu 44–48, ap. 8; tel. (21) 2100602; fax (21) 2113999; Ambassador ZURAB BERIDZE.

Germany: 011849 Bucharest, Str. Capt. Aviator Gh. Demetriade 6–8; tel. (21) 2029830; fax (21) 2305846; e-mail botschaft@deutschebotschaft-bukarest.ro; internet www.bukarest.diplo.de; Ambassador ROLAND LOHKAMP.

Greece: 021403 Bucharest, Bd. Pache Protopopescu 1–3, Sector 2; tel. (21) 2094170; fax (21) 2094175; e-mail grembassy@grembassy.ro; internet www.grembassy.ro; Ambassador GEORGIOS POUKAMISSAS.

Holy See: 010187 Bucharest, Str. Pictor C. Stahi 5–7; tel. (21) 3123883; fax (21) 3120316; e-mail nuntius@rdslink.ro; Apostolic Nuncio Most Rev. FRANCISCO-JAVIER LOZANO (Titular Archbishop of Penafiel).

Hungary: 020027 Bucharest, Str. Dimitrie Gerotă 63–65; tel. (21) 3120073; fax (21) 3120467; e-mail hunembro@ines.ro; internet hungaryemb.ines.ro; Ambassador JÁNOS TERÉNYI.

India: 020078 Bucharest 3, Str. Mihai Eminescu 183; tel. (21) 2115451; fax (21) 2110614; e-mail office@embassyofindia.ro; internet www.embassyofindia.ro; Ambassador DEBASHISH CHAKRAVARTI.

Indonesia: 010488 Bucharest 1, Str. Gina Patrichi 10; tel. (21) 3120742; fax (21) 3120214; e-mail indobuch@indonezia.ro; Ambassador NUNI TURNIJATI DJOKO.

Iran: 010633 Bucharest, Bd. Lascar Catargiu 39, Sector 1; tel. (21) 3120495; fax (21) 3120496; e-mail office@iranembassy.ro; internet www.iranembassy.ro; Ambassador HAMID REZA ARSHADI.

Iraq: 011834 Bucharest 1, Str. Venezuela 6–8; tel. (21) 2339008; fax (21) 2339007; e-mail bkremb@iraqmofamail.net; Ambassador ABDEL MURAD ALI.

Ireland: 011015 Bucharest 1, Str. Buzesti 50–52, 3rd Floor; tel. (21) 3102131; fax (21) 3112285; e-mail bucharestembassy@dfa.ie; Ambassador PÁDRAIC CRADOCK.

Israel: 040231 Bucharest 4, Bd. Dimitrie Cantemir 1, Bl. B2, 5th Floor; tel. (21) 3304149; fax (21) 3300750; e-mail israel.embassy@algoritma.ro; Ambassador OREN DAVID.

Italy: 010667 Bucharest, Str. Henri Coandă 7–9; tel. (21) 3052100; fax (21) 3120422; e-mail ambasciata.bucarest@esteri.it; internet www.ambbucarest.esteri.it; Ambassador DANIELE MANCINI.

Japan: 011141 Bucharest 1, America House East Wing, Şos. Nicolae Titulescu 4–8; tel. (21) 3191890; fax (21) 3191895; e-mail embassy@embjpn.ro; internet www.ro.emb-japan.go.jp; Ambassador KANJI TSUSHIMA.

Jordan: 020461 Bucharest 2, Str. Dumbrava Roşie 1; tel. (21) 2104705; fax (21) 2100320; e-mail jordan.embassy@pcnet.ro; Ambassador RASSEM YAQOUB HASHEM.

Kazakhstan: Bucharest, Str. Av. Traian Vasile 76, Sector 1; tel. (21) 6657828; fax (21) 2243512; Chargé d'affaires a.i. BAKYTZHAN ORDABAYEV.

Korea, Democratic People's Republic: 014103 Bucharest, Şos. Nordului 6; tel. and fax (21) 2329665; Ambassador HA PYONG GUK.

Korea, Republic: 012013 Bucharest, Bd. Mircea Eliade 14; tel. (21) 2307198; fax (21) 2307629; e-mail koerom@mofat.go.kr; Ambassador IHL SONG CHOI.

Kuwait: 011751 Bucharest 1, Str. Louis Blanc 19A-B; tel. (21) 2309980; fax (21) 2309992; e-mail kuwaitstampa@tiscalinet.it; internet www.kuwaitembassy.ro; Ambassador YAQOUB YOUSEF AL-ATEEQI.

Lebanon: 011817 Bucharest 1, Str. Paris 46, ap.1; tel. (21) 2309205; fax (21) 2307534; e-mail emblebanon@k.ro; Ambassador MUHAMMAD EL-DIB.

Libya: 010633 Bucharest 1, Bd. Lascar Catargiu 15; tel. (21) 2127832; fax (21) 3120232; Chargé d'affaires AHMAD IBRAHIM AL-FAQIH.

Lithuania: 011973 Bucharest, Bd. Primăverii, 51, Sector 1; tel. (21) 3115997; fax (21) 3115919; e-mail amb.ro@urm.lt; internet www.ro.mfa.lt; Ambassador VLADIMIR JARMOLENKO.

Macedonia, former Yugoslav Republic: 020083 Bucharest, Str. Mihai Eminescu 144; tel. (21) 2100880; fax (21) 2117295; e-mail ammakbuk@rdsmail.ro; Ambassador LJUPČO ARSOVSKI.

Malaysia: 020025 Bucharest 2, Str. Pta Cantacuzino 1, 3rd Floor, Rm 4; tel. (21) 2113801; fax (21) 2100270; e-mail mwbucrst@itcnet.ro; Ambassador DATIN PADUKA HALIMAH ABDULLAH.

Mexico: 020082 Bucharest, Str. Mihai Eminescu 124C, Rm 13–14, Sector 2; tel. (21) 2104577; fax (21) 2104713; internet www.embamex.ro; Chargé d'affaires a.i. LUIS ALBERTO BARRERO STAHL.

Moldova: 011824 Bucharest 1, Al. Alexandru 40; tel. (21) 2300474; fax (21) 2307790; e-mail ambasadamoldova@zappmobile.ro; Ambassador LIDIA GUŢU.

Morocco: 010459 Bucharest 1, Str. Dionisie Lupu 78; tel. (21) 2102945; fax (21) 2102767; e-mail ambamarbuc@ambasadamaroc.ro; internet www.ambasadamaroc.ro; Ambassador LAHCEN AZOULY.

Netherlands: 011823 Bucharest, Al. Alexandru 20; tel. (21) 2086030; fax (21) 2307620; e-mail bkr@minbuza.nl; internet www.olanda.ro; Ambassador JAAP L. WERNER.

Nigeria: 010449 Bucharest, POB 1–305, Str. Gina Patrichi 9; tel. (21) 3128685; fax (21) 3120622; e-mail nigeremb@canad.ro; Ambassador A. B. MAGASHI.

Norway: 020463 Bucharest, Str. Dumbrava Roşie 4; tel. (21) 2100274; fax (21) 2100275; e-mail emb.bucharest@mfa.no; internet www.norvegia.ro; Ambassador ØYSTEIN HOVDKINN.

Pakistan: 011352 Bucharest 1, Str. Barbu Delavrancea 22; tel. (21) 3187873; fax (21) 3187874; e-mail parepbuc@k.ro; Ambassador SANAULLAH.

Peru: 011346 Bucharest 1, Şos. Pavel Kiseleff 18; tel. (21) 2231956; fax (21) 2231088; e-mail embaperu@pcnet.ro; Ambassador ELARD ESCALA SANCHEZ-BARRETO.

Philippines: 050453 Bucharest 5, Str. Carol Davila 105–107, 5th Floor, Rm 10–11; tel. (21) 3198252; fax (21) 3198253; e-mail bucharestpe@rdsmail.ro; Ambassador TERESITA C. DAZA.

Poland: 011821 Bucharest 1, Al. Alexandru 23; tel. (21) 2302330; fax (21) 2307832; e-mail ambasada@bukareszt.ro; Ambassador JACEK PALISZEWSKI.

Portugal: 011815 Bucharest 1, Str. Paris 55; tel. (21) 2304136; fax (21) 2304117; e-mail secretariat@embportugal.ro; internet www.embportugal.ro; Ambassador ALEXANDRE VASSALO.

Qatar: 011834 Bucharest, Str. Venezuela 10A; tel. (21) 2304741; fax (21) 2305446; e-mail qtr_ambassador@b.astral.ro; Ambassador SALEM ABDULLAH SULTAN AL-JABER.

Russia: 011341 Bucharest 1, Şos. Kiseleff 6; tel. (21) 2223170; fax (21) 2229450; e-mail rab@mb.roknet.ro; internet www.romania.mid.ru; Ambassador ALEKSANDR A. CHURILIN.

ROMANIA

Saudi Arabia: 010501 Bucharest 1, Str. Polonă 6; tel. (21) 2109109; fax (21) 2107093; Chargé d'affaires AHMAD M. AL-ZUGHAIBI.

Serbia: 010573 Bucharest 1, Calea Dorobanților 34; tel. (21) 2119871; fax (21) 2100175; e-mail ambiug@ines.ro; Ambassador DUŠAN CRNOGORCEVIĆ.

Slovakia: 020977 Bucharest 2, Str. Ofetari 3; tel. (21) 3006100; fax (21) 3006101; e-mail embassy@bukurest.mfa.sk; internet www.bucharest.mfa.sk; Ambassador HILDEGARD BUNČÁKOVÁ.

Slovenia: Bucharest, Str. Puskin Alexandru 10, Sector 1; tel. (21) 3002780; fax (21) 3150927; e-mail vbk@gov.si; internet www.bukaresta.veleposlanistvo.si; Chargé d'affaires a.i. MARCEL KOPROL.

South Africa: 010113 Bucharest, Str. Ştirbei Vodă 26–28, Sector 1; tel. (21) 3133725; fax (21) 3133795; Ambassador JOHANNES HENDRIK KOTZE.

Spain: 011827 Bucharest, Str. Tirana 1; tel. (21) 2339190; fax (21) 2307626; e-mail embespro@mail.mae.es; internet www.spania.xnet.ro; Ambassador JUAN PABLO GARCÍA-BERDOY Y CEREZO.

Sudan: 011941 Bucharest 1, Str. Pictor Negulici 3; tel. (21) 2339189; fax (21) 2339188; e-mail sudanbuc@sudanembassy.ro; Ambassador ABDELAZIZ MARHOUM AHMED.

Sweden: 011343 Bucharest, Şos. Kiseleff 43, Sector 1; tel. (21) 4067100; fax (21) 4067124; e-mail ambassaden.bukarest@foreign.ministry.se; Ambassador MATS O. ÅBERG.

Switzerland: 010626 Bucharest, Str. Grigore Alexandrescu 16–20; tel. (21) 2061600; fax (21) 2061620; e-mail vertretung@buc.rep.admin.ch; internet www.eda.admin.ch/bucarest; Ambassador LIVIO HÜRZELER.

Syria: 010673 Bucharest, Bd. Lascar Catargiu 50; tel. (21) 3192467; fax (21) 3129554; Ambassador Dr WALID ALI OSMAN.

Thailand: 020953 Bucharest, Str. Vasile Conta 12; tel. (21) 3110031; fax (21) 3110044; e-mail thaibuh@speedmail.ro; Ambassador RUSHDA THAVARAVEJ.

Tunisia: 010517 Bucharest 1, Str. Mihai Eminescu 50–54, 4th Floor, Rm 10; tel. (21) 2101197; fax (21) 2101114; Ambassador SALOUA BAHRI.

Turkey: 010575 Bucharest, Calea Dorobanților 72; tel. (21) 2063700; fax (21) 2063737; e-mail bukres.be@mfa.gov.tr; Ambassador AYŞE SINIRLIOGLU.

Ukraine: 010572 Bucharest, Bd. Aviatorilor 24, Sector 1; tel. (21) 2303660; fax (21) 2303661; e-mail emb_ukr@itcnet.ro; Ambassador YURIY MALKO.

United Kingdom: 010463 Bucharest, Str. Jules Michelet 24; tel. (21) 2017200; fax (21) 2017299; e-mail press@bucharest.mail.fco.gov.uk; internet www.britishembassy.gov.uk/romania; Ambassador ROBIN BARNETT.

USA: 020942 Bucharest, Str. Tudor Arghezi 7–9; tel. (21) 2003300; fax (21) 2003442; internet www.usembassy.ro; Ambassador NICHOLAS TAUBMAN.

Venezuela: 011396 Bucharest 1, Str. G.D. Mirea, pictor 18; tel. (21) 2225874; fax (21) 2225073; e-mail embavero@pcnet.ro; Chargé d'affaires a.i. MARGOT J. MÁRQUEZ GARCÍA.

Viet Nam: 020011 Bucharest, Str. C. A. Rosetti 35; tel. (21) 3111604; fax (21) 3121626; e-mail viethuru@b.astral.ro; internet www.vietnamembassy-romania.org; Ambassador LE MANH HUNG.

Judicial System

In preparation for its entry into the European Union on 1 January 2007, Romania implemented a programme of judicial reform, with a particular emphasis on guaranteeing the independence of the judiciary.

High Court of Cassation and Justice
(Înalte Curte de Casație și Justiție a României)

020936 Bucharest 2, Str. Batiște 2; tel. (21) 3137656; fax (21) 3137655; internet www.scj.ro.

The High Court of Cassation and Justice, which was reorganized in June 2004, exercises control over the judicial activity of all courts. It ensures the correct and uniform application of the law. The Court includes sections dealing with: civil and intellectual property law; criminal law; commercial law; and administrative and fiscal regulations.

President: NICOLAE POPA.

Constitutional Court of Romania (Curtea Constituțională a României): 050725 Bucharest, Palatul Parlamentului, Calea 13 Septembrie 2, Sector 5; tel. (21) 4022121; fax (21) 3124359; e-mail ccr@ccr.ro; internet www.ccr.ro; f. 1992; Pres. IOAN VIDA.

Office of the Prosecutor-General: 050706 Bucharest 5, Bd. Libertății 14; tel. (21) 4102727; fax (21) 3113939; e-mail pg@kappa.ro; Prosecutor-General LAURA CODRUTA KOVESI.

COUNTY COURTS AND LOCAL COURTS

The judicial organization of courts at the county and local levels was established by Law 92 of 4 August 1992. In each of the 40 counties of Romania there is a county court and between three and six local courts. The county courts also form 15 circuits of appeal courts, where appeals against sentences passed by local courts are heard, which are generally considered courts of first instance. There is also a right of appeal from the appeal courts to the Supreme Court. In both county courts and local courts the judges are professional magistrates.

Religion

In Romania there are 15 religious denominations and more than 400 religious associations recognized by the state. According to census figures, about 87% of the population belonged to the Romanian Orthodox Church in January 1992.

State Secretariat for Religious Affairs: 020962 Bucharest, Str. Nicolae Filipescu 40; tel. (21) 2118116; fax (21) 2109471; e-mail ssc@mediasat.ro; f. 1990; State Sec. LAURENȚIU TĂNASE.

CHRISTIANITY
The Romanian Orthodox Church

The Romanian Orthodox Church is the major religious organization in Romania (with more than 19m. believers) and is organized as an autocephalous patriarchate, led by the Holy Synod and headed by a patriarch. The Patriarchate comprises five metropolitanates, 10 archdioceses and 13 dioceses.

Romanian Patriarchate
(Patriarhia Română)

040163 Bucharest, Al. Dealul Mitropoliei 25; tel. (21) 3374035; fax (21) 3370097; e-mail externe@patriarhia.ro; internet www.patriarhia.ro.

Patriarch, Metropolitan of Muntênia and Dobrogea and Archbishop of Bucharest: DANIEL (CIOBOTEA), 040161 Bucharest, Str. Patriarhiei 21; tel. (21) 3372776.

Metropolitan of Banat and Archbishop of Timişoara and Caransebeş: Dr NICOLAE (CORNEANU), 300021 jud. Timiş, Timişoara, Bd. Constantin Diaconovici Loga 7; tel. (256) 190960; internet www.mitropolia-banatului.home.ro.

Metropolitan of Cluj, Alba, Crişana and Maramureş and Archbishop of Vad, Feleac and Cluj: Bartolomeu, 400117 jud. Cluj, Cluj-Napoca, Piaţa Avram Iancu 18; tel. (264) 593944; fax (264) 595184; e-mail bartolomeu@arhiepiscopia-ort-cluj.org; internet www.arhiepiscopia-ort-cluj.org.

Metropolitan of Moldova and Bucovina and Archbishop of Iaşi: TEOFAN, 700064 jud. Iaşi, Iaşi, Bd. Ştefan cel Mare şi Sfânt 16; tel. (232) 214771; fax (232) 212656; e-mail iecum@mail.dntis.ro; internet www.mmb.ro.

Metropolitan of Oltenia and Archbishop of Craiova: (vacant), 200381 jud. Dolj, Craiova, Str. Mitropolit Firmilian 3; tel. (251) 415054; fax (251) 418369; internet www.m-ol.ro.

Metropolitan of Transylvania and Archbishop of Sibiu: LAURENȚIU, 550179 jud. Sibiu, Sibiu, Str. Mitropoliei 24; tel. (269) 412867.

The Roman Catholic Church

Roman Catholics in Romania include adherents of the Armenian, Latin and Romanian (Byzantine) Rites.

Bishops' Conference: 010804 Bucharest, via Popa Tatu 68; tel. (21) 3111289; fax (21) 3111591; e-mail budau@b.astral.ro; f. 1993; Pres. Most Rev. IOAN ROBU (Archbishop of Bucharest).

Latin Rite

There are two archdioceses (including one directly subordinate to the Holy See) and four dioceses. At 31 December 2005 there were 1,220,574 adherents of the Latin Rite (about 5.1% of the total population).

Archbishop of Alba Iulia: Most Rev. GYÖRGY-MIKLÓS JAKUBÍNYI, 510010 jud. Alba, Alba Iulia, Str. Mihai Viteazul 21; tel. (258) 811689; fax (258) 811454; e-mail albapress@gyrke.uab.ro.

Archbishop of Bucharest: Most Rev. IOAN ROBU, 010164 Bucharest, Str. Gen. Berthelot 19; tel. (21) 3158349; fax (21) 3121208; e-mail secretariat@arcb.ro.

Romanian Rite

There is one archbishopric—major and four dioceses. At 31 December 2005 there were 758,083 adherents of the Romanian Rite (about 3.5% of the total population).

Archbishop—Major of Făgăraş and Alba Iulia: Most Rev. LUCIAN MUREŞAN, 515400 jud. Alba, Blaj, Str. Petru Pavel Aron 2; tel. (258) 712057; fax (258) 713602; e-mail mitropolia@bru.ro.

Armenian Rite

There were 842 adherents of the Armenian Rite in Romania at 31 December 2005, represented by an Ordinariate.

Reformed (Calvinist) Church

The Reformed (Calvinist) Church has some 700,000 mems. There are two bishoprics.

Bishop of Oradea: 410210 jud. Bihor, Oradea, Str. J. Calvin 1; tel. (259) 432837; e-mail partium@rdsor.ro; internet www.kiralyhagomellek.ro; Bishop LÁSZLÓ TŐKÉS.

Bishop of the Transylvanian Reformed Church District: 400079 jud. Cluj, Cluj-Napoca, Str. I. C. Brătianu 51; tel. (264) 597472; fax (264) 595104; e-mail office@reformatus.ro; internet www.reformatus.ro; Bishop Rev. Dr GÉZA PAP.

Other Protestant Churches

Evangelical-Lutheran Church in Romania: 400105 jud. Cluj, Cluj-Napoca, Bd. 21 Decembrie 1989 1; tel. (264) 596614; fax (264) 593897; internet www.lutheran.ro; comprises about 27,100 Hungarians, 4,600 Slovaks and 340 Romanians; Superintendent Bishop ZOLTÁN ADORJANI DEZSŐ.

Romanian Evangelical Church (Biserica Evanghelica România): 050454 Bucharest, Str. Carol Davila 48; tel. (21) 4119622; fax (21) 4103652; e-mail ber@fx.ro; internet www.ber.ro.

Unitarian Church in Transylvania: 400105 jud. Cluj, Cluj-Napoca, Str. 21 Decembrie 1989 9; tel. (264) 593236; fax (264) 595927; e-mail ekt@unitarius.com; internet www.unitarius.com; f. 1568; comprises about 75,000 mems, principally of Hungarian ethnicity; 125 churches and 30 fellowships; Bishop ÁRPÁD SZABÓ.

Other Christian Churches

Belaya Krinitsa Old Believers' Orthodox Church: 810140 jud. Brăila, Brăila, Str. Zidari 5; tel. (239) 647023; Metropolitan LEONTY IZOTOV.

Pentecostal Church: 050453 Bucharest, Str. Carol Davila 81; tel. (21) 2126419; fax (21) 2204303; e-mail cuvadev@fx.ro; f. 1922; 2,455 churches, 525 pastors (Dec. 2001); 450,000 mems; Pres. Rev. RIVIS TIPEI PAVEL; Gen. Sec. Rev. IOAN GURĂU.

Seventh-day Adventist Church: 077190 jud. Ilfov, Voluntari, Str. Erou Iancu Nicolae 38; tel. (21) 4908590; fax (21) 4908570; e-mail communicatii@adventist.ro; internet www.adventist.ro; f. 1920; 67,000 mems; Pres. of the Union Rev. ADRIAN BOCANEANU; Sec.-Gen. TEODOR HUTANU.

ISLAM

The Muslim Community comprises some 55,000 members, mostly of Turkish-Tatar origin.

Muftiatul Cultului Musulman din Romania: Grand Mufti OSMAN NEGEAT, 900742 jud. Constanţa, Constanţa, Bd. Tomis 41; tel. (241) 611390.

JUDAISM

In 1999 there were about 14,000 Jews, organized in some 70 communities, in Romania.

Federation of Jewish Communities: 030202 Bucharest 3, Str. Sf. Vineri 9–11; tel. (21) 3132538; fax (21) 3120869; e-mail vainer@jewish.ro; Chief Rabbi AUREL MENACHEM VAINER HACOHEN.

The Press

The Romanian press is highly regionalized, with newspapers and periodicals appearing in all of the administrative districts. In 2005 there were a total of 80 daily newspapers and 2,044 periodicals in circulation. In 2002 some 10 newspapers and 207 periodicals were published in the languages of ethnic minorities in Romania, including Hungarian, German, Serbian, Ukrainian, Armenian and Yiddish.

The publications listed below are in Romanian, unless otherwise indicated.

PRINCIPAL DAILY NEWSPAPERS

Adevărul (The Truth): 013701 Bucharest, Piaţa Presei Libere 1; tel. (21) 2240067; fax (21) 2243612; e-mail redactia@adevarul.kappa.ro; internet www.adevarulonline.ro; f. 1888; daily except Sun.; independent; Dir CHRISTIAN TUDOR POPESCU; circ. 200,000.

Azi (Today): 010062 Bucharest, Calea Victoriei 39A, CP 45–49; tel. (21) 3144215; fax (21) 3120128; e-mail redactie@azi.ro; internet www.azi.ro; f. 1990; independent; Editor-in-Chief ANA MOD.

Cotidianul (The Daily): 020922 Bucharest 2, Bd. Carol I 34–36; tel. (21) 3173192; fax (21) 3173124; e-mail rhpress@cotidianul.ro; internet www.cotidianul.ro; f. 1991; daily except Sun.; Editorial Dir DORU BUSCU; Editor-in-Chief CAROL SEBASTIAN; circ. 120,000.

Cronica Română: 013701 Bucharest 1, POB 33, Piaţa Presei Libere 1, corp. C, etaj 1, camera 31; tel. (21) 3179165; fax (21) 3179169; internet www.cronicaromana.ro; f. 1992; daily; Dir HORIA ALEXANDRESCU; Editor-in-Chief DAN OLTEANU; circ. 29,000.

Curierul Naţional (The National Courier): 010024 Bucharest, Str. Cristian Popişteanu 2–4; tel. (21) 3159512; fax (21) 3121300; internet www.curierulnational.ro; f. 1991; Editor-in-Chief CRISTINA OROVEANU; circ. 55,000.

Evenimentul Zilei (The Event of the Day): 020337 Bucharest 2, Bd. Dimitrie Pompeiu 6; tel. (21) 2226381; fax (21) 2226382; internet www.evz.ro; f. 1991; owned by Ringier (Switzerland); tabloid; Bucharest, Transylvania and western regional editions; Editor-in-Chief RAZVAN IONESCU; circ. 200,000.

Gândul: 013701 Bucharest 1, Piaţa Presei Libere 1, Corp. A3–A4; tel. (21) 2053125; fax (21) 2053188; e-mail redactia@gandul.info; internet www.gandul.info; f. 2005; independent; Editor-in-Chief ADRIAN URSU.

Gazeta Sporturilor (Sports Gazette): 051431 Bucharest 1, Şos. Bucuresti–Ploieşti 17; tel. (21) 2087460; fax (21) 2087484; e-mail gazeta@gsp.ro; internet www.gazetasporturilor.ro; f. 1924; daily except Sun.; independent; Editor-in-Chief CATALIN TOLONTAN; circ. 50,000.

Jurnalul National (The National Journal): 013701 Bucharest 1, Piaţa Presei Libere 1, Corp. D, etaj 8; tel. (21) 2243701; fax (21) 2243351; e-mail off@jurnalul.ro; internet www.jurnalul.ro; f. 1993; Editor-in-Chief MARIUS TUCĂ; circ. 70,000.

Libertatea (Freedom): 020337 Bucharest, Bd. Dimitrie Pompeiu 6, Sector 2; tel. (21) 2030940; fax (21) 2030832; internet www.libertatea.ro; f. 1989; owned by Ringier (Switzerland); daily; Sunday edition, *Libertatea de Duminica*, launched in 2002; tabloid; morning paper; Editor-in-Chief ADRIAN HALPERT; circ. 140,000.

ProSport: 020337 Bucharest 2, Bd. Dimitrie Pompeiu 6, Novo Parc; internet www.prosport.ro; f. 1997; owned by Ringier (Switzerland); sports news.

România Libera (Free Romania): 013701 Bucharest, Piaţa Presei Libere 1, Corp. C, etaj 4; tel. (21) 2224770; fax (21) 2232071; e-mail redactia@romanialibera.ro; internet www.romanialibera.ro; f. 1877; daily except Sun.; independent; Editor-in-Chief BOGDAN FICEAC; circ. 100,000.

Ziarul Financiar: 030195 Bucharest, Str. Bărăţiei 31; tel. (31) 8256235; fax (31) 8256285; e-mail zf@zf.ro; internet www.zf.ro.

Ziua (The Day): 010036 Bucharest, Str. Ion Câmpineanu 4; tel. and fax (21) 3113155; e-mail ziua@ziua.ro; internet www.ziua.net; f. 1930; Dir SORIN ROSCA STANESCU.

DISTRICT NEWSPAPERS

Alba

Unirea (The Union): 510093 jud. Alba, Alba Iulia, Str. Decebal 27; tel. and fax (258) 811420; e-mail unirea@unirea-pres.ro; internet www.ziarulunirea.ro; f. 1891; independent; daily except Sun.; Gen. Man. GHEORGHE CIUL; Editor-in-Chief MARIA LUCIA MUNTEANU; circ. 32,000.

Arad

Adevărul (The Truth): 310130 jud. Arad, Arad, Bd. Revoluţiei 81; tel. (257) 281802; fax (257) 280904; e-mail adevarul@arad.ro; internet www.adevarul.arad.ro; f. 1989; independent; daily; Dir DOREL ZAVOIANU; circ. 25,900.

Argeş

Argeşul Liber (Free Argeş): 110177 jud. Argeş, Piteşti, Str. Republicii 88; tel. (276) 30490; e-mail argesul@rdspt.ro; internet www.cotidianul-argesul.ro; f. 1990; independent; daily; Editor-in-Chief MARIN MANOLACHE.

Bacău

Deşteptarea (The Awakening): 600010 jud. Bacău, Bacău, Str. Vasile Alecsandri 41; tel. (234) 511272; fax (234) 524927; e-mail dsa@desteptarea.ro; internet www.desteptarea.ro; f. 1989; Editor-in-Chief DORIAN POCOVNICU; circ. 50,000.

Bihor

Erdélyi Napló: 400750 jud. Bihor, Oradea, POB 1320, Of. p. 1.; tel. (264) 420773; fax (259) 417126; e-mail erdelyinaplo@cluj.astral.ro; internet www.hhrf.org/erdelyinaplo; in Hungarian; weekly; Editor-in-Chief LÁSZLÓ DÉNES.

ROMANIA

Bistriţa-Năsăud

Mesagerul de Bistriţa-Năsăud: 420074 jud. Bistriţa-Năsăud, Bistriţa, Str. Ursului 14; tel. (402) 63234688; fax (402) 63234689; e-mail mesagerul@mesagerul.ro; internet www.mesagerul.ro; daily.

Botoşani

Monitorul de Botoşani: 710210 jud. Botoşani, Botoşani, Str. Mihail Kogălniceanu 4; tel. (231) 515053; fax (231) 515130; e-mail monitorul@monitorulbt.ro; internet www.monitorulbt.ro; Editor-in-Chief Catalin Moraru.

Braşov

Bună Ziua Braşov (Good Afternoon Braşov): 500090 jud. Braşov, Braşov, Str. Mihai Kogalniceanu 19, etaj 7; tel. (268) 411073; fax (268) 314692; e-mail bzb@bzb.ro; internet www.bzb.ro; f. 1995; Dir Ovidiu Fodor; circ. 30,000.

Gazeta de Transilvania (Transylvanian Gazette): 550030 jud. Braşov, Braşov, Str. M. Sadoveanu 3; tel. (268) 8142029; fax (268) 8152927; f. 1838; ceased publication 1946, re-established 1989; daily except Mon.; independent; Editor-in-Chief Eduard Huidan.

Buzău

Opinia (Opinion): jud. Buzău, Buzău; tel. (238) 412764; fax (238) 711063; internet opinia.buzau.ro; f. 1990; independent; daily; Editor-in-Chief Calin Bostan.

Călăraşi

Pământul (Free Earth): 991048 jud. Călăraşi, Călăraşi, Str. Bucureşti 187; tel. (2911) 15840; fax (2911) 313630; f. 1990; socio-political; weekly; Editor-in-Chief Gheorghe Frangulea.

Caraş-Severin

Timpul (The Times): 320026 jud. Caraş-Severin, Reşiţa, Piaţa Republicii 7; tel. (55) 212739; fax (55) 216709; e-mail redactia@timpul-cs.ro; internet www.timpul-cs.ro; f. 1990; independent; daily; Editor-in-Chief Gheorghe Jurma.

Cluj

Făclia de Cluj (Cluj Torch): 401050 jud. Cluj, Cluj-Napoca, Str. Napoca 16; tel. and fax (264) 597418; e-mail redactia@ziarulfaclia.ro; internet www.ziarulfaclia.ro; f. 1989; daily; fmrly Adevărul de Cluj (Cluj Truth); present name adopted 2007; independent; Editor-in-Chief Ilie Călian; circ. 200,000.

Szabadság (Freedom): 400009 jud. Cluj, Cluj-Napoca, Str. Napoca 16, POB 340; tel. (264) 598985; fax (264) 597206; e-mail szabadsag@szabadsag.dntcj.ro; internet www.szabadsag.ro; f. 1989; Minerva Cultural Asscn (non-governmental org.); daily except Sun.; in Hungarian; online edition in parallel since 1995 (up to 5,000 readers); covers five counties; Editor-in-Chief Aron Balló; circ. 10,000.

Constanţa

Cuget Liber (Free Thinking): 900711 jud. Constanţa, Constanţa, Şos. I. C. Brătianu 5; tel. (241) 582120; fax (241) 619524; internet www.cugetliber.ro; f. 1989; independent; daily; Editor-in-Chief Ion Tiţa Călin.

Covasna

Cuvântul nou (New Word): 520064 jud. Covasna, Sfântu Gheorghe, Str. Pieţei 8; tel. (240) 2311388; f. 1968; new series 1990; daily except Mon.; Editor-in-Chief Dumitru Mânolăchescu.

Háromszék (Three Chairs): 520064 jud. Covasna, Sfântu Gheorghe, Str. Presei 8A; tel. (240) 67351504; fax (240) 67351253; e-mail hpress@3szek.ro; internet www.3szek.ro; f. 1989; socio-political; daily; in Hungarian; Editor-in-Chief Farkas Árpád.

Dâmboviţa

Dâmboviţa: 130082 jud. Dâmboviţa, Târgovişte, Bul. Unirii 32; f. 1990; independent; daily; Editor-in-Chief Alexandru Ilie.

Dolj

Cuvântul Libertăţii (Word of Liberty): 200020 jud. Dolj, Craiova, Str. Lyon 8; tel. (251) 2457; fax (251) 4141; f. 1989; daily except Sun.; Editor-in-Chief Dan Lupescu; circ. 40,000.

Galaţi

Viaţa Libera (Free Life): 800215 jud. Galaţi, Galaţi, Str. Domnească 68; tel. (23) 460620; fax (23) 471028; e-mail redactie@viata-libera.galati.ro; internet www.vlg.sisnet.ro; f. 1990; independent; daily; Dir Radu Macovei.

Giurgiu

Cuvântul Liber (Free Word): 080195 jud. Giurgiu, Giurgiu, Str. 1 Decembrie 1918 60A; tel. (2912) 21227; f. 1990; weekly; Editor-in-Chief Ion Gaghii; circ. 10,000.

Gorj

Gorjanul: 210192 jud. Gorj, Târgu Jiu, Str. Constantin Brâncuşi 15; tel. (2929) 17464; f. 1990; daily; Editor-in-Chief Nicolae Brînzan.

Harghita

Adevărul Harghitei (Harghita Truth): 530190 jud. Harghita, Miercurea-Ciuc, Str. Leliceni 45; tel. (266) 171805; fax (266) 172065; f. 1990; independent; daily; Editor-in-Chief Mihai Groza.

Hargita Népe: 530190 jud. Harghita, Miercurea-Ciuc, Str. Leliceni 45; tel. and fax (266) 171322; e-mail hargitanepe@topnet.to; internet www.topnet.ro/hargitanepe; daily; in Hungarian; Dir László Borbely.

Hunedoara

Cuvântul Liber (The Free Word): 330005 jud. Hunedoara, Deva, Str. 22 Decembrie 37A; tel. (256) 211275; fax (256) 218061; e-mail cuvlib@rdslink.ro; internet cuvlibdeva.recep.ro/ziar.htm; f. 1949; daily except Mon.; Editor-in-Chief Cornel Poenar; circ. 25,000.

Ialomiţa

Tribuna Ialomiţei (Ialomiţa Tribune): 920033 jud. Ialomiţa, Slobozia, Str. Dobrogeanu-Gherea 2; f. 1969; weekly; Editor-in-Chief Titus Niţu.

Iaşi

Evenimentul: 700497 jud. Iaşi, Iaşi, Stradelă Ştefan cel Mare şi Sfânt 4; tel. (232) 112023; fax (232) 112025; internet www.evenimentul.ro/sectiune/iasi.html; f. 1991; daily; Editor-in-Chief Constantin Paladuta.

Monitorul de Iaşi (Monitor): 700237 jud. Iaşi, Iaşi, Şos. Naţională 45; tel. (232) 802709; fax (232) 802710; e-mail redactia@monitorulis.ro; internet www.monitorulis.ro; f. 1991; daily; Editor-in-Chief Cătălina Terchea.

Ziarul de Iaşi: 700399 jud. Iaşi, Iaşi, Str. Smârdan 5; tel. (232) 271271; fax (232) 270415; e-mail ziaruldeiasi@ziaruldeiasi.ro; internet www.ziaruldeiasi.ro; daily.

Maramureş

Bányavidéki Új Szó (Miners' New Word): 430051 jud. Maramureş, Baia Mare, Bd. Bucureşti 25; tel. (262) 274465; fax (262) 432585; e-mail genius@sintec.ro; f. 1989; weekly; in Hungarian; Editor-in-Chief Maria Szilveszter.

Graiul Maramureşului (The Voice of Maramureş): 430051 jud. Maramureş, Baia Mare, Bd. Bucureşti 25; tel. (262) 221017; fax (262) 224871; e-mail graiul@graiul.ro; internet www.graiul.ro; f. 1989; independent; daily except Sun.; Editor-in-Chief Augustin Cozmuţa; circ. 10,000.

Mehedinţi

Datina (Tradition): 220134 jud. Mehedinţi, Drobeta-Turnu Severin, Str. Trâian 89; tel. (2978) 119950; f. 1990; independent; daily; Editor-in-Chief Gheorghe Bureţea.

Mureş

Cuvântul Liber (Free Word): 540015 jud. Mureş, Târgu Mureş, Str. Gh. Doja 9; tel. (265) 36636; f. 1990; independent; daily; Editor-in-Chief Lazăr Ladariu.

Népújság (People's Journal): 540015 jud. Mureş, Târgu Mureş, Str. Gh. Doja 9; tel. (265) 266780; fax (265) 266270; e-mail nepujsag@e-nepujsag.ro; internet www.hhrf.org/nepujsag; f. 1990; daily; in Hungarian; Editor-in-Chief János Makkai.

Neamţ

Ceahlăul: 610263 jud. Neamţ, Piatra-Neamţ, Al. Tiparului 14; tel. and fax (233) 625282; f. 1989; daily; Editor-in-Chief Viorel Tudose; circ. 20,000.

Olt

Olt Press: 230083 jud. Olt, Slatina, Str. G. Poboran 5; tel. (244) 439441; f. 1990; fmrly Glasul Adevărului (Voice of Truth); 5 a week.

ROMANIA

Prahova

Prahova: 100066 jud. Prahova, Ploieşti, Bd. Republicii 2; tel. (244) 141245; fax (244) 111206; internet www.ziarulprahova.ro; f. 1870; Editor-in-Chief DUMITRU CÂRSTEA; circ. 17,000.

Sălaj

Graiul Sălajului (Voice of Sălaj): 450042 jud. Sălaj, Zalău, Piaţa Unirii 7; tel. (299) 614120; f. 1990; daily; Editor-in-Chief IOAN LUPA.

Szilágyaság (Word from Sălaj): 450042 jud. Sălaj, Zalău, Piaţa Libertăţii 9, POB 68; tel. (299) 633736; e-mail szilagysag@zappmobile.ro; f. 1990; organ of Hungarian Democratic Union of Romania; weekly; Editor-in-Chief JÁNOS KUI.

Satu Mare

Szatmári Friss Újság: 440030 jud. Satu Mare, Satu Mare, Str. M. Viteazu 32; tel. (261) 712024; fax (261) 714654; e-mail szfu@multiarea.ro; internet www.hhrf.org/frissujsag; f. 1990; daily except Sun.; in Hungarian; Editor-in-Chief VERES ISTVÁN.

Sibiu

Tribuna: 550013 jud. Sibiu, Sibiu, Str. Gheorghe Coşbuc 38; tel. (269) 2113333; fax (269) 216603; e-mail red@tribuna.ro; internet www.tribuna.ro; f. 1884; daily; independent; Editor-in-Chief MIRCEA BITU; circ. 17,000.

Suceava

Crai nou: 720059 jud. Suceava, Suceava, Str. Mihai Viteazul 32; tel. (230) 214723; fax (230) 530285; e-mail redactie@crainou.ro; internet www.crainou.ro; f. 1990; daily; Editor-in-Chief DUMITRU TEODORESCU.

Teleorman

Teleormanul Liber (Free Teleorman): 140033 jud. Teleorman, Alexandria, Str. Ion Creangă 63; tel. (247) 311950; fax (247) 323871; e-mail etl@starnets.ro; f. 1990; daily; Editor-in-Chief GHEORGHE FILIP.

Timiş

Renaşterea Bănăţeană: 300024 jud. Timiş, Timişoara, Bd. Revoluţiei 1989 8; tel. (256) 490145; fax (256) 495317; e-mail renasterea@renasterea.ro; internet www.renasterea.ro; f. 1990; daily; independent; tabloid; Editor-in-Chief ADRIAN POP; circ. 19,000.

Timişoara: 300012 jud. Timiş, Timişoara, Str. Brediceanu 37A; tel. (256) 264546; fax (256) 146170; e-mail timisoara@rdstm.ro; internet www.cotidianultimisoara.ro; f. 1990; daily; Editor-in-Chief OSCAR BERGER.

Tulcea

Delta (The Delta): 820180 jud. Tulcea, Tulcea, Str. Spitalului 4; tel. (2405) 12406; fax (2405) 16616; f. 1885; new series 1990; daily except Mon.; Editor-in-Chief NECULAI AMIHULESEI.

Vâlcea

Curierul de Vâlcea (Courier of Vâlcea): 240165 jud. Vâlcea, Râmnicu Vâlcea, Calea lui Traian 127; tel. (250) 702942; fax (250) 702941; e-mail office@curierul.ro; internet www.curierul.ro; f. 1990; independent; daily except Mon.; commerce; Dir IOAN BARBU.

Vaslui

Adevărul (The Truth): 730168 jud. Vaslui, Vaslui, Str. Ştefan cel Mare 79; tel. (2983) 12203; socio-cultural publication; twice weekly; f. 1990; Editor-in-Chief TEODOR PRAXIU.

Vrancea

Milcovul Liber (Free Milcov): 620095 jud. Vrancea, Focşani, Bd. Unirii 18; tel. (237) 614579; fax (237) 613588; f. 1989; weekly; Dir OVIDIU BUTUC.

PRINCIPAL PERIODICALS

Bucharest

22: 010093 Bucharest, Calea Victoriei 120; tel. (21) 3141776; fax (21) 3112208; e-mail r22@r22.sfos.ro; f. 1990; weekly; Editor-in-Chief GABRIELA ADAMEŞTEANU; circ. 13,000.

Academia Caţavencu (Caţavencu Academy): 030016 Bucharest 2, Bd. Regina Elisabeta 7–9, et. 6; tel. (21) 4209459; fax (21) 3140258; internet www.catavencu.ro; f. 1991; weekly; satirical; Editor DORU BUŞCU; circ. 85,000.

Bursa: 010804 Bucharest 1, Str. Popa Tatu 7; tel. (21) 3154356; fax (21) 3124556; e-mail marketing@bursa.ro; internet www.bursa.ro; f. 1990; finance; Editor-in-Chief FLORIAN GOLDSTEIN; circ. 35,000.

Capital: 020337 Bucharest 2, Bd. Dimitrie Pompeiu 6, Novo Park; tel. (21) 2030802; fax (21) 2035632; e-mail office@capital.ro; internet www.capital.ro; f. 1992; owned by Ringier (Switzerland); weekly; economic and financial magazine; Editor-in-Chief IONUT POPESCU; circ. 60,000.

Contemporanul—Ideea Europeană (The Contemporary–The European Idea): 014780 Bucharest 1, Piaţa Amzei, European Idea Cultural Foundation, POB 113, Of. p. 22; tel. (21) 2125692; fax (21) 3106618; e-mail contemporanul@ideeaeuropeana.ro; internet www.ideeaeuropeana.ro/cod/public/revista.php; f. 1881; monthly; cultural, political and scientific review; published by the European Idea Cultural Foundation; Editor-in-Chief AURA CHRISTI.

Economistul (The Economist): 010702 Bucharest 1, Calea Griviţei 21, 7th Floor; tel. (21) 6507820; fax (21) 3129717; e-mail edeconomica@edeconomica.com; internet www.edecon.ro; f. 1990; daily; Editor-in-Chief IOAN ERHAN.

Femeia Moderna (Modern Woman): 013701 Bucharest, Piaţa Presei Libere 1, Corp. C, etaj 4, Rm 405–408; tel. (21) 2029193; fax (21) 2029194; e-mail redactia@femeia.ro; internet www.femeia.ro; f. 1868; monthly; Dir VASILE TINCU.

Flacăra (The Flame): 013701 Bucharest 1, Piaţa Presei Libere 1; tel. (21) 2243688; fax (21) 2273713; e-mail redactia@flacara21.ro; internet www.flacara21.ro; f. 1911; monthly; Editor-in-Chief ALEXANDRU ARION; circ. 30,000.

Jurnalul Afacerilor (Romanian Business Journal): 013701 Bucharest 1, Piaţa Presei Libere 1, Corp. 3, 3rd Floor, Rm 317–321; tel. (21) 2246897; fax (21) 2246896; e-mail rbj@euroweb.ro; f. 1990; Dir MARCEL BARBU; circ. 25,000.

Luceafărul (The Morning Star): 010071 Bucharest, Calea Victoriei 133; tel. (21) 596760; f. 1958; weekly; published by the Writers' Union; Dir LAURENTIU ULICI.

Magazin (The Magazine): 013701 Bucharest, Piaţa Presei Libere 1; tel. (21) 2225111; fax (21) 2230866; f. 1958; Dir FILIP DUMITRU.

Magazin istoric (Historical Magazine): 010155 Bucharest, Piaţa Valter Mărăcineanu 1–3; tel. (21) 3126877; fax (21) 3150991; e-mail mistoric@itcnet.ro; internet magazinistoric.itcnet.ro; f. 1967; monthly; review of historical culture; Chief Editor DORIN MATEI; circ. 25,000 (2007).

Meridian: 021875 Bucharest 2, Laurentiu Claudian 9; tel. (21) 2500030; fax (21) 2501261; e-mail office@libripress.ro; internet www.libripress.ro; f. 1993; monthly; tourism.

Panoramic Radio-TV: 011964 Bucharest, Str. Jean Baptiste Molière dramaturg 2–4; tel. (21) 2307501; fax (21) 156992; e-mail micara.dumutrescu@tvr.ro; f. 1990; weekly; Dir STEFAN DIMITRIU; Editor-in-Chief ADRIAN IONESCU; circ. 50,000.

PC World Romania: 011455 Bucharest, Bd. Mareşal Averescu 8–10, Sector 1; tel. (21) 3161132; fax (21) 3162621; e-mail office@idg.ro; internet www.pcworld.ro; f. 1993; monthly; computing; Editor-in-Chief OANA BURGHELEA; circ. 15,000.

Practic in bucătărie: 010652 Bucharest 1, Str. Ciprian Porumbescu 10; tel. (21) 3170610; e-mail secretariat@casalux.ro; internet www.practic.ro; owned by Hubert Burda Media (Germany); monthly; cookery and kitchen-design magazine; Editor-in-Chief CRISTINA BUNEA.

Revista Română de Statistică (Romanian Statistical Review): 050706 Bucharest, Bd. Libertăţii 16; tel. and fax (21) 3171110; e-mail rrs@insse.ro; internet www.revistadestatistica.ro; f. 1952; monthly; organ of the National Institute of Statistics; Editor-in-Chief ŞTEFAN DORGOŞAN.

România Literară (Literary Romania): 010071 Bucharest, Calea Victoriei 133; tel. (21) 6506286; fax (21) 6503369; e-mail romlit@romlit.ro; internet www.romlit.ro; f. 1968; weekly; literary, artistic and political magazine; published by the Fundation România Literară (Writers' Union); Dir NICOLAE MANOLESCU; Editor-in-Chief ALEX ŞTEFĂNESCU.

România Mare (Greater Romania): 010062 Bucharest, Calea Victoriei 39A; tel. (21) 6156093; fax (21) 3125396; f. 1990; weekly; nationalist; Editor-in-Chief CORNELIU VADIM TUDOR; circ. 90,000.

Romanian Panorama: Bucharest; tel. (21) 2242162; e-mail rps@dial.kappa.ro; f. 1955; monthly; in English, French, German, Russian and Spanish; economy, politics, social affairs, science, history, culture, sport, etc.; published by the Foreign Languages Press Group; Dir NICOLAE ŞARAMBEI; circ. 166,000.

Super Magazin: 013701 Bucharest, Piaţa Presei Libere 1; tel. (21) 2223323; fax (21) 2226382; f. 1993; Editor-in-Chief GHEORGHE VOICU; circ. 200,000.

Tehnium: 013701 Bucharest, Piaţa Presei Libere 1; tel. (21) 2223374; f. 1970; monthly; hobbies; Editor-in-Chief Ing. ILIE MIHĂESCU; circ. 100,000.

ROMANIA

Tribuna economică (Economic Tribune): 010336 Bucharest, Bd. Magheru 28–30; tel. (21) 2127938; fax (21) 3102934; e-mail tribunae@tribunaeconomica.ro; internet www.tribunaeconomica.ro; f. 1899; weekly; Editor-in-Chief EMILIAN STANCU; circ. 10,000.

Vânătorul și Pescarul Român (The Romanian Hunter and Angler): 020882 Bucharest, Calea Moșilor 128; tel. (21) 3133363; fax (21) 3136804; f. 1948; monthly review; Editor-in-Chief GABRIEL CHEROIU.

Cluj-Napoca

Korunk (Our Time): 400304 jud. Cluj, Cluj-Napoca, Str. Gen. Eremia Grigorescu 52; tel. (264) 375035; fax (264) 375093; e-mail korunk@gmail.com; internet www.korunk.org; f. 1926; monthly; social review; in Hungarian; Editor-in-Chief LAJOS KÁNTOR; circ. 1,500 (2006).

Napsugár (Sun Ray): 401050 jud. Cluj, Cluj-Napoca, Str. L. Rebreanu 58/28, POB 137; tel. and fax (264) 418001; e-mail naps.sziv@napsugar.ro; internet www.napsugar.ro; f. 1956; monthly; illustrated literary magazine for children aged 7–12 years; in Hungarian; Editor-in-Chief EMESE ZSIGMOND; circ. 18,500 (2007).

Szivárvány (Rainbow): 401050 jud. Cluj, Cluj-Napoca, Str. L. Rebreanu 58/28, POB 137; tel. and fax (264) 418001; e-mail naps.sziv@napsugar.ro; f. 1980; monthly; illustrated literary magazine for children aged 3–6 years; in Hungarian; Editor-in-Chief EMESE ZSIGMOND; circ. 20,000 (2007).

Tribuna: 400091 jud. Cluj, Cluj-Napoca, Str. Universității 1; tel. (264) 117548; f. 1884; weekly; cultural review; Editor-in-Chief AUGUSTIN BUZURA.

Iași

Cronica: 700037 jud. Iași, Iași, Str. I. C. Brătianu 22; tel. and fax (232) 262140; f. 1966; monthly; cultural review; Editor-in-Chief VALERIU STANCU; circ. 5,000.

Timișoara

Orizont (Horizon): 300085 jud. Timiș, Timișoara, A. Pacha 1; tel. and fax (256) 294893; internet www.revistaorizont.com; f. 1949; monthly; review of the Writers' Union (Timișoara br.); Editor-in-Chief MIRCEA MIHAIEȘ.

Târgu Mureș

Erdélyi Figyelő (Transylvanian Observer): 540026 jud. Mureș, Târgu-Mureș, Str. Primăriei 1; tel. (265) 166910; fax (265) 168688; f. 1958; fmrly Uj Élet; trimestrial; illustrated magazine; in Hungarian; Editor-in-Chief JÁNOS LÁZOK.

NEWS AGENCIES

Mediafax: 020941 Bucharest 2, Str. Tudor Arghezi 3B; tel. (31) 8256100; fax (31) 8256140; e-mail customer@mediafax.ro; internet www.mediafax.ro; f. 1991; largest independent news agency in Romania; Editor-in-Chief CRISTIAN DIMITRIU.

Rompres (Romanian National News Agency): 013701 Bucharest, Piața Presei Libere 1; tel. (21) 2228340; fax (21) 2220089; e-mail webmaster@rompres.ro; internet www.rompres.ro; f. 1949; fmrly Agerpres; provides news and photo services; in English and French; Gen. Man. CONSTANTIN BADEA.

PRESS ASSOCIATIONS

Society of Romanian Journalists—Federation of All Press Unions (Societatea Ziariștilor din România—Federația Sindicatelor din Întreaga Presă): 013701 Bucharest, Piața Presei Libere 1; tel. (21) 2228351; fax (21) 2224266; f. 1990; affiliated to International Organization of Journalists and to International Federation of Journalists; Pres. RADU SORESCU; 5,000 mems.

Publishers

Editura Academiei Române (Publishing House of the Romanian Academy): 050711 Bucharest, Calea 13 Septembrie 13; tel. (21) 4119008; fax (21) 4103983; e-mail edacad@ear.ro; internet www.ear.ro; f. 1948; books and periodicals on original scientific work; 80 periodicals in Romanian and foreign languages; Gen. Man. DUMITRU RADU POPESCU.

Editura Albatros: 013701 Bucharest, Piața Presei Libere 1, Of. 33; tel. and fax (21) 2228493; f. 1969; Romanian literature and culture; Editor-in-Chief GEORGETA DIMISIANO.

Editura Artemis (Artemis Publishing House): 013701 Bucharest, Piața Presei Libere 1; tel. (21) 2226661; f. 1991; fine arts, fiction, children's literature, history; Dir MIRELLA ACSENTE.

Editura Cartea Românească (Publishing House of the Romanian Book): 010071 Bucharest 1, Calea Victoriei 115; tel. (21) 2315237; fax (21) 2244829; e-mail ecr@cartearomaneasca.ro; internet www.cartearomaneasca.ro; f. 1969; Romanian contemporary literature; Dir DAN CRISTEA.

Editura Ceres: 013701 Bucharest, Piața Presei Libere 1; tel. (21) 2224836; f. 1953; books on agriculture and forestry; Dir MARIA DAMIAN.

Editura Dacia (Dacia Publishing House): 400660 jud. Cluj, Cluj-Napoca, Str. Ospatariei 4; tel. and fax (264) 429675; e-mail office@edituradacia.ro; internet www.edituradacia.ro; f. 1969; classical and contemporary literature, science fiction, academic, technical, philosophical and scientific books; in Romanian and Hungarian; Gen. Man. IOAN VĂDAN.

Editura Didactică și Pedagogică (Educational Publishing House): 010176 Bucharest, Str. Spiru Haret 12; tel. and fax (21) 3122885; internet www.edituradp.ro; f. 1951; school, university, technical and vocational textbooks, pedagogic literature and methodology, teaching materials; Gen. Man. Prof. MIHAELA ZĂRNESCU-ENCEANU.

Editura Eminescu (Eminescu Publishing House): 020982 Bucharest 2, Str. Sfantul Spiridon 8; tel. and fax (21) 2123588; e-mail info@edituraeminescu.ro; internet www.edituraeminescu.ro; f. 1969; contemporary original literary works and translations of world literature; Dir SILVIA CINCA.

Editura Enciclopedică (Encyclopedia Publishing House): 013701 Bucharest, Piața Presei Libere 1; tel. and fax (21) 3179035; e-mail enciclopedica2006@yahoo.com; f. 1968; encyclopedias, dictionaries, monographs, reference books and children's books; Dir MARCEL POPA.

Editura Humanitas (Humanitas Publishing House): 013701 Bucharest, Piața Presei Libere 1; tel. (21) 3171819; fax (21) 3171824; e-mail secretariat@humanitas.ro; internet www.humanitas.ro; f. 1990; philosophy, religion, political and social sciences, economics, history, fiction, textbooks, art, literature, practical books; Dir GABRIEL LIICEANU.

Editura Junimea (Junimea Publishing House): 700506 jud. Iași, Iași, Bd. Carol 3–5; tel. (232) 410427; e-mail office@editurajunimea.ro; internet www.editurajunimea.ro; f. 1969; Romanian literature, art books, translations, scientific and technical books; Dir CEZAR IVĂNESCU.

Editura Kriterion (Kriterion Publishing House): 030104 Bucharest, str. Franceză 6/1; tel. and fax (21) 3146246; e-mail krit@dnt.ro; internet www.kriterion.ro; f. 1969; classical and contemporary literature, reference books in science and art; in Hungarian, German, Romanian, Russian, Serbian, Slovak, Tatar, Turkish, Ukrainian and Yiddish; translations in Romanian, Hungarian and German; Dir GYULA H. SZABÓ.

Editura Litera Internațional (International Letter Publishing House): 011422 Bucharest, Str. Emanoil Porumbaru 31A, et. 1, ap. 3; tel. (21) 3196393; fax (21) 3196390; e-mail info@litera.ro; internet www.litera.ro; f. 1989; original literature; Dir-Gen. DAN VIDRASCU.

Editura Medicală SA (Medical Publishing House): 021411 Bucharest 2, Bd. Protopescu Pache 131; tel. (21) 2525188; fax (21) 3124879; e-mail ed-medicala@b.astral.ro; internet www.ed-medicala.ro; f. 1954; medical literature; Dir Prof. AL C. OPROIU.

Editura Militară (Military Publishing House): 061353 Bucharest 6, Drumul Taberei 9–11; tel. and fax (21) 3149161; e-mail adrian.pandea@edituramilitara.ro; internet www.edituramilitara.ro; f. 1950; military history, theory, science, technics, medicine and fiction; Dir ADRIAN PANDEA.

Editura Muzicală (Musical Publishing House): 010071 Bucharest, Calea Victoriei 141; tel. and fax (21) 3129867; e-mail em@edituramuzicala.ro; internet www.edituramuzicala.ro; f. 1957; books on music, musicology and musical scores; Dir MARIUS VASILEANU.

Editura Polirom: 700505 jud. Iași, Iași, Bd. Carol I 4, etaj 4, POB 266; tel. (232) 214100; fax (232) 214111; e-mail office@polirom.ro; internet www.polirom.ro; f. 1995; Dir SILVIU LUPESCU.

Editura Tehnică (Technical Publishing House): 024056 Bucharest 2, Str. Olari 213; tel. (21) 2522366; fax (21) 2525077; e-mail tehnica@edituratehnica.ro; internet www.edituratehnica.ro; f. 1950; technical and scientific books, technical dictionaries; Dir ROMAN CHIRILĂ.

Editura Univers: 010209 Bucharest, Str. Ionel Perlea 8; tel. (21) 3110201; fax (21) 2243765; e-mail univers@rnc.ro; f. 1961; translations from world literature, criticism, essays, literary history, philosophy of culture, educational; Dir DIANA CRUPENSCHI.

Editura de Vest (Publishing House of the West): 300085 jud.Timiș, Timișoara, Piața Sfântul Gheorghe 2; tel. (256) 18218; fax (256) 14212; f. 1972 as Editura Facla; socio-political, technical, scientific and literary works; in Romanian, Hungarian, German and Serbian; Dir VASILE POPOVICI.

ROMANIA   Directory

Rao International Publishing Co: 011322 Bucharest, Str. Turda 117–119/6; tel. (21) 2241231; fax (21) 2241472; e-mail office@raobooks.com; internet www.raobooks.com.

PUBLISHERS' ASSOCIATIONS

Romanian Publishers' Asscn (Asociaţia Editorilor din România): 010326 Bucharest, Bd. Magheru 35, 4th Floor, ap. 42; tel. (21) 2125162; fax (21) 2125178; e-mail info@aer.ro; internet www.aer.ro; f. 1993; 57 mems; Pres. GABRIEL LIICEANU.

Broadcasting and Communications

TELECOMMUNICATIONS

Regulatory Authority

National Regulatory Authority for Communications (Autoritatea Naţionala de Reglementare in Comunicaţii—ANRC): 050706 Bucharest 5, Bd. Libertăţii 14; tel. (21) 3075400; fax (21) 3075402; e-mail anrc@anrc.ro; internet www.anrc.ro; f. 2002.

Service Providers

Cosmote Romanian Mobile Telecommunications SA: 011141 Bucharest 1, Şos. Nicolae Titulescu 4–8; tel. (21) 4041234; fax (21) 4137530; e-mail info@cosmote.ro; internet www.cosmote.ro; f. 2000; fmrly CosmoROM; owned by COSMOTE (Greece); mobile cellular telecommunications services; Chief Exec. NIKOLAOS TSOLAS.

Orange Romania SA: 010665 Bucharest 1, Bd. Lascar Catargiu 51–53, Europe House; tel. (21) 2033030; fax (21) 2033413; e-mail infocorporate@orange.ro; internet www.orange.ro; f. 1996; fmrly Mobil-Rom; owned by Orange (France); mobile cellular telecommunications services; Exec. Dir PIERRE MATTEI; 5m. subscribers (2005).

Romtelecom SA: 050706 Bucharest 5, Bd. Libertăţii 14–16; tel. (21) 4001212; fax (21) 4105581; e-mail contact@romtelecom.ro; internet www.romtelecom.ro; f. 1933; fmr state monopoly; 54% owned by Hellenic Telecommunications Organization (Greece); Dir-Gen. GEORGIOS IOANNIDIS.

Telemobil SA (Zapp): 077015 jud. Ilfov, Baloteşti, Str. Bucureşti 2 Bis; tel. (21) 4024444; fax (21) 4024456; internet www.telemobil.ro; f. 1999; operates mobile cellular telephone network; Man. Dir and Chief Exec. DIWAKER SINGH.

Vodafone Romania: 061344 Bucharest 6, Bd. Vasile Milea 4A; tel. (21) 3021111; fax (21) 3021413; e-mail contact@connex.ro; internet www.connex.ro; f. 2005 by acquisition of Connexnis; fmrly Connex (Mobifon); operates mobile cellular telephone network and third-generation (GSM) services, and provides internet services; 99% owned by Vodafone Group PLC; 5.2m. customers (June 2005); Pres. AL TOLSTOY.

BROADCASTING

Radio

Societatea Româna de Radiodifuziune (SRR) (Romanian Radio Corpn): 010171 Bucharest, Str. Gen. Berthelot 60–64, POB 63-1200; tel. (21) 3031432; fax (21) 3121057; e-mail mesaje@rornet.ro; internet www.srr.ro; f. 1928; 39 transmitters on medium-wave, 69 transmitters on VHF; 114 relays; operates the Radio Romania and Radio Romania International stations: news, cultural, youth and music programmes, plus two local and six regional programmes; foreign broadcasts on one medium-wave and eight short-wave transmitters in Arabic, Bulgarian, Chinese, English, German, Greek, Hungarian, Italian, Portuguese, Romanian, Russian, Serbian, Spanish, Turkish and Ukrainian; Pres. MARIA TOGHINA.

Kiss FM: 060022 Bucharest 6, Spl. Independenţei 202A; tel. (21) 3188000; fax (21) 3125346; e-mail kissfm@kissfm.ro; internet www.kissfm.ro; owned by SBS Broadcasting Sa.r.l.

Pro FM: 021409 Bucharest 2, Bd. Protopopescu Pache 109, etaj 6; tel. (21) 2501430; internet www.profm.ro; f. 1993; owned by Central European Media Enterprises Ltd (Bermuda); Gen. Dir ADRIAN SARBU.

Radio Europa FM: 010541 Bucharest 1, Intr. Camil Petrescu 5; tel. (21) 2010500; fax (21) 2010519; e-mail europafm@europafm.ro; internet www.europafm.ro; Gen. Dir ILIE NĂSTASE.

Radio Nord-Est: 700479 jud. Iaşi, Iaşi, Str. Codrescu 1; tel. and fax (232) 211570; e-mail rneiasi@dntis.ro; f. 1992; independent; Man. MIHAI GRETY.

Societatea Naţională de Radiocomunicaţii, SA (National Radiocommunications Co): 050706 Bucharest 5, Bd. Libertăţii 14; tel. (21) 3073007; fax (21) 3149798; e-mail info@snr.ro; internet www.snr.ro; f. 1991 through the reorganization of Rom Post Telecom; state-owned; radio and television broadcasting (including digital), high-speed internet and broadband services, video conferencing, satellite communications; 2,445 employees.

Television

Televiziunea Română (TVR) (Romanian Television): 015089 Bucharest, Calea Dorobanţilor 191, POB 63-1200; tel. (21) 2312704; fax (21) 2307514; e-mail tvr@tvr.ro; internet www.tvr.ro; f. 1956; state-owned; public broadcasting service; four channels broadcasting 24 hours; Pres. and Dir-Gen. GIURGIU TUDOR.

Antena 1: 013682 Bucharest, Şos. Bucureşti-Ploieşti 25–27; tel. (21) 2121844; internet www.antena1.ro; f. 1993; independent commercial television station.

Prima TV: 040204 Bucharest 4, Calea Serban Voda 95–101; tel. (21) 3359341; e-mail focus@primatv.ro; internet www.primatv.ro; f. 1997; owned by SBS Broadcasting SA.

Pro TV: 021409 Bucharest 2, Bd. Pache Protopopescu 109, etaj 6; tel. (21) 2505063; fax (21) 2501951; e-mail info@protv.ro; internet www.protv.ro; f. 1995; owned by Central European Media Enterprises Ltd (CME), Bermuda; commercial station; Gen. Dir ADRIAN SARBU.

Realitatea TV: 033091 Bucharest, Şos. Dudesti Pantelimon 1–3; tel. and fax (21) 2552665; e-mail office@realitatea.tv; internet www.realitatea.tv; f. 2001; 24 hours; primarily news content.

Finance

(cap. = capital; res = reserves; dep. = deposits; m. = million;
brs = branches; amounts in new lei, unless otherwise indicated)

BANKING

Central Bank

National Bank of Romania (Banca Naţională a României): 030031 Bucharest 3, Str. Lipscani 25; tel. (21) 3130410; fax (21) 3123831; e-mail info@bnro.ro; internet www.bnro.ro; f. 1880; central bank and bank of issue; manages monetary policy; supervises commercial banks and credit business; cap. 30m., res 3,539.50m., dep. 36,646.8m. (Dec. 2005); Gov. MUGUR CONSTANTIN ISĂRESCU; 22 brs.

Other Banks

Alpha Bank Romania SA: 010566 Bucharest 1, Calea Dorobanţilor 237B; tel. (21) 2092100; fax (21) 2316570; e-mail bbr@alphabank.ro; internet www.alphabank.ro; f. 1994 as Banca Bucureşti SA; present name since 2000; 99% owned by Alpha Bank AE (Greece), 1% owned by Alpha Finance AXEEY (Greece); cap. 559.8m., res 176.2m., dep. 6,041.8m. (Dec. 2006); Pres. SERGIU BOGDAN OPRESCU.

ATE Bank Romania SA: 010732 Bucharest 1, Calea Grivitei 24; tel. (21) 3030700; fax (21) 3030732; e-mail atebank@atebank.ro; internet www.atebank.ro; f. 1990; cap. 358.1m., res 10.9m., dep. 197.3m. (Dec. 2006); Chair. SERGIU IOAN MANEA; 12 brs.

Banca Comercială Carpatica SA (BCC): 550135 jud. Sibiu, Sibiu, Str. Autogarii 1; tel. (269) 233815; fax (269) 233371; e-mail extern@carpatica.ro; internet www.carpatica.ro; f. 1999; cap. 103.3m., res 28.1m., dep. 717.0m. (Dec. 2005); Pres. and Chair. NICOLAIE HOANTA.

Banca Comercială Română SA—BCR (Romanian Commercial Bank): 030016 Bucharest 3, Bd. Regina Elisabeta 5; tel. (21) 3126185; fax (21) 3122096; internet www.bcr.ro; f. 1990; 69.15% owned by Erste Bank (Austria); cap. 2,119.7m., res 1,044.4m., dep. 42,003.0m. (Dec. 2006); Pres. ANDREAS TREICHL; CEO NICOLAE DĂNILĂ; 372 brs and sub-brs.

Banca C. R. Firenze Romania SA: 030826 Bucharest 3, Bd. Unirii 55, Bloc E4A, Tronson 1, Parter; tel. (21) 2011930; fax (21) 2011931; e-mail office@bancacrfirenze.ro; internet www.bancacrfirenze.ro; f. 1996 as Banca Daewoo (Romania) SA; name changed as above in 2006; 56.2% owned by Banca Cassa di Risparmio di Firenze (Italy); cap. 37.0m., res 1.9m., dep. 155.2m. (Dec. 2005); Pres. MIHAIL MICU; 10 brs.

Banca de Export-Import a României—Eximbank SA: 050092 Bucharest 5, Str. Splaiul Independenţei 15; tel. (21) 3192971; fax (21) 3192999; e-mail pr@eximbank.ro; internet www.eximbank.ro; f. 1992; 87.4% owned by State Privatization Agency; cap. 1,652.3m., dep. 1,439.9m. (Dec. 2006); Chair. and Chief Exec. CARMEN RADU; 7 brs.

Banca Românească SA (Romanian Bank): 030822 Bucharest 3, Bd. Unirii 35, Bloc A3; tel. (21) 3059300; fax (21) 3059550; e-mail office@brom.ro; internet www.brom.ro; f. 1993; 88.7% owned by National Bank of Greece SA (NBG); cap. 479.9m., res 87.0m., dep. 2,819.3m. (Dec. 2006); Gen. Man. ANDREAS MARAGKOUDAKIS.

Banca Transilvania SA (Transylvanian Bank): 400027 jud. Cluj, Cluj-Napoca, Str. G. Baritiu 8; tel. (264) 407150; fax (264) 407179; e-mail bancatransilvania@bancatransilvania.ro; internet www.bancatransilvania.ro; f. 1994; cap. 483.3m., res 274.3m., dep. 7,028.8m. (Dec. 2006); Chair. HORIA CIORCILA; Chief Exec. ROBERT C. REKKERS; 55 brs.

Bancpost SA: 031296 Bucharest 3, Calea Vitan 6–6A; tel. (21) 3080901; fax (21) 3268520; e-mail bpt@bancpost.ro; internet www

.bancpost.ro; f. 1991; Banc Post SA until 2004; 77.6% owned by EFG Eurobank Ergasias SA (Greece); cap. 372.6m., res 448.7m., dep. 4,640.9m. (Dec. 2005); Chair. MIHAI BOGZA; Gen. Man. MANUELA PLAPCIANU.

BRD-Groupe Société Générale SA (Romanian Bank for Development): 011171 Bucharest 1, Bd. Ion Mihalache 1–7; tel. (21) 3016100; fax (21) 3016636; e-mail communication@brd.ro; internet www.brd.ro; f. 1990 to replace Investment Bank of Romania (f. 1923); name changed in 2004 from Banca Română Pentru Dezvoltare SA-Groupe Société Générale (BRD); financial and banking services and operations to individual and private and small cos, etc.; 58.3% owned by Société Générale (France); cap. 2,515.6m., res 3.0m., dep. 21,170.5m. (Dec. 2006); Chair. and Chief Exec. PATRICK GELIN; 191 brs.

Casa de Economii și Consemnațiuni—CEC SA (Savings and Consignation Bank): 030022 Bucharest 3, Calea Victoriei 11–13; tel. (21) 3111119; fax (21) 3143970; e-mail office@cec-sa.ro; internet www.cec-sa.ro; f. 1864; state-owned; scheduled for privatization; handles private savings, loans for the inter-banking market and mortgages; cap. 149.7m., res 180.6m., dep. 4,952.0m. (Dec. 2005); Chair. and Chief Exec. RADU GRATIAN GHETEA; 42 brs.

Citibank Romania SA: 011742 Bucharest 1, Bd. Iancu de Hunedoara 8, POB 63-5; tel. (21) 2035550; fax (21) 2035565; internet www.citibank.ro; f. 1996; 99.6% owned by Citigroup Overseas Investment Corpn (USA); cap. 99.5m., dep. 2,241.0m. (Dec. 2005); County Officer SHAHMIR KHALIQ.

Credit Europe Bank (Romania) SA: 040034 Bucharest 4, Str. Splaiul Unirii 12, Bloc B6; tel. (21) 3017100; fax (21) 3310970; e-mail office@crediteurope.ro; internet www.crediteurope.ro; f. 1993 as Banca de Credit Industrial si Comercial SA; name changed to Finansbank (Romania) in 2000; name changed as above in March 2007; 89.8% owned by Fiba International Holding (Netherlands); cap. 249.4m., res 23.8m., dep. 1,607.2m. (Dec. 2006); Pres. TAMER OZATAKUL; 85 brs.

Libra Bank SA: 011885 Bucharest 1, Str. Grigore Mora 11; tel. (21) 2088000; fax (21) 2306565; e-mail info@librabank.ro; internet www.librabank.ro; f. 1996 as Banca Română Pentru Relansare Economica SA (Romanian Bank for Economic Revival); present name adopted March 2005; cap. 108.5m., dep. 302.5m. (Dec. 2005); Pres. EMILIAN BITULEANU.

MKB Romexterra Bank SA: 540447 jud.Mureș, Târgu Mureș, Bd. 1 Decembrie 1918 93; tel. (265) 266640; fax (265) 266047; e-mail info@romexterra.ro; internet www.romexterra.ro; f. 1993; 75.49% owned by MKB Bank Nyrt (Hungary); present name adopted 2007; cap. 200.0m., res 29.3m., dep. 1,057.2m. (Dec. 2006); CEO ADRIAN RADU; 68 brs.

OTP Bank Romania SA: 011017 Bucharest 3, Str. Buzesti 66–68; tel. (21) 3075700; fax (21) 3075736; e-mail office@otpbank.ro; internet www.otpbank.ro; f. 1995; named changed in 2005 from Banca Comercială Robank SA; 99.99% owned by OTP Bank Ltd (Hungary); cap. 367.5m., res 42.8m., dep. 1,594.2m. (Dec. 2006); Chair. of Bd Dr ANTAL PONGRACZ.

Piraeus Bank Romania SA: 020922 Bucharest 2, Bd. Carol I 34–36, International Business Centre, 3rd Floor; tel. (21) 3036900; fax (21) 2501799; e-mail office@piraeusbank.ro; internet www.piraeusbank.ro; f. 1995; present name adopted 2000; 87.97% owned by Piraeus Bank (Greece); cap. 116.9m., res 18.2m., dep. 933.4m. (Dec. 2005); Pres. EMANUEL ODOBESCU; 3 brs.

ProCredit Bank SA: 011017 Bucharest 1, Str. Buzesti 62–64; tel. (21) 2016000; fax (21) 2016002; e-mail headoffice@procreditbank.ro; internet www.procreditbank.ro; f. 2002 as Banca de Microfinantare Miro SA; 25.62% owned by ProCredit Holding AG (Germany), 20.03% owned by Commerzbank AG (Germany); cap. €14.7m., res €0.9m., dep. €77.8m. (Dec. 2005); Gen. Man. MICHAEL KOWALSKI.

Raiffeisen Bank SA: 011857 Bucharest 1, Piața Charles de Gaulle 15; tel. (21) 3061000; fax (21) 2300700; e-mail centrala@rzb.ro; internet www.raiffeisen.ro; f. 2002; 99.5% owned by Raiffeisen International Beteiligungs AG (Austria); cap. 1,196.3m., res 4.9m., dep. 9,586.7m. (Dec. 2005); Pres. STEVEN VAN GRONINGEN; 329 brs.

Sanpaolo IMI Bank Romania SA: 310025 jud. Arad, Arad, Bd. Revoluției 88; tel. (257) 308200; fax (257) 285335; e-mail headoffice@sanpaoloimi.ro; internet www.sanpaoloimi.ro; f. 1996 as Banca Comercială West Bank SA; present name adopted Sept. 2003; 98.7% owned by Sanpaolo IMI Internazionale SpA (Italy); cap. 180.2m., res 11.5m., dep. 692.9m. (Dec. 2006); Pres. GIOVANNI RAVASIO; Gen. Man. NICOLA CALABRO.

UniCredit Tiriac Bank SA: 014106 Bucharest, Str. Ghetarilor 23–25, Sector 1; tel. (21) 2002000; fax (21) 2002002; e-mail office@unicredittiriac.ro; internet www.unicredit-tiriac.ro; f. 1991 as Banca Tiriac; name changed as above in June 2007, with merger of Banca Comercială HVB Tiriac and UniCredit Romania SA; cap. 2,296,370m., res 4,996m., dep. 9,941,483m. (Dec. 2006); Chair. DAN PASCARIU; CEO RADU RASVAN; 50 brs.

Volksbank România SA: 021323 Bucharest 2, Șos. Mihai Bravu 171; tel. (21) 2094400; fax (21) 2094490; e-mail marketing@volksbank.com.ro; internet www.volksbank.com.ro; f. 2000; 97.89% owned by Volksbank International AG (Austria); cap. 169.7m., res 194.8m., dep. 1,453.6m. (Dec. 2005); Pres. GERALD SCHREINER.

BANKING ASSOCIATION

Romanian Banking Association (Asociația Română a Băncilor): 030205 Bucharest 3, Str. Sfanta Vineri 34, Bloc A6; tel. (21) 3212078; fax (21) 3212095; e-mail arb@arb.ro; internet www.arb.ro; f. 1991; 39 mems; Chair. RADU GRAȚIAN GHEȚEA; Sec.-Gen. RADU NEGREA.

STOCK EXCHANGE

Bucharest Stock Exchange (Bursa de Valori București): 020922 Bucharest 2, Bd. Carol I 34–36, 14th Floor; tel. (21) 3079500; fax (21) 3079519; e-mail bvb@bvb.ro; internet www.bvb.ro; f. 1882; reopened 1995 (ceased operations 1948); 128 listed cos; Pres. SERGIU OPRESCU; Gen. Man. STERE FARMACHE.

COMMODITIES EXCHANGE

Romanian Commodities Exchange (Bursa Română de Mărfuri): 013701 Bucharest 1, Piața Presei Libere 1; tel. (21) 2244560; fax (21) 2242878; e-mail bursa@brm.ro; internet www.brm.ro; Pres. MIRCEA FILIPOIU.

INSURANCE

In 2003 there were 46 insurance companies.

Allianz-Tiriac Asigurări: 010616 Bucharest, Str. Căderea Bastiliei 80–84; tel. (21) 2082222; fax (21) 2082211; e-mail office@allianztiriac.ro; internet www.allianztiriac.ro.

Asigurarea Româneasca SA (ASIROM) (Romanian Insurance): 020912 Bucharest 2, Bd. Carol I 31–33; tel. (21) 2504271; fax (21) 2504145; internet www.asirom.com.ro; f. 1991 following the restructuring of the state insurance monopoly ADAS into three JSCs; 40.55% owned by InterAgro (Romania-UK); all types of insurance, including life insurance; Dir-Gen. ION GHEORGHE BRATULESCU; 41 brs.

Astra SA: 011996 Bucharest 1, Str. Pușkin 10–12; tel. (21) 2318080; fax (21) 2305248; e-mail info@astrasig.ro; internet www.astrasig.ro; f. 1991 following the restructuring of the state insurance monopoly ADAS into three JSCs; Gen. Man. DAN ADAMESCU.

Certasig SA: 011013 Bucharest 1, Str. Buzesti 75, 1st Floor; tel. (21) 3133375; fax (21) 3133376; e-mail office@certasig.ro; internet www.certasig.ro; formerly Fortuna SA; merged with Romanian-Canadian Insurance Co (AROCA) in 2003; insurance and reinsurance; Pres. ROBERT-SARBINIU SERBAN.

ING Asigurări de Viața SA: 050552 Bucharest 3, Str. Costache Negri 1–5, Opera Centre; tel. (21) 4028580; fax (21) 4028581; e-mail client@ingasigurari.ro; internet www.ingasigurari.ro; f. 1997; life insurance; Gen. Man. BRAM BOON.

Omniasig SA: 011862 Bucharest 1, Bd. Aviatorilor 28; tel. (21) 2315040; fax (21) 2315029; e-mail secretary@omniasig.ro; internet www.omniasig.ro; f. 1994; insurance and reinsurance co; 70.7% owned by TBI Financial Services Group (Netherlands); Chair. CONSTANTIN TOMA.

Unita: 010413 Bucharest 1, Bd. Dacia 30; tel. (21) 2120852; fax (21) 2120843; e-mail unita@unita.ro; internet www.unita.ro; f. 1990; mem. of Wiener Stadtische Group (Austria); Dir DAN ODOBESCU.

Insurance Association

Uniunea Națională a Societăților de Asigurare și Reasigurare din România (National Association of Insurance and Reinsurance Companies of Romania): 040129 Bucharest 4, Bd. Libertății 12, Bloc 114, sc. 3, 4th Floor, ap. 68; tel. (21) 3351269; fax (21) 3372243; e-mail unsar@dnt.ro; internet www.unsar.ro; f. 1994; 22 mems; Pres. CRISTIAN CONSTANTINESCU; Gen. Sec. FLORENTINA ALMAJANU.

Trade and Industry

GOVERNMENT AGENCIES

Agency for Small and Medium Enterprises and Co-operatives (Agenția Naționala pentru Întreprinderi Mici și Mijlocii și Cooperație): 040263 Bucharest 4, Str. Poterași 11; tel. (21) 3352620; fax (21) 3361843; e-mail mariana.spranceana@mimmc.ro; internet www.mimmc.ro; Pres. (vacant).

Authority for the Capitalization of State Assets (Autoritatea pentru Valorificarea Activelor Statului—AVAS): 715151 Bucharest 1, Str. Capt. A. Șerbănescu 50; tel. (21) 3036122; fax (21) 3036521; e-mail infopublic@avas.gov.ro; internet www.avas.gov.ro; created by

ROMANIA

Directory

merger of the Banking Assets Resolution Agency (AVAB) and the Authority for Privatization and Management of State Ownership (APAPS); successor org. to the State Ownership Fund; Gen. Dir GILIOLA CIORTEANU (acting).

Romanian Agency for Foreign Investment: 011974 Bucharest 1, Bd. Primaverii 22; tel. (21) 2339103; fax (21) 2339104; e-mail aris@arisinvest.ro; internet www.arisinvest.ro; f. 2002; Vice-Pres. MONICA BARBULETIU; Sec.-Gen. FLORIN VASILACHE.

Romanian Trade Promotion Centre (Centrul Român pentru Promovarea Comertului—RTPC): 050741 Bucharest 5, Str. Apolodor 17, POB 1/756; tel. (21) 3185050; fax (21) 3111491; e-mail office@traderom.ro; internet www.traderom.ro; f. 1995.

CHAMBER OF COMMERCE

Chamber of Commerce and Industry of Romania and the Municipality of Bucharest: 030982 Bucharest 3, Bd. Octavian Goga 2; tel. (21) 3229536; fax (21) 3229542; e-mail ccir@ccir.ro; internet www.ccir.ro; f. 1868; non-governmental organization; Pres. GHEORGHE COJOCARU.

EMPLOYERS' ASSOCIATIONS

Alliance of Employers' Confederations of Romania (ACPR) (Alianţa Confederaţiilor Patronale din România): 030982 Bucharest 3, Str. Octavian Goga 2, floor 10; tel. (21) 3211381; fax (21) 3211443; internet www.acpr.ro; f. 2004; includes the National Confederation of Romanian Employers (CNPR), the Employer Confederation of Romanian Industry (CONPIROM) and four others; Pres. GHEORGHE COPOS.

National Confederation of Romanian Employers (Confederaţia Naţională a Patronatului Român—CNPR): 020982 Bucharest 3, Bd. Octavian Goga 2; tel. (21) 3212074; fax (21) 3212075; e-mail cnpr@untrr.ro; internet www.cnpr.org.ro; Pres. DINU PATRICIU; Dir-Gen. CRISTIAN PARVAN.

Romanian Private Farmers' Federation (Federaţia agricultorilor privatizaţi din România): 010043 Bucharest 1, Bd. Nicolae Bălcescu 17–19; tel. (21) 6131869; fax (21) 6133043; f. 1991; represents 4,000 farming co-operatives and 41 district unions; Pres. GHEORGHE PREDILA.

Union of Romanian Employers (Uniunea Patronatelor din România—UPR): 020361 Bucharest 2, Str. Luigi Galvani 17–19, c/o Romanian Employers' Organization (PR); tel. (21) 2111246; fax (21) 2103075; e-mail office@patronatulroman.ro; internet www.patronatulroman.ro; f. 2004; consists of 6 nationally representative employers' organizations; Pres. OVIDIU TENDER.

UTILITIES

Regulatory Authority

National Energy Regulatory Authority (Autoritatea Nationala de Reglementare in domeniul Energiei—ANRE): 020995 Bucharest 2, Str. Constantin Nacu 3; tel. (21) 3112244; fax (21) 3124365; internet www.anre.ro; f. 1999; Pres. NICOLAE OPRIS.

National Regulatory Authority for the Natural Gas Sector (Autoritatea Nationala de Reglementare in domeniul Gazelor Naturala—ANRGN): 060114 Bucharest 6, Şos. Cotroceni 4; tel. (21) 3033800; fax (21) 3033808; e-mail anrgn@anrgn.ro; internet www.anrgn.ro; f. 2000; Pres. STEFAN COSMEANU.

Electricity

Electrica SA: 010621 Bucharest, Str. Grigore Alexandrescu 9, Sector 1; tel. (21) 2085999; fax (21) 2085998; internet www.electrica.ro; f. 2002 following the reorganization of the National Electricity Company, CONEL; electricity distributor and supplier; 8 regional branches; two regional branches, Electrica Banat and Electrica Dobrogea, divested to ENEL (Italy) in 2005; Electrica Muntenia Sud—EMS (the largest regional distributor) was also acquired in 2006; 51% of Electric Oltenia was acquired by CEZ (Czech Republic) and 51% in Electric Moldova by E.ON Energie (Germany) in 2005; Chair. CRISTIAN ISTODORESCU.

Hidroelectrica SA: 020995 Bucharest, Str. Constantin Nacu 3, Sector 2; tel. (21) 3112231; fax (21) 3111174; e-mail generala@hidroelectrica.ro; internet www.hidroelectrica.ro; state-owned; administers 120 hydropower plants and 4 pumping stations through 10 regional subsidiaries; Gen. Man. EUGEN PENA.

Nuclearelectrica SA: 010494 Bucharest 1, POB 22–102, Str. Polonă 65; tel. (21) 2038251; fax (21) 3169400; e-mail office@nuclearelectrica.ro; internet www.nuclearelectrica.ro; f. 1998; electrical and thermal power generation; production of nuclear fuel; Gen. Dir Dr IOAN ROTARU; 2,308 employees (2003).

Transelectrica SA: 010325 Bucharest 1, Bd. Gen. Gh. Magheru 33; tel. (21) 3035611; fax (21) 3035820; e-mail office@transelectrica.ro; internet www.transelectrica.ro; f. 2000; fmrly part of the National Electricity Company, CONEL; 73.7% state-owned; transmission system operator of the Romanian power system; includes 9 brs and 6 subsidiaries; Chair. and Gen. Dir STELIAN ALEXANDRU GAL; 2,184 employees.

Gas

SC DistriGaz Nord SA: 540049 jud. Mureş, Târgu Mureş, Piaţa Trandafirilor 21; tel. and fax (265) 267229; e-mail dgnm@distrigaznord.ro; internet www.distrigaznord.ro; f. 1975; privatized in 2004/05; 51% owned by E.ON Ruhrgas (Germany); natural gas distributor.

DistriGaz Sud SA: 040254 Bucharest 4, Bd. Mărăşeşti 4–6; tel. (21) 3012000; fax (21) 3012151; e-mail contact@distrigazsud.ro; internet www.distrigazsud.ro; privatized 2004/05; 30% owned by Gaz de France (France); natural gas distributor.

SNTGN Transgaz SA (Societăţii Naţionale de transport Gaze Naturale Transgaz SA): 551130 jud. Sibiu, Mediaş, Piaţa Constantin I. Moţaş 1; tel. (269) 803333; fax (269) 839031; e-mail cabinet@transgaz.ro; internet www.transgaz.ro; 75% state-owned; exploration, transmission and distribution of natural gas; Gen. Dir IOAN RUSU.

TRADE UNIONS

National Trade Union Confederation Cartel Alfa (Confederaţia Naţionala Sindicală Cartel Alfa—CNS Cartel Alfa): 060041 Bucharest 6, Spl. Independenţiei 202A, 2nd Floor; tel. (21) 3171040; fax (21) 3123481; e-mail alfa@cartel-alfa.ro; internet www.cartel-alfa.ro; f. 1990; 1m. mems; 38 professional affiliations; Pres. BOGDAN IULIU HOSSU.

Confederation of Democratic Trade Unions of Romania (Confederaţia Sindicatelor Democratice din România—CSDR): 010155 Bucharest 1, Piaţa Walter Maracineanu 1–3; tel. (21) 3156542; e-mail csdr@b.astral.ro; f. 1994; 20 professional federations; 640,000 mems; Pres. IACOB BACIU.

National Confederation of Free Trade Unions of Romania 'Brotherhood' (Confederaţia Naţională a Sindicatelor Libere din România Frăţia—CNSLR Frăţia): 010024 Bucharest 1, Str. Cristian Popisteanu 1–3; tel. and fax (21) 3151632; e-mail birourpresa@cnslr-fratia.ro; internet www.cnslr-fratia.ro; merged with the National Trade Union Bloc (Blocul Naţional Sindical—f. 1991) in 2004; 800,000 mems; 44 professional federations; Pres. MARIUS PETCU.

Meridian National Trade Union Confederation (MNTUC) (Confederaţia Sindicala Nationala Meridian): 010366 Bucharest 1, Str. D. I. Mendeleev 36–38; tel. (21) 3168017; fax (21) 3168018; e-mail csnmeridian@csnmeridian.ro; internet www.csnmeridian.ro; f. 1994; 27 br. federations; Gen. Sec. ION ALBU.

Transport

RAILWAYS

In 2003 there were 11,077 km of track in operation (of which 3,965 km were electrified). In September 1998 the Societatea Nationale a Căilor Ferate Române (SNCFR—National Romanian Railway Company) was divided into five companies.

Romanian Railway Authority (Autoritatea Feroviara Româna—AFER): 010719 Bucharest 1, Calea Grivitei 393; tel. (21) 3077900; fax (21) 2241832; e-mail secretariat@afer.ro; internet www.afer.ro; f. 1998; under the jurisdiction of the Ministry of Transport, Construction and Tourism; Gen. Dir VASILE BELIBOU.

National Railways Company for Freight Traffic (Societatea Naţională de Transport Feroviar de Marfă) (CFR Marfă SA): 010873 Bucharest, Bd. Dinicu Golescu 38; tel. (21) 2249336; fax (21) 3124700; e-mail vtulbure@marfa.cfr.ro; internet www.cfrmarfa.cfr.ro; f. 1998 after the reorganization of the SNCFR; main railway freight transport operator in Romania; Gen. Man. LIVIU BOBAR.

National Passenger Railway Transport Co (Societatea Naţională de Transport Feroviar de Călători—CFR Călători SA): 010873 Bucharest, Bd. Dinicu Golescu 38; tel. (21) 3190322; fax (21) 4112054; e-mail marketing.calatori@cfr.ro; internet www.cfr.ro/calatori/; f. 1998; divided into eight regional administrations since 1999; reorganized in Feb. 2001 and merged with eight regional companies; operates all local, regional, long-distance and international passenger rail services; Chair. and Chief Exec. ALEXANDRU NOAPTES.

National Railways Company (CFR SA): 010873 Bucharest, Bd. Dinicu Golescu 38; tel. (21) 3192400; fax (21) 3123200; e-mail virgil.daschievici@cfr.ro; internet www.cfr.ro; management of railway infrastructure; Gen. Dir CONSTANTIN AXINIA; 28,936 employees.

City Underground Railway

The Bucharest underground railway network totals 63.5 km in length.

ROMANIA

Metrorex SA—Societatea Comercială de Transport cu Metroul București: 010873 Bucharest 1, Bd. Dinicu Golescu 38; tel. (21) 2248975; fax (21) 3125149; e-mail contact@metrorex.ro; internet www.metrorex.ro; f. 1977; Gen. Man. Marius Ionel Lăpădat.

ROADS

In 2004 the total length of the national road network was 198,817 km, of which only 30.2% was paved; there were 14,809 km of highways and 36,010 km of secondary roads. A Bucharest–Constanța motorway was due to be completed by 2010. A project to construct the Bucharest–Brașov–Bors motorway was also under way. A further project, scheduled for completion in 2014, aimed to connect Bucharest with Nadlac.

National Administration of Roads (Administrația Națională a Drumurilor RA—AND): Ministerul Transporturilor, 010873 Bucharest 1, Bd. Dinicu Golescu 38; tel. (21) 2232606; fax (21) 3120984; e-mail and@andnet.ro; internet www.andnet.ro; Gen. Dir Mihai Grecu.

INLAND AND OCEAN SHIPPING

The Danube–Black Sea Canal was officially opened to traffic in 1984, and has an annual handling capacity of 80m. metric tons. Romania's principal ports are at Constanța, on the Black Sea; and Tulcea, Galați, Brăila and Giurgiu, on the Danube. In 1995 Romania launched its first ferry service to Turkey, operating between Constanța and Samsun. In 2006 Romania's merchant fleet had 193 vessels, with a combined aggregate displacement of 272,128 grt.

River Administration of the Lower Danube–Galați (Administrația Fluvială a Dunării de Jos RA–Galați): 800025 jud. Galați, Galați, Str. Portului 28–30; tel. (236) 460812; fax (236) 460847; e-mail secretariat@afdj.ro; internet www.afdj.ro; 2 brs and 3 agencies; Gen. Man. Mihai Ochialbescu.

Maritime Port Administration of Constanța SA (NC MPA SA): 900125 jud. Constanța, Constanța, Portului Incinta, Gara Maritima; tel. (241) 611540; fax (241) 619512; internet www.portofconstantza.com; f. 1991; largest port in the Black Sea; one of the main distribution centres for Central and Eastern Europe; also administrates Midia and Mangalia ports, and Tomis marina; Gen. Man. Gheorghe Moldoveanu.

National Co for the Administration of Maritime Ports on the Danube (CN APDM SA) (CN Administrația Porturilori Dunării Maritime SA–Galați): 800025 jud.Galați, Galați, Str. Portului 34; tel. (236) 460660; fax (236) 460140; e-mail apdm@apdm.galati.ro; internet apdm.galati.ro; f. 1998; manages the Maritime Danube Ports Galați, Brăila and Tulcea and the smaller ports: Chilia, Sulina and Sf. Gheorghe; a marina at Tulcea was under construction in 2006; Gen. Man. Carmen Costache.

Administration of Navigable Canals SH (Administrația Canalelor Navigabile SA): 907015 jud. Constanța, Constanța, Str. Ecluzei Agigea 1; tel. (241) 738505; fax (241) 702705; e-mail compania@acn.ro; internet www.acn.ro; fmrly Constanța Corpn for Navigable Channels; Gen. Man. Sevastian Stefan.

National Co for the Administration of River Ports on the Danube (Compania Națională Administrația Porturilor Dunării Fluviale SA); CN APDF SA: 080011 jud. Giurgiu, Giurgiu, Șos. Portului 1; tel. (246) 213003; fax (21) 3110521; internet www.apdf.ro; f. 1998; Gen. Man. Cristian Nemtescu.

NAVROM—Romanian River Navigation Co (Compania de Navigatie Fluviala Romana SA—NAVROM): 800025 jud. Galați, Galați, Str. Portului 34; tel. (236) 460706; fax (236) 460190; e-mail navrom@rls.roknet.ro; owned by Transport Trade Services SA; Romania's leading private river shipping company; fleet of over 400 barges and tugs on the Danube River.

Petromin Shipping Co (CNM Petromin SA): 900125 jud. Constanța, Constanța, Portului Incinta, Poarta 2; tel. (241) 617802; fax (241) 619690; e-mail office@petromin.cunet.ro; undergoing privatization; merchant fleet of 30 ships and tankers; Chair. Andrei Caraiani.

CIVIL AVIATION

There are two international airports at Bucharest: Aurel Vlaicu International (at Băneasa, renamed in 2004) and the largest, Henri Coandă International (at Otopeni, also renamed in 2004). There are other international airports at M. Kogălniceanu-Constanța, Timișoara, Sibiu and Cluj-Napoca. Domestic airports include those at Arad, Bacau, Iași and Oradea.

Romanian Civil Aeronautic Authority (Regia Autonomă Autoritatea Aeronautică Civilă Română): 715621 Bucharest, District 1, Șos. București-Ploiești 38–40; tel. (21) 2081508; fax (21) 2081572; internet www.caa.ro; Gen. Man. Aurelian Botezatu.

Acvila Air: 010301 Bucharest 1, Str. Gheorghe Enescu 7; tel. (21) 3126085; fax (21) 3120069; e-mail info@acvila-air.ro; internet www.acvila-air.ro; f. 1993; cargo and passenger flights to Italy, Portugal, Spain, Egypt and the United Arab Emirates; Pres. Ion Menciu.

Blue Air Transport Aerian: 013695 Bucharest, Șos. București-Ploiești 40, Aeroport București-Băneasa-Aurel Vlaicu International; tel. (21) 2088686; e-mail info@blue-air.ro; internet www.blueair-web.com; f. 2004; low-cost charter-flight co; flies to 12 European destinations; Gen. Dir Gheorghe Racaru.

Carpatair: 307201 jud. Timiș, Timișoara, Timișoara International Airport; tel. (256) 306933; fax (256) 306962; e-mail timisoara@carpatair.com; internet www.carpatair.ro; f. 1999 as Veg Air; assumed present name in 1999; scheduled domestic and regional flights to 28 destinations in six countries; Pres. Nicolae Petrov.

Romavia Romanian Aviation Co: 040231 Bucharest, Bd. Dimitrie Cantemir 1; tel. (21) 3169961; fax (21) 3169957; e-mail office@romavia.ro; internet www.romavia.ro; f. 1991; owned by Ministry of National Defence; state VIP and chartered and scheduled passenger and cargo flights on the routes: Bucharest–Strasbourg (France); Bucharest–Tel Aviv (Israel); and Bucharest–Târgu Mureș–Nuremberg (Germany); Man. Dir Iuliu-Adrian Goleanu.

Tarom—Compania Nationala de Transporturi Aeriene Romane SA (TAROM): 013697 Bucharest, Șos. București–Ploiești, km 16.5, Henri Coandă International (Otopeni) Airport; tel. (21) 2322494; fax (21) 3125686; e-mail secrgen@tarom.ro; internet www.tarom.ro; f. 1954; joint-stock co; services throughout Europe, the Middle East, Asia, the USA and domestically; Pres. Gheorghe Racaru.

Tourism

The Carpathian Mountains, with their numerous painted monasteries, the Danube delta and the Black Sea resorts (Mamaia, Eforie, Mangalia and others) are the principal attractions. In 2005 there were 5.8m. foreign tourist arrivals. Receipts from tourism (including passenger transport) totalled US $1,310m. in 2005, compared with $607m. in 2004.

National Tourism Authority: 010873 Bucharest 1, Bd. Dinicu Golescu 38; tel. (21) 3149957; fax (21) 3149960; e-mail promovare@mturism.ro; internet www.romaniatravel.com; govt org.; Pres. Iuliu Marian Ovidiu.

THE RUSSIAN FEDERATION

Introductory Survey

Location, Climate, Language, Religion, Flag, Capital

The Russian Federation, or Russia, constituted the major part of the USSR, providing some 76% of its area and approximately 51% of its population in 1989. It is bounded by Norway, Finland, Estonia and Latvia to the north-west and by Belarus and Ukraine to the west. The southern borders of European Russia are with the Black Sea, Georgia, Azerbaijan, the Caspian Sea and Kazakhstan. The Siberian and Far Eastern regions have southern frontiers with the People's Republic of China, Mongolia and the Democratic People's Republic of Korea. The eastern coastline is on the Sea of Japan, the Sea of Okhotsk, the Pacific Ocean and the Barents Sea, and the northern coastline is on the Arctic Ocean. The region around Kaliningrad (formerly Königsberg in East Prussia), on the Baltic Sea, became part of the Russian Federation in 1945. Separated from the rest of Russia by Lithuania and Belarus, it borders Poland to the south, Lithuania to the north and east and has a coastline on the Baltic Sea. The climate of Russia is extremely varied, ranging from extreme Arctic conditions in northern areas and much of Siberia to generally temperate weather in the south. The average temperature in Moscow in July is 19°C (66°F); the average for January is −9°C (15°F). Average annual rainfall in Moscow is 575 mm (23 ins). The official language is Russian, but many other languages are also used. Christianity is the major religion, with the Russian Orthodox Church (Moscow Patriarchate) the largest denomination. The main concentrations of adherents of Islam are among the Tatar, Bashkir and Chuvash peoples of the middle Volga, and the peoples of the northern Caucasus, including the Chechen, Ingush, Kabardins and the peoples of Dagestan. Buddhism is the main religion of the Buryats, the Tyvans and the Kalmyks. The large pre-1917 Jewish population has been depleted by war and emigration, but some 230,000 Jews remained in the Russian Federation in 2002, according to census results. The national flag (proportions 2 by 3) consists of three equal horizontal stripes of (from top to bottom) white, blue and red. The capital is Moscow (Moskva).

Recent History

By the late 19th century the Russian Empire extended throughout vast territories in eastern Europe, and included much of northern and central Asia, a result of the territorial expansionism of the Romanov dynasty, which had ruled Russia as an autocracy since 1613. Growing dissatisfaction with economic conditions in urban areas, combined with the adverse effect of defeats in the Russo–Japanese War (1904–05), led Tsar Nicholas (Nikolai) II (1894–1917) to issue a manifesto in October 1905, which promised respect for civil liberties and the introduction of some constitutional order, although the ensuing attempt at reforms failed to placate the increasingly restive workers and peasants. In 1917 there were strikes and demonstrations in the capital, Petrograd (as St Petersburg had been renamed in 1914). In March 1917 the Tsar was forced to abdicate and a liberal Provisional Government, composed mainly of landowners, took power. However, most real authority lay with the soviets (councils), composed largely of workers and soldiers, which were attracted to socialist ideas.

The inability of the Provisional Government, led first by Prince Georgii Lvov and then by the moderate socialist Aleksandr Kerenskii, to implement land reforms, or to effect a withdrawal from the First World War, allowed more extreme groups, such as the Bolshevik faction of the Russian Social Democratic Labour Party (RSDLP) led by Vladimir Ulyanov (Lenin), to attain prominence. On 7 November 1917 (25 October in the Old Style calendar, which remained in use until February 1918) the Bolsheviks, who had come to dominate the Petrograd Soviet, seized power in the capital, with minimal use of force, and proclaimed the Russian Soviet Federative Socialist Republic (RSFSR or Russian Federation). The Bolsheviks subsequently adopted the name All-Russian Communist Party (Bolsheviks).

The Bolsheviks asserted that they would respect the self-determination of the former Empire's many nations. Poland, Finland and the Baltic states of Estonia, Latvia and Lithuania achieved independence, but other independent states established in 1917–18 were forced, militarily, to declare themselves Soviet Republics. These were proclaimed as independent republics, in alliance with the RSFSR, but the laws, Constitution and Government of the Federation were supreme in all of them. However, in 1922 the RSFSR joined the Belarusian, Ukrainian and Transcaucasian republics as constitutionally equal partners in a Union of Soviet Socialist Republics (USSR, or Soviet Union), and institutions of the RSFSR were re-formed as institutions of the new Union. The USSR eventually numbered 15 constituent Soviet Socialist Republics (SSRs). Moscow, the RSFSR's seat of government since 1918, became the capital of the USSR.

The RSFSR, in common with the other republics, experienced hardship as a result of the collectivization campaign of the early 1930s and the widespread repression under Iosif Dzhugashvili (Stalin), who established a brutal dictatorship after the death of Lenin in 1924. The Five-Year Plans, introduced in the late 1920s, effected rapid industrialization, a process that was reinforced by the removal of strategic industries from the west of the republic to the Ural regions during the Second World War (or 'Great Patriotic War'), which the USSR was drawn into in 1941. Under the Nazi German-Soviet Treaty of Non-Aggression (the 'Molotov-Ribbentrop Pact') of August 1939, the USSR annexed the Baltic states as well as other territories. Victory in the war in 1945 led to further territorial gains for the Russian Federation. In the west it gained part of East Prussia around Königsberg (now Kaliningrad) from Germany, a small amount of territory from Estonia and Latvia and those parts of Finland annexed during the Soviet–Finnish War (1939–40). In the east it acquired the Kurile Islands from Japan. The nominally independent People's Republic of Tuva (Tyva), situated between the USSR and Mongolia, was annexed in 1944. In 1954 the peninsula of Crimea was ceded by the Russian Federation to the Ukrainian SSR.

Shortly after the death of Stalin in 1953, Nikita Khrushchev became First Secretary of the Communist Party of the Soviet Union (CPSU—as the Communist Party had been renamed in 1952), and gradually assumed predominance over his rivals. The most brutal aspects of the regime were ended, and in 1956 Khrushchev admitted the existence of large-scale repression under Stalin. Khrushchev was dismissed in 1964. He was replaced as First Secretary (later General Secretary) of the CPSU by Leonid Brezhnev. During the 1970s relations with the West, which had, since the late 1940s, been generally characterized by the intense mutual hostility of the 'Cold War', experienced a considerable *détente*; however, this was ended by the Soviet invasion of Afghanistan in 1979. Brezhnev's successor as CPSU General Secretary, following his death in 1982, was Yurii Andropov. He was succeeded upon his death, in February 1984, by Konstantin Chernenko, who, in turn, died in March 1985.

Chernenko's successor as General Secretary was Mikhail Gorbachev. A policy of glasnost (openness) provided a greater degree of freedom for the mass media. In November 1987, however, supporters of perestroika (restructuring), as Gorbachev's reform programme was known, seemed to suffer a reverse, with the dismissal from the Politburo (the executive committee of the CPSU) of Boris Yeltsin. In June 1988 Gorbachev announced plans for the introduction of a two-tier legislature, elected largely by competitive elections. In elections to the new USSR Congress of People's Deputies, held in March 1989, many reformist politicians, including Yeltsin, were successful in achieving election. In May the Congress elected Gorbachev to the new post of executive President of the USSR.

Within the USSR the RSFSR was clearly pre-eminent, both economically and politically, and ethnic Russians dominated the Soviet élite. However, this prominence meant that Russia developed few autonomous institutions. The initial stage in the process of instituting Russian sovereignty was the election of the RSFSR Congress of People's Deputies in March 1990 by largely free and competitive elections. In May the Congress elected Yeltsin to the highest state post in the RSFSR, the Chairman of the Supreme Soviet (the permanent working body of the Congress). On 12 June the Congress adopted a declaration asserting the sovereignty of the RSFSR in which the federation laws had primacy over all-Union legislation. In March 1991, when a referendum was held in nine republics to determine whether a restructured USSR should be retained, voters in the RSFSR also approved an additional question on the introduction of a Russian presidency. A direct presidential election, held in June, was won by Yeltsin and his Vice-President, Aleksandr Rutskoi, with 57.3% of the votes cast.

On 19 August 1991, one day before the new union treaty was due to be signed, the conservative communist 'State Committee for the State of Emergency' (SCSE), led by the Soviet Vice-President, Gennadii Yanayev, seized power in Moscow, taking advantage of Gorbachev's absence from the city. The attempted coup collapsed within three days, and Yeltsin asserted control over all-Union bodies, appointing RSFSR ministers to head central institutions.

In October 1991 Yeltsin announced a programme of radical economic reforms. In November a new Government was announced, with Yeltsin as Chairman (Prime Minister). The CPSU was banned. In November 1991 the Congress granted Yeltsin special powers for one year, including the right to issue decrees with legislative force and to appoint government ministers without parliamentary approval, and elected Ruslan Khasbulatov, hitherto First Deputy Chairman of the Supreme Soviet, to succeed Yeltsin as Chairman.

On 8 December 1991 the leaders of Belarus, Ukraine and Russia announced the annulment of the 1922 Union Treaty creating the USSR; the Commonwealth of Independent States (CIS, see p. 215), defined as a co-ordinating organization, was created in its place. The CIS was formally established by the Alma-Ata (Almaty) Declaration, signed on 21 December 1991. Of the former Soviet republics, only Georgia, Estonia, Latvia and Lithuania remained outside the new body. (Georgia acceded to the CIS in December 1993.) On 25 December 1991 Gorbachev resigned as President of the USSR, and the Russian Supreme Soviet formally changed the name of the RSFSR to the Russian Federation.

In June 1992 Yeltsin appointed Yegor Gaidar, an advocate of radical economic reform, as acting Chairman, and in the same month the Supreme Soviet adopted legislation permitting large-scale privatization. In December the Congress of People's Deputies refused to endorse Gaidar's nomination, and Yeltsin was forced to appoint a new, substantially less reformist, premier, Viktor Chernomyrdin. Following the annulment, in March 1993, of an agreement on constitutional reform by the Congress, Yeltsin announced that he would rule by decree prior to the holding of a referendum on a draft constitution, which was held on 25 April 1993. A question on confidence in Yeltsin as President received a positive response from 57.4% of voters, while 53.7% of voters expressed support for Yeltsin's socio-economic policies. Support for early presidential elections was only 49.1%, but 70.6% of voters favoured early elections to the Congress of People's Deputies.

In July 1993 the Constitutional Conference approved a draft that provided for a presidential system with a bicameral parliament—the Federalnoye Sobraniye (Federal Assembly)—comprising a lower chamber (Gosudarstvennaya Duma—State Duma) and an upper chamber (Sovet Federatsii—Federation Council); however, the Congress of People's Deputies rejected this draft. The long-standing impasse between the presidential administration and the legislature eventually resulted in violent confrontation. On 21 September Yeltsin suspended the Congress of People's Deputies and the Supreme Soviet, and scheduled elections to the Federalnoye Sobraniye for December. The Supreme Soviet consequently voted to dismiss Yeltsin as President, announcing the appointment of Rutskoi in his place; an emergency session of the Congress of People's Deputies confirmed this appointment, and voted to impeach Yeltsin. On 27 September government troops surrounded the parliament building: some 180 deputies remained inside, with armed supporters. Conflict erupted in early October, as supporters of the rebel deputies attempted to seize control of strategic buildings in Moscow, and Yeltsin declared a state of emergency in the capital. On 4 October army tanks bombarded the parliament building, forcing the surrender of the rebels. The leaders of the rebellion were imprisoned and charged with inciting mass disorder. According to official figures, 160 people were killed in the fighting.

The new draft constitution, which strengthened the powers of the President, was submitted to a referendum on 12 December 1993, held concurrently with elections to the Federalnoye Sobraniye. Of the 54.8% of the registered electorate that participated in the plebiscite, 58.4% endorsed the draft. In the elections to the Gosudarstvennaya Duma, Vladimir Zhirinovskii's nationalist Liberal Democratic Party of Russia (LDPR) secured a total of 64 seats, the largest number obtained by any single party or alliance. (Of the 450 members of the lower chamber, 225 were elected by proportional representation on the basis of party lists, and 225 within single-member constituencies.) Russia's Choice, an alliance of pro-reform groups, led by Gaidar, secured 58 seats. The Communist Party of the Russian Federation (CPRF), which had been founded earlier in the year, took 48 seats, while the Agrarian Party of Russia (APR) won 33 seats. With the ensuing alignment of parties and the 130 independents into parliamentary factions, Russia's Choice emerged as the largest group in the Duma, although no coherent pro-Government majority was established. The Sovet Federatsii was to comprise two representatives from each of Russia's 89 federal subjects (as the constituent territories of the Federation were known), although in December representatives were not elected in the separatist republics of Tatarstan and Chechnya, owing to a voter boycott. The majority of the Council's members were non-partisan republican or regional leaders. A new Government was appointed in January 1994. In February the Duma voted in favour of granting amnesties to Rutskoi, Khasbulatov and other leaders of the 1993 rebellion, as well as to the SCSE.

In October 1994 a sudden decline in the value of the rouble prompted the resignation or dismissal of government members and the Chairman of the Central Bank, Viktor Gerashchenko. In November the reformist Anatolii Chubais, who had hitherto been responsible for the privatization programme, was promoted to the post of First Deputy Chairman, although other government appointments appeared to advance those opposed to further economic liberalization.

In late 1994 Russia commenced military intervention in the separatist Chechen Republic (Chechnya); an apparent lack of progress there, together with the continued deterioration of the economy, were instrumental in the approval by the Duma, in June 1995, of a motion expressing no confidence in the Government. Yeltsin subsequently dismissed a number of ministers, and in July a second vote of no confidence (as required by the Constitution) failed to secure the necessary majority.

Elections to the Duma took place on 17 December 1995. In accordance with a new electoral law, which introduced a minimum requirement of 5% of the votes cast for seats allocated on the basis of party lists, only four parties—the CPRF, the LDPR, Chernomyrdin's Our Home is Russia (OHR) and the liberal Yabloko—secured representation on this basis, while an additional 10 parties and 77 independent candidates obtained seats through voting in single-member constituencies. The CPRF emerged as the largest single party in the Duma, with 157 of the 450 deputies. OHR won 55 seats, the LDPR 51 and Yabloko 45.

In January 1996 Yeltsin dismissed Chubais as First Deputy Chairman. In the same month the Duma elected Gennadii Seleznev, a CPRF deputy, as its Chairman. In the first round of presidential voting, held on 16 June, and contested by 10 candidates, Yeltsin, with 35.8% of the votes cast, narrowly defeated Gennadii Zyuganov (of the CPRF), with 32.5%. Gen. Aleksandr Lebed, who had until recently commanded Russian forces in the separatist Transnistria (Pridnistrovie) region of Moldova, was placed third, with 14.7%. Since neither had received the 50% of the votes required for outright victory, Yeltsin and Zyuganov proceeded to a second round of voting. Yeltsin subsequently appointed Lebed as Secretary of the Security Council and National Security Adviser, and granted him particular responsibility for resolving the crisis in Chechnya. Despite increasingly infrequent public appearances, apparently a result of poor health, Yeltsin was re-elected as President in the second ballot, on 3 July, with 54% of the total votes cast. Chernomyrdin was subsequently re-appointed as premier, and Chubais was promoted to head the Presidential Administration. Despite the successful negotiation of a cease-fire agreement in Chechnya in August, in October Yeltsin dismissed Lebed. In November Yeltsin underwent heart surgery, reassuming full presidential duties in December, although he was again hospitalized shortly afterwards, and there was growing pressure for his resignation.

Although Yeltsin delivered a vehement criticism of the Government in his annual address to the Federalnoye Sobraniye in March 1997, in a subsequent government reorganization Chernomyrdin retained his post, thereby avoiding the need to seek parliamentary approval of the new, broadly reformist, cabinet.

Chubais was appointed First Deputy Chairman and Minister of Finance, and Boris Nemtsov was appointed as First Deputy Chairman, with responsibility for dismantling state monopolies, particularly in the areas of fuel and energy; a priority was to increase tax revenue in order to settle wages and pensions arrears. (In March some 2m. people had participated in demonstrations protesting at the non-payment of wages and pensions.) In November Nemtsov lost the fuel and energy portfolio, and Chubais was dismissed as Minister of Finance, although both retained their posts as First Deputy Chairmen.

In March 1998 Yeltsin removed Chernomyrdin from office. The Duma confirmed the appointment of Sergei Kiriyenko, the hitherto Minister of Fuel and Energy, as Chairman in mid-April. Several ministers, including Nemtsov, retained their portfolios in the new Government formed during April–May. Chubais, meanwhile, was appointed Chairman of the electricity monopoly, Unified Energy System of Russia. An attempt by the CPRF to initiate impeachment charges against Yeltsin was ruled unconstitutional by a parliamentary commission in late July. In mid-August, however, the Duma succeeded in approving a resolution demanding the voluntary resignation of Yeltsin.

In August 1998 mounting political instability was exacerbated by severe economic difficulties. Yeltsin dismissed Kiriyenko and his Government, reappointing Chernomyrdin as Chairman. However, Chernomyrdin's candidacy to the premiership was twice rejected by the Duma. In mid-September Yeltsin (aware that should his candidate be rejected for a third time he would be constitutionally obliged to dissolve the Duma) nominated Yevgenii Primakov (Minister of Foreign Affairs since 1996, and a former Director of the Foreign Intelligence Service) as Chairman, a candidacy that was endorsed by a large majority.

In May 1999 Yeltsin dismissed Primakov. Sergei Stepashin, hitherto First Deputy Chairman and Minister of Internal Affairs, was appointed as Chairman, and a new Government was formed later in the month. However, Yeltsin dismissed Stepashin in August. Later in the month the Duma endorsed his replacement by Vladimir Putin, a former colonel in the Soviet Committee for State Security (KGB), First Deputy Chairman of St Petersburg City Government in 1994–96, and hitherto head of the Federal Security Service (FSB) and Secretary of the Security Council.

Following a number of incursions by Chechen militants into the neighbouring Republic of Dagestan in August 1999, tensions resurfaced relating to the unresolved status of Chechnya and the emergence there, from the mid-1990s, of militant Islamist groups. Moreover, Putin attributed to Chechen militant groups a series of bomb explosions in Moscow, in Dagestan and in Rostov Oblast, which took place in August–September, killing more than 300 people. Citing the threat posed by militants in the separatist republic, Putin announced that military action was to recommence and, prior to the large-scale deployment of ground troops, the aerial bombardment of Chechnya began on 23 September.

In the months preceding Duma elections in December 1999 several new political alliances were formed; in August Fatherland-All Russia (FAR) was formed by the merger of the centrist party of the Mayor of Moscow, Yurii Luzhkov, with a grouping of regional governors. In September a pro-Government bloc, Unity, was formed under the leadership of Sergei Shoigu, the civil defence and emergencies minister, while Kiriyenko and Nemtsov were among the leaders of a new pro-market bloc, the Union of Rightist Forces (URF).

Some 29 parties and blocs contested the elections to the Gosudarstvennaya Duma on 19 December 1999, in which 62% of the electorate participated. Six parties obtained representation on the basis of party lists; a further eight parties and blocs, and 106 independent candidates, secured representation from single-member constituency ballots. The CPRF, with 24.3% of the votes, again obtained the largest representation, with 113 seats. Unity, which received 23.3% of the votes cast, was the second largest party in the Duma, with 72 seats; FAR won 67, the URF 29, Yabloko 21 and the Zhirinovskii bloc (chiefly comprising the LDPR) won 17 seats.

On 31 December 1999 Boris Yeltsin unexpectedly resigned as President. Putin assumed the presidency in an acting capacity. He granted Yeltsin immunity from prosecution, and removed from office principal members of Yeltsin's administration. When the new Duma convened in mid-January 2000, the CPRF and Unity factions formed an alliance; thus, for the first time since the dissolution of the USSR, pro-Government forces held a majority in the legislature.

Putin received 52.9% of the votes cast in the presidential election held on 26 March 2000, having received the support of FAR, as well as Unity. His closest rival was Zyuganov, of the CPRF, with 29.2%. Putin was inaugurated as President on 7 May. In mid-May Mikhail Kasyanov, hitherto First Deputy Chairman and Minister of Finance, was approved as Chairman of the Council of Ministers. A new Government was appointed shortly afterwards.

Concerns regarding the freedom of the media in Russia were heightened following the presidential approval in September 2000 of a new information doctrine and by the severe restrictions imposed over coverage of the conflict in Chechnya. Meanwhile, Vladimir Gusinskii, the owner of the Mediya-Most holding company (which included Russia's only wholly independent national television broadcaster, NTV), was arrested in June and charged with fraud. Although all charges were withdrawn in July, Gusinskii fled to Spain. In September the state-controlled gas monopoly, Gazprom (to which Mediya-Most was heavily indebted), brought charges of criminal embezzlement against Mediya-Most's management. Gusinskii lost control of the company in November, and the deal reached with Alfred Kokh, the head of the Gazprom subsidiary, Gazprom-Mediya, effectively gave the State a controlling stake in all Mediya-Most enterprises, with the exception of NTV. In December the Moscow fiscal authorities demanded that Mediya-Most be closed, on grounds of insolvency, and Gusinskii was detained in Spain in the same month. Following the refusal of the Spanish authorities to extradite Gusinskii to Russia, in April 2001 he took up residence in Israel (where he held dual citizenship). None the less, Russia issued a fresh warrant for Gusinskii's arrest, on charges of money laundering. In October 2003, following Gusinskii's arrest in Greece, a Greek court ruled against his extradition to Russia.

Meanwhile, other prominent businessmen were subjected to examinations of their business affairs, in what was interpreted as an attempt by the Government to reduce the powers of the 'oligarchs', as a number of wealthy businessmen, who in many cases had acquired control of formerly nationalized industries in the 1990s, were widely known. In July 2000 Boris Berezovskii, a prominent business executive and former Deputy of the Security Council and Executive Secretary of the CIS (who had played a major role in promoting Putin's candidacy as President), relinquished his seat in the Duma and, therefore, his immunity from prosecution, accusing Putin of having adopted an increasingly authoritarian style of governance. In September Berezovskii announced his intention to relinquish his 49% of shares in the state-controlled television station, ORT, claiming that he had received an ultimatum that he should surrender his holding to the state or risk imprisonment; the sale finally took place in February 2001. None the less, a warrant for Berezovskii's arrest was issued in November 2000, after he failed to return to Russia from France to answer questions relating to charges of money laundering and illegal entrepreneurship in a case which had recently been reopened.

Putin introduced significant changes to regional governance during 2000. In May, as part of measures intended to promote structures of 'vertical power', seven Federal Okrugs (Districts) were created, each of which was headed by a presidential appointee, to whom regional governments and governors were to be answerable. A new consultative body, the State Council, comprising the heads of the federal subjects, was created by presidential decree in September.

In March 2001 Putin implemented a minor ministerial reorganization, appointing Boris Gryzlov, the head of the Unity faction in the Duma, as Minister of Internal Affairs, and Sergei Ivanov (hitherto Secretary of the Security Council and a former deputy head of the FSB) as Minister of Defence. In April it was announced that the Unity faction in the Duma was, henceforth, to form an alliance with FAR, in preference to the CPRF.

Meanwhile, in early April 2001 NTV was acquired by Gazprom-Mediya. Following the dismissal of NTV's management, Yevgenii Kiselyev, the company's former Director-General and Editor-in-Chief, was appointed to head a small television channel owned by Berezovskii, TV6, to which the majority of the former NTV journalists transferred. Later in the year Berezovskii, who remained outside Russia, announced the formation of a political party, Liberal Russia. Meanwhile, in July the legislature approved a new law, which banned foreign citizens, as well as those Russians holding dual citizenship, from acquiring a majority stake in Russian television channels.

In July 2001 Putin signed a law imposing new conditions on political parties; henceforth, parties would be required to have a minimum of 10,000 members, including no fewer than 100 members in at least 50 of the 89 federal subjects, in order to be permitted to participate in elections. At the beginning of December the first congress of Unity and Fatherland-United Russia (subsequently known simply as United Russia—UR), formed by the merger of FAR and Unity, marked the formal establishment of the party, which held a majority of seats in both parliamentary houses. Although not a member of that party or of any other, Putin attended the founding congress.

In January 2002 TV6 ceased transmissions, following a court case brought by a minority shareholder, a subsidiary of the state-controlled petroleum company LUKoil, which had demanded the television company's liquidation on the grounds of unprofitability. In March it was announced that a new, non-profit organization, Mediya-Sotsium, associated with Primakov, had been awarded the contract to broadcast formerly held by TV6; Kiselyev and many journalists from that station transferred to the new channel, which commenced operations under the name TVS. Meanwhile, Berezovskii presented a video-recording in London, United Kingdom, which purported to demonstrate the FSB's involvement, and Putin's acquiescence, in the apartment block bombings of mid-1999.

Meanwhile, in January 2002 a new session of the Sovet Federatsii, chaired by Sergei Mironov, an ally of Putin, opened, with a reformed composition. In place of regional leaders and chairmen of regional legislative assemblies, the Council comprised their full-time appointees; the formation of political factions and groups in the Council was to be prohibited.

In October 2002 Berezovskii was charged, *in absentia*, with defrauding the state. In November the Russian authorities requested Berezovskii's extradition from the United Kingdom, where he was resident. (In March 2003 Berezovskii was arrested in London, in response to the extradition request. In September of that year he was granted political asylum, and the extradition proceedings were dismissed.) Meanwhile, in mid-October 2002, following the publication of an interview in a nationalist journal in which Berezovskii appeared to support the formation of a united opposition front by liberal and left-wing forces, he was suspended from Liberal Russia; one week later the Ministry of Justice agreed to register the party, which had hitherto been denied registration on several occasions, and which had obtained only negligible public support.

In late October 2002, following the deaths of at least 129 people as the result of an armed siege at a Moscow theatre by heavily armed militants, linked to Chechen extremists (see below), the Government implemented a number of personnel changes in Chechnya, and in mid-November Stanislav Ilyasov, hitherto the Prime Minister of Chechnya, was appointed to the federal Government as Minister without Portfolio, responsible for the Social and Economic Development of the Chechen Republic.

In March 2003 presidential decrees provided for the transfer of powers from various other organs of state to the FSB and to the Ministry of Internal Affairs. In mid-April one of the co-chairmen of Liberal Russia, Sergei Yushenkov, was assassinated in Moscow (another deputy of the party, Vladimir Golovlev, had been murdered in August 2002); in June 2003 a party member, Mikhail Kodanev, was arrested on suspicion of involvement in the killing of Yushenkov, along with three others. (In late March 2004 Kodanev was sentenced to 20 years' imprisonment for organizing the assassination; the three other suspects each received custodial sentences of between 11 and 20 years.) In June the Ministry of the Press, Broadcasting and Mass Media ordered the closure of TVS, purportedly as a result of financial difficulties experienced by the station, the broadcasts of which were replaced by a newly established, state-controlled sports channel.

Meanwhile, on 18 June 2003 the Duma failed to approve a motion of no confidence in the Government that had been presented by the CPRF and Yabloko factions. Meanwhile attacks against civilian targets by militants associated with Chechen separatist, or Islamist, rebels continued to occur, particularly in regions of southern Russia near Chechnya and in Moscow. In July at least 18 people were killed following two suicide bombings at a music festival near Moscow. A suicide bombing, in early December, on a train in southern Russia killed at least 42 people, and injured some 200 others. On 9 December, two days after the legislative elections (see below), a suicide bombing in central Moscow resulted in at least six deaths. In early February 2004 at least 39 people were killed and more than 100 injured in a further bomb attack on a train on the Moscow Metro.

During the latter half of 2003 several court cases and judicial investigations were instigated against senior officials of the prominent privately owned petroleum company, Yukos, and its subsidiary companies. The chief executive of the company, Mikhail Khodorkovskii (who was believed to be the wealthiest person in Russia) had recently announced that he was providing financial support to Yabloko and the URF. On 25 October Khodorkovskii was arrested by FSB officers; he was subsequently charged with tax evasion and fraud, and imprisoned pending further investigations. At the end of the month it was announced that a significant stake in the company had been 'frozen' by the authorities. (In early November Khodorkovskii resigned as head of Yukos, and at the end of the month it was announced that the proposed merger of Yukos with another prominent petroleum company, Sibneft, had been suspended.) On 30 December 2003 charges of tax evasion worth US $3,300m. were brought against Yukos.

Elections to the Duma, held on 7 December 2003, were contested by 32 parties and blocs. Only four of these groupings received the minimum 5% share of votes cast required to obtain representation on the basis of federal party lists: UR obtained an absolute majority of seats in the new legislature, with 226 seats, while the representation of the CPRF was substantially reduced, to 53 seats. The LDPR obtained 38 seats, while a recently formed electoral bloc, Motherland—People's Patriotic Union (Motherland), which comprised several communist and nationalist groups, received 37 seats. Nine other groups and 57 independent deputies achieved representation in the new Duma on the basis of constituency voting. The failure of the URF and Yabloko to obtain representation on the basis of proportional representation (the two parties obtained around 8% of the votes between them, and a total of seven deputies) was regarded as a serious reverse for the parliamentary representation of pro-Western reformists. The URF, Yabloko and the CPRF alleged that electoral fraud had been perpetrated, and electoral observers of the Organization for Security and Co-operation in Europe (OSCE, see p. 354) expressed concern that UR, which had become increasingly identified with the presidential administration, had benefited from the use of state administrative resources in support of the party. Moreover, several members of the Government held senior positions in UR, in apparent defiance of a constitutional clause prohibiting ministers from holding membership of political parties, and the party had effectively received the endorsement of Putin on several occasions. Gryzlov, the Chairman of the Supreme Council of UR, was elected as the Chairman of the Duma on 24 December. (He was replaced as Minister of Internal Affairs by Col-Gen. Rashid Nurgaliyev.)

Campaigning for the presidential election held on 14 March 2004 was characterized by an absence of prominent or credible challengers to Putin, who contested the election as an independent candidate, and refused to participate in televised debates with other candidates. In place of their leaders, who had contested the presidential elections in 1996 and 2000, the CPRF and LDPR presented relatively obscure figures, nominating Nikolai Kharitonov and Oleg Malyshkin, respectively, as their candidates. The URF's refusal to endorse the presidential candidacy of one of its leading members, Irina Khakamada, obliged her to campaign as an independent candidate; Khakamada and Nemtsov both subsequently announced their resignations from the URF. Meanwhile, the candidacy of Sergei Glazyev, an economist who had been regarded as the principal instigator of the Motherland electoral bloc, failed to obtain the support of any of its constituent parties, and he therefore contested the election as an independent candidate. Mironov contested the election, as the candidate of his party, the Russian Party of Life (RPL), but none the less expressed support for Putin. (A further candidate, Ivan Rybkin, an ally of Berezovskii, withdrew his candidacy in early March, after he had apparently been taken hostage in Ukraine for several days.) Meanwhile, the leader of Yabloko, Grigorii Yavlinskii, announced that his party was to boycott the presidential election. On 24 February Putin dismissed the Government, and on 1 March Putin announced the nomination of Mikhail Fradkov, hitherto the permanent representative of Russia to the European Communities, as the new Chairman of the Government. The appointment of Fradkov, widely regarded as a 'technocrat', without significant political support of his own, was subsequently approved by the Duma, and on 9 March the formation of a new Government was announced; the number of ministers was significantly reduced to 17, compared with 31 in the outgoing administration. Although most of the principal positions within the Government remained unchanged, a new

Minister of Foreign Affairs, Sergei Lavrov, hitherto ambassador to the UN, was appointed.

On 14 March 2004 Putin was re-elected, as had been widely anticipated, for a second, and, in accordance with the Constitution, final term of office, receiving 71.3% of the votes cast. His nearest rival, Kharitonov, took 13.7%. The rate of participation was 64.4%. Putin's inauguration took place on 7 May.

Violent attacks on Russian civilians, attributed to extremist Chechen separatists, culminated in a series of incidents in mid-2004, which intensified following the assassination of the President of the Republic in May (see below). On 24 August two passenger planes, both flying from Moscow's Domodedovo airport, crashed, killing all 89 people on board. Both crashes were subsequently attributed to Chechen suicide bombers. On 1 September, the first day of the school year, armed militants occupied a school in Beslan, in the Republic of North Osetiya—Alaniya, taking at least 1,100 children, parents and teachers hostage. On 3 September troops stormed the building, reportedly in reaction to a series of explosions. Some 350 hostages, including 186 children, died in the ensuing battle, according to official figures. The militant Chechen leader, Shamil Basayev, subsequently claimed responsibility for the hostage-taking operation.

Apparently in reaction to this event, President Putin announced a series of proposed political reforms, chief among which was the introduction of a system whereby all regional governors would be appointed by the federal president, subject to the approval of the appropriate regional legislature. (Directly elected governors had become almost universal across the subjects of the Russian Federation in the second half of the 1990s.) Putin signed legislation to this end on 12 December, following its approval by both chambers of the Federalnoye Sobraniye. The final scheduled gubernatorial election in the Federation took place on 6 February 2005, and henceforth all regional governors were appointed in accordance with the new system. Putin also announced proposals that all 450 members of the Duma be elected on the basis of proportional representation and party lists. Moreover, the minimum membership required of a political party for it to be eligible for registration was to be increased from 10,000 to 50,000; this requirement was to take effect from January 2006. The quota for representation in the Duma on the basis of federal party lists was also to be increased from 5% of the total votes cast to 7%.

Meanwhile, in June 2004 the trial of Khodorkovskii and his business associate, Platon Lebedev, the Chairman of the Menatep financial group, began in Moscow, on seven charges, including tax evasion, forgery and fraud. While the trial was in progress, the state authorities presented Yukos with a series of demands for unpaid taxes for 2000–03, totalling some US $27,500m. In order that this sum be paid, the authorities demanded that the principal production subsidiary of Yukos, Yuganskneftegaz, be brought to auction. In December Yuganskneftegaz was sold for $9,350m. to a previously unknown company, Baikalfinansgrup, which was acquired by the state-owned petroleum company Rosneft shortly after the auction. Meanwhile, in closing statements in late March, the prosecution in the trial of Lebedev and Khodorkovskii demanded sentences of 10 years' imprisonment for the accused. At the end of May both Khodorkovskii and Lebedev were sentenced to nine years' imprisonment, having each been found guilty of six charges, including tax evasion and embezzlement. These sentences were confirmed on appeal in September. (In February 2007 state prosecutors brought further charges of money laundering and embezzlement against Khodorkovskii.)

Meanwhile, in January 2005 a series of demonstrations took place across Russia in protest at the introduction of social welfare reforms, most notably the replacement of pensioners' entitlements to free public transport and medicine with a system of monetary payments. Putin subsequently stated that mistakes had been made in the implementation of the reforms, and several conciliatory measures were announced.

In July 2005 a criminal investigation, on charges of corruption related to the illicit acquisition of a state property, was opened against former premier Kasyanov, amid widespread speculation that the charges were politically motivated; in mid-September Kasyanov announced that he intended to contest the presidential election scheduled for early 2008. Meanwhile, liberal-democratic and pro-Western opposition to the Putin administration was increasingly expressed by the '2008 Free Choice Committee' (which subsequently formed a larger group, known as the United Civil Front), led by the former international chess champion, Garri Kasparov. Putin repeatedly rejected speculation that he intended to seek a third term of office, in defiance of the Constitution, or that he would amend the Constitution to ensure that he retained substantial powers after 2008.

On 14 November 2005 President Putin announced a government reorganization. Dmitrii Medvedev, the Chairman of the Board of Directors of Gazprom and hitherto Chief of the Presidential Staff, was appointed to the newly created post of First Deputy Chairman (Medvedev was, additionally, to retain his position at Gazprom). Sergei Ivanov, while retaining his responsibilities as Minister of Defence, was also to serve as one of two Deputy Chairmen of the Government.

A major focus of parliamentary activity during the second half of 2005 was the development of measures intended to result in greater government supervision and regulation of civil society and non-governmental organizations (NGOs); at least in part, demands for increased control in these areas had evolved in response to apparent concern that the so-called 'colour revolutions' that had taken place in Georgia in 2003, Ukraine in 2004 and Kyrgyzstan earlier in 2005 had been, to a certain extent, facilitated by externally financed NGOs. After several months of discussions, new legislation that, *inter alia*, permitted the authorities to close NGOs deemed to infringe Russia's sovereignty, unity or cultural heritage, was signed into law by President Putin in mid-January 2006. On 12 March, after the restrictions on party registration entered into effect on 1 January, the first 'unified election day' (for elections to various levels of government, or to certain local and regional assemblies in the Federation) took place. (Henceforth, the overwhelming majority of such elections were to take place on the second Sundays of March and of October in each year.) UR performed strongly, winning control of the overwhelming majority of regional assemblies to which elections were conducted, a pattern that was repeated at the following two unified election days, although the rate of voter participation was relatively low. In June Putin nominated the Minister of Justice, Yurii Chaika, to serve as Prosecutor-General; he was succeeded as Minister of Justice by Vladimir Ustinov, who had been dismissed as Prosecutor-General at his own request earlier in the month. In October Motherland, the RPL and the Russian Pensioners' Party united to form a new political party, A Just Russia (AJR). Mironov was elected as Chairman of AJR (which absorbed another small party, the People's Party, in April 2007).

In October 2006 a journalist of the independent newspaper *Novaya Gazeta*, Anna Politkovskaya, a leading critic of the Russian military campaigns in Chechnya and the official Chechen leadership, was shot dead at her apartment building in Moscow. Her death attracted international attention, amid widespread speculation that the Chechen authorities may have been implicated in her killing. (According to independent estimates, at least 13 journalists had been murdered in Russia since 2000; a substantially greater number of journalists had been killed in suspicious circumstances during the 1990s.) In November 2006 Aleksandr Litvinenko, a former officer in the FSB and exile to the United Kingdom, died in a London hospital as a result of radiation poisoning, having publicly accused Putin of responsibility for his sickness. Medical tests concluded that Litvinenko had been exposed to the radioactive substance Polonium-210. Police investigations into the killing of Litvinenko, who had been a close associate of Berezovskii, and had published a book accusing elements within the FSB of committing the apartment bombings of September 1999 (see below), commenced in both the United Kingdom and Russia. The Russian authorities subsequently refused to accede to a request by the British Government for the extradition of the principal suspect, Andrei Lugovoi, who had met with Litvinenko in London around the time of his poisoning, on the grounds that it convened the Constitution. (In December 2007 Lugovoi was elected to the Gosudarstvennaya Duma, thereby securing immunity from prosecution within Russia.)

In early December 2006 Putin signed into law further amendments to electoral legislation, including the abolition of the minimum voter-turnout requirement for elections at every level. At the end of that month the Chairman of the Central Electoral Commission (CEC), Aleksandr Veshnyakov, announced that the forthcoming presidential election would take place on 9 March 2008, on the expiry of Putin's second four-year term. On 15 February 2007 Putin reorganized the Government, appointing Sergei Ivanov to the office of First Deputy Chairman (thereby granting him equal status to Medvedev). Anatolii Serdyukov, hitherto the head of the Federal Tax Service, replaced Ivanov as Minister of Defence, becoming the first appointee to that position not to have a background in the military or security services. Putin also appointed the President of the Chechen Republic, Maj.-Gen. Alu Alkhanov, to the post of deputy justice minister in the federal Government, enabling the controversial Prime Minister of that territory, Ramzan Kadyrov, to become acting President of the Republic (see below). In early March a mass opposition rally was organized in St Petersburg by Another Russia, a coalition of both left- and right-wing groups opposing Putin; leaders of Another Russia included Kasparov, Kasyanov, and the leader of the extremist and prohibited National Bolshevik Party, Eduard Limonov. The subsequent removal of Veshnyakov from the post of Chairman of the CEC was attributed in the Russian media to his public criticism of the pro-Government parties and the amendments to the electoral legislation. Later in March, following continued speculation (repeatedly denied by the President) that Putin would contrive to serve a third presidential term, Mironov proposed to the Sovet Federatsii that the constitutional restriction to two consecutive four-year terms be abolished.

In April 2007, after Berezovskii declared to the British newspaper, *The Guardian*, that he planned the forcible ousting of the Putin Administration, Minister of Foreign Affairs Lavrov reiterated demands for his extradition from the United Kingdom and announced further criminal proceedings against him. The insistence of the British authorities that Berezovskii was immune from extradition, owing to his political asylum status, further exacerbated diplomatic relations between the two countries (which had been particularly strained by the death of Litvinenko). In mid-April Another Russia organized anti-Government demonstrations in Moscow and St Petersburg, which were violently suppressed by troops associated with the Ministry of the Interior (OMON). Some 350 protesters, including Kasparov and Kasyanov, were briefly detained in Moscow. EU and US officials expressed concern at the security operation implemented by the Russian authorities, and a state investigation into the measures taken against demonstrators by the OMON was initiated. (In November Berezovskii was sentenced *in absentia* by a Moscow district court to six years' imprisonment for embezzlement; a number of criminal cases against him were pending.)

On 14 September 2007, following the resignation of Fradkov and his Government, the Gosudarstvennaya Duma approved Putin's nomination of Viktor Zubkov, hitherto head of the Federal Financial Monitoring Service, as Chairman. Later that month Putin announced a government reorganization; three new ministers were appointed, including Elvira Nabiullina, who received the economic development and trade portfolio, while the Minister of Finance, Aleksei Kudrin, also became a Deputy Chairman. At the beginning of October Putin announced, in a statement made at UR's party congress, that he would head the party's list of candidates in the forthcoming legislative elections on 2 December and that he viewed favourably a proposal by delegates that he, eventually, become Chairman of the Government. Popular support for Putin's continued leadership increased during campaigning, and a number of regional organizations that had staged rallies in favour of a third presidential term for him grouped in November to form a 'For Putin' movement. In the same month Another Russia organized demonstrations in Moscow and St Petersburg, which resulted in the temporary detention of opposition leaders, including Kasparov. In November the Office for Democratic Institutions and Human Rights (ODIHR) of the OSCE announced the abandonment of plans to monitor the elections, after Russia imposed restrictions on the number of observers who would be invited; however, the Parliamentary Assemblies of the OSCE and Council of Europe dispatched small monitoring missions. At the elections to the Gosudarstvennaya Duma on 2 December, UR won a substantial majority, winning 64.3% of the votes cast, according to official results, and secured 315 seats; the CPRF received 11.6% of votes and 57 seats, the LDPR 8.1% and 40 seats, and A Just Russia 7.7% and 38 seats. Voter turn-out was 63.7% of the electorate. Reports emerged that students and public-sector workers had been placed under considerable pressure by the authorities to vote in favour of UR. The Russian Government dismissed a subsequent joint statement by the OSCE and Council of Europe that the conduct of the elections had failed to meet international standards for democracy, following widespread allegations of media bias in favour of UR and voting irregularities. (A report by CIS observers upheld the organization of the elections.) On 10 December Putin announced his support for the nomination by four parties (UR, AJR, the APR and the newly established Civic Force) of Medvedev as a candidate in the forthcoming presidential election on 2 March 2008. Putin subsequently indicated approval of a proposal made by Medvedev that he serve as premier in the event that Medvedev be elected to the presidency.

In December 2007, amid continuing strained relations with the United Kingdom, Russia ordered the closure of two regional offices of a British state cultural and educational organization, the British Council, from January 2008, on the grounds that it was operating illegally. After the British Government insisted that the offices remain open, in defiance of the demand, a number of the British Council's Russian employees were questioned by the FSB, and the head of the Council in St Petersburg was briefly detained on an alleged traffic offence. On 17 January the British Council suspended operations at the two offices. In a press interview in February, Medvedev reiterated allegations that the British Council was involved in espionage. In March the Council confirmed its intention to continue its operations in Moscow.

In January 2008 the CEC rejected the presidential candidacy of Kasyanov, ruling that a number of the signatures collected in his support were invalid; he subsequently urged a boycott of the poll. In early February the ODIHR again announced that it would not dispatch a monitoring mission to Russia, on the grounds that a stipulation by the Russian authorities that 70 observers be invited only three days before the poll would prevent adequate monitoring of the elections. On 2 March, as widely anticipated, Medvedev (following his endorsement by Putin) was overwhelmingly elected to the presidency, with some 70.3% of votes cast, according to final official results; Zyuganov of the CPRF received 17.7% of votes, and Zhirinovskii of the LDPR about 9.4% of votes. Official voter turnout was estimated at about 69.8%. Observers from the Parliamentary Assembly of the Council of Europe acknowledged popular support for Medvedev, but reported that aspects of the electoral campaign had failed to meet democratic principles. At a UR congress in April Putin formally accepted an invitation to assume the new post of Chairman of the party, although it was confirmed that Putin would not become a member of the party. Medvedev was inaugurated as President on 7 May (when Putin, on relinquishing the presidency, officially became Chairman of UR). Shortly afterwards Medvedev nominated Putin as Chairman of the Government; on 8 May the Gosudarstvennaya Duma approved his nomination to the office by an overwhelming majority (with only CPRF deputies opposing it). On 12 May Putin announced a government reorganization, in which an additional three ministries were created. Zubkov became First Deputy Chairman, and was to assume particular responsibility for the agricultural sector, while a senior presidential aide, Igor Shuvalov, was also accorded the post of First Deputy Chairman. Igor Sechin, the Chairman of Rosneft and hitherto deputy head of the presidential administration, was appointed to the Government as Deputy Chairman and was to supervise industrial development programmes. Ivanov remained in the new administration as a Deputy Chairman; other principal ministers, including Kudrin, Lavrov and Serdyukov, retained their posts.

In the early 1990s the Russian Federation encountered difficulties in attempting to satisfy the aspirations of its many minority ethnic groups for self-determination. In March 1992 some 18 of Russia's 20 nominally autonomous republics signed a federation treaty. The two dissenters, both predominately Islamic and petroleum-producing regions, were Tatarstan, which had voted for self-rule earlier in the month, and the Checheno-Ingush Republic, which had declared independence from Russia in November 1991 (as the Chechen Republic—Chechnya). The new treaty granted the republics greater authority, including control of natural resources and formal borders, and allowed them to conduct their own foreign trade. An agreement signed with the Russian Government in February 1994 accorded Tatarstan a considerable measure of sovereignty. Other power-sharing agreements, granting varying degrees of sovereignty, were eventually signed by some 42 of the 89 federal subjects during Yeltsin's presidency, although from 2000 Putin implemented a number of measures intended to curtail the power of regional governors, which led to the rescission of the vast majority of the power-sharing treaties by mid-2002. In May 2000 the Gosudarstvennaya Duma approved legislation according the President the right to dismiss regional governors, a prerogative that was extended to governors with regard to those elected officials subordinate to them; however, by 2004 these powers had been seldom used, although as a result of legislation approved in

December (see above), the appointment of regional governors (the election of whom had become almost universal across the Federation by the late 1990s) by the federal President, subject to the approval of regional legislatures, became the norm from early 2005.

In March 1992, in response to the unilateral declaration of independence by Chechnya, the Ingush inhabitants of the former Checheno-Ingush Republic demanded the establishment of a separate republic. The formation of the new republic, Ingushetiya, was approved by the federal Supreme Council in June. Additionally, Ingush activists claimed territories in neighbouring North Osetiya, which had formed part of the Ingush Republic prior to the Second World War, when the Ingush (and Chechens, in common with several other nationalities of the USSR) were deported *en masse* to Central Asia. In October 1992 violent conflict broke out in the disputed Prigorodnyi district in North Osetiya. By November more than 300 people had died in the conflict and some 50,000 Ingush had fled the region. In September 1997, following mediation by Yeltsin, a treaty on normalizing relations was signed by the republican Governments of North Osetiya and Ingushetiya.

In late 1993 armed hostilities commenced in Chechnya between forces loyal to the republican authorities and those of the separatist leader, Gen. Dzhokhar Dudayev (who had been elected President of the Republic in October 1991, following a coup against the republic's communist Government, led by Doku Zavgayev). Chechnya boycotted the Russian general election and referendum of December 1993; in August 1994 an unsuccessful attempt to overthrow the Dudayev regime was reputedly aided by the federal security services. Following the defeat of a further offensive in November, federal troops entered Chechnya in December. The troops rapidly gained control of the lowland area of northern Chechnya. Dudayev's forces, estimated to number some 15,000 irregular troops, were concentrated in the Chechen capital, Groznyi, a city upon which federal troops launched an assault in late December, following heavy bombardment from the air. Despite sustaining significant casualties, federal troops gradually took control of the city and seized the presidential palace (the headquarters of Dudayev's forces) in January 1995. Groznyi suffered great devastation during the assault, and there were reported to be thousands of civilian casualties. In June 1995 Chechen gunmen engaged local security forces in Budennovsk, some 200 km from the border with Chechnya, and took hostage more than 1,000 people in the city hospital. The rebels demanded that the Russian Government initiate talks with Dudayev on the immediate withdrawal of troops from Chechnya. Following the failure of attempts by federal army units to free the hostages, telephone negotiations were conducted between the rebel leader, Shamil Basayev, and federal premier Chernomyrdin, by which time some 100 people had reportedly been killed. Subsequently, as a cease-fire took effect in Chechnya, the rebels began gradually to release hostages. Peace talks between a delegation from the federal Government and the Chechen leadership commenced in Groznyi in late June, and a cease-fire agreement was formalized in July.

In October 1995, following an assassination attempt on the commander of the federal forces in Chechnya, the federal Government announced a temporary suspension of the July agreement. In response, the Chechen leadership announced its complete rejection of the accord. In December elections took place in the Republic, both to the Duma and to the Chechen presidency. Zavgayev was elected republican President, reportedly receiving some 93% of the votes cast in elections that Dudayev rejected as invalid.

In January 1996 Chechen militants seized about 2,000 civilians in Kizlyar, Dagestan, and held them hostage in a hospital. Following negotiations, most were released, and the rebels departed, accompanied by some 150 hostages, for Chechnya. Federal troops halted the rebels in the border village of Pervomaiskoye and demanded the release of the remaining hostages. After further negotiations failed, federal forces attacked and captured the village. Although the rebels' leader, Salman Raduyev, escaped to Chechnya with some of his forces and around 40 hostages, some 150 rebels, and a number of their captives, were reportedly killed in the assault. In April Dudayev was killed in a missile attack. He was succeeded as leader of the separatists by Zemlikhan Yandarbiyev, who subsequently developed an association with the Islamist Taliban regime in Afghanistan. Sporadic fighting persisted, but a new cease-fire agreement between the federal authorities and Yandarbiyev was reached in May. A formal military agreement, concluded in June, envisaged a withdrawal of the federal troops by the end of August and the disarmament of the separatist fighters. In August separatist forces, led by Basayev, launched a sustained offensive against Groznyi, routing many of the federal troops stationed in the city and trapping thousands of civilians. Yeltsin granted Gen. Lebed, the recently appointed Secretary of the Security Council, extensive powers to co-ordinate federal operations in the republic and to conduct a negotiated settlement. Following discussions involving Yandarbiyev and the Chechen military leader, Gen. Khalid ('Aslan') Maskhadov, a fresh cease-fire was brokered in mid-August. Following further negotiations, the withdrawal of troops commenced, and on 31 August Lebed and Maskhadov signed a conclusive peace agreement (known as the Khasavyurt Accords) in Dagestan, according to which any decision regarding Chechnya's future political status was to be deferred until December 2001. The withdrawal of federal troops and the exchange of prisoners of war began, and the cease-fire was largely respected. In September 1996 a Chechen Government was created, with Maskhadov as Prime Minister, and Yandarbiyev as Chairman of the cabinet. Nevertheless, sporadic violence continued: by early 1997 it was estimated that the conflict had caused some 80,000 deaths, and resulted in the displacement of 415,000 civilians.

All federal troops were withdrawn before the republican presidential and legislative elections, held on 27 January 1997. Maskhadov was elected President, with some 59.3% of the total votes cast. Of the 12 remaining candidates, Basayev won 23.5% of the votes, and Yandarbiyev 10.1%. The rate of voter participation was reported to be 79.4%, and international observers reported no serious discrepancies in the electoral process. Maskhadov declined his seat in the Sovet Federatsii, and affirmed his support for Chechen independence. Elections to the Chechen legislature were inconclusive and, after a second round of voting, only 45 of the 63 seats had been filled; further rounds were held in May and June. On 12 May Yeltsin and Maskhadov signed a formal peace treaty, defining the principles of future relations between Chechnya and the Russian Federation, and renouncing the use of violence as a means of resolving differences. The treaty, however, did not address the issue of Chechnya's constitutional status and, moreover, was refused ratification by the Gosudarstvennaya Duma.

Attacks and, in particular, hostage-taking, continued to be perpetrated by rebels opposed to the peace agreement. Meanwhile, Chechnya's introduction of elements of *Shari'a* (Islamic religious) law in 1997, in particular the holding of public executions, was strongly opposed by the federal authorities. In January 1998 Maskhadov dismissed his cabinet and entrusted Basayev (who had been indicted by the federal authorities on charges of terrorism), hitherto Chechen First Deputy Prime Minister, but now acting Prime Minister, with the formation of a new government. In late March the republican parliament announced that the territory was henceforth to be known as the 'Chechen Republic of Ichkeriya'. Increasing lawlessness and militancy was reported in the republic. In May Chechen rebels kidnapped Yeltsin's special representative to Chechnya, Vladimir Vlasov; he was freed in November by interior ministry troops. Four employees of a British telecommunications company were kidnapped in Chechnya in October; their decapitated bodies were found several weeks later. As disorder increased, Maskhadov dismissed the entire Chechen administration in October, and declared a further state of emergency in December. It became apparent that militant Islamist groups, including a faction led in Chechnya by Omar ibn al-Khattab (believed to be of Saudi or Jordanian origin), were increasingly implicated in the violence in Chechnya.

In August–September 1999 Islamist factions associated with Basayev launched a series of attacks on Dagestan from Chechnya, with the aim of protecting and extending the jurisdiction of a 'separate Islamic territory' in Dagestan, over which rebels had obtained control in the previous year. (The territory was returned to federal rule in mid-September.) Federal troops were dispatched to the area, and after two weeks of fighting and aerial bombardment the rebels withdrew. However, there were renewed incursions and fighting in September. Meanwhile, in mid-August Maskhadov declared a one-month state of emergency in Chechnya, following threats by the federal authorities to bomb alleged terrorist bases in the republic. A series of bomb explosions in August and September in Moscow, Dagestan and Volgodonsk (Rostov Oblast), including two that destroyed entire apartment blocks, officially attributed by the Government to Chechen separatists, killed almost 300 people, prompting the redeployment of federal armed forces in the Republic from late

September; the recently inaugurated premier, Putin, described the deployment as an 'anti-terrorist operation'. Allegations persisted that sources associated with the FSB had ordered the attacks, in order to justify a renewed military campaign in Chechnya; notably, the discovery of an apparent attempt to initiate a further bombing in an apartment block in Ryazan heightened concerns of FSB involvement, although the authorities insisted that the incident was simply an exercise designed to ensure a heightened state of public vigilance. (In January 2004 two men were sentenced to life imprisonment for their part in the attacks.) Following air and ground offensives, federal troops had advanced to within 10 km of Groznyi by late October 1999, and both sides claimed to have inflicted heavy losses on the other. In December many republican and federal administrative bodies were relocated to Gudermes, the Republic's second city. In February 2000 federal forces obtained control of Groznyi and proceeded to destroy much of the city.

In May 2000 President Putin decreed that, henceforth, Chechnya would be governed federally. Mufti Akhmad haji Kadyrov was inaugurated as administrative leader (Governor) of the republic in June. Kadyrov, a former ally of Maskhadov, was to be directly responsible to the federal authorities. In January 2001 Putin signed a decree transferring control of operations in Chechnya from the Ministry of Defence to the FSB, and announced the intention of withdrawing the majority of the 80,000-strong federal forces from the region, in order to leave a 15,000-strong infantry division and 7,000 interior ministry troops. The local administration in Chechnya was restructured, and Stanislav Ilyasov, a former Governor of Stavropol Krai, was appointed as the Chechen premier. Despite claims that federal military operations had effectively ended, guerrilla attacks showed no sign of abating, and concern escalated among international human rights organizations about the conduct of 'cleansing' operations by federal troops, in which entire towns or areas were searched for rebels; in 2001–02 the discovery of a number of mass graves, containing severely mutilated corpses, prompted outrage internationally.

In early 2001 a number of violent incidents outside Chechnya were staged by rebels, with the intention of drawing attention to the ongoing conflict. In mid-March three armed Chechen rebels hijacked a passenger aeroplane en route from Istanbul, Turkey, to Moscow, causing it to be diverted to Medina, Saudi Arabia. The rebels demanded that federal forces withdraw from Chechnya. Following the intervention of Saudi security forces, three hijackers were detained; three people, including one of the hijackers, were killed in the struggle. Later in the month 23 people were killed, and more than 140 were injured in three simultaneous bomb attacks in southern Russia, which were attributed to associates of Khattab.

In early May 2001 the continuing disorder in Chechnya was demonstrated by the announcement that the withdrawal of troops from the province had been terminated; by this time only 5,000 federal troops had left Chechnya. Meanwhile, tensions increased between federal forces and the Governor of Chechnya, and in August, writing in the federal parliamentary journal, *Parlamentskaya Gazeta*, Kadyrov called for an expedited end to the Government's campaign. In early September 2001 a bomb was detonated in the offices of the republican Government, which had, by this time, returned to Groznyi; both Kadyrov and Ilyasov escaped unharmed.

In mid-November 2001 the first direct negotiations between the warring factions since the renewal of hostilities in 1999, held in Moscow between the presidential representative to the Southern Federal Okrug, Col-Gen. Viktor Kazantsev and Maskhadov's deputy, Akhmed Zakayev, reached no substantive agreement, and no further high-level meetings took place. In late December Raduyev, the only prominent Chechen rebel leader to have been captured by federal forces, was sentenced to life imprisonment, having been guilty of 10 charges, including murder, terrorism and hostage-taking. (Raduyev died in prison in December 2002.)

In April 2002 Khattab was killed by federal forces. Rebel activity increased markedly in the months that followed; although the political authority of Maskhadov had dwindled, his military leadership of what was known as the State Defence Committee became increasingly prominent as a focus for resistance to the federal troops. In July it was reported that Basayev had been appointed to a senior position on the Committee. Meanwhile, on 9 May, during celebrations in Kaspiisk, Dagestan, to mark 'Victory Day', some 45 people were killed and more than 130 injured in an explosion, which the federal authorities attributed to Chechen rebels. In mid-August federal forces experienced their single largest loss of life since the recommencement of operations in 1999, when a military helicopter was shot down by rebels in Groznyi, killing some 118 troops; at the end of the month a second federal helicopter was attacked, killing its two crew members, and two further helicopters had been shot down by early November. Meanwhile, in late September rebels staged incursions into Ingushetiya; at least 17 deaths were reported in fighting. Moreover, an explosion outside a police station in Groznyi in mid-October resulted in the deaths of at least 24 people.

On 23–26 October 2002 over 40 heavily armed rebels, led by Movsar Barayev, the cousin of a Chechen rebel leader who had been killed by federal troops in 2001, held captive more than 800 people in a Moscow theatre, and demanded the withdrawal of federal troops from the republic. The rebels described themselves as members of a 'suicide battalion'. The siege ended when élite federal forces stormed the theatre, having initially filled the building with an unidentified incapacitating gas. The rebels were killed, and it subsequently emerged that at least 129 hostages had also died, in almost all cases owing to the toxic effects of the gas. Maskhadov issued a statement condemning the rebels' use of terrorist methods, but, despite denials by the rebel Chechen leadership of their involvement in the incident, Zakayev was arrested in late October, reportedly on the orders of the federal Government, in Denmark. In early December the Danish authorities refused to extradite Zakayev to Russia, citing a lack of credible evidence of his involvement in terrorist activities. Zakayev's presence in Denmark resulted in the relocation to Brussels, Belgium, of the EU-Russia summit that had been scheduled to take place in Copenhagen in November. Zakayev subsequently fled to the United Kingdom, where extradition proceedings commenced in late January 2003. (However, it was announced in late November that Zakayev had been granted political asylum in the United Kingdom, following the dismissal of the Russian request for his extradition.)

In mid-November 2002 Ilyasov was removed from his position as Prime Minister of Chechnya and, in what was widely perceived as a promotion, appointed as a minister in the federal Government, in which capacity he was to be responsible for the social and economic development of Chechnya; Ilyasov was succeeded as the premier of Chechnya by Capt. (retd) Mikhail Babich, who had previously held senior positions in two regional administrations elsewhere in Russia. In late November Ilyasov announced that a referendum on a new draft Chechen constitution, which would, *inter alia*, determine the status of the republic within the Russian Federation, was to be held in March 2003. At the end of December at least 83 people died, and more than 150 others were injured, when suicide bombers detonated bombs in two vehicles stationed outside the headquarters of the republican Government in Groznyi; no senior officials were killed. (Basayev subsequently claimed responsibility for the attack.) By late December 2002 federal losses during the campaign, according to official figures, were put at 4,572 dead and 15,549 wounded, with 29 missing, although Chechen estimates were considerably higher. (It was also estimated that more than 14,000 rebel fighters had been killed since September 1999.) In late January 2003 Babich resigned as premier. On 10 February Anatolii Popov, the hitherto deputy chairman of the state commission for the reconstruction of Chechnya, was appointed as the new republican premier.

The referendum on the draft constitution for Chechnya, describing the republic (which was to be renamed the Chechen—Nokchi Republic) as both a sovereign entity, with its own citizenship, and as an integral part of the Russian Federation, proceeded, as scheduled, on 23 March 2003, despite concerns that the instability of the republic would prevent the poll from being free and fair. The draft constitution also provided for the holding of fresh elections to a strengthened republican presidency and legislature. According to the official results, some 88.4% of the electorate participated in the plebiscite, of whom 96.0% supported the draft constitution. Two further questions, on the method of electing the President and the Parliament of the Chechnya, were supported by 95.4% and 96.1% of participants, respectively. However, independent observers challenged the results, reporting that the rate of participation by the electorate had been much lower than officially reported.

Political violence continued to dominate Chechen affairs after the referendum; in early April 2003 at least 22 people were killed in two separate incidents when their vehicles detonated landmines. In early May at least 59 people were killed when suicide bombers attacked government offices in the north of Chechnya. Two days later another suicide bombing at a religious festival attended by Kadyrov resulted in at least 14 deaths, although Kadyrov escaped unhurt; Basayev claimed responsibility for the organization of both attacks. On 21 June Kadyrov inaugurated an interim legislative body, the State Council, comprising the head of, and an appointed representative of, each administrative district. In July Putin announced that presidential elections in Chechnya would be held in October. None the less, clashes continued, and in August at least 50 people were killed in an attack on a military hospital in the neighbouring North Osetiya.

From 1 September 2003 control of military operations in Chechnya was transferred from the FSB to the federal Ministry of Internal Affairs; such operations were no longer regarded as having an 'anti-terrorist' character but were, rather, to form part of an 'operation to protect law and constitutional order'. Meanwhile, campaigning for the presidential election commenced, and by mid-August 11 valid applications for candidacies had been made. However, the subsequent withdrawal of Aslanbek Aslakhanov, a representative of Chechnya in the Gosudarstvennaya Duma, and the debarring of a business executive, Malik Saidullayev, effectively removed any major challenges to Kadyrov's candidacy. As had been widely anticipated, on 5 October Kadyrov was elected as President, receiving 87.7% of the votes cast, according to official figures. The rate of participation by the electorate was stated to be 82.6%. In mid-December at least 12 people were killed in clashes that followed incursions by heavily armed Chechen rebels into Dagestan, resulting in the imposition of a state of emergency in the region. An explosion in a Moscow Metro train on 6 February 2004, which resulted in the deaths of at least 39 people, was attributed to Chechen militants. In mid-February Yandarbiyev was killed by a car bomb in Doha, Qatar (two Russian intelligence agents were subsequently tried for Yandarbiyev's murder by a Qatari court, and sentenced to life imprisonment; however, they were returned to Russia to serve out their sentences in December, and in early 2005 it was reported that they were no longer being held in detention). In early March 2004 another influential rebel leader, Ruslan Gelayev, was reported to have been killed in clashes with federal troops in Dagestan. In mid-March Popov was formally dismissed as premier of Chechnya, following a period of ill health; he was replaced by Sergei Abramov, who had previously worked in the republican Ministry of Finance. In accordance with the provisions of the constitutional referendum held in the previous year, his appointment required, and duly obtained, the endorsement of the republican State Council.

An explosion in Groznyi on 9 May 2004, at a celebration to mark 'Victory Day', resulted in the deaths of several senior officials, including Kadyrov and Khusain Isayev, the head of the republican legislature. (Basayev subsequently claimed responsibility for the attack.) Abramov assumed presidential responsibilities in an acting capacity, pending elections, while Ramzan Kadyrov, the son of the assassinated President and the leader of the presidential security service (often known as the *Kadyrovtsi* and which was widely believed to have been implicated in several unexplained 'disappearances'), was appointed as First Deputy Prime Minister. Chechen militants were suspected of involvement in a series of raids on interior ministry targets in the neighbouring republic of Ingushetiya, which took place in June. In the presidential election held on 29 August, Maj.-Gen. Alu Alkhanov, an officer in the interior ministry troops, and generally acknowledged to be the candidate favoured by the federal Government, was elected President, receiving 73.7% of the votes cast, according to official figures, which evaluated the rate of participation at 85.3%. The Council of Europe described the elections as undemocratic. Alkhanov retained Abramov as Prime Minister, while Ramzan Kadyrov was retained both as First Deputy Prime Minister and as head of the presidential security service. In the period immediately before and after the election, attacks on Russian civilians, attributed to extremist Chechen separatists, intensified, with the destruction, apparently by suicide bombers, of two passenger planes, the explosion of a bomb outside a Moscow Metro station, and the occupation of a school in Beslan, in the Republic of North Osetiya—Alaniya, on 1–3 September (see above). Basayev subsequently released a statement claiming that the attacks had occurred under his orchestration, and describing the demands of the Beslan hostage-takers as the complete withdrawal of federal troops from Chechnya and the resignation of President Putin.

In February 2005 Maskhadov announced that he had ordered separatist fighters to observe a unilateral one-month cease-fire, in what he described as a 'goodwill gesture' towards the Russian authorities. On 8 March Russian media reported that Maskhadov had been killed during a special operation by FSB forces north of Groznyi. Footage of what appeared to be Maskhadov's corpse was broadcast on national television later that day. Maskhadov was replaced as leader of the State Defence Committee by his chosen successor, Abdul-Khalim Sadulayev. Sadulayev, like Maskhadov before him, announced his willingness to enter into negotiations with the federal authorities, but maintained that the use of force was legitimate in the absence of such negotiations. In June Sadulayev issued a decree appointing Doku Umarov, a radical Islamist believed to be a close associate of Basayev (who had, earlier in the year, stated that Chechen militants would launch large-scale operations in other regions of Russia as part of a so-called 'Caucasus Front') as vice-president of the rebel leadership; he also issued a statement to the effect that the expulsion of Russian forces from Chechnya would not constitute an end to the conflict, as the Chechens would be obligated to take vengeance against 'unbelievers' (i.e. non-Muslims) for their actions in Chechnya. In mid-July at least 15 people were killed following the detonation of a car bomb in Znamenskoye. In mid-August Sadulayev dismissed the rebel Chechen 'parliament-in-exile' and a network of 'ambassadors', which he collectively accused of financial malpractice and incompetence; he also appointed a new rebel 'Government' at the end of the month, to which, notably, Basayev was appointed as 'First Deputy Prime Minister', while Zakayev was appointed to represent the rebel authorities internationally. In early September Basayev was interviewed by a US television station, and stated that he accepted his designation as a 'terrorist', but that he regarded his use of violence as justified. In early October a co-ordinated series of attacks by some 100 militants against law-enforcement bodies in Nalchik, the capital of the Kabardino-Balkar Republic, in the western North Caucasus, resulted in the deaths of at least 130 people; Basayev claimed responsibility for the organization of the attack. An Islamist group active in the Kabardino-Balkar Republic, the Yarmuk Dzhamaat, also claimed to have participated in the attacks, as part of the 'Caucasus Front'. Meanwhile, tensions between Chechens and the most numerous ethnic group in neighbouring Dagestan, the Avars, were also heightened on several occasions from the first half of 2005, as a result of security forces associated with the Chechen authorities (most notably members of the *Kadyrovtsi*) making incursions into Dagestan, apparently in response to Chechen rebels taking refuge in the neighbouring Republic. Clashes were also reported between those troops loyal to Ramzan Kadyrov and those loyal to the federal authorities.

On 27 November 2005 elections were held in Chechnya to a new, bicameral legislature, comprising the 18-seat Council of the Republic (the upper chamber) and the 40-seat People's Assembly (the lower chamber). The federal Government cited the ballot as evidence that normality was returning to Chechnya, although no candidates advocating Chechen independence were allowed to stand. The rate of participation by the electorate was estimated as some 60%, well above the 25% required to validate the election; however, international observers expressed doubt that the vote was free and fair. As predicted, the majority of deputies in the new parliament (33 out of 58) were from UR. The CPRF, the pro-market URF and the Eurasian Union also obtained representation, as did 14 deputies with no party affiliation. Thus the position of Kadyrov, a member of UR and for a long time perceived as de facto leader of the Chechen Government, was consolidated; furthermore, Kadyrov at this time held the position of acting premier, after Abramov sustained injuries in an automobile accident earlier in the month.

On 28 February 2006 Abramov resigned as Prime Minister of Chechnya. On 4 March the republican legislature unanimously approved the appointment of Kadyrov as his successor. Although this appointment effectively confirmed the distribution of power that had been in place in the Republic for several months, it was not without controversy. As acting Prime Minister, Kadyrov had spoken in favour of permitting men to marry up to four women, although this would be in clear breach of the family code; moreover, before being overruled by Alkhanov, Kadyrov had prohibited a Danish humanitarian relief organization from operating in Chechnya, as part of international protests by Muslims that followed the publication of cartoons depicting the Islamic Prophet Muhammad, initially in a Danish newspaper (and their circulation, by a group of imams, alongside several more inflammatory images, in various countries of the Middle East), which were deemed to be offensive towards Islam.

In June Sadulayev was killed in an operation by special forces in Chechnya. He was succeeded as leader of the separatist Chechen rebels by Umarov. In July Basayev was killed, in an explosion in Ingushetiya (for which the FSB claimed responsibility). In October Kadyrov reached 30 years of age (the minimum age for eligibility to serve as Chechen President). On 15 February 2007 Putin's transferral of Alkhanov to the federal Government (see above) allowed Kadyrov, as Chairman of the republican Government, to assume the duties of President, in an acting capacity. Later in the month it was confirmed that he was the federal authorities' preferred nominee to become President; his appointment was endorsed by the republican legislature on 2 March. In October a federal military commander announced that the number of federal troops in Chechnya would not be reduced in the immediate future, despite Kadyrov having expressed support for a gradual withdrawal. Later that month Umarov issued a statement proclaiming himself emir of a 'North Caucasus Islamic state', thereby precipitating a split in the separatist movement between Islamist and nationalist elements. In early November the rebel Chechen 'parliament-in-exile' announced that Umarov's powers as 'President' of the 'Chechen Republic of Ichkeriya' had been formally removed. The rebel 'Minister of Foreign Affairs' based in London, United Kingdom, Zakayev, condemned Umarov's statement, and subsequently received the support of senior rebel commanders. Later in October the chairman of the 'parliament-in-exile' issued a decree appointing Zakayev as 'Prime Minister', although this appointment was not recognized by supporters of Umarov.

Following the dissolution of the USSR in December 1991, Russia's most immediate foreign policy concerns were with the other former Soviet republics, generally referred to in Russia as the 'near abroad'. Relations with Ukraine were, initially, dominated by a dispute over the division of the former Soviet Black Sea Fleet, based mainly in Sevastopol, on the Crimean peninsula (Ukraine). Russia and Ukraine signed an agreement on the division of the Fleet in June 1995, but Russia subsequently refused to implement the accord, owing to continued disagreement concerning the status of Sevastopol. In May 1997 an agreement was concluded with Ukraine, whereby Russia was to lease part of the city's naval base for a period of 20 years, and was to provide financial compensation for ships and equipment received from Ukraine. (Upon expiry, the treaty could be renewed for five years, should both parties agree, but would then be subject to renegotiation.) A Treaty on Friendship, Co-operation and Partnership was signed by the two countries in that month. In January 2003 a treaty delineating the land boundary between Russia and Ukraine (which remained largely unmarked and unregulated) was signed by Putin and President Leonid Kuchma of Ukraine, although discussions on the status of the Sea of Azov, which lies between the two countries, remained unresolved. Work on the construction of a dam in the Sea, which commenced, apparently at the instigation of the regional authorities in Krasnodar Krai, in September, precipitated considerable controversy, and raised concerns that the territorial integrity of Ukraine was being violated. In late December the Presidents of the two countries signed an agreement on the use of the Sea of Azov, the entirety of which was defined as comprising the internal waters of both countries. Agreement was also reached on the maritime state boundary of Russia and Ukraine in the region.

Relations with Ukraine were damaged by the circumstances of the disputed 2004 presidential election in that country (see the chapter on Ukraine), as Putin openly supported the candidacy of the incumbent Prime Minister, Viktor Yanukovych, whose reported victory in the second round was subsequently overturned following large public protests over the conduct of the poll. Notably, Putin visited Ukraine twice during the campaign, appearing publicly with Yanukovych on both occasions, and telephoned Yanukovych to congratulate him on his victory before the official (and later discredited) results had been announced. Putin also described the protests that led to the election being repeated, and which became known as the 'orange revolution', as a violation of constitutional order. In a move widely interpreted as acknowledging the necessity of continued co-operation between the two countries (and reflecting the substantial ethnic Russian and Russian-speaking population of Ukraine), the newly elected President, Viktor Yushchenko, visited Moscow the day after his inauguration in January 2005. However, relations between the two countries were again strained later in 2005, following the announcement by the Russian state-controlled company, Gazprom, that it intended to charge Ukraine market prices for the supply of natural gas, which had hitherto been supplied at a subsidized rate. After failing to negotiate new terms, on 1 January 2006 Gazprom halted supplies to Ukraine, a measure that resulted in a reduced output of gas in several countries in central and western Europe supplied by pipelines crossing Ukraine. Supplies were restored on 4 January, following agreement on new terms of supply less favourable to Ukraine. In October 2007 Gazprom threatened again to suspend natural gas supplies to Ukraine, stating that it was owed $1,300m.; a few days later it was announced that a compromise agreement had been reached, whereby Ukraine was to repay $1,200m. by transferring gas from underground storage facilities in Ukraine to Gazprom for further export. In February 2008 Gazprom warned that it would reduce supplies to Ukraine, in response to debts incurred during the previous month; it was subsequently announced that Ukraine and Russia had reached a debt settlement, and also agreed to discontinue use of the intermediary trading company in gas supplies to Ukraine, the Swiss-registered RosUkrEnergo. Later in February, however, Gazprom claimed that Ukraine had failed to sign the negotiated agreements. After further discussions, in April the Ukrainian Government announced that agreement had been reached on a new payment scheme; at the insistence of the Russian authorities, RosUkrEnergo was to remain the intermediary company, operating within Russia.

In April 1996 Russia and Belarus signed an agreement creating a 'Community of Russia and Belarus', according to which the two countries would pursue economic integration and close co-ordination of foreign and defence policies. In May 1997 a 'Charter of the Union of Belarus and Russia' was concluded, which, while promoting greater co-operation between the two countries, moved away from advocating full union, although in June the first official session of the Union's joint Parliamentary Assembly was convened. During 1998 the Union was strengthened by the decision to grant joint citizenship to residents, and the establishment of a joint legislative and representative body to deal with union issues. A treaty on unification, which came into force on 26 January 2000, when the President of Belarus, Alyaksandr Lukashenka, was appointed Chairman of the High State Council of the Union, did not satisfy the Belarusian President's wishes for the formation of a single state. A union budget was passed at a session of the Parliamentary Assembly (established under the 1996 Treaty, and comprising 36 members from the legislature of each country) in May. Although agreement was reached in March 2002 on the harmonization of the two countries' customs and tax laws, and on the removal of trade barriers, Putin was increasingly dismissive of Lukashenka's proposals for a closer union of the two states. In August Putin presented Lukashenka with a new unification plan, which effectively provided for the absorption of Belarus' seven oblasts (regions) into the Russian Federation. The proposals were, however, rejected by Lukashenka, who stated that the introduction of such measures would undermine Belarusian sovereignty.

Concern at the treatment and status of ethnic Russians in Estonia and Latvia remained a particular source of tension, and the demarcation of mutual frontiers also created difficulties. In the early 2000s Russia expressed particular concern for its citizens in the Russian exclave of Kaliningrad, which is separated from the remainder of the Russian Federation by Belarus and Lithuania. Russian premier Kasyanov attempted to ensure that residents of the exclave would be exempted from visa requirements that were to be imposed by Lithuania and Poland prior to the two countries' accession to the EU (which took effect from 1 May 2004). In November 2002, at an EU-Russia summit meeting, held in Brussels, Russia finally agreed to an EU proposal for simplified visa arrangements. According to the compromise accord, multiple-transit travel documentation would be made available to residents of the exclave travelling by motor vehicle; the new regulations came into effect on 1 July 2003. In 2006 President Putin inaugurated a railway ferry service, initially servicing only cargo, connecting the exclave to metropolitan Russia.

Following the dissolution of the USSR, Russia maintained significant political and military influence in many former Soviet republics, especially in those areas involved in civil or ethnic conflicts. Russian troops were deployed in Tajikistan to support the Tajikistani Government against rebel forces during the civil war of 1992–97, and remained thereafter to ensure the security of the Tajikistani–Afghan border. In 2004 it was announced that Russian troops were to transfer responsibility for border security to the Tajikistani military; in October, meanwhile, it was announced that Russia had been formally granted a permanent military base in Tajikistan. In October 2003 a Russian military base commenced operations in Kyrgyzstan, the first to be established outside Russia subsequent to the dissolution of the USSR; the base was intended to meet the requirements of the Collective Security Treaty Organization (CSTO, see p. 423), inaugurated in April to succeed the CIS Collective Security Treaty. In November 2005 Putin and President Islam Karimov of Uzbekistan signed a defence pact, which provided for mutual support in the event that one of the countries came under attack; this measure followed the departure of US troops from a base in Uzbekistan, on the orders of Karimov, following US (and widespread international) criticism of the use of violence by Uzbekistani troops against demonstrators in the city of Andijon in May of that year (see the chapter on Uzbekistan). Russia, together with Belarus, Kazakhstan, Kyrgyzstan and Tajikistan, was a founding member of the Eurasian Economic Community (EURASEC, see p. 412), which was formally established in 2001. In October 2007 EURASEC leaders approved the legal basis for the establishment of a new customs union that was initially to comprise Belarus, Kazakhstan and Russia, with Kyrgyzstan, Tajikistan and Uzbekistan expected to join by 2011.

Considerable controversy arose from the 1990s because of the Russian Government's provision of support for separatist factions in Moldova and Georgia. In 1999 it was announced that all Russian troops in the separatist Transnistria region of Moldova were to be withdrawn by the end of 2002; however, this was subsequently postponed, and in February 2004 the Russian Minister of Defence, Sergei Ivanov, indicated that Russia intended to maintain a military presence in the region. Meanwhile, in December 1998 Russia and Georgia signed an agreement that provided for the incremented transfer of the control of their mutual frontiers, from Russian to Georgian guards. (Control of the frontier was, however, complicated by the existence of separatist and rebel-controlled regions on both sides of the border—Chechnya within Russia, and Abkhazia and South Ossetia within Georgia). In November 1999 it was agreed that two of the four Russian bases on Georgian territory would be closed by mid-2001. Russian troops had left the two bases in Georgia by November 2001. (An agreement signed between Russia and Georgia in March 2006 provided for a Russian withdrawal from the military base that it maintained at Akhalkalaki and headquarters at Tbilisi by the end of 2007, and from the second base at Batumi in 2008; in the event, the withdrawal of Russian forces from the military bases was completed in November 2007, earlier than scheduled.) In September 2002 the Russian authorities accused Georgia of permitting Chechen rebels to operate from bases within its territory, and declared that Russia reserved the right to instigate 'pre-emptive' military action, in self-defence, should the situation persist. However, in early October tensions abated somewhat, when Russia and Georgia agreed to commence joint patrols of their common border. Putin attended talks in Moscow with the recently inaugurated President of Georgia, Mikheil Saakashvili, in February 2004, when progress was reportedly made towards the planned signature of a framework agreement between the two countries on matters of concern, including, notably, co-operation on measures to combat terrorism. Relations between the two countries continued to be complicated, however, by Russian support for the secessionist regimes in Abkhazia and South Ossetia and, in particular, by the granting of Russian citizenship to those resident in the separatist regions.

In October 2006 Russia temporarily withdrew its ambassador and closed all transport, postal and banking communications with Georgia, following the detention, in late September, of four Russian military officers in Georgia, on charges of espionage. In subsequent weeks large numbers of Georgian citizens residing illegally in Russia were deported. In August 2007 the Georgian authorities protested at an alleged incident, in which two military jets had entered Georgian airspace from Russia and launched a missile on its territory, near South Ossetia. The Russian Government strongly denied the allegations; however, international experts subsequently confirmed that at least one aircraft had violated Georgian airspace from Russia. Shortly after the declaration of independence of Kosovo from Serbia in February 2008 (see below), prompting international concern regarding other secessionist regions, Russia stated that it upheld the territorial integrity of Georgia and Moldova. In April, however, a Russian presidential decree providing for increased co-operation in trade and culture with Abkhazia and South Ossetia, and protection to Russian citizens living in those regions, was strongly criticized by the international community. Also in April, following the resumption of direct air links with Georgia in March, the Russian authorities announced the restoration of postal services between the two countries and envisaged the removal of other sanctions. Tension between the two countries increased later in April, after a Georgian reconnaissance aeroplane was shot down over Abkhazia, allegedly by a Russian military aircraft; although Russia denied involvement in the incident, the Georgian Government condemned it as an act of aggression and announced that it was to demand an emergency meeting of the UN Security Council in response. Meanwhile, at a NATO summit meeting, which was convened in Bucharest, Romania, on 2 April, leaders indicated that Ukraine and Georgia would be offered Membership Action Plans in the future; Russia's permanent representative at NATO had criticized US support for the aspirations towards NATO accession of those countries. Putin had warned that, in the event that Ukraine join NATO and agree to the deployment on its territory of part of the planned US national missile defence system, Russia would be prepared to target its missiles at Ukraine.

After December 1991 the Russian Federation was recognized as the successor to the USSR. It was granted the USSR's permanent seat on the UN Security Council and, additionally, was to be responsible for the receipt and destruction of all nuclear weapons of the former USSR located in other newly independent republics (Belarus, Kazakhstan and Ukraine), a process that was successfully completed by the mid-1990s. In January 1993 Russia and the USA signed the second Strategic Arms Reduction Treaty (START II), which envisaged a reduction in the strategic nuclear weapons of both powers. The Russian legislature ratified START II in April 2000. Following the first meeting of President Putin and President George W. Bush of the USA, in Ljubljana, Slovenia, in June 2001, relations appeared to improve markedly. Putin assumed a notably measured approach towards the proposed abrogation by the USA of the Anti-Ballistic Missile (ABM) treaty (signed with the USSR in 1972), which formed a principal part of the Bush Administration's foreign defence policy.

Russia offered assistance and gave support to the USA in its attempts to form a global coalition against militant Islamist terrorism, after the suicide air attacks against the USA of 11 September 2001 (see the chapter on the USA). Although Russia refused to commit troops to participate in the military campaign against targets of the Taliban regime in Afghanistan, which commenced on 7 October, it provided military intelligence, and allowed the coalition access to its airspace. Russia also increased logistical and military support to the anti-Taliban forces of the United Islamic Front for the Salvation of Afghanistan.

In mid-November 2001, at a meeting in Crawford, Texas, Bush and Putin announced that significant reductions would be made to their countries' nuclear arsenals over the following decade; Putin did not specify how many weapons would be destroyed, and emphasized his desire to formalize the agreement by means of a treaty, together with clear verification procedures, in contrast to the more informal measures envisaged by Bush. In mid-December, following the USA's announcement that it was to withdraw unilaterally from the ABM treaty, with effect from June 2002, Putin reiterated earlier claims that, while he did not support the abrogation of the treaty, its abandonment did not pose a security threat to Russia. In mid-May 2002 Russia and the USA announced that agreement had been reached on the reduction of their nuclear arsenals by approximately two-thirds, and a nuclear accord and a declaration on strategic partnership were duly signed by Presidents Putin and Bush on 24 May. The USA withdrew from the ABM treaty on 13 June, and the following day Russia withdrew from START II, which had been superseded by the treaty signed with the USA in the previous month.

The Russian Government consistently condemned intermittent US-led missile attacks on Iraq during the 1990s and early 2000s; additionally, in 1996, in contravention of a UN embargo, Russia concluded an agreement with Iraq on the development of petroleum fields in that country. In late 1997, following Iraq's refusal to permit weapons inspectors of the UN Special Commission (UNSCOM) access to contentious sites, the Russian Government intervened in an attempt to avert a renewal of hostilities, and the conclusion of an agreement between the UN and Iraq in late February 1998 was regarded by Russia as a significant diplomatic success. Russia resumed scheduled flights to Iraq in late 2000, in contravention of UN sanctions. In mid-2001 Russia, which supported Iraq in its demands that the sanctions regime in force since 1990 should be revoked, effectively obstructed a

British-drafted proposal before the Security Council for the introduction of a new, US-advocated, programme of 'smart' sanctions. As the US Administration of George W. Bush, from the second half of 2002, utilized increasingly bellicose rhetoric against Iraq, Russia urged the USA to avoid the use of unilateral force, and encouraged Iraq's compliance with UN demands regarding weapons inspections, so as to facilitate the lifting of sanctions. Although Russia voted to support UN Security Council Resolution 1441, approved in November 2002, which provided for the expedited return of weapons inspectors to Iraq under the auspices of the UN Monitoring, Verification and Inspection Commission (UNMOVIC), it was a leading opponent of attempts, led by the USA and the United Kingdom in February–March 2003, to approve a further Security Council resolution explicitly to endorse military action in Iraq, and President Putin described the conflict, which commenced in mid-March, as a 'political mistake'. Although senior members of the US Government criticized various aspects of Russian policy (including, notably, progress towards establishing democratic governance and the rule of law in Russia) during 2003, Putin, in particular, emphasized the importance of maintaining co-operative relations with the USA. Observers speculated that Russia's commitment to renew exports of nuclear fuel to Iran in early 2005 (see below), and seeming pursuit of closer ties with Syria (with reports in 2005 suggesting that Russia was to sell missiles to Syria), could be harmful to relations with the USA, the foreign policy of which was notably hostile towards those countries.

In early 2007 the Russian Government declared emphatically its opposition to the establishment of a radar installation in the Czech Republic and missile interceptors in Poland by 2011–12 as part of the USA's proposed National Missile Defence programme, despite repeated US assurances that the plan was not intended to threaten Russian interests. Russia warned that it would take retaliatory measures against the US programme, including withdrawal from the Conventional Forces in Europe (CFE) Treaty, prompting the Czech and Polish Governments to demand security and legal guarantees from the USA and further exacerbating strained relations with the West. At a conference on security policy, held in Munich, Germany, in February 2007, President Putin strongly criticized the US Administration for its stance on defence, which he described as being against the fundamental principles of international law. Legislation providing for Russia's suspension of the CFE Treaty was formally adopted by both parliamentary chambers in November, and, after its endorsement by Putin, entered into effect in early December. At the NATO summit meeting in early April 2008 (see above), member states endorsed US plans to position missile defence bases in the Czech Republic and Poland (a previous suggestion by Putin that bases in Azerbaijan be used having been rejected by the USA). Despite the continuing lack of agreement on the US defence plan, a subsequent meeting between President Bush and Putin in the Russian Black Sea town of Sochi (the last before Putin relinquished office as President) was reported as cordial.

In June 1994 Russia joined the North Atlantic Treaty Organization's (NATO) 'Partnership for Peace' (see p. 342) programme of military co-operation with former Eastern bloc states. A 'Founding Act on Mutual Relations, Co-operation and Security between NATO and the Russian Federation' was signed in May 1997. The Act provided for enhanced Russian participation in all NATO decision-making activities, equal status in peace-keeping operations and representation at the Alliance headquarters at ambassadorial level. A NATO-Russian Permanent Joint Council was established. Russia's relations with NATO became increasingly strained in 1999, in particular after the situation in the province of Kosovo, in the Republic of Serbia, then Yugoslavia, precipitated the aerial bombardment of Yugoslav targets by NATO forces in late March (see chapter on Serbia). Russia condemned the air offensive, and suspended its relations with the Alliance. Following the capitulation of Yugoslav forces in mid-June, and their withdrawal from Kosovo, Russian troops were the first to enter the province, before NATO forces. Contacts were resumed between Russia and NATO in February 2000. In July 2001 Putin called for a pan-European security pact to be established in place of NATO, to incorporate Russia. On 28 May 2002 Putin and the heads of state and of government of the 19 NATO member states, meeting in Italy, signed the Rome Declaration, inaugurating a new NATO-Russia Council to replace the Permanent Joint Council. The new Council would enable Russia to enter into negotiations with its members on a range of issues, including terrorism, non-proliferation, defence and peace-keeping. Although Russia had expressed concern at the expansion of NATO to include seven eastern European countries, including the three Baltic states, from early 2004, Putin emphasized that the expansion would not have negative consequences for the Alliance's relations with Russia. The Russian Government expressed support for Serbia in opposing a proposal, presented to the UN Security Council by UN special envoy Martii Ahtisaari at the end of March 2007, to grant internationally supervised independence to Kosovo. In July UN Security Council draft resolutions on the future status of Kosovo were abandoned, owing to Russia's insistence that it would veto any resolution that was not acceptable to the Serbian Government. A further series of negotiations between Serbian and Kosovan delegations, beginning in August, were mediated by US, EU and Russian envoys, but again ended in failure. Following Kosovo's unilateral declaration of independence on 17 February 2008 (see the chapter on Kosovo), Russia demanded at an emergency meeting of the UN Security Council that Kosovo's declaration of sovereignty be annulled. Meanwhile, in late January relations between Russia and Serbia were consolidated with the signature of an agreement whereby Serbia was to join Russia's 'South Stream' pipeline project (see below), and Gazprom acquired a 51% share in the Serbian state-owned oil enterprise, Naftna Industrija Srbije.

In January 1996 Russia was admitted as a member of the Council of Europe (see p. 225). As a condition of membership, Russia was to abolish the death penalty by the end of February 1999. However, the Duma has yet to approve its abolition, although capital punishment has been subject to a moratorium since Russia's admission to the organization. Russia's voting rights were suspended between April 2000 and January 2001, as a result of allegations of human rights abuses committed during Russia's renewed military campaign in Chechnya. In April 2003 the Parliamentary Assembly of the Council of Europe voted, by a large majority, in favour of the establishment of an international tribunal to try those suspected of war crimes in the republic. In February 2005 the European Court of Human Rights, a subsidiary institution of the Council of Europe, in ruling on cases brought by six Chechen citizens, concluded that serious human rights abuses had been committed by the Russian military in Chechnya and ordered the Russian Government to pay compensation to the victims' relatives. In 2006 Russia became the rotating chairman of the Group of Eight leading industrialized nations (G-8), to which it had been admitted in 2000.

In November 2004, following approval by both chambers of the legislature, President Putin signed a bill ratifying the Kyoto Protocol to the United Nations Framework Convention on Climate Change, thereby bringing the Protocol into force for its signatories. Observers suggested that the decision to approve the protocol may have been motivated by the Russian Government's ongoing pursuit of membership of the World Trade Organization (WTO, see p. 396). In May 2007, following a deterioration in relations with Estonia (see above), the EU announced that it would not support Russia's application to join the WTO unless the Government demonstrated commitment to resolving political issues.

Russia's relations with Iran in the late 1990s and early 2000s were a cause of concern for the USA. In mid-1997 Iran and Russia held discussions on nuclear co-operation, primarily focusing on the development of a nuclear power plant in Bushehr, Iran. In December 2000 Igor Sergeyev, the Russian Minister of Defence, paid the first official visit to Iran by a Russian official since the Islamic Revolution in that country of 1979, with a view to increasing military and technical co-operation. In March 2001, during a visit to Moscow by the Iranian President, Muhammad Khatami, Russia agreed to resume the sale of conventional weapons to Iran and to assist with the construction of the Bushehr power plant; an agreement for arms sales worth some US $300m., the first such agreement between the two countries since 1995, was signed in October. Although in December 2002 it was announced that Russia was to increase its nuclear co-operation with Iran, the Russian Minister of Foreign Affairs, Igor Ivanov, reiterated that this co-operation was of a civilian nature and that Russia remained opposed to Iran's potential development of nuclear weapons. In mid-2003 Russia announced that it was to suspend exports of nuclear fuel to Iran; however, in February 2005 a new agreement was reached between the two countries on the provision of nuclear fuel (which would, however, be returned to Russia, once it was spent). In February 2006 Russia was one of 27 countries represented on the 35-member Board of Governors of the International Atomic Energy Agency (IAEA) to vote in favour of Iran's referral to the UN Security Council, after it was discovered not to have complied with the conditions of an agreement reached with the IAEA; none the less, Russia remained opposed to the use of military force against Iran to bring it into compliance. In October 2007 Putin visited the Iranian capital, Tehran, to attend a summit meeting of the five Caspian state leaders. The declaration adopted by the parties at the end of the summit postponed settlement of territorial issues, but asserted that they each country would not allow its territory to be used by other states for the purposes of a military attack against another state.

Relations with Japan were complicated by a continuing dispute over the status of the Kurile Islands (in Sakhalin Oblast, and known in Japan as the Northern Territories), which became part of the USSR at the end of the Second World War; Japan maintained its long-standing demand that four of the islands be returned to Japanese sovereignty. Discussions on the territorial dispute between the leaderships of Russia and Japan from the late 1990s, but resulted in little progress. Despite Russian President Vladimir Putin's repudiation of Japan's claim to any of the islands during his first official visit to Tokyo in September 2000, Russia subsequently offered to abide by a 1956 declaration that it would relinquish two of the islands after the signature of a peace treaty, but Japan rejected this partial solution. In August 2006 Russian security troops killed one Japanese fisherman and detained three others who had allegedly been fishing illegally in Russian waters; the captain of the Japanese vessel subsequently received a fine for intrusion into Russian waters and poaching. The revocation, in the following month, of an environmental permit associated with the Sakhalin-2 natural gas project, and the subsequent enforced reduction of the share held in the project by Japanese companies (see Economy Affairs), was a further cause of heightened tensions between Russia and Japan. In April 2008, during an official visit by Japanese Prime Minister Yasuo Fukuda to Russia, he and President Putin agreed that further discussions would be conducted, in an effort to resolve the territorial dispute; pledges for increased bilateral co-operation were also made.

Relations with the People's Republic of China improved significantly during the 1990s. In 1999 several agreements on bilateral economic and trade co-operation, and a final accord on the demarcation of a common border between the two countries, were signed. Meanwhile, negotiations in the mid-1990s that initially focused on defining the mutual borders of China, Kazakhstan, Kyrgyzstan, Russia and Tajikistan appeared to be instrumental in bringing about closer co-operation between these countries, which in 1996 formed the so-called Shanghai Five group. The group subsequently broadened its areas of activity to include trade, cultural, military and security co-operation; in June 2001 Uzbekistan joined the grouping, which was renamed the Shanghai Co-operation Organization (see p. 425). In September 2003 the Organization announced its intention to establish a joint anti-terrorism centre, to be located in Tashkent, Uzbekistan, and a secretariat, in the Chinese capital, Beijing. Kasyanov visited Beijing in August 2002, to discuss strategic issues, and Putin visited China in December, when he met President Jiang Zemin and his appointed successor, Hu Jintao. The two countries issued a joint declaration on a number of global strategic issues, particularly urging a peaceful resolution to the USA's diplomatic crisis with Iraq. Russia also participated in multilateral negotiations in China in mid-2003, attended by representatives of the Governments of China, the Democratic People's Republic of Korea (DPRK—North Korea), Japan, the Republic of Korea (South Korea) and the USA, which were intended to encourage the DPRK to abandon its nuclear weapons programme. In October 2004 a treaty was signed by Presidents Putin and Hu settling a long-running dispute over the course of the border between the two states. In 2005 Russia and China conducted joint military manoeuvres for the first time.

Government

Under the Constitution of December 1993, the Russian Federation is a democratic, federative, multi-ethnic republic, in which state power is divided between the legislature, executive and judiciary, which are independent of one another. The President of the Russian Federation is Head of State and Commander-in-Chief of the Armed Forces, and also holds broad executive powers. The President, who is elected for a term of four years, renewable once, by universal direct suffrage, appoints the Chairman of the Government (Prime Minister). Supreme legislative power is vested in the bicameral Federalnoye Sobraniye (Federal Assembly). The upper chamber is the Sovet Federatsii (Federation Council), which comprises two representatives from each of the country's federal territorial units (appointed by the legislature and the executive in each region); its lower chamber is the 450-member Gosudarstvennaya Duma (State Duma), which is elected by direct universal suffrage for a period of four years.

For much of the 1990s and the first half of the 2000s the Russian Federation comprised 89 federal territorial units ('federal subjects'). From the mid-2000s a number of territorial mergers took place, comprising the absorption of nominally Autonomous Okrugs into the territories of which they had hitherto formed part, while remaining as federal subjects in their own right. By March 2008 the number of territorial subjects had been reduced to 83, comprising 21 republics, nine krais (provinces), 46 oblasts (regions), two cities of federal status, one autonomous oblast and four autonomous okrugs (districts). The republics and the autonomous oblast and okrugs are nominally representative of ethnic groups, and the administrative oblasts and krais of geographic regions. In May 2000 the federal subjects were grouped into seven federal okrugs, each headed by a presidential appointee. In December 2004 the federal legislature approved proposals, initially presented by President Putin, in accordance with which governors of all federal subjects were henceforth to be appointed by the federal authorities, subject to approval by regional legislatures.

Defence

In May 1992 the Russian Federation established its own armed forces, on the basis of former Soviet forces on the territory of the Russian Federation, and former Soviet forces outside its territory not subordinate to other former republics of the USSR. As assessed at November 2007, the total Russian active armed forces numbered an estimated 1,027,000, with an estimated 20,000,000 reserves. These included an estimated 80,000 permanent members of the Strategic Deterrent Forces, an estimated 395,000 in the army (including some 190,000 conscripts), 142,000 in the navy, and an estimated 160,000 in the air force, following its merger with the air defence troops. There were a further estimated 419,000 paramilitary troops. A presidential decree in March 2007 reduced the length of compulsory military service (for males over the age of 18 years) from two years to one, starting on 1 January 2008. (Those drafted as of 1 January 2007 were to serve for 18 months as an interim measure.) The defence budget for 2007 allocated 821,000m. roubles to defence.

Economic Affairs

In 2006, according to estimates by the World Bank, Russia's gross national income (GNI), measured at average 2004–06 prices, was US $822,364m., equivalent to $5,780 per head (or $11,630 per head on an international purchasing-power parity basis). Between 1996 and 2006, it was estimated, the population declined by an annual average of 0.4%, while gross domestic product (GDP) per head increased, in real terms, at an average annual rate of 5.3%. According to the World Bank, overall GDP increased, in real terms, at an average annual rate of 4.9% in 1996–2006. Real GDP increased by 6.4% in 2005 and by 6.7% in 2006.

Agriculture (including forestry and fishing) contributed 4.6% of GDP in 2007. In 2006, according to the ILO, 10.0% of the employed labour force were engaged in the agricultural sector. The principal agricultural products are grain, potatoes and livestock. In 1990 the Russian Government began a programme to encourage the development of private farming, to replace the state and collective farms. Legislation to permit the sale and purchase of agricultural land from 2003 was approved by the Gosudarstvennaya Duma in June 2002. According to World Bank estimates, real agricultural GDP increased at an average annual rate of 3.7% in 1996–2005; the GDP of the sector increased by 2.9% in 2004 and by 1.1% in 2005.

Industry contributed 37.4% of GDP in 2007. In 2006 the industrial sector (including mining, manufacturing, construction and utilities) provided 29.3% of employment. According to estimates by the World Bank, industrial GDP increased, in real terms, by an annual average of 5.1% in 1996–2005. Industrial GDP increased by 6.9% in 2004 and by 4.1% in 2005.

Mining and quarrying contributed 10.1% of GDP in 2007 and employed 1.7% of the employed labour force in 2006. Russia has considerable reserves of energy-bearing minerals, including one-third of the world's natural gas reserves and substantial deposits of petroleum, coal and peat. It also has large supplies of palladium, platinum and rhodium. Other minerals exploited include bauxite, cobalt, copper, diamonds, gold, iron ore, mica, nickel and tin.

The manufacturing sector contributed 18.5% of GDP in 2007, and the sector provided 18.1% of employment in 2006.

Electric energy is derived from petroleum-, gas- and coal-fired power stations, nuclear power stations and hydroelectric installations. In 2004 Russia's 29 nuclear reactors supplied some 15.6% of total electricity generation, while coal accounted for some 17.3% of Russia's generating capacity; hydroelectric power accounted for 18.9% of electricity production, and 45.3% of the country's generating capacity originated from natural gas. Russia is a major exporter of natural gas and crude petroleum, and Russia's largest company, Gazprom, is also the world's largest producer of natural gas. Countries of the CIS remain highly dependent on Russia for imports of these fuels. From the late 1990s Russia sought to increase its exports of mineral fuels to other countries, particularly in central and western Europe. The construction of the 'Blue Stream' pipeline, which was to carry natural gas from Novorossiisk, Krasnodar Krai, in southern Russia, to Ankara, Turkey, was completed in October 2002, and was expected to facilitate further growth in Russia's energy exports (see below). In early 2005 it was announced that a pipeline would be constructed from eastern Siberia to the port of Nakhodka on the Pacific Coast, enabling exports to Japan and the wider Pacific region; this route was chosen in favour of a long-discussed alternative route to the People's Republic of China (see above). Imports of fuel comprised just 1.6% of the value of Russia's total merchandise imports in 2004.

The services sector contributed 57.9% of GDP in 2007, and provided 60.7% of employment in 2006. According to estimates by the World Bank, the GDP of the services sector increased, in real terms, at an average annual rate of 4.4% in 1996–2005. The GDP of the sector increased by 7.8% in 2004 and by 7.6% in 2005.

In 2006 Russia recorded a visible trade surplus of US $139,234m., and there was a surplus of $95,323m. on the current account of the balance of payments. In 2006 the most significant source of imports was Germany (accounting for 13.4% of the total), followed by the People's Republic of China (9.4%), Ukraine (6.7%) and Japan (5.7%). The largest market for Russian exports in 2006 was the Netherlands (purchasing 11.9% of the total), followed by Italy (8.3%), Germany (8.1%), the People's Republic of China (5.2%). The principal exports in 2006 were mineral fuels (comprising 65.9% of Russia's total exports), followed by metals, precious stones, and articles thereof (16.4%), machinery, vehicles and transport equipment (5.8%) and chemical products and rubber (5.6%). The principal imports in that year were machinery and transport equipment (accounting for 47.7% of total imports), followed by chemical products and rubber (15.9%), foodstuffs and agricultural raw materials, excluding textiles (15.7%) and metals, precious stones, and articles thereof (7.7%).

In 2005 Russia recorded a surplus on the federal budget of 278,111.8m. roubles, equivalent to 1.3% of GDP. At the end of 2005 the country's total external debt was US $229,042m., of which $75,359m. was long-term public debt. In that year the cost of debt-servicing was equivalent to 14.6% of the value of exports of goods and services. In 1995–2005 the average annual rate of inflation was 25.5%. Following the collapse of the rouble in 1998, the rate of inflation was 85.7% in 1999, but it declined thereafter. The rate of inflation was 10.9% in 2005 and 9.0% in 2006. In November 2006 some 5.3m. people (7.2% of the labour force) were unemployed.

Russia became a member of the World Bank and the IMF in 1992. Russia is also a member (as a 'Country of Operations') of the European Bank for Reconstruction and Development (EBRD, see p. 239). In 1994 Russia signed an agreement of partnership and co-operation with the European Union (EU, see p. 244). Russia is also pursuing membership of the World Trade Organization (WTO, see p. 396). Russia joined the Asia-Pacific Economic Co-operation forum (APEC, see p. 176) in 1998.

After the dissolution of the USSR, a programme of economic reforms was initiated to effect the transition to a market-orientated system. Following a financial crisis in August 1998, Russia recorded sustained growth, largely attributable to high international prices for petroleum, natural gas and metals, Russia's principal exports. The regime of President Vladimir Putin introduced significant reforms in the areas of land ownership, fiscal procedure and banking introduced in 2001–03, while a decline in both the rate of inflation and the unemployment rate appeared to mark the onset of relative stability. The merger in early 2003 of two Russian petroleum companies, Sidanco and Tyumen Oil Co (TNK), with the Russian interests of BP (United Kingdom), to form TNK-BP, represented an unprecedented level of co-operation between Russian and foreign investors in the Russian petroleum sector. However, the dismantling, in late 2004, of the privately owned petroleum company Yukos, and the effective renationalization of its most productive subsidiary, Yuganskneftegaz, through its effective acquisition by the state-owned petroleum company Rosneft (see Recent History), and the approval in 2005 of legislation that limited the degree of involvement permitted to foreign companies in the exploitation of natural resources in certain designated regions and projects, demonstrated a reverse from the free market principles that Putin had previously appeared to endorse and raised concerns that Russia was becoming less hospitable to foreign investors. In late 2006 the state-controlled Gazprom acquired a 50%-plus-one-share stake in the Sakhalin-2 petroleum and natural-gas project, in the Far East of Russia, thereby markedly reducing the share in the project held by an international consortium. Meanwhile, Russia has moved to expand its network of international pipelines, with construction of the East Siberian–Pacific Ocean pipeline, intended to transport Russian petroleum to markets in East Asia, commencing in late 2006. In November 2007 Gazprom and Italian energy company Eni signed an agreement creating the 'South Stream' joint venture for the construction of a pipeline to transport Russian natural gas to Italy; Bulgaria, Hungary and Serbia subsequently agreed to participate in the project. In December 2007 Gazprom began production at the Yuzhnoye-Russkoye natural gas field, which was expected to be a major supplier of a planned gas pipeline under the Baltic Sea to Germany. Concerns persisted that the successes of the fossil fuel sector were obscuring the relative lack of progress in other sectors of the economy. Moreover, surveys by the German-based NGO Transparency International indicated that Russia continued to be perceived as a highly corrupt country in 2007, and a Russian organization, the National Strategy Institute, stated in 2008 that the 'shadow' economy continued to account for more than 40% of GDP. Growth in 2007 was recorded at 8.1%, though the IMF anticipated that the rate of growth would fall to 6.7% in 2008.

Education

Education is compulsory for nine years, to be undertaken between the ages of six and 15 years. State education is generally provided free of charge, although in 1992 some higher education establishments began charging tuition fees. Students of selected courses in higher education receive a small stipend from the state. Primary education usually begins at six years of age and lasts for four years. Secondary education lasts for seven years, comprising a first cycle of five years and a second of two years. In 2005 enrolment at primary schools included 92.2% of pupils in the relevant age-group. In that year Secondary enrolment in that year was equivalent to 91.9% of children in the appropriate age-group.

The level of education in the Russian Federation is relatively high, and 7.3m. students were enrolled at institutes of higher education in 2006/07. Although Russian is the principal language used in educational establishments, a number of local languages are also in use. Budgetary expenditure on education (excluding scientific research and technology) in 2005 was an estimated 155,338.0m. roubles (representing 5.1% of total federal government expenditure).

All educational institutions were state-owned under Soviet rule, but a wide range of independent schools and colleges commenced operations in the early 1990s. In 2000/01 there were some 635 independent schools and 358 independent higher education institutions.

Public Holidays

2008: 1–8 January (for New Year and Orthodox Christmas), 25 February (for Defenders of the Fatherland Day), 10 March (for International Women's Day), 1–2 May (Spring Holiday and Labour Day), 9 May (Victory Day), 12 June (Russia Day), 3–4 November (National Unity Day).

2009: 1–5 January (for New Year), 7–8 January (Orthodox Christmas), 23 February (Defenders of the Fatherland Day), 9 March (for International Women's Day), 1–2 May (Spring Holiday and Labour Day), 9 May (Victory Day), 12 June (Russia Day), 3–4 November (National Unity Day).

Weights and Measures

The metric system is in force.

THE RUSSIAN FEDERATION   Statistical Survey

Statistical Survey

Source (unless otherwise indicated): Federal Service of State Statistics103450 Moscow, ul. Myasnitskaya 39; tel. (495) 207-49-02; fax (495) 207-40-87; e-mail stat@gks.ru; internet www.gks.ru.

Area and Population

AREA, POPULATION AND DENSITY

Area (sq km)	17,075,400*
Population (census results)	
12 January 1989	147,021,869
9–16 October 2002	
Males	67,605,133
Females	77,561,598
Total	145,166,731
Population (official estimates at 1 January)	
2006	142,753,551
2007	142,220,968
2008	142,008,838
Density (per sq km) at 1 January 2008	8.3

*6,592,850 sq miles.

POPULATION BY ETHNIC GROUP
(census of 9–16 October 2002)

	'000	%
Russian[1]	115,889.1	79.83
Tatar[2]	5,554.6	3.83
Ukrainian	2,943.0	2.03
Bashkir	1,673.4	1.15
Chuvash	1,637.1	1.13
Chechen[3]	1,360.2	0.94
Armenian	1,130.5	0.78
Mordovian[4]	843.4	0.58
Avar[5]	814.5	0.56
Belarusian	808.0	0.56

—continued	'000	%
Kazakh	654.0	0.45
Udmurt	636.9	0.44
Azeri	621.8	0.43
Mari[6]	604.3	0.42
German	597.2	0.41
Kabardin	520.1	0.36
Osetiyan[7]	514.9	0.35
Dargin[8]	510.2	0.35
Others[9]	7,853.5	5.41
Total	145,166.7	100.00

[1] Including Cossacks (140,028) and Pomors (6,571).
[2] Including Astrakhan Tatars (2,003), Kryashens (Christian Tatars, 24,668) and Siberian Tatars (9,611), but excluding Crimean Tatars (4,131).
[3] Including Chechen-akkintsy (218).
[4] Including Erzya-Mordovians (84,407) and Moksha-Mordovians (49,624).
[5] Including Akhvakhtsy (6,376), Andiitsy (21,808), Archintsy (89), Bagulaly (40), Bezhtintsy (6,198), Botlikhtsy (16), Chamalaly (12), Didoitsy (15,256), Ginukhtsy (531), Godoberintsy (39), Gunzibtsy (998), Karatintsy (6,052), Khvarshiny (128) and Tindaly (44).
[6] Including Lugovo-Vostochnye Mari (56,119) and Mountain Mari (18,515).
[7] Including Digor-Osetiyans (607) and Irontsy-Osetiyans (97).
[8] Including Kaitagtsy (5) and Kubachintsy (88).
[9] Including 1,460,751 respondents (1.01% of the total) who did not state their nationality or ethnic group.

ADMINISTRATIVE DIVISIONS
(1 January 2008, official estimates, except where otherwise stated)

Federal territory	Area ('000 sq km)	Population	Density (per sq km)	Capital (with population, '000)[1]
Central Federal Okrug	650.7	37,150,741	57.1	Moscow
Moscow City	1.0	10,470,318	10,470.3	Moscow (10,406.6)
Belgorod Oblast	27.1	1,519,137	56.1	Belgorod (340.9)
Bryansk Oblast	34.9	1,308,479	37.5	Bryansk (424.1)
Ivanovo Oblast	21.8	1,079,605	49.5	Ivanovo (418.2)
Kaluga Oblast	29.9	1,005,648	33.6	Kaluga (329.5)
Kostroma Oblast	60.1	697,043	11.6	Kostroma (275.9)
Kursk Oblast	29.8	1,162,475	39.0	Kursk (406.4)
Lipetsk Oblast	24.1	1,168,814	48.5	Lipetsk (503.1)
Moscow Oblast	46.0	6,672,773	145.1	Moscow[2]
Orel Oblast	24.7	821,934	33.3	Orel (329.4)
Ryazan Oblast	39.6	1,164,530	29.4	Ryazan (515.9)
Smolensk Oblast	49.8	983,227	19.7	Smolensk (319.3)
Tambov Oblast	34.3	1,106,035	32.2	Tambov (287.2)
Tula Oblast	25.7	1,566,295	60.9	Tula (465.9)
Tver Oblast	84.1	1,379,542	16.4	Tver (406.7)
Vladimir Oblast	29.0	1,449,475	50.0	Vladimir (310.5)
Voronezh Oblast	52.4	2,280,406	43.5	Voronezh (848.8)
Yaroslavl Oblast	36.4	1,315,005	36.1	Yaroslavl (605.2)
North-Western Federal Okrug	1,677.9	13,501,038	8.0	St Petersburg
St Petersburg City	0.6	4,568,047	7,613.4	St Petersburg (4,600.0)
Republic of Kareliya	172.4	690,653	4.0	Petrozavodsk (266.0)
Republic of Komi	415.9	968,164	2.3	Syktyvkar (228.9)
Archangel Oblast	587.4	1,271,877	2.2	Archangel (351.6)
Nenets Autonomous Okrug	176.7	42,019	0.2	Naryn-Mar (19.0)
Kaliningrad Oblast	15.1	937,404	62.1	Kaliningrad (425.6)
Leningrad Oblast	85.3	1,633,350	19.1	St Petersburg[2]
Murmansk Oblast	144.9	850,929	5.9	Murmansk (325.1)
Novgorod Oblast	55.3	652,437	11.8	Velikii Novgorod (218.8)
Pskov Oblast	55.3	705,289	12.8	Pskov (200.1)
Vologda Oblast	145.7	1,222,888	8.4	Vologda (288.4)
Southern Federal Okrug	589.2	22,835,216	38.8	Rostov-on-Don
Republic of Adygeya	7.6	441,176	58.0	Maikop (157.2)

THE RUSSIAN FEDERATION

Statistical Survey

Federal territory—*continued*	Area ('000 sq km)	Population	Density (per sq km)	Capital (with population, '000)[1]
Chechen (Nokchi) Republic[3]	n.a.	1,209,040	n.a.	Groznyi (215.7)
Republic of Dagestan	50.3	2,687,822	53.4	Makhachkala (465.0)
Republic of Ingushetiya[3]	n.a.	499,502	n.a.	Magas (0.3)
Kabardino-Balkar Republic	12.5	891,338	71.3	Nalchik (272.8)
Republic of Kalmykiya	75.9	285,541	3.8	Elista (103.3)
Karachai-Cherkess Republic	14.1	427,418	30.3	Cherkessk (117.1)
Republic of North Osetiya—Alaniya	8.0	702,456	87.8	Vladikavkaz (314.5)
Krasnodar Krai	76.0	5,121,799	67.4	Krasnodar (715.4)
Stavropol Krai	66.5	2,705,067	40.7	Stavropol (355.9)
Astrakhan Oblast	44.1	1,000,874	22.7	Astrakhan (501.3)
Rostov Oblast	100.8	4,254,421	42.2	Rostov-on-Don (1,058.0)
Volgograd Oblast	113.9	2,608,762	22.9	Volgograd (999.1)
Volga Federal Okrug	1,038.0	30,241,581	29.1	Nizhnii Novgorod
Republic of Bashkortostan	143.6	4,052,731	28.2	Ufa (1,036.0)
Chuvash Republic	18.3	1,282,567	70.1	Cheboksary (442.6)
Republic of Marii-El	23.2	703,220	30.3	Yoshkar-Ola (253.4)
Republic of Mordoviya	26.2	840,391	32.1	Saransk (299.2)
Republic of Tatarstan	68.0	3,762,809	55.3	Kazan (1,110.0)
Udmurt Republic	42.1	1,532,736	36.4	Izhevsk (623.4)
Perm Krai[4]	160.6	2,718,227	16.9	Perm (989.5)
Kirov Oblast	120.8	1,413,257	11.7	Kirov (448.5)
Nizhnii Novgorod Oblast	76.9	3,359,816	43.7	Nizhnii Novgorod (1,289.5)
Orenburg Oblast	124.0	2,119,003	17.7	Orenburg (538.6)
Penza Oblast	43.2	1,388,021	32.1	Penza (512.9)
Samara Oblast	53.6	3,172,787	59.2	Samara (1,133.4)
Saratov Oblast	100.2	2,583,808	25.8	Saratov (858.0)
Ulyanovsk Oblast	37.3	1,312,208	35.2	Ulyanovsk (623.1)
Urals Federal Okrug	1,788.9	12,240,382	6.8	Yekaterinburg
Chelyabinsk Oblast	87.9	3,510,990	39.9	Chelyabinsk (1,095.1)
Kurgan Oblast	71.0	960,410	13.5	Kurgan (334.3)
Sverdlovsk Oblast	194.8	4,395,617	22.6	Yekaterinburg (1,304.3)
Tyumen Oblast	1,435.2	3,373,365	2.4	Tyumen (538.3)
Khanty-Mansii Autonomous Okrug—Yugra	523.1	1,505,248	2.9	Khanty-Mansiisk (57.3)
Yamalo-Nenets Autonomous Okrug	750.3	542,732	0.7	Salekhard (38.3)
Siberian Federal Okrug	5,114.8	19,553,461	3.8	Novosibirsk
Altai Republic	92.6	207,122	2.2	Gorno-Altaisk (52.8)
Republic of Buryatiya	351.3	959,892	2.7	Ulan-Ude (352.6)
Republic of Khakasiya	61.9	537,230	8.7	Abakan (164.7)
Republic of Tyva	170.5	311,619	1.8	Kyzyl (108.1)
Altai Krai	169.1	2,508,478	14.8	Barnaul (631.2)
Krasnoyarsk Krai[5]	2,339.7	2,890,350	1.2	Krasnoyarsk (917.2)
Chita Oblast[6]	431.5	1,118,931	2.6	Chita (308.5)
Aga-Buryat Autonomous Okrug[6]	19.0	76,383	4.0	Aginskoye (12.6)
Irkutsk Oblast[7]	767.9	2,507,676	3.3	Irkutsk (582.5)
Kemerovo Oblast	95.5	2,823,539	29.6	Kemerovo (522.6)
Novosibirsk Oblast	178.2	2,635,642	14.8	Novosibirsk (1,405.6)
Omsk Oblast	139.7	2,017,997	14.4	Omsk (1,142.9)
Tomsk Oblast	316.9	1,034,985	3.3	Tomsk (487.4)
Far Eastern Federal Okrug	6,215.9	6,486,419	1.0	Khabarovsk
Republic of Sakha (Yakutiya)	3,103.2	951,436	0.3	Yakutsk (235.6)
Kamchatka Krai[8]	472.3	345,669	0.7	Petropavlovsk-Kamchatskii (196.0)
Khabarovsk Krai	788.6	1,403,712	1.8	Khabarovsk (579.0)
Maritime (Primorskii) Krai	165.9	1,995,828	12.0	Vladivostok (586.8)
Amur Oblast	363.7	869,617	2.4	Blagoveshchensk (217.7)
Magadan Oblast	461.4	165,820	0.4	Magadan (99.8)
Sakhalin Oblast	87.1	518,539	6.0	Yuzhno-Sakhalinsk (173.6)
Jewish Autonomous Oblast	36.0	185,535	5.2	Birobidzhan (76.6)
Chukot Autonomous Okrug	737.7	50,263	0.1	Anadyr (10.9)
Russian Federation	17,075.4	142,008,838	8.3	Moscow

[1] Official estimates at 1 January 2005.
[2] Although Moscow and St Petersburg are the administrative centres of Moscow and Leningrad Oblasts, respectively, the cities themselves do not form part of the oblasts.
[3] Before 1992 the territories of the Chechen (Nokchi) Republic and the Republic of Ingushetiya were combined in the Checheno-Ingush Autonomous Republic (area 19,300 sq km).
[4] Perm Krai was formed on 1 December 2005 by the merger of Perm Oblast and the Komi-Permyak Autonomous Okrug.
[5] Krasnoyarsk Krai was formally merged with the Evenk and Taimyr (Dolgano-Nenets) Autonomous Okrugs with effect from 1 January 2007.
[6] Chita Oblast and the Aga-Buryat Autonomous Okrug merged to form Transbaikal Krai on 1 March 2008.
[7] Irkutsk Oblast was formally merged with the Ust-Orda Buryat Autonomous Okrug with effect from 1 January 2008.
[8] Kamchatka Krai was formed on 1 July 2007 by the merger of Kamchatka Oblast and the Koryak Autonomous Okrug.

THE RUSSIAN FEDERATION

PRINCIPAL TOWNS
(1 January 2005, official estimates)

Town	Population	Town	Population
Moskva (Moscow, the capital)	10,406,600	Naberezhnye Chelnyi	507,900
Sankt-Peterburg (St Petersburg)*	4,600,000	Lipetsk	503,100
Novosibirsk	1,405,600	Astrakhan	501,300
Yekaterinburg*	1,304,300	Tomsk	487,400
Nizhnii Novgorod*	1,289,500	Tula	465,900
Omsk	1,142,900	Makhachkala	465,000
Samara*	1,133,400	Kirov*	448,500
Kazan	1,110,000	Cheboksary	442,600
Chelyabinsk	1,095,100	Kaliningrad	425,600
Rostov-na-Donu (Rostov-on-Don)	1,058,000	Bryansk	424,100
Ufa	1,036,000	Ivanovo	418,200
Volgograd	999,100	Magnitogorsk	416,700
Perm	989,500	Tver*	406,700
Krasnoyarsk	917,200	Kursk	406,400
Saratov	858,000	Nizhnii Tagil	383,100
Voronezh	848,800	Stavropol	355,900
Krasnodar	715,400	Ulan-Ude	352,600
Tolyatti	704,800	Arkhangelsk (Archangel)	351,600
Barnaul	631,200	Belgorod	340,900
Izhevsk*	623,400	Kurgan	334,300
Ulyanovsk*	623,100	Kaluga	329,500
Yaroslavl	605,200	Orel	329,400
Vladivostok	586,800	Sochi	328,500
Irkutsk	582,500	Murmansk	325,100
Khabarovsk	579,000	Smolensk	319,300
Novokuznetsk	563,300	Vladikavkaz*	314,500
Orenburg	538,600	Vladimir	310,500
Tyumen	538,300	Cherepovets	309,500
Kemerovo	522,600	Volzhskii	309,400
Ryazan	515,900	Chita	308,500
Penza	512,900		

* Some towns that were renamed during the Soviet period have reverted to their former names: St Petersburg (Leningrad); Nizhnii Novgorod (Gorkii); Yekaterinburg (Sverdlovsk); Samara (Kuibyshev); Izhevsk (Ustinov); Naberezhnye Chelny (Brezhnev); Tver (Kalinin); Vladikavkaz (Ordzhonikidze). The towns of Ulyanovsk and Kirov, which retained their Soviet-era names in the mid-2000s, are sometimes unofficially referred to by their pre-Soviet designations, of Simbirsk and Vyatka, respectively.

Note: Figures are rounded.

BIRTHS, MARRIAGES AND DEATHS

	Registered live births Number	Rate (per 1,000)	Registered marriages Number	Rate (per 1,000)	Registered deaths Number	Rate (per 1,000)
1999	1,214,689	8.3	911,162	6.2	2,144,316	14.7
2000	1,266,800	8.7	897,327	6.2	2,225,332	15.3
2001	1,311,604	9.0	1,001,589	6.9	2,254,856	15.6
2002	1,396,967	9.7	1,019,762	7.1	2,332,272	16.2
2003	1,477,301	10.2	1,091,778	7.6	2,365,826	16.4
2004	1,502,477	10.4	979,667	6.8	2,295,402	16.0
2005	1,457,376	10.2	1,066,366	7.5	2,303,935	16.1
2006*	1,476,200	10.4	1,113,700	7.8	2,165,700	15.1

* Numbers are rounded to the nearest 100.

Expectation of life (years at birth, WHO estimates): 65.2 (males 58.7; females 72.4) in 2005 (Source: WHO, *World Health Statistics*).

IMMIGRATION AND EMIGRATION

	2005	2006	2007
Immigrants	177,230	186,380	286,879
Emigrants	69,798	54,061	47,012

Statistical Survey

ECONOMICALLY ACTIVE POPULATION
(sample surveys, '000 persons aged 15 to 72 years, at November, excl. Chechen Republic)

	2004	2005	2006
Agriculture, hunting and forestry	6,627	6,769	6,685
Fishing	205	166	176
Mining and quarrying	1,212	1,236	1,196
Manufacturing	12,674	12,534	12,470
Electricity, gas and water supply	2,001	1,959	2,063
Construction	4,127	4,575	4,460
Wholesale and retail trade; repair of motor vehicles and motorcycles and personal and household goods	10,131	10,383	10,594
Restaurants and hotels	1,223	1,297	1,392
Transport, storage and communications	6,261	6,249	6,212
Financial intermediation	918	962	1,060
Real estate, renting and business activities	4,119	4,039	4,146
Public administration and defence; compulsory social security	4,702	4,815	4,875
Education	6,142	6,204	6,196
Health and social work	4,833	4,701	4,894
Other community, social and personal service activities	2,100	2,247	2,389
Private households with employed persons	—	26	21
Extra-territorial organizations and bodies	1	4	4
Total employed	67,275	68,169	68,834
Males	34,181	34,549	34,685
Females	33,094	33,620	34,149
Unemployed	5,675	5,263	5,312
Total labour force	72,950	73,432	74,146

Source: ILO.

Health and Welfare

KEY INDICATORS

Total fertility rate (children per woman, 2005)	1.4
Under-5 mortality rate (per 1,000 live births, 2005)	14
HIV/AIDS (% of persons aged 15–49, 2005)	1.1
Physicians (per 1,000 head, 2003)	4.25
Hospital beds (per 1,000 head, 2005)	9.7
Health expenditure (2004): US $ per head (PPP)	582.7
Health expenditure (2004): % of GDP	6.0
Health expenditure (2004): public (% of total)	61.3
Access to water (% of persons, 2004)	97
Access to sanitation (% of persons, 2004)	87
Human Development Index (2005): ranking	67
Human Development Index (2005): value	0.802

For sources and definitions, see explanatory note on p. vi.

Agriculture

PRINCIPAL CROPS
('000 metric tons)

	2004	2005	2006
Wheat	45,412.7	47,697.5	45,006.3
Rice (paddy)	471.1	574.6	686.4
Barley	17,179.7	15,791.4	18,153.6
Maize	3,515.7	3,210.8	3,668.6
Rye	2,871.9	3,628.4	2,965.1
Oats	4,954.8	4,564.5	4,880.3
Millet	1,117.2	455.9	600.4
Buckwheat	649.6	605.6	865.5
Potatoes	35,914.2	37,279.8	38,572.6
Sugar beet	21,848.3	21,420.1	30,861.2
Dry peas	1,242.5	1,126.8	1,157.6
Soybeans (Soya beans)	555.3	688.7	806.6
Sunflower seed	4,800.7	6,440.9	6,752.9
Rapeseed	275.9	302.7	522.2

THE RUSSIAN FEDERATION

—continued	2004	2005	2006
Cabbages	4,067.7	4,051.1	4,073.2
Tomatoes	2,017.9	2,295.9	2,414.9
Cucumbers and gherkins	1,321.9	1,414.0	1,423.2
Dry onions	1,673.4	1,758.7	1,788.8
Garlic	236.2	257.3	255.9
Carrots	1,762.0	1,793.3	1,918.4*
Watermelons	920.4	964.6	985.5
Apples	2,030†	1,773*	1,617*
Sweet cherries	100	90	47
Sour (Morello) cherries*	225	230	111
Plums	178†	168*	98*
Strawberries	215†	228*	235*
Raspberries	170†	181*	184*
Currants	396†	432*	435*
Grapes	318.3	333.3	243.5

* FAO estimate(s).
† Unofficial figure.

Aggregate production ('000 metric tons, may include official, semi-official or estimated data): Total cereals 76,231.4 in 2004, 76,563.6 in 2005, 76,866.1 in 2006; Total roots and tubers 35,914.2 in 2004, 37,279.8 in 2005; 38,572.6 in 2006; Total oilcrops 5,753.4 in 2004, 7,559.3 in 2005, 8,192.3 in 2006; Total pulses 1,875.4 in 2004, 1,630.1 in 2005, 1,763.5 in 2006; Total vegetables (incl. melons) 14,808.4 in 2004; 15,404.0 in 2005; 15,929.9 in 2006; Total fruits (excl. melons) 3,941.0 in 2004, 3,712.7 in 2005, 3,189.3 in 2006.

Source: FAO.

LIVESTOCK
('000 head at 1 January)

	2004	2005	2006
Horses	1,499	1,409	1,319
Cattle	24,935	22,988	21,474
Pigs	15,980	13,413	13,455
Sheep	14,669	15,494	16,074
Goats	2,361	2,277	2,138
Chickens	328,338	328,707	343,030
Turkeys	9,823	8,518	9,434
Geese*	2,800	2,750	2,850

* FAO estimates.
Source: FAO.

LIVESTOCK PRODUCTS
('000 metric tons)

	2004	2005	2006
Cattle meat	1,951.2	1,793.4	1,755.2
Sheep meat	125.4	134.4	135.8
Pig meat	1,643.4	1,520.1	1,602.1
Chicken meat	1,152.2	1,345.7	1,534.4
Cows' milk	31,904.2	30,889.9	31,074.0
Goats' milk	268.2	253.7	256.0
Hen eggs	1,991.5	2,049.9	2,100.0
Honey	52.7	52.1	55.0
Wool: greasy	47.1	48.0	48.0

Source: FAO.

Forestry

ROUNDWOOD REMOVALS
('000 cubic metres, excl. bark)

	2004	2005	2006
Sawlogs, veneer logs and logs for sleepers	67,900	70,400	73,800
Pulpwood	48,000	53,500	56,000
Other industrial wood	14,700	14,100	14,800
Fuel wood	47,800	47,000	46,000
Total	178,400	185,000	190,600

Source: FAO.

SAWNWOOD PRODUCTION
('000 cubic metres, incl. railway sleepers)

	2004	2005	2006
Coniferous (softwood)	18,770	19,770	19,800
Broadleaved (hardwood)	2,585	2,730	2,700
Total	21,355	22,500	22,500

Source: FAO.

Fishing
('000 metric tons, live weight)

	2003	2004	2005
Capture	3,281.4	2,941.5	3,190.9
Pink (humpback) salmon	188.1	114.8	202.3
Atlantic cod	186.2	205.0	203.7
Alaska (Walleye) pollock	1,055.9	849.6	961.7
Blue whiting (Poutassou)	360.2	346.8	332.2
Atlantic herring	144.2	123.3	140.1
Pacific herring	190.8	194.4	205.4
Aquaculture	108.7	109.8	114.8
Total catch	3,390.1	3,051.3	3,305.7

Note: Figures exclude seaweeds and other aquatic plants ('000 metric tons): 39.1 (capture 39.1, aquaculture 0.1) in 2003; 58.2 (capture 58.0, aquaculture 0.2) in 2004; 50.5 (capture 50.3, aquaculture 0.2) in 2005. Also excluded are aquatic mammals, recorded by number rather than weight. The number of whales caught was: 195 in 2003; 139 in 2004; 131 in 2005. The number of seals (incl. walrus) caught was: 48,412 in 2003; 14,855 in 2004; 28,379 in 2005.

Source: FAO.

Mining
('000 metric tons, unless otherwise indicated)

	2003	2004	2005
Iron ore: gross weight	91,760	96,980	96,764
Copper ore*†	675	675	700
Nickel ore*†	260	261	266
Bauxite	5,442	6,000*	6,400*
Lead ore*†	24.0	23.0	36.0
Zinc ore*†	159	179	180
Tin (metric tons)*†	2,000	2,500	3,000
Manganese ore*†	23	23	23
Chromium ore	116.5	320.2	772.0
Tungsten concentrates (metric tons)*†	5,450	5,500	600
Molybdenum (metric tons)*	2,900	2,900	2,900
Cobalt ore (metric tons)*†	4,800	4,700	5,000
Mercury (metric tons)*	50	50	50
Silver (metric tons)*†	700	1,277	1,350
Uranium concentrate (metric tons)*†	3,150	3,200	3,430
Gold (metric tons)*†	170.1	163.1	169.3
Platinum (metric tons)*	28	28	30
Palladium (metric tons)*	97	97	97
Kaolin (concentrate)*	45	45	45
Magnesite*	1,200	1,200	1,200
Phosphate rock (Apatite)*‡	4,121	4,120	4,200
Potash*§	4,740	5,000	5,000
Native sulphur*	50	50	50
Fluorspar (concentrate)	170	226	246
Barite (Barytes)*	78	63	63

THE RUSSIAN FEDERATION

—continued	2003	2004	2005
Salt (unrefined)*	2,800	2,800	2,800
Diamonds: gems ('000 metric carats):			
gem*	20,000	21,400	23,000
industrial*	13,000	14,200	15,000
Gypsum (crude)*	1,750	2,077	2,200
Asbestos	878	923	925*
Mica*	100	100	100
Talc*	100	100	100
Feldspar*	45	45	45
Peat (horticulture and fuel use)	1,000	1,500	1,500

* Estimated production.
† Figures refer to the metal content of ores.
‡ Figures refer to the phosphoric acid content. The data exclude sedimentary rock (estimates, '000 metric tons): 300 per year in 2002–05.
§ Figures refer to the potassium oxide content.

Source: US Geological Survey.

Crude petroleum (incl. gas condensate, '000 metric tons): 379,563 in 2002; 421,341 in 2003; 459,318 in 2004; 470,175 in 2005.

Natural gas (million cu m): 595,106 in 2002; 620,234 in 2003; 632,623 in 2004; 640,801 in 2005.

Coal ('000 metric tons): 255,754 in 2002; 276,664 in 2003; 281,744 in 2004; 298,500 in 2005.

Industry

SELECTED PRODUCTS
('000 metric tons, unless otherwise indicated)

	2005	2006	2007
Flour	10,356	10,364	10,095
Granulated sugar	5,600	5,833	6,069
Cotton fabrics (million sq metres)	2,225	2,222	2,143
Woollen fabrics (million sq metres)	30.3	29.0	28.5
Linen fabrics (million sq metres)	122	124	101
Footwear, excl. rubber footwear ('000 pairs)	47,200	57,300	50,800
Plywood ('000 cubic metres)	2,556	2,615	2,763
Particle board ('000 cubic metres)	3,750	3,880	4,020
Newsprint	1,753	1,716	2,087
Cardboard	3,125	3,396	3,496
Paper	4,001	4,038	4,063
Sulphuric acid	9,452	9,379	9,652
Soda ash (sodium carbonate)	2,582	2,938	2,940
Mineral fertilizers	16,625	16,207	17,655
Synthetic ammonia	12,473	12,954	13,005
Gasoline	32.0	34.4	35.1
Rubber tyres ('000)	41,436	40,413	43,214
Rubber footwear ('000 pairs)	16,100	17,400	22,100
Cement	48,500	54,700	59,900
Pig-iron	49,175	52,362	51,523
Steel	66,262	70,816	72,389
Steel pipes	6,695	7,898	8,706
Rolled metal products	54,661	58,215	59,635
Tractors (number)	8,600	10,900	13,500
Refrigerators and freezers ('000)	2,777	2,995	3,573
Domestic washing machines ('000)	1,582	2,016	2,708
Televisions ('000)	6,278	4,601	6,154
Electric vacuum cleaners ('000)	890	584	626
Passenger motor cars ('000)	1,069	1,178	1,290
Electric energy (million kWh)	953,000	996,000	1,016,000

Finance

CURRENCY AND EXCHANGE RATES

Monetary Units
100 kopeks = 1 Russian rubl (ruble or rouble).

Sterling, Dollar and Euro Equivalents (31 December 2007)
£1 sterling = 49.176 roubles;
US $1 = 24.546 roubles;
€1 = 36.134 roubles;
1,000 roubles = £20.34 = $40.74 = €27.67.

Average Exchange Rate (roubles per US dollar)
2005 28.2844
2006 27.1910
2007 25.5808

Note: On 1 January 1998 a new rouble, equivalent to 1,000 of the former units, was introduced. Figures in this Survey are expressed in terms of new roubles, unless otherwise indicated.

FEDERAL BUDGET
(million roubles)

Revenue	2003	2004	2005
Tax revenue	1,892,363.7	2,071,384.5	3,151,745.6
Taxes on corporate profit and capital gains	179,550.5	164,587.4	259,003.3
Taxes on goods and services	1,178,971.2	1,088,389.6	791,822.6
Value added tax	946,218.5	988,389.6	713,226.9
Excise duties	227,708.8	94,357.7	78,595.7
Natural gas	133,112.1	20,000.0	—
Taxes on the use of natural resources	183,129.5	279,381.1	483,035.6
Taxes on international trade and transactions	335,975.5	532,538.2	919,093.8
Customs duties on imports	150,355.9	180,613.5	249,762.0
Customs duties on exports	185,619.6	351,924.7	618,207.0
Non-tax revenue	145,721.8	219,194.4	174,295.5
Income from state property and activities	83,158.8	165,612.1	73,004.0
Special budgetary funds	14,066.3	14,061.5	—
Contribution of unified social tax to federal budget	365,640.0	438,210.0	—
Total	2,417,791.8	2,742,850.4	3,326,041.1

Expenditure	2003	2004	2005
State administration	66,506.9	76,967.2	123,353.1
Judicial system	25,481.9	33,250.8	36,769.0
National defence	219,884.6	255,390.2	531,139.2
Public order and state security	190,080.1	250,025.3	398,889.5
Education	97,672.0	117,791.9	155,338.0
Health and sport	39,344.8	47,097.8	85,672.2
Social security and welfare	150,685.0	161,193.5	167,360.9
Servicing of government debt	277,510.1	287,570.6	244,150.4
Federal transfers	714,600.2	813,969.8	954,545.2
Total (incl. others)	2,123,424.9	2,400,751.2	3,047,929.3

2005 ('000 million roubles, budget execution excl. deficit financing): *Revenue:* Tax revenue 3,188.2 (Value added tax 1,472.2, Profit tax 377.6, Excise taxes 107.2, Social Tax (ST) revenues 267.5, Other 963.6); Non-tax revenue 1,936.9 (Customs duties 1,622.8, Other non-tax revenues 314.1); Total 5,125.1. *Expenditure:* Debt service 208.4 (Domestic 53.4, Foreign 154.9); Non-interest expenditure 3,303.8 (State administration 290.9, Defence, law and order 1,031.2, Social and cultural sphere 475.9, National economy 260.1, Financial aid to regions 486.7, Transfers to extrabudgetary accounts 758.9); Total 3,512.2.

2006 ('000 million roubles, budget execution excl. deficit financing): *Revenue:* Tax revenue 3,673.0 (Value added tax 1,510.9, Profit tax 509.9, Excise taxes 110.5, Social Tax (ST) revenues 315.8, Other 1,225.9); Non-tax revenue 2,603.3 (Customs duties 2,237.4, Other non-tax revenues 365.9); Total 6,276.3. *Expenditure:* Debt service 169.1 (Domestic 49.8, Foreign 119.3); Non-interest expenditure 4,112.3 (State administration 360.6, Defence, law and order 1,232.0, Social and cultural sphere 616.4, National economy 404.4, Financial aid to regions 584.6, Transfers to extrabudgetary accounts 914.3); Total 4,281.3.

Source: Ministry of Finance, Moscow.

THE RUSSIAN FEDERATION

INTERNATIONAL RESERVES
(US $ million at 31 December)

	2005	2006	2007
Gold (national valuation)	6,349.0	8,164.4	12,011.9
IMF special drawing rights	5.6	7.1	0.8
Reserve position in IMF	195.9	283.3	373.9
Foreign exchange	175,689.9	295,277.1	464,004.3
Total	182,240.4	303,731.9	476,390.9

Source: IMF, *International Financial Statistics*.

MONEY SUPPLY
('000 million roubles at 31 December)

	2005	2006	2007
Currency outside banks	2,009.2	2,785.2	3,702.2
Demand deposits at banks	1,805.7	2,754.4	3,825.9
Total money (incl. others)	3,858.5	5,598.4	7,582.1

Source: IMF, *International Financial Statistics*.

COST OF LIVING
(Consumer Price Index; base: previous year = 100)

	2004	2005	2006
Food and beverages	112.3	109.6	108.7
Other consumer goods	107.4	106.4	106.0
Services	117.7	121.0	113.9
All items	111.7	110.9	109.0

NATIONAL ACCOUNTS
('000 million roubles at current prices)

Expenditure on the Gross Domestic Product

	2005	2006	2007
Final consumption expenditure	14,318.9	17,616.0	21,810.9
Households	10,590.0	12,880.9	15,815.5
Non-profit institutions serving households	138.2	159.0	175.0
General government	3,590.7	4,576.1	5,820.4
Gross capital formation	4,338.7	5,736.8	8,102.0
Gross fixed capital formation. Acquisitions, less disposals, of valuables	3,836.9	4,968.4	6,951.1
Changes in inventories	501.8	768.4	1,150.9
Total domestic expenditure	18,657.6	23,352.8	29,912.9
Exports of goods and services	7,607.3	9,079.3	10,057.2
Less Imports of goods and services	4,648.3	5,656.8	7,186.7
Sub-total	21,616.6	26,775.3	32,783.4
Statistical discrepancy*	8.8	104.5	204.0
GDP in market prices	21,625.4	26,879.8	32,987.4

* Referring to the difference between the sum of the expenditure components and official estimates of GDP, compiled from the production approach.

Gross Domestic Product by Economic Activity

	2005	2006	2007
Agriculture, hunting and forestry	962.4	1,096.1	1,275.9
Fishing	65.5	68.3	72.8
Mining and quarrying	2,084.9	2,556.8	2,952.8
Manufacturing	3,521.0	4,185.6	5,387.4
Electricity, gas and water supply	632.5	754.8	886.2
Construction	1,012.0	1,211.4	1,671.0
Wholesale and retail trade; repair of motor vehicles, motorcycles and personal and household goods	3,649.4	4,761.9	5,840.9
Hotels and restaurants	170.6	199.4	256.9
Transport, storage and communication	1,925.1	2,282.2	2,669.6
Financial intermediation	759.0	1,050.1	1,347.9
Real estate, renting and business activities	1,848.2	2,344.8	2,936.9
Public administration and defence; compulsory social security	959.1	1,189.2	1,495.4
Education	494.1	621.8	790.1
Health and social work	566.3	770.2	968.8
Other community, social and personal services	326.0	428.4	548.3
Sub-total	18,976.4	23,521.0	29,100.9
Less Financial intermediation services indirectly measured	442.9	578.6	772.3
Gross value added in basic prices	18,533.3	22,942.5	28,328.6
Taxes, *less* subsidies, on products	3,092.1	3,937.3	4,658.7
GDP in market prices	21,625.4	26,879.8	32,987.4

BALANCE OF PAYMENTS
(US $ million)

	2004	2005	2006
Exports of goods f.o.b.	183,207	243,798	303,926
Imports of goods f.o.b.	−97,382	−125,434	−164,692
Trade balance	85,825	118,364	139,234
Exports of services	20,595	24,963	30,927
Imports of services	−33,287	−38,863	−44,739
Balance on goods and services	73,133	104,464	125,422
Other income received	11,998	17,382	29,010
Other income paid	−24,767	−36,371	−57,573
Balance on goods, services and income	60,364	85,475	96,860
Current transfers received	3,467	4,490	6,403
Current transfers paid	−4,317	−5,528	−7,940
Current balance	59,514	84,437	95,323
Capital account (net)	−1,624	−12,764	191
Direct investment abroad	−13,782	−12,767	−22,657
Direct investment from abroad	15,444	12,886	30,827
Portfolio investment assets	−3,820	−10,666	6,248
Portfolio investment liabilities	4,406	−828	9,124
Financial derivatives assets	758	858	1,242
Financial derivatives liabilities	−857	−1,091	−1,342
Other investment assets	−26,044	−32,623	−47,857
Other investment liabilities	19,331	45,846	30,340
Net errors and omissions	−6,436	−8,320	6,027
Overall balance	46,890	64,968	107,466

Source: IMF, *International Financial Statistics*.

THE RUSSIAN FEDERATION

External Trade

PRINCIPAL COMMODITIES
(US $ '000 million)

Imports	2004	2005	2006
Foodstuffs and agricultural raw materials (excl. textiles)	13.9	17.4	21.6
Mineral products	3.0	3.0	3.3
Chemical products and rubber	12.0	16.3	21.8
Leather, fur, and articles thereof	0.2	0.3	0.4
Wood, pulp and paper products	2.9	3.3	4.0
Textiles, textile articles and footwear	3.3	3.6	5.5
Metals, precious stones, and articles thereof	6.0	7.6	10.6
Machinery, vehicles and transport equipment	31.1	43.4	65.6
Other	3.2	3.7	4.9
Total	**75.6**	**98.7**	**137.5**

Exports	2004	2005	2006
Foodstuffs and agricultural raw materials (excl. textiles)	3.3	4.5	5.5
Mineral products	105.0	156.0	199.0
Chemical products and rubber	12.0	14.4	16.9
Leather, fur, and articles thereof	0.4	0.3	0.4
Wood, pulp and paper products	7.0	8.3	9.5
Textiles, textile articles and footwear	1.1	0.9	0.9
Metals, precious stones, and articles thereof	36.7	40.9	49.5
Machinery, vehicles and transport equipment	14.1	13.5	17.5
Other	2.1	2.5	3.1
Total	**181.7**	**241.5**	**302.0**

PRINCIPAL TRADING PARTNERS
(US $ million)

Imports	2004	2005	2006
Austria	918	1,211	1,840
Belarus	6,485	5,716	6,850
Belgium	1,176	1,476	2,169
Brazil	1,370	2,346	2,986
China, People's Republic	4,746	7,265	12,889
Czech Republic	835	989	1,528
Denmark	717	921	1,346
Finland	2,336	3,100	3,998
France	3,071	3,673	5,852
Germany	10,556	13,272	18,436
Hungary	740	1,100	1,866
India	651	784	968
Italy	3,199	4,416	5,719
Japan	3,941	5,834	7,779
Kazakhstan	3,429	3,225	3,839
Korea, Republic	2,026	4,005	6,774
Netherlands	1,375	1,941	2,680
Poland	2,310	2,747	3,400
Spain	879	1,227	1,950
Sweden	1,612	1,861	2,141
Turkey	1,231	1,738	2,670
Ukraine	6,100	7,819	9,218
United Kingdom	2,067	2,776	3,671
Uzbekistan	613	904	1,289
USA	3,200	4,563	6,397
Total (incl. others)	**75,569**	**98,707**	**137,548**

Exports	2004	2005	2006
Austria	1,115	2,353	3,353
Belarus	11,219	10,118	13,084
Belgium	1,820	2,464	2,633
China, People's Republic	10,105	13,048	15,751
Cyprus	5,710	5,096	4,551
Czech Republic	2,280	3,817	4,665
Finland	5,828	7,651	9,201
France	4,424	6,111	7,602
Germany	13,302	19,736	24,493
Greece	1,262	1,930	2,757
Hungary	3,254	5,004	6,229
India	2,502	2,314	2,988
Israel	1,437	1,538	1,558
Italy	12,086	19,053	25,111
Japan	3,404	3,740	4,670
Kazakhstan	4,664	6,526	8,969
Korea, Republic	1,963	2,359	2,527
Netherlands	15,272	24,614	35,862
Poland	5,700	8,623	11,479
Romania	1,819	3,041	3,272
Slovakia	2,423	3,190	4,582
Spain	1,748	2,823	460
Sweden	1,565	2,320	2,195
Switzerland	7,707	10,774	12,068
Taiwan	1,987	1,438	934
Turkey	7,440	10,841	14,377
Ukraine	10,770	12,402	14,979
United Kingdom	5,640	8,280	10,362
USA	6,624	6,323	8,922
Total (incl. others)	**181,662**	**241,473**	**301,976**

Transport

RAILWAYS
(traffic)

	2004	2005	2006
Paying passengers ('000 journeys)	1,335,000	1,339,000	1,337,000
Freight carried ('000 metric tons)	1,221,000	1,273,000	1,311,000
Passenger-km (million)	164,300	172,200	177,400
Freight ton-km (million)	1,802,000	1,858,000	1,951,000

ROAD TRAFFIC
(motor vehicles in use)

	1998	1999	2000
Passenger cars	18,819,600	19,717,800	20,353,000
Buses and coaches	627,500	633,200	640,100
Lorries and vans	4,260,000	4,387,800	4,400,600
Motorcycles and mopeds	7,165,900	6,328,600	n.a.

Source: IRF, *World Road Statistics*.

SHIPPING

Merchant Fleet
(registered at 31 December)

	2004	2005	2006
Number of vessels	3,802	3,722	3,656
Total displacement ('000 grt)	8,638.9	8,334.5	8,046.0

Source: Lloyd's Register-Fairplay, *World Fleet Statistics*.

International Sea-borne Freight Traffic
('000 metric tons, rounded data)

	2004	2005	2006
Goods loaded	8,200	9,100	7,700
Goods unloaded	1,100	700	400

Note: Annual data extrapolated from monthly averages.

Source: UN, *Monthly Bulletin of Statistics*.

THE RUSSIAN FEDERATION

CIVIL AVIATION
(traffic on scheduled services)

	2001	2002	2003
Kilometres flown (million)	568	653	602
Passengers carried ('000)	20,301	20,892	22,723
Passenger-km (million)	48,321	49,890	53,894
Total ton-km (million)	5,292	5,580	6,018

Source: UN, *Statistical Yearbook*.

Tourism

FOREIGN VISITOR ARRIVALS
('000, incl. excursionists)

Country of origin	2003	2004	2005
Armenia	331.9	377.3	386.5
Azerbaijan	826.0	823.5	824.6
China, People's Republic	679.6	813.1	798.7
Estonia	406.0	521.1	510.3
Finland	1,154.1	1,092.3	1,115.5
Georgia	737.9	320.8	229.0
Germany	516.2	567.2	550.8
Kazakhstan	2,674.9	2,761.5	2,453.2
Kyrgyzstan	272.0	306.6	293.6
Latvia	345.0	371.1	709.3
Lithuania	873.8	949.6	1,251.5
Moldova	751.6	804.9	837.1
Poland	1,232.9	1,128.5	1,195.9
Tajikistan	366.9	456.4	466.5
Ukraine	7,686.2	6,683.2	6,416.9
USA	280.8	308.3	280.9
Uzbekistan	554.0	677.0	660.6
Total (incl. others)	22,521.1	22,064.2	22,200.6

Receipts from tourism (US $ million, incl. passenger transport): 5,879 in 2003; 6,958 in 2004; 7,402 in 2005.

Source: World Tourism Organization.

Communications Media

	2003	2004	2005
Telephones ('000 main lines in use)	36,993	39,616	40,100
Mobile cellular telephones ('000 subscribers)	36,500	74,420	120,000
Personal computers ('000 in use)	15,364	15,000	17,400
Internet users ('000)	10,000	18,500	21,800
Broadband subscribers ('000)	343.0	675.0	1,589.0

2006: Internet users ('000) 25,689.

Source: International Telecommunication Union.

Television receivers ('000 in use): 79,000 in 2000.

Radio receivers ('000 in use): 61,500 in 1997.

Facsimile machines (number in use): 52,900 in 1998.

Book production (including pamphlets): 36,237 titles in 1996 (421,387,000 copies).

Daily newspapers: 285 in 1996 (average circulation 15,517,000 copies); 333 in 2000.

Non-daily newspapers: 4,596 in 1996 (average circulation 98,558,000 copies); 10,188 in 2000.

Other periodicals: 2,751 in 1996 (average circulation 387,832,000 copies).

Sources: UNESCO, *Statistical Yearbook*; and UN, *Statistical Yearbook*.

Education

(2006/07, except where otherwise specified)

	Institutions	Students*	Teachers
Pre-primary	46,200	4,713,000	610,828†
Primary and general secondary	61,042	14,798,000	1,537,000*
Vocational secondary	2,847	2,514,000	136,400
Higher	1,090	7,310,000	387,300*‡

* Rounded figure(s).
† 2004/05.
‡ 2005/06.

Adult literacy rate (UNESCO estimates): 99.4% (males 99.7%; females 99.2%) in 2002 (Source: UNNESCO Institute for Statistics).

Directory

The Constitution

The current Constitution of the Russian Federation came into force on 12 December 1993, following its approval by a majority of participants in a nation-wide plebiscite. It replaced the Constitution originally adopted on 12 April 1978, but amended many times after 1990.

THE PRINCIPLES OF THE CONSTITUTIONAL SYSTEM

The Russian Federation (Russia) is a democratic, federative, law-based state with a republican form of government. Its multi-ethnic people bear its sovereignty and are the sole source of authority. State power is divided between the legislative, executive and judicial branches, which are independent of one another. Ideological pluralism and a multi-party political system are recognized. The state is secular.

HUMAN AND CIVIL RIGHTS AND FREEDOMS

Basic human rights and freedoms of the Russian citizen are guaranteed regardless of sex, race, ethnicity or religion. The rights to life and to freedom and personal inviolability are guaranteed. The principles of freedom of movement, freedom of expression and freedom of conscience are upheld. Censorship is prohibited. Citizens are guaranteed the right to vote in and to contest state and local elections and to participate in referendums. Individuals shall have equal access to state employment, and may establish trade unions and public associations. The State is committed to the protection of motherhood and childhood and the granting of social security, state pensions and social benefits. Each person has the right to housing. Health care and education are free of charge. Basic general education is compulsory. Citizens are guaranteed the right to receive qualified legal assistance. Payment of statutory taxes and levies is obligatory, as is military service.

THE ORGANIZATION OF THE FEDERATION

The federal subjects (territorial units) of the Federation are named. Russian is declared the state language, but all peoples of the Federation are guaranteed the right to preserve their native tongue. The state flag, emblem and anthem of the Federation are established by constitutional law. The separate roles of the authority of the Federation, as distinct from that of the joint authority of the Federation and the federal subjects, are defined. The powers of the federal executive bodies and the executive bodies of the members of the Federation are defined.

THE PRESIDENT OF THE RUSSIAN FEDERATION

The powers and responsibilities of the Head of State, the President of the Russian Federation, are defined. The President, who must be aged at least 35 years, and have been resident in Russia for at least 10 years, is elected to office for a term of four years by universal, direct suffrage, for no more than two consecutive terms. The President appoints the Chairman of the Government (Prime Minister) of the Russian Federation, with the approval of the Gosudarstvennaya Duma (State Duma), and may dismiss the Government. The President is entitled to chair sessions of the Government. The President's responsibilities include scheduling referendums and elections to the Gosudarstvennaya Duma, dissolving the Gosudarstvennaya Duma, submitting legislative proposals to the Gosudarstvennaya Duma, promulgating federal laws and nominating candidates, subject to approval by the Federalnoye Sobraniye, to the posts of Chairman of the Central Bank, judges of the Constitutional Court, the Supreme Court and the Supreme Arbitration Court, and of Prosecutor-General. The President forms and heads the Security Council, the status of which is determined by federal law. The President is responsible for the foreign policy of the Russian Federation. The President is Commander-in-Chief of the Armed Forces and may introduce martial law or a state of emergency under certain conditions.

If the President is unable to carry out the presidential duties, these will be assumed by the Chairman of the Government. The acting President, however, will not possess the full powers of the President, such as the right to dissolve the Gosudarstvennaya Duma or to order a referendum. The President may only be removed from office by the Sovet Federatsii (Federation Council) on the grounds of a serious accusation by the Gosudarstvennaya Duma.

THE FEDERALNOYE SOBRANIYE

The Federalnoye Sobraniye (Federal Assembly) is the highest representative and legislative body in the Russian Federation. It comprises two chambers: the Sovet Federatsii (upper chamber) and the Gosudarstvennaya Duma (lower chamber). The Sovet Federatsii comprises two representatives from each member of the Russian Federation, one appointed by its legislative and one by its executive body. The Gosudarstvennaya Duma is composed of 450 deputies, elected for a term of four years. The deputies of the Russian Federation must be over 21 years of age and may not hold government office or any other paid job.

Both chambers of the Federalnoye Sobraniye elect their Chairman and Deputy Chairmen. The powers of the Sovet Federatsii include the approval of the President's decrees on martial law and a state of emergency, the scheduling of presidential elections and the impeachment of the President. The Gosudarstvennaya Duma has the power to approve the President's nominee to the office of Chairman of the Government. Both chambers of the Federalnoye Sobraniye adopt resolutions by a majority vote of the total number of members. All federal and federal constitutional laws are adopted by the Gosudarstvennaya Duma and submitted for approval first to the Sovet Federatsii and then to the President. If the Sovet Federatsii or the President reject proposed legislation it is submitted for repeat consideration to one or both chambers of the Federalnoye Sobraniye.

The Gosudarstvennaya Duma may be dissolved by the President if it adopts two successive votes of 'no confidence' in the Government. If the Gosudarstvennaya Duma rejects three candidates to the office of Chairman, the President will appoint the Chairman, dissolve the Gosudarstvennaya Duma and order new elections. However, it may not be dissolved during a period of martial law or a state of emergency or in the case of charges being lodged against the President. A newly elected Gosudarstvennaya Duma should be convened no later than four months after dissolution of the previous parliament.

THE GOVERNMENT OF THE RUSSIAN FEDERATION

The executive authority of the Russian Federation is vested in the Government, which comprises the Chairman, the Deputy Chairmen and federal ministers. The Chairman is appointed by the President and his nomination approved by the Gosudarstvennaya Duma. The Government submits the federal budget to the Gosudarstvennaya Duma and supervises its execution, guarantees the implementation of a uniform state policy, conducts foreign policy, ensures the country's defence and security.

Regulations for the activity of the Government are determined by a federal constitutional law. The Government adopts resolutions and directives, which may be vetoed by the President. The Government must submit its resignation to a newly elected President of the Russian Federation, which the President may accept or reject. A vote of 'no confidence' in the Government may be adopted by the Gosudarstvennaya Duma. The President can reject this decision or demand the Government's resignation. If the Gosudarstvennaya Duma adopts a second vote of 'no confidence' within three months, the President will announce the Government's resignation or dissolve the Gosudarstvennaya Duma.

JUDICIAL POWER

Justice is administered by means of constitutional, civil, administrative and criminal judicial proceedings. Judges in the Russian Federation must be aged 25 or over, have a higher legal education and have a record of work in the legal profession of no less than five years. Judges are independent, irremovable and inviolable. Proceedings in judicial courts are open. No criminal case shall be considered in the absence of a defendant. Judicial proceedings may be conducted with the participation of a jury.

The Constitutional Court comprises 19 judges. The Court decides cases regarding the compliance of federal laws and enactments, the constitutions, statutes, laws and other enactments of the federal subjects, state treaties and international treaties that have not yet come into force. The Constitutional Court settles disputes about competence among state bodies. Enactments or provisions thereof that have been judged unconstitutional by the Court are invalid. At the request of the Sovet Federatsii, the Court will pronounce its judgment on bringing an accusation against the President of the Russian Federation.

The Supreme Court is the highest judicial authority on civil, criminal, administrative and other cases within the jurisdiction of the common plea courts. The Supreme Arbitration Court is the highest authority in settling economic and other disputes within the jurisdiction of the courts of arbitration.

The judges of the three higher courts are appointed by the Federation Council on the recommendation of the President. Judges of other federal courts are appointed by the President.

The Prosecutor's Office is a single centralized system. The Prosecutor-General is appointed and dismissed by the Sovet Federatsii on the recommendation of the President. All other prosecutors are appointed by the Prosecutor-General.

LOCAL SELF-GOVERNMENT

The exercise of local self-government is provided for through referendums, elections and through elected and other bodies. The responsibilities of local self-government bodies include: independently managing municipal property; forming, approving and executing the local budget; establishing local taxes and levies; and maintaining law and order.

CONSTITUTIONAL AMENDMENTS AND REVISION OF THE CONSTITUTION

No provision contained in Chapters One (on The Principles of the Constitutional System), Two (on Human and Civil Rights and Freedoms) and Nine (on Constitutional Amendments and Revision of the Constitution) may be reviewed by the Federalnoye Sobraniye, while amendments to the remaining Chapters may be passed in accordance with the procedure for a federal constitutional law. If a proposal for a review of the provisions of Chapters One, Two and Nine wins a three-fifths' majority in both chambers, a Constitutional Assembly will be convened.

CONCLUDING AND TRANSITIONAL PROVISIONS

Should the provisions of a federal treaty contravene those of the Constitution, the constitutional provisions will apply. All laws and other legal acts enforced before the Constitution came into effect will remain valid unless they fail to comply with the Constitution.

The Government

HEAD OF STATE

President of the Russian Federation: Dmitrii A. Medvedev (elected 2 March 2008; inaugurated 7 May).

THE GOVERNMENT
(May 2008)

Chairman: Vladimir V. Putin.

First Deputy Chairman: Viktor A. Zubkov.

First Deputy Chairman: Igor I. Shuvalov.

Deputy Chairman: Aleksandr D. Zhukov.

Deputy Chairman: Sergei B. Ivanov.

Deputy Chairman, Minister of Finance: Aleksei L. Kudrin.

Deputy Chairman: Igor I. Sechin.

Deputy Chairman, Head of the Government Staff: Sergei S. Sobyanin.

First Deputy Chairman of the Military-Industry Commission, Minister: Vladislav N. Putilin.

Minister of Agriculture: Aleksei V. Gordeyev.

Minister of Civil Defence, Emergencies and Clean-up Operations: Col-Gen. Sergei K. Shoigu.

Minister of Communications and the Mass Media: Igor O. Shchegolev.

Minister of Culture: Aleksandr A. Abdeyev.

Minister of Defence: Anatolii E. Serdyukov.

Minister of Economic Development: Elvira S. Nabiullina.

Minister of Education and Science: Andrei A. Fursenko.

Minister of Energy: Sergei I. Shmatko.

THE RUSSIAN FEDERATION

Minister of Foreign Affairs: SERGEI V. LAVROV.
Minister of Health and Social Development: TATYANA A. GOLIKOVA.
Minister of Industry and Trade: VIKTOR V. KHRISTENKO.
Minister of Information and Communications Technologies: LEONID D. REIMAN.
Minister of Internal Affairs: Col-Gen. RASHID G. NURGALIYEV.
Minister of Justice: ALEKSANDR V. KONOVALOV.
Minister of Natural Resources and Ecology: YURII P. TRUTNEV.
Minister of Regional Development: DMITRII N. KOZAK.
Minister of Sport, Youth and Tourism: VITALII L. MUTKO.
Minister of Transport: IGOR YE. LEVITIN.

MINISTRIES

Office of the President: 103132 Moscow, Staraya pl. 4; tel. (495) 925-35-81; fax (495) 206-07-66; e-mail president@gov.ru; internet www.kremlin.ru.

Office of the Government: 103274 Moscow, Krasnopresnenskaya nab. 2; tel. (495) 205-57-35; fax (495) 205-42-19; internet www.government.ru.

Ministry of Agriculture: 107139 Moscow, Orlikov per. 1/11; tel. (495) 207-83-86; fax (495) 207-95-80; e-mail info@mcx.ru; internet www.mcx.ru.

Ministry of Civil Defence, Emergencies and Clean-up Operations: 109012 Moscow, Teatralnyi proyezd 3; tel. (495) 926-39-01; fax (495) 923-57-45; e-mail info@mchs.gov.ru; internet www.mchs.gov.ru.

Ministry of Communications and the Mass Media: Moscow.

Ministry of Culture: 109074 Moscow, Kitaigorodskii proyezd 7; tel. (495) 625-11-95; internet www.mkmk.ru.

Ministry of Defence: 105175 Moscow, ul. Myasnitskaya 37; tel. (495) 293-38-54; fax (495) 296-84-36; internet www.mil.ru.

Ministry of Economic Development: 125993 Moscow, ul. 1-ya Tverskaya-Yamskaya 1/3; tel. (495) 200-03-47; e-mail presscenter@economy.gov.ru; internet www.economy.gov.ru.

Ministry of Education and Science: 103905 Moscow, ul. Tverskaya 11; tel. (495) 237-97-63; internet www.mon.gov.ru.

Ministry of Energy: Moscow.

Ministry of Finance: 109097 Moscow, ul. Ilinka 9; tel. (495) 298-91-01; fax (495) 925-08-89; internet www.minfin.ru.

Ministry of Foreign Affairs: 119200 Moscow, Smolenskaya-Sennaya pl. 32/34; tel. (495) 244-16-06; fax (495) 230-21-30; e-mail ministry@mid.ru; internet www.mid.ru.

Ministry of Health and Social Development: 127994 Moscow, Rakhmanovskii per. 3/25; tel. (495) 927-28-48; fax (495) 928-58-15; internet www.mzsrrf.ru.

Ministry of Industry and Trade: 109074 Moscow, Kitaigorodskii proyezd 7; tel. (495) 710-55-00; fax (495) 710-57-22; e-mail info@mte.gov.ru; internet www.minprom.gov.ru.

Ministry of Information and Communications Technologies: 125375 Moscow, ul. Tverskaya 7; tel. (495) 771-81-00; fax (495) 771-87-18; internet www.minsvyaz.ru.

Ministry of Internal Affairs: 119049 Moscow, ul. Zhitnaya 16; tel. (495) 239-69-71; fax (495) 293-59-98; e-mail mvd12@mvdrf.ru; internet www.mvd.ru.

Ministry of Justice: 119991 Moscow, ul. Zhitnaya 14; tel. (495) 955-59-99; fax (495) 916-29-03; internet www.minjust.ru.

Ministry of Natural Resources and Ecology: 123242 Moscow, ul. B. Gruzinskaya 4/6; tel. (495) 254-48-00; fax (495) 254-43-10; e-mail admin@mnr.gov.ru; internet www.mnr.gov.ru.

Ministry of Regional Development: 127994 Moscow, ul. Sadovaya-Samotechnaya 10/23/1; tel. (495) 980-25-47; fax (495) 699-38-41; e-mail info@minregion.ru; internet www.minregion.ru.

Ministry of Sport, Youth and Tourism: Moscow.

Ministry of Transport: 109012 Moscow, ul. Rozhdestvenka 1/1; tel. (495) 926-10-00; fax (495) 200-33-56; e-mail mcc@morflot.ru; internet www.mintrans.ru.

President

Presidential Election, 2 March 2008

Candidates	Votes	%
Dmitrii A. Medvedev (United Russia)	52,530,712	70.28
Gennadii A. Zyuganov (Communist Party of the Russian Federation)	13,243,550	17.72
Vladimir V. Zhirinovskii (Liberal Democratic Party of Russia)	6,988,510	9.36
Andrei V. Bogdanov (Independent)	968,344	1.30
Total*	74,746,649	100.00

*Including 1,005,533 invalid votes, equivalent to 1.34% of the total.

Legislature

The Federalnoye Sobraniye (Federal Assembly) is a bicameral legislative body, comprising the Sovet Federatsii (Federation Council) and the Gosudarstvennaya Duma (State Duma).

Sovet Federatsii (Federation Council)

103426 Moscow, ul. B. Dmitrovka 26; tel. (495) 203-90-74; fax (495) 203-46-17; e-mail post_sf@gov.ru; internet www.council.gov.ru.

The Sovet Federatsii is the upper chamber of the Federalnoye Sobraniye. It comprises two deputies appointed from each of the constituent members (federal territorial units) of the Russian Federation, representing the legislative and executive branches of power in each republic and region.

Chairman: SERGEI M. MIRONOV.

Gosudarstvennaya Duma (State Duma)

103265 Moscow, Okhotnyi ryad 1; tel. (495) 292-83-10; fax (495) 292-94-64; e-mail www@duma.ru; internet www.duma.ru.

Chairman: BORIS V. GRYZLOV.

General Election, 2 December 2007

Parties and blocs	Votes	%	Seats
United Russia	44,714,241	64.30	315
Communist Party of the Russian Federation	8,046,886	11.57	57
Liberal Democratic Party of Russia	5,660,823	8.14	40
A Just Russia: Motherland/Pensioners/Life	5,383,639	7.74	38
Agrarian Party of Russia	1,600,234	2.30	—
Yabloko	1,108,985	1.59	—
Civic Force	733,604	1.05	—
Union of Rightist Forces	669,444	0.96	—
Patriots of Russia	615,417	0.89	—
Party of Social Justice	154,083	0.22	—
Democratic Party of Russia	89,780	0.13	—
Invalid votes	759,929	1.09	—
Total	69,537,065	100.00	450

Election Commission

Central Electoral Commission of the Russian Federation (Tsentralnaya izbiratelnaya komissiya Rossiiskoi Federatsii): 109012 Moscow, B. Cherkassii per. 9; tel. (495) 606-79-57; e-mail info@cikrf.ru; internet www.cikrf.ru; Chair. VLADIMIR CHUROV.

Political Organizations

Legislation approved by President Vladimir Putin in July 2001 required each political party to have at least 10,000 members, including no fewer than 100 members in at least 50 of the 89 subjects of the Russian Federation, in order to register and to function legally. The elections to the Gosudarstvennaya Duma (State Duma), held on 7 December 2003, were contested by 27 electoral associations (parties) and five electoral blocs. In December 2004 President Putin signed into law a series of amendments to the legislation of 2001, notably increasing the minimum membership required for registration of a political party to 50,000, with the additional requirement that at least 500 members of the party must be resident in more than one-half of the subjects (territorial units)

THE RUSSIAN FEDERATION

of the Federation, with at least 250 members in each of the remaining regions. Parties previously registered under the original legislation were obliged to meet the new membership requirements by 1 January 2006. In July 2005 new legislation increased the threshold for parties to obtain representation in the Gosudarstvennaya Duma from 5% to 7%, while single-mandate constituencies (which hitherto provided one-half of deputies) were to be abolished. Based on the requirements of the amended legislation. only 11 parties were officially registered to contest elections to the Gosudarstvennaya Duma in December 2007.

Agrarian Party of Russia (APR) (Agrarnaya partiya Rossii): 107045 Moscow, per. B. Golovin 20/1; tel. (495) 207-99-51; fax (495) 207-99-01; e-mail press@agroparty.ru; internet www.agroparty.ru; f. 1993; left-wing, supports the agricultural sector; Chair. VLADIMIR N. PLOTNIKOV; 167,580 mems (2006).

Civic Force (Grazhdanskaya sila): 101000 Moscow, ul. Myasnitskaya 16; tel. (495) 229-32-09; fax (495) 777-27-62; e-mail fps@gr-sila.ru; internet www.gr-sila.ru; f. 2004 by fmr mems of the Union of Rightist Forces (q.v.); fmrly Free Russia (Svobodnaya Rossiya); name changed as above 2007; Leader MIKHAIL YU. BARSHCHEVSKII.

Communist Party of the Russian Federation (CPRF) (Kommunisticheskaya partiya Rossiiskoi Federatsii—KPRF): 103051 Moscow, per. M. Sukharevskii 3/1; tel. (495) 628-04-90; fax (495) 292-90-50; e-mail kprf2005@yandex.ru; internet www.kprf.ru; f. 1993; claims succession to the Russian Communist Party, which was banned in 1991; membership of the People's Patriotic Union of Russia (Narodno-patrioticheskii soyuz Rossii—NPSR) in dispute following split in party between factions headed by Zyuganov and Gennadii Semigin at 10th Party Congress in July 2004; Chair. of Central Committee GENNADII A. ZYUGANOV; 184,181 mems (2006).

Democratic Party of Russia (Demokraticheskaya partiya Rossiya): 127287 Moscow, ul. Poltavskaya 18; tel. (495) 611-30-11; fax (495) 611-56-70; internet www.democrats.ru; f. 1990; liberal-conservative; Chair., Central Committee ANDREI V. BOGDANOV; Chair., Exec. Committee VYACHESLAV N. SMIRNOV; 82,183 mems (2006).

A Just Russia (AJR) (Spravedlivaya Rossiya): 107031 Moscow, ul. B. Dmitrovka 32/1; tel. (495) 650-38-80; e-mail nfo@spravedlivo.ru; internet www.spravedlivo.ru; f. 2006 by merger of Motherland, Russian Party of Life and Russian Pensioners' Party; absorbed People's Party of the Russian Federation in Apr. 2007; statist, patriotic party; Chair. SERGEI M. MIRONOV.

Liberal Democratic Party of Russia (LDPR) (Liberalno-demokraticheskaya partiya Rossii): 103045 Moscow, Lukov per. 9; tel. (495) 692-11-95; fax (495) 692-92-42; e-mail info@ldpr.ru; internet www.ldpr.ru; f. 1988; nationalist; generally supportive of Pres. Putin; Chair. VLADIMIR V. ZHIRINOVSKII; 116,387 mems (2006).

Party of Social Justice (Partiya Sotsialnoi Spravedlivosti): 109147 Moscow, ul. Taganskaya 31/22; tel. (499) 763-36-86; e-mail region@nasled.ru; internet www.pp-pss.ru; f. 2002; nationalist, statist; contested 2003 elections to the Gosudarstvennaya Duma in electoral bloc with Russian Pensioners' Party; Leader ALEKSEI I. PODBEREZKIN; 60,446 mems (2006).

Patriots of Russia (Patrioty Rossii): 119121 Moscow, Smolenskii bulv. 11/2; tel. (495) 692-15-50; fax (495) 692-15-50; e-mail partia-korn@rambler.ru; internet www.patriot-rus.ru; f. 2002; fmrly Russian Party of Labour; Leader GENNADII YU. SEMIGIN.

Union of Rightist Forces (URF) (Soyuz pravykh sil—SPS): 109544 Moscow, ul. M. Andronyevskaya 15; tel. (495) 232-04-06; e-mail edit@sps.ru; internet www.sps.ru; f. 1999 as alliance of nine movements, which merged to form one party in 2001; pro-market, economically liberal; Exec. Dir OLEG N. PERMYAKOV; Chair. of the Federal Political Council NIKITA YU. BELYKH; 14,646 mems (2005).

United Russia (UR) (Yedinaya Rossiya): 129110 Moscow, Pereyaslavskii per. 4; tel. (495) 786-82-89; fax (495) 975-30-78; e-mail centrpr@edinros.ru; internet www.er.ru; f. 2001 as Unity and Fatherland—United Russia, on the basis of Unity (f. 1999, incorporating Our Home is Russia), Fatherland (f. 1999, and led by Mayor of Moscow YURII LUZHKOV) and the All Russia grouping of regional governors; pragmatic centrist grouping that promotes moderate economic reforms and a strong state; Chair VLADIMIR V. PUTIN; Chair of Supreme Council BORIS V. GRYZLOV; 659,654 mems (2006).

Yabloko Russian Democratic Party (Rossiiskaya demokraticheskaya partiya 'Yabloko'): 119034 Moscow, per. M. Levshinskii 7/3; tel. (495) 201-43-79; fax (495) 292-34-50; e-mail admin@yabloko.ru; internet www.yabloko.ru; f. 1993 on the basis of the Yavlinskii-Boldyrev-Lukin electoral bloc; democratic, politically and socially liberal; Chair. GRIGORII A. YAVLINSKII; 60,440 mems (2006).

Diplomatic Representation

EMBASSIES IN RUSSIA

Afghanistan: 121069 Moscow, ul. Povarskaya 42; tel. (495) 290-16-80; fax (495) 290-01-46; e-mail safarat_moscow@yahoo.com; Ambassador ZALMAI AZIZ.

Albania: 119049 Moscow, ul. Mytnaya 3/8; tel. (495) 230-77-32; fax (495) 230-76-35; e-mail embassy.moscow@mfa.gov.al; Ambassador TEODOR LACO.

Algeria: 103051 Moscow, Krapivinskii per. 1A; tel. (495) 937-46-00; fax (495) 937-46-25; e-mail algamb@ntl.ru; internet www.algerianembassy.ru; Ambassador AMAR ABBA.

Angola: 119590 Moscow, ul. U. Palme 6; tel. (495) 939-95-18; fax (495) 956-18-80; e-mail angomosc@col.ru; Ambassador SAMUEL TITO ARMANDO.

Argentina: 119017 Moscow, ul. B. Ordynka 72; tel. (495) 502-10-20; fax (495) 502-10-21; e-mail efrus@co.ru; Ambassador LEOPOLDO BRAVO.

Armenia: 101990 Moscow, Armyanskii per. 2; tel. (495) 924-32-43; fax (495) 924-45-35; e-mail info@armen.ru; internet www.armenianembassy.ru; Ambassador ARMEN B. SMBATIAN.

Australia: 109028 Moscow, Podkolokolii per. 10A/2; tel. (495) 956-60-70; fax (495) 956-61-70; e-mail austembmos@dfat.gov.au; internet www.russia.embassy.gov.au; Ambassador ROBERT TYSON.

Austria: 119034 Moscow, Starokonyushennyi per. 1; tel. (495) 502-95-12; fax (495) 937-42-69; e-mail moskau-ob@bmeia.gv.at; internet www.aussenministerium.at/moskau; Ambassador Dr MARTIN VUKOVICH.

Azerbaijan: 125009 Moscow, Leontyevskii per. 16; tel. (495) 629-43-32; fax (495) 220-50-72; e-mail azerirus@cnt.ru; internet www.azembassy.msk.ru; Ambassador POLAD BULBULOĞLU.

Bahrain: 109017 Moscow, ul. B. Ordynka 18/1; tel. (495) 953-00-22; fax (495) 953-74-74; e-mail moscowbah@yahoo.com; Ambassador ABDULHAMEED ALI HASAN ALI.

Bangladesh: 119121 Moscow, Zemledelcheskii per. 6; tel. (495) 246-78-04; fax (495) 248-31-85; e-mail moscow.bangla@com2com.ru; internet www.bangladeshembassy.ru; Ambassador AMIR HUSSAIN SIKDER.

Belarus: 101990 Moscow, ul. Maroseika 17/6; tel. (495) 777-66-44; fax (495) 777-66-33; e-mail mail@embassybel.ru; internet www.embassybel.ru; Ambassador VASIL DALHALYOV.

Belgium: 121069 Moscow, ul. M. Molchanovka 7; tel. (495) 780-03-31; fax (495) 780-03-32; e-mail moscow@diplobel.org; internet www.diplomatie.be/moscow; Ambassador VINCENT MERTENS DE WILMARS.

Benin: 127006 Moscow, Uspenskii per. 7; tel. (495) 299-23-60; fax (495) 200-02-26; e-mail ambabeninmoscou@hotmail.com; Ambassador VISSINTO AYI D'ALMEIDA.

Bolivia: 115191 Moscow, ul. Serpukhovskii Val 8/135–137; tel. (495) 954-06-30; fax (495) 958-07-55; e-mail embolrus@online.ru; internet www.emborus.com; Ambassador SERGIO SÁNCHEZ BALLIVIÁN.

Bosnia and Herzegovina: 119590 Moscow, ul. Mosfilmovskaya 50/1/484; tel. (499) 147-64-88; fax (499) 147-64-89; e-mail embassybih@mail.ru; Ambassador ENVER HALILOVIĆ.

Brazil: 121069 Moscow, ul. B. Nikitskaya 54; tel. (495) 363-03-66; fax (495) 363-03-67; e-mail brasrus@brasemb.ru; internet www.brasemb.ru; Ambassador CARLOS AUGUSTO REGO SANTOS-NEVES.

Brunei: 121059 Moscow, Berezhkovskaya nab. 2, Radisson-Slavyanskaya Hotel, kom. 440–441; tel. (495) 941-82-16; fax (495) 941-82-14; e-mail moscow.russia@mfa.gov.bn; Ambassador JANIN BIN ERIH.

Bulgaria: 119590 Moscow, ul. Mosfilmovskaya 66; tel. (495) 143-67-00; fax (495) 232-33-02; e-mail bulemrus@bolgaria.ru; internet www.bolgaria.ru; Ambassador PLAMEN I. GROZDANOV.

Burundi: 119049 Moscow, Kaluzhskaya pl. 1/226–227; tel. (495) 230-25-64; fax (495) 230-20-09; e-mail bdiam@mail.cnt.ru; Ambassador RENOVAT NDAYIRUKIYE.

Cambodia: 121002 Moscow, Starokonyushennyi per. 16; tel. (495) 637-47-36; fax (495) 956-65-73; e-mail cambemoscow@stream.ru; Ambassador KHIEU THAVIKA.

Cameroon: 121069 Moscow, ul. Povarskaya 40, BP 136; tel. (495) 290-65-49; fax (495) 290-61-16; Ambassador ANDRÉ NGONGANG OUANDJI.

Canada: 119002 Moscow, Starokonyushennyi per. 23; tel. (495) 925-60-00; fax (495) 925-60-25; e-mail mosco@international.gc.ca; internet www.dfait-maeci.gc.ca/missions/russia-russie/menu.asp; Ambassador RALPH JAMES LYSYSHYN.

Central African Republic: 117571 Moscow, ul. 26-i Bakinskikh Kommissarov 9/124–125; tel. (495) 434-45-20; fax (495) 933-28-99; Ambassador CLAUDE BERNARD BELOUM.

THE RUSSIAN FEDERATION

Chad: 117393 Moscow, ul. A. Pilyugina 14/3/895–896; tel. (495) 936-17-63; fax (495) 936-11-01; Ambassador Djibrine Abdoul.

Chile: 119002 Moscow, Denezhnii per. 7/1; tel. (495) 241-01-45; fax (495) 241-68-67; e-mail echileru@col.ru; internet www.embachilerusia.ru; Ambassador Cesar Augusto Parra Muñoz.

China, People's Republic: 117330 Moscow, ul. Druzhby 6; tel. (495) 956-11-68; fax (495) 956-11-69; e-mail chiemb@microdin.ru; internet ru.china-embassy.org; Ambassador Liu Guchang.

Colombia: 119121 Moscow, ul. Burdenko 20/2; tel. (495) 248-30-42; fax (495) 248-30-25; e-mail emoscu@cancilleria.gov.co; Ambassador Diego José Tóbon Echeverri.

Congo, Democratic Republic: 117556 Moscow, Simferopolskii bulv. 7A/49-50; tel. and fax (495) 113-83-48; e-mail rdcambamoscou@yahoo.fr; Ambassador Raphaël Mutombo Tshitambwe.

Congo, Republic: 119034 Moscow, Kropotinskii per. 12; tel. (495) 236-33-68; fax (495) 236-41-16; Ambassador Jean-Pierre Louyébo.

Costa Rica: 121615 Moscow, Rublevskoye shosse 26/1/23–24; tel. (495) 415-40-14; fax (495) 415-40-42; e-mail consulcr@rol.ru; Ambassador Isabel Montero de la Cámara.

Côte d'Ivoire: 119034 Moscow, Korobeinikov per. 14/9; tel. (495) 637-24-00; fax (495) 637-21-57; e-mail ambacimow@hotmail.com; internet ambaci-russie.org; Ambassador Gnagno Philibert Fagnidi.

Croatia: 119034 Moscow, Korobeinikov per. 16/10; tel. (495) 637-38-68; fax (495) 637-46-24; e-mail croemb.russia@mvpei.hr; internet ru.mvp.hr; Ambassador Božo Kovačević.

Cuba: 119017 Moscow, ul. B. Ordynka 66; tel. and fax (495) 933-79-57; e-mail embsecret@ecurusia.ru; Ambassador Jorge Martí Martínez.

Cyprus: 121069 Moscow, ul. Povarskaya 9; tel. (495) 744-29-44; fax (495) 744-29-45; e-mail moscowembassy@mfa.gov.cy; internet www.mfa.gov.cy/embassymoscow; Ambassador Leonidas Pantelides.

Czech Republic: 123056 Moscow, ul. Yu. Fuchika 12/14; tel. (495) 251-05-44; fax (045) 250-15-23; e-mail moscow@embassy.mzv.cz; internet www.mfa.cz/moscow; Ambassador Miroslav Kostelka.

Denmark: 119034 Moscow, Prechistenskii per. 9; tel. (495) 642-68-00; fax (495) 775-01-91; e-mail mowamb@um.dk; internet www.ambmoskva.um.dk; Ambassador Per Carlsen.

Ecuador: 103064 Moscow, Gorokhovskii per. 12; tel. (499) 261-55-27; fax (499) 267-70-79; e-mail embajada@ecuaemb.ru; internet www.ecuaemb.ru; Ambassador Patricio Chávez.

Egypt: 119034 Moscow, Kropotkinskii per. 12; tel. (495) 246-02-34; fax (495) 246-10-64; e-mail egyemb_moscow@yahoo.com; Ambassador Ezzat Saad As-Sayed Al-Buraey.

Equatorial Guinea: 119017 Moscow, Pogorelskii per. 7/1; tel. (495) 953-27-66; Ambassador Fausto Abeso Fuma.

Eritrea: 129090 Moscow, ul. Meshchanskaya 17; tel. (495) 631-06-20; fax (495) 631-37-67; Ambassador Teklay Minassie Asgedom.

Estonia: 125009 Moscow, M. Kislovskii per. 5; tel. (495) 737-36-40; fax (495) 737-36-46; e-mail embassy.moskva@mfa.ee; internet www.estemb.ru; Ambassador Marina Kaljurand.

Ethiopia: 129041 Moscow, Orlovo-Davydovskii per. 6; tel. (495) 680-16-16; fax (495) 680-66-08; e-mail eth-emb@col.ru; Ambassador Dr Teketel Forsido.

Finland: 119034 Moscow, Kropotkinskii per. 15/17; tel. (495) 787-41-74; fax (495) 247-33-80; e-mail sanomat.mos@formin.fi; internet www.finland.org.ru; Ambassador Harry Gustaf Helenius.

France: 119049 Moscow, ul. B. Yakimanka 45; tel. (495) 937-15-00; fax (495) 937-14-46; e-mail amba@ambafrance.ru; internet www.ambafrance.ru; Ambassador Stanislas Lefebvre de Laboulaye.

Gabon: 119002 Moscow, Denezhnyi per. 16; tel. (495) 241-00-80; fax (495) 244-06-94; Ambassador Paul Bié Eyené.

Georgia: 121069 Moscow, M. Rzhevskii per. 6; tel. (495) 291-13-59; fax (495) 291-21-36; e-mail ineza@got.mmtel.ru; Ambassador Irakli Chubinashvili.

Germany: 119285 Moscow, ul. Mosfilmovskaya 56; tel. (495) 937-95-00; fax (495) 938-23-54; e-mail germanmo@aha.ru; internet www.moskau.diplo.de; Ambassador Dr Walter Schmid.

Ghana: 121069 Moscow, Skaretrnyi per. 14; tel. (495) 202-18-71; fax (495) 202-18-89; e-mail embghmos@astelit.ru; Ambassador Air Vice-Marshall Edward A. Mantey.

Greece: 103009 Moscow, Leontiyevskii per. 4; tel. (495) 290-14-46; fax (495) 771-65-10; e-mail gremb.mow@mfa.gr; internet www.hellas.ru; Ambassador Ilias Klis.

Guatemala: 119049 Moscow, ul. Korovii Val 7/98; tel. (495) 238-22-14; fax (495) 238-14-46; e-mail embrusia@minex.gob.gt; Ambassador Lars Henrik Pira Pérez.

Guinea: 119034 Moscow, Pomerantsev per. 6; tel. (495) 201-36-01; fax (502) 220-21-38; Ambassador Lt-Col Amara Bangoura.

Guinea-Bissau: 117556 Moscow, Simferopolskii bulv. 7A/183; tel. and fax (495) 317-95-82; Ambassador Rogerio Araujo Adolpho Herbert.

Holy See: 127055 Moscow, Vadkovskii per. 7/37; tel. (495) 726-59-30; fax (495) 726-59-32; e-mail nuntius@cityline.ru; Apostolic Nuncio Most Rev. Antonio Mennini (Titular Archbishop of Ferentium).

Hungary: 119590 Moscow, ul. Mosfilmovskaya 62; tel. (495) 796-93-70; fax (495) 796-93-80; e-mail mow.missions@kum.hu; internet www.mfa.gov.hu/emb/moscow; Ambassador Árpád Székely.

Iceland: 121069 Moscow, Khlebnyi per. 28; tel. (495) 956-76-04; fax (495) 956-76-12; e-mail emb.moscow@mfa.is; internet www.iceland.org/ru; Ambassador Benedikt Ásgeirsson.

India: 101000 Moscow, ul. Vorontsovo Pole 6/8; tel. (495) 783-75-35; fax (495) 975-23-37; e-mail india@online.ru; internet www.indianembassy.ru; Ambassador Prabhat Shukla.

Indonesia: 109017 Moscow, ul. Novokuznetskaya 12; tel. (495) 951-95-50; fax (495) 230-64-31; e-mail kbrimos@online.ru; internet www.kbrimoskow.org; Ambassador (vacant).

Iran: 117292 Moscow, Pokrovskii bulv. 7; tel. (495) 917-72-82; fax (495) 230-28-97; Ambassador Gholmreza Shafehee.

Iraq: 119121 Moscow, ul. Pogodinskaya 12; tel. (495) 246-55-07; fax (495) 230-29-22; e-mail mosemb@iraqmofamail.net; Ambassador Dr Abdul-Karim Hashim.

Ireland: 129010 Moscow, Grokholskii per. 5; tel. (495) 937-59-11; fax (495) 680-06-23; e-mail moscowembassy@dfa.ie; Ambassador Justin Harman.

Israel: 115095 Moscow, ul. B. Ordynka 56; tel. (495) 660-27-00; fax (495) 660-27-68; e-mail info@moscow.mfa.gov.il; internet moscow.mfa.gov.il; Ambassador Anna Azari.

Italy: 121002 Moscow, Denezhnyi per. 5; tel. (495) 796-96-91; fax (495) 253-92-89; e-mail embitaly.mosca@esteri.it; internet www.ambmosca.esteri.it; Ambassador Vittorio Claudio Surdo.

Japan: 129090 Moscow, Grokholskii per. 27; tel. (495) 229-25-50; fax (495) 229-25-55; e-mail embjapan@mail.cnt.ru; internet www.ru.emb-japan.go.jp; Ambassador Yasuo Saito.

Jordan: 123001 Moscow, Mamonovskii per. 3; tel. (495) 699-12-42; fax (495) 699-43-54; e-mail emjordan@umail.ru; Ambassador Abdelilah Muhammad Ali al-Kurdi.

Kazakhstan: 101000 Moscow, Chistoprudnyi bulv. 3A; tel. (495) 927-17-01; fax (495) 608-15-49; e-mail kazembassy@kazembassy.ru; internet www.kazembassy.ru; Ambassador Nurtai A. Abykayev.

Kenya: 119034 Moscow, Lopukhinskii per. 5; tel. (495) 637-21-86; fax (495) 637-54-63; e-mail kenemb@kenemb.ru; internet www.kenemb.ru; Ambassador Dr Sospeter Magita Machage.

Korea, Democratic People's Republic: 107140 Moscow, ul. Mosfilmovskaya 72; tel. (499) 143-62-49; fax (499) 143-63-12; Ambassador Kim Yong Jae.

Korea, Republic: 131000 Moscow, ul. Plyushchikha 56/1; tel. (495) 783-27-27; fax (495) 783-27-77; e-mail info@koreaemb.ru; internet rus-moscow.mofat.go.kr; Ambassador Kim Jae-Sup.

Kuwait: 119285 Moscow, ul. Mosfilmovskaya 44A; tel. (499) 147-00-40; fax (495) 956-60-32; Ambassador Suleiman Ibrahim al-Morjan.

Kyrgyzstan: 119017 Moscow, ul. B. Ordynka 64; tel. (495) 237-48-82; fax (495) 951-60-62; e-mail embassy@embas-kyrg.msk.ru; Chargé d'affaires a.i. Raimkul A. Attakurov.

Laos: 121069 Moscow, ul. Kachalova 18; tel. (495) 203-14-54; fax (495) 203-01-58; e-mail thingsavanh_ph@yahoo.com; Ambassador Thongsavanh Phomvihane.

Latvia: 105062 Moscow, ul. Chaplygina 3; tel. (495) 232-97-60; fax (495) 232-97-50; e-mail embassy.russia@am.gov.lv; internet www.am.gov.lv/lv/moscow; Ambassador Andris Teikmanis.

Lebanon: 103051 Moscow, ul. Sadovaya-Samotechnaya 14; tel. (495) 200-00-22; fax (495) 200-32-22; Ambassador Dr Assem Jaber.

Libya: 131940 Moscow, ul. Mosfilmovskaya 38; tel. (495) 143-03-54; fax (495) 938-21-62; Ambassador Abdul-Adim Khimali.

Lithuania: 121069 Moscow, Borisoglebskii per. 10; tel. (495) 785-86-05; fax (495) 785-86-00; internet ru.mfa.lt; Ambassador Rimantas Šidlauskas.

Luxembourg: 119034 Moscow, Khrushchevskii per. 3; tel. (495) 203-53-81; e-mail moscou.amb@mae.etat.lu; Ambassador Carlo Krieger.

Macedonia, former Yugoslav republic: 117292 Moscow, ul. D. Ulyanova 16/2/8/509–510; tel. (495) 124-33-57; fax (495) 982-36-34; e-mail mkambmos@mail.tascom.ru; Ambassador Zlatko Lečevski.

Madagascar: 119034 Moscow, Kursovoi per. 5; tel. (495) 290-02-32; fax (495) 202-34-53; e-mail info@ambamadagascar.ru; internet www.ambamadagascar.ru; Ambassador Eloi Maxime Dovo.

THE RUSSIAN FEDERATION

Malaysia: 119192 Moscow, ul. Mosfilmovskaya 50; tel. (499) 147-15-14; fax (495) 937-96-02; e-mail malmoscow@kln.gov.my; Ambassador Dato' MUHAMMAD KHALIS ALI HASSAN.

Mali: 113184 Moscow, ul. Novokuznetskaya 11; tel. (495) 951-06-55; fax (495) 230-28-89; e-mail amaliru@mail.ru; Ambassador Gen. BRÉHIMA SIRÉ TRAORÉ.

Malta: 119049 Moscow, ul. Korovii Val 7/219; tel. (495) 237-19-39; fax (495) 237-21-58; e-mail maltaembassy.moscow@gov.mt; Ambassador Dr MARIO COSTA.

Mauritania: 119049 Moscow, ul. B. Ordynka 66; tel. (495) 237-37-92; fax (495) 237-28-61; e-mail m_embassy@oss.ru; Ambassador MUHAMMAD MAHMOUD OULD DAHI.

Mexico: 119034 Moscow, B. Levshinskii per. 4; tel. (495) 969-28-79; fax (495) 969-28-77; e-mail info@embamex.ru; Ambassador ALFREDO ROGERIO PÉREZ BRAVO.

Moldova: 107031 Moscow, ul. Kuznetskii most 18; tel. (495) 924-53-53; fax (495) 924-95-90; e-mail moscova@mfa.md; internet www.moldembassy.ru; Ambassador VASILE STURZA.

Mongolia: 121069 Moscow, Borisoglebskii per. 11; tel. (495) 290-67-92; fax (495) 291-46-36; e-mail mongolia@online.ru; Ambassador LUVSANDANDARYN KHANGAI.

Montenegro: 117049 Moscow, ul. Korovyi Val 7/97; tel. (495) 237-71-34; Chargé d'affaires a.i. MIODRAG KOLJEVIĆ.

Morocco: 121069 Moscow, bulv. B. Nikitskaya 51; tel. (495) 291-17-62; fax (495) 291-16-42; e-mail sifmamos@df.ru; Ambassador NOUREDDINE SEFIANI.

Mozambique: 129090 Moscow, ul. Gilyarovskogo 8/25; tel. (495) 684-40-07; fax (495) 684-36-54; e-mail embamocru@hotmail.com; Ambassador BERNARDO MARCELINO CHERINDA.

Myanmar: 119049 Moscow, ul. Korovii Val 7/135; tel. (495) 230-24-26; fax (495) 730-96-46; e-mail mofa.aung@mptmail.net.mm; Ambassador U TIN SOE.

Namibia: 113096 Moscow, 2-i Kazachii per. 7; tel. (495) 230-32-75; fax (495) 230-22-74; e-mail namembrf@online.ru; Ambassador Dr SAMUEL K. MBAMBO.

Nepal: 119121 Moscow, 2-i Neopalimovskii per. 14/7; tel. (495) 244-02-15; fax (495) 244-00-00; e-mail nepalemb@mtu-net.ru; internet www.nepalembassyrus.org; Chargé d'affaires a.i. ACHYUT BHAKTA POUDEL.

Netherlands: 125009 Moscow, Kalashnyi per. 6; tel. (495) 797-29-00; fax (495) 797-29-04; e-mail mos@minbuza.nl; internet www.netherlands-embassy.ru; Ambassador JAN-PAUL DIRKSE.

New Zealand: 121069 Moscow, ul. Povarskaya 44; tel. (495) 956-35-79; fax (495) 956-35-83; e-mail nzembmos@umail.ru; internet www.nzembassy.com/home.cfm?c=42; Ambassador CHRISTOPHER J. ELDER.

Nigeria: 121069 Moscow, ul. M. Nikitskaya 13; tel. (495) 290-37-83; fax (495) 956-28-25; e-mail ngrmosco@online.ru; Ambassador Air Cdre (retd) DAN SULEIMAN.

Norway: 131940 Moscow, ul. Povarskaya 7; tel. (495) 933-14-10; fax (495) 933-14-11; e-mail emb.moscow@mfa.no; internet www.norvegia.ru; Ambassador ØYVIND NORDSLETTEN.

Oman: 109180 Moscow, Staromonetnii per. 14/1; tel. (495) 230-15-87; fax (495) 230-15-44; e-mail amoman@ipc.ru; Ambassador ABDULLAH BIN ZAHER AL-HUSSNI.

Pakistan: 123001 Moscow, ul. Sadovaya-Kudrinskaya 17; tel. (495) 254-97-91; fax (495) 956-90-97; e-mail parepmoscow@yahoo.com; internet www.pakistanembassy.ru; Ambassador KHALID KHATTAK.

Panama: 119590 Moscow, ul. Mosfilmovskaya 50/1; tel. (495) 956-07-29; fax (495) 956-07-30; e-mail empanrus@aha.ru; Ambassador (vacant).

Peru: 121002 Moscow, Smolenskii bulv. 22/14/15; tel. (495) 248-27-66; fax (495) 230-20-00; e-mail leprumoscu@mtu-net.ru; Ambassador Dr HUMBERTO UMERES ALVARES.

Philippines: 121099 Moscow, Karmanitskii per. 6; tel. (495) 241-05-63; fax (495) 241-26-30; e-mail moscowpe@utsmail.ru; internet www.phil-embassy.ru; Ambassador ERNESTO V. LLAMAS.

Poland: 123557 Moscow, ul. Klimashkina 4; tel. (495) 231-15-00; fax (495) 231-15-15; e-mail embassy@polandemb.ru; internet www.moskwa.polemb.net; Ambassador JERZY BAHR.

Portugal: 129010 Moscow, Botanicheskii per. 1; tel. (495) 981-34-10; fax (495) 981-34-16; e-mail embptrus@moscovo.dgaccp.pt; Ambassador MANUEL MARCELO MONTIERO CURTO.

Qatar: 117049 Moscow, ul. Korovii Val 7/196–198; tel. (495) 980-69-18; fax (495) 980-69-17; e-mail moscow@mofa.gov.qa; Ambassador SAAD MUHAMMAD SAAD AL-KOBAISI.

Romania: 119590 Moscow, ul. Mosfilmovskaya 64; tel. (499) 143-04-24; fax (499) 143-04-49; e-mail ambasada@orc.ru; internet moscova.mae.ro; Ambassador MIHAIL GRIGORIE.

Saudi Arabia: 119121 Moscow, 3-i Neopalimovskii per. 3; tel. (495) 245-23-10; fax (495) 246-94-71; e-mail saudimoscow@yahoo.com; internet www.mofa.gov.sa/detail.asp?InServiceID=238; Chargé d'affaires a.i. GAZI SHERBINI.

Senegal: 119049 Moscow, ul. Korovii Val 7/193–194; tel. (495) 230-20-72; fax (495) 230-20-63; Ambassador Maj.-Gen. MOUNTAGA DIALLO.

Serbia: 119285 Moscow, ul. Mosfilmovskaya 46; tel. (499) 147-41-06; fax (499) 147-41-04; e-mail ambasada@co.ru; Ambassador STANIMIR VUKIĆEVIĆ.

Sierra Leone: 121615 Moscow, Rublevskoye shosse 26/1/58–59; tel. (495) 415-41-24; fax (495) 415-29-85; Ambassador MELROSE BEYOH KAI-BANYA.

Singapore: 121099 Moscow, per. Kamennoi Slobody 5; tel. (495) 241-39-13; fax (495) 241-78-95; e-mail singemb_mow@sgmfa.gov.sg; internet www.mfa.gov.sg/moscow; Ambassador MICHAEL TAY CHEOW ANN.

Slovakia: 123056 Moscow, ul. Yu. Fuchika 17/19; tel. (495) 250-10-70; fax (495) 250-15-91; e-mail embassy@moskva.mfa.sk; internet www.moscow.mfa.sk; Ambassador Dr AUGUSTÍN ČISÁR.

Slovenia: 127006 Moscow, ul. M. Dmitrovka 14/1; tel. (503) 737-63-55; fax (495) 694-15-68; e-mail vmo@gov.si; internet moskva.veleposlanistvo.si; Ambassador ANDREJ BENEDEJČIČ.

Somalia: 117556 Moscow, Simferopolskii bulv. 7A /145; tel. and fax (495) 317-06-22; e-mail somemb@nabad.org; Chargé d'affaires a.i. MOHAMED MOHAMED HANDULLE.

South Africa: 123001 Moscow, Granatnyi per. 1/9; tel. (495) 540-11-77; fax (495) 540-11-78; e-mail moscow.ambassador@foreign.gov.za; internet saembassy.ru; Ambassador Dr B. W. J. BHEKI LANGA.

Spain: 121069 Moscow, ul. B. Nikitskaya 50/8; tel. (495) 202-21-61; fax (495) 291-91-71; e-mail embespru@mail.mae.es; internet www.maec.es/embajadas/moscu; Ambassador FRANCISCO JAVIER ELORZA CAVENGT.

Sri Lanka: 129090 Moscow, ul. Shchepkina 24; tel. (495) 688-16-20; fax (495) 688-17-57; e-mail lankaemb@com2com.ru; Ambassador U. WEERATUNGA.

Sudan: 127006 Moscow, Uspenskii per. 4A; tel. (495) 299-54-61; fax (495) 299-33-42; e-mail sudmos@cityline.ru; Ambassador CHOL DENG ALAK.

Sweden: 119590 Moscow, ul. Mosfilmovskaya 60; tel. (495) 937-92-00; fax (495) 937-92-02; e-mail moscow.sweinfo@foreign.ministry.se; internet www.swedenabroad.com/moscow; Ambassador JOHAN MOLANDER.

Switzerland: 101000 Moscow, per. Ogorodnoi Slobody 2/5; tel. (495) 258-38-30; fax (495) 621-21-83; e-mail mos.vertretung@eda.admin.ch; internet www.eda.admin.ch/moscow; Ambassador ERWIN H. HOFER.

Syria: 119034 Moscow, Mansurovskii per. 4; tel. (495) 203-15-21; fax (495) 956-31-91; Ambassador WAHIB AL-FADEL.

Tajikistan: 103001 Moscow, Granatnyi per. 13; tel. (495) 290-38-46; fax (495) 291-89-98; e-mail embassy_moscow@tajikistan.ru; internet www.tajikistan.ru; Ambassador ABDULMAJID S. DOSTIYEV.

Tanzania: 109017 Moscow, ul. Pyatnitskaya 33; tel. (495) 953-82-21; fax (495) 956-61-30; e-mail tzmos@wm.west.call.com; Ambassador PATRICK SEGEJA CHOKALA.

Thailand: 129090 Moscow, ul. B. Spasskaya 9; tel. (495) 608-08-17; fax (495) 290-96-59; e-mail thaiemb@nnt.ru; internet www.thaiembassymoscow.com; Ambassador SUPHOT DHIRAKAOSAL.

Tunisia: 113105 Moscow, ul. M. Nikitskaya 28/1; tel. (495) 291-28-58; fax (495) 291-75-88; Ambassador MUHAMMAD BELLAGI.

Turkey: 119121 Moscow, 7-i Rostovskii per. 12; tel. (495) 956-55-95; fax (495) 956-55-97; e-mail turemb@co.ru; Ambassador KURTULUŞ TAŞKENT.

Turkmenistan: 119019 Moscow, Filippovskii per. 22; tel. (495) 291-66-36; fax (495) 291-09-35; Ambassador KHALNAZAR A. AGAKHANOV.

Ukraine: 103009 Moscow, Leontiyevskii per. 18; tel. (495) 629-35-42; fax (495) 629-46-81; e-mail emb_ru@mfa.gov.ua; internet www.mfa.gov.ua/russia; Ambassador OLEH O. DYOMIN.

United Arab Emirates: 101000 Moscow, ul. U. Palme 4; tel. (499) 147-00-66; fax (495) 234-40-70; e-mail uae@col.ru; Ambassador MUHAMMAD ALI AL-OSAIMI.

United Kingdom: 121099 Moscow, Smolenskaya nab. 10; tel. (495) 956-72-00; fax (495) 956-72-01; e-mail moscow@britishembassy.ru; internet www.britaininrussia.ru; Ambassador Sir ANTHONY BRENTON.

USA: 121099 Moscow, B. Devyatinskii per. 8; tel. (495) 728-50-00; fax (495) 728-50-90; e-mail pamoscow@pd.state.gov; internet moscow.usembassy.gov; Ambassador WILLIAM J. BURNS.

THE RUSSIAN FEDERATION

Uruguay: 119049 Moscow, ul. Mytnaya 3; tel. (495) 143-04-01; fax (495) 938-20-45; e-mail ururus@mrree.gub.uy; internet www.uruguay.org.ru; Ambassador Jorge Alberto Meyer Long.

Uzbekistan: 109017 Moscow, Pogorelskii per. 12; tel. (495) 230-00-76; fax (495) 238-89-18; e-mail info@uzembassy.ru; internet www.uzembassy.ru; Ambassador Bakhtiyor A. Islamov.

Venezuela: 115127 Moscow, B. Karetnyi per. 13/15; tel. (495) 699-40-42; fax (495) 956-61-08; e-mail info@embaven.ru; internet www.embaven.ru; Ambassador Dr Alexis Rafael Navarro Rojas.

Viet Nam: 119021 Moscow, ul. B. Pirogovskaya 13; tel. (495) 245-09-25; fax (495) 246-31-21; e-mail dsqvn@com2com.ru; Ambassador Nyugen Van Ngang.

Yemen: 119121 Moscow, 2-i Neopalimovskii per. 6; tel. (495) 246-15-40; fax (495) 230-23-05; Ambassador Abdulwahab Muhammad Ali Al-Rawhani.

Zambia: 129041 Moscow, pr. Mira 52A; tel. (495) 688-50-01; fax (495) 975-20-56; Ambassador Rev. Dr Peter L. Chintala.

Zimbabwe: 119121 Moscow, per. Serpov 6; tel. (495) 248-43-67; fax (495) 230-24-97; e-mail zimbabwe@rinet.ru; Ambassador Brig. (retd) Agrippah Mutambara.

Judicial System

In January 1995 the first section of a new code of civil law came into effect. It included new rules on commercial and financial operations, and on ownership issues. The second part of the code was published in January 1996. The Constitutional Court rules on the conformity of government policies, federal laws, international treaties and presidential enactments with the Constitution. Following its suspension in October 1993, the Court was reinstated, with a new membership of 19 judges, in April 1995. The Supreme Arbitration Court rules on disputes between commercial bodies. The Supreme Court oversees all criminal and civil law, and is the final court of appeal from lower courts. A system of Justices of the Peace, to deal with certain civil cases, and with criminal cases punishable by a maximum of two years' imprisonment, was established in 1998. In December 2001 President Putin approved several reforms to the judicial system, including the introduction of trials by jury across the Russian Federation, and procedures to guarantee the independence of judges. The majority of Russia's administrative regions introduced jury trials, in many cases only for the most serious crimes, during 2003.

Constitutional Court of the Russian Federation (Konstitutsionnyi Sud Rossiiskoi Federatsii): 190000 St Petersburg, pl. Dekabristov 1; e-mail ksrf@ksmail.rfnet.ru; internet www.ksrf.ru; f. 1991; Chair. Valerii D. Zorkin; Sec.-Gen. Yurii V. Kudyavtsev.

Office of the Prosecutor-General: 125993 Moscow, ul. B. Dmitrovka 15A; tel. (495) 692-26-82; fax (495) 292-88-48; internet www.genproc.gov.ru; Prosecutor-General Yurii Ya. Chaika.

Supreme Arbitration Court of the Russian Federation (Vysshii Arbitrazhnyi Sud Rossiiskoi Federatsii): 101000 Moscow, M. Kharitonevskii per. 12; tel. (495) 208-11-19; fax (495) 208-11-62; internet www.arbitr.ru; f. 1993; Chair. Anton A. Ivanov.

Supreme Court of the Russian Federation (Verkhovnyi Sud Rossiiskoi Federatsii): 103289 Moscow, ul. Ilinka 7/3; tel. (495) 924-23-47; fax (495) 202-71-18; e-mail gastello@ilinka.supcourt.ru; internet www.supcourt.ru; Chair. Vyacheslav M. Lebedev.

Religion

The majority of the population of the Russian Federation are adherents of Christianity, but there are significant Islamic, Buddhist and Jewish minorities.

In 1997 legislation restricted the operation of religious groups to those that were to prove that they had been established in Russia for a minimum of 15 years. Russian Orthodoxy, Islam, Buddhism and Judaism, together with some other Christian denominations, were deemed to comply with the legislation. Religious organizations failing to satisfy this requirement were, henceforth, obliged to register annually for 15 years, before being permitted to publish literature, hold public services or invite foreign preachers into Russia. Moreover, foreign religious groups were additionally obliged to affiliate themselves to Russian organizations.

CHRISTIANITY

The Russian Orthodox Church (Moscow Patriarchate)

The Russian Orthodox Church (Moscow Patriarchate) is the dominant religious organization in the Russian Federation, with an estimated 75m. adherents. In 2004 there were 12,638 parishes operating under the auspices of the Patriarchate in Russia.

Moscow Patriarchate: 115191 Moscow, Danilov Monastery, ul. Danilovskii Val 22; tel. (495) 954-04-54; fax (495) 633-72-81; e-mail es@mospatr.ru; internet www.mospat.ru; Patriarch of Moscow and all Rus Aleksei II Ridiger.

The Roman Catholic Church

At 31 December 2005 there were an estimated 775,900 Roman Catholics in the Russian Federation. In 1991 administrative structures of the Roman Catholic Church in Russia were restored. The organization of the Church in Russian comprises one archdiocese, three dioceses, one apostolic prefecture, and an apostolic exarchate for adherents of the Byzantine Rite.

Conference of Catholic Bishops of the Russian Federation 101031 Moscow, ul. Petrovka 19/5/35; tel. and fax (495) 923-16-97; e-mail ostastop@glasnet.ru; internet www.catholic.ru.

f. 1999; Pres. Most. Rev. Joseph Werth (Bishop of the Diocese of the Transfiguration at Novosibirsk).

Archbishop of the Archdiocese of the Mother of God at Moscow: Most Rev. Tadeusz Kondrusiewicz, 107078 Moscow, POB 116, ul. N. Basmannaya 16/31; tel. and fax (499) 261-67-14; e-mail cathmos@dol.ru.

Protestant Churches

Russian Church of Christians of the Evangelical Faith: 123363 Moscow, ul. Fabritsiusa 31A; tel. (495) 493-57-88; internet hve.ru; f. 1907, re-established 1990; fmrly known as Union of Christians of the Evangelical Faith-Pentecostalists in Russia; 1,600 parishes and more than 300,000 adherents in 2005; Elder Nazar P. Reshchikovets.

Russian Union of Evangelical Christians-Baptists: 117015 Moscow, Varshavskoye shosse 29/2; tel. (495) 958-13-36; fax (495) 975-23-67; e-mail bapt.un@g23.relcom.ru; internet baptist.org.ru; affiliated to the Euro-Asiatic Federation of Evangelical Christians-Baptists; Exec. Sec. Yurii Apatov.

Other Christian Churches

Armenian Apostolic Church: 123022 Moscow, ul. S. Makeyeva 10; tel. (495) 255-50-19.

Russian Orthodox Old Belief (Old Ritual) Church (Russkaya Pravoslavnaya Staroobryadcheskaya Tserkov): 109052 Moscow, ul. Rogozhskii pos. 1B/3; tel. (495) 361-51-92; e-mail expers2rpsc.ru; internet www.rpsc.ru; f. 1666 by separation from the Moscow Patriarchate; some 300 groups registered in 2005; divided into two main branches: the *popovtsi* (which have priests) and the *bespopovtsi* (which reject the notion of ordained priests and the use of all sacraments, other than that of baptism). Both branches are further divided into various groupings. The largest group of *popovtsi* are those of the Belokrinitskii Concord, under the Archbishop of Novozybkov, Moscow and All Rus, Kornilii (Titov); c. 250 parishes, seven bishops in Russia, Ukraine and Moldova; a further significant group of *popovtsi* Old Believers are those of the Beglopopovtsyi Concord.

Russian Autonomous Orthodox Church: 125212 Moscow, Church of the New Martyrs and Confessors of Russia, Golovinskoye shosse 13 A; tel. (495) 152-50-76; formally established in 1990 as the Free Russian Orthodox Church; re-registered in 1998 under above name following opposition by local, 'catacomb' priests to moves of reconciliation between the Russian Orthodox Church Abroad and the Moscow Patriarchate; 100 parishes in 2001; First Hierarch Metropolitan of Suzdal and Vladimir Valentin (Rusantsov).

ISLAM

Most Muslims in the Russian Federation are adherents of the Sunni sect. Islam is the predominant religion among many peoples of the North Caucasus, such as the Chechens, the Ingush and many smaller groups, and also in the Central Volga region, among them the Tatars, Chuvash and Bashkirs.

Central Muslim Spiritual Board for Russia and European Countries of the CIS: 450057 Bashkortostan, Ufa, ul. Tukaya 50; tel. (3472) 50-80-86; f. 1789; 27 regional branches in the Russian Federation, and one branch in Ukraine; Chair. (vacant).

Council of Muftis of Russia: 129090 Moscow, per. Vypolzov 7; tel. and fax (495) 681-49-04; e-mail mufty@muslim.ru; internet www.muslim.ru; Chair. Mufti Sheikh Ravil Khazrat Gainutdin.

JUDAISM

At the beginning of the 20th century approximately one-half of the world's Jews lived in the Russian Empire. Although many Jews emigrated from the USSR in the 1970s and 1980s, there is still a significant Jewish population (230,000 in late 2002, according to the official results of the census, although some estimates were considerably higher) in the Russian Federation.

THE RUSSIAN FEDERATION
Directory

Congress of Jewish Religious Communities and Organizations of Russia: 101000 Moscow, B. Spasoglinishevskii per. 10, Moscow Choral Synagogue; tel. (495) 917-95-92; fax (495) 740-12-18; e-mail keroor@mail.ru; f. 1996; co-ordinates activities of 120 Jewish communities throughout Russia; Chief Rabbi ADOLF SHAYEVICH; Dir ZINOVY KOGAN.

Federation of the Jewish Communities of Russia: 121099 Moscow, ul. Novyi Arbat 36/9/2; tel. (495) 290-75-18; fax (495) 290-86-49; e-mail office@fjc.ru; internet www.fjc.ru; unites 179 communities in Russia; affiliated to Federation of the Jewish Communities of the CIS and the Baltic States; Chief Rabbi of Russia, Chair. of Rabbinical Alliance of Russia and the CIS BEREL LAZAR.

Russian Jewish Congress: 101000 Moscow, B. Spasoglinishchevskii per. 9/1/936; tel. (495) 780-61-00; fax (495) 780-60-90; e-mail rjc@rjc.ru; internet www.rjc.ru; Pres. VYACHESLAV KANTOR.

BUDDHISM

Buddhism (established as an official religion in Russia in 1741) is most widespread in the Republic of Buryatiya, where the Traditional Buddhist Sangkha of Russia has its seat, the Republics of Kalmykiya and Tyva, in Transbaikal Krai (formerly Chita Oblast) and in Irkutsk Oblast.

Buddhist Traditional Sangkha of Russia (Buddiiskaya Traditsionnaya Sangkha Rossii): 670000 Buryatiya, Ulan-Ude, Ivolginskii datsan; e-mail buddhism@buryatia.ru; internet buddhism.buryatia.ru; Head Pandito Khambo Lama DAMBA AYUSHEYEV.

The Press

In 2004 there were 46,000 officially registered printed media, including some 26,000 newspapers. However, the number of titles in circulation was only around one-half of the total. The total print run of Russian newspapers in that year was 8,500m. copies, and that of magazines was around 600m. copies. At that time *Moskovskii Komsomolets*, with a circulation of 2.2m., was the best-selling daily, while the weekly, *Argumenty i Fakty*, which had a circulation of 2.9m. in 2007, was the best-selling newspaper overall.

Federal Agency for the Press and the Mass Media (Federalnoye Agentstvo po pechati i massovym kommunikatsiyam): 127994 Moscow, Strastnoi bulv. 5; tel. (495) 650-39-86; e-mail sekretarr@fapmc.ru; internet www.fapmc.ru; f. 2004; Chair. MIKHAIL V. SESLAVINSKII.

PRINCIPAL NEWSPAPERS

Moscow

Argumenty i Fakty (Arguments and Facts): 101000 Moscow, ul. Myasnitskaya 42; tel. (495) 923-35-41; fax (495) 925-61-82; e-mail n-boris@aif.ru; internet www.aif.ru; f. 1978; weekly; Editor-in-Chief NIKOLAI ZYATKOV; circ. 2.9m. (2007).

Gazeta (Newspaper): 123242 Moscow, ul. Zoologicheskaya 4; tel. (495) 787-39-99; fax (495) 787-39-98; e-mail info@gzt.ru; internet www.gzt.ru; f. 2001; Editor-in-Chief PETR YE. FADEYEV; circ. 726,000 (2005).

Gazeta.ru: 117152 Moscow, Zagorodnoye shosse 1/1; tel. (495) 785-09-76; internet www.gazeta.ru; online only; has no asscn with the newspaper *Gazeta*; Editor-in-Chief ALEKSANDR PISAREV.

Grani.ru: Moscow; tel. (495) 363-36-08; e-mail info@grani.ru; internet grani.ru; f. 2000; online only; Dir-Gen. YULIYA BEREZOVSKAYA; Editor-in-Chief VLADIMIR KORSUNSKII.

Gudok (The Horn): 105066 Moscow, ul. Staraya Basmannaya 38/2/3; tel. (495) 262-26-53; fax (495) 262-45-74; e-mail welcome@gudok.ru; internet www.gudok.ru; f. 1917 as newspaper of railway workers; daily; Editor-in-Chief IGOR T. YANIN; circ. 214,000 (2007).

Izvestiya (News): 127994 Moscow, ul. Tverskaya 18/1, POB 4; tel. (495) 209-05-81; fax (495) 933-64-62; e-mail info1@izvestia.ru; internet www.izvestia.ru; f. 1917; 50.19% owned by Gazprom Mediya, 49.81% by Prof-Mediya; Editor-in-Chief VLADIMIR MAMONTOV; circ. 130,000 (2007).

Kommersant (Businessman): 125080 Moscow, ul. Vrubelya 4/1; tel. (499) 943-97-71; fax (499) 943-97-28; e-mail kommersant@kommersant.ru; internet www.kommersant.com; f. 1989; daily; Editor ANDREI VASILYEV; circ. 119,322 (2007).

Komsomolskaya Pravda (Young Communist League Truth): 103287 Moscow, Staryi Petrovsko-Razumovskii proyezd 1/23/1; tel. (495) 257-51-39; fax (495) 200-22-93; e-mail kp@kp.ru; internet www.kp.ru; f. 1925; fmrly organ of the Lenin Young Communist League (Komsomol); independent; weekly supplements *KP-Tolstushka* (KP-Fat volume), *KP-Ponedelnik* (KP-Monday); managed by Prof-Mediya; Chair. OLEG RUDNOV; Editor VLADIMIR SUNGORKIN; circ. 700,000.

Krasnaya Zvezda (Red Star): 123007 Moscow, Khoroshevskoye shosse 38; tel. (495) 941-21-58; fax (495) 941-40-66; e-mail redstar@mail.cnt.ru; internet www.redstar.ru; f. 1924; organ of the Ministry of Defence; Editor N. N. YEFIMOV; circ. 80,000 (2000).

The Moscow News: 127018 Moscow, ul. Polkovaya 3/1; tel. (495) 234-32-23; fax (495) 232-62-29; internet www.moscowtimes.ru; f. 1930; weekly; in English; democratic, liberal; Chief Editor ROBERT BRIDGE.

Moscow Times: 127018 Moscow, ul. Polkovaya 3/1; tel. (495) 234-32-23; fax (495) 232-65-29; e-mail moscowtimes.editors@imedia.ru; internet www.themoscowtimes.com; f. 1992; daily; in English; Publr MAXINE MATERS; Editor ANDREW MCCHESNEY.

Moskovskaya Pravda (The Moscow Truth): 123846 Moscow, ul. 1905 Goda 7, POB D-22; tel. (495) 259-82-33; fax (495) 259-63-60; e-mail newspaper@mospravda.ru; internet www.mospravda.ru; f. 1918; fmrly organ of the Moscow city committee of the CPSU and the Moscow City Council; 5 a week; independent; Editor SHOD S. MULADZHANOV; circ. 400,000 (2007).

Moskovskii Komsomolets (MK): 123995 Moscow, ul. 1905 Goda 7; tel. (495) 259-50-36; fax (495) 259-46-39; e-mail letters@mk.ru; internet www.mk.ru; f. 1919 as *Moskovskii Komsomolets* (The Moscow Young Communist); 6 a week; independent; circ. 800,000 in Moscow, 2.2m. nation-wide (2004); Editor-in-Chief PAVEL GUSEV.

Nezavisimaya Gazeta (NG) (Independent Newspaper): 101000 Moscow, ul. Myasnitskaya 13; tel. (495) 645-61-54; e-mail info@ng.ru; internet www.ng.ru; f. 1990; 5 a week; regular supplements include *NG-Nauka* (NG-Science), *NG-Regiony* (NG-Regions), *NG-Politekonomiya* (NG-Political Economy), *NG-Dipkuryer* (NG-Diplomatic Courier); Gen. Man. and Editor-in-Chief KONSTANTIN REMCHUKOV; circ. 53,000 (2005).

Novaya Gazeta (New Newspaper): 101000 Moscow, Potapovskii per. 3; tel. and fax (495) 623-68-88; e-mail pr@novayagazeta.ru; internet www.novayagazeta.ru; f. 1993; weekly; Editor DMITRII A. MURATOV.

Novye Izvestiya (New News): 107076 Moscow, ul. Elektrozavodskaya 33; tel. (495) 783-06-36; fax (495) 783-06-37; e-mail webmaster@newizv.ru; internet www.newizv.ru; f. 2003 following the closure of the fmr *Novye Izvestiya* (f. 1997); daily; Editor-in-Chief VALERII YAKOV.

Parlamentskaya Gazeta (Parliamentary Newspaper): 125993 Moscow, ul. 1–ya Yamskogo Polya 28; tel. (495) 257-50-90; fax (495) 257-50-82; e-mail pg@pnp.ru; internet www.pnp.ru; f. 1998; 5 a week; organ of the Federanoye Sobraniye; Editor-in-Chief PETR A. KOTOV; circ. 50,000 (2005).

Polit.ru: 101000 Moscow, Krivokolennyi per. 10/6A; tel. (495) 624-80-09; e-mail edit@polit.ru; internet www.polit.ru; f. 1998; independent; online only; Editor-in-Chief ANDREI LEVKIN.

Pravda (Truth): 125867 Moscow, ul. Pravdy 24; tel. (499) 257-52-13; e-mail pravda2@cnt.ru; internet www.gazeta-pravda.ru; f. 1912; fmrly organ of the Cen. Cttee of the CPSU; independent; communist; Editor-in-Chief VALENTIN S. SHURCHANOV; circ. 100,300 (2007).

Pravda.ru: Moscow, ul. Staraya Basmannaya 16/2; tel. and fax (499) 261-48-85; e-mail home@pravda.ru; internet pravda.ru; f. 1999; online only, in Russian, English and Portuguese; has no asscn with the newspaper *Pravda*; Editor-in-Chief INNA S. NOVIKOVA.

Rossiiskaya Gazeta (Russian Newspaper): 125993 Moscow, ul. Pravdy 24, POB 40; tel. (495) 257-52-52; fax (495) 973-22-56; e-mail sekretar@rg.ru; internet www.rg.ru; f. 1990; organ of the Russian Govt; 6 a week; Gen. Man. ALEKSANDR N. GORBENKO; Editor-in-Chief VLADISLAV A. FRONIN; circ. 373,820 (2004).

Rossiiskiye Vesti (Russian News): 119034 Moscow, ul. Prechistenka 28; tel. (495) 933-06-47; fax (495) 201-51-02; e-mail mail@rosvesty.ru; internet www.rosvesty.ru; f. 1991; weekly; Editor-in-Chief ALEKSEI TITKOV.

Russkii Zhurnal (Russian Journal): 125009 Moscow, per. M. Gnezdnikovskii 9/8/3A; tel. and fax (495) 745-52-25; e-mail russ@russ.ru; internet www.russ.ru; f. 1997; online only; culture, politics, society; Editor-in-Chief and Publr GLEB PAVLOVSKII.

Selskaya Zhizn (Country Life): 125869 Moscow, ul. Pravdy 24, POB 137; tel. (495) 257-51-51; fax (495) 257-58-39; e-mail sg@sgazeta.ru; internet www.sgazeta.ru; f. 1918 as *Bednota* (Poverty), present name adopted in 1960; 2 a week; fmrly organ of the Cen. Cttee of the CPSU; independent; Editor-in-Chief and Gen. Man. SHAMUN M. KAGERMANOV; circ. 94,500.

Tribuna (Tribune): 125993 Moscow, ul. Pravdy 24, POB A-40; tel. (495) 257-59-13; fax (495) 973-20-02; e-mail tribuna@tribuna.ru; internet www.tribuna.ru; f. 1969; national industrial daily; Editor-in-Chief OLEG KUZIN.

Trud (Labour): 125993 Moscow, ul. Pravdy 24/5; tel. (495) 580-66-93; e-mail letter@trud.ru; internet www.trud.ru; f. 1921; 5 a week; Editor ALEKSANDR S. POTAPOV.

Vechernyaya Moskva (Evening Moscow): 123995 Moscow, ul. 1905 Goda 7, POB 5/22; tel. (495) 259-81-87; fax (495) 253-95-75; e-mail

THE RUSSIAN FEDERATION

post@vm.ru; internet www.vm.ru; f. 1923; Chair. Vladimir V. Zubkov.

Vedomosti (Gazette): 125212 Moscow, ul. Vyborgskaya 16; tel. (495) 232-32-00; fax (495) 956-07-16; e-mail vedomosti@media.ru; internet www.vedomosti.ru; f. 1999; independent business newspaper, publ. jointly with the *Financial Times* (United Kingdom) and the *Wall Street Journal* (USA); Editor-in-Chief Yelizabeta Osetinskaya.

Vremya Novosti (News Time): 115326 Moscow, ul. Pyatnitskaya 25; tel. (495) 231-18-77; e-mail nter@vremya.ru; internet www.vremya.ru; f. 2000; Editor-in-Chief Vladimir S. Gurevich.

Zhizn (Life): 125212 Moscow, ul. Vyborgskaya 16/1; tel. (495) 510-29-84; fax (495) 510-29-81; e-mail info@zhizn.ru; internet www.zhizn.ru; weekly; Editor-in-Chief Ruslan Sagayev; circ. 2.2.m. within Russia (2007).

St Petersburg

Peterburgskii Chas Pik (Petersburg Rush Hour): 191040 St Petersburg, Nevskii pr. 81; tel. (812) 579-25-65; fax (812) 579-19-12; e-mail nabor@chaspik.spb.ru; internet www.chaspik.spb.ru; f. 1990; weekly; owned by Gazprom-Mediya; Editor-in-Chief Larisa Afonina; circ. 30,000 (2005).

Novosti Peterburga (Petersburg News): 191084 St Petersburg, Mitrofanyevskoye shosse 29т; tel. (812) 334-27-21; e-mail pr@novosti.sp.ru; internet www.novostispb.ru; f. 1997; independent; Editor-in-Chief Kirill Metelev.

Sankt-Peterburgskiye Vedomosti (St Petersburg Gazette): 191025 St Petersburg, ul. Marata 25; tel. (812) 325-31-00; fax (812) 764-48-40; e-mail post@spbvedomosti.ru; internet www.spbvedomosti.ru; f. 1991 as revival of 1728–1917 title; re-established 1991; Editor-in-Chief and Gen. Man. Sergei A. Slobodskoi.

Smena (The Rising Generation): 191119 St Petersburg, ul. Marata 69; tel. (812) 315-04-76; fax (812) 315-03-53; e-mail info@smena.ru; internet www.smena.ru; f. 1919; 6 a week, controlled by Sistema Mass-Mediya; Editor-in-Chief Leonid Davydov; circ. 80,000 (2002).

The St Petersburg Times: 190000 St Petersburg, Isaakevskaya pl. 4; tel. and fax (812) 325-60-80; e-mail letters@sptimesrussia.com; internet www.sptimes.ru; f. 1993; 2 a week; in English; independent; Editor Tobin Auber.

Vechernii Peterburg (Evening Petersburg): 191023 St Petersburg, ul. Fontanka 59; tel. (812) 311-88-75; fax (812) 314-31-05; e-mail gazeta@vspb.spb.ru; internet vppress.ru; f. 1917; Editor Vladimir G. Gronskii.

PRINCIPAL PERIODICALS

Agriculture, Forestry, etc.

Ekologiya i Promlyshlennost Rossii (The Ecology and Industry of Russia): 119049 Moscow, Leninskii pr. 4; tel. (495) 913-80-94; fax (495) 247-23-08; e-mail ecip@kalvis.ru; internet ecip.kalvis.ru; f. 1996; monthly; environmental protection; Editor-in-Chief Prof. Dr V. D. Kalner.

Ekonomika Selskokhozyaistvennykh i Pererabatyvayushchikh Predpriyatii (Economics of Agricultural and Processing Enterprises): 107996 Moscow, ul. Sadovaya-Spasskaya 18/423; tel. (495) 207-15-80; fax (495) 207-18-56; internet www.reason.ru/economy; f. 1926; monthly; publ. by Ministry of Agriculture; Editor S. K. Devin.

Lesnaya Promyshlennost (Forest Industry): 101934 Moscow, Arkhangelskii per. 1/234; tel. (495) 207-91-53; f. 1926; 3 a week; publ. by the state forest industrial company, Roslesprom; Editor V. G. Zayedinov; circ. 250,000.

Veterinariya (Veterinary Science): 107996 Moscow, ul. Sadovaya-Spasskaya 18; tel. (495) 207-10-60; fax (495) 207-28-12; f. 1924; monthly; Editor V. A. Garkavtsev; circ. 4,860 (2000).

Zashchita i Karantin Rastenii (The Protection and Quarantine of Plants): 107996 Moscow, ul. Sadovaya-Spasskaya 18, GSB-6, B-78; tel. (495) 207-21-30; fax (495) 207-21-40; e-mail fitopress@ropnet.ru; internet www.z-i-k-r.ru; f. 1932; monthly; Editor Yurii N. Neipert; circ. 4,500 (2007).

Zemledeliye (Farming): 127434 Moscow, POB 9; tel. and fax (495) 976-11-93; e-mail zemledelie@mtu-net.ru; internet www.jurzemledelie.ru; f. 1939; 8 a year; publ. by Ministry of Agriculture, Russian Academy of Agricultural Sciences, Russian Scientific Research Institute of Farming; Editor Marianna G. Logvinova; circ. 2,500 (2005).

For Children

Koster (Campfire): 193024 St Petersburg, ul. Mytninskaya 1/20; tel. (812) 274-15-72; fax (812) 274-46-26; e-mail root@kostyor.spb.org; internet www.kostyor.ru; f. 1936; monthly; journal of the International Union of Children's Organizations (UPO-FCO); fiction, poetry, sport, reports and popular science; for ages 10–14 years; Editor-in-Chief N. B. Kharlampiyev; circ. 7,500 (2000).

Murzilka: 127015 Moscow, ul. Novodmitrovskaya 5а; tel. and fax (495) 685-18-81; e-mail murzilka@dateline.ru; internet www.murzilka.org; f. 1924; monthly; illustrated; for first grades of school; Editor Tatyana Androsenko; circ. 75,000 (2007).

Pionerskaya Pravda (Pioneers' Truth): 127994 Moscow, ul. Sushchevskaya 21; tel. and fax (495) 787-62-43; e-mail info@pionerka.ru; internet www.pionerka.ru; f. 1925; 4 a week; fmrly organ of the Union of Pioneer Organizations (Federation of Children's Organizations) of the USSR; Editor Mikhail N. Barannikov.

Veselye Kartinki (Merry Pictures): 127015 Moscow, POB 60, ul. Pravdy 24/830; tel. (495) 411-31-28; fax (495) 257-32-01; e-mail info@merrypictures.ru; internet www.merrypictures.ru; f. 1956; monthly; humorous, illustrated; for pre-school and first grades; Editor Marina Druzhininaya.

Yunyi Naturalist (Young Naturalist): 125015 Moscow, ul. Novodmitrovskaya 5а; tel. (495) 685-39-31; e-mail post@unnaturalist.ru; internet www.unnaturalist.ru; f. 1928; monthly; popular science for children of fourth–10th grades, who are interested in biology; Editor L. M. Samsonova.

Yunyi Tekhnik (Young Technician): 125015 Moscow, ul. Novodmitrovskaya 5а; tel. (495) 285-44-80; e-mail yt@got.mmtel.ru; internet jt-arxiv.narod.ru; f. 1956; monthly; popular science for children and youth; Editor Boris Cheremisinov.

Culture and Arts

Iskusstvo Kino (The Art of the Cinema): 125319 Moscow, ul. Usiyevicha 9; tel. (495) 151-56-51; fax (495) 151-02-72; e-mail filmfilm@mtu-net.ru; internet www.kinoart.ru/main.html; f. 1931; monthly; journal of the Russian Film-makers' Union; Editor Daniil Dondurei; circ. 5,000 (2004).

Knizhnoye Obozreniye (The Book Review): 129272 Moscow, ul. Sushchevskii Val 64; tel. (495) 681-62-66; fax (495) 681-51-45; internet www.knigoboz.ru; f. 1966; weekly; publ. of the Ministry of the Press, Broadcasting and Mass Media; summaries of newly published books; Editor-in-Chief Aleksandr F. Gavrilov; circ. 10,500 (2003).

Kultura (Culture): 127055 Moscow, ul. Novoslobodskaya 73; tel. (495) 285-06-40; fax (495) 200-32-25; e-mail kultura@dol.ru; internet www.kulturagz.ru; f. 1929; controlled by Sistema Mass-Mediya; weekly; Editor Yurii I. Belyavskii; circ. 29,200 (2002).

Literaturnaya Gazeta (Literary Newspaper): 109028 Moscow, Khokhlovskii per. 10/6; tel. and fax (499) 788-02-10; e-mail litgazeta@lgz.ru; internet www.lgz.ru; f. 1831; publ. restored 1929; weekly; literature, politics, society; controlled by Sistema Mass-Mediya; Editor-in-Chief Yu. M. Polyakov.

Literaturnaya Rossiya (Literary Russia): 103051 Moscow, Tsvetnoi bulv. 32/3; tel. and fax (495) 694-50-10; e-mail litrossia@litrossia.ru; internet www.litrossia.ru; f. 1958; weekly; essays, verse, literary criticism; Editor Vyacheslav Ogryzko; circ. 19,650 (2007).

Oktyabr (October): 125040 Moscow, ul. Pravdy 11/13; tel. (495) 214-62-05; fax (495) 214-50-29; internet magazines.russ.ru/october; f. 1924; monthly; independent literary journal; new fiction and essays by Russian and foreign writers; Editor-in-Chief Irina N. Barmetova.

Sem Dnei (Seven Days): 125871 Moscow, Leningradskoye shosse 5а; tel. (495) 195-92-76; fax (495) 753-41-32; e-mail 7days@7days.ru; internet www.7days.ru; f. 1967; celebrity news and television listings magazine; Editor V. V. Orlova; circ. 937,000 (2000).

Znamya (Banner): 103001 Moscow, ul. B. Sadovaya 2/46; tel. (495) 299-52-38; e-mail info@znamlit.ru; internet magazines.russ.ru/znamia; f. 1931; monthly; independent; novels, poetry, essays; Editor-in-Chief Sergei I. Chuprinin; circ. 5,300 (2004).

Economics and Finance

Chelovek i Trud (Man and Labour): 105064 Moscow, Yakovoapostolskii per. 6/3; tel. and fax (495) 917-76-36; e-mail chelt@yandex.ru; internet www.chelt.ru; monthly; f. 1956 as *Sotsialisticheskii trud* (Socialist Labour); present name adopted 1992; employment issues, unemployment, social policy, pensions, personnel management etc.; Editor-in-Chief M. A. Barinova; circ. 10,000 (2005).

D': 125866 Moscow, Bumazhnyi proyezd 14/1; tel. (495) 609-64-98; fax (495) 228-00-78; e-mail shu@expert.ru; internet www.expert.ru/printissues/d; f. 2005; personal finance; Chief Editor Tatyana Gurova; circ. 50,500 (2008).

Deloviye Lyudi (Business People): 123995 Moscow, ul. 1905 goda 7; tel. (495) 781-47-37; fax (495) 781-47-44; e-mail dl@mk.ru; internet www.dl.mk.ru; f. 1990; monthly; business, management and economics; Editor-in-Chief Andrei I. Lapik; circ. 50,000 (2007).

Dengi (Money): 125080 Moscow, ul. Vrubelya 4/1; tel. (499) 943-97-71; fax (499) 943-97-28; e-mail dengi@kommersant.ru; internet www

THE RUSSIAN FEDERATION

.kommersant.ru/k-money; weekly; publ. by the Kommersant Publishing House; Chief Editor Sergei Yakovlev.

Dengi i Kredit (Money and Credit): 107016 Moscow, ul. Neglinnaya 12; tel. (495) 771-99-87; fax (495) 771-99-93; e-mail ggv@cbr.ru; internet www.cbr.ru/publ/main.asp?Prtid=MoneyAndCredit; f. 1927; monthly; publ. by the Central Bank; all aspects of banking and money circulation; Chief Editor Vladimir S. Palevich; circ. 5,430 (2002).

Ekonomika i Zhizn (Economics and Life): 125319 Moscow, ul. Chernyakhovskogo 16; tel. and fax (495) 152-51-38; e-mail eg@ekonomika.ru; internet www.ekonomika.ru; f. 1918; weekly; fmrly *Ekonomicheskaya gazeta*; news and information about the economy and business; Editor Tatyana A. Ivanova; circ. 150,000 (2005).

Ekspert (Expert): 127137 Moscow, ul. Pravdy 24, Novyi Gazetnyi kor., POB 33; tel. (495) 510-56-43; fax (495) 510-56-39; e-mail ask@expert.ru; internet www.expert.ru; weekly; business and economics; financial and share markets; policy and culture; regional edns: *Ekspert Severo-Zapad* (St Petersburg and North-Western Russia), *Ekspert Sibir* (Siberia), *Ekspert Ural* (Urals), *Ekspert Volga* (The Volga region), *Ekspert Yug* (Southern Russia); Editor-in-Chief Valerii Fadeyev.

Finans (Finance): 127238 Moscow, Lokomotivnyi proyezd 21A; tel. and fax (495) 788-53-10; e-mail inform@finansmag.ru; internet www.fr.ru; f. 2003; weekly; economics, business, finance, society; Editor-in-Chief Oleg Anisimov; circ. 48,700 (2007).

Finansy (Finances): 125009 Moscow, ul. Tverskaya 22B; tel. (495) 699-44-27; fax (495) 699-96-16; e-mail finance@df.ru; internet www.df.ru/~finance; f. 1926; monthly; theory and information on finances; compilation and execution of the state budget, insurance, lending, taxation etc.; Editor Yu. M. Artemov; circ. 10,000 (2004).

Kompaniya (The Firm): 109544 Moscow, ul. B. Andronyevskaya 17; tel. (495) 745-84-10; e-mail ko@idr.ru; internet www.ko.ru; f. 1997; weekly; politics, economics, finance; Editor-in-Chief Andrei Grigoryev; circ. 78,000 (2007).

Mirovaya Ekonomika i Mezhdunarodniye Otnosheniya (World Economy and International Relations): 117859 Moscow, ul. Profsoyuznaya 23; tel. (495) 128-08-83; fax (495) 310-70-27; e-mail memojour@imemo.ru; internet www.imemo.ru; f. 1957; monthly; journal of the Institute of the World Economy and International Relations of the Russian Academy of Sciences; theory and practice of socio-economic development, international policies, economic co-operation; Editor A. V. Ryabov.

Profil (Profile): 109544 Moscow, ul. B. Andronyevskaya 17; tel. (495) 745-94-01; e-mail web@idr.ru; internet www.profil.orc.ru; f. 1996; weekly; Editor-in-Chief Mikhail Leontyev; circ. 83,000 in Russia and 27,600 in Ukraine (2007).

Rossiiskii Ekonomicheskii Zhurnal (Russian Economic Journal): 109542 Moscow, Ryazanskii pr. 99; tel. and fax (495) 377-25-56; internet www.e-rej.ru; f. 1958; monthly; economics; Editor A. Yu. Melentev; circ. 6,100 (2004).

Voprosy Ekonomiki (Questions of Economics): 117218 Moscow, Nakhimovskii pr. 32; tel. and fax (495) 124-52-28; e-mail mail@vopreco.ru; internet www.vopreco.ru; f. 1929; monthly; journal of the Institute of Economics of the Russian Academy of Sciences; theoretical problems of economic development, market relations, social aspects of transition to a market economy, international economics, etc.; Editor L. Abalkin; circ. 6,000 (2008).

Education

Semya (The Family): 107996 Moscow, Orlikov per. 5; tel. (495) 975-05-29; fax (495) 975-00-76; e-mail mail@semya.ru; internet www.semya.ru; f. 1988; weekly; Editor-in-Chief Sergei A. Abramov; circ. 50,000 (2004).

Semya i Shkola (Family and School): 129278 Moscow, ul. P. Korchagina 7; tel. (495) 683-82-21; fax (495) 683-86-14; e-mail mag7a@narod.ru; internet www.mag7a.narod.ru; f. 1871; monthly; for parents and children; Editor-in-Chief P. I. Gelazoniya; circ. 3,000 (2007).

Shkola i Proizvodstvo (School and Production): 127254 Moscow, ul. Sh. Rustaveli 10/3; tel. and fax (495) 219-83-80; e-mail sip@schoolpress.ru; internet www.schoolpress.ru/jornal/issues/sip/index.php; f. 1957; 8 a year; Chief Editor G. V. Pichugina; circ. 17,000 (2007).

Uchitelskaya Gazeta (Teachers' Gazette): 107045 Moscow, Ananyevskii per. 4/2/1; tel. (495) 928-82-53; fax (495) 928-82-53; e-mail ug@ug.ru; internet www.ug.ru; f. 1924; weekly; independent; Editor Petr Polozhevets; circ. 95,000 (2007).

International Affairs

Ekho Planety (Echo of the Planet): 103860 Moscow, Tverskoi bulv. 10/12; tel. (495) 202-67-48; fax (495) 290-59-11; e-mail echotex@itar-tass.com; internet www.explan.ru; f. 1988; weekly; publ. by ITAR—TASS; international affairs, economic, social and cultural; Editor-in-Chief Valentin Vasilets.

Mezhdunarodnaya Zhizn (International Life): 105064 Moscow, Gorokhovskii per. 14; tel. (495) 265-37-81; fax (495) 265-37-71; e-mail inter_affairs@mid.ru; f. 1954; monthly; Russian and English; publ. by the Pressa Publishing House; foreign policy and diplomacy; Editor-in-Chief B. D. Pyadyshev; circ. 70,000.

Novoye Vremya/The New Times: 125009 Moscow, Tverskoi bulv. 14/1; tel. and fax (495) 648-07-57; e-mail info@newtimes.ru; internet www.newtimes.ru; f. 1943; weekly; Russian, English; foreign and Russian affairs; Editor-in-Chief Aleksandr Pumpyanskii.

Russkii Reporter (Russian Reporter): 125866 Moscow, Bumazhnyi proyezd 14/1; tel. (495) 609-66-74; e-mail reporter@expert.ru; internet www.expert.ru/printissues/russian_reporter; f. 2007; monthly; domestic and international affairs and culture; Chief Editor Vitalii Leibin.

Language and Literature

Ex Libris-NG: 113935 Moscow, ul. Myasnitskaya 13; tel. (495) 928-48-50; fax (495) 975-23-46; e-mail info@ng.ru; internet exlibris.ng.ru; weekly; literature; Editor-in-Chief Igor Zotov.

Russkaya Literatura (Russian Literature): 199034 St Petersburg, nab. Makarova 4; tel. (812) 328-16-01; fax (812) 328-16-01; e-mail musliter@mail.ru; f. 1958; quarterly; journal of the Institute of Russian Literature of the Russian Academy of Sciences; development of Russian literature from its appearance up to the present day; Editor N. N. Skatov; circ. 1,099 (2004).

Voprosy Literatury (Questions of Literature): 125009 Moscow, B. Gnezdnikovskii per. 10; tel. (495) 629-49-77; fax (495) 629-64-71; e-mail vopli@arion.ru; internet magazines.russ.ru/voplit; f. 1957; 6 a year; publ. by Foundation for Literary Criticism; theory and history of modern literature and aesthetics; Editor L. I. Lazarev; circ. 2,500 (2007).

Leisure and Sport

Afisha (Poster): 103009 Moscow, per. B. Gnezdnikovskii 7/28/1; tel. (495) 785-17-00; fax (495) 785-17-01; e-mail info@afisha.net; internet www.afisha.ru; f. 1999; every 2 weeks; listings and reviews of events; 3 edns, for Moscow, St Petersburg, and the rest of Russia; Chief Editor Yurii Saprykin.

Avtopilot (Autopilot): 123308 Moscow, Khoroshevskoye shosse 41; tel. (495) 493-91-44; fax (495) 493-91-64; e-mail autopilot@kommersant.ru; internet autopilot.kommersant.ru; cars; publ. by the Kommersant Publishing House; Editor-in-Chief Aleksandr Fedorov.

Bolshoi Gorod (Big City): 125009 Moscow, B. Gnezdnikovskii per 7/28/1; tel. (495) 785-17-00; fax (495) 785-17-01; e-mail info@bg.ru; internet www.bg.ru; f. 2001; every two weeks; Moscow and St Petersburg edns; culture, travel, technology; Chief Editors Filipp Dzyadko ((Moscow edn)), Yuliya Tarnavskaya (St Petersburg edn).

Fizkultura i Sport (Exercise and Sport): 125130 Moscow, per. 6-i Novopodmoskovnii 3, POB 198; tel. (495) 786-60-62; fax (495) 786-61-39; e-mail fisemail@mtu-net.ru; internet www.fismag.ru; f. 1922; monthly; activities and development of Russian sports, health; Editor I. Sosnovskii.

Rossiiskaya Okhotnichya Gazeta (Russian Hunters' Magazine): 123848 Moscow, ul. 1905 Goda 7; tel. (495) 256-94-74; e-mail rog@mk.ru; internet www.mk.ru/blogs/idmk/ROG; weekly; hunting, shooting, fishing; Editor-in-Chief Oleg Malov.

Sport Ekspress (Sport Express): 123056 Moscow, ul. Krasina 27/2; tel. (495) 254-47-87; fax (495) 733-93-08; e-mail sport@sport-express.ru; internet www.sport-express.ru; f. 1991; daily; sport; Editor-in-Chief Vladimir Kuchmii; circ. in Moscow and St Petersburg 190,000 (2004).

Sovetskii Sport (Soviet Sport): 103287 Moscow, Staryi Petrovsko-Razumovskii proyezd 1/23/1; tel. (495) 637-64-33; fax (495) 637-64-24; e-mail sport@sovsport.ru; internet www.sovsport.ru; f. 1924; weekly; Editor-in-Chief Igor Kots.

Za Rulem (Behind The Wheel): 103045 Moscow, per. Selivyerstov 10; tel. (495) 607-23-82; fax (495) 737-43-07; e-mail stas@zr.ru; internet www.zr.ru; f. 1928; monthly; cars and motorsport; Editor-in-Chief Petr S. Menshikh.

Politics and Military Affairs

Litsa (People): 121099 Moscow, Smolenskaya pl. 13/21, POB 99; tel. (495) 241-37-92; e-mail litsa@aha.ru; f. 1996; monthly; Editor-in-Chief Artem Borovik; circ. 100,000 (2002).

Na Dne (The Lower Depths): 195112 St Petersburg, Novocherkasskii pr. 37/1A; tel. (812) 528-04-14; fax (812) 310-52-09; f. 1994; current affairs; social issues; 2 a month.

Nezavisimoye Voyennoye Obozreniye (Independent Military Review): 101000 Moscow, ul. Myasnitskaya 13; tel. and fax (495)

THE RUSSIAN FEDERATION

925-88-29; internet nvo.ng.ru; f. 1995; Editor VADIM SOLOVYEV; circ. 20,140 (2004).

Rossiya v Globalnoi Politike/Russia in Global Affairs: 103873 Moscow, ul. Mokhovaya 11/3v; tel. (495) 980-73-53; fax (495) 937-76-11; e-mail info@globalaffairs.ru; internet www.globalaffairs.ru; f. 2002; co-founded by the Russian Union of Industrialists and Entrepreneurs, the Council for Foreign and Defence Politics and the newspaper *Izvestiya*, in collaboration with the US journal, *Foreign Affairs*; 6 a year (Russian); 4 a year (English); online edns in Czech and Polish; Chair. of Editorial Bd SERGEI A. KARAGANOV; Editor-in-Chief FEDOR A. LUKYANOV.

Rossiiskaya Federatsiya Segodnya (The Russian Federation Today): 103800 Moscow, ul. M. Dmitrovka 3/10; tel. (495) 933-54-79; fax (495) 933-54-74; e-mail rfs@russia-today.ru; internet www.russia-today.ru; f. 1994; journal of the Gosudarstvennaya Duma; Editor YURII A. KHRENOV.

Russia Profile: 119021 Moscow, Zubovskii bulv. 4; tel. (495) 981-64-86; fax (495) 201-30-71; e-mail info@russiaprofile.org; f. 1966; monthly; in English; publ. by Independent Media for RIA-Novosti in association with the International Relations and Security Network (Zurich, Switzerland) and the Center for Defense Information (Washington, DC, USA); Editor ANDREI ZOLOTOV Jr.

Shchit i Mech (Shield and Sword): 127434 Moscow, Ivanovskii pr. 18; tel. (495) 976-66-44; fax (495) 619-80-90; e-mail gazeta@simech.ru; internet www.simech.ru; f. 1989; weekly; military, security, geopolitical concerns; publ. by the Ministry of Internal Affairs; Editor-in-Chief VALERII KULIK; circ. 50,000 (2004).

Sovershenno Sekretno (Top Secret): 121099 Moscow, Smolenskaya pl. 13/21, POB 255; tel. (495) 241-68-73; fax (495) 241-75-55; e-mail velekhov@topsecret.cnt.ru; internet sovsekretno.ru; f. 1989; monthly; Editor-in-Chief GALINA SIDOROVA.

Vlast (Power): 123308 Moscow, Khoroshevskoye shosse 41; tel. (499) 943-97-71; fax (499) 234-16-60; e-mail vlast@kommersant.ru; internet www.kommersant.ru/k-vlast; f. 1997; weekly; Chief Editor MAKSIM KOVALSKII.

Yezhenedelnyi Zhurnal (Weekly Magazine): 129110 Moscow, Pereyaslavskii per. 4; tel. (495) 785-82-50; fax (495) 785-82-51; e-mail info@ej.ru; internet www.ej.ru; f. 2001; Editor-in-Chief SERGEI PARKHOMENKO.

Zavtra (Tomorrow): 119146 Moscow, Frunzenskaya nab. 18/60; tel. (495) 726-54-83; e-mail zavtra@zavtra.ru; internet www.zavtra.ru; extreme left, nationalist; Editor-in-Chief ALEKSANDR A. PROGANOV.

Popular, Fiction and General

Inostrannaya Literatura (Foreign Literature): 109017 Moscow, ul. Pyatnitskaya 41; tel. (495) 953-51-47; fax (495) 953-50-61; e-mail inolit@rinet.ru; internet magazines.russ.ru/inostran; f. 1891; monthly; independent; Russian translations of modern foreign authors and literary criticism; Editor-in-Chief ALEKSEI SLOVESNII.

Molotok (Little Hammer): 125080 Moscow, vul. Vrubelya 4; tel. (495) 209-11-32; fax (495) 200-40-55; e-mail molotok@unity.kommersant.ru; internet www.zabey.ru; f. 2000; weekly; popular culture.

Nash Sovremennik (Our Contemporary): 127994 Moscow, Tsvetnoi bulv. 32/2; tel. (495) 200-24-24; fax (495) 200-24-12; e-mail mail@nash-sovremennik.ru; internet nash-sovremennik.ru; f. 1956; monthly; publ. by the Union of Writers of Russia; contemporary prose and 'patriotic polemics'; Editor STANISLAV KUNAYEV.

Novyi Krokodil (New Crocodile): 129090 Moscow, Potapovskii per. 3, POB 94; tel. (495) 956-37-17; e-mail crocodile@vf-m.ru; internet www.crocodile.su; f. 2005 to replace *Krokodil* (Crododile—founded 1922); monthly; satirical; Editor SERGEI MOSTOVSHCHIKOV.

Novyi Mir (New World): 103806 Moscow, M. Putinkovskii per. 1/2; tel. and fax (495) 200-08-29; e-mail nmir@aha.ru; internet magazines.russ.ru/novyi_mi; f. 1925; monthly; publ. by the Izvestiya (News) Publishing House; new fiction and essays; Editor ANDREI V. VASILEVSKII; circ.c. 8,000 (2005).

Ogonek (Beacon): 127055 Moscow, ul. Lesnaya 55/1–2; tel. (495) 660-94-47; fax (499) 973-14-30; e-mail ogoniok@ogoniokpress.ru; internet www.ogoniok.com/ f. 1899; weekly; politics, popular science, economics, literature; Editor VIKTOR LOSHAK; circ. 69,000 (2007).

Politicheskii Klass (The Political Class): 119002 Moscow, per. Sivtsev Vrazhek 29/16/415; tel. (495) 241-43-67; e-mail info@politklass.ru; internet politklass.ru; f. 2004; monthly; domestic and international affairs, philosophy and politics; Chief Editor V. T. TRETYAKOV.

Rodina (Motherland): 127025 Moscow, ul. Novyi Arbat 19; tel. (495) 203-75-98; fax (495) 203-47-45; e-mail istrodina@mail.ru; internet www.istrodina.com; f. 1989 as revival of 1879–1917 publication; monthly; publ. by Administration of the President of the Russian Federation and Government of the Russian Federation; popular historical; supplement *Istochnik* (Source), every two months, documents state archives; Chief Editor YURII BORISENOK; circ. 20,000 (2003).

Rodnaya Gazeta (Native Gazette): 125137 Moscow, ul. Pravdy 24/2; tel. (495) 789-44-00; fax (495) 789-44-01; e-mail info@rodgaz.ru; internet www.rodgaz.ru; f. 2003; weekly; politics, culture, nationalist, left-wing; Editor-in-Chief ALEKSANDR KOLODNYI.

Rossiiskii Kto Yest Kto (Russian Who's Who): 117335 Moscow, POB 81; tel. (495) 234-46-92; e-mail zhurnal@whoiswho.ru; internet www.whoiswho.ru; 2 a year; biographical and directory material; Editor-in-Chief SVYATOSLAV RYBAS; circ. 10,000.

Sobesednik (Interlocutor): 101484 Moscow, ul. Novoslobodskaya 73, POB 4; tel. (495) 685-56-65; fax (495) 973-20-54; e-mail info@sobesednik.ru; internet www.sobesednik.ru; f. 1984; weekly; Editor-in-Chief YURII PILIPENKO.

SPID-Info: 125284 Moscow, POB 42; tel. (495) 255-02-99; fax (495) 252-09-20; e-mail mail@si.ru; internet www.s-info.ru; f. 1991; two a month; popular; Editor-in-Chief OLGA BELAN; circ. 1,200,000 (2005).

Versiya (Possibility): 121099 Moscow, Smolenskaya pl. 13/21, POB 255; tel. (495) 291-23-76; e-mail versia@topsecret.cnt.ru; internet www.versiasovsek.ru; f. 1998; weekly; Editor-in-Chief A. V. BOKSHITSKAYA.

Vokrug Sveta (Around the World): 125015 Moscow, ul. Argunovskaya 12/1/6A; tel. (495) 491-96-45; fax (495) 490-57-25; e-mail editor@vokrugsveta.ru; internet www.vokrugsveta.ru; f. 1861; monthly; geographical, travel and adventure; illustrated; Chief Editor YELENA KNYAZEVA (acting).

Zvezda (Star): 191028 St Petersburg, ul. Mokhovaya 20; tel. (812) 272-71-38; fax (812) 273-52-56; e-mail mail@zvezdaspb.ru; internet zvezdaspb.ru; f. 1923; monthly; publ. by the Zvezda Publishing House; novels, short stories, poetry and literary criticism; Editors A. YU. ARYEV, YA. A. GORDIN.

Popular Scientific

Meditsinskaya Gazeta (Medical Gazette): 129090 Moscow, B. Sukharevskaya pl. 1/2; tel. (495) 608-86-95; fax (495) 208-69-80; e-mail inform@mgzt.ru; internet www.mgzt.ru; f. 1938; 2 a week; professional international periodical; Editor ANDREI POLTORAK.

Nauka i Zhizn (Science and Life): 101990 Moscow, ul. Myasnitskaya 24; tel. (495) 624-18-35; fax (495) 200-22-59; e-mail mail@nkj.ru; internet www.nkj.ru; f. 1890, resumed 1934; monthly; recent developments in all branches of science and technology; Chief Editor I. K. LAGOVSKII; circ. 46,000 (2007).

PC Week: 109047 Moscow, ul. Marksistskaya 34/10; tel. (495) 974-22-60; fax (495) 974-22-63; e-mail editorial@pcweek.ru; internet www.pcweek.ru; f. 1995; 48 a year; Editor-in-Chief EDUARD PROYDAKOV.

Priroda (Nature): 117810 Moscow, Maronovskii per. 26; tel. (495) 238-24-56; fax (495) 238-26-33; f. 1912; monthly; publ. by the Nauka (Science) Publishing House; journal of the Presidium of the Academy of Sciences; natural sciences; Editor A. F. ANDREYEV.

Radio: 107045 Moscow, per. Seliverstov 10/1; tel. (495) 207-31-18; fax (495) 208-77-13; internet www.radio.ru; f. 1924; monthly; audio, video, communications, practical electronics, computers; Editor Y. I. KRYLOV.

Tekhnika-Molodezhi (Engineering—For Youth): 127051 Moscow, ul. Petrovka 26/3, POB 94; tel. (495) 625-17-41; fax (495) 628-34-79; e-mail post@tm-magazin.ru; internet www.tm-magazin.ru; f. 1933; monthly; engineering and science; Editor A. N. PEREVOZCHIKOV.

Vrach (Physician): 119991 Moscow, ul. Trubetskaya 8/2; tel. and fax (499) 766-07-57; e-mail rvrach@mmascience.ru; internet www.rusvrach.ru; f. 1990; monthly; medical, scientific and socio-political; illustrated; Editor-in-Chief I. N. DENISOV; circ. 3,700 (2004).

Zdorovye (Health): 127994 Moscow, Bumazhnyi proyezd 14/1; tel. (495) 250-58-28; fax (495) 257-32-51; e-mail zdorovie@zdr.ru; internet www.zdr.ru; f. 1955; monthly; Editor TATYANA YEFIMOVA; circ. 170,000 (2006).

The Press, Printing and Bibliography

Bibliografiya (Bibliography): 119019 Moscow, Kremlevskaya nab. 1/9; tel. (499) 766-00-85; e-mail bibliogr@bookchamber.ru; internet www.bookchamber.ru/international/bibliography_mag.html; f. 1929; 6 a year; theoretical, practical and historical aspects of bibliography; Editor K. M. SUKHORUKOV; circ. 2,300 (2005).

Poligrafist i Izdatel (Printer and Publisher): 119313 Moscow, Leninskii pr. 87/392-395; tel. (499) 134-78-43; fax (495) 288-94-44; e-mail mediarama@mediarama.ru; internet www.mediarama.ru/pp/pp.html; f. 1994; monthly; Editor A. I. OVSYANNIKOV; circ. 3,000 (2008).

Poligrafiya (Printing): 129272 Moscow, ul. Sushchevskii Val 64; tel. and fax (495) 681-74-81; e-mail polimag@aha.ru; internet www.polimag.ru; f. 1924; 6 a year; equipment and technology of the printing industry; Dir N. N. KONDRATIYEVA; circ. 5,000 (2007).

THE RUSSIAN FEDERATION

Zhurnalist (Journalist): 125190 Moscow, Chezniyahovskogo ul. 16; tel. (495) 152-88-71; e-mail jour-nal@yandex.ru; internet www.journalist-virt.ru; f. 1920; monthly; publ. by Ekonomicheskaya Gazeta Publishing House; Editor G. P. MALTSEV; circ. 10,150 (2007).

Religion

Bratskii Vestnik (Herald of the Brethren): 109028 Moscow, M. Vuzovskii per. 3; tel. (495) 917-96-26; internet moscowseminary.ru/bv/index.html; f. 1945; 6 a year; organ of the Russian Union of Evangelical Christians-Baptists; Chief Editor VITALII KULIKOV.

Istina i Zhizn (Truth and Life): 105264 Moscow, ul. 7-aya Parkovaya 26/1/303; tel. and fax (495) 786-35-89; e-mail istina@aha.ru; internet istina.religare.ru; f. 1990; inter-confessional magazine of Christian culture; monthly; Editor Fr ALEKSANDR KHMELNITSKII.

Mezhdunarodnaya Yevreyskaya Gazeta (International Jewish Newspaper): 107005 Moscow, Pleteshkovskii per. 3A; tel. and fax (495) 225-44-84; e-mail meg@spacenet.ru; internet www.jig.ru; f. 1989; weekly; Dir-Gen. YAKOV POLISCHUK; circ. 15,000 (2002).

NG-Religii (The Independent-Religions): 101000 Moscow, ul. Myasnitskaya 13; tel. (495) 923-42-40; fax (495) 921-58-47; e-mail ngr@ng.ru; internet religion.ng.ru; f. 1997; analysis of religious affairs and their domestic and global social and political implications; 2 a month; Editor-in-Chief MAKSIM SHEVCHENKO.

Tserkovnyi Vestnik (Church Herald): 119435 Moscow, ul. Pogodinskaya 20/2; tel. and fax (495) 246-01-65; e-mail info03@rop.ru; internet www.tserkov.info; f. 1989; 24 a year; organ of the Russian Orthodox Church (Moscow Patriarchate); Editor-in-Chief Very Rev. VLADIMIR SILOVYEV; circ. 30,000 (2005).

Yevreiskoye Slovo (The Jewish Word): 127018 Moscow, 2-i Vysheslavtsev per. 5A; tel. (495) 792-31-13; e-mail redaktor@e-slovo.ru; internet www.e-slovo.ru; f. 2000; Editor-in-Chief VLADIMIR DYNKIN.

Zhurnal Moskovskoi Patriarkhii (Journal of the Moscow Patriarchate): 119435 Moscow, ul. Pogodinskaya 20/2; tel. (495) 246-98-48; fax (495) 246-21-41; e-mail eugpol@rop.ru; internet www.jmp.ru; f. 1934; monthly; official publication of the Russian Orthodox Church (Moscow Patriarchate); Editor Archpriest VLADIMIR (SILOVYEV).

Transport and Communication

Grazhdanskaya Aviatsiya (Civil Aviation): 125993 Moscow, Leningradskii pr. 37; tel. (495) 155-59-23; fax (495) 155-51-64; f. 1931; monthly; journal of the Union of Civil Aviation Workers; development of air transport; utilization of aviation in construction, agriculture and forestry; Editor A. M. TROSHIN.

Radiotekhnika (Radio Engineering): 103031 Moscow, Kuznetskii most 20/6/31; tel. (495) 921-48-37; fax (495) 925-92-41; e-mail iprzhr@online.ru; f. 1937; monthly; publ. by the Svyaz (Communication) Publishing House; journal of the A. S. Popov Scientific and Technical Society of Radio Engineering, Electronics and Electrical Communication; theoretical and technical problems of radio engineering; other publications include Advances in Radio Science, Radio Systems and Antennae; Editor YU. V. GULYAYEV.

Vestnik Svyazi (Herald of Communication): 101000 Moscow, Krivokolennyi per. 14/1; tel. (495) 625-42-57; fax (495) 621-27-97; e-mail vs@vestnik-sviazy.ru; internet www.vestnik-sviazy.ru; f. 1917; monthly; telecommunications; Editor E. B. KONSTANTINOV.

Women's Interest

Domovoi (House-Sprite): 113035 Moscow, ul. B. Ordynka 16; tel. (495) 675-52-48; e-mail dom@kommersant.ru; internet www.domovoy.ru; monthly; Chief Editor VALERIYA KUDRYAVTSEVA.

Elle: 115162 Moscow, ul. Shabolovka 31B; tel. (495) 891-39-10; e-mail achukovskaya@hfs.ru; internet www.elle.ru; f. 1996; monthly; fashion; Editor-in-Chief YELENA SOTNIKOVA.

Krestyanka (Peasant Woman): 127994 Moscow, Bumazhnyi proyezd 14; tel. (495) 257-39-39; fax (495) 257-39-63; e-mail mail@krestyanka.ru; internet www.krestyanka.ru; f. 1922; monthly; publ. by the Krestyanka Publishing House; popular; supplements *Khozyayushka* (Dear Hostess), *On i ona* (He and She), *Moda v dome* (Fashion at Home), *Samochuvstviye* (Health), *Nasha Usadba* (Our Garden), *Pyatnashki* (Game of Tag); Pres and Editor-in-Chief ANASTASIYA V. KUPRIYANOVA; circ. 85,000 (2004).

Mir Zhenshchiny (Woman's World): 101999 Moscow, Glinishchevskii per. 6; tel. and fax (495) 209-95-33; f. 1945; monthly; fmrly *Zhenshchina* (Woman); in Russian, Chinese, English, French, German and Spanish; fmrly publ. by the Soviet Women's Committee and the General Confederation of Trade Unions; popular; illustrated; Editor-in-Chief V. I. FEDOTOVA.

Rabotnitsa (Working Woman): 101458 Moscow, Bumazhnyi proyezd 14; tel. (495) 257-36-49; fax (495) 956-90-94; e-mail webmaster@rabotnitsa.ru; internet www.rabotnitsa.ru; f. 1914; monthly; popular; Editor ZOYA P KRYLOVA.

Youth

Rovesnik (Contemporary): 125015 Moscow, ul. Novodmitrovskaya 5A; tel. (495) 285-89-20; fax (495) 285-06-27; e-mail rovesnik@rovesnik.ru; internet www.rovesnik.ru/dom/rovesnik.asp; f. 1962; popular illustrated monthly of fiction, music, cinema, sport for 10–19 year olds; Editor I. A. CHERNYSHKOV; circ. 70,000 (2007).

Smena (The Rising Generation): 127994 Moscow, Bumazhnyi proyezd 19/2; tel. (495) 612-15-07; fax (495) 250-59-28; e-mail jurnal@smena-id.ru; internet www.smena-id.ru; f. 1924; monthly; popular illustrated, short stories, essays and problems of youth; Editor-in-Chief M. G. KIZILOV.

Yunost (Youth): 125047 Moscow, ul. Tverskaya-Yamskaya 8/1, POB 182; tel. and fax (495) 250-40-74; e-mail unost-contact@mail.ru; internet www.unost.org; f. 1955; monthly; novels, short stories, essays and poems by beginners; Editor TAMARA ANDREYEVA.

NEWS AGENCIES

ANP—Agentstvo novostei i prognozy (News and Forecasting Agency): 103009 Moscow, Kalashnyi per. 10/2; tel. (495) 782-33-71; fax (495) 153-57-45; e-mail aninons@online.ru; f. 2001 on basis of ANI News and Information Agency (f. 1991); Editor-in-Chief ALEKSEI SHCHAVELEV.

Interfax: 127006 Moscow, ul. 1-aya Tverskaya-Yamskaya 2; tel. (495) 250-98-40; fax (495) 250-97-27; e-mail info@interfax.ru; internet www.interfax.ru; f. 1989; independent information agency; Chief Exec. MIKHAIL KOMISSAR.

ITAR—TASS (Information Telegraphic Agency of Russia—Telegraphic Agency of the Sovereign Countries): 125993 Moscow, Tverskoi bulv. 10/12; tel. (495) 202-29-81; fax (495) 202-54-74; e-mail worldmarket@itar-tass.com; internet www.itar-tass.com; f. 1904 as St Petersburg Telegraph Agency, renamed as TASS (Telegraph Agency of the Soviet Union) in 1925; present name adopted 1992; state information agency; 74 bureaux in Russia and the states of the former USSR, 65 foreign bureaux outside the former USSR; Dir-Gen. VITALII N. IGNATENKO.

Prima Human Rights News Agency: 111399 Moscow, POB 5; tel. and fax (495) 455-30-11; e-mail prima@prima-news.ru; internet www.prima-news.ru; f. 2000; Editor-in-Chief ALEKSANDR PODRABINEK.

RIA—Novosti (Russian Information Agency—News): 103786 Moscow, Zubovskii bulv. 4; tel. (495) 201-82-09; fax (495) 201-45-45; e-mail marketing@rian.ru; internet www.rian.ru; f. 1961 as Agenstvo Pechati 'Novosti' (APN); present name adopted 1991; collaborates by arrangement with foreign press and publishing organizations in 110 countries; provider of Russian news features and photographs; Chair. SVETLANA MIRONYUK.

RosBalt Information Agency: 190000 St Petersburg, Konnogvardeiskii bulv. 7; tel. (812) 320-50-30; fax (812) 320-50-31; e-mail rosbalt@rosbalt.ru; internet www.rosbalt.ru; news coverage of European Russia and other countries in northern Europe; Chair. NATALIYA CHERKESOVA.

Rossiiskoye Informatsionnoye Agentstvo 'Oreanda' (RIA 'Oreanda'): 117342 Moscow, POB 21; tel. (495) 330-98-50; fax (495) 23-04-39; e-mail info@oreanda.ru; internet www.oreanda.ru; f. 1994.

Strana.Ru (Country-Russia): 119021 Moscow, Zubovskii bulv. 4, podyezd 8; tel. (495) 981-62-52; fax (495) 981-62-53; e-mail mail@strana.ru; internet www.strana.ru; f. 2000; news agency; central bureau in Moscow, regional bureaux in Groznyi (Chechen—Nokchi Republic) and in Kyiv, Ukraine; controlled by the All-Russian State Television and Radio Broadcasting Company (VGTRK); Editor-in-Chief YULIYA PANFILOVA.

PRESS ASSOCIATIONS

Russian Guild of Publishers of Periodical Press: 125047 Moscow, ul. Lesnaya 20/6-211; tel. and fax (495) 978-41-89.

Union of Journalists of Russia: 119021 Moscow, Zubovskii bulv. 4; tel. (495) 201-51-01; fax (495) 201-35-47; f. 1991; Sec.-Gen. IGOR YAKOVENKO.

Publishers

Ad Marginem-Ad Patres: Moscow; f. 1994; fiction, philosophy, artistic and literary criticism; Dir ALEKSANDR IVANOV.

Aleteiya (Aletheia): 193019 St Petersburg, pr. Obukhovskoi oborony 13; tel. (812) 567-22-39; e-mail aletheia@rol.ru; internet www.orthodoxia.org/aletheia; f. 1992; classics, ancient and medieval history, social sciences; Dir-Gen. I. A. SAVKIN.

AST: 129085 Moscow, Zvezdnyi bulv. 21; tel. (495) 215-01-01; fax (495) 215-51-10; e-mail astpub@aha.ru; internet www.ast.ru; original and translated fiction and non-fiction, children's and schoolbooks.

Avrora (Aurora): 191065 St Petersburg, Nevskii pr. 7/9; tel. (812) 312-37-53; fax (812) 312-54-60; e-mail aurora@mail.nevalink.ru; f. 1969; fine arts; Dir ZENOBIUS SPETCHINSKII.

Azbuka (Alphabet): 196105 St Petersburg, ul. Reshetnikova 15, POB 192; tel. (812) 327-04-55; fax (812) 327-01-60; e-mail post@azbooka.spb.ru; internet www.azbooka.ru; literary fiction, including translations; f. 1995; Dir-Gen. MAKSIM I. KRYUTCHENKO.

Bolshaya Rossiiskaya Entsiklopediya (The Great Russian Encyclopedia): 109028 Moscow, Pokrovskii bulv. 8; tel. (495) 917-90-00; fax (495) 916-01-22; e-mail secretar@greatbook.ru; internet www.greatbook.ru; f. 1925; encyclopedias and reference; Dir-Gen. NIKOLAI S. ARTEMOV.

Detskaya Entsiklopediya (Children's Encyclopedia): 107042 Moscow, ul. Bakuninskaya 55; tel. (495) 269-52-76; f. 1933; science fiction, literature, poetry, biographical and historical novels.

Drofa: 127018 Moscow, ul. Sushchevskii Val 49; tel. (495) 795-05-50; fax (495) 795-05-44; e-mail info@drofa.ru; internet www.drofa.ru; f. 1991; school textbooks, children's fiction; Dir-Gen. ALEKSANDR F. KISELEV.

Ekonomika (Economy): 123955 Moscow, Berezhkovskaya nab. 6; tel. (499) 240-58-18; fax (499) 240-48-178; e-mail info@economizdat.ru; internet www.economizdat.ru; f. 1963; various aspects of economics, management and marketing; Dir YELIZABETA V. POLIYEVKTOVA.

Eksmo: 127299 Moscow, ul. K. Tsetkina 18/5; tel. and fax (495) 411-68-86; e-mail info@eksmo.ru; internet www.eksmo.ru; f. 1991; fiction; Gen. Dir OLEG YE. NOVIKOV.

Energoatomizdat (Atomic Energy Press): 113114 Moscow, Shluzovaya nab. 10; tel. (495) 925-99-93; f. 1981; different kinds of energy, nuclear science and technology; Dir A. P. ALESHKIN.

Finansy i Statistika (Finance and Statistics): 101000 Moscow, ul. Pokrovka 7; tel. (495) 625-47-08; fax (495) 625-09-57; e-mail mail@finstat.ru; internet www.finstat.ru; f. 1924; education, economics, tourism, finance, statistics, banking, insurance, accounting, computer science; Dir Dr ALEVTINA N. ZVONOVA.

Forum: 101000 Moscow, Kolpachnyi per. 9A; tel. and fax (495) 625-52-43; e-mail mail@forum-books.ru; internet www.forum-books.ru; f. 2001; general and professional educational textbooks; Gen. Man. SVETLANA P. SILVANOVICH.

Galart: 125319 Moscow, ul. Chernyakhovskogo 4; tel. and fax (495) 151-25-02; e-mail galart@m9com.ru; internet www.galart-moscow.ru; f. 1969; fmrly Sovetskii Khudozhnik (Soviet Artist); art reproduction, art history and criticism; Gen. Dir A. D. SARABYANOV.

Gorodets: 109386 Moscow, ul. Krasnodonskaya 20/2; tel. and fax (495) 351-55-80; e-mail info@gorodets.com; internet www.gorodets.com; f. 1996; law, politics, international relations, economics.

INFRA-M: 127282 Moscow, ul. Polyarnara 31B; tel. and fax (495) 363-42-60; e-mail books@infra-m.ru; internet www.infra-m.ru; f. 1992; economics, law, computing, history, reference works, encyclopedias; Man. Dir VADIM D. SINYANSKII.

Izobrazitelnoye Iskusstvo (Fine Art): 129272 Moscow, ul. Sushchevskii Val 64; tel. (495) 681-65-48; fax (495) 681-41-11; e-mail iskusstvo@id.ru; reproductions of pictures, pictorial art, books on art, albums, calendars, postcards; Dir G. SH. YERITSYAN.

Khimiya (Chemistry): 107976 Moscow, ul. Strominka 21/2; tel. (495) 268-29-76; f. 1963; chemistry and the chemical industry; Dir BORIS S. KRASNOPEVTSEV.

Khudozhestvennaya Literatura (Fiction): 107078 Moscow, ul. Novobasmannaya 19; tel. (499) 261-88-65; fax (499) 261-83-00; fiction and works of literary criticism, history of literature, etc.; Dir A. N. PETROV; Editor-in-Chief V. S. MODESTOV.

Kolos (Ear of Corn): 107996 Moscow, ul. Sadovaya-Spasskaya 18/1; tel. (495) 207-19-45; fax (495) 207-28-70; internet www.koloc.ru; f. 1999; all agricultural production; Dir ANATOLII M. ULYANOV.

Kompozitor (Composer): 119034 Moscow, M. Levshinskii per. 7/2; tel. (495) 955-19-66; fax (495) 209-54-98; e-mail komp@kompubl.com; internet www.idk.su; f. 1957; music and music criticism; Dir GRIGORII A. VORONOV.

Meditsina (Medicine): 101838 Moscow, Petroverigskii per. 6/8; tel. (495) 924-87-85; fax (495) 928-60-03; e-mail meditsina@iname.com; internet www.medlit.ru; f. 1918; state-owned; imprint of Association for Medical Literature; books and journals on medicine and health; Dir A. M. STOCHIK.

Mezhdunarodnye Otnosheniya (International Relations): 107078 Moscow, ul. Sadovaya-Spasskaya 18/709; tel. (495) 207-67-93; fax (495) 200-22-04; e-mail info@inter-rel.ru; internet www.inter-rel.ru; f. 1957; international relations, economics and politics of foreign countries, foreign trade, international law, foreign language textbooks and dictionaries, translations and publications for the UN and other international organizations; Dir B. P. LIKHACHEV.

Molodaya Gvardiya (The Young Guard): 127994 Moscow, ul. Sushchevskaya 21; tel. (495) 972-05-46; fax (495) 972-05-82; e-mail dsel@gvardiya.ru; f. 1922; books, magazines; Gen. Dir V. F. YURKIN.

Moscow M. V. Lomonosov State University Press: 119899 Moscow, ul. Khokhlova 11; tel. (495) 939-33-23; fax (495) 203-66-71; e-mail kd_mgu@rambler.ru; internet www.msu.ru/depts/MSUPubl2005; f. 1756; scientific, educational and reference, books and journals; Dir YURIY YU. PETRUNIN.

Muzyka (Music): 127051 Moscow, ul. Petrovka 26; tel. (495) 921-51-70; fax (495) 928-33-04; e-mail muz-sekretar@yandex.ru; f. 1861; sheet music, music scores and related literature; Dir MARK ZILBERQUIT.

Mysl (Thought): 117071 Moscow, Leninskii pr. 15; tel. (495) 955-04-58; f. 1963; science, popular science, philosophy, history, political science, geography; Dir YEVGENYI A. TIMOFEYEV.

Nauka (Science): 117997 Moscow, ul. Profsoyuznaya 90; tel. (495) 334-71-51; fax (495) 420-22-20; e-mail secret@naukaran.ru; internet www.naukaran.ru; f. 1923; publishing house of the Academy of Sciences; general and social science, mathematics, physics, chemistry, biology, earth sciences, oriental studies, books in foreign languages, university textbooks, scientific journals, translation, export, distribution, typesetting and printing services; Dir-Gen. V. VASILIYEV.

Nauka i Tekhnologiya (Science and Technology): 107076 Moscow, Stromynskii per. 4; tel. (495) 269-51-96; fax (495) 269-49-96; e-mail admin@nauka-technologiy.ru; f. 2000; journals on chemistry, electronics and telecommunications; Gen. Dir MAKSIM A. KOVALEVSKII.

Nedra Biznestsentr (Natural Resources Business Centre): 125047 Moscow, pl. Tverskoi Zastavy 3; tel. (495) 251-31-77; fax (495) 250-27-72; e-mail business@nedrainform.ru; internet www.nedrainform.ru; f. 1964; geology, natural resources, mining and coal industry, petroleum and gas industry; Dir V. D. MENSHIKOV.

Nezavisimaya Gazeta ('Independent Newspaper' Publishing House): 101000 Moscow, ul. Myasnitskaya 13/10; tel. and fax (495) 981-61-53; e-mail ngbooks@ng.ru; internet www.ng.ru/izdatelstvo; f. 1991; books on history, literary essays, poetry, history of literature and of art, biography, dictionaries, encyclopaedias; Dir VIKTOR A. OBUKHOV.

Pedagogika Press (Pedagogy Press): 119034 Moscow, Smolenskii bulv. 4; tel. and fax (495) 246-59-69; f. 1969; scientific and popular books on pedagogics, didactics, psychology, developmental physiology; young people's encyclopaedia, dictionaries; Dir I. KOLESNIKOVA.

Pressa (The Press): 127137 Moscow, ul. Pravdy 24; tel. (495) 257-46-22; fax (499) 257-09-38; e-mail adm@media-pressa.ru; internet www.media-pressa.ru; f. 1934 as Pravda (Truth) Publishing House; booklets, newspapers and periodicals; Dir I. V. POLTAVTSEV.

Profizdat (Professional Publishers): 101000 Moscow, ul. Myasnitskaya 13/18; tel. (495) 924-57-40; fax (495) 975-23-29; e-mail profizdat@profizdat.ru; f. 1930; books and magazines; Gen. Dir VLADIMIR SOLOVYEV.

Progress (Progress): 119992 Moscow, Zubovskii bulv. 17; tel. (495) 246-90-32; fax (495) 230-24-03; e-mail progress@mcn.ru; f. 1931; translations of Russian language books into foreign languages and of foreign language books into Russian; political and scientific, fiction, literature for children and youth; encyclopedias; Dir-Gen. SARKIS V. OGANIAN.

Prosveshcheniye (Enlightenment): 127521 Moscow, 3-i proyezd Maryinoi roshchi 41; tel. (495) 789-30-40; fax (495) 789-30-41; e-mail prosv@prosv.ru; internet www.prosv.ru; f. 1930; school textbooks, dictionaries, atlases, reference and scientific books, educational materials; Dir ALEKSANDR M. KONDAKOV.

Raduga (Rainbow): 129090 Moscow, Grokholskii per. 32/2; tel. and fax (495) 680-12-39; e-mail radugarel@sumail.ru; internet www.raduga-publ.ru; f. 1982; translations of Russian fiction into foreign languages and of foreign authors into Russian; Gen. Dir KSENIYA ATAROVA.

Respublika (Republic): 125811 Moscow, Miusskaya pl. 7; tel. and fax (495) 656-09-70; e-mail respublik@dataforce.net; internet www.republik.ru; f. 1918; fmrly Politizdat (Political Publishing House); dictionaries, books on politics, human rights, philosophy, history, economics, religion, fiction, arts, reference; Dir VLADIMIR V. AKIMOV.

Rosmen (Rosman): 127018 Moscow, ul. Oktyabskaya 4/2; tel. (495) 933-70-70; fax (495) 933-71-36; e-mail rosman@rosman.ru; internet www.rosman.ru; children's literature, general, popular science; Dir-Gen. OLEG V. ZHIVYKH.

Rosspen Publishing House—Russian Political Encylopedia: 117393 Moscow, ul. Profsoyuznaya 82; tel. and fax (495) 334-81-62; e-mail rosspen@rosspen.com; internet www.rosspen.com; f. 1992;

politics, history, other academic and reference publishing; Dir-Gen. A. K. Sorokin.

Russkii Yazyk (Russian Language): 117303 Moscow, ul. M. Yushunski 1; tel. (495) 319-83-13; fax (495) 319-83-16; e-mail rlm@tpost.net; f. 2001; textbooks, reference, dictionaries; Dir Elizabet Braterskaya.

Shkola-Press (School-Press): 127254 Moscow, ul. Sh. Rustaveli 10/3; tel. and fax (495) 219-83-80; e-mail marketing@schoolpress.ru; internet www.schoolpress.ru; books on psychology, pedagogy, magazines.

Slovo (Word): 109147 Moscow, ul. Vorontsovskaya 41; tel. and fax (495) 911-61-33; internet www.slovo-online.ru; f. 1989; illustrated books on art, world literature in translation; Gen-Dir. Nataliya Avetisyan.

Stroyizdat (Construction Publishing House): 101442 Moscow, ul. Kalyayevskaya 23A; tel. (495) 251-69-67; f. 1932; building, architecture, environmental protection, fire protection and building materials; Dir V. A. Kasatkin.

Tekst (Text): 127299 Moscow, ul. Kosmonavta Volkova 7; tel. and fax (495) 150-0472; e-mail textpubl@yandex.ru; internet www.textpubl.ru; f. 1988; foreign poetry and prose fiction in translation, Russian poetry and prose, children's literature, social sciences, history, law; Dir Olget M. Libkin.

Vagrius: 125993 Moscow, ul. Nikoloyamskaya 1; tel. (495) 221-61-80; fax (495) 510-56-10; e-mail vagrius@vagrius.com; internet www.vagrius.com; f. 1992; fiction, politics, history; Pres. and Dir-Gen. Gleb Uspenskii.

Ves Mir (The Whole World): 101000 Moscow, Kolpachnyi per. 9A; tel. (495) 623-68-39; fax (495) 625-42-69; e-mail info@vesmirbooks.ru; internet www.vesmirbooks.ru; f. 1994; university textbooks, scholarly works in social sciences and humanities; Dir Dr Oleg A. Zimarin.

Vysshaya Shkola (Higher School): 127994 Moscow, ul. Neglinnaya 29/14; tel. (495) 200-04-56; fax (495) 200-34-86; e-mail info_vshkola@mail.ru; internet www.vshkola.ru; f. 1939; textbooks for higher-education institutions; Dir Mikhail L. Zorin.

Yuridicheskaya Literatura (Legal Literature): 121069 Moscow, ul. M. Nikitskaya 14; tel. (495) 203-83-84; fax (495) 291-98-83; internet www.jurizdat.ru; f. 1917; legal; official publishers of enactments of the Russian President and Govt; Dir Ivan A. Bunin.

Znaniye (Knowledge): 101835 Moscow, proyezd Serova 4; tel. (495) 928-15-31; f. 1951; popular books and brochures on politics and science; Dir V. K. Belyakov.

Broadcasting and Communications

TELECOMMUNICATIONS

Golden Telecom: 115114 Moscow, Kozhevnicheskii proyezd 1; tel. (495) 797-93-00; fax (495) 797-93-32; e-mail publicrelations@gldn.net; internet www.goldentelecom.ru; f. 1994; operates mobile cellular telecommunications network in cities across the Russian Federation, and in Almaty (Kazakhstan) and Kyiv (Ukraine); Chief Exec. Jean-Pierre Vandromme.

Megafon: 119435 Moscow, Savvinskaya nab. 15; tel. (495) 504-50-20; fax (495) 504-50-21; e-mail aklimov@megafon.ru; internet www.megafon.ru; f. 2002; operates mobile cellular communications networks across Russia; 6 regional cos; 15.6m. subscribers (March 2005); Gen. Dir Sergei Soldatenkov.

Mobilnye TeleSistemi/Mobile TeleSystems (MTS): 109147 Moscow, ul. Marksistskaya 4; tel. (495) 766-01-77; e-mail info@mts.ru; internet www.mts.ru; f. 1993; provides mobile cellular telecommunications in 82 regions of Russia; majority-owned by Sistema Telecom; 35.1% owned by Deutsche Telekom (Germany); Pres. Leonid A. Melamed; over 85m. subscribers (incl. subsidiary cos in Armenia, Belarus, Turkmenistan, Ukraine and Uzbekistan) (2008).

Moscow City Telephone Network (MGTS—Moskovskaya Gorodskaya Telefonnaya Set): 103051 Moscow, Petrovskii bulv. 12/3; tel. (495) 950-00-00; fax (495) 950-06-18; e-mail mgts@mgts.ru; internet www.mgts.ru; f. 1882; provides telecommunications services in Moscow City; Gen. Man. Nikolai A. Maksimenka.

Petersburg Telephone Network (PTS—Peterburgsskaya Telefonnaya Set): 119186 St Petersburg, ul. B. Morskaya 24; tel. (812) 314-15-50; fax (812) 110-68-34; e-mail office@ptn.ru; internet www.ptn.ru; f. 1993; Dir Igor N. Samylin.

Rostelekom (Rostelecom): 125047 Moscow, ul.1-aya Tverskaya-Yamskaya 14; tel. (495) 787-28-49; fax (495) 972-82-83; e-mail info@rostelecom.ru; internet www.rt.ru; 50.7% owned by Svyazinvest; dominant long-distance and international telecommunications service provider; 7 regional cos based in St Petersburg, Samara, Novosibirsk, Yekaterinburg, Khabarovsk, Moscow and Rostov-on-Don; Dir Dmitrii Yerokhin.

Svyazinvest: 119121 Moscow, ul. Plyushchikha 55/2; tel. (495) 248-24-71; fax (495) 248-24-53; e-mail dms@svyazinvest.ru; internet www.sinvest.ru; f. 1995; 75%-state-owned; holds controlling stakes in 7 'mega-regional' telecommunications operators, 1 international and domestic long-distance operator, and 2 local telecommunications cos, and non-controlling stakes in 2 city telecommunications cos; Chair. Leonid D. Reiman.

VympelKom-Bilain (Vympelcom-Beeline): 127006 Moscow, ul. Krasnoproletarskaya 4; tel. (495) 725-07-00; fax (495) 991-79-03; e-mail info@beeline.ru; internet www.beeline.ru; operates mobile cellular telecommunications in 78 regions of Russia, and in Armenia, Georgia, Kazakhstan, Tajikistan, Ukraine and Uzbekistan; 26.6% owned by Telenor (Norway); Chief Exec. Aleksandr V. Izosimov.

BROADCASTING

Pervyi Kanal (First Channel), operated by Public Russian Television (ORT) is received throughout Russia and many parts of the CIS. The All-Russian State Television Company (VGTRK) broadcasts Telekanal 'Rossiya', which reaches some 92% of the Russian population, and Telekanal 'Kultura' and Telekanal 'Sport'. In addition to the nation-wide television channels, there are local channels, and the NTV (Independent Television) channel (65% owned by the gas utility, Gazprom, in which the Government holds a majority stake) is broadcast in most of Russia. In the regions, part of Rossiya's programming is devoted to local affairs, with broadcasts in minority languages. A state-supported international English-language TV station, Russia Today, commenced broadcasts in 2006. In mid-2005 there were four nation-wide radio stations, as well as 11 urban radio networks and more than 200 regional stations. At that time Radio Rossiya had more listeners than any other state-run channel, but the commercial music station, Russkoye Radio, established in 1995, was the most popular station overall.

Association of Regional State Television and Radio Broadcasters: 113326 Moscow, ul. Pyatnitskaya 25/226; tel. and fax (495) 950-60-28; e-mail fstratyv@rzn.rosmail.com; Chair. of Bd Aleksandr N. Levchenko.

Regulatory Authority

Russian Television and Radio Broadcasting Network: 113326 Moscow, ul. Pyatnitskaya 25; tel. (495) 233-66-03; fax (495) 233-28-93; f. 2001; Gen. Man. Gennadii I. Sklyar.

Radio

All-Russian State Television and Radio Broadcasting Company (VGTRK): 125040 Moscow, ul. 5-aya Yamskogo Polya 19/21; tel. (495) 745-39-78; fax (495) 975-26-11; e-mail rtrinterdep@rfn.ru; internet www.tvradio.ru; f. 1991; broadcasts 'Rossiya', 'Kultura', 'Sport' and 'Planeta' television channels, 89 regional television and radio cos, and national radio stations 'Radio Rossiya', 'Radio Mayak' and 'Radio Nostalzhi'; Chair. Oleg Dobrodeyev.

Radio Mayak (Radio Beacon): 113326 Moscow, ul. Pyatnitskaya 25; tel. (495) 950-67-67; fax (495) 959-42-04; e-mail inform@radiomayak.ru; internet www.radiomayak.ru; f. 1964; state-owned; Chair. Irina A. Gerasimova.

Radio Nostalzhi (Radio Nostalgia): 113162 Moscow, ul. Shabolovka 37; tel. (495) 955-84-00; e-mail nostalgie@vimain.vitpc.com; f. 1993; Gen. Man. Irina A. Gerasimova.

Radio Rossiya (Radio Russia): 125040 Moscow, ul. 5-aya Yamskogo Polya 19/21; tel. (495) 234-85-94; fax (495) 730-42-77; e-mail direction@radiorus.ru; internet www.radiorus.ru; f. 1990; broadcasts information, social, political, musical, literary and investigate progamming; Dir-Gen. Aleksei V. Abakumov.

Ekho Moskvy (Moscow Echo): 119992 Moscow, ul. Novyi Arbat 11; tel. (495) 202-92-29; e-mail info@echo.msk.ru; internet www.echo.msk.ru; f. 1990; stations in Moscow, St Petersburg, Rostov-on-Don and Vologda; also broadcasts from Moscow to Chelyabinsk, Krasnoyarsk, Novosibirsk, Omsk, Perm, Saratov and Yekaterinburg; 66% owned by Gazprom-Mediya, 34% staff-owned; Gen. Man. Yurii Fedutinkov.

Golos Rossii (The Voice of Russia): 113326 Moscow, ul. Pyatnitskaya 25; tel. (495) 950-64-40; fax (495) 230-28-28; e-mail letters@vor.ru; internet www.vor.ru; fmrly Radio Moscow International; international broadcasts in 31 languages; Man. Dir Armen G. Oganesian.

Russkoye Radio (Russian Radio): 105064 Moscow, ul. Kazakova 16; tel. (495) 232-16-36; fax (495) 956-13-60; internet www.rusradio.ru; f. 1995; owned by Russkaya Mediyagruppa (Russian Media Group); nation-wide commercial music station; broadcasts to more than 700 towns in Russia, Ukraine, Kazakhstan, Moldova, Kyrgyzstan, the Baltic Republics and the USA; also *Russkoye Radio 2*,

THE RUSSIAN FEDERATION

principally news and talk programming, broadcast to Moscow; Dir-Gen. SERGEI KOZHEVNIKOV.

Serebryanyi Dozhd (Silver Rain): 127083 Moscow, Petrovsko-Razumovskaya alleya 12A; tel. (495) 925-10-01; internet www.silver.ru; f. 1995; commercial station broadcasting information and entertainment programming; broadcasts to 98 cities in Russia and the 'near abroad'; Dir-Gen. DMITRII SAVITSKII.

Yevropa Plyus (Europa Plus): 127427 Moscow, ul. Akademika Koroleva 19; tel. (495) 217-82-57; fax (495) 956-35-08; e-mail main@europaplus.ru; internet www.europaplus.ru; FM station, broadcasting music, entertainment and information programmes to 500 cities; Pres. ZHORZH POLINSKI.

Television

All-Russian State Television and Radio Broadcasting Company (VGTRK): 125040 Moscow, ul. 5-aya Yamskogo Polya 19/21; tel. (495) 745-39-78; fax (495) 975-26-11; e-mail rtrinterdep@rfn.ru; f. 1991; broadcasts 'Rossiya' 'Kultura', 'Sport' and 'Planeta' television channels, 89 regional television and radio cos, and national radio stations 'Radio Rossiya', 'Radio Mayak' and 'Radio Nostalzhi'; Chair. OLEG DOBRODEYEV.

Telekanal 'Kultura' (Television Channel 'Culture'): 123995 Moscow, ul. M. Nikitskaya 24; e-mail kultura@tvkultura.ru; internet www.tvkultura.ru; f. 1997; Gen. Dir ALEKSANDR S. PONOMAREV.

Telekanal 'Rossiya' (Television Channel 'Russia'): 115162 Moscow, ul. Shabolovka 37; tel. (495) 924-63-74; fax (495) 234-87-71; e-mail info@rutv.ru; internet www.rutv.ru; fmrly RTR-TV; name changed as above in 2002; Dir-Gen. ALEKSANDR S. PONAMAREV.

Telekanal 'Sport' (Television Channel 'Sport'): 113162 Moscow, ul. Shabolovka 37; e-mail info@rtr-sport.ru; internet news.sportbox.ru; f. 2003; Dir-Gen. VASILII KIKNADZE.

Telekanal 'Zvezda' (Television Channel 'Star'): 129110 Moscow, Suvorovskaya pl. 2; tel. (495) 631-58-83; internet www.tvzvezda.ru; f. 2005; Gen. Dir SERGEI V. SABUSHKIN.

NTV—Independent Television: 127427 Moscow, ul. Akademika Koroleva 12; tel. (495) 725-54-03; fax (495) 725-54-01; e-mail info@ntv.ru; internet www.ntv.ru; f. 1993; 65% owned by Gazprom-Mediya; also NTV World (NTV Mir), broadcasting to Russian communities in Israel, Europe and the USA; Dir-Gen. NIKOLAI YU. SENKEVICH.

Pervyi Kanal—First Channel (Channel One): 127427 Moscow, ul. Akademika Koroleva 12; tel. (495) 617-73-87; fax (495) 215-82-47; e-mail ort_int@ortv.ru; internet www.1tv.ru; f. 1995; fmrly ORT—Public Russian Television; name changed as above in 2002; 51% state-owned; 49% owned by private shareholders; Chair. MIKHAIL PYATKOVSKII; Dir-Gen. KONSTANTIN ERNST.

Ren-TV Network: 119843 Moscow, Zubovskii bulv. 17/510; tel. (495) 246-25-06; fax (495) 245-09-98; e-mail site@rentv.dol.ru; internet www.ren-tv.com; f. 1991; network of more than 100 television stations in the Russian Federation and 60 stations in republics of the CIS; Chair. LYUBOV SOVERSHAYEVA; Gen. Man. DMITRII A. LESNEVSKII.

STS—Network of Television Stations: 123298 Moscow, ul. 3-aya Khoroshevskaya 12; tel. (495) 797-41-73; fax (495) 797-41-01; e-mail www@ctc-tv.ru; internet www.ctc-tv.ru; f. 1996; owned by StoryFirst Communications (USA); broadcasts programmes of popular entertainment to 350 cities in Russia; Dir-Gen. ALEKSANDR YE. RODNYANSKII.

TNT—Territory of Our Viewers—TV Network: 127427 Moscow, ul. Akademika Koroleva 19; tel. (495) 217-81-88; fax (495) 748-14-90; e-mail info@tnt-tv.ru; internet www.tnt-tv.ru; f. 1997; cable television network broadcasting to 582 cities in Russia; Chief Exec. ALEKSANDR DYBAL; Dir-Gen. ROMAN PETRENKO.

TV-Tsentr (TVTs—TV-Centre): 113184 Moscow, ul. B. Tatarskaya 33/1; tel. (495) 959-39-87; fax (495) 959-39-66; e-mail info@tvc.ru; internet www.tvc.ru; f. 1997; broadcasting consortium for terrestrial cable and satellite television; receives funding from Govt of Moscow City; Pres. OLEG M. POPTSOV; Dir PAVEL V. KASPAROV.

Finance

(cap. = capital; res = reserves; dep. = deposits; m. = million; brs = branches; amounts in new roubles, unless otherwise stated)

BANKING

Central Bank

Bank Rossii—Central Bank of the Russian Federation: 107016 Moscow, ul. Neglinnaya 12; tel. (495) 771-91-00; fax (495) 621-64-65; e-mail webmaster@www.cbr.ru; internet www.cbr.ru; f. 1990; cap. 3,000m., res 303,732m., dep. 9,700,000m. (Jan. 2007); Chair. SERGEI M. IGNATIYEV; 79 brs.

Major Banks

Absolut Bank (Absolyut Bank): 127051 Moscow, Tsetnoi bulv. 18; tel. (495) 995-10-01; fax (495) 995-10-22; e-mail info@absolutbank.ru; internet www.absolutbank.ru; 95% owned by KBC Bank NV (Belgium); f. 1993; cap. 1,714.6., res 2,442.4m., dep. 56,896.5m. (Dec. 2006); Chair. ALEKSANDR SVETAKOV.

AK BARS Bank: 420066 Tatarstan, Kazan, ul. Dekabristov 1; tel. (843) 519-38-02; fax (843) 519-39-75; e-mail mail@akbars.ru; internet www.akbars.ru; f. 1993; cap. 25,244.0m., res 349.6m., dep. 60,303.4m. (Dec. 2006); Chair. of Bd ROBERT MINNEGALIYEV; 22 brs.

Alfa-Bank: 107078 Moscow, ul. Kalanchevskaya 27; tel. (495) 974-25-15; fax (495) 745-57-84; e-mail mail@alfabank.ru; internet www.alfabank.ru; f. 1990; cap. US $344.8m., res $26.0m., dep. $9,906.4m. (Dec. 2006); Chair. of Exec. Bd RUSHAN KHVESYUK; Pres. PETR AVEN.

Bank of Moscow (Bank Moskvy): 107996 Moscow, ul. Rozhdestvenka 8/15/3; tel. (495) 925-80-00; fax (495) 795-26-00; e-mail info@mmbank.ru; internet www.mmbank.ru; f. 1995 as Moscow Municipal Bank—Bank of Moscow; name changed as above 2004; 60% owned by Govt of Moscow City; cap. 14,786.8m., res 2,629.6m., dep. 348,161.8m. (Dec. 2006); Pres. and Chief Exec. ANDREI BORODIN; 117 brs.

Bank Petrocommerce (Bank Petrokommertz): 127051 Moscow, ul. Petrovka 24; tel. (495) 625-95-65; fax (495) 623-36-07; e-mail welcome@pkb.ru; internet www.pkb.ru; f. 1992; cap. 6,752.6m., res −9.7m., dep. 73,734.3m. (Dec. 2006); Pres. and Chair. of Bd VLADIMIR N. NIKITENKO.

Bank Rossiiskii Kredit (Russian Credit Bank): 119002 Moscow, Smolenskii bulv. 26/9; tel. (495) 967-34-43; fax (495) 247-39-39; e-mail info@roscredit.ru; internet www.roscredit.ru; f. 1990; cap. 7,520.9m., res 3,989.5m., dep. 2,871.7m. (Dec. 2005); Pres. DMITRII P. YEROPKIN; Chair. VYACHESLAV POPOV.

Bank Soyuz: 127006 Moscow, ul. Dolgorukovskaya 34/1; tel. (495) 729-55-00; fax (495) 729-55-05; e-mail info@banksoyuz.ru; internet www.banksoyuz.ru; f. 1993; cap. 4,413.7m., res 91.6m., dep. 53,146.0m. (Dec. 2006); Chair. STUART M. LAWSON.

Bank Uralsib: 119048 Moscow, ul. Yefremova 8; tel. (495) 705-90-39; fax (495) 745-70-10; e-mail pr@nikoil.ru; internet www.uralsib.ru; f. 1993; cap. 20,418.4m., res 4,040.2m., dep. 189,884.3m. (Dec. 2005); Chair. NIKOLAI TSVETKOV.

Bank VTB 24: 101000 Moscow, ul. Myasnitskaya 35; tel. (495) 771-78-78; fax (495) 980-46-66; e-mail info@vtb24.ru; internet www.vtb24.ru; f. 1991; cap. 17,611.9., res 658.8m., dep. 127,105.8m. (Dec. 2006); CEO MIKHAIL M. ZADORNOV; 44 brs.

Bank VTB Severo-Zapad (Bank VTB North-West): 191014 St Petersburg, ul. Kovenskii 17/18; tel. (812) 329-84-51; fax (812) 310-61-73; e-mail lider@icbank.ru; internet www.vtb-sz.ru; f. 1870 as Volga-Kama Bank; fmrly Industry and Construction Bank; present name adopted 2007; cap. 1,932.7m., res 2,477.6m., dep. 112,948.0m. (Dec. 2006); Chair. VLADIMIR SKATIN; 54 brs.

Bank Zenit: 129110 Moscow, Bannyi per. 9; tel. (495) 937-07-37; fax (495) 777-57-06; e-mail info@zenit.ru; internet www.zenit.ru; f. 1994; 26% owned by Tatneft; cap. US $392.9m., res $60.8m., dep. $3,216.3m. (Dec. 2006); Chair. of Bd ALEKSEI A SOKOLOV; 4 brs.

First Czech-Russian Bank (Pervyi Cheshsko-Rossiiskii Bank—PChRB): 119454 Moscow, ul. Lobachevskogo 27; tel. (495) 223-43-43; e-mail bank@pchrb.ru; internet www.pchrb.ru; f. 1996; cap. 3,510.2m., res 94.7m., dep. 6,832.9m. (Dec. 2006); 25.6% owned by Stroitransgaz Orel; Chair. ROMAN POPOV.

Gazprombank: 117420 Moscow, ul. Nametkina 16/1; tel. (495) 719-17-63; fax (495) 913-73-19; e-mail mailbox@gazprombank.ru; internet www.gazprombank.ru; f. 1990; 87.5% owned by Gazprom; cap. US $1,160.9m., res $1,824.3m., dep. $23,183.9m. (Dec. 2006); Chair. of Management Bd ANDREI I. AKIMOV; 32 brs.

Globeks Commercial Bank (GLOBEXBANK): 123242 Moscow, Novinskii bulv. 15; tel. (495) 785-22-22; fax (495) 795-13-08; e-mail post@globexbank.ru; internet www.globexbank.ru; f. 1992; cap. 10,084.4m., res 2,003.4m., dep. 37,662.8m. (Jan. 2007); Chair. ANDREI F. DUNAYEV; Pres. ANATOLII L. MOTYLEV; 5 brs.

Impexbank (Import-Export Bank): 125252 Moscow, ul. Novopeschanaya 20/10/1A; tel. and fax (495) 752-52-32; e-mail mail@impexbank.ru; internet www.impexbank.ru; f. 1993; cap. US $130.8m., res $35.4m. dep. $1,697.4m. (Dec. 2005); Chair. of Bd PAVEL I. LYSENKO; more than 400 brs in Moscow.

International Bank of St Petersburg (Mezhdunarodnyi Bank Sankt-Peterburga): 194044 St Petersburg, Krapivnyi per. 5; tel. (812) 541-82-17; fax (812) 541-83-93; e-mail mail@ibsp.ru; internet www.ibsp.ru; f. 1989; present name adopted 1999; cap. 621.5m., res

THE RUSSIAN FEDERATION

1,472.1m., dep. 15,211.8m. (Dec. 2005); Pres. SERGEI V. BAZHANOV; 2 brs.

International Moscow Bank (Mezhdunarodnyi Moskovskii Bank): 119034 Moscow, Prechistenskaya nab. 9; tel. (495) 258-72-00; fax (495) 258-72-72; e-mail imbank@imbank.ru; internet www.imb.ru; f. 1989; 47.4% owned by Bayerische Hypo- und Vereinsbank AG (Germany), 22.4% by Nordea Bank Finland, 20% by Banque Commerciale pour l'Europe du Nord—EUROBANK (France), 10.2% owned by European Bank for Reconstruction and Development—EBRD (UK); cap. US $348.2m., res $16.6m., dep. $8,205.0m. (Dec. 2006); Chair. of Bd of Dirs ERICH HAMPEL; 22 brs.

Khanty-Mansiiskii Bank: 628012 Tyumen obl., Khanty-Mansii AOk—Yugra, Khanty-Mansiisk, ul. Mira 38; tel. (34671) 302-10; fax (34671) 302-19; e-mail hmbank@khmb.ru; internet www.khmb.ru; f. 1992; cap. 5,787.3m., res 1,455.3m., dep. 60,521.5m. (Dec. 2006); Pres. DMITRII MIZGULIN; 16 brs.

MDM Bank (Moskovskiy Delovoy Mir—Moscow Business World): 115172 Moscow, Kotelnicheskaya nab. 33/1; tel. (495) 797-95-00; fax (495) 797-95-01; e-mail info@mdmbank.com; internet www.mdmbank.ru; f. 1993; cap. 1,736m., res 11,509m., dep. 207,443m. (Dec. 2006); Chair. VLADIMIR STOLIN; Chief Exec. MICHEL PERKHIRIN; 98 brs and sub-brs.

Mezhdunarodnyi Promyshlennyi Bank (International Industrial Bank): 125009 Moscow, ul. B. Dmitrovka 23/1; tel. (495) 626-44-46; fax (495) 692-82-84; e-mail mail@iib.ru; internet www.iib.ru; f. 1992; cap. 25,000m., res 405.6m., dep. 60,299.3m. (Dec. 2006); Chair. ALEKSANDR V. GNUSAREV; 5 brs.

Moscow Bank for Reconstruction and Development (Moskovskii Bank Rekonstruktsii i Razvitiya): 119034 Moscow, Yeropkinskii per. 5; tel. and fax (495) 101-28-00; fax (495) 232-27-54; e-mail mbrd@mbrd.ru; internet www.mbrd.ru; 60.66% owned by Sistema; cap. 943.4m., res 3,650.4m., dep. 52,301.5m. (Dec. 2006); Chair. of Bd SERGEI YE. CHEREMIN.

Nomos-Bank: 109240 Moscow, ul. Verkhnyaya Radishchevskaya 3/1; tel. (495) 737-73-55; fax (495) 797-32-50; e-mail nmosmail@online.ru; internet www.nomos.ru; f. 1992; cap. 5,318.1m., res 3,696.8m., dep. 87,539.8m. (Dec. 2006); Pres. DMITRII SOKOLOV; 8 brs.

Promsvyazbank: 109052 Moscow, ul. Smirnovskaya 10/2–3/22; tel. (495) 727-10-20; fax (495) 727-10-21; e-mail postmaster@psbank.ru; internet www.psbank.ru; f. 1995; cap. 6,188.8., res 5,679.8m., dep. 147,673.3m. (Dec. 2006); Chair. of Council DMITRII N. ANANIYEV; Pres. ALEKSANDR A. LEVKOVSKII; 11 brs.

Raiffeisenbank Austria ZAO: 129090 Moscow, ul. Troitskaya 17/1; tel. (495) 721-99-00; fax (495) 721-99-01; e-mail info@raiffeisen.ru; internet www.raiffeisen.ru; f. 1996; cap. 13,439.3m., res 1,368.1m., dep. 166,355.6m. (Dec. 2005); Chair. of Man. Bd JOHANN JONACH; 7 brs and sub-brs.

Rosbank: 107078 Moscow, ul. M. Poryvayevoi 11, POB 208; tel. (495) 921-01-01; fax (495) 725-05-11; e-mail mailbox@rosbank.ru; internet www.rosbank.ru; f. 1993; 70% by Interros, 20% by Société Générale; cap. US $1,070m., res $11,159m., dep. $7,773m. (Dec. 2006); Pres. and Chair. of Bd of Dirs ANDREI KLISHAS; Chief Exec. ALEKSANDR POPOV; 68 brs.

Russkii Standart Bank: 105066 Moscow, ul. Spartakovskaya 2/1/6; tel. (495) 748-15-19; fax (495) 797-84-04; e-mail nignatova@rs.ru; internet www.rs.ru; f. 1993; cap. 1,738.5m., res 809.7m., dep. 154,165.9m. (Dec. 2006); Chair. RUSTAM V. TARIKO; Chief Exec. DMITRII O. LEVIN.

Sberbank—Savings Bank of the Russian Federation: 117997 Moscow, ul. Vavilova 19; tel. (495) 957-58-62; fax (495) 957-57-31; e-mail sbrf@sbrf.ru; internet www.sbrf.ru; f. 1841 as a deposit-taking institution, reorganized as a joint-stock commercial bank in 1991; 60.6% owned by Bank Rossii—Central Bank of the Russian Federation; cap. 79,981m., res 25,360m., dep. 2,997,389m. (Dec. 2006); Chair. of Bd and Chief Exec. GERMAN O. GREF; 17 regional head offices, 823 brs and 19,307 sub-brs.

Svyaz-Bank (Interregional Bank for Settlements of the Telecommunications and Postal Services): 125375 Moscow, ul. Tverskaya 7; tel. (495) 771-32-60; fax (495) 771-32-76; e-mail MAV@sviaz-bank.ru; internet www.sviaz-bank.ru; f. 1991; cap. 5,745.8m., res —3.2m., dep. 56,230.2m. (Dec. 2006); Chair. of Bd of Dirs ANDREI KONOVAL.

TransKreditBank (TransCreditBank): 105066 Moscow, ul. N. Basmannaya 37A/1; tel. (495) 788-08-80; fax (495) 788-08-79; e-mail info@bnk.ru; internet www.tcb.ru; f. 1992; 75.0% state-owned; cap. 3,373.6m., res 2,602.9m., dep. 72,011.2m. (Dec. 2006); Pres. SERGEI N. PUSHKIN.

URSA Bank: 630102 Novosibirsk, ul. Inskaya 54; tel. (3832) 27–75–99; fax (3832) 34–00–25; e-mail secret@ursabank.ru; internet www.ursabank.ru; f. 1990; present name adopted 2006; cap. 1,434.9m., res 11,501.5m., dep. 90,690.2m. (Dec. 2006); Chair of Bd. of Dirs IGOR KIM.

Vneshekonombank (Bank for Foreign Economic Affairs): 107996 Moscow, pr. Sakharova 9; tel. (495) 207-10-37; fax (495) 975-21-43; e-mail info@veb.ru; internet www.veb.ru; f. 1924; dep. US $5,353m., total assets $6,373m. (Dec. 2005); Chair. VLADIMIR A. DMITRIYEV.

Vozrozhdeniye—V-Bank (Rebirth—Moscow Jt-Stock Commercial Bank Vozrozdeniye): 101999 Moscow, per. Luchnikov 7/4/1, POB 9; tel. (495) 777-08-88; fax (495) 620-19-99; e-mail vbank@co.voz.ru; internet www.vbank.ru; f. 1991; cap. US $293m., res $120m., dep. $2,687m. (Jul. 2007); Chair of Supervisory Bd YURII M. MARINICHEV; Chair. of Managing Bd DMITRII L. ORLOV; 160 brs.

VTB Bank: 190000 St Petersburg, ul. B. Morskaya 29; tel. (812) 314-60-59; fax (812) 312-78-18; e-mail info@vtb.ru; internet www.vtb.ru; f. 1990; frmly Bank for Foreign Trade; present name adopted 2007; 77.5% owned by Govt of Russian Federation; cap. US $2,500m., res $2,360m., dep. $39,140m. (Dec. 2006); Chair. of Bd and Chief Exec. ANDREI L. KOSLIN.

Bankers' Association

Association of Russian Banks (Assostiatsiya Rossiiskikh Bankov): 121069 Moscow, Skatertnyi per. 20/1; tel. (495) 291-66-30; fax (495) 291-66-66; e-mail arb@arb.ru; internet www.arb.ru; f. 1991; 755 mem. orgs, incl. 576 credit orgs (2007); Pres. GAREGIN A. TOSUNYAN.

INSURANCE

Agroinvest Insurance Co: 127422 Moscow, ul. Timiryazevskaya 26; tel. (495) 976-94-56; fax (495) 977-05-88; health, life and general insurance services; Pres. YURII I. MORDVINTSEV.

AIG Russia: 103009 Moscow, ul. Tverskaya 16/2; tel. (495) 935-89-50; fax (495) 935-89-52; e-mail aig.russia@aig.com; internet www.aigrussia.ru; f. 1994; mem. of the American International Group Inc; personal and business property insurance, also marine, life, financial etc.; Pres. GARY COLEMAN.

Allianz Insurance Co: 127473 Moscow, 3-i Samotechnii per. 3; tel. (495) 937-69-96; fax (495) 937-69-80; e-mail allianz@allianz.ru; internet www.allianz.ru; engineering, professional liability, life, medical, property, marine and private; Man. Dir MICHAEL HERGESELL.

Ingosstrakh Insurance Co: 115998 Moscow, ul. Pyatnitskaya 12/2; tel. (495) 232-32-11; fax (495) 959-45-18; e-mail ingos@ingos.ru; internet www.ingos.ru; f. 1947; undertakes all kinds of insurance and reinsurance; Chair. NATALIYA A. RAYEVSKAYA; Gen. Dir YEVGENII TUMANOV.

Medstrakh—Medical Insurance Fund of the Russian Federation: 107076 Moscow, pl. Preobrazhenskaya 7A/1; tel. (495) 964-84-27; fax (495) 964-84-21; e-mail mz@mcramn.ru; internet www.medstrah.ru; f. 1991; health, life, property, travel, liability; also provides compulsory medical insurance; Pres. PETR KUZNETSOV.

RESO-Garantiya Insurance Co: 125047 Moscow, ul. Gasheka 12/1; tel. (495) 730-30-00; fax (495) 956-25-85; e-mail reso@orc.ru; internet www.reso.ru; f. 1991; Dir-Gen. DMITRII G. RAKOVSHCHIK.

Rosgosstrakh—Russian State Insurance: 127994 Moscow, ul. Novoslobodskaya 23; tel. (495) 781-24-00; fax (495) 978-27-64; e-mail admin@rgs.ru; internet www.gosstrah.ru; majority state-owned; 49% stake transferred to private ownership in 2001; undertakes domestic insurance; subsidiary cos in 80 federal subjects (territorial units) of the Russian Federation; Chair. VLADISLAV REZNIK; Gen. Dir RUBEN VARDANIAN.

ROSNO—Russian National Society Insurance Co: 115184 Moscow, Ozerkovskaya nab. 30; tel. (495) 232-33-33; fax (495) 232-00-14; e-mail info@rosno.ru; internet www.rosno.ru; f. 1992; 100 brs and 186 agencies; 47% owned by AFK Sistema; 45.3% owned by Allianz AG (Germany); CEO LEONID MELAMED.

Russkiye Strakhovye Traditsii (Russian Traditions Insurance Co): 129366 Moscow, Raketnyi bulv. 13/2; tel. (495) 283-88-03; fax (495) 283-88-05; e-mail info@rustrad.ru; internet www.rustrad.ru; f. 1992; Pres. IVAN I. DAVYDOV.

SOGAZ—Insurance Co of the Gas Industry: 117997 Moscow, ul. Nametkina 16; tel. (495) 782-09-17; fax (495) 432-90-05; e-mail sogaz@sogaz.ru; internet www.sogaz.ru; f. 1993; owned by gas industry interests; Chair. of Bd of Dirs SERGEI A. LUKASH.

Soglasiye (Agreement) **Insurance Co:** 109017 Moscow, M. Tolmachevskii per. 8–11/3; tel. and fax (495) 959-46-32; e-mail official@soglasie.ru; internet www.soglasie.ru; f. 1993 as Interros-Soglasiye; owned by Interros; Gen. Man. IGOR ZHUK.

STOCK EXCHANGES

Moscow Stock Exchange (MSE) (Moskovskaya Fondovaya Birzha): 125047 Moscow, Miusskaya pl. 2/2; tel. (495) 771-35-80; fax (495) 250-17-34; e-mail mse@mse.ru; internet www.mse.ru; f. 1997; Pres. ROMAN N. MYLTSEV.

Siberian Stock Exchange: 630104 Novosibirsk, ul. Frunze 5, POB 233; tel. (3832) 21-60-67; fax (3832) 21-06-90; e-mail sibex@sibex.nsk.su; f. 1991; Pres. ALEKSANDR V. NOVIKOV.

COMMODITY EXCHANGES

Asiatic Commodity Exchange: 670000 Buryatiya, Ulan-Ude, ul. Sovetskaya 23/37; tel. and fax (3012) 22-26-81; f. 1991; Chair. ANDREI FIRSOV.

European-Asian Exchange (EAE): 101000 Moscow, ul. Myasnitskaya 26; tel. and fax (495) 787-58-93; e-mail info@eae.ru; internet www.eae.ru; f. 2000; Chair. of Council TATYANA S. SOKOLOVA; Gen. Man. ALEKSANDR B. YEREMIN.

Khabarovsk Commodity Exchange (KhCE): 680000 Khabarovsk; tel. and fax (4212) 33-65-60; f. 1991; Pres. YEVGENII V. PANASENKO.

Komi Commodity Exchange (KoCE): 167610 Komi, Syktyvkar, Oktyabrskii pr. 16; tel. (8212) 22-32-86; fax (8212) 23-84-43; f. 1991; Pres. PETR S. LUCHENKOV.

Kuzbass Commodity and Raw Materials Exchange (KECME): 650090 Kemerovo, ul. Novgorodskaya 19; tel. (3842) 23-45-40; fax (3842) 23-49-56; f. 1991; Gen. Man. FEDOR MASENKOV.

Moscow Commodity Exchange (MCE): 129223 Moscow, pr. Mira, Russian Exhibition Centre, Pavilion 69 (4); tel. (495) 187-86-14; fax (495) 187-88-76; f. 1990; organization of exchange trading (cash, stock and futures market); Pres. and Chair. of Bd YURII MILYUKOV.

Petrozavodsk Commodity Exchange (PCE): 185028 Kareliya, Petrozavodsk, ul. Krasnaya 31; tel. and fax (8142) 7-80-57; f. 1991; Gen. Man. VALERII SAKHAROV.

Russian Exchange (RE): 101000 Moscow, ul. Myasnitskaya 26; tel. (495) 787-84-34; fax (495) 262-57-57; e-mail ic@ci.re.ru; internet www.re.ru; f. 1990; Pres. PAVEL PANOV.

Russian Commodity Exchange of the Agro-Industrial Complex (RosAgroBirzha): 125080 Moscow, Volokolamskoye shosse 11; tel. (495) 209-52-25; f. 1990; Chair. of Exchange Cttee ALEKSANDR VASILIYEV.

St Petersburg Exchange: 199026 St Petersburg, Vasilyevskii Ostrov, 26-aya liniya 15; tel. (812) 322-44-11; fax (812) 322-73-90; e-mail spbex@spbex.ru; internet www.spbex.ru; f. 1991; Pres. and Chief Exec. VIKTOR V. NIKOLAYEV.

Udmurt Commodity Universal Exchange (UCUE): 426075 Udmurt Rep., Izhevsk, ul. Soyuznaya 107; tel. (3412) 37-08-88; fax (3412) 37-16-57; e-mail iger@udmnet.ru; f. 1991; Pres. N. F. LAZAREV.

Yekaterinburg Commodity Exchange (UCE): 620012 Sverdlovsk obl., Yekaterinburg, pr. Kosmonavtov 23; tel. (343) 234-43-01; fax (343) 251-53-64; f. 1991; Chair. of Exchange Cttee KONSTANTIN ZHUZHLOV.

Trade and Industry

GOVERNMENT AGENCY

Russian Federal Property Fund (Rossiiskii Fond Federalnogo Imushchestva): 119049 Moscow, Leninskii pr. 9; tel. (495) 236-71-15; fax (495) 956-27-80; e-mail rffi@dol.ru; internet www.fpf.ru; f. 1992 to ensure consistency in the privatization process and to implement privatization legislation; Chair. YURII A. PETROV.

NATIONAL CHAMBER OF COMMERCE

Chamber of Commerce and Industry of the Russian Federation (Torgovo-Promyshlennaya Palata RF): 109012 Moscow, ul. Ilinka 6; tel. (495) 929-00-09; fax (495) 929-03-60; e-mail dios-inform@tpprf.ru; internet www.tpprf.ru; f. 1991; Pres. YEVGENII M. PRIMAKOV.

REGIONAL CHAMBERS OF COMMERCE

In early 2002 there were a total of 148 regional chambers of commerce in the Russian Federation. The following are among the most important.

Astrakhan Chamber of Commerce: 414040 Astrakhan, ul. Zhelyabova 50; tel. (8512) 25-58-44; fax (8512) 28-14-42; e-mail cci@mail.astrakhan.ru; internet astrcci.astrakhan.ru; f. 1992; Pres. ALEKSEI D. KANTEMIROV.

Bashkortostan Chamber of Commerce: 450007 Bashkortostan, Ufa, ul. Vorovskogo 22; tel. (3472) 23-23-80; fax (3472) 51-70-79; e-mail office@tpprb.ru; internet www.tpprb.ru; f. 1990; Chair. BORIS A. BONDARENKO.

Central Siberian Chamber of Commerce: 660049 Krasnoyarsk, ul. Kirova 26; tel. (3912) 23-96-13; fax (3912) 23-96-83; e-mail cstp@krasmail.ru; internet www.cstpp.ru; f. 1985; Chair. VALERII A. KOSTIN.

East Siberian Chamber of Commerce: 664003 Irkutsk, ul. Sukhe-Batora 16; tel. (3952) 33-50-60; fax (3952) 33-50-66; e-mail info@ccies.ru; internet www.ccies.ru; f. 1974; Pres. KONSTANTIN S. SHAVRIN.

Far East Chamber of Commerce: 680670 Khabarovsk, ul. Sheronova 113; tel. (4210) 30-47-70; fax (4210) 30-54-58; e-mail dvtpp@fecci.khv.ru; f. 1970; Pres. MIKHAIL V. KRUGLIKOV.

Kaliningrad Chamber of Commerce and Industry: 236010 Kaliningrad, ul. Vatutina 20; tel. (4012) 95-68-01; fax (4012) 95-47-88; e-mail kaliningrad_cci@baltnet.ru; internet www.kaliningrad-cci.ru; f. 1990; Pres. IGOR V. TSARKOV.

Kamchatka Chamber of Commerce: 683000 Kamchatka obl., Petropavlovsk-Kamchatskii, ul. Leninskaya 38/208; tel. and fax (4152) 12-35-10; e-mail kamtpp@iks.ru; Pres. ALLA V. PARKHOMCHUK.

Krasnodar Chamber of Commerce: 350063 Krasnodar, ul. Kommunarov 8; tel. and fax (861) 268-22-13; e-mail tppkk@tppkuban.ru; internet www.tppkuban.ru; f. 1969; Chair. YURII N. TKACHENKO.

Kuzbass Chamber of Commerce: 650099 Kemerovo, pr. Sovetskii 63/407; tel. and fax (3842) 58-77-64; e-mail ktpp@mail.kuzbass.net; internet city.info.kuzbass.net/ktpp; f. 1991; Pres. TATYANA O. IVLEVA.

Maritime (Primorskii) Krai Chamber of Commerce: 690600 Maritime Krai, Vladivostok, Okeanskii pr. 13A; tel. (4232) 26-96-30; fax (4232) 22-72-26; e-mail palata@online.vladivostok.ru; internet www.ptpp.ru; f. 1964; Pres. VLADIMIR B. BREZHNEV.

Moscow Chamber of Commerce: 117393 Moscow, ul. Akademika Pilyugina 22; tel. (495) 132-07-33; fax (495) 132-75-03; e-mail extern@mtpp.org; internet www.mtpp.org; f. 1991; Chair. YURII I. KOTOV; Pres. LEONID V. GOVOROV.

Nizhnii Novgorod Chamber of Commerce: 603005 Nizhnii Novgorod, pl. Oktyabrskaya 1; tel. (8312) 19-42-10; fax (8312) 19-40-09; e-mail tpp@rda.nnov.ru; internet www.tpp.nnov.ru; f. 1990; Pres. GENNADII M. KHODYRYEV.

Northern Chamber of Commerce and Industry: 183766 Murmansk, per. Rusanova 10; tel. (8152) 47-29-99; fax (8152) 47-39-78; e-mail ncci@online.ru; internet www.ncci.ru; f. 1990; Pres. ANATOLII M. GLUSHKOV.

Novosibirsk Chamber of Commerce: 630064 Novosibirsk, pr. K. Marksa 1; tel. and fax (383) 346-41-50; e-mail org@ntpp.ru; internet www.ntpp.ru; f. 1991; Chair. BORIS V. BRUSILOVSKII; 315 mems (2002).

Omsk Chamber of Commerce: 644099 Omsk, ul. Krasnyi Put 18; tel. (3812) 23-05-23; fax (3812) 23-52-48; e-mail omtpp@omsknet.ru; internet www.omsknet.ru/cci; f. 1992; Pres. TATYANA A. KHOROSHAVINA.

Rostov Chamber of Commerce: 344022 Rostov-on-Don, ul. Pushkinskaya 176; tel. and fax (836) 264-45-47; e-mail tpp@rost.ru; internet www.tpp.tis.ru; f. 1992; Pres. NIKOLAI I. PRISYAZHNYUK.

Sakha (Yakutiya) Chamber of Commerce: 677000 Sakha (Yakutiya), Yakutsk, ul. Lenina 22/214; tel. (4112) 26-64-96; e-mail palata91@mail.ru; f. 1991; Chair. SERGEI G. BAKULIN.

Samara Chamber of Commerce: 443099 Samara, ul. A. Tolstogo 6; tel. (8462) 32-11-59; fax (8462) 70-48-96; e-mail ccisr@samara.ru; internet www.cci.samara.ru; f. 1988; Pres. BORIS V. ARDALIN.

Saratov Regional Chamber of Commerce and Industry: 410600 Saratov, ul. B. Kazachya 30; tel. (8452) 27-70-78; fax (8452) 27-70-82; e-mail srcci@sgtpp.ru; internet www.sgtpp.ru; f. 1986; Pres. MAKSIM A. FATEYEV.

Smolensk Chamber of Commerce: 214000 Smolensk, ul. K. Marksa 12; tel. (481) 255-41-42; fax (481) 223-74-50; e-mail smolcci@keytown.com; internet www.keytown.com/users/Torgpal; f. 1993; Pres. OLEG V. LUKIRICH.

South Urals Chamber of Commerce: 454080 Chelyabinsk, ul. S. Krivoi 56; tel. (351) 266-18-16; fax (351) 265-41-53; e-mail mail@uralreg.ru; internet www.uralreg.ru; f. 1992; Pres. FEDOR L. DEGTYAREV; 550 mems (2007).

St Petersburg Chamber of Commerce: 191123 St Petersburg, ul. Chaikovskogo 46–48; tel. (812) 273-48-96; fax (812) 273-48-96; e-mail spbcci@spbcci.ru; internet www.spbcci.ru; f. 1921; Pres. VLADIMIR I. KATENEV.

Stavropol Chamber of Commerce and Industry: 355003 Stavropol, ul. Lenina 384; tel. (8652) 94-53-34; fax (8652) 34-05-10; e-mail stcci@statel.stavropol.ru; f. 1991; Pres. VITALII S. NABATNIKOV.

Tatarstan Republic Chamber of Commerce and Industry: 420111 Tatarstan, Kazan, ul. Pushkina 18; tel. (843) 264-62-07; fax (843) 236-09-66; e-mail tpprt@tpprt.ru; internet www.tpprt.ru; f. 1992; Gen. Dir SHAMIL R. AGEYEV; 1,200 mems (2007).

Ulyanovsk Chamber of Commerce: 432600 Ulyanovsk, ul. Engelsa 19; tel. (8422) 31-45-23; fax (8422) 32-93-73; e-mail ultpp@mv.ru; f. 1992; Pres. YEVGENII S. BALANDIN.

Urals Chamber of Commerce and Industry: 620027 Sverdlovsk obl., Yekaterinburg, ul. Vostochnaya 6; tel. (343) 353-04-49; fax (343) 353-58-63; e-mail ucci@ucci.ur.ru; internet ucci.ur.ru; f. 1959; Pres. YURII P. MATUSHKIN.

THE RUSSIAN FEDERATION

Directory

Volgograd Chamber of Commerce: 400005 Volgograd, ul. 7-aya Gvardeiskaya 2; tel. (8442) 93-61-35; fax (8442) 34-22-02; e-mail cci@volgogradcci.ru; internet www.volgogradcci.ru; f. 1990; Pres. ALEKSANDR D. BELITSKII.

Vologda Chamber of Commerce and Industry: 160000 Vologda, ul. Lermontova 15; tel. and fax (8172) 72-46-87; e-mail grant@vologda.ru; internet www.vologdatpp.ru; f. 1992; Pres. GALINA D. TELEGINA.

Voronezh Chamber of Commerce: 394030 Voronezh, 'Voronezhnesh-servis', POB 63; tel. and fax (473) 252-49-38; e-mail mail@ooootpp.vm.ru; f. 1991; fmrly Central-Black Earth Chamber of Commerce and Industry; Pres. VYACHESLAV A. KONDRATYEV.

EMPLOYERS' ORGANIZATIONS

Co-ordinating Council of Employers' Unions of Russia (Koordinatsionnyi Sovet Obyedinenii Rabotodatelei Rossii—KSORR): 109017 Moscow, per. M. Tolmachevskii 8–11; tel. (495) 232-55-77; fax (495) 959-46-06; e-mail official@ksorr.ru; internet www.ksorr.ru; f. 1994; co-ordinates and represents employers in relations with government bodies and trade unions, and represents Russian employers in the ILO and the International Organization of Employers (IOE); Chair. OLEG V. YEREMEYEV; Gen. Dir SERGEI V. LUKONIN; unites 35 major employers' unions, including the following:

Agro-Industrial Union of Russia: 107139 Moscow, POB 139; tel. (495) 204-41-04; fax (495) 207-83-62; e-mail sva@gvs.aris.ru; Pres. VASILII A. STARODUBTSEV.

All-Russian Social Organization of Small and Medium-sized Businesses (OPORA Rossii) (Obshcherossiiskaya Obshchestvennaya Organizatsiya Malogo i Srednego Predprinimatelstva): 125047 Moscow, ul. 4-ya Tverskaya-Yamskaya 21/22/3; tel. (495) 775-81-11; fax (495) 775-81-91; internet www.opora.ru; f. 2002; Pres. SERGEI BORISOV.

Russian Union of Industrialists and Entrepreneurs (Employers) (RSPPR) (Rossiiskii Soyuz Promyshlennikov i Predprinimatelei): 103070 Moscow, Staraya pl. 10/4; tel. (495) 748-42-37; fax (495) 206-11-29; e-mail pr_dep@rspp.net; internet www.rspp.ru; f. 1991; Pres. ALEKSANDR SHOKHIN; Exec. Sec. NIKOLAI TONKOV.

UTILITIES

Electricity

Federal Energy Commission: 103074 Moscow, Kitaigorodskii proyezd 7; tel. (495) 220-40-15; fax (495) 206-81-08; e-mail fecrf@orc.ru; regulatory authority for natural energy monopolies; sole responsibility for establishing tariff rates for energy, transportation, shipping, postal and telecommunications industries in the Russian Federation from Sept. 2001; Chair. ANDREI ZADERNYUK.

Irkutskenergo (Irkutsk Energy Co): 664000 Irkutsk, ul. Sukhe-Batora 3; tel. (3952) 21-73-00; fax (3952) 21-78-99; e-mail idkan@irkutskenergo.ru; internet www.irkutskenergo.ru; f. 1954; generation and transmission of electrical and thermal energy; Dir-Gen. VLADIMIR V. KOLMOGOROV.

Mosenergo (Moscow Energy Co): 113035 Moscow, Raushskaya nab. 8; tel. (495) 957-35-30; fax (495) 957-34-70; e-mail press-centre@mosenergo.ru; internet www.mosenergo.ru; f. 1887; 49% owned by Unified Energy System of Russia; power generator and distributor; Chair. YURII A. UDALTSOV.

Rosenergoatom (Russian Atomic Energy Concern): 119017 Moscow, ul. B. Ordynka 24/26; tel. (495) 239-24-22; fax (495) 239-46-03; e-mail npp@rosatom.ru; internet www.rosenergoatom.ru; f. 1992; electricity generating co, manages Russia's 10 nuclear reactors; Dir-Gen. SERGEI OBOZOV.

Sverdlovenergo (Sverdlovsk Energy Co): 620219 Sverdlovsk obl., Yekaterinburg, pr. Lenina 38; tel. (343) 259-13-99; fax (343) 259-12-22; e-mail post@energo.pssr.ru; internet www.po.pssr.ru; f. 1942; Chair. of Bd ALEKSANDR V. CHIKUNOV; Gen. Man. VLADIMIR V. KALSIN.

Unified Energy System of Russia (RAO EES Rossii): 119526 Moscow, pr. Vernadskogo 101/3; tel. (495) 710-40-01; fax (495) 927-30-07; e-mail rao@elektra.ru; internet www.rao-ees.ru; f. 1992; operates national electricity grid; 52% state-owned; controls about 2.5m. km of transmission lines, holds shares in 43 power plants and 72 regional power cos, including Mosenergo and Lenenergo, accounting for more than 70% of Russia's electricity output; restructuring under way 2007; sales 797,300m. (2004); cap. 21,558,000m. (Dec. 2004). Chair. ALEKSANDR S. VOLOSHIN; Chief Exec. and Chair of Bd of Management ANATOLII B. CHUBAIS; 496,300 employees (2004).

Uralenergo (Ural Energy): 454006 Chelyabinsk, ul. Rossiiskaya 17; tel. (3512) 67-59-54; fax (3512) 67-59-48; e-mail info@uralenergo.com; internet www.uralenergo.com; manages 22 joint-stock cos; oversees 55 thermal power stations and 6 hydroelectric stations; total installed capacity of over 28,500m. kW; Dir ALEKSANDR S. NEMTSEV.

Gas

Gazprom: 117997 Moscow, ul. Nametkina 16; tel. (495) 719-30-01; fax (495) 719-83-33; e-mail gazprom@gazprom.ru; internet www.gazprom.ru; f. 1989 from assets of Soviet Ministry of Oil and Gas; became independent joint-stock co in 1992, privatized in 1994; 51% state-owned; Chair. of Exec. Bd (Chief Exec.) and Deputy Chair. of Bd of Dirs ALEKSEI B. MILLER; Chair. of Bd of Dirs DMITRII A. MEDVEDEV.

Mezhregiongaz (Inter-Regional Gas Co): 142770 Moscow Oblast, Leninskii raion, p/o Kommunarkap. Gazoprovod; tel. (495) 719-53-36; fax (495) 719-52-67; e-mail pr@mrg.gazprom.ru; internet www.mrg.ru; f. 1997; gas marketing co; subsidiary of Gazprom; brs in more than 60 federal subjects; Dir-Gen. KIRILL SELEZNEV.

Water

MosVodoKanal: 105005 Moscow, per. Pleteshkovskii 2; tel. (495) 763-34-9634; fax (495) 265-22-01; e-mail post@mosvodokanal.ru; internet www.mosvodokanal.ru; f. 1937; state-owned; provides water and sewerage services to Moscow and the surrounding region; Dir-Gen. STANISLAV KHRAMENKOV.

Vodokanal: 191015 St Petersburg, ul. Kavalergardskaya 42; tel. (812) 274-16-79; fax (812) 274-13-61; e-mail office@vodokanal.spb.ru; internet www.vodokanal.spb.ru; water and sewerage utility; Gen. Man. FELIKS V. KARMAZINOV.

TRADE UNIONS

In 1990 several branch unions of the All-Union Central Council of Trade Unions (ACCTU) established the Federation of Independent Trade Unions of the Russian Federation (FITUR), which took control of part of the property and other assets of the ACCTU. The ACCTU was re-formed as the General Confederation of Trade Unions of the USSR, which was, in turn, renamed the General Confederation of Trade Unions—International Organization in 1992.

All-Russian Labour Confederation: 103031 Moscow, ul. Rozhdestvenka 5/7; tel. (495) 785-21-30; fax (495) 915-83-67; e-mail vktrussia@online.ru; internet www.trud.org/guide/VKT.htm; f. 1995; unites five national trade unions and 40 regional orgs with 1,270,900 mems; Pres. ALEKSANDR N. BUGAYEV.

General Confederation of Trade Unions (VKP): 119119 Moscow, Leninskii pr. 42; tel. (495) 938-01-12; fax (495) 938-21-55; e-mail inter@vkp.ru; internet www.vkp.ru; f. 1992 to replace General Confederation of Trade Unions of the USSR; co-ordinating body for trade unions in CIS member states; unites nine national and 31 regional industrial orgs with 52m. mems; publishes *Profsoyuzy* (Trade Unions), weekly, *Vestnik profsoyuzov* (Herald of the Trade Unions), every two weeks, and *Inform-Contact*, in English and French, quarterly; Pres. MIKHAIL SHMAKOV; Sec.-Gen. VLADIMIR SCHERBAKOV.

Federation of Independent Trade Unions of Russia (FITUR) (Federatsiya Nezavisimykh Profsoyuzov Rossii—FNPR): 119119 Moscow, Leninskii pr. 42; tel. (495) 938-73-12; fax (495) 137-06-94; e-mail korneev@fnpr.ru; internet www.fnpr.ru; f. 1990; Pres. MIKHAIL V. SHMAKOV.

FITUR unites 48 national trade unions and 78 regional orgs (with c. 40m. mems), including the following::

All-Russian 'Electroprofsoyuz': 117119 Moscow, Leninskii pr. 42/3; tel. (495) 938-83-78; fax (495) 930-98-62; f. 1990; electrical workers; Pres. VALERII P. KUZICHEV.

Automobile and Farm Machinery Construction Industries Workers' Union: 117119 Moscow, Leninskii pr. 42/3; tel. (495) 938-76-13; fax (495) 938-86-15; Pres. YULII G. NOVIKOV.

Communication Workers' Union of Russia: 117119 Moscow, Leninskii pr. 42/3; tel. (495) 938-72-06; fax (495) 930-22-86; f. 1905; Pres. ANATOLII G. NAZEIKIN.

Construction and Building Materials Industry Workers' Union of the Russian Federation: 117119 Moscow, Leninskii pr. 42/1; tel. (495) 930-71-74; fax (495) 952-55-47; f. 1991; Pres. BORIS A. SOSHENKO.

Health Workers' Union of the Russian Federation: 117119 Moscow, Leninskii pr. 42/3; tel. (495) 938-84-43; fax (495) 938-81-34; e-mail ckprz@online.ru; f. 1990; Chair. MIKHAIL M. KUZMENKO.

Moscow Trade Unions Federation: 121205 Moscow, ul. Novyi Arbat 36/9; tel. (495) 290-82-62; fax (495) 202-92-70; e-mail main@mtuf.ru; f. 1990; largest regional branch of FITUR; Chair. MIKHAIL D. NAGAITSEV; 2.2m. mems.

Motor Transport and Road Workers' Union of Russia: 117218 Moscow, ul. Krzhizhanovskogo 20/30/5; tel. (495) 125-23-30; fax (495) 125-07-98; e-mail profavtodor@mtu.ru; f. 1990; Pres. VIKTOR I. MOKHNACHEV.

National Educational and Scientific Workers' Union of the Russian Federation: 117119 Moscow, Leninskii pr. 42/3; tel. (495) 938-87-77; fax (495) 930-68-15; f. 1990; Pres. VLADIMIR M. YAKOVLEV.

THE RUSSIAN FEDERATION

Oil, Gas and Construction Workers' Union: 119119 Moscow, Leninskii pr. 42/4; tel. (495) 930-69-74; fax (495) 930-11-24; e-mail rogwu@rogwu.ru; internet www.rogwu.ru; f. 1990; Pres. LEV A. MIRONOV.

Russian Chemical Industry Workers' Union: 117119 Moscow, Leninskii pr. 42/ 3; tel. (495) 930-69-93; fax (495) 938-21-55; e-mail rcwu@fnpr.ru; f. 1990; Pres. ALEKSANDR SITNOV (acting).

Russian Fishing Industry Workers' Union: 117119 Moscow, Leninskii pr. 42/3; tel. (495) 938-77-82; fax (495) 930-77-26; e-mail bfish@fnpr.ru; f. 1991; Pres. YURII V. SHALONIN.

Russian Independent Trade Union of Coal-industry Workers (Rosugleprof): 109004 Moscow, ul. Zemlyanoi Val 64/2; tel. (495) 915-28-52; fax (495) 915-30-77; Chair. IVAN I. MOKHNACHUK.

Russian Radio and Electronics Industry Workers Union: 109180 Moscow, 1-i Golutvinskii per. 3; tel. (495) 238-08-02; fax (495) 238-17-31; Pres. VALERII YE. MARKOV.

Russian Textiles and Light Industry Workers' Union: 117119 Moscow, Leninskii pr. 42/3; tel. (495) 938-78-24; fax (495) 938-84-05; f. 1990; Pres. TATYANA I. SOSNINA.

Russian Trade Union of Railwaymen and Transport Construction Workers (Rosprofzhel): 103064 Moscow, ul. Staraya Basmannaya 11; tel. (495) 262-58-73; fax (495) 923-88-31; e-mail iturr@orc.ru; Pres. ANATOLII B. VASILIYEV.

Shipbuilding Workers' Union: 117119 Moscow, Leninskii pr. 42/5; tel. (495) 938-88-72; fax (495) 938-84-74; Pres. VLADIMIR YE. MAKAVCHIK.

Timber Industry Workers' Union of the Russian Federation: 117119 Moscow, Leninskii pr. 42/1; tel. (495) 938-89-03; fax (495) 137-06-81; Pres. VALERII N. OCHEKUROV.

Union of Agro-industrial Workers of the Russian Federation: 119119 Moscow, Leninskii pr. 42/3; tel. (495) 938-77-35; fax (495) 938-82-63; e-mail info@profagro; f. 1919; Pres. NATALIYA N. AGAPOVA; 2.3m. mems (2007).

Union of Engineering Workers of the Russian Federation: 127486 Moscow, ul. Deguninskaya 1/2; tel. (495) 487-3507; fax (495) 487-56-37; Pres. YURII S. SPICHENOK.

Union of Food Industry and Production Co-operative Workers of the Russian Federation: 117119 Moscow, Leninskii pr. 42/3; tel. (495) 938-75-03; fax (495) 930-10-56; Pres. VALERII K. ZHOVTERIK.

Independent Trade Unions

Federation of Air Traffic Controllers' Unions of Russia (FPAR): 125993 Moscow, Leningradskii pr. 37/472, POB 3; tel. (495) 155-57-01; fax (495) 155-59-17; e-mail postmaster@fatcurus.ru; internet www.fatcurus.ru; f. 1989; Pres. SERGEI A. KOVALEV.

Metallurgical Industry Workers' Union: Moscow, ul. Pushkinskaya 5/6; left the FITUR in 1992 to form independent organization; Pres. BORIS MISNIK.

Transport

RAILWAYS

At the end of 2006 the total length of railway track in use was 84,821 km, around one-half of which was electrified.

Russian Railways OAO (RZhD) (Rossiiskiye zheleznyye dorogi): 107174 Moscow, ul. Novobasmannaya 2; tel. (495) 262-16-28; fax (495) 975-24-11; e-mail info@rzd.ru; internet www.rzd.ru; f. 2003; Pres. VLADIMIR YAKUNIN.

City Underground Railways

Moscow Metro: 129110 Moscow, pr. Mira 41/2; tel. (495) 622-10-01; fax (495) 631-37-44; e-mail info@mosmetro.ru; f. 1935; 12 lines (294 km) with 176 stations in 2007; Gen. Man. DMITRII V. GAYEV.

Nizhnii Novgorod Metro: 603002 Nizhnii Novgorod, pl. Revolutsii 7; tel. (8312) 44-17-60; fax (8312) 44-20-86; e-mail metro@sandy.ru; f. 1985; 15 km with 13 stations; Gen. Man. A. KUZMIN.

Novosibirsk Metro: 630099 Novosibirsk, ul. Serebrennikovskaya 34; tel. (3832) 90-81-10; fax (3832) 46-56-82; e-mail nsk@metro.snt.su; internet www.nsk.su/~metro; f. 1986; 2 lines (13.2 km) with 11 stations, and a further 6 km under construction; Gen. Man. V. I. DEMIN.

St Petersburg Metro: 190013 St Petersburg, Moskovskii pr. 28; tel. (812) 251-66-68; fax (812) 316-14-41; e-mail np@metro.spb.ru; internet www.metro.spb.ru; f. 1955; 4 lines (106 km) with 60 stations; Gen. Man. VLADIMIR A. GARYUGIN.

Short underground railways began to operate in Samara, Yekaterinburg and Kazan in 1987, 1991 and 2005, respectively. In 2008 the construction of underground railways was under way in Chelyabinsk, Krasnoyarsk and Omsk, and a light railway was scheduled to open in Sochi, prior to the holding of the Winter Olympics there in 2014.

ROADS

At the end of 2006 the total length of roads was 597,421 km, and 85.2% of roads were paved. In Siberia and the Far East there are few roads, and they are often impassable in winter, while the *rasputitsa*, or spring thaw, notoriously impedes rural road traffic, even in European Russia.

SHIPPING

The seaports of the Russian Federation provide access to the Pacific Ocean, in the east, the Baltic Sea and the Atlantic Ocean, in the west, and the Black Sea, in the south. Major eastern ports are at Vladivostok, Nakhodka, Vostochnyi, Magadan and Petropavlovsk. In the west St Petersburg and Kaliningrad provide access to the Baltic Sea, and the northern ports of Murmansk and Archangel (Arkhangelsk) have access to the Atlantic Ocean, via the Barents Sea. Novorossiisk and Sochi are the principal Russian ports on the Black Sea.

Principal Shipowning Companies

Baltic Shipping Co: 198035 St Petersburg, Mezhevoi kanal 5; tel. (812) 251-33-97; fax (812) 186-85-44; freight and passenger services; Chair. MIKHAIL A. ROMANOVSKII.

Baltic Transport Systems: 199106 St Petersburg, pl. Morskoi Slavy 1; tel. (812) 303-99-14; fax (812) 380-34-76; e-mail bts@baltics.ru; internet www.baltics.ru; f. 1994; freight and passenger services; Gen. Dir ALEKSEI E. SHUKLETSOV.

Far Eastern Shipping Co: 690019 Maritime (Primorskii) Krai, Vladivostok, ul. Aleutskaya 15; tel. (4232) 41-14-32; fax (4232) 52-15-51; e-mail 41401@41.fesco.ru; internet www.fesco.ru; f. 1880; Gen. Man. YEVGENII N. AMBROSOV.

Kamchatka Shipping Co: 683600 Kamchatka obl., Petropavlovsk-Kamchatskii, ul. Radiosvyazi 65; tel. (41522) 2-82-21; fax (41522) 2-19-60; f. 1949; freight services; Pres. NIKOLAI M. ZABLOTSKII.

Murmansk Shipping Co: 183038 Murmansk, ul. Kominterna 15; tel. (8152) 48-10-48; fax (8152) 48-11-48; e-mail postmaster@msco.ru; f. 1939; shipping and icebreaking services; Gen. Dir VYACHESLAV RUKSHA.

Northern Shipping Co (NSC Arkhangelsk) (Severnoye morskoye parokhodstvo OAO—SMP): 163000 Archangel, nab. Severnoi Dviny 36; tel. (8182) 63-72-03; fax (8182) 63-71-95; e-mail nsosnina@ansc.ru; internet www.ansc.ru; f. 1870; dry cargo shipping, liner services; Gen. Dir VIKTOR A. IZBITSKII.

Novorossiisk Shipping Co: 353900 Krasnodar Krai, Novorossiisk, ul. Svobody 1; tel. (8617) 25-31-26; fax (8617) 25-11-43; e-mail novoship@novoship.ru; internet www.novoship.ru; f. 1992; Chair. V. I. YAKUNIN.

Primorsk Shipping Corpn: 692900 Maritime (Primorskii) Krai, Nakhodka-4, Administrativnyi Gorodok; tel. (4236) 69-45-05; fax (4236) 69-45-75; e-mail psc@prisco.ru; internet www.prisco.ru; f. 1972; tanker shipowner; Dir-Gen. ALEKSANDR MIGUNOV.

Sakhalin Shipping Co: 694620 Sakhalin obl., Kholmsk, ul. Pobedy 16; tel. (42433) 6-62-07; fax (42433) 6-60-20; e-mail chief@sasco.sakhalin.ru; internet www.sasco.org; f. 1945; shipowners and managers, carriage of cargo and passengers; Pres. YAKUB ZH. ALEGEDPINOV.

Sovfrakht: 127944 Moscow, Rakhmanovskii per. 4, Morskoi Dom; tel. (495) 258-27-41; fax (495) 230-26-40; e-mail general@sovfracht.ru; internet www.sovfracht.ru; f. 1929; jt-stock co; chartering and broking of tanker, cargo and other ships; forwarding, booking and insurance agency; ship management; Dir-Gen. D. YU. PURIM; 120 employees (2003).

White Sea and Onega Shipping Co (Belomorsko-Onezhskoye parokhodstvo): 185005 Kareliya, Petrozavodsk, ul. Rigachina 7; tel. (8142) 71-12-01; fax (8142) 71-12-67; e-mail dir@bop.onego.ru; internet bop.onego.ru; f. 1940; cargo shipping, cargo-ship construction and repair; Gen. Dir STANISLAV ROZOLINSKII; Pres. ALEKSANDR LYALLYA.

CIVIL AVIATION

Until 1991 Aeroflot—Soviet Airlines was the only airline operating on domestic routes in the former USSR. In 1992–94 some 300 different independent airlines emerged on the basis of Aeroflot's former regional directorates. Several small private airlines were also established. In 2003 there were 451 airports in Russia.

Aeroflot-Don: 344009 Rostov-on-Don, pr. Sholokhova 272; tel. (863) 276-78-11; fax (863) 252-11-78; e-mail avia1@aeroflot-don.ru; internet www.aeroflot-don.ru; f. 1925; present name adopted 2000; 100% owned by Aeroflot—Russian Airlines; operates scheduled and chartered passenger and cargo flights to various domestic and international destinations (incl. Armenia, Austria, Egypt Germany,

Israel, Turkey, Ukraine, United Arab Emirates) from Rostov-on-Don, Moscow and Sochi, and betwen Moscow and Groznyi; Dir-Gen. MIKHAIL S. KRITSKII.

Aeroflot—Russian Airlines: 125167 Moscow, Leningradskii pr. 37/9; tel. and fax (495) 155-66-43; internet www.aeroflot.ru; f. 1923; 51% state-owned; operates flights to 108 destinations in 54 countries, and to 26 destinations in Russia; Gen. Dir VALERII M. OKULOV.

Domodedova Airlines: 142045 Moscow, Domodedova Airport; tel. (495) 504-03-00; fax (495) 787-86-18; e-mail ak_e3@tch.ru; internet www.akdal.ru; f. 1964; scheduled passenger flights to domestic and CIS destinations; chartered passenger and freight flights to domestic, CIS and international destinations; Gen. Dir ANDREI MASLOV.

Gazpromavia: 117997 Moscow, ul. Nametkina 16; tel. (495) 719-18-32; fax (495) 719-11-85; e-mail gazpromavia@gazprom.ru; internet gazpromavia.com; f. 1995; Dir-Gen. ANDREI S. OVCHARENKO.

KD Avia: 238315 Kaliningrad obl., Guryevskii raion, Khrabrovo, Aeroport; tel. (401) 235-51-75; e-mail info@kdavia.ru; internet www.kdavia.ru; f. 1945; present name adopted 2005; international and domestic flights from Kaliningrad; Dir-Gen. VALERII MIKHAILOV.

Kuban Airlines (Kubanskiye Avialinii): 350026 Krasnodar, Krasnodar—Pashkovskaya Airport; tel. (861) 237-06-00; fax (861) 237-38-11; e-mail info@kuban-airlines.com; internet www.kuban-airlines.de; f. 1932; regional and international flights.

Pulkovo Airlines: 196210 St Petersburg, ul. Pilotov 18/4; tel. (812) 324-36-34; fax (812) 104-37-02; internet www.pulkovo.ru; operates regular, direct flights from St Petersburg to domestic and international destinations; Gen. Dir B. G. DEMCHENKO.

S7 Airlines (Siberia Airlines): 633115 Novosibirsk obl., gorod Ob-4; tel. (3832) 59-90-11; fax (3832) 59-90-64; e-mail pr@s7.ru; internet www.s7.ru; fmrly Sibir Airlines; scheduled and charter flights to domestic, CIS, Asian, European and Middle Eastern destinations; Gen. Dir VLADISLAV FILEV.

SkyExpress: 119027 Moscow, Vnukovo, ul. Tsentralnaya 2/2; tel. (495) 580-93-60; fax (495) 980-74-61; e-mail info@skyexpress.ru; internet skyexpress.ru; 'low cost' airline operating passenger flights between Moscow (Vnukovo) and Murmansk, Rostov-on-Don and Sochi (Krasnodar Krai); f. 2007; Chief Exec. MARINA BUKALOVA.

Transaero Airlines: 121099 Moscow, 2-i Smolenskii per. 3/4; tel. (495) 937-84-71; fax (495) 937-84-64; e-mail info@transaero.ru; internet www.transaero.ru; f. 1991; Russia's largest privately owned airline; operates scheduled and charter passenger services to the CIS, Europe, Asia and Central America; Chief Exec. OLGA PLESHAKOVA.

Ural Airlines (Uralskiye Aviyalinii): 620910 Sverdlovsk obl., Yekaterinburg, ul. Sputnikov 6; tel. (343) 226-81-26; fax (343) 226-82-49; e-mail margarita@uralairlines.ru; internet www.uralairlines.ru; f. 1993; flights from Yekaterinburg to domestic and international destinations; Gen. Dir SERGEI SKURATOV.

Vladivostok Avia: 692756 Maritime (Primorskii) Krai, Artem, ul. Portovaya 41, Vladivostok Airport; tel. (4232) 30-73-33; fax (4232) 30-73-43; e-mail office@vladavia.ru; internet www.vladavia.ru; f. 1994; freight and scheduled passenger services from Vladivostok and Moscow to domestic and international destinations; Gen. Dir VLADIMIR SAIBEL.

Tourism

In 2005 there were 22,200,600 tourist arrivals in Russia, and receipts from tourism totalled US $7,402.

Intourist: 129366 Moscow, pr. Mira 150; tel. (495) 956-42-07; fax (495) 730-19-57; e-mail info@intourist.ru; internet www.intourist.ru; f. 1929; brs throughout Russia and abroad; Pres. NIKOLAI KAKORA.

RWANDA

Introductory Survey

Location, Climate, Language, Religion, Flag, Capital

The Rwandan Republic is a land-locked country in eastern central Africa, just south of the Equator, bounded by the Democratic Republic of the Congo to the west, by Uganda to the north, by Tanzania to the east and by Burundi to the south. The climate is tropical, although tempered by altitude. It is hot and humid in the lowlands, but cooler in the highlands. The average annual rainfall is 785 mm (31 ins). The main rainy season is from February to May. The population is composed of three ethnic groups: Hutu (85%), Tutsi (14%) and Twa (1%). French, English and Kinyarwanda, the native language, are all in official use, and Kiswahili is widely spoken. About one-half of the population adhere to animist beliefs. Most of the remainder are Christians, mainly Roman Catholics. There are Protestant and Muslim minorities. The national flag (proportions 1 by 2) has three unequal horizontal stripes, of blue, yellow and green, with a blue-ringed yellow disc (framed by 24 yellow rays) depicted near the fly end of the top stripe. The capital is Kigali.

Recent History

Rwanda, with the neighbouring state of Burundi, became part of German East Africa in 1899. In 1916, during the First World War, it was occupied by Belgian forces from the Congo. From 1920 Rwanda was part of Ruanda-Urundi, administered by Belgium under a League of Nations mandate and later as a UN Trust Territory. Long-standing dissension between the majority Hutu tribe and their former overlords, the Tutsi, caused a rebellion and the proclamation of a state of emergency in 1959. In September 1961 it was decided by referendum to abolish the monarchy and to establish a republic. Full independence followed on 1 July 1962. Serious tribal conflict erupted in December 1963, and massacres (of an estimated 20,000) were perpetrated by the Hutu against the Tutsi. During 1964–65 large numbers of displaced Rwandans were resettled in neighbouring countries. In 1969 Grégoire Kayibanda, the new Republic's first President, was re-elected, and all 47 seats in the legislature were retained by the governing party, the Mouvement démocratique républicain (MDR), also known as the Parti de l'émancipation du peuple Hutu (Parmehutu).

Tension between Hutu and Tutsi escalated again at the end of 1972 and continued throughout February 1973. In July the Minister of Defence and head of the National Guard, Maj.-Gen. Juvénal Habyarimana, led a bloodless coup against President Kayibanda, proclaimed a Second Republic and established a military administration. In August a new Council of Ministers, with Habyarimana as President, was formed. All political activity was banned until July 1975, when a new ruling party, the Mouvement révolutionnaire national pour le développement (MRND), was formed.

A national referendum in December 1978 approved a new Constitution, which was intended to return the country to democratically elected government (in accordance with an undertaking made by Habyarimana in 1973 to end the military regime within five years). Elections to the legislature, the Conseil national de développement (CND), took place in December 1981 and in December 1983; also in December 1983 Habyarimana was re-elected President. In December 1988 Habyarimana was again elected (unopposed) to the presidency, securing 99.98% of the votes cast. Elections to the CND were conducted in the same month.

In September 1990 a Commission was appointed to compile recommendations for a draft national charter, which was to provide for the establishment of a multi-party system. In April 1991, following the CND's revision of the Commission's proposals, a draft constitution was presented to an extraordinary congress of the MRND, at which the party was renamed the Mouvement républicain national pour la démocratie et le développement (MRNDD). On 10 June the reforms were promulgated by Habyarimana, and legislation regulating the formation of political parties was adopted; parties were to be non-tribal and independent, while members of the security forces and the judiciary were to be banned from political activity. (By June 1992 15 parties, among them the MRNDD and a revived MDR, had officially registered.) In October 1991 Sylvestre Nsanzimana, hitherto Minister of Justice, was appointed to the new post of Prime Minister, and in December he formed a transitional Government, in which all but two portfolios (assigned to the Parti démocratique chrétien—PDC) were allocated to members of the MRNDD. Opposition parties, which had been excluded from participation in the transitional Government for their rejection of a MRNDD Prime Minister, organized anti-Government demonstrations in late 1991 and early 1992, demanding the removal of Nsanzimana and the convening of a national conference. A series of negotiations between the Government and the major opposition parties was initiated in February 1992, and in April a protocol agreement was signed, providing for the establishment of a new transitional administration, with Dismas Nsengiyaremye of the MDR as Prime Minister. Habyarimana announced that multi-party elections would be conducted within one year of the installation of the new Government.

Relations with neighbouring Uganda were frequently strained, owing mainly to the presence of some 250,000 Rwandan refugees in Uganda (mainly members of Rwanda's Tutsi minority), who had fled their homeland following successive outbreaks of persecution by the Hutu regime in 1959, 1963 and 1973. In October 1990 rebel forces, based in Uganda, invaded northern Rwanda, occupying several towns. The 4,000-strong rebel army, known as the Front patriotique rwandais (FPR), which mainly comprised Rwandan Tutsi refugees, aimed to overthrow the Habyarimana regime and secure the repatriation of all Rwandan refugees. The Rwandan Government accused the Ugandan leadership of supporting the rebel forces (many of whom had served in the Ugandan armed forces), although this accusation was strenuously denied. With the assistance of French, Belgian and Zairean troops, the Rwandan army succeeded in repelling the FPR before it could reach Kigali. In late October the Government declared a cease-fire, although hostilities continued in northern Rwanda.

Unsuccessful negotiations took place during 1991 and early 1992, but further talks held in Arusha, Tanzania, in July resulted in an agreement on the implementation of a new cease-fire, effective from the end of that month, and the creation of a military observer group (GOM), sponsored by the Organization of African Unity (OAU—now the African Union, see p. 164, AU), to comprise representatives from both sides, together with officers from the armed forces of Nigeria, Senegal, Zimbabwe and Mali. However, subsequent negotiations failed to resolve outstanding problems concerning the creation of a proposed 'neutral zone' between the Rwandan armed forces and the FPR, the incorporation of the FPR in a future combined Rwandan national force, the repatriation of refugees, and FPR demands for full participation in a transitional government and legislature.

A resurgence in violence followed the breakdown of negotiations in February 1993. An estimated 1m. civilians fled southwards and into neighbouring Uganda and Tanzania, as the FPR advanced as far as Ruhengeri. France dispatched reinforcements to join a small military contingent that had been stationed in Kigali since October 1990 to protect French nationals. Meanwhile, the commander of the 50-member GOM declared that the group had inadequate manpower and resources to contain the FPR, and requested the deployment of an additional 400 troops from the OAU. In late February 1993 the Government accepted FPR terms for a cease-fire, in return for an end to attacks against FPR positions and Tutsi communities, and the withdrawal of foreign troops. Although fighting continued with varying intensity, fresh peace negotiations were convened in Arusha in March, and France subsequently began to withdraw its troops. Negotiations conducted during April failed to produce a solution to the crucial issue of the structure of a future single armed Rwandan force. In the same month the five participating parties in the ruling coalition agreed to a three-month extension of the Government's mandate, in order to facilitate the successful conclusion of a peace accord. Significant progress was made during renewed talks between the Government and the FPR during May, when a timetable for the demobilization of the 19,000-strong security forces was agreed. In June the UN Security

Council approved the creation of the UN Observer Mission Uganda-Rwanda (UNOMUR), to be deployed on the Ugandan side of the border, for an initial period of six months, in order to prevent the maintenance of a military supply line for the FPR.

In July 1993 President Habyarimana met with delegates from those political parties represented in the Government to seek a further extension of the coalition's mandate. However, the Prime Minister's insistence that the FPR should be represented in any new government exacerbated existing divisions within the MDR, prompting Habyarimana to conclude the agreement with a conciliatory group of MDR dissidents, including the Minister of Education, Agathe Uwilingiyimana, who was elected to the premiership.

In August 1993 a peace accord was formally signed in Arusha by Habyarimana and Col Alex Kanyarengwe of the FPR. A new transitional government, to be headed by a mutually approved Prime Minister, would be installed by 10 September, and multi-party elections would be conducted after a 22-month period. Failure to establish the transitional institutions by the stipulated deadline was attributed by the Government and the FPR to an increasingly precarious national security situation, and both sides urged the prompt dispatch of a neutral UN force to facilitate the implementation of the accord. In October the UN Security Council adopted Resolution 872, providing for the establishment of the UN Assistance Mission to Rwanda (UNAMIR), to be deployed in Rwanda for an initial period of six months, with a mandate to monitor observance of the cease-fire, to contribute to the security of the capital and to facilitate the repatriation of refugees. UNAMIR, which was to incorporate UNOMUR and GOM and to comprise some 2,500 personnel, was formally inaugurated on 1 November. In December the UN expressed the opinion that conditions had been sufficiently fulfilled to allow the inauguration of the transitional institutions.

On 5 January 1994 Habyarimana was invested as President of a transitional administration, for a 22-month period, under the terms of the Arusha accord. The inauguration of the transitional government and legislature was, however, repeatedly delayed, owing to political opposition to the proposed Council of Ministers, and to the insistence of Habyarimana that the list of proposed legislative deputies, presented in March, should be modified to include representatives of additional political parties, including the reactionary Coalition pour la défense de la République (CDR). Meanwhile, political frustration had erupted into violence in February, with the murder of the Minister of Public Works and Energy, Félicien Gatabazi of the Parti social-démocrate (PSD), who had been a prominent supporter of the Arusha accord and of the transitional administration. Within hours the CDR leader, Martin Bucyana, was killed in a retaliatory attack by PSD supporters, and a series of violent confrontations ensued.

On 6 April 1994 the presidential aircraft was fired on, above Kigali airport, and exploded, killing all 10 passengers, including Habyarimana. (The President of Burundi, Cyprien Ntaryamira, two Burundian cabinet ministers and the Chief of Staff of the Rwandan armed forces were among the other victims.) In Kigali the presidential guard immediately initiated a campaign of retributive violence against Habyarimana's political opponents, although it remained unclear who had been responsible for the attack on the aircraft. As politicians and civilians fled the capital, the brutality of the political assassinations was compounded by attacks on the clergy, UNAMIR personnel and members of the Tutsi tribe. Many Hutu civilians were reportedly forced to murder their Tutsi neighbours, and the mobilization of the Interahamwe unofficial militias (allegedly affiliated to the MRNDD and the CDR), committed to the massacre of Tutsi civilians and opponents of the Government, was encouraged by the presidential guard (with support from some factions of the armed forces) and by inflammatory radio broadcasts. The Prime Minister, the President of the Constitutional Court and the Ministers of Labour and Social Affairs and of Information were among the prominent politicians murdered (or declared missing and presumed dead) within hours of Habyarimana's death. On 8 April the Speaker of the CND, Dr Théodore Sindikubwabo, announced that he had assumed the office of interim President of the Republic, in accordance with the provisions of the 1991 Constitution. The five remaining participating political parties and factions of the Government selected a new Prime Minister, Jean Kambanda, and a new Council of Ministers (drawn largely from the MRNDD) from among their ranks. The legality of the new administration was immediately challenged by the FPR, which claimed that the terms of the Constitution regarding succession had been superseded by the terms of the Arusha accord. The legitimacy of the Government was subsequently rejected by several political parties and factions.

In mid-April 1994 the FPR resumed operations from its northern stronghold, with the stated aim of relieving its beleaguered battalion in Kigali, restoring order there and halting the massacre of civilians. The UN mediated a fragile cease-fire, during which foreign nationals were escorted out of Rwanda. Belgium's UNAMIR contingent of more than 400 troops was also withdrawn, having encountered increasing hostility as a result of persistent rumours of Belgian complicity in the attack on President Habyarimana's aircraft, and accusations that Belgian troops were providing logistical support to the FPR.

Members of the Rwandan Government embarked on a diplomatic offensive throughout Europe and Africa, seeking to enhance the credibility of the administration through international recognition of its legal status. However, this initiative achieved only limited success, and the FPR's refusal to enter into dialogue with the 'illegal' administration proved a major obstacle to attempts, undertaken by the UN and the Presidents of Tanzania and of Zaire, to sponsor a new cease-fire agreement in late April and early May 1994.

As the violent campaign initiated by the presidential guard and the estimated 30,000 Interahamwe gathered national momentum, the militia's identification of all Tutsi as political opponents of the State provoked tribal polarization and an effective pogrom. Reports of mass Tutsi graves and of unprovoked attacks on fleeing Tutsi refugees and those sheltering in schools, hospitals and churches provoked unqualified international outrage, and promises were made of financial and logistical aid for an estimated 2m. displaced Rwandans. By late May 1994 attempts to assess the full scale of the humanitarian catastrophe in Rwanda were complicated by reports that the FPR (who claimed to control more than one-half of the territory) was perpetrating retaliatory atrocities against Hutu civilians.

In view of the deteriorating security situation, in late April 1994 the UN Security Council approved a resolution to reduce UNAMIR to just 270 personnel. This was condemned by the Rwandan authorities, and in mid-May, following intense international pressure and the disclosure of the vast scale of the humanitarian crisis in the region, the Security Council approved Resolution 917, providing for the eventual deployment of some 5,500 UN troops with a revised mandate, including the protection of refugees in designated 'safe areas'. In early June the UN Security Council extended the mandate of what was designated UNAMIR II until December. However, the UN Secretary-General continued to encounter considerable difficulty in securing equipment and armaments requested by those countries that had agreed to participate.

By mid-June 1994 the emergence of confirmed reports of retributive murders committed by FPR members and the collapse of an OAU-brokered truce prompted the French Government to announce its willingness to lead an armed police action, endorsed by the UN, in Rwanda. Despite French insistence that its force (expected to total 2,000 troops) would maintain strict political neutrality, and operate, from the border regions, in a purely humanitarian capacity pending the arrival of a multinational UN force, the FPR was vehemently opposed to its deployment, citing the French Government's maintenance of high-level contacts with representatives of the self-proclaimed Rwandan Government as an indication of political bias. The UN Secretary-General welcomed the French initiative; however, the OAU expressed serious reservations as to the appropriateness of the action. In late June a first contingent of 150 French marine commandos launched 'Operation Turquoise', entering the western town of Cyangugu, in preparation for a large-scale operation to protect refugees in the area. By mid-July the French had relieved several beleaguered Tutsi communities, and had established a temporary 'safe haven' for the displaced population in the south-west, through which a massive exodus of Hutu refugees began to flow, prompted by fears that the advancing FPR forces were seeking violent retribution against the Hutu. An estimated 1m. Rwandans sought refuge in the Zairean border town of Goma, while a similar number attempted to cross the border elsewhere in the south-west. The FPR, meanwhile, swiftly secured all major cities and strategic territorial positions, but halted its advance several kilometres from the boundaries of the French-controlled neutral zone, requesting the apprehension and return for trial of those responsible for the recent atrocities. (In early July the UN announced the creation of a commission of inquiry to investigate allegations of genocide, following an initial report that as many as 500,000 Rwandans had been killed since April.)

On 19 July 1994 Pasteur Bizimungu, a Hutu, was inaugurated as President for a five-year term. On the same day the FPR announced the composition of a new Government of National Unity, with the leader of the MDR moderate faction, Faustin Twagiramungu, as Prime Minister. The majority of cabinet posts were assigned to FPR members (including the FPR military chief, Maj.-Gen. Paul Kagame, who became Minister of Defence and also assumed the newly created post of Vice-President), while the remainder were divided among the MDR, the PSD, the Parti libéral (PL) and the Parti démocratique chrétien (PDC). The new administration urged all refugees to return to Rwanda, and issued assurances that civilian Hutus could return safely to their homes. The new Government declared its intention to honour the terms of the Arusha accord within the context of an extended period of transition. In August, however, Twagiramungu declared the country to be effectively bankrupt, claiming that members of the former Government, who had fled abroad, had appropriated all exchange reserves. The claims to legitimacy of the exiled former administration were seriously undermined by recognition by the European Union (EU, see p. 244) of the new Government of National Unity in September.

Amid persistent rumours that the Rwandan armed forces were attempting to regroup and rearm in Zaire, in preparation for a counter-offensive against the FPR, in late August 1994 the UN initiated the deployment of some 2,500 UNAMIR II forces in the security zone (redesignated 'zone four'). French troops began to withdraw from the area (the final contingent departed in late September), prompting hundreds of thousands of internally displaced Hutu refugees within the zone to move to Zairean border areas. An estimated 500,000 refugees remained at camps in the former security zone at the end of August. The UNAMIR II mandate was extended for a further six months. (In June 1995, at the request of the Rwandan Government, the six-month mandate of the force, which was reduced from 5,586 to 2,330 personnel, was again renewed.)

In November 1994 a number of amendments to the terms of the August 1993 Arusha accord were adopted under a multi-party protocol of understanding. The most notable of the new provisions was the exclusion from the legislative process of those parties implicated in alleged acts of genocide during 1994. A 70-member National Transitional Assembly was formally inaugurated in December, with a composition including five representatives of the armed forces and one member of the national police force. On 5 May 1995 this legislature adopted a new Constitution, which was based on selected articles of the 1991 Constitution, the terms of the Arusha accord, the FPR's victory declaration of July 1994 and the November multi-party protocol.

A political crisis emerged in August 1995, after the Prime Minister expressed dissatisfaction with the Government's lack of adherence to the provisions of the Arusha accord regarding power-sharing, and with the security forces' repeated recourse to violence in their management of the refugee crisis. Twagiramungu and four other disaffected ministers were subsequently replaced. Pierre Célestin Rwigyema of the MDR, also Hutu and the former Minister of Primary and Secondary Education, was named as the new Prime Minister at the end of the month. The new Council of Ministers included representatives of both major ethnic groups and four political parties.

In late 1994 Hutu refugees within Rwanda and in neighbouring countries were continuing to resist the exhortations of the UN and the new Rwandan administration to return to their homes, despite the deteriorating security situation in many camps (which had, moreover, forced the withdrawal of a number of relief agencies). Hutu militias were reported to have assumed control of several camps, notably Katale in Zaire and Benaco in Tanzania. Reports also emerged that Hutu civilians intending to return to their homes had been subjected to violent intimidation by the Interahamwe. It was further alleged that male Hutu refugees were being forced to undergo military training in preparation for a renewed conflict. The reluctance of many refugees to return to their homes was also attributed to persistent allegations that the Tutsi-dominated FPR armed forces (the Armée patriotique rwandaise—APR) were conducting a systematic campaign of reprisal attacks against returning Hutus.

International scepticism regarding the Government's programme of refugee resettlement increased in early 1995, following a series of uncompromising initiatives to encourage the return of internally displaced Rwandans (including the interruption of food supplies to refugee camps), culminating in the forcible closure of the camps through military intervention. An attempt in April to dismantle the Kibeho camp in southern Rwanda provoked widespread international condemnation, after APR troops opened fire on refugees; independent sources estimated as many as 5,000 fatalities.

In August 1995, in response to requests made by the Rwandan Government, the UN Security Council voted to suspend the arms embargo to Rwanda (imposed in May 1994) for one year, in order to allow the Government to safeguard against the threat of a military offensive by Hutu extremists encamped in neighbouring countries. Meanwhile, the security situation in refugee camps along the Zairean border had deteriorated to such an extent that the Zairean Government initiated a programme of forcible repatriation, attracting widespread international concern. Despite a formal agreement between the office of the UN High Commissioner for Refugees (UNHCR) and the Zairean Government for a more regulated approach to the refugee crisis, APR attacks near the border with Zaire further deterred refugees. At a conference of the Great Lakes countries, convened in Cairo, Egypt, in late November President Mobutu of Zaire indicated that the forcible return of remaining refugees in early 1996 was no longer a realistic objective. The conference also accepted the Rwandan President's assertion that the participation of UNAMIR forces in peace-keeping operations in Rwanda was no longer necessary, but urged the Rwandan Government to accept the extension of a revised, three-month mandate for the forces to provide assistance in the refugee repatriation process. (A three-month mandate for a 1,200-strong force was thus renewed in December 1995, and the mission was formally terminated in April 1996.)

In February 1995 the UN Security Council adopted Resolution 977, whereby Arusha was designated the seat for the International Criminal Tribunal for Rwanda (ICTR), which was to investigate allegations made against some 400 individuals of direct involvement in the planning and execution of crimes against humanity perpetrated in Rwanda during 1994. The six-member Tribunal, to be headed by a Senegalese lawyer, Laïty Kama, was inaugurated in June for a four-year term. In October 1995 a Supreme Court was established by the Transitional National Assembly.

The ICTR began formal proceedings in November 1995. The first court session of the ICTR was convened in September 1996, but hearings concerning the first two (of 21) individuals indicted on charges of crimes against humanity were almost immediately postponed. Tribunal officials attributed the virtual collapse of proceedings to the escalating conflict in eastern Zaire, but widespread concern was expressed at the high number of administrative errors committed. In contrast, in January 1997 regional courts within Rwanda passed death sentences on five individuals accused of acts of genocide. (Whereas capital punishment would not be invoked by the ICTR, legislation published by the Rwandan authorities in September 1996 regarding penalties for crimes committed during 1994 made provision for the application of the death penalty.) In July 1997 former Prime Minister Jean Kambanda, two senior armed forces officers and a former government minister were arrested in Kenya and transferred for trial to Arusha. Later in July a Belgian journalist, who had worked for the extremist Radio Télévision Libre des Mille Collines at the time of the massacres, was arrested by the Kenyan authorities and similarly transferred for trial (becoming the first foreign national to be indicted by the ICTR).

Some 300 genocide suspects were tried by Rwandan courts during 1997, and an estimated 125,000 defendants were in detention awaiting trial; arrests reportedly continued at a rate of 1,000 per month. In late 1997, in an attempt to address the problem of severe overcrowding in prisons, the release was authorized of elderly, infirm or juvenile detainees. (This policy was denounced by organizations representing survivors of the 1994 massacres, and there were reports of attacks on freed genocide suspects.) The announcement that 23 people convicted of acts of genocide were to be publicly executed provoked international condemnation. Amnesty International and other human rights organizations expressed serious concerns that those convicted had been denied adequate opportunity to prepare a defence. The Rwandan authorities refuted such claims, and dismissed pleas for clemency. The public executions proceeded in April 1998.

Meanwhile, in August 1996, during a visit to Kigali by the Zairean Prime Minister, a bilateral agreement for the organized and unconditional repatriation of all Rwandan refugees in Zaire was concluded (without the participation of UNHCR officials).

During September, however, relations between the two countries were placed under renewed strain, when the attempts of the Interahamwe and the Zairean armed forces to displace large numbers of Zairean Banyamulenge (ethnic Tutsis) from eastern Zaire encountered large-scale armed resistance from the Banyamulenge, resulting in Zairean accusations of Rwandan support for the Banyamulenge, and culminating in a cross-border exchange of fire later that month. Throughout October, as the rebels made significant gains in the region, the Rwandan Government continued to deny Zairean allegations of its involvement in the Banyamulenge insurrection, and at the end of the month admitted that Rwandan troops had been deployed in eastern Zaire in response to an artillery attack on the Rwandan town of Cyangugu, allegedly made by the Zairean armed forces.

There was renewed international concern for the estimated 1m. refugees previously encamped in eastern Zaire, following reports that the regional conflict had resulted in the sudden exodus of some 250,000 refugees, and the interruption of food aid distribution. The rebel army in Zaire (known as the Alliance des forces démocratiques pour la libération du Congo-Zaïre—AFDL) declared a cease-fire for returning refugees, and later in the month announced the creation of a humanitarian corridor to the Rwandan border, with the intention that the estimated 700,000 Rwandan refugees now seeking shelter at the Mugunga camp, west of Goma, would return to Rwanda. The large-scale return of refugees was finally prompted by an AFDL attack on Interahamwe units operating from the camp. In April 1997 the AFDL leader, Laurent-Désiré Kabila, demanded that the UN complete full repatriation of the refugees within 60 days, after which time their return would be undertaken unilaterally by the rebels. The new Rwandan authorities, meanwhile, expressed concern that the UN was delaying the rapid repatriation of refugees from eastern Zaire. (By the end of May the AFDL had gained control of most of Zaire, which was renamed the Democratic Republic of Congo—DRC, and Kabila assumed power as Head of State.) Continuing ethnic unrest and violence, particularly in north-west Rwanda, throughout 1997 were exacerbated by the return from the DRC of large numbers of Hutus (see also the chapter on the DRC). Both the office of the UN High Commissioner for Human Rights and Amnesty International published reports in August, alleging that as many as 3,000 civilians had been killed by government troops in counter-insurgency operations since May. The Government denied having perpetrated massacres of civilians, and claimed that those killed had been Interahamwe militia. An extensive demobilization programme was undertaken from September, with the aim of reintegrating former combatants into civil society; some 57,500 personnel were to be demobilized over a three-year period.

The trial of genocide suspects continued in 1998, both in Rwanda and at the ICTR, and in early September the ICTR reached its first verdict. A former mayor of Taba, Jean-Paul Akayesu, was convicted and sentenced to life imprisonment; Kambanda, who had pleaded guilty to six charges of genocide and crimes against humanity, was also given a life sentence. Rwandan courts convicted and sentenced some 1,000 genocide suspects during 1998 (the authorities had aimed to hear 5,000 cases during the year). By June about 5,000 suspects in Rwandan prisons had pleaded guilty to acts of genocide in order to lessen their sentences, apparently in response to the public executions in April. In June Maj. Augustine Cyiza, the Vice-President of the Supreme Court and President of the Court of Cassation, resigned (he had been suspended for misconduct in March), and in October some controversy was caused by the decision to release at least 10,000 genocide suspects owing to lack of evidence against them. It was announced in November that 34,000 suspects had been freed since 1994.

In October 1998 the Transitional National Assembly approved the establishment of a fund to assist survivors of the genocide, and in the following month the Council of Ministers approved the establishment of two commissions, for human rights and for unity and reconciliation (both had been established by mid-1999). Between February and May 1999 some 16 deputies resigned, or were expelled, from the Transitional National Assembly for misconduct, incompetence or allegations of involvement in the genocide. In June the period of political transition, originally set at five years in 1994, was extended by a further four years, following agreement between the major political parties.

Voting in local elections (the first elections to be held since 1988) were conducted on a non-party basis on 29–31 March 1999. Voter participation was estimated to have been 95%, and at the end of the month the EU special envoy to the Great Lakes region commended the manner in which the elections were conducted. In June the Transitional National Assembly approved draft legislation establishing a commission that was to prepare a new constitution. Legislation establishing a national police force (which was to unify the existing national gendarmerie, and the communal and judicial police) was adopted in August.

During 1999 a number of prominent Hutu, including three former government ministers, were arrested on suspicion of involvement in the 1994 genocide and extradited to the ICTR. In May a former Rwandan mayor (the first Rwandan to be tried abroad for genocide) was convicted by a Swiss court on charges of inciting the killing of Tutsi civilians, and sentenced to life imprisonment. In June Navanethem Pillay succeeded Kama as President of the ICTR, and in September Carla del Ponte became UN Chief Prosecutor. In February 2000 legislation introducing a traditional system of justice, known as *gacaca* (on the grass), was adopted; certain categories of genocide crimes were to be tried under this system (by council in local communities), while the most serious genocide crimes would continue to be tried under the existing judicial system. It was hoped that the creation of the *gacaca* courts would alleviate the large number of cases awaiting trial and aid the process of national reconciliation.

In February 2000 the National Assembly voted in favour of investigating alleged abuses of power by Rwigyema. On 28 February he resigned from the office of Prime Minister, citing differences with the legislature. Bernard Makuza, hitherto the Rwandan ambassador in Germany, was appointed Prime Minister in March, and subsequently announced a government reorganization, in which six ministers were replaced. The new Government was the first since 1994 in which the parties were not represented in accordance with the 1993 Arusha peace accords. At its inauguration, Kagame (who remained Vice-President and Minister of Defence and National Security) failed to swear allegiance to the President. On 23 March Bizimungu resigned from office, owing to disagreement over the composition of the new Government, and Kagame was subsequently appointed interim President by the Supreme Court. On 17 April he was formally elected President of Rwanda by members of the Transitional National Assembly and the Government, securing 81 of 86 votes cast. He was inaugurated on 22 April (becoming the first Tutsi Head of State since 1959).

In July 2000 Rwigyema was removed from the leadership of the MDR by the party's political bureau, which accused him of acting contrary to its interests; he subsequently left the country. In December 2000 del Ponte announced that the ICTR was to commence investigations into members of the FPR for involvement in massacres of Hutu (having previously only instigated proceedings against Hutu supporters who had participated in the 1994 genocide of Tutsi).

In April 2001 an international warrant was issued for the arrest of Rwigyema, who had taken refuge in the USA, on suspicion of participating in the genocide of 1994. The trial of four Hutus (including two nuns), on charges of complicity in massacres in the southern Butare prefecture, commenced in Belgium later that month (under Belgian legislation permitting foreign nationals to be arraigned there for war crimes). In early June all four were sentenced to terms of imprisonment. Also in early June a former mayor became the first defendant to be acquitted by the ICTR (which at this time had convicted eight people on charges of involvement in the genocide). In July four Hutus, including a close associate of former President Habyarimana, Protais Zigiranyirazo, were arrested in western Europe and subsequently transferred to the ICTR (increasing the number of suspects held in detention there to more than 50). In the same month a Tribunal of First Instance officially banned the MRNDD and CDR for inciting violence in 1994.

On 4 October 2001 some 250,000 judges for the *gacaca* courts were elected in a national ballot. With the number of prisoners awaiting trial having increased to some 115,000, those suspected of lesser crimes relating to the genocide were henceforth to be tried by the *gacaca* system. In December a new national flag, emblem and anthem officially replaced those adopted at independence in 1962. In April 2002 the trial of Col Theoneste Bagosora, who was considered to be the principal organizer of the genocide, commenced at the ICTR. Bagosora, who had been in custody since his arrest in Cameroon in 1996, had allegedly planned the massacre of Tutsi civilians by the militia and had personally ordered the assassination of prominent politicians. He, and a further three former senior army officers on trial, refused to attend the initial session of the ICTR, on the grounds that their right to defence had been violated. Later in April security forces arrested former President Bizimungu (who had attempted to form an opposition political party in May 2001), and searched his residence. The authorities subsequently announced that Bizimungu had continued to engage in illegal political activity, and would be charged with endangering state security.

In early August 2002 Gen. Augustin Bizimungu, the army Chief of Staff in 1994, who had been indicted by the ICTR jointly with four other former military commanders, was arrested in Angola and transferred to the Tribunal. Later that month he pleaded not guilty to 10 charges, including that of genocide. In November trials by the *gacaca* court system officially commenced in large parts of the country. In the same month several principal ministers, including those responsible for the portfolios of foreign affairs and defence, were replaced in a government reorganization.

In January 2003, in an effort to reduce numbers in prisons, Kagame issued a decree providing for the provisional release of some 40,000 of those held in detention, including many who had pleaded guilty to charges related to the 1994 genocide. Although the Ministry of Justice maintained that legal proceedings against the released prisoners would continue, organizations representing survivors of the genocide criticized the measure. Most of the prisoners due for release were to be dispatched to 'solidarity camps', where they were to be prepared for reintegration into society. (By the end of 2003 some 25,000 suspects had been released.)

On 23 April 2003 the Transitional National Assembly adopted a new Constitution, which was to be submitted for approval at a national referendum. The draft Constitution provided for the establishment of a bicameral legislature (comprising an 80-member Chamber of Deputies and a 26-member Senate) and a President, who was to be elected by universal suffrage. At the national referendum, which took place on 26 May, the draft Constitution was endorsed by 93.4% of the electorate. The new Constitution entered into effect on 4 June; under its provisions, political associations formed on the basis of ethnicity, tribal or regional affiliation, religion or any other grounds for discrimination were prohibited. (Some existing political organizations were restructured to end such affiliations.) The presidential election was subsequently scheduled for 25 August, and was to be followed by legislative elections in late September. Kagame announced his intention to seek re-election, while former Prime Minister Twagiramungu returned to Rwanda from exile in Belgium in order to contest the presidency. (Twagiramungu of the MDR and Jean-Népomuscène Nayinzira, a former minister and President of the PDC, were both obliged to participate as independent candidates, owing to the dissolution of their political parties under the terms of the new Constitution.)

The first presidential election to take place in Rwanda since the single candidate poll of 1988 was conducted on 25 August 2003 (thereby marking the end of the nine-year transitional period). Kagame was returned to power, with 95.1% of votes cast, while Twagiramungu won 3.6%, and Nayinzira 1.3% of the votes. However, Twagiramungu accused the authorities of electoral malpractice, and submitted a challenge against the official results at the Supreme Court. EU monitors confirmed that irregularities had been noted, although a South African observer mission declared that the poll had been 'free and fair'. In early September the Supreme Court rejected Twagiramungu's appeal, and he announced that he would not pursue the claim further. Kagame was officially inaugurated on 12 September. Four political parties subsequently agreed to contest the forthcoming legislative elections in alliance with the FPR. Following the dissolution of the MDR, many of its former members joined the newly emerged Parti du progrès et de la concorde. In addition to the FPR-led coalition, the PSD, the PL and a number of independent candidates registered to contest the legislative elections. Elections to the Chamber of Deputies commenced on 29 September, with voting for seats allocated to one disabled and two youth representatives. The poll for the 53 seats contested by political parties and independent candidates followed on 30 September; the FPR-led coalition, with 73.8% of votes cast, secured 40 seats, while the PSD (12.3% of votes) won seven seats, and the PL (10.6%) six seats. The remaining 24 female representatives were selected at provincial level on 2 October. Kagame formed a new Council of Ministers on 19 October; Makuza was reappointed to the office of Prime Minister and most principal ministers retained their portfolios. Twagiramungu left the country in early November, after claiming that he faced detention owing to his opposition to Kagame's Government.

In August 2003, following a two-day mass trial, a *gacaca* court in the prefecture of Butare convicted 105 people of participation in the 1994 genocide, of whom 11 were sentenced to death. In early September a Gambian judge, Hassan Bubacar Jallow, was appointed Chief Prosecutor of the ICTR, replacing del Ponte. In early December the owners of Radio Télévision Libre des Mille Collines and the Hutu extremist newspaper *Kangura* were sentenced to life imprisonment at the ICTR, on charges relating to public incitement to commit genocide. By February 2004 the ICTR had convicted 18 and acquitted three defendants and in that month the Rwandan authorities urged those prisoners awaiting trial in connection with the genocide to qualify for a general amnesty by confessing to the charges against them. Meanwhile, at the ongoing trial of Bagosora at the ICTR, the testimony of a principal witness, a former Canadian UN commander, Gen. (retd) Romeo Dallaire, implicated French forces in failing to prevent the genocide.

In June 2004 former President Bizimungu (who had remained in detention since April 2002) was sentenced to a term of 15 years' imprisonment, after being convicted of corruption, inciting civil disobedience and criminal association; he was, however, acquitted of the principal charge of endangering state security through anti-Government activities. In July the Minister of Finance of the 1994 Government, Emmanuel Ndindabahizi, who had been arrested in Belgium in July 2001, received a sentence of life imprisonment at the ICTR on charges of genocide and two counts of crimes against humanity for his participation in the massacre of Tutsi refugees during that period. Proceedings for some of the large number of cases to be transferred from the ICTR to the *gacaca* courts commenced in early 2005. In February the Minister of Family and Women's Affairs of the 1994 Government became the first woman to be charged with genocide in connection with organized killings in the Butare prefecture. At the end of March the serving Minister of Defence, Gen. Marcel Gatsinzi, appeared before a *gacaca* court, where he pleaded not guilty to charges of failing to prevent troops under his command from perpetrating massacres in Butare.

In September 2005 a Belgian priest and former missionary was arrested on suspicion of having incited genocidal acts in 1994 (by republishing material from *Kangura*) and was initially arraigned before a *gacaca* court; following a request by the Belgian Government, his trial was transferred to Belgium in November. In early October the trial began of Zigiranyirazo (who had been extradited to the ICTR in October 2001); he pleaded not guilty to all charges relating to the genocide. (By late 2005 it was reported that some 4,162 cases, including those of several former officials, had been tried by the *gacaca* system.) In July 2006 phase two of the *gacaca* system began. While those charged with crimes related to the genocide were in prison in Rwanda, many of those suspected of issuing the orders had fled and were living in exile. However, an announcement was made in October 2006 that France, Belgium and the Netherlands had agreed to seek those who had taken up residence in those countries and bring them to trial. Frustrated at the slow progress being made by the ICTR—since 1997 only 29 of those responsible for the genocide had been convicted—the Rwandan Government wanted suspects transferred to face trial in Rwanda. Since the country maintained the death penalty suspects could not be extradited, but in July 2007 legislation to abolish this was officially promulgated; it was reported that those who had been sentenced to death would instead be subjected to terms of life imprisonment. Proceedings began in August to seek extradition orders.

Meanwhile, in October 2005 both legislative chambers approved a number of constitutional amendments, which principally provided for the reorganization of local government structures (reducing the number of provinces, formerly prefectures, from 12 to five) to allow greater decentralization; the territorial reforms entered into effect at the beginning of 2006. In February the Supreme Court upheld the 15-year sentence imposed on Bizimungu (who had submitted an appeal against the charges in October 2005). Also in February 2006 the Rwandan Government denied a request by Jallow for the transfer of the trial of a suspected Interahamwe military leader to Norway. In March a new Minister of Finance was appointed in a government reorganization, which was designed to assist efforts to reconstruct the economy; a new portfolio of science, information technology and research was also created. In April 2007 Bizimungu received a presidential pardon and was released from prison.

In 2003 the UN Security Council had mandated the ICTR to complete the first instance trials of genocide suspects by December 2008, and all appeals proceedings were to be completed by 2010. However, by early 2008 only 35 suspects had been tried and some 27 other cases were ongoing, while six suspects had yet to face trial. There were concerns that the trials would not be completed before the expiry of the ICTR's mandate and that too few of the suspected key perpetrators of the genocide had been prosecuted. In February 2008 draft legislation was being considered to grant *gacaca* courts the jurisdiction to try up to 90% of those suspects who would otherwise be required to be brought before the ICTR.

At the end of July 1998 Laurent-Désiré Kabila (the President of the DRC since 31 May 1997) announced that military co-operation with both Rwanda and Uganda was to end, and demanded that all foreign forces leave the DRC. Relations between Rwanda and the DRC subsequently deteriorated. Kabila claimed that a rebellion, which commenced in the east of the DRC in August, constituted a Rwandan invasion; the Rwandan Government denied any involvement, but in late 1998 conceded that Rwandan troops were present in the DRC to provide logistical support to the rebel-led action. The Rwandan Government participated in a series of regional peace negotiations, at which Kabila refused to negotiate directly with the rebels. Rwanda later denied reports that it was maintaining a joint military command with Uganda in the DRC (see also the chapter on the DRC).

Rwandan action in the DRC continued in 1999, although Rwanda's alliance with Uganda became increasingly unstable during that year. At the end of April Uganda temporarily recalled its ambassador to Rwanda, following an incident in the DRC, in which Rwandan troops killed a number of members of the Ugandan armed forces. A split within the rebel movement in the DRC, the Rassemblement congolais pour la démocratie (RCD), resulted in the creation of two factions, one supported by Rwanda and one by Uganda. Following further clashes in the DRC between Rwandan and Ugandan troops in Kisangani in August, both armies agreed to leave the city. In June the DRC instituted proceedings against Burundi, Rwanda and Uganda at the International Court of Justice (ICJ) in The Hague, Netherlands, accusing these countries of acts of armed aggression. (In early February 2001, however, the DRC abandoned proceedings against Burundi and Rwanda.)

In May 2000 Rwandan and Ugandan forces again clashed in the town of Kisangani (despite a cease-fire agreement, which had been reached by all forces involved in the conflict in April). After meeting a UN Security Council delegation, the Rwandan and Ugandan contingents agreed to the demilitarization of the town, and its transfer to the control of the UN Mission in the Democratic Republic of the Congo (MONUC, see p. 85) deployed in the country. Despite further fighting, it was confirmed at the end of June that all Rwandan and Ugandan forces had withdrawn from Kisangani. In December, however, the principal RCD faction, supported by Rwandan troops, succeeded in gaining control of the south-eastern town of Pweto. The Rwandan Government denied any involvement in the assassination of Kabila in January 2001 (see the chapter on the DRC). In February Kagame met the new DRC President, Joseph Kabila (the son of Laurent-Désiré), in Washington, DC, USA, to discuss the ongoing conflict. Later that month the groups involved in the conflict, under the aegis of the UN Security Council, agreed to a disengagement of their forces by mid-March, followed by a complete withdrawal of foreign troops from the DRC by mid-May. Although some military disengagement of forces took place accordingly in March, factions subsequently refused to continue until MONUC guaranteed security in the region. In April the Governments of Burundi, Rwanda and Uganda rejected the claims of a UN report that the forces of these countries had exploited the natural resources of the DRC. In June it was reported that Interahamwe militia, led by former members of the Rwandan army, had intensified incursions into north-western Rwanda from the DRC. Despite continued pressure from the UN Security Council, in August Kagame insisted that Kabila fulfil pledges to demobilize the Interahamwe (who were supporting DRC government forces), as a precondition to the withdrawal of Rwandan forces from the DRC.

At the end of July 2002, after further discussions mediated by the South African Government, a peace agreement was signed by Kabila and Kagame in Pretoria. Under the accord, Kabila pledged to arrest and disarm the Interahamwe militia in the DRC, while the Rwandan Government agreed to withdraw all troops from the country. In October it was announced that all 23,400 Rwandan troops had been withdrawn from the DRC. The Rwandan authorities denied reports that they planned to redeploy forces in the DRC, in response to the continued Ugandan involvement in hostilities there. In September 2003 the Governments of Rwanda and the DRC agreed to re-establish diplomatic links, and the improvement in relations between the two countries was further demonstrated by the visit to Rwanda of the DRC Minister of Foreign Affairs in October. In July 2004, however, a report by a UN commission contained accusations, which were denied by the Rwandan Government, of Rwandan support for an insurrection by dissident members of the armed forces in eastern DRC (see chapter on the DRC). Following a massacre of Banyamulenge refugees from the DRC at a border camp in Burundi in August, the Governments of Rwanda and Burundi claimed that the Interahamwe militia operating within the DRC were implicated and threatened to resume military engagement in the country. Repeated reports (confirmed by MONUC) that Rwandan troops had re-entered DRC territory ensued.

In November 2001 Kagame and the Ugandan Head of State, Lt-Gen. Yoweri Kaguta Museveni, met in London, United Kingdom, in an effort to resolve the increasing tension between the two nations, following the repeated clashes in the DRC. The Ugandan Government had accused Rwanda of supporting dissidents who intended to overthrow Museveni's administration, while Kagame claimed that Ugandan troops were amassing on the joint border between the two countries. In February 2002 further discussions between Kagame and Museveni, with mediation by the British Secretary of State for International Development, were conducted in Uganda. It was agreed that both Governments would urge the dissidents based in their respective countries to take refuge elsewhere, and the adoption of a mutual extradition treaty was envisaged. In July 2003 the Rwandan Government signed a tripartite agreement with the Ugandan authorities and UNHCR, providing for the voluntary repatriation of some 26,000 Rwandans resident in refugee camps in western Uganda. (Similar accords were signed between Rwanda and the Governments of Malawi, Togo, Zambia and Tanzania.) In February 2004 an improvement in diplomatic relations between Rwanda and Uganda (following progress in the situation in the DRC) was demonstrated by a bilateral agreement to strengthen co-operation in several fields.

Since 1994 the role of the international community in failing to avert the genocide has come under frequent scrutiny. In late 1997 the report of a Belgian Senate investigation concluded that the international community, and more specifically the UN and the Belgian authorities, was directly or indirectly responsible for certain aspects of the developments arising from the political violence from April 1994. Testifying before the ICTR in February 1998, the former UNAMIR commander stated that he had warned the UN in early 1994 of the impending ethnic catastrophe in Rwanda, but that the international community had lacked the will to intervene adequately. Suggestions that Kofi Annan, the head of UN peace-keeping operations at the time of the conflict, had failed to respond to such warnings prompted tensions between the UN Secretary-General (as Annan had subsequently become) and the Rwandan authorities in May 1998, as government officials refused to receive the Secretary-General in the course of a visit to Rwanda. Meanwhile, in February the OAU announced the establishment of a committee to investigate the genocide; the committee held its first meeting in October. In December a French parliamentary committee, established in March, presented its report on French involvement in events prior to and at the time of the genocide. (Despite evidence to the contrary, the French authorities have persistently denied allegations that France continued to supply military equipment and support to Rwanda after the imposition of the UN arms embargo in May 1994.) The report cleared France of any direct complicity in the genocide, although it conceded that 'Operation Turquoise' both delayed the accession to power of the FPR, and facilitated the escape of Hutu extremist forces into the DRC. The report attributed responsibility for the genocide to the international community as a whole, particularly to the USA (which had failed to support UN peace-keeping operations in Rwanda).

In March 1999 the UN Security Council approved a proposal for the establishment of a commission of inquiry into the actions of the UN prior to and during the genocide. The three-member commission of inquiry presented its report in December after a six-month investigation. The report criticized the UN for failing in its mission to prevent the genocide and for ignoring the warnings of the head of the peace-keeping mission. It also cited the UN Security Council's failure to deploy a sufficient peace-keeping force at the end of 1993. Following the report, Kofi Annan issued a personal apology for UN inaction at the time. In January 2000 it was announced that two Rwandan genocide survivors were to sue the UN for its 'complicity' in the genocide. In March a Canadian newspaper published a UN memorandum, stating that the FPR was responsible for the attack on the aircraft on 6 April 1994, which killed President Juvénal Habyarimana, and that Kagame had been in overall command of the force that carried out the attack. Kagame subsequently dismissed the allegations, claiming that the report was part of a UN attempt to absolve itself of blame for the genocide of 1994.

In August 2001 the French Minister of Foreign Affairs made an official visit to Rwanda (the first by a senior French official since 1994), in an effort to normalize bilateral relations. (Diplomatic links were restored in 2002.) In March 2002 the French Government (which, within the UN Security Council, had placed increasing pressure on Rwanda to withdraw forces from the DRC) protested that Rwandan troops had launched a major offensive in the east of that country. In March 2004 the results of an official French investigation into the destruction of President Habyarimana's aircraft alleged that Kagame, as leader of the FPR, had ordered the missile attack. Kagame again denied any responsibility, and claimed that French forces had, by training and arming the Hutu militia, supported the mass killings. In early April the French Secretary of State for Foreign Affairs curtailed his visit to Rwanda, after Kagame repeated these accusations at an official ceremony in Kigali commemorating the 10th anniversary of the genocide. On the following anniversary in April 2005 the Rwandan Government reiterated demands that the UN instigate legal proceedings against French officials for complicity in the genocide. In December a French military tribunal began to investigate claims by survivors of the genocide that French forces had facilitated attacks against Tutsi in 1994 (by failing to prevent massacres and then by allowing the perpetrators of the genocide to evade capture). In November 2006 Rwanda severed diplomatic relations with France, recalling the ambassador to that country and closing the French embassy. The move followed the order by the French judiciary to issue international arrest warrants against President Kagame and nine high-ranking Rwandan officials. In September 2007, for the first time since the severance of diplomatic ties, a delegation of French officials visited Kigali with the aim of making progress towards the restoration of normal relations. Despite the abolition of the death penalty in Rwanda in July 2007, the French Government had refused to extradite genocide suspects; however, in November a French court approved the extradition of one of the suspects currently resident in France. In January 2008 French Minister of Foreign and European Affairs Bernard Kouchner met briefly with President Kagame to resume dialogue with Rwanda, and in a press conference Kouchner admitted that France had made a political mistake in its response to the 1994 genocide; nevertheless, he denied any military responsibility.

Government

Under the terms of the Constitution, which entered into force on 4 June 2003, legislative power is vested in a bicameral Parliament, comprising a Chamber of Deputies and a Senate. The Chamber of Deputies has 80 deputies, who are elected for a five-year term. In addition to 53 directly elected deputies, 27 seats are allocated, respectively, to two youth representatives, one disabilities representative, and 24 female representatives, who are indirectly elected. The Senate comprises 26 members, of whom 12 are elected by local government councils in the 12 provinces, and two by academic institutions, while the remaining 12 are nominated (eight by the President and four by a regulatory body, the Parties' Forum). Members of the Senate serve for eight years. Executive power is exercised by the President (Head of State), assisted by an appointed Council of Ministers. The President is elected by universal suffrage for a seven-year term, and is restricted to two mandates.

Following territorial reforms, which entered into effect at the beginning of 2006, the country is divided into five provinces and subdivided into 30 districts, each administered by an elected mayor. Local government elections took place on a non-party basis in April 2001.

Defence

As assessed at November 2007, the total strength of the armed forces was estimated at 33,000: army 32,000, air force 1,000. In addition, there were local defence forces of about 2,000. Defence expenditure for 2007 was budgeted at 33,900m. Rwanda francs.

Economic Affairs

In 2006, according to estimates by the World Bank, Rwanda's gross national income (GNI), measured at average 2004–06 prices, was US $2,341m., equivalent to $250 per head (or $1,270 per head on an international purchasing-power parity basis). During 1996–2006, it was estimated, the population increased at an average annual rate of 5.0%, while gross domestic product (GDP) per head rose, in real terms, by an average of 1.7% per year. Overall GDP increased, in real terms, at an average annual rate of 6.8% in 1996–2006; growth in 2006 was 5.3%.

Agriculture (including forestry and fishing) contributed 41.0% of GDP in 2006. According to FAO estimates, 89.8% of the employed labour force were engaged in the sector (mainly at subsistence level) at mid-2005. The principal food crops are plantains, sweet potatoes, cassava, dry beans and sorghum. The principal cash crops are coffee (which provided 27.6% of total export earnings in 2003), tea (23.6%), pyrethrum and quinquina. Goats and cattle are traditionally the principal livestock raised. According to the World Bank, agricultural GDP increased by an average of 5.6% per year during 1996–2006, although it remained constant in 2006.

Industry (including mining, manufacturing, power and construction) accounted for 21.2% of GDP in 2006, while industrial activities engaged 2.8% of the employed labour force in 2002. According to the World Bank, industrial GDP increased at an average annual rate of 7.8% during 1996–2006. GDP in the industrial sector increased by 12.5% in 2006.

Mining and quarrying, it was estimated, contributed 0.6% of GDP in 2003. Cassiterite (a tin-bearing ore) is Rwanda's principal mineral resource. There are also reserves of wolframite (a tungsten-bearing ore), columbo-tantalite, gold and beryl, and work has begun on the exploitation of natural gas reserves beneath Lake Kivu, which are believed to be among the largest in the world. Mining GDP declined at an estimated average annual rate of 0.4% in 1990–2002, according to the Banque Nationale du Rwanda. Mining GDP increased by 16.6% in 2001, but declined by an estimated 5.7% in 2002.

Manufacturing accounted for 8.5% of GDP in 2006, while production activities engaged 1.3% of the employed labour force in 2002. The principal branches of manufacturing are beverages and tobacco, food products and basic consumer goods, including soap, textiles and plastic products. According to the World Bank, manufacturing GDP increased by an average of 4.1% per year during 1996–2006; GDP in the sector increased by 13.5% in 2006.

Electrical energy is derived almost entirely from hydroelectric power. In 1999 Rwanda imported 35.5% of its electricity, but subsequently benefited from the completion of the Ruzizi-II plant (a joint venture with Burundi and the Democratic Republic of the Congo—DRC). Imports of fuels and lubricants comprised 15.5% of the total value of merchandise imports in 2003.

The services sector contributed 37.8% of GDP in 2006, and engaged 8.6% of the employed labour force in 2002. According to the World Bank, the GDP of the services sector increased at an average annual rate of 7.7% during 1996–2006; growth in the services sector was 8.1% in 2006.

In 2006 Rwanda recorded a visible trade deficit of US $343.0m., and there was a deficit of $180m. on the current account of the balance of payments. In 2003 the principal source of imports (28.4%) was Kenya; other major suppliers were Belgium, Uganda, the United Arab Emirates and Tanzania. In the same year the principal market for exports was also Kenya (40.9%); other significant purchasers were Uganda, Tanzania and the United Kingdom. The principal exports in 2004 were coffee, tea, crude materials, and metalliferous ores (particularly ores and concentrates of tin, molybdenum, niobium and titanium). The main imports in that year were machinery and transport equipment, manufactured goods, mineral fuels (particularly petroleum products) and chemicals.

An overall budgetary deficit of 6,500m. Rwanda francs (equivalent to 0.4% of GDP) was recorded in 2006. At the end of 2005 Rwanda's external debt totalled US $1,518m., of which $1,420m. was long-term public debt. The cost of debt-servicing in that year was equivalent to 8.1% of the value of exports of goods and services. In 1996–2006 the average annual rate of inflation was 5.9%. Consumer prices increased by 8.8% in 2006.

Rwanda is a member of the Organization for the Management and Development of the Kagera River Basin (see p. 414) and, with Burundi and the DRC, is a founding member of the Economic Community of the Great Lakes Countries (see p. 412) and of the Common Market for Eastern and Southern

RWANDA

Statistical Survey

Africa (see p. 205). The country is also a member of the International Coffee Organization (see p. 408). In December 2006 Rwanda, together with Burundi, was admitted to the East African Community (EAC, see p. 412)

Rwanda has traditionally relied heavily on foreign aid, owing to an economic development impeded by ethnic and political unrest. The genocide of early 1994 (see Recent History) resulted in the destruction of the country's economic base and of prospects of attracting private and external investment. With assistance from the international financial community, the new Government, which was established in July, initiated measures to resettle more than 2m. displaced civilians and to reconstruct the economy. In 1998 a three-year Enhanced Structural Adjustment Facility was approved by the IMF, and by the end of 1999 Rwanda had made considerable progress in rehabilitating and stabilizing the economy. In late 2000, following a meeting with international financial donor institutions, Rwanda qualified for debt relief under the initiative of the IMF and World Bank for heavily indebted poor countries (HIPCs), and in August 2002 the IMF approved a further three-year credit arrangement under the Poverty Reduction and Growth Facility (PRGF). In 2005 Rwanda reached the completion point of the enhanced HIPC initiative, enabling the Government to save some US $48m. each year in debt-servicing for the subsequent 10 years, and in June 2006 the IMF approved a further three-year PRGF. Following the divestment of one of the country's largest telecommunications companies in mid-2005, the Government entered into partnership in 2006 with the Scottish firm Dane Associates, and announced plans to extract methane resources from Lake Kivu, which would be converted into electricity at a newly constructed plant. Meanwhile, it was hoped that the provision of low-interest loans to small and medium-sized enterprises via the 'Tradeline' scheme would hasten the delivery of goods and services and encourage further growth in the private sector. The World Bank approved a grant for $70m. in February 2008, aimed at assisting the Government with implementing key policies outlined under the PRGF. The Central Bank of Rwanda launched its own securities exchange in early 2008, based in the nation's capital, Kigali. Dealing initially with corporate and treasury bonds, it was hoped that the exchange would develop sufficiently to include shares and other products, potentially strengthening prospects of long term economic growth. GDP growth in Rwanda reached 6.0% in 2007 and was underpinned by expansion in the construction and services sectors, although the IMF noted a cyclical decline in agriculture. Growth was anticipated to remain at 6.0% in 2008, on the assumption that the Government could maintain macroeconomic stability concomitant with low inflation. Meanwhile, government revenue was expected to grow with mineral exports increasing by an estimated 57% in 2007, and the tourism sector continuing to expand.

Education

Primary education, beginning at seven years of age and lasting for six years, is officially compulsory. Secondary education, which is not compulsory, begins at the age of 14 and lasts for a further six years. In 2003, however, the Government announced plans to introduce a nine-year system of basic education, including three years of attendance at lower secondary schools. Schools are administered by the state and by Christian missions. In 2003/04 93.0% of children in the relevant age-group (males 91.5%, females 94.5%) were enrolled in primary schools, according to official estimates, while secondary enrolment was equivalent in 1999/2000 to only 12.1% of children in the appropriate age-group (males 12.4%, females 11.8%). Secondary enrolment was equivalent to 13.9% of children in that age-group in 2002. The Ministry of Education established 94 new secondary schools in 2003, and a further 58 in 2005. Rwanda has a university, with campuses at Butare and Ruhengeri, while some students attend universities abroad, particularly in Belgium, France or Germany. In 2003 the number of students at the six public higher education institutions was 12,211, with a further 8,182 attending about seven private higher institutions. Estimated total expenditure by the central Government in 2003/04 represented 23.0% of total public expenditure.

Public Holidays

2008: 1 January (New Year), 28 January (Democracy Day), 24 March (Easter Monday), 7 April (National Mourning Day), 1 May (Labour Day), 1 May (Ascension Day), 1 July (Independence Day), 1 August (Harvest Festival), 15 August (Assumption), 8 September (Culture Day), 25 September (Kamarampaka Day, anniversary of 1961 referendum), 1 October (Armed Forces Day), 1 November (All Saints' Day), 25 December (Christmas).

2009: 1 January (New Year), 28 January (Democracy Day), 7 April (National Mourning Day), 13 April (Easter Monday), 1 May (Labour Day), 21 May (Ascension Day), 1 July (Independence Day), 1 August (Harvest Festival), 15 August (Assumption), 8 September (Culture Day), 25 September (Kamarampaka Day, anniversary of 1961 referendum), 1 October (Armed Forces Day), 1 November (All Saints' Day), 25 December (Christmas).

Weights and Measures

The metric system is in force.

Statistical Survey

Source (unless otherwise stated): Office rwandais d'information, BP 83, Kigali; tel. 75724.

Area and Population

AREA, POPULATION AND DENSITY

Area (sq km)	26,338*
Population (census results)	
15 August 1991	7,142,755
16 August 2002†	
Males	3,879,448
Females	4,249,105
Total	8,128,553
Population (UN estimate at mid-year)‡	
2005	9,234,000
2006	9,464,000
2007	9,725,000
Density (per sq km) at mid-2007	369.2

* 10,169 sq miles.
† Provisional results.
‡ Source: UN, *World Population Prospects: The 2006 Revision*.

PREFECTURES
(1991 census)

	Area (sq km)	Population*	Density (per sq km)
Butare	1,830	765,910	418.5
Byumba	4,987	779,365	159.2
Cyangugu	2,226	517,550	232.5
Gikongoro	2,192	462,635	211.1
Gisenyi	2,395	728,365	304.1
Gitarama	2,241	849,285	379.0
Kibungo	4,134	647,175	156.5
Kibuye	1,320	472,525	358.0
Kigali	} 3,251	{ 921,050	} 355.2
Kigali-Ville		233,640	
Ruhengeri	1,762	765,255	434.3
Total	26,338	7,142,755	271.2

* Source: UN, *Demographic Yearbook*.

RWANDA

PRINCIPAL TOWNS
(population at 1978 census)

Kigali (capital)	117,749	Ruhengeri		16,025
Butare	21,691	Gisenyi		12,436

Mid-2007 (incl. suburbs, UN estimate): Kigali 860,000 (Source: UN, *World Urbanization Prospects: The 2007 Revision*).

BIRTHS AND DEATHS
(annual averages, UN estimates)

	1990–95	1995–2000	2000–05
Birth rate (per 1,000)	41.7	40.2	43.9
Death rate (per 1,000)	41.9	24.1	18.4

Source: UN, *World Population Prospects: The 2006 Revision*.

Expectation of life (years at birth, WHO estimates): 45.6 (males 44.5; females 46.7) in 2005 (Source: WHO, *World Health Statistics*).

ECONOMICALLY ACTIVE POPULATION
(persons aged 14 years and over, at census of August 2002)

	Males	Females	Total
Agriculture	1,218,181	1,731,411	2,949,592
Fishing	3,374	94	3,468
Industrial activities	3,692	1,636	5,328
Production activities	32,994	10,649	43,643
Electricity and water	2,390	277	2,667
Construction	41,641	1,244	42,885
Trade reconstruction	56,869	32,830	89,699
Restaurants and hotels	4,525	2,311	6,836
Transport and communications	29,574	1,988	31,562
Financial intermediaries	1,560	840	2,400
Administration and defence	22,479	5,585	28,064
Education	22,688	17,046	39,734
Health and social services	7,521	7,054	14,575
Activities not adequately defined	69,042	39,458	108,500
Total employed	1,516,530	1,852,423	3,368,953

Source: IMF, *Rwanda: Selected Issues and Statistical Appendix* (December 2004).

Mid-2005 (estimates in '000): Agriculture, etc. 4,376; Total labour force 4,873 (Source: FAO).

Health and Welfare

KEY INDICATORS

Total fertility rate (children per woman, 2005)	5.5
Under-5 mortality rate (per 1,000 live births, 2005)	203
HIV/AIDS (% of persons aged 15–49, 2005)	3.1
Physicians (per 1,000 head, 2004)	0.05
Hospital beds (per 1,000 head, 2004)	1.70
Health expenditure (2004): US $ per head (PPP)	125.9
Health expenditure (2004): % of GDP	7.5
Health expenditure (2004): public (% of total)	56.8
Access to water (% of persons, 2004)	74
Access to sanitation (% of persons, 2004)	42
Human Development Index (2005): ranking	161
Human Development Index (2005): value	0.452

For sources and definitions, see explanatory note on p. vi.

Agriculture

PRINCIPAL CROPS
('000 metric tons)

	2004	2005	2006
Maize	88.2	97.3	91.8
Sorghum	163.8	227.9	187.4
Potatoes	1,072.8	1,314.1	128.5
Sweet potatoes	908.3	885.6	777.0
Cassava (Manioc)	765.7	781.6	588.2
Taro (Coco yam)	136.4	136.9	125.4
Sugar cane*	70.0	70.0	70.0
Dry beans	198.2	199.6	283.4
Dry peas	16.8	18.9	14.2
Groundnuts (in shell)	10.8	10.1	9.0
Pumpkins, squash and gourds*	210.3	214.4	214.4
Plantains	2,469.7	2,593.1	2,653.3
Coffee (green)	20.0	18.6	21.0
Tea (made)	14.5	16.5	16.0

* FAO estimates.

Aggregate production ('000 metric tons, may include official, semi-official or estimated data): Total cereals 319 in 2004, 413 in 2005, 366 in 2006; Total roots and tubers 2,887 in 2004, 3,122 in 2005, 2,780 in 2006; Total pulses 215 in 2004, 219 in 2005, 298 in 2006; Total vegetables (incl. melons) 267 in 2004, 271 in 2005, 271 in 2006; Total fruits (excl. melons) 2,546 in 2004, 2,670 in 2005, 2,730 in 2006.

Source: FAO.

LIVESTOCK
('000 head, year ending September)

	2003	2004	2005
Cattle	991.7	1,003.7	1,004.1
Pigs	211.9	326.7	346.9
Sheep	371.8	470.0	464.3
Goats	941.1	1,264.0	1,339.7
Rabbits	498	520	519
Chickens	1,800*	2,042	2,000*

* FAO estimate.

2006: Figures assumed to be unchanged from 2005 (FAO estimates).

Source: FAO.

LIVESTOCK PRODUCTS
('000 metric tons, FAO estimates)

	2003	2004	2005
Cattle meat	23.6	23.0	23.1
Goat meat	3.3	4.5	4.7
Pig meat	3.9	6.0	6.4
Chicken meat	2.0	2.3	2.3
Game meat	11.0	11.0	11.0
Other meat	3.1	3.4	3.4
Cows' milk	112.5	121.4	120.0
Sheep's milk	1.8	1.9	1.9
Goats' milk	17.9	24.0	24.0
Poultry eggs	2.3	2.3	2.3

2006: Figures assumed to be unchanged from 2005 (FAO estimates).

Source: FAO.

Forestry

ROUNDWOOD REMOVALS
('000 cubic metres, excluding bark, FAO estimates)

	2003	2004	2005
Sawlogs, veneer logs and logs for sleepers	245	245	245
Other industrial wood	250	250	250
Fuel wood	5,000	5,000	5,000
Total	5,495	5,495	5,495

2006: Figures assumed to be unchanged from 2005 (FAO estimates).
Source: FAO.

SAWNWOOD PRODUCTION
('000 cubic metres, including railway sleepers)

	1997	1998	1999
Coniferous (softwood)	20	21	22
Non-coniferous (hardwood)	54	55	57
Total	74	76	79

2000–06: Figures assumed to be unchanged from 1999 (FAO estimates).
Source: FAO.

Fishing

(metric tons, live weight)

	2003	2004	2005*
Capture	7,400	7,826	7,800
Nile tilapia	2,800	3,120	3,100
Aquaculture	1,027	386	386
Nile tilapia	1,000	340	340
Total catch	8,427	8,212	8,186

*FAO estimates.
Source: FAO.

Mining

(metric tons, unless otherwise indicated)

	2004	2005	2006*
Tin concentrates†*	550	700	700
Tungsten concentrates†	113	401	400
Columbo-tantalite‡	220	276	280
Natural gas (million cubic metres)§	140	170	170

*Estimates.
† Figures refer to the metal content of ores and concentrates.
‡ Figures refer to the estimated production of mineral concentrates. The metal content (estimates, metric tons) was: Niobium (Columbium) 69 in 2004, 86 in 2005, 88 in 2006; Tantalum 49 in 2004, 61 in 2005, 62 in 2006.
§ Figures refer to gross output.
Source: US Geological Survey.

Industry

SELECTED PRODUCTS

	2001	2002	2003
Beer ('000 hectolitres)	479	539	412
Soft drinks ('000 hectolitres)	228	n.a.	n.a.
Cigarettes (million)	278	391	402
Soap (metric tons)	7,056	5,571	4,456
Cement (metric tons)	83,024	100,568	105,105
Electric energy (million kWh)	89.3	n.a.	n.a.

Source: IMF, *Rwanda: Statistical Annex* (August 2002) and IMF, *Rwanda: Selected Issues and Statistical Appendix* (December 2004).

Cement ('000 metric tons): 104.3 in 2004; 101.1 in 2005; 100.0 in 2006 (estimate) (Source: US Geological Survey).

Finance

CURRENCY AND EXCHANGE RATES

Monetary Units
100 centimes = 1 franc rwandais (Rwanda franc).

Sterling, Dollar and Euro Equivalents (29 December 2006)
£1 sterling = 1,077.00 Rwanda francs;
US $1 = 548.65 Rwanda francs;
€1 = 722.58 Rwanda francs;
10,000 Rwanda francs = £9.29 = $18.23 = €13.84.

Average Exchange Rate (Rwanda francs per US $)
2004 574.622
2005 555.841
2006 552.555

Note: Since September 1983 the currency has been linked to the IMF special drawing right (SDR). Until November 1990 the mid-point exchange rate was SDR 1 = 102.71 Rwanda francs. In November 1990 a new rate of SDR 1 = 171.18 Rwanda francs was established. This remained in effect until June 1992, when the rate was adjusted to SDR 1 = 201.39 Rwanda francs. The latter parity was maintained until February 1994, since when the rate has been frequently adjusted. In March 1995 the Government introduced a market-determined exchange rate system.

BUDGET
('000 million Rwanda francs)

Revenue*	1999	2000	2001†
Tax revenue	60.4	65.3	79.5
Taxes on income and profits	15.2	17.9	23.9
Company profits tax	7.4	10.0	14.4
Individual income tax	6.1	7.5	9.0
Domestic taxes on goods and services	33.6	35.2	41.0
Excise taxes	17.9	18.8	14.2
Turnover tax	12.9	13.8	24.2
Road fund	2.7	2.5	2.6
Taxes on international trade	11.0	11.6	14.0
Import taxes	8.4	9.3	11.1
Non-tax revenue	3.2	3.3	6.7
Total	63.6	68.7	86.2

RWANDA

Statistical Survey

Expenditure‡	1999	2000	2001†
Current expenditure	86.0	89.2	107.4
General public services	31.5	35.7	53.7
Defence	27.0	25.8	28.6
Social services	21.9	30.5	36.2
Education	17.2	24.0	29.8
Health	3.3	3.8	5.1
Economic services	2.6	2.1	4.9
Energy and public works	0.7	0.4	2.3
Interest on public debt	4.0	1.8	2.8
Adjustment	−1.1	−6.7	−18.8
Capital expenditure	40.8	42.0	50.0
Sub-total	126.8	131.2	157.5
Adjustment for payment arrears§	2.0	−1.2	31.7
Total	128.8	130.0	189.2

* Excluding grants received ('000 million Rwanda francs): 38.5 in 1999; 63.7 in 2000; 63.3† in 2001.
† Estimates.
‡ Excluding lending minus repayments ('000 million Rwanda francs): −0.4 in 1999; 0.5 in 2000; 0.6 in 2001†.
§ Minus sign indicates increase in arrears.

Source: IMF, *Rwanda: Statistical Annex* (August 2002).

2002 (estimates, '000 million Rwanda francs): *Revenue:* Tax revenue 94.6; Non-tax revenue 6.6; Total 101.2, excl. grants received (70.8). *Expenditure:* Current 123.7; Capital 56.4; Total 180.1, excl. net lending (11.5) (Source: IMF, *Rwanda: First Review Under the Three-Year Arrangement Under the Poverty Reduction and Growth Facility and Request for Waiver of Performance Criteria—Staff Report; Staff Statement; Press Release on the Executive Board Discussion; and Statement by the Executive Director for Rwanda*—June 2003).

2005 ('000 million Rwanda francs): *Revenue:* Tax revenue 162.6; Non-tax revenue 17.7; Total 180.3, excl. grants received (169.1). *Expenditure:* Current 214.9; Capital 121.4; Total 336.3, excl. net lending (4.4) (Source: IMF, *Rwanda: Third Review Under the Three-Year Arrangement Under the Poverty Reduction and Growth Facility and Request for Waiver of Nonobservance of Performance Criterion—Staff Report; Staff Supplement; Press Release on the Executive Board Discussion; and Statement by the Executive Director for Rwanda*—March 2008).

2006 ('000 million Rwanda francs): *Revenue:* Tax revenue 193.6; Non-tax revenue 14.6; Total 208.2, excl. grants received (167.8). *Expenditure:* Current 254.1; Capital 118.7; Total 372.9, excl. net lending (9.6) (Source: IMF, *Rwanda: Third Review Under the Three-Year Arrangement Under the Poverty Reduction and Growth Facility and Request for Waiver of Nonobservance of Performance Criterion—Staff Report; Staff Supplement; Press Release on the Executive Board Discussion; and Statement by the Executive Director for Rwanda*—March 2008).

INTERNATIONAL BANK RESERVES
(US $ million at 31 December)

	2004	2005	2006
IMF special drawing rights	30.20	25.91	22.85
Foreign exchange	284.44	379.85	416.82
Total	314.64	405.76	439.67

Source: IMF, *International Financial Statistics*.

MONEY SUPPLY
(million Rwanda francs at 31 December)

	2003	2004	2005
Currency outside banks	29,246	36,512	46,277
Demand deposits at deposit money banks	52,220	62,604	82,524
Total money (incl. others)	82,305	99,941	129,326

Source: IMF, *International Financial Statistics*.

COST OF LIVING
(Consumer Price Index for Kigali; base: 2000 = 100)

	2004	2005	2006
All items	126.6	138.1	150.3

Source: IMF, *International Financial Statistics*.

NATIONAL ACCOUNTS
('000 million Rwanda francs at current prices)

Expenditure on the Gross Domestic Product

	2004	2005	2006
Government final consumption expenditure	206.4	238.6	294.1
Private final consumption expenditure	945.9	1,109.6	1,357.9
Increase in stocks			
Gross fixed capital formation	171.0	209.1	250.7
Total domestic expenditure	1,323.3	1,557.3	1,902.7
Exports of goods and services	115.3	136.3	166.2
Less Imports of goods and services	300.7	362.0	437.4
GDP in purchasers' values	1,137.9	1,331.6	1,631.6
GDP at constant 1995 prices	667.0	n.a.	n.a.

Source: IMF, *International Financial Statistics*.

Gross Domestic Product by Economic Activity

	2001	2002	2003
Agriculture, hunting, forestry and fishing	305.2	341.6	373.9
Mining and quarrying	14.5	9.1	5.7
Manufacturing	73.9	80.5	80.3
Electricity, gas and water	3.4	3.4	3.6
Construction	71.2	82.9	103.1
Trade, restaurants and hotels	75.2	82.0	91.7
Transport, storage and communications	55.1	60.7	61.7
Public administration	54.2	55.8	64.8
Other services	101.6	109.0	120.4
GDP at market prices	754.3	825.0	905.3

Source: IMF, *Rwanda: Selected Issues and Statistical Appendix* (December 2004).

BALANCE OF PAYMENTS
(US $ million)

	2004	2005	2006
Exports of goods f.o.b.	98	128	145
Imports of goods f.o.b.	−276	−355	−488
Trade balance	−178	−227	−343
Exports of services	103	129	131
Imports of services	−240	−304	−243
Balance on goods and services	−315	−402	−455
Other income received	6	27	27
Other income paid	−39	−44	−48
Balance on goods, services and income	−349	−418	−476
Current transfers received	169	352	319
Current transfers paid	−18	−18	−23
Current balance	−198	−84	−180
Capital account (net)	61	93	1,323
Direct investment abroad	—	—	14
Direct investment from abroad	8	8	11
Other investment assets	8	−14	−30
Other investment liabilities	−37	−52	−1,199
Net errors and omissions	23	26	87
Overall balance	−168	−23	26

Source: IMF, *International Financial Statistics*.

2007 (US $ '000 million, projected figures): Exports of goods 169.6; Imports of goods −571.1; *Trade balance* −401.5; Services (net) −205.8; Income (net) −14.0; Current transfers (net) 460.4; *Current balance* −160.8; Capital account 112.2; Financial account 163.3; *Overall balance* 114.6. (Source: IMF, *Rwanda: Third Review Under the Three-Year Arrangement Under the Poverty Reduction and Growth Facility and Request for Waiver of Nonobservance of Performance Criterion—Staff Report; Staff Supplement; Press Release on the Executive Board Discussion; and Statement by the Executive Director for Rwanda*—March 2008).

RWANDA

External Trade

PRINCIPAL COMMODITIES
(US $ million)

Imports c.i.f.	2001	2002	2003
Food and live animals	46.5	31.7	24.5
Cereals and cereal preparations	24.0	13.5	10.6
Rice	12.2	4.1	3.2
Vegetables and fruit	5.9	6.2	4.2
Sugar, sugar preparations and honey	8.6	5.9	5.0
Crude materials, inedible, except fuels	12.5	12.8	15.2
Textile fibres and their wastes	7.7	8.3	10.3
Mineral fuels, lubricants and related materials	39.7	40.7	40.6
Petroleum, petroleum products and related materials	39.5	40.6	40.5
Motor spirit, incl. aviation spirit	17.0	16.5	15.5
Gas oils	9.7	9.6	10.1
Animal and vegetable oils, fats and waxes	8.7	6.7	4.3
Chemicals and related products	23.8	33.8	30.4
Medicinal and pharmaceutical products	8.5	13.7	12.8
Basic manufactures	36.3	37.3	43.8
Iron and steel	11.3	8.9	12.9
Machinery and transport equipment	60.0	63.2	75.0
Telecommunications, sound recording and reproducing equipment	19.2	7.2	10.9
Electric machinery, apparatus and appliances, and parts	8.3	8.6	10.2
Road vehicles	18.4	24.8	31.2
Miscellaneous manufactured articles	46.2	22.4	25.7
Total (incl. others)	276.1	251.2	261.2

Exports f.o.b.	2001	2002	2003
Food and live animals	31.6	25.9	26.2
Coffee	15.0	14.0	13.9
Tea	16.6	11.8	11.9
Crude materials, inedible, except fuels	22.7	18.8	15.4
Metalliferous ores and metal scrap	20.9	16.3	11.7
Tin ores and concentrates	2.2	1.4	5.1
Ores and concentrates of other non-ferrous base metals	18.7	14.9	6.0
Ores of molybdenum, niobium and titanium	9.5	14.5	5.6
Total (incl. others)	55.5	46.0	50.4

Source: UN, *International Trade Statistics Yearbook*.

PRINCIPAL TRADING PARTNERS
(US $ million)

Imports	2001	2002	2003
Belgium	55.3	32.9	31.9
Canada	2.4	2.9	4.1
China	6.3	5.0	5.0
Denmark	1.9	5.8	2.8
France (incl. Monaco)	6.1	6.4	7.4
Germany	6.6	7.2	11.2
India	6.4	6.8	9.0
Israel	4.8	2.9	2.0
Italy	7.5	3.1	3.0
Japan	7.2	6.4	8.4
Kenya	61.9	66.7	74.1
Netherlands	7.4	5.7	4.5
Singapore	1.6	0.8	0.6

Imports—continued	2001	2002	2003
South Africa	12.5	11.0	12.9
Switzerland-Liechtenstein	1.3	1.3	1.5
Tanzania	9.6	13.2	14.7
Uganda	8.1	11.1	20.0
UAE	19.5	22.0	19.9
United Kingdom	8.0	6.5	4.3
USA	10.4	6.1	2.0
Viet Nam	4.8	0.9	0.2
Zambia	3.4	2.2	0.5
Total (incl. others)	276.1	251.2	261.2

Exports	2001	2002	2003
Belgium	2.1	2.3	0.8
Germany	2.4	0.3	0.2
Hong Kong	1.3	4.6	0.3
Kenya	24.0	18.1	20.6
Netherlands	1.2	6.5	0.0
Pakistan	0.2	1.3	0.6
Russia	1.4	0.0	0.0
South Africa	6.2	0.3	0.5
Switzerland-Liechtenstein	4.2	7.1	0.8
Tanzania	4.8	0.3	4.1
Uganda	2.5	1.0	13.4
United Kingdom	0.3	0.8	3.1
USA	3.0	1.4	0.1
Total (incl. others)	55.5	46.0	50.4

Source: UN, *International Trade Statistics Yearbook*.

Transport

ROAD TRAFFIC
(estimates, motor vehicles in use at 31 December)

	1995	1996
Passenger cars	12,000	13,000
Lorries and vans	16,000	17,100

Source: IRF, *World Road Statistics*.

CIVIL AVIATION
(traffic on scheduled services)

	1992	1993	1994
Passengers carried ('000)	9	9	9
Passenger-km (million)	2	2	2

Source: UN, *Statistical Yearbook*.

Tourism

(by country of residence)

	2000	2001*
Africa	93,058	99,928
Burundi	20,972	9,455
Congo, Democratic Republic	10,450	28,514
Kenya	2,050	2,243
Tanzania	18,320	18,697
Uganda	38,897	38,472
Americas	2,250	2,785
Europe	6,412	8,395
Belgium	1,866	2,057
Total (incl. others)	104,216	113,185

* January–November.

Tourism receipts (US $ million, excl. passenger transport): 23 in 2000; 25 in 2001; 31 in 2002; 30 in 2003; 44 in 2004.

Source: World Tourism Organization.

RWANDA

Communications Media

	2004	2005	2006
Telephones ('000 main lines in use)	23.0	22.0	16.5
Mobile cellular telephones ('000 subscribers)	138.7	219.7	314.2
Internet users ('000)	38	50	65
Broadband subscribers ('000)	1.1	1.2	1.7

Radio receivers ('000 in use): 601 in 1997.

Facsimile machines (number in use): 900 in 1998.

Daily newspapers: 1 in 1998.

Sources: International Telecommunication Union; UN, *Statistical Yearbook*; UNESCO, *Statistical Yearbook*.

Education

(1998)

	Teachers	Males	Females	Total
Primary	23,730	644,835	643,834	1,288,669
Secondary: general		39,088	38,337	77,425
technical and vocational	3,413	6,859	6,935	13,794
Tertiary	412	n.a.	n.a.	5,678

Source: mainly UNESCO Institute for Statistics.

Adult literacy rate (UNESCO estimates): 64.9% (males 71.4%; females 59.8%) in 2000 (Source: UNESCO Institute for Statistics).

Directory

The Constitution

A new Constitution was approved at a national referendum on 26 May 2003 and entered into effect on 4 June. The main provisions are summarized below:

PREAMBLE

The state of Rwanda is an independent sovereign Republic. Fundamental principles are: the struggle against the ideology of genocide and all its manifestations; the eradication of all ethnic and regional divisions; the promotion of national unity; and the equal sharing of power. Human rights and personal liberties are protected. All forms of discrimination are prohibited and punishable by law. The state recognizes a multi-party political system. Political associations are established in accordance with legal requirements, and may operate freely, providing that they comply with democratic and constitutional principles, without harm to national unity, territorial integrity and state security. The formation of political associations on the basis of race, ethnicity, tribal or regional affiliation, sex, religion or any other grounds for discrimination is prohibited.

LEGISLATURE

Legislative power is vested in a bicameral Parliament, comprising a Chamber of Deputies and a Senate. The Chamber of Deputies has 80 deputies, who are elected for a five-year term. In addition to 53 directly elected deputies, 27 seats are allocated, respectively, to two youth representatives, one disabilities representative, and 24 female representatives, who are indirectly elected. The Senate comprises 26 members, of whom 12 are elected by local government councils in the 12 provinces, and two by academic institutions, while the remaining 12 are nominated (eight by the President and four by a regulatory body, the Parties' Forum). Members of the Senate serve for eight years.

PRESIDENT

The President of the Republic is the Head of State, protector of the Constitution, and guarantor of national unity. He is the Commander-in-Chief of the armed forces. Presidential candidates are required to be of Rwandan nationality and aged a minimum of 35 years. The President is elected by universal suffrage for a seven-year term, and is restricted to two mandates. He signs into law presidential decrees in consultation with the Council of Ministers.

GOVERNMENT

The President nominates the Prime Minister, who heads the Council of Ministers. Ministers are proposed by the Prime Minister and appointed by the President.

JUDICIARY

The judiciary is independent and separate from the legislative and executive organs of government. The judicial system is composed of the Supreme Court, the High Court of the Republic, and provincial, district and municipal Tribunals. In addition, there are specialized judicial organs, comprising *gacaca* and military courts. The *gacaca* courts try cases of genocide or other crimes against humanity committed between 1 October 1990 and 31 December 1994. Military courts (the Military Tribunal and the High Military Court) have jurisdiction in military cases. The President and Vice-President of the Supreme Court and the Prosecutor-General are elected by the Senate two months after its installation.

The Government

HEAD OF STATE

President: Maj.-Gen. PAUL KAGAME (took office 22 April 2000; re-elected 25 August 2003).

COUNCIL OF MINISTERS
(March 2008)

Prime Minister: BERNARD MAKUZA.
Minister of Defence: Gen. MARCEL GATSINZI.
Minister of Local Government, Good Governance, Community Development and Social Affairs: PROTAIS MUSONI.
Minister of Internal Security: MUSA FAZIL HERERIMANA.
Minister of Foreign Affairs and Co-operation: ROSEMARY MUSEMINARI.
Minister of Finance and Economic Planning: JAMES MUSONI.
Minister of Agriculture and Animal Resources: CHRISTOPHER BAZIVAMO.
Minister of Education: Dr DAPHROSE GAHAKWA.
Minister of Infrastructure: LINDA BIHIRE.
Minister of Trade and Industry: MONIQUE NSANZABAGANWA.
Minister of Natural Resources: STANISLAS KAMANZI.
Minister of Justice and Attorney-General: THARCISSE KARUGARAMA.
Minister of Public Service and Labour: MUREKEZI ANASTSE.
Minister of Health: Dr JEAN-DAMASCÈNE NTAWUKURIRYAYO.
Minister of Sports and Culture: JOSEPH HABINEZA.
Minister of Youth: PROTAIS MITALI KABANDA.
Minister in the Office of the President: SOLINA NYIRAHABIMANA.
Minister of Cabinet Affairs: CHARLES MURIGANDE.
Minister in the Office of the President, in charge of Science and Technology: Prof. ROMAIN MURENZI.
Minister in the Office of the Prime Minister, in charge of Family and Gender Promotion: Dr JEANNE D'ARC MUJAWAMARIYA.
Minister in the Office of the Prime Minister, in charge of Information: LOUISE MUSHIKIWABO.
Minister of the East African Community: MONIQUE MUKARULIZA.
Minister of State at the Ministry of Local Government, Good Governance, Community Development and Social Affairs, in charge of Community Development and Social Affairs: CHRISTINE NYATANYI.
Minister of State at the Ministry of Education, in charge of Primary and Secondary Education: THEONESTE MUTSINDASHYAKA.
Minister of State at the Ministry of Natural Resources, in charge of the Environment, Water and Mines: Prof. BIKORO MUNYANGANIZI.
Minister of State at the Ministry of Infrastructure, in charge of Energy: ALBERT BUTARE.
Minister of State at the Ministry of Agriculture and Animal Resources, in charge of Agriculture: AGNES KALIBATA.

RWANDA

Minister of State at the Ministry of Trade and Industry, in charge of Industry and Investment Promotion: VINCENT KAREGA.

MINISTRIES

Office of the President: BP 15, Kigali; tel. 59062000; fax 572431; e-mail info@presidency.gov.rw; internet www.presidency.gov.rw.

Office of the Prime Minister: Kigali; tel. 585444; fax 583714; e-mail primature@gov.rw; internet www.primature.gov.rw.

Ministry of Agriculture and Animal Resources: BP 621, Kigali; tel. 585008; fax 585057; internet www.minagri.gov.rw.

Ministry of Defence: Kigali; tel. 577942; fax 576969; internet www.minadef.gov.rw.

Ministry of Education: BP 622, Kigali; tel. 583051; fax 582161; e-mail info@mineduc.gov.rw; internet www.mineduc.gov.rw.

Ministry of Finance and Economic Planning: BP 158, Kigali; tel. 575756; fax 577581; e-mail mfin@rwanda1.com; internet www.minecofin.gov.rw.

Ministry of Foreign Affairs and Co-operation: blvd de la Révolution, BP 179, Kigali; tel. 574522; fax 572904; internet www.minaffet.gov.rw.

Ministry of Gender and the Promotion of Women: Kigali; tel. 577626; fax 577543.

Ministry of Health: BP 84, Kigali; tel. 577458; fax 576853; e-mail info@moh.gov.rw; internet www.moh.gov.rw.

Ministry of Infrastructure: tel. 585503; fax 585755; e-mail webmaster@mininfra.gov.rw; internet www.mininfra.gov.rw.

Ministry of Internal Security: BP 446, Kigali; tel. 86708.

Ministry of Justice: BP 160, Kigali; tel. 586561; fax 586509; e-mail mjust@minijust.gov.rw; internet www.minijust.gov.rw.

Ministry of Lands, Environment, Forestry, Water and Natural Resources: Kigali; tel. 582628; fax 582629; internet www.minitere.gov.rw.

Ministry of Local Government, Good Governance, Rural Development and Social Affairs: BP 790, Kigali; tel. 585406; fax 582228; e-mail webmaster@minaloc.gov.rw; internet www.minaloc.gov.rw.

Ministry of Public Service and Labour: BP 403, Kigali; tel. 585714; fax 583621; e-mail mifotra@mifotra.gov.rw; internet www.mifotra.gov.rw.

Ministry of Trade and Industry: BP 2378, Kigali; tel. 574725; fax 575465; internet www.minicom.gov.rw.

Ministry of Youth, Sports and Culture: BP 1044, Kigali; tel. 583527; fax 583518; e-mail minicult@rwanda1.com; internet www.mijespoc.gov.rw.

President and Legislature

PRESIDENT

Presidential Election, 25 August 2003

Candidate	Votes	% of votes
Paul Kagame	3,544,777	95.05
Faustin Twagiramungu	134,865	3.62
Jean-Népomuscène Nayinzira	49,634	1.33
Total*	3,729,274	100.00

* Excluding 49,634 invalid votes.

CHAMBER OF DEPUTIES

Speaker: ALFRED MUKEZAMFURA.

General Election, 29 September–3 October 2003

Party	Votes	% of votes	Seats
Front patriotique rwandais*	2,774,661	73.78	40
Parti social-démocrate	463,067	12.31	7
Parti libéral	396,978	10.56	6
Others	125,896	3.35	—
Total	3,760,602	100.00	80†

* Contested the elections in alliance with the Parti démocrate centriste, Parti démocratique idéal, Union démocratique du peuple rwandais and Parti socialiste rwandais.

† In addition to the 53 directly elected deputies, 27 seats are allocated, respectively, to two youth representatives, one disabilities representative and 24 female representatives, who are indirectly elected.

SENATE

Speaker: Dr VINCENT BIRUTA.

The Senate comprises 26 members, of whom 12 are elected by local government councils in the 12 provinces and two by academic institutions, while the remaining 12 are nominated (eight by the President and four by a regulatory body, the Parties' Forum).

Election Commission

Commission électorale nationale du Rwanda: BP 6449, Kigali; tel. 597800; fax 597851; e-mail comelena@rwanda1.com; internet www.comelena.gov.rw; f. 2000; independent; Chair. Prof. CHRYSOLOGUE KARANGWA.

Political Organizations

Under legislation adopted in June 2003, the formation of any political organization based on ethnic groups, religion or sex was prohibited.

Front patriotique rwandais (FPR): f. 1990; also known as Inkotanyi; comprises mainly Tutsi exiles, but claims multi-ethnic support; commenced armed invasion of Rwanda from Uganda in Oct. 1990; took control of Rwanda in July 1994; Chair. Maj.-Gen. PAUL KAGAME; Vice-Chair. CHRISTOPHE BAZIVAMO; Sec.-Gen. CHARLES MURIGANDE.

Parti démocrate centriste (PDC): BP 2348, Kigali; tel. 576542; fax 572237; f. 1990; fmrly Parti démocrate chrétien; Leader ALFRED MUKEZAMFURA.

Parti démocratique idéal (PDI): Kigali; f. 1991; fmrly Parti démocratique islamique; Leader ANDRÉ BUMAYA HABIB.

Parti démocratique rwandais (Pader): Kigali; f. 1992; Sec. JEAN NTAGUNGIRA.

Parti libéral (PL): BP 1304, Kigali; tel. 577916; fax 577838; f. 1991; restructured 2003; Chair. PROSPER HIGORO; Sec.-Gen. Dr ODETTE NYIRAMIRIMO.

Parti du progrès et de la concorde (PPC): f. 2003; incl. fmr mems of Mouvement démocratique républicain; Leader Dr CHRISTIAN MARARA.

Parti progressiste de la jeunesse rwandaise (PPJR): Kigali; f. 1991; Leader ANDRÉ HAKIZIMANA.

Parti républicain rwandais (Parerwa): Kigali; f. 1992; Leader AUGUSTIN MUTAMBA.

Parti social-démocrate (PSD): Kigali; f. 1991 by a breakaway faction of fmr Mouvement révolutionnaire national pour le développement; Leader Dr VINCENT BIRUTA.

Parti socialiste rwandais (PSR): BP 827, Kigali; tel. 576658; fax 83975; f. 1991; workers' rights; Leader Dr MEDARD RUTIJANWA.

Rassemblement travailliste pour la démocratie (RTD): BP 1894, Kigali; tel. 575622; fax 576574; f. 1991; Leader EMMANUEL NIZEYIMANA.

Union démocratique du peuple rwandais (UDPR): Kigali; f. 1992; Leader ADRIEN RANGIRA.

Other political organizations have been formed by exiled Rwandans and operate principally from abroad; these include:

Rassemblement pour le retour des réfugiés et la démocratie au Rwanda (RDR): Postbus 3124, 2280 GC, Rijswijk, Netherlands; tel. (31) 623075674; fax (31) 847450374; e-mail info@rdrwanda.org; internet www.rdrwanda.org; f. 1995; prin. opposition party representing Hutu refugees in exile; Pres. VICTOIRE UMUHOZA INGABIRE.

Union du peuple rwandais (UPR): Brussels, Belgium; f. 1990; Hutu-led; Pres. SILAS MAJYAMBERE; Sec.-Gen. EMMANUEL TWAGILIMANA.

Diplomatic Representation

EMBASSIES IN RWANDA

Belgium: rue Nyarugenge, BP 81, Kigali; tel. 575551; fax 573995; e-mail kigali@diplobel.be; Ambassador FRANÇOIS ROUX.

Burundi: rue de Ntaruka, BP 714, Kigali; tel. 575010; Chargé d'affaires a.i. (vacant).

Egypt: BP 1069, Kigali; tel. 82686; fax 82686; e-mail egypt@rwanda1.com; Ambassador AHMED RAMI AWWAD EL HOSENI.

Germany: 8 rue de Bugarama, BP 355, Kigali; tel. 575141; fax 502087; internet www.kigali.diplo.de; Ambassador Dr CHRISTIAN CLAGES.

Holy See: 49 ave Paul VI, BP 261, Kigali (Apostolic Nunciature); tel. 575293; fax 575181; e-mail nuntrw@rwandatel1.rwanda1.com;

RWANDA

Apostolic Nuncio Most Rev. ANSELMO GUIDO PECORARI (Titular Archbishop of Populonia).

Kenya: BP 1215, Kigali; tel. 583332; fax 510919; e-mail kigali@mfa.go.ke; Ambassador KETTER A. ALEX.

Korea, Democratic People's Republic: Kigali; Ambassador KIM PONG GI.

Libya: BP 1152, Kigali; tel. 576470; Secretary of the People's Bureau MOUSTAPHA MASAND EL-GHAILUSHI.

Russia: 19 ave de l'Armée, BP 40, Kigali; tel. 575286; fax 574818; e-mail ambruss@rwandatel1.rwanda1.com; Ambassador MIRGAYAS M. SHIRINSKII.

South Africa: 1370 blvd de l'Umuganda, POB 6563, Kacyiru-Sud, Kigali; tel. 583185; fax 511760; e-mail saemkgl@rwanda1.com; internet www.saembassy-kigali.org.rw; Ambassador Dr EZRA M. SIGWELA.

United Kingdom: Parcelle 1131, Blvd de l'Umuganda, Kacyiru, BP 576, Kigali; tel. 584098; fax 582044; e-mail embassy.kigali@fco.gov.uk; internet www.britishembassykigali.org.rw; Ambassador NICHOLAS CANNON.

USA: blvd de la Révolution, BP 28, Kigali; tel. 505601; fax 507143; e-mail irckigali@state.gov; internet kigali.usembassy.gov; Ambassador MICHAEL RAY ARIETTI.

Judicial System

The judicial system is composed of the Supreme Court, the High Court of the Republic, and provincial, district and municipal Tribunals. In addition, there are specialized judicial organs, comprising *gacaca* and military courts. The *gacaca* courts were established to try cases of genocide or other crimes against humanity committed between 1 October 1990 and 31 December 1994. Trials for categories of lesser genocide crimes were to be conducted by councils in the communities in which they were committed, with the aim of alleviating pressure on the existing judicial system. Trials under the *gacaca* court system formally commenced on 25 November 2002. Military courts (the Military Tribunal and the High Military Court) have jurisdiction in military cases. The President and Vice-President of the Supreme Court and the Prosecutor-General are elected by the Senate.

Supreme Court

Kigali; tel. 87407.

The Supreme Court comprises five sections: the Department of Courts and Tribunals; the Court of Appeals; the Constitutional Court; the Council of State; and the Revenue Court.

President of the Supreme Court: ALOYSIA CYANZAIRE.

Vice-President: Prof. SAM RUGEGE.

Prosecutor-General: MARTIN NGOGAEU MUCYO.

Religion

AFRICAN RELIGIONS

About one-half of the population hold traditional beliefs.

CHRISTIANITY

Union des Eglises Rwandaises: BP 79, Kigali; tel. 85825; fax 83554; f. 1963; fmrly Conseil Protestant du Rwanda.

The Roman Catholic Church

Rwanda comprises one archdiocese and eight dioceses. At 31 December 2005 the estimated number of adherents represented about 48.3% of the total population.

Bishops' Conference

Conférence Episcopale du Rwanda, BP 357, Kigali; tel. 575439; fax 578080; e-mail cerwanda@rwanda1.com.

f. 1980; Pres. Rt Rev. ALEXIS HABIYAMBERE (Bishop of Nyundo).

Archbishop of Kigali: Most Rev. THADDÉE NTIHINYURWA, Archevêché, BP 715, Kigali; tel. 575769; fax 572274; e-mail kigarchi@yahoo.fr.

The Anglican Communion

The Church of the Province of Rwanda, established in 1992, has nine dioceses.

Archbishop of the Province and Bishop of Kigali: Most Rev. EMMANUEL MUSABA KOLINI, BP 61, Kigali; tel. and fax 573213; e-mail sonja914@compuserve.com.

Provincial Secretary: Rt Rev. JOSIAS SENDEGEYA (Bishop of Kigali), BP 2487, Kigali; tel. and fax 514160; e-mail peer@rwandatel1.rwanda1.

Protestant Churches

Eglise Baptiste: Nyantanga, BP 59, Butare; Pres. Rev. DAVID BAZIGA; Gen. Sec. ELEAZAR ZIHERAMBERE.

There are about 250,000 other Protestants, including a substantial minority of Seventh-day Adventists.

BAHÁ'Í FAITH

National Spiritual Assembly: BP 652, Kigali; tel. 572550.

ISLAM

There is a small Islamic community.

The Press

Bulletin Agricole du Rwanda: OCIR—Café, BP 104, Kigali-Gikondo; f. 1968; quarterly; French; Pres. of Editorial Bd Dr AUGUSTIN NZINDUKIYIMANA; circ. 800.

L'Ere de Liberté: BP 1755, Kigali; fortnightly.

Etudes Rwandaises: Université Nationale du Rwanda, Rectorat, BP 56, Butare; tel. 30302; f. 1977; quarterly; pure and applied science, literature, human sciences; French; Pres. of Editorial Bd CHARLES NTAKIRUTINKA; circ. 1,000.

Hobe: BP 761, Kigali; f. 1955; monthly; children's interest; circ. 95,000.

Inkingi: BP 969, Kigali; tel. 577626; fax 577543; monthly.

Inkoramutima: Union des Eglises Rwandaises, BP 79, Kigali; tel. 85825; fax 83554; quarterly; religious; circ. 5,000.

Kinyamateka: 5 blvd de l'OUA, BP 761, Kigali; tel. 576164; f. 1933; fortnightly; economics; circ. 11,000.

La Lettre du Cladho: BP 3060, Kigali; tel. 74292; monthly.

The New Times: BP 635, Kigali; tel. 573409; fax 574166; monthly.

Nouvelles du Rwanda: Université Nationale du Rwanda, BP 117, Butare; every 2 months.

Nyabarongo—Le Canard Déchaîné: BP 1585, Kigali; tel. 576674; monthly.

Le Partisan: BP 1805, Kigali; tel. 573923; fortnightly.

La Patrie—Urwatubyaye: BP 3125, Kigali; tel. 572552; monthly.

La Relève: Office Rwandais d'Information, BP 83, Kigali; tel. 75665; f. 1976; monthly; politics, economics, culture; French; Dir CHRISTOPHE MFIZI; circ. 1,700.

Revue Dialogue: BP 572, Kigali; tel. 574178; f. 1967; bi-monthly; Christian issues; Belgian-owned; circ. 2,500.

Revue Médicale Rwandaise: Ministry of Health, BP 84, Kigali; tel. 576681; f. 1968; quarterly; French.

Revue Pédagogique: Ministry of Education, Science, Technology and Research, BP 622, Kigali; tel. 85697; quarterly; French.

Rwanda Herald: Kigali; f. Oct. 2000; owned by Rwanda Independent Media Group.

Rwanda Libération: BP 398, Kigali; tel. 577710; monthly; Dir and Editor-in-Chief ANTOINE KAPITENI.

Rwanda Renaître: BP 426, Butare; fortnightly.

Rwanda Rushya: BP 83, Kigali; tel. 572276; fortnightly.

Le Tribun du Peuple: BP 1960, Kigali; tel. 82035; bi-monthly; Owner JEAN-PIERRE MUGABE.

Ukuli Gacaca: BP 3170, Kigali; tel. 585239; monthly; Dir CHARLES GAKUMBA.

Umucunguzi: Gisenyi; f. 1998; organ of Palir; Kinyarwanda and French; Chief Editor EMILE NKUMBUYE.

Umuhinzi-Mworozi: OCIR—Thé, BP 1334, Kigali; tel. 514797; fax 514796; f. 1975; monthly; circ. 1,500.

Umusemburo—Le Levain: BP 117, Butare; monthly.

Umuseso: Kigali; independent Kinyarwanda language weekly newspaper; Editor CHARLES KABONERO.

Urunana: Grand Séminaire de Nyakibanda, BP 85, Butare; tel. 530793; e-mail wellamahoro@yahoo.fr; f. 1967; 3 a year; religious; Pres. WELLAS UWAMAHORO; Editor-in-Chief DAMIEN NIYOYIREMERA.

NEWS AGENCIES

Agence Rwandaise de Presse (ARP): 27 ave du Commerce, BP 83, Kigali; tel. 576540; fax 576185; e-mail cbohizi@yahoo.fr; f. 1975.

RWANDA

Office Rwandais d'Information (Orinfor): BP 83, Kigali; tel. 575735; fax 576539; internet www.orinfor.gov.rw; f. 1973; Dir JOSEPH BIDERI.

Publishers

Editions Rwandaises: Caritas Rwanda, BP 124, Kigali; tel. 5786; Man. Dir Abbé CYRIAQUE MUNYANSANGA; Editorial Dir ALBERT NAMBAJE.

Implico: BP 721, Kigali; tel. 573771.

Imprimerie de Kabgayi: BP 66, Gitarama; tel. 562252; fax 562345; e-mail imprikabgayi@yahoo.fr; f. 1932; Dir Abbé CYRILLE UWIZEYE.

Imprimerie de Kigali, SARL: 1 blvd de l'Umuganda, BP 956, Kigali; tel. 582032; fax 584047; e-mail impkig@rwandatel1.rwanda1.com; f. 1980; Dir ALEXIS RUKUNDO.

Imprimerie URWEGO: BP 762, Kigali; tel. 86027; Dir JEAN NSENGIYUNVA.

Pallotti-Presse: BP 863, Kigali; tel. 574084.

GOVERNMENT PUBLISHING HOUSES

Imprimerie Nationale du Rwanda: BP 351, Kigali; tel. 576214; fax 575820; f. 1967; Dir JUVÉNAL NDISANZE.

Régie de l'Imprimerie Scolaire (IMPRISCO): BP 1347, Kigali; tel. 85818; fax 85695; e-mail imprisco@rwandatel1.rwanda1.com; f. 1985; Dir JEAN DE DIEU GAKWANDI.

Broadcasting and Communications

TELECOMMUNICATIONS

Rwandatel: BP 1332, Kigali; tel. 576777; fax 573110; e-mail info@rwandatel.rw; internet www.rwandatel.rw; national telecommunications service; privatized mid-2005.

MTN Rwandacell: Telecom House, blvd de l'Umuganda, Kigali; f. 1998; provides mobile cellular telephone services; CEO FRANÇOIS DU PLESSIS.

BROADCASTING

Radio

Radio Rwanda: BP 83, Kigali; tel. 575665; fax 576185; f. 1961; state-controlled; daily broadcasts in Kinyarwanda, Swahili, French and English; Dir of Programmes DAVID KABUYE.

Deutsche Welle Relay Station Africa: Kigali; daily broadcasts in German, English, French, Hausa, Swahili, Portuguese and Amharic.

Television

Télévision rwandaise (TVR): Kigali; fax 575024; f. 1992; transmissions reach more than 60% of national territory; broadcasts for 10 hours daily in Kinyarwanda, French and English.

Finance

(cap. = capital; res = reserves; dep. = deposits; m. = million; brs = branches; amounts in Rwanda francs)

BANKING

Central Bank

Banque Nationale du Rwanda: ave Paul VI, BP 531, Kigali; tel. 574282; fax 572551; e-mail info@bnr.rw; internet www.bnr.rw; f. 1964; bank of issue; cap. 2,000m., res 13,905.9m., dep. 157,148.0m. (Dec. 2005); Gov. FRANÇOIS KANIMBA.

Commercial Banks

Following the privatization of two commercial banks, government control of the banking section was reduced from 45% in 2003 to 22% in 2005, although the three largest banks continued to control two-thirds of the system's assets, valued at US $365m. (equivalent to 34% of GDP).

Bancor SA: 3rd Floor, UTC Bldg, 1232 ave de la Paix, BP 2059, Kigali; tel. 500091; fax 575761; e-mail bancor@rwanda1.com; internet www.bancor.co.rw; f. 1995 as Banque à la Confiance d'Or; name changed as above in 2001 when acquired by private investors; cap. and res 3,417.1m., total assets 34,549.3m. (Dec. 2005); Pres. NICHOLAS WATSON.

Banque de Commerce, de Développement et d'Industrie (BCDI): ave de la Paix, BP 3268, Kigali; tel. 574437; fax 573790; e-mail info@bcdi.co.rw; internet www.bcdi.co.rw; cap. and res 3,158.4m., total assets 45,950.9m. (Dec. 2003); Pres. and Dir-Gen. ALFRED KALISA.

Banque Commerciale du Rwanda, SA: BP 354, 11 blvd de la Revolution, Kigali; tel. 575591; fax 573395; e-mail bcr@rwandatel1.rwanda1.com; internet www.bcr-rwanda.com; f. 1963; privatized Sept. 2004; cap. and res 2,420.0m., dep. 30,564.3m. (Dec. 2003); Pres. Dr NKOSANA MOYO; Man. Dir DAVID KUWANA; 6 brs.

Banque de Kigali, SA: 63 ave du Commerce, BP 175, Kigali; tel. 593100; fax 573461; e-mail bkig10@rwanda1.com; f. 1966; cap. 1,500.0m., res 4,330.1m., dep. 59,378.6m. (Dec. 2005); Chair. FRANÇOIS NGARAMBE; Gen. Man. JAMES GATERA; 6 brs.

Caisse Hypothécaire du Rwanda (CHR): BP 1034, Kigali; tel. 576382; fax 572799; cap. 778.2m., total assets 6,966.8m. (Dec. 2003); Pres. FRANÇOIS RUTISHASHA; Dir-Gen. PIPIEN HAKIZABERA.

Compagnie Générale de Banque: blvd de l'Umuganda, BP 5230, Kigali; tel. 503343; fax 503336; e-mail cogebank@rwanda1.com; cap. and res 1,210.8m., total assets 7,297.4m. (Dec. 2003); Pres. ANDRÉ KATABARWA.

Fina Bank, SA: 20 blvd de la Révolution, BP 331, Kigali; tel. 598600; fax 573486; e-mail info@finabank.co.rw; f. 1983 as Banque Continentale Africaine (Rwanda); name changed 2005; cap. 1,650m., res 1,028.7m., dep. 22,730m. (Dec. 2006); privatized; Chair. ROBERT BINYOU; Man. Dir STEPHEN CALEY; 5 brs.

Development Banks

Banque Rwandaise de Développement, SA (BRD): blvd de la Révolution, BP 1341, Kigali; tel. 575079; fax 573569; e-mail brd@brd.com.rw; internet www.brd.com.rw; f. 1967; 56% state-owned; cap. and res 4,104.6m., total assets 13,920.7m. (Dec. 2003); Man. Dir THÉOGÈNE TURATSINZE.

Union des Banques Populaires du Rwanda (Banki z'Abaturage mu Rwanda): BP 1348, Kigali; tel. 573559; fax 573579; e-mail ubpr@rwandatel1.rwanda1.com; f. 1975; cap. and res 1,180.5m., total assets 20,433.8m. (Dec. 2002); Pres. INNOCENT KAYITARE; 145 brs.

INSURANCE

Société Nationale d'Assurances du Rwanda (SONARWA): BP 1035, Kigali; tel. 573350; fax 572052; e-mail sonarwa@rwandatel1.rwanda1.com; f. 1975; cap. 500m.; Pres. FRANÇOIS NGARAMBE; Dir-Gen. HOPE MURERA.

Société Rwandaise d'Assurances, SA (SORAS): BP 924, Kigali; tel. 573716; fax 573362; e-mail sorasinf@rwanda1.com; f. 1984; cap. 1,002m. (2007); Pres. CHARLES MHORANYI; Dir-Gen. MARC RUGENERA.

Trade and Industry

GOVERNMENT AGENCIES

National Tender Board: ave de la Paix, POB 4276, Kigali; tel. 501403; fax 501402; e-mail ntb@rwanda1.com; internet www.ntb.gov.rw; f. 1998 to organize and manage general public procurement.

Rwanda Investment and Export Promotion Agency: Kimihurura, ave du Lac Muhazi, POB 6239, Kigali; tel. 510248; fax 510249; e-mail info@rwandainvest.com; internet www.rwandainvest.com; f. 1998 as Rwanda Investment Promotion Agency; Dir-Gen. FRANCIS GATARE.

Rwanda Revenue Authority: Kigali; f. 1998 to maximize revenue collection; Commissioner-Gen. EDWARD LARBI SIAW.

DEVELOPMENT ORGANIZATIONS

Coopérative de Promotion de l'Industrie Minière et Artisanale au Rwanda (COOPIMAR): BP 1139, Kigali; tel. 82127; fax 72128; Dir DANY NZARAMBA.

Institut de Recherches Scientifiques et Technologiques (IRST): BP 227, Butare; tel. 30396; fax 30939; Dir-Gen. CHRYSOLOGUE KARANGWA.

Institut des Sciences Agronomiques du Rwanda (ISAR): BP 138, Butare; tel. 30642; fax 30644; for the devt of subsistence and export agriculture; Dir MUNYANGANIZI BIKORO; 12 centres.

Office des Cultures Industrielles du Rwanda—Café (OCIR—Café): BP 104, Kigali; tel. 575600; fax 573992; e-mail ocircafe@rwandatel1.rwanda1.com; f. 1978; devt of coffee and other new agronomic industries; operates a coffee stabilization fund; Dir ANASTASE NZIRASANAHO.

Office des Cultures Industrielles du Rwanda—Thé (OCIR—Thé): BP 1344, Kigali; tel. 514797; fax 514796; e-mail ocirthé@rwanda1.com; devt and marketing of tea; Dir CÉLESTIN KAYITARE.

**Office National pour le Développement de la Commercialisation des Produits Vivriers et des Produits Animaux (OPRO-

RWANDA

VIA): BP 953, Kigali; tel. 82946; fax 82945; privatization pending; Dir DISMAS SEZIBERA.

Régie d'Exploitation et de Développement des Mines (REDEMI): BP 2195, Kigali; tel. 573632; fax 573625; e-mail ruzredem@yahoo.fr; f. 1988 as Régie des Mines du Rwanda; privatized in 2000; state org. for mining tin, columbo-tantalite and wolfram; Man. Dir JEAN-RUZINDANA MUNANA.

Société de Pyrèthre au Rwanda (SOPYRWA): BP 79, Ruhengeri; tel. and fax 546364; e-mail sopyrwa@rwanda1.com; f. 1978; cultivation and processing of pyrethrum; post-war activities resumed in Oct. 1994; current production estimated at 80% pre-war capacity; Dir SYLVAIN NZABAGAMBA.

CHAMBER OF COMMERCE

Chambre de Commerce et d'Industrie de Rwanda: rue de l'Umuganda, POB 319, Kigali; tel. 83534; fax 83532; Pres. T. RUJUGIRO.

INDUSTRIAL ASSOCIATIONS

Association des Industriels du Rwanda: BP 39, Kigali; tel. and fax 575430; Pres. YVES LAFAGE; Exec. Sec. MUGUNGA NDOBA.

Federation of the Rwandan Private Sector Associations: POB 319, Kigali; tel. 83538; fax 83532; e-mail frsp@rwanda1.com; f. 1999 to represent interests of private sector; Exec. Sec. EUGÈNE BITWAYIKI.

UTILITIES

Electrogaz: POB 537, Kigali; tel. 572392; fax 573802; state-owned water, electricity and gas supplier; Dir JOSEPH MUJENGA.

TRADE UNIONS

Centrale d'Education et de Coopération des Travailleurs pour le Développement/Alliance Coopérative au Rwanda (CECOTRAD/ACORWA): BP 295, Kigali; f. 1984; Pres. ELIE KATABARWA.

Centrale Syndicale des Travailleurs du Rwanda: BP 1645, Kigali; tel. 85658; fax 84012; e-mail cestrav@rwandatel1.rwanda1.com; Sec.-Gen. FRANÇOIS MURANGIRA.

Transport

RAILWAYS

There are no railways in Rwanda, although plans exist for the eventual construction of a line passing through Uganda, Rwanda and Burundi, to connect with the Kigoma–Dar es Salaam line in Tanzania. Rwanda has access by road to the Tanzanian railways system.

ROADS

In 2004 there were an estimated 14,008 km of roads, of which 2,662 km were paved. There are road links with Uganda, Tanzania, Burundi and the Democratic Republic of the Congo. Internal conflict during 1994 caused considerable damage to the road system and the destruction of several important bridges.

Office National des Transports en Commun (ONATRACOM): BP 609, Kigali; tel. 575564; Dir (vacant).

INLAND WATERWAYS

There are services on Lake Kivu between Cyangugu, Gisenyi and Kibuye, including two vessels operated by ONATRACOM.

CIVIL AVIATION

The Kanombe international airport at Kigali can process up to 500,000 passengers annually. There is a second international airport at Kamembe, near the border with the Democratic Republic of the Congo. There are airfields at Butare, Gabiro, Ruhengeri and Gisenyi, servicing internal flights.

Alliance Express Rwanda (ALEX): BP 1440, Kigali; tel. 82409; fax 82417; e-mail aev@aev.com.rw; f. 1998 to succeed fmr Air Rwanda as national carrier; 51% owned by Alliance Air (jtly owned by Govts of Uganda and South Africa and by South African Airways), 49% state-owned; domestic and regional passenger and cargo services; Chair. GERALD ZIRIMWABAGABO.

Rwandair Express: BP 3246, Kigali; tel. 577564; fax 577669; f. 1998; privately owned; operates two passenger aircraft; regional services; CEO PIERRE CLAVER KABERA (acting).

Tourism

Attractions for tourists include the wildlife of the national parks (notably mountain gorillas), Lake Kivu and fine mountain scenery. Since the end of the transitional period in late 2003, the Government has increased efforts to develop the tourism industry. In 1998 there were only an estimated 2,000 foreign visitors to Rwanda, but by 2001 the number of tourist arrivals had increased to 113,185. Total receipts from tourism were estimated at US $44m. in 2004.

Office Rwandais du Tourisme et des Parcs Nationaux (ORTPN): blvd de la Révolution 1, BP 905, Kigali; tel. 576514; fax 576515; e-mail webmaster@rwandatourism.com; internet www.rwandatourism.com; f. 1973; govt agency.

SAINT CHRISTOPHER* AND NEVIS

Introductory Survey

Location, Climate, Language, Religion, Flag, Capital

The Federation of Saint Christopher and Nevis is situated at the northern end of the Leeward Islands chain of the West Indies, with Saba and St Eustatius (both in the Netherlands Antilles) to the north-west, Barbuda to the north-east and Antigua to the south-east. Nevis lies about 3 km (2 miles) to the south-east of Saint Christopher, separated by a narrow strait. The tropical heat, varying between 17°C (62°F) and 33°C (92°F), is tempered by constant sea winds, and annual rainfall averages 1,400 mm (55 ins) on Saint Christopher and 1,220 mm (48 ins) on Nevis. English is the official language. The majority of the population are Christians of the Anglican Communion, and other Christian denominations are represented. The national flag (proportions 2 by 3) comprises two triangles, one of green (with its base at the hoist and its apex in the upper fly) and the other of red (with its base in the fly and its apex in the lower hoist), separated by a broad, yellow-edged black diagonal stripe (from the lower hoist to the upper fly) bearing two five-pointed white stars. The capital is Basseterre, on Saint Christopher.

Recent History

Saint Christopher, settled in 1623, was Britain's first colony in the West Indies. The French settled part of the island a year later, and conflict over possession continued until 1783, when Saint Christopher was eventually ceded to Britain under the Treaty of Versailles. Nevis was settled by the British in 1628, and remained one of the most prosperous of the Antilles until the middle of the 19th century. The island of Anguilla was first joined to the territory in 1816. The St Kitts-Nevis-Anguilla Labour Party, formed in 1932, campaigned for independence for the islands. In 1958 Saint Christopher-Nevis-Anguilla became a member of the West Indies Federation, remaining so until the Federation's dissolution in 1962. A new Constitution, granted to each of the British territories in the Leeward Islands in 1960, provided for government through an Administrator and an enlarged Legislative Council. After an abortive attempt to form a smaller East Caribbean Federation, Saint Christopher-Nevis-Anguilla attained Associated Statehood in February 1967, as part of an arrangement that gave five of the colonies full internal autonomy, while the United Kingdom retained responsibility for defence and foreign relations. The House of Assembly replaced the Legislative Council, the Administrator became Governor, and the Chief Minister, Robert Bradshaw, leader of the Labour Party, became the state's first Premier. Three months later Anguilla rebelled against government from Saint Christopher, and in 1971 reverted to being a de facto British dependency. Anguilla was formally separated from the other islands in 1980.

A general election in 1971 returned Robert Bradshaw to the premiership. In the 1975 election the Labour Party again won the largest number of seats, while the Nevis Reformation Party (NRP) once more took both the Nevis seats. Bradshaw died in May 1978 and was succeeded as Premier by Paul Southwell, hitherto Deputy Premier (and a former Chief Minister). Southwell died in May 1979, and was replaced by the party's leader, Lee L. Moore (hitherto the Attorney-General).

In February 1980 the Labour Party was removed from government for the first time in nearly 30 years: the Labour Party secured four seats in the legislative election, while the People's Action Movement (PAM) took three and the NRP retained the two Nevis seats. Although the Labour Party had won 58% of the popular vote, a PAM-NRP coalition Government was formed under PAM leader, Dr Kennedy A. Simmonds. The change of government led to the suspension of a timetable for independence, which had been scheduled for June 1980. In 1982 proposals for a greater degree of autonomy for Nevis and for independence for the whole state were approved by the House of Assembly, although the Labour Party opposed the plans, arguing that the coalition Government did not have a mandate for its independence policy. Disagreements concerning the content of the proposed independence constitution led to civil disturbances in 1982 and 1983. Nevertheless, Saint Christopher and Nevis became an independent state, under a federal Constitution, on 19 September 1983. The Labour Party denounced the special provisions for Nevis in the Constitution (see below) as giving the island a powerful role in government that was disproportionate to its size and population. Elections to the Nevis Island Assembly were held in August, at which the NRP, led by Simeon Daniel, won all five elective seats. Upon independence Saint Christopher and Nevis became a full member of the Commonwealth (see p. 206).

Early elections to an enlarged National Assembly (now with 11 elective seats) took place in June 1984, at which the ruling PAM-NRP coalition was returned to power. The PAM, which won a clear majority of the popular vote on Saint Christopher, secured six seats, while the NRP no longer held the balance of power in the National Assembly. The three Nevis seats were won by the NRP.

At an election to the Nevis Island Assembly in December 1987, the NRP retained four seats and the Concerned Citizens' Movement (CCM) secured one. At the general election of March 1989, however, the CCM took one of the three Nevis seats from the NRP. The PAM retained its six seats, and the Labour Party its two. Moore resigned as leader of the Labour Party and was succeeded by Denzil Douglas. The electoral success of the coalition Government under the leadership of Simmonds was attributed to its economic policies, and was achieved despite persistent rumours of official connivance in drugs-trafficking activities on the islands.

The CCM secured a majority in the Nevis Island Assembly at an election in June 1992, with three seats, while the NRP retained two. The leader of the CCM, Vance Amory, became Premier of the Nevis Island Administration.

At a general election in November 1993 neither the PAM nor the Labour Party managed to secure a majority in the National Assembly, with both parties winning four seats. On Nevis the CCM secured two seats, and the NRP one. Following the refusal of Amory to form a coalition government with either the PAM or the Labour Party, the Governor-General, Sir Clement Arrindell, invited Simmonds to form a minority government with the support of the NRP. Douglas protested against the decision and appealed for a general strike to support his demands for a further general election. Serious disturbances ensued, and in early December the Governor-General declared a 21-day state of emergency. Meanwhile, Simmonds withdrew from negotiations with Douglas, although an initial agreement to hold a further general election had been reached, in protest at Douglas's premature public revelation of the agreement.

In October 1994 six people were charged in connection with the murder, in Basseterre, of the head of the Saint Christopher special investigations police unit, Jude Matthew, who had been conducting an investigation into the recent disappearances of William Herbert, the country's Permanent Representative to the UN, and Vincent Morris, a son of the Deputy Prime Minister Sidney Morris. Preliminary investigations suggested that these events were connected to the discovery, at the same time as Morris's disappearance, of a large consignment of cocaine in Saint Christopher. In November Sidney Morris resigned, following the arrest of two other sons on charges related to drugs and firearms offences.

A 'forum for national unity' was convened in November 1994, at which representatives of all political parties, church organizations and tourism, trade, labour and law associations agreed to seek closer political co-operation in the months preceding an early general election, in order to halt the advance of drugs-related crime and the attendant erosion of investor confidence in the islands. None the less, fierce electoral campaigning culminated, in June 1995, in a violent clash between rival PAM and Labour Party supporters, which resulted in a number of serious injuries. The general election, conducted on 3 July, was won decisively by the Labour Party, and Denzil Douglas became Prime Minister. Simmonds was among prominent PAM politicians who lost their seats. Douglas resolved to address promptly the problems of increasingly violent crime and of deteriorating

---

*While this island is officially called Saint Christopher as part of the state, the name is usually abbreviated to St Kitts.

prison conditions. The Prime Minister also announced plans to draft proposals for constitutional reform that would provide for the establishment of separate governments for the two islands.

On 1 January 1996 Sir Cuthbert Montroville Sebastian succeeded Sir Clement Arrindell as Governor-General.

In June 1996 Amory announced that the Nevis Island Assembly was initiating proceedings (as detailed in the Constitution—see below) for the secession of Nevis from the federation with Saint Christopher. The announcement was made as plans proceeded for the establishment of a federal government office on Nevis (which Amory considered to be unconstitutional) and as the National Assembly considered a financial services bill that proposed referring all potential investors in Nevis to the federal administration for approval. The Nevis Island Assembly was reported to have interpreted both measures as serious infringements of its administrative rights. Despite the prompt intervention of a number of regional diplomatic initiatives to preserve the Federation, a secession bill for Nevis received its preliminary reading in the National Assembly in July. In October the NRP, while supportive of the right to secede, expressed concern at the precipitant nature of Amory's secession timetable, and in November the NRP representative in the National Assembly boycotted a second reading of the bill, forcing a postponement of the debate.

At elections to the Nevis Island Assembly in February 1997 Amory's CCM retained three of the five elective seats, while the NRP retained the remaining two. In October the Nevis Assembly voted unanimously in favour of secession; a referendum on the issue was held in August 1998, in which 61.7%, less than the two-thirds' majority required by the Constitution, voted for secession. The leaders of the two islands immediately announced that they would work to improve relations, and Douglas pledged to implement the principal recommendations of a constitutional review commission intended to augment inter-island affairs.

In July 1997 the National Assembly approved legislation to restore a full-time defence force, to include the coastguard, with the principal aim of strengthening the islands' anti-drugs operations. (The Simmonds administration had disbanded the army in 1981.) The Nevis administration and the PAM accused the Labour Government of seeking to enhance its authority by recruiting party loyalists to the force. In July 1998 a convicted murderer was executed—the first implementation of the death penalty in the country since 1985. The Attorney-General, Delano Bart, defended the reintroduction of capital punishment, against criticism from the Roman Catholic Church and the human rights organization Amnesty International, as part of the Government's strategy to reduce crime rates.

In March 1999 a Constitutional Task Force, chaired by former Governor Sir Fred Phillips, began work on the drafting of a new constitution. In August the Task Force submitted its report to the Prime Minister, who appointed a seven-member select committee, comprising representatives of all the major parties, to review its recommendations and to draft proposals for constitutional change.

At a general election in March 2000 the Labour Party won all eight seats available on Saint Christopher (with 65% of the votes cast), gaining the seat previously held by the PAM, which won 36% of the votes. There was no change in the position on Nevis, where the CCM retained its two seats and the NRP its one. In October Lindsay Grant, a lawyer, was elected the new leader of the PAM, replacing Simmonds.

The new Government sought to address the increasing crime rate on the islands, which was affecting the tourism industry. In February 2001 a curfew for all children under 15 was introduced in an effort to reduce youth crime, and in June the Government sought to persuade the US Navy to relocate one of its bases to Saint Christopher. Douglas stated his hope that the country would derive 'economic, social and financial' benefits from the US presence. The per-head murder rate in 2004 (22 murders per 100,000 people) was the third highest of the Caribbean Community and Common Market (CARICOM, see p. 196) countries, behind Jamaica and Belize, but ahead of both Guyana and Trinidad and Tobago. Although still alarmingly high by international standards, this rate had declined to 17 murders per 100,000 people by 2005. Compared with figures for 2005, Nevis island recorded a 7.2% decrease in the incidence of crime in 2006, while reporting a 4% increase in crime detection; it was hoped that the domestic security improvements these figures indicated would restore confidence and concomitantly promote tourism as the twin-island Federation continued its efforts towards greater economic diversification. It appeared that some success was being achieved in this area when, in April 2008, the World Travel and Tourism Council forecast that the country would register an increase in revenue from its tourist industry of 5.6% in that year, the second-highest in the region.

In elections to the Nevis Island Assembly in September 2001 the CCM, led by Amory, strengthened its control of the legislature, gaining a total of four elective seats. The NRP, under the leadership of Joseph Parry, took the remaining one seat.

In October 2002 Douglas, pronouncing on the recurring issue of greater autonomy for Nevis, said that, while he supported the constitutional right of Nevis to secede from the federation, the federal Government was willing to discuss ways to increase the autonomy of the Nevis Island Administration and Assembly. Amory, however, remained convinced that full autonomy and separate membership of the Organisation of Eastern Caribbean States (OECS, see p. 425) would be a better option for Nevis. In January 2004 an OECS Heads of Government meeting urged the Nevis administration to review its intention to campaign for independence in favour of preserving the status quo. CARICOM, in 2003, and the US Government, earlier in January 2004, also indicated their support for the existing federation.

The Labour Party was returned to office for a third consecutive term at a general election held on 25 October 2004. The incumbent administration, which campaigned on its social development record, won seven of the eight seats on Saint Christopher (with 60.4% of the votes cast—slightly fewer than in 2000); the PAM, whose leader, Lindsay Grant, narrowly failed to get elected, secured the other seat and attracted 37.8% of Saint Christopher's votes. The balance of power remained the same on Nevis where the CCM secured two seats (with 54% of the votes cast on Nevis) and the NRP secured one seat (and the remaining 46% of the island's votes). Turn-out on Saint Christopher was 62.2%, but was less than 50% overall, reflecting the dissatisfaction of many Nevisians with the current system. Although the voter-registration process was regarded as imperfect (not least because of a long-standing failure of the authorities to remove the names of dead or migrated people from the electoral list), the team of CARICOM observers monitoring the election reported the contest to be generally free and fair.

The NRP emerged from 15 years in opposition to secure a legislative majority at an election to the Nevis Island Assembly, on 10 July 2006. The party captured three of the five elective seats, while the CCM won the remaining two seats. The NRP's leader, Joseph Parry, took office as Nevis Island Premier later in the same month. The issue of secession was again foregrounded, with the participating parties presenting opposing stances on a move towards greater autonomy; the outgoing CCM had campaigned for independence from Saint Christopher, while the NRP indicated a preference for constitutional reform. In January 2007 Prime Minister Douglas encouraged the pursuit of greater collaboration between the two islands; by this time the possibility of an imminent referendum on Nevis, promulgated by the former CCM Government, seemed, once again, to have receded.

Remarks made by Commonwealth and CARICOM observers of the 2004 general election precipitated governmental discussions from that year towards electoral reform in an effort to achieve a more comprehensive and democratic system of voting and greater regulation of campaign practices. Amendments proposed under the 'Road Map for Electoral Reform', submitted to the National Assembly in August 2006, included: the supervision of campaign spending; the consideration of constitutional revisions to provide for more inclusive consultations, particularly with political organizations without parliamentary representation; and a review and possible redefinition of constituency boundaries to achieve more proportional representation of the electorate. It was also suggested that a national registration scheme be conducted to ensure that records of eligible voters were current and accurate, and proposals for a voter identification card initiative, first advanced by the St Kitts-Nevis Labour Party in 2000, were also resurrected. The Electoral Reform Consultative Committee (ERCC) was to conduct a public consultation and submit a report of its findings to the National Advisory Electoral Reform and Boundaries Commission (NAERBC) by 17 November 2006, following which the NAERBC would present its recommendations to a parliamentary committee. However, the initial ERCC report was only received on 1 February 2007, inciting opposition party consternation and public concern about the transparency and effectiveness of the reform process. Nevertheless, the Government began to implement new legislation in early 2008 when the National Identification Card was introduced for registered voters, who were to receive the card on re-

registering at an electoral office. The opposition again expressed dissatisfaction, claiming there were a number of discrepancies with the process, including the opportunity for voters to confirm their addresses in multiple constituencies.

Saint Christopher and Nevis is a member of CARICOM and of the OECS. In the late 1980s regional discussions were held on the issue of political unity in the East Caribbean. Saint Christopher and Nevis expressed interest in political unity only if the proposed merger included its Leeward Island neighbours and the Virgin Islands, where an estimated 10,000 Kittitians and Nevisians reside. From January 1990 the OECS agreed to relax restrictions on travel between member states. Moreover, in February 2002 it was agreed, with effect from March, to allow nationals of member states to travel freely within the OECS area and to remain in the territory of any other member state for up to six months. A CARICOM passport, designed to enhance a sense of community and facilitate intra- and extra-regional travel for citizens of participating nations, was launched in January 2005 and implemented by Saint Christopher and Nevis in October of that year; the initiative, declared as integral to economic integration within the Caribbean, was expected to have been effected by all 15 member governments by 2008. In early 2006 the Prime Minister indicated that Saint Christopher and Nevis would join CARICOM's Caribbean Single Market and Economy (CSME), which was established by six founding member states on 1 January, later in that year. The CSME was intended to enshrine the free movement of goods, services and labour throughout the CARICOM region, although no OECS countries were signatories to the new project from its inauguration. Subsequently, at the 27th CARICOM Heads of Government Conference held in Saint Christopher and Nevis on 6 July, the Government—together with those of five other Caribbean states—signed a declaration of participation in the CSME. The two-island Federation acceded to the Non-aligned Movement in September 2006, and, in the same month, became the 102nd state delegation to join the International Criminal Court (instituted in The Hague, Netherlands, in July 2002).

In September 2005 Douglas reiterated the Government's commitment to its lucrative diplomatic relationship with Taiwan. Saint Christopher and Nevis, along with Saint Vincent and the Grenadines, remained the only Caribbean countries still to recognize the statehood of Taiwan, which was losing a contest of so-called 'dollar diplomacy' in the region with the People's Republic of China. In January 2008 Saint Christopher and Nevis opened an embassy in Taiwan, the first embassy of a Caribbean country to be located in Asia. However, relations were briefly strained in April when the Government of Saint Christopher and Nevis failed to send a congratulatory message to the winner of Taiwan's presidential election, Ma Ying-jeou, until some two weeks after the ballot. Vice-President Annette Lu Hsu-lien claimed that diplomatic relations were fragile but the Chargé d'affaires of Saint Christopher and Nevis in Taiwan, Jasmine Huggins, denied the pronouncement and claimed that her message had not been sent earlier due to personal problems.

Government

Saint Christopher and Nevis is a constitutional monarchy. Executive power is vested in the British monarch, as Head of State, and is exercised locally by the monarch's personal representative, the Governor-General, who acts in accordance with the advice of the Cabinet. Legislative power is vested in Parliament, comprising the monarch and the National Assembly. The National Assembly is composed of the Speaker, three (or, if a nominated member is Attorney-General, four) nominated members, known as Senators (two appointed on the advice of the Premier and one appointed on the advice of the Leader of the Opposition), and 11 elected members (Representatives), who are chosen from single-member constituencies for up to five years by universal adult suffrage. The Cabinet comprises the Prime Minister, who must be able to command the support of the majority of the members of the National Assembly, the Attorney-General (ex officio) and four other ministers. The Prime Minister and the Cabinet are responsible to Parliament.

The Nevis Island legislature comprises the Nevis Island Assembly and the Nevis Island Administration, headed by the British monarch (who is represented on the island by the Deputy Governor-General). It operates similarly to the Saint Christopher and Nevis legislature but has power to secede from the Federation, subject to certain restrictions (see Constitution, below).

Defence

The small army was disbanded by the Government in 1981, and its duties were absorbed by the Volunteer Defence Force and a special tactical unit of the police. In July 1997 the National Assembly approved legislation to re-establish a full-time defence force. Coastguard operations were to be brought under military command; the defence force was also to include cadet and reserve forces. Saint Christopher and Nevis participates in the US-sponsored Regional Security System, comprising police, coastguards and army units, which was established by independent East Caribbean states in 1982. Budgetary expenditure on national security in 1998 was approximately EC $23.8m.

Economic Affairs

In 2006, according to estimates by the World Bank, Saint Christopher and Nevis's gross national income (GNI), measured at average 2004–06 prices, was US $428m., equivalent to $8,840 per head (or $12,690 per head on an international purchasing-power parity basis). During 1996–2006 the population increased by an average of 1.7% per year, while over the same period, it was estimated, gross domestic product (GDP) per head increased, in real terms, at an average annual rate of 1.9%. Overall GDP increased, in real terms, by an average of 3.7% annually in 1996–2006; according to the Eastern Caribbean Central Bank (ECCB, see p. 415), growth was 4.9% in 2006.

Agriculture (including forestry and fishing) contributed 2.4% of GDP in 2006. According to FAO estimates, some 19.0% of the working population were employed in the agriculture sector (including sugar manufacturing) in 2005. Major crops include coconuts and sea-island cotton, although some vegetables are also exported. Sugar and sugar products had dominated the economy since the 1960s, but the industry, which had accumulated a debt of US $141.5m. (mainly with the St Kitts-Nevis-Anguilla National Bank and the Development Bank of St Kitts and Nevis), closed after the 2005 harvest and workers at the St Kitts Sugar Manufacturing Corporation received their final payments in March 2006. In spite of a guaranteed European Union (EU, see p. 244) sugar price, which was well above world market levels, the sugar industry had survived only as a result of government subsidies, which were equivalent to 3.5% of GDP in 2001. Large areas formerly used for sugar have been redesignated for tourism and the Government was expected to make provision for the retraining of sugar industry employees. Other important crops include yams, sweet potatoes, groundnuts, onions, sweet peppers, cabbages, carrots and bananas. In 2004 the Government entered into a partnership with a Canadian corporation to cultivate Stevia—a herb used as a sweetener or dietary supplement. In addition, fishing is an increasingly important commercial activity. According to ECCB estimates, agricultural GDP decreased by an annual average of 2.9% in 1998–2006. The real value of agricultural GDP decreased by 21.2% in 2006.

Industry (including mining, manufacturing, construction and public utilities) provided 23.6% of GDP in 2006. Excluding sugar manufacturing, the sector employed 21.0% of the working population in 1994. The 2007 Cricket World Cup increased the demand for construction services, with much of the public sector work concentrated on the Warner Park sports complex. According to ECCB estimates, the construction sector expanded by 9.0% in 2006. Real industrial GDP increased by an estimated annual average of 7.7% in 1998–2006. In 2006 the GDP of the sector expanded by an estimated 2.4%.

Manufacturing provided 8.2% of GDP in 2006, and non-sugar manufacturing employed 7.8% of the working population in 1994. Apart from the sugar industry (the production of raw sugar and ethyl alcohol), the principal manufactured products are garments, electrical components, food products, beer and other beverages. The sector recorded estimated average annual growth of 3.5% during 1998–2006. In 2006, according to ECCB estimates, real manufacturing GDP declined by 4.2%.

The islands are dependent upon imports of fuel and energy (8.8% of total imports in 2005) for their energy requirements. In September 2005 the Government became one of 13 Caribbean administrations to sign the PetroCaribe accord, under which Saint Christopher and Nevis would be allowed to purchase petroleum from Venezuela at reduced prices. However, Venezuela reportedly made no shipments of petroleum to Saint Christopher and Nevis in 2007. In the 2008 budget address the Government signalled its intention to explore alternative energy sources and thereby decrease its dependency on costly fuel imports.

SAINT CHRISTOPHER AND NEVIS

The services sector contributed 74.1% of GDP in 2006, and employed 64.4% of the working population in 1994. Tourism is a major contributor to the economy. In 2002, mainly as a result of a contraction in the US tourism market and hurricane damage to the hotel stock, the number of stop-over arrivals fell by 10.1% and the number of cruise-ship passengers decreased by 34.0%. However, the sector stabilized in 2003, and in 2004 the sector built strongly on its recovery when the total number of visitors increased by 54.9%. In 2005 the number of stop-over tourists continued to increase, by 8.0% (to 127,025), although the number of cruise-ship passengers declined by 15.8% (to 214,218). This strong performance was not repeated in 2006, during which visitor arrivals were estimated to have declined by 2.4% (a result attributed mainly to the lower number of cruise-ship and yacht passengers visiting the island). The real GDP of the services sector increased at an average annual rate of 3.7% in 1998–2006; growth was an estimated 6.0% in 2006.

In 2006 Saint Christopher and Nevis recorded an estimated visible trade deficit of EC $435.52m. and there was a deficit of some $56.63m. on the current account of the balance of payments. The USA was the islands' principal trading partner in 2003, supplying 53.3% of imports and purchasing 78.5% of exports. Trade with the United Kingdom and with other Caribbean states is also important. In 2003 electrical machinery was the country's leading export (accounting for 73.0% of total export revenues in 2003), and the principal imports are machinery and transport equipment, basic manufactures and food and live animals.

In 2006 the central Government of Saint Christopher and Nevis recorded an estimated budgetary deficit of EC $49.7m., equivalent to 3.7% of GDP. In 2006 the Caribbean Development Bank (CBD) offered EC $12m., in tandem with a bond issue of approximately EC $150m., to consolidate national debt and fiscal sustainability. The country's total external debt was estimated to be US $301.1m. at the end of 2005, of which US $299.3m. was long-term public debt. In that year the cost of debt-servicing was equivalent to 22.8% of the value of exports of goods and services. Total public sector debt reached an estimated 107% of GDP in December 2007, although since 2005 the Government has negotiated no further loans from external financiers, preferring instead to borrow from an existing overdraft facility. The annual rate of inflation averaged 1.9% in 2000–05; consumer prices increased by 2.3% in 2004 and by 1.8% in 2005. There is, however, a recurring problem of labour shortages in the agricultural sector (which will be eased by the collapse of the sugar industry) and the construction industry, and the rate of unemployment (reported to be around 10% in early 2003) is mitigated by mass emigration, particularly from Nevis: remittances from abroad provide an important source of revenue.

Saint Christopher and Nevis is a member of the Caribbean Community and Common Market (CARICOM, see p. 196), and of the Organisation of Eastern Caribbean States (OECS, see p. 425). The ECCB is based in Basseterre. In 2001 a regional stock exchange, the Eastern Caribbean Securities Exchange, opened in Basseterre. Saint Christopher and Nevis is a party to the Cotonou Agreement (see p. 301), the successor agreement to the Lomé Convention, signed in June 2000 between the EU and a group of developing countries.

Successive Governments attempted to reduce economic dependence on the cultivation and processing of sugar cane, the traditional industry of the islands, and in 2005 the state-run industry was finally closed and its assets dismantled and recycled. The most rapidly developing industry has been tourism, which was estimated by the World Travel and Tourism Council to provide some 28.6% of the country's GDP and 29.1% of employment in 2005. Expansion of this crucial sector stimulated economic growth of 4.9% in 2005. In more recent years greater focus has been placed on upmarket tourism, with a number of luxury resorts and a Marina village scheduled for construction during 2007–09. The development of light manufacturing, particularly of electronic components and textiles, has also helped to broaden the islands' economic base. In addition, a small 'offshore' financial sector on Nevis, which, by 2004, had registered 15,000 International Business Companies and 950 trusts, has been developed. Unfortunately, the division of regulatory powers between the island administration on Nevis and the federal Government has at times been unclear. Partly for this reason, Saint Christopher and Nevis was, in June 2000, listed as a 'non-co-operative jurisdiction' by the Financial Action Task Force on Money Laundering (FATF—based at the Secretariat of the Organisation for Economic Co-operation and Development in Paris, France); however, the island was removed from this list in 2002, after instituting stricter regulatory controls. In April 2003 a report indicated that the islands' 'offshore' banking operations had been halved as a result of the FATF action and the subsequent financial reforms; nevertheless, the banking and insurance sector was estimated to have grown by 7.5% in 2005. In his December 2005 budget speech, the Prime Minister introduced several new taxation measures designed to strengthen government revenue in the near term, particularly in the period before the 2007 Cricket World Cup, to be jointly hosted by Saint Christopher and Nevis and several other Caribbean countries and territories. However, contrary to predictions, this event failed to stimulate growth in tourism revenue and receipts declined slightly in 2007. Following the announcement of the closure of the sugar industry in March 2005, the EU provided grants worth US $14.6m. to Saint Christopher and Nevis. A further €165m. was pledged in 2007. The EU planned to release the funds over an eight-year period to assist with structural adjustment and economic diversification. The total cost of the transition to a non-sugar-producing economy was estimated at some $50m. Real GDP increased by an estimated 3.3% in 2007 and the IMF predicted further growth of 3.5% for 2008.

Education

Education is compulsory for 12 years between five and 17 years of age. Primary education begins at the age of five, and lasts for seven years. Secondary education, from the age of 12, generally comprises a first cycle of four years, followed by a second cycle of two years. In 2004/05 enrolment at primary schools included 93.4% of children in the relevant age-group, while comparable enrolment at secondary schools included 86.1% of pupils. There are 30 state, eight private and five denominational schools. There is also a technical college. Budgetary expenditure on education by the central Government in 1998 was projected to be EC $25m. (6.7% of total government expenditure). In September 2000 a privately financed 'offshore' medical college, the Medical University of the Americas, opened in Nevis with 40 students registered. The Ross University of School of Veterinary Medicine and the International University of Nursing also operated on Saint Christopher. A Basic Education Project, funded by the Caribbean Development Bank, was in 2003 complemented by a $18.8m. Secondary Education Project, which was to include the construction of a new secondary school and Multi-Purpose Learning Complex in Saddlers.

Public Holidays

2008: 1 January (New Year's Day), 2 January (Carnival Last Lap), 21 March (Good Friday), 24 March (Easter Monday), 1 May (May Day), 12 May (Whit Monday), 11 June (Queen's Official Birthday), 4 August (August Monday), 5 August (Nevis only: Culturama Last Lap), 16 September (Heroes Day), 19 September (Independence Day), 25–26 December (Christmas).

2009: 1 January (New Year's Day), 2 January (Carnival Last Lap), 10 April (Good Friday), 13 April (Easter Monday), 4 May (May Day), 1 June (Whit Monday), 11 June (Queen's Official Birthday), 3 August (August Monday), 7 August (Nevis only: Culturama Last Lap), 17 September (Heroes Day), 19 September (Independence Day), 25–26 December (Christmas).

Weights and Measures

The imperial system is used.

Statistical Survey

Source (unless otherwise stated): St Kitts and Nevis Information Service, Government Headquarters, Church St, POB 186, Basseterre; tel. 465-2521; fax 466-4504; e-mail skninfo@caribsurf.com; internet www.stkittsnevis.net.

AREA AND POPULATION

Area (sq km): 269.4 (Saint Christopher 176.1, Nevis 93.3).

Population: 40,618 (males 19,933, females 20,685) at census of 12 May 1991; 45,841 (males 22,784, females 23,057) at census of 14 May 2001. *2006:* 49,995 (mid-year estimate). Sources: UN, *Population and Vital Statistics Report* and Eastern Caribbean Central Bank.

Density (mid-2006): 185.6 per sq km.

Principal Town (estimated population incl. suburbs, mid-2003): Basseterre (capital) 13,262. Source: UN, *World Urbanization Prospects: The 2003 Revision*.

Births and Deaths (2001): Registered live births 803 (birth rate 17.4 per 1,000); Registered deaths 352 (death rate 7.6 per 1,000). *2003:* Crude birth rate 15.6 per 1,000; Crude death rate 7.6 per 1,000 (Source: Caribbean Development Bank, *Social and Economic Indicators*).

Expectation of life (years at birth, WHO estimates): 70.8 (males 69.4; females 72.2) in 2005. Source: WHO, *World Health Statistics*.

Employment (labour force survey, 1994): Sugar cane production/manufacturing 1,525; Non-sugar agriculture 914; Mining and quarrying 29; Manufacturing (excl. sugar) 1,290; Electricity, gas and water 416; Construction 1,745; Trade (except tourism) 1,249; Tourism 2,118; Transport and communications 534; Business and general services 3,708; Government services 2,738; Other statutory bodies 342; *Total* 16,608 (Saint Christopher 12,516, Nevis 4,092). Source: IMF, *St Kitts and Nevis: Recent Economic Developments* (August 1997).

HEALTH AND WELFARE
Key Indicators

Total Fertility Rate (children per woman, 2005): 2.3.

Under-5 Mortality Rate (per 1,000 live births, 2005): 20.

Physicians (per 1,000 head, 1997): 1.19.

Hospital Beds (per 1,000 head, 2005): 5.5.

Health Expenditure (2004): US $ per head (PPP): 709.6.

Health Expenditure (2004): % of GDP: 5.2.

Health Expenditure (2004): public (% of total): 63.2.

Access to Water (% of persons, 2004): 100.

Access to Sanitation (% of persons, 2004): 95.

Human Development Index (2005): ranking: 54.

Human Development Index (2005): value: 0.821.

For sources and definitions, see explanatory note on p. vi.

AGRICULTURE, ETC.

Principal Crops ('000 metric tons, 2005): Sugar cane 100.0; Coconuts 1.0. *Aggregate Production* ('000 metric tons, may include official, semi-official or estimated data): Roots and tubers 1.0; Vegetables (incl. melons) 0.6; Fruits (excl. melons) 1.3. *2006:* Figures for aggregate production assumed to be unchanged from 2005 (FAO estimates).

Livestock ('000 head, 2005): Cattle 4.8; Sheep 12.5; Goats 16.0; Pigs 2.0 (FAO estimate). Note: Data for 2006 were not available.

Livestock Products ('000 metric tons, 2005, FAO estimates unless otherwise indicated): Pig meat 0.1; Chicken meat 0.2; Hen eggs 0.2 (official figure). Note: Data for 2006 were not available.

Fishing (metric tons, live weight, 2005, FAO estimates): Groupers 25; Snappers 70; Grunts, sweetlips 10; Goatfishes, red mullets 80; Parrotfishes 45; Surgeonfishes 40; Triggerfishes, durgons 20; Caribbean spiny lobster 40; Stromboid conchs 90; *Total catch* (incl. others) 450.

Source: FAO.

INDUSTRY

Production: Raw sugar 10,700 metric tons in 2005; Electric energy 212.5 million kWh in 2006. Sources: IMF, *St Kitts and Nevis: Statistical Appendix* (April 2008) and Eastern Caribbean Central Bank.

FINANCE

Currency and Exchange Rates: 100 cents = 1 Eastern Caribbean dollar (EC $). *Sterling, US Dollar and Euro Equivalents* (30 November 2007): £1 sterling = EC $5.579; US $1 = EC $2.700; €1 = EC $3.985; EC $100 = £17.92 = US $37.04 = €25.09. *Exchange Rate*: Fixed at US $1 = EC $2.70 since July 1976.

Budget (EC $ million, 2007, estimates): *Revenue:* Revenue from taxation 319.9 (Taxes on income 96.1, Taxes on property 7.6, Taxes on domestic goods and services 50.0, Taxes on international trade and transactions 166.2); Other current revenue 91.3; Capital revenue 4.1; Foreign grants 20.0; Total 435.3. *Expenditure:* Current expenditure 385.7 (Personal emoluments and wages 148.1, Goods and services 94.5, Interest payments 83.7, Transfers and subsidies 59.3); Capital expenditure and net lending 99.3; Total 485.0.

International Reserves (US $ million at 31 December 2006): Reserve position in IMF 0.12; Foreign exchange 88.57; Total 88.70. Source: IMF, *International Financial Statistics*.

Money Supply (EC $ million at 31 December 2006): Currency outside banks 55.10; Demand deposits at deposit money banks 175.00; Total money 230.12. Source: IMF, *International Financial Statistics*.

Cost of Living (Consumer Price Index; base: 2000 = 100): 106.6 in 2003; 109.0 in 2004; 111.0 in 2005. Source: IMF, *International Financial Statistics*.

Gross Domestic Product (EC $ million at constant 1990 prices): 718.80 in 2004; 753.10 in 2005; 801.08 in 2006. Source: Eastern Caribbean Central Bank.

Expenditure on the Gross Domestic Product (EC $ million at current prices, 2006): Government final consumption expenditure 239.73; Private final consumption expenditure 710.53; Gross fixed capital formation 551.34; *Total domestic expenditure* 1,501.60; Exports of goods and services 583.27; *Less* Imports of goods and services 748.31; *GDP at market prices* 1,336.56. Source: Caribbean Development Bank.

Gross Domestic Product by Economic Activity (EC $ million at current factor cost, 2006): Agriculture, hunting, forestry and fishing 28.13; Mining and quarrying 3.00; Manufacturing 98.00; Electricity and water 28.57; Construction 152.26; Wholesale and retail trade 130.93; Restaurants and hotels 95.23; Transport 110.07; Communications 62.48; Finance and insurance 226.91; Real estate and housing 26.74; Government services 189.08; Other community, social and personal services 44.68; *Sub-total* 1,196.08; *Less* Financial intermediation services indirectly measured 116.47; *Total in basic prices* 1,079.61; Taxes, less subsidies, on products 256.95 *GDP at market prices* 1,336.56. Source: Eastern Caribbean Central Bank.

Balance of Payments (EC $ million, 2006): *Trade balance* –435.52; *Services* (net) 179.23; *Balance on goods and services* –256.29; Other income received (net) –87.32; *Balance on goods, services and income* –343.61; Current transfers received (net) 86.97; *Current balance* –256.63; Capital account (net) 35.53; Direct investment from abroad (net) 298.12; Portfolio investment (net) –56.60; Other investment (net) 0.43; Net errors and omissions 25.46; *Overall balance* 46.30. Source: Eastern Caribbean Central Bank.

EXTERNAL TRADE

Principal Commodities (US $ million, 2003): *Imports c.i.f.:* Food and live animals 27.8; Mineral fuels, lubricants, etc. 17.7 (Refined petroleum products 16.5); Chemicals 14.1; Basic manufactures 44.3 (Iron and steel manufactures 9.8); Machinery and transport equipment 58.5 (Road vehicles 12.7); Total (incl. others) 204.8. *Exports f.o.b.:* Food and live animals 8.0 (Raw sugar 7.2); Basic manufactures 0.6 (Metal manufactures 0.3); Machinery and transport equipment 37.3 (Electrical machinery 35.3); Miscellaneous manufactures 1.4 (Printed matter 0.8); Total (incl. others) 48.3. Source: UN, *International Trade Statistics Yearbook*. 2005 (EC $ million): Total imports 568.3; Total exports 147.0. 2006 (EC $ million): Total imports 673.7; Total exports 158.2 (Source: Eastern Caribbean Central Bank).

Principal Trading Partners (US $ million, 2003): *Imports:* Barbados 4.7; Canada 18.8; France 1.2; Japan 6.5; Netherlands 0.6; Trinidad and Tobago 26.5; United Kingdom 18.7; USA 109.2; Total (incl. others) 204.8. *Exports* (excl. re-exports): Dominica 0.3; United Kingdom 8.2; USA 37.9; Total (incl. others) 48.3. Source: UN, *International Trade Statistics Yearbook*.

SAINT CHRISTOPHER AND NEVIS

TRANSPORT

Road Traffic (registered motor vehicles): 11,352 in 1998; 12,432 in 1999; 12,917 in 2000.

Shipping: *Arrivals* (2000): 1,981 vessels. *International Sea-borne Freight Traffic* ('000 metric tons, 2000): Goods loaded 24.7; Goods unloaded 234.2. *Merchant Fleet* (vessels registered at 31 December 2006): Number 136; Total displacement 473,191 grt (Source: Lloyd's Register-Fairplay, *World Fleet Statistics*).

Civil Aviation (aircraft arrivals): 24,800 in 1998; 23,500 in 1999; 19,400 in 2000.

TOURISM

Visitor Arrivals: 382,290 (117,638 stop-over visitors, 3,045 excursionists, 7,072 yacht passengers, 254,535 cruise-ship passengers) in 2004; 350,737 (127,025 stop-over visitors, 3,471 excursionists, 6,023 yacht passengers, 214,218 cruise ship passengers) in 2005 (estimate); 342,165 (132,321 stop-over visitors, 3,893 excursionists, 2,876 yacht passengers, 203,075 cruise ship passengers) in 2006 (estimate).

Tourism Receipts (EC $ million): 277.1 in 2004; 309.2 in 2005 (estimate); 314.1 in 2006 (estimate).

Source: Eastern Caribbean Central Bank.

COMMUNICATIONS MEDIA

Radio Receivers ('000 in use, 1997): 28.

Television Receivers ('000 in use, 1999): 10.

Telephones ('000 main lines in use, 2005): 25.

Facsimile Machines (1996): 450.

Mobile Cellular Telephones (subscribers, 2004): 10,000.

Personal Computers (2004): 11,000.

Internet Users (2004): 10,000.

Broadband Subscribers (2004): 500.

Non-daily Newspapers (2000): Titles 4; Circulation 34,000 (1996).

Sources: mainly UNESCO, *Statistical Yearbook*; UN, *Statistical Yearbook*; International Telecommunication Union.

EDUCATION

Pre-primary (2003/04 unless otherwise indicated): 77 schools; 315 teachers (2004/05); 1,910 pupils.

Primary (2004/05 unless otherwise indicated): 23 schools (2003/04); 360 teachers; 6,350 pupils.

Secondary (2004/05 unless otherwise indicated): 7 schools (2003/04); 397 teachers; 3,939 pupils.

Tertiary (2003/04): 1 institution; 79 teachers; 751 students.

Adult Literacy Rate: 97.8% in 2004 (Source: UN Development Programme, *Human Development Report*).

Source: mostly UNESCO Institute for Statistics.

Directory

The Constitution

The Constitution of the Federation of Saint Christopher and Nevis took effect from 19 September 1983, when the territory achieved independence. Its main provisions are summarized below:

FUNDAMENTAL RIGHTS AND FREEDOMS

Regardless of race, place of origin, political opinion, colour, creed or sex, but subject to respect for the rights and freedoms of others and for the public interest, every person in Saint Christopher and Nevis is entitled to the rights of life, liberty, security of person, equality before the law and the protection of the law. Freedom of conscience, of expression, of assembly and association is guaranteed, and the inviolability of personal privacy, family life and property is maintained. Protection is afforded from slavery, forced labour, torture and inhuman treatment.

THE GOVERNOR-GENERAL

The Governor-General is appointed by the British monarch, whom the Governor-General represents locally. The Governor-General must be a citizen of Saint Christopher and Nevis, and must appoint a Deputy Governor-General, in accordance with the wishes of the Premier of Nevis, to represent the Governor-General on that island.

PARLIAMENT

Parliament consists of the British monarch, represented by the Governor-General, and the National Assembly, which includes a Speaker, three (or, if a nominated member is Attorney-General, four) nominated members (Senators) and 11 elected members (Representatives). Senators are appointed by the Governor-General; one on the advice of the Leader of the Opposition, and the other two in accordance with the wishes of the Prime Minister. The Representatives are elected by universal suffrage, one from each of the 11 single-member constituencies.

Every citizen over the age of 18 years is eligible to vote. Parliament may alter any of the provisions of the Constitution.

THE EXECUTIVE

Executive authority is vested in the British monarch, as Head of State, and is exercised on the monarch's behalf by the Governor-General, either directly or through subordinate officers. The Governor-General appoints as Prime Minister that Representative who, in the Governor-General's opinion, appears to be best able to command the support of the majority of the Representatives. Other ministerial appointments are made by the Governor-General, in consultation with the Prime Minister, from among the members of the National Assembly. The Governor-General may remove the Prime Minister from office if a resolution of 'no confidence' in the Government is passed by the National Assembly and if the Prime Minister does not resign within three days or advise the Governor-General to dissolve Parliament.

The Cabinet consists of the Prime Minister and other Ministers. When the office of Attorney-General is a public office, the Attorney-General shall, by virtue of holding that office, be a member of the Cabinet in addition to the other Ministers. The Governor-General appoints as Leader of the Opposition in the National Assembly that Representative who, in the Governor-General's opinion, appears to be best able to command the support of the majority of the Representatives who do not support the Government.

CITIZENSHIP

All persons born in Saint Christopher and Nevis before independence who, immediately before independence, were citizens of the United Kingdom and Colonies automatically become citizens of Saint Christopher and Nevis. All persons born in Saint Christopher and Nevis after independence automatically acquire citizenship, as do those born outside Saint Christopher and Nevis after independence to a parent possessing citizenship. There are provisions for the acquisition of citizenship by those to whom it is not automatically granted.

THE ISLAND OF NEVIS

There is a Legislature for the island of Nevis which consists of the British monarch, represented by the Governor-General, and the Nevis Island Assembly. The Assembly consists of three nominated members (one appointed by the Governor-General in accordance with the advice of the Leader of the Opposition in the Assembly, and two appointed by the Governor-General in accordance with the advice of the Premier) and such number of elected members as corresponds directly with the number of electoral districts on the island.

There is a Nevis Island Administration, consisting of a premier and two other members who are appointed by the Governor-General. The Governor-General appoints the Premier as the person who, in the Governor-General's opinion, is best able to command the support of the majority of the elected members of the Assembly. The other members of the Administration are appointed by the Governor-General, acting in accordance with the wishes of the Premier. The Administration has exclusive responsibility for administration within the island of Nevis, in accordance with the provisions of any relevant laws.

The Nevis Island Legislature may provide that the island of Nevis is to cease to belong to the Federation of Saint Christopher and Nevis, in which case this Constitution would cease to have effect in the island of Nevis. Provisions for the possible secession of the island contain the following requirements: that the island must give full and detailed proposals for the future Constitution of the island of Nevis, which must be laid before the Assembly for a period of at least six months prior to the proposed date of secession; that a two-thirds majority has been gained in a referendum which is to be held after the Assembly has passed the motion.

SAINT CHRISTOPHER AND NEVIS

The Government

HEAD OF STATE

Monarch: HM Queen Elizabeth II.
Governor-General: Sir Cuthbert Montroville Sebastian (took office 1 January 1996).

CABINET
(April 2008)

Prime Minister and Minister of Finance, Sustainable Development, Information and Technology, Tourism, Culture and Sport: Dr Denzil Llewellyn Douglas.
Deputy Prime Minister and Minister of Education, Youth, Social and Community Development and Gender Affairs: Sam Terrence Condor.
Minister of Public Works, Utilities, Transport and Postal Services: Dr Earl Asim Martin.
Minister of National Security, Immigration and Labour: Gerald Anthony Dwyer Astaphan.
Minister of Health: Rupert Emmanuel Herbert.
Minister of Foreign Affairs, International Trade, Industry and Commerce: Timothy Sylvester Harris.
Minister of Housing, Agriculture and Fisheries and Consumer Affairs: Cedric Roy Liburd.
Attorney-General and Minister of Justice and of Legal Affairs: Dennis Merchant.
Minister of State in the Ministry of Finance, Sustainable Development, Information and Technology: Sen. Nigel Alexis Carty.
Minister of State in the Ministry of Tourism, Culture and Sport: Sen. Richard Oliver Skerritt.

MINISTRIES

Office of the Governor-General: Government House, Basseterre; tel. 465-2315.
Government Headquarters: Church St, POB 186, Basseterre; tel. 465-2521; fax 466-4505; e-mail infocom@sisterisles.kn; internet www.gov.kn.
Prime Minister's Office: Government Headquarters, Church St, POB 186, Basseterre; tel. 465-9698; fax 465-9997; e-mail sknpmpresssec@cuopm.com; internet www.cuopm.org.
Attorney-General's Office and Ministry of Legal Affairs: Church St, POB 164, Basseterre; tel. 465-2521; fax 465-5040; e-mail attorneygeneral@gov.kn.
Ministry of Education and Youth: Church St, POB 333, Basseterre; tel. 465-2521.
Ministry of Finance, Sustainable Development, Information and Technology: Church St, POB 186, Basseterre; tel. 465-2521; fax 465-0198; e-mail adminskbmof@caribsurf.com; internet gip.gov.kn/mp.asp?mp=7.
Ministry of Foreign Affairs, International Trade, Industry, Commerce and Consumer Affairs: Church St, POB 186, Basseterre; tel. 465-2521; fax 465-5202; e-mail foreigna@sisterisles.kn; internet gip.gov.kn/mp.asp?mp=6.
Ministry of Health: Church St, POB 186, Basseterre; tel. 465-2521.
Ministry of Housing, Agriculture and Fisheries: East Park Range, Basseterre; tel. 466-4701; fax 466-4702; e-mail nhcorp@hotmail.com.
Ministry of Justice: Pelican Mall, Basseterre; tel. 465-2521; fax 466-1896.
Ministry of National Security, Immigration and Labour: Pelican Mall, Basseterre; tel. 465-2521; fax 466-1896; e-mail natsec@caribsurf.com.
Ministry of Public Works, Utilities, Transport and Postal Services: Needsmust, Basseterre; tel. 465-2521; fax 465-5501.
Ministry of Tourism, Culture and Sport: POB 878, Port Zante, Basseterre; tel. 465-2521; fax 465-7075; e-mail culture@sisterisles.kn.

NEVIS ISLAND ADMINISTRATION

Premier: Joseph W. Parry.
There are also two appointed members.
Administrative Centre: Main St, POB 689, Charlestown, Nevis; tel. 469-1469; fax 469-0039; e-mail nevfin@caribsurf.com; internet www.gisnevis.com.

Legislature

NATIONAL ASSEMBLY

Speaker: Marcella Liburd.
Elected members: 11. Nominated members: 3. Ex officio members: 1.
Election, 25 October 2004

Party	% of votes	Seats
St Kitts-Nevis Labour Party	50.6	7
Concerned Citizens' Movement	8.8	2
People's Action Movement	31.7	1
Nevis Reformation Party	7.5	1
Total (incl. others)	100.0	11

NEVIS ISLAND ASSEMBLY

Elected members: 5. Nominated members: 3.
Elections to the Nevis Island Assembly took place in July 2006. The Nevis Reformation Party took three seats and the Concerned Citizens' Movement secured the remaining two seats.

Political Organizations

Concerned Citizens' Movement (CCM): Charlestown, Nevis; tel. 469-3519; e-mail renaissance_trust@yahoo.com; internet www.myccmparty.com; Leader Vance W. Amory.
Nevis Reformation Party (NRP): Government Rd, POB 480, Charlestown, Nevis; tel. 469-0630; e-mail JosephParry@VoteNRP.com; internet www.votenrp.com; f. 1970; Leader Joseph W. Parry; Sec. Dwight Cozier.
People's Action Movement (PAM): POB 1294, Basseterre; tel. 466-2726; fax 465-0857; e-mail pamdemocrat@pamdemocrat.org; internet www.pamdemocrat.org/party; f. 1965; Political Leader Lindsay Grant; Deputy Leaders Shawn Richards, Eugene Hamilton.
St Kitts-Nevis Labour Party (SKNLP): Masses House, Church St, POB 239, Basseterre; tel. 465-5347; fax 465-8328; e-mail wanda.connor@sknlabourparty.com; internet www.sknlabourparty.org; f. 1932; socialist party; Chair. Dr Timothy Harris; Leader Dr Denzil Llewellyn Douglas.

Diplomatic Representation

EMBASSIES IN SAINT CHRISTOPHER AND NEVIS

China (Taiwan): Taylor's Range, POB 119, Basseterre; tel. 465-2421; fax 465-7921; e-mail rocemb@caribsurf.com; Ambassador Rong-chuen Wu.
Cuba: 34 Bladen Housing Devt, POB 600, Basseterre; tel. 466-3374; fax 468-8072; e-mail cubask@caribsurf.com; Ambassador Ana María González Suárez.
Venezuela: Delisle St, POB 435, Basseterre; tel. 465-1078; fax 465-5452; e-mail frontado@caribsurf.com; Chargé d'affaires a.i. Nelson Manuel Camacho Rosales.
Diplomatic relations with other countries are maintained at consular level, or with ambassadors and high commissioners resident in other countries of the region, or directly with the other country.

Judicial System

Justice is administered by the Eastern Caribbean Supreme Court (ECSC), based in Saint Lucia and consisting of a Court of Appeal and a High Court. Two of the 16 puisne judges of the High Court are responsible for Saint Christopher and Nevis and preside over the Court of Summary Jurisdiction. One of two ECSC Masters, chiefly responsible for procedural and interlocutory matters, is also resident in the territory. The Magistrates' Courts deal with summary offences and civil offences involving sums of not more than EC $5,000. Saint Christopher and Nevis acceded to the International Criminal Court, administered in The Hague, Netherlands, in September 2006. In 1998 the death penalty was employed in Saint Christopher and Nevis for the first time since 1985.

Puisne Judges: Francis Belle, Ianthea Leigertwood-Octave (acting).
Master: Pearletta Lanns.
Registrar: Claudette Jenkins.
Magistrates' Office: Losack Rd, Basseterre; tel. 465-2170.

SAINT CHRISTOPHER AND NEVIS

Religion

CHRISTIANITY

St Kitts Christian Council: Victoria Rd, POB 48, Basseterre; tel. 465-2167; e-mail stgeorgessk@hotmail.com; Chair. Archdeacon VALENTINE HODGE.

The Anglican Communion

Anglicans in Saint Christopher and Nevis are adherents of the Church in the Province of the West Indies. The islands form part of the diocese of the North Eastern Caribbean and Aruba. The Bishop is resident in The Valley, Anguilla.

The Roman Catholic Church

The diocese of Saint John's-Basseterre, suffragan to the archdiocese of Castries (Saint Lucia), includes Anguilla, Antigua and Barbuda, the British Virgin Islands, Montserrat and Saint Christopher and Nevis. At 31 December 2005 the diocese contained an estimated 15,604 adherents. The Bishop participates in the Antilles Episcopal Conference (currently based in Port of Spain, Trinidad and Tobago).

Bishop of Saint John's-Basseterre: (vacant), POB 836, St John's, Antigua; e-mail djr@candw.ag; internet www.diocesesjb.com.

Other Churches

There are also communities of Methodists, Moravians, Seventh-day Adventists, Baptists, Pilgrim Holiness, the Church of God, Apostolic Faith and Plymouth Brethren.

The Press

The Democrat: Cayon St, POB 30, Basseterre; tel. 466-2091; fax 465-0857; e-mail thedemocrat@sisterisles.kn; internet www.pamdemocrat.org/Newspaper; f. 1948; weekly (Saturdays); organ of PAM; Man. Editor DENIECE ALLEYNE; circ. 3,000.

The Labour Spokesman: Masses House, Church St, POB 239, Basseterre; tel. 465-2229; fax 466-9866; e-mail skn.union@caribsurf.com; internet www.labourworksforme.com/spokesman; f. 1957; Wednesdays and Saturdays; organ of St Kitts-Nevis Trades and Labour Union; Editor DAWUD ST LLOYD BYRON; Man. WALFORD GUMBS; circ. 6,000.

The Leeward Times: Old Hospital Rd, Charlestown, POB 535, Nevis; tel. 469-1049; fax 469-0662; e-mail hbramble@caribsurf.com; weekly (Fridays); Editor HOWELL BRAMBLE.

The St Kitts and Nevis Observer: Cayon St, POB 657, Basseterre; tel. 466-4994; fax 466-4995; e-mail observsk@caribsurf.com; internet www.stkittsnevisobserver.com; weekly (Fridays); independent; Publr and Editor-in-Chief KENNETH WILLIAMS.

Publishers

Caribbean Publishing Co (St Kitts-Nevis) Ltd: Dr William Herbert Complex, Frigate Bay Rd, POB 745, Basseterre; tel. 465-5178; fax 466-0307; e-mail sbrisban@caribpub.com; internet www.caribpub.com.

MacPennies Publishing Co: 10A Cayon St East, POB 318, Basseterre; tel. 465-2274; fax 465-8668; e-mail mcpenltd@macpennies.com; internet www.macpennies.com; f. 1969.

St Kitts-Nevis Publishing Association Ltd: Government Rd, POB 510, Charlestown, Nevis; tel. 469-5907; fax 469-5891.

Broadcasting and Communications

TELECOMMUNICATIONS

Regulatory Authority

Eastern Caribbean Telecommunications Authority: internet www.ectel.int; f. 2000; based in Castries, Saint Lucia; regulates telecommunications in Saint Christopher and Nevis, Dominica, Grenada, Saint Lucia and Saint Vincent and the Grenadines; Dir (Saint Christopher and Nevis) BARCHELLE CROOKE.

Service Providers

Cable & Wireless St Kitts and Nevis: Cayon St, POB 86, Basseterre; tel. 465-1000; fax 465-1106; internet www.cw.com/stkitts_nevis; f. 1985; fmrly St Kitts and Nevis Telecommunications Co Ltd (SKANTEL); 65% owned by Cable & Wireless plc; 17% state-owned; CEO PATRICIA WALTERS.

Digicel St Kitts and Nevis: Wireless Ventures (Saint Kitts and Nevis) Ltd, The Cable Bldg, cnr Cayon and New Sts, POB 1033, Basseterre; e-mail customercarestkittsandnevis@digicelgroup.com; internet www.digicelstkittsandnevis.com; acquired Cingular Wireless' Caribbean operations and licences in 2005; owned by an Irish consortium; Chair. DENIS O'BRIEN; Eastern Caribbean CEO KEVIN WHITE.

UTS-CariGlobe (CHIPPIE): Basseterre; owned by United Telecom Services—UTS, of Curaçao, the Netherlands Antilles, and CariGlobe, a local operator that was granted a licence in May 2002 to provide mobile telecommunications network; CEO CLECTON PHILLIP.

BROADCASTING

Radio

Goodwill Radio FM 104.5: Lodge Village, POB 98, Basseterre; tel. 465-7795; fax 465-9556; e-mail info@goodwillfm.com; internet goodwillfm.com; Gen. Man. DENNIS HUGGINS-NELSON.

Radio One (SKNBC): Bakers Corner, POB 1773, Basseterre; tel. 466-0941; fax 465-0406; e-mail radio1941fm@yahoo.com; owned by St Kitts & Nevis Broadcasting Corpn; music and commentary; Man. Dir GUS WILLIAMS.

Radio Paradise: Bath Plains, POB 508, Nevis; tel. 469-1994; fax 469-1642; e-mail info@radioparadiseonline.com; internet www.radioparadiseonline.com; owned by Trinity Broadcasting Network (USA); Christian; Man. ANDRE GILBERT.

Sugar City Rock FM: Greenlands, Basseterre; tel. 466-1113; e-mail sugarcityrock@hotmail.com; internet www.sugarcityrock.com; Gen. Man. VAL THOMAS.

Voice of Nevis (VON) Radio 895 AM: Bath Plain, Bath Village, POB 195, Charlestown, Nevis; tel. 469-1616; fax 469-5329; e-mail gmanager@vonradio.com; internet www.vonradio.com; f. 1988; Nevis Broadcasting Co Ltd; Gen. Man. EVERED (WEBBO) HERBERT.

WINN FM: Unit C24, The Sands, Newtown Bay Rd, Basseterre; tel. 466-9586; fax 466-7904; e-mail info@winnfm.com; internet www.winnfm.com; owned by Federation Media Group; Chair. MICHAEL KING.

ZIZ Radio and Television: Springfield, POB 331, Basseterre; tel. 465-2622; fax 465-5624; e-mail info@zizonline.com; internet www.zizonline.com; f. 1961; television from 1972; commercial; govt-owned; Gen. Man. WINSTON MCMAHON.

Television

ZIZ Radio and Television: see Radio.

Finance

(cap. = capital; res = reserves; dep. = deposits; brs = branches)

BANKING

Central Bank

Eastern Caribbean Central Bank (ECCB): Headquarters Bldg, Bird Rock, POB 89, Basseterre; tel. 465-2537; fax 465-9562; e-mail info@eccb-centralbank.org; internet www.eccb-centralbank.org; f. 1965 as East Caribbean Currency Authority; expanded responsibilities and changed name 1983; responsible for issue of currency in Anguilla, Antigua and Barbuda, Dominica, Grenada, Montserrat, Saint Christopher and Nevis, Saint Lucia and Saint Vincent and the Grenadines; res EC $181.3m., dep. EC $1,132.8m., total assets EC $2,080.8m. (March 2007); Gov. and Chair. Sir K. DWIGHT VENNER; Country Dir WENDELL LAWRENCE.

Other Banks

Bank of Nevis Ltd: Main St, POB 450, Charlestown, Nevis; tel. 469-5564; fax 469-5798; e-mail bon@caribsurf.com; internet www.thebankofnevis.com; dep. EC $0.3m., total assets EC $0.4m. (Dec. 2006); Chair. IVAN BROWNE.

FirstCaribbean International Bank (Barbados) Ltd: The Circus, POB 42, Basseterre; tel. 465-2449; fax 465-1041; internet www.firstcaribbeanbank.com; f. 2002 following merger of Caribbean operations of Barclays Bank PLC and CIBC; Barclays relinquished its stake to CIBC in 2006; res EC $0.8m. (March 2006); Exec. Chair. MICHAEL MANSOOR; CEO CHARLES PINK.

RBTT Bank (SKN) Ltd: Main and Chappel Sts, POB 673, Charlestown, Nevis; tel. 469-5277; fax 469-1493; internet www.rbtt.com; f. 1955 as Nevis Co-operative Banking Co Ltd; acquired by Royal Bank of Trinidad and Tobago (later known as RBTT) in 1996; Group Chair. PETER J. JULY.

St Kitts-Nevis Anguilla National Bank Ltd: Central St, POB 343, Basseterre; tel. 465-2204; fax 466-1050; e-mail Webmaster@

sknanb.com; internet www.sknanb.com; f. 1971; Govt of St Kitts and Nevis owns 51%; cap. EC $81.0m., res EC $113.4m., dep. EC $1,142.0m. (June 2006); Chair. WALFORD GUMBS; Man. Dir EDMUND LAURENCE; 5 brs.

Development Bank

Development Bank of St Kitts and Nevis: Church St, POB 249, Basseterre; tel. 465-2288; fax 465-4016; e-mail info@skndb.com; internet www.skndb.com; f. 1981; cap. EC $10.8m., res EC $4.3m., dep. EC $26.4m. (Dec. 2005); Chair. ELVIS NEWTON; Gen. Man. LENWORTH HARRIS.

STOCK EXCHANGE

Eastern Caribbean Securities Exchange: Bird Rock, POB 94, Basseterre; tel. 466-7192; fax 465-3798; e-mail info@ecseonline.com; internet www.ecseonline.com; f. 2001; regional securities market designed to facilitate the buying and selling of financial products for the eight member territories—Anguilla, Antigua and Barbuda, Dominica, Grenada, Montserrat, Saint Christopher and Nevis, Saint Lucia and Saint Vincent and the Grenadines; Chair. K. DWIGHT VENNER; Gen. Man. TREVOR E. BLAKE.

INSURANCE

National Caribbean Insurance Co Ltd: Central St, POB 374, Basseterre; tel. 465-2694; fax 465-3659; internet www.nci-biz.com; f. 1973; subsidiary of St Kitts-Nevis Anguilla National Bank Ltd; Gen. Man. JUDITH ATTONG.

St Kitts-Nevis Insurance Co Ltd (SNIC): Central St, POB 142, Basseterre; tel. 465-2845; fax 465-5410; internet www.tdclimited.com/snic; St Kitts-Nevis Anguilla Trading & Devt Co Ltd (TDC).

Several foreign companies also have offices in Saint Christopher and Nevis.

Trade and Industry

GOVERNMENT AGENCIES

Central Marketing Corpn (CEMACO): Pond's Pasture, POB 375, Basseterre; tel. 465-2628; fax 465-7823; Man. VERNA HERBERT.

Frigate Bay Development Corporation (FBDC): Frigate Bay, POB 315, Basseterre; tel. 465-8339; fax 465-4463; promotes tourist and residential devts; Chair. JANET HARRIS; Man. Dir RANDOLPH MORTON.

Investment Promotion Agency: Pelican Mall, Bay Rd, POB 132, Basseterre; tel. 465-4040; fax 465-6968; f. 1987.

Social Security Board: Robert Llewellyn Bradshaw Bldg, Bay Rd, POB 79, Basseterre; tel. 465-2535; fax 465-5051; e-mail pubinfo@socialsecurity.kn; internet www.socialsecurity.kn; f. 1977; Dir SEPHLIN LAWRENCE.

CHAMBER OF COMMERCE

St Kitts-Nevis Chamber of Industry and Commerce: Horsford Rd, Fortlands, POB 332, Basseterre; tel. 465-2980; fax 465-4490; e-mail sknchamber@sisterisles.kn; internet www.stkittsnevischamber.org; incorporated 1949; 137 mems (2006); Pres. FRANKLIN BRAND; Exec. Dir WENDY PHIPPS.

EMPLOYERS' ORGANIZATIONS

Building Contractors' Association: Anthony Evelyn Business Complex, Paul Southwell Industrial Park, POB 1046, Basseterre; tel. 465-6897; fax 465-5623; e-mail sknbca@caribsurf.com; Pres. ANTHONY E. EVELYN.

Nevis Cotton Growers' Association Ltd: Charlestown, Nevis; Pres. IVOR STEVENS.

Small Business Association: Anthony Evelyn Business Complex, Paul Southwell Industrial Park, POB 367, Basseterre; tel. 465-8630; fax 465-6661; e-mail sb-association@caribsurf.com; Pres. EUSTACE WARNER.

UTILITIES

Nevis Electricity Company Ltd (Nevlec): POB 852, Charlestown, Nevis; tel. 469-7245; fax 469-7249; e-mail nevlec@caribsurf.com; Gen. Man. CARTWRIGHT FARRELL.

TRADE UNIONS

Nevis Teachers' Union: POB 559, Charlestown, Nevis; tel. 469-8465; fax 469-5663; e-mail nevteach@caribsurf.com; Pres. WAKELY DANIEL; Gen. Sec. BERNELLA CAINES HAMILTON.

St Kitts-Nevis Trades and Labour Union (SKTLU): Masses House, Church St, POB 239, Basseterre; tel. 465-2229; fax 466-9866; e-mail sknunion@caribsurf.com; f. 1940; affiliated to Caribbean Maritime and Aviation Council, Caribbean Congress of Labour, International Federation of Plantation, Agricultural and Allied Workers and International Trade Union Confederation; associated with St Kitts-Nevis Labour Party; Pres. WALFORD GUMBS; Gen. Sec. BATUMBA TAK; c. 3,000 mems.

St Kitts Teachers' Union: Green Tree Housing Devt, POB 545, Basseterre; tel. 465-1921; e-mail stkittsteachersunion@hotmail.com; Pres. CLYDE CHRISTOPHER; Gen. Sec. CARLENE HEMRY-MORTON.

Transport

RAILWAYS

There are 58 km (36 miles) of narrow-gauge light railway on Saint Christopher, serving the sugar plantations. The railway, complete with new trains and carriages, was restored and developed for tourist excursions and opened in late 2002.

St Kitts Scenic Railway: Basseterre; tel. 465-7263; e-mail scenicreservations@caribsurf.com; internet www.stkittsscenicrailway.com; f. 2002.

St Kitts Sugar Railway: St Kitts Sugar Manufacturing Corpn, POB 96, Basseterre; tel. 465-8099; fax 465-1059; e-mail agronomy@caribsurf.com; Gen. Man. J. E. S. ALFRED.

ROADS

In 1999 there were 320 km (199 miles) of road in Saint Christopher and Nevis, of which approximately 136 km (84 miles) are paved. In July 2001 the Caribbean Development Bank loaned US $3.75m. to the Nevis Government for a road improvement scheme. Further improvements were to be undertaken in 2006 in preparation for the Cricket World Cup, principally the construction of the West Basseterre Bypass Road, at an estimated cost of EC $20m. However, it was anticipated that only sections serving the Robert Llewellyn Bradshaw International airport would be complete as the cricket tournament commenced, with the remaining majority of the project scheduled for completion by mid-2008. Negotiations with private sector investors for the construction of a bridge linking the two islands were at a preliminary stage in early 2007.

SHIPPING

The Government maintains a commercial motor-boat service between the islands, and numerous regional and international shipping lines call at the islands. A deep-water port, Port Zante, was opened at Basseterre in 1981. In June 2003 the Government of Kuwait agreed to provide a loan of EC $15m. to help fund the development of the cruise-ship facilities at Port Zante.

St Christopher Air and Sea Ports Authority: Bird Rock, POB 963, Basseterre; tel. 465-8121; fax 465-8124; e-mail info@scaspa.com; internet www.scaspa.com; f. 1993 to combine St Kitts Port Authority and Airports Authority; Chair. LINKON MAYNARD; CEO and Gen. Man. ERROL DOUGLAS; Airport Man. DENZIL JONES; Sea Port Man. ROSEVELT TROTMAN.

Shipping Companies

Delisle Walwyn and Co Ltd: Liverpool Row, POB 44, Basseterre; tel. 465-2631; fax 465-1125; e-mail info@delislewalwyn.com; internet www.delislewalwyn.com; f. 1951; Chair KISHU CHANDIRAMANI; Man. Dir DENZIL V. CROOKE.

Sea Atlantic Cargo Shipping Corpn: Main St, POB 556, Charlestown, Nevis.

Tony's Ltd: Main St, POB 564, Charlestown, Nevis; tel. 469-5413.

CIVIL AVIATION

Robert Llewellyn Bradshaw (formerly Golden Rock) International Airport, 4 km (2½ miles) from Basseterre, is equipped to handle jet aircraft and is served by scheduled links with most Caribbean destinations, the United Kingdom, the USA and Canada. In 2005 Taiwan and the St Kitts-Nevis-Anguilla National Bank Ltd financed a US $17m. expansion and development project at the airport, completed in December 2006. Saint Christopher and Nevis is a shareholder in the regional airline, LIAT (see chapter on Antigua and Barbuda), which began operating a joint flight schedule with its troubled rival, Caribbean Star Airlines (also headquartered in Antigua and Barbuda) in February 2007; LIAT's full acquisition of Caribbean Star was completed in October 2007. Vance W. Amory International Airport (formerly Newcastle Airfield), 11 km (7 miles) from Charlestown, Nevis, has regular scheduled services to St Kitts and other islands in the region. A new airport, Castle Airport, was opened on Nevis in 1998. In September 2002 a US $5.9m. project to construct a new passenger terminal at Vance W. Amory Airport was completed.

St Kitts Air and Sea Ports Authority: see Shipping.

SAINT CHRISTOPHER AND NEVIS

Private Airlines

Air St Kitts-Nevis: Vance W. Amory International Airport, Newcastle, Nevis; tel. 465-8571.

LIAT (1974) Ltd: Robert Llewellyn Bradshaw International Airport; tel. 465-2098; fax 466-3168; e-mail customerrelations@liatairline.com; internet www.liatairline.com; f. 1956 as Leeward Islands Air Transport Services, jtly owned by 11 regional Govts; privatized in 1995; shares are held by the govts of Antigua and Barbuda, Montserrat, Grenada, Barbados, Trinidad and Tobago, Jamaica, Guyana, Dominica, Saint Lucia, Saint Vincent and the Grenadines and Saint Christopher and Nevis (30.8%), Caribbean Airlines (29.2%), LIAT employees (13.3%) and private investors (26.7%); merger negotiations with Caribbean Star Airlines were finalized in March 2007; deal was abandoned in July in favour of a buyout arrangement in which LIAT would acquire all remaining shares in Caribbean Star; scheduled passenger and cargo services to 19 destinations in the Caribbean; charter flights are also undertaken; Chair. JEAN STEWART HOLDER; CEO MARK DARBY.

Tourism

The introduction of regular air services to the US cities of Miami and New York has opened up the islands as a tourist destination. Visitors are attracted by the excellent beaches and the historical Brimstone Hill Fortress National Park on Saint Christopher, the spectacular mountain scenery of Nevis and the islands' associations with Lord Nelson and Alexander Hamilton. In 2006 there were an estimated 203,075 cruise-ship passengers and 132,321 stop-over visitors. Receipts from tourism were estimated at EC $314.1m. in that year. In 2005 the National Assembly approved the Cricket World Cup 2007 (Tourism Accommodation Incentives) Act; the Act was designed to encourage the construction and refurbishment of hotels and other tourist accommodation for the 2007 Cricket World Cup, hosted by several Caribbean nations, including Saint Christopher.

Nevis Tourism Authority: Main St, POB 917, Charlestown, Nevis; tel. 469-7550; fax 469-7551; e-mail info@nevisisland.com; internet www.nevisisland.com; CEO GARCIA THOMPSON-HENDRICKSON.

Nevis Tourism Bureau: Main St, Charlestown, Nevis; tel. 469-1042; fax 469-1066; e-mail nevtour@caribsurf.com; Dir ELMEADER BROOKES.

St Kitts Tourism Authority: Pelican Mall, Bay Rd, POB 132, Basseterre; tel. 465-4040; fax 465-8794; e-mail stkitts@stkittstourism.kn; internet www.stkittstourism.kn; CEO CHRISTINE WALWYN.

St Kitts-Nevis Hotel and Tourism Association: Liverpool Row, POB 438, Basseterre; tel. 465-5304; fax 465-7746; e-mail stkitnevhta@caribsurf.com; f. 1972; Pres. KISHU CHANDIRAMANI; Man. MICHAEL HEAD.

SAINT LUCIA

Introductory Survey

Location, Climate, Language, Religion, Flag, Capital

Saint Lucia is the second largest of the Windward Islands group of the West Indies, lying 40 km (25 miles) to the south of Martinique and 32 km (20 miles) to the north-east of Saint Vincent, in the Caribbean Sea. The island is volcanic, with spectacular mountain scenery—the Pitons, the island's twin, jungle-clad volcanic mountains were designated a UNESCO (see p. 137) World Heritage Site in June 2004. The average annual temperature is 26°C (79°F), with a dry season from January to April, followed by a rainy season from May to August. The average annual rainfall is 1,500 mm (60 ins) in the low-lying areas, and 3,500 mm (138 ins) in the mountains. The official language is English, although a large proportion of the population speak a French-based patois. Almost all of the island's inhabitants profess Christianity, and 64% are adherents of the Roman Catholic Church. The national flag (proportions 1 by 2) is blue, bearing in its centre a white-edged black triangle partly covered by a gold triangle rising from a common base. The capital is Castries.

Recent History

British settlers made an unsuccessful attempt to colonize the island (originally inhabited by a Carib people) in 1605. A further British party arrived in 1638 but were killed by the indigenous Carib population. France claimed sovereignty in 1642, and fighting between French and Caribs continued until 1660, when a peace treaty was signed. Control of Saint Lucia was transferred 14 times before it was ceded by the French and became a British colony in 1814. It remained under British rule for the next 165 years.

Representative government was introduced in 1924. The colony was a member of the Windward Islands, under a federal system, until December 1959. It joined the newly formed West Indies Federation in January 1958, and remained a member until the Federation's dissolution in May 1962. From January 1960 Saint Lucia, in common with other British territories in the Windward Islands, was given a new Constitution, with its own Administrator and an enlarged Legislative Council.

In 1951 the first elections under adult suffrage were won by the Saint Lucia Labour Party (SLP), which retained power until 1964, when John (later Sir John) Compton, of the newly formed conservative United Workers' Party (UWP), became Chief Minister. In March 1967 Saint Lucia became one of the West Indies Associated States, gaining full autonomy in internal affairs, with the United Kingdom retaining responsibility for defence and foreign relations only. The Legislative Council was replaced by a House of Assembly, the Administrator was designated Governor, and the Chief Minister became Premier.

In 1975 the Associated States agreed that they would seek independence individually. After three years of negotiations, Saint Lucia became independent on 22 February 1979, remaining within the Commonwealth. Compton became the country's first Prime Minister.

A general election in July 1979 returned the SLP to government with a clear majority, and its leader, Allan Louisy, succeeded Compton as Prime Minister. In February 1980 a new Governor-General, Boswell Williams, was appointed. This led to disputes within the Government and contributed to a split in the SLP. Louisy's resignation was demanded by 12 SLP members of the House of Assembly, who favoured his replacement by George Odlum, the Deputy Prime Minister. The controversy continued until April 1981, when Louisy was forced to resign after Odlum and three other SLP members of the House voted with the opposition against the Government's budget. In May Winston Cenac, the Attorney-General in the Louisy Government, took office as Prime Minister. In September the Cenac administration defeated by one vote a motion of 'no confidence', introduced jointly by UWP and Progressive Labour Party (PLP—formed by Odlum) members of the House, who accused the Government of political and economic mismanagement. In January 1982 a government proposal to alter legislation regarding the expenses of members of Parliament produced widespread accusations of corruption and provoked a series of strikes. Demands for the Government's resignation increased from all sectors of the community, culminating in a general strike. Cenac resigned, and an all-party interim administration was formed, under the deputy leader of the PLP, Michael Pilgrim, pending a general election that was scheduled for May. At the election the UWP was returned to power, and John Compton was re-elected Prime Minister. In December Sir Allen Lewis was reappointed Governor-General, following the dismissal of Boswell Williams because of his previous close association with the SLP.

In 1984 the opposition parties began to reorganize in order to present a more effective opposition to the UWP Government. At a general election to the 17-member House of Assembly in early April 1987, the UWP secured nine seats and the SLP eight. A further election took place at the end of the month, in the hope of a more decisive result, but the distribution of seats remained unchanged. In June the UWP's majority in the House was increased to three seats, when Cenac defected from the SLP. He was subsequently appointed Minister of Foreign Affairs.

In late October 1988 the Government introduced legislation whereby it assumed control of the banana industry for one year. Subsequently, the 1988 annual convention of the Saint Lucia Banana Growers' Association (SLBGA) was cancelled, and the Government dismissed the association's board of directors. The opposition parties alleged that these actions had been motivated by the fact that prominent supporters of the ruling UWP were the SLBGA's principal debtors. Despite continued protests, particularly by banana producers and the SLP, Government control was extended until July 1990.

At a general election in April 1992 the UWP won 11 seats and the SLP took the remaining six seats. The SLP attributed its defeat largely to a redefinition of constituency boundaries by the Government prior to the election. In October 1993 a three-day strike was organized by a new pressure group, the Banana Salvation Committee (BSC), in support of demands for an increase in the minimum price paid to local producers for bananas and for the dismissal of the board of directors of the SLBGA. Following recommendations made by a government appointed committee, the Government implemented price increases and dismissed the board of directors of the SLBGA, who were replaced by an interim board including representatives of the BSC. An announcement by the Government, in January 1994, that the SLBGA was to be placed into receivership provoked a strike by the BSC in March. The BSC organized further strikes by banana farmers in December and in February and July 1995, in support of demands for an extraordinary meeting of the SLBGA, and for an inquiry into the deaths of two demonstrators during the October 1993 strike. Further industrial action was undertaken by the BSC in February 1996, in protest at the monopoly on banana exports exercised by the state-run Windward Islands Banana Development and Exporting Co (Wibdeco), in the context of higher prices for produce being offered to banana growers by a US distributor. In September the House of Assembly approved a bill to revise the selection procedure for members of the SLBGA and the responsibilities of its general manager. The new legislation effectively transferred control of the Association from the Government to the banana growers, who would henceforth elect six members of the board of directors (while the Government would continue to nominate the remaining five). In October the BSC co-ordinated industrial action by banana growers in support of renewed demands for an end to the Wibdeco monopoly, and for reform of the industry's management and payment systems. Attempts by a number of farmers who opposed the strike to transport produce to ports resulted in violent clashes. Subsequent negotiations with a parliamentary review committee and with the Government (which promised to transfer some responsibility for the industry to the private sector) failed to appease the farmers.

In August 1995 the report of a commission of inquiry into allegations of the Government's involvement in the misappropriation, for electoral purposes, of some US $100,000 in UN contributions concluded that the former Permanent Representative to the UN, Charles Flemming, had been the sole perpetrator of the fraud. Flemming, who insisted that he had acted with the knowledge and endorsement of senior members of the UWP (including the Prime Minister), failed to return from a visit to the USA undertaken during the commission's hearings. The Minister of State with Responsibility for Financial Services and the National Development Corporation, Rufus Bousquet (who claimed to have been an unwitting recipient of the funds), had been dismissed in May, after he publicly questioned whether it was appropriate that the Government remain in office pending investigation of the affair.

A UWP party conference, convened in January 1996, endorsed the appointment of Vaughan Lewis, the former Director-General of the Organisation of Eastern Caribbean States (OECS, see p. 425), to the vacancy created by the Prime Minister's retirement from the party leadership. Lewis contested and won the Central Castries parliamentary by-election in February, and was subsequently appointed Minister without Portfolio. SLP leader Julian Hunte resigned later in the month, following criticism of the party's poor performance at the by-election; Kenny Anthony, a former SLP education and culture minister, replaced him. In late March Compton resigned the premiership, and was succeeded in early April by Lewis.

A general election in May 1997 was won decisively by the SLP, which was returned to power after 15 years, securing 16 of the 17 seats in the House of Assembly. Kenny Anthony was sworn in as the new Prime Minister. Among the nine ministers in his first Cabinet was George Odlum, who had rejoined the SLP in July 1996. Following his electoral defeat Lewis announced his intention to resign the leadership of the UWP; Sir John Compton (as he had become), the former UWP leader and former Prime Minister, replaced him in June 1998.

In August 1997 the Governor-General, Sir George Mallet, resigned. His appointment, in June 1996, had been opposed by the SLP, on the grounds that the post's tradition of neutrality would be compromised—Mallet had previously been Deputy Prime Minister, and his portfolio had included several influential ministries. Saint Lucia's first female Governor-General, Dr Pearlette Louisy, was appointed in September 1997.

In September 1997 the inquiry into allegations of corruption under the UWP, which had been promised by the SLP Government after its election, began. However, legal challenges to the impartiality of the sole commissioner, Monica Joseph, effectively stalled proceedings and she withdrew from the inquiry in March 1998. Sir Louis Blom-Cooper, a prominent British jurist, was appointed in her place. In August 1999 Blom-Cooper submitted his report to the Government. The report cleared Compton and Lewis of corruption, but noted instances of impropriety and a 'high degree of maladministration' in their Governments.

In September 1997 the directors of the SLBGA resigned, at Anthony's request: the Government was reportedly concerned that divisions at boardroom level were damaging the association's operations. Such divisions became increasingly pronounced as plans proceeded for the privatization of the SLBGA, one of the stated aims of the SLP Government. The Concerned Farmers Group (CFG), formed in December and led by the ousted Chairman, Rupert Gajadhar, which grouped larger farmers, expressed concern that the more numerous smaller producers in the BSC (whose secretary, Patrick Joseph, was also a government senator) would unduly dominate the new company, since decision-making was to be on the basis of one-member-one-vote. Members of the CFG threatened to establish their own company unless their concerns were addressed.

In July 1998 the SLBGA was privatized and the Saint Lucia Banana Corpn (SLBC) was created in its place. The Government agreed to assume the debts incurred by the dissolved SLBGA, equivalent to EC $44m. The CFG, which had refused to participate in the process, subsequently established a rival company, the Tropical Quality Fruit Co (TQF). In October a court judgment ruled that the SLBC did not enjoy monopoly rights in the banana trade. This ruling followed complaints from the TQF that Wibdeco had been refusing to accept its fruit for shipment. The TQF alleged that this refusal was owing to pressure exerted by the SLBC Chairman, Patrick Joseph, in his capacity as a member of the Wibdeco board.

In January 1999 the SLBC announced that it had incurred losses of EC $6m. in 1998 and would therefore be forced to reduce the price paid to farmers. The SLBC blamed its operating deficit primarily on the fact that, because banana production had been underestimated, Wibdeco had failed to obtain sufficient European Union (EU, see p. 244) licences, meaning that much of the fruit produced did not reach high-paying markets. The TQF also announced a deficit, but claimed that its lower operating costs had reduced its losses. The TQF further suggested that the SLBC had damaged its own profitability by keeping prices deliberately high in an attempt to force the TQF out of business.

In July 1999 the Government founded a Banana Industry Trust, which was to oversee the improvement of farming practices in the banana sector and manage the financial resources available to the industry, including EC $21m. in funds provided by the EU. In the same month the Government announced that it was to make official loans of $7m. to the SLBC and $1.9m. to the TQF. However, falling prices and the ongoing lack of confidence among growers led the Government to announce that it was to hold senior-level talks with representatives of Wibdeco and Geest Bananas in order to discuss future pricing arrangements, while the Chairman of the SLBC urged Wibdeco and Geest to release money from their emergency funds to farmers threatened with bankruptcy. In August Wibdeco agreed to finance a temporary subsidy on prices in order to alleviate hardship among growers. In late 1999, however, the company encountered increasing pressure from the SLBC and from the Government to deliver increased returns to farmers, and in January 2000, following the expiry of its agreement to sell through Wibdeco, the SLBC announced plans to sell directly to Geest, despite criticism from its other regional partners in Wibdeco. In March Wibdeco announced that it would not contest the SLBC's decision, although it suggested that it might itself bypass the SLBC by buying directly from farmers.

Disbursement of a £1m. bonus fund to banana growers became the centre of a dispute between Wibdeco and the SLBC in April 2000, when the SLBC refused to submit a list of its banana growers and suppliers to Wibdeco, stating instead that it would provide a breakdown of the total payments from either Wibdeco or Geest to the individual growers. SLBC accused Wibdeco of attempting to use SLBC's money to compete directly with growers aligned to the Corporation by making payments directly to the growers. In May the dispute was resolved when Wibdeco decided to pay the monies to the growers through the local banana associations in the four Windward Islands to whom the growers had sold their bananas in 1999.

In January 2001, following an increase in tourist cancellations, Prime Minister Anthony announced a series of measures intended to reduce the crime rate in Saint Lucia. These included the establishment of a National Anti-Crime Commission, the creation of a 10-member police 'rapid response unit', a review of the penal code, and reforms to the police service. In June Anthony announced the creation of four more rapid response units, a special task force to target known criminals, plans for more severe penalties for gun crimes, an increase in police patrols and an amnesty for holders of illegal firearms. A special joint session of Parliament convened in the following month to debate the increase in violent crime.

In March 2001 the Minister of Foreign Affairs and International Trade, George Odlum, left the Government and the SLP to join a new opposition grouping, the National Alliance (NA). The former premier, Sir John Compton, and the UWP leader, Morella Joseph, had founded the NA in advance of legislative elections due in 2002 but widely expected to be held in late 2001. Prime Minister Anthony stated that he had dismissed Odlum from his ministerial post, although Odlum himself claimed that he had resigned from the Government. Julian Hunte, a former Permanent Representative to the UN, replaced Odlum as foreign minister.

In October 2001 the NA's assembly elected Compton to head the party. However, Odlum rejected the decision and claimed the voting process was flawed. Later the same month the UWP withdrew from the Alliance and announced it would contest the elections as a single party. Odlum chose to retain the National Alliance name for his group.

As expected, the ruling SLP achieved another convincing victory at the 3 December 2001 general election, winning 14 of the 17 parliamentary seats (and 54% of the valid votes cast). The remaining seats were taken by the UWP. Joseph and Odlum, leaders of the UWP and the NA, respectively, both lost their seats. The voter turn-out rate was 53%. Joseph resigned as UWP leader and was replaced by Vaughan Lewis. Marius Wilson became the new parliamentary leader of the opposition in December 2001. Meanwhile, in the same month, Prime Minister Anthony announced a new 15-member cabinet.

In July 2003 Parliament approved a constitutional amendment abolishing the oath of allegiance to the British monarch; instead, elected members were to pledge loyalty to the Saint

Lucian people. In November the Government announced the establishment of a Constitutional Review Commission. The development, which was supported by the opposition, was designed to expand public participation in Saint Lucia's democracy. Meanwhile, also in November the Government passed a new Criminal Code, which included two particularly controversial clauses. The first, Section 361, provided for a two-year prison sentence for anyone convicted of spreading 'false news'. The clause provoked consternation among local media representatives and the UWP, whose parliamentary members absented themselves from the vote. The second controversial element of the Code, Section 166, allowed for the legalization of abortion, previously illegal in all circumstances, in cases of rape, incest and medical danger to the mother. The law prompted trenchant criticism from anti-abortion and religious groups, and in January 2004 led to the dismissal of Sarah Flood-Beaubrun from her post as Minister of Home Affairs and Gender Relations, following a vehement disagreement with her fellow ministers over the new legislation; she resigned from the SLP in March and later established a new political party—the Organization for National Empowerment.

Flood-Beaubrun's dismissal from the Government was part of a wider cabinet realignment in early 2004, which included the appointment of the erstwhile Minister of Agriculture, Forestry and Fisheries, Calixte George, as head of a new Ministry of Home Affairs and Internal Security. The new department was to oversee the police service, previously the responsibility of the Attorney-General's Office, and was charged with finding a solution to the island's spiralling crime rate. Nevertheless, in 2004 the number of murders reached a record level, 37, a rate maintained in 2005. In November 2005 an Interception of Communication bill, which granted extra powers to law enforcement authorities and attracted emphatic criticism from opposition parties, received senate approval. In the first 10 months of that year 154 illegal guns were recovered through police raids and under a new 'amnesty' scheme, compared with 48 in the whole of 2004. Despite the recruitment of 10 British police officers in November 2006 and renewed pledges by the Government for more rigorous anti-crime initiatives and deterrents, the murder rate escalated to 39 by the end of that year. In January 2006 Anthony pledged to make greater use of the death penalty as a weapon against the increasing problem of crime, a promise reiterated by his successor, Sir John Compton (see below), in early 2007.

In November 2003 the High Court ruled that the Government's approval of the refinancing of the construction of the Hyatt Hotel in 1997 was 'void and illegal'. The opposition criticized the Government for not having sought parliamentary approval for the authorization of the loan and called for the resignation of the Attorney-General, Petrus Compton, whose actions, it claimed, were particularly implicated by the judgment. In October 2004 the much-criticized Compton was moved to the Ministry of Foreign Affairs, International Trade and Civil Aviation. His predecessor, Julian Hunte, had been reappointed ambassador of Saint Lucia to the UN. Victor La Corbiniere was given the vacant role of Attorney-General and Minister of Justice. Meanwhile, in December 2004 Prime Minister Anthony announced his intention to stand for a third term in office at the forthcoming elections, constitutionally due in 2006.

In April 2004 Marcus Nicholas, a UWP deputy, withdrew his support for Arsene James, whose popularity had fallen in recent months. With the support of Marius Wilson, Nicholas became the new leader of a four-member opposition, leading the UWP hierarchy to cancel his party membership. In addition to James being the party's sole loyal supporter in the House of Assembly, the UWP remained unable to develop a strong party executive and in March 2005 elected veteran politician Sir John Compton to lead the party into the next general election, in preference to the incumbent candidate, Vaughan Lewis. In September 2006 Lewis resigned from the UWP and joined the SLP.

The election of Compton as party leader proved highly perspicacious, as the UWP celebrated an unprecedented and decisive victory in the 11 December 2006 general election: the party secured 11 of the 17 parliamentary seats contested (equivalent to 51.4% of votes cast), while the incumbent SLP secured the remaining six seats (with 48.2% of the vote). Turn-out of the estimated 139,958 eligible electorate was preliminarily put at approximately 60% and election monitors from the Organization of American States (see p. 360) declared the ballot free and fair. Compton, an octogenarian politician who had presided over the Saint Lucia Government twice before, including for a 29-year term spanning the country's transition to independence, was sworn in as premier on 15 December. The appointment of Rosemary Husbands-Mathurin as Senate President and Sarah Flood-Beaubrun as Speaker of the House of Assembly signalled women's advancing prestige within the public arena, and represented the first female appointments to parliamentary leadership roles in Saint Lucia's history.

Mindful of the significant public debt burden requiring the new Government's urgent attention, Prime Minister Compton announced in January 2007 that an audit commission was to be established to investigate considerable ministerial overspending on public sector projects. The inquiry followed reports of widespread financial irregularities and unexplained delays in implementation. Furthermore, proposals for policy reform of election campaign financing, both within Saint Lucia and the wider Caribbean community, were promulgated for consideration at the state opening of Parliament on 15 January; the motion was prompted by the high levels of spending in the months preceding the December 2006 election and fears that a continuing lack of regulation in campaign practice could expose the electoral process to corrupting influences.

The newly elected UWP administration also confirmed in January 2007 that proposals by the previous Government to grant an amnesty to Caribbean Community and Common Market (CARICOM, see p. 196) nationals residing in Saint Lucia illegally would be sustained, offering those concerned the opportunity to 'regularize' their citizenship status upon payment of a stipulated fee. It was estimated that approximately 1,000 Guyanese, in addition to Jamaican, Trinidadian and other CARICOM nationals would benefit from the agreement.

Compton suffered a series of minor strokes in late April 2007, and on 1 May departed Saint Lucia in order to seek medical treatment in New York, USA. Stephenson King, the Minister of Health and UWP Chairman, was appointed acting Prime Minister and remained in the post after Compton's return on 19 May. In early June Rufus Bousquet, Minister of External Affairs, International Financial Services, Information and Broadcasting, was dismissed from the Cabinet. Local news media reported that the decision had been taken as Bousquet had re-established diplomatic relations with Taiwan without the knowledge of Compton (see below). Compton died on 7 September after experiencing a further stroke. The remaining 10 elected members of the UWP designated King as Compton's permanent successor, and he was duly sworn in as Prime Minister on 9 September. The new premier announced his Cabinet three days later, in which he assumed the portfolios for finance, external affairs, home affairs and national security. Former health minister Edmund Estephane acquired the newly created post of Minister of Labour, Information and Broadcasting and Keith Mondesir became Minister of Health Wellness, Family Affairs, National Mobilisation, Human Services and Gender Relations. Later in the same month the National Development Movement, formed after the 2001 general election, was dissolved when its leader, Minister of Economic Affairs, Economic Planning, National Development and Public Service Ausbert d'Auvergne, announced his decision to join the UWP.

The SLBC entered into a dispute with Wibdeco in early 2008 when, in February, the latter announced plans to terminate its contract with the SLBC as it had not been certified by the Fairtrade Labelling Organization of the United Kingdom. The Chairman of the SLBC, Eustace Monrose, claimed that the company had not been given adequate notice to achieve fair trade status and instructed Wibdeco to withdraw its notice of termination. However, in late March Wibdeco signed a sales and purchase agreement with two other companies, one of which was the Windward Islands Farmers' Association, in order to bring the supply chain of the island's bananas into line with fair trade regulations. The SLBC, now faced with the threat of closure, was subsequently granted a court injunction preventing Wibdeco from effecting its termination notice.

Saint Lucia's most important export market is the United Kingdom, which receives most of the banana crop under the terms of the Cotonou Agreement (see p. 301), the successor agreement to the Lomé Convention, which expired in 2000. In July 1993 new regulations came into effect governing the level of imports of bananas by the European Community (now EU, of which the United Kingdom is a member). The regulations were introduced to protect traditional producers covered by the Lomé Convention from competition from the expanding Latin American producers. At the instigation of the Latin American producers, consecutive dispute panels were appointed by the General

SAINT LUCIA

Agreement on Tariffs and Trade (which was succeeded by the World Trade Organization—WTO, see p. 396) to rule on whether the EU's actions contravened GATT rules. Although the dispute panels ruled in favour of the Latin American producers, the rulings were not enforceable. In February 1996, with support from Ecuador, Guatemala, Mexico and Honduras, the USA renewed consultations, begun in September 1995, with the WTO concerning the EU's banana import quota regime. In March 1997 a WTO interim report appeared to uphold many of the charges of unfair discrimination brought by the plaintiffs. The WTO Appellate Body rejected representations by the EU against the ruling in September, and the EU was informed that it must formulate a new system for banana imports by early 1998; new arrangements were duly proposed by the EU in January 1998, under which it would apply a system of quotas and tariffs to both groups of producers, while retaining an import-licensing system.

The EU's new banana import regime was implemented on 1 January 1999 in compliance with the WTO ruling, though the USA criticized the reforms as negligible. Further discussions on the issue broke down in late January 1999 when Saint Lucia, backed by other countries, objected to any discussion of US demands for sanctions on EU goods. On 1 February the USA introduced punitive import duties on various EU goods, and in March the WTO disputes panel was asked to consider whether the EU had done enough to amend its import regime and whether the USA could legally impose retaliatory import tariffs of up to 100% on certain EU goods. In retaliation against this move, the banana-exporting countries threatened to withdraw their co-operation with the US campaign against drugs-trafficking, while banana-producers warned that they might switch to growing marijuana if they were forced out of business. On 6 April WTO arbitrators awarded damages against the EU, although at a lower level than the USA had been claiming. On 12 April the WTO again delivered a ruling criticizing aspects of the EU banana-importing regime, and which gave the USA permission to impose retaliatory tariffs on certain European goods. In April 2001 the USA agreed to suspend these sanctions from 1 July, after the dispute was resolved: following a transition period, a new, tariff-only regime was introduced from January 2006. Despite substantial government and EU assistance, augmented by the efforts of a Banana Emergency Recovery Unit and the Banana Industry Trust, the Saint Lucian banana industry continued to exhibit decline.

Saint Lucia is a member of the OECS, and, since May 1987, has been a prominent advocate of the creation of a unitary East Caribbean state. In 1988 however, Antigua and Barbuda expressed opposition to political union, thereby discouraging any participation by Montserrat or Saint Christopher and Nevis. The four English-speaking Windward Islands countries (Saint Lucia, Dominica, Grenada, and Saint Vincent and the Grenadines) thus announced plans to proceed independently towards a more limited union. In 1990 the leaders of the four countries established a Regional Constituent Assembly. Following a series of discussions, the Assembly issued its final report in late 1992, in which it stated that the four countries were committed to the establishment of economic and political union under a federal system. Saint Lucia has also been a full participating member of the CARICOM regional community since May 1974. In February 2006 the House of Assembly approved legislation allowing Saint Lucia to join the Caribbean Single Market and Economy and, together with five other Caribbean nations (Antigua and Barbuda, Dominica, Grenada, Saint Christopher and Nevis, and Saint Vincent and the Grenadines), the country was formally admitted to the initiative on 3 July (see Economic Affairs). An intra-regional common passport initiative, regarded as an integral component in the advance towards economic union and designed to facilitate travel for citizens of participating nations, was implemented in Saint Lucia on 16 January 2007; use of the CARICOM passport was expected to have been introduced by all 15 member governments by 2008.

In August 1997 the new SLP Government effected a significant reorientation of foreign policy when it was announced that diplomatic relations were to be established with the People's Republic of China; it was reported that China was to provide educational materials valued at US $1m. immediately, and was to finance the construction of a new national sports stadium, a cultural centre, a new highway and a free trade zone. Taiwan subsequently severed relations with Saint Lucia. By 2004 it was estimated that China had provided Saint Lucia with funds worth US $100m. throughout the seven years of their association. In late 2005 Prime Minister Anthony accused the UWP of jeopardizing Saint Lucia's profitable relationship with China after allegations emerged that Sir John Compton had secretly met the President of Taiwan in Saint Vincent and the Grenadines and sought to develop a relationship between the UWP and Taiwan. Such fears were partly allayed with the signing of a technical co-operation agreement between the premier and the Chinese Minister of Foreign Affairs, Li Zhaoxing, in September 2006, although the UWP's victory in the December general election precipitated renewed uncertainties about the future of bilateral relations. In February 2007 the new foreign affairs minister, Rufus Bousquet, reiterated his Government's intention to maintain links with China but in April he announced that the country would resume diplomatic relations with Taiwan; China subsequently suspended ambassadorial relations with Saint Lucia. During an official state visit to the island in January 2008, Taiwan's President Chen Shui-bian stated his commitment to provide aid and investment, including US $100,000 for repairs to an earthquake-damaged school and funds for the redevelopment of a hospital.

Together with 12 other Caribbean administrations, in September 2005 the Government signed the PetroCaribe accord, under which Saint Lucia would be allowed to purchase petroleum from Venezuela at reduced prices. However, owing to very limited storage facilities in the region, many of the signatories—including Saint Lucia—were unable to proceed further in accepting fuel shipments. In September 2006 Hess Oil (St Lucia) Ltd announced an arrangement with Venezuelan state-owned oil company PDVSA whereby its plant at Cul de Sac would be employed as a repository, enabling receipt of the 1,700 barrels per day of oil products under the terms of the initiative. However, following his accession to the premiership in December, Sir John Compton indicated that implementation of the PetroCaribe initiative would not be a priority of his Government and the enterprise was abandoned indefinitely.

On 19 November 2003 Parliament passed legislation enabling the Government to pledge US $2.5m. towards the establishment of the Caribbean Court of Justice (CCJ), to be headquartered in Trinidad. The CCJ, which replaced the Privy Council in the United Kingdom as the region's highest court, was inaugurated in April 2005.

Government

Saint Lucia is a constitutional monarchy. Executive power is vested in the British monarch, as Head of State, and is exercisable by the Governor-General, who represents the monarchy and is appointed on the advice of the Prime Minister. Legislative power is vested in Parliament, comprising the monarch, the 17-member House of Assembly, elected from single-member constituencies for up to five years by universal adult suffrage, and the Senate, composed of 11 members appointed by the Governor-General, including six appointed on the advice of the Prime Minister and three on the advice of the Leader of the Opposition. Government is effectively by the Cabinet. The Governor-General appoints the Prime Minister and, on the latter's recommendation, the other Ministers. The Prime Minister must have majority support in the House, to which the Cabinet is responsible.

Defence

The Royal Saint Lucia Police Force, which numbers about 300 men, includes a Special Service Unit for purposes of defence. Saint Lucia participates in the US-sponsored Regional Security System, comprising police, coastguards and army units, which was established by independent East Caribbean states in 1982. There are also two patrol vessels for coastguard duties.

Economic Affairs

In 2006, according to estimates by the World Bank, Saint Lucia's gross national income (GNI), measured at average 2004–06 prices, was US $848m., equivalent to $5,110 per head (or $6,970 per head on an international purchasing-power parity basis). During 1996–2006, it was estimated, the population increased by an annual average rate of 1.2%, while gross domestic product (GDP) per head rose by 1.7% per year during the same period. Overall GDP increased, in real terms, at an average annual rate of 2.9% in 1996–2006; according to the Saint Lucia Government Statistics Department, real GDP increased by 5.0% in 2006.

Agriculture (including hunting, forestry and fishing) accounted for 3.7% of GDP in 2006, according to preliminary figures. The sector employed some 15.9% of the active working population in 2004. Despite the decline in banana industry, the fruit remains Saint Lucia's principal cash crop, although in 2006 it accounted for an estimated 18.6% of the total value of merchandise exports, compared with 49.9% in 2002. Other important crops include coconuts, mangoes, citrus fruit, cocoa and spices. Commercial fishing was being developed and in August 2001 Japan granted US $10.6m. towards the rehabilitation and improvement of fishery facilities in the Choiseul and Soufrière districts. During 1997–2006 real agricultural GDP decreased by an annual average of 8.2%, largely as a result of a 10.7% decline in the banana sector. The agriculture sector contracted by 24.7% in 2005, but recovered somewhat in 2006 with growth of an estimated 9.8%.

Industry (including mining, manufacturing, public utilities and construction) accounted for 19.0% of GDP in 2006, according to preliminary figures, and the sector engaged an estimated 16.2% of the active working population in 2004. During 1997–2006 industrial GDP increased by an estimated annual average of 3.8%. In 2006 the sector's real GDP increased by 11.5%. Construction contributed 8.5% to GDP in 2006. The sector increased by an annual average of 3.9% in 1997–2006.

Manufacturing accounted for 5.7% of GDP in 2006, according to preliminary figures, and employed 7.0% of the employed population in 2004. The principal manufacturing industries, which have been encouraged by the establishment of 'free zones', include the processing of agricultural products, the assembly of electronic components and the production of garments, plastics, paper and packaging (associated with banana production), beer, rum and other beverages. During 1997–2006 the sector's real GDP increased by an annual average of 4.3%. Real manufacturing GDP increased by 6.7% in 2006.

Energy is traditionally derived from imported hydrocarbon fuels (mineral fuels and lubricants comprised an estimated 12.9% of total imports in 2006). There is a petroleum storage and transshipment terminal on the island. Saint Lucia was a signatory to the PetroCaribe accord, introduced in 2005, under which the country was allowed to purchase petroleum from Venezuela at reduced prices, although implementation of the initiative was postponed after Sir John Compton assumed the premiership in December 2006.

The services sector contributed 77.4% of GDP in 2006, according to preliminary figures, and engaged an estimated 61.8% of those employed in 2004. Tourism is the most important of the service industries, and in 2006 tourist receipts of EC $935.5m. were equivalent to some 79.4% of the value of total exports of goods and services. The number of tourist arrivals declined by 8.2% in 2005 and by a further 7.1% in 2006, owing largely to a drop in the number of excursionists and cruise-ship passengers visiting the island (there was an increase in both stop-over visitors and yacht passengers in 2005, although numbers declined in 2006). The real GDP of the hotels and restaurants sector increased by 6.3% in 2005, but decreased by 2.7% in 2006 following a decline in occupancy rates (attributed, in part, to the cessation of some charter flights in January of that year). During 1997–2006 the real GDP of the services sector increased by an annual average of 3.1%. The sector increased by 20.8% in 2006, largely reflecting expansion in the financial and public sectors.

In 2005 Saint Lucia recorded an estimated visible trade deficit of US $335.39m., and a deficit of some US $153.97m. on the current account of the balance of payments. The principal source of imports in 2006 was the USA (34.6% of the total); other important markets in that year were Trinidad and Tobago (16.9%) and the United Kingdom (6.9%). The principal market for exports is the United Kingdom, which received 36.4% of total exports in 2006; other major export markets were Trinidad and Tobago (16%) and the USA and Barbados (both of which received 10.6% of Saint Lucia's exports). The Caribbean Community and Common Market (CARICOM, see p. 196) member states accounted for 25.4% of imports and 48.0% of exports in that year. Refined petroleum was the principal export commodity in 2006, ahead of food and live animals (comprising mainly bananas sent to the United Kingdom), machinery and transport equipment and beverages and tobacco (mainly beer). The principal imports were machinery and transport equipment and food and live animals.

In 2006 there was an overall budgetary deficit of EC $156.9m., equivalent to 6.3% of GDP. Saint Lucia's total external debt at the end of 2005 was US $424.9m., of which US $248.9m. was long-term public debt. In 2005 the cost of debt-servicing was equivalent to 7.1% of the value of exports of goods and services. The annual rate of inflation averaged 2.3% in 2000–06; inflation averaged 3.9% in 2005 and 2.3% in 2006. In 2004 the average rate of unemployment was 16%.

Saint Lucia is a member of CARICOM, the Eastern Caribbean Central Bank, and of the Organisation of Eastern Caribbean States (OECS, see p. 425). Saint Lucia is also a member of the regional stock exchange, the Eastern Caribbean Securities Exchange (based in Saint Christopher and Nevis), established in 2001. Saint Lucia has been a strong advocate of closer political and economic integration within the Caribbean region and became a signatory to CARICOM's Caribbean Single Market and Economy (CSME) on 3 July 2006. The CSME, which was established by six founding member states on 1 January 2006, was to enshrine the free movement of goods, services and labour throughout most of the CARICOM region, and was scheduled for full implementation by 31 December 2008. Saint Lucia is party to the Caribbean Basin Initiative (CBI) and to the Cotonou Agreement (see p. 301), the successor accord to the Lomé Convention.

The Saint Lucia economy, which traditionally relied on the production of bananas for export, underwent considerable structural change at the end of the 20th century, with the emergence of service industries as the most important sectors of the economy, while investment in the island's infrastructure also benefited the tourism industry, which became the principal source of foreign exchange. In 2005 the World Travel and Tourism Council estimated that the tourism sector accounted for about 43% of Saint Lucia's GDP and employment. As part of its efforts to diversify the economy, the Government also attempted to establish Saint Lucia as a centre for international financial services; Saint Lucia's first 'offshore' bank opened in 2001. However, the agricultural sector remained a significant source of employment and the erosion of Saint Lucia's preferential access to European markets was of considerable concern. Banana production declined dramatically from the 1990s as a result of poor climatic conditions and the retrenchments in the industry caused by increased international competition and lower market prices. This sector encountered more difficulties during 2007–08: Hurricane Dean, which swept across the island in August 2007, wreaked severe damage to that year's banana crop. The industry was further threatened by the actions of the banana exporting company Wibdeco in early 2008 (see 'Recent History'). Moreover, tourism (the most dynamic sector of the economy in recent years) contracted by an estimated 7.4% in 2007, while its contribution to overall GDP declined to 11.7%, compared with 12.6% in 2006. According to official estimates, the economy grew by just 0.5% in that year. As joint host of the 2007 Cricket World Cup, it had been expected that Saint Lucia would benefit from a substantial increase in tourist arrivals. However, the island was forced to compete with other hosting nations, many of whom experienced an overall decline in visitor arrivals (the number of stop-over visitors and yacht passengers arriving in Saint Lucia reportedly declined by 5% and 10% respectively in that year). The Government hoped to address this decline by renewed marketing efforts overseas and by directing greater investment into more lucrative branches of tourism (particularly yachting). The 2008 budget provided almost EC $1,000m. for capital investment in this sector, to be spent mainly on a planned cruise-ship port at Castries.

Education

Education is compulsory for 10 years between five and 15 years of age. Primary education begins at the age of five and lasts for seven years. Secondary education, beginning at 12 years of age, lasts for five years, comprising a first cycle of three years and a second cycle of two years. Enrolment at primary schools in 2004/05 included 97.0% of children in the relevant age-group, while comparable enrolment in secondary level education included 68.4% of pupils in the relevant age category. Free education is provided in more than 90 government-assisted schools. Facilities for industrial, technical and teacher-training are available at the Sir Arthur Lewis Community College at Morne Fortune, which also houses an extra-mural branch of the University of the West Indies. In May 2002 it was announced that an additional US $19m. was to be invested in the education system during 2002–06. The project, to build two new secondary schools and renovate existing ones, was to be partially funded by the World Bank and UNESCO. The implementation of universal secondary education was a stated aim of the Saint Lucia Labour Party Government. Some EC $162.7m. was allocated to the Ministry of Education and

SAINT LUCIA

Culture in the 2007/08 budget (equivalent to 18.3% of total planned budgetary expenditure).

Public Holidays

2008: 1–2 January (New Year), 22 February (Independence Day), 21 March (Good Friday), 24 March (Easter Monday), 1 May (Labour Day), 12 May (Whit Monday), 22 May (Corpus Christi), 1 August (Emancipation Day), 6 October (Thanksgiving Day), 1 November (All Saints' Day), 2 November (All Souls' Day), 22 November (Feast of St Cecilia), 13 December (Saint Lucia Day), 25–26 December (Christmas).

2009: 1–2 January (New Year), 22 February (Independence Day), 10 April (Good Friday), 13 April (Easter Monday), 1 May (Labour Day), 1 June (Whit Monday), 11 June (Corpus Christi), 1 August (Emancipation Day), 5 October (Thanksgiving Day), 1 November (All Saints' Day), 2 November (All Souls' Day), 22 November (Feast of St Cecilia), 13 December (Saint Lucia Day), 25–26 December (Christmas).

Weights and Measures

The imperial system is in use.

Statistical Survey

Source (unless otherwise indicated): St Lucian Government Statistics Department, Block A, Government Bldgs, Waterfront, Castries; tel. 452-7670; fax 451-8254; e-mail statsdept@candw.lc; internet www.stats.gov.lc.

AREA AND POPULATION

Area: 616.3 sq km (238 sq miles).

Population: 135,685 (males 65,988, females 69,697) at census of 12 May 1991; 162,982 (males 79,877, females 83,105) at census of 22 May 2001 (including estimate for underenumeration). *2006:* 166,838 (mid-year estimate). *By District* (estimates at mid-2006): Castries 68,209; Anse La Raye 6,468; Canaries 1,920; Soufrière 8,037; Choiseul 6,376; Laborie 7,705; Vieux-Fort 15,942; Micoud 16,794; Dennery 13,458; Gros Islet 21,929.

Density (mid-2006): 270.7 per sq km.

Principal Town (population incl. suburbs, mid-2006): Castries (capital) 14,509.

Births, Marriages and Deaths (2005, provisional): Registered live births 2,215 (birth rate 13.5 per 1,000); Registered marriages 591; Registered deaths 1,107 (death rate 6.7 per 1,000).

Expectation of Life (years at birth, WHO estimates): 75.0 (males 72.1; females 78.0) in 2005. Source: WHO, *World Health Statistics*.

Economically Active Population (persons aged 15 years and over, labour survey for October–December 2004): Agriculture, hunting and forestry 9,810; Fishing 690; Manufacturing 4,590; Electricity, gas and water 410; Construction 5,650; Wholesale and retail trade; repair of motor vehicles, motorcycles and personal and household goods 9,710; Hotels and restaurants 9,840; Transport, storage and communications 3,440; Financial intermediation 1,760; Real estate, renting and business activities 2,950; Public administration and compulsory social security 8,470; Education 730; Health and social work 270; Other community, social and personal service activities 1,400; Private households with employed persons 2,150; Activities not adequately defined 200; Not reported 3,830; *Total employed* 65,900; Unemployed 14,700; *Total labour force* 80,600 (males 43,440, females 37,160).

HEALTH AND WELFARE
Key Indicators

Total Fertility Rate (children per woman, 2005): 2.2.

Under-5 Mortality Rate (per 1,000 live births, 2005): 20.

Physicians (per 1,000 head, 1999): 5.17.

Hospital Beds (per 1,000 head, 2003): 2.9.

Health Expenditure (2004): US $ per head (PPP): 301.6.

Health Expenditure (2004): % of GDP: 5.0.

Health Expenditure (2004): public (% of total): 65.0.

Access to Water (% of persons, 2004): 98.

Access to Sanitation (% of persons, 2004): 89.

Human Development Index (2005): ranking: 72.

Human Development Index (2005): value: 0.795.

For sources and definitions, see explanatory note on p. vi.

AGRICULTURE, ETC.

Principal Crops ('000 metric tons, 2005): Cassava 1.0 (FAO estimate); Yams 0.4; Coconuts 9.8 (FAO estimate); Bananas 32.8; Plantains 0.7; Citrus fruits 2.0. *Aggregate Production* ('000 metric tons, may include official, semi-official or estimated data): Roots and tubers 6.5; Vegetables (incl. melons) 1.0; Fruits (excl. melons) 40.7. *2006:* Figures for aggregate production assumed to be unchanged from 2005 (FAO estimates).

Livestock ('000 head, 2004, FAO estimates): Cattle 12.4; Sheep 12.5; Goats 9.8; Pigs 15.0; Horses 1.0; Asses, mules or hinnies 1.5; Poultry 270. *2005:* Cattle 12.4; Pigs 15.0. Note: Data for 2006 were not available.

Livestock Products ('000 metric tons, 2005, FAO estimates): Pig meat 1.1; Chicken meat 1.0 (official figure); Cows' milk 1.0; Hen eggs 1.4. Note: Data for 2006 were not available.

Fishing (metric tons, live weight, 2005): Capture 1,409 (Wahoo 169; Skipjack tuna 159; Blackfin tuna 126; Yellowfin tuna 172; Common dolphinfish 198; Stromboid conches 42); Aquaculture 1; Total catch 1,410. Figures exclude aquatic plants.

Source: FAO.

INDUSTRY

Production (2006, unless otherwise indicated): Electric energy 330.8 million kWh; Copra 1,094 metric tons (2004); Coconut oil (unrefined) 1.2m. litres; Coconut oil (refined) 88,700 litres; Coconut meal 499,300 kg; Rum 191,900 proof gallons.

FINANCE

Currency and Exchange Rates: 100 cents = 1 Eastern Caribbean dollar (EC $). *Sterling, US Dollar and Euro Equivalents* (30 November 2007): £1 sterling = EC $5.579; US $1 = EC $2.700; €1 = EC $3.985; EC $100 = £17.92 = US $37.04 = €25.09. *Exchange Rate:* Fixed at US $1 = EC $2.70 since July 1976.

Budget (EC $ million, 2006): *Revenue:* Tax revenue 603.8 (Taxes on income and profits 148.4; Taxes on property 4.7; Taxes on domestic goods and services 105.6; Taxes on international trade and transactions 345.2); Other current revenue 40.9; Capital revenue 0.9; Total 645.6 (excl. grants 3.3). *Expenditure:* Current expenditure 551.2 (Personal emoluments 253.9; Goods and services 103.6; Interest payments 77.6; Transfers and subsidies 116.0); Capital expenditure and net lending 251.3; Total 802.5. Source: Eastern Caribbean Central Bank.

International Reserves (US $ million at 31 December 2006): IMF special drawing rights 2.33; Reserve position in IMF 0.01; Foreign exchange 132.19; Total 134.54. Source: IMF, *International Financial Statistics*.

Money Supply (EC $ million at 31 December 2006): Currency outside banks 156.11; Demand deposits at deposit money banks 175.00; Total money 331.12. Source: IMF, *International Financial Statistics*.

Cost of Living (Consumer Price Index; base: 2000 = 100): 107.8 in 2004; 112.0 in 2005; 114.6 in 2006. Source: IMF, *International Financial Statistics*.

Gross Domestic Product (EC $ million at constant 1990 prices): 1,290.56 in 2004; 1,339.91 in 2005; 1,407.17 in 2006 (preliminary).

Expenditure on the Gross Domestic Product (EC $ million at current prices, 2006, preliminary): Government final consumption expenditure 414.43; Private final consumption expenditure 1,534.35; Gross capital formation 736.21; *Total domestic expenditure* 2,684.99; Exports of goods and services 1,150.92; *Less* Imports of goods and services 1,337.50; *GDP at market prices* 2,498.41.

Gross Domestic Product by Economic Activity (EC $ million at current factor cost, 2006, preliminary): Agriculture, hunting, forestry and fishing 80.75; Mining and quarrying 6.82; Manufacturing 125.35; Electricity and water 99.22; Construction 187.54; Wholesale and retail trade 248.65; Restaurants and hotels 277.82; Transport 233.20; Communications 165.22; Banking and insurance 201.38; Real estate and housing 188.75; Government services 302.38; Other services 89.16; *Sub-total* 2,206.24; *Less* Imputed bank service charge 161.45; *Total in basic prices* 2,044.80; Taxes, less subsidies, on products 453.61; *GDP at market prices* 2,498.41.

Balance of Payments (US $ million, 2005): Exports of goods f.o.b. 82.73; Imports of goods f.o.b. –418.12; *Trade balance* –335.39; Exports of services 410.09; Imports of services –171.10; *Balance on goods and services* –96.40; Other income received (net) –70.59; *Balance on goods, services and income* –166.99; Current transfers received 29.67; Current transfers paid –16.65; *Current balance* –153.97; Capital account (net) 5.34; Direct investment from abroad (net) 81.52; Portfolio investment (net) 10.74; Other investment (net) 58.61; Net errors and omissions –17.46; *Overall balance* –15.22. Source: IMF, *International Financial Statistics*.

EXTERNAL TRADE

Principal Commodities (EC $ million, 2006, provisional): *Imports c.i.f.:* Food and live animals 255.4 (Meat 54.5; Cereals 45.2); Beverages and tobacco 55.4 (Beverages 48.1); Mineral fuels, lubricants, etc. 206.0 (Refined petroleum products 192.8); Chemicals 109.6; Basic manufactures 283.5 (Metal manufactures 60.9); Machinery and transport equipment 413.5 (Telecommunications equipment 38.6; Road vehicles 164.1); Miscellaneous manufactured articles 226.5; Total (incl. others) 1,599.5. *Exports f.o.b.* (incl. re-exports): Food and live animals 188.3 (Bananas 47.2); Beverages and tobacco 41.0 (Beer 35.0); Mineral fuels, lubricants, etc. 54.7 (Refined petroleum products 54.7); Basic manufactures 17.6 (Paper products 12.7); Machinery and transport equipment 46.2 (Telecommunications equipment 11.6; Electric machinery, etc. 10.1; Road vehicles 4.0); Miscellaneous manufactured articles 29.3; Total (incl. others) 253.1.

Principal Trading Partners (EC $ million, 2006, provisional): *Imports c.i.f.:* Barbados 70.9; Canada 43.4; France 24.6; Germany 24.3; Grenada 9.6; Japan 100.9; Netherlands 17.2; Saint Vincent and the Grenadines 15.4; Trinidad and Tobago 270.0; United Kingdom 110.2; USA 552.8; Total (incl. others) 1,599.5 *Exports f.o.b.* (excl. re-exports): Antigua and Barbuda 3.6; Barbados 14.9; Dominica 9.1; Grenada 4.6; Saint Vincent and the Grenadines 5.2; Trinidad and Tobago 22.4; United Kingdom 51.0; USA 14.9; Total (incl. others) 140.3.

TRANSPORT

Road Traffic (registered motor vehicles, 2002): Goods vehicles 9,554; Taxis and hired vehicles 1,880; Motorcycles 797; Private vehicles 21,421; Passenger vans 3,439; Total (incl. others) 38,572.

Shipping: *Arrivals* (2006): 1,557 vessels. *International Sea-borne Freight Traffic* (metric tons, 2006): Goods loaded 15,957; Goods unloaded 622,976.

Civil Aviation (traffic at George F. L. Charles and Hewanorra airports, 2006, Jan.–Oct.): Aircraft movements 26,756; Passenger departures 312,047; Passenger arrivals 325,532; Cargo loaded (metric tons) 1,203.8; Cargo unloaded (metric tons) 1,315.5. Source: Saint Lucia Air and Sea Ports Authority.

TOURISM

Visitor Arrivals: 813,681 (298,431 stop-over visitors, 11,441 excursionists, 22,530 yacht passengers, 481,279 cruise-ship passengers) in 2004; 747,308 (317,939 stop-over visitors, 7,541 excursionists, 27,464 yacht passengers, 394,364 cruise-ship passengers) in 2005; 694,469 (302,510 stop-over visitors, 7,011 excursionists, 25,355 yacht passengers, 359,593 cruise-ship passengers) in 2006. *Stop-over visitors by country* (2006): USA 117,450; Canada 17,491; United Kingdom 73,312; France 3,764; Germany 2,569; Caribbean 78,465; Other countries 9,459.

Tourism Receipts (EC $ million): 879.3 in 2004; 961.1 in 2005; 935.5 in 2006.

Source: Eastern Caribbean Central Bank.

COMMUNICATIONS MEDIA

Radio Receivers ('000 in use, 1997): 111.

Television Receivers ('000 in use, 1999): 56.

Telephones ('000 main lines in use, 2006): 39.4.

Mobile Cellular Telephones ('000 subscribers, 2005): 105.7.

Personal Computers ('000 in use, 2004): 26.

Internet Users ('000 subscribers, 2006): 8.8.

Non-daily Newspapers (1996): Titles 5; Circulation 34,000.

Sources: UN, *Statistical Yearbook*; UNESCO, *Statistical Yearbook*; International Telecommunication Union; Eastern Caribbean Telecommunications Authority, *Annual Telecommunications Sector Review 2006*.

EDUCATION

Pre-primary (state institutions only, 2005/06): 148 schools; 480 teachers; 5,062 pupils.

Primary (state institutions only, 2005/06): 78 schools; 1,214 teachers; 23,969 pupils.

General Secondary (state institutions only, 2005/06): 19 schools; 738 teachers; 13,099 pupils.

Special Education (state institutions only, 2000/01): 5 schools; 39 teachers; 227 students.

Adult Education (state institutions only, 2000/01): 19 centres; 80 facilitators; 729 learners.

Tertiary (state institutions, including part-time, 2000/01): 127 teachers; 1,403 students.

Source: partly Caribbean Development Bank, *Social and Economic Indicators*.

Adult Literacy Rate (UNESCO estimates): 94.8% in 2004. Source: UN Development Programme, *Human Development Report*.

Directory

The Constitution

The Constitution came into force at the independence of Saint Lucia on 22 February 1979. Its main provisions are summarized below:

FUNDAMENTAL RIGHTS AND FREEDOMS

Regardless of race, place of origin, political opinion, colour, creed or sex but subject to respect for the rights and freedoms of others and for the public interest, every person in Saint Lucia is entitled to the rights of life, liberty, security of the person, equality before the law and the protection of the law. Freedom of conscience, of expression, of assembly and association is guaranteed and the inviolability of personal privacy, family life and property is maintained. Protection is afforded from slavery, forced labour, torture and inhuman treatment.

THE GOVERNOR-GENERAL

The British monarch, as Head of State, is represented in Saint Lucia by the Governor-General.

PARLIAMENT

Parliament consists of the British monarch, represented by the Governor-General, the 11-member Senate and the House of Assembly, composed of 17 elected Representatives. Senators are appointed by the Governor-General: six on the advice of the Prime Minister, three on the advice of the Leader of the Opposition and two acting on his own deliberate judgement. The life of Parliament is five years.

Each constituency returns one Representative to the House who is directly elected in accordance with the Constitution.

At a time when the office of Attorney-General is a public office, the Attorney-General is an ex officio member of the House.

Every citizen over the age of 21 is eligible to vote.

Parliament may alter any of the provisions of the Constitution.

THE EXECUTIVE

Executive authority is vested in the British monarch and exercisable by the Governor-General. The Governor-General appoints as Prime Minister that member of the House who, in the Governor-General's view, is best able to command the support of the majority of the members of the House, and other Ministers on the advice of the Prime Minister. The Governor-General may remove the Prime Minister from office if the House approves a resolution expressing 'no confidence' in the Government, and if the Prime Minister does not resign within three days or advise the Governor-General to dissolve Parliament.

The Cabinet consists of the Prime Minister and other Ministers, and the Attorney-General as an ex officio member at a time when the office of Attorney-General is a public office.

SAINT LUCIA

The Leader of the Opposition is appointed by the Governor-General as that member of the House who, in the Governor-General's view, is best able to command the support of a majority of members of the house who do not support the Government.

CITIZENSHIP

All persons born in Saint Lucia before independence who immediately prior to independence were citizens of the United Kingdom and Colonies automatically become citizens of Saint Lucia. All persons born in Saint Lucia after independence automatically acquire Saint Lucian citizenship, as do those born outside Saint Lucia after independence to a parent possessing Saint Lucian citizenship. Provision is made for the acquisition of citizenship by those to whom it is not automatically granted.

The Government

HEAD OF STATE

Monarch: HM Queen ELIZABETH II.
Governor-General: Dame PEARLETTE LOUISY (took office 17 September 1997).

CABINET
(April 2008)

Prime Minister and Minister for Finance, International Financial Services, and for External Affairs, and for Home Affairs and National Security: STEPHENSON KING.
Minister for Social Transformation, Public Service, Human Resource Development, Youth and Sports: LENARD SPIDER MONTOUTE.
Minister for Health Wellness, Family Affairs, National Mobilisation, Human Services and Gender Relations: Dr KEITH MONDESIR.
Minister for Physical Development, Housing, Urban Renewal and Local Government: RICHARD FREDRICK.
Minister for Education and Culture: ARSENE VIGIL JAMES.
Minister for Agriculture, Lands, Fisheries, and Forestry: EZECHIEL JOSEPH.
Minister for Trade (Domestic and International), Industry, Commerce and Consumer Affairs: GEORGE GUY MAYERS.
Minister for Communications, Works, Transport and Public Utilities: GUY EARDLEY JOSEPH.
Minister for Tourism and Civil Aviation: ALLEN CHASTANET.
Minister for Economic Affairs, Economic Planning, Investment and National Development: AUSBERT D'AUVERGNE.
Minister for Labour, Information and Broadcasting: EDMUND ESTEPHANE.
Attorney-General and Minister for Justice: Dr NICHOLAS FREDERICK.
Minister in the Office of the Prime Minister: TESSA MANGAL.
Minister in the Ministry of Education and Culture: GASPARD PETER DAVID CHARLEMAGNE.

MINISTRIES

Office of the Prime Minister: Greaham Louisy Administrative Bldg, 5th Floor, Waterfront, Castries; tel. 468-2111; fax 453-7352; e-mail admin@pm.gov.lc; internet www.pm.gov.lc.
Attorney-General's Office and Ministry of Justice: Old Education Bldg, Cnr Micoud and Laborie Sts, Castries; tel. 452-3772; fax 453-6315; e-mail atgen@gosl.gov.lc.
Ministry of Agriculture, Forestry and Fisheries: Stanislaus James Bldg, 5th Floor, Waterfront, Castries; tel. 452-2526; fax 453-6314; e-mail adminag@candw.lc; internet www.slumaffe.org.
Ministry of Communications, Works, Transport and Public Utilities: Williams Bldg, Bridge St, Castries; tel. 468-4300; fax 453-2769.
Ministry of Economic Affairs, Economic Planning, Investment and National Development: Greaham Louisy Administrative Bldg, 2nd Floor, Waterfront, Castries; tel. 468-2202; fax 453-1305.
Ministry of Education and Culture: Francis Compton Bldg, Waterfront, Castries; tel. 468-5203; fax 453-2299; e-mail mineduc@candw.lc; internet www.education.gov.lc.
Ministry of External Affairs, International Finance Services, Information and Broadcasting: Conway Business Centre, Waterfront, Castries; tel. 468-4501; fax 452-7427; e-mail foreign@candw.lc.
Ministry of Finance: Financial Centre, 2nd Floor, Bridge St, Castries; tel. 468-5520; fax 451-9231; e-mail minfin@gosl.gov.lc.
Ministry of Health Wellness, Family Affairs, National Mobilisation, Human Services and Gender Relations: Chaussee Rd, Castries; tel. 452-2859; fax 452-5655; e-mail health@candw.lc.
Ministry of Home Affairs and National Security: Erdiston's Pl., Manoel St, Castries; tel. 468-3600; fax 453-6315.
Ministry of Labour, Information and Broadcasting: Stanislaus James Administrative Bldg, POB 163, Waterfront, Castries.
Ministry of Physical Development, Housing, Urban Renewal and Local Government: Castries; internet www.planning.gov.lc.
Ministry of Social Transformation, Public Service, Human Resource Development, Youth and Sports: Greaham Louisy Administrative Bldg, 4th Floor, Waterfront, Castries; tel. 468-5101; fax 453-7921.
Ministry of Tourism and Civil Aviation: Sir Stanislaus James Bldg, 3rd Floor, Waterfront, Castries; tel. 468-4629; fax 451-6986; e-mail mitandt@candw.lc.
Ministry of Trade, Industry and Commerce: Heraldine Rock Bldg, 4th Floor, Waterfront, Castries; tel. 468-4202; fax 451-6986.

Legislature

PARLIAMENT

Senate

The Senate has nine nominated members and two independent members.
President: ROSEMARY HUSBANDS-MATHURIN.

House of Assembly

Speaker: SARAH FLOOD-BEAUBRUN.
Clerk: KURT THOMAS.
Election, 11 December 2006

Party	Seats
United Workers' Party	11
Saint Lucia Labour Party	6
Total	17

Election Commission

Election Commission: St Lucia Electoral Dept, 23 High St, POB 1074, Castries; tel. 452-3725; fax 451-6513; e-mail info@electoral.gov.lc; internet www.electoral.gov.lc; Election Commr CARSON RAGGIE.

Political Organizations

Organization for National Empowerment (ONE): POB 1496, Castries; f. 2004; Leader PETER ALEXANDER; Chair. ROSEMUND CLERY.
Saint Lucia Freedom Party: Castries; f. 1999; campaigns against the political establishment; Spokesman MARTINUS FRANÇOIS.
Saint Lucia Labour Party (SLP): Tom Walcott Bldg, 2nd Floor, Jeremie St, POB 427, Castries; tel. 451-8446; fax 451-9389; e-mail slp@candw.lc; f. 1946; socialist party; Leader Dr KENNY DAVIS ANTHONY; Chair. JULIAN HUNTE.
United Workers' Party (UWP): 9 Coral St, POB 1550, Castries; tel. 451-9103; fax 451-9207; e-mail unitworkers@netscape.net; f. 1964; right-wing; Chair. and Leader STEPHENSON KING.

Diplomatic Representation

EMBASSIES AND HIGH COMMISSION IN SAINT LUCIA

China (Taiwan): Reduit Beach Ave, Rodney Bay; tel. 452-8105; fax 458-0441; Ambassador TOM CHOU.
Cuba: Rodney Heights, Gros Islet, POB 2150, Castries; tel. 458-4665; fax 458-4666; e-mail embacubasantalucia@candw.lc; Ambassador HUGO RUIZ CABRERA.
France: French Embassy to the OECS, GPO Private Box 937, Vigie, Castries; tel. 455-6060; fax 455-6056; e-mail frenchembassy@candw.lc; internet www.ambafrance-lc.org; Ambassador MICHÈLE SAUTER-AUD.
United Kingdom: Francis Compton Bldg, Waterfront, POB 227, Castries; tel. 452-2484; fax 453-1543; e-mail britishhc@candw.lc; High Commissioner DUNCAN JOHN RUSHWORTH TAYLOR (resident in Barbados).

SAINT LUCIA

Venezuela: Vigie House, POB 494, Castries; tel. 452-4033; fax 453-6747; e-mail vembassy@candw.lc; Ambassador EDUARDO ALFONZO BARRANCO HERNÁNDEZ.

Judicial System

SUPREME COURT

Eastern Caribbean Supreme Court: Heraldine Rock Bldg, Block B, Waterfront, POB 1093, Castries; tel. 452-7998; fax 452-5475; e-mail appeal@candw.lc; the West Indies Associated States Supreme Court was established in 1967 and was known as the Supreme Court of Grenada and the West Indies Associated States from 1974 until 1979, when it became the Eastern Caribbean Supreme Court. Its jurisdiction extends to Anguilla, Antigua and Barbuda, the British Virgin Islands, Dominica, Grenada (which rejoined in 1991), Montserrat, Saint Christopher and Nevis, Saint Lucia and Saint Vincent and the Grenadines. It is composed of the High Court of Justice and the Court of Appeal. The High Court is composed of the Chief Justice, who is head of the judiciary, and 16 High Court Judges, three of whom are resident in Saint Lucia. The Court of Appeal is itinerant and presided over by the Chief Justice and three other Justices of Appeal. Additionally, there are two Masters whose principal responsibilities extend to procedural and interlocutory matters. Jurisdiction of the High Court includes fundamental rights and freedoms, membership of the parliaments, and matters concerning the interpretation of constitutions. Following the inauguration of the Caribbean Court of Justice in April 2005, appeals from the Court of Appeal would no longer be made to the Judicial Committee of the Privy Council, based in the United Kingdom, but to the new regional court.

Chief Justice: HUGH ANTHONY RAWLINS (acting).
Justices of Appeal: DENYS ARTHUR BARROW, OLA MAE EDWARDS.
Managing Judge: ESBON ANTHONY ROSS.
Chief Registrar: KIMBERLY CENAC PHULGENCE.
Puisne Judges: KENNETH ANDREW CHARLES BENJAMIN, SANDRA PRUNELLA MASON, BRIAN COTTLE.
Registrar: AISHA BAPTISTE.

Religion

CHRISTIANITY

The Roman Catholic Church

Saint Lucia forms a single archdiocese. The Archbishop participates in the Antilles Episcopal Conference (currently based in Port of Spain, Trinidad and Tobago). At 31 December 2004 there were an estimated 100,243 adherents, equivalent to some 63.5% of the population.

Archbishop of Castries: ROBERT RIVAS, Archbishop's House, Nelson Mandela Dr., POB 267, Castries; tel. 452-2416; fax 452-3697; e-mail secretaries@archdioceseofcastries.org; internet www.archdioceseofcastries.org.

The Anglican Communion

Anglicans in Saint Lucia are adherents of the Church in the Province of the West Indies, comprising eight dioceses. The Archbishop of the West Indies is the Bishop of Nassau and the Bahamas. Saint Lucia forms part of the diocese of the Windward Islands (the Bishop is resident in Kingstown, Saint Vincent).

Other Christian Churches

Seventh-day Adventist Church: St Louis St, POB 117, Castries; tel. 452-4408; e-mail adventist@candw.lc; internet www.tagnet.org/cacaosda; Pastor THEODORE JARIA.

Trinity Evangelical Lutheran Church: Gablewoods Mall, POB 858, Castries; tel. 458-4638; e-mail spiegelbergs@candw.lc; Pastor Rev. TOM SPIEGELBERG.

Baptist, Christian Science, Methodist, Pentecostal and other churches are also represented in Saint Lucia.

The Press

The Catholic Chronicle: POB 778, Castries; f. 1957; monthly; Editor Rev. PATRICK A. B. ANTHONY; circ. 3,000.

The Crusader: 19 St Louis St, Castries; tel. 452-2203; fax 452-1986; f. 1934; weekly (Saturday); circ. 4,000.

The Mirror: Bisee Industrial Estate, Castries; tel. 451-6181; fax 451-6197; e-mail webmaster@stluciamirror.com; internet www.stluciamirroronline.com; f. 1994; weekly (Friday); Man. Editor GUY ELLIS.

Directory

One Caribbean: POB 852, Castries; e-mail dabread@candw.lc; weekly; Editor D. SINCLAIR DABREO.

She Caribbean: Rodney Bay Industrial Estate, Massade, Gros Islet, POB 1146, Castries; tel. 450-7827; fax 450-8694; e-mail waynem@candw.lc; internet www.shecaribbean.com; quarterly; Publr and Editor-in-Chief MAE WAYNE.

The Star: Rodney Bay Industrial Estate, Gros Islet, POB 1146, Castries; tel. 450-7827; fax 450-8694; e-mail starpub@candw.lc; internet www.stluciastar.com; f. 1987; 3 a week (Monday, Wednesday and weekend edns); circ. 8,000; Propr RICK WAYNE.

Tropical Traveller: Rodney Bay Industrial Estate, Massade, Gros Islet, POB 1146, Castries; tel. 450-7827; fax 450-8694; e-mail staceystar@candw.lc; internet www.tropicaltraveller.com; f. 1989; monthly; Editorial Dir MAE WAYNE.

The Vanguard: Hospital Rd, Castries; weekly; Editor ANDREW SEALY; circ. 2,000.

Visions of St Lucia Tourist Guide: 7 Maurice Mason Ave, Sans Souci, POB 947, Castries; tel. 453-0427; fax 452-1522; e-mail visions@candw.lc; internet www.visionsofstlucia.com; f. 1989; official tourist guide; published by Island Visions Ltd; annual; Chair. and Man. Dir ANTHONY NEIL AUSTIN; circ. 120,000.

The Voice of St Lucia: Odessa Bldg, Darling Rd, POB 104, Castries; tel. 452-2590; fax 453-1453; internet www.thevoiceofstlucia.com; f. 1885; 2 a week; circ. 8,000.

The Weekend Voice: Odessa Bldg, Darling Rd, POB 104, Castries; tel. 452-2590; fax 453-1453; weekly (Saturdays); circ. 8,000.

PRESS ORGANIZATION

Eastern Caribbean Press Council (ECPC): Castries; f. 2003; independent, self-regulating body designed to foster and maintain standards in regional journalism, formed by 14 newspapers in the Eastern Caribbean and Barbados; Chair. Lady MARIE SIMMONS.

NEWS AGENCY

Caribbean Media Corporation: Bisee Rd, Castries; tel. 453-7162; e-mail admin@cmccaribbean.com; internet thecmconline.com; f. 2000 by merger of Caribbean News Agency and Caribbean Broadcasting Union.

Publishers

Caribbean Publishing Co Ltd: American Drywall Bldg, Vide Boutielle Highway, POB 104, Castries; tel. 452-3188; fax 452-3181; e-mail publish@candw.lc; f. 1978; publishes telephone directories and magazines.

Crusader Publishing Co Ltd: 19 St Louis St, Castries; tel. 452-2203; fax 452-1986.

Island Visions Ltd: 7 Maurice Mason Ave, Sans Soucis, POB 947, Castries; tel. 453-0472; fax 452-1522; e-mail visions@candw.lc; internet www.visionsofstlucia.com; f. 1989; Chair. and Man. Dir ANTHONY NEIL AUSTIN.

Mirror Publishing Co Ltd: Bisee Industrial Estate, POB 1782, Castries; tel. 451-6181; fax 451-6503; e-mail mirror@candw.lc; f. 1994; privately owned; weekly (Fridays); Man. Editor GUY ELLIS; circ. 3,900.

Star Publishing Co: Rodney Bay Industrial Estate, Massade, Gros Islet, POB 1146, Castries; tel. 450-7827; fax 450-8694; e-mail starpub@candw.lc; internet www.stluciastar.com; Propr RICK WAYNE.

Voice Publishing Co Ltd: Odessa Bldg, Darling Rd, POB 104, Castries; tel. 452-2590; fax 453-1453.

Broadcasting and Communications

TELECOMMUNICATIONS

Regulatory Authorities

Eastern Caribbean Telecommunications Authority (ECTEL): Vide Boutielle, POB 1886, Castries; tel. 458-1701; fax 458-1698; e-mail ectel@ectel.int; internet www.ectel.int; f. 2000 to regulate telecommunications in Saint Lucia, Dominica, Grenada, Saint Christopher and Nevis and Saint Vincent and the Grenadines; Chair. ISAAC SOLOMON; Dir (Saint Lucia) EMBERT CHARLES.

National Telecommunications Regulatory Commission (NTRC): Global Tile Bldg, Bois d'Orange, Gros Islet, POB GM 690, Castries; tel. 458-2035; fax 453-2558; e-mail ntrc_slu@candw.lc; internet www.ntrc.org.lc; f. 2000; regulates the sector in conjunction with ECTEL; Chair. THADDEUS ANTOINE.

SAINT LUCIA

Major Service Providers

Cable & Wireless St Lucia: Bridge St, POB 111, Castries; tel. 453-9720; fax 453-9700; e-mail talk2us@candw.lc; internet www.candw.lc; provides fixed-line, mobile, internet and cable-television services; CEO COLIN JAMES.

Digicel St Lucia: Rodney Bay, Gros Islet, POB GM 791, Castries; tel. 456-3400; fax 450-3872; e-mail customercare.stlucia@digicelgroup.com; internet www.digicelstlucia.com; f. 2003; owned by an Irish consortium; acquired operations of Cingular Wireless in Saint Lucia in 2006; Chair. DENIS O'BRIEN; Eastern Caribbean CEO KEVIN WHITE.

Saint Lucia Boatphone Ltd: POB 2136, Gros Islet; tel. 452-0361; fax 452-0394; e-mail boatphone@candw.lc; wholly owned by Cable & Wireless; subsidiary co of Cable & Wireless Caribbean Cellular.

BROADCASTING

Radio

Gem Radio Network: POB 1146, Castries; tel. 459-0609.

Radio Caribbean International: 11 Mongiraud St, POB 121, Castries; tel. 452-2636; fax 452-2637; e-mail rci@candw.lc; internet www.rcistlucia.com; operates Radio Caraïbes; English and Creole services; broadcasts 24 hrs; Pres. H. COQUERELLE; Station Man. WINSTON FOSTER.

Saint Lucia Broadcasting Corporation: Morne Fortune, POB 660, Castries; tel. 452-2337; fax 453-1568; govt-owned; Man. KEITH WEEKES.

Radio 100-Helen FM: Morne Fortune, POB 621, Castries; tel. 451-7260; fax 453-1737; e-mail hts@candw.lc; internet www.htsstlucia.com; Gen. Man. STEPHENSON ANIUS.

Radio Saint Lucia (RSL): Morne Fortune, POB 660, Castries; tel. 452-2337; fax 453-1568; e-mail rsl@candw.lc; internet www.rslonline.com; English and Creole services; Chair. EVARISTUS JN MARIE; Man. KEITH WEEKES.

Television

Cablevision: George Gordon Bldg, Bridge St, POB 111, Castries; tel. 453-9311; fax 453-9740.

Catholic Broadcasting TV Network (CBTN): Micoud St, Castries; tel. 452-7050.

Daher Broadcasting Service Ltd (DBS): Vigie, POB 1623, Castries; tel. 453-2705; fax 452-3544; e-mail dbstv@candw.lc; internet dbstelevision.com; Man. Dir LINDA DAHER.

Helen Television System (HTS): National Television Service of St Lucia, POB 621, The Morne, Castries; tel. 452-2693; fax 454-1737; e-mail hts@candw.lc; internet www.htsstlucia.com; f. 1967; commercial station; Gen. Man. STEPHENSON ANIUS.

National Television Network (NTN): Castries; f. 2001; operated by the Government Information Service; provides information on the operations of the public sector.

Finance

(cap. = capital; dep. = deposits; m. = million; brs = branches)

BANKING

The Eastern Caribbean Central Bank, based in Saint Christopher, is the central issuing and monetary authority for Saint Lucia.

Eastern Caribbean Central Bank—Saint Lucia Office: Financial Centre, 3rd Floor, Bridge St, POB 295, Castries; tel. 452-7449; fax 453-6022; e-mail eccbslu@candw.lc; Country Dir TREVOR BRATHWAITE; Rep. GREGOR FRANKLIN.

Local Banks

Bank of Saint Lucia Ltd: Financial Centre, 5th Floor, 1 Bridge St, POB 1862, Castries; tel. 456-6000; fax 456-6702; e-mail bankofstlucia@candw.lc; internet www.ecfh.com; f. 2001 by merger of National Commercial Bank of St Lucia Ltd and Saint Lucia Devt Bank; total assets EC $1,301m. (Dec. 2006); 35% state-owned; parent co is East Caribbean Financial Holding Co Ltd; Chair. VICTOR A. EUDOXIE; Man. Dir ROBERT NORSTROM; 7 brs.

1st National Bank Saint Lucia Ltd: 21 Bridge St, POB 168, Castries; tel. 455-7000; fax 453-1630; e-mail manager@1stnationalbankslu.com; inc. 1937 as Saint Lucia Co-operative Bank Ltd; name changed as above Jan. 2005; commercial bank; share cap. EC $5m., asset base EC $221.4m. (Dec. 2004); Man. Dir C. CARLTON GLASGOW; 4 brs.

FirstCaribbean International Bank (Barbados) Ltd: Bridge St, POB 335, Castries; tel. 456-2422; fax 452-3735; internet www.firstcaribbeanbank.com; f. 2002 following merger of Caribbean operations of Barclays Bank PLC and CIBC; CIBC acquired Barclays' 43.7% stake in 2006; Exec. Chair. MICHAEL MANSOOR; CEO CHARLES PINK.

RBTT Bank Caribbean Ltd: 22 Micoud St, POB 1531, Castries; tel. 452-2265; fax 452-1668; e-mail rbttslu.isd@candw.lc; internet www.rbtt.com; f. 1985 as Caribbean Banking Corpn Ltd, name changed as above in March 2002; owned by R and M Holdings Ltd; Chair. PETER JULY; Country Man. EARL P. CRICHTON; 4 brs.

STOCK EXCHANGE

Eastern Caribbean Securities Exchange: based in Basseterre, Saint Christopher and Nevis; e-mail info@ecseonline.com; internet www.ecseonline.com; f. 2001; regional securities market designed to facilitate the buying and selling of financial products for the eight member territories—Anguilla, Antigua and Barbuda, Dominica, Grenada, Montserrat, Saint Christopher and Nevis, Saint Lucia and Saint Vincent and the Grenadines; Chair. K. DWIGHT VENNER; Man. Dir MICHAEL MORTON.

INSURANCE

Local companies include the following:

Caribbean General Insurance Ltd: Laborie St, POB 290, Castries; tel. 452-2410; fax 452-3649.

Eastern Caribbean Insurance Ltd: Laborie St, POB 290, Castries; tel. 452-2410; fax 452-3393; e-mail cgi.ltd@candw.lc.

Saint Lucia Insurances Ltd: 48 Micoud St, POB 1084, Castries; tel. 452-3240; fax 452-2240; e-mail sl.ins@candw.lc; principal agents of Alliance Insurance Co Ltd.

Saint Lucia Motor and General Insurance Co Ltd: 38 Micoud St, POB 767, Castries; tel. 452-3323; fax 452-6072.

Trade and Industry

DEVELOPMENT ORGANIZATION

National Development Corporation (NDC): 1st Floor, Heraldine Rock Bldg, The Waterfront, POB 495, Castries; tel. 452-3614; fax 452-1841; e-mail devcorp@candw.lc; internet www.investstlucia.com; f. 1971 to stimulate, facilitate and promote investment opportunities for foreign and local investors and to promote the economic devt of Saint Lucia; owns and manages seven industrial estates; br. in New York, USA; Exec. Chair. NICHOLAS JOHN; CEO WAYNE VITALIS.

CHAMBER OF COMMERCE

Saint Lucia Chamber of Commerce, Industry and Agriculture: Vide Bouteille, POB 482, Castries; tel. 452-3165; fax 453-6907; e-mail info@stluciachamber.org; internet www.stluciachamber.org; f. 1884; 150 mems; Pres. LAURIE BARNARD; Exec. Dir BRIAN LOUISY.

INDUSTRIAL AND TRADE ASSOCIATIONS

Saint Lucia Banana Corporation (SLBC): 7 Manoel St, POB 197, Castries; tel. 452-2251; f. 1998 following privatization of Saint Lucia Banana Growers' Asscn (f. 1967); Chair. EUSTACE MONROSE; Sec. FREEMONT LAWRENCE.

Saint Lucia Industrial and Small Business Association: 2nd Floor, Ivy Crick Memorial Bldg, POB 312, Castries; tel. 453-1392; Pres. LEO CLARKE; Exec. Dir Dr URBAN SERAPHINE.

EMPLOYERS' ASSOCIATIONS

Saint Lucia Agriculturists' Association Ltd: Mongiraud St, POB 153, Castries; tel. 452-2494; fax 453-2693; distributor and supplier of agricultural, industrial and organic products; exporter of cocoa; Chair. CUTHBERT PHILLIPS; CEO KERDE M. SEVERIN.

Saint Lucia Coconut Growers' Association Ltd: Palmiste Rd, POB 269, Castries; tel. 459-7227; fax 459-7216; e-mail slcga1@candw.lc; Chair. EZEKIEL JOSEPH; Man. KENNETH CAZAUBON.

Saint Lucia Employers' Federation: c/o The Morgan Bldg, L'Anse Rd, POB 160, Castries; tel. 452-2190; fax 453-0370; e-mail slef@candw.lc; Pres. MALCOLM CHARLES.

Saint Lucia Fish Marketing Corpn: POB 91, Castries; tel. 452-1341; fax 451-7073; e-mail slfmc@candw.lc.

Saint Lucia Marketing Board (SLMB): Conway, POB 441, Castries; tel. 452-3214; fax 453-1424; e-mail slmb@candw.lc; Chair. DAVID DEMAQUE; Man. MICHAEL WILLIAMS.

Windward Islands Banana Development and Exporting Co (Wibdeco): POB 115, Castries; tel. 452-2411; fax 452-4165; e-mail wibdeco@candw.lc; internet www.geest-bananas.co.uk; f. 1994 in succession to the Windward Islands Banana Growers' Asscn (WINBAN); regional org. dealing with banana devt and marketing; jtly owned by the Windward govts and island banana asscns; Chair. EUSTACE MONROSE.

UTILITIES

Electricity

Caribbean Electric Utility Services Corpn (CARILEC): Desir Ave, Sans Soucis, POB CP 5907, Castries; tel. 452-0140; fax 452-0142; e-mail admin@carilec.org; internet www.carilec.com; f. 1989; Chair. TREVOR LOUISY.

St Lucia Electricity Services Ltd (LUCELEC): St Lucia Electricity Services Ltd, Sans Soucis, POB 230, Castries; tel. 457-4400; fax 457-4409; e-mail lucelec@candw.lc; internet www.lucelec.com; f. 1964; Canadian energy co Emera acquired a 19% share in LUCELEC in Jan. 2007; Chair. MARIUS ST ROSE; Man. Dir TREVOR LOUISY.

Water

Water and Sewerage Company (WASCO): L'Anse Rd, POB 1481, Castries; tel. 452-5344; fax 452-6844; e-mail wasco@candw.lc; f. 1999, as the Water and Sewerage Authority (WASA); legislation to privatize WASA was approved by Parliament in Feb. 2005; Chair. GORDON CHARLES; Man. Dir JOHN C. JOSEPH.

TRADE UNIONS

National Workers' Union (NWU): Bour Bon St, POB 713, Castries; tel. 452-3664; fax 453-2896; e-mail natwork3@hotmail.com; f. 1973; represents daily-paid workers; affiliated to World Federation of Trade Unions; Pres.-Gen. TYRONE MAYNARD; Sec.-Gen. GEORGE GODDARD, Jr; 3,200 mems (2005).

Saint Lucia Civil Service Association: Sans Soucis, POB 244, Castries; tel. 452-3903; fax 453-6061; e-mail csa@candw.lc; internet www.csastlucia.org; f. 1951; Pres. JOSEPH DOSSERIE; Gen. Sec. DAVID J. DEMACQUE; 2,381 mems.

Saint Lucia Medical and Dental Association: POB 1079, Castries; tel. 452-7255; e-mail kurlenecenac@gmail.com; internet www.slmda.org; f. 1969; Pres. Dr PETULA MONROSE-PETER; Gen. Sec. Dr KURLENE CENAC.

Saint Lucia Nurses' Association: POB 819, Castries; tel. 452-1403; fax 453-0121; e-mail slna1947@gmail.com; f. 1947; Pres. LUCY LOUIS JOSEPH; Gen. Sec. FRANCES LESMOND.

Saint Lucia Seamen, Waterfront and General Workers' Trade Union: L'Anse Rd, POB 166, Castries; tel. 452-1669; fax 452-5452; e-mail seamen@candw.lc; f. 1945; affiliated to International Trade Union Confederation, International Transport Federation and Caribbean Congress of Labour; Pres. ALEXIS ALCIDE; Sec. CECILIA W. ADOLPH; 1,000 mems.

Saint Lucia Teachers' Union: La Clery, POB 821, Castries; tel. 452-4469; fax 453-6668; e-mail sltu@candw.lc; f. 1934; Pres. JULIAN MONROSE; Gen. Sec. WAYNE CUMBERBATCH.

Saint Lucia Trade Union Federation: c/o Saint Lucia Teachers' Union, La Clery, POB 821, Castries; tel. 452-4469; fax 453-6668; e-mail cumbatch42@gmail.com; f. 2005; comprises nine trade unions of Saint Lucia, including the Civil Service Asscn, Saint Lucia Teachers' Union, Saint Lucia Medical and Dental Asscn, Saint Lucia Nurses' Asscn, Seamen and Waterfront General Workers' Union, National Farmers' Asscn, Police Welfare Asscn, Saint Lucia Fire Service Asscn and Vieux Fort General and Dock Workers' Union; Pres. JOSEPH DOSSERIRE; Gen. Sec. WAYNE CUMBERBATCH.

Saint Lucia Workers' Union: Reclamation Grounds, Conway, Castries; tel. 452-2620; f. 1939; affiliated to International Trade Union Confederation; Pres. GEORGE LOUIS; Sec. TITUS FRANCIS; 1,000 mems.

Vieux Fort General and Dock Workers' Union: New Dock Rd, POB 224, Vieux Fort; tel. 454-5128; e-mail dockworkersunion@hotmail.com; f. 1954; Pres. ATHANATIUS DOLOR; Gen. Sec. CLAUDIA AUGUSTE (acting); 846 mems (1996).

Transport

RAILWAYS

There are no railways in Saint Lucia.

ROADS

In 2000 there was an estimated total road network of 910 km, of which 150 km were main roads and 127 km were secondary roads. In that year only 5.2% of roads were paved. The main highway passes through every town and village on the island. The construction of a coastal highway, to link Castries with Cul de Sac Bay, was completed in February 2000. Further improvements to the road infrastructure included the East Coast Road Project, linking Castries to Praslin, a Castries to Gros Islet highway and a Tertiary Roads Programme, scheduled for completion in late 2006. In early 2007 the Caribbean Development Bank was preparing a programme for the renovation of 10.1 km of roads in Desruisseux and Salibus, while the Ministry of Communications, Works, Transport and Public Utilities was allocated EC $106.9m. in the 2006/07 budget. Internal transport is handled by private concerns and controlled by the Government.

SHIPPING

The ports at Castries and Vieux Fort have been fully mechanized. Castries has six berths with a total length of 2,470 ft (753 m). The two dolphin berths at the Pointe Seraphine cruise-ship terminal have been upgraded to a solid berth of 1,000 ft (305 m) and one of 850 ft (259 m). The port of Soufrière has a deep-water anchorage, but no alongside berth for ocean-going vessels. There is a petroleum transshipment terminal at Cul de Sac Bay. In 2005 394,431 cruise-ship passengers called at Saint Lucia. Regular services are provided by a number of shipping lines, including ferry services to neighbouring islands. In January 2007, Island Global Yachting Facilities Ltd (New York, USA) acquired the marina at Rodney Bay, and plans for substantial upgrade work to enhance facilities and operations were announced.

Saint Lucia Air and Sea Ports Authority (SLASPA): Manoel St, POB 651, Castries; tel. 452-2893; fax 452-2062; e-mail info@slaspa.com; internet www.slaspa.com; f. 1983; Chair. ISAAC ANTHONY; Gen. Man. SEAN MATTHEW; Dir of Airports FERGUSSON JEAN.

Saint Lucia Marine Terminals Ltd: POB VF 355, Vieux Fort; tel. 454-8742; fax 454-8745; e-mail slumarterm@candw.lc; f. 1995; private port management co.

CIVIL AVIATION

There are two airports in use: Hewanorra International (formerly Beane Field near Vieux Fort), 64 km (40 miles) from Castries, which is equipped to handle large jet aircraft and underwent expansion works in 2006 in preparation for the anticipated increase in traffic ahead of the Cricket World Cup in 2007; and George F. L. Charles Airport, which is at Vigie, in Castries, and which is capable of handling medium-range jets. Saint Lucia is served by scheduled flights to the USA, Canada, Europe and most destinations in the Caribbean. The country is a shareholder in the regional airline LIAT (see chapter on Antigua and Barbuda) which in late 2006 announced that it was to merge with its troubled rival Caribbean Star Airlines (headquartered in Antigua and Barbuda); the two airlines began operating a joint flight schedule from February 2007 under LIAT's airline designation code. The planned merger was subsequently abandoned in favour of negotiations towards LIAT's full acquisition of Caribbean Star which were completed in October 2007.

Saint Lucia Air and Sea Ports Authority: see Shipping.

Air Antilles: Laborie St, POB 1065, Castries; f. 1985; designated as national carrier of Grenada in 1987; flights to destinations in the Caribbean, the United Kingdom and North America; charter co.

Caribbean Air Transport: POB 253, Castries; f. 1975 as Saint Lucia Airways; local shuttle service, charter flights.

Eagle Air Services Ltd: George F. L. Charles Airport, POB 838, Castries; tel. and fax 452-9683; e-mail eagleairslu@candw.lc; charter flights; Man. Dir Capt. EWART F. HINKSON.

Helenair Corpn Ltd: POB 253, Castries; tel. 452-1958; fax 451-7360; e-mail helenair@candw.lc; internet www.stluciatravel.com.lc/helenair.htm; f. 1987; charter and scheduled flights to major Caribbean destinations; Man. ARTHUR NEPTUNE.

Tourism

Saint Lucia possesses spectacular mountain scenery, a tropical climate and sandy beaches. Historical sites, rich birdlife and the sulphur baths at Soufrière are other attractions. Visitor arrivals totalled 649,509 in 2006, representing a contraction of 7.1% in comparison with the previous year. Tourism receipts in that year were an estimated EC $935.5m. The USA is the principal market (38.8% of total stop-over visitors in 2006), followed by the United Kingdom (with 24.2%). There were some 3,600 hotel rooms in October 2005; increasing this figure by about 1,100 before the 2007 Cricket World Cup, hosted by several Caribbean states, including Saint Lucia, was a government priority.

Saint Lucia Hotel and Tourism Association (SLHTA): John Compton Hwy, POB 545, Castries; tel. 452-5978; fax 452-7967; e-mail slhta@candw.lc; internet www.stluciatravel.com.lc; f. 1963; Pres. COLIN HUNTE; Exec. Gen. Man. SILVANIUS FONTENARD.

Saint Lucia Tourist Board: Sureline Bldg, Top Floor, Vide Bouteille, POB 221, Castries; tel. 452-4094; fax 453-1121; e-mail slutour@candw.lc; internet www.stlucia.org; 2 brs overseas; Chair. COSTELLO MICHEL; Dir MARIA FOWELL.

SAINT VINCENT AND THE GRENADINES

Introductory Survey

Location, Climate, Language, Religion, Flag, Capital

Saint Vincent and the Grenadines is situated in the Windward Islands group, approximately 160 km (100 miles) west of Barbados, in the West Indies. The nearest neighbouring countries are Saint Lucia, some 34 km (21 miles) to the north-east, and Grenada, to the south. As well as the main volcanic island of Saint Vincent, the state includes the 32 smaller islands and cayes known as the Saint Vincent Grenadines, the northerly part of an island chain stretching between Saint Vincent and Grenada. The principal islands in that part of the group are Bequia, Canouan, Mustique, Mayreau, Isle D'Quatre and Union Island. The climate is tropical, with average temperatures of between 18°C and 32°C (64°F–90°F). Annual rainfall ranges from 1,500 mm (60 ins) in the extreme south, to 3,750 mm (150 ins) in the mountainous interior of the main island. English is the official language. Most of the inhabitants profess Christianity and are adherents of the Anglican, Methodist or Roman Catholic Churches. The national flag (proportions 2 by 3) has three unequal vertical stripes, of blue (at the hoist), yellow and green (at the fly), with three lozenges in green, in a 'V' formation, superimposed on the broad central yellow stripe. The capital is Kingstown, on the island of Saint Vincent.

Recent History

The islands were first settled by an Arawak people, who were subsequently conquered by the Caribs. The arrival of shipwrecked and escaped African slaves resulted in the increase of a so-called 'Black Carib' population, some of whose descendants still remain. Under the collective name of Saint Vincent, and despite the opposition of the French and the indigenous population, the islands finally became a British possession during the 18th century. With other nearby British territories, the Governor of the Windward Islands administered Saint Vincent, under a federal system, until December 1959. The first elections under universal adult suffrage took place in 1951. The islands participated in the West Indies Federation from its foundation in January 1958 until its dissolution in May 1962. From January 1960, Saint Vincent, in common with the other Windward Islands, had a new Constitution, with its own Administrator and an enlarged Legislative Council.

After the failure of negotiations to form a smaller East Caribbean Federation, most of the British colonies in the Leeward and Windward Islands became Associated States, with full internal self-government, in 1967. This change of status was delayed in Saint Vincent because of local political differences. At controversial elections to the Legislative Council in 1966, the ruling People's Political Party (PPP) was returned with a majority of only one seat. Further elections took place in May 1967, when the Saint Vincent Labour Party (SVLP) secured six of the nine seats in the Council. Milton Cato, leader of the SVLP, became Chief Minister, in succession to Ebenezer Joshua of the PPP. On 27 October 1969, despite objections from the PPP, Saint Vincent became an Associated State, with the United Kingdom retaining responsibility for defence and foreign relations only. The Legislative Council was renamed the House of Assembly, the Administrator was designated Governor, and the Chief Minister became Premier.

Elections were held in April 1972 for an enlarged, 13-seat House of Assembly. The PPP and the SVLP each obtained six seats, while James Mitchell, formerly a minister in the SVLP Government and standing as an independent, secured the remaining one. The PPP agreed to form a Government with Mitchell as Premier and Joshua as Deputy Premier and Minister of Finance. In September 1974 Joshua resigned after policy disagreements with the Premier. A motion expressing 'no confidence' in Mitchell's Government was approved, and the House was dissolved. In the ensuing election, which took place in December, the PPP and SVLP campaigned in a 'unity agreement'. The SVLP secured 10 of the 13 seats, and the PPP two. (Mitchell was again elected as an independent.) Cato became Premier again, at the head of a coalition with the PPP, and committed his Government to attaining full independence from the United Kingdom.

After a constitutional conference in September 1978, the colony became fully independent, within the Commonwealth, as Saint Vincent and the Grenadines, on 27 October 1979. The Governor became Governor-General, while Cato took office as the country's first Prime Minister.

Cato's position was reinforced in the general election of December 1979, when the SVLP obtained 11 of the 13 elective seats in the 19-member House of Assembly. In 1982 the leader of the opposition United People's Movement (UPM), Dr Ralph Gonsalves, resigned, accusing the UPM of harbouring Marxist tendencies, and founded a new party, the Movement for National Unity (MNU). In June 1984 Cato announced an early general election, hoping to take advantage of divisions within the opposition. However, the repercussions of scandals surrounding the Cato Government, and the economic and taxation policies of the SVLP, contributed to an unexpected victory for the centrist New Democratic Party (NDP) at the election in July. The NDP's leader, James Mitchell, became Prime Minister. Cato subsequently retired from politics and in the ensuing by-election the NDP gained another seat. Hudson Tannis replaced Cato as leader of the SVLP in January 1985; Vincent Beache succeeded him as party leader in August 1986.

At a general election conducted in May 1989 the NDP won all 15 elective seats in the newly enlarged House of Assembly. Mitchell remained as Prime Minister and formed a new Cabinet.

The NDP secured its third consecutive term of office at a general election in February 1994, obtaining 12 seats in the House of Assembly. An electoral alliance formed by the SVLP and the MNU and headed by Vincent Beache won the three remaining elective seats. In September 1994 the MNU and the SVLP announced their formal merger as the Unity Labour Party (ULP).

Opposition charges that the Government had failed to address problems presented by a marked decline in banana production, a crisis in the health and education sectors and persistent allegations that drugs-related activities were being conducted on the islands culminated in the defeat, by 10 votes to three, of a motion of 'no confidence' in the Government, brought by the opposition in August 1994. The execution, by hanging, of three convicted murderers in February 1995 provoked outrage from international human rights organizations, who expressed concern at the alacrity and secrecy with which the sentences had been implemented.

At a general election in June 1998 the NDP lost four seats, retaining eight, while the ULP obtained the remaining seven. The reverse sustained by the NDP was attributed to voter dissatisfaction with the state of the economy. Although the ULP had obtained around 55% of the vote, Mitchell claimed that the result was a mandate for his Government to undertake a record fourth term of office. The ULP leader, Vincent Beache, called on the NDP to hold fresh elections within nine months, and not to govern on the basis of a minority vote. The ULP also claimed to have obtained evidence of irregularities during the elections, particularly in the four seats won by the NDP with margins of between 27 and 109 votes. In early July, at the opening of the first session of the House of Assembly, several hundred protesters demonstrated against the new Government and two ministers were attacked as they tried to drive through the crowd.

In November 1998 members of the public and of the opposition demonstrated outside government offices to call for the resignation of Mitchell and Arnhim Eustace, the Minister of Finance and Public Services. The protests followed the announcement of the details of an agreement reached by the Government with the Government of Italy and a consortium of European financial institutions on the repayment of US $67m., incurred because the Government had guaranteed a loan of $50m. made to a company of Italian developers that subsequently went into liquidation. The loan had been made to finance the failed Ottley Hall marina and shipyard project, valued at only $5m. The new agreement stipulated that the shipyard should be sold and that repayments of $32m. of debt should begin immediately, with the remaining $30m. to be set aside.

In December 1998 Dr Ralph Gonsalves, the deputy leader of the ULP, was elected leader at the ULP party congress, following the resignation of Beache, who was to remain leader of the opposition in the House of Assembly.

In late November 1998 marijuana growers demonstrated outside the Prime Minister's office against plans to use regional and US troops to destroy the marijuana crop in the highlands of Saint Vincent. Mitchell refused to meet representatives of the protesters, telling them to take advantage of government schemes to promote economic diversification. In December US marines and troops provided by the Regional Security System destroyed crops during a two-week operation, despite opposition from growers. Mitchell subsequently warned the USA that, if Saint Vincent's banana producers were bankrupted by the US initiative to challenge the preferential treatment accorded by the European Union (EU, see p. 244) to banana exports from Caribbean and African states, it was likely that producers would turn instead to the cultivation of marijuana. In March 1999 Saint Vincent and the Grenadines was one of a number of Caribbean states to warn that, if the USA continued to threaten their economic stability by pursuing its case against the EU banana import regime at the World Trade Organization (see p. 396), they would withdraw co-operation with US-sponsored anti-drugs initiatives. (See the Recent History of Saint Lucia for further details of the trade dispute over bananas between the USA and the EU.) In December, however, a large-scale marijuana eradication exercise took place in Saint Vincent with backing from US marines.

In December 1999 a committee chaired by Dwight Venner, the Governor of the Eastern Caribbean Central Bank, recommended that members of the House of Assembly should receive increased salaries. The committee, however, suggested that the increases should not be awarded until legislation on political integrity had been implemented, and reforms of the public sector had been effected. The proposed increases were opposed by the ULP, which in late January 2000 threatened to introduce a motion of 'no confidence' in the Government, accusing it of corruption, excessive expenditure on development projects, a failure to reduce crime levels and of neglecting education. The Government's subsequent introduction in April of legislation increasing the salaries and benefits of members of the House of Assembly provoked protests throughout the islands, which were directed by the ULP and by public sector trade unions, who accused the Government of 'disregard and contempt' for ordinary workers. Members of the Saint Vincent Union of Teachers undertook industrial action in protest at the Government's behaviour and to demand wage increases, while the protesters, who were grouped under an umbrella Organization in Defence of Democracy (ODD), demanded the resignation of the Government and fresh elections. Despite appeals for dialogue from the Government, employers' associations and the Chamber of Industry and Commerce, the ODD undertook several days of public demonstrations at the end of April, culminating in a mass rally in Kingstown. In early May the Government and the ODD reached an agreement, known as the Grand Beach accord, whereby fresh legislative elections were to be called before March 2001; the accord also allowed for a national dialogue on constitutional reform.

In August 2000 Mitchell relinquished the post of NDP President in favour of the Minister of Finance and Public Services, Arnhim Eustace, who defeated Jeremiah Scott, the Minister of Agriculture and Labour, in a leadership election. On 27 October Eustace also succeeded Mitchell as Prime Minister, following the latter's retirement as Head of Government. Mitchell stayed on in the Cabinet as Senior Minister.

A general election was held on 28 March 2001. The ULP secured an overwhelming victory, winning 12 of the 15 parliamentary seats and 57% of the votes cast. The NDP, which had been in power since 1984, secured 41% of the votes cast and the remaining three House of Assembly seats. The new Government took office in mid-April, led by Gonsalves. In December 2002 Gonsalves established a 25-member Constitutional Review Commission, the first report of which was presented in late March 2004. Among the issues to be addressed were local government organization and finance, civil service reform and the electoral system.

In June 2002 the Governor-General, Sir Charles Antrobus, died. Sir Frederick Ballantyne was appointed as his successor in September.

In March 2004 the parliamentary opposition boycotted the House of Assembly and established an 'alternative parliament' at the NDP's headquarters; Eustace claimed that the parliamentary Speaker, Hendrick Alexander, had consistently demonstrated a pro-Government bias. In late February Eustace had led NDP members out of Parliament after the Prime Minister was allowed to present an amendment to a motion on a day when opposition business should have taken precedence. The opposition again boycotted the House of Assembly and re-established its 'alternative parliament' in March 2005. On this occasion, the NDP was particularly unhappy about constituency boundaries and the registration of voters before the next elections, which were due by March 2006.

Despite the concerns of the opposition, Gonsalves' Government maintained its popularity; however, in 2004–05 the issue of violent crime was increasingly prominent and it was widely held that the Government had devoted insufficient funds to attempting to resolve the problem. Moreover, Saint Vincent remained one of the largest cultivators of marijuana in the region and in 2003 the Government reported that 40% of prison inmates had been jailed for drugs-related offences. In November 2004 Gonsalves, who had previously expressed severe reservations about capital punishment, claimed that the use of the death penalty was necessary to reduce the influence of criminal gangs in the country. The comments were made in the House of Assembly, during the passage of the Firearm Amendment Act, which was to introduce stricter penalties for illegal possession of weapons.

At legislative elections, held on 7 December 2005, the ULP secured 12 of the 15 seats in the House of Assembly (the same figure as in the election of 2001) and 55% of the popular vote. The NDP again secured the remaining three legislative seats, although the party increased its share of the vote to 45%, compared with 41% in 2001. A third party, the newly formed Saint Vincent and the Grenadines Green Party, garnered just 34 votes from the four constituencies in which it competed. Registered votes were cast by 63.7% of the electorate. Monitoring teams from various international organizations described the contest as free and fair; none the less, the NDP claimed there had been electoral 'irregularities', such as missing ballots and people voting in constituencies in which they did not reside, and pledged to take legal and political action against the results in three closely fought constituencies.

Following the ULP's re-election Gonsalves reorganized and expanded the Cabinet: among other changes, Louis Straker, the Deputy Prime Minister, was given his former portfolio of foreign affairs, commerce and trade. The previous holder of that post, Michael Browne, meanwhile, was placed in charge of a wide-ranging new Ministry of National Mobilization, Social Development, NGO Relations, Family, Gender Affairs and Persons with Disabilities, and Julian Francis was appointed Minister of Housing, Informal Human Settlements, Physical Planning, Lands and Surveys. The Prime Minister also pledged to use the Government's new mandate to introduce constitutional reform, after popular consultation via referendums. In addition, Gonsalves announced his intention to ask the House of Assembly to approve legislation making the Caribbean Court of Justice (which had been inaugurated in Trinidad and Tobago in April 2005) the country's senior court of appeal, in place of the Privy Council in the United Kingdom.

Prime Minister Gonsalves and his ULP Government suffered a significant threat in February 2007 when the NDP marshalled a demonstration in Kingstown demanding the removal of the premier from office and requisitioning a general election. Public and opposition unrest had escalated during the preceding months following increased public concerns over crime, despite an announcement by the Criminal Investigation Department of Saint Vincent and the Grenadines in September 2006 that the overall crime rate had declined during that year and that a sustained decline had been recorded from 2001. The early release of a convicted drugs offender, Alex Lawrence, whose 22-month sentence, handed down in February 2006, had been curtailed by the Governor-General upon the recommendation of the Prerogative of Mercy Committee, caused particular disquiet. NDP leader Eustace contested that Gonsalves' endorsement of the decision and failure to provide an explanation had severely compromised the Government's integrity and had undermined public confidence. Eustace further suggested that the increasing prevalence of drugs-related and violent crime in the country was directly attributable to Gonsalves' inadequate enforcement of penal law, and that the Government was implicated in the alleged engagement of drugs magnates in the financing of political campaigns. The Prime Minister asserted that the decision to pardon Lawrence was justified in the interests of national security, but that to divulge the particular details was inherently hazardous in the same regard; he did, however, indicate that such details might be discussed with the opposition leader, subject to Eustace's agreeing to take an Oath of Secrecy, an offer derided by the NDP leader.

Tensions between the Government and opposition parties intensified during 2007 and early 2008. An inquiry into the failed Ottley Hall marina and shipyard development project remained ongoing in April 2008; the losses incurred under the scheme, according to sources, accounted for more than one-quarter of Saint Vincent's total external debt. The NDP attempted to increase its popularity by challenging government plans to increase taxation by the introduction of a value-added tax, and in January 2008 it accused Gonsalves of misleading teachers in a 'reclassification' exercise of the public sector pay grade structure. The NDP claimed that the remuneration benefits were not, in reality, as generous as Gonsalves had initially suggested and, on 9 and 10 January, more than 1,000 teachers went on strike in protest at the changes, supported by the Saint Vincent and the Grenadines Teachers' Union. In March Eustace wrote to the Prime Minister formally asking him to resign after two separate allegations of sexual assault were made against him; the first, by a female police officer, referred to an incident that allegedly took place in January of that year, and the second, by a Canadian lawyer with Vincentian citizenship, cited an incident that she claimed had taken place in 2004. However, after reviewing the evidence the Director of Public Prosecutions, Colin Williams, dismissed the charges, which Gonsalves claimed had been politically motivated.

There was some public unease during 2007 with regards to Saint Vincent and the Grenadines' burgeoning economic relations with Venezuela. Specific protest was made against a memorandum of understanding, signed by the Prime Minister in February 2007, subscribing to the principles of President Hugo Chávez's Bolivarian Alternative for Latin America (Alternativa Bolivariana para América Latina y El Caribe—ALBA, see below). Eustace cautioned that the accord conspicuously aligned the country with Venezuela at the possible expense of its diplomatic relationship with the USA. Gonsalves maintained that relations with these respective nations were not mutually exclusive and emphasized the importance of Venezuela's influence upon the progress of national development, citing the benefits of the recently implemented PetroCaribe initiative (under which the country could purchase oil from Venezuela at discounted prices) and the Venezuelan Government's contribution to the construction of an international airport. President Chávez had lambasted the USA during his visit to Saint Vincent and the Grenadines on 17 February, ostensibly to open a fuel storage facility financed by PetroCaribe, provoking vigorous public debate about the country's diplomatic obligations and future position within the international community.

Saint Vincent and the Grenadines is a member of the Caribbean Community and Common Market (CARICOM, see p. 196), of the Organisation of Eastern Caribbean States (OECS, see p. 425), and is a signatory of the Cotonou Agreement (see p. 301), the successor agreement to the Lomé Convention. In September 2001 Gonsalves appointed Joseph Bonadie, an NDP senator, as his adviser on issues related to further OECS integration and in February 2003 proposed that a union of Caribbean states should take the form of a confederal political arrangement similar to that of the EU. In February 2004 parliament passed legislation allowing nationals of OECS member states to travel freely within the OECS area and to remain in a foreign territory within the area for up to six months. During the election campaign of December 2005 Gonsalves described regional integration as the 'bedrock' of his Government's foreign policy. Saint Vincent and the Grenadines, together with five other Caribbean states, became a signatory to CARICOM's Caribbean Single Market and Economy (CSME) on 3 July 2006, which had been established by six founding member states on 1 January of that year. The CSME was intended to enshrine the free movement of goods, services and labour throughout the CARICOM region. Following an Inter-Sessional Conference of CARICOM heads of government in Saint Vincent and the Grenadines in February 2007, it was announced that the single economy component of the initiative was advancing in accordance with the scheduled completion dates. Two phases of implementation were to ensue: the first would be consolidation of the single market and initiation of the single economy by 1 January 2009; while the second phase, spanning 2010–15, would define and institute the single economy and regional monetary union. The Inter-American Development Bank pledged financial assistance to facilitate the regional integration process between 2007 and 2010.

An intra-regional common passport initiative, regarded as an integral component in the advance towards economic union and designed to facilitate travel for citizens of participating nations, was implemented in Saint Vincent and the Grenadines in April 2006; use of the CARICOM passport was expected to have been introduced by all 15 member governments by 2008.

In 1992 the islands established diplomatic relations with Cuba. The two countries signed accords pledging further co-operation in a number of areas, including health and education, in September 2001 and November 2002. Taiwan and Saint Vincent and the Grenadines celebrated 25 years of diplomatic relations in August 2006; in the same month the Taiwanese Government announced the donation of US $15m. and extension of a $10m. loan towards the construction of an international airport on the islands, while reiterating its commitment to assisting in the infrastructural and human resource development of the Caribbean nation.

In 2001 Libya granted the islands, in common with other eastern Caribbean countries, access to a US $2,000m. development fund. It was also reported in September that Libya had agreed to provide Saint Vincent and the Grenadines with a grant of $4.5m. (including an immediate disbursement of $1.5m), following Gonsalves' controversial visit to the Libyan capital, Tripoli, earlier in the month. Further controversy arose after Japan pledged to provide $6m. for the construction of a fish market. It was claimed that, in return for Japanese financial aid, Saint Vincent and the Grenadines would support the pro-whaling bloc at meetings of the International Whaling Commission (IWC); Gonsalves refuted the allegation, pointing out that the Government had abstained on crucial votes relating to the provision of whale sanctuaries in the South Atlantic and the Pacific. However, the controversy re-emerged at the IWC meeting in June 2006 when Saint Vincent and the Grenadines endorsed Japan's proposal to end a 20-year moratorium on commercial whaling, invoking the vehement criticism of prominent international trading partners and creating a potential threat to the region's crucial tourist industry. Moreover, the subsequent announcement of a new EC $33m. fisheries complex to be financed by the Japanese Government provoked allegations of diplomacy motivated by economic incentive.

Diplomatic relations with Venezuela were bolstered in February 2007 when Saint Vincent and the Grenadines, in addition to two other OECS states, signed a memorandum of understanding in recognition of the principles of ALBA, an economic integration initiative orchestrated by the Venezuelan President as a rival to the stagnant Free Trade Areas of the Americas proposal promulgated by the USA.

In February 2003 Saint Vincent and the Grenadines was admitted to the Non-Aligned Movement (see p. 424).

Government

Saint Vincent and the Grenadines is a constitutional monarchy. Executive power is vested in the British monarch, as Head of State, and is exercisable by the Governor-General, who represents the British monarch locally and who is appointed on the advice of the Prime Minister. Legislative power is vested in Parliament, comprising the Governor-General and the House of Assembly (composed of 21 members: six nominated Senators and 15 Representatives, elected for up to five years by universal adult suffrage). Senators are appointed by the Governor-General: four on the advice of the Prime Minister and two on the advice of the Leader of the Opposition. Government is effectively by the Cabinet. The Governor-General appoints the Prime Minister and, on the latter's recommendation, selects the other Ministers. The Prime Minister must be able to command the support of the majority of the House, to which the Cabinet is responsible.

Defence

Saint Vincent and the Grenadines participates in the US-sponsored Regional Security System, comprising police, coastguards and army units, which was established by independent East Caribbean states in 1982. Since 1984, however, the paramilitary Special Service Unit has had strictly limited deployment. In the 2008 budget, EC $17.9m. of capital funding (equivalent to 7.5% of total capital expenditure) was allocated for national security. The recurrent budget for 2008 allocated some 10.3% of total expenditure (projected at EC $517.5m.) for defence purposes.

Economic Affairs

In 2006, according to estimates by the World Bank, Saint Vincent and the Grenadines' gross national income (GNI), measured at average 2004–06 prices, was US $470m., equivalent to $3,930 per head (or $7,010 per head on an international purchasing-power parity basis). During 1996–2006, it was estimated, the population increased by an annual average rate of 0.5%, while gross domestic product (GDP) per head increased, in real terms, by an average of 2.6% per year. Overall GDP increased, in real terms, by an average annual rate of 3.1% in 1996–2006; according to the Eastern Caribbean Central Bank (ECCB, see p. 415), real GDP increased by 8.7% in 2006.

Agriculture (including forestry and fishing) contributed 7.1% of GDP in 2006. The sector employed an estimated 22.2% of the working population in 2005, according to FAO, and agricultural products account for the largest share of export revenue. The principal cash crop is bananas, which contributed an estimated 28.7% of the value of total exports in 2005. Other important crops are arrowroot, sweet potatoes, tannias, taro, plantains and coconuts. According to the ECCB, during 1997–2006 real agricultural GDP (growth of which is heavily reliant on weather conditions and banana production) decreased by an annual average of 0.3%. However, an increase of 7.6% was recorded in 2006.

Industry (including mining, manufacturing, electricity, water and construction) employed 21.1% of the working population in 1991, and contributed 23.5% of GDP in 2006. During 1998–2006 real industrial GDP increased by an annual average of 2.7%, according to the ECCB; the sector expanded by 6.2% in 2006. In September 2005 the Prime Minister announced that a Canadian company was conducting preliminary petroleum-exploration work in Saint Vincent and the Grenadines' territorial waters.

The manufacturing sector contributed 5.3% of GDP in 2006, and engaged 8.5% of the employed labour force in 1991. Apart from a garment industry and the assembling of electrical components, the most important activities involve the processing of agricultural products, including flour- and rice-milling, brewing, rum distillation, and processing dairy products. During 1998–2006 real manufacturing GDP decreased by an annual average of 0.4%, according to ECCB figures. However, the sector's real GDP expanded by 2.9% in 2006.

Energy is derived principally from the use of hydrocarbon fuels (mineral fuels and lubricants accounted for around 13.8% of total imports in 2005). The islands imported most of their energy requirements. There is, however, an important hydroelectric plant in Cumberland. In September 2005 the Government became one of 13 Caribbean administrations to sign the PetroCaribe accord, under which Saint Vincent and the Grenadines would be allowed to purchase petroleum from Venezuela at reduced prices.

The services sector contributed an estimated 69.4% of GDP in 2006 and engaged 53.8% of the employed population at the time of the 1991 census. Tourism is the most important activity within the sector, but is smaller in scale than in most other Caribbean islands; estimated tourism receipts were equivalent to some 22.6% of GDP in 2006. Tourist activity remains concentrated in the Grenadines and caters for the luxury market. Visitors aboard yachts have traditionally been the most important sector, although the numbers of stop-over and cruise-ship visitors have increased in recent years. In 2004 the number of visitor arrivals increased by 8.3% (the equivalent increase in the number of stop-over tourists was 10.4%). However, in 2005 visitor arrivals decreased by 3.2%, although the number of stop-over tourists continued to climb, by an estimated 9.5%. The sector recovered in 2006; arrivals increased by an estimated 19.7% in that year, owing largely to the greater number of yacht and cruise-ship passengers visiting the islands (which rose by 14.3% and 52.6% respectively). Aside from tourism, a small 'offshore' financial sector also contributes to the services sector. During 1998–2006 the real GDP of the services sector as a whole increased by an annual average of 4.7%, according to the ECCB; an estimated increase of 7.3% was recorded in 2006.

In 2005 Saint Vincent and the Grenadines recorded an estimated visible trade deficit of US $168.8m., while there was a deficit of $101.4m. on the current account of the balance of payments. The principal source of imports is the USA (accounting for an estimated 38.6% of the total in 2005). Other important suppliers in that year were Trinidad and Tobago and the United Kingdom. The United Kingdom is the principal market for exports (accounting for an estimated 25.8% of total exports in 2005). Other important markets in that year were the USA, Barbados, Trinidad and Tobago and Saint Lucia. The principal exports in 2005 were bananas (28.7%) and rice, while the principal imports were machinery and transport equipment (22.1%), basic manufactures and food and live animals.

In 2006 there was an estimated overall budget deficit of EC $57.4m., equivalent to 4.2% of GDP. Saint Vincent and the Grenadines' total external debt was US $282.4m. at the end of 2005, of which US $248.3m. was long-term public debt. The cost of debt-servicing was equivalent to 11.2% of the value of exports of goods and services in 2005. The average annual rate of inflation was 1.9% in 2000–06, and consumer prices increased by an estimated average of 3.0% in 2006. At the 1991 census 20.0% of the labour force were unemployed. In February 2002 the IMF estimated that the rate of unemployment remained at a similar level.

In May 2000 the Financial Stability Forum categorized Saint Vincent and the Grenadines' banking supervision in the lowest group. In June the Organisation for Economic Co-operation and Development (OECD) included Saint Vincent and the Grenadines in a report on countries with harmful tax policies and in the same month it was also included on a list of 'non-co-operative' governments in the fight against money-laundering, by the Financial Action Task Force (FATF—based at the Secretariat of OECD). In July the International Financial Services Authority revoked the licences of six 'offshore' banks in an immediate response to an advisory by the US Department of the Treasury. Following further government commitments to improving the transparency of its tax and regulatory systems, Saint Vincent and the Grenadines was removed from OECD's harmful tax policy list in February 2002. In May of that year the Government established a Financial Intelligence Unit to counter money-laundering and in June 2003 Saint Vincent and the Grenadines was finally removed from the FATF's blacklist. Only six licensed 'offshore' banks remained in 2006, compared with a peak of 30 in 2002. Some 6,632 International Business Companies were also registered in late 2005. In September 2004 the IMF noted significant improvements in the regulation of the sector; however, questions were raised over 'political involvement with licensing'.

Saint Vincent and the Grenadines is a member of the ECCB, the Caribbean Community and Common Market (CARICOM, see p. 196), which seeks to encourage regional development, particularly by increasing trade between member states, and of the Organisation of Eastern Caribbean States (OECS, see p. 425). The country is also a member of the regional stock exchange, the Eastern Caribbean Securities Exchange (based in Saint Christopher and Nevis), established in 2001. Saint Vincent and the Grenadines joined CARICOM's Caribbean Single Market and Economy (CSME) in July 2006.

Traditionally the dominant sector of the economy, agriculture declined in importance in the 1990s. The introduction of other crops reduced dependence on the vulnerable banana harvest, although performance is significantly affected by weather conditions. The passage of 'Hurricane Ivan', which struck the islands in September 2004, proved disastrous for the sector, destroying 20% of the banana crop. The erosion of the islands' preferential access to European markets, together with lower prices and poor climatic conditions, contributed to a decline in banana production after 1992. In 2004 exports of bananas represented just 38.3% of the total value of merchandise exports (compared with 52.2% in 1990), although this figure was an improvement on the 2003 figure of 33.1%. The decline of the industry, and a related increase in unemployment and poverty, appeared inevitable. Therefore, the prospects for long-term growth were dependent on economic diversification and a prolonged stabilization of the increasingly important tourism sector. This sector had previously been disadvantaged (relative to neighbouring countries) by the absence of an international airport; consequently, efforts had been made to increase cruise-ship traffic and visiting yacht passengers. The 2008 budget increased tourism-related expenditure and allocated a substantial portion of its capital outlay to the International Airport Project at Argyle (excavation works on the runway were scheduled to commence in early 2008). Preliminary estimates valued the project at EC $475m.—which was to be partially financed by the Governments of Venezuela and

SAINT VINCENT AND THE GRENADINES

Cuba—and it was hoped that the new facility would increase overall capacity and attract a greater number of stop-over arrivals (a more lucrative market than cruise-ship passengers). Increasing international commodity prices precipitated a sharp rise in inflation during 2008, which averaged 8.7% according to IMF estimates. Government measures seeking to address this included the repeal of value-added taxation (which had been introduced the previous year) on 75 staple items, as well as an increase in personnel emoluments (public sector wages, pension and public assistance).

Education

Free primary education, beginning at five years of age and lasting for seven years, is available to all children in government schools, although it is not compulsory and attendance is low. There are 61 government and five private primary schools. Secondary education, beginning at 12 years of age, comprises a first cycle of five years and a second, two-year cycle. However, government facilities at this level are limited, and much secondary education is provided in schools administered by religious organizations, with government assistance. There are also a number of junior secondary schools. There is a teacher-training college and a technical college. In 2004/05 enrolment at primary schools included an estimated 90.3% of children in the relevant age-group, while comparable enrolment in secondary schools included an estimated 63.9% of pupils. Expenditure on education by the central Government was projected at EC $126.5m. in 2008 (equivalent to some 17% of the total expenditure). The Government announced in 2005 that it had succeeded in instituting universal secondary education.

Public Holidays

2008: 1 January (New Year's Day), 21 March (Good Friday), 24 March (Easter Monday), 7 May (Labour Day/Fisherman's Day), 12 May (Whit Monday), 7 July (CARICOM Day), 8 July (Carnival Tuesday), 1 August (Emancipation Day), 27 October (Independence Day), 25–26 December (Christmas).
2009: 1 January (New Year's Day), 10 April (Good Friday), 13 April (Easter Monday), 7 May (Labour Day/Fisherman's Day), 1 June (Whit Monday), 6 July (CARICOM Day), 7 July (Carnival Tuesday), 1 August (Emancipation Day), 27 October (Independence Day), 25–26 December (Christmas).

Weights and Measures

The imperial system is used.

Statistical Survey

Sources (unless otherwise stated): Statistical Office, Ministry of Finance and Economic Planning, Administrative Centre, Bay St, Kingstown; tel. 456-1111; e-mail statssvg@vincysurf.com.

AREA AND POPULATION

Area: 389.3 sq km (150.3 sq miles). The island of Saint Vincent covers 344 sq km (133 sq miles).

Population: 97,914 at census of 12 May 1980; 106,499 (males 53,165, females 53,334) at census of 12 May 1991; 109,202 at preliminary census count of May 2001. *2007:* 120,000 (mid-year estimate). Source: UN, *Demographic Yearbook, Population and Vital Statistics Report* and *World Population Prospects: The 2006 Revision*.

Density (mid-2007): 308.2 per sq km.

Principal Town: Kingstown (capital), population 13,526 at preliminary census count of May 2001. *Mid-2007* (population incl. suburbs, UN estimate): Kingstown 26,000 (Source: UN, *World Urbanization Prospects: The 2007 Revision*).

Births, Marriages and Deaths (registrations, 2005): Live births 1,779 (birth rate 17.1 per 1,000); Marriages 576 (marriage rate 5.6 per 1,000); Deaths 813 (death rate 7.8 per 1,000) (Source: UN, *Demographic Yearbook*).

Expectation of Life (years at birth, WHO estimates): 69.8 (males 66.2; females 73.8) in 2005. Source: WHO, *World Health Statistics*.

Economically Active Population (persons aged 15 years and over, 1991 census): Agriculture, hunting, forestry and fishing 8,377; Mining and quarrying 98; Manufacturing 2,822; Electricity, gas and water 586; Construction 3,535; Trade, restaurants and hotels 6,544; Transport, storage and communications 2,279; Financing, insurance, real estate and business services 1,418; Community, social and personal services 7,696; *Total employed* 33,355 (males 21,656, females 11,699); Unemployed 8,327 (males 5,078, females 3,249); *Total labour force* 41,682 (males 26,734, females 14,948). Source: ILO, *Yearbook of Labour Statistics*.

HEALTH AND WELFARE
Key Indicators

Total Fertility Rate (children per woman, 2005): 2.2.
Under-5 Mortality Rate (per 1,000 live births, 2005): 20.
Physicians (per 1,000 head, 1997): 0.87.
Hospital Beds (per 1,000 head, 2004): 4.5.
Health Expenditure (2004): US $ per head (PPP): 417.6.
Health Expenditure (2004): % of GDP: 6.1.
Health Expenditure (2004): public (% of total): 63.2.
Access to Water (% of persons, 2000): 93.
Access to Sanitation (% of persons, 2000): 96.
Human Development Index (2005): ranking: 93.
Human Development Index (2005): value: 0.761.

For sources and definitions, see explanatory note on p. vi.

AGRICULTURE, ETC.

Principal Crops ('000 metric tons, 2006, FAO estimates): Maize 0.3; Cassava 0.5; Sweet potatoes 0.9; Yams 1.7; Sugar cane 20.0; Coconuts 2.6; Bananas 50.0; Plaintains 3.1; Oranges 1.5; Lemons and limes 1.1; Apples 1.3; Mangoes 1.5. *Aggregate Production* ('000 metric tons, may include official, semi-official or estimated data): Roots and tubers 12.9; Vegetables (incl. melons) 4.3; Fruits (excl. melons) 59.3.

Livestock ('000 head, year ending September 2006, FAO estimates): Cattle 5.0; Sheep 12.0; Goats 7.2; Pigs 9.2; Asses, mules or hinnies 1.3; Poultry 125.

Livestock Products ('000 metric tons, 2006, FAO estimates unless otherwise indicated): Pig meat 1.1; Chicken meat 1.0 (official figure); Cows' milk 1.0; Hen eggs 1.4.

Fishing (capture production, metric tons, live weight, 2005, unless otherwise indicated): Albacore 63; Yellowfin tuna 2,043; Other tuna-like fishes 3,089 (2004); *Total catch* (incl. others) 2,747.

Source: FAO.

INDUSTRY

Selected Products ('000 metric tons, 2005, unless otherwise stated): Copra 2 (FAO estimate); Raw sugar 2 (FAO estimate); Rum 9,000 hectolitres (2003); Electric energy 131.9 million kWh (preliminary). Sources: FAO, Eastern Caribbean Central Bank and UN, *International Commodity Statistics Yearbook*.

FINANCE

Currency and Exchange Rates: 100 cents = 1 Eastern Caribbean dollar (EC $). *Sterling, US Dollar and Euro Equivalents* (30 November 2007): £1 sterling = EC $5.579; US $1 = EC $2.700; €1 = EC $3.985; EC $100 = £17.92 = US $37.04 = €25.09. *Exchange Rate:* Fixed at US $1 = EC $2.70 since July 1976.

Budget (EC $ million, 2006): *Revenue:* Revenue from taxation 361.7 (Taxes on income 98.8; Taxes on goods and services 98.2; Taxes on property 2.6; Taxes on international trade and transactions 162.1); Other current revenue 31.6; Capital revenue 6.0; Foreign grants 5.5; Total 404.8. *Expenditure:* Current expenditure 355.4 (Personal emoluments 171.3; Other goods and services 75.8; Interest payments 43.2; Transfers and subsidies 65.2); Capital expenditure and net lending 101.3; Total 456.7. Source: Eastern Caribbean Central Bank.

International Reserves (US $ million at 31 December 2006): Reserve position in IMF 0.75; Foreign exchange 77.94; Total 78.69. Source: IMF, *International Financial Statistics*.

Money Supply (EC $ million at 31 December 2006): Currency outside banks 80.50; Demand deposits 302.90; Total money 383.40. Source: IMF, *International Financial Statistics*.

Cost of Living (Consumer Price Index; base: 2000 = 100): 104.9 in 2004; 108.8 in 2005; 112.1 in 2006. Source: IMF, *International Financial Statistics*.

Gross Domestic Product (EC $ million at constant 1990 prices): 835.35 in 2004; 865.68 in 2005; 941.11 in 2006. Source: Eastern Caribbean Central Bank.

Expenditure on the Gross Domestic Product (preliminary, EC $ million at current prices, 2006): Government final consumption expenditure 249.90; Private final consumption expenditure 868.97; Gross capital formation 470.58; *Total domestic expenditure* 1,589.45; Exports of goods and services 539.69; *Less* Imports of goods and services 775.38; *GDP at market prices* 1,353.76. Source: Eastern Caribbean Central Bank.

Gross Domestic Product by Economic Activity (EC $ million at current factor cost, 2006): Agriculture, hunting, forestry and fishing 84.22; Mining and quarrying 2.49; Manufacturing 62.99; Electricity and water 56.33; Construction 154.92; Wholesale and retail trade 211.00; Restaurants and hotels 22.87; Transport 156.52; Communications 56.84; Banking and insurance 122.66; Real estate and housing 22.40; Government services 203.75; Other services 21.89; *Sub-total* 1,178.88; *Less* Financial intermediation services indirectly measured 84.92; *Total in basic prices* 1,093.96; Taxes, less subsidies, on products 259.80; *GDP at market prices* 1,353.76. Source: Eastern Caribbean Central Bank.

Balance of Payments (US $ million, 2005): Exports of goods f.o.b. 43.61; Imports of goods f.o.b. −212.39; *Trade balance* −168.79; Exports of services 158.76; Imports of services −85.04; *Balance on goods and services* −95.06; Other income received 12.30; Other income paid −36.77; *Balance on goods, services and income* −119.53; Current transfers received (net) 18.12; *Current balance* −101.40; Capital account (net) 14.10; Financial account (net) 78.82; Net errors and omissions 5.60; *Overall balance* −2.88. Source: IMF, *International Financial Statistics*.

EXTERNAL TRADE

Principal Commodities (2005, estimates): *Imports c.i.f.* (EC $ million): Food 119.3; Beverages and tobacco 17.4; Crude materials 17.9; Mineral fuels, lubricants, etc. 90.0; Chemicals and related products 59.9; Basic manufactures 122.9; Machinery and transport equipment 143.3; Total (incl. others) 649.4. *Exports f.o.b.* (US $ million, incl. re-exports): Vegetables and fruit 17.8 (Bananas 11.9); Manufactured and processed goods 15.5 (Flour 5.0; Rice 3.1); Total (incl. others) 41.4.

Principal Trading Partners (US $ million, 2005, estimates): *Imports c.i.f.*: Barbados 9.5; Canada 9.2; Guyana 1.9; Japan 10.0; Trinidad and Tobago 56.8; United Kingdom 22.6; USA 78.5; Total (incl. others) 203.3. *Exports f.o.b.*: Antigua and Barbuda 2.5; Barbados 5.1; Dominica 2.9; Jamaica 0.8; Saint Lucia 4.4; Trinidad and Tobago 4.9; United Kingdom 10.7; USA 3.2; Total (incl. others) 41.4.

Source: IMF, *St Vincent and the Grenadines: Statistical Appendix* (November 2007).

TRANSPORT

Road Traffic (motor vehicles in use, 2002): Private cars 10,504; Buses and coaches 1,150; Lorries and vans 3,019; Road tractors 89. Source: International Road Federation, *World Road Statistics*.

Shipping: *Arrivals* (2000): Vessels 1,007. *International Sea-borne Freight Traffic* ('000 metric tons, 2000): Goods loaded 54; Goods unloaded 156. *Merchant Fleet* (vessels registered at 31 December 2006): Number 1,064; Total displacement 6,107,004 grt (Source: Lloyd's Register-Fairplay, *World Fleet Statistics*).

Civil Aviation (visitor arrivals): 89,631 in 2003; 99,657 in 2004; 104,221 in 2005 (estimate). Source: IMF, *St Vincent and the Grenadines: Statistical Appendix* (November 2007).

TOURISM

Visitor Arrivals: 261,469 (86,721 stop-over visitors, 12,936 excursionists, 84,227 yacht passengers, 77,585 cruise-ship passengers) in 2004; 256,075 (95,504 stop-over visitors, 8,928 excursionists, 81,890 yacht passengers, 69,753 cruise-ship passengers) in 2005; 306,578 (97,432 stop-over visitors, 9,034 excursionists, 93,638 yacht passengers, 106,474 cruise-ship passengers) in 2006 (preliminary). *Stop-over visitors by country* (2006): USA 28,598; Canada 6,542; United Kingdom 14,837; Caribbean 38,219; Other countries 9,236.

Tourism Receipts (EC $ million): 258.0 in 2004; 280.5 in 2005; 305.8 in 2006 (preliminary).

Source: Eastern Caribbean Central Bank.

COMMUNICATIONS MEDIA

Radio Receivers ('000 in use, 2000): 100.

Television Receivers ('000 in use, 2000): 50.

Telephones ('000 main lines in use, 2006): 22.6.

Facsimile Machines (1996): 1,500.

Mobile Cellular Telephones (subscribers, 2006): 87,600.

Personal Computers ('000 in use, 2004): 16.

Internet Users ('000, 2005): 10.

Broadband Subscribers ('000, 2005): 3.6.

Non-daily Newspapers (2000): Titles 8; Circulation 50,000.

Sources: mainly UNESCO, *Statistical Yearbook*; UN, *Statistical Yearbook*; and International Telecommunication Union.

EDUCATION

Pre-primary (2003/04 unless otherwise indicated): 97 schools (1993/94); 340 teachers (2004/05); 3,861 pupils.

Primary (2004/05 unless otherwise indicated): 60 schools (2000); 1,020 teachers; 17,858 pupils.

Secondary (2004/05 unless otherwise indicated): 21 schools (2000); 547 teachers; 9,780 pupils.

Teacher Training (2000): 1 institution; 10 teachers; 107 students.

Technical College (2000): 1 institution; 19 teachers; 187 students.

Community College (2000): 1 institution; 13 teachers; 550 students.

Nursing College (2000): 1 institution; 6 teachers; 60 students.

Source: partly Caribbean Development Bank, *Social and Economic Indicators* and UNESCO Institute for Statistics.

Adult Literacy Rate: 88.1% in 2004. Source: UN Development Programme, *Human Development Report*.

Directory

The Constitution

The Constitution came into force at the independence of Saint Vincent and the Grenadines on 27 October 1979. The following is a summary of its main provisions

FUNDAMENTAL RIGHTS AND FREEDOMS

Regardless of race, place of origin, political opinion, colour, creed or sex, but subject to respect for the rights and freedoms of others and for the public interest, every person in Saint Vincent and the Grenadines is entitled to the rights of life, liberty, security of the person and the protection of the law. Freedom of conscience, of expression, of assembly and association is guaranteed and the inviolability of a person's home and other property is maintained.

Protection is afforded from slavery, forced labour, torture and inhuman treatment.

THE GOVERNOR-GENERAL

The British Monarch is represented in Saint Vincent and the Grenadines by the Governor-General.

PARLIAMENT

Parliament consists of the British monarch, represented by the Governor-General, and the House of Assembly, comprising 15 elected Representatives (increased from 13 under the provisions of an amendment approved in 1986) and six Senators. Senators are appointed by the Governor-General—four on the advice of the Prime Minister and two on the advice of the Leader of the Opposition. The life of Parliament is five years. Each constituency returns one

SAINT VINCENT AND THE GRENADINES

Representative to the House who is directly elected in accordance with the Constitution. The Attorney-General is an ex officio member of the House. Every citizen over the age of 18 is eligible to vote. Parliament may alter any of the provisions of the Constitution.

THE EXECUTIVE

Executive authority is vested in the British monarch and is exercisable by the Governor-General. The Governor-General appoints as Prime Minister that member of the House who, in the Governor-General's view, is the best able to command the support of the majority of the members of the House, and selects other Ministers on the advice of the Prime Minister. The Governor-General may remove the Prime Minister from office if a resolution of 'no confidence' in the Government is passed by the House and the Prime Minister does not either resign within three days or advise the Governor-General to dissolve Parliament.

The Cabinet consists of the Prime Minister and other Ministers and the Attorney-General as an ex officio member. The Leader of the Opposition is appointed by the Governor-General as that member of the House who, in the Governor-General's view, is best able to command the support of a majority of members of the House who do not support the Government.

CITIZENSHIP

All persons born in Saint Vincent and the Grenadines before independence who, immediately prior to independence, were citizens of the United Kingdom and Colonies automatically become citizens of Saint Vincent and the Grenadines. All persons born outside the country after independence to a parent possessing citizenship of Saint Vincent and the Grenadines automatically acquire citizenship, as do those born in the country after independence. Citizenship can be acquired by those to whom it would not automatically be granted.

The Government

HEAD OF STATE

Monarch: HM Queen ELIZABETH II.
Governor-General: Sir FREDERICK BALLANTYNE (took office 2 September 2002).

CABINET
(April 2008)

Prime Minister and Minister of Finance and Economic Planning, National Security, Legal Affairs, Grenadines Affairs and Energy: Dr RALPH E. GONSALVES.
Deputy Prime Minister and Minister of Foreign Affairs, Commerce and Trade: LOUIS STRAKER.
Minister of Tourism: GLEN BEACHE.
Minister of National Mobilization, Social Development, Non-Governmental Organization (NGO) Relations, Family, Gender Affairs, Persons with Disabilities, Youth and Sports: MICHAEL BROWNE.
Minister of Education: GIRLYN MIGUEL.
Minister of Rural Transformation, Information, Public Service and Ecclesiastical Affairs: SELMON WALTERS.
Minister of Health and the Environment: Dr DOUGLAS SLATER.
Minister of Telecommunications, Science, Technology and Industry: Dr JERROL THOMPSON.
Minister of Urban Development, Labour, Culture and Electoral Matters: RENEÉ MERCEDES BAPTISTE.
Minister of Transportation and Works: CLAYTON BURGIN.
Minister of Agriculture, Forestry and Fisheries: MONTGOMERY DANIEL.
Minister of Housing, Informal Human Settlements, Physical Planning, Lands and Surveys, and Local Government: Sen. JULIAN EVERARD FRANCIS.
Minister of State in the Office of the Prime Minister: CONRAD SAYERS.
Attorney-General: JUDITH S. JONES-MORGAN.

MINISTRIES

Office of the Governor-General: Government House, Kingstown; tel. 456-1401; fax 457-9701.
Office of the Prime Minister: Administrative Bldg, 4th Floor, Bay St, Kingstown; tel. 451-2939; fax 457-2152; e-mail pmosvg@caribsurf.com.
Office of the Attorney-General and Ministry of Legal Affairs: Methodist Bldg, Grandby St, Kingstown; tel. 456-1111; fax 457-2898; e-mail office.ageneral@mail.gv.vc.

Ministry of Agriculture, Forestry and Fisheries: Richmond Hill, Kingstown; tel. 456-1410; fax 457-1688; e-mail office.agriculture@mail.gov.vc.
Ministry of Education: Halifax St, Kingstown; tel. 456-1877; fax 457-1114.
Ministry of Finance and Economic Planning: Administrative Bldg, Bay St, Kingstown; tel. 456-1111; fax 457-2152.
Ministry of Foreign Affairs, Commerce and Trade: Administrative Bldg, 3rd Floor, Bay St, Kingstown; tel. 456-2060; fax 456-2610; e-mail office.foreignaffairs@mail.gov.vc.
Ministry of Health and the Environment: Ministerial Bldg, 1st Floor, Bay St, Kingstown; tel. 456-1111; fax 457-2684; e-mail office.health@mail.gov.vc.
Ministry of Housing, Informal Human Settlements, Physical Planning, Lands and Surveys, and Local Government: Methodist Church Bldg, Granby St, Kingstown; tel. 451-2479; e-mail office.housing@mail.gov.vc.
Ministry of National Security: Ministerial Bldg, 3rd Floor, Halifax St, Kingstown; tel. 451-2707; fax 451-2820; e-mail office.natsec@mail.gov.vc.
Ministry of National Mobilization, Social Development, Non-Governmental Organization (NGO) Relations, Family, Gender Affairs and Persons with Disabilities: Egmont St, Kingstown; tel. 456-1111; fax 457-2476; e-mail office.socialdevelopment@mail.gov.vc.
Ministry of Rural Transformation, Information, Public Service and Ecclesiastical Affairs: Ministerial Bldg, 2nd Floor, Halifax St, Kingstown; tel. 451-2707; fax 451-2820; e-mail office.rutrans@mail.gov.vc; internet www.gov.vc/Govt/api1.
Ministry of Telecommunications, Science, Technology and Industry: Egmont St, Kingstown; tel. 456-1223; fax 457-2880; e-mail webunit.telecom@mail.gov.vc.
Ministry of Tourism, Youth and Sports: c/o Ministry of Tourism and Culture, Cruise Ship Terminal, Harbour Quay, POB 834, Kingstown; tel. 457-1502; fax 451-2425; e-mail tourism@caribsurf.com.
Ministry of Transportation and Works: Grenville St, Kingstown; tel. 457-2039; fax 456-2168; e-mail office.transport@mail.gov.vc.
Ministry of Urban Development, Labour, Culture and Electoral Matters: Marion House Bldg, Ground Floor, Murray's Rd, Kingstown; tel. 457-1789; fax 485-6737; e-mail office.elections@mail.gov.vc.

Legislature

HOUSE OF ASSEMBLY

Senators: 6.
Elected Members: 15.
Speaker: HENDRICK ALEXANDER.
Clerk: NICOLE HEBERT, House of Assembly, Kingstown; tel. 457-1872; fax 457-1825.

Election, 7 December 2005

Party	Votes	% of votes	Seats
Unity Labour Party	31,848	55.26	12
New Democratic Party	25,748	44.68	3
Saint Vincent and the Grenadines Green Party	34	0.06	—
Total	57,630	100.00	15

Election Commission

Electoral Office: Administrative Centre, Bay St, Kingstown; tel. 457-1762; fax 485-6844; e-mail electoraloffice@gov.vc; Supervisor of Elections RODNEY ADAMS.

Political Organizations

New Democratic Party (NDP): Democrat House, Murray Rd, POB 1300, Kingstown; tel. 456-2114; fax 457-2647; e-mail ndp@caribsurf.com; internet www.ndpsvg.com; f. 1975; democratic party supporting political unity in the Caribbean, social devt and free enterprise; Leader ARNHIM ULRIC EUSTACE; Gen. Sec. DANIEL E. CUMMINGS; 7,000 mems.

SAINT VINCENT AND THE GRENADINES

Directory

Saint Vincent and the Grenadines Green Party: POB 1707, Kingstown; tel. and fax 456-9579; e-mail mail@svggreenparty.org; internet www.svggreenparty.org; f. 2005; Leader IVAN O'NEAL.

Unity Labour Party (ULP): Beachmont, Kingstown; tel. 457-2761; fax 456-2811; e-mail ulpweb@aol.com; f. 1994 by merger of Movement for National Unity and the Saint Vincent Labour Party; moderate, social-democratic party; Leader Dr RALPH E. GONSALVES.

Diplomatic Representation

EMBASSIES IN SAINT VINCENT AND THE GRENADINES

China (Taiwan): Murray Rd, POB 878, Kingstown; tel. 456-2431; fax 456-2913; e-mail rocemsvg@caribsurf.com; Ambassador LEO LEE.

Cuba: Ratho Mill, Kingstown; tel. 458-5844; fax 456-9344; e-mail embacubasvg@gmail.com; internet www.embacu.cubaminrex.cu/sanvicenteing; Ambassador OLGA CHAMERO TRÍAS.

Venezuela: Baynes Bros Bldg, Granby St, POB 852, Kingstown; tel. 456-1374; fax 457-1934; e-mail embavenezsanvicente@vincysurf.com; Ambassador TIBISAY URDANETA TROCONIS.

Judicial System

Justice is administered by the Eastern Caribbean Supreme Court, based in Saint Lucia and consisting of a Court of Appeal and a High Court. Two Puisne Judges are resident in Saint Vincent and the Grenadines. There are five Magistrates, including the Registrar of the Supreme Court, who acts as an additional Magistrate.

Puisne Judges: FREDERICK BRUCE-LYLE, GERTEL THOM.

Office of the Registrar of the Supreme Court

Registry Dept, Court House, Kingstown; tel. 457-1220; fax 457-1888; e-mail svgregistry@caribsurf.com; Registrar TAMARA GIBSON-MARKS.

Chief Magistrate: SIMONE CHURAMAN.

Magistrates: DONALD BROWNE, ZOILA ELLIS-BROWNE, LESTER CAESAR.

Director of Public Prosecutions: COLIN WILLIAMS.

Religion

CHRISTIANITY

Saint Vincent Christian Council: Melville St, POB 445, Kingstown; tel. 456-1408; f. 1969; four mem. churches; Chair. Mgr RENISON HOWELL.

The Anglican Communion

Anglicans in Saint Vincent and the Grenadines are adherents of the Church in the Province of the West Indies, comprising eight dioceses. The Archbishop of the West Indies is the Bishop of Nassau and the Bahamas, and is resident in Nassau. The diocese of the Windward Islands includes Grenada, Saint Lucia and Saint Vincent and the Grenadines.

Bishop of the Windward Islands: Rt Rev. CALVERT LEOPOLD FRIDAY, Bishop's Court, POB 502, Kingstown; tel. 456-1895; fax 456-2591; e-mail diocesewi@vincysurf.com.

The Roman Catholic Church

Saint Vincent and the Grenadines comprises a single diocese (formed when the diocese of Bridgetown-Kingstown was divided in October 1989), which is suffragan to the archdiocese of Castries (Saint Lucia). The Bishop participates in the Antilles Episcopal Conference, currently based in Port of Spain, Trinidad and Tobago. At 31 December 2005 there were an estimated 8,176 adherents in the diocese, comprising about 7% of the population.

Bishop of Kingstown: Rt Rev. ROBERT RIVAS, Bishop's Office, POB 862, Edinboro, Kingstown; tel. 457-2363; fax 457-1903; e-mail rcdok@caribsurf.com.

Other Christian Churches

The Methodists, Seventh-day Adventists, Baptists and other denominations also have places of worship.

BAHÁ'Í FAITH

National Spiritual Assembly: POB 1043, Kingstown; tel. 456-4717.

The Press

DAILY

The Herald: Blue Caribbean Bldg, Kingstown; tel. 456-1242; fax 456-1046; e-mail info@heraldsvg; internet heraldsvg.com; daily; internationally distributed.

SELECTED WEEKLIES

The News: Frenches Gate, POB 1078, Kingstown; tel. 456-2942; fax 456-2941; e-mail thenews@caribsurf.com; weekly; Man. Dir SHELLEY CLARKE.

Searchlight: Interactive Media Ltd, POB 152, Kingstown; tel. 456-1558; fax 457-2250; e-mail search@caribsurf.com; internet www.searchlight.vc; weekly on Fridays; Chair. CORLITA OLLIVERRE; Man. Editor NORMA KEIZER.

The Vincentian: St George's Pl., Kingstown; tel. 456-1123; fax 457-2821; e-mail info@thevincentian.com; internet www.thevincentian.com; f. 1919; weekly; owned by the Vincentian Publishing Co; Man. Dir EGERTON M. RICHARDS; Editor-in-Chief TERRANCE PARRIS; circ. 6,000.

The Westindian Crusader: Kingstown; tel. 458-0073; fax 456-9315; e-mail crusader@caribsurf.com; weekly; Editor ELSEE CARBERRY; Man. Editor LINA CLARKE.

SELECTED PERIODICALS

Caribbean Compass: POB 175, Bequia; tel. 457-3409; fax 457-3410; e-mail tom@caribbeancompass.com; internet www.caribbeancompass.com; marine news; monthly; free distribution in Caribbean from Puerto Rico to Panama; circ. 12,000; Editor SALLY ERDLE.

Government Gazette: POB 12, Kingstown; tel. 457-1840; f. 1868; Govt Printer OTHNIEL WHITE; circ. 492.

Unity: Middle and Melville St, POB 854, Kingstown; tel. 456-1049; fortnightly; organ of the United Labour Party.

Publishers

CJW Communications: POB 1078, Frenches Gate, Kingstown; tel. 456-2942; fax 456-2941.

Great Works Depot: Commission A Bldg, Granby St, POB 1849, Kingstown; tel. 456-2057; fax 457-2055; e-mail gwd@caribsurf.com.

The Vincentian Publishing Co Ltd: St George's Pl., Kingstown; tel. 456-1123; fax 457-2821; e-mail info@thevincentian.com; internet www.thevincentian.com; Man. Dir EGERTON M. RICHARDS.

Broadcasting and Communications

TELECOMMUNICATIONS

Regulatory Authorities

Eastern Caribbean Telecommunications Authority (ECTEL): based in Castries, Saint Lucia; f. 2000 to regulate telecommunications in Saint Vincent and the Grenadines, Dominica, Grenada, Saint Christopher and Nevis and Saint Lucia.

National Telecom Regulatory Commission (NTRC): KCCU Financial Centre, Granby St, Kingstown; tel. 457-2279; fax 457-2834; e-mail info@ntrc.vc; internet www.ntrc.vc; f. 2001 by the Telecommunications Act to regulate the sector in collaboration with ECTEL (q.v.); Chair K. DOUGLAS.

Major Service Providers

Cable & Wireless (St Vincent and the Grenadines) Ltd: Halifax St, POB 103, Kingstown; tel. 457-1901; fax 457-2777; e-mail svdinfo@caribsurf.com; internet www.candw.vc; CEO DARYL JACKSON.

Digicel: Suite KO59, cnr Granby and Sharpe Sts, Kingstown; tel. 453-3000; fax 453-3010; e-mail customercaresvg@digicelgroup.com; internet www.digicelsvg.com; f. 2003; mobile cellular phone operator; owned by an Irish consortium; Chair. DENIS O'BRIEN; Eastern Caribbean CEO KEVIN WHITE.

BROADCASTING

National Broadcasting Corporation of Saint Vincent and the Grenadines: Richmond Hill, POB 705, Kingstown; tel. 457-1111; fax 456-2749; e-mail nbcsvgadmin@nbcsvg.com; internet www.nbcsvg.com; govt-owned; Chair. KENNETH BROWNE; Gen. Man. CORLITA OLLIVERRE.

SAINT VINCENT AND THE GRENADINES

Radio

NBC Radio: National Broadcasting Corpn, Richmond Hill, POB 705, Kingstown; tel. 457-1111; fax 456-2749; e-mail nbcsvgadmin@nbcsvg.com; internet www.nbcsvg.com; commercial; broadcasts BBC World Service (United Kingdom) and local programmes.

Television

National Broadcasting Corporation of Saint Vincent and the Grenadines: see Broadcasting

SVG Television (SGVTV): Dorsetshire Hill, POB 617, Kingstown; tel. 456-1078; fax 456-1015; e-mail svgbc@vincysurf.com; internet www.svgbc.com/svgtv.htm; f. 1980; broadcasts local, regional and international programmes; Man. Dir R. PAUL MACLEISH.

Television services from Barbados can be received in parts of the islands.

Finance

(cap. = capital; res = reserves; dep. = deposits; m. = million; brs = branches)

BANKING

The Eastern Caribbean Central Bank, based in Saint Christopher, is the central issuing and monetary authority for Saint Vincent and the Grenadines.

Eastern Caribbean Central Bank—Saint Vincent and the Grenadines Office: Frenches House, POB 839, Frenches; tel. 456-1413; fax 456-1412; e-mail eccbsvg@vincysurf.com; Country Dir ELRITHA DICK.

Regulatory Authority

Financial Intelligence Unit (FIU): POB 1826, Kingstown; tel. 451-2070; fax 457-2014; e-mail svgfiu@vincysurf.com; internet www.stvincentoffshore.com/fin_intl_unit.htm; f. 2002; Dir SHARDA SINANAN-BOLLERS.

Principal Banks

FirstCaribbean International Bank (Barbados) Ltd: Lower Halifax St, POB 212, Kingstown; tel. 457-1587; e-mail Earl.Crichton@firstcaribbeanbank.com; internet www.firstcaribbeanbank.com; f. 2002 following merger of Caribbean operations of Barclays Bank PLC and CIBC; CIBC acquired Barclays' 43.7% stake in 2006; Exec. Chair. MICHAEL MANSOOR; CEO CHARLES PINK; Man. EARL CRICHTON.

First St Vincent Bank Ltd: Lot 112, Granby St, POB 154, Kingstown; tel. 456-1873; fax 456-2675; e-mail firstvinbank@vincysurf.com; f. 1988; fmrly Saint Vincent Agricultural Credit and Loan Bank; Man. HENRY KEIZER.

National Commercial Bank (SVG) Ltd: Cnr Halifax and Egmont Sts, POB 880, Kingstown; tel. 457-1844; fax 456-2612; e-mail natbank@caribsurf.com; internet www.svgncb.com; f. 1977; govt-owned; share cap. EC $14.0m., dep. EC $520.7m., res EC $19.1m. (June 2006); CEO PHILIP H. HERNANDEZ; Chair. DESMOND MORGAN.

RBTT Bank Caribbean Ltd: 81 South River Rd, POB 81, Kingstown; tel. 456-1501; fax 456-2141; internet www.rbtt.com; f. 1985 as Caribbean Banking Corpn Ltd, name changed as above in 2002; Chair. PETER J. JULY.

Saint Vincent Co-operative Bank: Cnr Long Lane (Upper) and South River Rd, POB 886, Kingstown; tel. 456-1894; fax 457-2183.

'OFFSHORE' FINANCIAL SECTOR

Legislation permitting the development of an 'offshore' financial sector was introduced in 1976 and revised in 1996 and 1998. International banks are required to have a place of business on the islands and to designate a licensed registered agent. International Business Companies registered in Saint Vincent and the Grenadines are exempt from taxation for 25 years. Legislation also guarantees total confidentiality. By December 2005 the 'offshore' financial centre comprised 6,632 International Business Companies, 114 trusts and six banks.

International Financial Services Authority (IFSA): Browne's Business Centre, 2nd Floor, Grenville St, POB 356, Kingstown; tel. 456-2577; fax 457-2568; e-mail info@stvincentoffshore.com; internet www.stvincentoffshore.com; f. 1996; Chair. CLAUDE SAMUEL; Exec. Dir DOUGAL JAMES (acting).

Saint Vincent Trust Service: Trust House, 112 Bonadie St, POB 613, Kingstown; tel. 457-1027; fax 457-1961; e-mail trusthouse@saint-vincent-trust.com; internet www.saint-vincent-trust.com; br. in Liechtenstein; Pres. BRYAN JEEVES.

'Offshore' Banks

European Commerce Bank: The Financial Services Centre, Paul's Ave, POB 1822, Kingstown; tel. 456-1460; fax 456-1455; e-mail info@eurocombank.com; internet www.eurocombank.com.

Loyal Bank Ltd: Cedar Hill Crest, POB 1825, Kingstown; tel. 485-6705; fax 451-2757; e-mail ceo@loyalbank.com; internet www.loyalbank.com; f. 1997; CEO ADRIAN BARON.

Millennium Bank Inc: Financial Service Centre, Stoney Grounds, Kingstown; tel. 451-2100; fax 451-2101; e-mail client-service@minbank.com; internet www.minbank.com.

Safe Harbor Bank Ltd: Nanton's Bldg, Egmont St, POB 2630, Kingstown; tel. 451-2030; fax 451-2031; e-mail iofo@safeharborbank.com; internet www.safeharborbank.com.

Trend Bank Ltd: The Financial Services Centre, Paul's Ave, POB 1823, Kingstown; tel. 457-0548; fax 451-2672; internet www.trendb.com.

United Bank Ltd: Sutherland's Bldg, Murray Rd, POB 1341, Kingstown; tel. 456-1666; fax 485-6716; e-mail info@united-bank.net; internet www.united-bank.net.

STOCK EXCHANGE

Eastern Caribbean Securities Exchange: based in Basseterre, Saint Christopher and Nevis; tel. (869) 466-7192; fax (869) 465-3798; e-mail info@ecseonline.com; internet www.ecseonline.com; f. 2001; regional securities market designed to facilitate the buying and selling of financial products for the eight mem. territories—Anguilla, Antigua and Barbuda, Dominica, Grenada, Montserrat, Saint Christopher and Nevis, Saint Lucia, and Saint Vincent and the Grenadines; Chair. K. DWIGHT VENNER; Man. Dir MICHAEL MORTON.

INSURANCE

A number of foreign insurance companies have offices in Kingstown. Local companies include the following:

Abbott's Insurance Co: Cnr Sharpe and Bay St, POB 124, Kingstown; tel. 456-1511; fax 456-2462.

BMC Agencies Ltd: Sharpe St, POB 1436, Kingstown; tel. 457-2041; fax 457-2103.

Durrant Insurance Services: South River Rd, Kingstown; tel. 457-2426.

Haydock Insurances Ltd: Granby St, POB 1179, Kingstown; tel. 457-2903; fax 456-2952.

Metrocint General Insurance Co Ltd: St George's Pl., POB 692, Kingstown; tel. 456-1821.

Saint Hill Insurance Co Ltd: Bay St, POB 1741, Kingstown; tel. 457-1227; fax 456-2374.

Saint Vincent Insurances Ltd: Lot 69, Grenville St, POB 210, Kingstown; tel. 456-1733; fax 456-2225; e-mail vinsure@caribsurf.com.

Trade and Industry

DEVELOPMENT ORGANIZATIONS

National Investment Promotions Inc (NIPI): Administrative Bldg, 2nd Floor, POB 608, Kingstown; tel. 457-2159; fax 457-2943; e-mail info@svg-nipi.com; internet www.svg-nipi.com; f. 2003, by decree; assumed DEVCO's (q.v.) responsibilities for investment promotion and foreign direct investment; reports to the Office of the Prime Minister; board mems appointed from both public and private sectors by the Cabinet; Exec. Dir SUZANNE JOACHIM; Chair. EDMOND A. JACKSON.

Saint Vincent Development Corporation (DEVCO): Grenville St, POB 841, Kingstown; tel. 457-1358; fax 457-2838; e-mail devco@caribsurf.com; f. 1970; finances industry, agriculture, fisheries, tourism; Chair. SAMUEL GOODLUCK; Man. CLAUDE M. LEACH.

CHAMBER OF COMMERCE

Saint Vincent and the Grenadines Chamber of Industry and Commerce (Inc): Corea's Bldg, Hillsborough St, POB 134, Kingstown; tel. 457-1464; fax 456-2944; e-mail info@svg-cic.com; internet www.svg-cic.com; f. 1925; Pres. MARTIN BOLLERS; Exec. Dir JOYLYN DENNIS.

INDUSTRIAL AND TRADE ASSOCIATION

Saint Vincent Marketing Corporation: Upper Bay St, POB 873, Kingstown; tel. 457-1603; fax 456-2673; e-mail svmc@caribsurf.com; f. 1959; CEO SONNY WILLIAMS.

EMPLOYERS' ORGANIZATIONS

Saint Vincent Arrowroot Industry Association: Upper Bay St, POB 70, Kingstown; tel. 457-1511; fax 457-2151; e-mail info@svgarrowroot.com; internet www.svgarrowroot.com; f. 1930; producers, manufacturers and sellers; 186 mems; Chair. GEORGE O. WALKER.

Saint Vincent Banana Growers' Association: Sharpe St, POB 10, Kingstown; tel. 457-1605; fax 456-2585; internet www.svbga.com; f. 1955; over 7,000 mems; Chair. LESLINE BEST; Gen. Man. HENRY KEIZER.

Saint Vincent Employers' Federation: Middle St, POB 348, Kingstown; tel. 456-1269; fax 457-2777; e-mail svef@caribsurf.com; Pres. DON PROVIDENCE; Exec. Dir CECIL JACKSON.

Windward Islands Farmers' Association (WINFA): POB 817, Kingstown; tel. 456-2704; fax 456-1383; e-mail winfa@winfa.org; f. 1982; Co-ordinator RENWICK ROSE.

UTILITIES

Electricity

Saint Vincent Electricity Services Ltd (VINLEC): Paul's Ave, POB 856, Kingstown; tel. 456-1701; fax 456-2436; e-mail vinlec@vinlec.com; internet www.vinlec.com; 100% state-owned; country's sole electricity supplier; Chair. DOUGLAS COLE; CEO THORNLEY O. A. O. MYERS; 275 employees.

Water

Central Water and Sewerage Authority (CWSA): New Montrose, POB 363, Kingstown; tel. 456-2946; fax 456-2552; e-mail cwsa@caribsurf.com; f. 1961; Gen. Man. GARTH SAUNDERS.

CO-OPERATIVES

There are 26 Agricultural Credit Societies, which receive loans from the Government, and five Registered Co-operative Societies.

TRADE UNIONS

Commercial, Technical and Allied Workers' Union (CTAWU): Lower Middle St, POB 245, Kingstown; tel. 456-1525; fax 457-1676; e-mail ctawu@vincysurf.com; f. 1962; affiliated to CCL, ICFTU and other international workers' orgs; Pres. ALICE MANDEVILLE; Gen. Sec. LLOYD SMALL; 2,500 mems.

National Labour Congress: POB 875, Kingstown; tel. 457-1801; fax 457-1705; five affiliated unions; Pres. CECIL JACK.

National Workers' Movement: Burkes Bldg, Grenville St, POB 1290, Kingstown; tel. 457-1950; fax 456-2858; e-mail natwok@karicable.com; Gen. Sec. NOEL C. JACKSON.

Public Services Union of Saint Vincent and the Grenadines: McKie's Hill, POB 875, Kingstown; tel. 457-1950; fax 456-2858; e-mail psuofsvg@caribsurf.com; f. 1943; Pres. AUBREY BURGIN; Gen. Sec. ELROY BOUCHER; 738 mems.

Saint Vincent and the Grenadines Teachers' Union: POB 304, Kingstown; tel. 457-1062; fax 456-1098; e-mail svgtu@caribsurf.com; f. 1952; mems of Caribbean Union of Teachers affiliated to FISE; Pres. OSWALD ROBINSON; Gen. Sec. JOY MATTHEWS; 1,250 mems.

Transport

RAILWAYS

There are no railways in the islands.

ROADS

In 2003 there was an estimated total road network of 829 km (515 miles), of which 580 km (360 miles) was paved. A government plan to extend and rehabilitate the Windward Highway was well advanced by mid-2008, while the first stage of a three-phase project to link Troumaca with Fergusson Gap was completed in 2007, at a cost of EC $2.5m.

SHIPPING

The deep-water harbour at Kingstown can accommodate two ocean-going vessels and about five motor vessels. There are regular motor-vessel services between the Grenadines and Saint Vincent. Geest Industries, formerly the major banana purchaser, operated a weekly service to the United Kingdom. Numerous shipping lines also call at Kingstown harbour. Some exports are flown to Barbados to link up with international shipping lines. A new marina and shipyard complex at Ottley Hall, Kingstown, was completed in 1995. A new container port at Campden Park, near Kingstown, was opened in the same year. A new dedicated Cruise Terminal opened in 1999, permitting two cruise ships to berth at the same time.

Saint Vincent and the Grenadines Port Authority: POB 1237, Kingstown; tel. 456-1830; fax 456-2732; e-mail port-svg@caribsurf.com; internet www.svgpa.com; Port Dir PAUL KIRBY.

CIVIL AVIATION

There is a civilian airport, E. T. Joshua Airport, at Arnos Vale, situated about 3 km (2 miles) south-east of Kingstown, that does not accommodate long-haul jet aircraft. The island of Canouan has a small airport with a recently upgraded runway and passenger terminal; construction of a jet airport began in October 2006 and was completed, at a reported cost of US $21.5m., in May 2008 when it commenced operations. Mustique island has a landing strip for light aircraft only. In August 2005 Prime Minister Gonsalves pledged to build an international airport on Saint Vincent. Construction of the facility—located at Argyle, 13 miles east of Kingstown, at an estimated cost of EC $480m.—was due to be completed in 2011. Cuba, Taiwan and Venezuela were committed to providing funding for the project, and several other countries had been approached for assistance.

American Eagle: POB 1232, E. T. Joshua Airport, Arnos Vale; tel. 456-5555; fax 456-5616.

Mustique Airways: POB 1232, E. T. Joshua Airport, Arnos Vale; tel. 458-4380; fax 456-4586; e-mail info@mustique.com; internet www.mustique.com; f. 1979; charter and scheduled flights; Chair. JONATHAN PALMER.

Saint Vincent and the Grenadines Air Ltd (SVG Air): POB 39, Arnos Vale; tel. 457-5124; fax 457-5077; e-mail info@svgair.com; internet www.svgair.com; f. 1990; charter and scheduled flights; CEO MARTIN BARNARD.

Tourism

The island chain of the Grenadines is the country's main tourism asset. There are superior yachting facilities, but the lack of major air links with countries outside the region has resulted in a relatively slow development for tourism. In 2006 Saint Vincent and the Grenadines received an estimated 106,474 cruise-ship passengers and 97,432 stop-over tourists. Tourism receipts were estimated to total EC $305.8m. in that year. There were 1,762 hotel rooms on the islands in 2001, although extensive developments were undertaken prior to the islands' joint hosting of the 2007 Cricket World Cup. In early 2008 the Government announced it would invest €5m. in a Tourism Development Project. The plan would involve an upgrade of tourism and airport facilities.

Department of Tourism: Cruise Ship Terminal, Upper Bay St, POB 834, Kingstown; tel. 457-1502; fax 451-2425; e-mail tourism@caribsurf.com; internet www.svgtourism.com; Dir VIDA BERNARD.

Saint Vincent and the Grenadines Hotel and Tourism Association (SVGHTA): E. T. Joshua International Airport, Arnos Vale; tel. 458-4379; fax 456-4456; e-mail office@svghotels.com; internet www.svghotels.net; f. 1968 as Saint Vincent Hotel Asscn; renamed as above in 1999; non-profit org.; mem. of the Caribbean Hotels Asscn; Pres. LEROY LEWIS; Exec. Dir DAWN SMITH; 71 mems.

SAMOA

Introductory Survey

Location, Climate, Language, Religion, Flag, Capital

The Independent State of Samoa (formerly Western Samoa) lies in the southern Pacific Ocean, about 2,400 km (1,500 miles) north of New Zealand. Its nearest neighbour is American Samoa, to the east. The country comprises two large and seven small islands, of which five are uninhabited. The climate is tropical, with temperatures generally between 23°C (73°F) and 30°C (86°F). The rainy season is from November to April. The languages spoken are Samoan (a Polynesian language) and English. Almost all of the inhabitants profess Christianity, and the major denominations are the Congregational, Roman Catholic and Methodist Churches. The national flag (proportions 1 by 2) is red, with a rectangular dark blue canton, containing five differently sized white five-pointed stars in the form of the Southern Cross constellation, in the upper hoist. The capital is Apia.

Recent History

The islands became a German protectorate in 1899. During the First World War (1914–18) they were occupied by New Zealand forces, who overthrew the German administration. In 1919 New Zealand was granted a League of Nations mandate to govern the islands. In 1946 Western Samoa (as it was known until July 1997) was made a UN Trust Territory, with New Zealand continuing as the administering power. From 1954 measures of internal self-government were gradually introduced, culminating in the adoption of an independence Constitution in October 1960. This was approved by a UN-supervised plebiscite in May 1961, and the islands became independent on 1 January 1962. The office of Head of State was held jointly by two traditional rulers but, upon the death of his colleague in April 1963, Malietoa Tanumafili II became sole Head of State for life, performing the duties of a constitutional monarch.

Fiame Mata'afa Mulinu'u, Prime Minister since 1959, lost the general election in 1970, and a new Cabinet, led by Tupua Tamasese Lealofi, was formed. Mata'afa regained power in 1973, following another general election, and remained in office until his death in May 1975. He was again succeeded by Tamasese, who, in turn, lost the general election in March 1976 to his cousin, Tupuola Taisi Efi. The previously unorganized opposition members formed the Human Rights Protection Party (HRPP) in 1979, and won the elections in February 1982, with 24 of the 47 seats in the Fono (Legislative Assembly). Va'ai Kolone was appointed Prime Minister, but in September he was removed from office as a result of past electoral malpractice. His successor, Tupuola Efi, with much popular support, sought to nullify an earlier agreement between Kolone and the New Zealand Government which, in defiance of a ruling by the British Privy Council, denied automatic New Zealand citizenship to all Western Samoans except those already living in New Zealand. However, Tupuola Efi resigned in December 1982, after the Fono had rejected his budget, and was replaced by the new HRPP leader, Tofilau Eti Alesana. At elections in February 1985 the HRPP won 31 of the 47 seats, increasing its majority in the Fono from one to 15 seats; the newly formed Christian Democratic Party (CDP), led by Tupuola Efi, obtained the remaining 16 seats. In December Tofilau Eti resigned, following the rejection of the proposed budget by the Fono and the Head of State's refusal to call another general election. Va'ai Kolone, with the support of a number of CDP members and HRPP defectors, was appointed Prime Minister of a coalition Government in January 1986.

At the February 1988 general election the HRPP and an alliance composed of independents and the CDP (later known as the Samoa National Development Party—SNDP) both initially gained 23 seats, with votes in the remaining constituency being tied. After two recounts proved inconclusive, a judge from New Zealand presided over a third and declared the CDP candidate the winner. However, before a new government could be formed, a newly elected member of the Legislative Assembly defected from the SNDP alliance to the HRPP. In April Tofilau Eti was re-elected Prime Minister, and a new Government, composed of HRPP members, was appointed.

Legislation proposed in early 1990 which would permit local village councils to fine or to impose forced labour or exile on individuals accused of offending communal rules was widely perceived as an attempt by the Government to ensure the support of the Matai (elected clan chiefs) at the next general election. Of the 47 seats in the Fono, 45 were traditionally elected by holders of Matai titles. However, the political importance of the Matai had been increasingly diminished by the procurement of Matai titles by those seeking to be elected to the Fono. This practice was believed to have undermined the system of chief leadership to such an extent that universal suffrage would have to be introduced to decide all of the seats in the Fono. A referendum was conducted in October 1990, at which voters narrowly accepted government proposals for the introduction of universal suffrage. A second proposal, to create an upper legislative chamber composed of the Matai, was rejected. A bill to implement universal adult suffrage was approved by the Fono in December 1990, despite strong opposition from the SNDP.

A general election was held in April 1991 (the election had been postponed from February, owing to the need to register an estimated 80,000 newly enfranchised voters). In the following weeks petitions were filed with the Supreme Court against 11 newly elected members of the Fono who were accused of corrupt or illegal electoral practices. Moreover, subsequent political manoeuvring resulted in the HRPP increasing its parliamentary representation from an initial 26 to 30 seats, while the SNDP ultimately secured only 16 seats in the Fono, and the remaining seat was retained by an independent. At the first meeting of the new Fono, convened in early May, Tofilau Eti was re-elected for what, he later announced, would be his final term of office as Prime Minister. In November the Fono approved legislation to increase the parliamentary term from three to five years and to create an additional two seats in the Fono. These seats were contested in early 1992 and won by the HRPP.

The introduction of a value-added tax on goods and services in January 1994 (which greatly increased the price of food and fuel in the country) provoked a series of demonstrations and protest rallies, as well as demands for the resignation of the Prime Minister. As a result of overwhelming opposition to the new regulations, the Government agreed, in March, to amend the most controversial aspects of the tax. Meanwhile, four members of the Fono (including three recently expelled HRPP members), who had opposed the financial reforms, established a new political organization, the Samoa Liberal Party, under the leadership of the former Speaker, Nonumalo Leulumoega Sofara.

In May 1994 treasury officials warned the Government that a financial crisis at Polynesian Airlines, the national carrier, was threatening the country's economic stability. It was estimated that the company's debts totalled more than 45m. tala. A report by the Chief Auditor, Tom Overhoff, accused the Government of serious financial mismanagement relating to a series of decisions to commit public funds to the airline, and charged seven cabinet ministers with fraud and negligence in their handling of government resources. An inquiry into the allegations conducted in late 1994 cleared the ministers in question of all the charges, although its findings were harshly criticized by Overhoff, who claimed that the inquiry had been neither independent nor impartial. (In 2005 Polynesian Airlines established a joint venture with Australia's Virgin Blue to form Polynesian Blue—see Economic Affairs.)

Protests against the value-added tax on goods and services continued in early 1995, following the Government's decision to charge two prominent members of the Tumua ma Pule group of traditional leaders and former members of the Fono with sedition, for organizing demonstrations against the tax during 1994. In March 1995 3,000 people delivered a petition to the Prime Minister, bearing the signatures of 120,000 people (some 75% of the population), that demanded that the tax be revoked. The Prime Minister questioned the authenticity of the signatures and appointed a 14-member committee to investigate the matter. In late June the case against the two members of Tumua ma Pule, which had attracted attention from several international non-governmental organizations (including the World Council of Churches and Amnesty International) was dismissed on the grounds of insufficient evidence.

In December 1995 the HRPP unanimously re-elected Tofilau Eti as the leader of the party, despite concern over the Prime Minister's deteriorating health, as well as a previous declaration that he would retire from politics upon completion of his current term in office. In March 1996 one of the two female members of the Fono, Matatumua Naimoaga, left the HRPP in order to form the Samoa All-People's Party. The formation of the new party, in preparation for the forthcoming general election, was reportedly a result of dissatisfaction with the Government's alleged mismanagement of public assets together with concern over corruption. Legislation introduced in April attempted to distinguish between the traditional Samoan practice of exchanging gifts and acts of bribery, amid numerous reports that voters were demanding gifts and favours from electoral candidates in return for their support.

A general election took place on 26 April 1996. The opposition was highly critical of the delay in the counting of votes (which took some three weeks in total), claiming that the length of time involved allowed the HRPP to recruit successful independent candidates in an attempt to gain a majority of seats in the Fono. It was eventually announced in mid-May that the HRPP had secured a total of 28 seats (with the recruitment of several independent members to their ranks), the SNDP had won 14 seats and independent candidates had secured seven. Tofilau Eti was subsequently re-elected as Prime Minister, defeating the Leader of the Opposition, Tuiatua Tupua Tamasese, with 34 votes to 14.

In May 1997 the Prime Minister proposed a constitutional amendment in the Fono to change the country's name to Samoa. (The country has been known simply as Samoa at the UN since its admission to the organization in 1976.) In July the Fono voted by 41 votes to one to approve the change, which took effect on the next day. However, the neighbouring US territory of American Samoa expressed dissatisfaction with the change (which was believed to undermine the Samoan identity of its islands and inhabitants), and in September introduced legislation to prohibit recognition of the new name within the territory. In March 1998 the House of Representatives in American Samoa voted against legislation that proposed not to recognize Samoan passports (thereby preventing Samoans from travelling to the territory), but decided to continue to refer to the country as Western Samoa and to its inhabitants as Western Samoans. Nevertheless, in January 2000 Samoa and American Samoa signed a memorandum of understanding, increasing co-operation in areas including health, trade and education.

A series of reports in *The Samoa Observer* in mid-1997 alleged that a serious financial scandal involving the disappearance of some 500 blank passports, and their subsequent sale to Hong Kong Chinese purchasers for up to US $26,000 each, had occurred. The Government refused to comment on the newspaper's allegations, stating only that several senior immigration officials had been suspended pending the outcome of an investigation into the affair. Moreover, the Government subsequently brought charges of defamatory libel against the editor, Savea Sano Malifa, for publishing a letter criticizing the Prime Minister (who was reported to have told the Fono of his intention to change legislation governing business licences, such that publications could have their licences withdrawn for publishing dissenting material). The regional Pacific Islands News Association also condemned the Prime Minister's comments as an attack on freedom of information and expression. The continued existence of the newspaper was placed in jeopardy when Savea Sano Malifa was found guilty of defaming the Prime Minister in two libel cases in July and September 1998, and was ordered to pay a total of some $17,000 in costs. The newspaper had alleged that public funds had been used to construct a hotel owned by the Prime Minister and had criticized the allocation of $0.25m. in the 1998 budget to Tofilau Eti's legal costs. The Government's increasingly autocratic style, its apparent intolerance of dissent and the perceived lack of accountability of its members, coupled with its poor economic record, resulted in frequent expressions of popular discontent during 1997. These culminated in a series of protest marches in late 1997 and early 1998, organized by the Tumua ma Pule group of chiefs and attended by several thousand people, which aimed to increase pressure on the Prime Minister to resign.

A long-standing dispute over land rights near Faleolo airport appeared to be the cause of violent activity in June 1998, when villagers shot a government official, burnt buildings and slaughtered or stole hundreds of cattle on a government estate. However, it was subsequently revealed that the incidents had been perpetrated by members of a gang styling themselves as Japanese Ninja warriors, who were believed to be involved in the cultivation of marijuana and cattle theft. Some 38 men, thought to be members of the gang, were later arrested. The dispute, which originated in a land survey carried out in 1871, re-emerged in January 2003 when villagers presented the Government with a petition and a list of demands relating to land rights and revenue from the airport. In July 2005 the Government stated that it wanted all families living on the disputed land to vacate the area (covering about 22 acres) and move to a nearby and larger plot of government land. One of the official reasons given for the request was in order to comply with health and safety regulations. However, the villagers resolved to resist the Government's request, restating their original demand for the return of 6,000 acres close to the airport, which they claimed had been wrongfully taken from them at the end of the 19th century. They were led in their resistance by senior Matai and former Minister of Civil Aviation, Toalepaiali'i Toeolesulusulu Suafaiga Siueva Pose Salesa III, who claimed that during his tenure in the Cabinet the Government had revealed its desire to remove the villagers' coconut trees in order to create a clearer flight path for aircraft and that this remained their motivation for moving the families.

In November 1998 Tofilau Eti Alesana resigned as Prime Minister, owing to ill health. He was replaced by the Deputy Prime Minister, Tuila'epa Sailele Malielegaoi, and, at the same time, the Cabinet was reorganized. Tofilau Eti Alesana died in March 1999.

In July 1999 the Minister of Public Works, Luagalau Levaula Kamu, was shot dead while attending an event commemorating the 20th anniversary of the foundation of the ruling HRPP. Speculation followed that the killer's intended target had been the Prime Minister, but this was denied both by Tuila'epa Sailele and by the New Zealand police officers sent to the island to assist in the investigation. The son of the Minister of Women's Affairs, Leafa Vitale, was later convicted of the murder and sentenced to death (subsequently commuted to a life sentence). Leafa Vitale was subsequently charged with the murder of Luagalau, together with the former Minister for Telecommunications, Toi Akuso, who faced additional charges of inciting others to murder Luagalau and Prime Minister Tuila'epa Sailele. In mid-April 2000 the two former ministers were found guilty of murdering Luagalau and were sentenced to death, which was similarly commuted to life imprisonment. It later emerged that Luagalau had been killed in an attempt to prevent him from uncovering cases of corruption and bribery in which the two ministers had become involved.

Meanwhile, in November 1999 the ruling HRPP increased its number of seats in the Fono to 34 (out of a possible 49) following the defection of an independent candidate to the HRPP. By-elections for the two imprisoned former ministers' seats were held in June 2000, and HRPP candidates were successful in both constituencies.

In August 2000 a supreme court ruling ordered the Government to allow opposition politicians access to the state-controlled media. For several years the opposition had been denied free access to the media.

At a general election on 2 March 2001 the HRPP won 22 seats, the SNDP secured 13 seats and independent candidates took 14 seats. On 16 March Tuila'epa Sailele won 28 votes in the Fono, after securing the support of six independents, to be re-elected Prime Minister. However, the opposition mounted a number of legal challenges to his election. In August eight elected members of Parliament, including the Deputy Prime Minister, the Minister of Health and the Minister of Internal Affairs, Women's Affairs and Broadcasting, faced charges of electoral malpractice in the Supreme Court. None of the cabinet ministers was found guilty, and by-elections for the vacant parliamentary seats were held in October and November. The HRPP won all four contested seats.

An Electoral Commission, established shortly after the March elections, published its recommendations in October 2001, urging the replacement of the two Individual Voters Roll seats with two Urban Seats and that government employees who wished to stand for Parliament should first be obliged to resign from their offices.

In mid-2003 members of the medical profession expressed alarm at the increasing numbers of qualified medical staff choosing to emigrate or to leave the profession. It was estimated that one-third of Samoa's nurses had left the profession between 2002 and 2003, while half of all doctors' positions remained vacant. The situation was attributed to relatively low levels of pay. In September 2005 Samoan doctors went on strike in protest against entry-level rates of pay and working conditions. When doctors refused to return to work, the Government was forced to recruit temporary staff from overseas. In late November some 1,500 people marched through the streets of Apia in support of 23 doctors who had resigned earlier that month as part of the continuing protest. A petition was presented to the Prime Minister's Department, whereupon two cabinet ministers stated that the issue would be addressed. A commission of inquiry made recommendations for changes, to which the Government then agreed, but no increase in doctors' starting salaries, as demanded by protesters, was forthcoming. By January 2006 four of the doctors involved in the protests had relocated overseas; 11 others returned to government employment.

Concern was expressed in early 2005 that the proliferation of Matai titles was leading to the making of hasty and undesirable decisions by village councils. A senior village chief and member of the Fono, Leva'a Sauaso, claimed that many of the new title-holders were lacking in knowledge and experience of village affairs and that these clan leaders were consequently making decisions that were detrimental to Samoan society.

The general election held on 31 March 2006 was contested by a total of 211 candidates, including 18 women. The ruling HRPP regained power, securing 33 of the 49 parliamentary seats, thus decisively defeating the Samoa Democratic United Party (SDUP, formed upon the merger of the SNDP and the Samoa Independent Party), which won 10 seats. The remaining seats were taken by independent candidates. However, vtiolence ensued when it was declared that the Minister for Public Works, Faumui Liuga, had defeated Letagaloa Pita, a senior-ranking Matai, in the constituency of Savai'i. In late August 2006 the opposition SDUP announced the appointment of a new leader, Asiata Sale'imoa Va'ai. The party's long-standing leader, Lemamea Mualia, initially disputed his replacement but formally resigned in late September, subsequently sitting as an independent member of the Fono.

The Samoan Head of State, Malietoa Tanumafili II, died in May 2007 at the age of 95. He had served as sole Head of State, for life, since 1963. His funeral was attended by regional leaders, including the King of Tonga and the New Zealand Prime Minister. In June 2007 the Fono unanimously elected former Prime Minister Tuiatua Tupua Tamasese Efi as Head of State, for a term of five years.

Despite independence, Samoa maintains strong links with New Zealand, where many Samoans live and many more receive secondary and tertiary education. In June 2002 New Zealand formally apologized for injustices it had committed against its former colony during its administration between 1914 and 1962. These included carelessness in allowing the 1918 influenza pandemic to kill 22% of Samoa's population (the virus having been brought in on a ship from New Zealand); the murder of a Samoan paramount chief and independence leader, Tupua Tamasese Lealofi III, and the killing of nine other supporters of the pacifist Mau movement during a non-violent protest in 1929; and the banishment of native leaders, who were also stripped of their chiefly titles. The apology, while accepted, attracted mixed reactions from Samoans, many of whom were more concerned with the issue of the restoration of their rights to New Zealand citizenship (which had been severely curtailed by the Citizenship Western Samoa Act of 1982). Moreover, in March 2003 large protest marches took place in Samoa and New Zealand demanding the repeal of the 1982 law. In May 2004 a parliamentary select committee rejected a 100,000-signature petition seeking a repeal of the law and upheld the principles of the 1982 ruling. In 2004 the number of Samoans applying for New Zealand citizenship under a quota scheme increased by more than 50% to some 8,600.

In September 2004 the Samoan Government announced that it was seeking to formalize its maritime boundary with American Samoa, owing to a number of recent, unspecified incidents. Discussions began in Apia in March 2005. In January 2006 the Samoan Government announced that it was to open a consulate in the American Samoan capital of Pago Pago. In February it was announced that Samoa had established diplomatic relations with Brunei, and in October 2007 diplomatic relations were established with Cuba. In May 2007 Samoa hosted a regional meeting attended by ministers from countries including New Zealand, Solomon Islands and Tonga, in order to discuss maritime issues.

Samoa hosted the 13th South Pacific Games in August–September 2007, in which 22 Pacific island nations participated. The Government of the People's Republic of China financed much of the cost of Samoa's preparations, including a US $12.7m. aquatic centre and the reconstruction of Apia Park Stadium, at a cost of $6.9m. However, the total cost was estimated at approximately $92m., and in September Deputy Prime Minister Misa Telefoni acknowledged that preparations for the event had left Samoa in debt. The Chinese Government was also financing the construction of buildings for the legislature and the judiciary in 2007.

Government

The Constitution provides for the Head of State to be elected by the Legislative Assembly for a term of five years. Until 2007 the Head of State held office for life. The Legislative Assembly is composed of 49 members, all of whom are elected by universal suffrage. A total of 47 members are elected from among holders of Matai titles (elected clan chiefs), and two are selected from non-Samoan candidates. Members hold office for five years. Executive power is held by the Cabinet, comprising the Prime Minister and other selected members of the Assembly. The Prime Minister is appointed by the Head of State with the necessary approval of the Assembly.

Defence

In August 1962 Western Samoa and New Zealand signed a Treaty of Friendship, whereby the New Zealand Government, on request, acts as the sole agent of the Samoan Government in its dealings with other countries and international organizations.

Economic Affairs

In 2006, according to estimates by the World Bank, Samoa's gross national income (GNI), measured at average 2004–06 prices, was US $421m., equivalent to $2,270 per head (or $6,400 per head on an international purchasing-power parity basis). During 1996–2006, it was estimated, the population increased at an average annual rate of 0.9%, while during the same period gross domestic product (GDP) per head increased, in real terms, by an average of 2.7% per year. Overall GDP increased, in real terms, at an average annual rate of 3.6% in 1996–2006. According to the Asian Development Bank (ADB), growth was 2.6% in 2006, rising to 4.0% in 2007.

Agriculture (including hunting, forestry and fishing) accounted for 11.3% of GDP in 2006 and engaged some 40.6% of the employed labour force in 2001. Some 29.9% of the economically active population were employed in agriculture at mid-2005, according to FAO. The principal cash crops are coconuts and taro (also the country's primary staple food). Breadfruit, yams, maize, passion fruit and mangoes are cultivated as food crops. Exports of breadfruit and papaya to New Zealand increased significantly following the installation in early 2003 of a treatment facility to eradicate fruit fly from the produce. Plans to expand fresh fruit exports to include pineapples, mangoes and limes were announced in early 2005. Pigs, cattle, poultry and goats are raised, mainly for local consumption. The country's commercial fishing industry expanded considerably from the late 1990s; revenue from exports of fresh fish totalled US $15.5m. in 2006. Exports of food and live animals earned 60.0m. tala (27.6% of total export receipts) in 2001, but only 28.2m. tala (11.1% of all exports) in 2007. Between 1996 and 2005, according to figures from the World Bank, the GDP of the entire agricultural sector decreased, in real terms, at an average annual rate of 3.2%. In real terms, compared with the previous year, agricultural GDP decreased by 4.1% in 2006, but increased by 1.9% in 2007, according to the ADB.

Industry (comprising manufacturing, mining, construction and power) employed 20.0% of the employed labour force in 2001 and provided 26.2% of GDP in 2006. According to World Bank figures, between 1996 and 2005 industrial GDP increased, in real terms, at an average annual rate of 3.6%. The GDP of the industrial sector contracted by 2.8% in 2006, before increasing by 5.4% in 2007, according to the ADB.

Manufacturing (including handicrafts) provided 14.8% of GDP in 2006 and employed 12.8% of the employed labour force in 2001.

The manufacturing sector expanded considerably in the early 1990s with the establishment of a Japanese-owned factory producing electrical components for road vehicles. By 1996 the Yazaki Samoa factory, which assembled wire harnessing systems for export to car-manufacturing plants, engaged about 2,500 workers, making it the largest private sector employer in the country. However, by 2005 reductions in the factory's operations were being recorded. Other products of the manufacturing sector include beverages (beer—which accounted for 13.1% of exports in 2004—and soft drinks), coconut-based products and cigarettes. The clothing industry has expanded, and in 2004 garments accounted for 40.1% of total export earnings. Between 1996 and 2005, according to the World Bank, manufacturing GDP increased, in real terms, at an average annual rate of 1.4%. However, the GDP of the manufacturing sector contracted by 0.5% in 2004 and by 3.5% in 2005.

Energy is derived principally from hydroelectric power and thermal power stations. Imports of mineral fuels accounted for 18.6% of the value of total imports in 2007. In 2005 a US company announced plans to begin conducting exploration activity in Samoan waters, hoping to find new sources of petroleum and natural gas.

The services sector provided 62.5% of GDP in 2006 and engaged 39.4% of the employed labour force in 2001. Between 1996 and 2005, according to World Bank figures, the sector's GDP increased at an average annual rate of 6.2%. Compared with the previous year, the GDP of the services sector expanded by 6.2% in 2006 and by 3.8% in 2007, according to the ADB. Tourism makes a significant contribution to the economy, with revenue from this source rising to US $78m. in 2005. Tourist arrivals were reported to have increased from 115,882 in 2006 (when 37.1% of visitors were from New Zealand) to 122,250 in 2007. 'Offshore' banking was introduced to the islands in 1989, and by July of that year more than 30 companies had registered in Apia. A large proportion of the islands' revenue is provided by remittances from nationals working abroad, which reached the equivalent of 24.6% of GDP in 2006.

In 2006 the country recorded a visible trade deficit of US $208.5m., and a deficit of $51.2m. on the current account of the balance of payments. In 2007, when imports totalled 694.2m. tala and exports reached 253.8m. tala, New Zealand was Samoa's principal supplier of imports, providing 30.7% of the total. Australia was the dominant buyer of Samoan goods, accounting for 81.4% of exports. The USA was also an important trading partner in that year, accounting for 12.8% of imports and purchasing 2.5% of total exports. The principal exports are fish, garments, coconut cream, copra and beer. The main imports are food and beverages, industrial supplies and fuels.

The large budget deficits of the early 2000s reflected an increase in development spending financed by external borrowing and a decrease in lending to the domestic banking system. Deficits were financed by means of concessional loans, with the remainder being provided through the issuance of government securities. However, in the year ending 30 June 2007 an overall budget surplus, including external funding, of 15.3m. tala was projected, the surplus being estimated at the equivalent of 1.2% of GDP. Aid from Australia and New Zealand is a major source of revenue. An estimated $A23.3m. was to be provided by Australia in 2007/08, with $NZ10.0m. to be supplied by New Zealand in that year. At the end of 2005 the country's total external debt was US $656.3m., of which $177.3m. was long-term public debt. The cost of debt-servicing in that year was equivalent to 17.3% of the value of exports of goods and services. In 2000–07 the annual rate of inflation averaged 5.6%. According to the ADB, consumer prices increased by 3.8% in 2006 and by 6.1% in 2007.

Samoa is a member of the Pacific Islands Forum (see p. 380), the Pacific Community (see p. 377), the Asian Development Bank (ADB, see p. 182) and the UN Economic and Social Commission for Asia and the Pacific (ESCAP, see p. 35), and is a signatory to the Lomé Conventions and the successor Cotonou Agreement (see p. 301) with the European Union (EU).

The Samoan economy was adversely affected by Cyclone Heta, which struck in January 2004, causing damage to buildings, infrastructure and the agricultural sector. Economic growth in 2004, therefore, was largely due to increased activity in the construction industry. Expansion in this sector was dominated by rehabilitation projects in the aftermath of the cyclone, by continued private sector hotel development and by the construction of facilities in preparation for the South Pacific Games, which Samoa hosted in mid-2007. GDP growth in 2005 resulted mainly from momentum in the areas of tourism, agriculture, transport, communications and construction. However, the establishment of a joint venture between Polynesian Airlines and Virgin Blue, the Australian carrier, to form Polynesian Blue in 2005 resulted in many job losses among the employees of Polynesian Airlines, with the majority of redundancies reportedly involving administrative staff. The new airline, in which the Samoan Government retained a shareholding of 49%, began operations at the end of October. The Government's settlement of the debts of Polynesian Airlines contributed to an increase in the balance-of-payments deficit in 2006. The economy remained vulnerable to external factors, notably variations in world commodity prices. In 2006 the cost of Samoa's imports rose substantially, as a result of high international prices for petroleum, while revenue from the country's exports of fish, coconut cream and other agricultural products declined. However, in 2007 the impact of rising petroleum prices was partly offset by an increase in the country's earnings from exports of fish. GDP growth in 2007 was supported by Samoa's hosting of the South Pacific Games in August of that year, with attendant gains in the tourism sector. Remittances from overseas emigrants were expected to continue sustaining growth in 2008, along with the tourism industry. The ADB forecast that GDP growth would decelerate to around 3.0% in 2008.

Education

The education system is based on that of New Zealand. About 97% of the adult population are literate in Samoan. In 2003/04 enrolment at primary schools included an estimated 90.4% of children in the relevant age-group, while enrolment at secondary level included an estimated 65.7% of pupils of the relevant age. In 1988 a national university was established, with an initial intake of 328 students. Faculties of arts and commerce, science, nursing and education exist. A project to upgrade the university campus was completed in early 1997. In 1992 the Government decided to reintroduce bonds for students awarded government scholarships for overseas study. Expenditure on education by the central Government in 2005 was an estimated 52.0m. tala (20.8% of total budgetary expenditure).

Public Holidays

2008: 1 January (New Year's Day), 2 January (Holiday for New Year), 21–24 March (Easter), 12 May (Whit Monday/Mother's Day), 2 June (Independence Celebrations), 11 August (Father's Day), 13 October (White Monday), 3 November (Arbor Day), 19 November (National Women's Day), 25 December (Christmas Day), 26 December (Boxing Day).

2009: 1 January (New Year's Day), 2 January (Holiday for New Year), 10–13 April (Easter), 11 May (Mother's Day), 1 June (Whit Monday), 1–3 June (Independence Celebrations), 10 August (Father's Day), 12 October (White Monday), November (National Women's Day), 6 November (Arbor Day), 25 December (Christmas Day), 26 December (Boxing Day).

Weights and Measures

The metric system of weights and measures is now the primary system in force, although the imperial system is still used in limited areas.

Statistical Survey

Source (unless otherwise indicated): Statistical Service Division, Ministry of Finance, Government Building (MFMII), P.O. Box 1151, Apia; tel. (685) 24384; fax (685) 24675; e-mail info.stats@mof.gov.ws; internet http://www.spc.int/prism/country/ws/stats.

AREA AND POPULATION

Area: Savai'i and adjacent small islands 1,708 sq km, Upolu and adjacent small islands 1,123 sq km; Total 2,831 sq km (1,093 sq miles).

Population: 176,710 at census of 5 November 2001; 179,186 (males 92,961, females 86,225) at census of 5 November 2006 (provisional results). *By Island* (2006 census, provisional): Savai'i 43,103; Upolu 136,083.

Density (2006 census): 63.3 per sq km.

Principal Towns (population at 2006 census): Apia (capital) 37,237 (urban area); Vaitele 6,294; Faleasi'u 3,548; Vailele 3,174; Le'auva'a 3,015.

Births, Marriages and Deaths (registrations, 2001): Live births 3,516; Marriages 821; Deaths 339. *2004:* Live births 1,679; Deaths 547. Note: Registration is incomplete. *2000–05* (annual averages, UN estimates): Birth rate 29.4 per 1,000; Death rate 5.7 per 1,000 (Source: UN, *World Population Prospects: The 2006 Revision*).

Expectation of Life (years at birth, WHO estimates): 67.8 (males 65.6; females 70.2) in 2005. Source: WHO, *World Health Statistics*.

Economically Active Population (persons aged 15 years and over, 2001 census): Agriculture, hunting and forestry 17,514; Fishing 2,562; Manufacturing and handicrafts 7,327; Electricity, gas and water supply 905; Construction 1,669; Wholesale and retail trade; repair of motor vehicles, motorcycles and personal and household goods 2,753; Hotels and restaurants 1,522; Transport, storage and communications 1,928; Financial intermediation 1,080; Real estate, renting and business activities 268; Public administration and defence; compulsory social security 3,321; Education 2,341; Health and social work 842; Other community, social and personal service activities 2,090; Private households with employed persons 2,877; Extra-territorial organizations and bodies 472; Activities not adequately defined 853; *Total employed* 50,325 (males 35,118, females 15,207); Unemployed 2,620 (males 1,621, females 999); *Total labour force* 52,945 (males 36,739, females 16,206). *Mid-2005* (estimates): Agriculture, etc. 20,000; Total labour force 67,000 (Source: FAO).

HEALTH AND WELFARE
Key Indicators

Total Fertility Rate (children per woman, 2005): 4.2.
Under-5 Mortality Rate (per 1,000 live births, 2005): 29.
Physicians (per 1,000 head, 1999): 0.70.
Hospital Beds (per 1,000 head, 2002): 1.5.
Health Expenditure (2004): US $ per head (PPP): 217.7.
Health Expenditure (2004): % of GDP: 5.3.
Health Expenditure (2004): public (% of total): 76.8.
Human Development Index (2005): ranking 77.
Human Development Index (2005): value 0.785.

For sources and definitions, see explanatory note on p. vi.

AGRICULTURE, ETC.

Principal Crops ('000 metric tons, 2006, FAO estimates): Taro 17; Yams 3.0; Other roots and tubers 3.3; Coconuts 153; Copra 11; Bananas 24.3; Papayas 2.7; Pineapples 4.7; Guavas and mangoes 4.0; Avocados 1.1; Other fruits 9.7; Vegetables 1.0; Cocoa beans 0.5.

Livestock ('000 head, year ending September 2006, FAO estimates): Pigs 201; Cattle 29; Asses 7.0; Horses 1.8; Chickens 450.

Livestock Products (metric tons, 2006, FAO estimates): Cattle meat 1,000; Pig meat 3,587; Chicken meat 410; Cows' milk 1,500; Hen eggs 260; Honey 417.

Forestry ('000 cubic metres, 1979): *Roundwood Removals* (excl. bark): Sawlogs and veneer logs 58; Other industrial roundwood 3; Fuel wood 70; Total 131. *Sawnwood Production* (incl. sleepers): 21. *1980–2006* (FAO estimates): Annual output as in 1979.

Fishing (metric tons, live weight, 2005): Albacore 1,263; Sharks, rays, skates, etc. 250 (FAO estimate); Other marine fishes 1,337; Marine crustaceans 200 (FAO estimate); Marine molluscs 800 (FAO estimate); Sea-urchins and other echinoderms 600 (FAO estimate); Total catch (incl. others) 4,501 (FAO estimate).

Source: FAO.

INDUSTRY

Electric Energy (million kWh): 123.3 in 2004; 128.9 in 2005; 113.5 in 2006. Note: Figures relate only to government-owned power schemes. Source: Treasury Department of Samoa.

FINANCE

Currency and Exchange Rates: 100 sene (cents) = 1 tala (Samoan dollar). *Sterling, US Dollar and Euro Equivalents* (31 December 2007): £1 sterling = 5.19251 tala; US $1 = 2.5582 tala; €1 = 3.7659 tala; 100 tala = £19.51 = US $39.09 = €26.55. *Average Exchange Rate* (tala per US $): 2.7103 in 2005; 2.7793 in 2006; 2.6166 in 2007.

Budget (million tala, year ending 30 June 2006): *Revenue:* Tax revenue 273.1 (Income tax 47.2; Excise tax 69.0; Taxes on international trade 40.9; Value-added gross receipts and services tax 108.6); Other revenue 42.2; Total 315.4, excl. external grants received (71.8). *Expenditure:* Current expenditure 281.9 (General administration 69.5, Law and order 20.2, Education 55.3, Health 47.3, Social security and pensions 14.0, Agriculture 11.7, Public works 29.6, Natural resources 12.4, Other economic services 2.6, Interest on public debt 4.3, Other purposes 29.7, *Less* Value-added gross receipts and services tax payable by government 14.7); Development expenditure 86.1; Total 368.0, excl. net lending (23.7) (Source: IMF, *Samoa: Selected Issues and Statistical Appendix—June 2007*). *2006/07* (million tala, provisional): Total revenue 487.6 (Domestic receipts 389.2, External grants 98.5); Total expenditure 472.3 (Domestically financed 372.6, Externally financed development 123.7, Capital expenditure and net lending −21.1) (Source: Ministry of Finance, *Quarterly Economic Review—July–September 2007*).

International Reserves (US $ million at 31 December 2007): IMF special drawing rights 4.08; Reserve position in IMF 1.10; Foreign exchange 106.52; Total 111.69. Source: IMF, *International Financial Statistics*.

Money Supply (million tala at 31 December 2007): Currency outside banks 54.87; Demand deposits at banks 124.26; *Total money* 179.13. Source: IMF, *International Financial Statistics*.

Cost of Living (Consumer Price Index, excluding rent; base: 2000 = 100): 133.1 in 2005; 138.1 in 2006; 146.6 in 2007. Source: IMF, *International Financial Statistics*.

Gross Domestic Product (million tala at constant 2002 prices): 943.3 in 2004; 991.8 in 2005; 1,017.2 in 2006. Source: Asian Development Bank.

Gross Domestic Product by Economic Activity (million tala at current prices, 2006): Agriculture and fishing 142.3; Manufacturing 161.6; Electricity, gas and water 58.2; Construction 112.0; Trade 304.0; Transport and communications 153.1; Finance 117.2; Public administration 104.4 Other services 111.3; *Sub-total* 1,264.2; *Less* Imputed bank service charges 14.8; *Total* 1,249.4.

Balance of Payments (US $ million, 2006): Exports of goods f.o.b. 10.3; Imports of goods f.o.b. −218.9; *Trade balance* −208.5; Exports of services 134.1; Imports of services −56.8; *Balance on goods and services* −131.2; Other income received 4.1; Other income paid −17.5; *Balance on goods, services and income* −144.7; Current transfers received 106.7; Current transfers paid −13.2; *Current balance* −51.2; Capital account (net) 41.6; Direct investment from abroad 20.7; Portfolio investment assets −0.0; Portfolio investment liabilities 0.3; Other investments assets 2.5; Other investment liabilities −15.9; Net errors and omissions −3.3; *Overall balance* −5.2. Source: IMF, *International Financial Statistics*.

EXTERNAL TRADE

Principal Commodities (million tala, 2007): *Imports c.i.f.:* Food and live animals 133.1; Crude materials (excl. fuels) 20.3; Mineral fuels, etc. 129.2; Chemicals 45.3; Basic manufactures 148.2; Machinery and transport equipment 132.7 Miscellaneous manufactured articles 63.9; Total (incl. others) 694.2. *Exports f.o.b.:* Food and live animals 28.2; Beverages and tobacco 5.3; Basic manufactures 8.5; Machinery and transport equipment 202.1; Total (incl. others) 253.8.

Principal Trading Partners (million tala, 2007): *Imports:* Australia 108.7; China, People's Republic 20.7; Japan 33.8; New Zealand 213.1; USA 88.7; Total (incl. others) 694.2. *Exports:* Australia 206.5; New Zealand 22.7; USA 6.4; Total (incl. others) 253.8.

TRANSPORT

Road Traffic (motor vehicles registered, 2005): Private cars 4,638; Pick-ups 3,724; Taxis 1,286; Trucks 872; Buses 298; Motorcycles 93; Tractors 32; Total (incl. others) 14,238.

International Shipping (freight traffic, '000 metric tons, 2006): Goods loaded 211.1; Goods unloaded 52.6. *Merchant Fleet* (total displacement, '000 grt at 31 December 2006): 10.5; vessels 10 (Source: Lloyd's Register-Fairplay, *World Fleet Statistics*).

Civil Aviation (traffic on scheduled services, 2003): Kilometres flown 4 million; Passengers carried 198,000; Passenger-kilometres 279 million; Total ton-kilometres 27 million. Source: UN, *Statistical Yearbook*.

TOURISM

Visitor Arrivals: 98,155 in 2004; 101,807 in 2005; 115,882 in 2006.

Visitor Arrivals by Country (2006): American Samoa 26,183; Australia 23,603; Fiji 2,740; New Zealand 42,966; USA 8,682; Total (incl. others) 115,882.

Tourism Receipts (US $ million, incl. passenger transport): 71 in 2004; 78 in 2005.

Source: World Tourism Organization.

COMMUNICATIONS MEDIA

Telephones (2006): 19,500 main lines in use*.

Facsimile Machines (1999): 500 in use*.

Personal Computers (2002): 1,000*.

Internet Users (2006): 8,000*.

Broadband Subscribers (2006): 100*.

Mobile Cellular Telephones (2006): 24,000 subscribers*.

Radio Receivers (1997): 410,000 in use†.

Television Receivers (2001): 26,000 in use*.

Non-daily Newspapers (1988): 5 (estimated circulation 23,000)†.

* Source: International Telecommunication Union.
† Source: UNESCO, *Statistical Yearbook*.

EDUCATION

Primary (2005): 167 schools; 1,392 teachers; 40,074 pupils.

Secondary (2001): 1,064 teachers; 22,185 pupils.

Universities and other Higher (2001): 140 teachers; 1,179 students.

Source: mostly UN, *Statistical Yearbook for Asia and the Pacific*.

Adult Literacy Rate (UNESCO estimates): 98.6% (males 98.9%; females 98.3%) in 2004. Source: UNESCO Institute for Statistics.

Directory

The Constitution

A new Constitution was adopted by a constitutional convention on 28 October 1960. After being approved by a UN-supervised plebiscite in May 1961, the Constitution came into force on 1 January 1962, when Western Samoa became independent. A constitutional amendment adopted in July 1997 shortened the country's name to Samoa. The main provisions of the Constitution are summarized below:

HEAD OF STATE

The office of Head of State was occupied (from 5 April 1963, when his co-ruler died) by HH Malietoa Tanumafili II, who held this post until his death in May 2007. After that the Head of State was to be elected by the Fono (Legislative Assembly) for a term of five years.

EXECUTIVE

Executive power lies with the Cabinet, consisting of the Prime Minister, supported by the majority in the Fono, and ministers selected by the Prime Minister. Cabinet decisions are subject to review by the Executive Council, which is made up of the Head of State and the Cabinet.

LEGISLATURE

The Fono consists of 49 members. It has a five-year term and the Speaker is elected from among the members. Beginning at the election of 5 April 1991, members are elected by universal adult suffrage: 47 members of the Assembly are elected from among the Matai (elected clan leaders) while the remaining two are selected from non-Samoan candidates.

The Government

HEAD OF STATE

O le Ao o le Malo: TUIATUA TUPUA TAMASESE EFI (elected by the Fono 15 June 2007).

CABINET
(April 2008)

Prime Minister and Minister of Foreign Affairs and Trade: TUILA'EPA SAILELE MALIELEGAOI.

Deputy Prime Minister and Minister of Commerce, Industry and Labour: MISA TELEFONI RETZLAFF.

Minister of Women, Community and Social Development: FIAME NAOMI MATA'AFA.

Minister of Police, Prisons and Fire Services: TOLEAFOA APULU FAAFISI.

Minister of Works, Transport and Infrastructure: TUISUGALETAUA SOFARA AVEAU.

Minister of Natural Resources and Environment: FAUMUINA TIATIA LIUGA.

Minister of Finance: NIKO LEE HANG.

Minister of Revenue: TUU'U ANASI'I LEOTA.

Minister of Health: GATOLOAIFAANA AMATAGA ALESANA GIDLOW.

Minister of Communications and Information Technology: SAFUNEITUUGA PA'AGA NERI.

Minister of Education, Sports and Culture: TOOMATA ALAPATI POESE TOOMATA.

Minister for Justice and Courts Administration: UNASA MESI GALO.

Minister of Agriculture: TAUA TAVAGA KITIONA SEUALA.

MINISTRIES AND MINISTERIAL DEPARTMENTS

Prime Minister's Department: POB L 1861, Apia; tel. 63122; fax 21339; e-mail pmdept@ipasifika.net.

Ministry of Agriculture, Forestry, Fisheries and Meteorology: POB 1874, Apia; tel. 22561; fax 21865; e-mail maffm@lesamoa.net.

Broadcasting Department: POB 200, Apia; tel. 21420.

Ministry of Commerce, Industry and Labour: Apia; tel. 20441; fax 20443; e-mail mpal@mcil.gov.ws; internet www.mcil.gov.ws.

Ministry of Communications and Information Technology: Private Bag, Apia; tel. 26117; fax 24671; e-mail mcit@mcit.gov.ws; internet www.mcit.gov.ws.

Customs Department: POB 44, Apia; tel. 21561.

Economic Affairs Department: POB 862, Apia; tel. 20471.

Ministry of Education, Sports and Culture: POB 1869, Apia; tel. 21911; fax 21917; e-mail samoamesc@lesamoa.net; internet www.mesc.gov.ws.

Ministry of Finance: Private Bag, Apia; tel. 34333; fax 21312; e-mail information@mof.gov.ws; internet www.mof.gov.ws.

Ministry of Foreign Affairs and Trade: POB L 1859, Apia; tel. 63333; fax 21504; e-mail mfat@mfat.gov.ws; internet www.mfat.gov.ws.

Ministry of Health: Private Bag, Apia; tel. 21212; fax 21440; e-mail DG@health.gov.ws; internet www.health.gov.ws.

Inland Revenue Department: POB 209, Apia; tel. 20411.

Ministry of Justice and Courts Administration: POB 49, Apia; tel. 22671; fax 21050.

Lands, Survey and Environment Department: Private Bag, Apia; tel. 22481; fax 23176.

Ministry of Natural Resources and Environment: PMB, Apia; tel. 23800; fax 23176; e-mail info@mnre.gov.ws; internet www.mnre.gov.ws.

Ministry of Police: Apia; tel. 28055; fax 21319.

Public Works Department: Private Bag, Apia; tel. 20865; fax 21927; e-mail pwdir@lesamoa.net.

Ministry for Revenue: Apia; tel. 22244; fax 23876; internet www.revenue.gov.ws.

Statistics Department: POB 1151, Apia; tel. 21371; fax 24675.

Ministry of Women, Community and Social Development: PMB, Apia; tel. 63410; fax 23639; internet www.mwcsd.gov.ws.

Ministry of Works, Transport and Infrastructure: Apia; tel. 24031; fax 20964.

Legislature

FONO
(Legislative Assembly)

The Assembly has 47 Matai members, representing 41 territorial constituencies, and two individual members. Elections are held every five years. At a general election on 31 March 2006, the Human Rights Protection Party (HRPP) won 33 seats, the Samoa Democratic United Party (SDUP) won 10 seats and independent candidates secured six seats.

Speaker: TOLOFUAIVALELEI FALEMOE LEIATAUA.

Political Organizations

Human Rights Protection Party (HRPP): c/o The Fono, Apia; f. 1979; Western Samoa's first formal political party; Leader TUILA'EPA SAILELE MALIELEGAOI; Gen. Sec. LAULU DAN STANLEY.

Samoa Democratic United Party (SDUP): POB 1233, Apia; tel. 23543; fax 20536; f. 1988; est. as Samoa National Development Party (SNDP); coalition party comprising the Christian Democratic Party (CDP) and several independents; assumed present name after the 2001 election following merger of the SNDP and the Samoa Independent Party; Leader Hon. ASIATA SALE'IMOA VA'AI; Sec. VALASI TAFITO.

Diplomatic Representation

EMBASSIES AND HIGH COMMISSIONS IN SAMOA

Australia: Beach Rd, POB 704, Apia; tel. 23411; fax 23159; internet www.samoa.embassy.gov.au; High Commissioner MATT ANDERSON.

China, People's Republic: Private Bag, Vailima, Apia; tel. 22474; fax 21115; e-mail tce@samoa.ws; Ambassador SHI LONGZHUANG.

New Zealand: Beach Rd, POB 1876, Apia; tel. 21711; fax 20086; e-mail nzhcapia@samoa.ws; High Commissioner CAROLINE BILKEY.

USA: POB 3430, Apia; tel. 21631; fax 22030; e-mail usembassy@samoa.net; internet samoa.usembassy.gov; Chargé d'affaires GEORGE W. COLVIN, Jr.

Judicial System

Attorney-General: MING LEUNG WAI.

The Supreme Court
Presided over by the Chief Justice. It has full jurisdiction for both criminal and civil cases. Appeals lie with the Court of Appeal.

Chief Justice: PATU TIAVA'ASU'E FALEFATU SAPOLU.

Secretary for Justice: FAAITAMAI P. F. MEREDITH.

The Court of Appeal: consists of the President (the Chief Justice of the Supreme Court), and of such persons possessing qualifications prescribed by statute as may be appointed by the Head of State. Any three judges of the Court of Appeal may exercise all the powers of the Court.

The District Courts
Replaced the Magistrates' Court in 1998.

Judges: LESATELE RAPI VAAI, TAGALOA ENOKA FERETI PUNI.

The Land and Titles Court
Has jurisdiction in respect of disputes over Samoan titles. It consists of the President (who is also a judge of the Supreme Court) and three Deputy Presidents, assisted by Samoan judges and Assessors.

President of the Land and Titles Court: PATU TIAVA'ASU'E FALEFATU SAPOLU.

Religion

Almost all of Samoa's inhabitants profess Christianity.

CHRISTIANITY

Fono a Ekalesia i Samoa (Samoa Council of Churches): POB 574, Apia; f. 1967; four mem. churches; Sec. Rev. EFEPAI KOLIA.

The Anglican Communion

Samoa lies within the diocese of Polynesia, part of the Church of the Province of New Zealand. The Bishop of Polynesia is resident in Fiji, while the Archdeacon of Tonga and Samoa is resident in Tonga.

Anglican Church: POB 16, Apia; tel. 20500; fax 24663; Rev. PETER E. BENTLEY.

The Roman Catholic Church

The islands of Samoa constitute the archdiocese of Samoa-Apia. At 31 December 2005 there were an estimated 39,552 adherents in the country. The Archbishop participates in the Catholic Bishops' Conference of the Pacific, based in Fiji.

Archbishop of Samoa-Apia: Cardinal ALAPATI L. MATA'ELIGA, Archbishop's House, Fetuolemoana, POB 532, Apia; tel. 20400; fax 20402; e-mail archdiocese@samoa.ws.

Other Churches

Church of Jesus Christ of Latter-day Saints (Mormon): Samoa Apia Mission, POB 1865, Apia; tel. 64210; fax 64222; f. 1888; Pres. RENDAL V. BROOMHEAD; f. 1888; 65,000 mems.

Congregational Christian Church in Samoa: Tamaligi, POB 468, Apia; tel. 22279; fax 20429; e-mail cccsgsec@lesamoa.net; f. 1830; 100,000 mems; Gen. Sec. Rev. MAONE F. LEAUSA.

Congregational Church of Jesus in Samoa: 505 Borie St, Honolulu, HI 96818, USA; Rev. NAITULI MALEPEAI.

Methodist Church in Samoa (Ekalesia Metotisi i Samoa): POB 1867, Apia; tel. 22282; f. 1828; 36,000 mems; Pres. Rev. SIATUA LEULUAIALII; Sec. Rev. FAATOESE AUVAA.

Seventh-day Adventist Church: POB 600, Apia; tel. 20451; f. 1895; covers Samoa and American Samoa; 5,000 mems; Pres. Pastor SAMUELU AFAMASAGA; Sec. UILI SOLOFA.

BAHÁ'Í FAITH

National Spiritual Assembly: POB 1117, Apia; tel. 23348; fax 21363.

The Press

Newsline: POB 2441, Apia; tel. 24216; fax 23623; twice a week; Editor PIO SIOA.

Samoa News: POB 1160, Apia; daily; merged with the weekly *Samoa Times* (f. 1967) in Sept. 1994; Publr LEWIS WOLMAN.

The Samoa Observer: POB 1572, Apia; tel. 21099; fax 21195; e-mail sanomalifa@yahoo.com; internet www.samoaobserver.ws; f. 1979; five times a week; independent; English and Samoan; also publ. in New Zealand twice a week; Editor AUMA'AGAOLU ROPETA'ALI; circ. 4,500.

Samoa Weekly: Saleufi, Apia; f. 1977; weekly; independent; bilingual; Editor (vacant); circ. 4,000.

Savali: POB L1861, Apia; publ. of Lands and Titles Court; monthly; govt-owned; Samoan edn f. 1904; Editor FALESEU L. FUA; circ. 6,000; English edn f. 1977; circ. 500; bilingual commercial edn f. 1993; circ. 1,500; Man. Editor (vacant).

South Seas Star: POB 800, Apia; tel. 23684; weekly.

Broadcasting and Communications

TELECOMMUNICATIONS

Digicel Samoa Ltd: Apia; fax 28005; internet www.digicelsamoa.com; f. 2006 following the acquisition of Telecom Samoa by the Digicel Group; 90% owned by the Digicel Group, 10% govt-owned; Commercial Man. PEPE CHRISTIAN FRUEAN.

SamoaTel: Maluafou, Private Bag, Apia; tel. 60000; fax 61000; internet www.samoatel.ws; corporatized in July 1999; telecommunications and postal services provider; CEO MIKE JOHNSTONE.

BROADCASTING

Radio and Television

Samoa Broadcasting Corpn: Apia; tel. 21420; fax 21072; f. 1948; govt-controlled with commercial sponsorship; operates SBC Radio 1 and SBC Television 1; CEO Faiasea Lei Sam Matafeo.

Magik 98 FM: POB 762, Apia; tel. 25149; fax 25147; e-mail magic98fm@samoa.net; f. 1989; privately-owned; operates on FM wavelengths 98.1 and 99.9 MHz; Man. Corey Keil.

Graceland Broadcasting Network: POB 3444, Apia; tel. 20197; fax 25487; e-mail gbn@lesamoa.net; f. 1992; telecommunications, television and radio.

Finance

(cap. = capital; res = reserves; dep. = deposits; m. = million; brs = branches; amounts in tala, unless otherwise indicated)

BANKING

Central Bank

Central Bank of Samoa: Private Bag, Apia; tel. 34100; fax 20293; e-mail cbs@lesamoa.net; internet www.cbs.gov.ws; f. 1984; cap. 10.0m., res 16.9m., dep. 104.5m. (June 2004); Gov. Papali'i Tommy Scanlan.

Commercial Banks

ANZ Bank (Samoa) Ltd: Beach Rd, POB L 1885, Apia; tel. 69999; fax 24595; internet www.anz.com/samoa/; f. 1959; est. as Bank of Western Samoa, name changed 1997; 100% owned by ANZ Funds Pty Ltd; cap. 1.5m., res 28.4m., dep. 246.1m. (Sept. 2001); Dir R. G. Lyon; Man. Dir Mandy R. Simpson; 1 br.

Industrial Bank Inc: POB 3271, Lotemau Centre, Vaea St, Apia; tel. 21878; fax 21869; f. 1995; owned by Industrial Pacific Investments Ltd; Chair. and Pres. Ian Bystrov.

International Business Bank Corporation Ltd: Chandra House, Convent St, Apia; tel. 20660; fax 23253; e-mail ibb@samoa.net; f. 1991; 46.7% owned by ELECS Investment Ltd, 22.5% by Tidal Funds Co Ltd; Chair. Ilia Karas; Exec. Dir Serguei Grebelski.

National Bank of Samoa: POB 3047L, Apia; tel. 26766; fax 23477; e-mail info@nationalbanksamoa.com; internet www.nationalbanksamoa.com; f. 1995; owned by consortium of private interests in Samoa, American Samoa and the USA; Chair. Sala Epa Tuioti; CEO Douglas M. Crombie; 15 agencies; 4 brs.

Samoa Commercial Bank: POB L602, Matafele; tel. 31233; fax 30250; e-mail info@scbl.ws; internet www.scbl.ws; f. 2003; CEO Ray Ah Liki.

Westpac Bank Samoa Ltd: Beach Rd, POB 1860, Apia; tel. 20000; fax 22848; e-mail westpac@samoa.com.ws; f. 1977; est. as Pacific Commercial Bank Ltd, current name adopted 2001; first independent bank; 93.5% owned by Westpac Banking Corpn (Australia); cap. 1.2m., res 5.5m., dep. 99.8m. (Sept. 2004); Chair. Alan Walter; Gen. Man. Shane Smith; 3 brs.

Development Bank

Development Bank of Samoa: POB 1232, Apia; tel. 22861; fax 23888; internet www.dbsamoa.ws; f. 1974; est. by Govt to foster economic and social development; Gen. Man. Falefa Lima.

INSURANCE

National Pacific Insurance Ltd: DBS Bldg, Level 5, Private Bag, Apia; tel. 20481; fax 23374; f. 1977; Gen. Man. Darryl Williamson.

Progressive Insurance Company: POB 620, Lotemau Centre, Apia; tel. 26110; fax 26112; e-mail progins@samoa.ws; f. 1993; Gen. Man. I. O. Filemu.

Western Samoa Life Assurance Corporation: POB 494, Apia; tel. 23360; fax 23024; f. 1977; Gen. Man. A. S. Chan Ting.

Trade and Industry

CHAMBER OF COMMERCE

Chamber of Commerce and Industry: Level one, Lotemau Centre, Convent St, POB 2014, Apia; tel. 31090; fax 31089; internet www.samoachamber.com; f. 1938; Pres. Sina Retzlaff-Lima; Vice-Pres. Daryl Clarke.

INDUSTRIAL AND TRADE ASSOCIATIONS

Samoa Coconut Products: Apia.

Samoa Forest Corporation: Apia.

UTILITIES

Electricity

Electric Power Corporation: POB 2011, Apia; tel. 22261; fax 23748; e-mail epcgm@samoa.ws; internet www.epc.ws; f. 1972; autonomous govt-owned corpn; part of Public Works Dept, known as Electric Power Scheme, until 1972; Gen. Man. Muaausa Joseph Walter.

Water

Samoa Water Authority: POB 245, Apia; tel. 20409; fax 21298; e-mail taputoa@swa.gov.ws; internet www.swa.gov.ws; Man. Dir Mafaa'uo Taputoa Titimaea.

TRADE UNIONS

Journalists' Association of Samoa: Government Bldg, Apia; tel. 26397; fax 24712; internet www.jawsamoa.blogspot.com; Pres. Uale Papalii Tamalelagi.

Samoa Association of Manufacturers and Exporters (SAME): POB 3428, Apia; tel. 23377; fax 26895; e-mail info@same.org.ws; internet www.same.org.ws; f. 1981; Pres. Eddie Wilson.

Samoa Nurses' Association (SNA): POB 3491, Apia; Pres. Faamanatu Nielsen; 252 mems.

Samoa Trade Union Congress (STUC): POB 1515, Apia; tel. 24134; fax 20014; f. 1981; affiliate of ITUC; Pres. Falefata Tuaniu Petaia; Dir Matafeo R. Matafeo; 5,000 mems.

Transport

Public Works Department: see under The Government; Dir of Works Isikuki Punivalu.

ROADS

In 1999 there were 790 km of roads on the islands, of which some 42% were paved. In mid-2004 the Government announced a programme of road-building, including new roads from Apia to the airport and to the inter-island wharves. New four-lane roads were also to be constructed in the capital in response to increased vehicle numbers, estimated to have risen by some 7% annually in the previous 10 years.

SHIPPING

There are deep-water wharves at Apia and Asau. A programme of improvements to port facilities at Apia, funded by Japanese aid, was completed in 1991. Regular cargo services link Samoa with Australia, New Zealand, American Samoa, Fiji, New Caledonia, Solomon Islands, Tonga, US Pacific coast ports and various ports in Europe.

Samoa Ports Authority: POB 2279, Apia; tel. 23552; fax 25870; e-mail spa@spasamoa.ws; internet www.spasamoa.ws; f. 1999; Gen. Man. Toleafoa Elon Betham.

Samoa Shipping Services Ltd: POB 1884, Apia; tel. 20790; fax 20026; e-mail sss@lesamoa.net; internet www.sssl.ws.

Samoa Shipping Corporation Ltd: Private Bag, Shipping House Matautu-tai, Apia; tel. 20935; fax 22352; e-mail ssc@samoa.net; internet www.samoashipping.com; Gen. Man. Oloialii Koki Tuala.

CIVIL AVIATION

There is an international airport at Faleolo, about 35 km from Apia and an airstrip at Fagali'i, 4 km east of Apia Wharf, which receives light aircraft from American Samoa. In mid-1999 US $19.4m. was allocated by the World Bank to improve facilities at Faleolo airport.

Polynesian Blue: internet www.polynesianblue.com; f. 2005; 49% owned by the Samoan Govt, 49% owned by Virgin Blue, 2% owned by independent Samoan shareholder; flies between Samoa, Australia and New Zealand; replaced the services of Polynesian Airlines upon that carrier's cessation of international operations in 2005; CEO John Bartlett.

Polynesian Ltd: 2nd Floor, SNPF Bldg, Beach Rd, POB 599, Apia; tel. 21261; fax 20023; e-mail enquiries@polynesianairlines.com; internet www.polynesianairlines.com; f. 1959; 100% govt-owned; operates service to American Samoa and international flights between Samoa and Tonga and also American Samoa and Tonga; operates codeshare services between Samoa and Fiji; Domestic Poly Link, also formed in 2005, manages domestic services between islands of Upolu and Savai'i; Chair. Tuila'epa Sailele Malielegaoi; CEO Taua Fatu Tielu.

Tourism

The principal attractions are the scenery and the pleasant climate. Samoa has traditionally maintained a cautious attitude towards tourism, fearing that the Samoan way of life might be disrupted by an influx of foreign visitors. A major project to construct a 400-room resort on Taumeasina island, off Apia, began in September 2004. Tourist arrivals were reported to have risen from 115,882 in 2006 to 122,250 in 2007. Most visitors come from New Zealand, American Samoa, Australia and the USA. Tourist receipts totalled US $78m. in 2005.

Samoa Tourism Authority: POB 2272, Apia; tel. 63500; fax 20886; e-mail info@visitsamoa.ws; internet www.visitsamoa.ws; CEO MATATAMALI'I SONJA HUNTER.

Samoa Hotel Association: POB 3973, Apia; tel. 30160; fax 30161; e-mail administration@samoahotels.ws; internet www.samoa-hotels.ws; f. 1999; owned by Asscn of Accommodation Providers; Pres. STEVE YOUNG.

SAN MARINO

Introductory Survey

Location, Climate, Language, Religion, Flag, Capital

The Republic of San Marino lies in southern Europe. The country is situated on the slopes of Mount Titano, in the Apennines, bordered by the central Italian region of Emilia-Romagna to the north, and the Marches region to the south. San Marino has cool winters and warm summers, with temperatures generally between −2°C (28°F) and 30°C (86°F). Average annual rainfall totals 880 mm (35 ins). The language is Italian. Almost all of the inhabitants profess Christianity, and the state religion is Roman Catholicism. The civil flag (proportions 3 by 4) has two equal horizontal stripes, of white and light blue. The state flag has, in addition, the national coat of arms (a shield, framed by a yellow cartouche, bearing three green mountains—each with a white tower, surmounted by a stylized ostrich feather, at the summit—the shield being surmounted by a bejewelled crown and framed by branches of laurel and oak, and surmounting a white ribbon bearing, in black, the word 'libertas') in the centre. The capital is San Marino.

Recent History

San Marino evolved as a city-state in the early Middle Ages and is the sole survivor of the numerous independent states that existed in Italy prior to its unification in the 19th century. A treaty of friendship and co-operation with Italy was signed in 1862, renewed in March 1939 and revised in September 1971.

From 1945 to 1957 San Marino was ruled by a left-wing coalition of the Partito Comunista Sammarinese (PCS) and the Partito Socialista Sammarinese (PSS). Defections from the PCS in 1957 led to a bloodless revolution, after which a coalition of the Partito Democratico Cristiano Sammarinese (PDCS) and the Partito di Democrazia Socialista came to power. In early 1973 an internal dispute over economic policy led to the resignation of the Government, and a new Government was formed by an alliance between the PDCS and the PSS. The PSS withdrew from the coalition in November 1975, resulting in the collapse of the Government. The Captains-Regent took over the administration until March 1976, when a new coalition between the PDCS and the PSS was formed. This Government collapsed in late 1977 but continued in an interim capacity until a new administration was formed. Attempts by the PCS to form a government were frustrated by the lack of a clear majority in the unicameral legislature, the Great and General Council (Consiglio Grande e Generale). Eventually the Council agreed to a dissolution and elections were held in May 1978, when the PDCS secured 26 of the 60 seats. However, they were still unable to form an administration and the three left-wing parties, the PCS, PSS and the Partito Socialista Unitario, which together held 31 seats, agreed to form a coalition Government led by the PCS. San Marino thus became the only Western European country with a communist-led government. A left-wing coalition again formed the administration following the May 1983 elections.

In 1986 a political crisis, resulting from a financial scandal which allegedly involved several prominent PSS members, led to the formation of a new coalition Government, the first to be composed of the PDCS and the PCS. The coalition was renewed in June 1988, following a general election in May. In 1990 the PCS was renamed the Partito Progressista Democratico Sammarinese (PPDS). In 1992 the PDCS negotiated the formation of a coalition Government with the PSS.

At the general election of May 1993 the PDCS and the PSS obtained 26 and 14 seats, respectively. The election was regarded as a defeat for the PPDS, which secured only 11 seats, and was also notable for the success of three recently formed parties, the Alleanza Popolare dei Democratici Sammarinese (known as the Alleanza Popolare—AP), the Movimento Democratico and the Rifondazione Comunista Sammarinese (RCS). In June the PDCS and the PSS agreed to form a coalition Government. The PDCS and the PSS were again dominant at the general election of 31 May 1998, winning 25 and 14 seats, respectively. The PPDS won 11 seats, the AP six, and the RCS two. The remaining two seats were secured by a new grouping, Socialisti per le Riforme, which had been founded in 1997. A coalition Government was formed by the PDCS and the PSS in July 1998. In February 2000 the PSS left the Government, and in March a new coalition Government was formed, with six members of the PDCS, three members of the PPDS and one member of the Socialisti per le Riforme; it also had parliamentary support from Idee in Movimento (as the Movimento Democratico had been renamed in 1998). In March 2001 the Partito dei Democratici Sammarinese (PdD) was formed, following an alliance between Idee in Movimento, the PPDS and the Socialisti per le Riforme; the PPDS Secretary-General, Claudio Felici, was appointed as the PdD's Secretary-General.

At legislative elections held on 10 June 2001, the PDCS secured 25 seats, and the PSS obtained 15 seats. The two parties subsequently formed a coalition Government. The PdD won 12 seats, while the AP secured five seats, the RCS two seats and the Alleanza Nazionale Sammarinese one seat.

In June 2002 the PDCS-PSS coalition Government collapsed after the PSS withdrew its support, ending the long-term domination of Sammarinese politics by the PDCS. A new coalition Government was formed on 25 June, incorporating five members of the PSS, three of the PdD and two members of the AP. By December, however, the alliance between the PSS and the PDCS had been renewed, and a new coalition Government was instituted on 17 December, with five members from each party. In January 2003 a new political party, Sammarinesi per la Libertà, was formed. In December the coalition Government collapsed owing to disagreements between the two ruling parties, and a new coalition comprising four PDCS members and two each from the PSS and the PdD was installed. In early 2005 the PSS and the PdD merged to form the Partito dei Socialisti e dei Democratici (PSD). Former members of the PSS founded a new party, the Nuovo Partito Socialista, in November.

On 4 June 2006 a general election took place, at which the PDCS won 32.9% of the valid votes cast (21 of the 60 seats in the Great and General Council). However, the PSD, which secured 31.8% of the votes (20 seats), subsequently formed a coalition Government with the AP and the Sinistra Unita (SU, an alliance of the RCS and Zona Franca), which received 12.1% (seven seats) and 8.7% (five seats), respectively. The abstention rate was 28.2%. The new Government, comprising six members of the PSD and two each from the AP and the SU, took office on 29 July. In March 2007 a new political party, the Democratici di Centro (DdC), was formed by disaffected former members of the PDCS.

In late October 2007 the coalition collapsed after a government bill regarding judicial reform was narrowly rejected by the Great and General Council. In November a new four-party coalition, comprising the PSD (five members), the AP, the SU (each two) and the DdC (one), was formed.

San Marino became a member of the UN in 1992. In early 2006 San Marino was represented at a conference of small European states, held in Monaco.

Government

San Marino is divided into nine 'Castles' (Castelli) corresponding to the original parishes of the Republic. Each 'Castle' is governed by a Castle-Captain (Capitano di Castello), who holds office for two years, and a Castle Board (Giunta di Castello), which holds office for five years.

Legislative power is vested in the unicameral Great and General Council (Consiglio Grande e Generale), with 60 members elected by universal adult suffrage, under a system of proportional representation, for five years (subject to dissolution). The Council elects two of its members to act jointly as Captains-Regent (Capitani Reggenti), with the functions of Head of State and Government, for six months at a time (ending in March and September). Executive power is held by the Congress of State (Congresso di Stato), with 10 members elected by the Council for the duration of its term. The Congress is presided over by the Captains-Regent.

Defence

There are combined Voluntary Military Forces. There is no obligatory military service but citizens between 16 and 55 years may be enlisted, in certain circumstances, to defend the state.

SAN MARINO

Economic Affairs

San Marino's gross national income (GNI) was €844m. in 2004, equivalent to €27,460 per head. Annual GDP growth averaged 3.4% in 2000–2006; GDP increased by an estimated 4.5% in 2007.

Agriculture contributed only 0.1% of GDP in 2007 and engaged 0.2% of the employed population (excluding the self-employed) in that year. The principal crops are wheat, barley, maize, olives and grapes. Livestock-rearing and dairy farming are also significant. Olive oil and wine are produced for export.

Industry (including manufacturing and construction) contributed 44.5% of GDP in 2007 and engaged 39.8% of the employed population (excluding the self-employed) in that year. Stonequarrying is the only mining activity in San Marino, and is an important export industry. Manufacturing contributed 38.0% of GDP in 2007 and engaged 32.0% of the employed population (excluding the self-employed) in that year. The most important branches of manufacturing are the production of cement, synthetic rubber, leather, textiles and ceramics. The sector is largely export orientated, owing to integration with firms in Italy.

Energy is derived principally from gas (more than 75%). San Marino is dependent on the Italian state energy companies for much of its energy requirements.

The services sector contributed 51.1% of GDP in 2004 and engaged 60.0% of the employed population (excluding the self-employed) in 2007. Tourism is a significant source of government revenue. In 2004 the number of visitor arrivals was 2,127,573; however, of that number, only 41,546 stayed at least one night. Total visitor arrivals numbered 2,163,858 in 2007. Tourism receipts totalled an estimated €27,620m. in 2003. The sale of coins and postage stamps, mainly to foreign collectors, is also a significant source of foreign exchange. San Marino, along with the Vatican and Monaco, was granted special dispensation to mint its own euro coins in 2002, with a view to providing for this specialist market. The sale of uncirculated minted coins to collectors plays a significant role in San Marino's economy and it was permitted to continue to mint gold scudi as a legal tender for San Marino only. The financial sector is increasingly important, contributing an estimated 20.3% of GDP in 2003–04, according to IMF data.

In 2002, according to official figures, San Marino recorded a trade deficit of €96.2m. In the same year, according to the IMF, there was a deficit of €302.5m. on the current account of the balance of payments. Data concerning imports and exports are included in those of Italy, with which San Marino maintains a customs union. A customs union is also maintained with the European Union (EU, see p. 244). The principal source of imports (estimated at 87%) is Italy, upon which the country is dependent for its supply of raw materials. The major exports are wine, woollen goods, furniture, ceramics, building stone and artisan- and hand-made goods.

San Marino receives a subsidy from the Italian Government, under the *Canone Doganale*, amounting to about €11m. annually, in exchange for the Republic's acceptance of Italian rules concerning exchange controls and the renunciation of customs duties. In January 1999 San Marino adopted the European single currency, the euro, which became the sole currency in circulation at the start of 2002.

No consolidated general government accounts are published by San Marino, and separate accounts and budgets are prepared by the central administration, the Social Security Institute, and each of the public enterprises, on an accrual basis. Figures published by the IMF, on a cash basis, for the budget of the central administration indicated a surplus of €71.7m. for 2005 (equivalent to some 6.5% of GDP). The annual rate of inflation averaged 1.8% in 2002–06; consumer prices increased by 2.1% in 2006. In 2007 477 people were unemployed—equivalent to 2.4% of the total labour force (excluding the self-employed). An increasingly large proportion of the work-force (31.0% of the employed labour force, excluding the self-employed, in 2005, compared with 10.8% in 1991) are cross-border workers, mainly Italians from the surrounding regions.

San Marino's economy is linked to that of its neighbour, Italy, with which it shares a monetary and customs union. Owing to its size, it is extremely vulnerable to economic developments in Italy and the wider EU. Although traditionally manufacturing was the principal sector of the economy, its contribution to GDP has been in decline and the financial sector, which benefited from alternative taxation and regulation structures, is becoming increasingly significant, accounting for about one-fifth of GDP in 2004. Tourism and commerce were also increasing in importance. Growth in the financial sector was also stimulated by advantageous banking confidentiality, which aroused some concern from the Organisation for Economic Co-operation and Development (OECD) that this would encourage money-laundering. However, commitment was expressed in 2000 to adherence to OECD guidelines on 'harmful tax competition'. In November 2004 the EU reached an agreement with San Marino on the adoption by the latter of measures equivalent to those contained in the EU's savings tax directive, which aimed to prevent EU citizens from avoiding taxes on savings by keeping their money in foreign bank accounts. Under the agreement, which took effect in July 2005, the Sammarinese authorities were to levy a withholding tax on interest payments made to residents of the EU, part of which was to be transferred to investors' states of residence. As an alternative, tax-payers could opt to permit the disclosure of the income to their member states of residence for tax purposes. GDP growth, which slowed in the early 2000s following a rapid rate of growth in the 1990s, improved later in the decade, owing to higher growth rates in Italy and the euro area and the continued success of the financial sector. Supervisory structures in the financial sector were being strengthened in the mid-2000s, following the transfer of supervisory responsibility from the Government to the central bank, which was also implementing reforms to modernize the sector. Plans to extend activities in mutual funds and insurance were being developed in 2007–08. Successive budget surpluses were achieved from 2003–06, reversing years of budget deficits, as a result of spending restraint, notably on public sector wages and health care. Although the budget surplus was expected to be reduced in 2007–09, partly by the need to maintain low taxes to attract investment, public debt remained low. Pension reforms were introduced in 2006 to address the fiscal problems associated with an ageing population. Labour market reforms and tax cuts exerted a positive effect on competitiveness and encouraged higher levels of growth, with estimated real GDP growth of 4.5% in 2007.

Education

Education is compulsory for 10 years between the ages of six and 16 years. Primary education begins at six years of age and lasts for five years. Secondary education begins at the age of 11 and may last for up to eight years: a first cycle of three years, a second of two years and a third, non-compulsory, cycle of three years. A state-administered university was inaugurated in 1987. Government expenditure on education was €38.5m. in 2004, equivalent to 8.1% of public spending.

Public Holidays

2008: 1 January (New Year's Day), 6 January (Epiphany), 5 February (Liberation Day and St Agatha's Day), 19 March (St Joseph's Day), 24 March (Easter Monday), 25 March (Anniversary of the Arengo), 1 April (Investiture of the new Captains-Regent), 1 May (Labour Day), 22 May (Corpus Christi), 28 July (Fall of Fascism), 15 August (Assumption), 3 September (San Marino Day and Republic Day), 1 October (Investiture of the new Captains-Regent), 1 November (All Saints' Day), 2 November (Commemoration of the Dead), 8 December (Immaculate Conception), 25 December (Christmas Day), 26 December (St Stephen's Day).

2009: 1 January (New Year's Day), 6 January (Epiphany), 5 February (Liberation Day), 19 March (St Joseph's Day), 25 March (Anniversary of the Arengo), 1 April (Investiture of the new Captains-Regent), 13 April (Easter Monday), 1 May (Labour Day), 11 June (Corpus Christi), 28 July (Fall of Fascism), 15 August (Assumption), 3 September (San Marino Day and Republic Day), 1 October (Investiture of the new Captains-Regent), 1 November (All Saints' Day), 2 November (Commemoration of the Dead), 8 December (Immaculate Conception), 25 December (Christmas Day), 26 December (St Stephen's Day).

Weights and Measures

The metric system is in force.

SAN MARINO

Statistical Survey

Source (unless otherwise stated): Ufficio Programmazione Economica e Centro Elaborazione Dati e Statistica, Viale Antonio Onofri 109, 47890 San Marino; tel. 0549 885150; fax 0549 885154; e-mail statistica.upeceds@pa.sm; internet www.upeceds.sm.

AREA AND POPULATION

Area: 61.2 sq km (23.6 sq miles).

Population: 30,792 (males 15,122, females 15,670) at 31 December 2007 (*of which* Sammarinese 26,555, Others 4,237).

Density (at 31 December 2007): 503.1 per sq km.

Principal Towns (population at 31 December 2007): Serravalle 9,966; Borgo Maggiore 6,162; San Marino (capital) 4,386.

Births, Marriages and Deaths (registrations, 2006 unless otherwise indicated): Live births 284 in 2005 (birth rate 10.1 per 1,000, 2000–06); Marriages 216 (marriage rate 7.2 per 1,000, 2002–06); Deaths 225 (death rate 7.1 per 1,000, 2002–06).

Expectation of Life (years at birth, official estimates): Males 79.6, females 85.3 in 2007.

Economically Active Population (2007): Agriculture 37; Manufacturing 6,186; Construction 1,508; Trade and hospitality 2,819; Communication and transport 475; Finance 899; Real estate, information technology and business services 2,241; Public sector 4,125; Other services 1,047; *Total employed* 19,337 (males 11,125, females 8,214); *Unemployed* 477 (males 128, females 349); *Total labour force* 19,816 (males 11,253, females 8,563). Note: Figures exclude self-employed (2,074).

HEALTH AND WELFARE

Key Indicators

Total Fertility Rate (children per woman, 2005): 1.3.

Under-5 Mortality Rate (per 1,000 live births, 2005): 3.

Physicians (per 1,000 head, 1990): 47.35.

Hospital Beds (per 1,000 head, 1990): 7.16.

Health Expenditure (2004): US $ per head (PPP): 3,197.8.

Health Expenditure (2004): % of GDP: 7.4.

Health Expenditure (2004): public (% of total): 79.0.

For sources and definitions, see explanatory note on p. vi.

FINANCE

Currency and Exchange Rates: Italian currency: 100 cent = 1 euro (€). *Sterling and Dollar Equivalents* (31 December 2007): £1 sterling = 1.3609 euros; US $1 = 0.6793 euros; €10 = £7.35 = $14.72. *Average Exchange Rates* (euros per US $): 0.8041 in 2005; 0.7971 in 2006; 0.7306 in 2007. Note: The local currency was formerly the Italian lira (plural = lire). From the introduction of the euro, with Italian participation, on 1 January 1999, a fixed exchange rate of €1 = 1,936.27 lire was in operation. Euro notes and coins were introduced on 1 January 2002. The euro and local currency circulated alongside each other until 28 February, after which the euro became the sole legal tender.

General Budget (€ million, 2005, provisional): *Revenue:* Tax revenue 243.2 (Taxation on individuals 101.8; Taxes on goods and services 118.9); Social contributions 107.6; Grants 4.6; Other revenue 149.3; Total revenue 504.8. *Expenditure:* Compensation of employees 153.3; Use of goods and services 98.3; Consumption of fixed capital 14.5; Interest 2.8; Subsidies 16.9; Social benefits 132.2; Other expense 15.1; Total expenditure 433.1. Source: IMF, *Government Finance Statistics Yearbook*.

International Reserves (US $ million at 31 December 2006): IMF special drawing rights 1.20; Reserve position in IMF 6.17; Foreign exchange 471.77; *Total* 479.14. Source: IMF, *International Financial Statistics*.

Money Supply (€ '000 at 31 December 2006): Demand deposits at banks 907,389. Source: IMF, *International Financial Statistics*.

Cost of Living (Consumer Price Index for the families of workers and employees; base: December 2002 = 100): All items 105.1 in 2005; 107.3 in 2006.

Gross Domestic Product (€ million at constant 1995 prices): 882.0 in 2005; 916.0 in 2006; 957.0 in 2007 (estimate).

Expenditure on the Gross Domestic Product (€ million at current prices, 2006): Final consumption expenditure 553.0; Increase in stocks 23.0; Gross fixed capital formation 598.0; *Total domestic expenditure* 1,174.0; Exports of goods and services 2,307.0; *Less* Imports of goods and services 2,310.0; *GDP in purchasers' values* 1,171.0.

Gross Domestic Product by Economic Activity (€ million at current prices, 2004): Agriculture 1.2; Manufacturing 438.5; Construction 78.8; Services 542.9 (Trade 107.8, Transport and communications 15.5, Finance and insurance 174.8, Public sector 145.2, Other services 99.6); Total 1,061.4.

Balance of Payments (US $ million, 1996, estimates): Merchandise exports f.o.b. 1,741,9; Merchandise imports c.i.f. −1,719.3; *Trade balance* 22.6; Exports of services 120.4; Imports of services −102.2; *Balance on goods and services* 40.9; Interest payments 63.5; Net labour income −57.9; Other capital income −45.5; *Balance on goods, services and income* 1.0; Net transfers 9.7; *Current balance* 10.7; Capital account (net) 218.5; Errors and omissions −219.8; *Overall balance* 9.4. Source: IMF, *San Marino: Recent Economic Developments* (April 1999).

EXTERNAL TRADE

Data concerning imports and exports are included in those of Italy, with which San Marino maintains a customs union.

TRANSPORT

Road Traffic (registered motor vehicles, 2005): Motorcycles 10,268; Passenger cars 31,747; Buses and coaches 3,421; Agricultural vehicles 1,015; Total (incl. others) 47,876.

TOURISM

Visitor Arrivals (incl. excursionists): 2,107,092 in 2005; 2,135,589 in 2006; 2,163,858 in 2007.

Tourist Arrivals (staying at least one night): 45,508 in 2002; 40,686 in 2003; 41,546 in 2004.

COMMUNICATIONS MEDIA

Radio Receivers (1998): 35,100 in use.

Television Receivers (1999): 23,000 in use.

Telephones (2006): 21,000 main lines in use.

Facsimile Machines (1998): 5,800 in use.

Mobile Cellular Telephones (subscribers, 2006): 17,400.

Internet Users (2005): 15,200.

Broadband Subscribers (2006): 1,500.

Daily Newspapers (1998): 3 titles; 2,000 copies circulated.

Non-Daily Newspapers (1998): 8 titles; 12,000 copies circulated.

Periodicals (1998): 17 titles; 10,000 copies circulated.

Sources: Direzione Generale Poste e Telecomunicazioni; International Telecommunication Union.

EDUCATION

Pre-primary (2007/08): 14 schools; 137 teachers; 1,028 pupils.

Primary (2007/08): 14 schools; 248 teachers; 1,573 pupils.

Secondary (Scuola Media) (2007/08): 3 schools; 152 teachers; 860 pupils.

Secondary and Vocational (Scuola Secondaria Superiore e Formazione Professionale): 4 schools (2004/05); 77 teachers (2004/05); 603 pupils (2007/08—a further 760 pupils were studying outside San Marino).

University (2007/08): 1 university, 31 students (a further 929 students were attending courses outside San Marino).

Directory

The Constitution

San Marino, founded in 301 AD, is reputed to be the world's oldest surviving republic. In 1243 the first two Capitani Reggenti (Captains-Regent) were elected to serve as Heads of State by the Consiglio Grande e Generale (Great and General Council). The *Leges Statutae Sancti Marini* date back to 1600 and outline the main administrative posts and legal basis of the state. Electoral legislation dates from 1926.

San Marino is divided into nine Castelli ('Castles') corresponding to the original parishes of the Republic. Each Castello is governed by a Capitano di Castello (Castle-Captain), who holds office for two years, and a Giunta di Castello (Castle Board), which holds office for five years. Legislative power is vested in the unicameral Consiglio Grande e Generale, with 60 members elected by universal adult suffrage, under a system of proportional representation, for five years (subject to dissolution). The Consiglio elects two of its members to act jointly as Capitani Reggenti, with the functions of Head of State and Government, for six months at a time (ending in March and September). Executive power is held by the Congresso di Stato (Congress of State), with 10 members elected by the Consiglio for the duration of its term. The Congresso is presided over by the Capitani Reggenti.

The Government

HEADS OF STATE

Capitani Reggenti (Captains-Regent): ROSA ZAFFERANI (DdC), FEDERICO PEDINI AMATI (PSD) (April–September 2008).

CONGRESSO DI STATO
(Congress of State)
(April 2008)

A coalition of the Partito dei Socialisti e dei Democratici (PSD), the Alleanza Popolare dei Democratici Sammarinesi (AP), the Sinistra Unita (SU) and the Democratici di Centro (DdC).

Secretary of State for Foreign and Political Affairs and Economic Planning: FIORENZO STOLFI (PSD).

Secretary of State for Internal Affairs, Civil Protection and Implementation of the Government Programme: VALERIA CIAVATTA (AP).

Secretary of State for Finance, the Budget, Post and Relations with the Azienda Autonoma di Stato Filatelica e Numismatica (AASFN): STEFANO MACINA (PSD).

Secretary of State for Industry, Handicrafts, Trade, Research and Relations with the Azienda Autonoma di Stato per i Servizi Pubblici (AASS): TITO MASI (AP).

Secretary of State for Territory, Environment, Agriculture and Relations with the Azienda Autonoma di Stato di Produzione (AASP): MARINO RICCARDI (PSD).

Secretary of State for Tourism, Sport, Telecommunications, Transport and Economic Co-operation: ANTONELLO BACCIOCCHI (PSD).

Secretary of State for Health, Social Security and Equal Opportunities: MAURO CHIARUZZI (PSD).

Secretary of State for Education, Culture, the University and Social Affairs: FRANCESCA MICHELOTTI (SU).

Secretary of State for Labour, Co-operation and Youth Policies: PIER MARINO MULARONI (DdC).

Secretary of State for Justice, Relations with the Castle Boards, Information and Peace: IVAN FOSCHI (SU).

MINISTRIES

Secretariat of State for Education, Culture, the University and Social Affairs: Contrada Omerelli, 47890 San Marino; tel. 0549 882548; fax 0549 882301; e-mail segreteria.ic@gov.sm; internet www.educazione.sm.

Secretariat of State for Finance, the Budget, Post and Relations with the Azienda Autonoma di Stato Filatelica e Numismatica (AASFN): Palazzo Begni, Contrada Omerelli, 47890 San Marino; tel. 0549 882242; fax 0549 882244; e-mail federica.renzi.finanze@gov.sm; internet www.finanze.sm.

Secretariat of State for Foreign and Political Affairs and Economic Planning: Palazzo Begni, Contrada Omerelli, 47890 San Marino; tel. 0549 882312; fax 0549 882814; e-mail segretariadistato@esteri.sm; internet www.esteri.sm.

Secretariat of State for Health, Social Security and Equal Opportunities: Via V. Scialoia, 47895 Cailungo; tel. 0549 883040; fax 0549 883041; e-mail dic.sanita@omniway.sm; internet www.sanita.segreteria.sm.

Secretariat of State for Industry, Handicrafts, Trade, Research and Relations with the Azienda Autonoma di Stato per i Servizi Pubblici (AASS): Palazzo Mercuri, Contrada del Collegio, 47890 San Marino; tel. 0549 882528; fax 0549 882529.

Secretariat of State for Internal Affairs, Civil Protection and Implementation of the Government Programme: Parva Domus, Piazza della Libertà, 47890 San Marino; tel. 0549 882425; fax 0549 885080; e-mail segreteria.interni@gov.sm; internet www.interni.segreteria.sm.

Secretariat of State for Justice, Relations with the Castle Boards, Information and Peace: Via A. di Superchio 16, 47893 Borgo Maggiore; tel. 0549 883779; fax 0549 883766; e-mail info.giustizia@gov.sm; internet www.giustizia.sm.

Secretariat of State for Labour, Co-operation and Youth Policies: Palazzo Mercuri, Contrada del Collegio 38, 47890 San Marino; tel. 0549 882532; fax 0549 882535; e-mail segr.lavoro@omniway.sm; internet www.lavoro.segreteria.sm.

Secretariat of State for Territory, Environment, Agriculture and Relations with the Azienda Autonoma di Stato di Produzione (AASP): Contrada Omerelli, 47890 San Marino; tel. 0549 882470; fax 0549 882473; e-mail segr.territorio@omniway.sm.

Secretariat of State for Tourism, Sport, Telecommunications, Transport and Economic Co-operation: Palazzo del Turismo, Contrada Omagnano, 47890 San Marino; tel. 0549 883158; fax 0549 885399; e-mail segreteria.turismo@gov.sm; internet www.visitsanmarino.com.

Legislature

Consiglio Grande e Generale
(Great and General Council)

Palazzo Pubblico, Piazza della Libertà, 47890 San Marino; tel. 0549 882259; fax 0549 882389; e-mail info.segristituzionale@pa.sm; internet www.consigliograndeegenerale.sm.

Election, 4 June 2006

Party	% of valid votes*	Seats
Partito Democratico Cristiano Sammarinese (PDCS)	32.91	21
Partito dei Socialisti e dei Democratici (PSD)	31.83	20
Alleanza Popolare dei Democratici Sammarinesi (AP)	12.05	7
Sinistra Unita (SU)	8.67	5
Nuovo Partito Socialista (NPS)	5.41	3
Noi Sammarinesi	2.53	1
Popolari Sammarinesi (PS)	2.43	1
Alleanza Nazionale Sammarinese (ANS)	2.33	1
Sammarinesi per la Libertà	1.84	1
Total	**100.00**	**60**

* The total number of votes cast, including invalid votes, was 22,816.

Political Organizations

Alleanza Nazionale Sammarinese (ANS) (San Marino National Alliance): Via Ventotto Luglio 187, 47893 Borgo Maggiore; tel. 0549 907815; fax 0549 875203; e-mail anrsm@omniway.sm; internet www.alleanzanazionalersm.sm; right-wing; Pres. ENNIO VITTORIO PELLANDRA; Political Sec. GLAUCO SANSOVINI.

Alleanza Popolare dei Democratici Sammarinesi (AP) (Popular Alliance of Sammarinese Democrats): Via Luigi Cibrario 25, 47893 Cailungo; tel. 0549 907080; fax 0549 907082; e-mail ap@alleanzapopolare.net; internet www.alleanzapopolare.net; f. 1993; also known as Alleanza Popolare (AP); advocates a constitution and institutional reform; Pres. CARLO FRANCIOSI; Co-ordinator MARIO VENTURINI.

Democratici di Centro (DdC) (Democrats of the Centre): Via Cà Franceschino 2, Borgo Maggiore; tel. (0549) 909884; fax (0549) 972855; e-mail gruppo.dc@omniway.sm; internet www.democraticidicentro.sm; f. 2007 by fmr mems of the Partito

SAN MARINO

Democratico Cristiano Sammarinese (PDCS); Pres. Orazio Mazza; Co-ordinator Giovanni Lonfernini.

Europopolari per San Marino (EPS) (European People for San Marino): Via dei Pini 1, 47895 Domagnano; tel. 0549 906622; fax 0549 902431; e-mail europopolari@omniway.sm; internet www.europopolari.sm; f. 2007 by fmr mems of the PDCS; Pres. Gian Marco Marcucci; Political Sec. Lorenzo Lonfernini.

Noi Sammarinesi (We Sammarinese): Via XXVIII Luglio 160, 47893 Borgo Maggiore; tel. and fax 0549 902591; e-mail info@noisammarinesi.com; internet www.noisammarinesi.com; f. 2006; Spokesman Marco Arzilli.

Nuovo Partito Socialista (NPS) (New Socialist Party): Via XXV Marzo 36, 47895 Domagnano; tel. 0549 980093; fax 0549 902212; e-mail nuovopartitosocialista@omniway.sm; internet www.nuovopartitosocialista.sm; f. 2005 by fmr mems of the Partito Socialista Sammarinese (PSS); Pres. Antonio Volpinari; Political Sec. Augusto Casali.

Partito Democratico Cristiano Sammarinese (PDCS) (San Marino Christian Democrat Party): Via delle Scalette 6, 47890 San Marino; tel. 0549 991193; fax 0549 992694; e-mail pdcs@omniway.sm; internet www.pdcs.sm; f. 1948; in 2007 four representatives to the Consiglio Grande e Generale left the party to form the Democratici di Centro; Political Sec. Pasquale Valentini; 2,400 mems.

Partito dei Socialisti e dei Democratici (PSD) (Party of Socialists and Democrats): Via Ordelaffi 46, 47893 Borgo Maggiore; tel. 0549 903806; fax 0549 906438; e-mail info@democratici.sm; internet www.socialistiedemocratici.sm; f. 2005 by merger of the Partito dei Democratici (PdD) and the Partito Socialista Sammarinese (PSS); Pres. Patrizia Busignani; Sec.-Gen. Paride Andreoli.

Popolari Sammarinesi (PS) (Sammarinese People): Via XXV Marzo 19B, 47895 Domagnano; tel. 0549 907776; fax 0549 944431; e-mail info@popolarisammarinesi.sm; internet www.popolarisammarinesi.sm; Pres. Antonio Putti; Political Sec. Angela Venturini.

Sammarinesi per la Libertà (Sammarinese for Liberty): Via Ca' dei Lunghi 16, 47893 Borgo Maggiore; tel. 0549 908400; fax 0549 905970; e-mail info@sammarinesiperlaliberta.sm; internet www.sammarinesiperlaliberta.sm; f. 2002; Pres. Giuseppe Rossi.

Sinistra Unita (SU) (United Left): Via delle Tamerici 1A, 47893 Domagnano; tel. 0549 907656; fax 0549 944397; e-mail sinistraunita@omniway.sm; internet www.sxun.org; f. 2006; left-wing coalition, comprising RCS and Zona Franca, formed to contest 2006 general election.

Rifondazione Comunista Sammarinese (RCS) (San Marino Communist Refoundation): Via Ca' dei Lunghi 70A, 47893 Borgo Maggiore; tel. and fax 0549 906682; e-mail rcs@omniway.sm; internet www.rifondazionecomunista-rsm.org; f. 1992; communist; Political Sec. Angelo Della Valle.

Diplomatic Representation

By September 2007 San Marino had established full diplomatic relations with 93 countries, five of which maintained a consular office in San Marino.

EMBASSIES IN SAN MARINO

Holy See: Domus Plebis 1, 47890 San Marino; tel. 0549 992448; Apostolic Nuncio Most Rev. Giuseppe Bertello (Titular Archbishop of Urbs Salvia) (resident in Rome, Italy).

Italy: Viale Antonio Onofri 117, 47890 San Marino; tel. 0549 991146; fax 0549 992229; e-mail ambasciata.sanmarino@esteri.it; internet www.ambsanmarino.esteri.it; Ambassador Fabrizio Santurro.

Judicial System

The administration of justice is entrusted to foreign judges, with the exception of the Justice of the Peace, who must be of San Marino nationality, and who judges minor civil suits. The major judicial institutions are as follows:

Tribunale Commissariale Civile e Penale (Civil and Criminal Commissionary Tribunal): Salita alla Rocca 44, San Marino; tel. 0549 882626; fax 0549 8825980; e-mail tribunale@omniway.sm.

Commissario della Legge (Law Commissioner): deals with civil and criminal cases where the maximum sentence does not exceed three years' imprisonment.

Giudice Penale di Primo Grado (Criminal Judge of the Primary Court of Claims): deals with criminal cases that are above the competence of the Law Commissioner.

Giudice Amministrativo di Appello (Court of Appeal): two judges, who deal with civil and criminal proceedings.

Consiglio dei XII (Council of Twelve): has authority as a Supreme Court of Appeal, for civil proceedings only.

Religion

CHRISTIANITY

The Roman Catholic Church

Roman Catholicism is the official state religion of San Marino. The Republic forms part of the diocese of San Marino-Montefeltro (comprising mainly Italian territory), suffragan to the archdiocese of Ravenna-Cervia.

Bishop of San Marino-Montefeltro: Rt Rev. Luigi Negri, Curia Vescovile, Piazza Giovanni Paolo II 1, 61016 Pennabilli, Pesaro, Italy; tel. (0541) 913721; fax (0541) 928832; e-mail vescovo.negri@diocesi-sanmarino-montefeltro.it; internet www.diocesi-sanmarino-montefeltro.it.

The Press

Argomenti: c/o CSdL, Via V Febbraio 17, Fiorina C-3, 47895 Domagnano; tel. 0549 962060; fax 0549 962075; organ of the Confederazione Sammarinese del Lavoro (CSdL); periodical; Dir Andrea Leardini; circ. 5,000.

Corriere di Informazione Sammarinese: Via Piana, 47890 San Marino; tel. 0549 995147; fax 0549 879021; e-mail corriere@rimini.com; daily.

Fixing: Via G. Giacomini 37, 47890 San Marino; e-mail fixing@omniway.sm; periodical.

Il San Marino: Via delle Scalette 6, 47890 San Marino; tel. 0549 991193; fax 0549 992694; e-mail pdcs@omniway.sm; internet www.pdcs.sm; periodical; organ of the PDCS; quarterly; Dir Jerome Cellarosi.

San Marino Oggi: Via dei Boschetti 53, 47893 Borgo Maggiore; tel. 0549 906607; fax 0549 906556; e-mail sanmarinooggi@omniway.sm; f. 1997; daily; circ. 750; Dir. Renato Cornacchia.

La Tribuna Sammarinese: Via Gino Giacomini 86A, 47890 San Marino; tel. 0549 990420; fax 0549 990398; e-mail direttore@latribunasammarinese.net; internet www.latribunasammarinese.net; daily; Dir Davide Graziosi.

Publishers

AIEP Editore: Via III Settembre 72, 47891 Dogana; tel. 0549 941457; fax 0549 973164; e-mail info@aiepeditore.net; internet www.aiepeditore.net; f. 1980; general book publishing; Man. Giuseppe Maria Morganti.

Guardigli Editore: Via Istriani 94, 47890 San Marino; tel. 0549 995144; fax 0549 990454; e-mail guardiglieditore@omniway.sm; f. 1991; book publishing; Man. Dir Pier Paolo Guardigli.

Broadcasting and Communications

TELECOMMUNICATIONS

Direzione Generale Poste e Telecomunicazioni: Contrada Omerelli 17, 47890 San Marino; tel. 0549 882555; fax 0549 992760; e-mail federico.valentini.telecomunicazioni@pa.sm; state body responsible for telecommunications; Dir-Gen. Dott. Rosa Zafferani.

Telecom Italia San Marino, SpA: Strada degli Angariari 3, 47031 Falciano; tel. 0549 886111; fax 0549 886188; e-mail secretary@telecomitalia.sm; internet www.telecomitalia.sm; f. 1992; provides international telecommunications services; Pres. and Man. Dir Andrea Cendali Pignatelli.

Telefonia Mobile Sammarinese, SpA (TMS): Via XXVIII Luglio 148, 47893 Borgo Maggiore; tel. 0549 980222; fax 0549 980044; e-mail info@tms.sm; internet www.tms.sm; f. 1999; mobile services.

SAN MARINO

BROADCASTING

In 1987 a co-operation agreement with Italy, preventing San Marino from operating its own broadcasting services, was abrogated, and a joint venture between San Marino and the Italian state-owned radio and television corporation, Radiotelevisione Italiana (RAI), was established in order to operate an independent broadcasting station for 15 years. RAI (see the chapter on Italy) broadcasts a daily information bulletin about the Republic under the title 'Notizie di San Marino'. San Marino RTV began broadcasting in mid-1993.

Radio

San Marino RTV (Radiotelevisione della Repubblica de San Marino): Viale Kennedy 13, 47890 San Marino; tel. 0549 882000; fax 0549 882855; e-mail redazione@sanmarinortv.sm; internet www.sanmarinortv.sm; f. 1991; Pres. STEFANO VALENTINO PIVA; Dir-Gen. MICHELE MANGIAFICO.

Radio San Marino: San Marino; tel. 0549 995013; e-mail redazione@radiosanmarino.sm; internet www.radiosanmarino.sm.

Radio Titano: Via delle Carrare 35, Frazione Murata, 47890 San Marino; tel. 0549 997251; Dir P. FAETANINI.

Television

San Marino RTV (Radiotelevisione della Repubblica de San Marino): (see Radio).

Finance

(cap. = capital; res = reserves; dep. = deposits; m. = million; brs = branches; amounts in euros)

In September 2005 there were 12 banks and 42 other financial institutions operating in San Marino.

BANKING

Central Bank

Banca Centrale della Repubblica di San Marino: Via del Voltone 120, 47890 San Marino; tel. 0549 882325; fax 0549 882328; e-mail info@bcsm.sm; internet www.bcsm.sm; f. 2003; formed by a merger between the Istituto di Credito Sammarinese and the Ispettorato per il Credito e le Valute; manages both state and public-sector deposits; cap. 12.9m., res 9.8m., dep. 253.2m. (Dec. 2005); Chair. ANTONIO VALENTINI; Dir-Gen. LUCA PAPI.

Commercial Banks

Banca Agricola Commerciale della Repubblica di San Marino SA: Piazza Marino Tini 26, 47891 Dogana; tel. 0549 871111; fax 0549 871222; internet www.bac.sm; f. 1920; cap. 16.8m., res 71.2m., dep. 1,301.7m (Dec. 2006); Pres. LUIGI LONFERNINI; Dir PIER PAOLO FABBRI; 8 brs.

Banca di San Marino, SpA: Strada della Croce 39, 47896 Faetano; tel. 0549 873411; fax 0549 873401; e-mail info@bsm.sm; internet www.bsm.sm; f. 1920 as Cassa Rurale Depositi e Prestiti di Faetano, Scrl; changed name as above in 2001; cap. 114.6m., res 31.0m., dep. 1,300.5m. (Dec. 2006); Chair. FAUSTO MULARONI; Gen. Man. WALTER ZANOTTI; 9 brs.

Cassa di Risparmio della Repubblica di San Marino: Piazzetta del Titano 2, 47890 San Marino; tel. 0549 872311; fax 0549 872700; e-mail info@carisp.sm; internet www.carisp.sm; f. 1882; cap. 350m., res 59.5m., dep. 2,611.7m. (Dec. 2005); Pres. Dott. GILBERTO GHIOTTI; CEO MARIO FANTINI; 16 brs.

Credito Industriale Sammarinese: Piazza Bertoldi 8, 47899 Serravalle; tel. 0549 8740; fax 0549 874116; e-mail info@cis.sm; internet www.cis.sm; f. 1933; owned by Banca Carim (Italy); cap. 35.0m., res 41.8m., dep. 508.8m. (Dec. 2006); Chair. FRANCO CAPICCHIONI; Man. Dir GIOVANNI PACCAPELO; 3 brs.

Euro Commercial Bank SpA: Strada dei Censiti 21, 47891 Rovereta; tel. 0549 943711; fax 0549 943737; e-mail info@ecb.sm; internet www.ecb.sm; f. 2000; cap. and res 26.9m., total assets 242.1m. (2006); Dir-Gen. GIUSEPPE GUIDI; 2 brs.

Istituto Bancario Sammarinese SpA: Via III Settembre 99, 47891 Dogana; tel. 0549 872011; fax 0549 872050; e-mail direzione@ibs.sm; internet www.ibs.sm; f. 2000 as Merchant Bank di San Marino SpA; changed name in 2001 following expansion into commercial banking; Pres. and Man. Dir Dott. GIOVANNI MERCADINI; 7 brs.

INSURANCE

Several major Italian insurance companies have agencies in San Marino.

Trade and Industry

GOVERNMENT AGENCIES

Azienda Autonoma di Stato Filatelica e Numismatica (AASFN): Piazza Garibaldi 5, 47890 San Marino; tel. 0549 882370; fax 0549 882363; e-mail aasfn3@omniway.sm; internet www.aasfn.sm; autonomous public enterprise; responsible for production and distribution of postage stamps and coins; Pres. PIGNATTA ORAZIO; Dir Gen. Dott. OTTAVIANO ROSSI.

Azienda Autonoma di Stato di Produzione (AASP): Via Ventotto Luglio 50, 47031 Borgo Maggiore; tel. 0549 883111; fax 0549 883600; e-mail aasp@omniway.sm; civil engineering works, road works, land reclamation; Pres. PAOLO RONDELLI; Dir FABIO BERARDI.

Azienda Autonoma di Stato per la gestione della Centrale del Latte: Strada Genghe di Atto 71, 47031 Acquaviva; tel. 0549 999207; fax 0549 999606; operates state monopoly in production and distribution of dairy products; Pres. TIZIANO CANINI; Dir PAOLO MUSCI.

CHAMBER OF COMMERCE

Camera di Commercio, Industria, Artigianato e Agricoltura di San Marino (CCIAA): Piazza Mercatale 29, 47893 Borgo Maggiore; tel. 0549 980380; fax 0549 944554; e-mail info@cc.sm; internet www.cc.sm; f. 2004; Dir Dott. MASSIMO GHIOTTI.

INDUSTRIAL AND TRADE ASSOCIATIONS

Associazione Nazionale dell'Industria Sammarinese (ANIS) (National Association for Industry): Via Gino Giacomini 39, 47890 San Marino; tel. 0549 873911; fax 0549 992832; e-mail anis@omniway.sm; internet www.anis.sm; Pres. PIER GIOVANNI TERENZI; Sec.-Gen. CARLO GIORGI.

Associazione Sammarinese Coltivatori Diretti, Affittuari e Mezzadri (ASCDAM): San Marino; tel. 0549 998222; farmers' association.

Associazione Sammarinese Produttori Agricoli (ASPA): Serrabolino 42, 47893 Borgo Maggiore; tel. 0549 902617; agricultural producers' association.

Consorzio San Marino 2000 srl: Via Piana 103, 47890 San Marino; tel. 0549 995031; fax 0549 990573; e-mail info@sanmarino2000.sm; internet www.sanmarino2000.sm; f. 1998; fmrly Unione Sammarinese Operatori Turistici (USOT); hotels and restaurants association.

Organizzazione Sammarinese degli Imprenditori (OSLA): Via N. Bonaparte 75, 47890 San Marino; tel. 0549 992885; fax 0549 992620; e-mail osla@omniway.sm; internet www.osla.sm; f. 1985; organization for the self-employed; Pres. MARIA TERESA VENTURINI.

Unione Nazionale Artigiani di San Marino (UNAS): Piazzale M. Giangi 2, San Marino; tel. 0549 992148; e-mail unas@omniway.sm; artisans' association; Pres. GIANFRANCO TERENZI.

Unione Sammarinese Commercianti (USC): Via Piana 111, 47890 San Marino; tel. 0549 992892; shopkeepers' association; Pres. MARCO ARZILLI.

UTILITIES

All utilities are imported from Italy.

Azienda Autonoma di Stato per i Servizi Pubblici (AASS): Via Andrea di Superchio 16, 47031 Cailungo; tel. 0549 883782; fax 0549 883720; e-mail info@aass.sm; internet www.aass.sm; f. 1981; autonomous state service company; distributes electricity, gas and water within San Marino; Pres. Dott. MARCO PODESCHI; Dir-Gen. EMANUELE VALLI.

TRADE UNIONS

Centrale Sindacale Unitaria (CSU): Via Cinque Febbraio 17, 47895 Domagnano; tel. 0549 962011; fax 0549 962055; e-mail csu@omniway.sm; internet www.csu.sm; f. 1976; Pres. LUCIANO NICOLINI.

Confederazione Democratica dei Lavoratori Sammarinesi (CDLS): Via V Febbraio 17, 47895 Domagnano; tel. 0549 962011; fax 0549 962095; e-mail boss@cdls.sm; internet www.cdls.sm; f. 1957; affiliated to ITUC and ETUC; Sec.-Gen. MARCO BECCARI; 4,960 mems.

Confederazione Sammarinese del Lavoro (CSdL): Via V Febbraio 17, 47895 Domagnano; tel. 0549 962060; fax 0549 962075; e-mail info@csdl.sm; internet www.csdl.sm; f. 1943; Sec.-Gen. GIOVANNI GHIOTTI; 5 mem. feds; 4,500 individual mems.

Transport

The capital, San Marino, is connected with Borgo Maggiore, about 1.5 km away, by funicular. There is also a bus service, and a highway down to the Italian coast at Rimini, about 24 km away. San Marino has an estimated 220 km of roads. The nearest airport to the Republic is at Rimini. There are no frontier or customs formalities.

Azienda Autonoma di Stato per i Servizi Pubblici (AASS): (see Utilities); numerous responsibilities include public transport and funicular railway.

Tourism

The mild climate attracts many visitors to San Marino each year, as do the contrasting scenery and well-preserved medieval architecture. In 2006 San Marino received 2.1m. visitors (including excursionists). Tourism receipts totalled an estimated €27,620m. in 2003.

Ufficio di Stato per il Turismo (State Tourist Board): Contrada Omagnano 20, 47890 San Marino; tel. 0549 882914; fax 0549 882575; e-mail info@visitsanmarino.com; internet www.visitsanmarino.com; Dir ANTONIO MACINA.

SÃO TOMÉ AND PRÍNCIPE

Introductory Survey

Location, Climate, Language, Religion, Flag, Capital

The Democratic Republic of São Tomé and Príncipe lies in the Gulf of Guinea, off the west coast of Africa. There are two main islands, São Tomé and Príncipe, and the country also includes the rocky islets of Caroço, Pedras and Tinhosas, off Príncipe, and Rôlas, off São Tomé. The climate is warm and humid, with average temperatures ranging between 22°C (72°F) and 30°C (86°F). The rainy season extends from October to May, and average annual rainfall varies from 500 mm (20 ins) in the southern highlands to 1,000 mm (39 ins) in the northern lowlands. Portuguese is the official language and native dialects are widely spoken. Almost all of the inhabitants profess Christianity, and the overwhelming majority (some 83%) are adherents of the Roman Catholic Church. The national flag (proportions 1 by 2) has three horizontal stripes, of green, yellow (one-half of the depth) and green, with a red triangle at the hoist and two five-pointed black stars on the yellow stripe. The capital is the town of São Tomé, on São Tomé island.

Recent History

A former Portuguese colony, São Tomé and Príncipe became an overseas province of Portugal in 1951 and received local autonomy in 1973. A nationalist group, the Comissão de Libertação de São Tomé e Príncipe, was formed in 1960 and became the Movimento de Libertação de São Tomé e Príncipe (MLSTP) in 1972, under the leadership of Dr Manuel Pinto da Costa. Based in Libreville, Gabon, the MLSTP was recognized by the Organization of African Unity (now the African Union—AU, see p. 164) in 1973.

Following the military coup in Portugal in April 1974, the Portuguese Government recognized the right of the islands to independence. Negotiations began in November, at which Portugal recognized the MLSTP as the sole representative of the people. On 12 July 1975 independence was achieved, with da Costa as the country's first President and Miguel dos Anjos da Cunha Lisboa Trovoada as Prime Minister. In December a legislative Assembleia Popular Nacional (National People's Assembly) was elected.

In March 1978 the Prime Minister stated that an attempted coup by foreign mercenaries, orchestrated from Gabon by Carlos Alberto Monteiro Dias da Graça, an exiled former Minister of Health, had been suppressed. Angolan troops were called in to support the Government, and in March 1979 the alleged conspirators were sentenced to terms of imprisonment. President da Costa took over the post of Prime Minister, and Trovoada was arrested in September and charged with complicity in the coup attempt. He was released and allowed to go into exile in 1981.

Worsening economic conditions, following a severe drought in 1982, prompted the Government to review the country's close ties with communist regimes and its consequent isolation from major Western aid sources. In late 1984 da Costa declared São Tomé and Príncipe to be politically non-aligned.

In October 1987 the Central Committee of the MLSTP announced major constitutional reforms, including the election by universal adult suffrage of the President of the Republic and of members of the Assembleia Popular Nacional. The amended Constitution also allowed 'independent' candidates to contest legislative elections, although the President of the MLSTP, chosen by the MLSTP Congress from two candidates proposed by the Central Committee, would continue to be the sole candidate for the presidency of the Republic. In January 1988 the premiership was restored, and Celestino Rochas da Costa, hitherto Minister of Education, Labour and Social Security, was appointed as Prime Minister.

In March 1990 a joint meeting of the Assembleia Popular Nacional and the MLSTP Central Committee approved a new draft Constitution, which provided for the establishment of a multi-party system, limited the President's tenure of office to two five-year terms, and permitted independent candidates to participate in legislative elections. In May 1990 Trovoada returned from exile to contest the forthcoming presidential election. On 22 August, in a national referendum, 72% of the electorate endorsed the new Constitution. In the following month new legislation on the formation of political parties came into effect. Delegates to the MLSTP Congress in October voted to replace da Costa as party President, appointing da Graça to the new post of Secretary-General. The party's name was amended to the Movimento de Libertação de São Tomé e Príncipe—Partido Social Democrata (MLSTP—PSD).

In January 1991 elections to the new Assembleia Nacional resulted in defeat for the MLSTP—PSD, which secured only 21 seats in the 55-member legislature, while the Partido de Convergência Democrática—Grupo de Reflexão (PCD—GR) won 33 seats. The Partido Democrático de São Tomé e Príncipe—Coligação Democrático da Oposição (PDSTP—CODO) took the remaining seat. In February a transitional Government, headed by the Secretary-General of the PCD—GR, Daniel Lima dos Santos Daio, was installed. In the same month President da Costa announced that he would not be contesting the presidential election, to be held in March. The MLSTP—PSD did not present an alternative candidate. In late February two of the three remaining presidential candidates withdrew from the election. Miguel Trovoada, who stood as an independent candidate (with the support of the PCD—GR), was thus the sole contender, and on 3 March he was elected President with the support of 81% of those who voted. He took office on 3 April. The transitional Government resigned in mid-April and was reappointed shortly afterwards.

In April 1992, following demonstrations demanding the resignation of the Daio Government due to the unpopular imposition of stringent austerity measures, Trovoada dismissed the Daio administration. The PCD—GR was invited to designate a new Prime Minister, and in May Norberto Costa Alegre (hitherto Minister of Economy and Finance) was chosen as Prime Minister. A new Government was named shortly afterwards.

In April 1994 the Assembleia Nacional adopted legislation, drafted by the MLSTP—PSD, reinforcing the rights of the parliamentary opposition. All opposition parties represented in the legislature were to be consulted on major political issues, including defence, foreign policy and the budget. In the same month deputies began discussion of a draft bill providing for a degree of autonomy for the island of Príncipe, to include the creation of a regional council. The proposed legislation was prompted by concern among inhabitants of Príncipe that the island had been neglected by the central administration.

Meanwhile, relations between the Government and the presidency deteriorated, and in April 1994 Trovoada publicly dissociated himself from government policy. Political tension increased in June, when the PCD—GR accused Trovoada of systematic obstruction of the government programme. In that month opposition parties petitioned the President to dismiss the Government, conduct early legislative elections and appoint foreign auditors to investigate the management of public finances under the PCD—GR administration. In July Trovoada dismissed the Alegre Government and appointed Evaristo do Espírito Santo de Carvalho (the Minister of Defence and Security in the outgoing administration) as Prime Minister. The PCD—GR, refusing to participate in an administration formed on presidential initiative, subsequently expelled Carvalho from the party. An interim Government, comprising principally technocrats and senior civil servants, was appointed. Shortly afterwards Trovoada dissolved the Assembleia Nacional, thus preventing the PCD—GR from using its parliamentary majority to declare the new Government unconstitutional.

Legislative elections were held on 2 October 1994, at which the MLSTP—PSD secured 27 seats, one short of an absolute majority. The PCD—GR and Acção Democrática Independente (ADI) each obtained 14 seats; da Graça was subsequently appointed Prime Minister. Despite initial efforts to involve opposition parties in a government of national unity, his Council of Ministers was dominated by members of the MLSTP—PSD.

In March 1995 the first elections to a new seven-member regional assembly and five-member regional government were conducted on Príncipe, which had been granted local autonomy by the Assembleia Nacional in 1994. The elections resulted in an absolute majority for the MLSTP—PSD; the ADI and the PCD—

GR did not present candidates, supporting instead a local opposition group. The new regional Government began functioning in April 1995.

In mid-August 1995 a group of some 30 soldiers, led by five junior officers, seized control of the presidential palace in a bloodless coup. Trovoada was detained at the headquarters of the armed forces and da Graça was placed under house arrest. The legislature was disbanded, the Constitution suspended and a curfew imposed. Following talks mediated by an Angolan delegation, the insurgents and the Government signed a 'memorandum of understanding', providing for the reinstatement of Trovoada and the restoration of constitutional order. In return, the Government gave an undertaking to restructure the armed forces, and the Assembleia Nacional granted a general amnesty to all those involved in the coup.

In late December 1995 Armindo Vaz d'Almeida was appointed Prime Minister, by presidential decree, to head a Government of National Unity. The new administration included six members of the MLSTP—PSD, four members of the ADI and one of the PDSTP—CODO. The three parties had signed a political pact, with the aim of ensuring political stability. In February 1996, at the request of the Comissão Eleitoral Nacional (National Electoral Commission), the forthcoming presidential election, which had been set for March, was postponed, pending the satisfactory completion of the electoral rolls. The date of the election was subsequently rescheduled for 30 June. In March Pinto da Costa was selected as the presidential candidate of the MLSTP—PSD, while Francisco Fortunato Pires was appointed Secretary-General of the party, replacing the more moderate da Graça. In April Trovoada declared his candidacy for the presidential election, supported by the ADI and the PDSTP—CODO.

At the presidential election of 30 June 1996 no candidate secured an absolute majority. The two leading candidates thus proceeded to a second round of voting on 21 July, at which Trovoada won 52.7% of the votes, defeating Pinto da Costa. In late July da Costa, who had initially acknowledged Trovoada's victory, claimed that irregularities had occurred in the registration process; however, on 20 August Trovoada was confirmed as President. Although he did not command majority support in the Assembleia Nacional, Trovoada dismissed the possibility of new legislative elections, announcing instead his intention to seek a broadly based government of national consensus. In September the Vaz d'Almeida administration was dissolved, following its defeat in a confidence motion in the Assembleia Nacional. The motion had been proposed by Vaz d'Almeida's own party, the MLSTP—PSD, which accused the Government of inefficiency and corruption, and had received the support of the PCD—GR. Vaz d'Almeida remained as Prime Minister in an interim capacity until November, when Raul Wagner da Conceição Bragança Neto, Assistant Secretary-General of the MLSTP—PSD, was appointed Prime Minister. A new coalition Government, including five members of the MLSTP—PSD, three members of the PCD—GR and one independent, was inaugurated later that month.

At an extraordinary congress of the MLSTP—PSD in May 1998, Pinto da Costa was elected unopposed as President of the party. (The ruling party of Angola, the Movimento Popular de Libertação de Angola (MPLA), had made the resumption of financial support for the MLSTP—PSD conditional on da Costa's election; following his defeat in the 1996 presidential election, the MPLA had ceased payments, creating serious problems for the MLSTP—PSD.) New party statutes were approved, creating the position of party President, together with three vice-presidential posts.

At legislative elections held on 8 November 1998 the MLSTP—PSD secured a majority, with 31 seats, while the ADI won 16 seats and the PCD—GR obtained the remaining eight seats. In December Guilherme Pósser da Costa (a Vice-President of the MLSTP—PSD and former Minister of Foreign Affairs and Co-operation) was appointed Prime Minister. However, the MLSTP—PSD accused Trovoada of interfering in areas outside his jurisdiction when, later that month, he vetoed Pósser da Costa's initial nominations for the Council of Ministers. A revised Council of Ministers was finally installed on 5 January 1999.

A presidential election took place on 29 July 2001. Among the five candidates to succeed Trovoada were former President Manuel Pinto da Costa, the leader of the MLSTP—PSD, and Fradique de Menezes, a businessman standing for the ADI. In the event, de Menezes was elected to the presidency, winning 56.3% of the votes cast, while da Costa secured 38.7%. De Menezes was inaugurated as President on 3 September. Following the dissolution by de Menezes of Pósser da Costa's administration (owing to disagreements over the distribution of ministerial positions), a new Government of 'presidential initiative', which did not include any members of the MLSTP—PSD, was appointed in late September. The new Council of Ministers, led by Evaristo de Carvalho as Prime Minister, was composed of members of the ADI, the PCD (which had voted to remove the suffix Grupo de Reflexão from its official name at a recent congress) and one independent. In early December de Menezes dissolved the Assembleia Nacional and announced that legislative elections would be held in March 2002, after which a new, more broadly based Government would be formed, according to an agreement reportedly signed by the President and representatives of political parties. In January 2002 the PCD formed an electoral alliance with the Movimento Democrático Força da Mudança (MDFM), which had been created in December by supporters of de Menezes.

At legislative elections, held on 3 March 2002, no party obtained an absolute majority in the Assembleia Nacional. Provisional results indicated that the MLSTP—PSD and the MDFM-PCD alliance had each secured 23 of the 55 seats, while the remaining nine seats had been won by Uê Kédadji (UK), an alliance of the ADI and four minor parties. However, following a re-run of voting in one district, the MLSTP—PSD secured an extra seat, to the cost of the UK alliance, and was proclaimed victorious. Gabriel da Costa, the former ambassador to Portugal, was subsequently appointed as the nominally independent Prime Minister, and in April a new coalition Government of National Unity, which included representatives of the MLSTP—PSD, the MDFM-PCD and UK, as well as a number of independents, was installed.

In late September 2002 da Costa's Government was dismissed by de Menezes, who appointed Maria das Neves de Souza, of the MLSTP—PSD, hitherto Minister of Trade, Industry and Tourism, as Prime Minister in early October. A new Government of National Unity, with six representatives from the MLSTP—PSD, five from the MDFM-PCD alliance, two from the UK alliance and one independent, was formed. In December the first MDFM congress elected Tomé Vera Cruz as Secretary-General of the party.

Meanwhile, in November 2002 the Assembleia Nacional approved a resolution for constitutional reform, altering the structure of the semi-presidential system to reduce presidential power. However, the draft revisions caused a political crisis over President de Menezes' delays in their promulgation and his repeated threats to veto them, according to powers vested in him by the Constitution of 1990. An apparent consensus was reached in December 2002, but the situation deteriorated further in early 2003, and in mid-January the President vetoed the new draft Constitution on the grounds that it should be endorsed by public referendum before coming into force. De Menezes dissolved the Assembleia Nacional by presidential decree later that month and called early elections for 13 April. However, Prime Minister das Neves vowed to continue working and transferred the Government of National Unity to the island of Príncipe. Following negotiations between the Government and the President, de Menezes reversed his decree, reinstating the Government, and a 'memorandum of understanding' was signed by de Menezes and the Assembleia Nacional, which provided for the immediate promulgation of the new Constitution, but called for a referendum to take place in March–April 2006 on the system of government.

The new Constitution, which took effect in March 2003, provided for the establishment of an advisory Council of State and a Constitutional Tribunal, with jurisdiction over issues of constitutionality. The President's right to veto constitutional amendments was removed. The changes were regarded as significantly reducing the executive power of the President, although maintaining a semi-presidential system pending the referendum.

On 16 July 2003, while de Menezes was in Nigeria, Maj. Fernando Pereira 'Cobo', together with Sabino dos Santos and Alércio Costa, the leaders of a small political party, the Frente Democrata Cristã (FDC), took power in a bloodless *coup d'état*. They formed a Junta Militar de Salvação Nacional and detained government ministers. The coup was condemned by the international community, which demanded a return to civilian rule. Following successful regional mediation efforts, co-ordinated by Rodolphe Adada, the Republic of the Congo's Minister of Foreign Affairs, Co-operation and Francophone Affairs, on 22 July de

Menezes returned to São Tomé, accompanied by President Olusegun Obasanjo of Nigeria. On the same day de Menezes, Pereira and Adada signed a 'memorandum of understanding', which provided for the restoration of de Menezes to the presidency, an amnesty for the coup leaders, a more transparent system of government finance, and the formation of a new government. The army was also to be privy to government information on the petroleum sector. A commission to monitor the implementation of these measures was created. In accordance with the conditions of the memorandum, Prime Minister das Neves resigned. She was subsequently reappointed by de Menezes to head a new Government of National Unity, comprising representatives of the MLSTP—PSD, the MDFM and the ADI. Vera Cruz was appointed to the increasingly significant post of Minister of Natural Resources and the Environment, and Lt-Col Óscar Sousa, an independent reportedly with close ties to de Menezes, became Minister of Defence and Internal Affairs.

In March 2004 tension increased between das Neves and de Menezes. Das Neves had repeatedly requested the dismissal of Vera Cruz and of Mateus Rita, the Minister of Foreign Affairs and Co-operation, claiming that she had not been appropriately consulted by either minister on government decisions. The subsequent resignations of Rita and Vera Cruz—both members of the MDFM—prompted the remaining two MDFM ministers, responsible for health and justice, to resign in protest. Agreements that Vera Cruz had signed with Canadian and South African mining companies were subsequently annulled. Later that month members of the ADI were appointed to head the ministries of health and of natural resources and the environment, while Elsa Pinto of the MLSTP—PSD became Minister of Justice, State Reform and Public Administration, and an independent, Ovídio Manuel Barbossa Pequeno, was appointed Minister of Foreign Affairs and Co-operation.

In April 2004 Leonel Mário d'Alva was elected President of the PCD, while later that month Vera Cruz was re-elected as Secretary-General of the MDFM, which was renamed the MDFM—Partido Liberal (PL), although it subsequently reverted to its original name. In May 11 presidential advisors, holding positions corresponding to government ministries, were appointed by de Menezes. The President denied claims that he had formed a shadow executive, insisting that the advisors would improve his capacity to evaluate government policies.

In early September 2004 a report issued by the Auditor-General, Adelino Pereira, accused the das Neves Government of the embezzlement of funds provided by foreign donors and also revealed a series of financial irregularities during 2001–04, including illicit transfers of funds to the Ministry of Finance. Following requests by the MDFM and UK (the latter resigned from the Government in mid-September) for the removal of the das Neves Government, President de Menezes held a series of meetings with the main political parties in an attempt to establish a consensus. Das Neves and her Council of Ministers were dismissed in September, and Damião Vaz de Almeida, hitherto Minister of Labour, Employment and Security and Vice-President of the MLSTP—PSD, was asked to form a new administration. The new 14-member Government was a coalition of the MLSTP—PSD, the ADI and independents and comprised six members of the previous administration.

In late September 2004 Diógenes Moniz, the former Director of the Gabinete de Gestão das Ajudas (GGA—a department attached to the Ministry of Trade, Industry and Tourism responsible for the administration of food aid counterpart funds) was arrested on charges of embezzlement. In October das Neves was among a number of former ministers questioned by the Public Prosecutor about their involvement with the GGA.

In January 2005 an attempt by de Menezes to sue das Neves for libel was rejected by the Assembleia Nacional, on the grounds that das Neves enjoyed parliamentary immunity. (In September 2004, following her dismissal from the premiership, she had accused de Menezes and other members of the Government of corruption.) However, in February 2005 the Assembleia voted to remove parliamentary immunity from the former Prime Minister, Guilherme Pósser da Costa, in order that he be questioned regarding an alleged assault on Pereira in November 2004. (Pósser da Costa received a suspended sentence in March 2005.) A further four members of the Assembleia, including das Neves, also had their immunity lifted, thus providing for the possibility of them being tried in connection with the GGA case. In May das Neves and Arzemiro dos Prazeres, a former Minister of Trade, Industry and Tourism, were charged with embezzlement. Meanwhile, in late February Pósser da Costa was elected President of the MLSTP—PSD.

In April 2005 trade unions representing public sector workers demanded a significant increase in the minimum salaries of their members. The Government, however, citing budgetary constraints, was unable to accede to the unions' demands and in late May the unions commenced a five-day general strike. Following declarations by de Menezes that the Government was responsible for the action, Prime Minister Vaz de Almeida abruptly resigned, accusing the President of a lack of institutional solidarity with the Government. On 9 June a new MLSTP—PSD Council of Ministers, led by Maria do Carmo Silveira, hitherto the Governor of the central bank, took office, and in late July the Assembleia Nacional approved the new Government's budget and a preliminary agreement on a pay rise for public sector workers was reached. Relations between de Menezes and the Government remained strained, however.

Voting in the legislative elections began as scheduled on 26 March 2006; however, owing to boycotts and protests against continuing poor living conditions, voting at 26 polling stations was rescheduled for 2 April when it proceeded without incident. According to results released by the Constitutional Court on 18 April, the renewed MDFM-PCD alliance won 23 seats in the Assembleia Nacional, the MLSTP—PSD took 20 and the ADI 11, while a newly formed party, the Novo Rumo, secured the remaining seat. The Secretary-General of the MDFM, Tomé Vera Cruz, was subsequently appointed Prime Minister (also assuming the media and regional integration portfolios) while Maria dos Santos Tebús Torres of the PCD became Deputy Prime Minister, with responsibility for finance and planning. The new 12-member Government took office on 21 April.

In April 2006 President de Menezes announced that a presidential election would be held on 30 July. De Menezes was re-elected to the presidency on that date after securing 60.58% of the votes cast. His nearest rival, Patrice Emery Trovoada, of the ADI, received 38.83%. International observers deemed the election, at which voter turn-out was 64.9%, to have been transparent and fair. In late August, at the first local elections to be held on the islands since 1992, the MDFM-PCD alliance won six of the seven constituencies on São Tomé and secured an absolute majority in five of the six local assemblies. Supported by the ruling MDFM-PCD, the União para a Mudança e Progresso do Príncipe won all seven seats in the Assembleia Regional on Príncipe.

At an extraordinary party congress in February 2007, the MLSTP—PSD elected Rafael Branco as party President; he defeated António Quintas by 675 votes to 221. Prime Minister Vera Cruz was re-elected Secretary-General of the MDFM at a convention in May; at the same time President de Menezes was elected Chairman of that party, despite a provision in the Constitution preventing the Head of State from accepting other public roles. De Menezes stated that he would not assume the role publicly while he remained President.

In November 2007 a ministerial reorganization was effected in which Ovídio Barbosa Pequeno assumed responsibility for the foreign affairs, co-operation and communities portfolio, while Arlindo Carvalho was named as the new Minister of Planning and Finance. Valdimira Tavares was appointed Minister of the Economy.

On 7 February 2008 Vera Cruz announced his resignation as Prime Minister after the Assembleia Nacional failed to approve his Government's budget for 2008. He was replaced by Patrice Emery Trovoada, who was sworn in on 14 February. Trovoada's ADI had agreed to form a coalition government with the MDFM-PCD on the condition that his party was awarded, *inter alia*, the premiership and the natural resources and environment portfolio. Trovoada named a Council of Ministers, which included Raul Cravid as Minister of Planning and Finance, while both Pequeno and Carvalho retained the portfolios assigned to them in November 2007.

São Tomé and Príncipe maintains cordial relations with the other former Portuguese African colonies and with Portugal. In July 1996 São Tomé and Príncipe was among the five lusophone African countries that, together with Portugal and Brazil, formed the Comunidade dos Países de Língua Portuguesa (CPLP, see p. 423), a Portuguese-speaking commonwealth seeking to achieve collective benefits from co-operation in technical, cultural and social matters. In February 2004 Angola and São Tomé and Príncipe signed an agreement on the creation of a permanent joint commission on parliamentary co-operation.

SÃO TOMÉ AND PRÍNCIPE

Introductory Survey

São Tomé and Príncipe has important trade links with the nearby mainland states of Gabon, Cameroon and Equatorial Guinea. In November 1999 São Tomé and Príncipe was a founder of the seven-member Gulf of Guinea Commission; it was hoped that the commission would assist in solving inter-state conflicts within the region.

In 2000 São Tomé and Príncipe and Nigeria agreed to establish a joint development zone (JDZ) for the exploitation of petroleum resources. A further accord, on the joint exploitation of a variety of mineral resources, was signed in February 2001; Nigeria was to receive 60% of revenues and São Tomé and Príncipe 40%. In January 2002 the Presidents of both countries inaugurated a development authority to oversee the affairs of the JDZ. Disagreements developed during 2002, however, over Nigeria's commitment to provide São Tomé and Príncipe with 60,000 barrels of petroleum per day (reduced to 40,000 in September, and to 10,000 in October) and the relative lack of Santomean representation in the development authority. In November de Menezes refused to continue with the proposed sale of oil blocs until the issue was resolved; he was supported in this by a report from the World Bank, which suggested that the division of profits was unfair to São Tomé and Príncipe. By 2003, however, issues had been resolved sufficiently for bids for exploration rights in the first nine of the 25 blocs in the JDZ to open in October.

Government

Under the 2003 Constitution, legislative power is vested in the Assembleia Nacional, which comprises 55 members, elected by universal adult suffrage for a term of four years. No limit is placed on the number of political parties permitted to operate. Executive power is vested in the President of the Republic, who is Head of State, and who governs with the assistance of an appointed Council of Ministers, led by the Prime Minister. The Council of State acts as an advisory body to the President, who is elected by universal suffrage for a term of five years. The President's tenure of office is limited to two successive terms. The Prime Minister, who is appointed by the President, is, in theory, nominated by the deputies of the Assembleia Nacional.

In 1994 the Assembleia Nacional granted political and administrative autonomy to the island of Príncipe. Legislation was adopted establishing a seven-member Assembleia Regional and a five-member regional government; both are accountable to the Government of São Tomé and Príncipe.

Defence

In 1992 a reorganization was initiated of the islands' armed forces (estimated to comprise some 600 men in 1995) and the police into two separate police forces, one for public order and another for criminal investigation. In the budget for 2000 expenditure on defence amounted to 1,100m. dobras.

Economic Affairs

In 2006, according to estimates by the World Bank, São Tomé and Príncipe's gross national product (GNI), measured at average 2004–06 prices, was US $124m., equivalent to $780 per head. During 1996–2006, it was estimated, the population increased at an average annual rate of 2.1%, while gross domestic product (GDP) per head, in real terms, increased at an average annual rate of 0.8% in 1995–2005. Overall GDP increased, in real terms, at an average annual rate of 3.5% in 1998–2005; growth was 3.0% in 2005.

Agriculture (including fishing) contributed an estimated 21.8% of GDP in 2005, and accounted for an estimated 61.6% of the labour force in mid–2005, according to FAO. The principal cash crop is cocoa, which accounted for 91.4% of export earnings in 2004. Secondary cash crops include coconuts and coffee. Staple crops for local consumption include bananas, taro, tomatoes and cassava. Agricultural production is principally concentrated on export commodities, although smallholder agriculture has become increasingly important. An agricultural policy charter, the Carta de Política e Desenvolvimento Rural, which was introduced in 2000, aimed to emphasize private sector involvement and diversification into areas such as ylang ylang, pepper, vanilla, fruits, vegetables and flowers. Fishing is also a significant activity. The sale of fishing licences to foreign fleets is an important source of income. According to the World Bank, agricultural GDP increased at an average annual rate of 3.6% in 1995–2005; growth in 2005 was 3.8%.

Industry (including manufacturing, construction and power) contributed an estimated 18.6% of GDP in 2005, and employed 17.0% of the employed population in 2001. According to the World Bank, industrial GDP increased by an average of 2.8% per year in 1995–2003; growth in 2003 was 4.6%.

There are no mineral resources on the islands, but offshore prospecting for hydrocarbons resulted in the discovery of significant quantities of petroleum in 1998, including an estimated 4,000m. barrels in the joint development zone (JDZ) with Nigeria (see Recent History), as well as higher-risk resources in São Tomé's exclusive economic zone (EEZ). More than 20 companies lodged bids for exploration rights in the first nine of the 25 blocs in the JDZ in October 2003. In February 2005 a consortium led by ChevronTexaco was awarded a concession to exploit the first section of the JDZ. However negotiations regarding the granting of concessions for a further five blocs in the JDZ were delayed by conflict and allegations of corruption within the Government, and a preliminary agreement was not reached until August. It was anticipated that revenue generated from the first bloc would amount to US $49.4m. and some $113.2m. from the other five blocs. Negotiations were also taking place with Galp Energia (Portugal) in late 2005 in connection with the exploitation of São Tomé's EEZ.

The manufacturing sector consists solely of small processing factories, producing soap, soft drinks, textiles and beer. Manufacturing, including electricity, gas and water, contributed an estimated 6.4% of GDP in 2005. According to the World Bank, manufacturing GDP increased at an average annual rate of 2.4% in 1995–2003; growth in 2003 was 4.5%.

In 2000 some 74% of electricity generation was derived from thermal sources and 26% from hydroelectric sources. Imports of petroleum products comprised 15.0% of the value of merchandise imports in 2004. In late 2004 the national utility company was privatized. In early 2006 it was announced that a thermal power plant, which would increase São Tomé's energy production by 70%, was to be built by a Nigerian company.

The services sector contributed an estimated 59.6% of GDP in 2005, and engaged 51.5% of the employed population in 2001. According to the World Bank, the GDP of the services sector increased by an average of 2.3% per year in 1995–2003; growth in 2003 was 4.4%.

In 2005 São Tomé and Príncipe recorded a trade deficit of US $38.3m. and a deficit of $23.2m. on the current account of the balance of payments. In 2004 the principal source of imports (60.5%) was Portugal; other major suppliers were Angola, Belgium and Japan. The principal market for exports in that year were Portugal (62.3%), the Netherlands, Belgium and the USA. The principal export in 2004 was cocoa. The principal imports in that year were foodstuffs, beverages, petroleum and petroleum products, equipment, transport equipment and construction materials.

In 2005, largely as a result of significant oil signatures bonuses, there was a budgetary surplus of 426,700m. dobras (equivalent to some 57% of GDP). São Tomé's total external debt was US $336.4m. at the end of 2005, of which $326.7m. was long-term public debt. In 2003 the cost of debt-servicing was equivalent to 31.4% of the total value of exports of goods and services. Annual inflation averaged 21.8% in 1996–2005. Consumer prices increased by an average of 15.2% in 2004 and by 17.2 in 2005. According to official figures, 27.4% of the labour force were unemployed in 1993.

São Tomé and Príncipe is a member of the International Cocoa Organization (see p. 408) and of the Communauté économique des états de l'Afrique centrale (see p. 411).

São Tomé and Príncipe's economy has traditionally been dominated by cocoa production and is therefore vulnerable to adverse weather conditions and to fluctuations in international prices for that commodity. While the discovery of petroleum in Santomean waters, and the anticipated increase in government revenues the sale of that commodity would provide, was a welcome development, concerns were raised by international institutions regarding the lack of transparency and accountability in the petroleum sector. Thus, in mid-2004 the Government agreed to establish a National Petroleum Fund into which all petroleum earnings were to be deposited, and which was to be subject to annual independent audits; it was also announced that 65% of the total revenue from petroleum was to be allocated to the upgrading of infrastructure and to improvements in the health care and education sectors. Despite ongoing investigations into the misappropriation of donor funds, São Tomé and Príncipe continued to be a major recipient of external assistance. In 2005 the Group of Eight leading industrial nations (G-8) announced that São Tomé and Príncipe was among nine 'second wave' countries deemed eligible for the cancellation of their debts

SÃO TOMÉ AND PRÍNCIPE

owed to the IMF, the World Bank and the ABD. In late 2005 the construction of a free trade zone was begun on the island of Príncipe, while in August, following a series of missions since the suspension of the Poverty Reduction and Growth Facility (PRGF) arrangement in 2000, the IMF announced a new three-year PRGF, worth US $4.3m. At the third review of the PRGF in January 2007 the Fund commended the Government for implementing a number of vital structural reforms, and in March the IMF announced that São Tomé and Príncipe had reached completion point of the enhanced initiative for heavily indebted poor countries, thus qualifying for debt relief equivalent to $314m. In early 2008 Nigeria provided some US $1m. in financial aid for São Tomé and Príncipe for investment in security and defence, while additionally undertaking social projects on the islands. GDP was estimated to have increased by 6.0% in 2006, sustained by oil exploration in the JDZ and continued buoyant construction activity. Although preliminary estimates suggested growth in 2007 had reached 8.0%, it was forecast to decline in 2008, returning to around 6.0%. The rate of inflation was forecast to reach 14.0% in that year, owing to higher fuel prices.

Education

Primary education is officially compulsory for a period of four years between six and 14 years of age. Secondary education lasts for a further seven years, comprising a first cycle of four years and a second, pre-university, cycle of three years. In 2001 the country had 73 primary schools, with a total enrolment of 20,858 pupils. There were 13 secondary schools (including two devoted to vocational training) in that year, with a total enrolment of 13,874 pupils. There was one polytechnic institute (with an enrolment of 117 in 2000/01). According to UNESCO estimates, in 2003/04 enrolment at primary schools included 98% of children in the relevant age-group (males 98%; females 98%), while the comparable ratio for secondary enrolment in that year was 26% (males 25%; females 27%). In 2000 public investment in education (including culture and sport) amounted to US $1.3m., equivalent to 6.7% of total public investment.

Public Holidays

2008: 1 January (New Year), 4 January (King Amador Day), 3 February (Martyrs' Day), 1 May (Labour Day), 12 July (Independence Day), 6 September (Armed Forces Day), 30 September (Agricultural Reform Day), 21 December (São Tomé Day), 25 December (Christmas Day).

2009: 1 January (New Year), 4 January (King Amador Day), 3 February (Martyrs' Day), 1 May (Labour Day), 12 July (Independence Day), 6 September (Armed Forces Day), 30 September (Agricultural Reform Day), 21 December (São Tomé Day), 25 December (Christmas Day).

Weights and Measures

The metric system is in force.

Statistical Survey

Source (unless otherwise stated): Instituto Nacional de Estatística, CP 256, São Tomé; tel. 221982.

AREA AND POPULATION

Area: 1,001 sq km (386.5 sq miles); São Tomé 859 sq km (331.7 sq miles), Príncipe 142 sq km (54.8 sq miles).

Population: 117,504 at census of 4 August 1991; 137,599 (males 68,236, females 69,363) at census of September 2001; 158,000 in 2007 (UN estimate at mid-year) (Source: UN, *World Population Prospects: The 2006 Revision*).

Density (mid-2007): 157.8 per sq km.

Population by District (census of 2001): Água-Grande 51,886, Mé-Zochi 35,105, Cantagolo 13,258, Caué 5,501, Lembá 10,696, Lobata 15,157, Pagué (Príncipe) 5,966; Total 137,599.

Principal Towns (population at census of 1991): São Tomé (capital) 42,300; Trindade 11,400; Santana 6,200; Santo Amaro 5,900; Neves 5,900. Source: Stefan Helders, *World Gazetteer* (internet www.world-gazetteer.com). *Mid-2007* (incl. suburbs): São Tomé (capital) 58,000 (Source: UN, *World Urbanization Prospects: The 2007 Revision*).

Births, Marriages and Deaths (2000): Registered live births 4,078 (birth rate 29.20 per 1,000); Registered marriages 210 (marriage rate 1.5 per 1,000); Registered deaths 1,030 (death rate 7.51 per 1,000). *2006:* Birth rate 32.5 per 1,000; Death rate 8.32 per 1,000 (Source: African Development Bank).

Expectation of Life (years at birth, WHO estimates): 58.7 (males 57.1; females 60.3) in 2005. (Source: WHO, *World Health Statistics*).

Economically Active Population (census of 2001): Agriculture and fishing 13,518; Industry, electricity, gas and water 2,893; Public works and civil construction 4,403; Trade, restaurants and hotels 8,787; Transport, storage and communications 792; Public administration 3,307; Health 776; Education 1,373; Other activities 7,088; Total employed 42,937. *Mid-2005* (estimates in '000): Agriculture, etc. 45; Total labour force 73 (Source: FAO).

HEALTH AND WELFARE
Key Indicators

Total Fertility Rate (children per woman, 2005): 3.8.

Under-5 Mortality Rate (per 1,000 live births, 2005): 118.

Physicians (per 1,000 head, 2004): 0.49.

Hospital Beds (per 1,000 head, 2003): 3.20.

Health Expenditure (2004): US $ per head (PPP): 141.4.

Health Expenditure (2004): % of GDP: 11.5.

Health Expenditure (2004): public (% of total): 86.2.

Access to Water (% of persons, 2004): 79.

Access to Sanitation (% of persons, 2004): 25.

Human Development Index (2005): ranking: 123.

Human Development Index (2005): value: 0.654.

For sources and definitions, see explanatory note on p. vi.

AGRICULTURE, ETC.

Principal Crops (metric tons, 2006, FAO estimates): Bananas 27,000; Maize 2,700; Cassava (Manioc) 6,890; Taro 28,000; Yams 1,547; Cocoa beans 3,534; Coconuts 26,277; Oil palm fruit 43,458; Coffee (green) 29; Cinnamon 30.

Livestock (head, 2006, FAO estimates): Cattle 4,600; Sheep 3,000; Goats 5,000; Pigs 2,500; Poultry 350,000.

Livestock Products (metric tons, 2006, FAO estimates): Cattle meat 122; Pig meat 75; Sheep meat 6; Goat meat 18; Chicken meat 667; Hen eggs 385; Cows' milk 144.

Forestry ('000 cubic metres, 1988): Roundwood removals 9; Sawnwood production 5. *1989–2006:* Annual output assumed to be unchanged since 1988.

Fishing (metric tons, live weight, estimates, 2005): Total catch 3,600 (Croakers and drums 110; Pandoras 160; Threadfins and tasselfishes 120; Wahoo 300; Little tunny 120; Atlantic sailfish 200; Flyingfishes 800; Jacks and crevalles 160; Sharks, rays and skates 170).

Source: FAO.

INDUSTRY

Production (metric tons, unless otherwise indicated): Bread and biscuits 3,768 (1995); Soap 261.1 (1995); Beer (litres) 529,400 (1995); Palm oil 2,000 (2006, FAO estimate); Electric energy (million kWh) 37.2 (2002). Sources: IMF, *Democratic Republic of São Tomé and Príncipe: Selected Issues and Statistical Appendix* (September 1998, February 2002, April 2004 and September 2006), and FAO.

FINANCE

Currency and Exchange Rates: 100 cêntimos = 1 dobra (Db). *Sterling, Dollar and Euro Equivalents* (29 December 2006): £1 sterling = 25,664.0 dobras; US $1 = 13,073.9 dobras; €1 = 17,218.3 dobras; 100,000 dobras = £3.90 = $7.65 = €5.81. *Average Exchange Rate* (dobras per US $): 9,902.3 in 2004; 10,558.0 in 2005; 12,445.4 in 2006.

Budget ('000 million dobras, 2005, estimates): *Revenue:* Taxation 184.0 (Direct 54.3, Indirect 129.7); Non-tax revenue 42.6; Grants 184.1; Oil signature bonuses 561.5; Total 972.2. *Expenditure:* Current expenditure 320.4 (Personnel costs 103.3, *of which* Wages and salaries 90.4, Goods and services 65.5, Interest on external debt 33.7. Interest on internal debt 1.9, Transfers 89.8, Other current expenditure 26.2); Capital expenditure 193.4; HIPC-related social expenditure 31.7; Total 545.5. Source: IMF, *Democratic Republic of São Tomé and Príncipe: Selected Issues and Statistical Appendix* (September 2006).

International Reserves (US $ million at 31 December 2006): IMF special drawing rights 0.07; Foreign exchange 34.12; Total 34.19. Source: IMF, *International Financial Statistics*.

Money Supply (million dobras at 31 December 2006): Currency outside banks 92,313; Demand deposits at commercial banks 341,746; Total money (incl. others) 435,181. Source: IMF, *International Financial Statistics*.

Cost of Living (Consumer Price Index; base: 1996 = 100): 437.2 in 2003; 503.8 in 2004; 590.5 in 2005. Source: IMF, *Democratic Republic of São Tomé and Príncipe: Selected Issues and Statistical Appendix* (September 2006).

Expenditure on the Gross Domestic Product (US $ million at current prices, 2006): Government final consumption expenditure 37.97; Private final consumption expenditure 57.24; Gross capital formation 65.91; *Total domestic expenditure* 160.42; Exports of goods and services 26.86; *Less* Imports of goods and services 104.14; *GDP in purchasers' values* 83.84. Source: African Development Bank.

Gross Domestic Product by Economic Activity ('000 million dobras at current prices, 2004, preliminary): Agriculture 83.7; Fishing 18.6; Manufacturing, electricity, gas and water 26.3; Construction 61.1; Trade and transport 175.0; Public administration 190.6; Financial institutions 69.4; Other services 4.4; *Total* 629.3. Source: IMF, *Democratic Republic of São Tomé and Príncipe: Selected Issues and Statistical Appendix* (September 2006).

Balance of Payments (US $ million, 2005, estimates): Exports of goods f.o.b. 3.8; Imports of goods f.o.b. –42.1; *Trade balance* –38.3; Net of service and income accounts –5.3; *Balance on goods, services and income* –43.6; Private transfers (net) 2.0; Official transfers (net) 18.4; *Current balance* –23.2; Project loans 3.9; Program loans 1.7; Oil signatures bonuses 49.2; Direct foreign investment 3.5; Other investment –0.6; Amortization –8.9; Short-term capital and errors and omissions 0.8; *Overall balance* 26.6. Source: IMF, *Democratic Republic of São Tomé and Príncipe: Selected Issues and Statistical Appendix* (September 2006).

EXTERNAL TRADE

Principal Commodities (US $ million, 2004): *Imports f.o.b.*: Foodstuffs 10.3; Beverages 5.0; Petroleum and petroleum products 6.2; Equipment 4.9; Transport equipment 4.4; Construction materials 2.9; Total (incl. others) 41.4. *Exports f.o.b.*: Cocoa 3.2; Coconuts 0.1; Total (incl. others) 3.5.

Principal Trading Partners (US $ million, 2004): *Imports c.i.f.*: Angola 6.6; Belgium 3.6; Gabon 0.6; Japan 2.5; Netherlands 0.4; Portugal 25.0; Total (incl. others) 41.3. *Exports f.o.b.*: Belgium 0.3; Gabon 0.1; Netherlands 1.8; Portugal 2.2; USA 0.2; Total (incl. others) 3.5. Source: Banco Central de São Tomé e Príncipe.

TRANSPORT

Road Traffic (registered vehicles, 1996, estimates): Passenger cars 4,000; Lorries and vans 1,540. Source: International Road Federation, *World Road Statistics*.

Shipping: *International Freight Traffic* (estimates, metric tons, 1992): Goods loaded 16,000; Goods unloaded 45,000. *Merchant Fleet* (registered at 31 December 2006): Number of vessels 34; Total displacement 32,659 grt (Source: Lloyd's Register-Fairplay, *World Fleet Statistics*).

Civil Aviation (traffic on scheduled services, 2003): Passengers carried ('000) 36; Passenger-km (million) 15; Total ton-km (million) 1. Source: UN, *Statistical Yearbook*.

TOURISM

Foreign Tourist Arrivals: 5,584 in 1998; 5,710 in 1999; 7,137 in 2000. Source: Tourism and Hotels Bureau.

Arrivals by Country of Residence (2005): Angola 552; Cape Verde 336; France 1,242; Gabon 286; Nigeria 473; Portugal 5,469; Spain 318; USA 154; Total (incl. others) 10,518. Source: World Tourism Organization.

Tourism Receipts (US $ million, excl. passenger transport): 10 in 2000; 10 in 2001; 10 in 2002. Source: World Tourism Organization.

COMMUNICATIONS MEDIA

Radio Receivers (1998): 45,000 in use. Source: UNESCO, *Statistical Yearbook*.

Television Receivers (1999): 33,000 in use. Source: UNESCO, *Statistical Yearbook*.

Newspapers and Periodicals (2000): Titles 14 (1997); Average circulation 18,500 copies.

Telephones ('000 main lines, 2006): 7.6 in use. Source: International Telecommunication Union.

Mobile Cellular Telephones ('000 subscribers, 2006): 18.4. Source: International Telecommunication Union.

Facsimile Machines (2000): 372 in use.

Internet Users (2006): 29,000. Source: International Telecommunication Union.

EDUCATION

Pre-primary (2001): 18 schools; 2,376 pupils.

Primary (2001): 73 schools; 623 teachers; 20,858 pupils.

General Secondary and Pre-university (2001): 11 schools; 630 teachers; 13,874 (including vocational education) pupils. There are also 2 vocational secondary schools.

Tertiary (2000/01): 1 polytechnic; 29 teachers; 117 pupils.

Source: mainly *Carta Escolar de São Tomé e Príncipe,* Ministério de Educação de Portugal.

Adult Literacy Rate (UNESCO estimates): 84.9% (males 92.2; females 77.9) in 2001. Source: UNESCO Institute for Statistics.

Directory

The Constitution

A new Constitution came into force on 4 March 2003, after the promulgation by the President of a draft approved by the Assembleia Nacional (National Assembly) in December 2002. A 'memorandum of understanding', which was signed in January 2003 by the President and the Assembleia Nacional, provided for the scheduling of a referendum on the system of governance in early 2006. However, the referendum did not take place. The following is a summary of the main provisions of the Constitution:

The Democratic Republic of São Tomé and Príncipe is a sovereign, independent, unitary and democratic state. Sovereignty resides in the people, who exercise it through universal, equal, direct and secret vote, according to the terms of the Constitution. There shall be complete separation between Church and State. There shall be freedom of thought, expression and information and a free and independent press, within the terms of the law.

Executive power is vested in the President of the Republic, who is elected for a period of five years by universal adult suffrage. The President's tenure of office is limited to two successive terms. He is the Supreme Commander of the Armed Forces and is accountable to the Assembleia Nacional. In the event of the President's death, permanent incapacity or resignation, his functions shall be assumed by the President of the Assembleia Nacional until a new President is elected.

The Council of State acts as an advisory body to the President and comprises the President of the Assembleia Nacional, the Prime Minister, the President of the Constitutional Tribunal, the Attorney-General, the President of the Regional Government of Príncipe, former Presidents of the Republic who have not been dismissed from their positions, three citizens of merit nominated by the President and three elected by the Assembleia Nacional. Its meetings are closed and do not serve a legislative function.

Legislative power is vested in the Assembleia Nacional, which comprises 55 members elected by universal adult suffrage. The Assembleia Nacional is elected for four years and meets in ordinary session twice a year. It may meet in extraordinary session on the proposal of the President, the Council of Ministers or of two-thirds of its members. The Assembleia Nacional elects its own President. In the period between ordinary sessions of the Assembleia Nacional its functions are assumed by a permanent commission elected from among its members.

SÃO TOMÉ AND PRÍNCIPE

The Government is the executive and administrative organ of State. The Prime Minister is the Head of Government and is appointed by the President. Other ministers are appointed by the President on the proposal of the Prime Minister. The Government is responsible to the President and the Assembleia Nacional.

Judicial power is exercised by the Supreme Court and all other competent tribunals and courts. The Supreme Court is the supreme judicial authority and is accountable only to the Assembleia Nacional. Its members are appointed by the Assembleia Nacional. The right to a defence is guaranteed.

The Constitutional Tribunal, comprising five judges with a mandate of five years, is responsible for jurisdiction on matters of constitutionality. During periods prior to, or between, the installation of the Constitutional Tribunal, its function is assumed by the Supreme Court. The Constitution may be revised only by the Assembleia Nacional on the proposal of at least three-quarters of its members. Any amendment must be approved by a two-thirds' majority of the Assembleia Nacional. The President does not have right of veto over constitutional changes.

Note: In 1994 the Assembleia Nacional granted political and administrative autonomy to the island of Príncipe. Legislation was adopted establishing a seven-member Assembleia Regional and a five-member Regional Government; both are accountable to the Government of São Tomé and Príncipe.

The Government

HEAD OF STATE

President and Commander-in-Chief of the Armed Forces: FRADIQUE DE MENEZES (took office 3 September 2001; re-elected 30 July 2006).

COUNCIL OF MINISTERS
(March 2008)

The Government comprises members of the Movimento Democrático Força da Mudança, the Partido de Convergência Democrática and independents.

Prime Minister: PATRICE EMERY TROVOADA.

Minister of Defence and Internal Order: Lt-Col ÓSCAR AGUÍAR SACRAMENTO E SOUSA.

Minister of Foreign Affairs, Co-operation and Communities: OVÍDIO BARBOSA PEQUENO.

Minister of Planning and Finance: RAUL CRAVID.

Minister of Justice and Parliamentary Affairs: JOSÉ CARLOS BARREIROS.

Minister of Public Works, Infrastructure and Town Planning: ARZEMIRO DOS PRAZERES.

Minister of Public Administration, State Reform and Territorial Administration: MARIA DE CRISTO CARVALHO.

Minister of Commerce, Industry and Tourism: FRANCISCO RITA.

Minister of Education, Culture and Sport: MARIANA RUTE LEAL.

Minister of Health: MARTINHO DO NASCIMENTO.

Minister of Natural Resources and the Environment: JOSÉ DA GRAÇA DIOGO.

Minister of Labour and Solidarity: MARIA TOMÉ.

Minister of Agriculture and Rural Development: VALDEMIRA TAVARES.

Secretary of State for Social Communication: ADELINO LUCAS.

Provisional Government of the Autonomous Region of Príncipe
(March 2008)

President: JOÃO PAULO CASSANDRA.

Secretary for Social and Cultural Affairs: FELÍCIA FONSECA DE OLIVEIRA E SILVA.

Secretary for Economic and Financial Affairs: HÉLIO LAVRES.

Secretary for Infrastructure and the Environment: TIAGO ROSAMONTE.

Secretary for Political, Organizational and Institutional Affairs: CARLOS GOMES.

MINISTRIES

Office of the President: Palácio Presidêncial, São Tomé; internet www.presidencia.st.

Office of the Prime Minister: Rua do Município, CP 302, São Tomé; tel. 223913; fax 224679; e-mail gpm@cstome.net.

Ministry of Agriculture and Rural Development: Avda Marginal 12 de Julho, Edif. Ministério da Agricultura, 1° andar, CP 47, São Tomé; tel. 222714; fax 222347.

Ministry of Commerce, Industry and Tourism: São Tomé.

Ministry of Defence and Internal Order: Av. 12 de Julho, CP 427, São Tomé; tel. 222041; e-mail midefesa@cstome.net; internet www.mindefordInterna.gov.st.

Ministry of Education, Culture and Sport: Rua Misericórdia, CP 41, São Tomé; tel. 222861; fax 221466; e-mail mineducal@cstome.net; internet www.minecjdesportos.gov.st.

Ministry of Foreign Affairs, Co-operation and Communities: Av. 12 de Julho, CP 111, São Tomé; tel. 221017; fax 222597; e-mail minecoop@cstome.net; internet www.mnecc.gov.st.

Ministry of Health: Av. Patrice Lumumba, CP 23, São Tomé; tel. 241200; fax 221306; e-mail msaude@cstome.net.

Ministry of Justice and Parliamentary Affairs: Av. 12 de Julho, CP 4, São Tomé; tel. 222318; fax 222256; e-mail emilioma@cstome.net.

Ministry of Labour and Solidarity: Rua Município, Edif. Ministério do Trabalho, São Tomé; tel. 221466.

Ministry of Natural Resources and the Environment: CP 1093, São Tomé; tel. 225272; fax 226262; e-mail mirecurna@cstome.net; internet www.minrecnatambiente.gov.st.

Ministry of Planning and Finance: Largo Alfândega, CP 168, São Tomé; tel. 224173; fax 222683; e-mail mpfc@cstome.net; internet www.minfinancas.gov.st.

Ministry of Public Administration, State Reform and Territorial Administration: Av. Kwame Nkrumah, CP 136, São Tomé; tel. 224750; fax 222824.

Ministry of Public Works, Infrastructure and Town Planning: São Tomé.

President and Legislature

PRESIDENT

Presidential Election, 30 July 2006

Candidate	Votes	% of votes
Fradique de Menezes	34,859	60.58
Patrice Emery Trovoada	22,339	38.82
Nilo de Oliveira Guimarães	340	0.59
Total	**57,538**	**100.00**

There were, in addition, 1,640 blank and other invalid votes

ASSEMBLEIA NACIONAL

Assembleia Nacional: Palácio dos Congressos, CP 181, São Tomé; tel. 222986; fax 222835; e-mail romao.couto@parlamento.st; internet www.parlamento.st.

President: FRANCISCO DA SILVA.

General Election, 26 March and 2 April 2006

Party	% of valid votes	Seats
Movimento Democrático Força da Mudança–Partido de Convergência Democrática	36.79	23
Movimento de Libertação de São Tomé e Príncipe—Partido Social Democrata	29.47	20
Acção Democrática Independente (ADI)	20.00	11
Novo Rumo (NR)	4.71	1
Others	9.03	—
Total	**100.00**	**55**

Election Commission

Comissão Eleitoral Nacional (CEN): Av. Amílcar Cabral, São Tomé; tel. 227828; fax 224116; Pres. JOSÉ CARLOS BARREIRO.

Political Organizations

Acção Democrática Independente (ADI): Av. Marginal 12 de Julho, Edif. C. Cassandra, São Tomé; tel. 222201; f. 1992; Sec.-Gen. EVARISTO CARVALHO.

SÃO TOMÉ AND PRÍNCIPE

Directory

Frente Democrata Cristã—Partido Social da Unidade (FDC—PSU): São Tomé; f. 1990; Pres. Arlécio Costa; Vice-Pres. Sabino dos Santos.

Geração Esperança (GE): São Tomé; f. 2005; Leader Edmilza Bragança.

Movimento Democrático Força da Mudança (MDFM): São Tomé; f. 2001; formed alliance with PCD to contest legislative elections in 2006; Chair. Fradique de Menezes; Sec.-Gen. Tomé Soares Vera Cruz.

Movimento de Libertação de São Tomé e Príncipe—Partido Social Democrata (MLSTP—PSD): Estrada Riboque, Edif. Sede do MLSTP, São Tomé; tel. 222253; f. 1972 as MLSTP; adopted present name in 1990; sole legal party 1972–90; Pres. Rafael Branco; Sec.-Gen. José Viegas.

Novo Rumo: São Tomé; f. 2006 by citizens disaffected by current political parties; Leader João Gomes.

Partido de Convergência Democrática (PCD): Av. Marginal 12 de Julho, CP 519, São Tomé; tel. and fax 223257; f. 1990 as Partido de Convergência—Grupo de Reflexão; formed alliance with MDFM to contest legislative elections in 2006; Pres. Leonel Mário d'Alva; Sec.-Gen. Delfim Santiago das Neves.

Partido de Coligação Democrática (CÓDÓ): São Tomé; f. 1990 as Partido Democrático de São Tomé e Príncipe—Coligação Democrática da Oposição; renamed as above June 1998; Leader Manuel Neves e Silva.

Partido Social e Liberal (PSL): São Tomé; f. 2005; promotes development and anti-corruption; Leader Agostinho Rita.

Partido Popular do Progresso (PPP): São Tomé; f. 1998; Leader Francisco Silva.

Partido de Renovação Democrática (PRD): São Tomé; tel. 903109; e-mail prd100@hotmail.com; f. 2001; Pres. Armindo Graça.

Partido Social Renovado (PSR): São Tomé; f. 2004; Leader Hamilton Vaz.

Partido Trabalhista Santomense (PTS): CP 254, São Tomé; tel. 223338; fax 223255; e-mail pascoal@cstome.net; f. 1993 as Aliança Popular; Leader Anacleto Rolin.

União para a Democracia e Desenvolvimento (UDD): São Tomé; f. 2005; Leader Manuel Diogo.

União Nacional para Democracia e Progresso (UNDP): São Tomé; f. 1998; Leader Paixão Lima.

The União para a Mudança e Progresso do Príncipe (UMPP) operates on the island of Príncipe and there is also a local civic group, O Renascimento de Água Grande, in the district of Agua Grande, which includes the city of São Tomé.

Diplomatic Representation

EMBASSIES IN SÃO TOMÉ AND PRÍNCIPE

Angola: Av. Kwame Nkrumah 45, CP 133, São Tomé; tel. 222400; fax 221362; e-mail embrang@cstome.net; Ambassador Pedro Fernando Mavunza.

Brazil: Av. Marginal de 12 de Julho 20, São Tomé; tel. 226060; fax 226895; e-mail brasembsaotome@cstome.net; Ambassador Manuel Innocencio de Lacerda Santos, Jr.

China (Taiwan): Av. Marginal de 12 de Julho, CP 839, São Tomé; tel. 223529; fax 221376; e-mail rocstp@cstome.net; Ambassador Yang Ching-yuen.

Equatorial Guinea: Rua Ex-Adriano Moreira, São Tomé; tel. 225427.

Gabon: Rua Damão, CP 394, São Tomé; tel. 224434; fax 223531; e-mail ambagabon@cstome.net; Ambassador Bekalé Michel.

Nigeria: Av. Kwame Nkrumah, CP 1000, São Tomé; tel. 225404; fax 225406; e-mail nigeria@cstome.net; Ambassador Sunday Dogonyaro Oon.

Portugal: Av. Marginal de 12 de Julho, CP 173, São Tomé; tel. 221130; fax 221190; e-mail eporstp@cstome.net; Ambassador Fernando José Rodrigues Ramos Machado.

Judicial System

Judicial power is exercised by the Supreme Court of Justice and the Courts of Primary Instance. The Supreme Court is the ultimate judicial authority. There is also a Constitutional Court, which rules on election matters.

Supremo Tribunal de Justiça: Av. Marginal de 12 de Julho, São Tomé; tel. and fax 222329; e-mail tsupremo@cstome.net; Pres. Maria Alice Vera Cruz de Carvalho.

Religion

According to the 2001 census more than 80% of the population are Christians, almost all of whom are Roman Catholics.

CHRISTIANITY

The Roman Catholic Church

São Tomé and Príncipe comprises a single diocese, directly responsible to the Holy See. At 31 December 2005 an estimated 73.0% of the population were adherents. The bishop participates in the Episcopal Conference of Angola and São Tomé (based in Luanda, Angola).

Bishop of São Tomé and Príncipe: Rt Rev. Manuel António Mendes dos Santos, Centro Diocesano, CP 104, Rua P. Pinto da Rocha 1, São Tomé; tel. 223455; fax 227348; e-mail diocese@cstome.net.

Other Churches

Igreja Adventista do 7° Dia (Seventh-Day Adventist Church): Rua Barão de Água Izé, São Tomé; tel. 223349.

Igreja Evangélica: Rua 3 de Fevereiro, São Tomé; tel. 221350.

Igreja Evanélica Assembleia de Deus: Rua 3 de Fevereiro, São Tomé; tel. and fax 222442; e-mail iead@cstome.net.

Igreja Maná: Av. Amílcar Cabral, São Tomé; tel. and fax 224654; e-mail imana@cstome.net.

Igreja do Nazareno: Vila Dolores, São Tomé; tel. 223943; e-mail nszst@cstome.net.

Igreja Nova Apostólica: Fruta Fruta, São Tomé; tel. and fax 222406; e-mail inasaotome@cstome.net.

Igreja Universal do Reino de Deus: Travessa Imprensa, São Tomé; tel. 224047.

The Press

Correio da Semana: Av. Amílcar Cabral 382, São Tomé; tel. 225299; f. 2005; weekly; Publr Rafael Branco; Dir Juvenal Rodrigues; circ. 3,000.

Diário da República: Cooperativa de Artes Gráficas, Rua João Devs, CP 28, São Tomé; tel. 222661; internet dre.pt/stp; f. 1836; official gazette; Dir Oscar Ferreira.

Jornal Maravilha: São Tomé; tel. 911690; f. 2006; Dir Nelson Signo.

Jornal Tropical: Rua Padre Martinho Pinto da Rocha, São Tomé; tel. 923140; e-mail jornaltropical06@hotmail.com; internet www.jornaltropical.st; Dir Octávio Soares.

O País: Av. Amílcar Cabral, CP 361, São Tomé; tel. 223833; fax 221989; e-mail iucai@cstome.net; f. 1998; Dir Francisco Pinto da Silveira Rita.

O Parvo: CP 535, São Tomé; tel. 221031; f. 1994; weekly; Publr Ambrósio Quaresma; Editor Armindo Cardoso.

Piá: Edif. Centro Cultural Português 1c, CP 600, São Tomé; tel. 226332; e-mail doriadesign@hotmail.com; f. 2002; monthly; Dir Nilton Dória.

Téla Nón: Largo Água Grande, Edif. Complexo Técnico da CST, São Tomé; tel. 225099; e-mail diario_digital@cstome.net; internet www.cstome.net/diario; f. 2000; provides online daily news service; Chief Editor Abel Veiga.

Online newspapers include the Jornal de São Tomé e Príncipe (www.jornal.st) and Jornal Horizonte (www.cstome.net/jhorizonte).

PRESS ASSOCIATION

Associação Nacional de Imprensa (ANI): São Tomé; Pres. Manuel Barreto.

NEWS AGENCY

STP-Press: Av. Marginal de 12 de Julho, CP 112, São Tomé; tel. 223431; fax 221973; e-mail stp_press@cstome.net; internet www.cstome.net/stp-press; f. 1985; operated by the radio station in asscn with the Angolan news agency ANGOP; Dir Manuel Dênde.

Broadcasting and Communications

TELECOMMUNICATIONS

Companhia Santomense de Telecomunicações, SARL (CST): Av. Marginal 12 de Julho, CP 141, São Tomé; tel. 222273; fax 222500; e-mail webmaster@cstome.net; internet www.cstome.net; f. 1989 by Govt of São Tomé (49%) and Grupo Portugal Telecom (Portugal, 51%) to facilitate increased telecommunications links and television reception via satellite; in March 1997 CST introduced internet services; Rádio Marconi's shares subsequently assumed by Portugal Telecom SA; introduced mobile cellular telephone service in 2001; Pres. Felisberto Afonso L. Neto; Sec. Jorge M. Tavares Magro.

SÃO TOMÉ AND PRÍNCIPE

BROADCASTING

Portuguese technical and financial assistance in the establishment of a television service was announced in May 1989. Transmissions commenced in 1992 and the service currently broadcasts seven days a week. In 1995 Radio France Internationale and Rádio Televisão Portuguesa Internacional began relaying radio and television broadcasts, respectively, to the archipelago. In 1997 Voice of America, which had been broadcasting throughout Africa since 1993 from a relay station installed on São Tomé, began local transmissions on FM. In 2004 there were plans for Televisão Pública de Angola to begin transmitting by the end of the year. The liberalization of the sector was approved by the Government in early 2005 and Rádio Jubilar, Rádio Tropicana (operated by the Roman Catholic Church) and Rádio Viva FM subsequently began broadcasting. The French television channel, TV5, began broadcasting in 2007.

Radio

Rádio Nacional de São Tomé e Príncipe: Av. Marginal de 12 de Julho, CP 44, São Tomé; tel. 223293; fax 221973; e-mail rnstp@cstome.net; f. 1958; state-controlled; home service in Portuguese and Creole; Dir MÁXIMO CARLOS.

Rádio Jubilar: Rua Padre Martinho Pinto da Rocha, São Tomé; tel. 223455; f. 2005; operated by the Roman Catholic Church; Dir FERNANDO CORREIA.

Rádio Tropicana: Travessa João de Deus, CP 709, São Tomé; tel. 226856; f. 2005; Dir AGUINALDO SALVATERRA.

Television

Televisão Santomense (TVS): Bairro Quinta de Santo António, CP 393, São Tomé; tel. 221041; fax 221942; state-controlled; Dir MATEUS FERREIRA.

Finance

(cap. = capital; res = reserves; dep. = deposits; m. = million; br(s). = branch(es); amounts in dobras, unless otherwise indicated)

BANKING

Central Bank

Banco Central de São Tomé e Príncipe (BCSTP): Praça da Independência, CP 13, São Tomé; tel. 221300; fax 222777; e-mail bcstp@bcstp.st; internet www.bcstp.st; f. 1992 to succeed fmr Banco Nacional de São Tomé e Príncipe; bank of issue; cap. 100m., res 91,623m., dep. 125,154m.; Gov. ARLINDO AFONSO DE CARVALHO.

Commercial Banks

Afriland First Bank/STP: Praça da Independência, CP 202, São Tomé; tel. 226749; fax 226747; e-mail firstbank@afriland-firstbank.com; internet www.afrilandfirstbank.com; f. 2003; private bank; owned by Afriland First Bank, SA, Cameroon; cap. US $1.8m.; Gen. Man. AUGUSTIN DIAYO; Administrator-Delegate JOSEPH TINDJOU.

Banco Equador: Rua Moçambique 3, CP 361, São Tomé; tel. 226150; fax 226149; e-mail be@bancoequador.st; internet www.bancoequador.st; f. 1995 as Banco Comercial do Equador; restructured and name changed to above in 2003; owned by Monbaka (Angola) (40%) and Grupo António Mbakassi (40%); cap. US $3m.; Pres. DIONÍSIO MENDONÇA; Gen. Man. DOUGLAS PETERSEN; 1 br.

Banco Internacional de São Tomé e Príncipe (BISTP) (International Bank of São Tomé and Príncipe): Praça da Independência, CP 536, São Tomé; tel. 243100; fax 222427; e-mail bistp@cstome.net; f. 1993; 48% govt-owned, 30% owned by Banco Totta e Açores, SA (Portugal), 22% by Caixa Geral de Depósitos (Portugal); cap. US $3.0m., res $3.1m., dep. $22.2m. (2004); Pres. MANUEL FERNANDO MONTEIRO PINTO; 3 brs.

Commercial Bank—São Tomé e Príncipe: Av. Marginal 12 de Julho, CP 1109, São Tomé; tel. 227678; fax 227676; e-mail gi_sandjon@hotmail.com; f. 2005; subsidiary of Groupe Bancaire Commercial Bank (Cameroon); cap. US $3m. (2005); Chair. YVES MICHEL FOTSO; Gen. Man. JAQUES PAUL WOUENDJI.

Ecobank São Tomé: Edificio HB, Traversa de Pelorinho, CP 316, São Tomé; tel. 222141; fax 222672; e-mail ecobankstp@cstome.net; f. 2007; cap. US $1.5m.

Island Bank, SA: Rua de Guiné, CP 1044, São Tomé; tel. 222521; f. 2005; cap. US $1.8m. (2005); Pres. MARC WABARA; Dir CHRIS U. MMEJE.

INVESTMENT BANK

National Investment Bank: Rua de Angola, São Tomé; tel. 908221; internet www.ni-bank.com; f. 2004; acquired by Superior Investments in 2005; cap. US $3.4m. (Dec. 2006); Chair. PAULO MIRPURI.

INSURANCE

Instituto de Segurança Social: Rua Soldado Paulo Ferreira, São Tomé; tel. 221382; e-mail inss@cstome.net; f. as Caixa de Previdência dos Funcionários Públicos, adopted present name 1994; insurance fund for civil servants; Pres. of Admin. Bd ALBINO GRAÇA DA FONSECA; Dir JUVENAL DO ESPÍRITO SANTO.

SAT INSURANCE: Av. 12 de Julho, CP 293, São Tomé; tel. 226161; fax 226160; e-mail satinsuran@cstome.net; f. 2001; general insurance; cap. US $0.6m.; Dir MICHEL SOBGUI.

Trade and Industry

GOVERNMENT AGENCIES

Agência Nacional do Petróleo de São Tomé e Príncipe (ANP—STP): Av. Nações Unidas, CP 1048, São Tomé; tel. 226940; fax 226937; e-mail anp_geral@cstome.net; internet www.anp-stp.gov.st; f. 2004; manages and implements govt policies relating to the petroleum sector; Exec. Dir LUÍS PRAZERES.

Nigeria-São Tomé and Príncipe Joint Development Authority (JDA): Plot 1101, Aminu Kano Cres., Wuse II, Abuja, Nigeria; Praça da UCCLA, São Tomé; tel. (234) 95241069; fax (234) 95241061; e-mail enquiries@nigeriasaotomejda.com; internet www.nigeriasaotomejda.com; f. 2002; manages development of petroleum and gas resources in Joint Development Zone; Chair. and Exec. Dir ADO YAKUBA WANKA.

DEVELOPMENT ORGANIZATION

Instituto para o Desenvolvimento Económico e Social (INDES): Travessa do Pelourinho, CP 408, São Tomé; tel. 222491; fax 221931; e-mail indes@cstome.net; f. 1989 as Fundo Social e de Infrastructuras; adopted present name 1994; channels foreign funds to local economy; Dir HOMERO JERÓNIMO SALVATERRA.

CHAMBER OF COMMERCE

Câmara do Comércio, Indústria, Agricultura e Serviços (CCIAS): Av. Marginal de 12 de Julho, CP 527, São Tomé; tel. 222723; fax 221409; e-mail ccias@cstome.net; Pres. ABÍLIO AFONSO HENRIQUES.

UTILITIES

Electricity and Water

Empresa de Água e Electricidade (EMAE): Av. Água Grande, CP 46, São Tomé; tel. 222096; fax 222488; e-mail emae@cstome.net; f. 1979; Synergie Investments (UK); state electricity and water co; privatized in 2004; Dir JÚLIO SILVA.

TRADE UNIONS

Federação Nacional dos Pequenos Agricoltores (FENAPA): Rua Barão de Agua Izé, São Tomé; tel. 224741; Pres. TEODORICO CAMPOS.

Organização Nacional de Trabalhadores de São Tomé e Príncipe (ONTSTP): Rua Cabo Verde, São Tomé; tel. 222431; e-mail ontstpdis@cstome.net; Sec.-Gen. JOÃO TAVARES.

Sindicato de Jornalistas de São Tomé e Príncipe (SJS): São Tomé; Pres. AMBRÓSIO QUARESMA.

Sindicato dos Trabalhadores do Estado (STE): São Tomé; Sec.-Gen. AURÉLIO SILVA.

União Geral dos Trabalhadores de São Tomé e Príncipe (UGSTP): Av. Kwame Nkrumah, São Tomé; tel. 222443; e-mail ugtdis@cstome.net; Sec.-Gen. COSTA CARLOS.

Transport

RAILWAYS

There are no railways in São Tomé and Príncipe.

ROADS

In 1999 there were an estimated 320 km of roads, of which 218 km were asphalted. In 2005 the European Union granted €930,000 towards upgrading the road network.

SHIPPING

The principal ports are at São Tomé city and at Neves on São Tomé island. At December 2006 São Tomé and Príncipe's registered merchant fleet comprised 34 vessels, totalling 32,659 grt.

SÃO TOMÉ AND PRÍNCIPE   *Directory*

Companhia Santomense de Navegação, SA (CSN): CP 49, São Tomé; tel. 222657; fax 221311; e-mail csn@setgrcop.com; internet www.navegor.pt; shipping and freight forwarding.

Empresa Nacional de Administração dos Portos (ENAPORT): Largo Alfândega, São Tomé; tel. 221841; fax 224949; e-mail enaport@cstome.net; Dir-Gen. DEODATO RODRIGUES.

Navetur-Navegação e Turismo, Lda: CP 147, Rua Viriato da Cruz, São Tomé; tel. 223781; fax 222122; e-mail navequatur@cstome.net; internet www.navetur-equatour.st.

Transportes e Serviços, Lda (TURIMAR): Rua Patrice Lumumba, CP 48, São Tomé; tel. 221869; fax 222162; e-mail turimar@cstome.net.

CIVIL AVIATION

The international airport is at São Tomé.

Empresa Nacional de Aeroportos e Segurança Aérea (ENASA): Aeroporto, CP 703, São Tomé; tel. 221878; fax 221154; e-mail enasa@cstome.net; Dir JORGE COELHO.

Linhas Aéreas São-tomenses (LAS): Rua Santo António do Príncipe, São Tomé; tel. 227282; fax 227281; e-mail hba.saotome@gmail.com; f. 2002; owned by Aerocontractors, Nigeria; Dir ANTÓNIO AGUIAR.

STP-Airways: Av. Marginal 12 de Julho, São Tomé; tel. 221160; fax 223449; e-mail stp-airways@cstome.net; f. 2006; 35% govt-owned; Dir FELISBERTO NETO.

Tourism

The islands benefit from spectacular mountain scenery, unspoilt beaches and unique species of flora and wildlife. Although still largely undeveloped, tourism is currently the sector of the islands' economy attracting the highest level of foreign investment. However, the high level of rainfall during most of the year limits the duration of the tourist season, and the expense of reaching the islands by air is also an inhibiting factor. There were 10,518 tourist arrivals in 2005, and receipts totalled some US $10m. in 2002.

SAUDI ARABIA

Introductory Survey

Location, Climate, Language, Religion, Flag, Capital

The Kingdom of Saudi Arabia occupies about four-fifths of the Arabian peninsula, in south-western Asia. It is bordered by Jordan, Iraq and Kuwait to the north, by Yemen to the south, by Oman to the south and east, and by Qatar and the United Arab Emirates to the north-east. Saudi Arabia has a long western coastline on the Red Sea, facing Egypt, Sudan and Eritrea, and a shorter coastline (between Kuwait and Qatar) on the Persian (Arabian) Gulf, with the Bahrain archipelago just off shore and Iran on the opposite coast. Much of the country is arid desert, and some places are without rain for years. In summer average temperatures in coastal regions range from 38°C to 49°C, and humidity is high. Temperatures sometimes reach 54°C in the interior. Winters are mild, except in the mountains. Annual rainfall averages between 100 mm and 200 mm in the north, and is even lower in the south. The official language is Arabic, which is spoken by almost all of the population. Except for the expatriate community (estimated to represent some 27% of the total population in 2007), virtually all of the inhabitants are adherents of Islam, the official religion. About 85% of the population are Sunni Muslims, and most of the indigenous inhabitants belong to the strictly orthodox Wahhabi sect. About 15% of the population are Shi'a Muslims, principally in the east of the country. The national flag (proportions 2 by 3) is green and bears, in white, an Arabic inscription ('There is no God but Allah and Muhammad is the Prophet of Allah') above a white sabre. The capital is Riyadh.

Recent History

The whole of the Arabian peninsula became part of Turkey's Ottoman Empire in the 16th century. Under the suzerainty of the Ottoman Sultan, the local tribal rulers enjoyed varying degrees of autonomy. The Wahhabi movement, dedicated to the reform of Islam, was launched in the Najd (Nejd) region of central Arabia in the 18th century. A Wahhabi kingdom, ruled by the House of Sa'ud from its capital at Riyadh, quickly expanded into the Hedjaz region on the west coast of Arabia. In 1890 the rival Rashidi family seized control of Riyadh, but in 1902 a member of the deposed Sa'udi family, Abd al-Aziz ibn Abd ar-Rahman, expelled the Rashidi dynasty and proclaimed himself ruler of Najd. In subsequent years he recovered and consolidated the outlying provinces of the kingdom, defeating Turkish attempts to subjugate him. Having restored the House of Sa'ud as a ruling dynasty, Abd al-Aziz became known as Ibn Sa'ud. In order to strengthen his position, he instituted the formation of Wahhabi colonies, known as Ikhwan ('Brethren'), throughout the territory under his control.

During the First World War, in which Turkey was allied with Germany, the Arabs under Ottoman rule rebelled. In 1915 the United Kingdom signed a treaty of friendship with Ibn Sa'ud, who was then master of central Arabia, securing his co-operation against Turkey. Relations subsequently deteriorated as a result of the British Government's decision to support Hussein ibn Ali, who proclaimed himself King of the Hedjaz in 1916, as its principal ally in Arabia. Hussein was also Sharif of Mecca (the holiest city of Islam), which had been governed since the 11th century by his Hashimi (Hashemite) family, rivals of the House of Sa'ud. At the end of the war, following Turkey's defeat, the Ottoman Empire was dissolved. Continuing his conquests, Ibn Sa'ud successfully campaigned against the rulers of four Arabian states (the Hedjaz, Asir, Hayil and Jauf) between 1919 and 1925. In September 1924 his forces captured Mecca, forcing Hussein to abdicate, and in 1925 they overran the whole of the Hedjaz. In January 1926 Ibn Sa'ud was proclaimed King of the Hedjaz and Sultan of Najd. On 23 September 1932 the dual monarchy ended when the two areas were merged as the unified Kingdom of Saudi Arabia.

Commercially exploitable deposits of petroleum (the basis of Saudi Arabia's modern prosperity) were discovered in the Eastern Province in 1938, and large-scale exploitation of the kingdom's huge reserves of petroleum began after the Second World War. Petroleum royalties were used to develop and modernize the country's infrastructure and services.

Ibn Sa'ud remained in power until his death in November 1953; all subsequent rulers of Saudi Arabia have been sons of his. The kingdom has remained an absolute monarchy and a traditional Islamic society. The King is the supreme religious leader as well as the Head of State, and governs by royal decree. In foreign affairs, Saudi Arabia has historically allied itself with the USA and other Western countries.

Ibn Sa'ud was succeeded by the Crown Prince, Sa'ud ibn Abd al-Aziz. Another of the late King's sons, Faisal ibn Abd al-Aziz, replaced Sa'ud as Crown Prince and Prime Minister. In 1958, bowing to pressure from the royal family, King Sa'ud conferred on Crown Prince Faisal full powers over foreign, internal and economic affairs. In March 1964 King Sa'ud relinquished power to Crown Prince Faisal, and in November was forced by the royal family to abdicate in his favour. The new King Faisal retained the post of Prime Minister, and appointed his halfbrother, Khalid ibn Abd al-Aziz, to be Crown Prince in 1965. In the Six-Day War of June 1967 Saudi Arabian forces collaborated with Iraqi and Jordanian troops in action against Israel. As a result of the Arab–Israeli War of October 1973, Saudi Arabia led a movement by Arab petroleum producers to exert pressure on Western countries by reducing supplies of crude oil.

In March 1975 King Faisal was assassinated by one of his nephews, and was immediately succeeded by Crown Prince Khalid. The new King also became Prime Minister, and appointed his brother, Fahd ibn Abd al-Aziz (Minister of the Interior since 1962), as Crown Prince and First Deputy Prime Minister.

The religious fervour that the Middle East experienced in the wake of the Iranian Revolution also arose in Saudi Arabia in late 1979, when an armed group of about 250 Sunni Muslim extremists attacked and occupied the Grand Mosque in Mecca, the most important centre of pilgrimage for Muslims. There was also a riot by Shi'a Muslims in the Eastern Province. In response to the unrest, Crown Prince Fahd announced in early 1980 that a consultative assembly would be formed to act as an advisory body, although the assembly was not inaugurated until December 1993 (see below).

King Khalid died in June 1982 and was succeeded by Crown Prince Fahd, who, following precedent, became Prime Minister and appointed a half-brother, Abdullah ibn Abd al-Aziz (Commander of the National Guard since 1962), to be Crown Prince and First Deputy Prime Minister.

As a result of its position as the world's leading exporter of petroleum, Saudi Arabia is a dominant member of the Organization of the Petroleum Exporting Countries (OPEC, see p. 373) and one of the most influential countries in the Arab world. In May 1981 the kingdom joined five neighbouring states in establishing the Co-operation Council for the Arab States of the Gulf (the Gulf Co-operation Council—GCC, see p. 219). In August Crown Prince (subsequently King) Fahd announced an eight-point plan for the settlement of the Arab–Israeli conflict. His proposals, by implication, recognized Israel as a legitimate state. At a summit conference of Arab states in September 1982, the so-called 'Fahd Plan' formed the basis of an agreed proposal for the achievement of peace in the Middle East, and during 1983 Saudi Arabia sponsored repeated diplomatic initiatives within the region. In November 1987 Saudi Arabia resumed full diplomatic relations with Egypt. Relations had been severed in 1979, following the signing of the peace treaty between Egypt and Israel.

Relations with Iran, already strained as a result of Saudi Arabia's support for Iraq in the Iran–Iraq War, deteriorated further in July 1987 following fierce clashes between Iranian pilgrims and Saudi security forces during the *Hajj*, in which 402 people, including 275 Iranians, were killed. Mass demonstrations took place in Tehran, where the Saudi Arabian embassy was sacked, and Iranian leaders vowed to avenge the pilgrims' deaths by overthrowing the Saudi ruling family. In March 1988 the Government announced its intention to limit the number of foreign pilgrims during the *Hajj* season by allocating national quotas. Saudi Arabia severed diplomatic relations with Iran, which subsequently refused to send pilgrims on that year's *Hajj*.

In July 1988, after the US Congress had refused to sanction an agreement to supply military equipment to Saudi Arabia (following the delivery of an unspecified number of medium-range missiles from the People's Republic of China to Saudi Arabia earlier that year), the Government signed a large-scale defence procurement agreement with the United Kingdom, which as a result superseded the USA as Saudi Arabia's main supplier of military equipment.

Widely held misgivings regarding national defence capabilities, and fears of Iraqi expansionist policy (a pact of non-aggression was signed with Iraq in March 1989), were exacerbated in August 1990, when Iraq invaded and annexed Kuwait and proceeded to deploy armed forces along the Kuwaiti–Saudi Arabian border. King Fahd requested that US forces be deployed in Saudi Arabia, as part of a multinational force, in order to deter a possible attack by Iraq. The dispatch of US combat troops and aircraft to Saudi Arabia signified the beginning of 'Operation Desert Shield' for the defence of Saudi Arabia, in accordance with Article 51 of the UN Charter. By the beginning of 1991 some 30 countries had contributed ground troops, aircraft and warships to the US-led multinational force based in Saudi Arabia and the Gulf region. The entire Saudi Arabian armed forces (numbering about 67,500 men) were mobilized. In January, following the failure of international diplomatic efforts to secure Iraq's withdrawal from Kuwait, the multinational force launched a military campaign ('Operation Desert Storm') to liberate Kuwait. As part of its response to the initial aerial bombardment, Iraq launched *Scud* missiles against targets in Saudi Arabia. However, fighting on Saudi Arabian territory was confined to a few minor incidents. In February Iraq formally severed diplomatic relations with Saudi Arabia.

Following the liberation of Kuwait in February 1991, the ministers responsible for foreign affairs of the GCC met their Syrian and Egyptian counterparts in Damascus, Syria, in March in order to discuss regional security issues. The formation of an Arab peace-keeping force, comprising mainly Egyptian and Syrian troops, was subsequently announced. In May, however, following the endorsement by the GCC member states of US proposals for an increased Western military presence in the Gulf region, Egypt announced its decision to withdraw all of its forces from the region, casting doubt on the future of joint Arab regional security arrangements. Diplomatic relations between Saudi Arabia and Iran were re-established in March, and Iranian pilgrims resumed attendance of the *Hajj*, their numbers regulated in accordance with the quota system.

In March 1992 King Fahd announced by royal decree the imminent creation of an advisory Consultative Council (Majlis ash-Shoura), with 60 members to be selected by the King every four years. Two further decrees provided for the establishment of regional authorities, and a 'basic law of government', equivalent to a written constitution. In September Sheikh Muhammad al-Jubair, hitherto Minister of Justice, was appointed Chairman of the Majlis. The Majlis was inaugurated by King Fahd at the end of 1993. (Its membership was increased to 90 in July 1997, to 120 in May 2001 and to 150 in April 2005—see below.)

In September 1992 Qatar accused a Saudi force of attacking a Qatari border post, killing two border guards and capturing a third. As a result, Qatar suspended a 1965 border agreement with Saudi Arabia, which had never been fully ratified. In December 1992, following mediation by President Hosni Mubarak of Egypt, the Qatari Amir, Sheikh Khalifa, signed an agreement in Medina with King Fahd to establish a committee to demarcate the disputed border. In June 1999 officials of the two countries met in Riyadh to sign the maps defining their joint border, and a final land and maritime demarcation agreement was signed in Doha, Qatar, in March 2001. The border agreement provided for a joint Saudi-Qatari committee, charged with ensuring full implementation of the 1965 accord. In October 2002 the Saudi ambassador to Qatar returned to Riyadh for unspecified 'consultations', apparently following broadcasts by the Qatari television news channel Al-Jazeera that were deemed to be critical of the Saudi regime. Saudi-Qatar relations were also reported to be strained over competition to influence the USA in its plans to attack the regime of Saddam Hussain in Iraq.

In May 1993 the Saudi authorities disbanded the Committee for the Defence of Legitimate Rights (CDLR), recently established by a group of six prominent Islamist scholars and lawyers. The organization's founders were also dismissed from their positions, and their spokesman, Muhammad al-Masari, was arrested. In April 1994 it was reported that members of the CDLR, including al-Masari (who had recently been released from custody), had relocated their organization to the United Kingdom. In January 1996 the British authorities ordered the deportation of al-Masari to Dominica: prominent British defence and aerospace companies were believed to have exerted pressure on their Government to concede to Saudi Arabia's demands that al-Masari be expelled in order to secure the continuation of lucrative trade agreements with Saudi Arabia. However, the Chief Immigration Adjudicator in the United Kingdom rejected the deportation order, recommending that the Government should reconsider al-Masari's application for political asylum, and in April al-Masari was granted exceptional leave to remain in the United Kingdom for a period of at least four years, although he was not granted asylum.

In September 1994 the CDLR was among organizations to report the arrest of more than 1,000 people, including clerics and academics, most of whom had attended a demonstration in Buraidah, north-west of Riyadh, to protest at the arrest of two religious leaders who had allegedly been agitating for the stricter enforcement of *Shari'a* (Islamic) law. The Government announced in October that 130 of the 157 people arrested in September had since been released. Also in October the King approved the creation of a Higher Council for Islamic Affairs, under the chairmanship of Prince Sultan ibn Abd al-Aziz, the Second Deputy Prime Minister and Minister of Defence and Civil Aviation, in a measure apparently aimed at limiting the influence of militant clerics and at diminishing the authority of the powerful 18-member Council of Ulema (Saudi Arabia's most senior Islamic authority). In mid-1995 King Fahd replaced six of the seven University chancellors and more than one-half of the members of the Council of Ulema, in an attempt to counter the perceived spread of Islamist fundamentalism.

In June 1995 an opposition activist, Abdullah Abd ar-Rahman al-Hudaif, was sentenced to 20 years' imprisonment for his part in an attack on a security officer and for maintaining links with the CDLR in the United Kingdom. In August al-Hudaif was reported to have been executed; no explanation was given for the alteration of his sentence, nor were details of his trial revealed. A further nine opposition activists reportedly received prison sentences ranging from three to 18 years; according to prominent human rights organization Amnesty International, as many as 200 'political suspects' remained in detention in Saudi Arabia.

In August 1995 the King announced the most far-reaching reorganization of the Council of Ministers for two decades, although no changes were made to the portfolios held by members of the royal family. The strategic portfolios of finance and national economy and of petroleum and mineral resources were allocated to younger, though highly experienced, officials.

A Supreme Economic Council, established by royal decree, convened for the first time in October 1997 under the chairmanship of the Crown Prince. A Supreme Petroleum and Minerals Council was established by royal decree in January 2000. In April the Government approved broad guide-lines for the issuing of tourist visas, and the creation of a supreme commission to promote foreign tourism in Saudi Arabia was announced. The Government declared in May that ministers were to lose their right to hold company posts while in office, with the exception of employees of the state-owned Saudi Aramco petroleum corporation. In June the inaugural session was held of the newly formed Royal Family Council, an officially apolitical body to be chaired by Crown Prince Abdullah.

King Fahd announced a restructured 27-member Council of Ministers in April 2003; this was only the third reorganization of the Government in almost 30 years. Reformists were disappointed that most of the key positions were unchanged, and that all the senior ministers belonging to the ruling as-Sa'ud family remained in post.

Following reports in the early part of 2003 that the Saudi Government intended to follow the example of Bahrain and hold elections to the Majlis ash-Shoura in 2005, in October 2003, at a human rights conference in Riyadh, the Government disclosed plans to create municipal councils and hold local elections by October 2004. The news was received with some scepticism among Saudi reformists, who noted that one-half of the councillors would be centrally appointed and that there had been no suggestion in the official announcement that suffrage would be extended to women. The decision by the authorities to introduce a degree of democracy to the kingdom came amid huge pressure both from inside and outside the country to implement social, economic, political and constitutional reforms. In November 2003 King Fahd issued a decree widening the legislative power of the Majlis. Under the new regulations, the Majlis was to be allowed to propose new laws and amendments to existing legislation without first asking permission from the King. In addition, the Council of Ministers was to be obliged to return laws to the Majlis for amendment should there be disagreement on an issue. (Under the previous system, whereby the Majlis was a purely advisory body, the matter would be resolved by the King.) In April 2005 a royal decree increased the membership of the Majlis to 150; the expansion prompted renewed demands for the introduction of a partially elected membership.

In February 2004 a reported 251 *Hajj* pilgrims died and some 244 others were injured in a stampede close to the Jamarat Bridge in Mina, near Mecca. Some 345 pilgrims were killed and a further 289 were injured in another stampede near the foot of the bridge in January 2006. Amid growing concerns among the Saudi authorities about safety during the *Hajj*, it was subsequently announced that the Jamarat Bridge area was scheduled to be restructured by 2009, at a cost of some US $1,400m.

The first stage of the elections for 178 municipal authorities in all 13 of the kingdom's provinces eventually took place on 10 February 2005 in Riyadh, having been postponed from September 2004; disappointingly for reformists, suffrage was not extended to women. In excess of 1,800 candidates stood for the 592 contested seats in the 178 councils; however, reportedly only about one-quarter of eligible voters in the capital had registered for the elections. Some analysts attributed this apathy to public dissatisfaction with the magnitude of the legislative reforms, which were widely seen merely as token measures. The second phase of the elections took place in the Eastern, Aseer, Jazan, Najran and al-Baha provinces on 3 March. According to the local chamber of commerce, only around 12% of the local male population in the Eastern province had registered to vote. The final phase, in the northern border provinces, was held on 21 April. Nationally, Islamist candidates secured a comfortable majority of the council seats. Meanwhile, later in the year women were allowed to campaign openly for elected positions on the 18-member board of the Jeddah Chamber of Commerce and Industry; two women secured seats on the board. In December a female candidate secured an elected position on the 10-member board of the Saudi Engineers' Council.

In May 2005 the increasingly frail King Fahd was declared to have been admitted to hospital in Riyadh suffering from pneumonia. The King died on 1 August and was succeeded by his half-brother, Crown Prince Abdullah, also aged 84, who had been the de facto ruler of the kingdom since King Fahd suffered a stroke in 1995. The Second Deputy Prime Minister, Minister of Defence and Civil Aviation and Inspector General, Prince Sultan, a full brother of King Fahd and also in his eighties, was named as the new Crown Prince. The Council of Ministers remained essentially unchanged; in accordance with the Constitution, King Abdullah assumed the role of Prime Minister and the Crown Prince was appointed Deputy Prime Minister. No replacement was named for the position of Second Deputy Prime Minister, however, which increased the speculation surrounding the succession to the throne after Crown Prince Sultan. Some observers believed that the succession would miss a generation and that one of King Ibn Sa'ud's many grandsons would emerge as a viable heir, but the mostly likely candidate to succeed Sultan, should he become King, remained another of King Fahd's full brothers. In October 2005 it was announced that a National Security Council (NSC), chaired by King Abdullah, was to be established. Among its extensive powers, the NSC was to: have the power to declare states of emergency and war; be given control over diplomatic relations; and be tasked with combating public corruption and mismanagement. Meanwhile, in December the Crown Prince announced that popular elections to the Majlis were not necessary on the basis that its existing members were highly capable; he claimed, however, not to be opposed to legislative elections in principle.

In May 2006 the Ministry of the Interior announced that the authority of the national religious police force—the Commission for the Promotion of Virtue and the Prevention of Vice—was to be reduced: those arrested on suspicion of moral offences were henceforth to be tried by a public prosecutor. On 20 October a constitutional amendment—first proposed by King Abdullah while he was still Crown Prince—was adopted that removed the monarch's power to choose his successor. Following the forthcoming accession to the throne of Crown Prince Sultan, subsequent heirs were to be elected by the Bay'ah Council (comprising senior members of the royal family). In May 2007 the Crown Prince stated that in the future it was intended that one-third of Saudi government posts would be allocated to women. Following Saudi Arabia's accession to the World Trade Organization (WTO, see p. 396) in December 2005 (see below), in early October 2007 King Abdullah issued a royal decree allowing for the creation of a supreme court in Riyadh and special tribunals intended to settle commercial and labour grievances, as well as the introduction of appeal courts in each of the country's 13 regions, which were to be granted the legal authority to overrule the judgments of lower courts. The new Judiciary Law also included provision for the modernization of the judicial system and improved training opportunities for court employees. In early March 2008 the Minister of Commerce and Industry, Dr Hashem ibn Abdullah Yamani, tendered his resignation; he was replaced by Abdullah ibn Ahmad Zainal Alireza shortly afterwards.

Saudi Arabia's human rights record has for many years been the focus of international scrutiny, particularly regarding the use of public beheading in the Saudi judicial system. A report issued by Amnesty International in March 2000 alleged that Saudi Arabia was guilty of widespread human rights abuses, including use of torture and refusal to allow prisoners access to family members and lawyers. A document published by Amnesty International in September accused the Saudi authorities of widespread discrimination against women and cited serious abuses of their human rights, including arbitrary detention and torture. The organization also reiterated its criticism of the Saudi judiciary for failing to conduct trials in compliance with internationally recognized standards. However, it was reported in late 2000 that Saudi Arabia had agreed to sign the UN Convention on the Elimination of All Forms of Discrimination against Women, although it stated that it would lodge reservations regarding any section deemed to contravene *Shari'a* law. In October 2003 Saudi Arabia held its first human rights conference in Riyadh; Western human rights bodies, however, were not invited. Several hundred protesters took part in an illegal demonstration, organized by the British-based Movement for Islamic Reform, outside the conference, demanding widespread reforms including the removal of the House of Sa'ud. Reports indicated that around 150 people were arrested the following day in connection with the demonstration. In January 2005 15 people were sentenced to short prison sentences and 150–200 lashes each after having taken part in an anti-monarchy demonstration in December 2004. In May 2005 three Saudi reformists were sentenced to terms of imprisonment ranging from six to nine years for having called for the establishment of a constitutional monarchy; however, the three dissidents were pardoned in October. In the same month the Government announced the establishment of a human rights watchdog headed by Turki ibn Khalid as-Sudairi, who would be given the equivalent rank to that of a government minister. Nevertheless, pressure for real liberalization, from both inside and outside the administration, was limited. One of the reformists pardoned in October 2005 received a six-month prison sentence in early November 2007, having been convicted of encouraging women to demonstrate against the arrest of their relatives in 2004, as part of a large security operation by the authorities against alleged Islamist militants in the kingdom.

Numerous bombings and terrorist attacks, often targeted against foreign civilians, have taken place in recent years. In November 1995 a car bomb exploded outside the offices of the Saudi Arabian National Guard in Riyadh, which was being used by US civilian contractors to train Saudi personnel. Seven foreign nationals (including five US citizens) were killed in the explosion, responsibility for which was claimed by several organizations, including the Islamic Movement for Change, which earlier in the year had warned that it would initiate attacks if non-Muslim Western forces did not withdraw from the Gulf region. In May 1996 four Saudi nationals were executed, having been convicted of involvement in the attack.

In June 1996 19 US military personnel were killed, and as many as 400 others (including 147 Saudi, 118 Bangladeshi and 109 US citizens) were injured, when an explosive device attached to a petroleum tanker was detonated outside a military housing complex in al-Khobar, near Dhahran. By late 1996 there was speculation that the investigating authorities were holding Saudi Shi'a groups with possible links to Iran responsible for the atrocity, rather than the same Sunni extremist factions that were widely blamed for the November 1995 bombing. The Iranian Government, however, repeatedly denied any involvement in the incident. In March 1997 the Canadian intelligence service announced the detention, in Ottawa, of Hani Abd ar-Rahim as-Sayegh, a Saudi Shi'a Muslim implicated in the al-Khobar attack and who was alleged to have links with the militant Hezbollah. In June as-Sayegh was extradited from Canada to stand trial in the USA, but in September US officials announced that there was insufficient evidence to secure a conviction. Saudi Arabia subsequently applied for as-Sayegh's extradition. In May 1998 Saudi Arabia's Minister of the Interior stated that there was no indication of a foreign role in the bombing, despite continuing US assertions of Iranian involvement. There were reports in June that US investigations into the bombing had collapsed and that the USA had withdrawn the majority of its investigators from Saudi Arabia. In October 1999, however, as-Sayegh was extradited from the USA to Saudi Arabia, shortly after the Saudi Minister of the Interior stated that the country's security services possessed information regarding as-Sayegh's involvement in the attack. Several Saudi nationals were arrested in January 2001 in connection with the bombing. In June US investigators indicted 14 individuals on charges relating to the explosion, although three of them remained at large in June 2002 when the Saudi authorities announced that sentences had been imposed on a number of the detainees. Meanwhile, as-Sayegh remained in custody in Saudi Arabia.

In October 2000 a Saudi Arabian Airlines passenger flight, en route from Jeddah to the United Kingdom and carrying some 40 British citizens, was hijacked by two armed Saudi nationals. The aircraft finally landed in the Iraqi capital, Baghdad, where the hijackers (who were reportedly protesting against human rights abuses in Saudi Arabia and the presence of US and British troops on Saudi territory) were detained by the Iraqi authorities. One British national died and three were injured in November, as a result of two separate car bomb attacks in Riyadh. No group claimed responsibility for the blasts, although they were initially believed to have been perpetrated by militant Islamists in protest at the role of Western states in the Israeli–Palestinian crisis. In December it was reported that a US citizen was among several foreign nationals arrested for questioning in relation to the bombings; Saudi officials suggested that the attacks may not have been politically motivated. A third bomb was detonated in al-Khobar in that month, and was followed by several more attacks throughout 2001. In February four expatriates (three British nationals and a Belgian) were detained by the Saudi authorities. Saudi television subsequently broadcast alleged confessions by the three British men relating to their involvement in the November bomb explosions, an admission punishable by the death penalty. By August three more Britons had been detained and their alleged confessions broadcast on Saudi television. The confessions, however, were later withdrawn amid allegations that the accused had been tortured.

In December 2002 one of four British nationals who had in December 2000 been sentenced to 12 years' imprisonment for the al-Khobar bombing admitted responsibility for the attack as part of a wider bombing campaign, which was said to be related to gang warfare over illegal trade in alcohol. (The man's family claimed that his confession had been extracted under torture and that Islamist dissidents were responsible for the bombings.) Meanwhile, another Briton was detained (but not charged) in November 2002 for the alleged murder of a German national in a car bomb attack in September. A total of six Britons were convicted in connection with the bombing campaign (two were sentenced to death; the remainder were given prison terms, although in February 2003 a report by the Special Rapporteur of the UN Commission on Human Rights on the independence of judges and lawyers, which cited 'substantial procedural irregularities' and noted that the men's descriptions of torture were 'consistent', cast considerable doubt on the validity of their trials. (In May one of the men was released from prison.) In August the six Britons, the Belgian and the British expatriate arrested in November 2002 for the killing of the German national were released, having been granted a royal pardon; the decision was seen as a tacit admission by the authorities that militant Islamists were the more likely perpetrators of the recent wave of bombings. Following the murders of a British defence contractor in February 2003 and of two North Americans in March, fears of intensified attacks against Westerners proved well-founded when a series of co-ordinated suicide attacks devastated an expatriate housing compound in Riyadh on 12 May (see below).

In late 1997, as the crisis developed regarding access to sites in Iraq by weapons inspectors of the UN Special Commission (UNSCOM, see p. 110), Saudi Arabia firmly advocated a diplomatic solution. During February 1998 Saudi officials stated that they would not allow the USA to use Saudi territory as a base for air-strikes against Iraq, although it was later claimed that discreet support had been given which included the use of Saudi bases. In September 2000 Iraq accused Saudi Arabia and Kuwait of inflicting (through the maintenance of the sanctions regime) suffering on the Iraqi population, and alleged that Saudi Arabia was appropriating Iraqi petroleum transported under the oil-for-food programme. Saudi Arabia, encouraged by the mediation of the League of Arab States (the Arab League, see p. 332), indicated at the beginning of 2002 that it was ready for a cautious rapprochement with Iraq. In October the border crossing from Saudi Arabia to Iraq was reopened, providing a fifth land route for Iraqi trade under the UN oil-for-food arrangement. Following the US-led military campaign to remove Saddam Hussain's regime in Iraq in 2003 (see below), Saudi Arabia reopened its embassy in Baghdad in February 2007. (Diplomatic relations between Iraq and Saudi Arabia had been severed in 1991, following Iraq's invasion of Kuwait.) However, relations between the Saudi regime and the Iraqi Government under Shi'a Prime Minister Nuri al-Maliki remained difficult in early 2008.

Relations between Saudi Arabia and Iran, which were particularly strained by suspicions of Iranian involvement in the 1996 al-Khobar bombing (see above), improved considerably following the election of Muhammad Khatami to the Iranian presidency in 1997. Co-operation was notably strengthened following the September 2001 attacks on New York and Washington, DC, for which the USA held the al-Qa'ida (Base) organization of the Saudi-born militant Islamist Osama bin Laden to be principally responsible, as Saudi Arabia and Iran sought to counter the emergence of anti-Islamic sentiment in the West. The election of Mahmoud Ahmadinejad to the Iranian presidency in June 2005, however, proved somewhat damaging to bilateral relations, with the Saudi Government becoming increasingly concerned by what it perceived to be Ahmadinejad's destabilizing effect on the region. However, in January 2007 the two states were reported to be conducting negotiations to seek an end to the political impasse in Lebanon (q.v.). Furthermore, President Ahmadinejad was unexpectedly granted an audience with King Abdullah in Riyadh in March, which was widely seen as an implicit snub by the Saudi monarch of the US policy of exclusion towards Iran. The two leaders concurred that the greatest danger facing Muslims world-wide was the deliberate exacerbation by unnamed aggressors of divisions between the Sunni and Shi'ite factions. However, despite an exchange of public expressions of goodwill between King Abdullah and Ahmadinejad, the visit did not appear to have resulted in the establishment of any joint initiatives.

In December 1994 Yemen accused Saudi Arabia of erecting monitoring posts and constructing roads on Yemeni territory. Relations had been strained as a result of Saudi Arabia's apparent support for secessionist forces in Yemen earlier in the year (q.v.). In January 1995 the two countries failed to renew the 1934 Ta'if agreement (renewable every 20 years), delineating their de facto frontier. Following military clashes between Saudi and Yemeni forces, and intense mediation by Syria, a joint statement was issued in which the two sides undertook to halt all military activity in the disputed border area. In February the Saudi and Yemeni Governments signed a memorandum of understanding that reaffirmed their commitment to the legitimacy of the Ta'if agreement and provided for the establishment of six joint committees to delineate the land and sea borders and to develop economic and commercial ties. The two countries signed a border security agreement in July 1996. In May 1998, however, Saudi Arabia invaded the disputed island of Huraym in the Red Sea and was reported to have sent a memorandum to the UN stating that it did not recognize the 1992 border agreement between Yemen and Oman, claiming that parts of the area involved were Saudi Arabian territory. The Saudi objection to the accord was widely believed to be related to its attempts to gain land access to the Arabian Sea, via a corridor between Yemen and Oman, which it had thus far been denied in its negotiations with Yemen.

Yemen submitted a memorandum to the Arab League in July 1998, refuting the Saudi claim to the land and stating that the Saudi protests contravened the Ta'if agreement signed by that country. Further clashes were reported close to the land and sea border between Yemen and Saudi Arabia in June, and in July three Yemeni troops were killed during fighting with a Saudi border patrol on the disputed island of Duwaima in the Red Sea; Saudi Arabia claimed its actions there were in self-defence and that, under the Ta'if agreement, three-quarters of the island was Saudi territory. In January 2000 both countries denied further reports of armed confrontations in the border area, and a meeting of a joint military committee began in San'a in February. Talks on the border issue continued meanwhile, and in June, during a visit to Saudi Arabia by President Saleh, a final agreement delineating land and sea borders was signed. As part of the accord, which incorporated the 1934 Ta'if agreement and much of the 1995 memorandum of understanding, both sides agreed to promote economic, commercial and cultural relations, and each undertook not to permit on its territory activities against the other by opposition groups. The agreement did not demarcate sections of the eastern border, and in August 2000 three Saudi border guards and one Yemeni soldier were reportedly killed in border clashes. Nevertheless, the first meeting of the Saudi-Yemen Co-operation Council for more than a decade took place in December; a further meeting followed in June 2001. Meanwhile, it was reported that the withdrawal from the border region of troops of both countries, in accordance with the border agreement, was almost complete. However, relations deteriorated again in early 2004 after the Saudi Government began construction of a 'security fence' along the border that risked violating the border demarcation treaty signed in June 2000. The construction of the barrier reflected a profound lack of trust on the part of the Saudi authorities in Yemen's ability to prevent weapons smugglers from infiltrating Saudi territory. In June 2006 the Saudi and Yemeni ministers responsible for internal affairs signed an agreement on the final demarcation of their shared border.

In July 1995 officials from Saudi Arabia and Oman signed documents to demarcate their joint border. In March 1999 Saudi Arabia held talks with Iran in an effort to mediate in its dispute with the United Arab Emirates (UAE) over the Tunb islands. Following a statement by the GCC condemning both Iran's recent military exercises near the islands and its claim to them and emphasizing UAE sovereignty of the islands, the Iranian President cancelled a planned visit to Saudi Arabia (the visit proceeded in May). Saudi Arabia's rapprochement with Iran had resulted in a deterioration in its relations with the UAE, and in March the UAE boycotted a meeting of GCC ministers responsible for petroleum production in protest at Saudi exploration of an oilfield in disputed territory prior to an agreement being reached. In September 2000 the Saudi Government approved an agreement, signed in July, which ended the long-standing dispute with Kuwait regarding their mutual sea border. Final maps delineating that border were signed by officials from both sides in January 2001.

Saudi Arabia severed diplomatic relations with the Taliban regime in Afghanistan in September 2001, in response to the suicide attacks on the mainland USA. Saudi Arabia was only one of three countries (along with Pakistan and the UAE) to have recognized the Taliban administration in Afghanistan. Although the USA's principal suspect in the attacks, Osama bin Laden (who was at that time based in Afghanistan), was born to a wealthy Saudi Arabian family, the Saudi authorities emphasized that bin Laden had been exiled since 1991 and his nationality revoked because of his subversive activities against the royal family. It was later revealed that 15 of the 19 hijackers were also of Saudi descent (although many of the identities were forged or stolen). Visiting Washington shortly after the attacks, Saudi Arabia's Minister of Foreign Affairs stated that he had conveyed to the US Secretary of State, Colin Powell, the support of the Saudi people for efforts to eliminate terrorism. Saudi Arabia also agreed to investigate alleged Saudi funding of bin Laden's al-Qa'ida network, said to be raised through certain charitable organizations and individual donations. However, the Saudi regime, under pressure from internal Islamist groups implacably opposed to the US military presence on Saudi territory and to any military action against another Islamic state, subsequently refused permission for the use of its airbases for military action against Afghanistan (although an air 'command and control' base in the kingdom was made available to support the military operation).

Following the launch of military attacks against Afghanistan by the US-led 'coalition against terror' in October 2001, the USA briefly closed its embassy in Saudi Arabia because of fear of reprisals. Later that month Crown Prince Abdullah accused the US media of conspiring to damage Saudi Arabia's reputation following the publication of articles highly critical of Saudi Arabia's perceived lack of co-operation after the September attacks. Although official statements by the US Administration continued to praise the Saudi regime, rumours of a deterioration in their relationship persisted, and in January 2002 there was speculation that Saudi Arabia was considering demanding the withdrawal of all US forces from its territory. Both Governments denied that a formal request had been issued. In the same month the Saudi authorities asked for the return of all Saudi citizens (reported to number more than 100 detainees), captured in Afghanistan while apparently fighting for the Taliban, who were imprisoned at Camp X-Ray, Guantánamo Bay, Cuba. This request was denied by the US authorities, but in June a delegation of officials of the Saudi Ministries of the Interior and of Foreign Affairs was reported to have been allowed access to the Saudi prisoners.

Relations between Saudi Arabia and the USA were placed under renewed strain in August 2002, after a group representing 900 relatives of victims of the September 2001 attacks filed a civil suit in Washington, DC, against senior Saudi ministers and institutions (and the Government of Sudan) seeking compensation amounting to US $1,000,000m. for their alleged funding of al-Qa'ida activities. Saudi investors reacted angrily to the suit, threatening in response to withdraw from the USA some $750,000m. in Saudi investments. In late 2002 Saudi Arabia was criticized by the USA for ignoring the funding of alleged terrorist organizations by Saudi nationals, and in November US media reports claimed that a charitable donation from the Saudi royal family had assisted two hijackers responsible for the suicide attacks on the USA. The allegations were strenuously denied by the Saudi authorities, and the US Administration was swift to defend the role Saudi Arabia had played in President George W. Bush's 'war on terror'. Nevertheless, it emerged that the US authorities were investigating the affairs of a number of wealthy Saudis in connection with alleged sponsorship of Islamist extremists, including al-Qa'ida. Saudi Arabia countered that it was being unfairly maligned, reiterating that it had begun auditing all charitable organizations operating in the country and that it had frozen three bank accounts allegedly linked to radical Islamist groups. Also in November the Saudi authorities, hitherto reluctant to admit to an al-Qa'ida presence in the country, conceded that some 100 Saudis had been detained under suspicion of involvement with the organization and that a further 700 people had been questioned. The Minister of the Interior, Prince Nayef ibn Abd al-Aziz as-Sa'ud, subsequently confirmed that 90 suspects were referred for trial in February 2003, while 250 people remained under investigation.

Despite the Saudi–US tensions, in September 2002, following intense pressure from the USA and the United Kingdom, the Saudi Minister of Foreign Affairs indicated that Saudi Arabia might be prepared to approve the use of military bases in Saudi Arabia for a future US-led attack on the regime of Saddam Hussain in Iraq. However, he emphasized that Saudi co-operation would only be forthcoming if the Iraqi authorities continued to reject UN resolutions demanding the unconditional return of weapons inspectors to Iraq and if such a military undertaking was to be conducted under UN auspices. It was established in December that the highly equipped Prince Sultan airbase would be made available to the US military, and that, although combat aircraft would not be allowed to fly offensive missions from the base with the primary aim of bombing Iraqi targets, aircraft launched from Iraqi soil would be permitted to open fire or release bombs in self-defence. In January 2003 Saudi Arabia attempted to secure support for a plan to persuade Saddam Hussain to relinquish power and go into exile in order to avert a US-led war to oust his regime. In the following month, however, as conflict appeared increasingly inevitable, the Saudi authorities deployed warships, troops and military helicopters to Kuwait, in order to strengthen the emirate's defences. In late April, after most of the USA's principal military objectives in Iraq had been achieved, it was announced that all but 400 of the 5,000 US military personnel in the country were to be withdrawn from Saudi Arabia by the end of August. Those troops that remained were to assist in training the Saudi armed forces.

On 12 May 2003 suicide bomb attacks on three expatriate residential compounds in Riyadh killed 34 people. The Minister of Foreign Affairs indicated that 19 people, including 17 Saudis, were believed to have been responsible for the attacks. The bombings, widely held to be the work of al-Qa'ida, provoked further US criticism of Saudi security measures, and led to the withdrawal of most of the US diplomats stationed in the kingdom. It emerged after the attacks that the Saudi authorities had made an unsuccessful attempt to apprehend the perpetrators in the week prior to 12 May. The Saudi leadership responded to the bombings by acknowledging more openly that the threat presented by al-Qa'ida was indeed serious and pledged to take effective action against the terrorist network, including those fundamentalist Islamic figures suspected of converting Saudis to al-Qa'ida's cause. In August the Crown Prince announced that the kingdom was engaged in a 'decisive battle' against terrorism, and throughout mid-2003 security forces intensified their campaign against militants, in particular against those linked to the recent suicide bombings.

In total, between 12 May 2003 and late October, at least 600 suspected militant Islamists were arrested, 70–90 of whom were charged, and more than 2,000 people were interrogated. In addition, in June some 1,000 Muslim clergy were suspended and ordered to undergo retraining aimed at eliminating Islamist militancy from the profession. Despite these measures, the terrorist violence reached new levels of intensity from late 2003. On 8 November al-Qa'ida apparently struck again when 17 people were killed and more than 120 others were injured in a suicide attack on a housing complex, mostly populated by Arab expatriates, in Riyadh. At a human rights conference held in Riyadh in October, delegates from the US, German and British embassies had warned that their intelligence agencies had received evidence of a planned terrorist attack on Riyadh's two main skyscrapers; Western governments issued further warnings against non-essential travel to Riyadh later in the same month. In December the Government stated that, according to DNA evidence, two Saudi nationals, both of whom had been pursued by the authorities on security charges, had carried out the 8 November suicide bombing.

On 21 April 2004 a car bomb exploded close to one of the headquarters of Riyadh's security services, killing five people and wounding up to 150. A militant Islamist group called the al-Haramain Brigades (alleged to have links to al-Qa'ida) claimed responsibility for the attack, which was regarded as the first direct assault on the Saudi regime. On 1 May gunmen in the Red Sea port of Yanbu killed at least one Saudi and five Western petroleum industry workers. On 29 May an attack by a minimum of four militants against a compound housing oil workers at al-Khobar resulted in the deaths of three Saudis and 19 expatriate workers. The compound was eventually surrounded by Saudi police, which resulted in a 25-hour siege. Despite an attempt by security forces to storm the compound, three of the attackers managed to escape. It was alleged that the militants had agreed a deal with police officers sympathetic to al-Qa'ida, an accusation that was angrily denied by the Saudi ambassador to the United Kingdom, Prince Turki al-Faisal. On 2 June two of those responsible for the atrocity were reported to have been killed by Saudi forces near Mecca. One of the men was believed to be Abd ar-Rahman Muhammad Yazji, one of the kingdom's most wanted militants. On 23 June, during a public address broadcast on Saudi television, the Crown Prince announced that a dozen named individuals with alleged ties to al-Qa'ida would not face the death penalty should they surrender to the security forces within one month. The Saudi authorities were particularly keen to obtain the surrender of Saleh Muhammad al-Oufi, regarded as the overall leader of al-Qa'ida in the kingdom following the death of Abd al-Aziz al-Muqrin in a police raid in June. It was, however, reported on 1 November that al-Qa'ida had appointed Saud bin Hamoud al-Otaibi as the new leader of its Saudi network; some commentators presumed that this confirmed suspicions that al-Oufi had been killed by security forces in July. In December seven expatriates and five Saudis died when gunmen attacked the US consulate in Jeddah. Significant militant activity and regular reprisals from security forces continued into early 2006, including an attempted suicide bombing on 24 February at the strategically important Abqaiq oil facility, which produces some 4% of the kingdom's petroleum output. Four suspected al-Qa'ida operatives were killed in government reprisals three days later. Meanwhile, in February 2005 the Government launched a national awareness campaign to mobilize people against militant activity.

In June 2006 Saudi security forces killed six suspected members of al-Qa'ida when they raided a property in Riyadh; a seventh suspect was injured in the gun battle, and was arrested at the scene. In the same month Saudi authorities announced that 42 people had been detained on suspicion of involvement in militant Islamism during the previous few months. In August security forces pursued four armed men into a building in the Al-Jamea district of Jeddah; the ensuing siege ended with the surrender and subsequent arrest of the men on the following day. The incident was believed to be connected to the recent arrest of seven suspected militants in the Al-Jawad quarter of Jeddah. Also in August it was announced that the Saudi authorities had released more than 700 alleged al-Qa'ida sympathizers after they underwent a 'correction' programme intended to uproot their belief in Islamist fundamentalism. In October the Deputy Minister of the Interior announced that trials of suspected Islamist militants in Islamic courts had commenced and that many defendants had already been sentenced and 'finished with'; no confirmation or denial was offered as to whether this meant that some had been executed. In February 2007 Saudi security forces detained several people on suspicion of fund-raising on behalf of foreign terrorist organizations, and in April it was reported that a further 172 people had been arrested for allegedly plotting attacks against public figures, oil refineries and military targets in Saudi Arabia and other neighbouring countries. In an effort to ensure that Saudi oil installations were protected from the real threat of potentially devastating terrorist attacks, it was revealed in August that the Government had begun to establish an Industrial Security Force of some 35,000 personnel specifically charged with providing security at the country's petroleum facilities; by mid-November an estimated 9,000 members had been deployed, and a further 8,000 were expected to be deployed each year. In late November the Ministry of the Interior declared that 208 suspected al-Qa'ida-affiliated militants (including a number of other Arab nationals) had been detained in recent months, again for allegedly planning attacks against various Saudi targets. A reported 28 people, most of whom were Saudi citizens, were arrested in late December, on suspicion of preparing terrorist actions in the holy cities of Mecca and Medina during the *Hajj*.

In what was described as a terrorist attack by the Saudi authorities, and the first attack resulting in foreign fatalities since 2004, three French nationals were shot dead near the town of Tabuk reportedly while travelling on a pilgrimage to Mecca in February 2007; a fourth died later in hospital from injuries sustained in the ambush. Meanwhile, in July 2006 Saudi Arabia and France signed an agreement pledging to increase defence co-operation, and officials confirmed that negotiations concerning the possible sale of French military aircraft to the kingdom were in their advanced stages. In August Saudi Arabia reached agreement with the United Kingdom regarding the purchase of 72 *Eurofighter Typhoon* military aircraft as part of efforts to establish 'a greater partnership to modernize the Saudi Arabian armed forces'; the deal was confirmed by the Saudi authorities in mid-September 2007. King Abdullah, accompanied by a large delegation of senior Saudi officials, began a high-profile state visit to the United Kingdom in late October, during which protests were held by those angered at what they deemed to be Saudi Arabia's poor record on human rights and curbing Islamist extremism. Early in the following month King Abdullah undertook a landmark visit to the Vatican City, where he became the first Saudi monarch to hold discussions with a Supreme Pontiff of the Roman Catholic Church; the talks with Pope Benedict XVI were reported to have focused on how to promote peace between Christians, Muslims and Jews worldwide and to achieve a just solution to the Israeli–Palestinian conflict. In March 2008 discussions were said to be ongoing between Saudi and Vatican officials concerning the possibility of the first Catholic church being built in the kingdom.

Although relations remained cool, Saudi Arabia was keen to improve its ties with the USA. On 28 July 2004, during a visit to Jeddah by Secretary of State Powell, Crown Prince Abdullah raised the possibility of Saudi Arabia taking a leading role in the formation of a Muslim security force for Iraq. Meanwhile, Saudi Arabia and Iraq announced that their embassies in

Baghdad and Riyadh, respectively, would be reopened for the first time since 1990. The move attracted predictable criticism from Islamist groups. In mid-2004 the deteriorating domestic security situation reportedly led some US companies to scale back their operations in the kingdom. The December attack by militants on the US consulate in Jeddah led to a further decline in bilateral relations. In February 2006, following the victory of the Islamic Resistance Movement (Hamas) in the Palestinian legislative elections of the previous month, the Saudi Government incurred US displeasure when it refused to support a US-led plan to deny regional aid to the new Hamas-led administration. During 2007 and early 2008 Saudi Arabia continued to play a mediatory role in both the dispute between the rival Palestinian factions Fatah and Hamas—and particularly following Hamas's takeover of the Gaza Strip in mid-June 2007—and the negotiations between the various feuding parties in Lebanon following that country's failure to elect a successor to President Emile Lahoud. Meanwhile, during a visit to Riyadh in November 2006, US Vice-President Dick Cheney was reportedly warned by King Abdullah that the Saudi Government would lend its support to the Sunni Muslims in the event of a US military withdrawal from Iraq; however, the comments were dismissed by the Bush Administration. In the following month Prince Turki al-Faisal, who had been transferred from the United Kingdom to the post of Saudi ambassador to the USA just 15 months previously, abruptly announced his resignation, providing a stark contrast to his immediate predecessor, who had remained in the post for over two decades; the reason behind al-Faisal's decision was uncertain, with some suggesting that it was purely for personal reasons, but others insinuating that it was symptomatic of deteriorating relations between Saudi Arabia and the USA or of divisions within the Saudi royal family concerning foreign policy issues such as Iran and Iraq. During a wider tour of the Middle East by President Bush in mid-January 2008, the US President visited Riyadh, where he reiterated his intention to pursue a controversial arms agreement with the Saudi Government, at an estimated cost of US $20,000m.; the deal formed part of a broader package of US military aid to its allies in the Gulf region, in an effort to counter any increased Iranian military strength. Bush's visit to Riyadh, was marred, however, by Saudi demands that the US Administration hand over to the kingdom 13 of its citizens currently being held in the US detention camp at Guantánamo Bay.

Meanwhile, at a summit meeting of the Arab League Council in March 2003, Libya was strongly critical of Saudi Arabia for hosting US forces on its territory. Relations deteriorated further when, in July 2004, allegations were made in the Saudi-owned pan-Arab daily *al-Sharq al-Aswat* concerning a Libyan plot to assassinate Crown Prince Abdullah. In December Saudi Arabia recalled its ambassador to Tripoli over the alleged conspiracy and expelled the Libyan ambassador to Riyadh, Dr Muhammad Sa'id al-Qashshat, from the kingdom. However, the respective embassies remained open during the dispute, and relations were normalized in late 2005. Al-Qashshat duly resumed his position in Riyadh in January 2006.

In February 2002 Crown Prince Abdullah put forward a proposal, based on the 1981 'Fahd Plan', to end the escalating conflict between Israel and the Palestinians based on the principle of 'land-for-peace'. In return for a collective Arab recognition of the State of Israel, the plan insisted on Israel's complete withdrawal from Arab territories occupied since 1967. The Crown Prince also urged the US Administration to exert pressure on Israel to withdraw its forces from the West Bank. The Saudi peace initiative was unanimously endorsed at a summit conference of the Arab League Council held in March 2002 in Beirut (see the chapter on Lebanon), but was categorically rejected by Israel. During a summit meeting with US President George W. Bush in Crawford, Texas, in late April, Crown Prince Abdullah reiterated his call for the USA to restrain Israel's actions against the Palestinians. Saudi Arabia's accession to the WTO (see p. 396) in December 2005 was expected to lead to a reconsideration of the kingdom's boycott of trade with Israel (in line with the Arab League).

In 2005 relations deteriorated between Saudi Arabia and three of its Gulf neighbours: Bahrain, Oman and the UAE. Bahrain and Oman had signed free trade agreements with the USA in September 2004 and October 2005, respectively, and in April 2006 the UAE was involved in negotiations with a view to signing a similar accord. Saudi Arabia, which argued that the GCC should negotiate a trade deal as a single body, claimed that the agreements contravened the GCC's external tariff treaty. In December relations with the UAE were further strained by a border dispute relating to the Shaybah oilfield in the Rub al-Khali desert region, which dated back to the 1970s and which formed the focal point of discussions between the UAE President, Sheikh Khalifa bin Zayed an-Nahyan, and the Saudi Minister of the Interior, Prince Nayef ibn Abd al-Aziz as-Sa'ud, in June 2006.

King Abdullah visited China in January 2006—the first such visit by a Saudi monarch since the formal establishment of diplomatic relations in 1990—whereupon he signed a bilateral agreement to co-operate in the petroleum and natural gas sectors. With the deterioration in Saudi–US relations, the kingdom was keen to diversify its international trade, and China, as the world's second largest petroleum consumer, was an ideal candidate for partnership. In the same month Abdullah also became the first Saudi monarch to visit India since 1955. In February 2006 a visit to Pakistan further bolstered traditionally strong bilateral relations, with the signing of five agreements aimed at increasing co-operation on the economy, education, investment, science and technology. In April Crown Prince Sultan embarked upon a tour of the Far East, visiting Japan, Singapore and China. This 'look-east' policy, the importance of which the Crown Prince explicitly underlined in early 2006, was adopted principally for economic gain, but it also served as a demonstration of Saudi independence from the USA.

In March 2007 King Abdullah publicly emphasized Saudi opposition to foreign intervention in Iraqi domestic affairs, insisting that Iraq's sovereignty and independence must be safeguarded. Later that month Riyadh hosted the 19th annual summit meeting of the Arab League Council, at which negotiations were dominated by the situations in Iraq and Lebanon and by the Israeli–Palestinian conflict. The Council reaffirmed its endorsement of the 'land-for-peace' offer extended to Israel in 2002, which had been amassing increasing levels of support in the run-up to the summit, and which Israeli Prime Minister Ehud Olmert had conceded might provide an initial basis for the renewal of formal peace discussions with Arab leaders. A proposed military pact to assist the 22 member states to resolve regional conflicts without the need for external intervention was also discussed. Saudi Arabia agreed to participate in the US-sponsored international peace meeting held at Annapolis, Maryland, in late November 2007, at which negotiations towards a resolution of the Israeli–Palestinian conflict were officially relaunched.

Government

Saudi Arabia is an absolute monarchy, with no legislature or political parties. Constitutionally, the King rules in accordance with the *Shari'a*, the sacred law of Islam. He appoints and leads a Council of Ministers, which serves as the instrument of royal authority in both legislative and executive matters. Decisions of the Council are reached by majority vote, but require royal sanction. A Consultative Council (Majlis ash-Shoura) was officially inaugurated in December 1993. Members of the Majlis are chosen by the King. Membership of the Majlis was increased from 60 to 90 in July 1997, to 120 in May 2001 and to 150 in April 2005.

The organs of local government are the General Municipal Councils and the tribal and village councils. A General Municipal Council is established in the towns of Mecca, Medina and Jeddah. Its members are proposed by the inhabitants and must be approved by the King. Functioning concurrently with each General Municipal Council is a General Administration Committee, which investigates ways and means of executing resolutions passed by the Council. Every village and tribe has a council with the power to enforce regulations; it is composed of the presiding sheikh, his legal advisers and two other prominent personages. A system of provincial government was announced in late 1993 by royal decree: this defined the nature of government for 13 newly created regions, as well as the rights and responsibilities of their governors, and appointed councils of prominent citizens for each region to monitor development and advise the government. Each council was to meet four times a year under the chairmanship of a governor, who would be an emir with ministerial rank. A royal decree, issued in April 1994, further divided the 13 regions into 103 governorates. In October 2003 it was announced that new municipal councils, of which one-half of the membership would be elected by universal suffrage and one-half appointed by the central Government, would be introduced. Municipal elections took place in early 2005 (for further details, see Recent History).

Defence

As assessed at November 2007, the active armed forces totalled an estimated 114,500 men: army 75,000, air force 20,000, navy 15,500 (including 3,000 marines); air defence forces 4,000. There were also paramilitary forces totalling more than 15,500 men, which included a frontier force of 10,500 and a 4,500-strong coastguard. There was a National Guard, comprising 75,000 active personnel and 25,000 tribal levies, and an Industrial Security Force, numbering 9,000, which was established in 2007 to protect petroleum and other important installations; the force was to expand by an additional 8,000 personnel each year, until reaching its maximum intended capacity of 35,000. The GCC's Peninsula Shield Force, based in Saudi Arabia, comprised some 9,000 troops in 2006; however, plans by the GCC to expand the force to comprise some 22,000 personnel based in the various member states were under discussion in early 2008. Military service is voluntary. The allocation for defence and security in the budget for 2007 was SR 132,922m.

Economic Affairs

In 2005, according to estimates by the World Bank, Saudi Arabia's gross national income (GNI), measured at average 2003–05 prices, was US $289,194m., equivalent to $12,510 per head (or $16,620 per head on an international purchasing-power parity basis). During 1996–2006, it was estimated, the population increased by an average annual rate of 2.2%, while gross domestic product (GDP) per head increased, in real terms, by an average of 1.0% per year during 1996–2005. Overall GDP increased, in real terms, at an average annual rate of 3.3% in 1996–2005; according to official figures, real GDP increased by 3.2% in 2006 and by a preliminary 3.4% in 2007.

Agriculture (including forestry and fishing) contributed 2.8% of GDP in 2007, according to preliminary figures, and employed 4.0% of the economically active population in 2006, according to ILO. The principal crop is wheat, the production of which depends almost entirely on irrigation. Saudi Arabia has exported a large wheat surplus since the late 1980s; however, the kingdom planned gradually to reduce output of the crop (with production scheduled to cease entirely by 2016), owing to the increasing scarcity of water resources. Sorghum, barley, potatoes, tomatoes, watermelons and dates are also significant crops. Saudi Arabia is self-sufficient in many dairy products, and in eggs and broiler chickens. Agricultural GDP increased by an average of 1.6% per year in 1997–2007; the sector's GDP increased by an estimated 1.0% in 2007.

Industry (including mining, manufacturing, construction and power) provided 65.1% of GDP in 2007, according to preliminary figures, and employed 20.3% of the active labour force in 2006, according to ILO. During 1997–2007, it was estimated, industrial GDP increased at an average annual rate of 3.9%; the sector expanded by 13.2% in 2007.

Mining and quarrying contributed 50.3% of GDP in 2007, according to preliminary figures, but engaged only 1.4% of the employed population in 2006, according to ILO. The sector is dominated by petroleum and natural gas, which provided a preliminary 50.0% of GDP in that year. Saudi Arabia remained the world's largest petroleum producer in 2007, and mineral products provided an estimated 89.3% of total export revenue in 2006. At the end of 2006 Saudi Arabia's proven recoverable reserves of petroleum were 264,300m. barrels, equivalent to 21.9% of the world's proven oil reserves. Crude petroleum production averaged 10.9m. barrels per day (b/d) in 2006. As a member of the Organization of the Petroleum Exporting Countries (OPEC, see p. 373), Saudi Arabia is subject to production quotas agreed by the Organization's Conference. The Ministry of Petroleum and Mineral Resources announced in early 2007 that it planned to increase oil production capacity from 11.3m. b/d to 12.5m. b/d by the end of 2009. It was reported in April 2008 that the Government had no plans significantly to increase capacity beyond this target. Observers conjectured that Saudi Arabia was not providing accurate information pertaining to its recoverable reserves and, moreover, that the country might not possess sufficient petroleum to meet demand in the long term. Gas reserves, mostly associated with petroleum, totalled 7,070,000m. cu m at the end of 2006. In 2002 the world's largest natural gas plant was opened at Hawiya; the plant, which was the first Saudi project to produce gas not associated with petroleum, was expected to increase the country's production of gas by more than 30%. Further non-associated gas reserves are yet to be fully exploited. Other minerals produced include limestone, gypsum, marble, clay and salt, while there are substantial deposits of phosphates, bauxite, gold and other metals. The GDP of the mining sector increased at an average annual rate of 1.7% in 1997–2007; the rate of growth was an estimated 0.2% in 2007.

Manufacturing contributed 9.5% of GDP in 2007, according to preliminary figures, and provided 6.7% of employment in 2006, according to ILO. The most important activity is the refining of petroleum, which contributed a preliminary 3.2% of GDP in 2007. The production of petrochemicals, fertilizers, construction materials (particularly steel and cement), and food- and drink-processing are also important activities. Manufacturing GDP increased by an estimated average of 1.7% per year in 1997–2007; the GDP of the sector increased by just 0.2% in 2007.

Electrical energy is generated by thermal power stations, using Saudi Arabia's own petroleum resources, although an increasing amount of electricity is now produced in association with sea-water desalination. Electricity expansion projects were planned in the early part of the 21st century to satisfy increased demand.

The services sector contributed 32.1% of GDP in 2007, according to preliminary figures, and engaged 75.6% of the employed labour force in 2006, according to ILO. The GDP of the services sector increased by an estimated average of 3.6% per year in 1997–2007; the rate of growth was 5.5% in 2004.

In 2006 Saudi Arabia recorded a visible trade surplus of US $147,391m., and a surplus of $99,066m. on the current account of the balance of payments. In 2007 the principal source of imports (13.6%) was the USA; other important suppliers were the People's Republic of China, Germany and Japan. Japan was the principal market for exports (16.5%) in 2006; other major markets in that year were the USA, the Republic of Korea (South Korea), China and India. In 2006 the dominant exports were mineral products, chemicals products and plastic products. According to provisional figures, the principal imports in 2007 were electrical machines, equipment and tools; transport equipment and spare parts; base metals and metal products; and chemical products.

A budgetary surplus of SR 55,000m. was forecast for 2006; however, revised figures indicated a surplus of SR 280,360m. A smaller budget surplus, of SR 20,000m., was forecast for 2007. Consumer prices increased by an annual average of 0.4% in 1997–2007, and by 4.1% in 2007. Unemployment was estimated to stand at around 20% of Saudi nationals in 2005; the rate was reported to be higher among the female population. However, ILO figures indicated an unemployment rate of 6.3% in 2006. In 2001 non-Saudi nationals comprised 52.1% of the labour force, although the *Middle East Economic Digest* indicated that the total was 65.4% in 2002. The Government approved legislation in 2005 to reduce the number of foreign workers to 20% of the population by 2015; the new law was also to provide maternity-leave rights and childcare facilities, in order to boost female participation in the work-force.

In addition to its membership of OPEC, Saudi Arabia is a member of the Islamic Development Bank (see p. 329), and the Organization of Arab Petroleum Exporting Countries (OAPEC, see p. 366). Saudi Arabia is the major aid donor in the region, disbursing loans to developing countries through the Arab Fund for Economic and Social Development (AFESD, see p. 174), the Arab Bank for Economic Development in Africa (BADEA, see p. 333) and other organizations. The kingdom acceded to the World Trade Organization (WTO, see p. 396) in December 2005. Saudi Arabia is also a member of the Co-operation Council for the Arab States of the Gulf (GCC, see p. 219), which created a unified regional customs tariff in January 2003 and agreed to establish a single market and currency no later than January 2010. The economic convergence criteria for the proposed monetary union were agreed at a heads of state meeting in Abu Dhabi, the UAE, in December 2005, and in January 2008 the GCC launched its common market.

Saudi Arabia's prosperity is based on exploitation of its petroleum reserves. Although the country remained the world's largest oil producer at the beginning of the 21st century, and continued to play a crucial role in determining OPEC production levels and thus world prices, the decline in the price of petroleum in the early 1990s caused the Government to seek alternative sources of revenue. Since 2000 the Saudi authorities have aimed to increase private investment and growth in the private and non-oil sectors, and sought to expand employment opportunities for the rapidly expanding Saudi population. The Manpower Development Fund was launched in April 2002 to promote the 'Saudiization' of the work-force, and the Eighth Five-Year Development Plan (for the period 2005–09) aimed to increase the participation of Saudi women in the labour force. As part of a process of structural and administrative reform, two new policy-making bodies, the Supreme Economic Council and the Supreme Petroleum and Minerals Council, have been established (the latter accompanied by the creation of the Saudi Electricity Company), and, as part of the deregulation process, two independent supervisory authorities for the electricity and telecommunications sectors were created in 2001. In addition to the liberalization of the telecommunications sector in 2004, plans to deregulate the water sector and to introduce elements of competition into the reorganized electricity industry were in progress in 2007. Tourism, regarded as hugely underdeveloped in the kingdom, was another sector that the authorities sought to stimulate. To this end, a Supreme Commission for Tourism was established in 2001 with the primary aim of increasing the number of visitors to the kingdom to 21m. by 2020. Plans for the construction of the new King Abdullah Economic City, situated on the west coast between Jeddah and Rabigh, were significantly expanded in late 2006; the project was expected to cost up to US $50,000m. A further five 'economic cities' were planned for other regions of the kingdom, as its huge petroleum revenues were utilized to increase private sector growth, establish new industries and create jobs. However, economic diversification was likely significantly to increase domestic energy demand, which—given the growing reliance on petroleum for generating electricity—would diminish resources available for export. In 2007 the US Energy Information Administration projected that, by 2020, one-third of oil produced in Saudi Arabia would be used domestically. None the less, there has been a strategic shift within the petroleum sector towards production of heavy crude oil as global demand increases. Despite output being negligible in late 2006, officials at the state-owned oil firm Saudi Aramco projected heavy crude oil production of 1.05m. b/d by 2010. Rising international prices for petroleum have greatly improved government revenues in recent years, and large fiscal deficits were recorded in 2006–07. The 2008 budget assumed that prices would remain high, and capital expenditure was scheduled to increase by 17.5% in that year owing to a number of outstanding infrastructure projects. Inflation rose sharply in 2007 (see above), reflecting the global food shortage. In its eagerness to appease the sizeable (and relatively mobile) expatriate population, as well as to provide for low-income households, the Government increased subsidies on a number of essential agricultural goods, including rice, barley and maize.

Education

Elementary, secondary and higher education are available free of charge, but education is not compulsory. Primary education begins at six years of age and lasts for six years. From the age of 12 there are three years of intermediate education, followed by three years of secondary schooling. According to UNESCO estimates, primary enrolment was equivalent to 90.7% of pupils in the relevant age-group in 2004/05; the comparable ratio at the secondary level was 87.6%. The proportion of females enrolled in Saudi Arabian schools increased from 25% of the total number of pupils in 1970 to 47.7% in 2004. In 2005 the Ministry of Education introduced a new 'open school' system offering greater flexibility to students, who were henceforth able to select the subjects they studied and to devise their own class schedules. Only a few schools were invited to adopt the new system in its first year; however, following the success of its implementation, the Ministry of Education was reported to be considering an expansion of the system to incorporate a greater number of schools. In 2004 573,736 students were enrolled in higher education. In 2006 the number of new students admitted to universities increased to about 110,000, compared with 68,000 in 2003. Tertiary institutions in 2006 included 110 university colleges and 87 colleges exclusively for women. Construction of the first private university, King Faisaliyah University, in partnership with a US technology institute, commenced in 2006. Education was reportedly allocated 24.5% of total expenditure in the 2006 budget, equivalent to SR 87,300m.

Public Holidays

2008: 23 September (National Day), 26 September–6 October* (Id al-Fitr, end of Ramadan), 5–13 December* (Id al-Adha, Feast of the Sacrifice).

2009: 15–25 September* (Id al-Fitr, end of Ramadan), 23 September (National Day), 23 November–1 December* (Id al-Adha, Feast of the Sacrifice).

* These holidays are dependent on the Islamic lunar calendar and may vary by one or two days from the dates given.

Weights and Measures

The metric system is in force.

SAUDI ARABIA

Statistical Survey

Sources (unless otherwise indicated): Central Department of Statistics, Ministry of Economy and Planning, POB 358, University St, Riyadh 11182; tel. (1) 401-3333; fax (1) 401-9300; e-mail info@cds.gov.sa; internet www.cdsi.gov.sa; Saudi Arabian Monetary Agency, *Annual Report* and *Statistical Summary*.

Area and Population

AREA, POPULATION AND DENSITY

Area (sq km)	2,240,000*
Population (census results)	
27 September 1992	16,948,388†
15 September 2004	
Males	12,557,240
Females	10,121,022
Total	22,678,262
Population (official estimates at mid-year)	
2005	23,118,994
2006	23,678,849
2007	24,242,578‡
Density (per sq km) at mid-2007	10.6

* 864,869 sq miles.

† Of the total population at the 1992 census, 12,310,053 (males 6,215,793, females 6,094,260) were nationals of Saudi Arabia, while 4,638,335 (males 3,264,180, females 1,374,155) were foreign nationals.

‡ Comprising an estimated 17,691,336 Saudi nationals and 6,551,242 foreign nationals.

Saudi Arabia-Iraq Neutral Zone: The Najdi (Saudi Arabian) frontier with Iraq was defined in the Treaty of Mohammara in May 1922. Later a Neutral Zone of 7,044 sq km was established adjacent to the western tip of the Kuwait frontier. No military or permanent buildings were to be erected in the zone and the nomads of both countries were to have unimpeded access to its pastures and wells. A further agreement concerning the administration of this zone was signed between Iraq and Saudi Arabia in May 1938. In July 1975 Iraq and Saudi Arabia signed an agreement providing for an equal division of the diamond-shaped zone between the two countries, with the border following a straight line through the zone.

Saudi Arabia-Kuwait Neutral Zone: A Convention signed at Uqair in December 1922 fixed the Najdi (Saudi Arabian) boundary with Kuwait. The Convention also established a Neutral Zone of 5,770 sq km immediately to the south of Kuwait in which Saudi Arabia and Kuwait held equal rights. The final agreement on this matter was signed in 1963. Since 1966 the Neutral Zone, or Partitioned Zone as it is sometimes known, has been divided between the two countries and each administers its own half, in practice as an integral part of the State. However, the petroleum deposits in the Zone remain undivided and production from the onshore oil concessions in the Zone is shared equally between the two states' concessionaires.

ADMINISTRATIVE REGIONS
(demographic survey for 2007)*

Riyadh	5,835,613	Ha'il	551,523
Makkah	6,097,077	Northern Borders	294,896
Al-Madinah	1,614,644	Jazan	1,253,089
Qassim	1,077,068	Najran	449,186
Eastern	3,545,644	Al-Baha	387,717
Aseer	1,756,625	Al-Jouf	382,070
Tabouk	735,682	**Total**	**23,980,834**

* Islamic year AH 1428, which corresponds to the period 20 January 2007 to 9 January 2008 in the Gregorian calendar.

PRINCIPAL TOWNS
(population at 1992 census)

Riyadh (royal capital)	2,776,096	Khamis-Mushait	217,870
Jeddah (administrative capital)	2,046,251	Ha'il (Hayil)	176,757
Makkah (Mecca)	965,697	Al-Kharj	152,071
Al-Madinah (Medina)	608,295	Al-Khubar	141,683
Dammam	482,321	Jubail	140,828
At-Ta'if	416,121	Hafar al-Batin	137,793
Tabouk	292,555	Yanbu	119,819
Buraidah	248,636	Abha	112,316
Hufuf	225,847	Ar Ar	108,055
Al-Mobarraz	219,123	Al-Qatif	98,920

Mid-2007 ('000, incl. suburbs, UN estimates): Riyadh 4,465; Jeddah 3,012; Mecca 1,385; Medina 1,010; Dammam 822 (Source: UN, *World Urbanization Prospects: The 2007 Revision*).

BIRTHS AND DEATHS
(UN estimates, annual averages)

	1990–95	1995–2000	2000–05
Birth rate (per 1,000)	33.5	29.5	26.5
Death rate (per 1,000)	4.6	4.0	3.8

Source: UN, *World Population Prospects: The 2006 Revision*.

Expectation of life (years at birth, WHO estimates): 70.6 (males 68.4; females 73.6) in 2005 (Source: WHO, *World Health Statistics*).

ECONOMICALLY ACTIVE POPULATION
(persons aged 15 years and over, April)

	2006
Agriculture, hunting, forestry and fishing	299,494
Mining and quarrying	102,178
Manufacturing	505,107
Electricity, gas and water	79,466
Construction	836,898
Wholesale and retail trade	1,210,079
Restaurants and hotels	241,378
Transport and communications	291,290
Financial intermediation	86,571
Real estate, renting and business activities	252,603
Public administration and defence	1,425,995
Education	907,173
Health and social work	325,494
Other community and personal services	169,152
Private households with employed persons	781,540
Extra-territorial organizations	8,566
Total employed	**7,522,984**
Unemployed	501,898
Total labour force	**8,024,882**

Source: ILO.

SAUDI ARABIA

Health and Welfare

KEY INDICATORS

Total fertility rate (children per woman, 2005)	3.8
Under-5 mortality rate (per 1,000 live births, 2005)	26
Physicians (per 1,000 head, 2004)	1.37
Hospital beds (per 1,000 head, 2004)	2.30
Health expenditure (2004): US $ per head (PPP)	601.1
Health expenditure (2004): % of GDP	3.9
Health expenditure (2004): public (% of total)	76.5
Access to water (% of persons, 2002)	90
Human Development Index (2005): ranking	61
Human Development Index (2005): value	0.812

For sources and definitions, see explanatory note on p. vi.

Agriculture

PRINCIPAL CROPS
('000 metric tons)

	2004	2005	2006*
Wheat	2,776	2,648	2,400
Barley	67	47	138
Maize	54	91	91
Millet	9	7	8
Sorghum	284	205	244
Potatoes	387	441	441
Tomatoes	480	496	496
Pumpkins, squash and gourds	127	135	135
Cucumbers and gherkins	217	212	212
Aubergines (Eggplants)	72	74	74
Dry onions	92	73	73
Carrots	65	56	56
Okra	52	46	46
Watermelons	331	364	364
Cantaloupes and other melons	246	230*	230
Grapes	114	132	132
Dates	941	970	970

* FAO estimate(s).

Aggregate production ('000 metric tons, may include official, semi-official or estimated data): Total cereals 3,189 in 2004, 2,999 in 2005, 2,881 in 2006; Total roots and tubers 387 in 2004, 441 in 2005, 441 in 2006; Total vegetables (incl. melons) 2,081 in 2004, 2,084 in 2005, 2,084 in 2006; Total fruits (excl. melons) 1,408 in 2004, 1,458 in 2005, 1,458 in 2006.

Source: FAO.

LIVESTOCK
('000 head, year ending September)

	2003	2004	2005
Asses, mules or hinnies*	100	100	100
Camels*	260	260	260
Cattle	332	342	352
Sheep*	7,000	7,000	7,000
Goats*	2,200	2,200	2,200
Chickens*	135,000	137,000	141,000

* FAO estimates.

2006: Figures assumed to be unchanged from 2005 (FAO estimates).

Source: FAO.

LIVESTOCK PRODUCTS
('000 metric tons)

	2004	2005	2006*
Cattle meat	22.2	22.4	22.4
Sheep meat*	76.0	76.0	76.0
Goat meat*	22.5	22.5	22.5
Chicken meat	528.0†	544.5†	544.5
Camel meat	42.0	41.1	41.1
Cows' milk*	900.0	n.a.	940.0
Sheep's milk*	82.5	82.5	82.5
Goats' milk*	76.5	76.5	76.5
Camels' milk*	90.0	90.0	90.0
Hen eggs	140.0	143.0*	143.0
Wool: greasy*	10.8	10.8	10.8

* FAO estimate(s).
† Unofficial figure(s).

Source: FAO.

Fishing

(metric tons, live weight)

	2003	2004	2005
Capture	55,440	55,418	60,403
Groupers and seabasses	1,229	1,936	5,413
Pink ear emperors	2,526	2,238	n.a.
Emperors (Scavengers)	4,260	4,459	8,546
Spinefeet (Rabbitfishes)	2,151	2,276	2,402
Narrow-barred Spanish mackerel	6,023	5,365	5,547
Indian mackerel	3,297	3,111	3,003
Green tiger prawns	4,487	6,568	n.a.
Aquaculture	11,824	11,172	14,375*
Nile tilapia	2,400	2,276	2,700*
Indian white prawn	9,160	8,705	11,259
Total catch	67,264	66,590	74,778*

* FAO estimate.

Source: FAO.

Mining

('000 metric tons, unless otherwise indicated)

	2004	2005	2006
Crude petroleum (million barrels)*	3,151	3,309	3,253†
Natural gas (million cu metres)*‡	68,000	68,547	70,878†
Silver (kilograms)§	14,494	13,501	9,100
Gold (kilograms)§	8,268	7,456	5,180†
Salt (unrefined)	1,530	1,738	1,752†
Gypsum (crude)	641	713	2,200†
Pozzolan	320	372	400†

* Including 50% of the total output of the Neutral or Partitioned Zone, shared with Kuwait.
† Preliminary.
‡ On a dry basis.
§ Figures refer to the metal content of concentrate and bullion.

Source: US Geological Survey.

SAUDI ARABIA   Statistical Survey

Industry

SELECTED PRODUCTS
(including 50% of the total output of the Neutral Zone; estimates, '000 barrels, unless otherwise indicated)

	2004	2005	2006
Phosphatic fertilizers ('000 metric tons)*†	295	300	300
Nitrogenous fertilizers‡	1,242	n.a.	n.a.
Motor spirit (petrol) and naphtha	198,570	198,870	186,420†
Jet fuel and kerosene	66,980	80,910	77,330†
Gas-diesel (distillate fuel) oils	234,890	236,370	241,790†
Residual fuel oils	172,790	177,970	181,000†
Petroleum bitumen (asphalt)	10,000	n.a.	n.a.
Liquefied petroleum gas	13,400	12,740	14,730†
Cement ('000 metric tons)	25,370	26,064	27,055†
Crude steel ('000 metric tons)	3,902	4,185	4,000†
Electric energy (million kWh)	145,385	153,283	163,151

* Production in terms of phosphoric acid.
† Estimate(s).
‡ Production in terms of nitrogen.

2007: Electric energy (million kWh) 169,303.

Source: mainly US Geological Survey.

Finance

CURRENCY AND EXCHANGE RATES

Monetary Units
100 halalah = 20 qurush = 1 Saudi riyal (SR).

Sterling, Dollar and Euro Equivalents (31 December 2007)
£1 sterling = 7.503 riyals;
US $1 = 3.745 riyals;
€1 = 5.513 riyals;
100 Saudi riyals = £13.33 = $26.70 = €18.39.

Exchange Rate: Since June 1986 the official mid-point rate has been fixed at US $1 = 3.75 riyals.

BUDGET ESTIMATES
(million riyals)

Revenue	2005	2006	2007
Petroleum revenues	220,000	320,000	330,000
Other revenues	60,000	70,000	70,000
Total	280,000	390,000	400,000

Expenditure	2005	2006	2007
Human resource development	69,899	87,164	96,483
Transport and communications	8,629	9,804	11,329
Economic resource development	10,516	12,454	13,902
Health and social development	23,057	26,798	31,010
Infrastructure development	3,292	4,555	5,188
Municipal services	8,976	11,588	13,576
Defence and security	95,146	110,779	132,922
Public administration and other government spending	51,665	62,814	61,756
Government lending institutions*	502	575	1,026
Local subsidies	8,318	8,469	12,808
Total	280,000	335,000	380,000

* Including transfers to the Saudi Fund for Development (SFD).

2004 (revised figures, million riyals): Total revenue 392,291 (Petroleum revenue 330,000, Other revenue 62,291); Total expenditure 285,200.

2005 (revised figures, million riyals): Total revenue 564,335 (Petroleum revenue 504,540, Other revenue 59,795); Total expenditure 346,474.

2006 (revised figures, million riyals): Total revenue 673,682 (Petroleum revenue 604,470, Other revenue 69,212); Total expenditure 393,322.

INTERNATIONAL RESERVES
(US $ million in December)

	2005	2006	2007
Gold*	230	242	254
IMF special drawing rights	550	640	721
Reserve position in IMF	1,906	912	731
Foreign exchange	24,074	25,971	32,308
Total	26,760	27,765	34,014

* Valued at US $50 per troy ounce at 31 December 2007.

Source: IMF, *International Financial Statistics*.

MONEY SUPPLY
('000 million riyals in December)

	2005	2006	2007
Currency outside banks	64.29	69.32	72.19
Demand deposits at commercial banks	220.28	243.62	311.92
Total money	284.57	312.94	384.11

Source: IMF, *International Financial Statistics*.

COST OF LIVING
(Consumer Price Index for all cities; base: 1999 = 100)

	2005	2006	2007
Food and beverages	106.5	112.2	120.1
Housing, fuel and water	100.0	101.0	109.2
Textiles and clothing (incl. footwear)	88.3	87.7	85.6
House furnishing	94.9	95.2	96.4
Medical care	101.4	102.7	107.0
Transport and communications	91.8	89.9	88.1
Entertainment and education	98.4	98.7	98.9
All items (incl. others)	99.6	101.8	106.0

NATIONAL ACCOUNTS

Expenditure on the Gross Domestic Product
(million riyals at current prices)

	2005	2006	2007*
Government final consumption expenditure	262,650	311,082	322,086
Private final consumption expenditure	312,957	354,913	404,574
Increase in stocks	20,055	26,437	25,711
Gross fixed capital formation	195,632	233,065	286,244
Total domestic expenditure	791,294	925,497	1,038,615
Exports of goods and services	719,898	835,122	936,811
Less Imports of goods and services	328,678	425,038	544,879
GDP in purchasers' values	1,182,514	1,335,581	1,430,547
GDP at constant 1999 prices	762,277	786,348	813,005

Gross Domestic Product by Economic Activity
(million riyals at current prices)

	2005	2006	2007*
Agriculture, forestry and fishing	38,280	39,373	40,154
Mining and quarrying:			
crude petroleum and natural gas	567,992	665,278	719,170
other	3,016	3,145	3,292
Manufacturing:			
petroleum refining	39,453	43,710	46,418
other	71,253	80,202	89,818
Electricity, gas and water	11,020	11,664	12,419
Construction	54,946	59,139	65,017
Trade, restaurants and hotels	62,759	67,868	73,990

SAUDI ARABIA

—continued

	2005	2006	2007*
Transport, storage and communications	38,429	41,367	45,087
Finance, insurance, real estate and business services:			
ownership of dwellings	50,012	52,223	54,778
other	47,772	52,575	55,948
Government services	176,350	196,386	200,306
Other community, social and personal services	27,855	29,203	30,631
Sub-total	1,189,137	1,342,133	1,437,028
Import duties	10,115	11,025	11,801
Less Imputed bank service charge	16,739	17,575	18,280
GDP in purchasers' values	1,182,514	1,335,581	1,430,547

*Preliminary figures.

BALANCE OF PAYMENTS
(US $ million)

	2004	2005	2006
Exports of goods f.o.b.	125,998	180,712	211,305
Imports of goods f.o.b.	−41,050	−54,595	−63,914
Trade balance	84,947	126,117	147,391
Exports of services	5,852	6,677	7,297
Imports of services	−25,696	−28,639	−40,552
Balance on goods and services	65,103	104,155	114,136
Other income received	4,278	4,964	10,376
Other income paid	−3,800	−4,963	−9,734
Balance on goods, services and income	65,581	104,156	114,777
Current transfers paid	−13,655	−14,096	−15,711
Current balance	51,926	90,060	99,066
Direct investment from abroad	−334	464	660
Portfolio investment assets	−26,654	−67,420	−78,567
Other investment assets	−21,955	−28,717	−17,664
Other investment liabilities	1,516	5,149	−2,601
Overall balance	4,498	−465	894

Source: IMF, *International Financial Statistics*.

External Trade

PRINCIPAL COMMODITIES
(million riyals)

Imports c.i.f.	2005	2006	2007*
Live animals and animal products	10,614	10,316	11,974
Vegetable products	11,288	12,155	17,765
Prepared foodstuffs, beverages, spirits, vinegar and tobacco	9,653	11,497	12,983
Chemical products	18,208	20,965	25,517
Textiles and textile articles	9,664	10,281	11,640
Base metals and articles of base metal	23,773	38,626	50,829
Electrical machines, equipment and tools	54,168	67,302	99,740
Transport equipment and spare parts	46,704	50,453	59,440
Total (incl. others)	222,985	261,402	338,088

Exports†	2004	2005	2006
Mineral products	415,696	606,371	706,486
Chemical products	18,673	24,329	26,563
Plastic products	12,455	17,726	19,373
Total (incl. others)	472,491	677,144	791,339

*Preliminary figures.
† Including re-exports (million riyals): 9,229 in 2004; 10,773 in 2005; 14,809 in 2006.

PRINCIPAL TRADING PARTNERS
(million riyals)

Imports c.i.f.	2005	2006	2007
Australia	6,270	7,734	7,296
Belgium	3,261	3,376	4,109
Brazil	4,992	5,490	6,564
Canada	1,940	2,563	3,584
China, People's Republic	16,521	22,391	32,664
France	7,687	10,082	11,499
Germany	18,238	21,223	30,022
India	6,884	9,864	11,529
Indonesia	2,030	2,354	3,516
Italy	8,468	10,550	15,381
Japan	20,093	21,146	29,563
Korea, Republic	8,138	9,900	15,162
Malaysia	2,045	2,206	3,225
Netherlands	3,703	3,865	4,552
Spain	2,510	2,880	4,429
Sweden	3,622	4,004	4,768
Switzerland	4,807	4,176	5,318
Syria	1,945	1,724	1,866
Thailand	3,817	4,946	5,582
Turkey	3,139	3,183	4,699
United Arab Emirates	5,862	7,167	8,437
United Kingdom	10,443	10,318	13,170
USA	32,952	37,802	45,852
Total (incl. others)	222,985	261,402	338,088

Exports (incl. re-exports)	2004	2005	2006
Bahrain	11,507	18,637	22,717
China, People's Republic	22,787	40,519	49,556
France	12,335	16,102	15,420
Greece	6,430	8,461	8,758
India	27,625	40,237	48,520
Indonesia	6,871	9,170	11,484
Italy	12,553	20,145	19,359
Japan	67,006	105,580	130,369
Jordan	6,852	10,238	12,148
Korea, Republic	40,382	57,368	72,570
Netherlands	18,216	24,308	24,331
Pakistan	7,979	9,435	11,363
Philippines	5,130	8,544	10,751
Singapore	22,147	35,488	37,405
South Africa	8,876	n.a.	n.a.
Spain	8,382	11,134	13,417
Taiwan	15,396	24,366	29,044
Thailand	8,365	12,016	13,264
United Arab Emirates	12,230	18,027	25,488
United Kingdom	6,353	6,855	3,843
USA	81,360	104,746	119,239
Total (incl. others)	472,491	677,144	791,339

Transport

RAILWAYS
(traffic)

	1999	2000	2001
Passenger journeys ('000)	770.4	853.8	790.4
Freight carried ('000 metric tons)	1,800	1,600	1,500

ROAD TRAFFIC
(motor vehicles in use at 31 December)

	1989	1990	1991
Passenger cars	2,550,465	2,664,028	2,762,132
Buses and coaches	50,856	52,136	54,089
Goods vehicles	2,153,297	2,220,658	2,286,541
Total	4,754,618	4,936,822	5,103,205

1996 (estimates): Passenger cars 1,744,000; Buses and coaches 23,040; Goods vehicles 1,169,000; Total 2,935,000.

Source: IRF, *World Road Statistics*.

SAUDI ARABIA

SHIPPING

Merchant Fleet
(vessels registered at 31 December)

	2004	2005	2006
Oil tankers:			
vessels	30	26	25
displacement ('000 grt)	907	231	153
Others:			
vessels	262	274	279
displacement ('000 grt)	771	797	869
Total vessels	292	300	304
Total displacement ('000 grt)	1,678	1,028	1,022

Source: Lloyd's Register-Fairplay, *World Fleet Statistics*.

International Sea-borne Freight Traffic
('000 metric tons)*

	1988	1989	1990
Goods loaded	161,666	165,989	214,070
Goods unloaded	42,546	42,470	46,437

* Including Saudi Arabia's share of traffic in the Neutral or Partitioned Zone.

Source: UN, *Monthly Bulletin of Statistics*.

2001 ('000 metric tons, excluding crude oil): Goods loaded 68,894; Goods unloaded 31,668.

CIVIL AVIATION
(traffic on scheduled services)

	2001	2002	2003
Kilometres flown (million)	126	124	125
Passengers carried ('000)	12,836	13,564	13,822
Passenger-kilometres (million)	20,217	20,804	20,801
Total ton-km (million)	2,633	2,748	2,739

Source: UN, *Statistical Yearbook*.

2004 (Saudi Arabian airlines): Passengers carried ('000) 15,800; Number of flights 127,798; Cargo carried ('000 metric tons) 293.

2005 (Saudi Arabian airlines): Passengers carried ('000) 16,900; Number of flights 130,942; Cargo carried ('000 metric tons) 295.

2006 (Saudi Arabian airlines): Passengers carried ('000) 17,800; Number of flights 141,964; Cargo carried ('000 metric tons) 296.

Tourism

Country of nationality	2003	2004	2005
Bahrain	281,875	277,618	356,163
Bangladesh	209,560	255,402	52,633
Egypt	787,277	976,931	799,665
India	362,609	474,467	117,101
Indonesia	396,709	486,869	226,037
Iran	618,897	386,507	519,865
Jordan	240,356	306,495	279,288
Kuwait	971,341	1,238,382	1,462,879
Pakistan	539,471	654,059	351,672
Qatar	388,239	434,944	511,143
Sudan	108,742	157,548	130,098
Syria	541,894	726,752	576,950
Turkey	177,467	236,267	100,167
United Arab Emirates	189,471	238,536	1,043,076
Yemen	212,292	220,759	261,520
Total (incl. others)	7,332,233	8,599,430	8,036,613

Tourism receipts (US $ million, incl. passenger transport): 3,418 in 2003; 6,486 in 2004; 5,181 in 2005.

Source: World Tourism Organization.

PILGRIMS TO MECCA FROM ABROAD*

	2003/04	2004/05	2005/06
Total	1,419,706	1,534,769	1,557,447

* Figures relate to Islamic lunar years. The equivalent dates in the Gregorian calendar are: 5 March 2003 to 21 February 2004; 22 February 2004 to 9 February 2005; 10 February 2005 to 30 January 2006.

Communications Media

	2004	2005	2006
Telephones ('000 main lines in use)	3,695.1	3,844.0	3,951.0
Mobile cellular telephones ('000 subscribers)	9,175.8	14,164.2	19,662.6
Personal computers ('000 in use)	8,476	8,476	n.a.
Internet users ('000)	2,360.0	3,000.0	4,700.0
Broadband subscribers ('000)	68.7	67.8	218.2

1995 (estimate): 150,000 facsimile machines in use.

1996: 13 daily newspapers; 185 non-daily newspapers.

1997: 6,250,000 radio receivers in use; Book titles published 3,780.

Sources: UNESCO, *Statistical Yearbook*; International Telecommunication Union.

Education

(2005, unless otherwise indicated)

	Institutions	Teachers	Students
Pre-primary*	893	7,703	85,484
Primary	13,163	213,355	2,417,811
Intermediate	7,086	104,675	1,071,747
Secondary (general)	4,215	79,754	954,141
Teacher training†	18	2,215	29,989
Technical and vocational	96	6,375	74,101
University colleges†	108	11,627	211,430

* Figures refer to 1996/97 (Source: UNESCO, *Statistical Yearbook*).
† 2003 figures.

Adult literacy rate (UNESCO estimates): 82.9% (males 87.5%; females 76.3%) in 2004 (Source: UNESCO Institute for Statistics).

Directory

The Constitution

The Basic Law of Government was introduced by royal decree in 1992.

Chapter 1 defines Saudi Arabia as a sovereign Arab, Islamic state. Article 1 defines God's Book and the Sunnah of his prophet as the constitution of Saudi Arabia. The official language is Arabic. The official holidays are Id al-Fitr and Id al-Adha. The calendar is the Hegira calendar.

Chapter 2 concerns the system of government, which is defined as a monarchy, hereditary in the male descendants of Abd al-Aziz ibn Abd ar-Rahman al-Faisal as-Sa'ud. It outlines the duties of the Heir Apparent. The principles of government are justice, consultation and equality in accordance with Islamic law (*Shari'a*).

Chapter 3 concerns the family. The State is to aspire to strengthen family ties and to maintain its Arab and Islamic values. Article 11 states that 'Saudi society will be based on the principle of adherence to God's command, on mutual co-operation in good deeds and piety and mutual support and inseparability'. Education aims to instil the Islamic faith.

Chapter 4 defines the economic principles of the State. All natural resources are the property of the State. The State protects public money and freedom of property. Taxation is only to be imposed on a just basis.

Chapter 5 concerns rights and duties. The State is to protect Islam and to implement the *Shari'a* law. The State protects human rights in accordance with the *Shari'a*. The State is to provide public services and security for all citizens. Punishment is to be in accordance with the *Shari'a*. The Royal Courts are open to all citizens.

Chapter 6 defines the authorities of the State as the judiciary, the executive and the regulatory authority. The judiciary is independent, and acts in accordance with *Shari'a* law. The King is head of the Council of Ministers and Commander-in-Chief of the Armed Forces. The Prime Minister and other ministers are appointed by the King. It provides for the establishment of a Consultative Council (Majlis ash-Shoura).

Chapter 7 concerns financial affairs. It provides for the annual presentation of a state budget. Corporate budgets are subject to the same provisions.

Chapter 8 concerns control bodies. Control bodies will be established to ensure good financial and administrative management of state assets.

Chapter 9 defines the general provisions pertaining to the application of the Basic Law of Government.

The Government

HEAD OF STATE

King: HM King ABDULLAH IBN ABD AL-AZIZ AS-SA'UD (acceded to the throne 1 August 2005).
Crown Prince: SULTAN IBN ABD AL-AZIZ AS-SA'UD.

COUNCIL OF MINISTERS
(April 2008)

Prime Minister and Commander of the National Guard: King ABDULLAH IBN ABD AL-AZIZ AS-SA'UD.
Deputy Prime Minister, Minister of Defence and Civil Aviation and Inspector General: Crown Prince SULTAN IBN ABD AL-AZIZ AS-SA'UD.
Minister of Municipal and Rural Affairs: Prince MUTAIB IBN ABD AL-AZIZ AS-SA'UD.
Minister of the Interior: Prince NAYEF IBN ABD AL-AZIZ AS-SA'UD.
Minister of Foreign Affairs: Prince SA'UD AL-FAISAL AS-SA'UD.
Minister of Petroleum and Mineral Resources: Eng. ALI IBN IBRAHIM AN-NUAIMI.
Minister of Labour: GHAZI AL-GOSAIBI.
Minister of Social Affairs: Dr ABD AL-MOHSEN IBN ABD AL-AZIZ AL-AKKAS.
Minister of Agriculture: Dr FAHD IBN ABD AR-RAHMAN IBN SULAIMAN BALGHUNAIM.
Minister of Water and Electricity: ABDULLAH AL-HUSSEIN.
Minister of Education: Dr ABDULLAH IBN SALIH IBN UBAYD.
Minister of Higher Education: Dr KHALID IBN MUHAMMAD AL-ANGARI.
Minister of Communications and Information Technology: MUHAMMAD IBN JABIL IBN AHMAD MULLA.
Minister of Finance: Dr IBRAHIM IBN ABD AL-AZIZ AL-ASSAF.
Minister of Economy and Planning: KHALED IBN MUHAMMAD AL-QUSAIBI.
Minister of Information and Culture: Dr IYAD IBN AMIN MADANI.
Minister of Commerce and Industry: ABDULLAH IBN AHMAD ZAINAL ALIREZA.
Minister of Justice: Dr ABDULLAH IBN MUHAMMAD IBN IBRAHIM ASH-SHEIKH.
Minister of Pilgrimage (Hajj) Affairs: FOUAD IBN ABD AS-SALAM IBN MUHAMMAD FARSI.
Minister of Awqaf (Religious Endowments), Dawa, Mosques and Guidance Affairs: SALEH IBN ABD AL-AZIZ MUHAMMAD IBN IBRAHIM ASH-SHEIKH.
Minister of Health: Dr HAMAD IBN ABDULLAH AL-MANE.
Minister of the Civil Service: Dr MUHAMMAD IBN ALI AL-FAYEZ.
Minister of Transport: Dr JUBARAH IBN EID AS-SURAISERI.
Ministers of State: Dr MUTLIB IBN ABDULLAH AN-NAFISA, Dr MUSAID IBN MUHAMMAD AL-AYBAN, Dr ABD AL-AZIZ AL-ABDULLAH AL-KHUWAITER, Prince ABD AL-AZIZ IBN FAHD AS-SA'UD, ABDULLAH IBN AHMAD IBN YOUSUF ZAINAL, NIZAR MADANI.

MINISTRIES

Most ministries have regional offices in Jeddah.

Council of Ministers: Murabba, Riyadh 11121; tel. (1) 488-2444.
Ministry of Agriculture: Airport Rd, Riyadh 11195; tel. (1) 401-6666; fax (1) 403-1415; e-mail info@agrwat.gov.sa; internet www.agrwat.gov.sa.
Ministry of Awqaf (Religious Endowments), Dawa, Mosques and Guidance Affairs: Riyadh 11232; tel. (1) 473-0401; internet www.islam.org.sa.
Ministry of the Civil Service: POB 18367, Riyadh 11114; tel. (1) 402-6666; fax (1) 403-5665; e-mail mcswebmaster@mcs.gov.sa; internet www.mcs.gov.sa.
Ministry of Commerce and Industry: POB 1774, Airport Rd, Riyadh 11162; tel. (1) 401-2222; fax (1) 403-8421; e-mail info@commerce.gov.sa; internet www.commerce.gov.sa.
Ministry of Communications and Information Technology: Intercontinental Rd, Riyadh 11112; tel. (1) 463-7225; fax (1) 405-2310.
Ministry of Defence and Civil Aviation: POB 26731, Airport Rd, Riyadh 11165; tel. (1) 478-5900; fax (1) 401-1336.
Ministry of Economy and Planning: POB 358, 44 University St, Riyadh 11182; tel. (1) 404-9212; fax (1) 405-2051; e-mail minister@planning.gov.sa; internet www.mep.gov.sa.
Ministry of Education: POB 3734, Airport Rd, Riyadh 11148; tel. (1) 404-2888; fax (1) 401-2365; e-mail webmaster@moe.gov.sa; internet www.moe.gov.sa.
Ministry of Finance: Airport Rd, Riyadh 11177; tel. (1) 405-0000; fax (1) 405-9202; e-mail info@mof.gov.sa; internet www.mof.gov.sa.
Ministry of Foreign Affairs: POB 55937, Riyadh 11544; tel. (1) 405-5000; fax (1) 403-0645; e-mail admin.dep@mofa.gov.sa; internet www.mofa.gov.sa.
Ministry of Health: Airport Rd, Riyadh 11176; tel. (1) 401-2220; fax (1) 402-9876; e-mail f_otaibi@moh.gov.sa; internet www.moh.gov.sa.
Ministry of Higher Education: King Faisal Hospital St, Riyadh 11153; tel. (1) 464-4444; fax (1) 441-9004; e-mail contact@mohe.gov.sa; internet www.mohe.gov.sa.
Ministry of Information and Culture: POB 570, Nasseriya St, Riyadh 11161; tel. (1) 401-4440; fax (1) 402-3570; e-mail samirad@saudinf.com; internet www.saudinf.com.
Ministry of the Interior: POB 2933, Airport Rd, Riyadh 11134; tel. (1) 401-1111; fax (1) 403-1185; internet www.moi.gov.sa.
Ministry of Justice: University St, Riyadh 11137; tel. (1) 405-7777; internet www.moj.gov.sa.
Ministry of Labour: Omar bin al-Khatab St, Riyadh 11157; tel. (1) 477-1480; fax (1) 477-7336; e-mail webmaster@mol.gov.sa; internet www.mol.gov.sa.
Ministry of Municipal and Rural Affairs: POB 955, Nasseriya St, Riyadh 11136; tel. (1) 456-9999; fax (1) 456-3196; e-mail info@momra.gov.sa; internet www.momra.gov.sa.
Ministry of Petroleum and Mineral Resources: POB 247, King Abd al-Aziz Rd, Riyadh 11191; tel. (1) 478-1661; fax (1) 478-1980; e-mail info@mopm.gov.sa; internet www.mopm.gov.sa.
Ministry of Pilgrimage (Hajj) Affairs: Al-Maazar St, Riyadh 11183; tel. (1) 404-3003; fax (1) 402-2555; internet www.hajinformation.com.

SAUDI ARABIA

Ministry of Social Affairs: Omar bin al-Khatab St, Riyadh 11157; tel. (1) 477-1480; fax (1) 477-7336; internet www.mosa.gov.sa.

Ministry of Transport: Airport Rd, Riyadh; tel. (1) 404-2928; fax (1) 403-1401.

Ministry of Water and Electricity: Riyadh; tel. (1) 205-2981; fax (1) 205-0557; internet www.mow.gov.sa.

MAJLIS ASH-SHOURA
(Consultative Council)

In March 1992 King Fahd issued a decree to establish a Consultative Council of 60 members, whose powers include the right to summon and question ministers. The composition of the Council was announced by King Fahd in August 1993, and it was officially inaugurated in December. Each member serves a term of four years. The Council's membership was increased to 90 when its second term began in July 1997; it was increased further, to 120, in May 2001, and to 150 in April 2005. King Fahd issued a decree extending the legislative powers of the Council in November 2003, including the right to propose new legislation.

Chairman: Dr SALIH IBN HUMAYD.

Vice-Chairman: ABDULLAH IBN UMAR IBN MUHAMMAD IBN NASIF.

Secretary-General: Dr HAMOUD IBN ABD AL-AZIZ AL-BADR.

Diplomatic Representation

EMBASSIES IN SAUDI ARABIA

Afghanistan: POB 93337, Riyadh 11673; tel. (1) 480-3459; fax (1) 480-3451; e-mail afgembriyad@hotmail.com; Ambassador KABIR FARAHI.

Algeria: POB 94388, Riyadh 11693; tel. (1) 488-7171; fax (1) 482-1703; Ambassador ABD AL-KARIM GHARIB.

Argentina: POB 94369, Riyadh 11693; tel. (1) 465-2600; fax (1) 465-3057; e-mail earab@nesma.net.sa; Ambassador ENRIQUE ANTONIO PAREJA.

Australia: POB 94400, Riyadh 11693; tel. (1) 488-7788; fax (1) 488-7973; internet www.saudiarabia.embassy.gov.au; Ambassador KEVIN MAGEE.

Austria: POB 94373, Riyadh 11693; tel. (1) 480-1217; fax (1) 480-1526; e-mail riyadh-ob@bmeia.gv.at; internet www.bmeia.gv.at/riyadh; Ambassador Dr FRIEDRICH STIFT.

Azerbaijan: 59 Al-Worood Quarter St, off Amir Failsal bin Sa'ud Abd ar-Rahman, Aloroba Rd, Riyadh; tel. (1) 419-2382; fax (1) 419-2260; e-mail asim67@awalnet.net.sa; Ambassador ELMAN ARASLI.

Bahrain: POB 94371, Riyadh 11693; tel. (1) 488-0044; fax (1) 488-0208; Ambassador RASHID SAAD AD-DOSERI.

Bangladesh: POB 94395, Riyadh 11693; tel. (1) 419-6665; fax (1) 419-3555; e-mail bdootriyadh@zajil.net; Ambassador MUHAMMAD AKRAM UL-HAQ.

Belgium: POB 94396, Riyadh 11693; tel. (1) 488-2888; fax (1) 488-2033; e-mail ambelriyad@nesma.net.sa; Ambassador MICHEL LASTSCHENKO.

Bosnia and Herzegovina: POB 94301, Riyadh 11693; tel. (1) 456-7914; fax (1) 454-4360; e-mail baembsaruh@awalnet.net.sa; Ambassador RAZIM ČOLIĆ.

Brazil: POB 94348, Riyadh 11693; tel. (1) 488-0018; fax (1) 488-1073; e-mail arabras@shabakah.net.sa; Ambassador LUÍS SÉRGIO GAMA FIGUEIRA.

Brunei: POB 94314, al-Warood, Area 29, al-Fujairah St, Riyadh 11693; tel. (1) 456-0814; fax (1) 456-1594; e-mail brunei@shabakah.net.sa; Ambassador Pengiran Haji JABARUDDIN BIN Pengiran Haji MUHAMMAD SALLEH.

Burkina Faso: POB 94330, Riyadh 11693; tel. (1) 465-2244; fax (1) 465-3397; e-mail burkinafaso.ksa@arab.net.sa; Ambassador OUMAR DIAWARA.

Cameroon: POB 94336, Riyadh 11693; tel. (1) 488-0022; fax (1) 488-1463; e-mail ambacamriyad@ifrance.com; internet www.ambacamriyad.org.sa; Ambassador Dr MOHAMADOU LABARANG.

Canada: POB 94321, Riyadh 11693; tel. (1) 488-2288; fax (1) 488-1997; e-mail ryadh@international.gc.ca; internet www.saudiarabia.gc.ca; Ambassador RODERICK BELL.

Chad: POB 94374, Riyadh 11693; tel. and fax (1) 465-7702.

China, People's Republic: POB 75231, Riyadh 11578; tel. (1) 483-2126; fax (1) 281-2070; e-mail chinaemb_sa@mfa.gov.cn; internet www.chinaembassy.org.sa; Ambassador YANG HONGLIN.

Côte d'Ivoire: POB 94303, Riyadh 11693; tel. (1) 482-5582; fax (1) 482-9629; e-mail ambciryd@digi.net.sa; Ambassador LANCINA DOSSO.

Directory

Denmark: POB 94398, Riyadh 11693; tel. (1) 488-0101; fax (1) 488-1366; e-mail ruhamb@um.dk; internet www.ambriyadh.um.dk; Ambassador HANS KLINGENBERG.

Djibouti: POB 94340, Riyadh 11693; tel. (1) 454-3182; fax (1) 456-9168; e-mail dya_bamakhrama@hotmail.com; Ambassador DYA-EDDINE SAID BAMAKHRAMA.

Egypt: POB 94333, Riyadh 11693; tel. (1) 481-0464; fax (1) 481-0463; Ambassador MUHAMMAD ABD AL-HAMID KASSEM.

Ethiopia: POB 94341, Riyadh 11693; tel. (1) 477-5285; fax (1) 476-8020; e-mail ethiopian@naseej.com.sa; Ambassador Ato MUHAMMAD ALI.

Finland: POB 94363, Riyadh 11693; tel. (1) 488-1515; fax (1) 488-2520; e-mail sanomat.ria@formin.fi; Ambassador MARTTI ISOARO.

France: POB 94367, Riyadh 11693; tel. (1) 488-1255; fax (1) 488-2882; e-mail diplomatie@ambafrance.org.sa; internet www.ambafrance.org.sa; Ambassador BERTRAND BESANCENOT.

Gabon: POB 94325, Riyadh 11693; tel. (1) 456-7171; fax (1) 453-6121; e-mail ambagabonriyad@yahoo.com; Ambassador NABIL KOUSSOU INAMA.

Gambia: POB 94322, Riyadh 11693; tel. (1) 205-2158; fax (1) 456-2024; e-mail gamextriyadh@yahoo.com; Ambassador LAMIN JABANG.

Germany: POB 94001, Riyadh 11693; tel. (1) 488-0700; fax (1) 488-0660; e-mail info@riad.diplo.de; internet www.riad.diplo.de; Ambassador JÜRGEN KRIEGHOFF.

Ghana: POB 94339, Riyadh 11693; tel. (1) 454-5122; fax (1) 450-9819; e-mail ghanaemb@naseej.com; Ambassador Alhaji RASHID BAWA.

Greece: POB 94375, Riyadh 11693; tel. (1) 480-1975; fax (1) 480-1969; e-mail gremb.ria@mfa.gr; Ambassador IOANNIS-THEODOROS ECONOMOU.

Guinea: POB 94326, Riyadh 11693; tel. (1) 488-1101; fax (1) 482-6757; Ambassador el-Hadj ABOUL KARIM DIOUBATÉ.

Hungary: POB 94014, al-Waha District, Ahmad Tonsy St 23, Riyadh 11693; tel. (1) 454-6707; fax (1) 456-0834; e-mail huemb.ryd@nournet.com.sa; Ambassador ISTVÁN TÖLLI.

India: POB 94387, Riyadh 11693; tel. (1) 488-4144; fax (1) 488-4189; e-mail info@indianembassy.org.sa; internet www.indianembassy.org.sa; Ambassador M. O. H. FAROUK.

Indonesia: POB 94343, Riyadh 11693; tel. (1) 488-2800; fax (1) 488-2966; e-mail contact@kbri-riyadh.org.sa; internet www.kbri-riyadh.org.sa; Ambassador Dr ISMAIL SUNY.

Iran: POB 94394, Riyadh 11693; tel. (1) 488-1916; fax (1) 488-1890; Ambassador SAYED MUHAMMAD HOSSEINI.

Iraq: Riyadh.

Ireland: POB 94349, Riyadh 11693; tel. (1) 488-2300; fax (1) 488-0927; e-mail riyadhembassy@dfa.ie; internet www.embassyofireland-riyadh.com; Ambassador TOM RUSSELL.

Italy: POB 94389, Riyadh 11693; tel. (1) 488-1212; fax (1) 480-6964; e-mail segreteria1.riad@esteri.it; internet www.ambriad.esteri.it; Ambassador EUGENIO D'AURIA.

Japan: POB 4095, Riyadh 11491; tel. (1) 488-1100; fax (1) 488-0189; e-mail info@jpn-emb-sa.com; internet www.ksa.emb-japan.go.jp; Ambassador SHIGERU NAKAMURA.

Jordan: POB 94316, Riyadh 11693; tel. (1) 488-0051; fax (1) 488-0072; e-mail jordan.embassy@nesma.net.sa; Ambassador HANI KHALIFAH.

Kazakhstan: POB 94012, Riyadh 11693; tel. (1) 480-6406; fax (1) 480-9106; e-mail office@kazembgulf.net; internet www.kazembgulf.net; Ambassador MUHAMMED KHOJAMUHAMEDOVICH ABALAKOV.

Kenya: POB 94358, Riyadh 11693; tel. (1) 488-1238; fax (1) 488-2629; Ambassador YUSUF ABD AR-RAHMAN NZIBO.

Korea, Republic: POB 94399, Riyadh 11693; tel. (1) 488-2211; fax (1) 488-1317; Ambassador KANG GWANG-WON.

Kuwait: POB 94304, Riyadh 11693; tel. (1) 488-3401; fax (1) 488-3682; Ambassador Sheikh HAMAD JABER AL-ALI AS-SABAH.

Kyrgyzstan: POB 75871, 32 Muhammad Khamid al-Fikki St, Riyadh; tel. (1) 229-3272; fax (1) 229-3274; Ambassador ZHUSUPBEK SHARIPOV.

Lebanon: POB 94350, Riyadh 11693; tel. (1) 480-4060; fax (1) 480-4703; Ambassador MERWAN ZAID.

Libya: POB 94365, Riyadh 11693; tel. (1) 488-9757; fax (1) 488-3252; Ambassador MUHAMMAD SA'ID AL-QASHAT.

Malaysia: POB 94335, Riyadh 11693; tel. (1) 488-7100; fax (1) 482-4177; e-mail malriyadh@kln.gov.my; internet www.kln.gov.my/perwakilan/riyadh; Ambassador Datuk ISMA'IL IBRAHIM.

Mali: POB 94331, Riyadh 11693; tel. (1) 464-5640; fax (1) 419-5016; Ambassador MUHAMMAD MAHMOUD OULD BOUYA.

SAUDI ARABIA

Malta: POB 94361, Riyadh 11693; tel. (1) 463-2345; fax (1) 463-3993; e-mail maltaembassy.riyadh@gov.mt; Ambassador GODWIN MONTANARO.
Mauritania: POB 94354, Riyadh 11693; tel. (1) 464-6749; fax (1) 465-8355; Ambassador MUHAMMAD WALAD MUHAMMAD FAL.
Mexico: POB 94391, Riyadh 11693; tel. (1) 480-8822; fax (1) 480-8833; e-mail embasaudita@sre.gob.mx; Ambassador RAÚL LÓPEZ LIRA NAVA.
Morocco: POB 94392, Riyadh 11693; tel. (1) 481-1858; fax (1) 482-7016; e-mail moembassy@hotmail.com; Ambassador ABD AL-KRIM SEMMAR.
Nepal: POB 94384, Riyadh 11693; tel. (1) 461-1108; fax (1) 464-0690; e-mail neksa@zajil.net; internet www.neksa.org; Ambassador HAMID ANSARI.
Netherlands: POB 94307, Riyadh 11693; tel. (1) 488-0011; fax (1) 488-0544; e-mail riy@minbuza.nl; internet www.mfa.nl/riy-en; Ambassador NICOLAAS BEETS.
New Zealand: POB 94397, Riyadh 11693; tel. (1) 488-7988; fax (1) 488-7912; e-mail info@nzembassy.org.sa; Ambassador TREVOR MATHESON.
Niger: POB 94334, Riyadh 11693; tel. and fax (1) 464-2931.
Nigeria: POB 94386, Riyadh 11693; tel. (1) 482-3024; fax (1) 482-4134; e-mail nigeria@nigeriariyadh.com; internet www.nigeriariyadh.com; Ambassador ALHAJI A. GARBA AMINCI.
Norway: POB 94380, Riyadh 11693; tel. (1) 488-1904; fax (1) 488-0854; e-mail emb.riyadh@mfa.no; internet www.al-norwige.org.sa; Ambassador JAN BUGGE-MAHRT.
Oman: POB 94381, Riyadh 11693; tel. (1) 482-3120; fax (1) 482-3738; Ambassador HAMAD H. AL-MO'AMARY.
Pakistan: POB 94007, Riyadh 11693; tel. (1) 488-7272; fax (1) 488-7953; Ambassador Adm. (retd) ADUL AZIZ MIRZA.
Philippines: POB 94366, Riyadh 11693; tel. (1) 482-0507; fax (1) 488-3945; e-mail filembry@sbm.net.sa; Ambassador ANTONIO P. VILLAMOR.
Portugal: POB 94328, Riyadh 11693; tel. (1) 462-2115; fax (1) 462-2105; e-mail portriade@nesma.net.sa; Ambassador Dr HENRIQUE M. V. DE SILVEIRA BORGES.
Qatar: POB 94353, Riyadh 11461; tel. (1) 482-5544; fax (1) 482-5394; Ambassador ALI ABDULLAH AL-MAHMOUD.
Russia: POB 94308, Riyadh 11693; tel. (1) 481-1875; fax (1) 481-1890; Ambassador IGOR A. MELIKHOV.
Rwanda: POB 94383, Riyadh 11693; tel. (1) 454-0808; fax (1) 456-1769; Ambassador SIMON INSONERE.
Senegal: POB 94352, Riyadh 11693; tel. (1) 488-0146; fax (1) 488-3804; Ambassador MOUHAMADOU DOUDOU LO.
Sierra Leone: POB 94329, Riyadh 11693; tel. (1) 464-3982; fax (1) 464-3662; e-mail slembrdh@zajil.net; Ambassador Alhaji AMADU DEEN TEJAN-SIE.
Singapore: POB 94378, Riyadh 11693; tel. (1) 480-3855; fax (1) 483-0632; e-mail singemb_ruh@sgmfa.gov.sg; internet www.mfa.gov.sg/riyadh; Ambassador V. P. HIRUBALAN.
Somalia: POB 94372, Riyadh 11693; tel. (1) 464-3456; fax (1) 464-9705; Ambassador ABD AR-RAHMAN A. HUSSEIN.
South Africa: POB 94006, Riyadh 11693; tel. (1) 456-2923; fax (1) 454-3718; e-mail saconsul@gmail.com; internet www.southafrica.com.sa; Ambassador ABD AL-HAMID KHUBAIR.
Spain: POB 94347, Riyadh 11693; tel. (1) 488-0606; fax (1) 488-0420; e-mail embespsa@mail.mae.es; Ambassador MANUEL ALBERT FERNÁNDEZ KABAD.
Sri Lanka: POB 94360, Riyadh 11693; tel. (1) 460-8689; fax (1) 460-8846; e-mail lankaemb@shabakah.net.sa; Ambassador ADAM JAAFAR SADIQ.
Sudan: POB 94337, Riyadh 11693; tel. (1) 488-7979; fax (1) 488-7729; Ambassador Dr MUHAMMAD AMIN ABDULLAH AL-KARB.
Sweden: POB 94382, Riyadh 11693; tel. (1) 488-3100; fax (1) 488-0604; e-mail ambassaden.riyadh@foreign.ministry.se; internet www.swedenabroad.se/riyadh; Ambassador JAN THESLEFF.
Switzerland: POB 94311, Riyadh 11693; tel. (1) 488-1291; fax (1) 488-0632; e-mail vertretung@rya.rep.admin.ch; Ambassador MAURICE DARIER.
Syria: POB 94323, Riyadh 11693; tel. (1) 482-6191; fax (1) 482-6196; Ambassador MUHAMMAD KHALID AT-TALL.
Tanzania: POB 94320, Riyadh 11693; tel. (1) 454-2839; fax (1) 454-9660; e-mail tzriyad@deltasa.com; Ambassador Prof. A. A. SHAREEF.
Thailand: POB 94359, Riyadh 11693; tel. (1) 488-1174; fax (1) 488-1179; e-mail thaiemryadsl@awalnet.net.sa; internet www.thaiembassy.org/riyadh; Chargé d'affaires a.i. CHARN JULLAMON.
Tunisia: POB 94368, Riyadh 11693; tel. (1) 488-7900; fax (1) 488-7641; Ambassador KACEM BOUSNINA.
Turkey: POB 94390, Riyadh 11693; tel. (1) 482-0101; fax (1) 488-7823; e-mail turkishembassy@sps.net.sa; Ambassador UGUR DOGAN.
Uganda: POB 94344, Riyadh 11693; tel. (1) 454-4910; fax (1) 454-9264; e-mail ugariyadh@hotmail.com; Ambassador IBRAHIM MUKAIBI.
United Arab Emirates: POB 94385, Riyadh 11693; tel. (1) 482-9652; fax (1) 482-7504; Ambassador ISSA K. AL-HURAIMIL.
United Kingdom: POB 94351, Riyadh 11693; tel. (1) 488-0077; fax (1) 488-1209; e-mail PressOffice.Riyadh@fco.gov.uk; internet www.britishembassy.gov.uk/saudiarabia; Ambassador WILLIAM PATEY.
USA: POB 94309, Riyadh 11693; tel. (1) 488-3800; fax (1) 488-7360; e-mail riyadhniv@state.gov; internet riyadh.usembassy.gov; Ambassador FORD M. FRAKER.
Uruguay: POB 94346, Riyadh 11693; tel. (1) 462-0739; fax (1) 462-0648; e-mail ururia@nesma.net.sa; Ambassador CARLOS A. CLULOW.
Uzbekistan: POB 94008, Riyadh 11693; tel. (1) 263-5223; fax (1) 263-5105; Ambassador ULUGBEK A. ISROILOV.
Venezuela: POB 94364, Riyadh 11693; tel. (1) 480-7141; fax (1) 480-0901; e-mail embvenar@embvenar.org.sa; Ambassador RAMÓN HERRERA NAVARRO.
Yemen: POB 94356, Riyadh 11693; tel. (1) 488-1769; fax (1) 488-1562; Ambassador MUHAMMAD ALI MOHSEN AL-AHWAL.

Judicial System

Judges are independent and governed by the rules of Islamic *Shari'a*. Although a new Judicial Law introduced in October 2007 provided for a number of significant changes to the courts system (see Recent History), the following courts currently operate:

Supreme Council of Justice: consists of 11 members and supervises work of the courts; reviews legal questions referred to it by the Minister of Justice and expresses opinions on judicial questions; reviews sentences of death, cutting and stoning; Chair. Sheikh SALIH BIN MUHAMMAD AL-LUHAIDAN.

Court of Cassation: consists of Chief Justice and an adequate number of judges; includes department for penal suits, department for personal status and department for other suits.

General (Public) Courts: consist of one or more judges; sentences are issued by a single judge, with the exception of death, stoning and cutting, which require the decision of three judges.

Summary Courts: consist of one or more judges; sentences are issued by a single judge.

Specialized Courts: Article 26 of the judicial system stipulates that the setting up of specialized courts is permissible by Royal Decree on a proposal from the Supreme Council of Justice.

Religion

ISLAM

Arabia is the centre of the Islamic faith, and Saudi Arabia includes the holy cities of Mecca and Medina. Except in the Eastern Province, where a large number of people follow Shi'a rites, the majority of the population are Sunni Muslims, and most of the indigenous inhabitants belong to the strictly orthodox Wahhabi sect. The Wahhabis originated in the 18th century, but first became unified and influential under Abd al-Aziz (Ibn Sa'ud), who became the first King of Saudi Arabia. They are now the keepers of the holy places and control the pilgrimage to Mecca. In 1986 King Fahd adopted the title of Custodian of the Two Holy Mosques; the title passed to King Abdullah upon his accession to the throne in August 2005. The country's most senior Islamic authority is the Council of Ulema.

Mecca: Birthplace of the Prophet Muhammad, seat of the Grand Mosque and Shrine of Ka'ba, visited by 1,557,447 Muslims in the Islamic year 1424 (2005/06).

Medina: Burial place of Muhammad, second sacred city of Islam.

Grand Mufti and Chairman of Council of Ulema: Sheikh ABD AL-AZIZ IBN ABDULLAH ASH-SHEIKH.

CHRISTIANITY

The Roman Catholic Church

A small number of adherents, mainly expatriates, form part of the Apostolic Vicariate of Arabia. The Vicar Apostolic is resident in the United Arab Emirates.

The Anglican Communion

Within the Episcopal Church in Jerusalem and the Middle East, Saudi Arabia forms part of the diocese of Cyprus and the Gulf. The

SAUDI ARABIA *Directory*

Anglican congregations in the country are entirely expatriate. The Bishop in Cyprus and the Gulf is resident in Cyprus, while the Archdeacon in the Gulf is resident in Bahrain.

Other Denominations

The Greek Orthodox Church is also represented.

The Press

Since 1964 most newspapers and periodicals have been published by press organizations, administered by boards of directors with full autonomous powers, in accordance with the provisions of the Press Law. These organizations, which took over from small private firms, are privately owned by groups of individuals experienced in newspaper publishing and administration (see Publishers).

There are also a number of popular periodicals published by the Government and by the Saudi Arabian Oil Co, and distributed free of charge. The press is subject to no legal restriction affecting freedom of expression or the coverage of news.

DAILIES

Arab News: POB 10452, SRP Bldg, Madinah Rd, Jeddah 21433; tel. (2) 639-1888; fax (2) 639-3223; e-mail arabnews@arabnews.com; internet www.arabnews.com; f. 1975; English; publ. by Saudi Research and Publishing Co; Editor-in-Chief KHALED AL-MAEENA; circ. 110,000.

Al-Bilad (The Country): POB 6340, Jeddah 21442; tel. (2) 672-3000; fax (2) 671-2545; f. 1934; Arabic; publ. by Al-Bilad Publishing Organization; Editor-in-Chief QUINAN AL-GHOMDI; circ. 66,210.

Al-Eqtisadiah: POB 10452, Jeddah 21433; tel. (2) 651-1333; fax (2) 667-6212; internet www.aleqt.com; f. 1992; publ. by Saudi Research and Publishing Co; Editor-in-Chief ABD AL-WAHAB FAYEZ.

Al-Jazirah (The Peninsula): POB 354, Riyadh 11411; tel. (1) 487-0000; fax (1) 487-1017; e-mail aljazirah@al-jazirah.com; internet www.al-jazirah.com; f. 1972; publ. by Al-Jazirah Corpn for Press, Printing and Publishing; Arabic; Gen. Man. ABD AR-RAHMAN BIN FAHD AR-RASHAD; Editor-in-Chief KHALID BIN HAMAD AL-MALIK; circ. 110,000.

Al-Madina al-Munawara (Medina—The Enlightened City): POB 807, Makkah Rd, Jeddah 21421; tel. (2) 671-2100; fax (2) 671-1877; e-mail webmaster@al-madina.com; internet www.almadinapress.com; f. 1937; Arabic; publ. by Al-Madina Press Establishment; Chief Editor FAHD HASSAN AL-AQRAN; circ. 46,370.

An-Nadwah (The Council): POB 5803, Jarwal Sheikh Sayed Halabi Bldg, Mecca; tel. (2) 520-0111; fax (2) 520-3055; e-mail info@al-nadwah.com; internet www.al-nadwah.com; f. 1958; Arabic; publ. by Makkah Printing and Information Establishment; Editor Dr ABD AR-RAHMAN AL-HARTHI; circ. 35,000.

Okaz: POB 1508, Seaport Rd, Jeddah 21441; tel. (2) 672-7621; fax (2) 672-4297; e-mail 104127.266@compuserve.com; internet www.okaz.com.sa; f. 1948; publ. by Okaz Organization for Press and Publication; Arabic; Editor-in-Chief Dr ABDUL HASHIM; circ. 110,000.

Ar-Riyadh: POB 2943, Riyadh 11476; tel. (1) 487-1000; fax (1) 441-7417; internet www.alriyadh.com.sa; f. 1965; Arabic; publ. by Al-Yamama Press Establishment; Editor TURKI A. AS-SUDARI; circ. 150,000 (Sat.–Thur.), 90,000 (Fri.).

Saudi Gazette: POB 5576, Jeddah 21432; tel. (2) 676-0000; fax (2) 672-7621; e-mail news@saudigazette.com.sa; internet www.saudigazette.com.sa; f. 1976; English; publ. by Okaz Organization for Press and Publication; Editor-in-Chief Dr AHMAD AL-YOUSUF; circ. 15,000.

Al-Watan: POB 15156, Airport Road, Abha; tel. (7) 227-3333; fax (7) 227-3756; internet www.alwatan.com.sa; f. 1998; publ. by Assir Establishment for Press and Publishing; Dir-Gen. HATEM HAMID; Editor-in-Chief OTHMAN MAHMOUD AS-SINI; circ. 150,000.

Al-Yaum (Today): POB 565, Dammam 31421; tel. (3) 858-0800; fax (3) 858-8777; e-mail mail@alyaum.com; internet www.alyaum.com; f. 1965; publ. by Dar al-Yaum Press, Printing and Publishing Ltd; Editor-in-Chief MUHAMMAD ABDULLAH AL-WAEEL; circ. 40,000.

WEEKLIES

Al-Muslimoon (The Muslims): POB 13195, Jeddah 21493; tel. (2) 669-1888; fax (2) 669-5549; f. 1985; Arabic; cultural and religious affairs; publ. by Saudi Research and Publishing Co; Editor-in-Chief Dr ABDULLAH AR-RIFA'E; circ. 68,665.

Saudi Arabia Business Week: POB 2894, Riyadh; English; trade and commerce.

Saudi Economic Survey: POB 1989, Jeddah 21441; tel. (2) 657-8551; fax (2) 657-8553; e-mail info@saudieconomicsurvey.com; internet www.saudieconomicsurvey.com; f. 1967; English; review of Saudi Arabian economic and business activity; Publr SAIFUDDIN A. ASHOOR; Gen. Man. WALID S. ASHOOR; circ. 6,000.

Sayidati (My Lady): POB 4556, Madina Rd, Jeddah 21412; tel. (2) 639-1888; fax (2) 669-5549; Arabic; women's magazine; publ. by Saudi Research and Publishing Co; Editor-in-Chief MATAR AL-AHMADI.

Ash-Shams (The Sun): Riyadh; f. 2005; tabloid format; sports, culture, entertainment; publishing licence revoked by the Govt in Feb. 2006.

Al-Yamama: POB 851, Riyadh 11421; tel. (1) 442-0000; fax (1) 441-7114; f. 1952; literary magazine; Editor-in-Chief ABDULLAH AL-JAHLAN; circ. 35,000.

OTHER PERIODICALS

Ahlan Wasahlan (Welcome): POB 8013, Jeddah 21482; tel. (2) 686-2349; fax (2) 686-2006; monthly; flight journal of Saudi Arabian Airlines; Gen. Man. and Editor-in-Chief YARUB A. BALKHAIR; circ. 150,000.

Al-Faysal: POB 3, Riyadh 11411; tel. (1) 465-3027; fax (1) 464-7851; monthly; f. 1976; Arabic; culture, education, health, interviews; Man. Editor ABDULLAH Y. AL-KOWAILEET.

Majallat al-Iqtisad wal-Idara (Journal of Economics and Administration): King Abd al-Aziz University, POB 9031, Jeddah 21413; twice a year; Chief Editor Prof. ABD AL-AZIZ A. DIYAB.

Al-Manhal (The Spring): POB 2925, Jeddah; tel. (2) 643-2124; fax (2) 642-8853; f. 1937; monthly; Arabic; cultural, literary, political and scientific; Editor NABIH ABD AL-QUDOUS ANSARI.

The MWL Journal: Press and Publications Department, Rabitat al-Alam al-Islami, POB 537, Mecca; fax (2) 544-1622; e-mail info@themwl.org; internet www.themwl.org; monthly; English; Dir MURAD SULAIMAN IRQISOUS.

Ar-Rabita: POB 537, Mecca; tel. (2) 560-0919; fax (2) 543-1488; e-mail info@themwl.org; internet www.themwl.org; Arabic; Chief Editor Dr OSMAN ABUZAID.

Saudi Review: POB 4288, Jeddah 21491; tel. (2) 651-7442; fax (2) 653-0693; f. 1966; English; monthly; newsletter from Saudi newspapers and broadcasting service; publ. by International Communications Co; Chief Editor SAAD AL-MABROUK; circ. 5,000.

Ash-Sharkiah-Elle (Oriental Elle): POB 6, Riyadh; monthly; Arabic; women's magazine; Editor SAMIRA M. KHASHAGGI.

As-Soqoor (Falcons): POB 2973, Riyadh 11461; tel. (1) 476-6566; f. 1978; 2 a year; air-force journal; cultural activities; Editor HAMAD A. AS-SALEH.

At-Tadhamon al-Islami (Islamic Solidarity): Ministry of Pilgrimage (Hajj) Affairs, Omar bin al-Khatab St, Riyadh 11183; monthly; Editor Dr MUSTAFA ABD AL-WAHID.

At-Tijarah (Commerce): POB 1264, Jeddah 21431; tel. (2) 651-5111; fax (2) 651-7373; e-mail jcci@mail.gcc.com.bh; f. 1960; monthly; publ. by Jeddah Chamber of Commerce and Industry; Chair. Sheikh ISMAIL ABU DAUD; circ. 8,000.

NEWS AGENCIES

International Islamic News Agency (IINA): POB 5054, Jeddah 21422; tel. (2) 665-2056; fax (2) 665-9358; e-mail iina@islamicnews.org.sa; internet www.islamicnews.org.sa; f. 1972; operates under the auspices of the Organization of the Islamic Conference; Dir-Gen. ABD AL-WAHAB KASHIF.

Saudi Press Agency (SPA): POB 7186, King Fahd Rd, Riyadh 11171; tel. (1) 419-5485; fax (1) 419-5685; e-mail wass@spa.gov.sa; internet www.spa.gov.sa; f. 1970; the Govt planned to transform the SPA into a public corpn; Dir-Gen. ABD AL-AZIZ BIN SAAD AL-GHAMDI.

Publishers

Assir Establishment for Press and Publishing: POB 15156, Abha; tel. (7) 227-3333; fax (7) 227-3590; f. 1998; publishes Al-Watan; cap. SR 200m.; Chair. FAHD AL-HARITHI.

Al-Bilad Publishing Organization: POB 6340, As-Sahafa St, Jeddah 21442; tel. (2) 672-3000; fax (2) 671-2545; publishes Al-Bilad and Iqra'a; Dir-Gen. AMIN ABDULLAH AL-QARQOURI.

Dar al-Maiman Publishers and Distributors: POB 90020, Riyadh 11613; tel. and fax (1) 4880806.

Dar ash-Shareff for Publishing and Distribution: POB 58287, Riyadh 11594; tel. (1) 403-4931; fax (1) 405-2234; f. 1992; fiction, religion, science and social sciences; Pres. IBRAHIM AL-HAZEMI.

Dar al-Yaum Press, Printing and Publishing Ltd: POB 565, Dammam 31421; tel. (3) 858-0800; fax (3) 858-8777; e-mail salhumaidan@alyaum.com; f. 1964; publishes Al-Yaum.

SAUDI ARABIA

International Publications Agency (IPA): POB 70, Dhahran 31942; tel. and fax (3) 895-4925; publishes material of local interest; Man. SAID SALAH.

Al-Jazirah Corpn for Press, Printing and Publishing: POB 354, Riyadh 11411; tel. (1) 441-9999; fax (1) 441-2536; e-mail marketing@al-jazirah.com; f. 1964; 42 mems; publishes Al-Jazirah and Al-Masaeyah (both dailies); Dir-Gen. SALAH AL-AJROUSH; Editor-in-Chief KHALID EL-MALEK.

Al-Madina Press Establishment: POB 807, Jeddah 21421; tel. (2) 671-2100; fax (2) 671-1877; f. 1937; publishes Al-Madina al-Munawara; Gen. Man. AHMAD SALAH JAMJOUM.

Makkah Printing and Information Establishment: POB 5803, Jarwal Sheikh Sayed Halabi Bldg, Mecca; tel. (2) 542-7868; publishes An-Nadwah daily newspaper.

Okaz Organization for Press and Publication: POB 1508, Jeddah 21441; tel. (2) 672-2630; fax (2) 672-8150; publishes Okaz and Saudi Gazette.

Saudi Publishing and Distributing House: Umm Aslam District, nr Muslaq, POB 2043, Jeddah 21451; tel. (2) 629-4278; fax (2) 629-4290; e-mail info@spdh-sa.com; internet www.spdh-sa.com; f. 1966; publishers, importers and distributors of English and Arabic books; Chair. MUHAMMAD SALAHUDDIN.

Saudi Research and Publishing Co: POB 478, Riyadh 11411; tel. (1) 441-9933; fax (1) 442-9555; internet www.srpc.com; publs incl. Arab News, Asharq al-Awsat, Al-Majalla, Al-Muslimoon and Sayidati; Chair. Prince FAISAL BIN SALMAN BIN ABD AL-AZIZ.

Al-Yamama Press Establishment: POB 2943, Riyadh 11476; tel. (1) 442-0000; fax (1) 441-7116; publishes Ar-Riyadh and Al-Yamama; Dir-Gen. SAKHAL MAIDAN.

Broadcasting and Communications

TELECOMMUNICATIONS

Communications and Information Technology Commission (CITC): Riyadh; tel. (1) 461-8000; fax (1) 461-8002; internet www.citc.gov.sa; f. 2001 under the name Saudi Communications Commission; present name adopted in 2003; ind. regulatory authority; Gov. ABD AR-RAHMAN BIN AHMAD AL-JAAFARI.

Ettihad Etisalat: Al-Malaka Trade Centre 23088, Riyadh 11321; tel. (1) 211-8015; fax (1) 211-8029; e-mail PRD@etisalat.ae; internet www.etisalat.co.ae; f. 2004; owned by a consortium led by Emirates Telecommunications Corpn (United Arab Emirates); awarded the second licence to provide mobile phone services in 2004; operates under the brand name Mobily (launched 2005); CEO KHALID AL-KAF.

Saudi Telecommunications Co—Saudi Telecom (STC): POB 87912, Riyadh 11652; tel. (1) 215-3030; fax (1) 215-2734; e-mail ecare@stc.com.sa; internet www.stc.com.sa; f. 1998; provides telecommunications services in Saudi Arabia; partially privatized in 2002; cap. SR 12,000m.; Chair. Dr MUHAMMAD BIN SULIMAN AL-JASER; Pres. Eng. SA'UD BIN MAJID AD-DAWEESH.

BROADCASTING

Radio

Saudi Arabian Broadcasting Service: c/o Ministry of Information and Culture, POB 60059, Riyadh 11545; tel. (1) 401-4440; fax (1) 403-8177; 24 medium- and short-wave stations, incl. Jeddah, Riyadh, Dammam and Abha, broadcast programmes in Arabic and English; 23 FM stations; overseas service in Bengali, English, Farsi, French, Hausa, Indonesian, Somali, Swahili, Turkestani, Turkish and Urdu; Dir-Gen. MUHAMMAD AL-MANSOOR.

Saudi Aramco FM Radio: Bldg 3030 LIP, Dhahran 31311; tel. (3) 876-1845; fax (3) 876-1608; f. 1948; English; private; for employees of Saudi Aramco; Man. ESSAM Z. TAWFIQ.

Television

Saudi Arabian Government Television Service: POB 7971, Riyadh 11472; tel. (1) 401-4440; fax (1) 404-4192; began transmission 1965; 112 stations, incl. six main stations at Riyadh, Jeddah, Medina, Dammam, Qassim and Abha, transmit programmes in Arabic and English; Dir-Gen. ABD AL-AZIZ AL-HASSAN (Channel 1).

Saudi Arabian Government Television Service Channel 2: POB 7959, Riyadh 11472; tel. (1) 442-8400; fax (1) 403-3826; began transmission 1983; Dir-Gen. ABD AL-AZIZ S. ABU ANNAJA.

Directory

Finance

(cap. = capital; res = reserves; dep. = deposits; m. = million; brs = branches; amounts in Saudi riyals unless otherwise stated)

BANKING

In 2007 the Saudi Arabian banking system consisted of: the Saudi Arabian Monetary Agency, as central note-issuing and regulatory body; 11 local commercial banks; 13 foreign banks; and six specialist banks. There is a policy of 'Saudiization' of the foreign banks.

Central Bank

Saudi Arabian Monetary Agency (SAMA): POB 2992, Riyadh 11169; tel. (1) 463-3000; fax (1) 466-2966; e-mail info@sama.gov.sa; internet www.sama.gov.sa; f. 1952; functions include stabilization of currency, administration of monetary reserves, regulation of banking and issue of notes and coins; dep. 340,651.3m., total assets 653,263.5m. (June 2006); Gov. Sheikh HAMAD SA'UD AS-SAYARI; 10 brs.

National Banks

National Commercial Bank (NCB): POB 3555, King Abd al-Aziz St, Jeddah 21481; tel. (2) 649-3333; fax (2) 644-6468; e-mail contact@alahli.com; internet www.alahli.com; f. 1950; 69.3% govt-owned; cap. 9,000.0m., res 14,852.1m., dep. 127,028.7m. (Dec. 2006); Chair. and Man. Dir Sheikh ABDULLAH SALIM BAHAMDAN; CEO ABD AL-KAREEM ABU AN-NASR; 258 brs.

Ar-Rajhi Banking and Investment Corpn (Ar-Rajhi Bank): POB 28, Al-Akariya Bldg, Oleya St, Riyadh 11411; tel. (1) 211-6000; fax (1) 460-0922; e-mail contactus@alrajhibank.com.sa; internet www.alrajhibank.com.sa; f. 1988; operates according to Islamic financial principles; cap. 6,750.0m., res 7,881.8m., dep. 80,887.0m. (Dec. 2006); Chair. and Man. Dir Sheikh SULAYMAN BIN ABD AL-AZIZ AR-RAJHI; CEO ABDULLAH SULAIMAN AR-RAJHI; 385 brs.

Riyad Bank Ltd: POB 22601, King Abd al-Aziz St, Riyadh 11416; tel. (1) 401-3030; fax (1) 404-1255; internet www.riyadbank.com.sa; f. 1957; cap. 6,250.0m., res 5,448.3m., dep. 79,229.5m. (Dec. 2006); Chair. RASHED A. AR-RASHED; Pres. and CEO TALAL I. AL-QUDAIBI; 180 brs.

Specialist Bank

Arab Investment Co SAA (TAIC): POB 4009, King Abd al-Aziz St, Riyadh 11491; tel. (1) 476-0601; fax (1) 476-0514; e-mail taic@taic.com; internet www.taic.com; f. 1974 by 17 Arab countries for investment and banking; cap. US $500.0m., res $193.0m., dep. $2,625,429m. (Dec. 2006); Chair. Dr MUHAMMAD SULAYMAN AL-JASSER; Dir-Gen. Dr SALIH AL-HUMAIDAN; 1 br.

Banks with Foreign Interests

Arab National Bank (ANB): POB 56921, King Faisal St, North Murabba, Riyadh 11564; tel. (1) 402-9000; fax (1) 402-7747; e-mail info@anb.com.sa; internet www.anb.com.sa; f. 1980; ownership: Arab Bank plc, Jordan, 40%, Saudi shareholders 60%; cap. 3,250.0m., res 4,470.0m., dep. 64,872.0m. (Dec. 2006); Chair. ABDULLATIF H. AL-JABR; Man. Dir and CEO Dr ROBERT EID; 143 brs.

Bank al-Jazira: POB 6277, Khalid bin al-Waleed St, Jeddah 21442; tel. (2) 651-8070; fax (2) 653-2478; e-mail info@baj.com.sa; internet www.baj.com.sa; 94.17% Saudi-owned; cap. 1,125.0m., res 1,636,944m., dep. 11,090.6m. (Dec. 2006); Chair. ABD AL-MOHEM AR-RASHID; Gen. Man. and CEO MISHARI I. AL-MISHARI; 23 brs.

Banque Saudi Fransi (Saudi French Bank): POB 56006, Ma'ather Rd, Riyadh 11554; tel. (1) 404-2222; fax (1) 404-2311; e-mail communications@alfransi.com.sa; internet www.alfransi.com.sa; f. 1977; name changed as above in 2002; Saudi shareholders 68.9%, Calyon, Paris La Défense 31.1%; cap. 3,375.0m., res 5,991.8m., dep. 65,454.4m. (Dec. 2006); Chair. IBRAHIM A. AT-TOUQ; Man. Dir JEAN MARION; 68 brs.

SAMBA Financial Group: POB 833, Riyadh 11421; tel. and fax (1) 477-4770; e-mail sambacare@samba.com; internet www.samba.com.sa; f. 1980; 96.4% owned by Saudi nationals; merged with United Saudi Bank in 1999; cap. 6,000.0m., res 6,305.8m., dep. 102,666.3m. (Dec. 2006); Chair. SAUD A. AL-GOSAIBI; Man. Dir and CEO EISA AL-EISA; 63 brs.

Saudi British Bank: POB 9084, Prince Abdulaziz bin Mossaid bin Jalawi St, Riyadh 11413; tel. (1) 405-0677; fax (1) 405-0660; e-mail sabb@sabb.com; internet www.sabb.com.sa; f. 1978; 60% owned by Saudi nationals, 40% by HSBC Holdings BV; cap. 3,750.0m., res 4,711.0m., dep. 65,470.2m. (Dec. 2006); Chair. Sheikh ABDULLAH MUHAMMAD AL-HUGAIL; Man. Dir JOHN COVERDALE; 78 brs.

Saudi Hollandi Bank (Saudi Dutch Bank): POB 1467, Head Office Bldg, adh-Dhabab St, Riyadh 11431; tel. (1) 406-7888; fax (1) 403-1104; e-mail csc@shb.com.sa; internet www.shb.com.sa; f. 1977 to assume activities of Algemene Bank Nederland NV in Saudi Arabia;

3892

… SAUDI ARABIA — Directory

a jt-stock co; ownership: ABN AMRO Bank (Netherlands) 40%, Saudi citizens 60%; cap. 1,260.0m., res 2,404.0m., dep. 34,361.5m. (Dec. 2005); Chair. Sheikh MUBARAK ABDULLAH AL-KHAFRAH; Man. Dir GEOFFREY CALVERT; 40 brs.

Saudi Investment Bank (SAIB): POB 3533, Riyadh 11481; tel. (1) 478-6000; fax (1) 477-6781; e-mail info@saib.com.sa; internet www.saib.com.sa; f. 1976; provides a comprehensive range of traditional and specialized banking services; cap. 2,406.3m., res 2,089.3m., dep. 32,378.0m. (Dec. 2006); Chair. Dr ABD AL-AZIZ O'HALI; Pres. and Gen. Man. SA'UD AS-SALEH; 21 brs.

Government Specialized Credit Institutions

Real Estate Development Fund (REDF): POB 5591, Riyadh 11139; tel. (1) 479-2222; fax (1) 479-0148; f. 1974; provides interest-free loans to Saudi individuals and cos for private or commercial housing projects; loans granted amounted to 1,900m. in 2000; Gen. Dir AHMAD AL-AKEIL; 25 brs.

Saudi Arabian Agricultural Bank (SAAB): POB 1811, Riyadh 11126; tel. (1) 402-3911; fax (1) 402-2359; f. 1963; loans disbursed amounted to 803.9m. in 2000; Controller-Gen. ABDULLAH SAAD AL-MENGASH; Gen. Man. ABD AL-AZIZ MUHAMMAD AL-MANQUR; 70 brs.

Saudi Credit Bank: POB 3401, Riyadh 11471; tel. (1) 402-9128; f. 1973; provides interest-free loans for specific purposes to Saudi citizens of moderate means; loans disbursed amounted to 321.3m. in 2000; Chair. SAID IBN SAIED; Dir-Gen. MUHAMMAD AD-DRIES; 24 brs.

STOCK EXCHANGE

The Saudi Arabian Monetary Agency (see Central Bank) operates the Electronic Securities Information System. In mid-2005 shares in 75 companies were being traded. A total of 57,829m. shares were traded in 2007, amounting to SR 2,557,712m.

INSURANCE

In 2004 22 insurance companies operated in Saudi Arabia.

Amana Gulf Insurance Co (E.C.): POB 6559, Jeddah 21452; tel. and fax (2) 665-5692.

Arabia Ace Insurance Co Ltd (E.C.): POB 276, Dammam 31411; tel. (3) 832-4441; fax (3) 834-9389; cap. US $1m.; Chair. Sheikh ABD AL-KARIM AL-KHEREIJI; Man. Dir TAJUDDIN HASSAN.

Independent Insurance Co of Saudi Arabia Ltd: POB 1178, Jeddah 21431; tel. (2) 651-7732; fax (2) 651-1968; f. 1977; all classes of insurance; cap. US $1m.; Pres. KHALID TAHER; Man. JULIAN D. SHARPE.

Insaudi Insurance Co (E.C.): POB 3984, Riyadh 11481; tel. (1) 476-7711; fax (1) 476-1213.

Islamic Arab Insurance Co: POB 122392, Jeddah 21332; tel. (2) 664-7877; fax (2) 664-7387; e-mail iaic.ksa@islamicarab.com.

Al-Jazira Insurance Co Ltd: POB 153, al-Khobar 31952; tel. and fax (3) 895-3445.

Ar-Rajhi Insurance Co: POB 22073, Jeddah 21495; tel. (2) 651-1017; fax (2) 651-1797.

Ar-Rajhi Islamic Co for Co-operative Insurance: POB 42220, Jeddah 21541; tel. (2) 651-4514; fax (2) 651-3185.

Red Sea Insurance Group of Cos: POB 5627, Jeddah 21432; tel. (2) 660-3538; fax (2) 665-5418; e-mail redsea@anet.net.sa; f. 1974; insurance, devt and reinsurance; Chair. KHALDOUN B. BARAKAT.

Royal & Sun Alliance Insurance (Middle East) Ltd (E.C.): POB 2374, Jeddah 21451; tel. (2) 671-8851; fax (2) 671-1377; managed by Royal & Sun Alliance Insurance Group, London; total assets US $73.0m. (2002); Chair. WAHIB S. BINZAGR; Man. Dir P. W. HEAD; Country Man. W. J. DAVIES.

Saudi Continental Insurance Co: POB 2940, Riyadh; tel. (1) 479-2141; fax (1) 476-9310; f. 1983; all classes of insurance; cap. US $3m.; Chair. OMAR A. AGGAD; Gen. Man. J. A. MCROBBIE.

Saudi National Insurance Co (E.C.): POB 5832, Jeddah 21432; tel. (2) 660-6200; fax (2) 667-4530; Gen. Man. OMAR S. BILANI.

Saudi Union National Insurance Corpn: POB 2357, Jeddah 21451; tel. (2) 667-0648; fax (2) 667-2084.

Saudi United Insurance Co Ltd: POB 933, al-Khobar 31952; tel. (3) 894-9090; fax (3) 894-9428; f. 1976; all classes of insurance and reinsurance except life; majority shareholding held by Ahmad Hamad al-Gosaibi & Bros; cap. US $5m.; Chair. and Man. Dir Sheikh ABD AL-AZIZ HAMAD AL-GOSAIBI; Dir and Gen. Man. ABD AL-MOHSIN AL-GOSAIBI; 6 brs.

Tawuniya (NCCI): POB 86959, Riyadh 11632; tel. (1) 218-0100; fax (1) 218-0102; e-mail info@tawuniya.com.sa; internet tawuniya.com.sa; f. 1985 by royal decree under the name National Co for Co-operative Insurance; owned by three govt agencies; proposed privatization approved by the Supreme Economic Council in May 2004; initial public offering of shares in Dec. 2004; auth. cap. 500m.; Chair. SULAYMAN AL-HUMMAYYD; Man. Dir and Gen. Man. ALI A. AS-SUBAIHIN; 13 brs.

U.C.A. Insurance Co (E.C.): POB 5019, Medina Rd, Jeddah 21422; tel. (2) 653-0068; fax (2) 651-1936; e-mail jeddah@uca.com.sa; internet www.uca.com.sa; f. 1974 as United Commercial Agencies Ltd; all classes of insurance; cap. US $14m.; Chair. ABU BAKER AL-HAMED; Senior Vice-Pres. MACHAAL A. KARAM.

Al-Yamamah Insurance Co Ltd: POB 41522, Riyadh 11531; tel. (1) 477-4498; fax (1) 477-4497.

Trade and Industry
(Figures for weight are in metric tons)

DEVELOPMENT ORGANIZATIONS

Arab Petroleum Investments Corpn: POB 9599, Dammam 31423; tel. (3) 847-0444; fax (3) 847-0011; e-mail apicorp@apicorp-arabia.com; internet www.apicorp-arabia.com; f. 1975; affiliated to the Organization of Arab Petroleum Exporting Countries; specializes in financing petroleum and petrochemical projects and related industries in the Arab world and in other developing countries; shareholders: Kuwait, Saudi Arabia and the United Arab Emirates (17% each), Libya (15%), Iraq and Qatar (10% each), Algeria (5%), Bahrain, Egypt and Syria (3% each); auth. cap. US $1,200m.; cap. $550m. (Dec. 2006); Chair. ABDULLAH A. AZ-ZAID; Gen. Man. and CEO AHMAD BIN HAMAD AN-NUAIMI.

General Investment Fund: c/o Ministry of Finance, Airport Rd, Riyadh 11177; tel. (1) 405-0000; f. 1970; provides the Govt's share of capital to mixed capital cos; 100% state-owned; cap. 1,000m. riyals; Chair. Dr IBRAHIM IBN ABD AL-AZIZ AL-ASSAF; Sec.-Gen. SULAYMAN MANDIL.

National Agricultural Development Co (NADEC): POB 2557, Riyadh 11461; tel. (1) 404-0000; fax (1) 405-5522; e-mail info@nadec-sa.com; internet www.nadec.com.sa; f. 1981; interests include four dairy farms, 40,000 ha for cultivation of wheat, barley, forage and vegetables and processing of dates; the Govt has a 20% share; chief agency for agricultural devt; cap. 400m. riyals; Chair. SULAYMAN ABD AL-AZIZ AR-RAJHI; Pres. and Gen. Man. ABD AL-AZIZ AL-BABTAIN.

National Industrialization Co (NIC): POB 26707, Riyadh 11496; tel. (1) 476-7166; fax (1) 477-0898; e-mail general@nic.com.sa; internet www.nic.com.sa; f. 1985 to promote and establish industrial projects in Saudi Arabia; cap. 785m. riyals; 100% owned by Saudi nationals; Chair. MUBARAK BIN ABDULLAH AL-KHAFRAH; CEO MOAYYED AL-QURTAS.

Saudi Arabian General Investment Authority (SAGIA): POB 1267, Riyadh 11431; tel. 448-4533; fax 448-1234; internet www.sagia.gov.sa; f. 2000 to promote foreign investment; Gov. AMIR BIN ABDULLAH AD-DABBAGH.

Saudi Fund for Development (SFD): POB 50483, Riyadh 11523; tel. (1) 464-0292; fax (1) 464-7450; e-mail info@sfd.gov.sa; internet www.sfd.gov.sa; f. 1974 to help finance projects in developing countries; owned by Saudi Govt; had financed 417 projects by 2007; total commitments amounted to 27,728.36m. riyals; Chair. Dr IBRAHIM IBN ABD AL-AZIZ AL-ASSAF (Minister of Finance); Vice-Chair. and Man. Dir E. YOUSUF I. AL-BASSAM.

Saudi Industrial Development Fund (SIDF): POB 4143, Riyadh 11149; tel. (1) 477-4002; fax (1) 479-0165; e-mail sidf@sidf.gov.sa; internet www.sidf.gov.sa; f. 1974; supports and promotes local industrial devt, providing medium-term interest-free loans; also offers marketing, technical, financial and administrative advice; loans disbursed amounted to 1,100m. riyals in 2000; Chair. YOUSUF BIN IBRAHIM AL-BASSAM; Dir-Gen. ABDULLAH MUHAMMAD AL-OBOUDI.

CHAMBERS OF COMMERCE

Council of Saudi Chambers of Commerce and Industry: POB 16683, Riyadh 11474; tel. (1) 405-3200; fax (1) 402-4747; e-mail council@saudichambers.org.sa; internet www.saudichambers.org.sa; comprises one delegate from each of the chambers of commerce in the kingdom; Chair. ABD AR-RAHMAN RASHID AR-RASHID; Sec.-Gen. Dr FAHD AS-SULTAN.

Abha Chamber of Commerce and Industry: POB 722, Abha; tel. (7) 227-1818; fax (7) 227-1919; e-mail bhachamber@arab.net.sa; Pres. ABDULLAH SAID AL-MOBTY; Sec.-Gen. Dr MUHAMMAD Y. AL-MIZHIR.

Al-Ahsa Chamber of Commerce and Industry: POB 1519, al-Ahsa 31982; tel. (3) 852-0458; fax (3) 857-5274; Pres. SULAYMAN A. AL-HAMAAD.

Ar'ar Chamber of Commerce and Industry: POB 440, Ar'ar; tel. (4) 662-6544; fax (4) 662-4581; Sec.-Gen. THANI B. AL-ANEZI.

SAUDI ARABIA

Al-Baha Chamber of Commerce and Industry: POB 311, al-Baha; tel. (7) 727-0291; fax (7) 828-0146; Pres. SAAD A. ZOWMAH; Sec.-Gen. YAHYA AZ-ZAHRANI.

Eastern Province Chamber of Commerce and Industry: POB 719, Dammam 31421; tel. (3) 857-1111; fax (3) 857-0607; e-mail info@chamber.org.sa; internet www.chamber.org.sa; f. 1952; Pres. ABD AR-RAHMAN RASHID AR-RASHID; Sec.-Gen. IBRAHIM ABDULLAH AL-OLAYAN.

Federation of Gulf Co-operation Council Chambers (FGCCC): POB 2198, Dammam 31451; tel. (3) 826-5943; fax (3) 826-6794; e-mail fgccc@zajil.net; Pres. SALIM H. ALKHALILI; Sec.-Gen. MUHAMMAD A. AL-MULLA.

Ha'il Chamber of Commerce and Industry: POB 1291, Ha'il; tel. (6) 532-1060; fax (6) 533-1366; e-mail info@hail_chamber.org.sa; Pres. KHALID A. AS-SAIF.

Jeddah Chamber of Commerce and Industry: POB 1264, Jeddah 21431; tel. (2) 651-5111; fax (2) 651-7373; e-mail customerservice@jcci.org.sa; internet www.jcci.org.sa; f. 1946; 26,000 mems; Pres. SALEH ALI AT-TURKI; Sec.-Gen. Dr MUSTAFA K. SABRI.

Jizan Chamber of Commerce and Industry: POB 201, Jizan; tel. (7) 322-5155; fax (7) 322-3635; Pres. Eng. FAHD A. QALM.

Al-Jouf Chamber of Commerce and Industry: POB 585, al-Jouf; tel. (4) 624-9060; fax (4) 624-0108; Pres. MARZOUK S. AL-RASHID; Sec.-Gen. AHMAD KHALIFA AL-MUSALLAM.

Al-Majma' Chamber of Commerce and Industry: POB 165, al-Majma' 11952; tel. (6) 432-0268; fax (6) 432-2655; Pres. FAHD MUHAMMAD AR-RABIAH; Sec.-Gen. ABDULLAH IBRAHIM AL-JAAWAN.

Mecca Chamber of Commerce and Industry: POB 1086, Mecca; tel. (2) 534-3838; fax (2) 534-2904; f. 1947; Pres. ADEL ABDULLAH KA'AKI; Sec.-Gen. ABDULLAH ABD AL-GAFOOR TOUJAR-ALSHAHI.

Medina Chamber of Commerce and Industry: POB 443, King Abd al-Aziz Rd, Medina; tel. (4) 838-8909; fax (4) 838-8905; e-mail info@mcci.org.sa; internet www.mcci.org.sa; Pres. SALEH R. AS-SOHIME; Sec.-Gen. Dr LOUI BAKUR AT-TAYAR.

Najran Chamber of Commerce and Industry: POB 1138, Najran; tel. (7) 522-2216; fax (7) 522-3926; Sec.-Gen. ALI H. AL-ABAAS.

Al-Qassim Chamber of Commerce and Industry: POB 444, Buraydah, Qassim; tel. (6) 381-4000; fax (6) 381-2231; e-mail info@qcc.org.sa; internet www.qcc.org.sa; Pres. ABDULLAH S. AL-OTHIM.

Al-Qurayat Chamber of Commerce and Industry: POB 416, al-Qurayat; tel. (4) 642-6200; fax (4) 642-3172; Pres. OTHMAN ABDULLAH AL-YOUSUF; Sec.-Gen. JAMAL ALI AL-GHAMDI.

Riyadh Chamber of Commerce and Industry: POB 596, Riyadh 11421; tel. (1) 404-0044; fax (1) 402-1103; internet www.riyadhchamber.com; f. 1961; acts as arbitrator in business disputes, information centre; Pres. ABD AR-RAHMAN ALI AL-JERAISY; Sec.-Gen. HUSSEIN ABD AR-RAHMAN AL-AZAL; 23,000 mems.

Tabouk Chamber of Commerce and Industry: POB 567, Tabouk; tel. (4) 422-2736; fax (4) 422-7387; Pres. MUHAMMAD H. AL-WABSI; Sec.-Gen. AWADH AL-BALAWI.

Ta'if Chamber of Commerce and Industry: POB 1005, Ta'if; tel. (2) 736-6800; fax (2) 738-0040; e-mail info@taifchamber.org.sa; internet www.taifchamber.org.sa; Pres. NAIF A. AL-ADWANI; Sec.-Gen. Eng. YOUSUF MUHAMMAD ASH-SHAFI.

Yanbu Chamber of Commerce and Industry: POB 58, Yanbu; tel. (4) 322-7878; fax (4) 322-6800; f. 1979; publishes quarterly magazine; 5,000 members; Pres. Dr MANSOUR M. AL-ANSARI; Sec.-Gen. OSMAN NAIM AL-MUFTI.

STATE HYDROCARBONS COMPANIES

General Petroleum and Mineral Organization (PETROMIN JET): POB 7550, 21472 Jeddah; tel. (2) 685-7666; fax (2) 685-7545; works in conjunction with the Ministry of Petroleum and Mineral Resources to oversee petroleum industry; Chair. and Exec. Asst ABDULLAH O. ATTAS (acting).

Arabian Drilling Co: POB 708, Dammam 31421; tel. (3) 887-2020; fax (3) 882-6588; e-mail adcgen@al-khobar.oilfield.slb.com; f. 1964; PETROMIN shareholding 51%, remainder French private cap; undertakes contract drilling for oil (on shore and off shore), minerals and water both inside and outside Saudi Arabia; Chair. SULAYMAN J. AL-HERBISH; Man. Dir SAAD ABDULLAH SAAB.

Arabian Geophysical and Surveying Co (ARGAS): POB 535, al-Khobar 31952; tel. (3) 882-9122; fax (3) 882-9060; f. 1966; PETROMIN shareholding 51%; remainder provided by Cie Générale de Géophysique; geophysical exploration for petroleum, other minerals and groundwater, as well as all types of land, airborne and marine surveys; Chair. AHMAD MUHAMMAD GHAZZAWI; Man. Dir HABIB M. MERGHELANI.

Petromin Marketing (PETMARK): POB 50, Dhahran Airport 31932; tel. (3) 890-3883; f. 1967; operates the installations and facilities for the distribution of petroleum products in the Eastern, Central, Southern and Northern provinces of Saudi Arabia; Pres. and CEO HUSSEIN A. LINJAWI.

Saudi Arabian Oil Co (Saudi Aramco): POB 5000, Dhahran 31311; tel. (3) 872-0115; fax (3) 873-8190; e-mail webmaster@aramco.com.sa; internet www.saudiaramco.com; f. 1933; previously known as Arabian-American Oil Co (Aramco); in 1993 incorporated the Saudi Arabian Marketing and Refining Co (SAMAREC, f. 1988) by merger of operations; holds the principal working concessions in Saudi Arabia; operates five wholly owned refineries (at Jeddah, Rabigh, Ras Tanura, Riyadh and Yanbu) with total capacity of more than 1m. barrels per day; Pres. and CEO ABDULLAH S. JUM'AH; Exec. Vice-Pres. (Operations) KHALID A. AL-FALIH.

Saudi Arabian Lubricating Oil Co (PETROLUBE): POB 1432, Jeddah 21431; tel. (2) 661-3333; fax (2) 661-3322; e-mail info@petrominoils.com; internet www.petrominoils.com; f. 1968; 71% owned by Saudi Aramco, 29% by Mobil; for the manufacture and marketing of lubricating oils and other related products; production 140m. litres (2002); cap. 110m. riyals; Chair. Eng. ALI A. AL-MUHAREB; Pres. and CEO Eng. SALEM H. SHAHEEN.

Saudi Aramco Lubricating Oil Refining Co (LUBEREF): POB 5518, Jeddah 21432; tel. (2) 638-5040; fax (2) 636-6932; f. 1975; owned 70% by Saudi Aramco and 30% by Mobil; production 3,800,000 barrels; Chair. SALIM S. AL-AYDH; Pres. and CEO MUHAMMAD ALI AL-HARAZY.

Saudi Aramco Mobil Refinery Co Ltd (SAMREF): POB 30078, Yanbu; tel. (4) 396-4000; fax (4) 396-0942; f. 1981; operated by Saudi Aramco and Mobil, capacity 360,000 b/d; Pres. and CEO MUHAMMAD A. MISFER.

Saudi Aramco Shell Refinery Co (SASREF): POB 10088, Madinat al-Jubail, as-Sinaiyah 31961; tel. (3) 357-2000; fax (3) 357-2525; e-mail info@sasref.com.sa; internet www.sasref.com.sa; operated by Saudi Aramco and Shell; capacity 300,000 b/d; exports began in 1985; Chair. HAMID T. AS-SAUDOON.

Saudi Basic Industries Corpn (SABIC): POB 5101, Riyadh 11422; tel. (1) 225-8000; fax (1) 225-9000; internet www.sabic.com; f. 1976 to foster the petrochemical industry and other hydrocarbon-based industries through jt ventures with foreign partners, and to market their products; 70% state-owned; production 38.79m. tons (2002); Chair. Prince SA'UD BIN THUNAYAN AS-SA'UD; Vice-Chair. and CEO MUHAMMAD AL-MADY.

Projects include:

Al-Jubail Petrochemical Co (Kemya): POB 10084, Jubail 31961; tel. (3) 357-6000; fax (3) 358-7858; f. 1980; began production of linear low-density polyethylene in 1984, of high-density polyethylene in 1985, and of high alfa olefins in 1986, capacity of 330,000 tons per year of polyethylene; jt venture with Exxon Corpn (USA) and SABIC; Pres. ABD AL-AZIZ I. AL-AUDAH; Exec. Vice-Pres. CLAY LEWIS.

Arabian Petrochemical Co (Petrokemya): POB 10002, Jubail 31961; tel. (3) 358-7000; fax (3) 358-4480; e-mail otaibifr@petrokemya.sabic.com; produced 2.4m. tons of ethylene, 135,000 tons of polystyrene, 100,000 tons of butene-1; 570,000 tons of propylene, 100,000 tons of butadiene and 150,000 tons of benzene in 2001; wholly owned subsidiary of SABIC; owns 50% interest in ethylene glycol plant producing 610,000 tons per year of monoethylene glycol, 65,000 tons per year of diethylene glycol and 3,900 tons per year of triethylene glycol; Chair. HOMOOD AT-TUWAIJRI; Pres. KHALID S. AR-RAWAF.

Eastern Petrochemical Co (Sharq): POB 10035, Jubail 31961; tel. (3) 357-5000; fax (3) 358-0383; f. 1981 to produce linear low-density polyethylene, ethylene glycol; total capacity 660,000 tons of ethylene glycol and 280,000 tons of polyethylene per year; a SABIC jt venture; Pres. IBRAHIM S. ASH-SHEWEIR.

National Industrial Gases Co (Gas): POB 10110, Jubail 31961; tel. (3) 357-5700; fax (3) 358-5542; total capacity of 876,000 tons of oxygen and 492,750 tons of nitrogen per year; jt venture with Saudi private sector; Pres. ABDULLAH MUJBEL AL-JALAWI.

National Plastic Co (Ibn Hayyan): POB 10002, Jubail 31961; tel. (3) 358-7000; fax (3) 358-4736; f. 1984; produces 390,000 tons per year of vinylchloride monomer and 24,000 tons per year of polyvinylchloride; jt venture with Lucky Group (Republic of Korea), SABIC and three other cos; Pres. KHALED AR-RAWAF.

Saudi-European Petrochemical Co (Ibn Zahr): POB 10330, Jubail 31961; tel. (3) 341-5060; fax (3) 341-2966; f. 1985; annual capacity 1.4m. tons of methyl-tertiary-butyl ether (MTBE), 0.3m. tons of propylene; SABIC has a 70% share, Ecofuel, Nesté Corpn and APICORP each have 10%; Pres. SAMI AS-SUWAIGH.

Saudi Methanol Co (ar-Razi): POB 10065, Jubail Industrial City 31961; tel. (3) 357-7820; fax (3) 358-0838; e-mail emt@arrazi.com; f. 1979; capacity of 3,158,000 tons per year of chemical-grade methanol; total methanol exports in 2001 were 3,248,000 tons; jt venture with a consortium of Japanese cos; Pres. NABIL A. MANSOURI; Exec. Vice-Pres. H. MIZUNO.

SAUDI ARABIA

Saudi Petrochemical Co (Sadaf): POB 10025, Jubail 31961; tel. (3) 357-3000; fax (3) 357-3142; f. 1980 to produce ethylene, ethylene dichloride, styrene, crude industrial ethanol, caustic soda and methyl-tertiary-butyl-ether (MTBE); total capacity of 4,710,000 tons per year; Shell (Pecten) has a 50% share; Pres. MOSAED S. AL-OHALI.

Saudi Yanbu Petrochemical Co (Yanpet): POB 30139, Yanbu; tel. (4) 396-5000; fax (4) 396-5006; f. 1980 to produce 820,000 tons per year of ethylene, 600,000 tons per year of high-density polyethylene and 340,000 tons per year of ethylene glycol; total capacity 1,692,200 tons per year by 1990; Mobil and SABIC each have a 50% share; Pres. ALI AL-KHURAIMI; Exec. CEO P. J. FOLEY.

Foreign Concessionaires

Arabian Oil Co Ltd (AOC): POB 256, Ras al-Khafji 31971; tel. (3) 766-0555; fax (3) 766-2001; internet www.aoc.co.jp; f. 1958; holds concession (2,200 sq km at Dec. 1987) for offshore exploitation of Saudi Arabia's half-interest in the Saudi Arabia-Kuwait Neutral Zone; Pres. KEIICHI KONAGA; Chief Exec. Gen. Affairs AHMAD IBRAHIM AL-ASFOUR.

Saudi Arabian Texaco Inc: POB 363, Riyadh; tel. (1) 462-7274; fax (1) 464-1992; also office in Kuwait; f. 1928; fmrly Getty Oil Co; holds concession (5,200 sq km at Dec. 1987) for exploitation of Saudi Arabia's half-interest in the Saudi Arabia-Kuwait Neutral Zone.

UTILITIES

Utilities Co (Uco): Jubail; f. 1999; owned equally by Royal Commission for Jubail and Yanbu, Public Investment Fund, Saudi Aramco and SABIC; cap. 2,000m. riyals; provides utilities in industrial cities of Jubail and Yanbu.

Electricity

Electricity and Co-generation Regulatory Authority (ECRA): PO Box 4540, Riyadh 11412; tel. (1) 201-9045; e-mail public@ecra.gov.sa; internet www.ecra.gov.sa; f. 2001 to regulate the power industry and to recommend tariffs for the sector; Gov. Dr FAREED M. ZEDAN.

Saudi Electricity Co (SEC): POB 57, Riyadh 11411; tel. (1) 403-2222; fax (1) 405-1191; internet www.se.com.sa; f. 1999 following merger of 10 regional cos, to organize the generation, transmission and distribution of electricity into separate operating cos; jt-stock co; cap. 33,758m.; Chair. GHAZI AL-GOSAIBI; CEO ALI SALEH AL-BARRAK.

Water

Saline Water Conversion Corpn (SWCC): POB 4931, 21412 Jeddah; tel. (2) 682-1240; fax (2) 682-0415; privatization under consideration in 2006; provides desalinated water; 24 plants; Gov. FAHID ASH-SHARIF; Dir-Gen. ABD AL-AZIZ OMAR NASSIEF.

TRADE UNIONS

Trade unions are illegal in Saudi Arabia.

Transport

RAILWAYS

Saudi Arabia has the only rail system in the Arabian peninsula. The Saudi Government Railroad comprises 719 km of single and 157 km of double track. In addition, the total length of spur lines and sidings is 348 km. The main line, which was opened in 1951, is 578 km in length; it connects Dammam port, on the Gulf coast, with Riyadh, and passes Dhahran, Abqaiq, Hufuf, Harad and al-Kharj. A 310-km line, linking Hufuf and Riyadh, was inaugurated in May 1985. New 950-km and 115-km lines, connecting Riyadh with Jeddah and Dammam with Jubail, respectively, known as the Saudi Landbridge Project, were planned in 2006. The revamped network was to connect the Red Sea with the Persian (Arabian) Gulf and was to be closely linked with Jeddah Islamic Port and King Abd al-Aziz Port (at Dammam). The scheme was presented to potential investors in January 2005. Concessions to build a 570-km 'Western Region' line, connecting the west-coast centres of Jeddah, Mecca, Medina and Yanbu, and a 1,300-km 'North–South' line, connecting Riyadh, Qassim, Ha'il, az-Zubayrah and al-Jalamid, were to be tendered at a later stage. A US $400m. project to construct two light urban lines in Riyadh was also planned in 2006; the project was scheduled for completion in 2013. A total of 1.3m. passengers travelled by rail in the kingdom in 2004.

Saudi Railways Organization (SRO): POB 36, Dammam 31241; tel. (3) 871-3000; fax (3) 827-1130; e-mail sro@sro.org.sa; internet www.saudirailways.org; Pres. ABD AL-AZIZ BIN MUHAMMAD AL-HOQAIL.

ROADS

Asphalted roads link Jeddah to Mecca, Jeddah to Medina, Medina to Yanbu, at-Ta'if to Mecca, Riyadh to al-Kharj, and Dammam to Hufuf, as well as the principal communities and certain outlying points in Saudi Aramco's area of operations. The trans-Arabian highway links Dammam, Riyadh, at-Ta'if, Mecca and Jeddah. The construction of an 810-km road connecting Qassim, Medina, Yanbu, Rabigh and Thuwal, at a cost of some SR 5,350m., was under way, and in February 2006 the long-considered project to build a causeway between Saudi Arabia and Egypt across the Straits of Tiran was revived. Tenders for the latter project were expected to be invited by the end of 2008. In 2006 there were 174,429 km of roads, of which 15,548 km were main roads (including motorways), 9,098 km were secondary roads and 25,845 km were asphalted agricultural roads. Metalled roads link all the main population centres.

Saudi Public Transport Co (SAPTCO): POB 10667, Riyadh 11443; tel. (1) 454-5000; fax (1) 454-2100; e-mail info@saptco.com.sa; internet www.saptco.com.sa; f. 1979; operates a public bus service throughout Saudi Arabia and to neighbouring countries; the Govt holds a 30% share; Chair. Dr NASIR AS-SALOOM; CEO Dr ABD AL-AZIZ AL-OHALY.

National Transport Co of Saudi Arabia: POB 7280, Queen's Bldg, Jeddah 21462; tel. (2) 643-4561; specializes in inward clearance, freight forwarding, general and heavy road haulage, re-export, charter air freight and exhibitions; Man. Dir A. D. BLACKSTOCK; Operations Man. I. CROXSON.

SHIPPING

Responsibility for the management, operation and maintenance of the commercial ports of Jeddah, Dammam, Yanbu, Dhiba and Jizan, the King Fahd Industrial Ports of Jubail and Yanbu, and the oil port of Ras Tanura, as well as a number of minor ports, began to be transferred to the private sector after 1997, but all ports remain subject to regulation and scrutiny by the Ports Authority. Some 98% of Saudi Arabia's imports and exports passed through the country's sea ports, which received 10,163 vessels in, 2004. In 2002 there were 183 mechanized and organized berths. In 2004 the total cargo handled by Saudi Arabian ports, excluding crude petroleum, was 119.9m. metric tons, compared with 68.2m. tons in 1990/91. Some 2.1m. passengers were also embarked and disembarked in that year.

Jeddah is the principal commercial port and the main point of entry for pilgrims bound for Mecca. It has berths for general cargo, container traffic, 'roll on, roll off' (ro-ro) traffic, livestock and bulk grain shipments, with draughts ranging from 8 m to 16 m. The port also has a 200-ton floating crane, cold storage facilities and a fully equipped ship-repair yard. In 2004 a total of 4,654 vessels called at Jeddah Islamic Port, and some 33.5m. tons of cargo, excluding crude petroleum, were handled and 1.1m. passengers were processed.

Dammam is the second largest commercial port and has general cargo, container, ro-ro, dangerous cargo and bulk grain berths. Draughts at this port range from 8 m to 13.5 m. It has a 200-ton floating crane and a fully equipped ship-repair yard. In 2004 a total of 2,028 vessels called at King Abd al-Aziz Port in Dammam and some 14.0m. tons of cargo, excluding crude petroleum, were handled.

Jubail has one commercial and one industrial port. The commercial port has general cargo, bulk grain and container berths with ro-ro facilities, and a floating crane. Draughts at this port range from 12 m to 14 m. In 2004 a total of 157 vessels called at Jubail Commercial Port, and 2.1m. tons of goods, excluding crude petroleum, were handled. The industrial port has bulk cargo, refined and petrochemical and ro-ro berths, and an open sea tanker terminal suitable for vessels up to 300,000 dwt. Draughts range from 6 m to 30 m. In 2004 a total of 1,284 vessels called at King Fahd Industrial Port in Jubail; 36.4m. tons of cargo, excluding crude petroleum, were handled in that year.

Yanbu, which comprises one commercial and one industrial port, is Saudi Arabia's nearest major port to Europe and North America, and is the focal point of the most rapidly growing area, in the west of Saudi Arabia. The commercial port has general cargo, ro-ro and bulk grain berths, with draughts ranging from 10 m to 12 m. It also has a floating crane, and is equipped to handle minor ship repairs. A total of 113 vessels called at Yanbu Commercial Port, and less than 1.0m. tons of cargo, excluding crude petroleum, were handled in 2004. The industrial port has berths for general cargo, containers, ro-ro traffic, bulk cargo, crude petroleum, refined and petrochemical products and natural gas liquids, and a tanker terminal on the open sea. In 2004 a total of 1,447 vessels called at King Fahd Industrial Port in Yanbu; the port handled 32.0m. tons of cargo, excluding crude petroleum, in that year.

Jizan is the main port for the southern part of the country. It has general cargo, ro-ro, bulk grain and container berths, with draughts ranging from 8 m to 11 m. It also has a 200-ton floating crane. In 2004 a total of 31 vessels called at Jizan Port; 0.6m. tons of cargo, excluding crude petroleum, were handled in the same year.

Dhiba port, on the northern Red Sea coast, serves the Tabouk region. It has three general cargo berths with a ro-ro ramp, and passenger-handling facilities. Maximum draught is 10.5 m. In 2004 a total of 899 vessels called at Dhiba; 0.4m. tons of cargo, excluding crude petroleum, were handled in that year.

In addition to these major ports, there are a number of minor ports suitable only for small craft, including Khuraiba, Haql, al-Wajh, Umlujj, Rabigh, al-Lith, Qunfoudah, Farasan and al-Qahma on the Red Sea coast and al-Khobar, al-Qatif, Uqair, Darin and Ras al-Khafji on the Gulf coast. Ras Mishab, on the Gulf coast, is operated by the Ministry of Defence and Civil Aviation.

Saudi Ports Authority: POB 5162, Riyadh 11422; tel. (1) 405-0005; fax (1) 405-3508; e-mail info@ports.gov.sa; internet www.ports.gov.sa; f. 1976; regulatory authority; Pres. Dr KHALED AHMAD ABD AR-RAHMAN BUBSHAIT.

Dammam: POB 28062, Dammam 31188; tel. (3) 858-3900; fax (3) 857-1727; Dir-Gen. NAEEM IBRAHIM AN-NAEEM.

Dhiba: POB 190, Dhiba; tel. (4) 432-1060; fax (4) 432-2679; Dir-Gen. MUHAMMAD ASH-SHAREEF.

Jeddah: POB 9285, Jeddah 21188; tel. (2) 647-1200; fax (2) 647-7411; Dir-Gen. SAHIR M. TAHLAWI.

Jizan: POB 16, Jizan; tel. (7) 317-1000; fax (7) 317-0777; Dir-Gen. ALI HAMOUD BAKRI.

Jubail: POB 547, Jubail 31951; tel. (3) 357-8000; fax (3) 357-8011; Dir-Gen. MUTHANNA ISA AL-QURTAS.

Yanbu: POB 30325, Yanbu; tel. (4) 396-7000; fax (4) 396-7037; Dir-Gen. Dr HUMOOD SAADI.

Arabian Petroleum Supply Co Ltd: POB 1408, Al-Qurayat St, Jeddah 21431; tel. (2) 637-1120; fax (2) 636-2366; Chair. Sheikh MUHAMMAD YOUSSUF ALI REZA; Gen. Man. E. D. CONNOLLY.

Baaboud Trading and Shipping Agencies: POB 7262, Jeddah 21462; tel. (2) 627-0000; fax (2) 627-1111; e-mail info@baaboud.net; Chair. AHMAD M. BAABOUD; Man. Dir AHMED ABOUD BAABOUD.

Bakry Navigation Co Ltd: POB 3757, Jeddah 21481; tel. (2) 651-9995; fax (2) 651-2908; Chair. Sheikh A. K. AL-BAKRY; Man. Dir G. A. K. AL-BAKRY.

National Shipping Co of Saudi Arabia (NSCSA): POB 8931, Riyadh 11492; tel. (1) 478-5454; fax (1) 477-8036; e-mail info@nscsa.com.sa; internet www.nscsa.com; f. 1979; transportation of crude petroleum and petrochemical products; routes through Red Sea and Mediterranean to USA and Canada; operates a fleet of 37 ships; Chair. ABDULLAH SULAIMAN AR-RUBAIAN; CEO HUMOUD AL-AJLAN.

Saudi Lines: POB 66, Jeddah 21411; tel. (2) 642-3051; regular cargo and passenger services between Red Sea and Indian Ocean ports; Pres. M. A. BAKHASHAB PASHA; Man. Dir A. M. BAKHASHAB.

Saudi Shipping and Maritime Services Co Ltd (TRANSHIP): POB 7522, Jeddah 21472; tel. (2) 642-4255; fax (2) 643-2821; e-mail transhp@tri.net.sa; Chair. Prince SA'UD IBN NAYEF IBN ABD AL-AZIZ; Man. Dir Capt. MUSTAFA T. AWARA.

Shipping Corpn of Saudi Arabia Ltd: POB 1691, Arab Maritime Center, Malik Khalid St, Jeddah 21441; tel. (2) 647-1137; fax (2) 647-8222; e-mail arablines@arabjeddah.com; Pres. and Man. Dir ABD AL-AZIZ AHMAD ARAB.

CIVIL AVIATION

King Abd al-Aziz International Airport (KAIA), in Jeddah, which was opened in 1981, has three terminals, one of which is specifically designed to cope with the needs of the many thousands of pilgrims who visit Mecca and Medina each year. Construction work on two new terminals and improvements at KAIA commenced in late 2004. The project, scheduled for completion by 2009 (at an estimated cost of US $600m.), was expected to increase the airport's annual passenger capacity from about 10.5m. to 25m. King Khalid International Airport, in Riyadh, opened in 1983 with four terminals. It handled 8.7m. passengers in 2001. A third major airport, King Fahd International Airport (with an initial handling capacity of 5.2m. passengers per year), opened in the Eastern Province in 1994. Some 2.7m. passengers used the airport in 2001. Overall, the country's airports were used by some 36m. passengers in 2006. There are 27 commercial airports in the kingdom. Plans to privatize the kingdom's airports were announced in October 2003. In March 2005 British Airways suspended its London–Jeddah and London–Riyadh services, stating that the routes were unprofitable. However, another British company, British Midland Airways, began operating three weekly London–Riyadh flights from September.

General Authority of Civil Aviation (GACA): POB 887, Jeddah 21165; tel. (2) 640-5000; fax (2) 640-2444; e-mail feedback@pca.gov.sa; internet www.gaca.gov.sa; fmrly the Presidency of Civil Aviation; Pres. Dr ALI ABD AR-RAHMAN AL-KHALAF.

National Air Services Co: Riyadh; f. 1998; privately owned; cap. 60m. riyals; Chair. YOUSUF AL-MAIMANI.

Sama Airlines: POB 361662, Riyadh 11313; tel. (1) 263-9500; fax (1) 454-8720; e-mail contact@flysama.com; internet www.flysama.com; f. 2006; low-cost airline providing domestic services; Chair. Prince BANDAR BIN KHALID AL FAISAL; Man. Dir ANDREW COWEN.

Saudi Arabian Airlines: POB 620, Jeddah 21231; tel. (2) 686-4588; fax (2) 686-4587; internet www.saudiairlines.com; f. 1945; began operations in 1947; carried 15.4m. passengers in 2004; regular services to 25 domestic and 52 international destinations; scheduled for privatization; Chair. Prince SULTAN IBN ABD AL-AZIZ; Dir-Gen. KHALID AL-MULHIM; Exec. Vice-Pres. (Operations) ADNAN AD-DAB-BAGH.

Tourism

All devout Muslims try to make at least one visit to the holy cities of Medina, the burial place of Muhammad, and Mecca, his birthplace. In 2000 the Government decided to issue tourist visas for the first time. A Supreme Commission for Tourism (SCT—now known as the General Commission for Tourism and Antiquities), to develop the tourism industry in Saudi Arabia, was subsequently established. In 2005 the SCT announced plans to increase the kingdom's supply of hotel rooms to 150,000 by 2013 (from the present 95,000). Tourist numbers increased to 8.6m. in 2004 (compared with 7.3m. in 2003), but declined to 8.0m. in 2005. Receipts from tourism amounted to US $5,181. in 2005. A total of 1,557,447 foreign pilgrims visited Mecca in the Islamic year ending 30 January 2006.

General Commission for Tourism and Antiquities (GCTA): POB 66680, Riyadh 11586; tel. (1) 880-8855; fax (1) 880-8844; internet www.gcta.gov.sa; f. 2001 as the Supreme Commission for Tourism; Sec-Gen. Prince SULTAN IBN SALMAN IBN ABD AL-AZIZ AS-SA'UD.

Saudi Hotels and Resort Areas Co (SHARACO): POB 5500, Riyadh 11422; tel. (1) 481-6666; fax (1) 480-1666; f. 1975; Saudi Govt has a 40% interest; Chair. MUSAAD AS-SENANY; Dir-Gen. ABD AL-AZIZ AL-AMBAR.

SENEGAL

Introductory Survey

Location, Climate, Language, Religion, Flag, Capital

The Republic of Senegal lies on the west coast of Africa, bordered to the north by Mauritania, to the east by Mali, and to the south by Guinea and Guinea-Bissau. In the southern part of the country The Gambia forms a narrow enclave extending some 320 km (200 miles) inland. The climate is tropical, with a long dry season followed by a short wet season—from June to September in the north, and from June to October in the south. Average annual temperatures range from 22°C (72°F) to 28°C (82°F). French is the official language; the most widely spoken national languages at the time of the 1988 census were Wolof (spoken by 49.2% of the population), Peul (22.2%), Serer (12.8%) and Diola (5.1%). At the 1988 census almost 94% of the population were Muslims, and some 4% Christians, mostly Roman Catholics; a small number followed traditional beliefs. The national flag (proportions 2 by 3) has three equal vertical stripes, of green, yellow and red, with a five-pointed green star in the centre of the yellow stripe. The capital is Dakar. In July 2005 the Assemblée nationale approved legislation providing for the creation of a new administrative capital, near Kébèmer, on the Atlantic littoral.

Recent History

After 300 years as a French colony, Senegal became a self-governing member of the French Community in November 1958. The Mali Federation, linking Senegal with Soudan (later the Republic of Mali), had only two months of independence before being dissolved when Senegal seceded, to become a separate independent state, on 20 August 1960. The Republic of Senegal was proclaimed on 5 September, with Léopold Sédar Senghor, leader of the Union progressiste sénégalaise (UPS), as the country's first President.

In late 1962, following the discovery of a coup attempt led by the Prime Minister, Mamadou Dia, Senghor assumed the premiership; other political parties were gradually absorbed into the UPS or outlawed, effectively creating a one-party state by 1966. In 1970 the office of Prime Minister was restored and assigned to a provincial administrator, Abdou Diouf, who in 1976 was made Senghor's constitutional successor. In 1973 Senghor, the sole candidate, was re-elected President. Senghor amended the Constitution in March 1976 to allow three parties to contest elections—the UPS, renamed the Parti socialiste (PS), the Parti démocratique sénégalais (PDS) and the Parti africain de l'indépendance (PAI). The first national elections under the three-party system took place in February 1978; the PS won 83 of the 100 seats in the Assemblée nationale, the remainder being won by the PDS. In the concurrent presidential election, Senghor overwhelmingly defeated the leader of the PDS, Abdoulaye Wade.

Senghor was succeeded as President by Diouf in January 1981. An amnesty was declared for political dissidents, and the Constitution was amended to allow the existence of an unlimited number of political parties. At elections in February 1983 Diouf received 83.5% of the presidential vote (compared with 14.8% for his nearest rival, Wade), while in legislative elections the PS won 111 of the 120 seats. In April Diouf abolished the post of Prime Minister, which had latterly been held by Habib Thiam.

When preliminary results of the February 1988 presidential and legislative elections indicated clear victories for both Diouf and the PS, opposition parties alleged fraud on the part of the ruling party, and, following the outbreak of rioting in Dakar, a state of emergency was imposed. Various opposition members, including Wade and Amath Dansokho, the leader of the Parti de l'indépendance et du travail (PIT), were arrested. According to the official results of the presidential election, contested by four candidates, Diouf obtained 73.2% of the votes cast, and Wade 25.8%. In the legislative elections, the PS won 103 seats, and the PDS the remaining 17.

In October 1989 changes to the electoral code were approved by the Assemblée nationale; a partial system of proportional representation was to be introduced for legislative elections, and access to the state-owned media was to be granted to opposition parties.

In March 1991 the legislature approved several amendments to the Constitution, notably the restoration of the post of Prime Minister, to which post Thiam was again named in the following month. Thiam's Government included four representatives of the PDS (including Wade, as Minister of State, effectively the most senior post in the Government other than the Prime Minister); Dansokho became Minister of Town Planning and Housing. In September 1991 the Assemblée nationale adopted further amendments to the electoral code. Presidential elections would henceforth take place, in two rounds if necessary (to ensure that the President would be elected by an absolute majority of votes cast), every seven years, with a mandate that would be renewable only once. Legislative voting would, however, continue to take place at five-yearly intervals.

In October 1992 Wade and his three PDS colleagues resigned from the Council of Ministers, protesting that they had been excluded from the governmental process. Eight candidates contested the presidential election, which took place in February 1993. Despite some irregularities, voting was reported to be orderly in most areas, outwith Casamance (see below). The opposition denounced the preliminary results, which indicated that Diouf had won a clear majority. In March the Constitutional Council announced that Diouf had been re-elected with 58.4% of the votes cast (51.6% of the electorate had voted); Wade secured 32.0% of the votes.

Elections to the Assemblée nationale took place in May 1993, in which the PS won 84 of the 120 elective seats; the PDS took 27 seats. The rate of participation by voters was 40.7%. Shortly after the announcement of the results the Vice-President of the Constitutional Council, Babacar Sèye, was assassinated. Wade and three other PDS leaders were detained for three days in connection with the killing. Thiam formed a new Government in June. Dansokho, who had supported Diouf's presidential campaign, retained his portfolio, while Abdoulaye Bathily, the leader of the Ligue démocratique—Mouvement pour le parti du travail (LD—MPT), who had also contested the presidency, received a ministerial post. In October Wade was charged with complicity in the assassination of Sèye; Wade's wife and a PDS deputy were also charged in connection with the killing. In November Ousmane Ngom, the PDS parliamentary leader, and Landing Savané, the leader of And Jëf—Parti africain pour la démocratie et le socialisme (AJ—PADS), were among those detained following a protest in Dakar to demand the cancellation of austerity measures. Ngom, Savané and some 87 others were convicted of participating in an unauthorized demonstration, and received suspended prison sentences.

Following the devaluation of the CFA franc, in January 1994, emergency measures were adopted to offset the immediate adverse economic effects and consequent hardship. In February a demonstration in Dakar to denounce the devaluation degenerated into serious rioting, as a result of which eight people were killed. Wade and Savané were among those subsequently charged in association with the unrest. Charges against Wade and his opposition associates in connection with the murder of Sèye were dismissed in May 1994, although Wade and Savané remained in custody until July, in connection with the post-devaluation violence. In October three of Sèye's alleged assassins were convicted and sentenced to 18–20 years' imprisonment.

Five members of the PDS, including Wade, as Minister of State at the Presidency, were appointed to a new Council of Ministers in March 1995. Djibo Kâ, a long-serving government member who, as Minister of the Interior, had been associated with the legal proceedings against Wade and other opposition leaders, left the Government. In September Dansokho and another PIT member were dismissed from the Council of Ministers. In January 1996 Diouf announced that a second legislative chamber, the Sénat, was to be established.

In February 1998 Wade appealed to the Constitutional Council to reject an amendment to the electoral code whereby the number of deputies in the Assemblée nationale was to be increased to 140; later in the month the Council annulled the proposed increase, the first occasion on which the Council had ruled against a decision of the legislature. In March, however, the Assemblée nationale again voted to increase the number of deputies. In April Kâ resigned from the PS to present his own list of candidates, as the Union pour le renouveau démocratique (URD).

Some 18 parties and coalitions contested the legislative elections on 24 May 1998. Outwith Casamance, voting was reported to have taken place generally in an atmosphere of calm. The PS obtained 93 seats in the enlarged assembly, with 50.2% of the valid votes cast, while the number of PDS deputies was reduced to 23; Kâ's URD, in alliance with the Alliance pour le progrès et la justice—Jëf-Jël (APJ—JJ), secured 11 seats. The rate of participation by voters was 39% of the registered electorate. In July Thiam resigned as Prime Minister, and was replaced by Mamadou Lamine Loum. A new Council of Ministers was named shortly afterwards, in which most ministers in the outgoing administration, with the notable exception of Moustapha Niasse, hitherto Minister of Foreign Affairs and Senegalese Abroad, retained their portfolios. Serigne Diop, the leader of the Parti démocratique sénégalais—Rénovation (which had broken away from the PDS in 1997) was the only non-PS member of the Government.

In August 1998 the Assemblée nationale voted to revise the Constitution to remove the clause restricting the Head of State to a maximum of two terms of office, thus permitting Diouf to contest the next presidential election, in 2000. A requirement that the President be elected by more than 25% of all registered voters was also abandoned. The opposition parties, condemning the amendments, boycotted the vote.

The PS won all 45 elective seats in the first, indirect, elections to the Sénat in January 1999; these 45 members were chosen by an electoral college of deputies, local, municipal and regional councillors. Only the PS, the Parti libéral du Sénégal (formed in 1998 by Ngom, leading a breakaway movement from the PDS), and a coalition of the PIT and AJ—PADS contested the elections; the PDS and other opposition parties were opposed to the introduction of an additional parliamentary chamber. A further 12 senators were appointed by the President of the Republic, including two opposition figures, and three were elected by Senegalese resident abroad. One of the 12 senators nominated by Diouf, Abdoulaye Diack, a prominent member of the PS, was elected President of the new body.

In March 1999 an alliance of AJ—PADS, the PIT, the PDS and the LD—MPT agreed to nominate Wade, who had resigned from the Assemblée nationale in mid-1998, as their joint candidate in the presidential election scheduled for 2000. In April 1999 the PDS began a boycott of the Assemblée nationale, accusing the Government of seeking to manipulate the voters' register for the presidential election. In June Niasse announced his intention of contesting the presidential election, and published a document accusing Diouf and the PS of corruption; Niasse was consequently expelled from the PS and subsequently formed the Alliance des forces de progrès (AFP).

Although Diouf won the largest proportion of votes cast (41.3%) at the election, held on 27 February 2000, his failure to secure an absolute majority of votes cast necessitated a second round of voting, between Diouf and Wade (who had secured 31.0% of votes cast). Of the remaining candidates, Niasse received 16.8% of votes cast, while Kâ took 7.1%. Prior to the second round of voting, Wade received the endorsement of Niasse, and of the majority of the candidates defeated in the first round, with the notable exception of Kâ, who defied the wishes of his party and gave public support to Diouf. At the second round, on 19 March, Wade won 58.5% of the total votes cast, thus taking the presidency from the PS for the first time. Turn-out in the second round was estimated at 60.1%, marginally lower than in the first round.

Wade was sworn in as President on 1 April 2000, at a public ceremony attended by seven African Heads of State. Niasse was named Prime Minister in the 29-member Council of Ministers appointed later in the month, and several other opposition leaders, including Savané of AJ—PADS and Bathily of the LD—MPT, and representatives of civil society received ministerial portfolios. Wade announced that he did not envisage governing alongside an Assemblée nationale dominated by the PS, and that he therefore intended to hold fresh legislative elections, following a constitutional referendum initially scheduled for 27 November 2000. Among the proposed changes, the President would gain the power to dissolve the Assemblée nationale, while other presidential powers would be transferred to the Prime Minister, and the presidential mandate would again be reduced from seven to five years, renewable only once. Furthermore, the Sénat was to be abolished.

The constitutional referendum was held, following several postponements, on 7 January 2001. Some 94.0% of votes cast in the plebiscite supported the new Constitution; 65.8% of the registered electorate voted. Most provisions of the Constitution, including the abolition of the Sénat and the Economic and Social Council, took immediate effect, following its promulgation by the President, with only those sections relating to the legislature necessitating new elections before their implementation. Future presidential mandates would be reduced from seven to five years, and the number of deputies in the Assemblée nationale was reduced from 140 to 120.

The President dissolved the Assemblée nationale in mid-February 2001 and announced that the new legislature, which was to be elected in April, would consist of 65 seats elected by majority voting in departments, and 55 by proportional representation using national lists. In March Wade appointed Mame Madior Boye, a politically unaffiliated magistrate, and hitherto Minister of Justice, as Prime Minister. In the ensuing reshuffle Niasse and other members of the AFP were removed from office, in what was regarded as an attempt by Wade to create a more unified Government, which incorporated greater representation for the PDS and its allies, prior to the legislative elections.

Legislative elections duly took place on 29 April 2001, in conditions that were widely praised for their democracy and transparency; outbreaks of violence in Casamance were none the less reported. Apart from the pro-Wade Sopi (Change) coalition (comprising 40 parties, led by the PDS), a further 24 parties contested the polls. The Sopi coalition won 49.6% of votes cast, and 89 of the 120 seats in the Assemblée nationale. The AFP obtained 11 seats, with 16.1% of the vote. The PS, despite receiving a slightly larger share of the vote than the AFP (17.4%), secured only 10 seats. The rate of electoral participation was 67.5%. Boye was reappointed as Prime Minister on 10 May. The new 24-member Government comprised 11 members of the PDS (who obtained most principal posts), nine representatives of civil society, and two members each of AJ—PADS and the LD—MPT.

Following the elections, nine parties, including the AFP, the APJ—JJ and the URD, announced that they were to join the PS in an informal opposition alliance. In August 2001 some 25 parties, led by the PDS, formed a pro-presidential electoral alliance, the Convergence des actions autour du Président en perspective du 21ième siècle (CAP-21), in advance of local and municipal elections (initially scheduled for November, but subsequently postponed); meanwhile, opposition groups also formed an electoral alliance, the Cadre permanent de concertation. In February 2002 the three men convicted of the assassination of Babacar Sèye in 1993 were granted presidential pardons and subsequently released from prison, provoking renewed controversy about the case. In the delayed local and municipal elections, which were eventually held on 12 May 2002, CAP-21 won control of nine of the 11 regional governments, as well as a majority of municipal and communal seats.

The sinking of a state-owned passenger ferry, the MV *Joola*, in late September 2002, en route from Ziguinchor, the principal city of Casamance, to Dakar led to a national political crisis, even before the final death toll of the accident, subsequently enumerated at more than 1,800 people, became apparent. In early October the Minister of Equipment and Transport, Youssouph Sakho, and the Minister of the Armed Forces, Yoba Sambou, resigned in response to the tragedy, as it became clear that the vessel had been severely overloaded; only 64 survivors were reported. Later in the month the head of the navy was dismissed, and Wade announced that the Government accepted responsibility for the disaster. In early November Wade dismissed Boye and her Government; although no official reason for the dismissal was given, it was widely believed to have been prompted by the Government's response to the disaster. Shortly after Boye's dismissal, an inquiry into the incident found that safety regulations had been widely violated on the *Joola*, and that the dispatch of rescue equipment and staff to the ship by the armed forces had been inexplicably delayed. Idrissa Seck, the Mayor of Thiès, a close ally of Wade and previously a senior official in the PDS, was appointed as the new Prime Minister; several principal posts in the new Government remained unchanged. In August 2003 the Chief of Staff of the Armed Forces and the Chief of Staff of the Air Force were dismissed as a result of disciplinary action related to the response to the sinking of the *Joola*.

Political tensions intensified in early 2004 as several parties that had supported Wade's candidacy in the presidential election of 2000 and had ministerial representation in the Government, including the LD—MPT and AJ—PADS, declined to participate in celebrations organized to mark the fourth anniversary of Wade's accession to power. Moreover, while the President continued to announce his intention of forming a broadly based Government, most opposition parties reiterated their reluctance to participate in any such administration. In late April Wade dismissed Seck's Government, appointing Macky Sall, hitherto Minister of State, Minister of the Interior and Local Communities, Government Spokesperson, as premier. Although the allocation of most strategic portfolios in the new Council of Ministers remained largely unchanged, Cheikh Sadibou Fall was accorded the post of Minister of the Interior. In November Wade reorganized the Government, dismissing Fall from his position as Minister of the Interior and replacing him with Ngom (who had been appointed as Minister of Trade in July). In December the Assemblée nationale approved legislation abolishing the death penalty in Senegal (the bill had previously been unanimously adopted by the Government in July).

In January 2005 the Assemblée nationale approved controversial legislation granting amnesty from prosecution to those suspected of 'politically motivated' offences committed between 1 January 1983 and 31 December 2004, and specifically those implicated in the murder, in 1993, of Babacar Sèye. The Constitutional Council ruled that the proposed amnesty did not contradict the Constitution, although its ruling did invalidate the separate article granting amnesty to those involved in the Sèye case. The law was subsequently promulgated by President Wade in mid-February 2005. In March Wade effected a further government reshuffle, replacing two members of the LD—MPT with affiliates of the PDS leaving AJ—PADS as the only party (other than the PDS) to retain ministerial representation from the alliance that supported Wade's presidential candidacy in 2000. The dismissals followed several months of discord between the PDS and the LD—MPT over the latter's criticism of Wade's presidency and its opposition to the amnesty legislation. In late April 12 PDS deputies, who were reported to be close to former Prime Minister Seck, resigned from the majority parliamentary group, and formed their own group within the Assemblée nationale, the Forces de l'alternance (FAL), led by Oumar Sarr. Amid ongoing tensions within the PDS, a further reorganization of the Government in May was interpreted as an attempt to strengthen support for the President.

In late May 2005 opposition leaders condemned the detention of Abdourahim Agne, the Secretary-General of a minor opposition party, the Parti de la réforme, who was charged with threatening state security after he called for street demonstrations against the President. Meanwhile, following a meeting between Wade and the 12 dissident PDS deputies, at which the President promised to address their grievances, the FAL was disbanded. Wade appointed members to a new Commission électorale nationale autonome in early June; however, the opposition expressed concern at the composition of the body. Further minor reorganizations of the Government took place in June, July and August.

Seck was questioned by police in mid-July 2005, after he was accused by President Wade of overspending on work to upgrade roads in Thiès, where he served as mayor. The former Prime Minister, whose house had been attacked in May, refuted any suggestion that he had embezzled government funds from the project. Later that month Seck was formally charged with endangering national security; there was no immediate explanation of the charges, which Seck's defence lawyers claimed to be politically motivated. In early September the Assemblée nationale ruled that Seck should be brought to trial on charges of embezzlement at the High Court of Justice, which was reserved for cases concerning crimes committed by members of the Government in the exercise of their duties. Meanwhile, the Assemblée nationale adopted legislation providing for the eventual creation of a new administrative and political capital some 150 km north-east of Dakar, near Kébèmer (rather than at Mékhé-Pékesse, which had been the location proposed in December 2002).

In mid-December 2005 the Assemblée nationale approved legislation, supported by President Wade, that delayed the legislative elections, which had been scheduled for mid-2006, until 2007, when they were to be held concurrently with presidential voting. Wade justified this postponement (which was condemned by the parliamentary opposition) on financial grounds, stating that the Government had recently been obliged to make unplanned spending on mitigating the effects of flooding. (The legislative elections were later postponed further until June 2007.) Further minor governmental reorganizations took place in early February and mid-March 2006.

Meanwhile, in early February 2006 Seck was released from detention, following the partial dismissal of the charges of corruption and embezzlement against him (some minor charges remained against him, however); the charges of endangering state security had been dropped in the previous month.

In November 2006 President Wade effected a reshuffle of the Council of Ministers in which five new ministers from the opposition were appointed, including Abdourahim Agne, who became Minister of Micro-finance and Decentralized Co-operation. In mid-November, prior to the forthcoming presidential election, the Assemblée nationale adopted new legislation ending the obligation for a candidate to receive votes from one-quarter of the total registered electorate to be elected in the first round. Under the new law it became possible for a candidate to secure victory in the first round by obtaining a majority of more than 50% of recorded votes.

The presidential election took place on 25 February 2007. President Wade secured a second five-year mandate in the first round, winning 55.90% of votes cast; his closest rival, with 14.92% of the votes, was Seck. Two days after the elections five ministers resigned and a government reorganization was implemented. Those who left the Government were members of AJ—PADS, hitherto an ally of the ruling PDS, and cited changes in the relationship with the ruling party as reasons for their resignations.

Legislative elections were held on 3 June 2007, at which President Wade's Sopi Coalition (comprising some 40 parties and movements, led by the PDS) secured 131 of the 150 available seats. However, many of the principal opposition parties chose to boycott the ballot when their demands for the establishment of an independent electoral commission were not met, and voter turn-out was estimated at just 34.7%. Later that month Prime Minister Sall resigned and was replaced by Cheikh Hadjibou Soumaré, hitherto Minister-delegate at the Office of the Minister of State of the Economy and Finance, responsible for the Budget. Soumaré subsequently named a new Government, which included 13 new appointments, eight of whom were women; the key portfolios remained unaltered.

Meanwhile, in May 2007 the Assemblée nationale voted to reinstate the Sénat, which had been dissolved in 2001 by President Wade owing to financial constraints. Opposition members who had contested the inauguration of the second chamber in 1999 accused President Wade of proposing contradictory policies. On 19 August 2007 parliamentarians and local officials elected 35 of the 100 senators; 34 of those seats were secured by PDS members. President Wade appointed the remaining 65 members, prompting concern that balance in the newly restored chamber would weigh in favour of the ruling party. The Sénat was officially installed in September; Pape Diop was elected President of that body and was replaced as President of the Assemblée nationale by former Prime Minister Sall. In early December Soumaré effected a number of minor changes to the composition of the Council of Ministers.

Long-standing resentment against the Government of Senegal in the southern province of Casamance (which is virtually cut off from the rest of the country by the enclave of The Gambia) was embodied from the early 1980s by the separatist Mouvement des forces démocratiques de la Casamance (MFDC). By April 1991 at least 100 people had reportedly died as a result of violence in the region, while more than 300 Casamançais were awaiting trial for sedition. The announcement in May 1991 of the imminent release of more than 340 detainees (including the Secretary-General and executive leader of the MFDC, Fr Augustin Diamacouné Senghor) who had been arrested in connection with unrest in Casamance facilitated the conclusion, shortly afterwards in Guinea-Bissau, of a cease-fire agreement by representatives of the Senegalese Government and of the MFDC. An amnesty was approved by the Assemblée nationale later in June, and some 400 detainees were released. A period of relative calm ensued.

In January 1992 a peace commission, comprising government representatives and members of the MFDC, was established, with mediation by Guinea-Bissau. A resurgence of violence in Casamance from July prompted the Government to redeploy armed forces in the region, giving rise to MFDC protests that the 'remilitarization' of Casamance contravened the truce. Contradictory statements made by MFDC leaders regarding their commitment to the peace accord evidenced a split within the movement. The 'Front nord' and the MFDC Vice-President, Sidi Badji, appealed to the rebels to lay down their arms; meanwhile, the 'Front sud', led by Diamacouné Senghor (who was now based in Guinea-Bissau), appeared determined to continue the armed struggle. After an escalation of the conflict in late 1992 and early 1993, in which more than 500 people were killed, hundreds injured and tens of thousands forced to leave their homes, a new round of negotiations resulted in the signing, in July 1993, of a cease-fire agreement, known as the Ziguinchor Accord, between the Government and Diamacouné Senghor (who had returned to Ziguinchor in March). Guinea-Bissau was to act as a guarantor of the agreement, and the Government of France was to be asked to submit an historical arbitration regarding the Casamance issue. In December France issued its judgment that Casamance had not existed as an autonomous territory prior to the colonial period, and that independence for the region had been neither demanded nor considered at the time of decolonization.

From early 1995, renewed violence indicated a re-emergence of divisions between the two factions of the MFDC. Rebels in the south accused the Senegalese armed forces of violating the provisions of the 1993 cease-fire accord. In June MFDC rebels announced an end to the cease-fire, again accusing government forces of having violated the 1993 accord. Although Diamacouné Senghor appealed to the rebels not to break the truce, renewed violence in the south-west resulted in some 60 deaths.

In September 1995 a Commission nationale de paix (CNP) was established and members of the commission reportedly sought a dialogue with Diamacouné Senghor and the MFDC's four other political leaders (all of whom remained under house arrest). During October, renewed rebel attacks on government forces were accompanied by a major army offensive in the south-west. By the end of the November it was reported that about 150 separatists and 15 members of the armed forces had been killed in clashes. In December Diamacouné Senghor made a televised appeal to the rebels to lay down their arms. He proposed that preliminary talks between the MFDC and the CNP take place in January 1996, to be followed by peace negotiations, in a neutral country, three months later. The members of the MFDC 'political bureau' were released from house arrest at the end of December 1995. Peace talks, scheduled to begin in Ziguinchor in April, were postponed indefinitely, following the refusal of Diamacouné Senghor and other MFDC leaders to attend, citing the failure of the Government to meet a number of their conditions, and renewed violence was reported in the region. During a visit to Ziguinchor in May, Diouf expressed his commitment to the pursuit of peace, stating that the ongoing process of administrative decentralization would afford greater autonomy to the region, but as an integral part of Senegal.

There was renewed optimism regarding the possible resumption of negotiations between a united MFDC and the authorities, following discussions in July 1996 between Diamacouné Senghor and Diouf's personal Chief of Staff in Ziguinchor. However, in March 1997 more than 40 rebels and two members of the armed forces were killed in clashes near the border with Guinea-Bissau. The MFDC denied that it had ended its cease-fire, stating that it would investigate these incidents.

While both the Senegalese authorities and the MFDC leadership appeared committed to reviving the peace process, the deaths of 25 soldiers in August 1997 near Ziguinchor prompted fears of a revival of the conflict. In September the armed forces launched a new offensive, in which rebel forces were reported to have sustained heavy losses. A further armed forces offensive in October, the largest such operation in Casamance since the 1995 cease-fire, involved as many as 3,000 soldiers and resulted in the deaths of 12 soldiers and 80 rebels in clashes near the border with Guinea-Bissau, according to Senegalese military sources. Salif Sadio, the MFDC's military leader, stated that the organization remained committed to the peace process, but maintained that its forces were justified in defending themselves against armed attack.

In January 1998 Diamacouné Senghor appealed for a cease-fire, indicating that his organization would be prepared to abandon its demand for independence, subject to the Government instituting measures to ensure greater economic and social development in Casamance. Nevertheless, rebel violence continued intermittently throughout the second half of 1998.

In June 1999 talks between several MFDC factions began in Banjul, The Gambia, although several leaders of military and exiled factions of the MFDC did not attend, claiming that Diamacouné Senghor was effectively a hostage of the Senegalese Government. At the meeting, Léopold Sagna was confirmed as the head of the armed forces of the MFDC, replacing Sadio, who was reportedly less prepared to compromise with government demands. The Senegalese authorities subsequently acceded to the MFDC's demand that Diamacouné Senghor be released from house arrest; his movements were, however, to remain restricted.

In November 1999 Diamacouné Senghor agreed to recommence negotiations with the Senegalese Government, demanding, however, that the safety of MFDC negotiators be guaranteed, and that representatives of Casamançais civil society be included in the negotiations. At the meeting, held in Banjul in late December, the Senegalese Government and the MFDC agreed to an immediate cease-fire and to create the conditions necessary to bring about lasting peace; the Governments of The Gambia and of Guinea-Bissau were to monitor the situation in the region. A further meeting between the two parties took place in January 2000.

In early February 2000 a joint mission of the Senegalese Government and the MFDC was established to oversee the cease-fire. Despite the presence of the mission and of increased security designed to prevent the disturbance of the Senegalese presidential election, violent incidents, in which three soldiers and two civilians were killed, were reported in February. Following his election as President in early March, Abdoulaye Wade announced that he was to continue the process of negotiations, but that his preference was to conduct direct dialogue with the MFDC. Wade further announced that Diamacouné Senghor would be permitted total freedom of movement. However renewed clashes were subsequently reported. In August Senegal and Guinea-Bissau announced that they would undertake joint military border patrols in order to restrict rebel activities in the region.

In November 2000 members of a peace commission, headed by the Minister of the Interior, Maj.-Gen. Mamadou Niang, and by Diamacouné Senghor, signed a joint statement that envisaged a series of official meetings between the Senegalese Government and the MFDC, the first of which would convene on 16 December. The Government simultaneously warned that full legal action would be taken against any person promoting or distributing speeches in favour of separatism. The discussions in mid-December were boycotted by representatives of the Front sud of the MFDC, led by Ali Badji. However, a senior MFDC official present at the onset of negotiations, Alexandre Djiba (who had long been resident outside Senegal), subsequently reportedly met Ali Badji's representatives in Guinea-Bissau. The Senegalese Minister of the Armed Forces, Yoba Sambou, himself a native of Casamance, meanwhile stated that the Government preferred the rebels to unite into a single faction, so that more militant factions within the MFDC would not dispute the peace talks. As a result of renewed unrest, however, the MFDC postponed a proposed meeting in Banjul, to be held in January 2001, which had been intended to establish a common position between its various factions.

The overwhelming support in Casamance for the new Constitution, which was endorsed by 96% of voters in the region at the referendum in January 2001, prompted Wade to announce that Casamance had definitively voted to remain part of Senegal. In mid-January the Guinea-Bissau armed forces reportedly destroyed all the Casamance rebel bases in that country, in response to clashes between rival MFDC factions there. Continued unrest in the region south-west of Ziguinchor further delayed the signature of a cease-fire agreement, originally intended to take place at the meeting of mid-December, which had been rescheduled to occur in Dakar in early February.

In February 2001 Diamacouné Senghor announced that, in order to accelerate the peace process in Casamance, several senior members of the MFDC, including Sidi Badji and Djiba, had been removed from their positions. However, Sidi Badji, who had served as Military Affairs Adviser to Diamacouné Senghor, rejected the legitimacy of his dismissal. Also in mid-February, in what was reportedly the most serious attack on civilian targets in Casamance for several years, separatist rebels killed some 13 civilians in an ambush. Both Sidi Badji and Diamacouné Senghor denied any knowledge of their supporters' involvement and condemned the attack, into which Wade announced the opening of a judicial inquiry. In mid-March the Senegalese Government issued an international arrest warrant for Sadio, who had recently been removed from Guinea-Bissau, and announced that a reward of some US $200,000 would be paid for his capture.

In mid-March 2001 Niang and Diamacouné Senghor signed a cease-fire agreement at a meeting in Ziguinchor, which provided for the release of detainees, the return of refugees, the removal of landmines (which had been utilized in the region since 1998) and for economic aid to reintegrate rebels and to ameliorate the infrastructure of Casamance. Some 16 prisoners were released several days after the accord was signed. The Gambian Government issued a communiqué in mid-March, in which it promised to prevent armed rebel groups from operating on Gambian territory; it was suspected that the renewed violence had been co-ordinated by groups based in The Gambia. Later in March Niang and Diamacouné Senghor signed a further agreement, which provided for the disarmament of rebel groups and the confinement to barracks of military forces in Casamance. In April Wade and Sambou participated in negotiations with Diamacouné Senghor, at which other MFDC leaders, including Sidi Badji, were also present.

As a result of the renewed conflict, Diamacouné Senghor announced, in late May 2001, that a proposed reconciliation forum, intended to unite the various factions of the MFDC, had been postponed indefinitely, and a number of members of the movement, including Djiba, were reportedly expelled. None the less, Diamacouné Senghor and Sidi Badji attended a meeting convened by the Gambian Government in Banjul in early June, in an attempt to overcome the impasse. As tensions between factions within the MFDC intensified, with further clashes reported in June and July, Diamacouné Senghor was removed from the position of Secretary-General of the MFDC in August, at the much-delayed reconciliation forum, and appointed as honorary President. Jean-Marie François Biagui, who had previously been involved in the French-based section of the MFDC, became Secretary-General and de facto leader. Sidi Badji, who continued to question the tactics of Diamacouné Senghor, was appointed as the organization's head of military affairs. Biagui not only demonstrated considerable reluctance to play a leadership role, but was also apparently unable to prevent Sadi Badji, who was reputed to have support from the authorities in The Gambia, from becoming the dominant force in the movement.

Despite these personnel changes within the MFDC, President Wade met Diamacouné Senghor at the presidential palace in Dakar in September 2001; both leaders reiterated the importance of implementing the cease-fire agreement. In response to this meeting, it was reported that the new leadership of the MFDC had suspended all further negotiations with the Government. Following further attacks by rebels, Biagui resigned as Secretary-General in early November. Sidi Badji was announced as Biagui's successor, in an acting capacity, although Diamacouné Senghor rejected this appointment, and reappointed Biagui as Secretary-General. In November MFDC rebels launched numerous attacks on civilians in Casamance and the following month violence in the province intensified. In an attempt to quell the rebellion, Diamacouné Senghor appointed an envoy, his nephew, Laurent Diamacouné, to seek negotiations with Sidi Badji, but with only limited success. In mid-December Diamacouné Senghor's position was further undermined, when an episcopal conference declared that his leadership of a movement that was using armed struggle to attain its ends was incompatible with his role as a Roman Catholic priest.

In mid-January 2002 Niang held talks with Diamacouné Senghor and Sidi Badji, although no date for the resumption of peace negotiations with the Government was forthcoming. In late March mediators from The Gambia and Guinea-Bissau met with MFDC representatives, with the intention of establishing a timetable for the resumption of peace talks. Following continued fighting, some 9,000 Casamançais were reported to have fled to The Gambia by the end of June.

In August 2002, following a joint declaration signed by Diamacouné Senghor and Sidi Badji urging the resumption of peace talks between the rebels and the Government, Wade appointed an official delegation, chaired by the Second Vice-President of the Assemblée nationale and President of Ziguinchor Regional Council, Abdoulaye Faye, and including among its membership Niang and Sambou, to undertake negotiations with the MFDC. Meanwhile, the holding of an intra-Casamance conference, in early September, appeared to indicate a decline in support for separatist aspirations, as the conference produced a declaration, signed by representatives of 10 ethnic groups resident in the region, in favour of a 'definitive peace in Casamance', and which referred to the region as 'belonging to the great and single territory of Senegal'. Moreover, the absence from the meeting of the MFDC faction loyal to Sidi Badji appeared to refute reports that the various wings of the MFDC had effectively reunited. In mid-September a further meeting between Faye and Niang, representing the Government, and Diamacouné Senghor and Sidi Badji, for the MFDC, was held in Ziguinchor. In late September five civilians, including the brother of Sambou, were killed in an attack attributed to separatist rebels north of Ziguinchor. The internal disunity of the MFDC was emphasized in mid-October, when Biagui, announcing that the conflict had definitively ended, publicly demanded forgiveness from the people of Casamance and Senegal for the actions of the organization and acknowledged that the MFDC was responsible for causing suffering to the populace; this statement was emphatically rejected by Sidi Badji. In spite of further discussions between the government commission and Diamacouné Senghor and Sidi Badji in January 2003, intermittent conflict and banditry continued to be reported in Casamance in early 2003, although by the end of April all members of the MFDC who had been imprisoned on charges other than murder had been released on bail.

In early May 2003 President Wade announced that several substantive measures towards the normalization of the political and economic situation in Casamance were to be implemented, notably major infrastructural projects and the rehabilitation of damaged villages. The Assemblée nationale was to consider an amnesty for all those implicated in crimes related to the conflict, following a convention of the MFDC, to be held, at an unspecified date, in Guinea-Bissau, prior to the conclusion of final peace talks between the MFDC and the Government. Wade also announced that the Government intended to accede to a further MFDC demand, by dismissing those implicated in the failed attempt to rescue the passengers of the stricken *Joola* ferry in September 2002 (see above), and arranging the provision of a replacement for the vessel, which had provided a key transport link between the Casamance region and Dakar. Mine-clearing operations, to involve both regular members of the army and former rebel fighters, were also to commence. Meanwhile, Diamacouné Senghor reiterated on several occasions that the Casamance conflict had concluded; reports suggested that the apparent death of Sadio, regarded as a leading opponent of compromise within the MFDC, had been a major factor in facilitating the improved relationship between the organization and the Government. (However, no clear proof of Sadio's death was presented.)

In late May 2003 Diamacouné Senghor announced that the MFDC convention, comprising 460 participants from the various factions of the organization, was to be held in Guinea-Bissau in early June, although it was reported that factions opposed to the proposed peace agreement would refuse to attend the gathering. Following the death of Sidi Badji, from natural causes, in late May, the convention was postponed, initially to late July. However, the Guinea-Bissau authorities announced that they would be unable to provide sufficient guarantees of security for participants, and the meeting was again postponed, until early October, when the gathering was held in Ziguinchor. On this occasion, which was not attended by hardline factions of the MFDC loyal to Djiba, both Diamacouné Senghor and Biagui issued statements confirming that the conflict had ended, and announced that what was termed the emancipation of Casamance did not, as a matter of course, necessarily entail its independence from Senegal. Following the restoration of peace in Casamance, it was anticipated that some 15,000 displaced persons would return to their home villages in the Ziguinchor administrative region, while demining operations commenced in July.

In mid-March 2004 unconfirmed reports suggested that Diamacouné Senghor had removed Biagui from the post of Secretary-General of the MFDC. The organization held a convention in Ziguinchor in early May, at which it proposed the cantonment of its combatants while observing a unilateral one-month cease-fire, in return for the withdrawal of government troops deployed in Casamance since 1982. In July the Assemblée nationale adopted legislation providing for an amnesty for all MFDC combatants; however, MFDC leaders claimed that their members had done nothing from which they required amnesty and urged the Government to engage in negotiations with the organization.

In September 2004 it was reported that an extraordinary general assembly of the MFDC had dismissed Diamacouné Senghor as the organization's leader and, as in 2001, appointed him Honorary President, while Biagui was reappointed Secretary-General and de facto leader. Biagui subsequently announced that the MFDC intended to transform itself into a legitimate political party and contest national elections; however, his status as leader was rejected by the MFDC's military wing, which issued a statement declaring its continuing recognition of Diamacouné Senghor as the movement's leader, while also reaffirming its commitment to full independence for Casamance. (The Senegalese Government was also reported to regard Diamacouné Senghor as remaining the MFDC's legitimate leader for the purposes of negotiations.) Following talks in Paris, France, between representatives of the Government and the external wing of the MFDC, plans were announced for the signing of a cease-fire between the two parties in late December 2004, to be followed by detailed negotiations towards a peaceful political settlement, although the Government's representatives insisted that there would be no concessions offered on the issue of independence for the region. Concerns persisted, however, over internal divisions within the MFDC: Diamacouné Senghor's appeal for a general assembly of the movement in late November, intended to reconcile the various factions in advance of the signing of the cease-fire, was reportedly rejected by his rivals in the movement's political wing, while Abdoulaye Diedhiou, leader of the military wing Atika ('arrow'), insisted that independence remained the MFDC's primary aim and criticized Diamacouné Senghor for making excessive concessions to the Senegalese Government.

On 30 December 2004 a 'General Peace Accord' was signed in Ziguinchor by the Minister of the Interior, on behalf of the Government, and Diamacouné Senghor, representing the MFDC. President Wade also signed the accord, which was, however, rejected by several factions of the MFDC, including Atika, the Front nord and elements of the movement's international wing. Negotiations aimed at achieving a definitive resolution of the conflict in Casamance were opened by Prime Minister Sall on 1 February 2005 in the town of Foundiougne, some 160 km south-east of Dakar, but were boycotted by Biagui and Diédhiou, who reportedly favoured further dialogue within the MFDC before engaging in talks with the Government. Both sides agreed to establish joint technical commissions to address reconstruction, economic and social development, and disarmament, demobilization and demining. Meanwhile, Diamacouné Senghor appointed Ansoumana Badji, formerly the MFDC's representative in Portugal, as Secretary-General of the movement; Badji stated that he aimed to persuade as many MFDC members as possible to join the peace process. Biagui rejected the legitimacy of Badji's appointment.

Since the signing of the 2004 peace agreement, outbreaks of violence had been sporadic. However, in August 2006 violent incidents between the Senegalese armed forces and the MFDC in Casamance began to escalate and by mid-August fighting resumed. Although the fighting spread north towards The Gambia, there were no reports of the conflict crossing the border. Nevertheless, many civilians fled to that country, seeking refuge and medical treatment. By October the violence began to subside as the army took control of the rebels' base. However, many civilians refused to return to the region until the security forces had departed. In 2007 small-scale operations were conducted to clear the region of landmines and the people of Casamance slowly began to return to their homes. However, having been empty for over a decade, many of the villages were uninhabitable with no water supplies and there was severe infrastructural damage. Tensions persisted between the MFDC and the Government and a rebel faction of the MFDC had been blamed for sabotaging demining efforts. Consequently, reconstruction work in villages across Casamance was yet to begin, leaving little to which the Casamançais could return.

From 1989 Senegal's regional relations underwent a period of considerable strain. A long-standing border dispute with Mauritania, which also involved ethnic and economic rivalries, was exacerbated by the deaths, in April of that year, of two Senegalese farmers, who had been involved in a dispute regarding grazing rights with Mauritanian livestock-breeders. Mauritanian nationals residing in Senegal were attacked, and their businesses looted, while Senegalese nationals in Mauritania suffered similar aggression. By early May it was believed that several hundred people, mostly Senegalese, had been killed. Operations to repatriate nationals of both countries commenced, with international assistance. Diplomatic relations, which had been suspended in August 1989, were fully restored in April 1992, and the process of reopening the border began in May, although the contentious issues that had hitherto impeded the normalization of relations remained largely unresolved. In December 1994, however, the Governments of Senegal and Mauritania agreed new co-operation measures, including efforts to facilitate the free movement of goods and people between the two countries.

In January 1995 the Governments of Senegal, Mauritania and Mali undertook to co-operate in resolving joint border issues and in combating extremism, arms-smuggling and drugs-trafficking. In July the office of the UN High Commissioner for Refugees (UNHCR) began a census of Mauritanian refugees in Senegal, estimated to number some 66,000, as part of initiatives for their eventual repatriation. In May 1998 the Ministers of the Interior of Mauritania, Mali and Senegal met to discuss border security, following reports of increased cross-border banditry, particularly in eastern Senegal. The unrest in the region was blamed by the Senegalese press on the continued presence there of Mauritanian refugees; in September it was reported that the Senegalese authorities had ceased to issue the refugees with travel documents. In May 1999 the two countries signed a further agreement on the joint exploitation of fisheries. In mid-2000, however, a dispute over water rights resulted in a period of substantial tension between Senegal and Mauritania. Following renewed negotiations, the visit of President Taya of Mauritania to Dakar in April, as the guest of honour at a ceremony to commemorate the 41st anniversary of the independence of Senegal, was widely regarded as indicating an improvement in relations between the countries. Presidents Taya and Wade met again in July 2003, when negotiations were conducted on a range of bilateral and international issues; Wade reiterated his support for Taya's administration, following an attempted *coup d'état* in Mauritania in the previous month. The extradition of one of the suspected coup plotters from Senegal to Mauritania was also interpreted as an indication of improved relations between the countries, as was the Mauritanian Government's decision to accord 270 temporary fishing licences to Senegalese fishermen in June 2004. According to provisional figures, 19,630 UNHCR-assisted Mauritanian refugees remained in Senegal at the end of 2006.

In October 1993 Senegal and Guinea-Bissau signed an agreement regarding the joint exploitation and management of fishing and petroleum resources in their maritime zones. This treaty was ratified in December 1995, to the effect that fishing resources were to be shared equally between the two countries, while Senegal was to benefit from an 85% share of revenue obtained from petroleum deposits. During bilateral contacts in 1995–97 Senegal and Guinea-Bissau pledged co-operation in matters of joint defence and security. It was hoped that the movement of refugees from the conflict in Casamance to Guinea-Bissau, which began, under the auspices of UNHCR, in February 1996, would expedite efforts to restore security in the border region between the countries. In January 1998 it was announced that the authorities in Guinea-Bissau had intercepted a consignment of armaments destined for MFDC rebels, and that some 15 officers of the Guinea-Bissau armed forces had been arrested and suspended from duty, including the head of the armed forces, Brig. (later Gen.) Ansumane Mané. In June, however, troops loyal to Mané rebelled against President Commdr João Vieira of Guinea-Bissau, and civil war broke out in that country. Senegalese troops intervened in support of the armed forces loyal to Vieira. By the end of the month refugees from the conflict were crossing into Casamance, exacerbating security concerns in the province, while it was also reported that members of the MFDC were fighting alongside the rebels against the Government of Guinea-Bissau and Senegalese forces. From December, as a result of a peace-keeping agreement brokered by the Economic Community of West African States (ECOWAS, see p. 232), Senegalese troops began to depart from Guinea-Bissau, but strengthened their presence in the border area, while the ECOWAS peace-keeping force, ECOMOG (see p. 235), assumed positions on the Guinea-Bissau side of the frontier with Casamance.

In May 1999 fighting again broke out in Guinea-Bissau, and Vieira was overthrown. Tensions between the two countries resurfaced in April 2000, when an armed group, reportedly composed of members of the MFDC operating from within Guinea-Bissau, attacked a Senegalese border post, killing three soldiers, and later that month the border between the two countries was temporarily closed. In August the terms of the agreement concerning the joint exploitation of maritime resources by the two countries was revised; henceforth, Guinea-Bissau was to receive 20% rather than 15% of the revenue generated from petroleum deposits. In early September, following clashes near the border in Guinea-Bissau, attributed to an armed faction of the MFDC, the Senegalese Government closed all border posts between the two countries. Following the killing of Mané in November 2000, during an attempted *coup d'état*, relations between Senegal and Guinea-Bissau improved significantly.

In August 1989 Diouf announced the withdrawal of Senegalese troops from The Gambia, in protest at a request by President Jawara of that country that The Gambia be accorded more power within the confederal agreement of Senegambia that had been formed by the two countries in 1982. Diouf subsequently stated that, in view of The Gambia's reluctance to proceed towards full political and economic integration with Senegal, the functions of the Confederation would be suspended. The Confederation was dissolved in September. In January 1991 the two countries signed a bilateral treaty of friendship and co-operation. Senegal's abrupt decision to close the Senegalese–Gambian border in September 1993, apparently to reduce smuggling between the two countries, again strained relations, although subsequent negotiations sought to minimize the adverse effects of the closure on The Gambia's regional trading links. Since the *coup d'état* in The Gambia in July 1994 Senegal has fostered cordial relations with the Government of President Jammeh and in June 1996 the two countries agreed to take joint measures to combat insecurity, illegal immigration, arms-trafficking and drugs-smuggling. In early 1998 Jammeh offered to act as a mediator between the Senegalese Government and the MFDC, and subsequently held regular meetings with MFDC representatives. None the less, intermittent disputes relating to transportation issues between the two countries have occurred, and tensions between the two countries again heightened in mid-2005, following a 100% increase in transportation fees on the ferry across the Gambia river by the Gambian port authorities. Senegalese trade unionists blockaded border crossings between Senegal and The Gambia to protest at the increase, and the Senegalese Government granted fuel subsidies to drivers who used a longer, alternative route between the southern and northern parts of Senegal, avoiding The Gambia. Although tensions lessened later in the year, when the port authority reduced the ferry charges by 15%, in what was described as a gesture of goodwill, there was increasing speculation that the Senegalese authorities were considering the construction of a tunnel to link the southern and northern parts of Senegal. Bilateral relations were again strained in March 2006, however, following allegations of Senegalese complicity in an abortive coup in The Gambia. One of those arrested in connection with the plot reportedly claimed to have been instructed by the alleged leader of the coup (who was believed to have fled to Senegal) to liaise with the Senegalese embassy in The Gambia. The Senegalese Government denied any involvement in the plot, which it condemned, and recalled its ambassador to The Gambia for consultations; a new ambassador was appointed in June.

Since his election in March 2000, President Wade has on several occasions promoted greater democratization in other West African countries and encouraged an expansion in the international political engagement of African countries. Notably, Wade's well-publicized condemnation, at an international conference on racism and xenophobia held under the auspices of the office of the UN High Commissioner for Human Rights in Dakar in January 2001, of the increasing importance of ethnically based politics in Côte d'Ivoire prompted violent demonstrations across Côte d'Ivoire. At the UN World Conference against Racism, Racial Discrimination, Xenophobia and Related Intolerance, held in Durban, South Africa, in August–September, Wade, notably among African leaders, condemned the notion that reparations should be paid by Western nations to the descendants of slaves.

President Wade was one of the four African leaders most closely involved in the initial development of the New Partnership for Africa's Development (NEPAD, see p. 169), a long-term plan for socio-economic recovery in Africa that was launched in October 2001 in accordance with a decision of the Organization of African Unity (OAU, now the African Union, see p. 164) summit of heads of state and government held in Lusaka, Zambia, in July of that year.

Relations with France have remained particularly strong since independence, and the existing defence arrangements between France and Senegal remained substantially unaltered following the major restructuring of the French armed forces undertaken by the administration of Jacques Chirac in the late 1990s and early 2000s. Relations between Senegal and France were strengthened in September 2006 when the two countries signed an agreement, which provided for, *inter alia*, a relaxation of visa regulations between the two countries and the provision of €2.5m. to fund development projects.

In late 2005 Senegal announced that it was to terminate its diplomatic relations with Taiwan in order to resume relations with the People's Republic of China. The respective embassies in Dakar and Beijing were re-opened, and ambassadors were exchanged between the two countries in early 2006.

Senegal is an active participant in regional and international peace-keeping operations. In February 1998 Senegal, with Mali and Mauritania, was among the principal participants in multinational military exercises conducted in eastern Senegal under the auspices of the UN and the OAU, as part of efforts to establish a regional crisis-intervention force. The exercise was organized by France and involved almost 3,500 troops from eight West African countries, as well as units from the USA, the United Kingdom and Belgium. Senegal is a member of the Accord de Non-agression et d'assistance en matière de défense, which in April 1999 adopted a draft protocol on the setting up of a peace-keeping force in the region. In September 1999 a Senegalese contingent joined the international peace-keeping operation in the Kosovo and Metohija province of Yugoslavia (now Serbia and Montenegro). In April 2001 more than 500 Senegalese soldiers joined UN observer missions in the Democratic Republic of the Congo. In early 2003 it was announced that Senegal was to contribute some 650 troops to the ECOWAS military mission in Côte d'Ivoire (ECOMICI); Senegalese troops were also expected to play a prominent role in the UN Operation in Côte d'Ivoire (UNOCI, see p. 87) that assumed the responsibilities of ECOMICI from April 2004. Meanwhile, in August 2003 some 260 Senegalese troops were dispatched to serve in the ECOWAS Mission in Liberia (ECOMIL), which was replaced by the UN Mission in Liberia (UNMIL, see p. 83) in October.

Government

Under the terms of the Constitution, approved by popular referendum in January 2001, executive power is held by the President, who is directly elected for a mandate of five years, which is renewable only once. (President Wade will, however, complete the seven-year mandate to which he was elected in March 2000 by the terms of the former Constitution). Legislative power rests with the Assemblée nationale, with 120 members elected for five years by universal adult suffrage. (In late 2005 the existing legislature voted to extend its mandate, exceptionally, by one further year.) The formation of parties on an ethnic, religious or geographical basis is prohibited. The President appoints the Prime Minister, who, in consultation with the President, appoints the Council of Ministers. Senegal comprises 11 regions, each with an appointed governor, an elected local assembly and a separate budget.

Defence

As assessed at November 2007, Senegal's active armed forces totalled 13,620 men: army 11,900, navy 950, air force 770. There was also a 5,000-strong paramilitary gendarmerie. Military service is by selective conscription and lasts for two years. France and the USA provide technical and material aid, and in November 2007 there were 840 French troops stationed in Senegal. The defence budget for 2007 was 80,000m. francs CFA.

Economic Affairs

In 2006, according to estimates by the World Bank, Senegal's gross national income (GNI), measured at average 2004–06 prices, was US $8,909m., equivalent to $750 per head (or $1,840 on an international purchasing-power parity basis). During 1996–2006, it was estimated, the population increased at an average annual rate of 2.5%, while gross domestic product (GDP) per head increased by an average of 1.8% per year. Overall GDP increased, in real terms, at an average annual rate of 4.3% per year in 1996–2006; growth in 2006 was 3.3%.

Agriculture (including forestry and fishing) contributed an estimated 16.7% of GDP in 2006; in 2005 some 72.2% of the labour force were engaged in the sector, according to FAO estimates. The principal cash crops are groundnuts and cotton. In the late 1990s Senegal began to export mangoes, melons, asparagus and green beans to European markets. Groundnuts, millet, sorghum, rice, maize and vegetables are produced for domestic consumption, although Senegal has yet to achieve self-sufficiency in basic foodstuffs. In 2004 Senegal's agricultural output was decreased by the swarms of locusts that invaded the

Sahel region of Africa from mid-year; however, the swarms only affected crops in the north of the country, while the primary crop-growing regions of the south were undamaged. The fishing sector makes an important contribution to both the domestic food supply and export revenue: fish and fish products had become Senegal's principal export commodity by the mid-1980s, and provided 23.8% of export earnings in 2004. The sale of fishing licences to the European Union (EU, see p. 244) was an important source of revenue from the late 1990s. Senegalese concerns at the dwindling fish stocks in its waters were addressed in an agreement signed with the EU in 2002, with an annual two-month moratorium on fishing. According to the World Bank, during 1996–2006 agricultural GDP increased by an average of 3.4% per year; agricultural GDP increased by 6.0% in 2006.

Industry (including mining, manufacturing, construction and power) contributed an estimated 24.6% of GDP in 2006. The principal activities are the processing of fish and agricultural products and of phosphates, while the production of cement is of increasing importance. According to the World Bank, during 1996–2006 industrial GDP increased at an average annual rate of 5.5%. Industrial GDP increased by 4.1% in 2005.

Mining contributed an estimated 1.1% of GDP in 2006. The principal mining activity is the extraction of calcium phosphates (aluminium phosphates are also mined in smaller quantities). Deposits of salt, fuller's earth (attapulgite), clinker and natural gas are also exploited, and investigations are under way into the feasibility of mining copper, alluvial diamonds and iron ore. Explorations at Sabodala have revealed gold reserves estimated at 30 metric tons. Offshore deposits of petroleum are also to be developed, in co-operation with Guinea-Bissau. According to IMF estimates, the GDP of the mining sector declined by an average of 4.0% per year in 1992–99; the GDP of the sector fell by 2.0% in 1998, but increased by 20.8% in 1999.

Manufacturing contributed an estimated 15.2% of GDP in 2006. The most important manufacturing activities are food-processing (notably fish, groundnuts and sugar), chemicals, textiles and petroleum-refining (using imported crude petroleum). According to the World Bank, manufacturing GDP increased at an average annual rate of 3.6% in 1996–2006; growth in 2006 was just 0.4%.

In 2004 75.0% of Senegal's electrical energy was derived from petroleum. The Manantali hydroelectric power installation (constructed under the auspices of the Organisation pour la mise en valeur du fleuve Sénégal—OMVS) commenced operations in December 2001; it was anticipated that Senegal would receive approximately one-third of the energy generated by the installation. Imports of fuels accounted for 22.9% of the value of merchandise imports in 2005.

The services sector contributed a provisional 43.7% of GDP in 2006. Tourism is a major source of foreign exchange, generating some US $287,000m. in 2004. About 4,500 people are directly employed (and some 15,000 indirectly employed) in the sector. Dakar's port is of considerable importance as a centre for regional trade. According to the World Bank, the GDP of the services sector increased by an average of 5.3% per year in 1996–2006. The GDP of the sector increased by 6.1% in 2006.

In 2006 Senegal recorded an estimated visible trade deficit of 864,000m. francs CFA, while there was a deficit of $485,000m. on the current account of the balance of payments. In 2004 the principal source of imports (24.3%) was France; other major suppliers were Nigeria and Thailand. India and Mali were the principal market for exports in that year (taking 13.9% and 13.7% of the total, respectively); France, Italy and Spain were also important purchasers. The principal exports in 2004 were food and live animals (accounting for 31.7% of the total, and principally comprising fish), chemicals and chemical products (25.6%) and mineral fuels and lubricants (19.4%, chiefly refined petroleum products). The principal imports in that year were food and live animals (amounting to 23.2% of total imports), machinery and transport equipment (18.6%), mineral fuels and lubricants, basic manufactures and chemicals and related products.

Senegal recorded an overall budget deficit of 295,000m. francs CFA (equivalent to 6.1% of GDP) in 2006. Total external debt was US $3,793m. at the end of 2005, of which $3,467m. was long-term public debt. In 2004 the cost of debt-servicing was equivalent to 11.8% of the value of exports of goods and services. In 1990–93 consumer prices declined by an annual average of 0.8%. However, following the 50% devaluation of the CFA franc, inflation averaged 32.3% in 1994; inflation subsequently slowed to an annual average of 1.4% in 1996–2006. Consumer prices increased by 2.1% in 2006. In early 1999 some 157,063 people were registered as unemployed.

Senegal is a member of the Economic Community of West African States (ECOWAS, see p. 232), of the West African organs of the Franc Zone (see p. 307), of the African Groundnut Council (see p. 407), of the West Africa Rice Development Association (see p. 410), of the Gambia River Basin Development Organization (see p. 412) and of the OMVS (see p. 413).

The attainment of sustained economic growth has been impeded by Senegal's dependence on revenue from a narrow export base, and by its consequent vulnerability to fluctuations in international prices for its principal commodities. Senegal has generally enjoyed good relations with the IMF; following an agreement under the Poverty Reduction and Growth Facility (PRGF) between 1998 and 2002, in April 2003 a further PRGF arrangement, amounting to some US $33m., was concluded with the IMF in support of the Government's economic reform programme for 2003–06. In July 2005 Senegal was among 18 countries to be granted 100% debt relief on multilateral debt agreed by the Group of Eight leading industrialized nations (G-8), subject to the approval of the lenders. The involvement of President Wade in the creation and promotion of the New Partnership for Africa's Development (NEPAD) has served to increase Senegal's international profile as a country committed to thorough economic reform and transparency. The Government was keen to develop Senegal's considerable potential for tourism, planning to double receipts from that sector by 2010. However, the continued prosperity of the fishing sector—traditionally Senegal's primary source of foreign currency income—was endangered by ageing equipment and the depletion of stocks as a result of unregulated overfishing. Also of concern was the fate of the state-controlled phosphate company, Industries Chimiques du Sénégal, which declared bankruptcy in 2006, following allegations of mismanagement and declining export revenues. The loss of this key industry coupled with high petroleum prices contributed to slowing economic growth and increasing budgetary deficits, which have, in turn, led to a lack of funding in the health and education sectors. It was estimated that by mid-2007 the deficit had grown to around 6% of GDP. However, more encouragingly, the Government launched the 'Return to Agriculture' project in mid-2006, as a means by which to stimulate entrepreneurial activities in the rural sector. The scheme was also expected to increase job opportunities in the agro-industrial sector and to reduce the migration of young Senegalese to Europe. In late 2007 government officials met with development partners at a summit in Paris, France, the result of which was an agreement to finance two development programmes, focusing particularly on budget transparency and poverty reduction. In 2005 the proportion of households living below the poverty line was 42.6%, compared with 48.5% in 2002. The Government aims to decrease that figure to below 30% by 2015. The IMF estimated GDP growth of 5.0% in 2007 and forecast it to increase slightly in 2008, to 5.4%.

Education

Primary education, which usually begins at seven years of age, lasts for six years and is officially compulsory. In 2003/04 primary enrolment included 66% of children in the relevant age-group (males 68%; females 64%), according to UNESCO estimates. The 1995–2008 Educational and Training Plan places special emphasis on increasing levels of female enrolment, and is intended to raise overall levels of pupil enrolment by 5% annually. Secondary education usually begins at the age of 13, and comprises a first cycle of four years (also referred to as 'middle school') and a further cycle of three years. According to UNESCO estimates, in 2003/04 secondary enrolment was equivalent to only 15% of children in the relevant age-group (males 18%; females 13%). There are three universities in Senegal, the Université Cheikh Anta Diop and the Université du Sahel in Dakar and the Université Gaston Berger in Saint-Louis. Since 1981 the reading and writing of national languages has been actively promoted, and is expressly encouraged in the 2001 Constitution. Current government expenditure on education in 2000 was some 100,400m. francs CFA (representing 24.4% of total current expenditure). Some 40% of the Senegalese budget for 2005 was designated for the educational sector.

Public Holidays

2008: 1 January (New Year's Day), 19 January* (Ashoura), 20 March* (Mouloud, Birth of the Prophet), 21 March (Good Friday), 24 March (Easter Monday), 4 April (National Day),

SENEGAL

1 May (Labour Day and Ascension Day), 12 May (Whit Monday), 14 July (Day of Association), 15 August (Assumption), 1 October* (Korité, end of Ramadan), 1 November (All Saints' Day), 9 December* (Tabaski, Feast of the Sacrifice), 25 December (Christmas).

2009: 1 January (New Year's Day), 7 January*† (Ashoura), 9 March* (Mouloud, Birth of the Prophet), 4 April (National Day), 10 April (Good Friday), 13 April (Easter Monday), 1 May (Labour Day), 21 May (Ascension Day), 1 June (Whit Monday), 14 July (Day of Association), 15 August (Assumption), 20 September* (Korité, end of Ramadan), 1 November (All Saints' Day), 27 November* (Tabaski, Feast of the Sacrifice), 25 December (Christmas), 27 December† (Ashoura).

* These holidays are determined by the Islamic lunar calendar and may vary by one or two days from the dates given.

† This festival occurs twice (in the Islamic years AH 1430 and 1431) within the same Gregorian year.

Weights and Measures

The metric system is in force.

Statistical Survey

Source (unless otherwise stated): Agence nationale de la Statistique et de la Démographie, blvd de l'Est, Point E, BP 116, Dakar; tel. 33-824-0301; fax 33-824-9004; e-mail statsenegal@yahoo.fr; internet www.ansd.org.

Area and Population

AREA, POPULATION AND DENSITY

Area (sq km)	197,021*
Population (census results)†	
27 May 1988	6,896,808
8 December 2002	
Males	4,846,126
Females	5,009,212
Total	9,855,338
Population (UN estimates at mid-year)	
2005	11,770,000
2006	12,072,000
2007	12,379,000
Density (per sq km) at mid-2007	62.8

* 76,070 sq miles.

† Figures for 1988 and 2002 refer to the *de jure* population. The de facto population at the 1988 census was 6,773,417, and at the 2002 census was 9,552,442.

POPULATION BY ETHNIC GROUP
(at 1988 census)

Ethnic group	Number	%
Wolof	2,890,402	42.67
Serere	1,009,921	14.91
Peul	978,366	14.44
Toucouleur	631,892	9.33
Diola	357,672	5.28
Mandingue	245,651	3.63
Rural-Rurale	113,184	1.67
Bambara	91,071	1.34
Maure	67,726	1.00
Manjaag	66,605	0.98
Others	320,927	4.74
Total	**6,773,417**	**100.00**

Source: UN, *Demographic Yearbook*.

REGIONS
(2002 census)

	Area (sq km)	Population	Density (per sq km)
Dakar	547	2,167,793	3,963.1
Diourbel	4,903	1,053,856	214.9
Fatick	7,910	609,853	77.1
Kaolack	15,449	1,069,880	69.3
Kolda	21,112	817,714	38.7
Louga	25,254	677,750	26.8
Matam	29,041	424,106	14.6
Saint-Louis	19,241	695,498	36.1
Tambacounda	59,542	612,288	10.3
Thiès	6,670	1,317,067	197.5
Ziguinchor	7,352	409,533	55.7
Total	**197,021**	**9,855,338**	**50.0**

PRINCIPAL TOWNS
(2002 census, provisional results)

Dakar (capital)	955,897	Mbour	153,503
Pikine	768,826	Diourbel	95,984
Rufisque	284,263	Louga	73,662
Guediawaye	258,370	Tambacounda	67,543
Thiès	237,849	Kolda	53,921
Kaolack	172,305	Mbacké	51,124
Saint-Louis	154,555		

Note: Data given pertains to communes, except for Dakar, Pikine, Rufisque and Guediawaye, where the population figure given is that of the département.

Mid-2007 ('000, incl. suburbs, UN estimate): Dakar 2,604 (Source: UN, *World Urbanization Prospects: The 2007 Revision*).

BIRTHS AND DEATHS
(annual averages, UN estimates)

	1990–95	1995–2000	2000–05
Birth rate (per 1,000)	41.5	39.0	37.6
Death rate (per 1,000)	11.8	10.6	9.8

Source: UN, *World Population Prospects: The 2006 Revision*.

Expectation of life (years at birth, WHO estimates): 55.8 (males 54.4; females 57.2) in 2005 (Source: WHO, *World Health Statistics*).

ECONOMICALLY ACTIVE POPULATION
('000 persons, 1990, ILO estimates)

	Males	Females	Total
Agriculture, hunting, forestry and fishing	1,319	1,190	2,508
Industry	195	51	246
Manufacturing	177	50	227
Services	370	145	516
Total	**1,884**	**1,386**	**3,269**

Source: ILO.

Unemployed (general survey, February–March 1999): 157,063 (males 99,892, females 57,171).

Mid-2005 (estimates in '000): Agriculture, etc. 3,746; Total labour force 5,189 (Source: FAO).

SENEGAL

Health and Welfare

KEY INDICATORS

Total fertility rate (children per woman, 2005)	4.8
Under-5 mortality rate (per 1,000 live births, 2005)	136
HIV/AIDS (% of persons aged 15–49, 2005)	0.9
Physicians (per 1,000 head, 2004)	0.06
Hospital beds (per 1,000 head, 1998)	0.40
Health expenditure (2004): US $ per head (PPP)	72.1
Health expenditure (2004): % of GDP	5.9
Health expenditure (2004): public (% of total)	40.3
Access to water (% of persons, 2004)	76
Access to sanitation (% of persons, 2004)	57
Human Development Index (2005): ranking	156
Human Development Index (2005): value	0.499

For sources and definitions, see explanatory note on p. vi.

Agriculture

PRINCIPAL CROPS
('000 metric tons)

	2004	2005	2006
Rice (paddy)	201.7	279.1	190.5*
Maize	400.6	400.0	181.6*
Millet	323.8	608.6	494.3*
Sorghum	126.5	144.0	121.0*
Cassava (Manioc)	401.4	281.5	120.8*
Sugar cane	828.5	n.a.	829.5*
Cashew nuts*	6.5	7.7	4.5
Groundnuts (in shell)	602.6	703.4	460.5*
Oil palm fruit*	72	74	70
Cottonseed	30*	30†	33*
Tomatoes	81.5	114.1	104.8*
Dry onions*	40.0	45.0	60.0
Watermelons	275.8	241.4	225.9*
Oranges	24.4	35.5	38.6*
Guavas, mangoes and mangosteens	65.8	61.6	82.2*
Cotton (lint)†	21.7	18.0	19.0

* FAO estimate(s).
† Unofficial figure(s).

Aggregate production ('000 metric tons, may include official, semi-official or estimated data): Total cereals 1,053.6 in 2004, 1,432.8 in 2005, 988.3 in 2006; Total pulses 12.3 in 2004, 93.2 in 2005, 53.2 in 2006; Total roots and tubers 435.2 in 2004, 314.5 in 2005, 165.14 in 2006; Total vegetables (incl. melons) 576.1 in 2004, 532.4 in 2005, 595.3 in 2006; Total fruits (excl. melons) 135.6 in 2004, 146.0 in 2005, 173.8 in 2006.

Source: FAO.

LIVESTOCK
('000 head, year ending September)

	2004	2005	2006
Cattle	3,039	3,091	3,137
Sheep	4,739	4,872	4,863
Goats	4,025	4,144	4,263
Pigs	300	309	318
Horses	504	514	518
Asses, mules or hinnies	412	413	415
Camels	4	4	4
Chickens	26,245	26,959	29,243

Source: FAO.

Statistical Survey

LIVESTOCK PRODUCTS
('000 metric tons)

	2004	2005	2006*
Cattle meat	43.1	47.2	48.3
Sheep meat	15.2	17.1	17.1
Goat meat	9.9	11.2	11.5
Pig meat	9.3	9.8	10.3
Horse meat*	6.9	7.0	7.1
Chicken meat	26.0	29.0	28.9
Cows' milk	95.9	97.3	98.8
Sheep's milk	8.1	8.3	8.7
Goats' milk	10.3	10.6	10.7
Hen eggs*	24	27	28

* FAO estimates.

Source: FAO.

Forestry

ROUNDWOOD REMOVALS
('000 cubic metres, excl. bark, FAO estimates)

	2004	2005	2006
Sawlogs, veneer logs and logs for sleepers*	40	40	40
Other industrial wood†	754	754	754
Fuel wood	5,243	5,276	5,306
Total	6,037	6,070	6,100

* Annual output assumed to be unchanged since 1986 (FAO estimates).
† Annual output assumed to be unchanged since 1999 (FAO estimates).

Source: FAO.

SAWNWOOD PRODUCTION
('000 cubic metres, incl. railway sleepers)

	1989	1990	1991
Total (all broadleaved)	15	22	23

1992–2006: Annual production as in 1991 (FAO estimates).

Source: FAO.

Fishing

('000 metric tons, live weight)

	2003	2004	2005
Capture*	478.5	445.3	405.1
Freshwater fishes*	38.4	38.4	38.4
Sea catfishes	8.6	18.8	18.8
Round sardinella	107.6	137.6	114.0
Madeiran sardinella	149.0	115.3	118.4
Bonga shad	23.6	21.8	19.2
Octopuses	10.9	5.0	1.8
Aquaculture	0.1	0.2	0.2
Total catch*	478.6	445.5	405.3

* FAO estimates.

Source: FAO.

Mining

('000 metric tons, unless otherwise stated)

	2003	2004*	2005*
Cement, hydraulic	1,694	1,700	1,700
Gold (kg)†	600	600	600
Calcium phosphates	1,761	1,576	1,451
Aluminium phosphates	4	4	4
Fuller's earth (attapulgite)	195	200	200
Salt (unrefined)	235	240	240

* Estimates.
† Government estimate of unreported production of artisanal gold.

Source: US Geological Survey.

Industry

PETROLEUM PRODUCTS
('000 metric tons)

	2002	2003	2004
Jet fuels	72	126	132
Motor gasoline (petrol)	140	151	148
Kerosene	23	26	19
Gas-diesel (distillate fuel) oils	375	463	471
Residual fuel oils	255	316	327
Lubricating oils	5	5	5
Liquefied petroleum gas	9	12	10

Source: UN, *Industrial Commodity Statistics Yearbook*.

SELECTED OTHER PRODUCTS
('000 metric tons, unless otherwise indicated)

	2001	2002	2003
Raw sugar	95.0*	95.0†	95.0†
Sugar cubes	27.2	19.8	23.2
Tobacco products (tons)	2,132	2,245	2,218
Groundnut oil—crude	125.3	98.1	39.2
Vegetable oil—refined	70.6	78.5	75.7
Canned tuna	12.1	10.7	6.9
Footwear (million pairs)	0.6	n.a.	n.a.
Cotton yarn (tons)	411	n.a.	n.a.
Soap	38.6	34.8	33.4
Paints and varnishes	4.6	4.3	4.6
Cement	1,539.0	1,653.2	1,693.9
Metal cans (million)	113.2	185.2	182.2
Electricity (million kWh)	1,651.2	1,557.3	1,855.5

* Unofficial figure.
† FAO estimate.

Source: mainly IMF, *Senegal: Selected Issues and Statistical Appendix* (May 2005).

Nitrogenous fertilizers (nitrogen content, '000 metric tons, unofficial figures): 38.8 in 1998; 24.5 in 1999; 19.4 in 2000 (Source: FAO).

Phosphate fertilizers (phosphoric acid content, '000 metric tons, unofficial figures): 67.5 in 1998; 45.0 in 1999; 32.4 in 2000 (Source: FAO).

Source: IMF, *Senegal: Statistical Appendix* (June 2003).

Cement ('000 metric tons, estimates): 1,700 annually in 2004–06 (Source: US Geological Survey).

Electric energy (million kWh): 2,351 in 2004 (Source: UN, *Industrial Commodity Statistics Yearbook*).

Finance

CURRENCY AND EXCHANGE RATES

Monetary Units
100 centimes = 1 franc de la Communauté financière africaine (CFA).

Sterling, Dollar and Euro Equivalents (31 December 2007)
£1 sterling = 892.702 francs CFA;
US $1 = 445.593 francs CFA;
€1 = 655.957 francs CFA;
10,000 francs CFA = £11.21 = $22.44 = €15.24.

Average Exchange Rate (francs CFA per US $)
2005   527.47
2006   522.89
2007   479.27

Note: An exchange rate of 1 French franc = 50 francs CFA, established in 1948, remained in force until January 1994, when the CFA franc was devalued by 50%, with the exchange rate adjusted to 1 French franc = 100 francs CFA. This relationship to French currency remained in effect with the introduction of the euro on 1 January 1999. From that date, accordingly, a fixed exchange rate of €1 = 655.957 francs CFA has been in operation.

BUDGET
('000 million francs CFA)

Revenue*	2004	2005	2006†
Tax revenue	739	851	922
Taxes on goods and services (excl. petroleum)	462	444	533
Taxes on imports (excl. petroleum)	174	178	219
Taxes on petroleum products	113	117	170
Non-tax revenue	38	29	41
Total	**777**	**880**	**963**

Expenditure‡	2004	2005	2006†
Current expenditure	565	632	829
Wages and salaries	218	255	286
Other operational expenses	301	336	500
Transfers and subsidies	147	165	308
Goods and services	148	163	186
Capital expenditure	410	455	475
Domestically financed	221	287	337
Externally financed	189	168	138
Total	**976**	**1,087**	**1,304**

* Excluding grants received ('000 million francs CFA): 88 in 2004; 76 in 2005; 73 in 2006 (estimate).
† Estimates.
‡ Excluding net lending ('000 million francs CFA): 12 in 2004; 17 in 2005; 27 in 2006 (estimate).

Source: IMF, *Senegal: Request for a Three-Year Policy Support Instrument—Staff Report; Staff Statement; Press Release on the Executive Board Discussion; and Statement by the Executive Director for Senegal* (November 2007).

INTERNATIONAL RESERVES
(excluding gold, US $ million at 31 December)

	2005	2006	2007
IMF special drawing rights	1.4	0.1	0.1
Reserve position in IMF	2.2	2.4	2.6
Foreign exchange	1,187.4	1,331.8	1,657.3
Total	**1,191.0**	**1,334.2**	**1,660.0**

Source: IMF, *International Financial Statistics*.

SENEGAL

Statistical Survey

MONEY SUPPLY
('000 million francs CFA at 31 December)

	2005	2006	2007
Currency outside banks	378.6	451.9	483.6
Demand deposits at deposit money banks	576.0	633.8	759.7
Checking deposits at post office	7.6	12.5	22.7
Total money (incl. others)	962.7	1,098.7	1,266.6

Source: IMF, *International Financial Statistics*.

COST OF LIVING
(Consumer Price Index; base: 2000 = 100)

	2004	2005	2006
Food (incl. tobacco)	110.3	114.5	116.0
Clothing	90.3	87.3	85.9
Electricity, gas and other fuels	114.9	113.7	n.a.
Rent	103.4	104.6	108.2
All items (incl. others)	105.9	107.7	110.0

Source: ILO.

NATIONAL ACCOUNTS
('000 million francs CFA at current prices)

Expenditure on the Gross Domestic Product

	2004	2005*	2006†
Final consumption expenditure	3,862.4	4,106.2	4,332.7
Households / Non-profit institutions serving households	3,280.1	3,479.5	3,665.9
General government	582.3	626.7	666.8
Gross capital formation	884.6	995.2	1,085.1
Gross fixed capital formation	961.9	1,038.4	1,123.8
Changes in inventories / Acquisitions, less disposals, of inventories	−77.3	−43.2	−38.7
Total domestic expenditure	4,747.0	5,101.4	5,417.8
Exports of goods and services	1,121.7	1,185.4	1,261.0
Less Imports of goods and services	1,670.2	1,790.5	1,962.5
Statistical discrepancy	—	64.9	182.8
GDP in purchasers' values	4,198.5	4,561.2	4,899.1
GDP in constant 1999 prices	3,874.0	4,109.1	4,316.0

* Estimates.
† Provisional.

Gross Domestic Product by Economic Activity

	2004	2005*	2006†
Agriculture, hunting, forestry and fishing	589.5	668.3	714.9
Mining and quarrying	48.3	45.2	48.2
Manufacturing	606.4	631.6	648.7
Electricity, gas and water	92.1	106.3	114.3
Construction	179.8	207.3	240.1
Trade	674.6	715.9	756.4
Transport, storage and communications	363.7	409.6	457.6
Education and training	142.3	156.1	166.5
Health and social services	58.0	61.2	64.7
Government services	291.0	322.2	349.7
Other services	627.9	664.2	714.8
Sub-total	3,673.6	3,987.9	4,275.9
Import taxes and duties	524.9	573.4	623.1
GDP in purchasers' values	4,198.5	4,561.2	4,899.1

* Estimates.
† Provisional.

BALANCE OF PAYMENTS
('000 million francs CFA)

	2005	2006*	2007†
Exports of goods f.o.b.	832	798	821
Imports of goods f.o.b.	−1,524	−1,661	−1,770
Trade balance	−691	−864	−949
Exports of services and incomes received	518	541	562
Imports of services and incomes paid	−588	−627	−649
Balance on goods, services and income	−762	−949	−1,036
Current transfers (net)	405	465	532
Current balance	−356	−485	−504
Capital account (net)	69	1,234	85
Direct investment (net)	28	47	143
Portfolio investment (net)	14	−3	32
Other investment (net)	117	−734	317
Net errors and omissions	6	−2	—
Overall balance	−122	57	71

* Estimates.
† Projected.

Source: IMF, *Senegal: Request for a Three-Year Policy Support Instrument—Staff Report; Staff Statement; Press Release on the Executive Board Discussion; and Statement by the Executive Director for Senegal* (November 2007).

External Trade

PRINCIPAL COMMODITIES
(distribution by SITC, US $ million)

Imports c.i.f.	2002	2003	2004
Food and live animals	449.2	563.5	661.3
Cereals and cereal preparations	257.4	297.9	349.3
Rice	184.4	217.2	243.2
Rice, broken	183.9	216.0	236.6
Crude materials (inedible) except fuels	41.6	87.5	110.0
Mineral fuels, lubricants, etc.	729.7	444.7	522.1
Petroleum, petroleum products, etc.	688.4	399.4	460.7
Crude petroleum oils, etc.	417.4	276.3	333.0
Petroleum products, refined	266.3	117.8	115.8
Animal and vegetable oils, fats and waxes	40.2	86.7	98.4
Fixed vegetable oils and fats	32.6	74.2	82.3
Chemicals and related products	191.9	255.2	325.8
Medicinal and pharmaceutical products	64.6	79.7	99.9
Medicaments (incl. veterinary)	59.3	71.2	90.5
Basic manufactures	224.8	304.2	403.5
Iron and steel	49.5	75.1	137.6
Machinery and transport equipment	248.1	486.8	530.2
General industrial machinery, equipment and parts	34.7	89.7	98.9
Road vehicles and parts (excl. tyres, engines and electrical parts)	108.6	160.9	146.9
Passenger motor vehicles (excl. buses)	61.0	83.1	70.6
Miscellaneous manufactured articles	65.1	105.8	152.2
Total (incl. others)	2,031.0	2,391.5	2,848.8

SENEGAL

Exports f.o.b.	2002	2003	2004
Food and live animals	50.5	343.1	417.8
Fish, crustaceans and molluscs, and preparations thereof	0.4	282.0	314.3
Fish, fresh, chilled or frozen	0.2	104.1	166.9
Fish, fresh or chilled, excl. fillets	—	14.5	82.1
Fish, frozen, excl. fillets and minced fish	—	62.3	76.8
Crustaceans and molluscs, fresh, chilled, frozen, salted, etc	—	142.0	118.9
Crustaceans, frozen	—	41.2	43.8
Shrimps and prawns, frozen	—	38.7	42.7
Molluscs and aquatic invertebrates, fresh, frozen, dried, etc.	—	100.8	74.3
Cuttlefish, octopus and squid, frozen, dried, salted or in brine	—	97.0	70.2
Beverages and tobacco	11.2	46.7	14.7
Tobacco and tobacco manufactures	10.4	36.8	13.5
Tobacco, manufactured (whether or not containing tobacco substitutes)	10.1	36.4	11.4
Crude materials (inedible) except fuels	63.5	77.1	86.5
Crude fertilizers and crude minerals	36.0	31.3	37.8
Mineral fuels, lubricants, etc.	157.5	231.5	256.3
Petroleum, petroleum products, etc.	156.8	230.7	255.4
Crude petroleum and oils obtained from bituminous materials	21.2	43.5	37.7
Refined petroleum products	133.7	184.4	215.3
Animal and vegetable oils, fats and waxes	53.5	37.4	27.3
Fixed vegetable oils and fats	53.4	36.9	26.8
Crude fixed vegetable oils and fats	53.0	36.5	26.0
Chemicals and related products	267.7	260.6	337.4
Inorganic chemicals	171.2	139.9	180.4
Phosphorus pentoxide and phosphoric acids	170.3	138.0	179.4
Oils and perfume materials; toilet and cleansing preparations	28.9	39.0	47.9
Manufactured fertilizers	37.5	49.7	69.0
Nitrogen-phosphorus-potassium fertilizer	35.1	48.0	62.6
Basic manufactures	40.8	55.4	87.6
Machinery and transport equipment	24.2	48.2	50.9
Miscellaneous manufactured articles	26.0	51.0	40.5
Total (incl. others)	694.7	1,151.2	1,319.2

Source: UN, *International Trade Statistics Yearbook*.

PRINCIPAL TRADING PARTNERS
(US $ million)

Imports c.i.f.	2002	2003	2004
Argentina	37.0	26.1	25.5
Belgium	55.5	67.1	81.8
Brazil	34.7	70.9	108.1
China, People's Republic	41.9	64.2	97.1
Côte d'Ivoire	75.0	86.1	100.4
France (incl. Monaco)	427.0	588.9	691.1
Germany	50.0	82.4	78.3
India	39.3	52.6	40.6
Ireland	28.0	28.7	45.7
Italy	85.2	86.0	89.9
Japan	36.6	57.8	68.9
Netherlands	76.8	71.3	73.8
Nigeria	385.4	280.7	334.3

Imports c.i.f.—continued	2002	2003	2004
Russia	22.9	42.4	30.1
Saudi Arabia	26.8	14.3	6.2
South Africa	20.4	24.1	40.4
Spain	67.4	103.5	117.5
Thailand	151.0	173.9	177.2
Ukraine	—	16.2	65.5
United Kingdom	31.3	49.2	52.4
USA	35.0	86.0	88.7
Viet Nam	20.5	21.9	53.9
Total (incl. others)	2,031.0	2,391.5	2,848.8

Exports f.o.b.	2002	2003	2004
Benin	21.8	32.7	24.3
Burkina Faso	6.3	29.5	23.0
China, People's Republic	0.6	15.3	6.4
Côte d'Ivoire	28.1	61.4	40.2
France (incl. Monaco)	53.5	137.5	125.1
The Gambia	33.8	42.8	65.9
Greece	—	16.6	27.5
Guinea	17.7	59.9	38.7
Guinea-Bissau	21.2	—	46.2
India	196.0	147.2	183.1
Italy	22.5	95.6	92.6
Mali	86.1	114.9	180.6
Mauritania	30.9	33.3	32.0
Netherlands	14.4	9.8	11.3
Spain	2.2	56.3	88.0
Togo	8.5	14.9	18.7
Total (incl. others)	694.7	1,151.2	1,319.9

Source: UN, *International Trade Statistics Yearbook*.

Transport

RAILWAYS
(traffic)

	2002	2003	2004
Passenger-km (million)	105	129	122
Net ton-km (million)	345	375	358

Passengers ('000): 4,789 in 1999.

Freight carried ('000 metric tons): 2,017 in 1999.

ROAD TRAFFIC
(motor vehicles in use)

	1997	1998	1999
Passenger cars	76,971	85,805	98,260
Buses and coaches	9,236	9,974	10,477
Lorries and vans	21,693	23,851	25,276
Road tractors	2,110	2,278	2,458
Motorcycles and mopeds	3,624	4,155	4,515

Source: IRF, *World Road Statistics*.

SHIPPING

Merchant Fleet
(vessels registered at 31 December)

	2004	2005	2006
Number of vessels	178	181	183
Total displacement ('000 grt)	40.8	41.6	42.5

Source: Lloyd's Register-Fairplay, *World Fleet Statistics*.

International Sea-borne Freight Traffic
('000 metric tons)

	2003	2004	2005
Goods loaded	3,028	2,875	2,911
Goods unloaded	7,521	7,144	8,026

Source: Port Autonome de Dakar.

CIVIL AVIATION
(traffic on scheduled services)*

	2001	2002	2003
Kilometres flown (million)	4	7	6
Passengers carried ('000)	176	231	130
Passenger-km (million)	319	572	388
Total ton-km (million)	116	20	35

*Including an apportionment of the traffic of Air Afrique.

Source: UN, *Statistical Yearbook*.

Tourism

FOREIGN TOURIST ARRIVALS BY NATIONALITY*

	2003	2004	2005
African states	85,664	89,660	87,565
Belgium, Luxembourg and the Netherlands	17,025	16,160	21,712
East Asian and Pacific states	2,273	3,705	3,837
France	181,470	172,878	191,580
Germany	7,985	8,374	9,615
Italy	9,279	9,413	11,493
Spain	12,680	13,415	15,353
United Kingdom	3,063	4,092	4,380
USA	8,518	10,422	11,080
Total (incl. others)	353,539	363,490	386,564

*Figures refer to arrivals at hotels and similar establishments.

Receipts from tourism (US $ million, excl. passenger transport): 269 in 2003; 287 in 2004; n.a. in 2005.

Source: World Tourism Organization.

Communications Media

	2004	2005	2006
Telephones ('000 main lines in use)	244.9	266.6	282.6
Mobile cellular telephones ('000 subscribers)	1,121.3	1,730.1	2,982.6
Personal computers ('000 in use)	242	n.a.	n.a.
Internet users ('000)	482	540	650
Broadband subscribers ('000)	7.7	18.0	28.9

Television receivers ('000 in use): 380 in 2000.

Radio receivers ('000 in use): 1,240 in 1997.

Daily newspapers: 1 (average circulation 45,000 copies) in 1996; 13 in 2004.

Non-daily newspapers: 6 (average circulation 37,000 copies) in 1995.

Sources: mainly International Telecommunication Union; UNESCO, *Statistical Yearbook*, UNESCO Institute for Statistics.

Education

(2004/05, unless otherwise indicated)

	Institutions*	Teachers	Males	Females	Total
Pre-primary	460	2,171	20.7	22.5	43.2
Primary	5,670	34,656	741.7	702.4	1,444.2
Secondary	591	15,394	233.6	172.3	405.9
Tertiary	n.a.	n.a.	n.a.	n.a.	59.1

(Students ('000))

*2002/03 (Source: Ministry of Education, Dakar).

Source: UNESCO Institute for Statistics.

Adult literacy rate (UNESCO estimates): 39.3% (males 51.1%; females 29.2%) in 2002 (Source: UNESCO Institute for Statistics).

Directory

The Constitution

The Constitution of the Republic of Senegal was promulgated following its approval by popular referendum on 7 January 2001, and entered into force thereafter, with the exception of those sections relating to the Assemblée nationale and the relations between the executive and legislative powers (articles 59–87), which took effect following legislative elections on 29 April 2001. The main provisions are summarized below:

PREAMBLE

The people of Senegal, recognizing their common destiny, and aware of the need to consolidate the fundaments of the Nation and the State, and supporting the ideals of African unity and human rights, proclaim the principle of national territorial integrity and a national unity respecting the diverse cultures of the Nation, reject all forms of injustice, inequality and discrimination, and proclaim the will of Senegal to be a modern democratic State.

THE STATE AND SOVEREIGNTY

Articles 1–6: Senegal is a secular, democratic Republic, in which all people are equal before the law, without distinction of origin, race, sex or religion. The official language of the Republic is French; the national languages are Diola, Malinké, Pular, Sérère, Soninké, Wolof and any other national language that may be so defined. The principle of the Republic is 'government of the people, by the people and for the people'. National sovereignty belongs to the people who exercise it, through their representatives or in referenda. Suffrage may be direct or indirect, and is always universal, equal and secret. Political parties and coalitions of political parties are obliged to observe the Constitution and the principles of national sovereignty and democracy, and are forbidden from identifying with one race, one ethnic group, one sex, one religion, one sect, one language or one region. All acts of racial, ethnic or religious discrimination, including regionalist propaganda liable to undermine the security or territorial integrity of the State are punishable by law. The institutions of the Republic are: the President of the Republic; the Assemblée nationale; the Government and the Constitutional Council; the Council of State; the Final Court of Appeal (Cour de Cassation); the Revenue Court (Cour de Comptes); and Courts and Tribunals.

PUBLIC LIBERTIES AND THE HUMAN PERSON; ECONOMIC AND SOCIAL RIGHTS AND COLLECTIVE RIGHTS

Articles 7–25: The inviolable and inalienable rights of man are recognized as the base of all human communities, of peace and justice in the world, and are protected by the State. All humans are equal before the law. The Republic protects, within the rule of law, the right to free opinion, free expression, a free press, freedom of association and of movement, cultural, religious and philosophical freedoms, the right to organize trade unions and businesses, the right to education and literacy, the right to own property, to work, to health, to a clean environment, and to diverse sources of information. No prior authorization is required for the formation of an organ of the press. Men and women are guaranteed equal rights to possess property.

Marriage and the family constitute the natural and moral base of the human community, and are protected by the State. The State is obliged to protect the physical and moral health of the family, in particular of the elderly and the handicapped, and guarantees to alleviate the conditions of life of women, particularly in rural areas. Forced marriages are forbidden as a violation of individual liberty. The State protects youth from exploitation, from drugs, and from delinquency.

All children in the Republic have the right to receive schooling, from public schools, or from institutions of religious or non-religious communities. All national educational institutions, public or private, are obliged to participate in the growth of literacy in one of the national languages. Private schools may be opened with the authorization of, and under the control of, the State.

Freedom of conscience is guaranteed. Religious communities and institutions are separate from the State.

All discrimination against workers on grounds of origins, sex, political opinions or beliefs are forbidden. All workers have the right to join or form trade or professional associations. The right to strike is recognized, under legal conditions, as long as the freedom to work is not impeded, and the enterprise is not placed in peril. The State guarantees sanitary and human conditions in places of work.

THE PRESIDENT OF THE REPUBLIC

Articles 26–52: The President of the Republic is elected, for a term of five years, by universal direct suffrage. The mandate may be renewed once. Candidates for the presidency must be of solely Senegalese nationality, enjoy full civil and political rights, be aged 35 years or more on the day of elections, and must be able to write, read and speak the official language fluently. All candidates must be presented by a political party or a legally constituted coalition of political parties, or be accompanied by a petition signed by at least 10,000 electors, including at least 500 electors in each of six administrative regions. Candidates may not campaign predominately on ethnic or regional grounds. Each political party or coalition of political parties may present only one candidate. If no candidate receives an absolute majority of votes cast in the first round, representing the support of at least one-quarter of the electorate, a second round of elections is held between the two highest-placed candidates in the first round. In the case of incapacity, death or resignation, the President's position is assumed by the President of the Assemblée nationale, and in the case of his or her incapacity, by one of the Vice-Presidents of the Assemblée nationale, in all cases subject to the same terms of eligibility that apply to the President. The President presides over the Council of Ministers, the Higher Council of National Defence, and the National Security Council, and is the Supreme Chief of the Armed Forces. The President appoints a Prime Minister, and appoints ministers on the recommendation of the Prime Minister.

THE GOVERNMENT

Articles 53–57: The head of the Government is the Prime Minister. In the event of the resignation or removal from office of a Prime Minister, the entire Government is obliged to resign.

THE OPPOSITION

Article 58: The Constitution guarantees the right to oppose to political parties that are opposed to Government policy, and recognizes the existence of a parliamentary opposition.

THE ASSEMBLÉE NATIONALE

Article 59–66: Deputies of the Assemblée nationale are elected by universal direct suffrage, for a five-year mandate, subject only to the dissolution of the Assemblée nationale. Any serving deputy who resigns from his or her party shall have his or her mandate removed. Deputies enjoy immunity from criminal proceedings, except with the authorization of the bureau of the Assemblée nationale. The Assemblée nationale votes on the budget. Deputies vote as individuals and must not be obligated to vote in a certain way. Except in exceptional and limited circumstances, sessions of the Assemblée nationale are public.

RELATIONS BETWEEN THE EXECUTIVE AND LEGISLATIVE POWERS

Articles 67–87: The Assemblée nationale is the sole holder of legislative power, votes on the budget and authorizes a declaration of war. The President of the Republic may, having received the opinion of the Prime Minister and the President of the Assemblée nationale, pronounce by decree the dissolution of the Assemblée nationale, except during the first two years of any Assemblée.

INTERNATIONAL TREATIES

Articles: 88–91: The President of the Republic negotiates international engagements, and ratifies or approves them with the authorization of the Assemblée nationale. The Republic of Senegal may conclude agreements with any African State that would comprise a partial or total abandonment of national sovereignty in order to achieve African unity.

JUDICIAL POWER

Articles 92–98: The judiciary is independent of the legislature and the executive power. The judiciary consists of the Constitutional Council, the Council of State, the Court of Final Appeal, the Revenue Court and Courts and Tribunals. The Constitutional Council comprises five members, including a President, a Vice-President and three judges. Each member serves for a mandate of six years (which may not be renewed) with partial renewals occurring every two years. The President of the Republic appoints members of the Constitutional Council, whose decisions are irreversible.

THE HIGH COURT OF JUSTICE

Articles 99–101: A High Court of Justice, presided over by a magistrate and comprising members elected by the Assemblée nationale, is instituted. The President of the Republic can only be brought to trial for acts accomplished in the exercise of his duties in the case of high treason. The High Court of Justice tries the Prime Minister and other members of the Government for crimes committed in the exercise of their duties.

LOCAL GOVERNMENT

Article 102: Local government bodies operate independently, by means of elective assemblies, in accordance with the law.

ON REVISION

Article 103: Only the President of the Republic or the deputies of the Assemblée nationale, of whom a three-quarters' majority must be in favour, may propose amending the Constitution. Amendments may be approved by referendum or, at the initiative of the President of the Republic, solely by approval by the Assemblée nationale, in which case a three-fifths' majority must be in favour.

The Government

HEAD OF STATE

President: ABDOULAYE WADE (took office 1 April 2000, re-elected 25 February 2007).

COUNCIL OF MINISTERS
(March 2008)

Prime Minister: CHEIKH HADJIBOU SOUMARÉ.

Minister of State, Minister of Foreign Affairs: CHEIKH TIDIANE GADIO.

Minister of State, Minister of the Economy and Finance: ABDOULAYE DIOP.

Minister of State, Keeper of the Seals, Minister of Justice: MADICKÉ NIANG.

Minister of State, Minister of the Interior: CHEIKH TIDIANE SY.

Minister of State, Minister of Mines, Industry and Small and Medium-sized Enterprises: OUSMANE NGOM.

Minister of State, Minister of the Environment, Conservation, Retention Basins and Man-made Lakes: DJIBO LEÏTY KÂ.

Minister of State, Minister of Infrastructure, Transport, Telecommunication and Information and Communication Technology: HABIB SY.

Minister of State, Minister of the Maritime Economy, Maritime Transport, Fisheries and Fishbreeding: SOULEYMANE NDÉNÉ NDIAYE.

Minister of State, Minister of the Armed Forces: BÉCAYE DIOP.

Minister of State, Minister of Town Planning, Housing, Urban Hydraulics, Public Hygiene and Sanitation: OUMAR SARR.

Minister of State, Minister of Decentralization and Local Communities: OUSMANE MASSECK NDIAYE.

Minister of Education and Technical and Professional Training: Prof. MOUSTAPHA SOURANG.

Minister of Land Settlement and Decentralized Co-operation: ABDOURAHIM AGNE.

Minister of the Family, Female Entrepreneurship and Microfinance: AWA NDIAYE.

Minister of Trade: MAMADOU DIOP.

Minister of Rural Hydraulics and the National Hydrographic Network: ADAMA SALL.

Minister of Culture, Protected National Heritage, National Languages and Francophone Affairs: MAME BIRAME DIOUF.

Minister of Health and Preventive Medicine: SAFIATOU THIAM.

Minister of Livestock: OUMOU KHAIRY GUEYE SECK.

Minister of Biofuels, Renewable Energy Resources and Scientific Research: CHRISTHIAN SINA DIATTA.

Minister of Crafts and Air Transport: FARBA SENGHOR.

Minister of Information and Relations with the Institutions, Spokesperson for the Government: ABDOU AZIZ SOW.

Minister of Sports and Leisure: Dr BACAR DIA.

Minister of Youth and Youth Employment: MAMADOU LAMINE KEÏTA.

Minister of Energy: SAMUEL AMÉTE SARR.

Minister of the Civil Service, Employment, Labour and Professional Organizations: INNOCENCE NTAP.
Minister of Senegalese Nationals Abroad and Tourism: AMINATA LÔ.
Minister of Agriculture: HAMATH SALL.
Minister-delegate at the Office of the Minister of State, Minister of the Economy and Finance, responsible for the Budget: IBRAHIMA SARR.

MINISTRIES

Office of the President: ave Léopold Sédar Senghor, BP 168, Dakar; tel. 33-823-1088; internet www.gouv.sn/institutions/president.html.

Office of the Prime Minister: Bldg Administratif, ave Léopold Sédar Senghor, BP 4029, Dakar; tel. 33-889-6969; fax 33-823-4479; internet www.gouv.sn.

Ministry of Agriculture and Stockbreeding: Bldg Administratif, BP 4005, Dakar; tel. 33-849-7000; fax 33-823-3268; internet www.agriculture.gouv.sn.

Ministry of the Armed Forces: Bldg Administratif, ave Léopold Sédar Senghor, BP 4041, Dakar; tel. 33-823-7612; fax 33-823-6338; internet www.forcesarmees.gouv.sn.

Ministry of Biofuels, Renewable Energy Resources and Scientific Research: 15 blvd Djily Mbaye, Dakar; tel. 33-889-5200.

Ministry of the Civil Service, Employment, Labour and Professional Organizations: Bldg Administratif, BP 4007, Dakar; tel. 33-849-7000; fax 33-823-7429; e-mail mineladiallo@yahoo.fr; internet www.fonctionpublique.gouv.sn.

Ministry of Crafts and Air Transport: Dakar; tel. 33-849-7512; fax 33-842-6763.

Ministry of Culture, Protected National Heritage, National Languages and Francophone Affairs: Bldg Administratif, ave Léopold Sédar Senghor, BP 4001, Dakar; tel. 33-822-4303; fax 33-822-1638; internet www.culture.gouv.sn.

Ministry of Decentralization and Local Communities: Bldg Administratif, ave Léopold Sédor Senghor, Dakar; tel. 33-849-7512; fax 33-849-6763.

Ministry of the Economy and Finance: ave Carde, Bâtiment CEPOD, Dakar; tel. 33-823-3427; fax 33-821-8312; e-mail i_diouf@minfinances.sn; internet www.finances.gouv.sn.

Ministry of Education: rue Docteur Calmette, BP 4025, Dakar; tel. 33-849-5454; fax 33-822-1463; internet www.education.gouv.sn.

Ministry of Energy: Bldg Administratif, BP 4021, Dakar; tel. 33-849-7300; fax 33-823-4470.

Ministry of the Environment, Conservation, Man-made Lakes and Retention Basins: Bldg Administratif, BP 4055, Dakar; tel. 33-889-0234; fax 33-822-2180; e-mail mepn@environnement.gouv.sn; internet www.environnement.gouv.sn.

Ministry of the Family, Female Entrepreneurship and Microfinance: Bldg Administratif, Dakar; tel. 33-849-7063; fax 33-822-9490; internet www.famille.gouv.sn.

Ministry of Foreign Affairs: pl. de l'Indépendance, BP 4044, Dakar; tel. 33-889-1300; e-mail maeuase@senegal.diplomatie.sn; internet www.diplomatie.gouv.sn.

Ministry of Health and Preventive Medicine: Fann Résidence, rue Aimé Césaire, BP 4024, Dakar; tel. 33-869-4242; fax 33-869-4269; e-mail mspmwebsante@sentoo.sn; internet www.sante.gouv.sn.

Ministry of Information and Relations with the Institutions: 58 blvd de la République, BP 4027, Dakar; tel. 33-823-1065; fax 33-821-4504; internet www.information.gouv.sn.

Ministry of Infrastructure, Transport, Telecomunication and Information and Communication Technology: Ex-Camp Lat Dior, Corriche, Dakar; tel. 33-823-8351; fax 33-823-8279; internet www.equipement.gouv.sn.

Ministry of the Interior: pl. Washington, BP 4002, Dakar; tel. 33-889-9100; fax 33-821-0542; e-mail mint@primature.sn; internet www.interieur.gouv.sn.

Ministry of Justice: Bldg Administratif, ave Léopold Sédar Senghor, BP 4030, Dakar; tel. 33-849-7000; fax 33-823-2727; e-mail justice@justice.gouv.sn; internet www.justice.gouv.sn.

Ministry of Land Settlement, Trade and Decentralized Cooperation: Bldg Administratif, Dakar; tel. 33-849-7100; fax 33-823-66735.

Ministry of the Maritime Economy, Maritime Transport, Fisheries and Fishbreeding: Bldg Administratif, BP 4050, Dakar; tel. 33-823-3426; fax 33-823-8720; e-mail abdoumbodj@yahoo.fr; internet www.ecomaritime.gouv.sn.

Ministry of Mining and Industry: 122 bis ave André Peytavin, BP 4037, Dakar; tel. 33-822-9994; fax 33-822-5594.

Ministry of Rural Hydraulics and the National Hydrographic Network: Bldg Administratif, ave Léopold Sédar Senghor, Dakar; tel. 33-889-1721; fax 33-842-5314.

Ministry of Senegalese Nationals Abroad and Tourism: VDN, Rue 50 X 23, Villa 23 bis, BP 45510, Dakar; tel. 33-867-0171; fax 33-867-0183; internet www.senex.gouv.sn.

Ministry of Sports and Leisure: rue Carnot 58, BP 4019, Dakar; tel. 33-822-4621; fax 33-822-4831; internet www.sports.gouv.sn.

Ministry of Technical and Professional Training: 23 rue Calmette, angle René Ndiaye, Dakar; tel. 33-822-2136; fax 33-821-7196.

Ministry of Town Planning, Housing, Urban Hydraulics, Public Hygiene and Sanitation: Ex Camp Lat Dior, Ave Peytavin, BP 4028, Dakar; tel. 33-823-9127; fax 33-823-6245; internet www.muat.gouv.sn.

Ministry of Youth and Youth Employment: Bldg Administratif, Dakar; tel. 33-869-1601; fax 33-822-9764; e-mail contact@jeunesse.gouv.sn; internet www.jeunesse-emploi.gouv.sn.

President and Legislature

PRESIDENT

Presidential Election, 25 February 2007

Candidate	Votes	% of valid votes
Abdoulaye Wade	1,914,403	55.90
Idrissa Seck	510,922	14.92
Ousmane Tanor Dieng	464,287	13.56
Moustapha Niasse	203,129	5.93
Robert Sagna	88,446	2.58
Abdoulaye Bathily	75,797	2.21
Landing Savané	70,780	2.07
Others	97,162	2.84
Total	**3,424,926**	**100.00**

LEGISLATURE

Assemblée nationale

pl. Soweto, BP 86, Dakar; tel. 33-823-1099; fax 33-823-6708; e-mail assnat@assemblee-nationale.sn; internet www.assemblee-nationale.sn.

President: MACKY SALL.

General Election, 3 June 2007

Party	Votes	% of votes	Seats
Sopi Coalition*	1,190,609	69.21	131
Takku Defaraat Sénégal Coalition	86,621	5.04	3
And Defar Sénégal Coalition	84,998	4.94	3
Waar Wi Coalition	74,919	4.35	3
Rassemblement pour le peuple (RP)	73,083	4.25	2
Front pour le socialisme et la démocratie—Benno Jubël (FSD—BJ)	37,427	2.18	1
Alliance Jëf-Jël	33,297	1.94	1
Convergence pour le renouveau et la citoyenneté (CRC)	30,658	1.78	1
Parti socialiste authentique (PSA)	26,320	1.53	1
Union nationale patriotique (UNP)	22,271	1.29	1
Mouvement de la réforme pour le développement social (MRDS)	20,041	1.16	1
Rassemblement des écologistes du Sénégal (RES)	17,267	1.00	1
Parti social-démocrate—Jant Bi (PSD—JB)	15,968	0.93	1
Rassemblement patriotique sénégalais—Jammi Rewmi (RPS—JR)	6,847	0.40	—
Total	**1,720,326**	**100.00**	**150**

* A coalition of some 40 parties and movements, led by the PDS.

SENEGAL

Sénat
President: PAPE DIOP.
Election, 19 August 2007

Party	Seats
Parti démocratique sénégalais (PPS)	34
And Jëf—Parti africain pour la démocratie et le socialisme (AJ—PADS)	1
Total	**100***

*The remaining 65 members are appointed by the President.

Election Commission

Commission électorale nationale autonome (CENA): Dakar; f. 2005; Pres. MAMADOU MOUSTAPHA TOURÉ.

Political Organizations

In mid-2007 there were 77 political parties registered in Senegal, of which the following were among the most important:

Alliance des forces de progrès (AFP): rue 1, angle rue A, point E, BP 5825, Dakar; tel. 33-825-4021; fax 33-864-0707; e-mail admin@afp-senegal.org; internet www.afp-senegal.org; f. 1999; mem. of opposition Cadre permanent de concertation (f. 2001); Sec.-Gen. MOUSTAPHA NIASSE.

Alliance Jëf Jël: Villa 5, rue 1, Castors Front de Terre, Dakar; tel. 77-652-2232; e-mail tallasylla@hotmail.com; f. 1997; mem. of opposition; Pres. TALLA SYLLA.

And Defar Sénégal Coalition: Kolda; Leader LANDING SAVANÉ.

And Jëf—Parti africain pour la démocratie et le socialisme (AJ—PADS): Villa 1, Zone B, BP 12136, Dakar; tel. 33-825-7667; fax 33-823-5860; e-mail webmaster@ajpads.org; internet x.ajpads.org; f. 1992; Sec.-Gen. LANDING SAVANÉ.

Bloc des centristes Gaïndé (BCG): Villa 734, Sicap Baobabs, Dakar; tel. 33-825-3764; e-mail issa_dias@sentoo.sn; f. 1996; Pres. and First Sec. JEAN-PAUL DIAS.

Convergence pour le renouveau et la citoyenneté (CRC): Leader ALIOU DIA.

Front pour le socialisme et la démocratie—Benno Jubël (FSD—BJ): contested 2001 election as mem. of Sopi Coalition; Leader ABDOULAYE DIÈYE.

Ligue démocratique—Mouvement pour le parti du travail (LD—MPT): ave Bourguiba, Dieuppeul 2, Villa 2566, BP 10172, Dakar Liberté; tel. 33-825-6706; fax 33-827-4300; regd 1981; social-democrat; Sec.-Gen. ABDOULAYE BATHILY.

Mouvement pour la démocratie et le socialisme—Naxx Jarinu (MDS—NJ): Unité 20, Parcelles Assainies, Villa 528, Dakar; tel. 33-869-5049; f. 2000; Leader OUMAR KHASSIMOU DAI.

Mouvement de la réforme pour le développement social (MRDS): HLM 4, Villa 858, Dakar; tel. 77-644-3170; f. 2000; Pres. IBRAHIMA DIENG; Sec.-Gen. Imam BABACAR NIANG.

Mouvement pour le socialisme et l'unité (MSU): HLM 1, Villa 86, Dakar; tel. 33-825-8544; f. 1981 as Mouvement démocratique populaire; mem. of opposition Cadre permanent de concertation (f. 2001); National Co-ordinator-Gen. MOUHAMADOU BAMBA N'DIAYE.

Mouvement républicain sénégalais (MRS): Résidence du Cap-Vert, 10e étage, 5 pl. de l'Indépendance, BP 4193, Dakar; tel. 33-822-0319; fax 33-822-0700; e-mail agaz@omnet.sn; Sec.-Gen. DEMBA BA.

Parti africain de l'indépendance (PAI): Maison du Peuple, Guediewaye, BP 820, Dakar; tel. 33-837-0136; f. 1957; reorg. 1976; Marxist; Sec.-Gen. MAJMOUT DIOP.

Parti démocratique sénégalais (PDS): blvd Dial Diop, Immeuble Serigne Mourtada Mbacké, Dakar; tel. 33-823-5027; fax 33-823-1702; e-mail cedobe@aol.com; internet www.sopionline.com; f. 1974; liberal democratic; Sec.-Gen. Me ABDOULAYE WADE.

Parti de l'indépendance et du travail (PIT): route front de terre, BP 10470, Dakar; tel. 33-827-2907; fax 33-820-9000; regd 1981; Marxist-Leninist; mem. of opposition Cadre permanent de concertation (f. 2001); Sec.-Gen. AMATH DANSOKHO.

Parti libéral sénégalais (PLS): 13 ave Malick Sy, BP 28277, Dakar; tel. and fax 33-823-1560; f. 1998 by breakaway faction of PDS; Leader Me OUSMANE NGOM.

Parti populaire sénégalais (PPS): Quartier Escale, BP 212, Diourbel; tel. 33-971-1171; regd 1981; populist; mem. of opposition Cadre permanent de concertation (f. 2001); Sec.-Gen. Dr OUMAR WANE.

Parti pour le progrès et la citoyenneté (PPC): Quartier Merina, Rufique; tel. 33-836-1868; absorbed Rassemblement pour le progrès, la justice et le socialisme in 2000; Sec.-Gen. Me MBAYE JACQUES DIOP.

Parti pour la renaissance africaine—Sénégal (PARENA): Sicap Dieuppeul, Villa 2685/B, Dakar; tel. 77-636-8788; fax 33-823-5721; e-mail mariamwane@yahoo.fr; f. 2000; Sec.-Gen. MARIAM MAMADOU WANE LY.

Parti de la renaissance et de la citoyenneté: Liberté 6, Villa 7909, Dakar; tel. 33-827-8568; f. 2000; supports Pres. Wade; Sec.-Gen. SAMBA DIOULDÉ THIAM.

Parti social-démocrate—Jant Bi (PSD—JB): Leader MAMOUR CISSE.

Parti socialiste authentique (PSA): Leader SOUTY TOURÉ.

Parti socialiste du Sénégal (PS): Maison du Parti Socialiste Léopold Sédar Senghor, Colobane, BP 12010, Dakar; tel. and fax 33-824-7744; e-mail senegalpartisocialiste@gmail.com; internet www.partisocialiste.sn; f. 1958 as Union progressiste sénégalaise; reorg. 1978; democratic socialist; First Sec. OUSMANE TANOR DIENG.

Rassemblement des écologistes du Sénégal—Les verts (RES): rue 67, angle rue 52, Gueule Tapée, BP 25226, Dakar-Fann; tel. and fax 33-842-3442; f. 1999; Sec.-Gen. OUSMANE SOW HUCHARD.

Rassemblement national démocratique (RND): Sacré-Coeur III, Villa no 972, Dakar; tel. 33-827-5072; f. 1976; legalized 1981; mem. of opposition Cadre permanent de concertation (f. 2001); Sec.-Gen. MADIOR DIOUF.

Rassemblement patriotique sénégalais—Jammi Rewmi (RPS—JR): Leader ELY MADIODO FALL FALL.

Rassemblement des travailleurs africains—Sénégal (RTA—S): Villa 999, HLM Grand Yoff, BP 13725, Dakar; tel. 33-827-1579; e-mail sambmomar@hotmail.com; f. 1997; Co-ordinator El Hadj MOMAR SAMBE.

Takku Defaraat Sénégal Coalition: VDN à côté de la Poste; tel. 33-860-5019; fax 33-860-5020; internet www.robertsagna.com; f. 2000; Leader ROBERT SAGNA.

Union nationale patriotique (UNP): Leader NDÈYE FATOU TOURÉ.

Union pour le renouveau démocratique (URD): Bopp Villa 234, rue 7, Dakar; tel. 33-820-5598; fax 33-820-7317; f. 1998 by breakaway faction of PS; mem. of opposition Cadre permanent de concertation (f. 2001); Sec.-Gen. DJIBO LEÏTY KÂ.

Waar Wi Coalition: Leader MOUDOU DIAGNE FADA.

In August 2001 some 25 pro-Government parties, which were formerly members of the Sopi (Change) Coalition that contested the legislative elections in April 2001, formed an electoral alliance, the **Convergence des actions autour du Président en perspective du 21ième siècle (CAP-21)** to contest municipal and local elections in May 2002. In May 2001 several opposition parties (numbering eight in February 2004 and led by the AFP) formed an opposition consultative framework, the **Cadre permanent de concertation (CPC)**, which was also to operate as an electoral alliance in the municipal and local elections.

The **Mouvement des forces démocratiques de la Casamance (MFDC)** was founded in 1947; it had paramilitary and political wings and formerly sought the independence of the Casamance region of southern Senegal. The MFDC is not officially recognized as a political party (the Constitution of 2001 forbids the formation of parties on a geographic basis) and waged a campaign of guerrilla warfare in the region from the early 1980s. Representatives of the MFDC have participated in extensive negotiations with the Senegalese Government on the restoration of peace and the granting of greater autonomy to Casamance, and in December 2004 a cease-fire agreement was signed between the two sides, pending further peace negotiations. The Honorary President of the MFDC, Fr AUGUSTIN DIAMACOUNÉ SENGHOR, died in January 2007; the post of Secretary-General was disputed between JEAN-MARIE FRANÇOIS BIAGUI and ANSOUMANA BADJI.

Diplomatic Representation

EMBASSIES IN SENEGAL

Algeria: 5 rue Mermoz, Plateau, Dakar; tel. 33-849-5700; fax 33-849-5701; e-mail ambalgdak@orange.sn; f. 1963; Ambassador Dr ABDELHAMID CHEBCHOUB.

Austria: 18 rue Emile Zola, BP 3247, Dakar; tel. 33-849-4000; fax 33-849-4370; e-mail dakar-ob@bmaa.gv.at; Ambassador GERHARD DOUJAK.

Belgium: ave des Jambaars, BP 524, Dakar; tel. 33-889-4390; fax 33-889-4398; e-mail ambeldak@orange.sn; internet www.diplomatie.be/dakar; Ambassador LUC WILLEMARCK.

Brazil: Immeuble Fondation Fahd, 4e étage, blvd Djily Mbaye, angle rue Macodou Ndiaye, BP 136, Dakar; tel. 33-823-1492; fax 33-823-7181; e-mail embdakar@sentoo.sn; Ambassador KÁTIA GODINHO GILABERTE DO NASCIMENTO BORGES.

Burkina Faso: Sicap Sacré Coeur III, Extension VDN No. 10628B, BP 11601, Dakar; tel. 33-864-5824; fax 33-864-5823; e-mail ambabf@sentoo.sn; Ambassador SALAMATA SAWADOGO.

Cameroon: 157–9 rue Joseph Gomis, BP 4165, Dakar; tel. 33-849-0292; fax 33-823-3396; Ambassador EMMANUEL MBONJO-EJANGUE.

Canada: rue Galliéni angle rue Amadou Cissé Dia, BP 3373, Dakar; tel. 33-889-4700; fax 33-889-4720; e-mail dakar@international.gc.ca; internet www.dakar.gc.ca; Ambassador JEAN-PIERRE BOLDUC.

Cape Verde: 3 blvd El-Hadji Djilly M'Baye, BP 11269, Dakar; tel. 33-822-4285; fax 33-821-0697; e-mail acvc.sen@metissacana.sn; Ambassador RAÚL JORGE VERA CRUZ BARBOSA.

China, People's Republic: rue 18 prolongée, BP 342, Dakar-Fann; tel. 33-864-7775; fax 33-864-7780; Ambassador LU SHAYE.

Congo, Democratic Republic: Fenêtre Mermoz, Dakar; tel. 33-825-1280; Chargé d'affaires a.i. FATAKI NICOLAS LUNGUELE MUSAMBYA.

Congo, Republic: Statut Mermoz, BP 5242, Dakar; tel. 77-634-5022; fax 33-825-7856; Ambassador VALENTIN OLLESSONGO.

Côte d'Ivoire: ave Birago Diop, BP 359, Dakar; tel. 33-869-0270; fax 33-825-2115; e-mail cmrci@ambaci-dakar.org; internet www.ambaci-dakar.org; Ambassador FATIMATA TANOE TOURÉ.

Cuba: 43 rue Aimé Césaire, BP 4510, Dakar-Fann; tel. 33-869-0240; fax 33-864-1063; e-mail embacubasen@sentoo.sn; Ambassador LLUSIF SADIN TASSE.

Egypt: 22 ave Brière de l'Isle, Plateau, BP 474, Dakar; tel. 33-889-2474; fax 33-821-8993; e-mail ambegydk@telecomplus.sn; Ambassador SANAA ISMAIL ATTA ALLAH.

Ethiopia: 18 blvd de la République, BP 379, Dakar; tel. 33-821-9896; fax 33-821-9895; e-mail ethembas@sentoo.sn; Ambassador ATO HASSEN ABDULKADIK.

France: 1 rue El Hadj Amadou Assane Ndoye, BP 4035, Dakar; tel. 33-839-5100; fax 33-839-5181; e-mail webmestre.dakar-amba@diplomatie.gouv.fr; internet www.ambafrance-sn.org; Ambassador JEAN-CHRISTOPHE RUFIN.

Gabon: ave Cheikh Anta Diop, cnr Fann Résidence, BP 436, Dakar; tel. 33-865-2234; fax 33-864-3145; Ambassador VINCENT BOULE.

The Gambia: 11 rue Elhadji Ismaïla Guèye (Thiong), BP 3248, Dakar; tel. 33-821-4416; fax 33-821-6279; Ambassador GIBRIL SEMAN JOOF.

Germany: 20 ave Pasteur, angle rue Mermoz, BP 2100, Dakar; tel. 33-889-4884; fax 33-822-5299; e-mail reg1@daka.auswaertiges-amt.de; internet www.dakar.diplo.de; Ambassador DORETTA LOSCHELDER.

Ghana: Lot 27, Parcelle B, Almadies, BP 25370, Dakar; tel. 33-869-1990; fax 33-820-1950; Ambassador FREDERICK DANIEL LARYEA.

Guinea: rue 7, angle B&D, point E, BP 7123, Dakar; tel. 33-824-8606; fax 33-825-5946; Ambassador HADJA KOUMBA DIAKITÉ.

Guinea-Bissau: rue 6, angle B, point E, BP 2319, Dakar; tel. 33-823-0059; fax 33-825-2946; Ambassador LANSANA TOURÉ.

Holy See: rue Aimé Césaire, angle Corniche-Ouest, Fann Résidence, BP 5076, Dakar; tel. 33-824-2674; fax 33-824-1931; e-mail vatemb@orange.sn; Apostolic Nuncio Most Rev. GIUSEPPE PINTO (Titular Archbishop of Anglona).

India: 5 rue Carde, BP 398, Dakar; tel. 33-822-5875; fax 33-822-3585; e-mail indiacom@sentoo.sn; internet www.ambassadeinde.sn; Ambassador PARBATI SEN VYAS.

Indonesia: ave Cheikh Anta Diop, BP 5859, Dakar; tel. 33-825-7316; fax 33-825-5896; e-mail kbri@sentoo.sn; internet www.indonesia-senegal.org; Ambassador AHZAM BAHDARI RAZIF.

Iran: rue AX8, point E, BP 735, Dakar; tel. 33-825-2528; fax 33-824-2314; e-mail ambiiran@telecomplus.sn; Ambassador MOHAMMAD HOSEINI.

Israel: Immeuble SDIH, 3 pl. de l'Indépendance, BP 2096, Dakar; tel. 33-823-7965; fax 33-823-6490; e-mail info@dakar.mfa.gov.il; internet dakar.mfa.gov.il; Ambassador DANIEL PINHASI.

Italy: rue Alpha Achamiyou Tall, BP 348, Dakar; tel. 33-822-0578; fax 33-821-7580; e-mail ambasciata.dakar@esteri.it; internet sedi.esteri.it/dakar; Ambassador AGOSTINO MATHIS.

Japan: blvd Martin Luther King, Corniche-Ouest, BP 3140, Dakar; tel. 33-849-5500; fax 33-849-5555; Ambassador AKIRA NAKAJIMA.

Korea, Republic: 4e étage, Immeuble Fayçal, 3 rue Parchappe, BP 3338, Dakar; tel. 33-822-5822; fax 33-821-6600; e-mail senegal@mofat.go.kr; internet www.mofat.go.kr/senegal; Ambassador JAE CHOL HAHN.

Kuwait: blvd Martin Luther King, Dakar; tel. 33-824-1723; fax 33-825-0899; Ambassador MUHAMMAD AZ-ZUWAIKH.

Lebanon: 56 ave Jean XXIII, BP 234, Dakar; tel. 33-822-0255; fax 33-823-5899; e-mail ambaliban@sentoo.sn; Ambassador MICHEL HADDAD.

Libya: route de Ouakam, Dakar; tel. 33-824-5710; fax 33-824-5722; Ambassador AL HADY SALEM HAMMAD.

Madagascar: Immeuble rue 2, angle Ellipse, Point E, BP 25395, Dakar; tel. 33-825-2666; fax 33-864-4086; e-mail ambadak@yahoo.fr; internet www.ambamad.sn; Ambassador LILA HANITRA RATSIFANDRIHAMANANA.

Malaysia: 7 Extension VDN, Fann Mermoz, BP 15057, Dakar; tel. 33-825-8935; fax 33-825-4719; e-mail mwdakar@sentoo.sn; Chargé d'affaires a.i. SHARWANA BIN IDRISS.

Mali: Fann Résidence, Corniche-Ouest, rue 23, BP 478, Dakar; tel. 33-824-6252; fax 33-825-9471; e-mail ambamali@sentoo.sn; Ambassador N'TJI LAÏCO TRAORÉ.

Mauritania: 37 blvd Charles de Gaulle, Dakar; tel. 33-823-5344; fax 33-823-5311; Ambassador MOHAMED EL-MOCTAR OULD MOHAMED YAHYA.

Morocco: 73 ave Cheikh Anta Diop, BP 490, Dakar; tel. 33-824-6927; fax 33-825-7021; e-mail ambmadk@sentoo.sn; Ambassador MOHA OUALI TAGMA.

Netherlands: 37 rue Jaques Bugnicourt, BP 3262, Dakar; tel. 33-849-0360; fax 33-821-7084; e-mail dak@minbuza.nl; internet www.nlambassadedakar.org; Ambassador Dr J. W. G. JANSING.

Nigeria: 8 ave Cheikh Anta Diop, BP 3129, Dakar; tel. 869-86-00; tel. 33-869-8600; fax 33-825-8136; e-mail info@nigeriandakar.sn; Ambassador AZUKA CECILIA UZOKA-EMEJULU.

Pakistan: Stèle Mermoz, Villa 7602, BP 2635, Dakar; tel. 33-824-6135; fax 33-824-6136; e-mail parepdkar@yahoo.com; Ambassador ABDUL MALIK ABDULLAH.

Poland: Villa 'Les Ailes', Fann Résidence, angle Corniche-Ouest, BP 343, Dakar; tel. 33-824-2354; fax 33-824-9526; e-mail ambassade.pl@sentoo.sn; internet www.ambassade-pologne.sn; Ambassador ANDRZEJ MICHAL LUPINA.

Portugal: 5 ave Carde, BP 281, Dakar; tel. 33-864-0317; fax 33-864-0322; e-mail ambportdakar@sentoo.sn; Ambassador ANTÓNIO AUGUSTO MONTENEGRO VIEIRA CARDOSO.

Qatar: 25 blvd Martin Luther King, BP 5150, Dakar; tel. 33-820-9559; fax 33-869-1012; Ambassador ALI ABDUL LATIF AHMED AL-MASALAMANI.

Romania: rue A prolongée, point E, BP 3171, Dakar; tel. 33-825-2068; fax 33-824-9190; e-mail romania@sentoo.sn; Ambassador SIMONA CORLAN-IOAN.

Russia: ave Jean Jaurès, angle rue Carnot, BP 3180, Dakar; tel. 33-822-4821; fax 33-821-1372; e-mail ambrus@sentoo.sn; Ambassador ALEKSANDR A. ROMANOV.

Saudi Arabia: route Corniche-Ouest, face Olympique Club, BP 3109, Dakar; tel. 33-864-0141; fax 33-864-0130; e-mail snemb@mofa.gov.sa; Chargé d'affaires a.i. FAHD NASSER AL BIHAIRAN.

South Africa: Memoz SUD, Lotissement Ecole de Police, BP 21010, Dakar-Ponty; tel. 33-865-1959; fax 33-864-2359; e-mail ambafsud@sentoo.sn; internet www.saesenegal.info; Ambassador T. C. MAJOLA-EMBALO.

Spain: 18–20 ave Nelson Mandela, BP 2091, Dakar; tel. 33-821-1178; fax 33-821-6845; e-mail ambespsn@mail.mae.es; Ambassador FERNANDO MORÁN CALVO-SOTELO.

Sudan: 31 route de la Pyrotechnie, Mermoz, BP 15033, Dakar-Fann; tel. 33-824-9853; fax 33-824-9852; e-mail sudembse@sentoo.sn; Ambassador MAHMOUD HASSAN EL-AMIN.

Sweden: 18 rue Emile Zola, BP 6087, Dakar; tel. 33-849-0333; fax 33-849-0340; e-mail ambassaden.dakar@foreign.ministry.se; internet www.swedenabroad.com/dakar; Ambassador AGNETA BOHMAN.

Switzerland: rue René N'Diaye, angle rue Seydou, BP 1772, Dakar; tel. 33-823-0590; fax 33-822-3657; e-mail dak.vertretung@eda.admin.ch; internet www.eda.admin.ch/dakar; Ambassador LIVIO HÜRZELER.

Syria: rue 1, point E, angle blvd de l'Est, BP 498, Dakar; tel. 33-824-6277; fax 33-825-1755; Ambassador HAMZEH DAWALIBI.

Thailand: 10 rue Léon Gontran Damas, BP 3721, Dakar-Fann; tel. 33-869-3290; fax 33-824-8458; e-mail thaidkr@sentoo.sn; internet www.mfa.go.th/web/2366.php; Ambassador ITTI DITBANJONG.

Tunisia: rue Alpha Hachamiyou Tall, BP 3127, Dakar; tel. 33-823-4747; fax 33-823-7204; Ambassador JALEL LAKHDAR.

Turkey: ave des Ambassadeurs, Fann Résidence, BP 6060, Etoile, Dakar; tel. 33-869-2542; fax 33-825-6977; e-mail trambdkr@sentoo.sn; Ambassador ALI SAVUT.

United Kingdom: 20 rue du Dr Guillet, BP 6025, Dakar; tel. 33-823-7392; fax 33-823-2766; e-mail britembe@orange.sn; internet www.britishembassy.gov.uk/senegal; Ambassador CHRIS TROTT.

SENEGAL   *Directory*

USA: ave Jean XXIII, angle rue Kleber, BP 49, Dakar; tel. 33-823-4296; fax 33-823-5163; e-mail usadakar@state.gov; internet dakar.usembassy.gov; Ambassador JANICE L. JACOBS.

Judicial System

In 1992 the Supreme Court was replaced by three judicial bodies. The Constitutional Council verifies that legislation and international agreements are in accordance with the Constitution. It decides disputes between the Executive and the Legislature, and determines the relative jurisdictions of the Council of State and the Court of Cassation. The Council of State judges complaints brought against the Executive. It also resolves electoral disputes. The Court of Cassation is the highest court of appeal, and regulates the activities of subordinate courts and tribunals. The Revenue Court supervises the public accounts.

Constitutional Council: BP 45732, Dakar; tel. 33-822-5252; fax 33-822-8187; e-mail magou_51@hotmail.com; internet www.gouv.sn/institutions/conseil_const.html; 5 mems; Pres. MIREILLE NDIAYE.

Council of State: rue Béranger Ferraut, Dakar; tel. 33-822-4786; internet www.gouv.sn/institutions/conseil_etat.html; Pres. ABDOU AZIZ BA.

Court of Cassation: blvd Martin Luther King, BP 15184, Dakar-Fann; tel. 33-889-1010; fax 33-821-1890; e-mail pasakho@yahoo.fr; internet www.gouv.sn/institutions/cour_cassation.html; First Pres. PAPA OUMAR SAKHO; Procurator-Gen. ABDOULAYE CRAYE; Sec.-Gen. MAMADOU BADIO CAMARA.

Revenue Court (Cour des Comptes): 15 ave Franklin Roosevelt, BP 9097, Peytavin, Dakar; tel. 33-849-4001; fax 33-849-4362; e-mail askonte@courdescomptes.sn; internet www.courdescomptes.sn; Pres. ABDOU BAME GUEYE; Sec.-Gen. El Hadji MALICK KONTE; Pres. of Chambers ABBA GOUDIABY, MOUSTAPHA GUEYE, MAMADOU HADY SARR; Chief Administrator ABDOURAHMANE DIOUKNANE.

High Court of Justice: Dakar; competent to try the Prime Minister and other members of the Government for crimes committed in the exercise of their duties; The President of the Republic may only be brought to trial in the case of high treason; mems elected by the Assemblée nationale.

Religion

At the time of the 1988 census almost 94% of the population were Muslims, while some 4% professed Christianity (the dominant faith being Roman Catholicism); a small number, mostly in the south, followed traditional beliefs.

ISLAM

There are four main Islamic brotherhoods active in Senegal: the Tidjanes, the Mourides, the Layennes and the Qadiriyas.

Association pour la coopération islamique (ACIS): Dakar; f. 1988; Pres. Dr THIERNAO KÂ.

Grande Mosquée de Dakar: Dakar; tel. 33-822-5648; Grand Imam El Hadj BAYE DAME DIÈNE.

CHRISTIANITY

The Roman Catholic Church

Senegal comprises one archdiocese and six dioceses. At 31 December 2005 there were an estimated 558,479 adherents of the Roman Catholic Church, representing about 5.3% of the total population.

Bishops' Conference

Conférence des Evêques du Sénégal, de la Mauritanie, du Cap-Vert et de Guinée-Bissau, BP 941, Dakar; tel. 33-836-3309; fax 33-836-1617; e-mail archevchedr@sentoo.sn.

f. 1973; Pres. Most Rev. JEAN-NOËL DIOUF (Bishop of Tambacounda).

Archbishop of Dakar: Cardinal THÉODORE-ADRIEN SARR, Archevêché, ave Jean XXIII, BP 1908, Dakar; tel. 33-889-0600; fax 33-823-4875; e-mail archevechedr@sentoo.sn.

The Anglican Communion

The Anglican diocese of The Gambia, part of the Church of the Province of West Africa, includes Senegal and Cape Verde. The Bishop is resident in Banjul, The Gambia.

Protestant Church

Eglise Protestante du Sénégal: 65 rue Wagane Diouf, BP 22390, Dakar; tel. 33-821-5564; fax 33-821-7132; f. 1862; Pastor ETITI YOMO DJERIWO.

BAHÁ'Í FAITH

National Spiritual Assembly: Point E, rue des Ecrivains, 2è impasse à droite après la Direction de la statistique, BP 1662, Dakar; tel. 33-824-2359; e-mail bahai@sentoo.sn; internet www.sn.bahai.org; regd 1975; Sec. ABOUBAKRINE BA.

The Press

DAILY NEWSPAPERS

L'Actuel: route du Front de Terre, angle ave Bourguiba, Immeuble Dramé, BP 11874, Dakar; tel. 33-864-2601; fax 33-864-2602; e-mail lactuel@sentoo.sn.

Dakar Soir: Dakar; tel. and fax 33-832-1093; f. 2000.

Dekeu Bi: Quartier Casier, Thiès; tel. 77-557-2915.

L'Evénement du Soir: Fann Résidence, rue A, angle rue 4, point E, BP 16060, Dakar; tel. 33-864-3430; fax 33-864-3600; evenings.

Frasques Quotidiennes: 51 rue du Docteur Thèze, BP 879, Dakar; tel. 33-842-4226; fax 33-842-4277; e-mail frasques@arc.sm.

L'Info 7: Sicap rue 10, BP 11357, Dakar; tel. and fax 33-864-2658; e-mail comsept@sentoo.sn; f. 1999.

Le Matin: route de l'Aéroport Léopold Sédar Senghor, BP 6472, Dakar; tel. 33-825-7359; fax 33-825-7358; e-mail lematin@metissacana.sn; daily; independent; Dir MAME LESS CAMARA; Editor-in-Chief ALIOUNE FALL.

La Pointe: Dakar; tel. 33-820-5035; fax 33-820-5043.

Le Populaire: 114 ave Peytavin, Immeuble Serigne Massamba Mbacké, Dakar; tel. 33-822-7977; fax 33-822-7927; f. 2000; Editor-in-Chief MAMADOU THIERNO TALLA.

Scoop: route du Service Géographique, BP 92, Dakar; tel. 33-859-5959; fax 33-859-6050.

Le Soleil: Société sénégalaise de presse et de publications, route du Service géographique, Hann, BP 92, Dakar; tel. 33-859-5940; fax 33-859-6050; e-mail lesoleil@lesoleil.sn; internet www.lesoleil.sn; f. 1970; Dir-Gen. and Dir of Publication MAMADOU SEYE; Editors-in-Chief HABIB DEMBA FALL, IBRAHIMA MBODJ; circ. 25,000 (2005).

Sud Quotidien: Immeuble Fahd, BP 4130, Dakar; tel. 33-821-3338; fax 33-822-5290; e-mail info@sudonline.sn; internet www.sudonline.sn; independent; Dir ABDOULAYE NDIAGA SYLLA; circ. 30,000.

Tract: 13 rue de Thann, BP 3683, Dakar; tel. and fax 33-823-4725; e-mail tract.sn@laposte.net; f. 2000.

Le Volcan: Dakar; tel. 33-820-5035; fax 33-820-5043.

Wal Fadjri/L'Aurore (The Dawn): Sicap Sacré-Coeur no 8542, BP 576, Dakar; tel. 33-824-2343; fax 33-824-2346; e-mail walf@walf.sn; internet www.walf.sn; f. 1984; Exec. Dir MBAYE SIDY MBAYE; circ. 15,000.

PERIODICALS

Afrique Médicale: 10 rue Abdou Karim Bourgi, BP 1826, Dakar; tel. 33-823-4880; fax 33-822-5630; f. 1960; 11 a year; review of tropical medicine; Editor P. CORREA; circ. 7,000.

Afrique Nouvelle: 9 rue Paul Holle, BP 283, Dakar; tel. 33-822-5122; f. 1947; weekly; devt issues; Roman Catholic; Dir RENÉ ODOUN; circ. 15,000.

Afrique Tribune: Dakar; tel. and fax 33-821-1592; monthly.

Amina: BP 2120, Dakar; e-mail amina@calva.net; monthly; women's magazine.

Le Cafard Libéré: 10 rue Tolbiac, angle Autoroute, Soumédioune, BP 7292, Dakar; tel. 33-822-8443; fax 33-822-0891; f. 1987; weekly; satirical; Editor PAPE SAMBA KANE; circ. 12,000.

Construire l'Afrique: Dakar; tel. 33-823-0790; fax 33-824-1961; f. 1985; six a year; African business; Dir and Chief Editor CHEIKH OUSMANE DIALLO.

Le Courrier du Sud: BP 190, Ziguinchor; tel. 33-991-1166; weekly.

Démocratie: Liberté V, 5375 M, 71 rue du rond-point Liberté V et VI; tel. 33-824-8669; fax 33-825-1879.

Eco Hebdo: 22 x 19 rue Médina, BP 11451, Dakar; tel. and fax 33-837-1414; weekly.

L'Equipe Sénégal: Dakar; tel. 33-824-0013; e-mail lequipesenegal@yahoo.fr; weekly; sports.

Ethiopiques: BP 2035, Dakar; tel. and fax 33-821-5355; f. 1974; literary and philosophical review; publ. by Fondation Léopold Sédar Senghor.

Le Journal de l'Economie: 15 rue Jules Ferry, BP 2851, Dakar; tel. 33-823-8733; fax 33-823-6007; weekly.

Journal Officiel de la République du Sénégal: Rufisque; f. 1856; weekly; govt journal.

SENEGAL

Momsareew: BP 820, Dakar; f. 1958; monthly; publ. by PAI; Editor-in-Chief MALAMINE BADJI; circ. 2,000.
Nord Ouest: Immeuble Lonase, BP 459, Louga; tel. 76-680-7943; e-mail lenordouest@yahoo.fr; regional monthly; Dir of Publication PAPE MOMAR CISSÉ.
Nouvel Horizon: Dakar; tel. and fax 33-822-7414; weekly.
Nuit et Jour: Dakar; tel. 33-832-1570; weekly.
Le Politicien: Dakar; tel. and fax 33-827-6396; f. 1977; weekly; satirical.
Promotion: BP 1676, Dakar; tel. 33-825-6969; fax 33-825-6950; e-mail giepromo@telecomplus.sn; f. 1972; fortnightly; Dir BOUBACAR DIOP; circ. 5,000.
République: BP 21740, Dakar; tel. 33-822-7373; fax 33-822-5039; e-mail replike@yahoo.fr; f. 1994.
Sénégal d'Aujourd'hui: Dakar; monthly; publ. by Ministry of Culture; circ. 5,000.
Sopi (Change): 5 blvd Dial Diop, Dakar; tel. 33-824-4950; fax 33-824-4700; f. 1988; weekly; publ. by PDS; Dir of Publishing JOSEPH NDONG; Editor CHEIKH KOUREYSSI BA.
Le Témoin: Gibraltar II, Villa no 310, Dakar; tel. 33-822-3269; fax 33-821-7838; f. 1990; weekly; Editor-in-Chief MAMADOU OUMAR NDIAYE; circ. 5,000.
Unir Cinéma: 1 rue Neuville, BP 160, Saint Louis; tel. 33-861-1027; fax 33-861-2408; f. 1973; quarterly African cinema review; Editor PIERRE SAGNA.
Vive La République: Sicap Amitié III, Villa no 4057, Dakar; tel. 33-864-0631; weekly.
Xareli (Struggle): BP 12136, Dakar; tel. 33-822-5463; fortnightly; publ. by AJ—PADS; circ. 7,000.

NEWS AGENCIES

Agence Panafricaine d'Information—PANA-Presse SA: ave Bourjuiba, BP 4056, Dakar; tel. 33-824-1395; fax 33-824-1390; e-mail marketing@panapress.com; internet www.panapress.com; f. 1979 as Pan-African News Agency (under the auspices of the Organization of African Unity), restructured as 75% privately owned co in 1997; Co-ordinator-Gen. BABACAR FALL.
Agence de Presse Sénégalaise: 58 blvd de la République, BP 117, Dakar; tel. 33-823-1667; fax 33-822-0767; e-mail aps@aps.sn; internet www.aps.sn; f. 1959; govt-controlled; Dir AMADOU DIENG.

PRESS ORGANIZATION

Syndicat des Professionnels de l'Information et de la Communication du Sénégal (SYNPICS): BP 21722, Dakar; tel. 33-842-4256; fax 33-842-0269; e-mail synpics@yahoo.fr; Sec.-Gen. DIATA CISSÉ.

Publishers

Africa Editions: BP 1826, Dakar; tel. 33-823-4880; fax 33-822-5630; f. 1958; general, reference; Man. Dir JOËL DECUPPER.
Agence de Distribution de Presse: km 2.5, blvd du Centenaire de la Commune de Dakar, BP 374, Dakar; tel. 33-832-0278; fax 33-832-4915; e-mail adpresse@telecomplus.sn; f. 1943; general, reference; Man. Dir PHILIPPE SCHORP.
Centre Africain d'Animation et d'Echanges Culturels Editions Khoudia: BP 5332, Dakar-Fann; tel. 33-821-1023; fax 33-821-5109; f. 1989; fiction, education, anthropology; Dir AÏSSATOU DIA.
Editions Clairafrique: 2 rue El Hadji Mbaye Guèye, BP 2005, Dakar; tel. 33-822-2169; fax 33-821-8409; f. 1951; politics, law, sociology, anthropology, literature, economics, devt, religion, school books.
Editions des Ecoles Nouvelles Africaines: ave Cheikh Anta Diop, angle rue Pyrotechnie, Stèle Mermoz, BP 581, Dakar; tel. 33-864-0544; fax 33-864-1352; e-mail eenas@sentoo.sn; youth and adult education, in French.
Editions Juridiques Africaines (EDJA): 18 rue Raffenel, BP 22420, Dakar-Ponty; tel. 33 821-6689; fax 33 823-2753; e-mail edja.ed@orange.sn; internet www.edja.sn; f. 1986; law; Dir NDÉYE NGONÉ GUÈYE.
Editions des Trois Fleuves: blvd de l'Est, angle Cheikh Anta Diop, BP 123, Dakar; tel. 33-825-7923; fax 33-825-5937; f. 1972; general non-fiction; luxury edns; Dir GÉRARD RAZIMOWSKY; Gen. Man. BERTRAND DE BOISTEL.
Enda—Tiers Monde Editions (Environmental Development Action in the Third World): 54 rue Carnot, BP 3370, Dakar; tel. 33-822-9890; fax 33-823-5157; e-mail editions@enda.sn; internet www.enda.sn; f. 1972; third-world environment and devt; Dir RAPHAËL NDIAYE; Exec. Sec. JOSÉPHINE OUÉDRAOGO.

Directory

Grande imprimerie africaine (GIA): 9 rue Amadou Assane Ndoye, Dakar; tel. 33-822-1408; fax 33-822-3927; f. 1917; law, administration; Man. Dir CHEIKH ALIMA TOURÉ.
Institut fondamental d'Afrique noire (IFAN)—Cheikh Anta Diop: BP 206, Campus universitaire, Dakar; tel. 33-825-9890; fax 33-824-4918; internet www.afrique-ouest.auf.org; f. 1936; scientific and humanistic studies of Black Africa, for specialist and general public.
Nouvelles éditions africaines du Sénégal (NEAS): 10 rue Amadou Assane Ndoye, BP 260, Dakar; tel. 33-822-1580; fax 33-822-3604; e-mail neas@telecomplus.sn; f. 1972; literary fiction, schoolbooks; Dir-Gen. SAYDOU SOW.
Per Ankh: BP 2, Popenguine; history.
Société africaine d'édition: 16 bis rue de Thiong, BP 1877, Dakar; tel. 33-821-7977; f. 1961; African politics and economics; Man. Dir PIERRE BIARNES.
Société d'édition 'Afrique Nouvelle': 9 rue Paul Holle, BP 283, Dakar; tel. 33-822-3825; f. 1947; information, statistics and analyses of African affairs; Man. Dir ATHANASE NDONG.
Société nationale de Presse, d'édition et de publicité (SONAPRESS): Dakar; f. 1972; Pres. OBEYE DIOP.
Sud-Communication: BP 4100, Dakar; operated by a journalists' co-operative; periodicals.
Xamal, SA: BP 380, Saint-Louis; tel. 33-961-1722; fax 33-961-1519; general literature, social sciences, in national languages and in French; Dir ABOUBAKAR DIOP.

GOVERNMENT PUBLISHING HOUSE

Société sénégalaise de presse et de publications—Imprimerie nationale (SSPP): route du Service géographique, BP 92, Dakar; tel. 33-832-4692; fax 33-832-0381; f. 1970; 62% govt-owned; Dir SALIOU DIAGNE.

Broadcasting and Communications

TELECOMMUNICATIONS

Regulatory Authority

Agence de Régulation des Télécommunications et des Postes (ARTP): route de Ngor Angle Dioulikayes, BP 14130, Dakar-Peytavin; tel. 33-869-0369; fax 33-869-0370; e-mail contact@artp.sn; internet www.artp.sn; f. 2001; Pres. Prof. ABDOULAYE SAKHO; Dir-Gen. DANIEL G. GOUMALO SECK.

Service Providers

Excaf Telecom: Domaine Industriel SODIDA, rue 14 Prolongée, BP 1656, Dakar; tel. 33-824-2424; fax 33-824-2191; internet www.excaf.com.
Sentel Sénégal GSM: ave Nelson Mandela, angle ave Moussé Diop, BP 146, Dakar; tel. 76-675-4202; fax 33-823-1873; internet www.sentel.sn; mobile cellular telephone operator in Dakar, most western regions, and in selected localities nation-wide; 75% owned by Millicom International Cellular (Luxembourg), 25% by Senegalese private investors; Gen. Man. YOUVAL ROSH; 250,000 subscribers (2003).
Société Nationale des Télécommunications du Sénégal (SONATEL): 46 blvd de la République, BP 69, Dakar; tel. 33-839-1118; fax 33-823-6037; internet www.sonatel.sn; f. 1985; 42.3% owned by France Câbles et Radio (France Télécom, France), 27.67% owned by Govt; Pres. MICHEL HIRSCH; Man. Dir CHEIKH TIDIANE MBAYE; 1,673 employees (2003).
  Alizé: 46 blvd de la République, BP 2352, Dakar; tel. 33-839-1700; fax 33-839-1754; e-mail webmaster@alize.sn; internet www.alize.sn; f. 1996 as Sonatel Mobiles.
Télécom Plus SARL: 20 rue Amadou Assane Ndoye, BP 21100, Dakar; tel. 33-839-9700; fax 33-823-4632; telecommunications products and services.

BROADCASTING

Regulatory Authority

Haut Conseil de l'Audiovisuel: Immeuble Fahd, Dakar; tel. and fax 33-823-4784; f. 1991; Pres. AMINATA CISSÉ NIANG.

Radio

Société nationale de la Radiodiffusion-Télévision Sénégalaise (RTS): Triangle sud, angle ave Malick Sy, BP 1765, Dakar; tel. 33-849-1212; fax 33-822-3490; e-mail rts@rts.sn; internet www.rts.sn; f. 1992; state broadcasting co; broadcasts two national and eight regional stations; Dir-Gen. DAOUDA NDIAYE.

SENEGAL   *Directory*

Radio Sénégal Internationale: Triangle sud, angle ave El Hadj Malick Sy, BP 1765, Dakar; tel. 33-849-1212; fax 33-822-3490; f. 2001; broadcasts news and information programmes in French, English, Arabic, Portuguese, Spanish, Italian, Soninké, Pulaar and Wolof from 14 transmitters across Senegal and on cable; Dir CHÉRIF THIAM.

RST1: Triangle sud, angle ave El Hadj Malick Sy, BP 1765, Dakar; tel. 33-849-1212; fax 33-822-3490; f. 1992; broadcasts in French, Arabic and six vernacular languages from 16 transmitters across Senegal; Dir MANSOUR SOW.

JDP FM (Jeunesse, Développement, Paix): BP 17040, Dakar; tel. 33-827-2097; fax 33-824-0741; e-mail sarrabdou@sentoo.sn.

Radio Nostalgie Dakar: BP 21021, Dakar; tel. 33-821-2121; fax 33-822-2222; e-mail nostafric@globeaccess.net; f. 1995; music; broadcasts in French and Wolof; Gen. Man. SAUL SAVIOTE.

Oxy-Jeunes: Fojes BP 18303, Pikine, Dakar; tel. 33-834-4919; fax 33-827-3215; e-mail cheikh_seck@eudoramail.com; f. 1999; youth and community radio station supported by the World Asscn of Community Radio Stations and the Catholic Organization for Development and Peace.

Radio PENC-MI: BP 51, Khombole; tel. 33-957-9103; fax 33-824-5898; e-mail rdoucoure@oxfam.org.uk.

Radio Rurale FM Awagna de Bignona: BP 72, Bignona; tel. 33-994-1021; fax 33-994-1909; e-mail mksonko2000@yahoo.fr.

Sud FM: Immeuble Fahd, 5e étage, BP 4130, Dakar; tel. 33-822-5393; fax 33-822-5290; e-mail info@sudonline.sn; f. 1994; operated by Sud-Communication; regional stations in Saint-Louis, Kaolack, Louga, Thiès, Ziguinchor and Diourbel; Man. Dir CHERIF EL-WAHIB SEYE.

Wal Fadjri FM: Sicap Sacré-Coeur no 8542, BP 576, Dakar; tel. 33-824-2343; fax 33-824-2346; f. 1997; Islamic broadcaster; Exec. Dir MBAYE SIDY MBAYE.

Broadcasts by the Gabonese-based Africa No. 1, the British Broadcasting Corporation and Radio France Internationale are received in Dakar.

Television

Radiodiffusion-Télévision Sénégalaise (RTS): see Radio; Dir of Television DAOUDA NDIAYE.

Canal Horizons Sénégal: 31 ave Albert Sarrault, BP 1390, Dakar; tel. 33-889-5050; fax 33-823-3030; e-mail infos@canalhorizons.sn; internet www.canalhorizons.com; f. 1990; private encrypted channel; 18.8% owned by RTS and Société Nationale des Télécommunications du Sénégal, 15% by Canal Horizons (France); Man. Dir JACQUES BARBIER DE CROZES.

Réseau MMDS-EXCAF Télécom: rue 14 prolongée, HLM 1, Domaine Industriel SODIDA, BP 1656, Dakar; tel. 33-824-2424; fax 33-824-2191; broadcasts selection of African, US, European and Saudi Arabian channels.

The French television stations, France-2, TV5 and Arte France, are also broadcast to Senegal.

Finance

(cap. = capital; res = reserves; dep. = deposits; m. = million; br(s). = branch(es); amounts in francs CFA)

BANKING

Central Bank

Banque centrale des états de l'Afrique de l'ouest (BCEAO): blvd du Général de Gaulle, angle Triangle Sud, BP 3159, Dakar; tel. 33-823-5384; fax 33-823-5757; e-mail akangni@bceao.int; internet www.bceao.int; f. 1962; bank of issue for mem. states of the Union économique et monétaire ouest africaine (UEMOA, comprising Benin, Burkina Faso, Côte d'Ivoire, Guinea-Bissau, Mali, Niger, Senegal and Togo); cap. 134,120m., res 949,521m., dep. 1,226,294m. (Dec. 2004); Gov. DAMO JUSTIN BARO (acting); Dir in Senegal SEYNI NDIAYE; brs at Kaolack and Ziguinchor.

Commercial Banks

Attijariwafa Bank Sénégal: 5 rue Victor Hugo, angle ave Léopold Sédar Senghor, Dakar; f. 2004; 100% owned by Attijariwafa Bank Maroc (Morocco); Pres. and Dir-Gen. SAÏD RAKI.

Bank of Africa—Sénégal: Résidence Excellence, 4 ave Léopold Sédar Senghor, BP 1992, Dakar; tel. 33-849-6240; fax 33-842-1667; e-mail information@boasenegal.com; internet www.bkofafrica.net/senegal.htm; f. 2001; 59.32% owned by African Financial Holding, 15.00% by Bank of Africa—Benin; cap. and res 1,661.2m., total assets 20,588.0m. (Dec. 2003); Pres. MAMADOU AMADOU AW; Dir-Gen. BERNARD PUECHALDOU; 1 br.

Banque Internationale pour le Commerce et l'Industrie du Sénégal (BICIS): 2 ave Léopold Sédar Senghor, BP 392, Dakar; tel. 33-839-0390; fax 33-823-3707; internet www.bicis.sn; f. 1962; 54.09% owned by Groupe BNP Paribas (France); cap. and res 15,638m., total assets 227,702m. (Dec. 2003); Pres. LANDING SANÉ; Dir-Gen. AMADOU KANE; 17 brs.

Citibank Dakar: Immeuble SDIH, 4e étage, 2 pl. de l'Indépendance, BP 3391, Dakar; tel. 33-849-1111; fax 33-823-8817; e-mail thioro.ba@citicorp.com; f. 1975; wholly owned subsidiary of Citibank NA (USA); cap. 1,626m., total assets 84,864m. (Dec. 2001); Pres. JOHN REED; Dir-Gen. MICHAEL GROSSMAN; 1 br.

Compagnie Bancaire de l'Afrique Occidentale (CBAO): 1 pl. de l'Indépendance, BP 129, Dakar; tel. 33-839-9696; fax 33-823-2005; e-mail cbao@cboa.sn; f. 1853; 76% owned by Groupe Mimran; cap. 9,000m., res 13,509m., dep. 307,312m. (Dec. 2005); Pres. JEAN CLAUDE MIMRAN; Dir-Gen. PATRICK MESTRALLET; 24 brs.

Compagnie Ouest Africaine de Crédit Bail (LOCAFRIQUE): Immeuble Coumaba Castel, 11 rue Galandou Diouf, BP 292, Dakar; tel. 33-822-0647; fax 33-822-0894; e-mail locafrique@are.sn; f. 1977; cap. 579m., total assets 1,241m. (Dec. 2003); Dir-Gen. IBRAHIMA SOUR.

Crédit Lyonnais Sénégal (CLS): blvd El Hadji Djily Mbaye, angle rue Huart, BP 56, Dakar; tel. 33-849-0000; fax 33-823-4430; e-mail cl_senegal@creditlyonnais.fr; internet www.creditlyonnais.sn; f. 1989; 95% owned by Calyon Global Banking (France); 5% state-owned; cap. 2,000m., res 8,018m., dep. 100,817m. (Dec. 2004); Pres. and Chair. BAUDOUIN MERLET; Dir-Gen. JEAN PAUL VERU; 1 br.

Crédit National du Sénégal (CNS): 7 ave Léopold Sédar Senghor, BP 319, Dakar; tel. 33-839-3486; fax 33-823-7292; f. 1990 by merger; 87% state-owned; cap. 1,900m., total assets 2,032m. (Dec. 1996); Pres. ABDOU NDIAYE.

Ecobank Sénégal: 8 ave Léopold Sédar Senghor, BP 9095, Dakar; tel. 33-849-2000; fax 33-823-4707; internet www.ecobank.com; 41.45% owned by Ecobank Transnational Inc (Togo, operating under the auspices of the Economic Community of West African States), 17.0% by Ecobank Bénin, 12.43% by Ecobank Côte d'Ivoire, 4.56% by Ecobank Niger, 4.56% by Ecobank Togo; cap. and res 3,181m., total assets 48,591m. (Dec. 2003); Pres. MAHENTA BIRIMA FALL; Dir-Gen. EVELYNE TALL.

Société Générale de Banques au Sénégal (SGBS): 19 ave Léopold Sédar Senghor, BP 323, Dakar; tel. 33-839-5500; fax 33-823-9036; e-mail sgbs@sentoo.sn; internet www.sgbs.sn; f. 1962; 57.72% owned by Société Générale (France), 35.23% owned by private Senegalese investors; cap. 4,528m., res 22,026m., dep. 325,030m. (Dec. 2004); Pres. PAPA-DEMBA DIALLO; Dir-Gen. SANDY GILLIOT; 30 brs and sub-brs.

Development Banks

Banque de l'Habitat du Sénégal (BHS): 69 blvd du Général de Gaulle, BP 229, Dakar; tel. 33-839-3333; fax 33-823-8043; e-mail bdld10@calva.com; internet www.bhs.sn; f. 1979; cap. and res 19,661.0m., total assets 132,554.6m. (Dec. 2003); Pres. AHMED YÉRO DIALLO; Dir-Gen. SOULEYMANE LY; 2 brs.

Banque Sénégalo-Tunisienne (BST): Immeuble Kebe, 97 ave André Peytavin, BP 4111, Dakar; tel. 33-849-6060; fax 33-823-8238; e-mail bst@bst.sn; internet www.banquesenegalotunisienne.com; f. 1986; 56.6% owned by Compagnie Africaine pour l'Investissement; cap. 4,200m., res 2,206m., dep. 81,587m. (Dec. 2004); Pres. and Chair. MAMADOU TOURÉ; Dir-Gen. ABDOUL MBAYE; 7 brs.

Caisse Nationale de Crédit Agricole du Sénégal (CNCAS): pl. de l'Indépendance, Immeuble ex-Air Afrique, 31–33 rue El Hadji Asmadou Assane Ndoye, angle ave Colbert, Dakar; tel. 33-839-3636; fax 33-821-2606; e-mail cncas@cncas.sn; internet www.cncas.sn; f. 1984; 23.8% state-owned; cap. 2,300m., res 3,952m., dep. 59,196m. (Dec. 2003); Pres. ABDOULAYE DIACK; Dir-Gen. ARFANG BOUBACAR DAFFE; 13 brs.

Société Financière d'Equipement (SFE): 2e étage, Immeuble Sokhna Anta, rue Dr Thèze, BP 252, Dakar; tel. 33-823-6626; fax 33-823-4337; 59% owned by Compagnie Bancaire de l'Afrique Occidentale; cap. and res 388m., total assets 6,653m. (Dec. 1999); Pres. ARISTIDE ORSET ALCANTARA; Dir-Gen. MOHAMED A. WILSON.

Islamic Bank

Banque Islamique du Sénégal (BIS): Immeuble Abdallah Fayçal, rue Huart, angle rue Amadou Ndoye, BP 3381, 18524 Dakar; tel. 33-849-6262; fax 33-822-4948; e-mail contact@bis-bank.com; internet www.bis-bank.com; f. 1983; 44.5% owned by Dar al-Maal al-Islami (Switzerland), 33.3% by Islamic Development Bank (Saudi Arabia), 22.2% state-owned; cap. 2,706m., res 4,120m., dep. 38,845m. (Dec. 2006); Pres. of Bd of Administration BADER EDDINE NOUIOUA; Dir-Gen. AZHAR S. KHAN; 4 brs.

SENEGAL

Banking Association

Association Professionnelle des Banques et des Etablissements Financiers du Sénégal (APBEF): 5 pl. de l'Indépendance, BP 6403, Dakar; tel. 33-823-6093; fax 33-823-8596; e-mail apbef@sentoo.sn; Pres. EVELYNE TALL (Dir-Gen. of Ecobank Sénégal).

STOCK EXCHANGE

Bourse Régionale des Valeurs Mobilières (BRVM): BP 22500, Dakar; tel. 33-821-1518; fax 33-821-1506; e-mail osane@brvm.org; internet www.brvm.org; f. 1998; national branch of BRVM (regional stock exchange based in Abidjan, Côte d'Ivoire, serving the member states of UEMOA); Man. OUSMANE SANE.

INSURANCE

AGF Sénégal Assurances: rue de Thann, angle ave Abdoulaye Fadiga, Dakar; tel. 33-849-4400; fax 33-823-1078; Dir-Gen. BERNARD GIRARDIN.

Les Assurances Conseils Dakarois A. Gueye et cie: 20 rue Mohamed V, BP 2345, Dakar; tel. 33-822-6997; fax 33-822-8680.

Assurances Générales Sénégalaises (AGS): 43 ave Albert Sarraut, BP 225, Dakar; tel. 33-839-3600; fax 33-823-3701; e-mail ags@metissacana.sn; f. 1977; cap. 2,990m.; Dir-Gen. IBRAHIM GUEYE.

AXA Assurances Sénégal: 5 pl. de l'Indépendance, BP 182, Dakar; tel. 33-849-1010; fax 33-823-4672; e-mail info@axa.sn; f. 1977; fmrly Csar Assurances; 51.5% owned by AXA (France); cap. 1,058m. (Mar. 2004); Pres. MOUSTAPHA CISSÉ; Dir-Gen. ALIOUNE NDOUR DIOUF.

V. Capillon Assurances: BP 425, Dakar; tel. 33-821-1377; fax 33-822-2435; f. 1951; cap. 10m.; Pres. and Man. Dir GILLES DE MONTALEMBERT.

Compagnie d'Assurances-Vie et de Capitalisation (La Nationale d'Assurances-Vie): 7 blvd de la République, BP 3853, Dakar; tel. 33-822-1181; fax 33-821-2820; f. 1982; cap. 80m.; Pres. MOUSSA DIOUF; Man. Dir BASSIROU DIOP.

Compagnie Sénégalaise d'Assurances et de Réassurances (CSAR): 5 pl. de l'Indépendance, BP 182, Dakar; tel. 33-823-2776; fax 33-823-4672; f. 1972; cap. 945m.; 49.8% state-owned; Pres. MOUSTAPHA CISSÉ; Man. Dir MAMADOU ABBAS BA.

Gras Savoye Sénégal: 15 blvd de la République, BP 9, Dakar; tel. 33-823-0100; fax 33-821-5462; e-mail olivier.destriau@grassavoye.sn; affiliated to Gras Savoye (France); Man. OLIVIER DESTRIAU.

Intercontinental Life Insurance Co (ILICO): BP 1359, Dakar; tel. 33-821-7520; fax 33-822-0449; f. 1993; life insurance; fmrly American Life Insurance Co; Pres. and Dir-Gen. MAGATTE DIOP.

Mutuelles Sénégalaises d'Assurance et de Transport (MSAT): Dakar; tel. 33-822-2938; fax 33-823-4247; f. 1981; all branches; Dir MOR ATJ.

La Nationale d'Assurances: 5 ave Albert Sarrault, BP 3328, Dakar; tel. 33-822-1027; fax 33-821-2820; f. 1976; fire, marine, travel and accident insurance; privately owned; Pres. AMSATA DIOUF; also La Nationale d'Assurances—Vie; life insurance.

La Sécurité Sénégalaise (ASS): BP 2623, Dakar; tel. 33-849-0599; e-mail ass.dk@sentoo.sn; f. 1984; cap. 500m. (2002); Pres. MOUSSA SOW; Man. Dir MBACKE SENE.

Société Africaine d'Assurances: Dakar; tel. 33-823-6475; fax 33-823-4472; f. 1945; cap. 9m.; Dir CLAUDE GERMAIN.

Société Nationale d'Assurances Mutuelles (SONAM): 6 ave Léopold Sédar Senghor, BP 210, Dakar; tel. 33-823-1003; fax 33-820-7025; f. 1973; cap. 1,464m.; Pres. ABDOULAYE FOFANA; Man. Dir DIOULDÉ NIANE.

Société Nouvelle d'Assurances du Sénégal (SNAS): rue de Thann, BP 2610, Dakar; tel. 33-823-4176; fax 33-823-1078; e-mail snas@telecomplus.sn; Dir-Gen. FRANÇOIS BURGUIERRE.

Société Sénégalaise de Courtage et d'Assurances (SOSECODA): 16 ave Léopold Sédar Senghor, BP 9, Dakar; tel. 33-823-5481; fax 33-821-5462; f. 1963; cap. 10m.; 55% owned by SONAM; Man. Dir A. AZIZ NDAW.

Société Sénégalaise de Réassurances SA (SENRE): 6 ave Léopold Sédar Senghor, angle Carnot, BP 386, Dakar; tel. 33-822-8089; fax 33-821-5652; cap. 600m.

Insurance Association

Syndicat Professionel des Agents Généraux d'Assurances du Sénégal: 43 ave Albert Sarraut, BP 1766, Dakar; Pres. URBAIN ALEXANDRE DIAGNE; Sec. JEAN-PIERRE CAIRO.

Trade and Industry

GOVERNMENT AGENCIES

Agence de Développement et d'Encadrement des Petites et Moyennes Entreprises (ADEPME): BP 333, Dakar-Fann; tel. 33-860-1363; e-mail adepme@sentoo.sn; f. 2001; assists in the formation and operation of small and medium-sized enterprises; Dir MARIE THÉRÈSE DIEDHIOU.

Agence nationale pour la promotion des investissements et des grands travaux (APIX): 52–54 rue Mohamed V, BP 430, 18524 Dakar; tel. 33-849-0555; fax 33-823-9489; e-mail contact@apix.sn; internet www.investinsenegal.com; f. 2000; promotes investment and major projects; Dir-Gen. AMINATA NIANE.

Agence Sénégalaise de Promotion des Exportations (ASEPEX): Dakar; f. 2005; promotes exports; Dir-Gen. MAIMOUNA SAVANÉ.

Société de Développement Agricole et Industriel (SODAGRI): BP 222, Dakar; tel. 33-821-0426; fax 33-822-5406; cap. 120m. francs CFA; agricultural and industrial projects; Pres. and Dir-Gen. AMADOU TIDIANE WANE.

Société de Gestion des Abattoirs du Sénégal (SOGAS): BP 14, Dakar; tel. 33-854-0740; fax 33-834-2365; e-mail sogas@sentoo.sn; f. 1962; cap. 619.2m. francs CFA; 28% state-owned; livestock farming; Dir-Gen. SOW SADIO.

Société Nationale d'Aménagement et d'Exploitation des Terres du Delta du Fleuve Sénégal et des Vallées du Fleuve Sénégal et de la Falémé (SAED): 200 ave Insa Coulibaly-Sor, BP 74, Saint-Louis; tel. 33-961-1563; fax 33-961-1463; e-mail saed@refer.sn; internet www.saed.sn; f. 1965; cap. 2,500m. francs CFA; 100% state-owned; controls the agricultural devt of more than 40,000 ha around the Senegal river delta; Dir-Gen. MAMOUDOU DEME.

Société Nationale d'Etudes et de Promotion Industrielle (SONEPI): Dakar; tel. 33-825-2130; fax 33-824-65465; f. 1969; cap. 150m. francs CFA; 28% state-owned; promotion of small and medium-sized enterprises; Chair. and Man. Dir HADY MAMADOU LY.

Société Nouvelle des Etudes de Développement en Afrique (SONED—AFRIQUE): 22 rue Moussé Diop, BP 2084, Dakar; tel. 33-823-9457; fax 33-823-4231; e-mail sonedaf@telecomplus.sn; f. 1974; cap. 150m. francs CFA; Pres. ABDOU WAHAB TALLA; Man. Dir El Hadj AMADOU WONE.

DEVELOPMENT ORGANIZATIONS

Agence Française de Développement (AFD): 15 ave Mandela, BP 475, Dakar; tel. 33-849-1999; fax 33-823-4010; e-mail afddakar@groupe-afd.org; Country Dir JEAN-MARC GRAVELLINI.

Association Française des Volontaires du Progrès (AFVP): BP 1010, route de la VDN, Sacré coeur 3, Villa no 9364, Dakar; tel. 33-827-4075; fax 33-827-4074; e-mail afvp@telecomplus.sn; internet www.afvp.org; f. 1972; Regional Delegate for Senegal, Cape Verde, Guinea, Guinea-Bissau, Mali and Mauritania JEAN-LOUP CAPDEVILLE; Nat. Delegate KARIM DOUMBIA.

Centre International du Commerce Extérieur du Sénégal: route de l'Aéroport, BP 8166, Dakar-Yoff, Dakar; tel. 33-827-5466; fax 33-827-5275; e-mail cices@metissacana.sn; Sec.-Gen. AMADOU SY.

Service de Coopération et d'Action Culturelle: BP 2014, Dakar; tel. 33-839-5305; administers bilateral aid from France; fmrly Mission Française de Coopération et d'Action Culturelle; Dir XAVIN ROZE.

CHAMBERS OF COMMERCE

Union Nationale des Chambres de Commerce, d'Industrie et d'Agriculture du Sénégal: 1 pl. de l'Indépendance, BP 118, Dakar; tel. 33-823-7169; fax 33-823-9363; f. 1888; restructured 2002; Pres. MAMADOU LAMINE NIANG.

Chambre de Commerce, d'Industrie et d'Agriculture de Dakar: 1 pl. de l'Indépendance, BP 118, Dakar; tel. 33-823-7189; fax 33-823-9363; e-mail cciad@sentoo.sn; internet www.cciad.sn; f. 1888; Pres. MAMADOU LAMINE NIANG; Sec.-Gen. ALY MBOUP (acting).

Chambre de Commerce, d'Industrie et d'Agriculture de Diourbel: BP 7, Diourbel; tel. 33-971-1203; fax 33-971-3849; e-mail ccdiour@cyg.sn; f. 1969; Pres. MOUSTAPHA CISSÉ LO; Sec.-Gen. MAMADOU NDIAYE.

Chambre de Commerce de Fatick: BP 66, Fatick; tel. and fax 33-949-1425; e-mail ccfatick@cosec.sn; Pres. BABOUCAR BOP; Sec.-Gen. SEYDOU NOUROU LY.

Chambre de Commerce et d'Industrie de Kaolack: BP 203, Kaolack; tel. 33-941-2052; fax 33-941-2291; e-mail cciak@netcourrier.com; internet www.cciak.fr.st; Pres. IDRISSA GUÈYE; Sec.-Gen. SALIMATA S. DIAKHATE.

Chambre de Commerce d'Industrie et d'Agriculture de Kolda: BP 23, Quartier Escale, Kolda; tel. 33-996-1230; fax 33-

996-1068; Pres. Amadou Mounirou Diallo; Sec.-Gen. Yaya Camara.

Chambre de Commerce, d'Industrie et d'Agriculture de Louga: 2 rue Glozel, BP 26, Louga; tel. 33-967-1114; fax 33-967-0825; e-mail ccial@orange.sn; Pres. Cheikh Macké Faye; Sec.-Gen. Doudou Niang.

Chambre de Commerce, d'Industrie et d'Agriculture de Matam: BP 95, Matam; tel. and fax 33-966-6591; Pres. Mamadou Ndiade; Sec.-Gen. Moussa Ndiaye.

Chambre de Commerce, d'Industrie et d'Agriculture de Saint-Louis: 10 rue Blanchot, BP 19, Saint-Louis; tel. 33-961-1088; fax 33-961-2980; f. 1879; Pres. El Hadj Abibou Dieye; Sec.-Gen. Moussa Ndiaye.

Chambre de Commerce, d'Industrie et d'Agriculture de Tambacounda: 120 blvd Diogoye, BP 127, Tambacounda; tel. 33-981-1014; fax 33-981-2995; Pres. Djiby Cissé; Sec.-Gen. Tenguella Ba.

Chambre de Commerce, d'Industrie et d'Agriculture de Thiès: 96 ave Lamine Guèye, BP 3020, Thiès; tel. 33-951-1002; fax 33-952-1397; e-mail ccthies@cosec.sn; f. 1883; 38 mems; Pres. Attou Ndiaye; Sec.-Gen. Abdoulkhadre Camara.

Chambre de Commerce, d'Industrie et d'Artisanat de Ziguinchor: rue du Gen. de Gaulle, BP 26, Ziguinchor; tel. 33-991-1310; fax 33-991-5238; f. 1908; Pres. Mamadou Diallo; Sec.-Gen. Alassane Ndiaye.

EMPLOYERS' ASSOCIATIONS

Chambre des Métiers de Dakar: route de la Corniche-Ouest, Soumbedioune, Dakar; tel. 33-821-7908; Sec.-Gen. Mbaye Gaye.

Confédération Nationale des Employeurs du Sénégal: Dakar; tel. 33-821-7662; fax 33-822-9658; e-mail cnes@sentoo.sn; Pres. Mansour Cama.

Conseil National du Patronat du Sénégal (CNP): 70 rue Jean Mermoz, BP 3537, Dakar; tel. 33-821-5803; fax 33-822-2842; e-mail cnp@sentoo.sn; Pres. Youssoupha Wade; Sec.-Gen. Mabousso Thiam.

Groupement Professionnel de l'Industrie du Pétrole du Sénégal (GPP): rue 6, km 4.5, blvd du Centenaire de la Commune de Dakar, BP 479, Dakar; tel. and fax 33-832-5212; e-mail noeljp@sentoo.sn; Sec.-Gen. Jean-Pierre Noël.

Organisation des Commerçants, Agriculteurs, Artisans et Industriels: Dakar; tel. 33-823-6794.

Rassemblement des Opérateurs Economiques du Sénégal (ROES): Dakar; tel. 33-825-5717; fax 33-825-5713.

Syndicat des Commerçants Importateurs, Prestataires de Services et Exportateurs de la République du Sénégal (SCIMPEX): 2 rue Parent, angle ave Abdoulaye Fadiga, BP 806, Dakar; tel. 33-821-3662; fax 33-842-9648; e-mail scimpex@orange.sn; f. 1943; Pres. Pape Alsassane Dieng.

Syndicat Patronal de l'Ouest Africain des Petites et Moyennes Entreprises et des Petites et Moyennes Industries: BP 3255, 41 blvd Djily M'Baye, Dakar; tel. 33-821-3510; fax 33-823-3732; e-mail moctarniang@yahoo.fr; f. 1937; Pres. Babacar Seye; Sec.-Gen. Moctar Niang.

Syndicat Professionnel des Entrepreneurs de Bâtiments et de Travaux Publics du Sénégal: ave Abdoulaye Fadiga, BP 593, Dakar; tel. 33-823-4373; f. 1930; 130 mems; Pres. Christian Virmaud.

Syndicat Professionnel des Industries du Sénégal (SPIDS): BP 593, Dakar; tel. 33-823-4324; fax 33-822-0884; e-mail spids@syfed.refer.sn; f. 1944; 110 mems; Pres. Christian Basse.

Union des Entreprises du Domaine Industriel de Dakar: BP 10288, Dakar-Liberté; tel. 33-825-0786; fax 33-825-0870; e-mail snisa@sentoo.sn; Pres. Aristide Tino Adediran.

Union Nationale des Chambres de Métiers: Domaine Industriel SODIDA, ave Bourguiba, BP 30040, Dakar; tel. 33-825-0588; fax 33-824-5432; f. 1981; Pres. El Hadj Seyni Seck; Sec.-Gen. Baboucar Diouf.

Union Nationale des Commerçants et Industriels du Sénégal (UNACOIS): BP 11542, 3 rue Valmy, Dakar; tel. 33-826-1519.

UTILITIES

Electricity

Société Nationale d'Electricité (SENELEC): 28 rue Vincent, BP 93, Dakar; tel. 33-839-3030; fax 33-823-1267; e-mail webmaster@senelec.sn; internet www.senelec.sn; f. 1983; 100% state-owned; Dir-Gen. Samuel Sarr.

Gas

Société Sénégalaise des Gaz: Dakar; tel. 33-832-8212; fax 33-823-5974.

Water

Société Nationale des Eaux du Sénégal (SONES): route de Front de Terre, BP 400, Dakar; tel. 33-839-7800; fax 33-832-2038; e-mail sones@sones.sn; internet www.sones.sn; f. 1995; water works and supply; state-owned; Pres. Abdoul Aly Kane; Dir-Gen. Amadou Ndiaye.

Sénégalaise des Eaux (SDE): BP 224, Dakar; tel. 33-839-3737; fax 33-839-3705; e-mail bdtt@sde.sn; f. 1996; subsidiary of Groupe Saur International (France); water distribution services; Pres. Abdoulaye Bouna Fall; Dir-Gen. Bernard Debenest.

TRADE UNIONS

Confédération Nationale des Travailleurs du Sénégal (CNTS): 7 ave du Président Laminé Gueye, BP 937, Dakar; tel. 33-821-0491; fax 33-821-7771; e-mail cnts@sentoo.sn; f. 1969; affiliated to PS; Sec.-Gen. Mody Guiro.

Confédération Nationale des Travailleurs du Sénégal—Forces de Changement (CNTS—FC): Dakar; f. 2002 following split from CNTS; Sec.-Gen Cheikh Diop; 31 affiliated asscns.

Confédération des Syndicats Autonomes (CSA): BP 10224, Dakar; tel. 33-835-0951; fax 33-893-5299; e-mail csasenegal@yahoo.com; organization of independent trade unions; Sec.-Gen. Mamadou Diouf.

Union Démocratique des Travailleurs du Sénégal (UDTS): BP 7124, Médina, Dakar; tel. 33-835-3897; fax 33-854-1070; 18 affiliated unions; Sec.-Gen. Alioune Sow.

Union Nationale des Syndicats Autonomes du Sénégal (UNSAS): BP 10841, HLM, Dakar; fax 33-824-8013; Sec.-Gen. Mademba Sock.

Transport

RAILWAYS

There are 922 km of main line including 70 km of double track. One line runs from Dakar north to Saint-Louis (262 km), and the main line runs to Bamako (Mali). All the locomotives are diesel-driven.

Société Nationale des Chemins de Fer du Sénégal (SNCS): BP 175A, Thiès; tel. 33-939-5300; fax 33-951-1393; f. 1905; state-owned; operates passenger and freight services on Dakar–Thiès and Djourbel–Kaoulack lines, following transfer of principal Dakar–Bamako (Mali) line to private management in 2003; suburban trains operate on Dakar–Thiès route as 'Le Petit Train Bleu', pending their proposed transfer to private management by 2006; Pres. Drame Alia Diene; Man. Dir Diouf Mbaye.

ROADS

In 2003 there were 13,576 km of roads, of which 4,216 km were main roads. Some 3,972 km of the network were paved. A 162.5 km road between Dialakoto and Kédougou, the construction of which (at a cost of some 23,000m. francs CFA) was largely financed by regional donor organizations, was inaugurated in March 1996. The road is to form part of an eventual transcontinental highway linking Cairo (Egypt) with the Atlantic coast, via N'Djamena (Chad), Bamako (Mali) and Dakar. In 1999 new highways were completed in the east of Senegal, linking Tambacounda, Kidira and Bakel.

Comité Executif des Transports Urbains de Dakar (CETUD): Résidence Fann, route du Front de Terre, Dakar; tel. 33-832-4742; fax 33-832-4744; e-mail cetud@telecomplus.sn; f. 1997; regulates the provision of urban transport in Dakar; Pres. Ousmane Thiam.

Dakar-Bus: Dakar; f. 1999; operates public transport services within the city of Dakar; owned by RATP (France), Transdev (France), Eurafric-Equipment (Senegal), Mboup Travel (Senegal) and Senegal Tours (Senegal).

INLAND WATERWAYS

Senegal has three navigable rivers: the Senegal, navigable for three months of the year as far as Kayes (Mali), for six months as far as Kaédi (Mauritania) and all year as far as Rosso and Podor, and the Saloun and the Casamance. Senegal is a member of the Organisation de mise en valeur du fleuve Gambie and of the Organisation pour la mise en valeur du fleuve Sénégal, both based in Dakar. These organizations aim to develop navigational facilities, irrigation and hydroelectric power in the basins of the Gambia and Senegal rivers, respectively.

SHIPPING

The port of Dakar is the second largest in West Africa, after Abidjan (Côte d'Ivoire), and the largest deep sea port in the region, serving Senegal, Mauritania, The Gambia and Mali. It handled more than 7m. metric tons of international freight in 1999. The port's facilities include 40 berths, 10 km of quays, and also 53,000 sq m of warehousing and 65,000 sq m of open stocking areas. There is also a container terminal with facilities for vessels with a draught of up to 11 m. In March 2005 the Governments of Mauritania, Morocco and Senegal agreed that a shipping line linking the three countries and to transport merchandise was to commence operations, following the completion of a tendering process.

Compagnie Sénégalaise de Navigation Maritime (COSENAM): Dakar; tel. 33-821-5766; fax 33-821-0895; f. 1979; 26.1% state-owned, 65.9% owned by private Senegalese interests, 8.0% by private French, German and Belgian interests; river and ocean freight transport; Pres. ABDOURAHIM AGNE; Man. Dir SIMON BOISSY.

Conseil Sénégalais des Chargeurs (COSEC): BP 1423, Dakar; tel. 33-849-0707; fax 33-823-1144; e-mail cosec@cyg.sn; Dir-Gen. AMADOU KANE DIALLO.

Dakarnave: Dakar; tel. 33-823-8216; fax 33-823-8399; e-mail commercial@dakarnave.sn; internet www.dakarnave.com; responsible for Senegalese shipyards; owned by Chantier Navals de Dakar, SA (Dakarnave), a subsidiary of Lisnave International, Portugal; Dir-Gen. JOSÉ ANTÓNIO FERREIRA MENDES.

Maersk Sénégal: route de Rufisque, BP 3836, Dakar; tel. 33-859-1111; fax 33-832-1331; e-mail senmkt@maersk.com; internet www.maersksealand.com/senegal; f. 1986.

SDV Sénégal: 47 ave Albert Sarrault, BP 233, Dakar; tel. 33-839-0000; fax 33-839-0069; e-mail sdv.shipping@sn.dti.bollore.com; f. 1936; 51.6% owned by Groupe Bolloré (France); shipping agents, warehousing; Pres. ANDRÉ GUILLABERT; Dir-Gen. BERNARD FRAUD.

Société pour le Développement de l'Infrastructure de Chantiers Maritimes du Port de Dakar (Dakar-Marine): Dakar; tel. 33-823-3688; fax 33-823-8399; f. 1981; privately controlled; operates facilities for the repair and maintenance of supertankers and other large vessels; Man. YORO KANTE.

Société Maritime de l'Atlantique (SOMAT): c/o Port Autonome de Dakar, BP 3195, Dakar; f. 2005; 51% owned by Compagnie Marocaine de Navigation, COMANAV (Morocco), 24.5% by Conseil Sénégalais des Chargeurs, COSEC, 24.5% by Société Nationale de Port Autonome de Dakar, PAD; operates foot passenger and freight ferry service between Dakar and Ziguinchor (Casamance).

Société Nationale de Port Autonome de Dakar (PAD): 21 blvd de la Libération, BP 3195, Dakar; tel. 33-823-4545; fax 33-823-3606; e-mail pad@sonatel.senet.net; internet www.portdakar.sn; f. 1865; state-owned port authority; Pres. and Dir-Gen. BARA SADY.

SOCOPAO-Sénégal: BP 233, Dakar; tel. 33-823-1001; fax 33-823-5614; f. 1926; warehousing, shipping agents, sea and air freight transport; Man. Dir GILLES CUCHE.

TransSene: 1 blvd de l'Arsenal, face à la gare ferroviaire, Dakar; tel. 33-821-8181; e-mail transsen@telecomplus.sn; internet www.transsene.sn.

Yenco Shipping: Fondation Fahd, blvd Djily Mbaye, Dakar; tel. 33-821-2726; fax 33-822-0781; e-mail yencoshi@sentoo.sn; f. 1988; Dir of Finance M. DIANKA; Dir of Shipping M. DIOKHANE.

CIVIL AVIATION

The international airport is Dakar-Léopold Sédar Senghor. There are other major airports at Saint-Louis, Ziguinchor and Tambacounda, in addition to about 15 smaller airfields. Facilities at Ziguinchor and Cap-Skirring were upgraded during the mid-1990s, with the aim of improving direct access to the Casamance region. In 1998 the Islamic Development Bank agreed to fund a new international airport at Tobor, Casamance. In 2000 work began to extend the runway at Saint-Louis in order to accommodate larger aircraft. The construction of a new international airport, at Ndiass, commenced in 2003.

Agence nationale de l'aviation civile du Sénégal (ANACS): BP 8184, Dakar; fax 33-820-0403; civil aviation authority; Dir-Gen. MATHIACO BESSANE.

Aeroservices: Dakar; f. 1996; charter flights; Sec.-Gen. El Hadj OMAR BA.

African West Air: Dakar; tel. 33-822-4538; fax 33-822-4610; f. 1993; services to western Europe and Brazil; Man. Dir J. P. PIEDADE.

Air Sénégal International (ASI): 45 ave Albert Serraut, Dakar; tel. 33-842-4100; e-mail resadkr@airsenegalinternational.sn; internet www.air-senegal-international.com; f. 2000; 51% owned by Royal Air Maroc, 43% state-owned; domestic, regional and international services; Dir-Gen. MOHAMED FATTAHI.

Tourism

Senegal's attractions for tourists include six national parks (one of which, Djoudj, is listed by UNESCO as a World Heritage Site) and its fine beaches. The island of Gorée, near Dakar, is of considerable historic interest as a former centre for the slave-trade. In 1993 the number of foreign tourist arrivals declined dramatically, largely as a result of the suspension of tourist activity in the Casamance region in that year. The sector recovered strongly from 1995 onwards, and in 2005 visitor arrivals of 386,564 were recorded; receipts from tourism in 2003 were US $201m.

Ministry of Tourism and Air Transport: rue Calmette, BP 4049, Dakar; tel. 33-821-1126; fax 33-822-9413; internet www.tourisme.gouv.sn.

SERBIA

Introductory Survey

Location, Climate, Language, Religion, Flag, Capital

The Republic of Serbia (formerly part of the State Union of Serbia and Montenegro, and prior to that the Federal Republic of Yugoslavia—FRY) is situated in the central Balkan Peninsula, in south-eastern Europe, and is landlocked. There are western borders (from south to north) with Montenegro, Bosnia and Herzegovina and Croatia, a border with Hungary to the north, with Romania and Bulgaria to the east, and with the former Yugoslav republic of Macedonia to the south. Kosovo (a former Serbian province, which made a declaration of independence in February 2008) also lies to the South. Serbia includes the province of Vojvodina. The climate is continental, with steady rainfall throughout the year. The average summer temperature in Belgrade is 22°C (71°F), the winter average being 0°C (32°F). The official language is Serbian, which is officially written in the Cyrillic script. Orthodox Christianity is predominant, the Serbian Orthodox Church being the largest denomination. Roman Catholicism is especially strong in Vojvodina. There is a small Jewish community. The national flag (proportions 1 by 2) has three equal horizontal stripes, of blue, white and red. Belgrade (Beograd) is the capital of Serbia.

Recent History

A movement for the union of the South Slav peoples, despite long-standing ethnic rivalries and cultural diversity, began in the early 19th century. However, it was not until the end of the First World War, and the collapse of the Austro-Hungarian empire (which ruled Croatia, Slovenia and Bosnia and Herzegovina), that the project for a Yugoslav ('south Slav') state could be realized. A pact between Serbia (which was under Ottoman Turkish rule until the 19th century) and the other South Slavs was signed in July 1917, declaring the intention to merge all the territories in a united state under the Serbian monarchy. Accordingly, when the First World War ended and Austria-Hungary was dissolved, the Kingdom of Serbs, Croats and Slovenes was proclaimed on 4 December 1918.

Prince Aleksandar, Regent of Serbia since 1914, accepted the regency of the new state, becoming King in August 1921. Following bitter disputes between Serbs and Croats, King Aleksandar assumed dictatorial powers in January 1929. He formally changed the country's name to Yugoslavia in October. Aleksandar's regime was Serb-dominated, and in October 1934 he was assassinated in France by Croat extremists. His brother, Prince Pavle, assumed power as Regent on behalf of King Petar II. Pavle's regime retained power with the support of the armed forces, despite internal unrest, particularly in Croatia. Among the anti-Government groups was the Communist Party of Yugoslavia (CPY), which had been officially banned in 1921, but continued to operate clandestinely. In 1937 the CPY appointed a new General Secretary, Josip Broz (Tito).

In March 1941 the increasingly pro-German regime of Prince Pavle was overthrown in a coup, and a Government that supported the Allied Powers was installed, with King Peter as Head of State. In April, however, German and Italian forces invaded, forcing the royal family and Government into exile. Resistance to the occupation forces was initially divided between two rival groups. The Yugoslav Army of the Fatherland (Cetniks) operated mainly in Serbia and represented the exiled Government, while the National Liberation Army (Partisans), led by the CPY, under Gen. (later Marshal) Tito, recruited supporters from Bosnia, Croatia, Montenegro and Slovenia. Rivalry between the two groups led to civil war, eventually won by the communist Partisans. On 29 November 1943 the Partisans proclaimed their own government in liberated areas. Attempts to reconcile the Tito regime with the exiled Government proved unsuccessful, and King Petar II was deposed in 1944.

After the war ended, elections were held, under communist supervision, for a Provisional Assembly. The Federative People's Republic of Yugoslavia was proclaimed on 29 November 1945, with Tito as Prime Minister. A Soviet-style Constitution, establishing a federation of six republics (Serbia, Montenegro, Croatia, Slovenia, Macedonia, and Bosnia and Herzegovina) and two autonomous provinces (Kosovo—with a substantial Albanian population, but also the location of the seat of the Serbian Orthodox Patriarchate, and Vojvodina—with a large Hungarian population, both within Serbia), was adopted in January 1946.

In 1948 Yugoslavia was expelled from the Soviet-dominated Cominform. The CPY was renamed the League of Communists of Yugoslavia (LCY) in November 1952, by which time it had established exclusive political control. A new Constitution was adopted in January 1953, with Tito becoming President of the Republic. Another Constitution, promulgated in April 1963, changed the country's name to the Socialist Federal Republic of Yugoslavia (SFRY). Links with the USSR were resumed in 1955, but Yugoslavia largely pursued a policy of non-alignment, the first conference of the Non-aligned Movement (see p. 424) being held in the Serbian and federal capital, Belgrade, in 1961.

In July 1971 President Tito introduced a system of collective leadership and regular rotation of personnel between posts, in an attempt to unify the various nationalities. A collective State Presidency, headed by Tito, was established. The two autonomous provinces within Serbia obtained substantially the same powers, with regard to representation at federal level, as the six republics, as a result of which three of the eight members of the rotating collective presidency represented Serbia and its provinces. A new Constitution, introduced in February 1974, granted Tito the presidency for an unlimited term of office, and in May he became Life President of the LCY. Tito died in 1980, and his responsibilities were transferred to the collective State Presidency and to the Presidium of the LCY.

Inter-ethnic tensions, largely suppressed during Tito's period in power, became increasingly evident in various regions of Yugoslavia. The most serious tensions were experienced in Kosovo, where a state of emergency was declared in 1981, following widespread demonstrations by ethnic Albanian nationalists, who supported the province being granted the status of a republic within the SFRY. Tensions were exacerbated in April 1987, when thousands of Serbs and Montenegrins protesting at Kosovo Polje (the site of a famous battle between Serbian forces and Osmanlı—Ottoman Turkish troops in 1389) against alleged harassment by the Albanian majority population clashed violently with the security forces. The perceived failure of the Serbian and federal leadership to curb Albanian nationalism led to the dismissal in September of the First Secretary of the League of Communists of Serbia (LCS—the Serbian branch of the LCY), Ivan Stambolić. His replacement, Slobodan Milošević, had denounced the Serbian leadership's policy on Kosovo (which was regarded as being too sympathetic to the demands of ethnic Albanians) and promised to reverse the emigration of Serbs from the area and halt the activities of Albanian nationalists.

During 1988 and 1989 ethnic unrest increased. Proposals to amend the Serbian Constitution to reduce the level of autonomy of the two provinces were supported by regular demonstrations by Serbs. Demonstrations against the local party leadership were organized by Milošević and his supporters in Vojvodina. In October 1988 protests by some 100,000 demonstrators in Novi Sad, the administrative centre of Vojvodina, forced the resignation of the Presidium of the League of Communists of Vojvodina, which had opposed some of the proposed constitutional amendments. Tension between the respective party leaderships of Kosovo and Serbia increased, and in November, following the resignation of several members of the Kosovo leadership, some 100,000 ethnic Albanians demonstrated in Prishtina (Prishtinë—Priština—the administrative capital of Kosovo) to demand their reinstatement. In Belgrade a further mass rally was staged by Serbs in protest at alleged discrimination against them by the ethnic Albanian population in Kosovo. Public demonstrations in Kosovo were banned in late November. In Montenegro continuing unrest resulted in the resignations of the members of the Montenegrin Presidency and of the republican party leadership in January 1989, and their replacement by leaders more sympathetic to Milošević. In May 1989 Milošević, who had become increasingly associated with the cause of Serbian nationalism, particularly with regard to Kosovo, was elected President of the State Presidency of Serbia.

Meanwhile, in May 1988 an emergency conference of the LCY took place. Radical economic and political reforms, including the separation of the powers of the LCY and the State, and greater democracy within the LCY, were proposed. In January 1989 Ante Marković, a member of the Croatian Presidency, was appointed to head a new federal Government. In September the Slovenian Assembly voted to adopt radical amendments to the Constitution of Slovenia, affirming its sovereignty and its right to secede from the SFRY. In early December Serbia imposed economic sanctions on Slovenia. In January 1990 the abolition of the LCY's constitutional monopoly of power and the introduction of a multi-party system were formally approved, but a proposal by Slovenia to award greater autonomy to the republican branches of the LCY was defeated. As a result, the Slovenian delegation left the Congress, which was then adjourned. The Congress resumed its work in May, but was not attended by delegations from Croatia, Slovenia or Macedonia, where the local communist parties had effectively seceded from the LCY.

Multi-party elections took place in Slovenia and Croatia in April and May 1990, respectively; in both cases opponents of Serbian nationalism and the regime of Milošević were elected to senior positions. In May, under the system of rotating leadership, Dr Borisav Jović of Serbia replaced Janez Drnovšek of Slovenia as President of the Federal Presidency. Jović promised to uphold Yugoslav territorial integrity and advocated the introduction of a stronger federal constitution. In Serbia a new Constitution, which entered into effect in September, included provisions removing the autonomous status of the provinces of Kosovo (officially renamed Kosovo and Metohija) and Vojvodina. The Kosovo Provincial Assembly and Government were dissolved by the Serbian authorities. In response, a group of 114 ethnic Albanian deputies to the Assembly attempted to declare Kosovo's independence from Serbia. Unrest continued, and in September a general strike was organized to protest against the mass dismissals of ethnic Albanian officials by the Serbian authorities. Criminal charges were brought against more than 100 members of the Provincial Assembly who attempted to re-establish the body, and several former ministers in the Government of Kosovo were charged with establishing an illegal separatist organization.

During November and December 1990 multi-party elections were held in four republics. In Bosnia and Herzegovina (in which republic no ethnic group represented a majority of the population) and in Macedonia nationalist parties were successful. In Montenegro the League of Communists (subsequently renamed the Democratic Party of Montenegrin Socialists—DPMS) was able to secure the Presidency and a majority of seats in the Skupština Republike Crne Gore (Assembly of the Republic of Montenegro). In Serbia, amid allegations of widespread irregularities, Milošević was re-elected President, overcoming a challenge by Vuk Drašković of the nationalist and anti-communist Serbian Renewal Movement (SRM). In the Narodna skupština Republike Srbije (National Assembly of the Republic of Serbia—as the republican legislature had been renamed) 194 of the 250 seats were won by the Socialist Party of Serbia (SPS—led by Milošević), which had been formed in July 1990 by the LCS and a smaller left-wing faction.

In October 1990 Croatia and Slovenia had proposed the transformation of the Yugoslav federation into a looser confederation, in which constituent republics would have the right to maintain armed forces and enter into diplomatic relations with other states. Serbia and Montenegro, however, advocated a centralized federal system, while Macedonia and Bosnia and Herzegovina supported the concept of a federation of sovereign states. Tension increased in December, when Croatia adopted a new Constitution, giving the republic the right to secede from Yugoslavia, while in Slovenia a majority voted in favour of secession at a referendum. In January 1991 Macedonia declared its sovereignty and right to secede from the SFRY.

In March 1991 mass demonstrations, led by Drašković's SRM, demanding the resignation of Milošević, were violently suppressed by the security forces. Jović resigned as President of the Federal Presidency, following his failure to secure approval from other members of the Presidency for emergency measures; his resignation was withdrawn following an appeal from the Narodna skupština Republike Srbije.

Meanwhile, in February 1991 Slovenia formally initiated its process of 'dissociation' from Yugoslavia, and Croatia asserted the primacy of its Constitution and laws over those of the federation. Later that month the self-proclaimed 'Serb Autonomous Region (SAR) of Krajina' (which subsequently formed part of a self-styled 'Republic of the Serb Krajina'—RSK) declared its separation from Croatia and the intention to unite with Serbia. In Croatia, in May the population voted in favour of independence at a referendum that was largely boycotted by the Serb minority, and armed clashes between Serbs and Croats ensued. Relations between Serbia and Croatia deteriorated further in that month, when Serbian representatives in the Federal Presidency refused to sanction the scheduled transfer of the Presidency to Stipe Mesić of Croatia. On 25 June Slovenia and Croatia declared independence. In response, federal troops (largely Serb-dominated) attacked a number of targets in Slovenia, including Ljubljana airport, resulting in 79 deaths, according to official figures. A cease-fire agreement, mediated by the European Community (EC—now European Union—EU, see p. 244), resulted in Serbia's acceptance of Mesić as President of the Federal Presidency. In early July agreement was reached on the immediate cessation of hostilities and on a three-month suspension in the implementation of dissociation by Croatia and Slovenia. The withdrawal of federal troops from Slovenia (which had a negligible Serb population) began almost immediately, but fighting intensified in Croatia, where federal troops increasingly identified openly with local Serb forces. By September Serb forces controlled almost one-third of Croatia's territory, and successive cease-fire agreements failed to end the conflict. In the same month, at a referendum in Macedonia, voters approved the establishment of an independent republic.

In late September 1991 the UN Security Council adopted Resolution 713, which imposed an armaments embargo on all governments within the territories that had formed part of the SFRY and urged that all hostilities end immediately. However, sporadic fighting continued in Croatia. In October Croatia and Slovenia formally ended their association with Yugoslavia, the moratoriums on independence (agreed in July) having expired. In the same month the Assembly of Bosnia and Herzegovina declared the republic's sovereignty, despite the objections of ethnic Serb deputies. The EC continued its negotiation efforts, and the UN also become directly involved. The Federal Prime Minister, Ante Marković, resigned, having been defeated in a vote of no confidence in the bicameral Savezna skupština (Federal Assembly, comprising the directly elected Veće gradana—Chamber of Citizens—and the indirectly elected Veće Republika—Chamber of Republics). In December, declaring that Yugoslavia had ceased to exist, Stipe Mesić resigned as President of the Federal Presidency. In January 1992 Slovenia and Croatia were recognized as independent states by the EC; numerous other countries followed. The deployment in Croatia of a UN contingent of 14,000 peace-keeping troops, the UN Protection Force UNPROFOR (agreed by the Federal Presidency in December 1991), commenced in February 1992.

Following the international recognition of the independence of Croatia and Slovenia, Serbia and Montenegro agreed to uphold the Yugoslav state. Macedonia's representative to the Federal Presidency had resigned in January, but EC recognition of Macedonian independence was delayed, owing to opposition from Greece (see the chapter on the former Yugoslav republic of Macedonia). In March Bosnia and Herzegovina declared its independence from the SFRY, the decision having been approved by the electorate in a referendum that had been largely boycotted by the large ethnic Serb population, some of whom had established several SARs during 1991. Later that month the 'Serb Republic (Republika Srpska) of Bosnia and Herzegovina' (renamed Republika Srpska in August 1992) was proclaimed, and a severe escalation in the Bosnian conflict ensued, as troops from Republika Srpska launched military action against Bosniaks and besieged several cities, including the capital of Bosnia and Herzegovina, Sarajevo.

In April 1992 the Savezna skupština adopted a new Constitution, formally establishing the Federal Republic of Yugoslavia (FRY), which comprised Serbia (including the provinces of Kosovo and Metohija and Vojvodina) and Montenegro, thereby effectively acknowledging the secession of the other four republics. (The Constitution was formally promulgated on 28 September.) In May elections to the Savezna skupština were held, the SPS enjoying considerable success as a result of an opposition boycott. In June Dobrica Ćosić became President of the FRY, and the collective Federal Presidency ceased to exist. In that month an alliance of opposition parties formed the Democratic Movement of Serbia (Depos), led by Drašković.

In May 1992 elections, declared to be illegal by the Serbian authorities, were held in Kosovo to establish a provincial

'Assembly', which described itself as the legislature of the self-proclaimed 'Republic of Kosovo'. In July Milan Panić was elected Federal Prime Minister by the Savezna skupština. At a conference on the former Yugoslavia, which took place in London, United Kingdom, in August 1992, Panić condemned the policy of 'ethnic cleansing', following the discovery of Serb-run concentration camps in Bosnia and Herzegovina, and reiterated the claim that there was no federal military involvement in the republic. In an attempt to force Milošević's removal from office, presidential and legislative elections were scheduled for December. In October Milošević retaliated by using Serbian police forces to seize control of the federal police headquarters in Belgrade, blockading the building for several weeks. In November Panić narrowly survived a second vote of no confidence in the Savezna skupština. The Federal Minister of Foreign Affairs resigned in September, in protest at Panić's policies; in November three more federal ministers resigned.

Presidential and parliamentary elections, at both federal and republican levels, took place on 20 December 1992. Ćosić was re-elected Federal President, with some 85% of the votes cast. Milošević was re-elected President of Serbia, receiving 57.5% of the votes cast, and the SPS secured 47 of the 138 seats in the Veće građana. Panić, who contested the Serbian presidency, winning some 35% of the votes, subsequently demanded that new elections be held, alleging widespread electoral malpractice on the part of the SPS. However, he was removed from the office of Federal Prime Minister on 29 December, after losing a third vote of no confidence. The SPS won 101 seats in the elections to the 250-member Narodna skupština Republike Srbije, while the extreme nationalist Serbian Radical Party (SRP) secured 73. In early February 1993 a new Federal Government, comprising the SPS and the DPMS, was established, with Radoje Kontić as Federal Prime Minister. In the same month the SPS formed a new Serbian Government, headed by Nikola Šainović. Depos, which had obtained 49 seats in the Narodna skupština, commenced a legislative boycott, claiming that the elections had been fraudulent.

On 1 June 1993 Ćosić (who was accused of conspiring with army generals to overthrow Milošević) was removed from office by a vote of no confidence in the Savezna skupština; the motion had been initiated by deputies of the SPS and the SRP, in what was widely regarded as an attempt by Milošević to consolidate his power. Ćosić's dismissal was followed by a large anti-Government demonstration in Belgrade. In late June the Savezna skupština appointed Zoran Lilić of the SPS, regarded as sympathetic to Milošević, as Federal President, and a reorganization of the Serbian Government in July followed. In August it was announced that the Supreme Defence Council was to assume responsibility for all military and defence duties, and that the republican defence ministries were to be abolished (a measure that was opposed by the Montenegrin Government).

By the second half of 1993 it appeared that the co-operation between Milošević and the SRP had ended; in October an attempt by the SRP to force a parliamentary vote expressing no confidence in the Šainović Government prompted Milošević to dissolve the Narodna skupština Republike Srbije. In response to SRP allegations that the Serbian leadership was betraying national interests by its involvement in attempts to end the conflict in Bosnia and Herzegovina, the party's leader, Dr Vojislav Šešelj, and his associates were accused of involvement in atrocities, and prominent members connected with its paramilitary wing were arrested.

In the elections to the Narodna skupština Republike Srbije, which took place on 19 December 1993, the SPS increased its representation to 123 deputies, winning 36.7% of the votes cast. Depos secured 45 seats, and the SRP took 39. In late February 1994 a new Serbian Government was formed, with the support of the six members of the New Democracy (ND) party, which had campaigned in the elections as a member of the Depos coalition. Mirko Marjanović, a pro-Milošević business executive, was appointed Prime Minister, replacing Šainović, who became a Deputy Prime Minister in the Federal Government. In September a new federal Government, in which Kontić retained the post of Prime Minister, was appointed. The results of the elections in Serbia and the defection of the ND to the Government permitted Milošević to distance himself further from his erstwhile allies in the nationalist opposition, notably the SRP, and to consolidate his political control in the FRY. Šešelj's personal position was further discredited when he was sentenced to a short term of imprisonment in September for assaulting the parliamentary Speaker.

In August 1995, in a military offensive, Croatian troops took control of the RSK, prompting a mass exodus of ethnic Serbs from the region. The Yugoslav leadership protested strongly against the Croatian action, demanding UN intervention and a withdrawal of Croatian troops from the area. However, President Milošević also blamed the leadership of the RSK, criticizing its reluctance to comply with international peace proposals. The Croatian offensive against the RSK resulted in the exodus of some 150,000 Serb refugees to Yugoslavia and Serb-controlled areas of Bosnia and Herzegovina. Many were settled in Vojvodina, prompting protests from ethnic Hungarians in that region.

In early November 1995 peace negotiations were convened in Dayton, Ohio, USA, with the aim of resolving the conflict in the former Yugoslavia. The conference, at which Milošević represented not only Yugoslavia, but also the Bosnian Serbs, resulted in an agreement on the future territorial and constitutional structure of Bosnia and Herzegovina, including the recognition of Republika Srpska as one of two constituent entities within Bosnia and Herzegovina. In response to Yugoslav acceptance of the plan, all UN sanctions against the FRY were suspended in late November. The SRP denounced the Dayton agreement, which was also criticized by the Democratic Party (DP), the Democratic Party of Serbia (DPS—founded in 1992 by former members of the DP) and the increasingly nationalist leadership of the Serbian Orthodox Church. However, the SRM supported the agreement. In late November Milošević dismissed several leading members of the SPS, who were known to be critical of the Dayton accord and supportive of militant factions within Republika Srpska. In June 1996 the Serbian Government was reorganized. All the new ministers appointed were members of the increasingly influential Yugoslav United Left (YUL), led by Milošević's wife, Mirjana Marković.

A number of new coalitions were formed in advance of elections held in late 1996, notably a grouping known as Together (Zajedno), which comprised the SRM, the DP, the DPS and the Civic Alliance of Serbia. The SPS established an alliance with the YUL and the ND, which became known as the United List. On 3 November municipal elections, and elections to the Veće građana and the Skupština Republike Crne Gore were held. At the elections to the Veće građana (which were boycotted by many Kosovo Albanians), the United List secured 64 seats, Together took 22, the DPMS 20 and the SRP 16; of the 138 elected deputies, 108 were from Serbia and 30 from Montenegro. Following a second round of voting in the Serbian municipal elections, provisional results indicated that Together had obtained control of 14 principal towns, including Belgrade. After the SPS challenged the results, however, most of the opposition victories were annulled by (SPS-dominated) municipal courts and electoral commissions, precipitating mass demonstrations.

In December 1996 opposition supporters continued to organize daily demonstrations (which had developed into general protests against the Milošević Government) in Belgrade and other towns. The Serbian Minister of Information resigned in protest at the Government's temporary closure of two independent radio stations, which had reported the demonstrations. Milošević denied government involvement in electoral malpractice and condemned the protests. In late December the demonstrations degenerated into violent clashes with members of the security forces in Belgrade; it was reported that two people had been killed and 58 injured. The Ministry of Internal Affairs subsequently ordered a ban on demonstrations, which the security forces attempted to enforce; nevertheless, anti-Government rallies continued. At the end of December a delegation from the Organization for Security and Co-operation in Europe (OSCE, see p. 354), which earlier that month had been invited by the Federal Minister of Foreign Affairs to visit Serbia, issued a report upholding the results of the municipal elections that had been invalidated. The international community consequently increased pressure on Milošević to comply with the OSCE ruling. In early February 1997 the violent suppression of anti-Government demonstrations attracted further international criticism. Shortly afterwards Milošević publicly instructed Marjanović to prepare emergency legislation providing for the official recognition of the results of the municipal elections, in accordance with the OSCE ruling. However, the leader of the DP, Zoran Đinđić, urged his supporters to continue protests until the election results were officially verified, further demanding that the electoral code and legislation governing the media be reformed and that members of the security forces involved in the violence earlier that month be charged. On 11 February the Narodna skupština Republike Srbije voted in favour of reinstating the annulled results (with deputies from the opposition and extreme nationalist parties boycotting the session); Together consequently obtained control of the municipal assemblies in Belgrade and 13 other towns. At the same time seven ministers were replaced in a reorganization of the Serbian Government. Later in February Đinđić was elected Mayor of Belgrade by Together members, who controlled 69 of the 110 seats in the city's municipal council.

In June 1997 it was announced that the SRM had withdrawn from the Together coalition. The SPS nominated Milošević as a candidate for the federal presidency and proposed constitutional amendments for the direct election of the President. Later that month a DPMS committee declared its support for Milošević's candidature (which was, however, strongly opposed by elements within the party, including Milo Đukanović, Prime Minister of Montenegro since 1991), but rejected the proposed amendments. On 25 June Lilić relinquished office; the Speaker of the Veće Republika, Srđan Božović, was to act as interim President, pending an election. In July supporters of Đukanović within the DPMS voted to remove Momir Bulatović, President of Montenegro since 1990 (who continued to demonstrate support for Milošević) from the party leadership. In mid-July Milošević was elected to the federal presidency by the Savezna skupština. Opposition deputies boycotted the vote in the Veće građana, which they subsequently declared to be invalid. On 23 July Milošević formally resigned from the office of President of Serbia and was inaugurated as Federal President.

In September 1997 students demonstrated in Belgrade in support of Đinđić, who, following the dissolution of Together, urged a boycott of the forthcoming Serbian presidential and legislative elections, on the grounds that they would be biased in favour of the incumbent administration. At the elections to the Narodna skupština Republike Srbije, held on 21 September, the United List coalition won 110 seats (failing to secure an outright majority); the SRP increased its representation to 82 seats and the SRM obtained 45 seats. In the concurrent presidential election, Lilić (the candidate of the United List) received 35.7% of the votes cast, while Šešelj, who contested the poll on behalf of the SRP, won 27.3% of the votes and Drašković 20.6%. Despite the boycott implemented by supporters of a number of opposition parties and Kosovo Albanians, some 62% of the electorate participated in the poll. Since none of the candidates had secured the requisite majority of more than one-half of the votes cast, a second round was scheduled to take place on 5 October. In early October SPS and SRP councillors in the Belgrade municipal assembly voted in support of an SRM initiative to remove Đinđić from the office of Mayor of Belgrade. Security forces subsequently suppressed protests in Belgrade by supporters of the DP, who demanded that further legislative and municipal elections be conducted. In the second round of voting in the Serbian presidential election on 5 October Šešelj won 49.1% and Lilić 47.9% of the votes cast. However, owing, in part, to the boycott organized by Đinđić, less than 50% of the electorate participated in the poll, which was consequently declared to be invalid. The Serbian authorities announced that a new presidential election would take place on 7 December.

Following his appointment as a Federal Deputy Prime Minister in November 1997, Lilić withdrew his candidacy to the Serbian presidency. In the Serbian presidential election, which was contested by seven candidates on 7 December, the United List coalition was represented by the Federal Minister of Foreign Affairs, Milan Milutinović, who secured 43.7% of the votes cast; Šešelj received 32.2% of the votes. In the ensuing second round, which took place on 21 December, Milutinović won 59.2% of the votes cast, while Šešelj obtained 37.5% of the votes. The Serbian Electoral Commission announced that about 50.1% of the electorate had participated in the poll, which was consequently pronounced to be valid. However, Šešelj claimed that the Serbian authorities had perpetrated electoral malpractice, particularly in Kosovo, where ethnic Albanians had again boycotted the polls. Later in December OSCE observers issued a report indicating that severe irregularities had taken place. On 29 December Milutinović was inaugurated as President of Serbia.

In February 1998 Milutinović reappointed Marjanović to the office of Serbian Prime Minister. Following protracted negotiations, the SPS formed an alliance with the SRP in March. Marjanović subsequently formed a new coalition Government, comprising 15 representatives of the SRP (including Šešelj, who became a Deputy Prime Minister), 13 representatives of the SPS, and four of the YUL. In May the Savezna skupština adopted a motion expressing no confidence in the federal Prime Minister, Kontić, which had apparently been initiated by DPMS deputies. Milošević's subsequent nomination of Bulatović to the office was approved by the Savezna skupština, and a new Federal Government was established. Đukanović, however, declared Bulatović's Government to be illegitimate. In June the Montenegrin legislature (which had been elected in the previous month, and in which supporters of Đukanović had obtained a majority) withdrew the 20 deputies representing the Republic from the Veće Republika and replaced them with members of Đukanović's coalition, to ensure that Milošević would not command the requisite two-thirds' majority for constitutional amendments. (Milošević, however, refused to allow deputies from Đukanović's coalition to assume seats in the Veće Republika.) In August a new Montenegrin Government, headed by Filip Vujanović of the DPMS, announced that it had suspended links with the federal Government until Bulatović agreed to resign from the office of Prime Minister in favour of a supporter of Đukanović.

During 1998 and early 1999 inter-ethnic hostilities in Kosovo further intensified, frequently resulting in violence, and, following the failure of internationally sponsored negotiations, culminated in the aerial bombardment of military, and subsequently certain civilian, targets in Serbia and Montenegro in March–June 1999 by North Atlantic Treaty Organization (NATO, see p. 340) forces, which sought to defend Kosovo Albanians from the Serbian security forces (see below). In late April Drašković was dismissed as Deputy Prime Minister of the FRY, after he publicly opposed Milošević's refusal to comply with NATO demands.

In May 1999 the International Criminal Tribunal for the former Yugoslavia (ICTY, see p. 18) indicted Milošević, together with Milutinović, Šainović, the former Serbian Minister of the Interior, Vlajko Stojiljković, and the Yugoslav Army Chief of Staff, Gen. Dragoljub Ojdanić, for crimes against humanity. In June SRP ministers and legislative deputies temporarily suspended participation in the Serbian Government, in protest at Milošević's acceptance of the peace plan for Kosovo, whereby NATO forces were to be deployed in the province under a peace-keeping mandate (see below). From July a series of demonstrations was conducted by a loose grouping of opposition associations, known as Alliance for Change, in support of Milošević's resignation. In early August Milošević reorganized the Federal Government. Also in August the Montenegrin Government presented proposals for the dissolution of the FRY, and its replacement with an 'Association of States of Serbia and Montenegro', and announced that a referendum on independence for the republic would be conducted if Milošević failed to agree to the demands. In September the Alliance for Change initiated a campaign against Milošević; however, Drašković refused to endorse the protest rallies. In January 2000, following inter-party discussions, leaders of the Alliance for Change presented unified demands for elections to be conducted in Serbia by the end of April.

In mid-January 2000 a notorious Serbian paramilitary leader and war crimes suspect, Željko Ražnatović ('Arkan'), was shot and killed in Belgrade. Speculation regarding his killing included the suggestion that, following his indictment by the ICTY in 1997, he had been prepared to implicate Milošević in war crimes. In February 2000 the Federal Minister of Defence, Pavle Bulatović, was also killed. Milošević subsequently appointed Gen. Ojdanić to the post. In July the Savezna skupština approved constitutional amendments removing limits on the President's tenure of office, providing for direct election to the presidency and the Veće Republika, and reducing Montenegro's status within the FRY. The amendments attracted immediate criticism from Serbian opposition parties and the international community. The Skupština Republike Crne Gore subsequently voted to reject the amendments, which Vujanović condemned as an attempt by Milošević to retain power. At the end of July Milošević announced that federal presidential and legislative elections were to take place on 24 September. The Montenegrin Government announced that the republic would not participate in the forthcoming elections, in protest at the amendments. In early August an alliance of 18 opposition parties, known as the Democratic Opposition of Serbia (DOS), presented the leader of the DPS, Dr Vojislav Koštunica, as their joint candidate to oppose Milošević in the presidential election.

Numerous allegations of electoral malpractice and intimidation emerged, both prior to and following the voting to the federal presidency and legislature on 24 September 2000. Preliminary results, released by the Federal Election Commission, indicated that Koštunica had won about 48% of the votes cast, compared with the 40% of the votes received by Milošević, and thereby

SERBIA

Introductory Survey

failed to obtain the 50% majority required to secure the presidency. Milošević subsequently insisted that a second round of voting be conducted on 8 October, while Koštunica rejected the results of the Commission as fraudulent, and claimed to have won the election outright. The international community declared its support for Koštunica and urged Milošević to accept defeat. The Yugoslav army announced that it would not intervene on Milošević's behalf, while the SRP and Serbian parties in Montenegro also acknowledged Koštunica's victory. Opposition supporters commenced a campaign of peaceful protest in Serbia (including a widely observed general strike from the beginning of October), in an effort to compel Milošević to resign. On 5 October protesters, who had gathered to stage a mass rally in Belgrade, overpowered security forces and seized control of the parliament building, the state television station and the official news agency, subsequently declaring Koštunica to be the elected President. On the following day, amid increasing international pressure, Milošević finally relinquished the presidency. Koštunica was officially inaugurated as President on 7 October. According to the final official results, Koštunica received 51.7% of the votes cast and Milošević 38.2%; in the concurrent legislative elections, the DOS secured 58 seats in the 138-member Veće građana, and the SPS 44. After the DOS negotiated an agreement with the SPS in mid-October, the Narodna skupština Republike Srbije was dissolved, and a transitional Government, in which the SPS retained the premiership, was installed later that month, pending legislative elections, which were brought forward to December. Since only about 30% of the Montenegrin electorate had participated in the voting, as a result of Đukanović's boycott, Koštunica was obliged to form an administration with the Socialist People's Party of Montenegro (SNP, led by Predrag Bulatović—the only Montenegrin party to be represented in the legislature). A member of that party, Zoran Žižić, was nominated to the post of Prime Minister, and a new federal Government, comprising representatives of the DOS and the SNP, was established in early November. Following the installation of the new Government, the normalization of relations between the FRY and the international community proceeded rapidly, and the country was formally admitted to the UN (from which it had been absent since the dissolution of the SFRY) on 1 November. In December Koštunica reorganized the armed forces, removing officers loyal to Milošević.

In the elections to the 250-member Narodna skupština Republike Srbije, held on 23 December 2000, the DOS secured a substantial majority, with 176 seats, while the SPS won 37 seats and the SRP 23. Later that month Đukanović announced proposals that the FRY become a loose union of two internationally recognized, separate states. At the end of December the People's Party of Montenegro, which supported a continued federation, withdrew from the governing coalition. Đukanović subsequently announced that elections to the Skupština Republike Crne Gore would take place in April 2001. In January Đinđić was elected to the Serbian premiership, and a new Government, comprising members of the DOS, was installed later that month.

In early 2001 the federal Government came under increasing pressure from the EU and USA to arrest Milošević and other war crimes suspects; Koštunica maintained that their extradition would contravene the Constitution. Following a warning by the USA that it would end financial aid to the FRY unless the new administration fully co-operated with the ICTY by the end of March 2001, Milošević was taken into custody on 1 April. The federal Public Prosecutor issued a series of charges against Milošević for abuses of power during his term of office (principally extensive embezzlement from state funds, and involvement in political assassinations, electoral malpractice and organized crime). Later that month Milošević, who was in detention in Belgrade, received the ICTY indictment. At the end of April Serbian courts authorized the extension of Milošević's period of detention for a further two months, despite an appeal that he be released on grounds of ill health. Koštunica, however, refused to comply with international demands that Milošević be dispatched for trial at the ICTY (apparently owing to concern that his extradition might prompt political unrest). Meanwhile, at the elections to the expanded 78-member Skupština Republike Crne Gore, which were conducted on 22 April, the pro-independence alliance, led by the DPMS, won 36 seats. Despite having failed to secure a decisive majority in the legislature, Đukanović announced that he would continue to pursue his aim of organizing a referendum on Montenegrin independence.

In June 2001, following continued international pressure for the authorities to co-operate with the ICTY, the Serbian Government approved a decree, providing for the extradition of Milošević and other indicted war criminals to the ICTY. Supporters of Milošević subsequently staged a large demonstration in Belgrade. The Serbian Government refused to comply with a ruling by the federal Constitutional Court that the decree was invalid, and on 29 June (shortly before an important international donor conference was to take place) Milošević was extradited to the ICTY. On the following day Žižić resigned from the office of federal Prime Minister, in protest at Milošević's extradition (which had been strongly opposed by the SNP). In July Koštunica appointed Dragiša Pešić, also a member of the SNP and hitherto Federal Minister of Finance, to the post. Later that month a reorganized federal Government, proposed by Pešić, was approved in the legislature. In August the division between Koštunica and Đinđić resulting from the Serbian Government's decision to extradite Milošević was further exacerbated by the killing in Belgrade of a security agent, who had reportedly been investigating alleged connections of prominent state officials to organized crime. Koštunica accused Đinđić's administration of failing to address widespread crime, and withdrew the DPS ministers from the Government.

In October 2001 the initial indictment against Milošević relating to Kosovo was amended, henceforth alleging that he had organized security-force operations against Kosovo Albanians, which had resulted in the expulsion of 80,000 civilians from the province. Also in October Milošević was further indicted in connection with war crimes perpetrated in Croatia in 1991–92; he was accused of ordering the forcible removal of the majority of the non-Serb population from one-third of the territory of Croatia, with the aim of incorporating the region into a Serb-dominated state. Four former naval officers were indicted for participation in an offensive against Dubrovnik, in Croatia, in late 1991. The former Commander of the Yugoslav Navy, Pavle Strugar, surrendered to the ICTY later in October 2001. In November Milošević (hitherto indicted for crimes against humanity, breaches of the 1949 Geneva Convention, and violations of the laws or customs of war) was charged with genocide, in connection with the atrocities perpetrated by Serb forces in Bosnia and Herzegovina in 1992–95. He continued to refuse to recognize the authority of the ICTY, and 'not guilty' pleas were submitted on his behalf for all three indictments. The trial of Milošević, who had decided to conduct his own defence, officially commenced on 12 February 2002.

In December 2001 the Speaker of the Narodna skupština Republike Srbije, Dragan Maršićanin, who was the deputy leader of the DPS and a close associate of Koštunica, resigned, having accused parties belonging to the DOS coalition of electoral malpractice. In January 2002 the federal Minister of Finance also tendered his resignation. In that month the Narodna skupština Republike Srbije voted in favour of partially restoring the autonomous status of Vojvodina. In March one of the Serbian Deputy Prime Ministers, Momčilo Perišić, was arrested, and subsequently resigned, after military intelligence sources claimed to have evidence that he had given classified information to a US diplomat. Đinđić rejected demands by Koštunica that he submit his resignation over the issue, and requested the dismissal of the head of the military security service responsible for Perišić's arrest. Perišić claimed that the charges had been fabricated, in an attempt to cause the dissolution of Đinđić's Government. In June the DPS withdrew from the Narodna skupština Republike Srbije, in protest at the expulsion of 21 DPS deputies. (The party was formally expelled from the ruling DOS coalition in the following month.) The Serbian Government was reorganized in the same month.

Following protracted negotiations on the issue of Montenegro's independence (which were mediated by the EU from November 2001), the government leaders of the FRY and the two republics signed a framework agreement on 14 March 2002, providing for the establishment of a State Union of Serbia and Montenegro. Under the accord, the two republics were to maintain separate economies, but have joint foreign and defence ministries, and elect a new, joint presidency and legislature. Montenegro was to retain the right to refer the issue of independence to a referendum after a period of three years. It was envisaged that, following endorsement of the agreement by the Savezna skupština and the legislatures of the two republics, a new constitution would be adopted, and elections to the new joint parliament would take place later that year. Later in March the Liberal Alliance of Montenegro (LAM) withdrew from Đukanović's coalition (thereby ending its narrow majority in the Skupština Republike Crne Gore), in protest at the agreement, which prompted widespread criticism from pro-independence supporters.

Meanwhile, the USA renewed pressure on the Federal Government to demonstrate co-operation with the ICTY. Following the expiry of a deadline for Yugoslav compliance with these demands, economic aid to the FRY was suspended at the end of March 2002. In April the Savezna skupština finally approved legislation providing for the extradition of indicted war crimes suspects, and the issue of arrest warrants for those who did not surrender to the ICTY. Shortly afterwards Stojiljković (the former Serbian Minister of the Interior who had been indicted in May 1999) committed suicide. Of 10 former Yugoslav state officials indicted, six (including Gen. Ojdanić and Šainović) agreed to surrender to the Tribunal. In early May 2002 Šainović was voluntarily transferred to the ICTY.

In late May 2002 the Savezna skupština officially approved the agreement on the creation of a State Union (which had been ratified by the legislatures of both republics in April). In July Lilić was arrested and extradited to the ICTY, having been subpoenaed as a prosecution witness in the trial of Milošević. He refused to testify unless he was guaranteed immunity from prosecution. It was announced that the presidential election in Serbia would be brought forward to 29 September, to allow the extradition of Milutinović to the ICTY.

At the Serbian presidential election, held on 29 September 2002, Koštunica won some 30.9% of the votes cast, while Miroljub Labus (the incumbent federal Deputy Prime Minister and Minister of Foreign Trade, who was supported by Đinđić) received 27.4% and Šešelj 23.2%; some 55.5% of the registered electorate voted. A second round of voting took place on 13 October between Koštunica and Labus, at which Koštunica secured some 68.4% of the votes cast. However, the election was declared invalid, owing to the participation of only 44.0% of the electorate, lower than the required minimum level of 50%. (Šešelj had urged his supporters not to participate in the poll, and it was reported that Đinđić had also unofficially supported a boycott).

On 6 December 2002 a 27-member commission on constitutional reform, comprising representatives of the principal parties of the two republics, submitted a draft of the new Constitutional Charter for the proposed State Union. A third presidential poll in Serbia on 8 December (in which Koštunica won just 57.7% of the votes) was again annulled, owing to a rate of participation of just 45.0%. On 30 December Milutinović was replaced, on an interim basis, by the President of the Narodna skupština Republike Srbije, Nataša Mićić. (Đukanović's pro-independence coalition, by now known as Democratic List for a European Montenegro, had obtained an overall majority in the republican legislature at elections held in Montenegro in late October, although presidential elections in the republic, held on 22 December were invalidated as a result of an insufficient level of participation by the electorate; a further vote was similarly declared invalid in mid-February 2003.)

On 20 January 2003 Milutinović was voluntarily transferred to the ICTY, where he subsequently pleaded not guilty to charges relating to crimes perpetrated during the 1999 conflict in Kosovo. The new Constitutional Charter, which provided for the creation of the State Union of Serbia and Montenegro, was approved by the Narodna skupština Republike Srbije on 27 January 2003 and by the Skupština Republike Crne Gore on 29 January. On 4 February both chambers of the Savezna skupština approved the Constitutional Charter, thereby officially replacing the FRY with the State Union of Serbia and Montenegro. Ethnic Albanians in Kosovo expressed their opposition to the province's inclusion in the new Union as part of Serbia, and continued to demand independence.

In February 2003 Šešelj surrendered to the ICTY, where he was charged in connection with the forcible removal of the non-Serb population from various regions of Bosnia and Herzegovina, Croatia and Serbia (Vojvodina) in 1991–95. On 25 February 2003, in accordance with the Constitutional Charter, the existing federal and republican legislatures elected a 126-member Skupština Srbije i Crne Gore (Assembly of Serbia and Montenegro), comprising 91 Serbian and 35 Montenegrin deputies. On 7 March a former Speaker of the Montenegrin legislature, Svetozar Marović, was elected unopposed as President of Serbia and Montenegro by the Skupština Srbije i Crne Gore. The President was also to chair a five-member Council of Ministers (with portfolios that included foreign affairs, defence, and human and minority rights), which was approved by the Skupština Srbije i Crne Gore on 18 March.

On 12 March 2003 Đinđić, having survived an apparent assassination attempt in February, was shot dead outside government buildings in Belgrade. Mićić immediately imposed a state of emergency in Serbia, and some 1,200 suspects, including a former Serbian Minister of Security, were arrested in connection with the assassination. The former federal Minister of Internal Affairs, Zoran Živković, was nominated by the DP to replace Đinđić as Serbian Prime Minister, and his nomination was approved by the Narodna skupština Republike Srbije on 18 March. At the end of March security forces discovered the remains of Ivan Stambolić, who had been abducted in August 2000. The Serbian authorities issued an international arrest warrant for Mirjana Marković and her son (who were in hiding in Russia), in connection with the killing of Stambolić; Milošević was subsequently also charged. In mid-April the Skupština Srbije i Crne Gore voted in favour of extending the state's co-operation with the ICTY, ending a stipulation that all war crimes suspects indicted by the Tribunal from that month be tried by domestic courts. Later that month the state of emergency in Serbia was ended and some 45 suspects, including Šešelj, were charged with alleged involvement in the assassination of Đinđić. Two former senior security advisers of Koštunica were also charged with conspiring to overthrow the Government in a coup, which, according to the Serbian authorities, was to have followed Đinđić's killing, with the aim of reinstating an administration opposed to co-operation with the ICTY. In early May two former heads of the Serbian security services and close associates of Milošević, already in detention in Belgrade in connection with Đinđić's assassination, were also indicted by the ICTY for war crimes.

In May Vujanović succeeded in being elected as President of Montenegro, following the abolition of the requirement that 50% of the electorate participate in polling; he subsequently pledged to hold a referendum on Montenegrin independence within three years. In June 2003 the former Serbian Minister of State Security, Jovica Stanišić, and his deputy, Franko Simatović, were extradited to the ICTY, having been indicted in May. Stanišić and Simatović had been arrested in connection with Đinđić's assassination. In August a senior naval officer, Vice-Adm. Miodrag Jokić, reached a compromise agreement with ICTY prosecutors, according to which he pleaded guilty to six charges relating to the bombardment of Dubrovnik. In the same month the Serbian Government issued arrest warrants for 44 people suspected of involvement in Đinđić's assassination, principally Milorad 'Legija' Luković, the leader of an organized criminal group and a prominent member of a paramilitary unit of Milošević's regime. In September the Serbian Government announced that Milošević would be arraigned at a special court on charges of ordering the killing of Stambolić. In October the ICTY issued indictments against four senior Serbian military and security officials, including the former Chief of General Staff of the Yugoslav Army, Col-Gen. Nebojsa Pavković (who had been removed from his post by Koštunica in June 2002), for war crimes perpetrated against the civilian population of Kosovo in 1998–99. Serbian leaders, including Živković, condemned the measure, claiming that they had been implicitly assured of indemnity from prosecution.

In November 2003, following long-standing dissension within the DOS, two small parties withdrew from the coalition, thereby ending its parliamentary majority. The DOS subsequently dissolved, and Živković scheduled fresh elections to the Narodna skupština Republike Srbije. Meanwhile, on 16 November a further presidential poll in Serbia (at which the acting leader of the SRP, Tomislav Nikolić, was placed first, securing 47.9% of the votes cast) was declared invalid, owing to a rate of electoral participation of only 38.8%. In December the trial began of 36 suspects charged in connection with Đinđić's assassination (15 of them, including Luković, in absentia). At the elections to the Narodna skupština Republike Srbije, held on 28 December, the SRP, with 28.0% of the votes cast, secured 82 seats, the DPS (18.0%) 53 seats, the DP (12.8%) 37 seats, a newly emerged reformist grouping known as G17 Plus (11.6%) 34 seats, an alliance of the SRM and New Serbia (NS—7.8%) 22 seats, and the SPS (7.7%) 22 seats. Candidates contesting parliamentary seats notably included four indicted war crimes suspects, two of whom (Milošević and Šešelj) were in detention at The Hague. Following lengthy inter-party discussions, the DPS formed a minority coalition with G17 Plus and the SRM-NS alliance, which was also, to the concern of the international community, reliant on the support of the SPS. On 4 February 2004 the DPS Vice-President, Maršićanin, was elected President of the Narodna skupština Republike Srbije (from which position he had resigned in December 2001), thereby replacing Mićić as the Republic's acting President. In that month the Narodna skupština voted to abolish the minimum rate of participation for elections to the republican presidency, as a means of ending the protracted political impasse. A new Council of Ministers, headed by Koštunica, was formed in March; owing to Maršićanin's inclusion in the administration as Minister of the Economy, he was replaced as President of the Narodna skupština Republike Srbije (and therefore acting President of Serbia) by the hitherto deputy speaker, Predrag Marković. In mid-April the Skupština Srbije i Crne Gore approved a reorganization of the state union Council of Ministers; Drašković received the foreign affairs portfolio, Prvoslav Davinić of G17 Plus replaced Boris Tadić as Minister of Defence, and Predrag Ivanović of the DPMS became Minister of Foreign Economic Relations. The principal suspect in the assassination of Đinđić, Luković, surrendered to the Serbian authorities in early May, subsequently denying all charges.

Some 15 candidates contested the elections to the presidency of Serbia, held on 13 June 2004. Nikolić secured 30.1% of the votes cast, and Tadić, the candidate (and leader) of the DP, won 27.7% of the votes. Bogoljub Karić, who was considered to be one of the most wealthy businessmen in Serbia, won 18.5% of the votes, and Maršićanin (having resigned his ministerial post, and contesting the election for a coalition of parties led by the DPS) 13.5%. Nikolić's narrow victory in the first round was attributed to the failure of the reformist parties to agree on a common candidate. A second round between Nikolić and Tadić was conducted on 27 June; Tadić, who benefited from the transferred support of the governing coalition parties, was elected to the presidency, receiving 54.0% of the votes. At his inauguration on 17 July, Tadić pledged commitment to the continuation of economic reforms and for the eventual integration of Serbia into the EU.

In early December 2004 a former Yugoslav Army officer, Gen. Dragoljub Milošević, surrendered to the Serbian authorities and was extradited to the ICTY, where he was charged with crimes relating to the blockade and bombardment of Sarajevo in 1994. In January 2005, however, the USA expressed dissatisfaction with the failure of Serbia and Montenegro to co-operate with the ICTY, and announced a reduction in financial aid and the withdrawal of US technical advisers from Serbian ministries. The EU subsequently indicated that the prospects for Serbia and Montenegro's eventual accession would be dependent on the extradition of the four former Serbian military and security officials who had been indicted in October 2003 for crimes committed during the conflict in Kosovo. Representatives of the international community repeatedly accused the Serbian authorities of aiding the continuing evasion from the Tribunal of the indictee associated with the former military of the Bosnian Serbs, Gen. Ratko Mladić, and also cited his extradition as essential for Serbia and Montenegro's accession to NATO's 'Partnership for Peace' (PfP, see p. 342) programme. In February 2005 one of those indicted, a former military commander in Prishtina, Gen. Vladimir Lazarević, agreed to surrender to the ICTY after meeting with Koštunica, and was subsequently extradited.

Amid increasing concern over the future of the State Union, in February 2005 Koštunica and Đukanović met for discussions on the scheduling of elections to the Skupština Srbije i Crne Gore. On 7 April, following mediation by the EU High Representative for Common Foreign and Security Policy, Javier Solana Madriaga, the Presidents agreed that the election of representatives to the Skupština Srbije i Crne Gore would take place concurrently with elections to the two republican legislatures; the Constitutional Charter was to be amended to allow the extension of the mandates of the incumbent deputies. The Montenegrin Government favoured the organization of a referendum on independence prior to elections, while supporters of the continuation of the State Union insisted that such a measure would require adherence to EU conditions and arbitration. Solana welcomed the agreement and commended Serbia's improved co-operation with the ICTY (following the transfer, between late 2004 and mid-2005, of 13 Serbian and Bosnian Serb war crime suspects, in surrenders mediated by the Koštunica Government). Shortly afterwards the European Commission indicated that sufficient progress had been made for Serbia and Montenegro to commence negotiations on a Stabilization and Association Agreement (SAA) with the EU. The surrender of Col-Gen. Pavković to the ICTY in late April demonstrated further progress towards improved relations between Serbia and the EU.

At the end of June 2005 the head of Milošević's secret service, Radomir Marković, together with Milorad Luković and three other former paramilitary members, were sentenced to terms of imprisonment for involvement in an assassination attempt against Drašković in 1999. In July 2005 Luković was sentenced to 40 years' and Marković to 15 years' imprisonment for the killing of Stambolić in August 2000; six former secret service officers also received custodial terms. In September 2005 a further international arrest warrant was issued for Mirjana Marković, who had failed to fulfil pledges to return from exile in Russia. On 10 October negotiations on the SAA officially commenced between the Government of Serbia and Montenegro and the EU. In early October five members of a former Serb paramilitary unit were charged in Serbia with the killing of six Muslims at Srebrenica, Bosnia and Herzegovina, following the release of video evidence of the killings; their trial commenced in December. Also in December some 14 members of a former Serb militia were sentenced by a Serbian court to terms of between five and 20 years for killing 200 Croat prisoners near the Croatian town of Vukovar in November 1991.

In November 2005 Milošević's trial at the ICTY was again adjourned on grounds of ill health; he subsequently rejected an attempt by the Tribunal to expedite proceedings. On 27 February 2006 a case submitted by Bosnia and Herzegovina against Serbia in 1993, demanding reparations for the alleged genocide of the Bosnian Muslim population in 1992–95, finally commenced at the International Court of Justice (ICJ, see p. 20) at the Hague. At the end of February the Montenegrin Government and opposition agreed that the planned referendum on Montenegrin's secession from the State Union would take place on 21 May.

On 11 March 2006 Milošević died while in custody at the ICTY. Preliminary autopsy results concluded that the cause of death was a heart attack, but supporters of Milošević immediately criticized the medical treatment that he had received in detention and the Tribunal's refusal in late February to grant a request for his transfer to hospital in Russia. (It emerged that shortly before his death Milošević had written to the Russian Minister of Foreign Affairs, claiming that he was being poisoned in detention.) The Serbian authorities refused to organize a state funeral, and members of Milošević's family, including Mirjana Marković (despite the temporary suspension of the international arrest warrant against her), failed to attend the ceremony, which took place at his family residence in the Serbian town of Pozarevac; although there were scenes of public mourning, former nationalist supporters at the funeral were reported to number only a few hundred. In April an independent investigation by Dutch pathologists confirmed that Milošević's death was the result of a heart attack.

In early 2006 the Serbian authorities came under increasing pressure from the EU to effect Mladić's extradition to the ICTY. In March the ICTY Prosecutor, Carla Del Ponte, visited Belgrade, with the aim of securing assurances that Mladić would be apprehended, and the EU issued an ultimatum that failure to arrest Mladić by 5 April would result in the suspension of the negotiations on the SAA. Discussions continued during that month, but were, however, suspended, after the Serbian Government failed to meet a further deadline, of 30 April, for Mladić's extradition. In early May Labus resigned from the post of Deputy Prime Minister of Serbia in protest at the failure of the authorities to apprehend Mladić. Labus subsequently resigned from the leadership of G17 Plus, after the party refused to withdraw other representatives from the Government. Ivana Dulić-Marković (hitherto Minister of Agriculture) was appointed Deputy Prime Minister in June.

At the referendum held in Montenegro on 21 May 2006 some 55.5% of votes were cast in favour of independence, narrowly exceeding the minimum requirement of 55% stipulated by the EU. Following Montenegro's subsequent declaration of independence on 3 June, the Narodna skupština Republike Srbije officially declared Serbia to be the successor state to the State Union of Serbia and Montenegro on 5 June. The Serbian Government announced that the central administration and other organs of the former State Union had ceased to exist. (Drašković and the hitherto Minister of Defence of Serbia and Montenegro, Zoran Stanković, retained their portfolios in an acting capacity, becoming ministers of the Republic of Serbia, without being officially appointed to its Government.) In mid-June the Serbian Government adopted a decision recognizing Montenegro's independence, and the Ministers of Foreign Affairs of the two countries signed a protocol on the establishment of diplomatic relations on 22 June. At the end of that month Tadić became the first Head of State to make an official visit to independent Montenegro.

In July 2006 the trial of six senior Serbian officials who had served under Milošević began at the ICTY: Milutinović, Šainović, Gen. Ojdanić, Col-Gen. Pavković, Gen. Lazarević, and Gen. Sretan Lukić were charged on five counts relating to human rights violations committed against ethnic Albanians in Kosovo during 1998–99. Meanwhile, the EU continued to adhere to its stipulation that Mladić be arrested before the resumption of SAA discussions, and in July Koštunica presented an 'action plan' for achieving full co-operation with the ICTY.

On 30 September 2006 the Narodna skupština Republike Srbije adopted a new draft Constitution by a unanimous vote (with 242 deputies attending); the draft was to be submitted for endorsement at a national referendum. The new Constitution included increased provisions for the guarantee of human and minority rights, and which notably referred to Kosovo and Metohija as an integral part of the Republic of Serbia, was approved by 53.0% of votes cast at the referendum, held on 29 October; it, duly entered into effect on 8 November. At the end of November NATO invited Serbia (together with Bosnia and Herzegovina and Montenegro) to join the PfP programme; Del Ponte strongly criticized Serbia's admission to the programme (which officially took place on 14 December), in view of the authorities' continued failure to extradite Mladić to the ICTY. In early December Šešelj (who had refused to attend the opening of his trial at the ICTY in November) ended a four-week hunger strike, after an appeals chamber at the Tribunal restored his right to defend himself. Also in December a SPS congress elected a former presidential candidate, Ivica Dačić, to replace Milošević as party leader. Two ethnic Albanian parties from the Preševo region established an alliance to contest the legislative elections, ending a boycott after the new Constitution no longer required minority parties to secure a minimum of 5% of the votes in order to obtain parliamentary representation.

At the elections to the Narodna skupština Republike Srbije, contested by 20 political parties and alliances on 21 January 2007, the SRP, with 29.1% of votes cast, obtained the largest number of seats (81), while the DP secured 23.1% of the votes (64 seats), and an alliance led by DPS 16.8% of the votes (47 seats). The representation of G17 Plus, which received 6.9% of votes cast, declined to 19 seats, and that of the SPS, with 5.7% of the votes, to 16 seats, while a new reformist alliance led by the Liberal Democratic Party won 5.4% of the votes and 15 seats. (The SRM, having undergone internal dissension, failed to secure any parliamentary representation.) After smaller parliamentary parties declared reluctance to enter into a minority administration with the SRP, Tadić engaged in consultations with party leaders regarding the establishment of a new coalition government. EU officials urged the establishment of a new administration in favour of democratic reforms, indicating that this would allow negotiations on a SAA to proceed (thereby abandoning the previous stipulation for the prior extradition of Mladić). However, the expected formation of a coalition between the DP and DPS was impeded by ideological differences between the two parties, compounded by resistance to a UN proposal for supervised independence for Kosovo (see below). It was reported that Koštunica insisted on remaining as Prime Minister, while Tadić favoured the nomination of Božidar Đelić to the office. Under the terms of the Constitution, following the inauguration of the Narodna skupština on 14 February, failure to form a new government by mid-May would require further elections to be held.

On 26 February 2007 the ICJ issued a decision on the case submitted by Bosnia and Herzegovina against Serbia, claiming reparations for the genocide of Bosnian Muslims in 1992–95. The ICJ ruled that the Serbian state was not directly responsible for genocide or complicity in genocide in Bosnia and Herzegovina in 1992–95; however, the Court declared that Serbia was in violation of its obligation under international law by having failed to prevent the 1995 massacre of more than 7,000 Bosnian Muslims in the east Bosnian town of Srebrenica and to act against its perpetrators. In April four members of a Serb paramilitary unit were sentenced to terms of imprisonment by a Belgrade court for the killing of six Muslims in south-eastern Bosnia and Herzegovina in 1995, after the emergence of video footage of the executions (which had been broadcast on Serbian television in 2005, prompting national outrage).

On 8 May 2007 Nikolić was elected President of the Narodna skupština Republike Srbije, after Koštunica instructed DPS deputies to support his nomination. However, Nikolić's appointment prompted international consternation (which coincided with Serbia's assumption of the rotational chairmanship of the Council of Europe), and EU officials offered Serbia strong incentives to form a pro-democracy Government. On 11 May Tadić announced that a coalition agreement had been reached between the DP, the DPS and New Serbia alliance, and G17 Plus, and that he had nominated Koštunica for a second term as Prime Minister. On 13 May Nikolić tendered his resignation from his new post. On 15 May, shortly before the expiry of the constitutional deadline, a coalition Government was approved by 133 votes in the Narodna skupština Republike Srbije; notably, the Government included the new position of a Minister of Kosovo and Metohija.

On 7 June 2007 the President of the European Commission invited Serbia to resume negotiations on a SAA, citing improved co-operation with the ICTY, following the arrest in Republika Srpska of a former Bosnian Serb army officer, Zdravko Tolimir, believed to be a close associate of Mladić and to be assisting his evasion of capture. Negotiations officially recommenced on 13 June; the EU (at the particular insistence of the Netherlands and Belgium) emphasized that conclusion of the Agreement continued to be conditional on full co-operation with the ICTY, resulting in the arrest and transfer of all ICTY indictees, including Mladić. In October the Government announced that it was to offer €1m. for information resulting in the arrest of Mladić.

In early December 2007 several laws, including legislation on the election of the President in accordance with the new Constitution, were adopted in the Narodna skupština Republike Srbije, allowing a pre-term presidential election to be scheduled for early 2008. At the first round of the election, which was contested by nine candidates on 20 January, Nikolić won about 40.0% of the votes cast and Tadić 35.4%. Later that month, in the absence of a finalized SAA, EU foreign ministers offered Serbia an interim political agreement, which provided for increased co-operation in trade and education, and relaxed visa requirements for Serbian nationals. Koštunica failed to transfer support to Tadić in the second round of the presidential election, after Tadić rejected his demand to pledge not to sign an SAA with the EU if the EU deployed a mission in Kosovo without UN authorization. Nevertheless, at the second round, which was conducted on 3 February, Tadić was re-elected to the presidency, securing about 50.3% of the votes cast, according to official figures, and narrowly defeating Nikolić. The rate of participation by the electorate was estimated at some 67%. EU officials welcomed the election results, which were widely viewed as an endorsement of Tadić's policy of favouring rapid EU integration. Tadić was inaugurated on 15 February. However, the ideological division between Tadić and Koštunica continued to impede effective governance; in early February Koštunica rejected the proposed political agreement with the EU, owing to his strenuous opposition to the EU's decision to establish EULEX Kosovo, a police and justice mission for Kosovo. The political agreement had been supported by Tadić as an opportunity for Serbia to benefit from closer relations with the EU.

Kosovo's declaration of independence on 17 February 2008, which was rapidly recognized by a number of EU nations (see below), presented a further obstacle to prospects for EU integration, since the United Kingdom, France and Germany (principal supporters of Kosovo's independence) indicated that Serbia would be required to relinquish its territorial claim on Kosovo for accession. In early March Koštunica declared support for a draft resolution, proposed in the Narodna skupština Republike Srbije by the SRP, which made further progress towards EU accession conditional on the rejection of Kosovo's independence by the Union. However, on 8 March Koštunica resigned from the premiership, citing irreconcilable differences within the ruling coalition over Kosovo and EU integration. On 13 March Tadić dissolved the Narodna skupština, at the request of the Government, and scheduled legislative elections for 11 May (when local elections and elections to the Vojvodina Assembly were also due to be conducted). After Belgium and the Netherlands reportedly ceded to pressure, in April EU foreign ministers reached a decision to sign the SAA with Serbia, an offer that was widely perceived as an effort to strengthen popular support for reformist parties contesting the forthcoming elections and to prevent nationalist groups from gaining ascendancy. On 29 April the EU signed the SAA, together with a provisional document whereby Serbia would be granted access to benefits based on the SAA before all EU members had ratified the Agreement;

however, its implementation was to be suspended until EU member states agreed unanimously on Serbia's full co-operation with the ICTY. Koštunica had continued to oppose signature of the SAA, maintaining that it implied Serbian acquiescence to the recognition of Kosovo by most EU member states, while the SRP announced that it would initiate impeachment proceedings against Tadić after the elections. In early May the Serbian authorities confirmed that Tadić had received threats against his life.

At the legislative elections on 11 May 2008, an electoral coalition of parties supporting EU integration formed by Tadić, known as For a European Serbia—Boris Tadić, won some 38.4% of the votes cast, according to preliminary results, increasing the DP and its allied parties' strength in the Narodna skupština Republike Srbije to 102 seats. The SRP secured about 29.4% of the votes and 78 seats, and the alliance between the DPS and New Serbia 11.6% of votes and 30 seats; a coalition of the SPS, the Party of United Pensioners of Serbia and United Serbia increased its joint representation in the chamber to 20 seats, with about 7.6% of the votes cast. The participation rate (including Serbs voting in Kosovo) was recorded at 60.1%. Following a number of complaints submitted by the SRP, the electoral commission announced that voting was to be repeated in three constituencies on 18 May, owing to irregularities. Neighbouring states, the EU and the USA welcomed the election results (which had followed predictions of success for the SRP) and urged the rapid formation of a new administration. (In view of continuing acrimony between Tadić and Koštunica during the electoral campaign, renewal of the DP governing coalition with the DPS was considered unlikely.) A few days after the poll, it was reported that the DP-led alliance and the SPS were engaged in negotiations towards a coalition agreement.

In early 1998 the USA and EU issued statements condemning the violent measures taken by the Serbian security forces in Kosovo to suppress the activities of the Kosovo Liberation Army (KLA), an ethnic Albanian paramilitary movement, while also criticizing the violence employed by the KLA, which had begun to launch attacks against Serbian forces in 1997 and had announced its intention to achieve independence for the province through armed resistance. The US Government announced that it was to withdraw the concessions that it had granted to the FRY in February, and threatened possible military intervention in Kosovo. The 'Contact Group', comprising the United Kingdom, France, Germany, Italy, Russia and the USA, which had been established in response to the conflict in Bosnia and Herzegovina, was convened in London; member nations envisaged the imposition of further sanctions against the FRY, including an embargo on armaments, unless the Serbian authorities acceded to a number of demands, including the withdrawal of security forces from Kosovo and the initiation of negotiations regarding the future status of the province. The British Government subsequently submitted a draft resolution to the UN Security Council for the imposition of an embargo on armaments against the FRY. Following a further meeting of the Contact Group, which took place in Bonn, Germany, later in March 1998, a statement was issued conceding that the Serbian authorities had achieved progress in reaching an agreement on education (see above), but continued to demand that they engage in negotiations regarding the future status of Kosovo. At the end of March the UN Security Council officially imposed an embargo on armaments against the FRY; of the member nations of the Council, only the People's Republic of China failed to endorse the resolution. The members of the Contact Group (apart from Russia) announced in April that Yugoslav assets abroad were to be 'frozen' and in May imposed a ban on foreign investment in Serbia.

In early July 1998 Milošević agreed that diplomatic observers from the EU, the USA and Russia would be allowed access to all regions of Kosovo to report on the activities of Serbian security forces. The Contact Group, which met in Bonn to discuss a peace settlement for Kosovo, recognized for the first time that it would be necessary to include KLA representatives in future negotiations on the status of the province. Meanwhile, Serbian security forces continued to initiate attacks against the KLA. Violence in the province continued during August, with further Serbian offensives against the KLA and killings of ethnic Albanian civilians.

In September 1998 the UN Security Council adopted Resolution 1199 (with the People's Republic of China abstaining), which demanded the immediate cessation of hostilities in Kosovo, the withdrawal of Serbian forces from the province, unrestricted access for humanitarian aid organizations, and the continuation of negotiations to determine the status of the province. NATO subsequently authorized its Supreme Allied Commander, Gen. Wesley Clark, to request member states to provide forces for possible military intervention. Despite an announcement by Serbian Prime Minister Marjanović at the end of September that Serbian security forces had suspended hostilities against the KLA, intensive fighting south of Prishtina (Prishtinë—Priština) was reported. NATO officially approved air bombardments against the FRY, and issued an ultimatum to Milošević that attacks would commence unless he complied with UN demands by a stipulated date later that month. (Russia continued to oppose military intervention against the FRY and had indicated that it would veto a further UN Security Council resolution authorizing such action.) Following intensive discussions with the US special envoy, Richard Holbrooke, Milošević agreed to the presence in Kosovo of a 2,000-member Organization for Security and Co-operation in Europe (OSCE) 'verification force' (to be known as the Kosovo Diplomatic Observer Mission), and to NATO surveillance flights in FRY airspace, to monitor the implementation of the UN Security Council's demands. Serbian leaders in Kosovo criticized Milošević's acceptance of the peace settlement, while the KLA considered the deployment of the OSCE monitors to be inadequate and continued to urge NATO military intervention. It was subsequently reported that the majority of federal army units had been withdrawn from Kosovo, but that some 11,600 members of the special Serbian security forces remained in the province. NATO urged further progress in the withdrawal of Serbian forces from Kosovo, but at the end of October suspended indefinitely the implementation of military action against the FRY.

In November 1998 the deployment of OSCE observers in Kosovo commenced; however, intermittent violations of the cease-fire were reported. Following the outbreak of heavy fighting between the KLA and Serbian forces in northern Kosovo in December, it became evident that the OSCE monitoring force was inadequate (and had no mandate) for peace-keeping operations. A 2,300-member NATO 'extraction force' was deployed in the former Yugoslav republic of Macedonia (FYRM), near the border with Kosovo, to effect the evacuation of the OSCE monitors in the event of attacks against them. In early January 1999 further clashes between Serbian and KLA forces were reported. In mid-January the discovery that some 45 ethnic Albanian civilians had been killed at the village of Reçak (Račak) prompted international condemnation of the Serbian authorities. OSCE observers dismissed claims by the Federal Government that those killed had been members of the KLA. At the end of January the 'Contact Group', meeting in London, decided that a peace conference should be convened at the French town of Rambouillet in early February. The British Secretary of State for Foreign and Commonwealth Affairs, Robin Cook, visited Belgrade to present the demands of the Contact Group (which he chaired) that Serbian, DAK and KLA leaders attend the negotiations on a draft peace agreement. Following international pressure, the KLA agreed that representatives of the movement would attend the conference, while in early February the Serbian legislature voted in favour of participation.

In early February 1999 the peace conference was convened in Rambouillet, as scheduled. Under the Contact Group's proposed peace plan, the Serbian authorities would be required to withdraw most of the 14,000 armed and security forces from Kosovo, while the KLA would be required to disarm within a period of three months. It was envisaged that NATO troops would be deployed in Kosovo to enforce the peace agreement. Negotiations at Rambouillet were extended, owing to the opposition of the Serbian delegation to the proposed deployment of the NATO force, and to the reluctance of elements of the KLA to accept the provisions in the agreement for disarmament. At the end of February, however, the ethnic Albanian delegation, including the KLA representatives, agreed, in principle, to accept the peace plan. Meanwhile, in early March it was reported that Serbian troops had forced several thousand ethnic Albanian civilians to flee from southern Kosovo, amid continued heavy fighting in the province. The peace conference was reconvened at Rambouillet in mid-March. The ethnic Albanian representatives signed the agreement; however, the Serbian delegation continued to present objections and proposed amendments to the peace plan, which were rejected by the Contact Group. It was subsequently reported that the Federal Government had deployed a further 30,000 Serbian forces in, or near, Kosovo. NATO reiterated threats of imminent air bombardments, despite continued opposition from the Russian Government, which attempted unsuccessfully to persuade Milošević to accept the peace plan. In the absence of a negotiated settlement to the conflict, the NATO Secretary-General ordered the commencement of air attacks against the FRY, in a campaign, codenamed Operation Allied Force, which was designed to force Milošević's capitulation to the demands of the Contact Group.

On 24 March 1999 NATO forces commenced an aerial bombardment of air defences and military installations across Serbia and Montenegro, notably in Belgrade, Novi Sad, Prishtina and Podgorica. The Federal Government declared a state of war (which, however, the Montenegrin administration refused to recognize), suspended diplomatic relations with the USA, France, Germany and the United Kingdom (the countries directly involved in the attacks), and ordered foreign journalists to leave the country. The People's Republic of China and Russia immediately condemned the air offensive (which NATO justified on humanitarian grounds, despite the lack of endorsement by a UN Security Council resolution). Serbian security forces in Kosovo subsequently intensified the campaign of mass expulsions and large-scale massacres of the ethnic Albanian civilian population, precipitating a continued exodus of refugees from the province. By early April some 140,000 ethnic Albanians had fled to the FYRM, 300,000 to Albania, and 32,000 to Montenegro. Some 12,000 NATO troops were stationed at the FYRM border with Kosovo, after the reinforcement of the extraction force.

During April 1999 the NATO air offensive intensified, with the extension of targets to include those of political and economic significance, including the Serbian state television station. The increasing number of civilian casualties was condemned by opponents of the air offensive; notably, NATO aircraft bombarded a convoy of ethnic Albanian refugees in Kosovo in mid-April, killing about 64, apparently owing to confusion over Serbian military targets. The Russian special envoy to the Balkans (and former premier), Viktor Chernomyrdin, became engaged in intensive mediation efforts with the Federal Government, while urging a suspension of the NATO air offensive. NATO, however, continued to demand the full withdrawal of Serbian forces from Kosovo, and the return of refugees with an international military presence, as a precondition to the suspension of air attacks. In early May the Group of Eight (G-8—comprising the seven Western industrialized nations and Russia), meeting in Bonn, agreed on general principles for a political solution to the conflict (which was referred to the UN Security Council), although differences over the composition of the international military force for Kosovo remained. Shortly afterwards, apparently owing to faulty military information, NATO forces bombarded the embassy of the People's Republic of China in Belgrade. Violent anti-NATO protests ensued in the Chinese capital, Beijing, and the Chinese Government, supported by Russia, demanded a cessation of the air offensive as a precondition to the discussion of the settlement at the UN Security Council. The Federal Government protested to the ICJ that the NATO air offensive was an illegal act of aggression, on the grounds that it had not received UN authorization. (The ICJ subsequently rejected the legal appeal.) At mid-May it was estimated that the NATO air campaign had resulted in the deaths of 1,200 civilians; about 600,000 ethnic Albanian refugees from Kosovo had fled to neighbouring countries.

In early 1999 the Federal Government announced that it had accepted the G-8 principles for a solution to the conflict. On 3 June, following mediation by the President of Finland, Martti Ahtisaari, the Narodna skupština Republike Srbije formally approved a peace plan presented to the Federal Government by EU and Russian envoys. The peace agreement provided for the withdrawal of Serbian forces from Kosovo, and the deployment of a joint NATO-Russian peace-keeping force of about 50,000 personnel. Ethnic Albanian refugees were to be allowed to return to Kosovo, and the province was to be granted some autonomy under an interim administration. On 9 June, following discussions between NATO and Yugoslav military commanders, which were conducted in the FYRM, a Military Technical Agreement, providing for the complete withdrawal of Serbian forces within 11 days, was signed. On the following day the UN Security Council adopted Resolution 1244 (with the People's Republic of China abstaining) approving the peace plan for Kosovo, and NATO announced the suspension of the air offensive, after it had been verified that the withdrawal of Serbian forces had commenced. NATO formally approved the establishment of a Kosovo Force (KFOR), and divided the province into five sectors (which were to be under the respective control of the United Kingdom, Germany, France, the USA and Italy). Shortly before NATO troops commenced deployment in Kosovo, however, about 200 Russian forces unexpectedly entered the province, and assumed control of the airport at Prishtina. Following discussions between the US Secretary of Defense, William Cohen, and his Russian counterpart, Igor Sergeyev, an agreement was reached whereby a Russian contingent, numbering about 3,600, would participate in KFOR (without controlling a separate sector as the Russian Government had previously demanded). Under the terms of the UN Resolution, the UN Interim Administration Mission in Kosovo (UNMIK, see p. 79) was established as the supreme legal and executive authority in Kosovo, with responsibility for civil administration, and for facilitating the reconstruction of the province as an autonomous region. A 3,100-member international police unit (which constituted part of UNMIK) was to supervise the creation of a new security force in Kosovo. The OSCE was allocated primary responsibility for installing democratic institutions, organizing elections in 2000 and monitoring human rights in the province. On 20 June 1999 NATO announced that the air campaign had officially ended, following the completion of the withdrawal of Serbian forces from Kosovo. The KLA subsequently signed an agreement with NATO, whereby the paramilitary organization was to disarm within a period of 90 days. On 24 June the Narodna skupština Republike Srbije formally ended the state of war in Serbia. Meanwhile, following the deployment of KFOR troops, nearly one-half of the ethnic Albanian refugees in neighbouring countries had returned to Kosovo by the end of the month, while an estimated 70,000 Serbian civilians had fled from the province, after reprisal attacks from KLA forces and members of the returning Albanian community. Investigators from the ICTY discovered increasing forensic evidence of large-scale massacres perpetrated by the Serbian forces against ethnic Albanian civilians during the conflict. Under a programme to establish partial provisional self-government in the province, elections to a Kosovo Assembly (Kuvendi i Kosovës/Skupština Kosova) were conducted in 2001 (see the chapter on Kosovo).

After the European Commission released a favourable report on Serbia and Montenegro in early April 2005, the resolution of Kosovo's future status became an increasingly pressing issue. The European Commission pledged to continue support for the eventual integration of Kosovo into European institutions, provided that the Kosovo Government demonstrated progress in meeting UN-endorsed standards of reform and democratic principles in eight areas. The process towards an agreement on a future status for Kosovo was expected to be problematic, since the authorities of Serbia and Montenegro strongly favoured conditions of increased autonomy, but less than total independence, while the Kosovo Albanian population insisted on unconditional independence; any final settlement was also to exclude any partition or border changes. In early June UN Secretary-General Kofi Annan appointed the Norwegian ambassador to NATO, Kai Eide, as the special envoy responsible for assessing standards in Kosovo, who was to undertake a comprehensive review of the provincial Government's commitment to democracy, good governance and human rights. A positive review would allow negotiations on the final status of the province to proceed; following their conclusion, a draft settlement (the 'Kosovo Accord'), would, together with a draft constitution prepared by the Kosovo Assembly, be submitted for endorsement by a UN-sponsored international conference. Later that month Eide conducted further discussions with leading members of the Serbian Government, including Tadić, to urge Serb participation in Kosovo's provisional institutions of government.

In September 2005 delegations from the Governments of Serbia and Kosovo met in Vienna, Austria, for preliminary discussions on decentralization and other technical issues. On 4 October Eide officially submitted the review on Kosovo to Annan; the report stated that the Government of Kosovo had made significant progress in establishing executive, legislative and judicial institutions, although efforts to maintain the rule of law and reduce the incidence of inter-ethnic attacks, violence and organized crime remained limited. On 24 October the UN Security Council endorsed the initiation of final status negotiations on Kosovo. In November the Serbian Government adopted a unanimous resolution rejecting any eventual proclamation of independence by Kosovo, while the Kosovo Assembly approved a motion stating that it would only accept independence as final status. Later that month a former Finnish President, Martti Ahtisaari, who had been appointed by Annan as the Special Envoy for the negotiations of Kosovo's future status, commenced separate discussions with Serbian and Kosovo leaders. Also in November the ICTY imposed a sentence (the first relating to crimes committed in Kosovo) of 13 years' imprisonment on a former KLA Commander who had been convicted of human rights abuses.

The first round of final status negotiations on Kosovo, which was conducted in Vienna on 20–21 February 2006, focused on issues related to decentralization, particularly the financing of ethnic Serb-majority municipalities. Serbia submitted a formal objection to the participation in the negotiations of the former KLA leader, Hashim Thaçi, accusing him of having committed crimes during the conflict in Kosovo. A third round of negotiations between the Kosovo Albanian and Serbian delegations again ended without agreement in April. After Montenegro's secession from the State Union of Serbia and Montenegro on 3 June (see above), the Serbian Government continued to resist strongly full independence for Kosovo, while agreeing to 'essential autonomy' for the province. At the instigation of Ahtisaari, direct high-level discussions, the first to involve the Presidents and Prime Ministers of Serbia and Kosovo since 1999, were conducted in Vienna in July 2006; the Kosovo delegation reiterated demands for full independence for the province by the end of that year, while the Serbian Prime Minister maintained that Serbia would not accept a loss of territory. The Kosovo delegation remained opposed to increased decentralization (including a Serbian proposal that a number of new Serb municipalities with autonomous powers be created), owing to concern that an effectively autonomous Serb polity would be established within the province. By the end of 2006 the two delegations had failed to reach any agreement on Kosovo's future status.

A new Serbian Constitution, which entered into effect in early November 2006, reaffirmed that Kosovo (again referred to as Kosovo and Metohija) was an integral part of the territory of Serbia, but that its status as an autonomous province entitled it to substantial autonomy. Following a subsequent announcement by the Serbian authorities that early legislative elections would take place on 21 January 2007, Ahtisaari declared that a proposed resolution for Kosovo's status (previously expected by the end of 2006) would be postponed until after the poll. Protests were subsequently staged in Kosovo, notably by supporters of an extreme ethnic-Albanian movement, Self-Determination (Vetevendosje), who attacked official buildings, including the Assembly and UNMIK headquarters. The province's authorities indicated that they would envisage a unilateral declaration of independence in the absence of a diplomatic resolution. On 2 February 2007 Ahtisaari presented his proposal for the future status of Kosovo to the Serbian and Kosovo authorities and invited the delegations to engage in consultations on the draft in Vienna. The discussions, which commenced on 21 February, ended on 10 March, with a meeting of the Serbian and Kosovo government leaders; Ahtisaari concluded that, in view of the failure of the delegations to compromise on previously stated positions, there was no further prospect of achieving a negotiated agreement. On 26 March Ahtisaari submitted to the UN Security Council the finalized Comprehensive Proposal for the Kosovo Status Settlement, which recommended independence, to be supervised and supported for an initial period by an international military and civilian presence. On 3 April, at the beginning of a debate in the UN Security Council, Prime Minister Koštunica declared that Serbia rejected the Proposal (following a vote in the Serbian legislature in February), and requested that a new mediator be appointed. On 5 April Ahtisaari's plan was approved by 100 of 101 votes cast in the Kosovo Assembly.

In August 2007, after Russia obstructed the adoption of a resolution based on Ahtisaari's plan at the UN Security Council, a further series of negotiations began between Serbian and Kosovo delegations, with mediation by the USA, the EU and Russia. On 7 December, shortly before the deadline stipulated by the UN, it was announced that the negotiations had failed to result in an agreement. On 26 December the Serbian legislature approved a resolution urging the Serbian Government to 'reconsider' diplomatic relations with any Western country that recognized Kosovo as independent. Relations between Russia and Serbia were consolidated in early 2008, with the signature of an agreement whereby Serbia was to join Russia's 'South Stream' pipeline project (see below), and Gazprom acquired a 51% share in the Serbian state-owned oil enterprise, Naftna Industrija Srbije.

In January 2008 Thaçi, who had become the new Prime Minister of Kosovo after elections there in November 2007 (see the chapter on Kosovo), announced his intention to achieve independence. On 17 February 2008 the Assembly of Kosovo adopted a declaration establishing the province as the Republic of Kosovo (Kosova), a sovereign state independent from Serbia, the resolution being based on Ahtisaari's Comprehensive Proposal for the Kosovo Status Settlement and in accordance with UN Security Council Resolution 1244 of 1999. Serbia, with the continued support of Russia, immediately protested that the declaration of independence contravened international law and demanded that it be annulled. On the following day the Serbian Ministry of the Interior issued arrest warrants against Thaçi and other Kosovo government officials for treason. KFOR reinforced the border between Kosovo and Serbia, after the destruction of two border posts by Serb protesters and reports that Serbian security forces had entered northern Kosovo. On 21 February Serb protesters rioted in Belgrade, attacking several embassies, including that of the United Kingdom and the USA. Several nations, including Albania, France, the USA and the United Kingdom, extended recognition to Kosovo on 18 February, followed by many others; Serbia immediately recalled its ambassadors based in those countries. In March the Serbian Government announced that it intended to submit a legal challenge against Kosovo's declaration of independence at the International Court of Justice and would also apply for international support at the UN General Assembly in September. By early May 39 UN member nations, including 19 EU member nations, had formally recognized Kosovo. In April UNMIK emphasized its opposition to plans by the Serbian Government to conduct polls in predominantly Serb municipalities when local elections took place in Serbia on 11 May, stating that this would violate UN Security Council Resolution 1244.

Government

On 5 June 2006 the Serbian legislature officially declared the Republic of Serbia to be the successor state to the State Union of Serbia and Montenegro (following Montenegro's declaration of independence on 3 June). Under the terms of a new Constitution, which officially entered into effect on 8 November, legislative power continued to be vested in the 250-member Narodna skupština Republike Srbije (National Assembly of the Republic of Serbia), which is directly elected for a period of four years. The President of the Republic, who is directly elected for a term of five years, nominates the Prime Minister for approval by the Narodna skupština. Executive power is vested in the Government, which is proposed to the Narodna skupština by the designated Prime Minister. The Narodna skupština is to be dissolved if it fails to appoint a new Government within 90 days of its inaugural session. The 11-member High Judicial Council ensures the independence of courts and judges, and is empowered to nominate or remove judges. Serbia formally comprises 24 administrative regions, including the seven regions of the province of Vojvodina, in the north of Serbia, which are divided into 170 municipalities; the territory of the former autonomous province of Kosovo, officially part of Serbia until 17 February 2008 (see Recent History), comprised seven regions.

Defence

Military service is compulsory for men, and lasts for six months. Voluntary military service for women was introduced in 1983. As assessed at November 2007, the estimated total strength of the armed forces was 24,257, of which the army accounted for 11,180 (including 1,724 conscripts) and the air force 4,155. Reserves totalled 54,249 personnel. In December Serbia was admitted to the 'Partnership for Peace' (see p. 342) programme of the North Atlantic Treaty Organization (NATO). The budget for 2007 allocated 57,000m. dinars to defence.

Economic Affairs

In 2006, according to estimates by the World Bank, the gross national income (GNI) of Serbia, measured at 2004–06 prices, was US $29,011m., equivalent to $3,910 per head. During 1998–2006, it was estimated, the population declined by an annual average of 0.2%, while gross domestic product (GDP) per head increased, in real terms, by 5.5% during 2000–06. Overall GDP increased, in real terms, at an average annual rate of 5.3% in 2000–06; growth was 5.8% in 2006.

Agriculture (including hunting, forestry and fishing) contributed 11.2% of GDP in 2006. In 2007 some 20.8% of the total employed labour force were engaged in the sector. Serbia's principal crops are maize, wheat, sugar beet and potatoes. The cultivation of fruit and vegetables is also important. Agricultural production (including Montenegro) decreased by an annual average of 1.4% in 2000–06, but increased by 2.2% in 2006.

Industry (including mining, manufacturing, construction and power) contributed 28.8% of GDP in 2006, and engaged 29.5% of the employed labour force in 2007. Industrial production (including Montenegro) increased by an annual average of 2.4% in 2000–06. According to figures from the World Bank, industrial output (including Montenegro) increased by 3.7% in 2006.

The mining and quarrying sector contributed 1.7% of GDP in 2006, and engaged 1.6% of the employed labour force in 2007. The principal minerals extracted are coal (mainly brown coal), copper ore and bauxite. Iron ore, crude petroleum, lead and zinc ore and natural gas are also produced. Sectoral output increased at an average annual rate of 3.7% in 2002–06. Production in the mining and quarrying sector of Serbia increased by 4.9% in 2006.

The manufacturing sector contributed an estimated 18.1% of GDP in 2006, and engaged 19.6% of the employed labour force in 2007. Manufacturing production in Serbia increased at an average annual rate of 1.9% per year in 2002–06, according to official figures. Manufacturing output declined by 0.1% in 2005, but increased by an estimated 5.6% in 2006.

Energy in Serbia (including Montenegro) is derived principally from coal (which provided about 69.9% of total electricity generated in 2003) and hydroelectric power (27.9%). Imports of mineral fuels accounted for 19.7% of the value of total imports to Serbia in 2006.

Services contributed 60.0% of GDP in 2006. Some 49.7% of the employed labour force were engaged in the sector in 2007. Services GDP (including Montenegro) increased by an annual average of 7.0% in 2000–06; GDP increased by 9.2% in 2006. Total foreign tourist arrivals in Serbia increased from 339,000 in 2003 to 469,000 in 2006.

In 2004 Serbia and Montenegro recorded a trade deficit of an estimated US $7,344m., and there was a deficit of an estimated $3,597m. on the current account of the balance of payments. In 2006 the principal source of imports to Serbia was Russia (accounting for 16.3% of the total); other major sources were Germany, Italy and the People's Republic of China. The principal market for exports in that year was Italy (taking 14.4% of all exports); other important purchasers were Bosnia and Herzegovina and Germany. (These figures excluded trade to or from Kosovo.) The main exports in 2006 were basic manufactures, food and live animals, miscellaneous manufactured articles, machinery and transport equipment, and chemicals. The principal imports in that year were machinery and transport equipment, basic manufactures, mineral fuels and lubricants, chemicals, and miscellaneous manufactured articles.

In 2007, according to projected figures, the overall budgetary surplus for Serbia and Montenegro was 24,600m. dinars. At the end of 2005 the total external debt of Serbia and Montenegro was $16,295m., of which $7,972m. was long-term public debt. In 2003 the cost of debt-servicing was equivalent to 7.8% of the value of exports of goods and services. In 1996–2004 the rate of inflation in Serbia and Montenegro increased by an annual average of 35.5%. Consumer prices in Serbia increased by 15.3% in 2006 and by 5.8% in 2007. The rate of unemployment in Serbia was estimated at 18.1% in 2007.

Following political changes in the Federal Republic of Yugoslavia (FRY) in September 2000, the country was admitted to the UN on 1 November. It was readmitted to the Organization for Security and Co-operation in Europe (OSCE, see p. 354) later in November, to the IMF in December and to the World Bank in May 2001. Serbia and Montenegro officially became a member of the Council of Europe (see p. 225) in April 2003.

Following the election of a new Government in September 2000, the FRY's integration into international institutions progressed rapidly. In October the European Union (EU, see p. 244) ended all sanctions against the FRY, and it was agreed that the country would receive aid under the EU's programme for Balkan reconstruction, development and stabilization. In December the FRY was readmitted to the IMF, and was granted emergency post-conflict assistance. The US Government officially ended economic sanctions against the FRY in January 2001; however, subsequent financial support from the USA was made conditional on the Yugoslav authorities' co-operation with the International Criminal Tribunal for the former Yugoslavia (ICTY, see p. 18). The establishment of the State Union of Serbia and Montenegro in February 2003 was expected to further the normalization of economic relations between the two republics, with the harmonization of trade, customs and tax systems in accordance with EU standards. In January 2005, however, the USA expressed dissatisfaction with Serbia and Montenegro's failure to co-operate with the ICTY, and announced punitive measures, including a reduction in financial aid. Following the extradition of a number of Serb war crimes suspects to the Tribunal, the European Commission indicated, in April, that sufficient progress had been made for Serbia and Montenegro to commence negotiations on a Stabilization and Association Agreement (SAA) with the EU, subject to continued reforms and ongoing co-operation with the ICTY. Negotiations officially commenced in October. Meanwhile, in February 2006 the IMF approved the completion of its extended three-year stand-by credit arrangement with Serbia and Montenegro, allowing the country to secure a final cancellation of outstanding debt, under the terms of an agreement made in 2001 with the 'Paris Club' of international creditors. In early 2006, however, the EU made the continuation of negotiations on the SAA increasingly conditional on the extradition of the principal Serb war crimes suspect, Ratko Mladić, to the ICTY, and at the beginning of May discussions were suspended, after the Serbian Government failed to comply with an ultimatum. On 5 June, after Montenegro officially declared its independence (see Recent History), Serbia officially declared itself to be the successor state to the State Union (thereby inheriting membership of international organizations). In early July the Serbian and Montenegrin Ministers of Finance and Central Bank Governors signed an agreement to divide financial rights and obligations of the two republics. Protracted failure to form a government an administration followed legislative elections in January 2007; in April a coalition Government of pro-democratic parties, again under the premiership of Dr Vojislav Koštunica, was finally established. The new Government was expected to introduce a restrictive budget in compliance with IMF recommendations, and initiate measures to address the extremely low level of foreign investment. According to the IMF, foreign direct investment increased in 2006 and, in addition to capital transfers, contributed 17% of GDP that year. (In early 2008, however, political instability following Kosovo's declaration of independence and the collapse of the coalition Government soon afterwards were expected further to limit foreign investment.) Negotiations on the SAA resumed in June 2007 and, despite the failure of the Government to arrest and extradite Mladić and other suspected war criminals, the Agreement was eventually signed with the EU in April 2008, fulfilling the promise of newly re-elected President Boris Tadić to create closer ties with Europe. However, implementation of the SAA was to be suspended until EU member states agreed unanimously on Serbia's full co-operation with the ICTY. The EU's decision was widely perceived as an effort to strengthen popular support for reformist parties contesting the legislative elections, which were brought forward to 11 May after the resignation of Koštunica's administration (see Recent History). The IMF estimated GDP growth of 7.3% in 2007 and forecast growth of 4.0% in 2008, the anticipated downturn being mainly attributed to political instability and the consequence of stalled economic reforms.

Education

Elementary education is free and compulsory for all children between the ages of seven and 15, when children attend the 'eight-year school'. Various types of secondary education are available to all who qualify, but the vocational and technical schools are the most popular. Alternatively, children may attend a general secondary school (gymnasium) where they follow a four-year course, prior to university entrance. At the secondary level there are also a number of art schools, apprentice schools and teacher-training schools. In 2000/01 some 95.8% of children in the appropriate age-group) were enrolled in primary schools, while enrolment at secondary schools was equivalent to 88.7% of students in the relevant age-group. In 2006/07 238,710 students were enrolled in higher education faculties. Serbia has seven state universities, including the University of Belgrade, which was established in 1863, and seven private universities.

Public Holidays

2008: 1–2 January (New Year), 7–8 January (Christmas), 15 February (National Day), 25–28 April (Orthodox Easter), 1–2 May (Labour Days), 9 May (Victory Day).
2009: 1–2 January (New Year), 7–8 January (Christmas), 15 February (National Day), 17–20 April (Orthodox Easter), 1–2 May (Labour Days), 9 May (Victory Day).

Weights and Measures

The metric system is in force.

SERBIA

Statistical Survey

Source (unless otherwise indicated): Statistical Office of the Republic of Serbia, 11000 Belgrade, Milana Rakića 5; tel. (11) 2412922; fax (11) 2411260; internet webrzs.statserb.sr.gov.yu/axd/en/index.php.

Note: Except where otherwise stated, figures in this survey include the province of Kosovo, which declared independence from Serbia on 17 February 2008. Certain figures pertain to the former Federal Republic of Yugoslavia (comprising Serbia and Montenegro), or to the State Union of those two republics that succeeded it in 2003, and that continued until Montenegro became independent in 2006.

Area and Population

AREA, POPULATION AND DENSITY

Area (sq km)	88,361*
Population (census results)†	
31 March 1991	7,576,837
31 March 2002	
Males	3,645,930
Females	3,852,071
Total	7,498,001
Population (official estimates at mid-year)†	
2004	7,463,157
2005	7,440,769
2006	7,411,569
Density (per sq km) at mid-2006†	95.7

* 34,116 sq miles; including Kosovo (10,887 sq km—4,203 sq miles).
† Excluding population and area of Kosovo.

Kosovo (population at 1991 census, unrevised figure): 1,956,196.

ADMINISTRATIVE DIVISIONS
(2002 census, excluding Kosovo)

	Area (sq km)	Population ('000)	Density (per sq km)	Principal city
Capital				
Belgrade	3,224	1,576,124	488.9	—
Okruzi (Districts)				
Bor	3,507	146,551	41.8	Bor
Braničevo	3,865	200,503	51.9	Požarevac
Jablanica	2,769	240,923	87.0	Leskovac
Kolubara	2,474	192,204	77.7	Valjevo
Mačva	3,268	329,625	100.9	Šabac
Moravica	3,016	224,772	74.5	Čačak
Nišava	2,729	381,757	139.9	Niš
Pčinja	3,520	227,690	64.7	Vranje
Pirot	2,761	105,654	38.3	Pirot
Podunavlje	1,248	210,290	168.5	Smederevo
Pomoravlje	2,614	227,435	87.0	Jagodina
Rasina	2,668	259,441	97.2	Kruševac
Raška	3,918	291,230	74.3	Kraljevo
Šumadija	2,387	298,778	125.2	Kragujevac
Toplica	2,231	102,075	45.8	Prokuplje
Zaječar	3,623	137,561	38.0	Zaječar
Zlatibor	6,140	313,396	51.0	Užice
Province				
Vojvodina	21,536	2,031,992	94.4	Novi Sad
Okruzi (Districts) within the Province of Vojvodina				
Central Banat	3,256	208,456	64.0	Zrenjanin
North Bačka	1,784	200,140	112.2	Subotica
North Banat	2,329	165,881	71.2	Kikinda
South Bačka	4,016	593,666	147.8	Novi Sad
South Banat	4,245	313,937	74.0	Pančevo
Srem	3,486	335,901	96.4	Sremska Mitrovica
West Bačka	2,420	214,011	88.4	Sombor
Total	77,498	7,498,001	96.8	—

PRINCIPAL TOWNS
(population at 2002 census unless otherwise indicated; excluding Kosovo)

Beograd (Belgrade, the capital)	1,576,124	Kraljevo	121,707
Novi Sad	299,294	Čačak	117,072
Niš	250,518	Smederevo	109,809
Kragujevac	175,802	Sombor	97,263
Leskovac	156,252	Valjevo	96,761
Subotica	148,401	Vranje	87,288
Zrenjanin	132,051	Loznica	86,413
Kruševac	131,368	Novi Pazar	85,996
Pančevo	127,162	Sremska Mitrovica	85,902
Šabac	122,893	Užice	83,022

Prishtina (Prishtinë—Priština) (Capital of Kosovo): 155,409 at 1991 census.

POPULATION BY ETHNIC GROUP
(2002 census, excluding Kosovo)

Ethnic group	Population ('000)	%
Serbs	6,213	82.9
Hungarians	293	3.9
Bosniaks	136	1.8
Roma	108	1.4
Yugoslavs	81	1.1
Croats	71	0.9
Montenegrins	69	0.9
Others	527	7.0
Total	**7,498**	**100.0**

1991 census ('000, including Montenegro and Kosovo): Serbs 6,504 (62.6%); Albanians 1,715 (16.5%); Montenegrins 520 (5.0%); Yugoslavs 350 (3.4%); Hungarians 344 (3.3%); Muslims 336 (3.2%).

BIRTHS, MARRIAGES AND DEATHS
(excluding Kosovo)

	Registered live births		Registered marriages		Registered deaths	
	Number	Rate (per 1,000)	Number	Rate (per 1,000)	Number	Rate (per 1,000)
1999	72,222	9.3	37,256	4.9	101,444	13.1
2000	73,764	9.6	42,586	5.7	104,042	13.6
2001	78,435	10.1	41,406	5.5	99,008	12.8
2002	78,101	10.4	41,947	5.6	102,785	13.7
2003	79,025	10.6	41,914	5.6	103,946	13.9
2004	78,186	10.5	42,030	5.6	104,320	14.0
2005	72,180	9.7	n.a.	n.a.	106,771	14.3
2006	70,997	9.6	n.a.	n.a.	102,884	13.9

SERBIA

ECONOMICALLY ACTIVE POPULATION
(labour force survey, persons aged 15 years and over, October 2007)*

	Males	Females	Total
Agriculture, forestry, fishing and water works	336,066	216,527	552,592
Mining and quarrying	31,566	9,695	41,261
Manufacturing	347,016	174,728	521,744
Electricity, gas and water	41,729	16,232	57,961
Construction	144,403	16,848	161,251
Wholesale and retail trade	186,511	211,958	398,470
Hotels and restaurants	34,882	37,435	72,317
Transport, storage and communications	135,584	34,185	169,769
Financial intermediation	17,358	25,687	43,044
Real estate and property	51,685	37,169	88,855
Public administration and social security	80,340	61,598	141,938
Education	38,337	79,727	118,064
Health and social work	38,202	128,203	166,405
Other community, social and personal services	61,207	52,914	114,121
Households with employed persons	389	6,046	6,435
Extra-territorial organizations and bodies	483	1,026	1,509
Total employed	1,545,758	1,109,979	2,655,736
Unemployed	289,803	295,669	585,472
Total labour force	1,835,561	1,405,648	3,241,208

* Excluding Kosovo.

Health and Welfare

KEY INDICATORS
(data for Serbia and Montenegro unless otherwise indicated)

Total fertility rate (children per woman, 2005, Serbia only)	1.8
Under-5 mortality rate (per 1,000 live births, 2005, Serbia only)	9
HIV/AIDS (% of persons aged 15–49, 2005)	0.2
Physicians (per 1,000 head, 2002)	2.06
Hospital beds (per 1,000 head, 2005, Serbia only)	5.9
Health expenditure (2003): US $ per head (PPP)	373
Health expenditure (2003): % of GDP	9.6
Health expenditure (2003): public (% of total)	75.5
Access to water (% of persons, 2004)	93
Access to sanitation (% of persons, 2004)	87

For sources and definitions, see explanatory note on p. vi.

Agriculture

(Data for Serbia and Montenegro)

PRINCIPAL CROPS
('000 metric tons)

	2004*	2005*	2006†
Wheat	2,761.0	2,009.7	1,875.3
Barley	409.0	311.1	275.6
Maize	6,579.0	7,095.0	6,016.8
Oats	119.4	91.0	84.4
Potatoes	1,108.0	1,102.4	930.3
Sugar beet	2,643.0	3,101.2	3,188.9
Dry beans	62.0	58.7	54.5‡
Soybeans (Soya beans)	317.8	368.0	429.6
Sunflower seed	437.6	350.8	384.9
Cabbages and other brassicas	383.0	297.2	324.7
Tomatoes	208.0	189.9	189.2
Chillies and green peppers	160.0	167.5	177.3
Dry onions	145.9§	133.1	140.3

—continued	2004*	2005*	2006†
Carrots and turnips	70.1	63.7	68.1
Watermelons	306.0	313.5	251.1
Apples	188.0	202.1	240.3
Pears	60.2	48.8	57.7
Sour (Morello) cherries	113.2	63.9	80.5
Peaches and nectarines	61.9	55.5	59.1
Plums and sloes	567.0	311.8	556.2
Raspberries and other berries	91.7	112.0	79.7
Grapes	467.0	277.6	359.5
Tobacco (leaves)	13.0	11.8	10.8

* Data for Serbia and Montenegro.
† Data for Serbia only.
‡ FAO estimate.
§ Unofficial figure.

Aggregate production (data for Serbia and Montenegro, unless otherwise indicated, '000 metric tons, may include official, semi-official or estimated data): Total cereals 9,893.0 in 2004, 9,533.9 in 2005, 8,277.4 in 2006 (Serbia only); Total roots and tubers 1,108.0 in 2004, 1,102.4 in 2005, 930.3 in 2006 (Serbia only); Total vegetables (incl. melons) 1,357.9 in 2004, 1,251.8 in 2005, 1,337.4 in 2006 (Serbia only); Total fruits (excl. melons) 1,668.6 in 2004, 1,162.5 in 2005, 1,524.1 in 2006 (Serbia only).

Source: FAO.

LIVESTOCK
('000 head, year ending 30 September)

	2004*	2005*	2006†
Horses	35	42	19
Cattle	1,276	1,213	1,096
Pigs	3,463	3,224	3,212
Sheep	1,838	1,866	1,609
Goats	195	139	139
Chickens	15,000‡	15,683§	17,905

* Data for Serbia and Montenegro.
† Data for Serbia only.
‡ Unofficial figure.
§ FAO estimate.

Source: FAO.

LIVESTOCK PRODUCTS
('000 metric tons)

	2004*	2005*	2006†
Cattle meat	161‡	156	83
Sheep meat	20	21	20
Pig meat	539	562	255
Chicken meat	65	67	75
Cows' milk	1,807	1,833	1,587
Sheep's milk	25	24	15
Hen eggs	76	77	73
Honey‡	4	4	4

* Data refer to Serbia and Montenegro.
† Data refer to Serbia only.
‡ Unofficial figure(s).

Source: FAO.

Forestry

(Data for Serbia and Montenegro)

ROUNDWOOD REMOVALS
('000 cubic metres, excl. bark)

	2003	2004	2005
Sawlogs, veneer logs and logs for sleepers	1,082	1,138	1,096
Pulpwood	106	196	168
Other industrial roundwood	66	89	52
Fuel wood	1,901	2,097	1,854
Total	3,155	3,520	3,170

2006: Figures assumed to be unchanged from 2005 (FAO estimates).

Source: FAO.

SERBIA

SAWNWOOD PRODUCTION
('000 cubic metres, including railway sleepers)

	2003	2004	2005
Coniferous (softwood)	158	207	154
Non-coniferous (hardwood)	356	368	343
Total	514	575	497

2006: Figures assumed to be unchanged from 2005 (FAO estimates).
Source: FAO.

Fishing
(Data for Serbia and Montenegro)

('000 metric tons, live weight)

	2003	2004	2005
Capture	1.8	2.4	2.5*
Freshwater fishes	1.0	1.6	1.7
Common carp	0.1	0.2	0.1*
Aquaculture	3.2	4.6	4.6*
Rainbow trout	2.6	4.0	n.a.
Total catch	5.0	7.0	7.0*

* FAO estimate.

Note: Figures exclude marine shells (metric tons): 3.1 in 2002; 3.1 in 2003; 3.0 in 2004; n.a. in 2005.
Source: FAO.

Mining

('000 metric tons unless otherwise indicated, excluding Kosovo)

	2004	2005	2006
Coal	34,786	35,635	37,327
Lignite	33,753	34,565	n.a.
Crude petroleum	653	648	654
Natural gas (million cubic metres)	317	282	283
Lead and zinc ore	111	162	n.a.
Copper ore	5,495	6,005	n.a.
Clay and kaolin	108	135	215

Industry

SELECTED PRODUCTS
('000 metric tons, unless otherwise indicated; excluding Kosovo)

	2004	2005	2006
Refined vegetable oils	101.6	102.7	110.4
Fruit and vegetable juices	126.0	167.9	181.2
Beer ('000 hectolitres)	5,328	5,206	6,568
Cigarettes (million)	15,107	17,324	27,581
Cotton yarn (metric tons)	1,048	765	1,239
Wool yarn (metric tons)	762	535	36
Hosiery ('000 pairs)	73,505	76,934	68,984
Underwear ('000 units)	9,463	7,398	7,270
Leather footwear ('000 pairs)	2,775	3,143	5,678
Parquet wooden flooring ('000 sq metres)	441.5	331.5	363.3
Paper and cardboard	106.6	102.6	92.3
Newsprint	42.2	37.7	45.9
Cement	2,240	2,276	2,565
Motor spirit (gasoline)	808	728	n.a.
Gas-diesel (distillate fuel) oil	1,005	876	n.a.
Residual fuel oil	714	900	n.a.

—continued	2004	2005	2006
Nitrogenous fertilizers	630.1	596.4	679.6
Rubber tyres for vehicles ('000)	7,839	8,114	13,230
Pig-iron	959.0	1,115.2	n.a.
Flat-rolled steel products	1,543.5	1,890.3	n.a.
Electric light bulbs ('000)	3,241	4,441	n.a.
Alternating current motors (units)	114,438	72,916	n.a.
Tractors (number)	5,392	4,356	2,387
Motor cars (number)	14,549	15,666	11,762
Kitchen wooden furniture ('000 units)	44.5	44.8	n.a.
Electric energy (million kWh)	33,874	36,474	36,495

Finance

CURRENCY AND EXCHANGE RATES (excluding Kosovo)

Monetary Units
100 para = 1 Serbian dinar.

Sterling, Dollar and Euro Equivalents (31 December 2007)
£1 sterling = 107.64 dinars;
US $1 = 53.73 dinars;
€1 = 79.10 dinars;
1,000 Serbian dinars = £9.29 = $18.61 = €12.64.

Average Exchange Rate (dinars per US $)
2005   66.71
2006   67.15
2007   58.45

CURRENCY AND EXCHANGE RATES (Kosovo)

Monetary Units
100 cent = 1 euro (€).

Sterling and Dollar Equivalents (31 December 2007)
£1 sterling = 1.3609 euros;
US $1 = 0.6793 euros;
€10 = £7.35 = $14.72.

Average Exchange Rate (euros per US $)
2005   0.8041
2006   0.7971
2007   0.7306.

Note: In September 1999 the UN decided to adopt the Deutsche Mark (DM) as the currency for official transactions in the Serbian province of Kosovo. Euro notes and coins were introduced on 1 January 2002, at an exchange rate of €1 = 1.95583 DM.

CONSOLIDATED BUDGET
('000 million dinars)

Revenue*	2005	2006	2007†
Current revenue	715.6	855.3	988.5
Personal income tax	94.3	118.6	115.0
Social security contributions	185.3	231.4	268.7
Corporate income tax	10.3	18.3	29.3
Retail sales tax; value added tax	216.0	225.2	270.0
Excises	71.3	86.9	99.8
Taxes on international trade and operations	39.0	45.3	58.9
Other taxes and non-tax revenue	99.5	129.6	146.9
Capital revenue	7.9	10.3	12.1
Total	723.5	865.6	1,000.6

SERBIA

Statistical Survey

Expenditure	2005	2006	2007†
Current expenditure	660.3	807.3	913.3
Wages and salaries	171.3	204.4	244.1
Expenditure on goods and services	125.5	156.6	183.1
Interest payments	24.9	30.2	21.7
Subsidies and other current transfers	338.5	416.1	464.3
Capital expenditure	45.0	80.4	101.4
Lending minus repayments	5.4	10.7	11.0
Total	**710.7**	**898.4**	**1,025.7**

* Excluding grants received ('000 million dinars): 1.1 in 2005; 1.9 in 2006; 0.5 in 2007 (projected).
† Projected figures.

Source: IMF, *Republic of Serbia: 2007 Article IV Consultation—Staff Report; Staff Statement; Public Information Notice on the Executive Board Discussion; and Statement by the Executive Director for the Republic of Serbia* (February 2008).

INTERNATIONAL RESERVES
(US $ million at 31 December)

	2005	2006	2007
Gold	147.0	235.9	323.2
IMF special drawing rights	30.2	8.8	0.8
Foreign exchange	5,597.7	11,638.9	13,891.8
Total	**5,774.9**	**11,883.6**	**14,215.8**

Source: IMF, *International Financial Statistics*.

MONEY SUPPLY
(million dinars at 31 December)

	2005	2006	2007
Currency outside banks	53,649.9	68,460.8	76,948.5
Demand deposits	85,310.5	122,143.7	161,945.9
Total money (incl. others)	**144,948.9**	**200,089.7**	**248,838.6**

Source: IMF, *International Financial Statistics*.

COST OF LIVING
(Consumer Price Index at January; base: 2004=100)

	2005	2006	2007
Food	92.0	108.1	111.2
Tobacco and beverages	94.5	107.4	128.4
Clothing (incl. footwear)	96.7	107.8	115.4
Rent	95.2	110.4	115.2
All items (incl. others)	**93.5**	**107.8**	**114.0**

NATIONAL ACCOUNTS
('000 million dinars at current prices)*

Expenditure on the Gross Domestic Product

	2004	2005	2006
Final consumption expenditure	1,296.0	1,536.0	1,785.7
Gross fixed capital formation	253.3	302.0	403.1
Changes in inventories	205.4	160.6	150.7
Statistical discrepancy	61.9	99.2	112.4
Total domestic expenditure	**1,816.6**	**2,097.8**	**2,451.9**
Exports of goods and services	341.2	484.2	627.0
Less Imports of goods and services	726.4	834.5	1,036.9
Gross domestic product at market prices	**1,431.3**	**1,747.5**	**2,042.0**

Gross Domestic Product by Economic Activity

	2004	2005	2006
Agriculture, hunting, forestry and water works	164.4	173.6	191.0
Fishing	0.4	0.5	0.6
Mining and quarrying	21.0	25.7	28.4
Manufacturing	208.4	252.2	310.7
Electricity, gas and water	53.0	59.6	74.2
Construction	57.0	65.3	81.4
Wholesale and retail trade; and repairs	116.0	177.1	218.3
Restaurants and hotels	13.3	17.7	22.6
Transport, storage and communications	94.8	125.5	138.4
Financial intermediation	48.6	57.9	70.9
Real estate, renting and business activities	188.1	230.7	280.2
Public administration and defence; compulsory social security	84.0	80.7	68.0
Education	51.0	64.5	79.0
Health and social work	69.2	83.5	98.8
Other community, social and personal services	30.5	41.5	51.8
Private households with employed persons	1.3	1.5	1.5
Gross value added in basic prices †	**1,201.2**	**1,457.4**	**1,715.6**
Taxes on products / *Less* Subsidies on products	230.1	290.1	326.4
GDP in market prices	**1,431.3**	**1,747.5**	**2,042.0**

* Excluding Kosovo.
† Deduction for financial intermediation services indirectly measured assumed to be distributed by sector.

BALANCE OF PAYMENTS
(including Montenegro, US $ million)

	2003	2004*
Exports of goods f.o.b.	3,054	4,044
Imports of goods c.i.f.	−7,941	−11,388
Trade balance	**−4,886**	**−7,344**
Exports of services	1,130	1,646
Imports of services	−795	−1,046
Balance on goods and services	**−4,552**	**−6,744**
Factor income received from abroad	70	81
Factor income paid abroad	−291	−352
Balance on goods, services and income	**−4,773**	**−7,015**
Private remittances and other transfers received from abroad	2,661	4,035
Private remittances and other transfers paid abroad	−422	−598
Adjustment	—	−19
Current balance (excl. grants)	**−2,543**	**−3,597**
Official grants	538	562
Foreign direct investment (net)	1,405	1,031
Medium- and short-term loans: disbursements	974	2,119
Medium- and long-term loans: amortization	−218	−513
Short-term loans and deposits (net)	66	393
Other capital inflows	281	58
Commercial banks (net)	31	88
Net errors and omissions	409	505
Overall balance	**943**	**646**

* Estimates.

Source: IMF, *Serbia and Montenegro: Sixth Review Under the Extended Arrangement, Financing Assurances Review, Request for Waivers of Non-observance of Performance Criteria, and Proposed Post-Program Monitoring—Staff Report; Press Release on the Executive Board Discussion; and Statement by the Executive Director for Serbia and Montenegro* (February 2006).

External Trade

PRINCIPAL COMMODITY GROUPS
(distribution by SITC, US $ million)*

Imports c.i.f.	2004	2005	2006
Food and live animals	625	591	649
Beverages and tobacco	162	115	160
Crude materials (inedible) except fuels	333	467	627
Mineral fuels, lubricants, etc.	1,634	2,029	2,595
Chemicals and related products	1,411	1,467	1,867
Basic manufactures	2,116	2,168	2,743
Machinery and transport equipment	3,388	2,693	3,376
Miscellaneous manufactured articles	1,023	879	1,098
Total (incl. others)	10,753	10,461	13,170

Exports f.o.b.	2004	2005	2006
Food and live animals	641	776	1,065
Crude materials (inedible) except fuels	196	198	278
Mineral fuels, lubricants, etc.	91	164	225
Chemicals and related products	385	494	650
Basic manufactures	1,184	1,595	2,418
Machinery and transport equipment	378	443	711
Miscellaneous manufactured articles	507	703	914
Total (incl. others)	3,523	4,482	6,427

* Excluding Kosovo.

Kosovo (US $ million, 1998): Total imports 117; total exports 38.

PRINCIPAL TRADING PARTNERS
(US $ million)*

Imports c.i.f.	2004	2005	2006
Austria	289	254	227
Bosnia and Herzegovina	235	292	343
Bulgaria	221	203	421
China, People's Republic	521	509	782
Croatia	205	258	334
Czech Republic	213	194	214
France	347	290	342
Germany	1,446	1,091	1,251
Greece	200	157	200
Hungary	311	267	306
Italy	1,039	909	1,100
Romania	202	274	437
Russia	1,396	1,669	2,142
Slovenia	332	285	308
Sweden	219	129	166
Turkey	198	211	256
Ukraine	275	284	289
USA	355	279	240
Total (incl. others)	10,753	10,461	13,170

Exports f.o.b.	2004	2005	2006
Bosnia and Herzegovina	626	744	749
Croatia	149	196	251
France	135	162	235
Germany	352	435	637
Greece	119	122	153
Hungary	120	131	188
Italy	448	652	926
Macedonia, former Yugoslav republic	257	261	300
Romania	123	130	177
Russia	153	225	311
Slovenia	155	189	253
Total (incl. others)	3,523	4,482	6,427

* Excluding figures for Kosovo.

Transport

RAILWAYS
(traffic)

	2004	2005	2006
Passengers carried ('000)	7,569	6,492	6,445
Passenger-kilometres (million)	821	713	684
Freight carried ('000 metric tons)	12,293	12,568	14,139
Freight ton-kilometres (million)	3,164	3,482	4,232

ROAD TRAFFIC
(motor vehicles in use)

	2004	2005	2006
Passenger cars	1,449,843	1,481,498	1,511,837
Buses and coaches	9,125	9,696	9,312
Goods vehicles	109,292	116,440	126,045
Special purpose vehicles			
Passenger	16,462	15,920	15,109
Cargo	109,292	116,440	n.a.
Articulated vehicles	91,546	101,465	103,859
Tractors	132,711	126,816	128,017
Motorcycles and mopeds	14,771	16,042	20,380

INLAND WATERWAYS

Traffic
('000 metric tons, national and international traffic at river ports, excl. transit)

	2004	2005	2006
Goods loaded	2,876	6,338	6,045
Goods unloaded	5,841	8,708	7,979

CIVIL AVIATION
(scheduled and non-scheduled services)

	2004	2005	2006
Kilometres flown (million)	19	17	18
Passengers carried ('000)	1,289	1,122	1,216
Passenger-kilometres (million)	1,387	1,219	1,252
Cargo carried (metric tons)	6,058	4,945	4,678
Total ton-kilometres (million)	8	6	5

Tourism

FOREIGN TOURIST ARRIVALS
('000 at accommodation establishments, excluding Kosovo)

Country of origin	2004	2005	2006
Bosnia and Herzegovina	45	49	54
Bulgaria	16	16	18
Croatia	25	29	34
Germany	25	29	28
Greece	19	25	27
Italy	24	28	28
Macedonia, former Yugoslav republic	29	30	26
Slovenia	42	56	54
Total (incl. others)	392	453	469

Tourism receipts (including Montenegro, US $ million, excl. passenger transport): 54 in 2001; 97 in 2002; 201 in 2003 (Source: World Tourism Organization).

Communications Media

	2003	2004	2005
Telephones (fixed network, '000 subscribers)	2,409.3	2,485.2	2,672.7
Mobile cellular telephones ('000 subscribers)	2,990.8	4,053.0	5,222.1

Education

(2005/06, unless otherwise indicated, excluding Kosovo)

	Institutions	Teachers	Students
Pre-primary	2,062	19,738	173,203
Regular primary	3,572	46,353	639,293
Special primary	245	1,606	7,707
Primary education of adults	19	235	2,653
Regular secondary	478	27,565	287,397
Special secondary	41		1,465
Accessory	100	n.a.	20,965
Higher*	272	6,304	238,710

* 2006/07, preliminary.

Adult literacy rate (including Montenegro): 96.4% (males 98.9%; females 94.1%) in 2002 (Source: UNESCO Institute for Statistics).

Directory

The Constitution

Serbia officially declared itself to be the successor state to the State Union of Serbia and Montenegro on 5 June 2006. A new Constitution of the Republic of Serbia was endorsed by national referendum on 28–29 October and entered into force on 8 November. Under the Constitution, the Province of Kosovo and Metohija is an integral part of Serbia and has substantial autonomy within Serbia. The Constitutions's main provisions are summarized below.

PRINCIPLES

The Republic of Serbia is a state of the Serb people and of all citizens who live in the Republic, based on the rule of law and social justice, principles of human rights and freedoms, and commitment to European principles and values. Sovereignty is vested in all citizens, who exercise it through referendums, people's initiatives, and by way of their freely elected representatives. Judicial power is independent. The territory of the Republic of Serbia is indivisible. The Republic of Serbia is a secular state. The right of citizens to provincial autonomy and local self-government is subject only to the terms of constitutionality and legality. The Constitution provides guarantees for human and minority rights and freedoms. There is no death penalty in the Republic of Serbia. Criminal prosecution or punishment for war crimes, genocide, or crimes against humanity is not subject to a statute of limitations. The economic system in the Republic of Serbia is based on the principles of the market economy. The official language is Serbian and the official script is Cyrillic. The official use of other languages and scripts shall be regulated by law.

ORGANIZATION OF GOVERNMENT

The Narodna skupština Republike Srbije (National Assembly of the Republic of Serbia) is the supreme representative body in the Republic of Serbia. The Narodna skupština comprises 250 deputies, who are directly elected for a term of four years. The Narodna skupština adopts decisions by a majority vote. The President of the Republic may dissolve the Narodna skupština, in response to a request by the Government. The Government may not propose the dissolution of the Narodna skupština if a proposal has been submitted for a vote of 'no confidence' in the Government. The Narodna skupština shall be dissolved if it fails to elect the Government within 90 days from the day of its inauguration.

The President of the Republic, who is directly elected for a term of five years, nominates the Prime Minister for approval by the Narodna skupština. In accordance with the law, the President commands the army, and appoints and dismisses army officers. Executive power is vested in the Government, which is proposed to the Narodna skupština by the nominee for Prime Minister.

Certain affairs of public administration may be delegated to the bodies of the autonomous provinces or to of local self-government. The Civic Defender, who shall be elected by the Narodna skupština, is empowered to protect citizens' rights and monitor the work of public administrative bodies.

The Supreme Court of Cassation, which is the Supreme Court of Serbia, is the highest court in the Republic; its President is elected for a five-year term by the Narodna skupština. The 11-member High Judicial Council is an independent body, which provides for and guarantees the independence and autonomy of courts and judges. The Narodna skupština elects judges on the proposal of the High Judicial Council, while the High Judicial Council elects permanent judges. The 15-member Constitutional Court protects constitutionality and legality, as well as human and minority rights and freedoms.

TERRITORIAL ORGANIZATION

Citizens have the right to provincial autonomy and local self-government. Autonomous provinces and local self-government units have the status of legal entities. The Skupština (Assembly) is the supreme body of the autonomous provinces and units of local self-government. In those autonomous provinces and local self-government units with an ethnically diverse population, the representation of national minorities in the relevant Skupština is assured. New autonomous provinces may be established, and existing ones may be revoked or merged, following the proceedings envisaged for amending the Constitution and subject to approval in a referendum. An autonomous province shall have direct revenue for financing its competencies.

AMENDING THE CONSTITUTION

Proposals to amend the Constitution may be submitted by at least one-third of the total number of parliamentary deputies, by the President of the Republic, by the Government or by at least 150,000 voters. Any amendment to the Constitution requires the approval of at two-thirds of the total number of deputies in the Narodna skupština. Additionally, at the request of the Narodna skupština, amendments may be subject to approval by a national referendum.

Note: Following the failure of UN-sponsored negotiations on its future status, Kosovo declared independence on 17 February 2008.

The Government

HEAD OF STATE

President of the Republic: BORIS TADIĆ (elected 27 June 2004; re-elected 3 February 2008; inaugurated 15 February 2008).

COUNCIL OF MINISTERS
(April 2008)

A coalition comprising representatives of the Democratic Party (DP), the Democratic Party of Serbia (DPS), New Serbia (NS) and G17 Plus.*

Prime Minister: Dr VOJISLAV KOŠTUNICA (DPS).
Deputy Prime Minister, in charge of European Integration: BOŽIDAR ĐELIĆ (DP).
Minister of Internal Affairs: DRAGAN JOČIĆ (DPS).
Minister of Finance: MIRKO CVETKOVIĆ (DP).
Minister of Defence: DRAGAN ŠUTANOVAC (DP).
Minister of Foreign Affairs: VUK JEREMIĆ (DP).
Minister of Justice: DUŠAN PETROVIĆ (DP).
Minister of Public Administration and Local Self-Government: MILAN MARKOVIĆ (DP).
Minister of Agriculture, Forestry and Water Management: SLOBODAN MILOSAVLJEVIĆ (DP).

SERBIA

Minister of the Economy and Regional Development: MLAĐAN DINKIĆ (G17 Plus).
Minister of Infrastructure: VELIMIR ILIĆ (NS).
Minister of Telecommunications and Information Technology: ALEKSANDRA SMILJANIĆ (DP).
Minister of Trade and Services: PREDRAG BUBALO (DPS).
Minister of Labour and Social Affairs: RASIM LJAJIĆ (DP).
Minister of Mining and Energy: ALEKSANDAR POPOVIĆ (DPS).
Minister of Science: ANA PEŠIKAN (G17 Plus).
Minister of Environmental Protection: SAŠA DRAGIN (DP).
Minister of Education: ZORAN LONČAR (DPS).
Minister of Youth and Sports: SNEŽANA MARKOVIĆ-SAMARDŽIĆ (G17 Plus).
Minister of Culture: VOJISLAV BRAJOVIĆ (DP).
Minister of Health: TOMICA MILOSAVLJEVIĆ (G17 Plus).
Minister of Religious Affairs: RADOMIR NAUMOV (DPS).
Minister of the Diaspora: MILICA ČUBRILO (DP).
Minister of Kosovo and Metohija: SLOBODAN SAMARDŽIĆ (DPS).
Minister without Portfolio, in charge of Co-ordinating the National Investment Plan: DRAGAN ĐILAS (DP).

* On 8 March 2008 Dr Vojislav Koštunica resigned from the premiership, following continuing dissension within the ruling coalition; the Narodna skupština Republike Srbije was subsequently dissolved, and early elections scheduled. After the alliance led by the Democratic Party of President Boris Tadić secured the highest number of votes in the legislative elections on 11 May, Tadić engaged in inter-party discussions to form a new coalition administration.

MINISTRIES

Office of the President: 11000 Belgrade, Andrićev venac 1; tel. (11) 3030866; fax (11) 3030868; e-mail kontakt.predsednik@predsednik.yu; internet www.predsednik.yu.

Office of the Prime Minister: 11000 Belgrade, Nemanjina 11; tel. (11) 3617719; fax (11) 3617609; e-mail predsednikvladesrbije@srbija.sr.gov.yu.

Ministry of Agriculture, Forestry and Water Management: 11000 Belgrade, Nemanjina 22–26; tel. (11) 3065038; fax (11) 3616272; e-mail office@minpolj.sr.gov.yu; internet www.minpolj.sr.gov.yu.

Ministry of Culture: 11000 Belgrade, Vlajkovićeva 3; tel. (11) 3398172; fax (11) 3398936; e-mail kabinet@min-cul.sr.gov.yu; internet www.kultura.sr.gov.yu.

Ministry of Defence: 11000 Belgrade, Birčaninova 5; tel. (11) 3006323; fax (11) 3117809; e-mail info@mod.gov.yu; internet www.mod.gov.yu.

Ministry of the Diaspora: 11000 Belgrade, Vase Čarapića 20; tel. (11) 2638033; fax (11) 2636815; e-mail info@mzd.sr.gov.yu; internet www.mzd.sr.gov.yu.

Ministry of the Economy and Regional Development: 11000 Belgrade, bul. Kralja Aleksandra 15; tel. (11) 3347231; fax (11) 3346770; e-mail officemprov@mpriv.sr.gov.yu; internet www.mpriv.sr.gov.yu.

Ministry of Education: 11000 Belgrade, Nemanjina 22–26; tel. (11) 3616489; fax (11) 3616491; e-mail webmaster@mps.sr.gov.yu; internet www.mps.sr.gov.yu.

Ministry of Environmental Protection: 11000 Belgrade, Omladinskih brigada 1; tel. (11) 3131357; fax (11) 3131394; internet www.ekoserb.sr.gov.yu.

Ministry of Finance: 11000 Belgrade, Kneza Miloša 20; tel. (11) 3619900; fax (11) 3618914; e-mail informacije@mfin.sr.gov.yu; internet www.mfin.sr.gov.yu.

Ministry of Foreign Affairs: 11000 Belgrade, Kneza Miloša 22–26; tel. (11) 3068351; fax (11) 3618052; e-mail msp@smip.sv.gov.yu; internet www.mfa.gov.yu.

Ministry of Health: 11000 Belgrade, Nemanjina 22–26; tel. (11) 3616251; fax (11) 3616596; e-mail kabinet.zdravlje@zdravlije.sr.gov.yu; internet www.zdravlje.sr.gov.yu.

Ministry of Infrastructure: 11000 Belgrade, Nemanjina 22–26; tel. (11) 3616431; fax (11) 3617486.

Ministry of Internal Affairs: 11000 Belgrade, Kneza Miloša 101; tel. (11) 3612410; fax (11) 3617814; e-mail muprs@mup.sr.gov.yu; internet www.mup.sr.gov.yu.

Ministry of Justice: 11000 Belgrade, Nemanjina 22–26; tel. (11) 3616548; fax (11) 3616419; e-mail kabinet@mpravde.sr.gov.yu; internet www.mpravde.sr.gov.yu.

Ministry of Kosovo and Metohija: 11000 Belgrade, Nemanjina 11; tel. (11) 3617717; fax (11) 3617693.

Ministry of Labour and Social Affairs: 11000 Belgrade, bul. Mihajla Pupina 2; tel. (11) 3112916; fax (11) 3114650; e-mail kabinet@minrzs.sr.gov.yu; internet www.minrzs.sr.gov.yu.

Ministry of Mining and Energy: 11000 Belgrade, Kralja Milana 36; tel. (11) 3346755; fax (11) 3616603; e-mail kabinet.mem@mem.sr.gov.yu; internet www.mem.sr.gov.yu.

Ministry of Public Administration and Local Self-Government: 11000 Belgrade, Birčaninova 6; tel. (11) 3613654; fax (11) 2685396; e-mail info.mpalsg@mpalsg.sr.gov.yu; internet www.mpalsg.sr.gov.yu.

Ministry of Religious Affairs: 11000 Belgrade, Nemanjina 11; tel. and fax (11) 3065960; e-mail kabinet.mv@mv.sr.gov.yu.

Ministry of Science: 11000 Belgrade, Nemanjina 22–26; tel. (11) 3616516; fax (11) 3616584; e-mail info@mntr.sr.gov.yu; internet www.mntr.sr.gov.yu.

Ministry of Telecommunications and Information Technology: 11000 Belgrade, Nemanjina 22–26; tel. (11) 3065698; fax (11) 3631645.

Ministry of Trade and Services: 11000 Belgrade, Nemanjina 22–26; tel. (11) 3618852; fax (11) 3610285; e-mail kabinet@mtu.sr.gov.yu; internet www.mtu.sr.gov.yu.

Ministry of Youth and Sports: Belgrade, bul. Mihajla Pupina 2; tel. (11) 3130912; fax (11) 3130915; e-mail sport@mos.sr.gov.yu; internet www.mos.sr.gov.yu.

President

Presidential Election, First Ballot, 20 January 2008

Candidate	Votes	% of votes
Tomislav Nikolić (Serbian Radical Party)	1,646,172	39.99
Boris Tadić (Democratic Party)	1,457,030	35.39
Velimir Ilić (New Serbia)	305,828	7.43
Milutin Mrkonjić (Socialist Party of Serbia)	245,889	5.97
Čedomir Jovanović (Liberal Democratic Party)	219,689	5.34
Others	163,765	3.69
Total*	**4,116,844**	**100.00**

* Including invalid votes.

Second Ballot, 3 February 2008

Candidate	Votes	% of votes
Boris Tadić (Democratic Party)	2,304,467	50.31
Tomislav Nikolić (Serbian Radical Party)	2,197,155	47.97
Total*	**4,580,428**	**100.00**

* Including invalid votes.

Legislature

Narodna skupština Republike Srbije
(National Assembly of the Republic of Serbia)
11000 Belgrade, Kralja Milana 14; tel. (11) 3222001; e-mail webmaster@parlament.sr.gov.yu; internet www.parlament.sr.gov.yu.

President: OLIVER DULIĆ.

Election, 11 May 2008, preliminary results

Parties	% of votes	Seats
For a European Serbia—Boris Tadić*	38.44	102
Serbian Radical Party	29.36	78
Democratic Party of Serbia-New Serbia	11.59	30
Socialist Party of Serbia-Party of United Pensioners of Serbia-United Serbia	7.60	20
Liberal Democratic Party	5.24	13
Hungarian Coalition—Ištvan Pastor†	1.83	4
Bosniak List for a European Sandžak—Dr Sulejman Ugljanin‡	0.92	2
Albanian Coalition from the Preševo Valley	0.39	1
Strength of Serbia Movement	0.54	—
Others	1.86	—
Total§	**100.00**	**250**

* Coalition, principally comprising the Democratic Party, G17 Plus, the Serbian Renewal Movement, the League of Social-Democrats of Vojvodina and the Sandžak Democratic Party.

SERBIA

† Coalition of the Alliance of Vojvodina Hungarians, the Democratic Fellowship of Vojvodina Hungarians and the Democratic Party of Vojvodina Hungarians.
‡ Coalition of five parties from the Sandžak region.
§ Including invalid votes.

Election Commission

Electoral Commission of the Republic of Serbia: 11000 Belgrade, Kralja Milana 14; tel. (11) 3222001; fax (11) 3617839; e-mail rik@parlament.sr.gov.yu; internet www.rik.parlament.sr.gov.yu; Chair. MIHAILO RUDIĆ.

Political Organizations

A total of 342 political parties were registered in early 2008.

Alliance of Vojvodina Hungarians (Vajdasági Magyar Szövetség/Savez Vojvođanskih Mađara): 24000 Subotica, Age Mamuzica 13; tel. (24) 553801; e-mail office@vmsz.org.yu; internet www.vmsz.org.yu; f. 1994; supports autonomous status for Vojvodina; contested legislative elections in May 2008 as part of the Hungarian Coalition—Ištvan Pastor; Chair. IŠTVAN PASTOR.

Democratic Party (DS) (Demokratska Stranka): 11000 Belgrade, Krunska 69; tel. (11) 3443003; fax (11) 2444864; e-mail info@ds.org.yu; internet www.ds.org.yu; f. 1990; led For a European Serbia—Boris Tadić coalition in legislative elections in May 2008; Pres. BORIS TADIĆ.

Democratic Party of Serbia (DSS) (Demokratska stranka Srbije): 11000 Belgrade, Pariska 13; tel. (11) 3204719; fax (11) 3204743; e-mail info@dss.org.yu; internet www.dss.org.yu; f. 1992 following split from Democratic Party; Leader Dr VOJISLAV KOŠTUNICA.

G17 Plus: 11000 Belgrade, trg Republike 5; tel. and fax (11) 3344930; e-mail office@g17plus.org.yu; internet www.g17plus.org.yu; f. 2003; contested legislative elections in May 2008 as part of the For a European Serbia—Boris Tadić coalition; Pres. MLAĐAN DINKIĆ.

League of Social-Democrats of Vojvodina (LSV) (Liga Socijaldemokrata Vojvodine): 21000 Novi Sad, trg Mladenaca 10; tel. (21) 529139; fax (21) 420628; e-mail office@lsv.org.yu; internet www.lsv.org.yu; Pres. NENAD ČANAK.

Liberal Democratic Party (Liberalno-demokratska Stranka): 11000 Belgrade, Simina 41; tel. (11) 3208300; e-mail ldpcis@gmail.com; internet www.ldpweb.org; f. 2005 by fmr mems of the Democratic Party; Leader ČEDOMIR JOVANOVIĆ.

New Serbia (Nova Srbija): 11000 Belgrade, Obilićev venac 4/1; tel. and fax (11) 3284766; fax (11) 2631748; e-mail nsbgd@eunet.yu; internet www.nova-srbija.org; Pres. VELIMIR ILIĆ.

Party of United Pensioners of Serbia (PUPS) (Partija Ujedinjenih Penzionera Srbije): 11000 Belgrade, Svetozara Markovića 32; tel. (11) 2131487; e-mail office@pups.org.yu; internet www.pups.org.yu; Leader JOVAN KRKOBABIĆ.

Roma Party (Romska Partija): represents Roma ethnic minority; Leader ŠAJN SRĐAN.

Roma Union of Serbia (Unija Roma Srbije): 11000 Belgrade, Sarajevska 11; tel. (11) 2681693; e-mail unijaromasrbije@hotmail.com; internet www.unijaromasrbije.org; f. 2004; represents Roma ethnic minority; Leader Dr RAJKO ĐURIĆ.

Serbian Radical Party (SRS) (Srpska Radikalna Stranka): 11080 Belgrade, Zemun, Magistratski trg 3; tel. (11) 3164621; e-mail info@srs.org.yu; internet www.srs.org.yu; f. 1991; extreme nationalist; advocates a 'Greater Serbian' state of territories inhabited by Serbs within and outside Serbia; leader Dr Vojislav Šešelj in detention at the International Criminal Tribunal for the former Yugoslavia; Leader TOMISLAV NIKOLIĆ (acting); Gen. Sec. ALEKSANDAR VUCIĆ.

Serbian Renewal Movement (SPO) (Srpski pokret obnove): 11000 Belgrade, Kneza Mihailova 48; tel. (11) 3283620; fax (11) 2628170; e-mail vuk@spo.org.yu; internet www.spo.org.yu; f. 1990; nationalist; Pres. VUK DRAŠKOVIĆ.

Social Democratic Party (SDP) (Socijaldemokratska Partija): 11000 Belgrade, Ruzveltova 45; tel. (11) 3290820; fax 911) 3294507; e-mail ncovic@sdp.org.yu; internet www.sdp.org.yu; f. 1997; Pres. Dr NEBOJŠA ČOVIĆ.

Social Democratic Union (Socijaldemokratska Unija): 11000 Belgrade, Kralja Milana 34/1; tel. and fax (11) 3613649; fax (11) 3620862; e-mail office@sdu.org.yu; internet www.sdu.org.yu; f. 1996; Pres. ŽARKO KORAĆ.

Socialist Party of Serbia (SPS) (Socijalistička partija Srbije): 11000 Belgrade, Studentski trg 15; tel. (11) 2627282; fax (11) 2627170; e-mail info.centar@sps.org.yu; internet www.sps.org.yu; f. 1990 by merger of League of Communists of Serbia and Socialist Alliance of Working People of Serbia; Pres. IVICA DAČIĆ.

Strength of Serbia Movement (Pokret snaga Srbije): 11040 Belgrade, bul. Mira 49; tel. (11) 3672805; fax (11) 3672906; e-mail info@snagasrbije.com; internet www.snagasrbije.com; f. 2004; Leader BOGOLJUB KARIĆ.

United Serbia: 35000 Jagodina, Nikčevićeva br. 2; tel. (81) 35233104; fax (81) 35252443; e-mail info@jedinstvenasrbija.org.rs; internet www.jedinstvenasrbija.org.rs; Leader DRAGAN MARKOVIĆ.

Diplomatic Representation

EMBASSIES IN SERBIA

Albania: 11000 Belgrade, bul. Kneza Aleksandra Karađorđevića 25A; tel. (11) 3066642; fax (11) 2665439; e-mail albembassy_belgrade@hotmail.com; Ambassador SPIRO KOÇI.

Algeria: 11000 Belgrade, Maglajska 26 B; tel. (11) 3671211; e-mail ambalg@eunet.yu; Ambassador BOUDJEMAA DELMI.

Angola: 11000 Belgrade, Vase Pelagića 32; tel. (11) 3690241; fax (11) 3690191; Ambassador ANTÓNIO MANUEL BENJAMIN.

Argentina: 11000 Belgrade, Kneza Mihajlova 24/I; tel. (11) 2623569; fax (11) 2622630; e-mail embaryu@eunet.yu; Ambassador MARIO EDUARDO BOSSI DE EZCURRA.

Australia: 11000 Belgrade, Čika Ljubina 13; tel. (11) 3303400; fax (11) 3303409; e-mail belgrade.embassy@dfat.gov.au; internet www.serbia.embassy.gov.au; Ambassador CLARE BIRGIN.

Austria: 11000 Belgrade, Kneza Sime Markovića 2; tel. (11) 3336500; fax (11) 635606; e-mail belgrade-ob@bmeia.gv.at; internet www.aussenministerium.at/belgrad; Ambassador GERHARD JANDL.

Belarus: 11000 Belgrade, Deligradska 13; tel. (11) 3616836; fax (11) 3616938; e-mail sam@belembassy.org; Chargé d'affaires a.i. SIARHEI CHICHUK.

Belgium: 11000 Belgrade, Krunska 18; tel. (11) 3230018; fax (11) 3244394; e-mail belgrade@diplobel.org; Ambassador DENISE DE HAUWERE.

Bosnia and Herzegovina: 11000 Belgrade, Krunska 9; tel. (11) 3241170; fax (11) 3241057; Chargé d'affaires a.i. AMIRA ARIFOVIĆ-HARMS.

Brazil: 11000 Belgrade, Krunska 14; tel. (11) 3239781; fax (11) 3230653; e-mail brasbelg@eunet.yu; Ambassador DANTE COELHO DE LIMA.

Bulgaria: 11000 Belgrade, Birčaninova 26; tel. (11) 3613980; fax 3611136; e-mail bulgamb@eunet.yu; Ambassador GEORGI DIMITROV.

Canada: 11000 Belgrade, Kneza Miloša 75; tel. (11) 3063000; fax (11) 3063042; e-mail bgrad@international.gc.ca; internet www.canada.org.yu; Ambassador ROBERT MCDOUGALL.

China, People's Republic: 11000 Belgrade, Augusta Cesarca 2v; tel. (11) 3695057; fax (11) 3066001; e-mail chinaemb_yu@mail.mfa.gov.cn; Ambassador LI GUOBANG.

Congo, Democratic Republic: 11000 Belgrade, Moravska 5; tel. and fax (11) 3446431; Chargé d'affaires a.i. PAUL EMILE TSHINGA AHUKA.

Croatia: 11000 Belgrade, Kneza Miloša 62; tel. (11) 3610535; fax (11) 3610032; e-mail croambg@eunet.yu; internet rs.mvp.hr; Ambassador TONČI STANIČIĆ.

Cuba: 11000 Belgrade, Ljube Jovanovića 9B; tel. (11) 3692441; fax (11) 3692442; e-mail emcubayu@eunet.yu; internet www.kubabeograd.org.yu; Ambassador JULIO CÉSAR CANCIO FERRER.

Cyprus: 11040 Belgrade, Diplomatska Kolonija 9; tel. (11) 3672725; fax (11) 3671348; e-mail cyprus@eunet.yu; Ambassador HOMER MAVROMMATIS.

Czech Republic: 11000 Belgrade, bul. Kralja Aleksandra 22; tel. (11) 3230133; fax (11) 3236448; e-mail belgrade@embassy.mzv.cz; internet www.mzv.cz/belgrade; Ambassador HANA HUBÁČKOVÁ.

Denmark: 11040 Belgrade, Neznanog Junaka 9A; tel. (11) 3679500; fax (11) 3679502; e-mail begamb@um.dk; internet www.ambbeograd.um.dk; Ambassador METTE KJUEL NIELSEN.

Egypt: 11000 Belgrade, Andre Nikolića 12; tel. (11) 2650585; fax (11) 2652036; Ambassador ADEL AHMED NAGUIB.

Finland: 11001 Belgrade, Birčaninova 29, POB 926; tel. (11) 3065400; fax (11) 3065375; e-mail sanomat.beo@formin.fi; Ambassador KARI JOHANNES VEIJALAINEN.

France: 11000 Belgrade, Pariska 11, POB 283; tel. (11) 3023500; fax (11) 3023510; e-mail amba_fr@eunet.yu; internet www.ambafrance-srb.org; Ambassador JEAN-FRANÇOIS TERRAL.

Germany: 11000 Belgrade, Kneza Miloša 76; tel. (11) 3064300; fax (11) 3064303; e-mail germany@sbb.co.yu; internet www.belgrad.diplo.de; Ambassador WOLFRAM JOSEF MAAS.

SERBIA

Directory

Ghana: 11000 Belgrade, Đorđa Vajferta 50; tel. (11) 3440856; fax (11) 3440071; e-mail ghana@eunet.yu; internet www.ghanaembelgrade.com; Ambassador Dr NYAHO NYAHO-TAMAKLOE.

Greece: 11000 Belgrade, Francuska 33; tel. (11) 3226523; fax 3344746; internet www.greekemb.co.yu; Ambassador CHRISTOS PANAGOPOULOS.

Guinea: 11000 Belgrade, Ohridska 4; tel. (11) 431830; fax (11) 451391; Ambassador El Hadj MUHAMMAD ISSIAGA KOUROUMA.

Holy See: 11000 Belgrade, Svetog Save 24; tel. (11) 3085356; fax (11) 3085216; e-mail nunbel@eunet.yu; Apostolic Nuncio Most Rev. EUGENIO SBARBARO (Titular Archbishop of Tiddi).

Hungary: 11000 Belgrade, Krunska 72; tel. (11) 2440472; fax (11) 3441876; e-mail hunemblg@eunet.yu; internet www.hunemblg.hu; Ambassador SÁNDOR PAPP.

India: 11040 Belgrade, Ljutice Bogdana 8,; tel. (11) 2661029; fax (11) 3674209; e-mail indemb@eunet.yu; internet www.embassyofindiabelgrade.org; Ambassador AJAY SWARUP.

Indonesia: 11000 Belgrade, bul. Kneza Aleksandra Karađorđevića 18; tel. (11) 3674062; fax (11) 3672984; e-mail kombeojo@eunet.yu; Ambassador MUHAMMAD ABDUH DALIMUNTHE.

Iran: 11000 Belgrade, Ljutice Bogdana 40; tel. (11) 3674360; fax (11) 3674363; Ambassador SEYED MIR HEYDARI.

Iraq: 11000 Belgrade, Neznanog Junaka 27A; tel. (11) 2662681; fax (11) 2668068; e-mail bgremb@iraqmofamail.net; Chargé d'affaires a.i. MAY KHALID OMRAN AL-BAYATI.

Israel: 11000 Belgrade, bul. Kneza Aleksandra Karađorđevića 47; tel. (11) 3672400; fax (11) 3670304; e-mail info@belgrade.mfa.gov.il; Ambassador ARTHUR KOLL.

Italy: 11000 Belgrade, ul. Birčaninova 11; tel. (11) 3066100; fax (11) 3249413; e-mail office@italy.org.yu; internet www.italy.org.yu; Ambassador ALESSANDRO MEROLA.

Japan: 11070 Novi Belgrade, Vladimira Popovića 6; tel. (11) 3012800; fax (11) 3118258; Ambassador TADASHI NGAI.

Korea, Republic: 11070 Belgrade, Užička 32; tel. (11) 3674225; fax (11) 3674229; Ambassador Dr KIM YOUNG-HEE.

Lebanon: 11000 Belgrade, Diplomatska kolonija 5; tel. (11) 3691178; fax (11) 3690155; e-mail ambaleb@eunet.yu; Ambassador CHÉHADÉ MOUALLEM.

Libya: 11000 Belgrade, Sime Lozanića 6; tel. (11) 2663445; fax (11) 3670805; e-mail libyaamb@eunet.yu; Chargé d'affaires a.i. HANAN KHALED ZOGHBIA.

Macedonia, former Yugoslav republic: 11000 Belgrade, Gospodar Jevremova 34; tel. (11) 3284924; fax (11) 3285076; e-mail macemb@eunet.yu; Ambassador ALEKSANDAR VASILEVSKI.

Mexico: 11000 Belgrade, Ljutice Bogdana 5, Savski venac; tel. (11) 3674170; fax (11) 3675013; e-mail embamex@net.yu; internet www.mexican-embassy.org.yu; Chargé d'affaires a.i. EDUARDO HÉCTOR MOGUEL FLORES.

Montenegro: Belgrade, Užička 1; tel. and fax (11) 2668975; e-mail ambasadacg@gmail.com; Ambassador ANKA VOJVODIĆ.

Morocco: 11000 Belgrade, Sanje Živanović 4; tel. (11) 3691866; fax (11) 3690499; e-mail sifamabe@eunet.yu; Ambassador KAMAL FAQIR BENAISSA.

Myanmar: 11000 Belgrade, Kneza Miloša 72; tel. (11) 3617165; fax (11) 3614968; e-mail mebel@sezampro.yu; Ambassador SOE NWE.

Netherlands: 11000 Belgrade, Simina 29, POB 489; tel. (11) 2023900; fax (11) 2023999; e-mail info@nlembassy.org.yu; internet www.nlembassy.org.yu; Ambassador RONALD JACOBUS PETRUS MARIE VAN DARTEL.

Norway: 11000 Belgrade, Užička 43; tel. (11) 3670404; fax (11) 3690158; Ambassador HÅKON BLANKENBORG.

Pakistan: 11000 Belgrade, bul. Kneza Aleksandra Karađorđevića 62; tel. (11) 2661676; fax (11) 2661667; e-mail ambpakistana@sbb.co.yu; internet www.pakistanembassy.org.yu; Ambassador MUHAMMAD NAWAZ CHAUDHRY.

Poland: 11000 Belgrade, Kneza Miloša 38; tel. (11) 2065318; fax (11) 3616939; e-mail ambrpfrj@eunet.yu; Ambassador MACIEJ SZYMAŃSKI.

Portugal: 11040 Belgrade, Vladimira Gaćinovića 4; tel. (11) 2662895; fax (11) 2662892; e-mail embporbg@yubc.net; Ambassador PAULO TIAGO JERÓNIMO DA SILVA.

Romania: 11000 Belgrade, Užička 10; tel. (11) 3675772; fax (11) 3675771; e-mail ambelgro@infosky.net; Ambassador ION MACOVEI.

Russia: 11000 Belgrade, ul. Deligradska 32; tel. (11) 3611323; fax (11) 3611900; e-mail ambarusk@eunet.yu; Ambassador ALEKSANDR V. KONUZIN.

Slovakia: 11070 Belgrade, bul. Umetnosti 18; tel. (11) 2223800; fax (11) 2223820; e-mail embassy@belehrad.mfa.sk; Ambassador IGOR FURDÍK.

Slovenia: Belgrade, Pariska 15; tel. (11) 3038477; fax (11) 3288657; e-mail vbg@gov.si; Ambassador MIROSLAV LUCI.

Spain: 11000 Belgrade, Prote Mateje 45; tel. (11) 3440231; fax (11) 3444203; e-mail embespyu@mail.mae.es; internet www.spanija.org.yu; Ambassador JOSÉ RIERA SIQUIER.

Sweden: 11040 Belgrade, Ledi Pedzet 2, POB 5; tel. (11) 2069200; fax (11) 2069250; e-mail ambassaden.belgrad@foreign.ministry.se; internet www.swedenabroad.se/belgrad; Ambassador NILS KRISTER BRINGÉUS.

Switzerland: 11000 Belgrade, Birčaninova 27; tel. (11) 3065820; fax (11) 2657253; e-mail vertretung@bel.rep.admin.ch; Ambassador WILHELM MEIER.

Syria: 11000 Belgrade, Aleksandra Stamboliskog 13; tel. (11) 2666124; fax (11) 2660221; e-mail syremb@net.yu; Ambassador Dr MAJED SHADOUD.

Tunisia: 11000 Belgrade, Vase Pelagića 19; tel. (11) 3691961; fax (11) 3690642; e-mail at.belgr@eunet.yu; Ambassador HOURIA FERCHICHI.

Turkey: 11000 Belgrade, Krunska 1; tel. (11) 3235431; fax (11) 3235433; e-mail turem@eunet.yu; Ambassador AHMET SUHA UMAR.

Ukraine: 11000 Belgrade, bul. Oslobođenja 87; tel. (11) 3978987; fax (11) 3978998; internet www.mfa.gov.ua/serbia; Ambassador ANATOLIY OLYNYK.

United Kingdom: 11000 Belgrade, Resavska 46; tel. (11) 3060900; fax (11) 3061077; e-mail belgrade.ppd@fco.gov.uk; internet www.britishembassy.gov.uk/serbia; Ambassador STEPHEN JOHN WORDSWORTH.

USA: 11000 Belgrade, Kneza Miloša 50; tel. (11) 3619344; fax (11) 3615489; internet www.belgrade.usembassy.gov; Ambassador CAMERON MUNTER.

Judicial System

The judicial system in the Republic of Serbia comprises the courts of regular competence (138 municipal courts, 30 district courts and the Supreme Court of Serbia) and courts of the special competence (17 commercial courts, High Commercial Court). A new Constitution, which entered into effect on 8 November 2006, provided for an 11-member independent High Judicial Council, which was to guarantee the independence and autonomy of courts and judges. The legislature was to elect judges on the proposal of the High Judicial Council, while the High Judicial Council was to elect permanent judges. The Constitutional Court, which was to comprise 15 judges, protects constitutionality and legality, as well as human and minority rights and freedoms.

Constitutional Court (Ustavni Sud Srbije): 11000 Belgrade, Nemanjina 26; tel. (11) 3616372; fax (11) 2658970; e-mail predsednik@ustavni.sud.sr.gov.yu; internet www.ustavni.sud.sr.gov.yu; f. 1963; Pres. SLOBODAN VUČETIĆ.

Supreme Court (Vrhovni Sud Srbije): 11000 Belgrade, Resavska 42; tel. (11) 3634240; fax (11) 3619376; e-mail vss@vrhovni.sud.sr.gov.yu; internet www.vrhovni.sud.srbija.yu; Pres. VIDA PETROVIĆ-SKERO.

Office of the Public Prosecutor of Serbia: 11000 Belgrade, Nemanjina 24–26; tel. (11) 658755; Public Prosecutor MILOMIR JAKOVLJEVIĆ.

Religion

Most of the inhabitants of Serbia are, at least nominally, Christian, but there is a significant Muslim minority. The main Christian denomination is Eastern Orthodox, but there is a strong Roman Catholic presence. There are also small minorities of Old Catholics, Protestants and Jews.

CHRISTIANITY

The Eastern Orthodox Church

Serbian Orthodox Church (Srpska Pravoslavna Crkva): 11001 Belgrade, Kralja Petra 5, POB 182; tel. (11) 3283997; fax (11) 182780; e-mail pravoslavlje@spc.yu; internet www.spc.yu; 11m. adherents; Patriarch of Serbia, Archbishop of Peć and Metropolitan of Belgrade-Karlovci PAVLE.

The Roman Catholic Church

Serbia comprises one archdiocese and two dioceses. There is also an apostolic exarchate of Serbia and Montenegro for Catholics of the Byzantine rite. At 31 December 2005 adherents of the Roman Catholic Church represented about 5.1% of the total population of

SERBIA

Serbia (including those adherents of the Byzantine rite resident within Montenegro).

International Bishops' Conference of SS Cyril and Methodius: 11000 Belgrade, Višegradska 23; tel. (11) 3032246; fax (11) 3032248; f. 2006; Pres. Most Rev. STANISLAV HOČEVAR (Archbishop of Belgrade).

Archbishop of Belgrade: Most Rev. STANISLAV HOČEVAR, 11000 Belgrade, Svetozara Markovića 20; tel. (11) 3032246; fax (11) 3032248; e-mail nadbisbg@eunet.yu.

Apostolic Exarch to Serbia and Montenegro for Catholics of the Byzantine Rite: ĐURA DŽUDŽAR (Titular Archbishop of Acrasso), 21000 Novi Sad, D. Magaraševića 18; tel. (21) 6371609; fax (21) 6371613; 22,720 adherents at 31 Dec. 2005.

Protestant Churches

Christian Reformed Church: 24323 Feketic, Bratsva 26; tel. and fax (24) 738070; f. 1919; 22,000 mems; Bishop ISTVAN CSETE-SZEMESI.

Evangelical Christian Church of the Augsburg (Lutheran) Confession in Serbia-Vojvodina: 24000 Subotica, Brace Radiča 17; tel. and fax (24) 721048; e-mail dolinsky@stcable.co.yu; internet www.lutheran.org.yu; Superintendent DOLINSKY ÁRPÁD.

Slovak Evangelical Church of the Augsburg (Lutheran) Confession: 21000 Novi Sad, Karadžićeva 2; tel. (21) 6611882; e-mail secav@eunet.yu; 50,000 mems (2002); Bishop Dr SAMUEL VRBOVSKY.

Union of Baptist Churches in Serbia: 11000 Belgrade, Slobodanke D. Savić 33; tel. and fax (11) 410964; f. 1992; Gen. Sec. Rev. AVRAM DEGA.

ISLAM

There are ethnic Slav Muslims (Bosniaks) in the part of Sandžak located in south-west Serbia, in particular in and around the town of Novi Pazar. Most Muslims in the country are Sunni.

Islamic Community of Serbia: Belgrade, G. Jevremova 11; tel. (11) 2622428; e-mail jus@beotel.yu; internet www.izs.org.yu.

Islamic Community of Vojvodina: 21000 Novi Sad, Futoška 61; tel. and fax (21) 6619444; internet www.islamvojvodina.com; Chair. ZIJA ZEKIR.

JUDAISM

Federation of Jewish Communities in Serbia: 11000 Belgrade, Kralja Petra 71 A/III, POB 512; tel. (11) 2624359; fax (11) 2621837; e-mail office@savezscg.net; f. 1919, revived 1944; Pres. ALEKSANDAR NEĆAK.

The Press

PRINCIPAL DAILIES

(In Serbian, except where otherwise stated)

Belgrade

Blic: 11000 Belgrade, Masarikova 5; tel. (11) 3619471; fax (11) 3619326; e-mail redakcija@blic.co.yu; internet www.blic.co.yu; f. 1996; Editor-in-Chief VESLIN SIMONOVIĆ; circ. 230,000.

Borba: 11000 Belgrade, trg Nikole Pašića 7; tel. (11) 334531; fax (11) 344913; e-mail borba@bits.net; internet www.borba.co.yu; f. 1922; morning; Editor-in-Chief SRDJAN PETKOVIĆ.

Glas Javnosti (Voice of the Public): 11000 Belgrade, Vlajkovićeva 8; tel. (11) 3249125; fax (11) 3225095; e-mail webmaster@glas-javnosti.co.yu; internet www.glas-javnosti.co.yu; f. 1874; Dir and Editor-in-Chief PETAR LAZIĆ.

Politika: 11000 Belgrade, Makedonska 29; tel. (11) 3373111; fax (11) 3373164; e-mail redakcija@politika.co.yu; internet www.politika.co.yu; f. 1904; Dir-Gen. DARKO RIBNIKOR; Editor-in-Chief MILON MIŠIĆ; circ. 130,000.

Politika Ekspres: 11000 Belgrade, Makedonska 29; tel. (11) 325630; evening; Editor-in-Chief MILE KORDIĆ; circ. 76,000.

Pregled: 11000 Belgrade, Toplicin venac 21/I; tel. and fax (11) 3282405; e-mail info@pregled.com; internet www.pregled.com; f. 1950; business and economics; Dir and Chief Editor SANDRA LABUDOVIĆ.

Večernje novosti (Evening News): 11000 Belgrade, trg Nikole Pašića 7; tel. (11) 3028000; e-mail internet@novosti.co.yu; internet www.novosti.co.yu; f. 1953; Dir and Editor-in-Chief MANOJLO MANJO VUKOTIĆ; circ. 270,000.

Niš

Narodne Novine (The People's News): 18000 Niš, Vojvode Gojka 14; internet www.narodne.com; morning.

Novi Sad

Dnevnik (Daily News): 21000 Novi Sad, bul. Oslobođenja 81; tel. (21) 421493; e-mail redakcija@dnevnik.co.yu; internet www.dnevnik.co.yu; f. 1942 as *Slobodna Vojvodina* (Free Vojvodina); morning; Editor-in-Chief PETAR PETROVIĆ.

Magyar Szó (Hungarian Word): 21000 Novi Sad, V. Mišića 1; tel. (21) 456066; fax (21) 456482; e-mail foszerk@magyar-szo.co.yu; internet www.magyar-szo.co.yu; f. 1944; morning; in Hungarian; Editor-in-Chief PETER KOKAI; circ. 15,000 (2006).

PERIODICALS

Belgrade

Ekonomist: Belgrade, Kneza Mihaila 2-4; tel. (11) 3284034; e-mail office@ekonomist.co.yu; internet www.ekonomist.co.yu; f. 1948; quarterly; journal of the Yugoslav Association of Economists; Editor Dr HASAN HADŽIOMEROVIĆ.

Ekonomska Politika (Economic Policy): 11000 Belgrade, trg Nikole Pašića 7; tel. (11) 3398298; fax (11) 3398300; e-mail office@ekopol.co.yu; internet www.ekopol.co.yu; f. 1952; weekly; Dir ČEDOMIR ŠOŠKIĆ; Editor-in-Chief SLAVKA KOVAČ.

Ilustrovana Politika: 11000 Belgrade, 29 Novembra 24; tel. (11) 3301442; fax (11) 3373346; f. 1958; weekly illustrated review; Gen. Dir DARKO RIBNIKAR; Editor-in-Chief GORDANA KNEŽEVIĆ; circ. 90,000.

Jisa Info: 11000 Belgrade, Zmaj Jovina 4; tel. (11) 2620374; fax (11) 2626576; e-mail jisa@jisa.org.yu; internet www.jisa.org.yu; f. 1993; publ. by Jisa (Jedinstveni informatički savez Srbije i Crne Gore—Union of ICT Societies of Serbia); computing, technology; Dir and Editor-in-Chief DUBRAVKA DURIĆ.

Međunarodni Problemi/International Problems: 11000 Belgrade, Institute of International Politics and Economics, Makedonska 25; tel. (11) 3373633; fax (11) 3373835; e-mail branam@gmail.com; internet www.diplomacy.bg.ac.yu/mpro.htm; f. 1949; quarterly; in Serbian and English; Editor BRANA MARKOVIĆ; circ. 1,000.

Mikro/PC World: 11030 Belgrade, PoŽeška 81A; tel. (11) 3055010; fax (11) 3058034; e-mail pisma@mikro.co.yu; internet www.mikro.co.yu; f. 1997; 11 a year; computing; Editorial Dir ALEKSANDAR SPASIĆ; circ. 23,000 (2007).

Nezavisna Svetlost: 34000 Kragujevac, Branka Radićevića 9; tel. and fax (34) 334746; e-mail nsvet@eunet.yu; internet www.svetlost.co.yu; f. 1995; weekly news; Editor-in-Chief MIROSLAV JOVANOVIĆ.

NIN—Nedeljne informativne novine (Weekly Informative News): 11000 Belgrade, Cetinjska 1, POB 208; tel. (11) 3373111; fax (11) 3373171; e-mail redakcija@nin.co.yu; internet www.nin.co.yu; f. 1935; politics, economics, culture; Dir DRAŠKO TANKOSIĆ; Editor-in-Chief SLOBODAN RELJIĆ; circ. 35,000.

Novi Glasnik (New Messenger): 11002 Belgrade, Balkanska 53; tel. (11) 645795; e-mail genstaffinfo@vj.yu; internet www.vj.yu/english/en_publikacije/glasnik.htm; f. 1993; 6 a year; publ. by Military Publishing Institute for the Armed Forces of Serbia and Montenegro; in Serbian and English; Editor-in-Chief Col MILAN SUMONJA.

Odbrana (Defence): 11002 Belgrade, Katanićeva 16; internet www.odbrana.mod.gov.yu; tel. (11) 3241258; fax (11) 3241363; f. 2005 to replace *Vojska* (Soldier); two a month; publ. by Ministry of Defence; Editor-in-Chief Lt-Col SLAVOLJUB M. MARKOVIĆ.

Ošišani Jež: 11000 Belgrade, Resavska 28; tel. (11) 3232211; fax (11) 3232423; internet www.jez.co.yu; f. 1935 as *Jež* (Hedgehog); fortnightly; satirical; Editor RADIVOJE BOJIČIĆ; circ. 50,000.

Politikin Zabavnik: Belgrade, 11000 Makedonska 29; f. 1939; weekly; comic; Editor RADOMIR ŠOŠKIĆ; circ. 41,000.

Pravoslavlje (Orthodoxy): 11000 Belgrade, Kralja Petra 5; tel. (11) 3282596; fax (11) 630865; e-mail pravoslavlje@spc.yu; internet www.pravoslavlje.com; f. 1967; fortnightly; Orthodox Christian.

Pregled Republika Srbija/Survey—Republic of Serbia: 11000 Belgrade, Dečanska 8, POB 677; tel. (11) 3233610; fax (11) 3240291; e-mail info@yusurvey.co.yu; internet www.yusurvey.co.yu; f. 1957 as *Jugoslovenski pregled/Yugoslav Survey*, renamed *Pregled SCG/Survey Serbia & Montenegro* in 2003, present name adopted 2006; quarterly; general reference publication of basic documentary information about Serbia; Serbian and English edns; Editor-in-Chief ILE KOVAČEVIĆ.

Svet Kompjutera (The World of the Computer): 11000 Belgrade, Cetinjska 1; tel. (11) 3301498; fax (11) 3373358; e-mail editors@sk.co.yu; internet www.sk.co.yu; f. 1984; monthly; computing; Editor ZORAN MOŠORINSKI.

Viva: 11000 Belgrade, Cetinjska 1v; tel. (11) 3220132; fax (11) 3220552; e-mail viva@politika.co.uk; monthly; health; Editor DRAGUTIN GREGORIĆ; circ. 25,000.

Vreme (Time): Belgrade, Mišarska 12–14; tel. (11) 3234774; fax (11) 3238662; internet www.vreme.com; Editor-in-Chief DRAGOLJUB ŽARKOVIĆ.

Yugoslav Journal of Operations Research: 11000 Belgrade, Faculty of Organizational Sciences, University of Belgrade, Jove Ilica 154; tel. (11) 3972383; fax (11) 461221; e-mail yujor@fon.fonbg.ac.yu; internet yujor.fon.bg.ac.yu; 2 a year; systems science and management science; Editor RADIVOJ PETROVIĆ; circ. 700.

Novi Sad

Letopis Matice Srpske: 21000 Novi Sad, Matice srpske 1; tel. (21) 527622; fax (21) 528901; e-mail ms@maticasrpska.org.yu; internet www.maticasrpska.org.yu/pages/izdanja/letopis.htm; f. 1824; monthly; literary review; Editors Dr DRAGAN STANIĆ, IVAN NEGRISORAC.

NEWS AGENCIES

Beta News Agency: 11000 Belgrade, Kraljana Milana 4; tel. (11) 3602400; fax (11) 642551; internet www.beta.co.yu; f. 1992; regional independent news service; Dir LJUBICA MARKOVIĆ; Editor-in-Chief DRAGAN JANJIĆ.

Tanjug News Agency (Novinska Agencija Tanjug): 11001 Belgrade, Obilićev Venac 2, POB 439; tel. (11) 3281608; fax (11) 633550; e-mail direkcija@tanjug.co.yu; internet www.tanjug.co.yu; f. 1943; press and information agency; in Serbian, English, French and Spanish; Dir and Editor-in-Chief DUŠAN ĐORĐEVIĆ.

PRESS ASSOCIATION

Independent Association of Journalists of Serbia: 11000 Belgrade, Resavska 28/II; tel. (11) 3343255; fax (11) 3343136; e-mail ijas@eunet.yu; internet www.nuns.org.yu; Pres. NEBOJŠA BUGARINOVIĆ.

Publishers

Alfa-Narodna knjiga (Alfa-People's Book): 11000 Belgrade, Šafarikova 11; tel. (11) 3227426; fax (11) 3227946; e-mail tea@eunet.yu; internet www.narodnaknjiga.co.yu; f. 1950; fiction, non-fiction, children's books and dictionaries; Gen. Man. MILIČKO MIJOVIĆ.

BIGZ (Beogradski izdavačko-grafički zavod) Publishing a.d. (Belgrade Publishing and Graphics Cp): 11000 Belgrade, bul. Vojvode Mišića 17/III; tel. (11) 3691259; fax (11) 3690519; internet www.bigz-publishing.co.yu; f. 1831; privately owned; literature and criticism, children's books, pocket books, popular science, philosophy, politics; Dir MIRJANA MILORADOVIĆ.

Dečje novine: 32300 Gornji Milanovac, T. Matijevića 4; tel. (32) 711195; fax (32) 711248; general literature, children's books, science, science fiction, textbooks; Gen. Dir MIROSLAV PETROVIĆ.

Forum Publishing House: 21000 Novi Sad, Vojvode Mišića 1, POB 200; tel. (21) 611300; f. 1957; newspapers, periodicals and books in Hungarian; Dir GYULA GOBBY.

Građevinska Knjiga (Citizens' Books) Publishing House: 11000 Belgrade, trg Nikole Pašica 8/II; tel. (11) 3233565; fax (11) 3233563; f. 1948; technical, scientific and educational textbooks; Dir LJUBINKO ANĐELIĆ.

Jugoslovenska knjiga (Yugoslav Books) Publishing House: 11000 Belgrade, trg Republike 5, POB 36; tel. (11) 621992; fax (11) 625970; art, economics and culture; Dir ZORAN NIKODIJEVIĆ.

Vuk Karadžič Publishing House: 11000 Belgrade, Kraljevića Marka 9, POB 762; tel. (11) 628066; fax (11) 623150; scientific and academic literature, popular science, children's books, general; Gen. Man. VOJIN ANČIĆ.

Matice srpske Publishing House: 21000 Novi Sad, trg Toze Markovića 2; tel. (21) 420199; fax (21) 27281; e-mail m.grujic@sezampro.yu; internet www.maticasrpska.org.yu; f. 1826; domestic and foreign fiction and humanities; Man. Dir MILORAD GRUJIĆ.

Medicinska knjiga (Medical Books) Publishing House: 11001 Belgrade, Mata Vidakovića 24–26; tel. (11) 458165; f. 1947; medicine, pharmacology, stomatology, veterinary; Dir MILE MEDIĆ.

Minerva Publishing House: 24000 Subotica, trg 29 Novembra 3; tel. (24) 25712; fax (24) 23208; novels and general; Dir LADISLAV ŠEBEK.

Naučna knjiga (Scientific Books) Publishing House: 11000 Belgrade, Uzun Mirkova 5; tel. (11) 637220; f. 1947; school, college and university textbooks, publications of scientific bodies; Dir Dr BLAŽO PEROVIĆ.

Nolit: 11000 Belgrade, Terazije 27; tel. (11) 3245017; fax (11) 627285; f. 1928; belles-lettres, philosophy and fine art; scientific and popular literature; Dir-Gen. RADIVOJE NEŠIĆ; Editor-in-Chief RADIVOJE MIKIĆ.

Prosveta (Education) Publishing House: 11000 Belgrade, Čika Ljubina 1; tel. (11) 629843; fax (11) 182581; f. 1944; general literature, art books, dictionaries, encyclopaedias, science, music; Dir BUDIMIR RUDOVIĆ.

Rad (Labour) Publishing House: 11000 Belgrade, Dečanska 12; tel. (11) 3239998; fax (11) 3230923; internet www.radbooks.co.yu; f. 1949; politics, economics, sociology, psychology, literature, biographies; Man. Dir SIMON SIMONOVIĆ; Editor-in-Chief NOVICA TADIĆ.

Savremena administracija (Contemporary Administration) Publishing House: 11000 Belgrade, Crnotravska 7–9; tel. (11) 667633; fax (11) 667277; e-mail m.jovic@savremena-ad.com; internet www.savremena-ad.com; f. 1954; economy, law, science university textbooks, encyclopedias and dictionaries; Dir MILUTIN PEJČIĆ.

Sportska knjiga (Sports Books) Publishing House: 11000 Belgrade, Makedonska 19; tel. (11) 320226; f. 1949; sport, chess, hobbies; Dir BORISLAV PETROVIĆ.

Srpska književna zadruga (Serb Publishing Collective): 11000 Belgrade, Srpskih Vladara 19/I; tel. (11) 330305; fax (11) 626224; f. 1892; works of classical and modern Serb writers, and translations of works of foreign writers; Pres. RADOVAN SAMARDŽIĆ; Editor RADOMIR RADOVANAĆ.

Svetovi: 21000 Novi Sad, Arse Teodorovića 11; tel. (21) 28032; fax (21) 28036; general; Dir JOVAN ZIVLAK.

Tehnička Knjiga (Technical Books) Publishing House: 11000 Belgrade, Vojvode Stepe 89; tel. (11) 468596; fax (11) 473442; f. 1948; technical works, popular science, reference books, hobbies; Dir RADIVOJE GRBOVIĆ.

Zavod za udžbenike i nastavna sredstva (Institute for School Books and Teaching Aids): 11000 Belgrade, Obilićev Venac 5; tel. (11) 638463; fax (11) 637426; e-mail press@zavod.co.yu; internet www.zavod.co.yu; f. 1957; textbooks and teaching aids; Dir RADOSLAV PETKOVIĆ.

PUBLISHERS' ASSOCIATIONS

Asscn of Publishers and Booksellers of Serbia (Udruženje izdavača i knjižara Srbije): 11000 Belgrade, Kneza Miloša 25, POB 570; tel. (11) 642533; fax (11) 646339; e-mail ognjenl@eunet.yu; f. 1954; organizes Belgrade International Book Fair; Dir OGNJEN LAKIĆEVIĆ; 116 mem. organizations.

Asscn of Publishers and Booksellers of Vojvodina (Poslovno udruženje izdavača i knjižara Vojvodine): 21000 Novi Sad; tel. and fax (21) 4720452; e-mail info@knjigavoj.co.yu; internet www.knjigavoj.co.yu; f. 2001; Dir ROMAN VEHOVEC; Chair. of Council ĐEZE BORDAS.

Broadcasting and Communications

TELECOMMUNICATIONS

063 Mobtel Srbija: 11070 Belgrade, bul. Nikole Tesle 42A; tel. (11) 3013267; e-mail pr@mobtel.co.yu; internet www.mobtel.co.yu; f. 1994; 51% owned by BK Trade Moscow (Russia), 49% by Telekom Srbija; provides mobile cellular telecommunications in Serbia.

Telekom Srbija (Telecom Serbia): 11000 Belgrade, Takovska 7; tel. (11) 3229991; internet www.telekomsrbija.com; 20% owned by OTE (Greece); provides fixed line and mobile cellular telecommunications services in Serbia; Dir-Gen. DRAŠKO PETROVIĆ.

BROADCASTING

Association of Independent Electronic Media: 11000 Belgrade, Maršala Birjuzova 3/IV; tel. and fax (11) 3034807; internet www.anem.org.yu; f. 1993; comprises 16 television and 28 radio stations, and 70 affiliated orgs; Chair. SLOBODAN STOJSIĆ.

Radio

Međunarodni Radio Srbija (International Radio Serbia): 11000 Belgrade, Hilandarska 2, POB 200; tel. (11) 3244455; fax (11) 3232014; e-mail radioyu@bitsyu.net; internet www.glassrbije.org; f. 1951; fmrly Radio Jugoslavija (Radio Yugoslavia); state-owned short-wave station; broadcasts daily in Serbian, English, French, German, Russian, Spanish, Hungarian, Chinese, Albanian, Greek, Italian and Arabic; Dir MILENA JOKIĆ.

Radio B92: 11000 Belgrade, bul. Avnoja 64; tel. (11) 3012000; fax (11) 3012001; internet www.b92.net; f. 1989; independent; Dir VERAN MATIĆ; Dir of Radio Programming GORICA NEŠOVIĆ.

Radio JAT: 11000 Belgrade, Svetog Save 1/XVI; tel. (11) 2440142; e-mail radio_jat@jat.com; internet www.radiojat.co.yu.

Radiotelevizija Košava: 11000 Belgrade, Masarikova 5; tel. (11) 3061491; fax (11) 3612135; internet www.kosava.co.yu; f. 1994; radio

SERBIA

station broadcasting popular music and talk programmes to most regions of Serbia.

Radiotelevizija Srbije (RTS) (Radio-Television of Serbia): 11000 Belgrade, Takovska 10; tel. (11) 3212200; fax (11) 3212211; e-mail rtstv@rts.co.yu; internet www.rts.co.yu; f. 1929; 5 radio programmes; comprises Radiotelevizija Beograd (Radio-Television of Belgrade), Radiotelevizija Novi Sad (Radio-Television of Novi Sad, Vojvodina) and Radiotelevizija Priština (Radio-Television of Priština, Kosovo); Dir-Gen. ALEKSANDAR TIJANIĆ.

Radio TV Bajina Basta: 31250 Bajina Basta, Svetosavska 34; tel. (31) 851688; fax (31) 853162; e-mail office@bajinabasta.org; internet www.bajinabasta.org; f. 1986; independent radio and television station; Dir BOBAN TOMIĆ.

Television

B92 Televizija: 11000 Belgrade, bul. Avnoja 64; tel. (11) 3012000; fax (11) 3012001; internet www.b92.net; f. 2000; independent; Dir VERAN MATIĆ; Dir of Programming IVA IVANIŠEVIĆ.

BK Telecom (BK): 11070 Belgrade, Nikole Tesle 42A; tel. (11) 3013555; fax (11) 3013526; internet www.bktv.com; f. 1994; independent television station; Dir-Gen. Dr TIMOHIR SIMIĆ; Editor-in-Chief MILOMIR MARIĆ.

Radiotelevizija Srbije: 11000 Belgrade, Takovska 10; tel. (11) 3212200; fax (11) 3212211; internet www.rts.co.yu; f. 1929; 5 radio programmes; comprises Radiotelevizija Beograd (Radio-Television of Belgrade), Radiotelevizija Novi Sad (Radio-Television of Novi Sad, Vojvodina) and Radiotelevizija Priština (Radio-Television of Priština, Kosovo); Dir-Gen. ALEKSANDAR TIJANIĆ.

RTV Pink: 11000 Belgrade, Neznanog Junaka 1; tel. (11) 3063400; fax (11) 3063500; internet www.rtvpink.com; f. 1993; leading private tv and radio broadcast co Pink International; Pres. and CEO ŽELJKO MITROVIĆ.

Finance

(cap. = capital; res = reserves; dep. = deposits; m. = million; amounts in Serbian dinars, unless otherwise stated; br. = branch)

BANKING

Central Banking System

In 2003, following the reconstitution of the Federal Republic of Yugoslavia as the State Union of Serbia and Montenegro, the National Bank of Yugoslavia became Serbia's central bank, and was renamed the National Bank of Serbia. In early 2008 there were 34 banks in Serbia.

National Bank of Serbia (Narodna banka Srbije): 11000 Belgrade, Kralja Petra 12, POB 1010; tel. (11) 3027100; fax (11) 3027113; e-mail kabinet@nbs.yu; internet www.nbs.yu; f. 1884; fmrly National Bank of Yugoslavia; cap. 8,608m., res 12,645m., dep. 292,783m. (Dec. 2005); Gov. RADOVAN JELAŠIĆ; 4 brs.

Other Banks

A Banka: 11030 Belgrade, Požeška 65B; tel. (11) 3050300; fax (11) 3540930; e-mail office@abanka.co.yu; f. 1996 as Alco Banka; present name adopted 2004; cap. 1,509.5m., res 15.1m., dep. 2,605.4m. (Dec. 2006); Pres. JAN VANHEVEL.

Alpha Bank Srbija AD: 11000 Belgrade, Kralja Milana 11; tel. (11) 3234931; fax (11) 3246840; e-mail alphabankserbia@alphabankserbia.com; internet www.alphabankserbia.com; f. 1956; fmrly Jubanka a.d. Beograd; present name adopted 2006; cap. 12,589.1m., res −2.9m., dep. 23,941.8m. (Dec. 2006); Chair. SPYROS N. FILARETOS; 23 brs.

Banca Intesa a.d. Beograd: 11070 Belgrade, Milentija Popovića 7B; tel. (11) 2011213; fax (11) 2011207; e-mail bi@bancaintesabeograd.com; internet www.bancaintesabeograd.com; f. 1991 as MB Delta Banka d.d.; name changed as above Nov. 2005; cap. 5,180.1m., res 5,726.6m., dep. 105,017.7m. (Dec. 2006); CEO DRAGINJA ĐURIĆ; 150 brs.

Erste Bank a.d. Novi Sad: 21000 Novi Sad, bul. Mihajla Pupina 3; tel. (21) 527733; fax (21) 529507; e-mail info@erstebank.co.yu; internet www.erstebank.co.yu; f. 1864 as Novosadska Banka a.d.; name changed as above Dec. 2005; cap. 9,629.7m., res 206.9m., dep. 15,839.7m. (Dec. 2006); Pres. SAVA DALBOKOV.

Hypo Alpe-Adria-Bank a.d. Beograd: 11070 Novi Beograd, bul. Mihajla Pupina 6; tel. (11) 2226000; fax (11) 2226555; e-mail office@hypo-alpe-adria.co.yu; internet www.hypo-alpe-adria.co.yu; f. 1991 as Depozitno-Kreditna Banka; merged with Hypo Alpe-Adria-Bank 2002; cap. 11,683.8m., res 2,159.9m., dep. 79,838.9m. (Dec. 2006); Chair. VLADIMIR ČUPIĆ.

Jubmes Banka—Jugoslovenska Banka Za Medjunarodnu Ekonomsku Saradnju (Yugoslav Bank for International Economic Co-operation): 11000 Belgrade, bul. Zorana Đinđića 121, POB 219; tel. (11) 3115270; fax (11) 3110217; e-mail jubmes@jubmes.co.yu; internet www.jubmes.co.yu; f. 1979; focuses on the financing of export-orientated and development projects; cap. 1,040.9m., res 967.6m., dep. 1,884.9m. (Dec. 2006); Pres. MILAN STEFANOVIĆ.

Komercijalna Banka a.d. Beograd: 11000 Belgrade, Svetog Save 14; tel. (11) 3080100; fax (11) 3441335; e-mail posta@kombank.com; internet www.kombank.com; f. 1970; cap. 12,662.9m., res 1,962.6m., dep. 83,157.4m. (Dec. 2006); Pres. IVICA SMOLIĆ.

Meridian Bank—Credit Agricole Group: 21000 Novi Sad, Futoški put 42–44; tel. (21) 4876876; fax (21) 4876976; e-mail meba@bankmeridian.com; internet www.bankmeridian.com; f. 1992 as Yuco Banka a.d.; name changed as above in 2006; cap. 2,376.0m., res 14.8m., dep. 15,425.1m. (Dec. 2006); Chair. DOMINIQUE TISSIER.

Metals Banka a.d. Novi Sad: 21000 Novi Sad, bul. Cara Lazara 7A; tel. (21) 450695; fax (21) 6350611; e-mail info@metals-banka.co.yu; internet www.metals-banka.co.yu; f. 1990; cap. 3,603.0m., res 232.4m., dep. 4,973.7m. (Dec. 2006); Gen. Man. ANANIJE PAVIĆEVIĆ.

NLB Continental Banka a.d. Novi Sad: 21000 Novi Sad, trg Mladenaca 1–3; tel. (21) 6615500; fax (21) 6616560; e-mail cont@cont.co.yu; internet www.cont.co.yu; f. 1991; renamed Continental Banka a.d. Novi Sad-NLB Group 2005, following acquisition by Nova Ljubljanska banka (Slovenia); present name adopted 2006; cap. 3,795.6m., res 779.0m., dep. 19,171.3m. (Dec. 2006); Chair. ANDREJ HAZABENT.

Panonska Banka a.d.: 21000 Novi Sad, bul. Oslobođenja 76, POB 351; tel. (21) 4887100; fax (21) 4887219; e-mail office@panban.co.yu; internet www.panban.co.yu; f. 1974; cap. 3,236.0m., res 72.2m., dep. 13,134.9m. (Dec. 2006); Gen. Man. SRĐAN PETROVIĆ; 12 brs.

Privredna Banka Beograd a.d.: 11000 Belgrade, bul. Vojske Jugoslavije 4; tel. (11) 2641255; fax (11) 2641894; e-mail office@pbbad.com; internet www.pbbad.com; f. 1973; cap. 971.0m., res 35.8m., dep. 3,603.2m. (Dec. 2005); Chair. ČEDO PETROVIĆ.

ProCredit Bank a.d. Beograd: 11000 Belgrade, bul. Despota Stefana 68C; tel. (11) 2077906; fax (11) 2077905; e-mail info@procreditbank.co.yu; internet www.procreditbank.co.yu; f. 2001 as Micro Finance Banka; present name adopted 2003; cap. €44.7m., dep. €244.4m. (Feb. 2007); Chair. DOERTE WEIDIG.

Raiffeisenbank a.d. Beograd: 11000 Belgrade, bul. Zorana Đinđića 64A; tel. (11) 3202100; fax (11) 2207080; e-mail rbj.contact@raiffeisenbank.co.yu; internet www.raiffeisenbank.co.yu; f. 2001; cap. 15,723.6m., dep. 116,541.5m. (Dec. 2006); Chair. and Gen. Man. OLIVER ROEGL.

UniCredit bank Serbia JSC: 11000 Belgrade, Rajiceva 27–29; tel. (11) 3344100; fax (11) 3204639; e-mail office@unicreditbank.co.yu; internet www.unicreditbank.co.yu; f. 2001 as HVB Banka Jugoslavija a.d.; name changed as above in 2007; cap. 6,517.6m., res 562.3m., dep. 26,486.8m. (Dec. 2006); Chair. ALEXANDER PICKER.

Vojvodjanska Banka, a.d. Novi Sad: 21000 Novi Sad, POB 391, trg Slobode 7; tel. (21) 4886700; fax (21) 611512; e-mail office@voban.co.yu; internet www.voban.co.yu; f. 1962; cap. 4,846.6m., res 1,661.3m., dep. 36,545.2m. (Dec. 2006); Pres. MARINOS STRATOPOULOS.

Banking Association

Association of Serbian Banks (Udruženje banaka Srbije): 11001 Belgrade, bul. Kralja Aleksandra 86; tel. (11) 3020760; fax (11) 3370179; e-mail ubs@ubs-asb.com; internet www.ubs-asb.com; f. 1955; association of business banks; works on improving inter-bank co-operation, organizes agreements of mutual interest for banks, gives expert assistance, establishes co-operation with foreign banks, other financial institutions and their associations, represents banks in relations with the Government and the National Bank of Serbia; Sec.-Gen. VEROLJUB DUGALIĆ.

STOCK EXCHANGE

Belgrade Stock Exchange (Beogradska Berza): 11070 Belgrade, Omladinskih brigada 1, POB 50; tel. (11) 3117297; fax (11) 3117304; internet www.belex.co.yu; Chair. of Bd DARKO ČUKIĆ.

INSURANCE

AMS Osiguranje (AMS Insurance): 11000 Belgrade, Ruzveltova 16; tel. (11) 3342755; e-mail info@ams.co.yu; internet www.ams.co.yu; non-life; Gen. Dir DRAGOLJUB RADOJEVIĆ.

DDOR Novi Sad: 21000 Novi Sad, Železnička 5; tel. (21) 4871000; internet www.ddor.co.yu; f. 1990; life and non-life insurance and reinsurance; Gen. Dir DARKO BOTIĆ.

Delta Generali Osiguranje: 11070 Novi Beograd, Milentija Popovića 7B; tel. (11) 2011720; fax (11) 2011727; e-mail kontakt@deltagenerali.co.yu; internet www.deltagenerali.co.yu; life and non-life insurance and reinsurance.

Dunav Osiguranje (Danube Insurance): 11000 Belgrade, Makedonska 4, POB 624; tel. (11) 3224001; fax (11) 2624652; e-mail info@dunav.com; internet www.dunav.com; f. 1974; life and non-life insurance and reinsurance; Gen. Man. MIRKO PETROVIĆ.

SIM Osiguranje (SIM Insurance): 11000 Belgrade, Oblakovska 28; tel. and fax (11) 3690110; e-mail simosg@eunet.yu.

Uniqa Osiguranje: 11000 Belgrade, Milutina Milankovića 134G; tel. (11) 2024100; e-mail info@uniqa.co.yu; internet www.uniqa.co.yu; fmrly Zepter Osiguranje; present name adopted 2006, following acquisition by Uniqa (Austria); life and non-life insurance; KONSTANTIN KLIJEN.

Trade and Industry

GOVERNMENT AGENCIES

Foreign Trade Institute (Institut za Spoljnu Trgovinu): 11000 Belgrade, Moše Pijade 8; tel. (11) 3235391; fax (11) 3235306; e-mail radovank@eunet.yu; Dir Dr SLOBODAN MRKŠA.

Investment and Export Promotion Agency of the Republic of Serbia (Agencija za strana ulaganja i promociju izvoza Republike Srbije—SIEPA): 11000 Belgrade, Vlajkovićeva 3; tel. (11) 3398550; fax (11) 3398814; e-mail office@siepa.sr.gov.yu; internet www.siepa.sr.gov.yu; f. 2001; Dir JASNA MATIĆ.

CHAMBER OF COMMERCE

Chamber of Commerce of Serbia (Privredna Komora Srbije): 11000 Belgrade, Gen. Zdanova 13–15; tel. (11) 3240611; fax (11) 3230949; e-mail pksrbije@pks.co.yu; internet www.pks.co.yu; Pres. RADOSLAV VESELINOVIĆ.

UTILITIES

Electricity

Elektroprivreda Srbije (EPS) (Serbia Electricity Corpn): 11000 Belgrade, Balkanska 13; tel. (11) 3610580; fax (11) 3611908; internet www.eps.co.yu; state-owned; production, transmission and distribution of electric power in Serbia (incl. Kosovo); Dir-Gen. VLADIMIR ĐORĐEVIĆ.

Gas

NIS-Energogas: 11070 Belgrade, Autoput 11; tel. (11) 2672033; fax (11) 602200; e-mail energogas@energogas.co.yu; internet www.energogas.co.yu; subsidiary of Naftna Industrija Srbije (Petroleum Industry of Serbia); transportation and distribution of natural gas and liquid petrol gas, civil engineering.

TRADE UNIONS

Association of Free and Independent Trade Unions: 11000 Belgrade, Karađorđeva 71; tel. and fax (11) 2623671; e-mail asns@asns.org.yu; internet www.asns.org.yu; Pres. RANKA SAVIĆ.

Confederation of Autonomous Trade Unions of Serbia (Savez Samostalnih Sindikata Srbije): 11000 Belgrade, trg Nikole Pašić 5; tel. (11) 3230922; fax (11) 3241911; 600,000 mems.

Transport

RAILWAYS

In 2006 there were 4,581 km of railway track in use in Serbia, excluding Kosovo, of which 1,196 km were electrified. In 2005 a major infrastructure project for the relocation of the central railway station in Belgrade was near completion and the rehabilitation of the capital's rail system was also under way.

Železnice Srbije (Serbian Railways): 11000 Belgrade, Nemanjina 6; tel. (11) 3614811; fax (11) 3616722; internet www.zeleznicesrbije.com; Dir MILE LOKAS; Dir-Gen. MILANKO SARANCIĆ.

ROADS

In 2001 there were an estimated 44,993 km of roads in Serbia and Montenegro, of which 28,031 km were paved.

INLAND WATERWAYS

About 3.7m. metric tons of freight were carried on inland water transport in Serbia and Montenegro in 2000.

SHIPPING

Jugoagent Pomorska—rečna Agencija (Yugo Maritime and Rivers Shipping Agency): 11070 Belgrade, bul. Mihaila Pupina 165A, POB 210; tel. (11) 2018700; fax (11) 3112070; e-mail office@jugoagent.net; internet www.jugoagent.net; f. 1947; fmrly Jugoslovenska Pomorska Agencija (Yugoslav Maritime Agency); charter services, liner and container transport, port agency, passenger service, air cargo service; Gen. Man. ZORAN NETKOVIĆ.

CIVIL AVIATION

There is an international airport at Belgrade, and several domestic airports.

Jat Airways: 11070 Belgrade, bul. Umetnosti 16; tel. (11) 3114222; fax (11) 3112853; e-mail pr@jat.com; internet www.jat.com; f. 1927 as Aeroput; fmrly Jugoslovenski Aerotransport (JAT—Yugoslav Airlines); 51% owned by Govt; flights between Serbia and destinations in Central, Western, Eastern and Southern Europe and the Middle East; Dir-Gen. PREDRAG VUJOVIĆ.

Tourism

Serbia's tourism industry is considered to have considerable potential for development, with notable attractions including the mountain scenery, traditional thermal spas, historical cultural cities, and heritage of monuments and monasteries. In 2006 tourist arrivals (excluding Kosovo) totalled some 469,000, and in 2003 tourism receipts (including Montenegro) amounted to US $201m.

National Tourism Organization of Serbia (Turistička Organizacija Srbije): 11000 Belgrade, POB 433, Dobrinska 11; tel. (11) 3612754; fax (11) 686804; e-mail ntos@eunet.yu; internet www.serbia-info.com/ntos; f. 1953; produces information and conducts market research and promotion in the field of tourism; Dir JOVAN POPESKU.

SEYCHELLES

Introductory Survey

Location, Climate, Language, Religion, Flag, Capital

The Republic of Seychelles comprises about 115 islands, widely scattered over the western Indian Ocean. Apart from the Seychelles archipelago, the country includes several other island groups, the southernmost being about 210 km (130 miles) north of Madagascar. The climate is tropical, with small seasonal variations in temperature and rainfall. The average temperature in Victoria is nearly 27°C (80°F) and average annual rainfall 236 cm (93 ins). In 1981 Seselwa, a creole spoken by virtually all Seychellois, replaced English and French as the official language. Almost all of the inhabitants are Christians, of whom more than 90% belong to the Roman Catholic Church. The national flag (proportions 1 by 2) has five rays, extending from the lower hoist corner, of blue, yellow, red, white and green. The capital is Victoria, on the island of Mahé.

Recent History

Seychelles was uninhabited until colonized by France in 1770. It was ceded to the United Kingdom in 1814 and administered as a dependency of Mauritius until 1903, when it became a Crown Colony.

During the 1960s political activity was focused on the centre-right Seychelles Democratic Party, led by James (later Sir James) Mancham, and the socialist-orientated Seychelles People's United Party (SPUP), led by Albert René. A ministerial system of government was introduced in 1970, and Seychelles proceeded to full independence, as a sovereign republic within the Commonwealth, on 29 June 1976, under a coalition Government with Mancham as President and René as Prime Minister. Under the independence agreement, the United Kingdom returned to Seychelles the islands of Aldabra, Farquhar and Desroches, detached in 1965 to form part of the British Indian Ocean Territory (q.v.) and subsequently leased to the USA. In 1982 the Aldabra group, which (including its lagoon) represents about one-third of Seychelles' total area, was designated by UNESCO as a world heritage site.

In June 1977 the SPUP staged an armed coup while Mancham was absent from the islands. René was declared President, the National Assembly was dissolved and the Constitution suspended. In May 1978 the SPUP was renamed the Seychelles People's Progressive Front (SPPF). A new Constitution, proclaimed in March 1979, established a one-party state. In June elections for a new National Assembly were held. René was the sole candidate in the concurrent presidential election and was re-elected in June 1984 and again in 1989 as sole candidate, for a third term of office, the maximum period permitted under the 1979 Constitution. During this period opponents of René's socialist Government made a number of attempts to overthrow the regime. The most serious assault took place in November 1981, when about 50 mercenaries, mainly South Africans posing as tourists, flew to join insurgents already on the islands. When the rebellion collapsed, most of the mercenaries escaped to South Africa, where several of their number were later tried and imprisoned. Further plots, discovered in October 1982 and November 1983, were ascribed to the same Seychellois exiles who had planned the 1981 coup attempt. In November 1985 Gérard Hoareau, the leader of an exiled opposition group, was shot dead in the United Kingdom. The incident formed one of a series of attacks on, and disappearances of, anti-René activists.

Until the early 1990s exiled opposition to René remained split among a number of small groups based principally in London, United Kingdom. In July 1991 five of these parties formed a coalition, the United Democratic Movement (UDM), under the leadership of Dr Maxime Ferrari, a former political associate of René, while ex-President Mancham established a 'Crusade for Democracy'. René, meanwhile, came under increasing pressure from France and the United Kingdom, the islands' principal aid donors, to restore a democratic political system. Internally, open opposition to the SPPF was fostered by the newly formed Parti Seselwa, or Parti Seychellois (PS), led by an Anglican clergyman, Wavel Ramkalawan. In August 1991 Ferrari returned from exile to organize support for the UDM, and in November the Government invited all political dissidents to return to the islands.

In December 1991 the SPPF agreed to surrender the party's monopoly of power. It was announced that, from January 1992, political groups numbering at least 100 members would be granted official registration, and that multi-party elections would take place in July for a constituent assembly, whose proposals for constitutional reform would be submitted to a national referendum, with a view to holding multi-party parliamentary elections before the end of 1992. In April Mancham returned from exile to lead the New Democratic Party (NDP). At the July elections for the 20-seat constitutional commission, the SPPF won 58.4% of the votes, while the NDP received 33.7%. The PS, which took 4.4% of the votes, was the only other political party to obtain representation on the commission.

The commission, which comprised 11 representatives from the SPPF, eight from the NDP (now renamed the Democratic Party—DP) and one from the PS, completed its work in October 1992. In the previous month, however, the DP withdrew its delegation, on the grounds that the SPPF had allegedly refused to permit a full debate of reform proposals. The DP also expressed objections that the commission's meetings had been closed to the public and news media. Following publication of the draft Constitution, the DP challenged the proposed voting arrangements for a new National Assembly, whose members were to be elected on a basis of one-half by direct vote and one-half by proportional representation. The latter formula was to reflect the percentage of votes obtained by the successful candidate in presidential election, and was intended to ensure a legislative majority for the President's party. Other sections of the proposed Constitution, relating to social issues, were strongly opposed by the Roman Catholic Church, to which more than 90% of the islanders belong.

The draft Constitution, which required the approval of at least 60% of voters, was endorsed by only 53.7% at a referendum held in November 1992. A second constitutional commission, whose meetings were opened to the public, began work in January 1993 on proposals for submission to a further referendum, unanimously agreeing on a new draft Constitution, in which a compromise plan was reached on the electoral formula for a new National Assembly. With the joint endorsement of René and Mancham, the draft document was submitted to a national referendum in June, approved by 73.9% of voters. Opponents of the new constitutional arrangements comprised the PS, the Seychelles National Movement (SNM) and the National Alliance Party (NAP). At the presidential and legislative elections that followed in July, René received 59.5% of the vote, against 36.7% for Mancham and 3.8% for Philippe Boullé, the candidate representing an electoral alliance of the PS, the Seychelles Christian Democrat Party (SCDP), the SNM and the NAP. In the legislative elections, the SPPF secured 21 of the 22 seats elected by direct vote, and the DP one seat. Of the 11 additional seats allocated on a proportional basis, the SPPF received a further seven seats, the DP three seats and the PS one seat.

Following the 1993 elections the Government began to promote a gradual transition from socialism to free-market policies, aimed at maximizing the country's potential as an 'offshore' financial and business centre. State-owned port facilities were transferred to private ownership in 1994, when plans were also announced for the creation of a duty-free International Trade Zone to provide transhipment facilities. Measures were introduced to implement the privatization of government activities in tourism, agriculture and tuna-processing.

In early 1995 tensions developed within the opposition DP, whose only directly elected MP, Christopher Gill, sought to remove Mancham from the party leadership on the grounds that the former President was insufficiently vigorous in opposing the policies of the René Government. Gill was suspended from the DP in June, and subsequently formed a breakaway 'New Democratic Party' with the aim of restructuring the DP under a new leader. The official registration of active political organizations, affording them corporate status, led to the formal amalgamation of the PS, the SNM, the SCDP and the NAP as a single party, the United Opposition (UO), under the leadership of Ramkalawan.

In the furtherance of its efforts to promote Seychelles as an international 'offshore' financial centre, the Government introduced, in November 1995, an Economic Development Act (EDA), under whose provisions investors of a minimum US $10m. would receive immunity in Seychelles from extradition or seizure of assets. It was feared in international financial circles, however, that the operation of the EDA would make Seychelles a refuge for the proceeds of drugs-trafficking and other crimes. Protest was led by the United Kingdom, France and the USA, and in February 1996 the EDA was described by the Financial Action Task Force on Money Laundering (see p. 416) as a 'serious threat to world financial systems.' The Government, while refusing to rescind the EDA, established an Economic Development Board under the chairmanship of René, to vet potential EDA investors. In April 1996 the Government introduced legislation aimed at preventing the use of the EDA for 'laundering' illicit funds. Following reports critical of Seychelles' financial sector from two international organizations, the EDA was finally repealed in July 2000.

In July 1996 the SPPF introduced a series of constitutional amendments, creating the post of Vice-President, to which James Michel, the Minister of Finance, Communications and Defence and a long-standing political associate of René, was appointed in the following month. The constitutional changes also provided for revisions in constituency boundaries, which were generally interpreted as favouring SPPF candidates in future parliamentary elections. Measures were also implemented whereby the number of seats in the National Assembly was to be increased (see Government).

In January 1998 René announced that the elections would be held in March, and that he was to seek the second of a maximum of three consecutive five-year terms as president permitted under the 1993 Constitution. The outcome of the elections provided the SPPF with a decisive victory. René obtained 66.7% of the presidential ballot, while his party secured 30 of the 34 seats in the enlarged National Assembly. Ramkalawan, with 19.5% of the presidential vote, substantially exceeded support for Mancham, who received 13.8%. In the National Assembly the UO increased its representation from one to three seats, with the DP losing three of the four seats previously held. Since the 1993 elections, effective opposition to the Government had increasingly been led by Ramkalawan's UO, as the DP opted to pursue a policy of 'reconciliation' with the SPPF. In mid-1998 the UO changed its name to the Seychelles National Party (SNP).

In July 2001 René declared a presidential election almost two years early, claiming that this was in order to reassure investors about the long-term stability of the country. On 31 August–2 September René was re-elected as President, but with the smallest mandate of his career, securing 54.2% of the valid votes cast. Ramkalawan, the SNP candidate, won 45.0% of the votes, but refused to accept the result, claiming serious irregularities in the electoral process, and subsequently filed a formal complaint with the Constitutional Court. Legislative elections, which were due in 2003, took place early, on 4–6 December 2002. The SPPF retained its majority in the National Assembly, but with a reduced margin, securing 23 of the 34 seats, while the SNP won the remaining 11 seats. In March 2003 René indicated during the congress of the SPPF that he would progressively relinquish control of certain presidential duties to Vice-President Michel, who was also designated as the party's candidate for the next presidential election.

On 14 April 2004 President René formally retired, having spent almost 27 years in office. He was succeeded by Vice-President Michel, who was inaugurated as President on the same day. René retained his position as President of the SPPF. Joseph Belmont was subsequently appointed Vice-President, retaining responsibility for tourism and transport. In July the portfolio for international trade and industry was subsumed into that of the Ministry of Economic Planning, which was to be headed by Jacquelin Dugasse.

In February 2005 President Michel reduced the number of government ministries from nine to seven. The Minister of Foreign Affairs, Jérémie Bonnelame, was appointed Permanent Representative to the United Nations and the USA and replaced by Patrick Pillay, hitherto Minister of Health. The health portfolio was merged with that of social affairs. The Minister of Manpower and Administration, Noellie Alexander, was also appointed elsewhere, but was not replaced; the areas of responsibility of the portfolio were reassigned to the Ministry of Education and Youth. Also in February Mancham resigned from the chairmanship of the DP; in March Paul Chow became the leader of the DP; Nichol Gabriel retained his post as party secretary. Chow was believed to favour an electoral alliance with the SNP.

In the weeks prior to the 2006 presidential election, tensions increased between supporters of the leading political parties contesting the vote, and there were reports of numerous violent incidents. Nevertheless, the election proceeded as scheduled on 28–30 July at which Michel secured victory with 53.73% of the valid votes cast; Ramkalawan received 45.71%. A voter turn-out of 88.7% was recorded. In mid-August a new Government was sworn in, including three new appointments to the 10-member administration. In October several high-ranking SNP officials, including Ramkalawan, were the victims of a violent attack by the paramilitary police. The incident occurred after Ramkalawan made a speech at the National Assembly denouncing a proposal to ban all political parties from establishing private radio stations. Ramkalawan was among three members of the SNP who were subsequently charged with attending an illegal demonstration. They were brought to trial that month; however, President Michel later suspended the charges in an attempt to quell rising violence among the political parties and their supporters. An independent inquiry into the incident was launched in March 2007, and in February 2008 the Government accepted responsibility for injuries caused during the protests. Attempts were made to settle the issue of compensation out of court; however, the Government's legal representatives insisted that an initial claim for some SR 1m. was inappropriate.

Meanwhile, the SNP threatened to boycott the parliamentary elections, scheduled to be held by the end of 2007, unless certain demands were met and in January Ramkalawan held talks with the Electoral Commissioner, Hendrick Gappy, and requested that the electoral register remain open up to two months prior to the ballot. President Michel announced in March that he would dissolve the National Assembly and called an early election, which was held on 10–12 May 2007. According to official results released later that month, the SPPF retained 23 seats and its majority in the National Assembly, securing 56.2% of the votes cast. Prior to the election the SNP and the DP announced that, for the first time since the re-emergence of multi-party politics in 1992, they would form an alliance and nominate common candidates to contest the ballot. The SNP-DP alliance received 43.8% of the votes, and secured the 11 remaining seats. International observers praised the country for the conduct of the elections, at which 85.9% of the registered electorate turned out to vote. In July President Michel reduced the number of government ministries from 10 to eight. Although the key ministers retained their positions, the Ministry of Finance was to encompass three separate departments for finance and commerce, the Treasury and the Revenue Authority, while the Ministry of Health became the Ministry of Social Development and Health.

Seychelles has traditionally pursued a policy of non-alignment in international affairs, and supports movements for the creation of a 'zone of peace' in the Indian Ocean area. Until 1983 all naval warships wishing to dock at Seychelles had to provide a guarantee that they were not carrying nuclear weapons. The British and US Governments refused to agree to this condition, and their respective naval fleets were therefore effectively banned from using Seychelles port facilities. This requirement was withdrawn in September 1983, although Seychelles continued, in theory, to refuse entry to ships carrying nuclear weapons.

Since the late 1980s Seychelles has expanded the scope of its formal diplomatic contacts. Relations have been established with the Comoros and with Mauritius, and agreements have been made with the latter for co-operation in health and economic development matters. In 1989 diplomatic relations were established with Morocco, Madagascar and Côte d'Ivoire, and in 1990 with Kenya. During 1992 formal relations were established with Israel and South Africa, and in 1998 Seychelles proposed to establish a diplomatic mission in Malaysia to expand its relations in Asia and Oceania. Libya opened a diplomatic mission in Seychelles in January 2000, and diplomatic ties were established with Sudan in October. Following years of minimal interaction between France and Seychelles, owing to Seychelles' accumulated debt to the Agence Française de Développement, the French Minister for Co-operation was the first minister in over four years to visit Seychelles in February 2001. It was hoped that a resolution to the situation could be found and a new schedule for repayments negotiated. In 2001 relations were restored with Japan, which granted a subsidy for fishery development to Seychelles; this was said to be a consequence of the reversal of Seychelles' whaling policy. President Michel paid a state visit to Mauritius in March 2005, as guest of honour at that country's annual celebration of independence; various economic and co-operative agreements between the two countries were also signed. In December 2005, as a result of the seventh session of the Seychelles-Mauritius Commission on Bilateral Co-operation, a further agreement was signed on the sharing of expertise in a wide range of fields. The Government also strengthened relations with the People's Republic of China, following a state visit to that country by Michel in November 2006.

Government

Under the 1993 Constitution, executive power is vested in the President, who is Head of State and Commander-in-Chief of the Armed Forces. The President, who is elected by direct popular vote, appoints and leads the Council of Ministers, which acts in an advisory capacity to him. The President also appoints the holders of certain public offices and the judiciary. The President may hold office for a maximum period of three five-year terms. The legislature is the unicameral National Assembly, presently comprising 34 members, of whom 25 are directly elected for five years and nine allocated on a proportional basis. Constitutional changes, introduced in July 1996, provide for an enlargement to 35 members: 25 directly elected and a maximum of 10 allocated on a proportional basis.

Defence

As assessed at November 2007, the army numbered 200 men, including a coastguard of 200. Paramilitary forces comprised a 250-strong national guard. The defence budget for 2007 allocated an estimated SR 80m. to defence. Seychelles was to contribute servicemen to the East African Stand-by Brigade, part of the African Union (see p. 164) stand-by peace-keeping force; the unit was intended to be ready for rapid response by 2010.

Economic Affairs

In 2006, according to estimates by the World Bank, Seychelles' gross national income (GNI), measured at average 2004–06 prices, was US $742m., equivalent to $8,650 per head (or $16,560 per head on an international purchasing-power parity basis). During 1996–2006, it was estimated, the population increased at an average annual rate of 1.2%, while gross domestic product (GDP) per head increased, in real terms, by an average of 1.0% per year. Overall GDP increased, in real terms, at an average annual rate of 2.2% in 1996–2006. Real GDP declined by 2.9% in 2004, but grew by 1.2% in 2005 and by 4.5% in 2006.

Agriculture (including forestry and fishing) contributed 2.3% of GDP in 2007, according to preliminary estimates, and accounted for 3.0% of total employment (excluding self-employed) in 2006. Much of Seychelles' production of coconuts has traditionally been exported in the form of copra, but exports dwindled in the late 1990s. Other cash crops include cinnamon bark (although production declined from 205 metric tons in 2004 to just nine tons in 2005, before recovering to 279 tons in 2006), tea, patchouli, vanilla and limes. Tea, sweet potatoes, cassava, yams, sugar cane, bananas, eggs and poultry meat are produced for local consumption. However, imports of food and live animals constituted an estimated 21.5% of the value of total imports in 2007. Fishing has become increasingly important since the 1980s, and exports of canned tuna alone contributed an estimated 50.6% of the value of total exports in 2007. Licence fees from foreign fishing vessels, allowed to operate in Seychelles' waters, contribute significantly to foreign exchange. A three-year fishing protocol, worth €3.48m., was signed with the European Union in 2001; a further six-year protocol was agreed in October 2004, and in December 2005 an agreement, valid until 2011, increased the payment for fishing rights to €4.12m. a year as well as raising the value of some licences, meaning that the Government could expect payments of some €6.0m. a year. Agricultural GDP increased at an average annual rate of 0.3% during 1996–2006, according to the World Bank; however, it declined by 2.6% in 2005 and by 2.0% in 2006.

Industry (including mining, manufacturing, construction and power) contributed an estimated 19.3% of GDP in 2007 and accounted for 23.4% of total employment (excluding self-employed) in 2006. Industrial GDP increased at an average annual rate of 3.0% during 1996–2006, according to the World Bank; the sector grew by 3.3% in 2004 but contracted by 2.0% in 2005 and by 2.0% in 2006.

The mining sector is small and mineral production consists mainly of quantities of construction materials, such as clay, coral, stone and sand. There are deposits of natural gas, and during the 1980s concessions were sold to several foreign companies, allowing exploration for petroleum. Exploratory drilling has so far proved unsuccessful; however, an agreement to renew exploration was made in 2005. A survey of offshore areas, initiated in 1980, revealed the presence of nodules, containing deposits of various metals, on the sea-bed. The possibility of renewed commercial exploitation of Seychelles' granite reserves is under investigation and the future development of offshore petroleum reserves is a possibility.

Manufacturing contributed an estimated 10.2% of GDP in 2007 and accounted for 11.3% of total employment in 2006. Apart from a tuna-canning plant (opened in 1987), the manufacturing sector consists mainly of small-scale activities, including boat-building, printing and furniture-making. According to the World Bank, manufacturing GDP increased at an average annual rate of 2.3% during 1996–2006. However, manufacturing GDP contracted by 2.0% in both 2005 and 2006.

Energy is derived principally from oil-fired power stations. In 2007 mineral fuels and lubricants accounted for an estimated 25.1% of the total value of imports. The vast majority of fuel imports are re-exported, mainly as bunker sales to visiting ships and aircraft—exports of refined petroleum products contributed 30.0% of total export earnings in 2004, and re-exports accounted for an estimated 44.7% of the value of total exports in 2007. It is envisaged that the proceeds from re-exports eventually will fund fully fuel imports.

Services provided an estimated 78.4% of GDP in 2007 and accounted for 73.6% of total employment (excluding self-employed) in 2006. Tourist arrivals totalled some 161,300 in 2007; income from tourism amounted to SR $885m. in 2006, according to central bank estimates. The majority of visitors were from western Europe, notably from France, Germany, Italy and the United Kingdom. The GDP of the services sector increased at an average annual rate of 1.9% during 1996–2006, according to the World Bank. Services GDP grew by 7.6% in 2006.

In 2006 Seychelles recorded a visible trade deficit of US $287.2m., and there was a deficit of $175.5m. on the current account of the balance of payments. The principal source of imports (24.8%) in 2007 was Saudi Arabia; other important suppliers were Germany, France, Singapore, Spain and South Africa. The principal market for domestic exports (excluding re-exports) in 2005 was the United Kingdom (45.4%; other significant purchasers were France, Italy and Germany. The principal export is canned tuna (following the expansion of the Indian Ocean Tuna Co in 1995 and increasing production thereafter); in 2007 canned tuna represented 91.4% of domestic exports. The main imports in 2007 were machinery and transport equipment, mineral fuels and lubricants, food and live animals, and basic manufactures.

In 2006 Seychelles recorded a budgetary surplus of SR 174.4m. (equivalent to 3.3% of GDP). Seychelles' total external debt was US $674.7m. at the end of 2005, of which $401.7m. was long-term public debt. In that year the cost of debt-servicing was equivalent to 7.4% of the value of exports of goods and services. According to the ILO, the annual rate of inflation averaged 2.9% in 1996–2006; consumer prices increased by an average of 0.9% in 2005, but declined by 0.3% in 2006. Some 8.3% of the labour force were registered as unemployed in 1993.

Seychelles is a member of the African Development Bank (see p. 162), of the Common Market for Eastern and Southern Africa (see p. 205) and of the Indian Ocean Commission (see p. 412), which aims to promote co-operation in the region. It was announced in December 1996 that Seychelles was to provide the headquarters of the Indian Ocean Tuna Commission.

Since the early 1970s tourism has been the mainstay of the Seychelles economy, and despite measures introduced in 1995 to develop Seychelles as an 'offshore' financial services centre (see Recent History), and to establish the islands as a centre for transhipment and air freight in the Indian Ocean area, the continuing dependence of the economy on tourism leaves the country highly vulnerable to outside economic influences, while the cost of servicing the external debt remains a major impediment to balanced growth. The new Government of President James Michel (who was also the Minister of Finance) from 2004, and his avowed commitment to the programme of economic reform gave rise to a degree of economic optimism, particularly with regard to privatization, and in late 2007 the Government announced its intention to develop Port Victoria and attract more maritime business in an effort to further diversify the country's economic base. However, a primary obstacle to relations with international donor institutions such as the IMF was the country's refusal to devalue the national currency, owing to its fears of incurring inflation (related to the country's dependence on imported items). It was argued, though, that the over-valuation of the rupee was a contributing factor to the ongoing shortage of foreign-exchange. In October 2007 the currency was eventually devalued to from 7.5 rupees per US dollar to 8.0 rupees. Meanwhile, in March 2006 the National Assembly approved a new investment code, drawn up with the advice of the World Bank and the UN, which aligned policy more closely with international regulations; the code allows investors to repatriate rupee earnings in the form of foreign exchange, provides an incentive structure and a dispute-settlement facility and protects against expropriation, but also protects certain local activities and services. The Government's priorities included the significant reduction of the country's public debt and the attraction of further foreign direct investment. In late 2007 the Government announced its aim to increase its budget surplus to some 5% of GDP in 2008, while it also hoped to double total GDP by 2015, focusing on growth in the financial services, tourism and fishing industries. The IMF forecast GDP growth of 4.6% for 2008, notwithstanding the island's vulnerability to rising fuel prices.

Education

In 1979 free and compulsory primary education was introduced for children between six and 16 years of age. A programme of educational reform, based on the British comprehensive schools system, was introduced in 1980. The language of instruction in primary schools is English. The duration of primary education is six years, while that of general secondary education is five years (of which the first four years are compulsory), beginning at 12 years of age. Pre-primary and special education facilities are also available. According to UNESCO estimates, in 2003/04 enrolment at primary schools included 96% of children in the relevant age-group (males 96%; females 97%), while the comparable ratio for secondary enrolment in that year was 93% (males 90%; females 96%). There were 1,837 students in post-secondary (non-tertiary) education in 2005. A number of students study abroad, principally in the United Kingdom. Government expenditure on education in 2006 was SR 189.2m., or about 8.2% of total expenditure.

Public Holidays

2008: 1–2 January (New Year), 21–22 March (Easter), 1 May (Labour Day), 22 May (Corpus Christi), 5 June (Liberation Day, anniversary of 1977 coup), 18 June (National Day), 29 June (Independence Day), 15 August (Assumption), 1 November (All Saints' Day), 8 December (Immaculate Conception), 25 December (Christmas Day).

2009: 1–2 January (New Year), 10–13 April (Easter), 1 May (Labour Day), 5 June (Liberation Day, anniversary of 1977 coup), 11 June (Corpus Christi), 18 June (National Day), 29 June (Independence Day), 15 August (Assumption), 1 November (All Saints' Day), 8 December (Immaculate Conception), 25 December (Christmas Day).

Weights and Measures

The imperial system is being replaced by the metric system.

Statistical Survey

Source (unless otherwise stated): Statistics and Database Administration Section, Management and Information Systems Division, POB 206, Victoria; e-mail misdstat@seychelles.net; internet www.nsb.gov.sc.

AREA AND POPULATION

Area: 455.3 sq km (175.8 sq miles), incl. Aldabra lagoon (145 sq km).

Population: 74,331 at census of 26 August 1994; 75,876 (males 37,589, females 38,287) at census of 29 August 1997. *Mid-2007* (official estimate): 85,032 (males 43,160, females 41,872).

Density (mid-2007): 186.8 per sq km.

Principal Town: Victoria (capital), estimated population 60,000 (incl. suburbs) in 1994. *Mid-2003* (incl. suburbs, UN estimate): Victoria 20,050. (Source: UN, *World Urbanization Prospects: The 2003 Revision*).

Births, Marriages and Deaths (registrations, 2007): Live births 1,499 (birth rate 17.6 per 1,000); Marriages (of residents) 405 (marriage rate 4.8 per 1,000); Deaths 630 (death rate 7.4 per 1,000).

Expectation of Life (years at birth, official estimates): 72.2 (males 68.9; females 75.7) in 2006.

Employment (2006, averages): Agriculture, forestry and fishing 1,189; Manufacturing 4,465; Electricity and water 1,089; Quarrying and construction 3,717; Trade, restaurants and hotels 7,978; Transport, storage and communications 3,366; Other services 17,758; *Total* 39,561. (Figures exclude self-employed persons, unpaid family workers and employees in private domestic services; total may not be equal to the sum of components, owing to rounding).

HEALTH AND WELFARE

Key Indicators

Total Fertility Rate (children per woman, 2007): 2.2.

Under-5 Mortality Rate (per 1,000 live births, 2005): 13.

Physicians (per 1,000 head, 2004): 1.51.

Hospital Beds (per 1,000 head, government establishments only, 2006): 4.93.

Health Expenditure (2004): US $ per head (PPP): 634.2.

Health Expenditure (2004): % of GDP: 6.1.

Health Expenditure (2004): public (% of total): 75.3.

Access to Water (% of persons, 2004): 88.

Human Development Index (2005): ranking: 50.

Human Development Index (2005): value: 0.843.

For sources and definitions, see explanatory note on p. vi.

AGRICULTURE, ETC.

Principal Crops (metric tons, 2006, FAO estimates): Coconuts 2,529; Vegetables (incl. melons) 1,946; Bananas 2,046; Other fruit 519; Tea (green leaf) 189; Cinnamon 279.

Livestock (head, 2006, FAO estimates): Cattle 1,400; Pigs 18,500; Goats 5,150.

Livestock Products (metric tons, 2006, FAO estimates): Pig meat 1,112; Chicken meat 1,147; Hen eggs 2,170.

Fishing ('000 metric tons, live weight, 2005): Capture 106.6 (Skipjack tuna 46.0; Yellowfin tuna 43.8; Bigeye tuna 10.4); Aquaculture 0.8 (Giant tiger prawn 0.8); *Total catch* 107.3.

Source: FAO.

INDUSTRY

Industrial Production (2007): Canned tuna 31,569 metric tons; Beer ('000 litres) 7,506; Soft drinks ('000 litres) 8,515; Cigarettes 33 million; Electric energy 271m. kWh.

FINANCE

Currency and Exchange Rates: 100 cents = 1 Seychelles rupee (SR). *Sterling, Dollar and Euro Equivalents* (30 November 2007): £1 sterling = 16.517 rupees; US $1 = 7.993 rupees; €1 = 11.799 rupees; 100 Seychelles rupees = £6.05 = $12.51 = €8.48. *Average Exchange Rate* (Seychelles rupees per US $): 5.5000 in 2004; 5.5000 in 2005; 5.5197 in 2006. Note: In November 1979 the value of the Seychelles rupee was linked to the IMF's special drawing right (SDR). In March 1981 the mid-point exchange rate was set at SDR 1 = 7.2345 rupees. This remained in effect until February 1997, when the fixed link with the SDR was ended.

Budget (SR million, 2006): *Revenue:* Taxation 1,245.6 (Taxes on income, etc. 297.0, Domestic taxes on goods and services 723.1, Import duties 225.5); Other current revenue 1,157.6; Total 2,403.2, excl. grants received (73.0). *Expenditure:* General government services 371.5; Community and social services 377.6; Education 189.2; Health 179.3; Economic services 47.7; Agriculture, environment and fishing 67.5; Transport and communications 62.8; Other purposes 199.7; Interest payments 405.9; Capital 403.8; Total 2,305.0, excl. lending minus repayments (–3.2). Note: Figures represent the consolidated accounts of the central Government, covering the operations of the Recurrent and Capital Budgets and of the Social Security Fund.

International Reserves (US $ million at 30 December 2006): IMF special drawing rights 0.0; Foreign exchange 112.92; Total 112.92. Source: IMF, *International Financial Statistics*.

Money Supply (SR million at 30 December 2006): Currency outside banks 392.8; Demand deposits at commercial banks 1,951.8; Total money (incl. others) 2,344.6. Source: IMF, *International Financial Statistics*.

Cost of Living (Consumer Price Index; base: 2001 = 100): All items 107.5 in 2004; 108.5 in 2005; 108.1 in 2006.

Expenditure on the Gross Domestic Product (US $ million at current prices, 2006): Government final consumption expenditure 172.68; Private final consumption expenditure 304.95; Gross fixed capital formation 152.39; *Total domestic expenditure* 630.02; Exports of goods and services 848.57; *Less* Imports of goods and services 732.23; *GDP in purchasers' values* 746.36. Source: African Development Bank.

Gross Domestic Product by Economic Activity (SR million at current prices, 2007, preliminary estimates): Agriculture, forestry and fishing 137.7; Manufacturing 608.7; Electricity and water 126.1; Construction 424.3; Trade, restaurants and hotels 1,180.0, Transport, storage and communications 1,174.2; Finance, insurance, real estate and business services 1,089.9; Education 229.8; Public administration and defence, and social security 545.5; Other services 476.8 *Sub-total* 5,993.0; Import duties, less subsidies 498.3; *Less* Imputed bank service charge 377.9; *GDP in purchasers' values* 6,113.2.

Balance of Payments (US $ million, 2006): Exports of goods f.o.b. 422.82; Imports of goods f.o.b. −710.05; *Trade balance* −287.23; Exports of services 430.60; Imports of services −311.63; *Balance on goods and services* −168.26; Other income received 10.27; Other income paid −53.95; *Balance on goods, services and income* −211.95; Current transfers received 46.56; Current transfers paid −10.10; *Current balance* −175.49; Capital account (net) 13.24; Direct investment abroad −8.01; Direct investment from abroad 145.82; Portfolio investment assets −0.05; Portfolio investment liabilities 198.21; Other investment assets −8.48; Other investment liabilities −74.03; Net errors and omissions 2.04; *Overall balance* 93.25. Source: IMF, *International Financial Statistics*.

EXTERNAL TRADE

Principal Commodities (distribution by SITC, SR million, 2007, provisional): *Imports c.i.f.:* Food and live animals 1,234.1; Mineral fuels 1,439.0; Basic manufactures 1,041.3; Machinery and transport 1,568.3; Total (incl. others) 5,728.4. *Exports f.o.b.:* Canned tuna 1,231.2; Fish (fresh/frozen) 13.9; Crustaceans 17.2; Fish meal 29.6; Medicaments, etc. 29.0; Total (incl. others) 2,435.3 (of which domestic exports SR 1,346.5m. and re-exports SR 1,088.7m).

Principal Trading Partners (SR million, 2007, provisional): *Imports c.i.f.:* France 445.2; Germany 545.1; Saudi Arabia 1,418.9; Singapore 486.4; South Africa 337.9; Spain 378.3; Total (incl. others) 5,728.4. *Exports f.o.b.:* Total 2,435.3 (of which domestic exports SR 1,346.5m. and re-exports SR 1,088.7m).

TRANSPORT

Road Traffic (registered motor vehicles, 2006): Private 6,766; Commercial 2,581; Taxis 304; Self-drive 1,125; Motor cycles 21; Omnibuses 215; *Total* 11,012.

Shipping: *Merchant Fleet* (registered at 31 December 2006): Vessels 47; Total displacement 115,616 grt (Source: Lloyd's Register-Fairplay, *World Fleet Statistics*); *International Sea-borne Freight Traffic* (2006): Freight ('000 metric tons): Imports 534; Exports 4,604; Transhipment (of fish) 74.

Civil Aviation (traffic on scheduled services, 2002): Kilometres flown 12 million; Passengers carried 518,000; Passenger-km 1,397 million; Total ton-km 153 million (Source: UN, *Statistical Yearbook*). *2006:* Aircraft movements 3,194; Passengers embarked 186,000; Passengers disembarked 189,000; Freight embarked 1,503 metric tons; Freight disembarked 5,380 metric tons.

TOURISM

Foreign Tourist Arrivals ('000): 128.7 in 2005; 140.6 in 2006; 161.3 in 2007.

Arrivals by Country of Residence (2005): CIS 4,248; France 27,592; Germany 17,011; Italy 18,377; South Africa 5,395; Switzerland 4,473; United Kingdom 16,497. Source: World Tourism Organization.

Tourism Receipts (SR million, central bank estimates): 818 in 2004; 824 in 2005; 885 in 2006; n.a. in 2007.

COMMUNICATIONS MEDIA

Radio Receivers (1997): 42,000 in use. Source: UNESCO, *Statistical Yearbook*.

Television Receivers (2000): 16,500 in use. Source: International Telecommunication Union.

Telephones (2007): 21,559 main lines in use.

Facsimile Machines (2002): 590 in use.

Mobile Cellular Telephones (2007): 83,293 subscribers.

Personal Computers (2004): 15,000 in use. Source: International Telecommunication Union.

Internet Users (2006): 3,872 accounts.

Broadband Subscribers (2006): 1,300. Source: International Telecommunication Union.

Book Production (1980): 33 titles (2 books, 31 pamphlets).

Daily Newspapers (2006): 1.

Non-daily Newspapers (2006): 3.

EDUCATION

Pre-primary (2007): 32 schools; 191 teachers; 2,825 pupils.

Primary (2007): 25 schools; 687 teachers; 8,802 pupils.

Secondary (2007): 13 schools; 588 teachers; 7,816 pupils.

Post-secondary (2007): 9 schools; 209 teachers; 1,906 pupils.

Vocational (2004): 7 institutions; 82 teachers; 1,099 pupils.

Adult Literacy Rate (official estimate): 96% (males 96%; females 96%) in 2007.

Directory

The Constitution

The independence Constitution of 1976 was suspended after the coup in June 1977 but reintroduced in July with substantial modifications. A successor Constitution, which entered into force in March 1979, was superseded by a new Constitution, approved by national referendum on 18 June 1993.

The President is elected by popular vote simultaneously with elections for the National Assembly. The President fulfils the functions of Head of State and Commander-in-Chief of the armed forces and may hold office for a maximum period of three consecutive five-year terms. The Assembly, elected for a term of five years, consists of 34 seats, of which 25 are filled by direct election and nine are allocated on a proportional basis. Constitutional amendments, introduced in July 1996, provided for an Assembly of 25 directly elected seats and a maximum of 10 proportionally allocated seats. There is provision for an appointed Vice-President. The Council of Ministers is appointed by the President and acts in an advisory capacity to him.

The President also appoints the holders of certain public offices and the judiciary.

The Government

HEAD OF STATE

President: JAMES MICHEL (took office 14 April 2004, elected 28–30 July 2006).

Vice-President: JOSEPH BELMONT.

COUNCIL OF MINISTERS
(March 2008)

President, with additional responsibility for Defence, the Police, Information and Public Relations, Legal Affairs and Risk and Disaster Management: JAMES MICHEL.

SEYCHELLES

Vice-President, Minister of Tourism, and Minister of Public Administration and Internal Affairs: JOSEPH BELMONT.
Minister of Finance: DANNY FAURE.
Minister of Foreign Affairs: PATRICK PILLAY.
Minister of National Development: JACQUELIN DUGASSE.
Minister of the Environment, Natural Resources and Transport: JOEL MORGAN.
Minister of Community Development, Youth, Sports and Culture: VINCENT MERITON.
Minister of Education: BERNARD SHAMLAYE.
Minister of Employment and Human Resources Development: MACSUZY MONDON.
Minister of Social Development and Health: MARIE-PIERRE LLOYD.

MINISTRIES

Office of the President: State House, POB 55, Victoria; tel. 224155; fax 224985.
Office of the Vice-President: State House, POB 1303, Victoria; tel. 225509; fax 225152; e-mail jbelmont@statehouse.gov.sc.
Ministry of Community Development, Youth, Sports and Culture: Oceangate House, POB 731, Victoria; tel. 225477; fax 225254; e-mail frevet@seychelles.net.
Ministry of Education: POB 48, Mont Fleuri; tel. 283283; fax 224859; e-mail pamedu@seychelles.net; internet www.education.gov.sc.
Ministry of Employment and Human Resources Development: Independence House, POB 1097, Victoria; tel. 676250; fax 610795; e-mail department@employment.gov.sc; internet www.employment.gov.sc.
Ministry of the Environment, Natural Resources and Transport: Independence House, POB 166, Victoria; tel. 611120; fax 225438; internet www.env.gov.sc.
Ministry of Finance: Liberty House, POB 113, Victoria; tel. 382004; fax 225265; e-mail psf@finance.gov.sc.
Ministry of Foreign Affairs: Maison Queau de Quincy, POB 656, Mont Fleuri; tel. 283500; fax 225398; e-mail dazemia@mfa.gov.sc; internet seychelles.diplomacy.edu.
Ministry of National Development: International Conference Centre, POB 648, Victoria; tel. 611200; fax 225374.
Ministry of Social Development and Health: POB 52, Mont Fleuri; tel. 388000; fax 226042.

President and Legislature

PRESIDENT

Election, 28–30 July 2006

Candidate	Votes	% of votes
James Michel (SPPF)	30,119	53.73
Wavel Ramkalawan (SNP)	25,626	45.71
Philippe Boullé (Independent)	314	0.56
Total	56,059	100.00

NATIONAL ASSEMBLY

Speaker: PATRICK HERMINIE.
Election, 10–12 May 2007

Party	Votes	% of votes	Seats*
Seychelles People's Progressive Front (SPPF)	30,571	56.2	23
Seychelles National Party (SNP)-Democratic Party (DP)	23,869	43.8	11
Total	54,440	100.0	34

* Of the Assembly's 34 seats, 25 were filled by direct election and nine by allocation on a proportional basis.

Election Commission

Electoral Commission: POB 741, Victoria; Suite 203, Aarti Bldg, Mont Fleuri; tel. 225847; fax 225474; e-mail hendrick@seychelles.net; Electoral Commissioner HENDRICK PAUL GAPPY.

Political Organizations

Democratic Party (DP): POB 169, Mont Fleuri; tel. 224916; fax 224302; internet www.dpseychelles.com; f. 1992; successor to the Seychelles Democratic Party (governing party 1970–77); Leader PAUL CHOW; Sec.-Gen. NICHOL GABRIEL.
Mouvement Seychellois pour la Démocratie: Mont Fleuri; tel. 224322; fax 224460; f. 1992; Leader JACQUES HODOUL.
Seychelles National Party (SNP): Arpent Vert, Mont Fleuri, POB 81, Victoria; tel. 224124; fax 225151; e-mail snpseychelles@gmail.com; internet www.snpseychelles.sc; f. 1995 as the United Opposition, comprising the fmr mem. parties of a coalition formed to contest the 1993 elections; adopted present name in 1998; Leader Rev. WAVEL RAMKALAWAN; Sec. ROGER MANCIENNE.
Seychelles People's Progressive Front (SPPF): POB 1242, Victoria; tel. 324622; fax 225070; e-mail people@sppf.sc; internet www.sppf.sc; fmrly the Seychelles People's United Party (f. 1964), which assumed power in 1977; renamed in 1978; sole legal party 1978–91; Pres. FRANCE ALBERT RENÉ; Sec.-Gen. JAMES MICHEL.

Diplomatic Representation

EMBASSIES AND HIGH COMMISSIONS IN SEYCHELLES

China, People's Republic: POB 680, St Louis; tel. 266588; fax 266866; e-mail china@seychelles.net; internet sc.china-embassy.org/eng/; Ambassador WANG WEIGUO.
Cuba: Belle Eau, POB 730, Victoria; tel. 224094; fax 224376; e-mail cubasey@seychelles.net; Ambassador DOMINGO ANGEL GARCÍA RODRÍGUEZ.
France: La Ciotat Bldg, Mont Fleuri, POB 478, Victoria; tel. 382500; fax 382510; e-mail ambafrance@intelvision.net; internet www.ambafrance-sc.org; Ambassador MICHEL TRÉTOUT.
India: Le Chantier, POB 488, Francis Rachel St, Victoria; tel. 610301; fax 610308; e-mail hicomind@seychelles.net; internet www.seychelles.net/hicomind; High Commissioner MALAY MISHRA.
Russia: Le Niol, POB 632, St Louis, Mahé; tel. 266590; fax 266653; e-mail rfembsey@seychelles.net; Ambassador ALEXANDER VLADIMIROV.
United Kingdom: 3rd Floor, Oliaji Trade Centre, POB 161, Victoria; tel. 283666; fax 283657; e-mail bhcvictoria@fco.gov.uk; internet www.bhcvictoria.sc; High Commissioner FERGUS COCHRANE-DYET.

Judicial System

The legal system is derived from English Common Law and the French Code Napoléon. There are three Courts, the Court of Appeal, the Supreme Court and the Magistrates' Courts. The Court of Appeal hears appeals from the Supreme Court in both civil and criminal cases. The Supreme Court is also a Court of Appeal from the Magistrates' Courts as well as having jurisdiction at first instance. The Constitutional Court, a division of the Supreme Court, determines matters of a constitutional nature, and considers cases bearing on civil liberties. There is also an industrial court and a rent tribunal.

Supreme Court: POB 157, Victoria; tel. 224071; fax 224197; Chief Justice VIVEKANAND ALLEEAR.
President of the Court of Appeal: STEPHEN BWANA (acting).
Justices of Appeal: ANNEL SILUNGWE, A. PILLAY, G. P. S. DE SILVA, K. P. MATADEEN.
Puisne Judges: RANJAN PERERA, D. KARUNAKARAN, N. JUDDOO.
Attorney-General: ANTHONY F. FERNANDO.

Religion

The majority of the inhabitants are Christians, of whom more than 90% are Roman Catholics and about 8% Anglicans. Hinduism, Islam, and the Bahá'í Faith are also practised, however.

CHRISTIANITY

The Anglican Communion

The Church of the Province of the Indian Ocean comprises six dioceses: four in Madagascar, one in Mauritius and one in Seychelles. The Archbishop of the Province is the Bishop of Antananarivo, Madagascar.

Bishop of Seychelles: Rt Rev. SANTOSH MARRAY, POB 44, Victoria; tel. 224242; fax 224296; e-mail angdio@seychelles.net.

SEYCHELLES

The Roman Catholic Church
Seychelles comprises a single diocese, directly responsible to the Holy See. At 31 December 2005 there were an estimated 70,424 adherents in the country, representing 85% of the total population.

Bishop of Port Victoria: Rt Rev. DENIS WIEHE, Bishop's House-Evêché, Olivier Maradan St, POB 43, Victoria; tel. 322152; fax 324045; e-mail rcchurch@seychelles.net.

Other Christian Churches
Pentecostal Assemblies of Seychelles: Victoria; tel. 224598; e-mail paos@seychelles.net; Pastor HERMITTE FREMINOT.

The Press

L'Echo des Iles: POB 12, Victoria; tel. 322262; fax 321464; monthly; French, Creole and English; Roman Catholic; Editor Fr EDWIN MATHIOT; circ. 2,800.

Le Nouveau Seychelles Weekly: Victoria; supports the Democratic Party.

The People: Maison du Peuple, Revolution Ave, Victoria; tel. 224455; owned by the SPPF; monthly; Creole, French and English; circ. 1,000.

Seychelles Nation: Information Technology and Communication Division, POB 800, Victoria; tel. 225775; fax 321006; e-mail seynat@seychelles.net; internet www.seychelles-online.com.sc; f. 1976; govt-owned; Mon.–Sat.; English, French and Creole; the country's only daily newspaper; Dir DENIS ROSE; circ. 3,500.

Seychelles Review: POB 29, Mahé, Victoria; tel. 241717; fax 241545; e-mail surmer@seychelles.net; monthly; business, politics, real estate and tourism; Editor ROLAND HOARAU.

Seychellois: POB 32, Victoria; f. 1928; publ. by Seychelles Farmers Asscn; quarterly; circ. 1,800.

Vizyon: Arpent Vert, Mont Fleuri, Victoria; tel. 224507; fax 224987; internet www.snpseychelles.sc/vizyon.htm; f. 2007; political fortnightly magazine of the opposition SNP; successor to weekly Regar; Creole, English and French; Editor ROGER MANCIENNE.

NEWS AGENCY
Seychelles Agence de Presse (SAP): Victoria Rd, POB 321, Victoria; tel. 224161; fax 226006.

Broadcasting and Communications

TELECOMMUNICATIONS
Cable and Wireless (Seychelles) Ltd: Mercury House, Francis Rachel St, POB 4, Victoria; tel. 284000; fax 322777; e-mail cws@seychelles.net; internet www.cwseychelles.com; f. 1990; Chief Exec. CHARLES HAMMOND.

Atlas (Seychelles) Ltd: POB 903, Victoria; tel. 304060; fax 324565; e-mail atlas@seychelles.net; internet www.seychelles.net; f. 1996 by a consortium of Space95, VCS and MBM; acquired by Cable and Wireless (Seychelles) Ltd in 2006; internet service provider; Gen. Man. ANTHONY DELORIE.

Telecom Seychelles Ltd (AirTel): POB 1358, Providence; tel. 345505; fax 345499; internet www.airtel.sc; f. 1998; 80% owned by private investors, 10% by Govt of Seychelles; provides fixed-line, mobile and satellite telephone and internet services; Chief Exec. RAJAN SWAROOP.

BROADCASTING

Radio
Seychelles Broadcasting Corpn (SBC): Hermitage, POB 321, Victoria; tel. 289600; fax 225641; e-mail sbcradtv@seychelles.sc; internet www.sbc.sc; f. 1983; reorg. as independent corpn in 1992; programmes in Creole, English and French; Man. Dir IBRAHIM AFIF.

SBC Radio: Union Vale, POB 321, Victoria; tel. 289600; fax 289720; e-mail sbcradtv@seychelles.sc; internet www.sbc.sc; f. 1941; programmes in Creole, English and French; Man. Dir IBRAHIM AFIF.

Television
Seychelles Broadcasting Corpn (SBC): see Radio.

SBC TV: Hermitage, POB 321, Mahé; tel. 224161; fax 225641; e-mail sbcradtv@seychelles.sc; f. 1983; programmes in Creole, English and French; Head of TV Production JUDE LOUANGE.

Directory

Finance
(cap. = capital; res = reserves; dep. = deposits; m. = million; brs = branches; amounts in Seychelles rupees)

BANKING

Central Bank
Central Bank of Seychelles (CBS): Independence Ave, POB 701, Victoria; tel. 225200; fax 224958; e-mail cbs@seychelles.sc; internet www.cbs.sc; f. 1983; bank of issue; cap. 1.0m., res 82.6m., dep. 830.6m. (Dec. 2005); Gov. FRANCIS CHANG-LENG; Gen. Man. (vacant).

National Banks
Development Bank of Seychelles: Independence Ave, POB 217, Victoria; tel. 294400; fax 224274; e-mail devbank@dbs.sc; internet www.dbs.sc; f. 1978; 55.5% state-owned; cap. 39.2m., res 43.7m., dep. 11.5m. (Dec. 2000); Chair. ANTONIO LUCAS; Man. Dir ROGER TOUSSAINT.

Seychelles International Mercantile Banking Corporation Ltd (Nouvobanq) (SIMBC): Victoria House, State House Ave, POB 241, Victoria; tel. 293000; fax 224670; e-mail nvb@nouvobanq.sc; f. 1991; 78% state-owned, 22% by Standard Chartered Bank (UK); cap. 50.0m., res 50.0m., dep. 1,664.9m. (Dec. 2004); Chair. VISWANATHAN SHANKAR; Pres. AHMED SAEED; 2 brs.

Seychelles Savings Bank Ltd (SSB): Kingsgate House, POB 531, Victoria; tel. 294000; fax 224713; e-mail ssb@savingsbank.sc; f. 1902; state-owned; term deposits, savings and current accounts; cap. and res 7.8m. (Dec. 1992), dep. 356.4m. (1999); Chair. JOSEPH NOURRICE; 4 brs.

Foreign Banks
Bank of Baroda (India): Trinity House, Albert St, POB 124, Victoria; tel. 323038; fax 324057; e-mail ce.seychelles@bankofbaroda.com; f. 1978; Man. M. S. PHOGAT.

Barclays Bank (Seychelles) Ltd (United Kingdom): Independence Ave, POB 167, Victoria; tel. 383838; fax 324054; e-mail barclays@seychelles.sc; f. 1959; Seychelles Dir M. P. LANDON; 3 brs and 4 agencies.

Habib Bank Ltd (Pakistan): Frances Rachel St, POB 702, Victoria; tel. 224371; fax 225614; e-mail habibsez@seychelles.net; f. 1976; Vice-Pres. and Chief Man. SOHAIL ANWAR.

Mauritius Commercial Bank (Seychelles) Ltd (MCB Seychelles): POB 122, Manglier St, Victoria; tel. 284555; fax 322676; e-mail contact@mcbseychelles.com; internet www.mcbseychelles.com; f. 1978 as Banque Française Commerciale (BFCOI); changed name in 2003; cap. 14.0m., res 14.0m., dep. 958.4m. (Dec. 2003); Man. Dir JOCELYN AH-YU; 5 brs.

INSURANCE
H. Savy Insurance Co Ltd (HSI): Maison de la Rosière, 2nd Floor, POB 887; Victoria; tel. 322272; fax 321666; e-mail insurance@mail.seychelles.net; f. 1995; all classes; majority-owned by Corvina Investments; Gen. Dir JEAN WEELING-LEE.

Seychelles Assurance Company Ltd (SACL): Pirate's Arms Bldg, POB 636, Victoria; tel. 225000; fax 224495; internet www.sacos.sc; f. 1980; state-owned; scheduled for privatization (excluding the Life Insurance Fund); all classes of insurance; subsidiaries include SUN Investments (Seychelles) Ltd, property-development company; fmrly State Assurance Corporation of Seychelles—SACOS; current name adopted 2006; Exec. Chair. ANTONIO A. LUCAS.

Trade and Industry

GOVERNMENT AGENCIES
Seychelles Fishing Authority (SFA): POB 449, Fishing Port, Victoria; tel. 670300; fax 224508; e-mail management@sfa.sc; internet www.sfa.sc; f. 1984; assessment and management of fisheries resources; Man. Dir RONDOLPH PAYET; Chair. FINLAY RACOMBO.

Seychelles Marketing Board (SMB): Latanier Rd, POB 634, Victoria; tel. 285000; fax 224735; e-mail mail@smb.sc; internet www.smb.sc; f. 1984; manufacturing and marketing of products, retailing, trade; CEO PATRICK VEL.

DEVELOPMENT ORGANIZATIONS
Indian Ocean Tuna Commission (IOTC) (Commission de Thons de l'Océan Indien): POB 1011, Victoria; tel. 225494; fax 224364; e-mail secretariat@iotc.org; internet www.iotc.org; f. 1997; an intergovernmental organization mandated to manage tuna and tuna-like species in the Indian Ocean and adjacent seas; to promote co-

operation among its members with a view to ensuring, through appropriate management, the conservation and optimum utilisation of stocks and encouraging sustainable development of fisheries based on such stocks; Exec. Sec. ALEJANDRO ANGANUZZI.

Seychelles Agricultural Development Co Ltd (SADECO): POB 172, Victoria; tel. 375888; f. 1980; Gen. Man. LESLIE PRÉA (acting).

Seychelles Industrial Development Corporation (SIDEC): POB 537, Victoria; tel. 323151; fax 324121; internet www.sidec.sc; f. 1988; promotes industrial development and manages leased industrial sites; CEO MAXWELL JULIE.

Seychelles International Business Authority (SIBA): Industrial Trade Zone, POB 991, Victoria; Bois de Rose Ave, Roche Caiman; tel. 380800; fax 380888; e-mail siba@seychelles.net; internet www.siba.net; f. 1995 to supervise registration of companies, transhipment and 'offshore' financial services in an international free-trade zone covering an area of 23 ha near Mahé International Airport; Chief Exec. and Man. Dir STEVE FANNY.

Seychelles Investment Bureau (SIB): POB 1167, Caravelle House, 2nd floor, Manglier St, Victoria; tel. 295500; fax 225125; e-mail sib@seychelles.sc; internet www.sib.sc; f. 2004; Chief Exec. JOSEPH NOURRICE.

CHAMBER OF COMMERCE

Seychelles Chamber of Commerce and Industry: Ebrahim Bldg, 2nd Floor, POB 1399, Victoria; tel. 323812; fax 321422; e-mail scci@seychelles.net; Chair. BERNARD POOL; Sec.-Gen. NICHOLE TIRANT-GHÉRARDI.

EMPLOYERS' ORGANIZATION

Federation of Employers' Associations of Seychelles (FEAS): POB 214, Victoria; tel. 324969; fax 324996; Chair. BASIL SOUNDY.

UTILITIES

Electricity

Public Utilities Corporation (Electricity Division): Electricity House, POB 174, Roche Caiman; tel. 678000; fax 321020; e-mail pmorin@puc.sc; Man. Dir PHILIPPE MORIN.

Water

Public Utilities Corporation (Water and Sewerage Division): Unity House, POB 34, Victoria; tel. 322444; fax 325612; e-mail pucwater@seychelles.net; Man. Dir STEPHEN ROUSSEAU.

TRADE UNION

Seychelles Federation of Workers' Unions (SFWU): Maison du Peuple, Latanier Rd, POB 154, Victoria; tel. 224455; fax 225351; e-mail sfwu@seychelles.net; f. 1978 to amalgamate all existing trade unions; affiliated to the Seychelles People's Progressive Front; 25,200 mems; Pres. OLIVIER CHARLES; Gen. Sec. ANTOINE ROBINSON.

Transport

RAILWAYS
There are no railways in Seychelles.

ROADS
In 2004 there were 498 km of roads, of which 478 km were surfaced. Most surfaced roads are on Mahé and Praslin.

SHIPPING
Privately owned ferry services connect Victoria, on Mahé, with the islands of Praslin and La Digue. At 31 December 2006 Seychelles' merchant fleet numbered 47 vessels, totalling 115,616 grt.

Port and Marine Services Division, Ministry of Tourism and Transport: POB 47, Mahé Quay, Victoria; tel. 224701; fax 224004; e-mail marineservices@seychellesports.sc; Dir-Gen. (Port of Victoria) Capt. W. ERNESTA.

Aquarius Shipping Agency Ltd: POB 865, Victoria; tel. 225050; fax 225043; e-mail aqua@seychelles.net; Gen. Man. ANTHONY SAVY.

Hunt, Deltel and Co Ltd: Victoria House, POB 14, Victoria; tel. 380300; fax 225367; e-mail hundel@seychelles.net; internet www.hundel.sc; f. 1937; Man. Dir E. HOUAREAU.

Mahé Shipping Co Ltd: Maritime House, POB 336, Victoria; tel. 380500; fax 380538; e-mail maheship@seychelles.net; shipping agents; Chair. Capt. G. C. C. ADAM.

Harry Savy & Co Ltd: POB 20, Victoria; tel. 322120; fax 321421; e-mail hsavyco@seychelles.net; shipping agents; Man. Dir GUY SAVY.

Seychelles Shipping Line Ltd: POB 977, Providence, Victoria; tel. 373737; fax 373647; e-mail ssl@gondwana.sc; f. 1994; operates freight services between Seychelles and Durban, South Africa; Chair. SELWYN GENDRON; Man. Dir HASSAN OMAR.

CIVIL AVIATION

Seychelles International Airport is located at Pointe Larue, 10 km from Victoria. A new international passenger terminal and aircraft parking apron were to be constructed by 2007 on land reclaimed in 1990; the existing terminal (which underwent SR 3m. in renovations in 2002) was to be converted into a cargo terminal. The airport also serves as a refuelling point for aircraft traversing the Indian Ocean. There are airstrips on several outlying islands.

Seychelles Civil Aviation Authority (SCAA): POB 181, Victoria; tel. 384000; fax 384009; e-mail dcaadmin@seychelles.net; formerly Directorate of Civil Aviation; offers ground and cargo handling and refuelling services, as well as holding responsibility for the Flight Information Region of 2.6m. sq km of Indian Ocean airspace; Chair. GERARD LAFORTUNE; Chief Exec. CONRAD BENOÎTON.

Air Seychelles: The Creole Spirit Bldg, Quincy St, POB 386, Victoria; tel. 224305; fax 225933; e-mail airseymd@seychelles.net; internet www.airseychelles.net; f. 1979; operates scheduled internal flights from Mahé to Praslin; also charter services to Bird, Desroches and Denis Islands and to outlying islands of the Amirantes group; international services to Europe, Far East, East and South Africa; Chief Exec. Capt. DAVID SAVY.

Emirates Airlines: 5th June Ave and Manglier St, Victoria; tel. 292700; f. 2005; Dir ABDULRAHMAN AL BALOOSHI.

Tourism

Seychelles enjoys an equable climate, and is renowned for its fine beaches and attractive scenery. There are more than 500 varieties of flora and many rare species of birds. Most tourist activity is concentrated on the islands of Mahé, Praslin and La Digue, although the potential for ecological tourism of the outlying islands received increased attention in the late 1990s. It is government policy that the development of tourism should not blight the environment, and strict laws govern the location and construction of hotels. In 1998 the Government indicated that up to 200,000 visitors (although not more than 4,000 at any one time) could be accommodated annually without detriment to environmental quality. However, several new luxury resorts were constructed in the early 2000s, and the yachting sector was also under development. Receipts from tourism totalled an estimated SR 885m. in 2006. In 2007 there were 161,300 tourist arrivals; most visitors (approximately 65.2% in 2005) are from Europe.

Compagnie Seychelloise de Promotion Hotelière Ltd: POB 683, Victoria; tel. 224694; fax 225291; e-mail cosproh@seychelles.net; promotes govt-owned hotels.

Seychelles Tourism Board (STB): POB 1262, Victoria, Mahe; tel. 671300; fax 620620; e-mail info@seychelles.com; internet www.seychelles.travel; f. 1998 as Seychelles Tourism Marketing Authority; merged with Seychelles Tourism Office in 2005; Chair. MAURICE LOUSTEAU-LALANNE.

SIERRA LEONE

Introductory Survey

Location, Climate, Language, Religion, Flag, Capital

The Republic of Sierra Leone lies on the west coast of Africa, with Guinea to the north and east, and Liberia to the south. The climate is hot and humid, with an average annual temperature of 27°C (80°F). The rainy season lasts from May to October. The average annual rainfall is about 3,436 mm (13.5 ins). English is the official language, while Krio (Creole), Mende, Limba and Temne are also widely spoken. The majority of the population follow animist beliefs, but there are significant numbers of Islamic and Christian adherents. The national flag (proportions 2 by 3) has three equal horizontal stripes, of green, white and blue. The capital is Freetown.

Recent History

Sierra Leone was formerly a British colony and protectorate. A new Constitution, which provided for universal adult suffrage, was introduced in 1951. In that year the Sierra Leone People's Party (SLPP) won the majority of votes in elections. The leader of the SLPP, Dr (later Sir) Milton Margai, became Chief Minister in 1953 and Prime Minister in 1958. On 27 April 1961 Sierra Leone achieved independence as a constitutional monarchy within the Commonwealth. Margai died in April 1964 and was succeeded as Prime Minister by his half-brother, Dr (later Sir) Albert Margai, previously the Minister of Finance.

In March 1967 the army assumed control and established a ruling body, the National Reformation Council. In April 1968 a further coup was staged by army officers, and power was subsequently transferred to a civilian Government; Dr Siaka Stevens, the leader of the All-People's Congress (APC), was elected as Prime Minister. In April 1971 a republican Constitution was introduced and Stevens became executive President.

The general election in May 1973 was not contested by the SLPP, and in 1976 Stevens, the sole candidate, was unanimously re-elected to the presidency for a second five-year term of office. A new Constitution, which provided for a one-party system, was adopted by the House of Representatives in June. The APC thus became the sole legitimate political organization. Stevens was inaugurated as President for a seven-year term on 14 June 1978. He subsequently released political detainees and allocated ministerial posts to several former SLPP members (who had joined the APC).

During the 1980s civil unrest, prompted by economic hardship, increased and in April 1985 Stevens announced that (contrary to earlier indications) he would not seek re-election to the presidency upon the expiry, in June, of his existing mandate. Stevens' term of office was subsequently extended for six months, to allow time for registration of voters and the nomination of a presidential candidate. At a conference of the APC in August, Maj.-Gen. Joseph Momoh, a cabinet minister and the Commander of the Army, was the sole candidate for the leadership of the party and for the presidential nomination. Momoh was elected to the national presidency in October, with 99% of the votes cast, and was inaugurated on 28 November. Although retaining his military status, Momoh appointed a civilian Cabinet, which included several members of the previous administration. Elections to the House of Representatives took place in May 1986.

Despite a campaign against financial malpractice in the public sector, Momoh's administration failed to improve the serious economic situation, and popular discontent continued. In March 1987 the Government announced that it had suppressed an attempted coup; more than 60 people were subsequently arrested, including the First Vice-President, Francis Minah. In October Minah and 15 other defendants were sentenced to death for plotting to assassinate Momoh and to overthrow the Government, and two defendants received custodial sentences on charges of treason. In October 1989 Minah and five others were executed, despite international appeals for clemency.

Following the outbreak of civil conflict in Liberia in December 1989, an estimated 125,000 Liberians took refuge in Sierra Leone. The Sierra Leonean Government contributed troops to the cease-fire monitoring group (ECOMOG) of the Economic Community of West African States (ECOWAS, see p. 232), which was dispatched to Liberia in August 1990. In November of that year Charles Taylor, the leader of the principal Liberian rebel faction, the National Patriotic Front of Liberia (NPFL), threatened to attack Freetown International Airport (alleged to be a base for ECOMOG offensives against rebel strongholds). In early April 1991, following repeated border incursions by members of the NPFL, government forces entered Liberian territory and launched a retaliatory attack against NPFL bases. By the end of that month, however, NPFL forces had advanced 150 km within Sierra Leone. The Momoh Government alleged that the rebel offensive had been instigated by Taylor, in an attempt to force Sierra Leone's withdrawal from ECOMOG, and also accused the Government of Burkina Faso of actively assisting the rebels. It was reported, however, that members of a Sierra Leonean resistance movement, known as the Revolutionary United Front (RUF), had joined the NPFL in attacks against government forces. In mid-1991 government troops, with the assistance of military units from Nigeria and Guinea, initiated a counter-offensive against the rebels, and succeeded in recapturing several towns in the east and south of the country.

In August 1990 Momoh conceded the necessity of electoral reforms, and announced an extensive revision of the Constitution, subsequently appointing a 30-member National Constitutional Review Commission. In March 1991 the Commission submitted a draft Constitution, which provided for the adoption of a multi-party system, for consideration by the Government. The new Constitution stipulated that the President, who was to appoint the Cabinet, was to be elected by a majority of votes cast nationally and by at least 25% of the votes cast in more than one-half of the electoral districts. Members of the legislature were to be elected by universal adult suffrage for a term of five years. The Government subsequently accepted the majority of the Commission's recommendations. In June the Government presented the draft Constitution to the House of Representatives, and announced that the parliamentary term, which was due to end that month, was to be extended until May 1992 to allow time for the transition to a multi-party system.

In early August 1991 the House of Representatives formally approved the new Constitution, and at a national referendum, which was conducted later in August, it was endorsed by 60% of voters, with 75% of the electorate participating. In the same month six newly created political associations formed an alliance, known as the United Front of Political Movements, which subsequently demanded that the forthcoming elections be monitored by international observers, and that the incumbent Government be dissolved and an interim administration established. On 23 September, following the resignation of the First Vice-President and Second Vice-President from both the APC and the Government, Momoh announced the formation of a new 18-member Cabinet, which retained only seven members of the previous Government. Later that month legislation that formally permitted the formation of political associations was introduced; several organizations were subsequently granted legal recognition.

On 29 April 1992 members of the armed forces, led by a five-member military junta, seized a radio station in Freetown and broadcast demands for improvements in conditions in the armed forces. The rebel troops later occupied the presidential offices, and the leader of the military junta, Capt. Valentine E. M. Strasser, announced that the Government had been overthrown. On the following day Momoh fled to Guinea, and Strasser announced the establishment of a governing council, to be known as the National Provisional Ruling Council (NPRC). Strasser affirmed the NPRC's commitment to the introduction of a multi-party system, and pledged to end the conflict in the country. On the same day the Constitution was suspended, the House of Representatives was dissolved and a state of emergency was imposed. On 1 May the NPRC (which principally comprised military officers), chaired by Strasser, was formed. Shortly afterwards a new 19-member Cabinet, which included a number of members of the NPRC, was appointed, and the Commander of the Armed Forces and the head of the security forces were replaced. On 6 May Strasser was inaugurated as Head of State.

In July 1992 Strasser replaced the three members of the NPRC in the Cabinet with civilians, and removed all civilian cabinet ministers from the NPRC. Later that month he announced extensive structural changes, which were designed to reduce the direct involvement of the NPRC in government administration: the NPRC was officially designated the Supreme Council of State, while the Cabinet was reconstituted as the Council of Secretaries (headed by the Chief Secretary of State), which was to be responsible for government administration, subject to the authority of the NPRC. In December Strasser announced a reorganization of the Council of Secretaries, in which the two remaining members of the Momoh administration were replaced. In the same month the Deputy Chairman of the NPRC, Capt. Solomon A. J. Musa, became Chief Secretary of State. Later in December, in an apparent attempt to regain public support, the Government established a 19-member National Advisory Council, comprising representatives of various non-governmental organizations, which was to draft a programme for transition to civilian rule.

At the end of December 1992 the Government announced that the security forces had suppressed a coup attempt. Shortly afterwards nine of those accused of involvement in the attempted coup were convicted by a special military tribunal, and, together with 17 prisoners who had been convicted in November on charges of treason, were summarily executed. Human rights organizations subsequently contested the Government's statement that a coup attempt had been staged, and condemned the trial by special military tribunal. In January 1993 the United Kingdom announced the suspension of economic aid to Sierra Leone in protest at the executions.

In April 1993 Strasser announced that a programme providing for a transition to civilian rule within a period of three years was to be adopted; in addition, all political prisoners were to be released, press restrictions would be relaxed, and the function of special military tribunals was to be reviewed. In July Musa was replaced as Deputy Chairman of the NPRC and Chief Secretary of State by Capt. Julius Maada Bio. Musa (who was widely believed to be responsible for the repressive measures undertaken by the Government) took refuge in the Nigerian high commission in Freetown, amid widespread speculation regarding his dismissal, and subsequently emigrated to the United Kingdom.

At the end of November 1993 Strasser announced the details of a two-year transitional programme, which provided for the installation of a civilian government by January 1996. The registration of political parties was to take place in June 1995, prior to a presidential election in November and legislative elections in December of that year. In December a five-member Interim National Electoral Commission was established to organize the registration of voters and the demarcation of constituency boundaries, in preparation for forthcoming local government elections. In the same month the National Advisory Council submitted constitutional proposals (which included a number of similar provisions to the 1991 Constitution, stipulating that: executive power was to be vested in the President, who was to be required to consult with the Cabinet, and was to be restricted to a tenure of two four-year terms of office; only Sierra Leonean nationals of more than 40 years of age were to qualify to contest a presidential election (thereby precluding Strasser and the majority of NPRC members, on grounds of age); the legislature was to comprise a House of Representatives, which was to be elected by universal adult suffrage for a term of five years, and a 30-member upper chamber, the Senate.

At the end of December 1993 the Government ended the state of emergency that had been imposed in April 1992 (although additional security measures remained in force). In April 1994 13 senior members of the armed forces were dismissed, following widespread criticism of the Government's failure to end continued conflict in the south-east of the country with the RUF, led by Foday Sankoh, which, in 1991, had joined Liberian rebels in attacks against government forces. In July it was reported that the RUF (which had been joined by disaffected members of the armed forces) had besieged the principal town of Kenema, near the border with Liberia, and was exploiting diamond reserves in the region.

In October 1994 a draft Constitution was submitted to the NPRC. In January 1995 the RUF gained control of the mining installations owned by the Sierra Leone Ore and Metal Company (SIEROMCO) and Sierra Rutile Ltd, and seized a number of employees of the two enterprises, including eight foreign nationals. Later in January seven Roman Catholic nuns, together with a number of Sierra Leonean citizens, were abducted following an attack by the RUF against the north-western town of Kambia. In the same month the RUF threatened to kill the British hostages if the Sierra Leonean authorities executed an officer, who had been convicted by military tribunal of collaborating with the rebels. In February the RUF rejected appeals by the UN and the Organization of African Unity (OAU, now the African Union, see p. 164) that peace negotiations be initiated, and demanded that all troops that had been dispatched by foreign Governments to assist the Strasser administration be withdrawn as a precondition to discussions. In mid-February government forces (which had succeeded in recapturing the mining installations owned by Sierra Rutile) launched an offensive against a principal rebel base in the Kangari region, east of Freetown. Meanwhile, continued atrocities perpetrated against civilians were increasingly attributed to disaffected members of the armed forces.

In February 1995 the military administration engaged 58 Gurkha mercenaries, who had previously served in the British army, prompting further concern regarding the safety of the British hostages in Sierra Leone. In March government forces regained control of the mining installations owned by SIEROMCO and the principal town of Moyamba, 100 km south-east of Freetown (which had been captured by the RUF earlier that month). Later that month the rebels released the seven nuns who had been abducted in January. Despite the successful counter-offensives by government forces, by April the RUF had advanced towards Freetown and had initiated a series of attacks against towns in the vicinity (including Songo, which was situated only 35 km east of Freetown), apparently prior to besieging the capital. Later in April the remaining foreign nationals who had been seized by the RUF were released.

In March 1995 the Council of Secretaries was reorganized to allow principal military officials in the Government to assume active functions within the armed forces (following the advance of RUF forces towards Freetown); Lt-Col Akim Gibril became Chief Secretary of State, replacing Bio, who was appointed Chief of Defence Staff. At the end of April, on the anniversary of the NPRC's assumption of power, Strasser formally announced that the ban on political activity was to be rescinded, and that a National Consultative Conference was to be convened to discuss the transitional process; he further indicated that elections were to take place by the end of that year, prior to the installation of a civilian government in January 1996, in accordance with the transitional programme. The ban on political activity was formally ended on 21 June; some 15 parties were subsequently granted registration (although the RUF failed to respond to government efforts to include the movement in the electoral process).

In May 1995 government forces initiated a number of counter-attacks against the RUF, and succeeded in recapturing Songo. By the end of June government forces had regained control of significant diamond-mining regions in the eastern Kono District, and part of Bo District, in a successful counter-offensive, which was generally attributed to the assistance of South African mercenaries. In September, however, the RUF launched further offensives in Bo District, while increasing reports of massacres and other violations of human rights perpetrated by the rebels against the civilian population emerged.

In December 1995 it was announced that the presidential and legislative elections were to take place concurrently on 26 February 1996. In January 1996, however, Strasser was deposed by military officers, led by Bio, in a bloodless coup. Bio, who assumed the office of Head of State, announced that the coup had been instigated in response to efforts by Strasser to remain in power. (It was reported that Strasser had intended to amend restrictions on the age of prospective candidates to enable himself to contest the elections.) Strasser (who had been expelled to Guinea) claimed, however, that the new military administration planned to delay the transition to civilian government. A reconstituted Supreme Council of State and Council of Secretaries were formed and it was announced that the elections were to take place as scheduled. The RUF indicated that it was prepared to enter into negotiations with the new Government, and declared a temporary cease-fire to allow voter registration to proceed throughout the country, but urged a postponement of the elections, pending a peace settlement that would allow the movement to participate in the democratic process. However, delegates at the National Consultative Conference, which was convened in early February, voted in favour of adherence to the scheduled date. The RUF subsequently abandoned the cease-fire and launched a series of attacks in various parts of the country, in an apparent attempt to undermine the electoral process.

On 26 February 1996 presidential and legislative elections took place as scheduled. However, some 27 people were killed in attacks by armed groups, particularly in Bo and parts of Freetown, which were generally attributed to the RUF; voting was consequently extended for a further day. The reconstituted SLPP secured 36.1% of votes cast in the legislative elections, while its presidential candidate, Ahmed Tejan Kabbah, also received most support, with 35.8% of votes. A second round of the presidential election, which took place on 15 March, was contested by Kabbah and the candidate of the United National People's Party (UNPP), John Karefa-Smart (who had obtained 22.6% of votes cast in the first round): Kabbah was elected President by 59.5% of the votes. Later in March seats in the new 80-member Parliament were allocated on a basis of proportional representation, with the SLPP securing 27, the UNPP 17, the People's Democratic Party 12 and the reconstituted APC only five seats; the 12 provincial districts were represented in the legislature by Paramount Chiefs. Kabbah was inaugurated on 29 March, when the military Government officially relinquished power to the new civilian administration. In April Kabbah appointed a new Cabinet, which was subsequently approved by the new Parliament.

Following the elections, the Government announced in March 1996 that the RUF had agreed to a cease-fire; at a meeting between Sankoh and Bio in Yamoussoukro, Côte d'Ivoire, later that month, the RUF undertook to observe the cease-fire for a period of two months and to continue negotiations with the newly elected civilian Government. Following discussions between Sankoh and Kabbah in April, the Government and RUF reaffirmed their commitment to a permanent cessation of hostilities, and announced the establishment of three joint committees, which would consider issues regarding the demobilization of rebel forces. However, Sankoh continued to refuse to recognize the legitimacy of the new Government, and demanded that a transitional administration be installed pending further elections. Despite the official cease-fire, sporadic attacks by the RUF were subsequently reported and further clashes occurred later that year between government forces and the Kamajors (traditional fighters reconstituted as an auxiliary defence force).

In July 1996 the Parliament adopted legislation that formally reinstated the Constitution of 1991. In September 1996 Kabbah ordered the compulsory retirement of some 20 officers, including Strasser and Bio, from the armed forces. Shortly afterwards it was reported that a conspiracy to overthrow the Government had been thwarted by senior military officers. About 17 members of the armed forces were arrested, of whom nine were subsequently charged with involvement in the conspiracy. Following reports of a further conspiracy to overthrow the Government in January 1997, Kabbah announced that an investigative mission from Nigeria had concluded that former members of the NPRC administration had instigated the coup attempt of September 1996.

In November 1996 Kabbah demanded that the RUF relinquish armaments within a period of two weeks, threatening that government forces would resume military operations. At the end of that month Kabbah and Sankoh signed a peace agreement in Abidjan, Côte d'Ivoire, whereby RUF forces were to be demobilized and the movement was to be reconstituted as a political organization, while all foreign troops were to be withdrawn from the country and replaced with foreign observers. A National Commission for the Consolidation of Peace was subsequently established to monitor the peace settlement. By February 1997 all foreign mercenaries had left Sierra Leone in accordance with the agreement, while the repatriation of Sierra Leonean refugees from Liberia had commenced. However, at the end of that month (when the implementation of the peace agreement was scheduled for completion) it was reported that members of the RUF had repeatedly violated the peace agreement and had failed to report to designated centres for disarmament. In March members of the political wing of the RUF issued a declaration that Sankoh had been removed as leader of the organization, owing to his failure to implement the peace accord. Later that month, however, RUF forces loyal to Sankoh kidnapped members of the movement who had supported his replacement, together with the Sierra Leonean ambassador to Guinea; the faction issued demands for the release of Sankoh, who had been detained in Nigeria earlier that month (being reportedly in possession of armaments).

On 25 May 1997 dissident members of the armed forces, led by Maj. Johnny Paul Koroma, seized power, deposing Kabbah, who fled to Guinea. The new authorities imposed a curfew in Freetown, following widespread violent looting by armed factions, and most foreign nationals were evacuated. In early June Nigerian forces initiated a naval bombardment of Freetown in an effort to force the new military leaders to resign. However, forces loyal to the coup leaders, assisted by RUF members, succeeded in repelling Nigerian attacks. Koroma announced the establishment of a 20-member Armed Forces Revolutionary Council (AFRC), with himself as Chairman and Sankoh (who remained in detention in Nigeria) as Vice-Chairman; the AFRC (which was not internationally recognized as the legitimate Government) included a further three members of the RUF and several civilians. All political activity, the existing Constitution and government bodies were suspended, although Koroma pledged that democratic rule would be restored. Nigeria reiterated that it intended to reinstate the ousted Government with the support of ECOWAS, and a further two Nigerian warships were dispatched to the region; further clashes between Nigerian troops, who had been serving under the mandate of ECOMOG in neighbouring Liberia (q.v.), and supporters of the new military leaders occurred at the international airport at Lungi. In mid-June the AFRC announced that it had suppressed a coup attempt, following the arrest of 15 people, including several senior military officers. In the same month it was reported that troops supporting the junta had repulsed an attack by Kamajors (who remained loyal to Kabbah) at the town of Zimmi, 250 km south-east of Freetown. On 17 June Koroma was formally inaugurated as the self-proclaimed Head of State. However, despite appeals from Koroma, a campaign of civil disobedience, organized by the labour congress in protest at the coup, continued.

By early July 1997 the new military Government had been completely isolated by the international community. The Commonwealth Ministerial Action Group on the Harare Declaration (CMAG—which had been established to ensure adherence to the principles of democracy by member states) suspended Sierra Leone from meetings of the Commonwealth, pending the restoration of constitutional order and the reinstatement of a democratically elected government. The UN Security Council also condemned the coup, and expressed support for ECOWAS efforts to resolve the situation. Meanwhile, a four-member ministerial committee, comprising representatives of Nigeria, Côte d'Ivoire, Guinea and Ghana, which had been established by ECOWAS, urged the Government to relinquish power during a series of negotiations with an AFRC delegation.

In mid-July 1997 Koroma formed a cabinet, known as the Council of Secretaries, comprising representatives of the RUF and the army, together with a number of civilians. Later that month, following further reports of clashes between Kamajors and forces loyal to the junta in the south of the country, AFRC representatives and the ECOWAS committee, meeting in Abidjan, agreed to an immediate cease-fire; negotiations were to continue, with the aim of restoring constitutional order. At the end of July continuing discussions between the ECOWAS committee and AFRC representatives in Abidjan were abandoned, after Koroma insisted that he retain power for a tenure of four years, and refused to restore the Constitution and to end the ban on political activity. Consequently, in late August an ECOWAS conference, which was convened at Abuja, Nigeria, officially endorsed the imposition of sanctions against Sierra Leone, with the aim of obliging the AFRC to relinquish power. ECOMOG was granted a mandate to monitor the cease-fire and to enforce the economic embargo; it was also agreed that the ECOWAS monitoring committee would henceforth include Liberia (following the election of a democratic Government in that country).

In September 1997 ECOMOG troops stationed at the airport at Lungi bombarded container vessels that were suspected of attempting to violate the sanctions, and staged aerial attacks against commercial and military targets in Freetown, killing about 50 civilians. In the same month CMAG voted in support of the decision of the ECOWAS committee to effect the reinstatement of the Kabbah administration. In early October the UN Security Council imposed sanctions on the import of armaments and petroleum products to Sierra Leone. Following further aerial bombardments of Freetown by ECOMOG troops (in which large numbers of civilians were killed), a mass demonstration was held in the capital to demand that the Nigerian Government withdraw its troops from Sierra Leone. Negotiations between the AFRC and the five-member committee continued, however, and later in October an agreement, which was signed in Conakry, Guinea, provided for an immediate cease-fire, and the reinstatement of Kabbah's Government by April 1998, together with immunity from prosecution for AFRC members; all troops loyal to the incumbent military administration and RUF members were to be demobilized, under the supervision of a disarmament committee, comprising representatives of the AFRC, ECOMOG and local forces loyal to Kabbah. In January 1998 ECOMOG forces again bombarded the port at Freetown (for the first time since the peace agreement in October), apparently with the aim of preventing merchant vessels from contravening the sanctions.

In early February 1998 further clashes erupted near Freetown between ECOMOG troops and supporters of the military junta. Nigerian troops belonging to ECOMOG subsequently launched an intensive bombardment against Freetown and succeeded in gaining control of the capital, after senior members of the AFRC, including Koroma, fled into hiding, or surrendered to the ECOMOG forces; some 100 civilians were killed in the fighting, while more than 3,000 took refuge in Guinea. About 50 members of the military junta were arrested in Monrovia, Liberia, prompting protests from the Liberian Government regarding the Nigerian military intervention. It was announced that the Government that had been ousted on 25 May 1997 was to be reinstated, and that all subsequent appointments were to be considered invalid. ECOMOG forces were to remain in the country to assist in the restructuring of the armed forces. Meanwhile, following reports that troops loyal to the former military junta, with the assistance of the RUF, had taken control of Bo, ECOMOG forces were deployed in the region to support the Kamajors, and rapidly succeeded in regaining control of most of the region (prompting speculation that the Nigerian military initiative had been undertaken with the aim of gaining access to Sierra Leone's mineral resources).

On 10 March 1998 Kabbah returned from exile and was officially reinstated as President; he subsequently appointed a Cabinet (which included a number of members of his previous administration). The new Government declared a state of emergency under which members of the former military junta could be detained for a maximum of 30 days without being formally charged. It was announced that some 1,500 civilians and members of the armed forces (including Momoh) had been placed in detention and were to be charged for their alleged connections with the former military junta. Also in March the UN Security Council voted to end its embargo on imports of petroleum products to Sierra Leone (which had resulted in severe fuel shortages), although an embargo on the supply of armaments was maintained. It was reported that ECOMOG forces had launched an offensive in the east of the country, in an effort to eradicate the remaining forces loyal to the former military junta and members of the RUF. In July the UN Security Council adopted a resolution establishing a UN Observer Mission in Sierra Leone (UNOMSIL), comprising 70 military observers, with an initial six-month mandate to monitor the security situation, supervise the disarmament of former combatants, and advise the authorities on the restructuring of the security forces. In the same month it was announced that the national army had been dissolved.

In late July 1998 the Nigerian Government returned Sankoh (who had been in detention in Nigeria since early 1997) to Sierra Leone, where he was charged with treason following his support for the military coup of May 1997. In August 16 civilians, including five journalists, were sentenced to death, after being convicted of supporting the former military junta. In October 24 army officers were publicly executed, following their conviction for involvement with the military junta, provoking condemnation from many foreign Governments and human rights organizations, which had appealed for clemency. Death penalties imposed against a further 10 officers were commuted to terms of life imprisonment. In November a further 15 civilians, including several ministers who had served in the AFRC Government, were sentenced to death for their part in the May 1997 coup; Momoh received a custodial term of 10 years for colluding with the military junta.

Meanwhile, ECOMOG continued efforts to suppress rebel activity, particularly in the north and east of the country, and in October 1998 transferred its operational headquarters from the Liberian capital, Monrovia, to Freetown. In that month the RUF intensified hostilities, after it was announced that Sankoh had been sentenced to death by the High Court on charges of treason. In November ECOMOG forces commenced aerial bombardments of rebel bases. By late December, however, RUF forces, together with supporters of the former military junta, had advanced towards Freetown, and had seized control of the principal town of Makeni, 140 km north-east of Freetown. The Governments of Nigeria and Ghana dispatched additional troops to reinforce the ECOMOG contingent (which henceforth numbered about 15,000). At the end of December the acting Commander of the RUF, Sam Bockarie, rejected a government invitation to enter into peace negotiations, and ECOMOG forces, supported by Kamajors, attempted to repulse rebel attacks in the outskirts of Freetown.

On 6 January 1999 rebel forces attacked Freetown (where thousands of civilians from the surrounding area had taken refuge), releasing a number of supporters of the former junta from the capital's prison and seizing the Nigerian High Commission and government offices; Kabbah and a number of cabinet ministers were obliged to flee to ECOMOG headquarters. (It was subsequently discovered that two ministers had been killed by the rebels.) Bockarie announced that Freetown was under the control of the RUF, and demanded that Sankoh be released from detention. ECOMOG troops initiated a counter-offensive, with an aerial bombardment of Freetown, forcing the rebels to retreat to the outskirts of the capital. It was estimated that about 3,000 people had been killed during the RUF occupation of the capital, and further large numbers of civilians were maimed by the rebels. By late January ECOMOG forces claimed to have regained control of Freetown, and a cease-fire was agreed, pending peace negotiations, which were convened in Conakry, with mediation by the Governments of Guinea, Côte d'Ivoire and Togo. It was reported that Sankoh (who had been allowed by the Sierra Leonean authorities to attend the peace discussions) demanded his release and the official recognition of the RUF as a political movement as preconditions to the cessation of hostilities. Some 100 members of ECOMOG were arrested, following claims by a UN report (which were denied by ECOMOG) that suspected rebels had been summarily executed; the Kamajors were also implicated in summary killings.

Following the rebel offensive in January 1999, a number of West African Governments, particularly those of Nigeria and Ghana, reiterated claims that the Liberian Government was supporting the RUF with mercenaries and illicit exports of armaments in exchange for diamonds. ECOMOG also accused Burkina Faso and Libya of assisting rebel operations. Charles Taylor (now the Liberian President) denied any connections with the RUF, dismissing the allegations as an attempt to destabilize his administration. In April the Nigerian President-elect, Olusegun Obasanjo, agreed that the Nigerian contingent (then numbering nearly 15,000) would remain in Sierra Leone until peace was restored, apparently in response to the influence of the international community; however, a gradual withdrawal of ECOMOG troops, to be completed by early 2000, was envisaged. Meanwhile, Kabbah authorized discussions between Sankoh and active RUF leaders to clarify RUF demands, and, following pressure from the Nigerian, US and British Governments, agreed to conduct formal peace negotiations with the rebels. In late April, following discussions between RUF leaders, formal negotiations between the RUF and a government delegation commenced in the Togolese capital, Lomé, with mediation by President Gnassingbé Eyadéma of Togo. In early May the Government and the RUF signed a cease-fire agreement, which came into effect later that month. Continuing negotiations on the proposed participation of the RUF in a coalition transitional administration, as part of a wider peace settlement, followed. In early July the Government and the RUF reached a power-sharing agreement, after government negotiators acceded to rebel demands that Sankoh be granted vice-presidential powers, with responsibility for the mineral resources industry, and the RUF be allocated a number of cabinet posts. The accord provided for the release of civilians who had been abducted by the rebels, and the disarmament and reintegration into the armed forces of former combatants; the RUF was to be reconstituted as a political organization. Following the completion of disarmament, legislative and presidential elections were to take place by February 2001.

In August 1999 former supporters of the AFRC junta kidnapped some 32 members of ECOMOG and UNOMSIL who had been abducted by the rebels, after attempting to negotiate the release of about 200 civilians, held by the rebels. The dissidents issued demands for the extension of the amnesty to supporters of the former junta, and the release of Koroma, who, they believed, had been detained by the RUF. Koroma was transported by the UN to Monrovia, where he urged his supporters to free the hostages. Following negotiations between the Sierra Leonean authorities and the rebels, with the assistance of British mediators, the ECOMOG and UNOMSIL hostages were subsequently released.

In early October 1999 Sankoh (who had been conducting discussions with Taylor) and Koroma returned to Freetown from Monrovia, and pledged to co-operate with Kabbah in the implementation of the Lomé peace accord. Later that month the UN Security Council adopted Resolution 1270, establishing a 6,000-member force, the UN Mission in Sierra Leone (UNAMSIL), which was granted a six-month mandate to supervise the implementation of the peace agreement, and to assist in a programme for the disarmament and reintegration of the former rebel factions; at the same time the mandate of UNOMSIL was terminated. The withdrawal of the ECOMOG contingent was to be completed following the deployment of UNAMSIL, although, in effect, the new peace-keeping force (which was to comprise 4,000 Nigerian troops and 2,000 principally Kenyan and Indian troops) would incorporate a number of the Nigerian forces belonging to ECOMOG. On 2 November a new coalition Cabinet was officially installed; four former members of the RUF and the AFRC junta were allocated ministerial posts. Sankoh became Chairman of a commission supervising the reconstruction of the mineral resources industry, with vice-presidential status, while Koroma was nominated Chairman of the Commission for the Consolidation of Peace. In the same month the Government announced the establishment of a Truth and Reconciliation Commission (TRC), which was to make recommendations regarding compensation for victims of human rights violations. However, reports of atrocities perpetrated against the civilian population by rebels continued, and in November division between the AFRC and RUF leadership emerged, apparently as a result of the former junta's dissatisfaction with its cabinet posts. The arrival of UNAMSIL troops in Sierra Leone commenced at the end of November.

In early 2000 reports emerged of RUF forces in the Kailahun District of eastern Sierra Leone (where illegal diamond-mining continued) resisting disarmament and the deployment of UNAMSIL troops. In February the UN Security Council adopted a resolution in favour of expanding UNAMSIL to number 11,100, and extended its mandate for six months. In March Kabbah established a commission to supervise the elections, which, under the terms of the peace agreement, were to take place following the disarmament of the former rebel factions. By the end of that month, however, only about 17,000 of the 45,000 former combatants had been disarmed.

In April 2000 UNAMSIL troops stationed in the eastern town of Kenema repulsed attacks from rebel forces. In early May, following a further dispute over disarmament, RUF forces attacked UNAMSIL troops in Makeni and the neighbouring town of Magburaka, killing at least four Kenyan members of the contingent, and seizing a number of UN personnel as hostages. Six civilian UN observers were subsequently released, following intervention by Taylor. However, rebel forces continued to hold about 300 members of UNAMSIL (principally Zambians) hostage, while a further Zambian contingent of the peace-keeping force, numbering about 200, was reported missing. The UN Secretary-General urged West African Heads of State to increase pressure on Sankoh to order the release of the hostages. Following a reported advance on Freetown by RUF forces, foreign nationals were advised to leave the country. The British Government dispatched a military task force to the region (stationing troops at the airport at Lungi, and in Senegal), which evacuated most European nationals. RUF supporters guarding Sankoh's residence in Freetown fired on civilian demonstrators, who were demanding that Sankoh comply with the peace agreement; some 20 protesters were killed. (UN officials were subsequently unable to contact Sankoh, who had fled from Freetown.) Sierra Leonean government forces, led by Koroma (who continued to support the Kabbah administration), were deployed to halt rebel advances, and claimed to have recaptured territory from the RUF. At an ECOWAS summit meeting in Abuja, Taylor was authorized to negotiate with the RUF regarding their release of the hostages; the redeployment of Nigerian troops under an ECOMOG mandate was considered. In late May Sankoh was arrested in Freetown by troops loyal to Kabbah. By the end of that month, following mediation by Taylor, the hostages held by the RUF were released. In early June, however, 21 Indian members of UNAMSIL were seized by the RUF at the eastern town of Pendembu, while a further 233 peace-keeping troops were surrounded by rebels at nearby Kailahun. By mid-June most of the British forces had withdrawn (with about 250 troops remaining in the country to train new members of the Sierra Leone armed forces, and to assist in establishing the operations of a British military advisory team).

In early July 2000 the UN Security Council adopted a resolution, proposed by the British Government, imposing an international embargo on the purchase of unauthenticated diamonds (in an effort to prevent illicit trade from RUF-held regions, thereby ending the rebels' principal source of funding for armaments); the Sierra Leonean Government was to implement a system whereby officially mined diamonds would be granted certification. In the same month government forces clashed with one of the most notorious militia groups, the West Side Boys (WSB), which had hitherto supported the former AFRC junta. In mid-July the battalion of (principally Indian) peace-keeping personnel, who had been besieged by the RUF at Kailahun, were rescued in a military operation by UNAMSIL; one member of the contingent was killed during the offensive. In early August the UN Security Council approved the establishment of an international tribunal, where Sankoh and others responsible for atrocities committed during the civil conflict would be placed on trial. The RUF leadership announced the nomination of Gen. Issa Sesay (who was reported to be a more moderate commander) to replace Sankoh. Later in August the WSB abducted 11 British military personnel and one member of the Sierra Leonean armed forces, subsequently issuing a number of demands as a precondition to releasing the hostages. Five of the British personnel were freed after negotiations, but additional British troops were dispatched to Sierra Leone, following the failure of government officials to secure an agreement on the remaining hostages. In early September about 150 British troops attacked the main WSB base, 48 km east of Freetown, and succeeded in rescuing the other seven hostages. One member of the British armed forces died during the military operation, while 25 members of the WSB were killed, and a further 18 (including the movement's leader, Foday Kallay) were captured.

In September 2000 the Indian Government announced that it was to withdraw its contingent (then numbering 3,073 troops) from UNAMSIL, despite a proposal by the UN Secretary-General that the maximum strength of the peace-keeping force be increased. In October several nations, notably Bangladesh, Ghana and Kenya, pledged to dispatch additional troops to replace those of India. The number of British troops in the country had been increased to 400, while a 500-member naval task force was deployed off Freetown to provide additional support to the UN peace-keeping operations. On 10 November, following further negotiations mediated by ECOWAS, the Government and the RUF signed a cease-fire agreement in Abuja, providing for the demobilization and disarmament of all militia forces, and the deployment of UNAMSIL throughout the country.

Meanwhile, civilians continued to flee from the country, and by August 2000 some 331,000 Sierra Leonean refugees were registered in Guinea. In September the Guinean President, Gen. Lansana Conté, claimed that Liberian and Sierra Leonean refugees were supporting the activity of rebels attempting to overthrow his Government (see the chapter on Guinea), and ordered them to leave the country. Following clashes on Guinea's border with Liberia, tripartite discussions between Guinea, Liberia and Sierra Leone commenced in October. In March 2001, however, Taylor expelled the ambassadors of Guinea and Sierra Leone from Liberia, on the stated grounds that they had been engaged in activity incompatible with their office. Kabbah retaliated by ordering the Liberian chargé d'affaires to leave the country, and announced the closure of the joint border with Liberia. As a result of the continued violence and the hostility of the Guinean authorities, large numbers of the refugees in Guinea began to return to Sierra Leone. (Diplomatic links between Liberia and Sierra Leone and Guinea were normalized in August, following a request to Taylor by ECOWAS Heads of State.)

In February 2001 the National Assembly unanimously approved a proposal by Kabbah that presidential and legislative elections, scheduled to take place in February and March, respectively, be postponed for six months, owing to the continued civil unrest in the country. At the end of March the UN Security Council adopted a resolution increasing the strength of UNAMSIL (which then numbered 9,500) to 17,500 troops. In April UNAMSIL began to deploy troops in northern regions of the country, including the towns of Lunsar and Makeni, formerly held by the RUF. In early May, however, it was reported that the pro-Government Kamajor militia, now known as the Civil Defence Forces (CDF), had attacked RUF positions in eastern towns. UNAMSIL accused the CDF, which had advanced within RUF-held territory, of instigating the hostilities. In mid-May the RUF and CDF signed an agreement, providing for the immediate cessation of hostilities and resumption of disarmament for both forces. In June UNAMSIL and (British-trained) government forces regained control of part of the significant diamond-mining regions and the eastern border with Guinea and Sierra Leone (thereby forestalling renewed rebel activity originating from the neighbouring countries). Further clashes between the RUF and CDF continued to impede the disarmament process, and in mid-July discussions regarding the implementation of the peace agreement were conducted at Bo; the Government, the RUF and UNAMSIL agreed to a ban on diamond-mining in eastern regions still controlled by the rebels, in order to facilitate the demobilization of combatants.

In early September 2001 the Government announced that presidential and legislative elections would take place, under the aegis of the UN, on 14 May 2002 (after a further postponement, owing to the continued uncertainty of the security situation). The RUF, however, protested at the delay and threatened to withdraw from the peace process unless an interim coalition administration replaced the incumbent Government. In November representatives of the Government, the RUF and civil society agreed that parliamentary deputies in the forthcoming elections were to be elected by district (rather than under the previous system of proportional representation). In December the UN Security Council extended its ban on trade in uncertified diamonds for a further 11 months (effective from 5 January 2002).

In preparation for the forthcoming elections, a three-week process of voter registration commenced in mid-January 2002. The disarmament of an estimated 45,000 former combatants was officially completed on 18 January. Later that month the UN and the Government reached agreement on the establishment of a war crimes tribunal, to be known as the Special Court, which was to be based in Sierra Leone; the Special Court had a three-year mandate to prosecute crimes perpetrated from the end of November 1996. Meanwhile, the continuing rebel insurgency in northern Liberia, which had advanced rapidly towards Monrovia by early 2002, prompted concern that the resumption of civil conflict there would cause further instability in Sierra Leone. Despite UN pressure on the Liberian Government to end assistance for the RUF, it was reported that Bockarie, supported by 4,000 rebel forces, continued to be based in Liberia.

Following the completion of disarmament, the RUF announced its reconstitution as a political organization, the Revolutionary United Front Party (RUFP), with the aim of contesting the elections. In early March 2002, however, Sankoh (who remained titular leader of the RUFP) was formally charged with murder, in connection with the killing of some 20 civilian protesters by his supporters in May 2000. (The trial of Sankoh, together with a further 49 former RUF members, commenced later in March.) In mid-March Kabbah was elected unopposed as the presidential candidate of the SLPP. A total of 24 political parties had officially registered by this time, notably the Peace and Liberation Party (PLP), led by Koroma. However, after the collapse of an opposition alliance, which had been established in late 2001, no serious challenge to the SLPP had emerged. In early April, after the authorities announced that Sankoh would not be permitted to contest the elections on behalf of the RUFP, the party's Secretary-General, Pallo Bangura, was nominated as its presidential candidate. By the end of that month an estimated 60,000 of the 150,000 Sierra Leonean refugees in Guinea and Liberia had returned voluntarily in order to participate in the elections.

Presidential and legislative elections took place peacefully on 14 May 2002. Kabbah was elected to a second term in office by 70.1% of the votes cast, while Ernest Bai Koroma of the APC received 22.4% of the votes. The SLPP also secured an outright majority in the expanded 124-member Parliament, with 83 seats, while the APC won 27 seats and the PLP two. Later that month Solomon Berewa (hitherto Minister of Justice) became the new Vice-President, and a reorganized Cabinet was installed.

In July 2002 the authorities announced that a seven-member TRC had been established. In August Pallo Bangura resigned his RUFP office, having secured less than 2% of votes cast in the presidential election. In September 2002 the UN Security Council adopted a resolution extending the mandate of UNAMSIL for a further six months, but also advocating that the contingent be reduced in size, while in December the UN embargo on illicit trade in diamonds was renewed for a further six months. In February 2003 a further 300 British troops were deployed in Sierra Leone, owing to concern that the intensification of hostilities between government and rebel Liberians United for Reconciliation and Democracy (LURD) forces in Liberia might destabilize the situation in Sierra Leone. (The British military presence in Sierra Leone had been reduced to number some 100 officers in July 2002.)

After the appointment of a British lawyer, Geoffrey Robertson, as President of the Special Court and a US lawyer, David Crane, as Chief Prosecutor, trial activities commenced at the end of 2002. In March 2003 the Special Court approved indictments for war crimes against seven former faction leaders, notably Sankoh, Koroma, the former RUF Commanders, Bockarie and Sesay, and the incumbent Minister of the Interior (and Kamajor leader), Sam Hinga Norman. Five of those indicted, including Hinga Norman, were taken into custody. Koroma went into hiding, following an attempt by the authorities to arrest him, while it was reported that Bockarie was supporting Liberian government forces against the LURD. In April Hinga Norman pleaded not guilty at the Special Court to charges relating to atrocities perpetrated during the civil war. Public hearings before the TRC commenced in mid-April. In early May the Liberian authorities announced that Bockarie had been killed near the border with Côte d'Ivoire, after clashing with Liberian troops attempting to arrest him, and ordered an investigation. Officials at the Special Court claimed that Bockarie and his immediate family had been captured and murdered by Liberian security forces, in an effort to prevent him from testifying against prominent regional figures. In June it was reported that Koroma had also been killed while at large in Liberia.

On 4 June 2003 the Special Court officially indicted Taylor for crimes against humanity, owing to his alleged long-standing support for the RUF, and an international warrant was issued for his arrest. The indictment against Taylor immediately precipitated a major offensive against the Liberian capital by rebels demanding his resignation (see the chapter on Liberia). The renewed humanitarian crisis in Liberia during June resulted in further large numbers of Liberian refugees fleeing to southern Sierra Leone. Having accepted an offer of asylum from the Nigerian Head of State, Olusegun Obasanjo, Taylor formally resigned his office and left for exile in Nigeria on 11 August, thereby evading arrest for the charges brought against him by the Special Court. Meanwhile, progress in the case against Sankoh was hindered by the deterioration of his state of health, and, after receiving medical treatment in hospital under UN custody from March, he died at the end of July. Also in July the UN Security Council adopted a resolution recommending the gradual withdrawal of UNAMSIL by the end of 2004, in view of improved security conditions.

In early February 2004 the five-year programme for 'disarmament, demobilization and reintegration' (in which 72,490 former combatants, including 6,845 children, had been disarmed) officially ended. In March Robertson was removed from the office of President of the Special Court, after being accused of demonstrating bias against the RUF in a book he had written concerning the atrocities committed during the civil conflict. At the end of that month, owing to renewed concern that the Sierra Leonean authorities would be unable to maintain stability, particularly in view of the security situations in Guinea and Côte d'Ivoire, the UN Security Council approved a resolution in favour of maintaining a reduced UNAMSIL contingent in the country until the end of September, with further extensions possible.

In June 2004 trials of prominent former combatants officially commenced at the Special Court. On 23 September UNAMSIL officially transferred primary responsibility for security in the remaining parts of the country where it was deployed, including Freetown, to government forces. The UN Security Council approved a further resolution in the same month, authorizing the contingent's continued presence in the country until the end of June 2005.

At the end of June 2005 the UN Security Council extended the mandate of UNAMSIL for a final six months, until the end of that year. In August a further resolution provided for the creation of United Nations Integrated Office in Sierra Leone (UNIOSIL). Following the complete withdrawal of UNAMSIL as scheduled, UNIOSIL was established on 1 January 2006, for an initial period of one year; the mission was authorized to support the consolidation of peace and assist the Government in strengthening state institutions, the rule of law, human rights, and the security sector, and the organization of presidential and legis-

SIERRA LEONE

lative elections, scheduled for July 2007. In December 2006 UNIOSIL's mandate was extended until 31 December 2007. In mid-December the UN Secretary-General recommended that UNIOSIL's mandate be extended for a further nine months, to assist the Government in conducting the forthcoming elections. A new, smaller office was to replace UNIOSIL after that time, which would continue to aid the Sierra Leonean authorities in consolidating peace in the country. At the end of December the UN Security Council approved the final, nine-month extension (until September 2008) of UNIOSIL's mandate.

Meanwhile, in early September 2005 Kabbah reorganized the Cabinet. Most notably, John Oponjo Benjamin replaced Joseph Dauda as Minister of Finance, while Pascal Egbenda assumed the internal affairs portfolio and Lloyd During was appointed Minister of Energy and Power.

In February 2006 the trial of Hinga Norman officially commenced at the Special Court; proceedings against him were expected to be highly controversial, owing to the popular support retained by the Kamajors. In early February 2007 Hinga Norman was taken to a hospital in Dakar, Senegal, for what was termed a routine procedure. On 22 February it was reported that he had collapsed and died in his hospital room. An autopsy report released the following month concluded that he died of natural causes, although Hinga Norman's family voiced their suspicions at the verdict and were believed to be considering initiating a private investigation into the circumstances surrounding his death.

In March 2006 Nigeria announced that it had received a formal request from the new Liberian Government (see chapter on Liberia) to extradite Taylor to the Special Court. Later that month Taylor fled from his residence in Nigeria in an attempt to evade custody, but was apprehended two days later, near the border with Cameroon, and dispatched to Liberia, from where he was immediately extradited by peace-keeping forces to the Special Court. In early April Taylor (who initially refused to accept the authority of the Court) pleaded not guilty to 11 charges relating to his involvement in the civil conflict in Sierra Leone. Tribunal officials subsequently requested that his trial be transferred to the International Criminal Court (see p. 314) at The Hague (while remaining under the jurisdiction of the Special Court), in the interests of regional stability. The Dutch authorities acceded to that request on the condition that any sentence handed down to Taylor was served in another country. The United Kingdom subsequently agreed to host Taylor should he be imprisoned and, following the unanimous approval of the UN Security Council, on 20 June Taylor was transferred to The Hague. Taylor's trial commenced in early April 2007. Taylor remained absent from the trial until July, at which time he offered no explanation for his decision to attend and spoke only to plead 'not guilty' to the charges against him. In August it was reported that the Special Court, intended only to function until 2005, was to cease operations by the end of 2009. In June 2007 the Special Court had handed down its first verdicts, finding three former AFRC members guilty of war crimes and crimes against humanity. The following month two of those convicted were sentenced to 50 years' imprisonment, while the third defendant received a prison term of 45 years.

Legislative and presidential elections, initially due to be held in July 2007, were postponed until August to allow more time for campaigning and logistical preparations; voting eventually took place on 11 August. Official results indicated that the opposition APC had secured the largest representation in Parliament, taking 59 of the 124 available seats. The SLPP returned 43 deputies and the People's Movement for Democratic Change, led by Charles Margai, the son of Sir Abert Margai, took 10 seats. In the presidential election Koroma, contesting the election on behalf of the APC, secured 44.34% of the vote, while Berewa, of the SLPP, received 38.28% and Margai 13.89%. As no candidate secured more than 50% of the vote, Koroma and Berewa contested a second round on 8 September, at which Koroma won 60.22% of the vote. The elections were conducted in a largely peaceful manner, despite a small number of disturbances and opposition claims of procedural irregularities. In October President Koroma, who stated the tackling of corruption as one of his priorities, named a partial cabinet list, which included Zainab Hawa Bangura as Minister of Foreign Affairs and David Carew as Minister of Finance and Development. Further appointments were announced later that month, including Abdul Serry Kamal, who assumed the position of Minister of Justice and Attorney-General, and Paolo Conteh, who was awarded the defence portfolio.

Government

Under the terms of the Constitution of 1991, executive power is vested in the President, who is directly elected by universal adult suffrage. The President appoints the Cabinet (subject to approval by the legislature). The maximum duration of the President's tenure of office is limited to two five-year terms. Legislative power is vested in a unicameral Parliament, which is elected for a five-year term and comprises 112 members elected by a system of proportional representation, in 14 constituencies, and 12 Paramount Chiefs, who represent the provincial districts.

The country is divided into four regions: the Northern, Eastern and Southern Provinces, and the Western Area, which comprise 12 districts. There are 147 chiefdoms, each controlled by a Paramount Chief and a Council of Elders, known as the Tribal Authority.

Defence

As assessed at November 2007, active members of the armed forces of the Republic of Sierra Leone numbered about 10,500, with a navy of 200. In October 1999 the UN Security Council adopted a resolution establishing the UN Mission in Sierra Leone (UNAMSIL), which was to supervise the implementation of a peace agreement between the Government and rebel forces, signed in July of that year. Following the completion of disarmament in January 2002, a new army, restructured with British military assistance, was established. Some 100 British troops remained in the country to support peace-keeping operations and to continue reorganization of the Sierra Leone armed forces. Following the completion of UNAMSIL's mandate, the United Nations Integrated Office in Sierra Leone (UNIOSIL) was established on 1 January 2006 for an initial period of one year (in accordance with a Security Council resolution of 31 August 2005), extended in December of that year until the end of 2007. In December 2007 UNIOSIL's mandate was extended for a further 12 months. Expenditure on defence in 2007 was budgeted at Le 75,000m.

Economic Affairs

In 2006, according to the World Bank, Sierra Leone's gross national income (GNI), measured at average 2004–06 prices, was US $1,357m., equivalent to $240 per head (or $850 per head on an international purchasing-power parity basis). During 1996–2006, it was estimated, the population increased at an average annual rate of 3.1%, while gross domestic product (GDP) per head rose, in real terms, by an average of 1.6% per year. Overall GDP increased, in real terms, at an average annual rate of 4.7% in 1996–2005; growth was 7.1% in 2006.

Agriculture (including forestry and fishing) contributed 46.6% of GDP in 2006, according to the World Bank. About 59.4% of the labour force were employed in the sector in 2005. The principal cash crops are cocoa beans and coffee. Staple food crops include cassava, rice and citrus fruit. Chickens, cattle and sheep are the principal livestock. During 1990–2003 the GDP of the agricultural sector declined at an average annual rate of 4.4%; however, growth in agricultural GDP was 6.7% in 2003.

According to the World Bank, industry (including mining, manufacturing, construction and power) contributed 25.1% of GDP in 2006, and employed 6.5% of the working population in 2004. The GDP of the industrial sector declined by an average of 2.9% per year in 1990–2003; however, industrial GDP increased by 8.5% in 2003.

Mining and quarrying contributed 17.5% of GDP in 1994/95, and employed 3.6% of the working population in 2004. The principal mineral exports are diamonds (which, according to official figures, accounted for 54.1% of total export earnings in 2006), rutile (titanium dioxide), bauxite and gold. The production of iron ore, previously an important mineral export, was suspended in 1985. In 1995 increased rebel activity effectively suspended official mining operations (although illicit exports of diamonds by rebel forces continued). In October 2000 official exports of diamonds were resumed under a certification scheme. Following reinvestment in a major kimberlite diamond field at Koidu, production commenced at the end of 2003. The Sierra Rutile mines (the largest source of private-sector employment and foreign-exchange earnings prior to 1995) resumed full mining operations in early 2006, while rehabilitation of the country's bauxite mine was completed in 2005, also allowing production to recommence in early 2006.

Manufacturing contributed 5.3% of GDP in 2004 and engaged 0.5% of the employed population in 2004. The manufacturing sector consists mainly of the production of palm oil and other agro-based industries, textiles and furniture-making. During 1990–96 the GDP of the manufacturing sector increased at an average annual rate of 2.5%. Manufacturing GDP declined by 9.9% in 1995, but increased by 1.7% in 1996.

Energy is derived principally from oil-fired thermal power stations. With the electricity sector continuing to deteriorate, the Government planned to bring a delayed hydroelectric project at Bumbuna, in the north of the country, into operation by 2006. Imports of mineral fuels comprised 37.3% of the value of total imports in 2006.

The services sector contributed 28.3% of GDP in 2006, according to the World Bank, and employed 26.4% of the engaged population in 2004. The GDP of the services sector declined by an average of 0.3% per year in 1990–2003, rising by 6.8% in 2003.

In 2006 Sierra Leone recorded an estimated trade deficit of US $78.3m., and there was a deficit of $146.1m. on the current account of the balance of payments. In 2003, according to official estimates, the principal source of imports (42.8%) was Germany; other major suppliers were the United Kingdom and France. Belgium was the principal market for exports (taking 57.0% of the total); the other significant purchaser was Germany. The principal export in 2006 was diamonds. The principal imports in that year were mineral fuels, machinery and transport equipment, food and live animals and basic manufactures.

The overall budget deficit for 2005 was Le 60,452m. Sierra Leone's external debt totalled US $1,682m. at the end of 2005, of which $1,420m. was long-term public debt. In that year the cost of debt-servicing was equivalent to 9.2% of the value of exports of goods and services. The annual rate of inflation averaged 13.2% in 1995–2005. Consumer prices increased by 14.2% in 2004 and by an estimated 12.0% in 2005. An estimated 50% of the labour force were unemployed in early 1990.

Sierra Leone is a member of the Economic Community of West African States (see p. 232) and of the Mano River Union (see p. 413), which aims to promote economic co-operation with Guinea and Liberia.

The civil conflict, which commenced in 1991, resulted in the progressive destruction of Sierra Leone's infrastructure, and severe disruption, or complete suspension, of traditional economic activities. However, since the end of the civil war in January 2002 the country has experienced substantial real economic growth and falling inflation. Additionally, improvements in fiscal control and considerable support from international financial institutions have resulted in some progress in reconstruction. Sierra Leone's economic prospects improved further with the post-war resumption of the production and export of rutile and bauxite in early 2006, resulting in an increase in exports of 28% in that year and a further 11% in 2007. In May 2006 the IMF approved a three-year US $46.3m. arrangement for Sierra Leone under the existing Poverty Reduction and Growth Facility (PRGF) for low income countries. The Fund praised the country's performance under the previous PRGF-supported programme and commended the Government's 2006–2008 economic programme, which aimed, *inter alia*, to target poverty reduction and improve revenue administration. At a visit to Sierra Leone by the IMF in February–March 2008, during which the mission met with President Ernest Bai Koroma, the importance of improving revenue collection in order to avoid risks to the macroeconomic stability of the country was again emphasized. Despite obvious economic progress and improved business confidence, Sierra Leone remained heavily dependent on international aid, and private sector investment projects were problematic. In late 2006, however, the IDA and the IMF announced that Sierra Leone had made sufficient macroeconomic progress to reach completion point of the initiative for heavily indebted poor countries, granting the country debt relief totalling $675.2m., thus reducing the country's external debts to $483m. at the end of that year. Nevertheless, Sierra Leone's population continues to suffer from extremely high levels of poverty (the country has one of the lowest per-head gross national incomes in the world, at just $240). According to the IMF, GDP was forecast to increase by 6.5% in 2008.

Education

Primary education in Sierra Leone begins at six years of age and lasts for six years. Secondary education, beginning at the age of 12, lasts for a further six years, comprising two three-year cycles. In 2003/04 85% of the total school-age population was enrolled at primary and secondary schools. There is one university, which comprises six colleges. A total of 8,795 students were enrolled in tertiary education in 2000/01. Following the onset of the civil conflict in 1991, large numbers of children were forced to join rebel militia, and to participate in atrocities. After peace was largely restored in July 1999, the reintegration of young former combatants into the community was a priority for the new administration. Education was allocated Le 30,700m. in the 2001 budget, increasing to a projected Le 36,400m. (equivalent to 5.2% of total expenditure) in 2002.

Public Holidays

2008: 1 January (New Year's Day), 20 March (Mouloud, Birth of the Prophet)*, 21–24 March (Easter), 27 April (Independence Day), 1 October (Id al-Fitr, end of Ramadan)*, 9 December* (Id al-Adha, Feast of the Sacrifice), 25–26 December (Christmas and Boxing Day).

2009: 1 January (New Year's Day), 9 March (Mouloud, Birth of the Prophet)*, 10–13 April (Easter), 27 April (Independence Day), 20 September (Id al-Fitr, end of Ramadan)*, 27 November (Id al-Adha, Feast of the Sacrifice)*, 25–26 December (Christmas and Boxing Day).

* These holidays are dependent on the Islamic lunar calendar and may vary by one or two days from the dates given.

Weights and Measures

The metric system is in force.

SIERRA LEONE

Statistical Survey

Source (unless otherwise stated): Central Statistics Office, PMB 595, Tower Hill, Freetown; tel. (22) 223287; fax (22) 223897; internet www.sierra-leone.org/cso.html and www.statistics-sierra-leone.org.

Area and Population

AREA, POPULATION AND DENSITY

Area (sq km)	71,740*
Population (census results)†	
14 December 1985	3,515,812
4 December 2004‡	
Males	2,412,860
Females	2,550,438
Total	4,963,298
Population (UN estimates at mid-year)§	
2005	5,586,000
2006	5,743,000
2007	5,866,000
Density (per sq km) at mid-2007	81.8

* 27,699 sq miles.
† Excluding adjustment for underenumeration, estimated to have been 9% in 1985.
‡ Provisional.
§ Source: UN, *World Population Prospects: The 2006 Revision*.

PRINCIPAL TOWNS
(population at 1985 census)

Freetown (capital)	384,499		Kenema	52,473
Koindu	82,474		Makeni	49,474
Bo	59,768			

Mid-2007 (incl. suburbs, UN estimate): Freetown 827,000 (Source: UN, *World Urbanization Prospects: The 2007 Revision*).

BIRTHS AND DEATHS
(annual averages, UN estimates)

	1990–95	1995–2000	2000–05
Birth rate (per 1,000)	47.5	47.1	46.9
Death rate (per 1,000)	26.3	24.5	23.5

Source: UN, *World Population Prospects: The 2006 Revision*.

Expectation of life (years at birth, WHO estimates): 38.6 (males 37.3; females 39.9) in 2005 (Source: WHO, *World Health Report*).

EMPLOYMENT
(persons aged 10 years and over, 2004 census)

	Male	Female	Total
Agriculture, hunting and forestry	618,335	654,507	1,272,842
Fishing	33,337	17,828	51,165
Mining and quarrying	59,403	9,674	69,077
Manufacturing	7,411	2,016	9,427
Electricity, gas and water supply	7,128	1,247	8,375
Construction	28,296	10,836	39,132
Wholesale and retail trade; Repair of motor vehicles, motorcycles and personal and household goods	102,425	167,463	269,888
Hotels and restaurants	2,626	2,318	4,944
Transport, communications and storage	14,476	1,262	15,738
Financial intermediation	4,001	2,948	6,949
Real estate, renting and business activities	5,479	5,312	10,791
Public administration and defence; compulsory social security	21,146	4,864	26,010
Education	23,318	11,345	34,663
Health and social work	9,878	9,997	19,875
Other community, social and personnel service activities	44,541	39,130	83,671
Households with employed persons	4,001	4,318	8,319
Extra-territorial organizations and bodies	2,516	1,341	3,857
Total employed	988,317	946,406	1,934,723

Source: ILO.

Unemployed: 68,252 at census of 2004 (males 45,936, females 22,316).

Mid-2005 (estimates in '000): Agriculture, etc. 1,249; Total labour force 2,103 (Source: FAO).

Health and Welfare

KEY INDICATORS

Total fertility rate (children per woman, 2005)	6.5
Under-5 mortality rate (per 1,000 live births, 2005)	282
HIV/AIDS (% of persons aged 15–49, 2005)	1.6
Physicians (per 1,000 head, 2004)	0.03
Hospital beds (per 1,000 head, 2006)	0.40
Health expenditure (2004): US $ per head (PPP)	34.1
Health expenditure (2004): % of GDP	3.3
Health expenditure (2004): public (% of total)	59.0
Access to water (% of persons, 2004)	57
Access to sanitation (% of persons, 2004)	39
Human Development Index (2005): ranking	177
Human Development Index (2005): value	0.336

For sources and definitions, see explanatory note on p. vi.

Agriculture

PRINCIPAL CROPS
('000 metric tons)

	2004	2005	2006
Rice (paddy)	542.0	738.0	1,062.0
Maize	32.1	39.1	48.8
Millet*	15	20	25
Sorghum†	15.9	14.1	14.1
Sweet potatoes†	25.5	26.0	26.0
Cassava (Manioc)†	390.0	390.0	350.0
Sugar cane†	70	70	70
Groundnuts (in shell)	91.1	104.7	115.2
Oil palm fruit†	174.9	166.1	166.1
Tomatoes†	15.1	15.1	15.1
Plantains†	30.8	30.5	30.5
Citrus fruit†	82.4	82.3	82.3
Coffee (green)†	16.4	15.5	15.5
Cocoa beans	9.7†	8.7†	13.9

* Unofficial figures.
† FAO estimate(s).

Aggregate production ('000 metric tons, may include official, semi-official or estimated data): Total cereals 608.4 in 2004, 814.6 in 2005, 115.4 in 2006; Total roots and tubers 418.1 in 2004, 418.6 in 2005, 378.6 in 2006; Total vegetables (incl. melons) 235.1 in 2004, 235.1 in 2005, 235.1 in 2006; Total fruits (excl. melons) 181.9 in 2004, 181.9 in 2005, 181.9 in 2006.

Source: FAO.

LIVESTOCK
('000 head, year ending September)

	2004	2005	2006
Cattle	200.0	250.0	350.0
Pigs*	52	52	52
Sheep	300	375	470
Goats	350	438	540
Chickens*	7,500	7,500	7,500
Ducks*	70	70	70

* FAO estimates.
Source: FAO.

LIVESTOCK PRODUCTS
('000 metric tons, FAO estimates)

	2003	2004	2005
Chicken meat	11.3	10.8	10.8
Pig meat	2.3	2.3	2.4
Game meat	2.5	2.5	2.5
Cows' milk	21.3	21.3	21.3
Hen eggs	8.3	8.3	8.3

2006: Figures assumed to be unchanged from 2005 (FAO estimates).
Source: FAO.

Forestry

ROUNDWOOD REMOVALS
('000 cubic metres, excl. bark, FAO estimates)

	2004	2005	2006
Sawlogs, veneer logs and logs for sleepers*	3.6	3.6	3.6
Other industrial wood†	120.0	120.0	120.0
Fuel wood	5,403.1	5,422.8	5,448.3
Total	5,526.7	5,546.4	5,571.9

* Annual output assumed to be unchanged since 1993.
† Annual output assumed to be unchanged since 1980.
Source: FAO.

SAWNWOOD PRODUCTION
('000 cubic metres, incl. railway sleepers)

	1991	1992	1993
Total (all broadleaved)	9.0	9.0*	5.3

* FAO estimate.
1994–2006: Annual production as in 1993 (FAO estimates).
Source: FAO.

Fishing

('000 metric tons, live weight of capture)

	2003	2004	2005
West African ilisha	1.5	3.1	3.5
Tonguefishes	1.2	1.0	1.1
Bobo croaker	5.8	7.3	7.9
Sardinellas	15.4	18.2	22.1
Bonga shad	28.5	51.0	52.7
Tuna-like fishes	0.8	2.5	2.0
Marine molluscs	3.1	1.3	1.9
Total catch (incl. others)	96.9	134.4	146.0

Source: FAO.

Mining

(metric tons, unless otherwise indicated)

	2003	2004	2005
Gypsum	4,000	—	—
Diamonds ('000 carats)	507	693	669
Salt	1,005	827	—

Source: US Geological Survey.

Industry

PETROLEUM PRODUCTS
('000 metric tons, estimates)

	2002	2003	2004
Jet fuels	20	20	21
Motor spirit (petrol)	31	31	32
Kerosene	10	10	10
Distillate fuel oils	74	74	n.a.
Residual fuel oils	55	55	55

Source: UN, *Industrial Commodity Statistics Yearbook*.

SELECTED OTHER PRODUCTS
('000 metric tons, unless otherwise indicated)

	2005	2006
Beer and stout ('000 cartons)	669	582
Malt drink ('000 cartons)	160	160
Soft drinks ('000 crates)	1,908	2,089
Confectionery ('000 lbs)	2,074	2,330
Soap (metric tons)	417	467
Paint ('000 gallons)	136	143
Cement	172	234
Flour	19	14

Source: Bank of Sierra Leone, *Annual Report*.

SIERRA LEONE

Finance

CURRENCY AND EXCHANGE RATES

Monetary Units
100 cents = 1 leone (Le).

Sterling, Dollar and Euro Equivalents (31 December 2007)
£1 sterling = 5,965.329 leones;
US $1 = 2,977.600 leones;
€1 = 4,383.323 leones;
10,000 leones = £3.46 = $6.94 = €4.71.

Average Exchange Rate (leones per US $)
2005   2,889.59
2006   2,961.91
2007   2,985.19

BUDGET
(Le million)

Revenue*	2003	2004	2005
Taxes on income and profit	73,046	93,963	110,153
Taxes on goods and services	63,742	85,257	103,501
Taxes on international trade	114,166	166,137	172,283
Other taxes	2,535	3,717	4,288
Non-tax revenue	4,168	7,893	25,756
Total	287,657	356,966	415,982

Expenditure	2003	2004	2005
Recurrent expenditure	485,368	555,046	620,728
Wages and salaries	152,003	178,751	229,440
Goods and services	222,088	191,172	202,468
Emergency defence	40,774	35,244	33,976
Subsidies and transfers	27,506	55,559	63,233
Education	19,000	21,187	20,549
Local government	417	—	15,508
Pensions/Others	8,088	34,372	27,176
Interest	83,771	129,564	125,588
Development Expenditure and net lending	112,631	133,046	207,575
Total	597,999	688,092	828,304

* Excluding grants received (Le million): 179,344 in 2003; 259,376 in 2004; 351,870 in 2005.

Source: IMF, *Sierra Leone: Statistical Appendix* (January 2007).

INTERNATIONAL RESERVES
(US $ million at 31 December)

	2005	2006	2007
IMF special drawing rights	32.8	29.2	30.7
Foreign exchange	137.7	154.7	185.8
Total	170.5	183.9	216.5

Source: IMF, *International Financial Statistics*.

MONEY SUPPLY
(Le million at 31 December)

	2005	2006	2007
Currency outside banks	231,274	275,405	309,837
Demand deposits at commercial banks	176,649	195,870	218,503
Total money (incl. others)	424,173	489,298	550,291

Source: IMF, *International Financial Statistics*.

COST OF LIVING
(Consumer Price Index for Freetown; base: 2000 = 100)

	2001	2002	2003
Food	105.2	104.4	112.2
All items (incl. others)	102.2	98.8	106.3

All items: 121.3 in 2004; 135.9 in 2005; 148.9 in 2006.

Source: IMF, *International Financial Statistics*.

NATIONAL ACCOUNTS

National Income and Product
(Le million at current prices, year ending 30 June)

	1992/93	1993/94	1994/95*
Compensation of employees	86,503.1	107,650.3	138,658.6
Operating surplus	313,873.8	352,605.6	467,380.1
Domestic factor incomes	400,376.9	460,255.8	606,038.7
Consumption of fixed capital	30,097.2	35,104.2	41,907.3
Gross domestic product (GDP) at factor cost	430,474.1	495,360.0	647,946.1
Indirect taxes, *less* subsidies	36,713.4	48,351.0	62,443.2
GDP in purchasers' values	467,187.5	543,711.0	710,389.3
Factor income received from abroad / *Less* Factor income paid abroad	−66,914.8	−70,237.5	−84,216.0
Gross national product (GNP)	400,272.7	473,473.5	626,173.3
Less Consumption of fixed capital	30,097.2	35,104.2	41,907.3
National income in market prices	370,175.5	438,369.3	584,265.9
Other current transfers received from abroad / *Less* Other current transfers paid abroad	11,483.0	12,438.6	15,067.8
National disposable income	381,658.5	450,807.9	599,333.7

* Provisional figures.

Expenditure on the Gross Domestic Product
(US $ million at current prices)

	2004	2005	2006
Government final consumption expenditure	145.25	163.36	182.96
Private final consumption expenditure	980.03	1,065.97	1,286.40
Gross capital formation	113.11	208.40	222.60
Total domestic expenditure	1,238.39	1,437.73	1,691.96
Exports of goods and services	239.02	291.08	399.38
Less Imports of goods and services	405.98	515.88	634.59
GDP in purchasers' values	1,071.43	1,212.94	1,456.74
GDP at constant 2000 prices	1,085.64	1,164.32	1,250.28

Source: African Development Bank.

Gross Domestic Product by Economic Activity
(Le million at current prices, year ending 30 June)

	1992/93	1993/94	1994/95*
Agriculture, hunting, forestry and fishing	162,194.6	188,884.1	275,327.5
Mining and quarrying	98,615.8	96,748.8	119,229.2
Manufacturing	39,567.0	47,816.7	61,475.3
Electricity, gas and water	469.8	757.3	2,816.8
Construction	4,655.4	12,544.4	15,788.2
Trade, restaurants and hotels	69,139.9	77,251.0	98,270.1
Transport, storage and communications	37,056.5	50,047.1	61,267.5
Finance, insurance, real estate and business services	15,947.0	17,988.0	14,732.2
Government services	14,500.0	17,884.0	19,844.9
Other community, social and personal services	8,998.3	9,769.0	12,308.9
Sub-total	451,144.3	519,690.4	681,060.6
Import duties	18,994.0	27,410.0	32,942.0
Less Imputed bank service charge	2,950.8	3,389.8	3,612.3
GDP in purchasers' values	467,187.5	543,711.0	710,389.3

* Provisional figures.

SIERRA LEONE

BALANCE OF PAYMENTS
(US $ million)

	2004	2005	2006
Exports of goods f.o.b.	154.1	183.6	272.9
Imports of goods f.o.b.	–274.3	–361.7	–351.2
Trade balance	–120.2	–178.0	–78.3
Exports of services	61.4	78.0	39.7
Imports of services	–92.3	–90.7	–83.1
Balance on goods and services	–151.2	–190.7	–121.6
Other income received	4.1	5.4	11.1
Other income paid	–71.1	–56.3	–52.0
Balance on goods, services and income	–218.2	–241.6	–162.5
Current transfers received	80.3	73.5	52.9
Current transfers paid	–2.8	–2.0	–36.5
Current balance	–140.8	–170.1	–146.1
Capital account (net)	18.4	36.8	50.5
Direct investment abroad	—	7.5	–0.1
Direct investment from abroad	61.2	83.2	58.5
Other investment assets	10.1	–1.9	–7.0
Other investment liabilities	5.0	–26.1	–16.1
Net errors and omissions	–53.5	–59.0	119.3
Overall balance	–99.7	–129.6	59.2

Source: IMF, *International Financial Statistics*.

External Trade

PRINCIPAL COMMODITIES
(US $ '000)

Imports c.i.f.	2004	2005	2006
Food and live animals	57,058.5	53,115.3	56,139.9
Beverages and tobacco	11,122.5	9,920.2	9,295.3
Crude materials (inedible) except fuels	7,578.3	8,754.2	21,702.7
Mineral fuels, lubricants, etc.	94,865.6	115,597.0	147,080.4
Animal and vegetable oils and fats	1,966.8	1,306.8	3,327.0
Chemicals	17,534.0	22,746.8	23,999.9
Basic manufactures	31,844.0	40,674.5	48,601.3
Machinery and transport equipment	50,861.3	71,824.1	69,111.0
Miscellaneous manufactured articles	13,634.1	17,125.1	15,571.3
Total	286,465.1	341,063.9	394,828.8

Exports f.o.b.	2004	2005	2006
Coffee	52.8	873.8	1,093.4
Cocoa beans	5,259.5	5,236.7	11,570.7
Diamonds	126,330.2	142,202.3	125,041.2
Total (incl. others)*	139,705.6	159,010.6	231,037.4

* Including re-exports: 3,980.7 in 2004; 7,189.5 in 2005; 28,399.8 in 2006.
Source: Bank of Sierra Leone.

PRINCIPAL TRADING PARTNERS

Imports c.i.f. (US $ million)	2002
Canada	23.0
China, People's Repub.	11.8
Côte d'Ivoire	129.1
Germany	9.1
India	13.2
Japan	14.9
Netherlands	19.4
United Kingdom	11.9
USA	17.4
Total (incl. others)	352.0

Source: UN, *International Trade Statistics Yearbook*.

Exports (Le million)	1992	1993	1994
Belgium	25,770	54	11,412
Germany	1,060	2,486	1,328
Guinea	1,315	817	1,331
Netherlands	5,307	1,201	2,815
Switzerland	7,546	486	215
United Kingdom	5,567	5,988	11,767
USA	13,832	17,564	30,431
Total (incl. others)	75,034	67,077	67,930

Source: Central Statistics Office, Freetown.

Transport

ROAD TRAFFIC
(motor vehicles in use at 31 December)

	2000	2001	2002
Passenger cars	2,045	2,263	11,353
Buses and coaches	2,597	3,516	4,050
Goods vehicles	2,309	2,898	3,565
Motorcycles	1,398	1,532	1,657

Source: IRF, *World Road Statistics*.

SHIPPING

Merchant Fleet
(registered at 31 December)

	2004	2005	2006
Number of vessels	46	69	194
Displacement (gross registered tons)	26,999	77,244	293,872

Source: Lloyd's Register-Fairplay, *World Fleet Statistics*.

International Sea-borne Freight Traffic
(estimates, '000 metric tons)

	1991	1992	1993
Goods loaded	1,930	2,190	2,310
Goods unloaded	562	579	589

Source: UN Economic Commission for Africa, *African Statistical Yearbook*.

CIVIL AVIATION
(traffic on scheduled services)

	2000	2001	2002
Kilometres flown (million)	1	1	1
Passengers carried ('000)	19	14	14
Passenger-km (million)	93	73	74
Total ton-km (million)	18	13	13

2003: Figures assumed to be unchanged from 2002.
Source: UN, *Statistical Yearbook*.

Tourism

	2003	2004	2005
Tourist arrivals	38,107	43,560	40,023
Tourism receipts (US $ million, excl. passenger transport)	60	58	64

Source: World Tourism Organization.

SIERRA LEONE

Communications Media

	2000	2001	2002
Television receivers ('000 in use)	64	65	n.a.
Telephones ('000 main lines in use)	19.0	22.7	24.0
Mobile cellular telephones ('000 subscribers)	11.9	26.9	67.0
Internet users ('000)	5	7	8

2003 ('000): Mobile cellular telephones (subscribers) 113.2; Internet users 9.

2004–05 ('000): Mobile cellular telephones (subscribers) 113.2 (estimates); Internet users 10.

Radio receivers ('000 in use): 1,120 in 1997.

Facsimile machines (number in use, year beginning 1 April): 2,500 in 1998.

Daily newspapers: 1 (average circulation 20,000) in 1996.

Sources: UNESCO, *Statistical Yearbook*; UN, *Statistical Yearbook*; and International Telecommunication Union.

Education

(2001/02)

	Schools	Teachers	Males	Females	Total
Primary	2,704	14,932	323,924	230,384	554,308
Secondary	246	5,264	66,745	41,031	107,776
University*	n.a.	n.a.	1,163	300	1,463

Number of pupils

* Full time undergraduate students in 1995.

2003/04: *Primary:* Pupils 1,158,399 (males 670,079, females 488,320) (Source: UNESCO Institute for Statistics).

Adult literacy rate (UNESCO estimates): 34.8% (males 46.7%; females 24.2%) in 2004 (Source: UNESCO Institute for Statistics).

Directory

The Constitution

Following the transfer of power to a democratically elected civilian administration on 29 March 1996, the Constitution of 1991 (which had been suspended since April 1992) was reinstated. The Constitution provided for the establishment of a multi-party system, and vested executive power in the President, who was to be elected by the majority of votes cast nationally and by at least 25% of the votes cast in each of the four provinces. The maximum duration of the President's tenure of office was limited to two five-year terms. The President was to appoint the Cabinet, subject to approval by the Parliament. The Parliament was elected for a five-year term and comprised 124 members, 112 of whom were elected by a system of proportional representation, in 14 constituencies, while 12 Paramount Chiefs also represented the provincial districts in the legislature. Members of the Parliament were not permitted concurrently to hold office in the Cabinet.

The Government

HEAD OF STATE

President and Commander-in-Chief of the Armed Forces: ERNEST BAI KOROMA (elected 8 September 2007; inaugurated 15 November 2007).

Vice-President: SAHR SAM-SUMANA.

CABINET
(March 2008)

Minister of Foreign Affairs: ZAINAB HAWA BANGURA.
Minister of Finance and Development: DAVID CAREW.
Minister of Defence: PAOLO CONTEH.
Minister of Information and Communications: Alhaji I. B. KARGBO.
Minister of Justice and Attorney-General: ABDUL SERRY-KAMAL.
Minister of Health: Dr SOCCOH KABIA.
Minister of Mineral Resources: Alhaji ABUBAKARR JALLOH.
Minister of Housing and Infrastructural Development: JOHN SAAB.
Minister of Agriculture: Dr SAM SESAY.
Minister of Internal Affairs, Local Government and Rural Development: DAUDA SULAIMAN KAMARA.
Minister of Lands, Country Planning and the Environment: BENJAMIN O. N. DAVIES.
Minister of Energy and Power: HAJA AFSATU KABBAH.
Minister of Marine Resources: Dr MOSES MOISA-KAPU.
Minister of Social Welfare, Gender and Children's Affairs: MUSU KANDEH.
Minister of Tourism and Cultural Affairs: HINDOLO TRYE.
Minister of Employment and Social Security: MINKAILU MANSARAY.
Minister of Education, Youths and Sports: Dr MINKAILU BAH.
Minister of Trade and Industry: ALIMAMY KOROMA.
Minister of Transport and Aviation: KEMOH SESAY.
Minister of Presidential and Public Affairs: ALPHA KANU.

MINISTRIES

Office of the President: Freetown; tel. (22) 232101; fax (22) 231404; e-mail info@statehouse-sl.org; internet www.statehouse-sl.org/president.html.
Ministry of Agriculture: Youyi Bldg, 3rd Floor, Brookfields, Freetown; tel. (22) 222242; fax (22) 241613.
Ministry of Defence: State Ave, Freetown; tel. (22) 227369; fax (22) 229380.
Ministry of Education, Youths and Sports: New England, Freetown; tel. (22) 240881; fax (22) 240137.
Ministry of Employment and Social Security: New England, Freetown; tel. (22) 241947.
Ministry of Energy and Power: Electricity House, Siaka Stevens St, Freetown; tel. (22) 226566; fax (22) 228199.
Ministry of Finance and Development: Secretariat Bldg, George St, Freetown; tel. (22) 225612; fax (22) 228472.
Ministry of Foreign Affairs: Gloucester St, Freetown; tel. (22) 223260; fax (22) 225615; e-mail mfaicsl@yahoo.com.
Ministry of Health: Youyi Bldg, 4th Floor, Brookfields, Freetown; tel. (22) 240187; fax (22) 241613; e-mail info@health.sl; internet www.health.sl.
Ministry of Housing and Infrastructural Development: New England, Freetown; tel. (22) 240937; fax (22) 240018.
Ministry of Information and Communications: Youyi Bldg, 8th Floor, Brookfields, Freetown; tel. (22) 240339; fax (22) 241757.
Ministry of Internal Affairs, Local Government and Rural Development: Liverpool St, Freetown; tel. (22) 226979; fax (22) 227727.
Ministry of Justice: Guma Bldg, Lamina Sankoh St, Freetown; tel. (22) 227444; fax (22) 229366.
Ministry of Lands, Country Planning and the Environment: Youyi Bldg, 4th Floor, Brookfields, Freetown; tel. (22) 242013.
Ministry of Marine Resources: Marine House, 11 Old Railway Line, Brookfields, Freetown; tel. (22) 242117.
Ministry of Mineral Resources: Youyi Bldg, 5th Floor, Brookfields, Freetown; tel. and fax (22) 240467; e-mail contact@mmr-sl.org; internet www.mmr-sl.org.
Ministry of Presidential and Public Affairs: State House, State Ave, Freetown; tel. (22) 229728; fax (22) 229799.
Ministry of Social Welfare, Gender and Children's Affairs: New England, Freetown; tel. (22) 241256; fax (22) 242076.

SIERRA LEONE

Ministry of Trade and Industry: Ministerial Bldg, George St, Freetown; tel. (22) 225211.

Ministry of Transport and Aviation: Ministerial Bldg, George St, Freetown; tel. (22) 221245; fax (22) 227337.

Ministry of Tourism and Cultural Affairs: Ministerial Bldg, George St, Freetown; tel. (22) 222588.

President and Legislature

PRESIDENT

Presidential Election, First Round, 11 August 2007

Candidate	Votes	% of votes
Ernest Bai Koroma (APC)	815,523	44.34
Solomon Berewa (SLPP)	704,012	38.28
Charles Margai (PMDC)	255,499	13.89
Andrew Turay (CPP)	28,610	1.56
Amadu Jalloh (NDA)	17,748	0.96
Kandeh Baba Conteh (PLP)	10,556	0.57
Abdul Kady Karim (UNPP)	7,260	0.39
Total	**1,839,208**	**100.00**

Presidential Election, Second Round, 8 September 2007

Candidate	Votes	% of votes
Ernest Bai Koroma (APC)	859,144	60.22
Solomon Berewa (SLPP)	567,449	39.78
Total	**1,426,593**	**100.00**

PARLIAMENT

Speaker: Justice E. K. COWAN.

General Election, 11 August 2007

Party	Seats
All-People's Congress (APC)	59
Sierra Leone People's Party (SLPP)	43
People's Movement for Democratic Change (PMDC)	10
Total	**112***

*A further 12 seats were allocated to Paramount Chiefs, who represented the 12 provincial districts.

Election Commission

National Electoral Commission (NEC): 15 Wellington Industrial Esate, Freetown; tel. 76547299; internet www.necsl.org; f. 2000; Chair. CHRISTIANA AYOKA MARY THORPE.

Political Organizations

A ban on political activity was rescinded in June 1995. Numerous political parties were officially granted registration, prior to elections in May 2002.

All-People's Congress (APC): 137H Fourah Bay Rd, Freetown; e-mail info@new-apc.org; internet apcparty.org; f. 1960; sole authorized political party 1978–91; merged with the Democratic People's Party in 1992; reconstituted in 1995; Leader ERNEST BAI KOROMA.

Citizens United for Peace and Progress (CUPP): e-mail info@cupp.org; internet www.cupp.org; f. 2002; Chair. ABUBAKARR YANSSANEH.

Grand Alliance Party (GAP): Freetown; f. 2002; Pres. Dr RAYMOND KAMARA.

Movement for Progress (MOP): Freetown; f. 2002; Pres. ZAINAB HAWA BANGURA.

National Alliance Democratic Party (NADP): Leader MOHAMED YAHYA SILLAH.

National Democratic Alliance (NDA): Leader Alhaji AMADU M. B. JALLOH.

National Unity Movement (NUM): Leader DESMOND LUKE.

National Unity Party (NUP): e-mail johnben@nupsl.org; internet www.nupsl.org; Leader JOHN OPONJO BENJAMIN (acting).

Peace and Liberation Party (PLP): Freetown; f. 2002; Leader JOHNNY PAUL KOROMA.

People's Democratic Party (PDP): Freetown; supported Sierra Leone People's Party in May 2002 elections; Leader OSMAN KAMARA.

People's Movement for Democratic Change (PMDC): Freetown; f. April 2006 by fmr mems of Sierra Leone People's Party; Leader CHARLES MARGAI; Sec.-Gen. ANSU LANSANA.

People's National Convention (PNC): Leader EDWARD JOHN KARGBO.

People's Progressive Party (PPP): Leader ABASS CHERNOR BUNDU.

Sierra Leone People's Party (SLPP): 15 Wallace Johnson St, Freetown; tel. and fax (22) 2256341; e-mail info@slpp.ws; internet www.slpp.ws; f. 1951; Nat. Chair. Alhaji U. N. S. JAH; Leader SOLOMAN BEREWA.

Social Democratic Party (SDP): Leader ANDREW VICTOR LUNGAY.

United National People's Party (UNPP): Leader Dr JOHN KAREFA-SMART.

Young People's Party (YPP): 19 Lewis St, Freetown; tel. (22) 232907; e-mail info@yppsl.org; internet www.yppsl.org; f. 2002; Leader SYLVIA BLYDEN; Sec.-Gen. ABDUL RAHMAN YILLA.

Diplomatic Representation

EMBASSIES AND HIGH COMMISSIONS IN SIERRA LEONE

China, People's Republic: 29 Wilberforce Loop, POB 778, Freetown; tel. and fax (22) 231797; e-mail chinaemb_sl@mfa.gov.cn; internet sl.china-embassy.org; Ambassador CHENG WENJU.

Egypt: 174C Wilkinson Rd, POB 652, Freetown; tel. (22) 231245; fax (22) 234297; Ambassador MAHMOUD YEHIA M. EZZAT.

The Gambia: 6 Wilberforce St, Freetown; tel. (22) 225191; fax (22) 226846; High Commissioner DEMBO BADJIE.

Ghana: 13 Walpole St, Freetown; tel. (22) 223461; fax (22) 227043; High Commissioner KABRAL BLAY-AMIHERE.

Guinea: 6 Wilkinson Rd, Freetown; tel. (22) 232584; fax (22) 232496; Ambassador MOHAMED LAMIN SOMPARE.

Lebanon: 22A Spur Rd, Wilberforce, Freetown; tel. (22) 222513; fax (22) 234665; Ambassador GHASSAN ABDEL SATER.

Liberia: 10 Motor Rd, Brookfields, POB 276, Freetown; tel. (22) 230991; Chargé d'affaires a.i. SAMUEL PETERS.

Libya: 1A and 1B P. Z. Compound, Wilberforce, Freetown; tel. (22) 235231; fax (22) 234514; Chargé d'affaires a.i. ALI TELLISI.

Nigeria: 37 Siaka Stevens St, Freetown; tel. (22) 224224; fax (22) 2242474; High Commissioner ADAMU A. ABBAS.

United Kingdom: 6 Spur Rd, Wilberforce, Freetown; tel. (22) 232565; fax (22) 232070; e-mail freetown.consular.enquiries@fco.gov.uk; internet www.britishhighcommission.gov.uk/sierraleone; High Commissioner SARAH MACINTOSH.

USA: Leicester, Freetown; tel. (22) 515000; fax (22) 515355; e-mail TaylorJB2@state.gov; internet freetown.usembassy.gov; Ambassador JUNE CARTER PERRY.

Judicial System

The Supreme Court

The ultimate court of appeal in both civil and criminal cases. In addition to its appellate jurisdiction, the Court has supervisory jurisdiction over all other courts and over any adjudicating authority in Sierra Leone, and also original jurisdiction in constitutional issues.

Chief Justice: UMU HAWA TEJAN JALLOH (acting).

Supreme Court Justices: C. A. HARDING, AGNES AWUNOR-RENNER.

The Court of Appeal

The Court of Appeal has jurisdiction to hear and determine appeals from decisions of the High Court in both criminal and civil matters, and also from certain statutory tribunals. Appeals against its decisions may be made to the Supreme Court.

Justices of Appeal: S. C. E. WARNE, C. S. DAVIES, S. T. NAVO, M. S. TURAY, E. C. THOMPSON-DAVIS, M. O. TAJU-DEEN, M. O. ADOPHY, GEORGE GELAGA KING, Dr A. B. Y. TIMBO, VIRGINIA A. WRIGHT.

High Court

The High Court has unlimited original jurisdiction in all criminal and civil matters. It also has appellate jurisdiction against decisions of Magistrates' Courts.

SIERRA LEONE   *Directory*

Judges: Francis C. Gbow, Ebun Thomas, D. E. M. Williams, Laura Marcus-Jones, L. B. O. Nylander, A. M. B. Tarawallie, O. H. Alghalli, W. A. O. Johnson, N. D. Alhadi, R. J. Bankole Thompson, M. E. T. Thompson, C. J. W. Atere-Roberts (acting).

Magistrates' Courts: In criminal cases the jurisdiction of the Magistrates' Courts is limited to summary cases and to preliminary investigations to determine whether a person charged with an offence should be committed for trial.

Local Courts have jurisdiction, according to native law and custom, in matters that are outside the jurisdiction of other courts.

Religion

A large proportion of the population holds animist beliefs, although there are significant numbers of Islamic and Christian adherents.

ISLAM

In 1990 Islamic adherents represented an estimated 30% of the total population.

Ahmadiyya Muslim Mission: 15 Bath St, Brookfields, POB 353, Freetown; Emir and Chief Missionary Khalil A. Mobashir.

Kankaylay (Sierra Leone Muslim Men and Women's Association): 15 Blackhall Rd, Kissy, POB 1168, Freetown; tel. (22) 250931; e-mail kankaylay@yahoo.com; f. 1972; 500,000 mems; Pres. Alhaji Ibrahim Alpha Turay; Lady Pres. Haja Mariam Turay.

Sierra Leone Muslim Congress: POB 875, Freetown; f. 1928; Pres. Alhaji Muhammad Sanusi Mustapha.

CHRISTIANITY

Council of Churches in Sierra Leone: 4A King Harman Rd, Brookfields, POB 404, Freetown; tel. (22) 240569; fax (22) 421109; f. 1924; 17 mem. churches; Pres. Rev. Moses B. Khanu; Gen. Sec. Alimamy P. Koroma.

The Anglican Communion

Anglicans in Sierra Leone are adherents of the Church of the Province of West Africa, comprising 12 dioceses, of which two are in Sierra Leone. The Archbishop of the Province is the Bishop of Koforidua, Ghana.

Bishop of Bo: Rt Rev. Samuel Sao Gbonda, MacRobert St, POB 21, Bo, Southern Province.

Bishop of Freetown: Rt Rev. Julius O. Prince Lynch, Bishopscourt, Fourah Bay Rd, POB 537, Freetown.

Baptist Churches

Sierra Leone Baptist Convention: POB 64, Lunsar; Pres. Rev. Joseph S. Mans; Sec. Rev. N. T. Dixon.

The Nigerian Baptist Convention is also active.

Methodist Churches

Methodist Church Sierra Leone: Wesley House, George St, POB 64, Freetown; tel. (22) 222216; autonomous since 1967; Pres. of Conf. Rev. Gershon F. H. Anderson; Sec. Rev. Christian V. A. Peacock; 26,421 mems.

United Methodist Church: Freetown; Presiding Bishop T. S. Bangura; 36,857 mems.

Other active Methodist bodies include the African Methodist Episcopal Church, the Wesleyan Church of Sierra Leone, the Countess of Huntingdon's Connexion and the West African Methodist Church.

The Roman Catholic Church

Sierra Leone comprises one archdiocese and two dioceses. At 31 December 2005 there were an estimated 257,557 adherents in the country, representing about 4.1% of the total population.

Inter-territorial Catholic Bishops' Conference of The Gambia and Sierra Leone

Santanno House, POB 893, Freetown; tel. (22) 228240; fax (22) 228252.

f. 1971; Pres. Rt Rev. George Biguzzi (Bishop of Makeni).

Archbishop of Freetown and Bo: Most Rev. Joseph Henry Ganda, Santanno House, POB 893, Freetown; tel. (22) 224590; fax (22) 224075; e-mail jhg3271@sierratel.sl.

Other Christian Churches

The following are represented: the Christ Apostolic Church, the Church of the Lord (Aladura), the Evangelical Church, the Missionary Church of Africa, the Sierra Leone Church and the United Brethren in Christ.

AFRICAN RELIGIONS

There is a diverse range of beliefs, rites and practices, varying between ethnic and kinship groups.

The Press

DAILIES

Daily Mail: 29–31 Rawdon St, POB 53, Freetown; tel. (22) 223191; f. 1931; state-owned; Editor Aiah Martin Mondeh; circ. 10,000.

For di People: Freetown; independent; Editor Paul Kamara.

PERIODICALS

African Crescent: 15 Bath St, POB 353, Brookfields, Freetown; Editor Maulana-Khalil A. Mobashir.

The Catalyst: Christian Literature Crusade Bookshop, 92 Circular Rd, POB 1465, Freetown; tel. (22) 224382; Editor Elias Bangura.

Concord Times: 139 Pademba Rd, Freetown; 3 a week; Editor Dorothy Gordon.

Leonean Sun: 49 Main Rd, Wellington, Freetown; tel. (22) 223363; f. 1974; monthly; Editor Rowland Martyn.

Liberty Voice: 139 Pademba Rd, Freetown; tel. (22) 242100; Editor A. Mahdieu Savage.

New Breed: Freetown; weekly; independent; Man. Editor (vacant).

New Citizen: 5 Hanna Benka-Coker St, Freetown; tel. (22) 241795; Editor I. Ben Kargbo.

The New Globe: 49 Bathurst St, Freetown; tel. (22) 228245; weekly; Man. Editor Sam Tumoe; circ. 4,000.

The New Shaft: 60 Old Railway Line, Brookfields, Freetown; tel. (22) 241093; 2 a week; independent; Editor Franklin Bunting-Davies; circ. 10,000.

The Pool Newspaper: 1 Short St, 5th Floor, Freetown; tel. and fax (22) 220102; e-mail pool@justice.com; internet www.poolnewspaper.tripod.com; f. 1992; 3 a week; independent; Man. Dir Chernor Ojuku Sesay; circ. 3,000.

Progress: 1 Short St, Freetown; tel. (22) 223588; weekly; independent; Editor Fode Kandeh; circ. 7,000.

Sierra Leone Chamber of Commerce Journal: Sierra Leone Chamber of Commerce, Industry and Agriculture, Guma Bldg, 5th Floor, Lamina Sankoh St, POB 502, Freetown; tel. (22) 226305; fax (22) 228005; monthly.

Unity Now: 82 Pademba Rd, Freetown; tel. (22) 227466; Editor Frank Kposowa.

The Vision: 60 Old Railway Line, Brookfields; tel. (22) 241273; Editor Siaka Massaquoi.

Weekend Spark: 7 Lamina Sankoh St, Freetown; tel. (22) 223397; f. 1983; weekly; independent; Editor Rowland Martyn; circ. 20,000.

Weekly Democrat: Freetown; Editor Jon Foray.

NEWS AGENCY

Sierra Leone News Agency (SLENA): 15 Wallace Johnson St, PMB 445, Freetown; tel. (22) 224921; fax (22) 224439; f. 1980; Man. Dir Abdul Karim Jalloh (acting).

Publishers

Njala University Publishing Centre: Njala University College, PMB, Freetown; science and technology, university textbooks.

Sierra Leone University Press: Fourah Bay College, POB 87, Freetown; tel. (22) 22491; fax (22) 224439; f. 1965; biography, history, Africana, religion, social science, university textbooks; Chair. Prof. Ernest H. Wright.

United Christian Council Literature Bureau: Bunumbu Press, POB 28, Bo; tel. (32) 462; books in Mende, Temne, Susu; Man. Dir Robert Sam-Kpakra.

Broadcasting and Communications

TELECOMMUNICATIONS

Celtel Sierra Leone: Celtel House, 42 Main Motor Rd, Wilberforce, Freetown; tel. (22) 233222; internet www.sl.celtel.com; f. 2000; Man. Dir Ted Sauti-Phiri.

Sierra Leone Telecommunications Co (SIERRATEL): 7 Wallace Johnson St, POB 80, Freetown; tel. (22) 222804; fax (22) 224439; state owned telecommunications operator.

SIERRA LEONE   *Directory*

BROADCASTING

Sierra Leone Broadcasting Service: New England, Freetown; tel. (22) 240403; f. 1934; state-controlled; programmes mainly in English and the four main Sierra Leonean vernaculars, Mende, Limba, Temne and Krio; weekly broadcast in French; television service established 1963; Dir-Gen. JEANA BANDATOMO.

Finance

(cap. = capital; res = reserves; dep. = deposits; m. = million; br(s). = branch(es); amounts in leones)

BANKING

Central Bank

Bank of Sierra Leone: Siaka Stevens St, POB 30, Freetown; tel. (22) 226501; fax (22) 224764; e-mail info@bankofsierraleone-centralbank.org; internet www.bankofsierraleone-centralbank.org; f. 1964; cap. 24,001.5m., res −177,362.3m., dep. 717,290.7m. (Dec. 2005); Gov. JAMES D. ROGERS; Dep. Gov. MOHAMED S. FOFANA; 1 br.

Other Banks

Guaranty Trust Bank: Sparta Bldg, 12 Wilberforce St, POB 1168, Freetown; tel. (22) 228493; fax (22) 228318; internet www.gtb.sl; f. Feb. 2002 through the acquisition of 90% of shareholding of First Merchant Bank of Sierra Leone by Guaranty Trust Bank of Nigeria; cap. 2,261.0m., total assets 17,769.0m. (Dec. 2003); Chair. TAYO ADERINOKUN.

National Development Bank Ltd: Leone House, 6th Floor, 21–23 Siaka Stevens St, Freetown; tel. (22) 226792; fax (22) 224468; f. 1968; 99% state-owned; provides medium- and long-term finance and tech. assistance to devt-orientated enterprises; cap. 1,604.3m., total assets 2,200m. (Dec. 2003); Chair. MURRAY E. S. LAMIN; Man. Dir MOHAMED M. TURAY; 3 brs.

Rokel Commercial Bank of Sierra Leone Ltd: 25–27 Siaka Stevens St, POB 12, Freetown; tel. (22) 222501; fax (22) 222563; internet www.rokelsl.com; f. 1971; cap. 1,119.7m., res 1,776.7m., dep. 141,581.1m. (Dec. 2005); 51% govt-owned; Chair. YAYAH TOBIAS SESAY; Man. Dir HENRY AKIN MACAULEY; 10 brs.

Sierra Leone Commercial Bank Ltd: 29–31 Siaka Stevens St, Freetown; tel. (22) 225264; fax (22) 225292; e-mail slcb@slcb.biz; internet www.slcb.biz; f. 1973; state-owned; cap. 1,000.0m., res 19,090.2m., dep. 148,960.7m. (Dec. 2005); Chair. VICTOR F. JAMINA; Man. Dir Alhaji ABDULAI KAKAY; 8 brs.

Standard Chartered Bank Sierra Leone Ltd: 9 and 11 Lightfoot-Boston St, POB 1155, Freetown; tel. (22) 225022; fax (22) 225760; f. 1971; cap. and res 13,073.0m., total assets 102,179.9m. (Dec. 2003); Chair. LLOYD A. DURING; Man. Dir LAMIN KEMBA MANJANG; 14 brs.

Union Trust Bank Ltd: Howe St, PMB 1237, Freetown; tel. (22) 226954; fax (22) 226214; fmrly Meridien BIAO Bank Sierra Leone Ltd; adopted present name in 1995; cap. and res 8,221.1m., total assets 29,025.0m. (Dec. 2003); Chair. S. B. NICOL-COLE; Man. Dir JOHN D. OKRAFO-SMART.

INSURANCE

Aureol Insurance Co Ltd: Kissy House, 54 Siaka Stevens St, POB 647, Freetown; tel. (22) 223435; fax (22) 229336; f. 1987; Man. Dir S. G. BENJAMIN.

National Insurance Co Ltd: 18–20 Walpole St, PMB 84, Freetown; tel. (22) 222535; fax (22) 226097; e-mail nic@sierratel.sl; f. 1972; state-owned; Chair. P. J. KUYEMBEH; CEO ARTHUR NATHANIEL YASKEY.

New India Assurance Co Ltd: 18 Wilberforce St, POB 340, Freetown; tel. (22) 226453; fax (22) 222494; e-mail niasl@sierratel.sl; Man. Dir A. CHOPRA.

Reliance Insurance Trust Corpn Ltd: 24 Siaka Stevens St, Freetown; tel. (22) 225115; fax (22) 228051; e-mail oonomake@yahoo.com; f. 1985; Chair. MOHAMED B. COLE; Man. Dir ALICE M. ONOMAKE.

Sierra Leone Insurance Co Ltd: 31 Lightfoot Boston St, POB 836, Freetown; tel. (22) 224920; fax (22) 222115; Man. Dir IDRISSE YILLE.

Trade and Industry

GOVERNMENT AGENCY

Government Gold and Diamond Office (GGDO): c/o Bank of Sierra Leone, Siaka Stevens St, Freetown; tel. (22) 222600; fax (22) 229064; f. 1985; govt regulatory agency for diamonds and gold; combats illicit trade; Chair. Alhaji M. S. DEEN.

CHAMBER OF COMMERCE

Sierra Leone Chamber of Commerce, Industry and Agriculture: Guma Bldg, 5th Floor, Lamina Sankoh St, POB 502, Freetown; tel. (22) 226305; fax (22) 228005; internet www.cocsl.com; f. 1961; 215 mems; Pres. Alhaji MOHAMED MUSA KING.

TRADE AND INDUSTRIAL ASSOCIATIONS

Sierra Leone Export Development and Investment Corpn (SLEDIC): 18–20 Walpole St, PMB 6, Freetown; tel. (22) 227604; fax (22) 229097; e-mail info@sledic-sl.org; internet www.sledic-sl.org; f. 1993; Man. Dir CHRIS JASABE.

Small-Medium Scale Businesses Association (Sierra Leone): O.A.U. Dr., Tower Hill, PMB 575, Freetown; tel. (22) 222617; fax (22) 224439; Dir ABU CONTEH.

EMPLOYERS' ORGANIZATIONS

Sierra Leone Employers' Federation: POB 562, Freetown; Chair. AMADU B. NDOEKA; Exec. Officer L. E. JOHNSON.

Sierra Leone Chamber of Mines: POB 456, Freetown; tel. (22) 226082; f. 1965; mems comprise the principal mining concerns; Pres. JOHN SISAY; Exec. Officer N. H. T. BOSTON.

UTILITIES

Electricity

National Power Authority: Electricity House, Siaka Stevens St, Freetown; tel. (30) 700000; fax (22) 227584; e-mail Sierra_Leone@iaeste.org; supplies all electricity in Sierra Leone.

Water

Guma Valley Water Co: Guma Bldg, 13/14 Lamina Sankoh St, POB 700, Freetown; tel. (22) 25887; e-mail gumasl@yahoo.co.uk; f. 1961; responsible for all existing water supplies in Freetown and surrounding villages, including the Guma dam and associated works.

TRADE UNIONS

Artisans', Ministry of Works Employees' and General Workers' Union: 4 Pultney St, Freetown; f. 1946; 14,500 mems; Pres. IBRAHIM LANGLEY; Gen. Sec. TEJAN A. KASSIM.

Sierra Leone Labour Congress: 35 Wallace Johnson St, POB 1333, Freetown; tel. (22) 226869; f. 1966; 51,000 mems in 19 affiliated unions; Pres. H. M. BARRIE; Sec.-Gen. KANDEH YILLA.

Principal affiliated unions:

Clerical, Mercantile and General Workers' Union: 35 Wallace Johnson St, Freetown; f. 1945; 3,600 mems; Pres. M. D. BENJAMIN; Gen. Sec. M. B. WILLIAMS.

Sierra Leone Association of Journalists: 31 Garrisson Street, Freetown; tel. 76605811; e-mail slajalone@hotmail.com; Pres. PHILIP NEVILLE.

Sierra Leone Dockworkers' Union: 165 Fourah Bay Rd, Freetown; f. 1962; 2,650 mems; Pres. ABDUL KANISURE; Gen. Sec. A. C. CONTEH.

Sierra Leone Motor Drivers' Union: 10 Charlotte St, Freetown; f. 1960; 1,900 mems; Pres. A. W. HASSAN; Gen. Sec. ALPHA KAMARA.

Sierra Leone Teachers' Union: Regaland House, Lowcost Step—Kissy, POB 477, Freetown; f. 1951; 18,500 mems; Pres. ABDULAI KOROMA; Sec.-Gen. DAVIDSON KUYATEH.

Sierra Leone Transport, Agricultural and General Workers' Union: 4 Pultney St, Freetown; f. 1946; 1,600 mems; Pres. S. O. SAWYERR-MANLEY; Gen. Sec. S. D. KARGBO.

United Mineworkers' Union: 35 Wallace Johnson St, Freetown; f. 1944; 6,500 mems; Gen. Sec. EZEKIEL DYKE.

Also affiliated to the Sierra Leone Labour Congress: **General Construction Workers' Union, Municipal and Local Government Employees' Union, Sierra Leone National Seamen's Union.**

Transport

RAILWAYS

There are no passenger railways in Sierra Leone.

Marampa Mineral Railway: Delco House, POB 735, Freetown; tel. (22) 222556; 84 km of track linking iron ore mines at Marampa (inactive since 1985) with Pepel port; Gen. Man. SYL KHANU.

ROADS

In 2002 there were an estimated 11,300 km of classified roads, including 2,138 km of main roads and 1,950 km of secondary roads; about 904 km of the total network was paved.

Sierra Leone Road Transport Corpn: Blackhall Rd, POB 1008, Freetown; tel. (22) 250442; fax (22) 250000; f. 1965; state-owned; operates transport services throughout the country; Gen. Man. DANIEL R. W. FAUX.

INLAND WATERWAYS

Established routes for launches, which include the coastal routes from Freetown northward to the Great and Little Scarcies rivers and southward to Bonthe, total almost 800 km. Although some of the upper reaches of the rivers are navigable only between July and September, there is a considerable volume of river traffic.

SHIPPING

Freetown, the principal port, has full facilities for ocean-going vessels.

Sierra Leone National Shipping Co Ltd: 45 Cline St, POB 935, Freetown; tel. (22) 229883; fax (22) 229513; f. 1972; state-owned; shipping, clearing and forwarding agency; representatives for foreign lines; Chair. Alhaji B. M. KOROMA; Man. Dir SYLVESTER B. FOMBA.

Sierra Leone Ports Authority: Queen Elizabeth II Quay, PMB 386, Cline Town, Freetown; tel. (22) 226480; fax (22) 226443; f. 1965; parastatal body, supervised by the Ministry of Transport and Communications; operates the port of Freetown.

Sierra Leone Shipping Agencies Ltd: Deep Water Quay, Clinetown, POB 74, Freetown; tel. (22) 223453; fax (22) 220021; e-mail slsa@sl.dti.bollore.com; f. 1949; Man. Dir MICHEL MEYNARD.

Silver Star Shipping Agency Ltd: PMB 1023, Freetown; tel. (22) 221035; fax (22) 226653; e-mail silver2_star@hotmail.com; Dir Capt. H. A. BLOOMER.

CIVIL AVIATION

There is an international airport at Lungi.

Directorate of Civil Aviation: Ministry of Transport and Communications, Ministerial Bldg, George St, Freetown; tel. (22) 221245; Dir T. T. A. VANDY.

Sierra National Airlines: Leone House, 25 Pultney St, POB 285, Freetown; tel. (22) 222075; fax (22) 222026; internet www.flysna.com; f. 1982; state-owned; operates domestic and regional services, and a weekly flight to Paris, France; operations resumed, following civil conflict, in Nov. 2000; Chair. TAMBA MATTURI; Man. Dir ADAM CORMACK.

Tourism

The main attractions for tourists are the coastline, the mountains and the game reserves. Civil conflict throughout most of the 1990s effectively suspended tourist activity. By 2005, however, according to the World Tourism Organization, tourist arrivals had increased to 40,023, compared with 10,615 in 1999. Receipts from tourism totalled an estimated US $64m. in 2005.

National Tourist Board of Sierra Leone: Cape Sierra Hotel, Room 100, Aberdeen, POB 1435, Freetown; tel. (22) 236620; fax (22) 236621; e-mail info@welcometosierraleone.org; internet www.visitsierraleone.org; f. 1990; Gen. Man. CECIL J. WILLIAMS.

SINGAPORE

Introductory Survey

Location, Climate, Language, Religion, Flag, Capital

The Republic of Singapore lies in South-East Asia. The country comprises one main island and some 64 offshore islands, situated approximately 137 km (85 miles) north of the Equator, off the southernmost tip of the Malay Peninsula, to which it is linked by a causeway. The climate is equatorial, with a uniformly high daily and annual temperature varying between 24°C and 27°C (75°F–80°F). Relative humidity is high (often exceeding 90%), and the average annual rainfall is 235 cm (93 ins). There are four official languages—Malay (the national language), Chinese (Mandarin), Tamil and English. The language of administration is English. Chinese dialects were spoken as a first language by 24% of the population in 2000. The principal religions are Daoism, Buddhism, Islam, Christianity and Hinduism. The national flag (proportions 2 by 3) has two equal horizontal stripes of red and white, with a white crescent moon and five white stars, arranged in a pentagram, in the upper hoist. The capital is Singapore City.

Recent History

In 1826 the East India Company formed the Straits Settlements by the union of Singapore and the dependencies of Penang and Malacca on the Malay Peninsula. They came under British rule in 1867 as a crown colony. Singapore was occupied by Japan for three years during the Second World War. At the end of the war, following Japan's defeat, Singapore was governed by a British military administration. When civil rule was restored in 1946, Singapore was detached from the other Straits Settlements and became a separate crown colony. A new Constitution, adopted in February 1955, introduced some measure of self-government, and in June 1959 the state achieved complete internal self-government, with Lee Kuan Yew as Prime Minister. The Federation of Malaysia came into being in September 1963, with Singapore as a constituent state. On 9 August 1965, following irreconcilable differences with the central Government in Malaysia, Singapore seceded from the federation and became an independent country. Singapore joined the UN in September and became a member of the Commonwealth in October. In December Singapore was proclaimed a republic, with a President as constitutional Head of State. In May 1973 the last major links with Malaysia, concerning currency and finance, were renounced. In September 1972 Lee Kuan Yew's ruling People's Action Party (PAP) won all 65 parliamentary seats in a general election.

After independence the Government supported a strong US military presence in South-East Asia. However, with the collapse of US influence in the area during 1974–75, at the end of the war in Viet Nam, Singapore adopted a conciliatory attitude towards the People's Republic of China and its communist neighbours. The Government urged the removal of foreign bases from member states of the Association of South East Asian Nations (ASEAN, see p. 185), and advocated a policy of neutrality. Singapore sought to consolidate its trade links with China, although diplomatic relations were not established until 1982.

At general elections in December 1976 and again in December 1980, the PAP won all 69 seats in the enlarged Parliament. The PAP's monopoly ended in October 1981, however, when the Secretary-General of the opposition Workers' Party, J. B. Jeyaretnam, won a by-election. This posed no direct threat, but, in order to reassert its authority, the Government increased its control over trade unions and restructured the ownership of major newspapers. The PAP was again returned to power in December 1984 with a large majority in Parliament (now expanded to 79 seats), but the party lost two seats to opposition parties, and its share of the total votes was reduced to 62.9% from 75% in 1980. A constitutional amendment approved in July 1984 provided for up to three 'non-constituency' parliamentary seats for the opposition (with restricted voting rights) if none was won in the election. One extra seat was subsequently offered to the losing opposition candidate with the highest percentage of votes. However, this seat was refused by the Workers' Party in January 1985. In March the state President, Devan Nair, resigned. A new President, Wee Kim Wee (hitherto the Chairman of the Singapore Broadcasting Corporation), was elected by Parliament in August.

During 1986 the Government exhibited signs of increasing intolerance towards its critics. In August amendments to the Parliament (Privileges, Immunities and Powers) Act were hurriedly adopted, enabling Parliament to fine, expel or imprison members who were deemed to have abused their parliamentary privileges. In the same month Parliament also approved a Newspaper and Printing Presses (Amendment) Act, which empowered the Government to restrict the distribution of foreign publications deemed to be interfering in domestic political affairs; the circulation of several foreign periodicals was subsequently restricted.

In November 1986 Jeyaretnam (one of the two opposition members of Parliament) was sentenced to one month's imprisonment and fined S $5,000 (enough, according to the Constitution, to deprive him of his parliamentary seat and prevent him from standing for election for five years), when the Supreme Court upheld a conviction for perjury in connection with bankruptcy proceedings brought against the Workers' Party four years previously. In February 1987 Jeyaretnam was also fined by a parliamentary committee for abuse of privilege, having made allegations of government interference in the judiciary; further fines were imposed on him for publishing 'distorted' accounts of an earlier hearing of the committee, and (in May) for alleged contempt of Parliament and abuse of parliamentary privilege. In October Jeyaretnam's removal from the Law Society register was ordered by a three-judge court. An appeal to the Judicial Committee of the Privy Council in the United Kingdom (then the highest court of appeal for Singapore) resulted, in October 1988, in his reinstatement as a practising lawyer. During the course of the appeal, investigations into Jeyaretnam's previous convictions found that they had been 'fatally flawed'. However, since the criminal case had been considered in the District Court, where there was no right of appeal to the Privy Council, the original convictions prevented Jeyaretnam from re-entering Parliament without a presidential pardon. This was refused by Wee Kim Wee in May 1989.

In May and June 1987 the Government detained a total of 22 people (including 10 Roman Catholic church workers and four members of the Workers' Party) without trial, under the Internal Security Act, for their alleged involvement in a 'Marxist conspiracy' to subvert state organizations. The arrests were denounced by Jeyaretnam, who claimed that the Government wished to intimidate Singaporeans so that they would not support opposition parties. In November the Government was also criticized by international human rights groups, including Amnesty International, for its refusal to present evidence of such a conspiracy in court. By December most of the alleged conspirators had been released, but eight of them were rearrested in April 1988, after complaining that they had been tortured while in detention. Four prisoners were released by June, and in December a further four detainees were released in accordance with a ruling by the Court of Appeal, based on a fault in their detention orders. They were immediately rearrested. However, the trial had established a precedent for the judicial review of cases brought under the Internal Security Act, including the acceptability to the courts of evidence used in warrants for the arrest of suspects. In January 1989 Parliament approved legislation ensuring that the judiciary could examine such detentions only on technical grounds, and abolishing the right of appeal to the Privy Council in cases brought under the Internal Security Act. In March three detainees were released. The two remaining prisoners (of the original 22) remained in detention until June 1990.

A general election was held in September 1988. The electoral system was altered so that 39 of the existing 79 constituencies were replaced by 13 'group representation constituencies', to be contested by teams of three representatives for each party, at least one of whom was to be a member of an ethnic minority (i.e. non-Chinese). The declared aim was to ensure the presence of racial minorities in Parliament; however, in practice opposition parties with few resources were restricted by the difficulty of presenting three candidates. The PAP won 80 of the elective seats (which now totalled 81); one was taken by the leader of the Singapore Democratic Party (SDP), Chiam See Tong. Two 'non-constituency' seats were offered to Francis Seow (Workers' Party) and Lee Siew Choh (Socialist Front). In December, however, while Seow (who had already been detained in May under the Internal Security Act for organizing a meeting between a US diplomat and lawyers critical of the Government) was undergoing medical treatment in the USA, he was convicted *in absentia* for tax evasion and fined S $19,000: he was thus debarred from taking his seat in Parliament.

In January 1989 Lee began his eighth term as Prime Minister, and announced that he would retire from the premiership before the expiry of the term. This announcement was followed by a statement from the First Deputy Prime Minister, Goh Chok Tong (Lee's chosen successor), that Lee was adopting a secondary and more advisory role in the government of the country. In August Parliament unanimously re-elected Wee Kim Wee for a further four-year term as President. In early 1990 Parliament approved legislation enabling the Government to nominate as many as six unelected MPs. The politically-neutral nominated MPs would be appointed for two years, and would be able to vote on all legislative proposals except those concerning financial and constitutional affairs.

On 28 November 1990 Lee was duly replaced as Prime Minister by Goh Chok Tong. Lee remained in the Cabinet as Senior Minister in the Prime Minister's Office, and retained the position of Secretary-General of the PAP, while Lee's son, Brig.-Gen. Lee Hsien Loong, was appointed as a Deputy Prime Minister.

In January 1991 the Constitution was amended to provide for a popularly elected presidency with extensive powers of veto on proposed financial legislation, a role as final arbiter in cases of detention for reasons of national security, and influence in civil and military appointments. The changes to the (hitherto highly ceremonial) functions of the President were initially proposed by Lee in 1984, and were criticized by members of opposition parties as being intended to accommodate the former Prime Minister. Under the amendment, Wee Kim Wee was to continue in office until October 1993. Legislation empowering him with the authority of an elected president took effect from 30 November 1991. Candidates for the presidency were limited to those who had held the post of a minister, chief justice or senior civil servant or were at the head of a large company. The candidates were to be scrutinized by a new presidential election committee, which was to comprise the head of the Society of Accountants, the Chairman of the Public Service Commission and a member of the Presidential Council of Human Rights. The last two officials were appointed by the Government, prompting fears that the selected candidates would be those favoured by the PAP. The constitutional amendment also included a clause increasing the number of candidates required to contest a 'group representation constituency' in a general election to a minimum of three and a maximum of four, one of whom was to be a member of an ethnic minority.

In early 1991 the Government promoted the acceptance of five 'shared values', based on Confucian philosophy, as the basis of a national ideology. Critics alleged that the ideology would be used to reinforce support for the PAP and to obviate opposition challenges. Goh attempted, in principle, to introduce a more 'open', consultative form of government. He instituted an extensive programme of community visits to assess popular opinion, showing solicitude for the views of the minority Malay and Indian communities. Although film censorship was relaxed, the Internal Security Act and restrictions on the foreign press remained in force. In early August, seeking a popular mandate for his style of government, Goh announced that there would be a general election at the end of the month. Under a plan conceived by Chiam, the opposition parties contested only 40 of the 81 seats, thus guaranteeing an absolute majority for the incumbent PAP. Chiam issued an appeal to the electorate to take the opportunity to elect a strong opposition. Goh indicated that a failure to receive a popular endorsement would result in a return to a more authoritarian and paternalistic form of government. At the election, held on 31 August, the PAP's share of the vote was 61.0% (compared with 63.2% in 1988), and the party won 77 seats (compared with 80 in 1988). Chiam's SDP secured three seats, and the Workers' Party one seat. Jeyaretnam was unable to contest the election, as his disqualification remained in force until November. In response to Jeyaretnam's accusations that he had been deliberately excluded from the election, and also because the election schedule had prevented the PAP from presenting enough new candidates, Goh had announced, prior to the polls, that he would organize by-elections within 12–18 months of the general election.

In October 1991 Seow, who had remained in exile in the USA since 1988, was convicted *in absentia* of a further 60 offences involving tax evasion, rendering him ineligible to contest any potential by-election. Later that month Jeyaretnam paid S $392,838 in legal costs to Lee, thus avoiding bankruptcy, which would have prevented his candidacy. Lee had instituted a successful defamation suit against Jeyaretnam in 1990, over remarks made by Jeyaretnam at a 1988 election rally.

Following the general election, Lee, who had temporarily withdrawn from public attention after Goh's accession to the premiership, resumed a prominent role in domestic politics. He attributed the decline in PAP support to neglect of the Mandarin-educated ethnic Chinese majority, and advocated a greater emphasis on Chinese culture and language. In April 1991 Goh announced that the level of electoral support among residents would be one of the criteria used to determine the order in which refurbishments would be undertaken in public housing estates. Since about 86% of Singaporeans lived in public housing, this was widely interpreted as a warning against voting for the opposition in the forthcoming by-elections.

Prior to the convening of Parliament in September 1992 the Government appointed the maximum of six nominated MPs. This too was generally regarded as an attempt to discourage support for opposition candidates in the impending by-elections. In October the implementation of legislation prohibiting MPs from using the ground floors of public housing blocks as office space adversely affected all four opposition MPs, who, because of a shortage of party funds, were unable to afford commercial rents.

In November 1992 Goh announced to the Central Executive Committee of the PAP that the renewal of national leadership was the party's most urgent consideration. This statement was followed two days later by the public disclosure that both Deputy Prime Ministers, Lee Hsien Loong and Ong Teng Cheong, had been diagnosed as suffering from cancer. The revelation strengthened Goh's position as Prime Minister, since many had previously regarded his incumbency as an interim arrangement prior to Lee Hsien Loong's assumption of the premiership. In December Goh was unanimously elected to replace Lee Kuan Yew (who proposed his candidacy) as Secretary-General of the PAP.

In December 1992 Goh relinquished his parliamentary seat (which formed part of a four-member 'group representation constituency') in order to contest a by-election. Jeyaretnam was unable to contest the by-election as only three candidates from the Workers' Party registered with the authorities. The results of the by-election were regarded as an endorsement of Goh's leadership, as the four PAP candidates received 72.9% of the votes cast, while the opposition SDP secured 24.5%.

In March 1993 Chee Soon Juan, who contested the December by-election as a candidate for the SDP, was dismissed from his post as a lecturer at the National University of Singapore for 'dishonest conduct'. The Government denied that the dismissal was politically motivated, and defamation proceedings were initiated by university officials against Chee. In June, following a rejection by the SDP Central Committee of a motion of censure proposed by Chiam against Chee for bringing the party into disrepute, Chiam resigned as Secretary-General of the party. Chee replaced him as acting Secretary-General, pending party elections in early 1995. In August 1993 the SDP expelled Chiam for alleged indiscipline; however, a High Court ruling in December declared the expulsion 'illegal and invalid'. (This enabled Chiam to retain his seat in Parliament: under the Constitution a member of the legislature is obliged to relinquish his seat if he resigns or is expelled from the party he has been elected to represent.) The following month, under a judicial ruling, a 'breakaway' central executive committee, formed in 1993 by a faction of the SDP that remained loyal to Chiam, was declared void. Chee subsequently published a book entitled *Dare to Change*, which demanded greater democracy and was adopted as official party policy by the SDP in June 1994. Chee was formally elected Secretary-General of the SDP in January 1995.

Meanwhile, in August 1993 Ong Teng Cheong was elected President with 58.7% of the votes cast. However, contrary to expectation the only other candidate, Chua Kim Yeow, a former government official, who adopted an apolitical position, secured a substantial proportion (41.3%) of the vote. The candidacies of both Jeyaretnam and Tan Soo Phuan, another member of the Workers' Party, were rejected by the Presidential Election Committee on the grounds that they were unsuitable 'in regard to integrity, good character and reputation'.

In October 1996 Parliament approved amendments to the Constitution that redefined the role of the President and partially reformed the voting system. The President's powers were restricted by new provisions empowering the Government to call a referendum if the President vetoed certain constitutional amendments, and also enabling Parliament to overturn (by a two-thirds' majority) a presidential veto on senior civil service appointments. A further amendment expanded the number of 'group representation constituencies' and increased the maximum number of group candidates from four to six. The electoral reforms were opposed by the opposition parties on the grounds that the amendments favoured large, well-established parties such as the PAP, while smaller parties would have difficulty in finding and funding large numbers of candidates.

Prior to the general election, which took place on 2 January 1997, the success of the PAP was predetermined by the opposition parties' decision to contest only 36 of the 83 seats. Nevertheless, the PAP conducted a rigorous campaign in an effort to ensure that the party received two-thirds of the total votes cast, a margin regarded as sufficient endorsement of Goh and his administration. During the campaign, it was again announced that public housing improvements would be prioritized according to levels of electoral support for the PAP. The party secured a resounding victory, winning 65% of the votes and 81 seats (including all nine single-member constituencies). The remaining two elective seats were won by Chiam See Tong of the Singapore People's Party (for the fourth time, although previously he had been elected as a representative of the SDP) and Low Thia Khiang of the Workers' Party (for a second time). The Workers' Party, as the opposition party with the most votes but less than three seats, was also allocated a non-constituency seat; this was accepted by Jeyaretnam. The SDP lost the three seats it had previously held.

Seemingly a particular focus for attack by the PAP during the election campaign was Tang Liang Hong, a candidate of the Workers' Party. The PAP accused Tang of being anti-Christian, of promoting Chinese interests over those of Singapore's ethnic minorities and of attempting to foment discontent among the ethnic Chinese community. Tang, standing in the same 'group representation constituency' as Jeyaretnam, failed to secure election. (Goh, unopposed in a single-member constituency, personally campaigned against Tang in the group constituency.) Tang's public rebuttal of the accusations of the PAP leaders prompted them to issue writs against him for defamation. Tang fled to Malaysia in January 1997, claiming to have received anonymous death threats. Tang was found guilty of defamation by the High Court in March, as he failed to attend the trial and provide a defence, and was ordered in May to pay a record sum of S $8m. in libel damages to Goh and 10 senior PAP leaders. Tang appealed against the judgment in September on the grounds that it contained legal errors and that the cases had been brought for political motives. The Court of Appeal ruled in November that the damages awarded against Tang were disproportionate to the injury caused, and reduced the sum to S $4.53m. In February 1998, despite this concession, Tang, against whom a warrant for arrest had been issued on 33 counts of tax evasion, was declared bankrupt.

Goh and 10 senior PAP members also sued Jeyaretnam for alleged defamation following remarks made at an election rally concerning two police reports submitted by Tang accusing the PAP leadership of criminal conspiracy and lying. In September 1997 Jeyaretnam was ordered to pay damages of S $20,000; however, the award represented only 10% of the amount sought by the PAP leadership, and the judge, who criticized Goh's lawyers for their handling of the case, ordered that Jeyaretnam pay only 60% of the legal costs. During the trial Goh admitted under cross-examination that he had authorized the unofficial disclosure of the police reports to the press, and it was put to him that the legal suits were an attempt to bankrupt Jeyaretnam and thus disqualify him from Parliament. However, the Court of Appeal dismissed an appeal by Jeyaretnam in July 1998, increasing the damages to S $100,000, and awarding full costs against him. It was subsequently agreed, however, that Jeyaretnam would be permitted to pay the damages in five instalments, thereby enabling him to avoid bankruptcy proceedings and to continue as a legislator.

In November 1998 the Government revoked the remaining restrictions on the activities of the political activist Chia Thye Poh. Chia had been arrested in 1966, imprisoned for more than 22 years without trial under the Internal Security Act, confined to a fortress on an island off the coast of Singapore for a further three years, then permitted to reside in Singapore from 1992, although prohibited from taking part in any political activity. Despite this concession to Chia, government suppression of expressions of opposition continued. In January 1999 Chee was charged twice under the Public Entertainment Act for making unlicensed public speeches. Chee had deliberately refused to apply for licences to make the two public speeches, in which he criticized government policy, on the grounds that freedom of expression was guaranteed under the Constitution. During the first trial Chee was represented by Jeyaretnam, who attempted to expose the alleged use of the above Act to restrict political opposition. However, Chee was found guilty at the beginning of February, and was sentenced to seven days' imprisonment, owing to his refusal to pay a fine of S $1,400. Following his release, Chee appeared in court for a second time in February, and was sentenced, with the Assistant Secretary-General of the SDP, Wong Hong Toy, who had reportedly assisted Chee at the speech, to 12 days' imprisonment after Chee and Wong refused to pay respective fines of S $2,500 and S $2,400. The level of the fines automatically disqualified both men from seeking political office for five years; however, following an appeal, the two had their fines reduced to S $1,900 each, below the level that would have rendered them ineligible to stand for election. For its part, the Government maintained that opposition politicians had adequate opportunity to expound their views in Parliament or in the media (although in February 1998 the Government had banned political parties from producing videos and from promoting their opinions on television). In April 1999 it was reported that, subsequent to his release from prison after serving his second term of imprisonment, Chee had been fined S $600 for illegal sales of a book he had produced on Asian opposition leaders. In March members of the PAP filed a petition to close the Workers' Party, owing to its inability to pay more than S $280,000 in damages and costs awarded against it in a defamation case. The party's closure would force the resignation of its two parliamentary representatives. It was subsequently reported that the party had lost a judicial appeal against the award.

In May 2000 Jeyaretnam was declared bankrupt by the High Court after he failed to make payments of S $30,000 in libel damages arising from a lawsuit concerning an article that appeared in the Workers' Party newspaper, *The Hammer*, in 1995. The bankruptcy ruling would have disqualified Jeyaretnam from serving in Parliament, but the orders were set aside after the outstanding debt was paid, and he was authorized to retain his non-constituency seat. In January 2001, however, Jeyaretnam was once again declared bankrupt by the High Court, with a S $235,000 debt as a result of a defamation claim against a Workers' Party newsletter. The appeal against the bankruptcy ruling was dismissed in February. In May Jeyaretnam was replaced as Secretary-General of the Workers' Party by Low Thia Khiang. In July he finally lost his seat in Parliament when the Court of Appeals confirmed that it would not overturn the bankruptcy ruling against him.

Meanwhile, legislation introduced in May 1997 increased the number of nominated MPs from six to nine; the Constitution was amended accordingly in September. During the year nine Community Development Councils (CDCs) were formed. The CDCs encompassed all constituencies, including the two opposition wards, although opposition representatives would not be permitted to serve as council leaders and would have no power to disburse funds.

During 1999 Lee Hsien Loong, who had been appointed Chairman of the Monetary Authority of Singapore (MAS) in December 1997, began to assume a more prominent political role. George Yeo, hitherto the Minister for Information and the Arts, also gained prominence following his promotion to the trade and industry portfolio in a minor cabinet reorganization in June 1999. Singapore's second presidential election was scheduled to take place in August. President Ong, despite his PAP affiliation, had proved an independent President, whose determination to exercise the full powers of the elected presidency had resulted in strained relations with his former government colleagues. His allegations of government obstruction of his efforts to establish the details of the Republic's financial reserves (in order to fulfil his role of guardian of those reserves as specified in the constitutional amendments of 1991) had led to a rare display of disunity among senior PAP officials, involving public disputes with both Goh and Lee. Despite a medical report confirming that Ong was in complete remission from a cancer diagnosed in 1992, the PAP announced that, on the grounds of health, it would not support his candidacy should he choose to seek a second term of office. Ong, who was widely believed to command sufficient popular support to secure the presidency without a government endorsement, finally announced his decision not to contest the election in July, but unexpectedly proceeded to enumerate his political difficulties while in office. Despite Goh's expressed support for a more consultative style of governance, in mid-August a government-appointed committee declared that only one of three potential presidential candidates, S. R. Nathan (a former Singaporean ambassador to the USA whose presidential candidature was supported by the Cabinet), had fulfilled the criteria set by the committee; Nathan was subsequently nominated as the new President of Singapore on 18 August, and was formally appointed to the position on 1 September, prompting criticism of the Government's autocratic approach.

In September 2000 the Government appeared to have relaxed its strict control over public speaking, with the opening of a 'Speakers' Corner', theoretically allowing a forum for any citizen to air issues of concern. In practice, however, speakers were obliged to register with the police beforehand, and to refrain from speaking on certain racial issues. The opportunity to speak was taken up by members of two Singaporean policy centres, after they were refused a permit to organize a marathon run to protest against the Internal Security Act in December. The gathering of around 50 people was not dispersed, but a report on the event broadcast by the Radio Corporation of Singapore was later edited at the request of the management, and the presenter who publicized the re-editing was dismissed. In April 2001 the Government permitted a rare opposition political rally. It was the first authorized protest to be openly critical of the Government since independence. The rally, intended as a pro-democracy fund-raising event for Jeyaretnam, was attended by over 1,000 people.

In July 2001 four opposition parties—the Singapore People's Party, the Singapore Malay National Organization, the National Solidarity Party and the Singapore Justice Party—formed the Singapore Democratic Alliance (SDA). The new coalition was chaired by Chiam See Tong, and it was hoped that its formation would strengthen the fragmented political opposition to the PAP. In October President Nathan unexpectedly announced that a general election was to be held in early November 2001, significantly in advance of the August 2002 deadline. During the campaign the Government declared that the allocation of priority to public housing improvements would again be affected by levels of electoral support. Electoral boundaries were also redrawn, leading to the enlargement of 14 multi-member constituencies and to an increase in the number of parliamentary seats to 84, in order to accommodate a rise in the number of registered voters. The opposition protested that it had been disadvantaged by the rearrangements. When nominations closed in late October PAP candidates were unopposed for 55 of the 84 seats. The Government thus secured victory by default before the polls opened. The Prime Minister, however, urged voters to turn out on election day to decide the outcome of the contests for the remaining 29 seats, warning that Singapore faced its 'gravest challenge since independence'. He also officially announced that he would leave office upon the conclusion of his next term.

The elections were held on 3 November 2001. The level of voter participation was low, owing to the large number of uncontested seats. Despite speculation that the PAP would lose some ground in the election because of the deterioration in the economy, it succeeded in winning 82 seats and increasing its share of the votes cast to 75.3%. The remaining two seats went to Chiam See Tong, Chairman of the SDA, and Low Thia Khiang of the Workers' Party. Steve Chia of the SDA was awarded a non-constituency seat.

Shortly after the election it was reported that Lee and Goh were suing Chee Soon Juan of the SDP for defamation. Chee had alleged that the Government had lent more than S $17,000m. of public money to the Suharto administration in Indonesia during the 1997–98 financial crisis. He had issued a public apology for the comments soon afterwards and admitted fabricating the accusation, but had later retracted his statement, claiming that it had been made under duress. Goh claimed that, while the loan had been offered to the Suharto administration, it had never been disbursed. In February 2002 Chee faced further legal action after contravening the rule banning the discussion of racial and religious issues in 'Speakers' Corner'. He had criticized the Government's policy of banning Muslim girls from wearing headscarves in public schools and urged the promotion of cultural diversity. His comments followed the suspension of three Muslim girls from school for their wearing of headscarves.

In April 2002 Jeyaretnam made a public apology in the High Court in an attempt to bring to an end the series of defamation suits that had been brought against him by the Government; seven outstanding lawsuits were subsequently abandoned. In the same month Chee stated that he intended to defend the lawsuits against him. In May Chee and the Vice-Chairman of the SDP, Ghandi Ambalam, led an unauthorized rally outside the presidential palace demanding workers' rights. Following the rally, Chee and Ambalan were both sentenced to brief prison terms, having chosen not to pay the fines imposed upon them. However, Ambalan's family subsequently paid his fine, in order to enable his release from prison on the grounds of ill health. In August the High Court ordered Chee to pay damages of S $500,000 to Lee and Goh, after his request for a trial was rejected; the verdict was confirmed in January 2005. Meanwhile, a constitutional amendment was passed stipulating that any member of Parliament declared bankrupt or found guilty of a crime would be banned from speaking or voting in Parliament for the duration of any appeal. In February 2003 Ambalam's appeal against his fine (which was sufficient to prohibit him from standing for political office for five years) was rejected by the Chief Justice. In October 2004 the Jeyaretnam affair resumed when he again appealed for early discharge from bankruptcy in order to secure re-entry into the political arena. However, the Court of Appeal deemed him to have been dishonest about his assets, ruling that he had failed to declare property in Johor Baru worth more than S $350,000. Consequently, the Court's original decision was upheld and Jeyaretnam's application for clemency was denied. Jeyaretnam was discharged from bankruptcy in May 2007 after paying the damages he owed.

In April 2003, meanwhile, Prime Minister Goh announced a cabinet reorganization. The acting Minister for Information, Communications and the Arts, David Lim Tik En, resigned and was replaced by Dr Lee Boon Yang, the former Minister for Manpower, who was succeeded by Dr Ng Eng Hen. Khaw Boon Wan was appointed to be acting Minister for Health, replacing Lim Hng Kiang, who became a Minister in the Prime Minister's Office. Meanwhile, Deputy Prime Minister and former Minister for Defence Dr Tony Tan Keng Yam was appointed to the newly created position of Co-ordinating Minister for Security and Defence in the Prime Minister's Office (effective from August 2003). The defence portfolio was allocated to the former Minister for Education, Teo Chee Hean, who was to be succeeded in an acting capacity by Tharman Shanmugaratnam.

In August 2003 Prime Minister Goh announced that he intended to resign from his post at least two years prior to the country's next general election, scheduled to be held in 2007. He designated his deputy, Lee Hsien Loong, as his successor. In early 2004 Lee indicated that, following his accession to power, he would implement measures to reduce the control of the Government over Singaporean citizens and to promote a culture of political 'openness' in the country.

On 12 August 2004 Lee was formally sworn in as Prime Minister, amid claims that a dynastic succession had been contrived. Both former Prime Ministers were included within the new Cabinet: Goh was retained as Senior Minister, while Lee Kuan Yew was redesignated as Minister Mentor. Shanmugam Jayakumar became Singapore's first Deputy Minister of Indian origin, and Dr Tony Tan Keng Yam was also reappointed to this position. Lee retained the finance portfolio but, in an unexpected development, relinquished the chairmanship of the MAS to Goh. Wong Kan Seng remained the Minister for Home Affairs but was also designated as successor to Dr Tan as Deputy Prime Minister upon the latter's retirement, scheduled for June 2005. Brig.-Gen. George Yeo was named the new Minister for Foreign Affairs and Rear-Adm. Teo Chee Hean retained the defence portfolio, while Tharman Shanmugaratnam was confirmed in the permanent position of Minister for Education. Two women were appointed as Ministers of State: Lim Hwee Hua was named Minister of State for Finance and Transport, and Yu-Foo Yee Shoon became Minister for State for Community Development and Sports.

The reversal of the decline in Singapore's birth rate was immediately rendered a major government priority following Lee's inauguration. In late August 2004 Lee added responsibility for the revival of the country's population growth to the brief of Wong Kan Seng and implemented an array of measures aimed at increasing the birth rate, which since the 1960s had decreased sharply. Government bonuses were offered to parents producing a third or fourth child, maternity leave was lengthened and tax rebates were introduced for working mothers.

In April 2005 Prime Minister Lee announced that the Government was no longer opposed to the construction of two major casino resorts in Singapore, to be built at an estimated cost of US $3,000m. In the same month the Government approved a draft bill to legalize gambling on the island, thereby proposing to remove a ban that had been in place for 40 years. It was hoped that the resorts, which were expected to become operational by 2009, would significantly boost the country's tourism industry and contribute to the Government's campaign to double the number of tourist arrivals by 2015, as well as allowing Singapore to retain the money of its nationals who had hitherto been obliged to travel abroad in order to engage in gambling activities. However, the decision encountered widespread disapproval, particularly from religious groups, which accused the Government of prioritizing profit over the country's moral standing. The Minister for Trade and Industry, Lim Hng Kiang, suggested that the project itself would create as many as 30,000 new jobs.

Following a series of bomb attacks targeting commuters on the public transport network of the British capital city of London, in July 2005, and a series of attacks in neighbouring Indonesia by the Islamist militant organization Jemaah Islamiah (JI), Minister for Transport Yeo Cheow Tong announced the creation of the Singaporean Police Mass Rapid Transport (MRT) Unit, intended to protect the island's transport system from terrorist attack. The unit commenced random patrols in the following month.

Presidential elections were scheduled to be held in August 2005. However, of the four candidates who had applied for inclusion in the contest only the incumbent, S. R. Nathan, was granted a Certificate of Eligibility, the other three candidates being deemed to be lacking in political experience. Consequently, Nathan was returned unopposed for a second term in office; he was formally sworn in on 1 September. In October the Deputy Prime Minister, Co-ordinating Minister for National Security and Minister of Law, Shanmugam Jayakumar, announced the development of the Risk Assessment and Horizon Scanning programme, an early warning system intended to identify and monitor the activities of newly emerging threats to national and regional security. In April 2006, following months of speculation that Prime Minister Lee Hsien Loong was to call an early legislative election in order to take advantage of Singapore's strong economic position, it was announced that the poll (which had not been due until June 2007) would be held on 6 May. At the election, opposition parties contested 47 of the 84 parliamentary seats. The PAP won 82 seats, as it had done at the 2001 election, while the SDA and the Workers' Party secured one seat each. However, the PAP's share of the votes cast decreased to 66.6%, compared with 75.4% at the 2001 election.

In February 2006, meanwhile, Chee Soon Juan was declared bankrupt by the High Court, having failed to pay the stipulated damages of S $500,000 to Lee Kuan Yew and Goh Chok Tong for the comments he had made during the 2001 elections (see above). Under the bankruptcy order, Chee was forbidden from contesting legislative elections for five years and was required to seek official permission to travel overseas. In the following month Chee was convicted of contempt of court for his criticism of Singapore's judiciary during the February court hearing, and was ordered to pay a fine of S $6,000. Upon his refusal to pay the fine, Chee was imprisoned for seven days, after which he refused to pay and his imprisonment was subsequently extended for a further seven days. In April Chee and several other SDP officials were sued for defamation by Lee Kuan Yew and Lee Hsien Loong in connection with articles published in February in the party's newsletter, *The New Democrat*, which had compared the PAP Government's running of the country to the management of the National Kidney Foundation (NKF), which was embroiled in a corruption scandal. (The controversy at the NKF had emerged in July 2005; amid allegations of misuse of funds, the entire executive board of the charitable organization tendered its resignation and the wife of Senior Minister Gok Chok Tong, hitherto the patron of NKF, also relinquished her position.) Chee Soon Juan and his sister, Chee Siok Chin, were found guilty of defamation in September 2006 in a summary judgment by the High Court, their request for a trial having been rejected. In November Chee was sentenced to five weeks' imprisonment for not paying a fine for speaking in public without a government permit during the 2006 election period.

Human rights issues were brought to the fore in 2006/07 as the Government sought to curb freedom of expression, attempting to restrict public gatherings, political demonstrations and views portrayed over the internet. At the annual meeting of the IMF and the World Bank in September 2006 the Government prevented five activists from attending, although it had originally yielded to international pressure by allowing access to 22 others. Despite criticism from the President of the World Bank, the Government claimed that the activists posed a security threat and could endanger the attending delegates. In February 2007 the *Far Eastern Economic Review*, a Hong Kong-based journal, failed in its second attempt to have a defamation action dismissed after the publication in July 2006 of an article entitled 'Singapore's 'Martyr' Chee Soon Juan'. The *Review* vowed to defend itself vigorously against the suit filed by Prime Minister Lee Hsien Loong and Minister Mentor Lee Kuan Yew, over alleged negative comments made about them and the Government by Chee. In its defence, the journal argued that, as it was published in Hong Kong and employed no Singaporean journalists, it was not bound by Singaporean law. Distribution of the journal in Singapore had been banned by the Government in September 2006 on the grounds that it had failed to comply with media regulations.

The application of the death penalty also continued to be a contentious issue after the execution of two convicted drugs-smugglers, Iwuchukwu Amara Tochi from Nigeria and Okele Nelson Malachy from South Africa, in January 2007. The case drew international condemnation from various governments and human rights organizations, while Philip Alston, the UN Special Rapporteur on extra-judicial, summary or arbitrary executions, described it as failing to meet international legal standards for criminal prosecution.

In April 2007 it was reported by the Minister in Charge of the Civil Service, Teo Chee Hean, that cabinet ministers were to receive a salary increase of 60%, to be implemented by 2008. While the decision prompted large-scale public opposition, Prime Minister Lee argued that the increase was well deserved and a necessary precaution against corruption. (Lee himself was to donate his extra salary to various good causes.) Chee Soon Juan criticized the pay rises at an unauthorized forum on democracy in Asia and Europe organized by the SDP. Several members of the European Parliament, as well as two legislators from Cambodia and the Philippines, were denied permission to address the forum by the Singaporean authorities on the grounds that their contributions would constitute interference in Singaporean domestic politics and would not be in the public interest. In September the bankrupt Chee served a three-week prison sentence after failing to pay a fine for attempting to leave Singapore without permission in April 2006. Chee was arrested again in October 2007, together with three other members of the SDP, as they attempted to stage a protest outside the presidential palace in support of their demands for the full disclosure of investments by Singaporean state-controlled companies in Myanmar, following the recent violent suppression of anti-Government marches in that country.

From December 2007 the Minister for Education, Tharman Shanmugaratnam, a former Managing Director of the MAS, assumed additional responsibility for the finance portfolio, which had hitherto been held by Prime Minister Lee. In a cabinet reorganization announced in late March 2008, Tharman was retained as Minister for Finance, but relinquished the education portfolio to Ng Eng Hen, who was replaced as Minister of Manpower in an acting capacity by Gan Kim Yong. From May K. Shanmugam, a senior lawyer, was to succeed Shanmugam Jayakumar as Minister of Law, while also being appointed Second Minister for Home Affairs. Jayakumar would remain Deputy Prime Minister and Co-ordinating Minister for National Security. Meanwhile, some 30 people participated in an unauthorized demonstration organized to protest against rising consumer prices in mid-March; 12 of the protesters, including Chee Soon Juan, were detained.

Singapore's foreign policy has been dominated by its membership of the regional grouping, ASEAN (which comprised all 10 South-East Asian nations by mid-1999), although it has also maintained strong political and military links with more distant allies, including the USA. In November 2000 the fourth informal summit meeting of the ASEAN + 3 group of leaders was convened in Singapore. The summit comprised the leaders of all 10 ASEAN members, as well as those of the People's Republic of China,

Japan and the Republic of Korea. An outcome of the meeting was the commissioning of an East Asia Study Group to report on the feasibility of a larger East Asia political and economic grouping and free trade area. However, despite ASEAN's ongoing attempts to curb alleged human rights abuses by the Myanma Government, Singapore continued its support of the military regime in April 2007 when Minister for Foreign Affairs, George Yeo, visited the new administrative capital, Pyinmana (Nay Pyi Taw). This followed the revelation that several Singaporean firms had recently signed contracts to search for natural gas in Myanma waters, a decision seen as greatly reducing the impact of Western sanctions. Singapore hosted the 13th ASEAN summit and related meetings in November, having assumed the chairmanship of the Association for one year in August. The summit meeting was overshadowed to some extent by concerns regarding the violence used to quell anti-Government protests in Myanmar in September. Singapore had invited the UN envoy to Myanmar, Ibrahim Gambari, to address the meeting, but the Myanma Government, with the support of several other member states, succeeded in forcing the cancellation of his briefing. Achievements of the summit meeting included the adoption of a Declaration on Environmental Sustainability, which contained commitments related to environmental protection and management, climate change, and the conservation of natural resources; the approval of plans for the establishment of an Asian Economic Community by 2015; and the signature of an ASEAN Charter codifying the principles and purposes of the Association. In December Singapore became the first country to ratify the new Charter.

Singapore's relations with Indonesia improved in the late 1980s: the process of establishing joint military training facilities with Indonesia, which had begun in 1986, was accomplished in February and March 1989 by the signing of two agreements. In January 1995 the two countries launched a bilateral Defence Forum and signed a Defence Co-operation Pact. In June 1996 Singapore and Indonesia jointly opened the Bintan tourist resort in the Riau Islands. Following the resignation of President Suharto in May 1998, relations deteriorated, in part owing to Lee's criticism of the new President, Prof. Dr Ir B. J. Habibie. In February 1999 Habibie accused Singapore of racism for allegedly discriminating against its Malay minority. The principal problem was, however, Singapore's refusal to meet Indonesia's high expectations of aid in response to the regional economic crisis. In March the Singaporean Minister for Foreign Affairs, Shanmugam Jayakumar, eased tensions in relations between Singapore and Indonesia by declaring in Parliament that Singapore had a vested interest in the economic and political stability of the Indonesian archipelago and pledging the Singaporean Government's intention to co-operate with the Indonesian administration. Relations improved temporarily following Habibie's replacement as President by Abdurrahman Wahid in October 1999. In November 2000, however, Wahid jeopardized the relationship by accusing Singapore of discriminating against Malays, after Singapore rejected certain motions proposed by its neighbour at the ASEAN summit. Nevertheless, Singapore subsequently concluded an agreement with Indonesia to supply the city-state with natural gas for the next 22 years. In February 2002 bilateral relations deteriorated once more following the publication of an article in *The Straits Times* in which Lee Kwan Yew remarked that Singapore's national security was being compromised by the fact that terrorists remained at large in Indonesia. In response, the Indonesian Government summoned the Singaporean envoy to Jakarta and lodged an objection to the accusations, claiming that they were provocative and unsubstantiated. Meanwhile, Indonesian Islamic groups held protests outside Singapore's embassy in Jakarta. In March 2002 Abu Bakar Bashir, an Indonesian cleric accused of being linked to the international terrorist al-Qa'ida (Base) network, issued a writ of defamation against Lee in relation to his comments. In February 2006 the Indonesian authorities agreed to the deportation to Singapore of Mas Selamat Kastari, the alleged leader of the Singaporean branch of JI, following his rearrest in Indonesia on suspicion of immigration offences. Kastari, first arrested in Indonesia in 2003, also on charges of suspected illegal immigration, had been the subject of several previous extradition requests from Singapore, which accused Kastari of a central role in an alleged plot, thwarted in late 2001, to crash a hijacked aeroplane into Changi International Airport. The Indonesian Government had rejected those requests, on the grounds that Indonesia and Singapore had no formal extradition treaty; it was unclear why Indonesia subsequently chose to reverse its decision. In February 2008 Kastari escaped from a detention centre in Singapore, where he was being held under the Internal Security Act. Of considerable embarrassment to the Singaporean authorities, Kastari's escape prompted an increase in border security, amid fears that he would attempt to enter Indonesia or Malaysia. Meanwhile, fires resulting from uncontrolled 'slash and burn' land-clearing practices in Indonesia caused a prolonged haze in late 2006, affecting Singapore and other countries in the region. Singapore was reported to have suffered US $50m. in economic losses. Relations between the two nations came under further pressure in February 2007 after Indonesia imposed an outright ban on all sand exports to Singapore. Owing to the latter's land reclamation projects, as well as its burgeoning construction industry, large amounts of sand from Indonesia had been exported in deals worth millions of dollars. The Indonesian Government took the decision after independent environmental experts highlighted the extensive damage caused to the environment by sand exports. (Singapore had been importing sand from Indonesia after Malaysia banned all exports in 1997.) Myanmar later offered to be Singapore's long-term supplier of sand, cement, granite and other construction materials. It was hoped that relations between Singapore and Indonesia would improve following the signature of an extradition treaty and a new agreement on defence co-operation in April 2007. There had been speculation that Indonesia's recent ban on sand exports to Singapore had been introduced in protest at delays in the conclusion of the extradition treaty. Differences emerged in May, however, when Indonesia sought amendments to the defence accord regarding arrangements for Singaporean troops to use Indonesian military training facilities. With Singapore refusing to consider any revisions, the ratification of both the defence and extradition agreements remained indefinitely suspended in early 2008.

In September 1994 Singapore and Malaysia agreed to settle their long-standing dispute over the ownership of Pedra Branca Island (Batu Putih) by referring the case to the International Court of Justice (ICJ) in The Hague, the Netherlands. An agreement on the referral was finally signed in early 2003. The ICJ began deliberating its judgment in November 2007, following the conclusion of public hearings on the case. In August 1995 Singapore and Malaysia agreed on the permanent boundary of their territorial waters following 15 years of negotiations. In March 1997 Lee Kuan Yew provoked tension between the two countries by making disparaging comments about security in the Malaysian state of Johor. Lee subsequently made an apology to Malaysia, which was accepted. In April 1999 Singapore and Malaysia undertook joint defence exercises within the context of the regional Five-Power Defence Arrangements; Malaysia had withdrawn from similar exercises in 1998, citing tensions between the two countries as well as economic difficulties.

In February 1998 Goh made an official visit to Malaysia. In the latter half of 1998, however, relations between the two countries deteriorated as a result of conflict over a number of issues. In early August the Malaysian Prime Minister condemned Singapore for requesting that Malaysia transfer its customs, immigration and quarantine facilities from Tanjung Pagar, a railway station in central Singapore situated on land owned by the Malaysian Government; Malaysia subsequently decided to continue using its facilities at Tanjung Pagar, while Singapore moved its customs office to a new location. In September Malaysia announced its decision to insist on prior clearance for Singaporean military aircraft wishing to enter its airspace; combined operations and exercises between the two countries' air forces were also terminated. In the same month the publication of the memoirs of Lee Kuan Yew, which referred to the events surrounding the secession of Singapore from the Federation of Malaysia, exacerbated tensions in bilateral relations. An improvement in relations between the two countries was perceived in November, when Goh visited Malaysia at the invitation of Malaysian Prime Minister Mahathir. Lee Kuan Yew further angered Malaysian politicians in August 2000, however, when he publicly criticized Mahathir over his handling of the dismissal and detention of Malaysia's former Deputy Prime Minister, Anwar Ibrahim.

In September 2001 Lee Kuan Yew visited Malaysia and held talks with Mahathir to address the outstanding issues affecting the relationship between the two countries. A framework agreement was subsequently signed under which Malaysia agreed to relocate its facilities at Tanjung Pagar in return for Singapore's agreement to construct a railway tunnel under the strait. Lee also reported that the two countries would work together to construct a suspension bridge, which would enable the demolition of the causeway linking the two countries. However, in January 2002 the Malaysian Government denied the existence of such an agreement and proposed that Malaysia should build a suspension bridge and a railway swing bridge to replace its half of the road link, enabling the Malaysian half of the causeway to be demolished without Singapore's co-operation. Tension was also promoted by the ongoing renegotiation of the terms upon which Malaysia would continue to supply water to Singapore (based upon an agreement originally concluded in 1961 and due to expire in 2061). While an agreement had provisionally been reached in September 2001, the Malaysian Government was dissatisfied with its terms and continued to increase its demands. In March 2002 relations were further strained when Malaysia claimed that reclamation work being carried out by Singapore in the Tebrau Straits was too close to its border and was obstructing ships sailing into ports in Johor. Malaysia later applied to the International Tribunal for the Law of the Sea (see p. 324) for a suspension of the reclamation work. The issue was among those discussed when Deputy Prime Minister Lee Hsien Loong visited Malaysia in the same month. In July the two countries held talks in an attempt to find a solution to the ongoing water supply problem; further negotiations over the issue also took place in September and October of that year. While the Government wished to link resolution of the matter to other issues it considered to be a cause of tension in the bilateral relationship, Malaysia threatened to take Singapore to an international court of arbitration to seek a solution. In February 2003 Mahathir pledged that his country would continue to supply water to Singapore indefinitely. However, he stated that Malaysia would cease its provision of untreated water to the city-state upon the termination of an existing agreement in 2011 and provide filtered water instead, at what it considered to be a reasonable price. Singapore continued to insist that any proposed price was too high and that it received too little for the treated water that it supplied to Malaysia in return.

In October 2003 the International Tribunal for the Law of the Sea ruled that the land reclamation work being carried out by Singapore in the Tebrau Straits was in accordance with international law and could, therefore, proceed. The long-running dispute was ostensibly resolved in January 2005 when the respective Governments of Singapore and Malaysia issued a joint statement declaring their agreement that the Tebrau Straits constituted a shared body of water and that the two countries had 'a common interest in co-operating to protect the environment, including the monitoring of water quality'.

Meanwhile, following the accession of Abdullah Ahmad Badawi to the Malaysian premiership in October 2003, it was hoped that Singapore's relations with Malaysia would improve. In January 2004 Abdullah Badawi visited Singapore and held talks with Prime Minister Goh in an attempt to ease the tensions between the two countries. Moreover, the transfer of the premiership to Lee augured well for bilateral relations; in his first National Day Rally speech, in August 2004, the incoming Prime Minister stressed his deep commitment to working in close unison with Abdullah Badawi, whom he had known for many years, in order to consolidate Singapore's links with Malaysia. Discussions aimed at strengthening relations between the two countries were resumed in March 2005. In mid-2005 Abdullah announced the abandonment of his predecessor's plans for the construction of a replacement causeway linking Singapore and Malaysia. It was hoped that this decision would dissipate bilateral tensions. Further negotiations were held in September. However, in January 2006 Malaysia unexpectedly announced that it was to commence construction of its section of the new bridge, also referred to as the 'scenic bridge', in the hope that Singapore would agree in due course to the construction of its part. Construction of the Malaysian section of the bridge began in March, but was halted by Abdullah in the following month; the Malaysian Prime Minister announced that all negotiations with Singapore pertaining to the bridge were also to be abandoned. Prime Minister Lee Hsien Loong visited Malaysia in May 2007 for two days of informal talks with Abdullah Badawi. The main outcome of the discussions was a decision to form a joint ministerial committee to oversee collaboration on Malaysia's plan to establish a 2,217-sq-km economic development zone in its southern state of Johor, to be known as the Iskandar Development Region, with both leaders agreeing that outstanding issues of dispute, such as water sales to Singapore and the suspended construction of the bridge, should not be allowed to impede bilateral co-operation in other areas.

In November 1990 representatives of the Governments of the USA and Singapore signed an agreement providing the US navy and air force with increased access to existing bases in Singapore following the planned US withdrawal from military installations in the Philippines. In January 1992 the two countries reached an agreement, in principle, on the relocation of a naval logistic command headquarters from Subic Bay, in the Philippines. However, relations with the USA were occasionally strained by attacks on the authoritarian style of government in Singapore by the liberal US media. Following the terrorist attacks on the USA in September 2001 (see the chapter on the USA), Singapore affirmed its support for the US-led alliance against terrorism.

Following the 2001 terrorist attacks in the USA, a number of suspects with alleged links to al-Qa'ida and its regional affiliates Abu Sayyaf and JI were arrested in Singapore under the Internal Security Act; among those detained were two Singaporean nationals in 2003. Alleged members of the Moro Islamic Liberation Front (MILF) were also detained in November 2005 under the Internal Security Act. In the same month the Government announced that it had detained for a two-year period Mohammad Sharif Rahmat, an alleged member of JI. While JI's network seemed to have been severely damaged by the arrests, leading members of both groups remained at large in the region. In order to address the ensuing national security concerns, the Government announced the establishment of a national security secretariat, within the Ministry of Defence, intended to strengthen co-ordination between the security services of Singapore and the USA. In October 2007 Singapore's Parliament approved counter-terrorism legislation designed to give effect to the International Convention for the Suppression of Terrorist Bombings (adopted by the UN General Assembly in 1997). The new law provided for the extradition of those suspected of perpetrating terrorist bombings, even in the absence of an extradition treaty between Singapore and the other country, and gave Singapore the power to prosecute foreign nationals accused of committing terrorist offences within its territory.

In March 2003 the Government announced its support for the US-led military campaign to oust the regime of Saddam Hussain in Iraq. Security measures within Singapore were strengthened subsequently, as the conflict was perceived to have raised the level of the terrorist threat to the country. In an apparent display of approval for Singapore's firm stance on terrorism, the US Government dispatched Secretary of Homeland Security Tom Ridge to Singapore's National Day reception held in Washington, DC, in August 2004. It was the first time that a US official of cabinet rank had attended this annual event during the nine-year tenure of Singapore's ambassador to the USA, Chan Heng Chee.

In October 2004 officials from Bahrain, Bangladesh, Egypt, Jordan, Kuwait, Malaysia, Singapore and Thailand convened in Singapore and agreed to hold the inaugural Asia-Middle East Dialogue (AMED) in mid-2005. This diplomatic initiative had been instigated by former Prime Minister Goh owing to concern that terrorism was being equated with Islam and also out of respect for Middle Eastern states' general suspicion of dialogues initiated by the USA or Europe. It was to focus on improving political, economic and business links between the two regions, as well as on promoting a greater level of mutual cultural understanding. The meeting was held in Singapore in June and was attended by representatives of approximately 50 Asian and Middle Eastern states. It was agreed that AMED would convene on a biennial basis, at venues alternating between Asia and the Middle East. In January 2008 Singapore concluded negotiations with the Gulf Co-operation Council (comprising Bahrain, Kuwait, Oman, Qatar, Saudi Arabia and the United Arab Emirates) on its second free trade agreement in the Middle East, the first having been signed with Jordan in May 2004.

Despite the establishment of important economic links during the 1980s, Singapore's relations with the People's Republic of China were adversely affected by the perceived threat of Chinese domination, owing to the preponderance of ethnic Chinese in Singapore (76.8% in 2000). Relations were also strained by Singapore's close military and economic links with Taiwan. In October 1990, however, Singapore and the People's Republic of China established diplomatic relations at ambassadorial level. This development was prompted mainly by the resumption of diplomatic relations between the People's Republic of China and Indonesia, and followed a visit by the Chinese Premier, Li Peng, to Singapore in August. Nevertheless, Prime Minister Goh made his first official visit to Taiwan in October 1993. In October 1996 Singapore and Australia issued a joint communiqué urging the

SINGAPORE

integration of the People's Republic of China into the Asian regional security structure, and reaffirming their commitment to a co-operative dialogue with the People's Republic. However, a private visit to Singapore in January 1998 by the Taiwanese Vice-President, Lien Chan, during which he met with Goh and with Singaporean cabinet ministers, provoked the disapproval of the People's Republic. Relations improved in November 1998 when Goh made an official visit to the People's Republic, and in November 1999 the Chinese Premier, Zhu Rongji, made a reciprocal visit to Singapore. However, further visits to Taiwan, by Lee Kuan Yew in September 2000 and September 2002, and by Lee Hsien Loong in July 2004 shortly before he assumed the premiership, caused further damage to bilateral relations. The diplomatic furore caused by Lee's visit in 2004 served to delay the start of negotiations concerning a free trade pact between the People's Republic and Singapore, which had been due to commence in November 2004, despite Lee's insistence that his visit in no way weakened his country's commitment to the 'One China' policy that denied recognition of Taiwan. The Chinese Prime Minister, Wen Jiabao, and Lee consequently agreed to commence free trade talks as planned, but they withheld from offering any indication as to when negotiations might begin. In October 2005, at a meeting in Beijing of Singaporean and Chinese delegates, led by Lee Hsien Loong and Wen Jiabao, both countries affirmed their commitment to accelerating the holding of free trade negotiations. The two countries also agreed to work together to address the regional threats of terrorism and piracy in the Straits of Melaka (Malacca). China and Singapore held their first round of free trade talks in October 2006; several further sessions took place in 2007.

Government

Legislative power is vested in the unicameral Parliament, with 84 members who are elected by universal adult suffrage for five years (subject to dissolution—within three months of which a general election must be held) in single-member and multi-member constituencies. As many as three additional 'non-constituency' seats may be offered to opposition parties, and up to nine non-elected, neutral MPs may be nominated: all have restricted voting rights. The President is directly elected by universal adult suffrage for a six-year term as a constitutional Head of State, vested with limited powers of veto in financial matters, public appointments and detentions for reasons of national security. Effective executive authority rests with the Cabinet, led by the Prime Minister, which is appointed by the President and responsible to Parliament.

Defence

As assessed at November 2007, the Singapore armed forces had an estimated total active strength of 72,500 troops (including 35,000 conscripts): 50,000 in the army, an estimated 9,000 in the navy and 13,500 in the air force. The length of compulsory military service was 24 months. Paramilitary forces comprised a civil defence force (numbering an estimated 81,800) and a police force (numbering an estimated 8,500). Singapore is a participant in the Five-Power Defence Arrangements (with Australia, Malaysia, New Zealand and the United Kingdom). In 2007 the Government budgeted S $10,580m. for defence.

Economic Affairs

In 2006, according to estimates by the World Bank, Singapore's gross national income (GNI), measured at average 2004–06 prices, was US $128,816m., equivalent to US $29,320 per head (or US $31,710 per head on an international purchasing-power parity basis). During 1996–2006, it was estimated, the population increased at an average annual rate of 1.8%, while gross domestic product (GDP) per head increased, in real terms, at an average rate of 3.3% per year. Overall GDP increased, in real terms, at an average annual rate of 5.2% in 1996–2006. According to official figures, GDP expanded by 8.2% in 2006 and by an estimated 7.7% in 2007.

Agriculture (including fishing and quarrying—mainly of granite) contributed an estimated 0.1% of GDP in 2007 and, including utilities, engaged only 0.7% of the employed labour force in the same year. Vegetables, plants and orchid flowers are the principal crops. According to figures from the World Bank, agricultural GDP (again including fishing and quarrying) declined at an average annual rate of 0.5% during 1996–2006. According to official figures, agricultural GDP (including fishing and quarrying) expanded by 15.5% in 2006 and by an estimated 0.2% in 2007.

Industry (including manufacturing, construction and utilities) contributed an estimated 29.4% of GDP in 2007, and, excluding utilities, engaged 31.2% of the employed labour force in the same year. During 1996–2006, according to figures from the World Bank, industrial GDP increased at an average annual rate of 5.1%. According to official figures, the GDP of the sector expanded by 10.5% in 2006 and by an estimated 7.3% in 2007.

Manufacturing contributed an estimated 24.1% of GDP in 2007 and engaged 20.8% of the employed labour force in that year. The principal branches of manufacturing in 2004 (measured in terms of the value of output) were electronic products and components (which accounted for 38.8% of total manufacturing production), refined petroleum products, chemicals and chemical products, non-electrical machinery and equipment, biomedical and pharmaceutical products, and transport equipment (especially shipbuilding). According to figures from the World Bank, manufacturing GDP increased at an average annual rate of 6.3% in 1996–2006. The manufacturing sector's GDP increased by an estimated 5.8% in 2007, according to official figures.

Singapore relies on imports of hydrocarbons to fuel its three thermal power stations. In 2004 natural gas accounted for 68.8% of the total amount of electrical energy produced; petroleum accounted for 31.2%. In 2007 imports of crude petroleum accounted for 8.5% of merchandise imports.

The services sector contributed an estimated 70.5% of GDP in 2007, and engaged 68.1% of the employed labour force in that year. Financial and business services provided an estimated 24.9% of GDP in 2007, and in that year engaged 12.8% of the employed labour force. The GDP of the financial services sector increased by 10.6% in 2006 and by an estimated 16.9% in 2007. Singapore is an important foreign-exchange dealing centre in Asia and the Pacific. Banking is also a significant sector, with a total of 111 commercial banks in operation in April 2005. Tourism is a significant source of foreign exchange, and receipts from tourism amounted to approximately US $5,736m. in 2005. The number of tourist arrivals increased from 9.8m. in 2006 to 10.3m. in 2007. In 2007 transport, storage, information and communications contributed an estimated 13.0% of GDP. The GDP of the transport, storage, information and communications sector increased by 4.7% in 2006 and by an estimated 5.4% in 2007. Singapore is the world's busiest port in tonnage terms and has one of the largest merchant shipping registers in the world. According to figures from the World Bank, the GDP of the services sector increased at an average annual rate of 5.4% in 1996–2006. According to official figures, the sector expanded by 7.2% in 2006 and by an estimated 7.8% in 2007.

In 2007 Singapore recorded a visible trade surplus of an estimated US $74,097m., and there was a surplus of US $59,014m. on the current account of the balance of payments. In 2007 the principal sources of imports were Malaysia (13.1%), the USA (12.3%) and the People's Republic of China (12.1%); other major suppliers were Japan and Taiwan. Malaysia (12.9%), Hong Kong (10.5%) and China (9.7%) were the principal markets for exports in that year; other major purchasers were the USA and Japan. Principal imports in 2007 included machinery and equipment (notably electronic components and parts), mineral fuels, basic manufactures, miscellaneous manufactured articles and chemicals. Principal exports included machinery and equipment (notably electronic components and parts), mineral fuels (notably petroleum products), chemicals and miscellaneous manufactured articles. Singapore is an important entrepôt, and re-exports accounted for 47.9% of total exports in 2007.

The 2007/08 budget recorded an operating surplus of S $8,181m. A small deficit (projected at 0.3% of GDP) was forecast for 2008/09. According to the ADB, at the end of 2007 Singapore's external debt totalled US $326,086m. The annual rate of inflation averaged 0.7% in 1996–2006; consumer prices increased by 2.1% in 2007. The rate of unemployment declined to 2.1% of the labour force in 2007, the lowest level for 10 years.

Singapore is a member of the UN Economic and Social Commission for Asia and the Pacific (ESCAP, see p. 35), of the Asian Development Bank (ADB, see p. 182), of the Association of South East Asian Nations (ASEAN, see p. 185), of Asia-Pacific Economic Co-operation (APEC, see p. 176) and of the Colombo Plan (see p. 411). As a member of ASEAN, Singapore signed an accord in January 1992 pledging the creation of a free trade zone to be known as the ASEAN Free Trade Area (AFTA). A reduction of tariffs to between 0% and 5% was originally envisaged to be completed by 2008 but this was subsequently advanced to 2002, when AFTA was formally implemented. However, Malaysia applied for an extension of this date for its automotive industry, fearing direct competition. Target dates for the removal of all tariffs were brought forward from 2015 to 2010 in November 1999.

Singapore's economic success has been based largely on its central location in the region, efficient planning, advanced infrastructure and highly skilled work-force. The country has consolidated its position as a financial and trading centre through various reforms, including a programme to transfer many state-owned corporations to the private sector. However, as the programme of structural reforms continued, there was some concern with regard to the disparities in income levels that were becoming increasingly evident, as the real wage levels of less-skilled Singaporeans were failing to keep pace with those of the better-educated. Singapore embarked upon a series of free trade agreement (FTA) initiatives. By 2006 various FTAs had been concluded, among them agreements with New Zealand, Japan, the European Free Trade Association (EFTA, see p. 412), Australia, the USA, the Republic of Korea and the People's Republic of China. Foreign direct investment was reported to have increased from US $6,986m. in 2005 to $12,502m. in 2006, before declining slightly in 2007, to $11,837m. Confidence amongst property investors and developers was raised by the strong economic performance, and by the progress of plans for major projects, including a new business district, as well as the two casino resorts. The slight decline in GDP growth in 2007 was attributed to the weaker performance of the electronics sector and to lower production in the pharmaceutical sector. Thus, manufacturing growth decelerated to less than 6% in 2007, compared with almost 12% the previous year. However, the transport engineering sector performed very strongly in 2007, expanding by 23.5%. The property market also performed well, as did the construction industry. However, high rates of growth led to inflationary pressures. In particular, transport costs continued to rise as a result of increasing petroleum prices, and global prices for essential food commodities rose sharply in early 2008. The Government envisaged that the economy would further decelerate in 2008, as external demand weakened; it forecast GDP growth of between 4.5% and 6.5% in that year.

Education

Primary and secondary education is available in the four official languages of Malay, Chinese, Tamil and English. In 1978, as part of a policy of bilingualism, examinations in English and Mandarin Chinese became compulsory for pupils seeking to enter secondary education. In 1987 English became the medium of instruction in all schools. In 2003 the Government introduced a six-year period of compulsory education, covering the whole duration of primary education, which begins at six years of age. In 2004/05 enrolment at primary education was equivalent to 78% of children in the relevant age-group (males 78%; females 78%). Secondary education lasts for four or five years from the age of 12. In 2004/05 enrolment at secondary education was equivalent to 63% of children in the relevant age-group (males 62%, females 64%). Post-secondary education lasts for two or three years and provides pre-university instruction. Outside the school system there are several higher education centres and vocational institutes, providing craft and industrial training, and technical institutes providing advanced craft training. In 2004 57.8% of resident non-students aged 15 years and over held secondary or higher qualifications. According to UNESCO, in 1996 total enrolment in tertiary-level education was equivalent to 38.5% of those in the relevant age-group (males 41.5%; females 35.3%). At June 2005 a total of 59,441 students were enrolled at Singapore's four universities. A total of 67,667 students were enrolled at the country's five polytechnics in June 2006. Adult education courses are conducted by a statutory board. Operating expenditure on education by the central Government in 2007 was budgeted at S $6,567m. (21.0% of total spending).

Public Holidays

2008: 1 January (New Year's Day), 7–8 February (Chinese New Year), 21 March (Good Friday), 1 May (Labour Day), 19 May (Vesak Day), 9 August (National Day), 1 October* (Hari Raya Puasa, end of Ramadan), 28 October (Deepavali), 8 December* (Hari Raya Haji, Feast of the Sacrifice), 25 December (Christmas Day).

2009: 1 January (New Year's Day), 26–27 January (Chinese New Year), 10 April (Good Friday), 1 May (Labour Day), 2 May (Vesak Day), 9 August (National Day), 20 September* (Hari Raya Puasa, end of Ramadan), 17 October (Deepavali), 27 November* (Hari Raya Haji, Feast of the Sacrifice), 25 December (Christmas Day).

* These holidays are dependent on the Islamic lunar calendar and may vary by one or two days from the dates given.

Weights and Measures

The metric system is in force, but local units are also used.

Statistical Survey

Source (unless otherwise stated): Department of Statistics, 100 High St, 05-01 The Treasury, Singapore 179434; tel. 63327686; fax 63327689; e-mail info@singstat.gov.sg; internet www.singstat.gov.sg.

Area and Population

AREA, POPULATION AND DENSITY

Area (sq km)	699.4*
Population (census results)†	
30 June 1990	3,047,132‡
30 June 2000	
Males	2,061,800§
Females	1,955,900§
Total	4,017,733
Population (official estimates at mid-year)§	
2005	4,341,800
2006	4,483,900
2007	4,680,900
Density (per sq km) at mid-2007	6,692.7

* 270.0 sq miles.
† Includes non-residents, totalling 311,264 in 1990 and 754,524 in 2000.
‡ Includes resident population temporarily residing overseas.
§ Rounded figure(s).

ETHNIC GROUPS
(at census of 30 June 2000)*

	Males	Females	Total
Chinese	1,245,782	1,259,597	2,505,379
Malays	228,174	225,459	453,633
Indians	134,544	123,247	257,791
Others	21,793	24,613	46,406
Total	1,630,293	1,632,916	3,263,209

* Figures refer to the resident population of Singapore.

SINGAPORE

BIRTHS, MARRIAGES AND DEATHS*

	Registered live births		Registered marriages		Registered deaths	
	Number	Rate (per 1,000)	Number	Rate (per 1,000)	Number	Rate (per 1,000)
2000	46,997	14.4	22,561	5.6	15,693	4.8
2001	41,451	12.5	22,280	5.4	15,367	4.6
2002	40,760	12.1	23,198	5.6	15,820	4.7
2003	37,485	10.9	21,962	5.2	16,036	4.7
2004	37,174	10.1	22,189	5.2	15,860	4.3
2005	37,492	10.0	22,992	5.3	16,215	4.3
2006	38,317	10.1	23,706	n.a.	16,393	4.3
2007	39,375	n.a.	23,966	n.a.	17,052	n.a.

* Data are tabulated by year of registration, rather than by year of occurrence.

Expectation of life (years at birth, WHO estimates): 80.2 (males 78.2; females 82.3) in 2005 (Source: WHO, *World Health Statistics*).

EMPLOYMENT
('000 persons aged 15 years and over, at June of each year)

	2005	2006	2007
Agriculture, fishing, mining and quarrying, utilities, sewage and waste management	19.8	15.7	17.3
Manufacturing	485.1	495.3	543.5
Construction	184.4	244.2	271.9
Wholesale and retail trade; repair of motor vehicles, motorcycles and personal and household goods	350.6	353.0	373.7
Hotels and restaurants	124.2	135.8	152.2
Transport and storage	185.8	176.2	181.7
Information and communications	74.3	69.6	76.4
Financial intermediation	111.2	121.3	136.8
Real estate, renting and business activities	246.4	171.6	196.9
Public administration and defence; compulsory social security		107.3	119.3
Community, social and personal service activities; private households with employed persons and extra-territorial organizations and bodies	485.1	511.3	540.0
Total employed	2,266.7	2,401.4	2,609.7

Health and Welfare

KEY INDICATORS

Total fertility rate (children per woman, 2005)	1.3
Under-5 mortality rate (per 1,000 live births, 2005)	3
HIV/AIDS (% of persons aged 15–49, 2005)	0.3
Physicians (per 1,000 head, 2004)	1.40
Hospital beds (per 1,000 head, 2004)	2.79
Health expenditure (2004): US $ per head (PPP)	1,117.9
Health expenditure (2004): % of GDP	3.7
Health expenditure (2004): public (% of total)	34.0
Human Development Index (2005): ranking	25
Human Development Index (2005): value	0.922

For sources and definitions, see explanatory note on p. vi.

Agriculture

PRINCIPAL CROPS
('000 metric tons)

	2003	2004	2005
Groundnut oil*	4,891.7	3,678.8	3,678.8
Sesame oil*	2,726.0	2,294.5	2,294.5
Soybean oil*	3,114.2	3,545.3	3,545.3
Cabbages and other brassicas*	489.0	408.0	465.0
Spinach	1,548.0	1,786.0	1,722.0

* FAO estimates.

2006 ('000 metric tons): Cabbages and other brassicas 533.0; Spinach 1,704.0.

Total vegetables (incl. melons, '000 metric tons, may include official, semi-official or estimated data): 19.0 in 2003, 19.8 in 2004, 20.0 in 2005, 18.1 in 2006.

Source: FAO.

LIVESTOCK
('000 head, year ending September, FAO estimates)

	2002	2003	2004
Pigs	250	250	250
Chickens	2,000	2,000	2,000
Ducks	600	600	600

2005: Figures assumed to be unchanged from 2004 (FAO estimates).

Note: Data were not available for 2006.

Source: FAO.

LIVESTOCK PRODUCTS
('000 metric tons)

	2004	2005	2006
Pig meat	20.0	20.2	15.9
Chicken meat*	68.7	75.7	76.0
Hen eggs	22.7	20.6	21.3

* FAO estimates.
Source: FAO.

Forestry

SAWNWOOD PRODUCTION
('000 cubic metres, incl. railway sleepers, FAO estimates)

	1990	1991	1992
Coniferous (softwood)	5	10	5
Broadleaved (hardwood)	50	20	20
Total	55	30	25

1993–2006: Annual production assumed to be unchanged since 1992 (FAO estimates).

Source: FAO.

SINGAPORE

Fishing

(metric tons, live weight)

	2003	2004	2005
Capture	2,085	2,173	1,920
Prawns and shrimps	220	245	251
Aquaculture	5,024	5,406	5,917
Indonesian snakehead	525	428	416
Milkfish	1,492	1,839	1,500
Green mussel	2,362	2,391	2,958
Total catch	7,109	7,579	7,837

Note: Figures exclude crocodiles, recorded by number rather than by weight. The number of estuarine crocodiles caught was: 1,074 in 2003; 1,136 in 2004; 1,330 in 2005.

Source: FAO.

Industry

PETROLEUM PRODUCTS
('000 metric tons)

	2002	2003	2004
Liquefied petroleum gas	818	870	872
Naphtha	3,561	3,284	3,870
Motor spirit (petrol)	3,632	3,350	3,948
Kerosene	462	426	501
Jet fuel	5,361	6,735	6,481
Gas-diesel (distillate fuel) oils	10,775	9,938	11,711
Residual fuel oil	6,614	6,400	7,042
Lubricating oils	1,696	1,575	1,951
Petroleum bitumen (asphalt)	1,639	1,644	1,974

Source: UN, *Industrial Commodity Statistics Yearbook*.

SELECTED OTHER PRODUCTS

	1988	1989	1990
Paints ('000 litres)	48,103.6	52,746.9	58,245.9
Broken granite ('000 metric tons)	6,914.0	7,007.5	6,371.7
Bricks ('000 units)	103,136	116,906	128,386
Soft drinks ('000 litres)	269,689.4	252,977.6	243,175.1
Plywood, plain and printed ('000 sq m)	31,307.0	28,871.3	26,106.9
Vegetable cooking oil (metric tons)	75,022	103,003	102,854
Animal fodder (metric tons)	110,106	115,341	104,541
Electricity (million kWh)	13,017.5	14,039.0	15,617.6
Gas (million kWh)	681.1	722.4	807.1
Cassette tape recorders ('000 sets)	15,450	14,006	18,059

Source: UN, *Industrial Commodity Statistics Yearbook*.

Plywood ('000 cu m, estimates): 280 per year in 1991–2006 (Source: FAO).

Electric energy (million kWh): 38,213 in 2005; 39,442 in 2006; 41,138 in 2007 (Source: mainly Asian Development Bank, *Key Indicators of Developing Asian and Pacific Countries*).

Finance

CURRENCY AND EXCHANGE RATES

Monetary Units
100 cents = 1 Singapore dollar (S $).

Sterling, US Dollar and Euro Equivalents (31 December 2007)
£1 sterling = S $2.8873;
US $1 = S $1.4412;
€1 = S $2.1216;
S $100 = £34.63 = US $69.39 = €47.13.

Average Exchange Rate (Singapore dollars per US $)
2005   1.6644
2006   1.5890
2007   1.5071

BUDGET
(S $ million)

Revenue*	2005	2006	2007
Tax revenue	25,201	28,718	36,061
Income tax	12,655	14,948	16,410
Corporate and personal income tax	11,208	12,925	14,616
Contributions by statutory board	1,446	2,022	1,794
Assets taxes	1,819	2,052	2,432
Taxes on motor vehicles	1,438	1,723	2,101
Customs and excise duties	1,995	1,943	2,034
Betting taxes	1,531	1,548	1,665
Stamp duty	813	1,312	4,078
Goods and services tax	3,815	3,960	5,612
Others	1,136	1,232	1,729
Fees and charges	2,567	2,120	3,232
Total (incl. others)	28,117	31,072	39,516

Expenditure	2005	2006	2007
Operating expenditure	20,675	23,463	24,352
Security and external relations	10,443	11,973	11,309
Social development	8,548	9,685	10,996
Education	4,981	5,685	6,567
Health	1,671	1,764	2,016
Community development and sports	818	898	833
Environment and water resources	443	418	436
Economic development	924	954	1,117
Trade and industry	444	459	579
Transport	285	284	284
Government administration	759	852	931
Development expenditure	8,107	6,412	6,983
Total	28,782	29,875	31,335

*Figures refer to operating revenue only; the data exclude investment income and capital revenue.

INTERNATIONAL RESERVES
(US $ million at 31 December)

	2005	2006	2007
Gold and foreign exchange	116,172	136,259	162,957
IMF special drawing rights	285	316	350
Reserve position in the IMF	174	130	90
Total	116,631	136,706	163,397

Source: IMF, *International Financial Statistics*.

MONEY SUPPLY
(S $ million at 31 December)

	2005	2006	2007
Currency outside banks	14,585	15,285	16,669
Demand deposits at commercial banks	31,501	36,958	47,270
Total money	46,086	52,243	63,939

Source: IMF, *International Financial Statistics*.

COST OF LIVING
(Consumer Price Index; base: 2004 = 100)

	2005	2006	2007
Food	101.3	102.8	105.9
Transport and communication	97.8	96.4	98.3
Clothing and footwear	99.9	100.6	101.3
Housing	100.8	103.5	103.9
Education	102.0	104.0	105.3
Health	100.4	101.3	105.5
All items (incl. others)	100.4	101.4	103.5

SINGAPORE

Statistical Survey

NATIONAL ACCOUNTS
(S $ million at current prices)

National Income and Product

	2005	2006	2007*
Compensation of employees	82,746.7	89,984.4	100,174.2
Gross operating surplus	101,406.8	110,840.2	119,826.5
Gross domestic product (GDP) at factor cost	184,153.5	200,824.6	220,000.7
Taxes, less subsidies, on production and imports	14,578.5	15,149.7	21,292.6
Statistical discrepancy	642.8	1,020.2	1,875.5
GDP in market prices	199,374.8	216,994.5	243,168.8
Net primary incomes received from abroad	−18,072.0	−15,222.8	−8,602.7
Gross national income (GNI)	181,302.8	201,771.7	234,566.1

* Preliminary figures.

Expenditure on the Gross Domestic Product

	2005	2006	2007*
Government final consumption expenditure	21,369.8	24,288.0	25,440.7
Private final consumption expenditure	82,006.3	87,121.6	96,280.5
Change in inventories	−3,411.2	−5,770.7	−5,750.1
Gross fixed capital formation	43,148.9	49,225.1	60,604.8
Statistical discrepancy	−990.5	−2,624.2	−3,575.2
Total domestic expenditure	142,123.3	152,239.8	173,000.7
Trade in goods and services (net)	57,251.5	64,754.7	70,168.1
GDP in market prices	199,374.8	216,994.5	243,168.8
GDP at constant 2000 prices	196,645.6	212,711.5	229,123.1

* Preliminary figures.

Gross Domestic Product by Economic Activity

	2005	2006	2007*
Agriculture, fishing and quarrying	165.8	184.6	187.2
Manufacturing	51,123.4	56,659.1	57,683.6
Electricity, gas and water	3,344.1	3,534.8	3,732.3
Construction	7,226.6	7,595.8	9,083.9
Wholesale and retail trade	33,556.6	36,885.2	38,823.1
Hotels and restaurants	3,698.7	4,095.5	4,643.0
Transport and storage	19,459.3	20,289.0	22,574.3
Information and communications	7,700.8	8,245.8	8,620.1
Financial services	21,712.2	23,699.1	29,795.9
Business services	22,172.5	24,940.4	29,943.0
Owner-occupied dwellings	6,942.3	8,628.7	11,118.7
Other services	20,400.0	21,668.6	23,376.0
Sub-total	197,502.3	216,426.6	239,581.1
Less Financial intermediation services indirectly measured	9,076.4	10,681.8	12,924.1
Gross value added at basic prices	188,425.9	205,744.8	226,657.0
Taxes on products	10,948.9	11,249.7	16,511.8
GDP in market prices	199,374.8	216,994.5	243,168.8

* Preliminary figures.

BALANCE OF PAYMENTS
(US $ million)

	2005	2006	2007*
Exports of goods	387,348.5	437,122.6	456,378.9
Imports of goods	−325,619.3	−368,169.4	−382,282.3
Trade balance	61,729.2	68,953.2	74,096.6
Exports of services	88,156.3	97,012.8	105,108.5
Imports of services	−92,634.0	−101,211.3	−109,037.0
Balance on goods and services	57,251.5	64,754.7	70,168.1
Income (net)	−18,072.0	−15,222.8	−8,602.7
Balance on goods, services and income	39,179.5	49,531.9	61,565.4
Current transfers (net)	−2,104.0	−2,236.9	−2,551.5
Current balance	37,075.5	47,295.0	59,013.9
Capital account (net)	−335.6	−367.0	−390.5
Direct investment (net)	11,629.6	19,864.5	17,839.6
Portfolio investment (net)	−5,484.9	−14,207.2	−25,007.5
Other investments (net)	−27,237.6	−28,069.3	−20,545.3
Net errors and omissions	4,749.7	2,479.7	−1,612.6
Overall balance	20,396.7	26,995.7	29,297.6

* Preliminary figures.

External Trade

PRINCIPAL COMMODITIES
(S $ million)

Imports c.i.f.	2005	2006	2007
Mineral fuels, lubricants, etc.	59,145	74,645	83,367
Crude petroleum	30,820	32,404	33,830
Chemicals and related products	20,744	22,695	23,919
Basic manufactures	25,040	27,933	30,715
Machinery and equipment	185,980	207,372	208,400
Electronic components and parts	71,393	80,812	79,813
Miscellaneous manufactured articles	26,526	27,693	29,238
Total (incl. others)	333,191	378,924	395,973

Exports f.o.b.*	2005	2006	2007
Mineral fuels, lubricants, etc.	57,415	70,553	79,721
Petroleum products	45,881	55,736	61,374
Chemicals and related products	43,611	49,070	55,606
Basic manufactures	17,498	18,496	21,889
Machinery and equipment	224,980	249,241	247,628
Electronic components and parts	91,654	109,988	108,129
Miscellaneous manufactured articles	26,049	28,273	29,158
Total (incl. others)	382,532	431,559	450,587

* Including re-exports (S $ million); 175,084 in 2005; 204,181 in 2006; 215,713 in 2007.

SINGAPORE

PRINCIPAL TRADING PARTNERS
(S $ million)

Imports c.i.f.	2005	2006	2007
Australia	4,851	5,934	4,764
China, People's Republic	34,170	43,194	48,013
France	6,346	8,523	9,300
Germany	9,915	10,794	12,241
Hong Kong	7,009	6,507	5,804
India	6,788	7,755	8,814
Italy	3,594	4,160	4,708
Japan	32,034	31,640	32,423
Korea, Republic	14,323	16,636	19,254
Kuwait	6,138	7,163	7,635
Malaysia	45,527	49,481	51,809
Netherlands	3,007	3,266	4,422
Philippines	7,742	8,967	8,756
Saudi Arabia	14,894	14,767	13,241
Switzerland	3,835	2,920	3,440
Taiwan	19,720	24,207	23,306
Thailand	12,516	13,856	12,797
United Arab Emirates	4,242	6,636	6,910
United Kingdom	6,554	6,819	7,235
USA	38,793	47,474	48,651
Total (incl. others)	333,191	378,924	395,973

Exports f.o.b.*	2005	2006	2007
Australia	14,045	16,182	16,832
China, People's Republic	32,909	42,061	43,549
France	5,460	5,030	6,738
Germany	10,504	10,418	8,951
Hong Kong	35,849	43,335	47,155
India	9,817	12,166	15,046
Japan	20,874	23,590	21,630
Korea, Republic	13,412	13,877	15,958
Malaysia	50,612	56,372	58,099
Netherlands	9,129	8,635	8,626
Philippines	6,970	8,067	9,224
Taiwan	14,938	15,065	13,770
Thailand	15,662	17,945	18,653
United Arab Emirates	6,155	5,048	5,256
United Kingdom	10,525	11,540	12,259
USA	39,024	42,829	39,493
Viet Nam	7,364	8,665	9,802
Total (incl. others)	382,532	431,559	450,587

*Including re-exports (S $ million); 175,084 in 2005; 204,181 in 2006; 215,713 in 2007.

Transport

ROAD TRAFFIC
(registered vehicles)

	2005	2006	2007
Cars*	440,583	474,717	517,041
Motorcycles and scooters	139,434	142,736	144,340
Motor buses	13,494	14,120	14,530
Taxis	22,383	23,334	24,446
Goods and other vehicles (incl. private)	139,038	144,466	150,979
Total	754,992	799,373	851,336

*Including private, company, tuition and private hire cars.

SHIPPING
Merchant Fleet
(at 31 December)

	2004	2005	2006
Number of vessels	1,842	1,977	2,079
Displacement (grt)	26,282,777	30,989,786	32,173,922

Source: Lloyd's Register-Fairplay, *World Fleet Statistics*.

International Sea-borne Shipping

	2005	2006	2007
Vessels entered	130,318	128,922	128,568
Total cargo ('000 metric tons)	423,268	448,504	483,616

Source: Maritime and Ports Authority of singapore.

CIVIL AVIATION

	2005	2006	2007
Passengers:			
arrived	15,364,071	16,677,822	17,639,556
departed	15,356,295	16,690,277	17,581,646
in transit	1,710,490	1,664,984	1,480,353
Mail (metric tons):			
landed	8,809	8,921	10,801
dispatched	12,080	11,746	12,592
Freight (metric tons):			
discharged	892,141	952,876	963,873
loaded	941,580	958,341	930,896

Source: partly Civil Aviation Authority of Singapore.

Tourism

FOREIGN VISITOR ARRIVALS
('000, incl. excursionists)

Country of nationality	2005	2006	2007
Australia	620,237	691,632	768,490
China, People's Republic	857,792	1,037,197	1,113,948
Germany	154,775	161,122	164,898
Hong Kong	313,814	291,474	302,110
India	583,532	658,893	748,726
Indonesia	1,813,444	n.a.	n.a.
Japan	588,500	594,404	594,511
Korea, Republic	364,192	454,721	464,286
Malaysia*	577,882	n.a.	n.a.
Philippines	319,923	n.a.	n.a.
Taiwan	213,950	219,463	208,156
Thailand	379,013	n.a.	n.a.
United Kingdom	467,144	488,166	495,691
USA	371,422	399,782	408,875
Total (incl. others)*	8,942,408	9,750,952	10,284,410

*Data exclude arrivals of Malaysians by land.

Tourism receipts (US $ million, excl. passenger transport): 3,783 in 2003; 5,224 in 2004; 5,736 in 2005 (Source: World Tourism Organization).

Communications Media

(at 31 December)

	2004	2005	2006
Telephones ('000 main lines in use)	1,857.0	1,844.4	1,853.5
Mobile cellular telephones ('000 subscribers)	3,990.7	4,384.6	4,788.6
Personal computers ('000 in use)	2,590	n.a.	n.a.
Internet users ('000)	2,421.8	1,731.6	1,717.1
Broadband subscribers ('000)	545.5	665.6	796.5

Radio receivers ('000 in use): 2,550 in 1997.

Television receivers ('000 in use): 1,200 in 2000.

Facsimile machines ('000 in use, estimate): 100 in 1998.

Daily newspapers: 11 (with average circulation of 1,542,000 copies) in 2004.

Non-daily newspapers: 9 (with average circulation of 1,134,000 copies) in 2004.

Sources: mainly International Telecommunication Union; UNESCO, *Statistical Yearbook*; UNESCO Institute for Statistics; UN, *Statistical Yearbook*.

Education

(June 2006)

	Institutions	Students	Teachers
Primary	172	277,291	12,268
Secondary	155	200,291	10,570
Centralized institutes	13	29,176	2,131
Junior colleges			
Institute of Technical Education	3	23,636	1,502
Polytechnics	5	67,667	3,736
National Institute of Education	1	4,348	460
Universities*	3	62,918	3,414

*Student and teacher numbers are not available for Singapore's fourth university (SIM University) which opened in 2005.

Adult literacy rate (official estimate): 95.7% in 2007.

Directory

The Constitution

A new Constitution came into force on 3 June 1959, with the establishment of the self-governing State of Singapore. This was subsequently amended as a consequence of Singapore's affiliation to Malaysia (September 1963 to August 1965) and as a result of its adoption of republican status on 22 December 1965. The Constitution was also amended in January 1991 to provide for the election of a President by universal adult suffrage, and to extend the responsibilities of the presidency, which had previously been a largely ceremonial office. A constitutional amendment in October 1996 placed restrictions on the presidential right of veto. The main provisions of the Constitution are summarized below:

HEAD OF STATE

The Head of State is the President, elected by universal adult suffrage for a six-year term. He normally acts on the advice of the Cabinet, but is vested with certain functions and powers for the purpose of safeguarding the financial reserves of Singapore and the integrity of the Public Services.

THE CABINET

The Cabinet, headed by the Prime Minister, is appointed by the President and is responsible to Parliament.

THE LEGISLATURE

The Legislature consists of a Parliament of 84 elected members, presided over by a Speaker who may be elected from the members of Parliament themselves or appointed by Parliament although he may not be a member of Parliament. Members of Parliament are elected by universal adult suffrage for five years (subject to dissolution) in single-member and multi-member constituencies.* Additionally, up to three 'non-constituency' seats may be offered to opposition parties, in accordance with a constitutional amendment approved in 1984, while legislation approved in 1990, and amended in 1997, enables the Government to nominate up to nine additional, politically neutral members for a term of two years; these members have restricted voting rights.

A 21-member Presidential Council, chaired by the Chief Justice, examines material of racial or religious significance, including legislation, to see whether it differentiates between racial or religious communities or contains provisions inconsistent with the fundamental liberties of Singapore citizens.

CITIZENSHIP

Under the Constitution, Singapore citizenship may be acquired either by birth, descent or registration. Persons born when Singapore was a constituent State of Malaysia could also acquire Singapore citizenship by enrolment or naturalization under the Constitution of Malaysia.

*A constitutional amendment was introduced in May 1988, whereby 39 constituencies were merged to form 13 'group representation constituencies', which would return 'teams' of three Members of Parliament. At least one member of each team was to be of minority (non-Chinese) racial origin. In January 1991 the Constitution was further amended, stipulating that the number of candidates contesting 'group representation constituencies' should be a minimum of three and a maximum of four. The maximum was increased to six by constitutional amendment in October 1996.

The Government

HEAD OF STATE

President: SELLAPAN RAMANATHAN (S. R.) NATHAN (took office 1 September 1999).

CABINET
(May 2008)

Prime Minister: Brig.-Gen. (retd) LEE HSIEN LOONG.

Senior Minister in the Prime Minister's Office: GOH CHOK TONG.

Minister Mentor: LEE KUAN YEW.

Deputy Prime Minister and Co-ordinating Minister for National Security: Prof. SHANMUGAM JAYAKUMAR.

Deputy Prime Minister and Minister for Home Affairs: WONG KAN SENG.

Minister for Foreign Affairs: Brig.-Gen. (retd) GEORGE YONG-BOON YEO.

Minister for Finance: THARMAN SHANMUGARATNAM.

Minister for Trade and Industry: LIM HNG KIANG.

Minister for Information, Communications and the Arts: Dr LEE BOON YANG.

Minister for Education and Second Minister for Defence: NG ENG HEN.

Minister for Manpower: GAN KIM YONG (acting).

Minister for Health: KHAW BOON WAN.

Minister for Transport and Second Minister for Foreign Affairs: RAYMOND LIM SIANG KEAT.

Ministers in the Prime Minister's Office: LIM SWEE SAY, LIM BOON HENG.

Minister for National Development: MAH BOW TAN.

Minister for Community Development, Youth and Sports: Dr VIVIAN BALAKRISHNAN.

Minister for Defence: Rear-Adm. (retd) TEO CHEE HEAN.

Minister for the Environment and Water Resources and Minister-in-charge of Muslim Affairs: Dr YAACOB IBRAHIM.

Minister for Law and Second Minister for Home Affairs: K. SHANMUGAM.

SINGAPORE
Directory

MINISTRIES

Office of the President: The Istana, Orchard Rd, Singapore 238823; e-mail istana_general_office@istana.gov.sg; internet www.istana.gov.sg.

Office of the Prime Minister: The Istana, Orchard Rd, Singapore 238823; tel. 63327200; fax 63328983; e-mail lee_hsien_loong@pmo.gov.sg; internet www.pmo.gov.sg.

Ministry of Community Development, Youth and Sports: 512 Thomson Rd, MCYS Bldg, Singapore 298136; tel. 62589595; fax 63536695; e-mail mcys_email@mcys.gov.sg; internet www.mcys.gov.sg.

Ministry of Defence: Gombak Dr., off Upper Bukit Timah Rd, Mindef Bldg, Singapore 669645; tel. 67608844; fax 67646119; internet www.mindef.gov.sg.

Ministry of Education: 1 North Buona Vista Dr., MOE Bldg, Singapore 138675; tel. 68722220; fax 67755826; e-mail contact@moe.edu.sg; internet www.moe.gov.sg.

Ministry of the Environment and Water Resources: 40 Scotts Rd, Environment Bldg, 24-00, Singapore 228231; tel. 67327733; fax 67319456; e-mail mewr_feedback@mewr.gov.sg; internet www.mewr.gov.sg.

Ministry of Finance: 100 High St, 10-01 The Treasury, Singapore 179434; tel. 62259911; fax 63327435; e-mail mof_qsm@mof.gov.sg; internet www.mof.gov.sg.

Ministry of Foreign Affairs: MFA Bldg, Tanglin, off Napier Rd, Singapore 248163; tel. 63798000; fax 64747885; e-mail mfa@mfa.gov.sg; internet www.mfa.gov.sg.

Ministry of Health: 16 College Rd, College of Medicine Bldg, Singapore 169854; tel. 63259220; fax 62241677; e-mail moh_info@moh.gov.sg; internet www.moh.gov.sg.

Ministry of Home Affairs: New Phoenix Park, 28 Irrawaddy Rd, Singapore 329560; tel. 64787010; fax 62546250; e-mail mha_feedback@mha.gov.sg; internet www.mha.gov.sg.

Ministry of Information, Communications and the Arts: 140 Hill St, 02-02 MICA Bldg, Singapore 179369; tel. 62707988; fax 68379837; e-mail mica@mica.gov.sg; internet www.mica.gov.sg.

Ministry of Law: 100 High St, 08-02 The Treasury, Singapore 179434; tel. 63328840; fax 63328842; e-mail contact@mlaw.gov.sg; internet www.minlaw.gov.sg.

Ministry of Manpower: 18 Havelock Rd, 07-01, Singapore 059764; tel. 64385122; fax 65344840; e-mail mom_hq@mom.gov.sg; internet www.mom.gov.sg.

Ministry of National Development: 5 Maxwell Rd, 21/22-00 Tower Block, MND Complex, Singapore 069110; tel. 62221211; fax 63257254; e-mail mnd_hq@mnd.gov.sg; internet www.mnd.gov.sg.

Ministry of Trade and Industry: 100 High St, 09-01 The Treasury, Singapore 179434; tel. 62259911; fax 63327260; e-mail mti_email@mti.gov.sg; internet www.mti.gov.sg.

Ministry of Transport: 460 Alexandra Rd, 39-00 PSA Bldg, Singapore 119963; tel. 62707988; fax 63757734; e-mail mot@mot.gov.sg; internet www.mot.gov.sg.

President and Legislature

PRESIDENT

On 13 August 2005, at the end of his six-year term, the incumbent SELLAPAN RAMANATHAN (S. R.) NATHAN was again nominated as President by a state-appointed committee. S. R. Nathan was the sole candidate for the Presidency, following the rejection by the committee of three other potential candidates on the grounds of their insufficient experience. He was officially reappointed to the post on 1 September.

PARLIAMENT

Parliament House

1 Parliament Place, Singapore 178880; tel. 63326666; fax 63325526; e-mail parl@parl.gov.sg; internet www.parliament.gov.sg.

Speaker: ABDULLAH TARMUGI.

General Election, 6 May 2006

	Seats
People's Action Party	82*
Workers' Party	1
Singapore Democratic Alliance	1
Total	84

* 37 seats were unopposed.

Election Commission

Elections Department of Singapore (ELD): Prime Minister's Office, 11 Prinsep Link, Singapore 187949; fax 63323428; internet www.elections.gov.sg; govt body; Chair. ROBIN CHAN.

Political Organizations

National Solidarity Party: 397 Jalan Besar, 02-01A, Singapore 209007; tel. and fax 65366388; e-mail nsp-cec@yahoogroups.com; internet www.nsp.sg; f. 1987; joined Singapore Democratic Alliance (SDA) in July 2001; Pres. SEBASTIAN TEO; Sec.-Gen. LAW SIN LING.

People's Action Party (PAP): Blk 57B, PCF Bldg, 01-1402 New Upper Changi Rd, Singapore 463057; tel. 62444600; fax 62430114; e-mail paphq@pap.org.sg; internet www.pap.org.sg; f. 1954; governing party since 1959; 12-member Cen. Exec. Cttee; Chair. LIM BOON HENG; Sec.-Gen. LEE HSIEN LOONG.

Pertubuhan Kebangsaan Melayu Singapura (PKMS) (Singapore Malay National Organization): 218F Changi Rd, 4th Floor, PKM Bldg, Singapore 1441; tel. 64470468; fax 63458724; e-mail pkms_melayu@pacific.net.sg; internet www.geocities.com/pkms218; f. 1950 as the United Malay National Organization (UMNO) of Malaysia; renamed as UMNO Singapore in 1954 and as PKMS in 1967; seeks to advance the implementation of the special rights of Malays in Singapore, as stated in the Constitution, to safeguard and promote the advancement of Islam and to encourage racial harmony and goodwill in Singapore; joined Singapore Democratic Alliance (SDA) in July 2001; Pres. Haji BORHAN ARIFFIN.

Singapore Democratic Alliance (SDA): Singapore; f. 2001; est. to contest 2001 general election; coalition of Pertubuhan Kebangsaan Melayu Singapura (PKMS), Singapore People's Party (SPP), National Solidarity Party and the Singapore Justice Party; Chair. CHIAM SEE TONG.

Singapore Democratic Party (SDP): 1357A Serangoon Rd, Singapore 328240; tel. and fax 63981675; e-mail speakup@yoursdp.org; internet www.singaporedemocrat.org; f. 1980; 12-mem. Cen. Cttee; Chair. GANDHI AMBALAM; Sec.-Gen. CHEE SOON JUAN.

Singapore Justice Party: Singapore; f. 1972; joined Singapore Democratic Alliance (SDA) in July 2001; Pres. A. R. SUIB; Sec.-Gen. AMINUDDIN BIN AMI.

Singapore People's Party (SPP): Singapore; e-mail feedback@spp.org.sg; internet www.spp.org.sg; f. 1993; a breakaway faction of the SDP, espousing more moderate policies; joined Singapore Democratic Alliance (SDA) in July 2001; 12-mem. Cen. Exec. Cttee; Chair. SIN KEK TONG; Sec.-Gen. CHIAM SEE TONG.

Workers' Party: 216G Syed Alwi Rd 02-03, Singapore 207799; tel. 62984765; fax 64544404; e-mail wp@wp.org.sg; internet www.wp.org.sg; f. 1961; active as opposition party in Singapore since 1957, merged with Barisan Sosialis (Socialist Front) in 1988; seeks to establish a democratic socialist govt with a constitution guaranteeing fundamental citizens' rights; Chair. SYLVIA LIM SWEE LIAN; Sec.-Gen. LOW THIA KHIANG.

Other parties are the Alliance Party Singapura, the Democratic People's Party, the Democratic Progressive Party, the National Party of Singapore, the Partai Rakyat, the Parti Kesatuan Ra'ayat (United Democratic Party), the People's Front, the People's Republican Party, the Persatuan Melayu Singapura, the Singapore Chinese Party, the Singapore Indian Congress, the Singapore National Front, the United National Front, the United People's Front and the United People's Party.

Diplomatic Representation

EMBASSIES AND HIGH COMMISSIONS IN SINGAPORE

Angola: 9 Temasek Blvd, 44-03 Suntec Tower Two, Singapore 038989; tel. 63419360; fax 63419367; e-mail embangola@pacific.net.sg; Ambassador FLÁVIO SARAIVA DE CARVALHO FONSECA.

Australia: 25 Napier Rd, Singapore 258507; tel. 68364100; fax 67375481; e-mail public-affairs-sing@dfat.gov.au; internet www.australia.org.sg; High Commissioner MILES KUPA.

Bangladesh: 91 Bencoolen St, 6 Sunshine Plaza, Singapore 189652; tel. 62550075; fax 62551824; e-mail bdoot@signet.com.sg; internet www.bangladesh.org.sg; High Commissioner KAMRUL AHSAN.

Belgium: 8 Shenton Way, 14-01 Temasek Tower, Singapore 068811; tel. 62207677; fax 62226976; e-mail singapore@diplobel.org; internet www.diplomatie.be/singapore; Ambassador MARC A. M. CALCOEN.

Brazil: 101 Thomson Rd, 10-05 United Sq., Singapore 307591; tel. 62566001; fax 62564565; e-mail cinbrem@brazil.org.sg; internet www.brazil.org.sg; Ambassador PAULO ALBERTO DE SILVEIRA SOARES.

SINGAPORE

Directory

Brunei: 325 Tanglin Rd, Singapore 247955; tel. 67339055; fax 67375275; High Commissioner ABDUL GHAFAR BIN ISMAIL.

Cambodia: 400 Orchard Rd, 10-03/04 Orchard Towers, Singapore 238875; tel. 63419785; fax 63419201; e-mail cambodiaembasy@pacific.net.sg; internet www.recambodia.net; Ambassador SEREY SIN.

Canada: 1 George St 11-01, Singapore 049145; tel. 68545900; fax 68545930; e-mail echiesg@pacific.net.sg; internet www.dfait-maeci.gc.ca/singapore; High Commissioner ALAN VIRTUE.

Chile: 105 Cecil St, 25-00 The Octagon, Singapore 069534; tel. 62238577; fax 62250677; e-mail echilesg@pacific.net.sg; Ambassador GRACIELA MERCEDES FERNÁNDEZ SOBARZO.

China, People's Republic: 150 Tanglin Rd, Singapore 247969; tel. 64712117; fax 64795345; e-mail chinaemb_sg@fmprc.gov.cn; internet www.chinaembassy.org.sg; Ambassador ZHANG XIAOKANG.

Costa Rica: 271 Bukit Timah Rd, 04-08 Balmoral Plaza, Singapore 259708; tel. 67380566; fax 67380567; e-mail embassycostarica@singnet.com.sg; Ambassador JUAN FERNANDO CORDERO ARIAS.

Denmark: 101 Thomson Rd, 13-01/02 United Sq., Singapore 307591; tel. 63555010; fax 62533764; e-mail sinamb@um.dk; internet www.denmark.com.sg; Ambassador VIBEKE ROVSING LAURITZEN.

Egypt: 75 Grange Rd, Singapore 249579; tel. 67371811; fax 67323422; e-mail admin@egyptemb-sin.org; Ambassador MOHAMED ELZORKANY.

Finland: 101 Thomson Rd, 21-03 United Sq., Singapore 307591; tel. 62544042; fax 62534101; e-mail sanomat.sin@formin.fi; internet www.finland.org.sg; Ambassador SATU MATTILA.

France: 101–103 Cluny Park Rd, Singapore 259595; tel. 68807800; fax 68807801; e-mail ambassadeur@france.org.sg; internet www.france.org.sg; Ambassador PIERRE BUHLER.

Germany: 12-00 Singapore Land Tower, 50 Raffles Place, Singapore 048623; tel. 65336002; fax 65331132; e-mail germany@singnet.com.sg; internet www.sing.diplo.de; Ambassador FOLKMAR STOECKER.

Hungary: 250 North Bridge Rd, 29-01 Raffles City Tower, Singapore 179101; tel. 68830882; fax 68830177; e-mail mission.sin@kum.hu; internet www.mfa.gov.hu/emb/singapore; Ambassador TAMAS MAGDA.

India: 31 Grange Rd, India House, Singapore 239702; tel. 67376777; fax 67326909; e-mail indiahc@pacific.net.sg; internet www.embassyofindia.com; High Commissioner SUBRAHMANYAM JAISHANKAR.

Indonesia: 7 Chatsworth Rd, Singapore 249761; tel. 67377422; fax 67375037; e-mail info@kbrisingapura.com; internet www.kbrisingapura.com; Ambassador WARDANA.

Ireland: Ireland House, 541 Orchard Rd, 8th Floor, Liat Towers, Singapore 238881; tel. 62387616; fax 62387615; e-mail singaporeembassy@dfa.ie; internet www.embassyofireland.sg; Ambassador RICHARD O'BRIEN.

Israel: 24 Stevens Close, Singapore 257964; tel. 68349200; fax 67337008; e-mail press@singapore.mfa.gov.il; internet singapore.mfa.gov.il; Ambassador ILAN BEN-DOV.

Italy: 101 Thomson Rd, 27-02/03 United Sq., Singapore 307591; tel. 62506022; fax 62533301; e-mail ambitaly@italyemb.org.sg; internet www.italyemb.org.sg; Ambassador FOLCO DE LUCA GABRIELLI.

Japan: 16 Nassim Rd, Singapore 258390; tel. 62358855; fax 67331039; e-mail eojsingfv@vsystem.com.sg; internet www.sg.emb-japan.go.jp; Ambassador MAKOTO YAMANAKA.

Kazakhstan: 20 Raffles Place, 14-06 Ocean Towers, Singapore 048620; tel. 65366100; fax 64388990; e-mail office@kazakhstan.org.sg; internet www.kazakhstan.org.sg; Ambassador YERLAN BAUDARBEK-KOZHATAYEV.

Korea, Democratic People's Republic: 7500 Beach Rd, 09-320 The Plaza, Singapore 199591; tel. 64403498; fax 63482026; e-mail embdprk@singnet.com.sg; Ambassador JI JAE SUK.

Korea, Republic: 47 Scotts Rd, 08-00 Goldbell Towers, Singapore 228233; tel. 68362263; fax 62352581; e-mail info@koreaembassy.org.sg; internet www.koreaembassy.org.sg; Ambassador KIM JOONG-KEUN.

Kuwait: c/o The Ritz-Carlton Millenia Singapore, 7 Raffles Ave, Suite 3108, Singapore 039799; tel. 64345388; fax 64345387; Ambassador ABDULAZIZ AHMED S. AL-ADWANI.

Laos: 101 Thomson Rd, 03-05A United Sq., Singapore 307591; tel. 62506044; fax 62506014; e-mail laoembsg@singnet.com.sg; Ambassador THOUANE VORASARN.

Malaysia: 30 Hill St, 02-01, Singapore 179360; tel. 62350111; fax 67336135; e-mail mwspore@singnet.com.sg; High Commissioner Dato' NAGALINGAM PARAMESWARAN.

Maldives: 101 Thomson Rd, 30-01A, United Sq., Singapore 307591; tel. 67209012; fax 67209014; e-mail info@maldiveshighcommission.sg; High Commissioner HASSAN SOBIR.

Mexico: 152 Beach Rd, 06-07/08, 6th Floor, Gateway East Tower, Singapore 189721; tel. 62982678; fax 62933484; e-mail embamexsing@embamexsing.org.sg; internet www.embamexsing.org.sg; Ambassador JUAN JOSÉ GOMEZ CAMACHO.

Mongolia: 600 North Bridge Rd, 24-08 Parkview Sq., Singapore 188778; tel. 63480745; fax 63481753; e-mail consulmn@singnet.com.sg; internet www.mongoliaembassysingapore.com; Ambassador PÜREVJAVYN GANSÜKH (designate).

Myanmar: 15 St Martin's Drive, Singapore 257996; tel. 67350209; fax 67356236; e-mail ambassador@mesingapore.org.sg; internet www.mesingapore.org.sg; Ambassador WIN MYINT.

Netherlands: 541 Orchard Rd, 13-01 Liat Towers, Singapore 238881; tel. 67371155; fax 67371940; e-mail nlgovsin@singnet.com.sg; internet www.mfa.nl/sin; Ambassador CHRISTIAAN CORNELIS SANDERS.

New Zealand: 391A Orchard Rd, Tower A, 15-06/10 Ngee Ann City, Singapore 238873; tel. 62359966; fax 67339924; e-mail enquiries@nz-high-com.org.sg; internet www.nzembassy.com/singapore; High Commissioner Dr MARTIN WILFRED HARVEY.

Nigeria: 08-02 Anson House, 72 Anson Rd, Singapore 079911; tel. 67321743; fax 67321742; e-mail highcommission@nigeriahc.org.sg; internet www.nigeriahc.org.sg; High Commissioner Dr OZICHI J. ALIMOLE (acting).

Norway: 16 Raffles Quay, 44-01 Hong Leong Bldg, Singapore 048581; tel. 62207122; fax 62202191; e-mail emb.singapore@mfa.no; internet www.norway.org.sg; Ambassador JANNE JULSRUD.

Pakistan: 1 Scotts Rd, 24-02/04 Shaw Centre, Singapore 228208; tel. 67376988; fax 67374096; e-mail parep@singnet.com.sg; internet www.parep.org.sg; High Commissioner SAJJAD ASHRAF.

Panama: 16 Raffles Quay, 41-06 Hong Leong Bldg, Singapore 048581; tel. 62218677; fax 62240892; e-mail general@panamaemb.org.sg; Ambassador EDUARDO A. REAL.

Peru: 390 Orchard Rd, 12-03 Palais Renaissance, Singapore 238871; tel. 67388595; fax 67388601; e-mail embperu@pacific.net.sg; internet www.embassyperu.org.sg; Ambassador J. ARTURO MONTOYA.

Philippines: 20 Nassim Rd, Singapore 258395; tel. 67373977; fax 67339544; e-mail php@pacific.net.sg; internet www.philippine-embassy.org.sg; Ambassador BELEN FULE-ANOTA.

Poland: 435 Orchard Rd, 10-01/02 Wisma Atria, Singapore 238877; tel. 62359478; fax 62359479; e-mail polish_embassy@pacific.net.sg; internet www.singapore.polemb.net; Ambassador BOGUSLAW MARCIN MAJEWSKI.

Qatar: c/o Shangri-La Hotel, 22 Orange Grove Rd, Rms 1832 & 1833, Singapore 258350; tel. 67373644; fax 62134021; Ambassador RASHID BIN ALI HASSAN AL-KHATER.

Romania: 48 Jalan Harom Setangkai, Singapore 258827; tel. 64683424; fax 64683425; e-mail comofrom@starhub.net.sg; Chargé d'affaires a.i. SILVIU IONESCU.

Russia: 51 Nassim Rd, Singapore 258439; tel. 62351834; fax 67334780; e-mail rosposol@pacific.net.sg; internet www.singapore.mid.ru; Ambassador ANDREY N. ROZHKOV.

Saudi Arabia: 40 Nassim Rd, Singapore 258449; tel. 67345878; fax 67385291; e-mail enquiries@saudiembassy.org.sg; internet www.saudiembassy.org.sg; Ambassador Dr MOHAMAD AMIN KURDI.

South Africa: 331 North Bridge Rd, 15/01-06 Odeon Towers, Singapore 188720; tel. 63393319; fax 63396658; e-mail singhc@foreign.gov.za; internet www.southafrichc.org.sg; High Commissioner ZANELE MAKINA.

Spain: 7 Temasek Blvd, 39-00 Suntec Tower 1, Singapore 038987; tel. 67259220; fax 63333025; Ambassador ANTONIO SÁNCHEZ JARA.

Sri Lanka: 13-07/12 Goldhill Plaza, 51 Newton Rd, Singapore 308900; tel. 62544595; fax 62507201; e-mail slhcs@lanka.com.sg; internet www.lanka.com.sg; High Commissioner WINITHKUMAR SHEHAN RATNAVALE.

Sweden: 111 Somerset Rd, 05-01 Singapore Power Bldg, Singapore 238164; tel. 64159720; fax 64159747; e-mail ambassaden.singapore@foreign.ministry.se; internet www.swedenabroad.com/singapore; Ambassador PÄR AHLBERGER.

Switzerland: 1 Swiss Club Link, Singapore 288162; tel. 64685788; fax 64668245; e-mail sin.vertretung@eda.admin.ch; internet www.eda.admin.ch/singapore; Ambassador Dr DANIEL WOKER.

Thailand: 370 Orchard Rd, Singapore 238870; tel. 67372158; fax 67320778; e-mail thaisgp@singnet.com.sg; internet www.thaiembassy.sg; Ambassador NOPADOL GUNAVIBOOL.

Turkey: 2 Shenton Way 10-03, SGX Centre 1, Singapore 068804; tel. 65333390; fax 65333360; e-mail turksin@singnet.com.sg; internet www.turkishembassy.org.sg; Ambassador BÜLENT MERIÇ.

Ukraine: 50 Raffles Place, 16-05 Singapore Land Tower, Singapore 048623; tel. 65356550; fax 65352116; e-mail emb_sg@mfa.gov.ua;

internet www.embassy-ukraine.com; Ambassador Dr VIKTOR MASHTABEI.

United Arab Emirates: 600 North Bridge Road, 09-01/05 Parkview Sq., Singapore 188778; tel. 62388206; fax 62380081; e-mail emarat@singnet.com.sg; internet www.uaeembassy-sg.com; Chargé d'affaires a.i. ASIM MIRZA ALRAHMAH.

United Kingdom: 100 Tanglin Rd, Singapore 247919; tel. 64244200; fax 64244218; e-mail commercial.singapore@fco.gov.uk; internet www.britain.org.sg; High Commissioner PAUL MADDEN.

USA: 27 Napier Rd, Singapore 258508; tel. 64769100; fax 64769340; e-mail singaporeusembassy@state.gov; internet singapore.usembassy.gov; Ambassador PATRICIA LOUISE HERBOLD.

Uzbekistan: 5 Shenton Way 37-02, Rms 34 & 35, UIC Bldg, Singapore 068808; tel. 63251843; fax 63251844; e-mail uz-emb.sg@hotmail.com; Ambassador ALISHER A. KURMANOV.

Venezuela: 3 Killiney Rd, 07–03 Winsland House I, Singapore 239519; tel. 64911172; fax 62353167; e-mail embassy@embavenez.org.sg; Chargé d'affaires a.i. GEOMAR CATTAFI-ANDRADE.

Viet Nam: 10 Leedon Park, Singapore 267887; tel. 64625938; fax 64625936; e-mail vnemb@singnet.com.sg; Ambassador NGUYEN TRUNG THANH.

Judicial System

Supreme Court: 1 Supreme Court Lane, Singapore 178879; tel. 63360644; fax 63379450; e-mail supcourt_qsm@supcourt.gov.sg; internet www.supcourt.gov.sg.

The judicial power of Singapore is vested in the Supreme Court and in the Subordinate Courts. The Judiciary administers the law with complete independence from the executive and legislative branches of the Government; this independence is safeguarded by the Constitution. The Supreme Court consists of the High Court and the Court of Appeal. The Chief Justice is appointed by the President if the latter, acting at his discretion, concurs with the advice of the Prime Minister. The other judges of the Supreme Court are appointed in the same way, in consultation with the Chief Justice. Under a 1979 constitutional amendment, the position of judicial commissioner of the Supreme Court was created 'to facilitate the disposal of business in the Supreme Court'. A judicial commissioner has the powers and functions of a judge, and is appointed for such period as the President thinks fit.

The Subordinate Courts consist of District Courts and Magistrates' Courts. In addition, there are also specialized courts such as the Coroner's Court, Family Court, Juvenile Court, Mentions Court, Night Court, Sentencing Courts and Filter Courts. The Primary Dispute Resolution Centre and the Small Claims Tribunals are also managed by the Subordinate Courts. The Subordinate Courts have also established the Multi-Door Courthouse, which serves as a one-stop centre for the screening and channelling of any cases to the most appropriate forum for dispute resolution.

District Courts and Magistrates' Courts have original criminal and civil jurisdiction. District Courts try offences for which the maximum penalty does not exceed 10 years of imprisonment and in civil cases where the amount claimed does not exceed S $250,000. Magistrates' Courts try offences for which the maximum term of imprisonment does not exceed three years. The jurisdiction of Magistrates' Courts in civil cases is limited to claims not exceeding S $60,000. The Coroners' Court conducts inquests. The Small Claims Tribunal has jurisdiction over claims relating to a dispute arising from any contract for the sale of goods or the provision of services and any claim in tort in respect of damage caused to any property involving an amount that does not exceed S $10,000. The Juvenile Court deals with offences committed by young persons aged under 16 years.

The High Court has unlimited original jurisdiction in criminal and civil cases. In its appellate jurisdiction it hears criminal and civil appeals from the District Courts and Magistrates' Courts. The Court of Appeal hears appeals against the decisions of the High Court in both criminal and civil matters. In criminal matters, the Court of Appeal hears appeals against decisions made by the High Court in the exercise of its original criminal jurisdiction. In civil matters, the Court of Appeal hears appeals against decisions made by the High Court in the exercise of both its original and appellate jurisdiction.

With the enactment of the Judicial Committee (Repeal) Act 1994 in April of that year, the right of appeal from the Court of Appeal to the Judicial Committee of the Privy Council in the United Kingdom was abolished. The Court of Appeal is now the final appellate court in the Singapore legal system.

Attorney-General: Prof. WALTER WOONG CHEONG MING.

Chief Justice: CHAN SEK KEONG.

Judges of Appeal: V. K. RAJAH, ANDREW PHANG BOON LEONG, CHAO HICK TIN.

Judges of the High Court: KAN TING CHIU, LAI SIU CHIU, JUDITH PRAKASH, TAN LEE MENG, CHOO HAN TECK, BELINDA ANG, WOO BIH LI, TAY YONG KWANG, ANDREW ANG, LEE SEIU KIN, CHAN SENG ONN.

Religion

According to the 2000 census, 64.4% of ethnic Chinese, who constituted 76.8% of the population, professed either Buddhism or Daoism (including followers of Confucius, Mencius and Lao Zi) and 16.5% of Chinese adhered to Christianity. Malays, who made up 13.9% of the population, were 99.6% Muslim. Among Indians, who constituted 7.9% of the population, 55.4% were Hindus, 25.6% Muslims, 12.1% Christians and 6.3% Sikhs, Jains or adherents of other faiths. There are small communities of Zoroastrians and Jews. Freedom of worship is guaranteed by the Constitution.

BAHÁ'Í FAITH

The Spiritual Assembly of the Bahá'ís of Singapore: 110D Wishart Rd, Singapore 098733; tel. 62733023; fax 62732497; e-mail secretariat@bahai.org.sg; internet www.bahai.org.sg.

BUDDHISM

Buddhist Union: 28 Jalan Senyum, Singapore 418152; tel. 64435959; fax 64443280.

Singapore Buddhist Federation: 12 Ubi Ave 1, Singapore 408932; tel. 67444635; fax 67473618; e-mail buddhist@singnet.com.sg; internet www.buddhist.org.sg; f. 1948.

Singapore Buddhist Sangha Organization: 88 Bright Hill Drive, Singapore 579644.

CHRISTIANITY

National Council of Churches: 1 Coleman St, B1-27 The Adelphi, Singapore 179803; tel. 63368177; fax 63368178; e-mail admin@nccs.org.sg; internet www.nccs.org.sg; f. 1948; six mem. churches, six assoc. mems; Pres. Bishop ROBERT SOLOMON; Gen. Sec. LIM K. TAN.

Singapore Council of Christian Churches (SCCC): Singapore; f. 1956.

The Anglican Communion

The Anglican diocese of Singapore (also including Indonesia, Laos, Thailand, Viet Nam and Cambodia) is part of the Province of the Anglican Church in South-East Asia.

Bishop of Singapore: The Rt Rev. Dr JOHN HIANG CHEA CHEW, 4 Bishopsgate, Singapore 249970; tel. 64741661; fax 64791054; e-mail bpoffice@anglican.org.sg.

Orthodox Churches

The Orthodox Syrian Church and the Mar Thoma Syrian Church are both active in Singapore.

The Roman Catholic Church

Singapore comprises a single archdiocese, directly responsible to the Holy See. In December 2005 there were an estimated 170,223 adherents in the country, representing 3.9% of the total population.

Archbishop of Singapore: Most Rev. NICHOLAS CHIA, Archbishop's House, 31 Victoria St, Singapore 187997; tel. 63378818; fax 63334735; e-mail nc@veritas.org.sg.

Other Christian Churches

Brethren Assemblies: Bethesda Hall (Ang Mo Kio), 601 Ang Mo Kio Ave 4, Singapore 569898; tel. 64587474; fax 64566771; e-mail bethesdahall@gmail.com; internet www.bethesdahall.com; f. 1864; Hon. Sec. WONG TUCK KEONG.

Evangelical Fellowship of Singapore (EFOS): Singapore; f. 1980.

Methodist Church in Singapore: 70 Barker Rd, Singapore 309936; tel. 64784784; fax 64784794; e-mail episcopacy@methodist.org.sg; internet www.methodist.org.sg; f. 1885; 34,232 mems (Dec. 2006); Leader Bishop Dr ROBERT SOLOMON.

Presbyterian Church: 3 Orchard Rd, cnr Penang Rd, Singapore 238825; tel. 63376681; fax 63391979; e-mail orpcenglish@orpc.org.sg; internet www.orpc.org.sg; f. 1856; services in English, Chinese (Mandarin), Indonesian and German; 2,000 mems; Chair. Rev. DAVID BURKE.

Singapore Baptist Convention: 01 Goldhill Plaza, 03-19 Podium Blk, Singapore 308899; tel. 62538004; fax 62538214; e-mail info@baptistconvention.org.sg; internet www.baptistconvention.org.sg; f. 1974; Chair. Rev. EDWIN LAM HON MUN; Exec. Dir PETER TANG.

Other denominations active in Singapore include the Lutheran Church and the Evangelical Lutheran Church.

SINGAPORE

HINDUISM

Hindu Advisory Board: c/o 397 Serangoon Rd, Singapore 218123; tel. 62963469; fax 62929766; e-mail heb@pacific.net.sg; f. 1985; Chair. AJAIB HARI DASS; Sec. E. SANMUGAM.

Hindu Endowments Board: 397 Serangoon Rd, Singapore 218123; tel. 62963469; fax 62929766; e-mail heb@pacific.net.sg; internet www.heb.gov.sg; f. 1968; Chair. V. R. NATHAN; Sec. SATISH APPOO.

ISLAM

Majlis Ugama Islam Singapura (MUIS) (Islamic Religious Council of Singapore): 1 Lorong 6 Toa Payoh, Singapore 319376; tel. 62568188; fax 62537572; e-mail info@muis.gov.sg; internet www.muis.gov.sg; f. 1968; Pres. Haji MOHD ALAMI MUSA; Sec. ABDUL RAZAK MARICAR.

Muslim Missionary Society Singapore (JAMIYAH): 31 Lorong, 12 Geylang Rd, Singapore 399006; tel. 67431211; fax 67450610; e-mail info@jamiyah.org.sg; internet www.jamiyah.org.sg; Pres. Haji ABU BAKAR MAIDIN; Sec.-Gen. ISMAIL ROZIZ.

SIKHISM

Central Sikh Gurdwara Board (CSGB): c/o 2 Towner Rd, 03-01, Singapore 327804; tel. 62993855; e-mail csgb@sikhs.org.sg; internet www.sikhs.org.sg; Pres. KARPAL SINGH MEHLI.

The Press

Compulsory government scrutiny of newspaper management has been in operation since 1974. All newspaper enterprises must be public companies. The Newspaper and Printing Presses (Amendment) Act 1986 empowers the Government to restrict the circulation of foreign periodicals that are deemed to exert influence over readers on domestic political issues. An amendment to the Newspaper and Printing Presses Act was promulgated in October 1990. Under this amendment, all publications of which the 'contents and editorial policy were determined outside Singapore' and which dealt with politics and current events in South-East Asia would be required to obtain a ministerial licence, renewable annually. The permit would limit the number of copies sold and require a deposit in case of legal proceedings involving the publication. Permits could be refused or revoked without any reason being given. In November, however, a statement was issued exempting 14 of the 17 foreign publications affected by the amendment, which came into effect in December.

DAILIES

English Language

Business Times: 1000 Toa Payoh North, Podium Blk, Level 3, Singapore 318994; tel. 63196319; fax 63198277; e-mail btnews@sph.com.sg; internet business-times.asiaone.com; f. 1976; morning; Editor ALVIN TAY; circ. 30,400 in 2006 (Singapore only).

The New Paper: 1000 Toa Payoh North, Annexe Blk, Level 6, Singapore 318994; tel. 63196319; fax 63198266; e-mail tnp@asia1.com.sg; internet newpaper.asia1.com.sg; f. 1988; afternoon tabloid; Editor IVAN FERNANDEZ; circ. 111,400 in 2006 (Singapore only).

The Straits Times: 1000 Toa Payoh North, Singapore 318994; tel. 63196319; fax 63198282; e-mail sti@sph.com.sg; internet straitstimes.asiaone.com; f. 1845; morning; Editor-in-Chief PATRICK DANIEL; circ. 388,500 in 2006 (Singapore only).

Today: 24 Raffles Place, 28-01/06 Clifford Centre, Singapore 048621; tel. 62364889; fax 64812098; e-mail news@newstoday.com.sg; internet www.todayonline.com; f. 2000; merged with Streats newspaper, a rival free morning tabloid, in 2004; Editor P. N. BALJI; circ. 550,000.

Chinese Language

Lianhe Wanbao: 1000 Toa Payoh North, Podium Blk, Level 4, Singapore 318994; tel. 63196319; fax 63198133; e-mail wanbao@sph.com.sg; f. 1983; evening; Editor KOH LIN HOE; circ. 178,400 (week), 94,640 (Sun.) in 2006.

Lianhe Zaobao: 1000 Toa Payoh North, Podium Blk, Level 4, Singapore 318994; tel. 63196319; fax 63198119; e-mail cnzbmgt@sph.com.sg; internet www.zaobao.com; f. 1923; Editor LIM JIM KOON; circ. 183,000 (week), 191,300 (weekend) in 2006.

My Paper: Singapore; tel. 63192222; fax 63198115; e-mail mypaper@sph.com.sg; internet mypaper.sg; f. 2006; free tabloid aimed at bilingual working adults aged between 20 and 40 years old; Tues.-Sat; Editor GOH SIN TECK; circ. 120,000 (2006).

Shin Min Daily News (S) Ltd: 1000 Toa Payoh North, Podium Blk, Level 4, Singapore 318994; tel. 63196319; fax 63198166; e-mail shinmin@sph.com.sg; f. 1967; evening; Editor TOH LAM HHAT; circ. 120,800 (week), 122,600 (weekend) in 2006.

Malay Language

Berita Harian: 1000 Toa Payoh North, Singapore 318994; tel. 63195137; fax 63198255; e-mail aadeska@sph.com.sg; internet cyberita.asia1.com.sg; f. 1957; morning; Editor MOHD GUNTOR SADALI; circ. 62,500 in 2006.

Tamil Language

Tamil Murasu: 82 Genting Lane 06-07, Singapore 349567; tel. 63196319; fax 63194001; e-mail murasu4@cyberway.co.sg; internet tamilmurasu.asia1.com.sg; f. 1935; Editor CHITRA RAJARAM; circ. 10,200 (week), 17,600 (Sunday) in 2006.

WEEKLIES

English Language

The New Paper on Sunday: 1000 Toa Payoh North, Annexe Blk, Level 6, Singapore 318994; tel. 63196319; fax 63198266; e-mail tnp@asia1.com.sg; internet newpaper.asia1.com.sg; f. 1999; tabloid; Editor IVAN FERNANDEZ; circ. 145,300 in 2006.

The Sunday Times: 1000 Toa Payoh North, Singapore 318994; tel. 63195397; fax 67320131; e-mail sti@sph.com.sg; internet straitstimes.asiaone.com; f. 1931; Editor-in-Chief CHEONG YIP SENG; circ. 402,600 in 2006 (Singapore only).

Weekend Today: 24 Raffles Place, 28-01/06 Clifford Centre, Singapore 048621; tel. 62364889; fax 64812098; e-mail sales_enquiry@newstoday.com.sg; internet www.todayonline.com; f. 2002; Editor P. N. BALJI; circ. 300,000.

Malay Language

Berita Minggu: 1000 Toa Payoh North, Singapore 318994; tel. 63195665; fax 63198255; e-mail aadeska@sph.com.sg; internet cyberita.asia1.com.sg; f. 1960; Sunday; Editor MOHD GUNTOR SADALI; circ. 72,100 in 2006 (Singapore only).

SELECTED PERIODICALS

English Language

Accent: Accent Communications, 215 Intrepid Warehouse Complex, 4 Ubi Ave, Singapore 1440; tel. 67478088; fax 67472811; f. 1983; monthly; lifestyle; Senior Editor DORA TAY; circ. 65,000.

Cherie Magazine: 12 Everton Rd, Singapore 0208; tel. 62229733; fax 62843859; f. 1983; bi-monthly; women's; Editor JOSEPHINE NG; circ. 20,000.

8 Days: 10 Ang Mo Kio St 65, 01-06/08 Techpoint, Singapore 569059; tel. 62789822; fax 62724800; e-mail feedback@8daysonline.com; internet www.8days.sg; f. 1990; weekly; Editor-in-Chief TAN LEE SUN; circ. 113,258.

Her World: SPH Magazines Pte Ltd, 82 Genting Lane, Singapore 349567; tel. 63196319; fax 63196345; e-mail nguislc@sph.com.sg; internet www.herworld.com; f. 1960; monthly; women's; Editor CAROLINE NGUI; circ. 62,529.

Her World Brides: SPH Magazines Pte Ltd, 82 Genting Lane, Singapore 349567; tel. 63196319; fax 63196345; e-mail sphmag@sph.com.sg; f. 1998; quarterly; circ. 13,193.

Home and Decor: 82 Genting Lane, SPH Media Centre, 5th Floor, Singapore 349567; tel. 63196319; fax 63196345; e-mail hdecor@sph.com.sg; internet www.homeanddecor.com.sg; f. 1981; 6 a year; home-owners; Editor SOPHIE KHO; circ. 27,000.

LIME: 10 Ang Mo Kio St 65, 01-06/08 Techpoint, Singapore 569059; tel. 64837118; fax 64837286; internet lime.mediacorppublishing.com; f. 1996; Editor PAMELA QUEK; circ. 34,947.

Mondial Collections: Singapore; f. 1990; bimonthly; arts; Chair. CHRIS CHENEY; circ. 100,000.

NSman: SAFRA National Service Association, 5200 Jalan Bukit Merah, Singapore 159468; tel. 62786011; fax 63779898; e-mail hq@safra.org.sg; internet www.safra.sg; f. 1972; bi-monthly; publication of the SAF National Service; Gen. Man. TAN KEE BOO; circ. 130,000.

Republic of Singapore Government Gazette: SNP Corpn Ltd, 1 Kim Seng Promenade, 18-01 Great World City East Tower, Singapore 237994; tel. 68269600; fax 68203341; e-mail egazinfo@snpcorp.com; internet www.egazette.com.sg; weekly; Friday.

Reservist: 5200 Jalan Bukit Merah, Singapore 0315; tel. 62786011; fax 6273441; f. 1973; bi-monthly; men's; Editor SAMUEL EE; circ. 130,000.

Singapore Medical Journal: Singapore Medical Association, Level 2, Alumni Medical Centre, 2 College Rd, Singapore 169850; tel. 62231264; fax 62247827; e-mail smj@sma.org.sg; internet www.sma.org.sg/smj; monthly; Editor Prof. W. C. G. PEH; circ. 5,000.

SINGAPORE

Times Guide to Computers: 1 New Industrial Rd, Times Centre, Singapore 536196; tel. 62848844; fax 62850161; e-mail ttd@corp.tpl.com.sg; internet www.tpl.com.sg; f. 1986; annually; computing and communications; Vice-Pres. LESLIE LIM; circ. 30,000.

Visage: Ubi Ave 1, 02-169 Blk 305, Singapore 1440; tel. 67478088; fax 67472811; f. 1984; monthly; Editor-in-Chief TENG JUAT LENG; circ. 63,000.

WEEKENDeast: 82 Genting Lane, News Centre, Singapore 349567; tel. 67401200; fax 67451022; e-mail focuspub@cyberway.com.sg; f. 1986; Editor VICTOR SOH; circ. 75,000.

Woman's Affair: 140 Paya Lebar Rd, 04-10 A-Z Bldg, Singapore 1440; tel. 67478088; fax 67479119; f. 1988; 2 a month; Editor DORA TAY; circ. 38,000.

Young Parents: SPH Magazines Pte Ltd, 82 Genting Lane, Singapore 349567; tel. 63196319; fax 63196345; e-mail yparents@cyberway.com.sg; internet www.youngparents.com.sg; f. 1986; quarterly; family; Editor CRISPINA ROBERT; circ. 15,000.

Chinese Language

Characters: 1 Kallang Sector, 04-04/04-05 Kolam Ayer Industrial Park, Singapore 349276; tel. 67458733; fax 67458213; f. 1987; monthly; television and entertainment; Editor SAM NG; circ. 45,000.

The Citizen: People's Association, 9 Stadium Link, Singapore 397750; tel. 63405138; fax 63468657; monthly; English, Chinese, Tamil and Malay; Man. Editor OOI HUI MEI.

Icon: 82 Genting Lane, SPH Media Centre, Singapore 349567; tel. 63196319; f. 2005; Chinese language; lifestyle magazine.

i-weekly: 10 Ang Mo Kio St 65, 01-06/08 Techpoint, Singapore 569059; tel. 62789822; fax 62724811; e-mail feedback@i-weeklyonline.com; internet i-weekly.mediacorppublishing.com; f. 1981; weekly; radio and television; Editor-in-Chief LOKE TAI TAY; circ. 113,000.

Punters' Way: 4 Ubi View (off Ubi Rd 3), Pioneers and Leaders Centre, Singapore 408557; tel. 67458733; fax 67458213; e-mail pnlhldg@pnl-group.com; f. 1977; bi-weekly; English and Chinese; sport; Editor T. S. PHAN; circ. 90,000.

Racing Guide: 1 New Industrial Rd, Times Centre, Singapore 1953; tel. 62848844; fax 62881186; f. 1987; 2 a week; English and Chinese; sport; Editorial Consultant BENNY ORTEGA; Chinese Editor KUEK CHIEW TEONG; circ. 20,000.

Singapore Literature: Singapore Literature Society, 122B Sims Ave, Singapore 1438; quarterly; Pres. YAP KOON CHAN; Editor LUO-MING.

Tune Monthly Magazine: Henderson Rd 06-04, Blk 203A, Henderson Industrial Park, Singapore 0315; tel. 62733000; fax 62749538; f. 1988; monthly; women's and fashion; Editor CHAN ENG; circ. 25,000.

You Weekly: SPH Magazines Pte Ltd, 82 Genting Lane, Singapore 349567; tel. 63196319; fax 63196345; e-mail sphmag@sph.com.sg; f. 2001; weekly; entertainment; circ. 80,000.

Young Generation: SNP Panpac Pte Ltd, 97 Ubi Avenue 4, Singapore 408754; tel. 67412500; fax 67454129; e-mail yg@snpcorp.com; internet www.snpcorp.com; monthly; children's; Editor EVELYN TANG; circ. 80,000.

Malay Language

Manja: 10 Ang Mo Kio St 65, 01-06/08 Techpoint, Singapore 569059; tel. 64837118; fax 64812098; e-mail hello@manjaonline.com.sg; internet www.manja.sg; monthly; entertainment and lifestyle; Editor TUMINAH SAPAWI.

NEWS AGENCIES

Foreign Bureaux

Sixteen foreign bureaux operate in Singapore.

Publishers

ENGLISH LANGUAGE

Butterworths Asia: 1 Temasek Ave, 17-01 Millenia Tower, Singapore 039192; tel. 63369661; fax 63369662; e-mail sales@butterworths.com.sg; internet www.lexisnexis.com.sg/butterworths-online/; f. 1932; law texts and journals; Man. Dir GRAHAM J. MARSHALL.

Caldecott Publishing Pte Ltd: 10 Ang Mo Kio St 65, 01-06/08 Techpoint, Singapore 569059; tel. 64837118; fax 64837286; f. 1990; Editorial Dir MICHAEL CHIANG; Group Editor TAN LEE SUN.

EPB Publishers Pte Ltd: Blk 162, 04-3545 Bukit Merah Central, Singapore 150162; tel. 62780881; fax 62782456; e-mail epb@sbg.com.sg; fmrly Educational Publications Bureau Pte Ltd; textbooks and supplementary materials, general, reference and magazines; English and Chinese; Gen. Man. ROGER PHUA.

FEP International Pte Ltd: 11 Arnsal Chetty Rd, 03-02, Singapore 239949; tel. 67331178; fax 67375561; f. 1960; textbooks, reference, children's and dictionaries; Gen. Man. RICHARD TOH.

Flame of the Forest Publishing Pte Ltd: Blk 5, Ang Mo Kio Industrial Park 2A, 07-22/23, AMK Tech II, Singapore 567760; tel. 64848887; fax 64842208; e-mail mail@flameoftheforest.com; internet www.flameoftheforest.com; Man. Dir ALEX CHACKO.

Graham Brash Pte Ltd: 45 Kian Teck Drive, Blk 1, Level 2, Singapore 628859; tel. 62624843; fax 62621519; e-mail graham_brash@giro.com.sg; internet www.grahambrash.com.sg; f. 1947; general, academic, educational; English, Chinese and Malay; CEO CHUAN I. CAMPBELL; Dir HELENE CAMPBELL.

HarperCollins, Asia Pte Ltd: 970 Toa Payoh North, 04-24/26, Singapore 1231; tel. 62501985; fax 62501360; f. 1983; educational, trade, reference and general; Man. Dir FRANK FOLEY.

Institute of Southeast Asian Studies: 30 Heng Mui Keng Terrace, Pasir Panjang Rd, Singapore 119614; tel. 67780955; fax 67781735; e-mail admin@iseas.edu.sg; internet www.iseas.edu.sg; f. 1968; scholarly works on contemporary South-East Asia and the Asia-Pacific region; Chair. Prof. WANG GUNGWU; Dir K. KESAVAPANY.

Intellectual Publishing Co: 113 Eunos Ave 3, 04-08 Gordon Industrial Bldg, Singapore 1440; tel. 67466025; fax 67489108; f. 1971; Man. POH BE LECK.

Marshall Cavendish International (Singapore) Pte Ltd: Times Centre, 1 New Industrial Rd, Singapore 536196; tel. 62139300; fax 62854871; e-mail mca@sg.marshallcavendish.com; internet www.marshallcavendish.com/academic; f. 1957; fmrly Times Media Pte Ltd; academic texts; Group Publr ELSA TAN; Man. Editor ANTHONY THOMAS.

NUS Press (Pte) Ltd: National University of Singapore, 3 Arts Link, AS3–01–02, Singapore 117569; tel. 67761148; fax 67740652; e-mail nusbooks@nus.edu.sg; internet www.nus.edu.sg/npu; f. 1971; scholarly; Man. Dir PAUL KRATOSKA.

Pearson Education South Asia Pte Ltd: 23/25 First Lok Yang Rd, Jurong Town, Singapore 629733; tel. 63199388; fax 63199171; e-mail asia@pearsoned.com.sg; educational; Reg. Dir LOW CHWEE LEONG.

Simon & Schuster Asia Pte Ltd: 317 Alexandra Rd, 04-01 Ikea Bldg, Singapore 159965; tel. 64764688; fax 63780370; e-mail prenhall@signet.com.sg; f. 1975; educational; Man. Dir GUNAWAN HADI.

Stamford College Publishers: Colombo Court 05-11A, Singapore 0617; tel. 63343378; fax 63343080; f. 1970; general, educational and journals; Man. LAWRENCE THOMAS.

Times Editions Pte Ltd: Times Centre, 1 New Industrial Rd, Singapore 536196; tel. 62139288; fax 62844733; e-mail tpl@tpl.com.sg; internet www.tpl.com.sg; f. 1978; political, social and cultural books, general works on Asia; Chair. LIM KIM SAN; Pres. and CEO LAI SECK KHUI.

World Scientific Publishing Co Pte Ltd: 5 Toh Tuck Link, Singapore 596224; tel. 64665775; fax 64677667; e-mail wspc@wspc.com.sg; internet www.worldscientific.com; f. 1981; academic and research texts and science journals; Chair. and Editor-in-Chief Prof. K. K. PHUA; Man. Dir DOREEN LIU.

MALAY LANGUAGE

Malaysia Press Sdn Bhd (Pustaka Melayu): Singapore; tel. 62933454; fax 62911858; f. 1962; textbooks and educational; Man. Dir ABU TALIB BIN ALLY.

Pustaka Nasional Pte Ltd: 548 Changi Rd, Singapore 419931; tel. 67454321; fax 67452417; e-mail enquiry@pustaka.com.sg; internet www.pustaka.com.sg; f. 1963; Arabic, English, Malay and Islamic religious books and CD-Roms; Dir SYED ALI SEMAIT.

CHINESE LANGUAGE

Shanghai Book Co (Pte) Ltd: 231 Bain St, 02-73 Bras Basah Complex, Singapore 180231; tel. 63360144; fax 63360490; e-mail shanghaibook@pacific.net.sg; f. 1925; educational and general; Man. Dir MA JI LIN.

Shing Lee Publishers Pte Ltd: 120 Hillview Ave, 05-06/07 Kewalram Hillview, Singapore 2366; tel. 67601388; fax 67625684; e-mail shingleebook@sbg.com.sg; f. 1935; educational and general; Man. PEH CHIN HUA.

Union Book Co (Pte) Ltd: 231 Bain St, 03-01, Bras Basah Complex, Singapore 180231; tel. 63380696; fax 63386306; general and reference; Gen. Man. CHOW LI-LIANG.

TAMIL LANGUAGE

EVS Enterprises: Singapore; tel. 62830002; f. 1967; children's books, religion and general; Man. E. V. SINGHAN.

SINGAPORE   Directory

GOVERNMENT PUBLISHING HOUSE

SNP Corpn Ltd: 1 Kim Seng Promenade, 18-01 Great World City East Tower, Singapore 237994; tel. 68269600; fax 68203341; e-mail enquiries@snpcorp.com; internet www.snpcorp.com; f. 1973; printers and publishers; Pres. and CEO YEO CHEE TONG.

PUBLISHERS' ORGANIZATIONS

National Book Development Council of Singapore (NBDCS): 50 Geylang East Ave 1, Singapore 389777; tel. 68488290; fax 67429466; e-mail info@bookcouncil.sg; internet www.bookcouncil.sg; f. 1969; independent non-profit org.; promotes reading, writing and publishing and organizes the annual Asian Congress of Storytellers and Asian Children's Writers and Illustrators' Conference; offers professional training programmes through Centre for Literary Arts and Publishing; Chair. Prof. TOMMY KOH.

Singapore Book Publishers' Association: 86 Marine Parade Central 03–213, Singapore 440086; tel. 63447801; fax 64470897; e-mail twcsbpa@singnet.com.sg; internet www.publishers-sbpa.org.sg; Pres. TAN WU CHENG.

Broadcasting and Communications

TELECOMMUNICATIONS

Infocomm Development Authority of Singapore (IDA): 8 Temasek Blvd, 14-00 Suntec Tower Three, Singapore 038988; tel. 62110888; fax 62112222; e-mail info@ida.gov.sg; internet www.ida.gov.sg; f. 1999; formed as result of merger of National Computer Board and Telecommunication Authority of Singapore; the national policy maker; regulator of telecommunications and promoter of infocommunications in Singapore; CEO RONNIE TAY.

Netrust Pte Ltd: 70 Bendemeer Rd, 05-03, Luzerne, Singapore 339940; tel. 62121388; fax 62121366; e-mail infoline@netrust.net; internet www.netrust.net; f. 1997; the only licensed Certification Authority (CA) in Singapore, jtly formed by the National Computer Board and the Network for Electronic Transfers; the authority verifies the identity of parties doing business or communicating in cyberspace through the issuing of electronic identification certificates, in order to enable government organizations and private enterprises to conduct electronic transactions in a secure manner; CEO FOO JONG AI.

Singapore Technologies Telemedia: 51 Cuppage Rd, 10-11/17, Starhub Centre, Singapore 229469; tel. 67238777; fax 67207277; e-mail contactus@stt.st.com.sg; internet www.sttelemedia.com; Pres. and CEO LEE THENG KIAT.

Singapore Telecommunications Ltd (SingTel): 19-00 Comcentre, 31 Exeter Rd, Singapore 239732; tel. 68383388; fax 67383769; e-mail contact@singtel.com; internet www.singtel.com; f. 1992; a postal and telecommunications service operator and a holding company for a number of subsidiaries, serving both the corporate and consumer markets; 61.79%-owned by Temasek Holdings (Private) Ltd (a government holding company), 38.21% transferred to the private sector; Chair. CHUMPOL NALAMLIENG; Group CEO CHUA SOCK KOONG.

StarHub Pte Ltd: Head Office, 51 Cuppage Rd, 07-00 StarHub Centre, Singapore 229469; tel. 68255000; fax 67215000; e-mail corpcomms@starhub.com; internet www.starhub.com.sg; f. 2000; telecommunications service provider; consortium includes Singapore Technologies Telemedia Pte Ltd, Singapore Power Ltd, Nippon Telegraph and Telephone Corpn (NTT) and British Telecom (BT); Pres. and CEO TERRY CLONTZ.

BROADCASTING

Regulatory Authority

Media Development Authority (MDA): MITA Bldg 04-01, 140 Hill St, Singapore 179369; tel. 68379973; fax 63368023; internet www.mda.gov.sg; f. 1994; fmrly Singapore Broadcasting Authority, name changed as above in Jan. 2003; licenses and regulates the media industry in Singapore; encourages, promotes and facilitates the development of media industries in Singapore, ensures the provision of an adequate range of media services to serve the interests of the general public, maintains fair and efficient market conduct and effective competition in the media industry, ensures the maintenance of a high standard of media services, regulates public service broadcasting; Chair. Dr TAN CHIN NAM; CEO Dr CHRISTOPHER CHIA.

Radio

Far East Broadcasting Associates: 30 Lorong Ampas, 07-01 Skywaves Industrial Bldg, Singapore 328783; tel. 62508577; fax 62508422; e-mail febadmin@febasgp.com; f. 1960; Chair. GOH EWE KHENG; Exec. Dir Rev. JOHN CHANG.

Media Corporation of Singapore: Caldecott Broadcast Centre, Andrew Rd, Singapore 299939; tel. 63333888; fax 62515628; e-mail cherfern@mediacorpradio.com; internet www.mediacorp.com.sg; f. 1994; est. as Singapore International Media (SIM), following the corporatization of the Singapore Broadcasting Corpn; holding co for seven operating cos—Television Corpn of Singapore (TCS), Singapore Television Twelve (STV12), Radio Corpn of Singapore (RCS), MediaCorp Studios, MediaCorp News, MediaCorp Interactive and MediaCorp Publishing; Chair. HO KWON PING.

Radio Corpn of Singapore Pte Ltd (RCS): Caldecott Broadcast Centre, Radio Bldg, Andrew Rd, Singapore 299939; tel. 62518622; fax 62569533; e-mail feedback@rcs.com.sg; internet www.mediacorpradio.com; f. 1936; operates 12 domestic services—incl. in English (five), Chinese (Mandarin) (three), Malay (two) and Tamil (one)—and three international radio stations (manages Radio Singapore International (RSI)—services in English, Mandarin and Malay for three hours daily and service in Bahasa Indonesia for one hour daily); COO CHUA FOO YONG.

Rediffusion (Singapore) Pte Ltd: 6 Harper Rd, 04-01/08 Leong Huat Bldg, Singapore 369674; tel. 63832633; fax 63832622; e-mail md@rediffusion.com.sg; internet www.rediffusion.com.sg; f. 1949; commercial audio wired broadcasting service and wireless digital audio broadcasting service; broadcasts two programmes in Mandarin (18 hours daily) and English (24 hours daily); Man. Dir WONG BAN KUAN.

SAFRA Radio: Bukit Merah Central, POB 1315, Singapore 911599; tel. 63731924; fax 62783039; e-mail power98@pacific.net.sg; internet www.power98.com.sg; f. 1994; broadcasts in Chinese (Mandarin) and English.

Union Works Pte Ltd: Singapore; internet www.wrkz913.com; f. 1991; fmrly Radio Heart; name changed as above in 2000; first private radio station; broadcasts in English; 2 channels broadcasting a total of 336 hours weekly.

Television

CNBC Asia Business News (S) Pte Ltd: 10 Anson Rd, 06-01 International Plaza, Singapore 079903; tel. 63230488; fax 63230788; e-mail talk2us@cnbcasia.com; internet www.cnbcasia.com.sg; f. 1998; cable and satellite broadcaster of global business and financial news; US controlled; broadcasts in English (24 hours daily) and Mandarin; Pres. PAUL FRANCE.

Media Corporation of Singapore: see Radio.

Singapore Television Twelve Pte Ltd (STV12): 12 Prince Edward Rd, 05-00 Bestway Bldg, Singapore 079212; tel. 62258133; fax 62203881; internet www.stv12.com.sg; f. 1994; terrestrial television station; 2 channels—Suria (Malay, 58 hours weekly) and Central (110.5 hours weekly); COO WOON TAI HO.

SPH MediaWorks Ltd: 82 Genting Lane, Singapore 349567; tel. 63197988; fax 67443318; e-mail mwcc@sphmediaworks.com; internet www.sphmediaworks.com; f. 2000; subsidiary of Singapore Press Holdings Ltd (SPH); two channels—Channel U (Mandarin) and Channel i (English); also owns two radio stations; Exec. Dir WEE LEONG HOW.

Starhub CableVision Ltd: 51 Cuppage Rd 07-00, Singapore 229469; tel. 68255000; fax 67215000; internet www.starhub.com; f. 1992; fmrly Singapore CableVision Ltd; name changed as above in 2002 following acquisition by Starhub Ltd; broadcasting and communications co; subscription television service; launched cable service in June 1995; offers 83 digital channels (March 2005); offers broadband access services; CEO TERRY CLOONTZ.

Television Corpn of Singapore (TCS): Caldecott Broadcast Centre, Andrew Rd, Singapore 299939; tel. 62560401; fax 62538119; e-mail webmaster@mediacorptv.com; internet www.mediacorptv.com; f. 1994; est. following the corporatization of Singapore Broadcasting Corpn; four channels—TCS 5 (English), TCS 8 (Mandarin), Suria (Malay) and Central; teletext service on two channels; also owns TVMobile, Singapore's first digital television channel, and Digital TV; Chair. HO KWON PING; CEO LIM HUP SENG.

Finance

(cap. = capital; res = reserves; dep. = deposits; m. = million; brs = branches; amounts in Singapore dollars)

BANKING

The Singapore monetary system is regulated by the Monetary Authority of Singapore (MAS) and the Ministry of Finance. The MAS performs all the functions of a central bank and also assumed responsibility for the issuing of currency following its merger with the Board of Commissioners of Currency in October 2002. In May 2008 there were 113 commercial banks (six local, 107 foreign) and 44 representative offices in Singapore. Of the foreign banks, 25 had full

SINGAPORE

Directory

licences, 42 had wholesale licences and 40 had 'offshore' banking licences.

Government Financial Institution

Monetary Authority of Singapore (MAS): 10 Shenton Way, MAS Bldg, Singapore 079117; tel. 62255577; fax 62299491; e-mail webmaster@mas.gov.sg; internet www.mas.gov.sg; merged with Board of Commissioners of Currency Oct. 2002; cap. 100m., res 17,463m., dep. 8,441m. (March 2006); Chair. GOH CHOK TONG; Man. Dir HENG SWEE KEAT.

Domestic Full Commercial Banks

Bank of Singapore Ltd: 18 Church St, 01-00 OCBC Centre South, Singapore 049479; tel. 65863200; fax 64383718; e-mail clientservice@finatiq.com; internet www.finatiq.com; f. 1954; subsidiary of Oversea-Chinese Banking Corpn Ltd; Chair. DAVID PHILBRICK CONNER; CEO TAN NGIAP JOO.

DBS Bank (Development Bank of Singapore Ltd): 6 Shenton Way, DBS Bldg, Tower One, Singapore 068809; tel. 68788888; fax 64451267; e-mail dbs@dbs.com; internet www.dbs.com/sg; f. 1968; 29% govt-owned; merged with Post Office Savings Bank in 1998; cap. 12,096m., res 7,110m., dep. 121,662m. (Dec. 2006); Chair. S. DHANABALAN; Vice-Chair. and CEO JACKSON TAI; 107 local brs, 9 overseas brs.

Far Eastern Bank Ltd: 156 Cecil St, 01-00 FEB Bldg, Singapore 069544; tel. 62219055; fax 62242263; internet www.uobgroup.com; f. 1959; subsidiary of United Overseas Bank Ltd; cap. 100m., res 69.8m., dep. 645.7m. (Dec. 2006); Chair. and CEO WEE CHO YAW; Pres. WEE EE CHEONG; 3 brs.

Oversea-Chinese Banking Corpn (OCBC) Ltd: 65 Chulia St, 08-00 OCBC Centre, Singapore 049513; tel. 65357222; fax 65337955; e-mail info@ocbc.com.sg; internet www.ocbc.com.sg; f. 1932; merged with Keppel TatLee Bank Ltd in Aug. 2001; cap. 5,480.9m., res 7,923.3m., dep. 89,639.5m. (Dec. 2006); Chair. Dr CHEONG CHOONG KONG; CEO DAVID PHILBRICK CONNER; 63 local brs, 52 overseas brs.

United Overseas Bank Ltd: 80 Raffles Place, UOB Plaza, Singapore 048624; tel. 65394439; fax 65342334; internet www.uobgroup .com; f. 1935; merged with Overseas Union Bank Ltd in Jan. 2002 and Industrial and Commercial Bank Ltd in Aug. 2002; cap. 2,247.3m., res 8,001.3m., dep. 110,210.6m. (Dec. 2006); Chair. and CEO WEE CHO YAW; Pres. WEE EE CHEONG; 61 local brs, 21 overseas brs.

Foreign Banks

Full Commercial Banks

ABN AMRO Asia Merchant Bank (Singapore) Ltd (Netherlands): 63 Chulia St, Singapore 049514; tel. 62318888; fax 65323108; Chair. DAVID WONG SEE HONG; Man. Dir ROBERT R. DAVIS.

American Express Bank Ltd (USA): 16 Collyer Quay, Hitachi Tower, Singapore 049318; tel. 65384833; fax 65343022; Sr Country Exec. S. LACHLAN HOUGH.

Bangkok Bank Public Co Ltd (Thailand): 180 Cecil St, Bangkok Bank Bldg, Singapore 069546; tel. 62219400; fax 62255852; e-mail torpong.cha@bbl.co.th; Sr Vice-Pres. and Gen. Man. TORPHONG CHARUNGCHAREONVEJI.

Bank of America NA (USA): 9 Raffles Place, 18-00 Republic Plaza Tower 1, Singapore 048619; tel. 62393888; fax 62393068; CEO ALAN KOH; Man. Dir GOETZ EGGELHOEFER.

Bank of China (People's Republic of China): 4 Battery Rd, Bank of China Bldg, Singapore 049908; tel. 65352411; fax 65343401; Gen. Man. ZHU HUA.

Bank of East Asia Ltd (Hong Kong): 137 Market St, Bank of East Asia Bldg, Singapore 048943; tel. 62241334; fax 62251805; e-mail info@hkbea.com.sg; Gen. Man. KHOO KEE CHEOK.

Bank of India (India): 01-01 to 03-01, Hong Leong Centre, 138 Robinson Rd, Singapore 068906; tel. 62220011; fax 62254407; Chief Exec. VIJAY MEHTA; Gen. Man. B. RAMASUBRAMANIAM.

PT Bank Negara Indonesia (Persero) Tbk (Indonesia): 158 Cecil St, 01-00 to 04-00 Dapenso Bldg, Singapore 069545; tel. 62257755; fax 62254757; Gen. Man. MUHAMMAD YAZEED.

Bank of Tokyo-Mitsubishi UFJ Ltd (Japan): 9 Raffles Place, 01-01 Republic Plaza, Singapore 048619; tel. 65383388; fax 65388083; Gen. Man. HAKOTO NAKAGAWA; Dep. Gen. Man. HIDEMITSU OTSUKA.

BNP Paribas (France): 20 Collyer Quay, 18-01 Tung Centre, Singapore 049319; tel. 62101288; fax 62243459; internet www .bnpparibas.com.sg; Regional Man. JEAN-PIERRE BERNARD.

Calyon (France): 168 Robinson Rd, 22-01, Capital Tower, Singapore 068912; tel. 65354988; fax 65322422; internet www.calyon.com; formed through merger of Crédit Agricole Indosuez and Crédit Lyonnais.

Citibank NA (USA): Capital Square, 23 Church St, 01-01, Singapore 049481; tel. 62255225; fax 6325880; internet www.citibank.com.sg; Country Corporate Officer SANJIV MISRA.

HL Bank (Malaysia): 20 Collyer Quay, 01-02 and 02-02 Tung Centre, Singapore 049319; tel. 65352466; fax 65339340; Country Head GAN HUI TIN.

Hongkong and Shanghai Banking Corpn Ltd (Hong Kong): 01-00 HSBC Bldg, 21 Collyer Quay, Singapore 049320; tel. 65305000; fax 62214676; e-mail direct@hsbc.com.sg; internet www.hsbc.com .sg; CEO (Singapore) PAUL LAWRENCE.

Indian Bank (India): 3 Raffles Place, Bharat Bldg, Singapore 048617; tel. 65343511; fax 65331651; e-mail ceibsing@mbox3 .singnet.com.sg; Chief Exec. V. SRINIVASAN.

Indian Overseas Bank (India): 94 Serangoon Rd, Singapore 217999; tel. 62941385; fax 62970701; e-mail iobrem@iob.com.sg; Chief Exec. KONIDALA PERUMAL MUNIRATHNAM.

JP Morgan Chase Bank (USA): 168 Robinson Rd, 15th Floor, 14-01 Capital Tower, Singapore 068912; tel. 68822888; fax 68821756; Sr Country Officer RAYMOND CHANG.

Maybank (Malaysia): Maybank Tower, 2 Battery Rd 01-00, Singapore 049907; tel. 65507000; fax 65333071; e-mail cs@maybank.com .sg; internet www.maybank2u.com.sg; Country Head POLLIE SIM; 22 brs.

RHB Bank Bhd (Malaysia): 5th Floor, 90 Cecil St 05-00, Singapore 069531; tel. 62202736; fax 62216646; internet www.rhbbank.com .my/cbob/singapore.shtm; Country Head ANTHONY YEO.

Southern Bank Bhd (Malaysia): 39 Robinson Rd, 01-02 Robinson Point, Singapore 068911; tel. 65321318; fax 65355366; Dir YEAP LAM YANG.

Standard Chartered Bank (UK): 6 Battery Rd, Singapore 049909; tel. 62258888; fax 67893756; internet www.standardchartered.com .sg; Group Chair. BRYAN SANDERSON; Chief Exec. (Singapore) EULEEN GOH.

Sumitomo Mitsui Banking Corpn (Japan): 3 Temasek Ave, 06-01 Centennial Tower, Singapore 039190; tel. 68820001; fax 68870330; Gen. Man. MASAMI TASHIRO.

UCO Bank (India): 3 Raffles Place, 01-01 Bharat Bldg, Singapore 048617; tel. 65325944; fax 65325044; e-mail general@ucobank.com .sg; Chief Exec. P. K. TAGORE.

Wholesale Banks

Australia and New Zealand Banking Group Ltd (Australia): 10 Collyer Quay, 17-01/07 Ocean Bldg, Singapore 049315; tel. 65358355; fax 65396111; Gen. Man. BILL FOO.

Bank of Nova Scotia (Canada): 10 Collyer Quay, 15-01/09 Ocean Bldg, Singapore 049315; tel. 65358688; fax 65363325; Country Head, Vice-Pres. and Man. SEONG KOON WAH SUN.

Barclays Bank PLC (UK): 23 Church St, 13-08 Capital Sq., Singapore 049481; tel. 63953000; fax 63953139; Regional Head JAMES LOH; Country Man. QUEK SUAN KIAT.

Bayerische Hypo- und Vereinsbank AG (Germany): 30 Cecil St, 26-01 Prudential Tower, Singapore 049712; tel. 64133688; fax 65368591; Gen. Man. RICHARD LEE.

Bayerische Landesbank Girozentrale (Germany): 300 Beach Rd, 37-01 The Concourse, Singapore 199555; tel. 62933822; fax 62932151; e-mail sgblb@blb.de; Gen. Man. and Sr Vice-Pres. MANFRED WOLF; Exec. Vice-Pres. HEINZ HOFFMANN.

BNP Paribas Private Bank (France): 20 Collyer Quay, 18-01 Tung Centre, Singapore 049319; tel. 62101037; fax 62103671; internet www.bnpparibas.com.sg; CEO SERGE FORTI.

Commerzbank AG (Germany): 8 Shenton Way, 41-01 Temasek Tower, Singapore 068811; tel. 63110000; fax 62253943; Gen. Man. MICHAEL OLIVER.

Crédit Lyonnais (France): 3 Temasek Ave, 11-01 Centennial Tower, Singapore 039190; tel. 63336331; fax 63336332; Gen. Man. PIERRE EYMERY.

Crédit Suisse (Switzerland): 1 Raffles Link, 05-02, Singapore 039393; tel. 62126000; fax 62126200; e-mail ask.us@credit-suisse .com; internet www.cspb.com.sg; Br. Man. DIDIER VON DAENIKEN.

Crédit Suisse First Boston (Switzerland): 1 Raffles Link, 03/04-01 South Lobby, Singapore 039393; tel. 62122000; fax 62123100; Br. Man. ERIC M. VARVEL.

Deutsche Bank AG (Germany): 6 Shenton Way, 15-08 DBS Bldg, Tower Two, Singapore 068809; tel. 64238001; fax 62259442; Gen. Man. RONNY TAN CHONG TEE.

Dresdner Bank AG (Germany): 20 Collyer Quay, 22-00 Tung Centre, Singapore 049319; tel. 62228080; fax 62244008; Man. Dirs ANDREAS RUSCHKOWSKI, RAYMOND B. T. KOH, PIERS WILLIS; CEO BAUDOUIN GROONENBERGHS.

SINGAPORE

First Commercial Bank (Taiwan): 76 Shenton Way, 01-02 ONG Bldg, Singapore 079119; tel. 62215755; fax 62251905; e-mail fcbsin@singnet.com.sg; Gen. Man. TSENG CHI-LUNG.

Fortis Bank SA/NV (Belgium/Netherlands): 63 Market St, 21-01, Singapore 048942; tel. 65394988; fax 65394933; Gen. Man. PETER FOO.

Habib Bank Ltd (Pakistan): 3 Phillip St, 01-03 Commerce Pt, Singapore 048693; tel. 64380055; fax 64380644; e-mail gmhbl@singnet.com.sg; Regional Gen. Man. ASHRAF MAHMOOD WATHRA.

HSBC Republic Bank (Suisse) SA (Switzerland): 21 Collyer Quay, 21-01 HSBC Bldg, Singapore 049320; tel. 62248080; fax 62237146; CEO KENNETH SIT YIU SUN.

Industrial and Commercial Bank of China (People's Republic of China): 6 Raffles Quay, 12-01 John Hancock Tower, Singapore 048580; tel. 65381066; fax 65381370; e-mail icbcsg@icbc.com.sg; Chair. and Pres. JIANG JIANQING.

ING Bank NV (Netherlands): 9 Raffles Place, 19-02 Republic Plaza, Singapore 048619; tel. 65353688; fax 65338329; Country Head J. KESTEMONT.

Intesa Sanpaolo SpA (Italy): 6 Temasek Blvd, 42/04-05 Suntec Tower Four, Singapore 038986; tel. 63338270; fax 63338252; e-mail singapore.sg@intesasanpaolo.com; internet www.intesasanpaolo .com; fmrly San Paolo IMI SpA; Gen. Man. GIOVANNI FIORENDI.

KBC Bank NV (Belgium): 30 Cecil St, 12-01/08 Prudential Tower, Singapore 049712; tel. 63952828; fax 65342929; Gen. Man. THIERRY MEZERET.

Korea Exchange Bank (Republic of Korea): 30 Cecil St, 24-03/08 Prudential Tower, Singapore 049712; tel. 65361633; fax 65382522; e-mail kebspore@singnet.com.sg; Gen. Man. HO SUN YUN.

Landesbank Baden-Württemberg (Germany): 25 International Business Park, 01-72 German Centre, Singapore 609916; tel. 65627722; fax 65627729; Man. Dr WOLFHART AUER VAN HERRENKIRCHEN.

Mega International Commercial Bank Co Ltd (Taiwan): 80 Raffles Place, 23-20 UOB Plaza II, Singapore 048624; tel. 65366311; fax 65360680; Gen. Man. HSIANG YEN-PING.

Mizuho Corporate Bank Ltd (Japan): 168 Robinson Rd, 13-00 Capital Tower, Singapore 068912; tel. 64230330; fax 64230012; Gen. Man. TADAO OGOSHI.

Moscow Narodny Bank Ltd (UK): 50 Robinson Rd, MNB Bldg, Singapore 068882; tel. 62209422; fax 62250140; Man. Dir EVGENY MIKHAILOVICH GREVTSEV.

National Australia Bank Ltd (Australia): 5 Temasek Blvd, 15-01 Suntec City Tower Five, Singapore 038985; tel. 63380038; fax 63380039; Gen. Man. FRANK OLSSON.

National Bank of Kuwait SAK (Kuwait): 9 Raffles Place, 51-01/02 Republic Plaza, Singapore 048619; tel. 62225348; fax 62245438; Gen. Man. RICHARD MCKEGNEY.

Norddeutsche Landesbank Girozentrale (Germany): 6 Shenton Way, 16-08 DBS Bldg Tower Two, Singapore 068809; tel. 63231223; fax 63230223; e-mail nordlb.singapore@nordlb.com; Gen. Man. and Regional Head Asia/Pacific HEINZ WERNER FRINGS.

Northern Trust Company (USA): 1 George St, 12-06, Singapore 049145; tel. 64376666; fax 64376609; e-mail LA16@ntrs.com; internet www.northerntrust.com; f. 1889; Sr Vice-Pres. LAWRENCE AU.

Rabobank International (Netherlands): 77 Robinson Rd, 09-00 SIA Bldg, Singapore 068896; tel. 65363363; fax 65363236; Regional Man. (Asia) ROB VAN ZADELHOFF.

Royal Bank of Scotland PLC (UK): 50 Raffles Place, 08-00 Singapore Land Tower, Singapore 048623; tel. 64168600; fax 62259827; Gen. Man. ALAN ROY GOODYEAR.

Société Générale (France): 80 Robinson Rd, 25-00, Singapore 068898; tel. 62227122; fax 62252609; Chief Country Officer ERIC WORMSER.

State Street Bank and Trust Co (USA): 8 Shenton Way, 33-03 Temasek Tower, Singapore 068811; tel. 63299600; fax 62259377; Br. Man. LEE YOW FEE.

UBS AG (Switzerland): 5 Temasek Blvd, 18-00 Suntec City Tower, Singapore 038985; tel. 64318000; fax 64318188; e-mail rolf-w .gerber@wdr.com; Man. Dir and Head of Br. (Singapore) BRAD ORGILL.

UniCredito Italiano SpA (Italy): 80 Raffles Place, 51-01 UOB Plaza 1, Singapore 048624; tel. 62325728; fax 65344300; e-mail singaporebranch@gruppocredit.it; Gen. Man. MAURIZIO BRENTEGANI.

WestLB AG (Germany): 3 Temasek Ave, 33-00 Centennial Tower, Singapore 039190; tel. 63332388; fax 63332399; Gen. Man. TEO EE-NGOH.

Offshore Banks

ABSA Bank Ltd (South Africa): 9 Temasek Blvd, 40-01 Suntec Tower Two, Singapore 038989; tel. 63331033; fax 63331066; Gen. Man. DAVID MEADOWS.

Agricultural Bank of China (People's Republic of China): 80 Raffles Place, 27-20 UOB Plaza 2, Singapore 048624; tel. 65355255; fax 65387960; e-mail aboc@abchina.com.sg; Gen. Man. SUN MEIYU.

Arab Bank PLC (Jordan): 80 Raffles Place, 32-20 UOB Plaza 2, Singapore 048624; tel. 65330055; fax 65322150; e-mail abplc@pacific .net.com.sg; Exec. Vice-Pres. and Area Exec. Asia Pacific KIM EUN-YOUNG.

Banca Monte dei Paschi di Siena SpA (Italy): 10 Collyer Quay, 13-01 Ocean Bldg, Singapore 0104; tel. 65352533; fax 65327996; Gen. Man. GIUSEPPE DE GIOSA.

Banca di Roma (Italy): 9 Raffles Place, 20-20 Republic Plaza II, Singapore 048619; tel. 64387509; fax 65352267; e-mail bdrsi@singnet.com.sg; Gen. Man. MARIO FATTORUSSO.

Bank of Communications (People's Republic of China): 50 Raffles Place, 26-04 Singapore Land Tower, Singapore 048623; tel. 65320335; fax 65320339; Gen. Man. NIU KE RONG.

PT Bank Mandiri (Persero) (Indonesia): 16 Collyer Quay, 28-00 Hitachi Tower, Singapore 049318; tel. 65320200; fax 65320206; Gen. Man. MUHADJIR SANGIDU.

Bank of New York (USA): 1 Temasek Ave, 02-01 Millenia Tower, Singapore 039192; tel. 64320222; fax 63374302; in Dec. 2006 the Bank of New York announced the preliminary approval of plans to merge with Mellon Financial Corpn, to form the Bank of New York Mellon Corpn; merger expected to be completed by mid-2007; Sr Vice-Pres. and Man. Dir JAI ARYA.

Bank of New Zealand (New Zealand): 5 Temasek Blvd, 15-01 Suntec City Tower, Singapore 038985; tel. 63322990; fax 63322991; Gen. Man. VIVIEN KOH.

Bank of Taiwan (Taiwan): 80 Raffles Place, 28-20 UOB Plaza 2, Singapore 048624; tel. 65365536; fax 65368203; Gen. Man. CHIOU YE-CHIN.

Bumiputra Commerce Bank Bhd (Malaysia): 7 Temasek Blvd, 37-01/02/03 Suntec Tower One, Singapore 038987; tel. 63375115; fax 63371335; e-mail bpsp3700@pacific.net.sg; Gen. Man. DHANA SEGARAM.

Canadian Imperial Bank of Commerce (Canada): 16 Collyer Quay, 04-02 Hitachi Tower, Singapore 049318; tel. 65352323; fax 65357565; Br. Man. NORMAN SIM CHEE BENG.

Chang Hwa Commercial Bank Ltd (China): 1 Finlayson Green, 08-00, Singapore 049246; tel. 65320820; fax 65320374; Gen. Man. YANG JIH-CHENG.

China Construction Bank Corpn (People's Republic of China): 9 Raffles Place, 33-01/02 Republic Plaza, Singapore 048619; tel. 65358133; fax 65356533; e-mail enquiry@ccb.com.sg; internet www.ccb.com.sg; Gen. Man. KONG YONG XIN.

Commonwealth Bank of Australia (Australia): 22-04 Singapore Land Tower, 50 Raffles Place, Singapore 048623; tel. 62243877; fax 62245812; Gen. Man. ROBERT LEWIS BUCHAN.

Crédit Industriel et Commercial (France): 63 Market St, 15-01, Singapore 048942; tel. 65366008; fax 65367008; internet www.cic .com.sg; Gen. Man. JEAN-LUC ANGLADA.

Crédit Lyonnais (Suisse) SA (Switzerland): 3 Temasek Ave 11-01, Centennial Tower, Singapore 039190; tel. 68320900; fax 63338590; e-mail singaporebranch@creditlyonnais.ch; Man. Dir ANTOINE CANDIOTTI.

Deutsche Zentral Genossenschaftsbank (DZ Bank AG) (Germany): 50 Raffles Place, 40-01 Singapore Land Tower, Singapore 048623; tel. 64380082; fax 62230082; Gen. Man. KLAUS GERHARD BORIG.

Dexia Banque Internationale à Luxembourg (Luxembourg): 9 Raffles Place, 42-01 Republic Plaza, Singapore 048619; tel. 62227622; fax 65360201; Gen. Man. ALEXANDRE JOSSET.

DnB NOR (Norway): 8 Shenton Way, 48-02 Temasek Tower, Singapore 068811; tel. 62206144; e-mail dnb.singapore@dnb.no; internet www.dnbnor.no.

Hana Bank (Republic of Korea): 8 Cross St, 23-06 PWC Bldg, Singapore 048424; tel. 64384100; fax 64384200; Gen. Man. CHO YOUNG-SEOK.

Hang Seng Bank Ltd (Hong Kong): 21 Collyer Quay, 14-01 HSBC Bldg, Singapore 049320; tel. 65363118; fax 65363148; e-mail sgp@hangseng.com; Country Man. ANTHONY KAM PING LEUNG.

HSH Nordbank AG (Germany): 3 Temasek Ave, 32-03 Centennial Tower, Singapore 039190; tel. 65509000; fax 65509003; e-mail info@hsh-nordbank.com.sg; Gen. Man. and Regional Head KLAUS HEINER BORITZKA.

SINGAPORE

Directory

Hua Nan Commercial Bank Ltd (Taiwan): 80 Robinson Rd, 14-03, Singapore 068898; tel. 63242566; fax 63242155; Gen. Man. HUANG YUN-LUNG.

ICICI Bank Ltd (India): 9 Raffles Place, 50-01 Republic Plaza, Singapore 048619; tel. 67239288; fax 67239268; e-mail globalinvest@ icicibank.com; internet www.icicibank.com.sg; Chief. Exec. SUVEK NAMBIAR.

Korea Development Bank (Republic of Korea): 8 Shenton Way, 07-01 Temasek Tower, Singapore 068811; tel. 62248188; fax 62256540; Gen. Man. KIM BYOUNG SOO.

Krung Thai Bank Public Co Ltd (Thailand): 65 Chulia St, 32-05/08 OCBC Centre, Singapore 049513; tel. 65336691; fax 65330930; e-mail br.singapore@ktb.co.th; Gen. Man. PUMIN LEELAYOOVA.

Land Bank of Taiwan: UOB Plaza 1, 34-01 Raffles Place, Singapore 048624; tel. 63494555; fax 63494545; Gen. Man. WILSON W. B. LIN.

Lloyds TSB Bank PLC (UK): 1 Temasek Ave 18-01, Millenia Tower, Singapore 039192; tel. 65341191; fax 65322493; e-mail mktg@lloydstsb.com.sg; internet www.lloydstsb.com.sg; Country Head WALLACE WONG.

Mitsubishi Trust and Banking Corpn (Japan): 50 Raffles Place, 42-01/06 Singapore Land Tower, Singapore 048623; tel. 62259155; fax 62241857; Gen. Man. MIKIO KOBAYASHI.

Natexis Banques Populaires (France): 50 Raffles Place, 41-01, Singapore Land Tower, Singapore 048623; tel. 62241455; fax 62248651; Gen. Man. PHILIPPE PETITGAS.

Nedcor Bank Ltd (South Africa): 30 Cecil St, 10-05 Prudential Tower, Singapore 049712; tel. 64169438; fax 64388350; e-mail nedsing@nedcor.com; Gen. Man. BRIAN SHEGAR.

Nordea Bank Finland Plc (Finland): 3 Anson Rd, 22–01 Springleaf Tower, Singapore 079909; tel. 63176500; fax 63275616; e-mail singapore@nordea.com; Gen. Man. THOR ERLING KYLSTAD.

Norinchukin Bank (Japan): 80 Raffles Place, 53-01 UOB Plaza 1, Singapore 048624; tel. 65351011; fax 65352883; Gen. Man. AKITA KURIHARA.

Philippine National Bank (Philippines): 96 Somerset Rd, 04-01/04 UOL Bldg, Singapore 238183; tel. 67374646; fax 67374224; e-mail singapore@pnb.com.ph; Vice-Pres. and Gen. Man. RODELO G. FRANCO.

Raiffeisen Zentralbank Österreich Aktiengesellschaft (Austria): 50 Raffles Place, 45-01 Singapore Land Tower, Singapore 048623; tel. 62259578; fax 62253973; Gen. Man. RAINER SILHAVY.

Royal Bank of Canada (Canada): 20 Raffles Place, 27-03/08 Ocean Towers, Singapore 048620; tel. 65369206; fax 65322804; Gen. Man. TREVOR DAVID WYNN.

Shinhan Bank (Republic of Korea): 50 Raffles Place, 04-02/03 Singapore Land Tower, Singapore 048623; tel. 65361144; fax 65331244; merged with Chohun Bank 2006; Gen. Man. CHOI HEUNG MIN.

Siam Commercial Bank Public Company Ltd (Thailand): 16 Collyer Quay, 25-01 Hitachi Tower, Singapore 049318; tel. 65364338; fax 65364728; Gen. Man. BANDIT ROJANAVONGSE.

Skandinaviska Enskilda Banken AB Publ (Sweden): 50 Raffles Place, 36-01 Singapore Land Tower, Singapore 048623; tel. 62235644; fax 62253047; Gen. Man. SVEN BJÖRKMAN.

State Bank of India (India): 6 Shenton Way, 22-08 DBS Bldg Tower Two, Singapore 068809; tel. 62222033; fax 62253348; e-mail sbinsgsg@pacific.net.sg; CEO PADMA RAMASUBBAN.

Sumitomo Trust & Banking Co Ltd (Japan): 8 Shenton Way, 45-01 Temasek Tower, Singapore 068811; tel. 62249055; fax 62242873; Gen. Man. MASAYUKI IMANAKA.

Svenska Handelsbanken AB (publ) (Sweden): 65 Chulia St, 21-01/04 OCBC Centre, Singapore 049513; tel. 65323800; fax 65344909; Gen. Man. JAN BIRGER DJERF.

Toronto-Dominion (South East Asia) Ltd (Canada): 15-02 Millenia Tower, 1 Temasek Ave, Singapore 039192; tel. 64346000; fax 63369500; Br. Dir AKHILESHWAR LAMBA.

Union de Banques Arabes et Françaises (UBAF) (France): 6 Temasek Blvd, 25-04-05 Suntec Tower Four, Singapore 038986; tel. 63336188; fax 63336789; e-mail ubafsg@singnet.com.sg; Gen. Man. ERIC REINHART.

Westpac Banking Corpn (Australia): 77 Robinson Rd, 19-00 SIA Bldg, Singapore 068896; tel. 65309898; fax 65326781; e-mail yhlee@ westpac.wm.au; Gen. Man. CHRISTOPHER DAVID RAND.

Woori Bank (Republic of Korea): 5 Shenton Way, 17-03 UIC Bldg, Singapore 068808; tel. 62235855; fax 62259530; e-mail combksp@ singnet.com.sg; Gen. Man. PARK DONG YOUNG.

Bankers' Association

The Association of Banks in Singapore: 10 Shenton Way, 12-08 MAS Bldg, Singapore 079117; tel. 62244300; fax 62241785; e-mail banks@abs.org.sg; internet www.abs.org.sg; f. 1973; Chair. DAVID P. CONNOR.

STOCK EXCHANGE

Singapore Exchange Limited (SGX): 2 Shenton Way, 19-00 SGX Centre One, Singapore 068804; tel. 62368888; fax 65356994; e-mail webmaster@sgx.com; internet www.sgx.com; f. 1999; demutualized and integrated securities and derivatives exchange; Chair. J. Y. PILLAY; CEO HSIEH FU HUA; Chief Finance Officer LINUS KOH KIA MENG.

INSURANCE

The insurance industry is supervised by the Monetary Authority of Singapore (see Banking). In May 2008 there were 147 insurance companies, comprising 59 direct insurers (12 life insurance, 42 general insurance, five composite insurers), 25 professional re-insurers (three life reinsurers, 13 general reinsurers, nine composite reinsurers), five authorized reinsurers (one life reinsurer, three general reinsurers, one composite reinsurer) and 60 captive insurers.

Domestic Companies

Life Insurance

Aviva Ltd: 4 Shenton Way, 01-01, SGX Centre 2, Singapore 068807; tel. 68277988; fax 68277900; internet www.aviva-singapore.com.sg; f. 2002; Prin. Officer KEITH PERKINS.

Axa Life Insurance Singapore Pte Ltd: 143 Cecil St, 03-01/10 GB Bldg, Singapore 069542; tel. 68805500; fax 68805501; e-mail comsvc@axa-life.com.sg; internet www.axa-life.com.sg; Prin. Officer RICHARD MARC SHERMON.

China Life Insurance Co Ltd: 105 Cecil St, 18-00 and 19-00 The Octagon, Singapore 069534; tel. 62222366; fax 62221033; Prin. Officer SHEN NAN NING.

Friends Provident International Ltd (Singapore): 63 Market St, 06-05, Singapore 048942; tel. 63274019; fax 63274020; e-mail singapore.enquiries@fpiom.com; Prin. Officer CHRISTOPHER GAVIN GILL.

International Medical Insurers Pte Ltd: 585 North Bridge Rd, 13-00, Raffles Hospital, Singapore 188770; tel. 63111331; fax 63112396; e-mail enquiries@imi.sg; internet www.imi.sg; f. 1996; Prin. Officer Dr YII HEE SENG.

Manulife (Singapore) Pte Ltd: 491B River Valley Rd, 07-00 Valley Pt, Singapore 248373; tel. 67371221; fax 68362374; e-mail service@ manulife.com; internet www.manulife.com.sg; acquired John Hancock Life Assurance Co Ltd in Dec. 2004; Pres. and CEO DARREN THOMSON.

TM Asia Life Singapore Ltd: 80 Anson Rd, 14-00 Fuji Xerox Towers, Singapore 079907; tel. 62243181; fax 62239120; e-mail asialife@asialife.com.sg; internet www.tmasialife.com; f. 1948; fmrly The Asia Life Assurance Society Ltd; Man. Dir ARTHUR LEE KING CHI.

Transamerica Life (Singapore) Ltd: 1 Finlayson Green, 13-00, Singapore 049246; tel. 62120620; fax 62120621; internet www .transamerica.com.sg; wholly owned subsidiary of Transamerica Occidental Life Insurance Co; Prin. Officer LAURENCE WONG YUEN TIN.

Transamerica Occidental Life Insurance Co: 9 Raffles Place, 53-02, Republic Plaza, Singapore 048619; tel. 62362366; fax 62362123; internet www.transamerica.com.sg; Prin. Officer LAURENCE WONG YUEN TIN.

UOB Life Assurance Ltd: 156 Cecil St, 10-01 Far Eastern Bank Bldg, Singapore 069544; tel. 62278477; fax 62243012; e-mail uoblife@uobgroup.com; internet www.uoblife.com.sg; Man. Dir RAYMOND KWOK CHONG SEE.

Zurich International Life (Singapore) Ltd: 50 Raffles Place, 23-02, Singapore Land Tower, Singapore 048623; tel. 68766750; fax 68766751; Regional Dir CARLOS SABUGUEIRO.

General Insurance

Allianz Insurance Company of Singapore Pte Ltd: 3 Temasek Ave, 09-01 Centennial Tower, Singapore 039190; tel. 62972529; fax 62971956; e-mail askme@allianz.com.sg; internet www.allianz.com .sg; formed by merger between Allianz Insurance (Singapore) Pte Ltd and AGF Insurance (Singapore) Pte Ltd; Man. Dir ROWAN D'ARCY.

Asia Insurance Co Ltd: 2 Finlayson Green, 03-00 Asia Insurance Bldg, Singapore 049247; tel. 62243181; fax 62214355; e-mail asiains@asiainsurance.com.sg; internet www.asiainsurance.com.sg; f. 1923; Prin. Officer and Exec. Dir LARRY CHAN; Gen. Man. TAN KAH HO.

SINGAPORE

Asian Securitization and Infrastructure Assurance (Pte) Ltd: 9 Temasek Blvd, 38-01 Suntec Tower 2, Singapore 038989; tel. 63342555; fax 63342777; e-mail general@asialtd.com; Dir ELEANOR L. LIPSEY.

Aviva General Insurance Ltd: 4 Shenton Way, 21-01, SGX Centre 2, Singapore 068807; tel. 68277888; fax 68277800; e-mail service@aviva-gi.com; internet www.aviva-gi.com.sg; f.; subsidiary of Mitsui Sumitomo Insurance Co Ltd following acquisition in 2004.

Axa Insurance Singapore Pte Ltd: 143 Cecil St, 01-01 GB Bldg, Singapore 069542; tel. 68804741; fax 68804740; e-mail customer.service@axa.com.sg; internet www.axa.com.sg; CEO BERNARD MARSEILLE.

Cosmic Insurance Corpn Ltd: 410 North Bridge Rd, 04-01 Cosmic Insurance Bldg, Singapore 188726; tel. 63387633; fax 63397805; e-mail query@cosmic.com.sg; internet www.cosmic.com.sg; f. 1971; Gen. Man. SWEE LEE CHUN.

ECICS-COFACE Guarantee Co (Singapore) Ltd: 7 Temasek Blvd, 10-03 Suntec City Tower 1, Singapore 038987; tel. 63374779; fax 63389267; e-mail ecics@ecics.com.sg; internet www.ecics.com.sg; Chair. KWAH THIAM HOCK; Asst Vice-Pres. KIM LIN MIN.

First Capital Insurance Ltd: 6 Raffles Quay 21-00, Singapore 048580; tel. 62222311; fax 62223547; e-mail enquiry@first-insurance.com.sg; internet www.first-insurance.com.sg; CEO RAMASWAMY ATHAPPAN.

India International Insurance Pte Ltd: 64 Cecil St, 04-00/05-00 IOB Bldg, Singapore 049711; tel. 63476100; fax 62244174; e-mail insure@iii.com.sg; internet www.iii.com.sg; f. 1987; all non-life insurance; CEO J. K. GUPTA.

Kemper International Insurance Co (Pte) Ltd: 3 Shenton Way, 22-09 Shenton House, Singapore 068805; tel. 68369120; fax 68369121; e-mail vchia@kemper.com.sg; internet www.kemper.com.sg; Gen. Man. VIOLET CHIA.

Liberty Insurance Pte Ltd: 51 Club St, 03-00 Singapore 069428; tel. 62218611; fax 62263360; e-mail feedback@libertycitystate.com.sg; internet www.libertyinsurance.com.sg; division of Liberty Mutual Group (USA); fmrly Citystate Insurance Pte Ltd; Man. Dir A. K. CHER.

Mitsui Sumitomo Insurance (Singapore) Pte Ltd: 16 Raffles Quay, 24-01 Hong Leong Bldg, Singapore 048581; tel. 62209644; fax 62256371; internet www.ms-ins.com.sg; fmrly Mitsui Marine and Fire Insurance (Asia) Private Ltd; merged with The Sumitomo Marine and Fire Insurance Co Ltd and name changed as above in 2001; Prin. Officer TORU SATO.

Royal & Sun Alliance Insurance (Singapore) Ltd: 77 Robinson Rd, 17-00 SIA Bldg, Singapore 068896; tel. 64230888; fax 64230798; e-mail customer.service@sg.royalsun.com; internet www.royalsunalliance.com.sg; Man. Dir and CEO EDMUND LIM.

SHC Capital Ltd: 302 Orchard Rd, 09-01 Tong Bldg, Singapore 238862; tel. 68299199; fax 68299249; e-mail shccapital@shcsb.com.sg; internet www.shccapital.com.sg; f. 1956; fmrly The Nanyang Insurance Co Ltd; name changed as above following takeover in June 2004; Dir and Prin. Officer PETER KOH TIEN HOE.

Singapore Aviation and General Insurance Co (Pte) Ltd: 25 Airline Rd, 06-A Airline House, Singapore 819829; tel. 65423333; fax 65450221; f. 1976; Man. AMARJIT KAUR SIDHU.

Standard Steamship Owners' Protection and Indemnity Association (Asia) Ltd: 140 Cecil St, 10-02 PIL Bldg, Singapore 069540; tel. 62211060; fax 62211082; e-mail p&i.singapore@ctcplc.comcentral@ctg-ap.com; internet www.standard-club.com; Prin. Officer ROBERT DRUMMOND.

Tenet Insurance Co Ltd: 10 Collyer Quay, 04-01 Ocean Bldg, Singapore 049315; tel. 65326022; fax 65333871; Chair. ONG CHOO ENG.

The Tokio Marine & Fire Insurance Co (Singapore) Pte Ltd: 6 Shenton Way, 23-08 DBS Bldg Tower Two, Singapore 068809; tel. 62216111; fax 62240895; Man. Dir KYOZO HANAJIMA.

United Overseas Insurance Ltd: 156 Cecil St, 09-01 Far Eastern Bank Bldg, Singapore 069544; tel. 62227733; fax 63273870; e-mail contactus@uoi.com.sg; internet www.uoi.com.sg; f. 1971; Man. Dir DAVID CHAN MUN WAI.

Zürich Insurance (Singapore) Pte Ltd: 78 Shenton Way, 06-01, Singapore 079120; tel. 62202466; fax 62255749; Prin. Officer and Man. Dir RONALD CHENG JUE SENG.

Composite Insurance

American International Assurance Co Ltd: 1 Robinson Rd, AIA Tower, Singapore 048542; tel. 62918000; fax 65385802; internet www.aia.com.sg; Prin. Officer MARK O'DELL.

Great Eastern Life Assurance Co Ltd: 1 Pickering St, 13-01 Great Eastern Centre, Singapore 048659; tel. 62482000; fax 65322214; e-mail wecare@lifeisgreat.com.sg; internet www.lifeisgreat.com.sg; f. 1908; Dir and CEO TAN BENG LEE.

HSBC Insurance (Singapore) Pte Ltd: 3 Killiney Rd, 10-01/09, Winsland House 1, Singapore 239519; tel. 62256111; fax 62212188; internet www.insurance.hsbc.com.sg; Prin. Officer JASON DOMINIC SADLER.

NTUC Income Insurance Co-operative Ltd: 75 Bras Basah Rd, NTUC Income Centre, Singapore 189557; tel. 63363322; fax 63381500; e-mail inbox@income.wm.sg; internet www.income.com.sg; CEO TAN KIN LIAN; Gen. Man. ALOYSIUS TEO SENG LEE.

Overseas Assurance Corpn Ltd: 1 Pickering St, 13-01 Great Eastern Centre, Singapore 048659; tel. 62482000; fax 65322214; e-mail general@oac.com.sg; internet www.oac.com.sg; f. 1920; fully-owned subsidiary of Great Eastern Holdings; Chair. MICHAEL WONG PAKSHONG.

Prudential Assurance Co Singapore (Pte) Ltd: 30 Cecil St, 30-01 Prudential Tower, Singapore 049712; tel. 65358988; fax 65354043; e-mail customer.service@prudential.com.sg; internet www.prudential.com.sg; CEO TAN SUEE CHIEH.

Associations

General Insurance Association of Singapore: 112 Robinson Rd, 05-03 HB Robinson, Singapore 068902; tel. 62218788; fax 62272051; e-mail feedback@gia.org.sg; internet www.gia.org.sg; f. 1965; Pres. DEREK TEO; Exec. Dir WU SIONG YEN.

Life Insurance Association, Singapore: 20 Cross St, 02-07/08 China Court, China Sq. Central, Singapore 048422; tel. 64388900; fax 64386989; e-mail lia@lia.org.sg; internet www.lia.org.sg; f. 1967; Pres. MARK O'DELL.

Reinsurance Brokers' Association: 69 Amoy St, Singapore 069888; tel. 63723189; fax 62241091; e-mail secretariat@rbas.org.sg; internet www.rbas.org.sg; f. 1995; Chair. RICHARD AUSTEN.

Singapore Insurance Brokers' Association: 138 Cecil St, 15-00 Cecil Court, Singapore 069538; tel. 62227777; fax 62220022; e-mail siba@stcsamasmgt.com.sg; Pres. ANTHONY LIM; Vice-Pres. DAVID LUM.

Singapore Reinsurers' Association: 85 Amoy St, Singapore 069904; tel. 63247388; fax 62248910; e-mail secretariat@sraweb.org.sg; internet www.sraweb.org.sg; f. 1979; Chair. CHRISTOPHER HO SIOW SOONG.

Trade and Industry

GOVERNMENT AGENCIES

Housing and Development Board: 480 Lorong 6, Toa Payoh, Singapore 310480; tel. 64901111; fax 63972070; e-mail hdbmailbox@hdb.gov.sg; internet www.hdb.gov.sg; f. 1960; public housing authority; Chair. JAMES KOH CHER SIANG.

Singapore Land Authority (SLA): 8 Shenton Way, 26-01 Temasek Tower, Singapore 068811; tel. 63239829; fax 63239937; e-mail SLA_enquiry@sla.gov.sg; internet www.sla.gov.sg; responsible for management and development of state land resources; Chair. GREG SEOW.

Urban Redevelopment Authority (URA): 45 Maxwell Rd, URA Centre, Singapore 069118; tel. 62216666; fax 62275069; e-mail ura_email@ura.gov.sg; internet www.ura.gov.sg; statutory board; responsible for national planning; Chair. BOBBY CHIN; CEO CHEONG-CHUA KOON HEAN.

DEVELOPMENT ORGANIZATIONS

Agency for Science, Technology and Research (A*STAR): 20 Biopolis Way 01-03, Singapore 138668; tel. 68266111; fax 67771711; e-mail astar_contact@a-star.gov.sg; internet www.a-star.gov.sg; f. 1990; fmrly National Science and Technology Board; statutory board; responsible for the development of science and technology; Chair. LIM CHUAN POH; Man. Dir YENA LIM.

Applied Research Corpn (ARC): independent non-profit-making research and consultancy org. aiming to facilitate and enhance the use of technology and expertise from the tertiary institutions to benefit industry, businesses and joint institutions.

Asian Infrastructure Fund (AIF): Singapore; f. 1994; promotes and directs investment into regional projects; Chair. MOEEN QURESHI.

Economic Development Board (EDB): 250 North Bridge Rd, 24-00 Raffles City Tower, Singapore 179101; tel. 68326832; fax 68326565; e-mail webmaster@edb.gov.sg; internet www.edb.gov.sg; f. 1961; statutory body for industrial planning, development and promotion of investments in manufacturing, services and local business; Chair. LIM SIONG GUAN; Man. Dir KO KHENG HWA.

Government of Singapore Investment Corpn Pte Ltd (GIC): 168 Robinson Rd, 37-01 Capital Tower, Singapore 068912; tel.

SINGAPORE

Directory

68898888; fax 68898722; e-mail contactus@gic.com.sg; internet www.gic.com.sg; f. 1981; Exec. Dir Dr TONY TAN KENG YAM.

Infocomm Development Authority of Singapore (IDA): see under Telecommunications.

International Enterprise Singapore: 230 Victoria St, 07-00 Bugis Junction Office Tower, Singapore 188024; tel. 63376628; fax 63376898; e-mail enquiry@iesingapore.gov.sg; internet www.iesingapore.gov.sg; f. 1983; formed to develop and expand international trade; fmrly Trade Development Board; statutory body; Chair. EULEEN GOH; CEO LIT CHEONG CHONG.

Jurong Town Corpn (JTC): The JTC Summit, 8 Jurong Town Hall Rd, Singapore 609434; tel. 65600056; fax 65655301; e-mail askjtc@jtc.gov.sg; internet www.jtc.gov.sg; f. 1968; statutory body responsible for planning, promoting and developing industrial space; Chair. CEDRIC FOO; CEO OW FOONG PHENG.

Standards, Productivity and Innovation Board Singapore (SPRING): 2 Bukit Merah Central, Singapore 159835; tel. 62786666; fax 62786667; e-mail queries@spring.gov.sg; internet www.spring.gov.sg; f. 1996 as Singapore Productivity and Standards Board (PSB), following merger of Singapore Institute of Standards and Industrial Research and the National Productivity Board; name changed as above in 2001; carries out activities in areas including workforce development, training, productivity and innovation promotion, standards development, ISO certification, quality programmes and consultancy, technology application, product and process development, system and process automation services, testing services, patent information, development assistance for small and medium-sized enterprises; Chair. PHILIP YEO; Chief Exec. LOH KHUM YEAN.

CHAMBERS OF COMMERCE

Singapore Business Federation (SBF): 10 Hoe Chiang Rd, 22-01 Keppel Towers, 089315 Singapore; tel. 68276828; fax 68276807; e-mail webmaster@sbf.org.sg; internet www.sbf.org.sg; f. 2002 as result of restructuring of Singapore Federation of Chambers of Commerce and Industry; Chair. SAT PAL KHATTAR; mems include the following:

Singapore Chinese Chamber of Commerce and Industry: 47 Hill St, 09-00 Singapore 179365; tel. 63378381; fax 63390605; e-mail corporate@sccci.org.sg; internet www.sccci.org.sg; f. 1906; promotes trade and industry and economic development of Singapore; Pres. CHUA THIAN POH; Sec.-Gen. LIM SAH SOON.

Singapore Indian Chamber of Commerce and Industry: 101 Cecil St, 23-01/04 Tong Eng Bldg, Singapore 069533; tel. 62222855; fax 62231707; e-mail sicci@sicci.com; internet www.sicci.com; Chair. M. RAJARAM; Exec. Dir PREDEEP KUMAR MENON.

Singapore International Chamber of Commerce: 6 Raffles Quay, 10-01 John Hancock Tower, Singapore 048580; tel. 62241255; fax 62242785; e-mail general@sicc.com; internet www.sicc.com.sg; f. 1837; Chair. LEE TZU YANG.

Singapore Malay Chamber of Commerce: 72A Bussorah St, Singapore 199485; tel. 62979296; fax 63924527; e-mail smcci@smcci.org.sg; internet www.smcci.org.sg; Pres. Dato' MOHAMAD ZAIN ABDULLAH.

Singapore Manufacturers' Federation (SMa): The Enterprise 02-02, 1 Science Centre Rd, Singapore 609077; tel. 68263000; fax 68228828; e-mail hq@smafederation.org.sg; internet www.smafederation.org.sg; f. 1932 as Singapore Manufacturers' Association; renamed Singapore Confederation of Industries in 1996; name changed as above in 2002; Pres. LEW SYN PAU; Sec.-Gen. Dr ROGER LOW.

INDUSTRIAL AND TRADE ASSOCIATIONS

Association of Singapore Marine Industries (ASMI): 20 Science Park Rd, 02-04/05 TeleTech Park, Singapore Science Park II, Singapore 117674; tel. 62704730; fax 62731867; e-mail asmi@pacific.net.sg; internet www.asmi.com; f. 1968; 12 hon. mems, 70 assoc. mems, 51 ord. mems (Oct. 2003); Pres. MICHAEL CHEA; Exec. Dir WINNIE LOW.

Singapore Commodity Exchange (SICOM): 111 North Bridge Rd, 23-04/05 Peninsula Plaza, Singapore 179098; tel. 63385600; fax 63389116; e-mail marketing@sicom.com.sg; internet www.sicom.com.sg; f. 1968 as Rubber Association of Singapore; adopted present name 1994; to regulate, promote, develop and supervise commodity futures trading in Singapore, including the establishment and dissemination of official prices for various grades and types of rubber; provides clearing facilities; endorses certificates of origin and licences for packers, shippers and mfrs; Chair. LIM HOW TECK; Pres. JEFFREY TAN.

EMPLOYERS' ORGANIZATION

Singapore National Employers' Federation: Keppel Towers 22-00, 10 Hoe Chiang Rd, Singapore; tel. 68276827; fax 68276800; e-mail webmaster@snef.org.sg; internet www.sgemployers.com; f. 1948; Pres. STEPHEN LEE CHING YEN; Vice-Pres ALEX CHAN, BOB BENG HAI TAN, LANDIS W. HICKS.

UTILITIES

Electricity and Gas

Singapore Power Ltd: 111 Somerset Rd 10-01, Singapore Power Bldg, Singapore 238164; tel. 68238888; fax 68238188; e-mail corpcomms@singaporepower.com.sg; internet www.singaporepower.com.sg; incorporated in 1995 to take over the piped gas and electricity utility operations of the Public Utilities Board (see Water), which now acts as a regulatory authority for the privately owned cos; 100% owned by government holding company, Temasek Holdings Pte Ltd; subsidiaries include PowerGrid, PowerGas, Power Supply, Singapore Power International, Development Resources, Power Automation, SP E-Services, SP Systems, Singapore District Cooling and SP Telecommunications; Chair. NG KEE CHOE; CEO QUEK POH HUAT.

Water

Public Utilities Board: 40 Scotts Rd, 22-01, Singapore 228231; tel. 62358888; fax 67313020; e-mail pub_pr@pub.gov.sg; internet www.pub.gov.sg; statutory board responsible for water supply; manages Singapore's water system to optimize use of water resources, develops additional water sources; Chair. TAN GEE PAW.

TRADE UNIONS

At the end of 2003 there were 68 employees' trade unions and associations, with 417,166 members, and three employer unions, with 2,052 members.

National Trades Union Congress (NTUC): NTUC Centre, 1 Marina Blvd B1-01, Singapore 018989; tel. 62138008; fax 63273740; e-mail bizcentre@ntuc.org.sg; internet www.ntuc.org.sg; f. 1961; 62 affiliated unions, 7 affiliated associates and approx. 500,000 mems (2008); Pres. JOHN DE PAYVA; Sec.-Gen. LIM SWEE SAY.

Transport

RAILWAYS

In 1993 there was 26 km of 1-m gauge railway, linked with the Malaysian railway system and owned by the Malayan Railway Pentadbiran Keretapi Tanah Melayu—KTM. The main line crosses the Johor causeway (1.2 km) and terminates near Keppel Harbour. Branch lines link it with the industrial estate at Jurong.

The Mass Rapid Transit (MRT) system was completed in 1990. The system extends for 83 km and consists of two lines with 48 stations (32 elevated, 15 under ground and one at ground level). The construction of a further 20-km line, the North–East Line, began in 1997; the line has 16 stations and one depot, and was completed in 2003. In 2002 the extension of the East–West line to Changi Airport was completed; the Changi Airport Line (CAL) has one underground and one elevated station. In the early 2000s construction was under way on the Circle Line, a 33.3-km orbital line running entirely under ground which was to link all the radial lines into the city. The line was to start at Dhoby Ghaut and terminate at Harbour Front and was to be implemented in five stages, the last of which was scheduled for completion in 2010.

Singapore's first Light Rapid Transit (LRT) system, the Bukit Panjang LRT (a 7.8-km line with 14 stations), was completed in April 1998. In January 2003 an LRT line in Sengkang also became operational, and work on the first stage of a further LRT line, in Punggol, was completed in 2004. Construction of the 2.1-km Sentosa Express monorail system was completed in June 2006, and operations commenced in January 2007.

Land Transport Authority: 1 Hampshire Rd, Singapore 219428; tel. 63757100; fax 63757200; internet www.lta.gov.sg; Chair. MICHAEL LIM CHOO SAN; Chief Exec. YAM AH MEE.

ROADS

In 2006 Singapore had a total of 3,262 km of roads, of which 150 km were motorway; in that year 100% of the road network was paved. In 1990 the Government introduced a quota system to control the number of vehicles using the roads. A manual road-pricing system was introduced on one expressway in June 1996 and extended to two further expressways in May 1997. It was replaced by a system of Electronic Road Pricing (ERP) in 1998, whereby each vehicle was charged according to road use in congested areas. The ERP was first introduced on one expressway in April 1998, and was subsequently extended to include two other expressways and the Area Licensing Scheme gantry areas by early September of that year. In 2001 construction of the 12-km Kallang–Paya Lebar expressway began; an estimated 9 km of the expressway was to be under ground, which

SINGAPORE

would render it the longest underground expressway in South-East Asia. It was scheduled for completion in 2008, and was expected to cost approximately S $1,800m.

SHIPPING

The Port of Singapore is the world's busiest in tonnage terms; Singapore handled 128,922 vessels with a total displacement of 1,315.0m. grt in 2006.

The Port of Singapore Authority operates six cargo terminals: Tanjong Pagar Terminal, Keppel Terminal, Brani Terminal, Pasir Panjang Terminal, Sembawang Terminal and Jurong Port.

Tanjong Pagar Terminal and Keppel Terminal have the capacity to handle 10.7m. 20-foot equivalent units (TEUs).

The third container terminal, Brani, built on an offshore island connected to the mainland by a causeway, has a capacity of 5.5m. TEUs.

Pasir Panjang Terminal, Singapore's main gateway for conventional cargo (particularly timber and rubber), has five deep-water berths, eight coastal berths and 17 lighter berths.

Sembawang Terminal has three deep-water berths and one coastal berth. This terminal is the main gateway for car carriers as well as handling steel and timber products.

Jurong Port (which handles general and dry-bulk cargo, is situated in south-western Singapore, and serves the Jurong Industrial Estate) has 20 deep-water berths and one coastal berth.

A new container terminal, at Pasir Panjang, was officially opened in 2000, following the completion of the second of four planned phases of building work. Upon completion, scheduled for 2009, the terminal was to have 49 berths and a handling capacity of 35m. TEUs.

Maritime and Port Authority of Singapore: 460 Alexandra Rd, 18-00 PSA Bldg, Singapore 119963; tel. 63751600; fax 62759247; e-mail media_enquiries@mpa.gov.sg; internet www.mpa.gov.sg; f. 1996; regulatory body responsible for promotion and development of the port, overseeing all port and maritime matters in Singapore; Chair. PETER ONG BOON KWEE; Chief Exec. TAY LIM HENG.

PSA International Pte Ltd: 460 Alexandra Rd, 36-00 PSA Bldg, Singapore 119963; tel. 62747111; e-mail gca@psa.com.sg; internet www.internationalpsa.com; f. 1964 as a statutory board under the Ministry of Communications; est. as Port of Singapore Authority; changed name to above in 2003; made a corporate entity in 1997 in preparation for privatization; responsible for the provision and maintenance of port facilities and services; Chair. Dr YEO NING HONG; Pres. KHOO TENG CHYE.

Major Shipping Companies

American President Lines Ltd (APL): 456 Alexandra Rd, 08-00 NOL Bldg, Singapore 119962; tel. 62789000; fax 62742113; e-mail hung-song-goh@apl.com; internet www.apl.com; container services to North and South Asia, the USA and the Middle East; COO ED ALDRIDGE.

Glory Ship Management Private Ltd: 24 Raffles Place, 17-01/02, Clifford Centre, Singapore 048621; tel. 65361986; fax 65361987; e-mail gene@gloryship.com.sg.

Guan Guan Shipping Pte Ltd: 2 Finlayson Green, 13-05 Asia Insurance Bldg, Singapore 049247; tel. 65343988; fax 62276776; e-mail golden@golden.com.sg; f. 1955; shipowners and agents; cargo services to East and West Malaysia, Indonesia, Pakistan, Sri Lanka, Bengal Bay ports, Persian (Arabian) Gulf ports, Hong Kong and China; Man. Dir RICHARD THIO.

IMC Shipping Co Pte Ltd: 5 Temasek Blvd, 12-01 Suntec City Tower, Singapore 038985; tel. 63362233; fax 63379715; e-mail biz@imcpaa.com; internet www.imcshipping.com; Man. Dir PETER CHEW.

Nedlloyd Lines Singapore Pte Ltd: 138 Robinson Rd, 01-00 Hong Leong Centre, Singapore 068906; tel. 62218989; fax 62255267; f. 1963; Gen. Man. F. C. SCHUCHARD.

Neptune Orient Lines Ltd: 456 Alexandra Rd, 05-00 NOL Bldg, Singapore 119962; tel. 62789000; fax 62784900; e-mail nol_group_corp_comms@nol.com.sg; internet www.nol.com.sg; f. 1968; liner containerized services on the Far East/Europe, Far East/North America, Straits/Australia, South Asia/Europe and South-East Asia, Far East/Mediterranean routes; logistics services and terminals; Chair. CHENG WAI KEUNG; Group Pres. and CEO THOMAS HELD.

New Straits Shipping Co Pte Ltd: 51 Anson Rd, 09-53 Anson Centre, Singapore 0207; tel. 62201007; fax 62240785.

Ocean Tankers (Pte) Ltd: 37 Tuas Rd, Singapore 638503; tel. 68632202; fax 68639480; e-mail admin@oceantankers.com.sg; internet www.oceantankers.com.sg; Marine Supt V. LIM.

Osprey Maritime Ltd: 8 Cross St, 24-02/03 PWC Bldg, Singapore 048424; tel. 62129722; fax 65570450; CEO PETER GEORGE COSTALAS.

Pacific International Lines (Pte) Ltd: 140 Cecil St, 03-00 PIL Bldg, POB 3206, Singapore 069540; tel. 62218133; fax 62273933; e-mail sherry.chua@sgp.pilship.com; internet www.pilship.com; shipowners, agents and managers; liner services to South-East Asia, the Far East, India, the Red Sea, the Persian (Arabian) Gulf, West and East Africa; container services to South-East Asia; worldwide chartering, freight forwarding, container manufacturing, depot operators, container freight station operator; Exec. Chair. Y. C. CHANG; Man. Dir S. S. TEO.

Petroships Private Ltd: 460 Alexandra Rd, 25-04 PSA Bldg, Singapore 119963; tel. 62731122; fax 62732200; e-mail gen@petroships.com.sg; Man. Dir KENNETH KEE.

Singa Ship Management Private Ltd: 78 Shenton Way 16-02, Singapore 079120; tel. 62244308; fax 62235848; e-mail agency@singaship.com.sg; Chair. OLE HEGLAND; Man. Dir EILEEN LEONG.

Syabas Tankers Pte Ltd: 10 Anson Rd, 34-10 International Plaza, Singapore 0207; tel. 62259522.

Tanker Pacific Management (Singapore) Private Ltd: 1 Temasek Ave, 38-01 Millenia Tower, Singapore; tel. 63365211; fax 63375570; internet www.tanker.com.sg; Man. Dir ALASTAIR MCGREGOR.

CIVIL AVIATION

Singapore's international airport at Changi was opened in 1981. Construction on a terminal solely for the use of budget carriers was completed in January 2006, and became operational in March of that year, thereby increasing the airport's total capacity to 64m. passengers a year. Separate facilities for premium air travellers were opened in September 2006. Construction of a third main terminal was completed in January 2008. A second airport at Seletar operates as a base for charter and training flights.

Civil Aviation Authority of Singapore: Singapore Changi Airport, POB 1, Singapore 918141; tel. 65421122; fax 65421231; e-mail thennarasee_R@caas.gov.sg; internet www.caas.gov.sg; responsible for regulatory and advisory services, air services development, airport management and development and airspace management and organization; Chair. LIEW MUN LEONG; Dir-Gen. LIM KIM CHOON.

Jetstar Asia Airways: Singapore Changi Airport; internet www.jetstar.com; f. 2004; 49% owned by Qantas (Australia); service to regional destinations; merged with ValuAir in 2005; continues to operate under the Jetstar name; CEO CHONG PHIT LIAN.

SilkAir: 77 Robinson Rd, 25-01 SIA Bldg, Singapore 068896; tel. 65428111; fax 65426286; internet www.silkair.com; f. 1975; fmrly Tradewinds Private; wholly owned subsidiary of Singapore Airlines Ltd; began scheduled services in 1989; Chair. SOO KHIANG BEY; CEO YAU SENG CHIN.

Singapore Airlines Ltd (SIA): 7D Airline House, 25 Airline Rd, Singapore 819829; tel. 65415880; fax 65423002; e-mail investor_relations@singaporeair.com.sg; internet www.singaporeair.com; f. 1972; passenger services to over 90 destinations in about 40 countries; Chair. STEPHEN LEE CHING YEN; CEO CHEW CHOON SENG.

Tiger Airways: Singapore Changi Airport, POB 82, Singapore 918143; tel. 65384437; fax 65807564; internet www.tigerairways.com; f. 2003; 49% owned by Singapore Airlines, 24% owned by US co Indigo Partners, 11% owned by Temasek Holdings Pte Ltd; services to 10 regional destinations; Chair. WILLIAM FRANKE; CEO TONY DAVIS.

ValuAir: POB 323, Singapore 918144; tel. 68222288; e-mail feedback@valuair.com.sg; internet www.valuair.com.sg; f. 2003; regional destinations; merged with Jetstar Asia in 2005; continues to operate under the ValuAir name; Chair. LIM CHIN BENG.

Tourism

Singapore's tourist attractions include its blend of cultures and excellent shopping facilities. In April 2005 the Government approved draft legislation to permit gambling on the island for the first time in 40 years. The new law opened the way for the construction of two major casino resorts, at Marina Bay and on Sentosa Island. The resorts were scheduled to become operational by 2009 and were expected significantly to boost the number of visitors to Singapore. Tourist arrivals totalled 10,284,410 in 2007. Receipts from tourism (excluding passenger transport) totalled US $5,736m. in 2005, an increase of 9.8% compared with the previous year.

Singapore Tourism Board: Tourism Court, 1 Orchard Spring Lane, Singapore 247729; tel. 67366622; fax 67369423; e-mail feedback@stb.com.sg; internet www.stb.com.sg; f. 1964; Chair. SIMON ISRAEL; Dep. Chair. and Chief Exec. LIM NEO CHIAN.

SLOVAKIA

Introductory Survey

Location, Climate, Language, Religion, Flag, Capital

The Slovak Republic (formerly a constituent republic of the Czech and Slovak Federative Republic, or Czechoslovakia) is a landlocked state located in central Europe, bordered to the north by Poland, to the east by Ukraine, to the south by Hungary, to the west by Austria and to the north-west by the Czech Republic. The climate is typically continental, with cold, dry winters and hot, humid summers. Average temperatures in Bratislava range from −0.7°C (30.7°F) in January to 21.1°C (70.0°F) in July. Average annual rainfall in the capital is 649 mm (26 ins). The official language is Slovak, although Hungarian, Czech and other languages are also spoken. The major religion is Christianity, the Roman Catholic Church being the largest denomination, followed by the Evangelical Church of the Augsburg (Lutheran) Confession. The national flag (proportions 2 by 3) consists of three equal horizontal stripes, of white, blue and red; in the centre hoist there is a white-rimmed red shield containing a silver archiepiscopal (double-barred) cross surmounted on the central (and highest) of three blue hillocks. The capital is Bratislava.

Recent History

Slovaks and Czechs (who are closely related members of the western Slavic peoples) were first united in the ninth century AD, in the Great Moravian Empire, but were divided following the Empire's dissolution in 907. While the Slovaks came under Hungarian rule (which was to last, in different forms, until the early 20th century), the Czechs established a kingdom that remained an important political force until the incorporation of the Czech Lands into the Habsburg Empire in the 16th and 17th centuries.

A movement of nationalist revival, closely linked with a similar movement in the Czech Lands, evolved in Slovakia in the late 18th and 19th centuries. During the First World War (1914–18) Slovaks joined with Czechs in campaigning for an independent state, which would be composed of the Czech Lands and Slovakia. The Republic of Czechoslovakia was established on 28 October 1918, as one of the successor states to the Austro-Hungarian Empire. The country's boundaries were defined by the Treaty of Trianon of 1920, under which a large Hungarian minority was incorporated into Slovakia. Czechoslovakia's first Constitution, promulgated in 1920, made no provision for a proper federal system, and Slovak proposals for self-government were rejected by the central authorities in the capital, Prague. A further cause of Slovak disaffection was the fact that the Czech Lands were the focus of the country's economic development, while Slovakia remained comparatively undeveloped. There was also an ideological divide between the two parts of the country: while the majority of Slovaks were strict Roman Catholics, the central Government in Prague was professedly anticlerical.

In October 1938, following the Munich Agreement of 29 September (whereby the predominantly German-populated areas of Czechoslovakia were ceded to Germany), nationalists declared Slovak autonomy. On 14 March 1939, one day before Nazi armed forces occupied the Czech Lands, Adolf Hitler agreed to the establishment of a separate Slovak state, under the pro-Nazi 'puppet' regime of Fr Jozef Tiso. Under the wartime Slovak state, any opposition to the Tiso regime was ruthlessly suppressed, and the treatment of Jews was particularly severe. In August 1944 an armed resistance (the Slovak National Uprising) against Tiso's regime was begun, but it was suppressed within two months by German troops.

Following the restoration of the Czechoslovak state in 1945, at the end of the Second World War, certain concessions were made to Slovak demands for autonomy, including the establishment of a regional legislature with restricted powers (the Slovenská národná rada—Slovak National Council) and an executive, both in Bratislava, the Slovak capital. However, communists (led by Gustav Husák) seized power in Slovakia in late 1947, and in the whole of the country in 1948. In May 1948 a new Constitution was approved, which declared Czechoslovakia to be a 'people's democracy'. The communists' consolidation of power was completed in the following month with the election to the post of President of Klement Gottwald, a Czech and the leader of the Communist Party of Czechoslovakia (CPCz), who had been Prime Minister since 1946.

In the first years of communist rule there was widespread repression. Expressions of Slovak nationalism were harshly suppressed, and in 1954 Husák and other Slovaks were imprisoned on charges of separatism. The new Constitution of 1960 restricted Slovak autonomy: the executive in Bratislava was dissolved, and legislative authority was removed from the Slovenská národná rada. In January 1968 Alexander Dubček (a Slovak and hitherto the leader of the Communist Party of Slovakia—CPS) was appointed First Secretary of the CPCz. The wide-ranging political and economic reforms introduced by Dubček and the new Government included plans for the creation of a federal system of two equal republics. This period of political tolerance and freedom of expression (subsequently known as the 'Prague Spring') was abruptly ended in August 1968 by the armed intervention of some 600,000 troops of the USSR and its allies. Dubček was replaced by Husák as First (subsequently General) Secretary of the CPCz, and there was a purge of party members, in particular reformists and associates of Dubček. Nevertheless, the federal system was realized in January 1969: separate Czech and Slovak Socialist Republics were established, each with its own government and legislature (Národná rada—National Council). Supreme legislative and executive power, meanwhile, were vested in the Federal Assembly and the Federal Government, respectively. However, the reimposition of centralized communist rule, under the leadership of Husák, left the new regional institutions largely powerless.

In 1975 Husák was appointed President of Czechoslovakia. In December 1987 he was replaced as General Secretary of the CPCz by Miloš Jakeš, a Czech member of the CPCz Presidium. Although the administration publicly avowed its commitment to introduce political and economic reforms similar to those taking place in the USSR under Mikhail Gorbachev, political liberalization was not forthcoming. The Government continued its repressive treatment of both the Roman Catholic Church and the several dissident groups that had been established since the late 1970s (the most important being Charter 77). Nevertheless, the dissident movement was instrumental in organizing a series of anti-Government demonstrations, beginning in 1988, which were to culminate in the anti-communist revolution of late 1989 (see the chapter on the Czech Republic).

Elections to the Federal Assembly and to the Czech and Slovak National Councils on 8–9 June 1990 were the first to be held freely since 1946. Of the Slovak parties and movements, Public Against Violence (PAV), which, with its Czech counterpart, Civic Forum, had been the principal force in effecting the end of communist rule, emerged with the largest representation at both federal and republican level. A coalition Slovak Government, dominated by PAV, was subsequently formed, with Vladimír Mečiar as Prime Minister.

The future of Czech-Slovak relations emerged in the latter half of 1990 as the dominant topic of political debate. Although most Czech and Slovak citizens appeared to favour the preservation of a common state, there was increasing support in Slovakia for a more decentralized form of the existing federation. Among the Slovak political parties, the Christian Democratic Movement (CDM), which formed part of the Slovak coalition Government, advocated greater Slovak autonomy within a common state; however, more radical parties—most notably the Slovak National Party (SNP), which held seats in both the federal and republican legislatures—advocated the complete secession of Slovakia from the federation. The debate over the future of the country (which since April 1990 had been officially known as the Czech and Slovak Federative Republic) led to increasing political turmoil in Slovakia during 1991. In March Mečiar was forced to resign as Slovak Prime Minister, accused of harming Czech-Slovak relations by his increasingly strident advocacy of full autonomy for Slovakia. Mečiar left PAV and formed a new party, the Movement for a Democratic Slovakia (MDS). He was replaced as Prime Minister by Ján Carnogurský, the leader of the CDM. Proposals by the Czechoslovak President, Václav

Havel, for a referendum to determine the country's future were repeatedly rejected by the Federal Assembly.

Following elections to the federal and republican legislatures on 5–6 June 1992, the MDS emerged as the dominant Slovak party both in the Federal Assembly and the Slovenská národná rada. In the latter body the MDS won 74 of the 150 seats available, compared with only 18 won by the CDM and 15 by the SNP. The Party of the Democratic Left (PDL—the successor to the CPS) won the second largest representation (29 seats). In late June Mečiar was reinstated as Prime Minister, at the head of a new, MDS-dominated Slovak Government.

On 17 July 1992 the Slovenská národná rada approved a declaration of Slovak sovereignty, as a result of which the dismantling of the Czechoslovak federation appeared inevitable. In late July Mečiar and his Czech counterpart, Václav Klaus, reached agreement on the necessary measures to permit the separation of the two republics. On 1 September the new Slovak Constitution was adopted by the Slovenská národná rada. In November the Federal Assembly finally approved (albeit at the third attempt and by a margin of only three votes) legislation to permit the constitutional dissolution (to be effected on 1 January 1993) of Czechoslovakia.

During the remainder of 1992 there was an acceleration of the process of dividing federal assets and liabilities, as well as the armed forces, between the Czech and Slovak Republics. In December the two republics signed a co-operation agreement, and subsequently established formal diplomatic relations. With the dissolution of all federal structures at midnight on 31 December, the Czech Republic and the Slovak Republic came into existence. Recognition was rapidly accorded to the new countries by all those states that had maintained relations with Czechoslovakia, as well as by various international bodies.

Slovakia's MDS-dominated Government and legislature remained in place. In February 1993 the Národná rada Slovenskej republiky (National Council of the Slovak Republic, as the legislature was redesignated—Národná rada) elected Michal Kováč, Deputy Chairman of the MDS and former Chairman of Czechoslovakia's Federal Assembly, as President. Meanwhile, there were increasing internal divisions in the MDS, which culminated in March 1993 with the dismissal of Milan Kňažko, the strongest critic of Mečiar within the party, from his post of Deputy Prime Minister and Minister of Foreign Affairs. Kňažko subsequently formed a liberal party, the Alliance of Democrats of the Slovak Republic (ADSR), in opposition to Mečiar's Government. Also in March the SNP leader, Ludovít Černák, resigned as Minister of the Economy, leaving the Government (with the exception of two independent ministers) composed exclusively of members of the MDS. However, as a result of several defections, the party (plus affiliates) lost its majority in the legislature. A new coalition Government, in which the SNP held several principal portfolios, was formed in November. One of Mečiar's ministerial nominees was rejected by Kováč, who had become severely critical of the Prime Minister. In December Mečiar ignored a demand by the President for his resignation.

Mečiar's position was further undermined in early 1994. In February six SNP deputies left the party to form what became the National Democratic Party—New Alternative (NDP–NA), led by Černák. In the same month the Minister of Foreign Affairs, Jozef Moravčík, and the Deputy Prime Minister, Roman Kováč, resigned from the Government, subsequently establishing another new opposition party, the Democratic Union of Slovakia (DUS). In March the Národná rada approved a motion expressing no confidence in Mečiar's Government (the MDS and the SNP both abstained from voting). Following the resignation of Mečiar's administration, a new, five-party, interim coalition was installed in mid-March. The new Government, with Moravčík as Prime Minister, comprised members of the CDM and the PDL, as well as the three new formations: the NDP–NA, the DUS and the ADSR (the last was subsequently absorbed into the DUS). Early legislative elections were scheduled for September.

The MDS emerged as the leading party at elections to the Národná rada, held on 30 September and 1 October 1994 (with the participation of some 76% of the electorate). The renewed success of the MDS (which, in alliance with the Farmers' Party of Slovakia, secured 35.0% of the total votes cast and 61 seats) was attributed to Mečiar's populist election campaign. The Common Choice bloc (an alliance of left-wing parties, led by the PDL) won 10.4% of the votes cast and 18 seats, followed by a coalition of Hungarian parties (17) and the CDM (also 17). The remaining seats were taken by the DUS (15), the Association of Workers of Slovakia (AWS—formed earlier in the year, following a split in the PDL—13 seats) and the SNP (nine seats).

Subsequent inter-party negotiations proved inconclusive, and in late October 1994 Kováč requested that Mečiar form a Government. A coalition of the MDS, the SNP and the AWS was eventually announced in mid-December. In January 1995 the new Government attempted to annul all decisions on privatization made by the previous administration and overturn a presidential veto. However, in May the Constitutional Court declared the suspension of the privatization programme to be illegal. The personal enmity between Mečiar and Kováč culminated in an unsuccessful motion of no confidence in the President, following allegations that the Slovak Intelligence Service (SIS, which had been under presidential control until April) had provided Kováč with confidential information concerning the activities of political parties, in particular the MDS, and of state officials.

In February 1996 President Kováč claimed that there was evidence to suggest that the SIS had been responsible for the abduction of one of his sons (also called Michal) from Bratislava. Michal Kováč had subsequently been detained by police on an international arrest warrant in Austria, in connection with allegations of embezzlement, but later permitted to return to Slovakia. Mečiar alleged that the President had also been involved in the embezzlement affair, and that his son had organized his own abduction in order to divert attention from the financial scandal; President Kováč subsequently filed libel charges against Mečiar. However, investigations into both the alleged abduction and the libel suit were adjourned owing to lack of evidence. (Although in April 1999 Ivan Lexa, the former head of the SIS, was arrested in connection with Michal Kováč's abduction and other offences alleged to have been committed by the SIS, he was not convicted of any crime.)

The Ministers of the Economy, of Foreign Affairs and of the Interior were replaced in August 1996. Opposition deputies, meanwhile, campaigned for a referendum to be held on their proposals that the Head of State be elected by direct popular vote, rather than chosen by the legislature. President Kováč scheduled a referendum for 23–24 May 1997. However, when the poll took place, the question on presidential elections was omitted from the ballot papers. The majority of voters consequently boycotted the referendum, and the rate of electoral participation (at less than 10%) was too low to render the vote valid. The Minister of Foreign Affairs, Pavol Hamžík, resigned in protest at what he regarded as the Government's manipulation of the democratic process. In June several thousand people attended a rally to protest against the Government's intervention in the referendum. In February 1998, following a ruling by the Constitutional Court that government intervention had impeded citizens' rights to vote in the referendum, and in response to appeals from the opposition, Kováč announced that a new referendum would be held in April.

Meanwhile, the Slovak Democratic Coalition (SDC), a new grouping of five opposition parties (including the CDM and the DUS), demanded Mečiar's resignation, accusing his administration of endangering Slovakia's political and economic future, following the failure of Slovakia to be invited to join the North Atlantic Treaty Organization (NATO, see p. 340) or to be recommended by the European Commission for negotiations on membership of the European Union (EU, see p. 244) in mid-1997. In October, despite ongoing tension, Kováč and Mečiar issued a joint statement affirming Slovakia's commitment to future membership of the EU and other international organizations, amid increasing concern about the country's image abroad.

During January–March 1998 several attempts to elect a new President failed in the Národná rada, when candidates were unable to secure the required three-fifths' majority. The MDS had not contested the first rounds of voting, apparently confirming opposition fears that Mečiar was attempting to ensure that the presidency would remain vacant when Kováč left office, enabling him to assume a number of presidential powers. On 2 March Kováč's term expired, and certain presidential powers were transferred to the Government, in accordance with the Constitution. Mečiar immediately cancelled the referendum scheduled for April and announced the dismissal of some 28 of Slovakia's ambassadors abroad. He also granted an amnesty to various prisoners, including those suspected of abducting Kováč's son in 1995, and halted criminal proceedings relating to the May 1997 referendum. The Prime Minister's actions prompted a series of widely supported protest rallies organized by opposition parties, and were strongly criticized by the EU and the USA. In mid-April 1998 a further round of voting in the presidential election was contested for the first time by an MDS candidate; however, the Národná rada again failed to elect a new head of state. Subsequent attempts were also unsuccessful.

At the end of May 1998, in preparation for legislative elections scheduled for September, the Národná rada approved amendments to the electoral law, including a stipulation that political parties obtain at least 5% of the votes cast in order to secure parliamentary representation. Legislation was also approved that restricted pre-election campaigning to the state-run media. In June three ethnic Hungarian parties formally merged to create the Party of the Hungarian Coalition (PHC), and the SDC registered officially as a single party. In July a constitutional amendment providing for the transfer of a number of presidential powers to the Chairman of the Národná rada, in the event of the presidency becoming vacant, was supported by deputies from all parties.

The elections to the Národná rada were held, as scheduled, on 25–26 September 1998, with the participation of 84.2% of the electorate. The MDS narrowly retained its position as the strongest party in the legislature, winning 43 seats (with 27.0% of the votes cast), but was unable to form a government, with its only possible ally, the SNP, holding 14 seats. The SDC obtained 42 seats (26.3% of the votes), the PDL won 23 seats (14.7%), the PHC took 15 seats and the Party of Civic Understanding (PCU—formed earlier that year) won 13 seats. With a combined total of 93 seats, the SDC, the PDL, the PHC and the PCU agreed to attempt to form a new administration. Negotiations took place throughout October, and a new coalition Government, headed by Mikuláš Dzurinda, the leader of the SDC, was appointed at the end of the month. Jozef Migaš, of the PDL, was elected Chairman of the Národná rada. The opposition's victory was welcomed both by Western institutions and by neighbouring countries, which anticipated improved relations with Slovakia. Dzurinda emphasized the new Government's intention to pursue early membership of the EU and NATO, pledged to combat organized crime, and outlined measures to improve Slovakia's economic situation. In December the European Parliament adopted a resolution on Slovakia's application for membership of the EU, recommending that the European Commission consider initiating entry talks in 1999.

In January 1999 the Národná rada approved a government-sponsored constitutional amendment providing for the introduction of direct presidential elections. The ruling coalition nominated Rudolf Schuster, the Chairman of the PCU, as its presidential candidate. Nine candidates contested the first round of the presidential election, which was held on 15 May. Schuster won 47.4% of the votes cast, and Mečiar obtained 37.2%. (Kováč had withdrawn his candidature prior to the first round, in favour of Schuster.) Schuster defeated Mečiar in a second round of voting on 29 May, with 57.2% of the votes cast, and was duly inaugurated as President on 15 June, having resigned the chairmanship of the PCU.

In September 1999 a large demonstration was staged in Bratislava to protest against rising unemployment and declining living standards, resulting from a series of austerity measures implemented by the Government. In October Černák resigned as Minister of the Economy; his ministerial post was assumed by Lubomír Harach, the Chairman of the DUS. In January 2000, following several weeks of disputes over the future structure of the SDC, during which he had failed to consolidate the unity of the party, Dzurinda announced plans to form a new party, the Slovak Democratic and Christian Union (SDCU). The SDCU was officially registered in February, and was joined by several government ministers. Further SDC deputies subsequently resigned from the CDM and the DUS to join the SDCU. Following Dzurinda's election as SDCU Chairman at the party's opening congress in November, the SDC became effectively defunct. Meanwhile, in June Schuster underwent emergency surgery, and later that month was transferred to Austria for further medical treatment. The President resumed office in August.

In early 2001 discussions commenced in the Národná rada regarding proposed revisions to the Constitution, which, although opposed by the MDS and the SNP, were adopted by a narrow majority in the legislature in February. The revisions (which officially entered into effect on 1 July) redefined the relationship between national and international law, thereby facilitating the process of joining foreign alliances; strengthened the powers of the Constitutional Court; granted greater independence to the judiciary; and provided for public-administration reform. In May Schuster replaced Pavol Hamzik, the Deputy Prime Minister for European Integration, held responsible for the misuse of EU funds, which had led to the suspension of payments in the previous month. Also in May the Minister of the Interior tendered his resignation, following increasing criticism of an investigation into mismanagement under the Mečiar administration.

In July 2001 the Government pledged to introduce measures to restore public confidence in the security forces, after the death of a member of the Roma population in police custody. In the same month dissension increased between the government coalition parties over new legislation providing for the establishment of a higher level of regional self-administration. Following the adoption of the reforms, which provided for the creation of eight 'higher territorial units' (VUCs), local government elections took place in two rounds, on 1 and 15 December. In a reflection of increasing popular support, MDS representatives secured 146 of the 401 seats in the regional councils and six of the eight gubernatorial posts. (However, voter participation in the second round was estimated at only 22% of the registered electorate.)

In January 2002 the PDL demanded the resignation of the reformist Minister of Finance, Brigita Schmögnerová (a PDL member), after she allegedly withheld information regarding the privatization programme. Although Dzurinda initially refused to dismiss her, threats by the PDL to withdraw from the coalition finally resulted in her replacement. Schmögnerová subsequently left the PDL and formed a new political party, the Social Democratic Alternative (SDA). In February the Deputy Prime Minister for the Economy, Ivan Mikloš, who was principally responsible for a programme of extensive structural reforms, survived a second motion of no confidence in the Národná rada.

In July 2002 members of the MDS who had not been selected by the party to contest the forthcoming legislative elections established a new party, known as the Movement for Democracy. At the elections to the Národná rada on 20–21 September, the MDS received the highest proportion of the votes cast (19.5%), obtaining 36 mandates. The SDCU received 15.1% of the votes cast and 28 seats; a centre-right party, Direction (Smer), 13.5% and 25 seats; the PHC 11.2% and 20 seats; and the CDM 8.3% and 15 seats. The New Citizens' Alliance (NCA), established in 2001, won 8.0% of the votes and 15 seats, while the Slovak Communist Party (SCP) significantly increased its share, securing 6.3% and 11 seats. However, Mečiar subsequently proved unable to negotiate alliances with other parties in order to form a coalition government, and in late September Schuster invited Dzurinda to establish a new administration. A coalition agreement was signed in early October by four reformist, centre-right parties (the SDCU, the PHC, the CDM and the NCA), which together commanded a narrow majority, holding a total of 78 of the 150 seats in the Národná rada. On 16 October Schuster formally appointed a new coalition Government, comprising representatives of the four parties. The leader of the Democratic Party (DP), which had supported the SDCU in the elections, was also allocated a portfolio, although the party was not a coalition member. Mikloš was retained in the administration as the new Minister of Finance. The adoption of an austerity budget in November prompted popular protests, and the MDS urged deputies in the Národná rada to reverse the legislation. Local government elections took place on 6–7 December; mayoral offices were equally divided between the government coalition parties and the MDS.

In May 2003 a new party, the People's Union, was formed by disaffected members of the MDS. Former MDS Deputy Chairman Vojtech Tkáč was elected Chairman of the party. In the following month Mečiar was re-elected as Chairman of the MDS for a further two-year term. At the same time, MDS members approved changing the party's name to the People's Party—Movement for a Democratic Slovakia (PP—MDS). Tensions emerged within the ruling coalition in July, after the Národná rada approved legislative amendments proposed by the NCA, easing restrictions on abortion, which were strongly opposed by the CDM. In late July Schuster vetoed the legislation, fearing the collapse of the Government. In September the Deputy Prime Minister and Minister of the Economy, Robert Nemcsics, officially resigned his post, after losing the support of the NCA, following his criticism of Pavel Rusko, the Chairman of the party. Later that month Rusko was appointed as Deputy Prime Minister and Minister of the Economy. In October Juraj Liska was appointed as Minister of Defence, replacing Ivan Simko, who had been dismissed in September. A number of deputies subsequently left the SDCU to join Simko's newly formed Free Forum, rendering the ruling coalition a minority Government, with just

SLOVAKIA

Introductory Survey

68 parliamentary seats. In March 2004 Mikloš survived a further motion of no confidence, proposed by the PP—MDS.

In the first round of voting in the presidential election of 3 April 2004, former Prime Minister Vladimír Mečiar won 32.7% of the votes cast, followed by the Movement for Democracy leader (and former ally of Mečiar) Ivan Gašparovič, who won 22.3% of the votes. Eduard Kukan of the SDCU, the Minister of Foreign Affairs and the preferred candidate of Dzurinda's Government, took third place, with 22.1% of the votes, and was thus disqualified from the second round of voting. Schuster, the incumbent, obtained just 7.4% of the votes. The failure of Kukan's presidential bid prompted demands in the Národná rada for the resignation of Dzurinda, whereas Mečiar's success was seen as a potential threat to Slovakia's planned accession to the EU (due at the beginning of May). In the second round of voting, held on 17 April, Gašparovič was elected as President, receiving 59.9% of the votes cast; the rate of participation by the electorate in the second round was 43.5%. Gašparovič, who subsequently announced his resignation from the leadership of the Movement for Democracy, was inaugurated on 15 June, and pledged to co-operate with other EU states, while representing Slovakia's interests. Meanwhile, at Slovakia's first elections to the European Parliament in mid-June, a rate of participation by the electorate of just 17.0% was recorded—the lowest rate recorded in any EU member state. The SDCU received 17.1% of the votes, the PP—MDS 17.0%, Direction 16.9% and the CDM 16.2%; the four parties were each allocated three seats in the European Parliament. The PHC, which won 13.2% of votes, obtained two seats.

In January 2005 a new party, Direction-Social Democracy, was founded by the merger of Direction, the Social Democratic Party of Slovakia, the SDA and the PDL. In November 2004, meanwhile, the National Memory Institute had announced that it was to publish thousands of hitherto secret official files from Slovakia's communist era, detailing names of collaborators with the former regime; a deputy minister resigned in January 2005, after he was revealed to be a former agent of the communist security services.

In July 2005 Dzurinda survived a motion of no confidence in the Národná rada, which had been proposed by the Chairman of Direction-Social Democracy, Robert Fico, and supported by PP—MDS Chairman Vladimír Mečiar. Fico had criticized Dzurinda for his failure to combat corruption, and argued that his reforms had increased poverty. In August President Gašparovič dismissed Rusko from his post as Deputy Prime Minister and Minister of the Economy, after he was implicated in a loan scandal, which revealed an apparent conflict of interest between his private business activities and his ministerial duties. (Rusko had refused to comply with an earlier request that he tender his resignation, after the CDM threatened to withdraw its 15 deputies from the Národná rada if he remained in the Government.) Deputy Prime Minister and Minister of Finance Ivan Mikloš assumed the economy portfolio, in an acting capacity. Rusko, who remained leader of the NCA, subsequently urged Dzurinda to dismiss the Minister of Health, Rudolf Zajac (who had been nominated by the NCA, but was not a party member), and the Minister of Culture, František Tóth (an NCA member), both of whom had supported Rusko's removal. According to the coalition agreement, the NCA was authorized to nominate the Ministers of the Economy, of Culture and of Health; Rusko threatened to withdraw the NCA from the Government should Dzurinda refuse to replace the ministers, which he considered a breach of the coalition agreement. Members of the NCA opposed to Rusko's leadership, including two party Vice-Chairmen, Ľubomír Lintner and Jirko Malchárek, and Tóth, formed a splinter faction, led by Lintner. At the beginning of September the SDCU, the CDM and the PHC agreed to expel the NCA from the ruling coalition; Zajac and Tóth were permitted to retain their posts. Lintner's group of deputies pledged its co-operation with the governing parties, and proposed Malchárek for the post of Minister of the Economy. On 11 September the NCA expelled nine members from the party, including Tóth and five Vice-Chairmen (among them Lintner and Malchárek). The following day the Government signed a co-operation agreement with Lintner's group of deputies. Opposition parties boycotted the Národná rada, but after nine days, the Government narrowly managed to secure sufficient support to open a legislative session. In early October Gašparovič appointed Malchárek as Deputy Prime Minister and Minister of the Economy.

In October 2005 DP leader Ludovít Kaník resigned his post as Minister of Labour, Social Affairs and the Family. Kaník, who was replaced by Iveta Radičová, subsequently proposed a merger of the DP and the SDCU. In December a congress of the DP approved a draft agreement on the merger, which was confirmed in January 2006 at an extraordinary congress of the SDCU. The new political union was known as the SDCU-DP. Also in January Malchárek, Tóth and a former Deputy Minister of Health founded a new political party, Hope, which was officially registered in March.

Meanwhile, on 26 November and 10 December 2005 an estimated 18% of the electorate took part in local government elections. Just 11% of the electorate participated in the second round, the lowest rate of participation in Slovakia's history. Of the parties represented in the Národná rada, the CDM secured 87 of the 412 seats in the VÚCs, Direction-Social Democracy took 70 and the SDCU won 64.

In January 2006 the Minister of Defence, Juraj Liška, tendered his resignation, after a military aircraft crashed on the Hungarian–Slovak border, killing some 42 people. Although the cause of the accident was unknown, the Government had been criticized for its decision to modernize Soviet-manufactured aircraft, rather than buying new equipment. Liška was replaced by Martin Fedor. In February the CDM announced the withdrawal of its three ministers from the Government, following Dzurinda's refusal to submit for discussion a proposal to approve a treaty with the Vatican that would enable workers to refuse to perform duties on the basis of religious objections. Dzurinda argued that any such treaty would permit the Roman Catholic Church to interfere in civil affairs. The leader of the CDM subsequently resigned as Chairman of the Národná rada, and was replaced, in an acting capacity, by the PHC leader and Deputy Chairman of the legislature, Béla Bugár. As a result of the CDM's withdrawal, the ruling coalition controlled just 53 seats in the legislature, and three days later the Národná rada approved a proposal by Dzurinda for legislative elections, originally due to take place in September, to be held on 17 June. Gašparovič subsequently appointed Martin Pado of the SDCU-DP as Minister of the Interior, László Szigeti (of the PHC) as Minister of Education, and Lucia Žitňanská, an independent, as Minister of Justice. In early April Tóth was dismissed from his position as Minister of Culture, after being accused of misusing state funds; Rudolf Chmel, who held the position until May 2005, was subsequently re-appointed to the culture portfolio.

In legislative elections held on 17 June 2006 the majority of seats (a total of 50) were won by Fico's Direction-Social Democracy, which secured 29.1% of the votes cast. The SDCU-DP obtained 18.4% of the votes (31 seats), while the SNP and the PHC both won 11.7% (20 seats). Fifteen seats were allocated to the PP—MDS, which attracted 8.8% of the ballot, while the CDM secured 14 seats, with 8.3%. The rate of participation in the elections was 54.7%. Three days later Fico was invited by President Gašparovič to form a Government. On 28 June Direction-Social Democracy voted in favour of inviting the SNP and the PP—MDS to enter into a coalition; an agreement to this end was signed on 3 July. Fico's new administration predominantly comprised members of his own party, with the SNP and the PP—MDS being allocated just three and two cabinet posts, respectively. Neither Mečiar nor SNP Chairman Ján Slota were awarded cabinet positions. None the less, the Party of European Socialists (PES), in protest at Direction-Social Democracy's involvement with a far-right organization such as the SNP, voted temporarily to suspend the party's membership. (Direction-Social Democracy, whose contingent had been aligned with the PES in the European Parliament, was formally expelled from the PES in October.) Moreover, the European People's Party-European Democrats, the strongest conservative group within the European Parliament, agreed to create a monitoring team to observe developments in Slovakia, as proposed by Slovak MEPs within the group. Fico was formally appointed Prime Minister on 4 July; the new Národná rada was sworn in on the same day.

Assurances by Fico's administration that it would continue the foreign and domestic policies pursued by the previous Government, including those pertaining to Slovakia's planned accession to the euro zone (which was scheduled for 1 January 2009), were undermined in the weeks following the general election by highly contentious statements attributed to Slota in the domestic and international press on the issues of deportation and Slovakia's ethnic Hungarian population. While the PHC appealed to prosecutors to take legal action against Slota, the SNP threatened to sue controversial PHC deputy Miklos Duray for terming it a 'fascist' party. Following an attack in late August 2006 in the western town of Nitra by ultra-nationalists on a Hungarian student—one of a series of manifestations of anti-Hungarian sentiment—and subsequent pressure from the Hungarian Prime Minister, Ferenc Gyurcsány, Fico publicly condemned extremism in Slovakia. (Police later accused the student of fabricating the attack and abandoned their investigation into the incident.) An escalation in tension between Slovakia and Hungary prompted President Gašparovič to express his concerns regarding national intolerance in his country, but also to warn against excessive criticism of Slovakia. At the end of August the Chairman of the Parliamentary Assembly of the Council of Europe, Rane van der Linden, denounced the manifestations of racial intolerance in Slovakia. In early September Minister of Foreign Affairs Ján Kubiš and his Hungarian counterpart, Kinga Göncz, pledged to work together to improve bilateral relations. The head of the European Commission, José Manuel Barroso, also criticized the escalating tension in Slovakia with regard to its Hungarian minority, and reminded the country of its commitment to human rights as a member state of the EU. On 7 September the Národná rada adopted a declaration against extremism and intolerance (112 deputies voted in favour of the motion, while 28 abstained). In 2006 Slovakia granted asylum to just eight individuals, from a total of 2,871 applicants, the lowest figure since the country's inception in 1993.

Despite the turbulence of the first two months of his premiership, by the end of 2006 Fico appeared to have consolidated his position and introduced a period of political stability. Direction-Social Democracy performed well at the municipal elections of 2 December (in which 47.7% of the electorate participated). However, the appointment in that month of Radim Hreha, a strong supporter of Fico, as Director of Slovak Television (STV), prompted fears that the premier was applying pressure on the state media to adopt a pro-government stance, fears that were fuelled in January 2007 by Hreha's dismissal of Editor-in-Chief Roland Kyska, who had recently been involved in a public disagreement with Fico. In April an internal dispute erupted within the PHC when Duray accused outgoing Chairman Béla Bugár of co-operating with the communist-era secret police. (Bugár had been replaced as Chairman at the beginning of that month by Pál Csáky, whom many expected to adopt a more radical stance on Hungarian autonomy.)

In November 2007 the PP—MDS threatened to withdraw from the Government, in protest at Fico's dismissal of the Minister of Agriculture (a representative of that party), after evidence emerged of an illicit land sale agreement involving the Slovak State Land Fund. However, in December the Národná rada approved the budget for 2008, by 85 votes to 61, in a motion that was also regarded as expressing confidence in Fico's administration. In January 2008 the new Minister of Agriculture, Zdenka Kramplová, ordered the dismissal of the entire board of the Slovak State Land Fund. Later that month the Minister of Defence, František Kašický, resigned, following allegations that his ministry had overpriced tenders for the maintenance of military barracks; he was succeed by Jaroslav Baška, also of Direction-Social Democracy. In April President Gašparovič signed into law new regulations, to enter into effect in June, that were expected severely to restrict the activities of the print media; the new legislation had been drafted by the Minister of Culture, following ongoing government criticism of press statements, and had attracted objections from international organizations.

In 1997 Mečiar appealed to the Roma population not to seek asylum abroad, after a number of Roma were repatriated from the United Kingdom. However, Slovakia's Roma continued to seek political asylum abroad (largely unsuccessfully), prompting several countries to introduce mandatory visa requirements, on a temporary basis, for Slovak citizens. Although, according to the 2001 census, there were some 89,900 Roma in Slovakia, the community was unofficially estimated to number around 200,000. In January 2004 a report by the Council of Europe (see p. 225) concluded that Slovakia's Roma were frequently victims of racial prejudice and were disadvantaged socially. In the following month proposed reductions in social welfare prompted violent protests by the Roma minority, and some 1,000 troops were deployed to control rioting. In July new legislation was introduced prohibiting discrimination on the grounds of ethnicity. In November 2006 the European Monitoring Centre on Racism and Xenophobia, based in Vienna, Austria, criticized Slovakia, along with the Czech Republic and Hungary, for segregating its Roma populations, particularly in the education sector, but also with regard to housing and the labour market.

Slovakia's relations with Hungary have been strained by the issue of the large Hungarian minority (numbering some 520,500 at the 2001 census) resident in Slovakia, who are campaigning for cultural and educational autonomy. The two countries are also involved in a dispute over the Gabčíkovo-Nagymaros hydroelectric project, a scheme initiated by the Governments of Czechoslovakia and Hungary in 1977, which involved the construction of two dams and the diversion of the River Danube. Despite Hungary's decision in 1989 to abandon the project (following pressure by environmentalist groups), the Czechoslovak Government announced that it would proceed unilaterally with its part of the construction. In early 1993 Slovakia and Hungary agreed to forward the dispute to the International Court of Justice (ICJ) in The Hague, the Netherlands, and to operate a temporary water-management scheme in the mean time. In March 1995, none the less, an historic bilateral Treaty of Friendship and Co-operation was signed by the Prime Ministers of Hungary and Slovakia. The Treaty, notably, guaranteed the rights of ethnic minorities in each republic, while confirming the existing state border. However, the language law approved by the Slovak legislature in November, declaring Slovak the only official language and thereby potentially restricting the use of minority languages, was criticized both by Hungarian residents of Slovakia and by the Hungarian Government, as a violation of the Treaty. In August 1997 the Hungarian Prime Minister, Gyula Horn, and Mečiar agreed on the establishment of a joint commission to assess the implementation of the 1995 Treaty.

In September 1997 the ICJ pronounced its judgment on the Gabčíkovo-Nagymaros hydroelectric project, ruling that both countries had breached international law: Hungary was not justified in suspending work on the project, while the former Czechoslovakia should not have proceeded unilaterally. Both countries were to pay compensation for damages, and to negotiate regarding the realization of the original agreement. The participation of the PHC in the new Slovak Government, appointed in October 1998, improved prospects for the protection of minority rights. In February 1999 the first meeting of the joint minorities commission to monitor the implementation of the 1995 Treaty was held in Budapest, Hungary. In July 1999 the Národná rada approved legislation that provided for the use of an ethnic minority language in towns where the minority accounted for at least 20% of the population.

In December 1999 Hungary renounced any claim to a share of the hydroelectric energy produced by the Gabčíkovo-Nagymaros dam project, but requested an increase in the common flow of water along the Danube, for ecological reasons. In February 2001 Slovakia accepted that it had no legal means to compel Hungary to complete the project, but stated that it was to seek compensation. In December 2003 an intergovernmental commission was established to co-ordinate negotiations on the issue. (In December 2006 it was announced that negotiations on the project were to be resumed.) Meanwhile, in January 2002 relations between Slovakia and Hungary had again become acrimonious, following Hungary's adoption of legislation that granted ethnic Hungarians resident in six neighbouring states, including Slovakia, education, employment and medical benefits. The Slovak Government protested that the new legislation violated Slovakia's sovereignty, and demanded that it be cancelled or amended. In early March 2003 Hungary agreed to suspend the application of the law in Slovakia, and in December the Ministers of Foreign Affairs of Hungary and Slovakia signed an agreement on the issue. The provisions of the Hungarian 'status law' were effectively superseded by the accession of Hungary and Slovakia to the EU in May 2004 (see below). In February 2006 it was announced that Slovakia and Hungary had agreed to implement the 1997 ICJ ruling on the Gabčíkovo-Nagymaros hydroelectric project. The two Governments were to draft an agreement on the implementation of the ruling and amend the 1977 agreement on the construction and operation of the system.

Relations with neighbouring Austria were strained by the issue of the partially constructed, Soviet-designed nuclear power station at Mochovce (north-east of Bratislava), operated by Slovenské elektrárne (Slovak Electricity), the completion of which was opposed by the Austrian Government, owing to safety concerns. An agreement on completion of the project was signed in April 1996, with Western European, Russian and Czech companies, according to which the first reactor would be commissioned by July 1998 and the second by March 1999. Tension increased in June 1998, when the first reactor was activated, despite a request from the Austrian Government that Slovakia delay the opening of the plant until an international team of inspectors, who had visited Mochovce in May, had submitted a final report on the plant's safety. In late 1999 the Slovak Government announced its decision to close two existing reactors at Jaslovské-Bohunice between 2006 and 2008, further antagonizing Austria, which had favoured closure by 2000. In May 2004, shortly after Slovakia's accession to the EU, tensions between the two countries heightened, following the Slovak Government's announcement that it intended to complete work on the Mochovce plant. In August 2005 the Italian electricity group Enel, which had bought a majority stake in Slovenské elektrárne in February, agreed to invest some €1,600m. in Mochovce; Enel intended to complete the construction of the two unfinished reactors by 2010.

In December 1999 Slovakia was among six countries formally invited to commence talks on accession to the EU; entry negotiations opened in February 2000. Following the return to power of a reformist coalition Government in October 2002 (see above), at an EU summit meeting held in Copenhagen, Denmark, in December, Slovakia was one of 10 nations invited to become a member in 2004. At a national referendum, which was conducted on 16–17 May 2003, 92.5% of votes were cast in favour of membership of the EU; some 52% of the electorate participated in the ballot. Slovakia's Treaty of Accession was formally ratified by the Národná rada on 1 July, and the country became a full member of the EU on 1 May 2004. In December 2007 Slovakia, together with eight other EU member nations (including the Czech Republic, Hungary and Poland), implemented the Schengen Agreement on freedom of travel, effectively removing border controls between those states subject to the Agreement. In early 2008 the Slovak authorities announced a subsequent increase in the number of illegal immigrants detained. Following Kosovo's unilateral declaration of independence in February (see the chapter on Kosovo), Slovakia was among several EU member nations (including Spain, Romania and Cyprus) to refuse to recognize it as a sovereign state, although the Government offered it 'partnership'. In May 2008 the European Commission approved Slovakia's planned accession to the euro zone on 1 January 2009, with a final decision expected by EU finance ministers in July.

Meanwhile, in February 1994 Slovakia joined NATO's 'Partnership for Peace' programme (see p. 342). At a NATO summit meeting in Prague at the end of November 2002, Slovakia (together with six other countries) was formally invited to join the Alliance, and it became a full member on 29 March 2004. In May Slovakia hosted a plenary session of the NATO Parliamentary Assembly, and in February 2005 it hosted a summit meeting between US President George W. Bush and Russian President Vladimir Putin. President Bush praised the deployment of 100 Slovak troops to Iraq to participate in the US-led military operations there. However, in February 2007 Fico fulfilled one of his electoral promises by withdrawing his country's troops from Iraq. (This, in addition to controversial visits by the new premier to the People's Republic of China and Libya, was seen as an effort by Fico to distance himself from the pro-US stance of his predecessor.) Also in February it was agreed that some 60 Slovak troops stationed in Kabul, Afghanistan, as part of the NATO-led International Security Assistance Force (ISAF) mission, would be transferred to Kandahar, in the south of the country, by June. In March Slovakia joined the International Energy Agency (IEA).

Government

Supreme legislative power is vested in the Národná rada Slovenskej republiky (National Council of the Slovak Republic), the 150 members of which are elected for a term of four years by universal adult suffrage. The President of the Republic (Head of State) is directly elected by universal adult suffrage for a five-year term. The President, who is restricted to two consecutive terms of office, appoints the Prime Minister and, on the latter's recommendation, the other members of the Government (the supreme body of executive power). For administrative purposes, Slovakia is divided into eight 'higher territorial units' (VUCs), each with a regional council (together totalling 401 seats), and 79 electoral districts.

Defence

As assessed at November 2007, the total active strength of Slovakia's armed forces was 17,129: army 7,324, air force 4,280, and some 5,525 centrally controlled personnel, logistical and support staff. Reserve forces comprised 20,000 personnel. In July 2005 it was announced that compulsory military service was to be abandoned from 1 August, and in December the army became fully professional. Slovakia became a full member of the North Atlantic Treaty Organization (NATO, see p. 340) on 29 March 2004. The 2007 budget allocated 28,500m. koruny to defence.

Economic Affairs

In 2006, according to the World Bank, Slovakia's gross national income (GNI), measured at average 2004–06 prices, was US $53,168m., equivalent to $9,870 per head (or $17,600 per head on an international purchasing-power parity basis). During 1996–2006, it was estimated, the population remained constant, while gross domestic product (GDP) per head increased, in real terms, by an average of 4.1% per year. Overall GDP increased, in real terms, at an average annual rate of 4.1% in 1996–2006; real GDP increased by 8.3% in 2006.

In 2006 the agricultural sector (including hunting, forestry and fishing) contributed 4.0% of GDP and employed 4.4% of the labour force. The principal crops are sugar beet, wheat and maize. Livestock breeding is also important. During 1996–2006, according to the World Bank, the GDP of the agricultural sector increased, in real terms, by an average annual rate of 6.3%. Agricultural GDP increased by 2.6% in 2006.

Industry (including mining, manufacturing, construction and power) contributed 35.0% of GDP in 2006, when it engaged 38.8% of the employed labour force. According to the World Bank, the GDP of the industrial sector increased, in real terms, at an average annual rate of 5.3% during 1996–2006. Industrial GDP increased by 10.5% in 2006.

Mining and quarrying contributed 0.5% of GDP in 2006, and engaged 0.7% of the employed labour force in 2005. The principal minerals extracted include brown coal and lignite, copper, zinc, lead, iron ore and magnesite. There are also deposits of crude petroleum, natural gas and mercury, as well as materials used in construction (including limestone, gravel and brick loam). According to IMF estimates, the GDP of the mining and quarrying sector increased by an average annual rate of 2.5% in 1995–2001. Mining GDP declined by 9.2% in 2001.

The manufacturing sector contributed 21.9% of GDP in 2006, and engaged 26.7% of the employed labour force in 2005. The GDP of the manufacturing sector increased by an average annual rate of 7.9% in 1996–2006. Manufacturing GDP increased by 10.7% in 2006.

Energy is derived principally from nuclear power, which provided some 55.9% of electricity generated in 2004. In that year coal accounted for 20.0% of electricity production, and hydroelectric power for 13.5%. A nuclear power station at Jaslovské-Bohunice has been in operation since the early 1980s, although in 1999 the Government pledged to close two reactors there by 2008. In mid-1998 the first block of a new nuclear power installation, at Mochovce, commenced operations; construction work on two unfinished reactors there was due to be completed by 2010. Slovakia has been heavily dependent on imported fuel and energy products. According to preliminary data, fuels and related products accounted for 14.3% of the value of total merchandise imports in 2006.

The services sector contributed 61.1% of GDP in 2006, when the sector engaged 56.8% of the employed labour force. During 1996–2006, according to the World Bank, the GDP of the services sector increased, in real terms, by an average annual rate of 3.2%. Services GDP increased by 7.3% in 2006.

In 2006 Slovakia recorded a trade deficit of an estimated US $3,083m., and there was a deficit of some $4,562m. on the current account of the balance of payments. In 2006 the principal source of imports was Germany, which accounted for an estimated 20.4% of the total; other major suppliers were the Czech Republic and Russia. Germany was also the principal market for exports in that year (accounting for an estimated 23.6%); other important purchasers were the Czech Republic, Italy, Poland, Austria, and Hungary. The main exports in 2006 (according to preliminary figures) were machinery and transport equipment, intermediate manufactured products, miscellaneous manufactured articles, fuels, and chemicals and related products. The principal imports (according to provisional data) were machinery and transport equipment, intermediate manufactured products, fuels and related products, miscellaneous manufactured articles, and chemicals and related products.

Slovakia's overall budgetary deficit was 44,455m. koruny in 2006, equivalent to 2.7% of GDP. At the end of 2005 Slovakia's total external debt was US $23,654m., of which $3,340m. was long-term public debt. In 2003 the cost of debt-servicing was equivalent to 13.8% of the value of exports of goods and services. The annual rate of inflation averaged 6.9% in 1996–2006;

SLOVAKIA

Agriculture

PRINCIPAL CROPS
('000 metric tons)

	2004	2005	2006
Wheat	1,764.8	1,607.9	1,342.7
Barley	915.9	739.3	641.8
Maize	862.4	1,074.0	838.3
Rye	124.3	68.6	30.2
Oats	55.6	38.2	41.4
Triticale (wheat-rye hybrid)	65.8	52.4	30.4
Potatoes	381.9	301.2	263.1
Sugar beet	1,598.8	1,732.6	1,370.9
Dry peas	31.4	28.2	22.8
Sunflower seed	196.4	195.3	228.6
Rapeseed	262.7	235.1	259.7
Cabbages and other brassicas	85.2	84.5	87.7
Tomatoes	61.5	61.0	63.0
Chillies and green peppers	27.0	28.7	28.6
Cucumbers and gherkins	23.6	32.4	32.0
Onions	36.9	27.1	26.9
Carrots and turnips	41.6	37.6	37.8
Apples	31.1	36.3	30.8
Grapes	56.5	54.1	52.0
Watermelons	11.4	10.7	7.5
Tobacco (leaves)	1.3	1.0	0.7

Aggregate production ('000 metric tons, may include official, semi-official or estimated data): Total cereals 3,797.7 in 2004, 3,585.3 in 2005, 2,928.8 in 2006; Total roots and tubers 381.9 in 2004, 301.2 in 2005, 263.1 in 2006; Total vegetables (incl. melons) 341.2 in 2004, 338.9 in 2005, 333.0 in 2006; Total fruits (excl. melons) 95.8 in 2004, 99.3 in 2005, 95.0 in 2006.

Source: FAO.

LIVESTOCK
('000 head, year ending 30 September)

	2004	2005	2006
Cattle	593	540	528
Pigs	1,443	1,149	1,108
Sheep	325	321	320
Goats	39	39	40
Horses	8	8	8
Chickens	13,767	13,262	13,619

Source: FAO.

LIVESTOCK PRODUCTS
('000 metric tons, unless otherwise indicated)

	2004	2005	2006
Cattle meat	25.6	26.4	21.4
Pig meat	164.9	139.9	122.3
Chicken meat	84.5	87.2	86.1
Cows' milk	1,049.3	1,072.1	1,064.2
Goats' milk	8.9	8.9	8.9*
Hen eggs	63.3	62.9	70.3
Other poultry eggs	4.3	4.5*	4.5*

* FAO estimate.
Source: FAO.

Forestry

ROUNDWOOD REMOVALS
('000 cubic metres, excl. bark)

	2004	2005	2006
Sawlogs, veneer logs and logs for sleepers	3,119	4,845	4,102
Pulpwood	3,397	3,629	2,677
Other industrial wood	420	531	783
Fuel wood	304	297	307
Total	7,240	9,302	7,869

Source: FAO.

SAWNWOOD PRODUCTION
('000 cubic metres, incl. railway sleepers)

	2004	2005	2006
Coniferous (softwood)	1,251	1,984	1,760
Broadleaved (hardwood)	586	637	680
Total	1,837	2,621	2,440

Source: FAO.

Fishing

(metric tons, live weight)

	2003	2004	2005
Capture	1,646	1,603	1,693
Common carp	1,046	1,015	1,112
Northern pike	56	61	68
Pike-perch	78	78	83
Breams	98	98	105
Aquaculture	881	1,180	955
Common carp	139	345	169
Rainbow trout	682	818	742
Total catch (incl. others)	2,527	2,783	2,648

Source: FAO.

Mining

('000 metric tons, unless otherwise indicated)

	2003	2004	2005
Coal (brown and lignite)	3,077	2,952	2,511
Iron ore:			
gross weight	400	300	300
metal content	200	500	500
Crude petroleum	48	50	50
Natural gas (million cu metres)	210	200	200
Limestone and other calcareous stones for cement	3,453	4,501	6,034
Sands and gravel ('000 cubic metres)	1,300	1,300*	1,800

* Estimated production.
Source: US Geological Survey.

Industry

SELECTED PRODUCTS
('000 metric tons, unless otherwise indicated)

	2001	2002	2003
Wheat flour	312	333	320
Bread	145	138	140
Refined sugar	38	35	38
Beer ('000 hectolitres)	4,520	4,800	4,630
Wine ('000 hectolitres)	450	374	345
Distilled alcoholic beverages ('000 hectolitres)	123	111	109
Cotton yarn	3.6	6.3	5.4
Footwear, excl. rubber footwear ('000 pairs)	8,994	9,555	13,496
Paper and paperboard	988	994	n.a.
Paints and enamels	32.9	34.6	32.7
Black-coal coke	1,697	1,806	1,886
Residual fuel oils	718	620	635

SLOVAKIA

—continued	2001	2002	2003
Gas-diesel (distillate fuel) oil	2,406	2,341	2,351
Cement	3,123	3,141	3,147
Pig-iron*	3,255	3,533	3,892
Crude steel*	3,989	4,275	4,709
Alumina*	111.6	132.1	156.9
Household refrigerators and freezers ('000 units)	27	2	n.a.
Passenger motor cars ('000 units)	277	226	n.a.
Lorries (number)	70	n.a.	n.a.
Colour television receivers ('000 units)	594	712	n.a.
Electric energy	32,046	32,427	31,179

* Source: US Geological Survey.

Source: UN, *Industrial Commodity Statistics Yearbook*.

Black-coal coke ('000 metric tons): 1,883 in 2004 (Source: UN, *Industrial Commodity Statistics Yearbook*).

Residual fuel oils ('000 metric tons): 585 in 2004 (Source: UN, *Industrial Commodity Statistics Yearbook*).

Gas-diesel (distillate fuel) oil ('000 metric tons): 2,598 in 2004 (Source: UN, *Industrial Commodity Statistics Yearbook*).

Cement ('000 metric tons, estimate): 3,158 in 2004; 3,499 in 2005 (Source: US Geological Survey).

Pig-iron ('000 metric tons, estimate): 3,980 in 2004; 3,681 in 2005 (Source: US Geological Survey).

Crude steel ('000 metric tons, estimate): 4,564 in 2004; 4,242 in 2005 (Source: US Geological Survey).

Aluminium ingot, primary (metric tons, estimate): 175 in 2004 (estimate); 158 in 2005 (Source: US Geological Survey).

Electric energy (million kWh): 30,567 in 2004 (Source: UN, *Industrial Commodity Statistics Yearbook*).

Finance

CURRENCY AND EXCHANGE RATES

Monetary Units
100 halierov (singular: halier) = 1 slovenská koruna (Slovak crown or Sk).

Sterling, Dollar and Euro Equivalents (30 November 2007)
£1 sterling = 46.779 koruna;
US $1 = 22.638 koruna;
€1 = 33.416 koruna;
1,000 koruna = £21.38 = $44.17 = €29.93.

Average Exchange Rate (koruna per US $)
2004 32.257
2005 31.018
2006 29.697

Note: In February 1993 Slovakia introduced its own currency, the Slovak koruna, to replace (at par) the Czechoslovak koruna.

GOVERNMENT FINANCE
(general government transactions, non-cash basis, '000 million koruna)

Summary of Balances

	2004	2005	2006*
Revenue	503.78	529.55	573.65
Less Expense	513.92	551.75	604.91
Net operating balance	−10.13	−22.21	−31.27
Less Net acquisition of non-financial assets	31.69	29.20	29.95
Net lending/borrowing	−41.82	−51.41	−61.21

Revenue

	2004	2005	2006*
Taxes	244.32	265.60	283.76
Taxes on income, profits and capital gains	77.39	77.93	93.59
Taxes on goods and services	158.08	179.94	183.05
Social contributions	170.05	186.25	200.67
Grants	7.90	14.59	6.93
Other revenue	81.51	63.11	82.30
Total	503.78	529.55	573.65

Expense/Outlays

Expense by economic type	2004	2005	2006*
Compensation of employees	111.26	107.47	126.22
Use of goods and services	85.69	75.37	90.45
Consumption of fixed capital	—	—	—
Interest	29.44	25.49	26.95
Subsidies	24.62	27.40	30.15
Grants	8.71	10.43	14.64
Social benefits	224.19	249.22	269.46
Other expense	30.01	56.37	47.04
Total	513.92	551.75	604.91

Outlays by functions of government†	2004	2005	2006*
General public services	76.94	97.65	105.14
Defence	20.85	23.38	25.46
Public order and safety	26.49	30.00	32.23
Economic affairs	59.47	71.46	85.20
Environmental protection	9.53	10.50	11.46
Housing and community amenities	13.97	12.94	13.95
Health	120.17	95.79	107.02
Recreation, culture and religion	11.67	12.68	17.76
Education	53.71	57.42	62.73
Social protection	157.26	174.87	184.20
Statistical discrepancy	−4.46	−5.74	−10.27
Total	545.60	580.95	634.86

* Preliminary.
† Including net acquisition of non-financial assets.

Source: IMF, *Government Finance Statistics Yearbook*.

INTERNATIONAL RESERVES
(US $ million at 31 December)

	2005	2006	2007
Gold (national valuation)	579	717	944
IMF special drawing rights	1	1	2
Foreign exchange	14,901	12,647	18,032
Total	15,481	13,365	18,978

Source: IMF, *International Financial Statistics*.

MONEY SUPPLY
(million koruna at 31 December)

	2005	2006	2007
Currency outside banks	119,837	131,171	141,713
Demand deposits at commercial banks	347,941	397,554	456,579
Total money (incl. others)	468,041	528,978	598,607

Source: IMF, *International Financial Statistics*.

SLOVAKIA

Statistical Survey

COST OF LIVING
(Consumer Price Index; base December 2000 = 100)

	2004	2005	2006
Foodstuffs and non-alcoholic beverages	113.5	111.9	113.5
Alcoholic beverages and tobacco	137.2	136.3	140.8
Clothing and footwear	107.5	106.5	106.3
Housing, water, electricity, gas and other fuels	153.8	165.9	185.0
All items (incl. others)	127.0	130.5	136.3

NATIONAL ACCOUNTS
(million koruna at current prices)

Expenditure on the Gross Domestic Product

	2004	2005	2006
Final consumption expenditure	1,039,587	1,116,414	1,239,221
Households	754,351	829,771	927,159
Non-profit institutions serving households	14,506	14,409	14,620
General government	270,730	272,234	297,442
Gross capital formation	352,568	429,388	474,824
Gross fixed capital formation	327,087	394,618	432,084
Changes in inventories	25,481	34,770	42,740
Total domestic expenditure	1,392,155	1,545,802	1,714,045
Exports of goods and services	1,018,835	1,136,854	1,402,203
Less Imports of goods and services	1,055,728	1,211,525	1,478,204
Statistical discrepancy	—	—	−1,781
GDP in purchasers' values	1,355,262	1,471,131	1,636,263

Gross Domestic Product by Economic Activity

	2004	2005	2006
Agriculture, hunting, forestry and fishing	54,432	56,667	58,577
Mining and quarrying	7,181	7,938	7,718
Manufacturing	285,271	305,147	324,682
Construction	76,630	88,878	101,944
Electricity, gas and water supply	58,692	63,836	83,091
Wholesale and retail trade; repair of motor vehicles	165,830	187,575	229,672
Hotels and restaurants	16,673	17,596	20,120
Transport and storage	121,140	135,012	146,278
Financial intermediation	60,408	54,959	63,323
Real estate, renting and business activities	173,921	187,085	217,013
Public administration, defence and compulsory social security	70,126	72,801	79,874
Education	47,430	50,834	55,931
Health and social work	43,479	44,165	53,068
Other community, social and personal service activities	29,461	31,587	38,441
Sub-total	1,210,674	1,304,080	1,479,732
Taxes, less subsidies, on products	144,588	167,051	156,531
GDP in purchasers' values	1,355,262	1,471,131	1,636,263

BALANCE OF PAYMENTS
(US $ million)

	2004	2005	2006*
Exports of goods f.o.b.	27,621	32,026	41,696
Imports of goods f.o.b.	−29,157	−34,476	−44,778
Trade balance	−1,536	−2,450	−3,083
Exports of services	3,725	4,407	5,404
Imports of services	−3,458	−4,087	−4,740
Balance on goods and services	−1,269	−2,130	−2,418
Income (net)	−2,198	−1,976	−2,088
Balance on goods, services and income	−3,467	−4,106	−4,506
Current transfers	169	15	−55
Current balance	−3,298	−4,090	−4,562
Capital transfers	137	−18	−41
Direct foreign investment	3,052	1,951	3,797
Portfolio investment	866	−982	1,561
Other investment	858	4,245	−4,119
Financial derivatives	17	−34	−162
Net errors and omissions	1,130	−503	1,410
Overall balance	2,763	568	−2,115

*Preliminary.

Source: IMF, *Slovak Republic: 2007 Article IV Consultation - Staff Report; and Public Information Notice on the Executive Board Discussion* (July 2007).

External Trade

COMMODITY GROUPS
(million koruna)

Imports f.o.b.	2003	2004	2005
Prepared foodstuffs, beverages and tobacco	23,306	27,470	34,727
Mineral products	108,522	133,303	164,866
Products of the chemical or allied industries	63,989	74,879	80,905
Rubber and plastics, and articles thereof	57,007	59,877	63,622
Wood pulp, cellulose and paper, and articles thereof	22,662	24,173	24,847
Textiles and textile articles	42,545	42,510	42,977
Base metals and articles of base metal	74,163	94,233	106,423
Machinery and electrical equipment	217,842	240,687	275,950
Vehicles, aircraft, vessels and transport equipment	123,652	128,994	131,693
Optical, photographic, measuring and medical apparatus; clocks and watches; musical instruments	20,648	29,957	43,910
Total (incl. others)	826,673	940,471	1,069,517

SLOVAKIA

Exports f.o.b.	2003	2004	2005
Mineral products	48,405	64,816	78,976
Products of the chemical or allied industries	27,353	30,709	35,814
Rubber and plastics, and articles thereof	41,618	48,222	57,529
Wood pulp, cellulose and paper, and articles thereof	30,409	41,304	35,458
Textiles and textile articles	40,964	33,482	42,017
Base metals and articles of base metal	108,206	134,009	151,612
Machinery and electrical equipment	151,033	193,794	254,32
Vehicles, aircraft, vessels and transport equipment	233,225	214,439	194,811
Total (incl. others)	803,238	890,921	993,516

2006 (million koruna, preliminary): *Imports:* Food and live animals 57,665; Crude materials 41,492; Fuels and related products 190,882; Chemicals and related products 118,587; Intermediate manufactured products 227,886; Machinery and transport equipment 511,963; Miscellaneous manufactured articles 170,755; Total (incl. others) 1,333,489. *Exports:* Food and live animals 45,600; Crude materials 29,223; Fuels and related products 80,436; Chemicals and related products 68,329; Intermediate manufactured products 292,028; Machinery and transport equipment 603,072; Miscellaneous manufactured articles 116,384; Total (incl. others) 1,240,389.

PRINCIPAL TRADING PARTNERS
(million koruna)

Imports f.o.b.	2003	2004	2005
Austria	36,206	40,261	40,662
Belgium	13,947	15,737	15,215
China, People's Republic	20,437	25,665	34,462
Czech Republic	118,317	128,129	135,526
France	35,068	34,834	34,761
Germany	210,632	221,651	223,813
Hungary	28,379	32,135	38,690
Italy	50,995	52,732	50,958
Japan	15,636	18,801	20,150
Korea, Republic	7,076	16,959	28,139
Netherlands	13,627	14,366	14,527
Poland	29,150	37,642	44,053
Russia	89,595	88,368	114,893
Spain	22,420	18,925	18,611
Switzerland	9,593	8,857	8,862
Ukraine	8,586	13,269	15,818
United Kingdom	17,627	17,179	19,458
USA	16,106	15,246	14,943
Total (incl. others)	827,603	948,513	1,070,893

Exports f.o.b.	2003	2004	2005
Austria	59,726	70,651	70,283
Belgium	15,971	18,797	19,861
Czech Republic	103,649	121,724	140,359
France	28,196	32,645	38,811
Germany	247,680	256,843	259,277
Hungary	39,124	46,132	56,318
Italy	60,132	57,120	65,776
Netherlands	21,683	27,564	34,571
Poland	38,383	48,777	62,753
Russia	9,817	10,820	15,524
Spain	13,123	16,033	20,906
Switzerland	8,860	7,357	7,620
Ukraine	8,152	9,555	12,022
United Kingdom	16,960	26,149	30,902
USA	42,216	42,628	31,169
Total (incl. others)	803,238	898,096	994,571

2006 (million koruna, preliminary): *Imports:* Austria 44,982; Belgium 16,401; People's Republic of China 53,025; Czech Republic 163,863; France 43,101; Germany 272,433; Hungary 60,827; Italy 60,321; Netherlands 17,765; Poland 58,867; Russia 150,922; Spain 20,418; United Kingdom 19,692; USA 16,620; Total (incl. others) 1,333,489. *Exports:* Austria 74,945; Belgium 22,985; People's Republic of China 6,529; Czech Republic 173,440; France 53,396; Germany 292,127; Hungary 71,732; Italy 80,282; Netherlands 52,510; Poland 76,559; Russia 20,362; Spain 35,934; United Kingdom 48,214; USA 39,210; Total (incl. others) 1,240,389.

Transport

	2004	2005	2006
Railway transport:			
freight ('000 tons)	50,445	49,310	52,449
passengers ('000)	50,325	50,458	48,438
Public road transport:			
freight ('000 tons)	49,769	48,357	n.a.
passengers ('000)	461,772	449,456	403,270
Waterway transport: freight ('000 tons)	1,636	1,526	n.a.

ROAD TRAFFIC
(motor vehicles in use at 31 December)

	2004	2005	2006
Passenger cars ('000)	1,197	1,304	1,334
Buses and coaches ('000)	9	9	9
Goods vehicles ('000)	140	160	173

Civil Aviation
(traffic on scheduled services)

	2003	2004	2005
Passengers carried ('000)	428	974	1,716
Freight carried ('000 metric tons)	1	—	—

Tourism

FOREIGN TOURIST ARRIVALS
(visitors at accommodation facilities)

Country of origin	2003	2004	2005
Austria	51,365	55,609	55,630
Czech Republic	469,991	419,273	424,900
France	28,629	37,006	42,668
Germany	175,746	188,067	194,158
Hungary	100,546	111,065	121,615
Italy	37,996	50,201	59,344
Netherlands	24,487	27,114	28,838
Poland	215,383	179,078	198,479
Russia	22,681	18,074	19,779
United Kingdom	26,062	34,349	51,720
USA	25,383	28,665	32,593
Total (incl. others)	1,386,791	1,401,189	1,514,980

Tourism receipts (US $ million, incl. passenger transport): 876 in 2003; 932 in 2004; n.a. in 2005.

Source: World Tourism Organization.

Total foreign visitors at accommodation facilities ('000): 1,612 in 2006.

Communications Media

	2003	2004	2005
Telephones ('000 main lines in use)	1,294.7	1,250.4	1,197.0
Mobile cellular telephones ('000 subscribers)	3,678.8	4,275.2	4,540.4
Personal computers ('000 in use)	1,270	1,593	1,929
Internet users ('000)	1,375.8	1,652.2	1,905.2
Broadband subscribers ('000)	22.5	78.8	181.5
Newspapers: titles	463	455	426
Newspapers: circulation ('000 copies)	270,498	257,231	239,869
Periodicals: titles	1,076	948	962
Periodicals: circulation ('000 copies)	153,799	181,273	244,691

2006: Telephones ('000 main lines in use) 1,167.4; Mobile cellular telephones ('000 subscribers) 4,893.2; Internet users ('000) 2,255.6; Broadband subscribers ('000) 317.0.

Radio receivers (licensed): 1,255,624 in 1998; 1,368,863 in 1999; 1,347,477 in 2000.

Television receivers (licensed): 1,392,883 in 1998; 1,241,663 in 1999; 1,211,773 in 2000.

Book production (number of titles): 2,064 in 1997; 4,386 in 1998; 3,153 in 1999.

Facsimile machines (number registered): 54,037 in 1998.

Sources: partly International Telecommunication Union and UNESCO Institute for Statistics.

Education

(2006, unless otherwise indicated)

	Institutions	Teachers*	Students
Kindergarten	2,928	13,201	140,014
Primary (basic)	2,383	34,914	508,130
Secondary: grammar	246	7,568	101,090
Secondary: specialized	249	7,869	85,774
Secondary: vocational	210	3,254	60,621
Higher	30	10,220	198,770

*Data for 2005.

Directory

The Constitution*

On 1 September 1992 the Slovenská národná rada (Slovak National Council) adopted the Constitution of the Slovak Republic (which entered into force on 1 January 1993), the main provisions of which, as amended in January 1999, are summarized below:

FUNDAMENTAL PROVISIONS

The Slovak Republic is a democratic and sovereign state, ruled by law. It is bound neither to an ideology, nor to a religion. State power belongs to the people, who exercise it either through their representatives or directly. The state authorities shall act only on the basis of the Constitution and to the extent and in the manner stipulated by law.

The territory of the Slovak Republic is integral and indivisible. The conditions for naturalization or deprival of state citizenship of the Slovak Republic are regulated by law. No person may be deprived of citizenship against his or her will. The Slovak language is the state language in the republic. The use of languages other than the state language in administrative relations is regulated by law. The capital of the republic is Bratislava.

BASIC RIGHTS AND FREEDOMS

The people are free and equal, and the rights and freedoms of every citizen are guaranteed, irrespective of sex, race, colour, language, faith, political or other conviction, national or social origin, nationality or ethnic origin. No person may be tortured, nor be subjected to cruel, inhuman or humiliating treatment or punishment. Capital punishment is not practised.

Every person has the right to own property. The place of abode is inviolable. The freedom of migration and the freedom of domicile are guaranteed.

The freedom of expression and the right to information are guaranteed. Censorship is prohibited. The right to assemble peacefully is guaranteed. Every person has the right to be a member of a union, community, society or any other association. Citizens have the right to found political parties and movements. Such parties and movements, as well as other associations, are separate from the State.

The citizens have the right to participate in the administration of public affairs, either directly or through the free election of their representatives. The right to vote is universal, direct and equal and is exercised by secret ballot.

The universal advancement of citizens who are members of national minorities and ethnic groups is guaranteed, above all the right to develop their own culture, to broadcast and receive information in their mother tongue, to join national associations and to found and maintain educational and cultural institutions. The languages of national minorities may also be used in administrative relations.

Every person has the right to the free choice of profession and vocational training, as well as to do business and to perform other commercial activities. Employees are entitled to fair and satisfactory working conditions. Citizens may form free associations to protect their economic and social interests. Trade unions are independent of the State. The right to strike is guaranteed.

Every citizen is entitled to adequate old-age and disability benefits; widow's allowances; free health care; family support; and education.

NÁRODNÁ RADA SLOVENSKEJ REPUBLIKY

Supreme legislative power is vested in the Národná rada Slovenskej republiky (National Council of the Slovak Republic—Národná rada), which has 150 deputies, elected for a four-year term. The deputies represent the citizens and are elected by them in general, equal and direct elections, by secret ballot.

The Národná rada has the power to: adopt the Constitution, constitutional and other laws and supervise their execution; decide on proposals to call a referendum; prior to their ratification, give consent to international political, economic or other agreements; establish ministries and other bodies of state administration; supervise the activities of the Government and pass a vote of confidence or censure on the Government or its members; approve the state budget and supervise its execution; elect judges, including the Chairman and Vice-Chairmen of the Supreme Court and of the Constitutional Court; adopt a resolution to declare war if the Slovak Republic is attacked, or if such a declaration ensues from the obligations of international treaties.

THE PRESIDENT OF THE REPUBLIC

The President is the Head of State of the Slovak Republic. He or she is directly elected by universal adult suffrage for a five-year term. The President is responsible to the Národná rada. He/she may not be elected for more than two consecutive terms.

The President represents the Slovak Republic internationally; negotiates and ratifies international agreements; receives and gives credentials to envoys; convenes constituent sessions of the Národná rada; may dissolve the Národná rada; signs laws; appoints and recalls the Prime Minister and other members of the Government and receives their resignation; grants amnesty, pardons and commutes sentences imposed by courts; may declare a state of emergency on the basis of constitutional law; may declare a referendum.

THE GOVERNMENT

The Government of the Slovak Republic is the highest organ of executive power. It is composed of the Prime Minister and Ministers. The Prime Minister is appointed by the President of the Republic. On the Prime Minister's recommendation, the President appoints and recalls the members of the Government and puts them in charge of their ministries. For the execution of office, the Government is responsible to the Národná rada.

The Government has the power to prepare bills; issue decrees; adopt fundamental provisions for economic and social policy; authorize drafts for the state budget and closing account of the year; decide international agreements; decide principal questions of internal and international policy; submit bills to the Národná rada; request the legislature for a vote of confidence.

* Further revisions to the Constitution were approved in February 2001 and officially entered into effect on 1 July. The amendments redefined the relationship between national and international law, incorporated Slovakia's aim of joining foreign alliances, strengthened the powers of the Constitutional Court, granted greater independence to the judiciary (by the establishment of a new judicial council), and provided for public administration reform, with the creation of a higher level of regional self-government.

The Government

HEAD OF STATE

President of the Republic: IVAN GAŠPAROVIČ (elected 17 April 2004; inaugurated 15 June 2004).

GOVERNMENT
(April 2008)

The Government comprises members of Direction-Social Democracy, the Slovak National Party (SNP) and the People's Party—Movement for a Democratic Slovakia (PP—MDS).

Prime Minister: ROBERT FICO (Direction-Social Democracy).
Deputy Prime Minister for the Knowledge-Based Economy, European Affairs, Human Rights and Minorities: DUŠAN ČAPLOVIČ (Direction-Social Democracy).
Deputy Prime Minister and Minister of the Interior: ROBERT KALIŇÁK (Direction-Social Democracy).
Deputy Prime Minister and Minister of Education: JÁN MIKOLAJ (SNP).
Deputy Prime Minister and Minister of Justice: ŠTEFAN HARABIN (PP—MDS).
Minister of Finance: JÁN POČIATEK (Direction-Social Democracy).
Minister of Foreign Affairs: JÁN KUBIŠ (Direction-Social Democracy).
Minister of the Economy: ĽUBOMÍR JAHNÁTEK (Direction-Social Democracy).
Minister of Defence: JAROSLAV BAŠKA (Direction-Social Democracy).
Minister of Culture: MAREK MAĎARIČ (Direction-Social Democracy).
Minister of Health: IVAN VALENTOVIČ (Direction-Social Democracy).
Minister of Agriculture: ZDENKA KRAMPLOVÁ (PP—MDS).
Minister of Transport, Post and Telecommunications: ĽUBOMÍR VÁŽNY (Direction-Social Democracy).
Minister of Construction and Regional Development: MARIÁN JANUŠEK (SNP).
Minister of Labour, Social Affairs and the Family: VIERA TOMANOVÁ (Direction-Social Democracy).
Minister of the Environment: JAROSLAV IZÁK (SNP).

MINISTRIES

Office of the President: Hodžovo nám. 1, 810 00 Bratislava, POB 128; tel. (2) 5720-1121; fax (2) 5441-7010; e-mail informacie@prezident.sk; internet www.prezident.sk.
Office of the Government: nám. Slobody 1, 813 70 Bratislava; tel. (2) 5729-5111; fax (2) 5249-7595; e-mail urad@government.gov.sk; internet www.government.gov.sk.
Ministry of Agriculture: Dobrovičova 12, 812 66 Bratislava; tel. (2) 5926-6111; fax (2) 5926-6311; e-mail tlacove@land.gov.sk; internet www.land.gov.sk.
Ministry of Construction and Regional Development: Prievozská 2B, 825 25 Bratislava; tel. (2) 5831-7111; fax (2) 5293-1203; e-mail informacie@build.gov.sk; internet www.build.gov.sk.
Ministry of Culture: nám. SNP 33, 813 31 Bratislava; tel. (2) 5939-1155; fax (2) 5939-1174; e-mail mksr@culture.gov.sk; internet www.culture.gov.sk.
Ministry of Defence: Kutuzovova 7, 832 47 Bratislava; tel. (2) 4425-0320; fax (2) 4425-3242; e-mail iveta.viragova@mod.gov.sk; internet www.mosr.sk.
Ministry of the Economy: Mierová 19, 827 15 Bratislava; tel. (2) 4854-1111; fax (2) 4333-7827; e-mail info@economy.gov.sk; internet www.economy.gov.sk.
Ministry of Education: Stromová 1, 813 30 Bratislava; tel. (2) 5937-4111; fax (2) 5937-4335; e-mail kancmin@minedu.sk; internet www.minedu.sk.
Ministry of the Environment: nám. Ľ. Štúra 1, 812 35 Bratislava; tel. (2) 5956-1111; fax (2) 5956-2031; e-mail info@enviro.gov.sk; internet www.enviro.gov.sk.
Ministry of Finance: Štefanovičova 5, POB 82, 817 82 Bratislava; tel. (2) 5958-1111; fax (2) 5249-8042; e-mail podatelna@mfsr.sk; internet www.finance.gov.sk.
Ministry of Foreign Affairs: Hlboká cesta 2, 833 36 Bratislava; tel. (2) 5978-1111; fax (2) 5978-2213; e-mail informacie@foreign.gov.sk; internet www.mzv.sk.
Ministry of Health: Limbová 2, POB 52, 837 52 Bratislava; tel. (2) 5937-3111; fax (2) 5477-7983; e-mail office@health.gov.sk; internet www.health.gov.sk.
Ministry of the Interior: Pribinova 2, 812 72 Bratislava; tel. (2) 5094-1111; fax (2) 5094-4397; e-mail tokmv@minv.sk; internet www.minv.sk.
Ministry of Justice: Župné nám. 13, 813 11 Bratislava; tel. (2) 5935-3111; fax (2) 5935-3600; e-mail tlacove@justice.sk; internet www.justice.gov.sk.
Ministry of Labour, Social Affairs and the Family: Špitálska 4–6, 816 43 Bratislava; tel. (2) 5975-1617; fax (2) 5292-1258; e-mail tothova@employment.gov.sk; internet www.employment.gov.sk.
Ministry of Transport, Post and Telecommunications: nám. Slobody 6, 810 05 Bratislava; tel. (2) 5949-4111; fax (2) 5249-4794; e-mail info@telecom.gov.sk; internet www.telecom.gov.sk.

President

Presidential Election, First Ballot, 3 April 2004

Candidates	Number of votes	%
Vladimír Mečiar	650,242	32.74
Ivan Gašparovič	442,564	22.28
Eduard Kukan	438,920	22.10
Rudolf Schuster	147,549	7.43
František Mikloško	129,414	6.52
Martin Bútora	129,387	6.51
Others	48,138	2.42
Total	**1,986,214**	**100.00**

Second Ballot, 17 April 2004

Candidates	Number of votes	%
Ivan Gašparovič	1,079,592	59.91
Vladimír Mečiar	722,368	40.09
Total	**1,801,960**	**100.00**

Legislature

**Národná rada Slovenskej republiky
(National Council of the Slovak Republic)**
nám. Alexandra Dubčeka 1 1, 812 80 Bratislava; tel. (2) 5972-1111; fax (2) 5441-9529; e-mail info@nrsr.sk; internet www.nrsr.sk.

Chairman: PAVOL PAŠKA.

SLOVAKIA

General Election, 17 June 2006

Party	Votes	% of votes	Seats
Direction-Social Democracy	671,185	29.14	50
Slovak Democratic and Christian Union-Democratic Party	422,815	18.36	31
Slovak National Party	270,230	11.73	20
Party of the Hungarian Coalition	269,111	11.68	20
People's Party—Movement for a Democratic Slovakia	202,540	8.79	15
Christian Democratic Movement	191,443	8.31	14
Others	275,815	11.98	—
Total valid votes	**2,303,049**	**100.00**	**150**

Election Commission

Ústredná volebná komisia, Ministerstva vnútra (Central Elections Commission, Ministry of the Interior): Drieňova 22, 826 86 Bratislava; tel. (2) 4859-1111; fax (2) 4333-3175; e-mail ovr.svs@mvsr.vs.sk; internet www.civil.gov.sk; organ of the Ministry of the Interior; Chair. EVA GARBIAROVÁ.

Political Organizations

Christian Democratic Movement (CDM) (Krestanskodemokratické hnutie—KDH): Bajkalská 25, 821 09 Bratislava; tel. (2) 5057-4101; fax (2) 5057-4049; e-mail tlacove@kdh.sk; internet www.kdh.sk; f. 1990; conservative; supports Christian and family values; Chair. PAVOL HRUŠOVSKÝ.

Civic Conservative Party (Občianska konzervatívna strana—OKS): Panenská 26, Bratislava 811 03; tel. (2) 6207-48238; e-mail oks@oks.sk; internet www.oks.sk; f. and regd 2001; Chair. PETER TATÁR.

Communist Party of Slovakia (CPS) (Komunistická strana Slovenska—KSS): Ústredný výbor, Hattalova 12A, 831 03 Bratislava; tel. and fax (2) 4437-2540; e-mail sekr@kss.sk; internet www.kss.sk; f. 1992 following merger of two Marxist parties, the Union of Communists of Slovakia (Zväz komunistov Slovenska) and the Communist Party of Slovakia—91 (Komunistická strana Slovenska—91), which were established by Orthodox communists opposed to the transformation of the Communist Party of Slovakia into the non-Marxist Party of the Democratic Left (Strana demokratickej lavice); Pres. JOZEF ŠEVC; Gen. Sec. Dr LADISLAV JAČA; 10,000 mems.

Direction-Social Democracy (Smer-Sociálna demokracia): Súmračná 27, 821 02 Bratislava; tel. and fax (2) 4342-6297; e-mail sekretariat.fico@strana-smer.sk; internet www.strana-smer.sk; f. and regd in 1999 as Direction (Smer); absorbed the Party of Civic Understanding in 2003; merged with the Party of the Democratic Left in Dec. 2004, and name changed as above; Chair. ROBERT FICO.

Free Forum Party (Slobodné fórum) (SF): Bazová 9, 821 08 Bratislava; tel. (2) 5564-2494; fax (2) 5564-2496; e-mail sf@slobodneforum.sk; internet www.slobodneforum.sk; f. 2003; regd 2004; centre-right; in March 2006 reached agreement on co-operation with the Democratic Party of Slovakia, the Democratic Union of Slovakia and the Green Party, ahead of legislative elections in June; Chair. ZUZANA MARTINÁKOVÁ.

Green Party (Strana zelených): Sienkiewiczova 4, 811 09 Bratislava; tel. and fax (2) 5292-3231; e-mail sekretariat@stranazelenych.sk; internet www.stranazelenych.sk; f. 1989; regd 1991; in March 2006 reached agreement on co-operation with the Democratic Party of Slovakia, the Democratic Union of Slovakia and the Free Forum, ahead of legislative elections in June; Chair. PAVEL PETRÍK.

Movement for Democracy (Hnutie za demokraciu—HZD): Nevädzová 5, 821 01, Bratislava; tel. (2) 4828-7638; fax (2) 4828-7417; e-mail hzd@hzd.sk; internet www.hzd.sk; f. and regd 2002 by former mems of the Movement for a Democratic Slovakia; Chair. JOZEF GRAPA.

Left-wing Bloc (Lavicový blok): Nevädzova 5, 821 01 Bratislava; e-mail aparat@lavicovyblok.sk; internet www.lavicovyblok.sk; regd 2002; Chair. JOZEF KALMAN.

New Citizens' Alliance (NCA) (Aliancia nového občana—ANO): Drobného 27, 841 01 Bratislava; tel. (2) 6920-2918; fax (2) 6920-2920; e-mail ano@ano-aliancia.sk; internet www.ano-aliancia.sk; f. 2001; centre-right; pro-reform; Dir PAVEL RUSKO.

Party of the Hungarian Coalition (PHC) (Strana maďarskej koalície/Magyar Koalíció Pártja): Čajakova 8, 811 05 Bratislava; tel. (2) 5249-5164; fax (2) 5249-5264; internet www.mkp.sk; f. 1998 by merger of Coexistence (Spolužitie/Együttélés), the Hungarian Christian Democratic Movement and the Hungarian Civic Party; Chair. PÁL CSÁKY.

People's Party—Movement for a Democratic Slovakia (PP—MDS) (Ludová strana—Hnutie za Demokratické Slovensko—LS—HZDS): POB 49, Tomášikova 32A, 830 00 Bratislava; tel. (2) 4822-0203; fax (2) 4822-0223; e-mail krampl@hzds.sk; internet www.hzds.sk; f. 1991 as Movement for a Democratic Slovakia; present name adopted 2003; Chair. VLADIMÍR MEČIAR.

People's Union (Ludová únia—LU): Hanulova 5B, 841 01 Bratislava; tel. (2) 6428-8312; fax (2) 6428-7567; e-mail ludovaunia@ludovaunia.sk; f. 2003 by fmr mems of Movement for a Democratic Slovakia; regd 2003; Chair. GUSTÁV KRAJČI.

Slovak Democratic and Christian Union-Democratic Party (SDCU-DP) (Slovenská demokratická a krestanská únia-Demokratická strana—SDKÚ-DS): Ružinovská 28, 827 35 Bratislava; tel. (2) 4341-4102; fax (2) 4341-4106; e-mail sdku@sdkuonline.sk; internet www.sdkuonline.sk; f. and regd 2000 as the Slovak Democratic and Christian Union; name changed as above following merger with the Democratic Party in Jan. 2006; Leader MIKULÁŠ DZURINDA.

Slovak National Party (SNP) (Slovenská národná strana—SNS): Šafárikovo nám. 3, 814 99 Bratislava; tel. (2) 5292-4260; fax (2) 5296-6188; e-mail sns@sns.sk; internet www.sns.sk; f. 1871; regd 1990; right-wing; against ethnic-Hungarian representation in govt; Chair. JÁN SLOTA.

Diplomatic Representation

EMBASSIES IN SLOVAKIA

Angola: Mudroňova 47, 811 03 Bratislava 1; tel. (2) 5441-2164; fax (2) 5441-2182; e-mail embangola1@embangola.sk; Ambassador ALBERTO CORREIA NETO.

Austria: Ventúrska 10, 811 01 Bratislava; tel. (2) 5930-1500; fax (2) 5443-2486; e-mail pressburg-ob@bmeia.gv.at; internet www.rakusko.eu; Ambassador Dr HELMUT WESSELY.

Belarus: Kuzmányho 3A, 811 06 Bratislava; tel. (2) 5441-6325; fax (2) 5441-6328; e-mail slovakia@belembassy.org; internet www.belembassy.org/slovakia; Chargé d'affaires a.i. VIKTOR NAVROTSKY.

Belgium: Fraňa krála 5, 811 05 Bratislava; tel. (2) 5710-1211; fax (2) 5249-4296; internet www.diplomatie.be/bratislava; Ambassador ALAIN COOLS.

Bulgaria: Kuzmányho 1, 811 06 Bratislava; tel. (2) 5441-5308; fax (2) 5441-2404; e-mail bulharskoet@stonline.sk; internet www.bulgarianembassy.sk; Ambassador OGNIAN GALKOV.

China, People's Republic: Jančova 8, 811 02 Bratislava; tel. (2) 6280-3348; fax (2) 6280-4285; Ambassador HUANG ZHONGPO.

Croatia: Mišikova 21, 811 06 Bratislava; tel. (2) 5443-3647; fax (2) 5443-5365; e-mail croemb.bratislava@mvpei.hr; Ambassador TOMISLAV CAR.

Cuba: Somolického 1A, 811 05 Bratislava; tel. (2) 5249-2777; fax (2) 5249-4200; Ambassador DAVID PAULOVICH ESCALONA.

Czech Republic: POB 208, Hviezdoslavovo nám. 8, 810 00 Bratislava; tel. (2) 5920-3303; fax (2) 5920-3330; e-mail bratislava@embassy.mzv.cz; internet www.mzv.cz/bratislava; Ambassador VLADIMÍR GALUŠKA.

Denmark: Panská 27, 816 06 Bratislava; tel. (2) 5930-0200; fax (2) 5443-3656; e-mail btsamb@um.dk; internet www.denmark.sk; Ambassador JORGEN MUNK RASMUSSEN.

Finland: Palisády 29, 811 06 Bratislava; tel. (2) 5980-5111; fax (2) 5980-5120; e-mail sanomat.brt@formin.fi; internet www.finlandembassy.sk; Ambassador RAUNO VIEMERÖ.

France: Hlavné nám. 7, 812 83 Bratislava; tel. (2) 5934-7111; fax (2) 5934-7199; e-mail diplo@france.sk; internet www.france.sk; Ambassador HENRY CUNY.

Germany: Hviezdoslavovo nám. 10, 813 03 Bratislava; tel. (2) 5920-4400; fax (2) 5441-9634; e-mail info@germanembassy.sk; internet www.germanembassy.sk; Ambassador Dr JOCHEN TREBESCH.

Greece: Hlavné nám. 4, 811 01 Bratislava; tel. (2) 5443-4143; fax (2) 5443-4064; e-mail embassy@greece.sk; internet www.greece.sk; Ambassador KONSTANTINOS KARABETSIS.

Holy See: Nekrasovova 17, 811 04 Bratislava; tel. (2) 5479-3528; fax (2) 5479-3529; e-mail nunziatura@nunziatura.sk; Apostolic Nuncio (vacant).

Hungary: Sedlárska 3, 814 25 Bratislava; tel. (2) 5920-5200; fax (2) 5443-5484; e-mail pozsony@embhung.sk; Ambassador ANTAL HEIZER.

India: Dunajská 4, 811 08 Bratislava; tel. (2) 5296-2915; fax (2) 5296-2921; e-mail eindia@slovanet.sk; internet www.indianembassy.sk; Ambassador HOMAI SAHA.

SLOVAKIA

Indonesia: Mudroňova 51, 811 03 Bratislava; tel. (2) 5441-9886; fax (2) 5441-9890; e-mail indonesia@indonesia.sk; internet www.indonesia.sk; Ambassador LUTFI RAUF.

Ireland: Carlton Savoy Bldg, Mostavá 2, 811 02 Bratislava 1; tel. (2) 5930-9611; fax (2) 5443-0690; e-mail bratislava@dfa.ie; Ambassador DECLAN CONNOLLY.

Israel: Slávičie údolie 106, POB 6, 811 02 Bratislava; tel. (2) 5441-0557; fax (2) 5441-0850; e-mail cao-sec@bratislava.mfa.gov.il; Ambassador ZEEV BOKER.

Italy: Palisády 49, 811 06 Bratislava; tel. (2) 5980-0011; fax (2) 5441-3202; e-mail amb.bratislava@esteri.it; internet www.ambbratislava.esteri.it; Ambassador ANTONINO PROVENZANO.

Japan: Hlavné nám. 2, 813 27 Bratislava; tel. (2) 5980-0100; fax (2) 5443-2771; internet www.sk.emb-japan.go.jp; Ambassador MAKOTO WASHIZU.

Libya: Révova ul. 45, 811 02 Bratislava 1; tel. (2) 5441-0324; fax (2) 5441-0730; e-mail lpb@stonline.sk; Sec. of People's Bureau AHMED KHALIFA.

Netherlands: Frana Krála 5, 811 05 Bratislava; tel. (2) 5262-5081; fax (2) 5249-1075; e-mail info@holandskoweb.com; internet www.holandskoweb.com; Ambassador ROB SWARTBOL.

Norway: Palisády 29, 811 06 Bratislava; tel. (2) 5910-0100; fax (2) 5910-0115; e-mail emb.bratislava@mfa.no; internet www.norway.sk; Ambassador BRIT LØVSETH.

Poland: Hummelova 4, 814 91 Bratislava; tel. (2) 5441-3175; fax (2) 5441-3184; e-mail bratampl@nextra.sk; internet www.polskevelvyslanectvo.sk; Chargé d'affaires a.i. BOGDAN WRZOCHALSKI.

Romania: Fraňa Krála 11, 811 05 Bratislava; tel. (2) 5249-1665; fax (2) 5244-4056; e-mail ro-embassy@ba.sknet.sk; internet bratislava.mae.ro; Chargé d'affaires a.i. GHEORGHE ANGHEL.

Russia: Godrova 4, 811 06 Bratislava; tel. (2) 5441-4436; fax (2) 5443-4910; e-mail embrus@chello.sk; internet www.slovakia.mid.ru; Ambassador ALEKSANDR I. UDALTSOV.

Serbia: Búdková 38, 811 04 Bratislava; tel. (2) 5443-1927; fax (2) 5443-1933; e-mail info@embassyscg.sk; Ambassador DANKO PROKIĆ.

Slovenia: Moyzesova 4, 813 15 Bratislava; tel. (2) 5726-7700; fax (2) 5245-0009; e-mail vbs@gov.si; Ambassador MAJA MARIJA LOVRENČIČ SVETEK.

Spain: Prepoštská 10, 811 01 Bratislava; tel. (2) 5441-5724; fax (2) 5441-7565; e-mail embepsk@mail.mae.es; Ambassador MIGUEL AGUIRRE DE CÁRCER GARCÍA DEL ARENAL.

Sweden: Palisády 29, 4th Floor, 811 06 Bratislava; tel. (2) 5910-2200; fax (2) 5910-2233; e-mail ambassaden.bratislava@foreign.ministry.se; internet www.swedenabroad.com/bratislava; Ambassador MIKAEL WESTERLIND.

Switzerland: Tolstého 9, 811 06 Bratislava; tel. (2) 5930-1111; fax (2) 5930-1100; e-mail vertretung@bts.rep.admin.ch; internet www.eda.admin.ch/bratislava; Ambassador JOSEF AREGGER.

Turkey: Holubyho 11, 811 03 Bratislava; tel. (2) 5441-5504; fax (2) 5441-3145; e-mail testta@nextra.sk; Ambassador TUNÇ ÜGDÜL.

Ukraine: Radvaňská 35, 811 01 Bratislava; tel. (2) 5920-2810; fax (2) 5441-2651; Ambassador INNA OHNYIVETS.

United Kingdom: Panská 16, 811 01 Bratislava; tel. (2) 5998-2000; fax (2) 5998-2237; e-mail bebra@internet.sk; internet www.britishembassy.sk; Ambassador MICHAEL JOHN WYN ROBERTS.

USA: Hviezdoslavovo nám. 5, 811 02 Bratislava; tel. (2) 5443-3338; fax (2) 5443-0096; e-mail cons@usembassy-bratislava.sk; internet www.usembassy.sk; Ambassador VINCENT OBSITNIK.

Judicial System

The judicial system of Slovakia has three levels: district courts (55), regional courts (eight) and the Supreme Court. Regional courts serve as courts of appeal to the district courts, as well as serving as courts of first instance in some cases: the Supreme Court is the highest judicial authority in the country, operating as a court of cassation and appeal for Regional Courts. There is also a Constitutional Court to ensure compliance with the Constitution. In April 2002 an 18-member Judicial Council was elected, all of whom were lawyers, and nine of whom were judges. Three members are nominated by the President, three by the legislature, three by the Government, and eight are elected by the judges themselves. The final member is the Chairman of the Supreme Court. The Council proposes candidates for judgeships, decides on the assignment of judges, comments on the budget, and elects the Chief Justice of the Supreme Court.

Supreme Court of the Slovak Republic
(Najvyšší súd Slovenskej republiky)
Župné nám. 13, Bratislava 81 490; tel. (2) 5935-3111; fax (2) 5441-1535; internet www.nssr.gov.sk.

Chairman: MILAN KARABÍN.

Office of the Prosecutor-General: Štúrova ul. 2, 812 85 Bratislava; tel. (2) 5953-2505; fax (2) 5953-2653; e-mail generalna.prokuratura@genpro.gov.sk; internet www.genpro.gov.sk; Prosecutor-General DOBROSLAV TRNKA.

Constitutional Court of the Slovak Republic
(Ústavný súd Slovenskej republiky)
Hlavná 110, 042 65 Košice; tel. (55) 720-7211; fax (55) 622-7639; e-mail ochodni@concourt.sk; internet www.concourt.sk.

Chairman: IVETTA MACEJKOVÁ.

Religion

The principal religion in Slovakia is Christianity, of which the largest denomination (representing some 69% of the total population according to the census of May 2001) is the Roman Catholic Church. About 10% of the population profess no religious belief.

CHRISTIANITY

The Roman Catholic Church

In early 2008 changes to the organization of the Roman Catholic Church in Slovakia were implemented. Slovakia comprises four archdioceses and seven dioceses. At 31 December 2005 there were an estimated 3,984,267 adherents, equivalent to 73.5% of the total population.

Bishops' Conference: Kapitulská 11, 81 499 Bratislava; tel. (2) 5443-5234; fax (2) 5443-5913; e-mail kbs@kbs.sk; internet www.rcc.sk; Pres. Rt Rev. FRANTIŠEK TONDRA (Bishop of Spiš).

Latin Rite

Archbishop of Bratislava: Most Rev. STANISLAV ZVOLENSKÝ, Hollého 10, POB 78, 917 66 Trnava; tel. (33) 591-2111; fax (33) 591-2280; e-mail abu@abu.sk.

Archbishop of Košice: Most Rev. ALOJZ TKÁČ, Hlavná 28, 041 83 Košice; tel. (55) 682-8111; fax (55) 622-1034; e-mail abukosice@kbs.sk; internet www.rimkat.sk/rs/_index.php.

Archbishop of Trnava: Most Rev. JAN SOKOL, Jána Hollého 10, POB 78, 919 66 Trnava; tel. (33) 591-2111; fax (33) 591-2280; e-mail abu@abu.sk; internet www.abu.sk.

Slovak Rite

Archbishop of Prešov: Most Rev. JÁN BABJAK, Hlavná 1, POB 135, 081 35 Prešov; tel. (51) 773-4622; fax (51) 756-2625; e-mail mons.babjak@greckokat.sk; internet www.grkatpo.sk; 137,203 adherents, 166 parishes (Dec. 2005).

The Eastern Orthodox Church

Orthodox Church in the Czech Lands and Slovakia (Pravoslávna cirkev v českých krajinách a na Slovensku): Budovatelská 1, 080 01 Prešov; tel. (51) 773-2174; fax (51) 773-4045; e-mail dzugan@orthodox.sk; internet www.orthodox.sk; divided into two eparchies in Slovakia: Prešov and Michalovce (the first of which is an archbishopric); and two eparchies in the Czech Republic: Prague and Olomouc—Brno (q.v.); Archbishop of Prešov Rev. JÁN.

Protestant Churches

Apostolic Church in Slovakia (Apoštolská cirkev na Slovensku): Sreznevského 2, 831 03 Bratislava; tel. and fax (2) 4425-0913; e-mail rada@acs-net.sk; internet www.acs-net.sk; f. 1956; affiliated to international Assemblies of God; 4,000 mems; Pres. JÁN LACHO.

Baptist Union of Slovakia: Súľovská 2, 821 05 Bratislava; tel. and fax (2) 4342-1145; e-mail baptist@baptist.sk; internet www.baptist.sk; f. 1994; 1,973 mems (2005); Pres. Rev. TOMÁŠ KRIŠKA; Gen. Sec. Rev. Dr DARKO KRAJLIK.

Evangelical Church of the Augsburg (Lutheran) Confession in Slovakia (Evanjelická cirkev augsburského vyznania na Slovensku): Palisády 46, POB 289, 811 00 Bratislava; tel. (2) 5443-2842; fax (2) 5443-2940; e-mail tlac@ecav.sk; internet www.ecav.sk; 327 parishes in 14 seniorates and two districts; 374,000 mems (Nov. 2001); Bishop-Gen. JÚLIUS FILO; Inspector-Gen. JÁN HOLČÍK.

Reformed Christian Church of Slovakia: Synodal Office, Hlavné nám. 23, 979 01 Rimavská Sobota; tel. (47) 562-1936; fax (47) 563-3090; e-mail reformata@reformata.sk; internet www.reformata.sk; 109,735 mems and 325 parishes (2001); Bishop Dr GÉZA ERDÉLYI.

JUDAISM

Central Union of the Jewish Religious Communities in the Slovak Republic (Ústredný zväz židovských náboženských obcí v Slovenskej republike): Kozia ul. 21, 814 47 Bratislava; tel. (2) 5441-

SLOVAKIA

2167; fax (2) 5441-1106; e-mail uzzno@netax.sk; c. 3,000 mems; Exec. Chair. Fero Alexander; Rabbi Baruch Myers.

The Press

The publications listed below are in Slovak, unless otherwise indicated.

PRINCIPAL DAILIES

Banská Bystrica

Smer magazín (Direction Magazine): Horná 37, 97401 Banská Bystrica; tel. (48) 415-1582; e-mail hospodarka.bb@petitpress.sk; internet www.regionalnenoviny.sk/?sek=rn_sdm; f. 1948; independent; Editor-in-Chief Zita Suráková.

Bratislava

Hospodárske noviny (Economic News): POB 35, Seberíniho 1, 820 07 Bratislava 27; tel. (2) 5063-3627; fax (2) 5063-4724; e-mail hn@hnx.sk; internet www.hnonline.sk; morning; Editor-in-Chief Alica Durianová; circ. 40,000.

Nový čas (New Time): Gorkého 5, 812 78 Bratislava; tel. (2) 536-3070; fax (2) 536-3104; f. 1991; morning; Editor-in-Chief Zuzana Račková; circ. 230,000.

Pravda (Truth): Trnavská cesta 39A, 831 04 Bratislava; tel. (2) 4959-6111; internet www.pravda.sk; f. 1920; independent; left-wing; Editor-in-Chief Pavol Minarik; circ. 165,000.

Roľnícke noviny (Agricultural News): Dobrovičova 12, 813 78 Bratislava; tel. (2) 368-449; fax (2) 321-282; f. 1946; Editor-in-Chief Juraj Šestak; circ. 20,000.

Slovenská republika (Slovak Republic): Ružová dolina 6, 824 70 Bratislava; tel. (2) 5022-1505; fax (2) 5022-1500; e-mail redakcia@republika.sk; Editor-in-Chief Eduard Fašung; circ. 78,000.

Sme (We Are): Mytná 33, 810 05 Bratislava; tel. (2) 5923-3500; fax (2) 5923-3669; internet www.sme.sk; f. 1993; merged with Práca (Labour) in Oct. 2002; Editor-in-Chief Martin Simecka; circ. 95,613.

Šport (Sport): Svätoplukova 2, 819 23 Bratislava; tel. (2) 60-053; fax (2) 211-380; Editor-in-Chief Zdeno Simonides; circ. 85,000.

Új szó (New Word): nám. SNP 30, 814 64 Bratislava; tel. (2) 5923-3459; fax (2) 523-8321; internet www.ujszo.com; f. 1948; midday; in Hungarian; Editor-in-Chief Attila Lovász; circ. 42,000.

Večerník (Evening Paper): Dunajská 4, 811 08 Bratislava; tel. (2) 5710-4021; fax (2) 5292-0741; e-mail vecernik@vecernikba.sk; internet www.vecernikba.sk; f. 1956; evening; Editor-in-Chief Míchaela Conzarová; circ. 30,000.

Košice

Košický večer (Košice Evening): tr. SNP 24, 042 97 Košice; tel. (55) 429-820; fax (55) 421-214; f. 1990; Editor-in-Chief Mikuláš Jesenský; circ. 25,000.

Lúč (Ray): B. Němcovej 32, 042 62 Košice; tel. (55) 633-2117; fax (55) 359-090; f. 1992; Editor-in-Chief Edita Pačajová-Kardošová; circ. 15,000.

Slovenský východ (Slovak East): Letná 45, 042 66 Košice; tel. (55) 53-979; fax (55) 53-950; Editor-in-Chief Dušan Klinger; circ. 30,000.

Prešov

Prešovský večerník (Prešov Evening Paper): Jarkova 4, 080 01 Prešov; tel. (51) 772-4563; fax (51) 772-3398; internet www.vecernik.po.sk; f. 1990; Editor-in-Chief Dr Peter Ličák; circ. 13,000.

PRINCIPAL PERIODICALS

A Het (The Week): Bratislava; weekly; Hungarian-language magazine; Editor-in-Chief Attila Lovász.

Avízo: Seberíniho 1, 821 03 Bratislava 2; tel. and fax (2) 4823-2111; e-mail obchod@avizo.sk; internet www.avizo.sk; 3 a week; advertising and information; Gen. Dir Oto Lanc; circ. 70,000.

Domino Efekt: Hlavná 68, 040 01 Košice; tel. and fax (55) 622-7692; f. 1992; weekly; Editor-in-Chief Andrej Hrico; circ. 20,000.

Domino fórum: Panská 13, 811 01 Bratislava; tel. (2) 5930-4088; e-mail domino@dofo.sk; internet www.dominoforum.sk; politics, economy, culture; pro-reform.

Elektrón + Zenit: Pražská 11, 812 84 Bratislava; tel. (2) 417-225; fax (2) 493-385; monthly; science and technology for young people; Editor-in-Chief Ladislav Gyorffy; circ. 22,000.

Eurotelevízia (Eurotelevision): POB 47, 820 04 Bratislava 24; tel. (2) 5822-7124; fax (2) 5822-7143; e-mail eurotelevizia@eurotelevizia.sk; weekly TV and radio guide; Editor-in-Chief Elena Budinská; circ. 290,000.

Directory

Eva: Pribinova 25, 819 39 Bratislava; tel. (2) 5063-3340; fax (2) 5063-4128; e-mail eva@euroskop.sk; internet www.euroskop.ringier.sk; monthly; magazine for women; Editor-in-Chief Katarina Patvarošová; circ. 120,000.

International: Štúrova 4, 815 80 Bratislava; tel. (2) 367-808; fax (2) 326-685; weekly; current affairs; Editor-in-Chief Tatiana Jaglová; circ. 60,000.

Kamarát (Friend): POB 73, 820 14 Bratislava; tel. and fax (2) 240-8777; f. 1950; fortnightly; magazine for teenagers; Editor-in-Chief Vladimír Topercer; circ. 30,000.

Katolícke noviny (Catholic News): Kapitulská 20, 815 21 Bratislava; tel. (2) 533-1790; fax (2) 533-3178; f. 1849; weekly; Editor-in-Chief Mária Kotesová; circ. 116,000.

Krásy Slovenska (Beauties of Slovakia): Dúbravská cesta 9, POB 115, 840 05 Bratislava 45; tel. (2) 5465-2055; fax (2) 5465-2056; e-mail info@krasy-slovenska.sk; internet www.krasy-slovenska.sk; illustrated bi-monthly; Editor-in-Chief Milan Kubiš; circ. 10,000.

Línia: Pribišova 19A, 841 05 Bratislava; tel. (2) 6025-1123; fax (2) 6025-1130; monthly; lifestyle; Editor-in-Chief Ján Hanuška; circ. 25,000.

Móda (Fashion): Štefánikova 4, 812 64 Bratislava; tel. (2) 765-704; fax (2) 491-191; quarterly; Editor-in-Chief Dana Lapšanská; circ. 20,000.

Ohník (Little Flame): Pražská 11, 812 84 Bratislava; tel. (2) 417-233; monthly; youth; Editor-in-Chief Stanislav Bebjak; circ. 35,000.

Plus 7 dní: Ružová dolina 27, 825 06 Bratislava; tel. (2) 65-683; fax (2) 201-6309; weekly; social magazine; Editor-in-Chief Miloš Luknár; circ. 60,000.

Rodina (Family): Pribinova 25, POB 122, 810 11 Bratislava; tel. (2) 210-4027; monthly; family magazine; Editor-in-Chief M. Város; circ. 145,000.

Romano nevo ľil/Rómsky nový list (The New Romany Journal): Jarková 4, 080 01 Prešov; tel. (51) 772-5283; fax (51) 773-3439; e-mail redakcia@rnl.sk; internet www.rnl.sk; f. 1991; in Romany, Slovak and English; publ. by the Association Jekhetane-Spolu (Together); Chief Editors Jozef Ferenc, Denisa Havrľová, Daniela Hivešová-Šilanová, Roman Čonka; circ. 8,500.

Slovenka (Slovak Woman): Jaskový rad 5, 833 80 Bratislava; tel. (2) 5478-9652; fax (2) 5477-6118; e-mail slovenka@slovenka.sk; f. 1948; weekly; illustrated magazine; Editor-in-Chief Zuzana Krútka; circ. 220,000.

Slovenské národné noviny (Slovak National News): Matica slovenská, Mudroňova 1, 036 52 Martin; tel. and fax (43) 413-4060; internet www.matica.sk/snn/snn.html; f. 1845; weekly; organ of Matica slovenská cultural organization; Editor-in-Chief Peter Mišák; circ. 7,000.

Slovenský profit: Pribinova 25, 810 11 Bratislava; tel. (2) 563-3817; fax (2) 563-4581; economic weekly; Editor-in-Chief Iveta Seifertová; circ. 25,000.

Stop: Exnárova 57, 820 12 Bratislava; tel. (2) 4342-5052; fax (2) 4342-0554; e-mail stop@ba.telecom.sk; fortnightly; motoring; Editor-in-Chief Ľuboš Kríž; circ. 47,000.

Szabad újság (Free Journal): Michalská 9, 814 99 Bratislava; tel. (2) 333-012; fax (2) 330-519; f. 1991; Hungarian-language economic weekly; Editor-in-Chief Géza Szabó; circ. 40,000.

Trend: Rezedova 5, POB 31, 820 07 Bratislava; tel. (2) 2082-2222; fax (2) 2082-2223; e-mail redakcia@trend.sk; internet www.etrend.sk; f. 1991; weekly; for entrepreneurs; publ. by Trend Holding; Editor-in-Chief Radoslav Baťo; circ. 25,000.

Vasárnap (Sunday): SNP 30, 814 64 Bratislava 1; tel. (2) 5923-3235; fax (2) 5923-3295; e-mail reklama@ujszo.com; f. 1948; weekly; independent Hungarian-language magazine; Editor-in-Chief József Szilvássy; circ. 97,000.

Výber (Digest): Kominárska 2, 832 03 Bratislava; tel. (2) 203-4486; fax (2) 203-4521; f. 1968; weekly; digest of home and foreign press; Editor-in-Chief Miroslava Avramovová; circ. 15,000.

Život (Life): Pribinova 25, 819 37 Bratislava; tel. (2) 210-4135; fax (2) 210-4145; f. 1951; illustrated family weekly; Editor-in-Chief Milan Város; circ. 255,000.

Zmena (Change): Sabinovská 14, 821 02 Bratislava; tel. (2) 237-758; fax (2) 522-6420; f. 1989; weekly; independent; Editor-in-Chief Vladimír Mohorita; circ. 20,000.

NEWS AGENCIES

Rómska tlačová agentúra (Roma Press Agency): Slovenskej jednoty 44, 040 01 Košice; tel. (55) 632-1372; e-mail rpa@rpa.sk; internet www.rpa.sk; reports on matters relating to the Roma minority, and aims to bring attention to issues affecting the community; Dir Ivan Hriczko.

SLOVAKIA

SITA: Mýtna 15, 811 07 Bratislava; tel. (2) 5249-6106; fax (2) 5249-3466; e-mail slovakam@sita.sk; internet www.sita.sk; f. 1997; independent; Dir-Gen. PAVOL MUDRY.

Tlačová agentúra Slovenskej republiky (TASR) (News Agency of the Slovak Republic): Pribinova 23, 819 28 Bratislava; tel. (2) 5921-0152; fax (2) 5296-2468; e-mail market@tasr.sk; internet www.tasr.sk; f. 1992; has overseas bureaux in Belgium, Czech Republic, Germany and Russia; Dir PETER NEDAVSKA.

PRESS ASSOCIATIONS

Slovenský syndikát novinárov (Slovak Syndicate of Journalists): Župné nám. 7, 815 68 Bratislava; tel. (2) 5443-5071; fax (2) 5443-2438; e-mail krutka.zuzana@ssn.sk; internet www.ssn.sk; f. 1968; reorganized 1990; 2,600 mems; Chair. ZUZANA KRÚTKA.

Združenie slovenských novinárov (Association of Slovak Journalists): Šafárikovo nám. 4, 811 02 Bratislava; tel. and fax (2) 363-184; f. 1992; 700 mems; Chair. JÁN SMOLEC.

Publishers

Academic Electronic Press: Bajzova 7, 821 08 Bratislava; tel. and fax (2) 5556-4495; non-fiction.

Dajama: Ľubľanská 2, 831 02 Bratislava; tel. and fax (2) 4463-1702; e-mail info@dajama.sk; internet www.dajama.sk; guide books about Slovakia in Slovak, Hungarian, German, Polish, Russian and English.

Enigma: Javorová 4, 949 01 Nitra 1; tel. (87) 655-5551; e-mail enigma@enigma.sk; internet www.enigma.sk; f. 1991; textbooks, translations of children's books, illustrated books; Dir VLADIMIR PRELOZNIK.

Epos, Ing. Miroslav Mračko: Pečnianska 27, 851 01 Bratislava 5; tel. and fax (2) 6241-2357; e-mail epos@epos.sk; internet www.epos.sk; f. 1990; economics, law, non-fiction.

Kalligram, s.r.o.: Staromestská 6D, POB 223, 810 00 Bratislava 1; tel. and fax (2) 5441-5028; e-mail kalligram@kalligram.sk; internet www.kaligram.sk; f. 1990; Slovak and Central European and world literature, literary criticism, philosophy, religion, history, social sciences, science; Dir LÁSZLÓ SZIGETI.

Koloman Kertész Bagala (LCA Publishers Group): POB 99, 810 00 Bratislava 1; tel. (2) 5441-5366; fax (2) 5464-7393; e-mail lca@lca.sk; internet www.lca.sk; f. 1991; fiction; Dir KOLOMAN KERTÉSZ BAGALA.

Matica slovenská: J. C. Hronského, 036 52 Martin; tel. (43) 413-2454; fax (43) 413-3188; e-mail msba@matica.sk; internet www.matica.sk; f. 1863; literary science, bibliography, biography and librarianship; Chair. Ing. JOZEF MARKUŠ.

Poradca podnikateľa, spol. s.r.o. (Entrepreneur's Adviser): Martina Rázusa 23A, 010 01 Žilina; tel. (41) 705-3777; fax (41) 705-3214; internet www.epi.sk; books and CD-ROMs providing economic and legal information; Dir JÁN BRIGANT.

Príroda a.s. (Nature): Krížkova 9, 811 04 Bratislava; tel. (2) 396-335; fax (2) 397-564; e-mail priroda@priroda.bts.sk; f. 1949; school textbooks, encyclopedias, reference books, etc. for children and young people; Chair. Ing. EMILIA JANKOVITSOVÁ.

Slovenské pedagogické nakladetel'stvo—Mladé letá, s.r.o. (Slovak Educational Publishing House—Young Years): Sasinkova 5, 815 19 Bratislava; tel. (2) 5022-7312; fax (2) 5542-5758; e-mail spn@spn.sk; internet www.spn-mladeleta.sk; f. 1920; pedagogical literature, educational, school texts, dictionaries; Exec. Man. DARINA TOROKOVA.

Slovenský spisovatel a.s. (Slovak Writer): A. Plávku 12, 813 67 Bratislava; tel. and fax (2) 499-736; e-mail slovspis@slovspis.sk; fiction, poetry; Dir MARTIN CHOVANEC.

Smena (Change): Pražská 11, 812 84 Bratislava; tel. (2) 498-018; fax (2) 493-305; f. 1949; fiction, literature for young people, newspapers and magazines; Dir Ing. JAROSLAV SIŠOLÁK.

Šport: Vajnorská 100/A, 832 58 Bratislava; tel. (2) 69-195; sport, physical culture, guide books, periodicals; Dir Dr BOHUMIL GOLIAN.

Tatran: Michalská 9, 815 82 Bratislava; tel. (2) 5443-5849; fax (2) 5443-5777; f. 1949; fiction, art books, children's books, literary theory; Dir Dr EVA MLÁDEKOVÁ.

Veda (Science): Bradáčova 7, 852 86 Bratislava; tel. and fax (2) 832-254; f. 1953; publishing house of the Slovak Academy of Sciences; scientific and popular scientific books and periodicals; Man. EVA MAJESKÁ.

PUBLISHERS' ASSOCIATION

Publishers' and Booksellers' Asscn of the Slovak Republic (Združenie vydavateľov a kníhkupcov Slovenskej republiky): Gregorovej 8, 821 03 Bratislava; tel. and fax (2) 4333-6700; e-mail alex.aust@post.sk; Pres. Dr ALEX AUST.

Broadcasting and Communications

TELECOMMUNICATIONS

Regulatory Authority

Telecommunications Office of the Slovak Republic: Továrenská 7, POB 18, 810 06 Bratislava 16; tel. (2) 5788-1111; fax (2) 5293-2096; e-mail eduard.mracka@teleoff.gov.sk; internet www.teleoff.gov.sk; Chair. MILAN LUKNÁR.

Service Providers

Orange Slovensko (Orange Slovakia): Prievozská 6, 821 09 Bratislava; tel. (2) 5851-2345; e-mail info@orange.sk; internet www.orange.sk; f. 1997 as Globtel; present name adopted 2002; wholly owned by Orange (France); provides mobile cellular telecommunications services; Dir-Gen. PAVOL LANČARIČ.

T-Com, a.s.: nám. Slobody 6, 817 62 Bratislava 15; tel. (2) 5249-2324; fax (2) 5249-2492; e-mail sekr.gr@st.sk; internet www.t-com.sk; 51% owned by Deutsche Telekom (Germany), 34% owned by Ministry of Transport, Posts and Telecommunications, 15% owned by the National Property Fund of the Slovak Republic; formerly Slovenské Telekomunikácie; name changed to Slovak Telecom in Jan. 2004; name changed as above in March 2006; Pres. and Chief Exec. MIROSLAV MAJOROŠ.

T-Mobile Slovensko, a.s.: Vajnorská 100A, 831 03 Bratislava; tel. (2) 4955-1111; internet www.t-mobile.sk; f. 1997; 100% owned by T-Com; provides mobile cellular telecommunications services; Gen. Dir ROBERT CHVÁTEL.

BROADCASTING

Radio

Slovenský rozhlas (Slovak Radio): Mýtna 1, POB 55, 817 55 Bratislava; tel. (2) 5727-3560; fax (2) 5249-8923; e-mail interrel@slovakradio.sk; internet www.slovakradio.sk; f. 1926; Dir-Gen. MILOSLAVA ZEMKOVÁ.

Television

Slovenská televízia (STV) (Slovak Television): Mlynská dolina 28, 845 45 Bratislava; tel. (2) 6542-3001; fax (2) 6542-2341; internet www.stv.sk; f. 1956; public broadcasting co; Chair. of Council JAROSLAV FRANEK; Gen. Man. ŠTEFAN NIŽŇANSKÝ.

Slovenská Televizná Spoločnosť: tel. (2) 6827-4111; fax (2) 6595-6824; internet tv.markiza.sk; e-mail markiza@markiza.sk; f. 1996; broadcasts as Markiza TV; first privately owned television channel; owned by Central European Media Enterprises Ltd; Dir-Gen. VLADIMÍR REPČÍK.

TA3: Gagarinova 12, POB 31, 820 15 Bratislava; e-mail web@ta3.com; internet www.ta3.com; f. 2001; privately owned; Dir-Gen. MARTIN LENGYEL; Editor-in-Chief ZDENEK SAMAL.

TV Joj: Grešákova 10, 040 01 Košiče; tel. (55) 622-2664; fax (55) 622-1027; e-mail joj@joj.sk; internet www.joj.sk; f. 2002; privately owned subsidiary of Nova TV (Czech Republic); Dir-Gen. VLADIMÍR ŽELEZNÝ; Dir MILAN KNAŽKO.

TV Markíza: Bratislavská 1A, POB 7, 843 56 Bratislava 48; tel. (2) 6827-4111; fax (2) 6595-6824; e-mail markiza@markiza.sk; internet tv.markiza.sk; 80% owned by Central European Media Enterprises Ltd (USA); Dir-Gen. VÁCLAV MIKA.

Finance

(cap. = capital; res = reserves; dep. = deposits; m. = million; brs = branches; amounts in Slovak koruna, unless otherwise indicated)

BANKING

Central Bank

National Bank of Slovakia (Národná banka Slovenska): Imricha Karvaša 1, 813 25 Bratislava; tel. (2) 5787-1111; fax (2) 5787-1100; e-mail webmaster@nbs.sk; internet www.nbs.sk; f. 1993; res −49,994.0m., dep. 311,918.0m. (Dec. 2006); central bank and bank of issue; Gov. IVAN ŠRAMKO.

Commercial Banks

Citibank (Slovakia), a.s.: Mlynské nivy 43, 825 01 Bratislava; tel. (2) 5823-0111; fax (2) 5823-0200; e-mail citibank.slovakia@citibank

SLOVAKIA

Directory

.com; internet www.citibank.sk; f. 1995; cap. 1,650.0m., res 966.2m., dep. 35,707.1m. (Dec. 2006); Gen. Dir IGOR THAM; 3 brs.

Dexia banka slovensko, a.s.: Hodžova 11, 010 11 Žilina; tel. (41) 511-1111; fax (41) 562-4129; e-mail info@dexia.sk; internet www.dexia.sk; f. 1993; fmrly Prvá komunálna banka; name changed as above 2003; cap. 1,202.4m., res 517.3m., dep. 51,830.0m. (Dec. 2006); Pres. and Chair. PAVOL DURINIK; 52 brs.

Komerční Banka Bratislava, a.s.: Medená 6, POB 137, 811 02 Bratislava; tel. (2) 5927-7111; fax (2) 5296-4801; e-mail koba@koba.sk; internet www.koba.sk; f. 1995; cap. 500.0m., res 169.3m., dep. 4,742.5m. (Dec. 2006); Chair. JAROMÍR CHABR.

Ľudová banka, a.s. (People's Bank): Vysoká 9, POB 81, 810 00 Bratislava; tel. (2) 5965-1111; fax (2) 5441-2453; e-mail market@luba.sk; internet www.luba.sk; f. 1991; cap. 1,000.0m., res 2,973.2m., dep. 32,091.5m. (Dec. 2006); Chair. KURT KAPELLER; 12 brs.

OTP Banka Slovensko, a.s. (Investment and Development Bank): Štúrova 5, 813 54 Bratislava; tel. (2) 5979-1111; fax (2) 5296-3484; e-mail info@otpbanka.sk; internet www.otpbanka.sk; f. 1992 as Investičná a rozvojová banka; name changed as above in 2002; cap. 2,064.4m., res 449.8m., dep. 40,361.7m. (Dec. 2006); Pres. ERNÖ KELECSÉNYI; 72 brs.

Poštová banka, a.s. (Postal Bank): Prievozska 2B, 821 09 Bratislava; tel. (2) 5960-3333; fax (2) 5960-3344; e-mail postbank@pabk.sk; internet www.pabk.sk; f. 1993; cap. 2,449.1m., res 722.9m., dep. 22,821.5m. (Dec. 2006); Gen. Dir and Chair. ROMAN FECIK; 24 brs.

Privatbanka, a.s.: Suché Mýto 1, 811 03 Bratislava; tel. (2) 5920-6620; fax (2) 5443-3131; e-mail privatbanka@privatbanka.sk; internet www.privatbanka.sk; f. 1996; cap. 756.9m., res 46.6m., dep. 6,568.9m. (Dec. 2006); fmrly Banka Slovakia a.s.; name changed as above Nov. 2005; Chair. and CEO ĽUBOŠ ŠEVČÍK.

Tatra banka, a.s.: POB 42, Hodzovo nám. 3, 811 06 Bratislava; tel. (2) 5919-1111; fax (2) 5919-1110; e-mail tatrabanka@tatrabanka.sk; internet www.tatrabanka.sk; f. 1990; total assets 208,820.7m., dep. 184,249.1m. (Dec. 2006); Chair. and Gen. Man. IGOR VIDA; 30 brs.

UniCredit Bank, a.s.: Sancová 1A, 813 33 Bratislava; tel. (2) 4950-2112; fax (2) 4437-3975; internet www.unicreditbank.sk; f. 1990; name changed as above 2007; cap. 2,377.1m., res 1,323.5m., dep. 45,804.4m. (Dec. 2006); Chair. of Bd and CEO JOZEF BARTA; 10 brs.

Všeobecná úverová banka, a.s. (General Credit Bank): Mlynské Nivy 1, POB 90, 829 90 Bratislava; tel. (2) 5055-1111; fax (2) 5556-6650; internet www.vub.sk; f. 1990; sold to Banka Intesa (Italy) in 2001; cap. 12,978.0m., res 3,021.0m., dep. 216,168.0m. (Dec. 2006); Chair. and CEO IGNACIO JAQUOTOT; 240 brs.

Savings Banks

Prvá stavebná sporiteľňa, a.s.: Bajkalská 30, POB 48, 829 48 Bratislava; tel. (2) 5823-1111; fax (2) 5341-1131; internet www.pss.sk; f. 1992; cap. 1,000m.; Chair. of Bd IMRICH BÉREŠ.

Slovenská sporiteľňa, a.s. (Slovak Savings Bank): Suché mýto 4, 816 07 Bratislava; tel. (2) 5850-3111; fax (2) 5957-4009; e-mail info@slsp.sk; internet www.slsp.sk; f. 1842; fmrly state-owned; absorbed operations of Priemyselná banka (Industrial Bank) in 1999; 100% owned by Erste Bank (Austria) since 2001; dep. 270,661.0m., total assets 297,9082m. (Dec. 2006); Chair. and Gen. Dir REGINA OVESNY-STRAKA; 270 brs.

COMMODITY AND STOCK EXCHANGES

Bratislava Commodity Exchange (Komoditná burza Bratislava): 29 Augusta 2, 811 07 Bratislava; tel. (2) 5293-1010; fax (2) 5293-1007; e-mail burza@kbb.sk; internet www.kbb.sk; Gen. Sec. IVAN POLIAČIK.

Bratislava Stock Exchange (Burza cenných papierov v Bratislave, a.s.): Vysoká 17, POB 151, 814 99 Bratislava 1; tel. (2) 4923-6111; fax (2) 4923-6103; e-mail info@bsse.sk; internet www.bsse.sk; f. 1991; Dir-Gen. MÁRIA HURAJOVÁ; Chair. MARIÁN ŠEDO.

INSURANCE

Allianz—Slovak Insurance Co (Allianz—Slovenská poisťovňa, a.s.): Dostojevského rad 4, 815 74 Bratislava; tel. (2) 5963-1111; fax (2) 5963-2740; e-mail info@allianzsp.sk; internet www.allianzsp.sk; 84.5% owned by Allianz AG (Germany), 15% owned by European Bank for Reconstruction and Development; majority stake divested to Allianz AG (Germany) in 2002; name changed from Slovenská poisťovňa to Allianz—Slovenská poisťovňa in 2003; Chair. and Pres. RUDOLF JANÁČ; 2,900 employees.

Trade and Industry

GOVERNMENT AGENCIES

National Property Fund of the Slovak Republic (Fond Národného Majetku Slovenskej Republiky): Drieňová 27, 821 01 Bratislava; tel. (2) 4827-1111; fax (2) 4827-1289; e-mail fnm@natfund.gov.sk; internet www.natfund.gov.sk; f. 1993; supervises the privatization process; Pres. PETER ŠIMKO.

SARIO—Slovak Investment and Trade Development Agency (SARIO—Slovenská agentúra pre rozvoj investícií a obchodu): Martinčekova 17, 821 01 Bratislava; tel. (2) 5826-0100; fax (2) 5826-0109; e-mail sario@sario.sk; internet www.sario.sk; f. 1991; Gen. Dir MILAN JURÁŠKA.

CHAMBERS OF COMMERCE

Slovak Chamber of Commerce and Industry (Slovenská obchodná a priemyselná komora): Gorkého 9, 816 03 Bratislava; tel. (2) 5443-3291; fax (2) 5413-1159; e-mail sopkurad@scci.sk; internet www.scci.sk; Pres. Dr PETER MIHÓK.

Banská Bystrica Chamber of Commerce and Industry: Nám. Š. Moysesa 4, 974 01 Banská Bystrica; tel. (48) 412-5634; fax (48) 412-5636; e-mail sopkrbb@sopk.sk; internet www.bb.scci.sk.

Košice Chamber of Commerce and Industry: Floriánska 19, 040 01 Košice; tel. (55) 7279-160; fax (55) 7279-156; e-mail sopkrkke@scci.sk; internet www.sopk.sk/ko/sk; Dir IVAN PEZLÁR.

Trenčín Chamber of Commerce and Industry: ul. Jilemnického 2, 911 01 Trenčín; tel. (32) 652-3834; fax (32) 652-1023; e-mail sopkrktn@scci.sk; internet www.sopk.sk/tn/an/index.html.

Žilina Chamber of Commerce and Industry: ul. Halková 31, 010 01 Žilina; tel. (41) 723-5655; fax (41) 723-5653; internet www.sopk.sk/za/sk; Dir JÁN MIŠURA.

UTILITIES

Electricity

Slovenské elektrárne, a.s. (SE) (Slovak Electricity): Hraničná 12, 827 36 Bratislava 212; tel. (2) 5866-1111; fax (2) 5341-7525; e-mail info@hq.seas.sk; internet www.seas.sk; fmr state-owned utility; 66% share acquired by Enel (Italy) in April 2006; 34% owned by the Slovak National Property Fund; Dir-Gen. and Chair. PAOLO RUZZINI; Deputy Chair. MARCO ARCELLI.

Stredoslovenská energetika, a.s. (SSE) (Central Slovakia Energy): Republiky 5, 010 47 Žilina; tel. (41) 519-1111; fax (41) 519-2575; e-mail sse@sse.sk; internet www.sse.sk; 51% owned by the National Property Fund of the Slovak Republic, 49% by Eléctricité de France; regional electricity distributor; Gen. Dir PATRICK LUCCIONI.

Východoslovenská energetika, a.s. (VSE) (East Slovakia Energy): Mlynská 31, 042 91 Košice; tel. (55) 610-2111; fax (55) 678-6516; e-mail info@vse.sk; internet www.vse.sk; 51% owned by the National Property Fund of the Slovak Republic, 49% by RWE Energie AG (Germany); regional electricity distributor; Chair. and Gen. Dir NORBERT SCHÜRMANN.

Západoslovesnká energetika (ZSE) (West Slovakia Energy): Čulenova 6, 816 47 Bratislava; tel. (2) 5296-1741; fax (2) 5061-3901; e-mail kontakt@zse.sk; internet www.zse.sk; f. 1922; 51% owned by National Property Fund of the Slovak Republic, 40% by E.ON Energie AG (Germany) and 9% by the European Bank for Reconstruction and Development; regional electricity distributor; Chair. of Bd of Dirs KONRAD KREUZER; Dir of Man. Bd Dr JÁN ORLOVSKÝ.

Gas

Slovenský Plynárenský Priemysel (SPP) (Slovak Gas Co): Mlynské nivy 44A, 825 11 Bratislava; tel. (2) 5869-1111; fax (2) 5869-2765; e-mail spp@spp.sk; internet www.spp.sk; partially privatized in July 2002; Chair. Ing. JAN MASSMANN; Gen. Dir MIROSLAV LAPUNÍK.

TRADE UNIONS

Confederation of Trade Unions of the Slovak Republic (Konfederácia odborových zväzov Slovenskej republiky): Odborárské nám. 3, 815 70 Bratislava; tel. (2) 5557-6065; fax (2) 5023-9102; e-mail press@kozsr.sk; internet www.kozsr.sk; Pres. IVAN SAKTOR; 1.1m. mems; affiliated unions listed below.

Metalworkers' Federation (Odborový zväz kovo—OZ KOVO): Miletičova 24, 815 70 Bratislava; tel. (2) 5556-5383; fax (2) 5556-5387; e-mail oskovo@kovo.sk; internet www.ozkovo.sk; Pres. EMIL MACHYNA.

Trade Union of Workers in Agriculture: Vajnorská 1, 815 70 Bratislava; tel. (2) 542-4186; fax (2) 542-1673; Pres. SVETOZÁR KORBEĽ.

Trade Union of Workers in the Chemical Industry (Odborový zväz chémia Slovenskej Republiky): Osadná 6, 831 03 Bratislava 3; tel. (2) 4445-3941; fax (2) 4437-3538; e-mail ozchsr@ozchsr.sk; internet www.ozchsr.sk; f. 1993; Chair. JURAJ BLAHÁK.

Trade Union of Workers in Construction and Construction Materials: Vajnorská 1, 815 70 Bratislava; tel. (2) 5542-4180; fax (2) 5542-2764; e-mail stavba@nextra.sk; Pres. DUŠAN BARČÍK.

Trade Union of Workers in Cultural and Social Organizations: Vajnorská 1, 815 70 Bratislava 1; tel. and fax (2) 5542-3760; e-mail sozkaso@nextra.sk; Pres. MÁRIA KRIŠTOFIČOVÁ.

Trade Union of Workers in Education and Science (Odborový zväz pracovníkov školstva a vedy na Slovensku): Vajnorská 1, 815 70 Bratislava; tel. and fax (2) 5542-4448; e-mail dubekova@ozpsav.sk; internet www.ozpsav.sk; Chair. JÁN GAŠPERAN; 82,800 mems.

Trade Union of Workers in Energy: Vajnorská 1, 815 70 Bratislava; tel. and fax (2) 542-1622; f. 1992; Pres. VLADIMIR MOJŠ.

Trade Union of Workers in the Food-processing Industry: Vajnorská 1, 815 70 Bratislava; tel. (2) 5542-1575; fax (2) 566-2506; e-mail ozp@isnet.sk; Pres. MAGDALENA MELLENOVA.

Trade Union of Workers in the Glass Industry: ul. Matice Slovenskej 19, 911 05 Trenčín; tel. (32) 743-7200; Pres. MIROSLAV BUČEK.

Trade Union of Workers in Health and Social Services (Slovenský odborový zväz zdravotníctva a sociálnych služieb): Vajnorská 1, 815 70 Bratislava 3; tel. (2) 5024-0257; fax (2) 5542-5330; internet www.sozpzass.sk; f. 1990; Pres. ANDREJ KUČINSKÝ.

Trade Union of Workers in Radio, Television and Newspapers: Vajnorská 1, 815 70 Bratislava; tel. (2) 211-844; Pres. PETER JÁCHIN.

Trade Union of Workers in the Textile, Clothing and Leather Industry: Vajnorská 1, 815 70 Bratislava; tel. (2) 213-389; fax (2) 526-2570; Pres. Ing. KONŠTANTÍN BALÁŽ.

Trade Union of Workers in the Wood-working, Furniture and Paper Industries (Odborový zväz pracovníkov drevospracujúceho priemyslu, lesného a vodného hospodárstva na Slovensku): Vajnorská 1, 815 70 Bratislava; tel. (2) 5542-3660; fax (2) 5542-3163; e-mail sekretariat@ozdlv.sk; internet www.ozdlv.sk; Pres. BORISLAV MAJTÁN.

Transport

RAILWAYS

In 2004 the total length of railways in Slovakia was estimated at 3,660 km, of which 1,556 km were electrified. In June 2005 Slovakia agreed to modernize its railway network in order to meet European Union rail transport standards. The cost of the process, expected to be completed in 2020, was estimated at €2,000m.

Železničná spoločnosť Cargo Slovakia, a.s. (ZSSK Cargo): Drieňová 24, 820 09 Bratislava; e-mail infoservis@zscargo.sk; internet www.zscargo.sk; f. 2005, following division into two of the state railway company, Železničná spoločnost, a.s.; operation of rail freight transport and freight-related commercial activities; state-owned.

Železničná spoločnosť Slovensko, a.s.: Žabotova 14, 813 13 Bratislava; tel. (2) 5058-7015; fax (2) 5341-0128; e-mail info@slovakrail.sk; internet www.slovakrail.sk; f. 2005, following division into two of the state railway company, Železničná spoločnost, a.s.; passenger transport; state-owned; Dir-Gen. ONDREJ MATEJ.

Železnice Slovenskej republiky (Slovak State Railways): Klemensova 8, 813 61 Bratislava; tel. (2) 2029-1111; fax (2) 5296-2296; e-mail gr@zsr.sk; internet www.zsr.sk; f. 1993; became a joint-stock co with responsibility for management of rail infrastructure in 2001, when responsibility for operations was transferred to the newly established state-owned concern, Železničná spoločnost; Dir-Gen. ANDREJ EGYED.

Dopravný podnik Bratislava, a.s. (Bratislava Transport): Olejkárska 1, 814 52 Bratislava; tel. (2) 5950-1411; fax (2) 5950-1400; e-mail sekretariat.gr@dpb.sk; internet www.dpb.sk; tramway being upgraded to light-rail system; 11 routes with 154 stops; Dir-Gen. J. ZACHAR.

ROADS

In 2004 the total length of the road system (including motorways) was estimated at 43,000 km, of which 87.3% was paved.

Slovak Road Administration (Slovenská správa ciest): Miletičova 19, 826 19 Bratislava; tel. (2) 5025-5111; fax (2) 5556-7976; e-mail info@ssc.sk; internet www.ssc.sk; f. 1996; Dir-Gen. Ing. ROMAN ŽEMBERA.

INLAND WATERWAYS

The total length of navigable waterways in Slovakia (on the River Danube) is 172 km. The Danube provides a link with Germany, Austria, Hungary, Serbia, Bulgaria, Romania and the Black Sea. The main river ports are Bratislava and Komárno.

State Shipping Authority (Štátna plavebná správa): ul. Prístavná 10, 821 09 Bratislava; tel. (2) 5556-6336; fax (2) 5556-6335; e-mail sekretariat@sps.sk; internet www.sps.sk; Dir Ing. JÁN JURIA.

Slovak Shipping and Ports Co, a.s. (Slovenská plavba a prístavy, a.s.): Pribinova 24, 815 24 Bratislava; tel. (2) 5827-1111; fax (2) 5827-1114; e-mail spap@spap.sk; internet www.spap.sk; Chair. of Advisory Committee PETER PLANÝ; Chair. of Bd JOZEF BLAŠKO; Gen. Man. ANTON PRNO.

CIVIL AVIATION

There are five international airports in Slovakia: Bratislava (M. R. Štefánik Airport), Košice, Piešťany, Poprad and Sliač. Until Slovak Airlines, the national carrier, began operations in March 1998, Czech Airlines (CSA) provided air transport services for both Slovakia and the Czech Republic. In February 2006 the TwoOne consortium, led by Flughafen Wien (Austria), won a bid to purchase the Government's 66% stake in Bratislava and Košice airports. The privatization process was temporarily suspended later in February, pending legislative elections in June. The acquisition of the Government's stake in Košice airport was completed in October, at a cost to the TwoOne consortium of €23.7m. However, the acquisition of Bratislava airport was halted in August by the newly installed Government led by Robert Fico.

Air Slovakia: Pestovateľská ul. 2, 821 04 Bratislava; tel. (2) 4342-2744; fax (2) 4342-2742; e-mail airslovakia@airslovakia.sk; internet www.airslovakia.sk; f. 1993; scheduled passenger flights between Slovakia and Cyprus, India, Israel, Italy, Kuwait and the United Kingdom; charter and cargo services; Gen. Dir AUGUSTIN BERNAT.

SkyEurope Airlines, a.s.: Ivanská 26, POB 24, 821 04 Bratislava 21; tel. (2) 4850-1111; fax (2) 4850-1000; e-mail info@skyeurope.com; internet www.skyeurope.com; f. 2001; first budget airline in Central Europe; joint venture with Spanish and Belgian interests; scheduled and charter passenger and cargo services; domestic and international services; Chief Exec. CHRISTIAN MANDL; Chair. ALAIN SKOWRONEK.

Slovenské aerolínie, a.s. (Slovak Airlines): Letisko M. R. Štefánika, 820 01 Bratislava 21; tel. (2) 4445-0096; fax (2) 4445-0097; internet www.sll.sk; f. 1995; 62% stake acquired by Austrian Airlines (Austria) in Jan. 2005; scheduled and charter passenger and cargo services; scheduled international services between Bratislava and Brussels (Belgium) and Moscow (Russia); international charter services to Russia, Spain, Italy, Bulgaria, Cyprus, Turkey, Greece and Tunisia; Chair. CHRISTIANE BÖHM-MAYER.

Tatra Air: Banská Bystrica; tel. and fax (48) 412-4509; e-mail tatraair@tatraair.sk; internet www.tatraair.sk; f. 1990; scheduled passenger flights between Silac and Prague (Czech Republic), charter flights, air taxi service; Chair. ANDREJ KVASNA.

Tourism

Slovakia's tourist attractions include ski resorts in the High and Low Tatras and other mountain ranges, more than 20 spa resorts (with thermal and mineral springs), numerous castles and mansions, and historic towns, including Bratislava, Košice, Nitra, Bardejov, Kežmarok and Levoča. In 2005 1,514,980 foreign tourists visited Slovakia, compared with 975,105 in 1999. In 2004 revenue from tourism totalled US $932m.

Slovak Tourist Board: nám. L. Stura 1, POB 35, 974 05 Banská Bystrica; tel. (48) 413-6146; fax (48) 413-6149; internet www.slovakiatourism.sk.

SLOVENIA

Introductory Survey

Location, Climate, Language, Religion, Flag, Capital

The Republic of Slovenia is situated in south-central Europe. It is bounded by Austria to the north, Hungary to the north-east, Croatia to the south and east, and by Italy to the west, and it has a short western coastline on the Adriatic Sea. The climate is Alpine in the mountainous areas, Mediterranean along the coast and continental in the interior. Average temperatures range from between 0°C (32°F) and 22°C (71.6°F) inland, and between 2°C (35.6°F) and 24°C (75.2°F) on the coast. Average annual rainfall ranges from 800 mm (31.5 ins) in the east to 3,000 mm (118.1 ins) in the north-west. The official language is Slovene, and, in ethnically mixed regions, also Hungarian and Italian. The majority religion in Slovenia is Roman Catholicism, although there are small communities of other Christian denominations and of Muslims and Jews. The national flag (proportions 2 by 3) consists of three horizontal stripes of white, blue and red, with a shield in the upper hoist depicting a white three-peaked mountain (Triglav), below which are two horizontal wavy blue lines and above which are three six-pointed yellow stars. The capital is Ljubljana.

Recent History

Following the collapse of the Austro-Hungarian Empire, the Kingdom of Serbs, Croats and Slovenes was proclaimed on 4 December 1918. (The territory of Slovenia was formally ceded by Austria by the Treaty of Saint-Germain in 1919.) In 1929 the name of the country was changed to Yugoslavia. Yugoslavia collapsed under German attack in 1941 and, during the Second World War, Germany annexed lower Styria and Yugoslav Carinthia, while Italy annexed Istria and the territory around Ljubljana. (There was a continuing dispute with Italy over Istria; in 1954 Italy was awarded the city of Trieste, and Yugoslavia the remainder of the territory, giving Slovenia access to the sea.) Hungary occupied the plains along the Mura in north-eastern Slovenia.

The Slovene Liberation Front, formed in 1941, joined with the communist-led all-Yugoslav Partisan Army of Josip Broz (Tito), which was eventually recognized as an ally by the British and US Governments. Following the post-war proclamation of the Federal People's Republic of Yugoslavia (from 1963 the Socialist Federal Republic of Yugoslavia—SFRY), Slovenia became the most prosperous of the Yugoslav republics, but was increasingly suspicious of Serb domination. On 27 September 1989 the Slovene Assembly voted in favour of radical amendments to the Constitution of Slovenia, confirming Slovenia's sovereignty and its right to secede from the SFRY. The organization of multi-party elections was envisaged, and the establishment of opposition parties (the local League of Communists of Slovenia—LCS—having hitherto been the only legal party) was formally authorized. Slovenia was warned that the amendments contravened the Federal Constitution, and the Serbian leader, Slobodan Milošević, attempted to arrange protests in Slovenia against the Slovene leadership; however, the planned demonstrations were banned in November. Milošević subsequently instructed all Serbian enterprises to sever links with Slovenia, which retaliated by imposing reciprocal economic sanctions.

In January 1990 the Slovenian delegation withdrew from the 14th (Extraordinary) Congress of the League of Communists of Yugoslavia (LCY), following the overwhelming rejection of their proposals to reform the federal party and to give greater autonomy to the respective Leagues of Communists of the republics. The LCY suffered a further reverse in February, when its Central Committee was unable to secure the quorum necessary to set a date for the reconvening of the Congress. A boycott by the entire Slovene contingent was supported by members of the Leagues of Communists of Croatia and Macedonia. The LCS suspended its links with the LCY, and changed its name to the Party of Democratic Reform (PDR). In that month Štefan Korošec of Slovenia was removed from the position of Secretary of the Presidium of the LCY Central Committee, in advance of the expiry of his mandate, and was replaced by a Serb. In March Slovenia was redesignated the Republic of Slovenia. Meanwhile, opposition parties had been formed, and in December 1989 six of the main parties formed a coalition, the Democratic Opposition of Slovenia (DEMOS). In multi-party elections, held in April 1990, DEMOS won a majority in the republican parliament, and subsequently formed a Government under Lojze Peterle, the leader of the Slovenian Christian Democrats (SCD). However, the leader of the PDR, Milan Kučan (an opponent of Milošević), was elected President of the State Presidency, and the PDR remained the largest single party in the legislature.

On 2 July 1990 the Slovenian legislature declared the sovereignty of the Republic. An amendment to the republican Constitution, resolving that republican laws should take precedence over federal laws, was approved by the legislature on 27 September. Slovenia also assumed control over the local territorial defence force, thereby bringing the republic into direct confrontation with the Serb-dominated federal army, which attempted to reassert its authority by confiscating weapons and seizing the headquarters of the republican force. Slovenian and Croatian proposals to reform the Yugoslav Federation were rejected, and Serbia imposed economic sanctions on imports from the secessionist states. None the less, in a referendum held in Slovenia on 23 December 1990, some 89% of those who voted (about 94% of the electorate) endorsed Slovenian independence.

Relations between Slovenia and the SFRY deteriorated further in January 1991, when the Slovenian authorities refused to implement an order by the SFRY Presidency to disarm all paramilitary groups. In the same month Slovenia and Croatia signed friendship and military co-operation agreements. Although the Slovenian Government approved a programme for Slovenian dissociation from the SFRY in February, both Slovenia and Croatia remained willing to consider a federation of sovereign states. However, following the Serbian-led crisis in the Federal State Presidency in March (see the chapter on Serbia), the Slovenian Government became more resolved to withdraw from the federation. In May Slovenia declared its intention to secede before the end of June, and legislation was adopted that would enable eventual independence, including the establishment of a Slovenian army. Tensions with the federal authorities were exacerbated when Slovenia attempted to take control of the collection of customs duties.

Slovenia and Croatia declared their independence from the SFRY on 25 June 1991. In response, Serb-dominated federal troops were mobilized on 27 June, and tanks were dispatched from Belgrade, the Serbian and Yugoslav capital. Sporadic fighting ensued and, despite attempts by the European Community (EC—now European Union—EU, see p. 244) to arrange a cease-fire, there was an aerial bombardment of Brnik (Ljubljana) airport. On 7–8 July an EC-mediated cease-fire agreement between Slovenia and the SFRY ended all hostilities in Slovenia. According to official figures, 79 people were killed in the fighting in Slovenia. On 8 October (following the expiry of a three-month moratorium on dissociation, agreed as part of the EC cease-fire accord) Slovenia proclaimed its full independence, introduced its own currency, the tolar, and recalled all of its citizens serving in federal institutions. All federal army units had withdrawn from Slovenia by 26 October. A new Slovenian Constitution, providing for a bicameral legislature, was promulgated on 23 December. Slovenia was recognized by the EC in January 1992. The USA recognized the country in April, and withdrew sanctions against Slovenia (imposed on all states in the territory of the former SFRY in the previous year) in August. Slovenia was admitted to the UN in May.

Peterle's administration experienced increasing difficulties, as the struggle for independence became less of a unifying factor. In October 1991 the Slovenian Democratic Union, one of the larger and most influential DEMOS parties, split into two factions, both of which remained in the coalition. A liberal wing formed the Democratic Party (DP) under the Minister of Foreign Affairs, Dr Dmitrij Rupel, while the majority of the party's parliamentary delegates supported a more conservative programme and formed the National Democratic Party, led by the Minister of Justice and Administration, Dr Rajko Pirnat. DEMOS, undermined by such factionalism, was dissolved in December, although it was envisaged that the Peterle administration would remain in power pending the organization of elections (to take place under the terms of the new Constitution). However, the Government lost a parliamentary motion of no confidence in April 1992, and Peterle resigned. He was replaced by Dr Janez Drnovšek, the leader of the Liberal Democratic Party (LDP) and a former President of the SFRY Presidency.

Parliamentary and presidential elections took place on 6 December 1992. About 85% of the registered electorate participated in elections to the Državni zbor (National Assembly). Although the LDP returned the greatest number of deputies (22) to the 90-member body, it failed to secure a majority of seats in the legislature. Among the groupings that obtained representation were the SCD, with a total of 15 seats, the United List (a four-party electoral alliance), with 14 seats, and the extreme nationalist Slovenian National Party (SNP), which won 12 seats. In the presidential election, Kučan (standing as an independent candidate) was re-elected to what had become, under the terms of the 1991 Constitution, a largely ceremonial post, obtaining 63.9% of the votes cast. His nearest rival, Ivan Bizjak of the SCD, secured 21.1% of the votes. Voting was held concurrently for the 22 directly elected members of the advisory Državni svet (National Council); its remaining 18 members were chosen by an electoral college shortly afterwards.

In January 1993 Drnovšek formed a coalition Government, comprising members of the LDP, the SCD, the United List (later renamed the United List of Social Democrats—ULSD), the Greens of Slovenia and the Social Democratic Party of Slovenia (SDPS). Peterle was appointed Minister of Foreign Affairs, and Bizjak Minister of Internal Affairs. In July the Minister of Defence, Janez Janša, was among several senior politicians implicated in a scandal involving the sale of armaments to Bosnian Muslims (Bosniaks), in contravention of the UN embargo on the transfer of military equipment between the former Yugoslav republics. Earlier in the year Janša (the President of the SDPS) had accused Kučan of protecting former officials of the communist regime. Janša was dismissed from the Government in March 1994, after a ministerial commission found that security forces under the command of the Ministry of Defence had ill-treated a former ministry employee. The SDPS withdrew from the Government, protesting that the coalition agreement had been breached. In addition, the party cited as its reasons for leaving the Government continuing high-level corruption and the change in the coalition's structure, following the merger in March of the LDP with three other organizations to form a new party, Liberal Democracy of Slovenia (LDS). The LDS, led by Drnovšek, also included the DP and the Greens of Slovenia—Eco-Social Party (comprising the parliamentary members of the Greens of Slovenia), and numbered 30 deputies in the Državni zbor. Drnovšek subsequently formed a new coalition Government with the SCD and the ULSD. However, Bizjak resigned as Minister of Internal Affairs in May, following allegations that security forces controlled by his ministry had been involved in criminal activities in Austria. In September the appointment of an LDS member, Jožef Školjč, to the presidency of the Državni zbor prompted Peterle's resignation from the Government, in protest at what he regarded as the excessive concentration of authority among members of the LDS. Although the SCD remained within the government coalition, Drnovšek refused to accede to the party's demand that Peterle's successor should also be a member of the SCD. In January 1995 an agreement was finally reached whereby Zoran Thaler of the LDS was appointed Minister of Foreign Affairs, and Janko Deželak of the SCD assumed the post of Minister of Economic Relations and Development (a portfolio hitherto held by the LDS).

In January 1996 the ULSD withdrew from the governing coalition, following the Prime Minister's proposal to replace the ULSD Minister of Economic Affairs, Dr Maks Tajnikar. Tajnikar was subsequently replaced by an independent deputy, Metod Dragonja, and the three other positions left vacant by the ULSD withdrawal were allocated to one member of the LDS and two of the SCD. The coalition, which had lost its overall majority in the Državni zbor (it controlled 45 of the 90 seats), subsequently came under pressure to relax its economic austerity measures by a series of public-sector strikes for wage increases. In May Thaler was defeated in a motion of no confidence, prompted by his acceptance of a compromise solution to a dispute with Italy (which had prevented Slovenia's accession to associate membership of the EU—see below) opposed by the SCD.

At the elections to the Državni zbor, which took place on 10 November 1996, the LDS returned 25 deputies to the chamber, and subsequently increased its overall strength to 45 seats, having gained the support of the ULSD, the Democratic Party of Pensioners of Slovenia (DeSUS), the SNP and the representatives of the Hungarian and Italian minorities. A newly formed opposition alliance, Slovenian Spring, comprising the Slovenian People's Party (SPP), the SCD and the SDPS, also held 45 seats in the Državni zbor. Consequently, Kučan's nomination that Drnovšek be returned to the office of Prime Minister failed to obtain the requisite majority of more than one-half of the deputies. Following a protracted delay, an SCD deputy announced his withdrawal from the party to become an independent deputy, and agreed to support Drnovšek's candidacy, and in January 1997 Drnovšek was re-elected as Prime Minister. However, the continued absence of a majority in the Državni zbor impeded the formation of a new government, with the parties belonging to Slovenian Spring refusing to accept an administration headed by Drnovšek. Drnovšek consequently failed to secure sufficient support for his proposed new coalition administration, which was to include representatives of all the political parties in the legislature. In late February the SPP (which held 19 seats in the Državni zbor) finally agreed to join a coalition government with the LDS and DeSUS, which was subsequently approved by 52 votes in the Državni zbor.

Following an agreement in July 1997 by parliamentary party leaders to co-operate over the country's bid to join the EU, a two-thirds' majority of the Državni zbor voted to amend the Constitution, to allow foreigners to purchase land in Slovenia, thereby meeting the requirements for ratification of the EU association agreement. The agreement was ratified by the legislature on the following day. The European Commission subsequently recommended that the EU begin membership negotiations with Slovenia in 1998. Despite this positive development, in late July 1997 Thaler resigned as Minister of Foreign Affairs. Boris Frlec was appointed to the post in September.

A presidential election took place on 23 November 1997. Kučan won a second term of office, with 55.6% of the votes cast. His nearest rival, the President of the Državni zbor, Janez Podobnik, secured 18.4% of the votes. Indirect elections to the Državni svet followed on 26 November.

In January 2000 Frlec tendered his resignation as Minister of Foreign Affairs, following criticism of his failure to resolve longstanding disputes between the Governments of Slovenia and Croatia (particularly regarding the joint sea border between the two countries and over the Krško nuclear power station—see below). He was replaced in February by Dr Dmitrij Rupel. In March it was announced that, following lengthy negotiations between the SPP and the SCD, the two parties were to merge in the following month, and that the nine ministers belonging to the SPP would resign from the Government. In April Drnovšek attempted to form a new government. However, the proposed government was rejected by the Državni zbor, and Drnovšek was obliged to resign. The SPP and SCD merged as planned in mid-April, and subsequently formed a new alliance, Coalition Slovenia, with the SDPS. Coalition Slovenia nominated Andrej Bajuk as a candidate for the premiership, and in early May, after having twice been narrowly rejected by the Državni zbor, Bajuk was endorsed as Prime Minister. The Government, which was approved by the Državni zbor in June, notably included Peterle as Minister of Foreign Affairs and Janša as Minister of Defence.

In July 2000 the approval by 70 of the 90 deputies in the Državni zbor of constitutional amendments, providing for the introduction of a system of proportional representation in the forthcoming elections, resulted in division within the SPP. Bajuk (who had opposed the new legislation) announced his resignation from the reconstituted SPP and his intention of establishing a new breakaway party. Kučan subsequently declared that the legislative elections would take place in October; Bajuk's administration was to remain in office until then, despite the collapse of the government coalition. In August Bajuk was elected Chairman of the newly formed New Slovenia—Christian People's Party (NSi), which was also joined by Peterle. The elections to the Državni zbor on 15 October were conducted under the new system, whereby 88 deputies were elected on the basis of proportional representation, and the remaining two deputies were elected as representatives of the Italian and Hungarian minority communities. The LDS secured 34 seats (an increase of nine seats compared with 1996), while the SDPS won 14 seats, the ULSD 11 seats, the SPP nine seats, and the NSi eight seats. Consequently, Drnovšek was re-elected to the premiership by the Državni zbor in early November. Following inter-party negotiations, a coalition agreement was reached by the LDS, the ULSD, the SPP and DeSUS. A new Government, which included several prominent members of Drnovšek's previous administrations, was endorsed by the legislature at the end of November; the cabinet comprised eight representatives of the LDS, three of the ULSD and three of the SPP. Drnovšek announced that administrative reforms essential to EU requirements were to be expedited.

The presidential election on 10 November 2002 was contested by nine candidates. (Kučan was prohibited, under the terms of the Constitution, from seeking election for a third term.) Drnovšek won the highest proportion of votes, with 44.4%, but failed to secure an outright majority; a second round between him and Barbara Brezigar, a state prosecutor, who was supported by the SDPS and the NSi (who had received 30.8% of the votes) was scheduled for 1 December. At this second ballot Drnovšek was elected to the presidency, with 56.5% of the votes cast. Anton Rop, also a member of the LDS and hitherto Minister of Finance, was nominated to replace Drnovšek as Prime Minister, and on 19 December a new Government was approved by the Državni zbor. Drnovšek was inaugurated as President on 22 December. In September 2003 the SDPS was reconstituted as the Slovenian Democratic Party (SDP).

In early 2004 the Državni zbor approved legislation providing for the restoration of citizenship to 18,000 nationals of former Yugoslav republics, who (resident in Slovenia at the time of its independence) had been removed from population records and lost their residency rights. However, at a referendum, which was conducted in early April, following pressure from the SNP and three right-wing parties, some 94% of the votes cast by 31% of the electorate rejected adoption of the new legislation. Following the referendum, the SPP, the only party in the governing coalition to have supported the referendum, withdrew from the Government (which was subsequently reorganized). Following the accession of Slovenia to full membership of the EU on 1 May (see below), the first elections to the European Parliament took place on 13 June, although only about 28% of the electorate participated. In the elections, the NSi, the SDP and the LDS each obtained two mandates, while the ULSD received one seat. In July Rop dismissed Dimitrij Rupel as Minister of Foreign Affairs; Rupel had announced that he was transferring his support to the opposition SDP prior to forthcoming legislative elections. Ivo Vajgl, hitherto ambassador to Germany, was subsequently appointed to the post.

At the legislative elections on 3 October 2004 the centre-right SDP secured 29.1% of votes cast and 29 seats in the 90-member Državni zbor, defeating the ruling LDS (with 22.8% of the votes and 23 seats). Janša was appointed Prime Minister on 9 November. Following lengthy inter-party negotiations, the SDP reached a coalition agreement with the SPP, the NSi and DeSUS, and a new Government was approved by 51 votes in the Državni zbor on 3 December. In April 2005 the ULSD was reconstituted as the Social Democrats (SD).

In late November 2005 trade unions organized a mass demonstration in Ljubljana (the largest to be staged since 1991), in protest at government plans for extensive economic reforms, including the proposed introduction of a uniform rate of value-added tax. In December the Državni zbor approved the appointment of an economist as Minister without Portfolio; Jože Damijan was to head a newly established government development office and be responsible for the implementation of the reform strategy that was intended to facilitate Slovenia's adoption of the common European currency, the euro, in January 2007. Later that month this strategy was approved by the Državni zbor. In March 2006 Damijan announced his resignation, but Janša announced that the reforms would continue as planned. In December the Minister of Labour, Family and Social Affairs, Janez Drobnič of the NSi, was removed by the Državni zbor; his dismissal, following his refusal to resign, had been requested by Janša on the grounds that he had mismanaged dialogue over labour and social reforms.

In March 2007 a director of the telecommunications company Telekom Slovenije, Dr Žiga Turk, was appointed to the Government as Minister without Portfolio, responsible for Growth, fulfilling the duties previously held by Damijan. In the same month dissent between Drnovšek and the Državni zbor resulted in failure to appoint a new Governor of the national bank to replace Mitja Gaspari, whose second term in the post expired at the end of that month. (Consequently, Slovenia, which had joined the euro zone on 1 January, had no representative at the European Central Bank.) Drnovšek's nomination of Gaspari for a third term, and subsequently of his deputy, Andrej Rant, was rejected by the legislature. In June Janša finally agreed to support Drnovšek's nomination of a former Minister of Finance, Marko Kranjec, as Governor, which was subsequently approved by a substantial majority in the Državni zbor.

At a first round of voting in the presidential election on 21 October 2007, of the six candidates, Peterle, who contested the election as an independent with the support of the SDP, the SPP and the NSi, won 28.7% of the votes cast, while Danilo Türk, a former UN diplomat and independent candidate supported by DeSUS and the SD, won 24.5% and Gaspari obtained 24.1% of the votes cast. At the second round of voting, contested by Peterle and Türk on 11 November, Türk was elected President, with 68.0% of the votes cast. In mid-November the Government won a motion of confidence proposed by Janša, who had complained that opposition criticism was impeding preparations to adopt the rotational presidency of the EU. Türk was inaugurated on 22 December, upon the expiry of the mandate of Drnovšek (who had decided not to seek re-election and, following a period of prolonged ill health, died in early 2008).

Areas of disputed border territory with Croatia, most notably the maritime boundary in the Bay of Piran in Istria, undermined otherwise harmonious relations between the two countries following independence. In July 1993 tensions between the two countries prevented the signing of agreements on friendship and co-operation and on the regulation of bilateral payments, although protocols governing other issues, including trade and economic relations, were concluded. In November Slovenian proposals to decommission the country's nuclear power plant, at Krško (constructed by the former federal authorities to supply energy to both Slovenia and Croatia), prompted protests by Croatia, which was reliant on the installation for one-quarter of its energy requirements. Little progress was achieved during 1994 in efforts to delineate the joint border, and the resumption of construction by Croatia of border facilities on Slovenian territory provoked renewed protests by the Slovenian Government. In October the Croatian Government submitted a formal protest to Slovenia, following the approval of legislation providing for a reorganization of local government boundaries in Slovenia, as part of which four villages in the disputed area were to be included within the Slovenian municipality of Piran (Pirano). The Državni zbor subsequently agreed to delay implementation of the law (and thus the holding of elections) in three villages, pending a resolution of the border issue. In February 1995 a meeting of the Slovenian-Croatian joint border commission agreed that, since the process of delineating the border would be lengthy, this should be pursued separately from other bilateral concerns. In March Slovenia and Croatia agreed to divide ownership of the Krško nuclear station equally between the two countries. Tension between the two countries escalated in early 1998, with the arrest in January of two Slovenian military intelligence agents, who had entered Croatian territory with electronic surveillance equipment. (They were later released.) Negotiations on border issues and other areas of contention continued none the less, and in March the Slovenian Minister of Foreign Affairs met with his Austrian and Croatian counterparts in Split, Croatia, with the aim of developing trilateral links within the framework of the Central European Initiative (see p. 423).

In July 1998 Slovenia ceased distributing electricity generated at the Krško nuclear power plant to Croatia, claiming that it had failed to pay for power, valued at some US $14m., already supplied. In the same month Slovenia privatized its share of the Krško power plant. Croatia was reported to have resumed payments to Slovenia in August, and subsequently the transfer of electricity was restored. In November it was announced that the dispute over the Krško nuclear power plant would be resolved on the basis of co-ownership. Following the election of a new Government in Croatia in early 2000, bilateral relations improved significantly. After lengthy negotiations between Drnovšek and the Croatian Prime Minister, Ivica Račan, an agreement resolving the outstanding issues of contention between Slovenia and Croatia was signed in July 2001. The accord (which required endorsement by the legislatures of the two countries) granted Slovenia access to the Adriatic Sea through the Bay of Piran, and provided for continued joint management of the Krško nuclear installation; the four disputed border villages were to remain under Croatian sovereignty. In 2003 a further dispute erupted between Slovenia and Croatia, after the Croatian Government announced plans to establish an economic zone in the Adriatic Sea, which would remove Slovenia's direct access to international waters. The Slovenian Government temporarily withdrew its ambassador in Croatia.

In August 2005 it was announced that Croatia had withdrawn its ambassador to Slovenia, following the Slovenian Government's decision to declare a fishing zone in the border region. (The ambassador was returned by early September.) After the Državni zbor approved the Government's decision, Croatia declared the fishing zone to be illegitimate and demanded that the issue be referred to international arbitration. The Slovenian Government demonstrated reluctance to enter into international arbitration and, following the official opening of Croatia's accession negotiations with the EU earlier that month, threatened to obstruct Croatian membership. The Slovenian Government also continued to reject claims by Croatia that it was liable for outstanding debts owed to Croatian citizens by the former Ljubjlanska Banka of Slovenia. At the end of 2005 the Croatian national power utility submitted to an international centre for investment disputes a demand for compensation for undelivered electricity from the Krško installation. In January 2007 the dispute between Croatia and Slovenia over their joint maritime boundary was revived with a diplomatic protest by Slovenia that the Croatian Government had pre-empted a border demarcation by extending concessions for petroleum exploration in the disputed region. The Croatian Government reiterated demands that the dispute be referred to international arbitration. At the beginning of 2008 Croatia implemented legislation enforcing its environmental fishing zone in the Adriatic Sea, which it had declared in 2003 with the objective of protecting fishing stocks; Slovenia, together with Italy, opposed the measure, which would result in significant financial damage for their fleets. Slovenia (which had assumed the EU presidency—see below) indicated that the issue would impede Croatia's ongoing EU integration process. In March 2008, following continued pressure from the EU, Croatia agreed that implementation of the environmental fishing zone would be postponed until its anticipated accession to the Union.

Slovenia and Croatia are united in their opposition to movements for Istrian autonomy and to any revision to their detriment of the 1975 Treaty of Osimo, which had defined the borders between the SFRY and Italy, and had provided for the payment by the SFRY of compensation for Italian property transferred to Yugoslav sovereignty after 1947. In 1993 some 35,000 Italians were reported to be demanding compensation for, or the restitution of, property in Slovenia. Consequently, in July 1994 the Italian Government of Silvio Berlusconi stated that until the Slovenian authorities agreed to compensate Italian nationals who had fled after 1947 from territory now held by Slovenia, and whose property had been confiscated under communist rule, Italy would block efforts by Slovenia to achieve further integration with Western Europe. Italy thus prevented scheduled negotiations on an association agreement between Slovenia and the EU until March 1995, when the new Italian Government of Lamberto Dini withdrew the veto. However, it was not until May 1996 that Slovenia and Italy agreed to a compromise solution proposed by Spain, whereby Slovenia was to allow EU nationals to purchase property in Slovenia, on a reciprocal basis, within four years of the association agreement's ratification, and EU citizens who had previously permanently resided in Slovenia for a period of three years (thus including Italian nationals who had fled after the Second World War) would be permitted to buy immediately. In June Slovenia finally signed an association agreement with the EU, and simultaneously applied for full membership of the organization. In July 1997 the Državni zbor voted in favour of amending the Constitution in accordance with the agreement.

In April 1993 Slovenia signed a trade and economic co-operation accord with the EU, and it achieved associate membership of the organization in June 1996 (see above). Slovenia joined the Council of Europe (see p. 225) in May 1993, and in December was granted observer status at the Western European Union (see p. 426) conference in Paris, France. In March 1994 it was announced that Slovenia was to join the 'Partnership for Peace' (see p. 342) programme of the North Atlantic Treaty Organization (NATO). In January 1996 Slovenia was admitted to the Central European Free Trade Agreement (now Association). Formal accession negotiations with the EU commenced in November 1998. In December 2002, at a summit meeting in Copenhagen, Denmark, Slovenia was one of 10 nations officially invited to become members of the EU with effect from 2004. Meanwhile, at a summit meeting in Prague, Czech Republic, in November 2002, Slovenia was formally invited to join NATO in 2004. A national referendum on the issue of joining both organizations was conducted on 23 March 2003; some 89.6% of voters endorsed membership of the EU, and 66.1% membership of NATO. On 29 March 2004 Slovenia was officially admitted to NATO, together with Bulgaria, Estonia, Latvia, Lithuania, Romania and Slovakia, at a ceremony in Washington, DC. Slovenia's accession to the EU followed on 1 May. In early February 2005 the Državni zbor voted in favour of ratifying the EU draft constitutional treaty. In June 2006 EU leaders, meeting in Brussels, Belgium, approved Slovenia's application to adopt the European common currency, the euro, with effect from 1 January 2007. The decision was confirmed by EU Ministers of Finance on 11 July, and Slovenia joined the euro zone as scheduled. In December Slovenia implemented the EU's Schengen Agreement on freedom of travel, effectively removing border controls between those states subject to the Agreement. On 1 January 2008 Slovenia assumed the rotational EU presidency for a period of six months.

Government

Under the terms of the 1991 Constitution, as subsequently modified, legislative power is vested in the 90-member Državni zbor (National Assembly). Of the 90 deputies, who serve a term of four years, 88 are elected on the basis of proportional representation; two members are representatives of the Hungarian and Italian minorities. The Državni svet (National Council), which is elected for five years, comprises 22 directly elected members and 18 members chosen by an electoral college to represent various social, economic, trading, political and local interest groups; the Council's role is mainly advisory, but it is empowered to veto decisions of the Državni zbor. The Prime Minister, who is elected by the Državni zbor, nominates the Government (subject to the approval of the legislature). The President of the Republic has largely ceremonial powers, and is directly elected for a maximum of two five-year terms. For administrative purposes, Slovenia is divided into 193 municipalities, 11 of which are designated as city municipalities.

Defence

As assessed at November 2007, the active Slovenian armed forces numbered 5,973; reserve forces totalled 20,000. There was a paramilitary police force of 4,500 (with 5,000 reserves). In September 2003 the Government announced the abolition of compulsory military service, prior to the country's official accession to the North Atlantic Treaty Organization (NATO, see p. 340) on 29 March 2004. The budget for 2007 allocated 126,000m. SIT to defence.

Economic Affairs

In 2006, according to the World Bank, Slovenia's gross national income (GNI), measured at average 2004–06 prices, was US $37,730m., equivalent to $18,890 per head (or $23,970 per head on an international purchasing-power parity basis). During 1996–2006, it was estimated, the population neither increased nor declined, while gross domestic product (GDP) per head increased, in real terms, by an average of 4.0% per year. Overall GDP increased, in real terms, at an average annual rate of 4.1% in 1996–2006. Real GDP increased by 5.2% in 2006.

Agriculture (including hunting, forestry and fishing) contributed 2.3% of GDP in 2006. In 2005 the sector engaged 4.8% of the employed labour force. The principal crops are cereals (particularly maize and wheat), potatoes, sugar beet and fruits (especially grapes and apples). Slovenia's forests, which cover about one-half of the country, are an important natural resource. Agricultural GDP declined at an average rate of 0.3% per year during 1996–2006. The GDP of the sector decreased by 0.5% in 2005, and by 1.0% in 2006.

Industry (including mining, manufacturing, construction and power) contributed 33.7% of GDP in 2006 and engaged 38.4% of the employed labour force in 2005. Industrial GDP increased at an average rate of 5.5% per year in 1996–2006. Sectoral GDP increased by 9.3% in 2006.

Mining and quarrying contributed 0.5% of GDP in 2006 and engaged 0.5% of the employed labour force in 2005. The principal activity is coal-mining; lead and zinc are also extracted, together with relatively small amounts of natural gas, petroleum and salt. Slovenia also has small deposits of uranium. The GDP of the mining sector increased at an average rate of 2.0% per year in 1996–2006. Mining GDP increased by 7.5% in 2006.

Manufacturing contributed 24.6% of GDP in 2006 and engaged 28.5% of the employed labour force in 2005. Manufacturing GDP increased at an average rate of 4.9% per year in 1996–2006. GDP in the manufacturing sector increased by 8.5% in 2006.

A nuclear power station was constructed in Slovenia by the former Yugoslav authorities to provide energy for both Slovenia and Croatia (see Recent History). In 2004 nuclear power stations provided 35.7% of energy requirements, coal-fired electricity generating stations provided 34.0%, and hydroelectric power stations provided 26.8%. Imports of fuel products comprised 11.2% of the value of merchandise imports in 2006.

The services sector contributed 64.1% of GDP in 2006 and engaged 56.7% of the employed labour force in 2005. Tourism is a significant source of revenue; tourist activity was adversely affected by the political instability of 1991, but the number of arrivals recovered, reaching 2,395,000 in 2005. The GDP of the services sector increased at an average rate of 4.3% per year in 1996–2006. Growth in the services sector was 5.0% in 2006.

In 2006 Slovenia recorded a visible trade deficit of US $1,458m., and there was a deficit of $1,088m. on the current account of the balance of payments. In that year Slovenia's principal source of imports was Germany (accounting for 20.4% of the total); other major suppliers were Italy (18.6%), Austria (12.2%) and France (6.2%). Germany was also the principal market for exports (taking 19.7% of the total in that year); Italy (12.9%), Croatia (8.7%), Austria (8.7%) and France (6.8%) were also significant purchasers. The major imports in 2006 were machinery and transport equipment, basic manufactures, chemical products, miscellaneous manufactured articles, mineral fuels and crude materials. The principal exports in that year were machinery and transport equipment (particularly road vehicles and parts and electrical machinery), basic manufactures, miscellaneous manufactured articles and chemicals.

Slovenia's overall budgetary deficit for 2006 was 59,906m. SIT, equivalent to 0.8% of GDP. At the end of 2007 total central government debt amounted to US $10,866m. The annual rate of inflation averaged 6.1% in 1996–2006. Consumer prices increased by 2.5% in 2006. An estimated 10.3% of the total labour force were unemployed in 2005.

Slovenia has joined several international organizations, including the IMF, the World Bank and (as a 'Country of Operations') the European Bank for Reconstruction and Development (see p. 239). The country became a full member of the World Trade Organization (see p. 396) in July 1995 and acceded to full membership of the European Union (EU, see p. 244) on 1 May 2004.

By the mid-1990s important advances in the transformation of the economy had allowed Slovenia to gain a favourable position among the countries chosen to participate in negotiations to join the EU. At April 2003 Slovenia had achieved sustained convergence in per-head income to about 70% of the EU average. Slovenia formally acceded to the EU on 1 May 2004 and, following the successful adoption of measures to reduce inflation, achieved entry into the exchange rate mechanism (ERM 2) in June. The continued reduction of inflation in order to meet EU levels, with the aim of adopting the euro in January 2007, was central to government policy. In November 2005 the Government announced extensive economic reforms, including measures to increase competitiveness, reform the labour market and the pension and health systems, and resume the privatization of state-owned enterprises. Trade unions responded by organizing mass protests, in particular against plans to introduce a uniform rate of value-added tax, which they claimed would adversely affect the standard of living. Nevertheless, the economic reform strategy was officially approved by the legislature in December. Slovenia adopted the euro on 1 January 2007, with government policy primarily focused on ensuring a smooth transition. According to the International Labour Organization (ILO), inflation increased to some 3.6% in 2007. Observers largely attributed the rise in consumer prices to the rigid labour market, which placed constant upward pressure on wages and undermined the overall competitiveness of the economy. Consumer price inflation continued to increase, reaching an annual rate of 6.6% in March 2008, when Slovenia recorded the highest level of inflation in the euro zone. Meanwhile, the IMF warned that the increasing ageing population could threaten long-term stability if not addressed with appropriate structural reform. However, the weakening mandate of the Prime Minister, Janez Janša, was likely to impede the progress of any economic policy with the potential to engender popular discontent. GDP grew by an estimated 6.1% in 2007, supported largely by the strengthening export sector. The IMF forecast that GDP growth would fall to 4.1% in 2008, partly due to the global economic slowdown.

Education

Primary education is free and compulsory for all children between the ages of six and 15 years. In ethnically mixed regions, two methods of schooling have been developed: bilingual or with instruction in the minority languages. Various types of secondary education, beginning at 15 and lasting between two and five years, are also available. In 2002/03 93% of children in the relevant age-group (males 94%; females 93%) were enrolled at primary schools, while the equivalent rate for secondary education was also 93% of children of the appropriate age-group (males 93%; females 94%). Slovenia's two universities are situated in Ljubljana and Maribor, with 58,265 and 25,621 students, respectively, in 2004/05. Expenditure on education by all levels of government in 2003 was estimated at SIT 350,062m., representing 6.1% of total government spending.

Public Holidays

2008: 1–2 January (New Year), 8 February (Prešeren Day, National Day of Culture), 21–24 March (Easter), 27 April (Resistance Day), 1–2 May (Labour Day), 25 June (National Statehood Day), 15 August (Assumption), 31 October (Reformation Day), 1 November (All Saints' Day), 25 December (Christmas Day), 26 December (Independence Day).

2009: 1–2 January (New Year), 8 February (Prešeren Day, National Day of Culture), 10–13 April (Easter), 27 April (Resistance Day), 1–2 May (Labour Day), 25 June (National Statehood Day), 15 August (Assumption), 31 October (Reformation Day), 1 November (All Saints' Day), 25 December (Christmas Day), 26 December (Independence Day).

Weights and Measures

The metric system is in force.

Statistical Survey

Source (unless otherwise indicated): Statistical Office of the Republic of Slovenia, 1000 Ljubljana, Vožarski pot 12; tel. (1) 2415104; fax (1) 2415344; e-mail info.stat@gov.si; internet www.stat.si.

Area and Population

AREA, POPULATION AND DENSITY

Area (sq km)	20,273*
Population (census results)	
31 March 1991	1,913,355
31 March 2002	
Males	958,576
Females	1,005,460
Total	1,964,036
Population (official estimates at 31 December)†	
2004	1,997,590
2005	2,003,358
2006	2,010,377
Density (per sq km) at 31 December 2006	99.2

* 7,827 sq miles.
† Estimates are calculated on a *de jure* basis.

POPULATION BY ETHNIC GROUP
(2002 census)

Ethnic group	Number	%
Slovenes	1,631,363	83.06
Serbs	38,964	1.98
Croats	35,642	1.81
Bosniaks	21,542	1.10
Muslims*	10,467	0.53
Others	226,058	11.51
Total (incl. others)	1,964,036	100.00

* Including persons claiming Muslim ethnicity rather than religious adherence.

PRINCIPAL TOWNS
(population at 2002 census)

Ljubljana (capital)	265,881	Koper (Capodistria)	47,539
Maribor	110,668	Novo mesto	40,925
Kranj	51,225	Nova Gorica	35,640
Celje	48,081		

Mid-2005 ('000, incl. suburbs, UN estimate): Ljubljana 263 (Source: UN, *World Urbanization Prospects: The 2005 Revision*).

BIRTHS, MARRIAGES AND DEATHS

	Registered live births		Registered marriages		Registered deaths	
	Number	Rate (per 1,000)	Number	Rate (per 1,000)	Number	Rate (per 1,000)
1999	17,533	8.8	7,716	3.9	18,885	9.5
2000	18,180	9.1	7,201	3.6	18,588	9.3
2001	17,477	8.8	6,935	3.5	18,508	9.3
2002	17,501	8.8	7,064	3.5	18,701	9.4
2003	17,321	8.7	6,756	3.4	19,451	9.7
2004	17,961	9.0	6,558	3.3	18,523	9.3
2005	18,157	9.1	5,769	2.9	18,825	9.4
2006	18,932	n.a.	6,368	n.a.	18,180	9.1

Expectation of life (years at birth, WHO estimates): 77.5 (males 73.6; females 81.2) in 2005 (Source: WHO, *World Health Statistics*).

IMMIGRATION AND EMIGRATION

	2004	2005	2006
Long-term immigrants	10,171	15,041	20,016
Long-term emigrants	8,269	8,605	13,749

ECONOMICALLY ACTIVE POPULATION
('000 persons aged 15 years and over, December)

	2003	2004	2005
Agriculture, hunting, forestry and fishing	41	38	39
Mining and quarrying	5	5	4
Manufacturing	236	239	232
Electricity, gas and water supply	11	11	11
Construction	60	63	65
Wholesale and retail trade; repair of motor vehicles, motorcycles, and personal and household goods	106	107	107
Hotels and restaurants	30	30	31
Transport, storage and communications	50	50	50
Financial intermediation	20	20	21
Real estate, renting and business activities	60	59	65
Public administration and defence; compulsory social security	48	48	50
Education	56	56	58
Health and social work	47	47	50
Other social and personal services	28	28	29
Total employed (incl. others)	800	801	813
Unemployed	96	91	93
Total labour force	896	892	906

Health and Welfare

KEY INDICATORS

Total fertility rate (children per woman, 2005)	1.2
Under-5 mortality rate (per 1,000 live births, 2005)	4
HIV/AIDS (% of persons aged 15–49, 2005)	<0.1
Physicians (per 1,000 head, 2002)	2.25
Hospital beds (per 1,000 head, 2004)	4.80
Health expenditure (2004): US $ per head (PPP)	1,814.9
Health expenditure (2004): % of GDP	8.7
Health expenditure (2004): public (% of total)	75.6
Human Development Index (2005): ranking	27
Human Development Index (2005): value	0.917

For sources and definitions, see explanatory note on p. vi.

SLOVENIA

Agriculture

PRINCIPAL CROPS
('000 metric tons)

	2004	2005	2006
Wheat	146.8	141.3	134.4
Barley	59.7	61.2	61.6
Maize	357.6	351.2	276.1
Oats	5.3	7.6	6.3
Triticale (wheat-rye hybrid)	8.9	7.8	10.9
Potatoes	171.5	144.7	107.0
Sugar beet	213.1	260.1	262.0
Cabbages	24.4	25.0	26.1
Lettuce	7.4	7.4	8.4
Tomatoes	5.4	6.6	4.6
Chillies and green peppers	6.1	10.2	4.8
Dry onions	7.4	7.2	5.4
Apples	140.0	106.2	119.2
Pears	14.2	8.2	11.4
Peaches and nectarines	14.4	13.3	11.2
Plums	10.0	4.3	5.4
Grapes	134.8	120.7	105.5

Aggregate production ('000 metric tons, may include official, semi-official or estimated data): Total cereals 582.9 in 2004, 576.3 in 2005, 493.6 in 2006; Total roots and tubers 171.5 in 2004, 144.7 in 2005, 107.0 in 2006; Total vegetables (incl. melons) 83.6 in 2004, 89.1 in 2005, 80.3 in 2006; Total fruits (excl. melons) 320.5 in 2004, 260.0 in 2005, 260.2 in 2006.

Source: FAO.

LIVESTOCK
('000 head)

	2004	2005	2006
Cattle	450	451	453
Pigs	621	534	547
Sheep	106	119	129
Goats	23	23	25
Horses	18*	20	20
Chickens	4,534	4,811	4,811†
Ducks†	200	200	200
Geese†	270	270	270
Turkeys	130	150†	150†

† FAO estimate(s).
* Unofficial figure.
Source: FAO.

LIVESTOCK PRODUCTS
('000 metric tons)

	2003	2004	2005
Cattle meat	51.8	46.9	45.5*
Pig meat	63.6	71.3	70.0*
Sheep meat	1.2	1.1†	1.1†
Chicken meat	54.3	47.0*	51.0*
Duck meat†	1.2	1.2	1.2
Goose meat	3.4†	3.4†	n.a.
Turkey meat†	8.4	8.4	8.4
Cows' milk	642.4	651.0	654.0†
Hen eggs	18.2	20.0†	n.a.

* Unofficial figure.
† FAO estimate(s).
2006: Figures assumed to be unchanged from 2005 (FAO estimates).
Source: FAO.

Forestry

ROUNDWOOD REMOVALS
('000 cubic metres, excl. bark)

	2004	2005	2006
Sawlogs, veneer logs and logs for sleepers	1,372	1,403	1,712
Pulpwood	283	288	445
Other industrial wood	171	99	39
Fuel wood	725	943	984
Total	2,551	2,733	3,179

Source: FAO.

SAWNWOOD PRODUCTION
('000 cubic metres, incl. railway sleepers)

	2004	2005	2006
Coniferous (softwood)	339	387	446
Broadleaved (hardwood)	175	140	134
Total	514	527	580

Source: FAO.

Fishing

(metric tons, live weight)

	2003	2004	2005
Capture	1,282	1,023	1,227
Common carp	82	83	76
European pilchard (sardine)	771	374	327
European anchovy	58	238	438
Aquaculture	1,353	1,571	1,536
Common carp	201	199	241
Rainbow trout	861	1,001	995
European seabass	55	78	25
Mediterranean mussel	135	164	201
Total catch	2,635	2,594	2,763

Source: FAO.

Mining

(metric tons, unless otherwise indicated)

	2003	2004	2005
Brown coal ('000 metric tons)	608	611	594
Lignite ('000 metric tons)	4,222	4,198	3,945
Natural gas ('000 cubic metres)	4,900	4,500	4,335
Crude petroleum	482	344	298
Bentonite*	4,000	4,000	4,000
Quartz and quartzite (incl. glass sand)*	200,000	200,000	200,000
Sand and gravel (excl. glass sand)*	11,000	11,000	11,000
Pumice*	40,000	40,000	40,000
Salt*	125,000	125,000	125,000

* Estimates.
Source: US Geological Survey.

SLOVENIA

Statistical Survey

Industry

SELECTED PRODUCTS
('000 metric tons, unless otherwise indicated)

	2004	2005	2006
Wine ('000 hectolitres)	361	293	255
Footwear (excl. rubber) ('000 pairs)	3,599	3,108	3,150
Veneer sheets ('000 cubic metres)	48	64	64
Plywood ('000 cubic metres)*	27	27	29
Mechanical wood pulp*	32	50	50
Chemical wood pulp*	121	111	62
Newsprint*	31	116	116
Household and sanitary paper*	161	63	39
Wrapping and packaging paper and paperboard	105	105	99
Cement†‡	1,300	1,300	n.a.
Crude steel ingots (incl. crude steel for casting)§	566	583	628
Refined lead†	16.0	15.4	n.a.
Passenger motor cars ('000)	140	185	n.a.
Electric energy (million kWh)	15,272	15,117	15,115

* Source: FAO.
† Source: US Geological Survey.
‡ Estimated production.
§ Source: International Iron and Steel Institute (Brussels).

Finance

CURRENCY AND EXCHANGE RATES

Monetary Units
100 cent = 1 euro (€).

Sterling, Dollar and Euro Equivalents (31 December 2007)
£1 sterling = 1.3609 euros;
US $1 = 0.6793 euros;
€10 = £7.35 = $14.72.

Average Exchange Rate (euros per US $)
2005   0.8041
2006   0.7971
2007   0.7306

The tolar was introduced in October 1991, replacing (initially at par) the Yugoslav dinar. Slovenia participated in the common European currency, the euro, with effect from 1 January 2007; a fixed exchange rate of €1 = 239.640 tolars was in operation. The euro and the tolar circulated alongside each other until 14 January, after which time the euro (comprising 100 cent) became the sole legal tender.

BUDGET
(million tolars)*

Revenue†	2004	2005	2006
Tax revenue	2,446,899	2,608,230	2,818,643
Taxes on income and profits	506,878	537,260	655,486
Taxes on payroll, property etc.	157,189	166,931	158,656
Social security contributions	899,400	955,611	1,013,970
Domestic taxes on goods and services	856,610	938,118	977,082
Taxes on international trade and transactions	19,339	9,360	12,145
Other current revenue	162,154	151,756	151,767
Capital revenue and grants	22,628	29,354	41,258
Transferred revenues	7,536	8,140	10,259
Receipts from EU budget	43,838	72,469	83,494
Total	2,683,055	2,869,949	3,105,421

Expenditure‡	2004	2005	2006
Current expenditure (excl. transfers)	1,234,113	1,283,018	1,363,301
Interest payments	91,933	89,180	90,199
Current transfers	1,249,909	1,341,641	1,420,064
Capital expenditure (excl. transfers)	151,305	156,784	216,016
Capital transfers	92,464	91,874	96,956
Payments to EU budget	40,637	68,438	68,990
Total	2,768,427	2,941,756	3,165,327

* Figures represent a consolidation of the accounts of the central Government (State Budget, Pension Fund and Health Insurance Fund) and local administrative authorities.
† Excluding net financing (million tolars): 85,372 in 2004; 71,807 in 2005; 59,906 in 2006.
‡ Excluding net lending (million tolars): −8,203 in 2004; 6,078 in 2005; 11,096 in 2006.

2007 (€ '000): *Revenue:* Current 13,467,157 (Tax revenue 12,757,942, Non-tax revenue 709,216); Capital revenue and grants 148,423; Transferred revenue 51,579; Receipts from the EU budget 347,997; Total 14,015,156 (excl. net financing −90,649). *Expenditure:* Current 5,951,017 (Interest payments 356,983); Current transfers 6,145,937; Capital expenditure (excl. transfers) 1,130,453; Capital transfers 341,196; Payments to the EU budget 355,904; Total 13,924,506 (excl. net lending 463,260).

Source: Ministry of Finance, Ljubljana.

INTERNATIONAL RESERVES
(US $ million at 31 December)

	2004	2005	2006
Gold (market prices)	105.80	83.35	103.30
IMF special drawing rights	11.15	11.63	12.41
Reserve position in IMF	119.98	51.62	36.64
Foreign exchange	8,662.27	8,013.12	6,987.08
Total	8,899.20	8,159.72	7,139.43

2007 (US $ million at 31 December): IMF special drawing rights 12.59; Reserve position in IMF 25.17.

Source: IMF, *International Financial Statistics*.

MONEY SUPPLY
(million tolars at 31 December)

	2003	2004	2005
Currency outside banks	156,040	167,920	187,230
Demand deposits at commercial banks	608,480	808,110	917,310
Total money (incl. others)	767,700	982,240	1,107,390

Note: Figures are rounded to the nearest 10,000 tolars.

Source: IMF, *International Financial Statistics*.

COST OF LIVING
(Consumer Price Index for urban areas; base: 2000 = 100)

	2004	2005	2006
Food (incl. beverages)	124.2	124.3	127.2
Fuel and light	123.8	139.0	150.4
Clothing (incl. footwear)	114.4	113.2	112.4
Rent	177.8	187.7	195.9
All items (incl. others)	127.4	130.6	133.8

Source: ILO.

SLOVENIA

Statistical Survey

NATIONAL ACCOUNTS

National Income and Product
(million tolars at current prices)

	2004	2005	2006
Compensation of employees	3,315,011	3,505,598	3,750,357
Net operating surplus	724,754	764,277	901,376
Net mixed income	459,056	502,207	569,578
Domestic primary incomes	4,498,821	4,772,082	5,221,311
Consumption of fixed capital	991,431	1,047,434	1,100,667
Gross domestic product (GDP) at factor cost	5,490,252	5,819,516	6,321,978
Taxes on production and imports	1,027,736	1,084,897	1,132,347
Less Subsidies	125,004	136,147	157,698
GDP in market prices	6,392,985	6,768,266	7,296,627
Net primary income from abroad	−75,128	−58,391	−78,661
Gross national income	6,317,857	6,709,875	7,217,966
Less Consumption of fixed capital	991,431	1,047,434	1,100,667
Net national income	5,326,426	5,662,441	6,117,299
Net current transfers from abroad	−10,555	−34,525	−50,281
Net national disposable income	5,315,871	5,627,916	6,067,018

Expenditure on the Gross Domestic Product
(million tolars at current prices)

	2004	2005	2006
Final consumption expenditure	4,703,677	4,964,645	5,299,860
Households	3,402,044	3,586,849	3,823,605
Non-profit institutions serving households	71,246	66,401	72,712
General government	1,230,387	1,311,395	1,403,543
Gross capital formation	1,770,142	1,846,356	2,068,981
Gross fixed capital formation	1,625,676	1,727,813	1,907,462
Changes in inventories / Acquisitions, less disposals, of valuables	144,466	118,543	161,519
Total domestic expenditure	6,473,819	6,811,001	7,368,841
Exports of goods and services	3,764,718	4,263,893	4,916,115
Less Imports of goods and services	3,845,552	4,306,627	4,988,328
GDP in purchasers' values	6,392,985	6,768,266	7,296,627

Gross Domestic Product by Economic Activity
(million tolars at current prices)

	2004	2005	2006
Agriculture, hunting and forestry	145,623	148,331	144,224
Fishing	842	982	1,034
Mining and quarrying	30,521	30,425	32,431
Manufacturing	1,391,950	1,417,900	1,529,222
Electricity, gas and water supply	165,148	177,023	189,855
Construction	301,574	342,115	397,592
Wholesale and retail trade; repair of motor vehicles, motorcycles and personal and household goods	650,003	710,367	759,309
Hotels and restaurants	125,646	133,532	147,401
Transport, storage and communications	417,292	457,395	499,419
Financial intermediation	252,558	260,121	314,035
Real estate, renting and business activities	945,835	1,009,737	1,073,176
Public administration and defence; compulsory social security	346,385	365,414	386,548
Education	318,406	341,335	359,309
Health and social work	284,556	305,653	316,735
Other community, social and personal services	202,924	216,444	231,949
Private households with employed persons	1,356	1,155	1,208
Gross value added at basic prices	5,580,619	5,917,930	6,383,448
Taxes on products	843,801	885,608	946,332
Less Subsidies	31,436	35,271	33,153
GDP in market prices	6,392,985	6,768,266	7,296,627

BALANCE OF PAYMENTS
(US $ million)

	2004	2005	2006
Exports of goods f.o.b.	16,065	18,146	21,397
Imports of goods f.o.b.	−17,322	−19,404	−22,856
Trade balance	−1,258	−1,258	−1,458
Exports of services	3,455	3,976	4,344
Imports of services	−2,603	−2,915	−3,254
Balance on goods and services	−406	−198	−368
Other income received	667	781	1,135
Other income paid	−1,060	−1,143	−1,642
Balance on goods, services and income	−799	−560	−874
Current transfers received	698	878	988
Current transfers paid	−792	−998	−1,202
Current balance	−893	−681	−1,088
Capital account (net)	−123	−138	−169
Direct investment abroad	−550	−629	−905
Direct investment from abroad	831	540	649
Portfolio investment assets	−809	−2,100	−2,677
Portfolio investment liabilities	37	102	849
Financial derivatives assets	7	−13	−16
Other investment assets	−1,608	−1,899	−2,428
Other investment liabilities	2,793	4,842	4,399
Net errors and omissions	17	181	−270
Overall balance	−296	206	−1,656

Source: IMF, *International Financial Statistics*.

External Trade

PRINCIPAL COMMODITIES
(distribution by SITC, € million)

Imports c.i.f.	2004	2005	2006
Food and live animals	713.6	825.2	953.9
Crude materials (inedible) except fuels	720.1	833.8	1,028.6
Mineral fuels, lubricants, etc.	1,162.6	1,675.6	2,045.9
Petroleum, petroleum products, etc.	803.7	1,122.2	1,288.0
Chemicals and related products	1,849.6	2,028.1	2,228.8
Basic manufactures	3,293.2	3,571.3	4,213.7
Textile yarn, fabrics, etc.	412.6	458.6	446.8
Iron and steel	825.0	876.8	1,042.6
Non-ferrous metals	427.5	500.6	724.4
Other metal manufactures	526.5	576.6	747.8
Machinery and transport equipment	4,831.5	5,156.7	5,955.5
Machinery specialized for particular industries	379.8	437.3	539.7
General industrial machinery, equipment and parts	655.0	720.2	858.6
Electrical machinery, apparatus, etc.	867.6	904.8	1,021.2
Road vehicles (incl. air-cushion vehicles) and parts (excl. tyres, engines and electrical parts)	1,688.2	183.3	204.9
Miscellaneous manufactured articles	1,437.8	1,564.8	1,737.5
Clothing and accessories (excl. footwear)	290.2	302.3	341.1
Total (incl. others)	14,143.0	15,804.8	18,340.8

SLOVENIA

Exports f.o.b.	2004	2005	2006
Chemicals and related products	1,711.0	1,877.8	2,298.2
Medicinal and pharmaceutical products	855.4	913.9	1,161.3
Basic manufactures	3,279.2	3,621.4	4,313.5
Paper, paperboard and articles thereof	444.7	461.0	473.4
Textile yarn, fabrics, etc.	379.6	400.9	419.0
Iron and steel	473.0	562.5	668.9
Non-ferrous metals	442.6	532.8	733.8
Other metal manufactures	578.9	630.1	856.4
Machinery and transport equipment	4,839.6	5,647.2	6,395.8
General industrial machinery, equipment and parts	677.9	799.1	1,000.1
Electrical machinery, apparatus, etc.	1,471.2	1,514.3	1,664.8
Road vehicles (incl. air-cushion vehicles) and parts (excl. tyres, engines and electrical parts)	1,595.7	2,183.4	2,281.4
Miscellaneous manufactured articles	2,161.4	2,219.9	2,337.4
Furniture and parts; bedding mattresses, etc.	885.8	846.3	859.2
Clothing and accessories (excl. footwear)	271.8	283.8	270.5
Total (incl. others)	12,783.1	14,397.1	16,757.2

PRINCIPAL TRADING PARTNERS
(€ million)

Imports c.i.f.	2004	2005	2006
Austria	1,863.9	1,952.7	2,245.2
Belgium	267.9	336.5	409.8
China, People's Republic	150.0	196.8	245.8
Croatia	514.2	608.8	735.9
Czech Republic	345.1	379.7	399.5
France	1,166.2	1,156.6	1,128.8
Germany	2,871.7	3,163.2	3,743.4
Hungary	540.4	603.1	671.1
Italy	2,672.7	3,013.5	3,405.3
Japan	62.9	123.1	726.0
Netherlands	508.0	572.1	683.2
Poland	188.8	239.0	302.7
Russia	299.6	334.2	357.1
Slovakia	173.0	210.5	259.0
Spain	385.3	490.2	498.1
Sweden	145.9	126.2	144.7
Switzerland	229.4	205.0	255.8
Turkey	109.9	147.7	180.2
United Kingdom	242.8	235.7	302.0
USA	165.6	145.4	199.2
Total (incl. others)	14,143.0	15,804.8	18,340.8

Exports f.o.b.	2004	2005	2006
Austria	955.4	1,159.6	1,450.7
Belgium	140.7	158.7	185.6
Bosnia and Herzegovina	490.7	514.9	484.7
Croatia	1,166.7	1,304.2	1,464.4
Czech Republic	244.5	320.5	390.3
France	822.2	1,185.0	1,135.1
Germany	2,759.6	2,862.9	3,295.8
Hungary	248.9	284.3	385.1
Italy	1,663.9	1,818.5	2,157.0
Macedonia, former Yugoslav republic	139.2	134.1	125.7
Netherlands	190.5	207.4	235.5
Poland	343.7	364.0	487.9
Russia	420.2	467.5	599.5
Serbia	454.5*	261.8	509.0
Slovakia	173.7	213.4	272.1
Spain	194.7	257.9	320.8
Switzerland	138.6	187.8	155.2
United Kingdom	288.5	358.4	468.7
USA	399.7	294.0	384.0
Total (incl. others)	12,783.1	14,397.1	16,757.2

*Serbia and Montenegro.

Transport

RAILWAYS
(traffic)

	2004	2005	2006
Passenger journeys ('000)	14,835	15,742	16,131
Passenger-kilometres (million)	764	777	793
Freight carried ('000 metric tons)	16,196	16,344	17,052
Freight ton-kilometres (million)	3,149	3,245	3,373

ROAD TRAFFIC
(registered motor vehicles at 31 December)

	2004	2005	2006
Motorcycles	11,574	14,473	18,801
Mopeds	28,626	34,198	34,392
Passenger cars	933,941	960,213	980,261
Buses	2,269	2,255	2,277
Lorries	57,601	60,234	62,964
Agricultural tractors	70,694	85,021	86,306
Total (incl. others)	1,117,783	1,170,606	1,200,981

SHIPPING
Merchant Fleet
(at 31 December)

	2004	2005	2006
Number of vessels	6	5	6
Displacement (grt)	1,499	1,130	1,626

Source: Lloyd's Register-Fairplay, *World Fleet Statistics*.

International Sea-borne Freight Traffic
('000 metric tons)

	2004	2005	2006
Goods loaded	154	193	188
Goods unloaded	2,976	2,997	3,206

CIVIL AVIATION
(traffic)

	2004	2005	2006
Kilometres flown ('000)	15,783	17,814	19,367
Passengers carried ('000)	885	944	1,018
Passenger-kilometres (million)	896	1,019	1,043
Freight carried (metric tons)	3,530	3,035	4,193
Freight ton-kilometres ('000)	3,201	2,765	3,436

Tourism

FOREIGN TOURIST ARRIVALS
('000)*

Country of origin	2003	2004	2005
Austria	201.4	205.7	201.9
Belgium	25.0	27.7	27.7
Bosnia and Herzegovina	27.6	23.5	20.4
Croatia	93.6	92.0	93.9
Czech Republic	31.3	32.1	31.7
France	34.7	50.4	55.9
Germany	229.4	237.9	219.3
Hungary	37.1	38.0	41.9
Israel	39.9	35.4	31.9
Italy	288.5	313.4	338.3
Netherlands	46.8	56.2	53.6
Poland	20.4	18.7	18.1
Russia	16.0	14.7	16.3
Serbia and Montenegro	25.1	30.0	32.3
Spain	13.1	17.7	20.1
Switzerland	22.5	23.8	24.4
United Kingdom	50.2	76.3	90.9
USA	29.6	38.5	41.3
Total (incl. others)	2,246.1	2,341.3	2,395.0

* Figures refer to arrivals at accommodation establishments.

Receipts from tourism (US $ million, incl. passenger transport): 1,427 in 2003; 1,726 in 2004; 1,894 in 2005 (Source: World Tourism Organization).

Communications Media

	2004	2005	2006
Telephone subscribers ('000 main lines)*	812.3	816.4	837.5
Mobile cellular telephones ('000 subscribers)*	1,848.6	1,759.2	1,819.6
Television subscriptions ('000)	619	619	624
Personal computers ('000 in use)*	704	808	n.a.
Internet users ('000)*	950	1,090	1,251
Broadband subscribers ('000)*	115.1	196.6	263.7
Daily newspapers	5	9	9
Non-daily newspapers	250	267	226
Other periodicals	1,587	1,539	1,425
Book production (titles published, including pamphlets)	4,340	4,394	4,684

* Source: International Telecommunication Union.

Facsimile machines (subscribers): 8,850 in 2002.

Education

(2004/05, unless otherwise indicated)

	Institutions	Teachers	Males	Females	Total
Pre-primary	752	6,762	28,782	26,033	54,815
Elementary*†	477	17,613	92,378	86,868	179,246
Upper secondary*†	281	12,898	61,098	60,766	121,864
Higher education	49*	5,673*	37,066‡	54,163‡	91,229‡

* 2003/04.
† Including education of adults.
‡ Excluding post-graduate students.

Directory

The Constitution

The Constitution of the Republic of Slovenia was enacted on 23 December 1991. The following is a summary of the Constitution's main articles:

INTRODUCTION

Slovenia is a democratic republic, governed by the rule of law. Slovenia is a territorially indivisible state. Human rights and fundamental freedom—including the rights of the autochthonous Italian and Hungarian ethnic communities—are protected. Slovenia attends to the welfare of Slovenian emigrants and migrant workers abroad.

The separation of church and state is guaranteed. Religious groups enjoy equal rights under the law and are guaranteed freedom of activity.

The autonomy of local government in Slovenia is guaranteed. The capital of the republic is Ljubljana. The official language of Slovenia is Slovene. In those areas where Italian or Hungarian ethnic communities reside, the official language is also Italian or Hungarian.

HUMAN RIGHTS AND FUNDAMENTAL FREEDOMS

All persons are guaranteed equal human rights and fundamental freedoms, irrespective of national origin, race, sex, language, religion, political or other beliefs, financial status, birth, education or social status, and all persons are equal before the law. Human life is inviolable, and there is no capital punishment. No person may be subjected to torture, inhuman or humiliating punishment or treatment. The right of each individual to personal liberty is guaranteed.

Respect for the humanity and dignity of the individual is guaranteed in all criminal or other proceedings. Except for certain situations (as determined by statute), all court proceedings are conducted in public. Each person is guaranteed the right of appeal. Any person charged with a criminal offence is presumed innocent until proven guilty.

Each person has the right to freedom of movement. The right to own and to inherit property is guaranteed. Freedom of expression of thought, freedom of speech, freedom to associate in public, and the freedom of the press are guaranteed. The right to vote is universal and equal. Each citizen who has attained the age of 18 years is eligible both to vote and to stand for election.

The freedom of work is guaranteed. The State regulates compulsory health, pension, disability and other social insurance, and ensures the proper administration thereof. Education is free, and the State provides the opportunity for all citizens to obtain a proper education.

Each person is entitled freely to identify with his national grouping or ethnic community, to foster and give expression to his culture, and to use his own language and script. All incitement to ethnic, racial, religious or other discrimination, as well as the inflaming of ethnic, racial, religious or other hatred or intolerance, is unconstitutional, as is incitement to violence or to war. The autochthonous Italian and Hungarian ethnic communities are guaranteed the right freely to use their national symbols. These two communities have the right to education and schooling in their own languages. They are also entitled to establish autonomous organizations in order to exercise their rights. The Italian and Hungarian communities are directly represented, both at the local level and in the Državni zbor (National Assembly). The status and special rights of Gypsy (Roma) communities living in Slovenia are determined by statute.

ECONOMIC AND SOCIAL RELATIONS

The State is responsible for the creation of opportunities for employment. Each person has the right to a healthy environment, and the State is responsible for such an environment.

Free enterprise is guaranteed. The establishment of trade unions, and the operation and membership thereof, is free. Workers enjoy the right to strike. The State creates the conditions necessary to enable each citizen to obtain proper housing.

ADMINISTRATION OF THE STATE

The Državni zbor (National Assembly)

The Državni zbor consists of 90 deputies, who serve a four-year term; 88 deputies are elected on a proportional basis from within eight regions, each of which is subdivided into 11 constituencies (although not all constituencies will necessarily obtain a direct representative). The remaining two deputies are elected as representatives of the Italian and Hungarian ethnic communities of Slovenia. The President of the Državni zbor (Speaker) is elected by a majority vote of all elected deputies.

The Državni zbor enacts laws; makes other decisions; authorizes adherence to international agreements; may call a referendum; may proclaim a state of war or a state of emergency, at the initiative of the Government; may establish parliamentary inquiries with respect to matters of public importance.

The Državni svet (National Council)

The Državni svet represents social, economic, trade and professional and local interests. It is composed of 40 councillors: four representing employers; four representing employees; four representing farmers, small business persons and independent professional persons; six representing non-profit-making organizations; and 22 representing local interests. Councillors are elected for a five-year term.

The Državni svet may: propose the enactment of statutes by the Državni zbor; demand that the Državni zbor reconsider statutes prior to their proclamation; demand the holding of a referendum; and demand the establishment of a parliamentary inquiry. The Državni zbor may require the Državni svet to provide its opinions on specific matters. A councillor of the Državni svet may not be simultaneously a deputy of the Državni zbor.

The President of the Republic

The President of the Republic of Slovenia is Head of State and Commander-in-Chief of the Defence Forces. The President is elected on the basis of universal, equal and direct suffrage by secret ballot. The President's term of office is five years (with a maximum of two consecutive terms). Only a citizen of Slovenia may be elected President of the Republic. Presidential elections are called by the President of the Državni zbor. The office of President of the Republic is incompatible with other public offices or other employment. In the event that the President of the Republic is permanently incapacitated, dies, resigns or is otherwise permanently unable to perform his functions, the President of the Državni zbor temporarily occupies the office of the President of the Republic until such time as a replacement is elected.

The President of the Republic is empowered to: call elections to the Državni zbor; proclaim statutes; appoint state officers and functionaries; accredit, and revoke the accreditation of, Slovenian ambassadors to foreign states, and to accept the credentials of foreign diplomatic representatives; grant amnesties; and confer state honours, decorations and honorary titles.

If, in the course of carrying out his office, the President of the Republic acts in a manner contrary to the Constitution or commits a serious breach of the law, he may be brought before the Constitutional Court upon the request of the Državni zbor. The President may be dismissed from office upon the vote of no less than two-thirds of all of the judges of the Constitutional Court.

The Government

The Government is composed of the Prime Minister and ministers. The Government is independent, and individual ministers are independent within their own particular portfolios. Ministers are accountable to the Državni zbor. After consultations with the leaders of the various political groups within the Državni zbor, the President of the Republic proposes to the Državni zbor a candidate for the office of Prime Minister. The Prime Minister is elected by the Državni zbor by a majority vote. Ministers in the Government are appointed or dismissed by the Državni zbor, upon the proposal of the Prime Minister. The Prime Minister is responsible for the political unity, direction and administrative programme of the Government and for the co-ordination of the work of the various ministers. The Državni zbor may, upon the motion of no fewer than 10 deputies and by a majority vote, elect a new Prime Minister (such a vote is deemed a vote of 'no confidence' in the Government). Furthermore, the Državni zbor may bring the Prime Minister or any minister before the Constitutional Court to answer charges relating to breaches of the Constitution.

The Judiciary

Judges independently exercise their duties and functions in accordance with the Constitution and with the law. The Supreme Court is the highest court for civil and criminal cases in the republic. The Državni zbor elects judges upon the recommendation of the Judicial Council, which is composed of 11 members. The office of a judge is incompatible with office in any other state body, local government body or organ of any political party.

The Office of the Public Prosecutor

The Public Prosecutor is responsible for the preferment of criminal charges, for prosecuting criminal matters in court and for the performance of such other duties as are prescribed by statute.

LOCAL SELF-GOVERNMENT

Slovenians exercise local government powers and functions through self-governing municipalities and other local government organizations. A municipality may comprise a single community or a number of communities, whose inhabitants are bound together by common needs and interests. The State supervises the proper and efficient performance of municipalities and wider self-governing local administrative bodies. Municipalities raise their own revenue. Municipalities are at liberty to join other municipalities in establishing wider self-governing local administrative bodies or regional local government bodies to exercise administrative powers and to deal with matters of wider common interest. Citizens may join together and form self-governing local bodies to further their common interests.

PUBLIC FINANCE

The Bank of Slovenia is the central bank. It is independent in its operations and accountable to the Državni zbor. The Governor of the Bank of Slovenia is appointed by the Državni zbor.

THE CONSTITUTIONAL COURT

The Constitutional Court is composed of nine judges, elected by the Državni zbor, upon the nomination of the President of the Republic, for a single term of nine years. The President of the Constitutional Court is elected by the judges from among their own number to hold office for a period of three years.

The Constitutional Court is empowered to decide upon matters relating to: the conformity of statutes with the Constitution and with international agreements; complaints of breaches of the Constitution involving individual acts infringing human rights and fundamental freedoms; juridical disputes between the state and local government bodies or among such local government bodies; juridical disputes between the Državni zbor, the President of the Republic and the Government; and unconstitutional acts or activities of political parties.

The Government

HEAD OF STATE

President: Dr DANILO TÜRK (elected 11 November 2007; inaugurated 22 December 2007).

GOVERNMENT
(April 2008)

A coalition comprising representatives of the Slovenian Democratic Party (SDP), New Slovenia—Christian People's Party (NSi), the Slovenian People's Party (SPP) and the Democratic Party of Pensioners of Slovenia (DeSUS).

Prime Minister: JANEZ JANŠA (SDP).
Minister of Finance: Dr ANDREJ BAJUK (NSi).
Minister of Internal Affairs: DRAGUTIN MATE (SDP).
Minister of Foreign Affairs: Dr DIMITRIJ RUPEL (SDP).
Minister of Justice: Dr LOVRO ŠTURM (NSi).
Minister of Defence: KARL ERJAVEC (DeSUS).
Minister of Labour, Family and Social Affairs: MARJETA COTMAN (NSi).
Minister of the Economy: ANDREJ VIZJAK (SDP).
Minister of Agriculture, Forestry and Food: IZTOK JARC (SDP).
Minister of Culture: Dr VASKO SIMONITI (SDP).
Minister of the Environment and Physical Planning: JANEZ PODOBNIK (SPP).
Minister of Transport: RADOVAN ŽERJAV (SPP).
Minister of Education and Sport: Dr MILAN ZVER (SDP).
Minister of Health: ZOFIJA MAZEJ KUKOVIČ (SDP).
Minister of Public Administration: Dr GREGOR VIRANT (SDP).
Minister of Higher Education, Science and Technology: MOJCA KUCLER DOLINAR (NSi).
Minister without Portfolio, responsible for Local Self-Government and Regional Policy: Dr IVAN ŽAGAR (SPP).
Minister without Portfolio, responsible for Growth: Dr ŽIGA TURK (Independent).

MINISTRIES

Office of the President: 1000 Ljubljana, Erjavčeva 17; tel. (1) 4781222; fax (1) 4781357; e-mail gp.uprs@up-rs.si; internet www.up-rs.si.

Office of the Prime Minister: 1000 Ljubljana, Gregorčičeva 20; tel. (1) 4781000; fax (1) 4781721; e-mail gp.kpv@gov.si; internet www.kpv.gov.si.

Government Office for Growth: 1000 Ljubljana, Gregorčičeva 25; tel. (1) 4781180; fax (1) 4781191; e-mail go.svr@gov.si; internet www.svr.gov.si.

Government Office for Local Self-Government and Regional Policy: 1000 Ljubljana, Kotnikova 28; tel. (1) 3083178; fax (1) 4783619; e-mail gp.svlr@gov.si; internet www.svlr.gov.si.

Ministry of Agriculture, Forestry and Food: 1000 Ljubljana, Dunajska 56–58; tel. (1) 4789000; fax (1) 4789021; e-mail gp.mkgp@gov.si; internet www.mkgp.gov.si.

Ministry of Culture: 1000 Ljubljana, Maistrova 10; tel. (1) 3695900; fax (1) 3695901; e-mail gp.mk@gov.si; internet www.mk.gov.si.

Ministry of Defence: 1000 Ljubljana, Vojkova 55; tel. (1) 4712211; fax (1) 4712978; e-mail info@mors.si; internet www.mors.si.

Ministry of the Economy: 1000 Ljubljana, Kotnikova 5; tel. (1) 4003311; fax (1) 4001031; e-mail info.mg@gov.si; internet www.mg.gov.si.

Ministry of Education and Sport: 1000 Ljubljana, Kotnikova 38; tel. (1) 4784200; fax (1) 4784329; e-mail gp.mss@gov.si; internet www.mss.gov.si.

Ministry of the Environment and Physical Planning: 1000 Ljubljana, Dunajska cesta 48; tel. (1) 4787400; fax (1) 4787422; e-mail gp.mop@gov.si; internet www.mop.gov.si.

Ministry of Finance: 1502 Ljubljana, Župančičeva 3; tel. (1) 3696610; fax (1) 3696619; e-mail gp.mf@gov.si; internet www.mf.gov.si.

Ministry of Foreign Affairs: 1001 Ljubljana, Prešernova 25; tel. (1) 4782231; fax (1) 4782170; e-mail info.mzz@gov.si; internet www.mzz.gov.si.

Ministry of Health: 1000 Ljubljana, Štefanova 5; tel. (1) 4786001; fax (1) 4786058; e-mail gp.mz@gov.si; internet www.mz.gov.si.

Ministry of Higher Education, Science and Technology: 1000 Ljubljana, trg OF 13; tel. (1) 4784600; fax (1) 4784719; e-mail gp.mvzt@gov.si; internet www.mvzt.gov.si.

Ministry of Internal Affairs: 1501 Ljubljana, Štefanova 2; tel. (1) 4325125; fax (1) 2514330; e-mail gp.mnz@gov.si; internet www.mnz.gov.si.

Ministry of Justice: 1000 Ljubljana, Župančičeva 3; tel. (1) 3695200; fax (1) 3695783; e-mail gp.mp@gov.si; internet www.mp.gov.si.

Ministry of Labour, Family and Social Affairs: 1000 Ljubljana, Kotnikova 5; tel. (1) 3697700; fax (1) 3697832; e-mail gp.mddsz@gov.si; internet www.mddsz.gov.si.

Ministry of Public Administration: 1000 Ljubljana, Tržaška cesta 21; tel. (1) 4788330; fax (1) 4788331; e-mail gp.mju@gov.si; internet www.mju.gov.si.

Ministry of Transport: 1535 Ljubljana, Langusova 4; tel. (1) 4788000; fax (1) 4788139; e-mail gp.mpz@gov.si; internet www.mzp.gov.si.

President

Presidential Election, First Ballot, 21 October 2007

Candidate	Votes	% of votes
Lojze Peterle (Independent)	283,412	28.73
Danilo Türk (Independent)	241,349	24.47
Mitja Gaspari (Independent)	237,632	24.09
Zmago Jelinčič Plemeniti (Slovenian National Party)	188,951	19.16
Darko Krajnc (Youth Party of Slovenia)	21,526	2.18
Others	13,559	1.37
Total	**986,429**	**100.00**

Second Ballot, 11 November 2007

Candidate	Votes	% of votes
Danilo Türk (Independent)	677,333	68.03
Lojze Peterle (Independent)	318,288	31.97
Total	**995,621**	**100.00**

Legislature

The Slovenian legislature is bicameral, comprising the Državni zbor (National Assembly), the directly elected lower chamber, and the Državni svet (National Council), the indirectly elected upper chamber.

Državni zbor
(National Assembly)

1000 Ljubljana, Šubičeva 4; tel. (1) 4789400; fax (1) 4789845; e-mail france.cukjati@dz-rs.si; internet www.dz-rs.si.

President: Dr FRANCE CUKJATI.

General Election, 3 October 2004

	Votes	% of votes	Seats
Slovenian Democratic Party	281,710	29.08	29
Liberal Democracy of Slovenia	220,848	22.80	23
United List of Social Democrats	98,527	10.17	10
New Slovenia—Christian People's Party	88,073	9.09	9
Slovenian People's Party	66,032	6.82	7
Slovenian National Party	60,750	6.27	6
Democratic Party of Pensioners of Slovenia	39,150	4.04	4
Others*	113,682	11.73	2
Total	**968,772**	**100.00**	**90**

*Two of the 90 seats in the Državni zbor are reserved for representatives of the Italian and Hungarian minorities.

Državni svet
(National Council)

1000 Ljubljana, Šubičeva 4; tel. (1) 4789798; fax (1) 4789851; e-mail janez.susnik@ds-rs.si; internet www.ds-rs.si.

There are 40 councillors in the Državni svet, who are indirectly elected for a five-year term by an electoral college.

President: JANEZ SUŠNIK.

Election Commission

Republic Electoral Commission: 1000 Ljubljana, Slovenska 54; tel. (1) 4322002; fax (1) 4331269; e-mail rvk@gov.si; internet volitve.gov.si; Chair. MARKO GOLUBIĆ.

Political Organizations

Democratic Party of Pensioners of Slovenia (DeSUS) (Demokratična stranka upokojencev Slovenije): 1000 Ljubljana, Kersnikova 6; tel. (1) 4397350; fax (1) 4314113; e-mail desus@siol.net; internet www.desus.si; Pres. KARL VIKTOR ERJAVEC.

Greens of Slovenia (Zeleni Slovenije): 1000 Ljubljana, Komenskega 11; tel. (2) 7781071; fax (2) 7878543; e-mail zeleni@zeleni.si; internet www.zeleni.si; f. 1989; in 1993 the party split into two factions, one retaining the original name, the other, more radical, wing adopting the title, Greens of Slovenia—Eco-Social Party; Chair. Prof. VLADO ČUŠ.

Liberal Democracy of Slovenia (LDS) (Liberalna demokracija Slovenije): 1000 Ljubljana, trg Republike 3; tel. (1) 2000310; fax (1) 2000311; e-mail lds@lds.si; internet www.lds.si; f. 1994 by a merger of the Liberal Democratic Party, the Greens of Slovenia—Eco-Social Party, the Democratic Party and the Socialist Party of Slovenia; Chair. KATARINA KRESAL; 18,000 mems.

New Slovenia—Christian People's Party (NSi) (Nova Slovenija—Krščanska ljudska stranka): 1000 Ljubljana, Cankarjeva 11; tel. (1) 2416650; fax (1) 2416670; e-mail andrej.bajuk@nsi.si; internet www.nsi.si; f. 2000 by mems of the Slovenian People's Party; Pres. Dr ANDREJ BAJUK.

Slovenian Democratic Party (SDP) (Slovenska Demokratska Stranka—SDS): 1000 Ljubljana, Komenskega 11; tel. (1) 4345450; fax (1) 4345452; e-mail sekretar@sds.si; internet www.sds.si; f. 1989 as Social Democratic Party of Slovenia; name changed in 2003; centre-right; Pres. JANEZ JANŠA; Sec.-Gen. DUŠAN STRNAD; 20,000 mems.

Slovenian National Party (SNP) (Slovenska nacionalna stranka—SNS): 1000 Ljubljana, Tivolska 13; tel. (1) 2529020; fax (1) 2529022; e-mail info@sns.si; internet www.sns.si; f. 1991; right-wing nationalist party; Pres. ZMAGO JELINČIČ; Sec.-Gen. MIŠA GLAŽAR; 7,000 mems (2007).

Slovenian People's Party (SPP) (Slovenska ljudska stranka) (SLS): 1000 Ljubljana, Beethovnova 4; tel. (1) 2418820; fax (1) 2511741; e-mail tajnistvo@sls.si; internet www.sls.si; f. 1989 as the Slovenian Farmers' Assn; merged with the Slovenian Christian Democrats in April 2000; Pres. BOJAN ŠROT.

Social Democrats (SD) (Socialni demokrati): 1000 Ljubljana, Levstikova 15; tel. (1) 2444100; fax (1) 2444123; e-mail info@socialnidemokrati.si; internet www.socialnidemokrati.si; f. 1993; Pres. BORUT PAHOR; Gen. Sec. UROŠ JAUŠEVEC; 23,000 mems.

Diplomatic Representation

EMBASSIES IN SLOVENIA

Austria: 1000 Ljubljana, Prešernova cesta 23; tel. (1) 4790700; fax (1) 2521717; e-mail laibach-ob@bmaa.gv.at; internet www.aussenministerium.at/laibach; Ambassador Dr VALENTIN INZKO.

Belgium: 1000 Ljubljana, trg Republike 3/IX; tel. (1) 2006010; fax (1) 4266395; e-mail ljubljana@diplobel.org; internet www.diplomatie.be/ljubljanafr; Ambassador LOUIS MOURAUX.

Bosnia and Herzegovina: 1000 Ljubljana, Korlajeva 26; tel. (1) 2343259; fax (1) 2343261; Ambassador IZMIR TALIĆ.

Bulgaria: 1000 Ljubljana, Rožna dolina XV/18; tel. (1) 4265744; fax (1) 4258845; e-mail bgembassysl@siol.net; Ambassador VLADIMIR A. ATANASOV.

China, People's Republic: 1000 Ljubljana, Koblarjeva 3; tel. (1) 4202855; fax (1) 2822199; e-mail kitajsko.veleposlanistvo@siol.net; internet si.china-embassy.org; Ambassador ZHI ZHAOLIN.

Croatia: 1000 Ljubljana, Gruberjevo nabrežje 6; tel. (1) 4256220; fax (1) 4258106; e-mail croemb.slovenia@mvp.hr; internet si.mvp.hr; Ambassador Dr MARIO NOBILO.

Cyprus: 1000 Ljubljana, Komenskega 12; tel. (1) 2321542; fax (1) 2302002; e-mail embassy.cyprus@siol.net; Ambassador CHARALAMBOS PANAYIDES.

Czech Republic: 1000 Ljubljana, Riharjeva 1; tel. (1) 4202450; fax (1) 2839259; e-mail ljubljana@embassy.mzv.cz; internet www.mzv.cz/ljubljana; Ambassador IVANA HLAVSOVÁ.

Denmark: 1000 Ljubljana, Tivolska 48, EuroCenter; tel. (1) 4380800; fax (1) 4317417; e-mail ljuamb@um.dk; internet www.ambljubljana.um.dk; Ambassador ANITA HUGAU.

Finland: 1000 Ljubljana, Ajdovščina 4/8; tel. (1) 3002120; fax (1) 3002139; e-mail sanomat.lju@formin.fi; internet www.finland.si; Ambassador BIRGITTA STENIUS-MLADENOV.

France: 1000 Ljubljana, Barjanska cesta 1; tel. (1) 4790400; fax (1) 4790410; e-mail info@ambafrance.si; internet www.ambafrance.si; Ambassador CHANTAL DE GHAISNE DE BOURMONT.

Germany: 1000 Ljubljana, Prešernova cesta 27; tel. (1) 4790300; fax (1) 4250899; e-mail germanembassy-slovenia@siol.net; internet www.ljubljana.diplo.de; Ambassador Dr HANS-JOACHIM GOETZ.

Greece: 1000 Ljubljana, Trnovski Pristan 14; tel. (1) 4201400; fax (1) 2811114; e-mail emb.gr.slo@siol.net; Ambassador DIONYSSIOS COUNDOUREAS.

Holy See: 1000 Ljubljana, trg Krekov 1; tel. (1) 4339204; fax (1) 4315130; e-mail nunaplub@yahoo.com; Apostolic Nuncio Most Rev. ABRIL Y CASTELLÓ SANTOS (Titular Archbishop of Tamada).

Hungary: 1210 Ljubljana, ul. Konrada Babnika 5; tel. (1) 5121882; fax (1) 5121878; e-mail huemblju@siol.net; internet www.hu-embassy.si; Ambassador Dr JÓZSEF CZUKOR.

Italy: 1000 Ljubljana, Snežniška 8; tel. (1) 4262194; fax (1) 4253302; e-mail archivio.lubiana@esteri.it; internet www.amblubiana.esteri.it; Ambassador Dr DANIELE VERGA.

Japan: 1000 Ljubljana, trg Republike 3/XI; tel. (1) 2008281; fax (1) 2511822; internet www.si.emb-japan.go.jp; Ambassador TSUNESHIGE IIYAMA.

Latvia: 1000 Ljubljana, Ajdovščina 4; tel. (1) 4341620; fax (1) 4341622; e-mail juris.poikans@mfa.gov.lv; Chargé d'affaires a.i. AIVARS GROZA.

Lithuania: 1000 Ljubljana, Kongresni trg 3; tel. (1) 2442611; fax (1) 2442619; e-mail amb.si@urm.lt; Ambassador RIMUTIS KLEVEČKA.

Macedonia, former Yugoslav republic: 1000 Ljubljana, Prešernova cesta 2; tel. (1) 4210021; fax (1) 4210023; e-mail makamb@siol.net; Ambassador SAMOIL JOSIF FILIPOVSKI.

Montenegro: 1000 Ljubljana, Reseljeva cesta 40; tel. (1) 4395365; fax (1) 4395360; e-mail embamon-lj@t-2.net; Ambassador BRANKO PEROVIĆ.

Netherlands: 1000 Ljubljana, Palača Kapitelj, Polijanski nasip 6; tel. (1) 4201460; fax (1) 4201470; e-mail lju@minbuza.nl; internet www.netherlands-embassy.si; Ambassador J. C. M. GROFFEN.

Norway: 1000 Ljubljana, Ajdovščina 4/8; tel. (1) 3002140; fax (1) 3002150; Ambassador MAY BRITT BROFOSS.

Poland: 1000 Ljubljana, Bežigrad 10; tel. (1) 4364712; fax (1) 4362521; e-mail ambpol.si@siol.net; internet www.lublana.polemb.net; Ambassador PIOTR KASZUBA.

Portugal: 1000 Ljubljana, trg Republika 3/10; tel. (1) 4790540; fax (1) 4790550; Ambassador MARIA DO CARMO ALLEGRO DE MAGALHÃES.

Romania: 1000 Ljubljana, Smrekarjeva 33 A; tel. (1) 5058294; fax (1) 5055432; e-mail embassy.of.romania@siol.net; internet ljubljana.mae.ro; Ambassador DANA MANUELA CONSTANTINESCU.

Russia: 1000 Ljubljana, Tomšičeva 9; tel. (1) 4256875; fax (1) 4254141; e-mail ambrus.slo@siol.net; internet www.rus-slo.mid.ru; Ambassador MIKHAIL V. VANIN.

Serbia: 1000 Ljubljana, Slomškova 1; tel. (1) 4380111; fax (1) 4342688; e-mail amba.srbije.lju@siol.net; Ambassador PREDRAG FILIPOV.

Slovakia: 1000 Ljubljana, Tivolska cesta 4, POB 395; tel. (1) 4255425; fax (1) 4210524; e-mail embass@lublana.mfa.sk; internet lublana.mfa.sk; Ambassador Dr ROMAN PALDAN.

Spain: 1000 Ljubljana, Trnovski pristan 24; tel. (1) 4202330; fax (1) 4202333; e-mail emb.liubliana@maec.es; Ambassador CARMEN FONTES MUÑOZ.

Sweden: 1000 Ljubljana, Ajdovščina 4/8, POB 1680; tel. (1) 3000270; fax (1) 3000271; e-mail ambassaden.ljubljana@foreign.ministry.se; internet www.swedenabroad.com/ljubljana; Ambassador JOHN HAGARD.

Switzerland: 1000 Ljubljana, trg Republike 3/VI; tel. (1) 2008640; fax (1) 2008669; e-mail vertretung@lju.rep.admin.ch; internet www.eda.admin.ch/ljubljana; Ambassador STEFAN SPECK.

Turkey: 1000 Ljubljana, Livarska 4; tel. (1) 2364150; fax (1) 4365240; e-mail vrtucije@siol.net; internet www.turkish-embassy.si; Ambassador MELEK SINA BAYDUR.

Ukraine: 1000 Ljubljana, Teslova 23, WTC; tel. (1) 4210604; fax (1) 4210603; e-mail emb_si@mfa.gov.ua; Ambassador VADYM V. PRIMACHENKO.

United Kingdom: 1000 Ljubljana, trg Republike 3/IV; tel. (1) 2003910; fax (1) 4250174; e-mail info@british-embassy.si; internet www.british-embassy.si; Ambassador TIM SIMMONS.

USA: 1000 Ljubljana, Prešernova cesta 31; tel. (1) 2005500; fax (1) 2005555; internet slovenia.usembassy.gov; Chargé d'affaires a.i. MARYRUTH COLEMAN.

Judicial System

The Slovenian Constitution guarantees the independence of the judiciary.

The 44 district courts decide minor cases. The 11 regional courts act as courts of the first instance in all cases other than those for which the district courts have jurisdiction. Four regional courts act as courts of the second instance. There are, in addition, labour courts and social courts, which adjudicate in disputes over pensions, welfare allocations and other social benefits. A Higher Labour and Social Court has jurisdiction in the second instance. The Supreme Court is the highest authority for civil and criminal law. There is also a Constitutional Court, composed of nine judges, each elected for a single term of nine years.

Constitutional Court of the Republic of Slovenia (Ustavno sodišča Republike Slovenije): 1000 Ljubljana, Beethovnova 10; tel. (1) 4776400; fax (1) 2510451; e-mail info@us-rs.si; internet www.us-rs.si; Pres. Dr JANEZ ČEBULJ.

Supreme Court of the Republic of Slovenia (Vrhovno Sodišče Republike Slovenije): 1000 Ljubljana, Tavčarjeva 9; tel. (1) 3664200; fax (1) 3664301; e-mail franc.testen@sodisce.si; internet www.sodisce.si; Pres. FRANC TESTEN.

Office of the Public Prosecutor: 1511 Ljubljana, Dunajska 22; tel. (1) 2320396; fax (1) 4310381; e-mail dtrs@dt-rs.si; Public Prosecutor BARBARA BREZIGAR.

Religion

Most of the population are Christian, predominantly adherents of the Roman Catholic Church. There are few Protestant Christians, despite the importance of a Calvinist sect (the Church of Carniola) to the development of Slovene literature in the 16th century. At the census of 2002 some 57.8% of the population described themselves as Roman Catholics, 10.1% as atheists, 2.4% as Muslims, 2.3% as Orthodox Christians and 0.8% as Protestants. (22.8% of all respondents did not respond to the question requesting their religious allegiance.)

CHRISTIANITY

The Roman Catholic Church

The Roman Catholic Church in Slovenia comprises two archdioceses and four dioceses. At 31 December 2005 there were an estimated 1,605,384 adherents (equivalent to 80.2% of the total population).

Bishops' Conference

1000 Ljubljana, p.p. 121/III, Ciril Metodov trg 4; tel. (1) 2342600; fax (1) 2314169; e-mail ssk@rkc.si.
f. 1993; Pres. Rt Rev. FRANC KRAMBERGER (Archbishop of Maribor).
Archbishop of Ljubljana: Most Rev. ALOJZIJ URAN, 1001 Ljubljana, p.p. 1990, Ciril Metodov trg 4; tel. (1) 2342600; fax (1) 2314169; e-mail nadskofija.lubljana@rkc.si.
Archbishop of Maribor: Most Rev. FRANC KRAMBERGER, 2000 Maribor, Slomškov trg 19; tel. (2) 2290401; fax (2) 2523092; e-mail ordinariat@slomsek.net.

Protestant Church

Evangelical Lutheran Church of Slovenia: 9226 Moravske Toplice, 11 Levstikova; tel. (2) 5381323; fax (2) 5381324; e-mail evang.cerkev.si@siol.net; f. 1561; 20,000 mems; Chair. GEZA ERNIŠA.

The Press

The publications listed below are in Slovene, unless otherwise indicated.

PRINCIPAL DAILIES

Delo (Event): 1509 Ljubljana, Dunajska 5; tel. (1) 4727402; fax (1) 4737406; e-mail webmaster@delo.si; internet www.delo.si; f. 1959; morning; Editor-in-Chief PETER JANCIC; circ. 93,781.
Dnevnik (Daily): 1510 Ljubljana, Kopitarjeva 2; tel. (1) 3082100; fax (1) 3082189; e-mail info@dnevnik.si; internet www.dnevnik.si; f. 1951; evening; independent; Man. Dir BRANKO BERGANT; Editor-in-Chief ZLATKO ŠETINC; circ. 63,000.
Slovenske novice (Slovene News): 1509 Ljubljana, Dunajska 5; tel. (1) 1737700; fax (1) 1737352; f. 1991; Editor-in-Chief MARJAN BAUER; Man. Editor TIT DOBERSEK; circ. 80,000.
Večer (Evening): 2000 Maribor, Svetozarevska 14; tel. (2) 2353500; fax (2) 2353368; internet www.vecer.si; f. 1945; Dir BORIS CEKOV; Editor-in-Chief MILAN PREDAN; circ. 70,000.

PERIODICALS

Antena: 1000 Ljubljana, Slovenska 15; tel. (1) 1253418; fax (1) 1253367; f. 1965; weekly; youth magazine concerned with popular culture; Editor-in-Chief JASMIN PETAN MALACHOVSKY; circ. 20,000.
Ars Vivendi: 1000 Ljubljana, Poljanska 6; tel. and fax (1) 317058; f. 1987; quarterly; visual arts and design; publ. in Slovene and English; Editor-in-Chief SONJA TOMAŽIČ; circ. 10,000.
Avto magazin: 1000 Ljubljana, Dunajska 5; tel. (1) 1738251; fax (1) 1738220; f. 1967; fortnightly; cars, motorcycles and sports; Editor BOŠTJAN JEVŠEK; circ. 16,000.
Delavska enotnost: 1000 Ljubljana, Dalmatinova 4; tel. (1) 1310033; fax (1) 1313942; f. 1942; weekly; trade union issues; Dir and Editor-in-Chief MARJAN HORVAT; circ. 16,000.
Dolenjski list: 8000 Novo mesto, Glavni trg 24; tel. (7) 3323606; fax (7) 3322898; internet www.dol-list.si; f. 1950; weekly; general and local information; Editor-in-Chief MARJAN LEGAN; circ. 24,000.
Družina: 1000 Ljubljana, trg Krekov 1; tel. (1) 1316202; fax (1) 1316152; e-mail druzina@siol.net; internet www.druzina.si; f. 1952; Christian; Editor-in-Chief JANEZ GRIL; circ. 70,000.
Finance: 1509 Ljubljana, Dunajska 5; tel. (1) 1330137; fax (1) 1312223; internet www.finance.si; f. 1992; 2 a week; Editor-in-Chief JOŽE PETROVČIČ; circ. 8,500.
Flaneur: 1000 Ljubljana, Šaranovičeva 12; f. 1992; bi-monthly; in English; politics, economy, culture and leisure; Editor-in-Chief TADEJ ČATER; circ. 2,500.
Gea: 1536 Ljubljana, Slovenska 29; tel. (1) 2413230; fax (1) 1252836; e-mail gea@mkz-lj.si; f. 1990; monthly; popular science; Editor-in-Chief JANA LESKOVEC; circ. 23,000.
Gorenjski glas: 4000 Kranj, Zoisova 1; tel. (4) 2014200; fax (4) 2014213; internet www.gorenjskiglas.si; f. 1947; 2 a week; general and regional information; Editor-in-Chief MARIJA VOLEJAK; circ. 23,300.
Jana: 1509 Ljubljana, Dunajska 5; tel. (1) 319260; fax (1) 1334320; f. 1972; weekly; women's interest; Editor-in-Chief BERNARDA JEKLIN; circ. 62,000.
Kaj: 62000 Maribor, Svetozarevska 14; tel. (2) 26951; fax (2) 227736; f. 1984; weekly; popular; Editor-in-Chief MILAN PREDAN; circ. 16,500.
Kmečki glas: 1000 Ljubljana, p.p. 47, Železna 14; tel. (1) 1735350; fax (1) 1735376; internet www.kmeckiglas.com; weekly; general and agricultural news; Dir BORIS DOLNIČAR; circ. 38,000.
Lipov list: 1000 Ljubljana, Miklosičeva 38/6; tel. (1) 4341682; fax (1) 4341680; e-mail tzs@siol.net; monthly; Editor-in-Chief MARJETICA NOVAK.
Mag: 1000 Ljubljana, Njegoševa 14; tel. (1) 319480; fax (1) 1329158; f. 1995; weekly; news and politics; Editor-in-Chief JANEZ MARKES.
Mladina: 1000 Ljubljana, Resljeva 16; tel. (1) 1328175; fax (1) 1331239; internet www.mladina.si; f. 1942; weekly; news magazine; Editor-in-Chief JANI SEVER; circ. 30,000.
Moj mikro: 1509 Ljubljana, Dunajska 5; tel. (1) 4738261; fax (1) 4738109; e-mail marjan.kodelja@delo-revije.si; internet www.mojmikro.si; monthly; personal computers; Editor-in-Chief MARJAN KODELJA.
Muska: 1000 Ljubljana, Kersnikova 4; tel. (1) 1317039; fax (1) 322570; e-mail kaja.sivic@kiss.uni_lj.si; monthly; music; Editor-in-Chief KAJA SIVIČ.
Naš Čas (Our Time): 63320 Velenje, Foltova 10; tel. (3) 855450; fax (3) 851990; f. 1956; weekly; general and regional information; Editor-in-Chief STANE VOVK; circ. 6,250.
Nedeljski dnevnik (Weekly Record): 1000 Ljubljana, Kopitarieva 2; tel. (1) 3082100; fax (1) 3082469; e-mail info@nedeljski.si; internet www.nedeljski.si; f. 1961; weekly; popular; Editor-in-Chief ZLATKO ŠETINC; circ. 145,000 (2006).
Novi tednik (New Weekly): 3000 Celje, Prešernova 19; tel. (3) 442500; fax (3) 441032; internet www.novitednik.com; f. 1945; weekly; general and local information; Editor-in-Chief BRANE STAMEJČIČ; circ. 16,980.
Obrtnik: 1000 Ljubljana, Celovška 71; tel. (1) 5830507; fax (1) 5193496; e-mail revija.obrtnik@ozs.si; internet www.ozs.si; f. 1971; monthly; small businesses; Editor-in-Chief MIRAN JAREC; circ. 60,000.
Pavliha: 1000 Ljubljana, Slovenska 15; tel. (1) 221661; monthly; satire; Editor-in-Chief JOŽE PETELIN.
PIL: 1000 Ljubljana, Slovenska 29; tel. (1) 2413221; fax (1) 4252836; e-mail pil@mkz.si; internet www.pil-on.net; monthly; for children aged 9 to 12 years; Editor BARBARA JARC; circ. 21,000.
Podjetnik: 1000 Ljubljana, Dunajska 51; tel. (1) 1330102; fax (1) 1330450; internet www.podjetnik.si; f. 1992; monthly; business and management; Editor-in-Chief JOŽE VILFAN; circ. 8,500.
Primorske novice (News from the Primorska region): 6000 Koper, ul. OF 12; tel. (5) 6648100; fax (5) 6648110; e-mail editors@prim-nov.si; internet www.prim-nov.si; f. 1947; daily; general and regional information; Editor-in-Chief TINO MAMIĆ; circ. 23,000.
Profit: 1000 Ljubljana, Dunajska 7; tel. (1) 4304310; fax (1) 2318940; e-mail profit.uredmistvo@sid.net; 2 a month; business; Editor-in-Chief JOŽE SIMČIČ.
Rodna gruda (Native Breast): 1000 Ljubljana, Cankarjeva 1/II, Združenje Slovenska izseljenska matica; tel. (1) 2410288; fax (1) 4251673; e-mail rodna.gruda@zdruzenje-sim.si; internet www.zdruzenje-sim.si; f. 1951; monthly; national issues and news; Editor-in-Chief VIDA POSINKOVIĆ; circ. 2,100.
Slovenian Business Report: 1000 Ljubljana, Dunajska 5; tel. (1) 3091924; fax (1) 3091705; e-mail info@sbr.si; internet www.sbr.si; f. 1991; monthly; in English; economic affairs; Editor-in-Chief JOŽE PETROVČIČ; circ. 4,000.
Slovenija: 1000 Ljubljana, Cankarjeva 1/II; tel. (1) 2410284; fax (1) 4251673; e-mail sim@siol.net; f. 1987; quarterly; in English; news about Slovenia and Slovenes; Man. Editor JOŽE PREŠEREN; circ. 3,500.
Slovenske brazde (Slovenian Tracks): 1000 Ljubljana, Zarnikova 3; tel. (1) 4301891; fax (1) 4301871; f. 1990; weekly; Man. Editor NACE POTOCNIK.
Štajerski Tednik: 2250 Ptuj, Raičeva 6; tel. (2) 7493410; fax (2) 7493435; e-mail tednik@radio-tednik.si; internet www.radio-tednik.si; f. 1948; weekly; politics, local information; Editor-in-Chief JOŽE ŠMIGOC; circ. 12,000.
Stop: 1000 Ljubljana, Dunajska 5; tel. (1) 319190; fax (1) 1330403; f. 1967; weekly; leisure, film, theatre, pop music, radio and television programmes; Editor IGOR SAVIČ; circ. 44,600.
Tretji dan (Third Day): 1000 Ljubljana, Jurčičev trg 2; tel. (1) 1263071; fax (1) 223864; weekly; Editor-in-Chief Dr TONE JAMNIK.

SLOVENIA

Tribuna: 1000 Ljubljana, Kersnikova 4; tel. (1) 319496; fax (1) 319448; 3 a week; student newspaper; Editor-in-Chief BOJAN KORENINI.

Vestnik Murska Sobota (Murska Sobota Herald): 9000 Murska Sobota, ul. Arhitekta Novaka 13; tel. (2) 5311960; fax (2) 5321175; e-mail vestnik@eunet.si; internet www.p-inf.si; f. 1949; weekly; popular; Editor-in-Chief JANEZ VOTEK; circ. 20,000.

Zdravje (Health): 1000 Ljubljana, Smartinska 10; tel. (1) 2319360; monthly; Editor-in-Chief MARIJA MICA KOTNIK.

PRESS AGENCIES

Morel: 1000 Ljubljana, Reboljeva 13, statti Parmova 41–45; tel. (1) 4361222; fax (1) 4361223; e-mail morel@si21.com; internet www.morel.si; f. 1993; Dir and Chief Editor EMIL LUKANČIČ-MORI.

Slovenska Tiskovna Agencija (STA): 1000 Ljubljana, Cankarjeva 5, p.p. 145; tel. (1) 2410100; fax (1) 4266050; e-mail desk@sta.si; internet www.sta.si; f. 1991; Dir-Gen. IGOR VEZOVNIK; Editor-in-Chief TADEJA ŠERGAN.

Publishers

Cankarjeva Založba: 1000 Ljubljana, Kopitarjeva 2; tel. (1) 3603720; fax (1) 3603787; e-mail import.books@cankarjeva-z.si; internet www.cankarjeva-z.si; f. 1945; philosophy, science and popular science, dictionaries and reference books, Slovenian and translated literature, international co-productions; Dir-Gen. JOŽE KORINŠEK.

DZS d.d.: 1538 Ljubljana, Dalmatinova 2; tel. (1) 3069700; fax (1) 3069877; e-mail info@dzs.si; internet www.dzs.si; f. 1945; textbooks, manuals, world classics, natural sciences, art books, encyclopedias, dictionaries, educational CD-ROMs; Exec. Dir ANDREJ ZALOŽNIK.

Mladinska Knjiga Založba: 1000 Ljubljana, Slovenska 29; tel. (1) 2413288; fax (1) 4252294; e-mail intsales@mkz-lj.si; f. 1945; books for youth and children, including general, fiction, science, travel and school books, language courses, magazines and videos; Dir MILAN MATOS.

Slovenska Matica: 1000 Ljubljana, Kongresni trg 8; tel. and fax (1) 4224340; e-mail drago.jancar@siol.net; f. 1864; poetry, science, philosophy; Pres. Prof. Dr JOŽA MAHNIČ.

Založba Lipa Koper: 66000 Koper, Muzejski trg 7; tel. (5) 6274883; fiction; Dir Prof. JOŽE A. HOČEVAR.

Založba Obzorja d.d. Maribor: 2000 Maribor, Partizanska 3–5; tel. (2) 2348100; fax (2) 2348135; e-mail info@zalozba-obzorja.si; internet www.zalozba-obzorja.si; f. 1950; popular science, general literature, periodicals, etc.; Man. Dir GORAZD ZEMLJARIČ.

Broadcasting and Communications

TELECOMMUNICATIONS

Telecommunications Agency (Agencija za telekomunikacje, radiodifuzijo in pošto Republike Slovenije—ATRP): 1000 Ljubljana, Kotnikova 19A; tel. (1) 4734900; fax (1) 4328036; e-mail urst.box@gov.si; internet www.atrp.si; Dir JOŽE KLEŠNIK (acting).

Mobitel: 1537 Ljubljana, Vilharjeva 23; tel. (1) 4722200; fax (1) 4722990; e-mail info@mobitel.si; internet www.mobitel.si; f. 1991; 100% owned by Telekom Slovenije; mobile cellular telecommunications services; Chief Exec. KLAVDIJ GODNIČ.

Si.mobil—Vodafone: 1000 Ljubljana, Šmartinska cesta 134B; tel. (1) 5440000; fax (1) 5440099; e-mail info@simobil.si; internet www.simobil.com; f. 1999; subsidiary of Mobilkom Austria; Chair. of Bd DEJAN TURK; 370,000 subscribers (Mar. 2006).

T-2: 2000 Maribor, Streliška cesta 150; e-mail pr@t-2.net; internet www.t-2.net; f. 2004; mobile cellular telecommunications services.

Telekom Slovenije: 1000 Ljubljana, Cigaletova 15; tel. (1) 2341000; fax (1) 2314736; e-mail info@telekom.si; internet www.telekom.si; f. 1949; 65% state-owned, further privatization pending in 2008; Pres. BOJAN DREMELJ.

Tušmobil: 3000 Celje, Resljeva ulica 16; tel. (1) 6000999; fax (1) 6002021; internet www.tusmobil.si; f. 2007; mobile cellular telecommunications services.

BROADCASTING

Regulatory Authority

Slovenian Broadcasting Council (Svet za Radiodifuzijo—SRDF): 1000 Ljubljana, Parmova 53; tel. (1) 1363596; fax (1) 1363595; e-mail info.srdf@srd.gov.si; internet www.sigov.si/srd; f. 1994; nine mems; protects independence of radio and television programmes; supervises the activities of broadcasting and cable operators.

Radio

Radiotelevizija Slovenija (RTV Slo): 1550 Ljubljana, Kolodvorska 2; tel. (1) 4752154; fax (1) 4752150; e-mail webmaster@rtvslo.si; internet www.rtvslo.si/html/radio-slo; f. 1928; 3 radio programmes nationally; broadcasts in Slovene, Hungarian and Italian; Gen. Man. ALEKS ŠTAKUL.

Radio Koper Capodistria: 6000 Koper, ul. OF 15; tel. (5) 6485483; fax (5) 6485488; e-mail radio.koper@rtvslo.si; internet www.rtvslo.si; Dir DRAGOMIR MIKELIČ.

Radio Maribor: 2000 Maribor, Ilichova 33; tel. (2) 4299132; fax (2) 4299215; e-mail srecko.trglec@rtvslo.si; internet www.rtvslo.si; Editor SREČKO TRGLEC.

Television

Radiotelevizija Slovenija (RTV Slo): 1550 Ljubljana, Kolodvorska 2; tel. (1) 4752154; fax (1) 4752150; e-mail webmaster@rtvslo.si; internet www.rtvslo.si/html/radio-slo; f. 1928; 3 television programmes (TV1, TV2 and TV3) nationally; broadcasts in Slovene, Hungarian and Italian; Gen. Man. ANTON GUZEJ.

Kanal A: 1000 Ljubljana, Tivolska 50; tel. (1) 1334133; fax (1) 1334222; Pres. DOUGLAS FULTON.

Pop TV: 1000 Ljubljana, Kranjčeva 26; tel. (1) 1893200; fax (1) 1612222; Editor TOMAŽ PEROVIČ.

TV 3: 1210 Ljubljana, Štula 23; tel. (1) 1831200; fax (1) 1521512; Editor-in-Chief MLADEN SICHROVSKY.

Finance

BANKS

(cap. = capital; res = reserves; dep. = deposits; m. = million; amounts in Slovene tolars, unless otherwise indicated; brs = branches)

In January 1999 new banking legislation allowed foreign banks to establish branches in Slovenia for the first time.

National Bank

Banka Slovenije (Bank of Slovenia): 1505 Ljubljana, Slovenska 35; tel. (1) 4719000; fax (1) 2515516; e-mail bsl@bsi.si; internet www.bsi.si; formerly National Bank of Slovenia, as part of the Yugoslav banking system; assumed central bank functions in 1991; cap. and res 191,680.0m., dep. 971,932.0m. (Dec. 2006); Gov. Dr MARKO KRANJEC.

Selected Banks

Abanka Vipa d.d.: 1517 Ljubljana, Slovenska 58, POB 368; tel. (1) 4718100; fax (1) 4325165; e-mail info@abanka.si; internet www.abanka.si; f. 1955 as Ljubljana Branch of Yugoslav Bank for Foreign Trade; present name adopted 1989; cap. 5,500.0m., res 16,240.2m., dep. 486,023.8m. (Dec. 2006); Pres. ALES ZAJDELA; 32 brs.

Banka Celje d.d.: 3001 Celje, Vodnikova 2, POB 431; tel. (3) 4221000; fax (3) 4221100; e-mail info@banka-celje.si; internet www.banka-celje.si; cap. 3,369.6m., res 30,459.0m., dep. 289,963.0m. (Dec. 2006); Pres. NIKO KAČ.

Banka Koper d.d.: 6502 Koper, Pristaniška 14; tel. (5) 6661000; fax (5) 6662006; e-mail info@banka-koper.si; internet www.banka-koper.si; f. 1955; cap. 7,099m., res 35,441m., dep. 290,040m. (Dec. 2006); Pres. of the Management Bd VOJKO ČOK; 14 brs.

Deželna banka Slovenije d.d.: 1000 Ljubljana, Kolodvorska 9; tel. (1) 4727100; fax (1) 4727411; e-mail info@dbs.si; internet www.dbs.si; f. 1990 as Slovenska Zadružna Kmetijska Banka d.d. Ljubljana; changed name to above in 2004 following merger with Zveza HKS Slovenije; cap. 2,295.3m., res 6,458.1m., dep. 110,649.5m. (Dec. 2005); Pres. Dr DRAŠKO VESELINOVIČ; 10 brs.

Factor Banka d.d.: 1001 Ljubljana, Tivolska cesta 48; tel. (1) 2306600; fax (1) 2307760; e-mail info@factorb.si; internet www.factorb.si; f. 1993; cap. €12.8m., res €23.6m., dep. €270.8m. (Dec. 2006); Chair. BORIS PESJAK.

Gorenjska Banka d.d. Kranj: 4000 Kranj, Bleiweisova cesta 1, POB 147; tel. (4) 2084000; fax (4) 2021718; e-mail info@gbkr.si; internet www.gbkr.si; f. 1955; cap. 4,172.6m., res 56,285.2m., dep. 202,917.9m. (Dec. 2006); Pres. and Chief Exec. ZLATKO KAVČIČ; 5 brs.

Hypo Alpe-Adria-Bank d.d.: 1000 Ljubljana, Dunajska cesta 117; tel. (1) 5804000; fax (1) 5804001; e-mail hypo-bank@hypo.si; internet www.hypo-alpe-adria.si; f. 1999; cap. 22,535.0m., res 4,994.0m., dep. 235,224.6m. (Dec. 2006); Pres. BOŽIDAR ŠPAN.

Nova Kreditna Banka Maribor d.d. (Nova KBM): 2505 Maribor, Vita Kraigherja 4; tel. (2) 2292290; fax (2) 2524333; e-mail info@nkbm.si; internet www.nkbm.si; f. 1955; adopted present name 1994; 90.4% state-owned; cap. 5,839.5m., res 58,911.8m., dep. 794,373.0m. (Dec. 2006); Pres. and CEO. MATJAŽ KOVAČIČ; 81 brs and sub-brs.

Nova Ljubljanska Banka d.d. (NLB): 1520 Ljubljana, trg Republike 2; tel. (1) 4250155; fax (1) 4250331; e-mail info@nlb.si; internet www.nlb.si; f. 1994; commercial, investment and savings bank; 35.4% state-owned, 34% owned by KBC Bank NV (Belgium); cap. 15,364.0m., res 112,456.4m., dep. 2,143,300.6m. (Dec. 2006); Pres. Marjan Kramar; 198 brs.

Probanka d.d.: 2000 Maribor, Svetozarevska 12; tel. (2) 2520500; fax (2) 2526029; e-mail info@probanka.si; internet www.probanka.si; f. 1991; cap. 12,921.6m., res 1,995.3m., dep. 146,155.3m. (Dec. 2006); Pres. and Chair. Romana Pajenk.

Raiffeisen Krekova Banka d.d. Maribor: 2000 Maribor, Slomškov trg 18; tel. (2) 2293100; fax (2) 2223502; e-mail info@r-kb.si; internet www.r-kb.si; f. 1992; cap. 3,387.0m., res 9,844.0m., dep. 209,347.0m. (Dec. 2006); Chief Exec. Zoran Nemec (acting); 14 brs.

SKB Banka d.d.: 1000 Ljubljana, Ajdovščina 4; tel. (1) 4715918; fax (1) 4715513; e-mail info@skb.si; internet www.skb.si; f. 1978; 99.58% owned by Société Générale (France); cap. 12,649.2m., res 31,468.2m., dep. 479,992.5m. (Dec. 2006); Pres. and Chief Exec. Cvetka Selšek; 57 brs.

UniCredit Banka Slovenija d.d.: 1000 Ljubljana, Smartinska 140; tel. (1) 5876600; fax (1) 5411860; e-mail info@unicreditgroup.si; internet www.unicreditgroup.si; f. 1991; fmrly Bank Austria Creditanstalt d.d. Ljubljana; name changed as above Sept. 2007; cap. 3,898.9m., res 29,986.6m., dep. 482,666.7m., (Dec. 2006); Chair. France Arhar.

STOCK EXCHANGE

Ljubljana Stock Exchange (Ljubljanska Borza d.d.): 1000 Ljubljana, Slovenska 56; tel. (1) 4710211; fax (1) 4710213; e-mail info@ljse.si; internet www.ljse.si; f. 1989; operative 1990; Pres. and Chief Exec. Dr Marko Simoneti.

INSURANCE

Adriatic Insurance Co: 6503 Koper, Ljubljanska cesta 3 A; tel. (5) 6643100; fax (5) 6643303; e-mail info@adriatic.si; internet www.adriatic.si; f. 1990.

Grawe Insurance Co d.d.: 2000 Maribor, Gregorčičeva 39; tel. (2) 2285500; fax (2) 2285526; e-mail prima@prima.si.

Maribor Insurance Co: 2507 Maribor, Cankarjeva 3; tel. (2) 224111.

Merkur Insurance Co: 1000 Ljubljana, Dunajska 58; tel. (1) 3005450; fax (1) 4361092; e-mail info@merkur-zav.si; internet www.merkur-zav.si; f. 1992; Gen. Man. Denis Stroligo.

Triglav Insurance Co (Zavarovalnica Triglav d.d.): 1000 Ljubljana, Miklošičeva 19; tel. (1) 4747200; fax (1) 4326302; e-mail info-triglav@triglav.si; internet www.zav-triglav.si; Pres. of Management Bd Andrej Kocič; Chair. of Supervisory Bd Damjan Mihevc.

Trade and Industry

GOVERNMENT AGENCY

Agency of the Republic of Slovenia for Restructuring and Privatization (Agencija Republike Slovenije za Prestrukturiranje in Privatizacijo—ARSPIP): 1000 Ljubljana, Kotnikova 28; tel. (1) 1316030; fax (1) 1316011; e-mail webmaster@arspip.si; Dir Mira Puc.

CHAMBERS OF COMMERCE

Chamber of Commerce and Industry of Slovenia (Gospodarska Zbornica Slovenije): 1504 Ljubljana, Dimičeva 13; tel. (1) 5898313; fax (1) 5898317; e-mail infolink@gzs.si; internet www.gzs.si; Pres. Josko Cuk.

Chamber of Small Businesses of Slovenia: 1000 Ljubljana, Celovška 71; tel. (1) 4593241; fax (1) 4559270; Pres. Miha Grah; Sec. Anton Filipič; 50,000 mems.

UTILITIES

Electricity

Elektro-Slovenija d.o.o. (ELES): 1000 Ljubljana, Hajdrihova 2; tel. (1) 1301440; fax (1) 1250333; e-mail info@eles.si; internet www.eles.si; national electricity distributor; Chief Exec. Vekoslav Korošec.

Nuklearna Elektrarna p.o. (NEK): 8270 Krško, Vrbina 12; tel. (7) 4802000; fax (7) 4921006; e-mail nek@nek.si; internet www.nek.si; f. 1974; 50% owned by GEN energija Ljubljana, 50% owned by Hrvatska Elektroprivreda Zagreb (Croatia); production and distribution of electricity from nuclear power plant at Krško.

Gas

Geoplin d.o.o.: 1000 Ljubljana, Ljubljanska brigade 11; tel. (1) 5820600; fax (1) 5820601; e-mail info@geoplin.si; internet www.geoplin.si; f. 1975; national gas co; Gen. Man. Alojz Stana.

TRADE UNIONS

The Association of Independent Trade Unions of Slovenia: 1000 Ljubljana, Dalmatinova 4; tel. (1) 4317983; fax (1) 4318294; Pres. Dušan Semolič.

Independence—Confederation of New Trade Unions of Slovenia: 1000 Ljubljana, Linhartova 13; tel. (1) 4329141; fax (1) 4302868; Pres. France Tomšič.

Transport

RAILWAYS

Slovenske Železnice (SŽ) (Slovenian Railways): 1506 Ljubljana, Kolodvorska 11; tel. (1) 2914001; fax (1) 2914800; e-mail boris.zivec@slo-zeleznice.si; internet www.slo-zeleznice.si; Dir-Gen. Boris Zivec.

ROADS

In 2001 the country had 20,236 km of roads, of which 435 km were motorways and 1,101 km were highways, main or national roads. An 84-km motorway links Ljubljana with the coastal region in the southwest.

Directorate for Roads: Ministry of Transport, 1535 Ljubljana, Langusova 4; tel. (1) 1788000; fax (1) 1788139; e-mail drsc-info@gov.si.

SHIPPING

Slovenia's principal international trading port, at Koper, handles some 3m. tons of freight annually.

Luka Koper d.d.: 6501 Koper, Vojkovo nabrežje 38; tel. (5) 6656100; fax (5) 6395020; e-mail portkoper@luka-kp.si; internet www.luka-kp.si; f. 1957; Pres. of Management Bd Robert Casar.

Principal Shipping Company

Splošna Plovba: 6320 Portorož, Obala 55, POB 60; tel. (5) 6766000; fax (5) 6766130; e-mail plovba@5-plovba.si; transport of all types of cargo; regular liner service; Man. Dir Aldo Krejačič.

CIVIL AVIATION

There are three international airports in Slovenia, at Brnik (Ljubljana), Maribor and Portorož.

Adria Airways: 1000 Ljubljana, Kuzmičeva 7; tel. (1) 3691000; fax (1) 4369233; e-mail info@adria.si; internet www.adria.si; f. 1961; operates international scheduled services to destinations in Europe and the Middle East; Pres. Tadej Tufek.

Tourism

Slovenia offers a variety of tourist attractions, including Mediterranean resorts to the west, the Julian Alps and the lakes of Bled and Bohinj to the north and, in the south, the *karst* limestone regions, with more than 6,000 caves. The number of foreign tourist arrivals increased steadily from the mid-1990s, reaching 2,395,000 in 2005, when tourism receipts totalled US $1,894m.

Slovenian Tourist Board: 1000 Ljubljana, Dunajska 156; tel. (1) 5891840; fax (1) 5891841; e-mail info@slovenia.info; internet www.slovenia.info; f. 1996; Gen. Man. Dimitrij Piciga.

SOLOMON ISLANDS

Introductory Survey

Location, Climate, Language, Religion, Flag, Capital

Solomon Islands is a scattered Melanesian archipelago in the south-western Pacific Ocean, east of Papua New Guinea. The country includes most of the Solomon Islands (those to the north-west being part of Papua New Guinea), Ontong Java Islands (Lord Howe Atoll), Rennell Island and the Santa Cruz Islands, about 500 km (300 miles) to the east. The climate is equatorial, with small seasonal variations, governed by the trade winds. In Honiara the average temperature is about 27°C (81°F) and the average annual rainfall about 2,160 mm (85 ins). The official language is standard English, although pidgin English is more widely used and understood. More than 80 different local languages exist, and no vernacular is common to the whole country. More than 95% of the inhabitants profess Christianity, and most of the remainder follow traditional beliefs. The national flag (proportions 1 by 2) comprises two triangles, one of blue (with its base at the hoist and its apex in the upper fly) and one of dark green (with its base in the fly and its apex in the lower hoist), separated by a narrow yellow diagonal stripe (from lower hoist to upper fly), with five white five-pointed stars (arranged to form a diagonal cross) in the upper hoist. The capital is Honiara, on the island of Guadalcanal.

Recent History

The northern Solomon Islands became a German protectorate in 1885 and the southern Solomons a British protectorate in 1893. Rennell Island and the Santa Cruz Islands were added to the British protectorate in 1898 and 1899. Germany ceded most of the northern Solomons and Ontong Java Islands to the United Kingdom between 1898 and 1900. The whole territory, known as the British Solomon Islands Protectorate, was placed under the jurisdiction of the Western Pacific High Commission (WPHC), with its headquarters in Fiji.

The Solomon Islands were invaded by Japan in 1942, but, after a fierce battle on Guadalcanal, most of the islands were recaptured by US forces in 1943. After the Second World War the protectorate's capital was transferred from Tulagi Island to Honiara. In January 1953 the headquarters of the WPHC also moved to Honiara. Meanwhile, elected local councils were established on most of the islands, and by 1966 almost the whole territory was covered by such councils.

Under a new Constitution, introduced in October 1960, a Legislative Council and an Executive Council were established for the protectorate's central administration. Initially, all members of both bodies were appointed, but from 1964 the Legislative Council included elected members, and the elective element was gradually increased. Another Constitution, introduced in March 1970, established a single Governing Council of 17 elected members, three *ex-officio* members and (until the end of 1971) up to six public service members. A new Governing Council of 24 directly elected members was formed in 1973, when a ministerial system was introduced.

A further new Constitution, adopted in April 1974, instituted a single Legislative Assembly, containing 24 members who chose a Chief Minister with the right to appoint his own Council of Ministers. A new office of Governor of the Protectorate was also created, to assume almost all of the functions previously exercised in the territory by the High Commissioner for the Western Pacific. Solomon Mamaloni, leader of the newly founded People's Progressive Party (PPP), was appointed the first Chief Minister in August 1974. The territory was officially renamed the Solomon Islands in June 1975, although it retained protectorate status.

In January 1976 the Solomon Islands received internal self-government, with the Chief Minister presiding over the Council of Ministers in place of the Governor. In June elections were held for an enlarged Legislative Assembly, and in July the Assembly elected one of its new members, Peter Kenilorea, to the position of Chief Minister. Solomon Islands (as it was restyled) became an independent state, within the Commonwealth, on 7 July 1978. The Legislative Assembly became the National Parliament and designated Kenilorea the first Prime Minister. The main political issue confronting the new nation was the proposed decentralization of authority to the regions, support for which was particularly strong in the Western District, the most commercially developed part of the country. The first general election since independence took place in August 1980. Independent candidates won more seats than any of the three parties. Parliament again elected Kenilorea Prime Minister by an overwhelming majority. In August 1981, however, Parliament approved a motion expressing no confidence in Kenilorea, and chose Mamaloni, who now led the People's Alliance Party (PAP) following the merger of the PPP with the Rural Alliance Party in 1979, to succeed him as Prime Minister.

After legislative elections in October 1984, Sir Peter Kenilorea (as he had become) was again elected as Prime Minister. The new Government consisted of a coalition of nine members of Kenilorea's Solomon Islands United Party (SIUPA), three members of the newly formed Solomone Ano Sagufenua (SAS) party and three independents. The five provincial ministries, established by Mamaloni, were abolished, in accordance with Kenilorea's declared policy of restoring to central government control some of the powers held by the provincial governments.

In October 1985 a new political party, which sought a resolution of ongoing land disputes, the Nationalist Front for Progress (NFP), was formed, under the leadership of Andrew Nori. The SAS subsequently withdrew from the coalition, and Kenilorea formed a new Cabinet, comprising nine members of the SIUPA, three of the NFP and three independents. Kenilorea resigned following the approval of a motion of no confidence (two others having previously been defeated); in December Ezekiel Alebua, the former Deputy Prime Minister, assumed the premiership.

A report by a specially commissioned constitutional review committee, chaired by Mamaloni, was published in March 1988, and proposed that Solomon Islands become a federal republic within the Commonwealth, and that the President of the Republic be a native of the territory. In January 1989 the PAP announced that Solomon Islands would be declared a republic if the party won the next general election, scheduled to take place in February. At the election the PAP won 11 of the 38 seats, the largest representation obtained by any party, while Alebua's party, the United Party, won only four seats. In March Mamaloni was elected Prime Minister. His Cabinet included the former Governor-General of Solomon Islands, Sir Baddeley Devesi, and was described as the first since independence to comprise the members of a single party.

In October 1990 Mamaloni resigned as leader of the PAP, one week before Parliament was due to vote on another motion of no confidence in his premiership, declaring that he would remain as an independent Prime Minister. He dismissed five members of the Cabinet, replacing them with four members of the opposition and a PAP back-bencher. The Prime Minister defied persistent demands for his resignation by a majority of the members of Parliament. The remaining 10 ministers of the PAP were expelled from the party in February 1991, following their refusal to resign from their posts in the interests of party unity. Later that year, as a result of continuing economic decline, the Solomon Islands Council of Trade Unions issued an ultimatum demanding Mamaloni's resignation.

At elections to the recently enlarged National Parliament in May 1993 the Group for National Unity and Reconciliation (GNUR), led by Mamaloni, won 21 of the 47 seats. However, a newly formed coalition of opposition parties and independents, the National Coalition Partners (NCP), was successful in electing an independent member, Francis Billy Hilly, to the premiership in June. Hilly defeated Mamaloni by a single vote.

In October 1994 a constitutional crisis arose, following attempts by the Governor-General, Moses (later Sir Moses) Pitakaka, to dismiss Hilly on the grounds that he no longer held a parliamentary majority. Hilly remained in office, however, with the support of a High Court ruling, and confusion intensified when Pitakaka appointed the opposition leader, Mamaloni, to the position of Prime Minister. Hilly finally resigned at the end of October, and the post was declared vacant. In a parliamentary election to the premiership in early November, Mamaloni defeated the former Governor-General, Devesi, by 29 votes to 18.

In late 1995 and early 1996 Mamaloni's Government suffered a series of allegations of corruption and misconduct, particularly in relation to claims that seven ministers had received payments from foreign logging companies between 1993 and 1995, although in February 1996 all seven were acquitted.

Controversy arose in July 1996 when it was reported that members of the National Parliament had begun to present gifts to their constituencies in preparation for the general election scheduled for 1997. This followed the reinstatement of the controversial Constituency Development Fund, which entitled each member to US $66,000, and which had been widely used by members at the previous general election to secure re-election by purchasing gifts for voters. In September the regional trades union organization, the South Pacific and Oceanic Council of Trade Unions (SPOCTU), cited the prevalence of corruption as the greatest obstacle to the islands' development, and stated that, in consequence, investors and aid donors would remain reluctant to make financial commitments to Solomon Islands.

In early August 1996 the National Parliament approved legislation to reform the provincial government system, which the Government claimed was inefficient and costly to maintain. Under the new system, the legislative and administrative powers of the nine provincial governments were to be transferred to 75 area assemblies and councils, with financial control vested wholly in the central Government. In February 1997, however, the legislation, which had been vehemently opposed by the larger provinces, was declared invalid by the High Court.

In May 1997 Mamaloni announced his intention to hold an early general election, following which he would resign as leader of the GNUR. Meanwhile, Alebua resigned from the leadership of the NCP, following accusations of misconduct, and was replaced by Edward Hunuehu. A general election took place on 6 August to a legislature that had recently been enlarged to 50 seats. The GNUR won 24 seats and a new grouping, the Solomon Islands Alliance for Change Coalition (SIACC), secured the remainder. A period of intense political manoeuvring followed the election, in attempts to form a parliamentary majority. In late August Bartholomew Ulufa'alu was elected Prime Minister, defeating the newly elected leader of the GNUR, Danny Philip, by 26 votes to 22. The new Government announced a programme of extensive structural reforms, including a rationalization of the public sector, a reduction in the number of ministerial portfolios (from 16 to 10), and measures to expand the private sector and to encourage greater participation of non-governmental organizations in the country's socio-economic development. The measures aimed to restore a degree of economic stability to Solomon Islands and to attract increased foreign investment. Legislation proposing that a politician seeking to change party allegiance would automatically lose his or her seat and be subject to a by-election was similarly intended to increase political stability.

In early 1998 a shipment of weapons (including a helicopter gunship, two military aircraft and smaller armaments) ordered by the previous administration for use in defending the maritime border with Papua New Guinea, arrived from the USA. Ulufa'alu requested assistance from Australia in impounding the weapons, following widespread concern that unofficial organizations (particularly the Bougainville secessionist rebels within Papua New Guinea) might intercept the shipment. A dispute subsequently arose between Ulufa'alu and the former Prime Minister, Solomon Mamaloni, who had ordered the weapons. Mamaloni accused Ulufa'alu of treason for surrendering sovereign property to a foreign government, while the Prime Minister claimed that serious irregularities had occurred in procuring the arms, citing missing files and apparent overpayment.

In April 1998 Job Dudley Tausinga, whose Coalition for National Advancement (CNA) constituted the largest group outside the Government, was appointed Leader of the Opposition. Following the defection of six government members in July–August 1998, the opposition claimed to hold a parliamentary majority (with 25 of the 49 sitting members), and consequently sought to introduce a motion of no confidence in the Prime Minister. A vote eventually took place on 18 September, after the failure of an attempt by the Government to declare the vote unlawful in the High Court, but was deemed to have been defeated as an equal number of votes were cast for and against the motion. Three opposition members subsequently defected to the Government, thus increasing its representation to 27 members. The climate of ongoing political instability prompted the Government to reiterate its proposal for legislation to restrict the rights of elected members of the National Parliament to change party allegiance. In late September Solomon Mamaloni was elected Leader of the Opposition. Mamaloni died in January 2000 and was succeeded by Manasseh Sogavare, under whose leadership the CNA subsequently reverted to its original name of the PPP.

From April 1998 violent unrest in Honiara was attributed to ethnic tensions, mainly between the inhabitants of Guadalcanal and Malaita provinces. One underlying cause of the disturbances was the alienation of land by the Government since independence. Title to some land thus expropriated had been returned to Guadalcanal, but this had not allayed a widespread feeling of resentment in the province at the financial burden imposed by hosting the country's capital. It was reported that a group styling itself the 'Guadalcanal Revolutionary Army' (GRA) had begun a campaign of militancy to force the Government to relocate the capital. The unrest intensified in early 1999, prompting the Government to establish a peace committee for the province. In mid-1999 talks between the Premier of Guadalcanal Province, Ezekiel Alebua, and the Solomon Islands Prime Minister failed to alleviate inter-ethnic tensions in the province. Riots broke out in Honiara, and some 80 Malaitan immigrants were evacuated following threats by armed GRA militants. Following Ulufa'alu's demands that peace be restored to the province before the implementation of any further measures, the GRA ordered an immediate halt to its activities. The Guadalcanal Provincial Assembly subsequently declared that it had accepted an initial payment of SI $500,000 in compensation for accommodating the national capital. A reconciliation ceremony was held between the two parties, during which Alebua appealed to the GRA to lay down its arms. However, the Malaitans subsequently demanded that they too be compensated, to the sum of US $600,000, for damage to their property by the GRA militants.

Following an increase in violence during which three Malaitan immigrants were reported to have been killed, and an estimated 10,000 forced to flee their villages, in mid-June 1999 a state of emergency was declared in Guadalcanal. A leader of the Isatabu Freedom Movement (IFM, formerly the GRA, and also known in 1999 as the Isatabu Freedom Fighters—IFF), Andrew Te'e, announced that the movement was willing to surrender in return for a full amnesty for the militants; however, this was rejected by Ulufa'alu. The former Prime Minister of Fiji, Sitiveni Rabuka, was appointed Commonwealth Special Envoy, following a request for assistance by Ulufa'alu. After meeting with the parties concerned, Rabuka announced on 28 June that a peace agreement had been reached, and a UN delegation and police officers from Fiji and Vanuatu were dispatched to help implement the peace plan. As part of the Honiara Peace Accord, the Solomon Islands Government agreed to pay SI $2.5m. into a Reconciliation Trust Fund, which was to be jointly administered by Guadalcanal Province and the national Government, to compensate the victims of the unrest. In return, the IFM agreed to disarm and to abandon their demands for a full amnesty for their supporters. In early August, however, Rabuka and the UN monitoring team returned to the province, after four members of the IFM were reported to have been shot by police near Honiara. However, in mid-August a new peace agreement was signed by Rabuka, Alebua and others. The agreement, known as the Panatina Agreement, allowed for a reduction in police activity in the province followed by the eventual revocation of the state of emergency, in return for the surrender of weapons by the IFM. Despite the extension of the disarmament deadline into September, the state of emergency was ended in mid-October and, following negotiations in Honiara and the signing of an agreement in Fiji, a multinational peace-monitoring group from Fiji and Vanuatu, jointly funded by Australia and New Zealand, arrived in Guadalcanal in late October. In early December the peace-keeping force's mandate was extended into January 2000, and subsequently further extended by three months, following renewed outbreaks of violence and the emergence of a new guerrilla group, the Malaita Eagle Force (MEF), demanding US $40m. in compensation payments for loss of property incurred by Malaitans as a result of the conflict. Among their spokesmen was the former Minister of Finance, Andrew Nori.

Following further outbreaks of violence in the province that led to the death of four people, including two policemen, in February 2000, the Governor-General issued a decree outlawing membership of both the IFM and the MEF. Further clashes between the two rebel groups were reported in early March, and later that month riots took place in Honiara during which Malaitan immigrants stoned the headquarters of the Guadalcanal provincial government. Peace talks took place in May without members of the IFM and the MEF, both of which refused to attend in protest at the decision to outlaw them. However, a document, known as the Buala Peace Communiqué, was issued as the outcome of these talks on 5 May. Later that month the order that outlawed the groups was suspended. In early June members of the MEF, armed with weapons obtained in raids on police armouries, seized control of Honiara, placing Ulufa'alu under house arrest. The rebels demanded the immediate resignation of the Prime Minister, claiming that he, himself an ethnic Malaitan, had failed to compensate displaced Malaitans within the established deadline (allegedly set for that day) and also demanded the appointment of a new Commissioner of Police, the de facto head of national security. In renewed outbreaks of violence, up to 100 people were reportedly killed. The MEF, meanwhile, claimed to have gained control of the Police Force, 98% of the military-style weapons in the territory, broadcasting services and the telecommunications infrastructure. Ulufa'alu was released after four days, following an agreement between the MEF and government negotiators that a special parliamentary sitting would be convened during which Ulufa'alu would be subject to a motion of no confidence. A 14-day cease-fire was called to guarantee the safe passage of a Commonwealth monitoring team. In mid-June June Ulufa'alu resigned, one day before the scheduled no confidence vote, but remained as 'caretaker' Prime Minister for a 14-day transitional period during which negotiations between the MEF, the IFM and a Commonwealth Special Envoy, Professor Ade Adefuye of Nigeria, were to take place. However, negotiations foundered following the MEF's refusal to hand over its weapons, pending the appointment of a new Prime Minister, which was to occur in an extraordinary parliamentary session in late June. As this session failed to raise the necessary quorum, the election of a new Prime Minister was delayed until the end of June, when Sogavare, the Leader of the Opposition, defeated Rev. Leslie Boseto, incumbent Minister for Lands and Housing, by 23 votes to 21. (The third candidate, Hilly, withdrew in support of Boseto.) Sogavare declared that he would seek to establish peace without making significant changes to the policy of the previous Government. None the less, Sogavare announced a comprehensive reallocation of ministerial posts and restructuring of ministries. A new Ministry for National Unity, Reconciliation and Peace was established, and plans to create a Solomon Islands Defence Force and Ministry of Defence were announced. (Previously defence issues had fallen within the remit of the police service, which had become compromised because of alleged MEF infiltration, and by allegations that about 75% of officers were ethnic Malaitans.)

New cease-fire negotiations in August 2000 resulted in the declaration of a 90-day cease-fire between the IFM and the MEF, although intermittent violent disorder continued in Guadalcanal. In late August IFM dissidents kidnapped the brother of Deputy Prime Minister Allan Kemakeza, demanding that SI $6.5m. in compensation be paid to the displaced persons of Guadalcanal. Kemakeza was released unharmed after 10 days without the payment of a ransom. Logistical problems delayed the onset of further peace talks until early September, when a further communiqué concerning potential methods of advancing the peace process was issued. In mid-September a breakaway group from the IFM, which had reverted to the former name of the GRA under the leadership of Harold Keke, held an airline pilot hostage with a demand for SI $2m.; he was released unharmed without the demands being acceded to, although Keke later claimed that the Government had paid him US $200,000.

A further round of peace talks in Queensland, Australia, led to the signing on 15 October 2000 of a peace treaty known as the Townsville Agreement, by the MEF, the IFM, the Solomon Islands Government and the Provincial Governments of Malaita and Guadalcanal. An amnesty for all those involved in crimes associated with the ethnic conflict was to be granted, subject to the surrender of all weaponry within 30 days. The agreement also envisaged the creation of an international peace-monitoring team, and the repatriation to their home villages of all MEF and IFM soldiers at the expense of the Solomon Islands Government. Infrastructure and service in the two provinces would be restored and developed. The two provinces would also be granted a greater degree of administrative autonomy. Malaita Province was to receive additional funding to reflect the demands placed on the region by the influx of 20,000 displaced persons from Guadalcanal.

The implementation of the peace process, overseen by monitors from Australia and New Zealand, was threatened in mid-November 2000, when four people were killed in a shooting in Gizo, Western Province. Among the dead were two members of Papua New Guinea's Bougainville Revolutionary Army (BRA). Moreover, delays in the disarmament process involving the MEF and the IFM caused the deadline for the surrender of arms to be extended from 15 November until the end of that month, and then further until 15 December. In mid-November, following an announcement that the Guadalcanal Provincial Government headquarters, which had been occupied by members of the MEF since June, was to be rehabilitated as a symbol of national unity, arsonists, believed to be linked with the MEF, attacked the building. Despite a series of ceremonies in late November and early December, in which members of the IFM and MEF surrendered weapons, it was believed that at least 400 illegally held weapons remained in circulation at the end of December. The legislation granting immunity to those who had committed crimes during the conflict was approved by Parliament in mid-December, and was criticized by the prominent human rights organization, Amnesty International. In late December one man was injured in an attack on a motel, in Honiara, in which disarmed former IFM rebels recruited to join the police were resident. Responsibility for the attack was attributed to a group calling itself the Marau Eagle Force, from the eastern Marau region of Guadalcanal, which was subject to separate peace negotiations. The Guadalcanal Liberation Force (GLF) as it was restyled, led by Harold Keke, also announced that it had not accepted the cease-fire. In early January 2001 concerns were expressed that, as a result of the ongoing economic crisis and a larger number of rebels having opted to join the police than had been anticipated, the Government might be unable to pay the former rebels, thus prompting further concerns about security.

In early December 2000 new legislation had permitted the appointment of two further ministers, a Minister of Rehabilitation, Reconstruction and Redirection, and a Minister of Economic Reform and Structural Adjustment. In early January 2001 it was reported that the Government was contemplating an extension of the amnesty. Further violence broke out between Guadalcanal militants and members of the Marau Eagle Force. A peace agreement between the group and the IFM was signed in early February, although the Peace Monitoring Council observed that the infrastructure of the Marau region had been almost entirely destroyed since 1998 and that there was little immediate prospect of recovery. In early March 2001 peace in the Marau region appeared to be threatened following an incident in which police officers, in connection with a drink-driving charge, opened fire on a vehicle owned by a former commander of the Marau Eagle Force. It was also reported that two other former Marau commanders had demanded SI $100,000 from the Government, and that other Marau militants would refuse to surrender their arms, in conformity with the agreement signed in February, unless the GLF were also disarmed. In mid-March tensions heightened following a security operation against the GLF leader, Keke, in which a government patrol boat fired at villages on the western coast of Guadalcanal. In the same month police disarmed and arrested a group of villagers from Munda, Western Province. Further incidents in early April, in which a boat fired at coastal targets in southern Guadalcanal, led the international peace monitoring force from Australia to state that the cease-fire arrangement reached under the Townsville Agreement might have been breached. The Assistant Commissioner of Police Operations protested that the Townsville Agreement did not require the police to surrender their guns, although a report published in April claimed that some of the weapons used in the security operation should have been surrendered the previous year. In June the Premier of Guadalcanal, Ezekiel Alebua, was shot and seriously injured in an assassination attempt, apparently carried out on the orders of former leaders of the IFM. Harold Keke met the Deputy Prime Minister and the secretary of the Peace Monitoring Council in June and, in October, he voiced his support for the imminent general elections. However, the failure of former militia groups to surrender their guns was the main obstacle to a lasting peace throughout 2001, and officials estimated that there remained some 500 high-powered weapons in the community, in addition to hand-made weapons. The Government declared an 'arms amnesty' in April 2002. Militants surrendered some 2,000 guns with impunity. Weapons disposal began in June, coinciding with the International Peace Monitoring Team's departure from the country.

In the second half of 2000 Western, Choiseul, and Temutu provinces all declared themselves to be semi-autonomous states within Solomon Islands; on 1 September the legislature of the latter, representing 20,000 inhabitants, approved a bill allowing for a referendum on the province's proposed independence; the worsening economic situation caused by the conflict in Guadalcanal was believed to be a determining factor. Additionally, movements in Guadalcanal and Makira provinces demanding greater autonomy were reported to have gained strength at this time. In late November the Minister of Provincial Government and Rural Development Nathaniel Waena announced that legislation to amend the Constitution would be submitted in 2001, in order to institute a federal system of government. Controversy arose following an announcement by the Government, in mid-March 2001, that it intended to introduce legislation to extend the life of Parliament for a further year, to expire in August 2002, stating that the social and economic position of the islands would not facilitate the holding of elections as scheduled in August 2001. This proposal attracted widespread opposition, including that of churches, trade unions, all provincial premiers, and the principal overseas aid donors to Solomon Islands. When it became apparent that he would not possess a parliamentary majority to support the legislation, Sogavare withdrew the bill from Parliament in early May; later that month it was announced that the elections would be held, as scheduled, funded wholly from overseas. In September the National Parliament approved a bill to increase national general election registration fees by 150%; Walter Folotalu, former member of the National Parliament for Baegu, successfully challenged the proposed legislation in the High Court in October. In the same month the High Court also began hearing the case brought by former Prime Minister Bartholomew Ulufa'alu; he had challenged the legality of the Government, seeking a ruling that the coup and subsequent election that ousted him were unconstitutional (he lost the case in November 2001).

In October 2001 public services deteriorated as nation-wide power cuts resulted from the inability of the Solomon Islands Electricity Authority (SIEA) to pay for its supplies of diesel fuel. The Government announced the introduction of health charges in order to maintain medical services, and was forced to appeal to Australia and New Zealand for assistance in policing, as violent crime was becoming endemic. A storage container holding weapons relinquished under the Townsville peace agreement was broken into and, in November, the revelation that compensation totalling SI $17.4m. had been paid to former members of the MEF for alleged property damage precipitated a violent demonstration by protesters demanding similar recompense. The Prime Minister was prevented from leaving his office (to attend a session of the UN General Assembly in New York), and the house of the Deputy Prime Minister was vandalized.

Accusations and rumours of bribery and intimidation were rife during the campaigning that preceded the general election, held on 5 December 2001. The electoral grouping of the SIACC won 12 seats, the PAP secured nine and the PPP six, while 22 seats were won by independent candidates. In the absence of a clear SIACC leader, 11 elected members of the coalition convened with 11 elected independents to decide upon a satisfactory premier. Following various shifts in allegiances, Sir Allan Kemakeza (as he had become), leader of the PAP and former Deputy Prime Minister, was declared Prime Minister. Despite having been previously accused of misappropriating state funds, the former Minister of Finance, Snyder Rini, was appointed Deputy Prime Minister and Minister for National Planning.

However, the new Government was unable to improve the increasingly desperate political and economic situation on the islands. A peace summit, organized by the Peace Monitoring Council, scheduled to be held in March 2002 was postponed until June, and, as the security situation in the country deteriorated further, numerous international peace monitors began withdrawing from the islands. In March Kemakeza dismissed Michael Maina, the Minister of Finance, after Maina failed to consult the Cabinet prior to announcing a number of drastic budgetary measures, the most significant of which was his decision to devalue the national currency by 25%. Maina was replaced by Laurie Chan, who in early April revalued the currency.

There were reports of further disturbances on the western coast of Guadalcanal in early June 2002 during which it was claimed that 11 Malaitans, who were part of a force attempting to capture the GLF leader, Harold Keke, had been killed. In mid-July water and electricity supplies to the capital were interrupted after the SIEA was once again unable to purchase fuel to power its generators, and the Solomon Islands Water Authority (SIWA) had failed to pay rental arrears to the landowners of the Kongulai water source. The country was further adversely affected by a series of strikes in mid-August by public-sector workers in protest at the non-payment of their salaries. Later that month the Minister for Youth and Sports and Women's Affairs, Rev. Augustin Greve, was assassinated. It was subsequently reported that Harold Keke had claimed responsibility for the murder. In September a church deacon was found beheaded on a beach on Guadalcanal's southern coast, an area considered to be a stronghold of the GLF. In a separate incident in the same month a woman and three children were shot dead and 11 others wounded in an assault which local chiefs attributed to Keke's organization. In late September Kemakeza made a formal request to the UN for a peace-keeping force to address the increasing state of lawlessness in the country and in the following month a delegation of four UN officials visited the islands to assess the situation.

In mid-October 2002 the Cabinet approved the establishment of the National Peace Council, an interim body, to replace the Peace Monitoring Council, the mandate of which expired on 15 October under the terms of the Townsville Peace Agreement. A permanent body was to be established after 16 January 2003. It was confirmed, however, in the same month that more weapons were in circulation in the country than when the peace agreement was signed in October 2000. The National Peace Council expressed a belief that many of the weapons surrendered under the arms amnesty of April 2002 had been removed for use by police officers in their campaign to capture Keke.

In mid-December 2002 the Minister of Finance, Laurie Chan, resigned. The Government claimed that this action was in response to criticism of his budget, which had recently been approved by the Cabinet. However, Radio New Zealand reported that his resignation was in protest at the Government's decision to pay unscheduled allowances to the 'special constables' (former militants from the ethnic conflict who were allowed to join the police force as part of the peace agreement) who had demanded the payments with threats and violence. The latter had included an incident in which gunshots were fired at the Prime Minister's residence by a group of 'special constables'. The Government faced a serious challenge in mid-December when six independent members of Parliament resigned because of what they described as a 'leadership problem' within the coalition. However, the Government defeated an opposition motion of no confidence by 28 votes to 17.

The country's precarious peace process suffered a major reversal in February 2003 when a leading member of the National Peace Council, Sir Frederick Soaki, was assassinated. There was speculation that the killing might have been connected to his involvement in a 'demobilization' programme for 'special constables'. A report by the human rights organization, Amnesty International, in March 2003 claimed that the country's 'special constables' had tortured and killed numerous people in the operation against Harold Keke along the southern coast of Guadalcanal. In April three of Keke's close associates deserted him and reported that they had witnessed him carry out nine murders in recent weeks. The killings were mostly thought to have involved his own supporters whom he had suspected of collaborating with the police. In May it was reported that Keke had taken six missionaries hostage in southern Guadalcanal. In a separate incident on Malaita, in the same month, an Australian missionary was beheaded.

In early June 2003 Kemakeza travelled to the Australian capital of Canberra for a meeting with Prime Minister John Howard, at which he reiterated the Solomon Islands' request for direct foreign intervention in order to address the country's worsening law and order crisis. (Former Prime Minister Manasseh Sogavare had made a similar appeal for Australia to send troops to the country at the time of the signing of the Townsville Peace Agreement in October 2000, but the request had been rejected.) In mid-June senior officials from Australia and New Zealand arrived in Solomon Islands to assess the possibility of mounting a regional intervention in the country. At a meeting of the Pacific Islands Forum (see p. 380) in Sydney, Australia, later that month, delegates from the 16 nations agreed unanimously to send a multinational intervention force to Solomon Islands; eight island members stated their intention to commit personnel to the force. The proposed action was to constitute the largest armed intervention in the South Pacific region since the Second World War.

Meanwhile, reports of violence and intimidation by Harold Keke and his rebel forces continued during June 2003. At least 23 people (including 11 members of a religious order) were taken hostage and several more were killed. An estimated 1,000 villagers fled their homes after Keke took control of a police post, thereby expanding the area under his control. The rebel leader also burned two villages where he believed that local people had informed the authorities of his activities. Furthermore, in the same month his militia forced some 1,200 people at gun-point to stand along several stretches of beach in order to serve as a human shield and thereby prevent a planned police landing in the area. Atrocities continued in the following month when another settlement (of some 500 people) was burned on Keke's orders and a number of people (including several children) were beaten to death or beheaded.

Discussions continued throughout July 2003 regarding the nature of the proposed regional intervention force and its role in the country. The Australian Government presented a document to Kemakeza stating its requirements for the intervention to proceed, which included unhindered access to the country's financial records and the appointment of up to 100 foreign nationals to senior positions in the islands' public service and government sectors. The economic component of the proposed intervention would also provide for the payment of Solomon Islands' domestic and foreign debts through increased aid from Australia and New Zealand. Displaced villagers (estimated to total 20,000 since ethnic violence intensified in 2000) were to receive a specific allocation of $A100,000 in aid from Australia. The Solomon Islands Government unanimously approved legislation to allow the Australian-led force, the Regional Assistance Mission to Solomon Islands (RAMSI) as it became known, into the country. The Australian Cabinet approved the deployment, and the warship HMAS *Manoora* subsequently arrived in Honiara with 400 personnel. Howard had stated, in relation to the intervention, that it was 'not in Australia's interests to have a number of failed states in the Pacific', which led some commentators to speculate that Australia was acting out of fears for its own security rather than through concern for the people of Solomon Islands. In the following days a total of 2,225 troops and police arrived in the islands from various other countries including New Zealand, Papua New Guinea, Fiji, Tonga, Vanuatu and Samoa. In November 2004 Tuvalu sent two police officers to join the regional forces, bringing the number of countries involved in the operation to 11. The murder of an Australian soldier in the same month prompted Australia to increase the number of its defence personnel in Solomon Islands by 100.

In early August 2003 the UN Secretary-General, Kofi Annan, commended the Pacific island countries for their efforts to support Solomon Islands and stated that the UN was prepared to contribute actively to any future peace process in the country. On 13 August Harold Keke surrendered and was arrested, along with 10 of his close associates. Thousands of villagers gathered to watch as Keke handed over a large number of firearms and was taken away on HMAS *Manoora* for his own safety. Two days later the MEF surrendered around 100 weapons in a decommissioning ceremony presided over by Nick Warner, the senior diplomat in charge of the multinational force. Later that month a 17-member 'economic assistance team' arrived in Solomon Islands, some of whom were to assume strategic roles in government and the public service in order to implement major reforms. The Australian Prime Minister also made a one-day visit to the islands. By early September the regional forces announced that they had collected a total of 3,850 weapons since the start of a firearms amnesty a month earlier. Australia began to withdraw its troops in late October and by early December more than one-half of its personnel had left the islands.

The capture and arrest of members of various militia groups, including two individuals who had been signatories to the Townsville Peace Agreement, continued during late 2003. Two senior members of the MEF, including Police Superintendent Mannaseh Maelanga, who had served as its Supreme Commander, were arrested in November. Maelanga was sentenced to one year's imprisonment in March 2004. Meanwhile, Andrew Te'e, former Supreme Commander of the IFM, was arrested and charged with the murder of three people. Moreover, the trial of Keke and three of his closest associates on multiple charges of murder and abduction began in February 2004. Keke and two of his associates were found guilty of the murder in 2002 of Augustine Geve, a cabinet minister and Catholic priest. He was expected to stand trial for other alleged offences, including the murder of seven missionaries, in the following months.

The Government was subject to considerable embarrassment in December 2003 when the Minister for Communications, Aviation and Meteorology, Daniel Fa'afunua, was arrested and charged with the assault of his wife and of a female police officer, with being drunk and disorderly and with demanding money with menaces. The former minister was found guilty in February 2004 and received a lengthy prison sentence. In September of that year the Minister for Agriculture and Livestock, Alex Bartlett, was arrested on charges relating to violent offences that had occurred during 2000, when he was involved in the leadership of the MEF. In June 2004 Nathaniel Waena, the former Minister for National Unity, Reconciliation and Peace, was elected Governor-General, with 27 parliamentary votes, and in the following month was duly sworn in.

Further controversy within the Cabinet arose in early 2005 when the Minister for Provincial Government, Clement Rojumana, was arrested on 25 corruption charges and the Minister for Police, Michael Maina, was charged with theft. Both ministers were replaced in March. In April the former Minister for Finance, Francis Zama, was charged with official corruption over the alleged granting to himself of an exemption from the payment of goods tax during his period in office. Moreover, a police investigation in mid-2005 claimed that the Minister for Health, Benjamin Una, had been involved in two shooting incidents in 2004 that had targeted personnel from the regional intervention force, including the killing of an Australian officer. Una denied the allegations and accused the Australian-led intervention force of demonstrating a lack of respect towards Solomon Islands leaders, chiefs, customs and culture. In October 2005 the Minister for Fisheries and Marine Resources, Paul Maenu'u, was obliged to resign, following intense criticism of his decision to vote, at a meeting of the International Whaling Commission, in favour of a reintroduction of commercial whaling, in defiance of the Government's stated position. Mathias Taro was appointed to replace Maenu'u. In November Benjamin Una submitted his resignation as Minister for Health, having been arrested and charged with stealing aid funds that had been donated for a development project in his parliamentary constituency. Johnson Koli was named as the new Minister for Health. Alfred Sasako was appointed as Minister for Infrastructure and Development in the same month, but was dismissed in March 2006 following allegations of misconduct. In January 2006, meanwhile, Simeon Bouro was named as Minister for Mines and Energy.

In November 2005 the Prime Minister became involved in controversy with regard to the allocation of loans from a Taiwanese bank. It was claimed that during his tenure of the post of Minister for National Unity and Reconciliation in 2001, Sir Allan Kemakeza had received compensation of US $121,000 for personal losses incurred during ethnic unrest. Following an audit, it was revealed that millions of dollars could not be accounted for and that the Cabinet had remained unaware of the situation.

In the legislative election held on 5 April 2006 around one-half of the incumbent members of the National Parliament were reported to have lost their seats. It was believed that only 16 of the 50 incoming members had formally declared their party affiliation prior to the election, a situation that drew attention to the weaknesses of the political system prevailing in the country, whereby electors tended to vote for individuals rather than for representatives of specific political parties. It was subsequently reported that independents occupied 29 seats and that the recently formed Solomon Islands Party for Rural Advancement (SIPRA), led by Job Dudley Tausinga, held four seats, the National Party four seats, the PAP four seats and the Solomon Islands Democratic Party three seats, with the remainder being distributed among various other parties. Lobbying then began, in advance of a secret parliamentary ballot to elect the Prime Minister, with a view to the formation of a coalition Government. On 18 April three candidates participated in the contest for the post of Prime Minister, but none secured the requisite majority in the first session of voting in Parliament. Manasseh Sogavare was thus eliminated and a second ballot took place, at which Snyder Rini, leader of the Association of Independent Members of Parliament and former Deputy Prime Minister, received 27 parliamentary votes, while Job Dudley Tausinga won 23.

Rini's appointment as Prime Minister led to widespread protests. A group calling itself People's Power delivered a petition to the Governor-General demanding Rini's immediate resignation, claiming that he had been involved in corruption and bribery. It was variously alleged that Rini had accepted funding from the local Chinese business community and from both mainland Chinese and Taiwanese supporters who hoped to influence the electoral process. Snyder Rini was nevertheless sworn in on 20 April 2006. Public dissatisfaction culminated in two days of the most serious rioting witnessed in the country for many years. Much of the capital was left in ruins, and in particular many local Chinese businesses and homes were destroyed in arson attacks. It was reported that more than 300 citizens of the People's Republic of China had been evacuated from Honiara to their homeland. A curfew was imposed, and in an attempt to restore law and order in the capital Australia dispatched reinforcements of 110 soldiers and 70 police officers. Several opposition politicians were among those arrested in connection with the rioting. However, shortly before a parliamentary vote of no confidence was scheduled to take place, and after just eight days in the post of Prime Minister, Snyder Rini announced his decision to resign. The announcement led to scenes of jubilation in Honiara, although Rini remained in office in an acting capacity, pending a fresh parliamentary ballot to choose the next Prime Minister. On 4 May Manasseh Sogavare was elected, securing 28 votes; Fred Fono, who had briefly served as Deputy Prime Minister in the interim Government, received 22 votes. The majority of Solomon Islanders appeared to welcome the appointment of Manasseh Sogavare, who on the following day announced the composition of his Cabinet. Job Dudley Tausinga was appointed as Deputy Prime Minister, also assuming responsibility for the portfolio of forestry, environment and conservation. Bartholomew Ululfa'alu was named Minister for Finance and Treasury; Patteson Oti became Minister for Foreign Affairs; and Bernard Ghiro was appointed Minister for Home Affairs. Australia and New Zealand were highly critical of the appointments of Charles Dausabea, as Minister for Police and National Security, and of Nelson Ne'e, as Minister for Culture and Tourism; both had been charged in connection with their alleged incitement of the recent riots. (In June the two Ministers were replaced.)

Following his assumption of office, the new Prime Minister announced that the country's economic strategies were to be reorientated (see Economic Affairs) and that a new policy regarding the management of Taiwanese financial aid to Solomon Islands was to be formulated, to permit greater transparency in the use of such funds. In mid-May 2006 it was announced that Taiwan's first quarterly payment in relation to the Rural Constituency Development Fund (RCDF) had been released. Total Taiwanese aid was projected at US $2.9m. annually. Francis Billy Hilly was dismissed from the post of Minister of Commerce, Industries and Employment in August following his alleged refusal to denounce a memorandum of understanding signed by his National Party with China. In October a parliamentary no-confidence motion submitted by Fred Fono, the Leader of the Opposition, against Prime Minister Sogavare, failed to gain sufficient votes to succeed. Sogavare subsequently effected a minor reorganization of his cabinet, in which the Minister of Finance and Treasury, Bartholomew Ulufa'alu, was replaced by Gordon Darcy Lilo, hitherto Minister for National Reform and Aid Co-ordination, while Steve Abana became Minister for Planning and Aid Co-ordination. In December Deputy Prime Minister Job Tausinga resigned, apparently over a logging-related dispute, and was replaced by Toswell Kaua, who retained the agriculture and livestock portfolio.

In early April 2007 a large earthquake in the South Pacific caused a tsunami that resulted in more than 50 fatalities in Solomon Islands and destroyed the homes of thousands in the Western and Choiseul provinces. Aftershocks continued to hamper international and local relief efforts. Australia and Taiwan both supported emergency operations in the area.

Relations between Solomon Islands and Australia became increasingly strained in 2006 over the extradition of Julian Moti, an Australian citizen who in September had been appointed as the Attorney-General of Solomon Islands. Moti, who was wanted by the Australian authorities on a charge of statutory rape (allegedly committed in Vanuatu several years previously), had been arrested in Papua New Guinea but contravened the conditions of his bail and gained refuge in the Solomon Islands' High Commission in Port Moresby in October. Shortly thereafter he was flown, reportedly on an aircraft of the Papua New Guinea Defence Force, to Solomon Islands, where he was arrested by police officers serving under RAMSI and charged with illegal immigration. In mid-October Prime Minister Sogavare declared his unwillingness to give assent to any Australian extradition requests and claimed that Moti's detention was unlawful. Sogavare's threat to suspend the mandate for RAMSI and appraise Australia's role in the mission attracted criticism from the parliamentary opposition, and fears were raised about the repercussions of the dispute on the security and stability of Solomon Islands. Indeed, Australia suggested that its aid policy might be affected by the incident. The rift deepened when RAMSI officers carried out a forcible search of Sogavare's office to obtain evidence relating to the Moti case, while Sogavare was abroad attending a meeting of the Pacific Islands Forum meeting. At the meeting Australia was accused by both Sogavare and the Papua New Guinean Prime Minister, Sir Michael Somare, of violating the sovereignty of their respective countries; one of the conclusions of the summit meeting was the establishment of a commission to review RAMSI and its operations. Peter Shanel, the Minister for Commerce, Employment and Trade, was arrested for allegedly having given misleading information with regard to Moti's entry into Solomon Islands; it was reported that the dismissal of Police Commissioner Shane Castles, an Australian citizen, in December, was related in part to Shanel's arrest and to the raid on Sogavare's office. In mid-December immigration charges against Moti were dismissed. The Solomon Islands Government then proposed a dialogue between Moti and the Australian authorities. In January 2007 Australia appointed a new High Commissioner to succeed Patrick Cole, who had been expelled from Solomon Islands in September 2006 because of his alleged interference in domestic politics; Sogavare hailed his endorsement of the appointment of Peter Hooton in March as a means to a resolution of the problems between the two countries. However, RAMSI remained a point of contention: in February the Australian Minister for Foreign Affairs, in an open letter published in a Solomon Islands newspaper, appealed to the islanders to support the mission; in the same month the Solomon Islands Minister for Foreign Affairs, Patteson Oti, urged the formulation of an exit strategy for RAMSI. At the end of February a RAMSI official reacted positively to the Government's assertion that it would not arm its police force as previously intimated. In July, having been suspended for several months, Moti was sworn in as Attorney-General, an act that was described by John Howard as 'provocative and insensitive'. Sogavare, for his part, threatened to take Australia to the International Court of Justice, claiming that its pursuit of Moti was related to political interests. Australia applied for Moti's extradition, but was refused in September.

Meanwhile, in May 2007 the Minister for Public Service, Joses Sanga died. Sanga's portfolio was allocated to Deputy Prime Minister Toswell Kaua, while the agriculture and livestock portfolio, hitherto the responsibility of Kaua, was transferred to a new cabinet member, Severino Nuaiasi. In the same month Francis Zama was convicted of official corruption (see above), receiving a 20-month prison sentence. Zama's sentence was subsequently suspended, and in October he was appointed Minister for Justice and Legal Affairs, before being transferred to the finance and treasury portfolio, and later to education and human resources. In November Sir Allan Kemakeza, the former Prime Minister, was convicted of larceny, intimidation and demanding money with menaces, relating to the theft of vehicles from a local law firm, in 2002; he was later sentenced to two months' imprisonment. In August 2007 a motion of no confidence against Sogavare was withdrawn amid reports of bribery allegations against a member of the opposition. Sogavare faced a further challenge in November when 13 members of his Government, including Deputy Prime Minister Toswell Kaua, Minister for Education and Human Resources Development Derek Sikua and other cabinet ministers, resigned. Together with the opposition, the group urged Sogavare himself to resign owing to the lack of confidence in his leadership. With the prospect of another motion of no confidence, a protracted period of uncertainty ensued. Sogavare's non-attendance at a recent Pacific Islands Forum, along with his handling of the Moti affair, were criticized in some quarters. Both sides claimed to have the support of a parliamentary majority, and several defectors and members of the opposition reportedly joined the Government after being appointed to cabinet posts. However, in mid-December a no-confidence motion submitted against Sogavare succeeded by a narrow margin, and soon after, Derek Sikua was elected to replace him as Prime Minister. Sikua's Cabinet included several members of the Sogavare Government prior to the defections, including Toswell Kaua, who was appointed Minister for Law and Justice, and Gordon Darcy Lilo, who assumed responsibility for environment, conservation and meteorology. Other notable appointments included Fred Fono as Deputy Prime Minister and William Haomae as Minister for Foreign Affairs. By the end of the month Moti had been dismissed and extradited to Australia, as the new Government signalled an improvement in bilateral relations; the Government also aimed to scale down the number of political appointments in an attempt to curb government spending. In January 2008 the opposition was further weakened by the withdrawal of support of four of its members.

From 2004 the huge increase in the production of round logs in Solomon Islands led to considerable disquiet among community representatives, landowners and environmentalists. The total harvest of round logs in that year was estimated at more than 900,000 cu m, which was equivalent to five times the sustainable limit for timber production in the country. In November a petition of more than 1,000 signatures was delivered to the Government, demanding a reduction in the current rate of logging, increased regulation of logging activity by foreign companies and a greater role for local communities in decisions made about their forestry resources. The petition, which contained endorsements from every province in Solomon Islands, urged the Government to approve legislation known as the Forests Bill 2004, providing for the sustainable management of the forestry industry in the country. However, the Government postponed consideration of the proposed legislation, and it was reported that logging rates had increased yet further in anticipation of its introduction. Concerns were again aroused in late 2005, and in December the people of Maniwiriwiri village on Makira island staged a peaceful protest, successfully preventing bulldozers from passing through the village and gaining access to a logging project located near the site of the residents' water supply and dam. This was one of many peaceful protests in an area where the local community was taking an increasingly strong stance against logging operations.

In 1990 relations between Papua New Guinea and Solomon Islands deteriorated, following allegations by the Solomon Islands' Government that patrol boats from Papua New Guinea were interfering with the traditional crossing between Bougainville Island (Papua New Guinea) and the Shortland Islands, while the Papua New Guinea Government accused Solomon Islands of harbouring members of the rebel BRA and of providing them with supplies. Despite the signing that year of an agreement on joint border surveillance and arrangements to host peace negotiations between the BRA and the Papua New Guinea Government, relations worsened considerably in 1992 when Papua New Guinea forces carried out several unauthorized incursions into the Shortland Islands, in which a fuel depot was destroyed and two Solomon Islanders were killed. Alleging Australian involvement in the incursions, Mamaloni suspended surveillance flights by the Australian air force over its territory, and relations between the two countries deteriorated significantly. Despite the initiation of discussions between Solomon Islands and Papua New Guinea in January 1993, further incursions were reported in April. Following the election of a new Government in May in Solomon Islands, however, relations appeared to improve, and subsequent negotiations between the two countries resulted in an agreement to close the BRA office in Honiara. Tensions with Papua New Guinea, however, increased in 1996 as violence on Bougainville intensified. Numerous incursions by Papua New Guinea defence forces into Solomon Islands' waters were reported, while the Papua New Guinea Government repeated accusations that Solomon Islands was harbouring BRA activists. However, in June 1997 Papua New Guinea and Solomon Islands concluded a maritime border agreement, following several years of negotiations. The purpose of the agreement was not only to delineate the sea boundary between the two countries but also to provide a framework for co-operation in matters of security, natural disaster, customs, quarantine, immigration and conservation. In December 1997 the Prime Ministers of the two countries paid an extended visit to Bougainville to express support for the recently established truce agreement. Furthermore, the Governor of Bougainville was sympathetic to the problem of increasing numbers of Solomon Islanders from the Western Province crossing to Bougainville in late 2001. Many were trading goods in Bougainville in exchange for food and services. Discussions regarding the border of Papua New Guinea were held in April 2002; both Governments were concerned about the increase of weapons trafficking from Bougainville to the Western Province. Renewed border discussions took place between the two countries in June 2003. A development agreement that included joint infrastructural development, technical assistance and information sharing was signed by the two Governments in March 2005. In January 2008 it was reported that the Solomon Islands Prime Minister Derek Sikua was to visit Papua New Guinea to bolster relations between the two countries, which, he maintained, had been damaged by the Moti affair and its consequences.

In March 1988 Solomon Islands signed an agreement with Vanuatu and Papua New Guinea to form the Melanesian Spearhead Group. The new group regarded as its principal aims the preservation of Melanesian cultural traditions and the attainment of independence by the French Overseas Territory of New Caledonia. In March 1990 the Melanesian Spearhead Group admitted the Front de Libération Nationale Kanak Socialiste (FLNKS—the main Kanak, or Melanesian, political group in New Caledonia). In mid-1994 the group concluded an agreement regarded as the first stage in the establishment of a free trade area by the three countries. Fiji was admitted to the group in mid-1996. Solomon Islands announced its commitment to further economic integration with the countries of the Melanesian Spearhead Group in late 1997. The members of the Melanesian Spearhead Group signed a constitution in March 2007. In October 1995 Solomon Islands became a signatory of the Federated States of Micronesia Agreement on Regional Fisheries Access. In early 1997 Solomon Islands and Vanuatu agreed to undertake negotiations on the maritime boundaries between the two countries in an attempt to clarify uncertainty regarding fishing rights.

Solomon Islands attracted international criticism in mid-2003 for its practice of capturing and exporting large numbers of live dolphins. Police mounted a large-scale security operation around Honiara airport to prevent journalists from filming some 200 dolphins being loaded into a cargo aeroplane bound for Mexico. Several reports of harassment and violence against foreign journalists were received. It was believed that, owing to the high price commanded by the sale of the animals, senior Solomon Islands officials were likely to be involved. The trade in wild dolphins had been prohibited by most developed countries under a Convention on International Trade in Endangered Species of Wild Flora and Fauna. The trade was not only a cause for concern among foreigners, however, and in late 2003 one of the country's important traditional houses of chiefs, the Gela, expressed disquiet over the treatment that the animals had received. In December 2004 a consignment of dolphins was prevented from being exported after representatives from the fishing industry complained that the trade was harming the reputation of the islands' important tuna industry (widely perceived by Western countries to be 'dolphin-friendly'). The export of dolphins was subsequently banned upon the entry into force in November 2005 of a new law; those found to have contravened the regulations would face a minimum fine and the possibility of a prison sentence of six months. In June 2007, however, the ban was removed.

A seven-member parliamentary delegation, including five cabinet ministers, travelled to Taiwan in September 2004 to discuss mutual co-operation. One of the most important issues to be debated was the review of Taiwan's annual aid programe to Solomon Islands. In August 2006, during an official visit, the Solomon Islands Minister for Foreign Affairs, Patteson Oti, reaffirmed his country's strong links with Taiwan, and in December 2007 the new Prime Minister of Solomon Islands, Derek Sikua, pledged to continue his country's pro-Taiwan policy.

Solomon Islands' relations with Japan attracted international attention in mid-2005, when, following receipt of US $6.7m. from the Japanese Government for a major project to improve Honiara Airport, Solomon Islands voted with Japan (see above) to remove a 20-year moratorium on commercial whaling at a meeting of the International Whaling Commission (thereby reneging on a recent commitment to abstain from the vote). Its decision to support Japan's pro-whaling position resulted in the removal of Solomon Islands from a list of destinations promoted by several international diving organizations, which was likely to have a negative impact on the country's tourism industry.

Government

Under the 1978 Constitution, executive authority is vested in the British monarch, as Head of State, and is exercisable by the monarch's representative, the Governor-General, who is appointed on the advice of Parliament and acts on the advice of the Cabinet. Legislative power is vested in the unicameral National Parliament, with 50 members elected by universal adult suffrage for four years (subject to dissolution) in single-member constituencies. The Cabinet is composed of the Prime Minister, elected by Parliament, and other ministers appointed by the Governor-General on the Prime Minister's recommendation. The Cabinet is responsible to Parliament. The country comprises four Districts, within which there are nine local government councils, elected by universal adult suffrage. The

SOLOMON ISLANDS

Introductory Survey

Constitution provides for further devolution of power to provincial authorities.

Defence

Prior to the coup of June 2000, a unit within the Police Force, the Police Field Force, received technical training and logistical support from Australia and New Zealand. The Force latterly had two patrol boats and undertook surveillance activities in Solomon Islands' maritime economic zone. The Solomon Islands Peace Plan, signed in July 2000, provided for the establishment of a Ministry of Defence, which was to be independent of the Ministry of Police, Justice and Legal Affairs. The Ministry of Defence would, as one of its first tasks, introduce legislation to permit the establishment of a Solomon Islands Defence Force. A national reconnaissance and surveillance force was founded in 1995, and was also to become answerable to the new ministry.

Economic Affairs

In 2006, according to estimates by the World Bank, Solomon Islands' gross national income (GNI), measured at average 2004–06 prices, was US $331m., equivalent to US $680 per head (or $2,170 on an international purchasing-power parity basis). During 1996–2006, it was estimated, the population increased at an average annual rate of 2.7%, while gross domestic product (GDP) per head decreased, in real terms, at an average annual rate of 2.9%. Overall GDP decreased, in real terms, at an average annual rate of 0.3% in 1996–2006. According to the Asian Development Bank (ADB), GDP increased by 6.1% in 2006 and by 10.0% in 2007.

Agriculture (including hunting, forestry and fishing) contributed 31.3% of GDP in 2006, according to the ADB. In 2004 an estimated 28.7% of those working in the formal sector of the economy were involved in agriculture. The principal cash crops have traditionally included coconuts, cocoa, rice and oil palm. Earnings from copra (which was for many years the country's main export) decreased from SI $25.5m. in 2004 to SI $16.4m. in 2005, before increasing to more than SI $45.6m. in 2006. The value of cocoa exports declined from SI $64.3m. in 2005 to SI $30.3m. in 2006. Meanwhile, the rehabilitation of the palm oil industry involved plans to replant thousands of hectares of the former plantations; it was hoped that in due course as many as 3,000 new jobs would be created, with an area of 12,000 ha being cleared for new plantations. Spices are cultivated for export on a small scale, while from the 1990s the production of honey became increasingly important. The main subsistence crops are root crops, garden vegetables and fruit. Pigs and cattle are also reared. Seaweed farming has been introduced, and seashells are exported. Giant-clam farming became an important activity in the mid-1990s. Fish accounted for 15.9% of export earnings in 2006. In March 2006 a new agreement provided for an expansion of the islands' tuna production and progression towards supplying tuna in catering-sized cans for the previously impenetrable European market; operations were to be extended to encompass the production of fish meal. The forestry sector is an extremely important source of revenue, timber exports accounting for 70.2% of total export receipts in 2006. The dramatic increase in the production of timber from the early 1990s prompted several international organizations to express alarm at the rate of logging in the country (see Recent History). Nevertheless, the rate of logging continued to increase. Output of timber more than doubled between 2000 and 2005 alone. The ADB estimated that agricultural GDP grew by 20.3% in 2004, declining to just 2.9% in 2005 before increasing to 3.2% in 2006.

Industry (including mining, manufacturing, construction and power) contributed 26.8% of GDP in 2006 and employed 6.4% of wage-earners in 2004. The ADB estimated that industrial GDP growth increased from 1.3% in 2004 to 9.2% in 2005, before declining to 3.4% in 2006. The mining sector's contribution to GDP is negligible. Gold has been the sole mineral export of significance. The other (mainly undeveloped) mineral resources include deposits of copper, lead, zinc, silver, cobalt, asbestos, phosphates, nickel and high-grade bauxite. In early 2005 there was a surge of interest in mineral prospecting by potential overseas investors, and the Government received a large number of applications for the prospecting of gold, nickel and diamonds. An application for the renewal of nickel-prospecting licences submitted by Pacrim Resources, however, was rejected in August 2005 after the company failed to pay the fees required and to provide reports on its activities. The company had also invested less in the area than originally anticipated.

Manufacturing contributed 4.1% of GDP (at 1985 prices) in 2002, and employed 15.6% of wage-earners in 1995. The most important branches are food-processing (notably fish-canning), coconut-based products, brewing, saw-milling, logging and handicrafts. Compared with the previous year, the manufacturing sector's GDP contracted by 19.4% in 2001 and by 5.4% in 2002.

Energy is derived principally from hydroelectric power, with solar energy being increasingly utilized. Mineral fuels accounted for 28.3% of the total value of imports in 2006. Several potential petroleum-producing areas in the islands have been identified. Electricity output totalled 68m. kWh in 2006.

Service industries contributed 41.9% of GDP in 2006 and engaged 64.9% of wage-earners in 2004. Tourist arrivals increased from 11,482 in 2006 to 13,748 in 2007, with Australia providing 43.4% of the latter total. Earnings from the sector had declined from some US $13m. in 1998 to just $2m. in 2005. The ADB estimated that the GDP of the services sector increased by 0.3% in 2005 and by 7.5% in 2006.

In 2006 there was a visible trade deficit of US $72m. and a deficit of US $51m. on the current account of the balance of payments. In 2006 the principal sources of imports were Australia (which accounted for 24.5%), Singapore (23.7%), Japan and New Zealand, while the principal markets for exports were the People's Republic of China (46.1%), the Republic of Korea (13.5%), Japan (8.1%), Thailand, the Philippines and Italy. The principal exports in that year were timber, fish, copra, palm oil and cocoa. The principal imports were mineral fuels, foodstuffs, basic manufactures and beverages and tobacco.

The budget announced in February 2007 provided for significant increases in both revenue and expenditure, to SI $949m. (including grants) and SI $944m. respectively. According to the ADB, the fiscal surplus decreased from the equivalent of 2.5% of GDP in 2005 to 1.5% of GDP in 2006, before moving into a deficit equivalent to 1.2% of GDP in 2007. Aid from Australia was projected at $A223.9m. in 2007/08, while financial assistance from New Zealand was budgeted at $NZ30.8m. for the same year. In 2007, according to the ADB, the country's external debt totalled US $147m. and the cost of debt-servicing was equivalent to 4.3% of the value of exports of goods and services. The average annual rate of inflation in Honiara in 1996–2006 was 8.5%. Compared with the previous year, the rate of inflation was estimated by the ADB at 8.4% in 2006 and at 7.0% in 2007. The extent of the islands' informal sector impedes an accurate assessment of the rate of unemployment; however, youth unemployment, particularly in urban areas, has remained at a high level.

Solomon Islands is a member of the Pacific Community (see p. 377), the Pacific Islands Forum (see p. 380), the Asian Development Bank (see p. 182) and the UN Economic and Social Commission for Asia and the Pacific (ESCAP, see p. 35), and is a signatory to the Lomé Conventions and the successor Cotonou Agreement (see p. 301) with the European Union (EU). The country is also a member (with Fiji, Papua New Guinea and Vanuatu) of the Melanesian Spearhead Group, which provides for free trade among member countries.

The economy of Solomon Islands remains one of the least developed in the Pacific region. Progress has been impeded by weak governance, inadequate infrastructure and a very high rate of population growth. The country's major agricultural and forestry exports are vulnerable to inclement weather and to fluctuations in prices on international markets. Furthermore, the islands' dependence upon forestry, with logging being the prime constituent of both taxation and export revenues, has become a major concern. The regional intervention of 2003 (see Recent History) included an economic recovery programme involving increased assistance from Australia (totalling some $A1,000m. over 10 years). The destruction of numerous businesses (owned predominantly by Chinese entrepreneurs) in the rioting of early 2006 was a deterrent to potential investors. Upon taking office as Prime Minister in May 2006, Manasseh Sogavare announced his intention to reorganize budgetary strategy in order to address the issue of rural development, envisaging the implementation of a programme of land reform. He aimed to accelerate the process of decentralizing major development activities from Honiara to the country's provinces, with greater emphasis to be placed on the role of the private sector. The National Transport Plan, approved in September 2006, aimed to improve the country's infrastructure. The telecommunications sector was to be deregulated. However, Sogavare was replaced in December 2007 (see Recent History). With the important logging industry continuing its rapid expansion, in April 2008 the new Government announced various measures to counter the detrimental impact on the nation's forests. Henceforth all companies,

SOLOMON ISLANDS

including those engaged in the mining and agricultural sectors, were to be required to obtain a public environment report prior to commencing operations. In the longer term, the potential decline in future logging revenues was expected to lead the Government to adopt a more cautious programme of expenditure. The 2008/09 budget, approved in April 2008, projected total expenditure of SI $1,400m., of which SI $380m. was allocated to development projects. The ADB anticipated that GDP growth would decelerate to 6.0% in 2008. As the substantial rises in global prices for essential commodities such as rice, wheat and petroleum continued in early 2008, increasing inflationary pressures were expected to present a major challenge to the Government.

Education

Education is not compulsory in Solomon Islands. Primary education generally begins at six years of age and lasts for six years. Secondary education, normally beginning at the age of 12, lasts for up to five years. In 2005 enrolment at primary schools was equivalent to 97% of children in the relevant age-group (males 99%; females 95%) while enrolment at secondary schools was equivalent to 30% of children from the relevant age-group (males 32%; females 27%). In 1993 there were 523 primary schools, with a total of 87,770 pupils in 2004, while in 1993 there were 23 secondary schools, with a total of 46,082 pupils in 2002. In 1993 10 of the country's secondary schools were national secondary schools, which are run either by the Government or by one of the churches, and the remaining 13 were provincial secondary schools, which are run by provincial assemblies and provide courses of a practical nature, mainly in agriculture and development studies. There are two teacher-training schools and a technical institute. Scholarships are available for higher education at various universities overseas, which in 1987 were attended by 413 students from Solomon Islands. In 1977 the Solomon Islands Centre of the University of the Pacific opened in Honiara. Government expenditure on education was SI $51m. (9.7% of total spending) in 1998. In 2005 plans to construct several new educational centres were announced. In an attempt to reduce the number of pupils abandoning their studies each year, many new community high schools were to be built over a period of 15 years. The islands were also granted funding for nine new distance learning centres, one to be built in each of the provinces. In November 2005 it was also announced that the University of the South Pacific was to establish a fourth campus in Solomon Islands, thereby reducing the amount of government funding needed to send students overseas. In March 2006 eight schools, four in Western Province and four in South Malaita, were selected for funding to construct new class rooms and to provide, equipment, desks and other facilities.

Public Holidays

2008: 1 January (New Year's Day), 21–24 March (Easter), 12 May (Whit Monday), 13 June (Queen's Official Birthday), 7 July (Independence Day), 25 December (Christmas Day), 26 December (Boxing Day).

2009 (provisional): 1 January (New Year's Day), 10–13 April (Easter), 1 June (Whit Monday), 8 June (Queen's Official Birthday), 7 July (Independence Day), 25 December (Christmas Day), 26 December (Boxing Day).

Weights and Measures

The metric system is in force.

Statistical Survey

Source (unless otherwise indicated): National Statistics Office, Ministry of Finance, P.O. Box G6, Honiara; tel. (677) 27835; fax (677) 23951; e-mail Stats_management@mof.gov.sb; internet http://www.spc.int/prism/country/sb/stats.

AREA AND POPULATION

Area: 27,556 sq km (10,639 sq miles).

Population: 285,176 at census of 23–24 November 1986; 409,042 (males 211,381, females 197,661) at census of 21–22 November 1999. *Mid-2007*: 495,026 (males 255,063, females 239,963).

Density (mid-2007): 18.0 per sq km.

Ethnic Groups (census of November 1986): Melanesians 268,536; Polynesians 10,661; Micronesians 3,929; Europeans 1,107; Chinese 379; Others 564.

Principal Towns (population at 1999 census): Honiara (capital) 49,107; Noro 3,482; Gizo 2,960 (Source: Thomas Brinkhoff, *City Population*—internet www.citypopulation.de). *Mid-2005* (incl. suburbs, UN estimate) Honiara 61,000 (Source: UN, *World Urbanization Prospects: The 2005 Revision*).

Births and Deaths (annual averages, 2000–05, UN estimates): Birth rate 33.6 per 1,000; Death rate 87.9 per 1,000 (Source: UN, *World Population Prospects: The 2006 Revision*).

Expectation of Life (years at birth, WHO estimates): 70.1 (males 68.4; females 72.1) in 2005. Source: WHO, *World Health Statistics*.

Employment (excluding informal sector, 2004, estimates): Agriculture 6,342; Forestry 3,482; Fishing 5,114; Manufacturing (incl. mining and quarrying) 1,476; Electricity and water 469; Construction 1,397; Trade, restaurants and hotels 3,274; Transport, storage and communications 1,246; Finance, insurance, real estate and business services 806; Administration 6,758; Other community, social and personal service activities 21,757; *Total* 52,121. *2005* (excluding informal sector, estimate): Total employed 56,559. Source: IMF, *Solomon Islands: Statistical Appendix* (October 2006). *Mid-2005* ('000, FAO estimates): Agriculture etc. 178; Total labour force 250. Source: FAO.

HEALTH AND WELFARE
Key Indicators

Total Fertility Rate (children per woman, 2005): 4.1.

Under-5 Mortality Rate (per 1,000 live births, 2005): 29.

Physicians (per 1,000 head, 1999): 0.13.

Hospital Beds (per 1,000 head, 2003): 2.2.

Health Expenditure (2004): US $ per head (PPP): 114.0.

Health Expenditure (2004): % of GDP: 5.9.

Health Expenditure (2004): public (% of total): 94.5.

Access to Water (% of persons, 2004): 70.

Access to Sanitation (% of persons, 2004): 31.

Human Development Index (2005): ranking: 129.

Human Development Index (2005): value: 0.602.

For sources and definitions, see explanatory note on p. vi.

AGRICULTURE, ETC.

Principal Crops ('000 metric tons, 2006, FAO estimates): Coconuts 276; Oil palm fruit 162; Rice (paddy) 5.5; Cocoa beans 3.8; Sweet potatoes 89; Yams 30; Taro 40; Vegetables and melons 8.2; Fruits (excl. melons) 19.3.

Livestock ('000 head, year ending September 2006, FAO estimates): Cattle 13.5; Pigs 53; Chickens 230.

Livestock Products (metric tons, 2006, FAO estimates): Cattle meat 740; Pig meat 2,320; Chicken meat 304; Hen eggs 480; Cows' milk 1,365.

Forestry ('000 cu m, 2006, FAO estimate): *Roundwood Removals* (excl. bark): Industrial wood 1,130; Fuel wood 138 (FAO estimate); Total 1,268. *Sawnwood Production:* 12 (FAO estimate, all broadleaved, incl. railway sleepers).

Fishing (metric tons, live weight, 2005): Skipjack tuna 10,763; Yellowfin tuna 6,491; Bigeye tuna 1,000 (FAO estimate); Total catch (incl. others): 28,538 (excl. aquatic plants 120).

Source: FAO.

MINING

Production (kilograms, 2006): Gold 10. Source: US Geological Survey.

INDUSTRY

Production (metric tons, 2006): Copra 21,000; Coconut oil 59,000; Palm oil 36,000 (unofficial figure from FAO); Electric energy 68 million kWh. Source: Asian Development Bank, *Key Indicators of Developing Asian and Pacific Countries*, unless otherwise indicated.

FINANCE

Currency and Exchange Rates: 100 cents = 1 Solomon Islands dollar (SI $). *Sterling, US Dollar and Euro Equivalents (30 November 2007):* £1 sterling = SI $15.835; US $1 = SI $7.663; €1 = SI $11.311; SI $100 = £6.32 = US $13.05 = €8.84. *Average Exchange Rate* (SI $ per US $): 7.4847 in 2004; 7.5299 in 2005; 7.6095 in 2006.

Budget (SI $ million, 2006, estimates): *Revenue:* Taxes 680.5; Non-tax revenue 141.8; Grants 967.1; Total 1,789.4. *Expenditure:* Total 1,684.0 (Recurrent 718.2, Development 965.8). Note: Figures include development grants and grant-financed development spending administered by donors (SI $898.6m.). Source: IMF, *Solomon Islands: Tax Summary and Statistical Appendix* (September 2007).

Official Development Assistance (US $ million, 2000): Bilateral 22.1; Multilateral 46.3; Total 68.4 (Grants 69.7, Loans –1.3). Source: UN, *Statistical Yearbook for Asia and the Pacific.*

International Reserves (US $ million at 31 December 2007): Reserve position in IMF 0.87; Foreign exchange 118.18; Total 119.05. Source: IMF, *International Financial Statistics.*

Money Supply (SI $ million at 31 December 2007): Currency outside banks 231.87; Demand deposits at deposit money banks 674.43; Total money 906.30. Source: IMF, *International Financial Statistics.*

Cost of Living (Consumer Price Index for Honiara, average of quarterly figures; base: October–December 1992 = 100): 308.2 in 2005; 342.8 in 2006; 369.0 in 2007. Source: Central Bank of Solomon Islands, *Quarterly Review* (December 2007).

Gross Domestic Product (US $ million at constant 1990 prices): 248 in 2001; 238 in 2002; 243 in 2003. Source: UN, *Statistical Yearbook.*

Gross Domestic Product by Economic Activity (SI $ million at constant 1984/85 prices, 2002): Agriculture 130.1; Mining –0.6; Manufacturing 10.6; Electricity, gas and water 4.6; Construction 1.1; Trade 27.2; Transport and communications 11.2; Finance 15.2; Other services (including public administration) 61.2; *GDP at factor cost* 260.6. Source: Asian Development Bank, *Key Indicators of Developing Asian and Pacific Countries.*

Balance of Payments (US $ million, 2006): Exports of goods f.o.b. 120.41; Imports of goods f.o.b. –192.54; *Trade balance* –72.12; Exports of services and income 59.62; Imports of services and income –66.14; *Balance on goods, services and income* –78.64; Current transfers received 69.32; Current transfers paid –41.38; *Current balance* –50.70; Capital account (net) 29.41; Direct investment 18.99; Other investments –42.96; Net errors and omissions –6.27; *Overall balance* –51.53. Source: Asian Development Bank, *Key Indicators of Developing Asian and Pacific Countries.*

EXTERNAL TRADE

Principal Commodities (SI $ '000, 2006): *Imports c.i.f.:* Food and live animals 164,578; Mineral fuels, etc. 414,371; Basic manufactures 63,746; Machinery and transport equipment 199,866; Total (incl. others) 1,463,807. *Exports f.o.b.:* Fish 145,855; Copra 45,645; Palm oil 30,719; Timber 643,574; Cocoa 30,258; Total (incl. others) 916,352.

Principal Trading Partners (US $ million, 2006): *Imports:* Australia 62.21; China, People's Republic 5.51; Fiji 10.32; Japan 20.19; New Zealand 12.97; Papua New Guinea 10.03; Singapore 60.22; USA 6.27; Total (incl. others) 253.76. *Exports:* China, People's Republic 113.51; Italy 10.49; Japan 20.05; Korea, Republic 33.19; Philippines 10.80; Thailand 11.05 Total (incl. others) 246.22.

Source: Asian Development Bank, *Key Indicators of Developing Asian and Pacific Countries.*

TRANSPORT

Road Traffic (motor vehicles in use at 30 June 1986): Passenger cars 1,350; Commercial vehicles 2,026.

Shipping: *Traffic* (international traffic, '000 metric tons, 1990): Goods loaded 278; Goods unloaded 349 (Source: UN, *Monthly Bulletin of Statistics*). *Merchant Fleet* (registered at 31 December 2006): Vessels 31; Total displacement ('000 grt) 10.1 (Source: Lloyd's Register-Fairplay, *World Fleet Statistics*).

Civil Aviation (traffic on scheduled services, 2003): Kilometres flown 2 million; Passengers carried 68,000; Passenger-km 59 million; Total ton-km 6. Source: UN, *Statistical Yearbook.*

TOURISM

Visitor Arrivals by Country (2007): Australia 5,960; Japan 572; New Zealand 987; Papua New Guinea 1,007; United Kingdom 318; USA 953; Vanuatu 950; Total (incl. others) 13,748.

Tourism Receipts (US $ million, excl. passenger transport): 2 in 2003; 4 in 2004; 2 in 2005.

Source: World Tourism Organization.

COMMUNICATIONS MEDIA

Non-daily Newspapers (1996): 3; estimated circulation 9,000.

Radio Receivers (1997): 57,000 in use.

Television Receivers (2001): 12,000 in use.

Telephones (2006): 7,400 main lines in use.

Mobile Cellular Telephones (2006): 6,000 subscribers.

Personal Computers (2005): 22,000 in use.

Internet Users (2006): 8,000.

Broadband subscribers (2006): 400.

Facsimile Machines (1999): 764 in use.

Sources: UNESCO, *Statistical Yearbook*; International Telecommunication Union.

EDUCATION

Pre-primary (1994): 12,627 pupils.

Primary: 523 schools (1993); 2,514 teachers (1994); 87,770 pupils (2004).

Secondary: 23 schools (1993); 618 teachers (1994); 46,082 pupils (2002).

Overseas Centres (1988): 405 students.

Source: mainly UNESCO, *Statistical Yearbook.*

Adult Literacy Rate (estimate based on census data): 76.6% in 2003. Source: UN Development Programme, *Human Development Report.*

Directory

The Constitution

A new Constitution came into effect at independence on 7 July 1978.

The main provisions are that Solomon Islands is a constitutional monarchy with the British sovereign (represented locally by a Governor-General, who must be a Solomon Islands citizen) as Head of State, while legislative power is vested in the unicameral National Parliament composed of 50 members (increased from 47 in 1997), elected by universal adult suffrage for four years (subject to dissolution), and executive authority is exercised by the Cabinet, led by the Prime Minister. The Governor-General is appointed for up to five years, on the advice of Parliament, and acts in almost all matters on the advice of the Cabinet. The Prime Minister is elected by and from members of Parliament. Other ministers are appointed by the Governor-General, on the Prime Minister's recommendation, from members of Parliament. The Cabinet is responsible to Parliament. Emphasis is laid on the devolution of power, and traditional chiefs and leaders have a special role within these arrangements. Legislation approved in August 1996 provided for the abolition of the provincial government system and the transfer of legislative and administrative powers from the nine provincial governments to 75 area assemblies and councils controlled by central Government.

The Constitution contains comprehensive guarantees of fundamental human rights and freedoms, and provides for the introduction of a 'leadership code' and the appointment of an Ombudsman and a Public Solicitor. It also provides for 'the establishment of the underlying law, based on the customary law and concepts of the Solomon Islands people'. Solomon Islands citizenship was automatically conferred on the indigenous people of the islands and on other residents with close ties with the islands upon independence. The acquisition of land is reserved for indigenous inhabitants or their descendants.

In mid-1999 it was announced that two review committees had been established to amend the Constitution. They were expected to examine ways in which the traditions of the various ethnic groups could be better accommodated.

SOLOMON ISLANDS

The Government

HEAD OF STATE

Monarch: HM Queen ELIZABETH II.
Governor-General: Sir NATHANIEL WAENA (sworn in 7 July 2004).

CABINET
(April 2008)

Prime Minister: Dr DEREK SIKUA.
Deputy Prime Minister and Minister for Rural Development and Indigenous Affairs: FRED FONO.
Minister for Agriculture and Livestock: SELWYN RIUMANA.
Minister for Commerce, Industry and Employment: FRANCIS BILLY HILLY.
Minister for Communication, Aviation and Meteorology: VARIAN LONAMEI.
Minister for Culture and Tourism: SETH GUKUNA.
Minister for Development Planning and Aid Co-ordination: STEVE ABANA.
Minister for Education and Human Resources Development: JOB DUDLEY TAUSINGA.
Minister for Energy, Mines and Rural Electrification: EDWARD HUNI'EHU.
Minister for Environment and Conservation: GORDON DARCY LILO.
Minister for Finance and Treasury: SNYDER RINI.
Minister for Fisheries and Marine Resources: NOLLEN LENI.
Minister for Foreign Affairs: WILLIAM HAOMAE.
Minister for Forestry: Sir ALLAN KEMAKEZA.
Minister for Health and Medical Services: JOHNSON KOLI.
Minister for Home Affairs: JAMES TORA.
Minister for Infrastructure Development: STANLEY SOFU.
Minister for Lands, Housing and Survey: MARTIN MAGGA.
Minister for Law and Justice: TOSWELL KAUA.
Minister for National Peace and Reconciliation: SAM IDURI.
Minister for Police, National Security and Correctional Services: SAMUEL MANETOALI.
Minister for Provincial Government: DAVID DAY PACHA.
Minister for Public Service: MILNER TOZAKA.
Minister for Women, Youth and Children's Affairs: PETER TOM.

MINISTRIES

Office of the Prime Minister: POB G1, Honiara; tel. 21867; fax 26088; internet www.pmc.gov.sb.
Ministry of Agriculture and Livestock Development: POB G13, Honiara; tel. 27987; fax 28365; e-mail psagriculture@pmc.gov.sb.
Ministry of Commerce, Industry and Employment: Honiara; tel. 28614; fax 25084; e-mail pscommerce@pmc.gov.sb.
Ministry of Communication and Aviation: Honiara; tel. 28049; fax 28054.
Ministry of Culture and Tourism: Honiara; tel. 26848; fax 26875.
Ministry of Development, Planning and Aid Co-ordination: Honiara; tel. 28608; fax 30163.
Ministry of Education and Human Resources: POB G28, Honiara; tel. 28643; fax 22042; e-mail pseducation@pmc.gov.sb.
Ministry of Energy, Mines and Rural Electrification: Honiara; tel. 28609; fax 25811; e-mail psmines@pmc.gov.sb.
Ministry of Environment, Conservation and Meteorology: Honiara; tel. 28611; fax 28735; e-mail psforestry@pmc.gov.sb.
Ministry of Finance and Treasury: POB 26, Honiara; tel. 24102; fax 28619; e-mail psfinance@pmc.gov.sb.
Ministry of Fisheries and Marine Resources: Honiara; tel. 28604; e-mail psfisheries@pmc.gov.sb.
Ministry of Foreign Affairs and External Trade: POB G10, Honiara; tel. 28612; fax 20351; e-mail psforeign@pmc.gov.sb.
Ministry of Forestry: Honiara; tel. 28611; fax 28735.
Ministry of Health and Medical Services: POB 349, Honiara; tel. 20830; fax 20085.
Ministry of Home Affairs: Honiara; tel. 28602; fax 25591; e-mail psaffairs@pmc.gov.sb.
Ministry of Infrastructure Development: POB G30, Honiara; tel. 28605; fax 28705; e-mail kudu@mnpd.gov.sb.

Directory

Ministry of Justice and Legal Affairs: Honiara; tel. 21048; fax 28424; e-mail psjustice@pmc.gov.sb.
Ministry of Lands, Housing and Survey: Honiara; tel. 22750; fax 27298; e-mail pslands@pmc.gov.sb.
Ministry of National Unity, Reconciliation and Peace: Honiara; tel. 28616.
Ministry of Police, National Security and Correctional Services: POB 1723/404, Honiara; tel. 28607; fax 28423; e-mail pspolice@pmc.gov.sb.
Ministry of Provincial Government and Institutional Strengthening: POB G35, Honiara; tel. 28606; fax 28708.
Ministry of Public Service: Honiara; tel. 28617; fax 25559; e-mail pspublic@pmc.gov.sb.
Ministry of Rural Development and Indigenous Affairs: Honiara; tel. 25238; fax 22170.
Ministry of Women, Youth and Children's Affairs: Honiara; tel. 28602; fax 23547.

Legislature

National Parliament
POB G19, Honiara; tel. 21751; fax 23866.
Speaker: Sir PETER KENILOREA.

General Election, 5 April 2006

Party	Seats
Solomon Islands Party for Rural Advancement	4
National Party	4
People's Alliance Party	4
Solomon Islands Democratic Party	3
Social Credit Party	2
Solomon Islands Liberal Party	2
LAFARI Party	2
Independents and others	29
Total	**50**

Election Commission

Electoral Commission: Parliament House, POB G19, Honiara; tel. 20683; Dir MUSU KEVU.

Political Organizations

Parties in the National Parliament can have a fluctuating membership and an influence disproportionate to their representation. There is a significant number of independents who are loosely associated in the amorphous, but often decisive, 'Independent Group'. The following parties represent the main groupings:

LAFARI Party: c/o National Parliament, POB G19, Honiara; supports an increased role for tribal chiefs in society; Leader JOHN M. GARO.
National Party: c/o National Parliament, POB G19, Honiara; f. 1996; Leader FRANCIS BILLY HILLY.
People's Alliance Party (PAP): Honiara; f. 1979; est. by merger of People's Progressive Party (f. 1973) and Rural Alliance Party (f. 1977); advocates establishment of a federal republic; Leader CLEMENT KENGAVA; Sec. EDWARD KINGMELE.
Social Credit Party: c/o National Parliament, POB G19, Honiara; f. 2006; focuses on the underlying issues of communal tension and economic underdevelopment; Leader MANASSEH SOGAVARE.
Solomon Islands Democratic Party: c/o National Parliament, POB G19, Honiara; campaigns for self-reliance and for ending of country's dependence on external aid.
Solomon Islands Liberal Party (SILP): c/o National Parliament, POB G19, Honiara; f. 1976; est. as National Democratic Party (NADEPA); present name adopted in 1986; Leader JAPHET WAIPORA.
Solomon Islands Party for Rural Advancement (SIPRA): Honiara; f. 2006; advocates the decentralization of powers and the recognition of community governance structures and traditional values; Pres. and Leader JOB DUDLEY TAUSINGA; Sec.-Gen. SAM ALASIA.

Other parties that contested the 2006 election included the Christian Alliance Party, the Solomon Islands Labour Party, the Solomons First Party, the One Nation Party and the United Party.

Diplomatic Representation

EMBASSIES AND HIGH COMMISSIONS IN SOLOMON ISLANDS

Australia: Hibiscus Ave, POB 589, Honiara; tel. 21561; fax 23691; e-mail austhoniara.enquiries@dfat.gov.au; internet www.solomonislands.embassy.gov.au; High Commissioner PETER HOOTON.

China (Taiwan): Panatina Plaza, POB 586, Honiara; tel. 38050; fax 38060; e-mail embroc@solomon.com.sb; Ambassador GEORGE CHAN.

Japan: National Provident Fund Bldg, Mendana Ave, POB 560, Honiara; tel. 22953; fax 21006; Chargé d'affaires IWANDA AKIRA.

New Zealand: Mendana Ave, POB 697, Honiara; tel. 21502; fax 22377; e-mail nzhicom@.solomon.com.sb; High Commissioner DEBORAH PANCKHURST.

Papua New Guinea: POB 1109, Honiara; tel. 20561; fax 20562; High Commissioner PARAI TAMEI.

United Kingdom: Telekom House, Mendana Ave, POB 676, Honiara; tel. 21705; fax 21549; e-mail bhc@solomon.com.sb; High Commissioner RICHARD JOHN LYNE.

Judicial System

The High Court is a Superior Court of Record with unlimited original jurisdiction and powers (except over customary land) as prescribed by the Solomon Islands Constitution or by any law for the time being in force in Solomon Islands. The Judges of the High Court are the Chief Justice, resident in Solomon Islands and employed by its Government, and the Puisne Judges (of whom there are usually three). Appeals from this Court go to the Court of Appeal, the members of which are senior judges from Australia, New Zealand and Papua New Guinea. The Chief Justice and judges of the High Court are *ex officio* members of the Court of Appeal.

In addition there are Magistrates' Courts staffed by qualified and lay magistrates exercising limited jurisdiction in both civil and criminal matters. There are also Local Courts staffed by elders of the local communities, which have jurisdiction in the areas of established native custom, petty crime and local government by-laws. In 1975 Customary Land Appeal Courts were established to hear land appeal cases from Local Courts, which have exclusive original jurisdiction over customary land cases.

Office of the Registrar: High Court and Court of Appeal, POB G21, Honiara; tel. 21632; fax 22702; e-mail chetwynd@welkam.solomon.com.sb.

President of the Court of Appeal: Sir ALBERT ROCKY PALMER.

Chief Justice of the High Court: Sir ALBERT ROCKY PALMER.

Puisne Judges: Sir ALBERT ROCKY PALMER, JOHN RODNEY BROWN, FRANK KABUI.

Registrar and Commissioner of the High Court: DAVID CHETWYND.

Chief Magistrate: SEKOVE NAQIOLEVU.

Attorney-General: GABRIEL SURI.

Director of Public Prosecutions: FRANCIS MWANESALUA.

Solicitor-General: (vacant).

Auditor-General: AUGUSTINE FATAI.

Public Solicitor: KENNETH HALL AVERRE.

Chair of Law Reform Commission: (vacant).

Religion

More than 95% of the population profess Christianity, and the remainder follow traditional beliefs. According to the census of 1976, about 34% of the population adhered to the Church of Melanesia (Anglican), 19% were Roman Catholics, 17% belonged to the South Seas Evangelical Church, 11% to the United Church (Methodist) and 10% were Seventh-day Adventists. Most denominations are affiliated to the Solomon Islands Christian Association. In many areas Christianity is practised alongside traditional beliefs, especially ancestor worship.

CHRISTIANITY

Solomon Islands Christian Association: POB 1335, Honiara; tel. 23350; fax 26150; e-mail essica@solomon.com.sb; f. 1967; five full mems, seven assoc. mem. orgs; Chair. Most Rev. ADRIAN SMITH; Gen. Sec. EMMANUEL IYABORA.

The Anglican Communion

Anglicans in Solomon Islands are adherents of the Church of the Province of Melanesia, comprising eight dioceses: six in Solomon Islands (Central Melanesia, Malaita, Temotu, Ysabel, Hanuato'o and Central Solomons, which was established in May 1997) and two in Vanuatu (one of which also includes New Caledonia). The Archbishop is also Bishop of Central Melanesia and is based in Honiara. The Church had an estimated 180,000 members in 1988.

Archbishop of the Province of Melanesia: Most Rev. Sir ELLISON POGO, Archbishop's House, POB 19, Honiara; tel. 21892; fax 21098; e-mail epogo@comphq.org.sb.

General Secretary: GEORGE KIRIAU, Provincial Headquarters, POB 19, Honiara; tel. 21892; fax 21098; e-mail gkiriau@comphq.oeg.sb.

The Roman Catholic Church

For ecclesiastical purposes, Solomon Islands comprises one archdiocese and two dioceses. At 31 December 2005 there were an estimated 95,967 adherents in the country. The Bishops participate in the Bishops' Conference of Papua New Guinea and Solomon Islands (based in Papua New Guinea).

Archbishop of Honiara: Most Rev. ADRIAN THOMAS SMITH, Holy Cross, GPOB 237, Honiara; tel. 21943; fax 26426; e-mail chancery@solomon.com.sb.

Other Christian Churches

Assembly of God: POB 928, Honiara; tel. and fax 25512; f. 1971; Gen. Supt Rev. JERIEL OTASUI.

Christian Fellowship Church: Church, Paradise, Munda, Western Province; f. 1960; over 5,000 mems in 24 villages; runs 12 primary schools in Western Province.

Seventh-day Adventist Mission: POB 63, Honiara; tel. 21191; over 9,000 mems on Guadalcanal and over 6,800 on Malaita (Oct. 2000); Pres. of Western Pacific Region NEIL WATTS; Sec. Pastor J. PIUKI TASA.

South Seas Evangelical Church: POB 16, Honiara; tel. 22388; fax 20302; Pres. ERIC TAKILA; Gen. Sec. CHARLES J. RAFEASI.

United Church in Solomon Islands: POB 82, Munda, Western Province; tel. 61125; fax 61143; e-mail ucsihq@solomon.com.sb; a Methodist church; Bishop of Solomon Islands Region Rev. PHILEMON RITI; Gen. Sec. GINA TEBULU.

BAHÁ'Í FAITH

National Spiritual Assembly: POB 245, Honiara; tel. 22475; fax 25368; e-mail bahainsa@welkam.solomon.com.sb.

ISLAM

Solomon Islands Muslim League: POB 219, Honiara; tel. 21773; fax 24243; Gen. Sec. Dr MUSTAPHA RAMO; 66 mems.

The Press

Agrikalsa Nius (Agriculture News): POB G13, Honiara; tel. 21211; fax 21955; f. 1986; monthly; Editor ALFRED MAESULIA; circ. 1,000.

Citizens' Press: Honiara; monthly.

Link: Solomon Islands Development Trust, POB 147, Honiara; tel. 21130; fax 21131; pidgin and English; 3 or 4 a year.

Solomon Nius: POB 718, Honiara; tel. 22031; fax 26401; monthly; Dept of Information publication; Editor-in-Chief THOMAS KIVO; monthly; circ. 2,000.

Solomon Star: POB 255, Honiara; tel. 22913; fax 21572; e-mail solstar@solomon.com.sb; internet www.solomonstarnews.com; f. 1982; daily; English; Dir JOHN W. LAMANI; Editor PETER LOMAS (acting); circ. 4,000.

Solomon Times: POB 212, Honiara; tel. 39197; fax 39197; internet www.solomontimes.com; weekly; Chief Editor and Man. Dir EDWARD KINGMELE.

Solomon Voice: POB 1235, Honiara; tel. 20116; fax 20090; f. 1992; weekly; circ. 10,000; Editor CAROL COLVILLE.

Broadcasting and Communications

TELECOMMUNICATIONS

Telekom (Solomon Telekom Company Ltd): POB 148, Honiara; tel. 21576; fax 23110; e-mail sales@telekom.com.sb; internet www.solomon.com.sb; 64.74% owned by Solomon Islands National Provident Fund, 32.58% by Cable and Wireless plc, 2.68% by Investment Corpn of Solomon Islands; operates national and

SOLOMON ISLANDS

international telecommunications links; Chair. JOHN BEVERLEY; Chief Exec. MARTYN ROBINSON.

BROADCASTING

Radio

Solomon Islands Broadcasting Corporation: POB 654, Honiara; tel. 20051; fax 23159; e-mail sibcnews@solomon.com.sb; internet www.sibconline.com.sb; f. 1976; daily transmissions in English and Pidgin; broadcasts total 112 hours per week; Chair. FRANK PULE; Broadcast Operations Man. DAVID PALAPU; Gen. Man. DYKES ANGIKI; Editor WALTER NALANGU.

Finance

The financial system is regulated and monitored by the Central Bank of Solomon Islands. There are three commercial banks and a development bank. Financial statutory corporations include the Home Finance Corpn (which took over from the Housing Authority in 1990), the Investment Corporation of Solomon Islands (the state holding company) and the National Provident Fund. At the end of 1996 there were 142 credit unions, with some 17,000 members and total assets estimated at SI $18m.

BANKING

(cap. = capital; res = reserves; dep. = deposits; brs = branches; amounts in Solomon Islands dollars)

Central Bank

Central Bank of Solomon Islands: POB 634, Honiara; tel. 21791; fax 23513; e-mail cbsi-it@welkam.solomon.com.sb; internet www.cbsi.com.sb; f. 1983; sole bank of issue; cap. 2.6m., res 13.7m., dep. 431.3m. (Dec. 2004); Gov. RICK HOUWENIPWELA; Deputy Gov. DENTON RARAWA.

Development Bank

Development Bank of Solomon Islands: POB 911, Honiara; tel. 21595; fax 23715; e-mail dbsi@welkam.solomon.com.sb; f. 1978; declared insolvent in Sept. 2004; remained under the administration of the Central Bank of Solomon Islands in 2006; Chair. JOHN MICHAEL ASIPARA; Man. Dir LUKE LAYMAN ETA; 4 brs; 5 sub-brs.

Commercial Banks

Australia and New Zealand Banking Group Ltd (Australia): Mendana Ave, POB 10, Honiara; tel. 21835; fax 22957; Gen. Man. TAIT JENKIN.

Bank South Pacific Ltd (Papua New Guinea): tel. 21874; e-mail mcorcoran@bsp.com.sb; internet www.bsp.com.sb; fmrly National Bank of Solomon Islands Ltd; became br. of Bank of South Pacific Ltd following acquisition in 2007; Gen. Man. MARK CORCORAN.

Westpac Banking Corporation (Australia): 721 Mendana Ave, POB 466, Honiara; tel. 21222; fax 23419; e-mail gtaviani@westpac.com.au; Man. GIAN TAVIANI.

INSURANCE

About 10 major British insurance companies maintain agencies in Solomon Islands. In mid-1995 the Government announced a joint venture with an Australian insurance company to establish the Solomon Islands Insurance Company.

Trade and Industry

GOVERNMENT AGENCY

Investment Corporation of Solomon Islands: POB 570, Honiara; tel. 22511; fax 21263; holding company through which the Government retains equity stakes in a number of corporations; Chair. MATTHEW WALE.

DEVELOPMENT ORGANIZATION

Solomon Islands Development Trust (SIDT): POB 147, Honiara; tel. 21130; fax 21331; e-mail sidt@welkam.solomon.com.sb; f. 1982; development org.; Chief Officer ABRAHAM BALANISIA.

CHAMBER OF COMMERCE

Solomon Islands Chamber of Commerce and Industry: POB 650, Honiara; tel. 39542; fax 39544; e-mail chamberc@solomon.com.sb; internet www.solomonchamber.com; 69 member cos (July 2004); Chair. IVAN DYER; Gen. Sec. SALLY ZIKU.

INDUSTRIAL AND TRADE ASSOCIATIONS

Association of Mining and Exploration Companies: c/o POB G24, Honiara; f. 1988; Pres. NELSON GREG YOUNG.

Commodities Export Marketing Authority: POB 54, Honiara; tel. 22528; fax 21262; e-mail cema@solomon.com.sb; regulator of agricultural commodities such as coconut, cocoa, coffee, palm oil, spices and ngalinut products; agencies at Honiara, Noro and Yandina; Chair. MARTIN SOPAGE; Gen. Man. PITAKIA MOSES PELOMO.

Livestock Development Authority: POB 525, Honiara; tel. 29649; fax 22214; f. 1977; privatized 1996; Man. Dir WARREN TUCKER.

Solomon Islands Business Enterprise Centre: POB 972, Honiara; tel. 26651; fax 26650; e-mail simbec@solomon.com.sb.

Solomon Islands Forest Industries Association: POB 1617, Honiara; tel. 26026; fax 20267; Chair. and Sec. KAIPUA TOHI.

EMPLOYERS' ORGANIZATIONS

Chinese Association: POB 1209, Honiara; tel. 22351; fax 23480; assen of business people from the ethnic Chinese community.

Federation of Solomon Islands Business: POB 320, Honiara; tel. 22902; fax 21477.

UTILITIES

Electricity

Solomon Islands Electricity Authority (SIEA): POB 6, Honiara; tel. 39442; fax 39472; e-mail mike@siea.com.sb; internet www.siea.com.sb; f. 1961; autonomous, govt-owned entity responsible for generation, transmission, distribution and sale of electrical energy; Chair. Hon. FRANCIS ZAMA; CEO MICHAEL NATION.

Water

Solomon Islands Water Authority (SIWA): POB 1407; Honiara; tel. 23985; fax 20723; f. 1994; Gen. Man. DONALD MAKINI.

CO-OPERATIVE SOCIETIES

Central Co-operative Association (CCA): Honiara.

Salu Fishing Cooperative Association: POB 1041, Honiara; tel. 26550.

Solomon Islands Consumers Co-operative Society Ltd: Honiara; tel. 21798; fax 23640.

Solomon Islands Farmers and Producers Cooperative Association Ltd: Honiara; tel. 30908.

Western General Co-operative Association (WGCA): Gizo, Western Province.

TRADE UNIONS

There are 14 registered trade unions in Solomon Islands.

Solomon Islands Council of Trade Unions (SICTU): National Centre for Trade Unions, POB 271, Honiara; tel. 22566; fax 23171; f. 1986; Pres. DAVID P. TUHANUKU; Sec. BENEDICT ESIBAEA; the principal affiliated unions are:

Media Association of Solomon Islands (MASI): POB 654, Honiara; tel. 20051; fax 23300; e-mail sibcnews@welkam.solomon.com.sb; Pres. ROBERT IROGA.

Solomon Islands Medical Association: Honiara.

Solomon Islands National Teachers' Association (SINTA): POB 967, Honiara; f. 1985; Pres. K. SANGA; Gen. Sec. BENEDICT ESIBAEA.

Solomon Islands National Union of Workers (SINUW): POB 14, Honiara; tel. 22629; Pres. DAVID P. TUHANUKU; Gen. Sec. TONY KAGOVAI.

Solomon Islands Post and Telecommunications Union: Honiara; tel. 21821; fax 20440; Gen. Man. SAMUEL SIVE.

Solomon Islands Public Employees' Union (SIPEU): POB 360, Honiara; tel. 21967; fax 23110; Pres. MARTIN KARANI; Sec.-Gen. CLEMENT WAIWORI.

Solomon Islands Seamen's Association: POB G32, Honiara; tel. 24942; fax 23798.

Transport

ROADS

There are about 1,300 km of roads maintained by the central and provincial governments. In addition, there are 800 km of privately maintained roads mainly for plantation use. Honiara has a main road running about 65 km each side of it along the north coast of Guadalcanal, and Malaita has a road 157 km long running north of Auki and around the northern end of the island to the Lau Lagoon,

SOLOMON ISLANDS

where canoe transport takes over; and one running south for 35 km to Masa. On Makira a road links Kira Kira and Kakoranga, a distance of 35 km.

SHIPPING

Regular shipping services (mainly cargo) exist between Solomon Islands and Australia, New Zealand, Hong Kong, Japan, Singapore, Taiwan and European ports. The four main ports are at Honiara, Yandina, Noro and Gizo. A new wharf, constructed with funding from the European Union, was opened in Gizo in 2004. The construction of seven further wharves, with similar funding, was completed in 2005.

Solomon Islands Ports Authority: POB 307, Honiara; tel. 22646; fax 23994; e-mail ports@solomon.com.sb; f. 1956; responsible for the ports of Honiara and Noro; Chair. NELSON BOSO; Gen. Man. N. B. KABUI.

Sullivans (SI) Ltd: POB 3, Honiara; tel. 21643; fax 23889; e-mail shipping@sullivans.com.sb; shipping agents, importers, wholesalers; CEO MARK WILLIAM CARROLL.

Tradco Shipping Ltd: POB 114, Honiara; tel. 22588; fax 23887; e-mail tradco@solomon.com.sb; f. 1984; shipping agents; Man. Dir GERALD STENZEL.

CIVIL AVIATION

Two airports are open to international traffic and a further 25 serve internal flights. Air Niugini (Papua New Guinea), Air Nauru (restyled as Our Airline in September 2006) and Qantas (Australia) fly to Honiara International Airport (located 13 km from the capital), at which a major renovation project financed by Japan was completed in December 2005. In late 2004 Air Pacific (Fiji) resumed a weekly service to Honiara some 20 years after it last operated a regular flight to the country.

Director of Civil Aviation: DEMETRIUS T. PIZIKI.

Solomon Airlines Limited: POB 23, Honiara; tel. 20031; fax 20232; e-mail gzoleveke@solair.com.sb; internet solomonairlines.com.au; f. 1968; govt-owned; international and domestic operator; scheduled services between Honiara and Port Moresby (Papua New Guinea), Nadi (Fiji), Brisbane (Australia) and Port Vila (Vanuatu); Chair. RICK HOUWENIPWELA; CEO RON SUMSUM.

Tourism

The development of the tourism sector is hindered by the relative inaccessibility of the islands and the inadequacy of tourist facilities. In 2005 tourism receipts (excl. passenger transport) amounted to US $2m. Tourist arrivals were reported to have risen from 11,482 in 2006 to 13,748 in 2007.

Solomon Islands Visitors Bureau: POB 321, Honiara; tel. 22442; fax 23986; e-mail visitors@solomon.com.sb; internet www.visitsolomons.com.sb; f. 1980; Gen. Man. MICHAEL TOKURU; Marketing Man. ANDREW NIHOPARA.

SOMALIA

Introductory Survey

Location, Climate, Language, Religion, Flag, Capital

The Somali Democratic Republic lies on the east coast of Africa, with Ethiopia to the north-west and Kenya to the west. There is a short frontier with Djibouti to the north-west. Somalia has a long coastline on the Indian Ocean and the Gulf of Aden, forming the 'Horn of Africa'. The climate is generally hot and dry, with an average annual temperature of 27°C (80°F). It is hotter in the interior and on the Gulf of Aden, but cooler on the Indian Ocean coast. Average annual rainfall is less than 430 mm (17 ins). The national language is Somali, but Arabic is also in official use. English and Italian are widely spoken. The state religion is Islam, and the majority of Somalis are Sunni Muslims. There is a small Christian community, mostly Roman Catholics. The national flag (proportions 2 by 3) is pale blue, with a large five-pointed white star in the centre. The capital is Mogadishu.

Recent History

Somalia was formed by a merger of two former colonial territories: British Somaliland, in the north, and its larger and more populous neighbour, Italian Somaliland. The United Kingdom established a protectorate in British Somaliland in 1886. Italian Somaliland originated in 1889, when Italy concluded agreements with two local rulers, who placed their territories under Italian protection. Italy's occupation of the region was subsequently extended along the coast and inland, and Italian control was completed in 1927. Italian forces in Somaliland and Eritrea invaded and occupied neighbouring Abyssinia (Ethiopia) in 1935–36. During the Second World War British Somaliland was conquered temporarily by Italian troops, but in 1941 it was recaptured by a British counter-offensive, which also forced the Italians to withdraw from Eritrea, Italian Somaliland and Ethiopia. A British military administration was then established in British and Italian Somaliland.

Under the provisions of the post-war peace treaty of February 1947, Italy renounced all rights to Italian Somaliland. In December 1950, however, the pre-war colony became the UN Trust Territory of Somalia, with Italy returning as the administering power for a 10-year transitional period, prior to independence. The territory's first general election on the basis of universal adult suffrage was held in March 1959, when 83 of the 90 seats in the Legislative Assembly were won by the Somali Youth League (SYL), a pro-Western party led by the Prime Minister, Seyyid Abdullah Issa.

British Somaliland reverted to civilian rule in 1948. The British colonial authorities prepared the territory for self-government, and the first general election took place in March 1959. Fresh elections, for a new legislative council, were held in February 1960, with all parties in favour of early independence and the unification of all Somali territories. Representatives of British Somaliland and the Trust Territory of Somalia met in April and agreed on a merger of the two territories in an independent republic. British Somaliland was granted independence on 26 June, and the merger received unanimous approval by the legislature on the following day.

Accordingly, the union of former British and Italian Somaliland took effect on 1 July 1960, when the independent Somali Republic was proclaimed. Dr Aden Abdullah Osman, hitherto President of the legislature of the southern territory, was elected to be the first President of the new Republic, and the legislatures of the two Somali regions merged to create a single National Assembly. The two dominant parties in former British Somaliland joined with the SYL to form a tripartite coalition government. Dr Abd ar-Rashid Ali Shermarke of the SYL became Prime Minister. In June 1964 Shermarke resigned as Prime Minister and was replaced by Abd ar-Razak Hussein, who formed a cabinet exclusively from members of the SYL. In June 1967, however, Shermarke was elected by the National Assembly to replace President Osman. He appointed a new Cabinet, led by Mohamed Ibrahim Egal, the former Prime Minister of British Somaliland.

On 15 October 1969 President Shermarke was assassinated. Six days later the army seized control in a coup on the eve of a planned presidential election. Power was assumed by the armed forces Commander-in-Chief, Maj.-Gen. Mohamed Siad Barre. The 1960 Constitution was suspended, political parties were abolished and the National Assembly was dissolved. A new Government was formed by the Supreme Revolutionary Council (SRC), chaired by Siad Barre, which proclaimed the Somali Democratic Republic. In October 1970 Siad Barre declared Somalia a socialist state and began a revolutionary programme of national unification and social and economic reform. In July 1976 the SRC dissolved itself, and power was transferred to the newly formed Somali Revolutionary Socialist Party (SRSP), with Siad Barre as Secretary-General.

A new Constitution came into force in September 1979. Elections were held in December for a new legislature, the People's Assembly, which, in January 1980, elected Siad Barre as President of the Republic. Constitutional amendments, approved by the Assembly in November 1984, effectively transferred all powers of government to the President. Despite continuing internal unrest, at elections to the Assembly, in December, a single list of SRSP candidates was reportedly endorsed by 99.9% of voters.

A presidential election, at which Siad Barre was the sole candidate, took place in December 1986, confirming his presidency for a further seven-year term by 99.9% of a reported 4.9m. votes cast. Although Lt-Gen. Mohamed Ali Samater was appointed to the newly created post of Prime Minister in February 1987, the President continued to dominate Somalia's political life.

Meanwhile, in October 1981 the Somali Salvation Front formed the Democratic Front for the Salvation of Somalia (DFSS, later renamed the Somali Salvation Democratic Front—SSDF) with two other opposition groups. Together with another group founded in 1981, the Somali National Movement (SNM), and with substantial Ethiopian military support, DFSS guerrillas invaded the central border area of Somalia in July 1982. The invasion was contained by the Somali national forces but, despite US and Italian military aid, they failed to expel the rebel troops from the country. Following a meeting between Siad Barre and Lt-Col Mengistu, the Ethiopian leader, in January 1986, Ethiopian military support for the insurgent groups was reduced, particularly in respect of the DFSS.

Anti-Government demonstrations in Mogadishu in July 1989, in protest at the arrest of several leading Muslim clerics, were violently suppressed by the armed forces, resulting in the deaths of more than 400 demonstrators. Two recently created opposition groups, the United Somali Congress (USC—composed of Hawiye clan intellectuals) and the National United Front of Somalia (allegedly dominated by disaffected army officers), were thought to have orchestrated the demonstrations. In August there were reports of fighting between government troops and members of the Ogadeni clan in southern Somalia, and Western sources claimed that the only areas of the country that remained under government control were Mogadishu, parts of Hargeysa and Berbera.

Meanwhile, the USC gained support in the south, where its forces were fighting alongside those of the Somali Patriotic Movement (SPM). In the north the emergence of the Somali Democratic Alliance (SDA), led by Mohamed Farah Abdullah, intensified the challenge to Siad Barre's authority. The President responded to these pressures by dismissing the Government in January 1990 and offering posts (which were refused) in a successor administration to prominent opposition leaders. A new Government, headed by Samater, took office in February.

In July 1990 the Council of Ministers endorsed the proposals of August 1989 for the democratization of Somalia's political system. It was decided that, following a review by the People's Assembly, a new constitution would be submitted to a national referendum in October, and that multi-party legislative and local government elections would be held in February 1991. In August 1990 the USC, the SNM and the SPM agreed to co-ordinate their separate military campaigns to overthrow Siad Barre. In October the Government announced the immediate introduction of the new Constitution and a new electoral code. Siad Barre relinquished the post of Secretary-General of the SRSP, in accordance with the Constitution, which stipulated that the President should hold no responsibilities other than those of the presidency. Despite the apparent readiness of the new Government to hasten the process of political reform, the principal insurgent groups showed no signs of relaxing their military campaigns, and in November SPM forces seized control of Kismayu, in southern Somalia. On 25 December legislation was introduced to permit the establishment of political parties opposed to the Government.

On 1 January 1991 the USC announced that it had captured most areas of Mogadishu and that it had besieged the home of Siad Barre. On 27 January Siad Barre was reported to have fled the capital with those forces remaining loyal to him, and the USC took power. It immediately invited all former opposition groups to participate in a national conference to discuss the democratization of Somalia. On 29 January the USC appointed Ali Mahdi Mohamed (a government minister in the 1960s) as President, in a temporary capacity, and he, in turn, invited Umar Arteh Ghalib (a former foreign affairs minister) to form a government that would prepare the country for democracy. The provisional Government was approved by the President on 2 February.

By mid-March 1991, however, Somalia was close to anarchy. Opposition movements rejected the USC's invitation to take part in a national conference, and the SNM was reported to have formed an 11-member administration and a legislature to govern the former territory of British Somaliland. In May the SNM announced its official support for the secession of that territory, and later that month the SNM Central Committee elected Abd ar-Rahman Ahmed Ali 'Tur' as President of the self-proclaimed 'Republic of Somaliland'. In June the Committee approved a 17-member government to administer the territory for a period of two years, after which free elections were to be held.

The SNM declined an invitation issued by the USC to participate in a conference of national reconciliation in June 1991, stating that it did not concern 'Somaliland'. The conference, convened in Djibouti, was attended by representatives of the USC, the Somali Democratic Movement (SDM), the SPM and the DFSS, and mandated delegates from the four organizations to travel to 'Somaliland' to persuade the SNM to abandon its declaration of independence. The SNM insisted, however, that the secession of 'Somaliland' from Somalia was irreversible. At a second reconciliation conference in July the four groups that had met in June were joined by the United Somali Front (USF) and the SDA. The leaders of the six groups signed a manifesto, which, *inter alia*, committed them to defeat the forces of Siad Barre (which had regrouped as the Somali National Front—SNF), to readopt the 1960 Constitution, which Barre had suspended in 1969, and to implement a general cease-fire. The manifesto also confirmed Ali Mahdi in his position as Somalia's President for a period of two years pending free elections. Ali Mahdi was sworn in as President on 18 August 1991, and in September he reappointed Ghalib as Prime Minister; in October the latter announced the formation of a newly expanded Government, comprising 72 ministers and deputy ministers, in order to ensure equal representation for the six participating groups.

Meanwhile, in June 1991 a major rift had developed within the USC, and supporters of President Ali Mahdi clashed with those of the USC's military commander, Gen. Mohamed Farah Aidid, in Mogadishu. Aidid objected to Ali Mahdi's assumption of the presidency, since he had commanded the military campaign to overthrow Siad Barre. In July Aidid was elected Chairman of the USC. In October Aidid rejected the legitimacy of the Government appointed earlier that month, and in November his faction launched a major offensive on the President's positions in the capital. The fighting intensified, and in December Ali Mahdi appealed to the UN to send a peace-keeping force to intervene in the conflict. The UN responded by sending a special envoy to Mogadishu in January 1992. However, the envoy's attempts met with failure, and the mission was followed by an escalation in violence. In mid-January Aidid appointed his own, 21-member administration. By the end of March it was estimated that 14,000 people (mostly civilians) had been killed and 27,000 wounded in the hostilities in Mogadishu.

In January 1992 the UN imposed an embargo on the sale of armaments to Somalia. In the following month the UN, the Organization of African Unity (OAU, now the African Union—AU, see p. 164), the League of Arab States (the Arab League, see p. 332) and the Organization of the Islamic Conference (OIC, see p. 369) issued a joint appeal for a cease-fire, stating that it was a prerequisite for the granting of humanitarian aid to Somalia. Representatives from the rival factions in Mogadishu subsequently agreed to the terms of a cease-fire accord devised by the international organizations. In March, in discussions with a joint mission of the UN, the OAU, the OIC and the Arab League in Mogadishu, Aidid agreed to the monitoring of the cease-fire by a foreign observer mission. In April the UN Security Council approved the establishment of a 'UN Operation in Somalia' (UNOSOM), to comprise a 50-strong observer mission to monitor the cease-fire, while it also agreed, in principle, to dispatch a peace-keeping force to protect UN personnel and supplies at Mogadishu's port, and to escort food supplies to distribution points. However, the Security Council needed to obtain consent for the peace-keeping force from both parties involved in the conflict, and Aidid was opposed to the deployment of foreign military personnel in Somalia.

In April 1992 the SNF advanced on Mogadishu, with Siad Barre apparently intent on recapturing the capital. Forces of the SNF came to within 40 km of the capital, but Gen. Aidid's militias decisively repelled them, pursuing them to the south of the country. At the end of April the USC captured the town of Garba Harre, in the south-west, which had served as Siad Barre's base since his overthrow. Siad Barre fled, with some 200 supporters, to Kenya. (Siad Barre was refused political asylum in Kenya, and in May he moved to Nigeria, where he died in January 1995.) In May Aidid's forces and those of the SPM, the SDM and the Southern Somali National Movement (SSNM), with which he had formed a military alliance known as the Somali Liberation Army (SLA), captured Kismayu, which had been held by the SNF. By June the SLA was in control of the majority of central and southern Somalia, making Aidid the most powerful of the country's warlords. In late June the UN secured agreement from the principal factions in Mogadishu for the deployment of the 50-strong observer mission envisaged in the March cease-fire accord. In August Aidid agreed to the deployment of 500 UN troops entrusted with escorting food aid from Mogadishu's port and airport to distribution points.

Also in August 1992 the coalition of Gen. Aidid's faction of the USC with the SPM, the SDM and the SSNM was consolidated with the formation of the Somali National Alliance (SNA), of which Aidid was the leader. Meanwhile, Ali Mahdi strengthened ties with other armed groups hostile to Aidid, notably the SSDF and a faction of the SPM, and forged links with Gen. Mohamed Siad Hersi 'Morgan' (who had led the SNF since the departure of his father-in-law, Siad Barre).

In September 1992 'Somaliland' stated its categorical opposition to the deployment of UN troops within its borders. By early November UNOSOM's 500 armed troops still had not been deployed. However, later in the month UNOSOM secured Mogadishu's airport with the agreement of the clan controlling it. The USA subsequently offered to lead a military operation in the country, with a US contingent of up to 30,000 men. The proposed US operation was sanctioned by the Security Council in early December. Shortly afterwards an advance contingent of 1,800 US marines landed on the beaches of Mogadishu and took control of the port and airport. Aidid and Ali Mahdi had instructed their supporters that the US forces were amicable, and consequently they encountered little resistance. The arrival of the foreign force, however, provoked fierce fighting in Kismayu, Baidoa and the north-east, with rival factions attempting to gain territory before the expected imposition of a cease-fire. The US members of the Unified Task Force (UNITAF) were reinforced subsequently by troops from 21 other countries.

In January 1993 14 of Somalia's political organizations attended peace negotiations in Addis Ababa, Ethiopia, held under the auspices of the UN. The talks resulted in agreements on an immediate cease-fire, disarmament under UN supervision and the holding of a conference of national reconciliation in March. Despite the cease-fire agreement, hostilities were resumed in various parts of the country almost immediately. In mid-March the national reconciliation conference opened in Addis Ababa and later that month an accord providing for the establishment of a Transitional National Council as the supreme authority in Somalia, with a mandate to hold elections within two years was agreed upon. The Council was to comprise 74 members: one from each of the 15 organizations represented at the conference, three from each of the 18 proposed administrative regions (inclusive of 'Somaliland') and five from Mogadishu.

Agreement on the future government of Somalia was reached hours after the UN Security Council approved the establishment of UNOSOM II, which was to take over responsibility for maintaining security from UNITAF by 1 May 1993. UNOSOM II was to be the UN's largest ever peace-keeping operation, comprising 28,000 military personnel and 2,800 civilian staff, and its first where peace-enforcement without consent from parties within the country was authorized. UNOSOM II was, in addition, to be responsible for overseeing the rehabilitation of the country and the repatriation of Somali refugees. By April Gen. 'Morgan' appeared to be in control of Kismayu, with the SNA accusing UNITAF of supporting the SNF by failing to oppose its advances. In May the USA transferred responsibility for international efforts in Somalia to UNOSOM II whose forces embarked on a series of armed initiatives, including air strikes, against suspected strategic positions of the SNA. Despite the increased scale of UNOSOM operations, Aidid avoided injury or capture during June, prompting the Security Council to issue a formal warrant for his arrest. The violent deaths of three Italian UNOSOM soldiers in July provoked Italian media claims that the military emphasis of the mission, promoted by the USA in pursuit of Aidid, was threatening the security of UN personnel and jeopardizing diplomatic initiatives undertaken by the Italian Government. The situation was exacerbated by a US helicopter attack on a suspected pro-Aidid command centre, which resulted in the deaths of 50–100 Somalis, and the murder, in retaliation, of four foreign journalists by enraged Somali crowds.

Uncompromising media coverage of the aftermath of the deaths of three US soldiers in September 1993, and a violent exchange in the capital in October (which resulted in the deaths of some 300 Somalis, 18 US servicemen and the capture, by local militiamen, of a US helicopter pilot and a Nigerian soldier), prompted widespread public outrage in the USA. The US President, Bill Clinton, subsequently announced that all US troops were to be withdrawn by the end of March 1994, regardless of the outcome of attempts to negotiate a political settlement to the conflict by that date. Clinton's decision, announced in October, to withdraw the US Ranger élite forces (which had actively sought to apprehend Aidid) prompted speculation that the release of the US pilot and the Nigerian soldier, secured in mid-October following lengthy discussions between representatives of the US Government and Aidid, had been achieved as part of an undisclosed bilateral agreement. Despite Aidid's declaration of a unilateral cease-fire prior to the talks, and subsequent indications of his willingness to enter into negotiations with the USA (in preference to the UN), fighting between pro-Aidid and pro-Mahdi factions escalated. In December Aidid and Ali Mahdi (who in November reportedly assumed the leadership of the Somali Salvation Alliance—SSA, a coalition of 12 factions opposed to Aidid) attended negotiations in Addis Ababa, but discussions disintegrated with little progress.

In February 1994, in the context of the imminent withdrawal of UNOSOM contingents from the USA and several other Western nations, the UN Security Council revised UNOSOM's mandate, reducing the troop strength of the mission to a maximum of 22,000. In March, following protracted negotiations, initiated by the UN, an agreement on the restoration of peace was signed by Aidid and Ali Mahdi (on behalf of the SSA) in Nairobi, Kenya, committing both sides to a cease-fire, disarmament and the organization of a conference of national reconciliation in May to elect a president, vice-presidents and a prime minister. Electoral procedures and a future legislative structure were to be decided at a meeting of all signatories to the 1993 Addis Ababa agreement and the SNM, to be convened in April. By mid-1994, however, no such meeting had taken place, with accusations of failure to adhere to the terms of the Nairobi agreement proceeding from both Aidid and the SSA.

In June 1994 the UN Security Council agreed to renew UNOSOM's mandate by four months; in November it extended the mandate to a final date of 31 March 1995. As the deadline for UNOSOM's departure approached, the competition for control of installations currently held by the UN, in particular the port and airport, became the focus of factional hostility. In November 1994 UN forces began to withdraw from positions outside Mogadishu in the first stages of UNOSOM's departure. In December Harti and Marehan clansmen fought for control of Kismayu port in the wake of the UN's withdrawal from that town. 'Operation United Shield', to ensure the safe evacuation of the UN troops and civilian personnel, as well as most of the equipment brought in under UNOSOM, was organized and led by the USA. The USA stationed several thousand marines in warships off the Somali coast in December, and in early 1995 they were joined by a multinational force of naval and air force units in order to protect departing UN employees (by early 1995 some 136 members of UNOSOM had been killed since the beginning of the operation).

In late February 1995 1,800 US and 400 Italian marines landed on Mogadishu's beaches, and command of the remaining 2,400 UN troops and of the whole operation was passed from the UN to the US commander. The marines secured the port and airport, and evacuated the remaining UN soldiers. The departure of the last UN personnel on 2 March (almost one month ahead of schedule) was closely followed by that of the US and Italian marines themselves. Somali looters overran the airport, but armoured cars from Aidid's faction, reportedly accompanied by UN-trained police officers, took control of the area. Ali Mahdi's Abgal clansmen gained control of the eastern section of the airport, and skirmishes were reported between the two sides. Aidid and Ali Mahdi subsequently agreed on the reopening of the port and set out detailed terms for the 'technical peace committee' that was to administer the port and airport; however, the terms of the agreement were promptly violated by both sides, and fighting for control of the crucial sites resumed.

Significant divisions within the SNA became more apparent in June 1995, following an attempt by disaffected members to replace Aidid with his former aide, Osman Hassan Ali 'Ato', as Chairman of the party. SNA members loyal to Aidid immediately rejected the legitimacy of the actions of the Ali 'Ato' faction and announced the expulsion of the faction from the SNA. In mid-June a conference of reconciliation, convened in southern Mogadishu by representatives of 15 pro-Aidid factions, elected Aidid President of the Republic of Somalia for a three-year term. Five Vice-Presidents, representing the interests of distinct clans, were also elected, and the composition of a comprehensive cabinet was subsequently announced. However, Aidid's presidency and mandate to govern were immediately rejected in a joint statement issued by Ali Mahdi and Ali 'Ato'. In September Aidid's forces seized Baidoa.

Fighting between Gen. Aidid's supporters and those loyal to Ali 'Ato' intensified in early 1996. In July pro-Aidid factions clashed with supporters of Ali Mahdi in Mogadishu, resulting in some 90 fatalities. Aidid was wounded during the skirmishes, and on 1 August he died as a result of his injuries. Despite initial hopes that Aidid's death might result in a cessation of hostilities and the resumption of peace negotiations, on 4 August one of his sons, Hussein Mohamed Aidid (a former US marine and hitherto Aidid's chief of security), was appointed interim President by the SNA leadership council. Hussein Aidid (who was subsequently elected Chairman of the SNA) vowed to continue his father's struggle, and factional fighting quickly resumed.

In October 1996, during negotiations in Nairobi, Ali 'Ato', Hussein Aidid and Ali Mahdi agreed to a series of measures, including the cessation of hostilities; however, fighting resumed in late October and intensified in the following months. In December representatives of some 26 Somali factions (notably excluding the SNA) held protracted talks in Sodere, Ethiopia, under the auspices of the Ethiopian Government and the Intergovernmental Authority on Development (IGAD). The conference culminated in January 1997 in the formation of a 41-member National Salvation Council (NSC), with an 11-member executive committee and a five-member joint chairmanship committee, to act as an interim government charged with drafting a transitional charter and holding a national reconciliation conference. Aidid condemned the establishment of the NSC and accused the Ethiopian authorities of interfering in Somali affairs.

International mediation efforts continued, and in March 1997 representatives of Somali factions participated in talks in Cairo, Egypt, under the auspices of the Egyptian Government and the Arab League. In May Ali 'Ato' and Hussein Aidid were reported to have reaffirmed their commitment to the Nairobi agreement, during a meeting held in San'a, Yemen. Later in the month Aidid and Ali Mahdi signed a reconciliation agreement in Cairo. In December, moreover, at the culmination of negotiations that began in November, 26 Somali faction leaders (including Aidid and Ali Mahdi) signed an accord in Cairo, establishing an end to all hostilities and providing for the eventual formation of a transitional government, charged with holding a general election within three years. A condition of the accord was that a national reconciliation conference be held in Baidoa in February 1998 in order to elect a 13-member presidential council (three representatives from each of Somalia's four principal clans and one from a minority group), a prime minister and a 189-seat legislature. The conference was later postponed on two occasions, not least because troops loyal to Aidid remained stationed in Baidoa.

In September 1999 the UN Secretary-General, Kofi Annan, announced that the UN Security Council was to consider a solution to the Somalia problem, following a proposal made by the Somali Peace Alliance (under the chairmanship of 'Puntland' Leader Abdullahi Yussuf) that central authority in Somalia be gradually rebuilt, beginning with regionally based administrations. This proposal was, however, immediately rejected by the Mogadishu faction leaders and President Egal of 'Somaliland'. In October IGAD delegates met in Addis Ababa to discuss President Ismael Omar Gelleh of Djibouti's proposed peace plan for Somalia. In February 2000 IGAD member states endorsed Gelleh's plan, which envisaged the staging of a Somali national reconciliation conference in Djibouti in late April and early May, to be attended by up to 1,500 delegates from various cross-sections of Somali society. Under the plan they would elect members to a new national legislature to be based in Mogadishu, which would, in turn, elect a President. The President would be responsible for choosing a Prime Minister, subject to the approval of the legislature, who would lead a transitional government for a period of no longer than two years, during which time a national constitution would be drafted and a date for elections would be selected. However, although the peace plan was unanimously approved by OAU foreign ministers in March, and also won the approval of the UN and the USA, Egal announced that 'Somaliland' would refuse any attempts to unite it with Somalia.

The Somali national reconciliation conference opened in Arta, Djibouti, on 2 May 2000, with some 400 delegates, representing various Somali clans and political and armed groups, in attendance. By mid-June the number of delegates had risen to around 900, although notably only one of the principal Somali faction leaders, Ali Mahdi, was present. In early July the conference produced a draft national charter, which envisaged the Somali Republic adopting a federal system of government, after a three-year interim period, comprising 18 regional administrations. Furthermore, it provided for the creation of the Somali Transitional National Assembly (TNA), which would consist of 225 members, of whom 25 would be women. In mid-July the Charter was approved by 638 votes to four and the process of electing members to the TNA began. The Charter, which was to serve as the Somali constitution for the three-year interim period, guaranteed freedom of expression and association for all Somali citizens, as well as free access to health and education services. The Charter also distinctly separated the executive, legislative and judiciary and guaranteed the independence of the latter. Each of the four major Somali clans (Dir, Hawiye, Darod and Rahanwin) was allocated 44 parliamentary seats, and an alliance of small clans was to receive 24 seats; the remaining 25 seats were reserved for women from the four major clans and the alliance of small clans, each of which would receive five seats. However, disagreements between clans and sub-clans over the distribution of seats ensued, and in early August President Gelleh intervened, suggesting the appointment of a further 20 members to the assembly, thus increasing the total number to 245. Gelleh's proposal was accepted, and on 13 August the TNA held its inaugural session in Arta. On 26 August it was announced that Abdulkasim Salad Hasan, a member of the Hawiye clan, who had held several ministerial positions in the Siad Barre administration, had been elected President of Somalia by the members of the TNA. Hasan was sworn in as President on the following day at a ceremony in Arta.

On 30 August 2000 President Hasan returned to Mogadishu, where he was greeted by tens of thousands of Somalis. At the same time several Mogadishu faction leaders opposed to the outcome of the Djibouti conference, including Hussein Aidid, Ali 'Ato' and Hussein Haji Bod, met in San'a for talks with Yemeni President Ali Abdullah Saleh, who attempted to persuade them to lend their support to Hasan's administration. However, on his return to Somalia, Aidid implored the international community not to recognise the legitimacy of Hasan's appointment. On 8 October President Hasan appointed Ali Khalif Galaydh, a former Minister of Industry in the Siad Barre regime, to the post of Prime Minister; later that month Galaydh announced a 32-member Cabinet.

Relations between Somalia and Ethiopia deteriorated in January 2001, after Galaydh accused Ethiopia of providing arms to factions opposed to the Transitional National Government (TNG). Relations between the two countries were further strained in March, when the Ethiopian authorities allowed several Somali faction leaders to convene in Addis Ababa for a series of meetings, which resulted in the creation of the Somali Reconciliation and Restoration Council (SRRC), headed by Hussein Aidid.

In early May 2001 Galaydh appointed 25 members to a Peace and Reconciliation Committee (PRC), chaired by former Prime Minister Abd ar-Razak Hussein, which was charged with obtaining recommendations from a cross-section of Somali factions for ways of accelerating the reconciliation process, defining the most suitable means of establishing a federal system in the country and addressing property and land issues. In mid-July violent clashes were again reported to have taken place in Mogadishu between followers of Hussein Aidid and Ali 'Ato' and troops loyal to the TNG, resulting in numerous fatalities. In late July the new administration suffered a further major set-back after Abd ar-Razak Hussein resigned as Chairman of the PRC, claiming that Galaydh had demonstrated a lack of co-operation with the committee and had failed actively to support its work. Abdiqadir Muhammad Adan Zope was subsequently appointed acting Chairman of the PRC.

In mid-October 2001 a group of dissatisfied TNA members proposed a motion of 'no confidence' in the TNG, citing the administration's failure to promote the reconciliation process and its lack of progress regarding the constitution of regional administrations. Later that month 141 of the 174 TNA members participating in the vote approved the motion to dismiss the Galaydh administration.

In mid-November 2001 President Hasan appointed Col Hassan Abshir Farah, hitherto Minister of Water and Mineral Resources, as Prime Minister. Farah announced that his first priority was to implement a programme of national reconciliation, and thus the appointment of a new cabinet was delayed until after the conclusion of further peace talks between the SRRC and members of the TNA, which were scheduled to take place in Nairobi later that month. Although the talks were further postponed until mid-December, they were attended by senior members of the SNA (again with the notable exception of Hussein Aidid) and representatives of several other Mogadishu faction leaders. On 24 December, in the Kenyan town of Nakura, Farah, on behalf of the TNA, and Mowlid Ma'aneh Mohamed, the Secretary-General of the SRRC, signed a peace agreement, which provided for the formation of an 'all-inclusive government' to ensure equitable power-sharing among all Somali clans and the establishment of a Nairobi-based secretariat to oversee the implementation of the Somali peace process and to solicit funds for it.

In mid-February 2002 Farah formed a new 31-member Cabinet, which notably included Dr Hussein Mohamed Usman Jimbir, a former senior member of the SRRC, as Minister of Education. However, several members of factions that had signed the Nakura peace agreement in December 2001 were reported to have requested to be excluded from the new Government until a parliamentary committee, established to investigate a proposed increase in the number of parliamentary seats, had released its recommendations. The reconciliation process in Somalia was further endangered in early April 2002, when the Rahanwin Resistance Army (RRA) announced that it had established a new autonomous region in south-western Somalia, based in Baidoa, to be known as the 'State of South-western Somalia'. The Chairman of the RRA, Mohamed Hasan Nur, was elected as 'President' of the new region for a four-year period.

In late June 2002 the TNG confirmed that it would attend an IGAD-sponsored reconciliation conference scheduled to be held in Kenya in July. The conference was subsequently postponed until September, and early that month the authorities in 'Somaliland' announced that they would not attend the talks. Following a further delay, the conference opened in the Kenyan town of Eldoret in mid-October in the presence of representatives of the Governments of Ethiopia, Kenya, Uganda, Sudan, Djibouti and Eritrea. Some 350 delegates from various Somali factions attended the opening sessions, including a delegation from the TNG led by Prime Minister Farah. The conference was to be conducted in three phases and in late October, following the conclusion of the first phase, the TNG and a number of Somali factions signed a temporary cease-fire and agreed to abide by the final outcome of the conference; to establish an all-inclusive federal system of government; to combat terrorism; and to enhance the safety of aid workers in the country. Further progress was slowed by continuing deadlock over the allocation of seats to the plenary session of the conference. However, by early December the TNG and Mogadishu-based faction leaders Hussein Aidid, Mohammed Qanyare Afrah, Yalahow and Ali 'Ato' signed a declaration committing themselves to ending violence in the Somali capital. In January 2003, however, Yalahow announced that he would no longer participate in the conference. Yalahow's departure followed the earlier withdrawal of Qanyare Afrah from the proceedings. In February the conference was moved to Nairobi, and, despite a number of cease-fire violations, in the following month the TNG and the remaining faction leaders provisionally agreed on the formation of an administration for Mogadishu and further measures to bring peace to the capital.

In early July 2003 delegates at the Nairobi conference reached a provisional agreement on the formation of an interim government. The arrangement provided for a transitional unicameral parliament, whose 351 members would be selected by political leaders, and which would remain in operation for four years. The nomination of members of parliament was to be made by the signatories of the December 2002 cease-fire declaration and politicians who were originally, and officially, invited to the conference. However, President Hasan rejected the agreement, which had been signed by Farah, stating that it would divide the country, and in August 2003 divisions between Hasan and Farah intensified. Later that month, just days before the expiry of the three-year mandate of the TNG, Hasan reportedly dismissed Farah and the Speaker of the TNA. Hasan insisted that the current governing institutions would remain in place, despite the expiry of their mandate, until a new President, government and parliament had been installed. Dr Abdi Guled Mohamed, the Minister of Air and Land Transport, was appointed premier, in an acting capacity.

In November 2003 the Somali National Salvation Council, a recently formed alliance of 12 factions, chaired by Yalahow, pledged to boycott any further talks in Nairobi. Despite the expiry of his mandate in August 2003, President Hasan appointed Mohamed Abdi Yusuf, hitherto Deputy Speaker of the TNA, as Prime Minister in early December. In the following month the TNA approved the appointment of a new 37-member TNG, which included three Deputy Prime Ministers. Also in January 2004 talks reconvened in Nairobi with the aim of restoring the faltering peace process. Following a period of intense negotiations, during which Yalahow and the leaders of the Juba Valley Alliance (JVA), the RRA and the SNF rejoined the discussions, later that month representatives from more than 20 factions in attendance agreed to establish a new transitional parliament, comprising 275 members (rather than the 351 previously agreed), who would serve a five-year term. Once formed, the parliament would appoint a President, who, in turn, would nominate a Prime Minister to form a government. It was envisaged that each of the four major Somali clans would select 61 members of the new legislature, while a coalition of smaller clans would be responsible for choosing the remaining 31 members. However, several faction leaders expressed concern at perceived favouritism towards certain groups on the part of the Kenyan and Djiboutian authorities overseeing the talks.

In mid-June 2004 an arbitration committee was formed in Nairobi to oversee the nomination of members to the new parliament. The deadline for nominations of 21 July was not observed by the Darod and Dir clans; however, by mid-August the majority of the new members of the Transitional Parliament (TP) had been nominated and inauguration ceremonies commenced in Nairobi. On 15 September Shariff Hassan Sheikh Adan, a Mogadishu-based business executive, was elected Speaker of the TP and later that month nominations were invited for the position of President. Following two rounds of voting by the 275 members of the TP on 10 October two presidential candidates remained: Col Abdullahi Yussuf Ahmed, the President of the autonomous region of 'Puntland' (see below), and Abdallah Ahmed Addow, a former Somali ambassador to the USA. At a third round of voting held later that day, Yussuf secured 189 of the 268 votes cast and was sworn in as President of Somalia at a ceremony in Nairobi on 14 October. In early November Yussuf appointed Ali Mohammed Ghedi, a member of the Hawiye clan and a former AU official, as Prime Minister.

On 7 December 2004 Ghedi unveiled a new 31-member Cabinet. Hussein Aidid was appointed Deputy Prime Minister and Minister of the Interior and Security, while Qanyare Afrah became Minister of National Security. However, the following day a number of ministers resigned from the Government, maintaining that the new administration was too large and did not fairly distribute power among the major clans, and on 12 December the TP, which remained based in Nairobi, overwhelmingly approved a motion of 'no confidence' in Ghedi, effectively dissolving the new Government. Two days later President Yussuf reappointed Ghedi as Prime Minister and in late December that decision was endorsed by 229 members of the TP. Ghedi was tasked with forming a government that more accurately represented the major clans and in early January 2005 Ghedi announced an amended Cabinet, which comprised some 90 ministers, assistant ministers and state ministers. Aidid and Qanyare Afrah retained the posts previously awarded to them, while Salim Aliow Ibrow was appointed Deputy Prime Minister and Minister of Finance, and Mahmud Abdullahi Jama Deputy Prime Minister and Minister of Information. Later in January 2005 the new Cabinet was approved by the TP.

Shortly after he had taken office, President Yussuf had appealed to the AU and the UN to approve the deployment of a peace-keeping force of up to 20,000 troops to assist with the relocation of the TP and the Government to Mogadishu and to disarm militias in the Somali capital. However, ongoing violence in the city caused plans to be stalled. In early January 2005 the AU stated its readiness 'in principle' to deploy a contingent of peace-keepers to Somalia, although no indication was given of the size of the force or the likely date of its arrival in the country. In mid-January Ghedi announced that the Government would begin the relocation to Mogadishu by the end of that month and envisaged that with the support of international peace-keepers the entire Government and Parliament would be settled in the capital by early May. Despite further concerns over the security situation in the capital, plans for the relocation of the Government and the Parliament proceeded, and in early February a delegation of 30 members of the TP, led by the Minister of Trade, Muse Sudi Yalahow, arrived in Mogadishu followed by a further 50 parliamentarians, led by Sheikh Adan, a few days later. It was subsequently announced, however, that members of the Cabinet would travel to various parts of Somalia to establish possible locations for the Government's new base and that ministers remained deeply divided on the most suitable course of action. As an AU mission arrived in Mogadishu in mid-February to assess the security situation, thousands of people staged protests against the proposed peace-keeping force and a bomb exploded in the capital killing two people and seriously injuring six others. In late February Yussuf and Ghedi arrived in Somalia to head a delegation, which would investigate potential bases for the new Government; notably, the President and the Prime Minister did not visit Mogadishu as part of their tour. The delegation returned to Kenya in early March and Ghedi's special adviser announced that other towns were being considered as a temporary base for the new Government until violence in the capital subsided.

In mid-March 2005 IGAD defence ministers agreed to deploy a 10,000-strong peace-keeping force, the IGAD Peace Support Mission to Somalia (IGASOM) in the country from 30 April, to be replaced at an unspecified later date by an AU force. Demonstrations were held days later in Mogadishu opposing the deployment of peace-keeping troops from neighbouring countries, and members of the TP were involved in a violent confrontation following a vote to reject the planned deployment. In an attempt to allay fears in Somalia, the IGAD Council of Ministers proposed a compromise solution, in which a reduced IGASOM force of 6,800 would initially be deployed, comprised solely of Sudanese and Ugandan troops. In late March the Somali Government announced that it would temporarily relocate to Baidoa and Jowhar, 90 km north of Mogadishu. However, heavy fighting in Baidoa later in March between supporters of Yussuf and militia opposed to the relocation of the Government outside of Mogadishu resulted in at least 14 fatalities, and in late April the 80 parliamentarians situated in Mogadishu rejected calls from the President and the UN-led Joint Co-ordination and Monitoring Committee to return to Nairobi, stating that a return to exile would jeopardize ongoing efforts to 'pacify' the capital.

At the end of April 2005 a bomb exploded in Mogadishu, killing 15 people and injuring at least 50 others, at a rally attended by Ghedi. In early May 100 members of the TP opposed to Yussuf's relocation plans, including Sheikh Adan, boycotted a parliamentary vote in Nairobi, where supporters of the President approved the planned relocation to Baidoa and Jowhar and the deployment of the proposed peace-keeping force. Days later Qanyare Afrah, Yalahow and Ali 'Ato' undertook to combine their militias and to withdraw militiamen and armoured vehicles from Mogadishu, and a partial disarmament of their forces took place at a ceremony in the capital. Also in April, the AU approved plans to send 1,700 peace-keeping troops to Somalia but stated that the force would only arrive when its security could be guaranteed. In mid-May 30 members of the TP accompanied Sheikh Adan upon his return to Mogadishu, while a spokesman for the President announced that Jama had been removed from office. In late May up to 19 people were reportedly killed during heavy fighting in Baidoa between militia affiliated to two opposing members of the TP. In mid-June Ghedi and the remaining ministers and members of parliament left Nairobi and arrived in Jowhar, despite the opposition of local militia. Fears of renewed conflict between the opposing factions were raised in early July as Yussuf announced plans to gather a group of militiamen in Jowhar and in August tensions escalated when the Mogadishu-based members of the TP accused Yussuf of planning a civil war with military assistance from Ethiopia. In September, speaking before the UN General Assembly, Yussuf urged the UN Security Council to lift the arms embargo, which he claimed had hindered the establishment of a national security force and had prevented the deployment of peace-keepers in Somalia. A convoy carrying Ghedi on a visit to Mogadishu was attacked with grenades and a land mine in early November. Three people were killed in the apparent assassination attempt, although Ghedi was uninjured in the attack. Later that month 11 people were killed during fighting in Mogadishu after the Union of Islamic Courts (UIC) of Mogadishu, which had established a court system in the capital based on *Shari'a* (Islamic) law, attempted to seize control of cinemas it had accused of encouraging immoral and criminal behaviour.

In early January 2006 Yussuf and Sheikh Adan signed an agreement for the TP to meet in Somalia within 30 days, following further talks held in San'a, and in late January members of the group led by Sheikh Adan signalled their willingness to support a process of reconciliation. Despite the absence of Ali 'Ato', Yalahow and several other prominent ministers opposed to Yussuf, 205 parliamentarians assembled in Baidoa on 26 February as the TP met for the first time since returning from Kenya. In late February a number of formerly opposed faction leaders, including Qanyare Afrah and Yalahow, formed a new political alliance—the Alliance for the Restoration of Peace and Counter-Terrorism (ARPCT)—which aimed to combat Islamist extremism in Somalia. Militia supported by the ARPCT were in conflict with forces loyal to the UIC in the south of Mogadishu and at least 33 people were killed before a cease-fire was negotiated by Somali elders. However, some 140 people were killed and thousands fled the capital in late March as fighting resumed, and attempts by elders to renegotiate a cease-fire between the two factions continued. Unrest continued in the capital during early May with more than 80 people reported to have been killed in clashes between the two sides.

In early June 2006 the UIC claimed to have seized control of Mogadishu. Later that month, at a meeting convened by the Arab League in Khartoum, Sudan, the Government signed an agreement of mutual recognition with the UIC in an attempt to avert a potential attack on Baidoa. Also in June four cabinet ministers, including Qanyare Afrah, were dismissed for refusing to end ongoing battles with Islamist extremists. Shortly after the agreement was signed the UIC underwent a reorganization and was renamed the Somali Supreme Islamic Courts Council (SSICC). The US-led Contact Group on Somalia urged the Somali Government to enter further discussions with the SSICC to avoid more widespread conflict. Talks were initially scheduled for mid-July, but the Government requested their postponement, accusing the SSICC of breaching cease-fire agreements. President Yussuf subsequently agreed to meet with SSICC leaders; however, they, in turn, refused to negotiate. In late July and early August some 40 ministers and assistant ministers resigned, citing their dissatisfaction with Prime Minister Ghedi's apparent unwillingness to negotiate with the SSICC. On 28 July the Minister of Constitutional and Federal Affairs, Abdallah Derow Isaq, was shot dead outside a mosque in Baidoa and two days later Prime Minister Ghedi narrowly defeated a vote of 'no confidence' in the TP. However, President Yussuf dissolved the Cabinet on 7 August and instructed Ghedi to form a new administration. In late August Ghedi nominated 31 Ministers, 31 Assistant Ministers and five State Ministers to form a new Government. Among the most notable appointments were Bare Adan Shire (hitherto Minister of Reconstruction and Resettlement) as Minister of Defence and Isma'il Muhammad Hurre 'Buba' as Minister of Foreign Affairs.

Tensions continued between the Government and the SSICC and during late August 2006 SSICC forces took control of several towns to the north of Mogadishu, and continued to demand the withdrawal of all Ethiopian troops stationed in Somalia, the presence of whom had repeatedly been denied by both the Somali and the Ethiopian Governments. Further peace talks took place in Khartoum on 4 September under the auspices of the Arab League and the following day IGAD convened a meeting in Nairobi at which regional leaders agreed to deploy an international peace force to Somalia, despite continued opposition to the proposal from the SSICC. IGAD also increased pressure on the UN to remove the arms embargo, which would allow President Yussuf to form a national security force; many observers feared that lifting the embargo would lead to a resurgence of fighting. In late September the remaining port outside SSICC control, at Kismayu, was seized by that organization; pro-government militia did not resist and withdrew peacefully. In November a UN arms report claimed that the mobilization of an IGAD peace-keeping mission to Somalia, as demanded by Ethiopian forces, would exacerbate existing tensions (see below) and would only be effective if the UN arms embargo was properly enforced.

Meanwhile, in mid-September 2006 President Yussuf narrowly escaped an assassination attempt outside the Parliament buildings. In exchanges of fire that followed the explosion 11 people were killed, including Yussuf's brother, which served further to increase tensions between the weakened Government and the SSICC, although the latter denied any involvement in the incident. In mid-October Prime Minister Ghedi dismissed three ministers, including the State Minister of Information. Although no official reason was given, it was suggested that they had failed to demonstrate support for the Government's stance against the SSICC.

In mid-October 2006 the SSICC declared a *jihad* (holy war) on Ethiopia, which it accused of launching a military offensive against Islamist troops. The Ethiopian Government had hitherto denied any military presence in Somalia but later that month the Ethiopian Prime Minister, Meles Zenawi, announced that his country was at war with the Islamist forces. A US report claimed that Ethiopia had earlier breached the UN arms embargo by delivering a consignment of weapons to the Somali Government forces and that Ethiopia's military presence in Somalia could intensify Somali nationalism and provoke attacks against Ethiopians. It was also reported that Eritrea was supplying arms to the Islamist militia.

Further peace talks were scheduled to take place in Khartoum in October 2006, but the SSICC refused to enter into discussions while the Ethiopian military remained in Somalia, and in early November negotiations were postponed. The SSICC issued a peace initiative to the Somali Government on 11 November; however, the Government rejected this and the following day violent conflict erupted, igniting fears that the situation could escalate into a regional war. Later that month Ethiopian reinforcements arrived in Baidoa as the Islamists began to assemble their forces nearby. SSICC troops were also deployed to positions close to the Ethiopian border. In early December the Ethiopian Government reported attacks by insurgents who had crossed the border. At the same time, violence escalated in the area surrounding Baidoa as opposing troops sought to exert control over the seat of government. The UN Security Council hurriedly adopted a resolution (No. 1725) providing for peace-keeping missions from other African nations to enter Somalia in support of government forces. Meanwhile, the SSICC, while lacking military strength in their comparatively limited number of soldiers, was securing wider popular support. The SSICC claimed that the majority of the country, under Islamist control, remained peaceful and that international intervention was the cause of much of the conflict. Nevertheless, in mid-December the SSICC issued an ultimatum to the Ethiopian forces to leave Somalia within seven days or face a full-scale war. Ethiopia rejected these demands and civilians fled Baidoa and the surrounding areas as fighting broke out once more; the SSICC maintained that it was not at war with the Somali Government forces. During a meeting with the European Union (EU) Commissioner for Development and Humanitarian Aid on 20 December the SSICC declared that it would honour its commitment to attending peace talks in Sudan and there followed reports that fighting had begun to subside. However, Ethiopian troops advanced towards Mogadishu forcing the SSICC to retreat. Pro-Government forces began to regain control over the capital and popular support for the SSICC reportedly waned.

On 1 January 2007, with the SSICC forces driven out of the capital, Prime Minister Ghedi announced a three-day amnesty during which civilians were to turn in their weapons. The UN warned that the continued presence of Eritrean forces in Somalia remained a threat to the fragile peace, and as Ethiopia began to withdraw troops from Somalia there was increased pressure on the AU to establish a peace-keeping force in the region. Remaining pro-Government troops were subjected to guerrilla attacks in the weeks that followed, although these were reported to be small in scale, and the success of the peace process remained uncertain. The USA launched a series of air strikes against Islamists who continued to pose a threat in southern areas of Somalia. In early January five Somali cabinet ministers were arrested in Kenya, having addressed a press conference and demanded that Ethiopian troops leave their country. The Kenyan Government issued a statement declaring that it would not tolerate actions which could disrupt the peace process. Further violence was reported in Mogadishu during late January, following the visit of an AU delegation to the capital to attend further talks on the deployment of a peace-keeping mission, causing many civilians to flee the area.

In mid-January 2007 Sheikh Adan was dismissed as Speaker of the TP amid allegations that he supported the Islamist extremists and had failed to attend parliamentary meetings. Shaykh Adan Madobe was elected to replace Sheikh Adan on 31 January. Meanwhile, in mid-January 154 members of the TP voted in favour of declaring martial law, to be imposed for a period of three months from 31 January. Two faction leaders had opposed the motion, claiming that the situation would worsen with the establishment of military control.

At the end of January 2007 the AU summit convened in Addis Ababa, Ethiopia, concluded, having secured less than 4,000 troops of the 8,000 pledged to constitute the peace force. However, President Yussuf agreed to stage a national reconciliation conference with the aim of bringing an end to the conflict in the war-torn country and in early February a week of political leaders' meetings began in the capital. It was agreed that the reconciliation conference would be held in mid-April. Later in February the UN Security Council adopted a resolution (No. 1725) authorizing the establishment of the AU Mission to Somalia (AMISOM) with an initial mandate of six months. It was envisaged that this force would replace the withdrawing Ethiopian troops and provide support to the Government. However, in early March insurgents attacked the first AMISON contingent to arrive in Somalia. Days later a military plane carrying further peace-keeping personnel caught fire at an airport in Mogadishu, although no casualties were reported.

A tentative cease-fire was agreed on 22 March 2007 between elders of the Hawiye clan and Ethiopian military officials. However, it broke down almost immediately when Government forces attacked Islamist militia in the southern region of the capital in an attempt to consolidate their control and the fighting escalated into what many observers claimed was the most violent conflict in 15 years. Fighting continued into early April and by that time, according to the office of the UN High Commissioner for Refugees (UNHCR), some 47,000 people had fled Mogadishu and it was reported that some 1,500 people had been killed, while several thousand more had been injured. The reconciliation talks were postponed until June.

Meanwhile, in February 2007 Prime Minister Ghedi effected a cabinet reshuffle; four ministers were redesignated, including the Deputy Prime Minister and Minister of Interior and Security, Hussein Aidid, who was demoted to the position of Minister of Public Works and Housing. Further governmental changes were implemented in April, including the appointment of Husayn Elabe Fahiye as Minister of Foreign Affairs.

On 12 March 2007 the TP voted to relocate the Government and the following day the office of the President moved from Baidoa to the capital, Mogadishu. Cabinet ministers began preparations to transfer their offices to the capital but progress was hindered by continuing violence in the city. The Government announced in mid-March that additional security measures were to be implemented to quell the violence, including deploying trained Ethiopian and AU troops to the worst affected areas. A UN agency reported that by late April more than 300,000 people—almost one-third of the city's population—had left Mogadishu, and in May Hawiye clan elders conceded defeat in the capital and the Government urged the group to enter into negotiations over disarmament. Meanwhile, the UN insisted on the need for investigations into alleged war crimes and human rights violations in Somalia.

The much-delayed reconciliation conference, scheduled for 14 June 2007, was further postponed as violence continued in Mogadishu. In mid-May a number of explosions were reported, and the following month the Prime Minister's residence came under attack when a bomb exploded killing several people. Ghedi escaped unharmed, however. The incident occurred after militants based in the north of Somalia were reported to have been killed when the USA launched a missile attack on a Somali village being used as a base. The reconciliation conference finally began in mid-July amid further violence and bomb attacks. Among the most pressing issues for discussion were the holding of future elections and the resolution of clan divisions, and the international community encouraged the Government to include moderate Islamists in the conference. However, Islamists and Hawiye clan elders refused to attend the meeting on the grounds that while Ethiopian troops remained in the country, the conference would not provide a neutral base for discussions. The outcome of the seven-week conference, largely considered successful by Somali organizers, was undermined by the absence of key parties, according to international observers. The Islamists planned to hold a separate conference in Asmara, Eritrea, although analysts agreed that an all-inclusive conference was needed to secure a lasting peace. In late August AMISOM's mandate was extended for a further six months.

The opposition conference began in early September 2007, attended by Sheikh Hassan Dahir Aweys, Chairman of the SSICC, who had been in hiding since being driven from Mogadishu by Ethiopian forces earlier that year. At the meeting, also attended by UN and EU observers, SSICC and opposition leaders formed a coalition known as the Alliance for the Liberation of Somalia (ALS). The ALS aimed to remove the Ethiopian-backed Government and would be guided by a 191-member committee, to function as a Parliament led by the former Speaker of the TP, Sheikh Adan. A 10-member executive committee was elected, with Sheikh Aweys named as Chairman.

Relations between President Yussuf, a member of the Darod clan, and Prime Minister Ghedi of the Hawiye clan, had become increasingly strained in 2007. Ghedi had opposed suggestions by Yussuf that cabinet ministers no longer needed to be members of the TP, while the two had also clashed over the control of petroleum concessions in 'Puntland' and funding pledged by Saudi Arabia. In late October Prime Minister Ghedi tendered his resignation following further outbreaks of violence involving insurgents and Ethiopian troops. Nur Hassan Hussein, the Secretary-General of the Somali Red Crescent humanitarian organization and a Hawiye, was named as the new Prime Minister and sworn into office on 24 November. Earlier in that month fighting in Mogadishu escalated, forcing thousands of residents to flee the capital.

Prime Minister Hussein announced his new Cabinet in December 2007, but his nominations were criticized by the Ethiopian Government, particularly that of Minister of Foreign Affairs and International Co-operation Mohamed Ali Hamud, who was believed to have close ties to Arab governments. Shortly after their appointment, five ministers submitted their resignation, claiming that the composition of the new administration did not fully represent their clans. Having failed to gain approval for his first Cabinet, Hussein formed a new Government in mid-January 2008, which included Ibrow as Minister of Justice and Religious Affairs and Acting Minister of Labour and Social Affairs, Aydid Abdullahi Ilka Hanaf as Minister of Education and Culture and Acting Minister of Health, and Muhammad Abdisalan Adan as Minister of Information, Youth Affairs and Sports; all three were also awarded the status of Deputy Prime Minister.

In late January 2008 AU security officials submitted a proposal for measures to establish lasting peace and security. The plan included increased efforts towards achieving reconciliation; ensuring a safe environment for humanitarian aid workers; and fostering greater co-operation from the international community in peace-keeping operations. In February Prime Minister Hussein conceded that the Government was willing to meet opposition leaders in an attempt to revive the faltering reconciliation process. The UN was considering the deployment of a UN peace-keeping force to replace AMISOM, which by mid-April comprised only 2,450 troops and had largely been restricted to protecting transport facilities in Mogadishu and providing security for government officials. In February the UN Security Council had authorized the extension of AMISOM's mandate until late August.

In May 1993 Egal, who had been Somalia's Prime Minister in 1967–69, was elected as the new President of 'Somaliland'. In June Egal announced the composition of a 14-member council of ministers for 'Somaliland'. By late September a two-year transitional programme for reconstruction had been approved by a 47-member bicameral parliament (comprising a council of elders and a council of representatives). The administration's hopes that the prevailing atmosphere of peace in the north-western region would inspire the international community's prompt recognition of 'Somaliland' were largely frustrated, in October, by the OAU Secretary-General's rejection of the territory's independent status. Relations between the Egal administration and UNOSOM officials improved in late 1993, following the assurances of the UN Secretary-General that the mission would not interfere in the region's affairs but would provide funding for reconstruction and the rehabilitation of the police force. Nevertheless, in August 1994 Egal expelled UN representatives from 'Somaliland', accusing them of interfering in internal affairs. This was apparently precipitated by talks between the new UN Special Representative to Somalia, James Victor Gbeho (appointed in July), and Ahmed Ali 'Tur', who was courted by both the UN and Gen. Aidid following his disavowal of secession for 'Somaliland'. In October the rift between Egal and Ahmed Ali 'Tur' culminated in violent confrontations in Hargeysa between military units remaining loyal to Egal and those defecting to support Ahmed Ali 'Tur'. By mid-December it was estimated that three-quarters of the population of Hargeysa had fled, many thousands of them seeking refuge in Ethiopia (see below). Fighting spread to other parts of 'Somaliland', and in April government forces were in conflict with fighters from the Garhadji clan who had recently formed an alliance with Issa militiamen belonging to the anti-secessionist USF. Despite Egal's weakened position, he persevered with the introduction of a new currency for the territory, the 'Somaliland shilling'.

In August 1995 four sub-committees were established to draft a new constitution for 'Somaliland'. A provisional document was published in March 1996. Peace talks between the territory's warring factions were conducted in December 1995, and in May 1996 it was reported that rebel armed forces had surrendered their weapons at an official disarmament ceremony in Hargeysa. In February 1997, shortly after it was announced that the constitution had become effective for a three-year interim period, Egal was re-elected (by an electoral college) President of 'Somaliland' for a five-year term.

At a referendum held in late May 2001, according to official results, 91.7% of the voters in 'Somaliland' approved a new constitution for the territory, which contained a clause confirming the self-declared state's independence. However, the outcome appeared unlikely to persuade the international community to grant recognition to 'Somaliland'. In mid-January 2002 Egal's term of office, which had been due to expire at the end of February, prior to scheduled presidential and parliamentary elections, was extended for one year by the council of elders. In early May, however, Egal died from complications following surgery at a military hospital in South Africa; a seven-day period of national mourning was declared, and the Vice-President, Dahir Riyale Kahin, was inaugurated as President of 'Somaliland'. Kahin appointed Ahmed Yusuf Yassin as Vice-President later that month, and in July Kahin announced that a presidential election would be held in January 2003. The election was delayed on a number of occasions, but finally proceeded on 14 April. According to results published by the 'Somaliland' Election Commission, Kahin defeated his nearest rival, Ahmad Muhammad Silanyo, by just 80 votes, securing 205,595 (42.1%) of the total 498,639 votes cast. A third candidate, Faysal Ali Warabe, received 77,433 votes (15.5%). Silanyo immediately contested the result of the election and announced his intention to appeal against the outcome. However, in the following month the 'Somaliland' constitutional court confirmed the legitimacy of Kahin's victory, and he was sworn in as President on 16 May.

During 2004–05 'Somaliland' continued its attempts to secure international recognition and reiterated that it would not participate in ongoing peace negotiations taking place in Kenya (see above). Indeed, following the election of Yussuf to the Somali presidency in mid-October 2004, Kahin again stated the readiness of 'Somaliland' to defend its territorial integrity and that it would seek to retain its independent status. Elections to the lower chamber of the legislature, the House of Representatives, scheduled to be held in late March 2005, were postponed by Kahin. Members of parliament had objected to the allocation of seats in the new legislature by clan, rather than on a one-person, one-vote basis, and demanded a national census to determine voter eligibility. Nevertheless, an amended elections bill was approved by the House of Representatives in early April. On 29 September candidates from three political parties contested the 82 seats in the House of Representatives. Kahin's Unity, Democracy and Independence Party (UDUB) emerged as the largest of the three parties with 33 seats, the Peace, Unity and Development Party (KULMIYE) won 28 seats and the Justice and Development Party (UCID) 21. At the official opening of parliament in November a disagreement over the election of a speaker developed into a physical confrontation between members of the Council. The role was eventually allocated to Abdirahman Mohamed Abdullahi of the UCID, and in mid-December the 'Somaliland' parliament held its first full session.

In July 1998 Col Abdullahi Yussuf Ahmed, a former leader of the SSDF, announced the formation of 'Puntland', a new autonomous administration in north-eastern Somalia. In August Abdullahi Yussuf, as President of the new administration, appointed a cabinet, which was subsequently approved by the recently inaugurated 69-member parliament (empowered to act as the legislature for a three-year transitional period, prior to the holding of regional elections). A charter for 'Puntland', released shortly afterwards, precluded 'Puntland' from seceding from Somalia, while it envisaged the adoption of a federal system of national government, with similar regional governments emerging around the country. Hussein Aidid declared his opposition to the administration, accusing the Ethiopian authorities of encouraging 'Puntland' to secede. In late June 2001 Yussuf's mandate was controversially extended for a further three years by the 'Puntland' parliament, at the behest of clan elders. The legality of the decision was challenged by several opposition figures, and the 'Puntland' High Court issued a decree, effective from 1 July, placing all security services and other government institutions under its supervision. The Chief Justice of 'Puntland', Yussuf Haji Nur, subsequently proclaimed himself President of the territory; senior clan elders confirmed Haji Nur as acting President until 31 August. However, Yussuf rejected this decision, and heavy fighting ensued between followers of Yussuf and Haji Nur. In late August a general congress, attended by representatives of all major 'Puntland' clans, opened in Garowe, the region's capital, to elect a new President and Vice-President, as well as members to a new 'Puntland' assembly, and in mid-November Jama Ali Jama and Ahmad Mahmud Gunle were sworn in as President and Vice-President, respectively. Just days later violent clashes were reported to have taken place in Garowe between troops loyal to Yussuf and Ali Jama. In April 2002 Yussuf and Ali Jama met for talks in Ethiopia, but no agreement was reached. Fighting continued in 'Puntland' during 2002 and early 2003, with numerous casualties reported on both sides. In May 2003 Yussuf sought to stabilize 'Puntland' by concluding a power-sharing agreement with opposition forces, under the terms of which opposition members were granted a number of ministerial portfolios. In July 2004, following a presidential decree which reduced the Government's term in office from two years to six months, Yussuf formed a new 15-member Government. In October Yussuf was elected President of Somalia (see above) and Mohamed Abdi Hashi succeeded him as President of 'Puntland' in an acting capacity. In early January 2005 Gen. Mohamud Muse Hersi 'Adde', a former Somali diplomat, secured the support of 35 members of the 'Puntland' parliament, thus defeating Hashi, who won 30 votes, and was elected President of 'Puntland'. Hassan Dahir Afqurac was elected Vice-President. In late February 2006 an armed confrontation near the parliament building between security forces and a group loyal to the Minister for Planning, Abdirahman Farole, resulted in at least three deaths. Security forces had surrounded the building, which the group had occupied the previous day. In early March members of parliament approved a new Cabinet, in which incumbent ministers retained their portfolios, with the exception of Farole, whom Hersi had dismissed following the siege. Meanwhile, in October 2005 it emerged that 'Puntland' had issued mineral and oil exploration rights to Range Resources of Australia in an agreement that included the regions of Sanaag and Sool, disputed by 'Puntland' and the neighbouring region of 'Somaliland', prompting vociferous criticism from the 'Somaliland' administration. From September 2004 troops from both regions had reportedly been engaged in heavy fighting near the border between the two self-declared states. In July 2007 the Sanaag region declared its independence as a self-governing entity and renamed itself Maakhir. In December of that month Hersi effected a cabinet reshuffle in which Gen. Abdullahi Said Samatar was named Minister of Security. A new Ministry of Oil and Minerals was established.

The escalation of hostilities between the Siad Barre Government and the rebel forces increased the flow of refugees from Somalia to Ethiopia and Kenya. Following the SNM's assumption of control in northern Somalia in early 1991, thousands of refugees returned from Ethiopia. Many more returned to their home territory in 'Somaliland' in late 1991 and early 1992, as a result of the ethnic conflict in south-western Ethiopia. The intensification of hostilities in the south of Somalia from April 1992 precipitated a huge movement of refugees: by the end of 1992 there were approximately 400,000 Somali refugees in Kenya, more than 300,000 in Ethiopia, up to 100,000 in Yemen, and hundreds of thousands in the Persian (Arabian) Gulf region, in Europe and North America. In early 1993 the International Committee of the Red Cross estimated that three-quarters of Somalia's population had been internally displaced by the civil conflict, although by late 1994 many thousands had returned to their villages. However, in November some 30,000 civilians fled to Ethiopia to escape fighting in Hargeysa, 'Somaliland'. According to UNHCR, at the end of 2006 there were an estimated 464,253 Somali refugees world-wide, including 173,702 in Kenya, 91,587 in Yemen, 72,546 in the USA, 34,138 in the United Kingdom, and 16,576 in Ethiopia.

In April 1988 a decade of hostile relations between Somalia and Ethiopia, following the war in 1977–78 over the Ogaden area of Ethiopia (which is inhabited by ethnic Somalis), ended with a peace accord. It was agreed to re-establish diplomatic relations, to withdraw troops from border areas and to exchange prisoners of war. Following the overthrow of the Mengistu regime in May 1991, the new Government in Ethiopia declared itself neutral with regard to the factions fighting for control of Somalia. Ethiopia hosted peace conferences for the warring Somali factions in 1993, 1996 and 1997. The Egyptian, Kenyan and Libyan authorities also fostered peace initiatives for Somalia from the late 1990s.

In March 1998 Ethiopian troops reportedly occupied several towns in Somalia's Gedo region, following the capture of the SNF-controlled town of Elwak (in Kenya) by the Islamist, Somali-based group al-Ittihad al-Islam. In April 1999 the Ethiopian Government denied reports that its forces were occupying two districts in western Somalia, while Hussein Aidid and Ali Mahdi reiterated their claims that Ethiopia was encouraging the division of Somalia by providing armaments and ammunition to autonomous administrations in the country.

Following the outbreak of the Eritrean–Ethiopian border conflict in mid-1998, rival Somali factions were the recipients of increasingly large consignments of weapons from the two warring countries, which sought to secure Somali allegiance to their causes. Growing concern about the activities of Eritrean-supported Somali militias prompted Ethiopia to launch cross-border raids into Somalia against warlords, and in June 1999 the RRA, assisted by Ethiopian troops, captured the town of Baidoa from Hussein Aidid's SNA. Aidid's continuing support of the Eritrean Government and Ethiopian insurgent groups led neutral observers to believe that the conflict was in danger of spreading elsewhere in the Horn of Africa. The Ethiopian Government claimed, however, that its actions were merely attempts to protect the border from attacks initiated by Somali-based rebel opposition groups. In September Ali 'Ato' and Aidid attended a meeting with the Ethiopian Minister of Foreign Affairs, Seyoum Mesfin, in Libya where an agreement was reached whereby Aidid would withdraw support for Ethiopian Oromo rebels in return for Ethiopian disengagement from Somalia. In November the SNA announced that it had disarmed several hundred Oromo Liberation Front (OLF) rebels living in Somalia, had closed down their offices and had asked the OLF leaders to leave the country. It was, however, reported that Ethiopian incursions into Somalia continued in early 2000. During late 2000 and early 2001 relations between the two countries deteriorated after the Hasan administration accused Ethiopia of offering support to faction leaders hostile to the TNA (see above). Relations between the two countries improved following the visit of a Somali government delegation to Ethiopia in June 2001. However, in September it was reported that Ethiopia had ordered the closure of the common border, fearing an increase in terrorist activity in Somalia after the events of 11 September. In November the Prime Ministers of the two countries met for talks in Addis Ababa, at which Ethiopia reiterated its concern over the suspected presence of Islamist terrorist elements in Somalia. Nevertheless, both sides pledged to improve bilateral relations, and Ethiopia affirmed its support for a comprehensive reconciliation process in Somalia. In February 2003 relations between the two countries were again strained after the Ethiopian Prime Minister admitted sending Ethiopian troops into Somali territory in pursuit of members of al-Ittihad al-Islam.

Following the suicide attacks on New York and Washington, DC, on 11 September 2001, for which the USA held the al-Qa'ida (Base) organization of Osama bin Laden responsible, the USA 'froze' the foreign assets of Somalia's al-Barakat bank, as it suspected that much of the estimated US $500m. remitted from Somalis abroad to the bank was being funnelled to terrorist organizations. Furthermore, al-Ittihad al-Islam was among 27 groups designated as foreign terrorist organizations in September by the US Government, which believed that al-Ittihad al-Islam had links to al-Qa'ida. In November the new Somali Prime Minister, Hassan Abshir Farah, denied that his Government had any links to al-Ittihad al-Islam or to al-Qa'ida and stated that he would not object to the deployment of US troops inside Somalia to monitor and detect alleged terrorist activities. In the following month US officials were reported to have held talks with several Somali faction leaders regarding the possible existence of al-Qa'ida camps in areas under their control. US special forces raided a Mogadishu hospital in March 2003 and seized a suspected al-Qa'ida operative, who was believed to have been involved in the bombing of an Israeli-owned hotel in Mombasa, Kenya, in November 2002, which resulted in the deaths of 18 people. A report published by the UN in November 2003 stated that the al-Qa'ida cell that had launched the attack on the hotel had used Somalia as a base, and warned of the possibility of further acts of terrorism being plotted, after it discovered evidence of attempts by extremist groups to procure weapons in Mogadishu. US naval forces stationed in Djibouti and Bahrain conducted patrols along the coast of Somalia throughout 2005 following a reported increase in piracy, and in late January 2006 13 suspected pirates were captured following an armed pursuit near the coast involving a US guided missile destroyer.

Government

In July 2000 a Somali national reconciliation conference, sponsored by President Gelleh of Djibouti, approved a national Charter, which envisaged the Somali Republic adopting a federal system of government, comprising 18 regional administrations, after a three-year interim period. The Charter provided for the creation of a Transitional National Assembly (TNA), which was to exercise legislative power in Somalia during the interim period. The 245-member TNA, comprising members of the four major clans and of an alliance of smaller clans, as well as 20 influential Somalis, was inaugurated in August and elected a President of Somalia. In October the President nominated a Prime Minister, who formed a Cabinet. Despite the expiry of its mandate in August 2003, the TNA remained in place, pending the election of a new legislative body. In late January 2004, following protracted negotiations in Kenya, an agreement was signed that provided for the establishment of a new 275-member national parliament, to comprise 61 representatives from each of the four major clans and 31 from an alliance of smaller clans. Once established, the parliament elected a national President, who, in turn, nominated a Prime Minister to form a government.

Defence

Of total armed forces of 64,500 in June 1990, the army numbered 60,000, the navy 2,000 and the air force 2,500. In addition, there were 29,500 members of paramilitary forces, including 20,000 members of the People's Militia. Following the overthrow of the Siad Barre regime in January 1991, there were no national armed forces. Somalia was divided into areas controlled by different armed groups, which were based on clan, or sub-clan, membership. In March 1994 the UN announced that 8,000 former Somali police officers had been rehabilitated throughout the country, receiving vehicles and uniforms from the UN. Following the UN withdrawal from Somalia in early 1995, these police officers ceased receiving payment and their future and their hitherto neutral stance appeared uncertain. In December 1998 a 3,000-strong police force was established for the Banaadir region (Mogadishu and its environs). An additional 3,000 members (comprising former militiamen and police officers) were recruited to the force in early 1999; however, the force was disbanded within months. Following his election to the presidency in August 2000, Abdulkasim Salad Hasan announced his intention to recruit former militiamen into a new national force: by December some 5,000 Somalis had begun training under the supervision of Mogadishu's Islamic courts. However, efforts to establish a new national armed force have made little progress since the Government's return to Somalia from exile in 2005. In August 2004 the total armed forces of the self-proclaimed 'Republic of Somaliland' were estimated to number 7,000.

Economic Affairs

In 1990, according to estimates by the World Bank, Somalia's gross national income (GNI), measured at average 1988–90 prices, was US $946m., equivalent to $150 per head. According to UN figures, in 2001 gross domestic product (GDP) was $1,000m., equivalent to $110 per head. During 1996–2006, it was estimated, the population increased at an average annual rate of 2.9%. GDP declined, in real terms, at an average annual rate of 3.3% in 1990–99; however, growth of 2.1% was recorded in 1999.

Agriculture (including forestry and fishing) contributed 66% of GDP in 1990. According to FAO estimates, 68.8% of the working population were employed in agriculture in mid-2005. Agriculture is based on the breeding of livestock, which accounted for 49% of GDP in 1989 and 38.4% of the total value of exports in 1988. Bananas are the principal cash crop, accounting for 40.3% of export earnings in 1988. The GDP of the agricultural sector declined by an average of 4.1% per year in 1990–99; agricultural GDP increased by 12.0% in 1999. Although crop production in 1996 was reported to have increased by 50% compared with the previous year, output was still some 37% lower than it had been prior to the civil war. Severe flooding in southern Somalia during 1997 led to widespread crop failure and resulted in the loss of as many as 30,000 cattle. Total cereals production was 207,800 metric tons in 1999, the lowest annual yield since 1993, but recovered to an estimated 304,900 in 2002. Southern Somalia experienced severe drought in 2005, causing harvests to fail for the third consecutive year and provoking acute shortages of food among the population.

Industry (including mining, manufacturing, construction and power) contributed 8.6% of GDP in 1988, and employed an estimated 12.0% of the working population in 2002. The combined GDP of the mining, manufacturing and power sectors increased by an average of 2.3% per year in 1990–99; growth in 1999 was 13.8%. The GDP of the construction sector increased at an average annual rate of 0.8% in 1990–99; growth of 16.8% was recorded in 1999.

Mining contributed 0.3% of GDP in 1988. Somalia's mineral resources include salt, limestone, gypsum, gold, silver, nickel, copper, zinc, lead, manganese, uranium and iron ore. Deposits of petroleum and natural gas have been discovered, but remain unexploited: US petroleum companies were granted exploration rights covering two-thirds of the country by Siad Barre, and were expected to start investigations once there was a durable peace. In February 2001 it was reported that the French petroleum company TotalFinaElf had signed an agreement with the transitional Somali Government to carry out oil exploration in the south of the country. Discussions commenced in January 2003 between the 'Somaliland' administration and a British-based company regarding the possible granting of contracts for petroleum exploration. An Australian mining company, Range Resources, began mineral and petroleum exploration in 'Puntland' and in October 2005 it signed a contract with the 'Puntland' Government, granting it 50.1% of exploration rights for the entire region, including territory disputed by neighbouring 'Somaliland'. However, the Transitional Federal Government later declared the contract void.

Manufacturing contributed almost 5% of GDP in 1988. The most important sectors are food-processing, especially sugar-refining, the processing of hides and skins, and the refining of petroleum. Manufacturing GDP increased by an average of 2.0% per year in 1990–99; growth in 1999 was 18.0%.

Energy is derived principally from oil-fired generators. Imports of fuel products comprised 14% of the value of merchandise imports in 1990.

The services sector contributed 24.6% of GDP in 1988, and engaged an estimated 21.1% of the employed labour force in 2002. Tourism accounted for some 9.3% of GDP in 1988.

In 1989 Somalia recorded a visible trade deficit of US $278.6m., and there was a deficit of $156.7m. on the current account of the balance of payments. In 1982 the principal source of imports (34.4%) was Italy, while Saudi Arabia was the principal market for exports (86.5%). Other major trading partners in that year were the United Kingdom, the Federal Republic of Germany and Kenya. The principal exports in 1988 were livestock and bananas. The principal imports were petroleum, fertilizers, foodstuffs and machinery. Livestock and bananas remained the principal exports in the late 1990s, while the United Arab Emirates emerged as Somalia's main trading partner.

In 1988 Somalia recorded a budget deficit of 10,009.4m. Somali shillings. A provisional budget for 1991 was projected to balance at 268,283.2m. Somali shillings. Somalia's total external debt was US $2,838m. at the end of 2003, of which $1,936m. was long-term public debt. In 1990–2001 the average annual rate of inflation was 20.6%. Consumer prices increased by 11.5% in 2001. The rate of unemployment was estimated at 47.4% in 2002.

Somalia is a member of the African Development Bank (see p. 162) and the Islamic Development Bank (see p. 329).

Somalia's long history of civil unrest, together with unreliable climatic conditions, have undermined the traditional agricultural base of the economy. By the mid-1990s a significant recovery had been recorded in livestock numbers, sorghum output and exports of bananas, although the production and export of the last exacerbated factional fighting, with rival clansmen competing for control of the industry in order to fund their war efforts. Following the establishment of the Transitional National Assembly in August 2000, it was hoped that Somalia's economic situation would improve. On his appointment, President Hasan appealed for foreign donors to provide assistance with the rehabilitation of basic infrastructures and to finance development projects. However, the Government's attempts to establish control over the economy by issuing large quantities of currency notes resulted in a rapid rise in the rate of inflation and a further depreciation in the value of the shilling. Although the economy subsequently began to show signs of a recovery, in December 2001 the UN announced that Somalia was on the verge of an economic collapse unparalleled in modern history. This was attributed largely to the US Administration's decision to enforce the closure of the al-Barakat banking and telecommunications organization (see Recent History), owing to its suspected links to terrorist organizations, thus severing the remittance process on which so much of the country is heavily dependent. The formation of a new Government in late 2004 again raised hopes that central authority would be restored to the country, thus enabling the possible creation of financial institutions and providing a degree of stability, which would, in turn, encourage the development of the economy. Indeed, in July 2004 Coca-Cola opened a soft drinks plant in Mogadishu, representing the largest single investment in the country, and in February 2005 Somalia signed a trade agreement with Kenya providing for co-operation in various sectors, including livestock farming, fisheries, telecommunications and industry. In mid-2007 the China National Offshore Oil Corporation signed an agreement with the Somali Government, which allowed the former the opportunity to explore any land with potential reserves of natural resources. As of 2007 Somalia had no proven reserves of oil. The development was in contrast to the general policy of Western companies, which saw the exploitation of conflict areas as anathema to local interests. However, despite pledges of significant humanitarian aid by the international community, divisions within the Government and ongoing conflict continued to prevent the development of an economic infrastructure and analysts do not expect any real economic growth in the coming years. The escalation of hostilities in early 2007 between government forces and Islamist forces resulted in the displacement of some 300,000 Somalis from the capital alone and it was reported that humanitarian aid was failing to reach those in greatest need.

Education

All private schools were nationalized in 1972, and education is now provided free of charge. Primary education, lasting for seven years, is officially compulsory for children aged six to 13 years. However, in 2002 enrolment at primary schools was equivalent to only 16.9% of the school-age population (boys 20.8%; girls 12.7%). Secondary education, beginning at the age of 13, lasts for five years, but is not compulsory. In 1985 the enrolment at secondary schools included 3% of children (boys 4%; girls 2%) in the relevant age-group. Current expenditure on education in the Government's 1988 budget was 478.1m. Somali shillings (equivalent to 1.9% of total current spending). Following the overthrow of Siad Barre's Government in January 1991 and the descent of the country into anarchy, Somalia's education system collapsed. In January 1993 a primary school was opened in the building of Somalia's sole university, the Somali National University in Mogadishu (which had been closed in early 1991). The only other schools operating in the country were a number run by Islamist groups and some that had been reopened in 'Somaliland' in mid-1991.

SOMALIA

Public Holidays

2008: 1 January (New Year's Day), 19 January* (Ashoura), 20 March* (Mouloud, birth of the Prophet), 1 May (Labour Day), 26 June (Independence Day), 1 July (Foundation of the Republic), 1 October* (Id al-Fitr, end of Ramadan), 9 December* (Id al-Adha, Feast of the Sacrifice).

2009: 1 January (New Year's Day), 7 January*† (Ashoura), 9 March* (Mouloud, Birth of the Prophet), 1 May (Labour Day), 26 June (Independence Day), 1 July (Foundation of the Republic), 20 September* (Id al-Fitr, end of Ramadan), 27 November* (Id al-Adha, Feast of the Sacrifice), 27 December*† (Ashoura).

*These holidays are dependent on the Islamic lunar calendar and may vary by one or two days from the dates given.

†This festival occurs twice (in the Islamic years AH 1430 and 1431) within the same Gregorian year.

Weights and Measures

The metric and imperial systems are both used.

Statistical Survey

Sources (unless otherwise stated): Economic Research and Statistics Dept, Central Bank of Somalia, Mogadishu, and Central Statistical Dept, State Planning Commission, POB 1742, Mogadishu; tel. (1) 80385.

Area and Population

AREA, POPULATION AND DENSITY

Area (sq km)	637,657*
Population (census results)†	
7 February 1975	3,253,024
February 1986 (provisional)	
Males	3,741,664
Females	3,372,767
Total	7,114,431
Population (UN estimates at mid-year)‡	
2005	8,196,000
2006	8,445,000
2007	8,699,000
Density (per sq km) at mid-2007	13.6

* 246,201 sq miles.
† Excluding adjustment for underenumeration.
‡ Source: UN, *World Population Prospects: The 2006 Revision*.

PRINCIPAL TOWNS
(estimated population in 1981)

Mogadishu (capital)	500,000		Berbera	65,000
Hargeysa	70,000		Merca	60,000
Kismayu	70,000			

Mid-2007 ('000, including suburbs, UN estimate): Mogadishu 1,100 (Source: UN, *World Urbanization Prospects: The 2007 Revision*).

BIRTHS AND DEATHS
(annual averages, UN estimates)

	1990–95	1995–2000	2000–05
Birth rate (per 1,000)	45.7	47.7	45.8
Death rate (per 1,000)	23.5	20.3	18.5

Source: UN, *World Population Prospects: The 2006 Revision*.

Expectation of life (years at birth, WHO estimates): 45.1 (males 45.1; females 45.1) in 2005 (Source: WHO, *World Health Statistics*).

ECONOMICALLY ACTIVE POPULATION
(estimates, '000 persons, 1991)

	Males	Females	Total
Agriculture, etc.	1,157	1,118	2,275
Industry	290	46	336
Services	466	138	604
Total labour force	1,913	1,302	3,215

Source: UN Economic Commission for Africa, *African Statistical Yearbook*.

2002 (percentage distribution): Agriculture 66.9; Industry 12.0; Services 21.1 (Source: The World Bank and United Nations Development Programme, *Socio-Economic Survey 2002 Somalia*).

Mid-2005 (estimates in '000): Agriculture, etc. 2,572; Total labour force 3,737 (Source: FAO).

Health and Welfare

KEY INDICATORS

Total fertility rate (children per woman, 2005)	6.2
Under-5 mortality rate (per 1,000 live births, 2005)	225
HIV/AIDS (% of persons aged 15–49, 2005)	0.9
Physicians (per 1,000 head, 1997)	0.04
Hospital beds (per 1,000 head, 1997)	0.42
Health expenditure (2001): US $ per head (PPP)	18
Health expenditure (2001): % of GDP	2.6
Health expenditure (2001): public (% of total)	44.6
Access to water (% of persons, 2004)	29
Access to sanitation (% of persons, 2004)	26

For sources and definitions, see explanatory note on p. vi.

Agriculture

PRINCIPAL CROPS
('000 metric tons)

	2003	2004	2005
Rice (paddy)	12*	18*	11†
Maize	170*	202*	245†
Sorghum	121*	145*	150†
Sweet potatoes†	7	7	7
Cassava (Manioc)†	80	83	85
Sugar cane	n.a.	200*	n.a.
Groundnuts (in shell)	4*	9*	4†
Sesame seed†	30	25	24
Watermelons	6*	8*	6†
Grapefruit and pomelos†	6	6	6
Bananas	38*	37*	38†
Oranges†	9	9	9
Lemons and limes†	8	8	9
Dates†	12	11	11

* Unofficial figure.
† FAO estimate(s).

2006: Sorghum 145 (unofficial figure).

Aggregate production ('000 metric tons, may include official, semi-official or estimated data): Total cereals 403 in 2003, 366 in 2004, 407 in 2005, 402 in 2006; Total roots and tubers 87 in 2003, 90 in 2004, 92 in 2005; Total vegetables (incl. melons) 83 in 2003, 91 in 2004, 96 in 2005; Total fruits (excl. melons) 202 in 2003, 202 in 2004, 203 in 2005.

Source: FAO.

SOMALIA

LIVESTOCK
('000 head, year ending September, FAO estimates)

	2003	2004	2005
Cattle	5,350	5,350	5,350
Sheep	14,350	14,500	13,100
Goats	12,800	12,800	12,700
Pigs	4	4	4
Asses and mules	41	41	41
Camels	7,200	7,000	7,000
Chickens	3	3	3

Note: Data for 2006 were not available.
Source: FAO.

LIVESTOCK PRODUCTS
('000 metric tons, FAO estimates)

	2000	2001	2002
Cows' milk	530	557	557
Goats' milk	390	392	392
Sheep's milk	430	445	445
Cattle meat	59	63	62
Sheep meat	35	43	43
Goat meat	37	32	38
Hen eggs	3	3	3

2003–05: Figures assumed to be unchanged from 2002 (FAO estimates).
Note: Figures for 2006 were not available.
Source: FAO.

Forestry

ROUNDWOOD REMOVALS
('000 cubic metres, excl. bark, FAO estimates)

	2004	2005	2006
Sawlogs, veneer logs and logs for sleepers*	28	28	28
Other industrial wood	82	82	82
Fuel wood	10,466	10,803	11,127
Total	10,576	10,913	11,237

* Annual output assumed to be unchanged since 1975.
Source: FAO.

SAWNWOOD PRODUCTION
('000 cubic metres, incl. railway sleepers)

	1973	1974	1975
Total (all broadleaved)	15*	10	14

* FAO estimate.
1976–2006: Production assumed to be unchanged from 1975 (FAO estimates).
Source: FAO.

Fishing

('000 metric tons, live weight, FAO estimates)

	1999	2000	2001
Marine fishes	23.5	19.8	26.3
Total catch (incl. others)	24.8	20.8	27.5

2002–05: Figures assumed to be unchanged from 2001 (FAO estimates).
Source: FAO.

Mining

('000 metric tons, estimates)

	2002	2003	2004
Salt	1	1	1
Gypsum	2	2	2

Source: US Geological Survey.

Industry

SELECTED PRODUCTS
('000 metric tons, unless otherwise indicated)

	1986	1987	1988
Sugar*	30.0	43.3	41.2
Canned meat (million tins)	1.0	—	—
Canned fish	0.1	—	—
Pasta and flour	15.6	4.3	—
Textiles (million yards)	5.5	3.0	6.3
Boxes and bags	15.0	12.0	5.0
Cigarettes and matches	0.3	0.2	0.1
Petroleum products	128	44	30
Electric energy (million kWh)†	253	255‡	257‡

Sugar (unofficial estimates, '000 metric tons)*: 23 in 2003; 22 in 2004; 21 in 2005.
Electric energy (million kWh)†: 282 in 2002; 284 in 2003; 286 in 2004.
* Data from FAO.
† Source: UN, *Industrial Commodity Statistics Yearbook*.
‡ Provisional figure.

Finance

CURRENCY AND EXCHANGE RATES
Monetary Units
100 cents = 1 Somali shilling (So. sh.).

Sterling, Dollar and Euro Equivalents (30 November 2007)
£1 sterling = 29,769 Somali shillings;
US $1 = 14,406 Somali shillings;
€1 = 21,265 Somali shillings;
100,000 Somali shillings = £3.36 = $6.94 = €4.70.

Average Exchange Rate (Somali shillings per US $)
1987   105.18
1988   170.45
1989   490.68

Note: A separate currency, the 'Somaliland shilling', was introduced in the 'Republic of Somaliland' in January 1995. The exchange rate was reported to be US $1 = 2,750 'Somaliland shillings' in March 2000.

CURRENT BUDGET
(million Somali shillings)

Revenue	1986	1987	1988
Total tax revenue	8,516.4	8,622.4	12,528.1
Taxes on income and profits	1,014.8	889.7	1,431.0
Income tax	380.5	538.8	914.8
Profit tax	634.3	350.9	516.2
Taxes on production, consumption and domestic transactions	1,410.4	1,274.2	2,336.4
Taxes on international transactions	6,091.2	6,458.5	8,760.6
Import duties	4,633.2	4,835.2	6,712.1
Total non-tax revenue	6,375.2	8,220.4	7,623.4
Fees and service charges	274.1	576.1	828.8
Income from government property	633.4	656.4	2,418.9
Other revenue	5,467.2	6,987.9	4,375.7
Total	14,891.6	16,842.8	20,151.5

SOMALIA

Statistical Survey

Expenditure	1986	1987	1988
Total general services	11,997.7	19,636.7	24,213.6
Defence	2,615.9	3,145.0	8,093.9
Interior and police	605.0	560.7	715.4
Finance and central services	7,588.3	14,017.8	12,515.6
Foreign affairs	633.0	1,413.9	2,153.1
Justice and religious affairs	248.5	290.2	447.0
Presidency and general administration	93.0	148.0	217.4
Planning	189.0	24.9	24.3
National Assembly	25.0	36.2	46.9
Total economic services	1,927.6	554.1	600.3
Transportation	122.2	95.2	94.5
Posts and telecommunications	94.3	76.7	75.6
Public works	153.9	57.5	69.8
Agriculture	547.2	59.4	55.3
Livestock and forestry	459.0	89.5	109.9
Mineral and water resources	318.8	85.2	93.1
Industry and commerce	131.0	45.1	43.9
Fisheries	101.2	45.5	58.2
Total social services	1,050.5	900.1	930.8
Education	501.6	403.0	478.1
Health	213.8	203.5	255.2
Information	111.5	135.0	145.8
Labour, sports and tourism	139.6	49.3	51.7
Other	84.0	109.3	—
Total	14,975.8	21,091.0	25,744.7

1989 (estimates): Budget to balance at 32,429.0m. Somali shillings.
1990 (estimates): Budget to balance at 86,012.0m. Somali shillings.
1991 (estimates): Budget to balance at 268,283.2m. Somali shillings.

CENTRAL BANK RESERVES
(US $ million at 31 December)

	1987	1988	1989
Gold*	8.3	7.0	6.9
Foreign exchange	7.3	15.3	15.4
Total	15.6	22.3	22.3

* Valued at market-related prices.
Source: IMF, *International Financial Statistics*.

MONEY SUPPLY
(million Somali shillings at 31 December)

	1987	1988	1989
Currency outside banks	12,327	21,033	70,789
Private-sector deposits at central bank	1,771	1,555	5,067
Demand deposits at commercial banks	15,948	22,848	63,971
Total money	30,046	45,436	139,827

Source: IMF, *International Financial Statistics*.

COST OF LIVING
(Consumer Price Index; base: 2000 = 100)

	2001	2002	2003
All items	111.5	133.8	133.8

2004–06: Consumer prices assumed to be unchanged from 2003.
Source: African Development Bank.

NATIONAL ACCOUNTS
Expenditure on the Gross Domestic Product*
(estimates, million Somali shillings at current prices)

	1988	1989	1990
Government final consumption expenditure	33,220	58,530	104,760
Private final consumption expenditure	240,950	481,680	894,790
Increase in stocks	14,770	n.a.	n.a.
Gross fixed capital formation	44,780	134,150	240,030
Total domestic expenditure	333,720	674,360	1,239,580
Exports of goods and services	7,630	8,890	8,660
Less Imports of goods and services	49,430	57,660	58,460
GDP in purchasers' values	291,920	625,580	1,189,780

* Figures are rounded to the nearest 10m. Somali shillings.
Source: UN Economic Commission for Africa, *African Statistical Yearbook*.

Gross Domestic Product by Economic Activity
(million Somali shillings at constant 1985 prices)

	1986	1987	1988
Agriculture, hunting, forestry and fishing	54,868	59,378	61,613
Mining and quarrying	291	291	291
Manufacturing	4,596	4,821	4,580
Electricity, gas and water	77	62	57
Construction	3,289	3,486	2,963
Trade, restaurants and hotels	8,587	9,929	8,599
Transport, storage and communications	6,020	6,153	5,873
Finance, insurance, real estate and business services	3,743	4,095	3,890
Government services	1,631	1,530	1,404
Other community, social and personal services	2,698	2,779	2,863
Sub-total	85,800	92,524	92,133
Less Imputed bank service charges	737	748	748
GDP at factor cost	85,064	91,776	91,385
Indirect taxes, *less* subsidies	5,301	4,250	3,262
GDP in purchasers' values	90,365	96,026	94,647

GDP at factor cost (estimates, million Somali shillings at current prices): 249,380 in 1988; 500,130 in 1989; 923,970 in 1990 (Source: UN Economic Commission for Africa, *African Statistical Yearbook*).

BALANCE OF PAYMENTS
(US $ million)

	1987	1988	1989
Exports of goods f.o.b.	94.0	58.4	67.7
Imports of goods f.o.b.	−358.5	−216.0	−346.3
Trade balance	−264.5	−157.6	−278.6
Imports of services	−127.7	−104.0	−122.0
Balance on goods and services	−392.2	−261.6	−400.6
Other income paid	−52.0	−60.6	−84.4
Balance on goods, services and income	−444.2	−322.2	−485.0
Current transfers received	343.3	223.7	331.2
Current transfers paid	−13.1	—	−2.9
Current balance	−114.0	−98.5	−156.7
Investment liabilities	−22.8	−105.5	−32.6
Net errors and omissions	39.0	22.4	−0.8
Overall balance	−97.9	−181.7	−190.0

Source: IMF, *International Financial Statistics*.

External Trade

PRINCIPAL COMMODITIES
(million Somali shillings)

Imports*	1986	1987	1988
Foodstuffs	1,783.3	3,703.6	1,216.1
Beverages and tobacco	298.1	183.6	6.2
Manufacturing raw materials	230.0	626.9	661.4
Fertilizers	1.8	238.0	2,411.4
Petroleum	2,051.0	3,604.2	3,815.9
Construction materials	981.4	2,001.9	307.8
Machinery and parts	1,098.3	1,203.6	957.1
Transport equipment	1,133.8	1,027.6	195.2
Total (incl. others)	8,443.4	13,913.7	11,545.5

* Figures cover only imports made against payments of foreign currencies. The total value of imports in 1986 was 20,474 million Somali shillings.

Exports	1986	1987	1988
Livestock	4,420.3	7,300.0	3,806.5
Bananas	1,207.2	2,468.8	3,992.3
Hides and skins	294.0	705.2	492.0
Total (incl. others)	6,372.5	10,899.9	9,914.1

1992 (estimates, US $ million): Imports 150; Exports 80.

PRINCIPAL TRADING PARTNERS
('000 Somali shillings)

Imports	1980	1981	1982
China, People's Repub.	46,959	40,962	89,772
Ethiopia	43,743	146,853	155,775
Germany, Fed. Repub.	104,117	430,548	214,873
Hong Kong	5,351	13,862	3,972
India	41,467	19,638	4,801
Iraq	2,812	67,746	402
Italy	756,800	662,839	1,221,146
Japan	28,900	54,789	48,371
Kenya	86,515	105,627	198,064
Saudi Arabia	120,208	160,583	82,879
Singapore	18,569	15,592	73,652
Thailand	19,296	40,527	106,474
United Kingdom	172,613	935,900	238,371
USA	201,662	141,823	154,082
Total (incl. others)	2,190,627	3,221,715	3,548,805

Exports	1980	1981	1982
Djibouti	6,640	3,209	2,458
Germany, Fed. Repub.	11,376	1,956	20,086
Italy	107,661	58,975	77,870
Kenya	2,425	6,929	4,211
Saudi Arabia	583,768	803,631	1,852,936
United Kingdom	1,233	—	3,169
USA	1,301	—	6,970
Yemen, People's Dem. Repub.	3,182	—	—
Total (incl. others)	844,012	960,050	2,142,585

Source: the former Ministry of Planning, Mogadishu.

1986: *Imports* (estimates, million Somali shillings) USA 1,816; Japan 836; China, People's Repub. 553; United Kingdom 773; France 341; Germany, Fed. Repub. 1,481; Total (incl. others) 8,443; *Exports* (estimates, million Somali shillings) USA 5; China, People's Repub. 4; United Kingdom 31; France 27; Germany, Fed. Repub. 11; Total (incl. others) 6,373 (Source: UN Economic Commission for Africa, *African Statistical Yearbook*).

Transport

ROAD TRAFFIC
(estimates, '000 motor vehicles in use)

	1994	1995	1996
Passenger cars	2.8	2.0	1.0
Commercial vehicles	7.4	7.3	6.4

Source: International Road Federation, *World Road Statistics*.

SHIPPING

Merchant Fleet
(registered at 31 December)

	2004	2005	2006
Number of vessels	18	18	19
Total displacement ('000 grt)	7.3	2.8	10.3

Source: Lloyd's Register-Fairplay, *World Fleet Statistics*.

International Sea-borne Freight Traffic
('000 metric tons)

	1989	1990	1991
Goods loaded	325	324	n.a.
Goods unloaded	1,252*	1,118	1,007*

*Estimate.

Source: UN Economic Commission for Africa, *African Statistical Yearbook*.

CIVIL AVIATION
(traffic on scheduled services)

	1989	1990	1991
Kilometres flown (million)	3	3	1
Passengers carried ('000)	89	88	46
Passenger-km (million)	248	255	131
Freight ton-km (million)	8	9	5

Source: UN, *Statistical Yearbook*.

Tourism

	1996	1997	1998
Tourist arrivals ('000)	10	10	10

Source: World Bank.

SOMALIA   *Directory*

Communications Media

	1995	1996	1997
Radio receivers ('000 in use)	400	450	470
Television receivers ('000 in use)	124	129	135
Telephones ('000 main lines in use)*	15	15	15
Daily newspapers	1	2	n.a.

* Estimates.

2003: Mobile cellular telephones (subscribers) 200,000; Telephones (main lines in use, estimate) 100,000; Internet users 30,000.

2004: Mobile cellular telephones (subscribers) 500,000; Telephones (main lines in use, estimate) 100,000; Internet users 86,000.

2005: Mobile cellular telephones (subscribers) 500,000; Telephones (main lines in use, estimate) 100,000; Internet users 90,000.

2006: Internet users 94,000.

Sources: UNESCO, *Statistical Yearbook*; International Telecommunication Union.

Education

(1985, unless otherwise indicated)

	Institutions	Teachers	Pupils
Pre-primary	16	133	1,558
Primary	1,224	10,338	196,496
Secondary:			
general	n.a.	2,149	39,753
teacher training	n.a.	30*	613*
vocational	n.a.	637	5,933
Higher	n.a.	817†	15,672†

* Figure refers to 1984.
† Figure refers to 1986.

Source: UNESCO, *Statistical Yearbook*.

1990 (UN estimates): 377,000 primary-level pupils; 44,000 secondary-level pupils; 10,400 higher-level pupils.

1991: University teachers 549; University students 4,640.

Adult literacy rate (UNESCO estimates): 24.0% in 2002 (Source: UN Development Programme, *Human Development Report*).

Directory

The Constitution

The Constitution promulgated in 1979 and amended in 1990 was revoked following the overthrow of President Siad Barre in January 1991. In July 2000 delegates at the Somali national reconciliation conference in Arta, Djibouti, overwhelmingly approved a national Charter, which was to serve as Somalia's constitution for an interim period of three years. The Charter, which is divided into six main parts, guarantees Somali citizens the freedoms of expression, association and human rights, and distinctly separates the executive, the legislature and the judiciary, as well as guaranteeing the independence of the latter.

The Government

HEAD OF STATE

President: Col ABDULLAHI YUSSUF AHMED (took office 14 October 2004).

CABINET
(March 2008)

Prime Minister: NUR HASSAN HUSSEIN.

Deputy Prime Minister and Minister of Education and Culture, Acting Minister of Health: AYDID ABDULLAHI ILKA HANAF.

Deputy Prime Minister and Minister of Justice and Religious Affairs, Acting Minister of Labour and Social Affairs: SALIM ALIYOW IBROW.

Deputy Prime Minister and Minister of Information, Youth Affairs and Sports: MUHAMMAD ABDISALAN ADAN.

Minister of Defence: MUHYADIN MUHAMMAD HAJI IBRAHIM.

Minister of Trade, Industry and Tourism: HUSAYN ELABE FAHIYE.

Minister of Finance and Planning: MUHAMMAD ALI HAMUD.

Minister of Air and Land Transport and Ports: MUHAMMAD IBRAHIM HABSADE.

Minister of Foreign Affairs and International Co-operation: ALI AHMAD JAMA JINGILI.

Minister of Regional Development and Federal Affairs: ABDIRAZAK ASHKIR ABDI.

Minister of Minerals and Energy: MUHAMMAD ALI SALAH.

Minister of Posts and Communications: ABDI MUHAMMAD TARAH.

Minister of Internal Affairs and National Security: MUSE NUR AMIN.

Minister of Agriculture, Water and Rural Development: MUSTAFA DUHULOW.

Minister of Public Works and Construction: NUR IDOW DAYLE.

Minister of Gender Development and Family Affairs, Acting Minister of Livestock Husbandry and Fisheries: KHADIJA MUHAMMAD DIRIYE.

In addition, there are five Deputy Ministers.

MINISTRIES

Until mid-2005 the Somali Government was based in Nairobi, Kenya, for security reasons. The President, the Prime Minister and several ministers relocated to Jowhar, Somalia, in June; however, a significant number of ministers returned to Mogadishu in defiance of the President. The Transitional Parliament (TP) held its first meeting in Baidoa, some 250 km north-west of Mogadishu, in February 2006 and the town was subsequently declared the seat of government. In mid-March 2007 the TP voted to move the Cabinet to Mogadishu, and in January 2008, following the appointment of the new Cabinet, the relocation was implemented.

Legislature

TRANSITIONAL PARLIAMENT

Speaker: SHAYKH ADAN MADOBE.

In August 2000, following the successful completion of the Somali national reconciliation conference, which commenced in Arta, Djibouti, in May, a Transitional National Assembly (TNA), comprising 245 members, was established. Despite the expiry of its mandate in August 2003, the TNA remained in place, pending the election of a new legislative body. In late January 2004, following protracted negotiations in Kenya, an agreement was signed that provided for the establishment of a new 275-member transitional national parliament, to comprise 61 representatives from each of the four major clans and 31 from an alliance of smaller clans. Members were sworn in to the Transitional Parliament in late August.

Political Organizations

Alliance for the Liberation of Somalia (ALS): f. 2007; Chair. SHEIKH HASSAN DAHIR AWEYS.

Alliance Party: Hargeysa; f. 2001; Chair. SULAYMAN MAHMUD ADAN.

Islamic Party (Hizb al-Islam): radical Islamist party; Chair. Sheikh AHMAD QASIM.

Islamic Union Party (al-Ittihad al-Islam): aims to unite ethnic Somalis from Somalia, Ethiopia, Kenya and Djibouti in an Islamic state.

Juba Valley Alliance (JVA): f. 1999; alliance of militia and businessmen from the Habr Gedir and Marehan clans; Pres. BARE ADAN SHIRE.

National Democratic League: Beled Weyne; f. 2003; Chair. Dr ABDIRAHMAN ABDULLE ALI; Sec.-Gen. ABDIKARIM HUSAYN IDOW.

SOMALIA

Northern Somali Alliance (NSA): f. 1997 as alliance between the United Somali Front and the United Somali Party.

United Somali Front (USF): f. 1989; represents Issas in the north-west of the country; Chair. ABD AR-RAHMAN DUALEH ALI; Sec.-Gen. MOHAMED OSMAN ALI.

United Somali Party (USP): opposes the SNM's declaration of the independent 'Republic of Somaliland'; Leader MOHAMED ABDI HASHI.

Peace and Development Party: Mogadishu; f. 2002; Chair. ABDULLAHI HASAN AFRAH.

Rahanwin Resistance Army (RRA): guerrilla force active around Baidoa; Chair. MOHAMED HASAN NUR.

Somali Democratic Alliance (SDA): f. 1989; represents the Gadabursi ethnic grouping in the north-west; opposes the Isaaq-dominated SNM and its declaration of an independent 'Republic of Somaliland'; Leader MOHAMED FARAH ABDULLAH.

Somali Democratic Movement (SDM): represents the Rahanwin clan; movement split in early 1992, with this faction in alliance with Ali Mahdi Mohamed; Leader ABDULKADIR MOHAMED ADAN.

Somali Eastern and Central Front (SECF): f. 1991; opposes the SNM's declaration of the independent 'Republic of Somaliland'; Chair. HIRSI ISMAIL MOHAMED.

Somali National Alliance (SNA): f. 1992 as alliance between the Southern Somali National Movement (which withdrew in 1993) and the factions of the United Somali Congress, Somali Democratic Movement and Somali Patriotic Movement given below; Chair. HUSSEIN MOHAMED AIDID.

Somali Democratic Movement (SDM): represents the Rahanwin clan; Chair. ADAM UTHMAN ABDI; Sec.-Gen. Dr YASIN MA'ALIM ABDULLAHI.

Somali Patriotic Movement (SPM): f. 1989; represents Ogadenis (of the southern Darod clan); Chair. GEDI UGAS MADHAR.

United Somali Congress (USC): f. 1989; overthrew Siad Barre in 1991; party split in mid-1991, and again in mid-1995; Chair. OSMAN HASSAN ALI 'ATO'.

Somali National Front (SNF): f. 1991; guerrilla force active in southern Somalia, promoting Darod clan interests and seeking restoration of SRSP Govt; a rival faction (led by OMAR HAJI MASALEH) is active in southern Somalia; Leader Gen. MOHAMED SIAD HERSI 'MORGAN'.

Somali National Salvation Council: f. 2003; Chair. MUSE SUDI YALAHOW.

Somali Patriotic Movement (SPM): f. 1989 in southern Somalia; represents Ogadenis (of the Darod clan) in southern Somalia; this faction of the SPM has allied with the SNF in opposing the SNA; Chair. Gen. ADEN ABDULLAHI NOOR ('Gabio').

Somali Peace Loving Party: Mogadishu; f. 2002; Dr KHALID UMAR ALI.

Somali People's Democratic Union (SPDU): f. 1997; breakaway group from the SSDF; Chair. Gen. MOHAMED JIBRIL MUSEH.

Somali Reconciliation and Restoration Council (SRRC): f. 2001 by faction leaders opposed to the establishment of the Hasan administration; aims to establish a rival national govt; Co-Chair. HUSSEIN MOHAMED AIDID, HILOWLE IMAN UMAR, ADEN ABDULLAHI NOOR, HASAN MOHAMED NUR, ABDULLAHI SHAYKH ISMA'IL; Sec.-Gen. MOWLID MA'ANEH MOHAMED.

Somali Revolutionary Socialist Party (SRSP): f. 1976 as the sole legal party; overthrown in Jan. 1991; conducts guerrilla operations in Gedo region, near border with Kenya; Sec.-Gen. (vacant); Asst Sec.-Gen. AHMED SULEIMAN ABDULLAH.

Somali Salvation Democratic Front (SSDF): f. 1981 as the Democratic Front for the Salvation of Somalia (DFSS), as a coalition of the Somali Salvation Front, the Somali Workers' Party and the Democratic Front for the Liberation of Somalia; operates in cen. Somalia, although a smaller group has opposed the SNA around Kismayu in alliance with the SNF; Chair. MOHAMED ABSHIR MONSA.

Somali Solidarity Party: Mogadishu; f. 1999; Chair. ABD AR-RAHMAN MUSA MOHAMED; Sec.-Gen. SA'ID ISA MOHAMED.

Southern Somali National Movement (SSNM): based on coast in southern Somalia; Chair. ABDI WARSEMEH ISAR.

Supreme Somali Islamic Courts Council: formerly the Union of Islamic Courts; seeks to create a Somali state under the guiding principles of *Shari'a* (Islamic) law; Chair. Sheikh HASSAN DAHIR AWEYS.

United Somali Congress (USC): f. 1989 in cen. Somalia; overthrew Siad Barre in Jan. 1991; party split in 1991, with this faction dominated by the Abgal sub-clan of the Hawiye clan, Somalia's largest ethnic group; Leader ABDULLAHI MA'ALIN; Sec.-Gen. MUSA NUR AMIN.

United Somali Congress—Somali National Alliance (USC—SNA): f. 1995 by dissident mems of the SNA's USC faction; represents the Habr Gedir sub-clan of the Hawiye; Leader OSMAN HASSAN ALI 'ATO'.

United Somali Congress—Somali Salvation Alliance (USC—SSA): Leader MUSE SUDI YALAHOW.

Unity for the Somali Republic Party (USRP): f. 1999; the first independent party to be established in Somalia since 1969; Leader ABDI NUR DARMAN.

In November 1993 interim President Ali Mahdi Mohamed was reported to have assumed the leadership of the **Somali Salvation Alliance (SSA)**, a coalition of 12 factions opposed to Gen. Aidid, including the Somali African Muki Organization (SAMO), the Somali National Union (SNU), the USF, the SDA, the SDM, the SPM, the USC (pro-Mahdi faction), the SSDF, the Somali National Democratic Union (SNDU), the SNF and the SSNM. In May 1994 the SNU announced its intention to leave the alliance and join the SNA.

Diplomatic Representation

EMBASSIES IN SOMALIA

Note: Following the overthrow of Siad Barre in January 1991, all foreign embassies in Somalia were closed and all diplomatic personnel left the country. Some embassies were reopened, including those of France, Sudan and the USA, following the arrival of the US-led Unified Task Force (UNITAF) in December 1992; however, nearly all foreign diplomats left Somalia in anticipation of the withdrawal of the UN peace-keeping force, UNOSOM, in early 1995.

Cuba: Mogadishu.

Djibouti: Mogadishu.

Iran: Via al-Mukarah, POB 1166, Mogadishu; tel. (1) 80881.

Korea, Democratic People's Republic: Via Km 5, Mogadishu; Ambassador KIM RYONG SU.

Kuwait: First Medina Rd, Km 5, POB 1348, Mogadishu.

Libya: Via Medina, POB 125, Mogadishu; Ambassador MOHAMED ZUBEYD.

Pakistan: Via Afgoi, Km 5, POB 339, Mogadishu; tel. (1) 80856.

Sudan: Via al-Mukarah, POB 552, Mogadishu; Chargé d'affaires a.i. ALI HASSAN ALI.

Turkey: Via Km 6, POB 2833, Mogadishu; tel. (1) 81975.

United Arab Emirates: Via Afgoi, Km 5, Mogadishu; tel. (1) 23178.

Yemen: K4, Mogadishu; Ambassador AHMED HAMID ALI UMAR.

Judicial System

Constitutional arrangements in operation until 1991 provided for the Judiciary to be independent of the executive and legislative powers. Laws and acts having the force of law were required to conform to the provisions of the Constitution and to the general principles of Islam.

Attorney-General: ABDULLAH DAHIR BARRE.

Supreme Court: Mogadishu; the court of final instance in civil, criminal, administrative and auditing matters; Chair. Sheikh AHMAD HASAN.

Military Supreme Court: Mogadishu; f. 1970; tried mems of the armed forces.

National Security Court: Mogadishu; heard cases of treason.

Courts of Appeal: Mogadishu; sat at Mogadishu and Hargeysa, with two sections, General and Assize.

Regional Courts: There were eight Regional Courts, with two sections, General and Assize.

District Courts: There were 84 District Courts, with Civil and Criminal Divisions. The Civil Division had jurisdiction over all controversies where the cause of action had arisen under *Shari'a* (Islamic) Law or Customary Law and any other Civil controversies where the matter in dispute did not involve more than 3,000 shillings. The Criminal Division had jurisdiction with respect to offences punishable with imprisonment not exceeding three years, or fines not exceeding 3,000 shillings, or both.

Qadis: District Courts of civil jurisdiction under Islamic Law.

In September 1993, in accordance with Resolution 865 of the UN Security Council, a judiciary re-establishment council, composed of Somalis, was created in Mogadishu to rehabilitate the judicial and penal systems.

Judiciary Re-establishment Council (JRC): Mogadishu; Chair. Dr ABD AL-RAHMAN HAJI GA'AL.

Following the withdrawal of the UN peace-keeping force, UNOSOM, in early 1995, most regions outside Mogadishu reverted to clan-based fiefdoms where Islamic (*Shari'a*) law (comprising an Islamic Supreme Council and local Islamic high courts) prevailed. In October

SOMALIA   Directory

1996 Ali Mahdi Mohamed endorsed a new Islamic judicial system under which appeals could be lodged on all sentences passed by Islamic courts, and no sentence imposed by the courts could be implemented prior to an appeal court ruling. In August 1998 the Governor of the Banaadir administration announced the application of *Shari'a* law in Mogadishu and its environs thenceforth.

Religion

ISLAM

Islam is the state religion. Most Somalis are Sunni Muslims.

Imam: Gen. MOHAMED ABSHIR.

CHRISTIANITY

The Roman Catholic Church

Somalia comprises a single diocese, directly responsible to the Holy See. At 31 December 2005 there were an estimated 100 adherents.

Bishop of Mogadishu: (vacant), POB 273, Ahmed bin Idris, Mogadishu; tel. (1) 20184; e-mail evechcat@intnet.dj.

The Anglican Communion

Within the Episcopal Church in Jerusalem and the Middle East, the Bishop in Egypt has jurisdiction over Somalia.

The Press

The Country: POB 1178, Mogadishu; tel. (1) 21206; f. 1991; daily.

Dalka: POB 388, Mogadishu; tel. (1) 500533; e-mail dalka@somalinternet.com; internet www.dalka-online.com; f. 1967; current affairs; weekly.

Heegan (Vigilance): POB 1178, Mogadishu; tel. (1) 21206; f. 1978; weekly; English; Editor MOHAMOUD M. AFRAH.

Horseed: POB 1178, Mogadishu; tel. (1) 21206; e-mail horseednet@gmail.com; internet www.horseednet.com; weekly; in Somali and English.

Huuriya (Liberty): Hargeysa; daily.

Jamhuuriya (The Republic): Hargeysa; e-mail webmaster@jamhuuriya.info; internet www.jamhuuriya.info; independent; daily; Editor-in-Chief HASSAN SAÏD FAISAL ALI; circ. 2,500.

Al Mujeehid: Hargeysa; weekly.

New Era: POB 1178, Mogadishu; tel. (1) 21206; quarterly; in English, Somali and Arabic.

Qaran Press (Maalinle Madaxbannaan): Mogadishu; tel. (1) 215305; internet www.qaranpress.com; financial information; daily; in Somali; Editor ABDULAHI AHMED ALI; circ. 2,000.

Riyaaq (Happiness): Bossaso.

Sahan (Pioneer): Bossaso; Editor MUHAMMAD DEEQ.

Somalia in Figures: Ministry of National Planning, POB 1742, Mogadishu; tel. (1) 80384; govt statistical publ; 3 a year; in English.

Somalia Times: POB 555, Mogadishu BN 03040; e-mail info@somalpost.com; internet www.somaliatimes.com; Somali; weekly; circ. 50,000.

NEWS AGENCIES

Horn of Africa News Agency: Mogadishu; e-mail info@hananews.org; internet www.hananews.org; f. 1990.

Somali National News Agency (SONNA): POB 1748, Mogadishu; tel. (1) 24058; Dir MUHAMMAD HASAN KAHIN.

Publishers

Government Printer: POB 1743, Mogadishu.

Somalia d'Oggi: Piazzale della Garesa, POB 315, Mogadishu; law, economics and reference.

Broadcasting and Communications

TELECOMMUNICATIONS

Ministry of Information: POB 1748, Mogadishu; tel. (1) 999621; Dir-Gen. A. ALI ASKAR.

Somali Telecom (Olympic Telecommunications): Mogadishu.

Somaliland Telecommunications Corpn: Hargeysa; Dir MOHAMED ARWO.

Telcom Somaliland: Telcom Somaliland Bldg, Togdheer St, Hargeysa; tel. (2) 300161; fax (2) 300162; e-mail info@telcomsomaliland.com; internet www.telcomsomaliland.com; f. 2003; provides local, national long distance and int. telecommunications, mobile communications and data services.

BROADCASTING

Radio

Holy Koran Radio: Mogadishu; f. 1996; religious broadcasts in Somali.

Radio Awdal: Boorama, 'Somaliland'; operated by the Gadabursi clan.

Radio Banaadir: Tahlil Warsame Bldg, 4 Maka al-Mukarama Rd, Mogadishu; tel. (5) 944176; e-mail rbb@radiobanadir.com; internet www.radiobanadir.com; f. 2000; serves Mogadishu and its environs.

Radio Free Somalia: f. 1993; operates from Galacaio in north-eastern Somalia; relays humanitarian and educational programmes.

Radio Gaalkayco: operates from 'Puntland'.

Radio Hargeysa, the Voice of the 'Republic of Somaliland': POB 14, Hargeysa; tel. 155; e-mail radiohargeysa@yahoo.com; internet www.radiosomaliland.com/radiohargeisa.html; serves the northern region ('Somaliland'); broadcasts in Somali, and relays Somali and Amharic transmission from Radio Mogadishu; Dir of Radio IDRIS EGAL NUR.

Radio HornAfrique: Mogadishu; f. 1999; commercial independent station broadcasting music and programmes on social issues; Dir AHMAD ABDI SALAN HAJI ADAN.

Radio Mogadishu, Voice of the Masses of the Somali Republic: southern Mogadishu; f. 1993 by supporters of Gen. Aidid after the facilities of the fmr state-controlled radio station, Radio Mogadishu (of which Gen. Aidid's faction took control in 1991), were destroyed by UNOSOM; broadcasts in Somali, Amharic, Arabic, English and Swahili; Chair. FARAH HASAN AYOBOQORE.

Radio Mogadishu, Voice of Somali Pacification: Mogadishu; f. 1995 by supporters of Osman Hassan Ali 'Ato'; broadcasts in Somali, English and Arabic; Dir-Gen. MUHAMMAD DIRIYEH ILMI.

Radio Mogadishu, Voice of the Somali Republic: northern Mogadishu; f. 1992 by supporters of Ali Mahdi Mohamed; Chair. FARAH HASSAN AYOBOQORE.

Radio Somaliland: internet www.radiosomaliland.com.

Voice of Peace: POB 1631, Addis Ababa, Ethiopia; f. 1993; aims to promote peace and reconstruction in Somalia; receives support from UNICEF and the AU.

Some radio receivers are used for public address purposes in small towns and villages.

Note: In January 2007 the Transitional National Government was granted emergency powers to proscribe four media companies in an attempt to restore order in Mogadishu. HornAfrique Media and Shabelle Media were believed to have ceased operations although others condemned the ban and refused to close.

Television

A television service, financed by Kuwait and the United Arab Emirates, was inaugurated in 1983. Programmes in Somali and Arabic are broadcast for three hours daily, extended to four hours on Fridays and public holidays. Reception is limited to a 30-km radius of Mogadishu.

Somali Television Network (STN): Mogadishu; f. 1999; broadcasts 22 channels in Somali, English, French, Hindi, Gujarati, Bengali, Punjabi, Italian and Arabic; Man. Dir ABURAHMAN ROBLEY ULAYEREH.

Television HornAfrique: Mogadishu; f. 1999; broadcasts 6 channels in Somali and Arabic; CEO ALI IMAN SHARMARKEH.

Finance

(cap. = capital; res = reserves; m. = million; brs = branches; amounts in Somali shillings unless otherwise stated)

BANKING

Central Bank

Central Bank of Somalia (Bankiga Dhexe ee Soomaaliya): Corso Somalia 55, POB 11, Mogadishu; tel. (1) 657733; f. 1960; bank of issue; cap. and res 132.5m. (Sept. 1985); Gov. BASHIR ISSE ALI; Gen. Man MOHAMED MOHAMED NUR.

A central bank (with 10 branches) is also in operation in Hargeysa (in the self-proclaimed 'Republic of Somaliland').

Commercial Banks

Commercial Bank of Somalia: Via Primo Luglio, POB 203, Mogadishu; tel. (1) 22861; f. 1990 to succeed the Commercial and Savings Bank of Somalia; state-owned; cap. 1,000m. (May 1990); 33 brs.

Universal Bank of Somalia: Mogadishu; f. 2002; cap. US $10m.; Gen. Man. MAHAD ADAN BARKHADLE (acting).

Private Bank

Somali-Malaysian Commercial Bank: Mogadishu; f. 1997; cap. US $4m.

Development Bank

Somali Development Bank: Via Primo Luglio, POB 1079, Mogadishu; tel. (1) 21800; f. 1968; state-owned; cap. and res 2,612.7m. (Dec. 1988); Pres. MOHAMED MOHAMED NUR; 4 brs.

INSURANCE

Cassa per le Assicurazioni Sociali della Somalia: POB 123, Mogadishu; f. 1950; workers' compensation; Dir-Gen. HASSAN MOHAMED JAMA; 9 brs.

State Insurance Co of Somalia: POB 992, Mogadishu; f. 1974; Gen. Man. ABDULLAHI GA'AL; brs throughout Somalia.

Trade and Industry

DEVELOPMENT ORGANIZATIONS

Agricultural Development Corpn: POB 930, Mogadishu; f. 1971 by merger of fmr agricultural and machinery agencies and grain marketing board; supplies farmers with equipment and materials and purchases growers' cereal and oil seed crops; Dir-Gen. MOHAMED FARAH ANSHUR.

Livestock Development Agency: POB 1759, Mogadishu; f. 1966; Dir-Gen. HASSAN WELI SHEIKH HUSSEN; brs throughout Somalia.

Somali Co-operative Movement: Mogadishu; Chair. HASSAN HAWADLE MADAR.

Somali Oil Refinery: POB 1241, Mogadishu; Chair. NUR AHMED DARAWISH.

Water Development Agency: POB 525, Mogadishu; Dir-Gen. KHALIF HAJI FARAH.

CHAMBER OF COMMERCE

Chamber of Commerce and Industry: Somali Chamber Bldg, nr Banadir Hotel, Shibis District, Mogadishu; tel. (1) 643081; fax (1) 221560; e-mail info@somalicci.com; internet www.somalicci.com; f. 1970.

TRADE ASSOCIATION

National Agency of Foreign Trade: POB 602, Mogadishu; tel. (1) 120485; major foreign trade agency; state-owned; brs in Berbera and over 150 centres throughout Somalia; Dir-Gen. JAMA AW MUSE.

UTILITIES

Water Development Agency: POB 525, Mogadishu; Dir-Gen. KHALIF HAJI FARAH.

TRADE UNIONS

National Union of Somali Journalists (NUSOJ): Tree Biano Bldg, Via al-Mukarah Km 4, Mogadishu; fax (1) 859944; e-mail nusoj@nusoj.org; internet www.nusoj.org; f. 2002 as Somali Journalists' Network (SOJON); name changed as above in 2005; Sec.-Gen. OMAR FARUK OSMAN; 6 brs across Somalia.

Transport

RAILWAYS

There are no railways in Somalia.

ROADS

In 1999 there were an estimated 22,100 km of roads, of which some 11.8% were paved.

SHIPPING

Merca, Berbera, Mogadishu and Kismayu are the chief ports. An EU-sponsored development project for the port of Berbera (in 'Somaliland') was announced in February 1996. It was reported that the port of Mogadishu, which had been largely closed since 1995, was reopened to commercial traffic in August 2006. In 2005 the International Maritime Bureau warned ship operators to avoid the coast of Somalia following an increase in piracy.

Somali Ports Authority: POB 935, Mogadishu; tel. (1) 30081; Port Dir MOHAMED JUMA FURAH.

Juba Enterprises Beder & Sons Ltd: POB 549, Mogadishu; privately owned.

National Shipping Line: POB 588, Mogadishu; tel. (1) 23021; state-owned; Gen. Man. Dr ABDULLAHI MOHAMED SALAD.

Puntland Shipping Service: Bossaso.

Shosman Commercial Co Ltd: North-Eastern Pasaso; privately owned.

Somali Shipping Corpn: POB 2775, Mogadishu; state-owned.

CIVIL AVIATION

Mogadishu has an international airport. There are airports at Hargeysa and Baidoa and six other airfields. It was reported that a daily service had been inaugurated in April 1994 between Hargeysa (in the self-declared 'Republic of Somaliland') and Nairobi, Kenya. Mogadishu international airport (closed since 1995) was officially re-opened in mid-1998, but continuing civil unrest hampered services. In August 2006 the airport reopened to commercial flights.

Air Somalia: Mogadishu; f. 2001; operates internal passenger services and international services to destinations in Africa and the Middle East; Chair. ALI FARAH ABDULLEH.

Jubba Airways: POB 6200, 30th St, Mogadishu; tel. (1) 217000; fax (1) 227711; e-mail jubbaair@emirates.net.ae; internet www.jubba-airways.com; f. 1998; operates domestic flights and flights to destinations in Djibouti, Saudi Arabia, the United Arab Emirates and Yemen.

SOUTH AFRICA

Introductory Survey

Location, Climate, Language, Religion, Flag, Capital

The Republic of South Africa occupies the southern extremity of the African mainland. It is bordered by Namibia to the north-west, by Botswana and Zimbabwe to the north, by Mozambique to the north-east, and by Swaziland to the east. Lesotho is completely surrounded by South African territory. The climate is generally sub-tropical, but with considerable regional variations. Temperatures in Cape Town, on the south-west coast, vary from 7°C (45°F) to 26°C (79°F), with an annual average of about 17°C (63°F). Annual rainfall averages 510 mm (20 ins) at Cape Town, and 1,101 mm (43 ins) at Durban, on the east coast. The official languages are Sepedi, Sesotho, Setswana, siSwati, Tshivenda, Xitsonga, Afrikaans, English, isiNdebele, isiXhosa and isiZulu. About 79.0% of the population are black, 9.6% are white, 8.9% are Coloured (of mixed race), and 2.5% are Asian (mainly of Indian origin). Most of the inhabitants profess Christianity, although traditional African religions are still adhered to. There are also small minorities of Hindus (nearly all Asians) and Muslims (mainly Coloureds and Asians). The national flag (proportions 2 by 3) has a green 'Y' shape extending from the upper and lower hoist corners to the centre of the fly end, bordered in white on its outer edges, and in light orange on its inner edges near the hoist; the areas above and below the horizontal band of the 'Y' are red and blue respectively, with a black triangle at the hoist. The administrative capital is Pretoria, the legislative capital is Cape Town, and the judicial capital is Bloemfontein.

Recent History

On 31 May 1910 four British dependencies were merged to form the Union of South Africa, a dominion under the British Crown. In 1931 the British Parliament recognized the Union as an independent country within the Commonwealth. From the establishment of South Africa until 1984, national administration was the exclusive preserve of the white population.

The National Party (NP), which acceded to power in 1948, introduced the doctrine of apartheid (in theory the separate, but equal, development of all racial groups, in practice leading to white, particularly Afrikaner, supremacy). The principal opposition to government policy during the 1950s took the form of a campaign of civil disobedience, led by the multiracial African National Congress of South Africa (ANC). In 1959 some members of the ANC formed the exclusively black Pan-Africanist Congress (PAC). In 1960 the ANC and the PAC protested against the 'pass laws' (which required blacks to be in possession of special documentation in designated white urban areas); at one demonstration, in Sharpeville, 67 blacks were killed by security forces, prompting international outrage, and further demonstrations within South Africa, as a result of which the ANC and the PAC were declared illegal. Both movements subsequently formed military wings, based outside South Africa, to conduct campaigns of sabotage. An influential leader of the ANC, Nelson Mandela, was detained in 1962 and sentenced to life imprisonment on a charge of sabotage in 1964, but remained a focus for opposition to apartheid.

On 31 May 1961, following a referendum among white voters in October 1960, South Africa became a republic, and left the Commonwealth. Dr Hendrik Verwoerd was Prime Minister from 1958 until his assassination in September 1966. He was succeeded by the former Minister of Justice, Balthazar Johannes (B. J.) Vorster.

As an integral part of the policy of apartheid, the territorial segregation of African ethnic groups was enforced, on the grounds that the Native Reserves (comprising only 13% of national territory) constituted the historic 'homelands' (Bantustans) of different African nations. In 1963 Transkei was accorded 'self-governing' status, with an Executive Council, headed by a Chief Minister, to be elected by a Legislative Assembly. Bophuthatswana (June 1972), Ciskei (August 1972), Lebowa (October 1972), Gazankulu (February 1973), KwaZulu (April 1973), Qwaqwa (November 1974), KwaNdebele (October 1977), and KaNgwane (August 1984) were subsequently granted 'self-government'. Transkei was declared 'independent' in October 1976, Bophuthatswana in December 1977, Venda in September 1979 and Ciskei in December 1981. The population of the 'independent homelands' was not entitled to South African citizenship. The 'independent homelands' were not recognized by any government other than that of South Africa.

The numerous discriminatory laws regulating the lives of the country's black, 'Coloured' (a term used to denote people of mixed race) and 'Indian' (Asian) populations, combined with stringent security legislation, led to the detention without trial of many of the Government's opponents, the banning of black political organizations outside the 'homelands', and the forced removal of hundreds of thousands of blacks in accordance with the provisions of the Group Areas Act of 1966 (which imposed residential segregation of the races) and the 'homelands' policy. In June 1976 violent riots occurred in Soweto (South-Western Townships), near Johannesburg, and rapidly spread to other black urban areas. Vorster used the executive's virtually limitless powers, conferred by the newly adopted Internal Security Act, to suppress riots and strikes. Several hundred people died in confrontations with the security forces, and many more were detained without trial. Allegations of human rights violations by security forces culminated in international indignation at the death in detention of a black community leader, Steve Biko, in September 1977. In 1978 black, Coloured and Indian activists founded the Azanian People's Organization (AZAPO).

In September 1978 Vorster resigned as Prime Minister, and was succeeded by Pieter Willem (P. W.) Botha, hitherto the Minister of Defence. In February 1981 a new, 60-member advisory body, the President's Council, comprising representatives of the white, Coloured and Indian population, was formed to consider constitutional reform. Its recommendations to include Coloureds and Indians (but not blacks) in a three-chamber Parliament, with a multiracial government (led by an executive President), exacerbated inter-party differences: the 'verligte' (liberal) wing of the NP, led by Botha, advocated the establishment of a confederation of South Africa and the 'homelands', with separate citizenships but a common South African nationality, and was strongly opposed by the 'verkrampte' (uncompromising) wing of the party. In March 1982 16 extreme right-wing parliamentary deputies who had opposed the constitutional recommendations were expelled from the NP; they subsequently formed the Conservative Party of South Africa (CP), in conjunction with other right-wing elements.

Throughout 1983 and 1984 Botha pursued his policy of constitutional reform. The majority vote of the Coloured Labour Party (LP) in 1983 to participate in the reform programme caused divisions within the party. The constitutional body representing the Indian population, the South African Indian Council (SAIC), provisionally agreed to the proposals, subject to approval by an Indian community referendum. This decision was opposed by the Transvaal Anti-SAIC Committee, an organization that had been formed in 1981 in protest at participation in elections to the SAIC. In August 1983 the Committee established the United Democratic Front (UDF), to organize resistance on a national scale to Indian and Coloured participation in the constitutional reforms. The UDF rapidly became the principal legal opposition movement.

The constitutional reforms were approved by the House of Assembly in September 1983, and by about 66% of voters in an all-white referendum in November. In the same month the Progressive Federal Party (PFP) decided to take part in the reformed system. However, six 'homeland' leaders, including Chief Mangosuthu Gatsha Buthelezi, the Chief Minister of KwaZulu (who had consistently opposed the 'homelands' policy), rejected the constitutional reforms on the grounds that blacks remained excluded from participation in the central Government. Despite a previous pledge by the Prime Minister to assess Coloured and Indian opinion on the reforms, elections to the Coloured and Indian chambers of the new Parliament, known as the House of Representatives and the House of Delegates respectively, took place in August 1984, without prior referendums. As a result, the boycott that had been organized by the

UDF was widely observed: about 18% of the eligible Coloured population voted in the elections to the House of Representatives, with the LP winning 76 of the 80 directly elected seats, while only 16.6% of eligible Indian voters participated in the elections to the House of Delegates, with the National People's Party (NPP) winning 18 and the Solidarity Party 17 of the 40 directly elected seats. (The House of Assembly, as elected in 1981, remained in office.)

The new Constitution came into effect in September 1984. Under the terms of the Constitution, legislative power was vested in the State President and the tricameral Parliament, comprising the 178-member House of Assembly (for the representation of whites), the 85-member House of Representatives (for Coloureds) and the 45-member House of Delegates (for Indians). The post of Prime Minister was abolished and Botha was unanimously elected to the new office of State President (which combined the powers of Head of State and Prime Minister) by an electoral college, comprising members of all three parliamentary chambers. A President's Council, a new Cabinet and three Ministers' Councils (one for each population group) were subsequently established. The Cabinet comprised only two non-white members, the Chairmen of the Indian and Coloured Ministers' Councils, neither of whom was given a portfolio.

During 1985–86 a number of the laws on which apartheid was based were modified or repealed, prompting strong right-wing opposition. The Immorality Act (1927) and the Prohibition of Mixed Marriages Act (1949), which banned sexual relations and marriage between members of different races, were repealed in April 1985, and in the following month it was announced that the Prohibition of Political Interference Act (1967), prohibiting members of different racial groups from belonging to the same political party, was to be abrogated. In April 1986 the Government promulgated legislation that provided for the removal of a number of restrictions on the movement, residence and employment of blacks in white urban areas. On 1 July the 'pass laws' were officially repealed, with the introduction of uniform identity documents for all South African citizens. On the same day reforms concerning the structure of local and provincial government were implemented, and legislation granting blacks limited rights to own property in black urban areas entered into force. In the same month it was announced that citizens of the four 'independent homelands' who were residing and working permanently in South Africa were to regain South African citizenship; in effect, however, only a small proportion of the population of the 'homelands' was eligible. Following discussions, initiated by Buthelezi in April 1986, regarding the establishment of a joint authority for his 'homeland', KwaZulu, and the province of Natal, the Government agreed to the formation of an administrative body, the Joint Executive Authority (which was installed in November 1987).

The introduction of the new Constitution in September 1984 prompted severe rioting in the black townships. Factional clashes within the black community also occurred, notably between supporters of the ANC and of the Inkatha Movement, a Zulu organization led by Buthelezi. In July 1985 the Government declared a state of emergency in 36 districts; by March 1986 it was estimated that 757 people had been killed, and almost 8,000 arrested. In June of that year Botha declared a nation-wide state of emergency, on the grounds that national security was endangered by subversive elements. Press censorship subsequently became progressively stricter, and the powers of the security forces were extended. Opposition to the Government emerged from the influential Congress of South African Trade Unions (COSATU).

At a general election to the House of Assembly in May 1987, the NP secured 123 of the 166 directly-elective seats. The CP increased its representation from 17 to 22 elective seats, thereby replacing the PFP as the official opposition. In June the Government renewed the state of emergency, and further stringent press restrictions were imposed.

In January 1989 Botha withdrew from his official duties, owing to ill health; in February he resigned as leader of the NP, and was succeeded by Frederik Willem (F. W.) de Klerk, hitherto Minister of National Education. Despite almost unanimous demands from the party that he should share power with de Klerk before retiring at the next general election, Botha refused to allow his power as State President to be eroded, and in March he resumed his official duties. In April the PFP, the Independent Party (which had been formed by one of a number of 'verligte' defectors from the NP in 1988) and the National Democratic Movement (established by dissident PFP members in late 1987) merged to form the Democratic Party (DP).

The state of emergency was extended for a further 12 months in June 1989. In August Botha claimed that members of his Cabinet had omitted to inform him of a prospective visit by de Klerk to Zambia to meet with President Kenneth Kaunda (which he opposed, owing to Kaunda's support for the ANC). Following a confrontation with the Cabinet, Botha resigned as State President. Shortly afterwards de Klerk was appointed acting President.

Elections to the three Houses of Parliament took place in September 1989. The NP won 93 of the 166 elective seats in the House of Assembly, while the CP secured 39 seats, and the DP 33 seats. Less than 12% of the Coloured electorate voted in the general election to the House of Representatives, at which the LP won 69 of the 80 directly-elective seats. Some 20% of the Indian electorate voted in the general election to the House of Delegates: the Solidarity Party secured 16 of the 40 directly-elective seats, while the NPP won nine. In mid-September, following his inauguration as State President, de Klerk stated that the implementation of constitutional reforms was his highest priority.

On 2 February 1990 de Klerk announced several radical reforms, including the legalization of the ANC, the PAC, the South African Communist Party (SACP), the UDF and more than 30 other banned political organizations. Nelson Mandela and a further 120 political prisoners were to be released unconditionally. In addition, most emergency regulations restricting the media were to be removed, as were repressive measures imposed on former political detainees; detention without trial was to be limited to a maximum of six months. De Klerk confirmed that the Government intended to initiate negotiations with the black opposition, with the aim of drafting a new democratic constitution. Leaders of the extreme right-wing parties reacted to de Klerk's reforms with threats of violence.

Mandela's release from prison, on 11 February 1990, received much international attention. In March he was elected Deputy President of the ANC. In spite of appeals by Mandela for reconciliation between rival factions within the black community, the continuing violence in Natal between supporters of the Inkatha Movement and mainly Xhosa-speaking supporters of the ANC intensified in March and April, and unrest erupted in several black townships. The first formal discussions between the ANC and the de Klerk Government took place in early May. In mid-May legislation was introduced that granted temporary immunity from prosecution to political exiles who had committed crimes, including leaders of the ANC. In June de Klerk repealed the state of emergency in all provinces except Natal. In July Buthelezi reconstituted the Inkatha Movement as the Inkatha Freedom Party (IFP), in order to participate in future constitutional negotiations. At a second series of discussions in August, the ANC and the Government reached an agreement whereby, in preparation for constitutional negotiations, the ANC was to suspend its guerrilla activities, and the Government was to release more than 3,000 political prisoners and to facilitate the return to South Africa of an estimated 40,000 exiles. However, the ANC subsequently continued to train recruits for its military wing (known as Umkhonto we Sizwe—MK) and to stockpile ammunition, thereby contravening the terms of its cease-fire and causing the Government to delay the release of political prisoners and the repatriation of exiles.

During August 1990 factional fighting between supporters of the IFP and of the ANC escalated in the black townships surrounding Johannesburg; more than 500 people were reported to have been killed by the end of that month. Nevertheless, in October the state of emergency was revoked in Natal. Also that month the Separate Amenities Act of 1953 (which had imposed racial segregation with regard to public amenities) was repealed, prompting right-wing protests, particularly from the Afrikaanse Weerstandsbeweging (AWB), a paramilitary organization that had been formed in 1973 under the leadership of Eugene Terre'Blanche. During October the NP opened its membership to all races. In December Oliver Tambo, the President of the ANC, returned to South Africa after more than 30 years in exile.

In February 1991 de Klerk announced that he was to introduce draft legislation to repeal the principal remaining apartheid laws: the Land Acts of 1913 and 1936 (which stipulated that the black population was entitled to own only 13.6% of the land), the Group Areas Act, the Black Communities Act of 1984 (which enforced the separate status of black townships) and the Population Registration Act of 1950 (which decreed that all South

Africans should be registered at birth according to race) were subsequently abolished. In the same month the Government agreed to assume joint administrative powers in Ciskei, following increasing pressure within the 'independent homeland' for its reincorporation into South Africa and for the resignation of its military ruler. In mid-February the Government and the ANC reached agreement on the release of political prisoners, the return of exiles and the curtailment of activities by the MK. However, increasing township violence continued to impede constitutional negotiations.

In May 1991 Winnie Mandela, the wife of Nelson Mandela, was found guilty of assaulting and kidnapping a young ANC activist, Stompie Moeketsi Seipei, in 1988, and was sentenced to six years' imprisonment, causing considerable embarrassment for the ANC. (Winnie Mandela, who separated from Nelson Mandela in 1992, remained at liberty, pending an appeal against the verdict; in June 1993 the conviction for assault was overturned, and her sentence was commuted to a fine and a suspended term of imprisonment.) In July 1991, at a national congress of the ANC, Nelson Mandela was elected as its President and Cyril Ramaphosa, hitherto leader of the National Union of Mineworkers, was elected Secretary-General of the organization.

In August 1991 the Government declared an amnesty for all political exiles. During that month the UDF was dissolved. In September the Government, the ANC, the IFP and 23 other political organizations signed a national peace accord, in an attempt to end township violence; however, unrest continued to escalate. In October a judicial commission of inquiry was established to assess the causes of civil violence.

A multi-party conference on South Africa's future, known as the Convention for a Democratic South Africa (CODESA), was convened in December 1991. CODESA was attended by the Government and 18 political organizations, including the ANC, the NP, the DP, the LP, the NPP, New Solidarity (formerly the Solidarity Party) and representatives of the 'homelands' (including the IFP, which represented KwaZulu); the conference was boycotted by the PAC, AZAPO and the CP. The negotiating body's stated aim to create an undivided South Africa was rejected by the IFP, which favoured the concept of a South African federation of independent states, and by the Bophuthatswana administration, which demanded total independence from South Africa.

In March 1992 a referendum of the white population, aimed at determining the level of support for the negotiation of a democratic constitution, resulted in an overwhelming mandate for the continuation of the process of reform. In May, however, constitutional negotiations were suspended, owing to the Government's insistence on having a majority vote in CODESA. The ANC subsequently organized a campaign of mass protests. In June several residents of Boipatong, a black township, were massacred, apparently by Inkatha supporters and allegedly with the complicity of the security forces. Following a visit to the township by de Klerk, 30 demonstrators were killed as the security forces suppressed an anti-Government protest. The ANC subsequently withdrew from all bilateral discussions with the Government, pending the latter's agreement to a number of demands, including the immediate release of all remaining political prisoners and effective action to curtail township violence. In August the ANC, SACP and COSATU intensified their campaign of anti-Government protests. In the same month several parliamentary deputies belonging to the CP defected to form a new extreme right-wing party, the Afrikaner Volksunie (AVU).

In mid-1992 the ANC announced that it was to organize a series of demonstrations in protest against 'homeland' leaders who wished their territories (Bophuthatswana, Ciskei, KwaZulu and Qwaqwa) to retain a strong measure of autonomy in the future South Africa. In September Ciskei security forces killed 28 ANC demonstrators, and injured about 200, prompting international outrage. The ANC accused the South African security forces (some of whose members had been seconded to Ciskei) of complicity in the incident. In mid-September de Klerk announced that measures to reduce the 'independence' of the 'homelands' would be implemented. In late 1992 the leaders of Bophuthatswana, Ciskei and KwaZulu, in conjunction with the IFP, the AVU and the CP, formed a pressure group (the Concerned South Africans Group—COSAG) to campaign for a maximum degree of regional autonomy.

In late September 1992 a peace summit was held, at which the Government accepted the ANC's preconditions for the resumption of constitutional negotiations. A 'record of understanding' was signed, which stated that the new Constitution would be drafted by an elected constitutional assembly and that there would be a non-racial elected interim government. In October the Constitution was amended to permit blacks to serve in the Cabinet. Later in that month legislation was approved that granted immunity from prosecution to perpetrators of politically motivated offences committed prior to 8 October 1990. In December Buthelezi published a draft constitution for a planned state comprising the KwaZulu 'homeland' and the province of Natal, which would retain a strong measure of autonomy within a future South African federation.

In February 1993 the ANC and the Government agreed to the immediate resumption of multi-party discussions. In March, at a meeting between the Government and 25 delegations from national political parties (including the formerly unco-operative PAC, IFP and CP) and the 'homeland' Governments, it was decided that CODESA was to be reconstituted, with the PAC, the IFP and the CP granted equal status with the other representatives. In May an informal alliance was established of 21 right-wing organizations (including the AVU, the CP and the AWB), known as the Afrikaner Volksfront (AVF), to co-ordinate opposition to the negotiating process.

In June 1993 legislation providing for the abolition of the President's Council was approved by Parliament. In July the negotiating forum confirmed that the elections would take place on 27 April 1994. The IFP, CP and KwaZulu delegations subsequently withdrew from the negotiations, while the remaining representatives in the forum continued discussions on the precepts of a multiracial interim constitution, which was to remain in force pending the preparation and adoption of a permanent constitution. The interim Constitution, promulgated in July, entrenched equal rights for citizens regardless of race, and vested executive power in a President and a Cabinet, which was to comprise representatives of the political parties that held a stipulated number of seats in the legislature. Legislative authority was vested in a bicameral Parliament, comprising a 400-member National Assembly (to be elected by proportional representation) and a Senate (with 10 members elected by each regional legislature). The National Assembly and Senate formed the Constitutional Assembly, which was to draft a new constitution, with adherence to the principles stipulated by the negotiating forum. Failure to adopt the draft by a majority of two-thirds within a period of two years would require the new document to be submitted for approval at a national referendum. Although the interim Constitution included provisions for the establishment of regional legislatures, it was rejected by COSAG (while the IFP, KwaZulu and CP delegations continued to boycott negotiations).

In early September 1993 the negotiating forum approved legislation providing for the establishment of a multiracial Transitional Executive Council (TEC), which was to rule in conjunction with the existing Government pending the elections, thereby allowing blacks to participate in central government for the first time. The TEC was to comprise representatives of the groups involved in the negotiating process; however, the IFP, the CP, the governments of Bophuthatswana, Ciskei and KwaZulu, and the PAC refused to participate. Later in September Parliament adopted legislation providing for the installation of the TEC, and the establishment of an Independent Electoral Commission (IEC), and an independent media commission and broadcasting authority.

In October 1993 the constituent members of COSAG, together with the AVF, formed the Freedom Alliance (FA), with the stated objective of negotiating concessions regarding regional autonomy. The Bophuthatswana and Ciskei delegations subsequently withdrew from the negotiating forum. In November the negotiating forum repealed legislation providing for detention without trial. Later that month agreement was reached regarding the establishment of a new security force, which was to be under the control of both central and provincial government, and a reconstituted national defence force, which was to comprise members of the existing armed forces of South Africa and the 'independent homelands', and the military wings of political organizations.

On 18 November 1993, following intensive discussions, 19 of the 21 delegations remaining in the negotiating forum approved the interim Constitution, which incorporated several amendments to the draft promulgated in July. A number of significant compromises between the Government and the ANC had been achieved: the Government abandoned its demand that cabinet decisions require a two-thirds' majority (thereby accepting that power-sharing would not be constitutionally entrenched), while the ANC agreed to a fixed five-year period for transition to majority rule. The President was to be elected by the National Assembly, and was to exercise executive power in consultation with at least two Deputy Presidents, who were to be nominated by parties with a minimum of 80 seats in the National Assembly (equivalent to 20% of the national vote). A Constitutional Court was to be appointed by the President from a list of candidates nominated by an independent judicial commission. As a concession to the FA, the interim Constitution included a provision that entitled the legislatures of the nine redesignated provinces to draft their own constitutions, subject to the principles governing the national Constitution. Nevertheless, the FA, together with the PAC, rejected the interim Constitution.

In early December 1993 the negotiating forum reached agreement on the reincorporation of the four 'independent homelands' into South Africa on 27 April 1994, when the interim Constitution was to enter into force. On 1 January South African citizenship was to be restored to the population of the 'homelands', who would be entitled to vote in the elections. However, the governments of Bophuthatswana and Ciskei refused to recognize the decision. On 7 December 1993 the TEC commenced sessions, but was, as expected, boycotted by a number of delegations. In mid-December the IEC was established. On 22 December Parliament ratified the interim Constitution, thereby effecting its own dissolution as an organ of the apartheid regime.

In December 1993 the judicial commission of inquiry into political violence that had been established in October 1991 announced that several members of the KwaZulu security forces, who had been trained by the South African armed forces, had killed ANC members in Natal. In January 1994 the military wing of the PAC, the Azanian People's Liberation Army (APLA), was implicated in further indiscriminate killings of civilians; the PAC, however, denied responsibility for the violence and announced that it had suspended the activities of the APLA. In January the Ciskei government decided to join the TEC and subsequently withdrew from the FA.

In February 1994, in accordance with a decision by the TEC, de Klerk announced that the elections, which were to be monitored by international observers, would take place between 26 and 28 April. The ANC's list of candidates incorporated members of the SACP, COSATU, the 'homeland' governments and parties representing the Indian and Coloured communities; the inclusion of Winnie Mandela (who had been elected President of the ANC's Women's League in December 1993) attracted widespread criticism. The IFP confirmed that it intended to boycott the elections, after the Zulu tribal monarch, King Goodwill Zwelithini (who was Buthelezi's nephew), rejected the interim Constitution and declared sovereignty over the territory traditionally owned by the Zulus, prompting increased fears of civil conflict. In mid-February Nelson Mandela announced a number of proposed amendments to the interim Constitution. The FA, however, rejected the concessions, on the grounds that the powers of regional government remained inadequate, and refused to attend discussions on the proposed amendments, which were, nevertheless, adopted by the negotiating forum. During that month a series of bomb attacks, which were attributed to right-wing extremists, took place in Orange Free State and Transvaal. In early March, after the ANC and IFP agreed to accept international mediation regarding the issue of regional autonomy, Buthelezi announced that he was to register the IFP provisionally to contest the elections. The leader of the AVU, Gen. (retd) Constand Viljoen (who had increasingly dissociated himself from extreme right-wing elements in the AVF) also provisionally registered a new party, the Freedom Front (FF). Despite the insistence of the AVF that its constituent groups were to boycott the elections, the FF subsequently submitted a list of candidates, which included several prominent members of the CP. The IFP failed to present a list of candidates by the stipulated date, while Zwelithini continued to urge his followers to boycott the elections.

In March 1994 the President of Bophuthatswana, Lucas Mangope (a member of the FA), announced that the population of the 'homeland' would not participate in the elections. Following widespread protests in Bophuthatswana, Mangope fled from the capital, Mmabatho, after disaffected members of the security forces demanded that he allow participation in the elections and refused to take action against the demonstrators. At the apparent instigation of the AVF, some 5,000 armed right-wing extremists, principally members of the AWB, entered Bophuthatswana and occupied Mmabatho, with the aim of reinstating Mangope. Shortly afterwards the Government dispatched some 2,000 members of the armed forces to Bophuthatswana, which, together with disaffected local troops, regained control of the 'homeland'. The Government and the TEC formally deposed Mangope, whose removal signified the effective dissolution of the FA. Later in March members of the armed forces were deployed in Ciskei to maintain civil order, following the resignation of the 'homeland's' military ruler in response to a strike by reformist members of the security forces. (The TEC and the Government assumed joint responsibility for administration in Bophuthatswana and Ciskei pending the elections.)

In April 1994, following protracted negotiations between the Government, the ANC and the IFP, with international mediation, an agreement was reached whereby the IFP was to participate in the elections, in exchange for guarantees that the institutions of the Zulu monarch and kingdom were to be recognized in the interim Constitution. Under the terms of a proposed draft constitution for KwaZulu/Natal (as Natal had been redesignated in February), the Zulu monarch was to be granted additional territorial powers and sovereignty with regard to traditional law and custom. However, the AVF announced that it would continue to boycott the elections. At the end of April about 32 members of the AWB, including prominent party officials, were arrested in connection with a bombing offensive conducted during that month, in which a total of 21 people were killed. Terre'Blanche subsequently threatened that the campaign would continue unless the Government acceded to demands for Afrikaner self-determination. Under the terms of an accord between the Government, the ANC and the FF earlier in April, the level of support for the FF in the elections was to be used to determine whether a separate Afrikaner state might be established in any region with the approval of the majority of the resident population. Prior to the elections, the Government also reached an agreement with the PAC, which provided for the inclusion of members of the APLA in the new national defence force, in exchange for a guaranteed cessation of hostilities.

On 27 April 1994 the interim Constitution came into force, with voting commencing on the previous day, as scheduled. However, a number of logistical difficulties led to widespread delays. On 28 April voting was extended by one day in KwaZulu/Natal and other regions affected by administrative confusion. Although a number of reports of electoral malpractice emerged, the IEC declared that the elections had been free and fair. The promulgation of the official results was delayed, owing, in part, to disputed ballots in KwaZulu/Natal; following negotiations between the IFP and the ANC, it was agreed that the IFP would be allocated 50.3% of the vote in the province, thereby allowing it a majority of one seat in the regional legislature. On 2 May, after partial results indicated a substantial majority in favour of the ANC, de Klerk conceded defeat, prompting widespread jubilation. Shortly afterwards it was announced that the ANC had secured 62.7% of votes cast, while the NP had won 20.4%, the IFP 10.5% and the FF 2.2%. Consequently, the ANC narrowly failed to obtain a parliamentary majority of two-thirds, which, under the terms of the interim Constitution, would have allowed its members to draft and adopt the new constitution without consulting other parties. The NP, which secured a majority in the province of Northern Cape, received the stipulated percentage of the national vote entitling it to nominate a Deputy President. Mandela subsequently appointed a senior official of the ANC, Thabo Mbeki, as First Deputy President, while de Klerk was nominated as Second Deputy President.

Mandela was officially elected as President by the National Assembly on 9 May 1994, and was inaugurated on the following day at a ceremony that was attended by a large number of international heads of state. A Cabinet of National Unity, comprising 18 representatives of the ANC, six of the NP and three of the IFP, was subsequently formed, with Buthelezi allocated the portfolio of home affairs. The appointment of Winnie Mandela as a deputy minister was widely interpreted as an attempt to prevent her from criticizing the new administration. Later in May the provincial legislatures elected a 90-member Senate, comprising 60 representatives of the ANC, 17 of the NP, five of the IFP and FF, respectively, and three of the DP. The ANC consequently held a slightly higher majority in the Constitutional Assembly than in the National Assembly, but failed, nevertheless, to obtain a two-thirds' majority. The Secretary-General of the ANC, Cyril Ramaphosa, was subsequently elected Chairman of the Constitutional Assembly.

The new Government adopted a Reconstruction and Development Programme (RDP), which comprised extensive measures for social and economic development, including the reform of the education and health services. The Government also announced plans to establish a 'Truth and Reconciliation Commission' (TRC), composed of eminent citizens, which would investigate violations of human rights perpetrated under the apartheid regime; the TRC was to be empowered to grant indemnity to individuals who confessed to politically motivated crimes committed before 5 December 1993 (when the TEC was effectively installed). Although the FF had failed to obtain the level of support in the elections stipulated as a precondition to the consideration of its demands, the Government subsequently agreed to the establishment of a 'volkstaat council', in which Viljoen and other right-wing Afrikaners were to debate the issue of self-determination. Meanwhile, it was disclosed that de Klerk had authorized the transfer of state-owned land (comprising one-third of the territory of KwaZulu/Natal) to Zwelithini shortly before the elections. The ANC denied knowledge of the agreement.

In June 1994 it was announced that the new South African National Defence Force (SANDF) was to be constituted over a period of three years (to allow the integration of former members of the MK and APLA). In mid-June a cabinet committee decided that Zwelithini was to remain the statutory trustee of the territory in KwaZulu/Natal that had been transferred to his control prior to the elections. At the end of June nine former MK officials were allocated prominent positions within the SANDF. (The commander of the former defence forces, Gen. George Meiring, had been reappointed Chief of the SANDF in May.) In September the Government officially ended the state of emergency in KwaZulu/Natal that had been imposed in March. In October the IFP majority in the provincial legislature of KwaZulu/Natal adopted legislation that provided for the establishment of an advisory council of Zulu chiefs, the House of Traditional Leaders, in which Zwelithini would be equal in status to other chiefs (including Buthelezi).

In November 1994 the Government adopted legislation that formally restored the rights of land ownership to members of the black population who had been dispossessed following the introduction of discriminatory legislation beginning in 1913; the Restitution of Land Rights Act provided for the establishment of a special commission and court to investigate and arbitrate claims.

In January 1995 the National Intelligence Service (NIS) was replaced with two new bodies, incorporating elements of the ANC's security department and agencies of the former 'homelands': the South African Secret Service, under the command of the former head of the NIS, was to control international intelligence, while the National Intelligence Agency (NIA), headed by a former ANC security official, was to be responsible for internal intelligence. In the same month, amid reports of increasing political violence between ANC and IFP supporters in KwaZulu/Natal, Buthelezi was elected Chairman of the House of Traditional Leaders.

An 11-member Constitutional Court was installed in February 1995; the Court was to ensure that the executive, legislative and judicial organs of government adhered to the principles entrenched in the interim Constitution, and was to endorse a final constitutional text with respect to these principles. In the same month Mandela confirmed that he would not contest the elections in 1999.

In February 1995 Buthelezi claimed that the ANC and NP had reneged on a pledge (which had been made shortly before the elections in April 1994) to invite international mediators to arbitrate on IFP demands for the devolution of power to KwaZulu/Natal, and IFP deputies consequently suspended participation in Parliament and the Constitutional Assembly. At a special party congress, which took place in March, the IFP agreed to resume participation in Parliament and in the Constitutional Assembly, but issued a resolution to the effect that IFP deputies would resume the boycott if Mandela failed to invite international mediators for negotiations on the issue of regional autonomy. Meanwhile, in late March Mandela finally removed Winnie Mandela from the Cabinet, after she publicly criticized government expenditure on the visit to South Africa of the British monarch.

At a party conference on constitutional policy in April 1995, the ANC rejected NP proposals that the principle of power-sharing be entrenched in the final constitution, thereby extending the tenure of the coalition Government. The conference also failed to accept IFP demands for international mediation on regional autonomy, and adopted constitutional proposals that provided for a Senate comprising members of provincial legislatures, which would be empowered to veto provincial legislation. Buthelezi implemented his threat to suspend IFP participation in the Constitutional Assembly, and indicated that the IFP would not accept a constitution that had been drafted by the remaining parties in the Assembly. In late May Mandela consented to foreign mediation on constitutional discussions. In the same month the National Assembly approved draft legislation providing for the establishment of the TRC; only the FF deputies opposed the enactment of the legislation.

In September 1995 the Constitutional Court ruled that Mandela had exceeded his presidential powers in overruling electoral boundaries that had been determined by the Western Cape Provincial Government prior to the local elections in November. The Court declared an amendment to the Local Government Transition Act (which had granted the President authority to issue decrees regarding the local elections) to be unconstitutional; the legislation was amended accordingly at an emergency session of Parliament in October. Elections in KwaZulu/Natal were postponed until March 1996, owing to continuing violence in the region. Voting took place in some parts of Western Cape, but not in the metropolitan area of Cape Town, nor in some rural areas of the province, as a result of delays in the demarcation of electoral boundaries. At the local elections, which took place in most parts of the country on 1 November 1995, the ANC secured 66.4% of the votes cast and the majority of the seats on the local councils, while the NP won 16.2% and the FF 4.0%.

In November 1995 Gen. Magnus Malan, the Minister of Defence in 1980–91, and a further 10 prominent officials in the former armed forces were arrested on charges relating to the killing of 13 people in KwaMakutha (south of Durban) in 1987; they were accused of involvement in the establishment in 1985 of a military camp in Namibia where IFP commandos were trained to perpetrate attacks on prominent ANC supporters. The arrest and subsequent indictment of Gen. Malan and the other former officers provoked great controversy; Mandela was accused by members of the NP and FF of political bias in his refusal to grant temporary indemnity to the accused until their cases could be heard by the TRC, which was to commence sessions in April 1996. (In late November 1995 Archbishop Desmond Tutu was appointed as Chairman of the Commission.) Buthelezi was cited in the indictment as having in 1985 requested the assistance of the security forces in creating paramilitary units to combat the ANC.

Renewed violence in KwaZulu/Natal in December 1995 culminated in an attack by some 600 IFP supporters against the village of Shobashobane, an ANC enclave in the south of the province, in which some 19 people were killed. In early February 1996 the NP Minister of Provincial Affairs and Constitutional Development, Roelf Meyer, announced that he was to resign from the Government and would assume the new post of Secretary-General of the NP. Later in the month Abraham Williams, also of the NP, resigned from the post of Minister of Welfare and Population Development, following allegations that he had defrauded social security funds. In March Mandela was granted a divorce from Winnie Mandela (who subsequently became known as Winnie Madikizela-Mandela). Later that month, in a cabinet reorganization, Mandela appointed Trevor Manuel, hitherto the Minister of Trade and Industry, to the finance portfolio.

The trial of Gen. Malan and his 19 co-defendants began in Durban in early March 1996. (In May charges were abandoned against three of the former security force commanders, owing to insufficient evidence.) In mid-March the Government withdrew indemnity from prosecution that had been granted by de Klerk's Government to 73 ANC members, including Mbeki and Modise. In April the TRC, comprising Archbishop Tutu (who retired from the archbishopric in June) and 16 other members drawn from all racial groups and a variety of professions, commenced hearings, which were to continue for up to two years. The Commission was empowered to grant judicial amnesties to perpetrators of human rights violations committed during the apartheid era, if it was satisfied that a full disclosure had been made and that the crime in question had been politically motivated (depending on the gravity of the crime). The TRC was also to advise on appropriate reparations to the victims (or to their families) of crimes committed.

On 8 May 1996 Parliament approved the final version of the Constitution, with the NP voting in favour, in spite of its reservations over some provisions. The IFP maintained its boycott of the Constitutional Assembly, while the 10 FF deputies abstained; only the two deputies of the African Christian Democratic Party (ACDP) voted against the adoption of the Constitution. The new Constitution incorporated an extensive Bill of Rights, and provided for the establishment of a commission to guarantee the rights of the white minority. A National Council of Provinces was to replace the existing Senate, and was designed to increase the influence of the provinces on the policy of the central Government (although falling short of the provincial powers demanded by the IFP). De Klerk subsequently announced that the NP was to withdraw from the Government of National Unity, attributing the decision to the diminishing influence of his party on government policy, the refusal of the ANC to include power-sharing arrangements in the new Constitution, and the necessity, in the interests of democracy, for an effective opposition. The NP later withdrew from all the Provincial Governments except for that of Western Cape (where it was in the majority). Mandela appointed members of his own party to the ministerial portfolios vacated by NP members and abolished the position of Second Deputy President.

Following negotiations between the province's political leaders, the local elections in KwaZulu/Natal took place on 26 June, amid relative calm. The IFP won the largest share (44.5%) of the votes cast.

In late August 1996 Mbeki made a statement to the TRC regarding violations of human rights perpetrated during the apartheid era, including the execution of 34 people at the ANC's camps in Angola, asserting that these were justified in the context of the struggle against apartheid. De Klerk apologized before the TRC for the suffering that the apartheid policies of the NP had caused, but denied that any violations of human rights had been authorized during his time in government. Also in late August Eugene de Kock, a former commander of the notorious counter-insurgency 'hit squad', the Vlakplaas, was convicted of 89 charges relating to the activities of the unit, including six charges of murder. In September de Kock detailed to the Supreme Court his involvement in the apartheid regime's campaign against its opponents, claiming that de Klerk and Botha had both had full knowledge of these operations, which included assassinations.

In early September 1996 the Constitutional Court ruled that the new Constitution failed to adhere to the principles enshrined in the interim Constitution in a number of respects, notably with regard to the powers of the provinces, which the Court deemed insufficient. The Constitutional Assembly was to amend the document accordingly within a period of 90 days. The IFP (which had boycotted the Constitutional Assembly in the negotiations resulting in the adoption of the national Constitution) rejoined the negotiations in early October, but withdrew shortly afterwards. The amended Constitution was approved by both chambers of Parliament on 11 October, with the ANC and the NP having negotiated a slight increase in the powers of the provinces. The new Constitution was returned to the Constitutional Court for final endorsement, and was promulgated by the President at a ceremony in Sharpeville on 10 December.

In mid-October 1996 Gen. Malan and his co-defendants were acquitted of all charges in connection with the massacre in Kwa-Makutha. Although it was accepted that the killings had been committed by IFP supporters who had been trained by the former armed forces, the prosecution failed to prove that the attack had been authorized by military or political leaders. The judgment was regarded as a set-back for the TRC, with Gen. Malan urging former members of the armed forces not to seek amnesties from the TRC, but to submit to trial in the courts if charged (thus discouraging potential confessions to the Commission). Later in October the TRC proposed that the final date for indemnity be extended from 6 December 1993 to 10 May 1994 (the date of Mandela's inauguration as President). Shortly afterwards a former police commissioner submitted evidence to the TRC implicating Botha in an attack against the headquarters of the South African Council of Churches in 1988. Botha declared that he would not submit evidence to the Commission and denied involvement in any crimes for which he needed to apply for amnesty. Following discussions with Tutu, however, he agreed to co-operate with the TRC by means of correspondence. In late October Tutu criticized the ANC for failing to submit amnesty applications from its members, and subsequently threatened to resign from the TRC if such applications were not made. The ANC responded by assuring the TRC that applications by its members would be made where necessary.

On 13 December 1996 (the eve of the deadline for applications for amnesty from the TRC) Mandela announced that the final date for the period in which crimes had been committed and the deadline for the receipt of amnesty applications were to be extended, to 10 May 1994 and 10 May 1997, respectively. The ANC confirmed that some 360 of its members, including three cabinet ministers, had applied for amnesty.

From January 1997 South Africa's main political parties conducted discussions regarding possible inter-party co-operation. Mandela issued invitations to both the DP and the PAC to participate in the Government of National Unity (which, however, both parties subsequently declined). In late January the IFP appeared to be in crisis, following the resignations of the KwaZulu/Natal Premier, Frank Mdlalose, the IFP Secretary-General and the Chairman of the IFP in Gauteng. The new Constitution entered into force on 4 February 1997. On 6 February the inaugural session of the new National Council of Provinces, which replaced the Senate as the second chamber of Parliament, was held.

By the 10 May 1997 deadline nearly 8,000 amnesty applications had been received. In mid-May Meyer resigned from the NP and from the National Assembly, following opposition from within the NP to his proposal that the party be reconstituted in order to attract black support. Meyer, in alliance with Bantu Holomisa, the former ruler of Transkei (who, in 1996, had been dismissed from the Government and expelled from the ANC for indiscipline, in connection with allegations he had made at a hearing of the TRC), subsequently established a new political movement, the United Democratic Movement (UDM). Also in May 1997 de Klerk made a second appearance before the TRC; his continued insistence that he had been unaware of the violations of human rights perpetrated during the period of apartheid prompted an angry response from Tutu, who accused de Klerk of being responsible for abuses. The NP subsequently suspended co-operation with the TRC, and initiated legal action against the TRC on the grounds of political bias.

In June 1997 Terre'Blanche received a custodial term of six years for the attempted murder of a black employee, and a further one-year sentence for assault; he was released on bail pending an appeal against his conviction. In the same month Buthelezi invited the ANC to enter into negotiations with the aim of reaching an agreement to end political violence in KwaZulu/Natal. However, in July the killing of five ANC members, including two newly elected municipal councillors, in KwaZulu/Natal reflected the continuing political tensions in the province. In early August the IFP withdrew from the peace discussions, after it was alleged during hearings of the TRC that Buthelezi had been aware of political killings perpetrated by supporters of the IFP during apartheid. At the end of August de Klerk resigned from the leadership of the NP and retired from active politics; he was subsequently replaced by Marthinus van Schalkwyk.

In September 1997 five members of the former security forces appeared before the TRC to apply for amnesty for the killing of Steve Biko in 1977 (see below); it was admitted during the hearing that some of the evidence presented at the inquest into Biko's death had been fabricated. In the same month the publication of a book, based on statements by a former bodyguard of Madikizela-Mandela, Katiza Cebekhulu, attracted considerable publicity; Cebekhulu alleged that Madikizela-Mandela had been actively involved in the killing of Stompie Moeketsi Seipei in 1988, and that she had subsequently ordered that a physician who had examined the victim prior to his death be killed. Nevertheless, Madikizela-Mandela continued to receive widespread public support, and was nominated for the post of Deputy President of the ANC by the party's Women's League prior to the ANC's December 1997 congress. Later in September Madikizela-Mandela appeared before the TRC, having been implicated by previous applicants for amnesty in 18 incidences of human rights violations, including eight killings. The TRC subsequently acceded to Madikizela-Mandela's request that hearings of her testimony be conducted in public. In November representatives of the business community applied for amnesty for their involvement with the apartheid system; however, Tutu criticized the failure of much of the private business sector, including three multinational petroleum companies, to participate in the TRC. During hearings of the TRC regarding the allegations against Madikizela-Mandela later that month, a number of witnesses testified that she had assaulted and killed several people. Cebekhulu appeared before the TRC to reiterate the claims that had been published in September 1997. Madikizela-Mandela subsequently denied involvement in any violations of human rights, and initiated legal action against Cebekhulu for libel.

At the ANC congress in December 1997 Mandela resigned from the presidency of the party, as anticipated, and was succeeded by Mbeki, who was elected unopposed. Jacob Zuma was elected Deputy President of the party. Madikizela-Mandela, who had refused her nomination to contest the post of Deputy President, was, however, elected to the NEC.

In August 1998, following considerable delays, Botha, who had failed to comply with three subpoenas ordering him to testify at the TRC regarding his enforcement of apartheid through emergency rule in the 1980s, was convicted of being in contempt of the TRC, receiving a fine of R 10,000 and a one-year suspended sentence (which could be brought into effect if he failed to comply with a further TRC subpoena). In September Parliament adopted legislation guaranteeing employment equity, whereby corporations were required to employ a certain proportion of blacks, women and disabled people.

In October 1998 the TRC commenced reparation payments to victims of human rights violations under the apartheid system. De Klerk appealed to the Cape Town High Court to prevent the publication of sections of the TRC's report alleging that he had prior knowledge of the bomb attacks against anti-apartheid bodies in the 1980s. The TRC agreed to remove provisionally the sections concerned, which were to be contested at the High Court in early 1999. However, the Cape Town High Court dismissed a legal challenge by the ANC to the publication of findings that it had perpetrated human rights violations in armed opposition to apartheid, on the grounds that it had failed to appeal against previous drafts of the report. Tutu condemned the ANC's efforts to prevent the release of part of the report, which had been opposed by Mandela and had resulted in division within the party. At the end of October 1998 Tutu presented to Mandela the TRC's interim report detailing human rights violations committed in 1960–64, based on statements from some 21,000 victims of abuses and about 7,000 amnesty applicants. The report concluded that the apartheid system constituted a crime against humanity; it was alleged that, while the State was primarily accountable for violations of human rights, the ANC had also committed abuses in its legitimate struggle against apartheid (notably in the MK's torture and execution of suspected dissidents in detention camps outside South Africa). Botha, as President of the State Security Council in 1978–89, was considered to be responsible for an increase in killings of government opponents and to have ordered the bomb attacks by state agents in the 1980s. Buthelezi was deemed accountable for human rights violations perpetrated by the IFP (which was responsible for the highest proportion of killings in 1990–94). The report also cited Viljoen, Terre'Blanche, and Madikizela-Mandela as being responsible for serious violations of human rights. It was stated that the South African business community had benefited from the apartheid system, and the introduction of a 'wealth tax' to assist in social reconstruction was proposed. The prosecution of those responsible for human rights violations who had not applied for amnesty, or who had been denied amnesty, was recommended. Buthelezi and Viljoen dismissed the findings of the report as reflecting pro-ANC bias in the TRC, and Buthelezi subsequently threatened to prosecute the Commission, particularly with regard to the report's allegation that the IFP had colluded with the apartheid regime. In November 1998 one of the members of the security forces implicated in the 1977 killing of Steve Biko was refused amnesty, on the grounds that the killing was not politically motivated. Amnesty applications of the remaining four members of the security forces involved in the incident were rejected in early 1999. In December 1998 Mandela confirmed that perpetrators of crimes committed under the apartheid regime would not be granted a general amnesty, which had been urged by the NP, IFP and some members of the ANC. Under TRC regulations, applicants would only be granted amnesty after submitting a full confession and evidence that the crime was politically motivated. However, in October 2003 the Ministry of Justice and Constitutional Development announced that none of the men implicated in the killing of Steve Biko would be prosecuted, largely owing to insufficient evidence.

In January 1999 the Secretary-General of the UDM, Sifiso Nkabinde, was assassinated (apparently by ANC supporters) in KwaZulu/Natal. Some 11 ANC members were killed in a retaliatory attack by armed assailants. Further clashes between UDM and ANC supporters around Richmond were reported. Also in January a bomb attack at a Cape Town police station was widely attributed to an Islamist group, People Against Gangsterism and Drugs (PAGAD). Meanwhile, an increasing number of attacks against farmers by organized armed groups were reported. The South African Agricultural Union claimed that the attacks (in which more than 550 members of the farming community had been killed in 1994–98) were part of a campaign to force farmers to abandon their land. In May the ANC and IFP signed an agreement to end hostilities between their supporters in KwaZulu/Natal during the forthcoming electoral period.

More than 16m. voters participated in legislative elections, which took place peacefully, at national and provincial level, on 2 June 1999. Some 32 political parties had registered to contest the elections. The ANC secured 266 of the 400 seats in the National Assembly, with 66.4% of votes cast; the DP increased its representation in the Assembly from seven to 38 seats, while the IFP won 34, and the New National Party (NNP, as the NP had been reconstituted), which had lost much support to the DP, only 28 seats. The ANC subsequently formed a coalition with an Indian party, the Minority Front, thereby securing a two-thirds' majority in the National Assembly. The IFP reached a coalition agreement with the ANC in KwaZulu/Natal, where the IFP Premier retained his post. In Western Cape no party won a majority of seats in the provincial legislature, and, after intensive negotiations, the NPP and DP established a coalition Government to prevent the ANC, which had obtained the highest number of votes, from gaining power. On 16 June Mbeki was inaugurated as President, in a ceremony that also marked the formal retirement of Mandela. The IFP joined the ANC in a further coalition Government, in which Buthelezi remained Minister of Home Affairs. Zuma became Deputy President.

In June 1999 Botha's appeal against his conviction was upheld, on the technical grounds that the TRC's subpoena was invalid since its mandate had temporarily expired. In July the TRC released a report containing evidence from former members of the security forces that implicated Botha in the killing of eight anti-apartheid activists in 1988. (Botha died in October 2006.) In August the TRC granted amnesty to Vlok, the former Commissioner of Police, Gen. Johan van der Merwe, de Kock, and a further 14 members of the former security forces, in respect of ordering the bombing of the offices of the South African Council of Churches in 1988. In September the Minister of Justice announced that further cases were to be submitted to judges specially nominated by Mbeki. In October the trial of Wouter Basson, the head of the apartheid regime's chemical and biological armaments programme in 1982–92, on 64 charges (including responsibility for the killing of 200 members of the South West Africa People's Organisation of Namibia—SWAPO), commenced at the High Court in Pretoria. He was acquitted of 15 charges in June 2001, and the remaining charges in April 2002. Later in October 1999 the TRC granted amnesty to nine former members of the security forces, including de Kock, who had provided evidence regarding the bombing of the ANC offices in London in 1982. In December 1999 10 members of the AWB were granted amnesty for the bombing campaign in 1994.

In January 2000 the National Assembly adopted extensive legislation prohibiting discrimination on any grounds and the use of racist terms in language. Meanwhile, the principal opposition parties (the DP, NNP, UDM and the FA) announced their intention to form an alliance prior to local government elections due in November; the DP also signed an electoral agreement with the smaller ACDP. In February, however, seven senior UDM officials left the party to join the ANC (increasing the total number of defections from the UDM since late 1999 to 34). In March, following the rejection of an appeal in October 1999, Terre'Blanche was ordered by the Pretoria High Court to surrender to the authorities to serve the one-year sentence he had received for assault, pending a further appeal against his six-year sentence. He was subsequently released on parole from the shorter sentence, but the longer sentence was confirmed on appeal in March 2001. (Terre'Blanche was released on parole in June 2004 after serving three years of the sentence. In November 2003 he was also convicted of involvement in terrorist activities prior to the 1994 elections and received a further, suspended, six-year sentence.) In June 2000 it was announced that the NNP and DP were to form a new coalition, known as the Democratic Alliance (DA), to contest the local government elections.

In April 2001 a court began hearing a petition, made by a group of 39 pharmaceutical manufacturers, to invalidate legislation, passed in 1997 (but suspended following an interim court ruling in the companies' favour in 1998), that enabled South Africa to purchase less expensive generic versions of patented anti-AIDS drugs from third parties. However, following international criticism, the companies abandoned the action unconditionally before the conclusion of the hearing. In September 2001 the South African Medical Research Council reported that HIV/AIDS was the largest single cause of death in South Africa, responsible for approximately 40% of adult deaths, and estimated that, without effective treatment, up to 7m. people could die from the disease by 2010. Mbeki had attracted criticism in August 2001 after urging the Minister of Health to reduce the budget for HIV/AIDS treatment, citing mortality figures from 1995 (when the disease accounted for only 2.2% of deaths). In December the Ministry of Health lost a case brought by the Treatment Action Campaign (TAC), a group of AIDS activists, when the High Court in Pretoria ordered it to provide antiretroviral drugs to all pregnant women infected with HIV to reduce the chance of transmission to their children; the Government had argued that the drugs were toxic and excessively expensive to administer. (The Government lost its appeal against the ruling in April 2002.) In February 2002 Buthelezi, as Minister of Home Affairs, ordered the distribution of antiretroviral drugs in Kwazulu/Natal, in contravention of official government policy, and in March the High Court upheld the ruling that ordered state provision of antiretroviral drugs. The Government sought leave to appeal the ruling, but it was overturned by the Constitutional Court in July; in October the Government announced that it would investigate means of providing antiretroviral drugs through the public health system. In November 2003 the Government also announced that it would spend R 12,100m. on combating HIV/AIDS over the next four years; R 1,900m. was to be allocated for the provision of antiretroviral drugs. At that time the Government committed to providing free antiretroviral treatment to some 53,000 people by March 2004; however, by November of that year the number of people receiving treatment was estimated at only 18,500. In September 2004 the National Assembly approved legislation to regulate the country's 200,000 practitioners of traditional medicine, thereby granting them formal recognition; some 70% of the population were believed to consult traditional healers.

Meanwhile, in July 2001 the PAC drew attention to what it considered the Government's inadequate housing and land redistribution policies, by seizing land belonging to farmers and the Provincial Government in east Johannesburg and inviting thousands of homeless people to settle there; many constructed shacks, believing that they were part of a resettlement scheme. Within two weeks the Government had removed the estimated 7,000 squatters from the land, using armed police-officers. COSATU and affiliated unions organized a two-day general strike in August in protest at the proposed privatization of public assets, which, it claimed, would result in large-scale redundancies. COSATU estimated that 4m. workers had participated in the strike, a figure that the Government described as exaggerated.

In August 2001 Agri South Africa, an organization representing commercial farmers (mainly white) and 'emerging' black farmers, reported that there had been more than 6,000 attacks on South African farms since 1991, resulting in the deaths of more than 1,000 people; it was widely feared that the motivation for the attacks was land redistribution, as had been the case in Zimbabwe since the late 1990s. The South African Government declared land seizures illegal in August.

The leader of the NNP, van Schalkwyk, announced in October 2001 that the party was suspending its participation in the DA, following differences with the DP; the DP had dismissed the mayor of Cape Town, a prominent figure in the NNP, while the DP suspected the NNP of attempting to increase membership in an attempt to take overall control of the DA. Van Schalkwyk announced that the NNP would seek an accommodation with the ANC, as the IFP had done, retaining its independence, but holding positions in the Cabinet. In late November the ANC and NNP announced a power-sharing agreement in Western Cape (the only province not previously under ANC control), and the NNP also took seats in seven of the eight other Provincial Governments (all except Kwazulu/Natal, where the ANC had an agreement with the IFP). Discord within the NNP emerged when Gerald Morkel resigned as Premier of Western Cape in November, after publicly refusing to support closer co-operation with the ANC; he was replaced by Peter Marais. Meanwhile, in October COSATU accused the ANC of attempting to discredit it and suppress criticism of the Government, after a leaked report from the ANC national executive suggested that COSATU intended to establish a rival, extreme left-wing party. Marais resigned in May over allegations of sexual harassment and was replaced by van Schalkwyk.

A ruling by the Constitutional Court in late 2002, allowing national and provincial deputies to change parties without losing their seats, led to significant changes in the political landscape: in April 2003 the ANC secured a two-thirds' parliamentary majority when members of the UDM and the NNP defected to the ruling party, while the FA and the Afrikaner Eenheidsbeweging lost all their seats. At provincial level, members of the IFP defected to the ANC in KwaZulu/Natal and assumed further positions in the Cabinet, although the premiership of the province remained under IFP control. In April Madikizela-Mandela, who had been re-elected to the NEC of the ANC in December, was convicted of fraud and theft for obtaining bank loans using the fabricated names of employees of the ANC Women's League, and sentenced to five years' imprisonment.

The TRC's final report was presented to Mbeki in March 2003. The Commission had granted amnesty to 1,200 people, but had rejected more than 5,000 applications. Tutu recommended that some US $240m. ($12,000 each) be paid to the 20,000 people identified as victims of apartheid, and urged companies that had benefited through their involvement with the apartheid regime to contribute to the reparations process. Publication of the final report had been delayed by a legal challenge brought by the IFP, which was heavily implicated in the perpetration of human rights violations. In April, having rejected the suggestion that a special tax be imposed on companies that had gained from apartheid, Mbeki announced that those designated victims by the TRC would receive single payments of just over $3,800 each.

An empowerment charter for the financial sector, released in October 2003, envisaged that within four years 25% of all company executives would be non-white; and that 50% of goods bought by financial companies would be sourced from black-owned suppliers, rising to 70% by 2014. The mining sector had released a similar charter in March 2003: this pledged that 26% of mines would be black-owned within 10 years; the first conversions of mineral rights were expected by the end of 2004. In 1994 the Government had promised to transfer 30% of white-owned farms to non-whites over the next five years, but by 2004 only 2% had been transferred. In October of that year the Minister of Agriculture and Land Affairs, Angela Thoko Didiza, announced that some R 30,000m. would be required to settle outstanding land claims by the Government's 2005 deadline. In February 2007 the first order was given for the sale of a white-owned farm in the Northern Cape province.

Elections to the National Assembly and the provincial legislatures took place concurrently on 14 April 2004. Final results confirmed the overwhelming victory of the ANC, which won 279 of the National Assembly's 400 seats, with 69.7% of the valid votes cast. The DA took 50 seats, with 12.4% of votes cast, and the IFP 28, with 7.0%. The ANC secured overall control of seven of the nine provincial assemblies; although it failed to win outright majorities in Kwazulu/Natal and Western Cape, the ANC subsequently nominated premiers to head all nine provincial governments. The IEC declared the elections to have been free and fair. On 23 April members of the National Assembly voted unanimously to re-elect Mbeki to the presidency. President Mbeki was sworn in to serve a second term of office on 27 April, amid celebrations to mark 10 years of multi-racial democracy. Mbeki announced the composition of a new Cabinet, which included most senior members of the previous administration: Zuma was reappointed Deputy President, while Mantombanza (Manto) Tshabalala-Msimang retained the health portfolio despite the slow progress regarding the provision of antiretroviral drugs to combat HIV/AIDS. Kader Asmal was replaced as Minister of Education by G. Naledi Pandor and Buthelezi who had held the post of Minister of Home Affairs since 1994, was dismissed. The two IFP representatives who had been allocated ministerial portfolios did not take up their posts when the new Government was sworn in on 29 April.

In August 2004 van Schalkwyk announced that the NNP was to merge with ANC and that the NNP would be disbanded in September 2005. The NNP leader also stated his intention to join the ANC and urged all NNP members to do the same. Former President de Klerk subsequently announced his resignation from the NNP in protest at the decision. (The NNP officially ceased to exist at the end of February 2006.)

Meanwhile, in August 2003, the National Director of Public Prosecutions, Bulelani Ngcuka, had announced that Deputy President Zuma would not be prosecuted for alleged corruption in connection with an arms-procurement deal, despite an apparent recommendation from investigators that he be charged. This prompted accusations of government interference in the legal process and opposition demands for Zuma's resignation. Zuma repeatedly rejected the allegations against him; however, in early June 2005 his financial adviser, Schabir Shaik, was found guilty of corruption and fraud and sentenced to fifteen years' imprisonment by the Durban High Court. The Court found evidence of a corrupt relationship between Shaik and Zuma, and that a series of payments made by Shaik on behalf of Zuma were intended to influence Zuma to benefit Shaik's business. Although Zuma did not give evidence, the trial revealed that Zuma had been party to a bid to solicit a bribe from a French defence company involved in the arms-procurement deal. Shaik launched an appeal against his conviction but this was rejected by the Supreme Court of Appeal in November 2006.

President Mbeki came under increasing pressure to dismiss Zuma and on 14 June 2005 he announced that the Deputy President would be 'released' from his duties. Zuma was replaced by Phumzile Mlambo-Ngcuka, hitherto the Minister of Energy and Mineral Affairs; Lindiwe Hendricks assumed Mlambo-Ngucka's vacated portfolio. In early August it was reported that the new Deputy President advocated the forced expropriation of white farms to accelerate the process of land distribution. At an education conference later that month Mlambo-Ngcuka was also reported to have called for South Africa to model its land redistribution programme on that of Zimbabwe. Following a preliminary hearing in October, in mid-November Zuma was provisionally indicted at Durban Magistrates' Court; his trial commenced in the High Court in late July 2006. In mid-September the High Court judge dismissed the case, stating that Zuma had suffered social prejudice as a result of the publicity the case had received. The judge also cited failures of the State to hear legal challenges to raids carried out on the property of Zuma and his advisers, adding that further investigations into the case should have been conducted. Zuma's supporters believed that the result would increase the likelihood of him being elected to the presidency in 2009, and urged President Mbeki, who was constitutionally prohibited from serving a third term, to reinstate him as Deputy President. Nevertheless, tensions remained between Mbeki and Zuma and differences continued to divide the ANC.

In November 2005 it was also reported that Zuma was under investigation for the alleged rape of a female family friend; he was charged with the offence in early December but strenuously denied the allegation and was acquitted in early May 2006. In a separate investigation into missing funds 16 current and former ministers were found guilty of theft and fraud in October 2006. As much as R 17m. had been stolen and parliamentary travel privileges had been abused. Earlier that year an investigation was launched in Germany into allegedly corrupt arms-procurement deals in South Africa.

In May 2007 Helen Zille, the Mayor of Cape Town, was elected leader of the DA, replacing Tony Leon who had led the party since its formation in 2000. In June the ANC held a national policy conference following which it was announced that both Mbeki and Zuma could contest the leadership of the party at its national conference in December. Internal tensions had continued to divide the ruling tripartite coalition, although Mbeki warned in June that he would not be dictated to regarding government policies by the SACP. Zuma had secured the support of senior members of the SACP, which was considering contesting the 2009 general election independently from the ANC if Mbeki retained the leadership of that party. In September 2007 Zuma received the endorsement of COSATU for his leadership campaign, although a number of leading South African business executives expressed concern that if Zuma were to the national presidency, he would reverse Mbeki's economic policies.

As the leadership contest gained momentum senior members of the ANC exerted pressure on both Mbeki and Zuma to withdraw their candidatures, claiming that their rivalry was causing a major rift within the party. Neither candidate was prepared to concede and in December 2007 ANC members elected Zuma to the party presidency after he secured 2,329 votes to Mbeki's 1,505; Kgalema Motlanthe was appointed ANC Deputy President. However, later that month the National Prosecuting Authority (NPA) indicted Zuma on charges of corruption and fraud. The Supreme Court of Appeal had ruled in November that Zuma could again be tried in connection with the arms-procurement deal. Zuma once more denied the allegations; however, the trial was scheduled to commence in August 2008, thus endangering his potential accession to the national presidency. In early 2008 differences between Mbeki and Zuma continued, deepening divides within both the ANC and the Government. In February the DA and the Independent Democrats announced their intention to seek a vote of 'no confidence' in Mbeki and force an early general election.

In mid-January 2008 the NPA announced that it would bring charges of corruption and 'defeating the ends of justice' against the National Police Commissioner, Jacob Selebi, who was placed on indefinite leave and resigned from his position as President of the International Criminal Police Organisation. Selebi was a close ally of Mbeki, and had been under investigation for alleged links to organized crime.

Meanwhile, in December 2007 the National Union of Mineworkers (NUM) called a one-day strike over working conditions and safety standards; in 2007 some 200 workers had been killed in South Africa's mines. The NUM claimed that the mining companies were taking unnecessary risks to ensure a profit and demanded improved training and salary increases for the country's miners.

South Africa became increasingly isolated politically in southern Africa after Zimbabwe (formerly Rhodesia) underwent the transition to independence in April 1980. During the 1980s South Africa's continued occupation of Namibia resulted in frequent clashes between SWAPO guerrillas and South African troops (see the chapter on Namibia). In 1971 the International Court of Justice had declared South Africa's presence in Namibia to be illegal and the UN had, in 1973, recognized SWAPO as the 'authentic representative of the Namibian people'. Following the collapse of the semi-autonomous internal administration, South Africa resumed direct rule of Namibia in January 1983. In February 1984 South Africa and Angola agreed on a cease-fire along the Angola–Namibia border, and established a joint commission to monitor the withdrawal of South African troops from Angola. In May 1988 negotiations began between Angola, Cuba and South Africa, with the USA acting as mediator. On 22 December Angola, Cuba and South Africa signed a formal treaty designating 1 April 1989 as the commencement date for the process leading to Namibian independence, as well as a treaty requiring all 50,000 Cuban troops to be withdrawn from Angola by July 1991. Elections were held in Namibia in November 1989, and independence for the former South African territory was achieved on 21 March 1990, under a SWAPO-controlled Government. The strategic port of Walvis Bay and 12 offshore islands, to which Namibia laid claim, remained under South African jurisdiction until September 1991, when the two countries agreed to administer the disputed territories jointly. In August 1993 South Africa relinquished sovereignty over Walvis Bay and the 12 islands, which were officially transferred to Namibia in March 1994. In August 2001 the South African and Namibian foreign ministers met to discuss the issue of their joint border on the Orange river; Namibia claimed the border extended to the middle of the river, while South Africa claimed it lay on the northern bank, provoking differences over mineral and fishing rights.

In 1984 South Africa signed a mutual non-aggression pact with Mozambique (the Nkomati accord), which implied that South Africa would withdraw its covert support for the Resistência Nacional Moçambicana (Renamo), while Mozambique would prevent the ANC from using its territory as a base for attacks on South Africa. In September 1985 the South African Government conceded that there had been 'technical' violations of the accord. In May 1988 Mozambican and South African officials agreed to reactivate the Nkomati accord, and in September President Botha visited President Joaquim Chissano of Mozambique, his first state visit to a black African nation. Following his election as President, Mandela made an official visit to Mozambique in July 1994. In August of that year South Africa, Mozambique and Swaziland signed a security co-operation accord, in an effort to combat the continuing illicit transport of armaments. In February 1997 South Africa appealed to the Government of Swaziland to release Swazi trade union leaders from detention. The Swazi Government protested at action mounted by COSATU in support of its Swazi counterparts, stating that it represented interference in the internal affairs of Swaziland. In April 2006 protests were staged by COSATU, the SACP and its Youth League, and the Swaziland Solidarity Network in support of Swaziland's campaign for democracy and human rights. Demonstrators attempted to blockade several crossing points on the Swaziland border and more than 20 people were arrested.

SOUTH AFRICA

Introductory Survey

In 1979 the Southern African Development Co-ordination Conference (SADCC) was established by southern African countries, to work towards a reduction of their economic dependence on South Africa. SADCC reformed in August 1992 as the Southern African Development Community (SADC, see p. 386), which aimed to achieve closer economic integration between its member states. South Africa was admitted to SADC in August 1994. In April 1997 members of the South African armed forces participated in military training exercises in Zimbabwe, as part of a nascent SADC regional peace-keeping force. In September 1998 about 600 South African and 200 Botswanan troops were dispatched to restore order in the Lesotho capital, Maseru, under the aegis of SADC, following a coup attempt by junior military officers. About 750 South African troops, together with some 350 Botswanan troops, remained in Lesotho to maintain civil order, before their withdrawal in May 2000.

In April 2000 Mbeki, together with the Presidents of Namibia and Mozambique, visited Zimbabwe to increase pressure on President Robert Mugabe to prevent the illegal occupation of white-owned farmland (see the chapter on Zimbabwe). Despite international condemnation of Mugabe and requests by a number of countries, most notably the United Kingdom, for more unequivocal criticism of President Mugabe's actions from South Africa, President Mbeki attempted to maintain 'constructive engagement' towards Zimbabwe. Following Mugabe's re-election as President in March 2002, the ANC issued a statement endorsing the ballot, despite allegations that Mugabe's party, the Zimbabwe African National Union—Patriotic Front, had intimidated voters and engaged in electoral fraud. The South African Government's position strained relations with the United Kingdom and the USA, and the latter threatened to withdraw support for the New Partnership for Africa's Development (NEPAD, see below) if the Government did not condemn Mugabe. However, later in March Mbeki was part of a Commonwealth troika (also comprising the President of Nigeria and the Prime Minister of Australia) that decided to suspend Zimbabwe from meetings of that organization for a period of one year. Mbeki had previously ignored pleas from Morgan Tsvangirai, the leader of the main opposition party in Zimbabwe, the Movement for Democratic Change, to impose sanctions on Zimbabwe prior to the election. In March 2003 Donald (Don) McKinnon, the Secretary-General of the Commonwealth, stated that the troika had concluded that Zimbabwe's suspension from the organization's meetings should remain in force for a further nine months. However, South Africa subsequently denied that it had agreed to the extension of the suspension. Zimbabwe withdrew from the Commonwealth in December 2003, shortly before the conclusion of the organization's Heads of Government meeting, at which the country's suspension had been extended indefinitely. Mbeki had criticized the decision to maintain the suspension, claiming that some Commonwealth members had failed to understand the question of land ownership in Zimbabwe. The Commonwealth appointed South Africa to a six-member advisory panel charged with monitoring the situation in Zimbabwe. Mbeki met separately with Mugabe and Tsvangirai in that month in an unsuccessful attempt to persuade them to form a coalition government. Mbeki continued to mediate between Mugabe and Tsvangirai prior to the Zimbabwean presidential and legislative elections held in March 2008, and brokered the introduction of new election legislation requiring electoral officials to post the number of votes cast at individual polling stations. However, following the decision of the Zimbabwe Electoral Commission not to release the results of the presidential election, in April Mugabe boycotted an emergency SADC summit in Zambia called to discuss the situation in Zimbabwe. Mbeki travelled to Harare for talks with Mugabe, but the former's policy of 'quiet diplomacy' attracted criticism from a number of international observers, while Tsvangirai appealed for Mbeki to relinquish his role as mediator to Zambian President Levy Mwanawasa.

In November 1996 South Africa was criticized for its approval of a substantial sale of weapons to Rwanda, which was believed to be providing military support to rebels in eastern Zaire who were engaged in conflict with the Zairean army. In response to international pressure, the South African Government subsequently decided to suspend the sale of armaments to Rwanda. During 1996 South Africa supported efforts to achieve reconciliation in Angola and in early 1997 was involved in intensive diplomatic activity, along with other African countries, with the aim of negotiating an end to the civil war in Zaire. Following the assumption of power by Alliance des forces démocratiques pour la libération du Congo-Zaïre, led by Laurent-Désiré Kabila, in May, South Africa became the first foreign government to recognize the new regime and pledged to assist in reconstruction efforts and in the holding of elections in the renamed Democratic Republic of the Congo (DRC). In October 2001 South African soldiers were dispatched to Burundi (q.v.) as part of a proposed 700-member peace-keeping mission, in an effort to enforce national security and to support the formation of a multi-ethnic transitional government. Mandela had been instrumental in negotiating a peace accord (signed in August 2000), whereby the Hutu and Tutsi ethnic groups, which had been engaged in civil conflict since 1993, were each to hold the presidency for 18 months during a three-year transitional period. In May 2003 1,400 South African troops were deployed in the DRC as part of a UN peace-keeping mission, rising to 1,750 at January 2004. In November 2004 President Mbeki was mandated by the African Union (AU, see p. 164) to lead peace negotiations in Côte d'Ivoire (q.v), following the breakdown of a cease-fire between the Government of that country and rebels. In March 2005 South Africa dispatched some 300 troops to Darfur, Sudan (q.v.), as part of an AU mission to investigate and monitor events in the region.

Following the implementation of political reforms in South Africa from February 1990, international sanctions imposed during the 1980s were reviewed. During 1991 South Africa was readmitted to international sporting competition, after many years of exclusion. In July the USA officially withdrew economic sanctions (which were, however, retained by a number of US states and cities). In October Commonwealth Heads of Government endorsed the withdrawal of cultural sanctions against South Africa; however, sanctions on finance, arms and trade and investment remained. Japan ended all its sanctions during that month. In 1992 the EC withdrew a number of sanctions against South Africa. In September 1993, following the adoption of legislation providing for the installation of a multiracial transitional administration (see above), the international community ended the remaining economic sanctions against South Africa. The UN Security Council ended its mandatory embargo on armaments, following the establishment of an interim Government of National Unity in May 1994; South Africa subsequently established diplomatic relations with more than 165 countries. South Africa became a member of the Commonwealth on 1 June, and joined the Organization of African Unity (OAU—now the AU) later that month. The People's Republic of China refused to establish formal diplomatic links while South Africa maintained relations with Taiwan. In November 1996 President Mandela announced that South Africa's diplomatic relations with Taiwan were to be severed in favour of the People's Republic of China, with effect from the end of 1997. In response, Taiwan withdrew its ambassador indefinitely and announced that the majority of its aid projects in South Africa would be suspended.

In December 1995 a joint US-South African commission was established, chaired by Mbeki and the US Vice-President, Al Gore. In February 1998 it was announced that South Africa and the USA were to normalize their defence trade agreement, thereby allowing South African armaments companies to trade with their US counterparts for the first time. In August 1998 two people were killed, and about 27 injured, in a bomb attack on a US restaurant in Cape Town. A supporter of an organization styled Muslims Against Global Oppression (MAGO) claimed to have perpetrated the bombing, apparently in retaliation for US air attacks on Sudan and Afghanistan (although MAGO officially denied responsibility for the incident). Several members of PAGAD were subsequently arrested in connection with the bombing. A series of further bombings in the Cape Town area, and the killing of a local magistrate in July 2000, were also attributed by the authorities to PAGAD.

In March 1998, following four years of negotiations, the European Union (EU) approved the terms for a comprehensive free-trade agreement with South Africa. The agreement provisionally came into force on 1 January 2000; a continuing dispute with the Governments of Italy, Spain, Portugal and Greece, which had refused to sign the accord on wines and spirits, was resolved after South Africa agreed to discontinue the use of traditional European names for alcoholic drinks within five years. In December 2000 a framework agreement was reached on a free-trade accord with the Southern Common Market (known as Mercosur—Mercado Común del Sur, comprising Argentina, Brazil, Paraguay and Uruguay); trade negotiations were ongoing in early 2004.

In October 2001 the New Partnership for Africa's Development (NEPAD) was launched, as part of a long-term strategy for socio-economic recovery in Africa, in accordance with a decision taken at the OAU summit held in Lusaka, Zambia, in July. Mbeki formulated NEPAD's founding documents, in conjunction with the heads of state of Algeria, Egypt, Nigeria and Senegal, and South Africa was to host the Secretariat. In mid-2004 the AU agreed that the Pan-African Parliament (PAP) would be based in South Africa; the Government then announced that the PAP would be housed in Midrand (between Johannesburg and Pretoria). The second session of the PAP—its first in South Africa—took place at temporary headquarters in Midrand in mid-September that year.

In February 2007 South Africa signed a defence agreement with the Central African Republic committing to the provision of military training and the donation of surplus military supplies. The accord indicated that South Africa was becoming more lenient in its attitude towards involvement with countries threatened by regional conflict.

Government

Under the terms of the Constitution, which was adopted on 8 May 1996 and entered into force on 4 February 1997, legislative power is vested in a bicameral Parliament, comprising a National Assembly and a National Council of Provinces (formerly the Senate). The National Assembly is elected by universal adult suffrage under a system of proportional representation and has between 350 and 400 members. The 90-member National Council of Provinces comprises six permanent delegates and four special delegates from each of the provincial legislatures (see below). The President, who is elected by the National Assembly from among its members, exercises executive power in consultation with the other members of the Cabinet. Any party that holds a minimum of 80 seats in the National Assembly (equivalent to 20% of the national vote) is entitled to nominate an Executive Deputy President. A Constitutional Court ensures that the executive, legislative and judicial organs of government adhere to the provisions of the Constitution.

Each of the nine provinces has a legislature, which is elected under a system of proportional representation. Each legislature is entitled to draft a constitution for the province, subject to the principles governing the national Constitution, and to elect a Premier, who heads an Executive Council. Parties that hold a minimum of 10% of seats in the provincial legislature are entitled to a proportional number of portfolios in the Executive Council.

Defence

As assessed at November 2007, the South African National Defence Force (SANDF) totalled about 62,334: army 41,350, navy 5,801, air force 9,183 and a medical corps numbering 6,000. The SANDF comprised members of the former South African armed forces, together with personnel from the former military wings of the ANC and the Pan-Africanist Congress, and the former 'homelands'. Budgetary expenditure on defence was estimated at R 25,920m. in 2007.

Economic Affairs

In 2006, according to estimates by the World Bank, South Africa's gross national income (GNI), measured at average 2004–06 prices, was US $255,333m., equivalent to $5,390 per head (or $11,710 per head on an international purchasing-power parity basis). During 1996–2006, it was estimated, the population increased at an average annual rate of 1.7%, while gross domestic product (GDP) per head, in real terms, increased by 1.7%. Overall GDP increased, in real terms, at an average annual rate of 3.4% in 1996–2006, according to the World Bank; growth was 5.0% in 2006.

Agriculture (including forestry and fishing) contributed 2.7% of GDP in 2006. Some 8.7% of the employed labour force were engaged in the sector at September 2007. Maize (also the principal subsistence crop), fruit and sugar are exported, and livestock-rearing is also important; wool is another significant export. The GDP of the agricultural sector declined by an average of 0.4% per year in 1996–2006, according to the World Bank. Agricultural GDP increased by 5.4% in 2005, but declined by 13.2% in 2006.

Industry (including mining, manufacturing, construction and power) contributed 30.9% of GDP in 2006, and engaged 25.8% of the employed labour force at September 2007. Industrial GDP increased at an average annual rate of 2.4% in 1996–2006, according to the World Bank. Industrial GDP increased by 4.2% in 2006.

Mining contributed 7.9% of GDP in 2006, and engaged 3.4% of the employed labour force at September 2007. South Africa was the world's leading producer of gold in 2006, with the major mineral export accounting for about 11.8% of total world production. According to unofficial projections, China overtook South Africa as the world's leading producer of that commodity in 2007. Coal, platinum, iron ore, diamonds, chromium, manganese, vanadium, vermiculite, antimony, limestone, asbestos, fluorspar, uranium, copper, lead and zinc are also important mineral exports. There are reserves of petroleum, natural gas, sillimanite, titanium and zirconium. The GDP of the mining sector increased by an average of 0.5% per year in 1997–2007. An increase in industrial accidents impeded production in the non-gold sector in 2006; mining GDP contracted by an estimated 0.1% in that year, and by 0.6% in 2007.

Manufacturing contributed 18.2% of GDP in 2006, and engaged 13.5% of the employed labour force at September 2007. The GDP of the manufacturing sector increased at an average annual rate of 2.9% in 1996–2006, according to the World Bank. Manufacturing GDP increased by 4.8% in 2006.

Energy is derived principally from coal-based electricity (93.2% in 2004); this is supplemented by nuclear power and by hydroelectric power (5.5% and 0.9%, respectively). The construction of a plant to convert natural gas into liquid fuel was completed in 1992. Exploitation of petroleum reserves in oilfields located 140 km south-west of the Southern Cape commenced in 1997. In 2001 substantial reserves of natural gas were discovered off the Western Cape. Imports of mineral fuels and lubricants comprised 14.3% of the value of total imports in 2005.

The services sector contributed 66.4% of GDP in 2006, and engaged 55.1% of the employed labour force at September 2007. The real GDP of the services sector increased by an average of 4.1% per year in 1996–2006, according to the World Bank. Services GDP increased by 6.0% in 2006.

In 2006 South Africa recorded a visible trade deficit of US $6,175m., while there was a deficit of $16,276m. on the current account of the balance of payments. In 2004 the principal source of imports for the Southern African Customs Union (SACU, see below) was Germany (an estimated 14.2%); other major suppliers of imports were the USA, the People's Republic of China, Japan, the United Kingdom and Saudi Arabia. The principal market for exports in that year was also the USA (11.6%); other important purchasers were the United Kingdom, Japan and Germany. The principal exports in 2004 were basic manufactures (particularly iron and steel and diamonds), machinery and transport equipment, mineral fuels, chemical products, crude materials and food and live animals. The principal imports were machinery and transport equipment, mineral fuels (particularly petroleum), basic manufactures and chemical products.

In the financial year 2007/08 South Africa's estimated budget surplus was R 10,728.3m. At the end of 2005 South Africa's total foreign debt was US $30,632m., of which $20,922m. was long-term public debt. The cost of debt-servicing in that year was equivalent to 6.7% of the value of exports of goods and services. The annual rate of inflation averaged 5.6% in 1996–2006; consumer prices increased by 4.7% in 2006. According to official figures, 22.8% of the labour force were unemployed at September 2007.

South Africa is a member of SACU (with Botswana, Lesotho, Namibia and Swaziland), of the Southern African Development Community (SADC, see p. 386) and of the African Development Bank (see p. 162). The Secretariat of the New Partnership for Africa's Development (see p. 169) is located in South Africa.

Despite South Africa's mineral wealth and highly developed manufacturing sector, economic progress was hindered during the 1980s following the imposition of economic sanctions by the international community in protest at apartheid (see Recent History). In late 1993, in response to the Government's adoption of political reforms, the remaining economic sanctions were ended and relations with international financial institutions were normalized. Following democratic elections in April 1994, foreign Governments pledged considerable financial assistance to South Africa. As a result of a series of government programmes, by 1999 financial market conditions had improved considerably, resulting in lower inflation, increased real GDP and an increase in investor confidence. The country's economic progress continued in the mid-2000s: real GDP growth increased steadily, reaching 5.0% in 2006; public debt fell from 35.4% of GDP in 2003 to 31.4% in 2006 and was predicted further to contract; and business and consumer confidence continued to grow. However, despite the country's impressive economic stabilization since the end of apartheid, many problems remained.

Employment increased slightly in 2006, by 4.1%, however unemployment levels were still high, at 25.5% of the population. The distribution of income in the country remained one of the most unequal in the world with poverty still widespread among vast sections of the population, while the HIV/AIDS epidemic continued to have a devastating social and economic impact. The Government has implemented several initiatives aimed at reducing social disparities: the Black Empowerment Act was introduced in 2004 to redistribute the nation's wealth among the black population through affirmative action. Companies were required to restructure their ownership, and the Government pledged that 26% of businesses would be led by blacks by 2014. Additionally, the land reform initiative aimed to transfer 30% of commercial agricultural land to previously disadvantaged groups by 2014. The association football World Cup, due to be staged in the country in mid-2010, accelerated investment in infrastructure, and both the construction and transport sectors expanded considerably, creating additional employment. The Government's budget for 2008 forecast reduced growth of 4.0%, however this was projected to rise to 4.6% by 2010.

Education

School attendance is compulsory for children of all population groups between the ages of seven and 16 years. From 1991 state schools were permitted to admit pupils of all races, and in 1995 the right to free state education for all was introduced. According to UNESCO estimates, in 2002/03 enrolment at primary schools included 89% of pupils in the relevant age-group (males 88%; females 89%), while in 1999/2000 secondary enrolment included 62% of pupils in the relevant age-group (males 58%; females 65%). During the 1980s universities, which were formerly racially segregated, began to admit students of all races. In 2006 there were 11 universities, five universities of technology, and six comprehensive institutions. Budget estimates for 2007/08 indicated the allocation of R 16,000.9m. (3.0% of total expenditure) to education.

Public Holidays

2008: 1 January (New Year's Day), 21 March (Human Rights Day), 21 March (Good Friday), 24 March (Family Day), 27 April (Freedom Day), 1 May (Workers' Day), 16 June (Youth Day), 9 August (National Women's Day), 24 September (Heritage Day), 16 December (Day of Reconciliation), 25 December (Christmas Day), 26 December (Day of Goodwill).

2009: 1 January (New Year's Day), 21 March (Human Rights Day), 10 April (Good Friday), 13 April (Family Day), 27 April (Freedom Day), 1 May (Workers' Day), 16 June (Youth Day), 9 August (National Women's Day), 24 September (Heritage Day), 16 December (Day of Reconciliation), 25 December (Christmas Day), 26 December (Day of Goodwill).

Weights and Measures

The metric system is in use.

Statistical Survey

Source (unless otherwise indicated): Statistics South Africa, Private Bag X44, Pretoria 0001; tel. (12) 3108911; fax (12) 3108500; e-mail info@statssa.pwv.gov.za; internet www.statssa.gov.za.

Area and Population

AREA, POPULATION AND DENSITY*

Area (sq km)	1,219,090†
Population (census results)	
9 October 1996	40,583,573
9 October 2001	
Males	21,434,033
Females	23,385,737
Total	44,819,770
Population (official estimates at mid-year)	
2005	46,892,424
2006	47,391,029
2007	47,850,064
Density (per sq km) at mid-2007	39.3

*Excluding data for Walvis Bay (area 1,124 sq km or 434 sq miles, population 22,999 in 1991), sovereignty over which was transferred from South Africa to Namibia on 1 March 1994.
† 470,693 sq miles.

ETHNIC GROUPS
(at census of October 2001)*

	Number	% of total
Africans (Blacks)	35,416,164	79.02
Europeans (Whites)	4,293,638	9.58
Coloureds	3,994,507	8.91
Asians	1,115,461	2.49
Total	44,819,770	100.00

*Figures exclude the effect of additional deaths caused by HIV/AIDS.

PROVINCES
(official estimates at mid-2007)

	Area (sq km)	Population	Density (per sq km)	Capital
KwaZulu/Natal	92,100	10,014,500	108.7	Pietermaritzburg
Gauteng*	17,010	9,688,100	569.6	Johannesburg
Eastern Cape	169,580	6,906,200	40.7	Bisho
Limpopo†	123,910	5,402,900	43.6	Pietersburg
Western Cape	129,370	4,839,800	37.4	Cape Town
North-West	116,320	3,394,200	291.8	Mmabatho
Mpumalanga‡	79,490	3,536,300	44.5	Nelspruit
Free State§	129,480	2,965,600	22.9	Bloemfontein
Northern Cape	361,830	1,102,200	3.0	Kimberley
Total	1,219,090	47,849,800	39.33	

* Formerly Pretoria-Witwatersrand-Vereeniging.
† Known as Northern Province (formerly Northern Transvaal) until February 2002.
‡ Formerly Eastern Transvaal.
§ Formerly the Orange Free State.

Note: Figures for population are rounded estimates based on the cohort-component compilation method.

SOUTH AFRICA

PRINCIPAL TOWNS
(metropolitan areas, population at 2001 census)

Johannesburg	3,225,812	Springs	80,776
Durban	3,090,122	Vanderbiljpark	80,201
Cape Town*	2,893,247	Vereeniging	73,288
Pretoria*	1,985,983	Uitenhage	71,668
Port Elizabeth	1,005,779	Rustenburg	67,201
Soweto	858,649	Kimberley	62,526
Tembisa	348,687	Brakpan	62,115
Pietermaritzburg	223,518	Witbank	61,092
Botshabelo	175,820	Somerset West	60,609
Mdantsane	175,783	Klerksdorp	59,511
Boksburg	158,650	Midrand	44,566
East London	135,560	Newcastle	44,119
Bloemfontein*	111,698	Welkom	34,158
Benoni	94,341	Potchefstroom	26,725
Alberton	89,394	Carletonville	18,362
Krugersdorp	86,618	Westonaria	8,440

*Pretoria is the administrative capital, Cape Town the legislative capital and Bloemfontein the judicial capital.

Mid-2007 ('000, incl. suburbs, UN estimates): Johannesburg 3,435; Cape Town 3,215; East Rand (Ekurhuleni) 2,986; Durban 2,729; Pretoria 1,338; Vereeniging 1,074; Port Elizabeth 1,021 (Source: UN, *World Urbanization Prospects: The 2007 Revision*).

BIRTHS AND DEATHS
(annual averages, UN estimates)

	1990–95	1995–2000	2000–05
Birth rate (per 1,000)	27.7	25.3	24.1
Death rate (per 1,000)	8.2	9.2	13.5

Source: UN, *World Population Prospects: The 2006 Revision*.

Registered live births ('000): 1,433 in 2001; 1,518 in 2002; 1,677 in 2003.

Registered deaths: 413,969 in 2000; 451,936 in 2001; 499,268 in 2002.

Registered marriages: 134,581 in 2001; 177,002 in 2002; 178,689 in 2003.

Expectation of life (years at birth, UN estimates): 51.0 (males 49.9; females 52.1) in 2005 (Source: WHO, *World Health Statistics*).

IMMIGRATION AND EMIGRATION

	2001	2002	2003
Immigrants:			
Africa	1,419	2,472	4,961
Europe	1,714	1,847	2,567
Asia	1,289	1,738	2,328
Americas	213	244	354
Oceania	51	65	99
Total (incl. others and unspecified)	4,832	6,545	10,578
Emigrants:			
Africa	1,584	1,461	2,611
Europe	5,316	4,637	6,827
Asia	226	218	445
Americas	1,713	1,473	2,090
Oceania	2,912	2,523	3,248
Total (incl. others and unspecified)	12,260	10,890	16,165

Immigrants (2004): Africa 5,235; Europe 2,638; Asia 2,225; Americas 343; Oceania 2,638; Total (incl. others) 10,714.

ECONOMICALLY ACTIVE POPULATION
(household survey, '000 persons aged 15 to 65 years, September 2001)*

	Males	Females	Total
Agriculture, hunting, forestry and fishing	727	324	1,051
Mining and quarrying	470	17	487
Manufacturing	1,004	602	1,605
Electricity, gas and water	80	15	95
Construction	534	60	594
Trade, restaurants and hotels	1,186	1,212	2,397
Transport, storage and communications	448	94	543
Financing, insurance, real estate and business services	547	428	975
Community, social and personal services	878	1,110	1,988
Private households	150	905	1,055
Total employed (incl. others)	6,049	4,783	10,833
Unemployed†	2,139	2,386	4,525
Total labour force	8,188	7,169	15,358

*Figures have been assessed independently, so that totals are not always the sum of the component parts.

†Based on the official definition. According to the expanded definition, the number of unemployed (in '000) was 7,698 (males 3,280, females 4,418).

September 2005 ('000): Agriculture, hunting, forestry and fishing 925; Mining and quarrying 411; Manufacturing 1,706; Electricity, gas and water 100; Construction 935; Wholesale and retail 3,024; Transport, storage and communications 616; Financing, insurance, real estate and business services 1,296; Community, social and personal services 2,192; Total employed (incl. others) 12,301; Unemployed 4,487; Total labour force 16,788.

September 2006 ('000): Agriculture, hunting, forestry and fishing 1,088; Mining and quarrying 398; Manufacturing 1,737; Electricity, gas and water 119; Construction 1,024; Wholesale and retail 3,055; Transport, storage and communications 611; Financing, insurance, real estate and business services 1,309; Community, social and personal services 2,319; Total employed (incl. others) 12,800; Unemployed 4,391; Total labour force 17,191.

September 2007 ('000): Agriculture, hunting, forestry and fishing 1,164; Mining and quarrying 455; Manufacturing 1,799; Electricity, gas and water 116; Construction 1,066; Wholesale and retail 2,952; Transport, storage and communications 596; Financing, insurance, real estate and business services 1,340; Community, social and personal services 2,452; Total employed (incl. others) 13,324; Unemployed 3,945; Total labour force 17,269.

Health and Welfare

KEY INDICATORS

Total fertility rate (children per woman, 2005)	2.7
Under-5 mortality rate (per 1,000 live births, 2005)	68
HIV/AIDS (% of persons aged 15–49, 2005)	18.8
Physicians (per 1,000 head, 2004)	0.77
Health expenditure (2004): US $ per head (PPP)	748.0
Health expenditure (2004): % of GDP	8.6
Health expenditure (2004): public (% of total)	40.4
Access to water (% of persons, 2004)	88
Access to sanitation (% of persons, 2004)	65
Human Development Index (2005): ranking	121
Human Development Index (2005): value	0.674

For sources and definitions, see explanatory note on p. vi.

SOUTH AFRICA

Statistical Survey

Agriculture

PRINCIPAL CROPS
('000 metric tons)

	2004	2005	2006
Wheat	1,687.0	1,905.0	2,105.0
Barley	185.0	225.0	236.0
Maize	9,965	11,716	6,935
Oats	37.0	34.0	43.5
Sorghum	373.0	260.0	96.0
Potatoes	1,799.6	1,767.7	1,862.9
Sweet potatoes	54.8	54.3	47.0
Sugar cane	19,094.8	21,265.0	20,275.4
Dry beans	80.0	69.8	67.3
Soybeans	220.0	272.5	424.0
Groundnuts (in shell)	115.0	64.0	74.0
Sunflower seed	648.0	620.0	520.0
Cottonseed	46.2	39.1	24.6
Cabbages	173.2	155.3	141.5
Tomatoes	436.5	462.2	441.8
Pumpkins, squash and gourds	256.0	253.9	78.3
Onions (dry)	403.2	387.3	403.2
Carrots	132.8	127.1	127.5
Green corn (maize)	320	320	320
Watermelons	64.9	74.8	65.3
Bananas	279.8	351.6	343.7
Oranges	1,197.9	1,246.5	1,334.4
Tangerines, mandarins, clementines and satsumas	113.7	137.1	133.0
Lemons and limes	230.1	184.3	217.0
Grapefruit and pomelos	288.4	363.0	415.2
Apples	765.4	680.4	639.8
Pears	305.7	312.8	316.1
Apricots	97.8	43.7	83.6
Peaches and nectarines	183.7	172.6	167.0
Plums	67.5	53.6	39.0
Grapes	1,761.9	1,682.8	1,550.4
Mangoes	100.8	108.6	95.3
Avocados	56.9	105.9	61.4
Pineapples	164.4	180.6	166.3
Tobacco (leaves)	22.2	20.0	17.5

Aggregate production ('000 metric tons, may include official, semi-official or estimated data): Total cereals 12,028 in 2004, 14,176 in 2005, 9,453 in 2006; Total roots and tubers 1,854 in 2004, 1,822 in 2005, 1,910 in 2006; Total vegetables (incl. melons) 2,264 in 2004, 2,259 in 2005, 2,042 in 2006; Total fruits (excl. melons) 5,743 in 2004, 5,754 in 2005, 5,690 in 2006.

Source: FAO.

LIVESTOCK
('000 head, year ending September)

	2004	2005	2006
Cattle	13,512	13,790	13,790*
Pigs	1,651	1,656	1,623
Sheep	25,360	25,334	24,983
Goats	6,372	6,356	6,400
Horses*	270	270	270
Asses, mules or hinnies*	164	164	164
Chickens	145,000*	121,000	125,840
Ducks*	360	360	360
Geese*	130	130	130
Turkeys*	500	500	500

* FAO estimate(s).
Source: FAO.

LIVESTOCK PRODUCTS
('000 metric tons)

	2004	2005	2006
Cattle meat	655	705	804
Sheep meat	120	115	117
Goat meat*	36.4	36.5	36.5
Pig meat	145	147	151
Chicken meat	906	949	971
Cows' milk	2,699	2,871	2,971
Hen eggs	357	366	384
Wool: greasy*	44.2	44.2	45.0

* FAO estimates.
Source: FAO.

Forestry

(including Namibia)

ROUNDWOOD REMOVALS
('000 cubic metres, excl. bark, FAO estimates)

	2004	2005	2006
Sawlogs, veneer logs and logs for sleepers	5,237.1	2,282.8	2,131.1
Pulpwood	14,833.3	14,833.3	14,833.3
Other industrial wood	1,260.9	1,098.3	1,098.3
Fuel wood	12,000.0	12,000.0	12,000.0
Total	33,331.3	30,214.4	30,062.7

Source: FAO.

SAWNWOOD PRODUCTION
('000 cubic metres, incl. railway sleepers)

	2004	2005	2006
Coniferous (softwood)	2,689.0	2,014.7	2,011.3
Broadleaved (hardwood)	134.8	201.8	79.8
Total	2,823.8	2,216.5	2,091.1

Source: FAO.

Fishing

('000 metric tons, live weight)

	2003	2004	2005
Capture*	822.9	881.9	817.6
Cape hakes (Stokvisse)	139.2	153.3	144.0
Southern African pilchard	290.0	373.8	246.8
Whitehead's round herring	42.5	47.2	28.9
Southern African anchovy	258.9	190.1	282.7
Cape horse mackerel	28.3	34.1	35.1
Aquaculture	4.9	3.2	3.1
Total catch*†	827.8	885.1	820.7

* FAO estimate(s).
† Excluding aquatic plants ('000 metric tons, FAO): 20.2 in 2003; 25.6 in 2004; 9.6 in 2005.

Note: Figures exclude aquatic animals, recorded by number rather than weight. The number of Nile crocodiles captured was: 31,321 in 2003; 35,760 in 2004; 16,384 in 2005. The number of toothed whales caught was 70 in 2003; 77 in 2004; 77 in 2005.

Source: FAO.

SOUTH AFRICA

Mining

('000 metric tons, unless otherwise indicated)

	2003	2004	2005*
Hard coal	239,311	243,372	245,007
Crude petroleum ('000 barrels)	4,068	6,769	7,277
Natural gas†	2,230	2,011	2,000
Iron ore‡	24,200	24,800	24,900
Copper ore (metric tons)‡	120,800	102,574	103,856
Nickel ore (metric tons)‡	40,842†	39,851	42,392
Lead concentrates (metric tons)‡	39,941	37,485	42,159
Zinc ore (metric tons)‡	41,400	32,001	32,112
Manganese ore and concentrates (metallurgical and chemical)§	3,501	4,282	4,611
Chromium ore§	7,406	7,677	7,494
Vanadium ore (metric tons)‡	27,172	23,302	22,604
Zirconium concentrates (metric tons)†	300,000	400,000	410,000
Antimony concentrates (metric tons)‡	5,291	4,967	8,600†
Cobalt ore (metric tons)†‡	400	460	400
Silver (kg)	79,817	70,913	87,874
Uranium oxide (metric tons)	894	887	795
Gold (kg)	373,300	337,223	294,671
Platinum-group metals (kg)	266,150	276,401	302,981
Kaolin	86.4	81.9	59.4
Magnesite—crude	86.1	65.9	66.0†
Phosphate rock§	2,643	2,735	2,577
Fluorspar	235.0	265.0	245.0†
Salt	441.3	332.7	399.1
Diamonds ('000 carats)	12,684	14,295	15,776
Gypsum—crude	394.1	452.3	547.6
Asbestos	6.2	—	—
Mica (metric tons)	1,003	901	924
Talc (metric tons)	6,719	8,141	8,469
Pyrophyllite (metric tons)	14,350	28,987	60,267

* Preliminary figures.
† Estimate(s).
‡ Figures refer to metal content of ores and concentrates.
§ Gross weight.

Source: US Geological Survey.

Industry

SELECTED PRODUCTS
('000 metric tons, unless otherwise indicated)

	2002	2003	2004
Wheat flour*	1,898	1,943	2,016
Sugar—refined	1,141	1,653	n.a.
Footwear ('000 pairs)	19,699	17,317	n.a.
Chemical wood pulp	2,648	2,667	n.a.
Newsprint	338	336	336
Rubber tyres ('000)	12,038	12,804	n.a.
Motor spirit (petrol)	8,085	8,360	8,343
Kerosene	636	620	633
Jet fuel	1,637	1,874	1,778
Distillate fuel oils	7,383	7,593	7,141
Lubricating oils	412	446	376
Petroleum bitumen—asphalt	278	408	412
Cement (sales)†	9,624	10,163	13,784
Pig-iron†	5,823	6,234	6,011
Crude steel†	9,100	9,481	9,500
Refined copper—unwrought†	101.0	111.0	91.5
Colour television receivers ('000)	271	359	n.a.
Passenger motor cars—assembled ('000)	300	306	n.a.
Lorries—assembled ('000)	129	125	n.a.
Electric energy (million kWh)	217,712	234,229	244,607

* Twelve months ending September.
† Source: US Geological Survey.

2005 ('000 metric tons, data from US Geological Survey): Cement sales 14,500 (estimate); Pig-iron 6,130; Crude steel 9,493; Refined copper—unwrought 100.0 (estimate).

Source: mostly UN, *Industrial Commodity Statistics Yearbook*.

Finance

CURRENCY AND EXCHANGE RATES

Monetary Units
100 cents = 1 rand (R).

Sterling, Dollar and Euro Equivalents (31 December 2007)
£1 sterling = 13.64 rand;
US $1 = 6.81 rand;
€1 = 10.02 rand;
100 rand = £7.33 = $14.68 = €9.98.

Average Exchange Rate (rand per US $)
2005   6.3593
2006   6.7716
2007   7.0454

BUDGET
(million rand, year ending 31 March)

Revenue	2005/06	2006/07*	2007/08*
Tax revenue (gross)	417,334.0	489,662.0	556,562.0
Taxes on incomes and profits	230,803.6	247,300.0	312,150.0
Individuals	125,645.3	139,000.0	155,335.0
Companies (including secondary tax)	98,438.4	130,471.0	154,515.0
Retirement funds	4,783.1	2,750.0	—
Other	1,936.7	2,079.0	2,300.0
Taxes on payroll and workforce	4,872.0	5,850.0	6,500.0
Taxes on property	11,137.5	10,345.0	10,995.0
Domestic taxes on goods and services	151,361.9	174,667.0	199,210.0
Value-added tax	114,351.6	134,562.0	155,068.0
Excise duties	14,546.5	16,100.0	17,792.4
Levies on fuel	20,506.7	21,750.0	23,937.7
Air departure tax	458.2	500.0	520.0
Other	341.7	455.0	477.0
Stamp duties and fees	792.8	600.0	222.0
State Miscellaneous Revenue	—	—	—
Taxes on international trade and transactions	18,201.9	23,900.0	27,485.0
Other current revenue	7,642.3	9,532.5	9,185.2
Capital revenue	916.5	1,813.1	1,907.4
Sub-total	425,892.8	501,007.6	567,654.6
Less SACU payments†	14,144.9	25,172.0	23,053.0
Total	411,747.9	475,835.6	544,601.6

Expenditure	2005/06‡	2006/07*	2007/08*
Central government administration	25,054.1	35,372.6	40,798.7
The Presidency	190.1	238.9	254.7
Parliament	673.8	782.1	835.7
Foreign affairs	2,687.7	3,042.1	3,856.4
Home affairs	3,172.1	2,800.4	3,314.6
Provincial and local government	15,976.1	25,392.3	28,844.2
Public works	2,354.3	3,116.8	3,693.1
Financial and administrative services	17,013.2	18,807.6	21,718.1
Government communication and information system	253.6	294.6	375.8
National treasury	13,100.7	16,752.9	19,708.2
Public services and administration	197.0	442.4	357.3
Public service commission	91.1	97.0	105.4
SA management development institute	55.4	58.9	71.1
Statistics South Africa	643.9	1,161.8	1,100.3
Social services	80,295.4	91,919.1	102,686.2
Arts and culture	1,121.0	1,330.1	1,608.0
Education	12,436.8	14,299.2	16,000.9
Health	9,937.1	11,454.0	12,655.1
Labour	1,295.9	1,493.5	2,032.9
Social development	55,067.8	62,382.4	67,232.1
Sport and Recreation South Africa	436.8	959.9	3,157.2
Justice and protection services	67,710.5	72,800.1	79,940.8
Correctional services	9,631.2	9,831.5	10,742.3
Defence	23,510.5	23,902.9	25,922.3
Independent complaints directorate	54.5	65.9	80.9

SOUTH AFRICA

Statistical Survey

Expenditure—continued	2005/06‡	2006/07*	2007/08*
Justice and constitutional development	5,153.5	6,478.6	7,277.8
Safety and security	29,360.8	32,521.2	35,917.5
Economic services and infrastructure	34,345.8	47,286.8	54,034.0
Agriculture	1,906.8	2,367.6	2,281.2
Communications	1,034.4	1,322.3	1,423.5
Environmental affairs and tourism	1,775.7	2,061.8	2,590.8
Housing	5,248.8	7,333.7	8,877.6
Land affairs	2,876.9	3,730.2	5,678.5
Minerals and energy	2,191.6	2,635.1	2,966.1
Public enterprises	2,671.5	2,869.9	1,064.0
Science and technology	2,041.3	2,617.1	3,142.5
Trade and industry	3,056.4	3,942.0	4,845.6
Transport	10,409.9	13,746.8	15,857.9
Water affairs and forestry	3,804.0	4,660.3	5,306.3
Unallocated funds / Projected underspending	—	−2,100.0	—
Contingency reserve	—	—	3,000.0
Sub-total	224,419.1	264,086.5	302,177.7
State debt costs	50,912.0	52,588.1	52,916.0
Provincial equitable share	135,291.6	150,752.9	171,271.4
Skills levy and seats	4,883.3	5,500.0	6,000.0
Members' remuneration	211.7	229.2	242.4
Judges' salaries	1,040.1	1,071.1	1,263.5
President and deputy-president salary	2.0	2.2	2.2
Total	416,759.9	474,229.9	533,873.3

* Estimates.
† Payments to Botswana, Lesotho, Namibia and Swaziland, in accordance with Southern African Customs Union agreements.
‡ Preliminary outcome.
Source: National Treasury, Pretoria.

INTERNATIONAL RESERVES
(US $ million at 31 December)

	2004	2005	2006
Gold (national valuation)	1,578	2,051	2,530
IMF special drawing rights	346	319	355
Reserve position in IMF	1	1	1
Foreign exchange	12,794	18,260	22,720
Total	14,719	20,630	25,606

Source: IMF, *International Financial Statistics*.

MONEY SUPPLY
(million rand at 31 December)

	2004	2005	2006
Currency outside banks	39,080	43,419	49,951
Demand deposits at deposit money banks	204,947	248,103	287,612
Total (incl. others)	244,027	291,522	337,563

Source: IMF, *International Financial Statistics*.

COST OF LIVING
(Consumer Price Index; base: 2000 = 100)

	2004	2005	2006
Food	134.9	137.9	147.8
Housing	111.2	113.4	118.2
Electricity, gas and other fuels	129.0	135.7	141.9
All items (incl. others)	123.8	128.0	134.0

Source: ILO.

NATIONAL ACCOUNTS
(million rand at current prices, preliminary)

National Income and Product

	2004	2005	2006
Compensation of employees	627,411	679,206	740,435
Net operating surplus	426,122	469,015	544,233
Consumption of fixed capital	172,966	189,892	214,803
Gross domestic product (GDP) at factor cost	1,226,499	1,338,113	1,499,471
Taxes on production	177,820	210,219	238,921
Less Subsidies	6,162	9,079	11,704
GDP at market prices	1,398,157	1,539,253	1,726,688
Primary incomes received from abroad	20,973	29,550	40,234
Less Primary incomes paid abroad	48,823	60,975	75,990
Gross national income at market prices	1,370,307	1,507,828	1,690,932
Current transfers received from abroad	1,621	1,536	1,792
Less Current transfers paid abroad	12,947	14,311	18,978
Gross national disposable income at market prices	1,358,981	1,495,053	1,673,746

Expenditure on the Gross Domestic Product

	2004	2005	2006
Government final consumption expenditure	273,708	301,338	336,073
Private final consumption expenditure	870,806	963,291	1,080,074
Increase in stocks	20,989	18,484	30,027
Gross fixed capital formation	226,808	262,432	320,642
Residual item	11,301	7,892	18,012
Total domestic expenditure	1,403,612	1,553,437	1,784,828
Exports of goods and services	372,722	423,022	515,355
Less Imports of goods and services	378,177	437,206	573,495
GDP at market prices	1,398,157	1,539,253	1,726,688
GDP at constant 2000 prices	1,062,187	1,118,155	1,189,015

Gross Domestic Product by Economic Activity

	2004	2005	2006
Agriculture, forestry and fishing	39,432	37,625	41,632
Mining and quarrying	89,290	100,515	120,222
Manufacturing	237,100	254,993	278,793
Electricity, gas and water	29,645	31,574	33,579
Construction (contractors)	29,838	33,161	39,274
Wholesale and retail trade, catering and accommodation	175,738	191,549	213,233
Transport, storage and communication	122,240	131,955	145,044
Finance, insurance, real estate and business services	260,151	293,481	336,950
Government services	193,420	209,614	226,360
Other community, social and personal services	76,998	84,055	94,327
Gross value added at basic prices	1,253,852	1,368,522	1,529,413
Taxes, less subsidies, on products	144,305	170,731	197,275
GDP at market prices	1,398,157	1,539,253	1,726,688

Source: South African Reserve Bank.

SOUTH AFRICA

BALANCE OF PAYMENTS
(US $ million)

	2004	2005	2006
Exports of goods f.o.b.	48,237	55,280	63,767
Imports of goods f.o.b.	−48,518	−56,484	−69,941
Trade balance	−281	−1,204	−6,175
Exports of services	9,682	11,157	12,022
Imports of services	−10,328	−12,155	−14,291
Balance on goods and services	−928	−2,201	−8,444
Other income received	3,259	4,640	5,944
Other income paid	−7,576	−9,569	−11,238
Balance on goods, services and income	−5,246	−7,130	−13,737
Current transfers received	257	240	261
Current transfers paid	−2,015	−2,251	−2,800
Current balance	−7,003	−9,142	−16,276
Capital account (net)	52	30	30
Direct investment abroad	−1,305	−909	−6,496
Direct investment from abroad	701	6,133	−11
Portfolio investment assets	−950	−911	−2,021
Portfolio investment liabilities	7,357	5,698	21,814
Other investment assets	−216	−3,503	−7,301
Other investment liabilities	2,065	4,896	8,545
Net errors and omissions	5,623	3,474	5,427
Overall balance	6,324	5,766	3,711

Source: IMF, *International Financial Statistics*.

External Trade

PRINCIPAL COMMODITIES
(distribution by SITC, US $ million)

Imports c.i.f.	2002	2003	2004
Food and live animals	925.1	1,185.6	1,626.8
Crude materials (inedible) except fuels	843.2	1,098.9	1,497.0
Mineral fuels, lubricants, etc.	3,269.2	4,105.3	6,885.8
Petroleum, petroleum products, etc.	3,134.7	3,934.5	6,647.6
Crude petroleum oils, etc.	2,796.4	3,597.9	5,937.6
Chemicals and related products	3,181.3	3,813.9	4,771.8
Basic manufactures	3,191.8	4,172.1	5,320.9
Non-metallic mineral manufactures	825.9	1,082.6	1,276.4
Machinery and transport equipment	9,839.8	13,595.0	18,905.6
Power generating machinery and equipment	581.6	809.3	1,040.6
Machinery specialized for particular industries	1,335.9	1,712.8	2,196.3
General industrial machinery, equipment and parts	1,444.9	1,986.1	2,266.4
Office machines and automatic data-processing equipment	1,080.4	1,616.0	2,329.7
Telecommunications and sound equipment	1,613.5	1,722.7	2,614.7
Other electrical machinery, apparatus, etc.	1,184.9	1,542.6	1,883.7
Road vehicles	1,662.5	2,441.5	3,818.7
Passenger motor vehicles (excl. buses)	959.7	1,455.2	2,568.0
Other transport equipment	737.7	1,486.6	2,391.6
Miscellaneous manufactured articles	2,307.3	2,887.9	3,989.2
Total (incl. others)	26,212.1	34,543.1	47,794.3

Exports f.o.b.	2002	2003	2004
Food and live animals	1,898.9	2,381.5	2,670.4
Vegetables and fruit	846.4	1,238.0	1,548.2
Beverages and tobacco	482.1	670.1	786.6
Crude materials (inedible) except fuels	2,435.4	2,744.6	3,094.4
Metalliferous ores and metal scrap	1,305.5	1,348.8	1,650.3
Mineral fuels, lubricants, etc.	2,853.2	3,105.8	3,658.9
Coal, lignite and peat	1,839.0	1,804.8	2,432.6
Petroleum, petroleum products, etc.	1,009.6	1,296.9	1,217.4
Chemicals and related products	2,154.3	2,395.9	3,152.9
Basic manufactures	6,714.9	12,045.0	16,897.6
Non-metallic mineral manufactures	1,750.1	2,010.3	2,326.5
Pearl, precious and semi-precious stones, unworked or worked	1,550.9	1,764.0	2,008.2
Diamonds (non-industrial), not mounted or set	1,543.8	1,754.6	1,998.5
Iron and steel	2,411.4	3,877.4	5,642.0
Pig-iron, etc.	1,109.8	1,722.4	2,776.5
Non-ferrous metals	1,099.1	4,423.5	6,927.8
Silver, platinum and other platinum group metals	20.3	3,206.7	4,641.2
Platinum group metals, unwrought, unworked or semi-manufactured	0.1	3,196.1	4,631.2
Aluminium	887.8	956.5	1,386.4
Aluminium and aluminium alloys, unwrought	704.2	679.0	1,017.9
Machinery and transport equipment	5,260.4	6,544.2	7,927.4
General industrial machinery, equipment and parts	1,294.8	1,650.7	1,955.7
Road vehicles	2,396.7	3,114.5	3,540.6
Passenger motor vehicles (excl. buses)	1,614.5	2,099.3	2,451.9
Miscellaneous manufactured articles	1,193.5	1,487.0	1,664.7
Total (incl. others)	23,064.4	31,635.9	40,206.1

Source: UN, *International Trade Statistics Yearbook*.

2004 (million rand): Total imports 304,432; *Exports:* Gold 32,830; Total 296,080. Source: IMF, *International Financial Statistics*.

2005 (million rand): Total imports 349,181; *Exports:* Gold 27,023; Total 328,760. Source: IMF, *International Financial Statistics*.

2006 (million rand): Total imports 461,042; *Exports:* Total 396,760. Source: IMF, *International Financial Statistics*.

SOUTH AFRICA

PRINCIPAL TRADING PARTNERS
(US $ million)*

Imports f.o.b.	2002	2003	2004
Australia	741.1	797.8	1,128.4
Austria	279.0	364.2	429.6
Belgium-Luxembourg	371.2	506.0	599.2
Brazil	467.2	715.1	1,000.8
China, People's Repub.	1,358.9	2,218.8	3,589.2
France (incl. Monaco)	1,075.7	2,063.7	2,901.7
Germany	4,076.2	5,128.4	6,778.1
India	280.5	417.7	708.9
Iran	920.8	1,251.6	2,376.2
Ireland	290.4	376.5	634.0
Italy	943.8	1,128.9	1,444.8
Japan	1,818.6	2,433.9	3,270.0
Korea, Repub.	427.7	558.3	1,013.5
Malaysia	345.8	402.6	593.3
Netherlands	478.4	579.8	707.8
Nigeria	344.0	405.1	810.7
Saudi Arabia	1,299.5	1,966.3	2,665.6
Spain	337.3	511.8	673.1
Sweden	316.7	448.8	641.3
Switzerland-Liechtenstein	453.9	466.4	483.6
Thailand	283.0	426.3	666.0
United Kingdom	2,372.0	3,000.7	3,269.7
USA	3,084.0	3,425.6	4,128.8
Total (incl. others)	26,212.0	34,543.1	47,794.3

Exports f.o.b.	2002	2003	2004
Angola	322.6	447.3	481.2
Australia	486.6	745.3	1,025.4
Belgium-Luxembourg	865.6	985.3	1,124.7
China, People's Repub.	450.3	889.1	1,054.2
France (incl. Monaco)	664.4	743.0	892.5
Germany	1,883.6	2,439.7	3,231.9
Hong Kong	316.1	423.2	527.3
India	351.5	380.3	566.3
Israel	521.2	508.1	634.7
Italy	743.0	931.1	1,188.9
Japan	1,490.2	3,147.7	4,104.5
Korea, Repub.	478.1	580.1	697.5
Mauritius	255.0	271.3	269.3
Mozambique	600.8	745.5	786.4
Netherlands	1,188.8	1,508.7	1,838.0
Nigeria	258.8	334.1	443.9
Spain	641.6	830.8	1,109.2
Switzerland-Liechtenstein	240.5	762.8	1,125.1
United Kingdom	2,519.1	3,197.4	4,209.4
USA	2,439.2	3,844.2	4,682.8
Zimbabwe	692.3	858.6	927.7
Total (incl. others)	23,064.4	31,635.8	40,206.1

* Imports by country of origin; exports by country of destination.

Source: UN, *International Trade Statistics Yearbook*.

Transport

RAILWAYS
(traffic, year ending 31 March)*

	1997/98	1998/99	1999/2000
Passenger-km (million)	1,775	1,794	3,930
Net ton-km (million)	103,866	102,777	106,786

* Including Namibia.

Source: UN, *Statistical Yearbook*.

ROAD TRAFFIC
(registered motor vehicles)

	2002
Heavy load vehicles	326,798
Heavy passenger motor vehicles	164,369
Light load vehicles	1,875,234
Light passenger motor vehicles	4,135,037
Motorcycles	159,266
Special vehicles	296,518
Other vehicles	17,955
Total (incl. others)	6,975,177

SHIPPING

Merchant Fleet
(vessels registered at 31 December)

	2004	2005	2006
Number of vessels	246	243	242
Displacement ('000 grt)	170.0	180.6	173.1

Source: Lloyd's Register-Fairplay, *World Fleet Statistics*.

International Sea-borne Freight Traffic

	2003	2004	2005
Goods loaded (metric tons)	128,477,183	124,370,762	127,408,557
Goods unloaded (metric tons)	42,845,843	43,820,161	43,847,748
Containers loaded (TEU)	1,194,400	1,290,883	1,484,009
Containers unloaded (TEU)	1,220,167	1,341,888	1,530,227

Source: National Ports Authority of South Africa.

CIVIL AVIATION
(traffic on scheduled services)

	2001	2002	2003
Kilometres flown (million)	167	170	188
Passengers carried ('000)	7,948	8,167	9,160
Passenger-km (million)	22,061	22,914	24,666
Total ton-km (million)	2,746	2,853	3,125

Source: UN, *Statistical Yearbook*.

Tourism

FOREIGN VISITOR ARRIVALS*

Country of origin	2003	2004	2005
Botswana	797,315	806,820	798,455
France	130,365	111,636	103,674
Germany	261,194	249,564	253,471
Lesotho	1,291,242	1,479,802	1,668,826
Mozambique	474,790	405,579	648,526
Namibia	216,978	226,525	220,045
Netherlands	122,565	122,271	117,855
Swaziland	809,049	852,636	911,990
United Kingdom	463,021	463,176	476,627
USA	192,561	213,322	238,934
Zambia	115,650	122,512	128,390
Zimbabwe	568,626	558,093	783,100
Total (incl. others and unspecified)	6,640,095	6,815,202	7,517,258

* Figures include same-day visitors (excursionists), but exclude arrivals of South African nationals resident abroad. Border crossings by contract workers are also excluded.

Tourism receipts (US $ million, incl. passenger transport): 6,533 in 2003; 7,380 in 2004; 8,448 in 2005.

Source: World Tourism Organization.

Communications Media

	2004	2005	2006
Telephones ('000 main lines in use)	4,850.0	4,729.0	4,729.0
Mobile cellular telephones ('000 subscribers)	20,839.0	33,960.0	39,662.0
Internet users ('000)	3,566.0	5,100.0	5,100.0
Personal computers in use ('000)	3,740	3,966	n.a.
Broadband subscribers ('000)	60.0	165.3	165.3

2001: Radio receivers ('000 in use): 11,696; Television receivers ('000 in use): 7,708.

2004: Daily newspapers (average circulation, '000): 1,408.0, (titles) 18.

Facsimile machines (number in use): 150,000 in 1997.

Book production: 5,418 titles in 1995.

Sources: partly UNESCO, *Statistical Yearbook*; UN, *Statistical Yearbook*; International Telecommunication Union.

Education

(2004)*

	Institutions	Teachers	Students
Primary	16,286	177,861	6,320,479
Secondary	5,887	114,755	3,717,780
Combined	3,911	53,305	1,755,083
Intermediate and middle	795	11,416	383,049
ABET centres†	2,339	15,954	272,725
ELSEN centres‡	408	7,392	86,388
Further education and training§	50	6,477	394,027
ECD|	4,146	7,363	189,254
Higher education§	29	15,375	744,488

* Figures for public and independent institutions, unless otherwise indicated.
† Adult basic education and training.
‡ Education for learners with special needs.
§ Figures refer to public institutions only.
| Early childhood development.

Source: Department of Education.

Adult literacy rate (UNESCO estimates): 82.4% (males 84.1%; females 80.9%) in 1996 (Source: UNESCO Institute for Statistics).

Directory

The Constitution

The Constitution was adopted by the Constitutional Assembly (comprising the National Assembly and the Senate) on 8 May 1996, and entered into force on 4 February 1997. Its main provisions are summarized below:

FOUNDING PROVISIONS

The Republic of South Africa is one sovereign democratic state founded on the following values: human dignity, the achievement of equality and advancement of human rights and freedoms; non-racialism and non-sexism; supremacy of the Constitution and the rule of law; universal adult suffrage, a national common voters' roll, regular elections, and a multi-party system of democratic government, to ensure accountability, responsiveness and openness. There is common South African citizenship, all citizens being equally entitled to the rights, privileges and benefits, and equally subject to the duties and responsibilities of citizenship.

BILL OF RIGHTS

Everyone is equal before the law and has the right to equal protection and benefit of the law. The state may not unfairly discriminate directly or indirectly against anyone on one or more grounds, including race, gender, sex, pregnancy, marital status, ethnic or social origin, colour, sexual orientation, age, disability, religion, conscience, belief, culture, language and birth. The rights that are enshrined include: protection against detention without trial, torture or any inhuman form of treatment or punishment; the right to privacy; freedom of conscience; freedom of expression; freedom of assembly; political freedom; freedom of movement and residence; the right to join or form a trade union or employers' organization; the right to a healthy and sustainable environment; the right to property, except in the case of the Government's programme of land reform and redistribution, and taking into account the claims of people who were dispossessed of property after 19 June 1913; the right to adequate housing; the right to health care, food and water and social security assistance, if needed; the rights of children; the right to education in the official language of one's choice, where this is reasonably practicable; the right to use the language and to participate in the cultural life of one's choice, but not in a manner inconsistent with any provision of this Bill of Rights; access to state information; access to the courts; the rights of people who have been arrested or detained; and the right to a fair trial.

CO-OPERATIVE GOVERNMENT

Government is constituted as national, provincial and local spheres of government, which are distinctive, interdependent and interrelated. All spheres of government and all organs of state within each sphere must preserve the peace, national unity and indivisibility of the Republic; secure the well-being of the people of the Republic; implement effective, transparent, accountable and coherent government for the Republic as a whole; respect the constitutional status, institutions, powers and functions of government in the other spheres; not assume any power or function except those conferred on them in terms of the Constitution.

PARLIAMENT

Legislative power is vested in a bicameral Parliament, comprising a National Assembly and a National Council of Provinces. The National Assembly has between 350 and 400 members and is elected, in general, by proportional representation. National and provincial legislatures are elected separately, under a 'double-ballot' electoral system. Each provincial legislature appoints six permanent delegates and nominates four special delegates to the 90-member National Council of Provinces, which is headed by a Chairperson, who is elected by the Council and has a five-year term of office. Parliamentary decisions are generally reached by a simple majority, although constitutional amendments require a majority of two-thirds.

THE NATIONAL EXECUTIVE

The Head of State is the President, who is elected by the National Assembly from among its members, and exercises executive power in consultation with the other members of the Cabinet. No person may hold office as President for more than two terms. Any party that holds a minimum of 80 seats in the National Assembly (equivalent to 20% of the national vote) is entitled to nominate an Executive Deputy President. If no party, or only one party, secures 80 or more seats, the party holding the largest number of seats and the party holding the second largest number of seats in the National Assembly are each entitled to designate one Executive Deputy President from among the members of the Assembly. The President may be removed by a motion of no-confidence or by impeachment. The Cabinet comprises a maximum of 27 ministers. Each party with a minimum of 20 seats in the National Assembly (equivalent to 5% of the national vote) is entitled to a proportional number of ministerial portfolios. The President allocates cabinet portfolios in consultation with party leaders, who are entitled to request the replacement of ministers. Cabinet decisions are reached by consensus.

JUDICIAL AUTHORITY

The judicial authority of the Republic is vested in the courts, which comprise the Constitutional Court; the Supreme Court of Appeal; the High Courts; the Magistrates' Courts; and any other court established or recognized by an Act of Parliament. (See Judicial System.)

PROVINCIAL GOVERNMENT

There are nine provinces: Eastern Cape, Free State (formerly Orange Free State), Gauteng (formerly Pretoria-Witwatersrand-Vereeniging), KwaZulu/Natal, Limpopo (formerly Northern Transvaal, subsequently Northern Province), Mpumalanga (formerly Eastern Transvaal), Northern Cape, North-West and Western Cape. Each

SOUTH AFRICA

province is entitled to determine its legislative and executive structure. Each province has a legislature, comprising between 30 and 80 members (depending on the size of the local electorate), who are elected by proportional representation. Each legislature is entitled to draft a constitution for the province, subject to the principles governing the national Constitution, and elects a Premier, who heads a Cabinet. Parties that hold a minimum of 10% of seats in the legislature are entitled to a proportional number of portfolios in the Cabinet. Provincial legislatures are allowed primary responsibility for a number of areas of government, and joint powers with central government in the principal administrative areas.

LOCAL GOVERNMENT

The local sphere of government consists of municipalities, with executive and legislative authority vested in the Municipal Council. The objectives of local government are to provide democratic and accountable government for local communities; to ensure the provision of services to communities; to promote social and economic development, and a safe and healthy environment; and to encourage the involvement of communities and community organizations in the matters of local government. The National Assembly is to determine the different categories of municipality that may be established, and appropriate fiscal powers and functions for each category. Provincial Governments have the task of establishing municipalities, and of providing for the monitoring and support of local government in each province.

STATE INSTITUTIONS SUPPORTING CONSTITUTIONAL DEMOCRACY

The following state institutions are designed to strengthen constitutional democracy: the Public Protector (whose task is to investigate any conduct in state affairs, or in the public administration in any sphere of government, that is alleged or suspected to be improper); the Human Rights Commission; the Commission for the Protection and Promotion of the Rights of Cultural, Religious and Linguistic Communities; the Commission for Gender Equality; the Auditor-General; and the Electoral Commission.

TRADITIONAL LEADERS

The institution, status and role of traditional leadership, according to customary law, are recognized, subject to the Constitution. A traditional authority that observes a system of customary law may function subject to any applicable legislation and customs. National and provincial legislation may provide for the establishment of local or provincial houses of traditional leaders; the National Assembly may establish a national council of traditional leaders.

The Government

HEAD OF STATE

President: THABO MBEKI (inaugurated 16 June 1999; re-elected by vote of the National Assembly 23 April 2004).

Deputy President: PHUMZILE MLAMBO-NGCUKA (ANC).

THE CABINET
(March 2008)

The African National Congress of South Africa (ANC), the Azanian People's Organization (AZAPO) and the South African Communist Party (SACP) are represented in the Cabinet.

Minister of Agriculture and Land Affairs: LULAMA XINGWANA (ANC).
Minister of Arts and Culture: Dr Z. PALLO JORDAN (ANC).
Minister of Communications: IVY MATSEPE-CASABURRI (ANC).
Minister of Correctional Services: NGCONDE BALFOUR (ANC).
Minister of Defence: MOSIUOA LEKOTA (ANC).
Minister of Education: G. NALEDI PANDOR (ANC).
Minister of Environmental Affairs and Tourism: MARTHINUS VAN SCHALKWYK (ANC).
Minister of Finance: TREVOR A. MANUEL (ANC).
Minister of Foreign Affairs: NKOSAZANA C. DLAMINI-ZUMA (ANC).
Minister of Health: MANTOMBAZANA (MANTO) TSHABALALA-MSIMANG (ANC).
Minister of Home Affairs: NOSIVIWE MAPISA-NQAKULA (ANC).
Minister of Housing: LINDIWE NONCEBA SISULU (ANC).
Minister of Intelligence: RONNIE KASRILS (ANC).
Minister of Justice and Constitutional Development: BRIGITTE S. MABANDLA (ANC).
Minister of Labour: MEMBATHISI M. S. MDLADLANA (ANC).
Minister of Minerals and Energy: BUYELWA P. SONJICA (ANC).

Minister of Provincial and Local Government: F. SYDNEY MUFAMADI (ANC).
Minister of Public Enterprises: ALEC ERWIN (ANC).
Minister of Public Service and Administration: GERALDINE J. FRASER-MOLEKETI (ANC).
Minister of Public Works: ANGELA THOKO DIDIZA (ANC).
Minister of Safety and Security: CHARLES NQAKULA (SACP).
Minister of Science and Technology: MOSIBUDI MANGENA (AZAPO).
Minister of Social Development: ZOLA S. T. SKWEYIYA (ANC).
Minister of Sport and Recreation: Rev. MAKHENKESI STOFILE (ANC).
Minister of Trade and Industry: MANDISI B. M. MPAHLWA (ANC).
Minister of Transport: JEFFREY T. RADEBE (ANC).
Minister of Water Affairs and Forestry: LINDIWE HENDRICKS (ANC).
Minister in the Presidency: Dr ESSOP G. PAHAD (ANC).

MINISTRIES

The Presidency: Union Bldgs, West Wing, Government Ave, Pretoria 0001; Private Bag X1000, Pretoria 0001; tel. (12) 3005200; fax (12) 3238246; e-mail president@po.gov.za; internet www.gov.za/president/index.html.

Ministry of Agriculture and Land Affairs: Agriculture Bldg, 20 Beatrix St, Arcadia, Pretoria 0002; Private Bag X250, Pretoria 0001; tel. (12) 3197298; fax (12) 3218558; e-mail nanaz@nda.agric.za; internet www.nda.agric.za.

Ministry of Arts and Culture: 481 Church St, 10th Floor, cnr Church and Beatrix Sts, Kingsley Centre, Arcadia, Pretoria; Private Bag X899, Pretoria 0001; tel. (12) 32440968; fax (12) 3242687; e-mail sandile.memela@dac.gov.za; internet www.dac.gov.za.

Ministry of Communications: Nkululeko House, iParioli Office Park, 399 Duncan St, cnr Park St, Hatfield, Pretoria 0083; Private Bag X860, Pretoria 0001; tel. (12) 4278000; fax (12) 4278026; e-mail elna@doc.gov.za; internet www.doc.gov.za.

Ministry of Correctional Services: Poyntons Bldg, West Block, cnr Church and Schubart Sts, Pretoria 0002; Private Bag X853, Pretoria 0001; tel. (12) 3072000; fax (12) 3286149; e-mail communications@dcs.gov.za; internet www.dcs.gov.za.

Ministry of Defence: Armscor Bldg, Block 5, Nossob St, Erasmusrand 0181; Private Bag X161, Pretoria 0001; tel. (12) 3556321; fax (12) 3556398; e-mail info@mil.za; internet www.mil.za.

Ministry of Education: Sol Plaatje House, 123 Schoeman St, Pretoria 0002; Private Bag X895, Pretoria 0001; tel. (12) 3125911; fax (12) 3256260; internet www.education.gov.za.

Ministry of Environmental Affairs and Tourism: Fedsure Forum Bldg, North Tower, cnr Van der Walt and Pretorius Sts, Pretoria; Private Bag X447, Pretoria 0001; tel. (12) 3103911; fax (12) 3222682; internet www.environment.gov.za.

Ministry of Foreign Affairs: Union Bldgs, East Wing, 1 Government Ave, Arcadia, Pretoria 0002; Private Bag X152, Pretoria 0001; tel. (12) 3511000; fax (12) 3510253; e-mail minister@foreign.gov.za; internet www.dfa.gov.za.

Ministry of Health: DTI Bldg, Rm 1105, Prinsloo St, Pretoria 0001; Private Bag X828, Pretoria 0001; tel. (12) 3120000; fax (12) 3264395; e-mail masint@health.gov.za; internet www.health.gov.za.

Ministry of Home Affairs: 270 Maggs St, Watloo; Private Bag X114, Pretoria 0001; tel. (12) 3148911; fax (12) 3216491; internet www.home-affairs.gov.za.

Ministry of Housing: Govan Mbeki House, 240 Walker St, Sunnyside, Pretoria 0002; Private Bag X644, Pretoria 0001; tel. (12) 4211311; fax (12) 3418510; internet www.housing.gov.za.

Ministry of Intelligence: Bogare Bldg, 2 Atterbury Rd, Menlyn, Pretoria 0063; POB 37, Menlyn 0063; tel. (12) 3670700; fax (12) 3670749.

Ministry of Justice and Constitutional Development: Momentum Centre, 329 Pretorius St, cnr Pretorius and Prinsloo Sts, Pretoria 0001; Private Bag X276, Pretoria 0001; tel. (12) 3151332; fax (12) 3151749; e-mail znqayi@justice.gov.za; internet www.doj.gov.za.

Ministry of Labour: Laboria House, Schoeman St, Pretoria 0002; Private Bag X117, Pretoria 0001; tel. (12) 3094000; fax (12) 3094030; e-mail page.boikanyo@labour.gov.za; internet www.labour.gov.za.

Ministry of Minerals and Energy: Mineralia Centre, 391 Andries St, Pretoria 0002; Private Bag X59, Pretoria 0001; tel. (12) 3179000; fax (12) 3204327; internet www.dme.gov.za.

Ministry of Provincial and Local Government: 87 Hamilton St, Arcadia, Pretoria 0001; Private Bag X804, Pretoria 0001; tel. (12)

SOUTH AFRICA

3340600; fax (12) 3340603; e-mail enquiry@dplg.gov.za; internet www.dplg.gov.za.

Ministry of Public Enterprises: Infotech Bldg, Suite 401, 1090 Arcadia St, Hatfield, Pretoria 0083; Private Bag X15, Hatfield 0028; tel. (12) 4311000; fax (86) 5012624; e-mail vimla.maistry@dpe.gov.za; internet www.dpe.gov.za.

Ministry of Public Service and Administration: Batho Pele House, Proes St, Pretoria 0001; Private Bag X916, Pretoria 0001; tel. (12) 3361334; fax (12) 3361810; e-mail natasha@dpsa.gov.za; internet www.dpsa.gov.za.

Ministry of Public Works: Central Government Bldg, cnr Bosman and Vermeulen Sts, Pretoria 0002; Private Bag X65, Pretoria 0001; tel. (12) 3372000; fax (12) 3252856; internet www.publicworks.gov.za.

Ministry of Safety and Security: Van Erkom Bldg, 8th Floor, Van Erkom Arcade, 217 Pretorius St, Pretoria 0002; Private Bag X922, Pretoria 0001; tel. (12) 3392500; fax (12) 3392536; e-mail stratfordm@saps.org.za; internet www.gov.za/sss.

Ministry of Science and Technology: Oranje Nassau Bldg, 7th Floor, 188 Schoeman St, Pretoria 0001; Private Bag X727, Pretoria 0001; tel. (12) 3174302; fax (12) 3242687; e-mail nelvis.qekema@dst.gov.za; internet www.dst.gov.za.

Ministry of Social Development: HSRC Bldg, North Wing, 134 Pretorius St, Pretoria 0002; Private Bag X901, Pretoria 0001; tel. (12) 3127654; fax (12) 3127943; internet www.welfare.gov.za.

Ministry of Sport and Recreation: Oranje Nassau Bldg, 3rd Floor, 188 Schoeman St, Pretoria; Private Bag X896, Pretoria 0001; tel. (12) 3343220; fax (12) 3264026; e-mail greg@srsa.gov.za; internet www.srsa.gov.za.

Ministry of Trade and Industry: 77 Meintjies St, Sunnyside, Pretoria 0002; Private Bag X84, Pretoria 0001; tel. (12) 2549405; fax (12) 2549406; e-mail contactus@thedti.gov.za; internet www.thedti.gov.za.

Ministry of Transport: 159 Forum Bldg, 159 Struben St, Pretoria 0002; Private Bag X193, Pretoria 0001; tel. (12) 3093000; fax (12) 3285926; e-mail khozac@dot.gov.za; internet www.transport.gov.za.

Ministry of Water Affairs and Forestry: Sedibeng Bldg, 10th Floor, 185 Schoeman St, Pretoria 0002; Private Bag X313, Pretoria 0001; tel. (12) 3368733; fax (12) 3284254; internet www-dwaf.pwv.gov.za.

National Treasury: 40 Church Sq., Pretoria 0002; Private Bag X115, Pretoria 0001; tel. (12) 3155111; fax (12) 3155234; internet www.treasury.gov.za.

Legislature

PARLIAMENT

National Council of Provinces

Chairman: MOSIUOA LEKOTA.

The National Council of Provinces (NCOP), which replaced the Senate under the new Constitution, was inaugurated on 6 February 1997. The NCOP comprises 90 members, with six permanent delegates and four special delegates from each of the nine provinces.

National Assembly

Speaker: BALEKA MBETE.
General Election, 14 April 2004

Party	Votes	% of votes	Seats
African National Congress	10,878,251	69.68	279
Democratic Alliance	1,931,201	12.37	50
Inkatha Freedom Party	1,088,664	6.97	28
United Democratic Movement	355,717	2.28	9
Independent Democrats	269,765	1.73	7
New National Party	257,824	1.65	7
African Christian Democratic Party	250,272	1.60	6
Freedom Front Plus	139,465	0.89	4
United Christian Democratic Party	117,792	0.75	3
Pan-Africanist Congress of Azania	113,512	0.73	3
Minority Front	55,267	0.35	2
Azanian People's Organisation	41,776	0.27	2
Others	113,161	0.72	—
Total	**15,612,667**	**100.00**	**400**

Provincial Governments
(March 2008)

EASTERN CAPE
Premier: NOSIMO BALINDLELA (ANC).
Speaker of the Legislature: NOXOLO KIVIET (ANC).

FREE STATE
Premier: BEATRICE MARSHOFF (ANC).
Speaker of the Legislature: MXOLISI DUKWANA (ANC).

GAUTENG
Premier: MBHAZIMA SHILOWA (ANC).
Speaker of the Legislature: RICHARD MDAKANE (ANC).

KWAZULU/NATAL
Premier: SIBUSISO NDEBELE (ANC).
Speaker of the Legislature: WILLIES MCHUNU (ANC).

LIMPOPO
Premier: SELLO MOLOTO (ANC).
Speaker of the Legislature: Dr TSHENUWANI FARISANI (ANC).

MPUMALANGA
Premier: SAMPSON PHATHAGE (THABANG) MAKWETLA (ANC).
Speaker of the Legislature: YVONE (PINKY) PHOSA (ANC).

NORTHERN CAPE
Premier: DIPUO PETERS (ANC).
Speaker of the Legislature: CONNIE SEOPOSENGWE (ANC).

NORTH-WEST
Premier: EDNA MOLEWA (ANC).
Speaker of the Legislature: THANDI MODISE (ANC).

WESTERN CAPE
Premier: EBRAHIM RASOOL (ANC).
Speaker of the Legislature: SHAUN BYNEVELDT (ANC).

Election Commission

Independent Electoral Commission: Election House, 260 Walker St, Sunnyside, Pretoria; tel. (12) 4285700; fax (12) 4285863; internet www.elections.org.za; f. 1996; Chair. Dr BRIGALIA BAM.

Political Organizations

A total of 21 parties contested the elections to the National Assembly in April 2004, while 37 parties presented candidates in the concurrent provincial elections.

African Christian Democratic Party (ACDP): Stats Building, 1st Floor, 2 Fore St, POB 1677, Alberton; tel. (11) 8693941; fax (11) 8693942; e-mail office@acdp.org.za; internet www.acdp.org.za; f. 1993; Leader Rev. KENNETH MESHOE.

African National Congress of South Africa (ANC): 54 Sauer St, Johannesburg 2001; POB 61884, Marshalltown 2107; tel. (11) 3761000; fax (11) 3761134; e-mail nmtyelwa@anc.org.za; internet www.anc.org.za; f. 1912; in alliance with the South African Communist Party (SACP) and the Congress of South African Trade Unions (COSATU); governing party since April 1994; Pres. JACOB ZUMA; Deputy Pres. KGALEMA MOTLANTHE; Sec.-Gen. GWEDE MANTASHE.

Afrikaner Eenheidsbeweging (AEB) (Unity Movement): Pretoria; right-wing movement; Leader CASPERUS AUCAMP.

Afrikaner Weerstandsbeweging (AWB) (Afrikaner Resistance Movement): POB 274, Ventersdorp 2710, Johannesburg; tel. and fax (18) 2642516; e-mail awb@awb.co.za; internet www.awb.co.za; f. 1973; Afrikaner (Boer) nationalist group seeking self-determination for the Afrikaner people in South Africa; Leader EUGENE TERRE' BLANCHE.

Azanian People's Organization (AZAPO): 100 President St, 7th Floor, Balmoral House, Johannesburg 2001; POB 4230, Johannesburg 2000; tel. (11) 3363551; e-mail azapo@mweb.co.za; internet www.azapo.org.za; f. 1978; to seek the establishment of a unitary, democratic, socialist republic; excludes white mems; Pres. MOSIBLIDI MANGENA; Nat. Chair. ZITHULELE N. A. CINDI.

Blanke Bevrydingsbeweging (BBB) (White Protection Movement): f. 1987; extreme right-wing activist group; Leader Prof. JOHAN SCHABORT.

Boerestaat Party (Boer State Party): POB 4995, Luipaardsvlei 1743; tel. (11) 7623841; fax (11) 7623842; e-mail info@boerestaatparty.co.za; internet www.boerestaatparty.co.za; f. 1988; seeks the reinstatement of the Boer Republics in a consolidated Boerestaat; Leader COEN VERMAAK.

Cape Democrats: f. 1988; white support; liberal.

Democratic Alliance (DA): POB 1475, Cape Town 8000; tel. (21) 4651431; fax (21) 4615559; e-mail info@da.org.za; internet www.da.org.za; f. 2000 by opposition parties, incl. the Democratic Party, the Federal Alliance and the New National Party (NNP), to contest that year's municipal elections; NNP withdrew in late 2001; Leader HELEN ZILLE; Chair. JOE SEREMANE.

Democratic Reform Party (DRP): f. 1988; Coloured support; Leader CARTER EBRAHIM.

Democratic Workers' Party (DWP): Cape Town; f. 1984 by breakaway faction of the People's Congress Party; mainly Coloured support; Leader DENNIS DE LA CRUZ.

Freedom Front Plus (Vryheidsfront Plus—FF Plus/VF Plus): 203 Soutpansberg Ave, Rietondale, Pretoria; POB 74693, Lynnwood Ridge 0040; tel. (12) 3291220; fax (12) 3291229; e-mail info@vf.co.za; internet www.vryheidsfront.co.za; f. 1994 as Freedom Front; name changed after incorporating the Conservative Party and Afrikaner Eenheidsbeweging in Sept. 2003; right-wing electoral alliance, incl. mems of the CPSA; Leader Dr PIETER W. A. MULDER; Sec.-Gen. Col (retd) PIET UYS.

Freedom Party: Coloured support; Leader ARTHUR BOOYSEN.

Herstigte Nasionale Party (HNP): 199 Neethling St, Eloffsdal, POB 1888, Pretoria 0001; tel. (12) 3358523; fax (12) 3358518; e-mail info@hnp.org.za; internet www.hnp.org.za; f. 1969 by fmr mems of the National Party; advocates 'Christian Nationalism'; Leader WILLEM MARAIS; Gen. Sec. LOUIS J. VAN DER SCHYFF.

Independent Democrats (ID): Rm 28, Marks Bldg, Parliament Plein St, POB 751, Cape Town 8000; tel. (21) 4038696; fax (21) 4032350; e-mail id@id.org.za; internet www.id.org.za; f. 2003; Leader PATRICIA DE LILLE.

Inkatha Freedom Party (IFP): Albany House North, 4th Floor, Albany Grove, POB 4432, Durban 4000; tel. (31) 3651300; fax (31) 3010252; internet www.ifp.org.za; f. as Inkatha Movement, liberation movement with mainly Zulu support; reorg. in 1990 as a multiracial political party; Leader Chief MANGOSUTHU GATSHA BUTHELEZI; Nat. Chair. L. P. H. M. MTSHALI; Sec.-Gen. M. ZAKHELE KHUMALO.

Justice and Freedom Alliance (JAFA): ME Store Bldg, 4th Floor, 155 Smit St, Johannesburg; Private Bag X49, Johannesburg; tel. (11) 3397129; fax (11) 3396982; f. 1997; CEO BARRY NILSSON; Sec.-Gen. A. DLOMO.

Minority Front: Law Society Bldg, Suite 17, Chancery Lane, Pietermaritzburg; tel. (33) 3557667; internet www.mf.org.za; f. 1993; Indian support; formed political alliance with the ANC in June 1999; Leader AMICHAND RAJBANSI.

New Freedom Party of Southern Africa: 15 Eendrag St, Bellville 7530; Coloured support.

New Solidarity: POB 48687, Qualbert 4078; tel. (11) 3055692; fax (11) 3011077; f. 1989; Indian support; Leader Dr J. N. REDDY.

Pan-Africanist Congress of Azania (PAC): 10th Floor, Renaissance House, 16–22 New St, Ghandi Sq., Johannesburg; POB 6010, Johannesburg 2000; tel. (11) 3372193; fax (11) 3376400; e-mail pacazania@telkomsa.net; internet www.panafricanperspective.com/pac/index.html; f. 1959; Pres. Dr MOTSOKO PHEKO; Nat. Exec. Sec. MFANELO SKWATSHA.

Progressive Independent Party (PIP): Indian support; Leader FAIZ KHAN.

South African Communist Party (SACP): Cosatu House, 3rd Floor, 1 Leyds St, Braamfontein; POB 1027, Johannesburg 2000; tel. (11) 3393633; fax (11) 3396880; e-mail info@sacp.org.za; internet www.sacp.org.za; f. 1921; reorg. 1953; supports the ANC; Chair. (vacant); Gen. Sec. BLADE NZIMANDE.

Transvaal Indian Congress: f. 1902; reactivated 1983; Pres. Dr ESSOP JASSAT.

United Christian Democratic Party (UCDP): POB 3010, Mmabatho; tel. (18) 3815691; fax (18) 3817346; e-mail ucdpheadoff@ucdp.org.za; internet www.ucdp.org.za; f. 1972 as the Bophuthatswana Nat. Party; name changed to Bophuthatswana Dem. Party in 1974; present name adopted in 1991; multiracial; Leader KGOSI L. M. MANGOPE; Sec.-Gen. M. N. MATLADI; Nat. Chair. I. SIPHO MFUNDISI.

United Democratic Movement: Tomkor Bldg, 2nd Floor, cnr Vermeulen and Du Toit Sts, Pretoria; POB 26290, Arcadia 0007; tel. (12) 3210010; fax (12) 3210014; e-mail research@udm.org.za; internet www.udm.org.za; f. 1997; multiracial support; demands effective measures for enforcement of law and order; Pres. BANTU HOLOMISA.

United Democratic Reform Party: POB 14048, Reigerpark 1466; f. 1987 by merger; mainly Coloured and Indian support; Leader JAKOBUS (JAC) ALBERT RABIE; Nat. Chair. NASH PARMANAND.

Workers' Organization for Socialist Action (WOSA): c/o University of Cape Town, Private Bag, Rondebosch 7701; e-mail nalexand@humanities.uct.ac.za; f. 1990; Trotskyist; Chair. Dr NEVILLE ALEXANDER; Gen. Sec. C. BRECHER.

Diplomatic Representation

EMBASSIES AND HIGH COMMISSIONS IN SOUTH AFRICA

Algeria: 950 Arcadia St, Hatfield, Pretoria 0083; POB 57480, Arcadia 0007; tel. (12) 3425074; fax (12) 3426479; Ambassador MOURAD BENCHEIKH.

Angola: 1030 Schoeman St, Hatfield, Pretoria 0083; POB 8685, Pretoria 0001; tel. (12) 3420049; fax (12) 3427039; Ambassador MIGUEL GASPAR FERNANDES NETO.

Argentina: 200 Standard Plaza, 440 Hilda St, Hatfield, Pretoria 0083; POB 11125, Pretoria 0028; tel. (12) 4303524; fax (12) 4303521; e-mail argembas@global.co.za; Ambassador CARLOS SERSALE DI CERISANO.

Australia: 292 Orient St, Arcadia, Pretoria; Private Bag X150, Pretoria 0001; tel. (12) 4236000; fax (12) 3428442; e-mail pretoria.info@dfat.gov.au; internet www.australia.co.za; High Commissioner PHILIP GREEN.

Austria: Momentum Office Park, 1109 Duncan St, Brooklyn, Pretoria 0181; POB 95572, Waterkloof 0145; tel. (12) 4529155; fax (12) 4601151; e-mail pretoria-ob@bmeia.gv.at; internet www.bmeia.gv.at/pretoria; Ambassador Dr HELMUT FREUDENSCHUSS.

Bangladesh: 410 Farenden St, Sunnyside, Pretoria 0002; tel. (12) 3432105; fax (12) 3435222; e-mail bdoot@mweb.co.za; High Commissioner MD SHAHIDUL ISLAM.

Belarus: 327 Hill St, Arcadia, Pretoria 0083; POB 4107, Pretoria 0001; tel. (12) 4307664; fax (12) 3426280; e-mail sa@belembassy.org; Ambassador Dr ANATOLII AKHRAMCHUK.

Belgium: 625 Leyds St, Muckleneuk, Pretoria 0002; tel. (12) 4403201; fax (12) 4403216; e-mail pretoria@diplobel.org; internet www.diplomatie.be/pretoria; Ambassador JAN MUTTON.

Benin: 900 Park St, cnr Orient and Park Sts, Arcadia, Pretoria 0083; POB 26484, Arcadia 0007; tel. (12) 3426978; fax (12) 3421823; e-mail embbenin@yebo.co.za; Chargé d'affaires a.i. PAMPHILE C. GOUTONDJI.

Bosnia and Herzegovina: 25 Stella St, Brooklyn, Pretoria 0181; POB 11464, Hatfield 0028; tel. (12) 3465547; fax (12) 3462295; e-mail bih@mweb.co.za; Ambassador DRAGAN PJEVIĆ.

Botswana: 24 Amos St, Colbyn, Pretoria 0083; POB 57035, Arcadia 0007; tel. (12) 4309640; fax (12) 3421845; High Commissioner MOTLHAGODI MOLOMO.

Brazil: Hillcrest Office Park, Woodpecker Pl., 1st Floor, 177 Dyer Rd, Hillcrest, Pretoria 0083; POB 3269, Pretoria 0001; tel. (12) 3665200; fax (12) 3665299; e-mail pretoria@brazilianembassy.org.za; internet www.brazilianembassy.org.za; Ambassador JOSÉ VICENTE DE SÁ PIMENTEL.

Bulgaria: 1071 Church St, Hatfield, Pretoria 0083; POB 29296, Arcadia 0007; tel. (12) 3423720; fax (12) 3423721; e-mail embulgsa@iafrica.com; internet www.bulgarianembassy.co.za; Ambassador V. C. NEYKOV.

Burundi: 20 Glyn St, Colbyn, Pretoria 0083; POB 12914, Hatfield 0028; tel. (12) 3424881; fax (12) 3424885; Ambassador PATRICE RWIMO.

Cameroon: 924 Pretorius St, Arcadia, Pretoria 0083; POB 13790, Hatfield 0028; tel. (12) 3624731; fax (12) 3624732; e-mail hicocam@cameroon.co.za; High Commissioner NJOTEH ALBERT FOBATONG (acting).

Canada: 1103 Arcadia St, cnr Hilda St, Hatfield, Pretoria 0083; Private Bag X13, Hatfield 0028; tel. (12) 4223000; fax (12) 4223052; e-mail pret@international.gc.ca; internet www.dfait-maeci.gc.ca/southafrica/menu-en.asp; High Commissioner RUTH ARCHIBALD.

Chile: Brooklyn Gardens, cnr Veale St and Middle St, Block B, 1st Floor, New Muckleneuk, Pretoria; POB 2449, Brooklyn Sq. 0075; tel. (12) 4608090; fax (12) 4608093; e-mail chile@iafrica.com; internet www.embchile.co.za; Ambassador CLAUDIO E. HERRERA ALAMOS.

China, People's Republic: 965 Church St, Arcadia, Pretoria 0083; POB 95764, Waterkloof 0145; tel. (12) 3424194; fax (12) 3424154;

e-mail reception@chinese-embassy.org.za; internet www.chinese-embassy.org.za; Ambassador ZHONG JIANHUA.

Colombia: 1105 Park St, 3rd Floor, Hatfield, Pretoria 0083; POB 12791, Hatfield 0028; tel. (12) 3420211; fax (12) 3420216; e-mail info@embassyofcolombia.co.za; Ambassador CARLOS MOREÑO DE CARO.

Comoros: 817 Thomas St, cnr Church and Eastwood Sts, Arcadia, Pretoria 0083; tel. (12) 3439483; fax (12) 3420138; Chargé d'affaires BACAR SALIM.

Congo, Democratic Republic: 791 Schoeman St, Arcadia, Pretoria 0083; POB 28795, Sunnyside 0132; tel. (12) 3441478; fax (12) 3441510; e-mail rdcongo@lantic.net; Ambassador BENE M'POKO.

Congo, Republic: 960 Arcadia St, Arcadia, Pretoria 0083; POB 40427, Arcadia 0007; tel. (12) 3425508; fax (12) 3425510; Ambassador ROGER ISSOMBO.

Côte d'Ivoire: 795 Government Ave, Arcadia, Pretoria 0083; POB 13510, Hatfield 0028; tel. (12) 3426913; fax (12) 3426713; Ambassador BOUBAKAR KONE.

Croatia: 1160 Church St, Colbyn, Pretoria 0083; POB 11335, Hatfield 0028; tel. (12) 3421206; fax (12) 3421819; Ambassador IVAN PICUKARIĆ.

Cuba: 45 Mackenzie St, Brooklyn, Pretoria 0181; POB 11605, Hatfield 0028; tel. (12) 3462215; fax (12) 3462216; e-mail sudafri@iafrica.com; Ambassador ESTHER ARMENTEROS CÁRDENAS.

Cyprus: cnr Church St and Hill St, Arcadia, Pretoria 0083; POB 14554, Hatfield 0028; tel. (12) 3425258; fax (12) 3425596; e-mail cyprusjb@mweb.co.za; High Commissioner COSTA LEONTIOU.

Czech Republic: 936 Pretorius St, Arcadia, Pretoria 0083; POB 13671, Hatfield 0028; tel. (12) 4312380; fax (12) 4302033; e-mail pretoria@embassymzv.cz; Ambassador MARTIN POHL.

Denmark: iParioli Office Park, Block B2, Ground Floor, 1166 Park St, Hatfield, Pretoria; POB 11439, Hatfield 0028; tel. (12) 4309340; fax (12) 3427620; e-mail pryamb@um.dk; internet www.ambpretoria.um.dk; Ambassador DAN E. FREDERIKSEN.

Egypt: 270 Bourke St, Muckleneuk, Pretoria 0002; POB 30025, Sunnyside 0132; tel. (12) 3431590; fax (12) 3431082; e-mail egyptemb@global.co.za; Ambassador MONA OMAR MUHAMMAD ATTIA.

Equatorial Guinea: 48 Florence St, Colbyn, Pretoria; POB 12720, Hatfield 0028; tel. (12) 3429945; fax (12) 3427250; Ambassador JUAN ANTONIO BIBANG NCHUCHUMA.

Eritrea: 1281 Cobham Rd, Queenswood, Pretoria 0186; POB 11371, Queenswood 0121; tel. (12) 3331302; fax (12) 3332330; Ambassador TESFAMICAEL GERAHTU OGBAGHIORGHIS.

Ethiopia: 47 Charles St, Bailey's Muckleneuk, Brooklyn 0181; POB 11469, Hatfield 0028; tel. (12) 3463542; fax (12) 3463867; e-mail ethiopia@sentechsa.com; Ambassador MELESE MARIMO MARASSO.

Finland: 628 Leyds St, Muckleneuk, Pretoria 0002; POB 443, Pretoria 0001; tel. (12) 3430275; fax (12) 3433095; e-mail sanomat.pre@formin.fi; internet www.finland.org.za; Ambassador HEIKKI TUUNANEN.

France: 250 Melk St, cnr Melk and Middle Sts, New Muckleneuk, Pretoria 0181; tel. (12) 4251600; fax (12) 4251689; e-mail france@ambafrance-rsa.org; internet www.ambafrance-rsa.org; Ambassador DENIS PIETTON.

Gabon: 921 Schoeman St, Arcadia, Pretoria 0083; POB 9222, Pretoria 0001; tel. (12) 3424376; fax (12) 3424375; Ambassador MARCEL-JULES ODONGUI-BONNARD.

Germany: 180 Blackwood St, Arcadia, Pretoria 0083; POB 2023, Pretoria 0001; tel. (12) 4278900; fax (12) 3433606; e-mail GermanEmbassyPretoria@gonet.co.za; internet www.pretoria.diplo.de; Ambassador DIETER WALTER HALLER.

Ghana: 1038 Arcadia St, Hatfield, Pretoria 0083; POB 12537, Hatfield 0028; tel. (12) 3425847; fax (12) 3425863; High Commissioner Dr JIMMY B. HEYMANN.

Greece: 1003 Church St, Arcadia, Pretoria 0083; tel. (12) 3427136; fax (12) 4304313; e-mail embgrsaf@global.co.za; Ambassador ARISTIDIS SANDIS.

Guinea: 336 Orient St, Arcadia, Pretoria 0083; POB 13523, Hatfield 0028; tel. (12) 3420893; fax (12) 3427348; e-mail embaguinea@iafrica.com; Chargé d'affaires a.i. BOURAM-CIRÉ DIAKITE.

Haiti: 808 George St, Arcadia, Pretoria 0007; POB 14362, Hatfield 0028; tel. (12) 4307560; fax (12) 3427042; Ambassador YOLETTE AZOR-CHARLES.

Holy See: 800 Pretorius St, Arcadia, Pretoria 0083; POB 26017, Arcadia 0007; tel. (12) 3443815; fax (12) 3443595; e-mail nunziosa@iafrica.com; Apostolic Nuncio Most Rev. JAMES PATRICK GREEN.

Hungary: 959 Arcadia St, Hatfield, Pretoria 0083; POB 13843, Hatfield 0028; tel. (12) 4303020; fax (12) 4303029; e-mail huembprt@mweb.co.za; Ambassador ISTVÁN EMRI.

Iceland: iParioli Office Park, Phase II, Block A2, 1166 Park St, Pretoria; POB 14325 Hatfield 0028; tel. (12) 3425885; fax (12) 3420883; e-mail emb.pretoria@mfa.is; internet www.iceland.org/za; Ambassador Dr SIGRIDUR DUNA KRISTMUNDSDOTTIR.

India: 852 Schoeman St, Arcadia, Pretoria 0083; POB 40216, Arcadia 0007; tel. (12) 3425392; fax (12) 3425310; e-mail polinf@hicomind.co.za; High Commissioner R. K. BHATIA.

Indonesia: 949 Schoeman St, Arcadia, Pretoria 0082; POB 13155, Hatfield, Pretoria 0028; tel. (12) 3423350; fax (12) 3423369; e-mail fpanggabean@indonesia-pretoria.org.za; internet www.indonesia-pretoria.org.za; f. 1995; Ambassador SUGENG RAHARDJO.

Iran: 1002 Schoeman St, Hatfield, Pretoria 0083; POB 12546, Hatfield 0083; tel. (12) 3425880; fax (12) 3421878; internet www.iranembassy.org.za; Ambassador ASGHAR EBRAHIMI ASL.

Iraq: 803 Duncan St, Brooklyn, Pretoria 0181; POB 11089, Hatfield 0028; tel. (12) 3622048; fax (12) 3622027; Ambassador QASIM ABDL-BAQI SHAKIR.

Ireland: Southern Life Plaza, 1st Floor, 1059 Schoeman St, cnr Festival and Schoeman Sts, Arcadia, Pretoria 0083; POB 4174, Arcadia 0001; tel. (12) 3425062; fax (12) 3424752; e-mail pretoria@dfa.ie; internet www.embassyireland.org.za; Ambassador COLIN WRAFTER.

Israel: 428 King's Hwy, Elizabeth Grove St, Lynnwood, Pretoria; POB 3726, Pretoria 0001; tel. (12) 3480470; fax (12) 3488594; e-mail operator@pretoria.mfa.gov.il; internet pretoria.mfa.gov.il; Ambassador ILAN BARUCH.

Italy: 796 George Ave, Arcadia, Pretoria 0083; tel. (12) 4230000; fax (12) 4305547; e-mail segreteria.pretoria@esteri.it; internet www.ambpretoria.esteri.it; Ambassador ALESSANDRO CEVESE.

Jamaica: 1119 Burnett St, Hatfield, Pretoria 0083; tel. (12) 3626667; fax (12) 3668510; e-mail jhcpretoria@telkomsa.net; High Commissioner JOAN THOMAS (acting).

Japan: 259 Baines St, cnr Frans Oerder St, Groenkloof, Pretoria 0181; Private Bag X999, Pretoria 0001; tel. (12) 4521500; fax (12) 4603800; e-mail info@embjapan.org.za; internet www.japan.org.za; Ambassador AKIHIKO FURUYA.

Jordan: 252 Olivier St, Brooklyn, Pretoria 0075; POB 14730, Hatfield 0028; tel. (12) 346861517; fax (12) 3468611; e-mail embjordpta@telkomsa.net; Ambassador Dr MAZEN IZZEDINE TAL.

Kenya: 302 Brooks St, Menlo Park, Pretoria 0081; POB 35954, Menlo Park 0012; tel. (12) 3622249; fax (12) 3622252; e-mail info@kenya.org.za; High Commissioner TABITHA J. SEII.

Korea, Democratic People's Republic: 958 Waterpoort St, Faerie Glen, Pretoria; POB 1238, Garsfontein 0042; tel. (12) 9918661; fax (12) 9918662; e-mail dprkembassy@lantic.net; Ambassador AN HUI JONG.

Korea, Republic: Greenpark Estates, Bldg 3, 27 George Storrar Dr., Groenkloof, Pretoria 0081; POB 939, Groenkloof 0027; tel. (12) 4602508; fax (12) 4601158; Ambassador KIM KYUN-SEOP.

Kuwait: 890 Arcadia St, Arcadia, Pretoria 0083; Private Bag X920, Pretoria 0001; tel. (12) 3420877; fax (12) 3420876; e-mail safarku@global.co.za; Ambassador HASSAN BADER KAREEM AL-OQAB.

Lebanon: 290 Lawley St, Waterkloof, Pretoria 0081; POB 941, Groenkloof 0027; tel. (12) 3467020; fax (12) 3467022; Chargé d'affaires a.i. MICHEL KATRA.

Lesotho: 391 Anderson St, Menlo Park, Pretoria 0081; POB 55817, Arcadia 0007; tel. (12) 4607648; fax (12) 4607469; Chargé d'affaires a.i. M KUMI.

Liberia: Suite 9 Section 7, Schoeman St Forum, 1157 Schoeman St, Hatfield, Pretoria; POB 14082, Hatfield, Pretoria; tel. (12) 3422734; fax (12) 3422737; e-mail libempta@pta.lia.net; Ambassador LOIS LEWIS BRUTHUS.

Libya: 900 Church St, Arcadia, Pretoria 0083; POB 40388, Arcadia 0007; tel. (12) 3423902; fax (12) 3423904; Ambassador Dr ABDULLAH ABDUSSALAM AL-ZUBEDI.

Madagascar: 90B Tait St, Colbyn, Pretoria; POB 11722, Queenswood 0121; tel. (12) 3420983; fax (12) 3420995; e-mail consul@infodoor.co.za; Ambassador DENIS ANDRIAMANDROSO.

Malawi: 770 Government Ave, Arcadia, Pretoria 0083; POB 11172, Hatfield 0028; tel. and fax (12) 3421759; High Commissioner AGRINA MUSSA.

Malaysia: 1007 Schoeman St, Arcadia, Pretoria 0083; POB 11673, Hatfield 0028; tel. (12) 3425990; fax (12) 4307773; High Commissioner YAHAYA BIN ABDUL JABAR.

Mali: 876 Pretorius St, Arcadia 0083, POB 12978, Hatfield, Pretoria 0028; tel. (12) 3427464; fax (12) 3420670; Ambassador SINALY COULIBALY.

Mauritania: 146 Anderson St, Brooklyn, Pretoria; tel. (12) 3623578; fax (12) 3623304; e-mail rimambapretoria@webmail.co.za; Ambassador MOHAMMED LEMINE OULD MOHAMED SALEM OULD SELAMANE.

Mauritius: 1163 Pretorius St, Hatfield, Pretoria 0083; tel. (12) 3421283; fax (12) 3421286; e-mail mhcpta@mweb.co.za; High Commissioner MOHAMED ISMAEL DOSSA.

SOUTH AFRICA

Mexico: 1 Hatfield Sq., 3rd Floor, 1101 Burnett St, Hatfield, Pretoria 0083; POB 9077, Pretoria 0001; tel. (12) 3622822; fax (12) 3621380; e-mail embamexza@mweb.co.za; Ambassador LUIS CABRERA CUARON.

Morocco: 799 Schoeman St, cnr Farenden St, Arcadia, Pretoria 0083; POB 12382, Hatfield 0028; tel. (12) 3430230; fax (12) 3430613; e-mail sifmapre@mwebbiz.co.za; Chargé d'affaires HABIB DEFOUAD.

Mozambique: 529 Edmund St, Arcadia, Pretoria 0083; POB 40750, Arcadia 0007; tel. (12) 4010300; fax (12) 3266388; High Commissioner FERNANDO ANDRADE FAZENDA.

Myanmar: 201 Leyds St, Arcadia, Pretoria 0083; POB 12121, Queenswood 0121; tel. (12) 3415207; fax (12) 3413867; e-mail euompta@global.co.za; Ambassador U OHN THWIN.

Namibia: 197 Blackwood St, Arcadia, Pretoria 0083; POB 29806, Sunnyside 0132; tel. (12) 4819100; fax (12) 3445998; e-mail secretary@namibia.org.za; High Commissioner PHILEMON KAMBALA.

Netherlands: 825 Arcadia St, Arcadia, Pretoria 0083; POB 117, Pretoria 0001; tel. (12) 3443910; fax (12) 3439950; internet www.dutchembassy.co.za; Ambassador ROBERT GERARD DE VOS.

New Zealand: Block C, Hatfield Gardens, 1110 Arcadia St, Hatfield, Pretoria 0083; Private Bag X17, Hatfield 0028; tel. (12) 3428656; fax (12) 3428640; e-mail enquiries@nzhc.co.za; internet www.nzhc.co.za; High Commissioner MALCOLM MCGOUN.

Nigeria: 971 Schoeman St, Arcadia, Pretoria 0083; POB 27332, Sunnyside 0132; tel. (12) 3420805; fax (12) 3421668; High Commissioner M ZANNEH (acting).

Norway: iParioli Bldg, A2, 1166 Park St, Hatfield, Pretoria 0083; POB 11612, Hatfield 0028; tel. (12) 3426100; fax (12) 3426099; e-mail emb.pretoria@mfa.no; internet www.norway.org.za; Ambassador TOR CHRISTIAN HILDAN.

Oman: 42 Nicholson St, Muckleneuk, Pretoria 0081; POB 2650, Brooklyn 0075; tel. (12) 3460808; fax (12) 3461660; e-mail sult-oman@telkom.net; Ambassador. KHALID BIN SULAIMAN BIN ABDUL RAHMAN BA'OMAR.

Pakistan: 312 Brooks St, Menlo Park, Pretoria 0181; POB 11803, Hatfield 0028; tel. (12) 3624072; fax (12) 3623967; e-mail pareppretoria@worldonline.co.za; High Commissioner ASHRAF QURESHI.

Panama: Pretoria; Ambassador ROBERTO E. CORDOVEZ CASTILLA.

Paraguay: 189 Strelitzia Rd, Waterkloof Heights, Pretoria 0181; POB 95774, Waterkloof 0145; tel. (12) 3471047; fax (12) 3470403; Chargé d'affaires a.i. ARNALDO R. SALAZAR.

Peru: Brooklyn Gardens Bldg, Block A, 1st Floor, 235 Veale St, Cnr Middel St, Nieuw Muckleneuk, Pretoria 0181; POB 907, Groenkloof 0027; tel. (12) 3468744; fax (12) 3468886; e-mail embaperu2@telkomsa.net; Ambassador FÉLIX CÉSAR CALDERÓN.

Philippines: 54 Nicholson St, Muckleneuk, Pretoria 0181; POB 2562, Brooklyn Sq. 0075; tel. (12) 3460451; fax (12) 3460454; e-mail pretoriape@mweb.co.za; internet mzone.mweb.co.za/residents/pretoriape/; Ambassador VIRGILIO A. REYES, Jr.

Poland: 14 Amos St, Colbyn, Pretoria 0083; POB 12277, Queenswood 0121; tel. (12) 4302621; fax (12) 4302608; e-mail amb.pol@pixie.co.za; Ambassador ROMUALD SZUNIEWICZ.

Portugal: 599 Leyds St, Muckleneuk, Pretoria 0002; POB 27102, Sunnyside 0132; tel. (12) 3412340; fax (12) 3413975; e-mail portemb@global.co.za; Ambassador PAULO COUTO BARBOSA.

Qatar: 355 Charles St, Waterkloof, Pretoria 0181; Private Bag X13, Brooklyn Sq. 0075; tel. (12) 4521700; fax (12) 3466732; e-mail qatar-emb@lantic.net; Ambassador Dr BASHIR ISSA AL-SHIRAWI.

Romania: 117 Charles St, Brooklyn, Pretoria 0181; POB 11295, Hatfield 0028; tel. (12) 4606940; fax (12) 4606947; e-mail romembsa@global.co.za; Ambassador VALER GABRIEL PAUL POTRA.

Russia: 316 Brooks St, Menlo Park, Pretoria 0081; POB 6743, Pretoria 0001; tel. (12) 3621337; fax (12) 3620116; e-mail ruspospr@mweb.co.za; internet www.russianembassy.org.za; Ambassador ANATOLY A. MAKAROV.

Rwanda: 983 Schoeman St, Arcadia, Pretoria; POB 55224, Arcadia 0007; tel. (12) 3426536; fax (12) 3427106; e-mail ambapretoria@minaffet.gov.rw; Ambassador EUGÉNE MUNYAKAYANZA.

Saudi Arabia: 711 Duncan St, cnr Lunnon St, Hatfield, Pretoria 0083; POB 13930, Hatfield 0028; tel. (12) 3624230; fax (12) 3624239; Ambassador MOHAMMED MAHMOUD BIN ALI AL-ALI.

Senegal: Charles Manor, 57 Charles St, Baileys Muckleneuk, Pretoria 0181; POB 2948, Brooklyn Sq. 0075; tel. (12) 4605263; fax (12) 3460550; e-mail ambassenepta@telkomsa.za; Ambassador MAÏMOUNA DIOP SY.

Serbia: 163 Marais St, Brooklyn, Pretoria; POB 13026, Hatfield 0028; tel. (12) 4605626; fax (12) 4606003; e-mail info@scgembassy.org.za; internet www.scgembassy.org.za; Ambassador JOVAN MARIĆ.

Singapore: 980 Schoeman St, Arcadia, Pretoria 0083; POB 11809, Hatfield 0028; tel. (12) 4306035; fax (12) 3424425; e-mail sporehc@mweb.co.za; High Commissioner MOHIDEEN P. H. RUBIN.

Slovakia: 930 Arcadia St, Pretoria 0083; POB 12736, Hatfield 0028; tel. (12) 3422051; fax (12) 3423688; e-mail slovakemb@telkomsa.net; internet www.mfa.sk/zu; Ambassador PAVOL IVAN.

Spain: 337 Brooklyn Rd, Menlo Park, Pretoria 0181; POB 1633, Pretoria 0001; tel. (12) 4600123; fax (12) 4602290; e-mail emb.pretoria@mae.es; Ambassador RAMÓN GIL-CASARAES SATRÚSTEGUI.

Sri Lanka: 410 Alexander St, Brooklyn, Pretoria 0181; tel. (12) 4607690; fax (12) 4607702; e-mail srilanka@global.co.za; internet www.srilanka.co.za; High Commissioner A. RAJAKARUNA.

Sudan: 1203 Pretorius St, Hatfield, Pretoria 0083; POB 25513, Monument Park 0105; tel. (12) 3424538; fax (12) 3424539; internet www.sudani.co.za; Ambassador KUOL ALOR.

Suriname: Suite No. 4, Groenkloof Forum Office Park, 57 George Storrar Drive, Groenkloof, 0181 Pretoria; POB 149, Pretoria; tel. (12) 3467627; fax (12) 3460802; e-mail embsur@lantic.net; Ambassador EDWARD RUDOLF BRAAFHEID.

Swaziland: 715 Government Ave, Arcadia, Pretoria 0007; POB 14294, Hatfield 0028; tel. (12) 3441910; fax (12) 3430455; High Commissioner PHILLIP NHLANHLA MUNTU MSWANE.

Sweden: iParioli Bldg, 1166 Park St, Hatfield, Pretoria 0028; POB 13477, Hatfield 0028; tel. (12) 4266400; fax (12) 4266464; e-mail sweden@iafrica.com; internet www.swedenabroad.com/Sydafrika; Ambassador ANDERS MÖLLANDER.

Switzerland: 225 Veale St, Parc Nouveau, New Muckleneuk, Pretoria 0181; POB 2508, Brooklyn Sq. 0075; tel. (12) 4520660; fax (12) 3466605; e-mail vertretung@pre.rep.admin.ch; internet www.swissembassy.co.za; Ambassador VIKTOR CHRISTEN.

Syria: 963 Schoeman St, Arcadia, Pretoria 0083; POB 12830, Hatfield 0028; tel. (12) 3424041; fax (12) 3424049; e-mail syriaemb@telkomsa.net; Chargé d'affaires a.i. Dr M. KHODUR.

Tanzania: 822 George Ave, Arcadia, Pretoria 0007; POB 56572, Arcadia 0007; tel. (12) 3424393; fax (12) 4304383; e-mail thc@tanzania.org.za; internet www.tanzania.org.za; High Commissioner EMMANUEL A. MWAMBULUKUTU.

Thailand: 428 cnr Hill and Pretorius Sts, Arcadia, Pretoria 0028; POB 12080, Hatfield 0083; tel. (12) 3424600; fax (12) 3424805; e-mail info@thaiembassy.co.za; internet www.thaiembassy.co.za; Ambassador DOMEDEJ BUNNAG.

Trinidad and Tobago: Pretoria 258 Lawley St, Waterkloof, 0181 Pretoria; POB 95872, Waterkloof, Pretoria 0145; tel. (12) 4609688; fax (12) 3467302; e-mail tthepretoria@telkomsa.net; High Commissioner DONNA MARINA CARTER.

Tunisia: 850 Church St, Arcadia, Pretoria 0083; POB 56535, Arcadia 0007; tel. (12) 3426223; fax (12) 3426284; Ambassador ALI GOUTALI.

Turkey: 1067 Church St, Hatfield, Pretoria 0083; POB 56014, Arcadia 0007; tel. (12) 3426055; fax (12) 3426052; e-mail pretbe@global.co.za; internet www.turkishembassy.co.za; Ambassador FERHAT ATAMAN.

Uganda: 882 Church St, Pretoria 0083; POB 12442, Hatfield 0083; tel. (12) 3426031; fax (12) 3426206; e-mail ugacomer@mweb.co.za; High Commissioner KWERONDA RUHEMBA.

Ukraine: 398 Marais St, Brooklyn, Pretoria 0181; POB 36463, Menlo Park 0102; tel. (12) 4601943; fax (12) 4601944; e-mail emb_za@mfa.gov.ua; Chargé d'affaires a.i. TETIANA SUSHKO.

United Arab Emirates: 992 Arcadia St, Arcadia, Pretoria 0083; POB 57090, Arcadia 0007; tel. (12) 3427736; fax (12) 3427738; e-mail uae@mweb.co.za; Ambassador ISMAEL OBAID YUSUF AL-ALI.

United Kingdom: 255 Hill St, Arcadia, Pretoria 0002; tel. (12) 4217500; fax (12) 4217555; e-mail media.pretoria@fco.gov.uk; internet www.britain.org.za; High Commissioner PAUL BOATENG.

USA: 877 Pretorius St, Arcadia, Pretoria 0083; POB 9536, Pretoria 0001; tel. (12) 4314000; fax (12) 3422299; e-mail embassypretoria@state.gov; internet southafrica.usembassy.gov; Ambassador ERIC M. BOST.

Uruguay: 301 MIB House, 3rd Floor, Hatfield Sq., 1119 Burnett St, Hatfield, Pretoria 0083; POB 3247, Pretoria 0001; tel. (12) 3626521; fax (12) 3626523; Ambassador GUILLERMO JOSÉ POMI BARIOLA.

Venezuela: Hatfield Gables South Bldg, 1st Floor, Suite 4, 474 Hilda St, Pretoria 0083; POB 11821, Hatfield 0028; tel. (12) 3626593; fax (12) 3626591; e-mail embasudaf@icon.co.za; Ambassador ANTONIO MONTILLA-SALDIVIA.

Viet Nam: 87 Brooks St, Brooklyn, Pretoria 0181; POB 13692, Hatfield 0028; tel. (12) 3628119; fax (12) 3628115; e-mail embassy@vietnam.co.za; Ambassador Dr TRAN DUY THI.

Yemen: 329 Main St, Waterkloof 0181; POB 13343, Hatfield 0028; tel. (12) 4250760; fax (12) 4250762; e-mail info@yemenbassy.org.za; internet www.yemenbassy.org.za; Chargé d'affaires a.i. MOHAMED JAMIL MUHARRAM.

SOUTH AFRICA   *Directory*

Zambia: 570 Ziervogel St, Arcadia, Pretoria 0083; POB 12234, Hatfield 0028; tel. (12) 3261854; fax (12) 3262140; High Commissioner LESLIE SAINOT MBULA.

Zimbabwe: Zimbabwe House, 798 Merton St, Arcadia, Pretoria 0083; POB 55140, Arcadia 0007; tel. (12) 3425125; fax (12) 3425126; e-mail zimpret@lantic.net; Ambassador SIMON KHAYA MOYO.

Judicial System

The common law of the Republic of South Africa is the Roman-Dutch law, the uncodified law of Holland as it was at the time of the secession of the Cape of Good Hope in 1806. The law of England is not recognized as authoritative, although the principles of English law have been introduced in relation to civil and criminal procedure, evidence and mercantile matters.

The Constitutional Court, situated in Johannesburg, consists of a Chief Justice, a Deputy Chief Justice and nine other justices. Its task is to ensure that the executive, legislative and judicial organs of government adhere to the provisions of the Constitution. It has the power to reverse legislation that has been adopted by Parliament. The Supreme Court of Appeal, situated in Bloemfontein, comprises a President, a Deputy President and a number of judges of appeal, and is the highest court in all but constitutional matters. There are also High Courts and Magistrates' Courts. A National Director of Public Prosecutions is the head of the prosecuting authority and is appointed by the President of the Republic. A Judicial Service Commission makes recommendations regarding the appointment of judges and advises central and provincial government on all matters relating to the judiciary.

Constitutional Court: cnr Queen and Sam Hancock/Hospital Sts, Constitution Hill, Braamfontein 2017; tel. (11) 3597400; fax (11) 4036524; e-mail cases@concourt.org.za; internet www.constitutionalcourt.org.za; f. 1995; Chief Justice PIUS N. LANGA.

Supreme Court of Appeal: cnr Elizabeth and President Brand Sts, Bloemfontein 9301; POB 258, Bloemfontein 9300; tel. (51) 4304128; fax (51) 4478098; e-mail astreet@justice.gov.za; internet www.supremecourtofappeal.gov.za; f. 1996; Pres. CRAIG T. HOWIE.

Religion

Some 80% of the population profess the Christian faith. Other religions that are represented are Hinduism, Islam, Judaism and traditional African religions.

CHRISTIANITY

At mid-2000 there were an estimated 12.4m. Protestants and 18.7m. adherents of other forms of Christianity.

South African Council of Churches: POB 62098, Marshalltown 2107; tel. (11) 2417800; fax (11) 4921448; internet www.sacc.org.za; f. 1968; 26 mem. churches; Pres. Prof. RUSSEL BOTMAN; Gen. Sec. EDDIE MAKUE.

The Anglican Communion

Most Anglicans in South Africa are adherents of the Anglican Church of Southern Africa (formerly the Church of the Province of Southern Africa), comprising 25 dioceses (including Angola, Lesotho, Namibia, St Helena, Swaziland and two dioceses in Mozambique). The Church had an estimated 4.5m. communicant members at mid-2006.

Archbishop of Cape Town and Metropolitan of the Province of Southern Africa: Most Rev. THABO CECIL MAKGOBA, 20 Bishopscourt Dr., Bishopscourt, Claremont, Cape Town 7700; tel. (21) 7612531; fax (21) 7614193; e-mail archbish@bishopscourt-cpsa.org.za; internet www.anglicanchurchsa.org.

The Dutch Reformed Church (Nederduitse Gereformeerde Kerk–NGK)

In 2005/06, including confirmed and baptized members, the Dutch Reformed Churches in South Africa consisted of: the Dutch Reformed Church, with 1,155,001 (mainly white) members; the Uniting Reformed Church, with 1,039,606 (mainly Coloured and black) members; the Reformed Church in Africa, with 1,708 Indian members; and the Dutch Reformed Church in Africa, with an estimated 150,000 (mainly black) members. All congregations were desegregated in 1986.

General Synod: POB 13528, Hatfield, Pretoria 0028; tel. (12) 3420092; fax (12) 3420380; e-mail algemenesinode@ngkerk.org.za; internet www.ngkerk.org.za; Moderator Prof. PIET STRAUSS; Gen. Sec. Dr KOBUS GERBER.

The Lutheran Churches

Lutheran Communion in Southern Africa (LUCSA): POB 7170, Bonaero Park 1622; tel. (11) 9731873; fax (11) 3951615; e-mail info@lucsa.org; f. 1991; co-ordinating org. for the Lutheran churches in southern Africa, incl. Angola, Botswana, Malawi, Mozambique, Namibia, South Africa, Swaziland, Zambia and Zimbabwe; 1,618,720 mems (1999); Pres. Bishop C. K. MOENGA; Exec. Dir Bishop Dr A. MOYO.

Evangelical Lutheran Church in Southern Africa (ELCSA): POB 7231, 1622 Bonaero Park; tel. (11) 9731853; fax (11) 3951888; e-mail elcsaadmin@mweb.co.za; f. 1975 by merger of four non-white churches; Pres. Bishop LOUIS SIBIYA; 624,567 mems.

Evangelical Lutheran Church in Southern Africa (Cape Church): POB 3466, 7602 Matieland; tel. (21) 8869747; fax (21) 8869748; e-mail rohwernj@adept.co.za; Pres. Bishop NILS ROHWER; 4,108 mems.

Evangelical Lutheran Church in Southern Africa (N-T): Church Council, 24 Geldenhuys Rd, Bonaero Park, Johannesburg; POB 7095, Bonaero Park 1622; tel. (11) 9731851; fax (11) 3951862; e-mail elksant@elksant.co.za; internet www.elcsant.org.za; f. 1981; Pres. Bishop DIETER R. LILJE; 9,800 mems (2006).

Moravian Church in Southern Africa: POB 24111, Lansdowne 7779; tel. (21) 7614030; fax (21) 7614046; e-mail mcsa@iafrica.com; f. 1737; Pres. ANGELENE H. SWART; 100,000 mems (2002).

The Roman Catholic Church

South Africa comprises four archdioceses, 21 dioceses and one Apostolic Vicariate. At 31 December 2005 there were an estimated 3,170,846 adherents in the country, representing about 6.4% of the total population.

Southern African Catholic Bishops' Conference (SACBC) Khanya House, 140 Visagie St, Pretoria 0001; POB 941, Pretoria 0001; tel. (12) 3236458; fax (12) 3266218; e-mail sacbclib@wn.apc.org; internet www.sacbc.org.za.

f. 1947; mems representing South Africa, Botswana and Swaziland; Pres. Cardinal WILFRID NAPIER (Archbishop of Durban; until Jan. 2007); Pres. Archbishop BUTI TLHAGALE (Bishop of Johannesburg; from Jan. 2007); Sec.-Gen. Fr RICHARD MENATSI.

Archbishop of Bloemfontein: JABULANI ADATUS NXUMALO, Archbishop's House, 7A Whites Rd, Bloemfontein 9301; POB 362, Bloemfontein 9300; tel. (51) 4481658; fax (51) 4472420; e-mail bfnarch@mweb.co.za.

Archbishop of Cape Town: Most Rev. LAWRENCE HENRY, Cathedral Place, 12 Bouquet St, Cape Town 8001; POB 2910, Cape Town 8000; tel. (21) 4622417; fax (21) 4619330; e-mail archbishop@intekom.co.za; internet www.catholic-ct.co.za.

Archbishop of Durban: Cardinal WILFRID NAPIER, Archbishop's House, 154 Gordon Rd, Durban 4001; POB 47489, Greyville 4023; tel. (31) 3031417; fax (31) 3121848; e-mail vg@catholic-dbn.org.za.

Archbishop of Pretoria: Most Rev. GEORGE FRANCIS DANIEL, Jolivet House, 140 Visagie St, Pretoria 0002; POB 8149, Pretoria 0001; tel. (12) 3265311; fax (12) 3253994; e-mail ptadiocese@absamail.co.za.

Other Christian Churches

In addition to the following Churches, there are a large number of Pentecostalist groups, and more than 4,000 independent African Churches.

African Gospel Church: POB 32312, 4060 Mobeni; tel. (31) 9074377; Moderator Rev. F. D. MKHIZE; Gen. Sec. O. MTOLO; 100,000 mems.

Afrikaanse Protestantse Kerk (Afrikaans Protestant Church): POB 11488, Hatfield 0028; tel. (12) 3621390; fax (12) 3622023; f. 1987 by fmr mems of the Dutch Reformed Church (Nederduitse Gereformeerde Kerk) in protest at the desegregation of church congregations; c. 46,400 mems.

Apostolic Faith Mission of South Africa: POB 890197, 2106 Lyndhurst; tel. (11) 7868550; fax (11) 8871182; e-mail afmgens@mweb.co.za; f. 1908; Gen. Sec. Pastor M. G. MAHLABO; 136,000 mems.

Assemblies of God: POB 51065, Musgrave 4062; tel. (31) 231341; fax (31) 231342; f. 1915; Chair. Rev. ISAAC HLETA; Gen. Sec. Rev. C. P. WATT; 300,000 mems.

Baptist Union of Southern Africa: Private Bag X45, Wilropark 1731; tel. (11) 7685980; fax (11) 7685983; e-mail secretary@baptistunion.org.za; f. 1877; Pres. Dr ROLAND MYBURGH; Gen. Sec. Rev. ANGELO SCHEEPERS; 53,000 mems (2006).

Black Dutch Reformed Church: POB 137, Bergvlei 2012; Leader Rev. SAM BUTI; c. 1m. mems.

Church of England in South Africa: POB 2180 Clareinch 7740; tel. (21) 6717070; fax (21) 6712553; e-mail cameronb@cesa.org.za; internet www.cesa.org.za; Bishop Rt Rev. F. RETIEF (presiding),

SOUTH AFRICA

Bishop Rt Rev. M. Morrison, Bishop Rt Rev. Dr W. Cole-Edwardes, Bishop Rt Rev. D. Inglesby; 207 churches.

Evangelical Presbyterian Church in South Africa: POB 31961, Braamfontein 2017; tel. (11) 3391044; fax (11) 4034144; e-mail mobbie@epcsa.co.za; Gen. Sec. Rev. J. S. Ngobe; Treas. Rev. H. D. Masangu; 60,000 mems.

The Methodist Church of Southern Africa: Methodist Connexional Office, POB 50216, Musgrave 4062; tel. (31) 2024214; fax (31) 2017674; internet www.users.club.co.za/mco; f. 1883; Pres. Bishop I. M. Abrahams; Sec. Rev. Ross A. J. Oliver; 696,353 mems.

Nederduitsch Hervormde Kerk van Afrika: POB 2368, Pretoria 0001; tel. (12) 3228885; fax (12) 3203279; e-mail fanie@nhk.co.za; internet www.nhk.co.za; e-mail fanie@nhk.co.za; Gen. Sec. Dr S. P. Pretorius; 193,561 mems.

Nederduitse Gereformeerde Kerk in Afrika: Portland Pl., 37 Jorissen St, 2017 Johannesburg; tel. (11) 4031027; 6 synods (incl. 1 in Swaziland); Moderator Rev. S. P. E. Buti; Gen. Sec. W. Raath; 350,370 mems.

Presbyterian Church of Africa: POB 54840, Umlazi 4031; tel. (31) 9072366; f. 1898; 8 presbyteries (incl. 1 in Malawi and 1 in Zimbabwe); Chief Clerk Rev. S. A. Khumalo; 1,231,000 mems.

Reformed Church in South Africa (Die Gereformeerde Kerke): POB 20002, Noordbrug 2522, Potchefstroom; tel. (148) 2973986; fax (148) 2931042; f. 1859; Prin. Officer Dr C. J. Smit; 158,973 mems.

Seventh-day Adventist Church: POB 468, Bloemfontein 9300; tel. (51) 4478271; fax (41) 4488059; e-mail sau.president@adventist.org.za; internet www.adventist.org.za; Pres. Pastor F. Louw; Sec. Pastor T. Kunene; 150,000 mems.

United Congregational Church of Southern Africa: POB 96014, Brixton; tel. and fax (21) 6839665; e-mail dave@uccsa.co.za; internet www.uccsa.org.za; f. 1799; Pres. Rev. Ian Booth; Gen. Sec. Rev. Des van der Water; 400,000 mems in 350 churches.

Uniting Presbyterian Church in Southern Africa: POB 96188, Brixton 2019; tel. (11) 3392471; fax (11) 3396938; e-mail gensec@presbyterian.org.za; internet www.upcsa.org.za; f. 1999; Moderator Rt Rev W. D. Pool; Gen. Sec. Rev. V. S. Vellem; Clerk of the Assembly T. W. Coulter; 130,000 mems.

Zion Christian Church: Zion City, Moria; f. 1910; South Africa's largest black religious group; Leader Bishop Barnabas Lekganyane; c. 4m. mems.

ISLAM

In 2003 there were some 455 Mosques and 408 Muslim colleges in South Africa.

United Ulama Council of South Africa (UUCSA): POB 4118, Cape Town 8000; tel. (21) 6965150; fax (21) 6968502; f. 1994; Pres. Sheikh Ebrahim Gabriels; Sec.-Gen. Moulana Yusuf Patel.

JUDAISM

According to the South African Jewish Board of Deputies, in 2006 there were about 80,000 Jews in South Africa, and about 200 organized Jewish communities.

African Jewish Congress: POB 51663, Raedene 2124; tel. (82) 4402621; fax (86) 6146724; e-mail moshe@beyachad.co.za; internet www.africanjewishcongress.com; f. 1994; co-ordinating body representing Jewish communities in sub-Saharan Africa; Pres. Mervyn Smith; Spiritual Leader Rabbi Moshe Silberhaft.

South African Jewish Board of Deputies: POB 87557, Houghton 2041; tel. (11) 6452523; fax (11) 6452559; e-mail sajbod@iafrica.com; internet www.jewish.org.za; f. 1903; the representative institution of South African Jewry; Pres. Russell Gaddin; Chair. Michael Bagraim; Nat. Dir Wendy Kahn.

BAHÁ'Í FAITH

National Spiritual Assembly: 209 Bellairs Dr., North Riding 2169, POB 932, Banbury Cross 2164; tel. (11) 4620100; fax (11) 4620129; e-mail nsa.sec@bahai.org.za; internet www.bahai.org.za; f. 1956; Gen. Sec. Shohreh Rawhani; 11,000 mems resident in 320 localities.

The Press

Government Communication and Information System (GCIS): Midtown Bldg, cnr Vermeulen and Prinsloo Sts, Pretoria; Private Bag X745, Pretoria 0001; tel. (12) 3142911; fax (12) 3252030; e-mail govcom@gcis.gov.za; internet www.gcis.gov.za; govt agency; CEO Themba Maseko.

South African Press Ombudsman: POB 47221, Parklands 2121, Johannesburg; tel. (11) 7884837; fax (11) 7884990; e-mail pressombudsman@ombudsman.org.za; internet www.ombudsman.org.za; Ombudsman Joe Thloloe.

DAILIES

Eastern Cape

Die Burger (Oos-Kaap): 52 Cawood St, POB 525, Port Elizabeth 6001; tel. (41) 5036111; fax (41) 5036138; f. 1937; morning; Afrikaans; Editor Leon van der Vyver; circ. 23,849.

Daily Dispatch: 35 Caxton St, POB 131, East London 5200; tel. (43) 7022000; fax (43) 7022968; e-mail phyliciao@dispatch.co.za; internet www.dispatch.co.za; f. 1872; publ. by Dispatch Media (Pty) Ltd; afternoon; also publ. *Weekend Dispatch* (Sat.); English; Editor Phylicia Oppelt; circ. 33,338 (Mon.–Fri.), 27,927 (Sat.).

The Herald: Newspaper House, 19 Baakens St; POB 1117, Port Elizabeth 6000; tel. (41) 5047911; fax (41) 5853947; f. 1845; fmrly *Eastern Province Herald*; publ. by Johnnic Publishing Ltd; morning; English; Editor Ric Wilson; circ. 29,719 (Mon.–Fri.), 25,000 (Sat.).

Free State

Die Volksblad: 79 Voortrekker St, POB 267, Bloemfontein 9300; tel. (51) 4047600; fax (51) 4306949; e-mail nuus@volksblad.com; internet www.naspers.com; f. 1904; publ. by Media 24; morning; Afrikaans; Editor Jonathan Crowther; circ. 29,018 (Mon.–Fri.), 23,000 (Sat.).

Gauteng

Beeld: Media Park, Kingsway 69, Auckland Park, Johannesburg; POB 333, Auckland Park 2006; tel. (11) 7139000; fax (11) 7139960; e-mail ggrobler@beeld.com; f. 1974; publ. by Media 24; morning; weekly: *Kampus-Beeld*, student news and information, and *JIP* youth supplement; Afrikaans; Editor Peet Kruger; Gen. Man. Lucille van Niekerk; circ. 105,618 (Mon.–Fri.), 88,402 (Sat.).

Business Day: POB 1745, Saxonwold 2132; tel. (11) 2803000; fax (11) 2805505; internet www.bday.co.za; f. 1985; publ. by BDFM Publrs (Pty) Ltd; afternoon; English; financial; incl. *Wanted* arts and leisure magazine; Editor Jim Jones; circ. 40,451 (Mon.–Fri.).

The Citizen: POB 43069, Industria 2042; tel. (11) 2486000; fax (11) 2486213; e-mail news@citizen.co.za; f. 1976; publ. by Caxton Publrs & Printers Ltd; morning; English; Editor M Williams; circ. 76,183 (Mon.–Fri.), 57,935 (Sat.).

The Pretoria News: 216 Vermeulen St, Pretoria 0002; POB 439, Pretoria 0001; tel. (12) 3002000; fax (12) 3257300; f. 1898; publ. by Independent Newspapers Gauteng Ltd; afternoon; English; Editor Philani Mgwaba; circ. 28,690 (Mon.–Fri.), 17,406 (Sat.).

Sowetan: 61 Commando Rd, Industria West, Johannesburg 2000; POB 6663, Johannesburg 2000; tel. (11) 4714000; fax (11) 4748834; e-mail editor@sowetan.co.za; internet www.sowetan.co.za; f. 1981; publ. by New Africa Publs (NAP) Ltd; morning; English; Editor Z. Aggrey Klaaste; circ. 4,122,825 (Mon.–Fri.).

The Star: 47 Sauer St, POB 1014, Johannesburg 2000; tel. (11) 6339111; fax (11) 8343918; e-mail starnews@star.co.za; internet www.star.co.za; f. 1887; publ. by Independent Newspapers Gauteng Ltd; morning; English; also publ. *The Saturday Star*; Editor Moegsien Williams; circ. 166,461 (Mon.–Fri.), 137, 385 (Sat.).

KwaZulu/Natal

The Daily News: 18 Osborne St, Greyville 4001; POB 47549, Greyville 4023; tel. (31) 3082107; fax (31) 3082185; internet www.iol.co.za; f. 1878; Mon.–Fri., afternoon; English; Editor D. Pather; circ. 50,000.

The Mercury: 18 Osborne St, Greyville 4001; POB 47397, Greyville 4023; tel. (31) 3082472; fax (31) 3082662; e-mail mercnews@inl.co.za; internet themercury.co.za; f. 1852; publ. by Independent Newspapers KZN; morning; English; Editor David Canning; circ. 39,343 (Mon.–Fri.).

Witness: 45 Willowton Rd, POB 362, Pietermaritzburg 3200; tel. (33) 3551111; fax (33) 3551122; e-mail johnc@witness.co.za; internet www.witness.co.za; f. 1846; publ. by Natal Witness Printing and Publishing Co Ltd; morning; English; also publ. *Weekend Witness*; Editor J. Conyngham; circ. 23,700 (Mon.–Fri.), 29,000 (Sat.).

Northern Cape

Diamond Fields Advertiser: POB 610, cnr Bean and Villiers Sts, Kimberley 8300; tel. (53) 8326261; fax (53) 8328902; e-mail pbe@independent.co.za; internet www.iol.co.za; publ. by Independent Newspapers Gauteng Ltd; morning; English; Editor Kevin Ritchie; circ. 8,948 (Mon.–Fri.).

North-West

Rustenburg Herald: 13 Coetzer St, POB 2043, Rustenburg 0300; tel. (14) 5928329; fax (14) 5921869; e-mail mailbag@

SOUTH AFRICA

rustenburgherald.co.za; f. 1924; English and Afrikaans; Man. Editor C. THERON; circ. 20,368.

Western Cape

Die Burger: 40 Heerengracht, POB 692, Cape Town 8000; tel. (21) 4062222; fax (21) 4062913; f. 1915; publ. by Media 24; morning; Afrikaans; Editor E. DOMMISSE; circ. 104,102 (Mon.–Fri.), 117,092 (Sat.).

Cape Argus: 122 St George's St, POB 56, Cape Town 8000; tel. (21) 4884911; fax (21) 4884075; f. 1857; publ. by Independent Newspapers Cape Ltd; afternoon; English; also publ. *Weekend Argus*; Editor MOEGSIEN WILLIAMS; circ. 73,230 (Mon.–Fri.), 103,953 (Sat. and Sun.).

Cape Times: Newspaper House, 122 St George's Mall, Cape Town 8001; POB 56, Cape Town 8000; tel. (21) 4884911; fax (21) 4884744; e-mail tyrone.august@inl.co.za; internet www.capetimes.co.za; f. 1876; publ. by Independent Newspapers Cape Ltd; morning; English; Editor TYRONE AUGUST; circ. 49,526 (Mon.–Fri.).

WEEKLIES AND FORTNIGHTLIES

Eastern Cape

Weekend Post: Private Bag X6071, Port Elizabeth 6000; tel. (41) 5047251; fax (41) 5854966; e-mail weekend@johnnicec.co.za; internet www.weekendpost.co.za; publ. by Johnnic Publishing Co Ltd; English; Editor CHARMAIN NAIDOO; circ. 33,372 (Sat.).

Free State

Vista: POB 1027, Welkom 9460; tel. (57) 3571304; fax (57) 3532427; e-mail avaneck@volksblad.com; internet www.media24.com/eng/newspapers/vista.html; f. 1971; weekly; English and Afrikaans; Editor MARTI WILLN; circ. 38,000 (2005).

Gauteng

Benoni City Times en Oosrandse Nuus: 28 Woburn Ave, POB 494, Benoni 1500; tel. (11) 8451680; fax (11) 4224796; English and Afrikaans; Editor HILARY GREEN; circ. 32,000.

City Press: POB 3413, Johannesburg 2000; tel. (11) 7139002; fax (11) 7139977; e-mail news@citypress.co.za; f. 1983; publ. by RCP Media Bpk; weekly; English; Editor-in-Chief KHULU SIBIYA; circ. 173,922 (Sun.).

Financial Mail: Johncom Bldg, 4 Biermann Ave, Rosebank 2196; POB 1744, Saxenwold 2132; tel. (11) 2803016; fax (11) 2805800; e-mail fmmail@fm.co.za; internet www.financialmail.co.za; weekly; English; Editor BARNEY MTHOMBOTHI; circ. 33,000.

The Herald Times: POB 31015, Braamfontein 2017; tel. (11) 8876500; weekly; Jewish interest; Man. Dir R. SHAPIRO; circ. 5,000.

Mail and Guardian: POB 91667, Auckland Park 2006; tel. (11) 7277000; fax (11) 7277110; publ. by M&G Media (Pty) Ltd; weekly; English; CEO GOVIN REDDY; Editor PHILIP VAN NIEKERK; circ. 40,162 (Fri.).

Engineering News/Mining Weekly: POB 75316, Garden View 2047; tel. and fax (11) 6229350; e-mail newsdesk@engineeringnews.co.za; internet www.miningweekly.co.za; f. 1979; publ. by Creamer Media; weekly; circ. 10,000.

Die Noord-Transvaler: POB 220, Ladanna, Pietersburg 0704; tel. (152) 931831; fax (152) 932586; weekly; Afrikaans; Editor A. BUYS; circ. 12,000.

Noordwes Gazette: POB 515, Potchefstroom 2520; tel. (18) 2930750; e-mail potchherald@media24.com; weekly; English and Afrikaans; Editor H. STANDER; circ. 35,000.

Northern Review: 16 Grobler St, POB 45, Pietersburg 0700; tel. (152) 2959167; fax (152) 2915148; weekly; English and Afrikaans; Editor R. S. DE JAGER; circ. 10,300.

Potchefstroom and Ventersdorp Herald: POB 515, Potchefstroom 2520; tel. (18) 2930750; fax (18) 2930759; e-mail potchherald@media24.com; f. 1908; Friday; English and Afrikaans; Editor H. STANDER; Man. Dir RASSIE VAN ZYL; circ. 8,000.

Rapport: POB 333, Auckland Park 2006; tel. (11) 7139002; fax (11) 7139977; e-mail rapport@rapport.co.za; internet www.naspers.co.za/rapport; publ. by RCP Media; weekly; Afrikaans; Sr Gen. Man. and Publr SAREL DU PLESSIS; Editor IZAK DE VILLIERS; circ. 322,731 (Sun.).

South African Jewish Report: Suite 175, Postnet X10039, Randburg 2125; tel. (11) 8860162; fax (11) 8864202; e-mail geoffs@icon.co.za; weekly; publ. by SA Jewish Report (Pty) Ltd; Editor GEOFF SIFRIN.

Springs and Brakpan Advertiser: 48, 5th Ave, POB 761, Springs 1560; tel. (11) 8124800; fax (11) 8124823; e-mail springseditorial@caxton.co.za; f. 1916; English and Afrikaans; Editor CATHY GROSVENOR; circ. 13,000.

Sunday Times: POB 1742, Saxonwold 2132; tel. (11) 2805101; fax (11) 2805111; e-mail makhanyam@sundaytimes.co.za; internet www.sundaytimes.co.za; publ. by Johnnic Publishing Co Ltd; weekly; English; Editor MONDLI MAKHANYA; circ. 505,402 (Sun.).

Vaalweekblad: 27 Ekspa Bldg, D. F. Malan St, POB 351, Vanderbijlpark 1900; tel. (16) 817010; fax (16) 810604; weekly; Afrikaans and English; Editor W. J. BUYS; circ. 16,000.

Die Vrye Afrikaan: PO Box 675, Durbanville 7551; tel. (12) 3268646; e-mail redakteur@vryeafrikaan.co.za; f. 2004; weekly; Afrikaans; Editor JOHANN ROUSSOUW; circ. 13,000.

KwaZulu/Natal

Farmers' Weekly: 368 Jan Smuts Ave, Craighall, Johannesburg 2196; tel. (11) 8890836; fax (11) 8890862; e-mail farmersweekly@caxton.co.za; internet www.farmersweekly.co.za; f. 1911; weekly; agriculture and horticulture; Editor CHRIS BURGESS; circ. 17,000.

Ilanga: 19 Timeball Blvd, The Point, Durban 4001; POB 2159 Durban 4000; tel. (31) 3374000; fax (31) 3379785; e-mail peterc@ilanganews.co.za; f. 1903; publ. by Mandla Matla Publishing Co (Pty) Ltd; 2 a week; also publ *Ilanga Lange Sonto* (Sun. circ. 70,000); Zulu; Editor S. NGOBESE; circ. 107,000; circ. 100,000 (Mon. and Thurs.).

Kwana in the City: POB 35559, Northway 4065; tel. (31) 5641230; fax (31) 5649807; e-mail vrydag@eastcoast.co.za; internet www.kwana.co.za; f. 1995; publ. by Kwana Group; English; free community newspaper with focus on consumer and human rights issues; also publ. *Kwana on Track* (f. 2004, English and Zulu, circ. 50,000) aimed at rail commuters; Publr SHELLEY SEID; Editor Dr HILDA GROBLER; circ. 20,000.

Independent On Saturday: 18 Osborne St, Greyville 4001; POB 47397, Greyville 4023; tel. (31) 3082900; fax (31) 3082185; e-mail satmail@inl.co.za; internet www.nn.independent.co.za; f. 1878; publ. by Independent Newspapers KZN; English; Editor CLYDE BAWDEN; circ. 56,216.

Ladysmith Gazette: POB 10019, Ladysmith 3370; tel. (36) 6376801; fax (36) 6372283; f. 1902; weekly; English, Afrikaans and Zulu; Editor DIANA PROCTER; circ. 7,000.

Post: 18 Osborne St, Greyville, Durban 4000; POB 47397, Greyville 4023; tel. (31) 3082400; fax (31) 3082427; e-mail post@inl.co.za; internet www.iol.co.za; f. 1955 as *Golden City Post*; publ. by Independent Newspapers KZN; weekly; English; focus on the Indian community; Editor BRIJLALL RAMGUTHEE; circ. 45,500 (Wed.).

Sunday Tribune: 18 Osborne St, POB 47549, Greyville 4023; tel. (31) 3082911; fax (31) 3082662; e-mail tribnews@nn.independent.co.za; internet www.iol.co.za; f. 1937; publ. by Independent Newspapers KZN; weekly; English; Editor ALAN DUNN; circ. 109,774 (Sun.).

Umafrika: 35A Intersite Ave, Umgeni Business Park, Durban; tel. (31) 2684500; fax (31) 2684545; e-mail editor@umafrika.co.za; f. 1911; owned by Izimpoondo Communications; Friday; Zulu and English; Editor and Publisher CYRIL MADLALA; circ. 32,000.

Northern Cape

Die Gemsbok: POB 60, Upington 8800; tel. 27017; fax 24055; English and Afrikaans; Editor D. JONES; circ. 8,000.

Western Cape

Drum: Naspers Bldg, 7th Floor, 5 Protea Place, Sandown 2096; POB 653284, Benmore 2010; tel. (11) 3220888; fax (11) 3220891; e-mail pmdluli@media24.com; f. 1951; English and Zulu; Editor ESMARE WEIDEMAN; Publr JOHN RELIHAN; circ. 79,895 (2006).

Eikestadnuus: 44 Alexander St, POB 28, Stellenbosch 7600; tel. (2231) 72840; fax (2231) 99538; weekly; English and Afrikaans; Editor R. GERBER; circ. 7,000.

Fair Lady: POB 785266, Cape Town 2146; tel. (11) 3220858; fax (11) 8836611; e-mail flmag@fairlady.com; internet www.fairlady.com; fortnightly; English; Editor SUZY BROKENSHA; circ. 103,642.

Huisgenoot: 40 Heerengracht, POB 1802, Cape Town 8000; tel. (21) 4062279; fax (21) 4063316; e-mail eweidema@media24.com; internet www.huisgenoot.com; f. 1916; weekly; Afrikaans; Editor ESMARÉ WEIDEMAN; circ. 355,487.

Move! Magazine: Media City, 10th Floor, 1 Heerengracht St, Foreshore, Cape Town 8001; tel. (21) 4461232; fax (21) 4461206; e-mail move@media24.com; f. 2005; weekly; English; Editor SBU MPUNGOSE.

The Southern Cross: POB 2372, Cape Town 8000; tel. (21) 4655007; fax (21) 4653850; e-mail scross@global.co.za; internet www.thesoutherncross.co.za; f. 1920; publ. by Catholic Newspapers and Publishing Co Ltd; weekly; English; Roman Catholic interest; Editor GÜNTHER SIMMERMACHER; circ. 11,000 (Wed.).

tvplus: Media City, 10th Floor, 1 Heerengracht St, Cape Town 8001; POB 7197, Roggebaai 8012; tel. (21) 4461222; fax (21) 4461206;

SOUTH AFRICA

e-mail tvplus@media24.com; internet www.tvplus.co.za; f. 2000; weekly; English and Afrikaans; Editor WICUS PRETORIUS.

Tyger-Burger: 40 Heerengracht, POB 2271, Cape Town 8000; tel. (21) 4062121; fax (21) 4062913; weekly; Afrikaans and English; Editor ABIE VON ZYL.

Weekend Argus: 122 St George's Mall, POB 56, Cape Town 8000; tel. (21) 4884911; fax (21) 4884762; internet www.iol.co.za; f. 1857; Sat. and Sun.; English; Editor CHRIS WHITFIELD; circ. 108,294.

You Magazine: Naspers Bldg, 7th Floor, 40 Heerengracht St, Cape Town 8001; POB 7167, Roggebaai 8012; tel. (21) 4062166; fax (21) 4062937; e-mail you@you.co.za; internet www.you.co.za; f. 1987; weekly; English; Editor ESMARÉ WEIDEMAN; circ. 222,845 (2004).

MONTHLIES
Free State

Wamba: POB 1097, Bloemfontein; publ. in seven vernacular languages; educational; Editor C. P. SENYATSI.

Gauteng

Nursing News: POB 1280, Pretoria 0001; tel. (12) 3432315; fax (12) 3440750; f. 1978; English and Afrikaans; magazine of the Dem. Nursing Org; circ. 76,000.

KwaZulu/Natal

Bona: POB 32083, Mobeni 4060; tel. (31) 422041; fax (31) 426068; f. 1956; English, Sotho, Xhosa and Zulu; Editor DAIZER MQHABA; circ. 256,631.

Living and Loving: POB 218, Parklands, Johannesburg 2121; tel. (11) 8890621; fax (11) 8890668; e-mail livingandloving@caxton.co.za; internet www.livingandloving.co.za; publ. by Caxton Magazines; English; lifestyle magazine; Editor CARLIEN WESSELS; circ. 55,000.

Rooi Rose: POB 412982, Craighall 2024; tel. (11) 8890665; fax (11) 8890975; e-mail rooirose@caxton.co.za; internet www.rooirose.co.za; Afrikaans; women's interest; Editor MARTIE PANSEGROUW; circ. 122,296.

World Airnews: POB 35082, Northway 4065; tel. (31) 5641319; fax (31) 5637115; e-mail tom@airnews.co.za; internet www.airnews.co.za; f. 1973; aviation news; Man. Editor TOM CHALMERS; circ. 12,270 (2008).

Your Family: POB 473016, Parklands 2121; tel. (11) 8890749; fax (11) 8890642; e-mail yourfamily@caxton.co.za; internet www.yourfamily.co.za; f. 1973; English; cooking, crafts, DIY; Editor ANGELA WALLER-PATON; circ. 164,115.

Western Cape

Boxing World: 5A Dover St, Randburg, Gauteng; tel. (11) 8868558; e-mail info@boxingworld.co.za; f. 1976; Editor PETER LEOPENG; circ. 10,000.

Car: Ramsay, Son & Parker (Pty) Ltd, Digital Publishing, 3 Howard Dr., Pinelands, Cape Town; POB 180, Howard Place 7450; tel. (21) 5303100; fax (21) 5322698; e-mail car@rsp.co.za; internet www.cartoday.com; English; Editor J. WRIGHT; circ. 105,934 (2004).

Femina: 21 St. John's St, POB 3647, Cape Town 8000; tel. (21) 4646248; fax (21) 4612501; Editor ROBYNNE KAHN; circ. 68,591.

Reader's Digest (South African Edition): 5 Protea Pl., Protea Park, Sandown, Johannesburg 2146; POB 785266, Sandton 2146; tel. (11) 3220700; fax (11) 8839495; e-mail magazine.sa@readersdigest.com; internet www.readersdigest.co.za; f. 1948; English; Editor ANTHONY JOHNSON; circ. 62,399.

Sarie: POB 785266, Sandton 2146; tel. and fax (21) 4062366; e-mail mvanbre@sarie.com; internet www.natmags.com; monthly; Afrikaans; women's interest; Editor MICHELLE VAN BREDA; circ. 137,970 (2004).

South African Medical Journal: MASA House, Central House, Private Bag X1, Pinelands 7430; tel. (21) 5306520; fax (21) 5314126; f. 1884; publ. by the South African Medical Asscn; Editor DANIEL J. NCAYIYANA; circ. 20,000.

Die Unie: POB 196, Cape Town 8000; tel. (21) 4616340; fax (21) 4619238; e-mail saoukaap@jaywalk.com; f. 1905; educational; publ. by the South African Teachers' Union; Editor H. M. NEL; circ. 7,200.

Die Voorligter: Private Bag, Tyger Valley 7536; tel. (21) 9177000; fax (21) 9141333; e-mail lig@cnw-inter.net; internet www.christene.co.za; f. 1937; journal of the Dutch Reformed Church of South Africa; Editor Dr F. M. GAUM; circ. 50,000.

Wineland Magazine: VinPro, POB 1411, Suider-Paarl 7624; tel. (21) 8634524; fax (21) 8634851; e-mail cas@wineland.co.za; internet www.wineland.co.za; f. 1931; publ. by VinPro wine producers' org.; viticulture and the wine and spirit industry; incorporates *Wynboer* technical guide for wine producers; Editor CASSIE DU PLESSIS; circ. 10,000.

Directory

The Wisden Cricketer: POB 16368, Vlaeberg 8018; tel. (21) 4083813; e-mail aevlambi@touchline.co.za; internet www.wisdencricketer.co.za; f. 2005; Publr NIC WIDES; Editor ROB HOUWING.

Woman's Value: POB 1802, Cape Town 8000; tel. (21) 4062629; fax (21) 4062929; e-mail wvdited@womansvalue.com; internet www.women24.com/women24/womanswalue/wv_template; English; Editor and Publr TERENA LE ROUX; circ. 134,749.

PERIODICALS
Eastern Cape

African Journal of AIDS Research (AJAR): Centre for AIDS Development, Research and Evaluation, Institute of Social and Economic Research, Rhodes University, POB 94, Grahamstown 6140; tel. (46) 6038553; fax (46) 6038770; e-mail ajar@ru.ac.za; internet www.cadre.org.za; f. 2002; quarterly; Man. Editor KEVIN KELLY.

Gauteng

Africa Insight: Africa Institute of South Africa, POB 630, Pretoria 0001; tel. (12) 3049700; fax (12) 3238153; internet www.ai.org.za; f. 1960; quarterly; journal of the Africa Institute of South Africa; Editor DIANA COETZEE; circ. 1,200.

African Journal of Political Science: 195 Beckett St, Arcadia, Pretoria; POB 13995, The Tramshed 0126; tel. (12) 3430409; fax (12) 3443622; e-mail program@aaps.org.za; 2 a year; articles in English and French; Editor ADEKUNLE AMUWO.

Africanus: Unisa Press, POB 392, UNISA, 0003 Pretoria; tel. (12) 4292953; fax (12) 4293449; e-mail delpoa@unisa.ac.za; 2 a year; journal of the Centre for Development Studies, Unisa; African and Third World developmental issues; Editor LINDA CORNWELL.

Codicillus: Unisa Press, POB 392, UNISA, 0003 Pretoria; tel. (12) 4292953; fax (12) 4293449; e-mail delpoa@unisa.ac.za; 2 a year; journal of the School of Law at the Univ. of South Africa; South African and international law; Editor Prof. H. C. ROODT.

The Motorist: Highbury Monarch Pty, 8th Floor, Metlife Centre, 7 Coen Steytler Ave, Foreshore, 8001 Cape Town; tel. (21) 4160141; fax (21) 4187312; e-mail themotorist@monarchc.co.za; f. 1966; journal of the Automobile Asscn of SA; Editor FIONA ZERBST; circ. 131,584 (2000).

The ScienceScope: POB 395, Pretoria 0001; tel. (12) 8414625; fax (12) 8413789; e-mail edaconceicao@csir.co.za; internet www.csir.co.za; f. 1991 as *Technobrief*; quarterly; publ. by the South African Council for Scientific and Industrial Research; Editor EUNICE DA CONCEIÇÃO; circ. 6,000.

South African Journal of Chemistry: School of Chemistry, University of KwaZulu-Natal, Durban 4000; tel. (31) 2601096; fax (31) 2603091; e-mail taford@vodamail.co.za; internet search.sabinet.co.za/sajchem/; f. 1921; publ. by the South African Chemical Institute; digital; Co-ordinating Editor TONY FORD.

South African Journal of Economics: 4.45 EBW Bldg, University of Pretoria, Pretoria 0002; POB 73354, Lynnwood Ridge 0040; tel. (12) 4203525; fax (12) 3625266; e-mail saje@up.ac.za; internet www.essa.org.za; f. 1933; quarterly; English and Afrikaans; journal of the Economic Soc. of South Africa; publ. by Blackwells; Man. Editor P. A. BLACK.

Kwa/Zulu Natal

African Journal on Conflict Resolution: ACCORD, Private Bag X018, Umhlanga Rocks 4320; tel. (31) 5023908; fax (31) 5024160; e-mail info@accord.org.za; internet www.accord.org.za/ajcr/intro.htm; f. 1999; annually; conflict transformation in Africa; Chair. Prof. JAKES GERWEL; Man. Editor RICHARD KAMIDZA; Editor JANNIE MALAN.

Indilinga: African Journal of Indigenous Knowledge Systems (IAJIKS): POB 13789, Cascades, Pietermaritzburg 3202; tel. (31) 9077000; fax (31) 9073011; e-mail nmkabela@hotmail.com; internet www.indilinga.org.za; f. 2002; 1–2 a year; issues relating to the transmission of local or traditional knowledge; Editor-in-Chief QUEENETH MKABELA.

North-West

Historia: c/o Dept of Historical and Heritage Studies, Faculty of Humanities, Humanities Bldg (Main Campus), University of Pretoria, Pretoria 0002; tel. (12) 4202323; fax (12) 4202656; e-mail moutofa@unisa.ac.za; f. 1956; 2 a year; journal of the Historical Asscn of South Africa; South African and African history; Co-ordinating Editor ALEX MOULTON.

SOUTH AFRICA   *Directory*

Western Cape

African Finance Journal: African Finance Association, ACIA, University of Stellenbosch Business School, POB 610, Bellville 7535; tel. (21) 9184347; fax (21) 9184262; e-mail afa@acia.sun.ac.za; f. 1999; 2 a year; finance, accounting and economics; Exec. Editor NICHOLAS BIEKPE.

Economic Prospects: Bureau for Economic Research, Economics and Management Sciences Bldg, 7th Floor, Bosman St, Stellenbosch 7600; Private Bag 5050, Stellenbosch 7599; tel. (21) 8872810; fax (21) 8839225; e-mail hhman@sun.ac.za; quarterly; forecast of the South African economy for the coming 18–24 months; Man. Editor P. LAUBSCHER.

Ecquid Novi: c/o South African Journal for Journalism Research, POB 106, Stellenbosch 7599; tel. (21) 8082625; fax (21) 8083488; e-mail novi@sun.ac.za; internet www.sun.ac.za/ecquidnovi; f. 1980; 2 a year; focus on role of the media in southern Africa and Africa; Editor ARNOLD S. DE BEER.

South African Journal of Wildlife Research: POB 217, Bloubergstrand 7436; tel. (21) 5541297; e-mail elma@mweb.co.za; internet www.sawma.co.za; f. 1970; journal of the Southern African Wildlife Management Asscn; 2 a year; Editor Dr MICHAEL SOMERS.

South African Law Journal: Faculty of Law, University of Cape Town, Private Bag Rondebosch 7700; POB 24299, Lansdowne 7779; tel. (21) 7633600; fax (21) 7970121; e-mail salj@law.uct.ac.za; f. 1884; Editor C. H. LEWIS; circ. 1,000.

NEWS AGENCIES

East Cape News (ECN) Pty Ltd: POB 897, Grahamstown 6140; tel. (46) 6361050; e-mail editor@ecn.co.za; internet www.ecn.co.za; f. 1997; fmrly East Cape News Agencies; Dir MIKE LOEWE.

South African Press Association (SAPA): Cotswold House, Greenacres Office Park, cnr Victory and Rustenburg Rds, Victory Park; POB 7766, Johannesburg 2000; tel. (11) 7821600; fax (11) 7821587; e-mail comms@sapa.org.za; internet www.sapa.org.za; f. 1938; Man. WIM J. H. VAN GILS; Editor MARK A. VAN DER VELDEN; 40 mems.

PRESS ASSOCIATIONS

Foreign Correspondents' Association of South Africa: POB 1136, Auckland Park, 2006; tel. and fax (11) 4860490; e-mail fca@onwe.co.za; internet www.fcasa.co.za; represents 175 int. journalists; Chair. JOHN CHIAHEMEN; Sec. MARTINA SCHWIKOWSKI.

Newspaper Association of South Africa: Nedbank Gardens, 5th Floor, 33 Bath Ave, Rosebank 2196, Johannesburg; POB 47180, Parklands 2121; tel. (11) 7213200; fax (11) 7213254; e-mail na@printmedia.org.za; internet www.printmedia.org.za; f. 1882; represents 42 national daily and weekly newspapers, and 178 community newspapers; Pres. TREVOR NCUBE.

Print Media SA: 2nd Floor, 7 St David's, St David's Office Park, St David's Place, Parktown 2193; POB 47180, Parklands 2121; tel. (11) 7213200; fax (11) 7213254; e-mail mamosat@printmedia.org.za; internet www.printmedia.org.za; f. 1995 following the restructuring of the Newspaper Press Union of Southern Africa; represents all aspects of the print media (newspapers and magazines); over 700 mems; CEO INGRID LOUW.

Publishers

Acorn Books: POB 4845, Randburg 2125; tel. (11) 8805768; fax (11) 8805768; e-mail acorbook@iafrica.com; f. 1985; Africana, general, natural history; Propr and Publr ELEANOR-MARY CADELL.

Jonathan Ball Publishers: 10–14 Watkins St, Denver Ext. 4, Johannesburg 2094; POB 33977, Jeppestown 2043; tel. (11) 6222900; fax (11) 6227610; e-mail orders@jonathanball.co.za; acquired by Via Afrika (Naspers Group) in 1992; fiction, reference, bibles, textbooks, general; imprints incl. AD Donker (literature), Delta (general fiction and non-fiction) and Sunbird; Man. Dir JONATHAN BALL.

BLAC Publishing House: POB 17, Athlone, Cape Town; f. 1974; general fiction, poetry; Man. Dir JAMES MATTHEWS.

Bible Society of South Africa: POB 5500, Tyger Valley 7536; tel. (21) 9108777; fax (21) 9108799; e-mail biblia@biblesociety.co.za; internet www.biblesociety.co.za; f. 1820; bibles and religious material in 11 official languages; CEO Rev. G. S. KRITZINGER.

Brenthurst Press (Pty) Ltd: POB 87184, Houghton 2041; tel. (11) 6466024; fax (11) 4861651; e-mail orders@brenthurst.co.za; internet www.brenthurst.org.za; f. 1974; Southern African history; Dir MARCELLE GRAHAM.

Clever Books: POB 13186, Hatfield 0028; tel. (12) 3423263; fax (12) 432376; e-mail elizabeth@cleverbooks.co.za; f. 1981; subsidiary of MacMillan Publrs; Man. Dir STEVEN CILLIERS.

Christelike Uitgewersmaatskappy (CUM): POB 1599, Vereeniging 1930; tel. (16) 4407000; fax (16) 4211748; e-mail orders@cabooks.co.za; internet www.cum.co.za; religious fiction and non-fiction.

Fisichem Publishers: Private Bag X3, Matieland 7602; tel. (21) 8870900; fax (21) 8839635; e-mail fisichem@iafrica.com; science study guides; Man. RETHA JORDAAN.

Flesch Publications: 11 Peninsula Rd, Zeekoevlei, Cape Town 7941; POB 31353, Grassy Park 7888; tel. (21) 7054317; fax (21) 7060766; e-mail sflesch@iafrica.com; f. 1954; biography, cookery, aviation; CEO STEPHEN FLESCH.

Fortress Books: POB 2475, Knysna 6570; tel. (44) 3826805; fax (44) 3826848; e-mail fortress@iafrica.com; internet www.uys.com/fortress; f. 1973; military history, biographies, financial; Man. Dir I. UYS.

Heinemann Publishers (Pty) Ltd: Heinemann House, Grayston Office Park, Bldg 3, 128 Peter Rd, Atholl Ext. 12, Sandton 2196; POB 781940, Sandown, Sandton 2146; tel. (11) 3228600; fax (11) 3228715; e-mail customerliaison@heinemann.co.za; internet www.heinemann.co.za; educational; incl. imprints Lexicon, Isando and Centaur; Man. Dir ORENNA KRUT.

Home Economics Publishers (Huishoudkunde Uitgewers): POB 7091, Stellenbosch 7599; tel. and fax (21) 8864722; e-mail mcv1@sun.ac.za; Man. M. C. VOSLOO.

Juta and Co Ltd: POB 14373, Kenwyn 7790, Cape Town; tel. (11) (21) 7633600; fax (21) 7627424; e-mail books@juta.co.za; internet www.juta.co.za; f. 1853; academic, educational, law, electronic; imprints incl. Double Storey (general contemporary), and University of Cape Town Press (scholarly and academic); CEO R. J. WILSON.

LAPA Publishers (Lees Afrikaans Praat Afrikaans): 380 Bosman St, POB 123, Pretoria 0001; tel. (12) 4010700; fax (12) 3244460; f. 1996 as the publishing arm of the Afrikaans Language and Culture Asscn; present name adopted in 2000; Afrikaans; general fiction and non-fiction; CEO WIM DE WET.

Learning Matters Africa: 341 West St, Durban 4001; POB 466, Durban 4000; tel. (31) 3053791; fax (31) 3077356; e-mail padams@adamsbooks.co.za; educational; CEO BRYAN PHILLIPS.

Lemur Books (Pty) Ltd (The Galago Publishing (1999) (Pty) Ltd): POB 1645, Alberton 1450; tel. (11) 9072029; fax (11) 8690890; e-mail lemur@mweb.co.za; internet www.galago.co.za; f. 1980; military, political, history, hunting, general; Man. Dir F. STIFF.

LexisNexis Butterworths SA: 215 North Ridge Rd, Morningside, Durban 4001; POB 792, Durban 4000; tel. (31) 2683111; fax (31) 2683108; e-mail customercare@lexisnexis.co.za; internet www.lexisnexis.co.za; f. 1948 as Butterworths; adopted LexisNexis name in 2001; jtly owned by Reed Elsevier, USA, and Kagiso Media; law, tax, accountancy; Chair. W. ROGER JARDINE; CEO WILLIAM J. LAST.

Lux Verbi-BM: POB 1822, Cape Town 8000; tel. (21) 8648237; fax (21) 8648292; e-mail epi@luxverbi-bm.co.za; internet www.luxverbi-bm.com; f. 1818 as the Dutch Reformed Church Publishing Co; merged with Bible Media in 1999; subsidiary of the Naspers Group; imprints incl. Hugenote, NG Kerk Uitgewers, Protea, and Waterkant; Christian media; CEO H. S. SPIES; Editor-in-Chief D. FOURIE.

Maskew Miller Longman (Pty) Ltd: cnr Forest Dr. and Logan Way, Pinelands 7405; POB 396, Cape Town 8000; tel. (21) 5326000; fax (21) 5310716; e-mail tembela@mml.co.za; internet www.mml.co.za; f. 1893 as Miller Maskew; merged with Longman in 1983; jtly owned by Pearson Education and Caxton Publrs and Printers Ltd; imprints incl. Kagiso Publishing (f. 1994; fmrly De Jager-HAUM) and Phumelela Books; educational and general; CEO JAPIE PIENAAR.

Methodist Publishing House: POB 13128, Woodstock, Cape Town 7915; tel. (21) 4483640; fax (21) 4483716; e-mail george@methbooks.co.za; f. 1894; religion and theology; Gen. Man. GEORGE VINE (acting).

NB Publishers: Naspers Bldg, 12th Floor, 40 Heerengracht, Roggebai 8012; POB 5050, Cape Town 8000; tel. (21) 4063033; fax (21) 4063812; e-mail nb@nb.co.za; internet www.nb.co.za; English, Afrikaans, Xhosa and Zulu; Human & Rousseau (f. 1959; general, children's and youth literature, cookery and self-help), Kwela (f. 1994; fiction), Pharos (dictionaries), Tafelberg (f. 1950; fiction and non-fiction, politics, children's and youth literature) and Best Books (educational texts); Head of Publishing C. T. BREYTENBACH.

Nasou—Via Afrika: 40 Heerengracht, Cape Town 8001; POB 5197, Cape Town 8000; tel. (21) 4063005; fax (21) 4063086; e-mail mdewitt@nasou.com; internet www.nasou-viaafrika.com; f. 1963; subsidiary of Via Afrika (Naspers Group); educational; imprints incl. Acacia, Action Publrs, Afritech, Afro, Atlas, Era, Juta, KZN Books, Gariep, Idem, Phoenix Education, Shortland and Y-Press Grade R-3; CEO LOUISE NAUDÉ.

Oxford University Press: POB 12119, N1 City, Cape Town 7463; tel. (21) 5962300; fax (21) 5961234; e-mail oxford.za@oup.com; internet www.oxford.co.za; f. 1914; Man. Dir LIEZE KOTZE.

SOUTH AFRICA

Directory

Protea Book House: 1067 Burnett St, Hatfield, Pretoria; POB 35110, Menlo Park, 0102 Pretoria; tel. (12) 3623444; fax (12) 3625688; e-mail protea@intekom.co.za; internet www.proteaboekhuis.co.za; f. 1997; art and photography, Afrikaans fiction, South African history, spiritual, academic and general; Dir NICOL STASSEN.

Random House (Pty) Ltd South Africa: POB 2002, Houghton 2041; tel. (11) 4843538; fax (11) 4846180; e-mail mail@randomhouse.co.za; f. 1966; general fiction; Man. Dir S. E. JOHNSON.

Shuter & Shooter Publishers (Pty) Ltd: 21C Cascades Cres., KwaZulu-Natal 3201; POB 13016, Cascades, Pietermaritzburg 3202; tel. (33) 3476100; fax (33) 3476130; internet www.shuters.com; f. 1921; educational, general and African languages and trade books; Man. Dir PRIMI CHETTY.

Struik New Holland Publishing (South Africa) (Pty) Ltd: 80 Mckenzie St, Gardens, Cape Town 8001; POB 1144, Cape Town 8000; tel. (21) 4624360; fax (21) 4619378; e-mail inquiry@booksite.co.za; general fiction and non-fiction, religious, women's issues, maps; imprints incl. Books of Africa, New Holland, Oshun, Struik, Two Dogs and Zebra; CEO BRIAN D. WOOTON.

University of KwaZulu-Natal Press (UKZN Press): Private Bag X01, Scottsville 3209; tel. (33) 2605226; fax (33) 2605801; e-mail books@ukzn.ac.za; internet www.ukznpress.co.za; academic and scholarly; Publr GLENN COWLEY; Editor SALLY HINES.

Van Schaik Publishers: POB 12681, Hatfield 0028; tel. (12) 3422765; fax (12) 4303563; e-mail vanschaik@vanschaiknet.com; internet www.vanschaiknet.com; f. 1915; acquired by Nasionale Pers, latterly (Via Afrika-Naspers Group) in 1986; English and Afrikaans; academic and scholarly; CEO. LEANNE MARTINI.

Wits University Press: PO Wits, Johannesburg 2050; tel. (11) 4845910; fax (11) 4845971; e-mail Veronica.Klipp@wits.ac.za; internet witspress.wits.ac.za; f. 1922; general trade, non-fiction and scholarly; Publr VERONICA KLIPP.

PUBLISHERS' ASSOCIATION

Publishers' Association of South Africa: Suite 305, 2nd Floor, The Foundry, Prestwich St, Green Point, Cape Town 8005; tel. (21) 4252721; fax (21) 4213270; e-mail dudley@publishsa.co.za; internet www.publishsa.co.za; f. 1992; promotes and protects the rights and responsibilities of the independent publishing sector in South Africa; Exec. Dir. DUDLEY H. SCHROEDER.

Broadcasting and Communications

REGULATORY AUTHORITY

Independent Communications Authority of South Africa (ICASA): Pinmill Farm, Blocks A, B, C and D, 164 Katherine St, Sandton 2146; Private Bag X10002, Marlboro 2063; tel. (11) 5663000; fax (11) 4441919; e-mail info@icasa.org.za; internet www.icasa.org.za; f. 2000 as successor to the Independent Broadcasting Authority (f. 1993) and South African Telecommunications Regulatory Authority (f. 1996); regulates telecommunications and broadcasting; Chair. PARIS MASHILE.

TELECOMMUNICATIONS

Cell C (Pty) Ltd: 150 Rivonia Rd, Sandown 2196; Private Bag X36, Benmore 2010, Johannesburg; tel. (11) 3244000; fax (11) 3244009; e-mail customerservice@cellc.co.za; internet www.cellc.co.za; f. 2000; subsidiary of 3C Telecommunications (60% owned by Oger Telecom South Africa, 40% by CellSAf); mobile cellular telecommunications provider; Chair. TALAAT LAHAM; CEO JEFFREY HEDBERG.

Mobile Telephone Networks (Pty) Ltd (MTN): 3 Alice Lane, Ext. 38, PMB 9955, Sandton 2146; tel. (11) 3016000; fax (11) 3018448; internet www.mtn.co.za; f. 1994; mobile cellular telecommunications provider; operations in 21 countries in Africa and the Middle East; 11m. subscribers in South Africa (2006); Chair. MATAMELA CYRIL RAMAPHOSA; Group Pres. and CEO PHUTHUMA NHLEKO.

Telkom SA Ltd: Telkom Towers North, 152 Proes St, Pretoria 0002; POB 925, Pretoria 0001; tel. (12) 3111007; fax (12) 3114031; e-mail letlapll@telkom.co.za; internet www.telkom.co.za; f. 1991; 38% govt-owned; ICT solutions service provider; Chair. SHIRLEY LUE ARNOLD; Exec. Dir PAPI MOLOTSANE.

Virgin Mobile South Africa (Pty) Ltd (VMSA): Citicorp Bldg, 2nd Floor, 145 West St, Sandton, Johannesburg; POB 78331, Sandton 2146; tel. (11) 3244000; fax (11) 3244113; e-mail paia@virginmobile.co.za; internet www.virginmobile.co.za; f. 2006; jt venture btwn Cell C and Virgin Mobile Telecoms Ltd, United Kingdom; mobile cellular telecommunications provider; CEO SAJEED SACRANIE.

Vodacom Group (Pty) Ltd: Vodacom Corporate Park, 082 Vodacom Blvd, Vodavalley, Midrand 1685; tel. (11) 6535000; e-mail corporate.affairs@vodacom.co.za; internet www.vodacom.co.za; f. 1993; 50% owned by Telkom SA Ltd, 50% by Vodafone Group PLC, United Kingdom; subsidiaries in the DRC (f. 2002), Lesotho (f. 1996), Mozambique (f. 2003) and Tanzania (f. 1999); Chair. OYAMA MABANDLA.

BROADCASTING

Radio

South African Broadcasting Corpn (SABC)—Radio: Private Bag X1, Auckland Park 2006, Johannesburg; tel. (11) 7149111; fax (11) 7149744; e-mail rpsales@sabc.co.za; internet www.sabc.co.za; f. 1936; comprises 15 public radio stations and three commercial radio stations broadcasting in 11 languages; Chair. Prof. PAULUS ZULU; CEO CHARLOTTE MAMPANE.

Domestic Services

Radio South Africa; Afrikaans Stereo; Radio 5; Radio 2000; Highveld Stereo; Good Hope Stereo; Radio Kontrei; RPN Stereo; Jacaranda Stereo; Radio Algoa (regional services); Radio Lotus (Indian service in English); Radio Metro (African service in English); Radio Lebowa; Radio Ndebele; Radio Sesotho; Setswana Stereo; Radio Swazi; Radio Tsonga; Radio Xhosa; Radio Zulu.

External Service

Channel Africa Network: POB 91313, Auckland Park 2006; tel. (11) 7142255; fax (11) 7142072; e-mail ntentenit@sabc.co.za; internet www.channelafrica.org; f. 1966; external service of SABC; broadcasts 217 hours per week in English, French, Portuguese, Kiswahili, Chinyanja and Silozi; Exec. Editor THAMI NTENTENI.

Television

In February 2007 the Government announced that the country would begin digital terrestrial broadcasting in November 2008 and that the country's analogue signal would be switched off in 2011.

e.tv: 5 Summit Rd, Hyde Park, Johannesburg 2196; Private Bag, X9044, Sandton 2146; tel. (11) 5379300; e-mail info@etv.co.uk; internet www.etv.co.uk; f. 1998; CEO MARCEL GOLDING.

Naspers: 40 Heerengracht, Cape Town 8001; tel. (21) 406 2121; internet www.naspers.co.za; provides subscription television through Multichoice, M-Net and SuperSport packages; CEO COBUS STOFBERG.

South African Broadcasting Corpn (SABC)—Television: Private Bag X41, Auckland Park 2006; tel. (11) 7149111; fax (11) 7145055; e-mail enterpri@sabc.co.za; internet www.sabc.co.za; transmissions began in 1976; broadcasts television services in 11 languages over three channels; SABC1 broadcasts in English, isiZulu, isiXhosa, isiNdebele and siSwati; SABC2 broadcasts in English, Afrikaans, Sesotho, Setswana, Sepedi, Xitsonga and Tshivendi; SABC3 broadcasts documentaries, educational programmes and sport in English; Chair. Prof. PAULUS ZULU; CEO DALI MPOFU.

Finance

(cap. = capital; auth. = authorized; res = reserves; dep. = deposits; m. = million; brs = branches; amounts in rand)

BANKING

In 2006 there were 30 commercial banks and 1,354 microfinance institutions operating in South Africa. The five largest banks—Standard Bank, Nedbank, ABSA, FirstRand, and Investec—controlled some 86% of total banking assets.

Central Bank

South African Reserve Bank: 370 Church St, POB 427, Pretoria 0002; tel. (12) 3133911; fax (12) 3133197; internet www.resbank.co.za; f. 1921; cap. 2.0m., res 3,429.1m., dep. 71,821.9m. (March 2002); Gov. TITO T. MBOWENI; Sen. Dep. Gov. X. P. GUMA; 7 brs.

Commercial Banks

ABSA Bank Ltd: ABSA Towers East, 3rd Floor, 170 Main St, Johannesburg 2001; tel. (11) 3504000; fax (11) 3503768; e-mail absa@absa.co.za; internet www.absa.co.za; total assets 306,848m. (Mar. 2004); Chair. Dr DANIE CRONJÉ; CEO STEVE F. BOOYSEN; 726 brs.

African Bank Investments Ltd: 59 16th Rd, Private Bag X170, Midrand 1685; tel. (11) 2569000; fax (11) 2569217; internet www.abil.co.za; f. 1975; cap. 1,876.4m., res 186.7m., dep. 706.2m. (Sept. 2002); CEO LEONIDAS KIRKINIS; 268 brs.

Albaraka Bank Ltd: 134 Commercial Rd, 1st Floor, Durban 4001; POB 4395, Durban 4000; tel. (31) 3662800; fax (31) 3052631; internet

SOUTH AFRICA

www.albaraka.co.za; f. 1989; operates according to Islamic principles; cap. 41.0m., res 13.5m., dep. 551.7m. (Dec. 2002); Chair. A. A. SABBAHI; Deputy CEO M. G. MCLEAN.

AMB Holdings Ltd: 18 Fricker Rd, Illovo, Sandton 2196; POB 786833, Sandton 2146; tel. (11) 2152000; fax (11) 268886; e-mail asprague@amb.co.za; internet www.amb.co.za; Exec. Dir ZENZO LUSENGO; CEO ANDREW SPRAGUE.

Brait South Africa Ltd: 9 Fricker Rd, Illovo Blvd, Illovo, Sandton 2196; Private Bag X1, Northlands 2116; tel. (11) 5071000; fax (11) 5071001; internet www.brait.com; f. 1998; subsidiary of Brait SA, Luxembourg; total assets 802.3m. (Mar. 2004); CEO JOHN COULTER.

FirstRand Bank Ltd: 4 Merchant Place, 4th Floor, cnr Fredman Dr. and Rivonia Rd, Sandton 2196; POB 786273, Sandton 2146; tel. (11) 2821808; fax (11) 2828065; e-mail information@firstrand.co.za; internet www.firstrand.co.za; f. 1971 as First National Bank of Southern Africa; merged with Rand Bank in 1998; total assets 323,500m. (June 2004); Chair. GERRIT T. FERREIRA; CEO LAURITZ L. DIPPENAAR; 650 brs.

GBS Mutual Bank: 18–20 Hill St, Grahamstown 6139; POB 114, Grahamstown 6140; tel. (46) 6227109; fax (46) 6228855; e-mail gbs@gbsbank.co.za; internet www.gbsbank.co.za; f. 1877; total assets 301.1m. (Dec. 2003); Chair. C. K. M. STONE; Man. Dir T. C. S. TAGG; 1 br.

HBZ Bank Ltd: 135 Jan Hofmeyr Rd, Westville, Durban 3631; POB 1536, Wandsbeck 3631; tel. (31) 2674400; fax (31) 2671193; e-mail sazone@hbzbank.co.za; internet www.habibbank.com; f. 1995; subsidiary of Habib Bank Ltd; total assets 650.4m. (Dec. 2003); Chair. MUHAMMAD HABIB; CEO ZAFAR ALAM KHAN; 4 brs.

Imperial Bank Ltd: 140 Boeing Rd, East Elma Park, Edenvale, Gauteng 1610; POB 3567, Edenvale 1610; tel. (11) 8792000; fax (11) 8792234; e-mail phassim@imperialbank.co.za; internet www.imperialbank.co.za; f. 1996; 51.1% owned by Nedbank, 49.9% Imperial Holdings; total assets 12,955.0m. (Dec. 2003); Chair. W. G. LYNCH; CEO R. VAN WYK.

Meeg Bank Ltd: Meeg Bank Bldg, 60 Sutherland St, Umtata; POB 332, Umtata 5100; tel. (47) 5026200; fax (47) 5311098; internet www.meegbank.co.za; f. 1977; fmrly Bank of Transkei; name changed Oct. 1998; total assets 782.4m. (March 2003); Chair. Prof. WISEMAN LUMKILE NKUHLU; Man. Dir. EMIL G. KALTENBRÜNN; 5 brs.

Mercantile Bank Ltd: Mercantile Lisbon House, 142 West St, Sandown 2196; POB 782699, Sandton 2146; tel. (11) 3020300; fax (11) 3020729; internet www.mercantile.co.za; f. 1965; subsidiary of Mercantile Lisbon Bank Holdings; total assets 2,224.8m. (Dec. 2003); Chair. Dr JOAQUIM A. S. DE ANDRADE CAMPOS; CEO D. J. BROWN; 14 brs.

Nedbank Ltd: 135 Rivonia Rd, Sandown 2196, Johannesburg 2001; POB 1144, Johannesburg 2000; tel. (11) 2940999; fax (11) 2950999; e-mail nedbankgroupir@nedbank.co.za; internet www.nedbankgroup.co.za; f. 1988; name changed from Nedcor Bank Ltd Nov. 2002; subsidiary of Nedbank Group Ltd; cap. 14,400m., res 6,300m., dep. 271,200m. (June 2006); Chair. REUEL J. KHOZA; CEO TOM BOARDMAN; 459 brs.

Rennies Bank Ltd: Rennie House, 11th Floor, 19 Ameshoff St, Braamfontein 2001, Johannesburg; POB 185, Johannesburg 2000; tel. (11) 4073000; fax (11) 4073322; e-mail agent2@bank.rennies.co.za; internet www.renniesbank.co.za; f. 1850; subsidiary of Bidvest Group Ltd; foreign exchange, trade finance and related activities; total assets 313,772m. (June 2003); Chair. J. J. PAMENSKY; CEO DAVID WALKER; over 60 brs.

South African Bank of Athens Ltd: Bank of Athens Bldg, 116 Marshall St, Johannesburg 2001; POB 7781, Johannesburg 2000; tel. (11) 6344300; fax (11) 8381001; e-mail karenc@bankofathens.co.za; internet www.bankofathens.co.za; f. 1947; 99.46% owned by National Bank of Greece; cap. 94.5m., dep. 531.7m. (Dec. 2004); Chair. TAKIS ARAPOGLOU; CEO HECTOR ZARCA; 10 brs.

Standard Bank Ltd: Standard Bank Centre, 5 Simmonds St, Johannesburg 2000; POB 7725, Johannesburg 2000; tel. (11) 6369111; fax (11) 6364207; e-mail information@standardbank.co.za; internet www.standardbank.co.za; f. 1862; cap. 5,703.0m., res 9,472.0m., dep. 204,812.0m. (Dec. 2003); Chair. DEREK E. COOPER; CEO SIM TSHABALALA; 997 brs.

Teba Bank Ltd: Sanhill Park, 1 Eglin Rd, Sunninghill; Private Bag X101, Sunninghill 2157; tel. (11) 5185000; fax (11) 2031554; e-mail corpcomm@tebabank.com; internet www.tebabank.co.za; f. 2000; fmrly Teba Savings Fund; specializes in micro-finance and providing financial services to mining communities; total assets 2,200.0m. (Feb. 2006); Man. Dir ZIENZI MUSAMIRAPAMWE; 23 brs, 70 mine outlets and 29 agencies.

Merchant Bank

Marriott Merchant Bank Ltd: Kingsmead Office Park, Durban 4001; POB 572, Durban 4000; tel. (31) 3661010; fax (31) 3661222; e-mail info@marriott.co.za; internet www.marriott.co.za; f. 1994; CEO SIMON PEARSE.

Investment Banks

Cadiz Investment Bank Ltd: Fernwood House, 1st Floor, The Oval, 1 Oakdale Rd, Newlands 7700; POB 44547, Claremont 7735; tel. 6578300; fax 6578301; e-mail reception@cadiz.co.za; internet www.cadiz.co.za; f. 1993; 15% owned by Investec, 11% Makana Financial Services; total assets 298.1m. (Dec. 2003); Chair. COLIN HALL; CEO RAM BARKAI.

Investec Bank Ltd: 100 Grayston Dr., Sandown, Sandton 2196; POB 785700, Sandton 2146; tel. (11) 2867000; fax (11) 2867777; internet www.investec.com; f. 1974; cap. 12.6m., res 7.7m., dep. 70.0m. (Sept. 2006); CEO S. KOSEFF; 6 brs.

Sasfin Bank Ltd: Sasfin Pl., 13–15 Scott St, Waverley 2090; POB 95104, Grant Park 2051; tel. (11) 8097500; fax (11) 8872489; e-mail info@sasfin.com; internet www.sasfin.com; f. 1951; subsidiary of Sasfin Holdings Ltd; total assets 2,460m. (2006); Chair. MARTIN GLATT; CEO ROLAND SASSOON.

Development Bank

Development Bank of Southern Africa (DBSA): 1258 Lever Rd, Headway Hill; POB 1234, Halfway House, Midrand 1685; tel. (11) 3133911; fax (11) 3133086; e-mail info@dbsa.org; internet www.dbsa.org; total assets 23,684.5m. (March 2004); f. 1983; Chair. JAYASEELAN NAIDOO; CEO MANDLA S. V. GANTSHO.

Bankers' Association

Banking Council of South Africa: 17 Harrison St, 10th Floor, POB 61674, Marshalltown 2107; tel. (11) 3703500; fax (11) 8365509; e-mail banking@banking.org.za; internet www.banking.org.za; f. 1993; 15,000 mems; Chair. E. R. BOSMAN; CEO ROBERT S. K. TUCKER.

STOCK EXCHANGE

JSE Ltd: 2 Gwen Lane, Sandown, Sandton; Private Bag X991174, Sandton 2146; tel. (11) 5207000; fax (11) 5208584; internet www.jse.co.za; f. 1887 as Johannesburg Stock Exchange; present name adopted in 2005; in late 1995 legislation was enacted providing for the deregulation of the Stock Exchange; automated trading commenced in June 1996; demutualized in July 2005 and became a listed co in June 2006; CEO R. M. LOUBSER.

INSURANCE

In 2003 South Africa was served by 96 short-term and 69 long-term insurers, and six reinsurance firms.

Allianz Insurance Ltd: 40 Ashford Rd, Parkwood, Johannesburg 2001; POB 62228, Marshalltown 2107; tel. (11) 4421111; fax (11) 4421125; Chair. D. DU PREEZ; Man. Dir IAN BAIN.

Clientèle Life Assurance Co: Clientèle House, Morning View Office Park, cnr Rivonia and Alon Rds, Morningside, Johannesburg; POB 1316, Rivonia 2128; tel. (11) 3203333; e-mail services@clientelelife.com; internet www.clientelelife.com; f. 1997; subsidiary of Hollard Insurance Group; Chair. G. Q. ROUTLEDGE; Man. Dir G. J. SOLL.

Credit Guarantee Insurance Corpn of Africa Ltd: 31 Dover St, POB 125, Randburg 2125; tel. (11) 8897000; fax (11) 8861027; e-mail info@cgic.co.za; internet www.creditguarantee.co.za; f. 1956; Chair. ALWYN MARTIN; Man. Dir MIKE TRUTER.

Discovery: Discovery Bldg, 155 West St cnr Alice Lane, Sandton 2146; POB 786722, Sandton 2146; tel. (11) 5292888; fax (11) 5293590; e-mail worldinfo@discovery.co.za; internet www.discoveryworld.co.za; f. 1992; 64% owned by FirstRand; health and life assurance; Chair. LAURITZ L. DIPPENAAR; CEO ADRIAN GORE.

Liberty Life: Liberty Life Centre, 1 Ameshoff St, Braamfontein, Johannesburg 2017; POB 10499, Johannesburg 2000; tel. (11) 4083911; fax (11) 4082109; e-mail info@liberty.co.za; internet www.liberty.co.za; f. 1958; Chair. D. E. COOPER; CEO BRUCE HEMPHILL.

Metropolitan Life Ltd: Parc du Cap Complex, Mispel Rd, Cape Town; POB 2212, Bellville 7535; tel. (21) 9405911; fax (21) 9405730; e-mail info@metropolitan.co.za; internet www.metropolitan.co.za; Chair. D. E. MOSENEKE; Man. Dir P. R. DOYLE.

Momentum Life Assurers Ltd: 268 West Ave, Centurion, Gauteng 0157; POB 7400, Centurion 0046; tel. (12) 6718911; fax (12) 6636288; e-mail corporate@momentum.co.za; internet www.momentum.co.za; f. 1967; Chair. LAURIE DIPPENAAR; Man. Dir HILLIE P. MEYER.

Mutual & Federal Insurance Co Ltd: Mutual Federal Centre, 75 President St, POB 1120, Johannesburg 2000; tel. (11) 3749111; fax (11) 3742652; internet www.mf.co.za; f. 1970; Chair. K. T. M. SAGGERS; Man. Dir B. CAMPBELL.

Old Mutual (South African Mutual Life Assurance Society): Mutualpark, Jan Smuts Dr., POB 66, Cape Town 8001; tel. (21) 5099111; fax (21) 5094444; e-mail contact@oldmutual.com; internet

SOUTH AFRICA

www.oldmutual.com; f. 1845; Chair. MICHAEL J. LEVETT; CEO JAMES SUTCLIFFE.

Santam Ltd: Santam Head Office, 1 Sportica Cres., Bellville 7530; POB 3881, Tyger Valley 7536; tel. (21) 9157000; fax (21) 9140700; internet www.santam.co.za; f. 1918; Chair. M. H. DALING; Man. Dir STEFFEN GIBERT.

South African National Life Assurance Co Ltd (SANLAM): 2 Strand Rd, Bellville; POB 1, Sanlamhof 7532; tel. (21) 9165000; fax (21) 9479440; e-mail life@sanlam.co.za; internet www.sanlam.co.za; f. 1918; Chair. Dr J. VAN ZYL.

Zurich Insurance Co South Africa Ltd: 70 Fox St, Johannesburg 2001; tel. (11) 3709111; fax (11) 8368018; e-mail nick.beyers@zurich.co.za; internet www.saeagle.co.za; fmrly South African Eagle Insurance Co Ltd; rebranded as above in 2007; Chair. M. C. SOUTH; CEO N. V. BEYERS.

Association

South African Insurance Association (SAIA): JCC House, 3rd Floor, 27 Owl St, Milpark; POB 30619, Braamfontein 2017; tel. (11) 7265381; fax (11) 7265351; e-mail adele@saia.co.za; internet www.saia.co.za; f. 1973; represents short-term insurers; Chair. ADAM SAMIE; CEO BARRY SCOTT.

Trade and Industry

DEVELOPMENT ORGANIZATIONS

Business Partners Ltd: 5 Wellington Rd, Parktown, Johannesburg 2193; POB 7780, Johannesburg 2000; tel. (11) 4808700; fax (11) 6422791; e-mail enquiries@businesspartners.co.za; internet www.businesspartners.co.za; f. 1981 as Small Business Devt Corpn; invests in, and provides services to, small and medium enterprises; Chair. JOHANN RUPERT; Man. Dir JO' SCHWENKE.

Industrial Development Corpn of South Africa Ltd (IDC): 19 Fredman Dr., Sandown 2196; POB 784055, Sandton 2146; tel. (11) 2693000; fax (11) 2693116; e-mail callcentre@idc.co.za; internet www.idc.co.za; f. 1940; promotes entrepreneurship and competitiveness; total assets 36,593m.; Chair. Dr WENDY Y. N. LUHABE; CEO G. M. QHENA.

The Independent Development Trust: Glenwood Office Park, cnr Oberon and Sprite Sts, Faerie Glen, Pretoria; POB 73000, Lynnwood Ridge 0040; tel. (12) 8452000; fax (12) 3480939; f. 1990; advances the national. devt programme working with govt and communities in fields incl. poverty relief, infrastructure, empowerment, employment and capacity building; CEO THEMBI NWEDAMUSTWU.

National Productivity Institute: Private Bag 235, Midrand 1685; tel. (11) 8485300; fax (11) 8485555; e-mail info@npi.co.za; internet www.npi.co.za; f. 1968; Chair. Dr J. M. LAUBSCHER (acting); Exec. Dir Dr YVONNE DLADLA.

CHAMBER OF COMMERCE

South African Chamber of Business (SACOB): 24 Sturdee Ave, Rosebank, Johannesburg; POB 213, Saxonwold 2132; tel. (11) 4463800; fax (11) 4463850; e-mail info@sacob.co.za; internet www.sacob.co.za; f. 1990 by merger of Asscn of Chambers of Commerce and Industry and South African Federated Chamber of Industries; Pres. D. PENFOLD; Deputy Pres. Prof. A. LOUW.

CHAMBERS OF INDUSTRIES

Bloemfontein Chamber of Commerce and Industry: 1st Floor, Tourism Centre, 30 Park Rd, Bloemfontein; POB 87, Bloemfontein 9301; tel. (51) 4473369; fax (51) 4475064; internet www.bcci.co.za; Pres. MOSS MOTSHUMI; c. 550 mems (2006).

Cape Town Regional Chamber of Commerce and Industry: Cape Chamber House, 19 Louis Gradner St, Foreshore, Cape Town 8001; tel. (21) 4024300; fax (21) 4024302; e-mail info@capechamber.co.za; internet www.capechamber.co.za; f. 1804; Pres. JANINE MYBURGH; 4,632 mems.

Chamber of Commerce and Industry–Johannesburg: JCC House, 6th Floor, Empire Rd, Milpark; Private Bag 34, Auckland Park 2006; tel. (11) 7265300; fax (11) 4822000; e-mail info@jcci.co.za; internet www.jcci.co.za; f. 1890; CEO KEITH BREBNOR; 3,800 mems.

Durban Chamber of Commerce and Industry: POB 1506, Durban 4000; tel. (31) 3351000; fax (31) 3321288; e-mail chamber@durbanchamber.co.za; internet www.durbanchamber.co.za; CEO Prof. BONKE DUMISA; 3,500 mems.

Gauteng North Chamber of Commerce and Industry (GNCCI): Tshwane Events Centre, Soutter St, Pretoria; POB 2164, Pretoria 0001; tel. (12) 3271487; fax (12) 3271490; internet www.gncci.co.za; f. 1929; fmrly Pretoria Business and Agricultural Centre; merged with Pretoria Sakekamer in 2004; Chair. BERT BADENHORST; CEO WIM DU PLESSIS; over 900 mems.

Directory

Pietermaritzburg Chamber of Business (PCB): POB 11734, Dorpspruit, Pietermaritzburg 3206; tel. (33) 3452747; fax (33) 3944151; e-mail pcb@pcb.org.za; internet www.pcb.org.za; f. 2002 as successor to the Pietermaritzburg Chamber of Commerce and Industries (f. 1910); CEO ANDREW LAYMAN; 880 mems.

Port Elizabeth Regional Chamber of Commerce and Industry (PERCCI): 200 Norvic Dr., Greenacres, Port Elizabeth 6045; KPMG House, POB 63866, Greenacres 6057; tel. (41) 3731122; fax (41) 3731142; e-mail info@pechamber.org.za; internet www.percci.co.za; f. 1995; CEO ODWA MTATI; 814 mems.

Wesvaal Chamber of Business (WESCOB): POB 7167, Flamwood 2572; tel. (18) 4842952; fax (86) 6936365; e-mail chamber@gds.co.za; f. 1898; Pres. JOHAN SMIT; c. 320 mems.

INDUSTRIAL AND TRADE ORGANIZATIONS

Association of Cementitious Material Producers: POB 10181, Centurion 0046; tel. (12) 6635146; fax (12) 6636036; e-mail naudek.acmp@mweb.co.za; f. 2002; Chair. ORRIE FENN.

Cape Wools: POB 2191, Port Elizabeth 6056; tel. (41) 544301; fax (41) 546760; e-mail onav@capewools.co.za; internet www.capewools.co.za; f. 1997; Section 21 service company; seven mems: three appointed by wool producer orgs, two by the Wool Textile Council, one by Wool Brokers and Traders and one by Labour; Chair. GEOFF KINGWILL; Gen. Man. ANDRÉ STRYDOM.

Chamber of Mines of South Africa: Chamber of Mines Bldg, 5 Hollard St, POB 61809, Marshalltown 2107; tel. (11) 4987100; fax (11) 0865024757; e-mail webmaster@bullion.org.za; internet www.bullion.org.za; f. 1889; Pres. SIPHO NKOSI.

Clothing Trade Council (CloTrade): 35 Siemers Rd, 6th Floor, Doornfontein; POB 2303, Johannesburg 2000; tel. (11) 4020664; fax (11) 4020667; f. 2002; successor to the Clothing Fed. of South Africa; Pres. JACK KIPLING.

Grain Milling Federation: POB 7262, Centurion 0046; tel. (12) 6631660; fax (12) 6633109; e-mail info@grainmilling.org.za; internet www.grainmilling.org.za; f. 1944; Exec. Dir JANNIE DE VILLIERS.

Industrial Rubber Manufacturers' Association of South Africa: POB 91267, Auckland Park 2006; tel. (11) 4822524; fax (11) 7261344; f. 1978; Chair. Dr D. DUNCAN.

Master Builders South Africa (MBSA): POB 1619, Halfway House, Midrand 1685; tel. (11) 2059000; fax (11) 3151644; e-mail info@mbsa.org.za; internet www.mbsa.org.za; f. 1904; fmrly known as Building Industries Fed. South Africa; President EUNICE FORBES; CEO PIERRE FOURIE; 4,000 mems.

Master Diamond Cutters' Association of South Africa: Private Bag X1, Suite 105, Excom 2023; tel. (11) 3341930; fax (11) 3341933; e-mail info@masingita.co.za; f. 1928; Pres. MACDONALD TEMANE; 76 mems.

National Association of Automobile Manufacturers of South Africa: Nedbank Plaza, 1st Floor, cnr Church and Beatrix Sts, Pretoria 0002; POB 40611, Arcadia 0007; tel. (12) 3232980; fax (12) 3263232; e-mail naamsa@iafrica.com; f. 1935; Dir N. M. W. VERMEULEN; 18 full mems and 10 associate mems.

National Chamber of Milling, Inc: POB 7262, Centurion 0046; tel. (12) 6631660; fax (12) 6633109; e-mail info@grainmilling.org.za; internet www.grainmilling.org.za; f. 1936; Exec. Dir JANNIE DE VILLIERS.

National Textile Manufacturers' Association: POB 1506, Durban 4000; tel. (31) 3013692; fax (31) 3045255; f. 1947; Sec. PETER MCGREGOR; 9 mems.

Plastics Federation of South Africa: 18 Gazelle Rd, Corporate Park South, Old Pretoria Rd, Midrand; Private Bag X68, Halfway House, Midrand 1685; tel. (11) 3144021; fax (11) 3143764; internet www.plasticsinfo.co.za; f. 1979; Exec. Dir DAVID HUGHES; 10 mems.

Printing Industries Federation of South Africa (PIFSA): Printech Ave, Laser Park, POB 1084, Honeydew 2040; tel. (11) 6993000; fax (11) 6993010; e-mail pifsa@pifsa.org; internet www.pifsa.org; f. 1916; CEO C. W. J. SYKES; c. 900 mems (representing 65% of printers in South Africa); six additional regional bodies.

Retail Motor Industry Organization (RMI): POB 2940, Randburg 2125; tel. (11) 8866300; fax (11) 7894525; e-mail rmi@rmi.org.za; internet www.rmi.org.za; f. 1908; affiliates throughout southern Africa; CEO JEFF OSBORNE; 7,800 mems.

South African Dairy Foundation: POB 72300, Lynnwood Ridge, Pretoria 0040; tel. (12) 3485345; fax (12) 3486284; e-mail dairy-foundation@pixie.co.za; f. 1980; Sec. S. L. VAN COLLER; 59 mems.

South African Federation of Civil Engineering Contractors (SAFCEC): POB 644, Bedfordview 2008; tel. (11) 4551700; fax (11) 4501715; e-mail admin@safcec.org.za; internet www.safcec.org.za; f. 1939; Dir H. P. LANGENHOVEN; 300 mems.

South African Fruit and Vegetable Canners' Association (Pty) Ltd (SAFVCA): Hoofstraat 258 Main St, POB 6175, Paarl 7620; tel. (21) 8711308; fax (21) 8725930; e-mail jill@safvca.co.za; f. 1953; Gen. Man. JILL ATWOOD-PALM; 9 mems.

South African Inshore Fishing Industry Association (Pty) Ltd: POB 2066, Cape Town 8000; tel. (21) 251500; f. 1953; Chair. W. A. LEWIS; Man. S. J. MALHERBE; 4 mems.

South African Oil Expressers' Association: Cereal Centre, 6th Floor, 11 Leyds St, Braamfontein 2017; tel. (11) 7251280; f. 1937; Sec. Dr R. DU TOIT; 14 mems.

South African Paint Manufacturers' Association: POB 751605, Gardenview, Johannesburg 2047; tel. (11) 4552503; fax (11) 4552502; e-mail sapma@sapma.org.za; internet www.sapma.org.za; Chair. DERYCK SPENCE; 80 mems.

South African Petroleum Industry Association (SAPIA): ABSA Centre, 14th Floor, Adderley St, Cape Town 8001; POB 7082, Roggebai 8012; tel. (21) 4198054; fax (21) 4198058; internet www.sapia.co.za; f. 1994; represents South Africa's six principal petroleum cos; Chair. MONWABISI FANDESO; Dir CONNEL NGCUKANA.

South African Sugar Association (SASA): 170 Flanders Dr., POB 700, Mount Edgecombe 4300; tel. (31) 5087000; fax (31) 5087199; internet www.sugar.org.za; Exec. Dir M. K. TRIKAM.

Includes:

South African Sugar Millers' Association Ltd (SASMAL): POB 1000, Mt Edgecombe 4300; tel. (31) 5087300; fax (31) 5087310; e-mail sasmal@sasa.org.za; represents interests of sugar millers and refiners within the operations of SASA; Exec. Dir D. W. HARDY; 6 mem. cos.

Sugar Manufacturing and Refining Employers' Association (SMREA): POB 1000, Mount Edgecombe 4300; tel. (31) 5087300; fax (31) 5087310; e-mail sasmal@sasa.org.za; f. 1947; regulates relations between mems and their employees; participates in the Bargaining Council for the sugar manufacturing and refining industry; Chair. B. V. LANE; 6 mem. cos.

South African Wool Textile Council: POB 2201, North End, Port Elizabeth 6056; tel. (41) 4845252; fax (41) 4845629; Sec. BEATTY-ANNE STARKEY.

Steel and Engineering Industries Federation of South Africa (SEIFSA): POB 1338, Johannesburg 2000; tel. (11) 2989400; fax (11) 2989500; e-mail info@seifsa.co.za; internet www.seifsa.co.za; f. 1943; Exec. Dir. BRIAN ANGUS; 38 affiliated trade asscns representing 2,350 mems.

VinPro (SA): POB 1411, Suider-Paarl 7624; tel. (21) 8073322; fax (21) 8632079; e-mail lerouxj@vinpro.co.za; internet www.vinpro.co.za; f. 1979; represents wine producers; Chair. ABRIE BOTHA; Exec. Dir JOS LE ROUX.

UTILITIES

Electricity

Electricity Supply Commission (ESKOM): POB 1091, Johannesburg 2000; tel. (11) 8008111; fax (11) 8004390; e-mail PAIA@eskom.co.za; internet www.eskom.co.za; f. 1923; state-controlled; CEO P. J. MAROGA.

Gas

SASOL Gas: POB 4211, Randburg 2125; tel. (11) 8897600; fax (11) 8897955; internet www.sasol.com/gas; f. 1964; Man. Dir HANS NAUDÉ.

Water

Umgeni Water: 310 Burger St, Pietermaritzburg 3201; tel. (331) 3411111; fax (331) 3411167; e-mail info@umgeni.co.za; internet www.umgeni.co.za/; f. 1974; CEO MZIMKULU MSIWA.

Water Research Commission: Private Bag X03, Gezina 0031; tel. (12) 3300340; fax (12) 3312565; e-mail orders@wrc.org.za; internet www.wrc.org.za; Chair. Prof. H. C. KASAN; CEO Dr SNOWY KHOZA.

TRADE UNIONS

According to COSATU, some 40% of workers were unionized at March 2005. Under amendments to the Labour Relations Act (LRA), 1995, introduced in 2002, the Government sought to eliminate illegitimate trade unions and employers' organizations. The provisions of the LRA also stipulated that organizations that failed to provide annual audited financial accounts would be deregistered.

Trade Union Federations

Confederation of South African Workers' Unions: Constancia Bldg, 7th Floor, Room 701, 291 Andries St, Pretoria; POB 877, Pretoria 0001; tel. (12) 3224961; fax (12) 3224964; e-mail consawu@mweb.co.za; internet www.consawu.co.za; f. 2003; affiliated to World Confed. of Labour and Dem. Org. of African Workers' Trade Unions; Pres. JOEL MFINGWANA; Gen. Sec. KHULILE NKUSHUBANA.

Affiliates with 20,000 or more mems include:

National Union of Public Service and Allied Workers (NUPSAW): Mercedes Benz Bldg, 2nd Floor, 11 Schoemen St, Pretoria; POB 11459, Tramshed 0126; tel. (12) 3282236; fax (012) 3286410; e-mail nupsaw@mweb.co.za; internet www.nupsaw.co.za; f. 1998; Pres. EZRA MFINWANA; Gen. Sec. SUCCESS MATAITSANE; c. 42,000 (2005).

Other organizations affiliated to CONSAWU include: the Asscn of Metal, Iron and General Workers' Union; the Asscn Trade Union of South African Workers; the Brick and General Workers' Union; Building, Wood and Allied Workers' Union of South Africa; the Building Workers' Union; the Food and Gen. Workers' Union; the Commercial Workers' Union of South Africa; the Food, Cleaning and Security Workers' Union; the Fed. Council of Retail and Allied Workers'; the Hotel and Allied Restaurant Workers' Union; the Movement for Social Justice; the Nat. Certified Fishing and Allied Workers' Union; the Nat. Construction, Building and Allied Workers' Union; the Nat. Union of Tertiary Education of South Africa; the Professional Educators' Union; the Professional Employees' Trade Union of South Africa; the Progressive Gen. Employees Asscn of South Africa; the Progressive Trade Union of South Africa; Solidarity; the South African Building and Allied Workers' Org.; the South African Domestic and Gen. Workers' Union; the South African Food, Retail and Agricultural Workers' Union; the Transport Action, Retail and Gen. Workers' Union; the Trawler and Line Fishermen's Union; the Westcoast Workers' Union; and the Workers' Labour Council–South Africa.

Congress of South African Trade Unions (COSATU): COSATU House, 4th Floor, 1–5 Leyds St, Braamfontein; POB 1019, Johannesburg 2000; tel. (11) 3394911; fax (11) 3396940; internet www.cosatu.org.za; f. 1985; 21 trade union affiliates representing c. 1.8m. paid-up mems; Pres. SDUMO DLAMINI (acting); Gen. Sec. ZWELINZIMA VAVI.

Affiliates with 20,000 or more mems include:

Chemical, Energy, Paper, Printing, Wood and Allied Workers' Union (CEPPWAWU): Umoya House, 3rd Floor, 2–6 New St, South Ghandi Sq., Johannesburg 2001; POB 3219, Johannesburg 2000; tel. (11) 8332870; fax (11) 8332883; e-mail secretariat@ceppwawu.org.za; f. 1999 by merger of the Chemical Workers' Industrial Union and Paper, Printing, Wood and the Allied Workers' Union; represents workers in the petrochemical, consumer chemical, rubber, plastics, glass and ceramics, printing, pulp and paper, furniture and woodworking industries; Pres. PASCO DYANI; Gen. Sec. WELILE NOLINGO; Nat. Treas. MARY NXUMALO; 61,768 mems (2006).

Communication Workers' Union (CWU): 29 Rissik St, 3rd Floor, Johannesburg 2001; POB 10248, Johannesburg 2000; tel. (11) 8388188; fax (11) 8388727; e-mail membership@cwu.org.za; internet www.cwu.org.za; f. 1996 by merger of the Post Office Employees Asscn, the Post and Telecommunication Workers Asscn and the South African Post Telecommunication Employees Asscn; Pres. JOE CHAUKE; Gen. Sec. MACVICAR B. DYASOPU; 44,000 mems (2006).

Democratic Nursing Organisation of South Africa (DENOSA): 605 Church St, Pretoria 0001; POB 1280, Pretoria 0001; tel. (12) 3432315; fax (12) 3440750; internet www.denosa.org.za; f. 1996; Pres. EPHRAIM P. MAFALO; Gen.-Sec. THEMBEKA T. GWAGWA; 64,165 mems (2006).

Food and Allied Workers' Union (FAWU): Vuyisile Mini Centre, cnr NY1 and NY110, Guguletu, Cape Town; POB 1234, Woodstock 7915; tel. (21) 6379040; fax (21) 6379190; e-mail admin@fawu.org.za; affiliated to the Int. Union of Food, Agricultural, Hotel, Restaurant, Catering, Tobacco and Allied Workers' Asscns; Pres. (vacant); Gen. Sec. KATISHI MASEMOLA; 111,029 mems (2006).

National Education, Health and Allied Workers' Union (NEHAWU): 56 Marshall St, Marshalltown, Johannesburg; POB 10812, Johannesburg 2000; tel. (11) 8332902; fax (11) 8343416; e-mail bongi@nehawu.org.za; internet www.nehawu.org.za; f. 1987; affiliated to the Public Services Int.; Pres. NOLUTHANDO MAYENDE-SIBIYA; Gen. Sec. FIKILE MAJOLA; 192,739 mems (2006).

National Union of Metalworkers of South Africa (NUMSA): NUMSA Bldg, 153 Bree St, cnr Becker St, Newtown, Johannesburg 2001; POB 260483, Excom 2023; tel. (11) 6891700; fax (11) 8336408; internet www.numsa.org.za; affiliated to the Int. Metalworkers' Fed.; represents workers in the engineering, motor, tyre, rubber and automobile assembly industries; Pres. MTHUTHUZELI TOM; Gen. Sec. SILUMKO NONDWANGU; 216,808 mems (2006).

National Union of Mineworkers (NUM): 7 Rissik St, cnr Frederick St, Johannesburg 2000; POB 2424, Johannesburg 2000; tel. (11) 3772000; fax (11) 8360367; e-mail zmakue@num.org.za; internet www.num.org.za; f. 1982; represents workers in the mining, energy, construction, building material manufacturing, civil engineering and building industries; Pres. SENZENI ZOKWANA; Gen. Sec. FRANS BALENI; 262,042 mems (2006).

Police and Prisons Civil Rights Union (POPCRU): POPCRU House, 97–99 Simmonds St, Braamfontein; POB 8657, Johannesburg 2000; tel. (11) 4030406; fax (11) 4039377; Pres. ZIZAMELE CEBEKHULU; Gen. Sec. ABBEY WITBOOI; 95,864 mems (2006).

SASBO: The Finance Union: SASBO House, Fourmall Office Park West, 1 Percy St, Fourways; Private Bag X84, Bryanston 2021; tel. (11) 4670192; fax (11) 4670188; e-mail michelek@sasbo.org.za; internet www.sasbo.org.za; f. 1916 as the South African Soc. of Bank Officials; Gen. Sec. SHAUN OELSCHIG; 63,470 mems (2007).

Southern African Clothing and Textile Workers' Union (SACTWU): Industria House, 350 Victoria Rd, Salt River, Cape Town; POB 1194, Woodstock 7915; tel. (21) 4474570; fax (21) 4474593; e-mail aldenea@sactwu.org.za; affiliated to the Int. Textile, Garment and Leather Workers' Fed.; Pres. JOHN ZIKHALI; Gen. Sec. EBRAHIM PATEL; 110,216 mems (2006).

South African Commercial, Catering and Allied Workers Union (SACCAWU): SACCAWU House, 11 Leyds St, Braamfontein; POB 10730, Johannesburg 2000; tel. (11) 4038333; fax (11) 4030309; e-mail secretariatadmin@saccawu.org.za; f. 1975; affiliated to the Union Network Int.; represents workers in the service industry, commercial, catering, tourism, hospitality and finance sectors; Pres. AMOS MOTHAPO; Gen. Sec. BONES SKULU; 107,553 mems (2006).

South African Democratic Teachers' Union (SADTU): Matthew Goniwe House, cnr Goud and Marshall Sts, Johannesburg 2000; POB 6401, Johannesburg 2000; tel. (11) 3344830; fax (11) 3344836; e-mail tntshangase@sadtu.org.za; internet www.sadtu.org.za; f. 1990; affiliated to Education Int.; Pres. WILLIAM MADISHA; Gen. Sec. THULAS NXESI; 224,387 mems (2006).

South African Municipal Workers Union (SAMWU): Trade Union House, 8 Beverly St, Athlone, Cape Town; Private Bag X9, Athlone 7760; tel. (21) 6971151; fax (21) 6969175; e-mail soraya.solomon@samwu.org.za; internet www.samwu.org.za; f. 1987; affiliated to the Public Services Int.; Pres. PETRUS MASHISHI; Gen. Sec. MTHANDEKI NHLAPO; 118,973 (2006).

South African Transport and Allied Workers' Union (SATAWU): Marble Towers, 6th Floor, cnr Jeppe and Von Wielligh Sts, Johannesburg 2000; POB 9451, Johannesburg 2001; tel. (11) 3336127; fax (11) 3338918; e-mail cecilia@satawu.org.za; internet www.satawu.org.za; f. 2000; affiliated to the Int. Transport Workers' Fed.; Pres. EZROM MABYANA; Gen. Sec. RANDALL HOWARD; 134,000 mems (2006).

Other organizations affiliated to COSATU include: the Musicians' Union of South Africa; the Performing Arts Workers' Equity; the Public and Allied Workers' Union of South Africa; the South African Democratic Nurses' Union; the South African Football Players' Union; the South African Medical Association; and the South African State and Allied Workers' Union.

Federation of Unions of South Africa (FEDUSA): Fedusa House, 10 Kingfisher St, Horizon Park, Roodepoort 1725; POB 7779, Westgate 1734; tel. (11) 2791800; fax (11) 2791821; e-mail dennis@fedusa.org.za; internet www.fedusa.org.za; f. 1997 by merger of the Fed. of South African Labour Unions and Fed. of Civil Servants; 22 mem. unions representing 550,000 workers; politically non-aligned; affiliated to the Int. Trade Union Confed; proposed 'super fed.' with the Nat. Council of Trade Unions and Confed. of South African Workers' Unions delayed in 2006; Pres. MARY MALETE; Gen. Sec. DENNIS GEORGE.

Affiliated unions with 10,000 or more mems include:

Health and Other Services Personnel Trade Union of South Africa (HOSPERSA): POB 12266 Queenswood, Pretoria 0121; tel. (12) 3652021; fax (12) 3652043; internet www.hospersa.co.za; affiliated to the Public Services Int.; represents workers in the public and private health, welfare and services sectors, and the public safety and security and education sectors; Pres. GAVIN MOULTRIE; Gen. Sec. JOHAN STEYN; 62,272 mems (2005).

National Security and Unqualified Workers' Union (NASAWU): United Bldg, 10th Floor, 58 Field St, Durban; POB 63015, Bishopsgate, Durban 4008; tel. (31) 3059320; fax (31) 3059621; Gen. Sec. HAROLD MDINEKA; 13,000 mems (2006).

National Union of Leather and Allied Workers (NULAW): Mercury House, 6th Floor, Rm 67, 320 Smith St, Durban; POB 839, Durban 4000; tel. (31) 3076420; fax (31) 3043077; e-mail nulaw.mar@mweb.co.za; affiliated to the Int. Textile, Garment and Leather Workers' Fed.; Gen. Sec. MARTIN PAULSEN; 13,180 mems (2005).

Professional Transport Workers' Union (PTWU): Sable Centre, 3rd Floor, 41 De Korte St, Braamfontein, Johannesburg; POB 31415, Braamfontein 2017; tel. (11) 3394249; fax (11) 6820444; e-mail ptwu@wol.co.za; represents workers in the road freight, private security and cleaning sectors; Gen. Sec. PAUL WA MALEMA; c. 10,000 mems (2002).

South African Typographical Union (SATU): SATU House, 166 Visagie St, Pretoria 0001; POB 1993, Pretoria 0001; tel. (12) 3236097; fax (12) 3231284; e-mail martind@satu.co.za; f. 1982; represents workers in the printing, newspaper and packaging industries; Gen. Sec. MARTIN DEYSEL; 17,796 mems (2001).

Suid-Afrikaanse Onderwysersunie (SAOU) (South African Teachers' Union): SAOU Bldg, 278 Serene St, Garsfontein, Pretoria; POB 90120, Garsfontein 0042; tel. (12) 3489641; fax (12) 3482478; e-mail liezla@saou.co.za; internet www.saou.co.za; Pres. JOHANNES S. ROUX; CEO EDWARD H. DAVIES; 24,247 (2006).

United Association of South Africa (UASA): UASA Office Park, 42 Goldman St, Florida 1709; POB 565, Florida 1710; tel. (11) 4723600; fax (11) 6744057; e-mail jplbez@uasa.org.za; internet www.uasa.org.za; f. 1998 by merger of the Administrative, Technical and Electronic Asscn of South Africa and Officials' Asscn of South Africa; fed. of 31 unions incl. the fmr Nat. Employees' Trade Union; represents workers in the mining, motor, transport, manufacturing and engineering industries; CEO J. P. L. 'KOOS' BEZUIDENHOUT; c. 100,000 mems (2006).

Other organizations affiliated to FEDUSA include: the Airline Pilots' Association of South Africa; the Care, Catering and Retail Allied Workers Union of South Africa; the Construction and Engineering Industrial Workers Union; the Insurance and Banking Staff Association; the Internal Staff Association; the Jewellers and Goldsmiths Union; the Millennium Workers Union; the Mouth Peace Workers Union; the National Democratic Change and Allied Workers Union; the National Teachers Union; the National Union of Hotel, Restaurant, Catering, Commercial, Health and Allied Workers; the South African Communications Union; the South African Parastatal and Tertiary Institutions Union; the United National Public Servants Association of South Africa and Allied Workers Union; and the United Transport and Allied Trade Union.

National Council of Trade Unions (NACTU): Metropolitan Life Centre, 4th Floor, 108 Fox St, Johannesburg; POB 10928, Johannesburg 2000; tel. (11) 8331040; fax (11) 8331032; e-mail info@nactu.org.za; internet www.nactu.org.za; f. 1986 by merger of the Council of Unions of South Africa and Azanian Confed. of Trade Unions; fed. of 22 African trade unions; aligned to the Pan-Africanist Congress of Azania party; Pres. JOSEPH MAQHEKENI; Gen. Sec. MAHLOMOLA SKHOSANA; 327,000 mems (2004).

Affiliates with 10,000 or more mems include:

Building, Construction and Allied Workers' Union (BCAWU): Glencairn Bldg, 8th Floor, 73 Market St, Johannesburg; POB 96, Johannesburg 2000; tel. (11) 3339180; fax (11) 3339944; e-mail bcawu@netactive.co.za; f. 1974; affiliated to the Building and Wood Workers Int.; Gen. Sec. NARIUS MOLOTO; c. 25,000 mems (2003).

Media Workers' Association of South Africa (MWASA): North State Bldg, 5th Floor, cnr Market and Kruis Sts, Johannesburg; POB 11136, Johannesburg 2000; tel. (11) 3336306; fax (11) 3338616; f. 1978 as the Writers Asscn of South Africa, successor to the Union of Black Journalists; present name adopted in 1986; affiliated to the Int. Fed. of Journalists and Union Network Int.; applied to become a political party in 2005; Pres. TUWANI GUMANI; Sec.-Gen. THEMBA HLATSHWAYO; c. 27,000 mems (1998).

Metal and Electrical Workers' Union of South Africa (MEWUSA): Elephant House, 5th Floor, 107 Market St, Johannesburg; POB 3669, Johannesburg 2000; tel. (11) 3369369; fax (11) 3369120; e-mail mewusa@lantic.net; f. 1989; affiliated to the Int. Metalworkers' Fed.; Gen. Sec. NKRUMAH RAYMOND KGAGUDI; c. 10,000 paid-up mems (2005).

National Union of Food, Beverages, Wine, Spirit and Allied Workers (NUFBWSAW): 8 Stannic Bldg, 4th Floor, New St, South Ghandi Sq., Johannesburg; POB 5718, Johannesburg 2000; tel. (11) 8331140; fax (11) 8331503; Pres. ARMSTRONG NTOYAKHE; Nat. Organizer ANTHONY HENDRICKS; c. 10,000 mems (2005).

South African Chemical Workers' Union (SACWU): 29 Klerk St, btwn Harrison and Dirk Sts, 11th Floor, Johannesburg; POB 236, Johannesburg 2000; tel. (11) 8386581; fax (11) 8386622; e-mail samela@sacwu.co.za; Pres. JOSEPH MAQHEKENI; c. 40,000 mems (2003).

Other organizations affiliated to NACTU include: the Banking, Insurance and Finance Workers' Union; the Hospitality Industry and Allied Workers' Union; the Hotel, Liquor, Catering, Commercial and Allied Workers' Union of South Africa; the Municipality, Education, State, Health And Allied Workers' Union; the National Clothing and Textile Workers' Union of South Africa; the National Services and Allied Workers' Union; the National Union of Farm Workers; the National Union of Furniture and Allied Workers; the Parliamentary Staff Union; Transport and Allied Workers Union; and the Transport and Omnibus Workers' Union.

SOUTH AFRICA

Non-affiliated Union

Public Servants' Association of South Africa (PSA): PSA Head Office Bldg, 563 Belvedere St, Arcadia, Pretoria; POB 40404, Arcadia 0007; tel. (12) 3036500; fax (12) 3036652; e-mail ask@psa.co.za; internet www.psa.co.za; withdrew affiliation from FEDUSA in 2006; Chair. PAUL SELLO; Pres. KOOT MYBURGH; Gen. Man. DANNY ADONIS; 185,500 mems (2006).

Transport

Most of South Africa's railway network and the harbours and airways are administered by the state-owned Transnet Ltd. There are no navigable rivers. Private bus services are regulated to complement the railways.

Transnet Ltd: 8 Hillside Rd, Parktown, Johannesburg; POB 72501, Parkview 2122; tel. (11) 4887055; fax (11) 4887511; internet www.transnet.co.za; Chair. BONGANI AUG KHUMALO; CEO MARIA RAMOS.

RAILWAYS

With the exception of commuter services, the South African railways system is operated by Spoornet Ltd (the rail division of Transnet). The network comprised 31,400 track-km in 1996, of which 16,946 km was electrified. Extensive rail links connect Spoornet with the rail networks of neighbouring countries.

Spoornet: Paul Kruger Bldg, 30 Wolmarans St, Private Bag X47, Johannesburg 2001; tel. (11) 7735090; fax (11) 7733033; internet www.spoornet.co.za; CEO SIYABONGA GAMA.

ROADS

In 2001 there were an estimated 36,131 km of classified roads, including 239 km of motorways. In 2004 there were 7,200 km of main roads.

South African National Roads Agency Ltd (SANRAL): Ditsela Pl., 1204 Park St, cnr Duncan St, Hatfield, Pretoria; POB 415, Pretoria 0001; tel. (12) 4266000; fax (12) 3622116; e-mail info@nra.co.za; internet www.nra.co.za; f. 1998; responsible for design, construction, management and maintenance of 13,933 km of the national road network (2005); Chair. LOT NDLOVU; CEO NAZIR ALLI.

SHIPPING

The principal harbours are at Richards Bay, Durban, Saldanha, Cape Town, Port Elizabeth, East London Ngqura (Coega), and Mossel Bay. The deep-water port at Richards Bay has been extended and its facilities upgraded. Both Richards Bay and Saldanha Bay are major bulk-handling ports, while Saldanha Bay also has an important fishing fleet. More than 30 shipping lines serve South African ports.

National Ports Authority (NPA): POB 32696, Braamfontein 2017; tel. (11) 2424022; fax (11) 2424027; internet www.npa.co.za; f. 2000; fmrly part of Portnet; subsidiary of Transnet; controls and manages the country's eight major seaports; CEO KHOMOTSO PHIHLELA (acting).

South African Maritime Safety Authority: Block E, Hatfield Gardens, 333 Grosvenor St, Hatfield, Pretoria; SAMSA, POB 13186, Hatfield 0028; tel. (12) 3423049; fax (12) 3423160; e-mail samsa@iafrica.com; advises the Govt on matters connected with sea transport to, from or between South Africa's ports, incl. safety at sea, and prevention of pollution by petroleum; CEO Capt. B. R. WATT.

South African Port Operations (SAPO): Marine Parade, POB 10124, Durban 4056; tel. (31) 3088333; fax (31) 3088352; e-mail webmaster@saportops.co.za; internet www.saponet.co.za; f. 2000; fmrly part of Portnet; subsidiary of Transnet; operates 13 container, bulk, breakbulk and car terminals at six of the country's major ports; CEO TAU MORWE.

CIVIL AVIATION

Civil aviation is controlled by the Minister of Transport. The Chief Directorate: Civil Aviation Authority at the Department of Transport is responsible for licensing and control of domestic and international air services.

Airports Company South Africa (ACSA): 24 Johnson Rd, Riverwoods, Bedfordview 2008; POB 75480, Gardenview 2047; tel. (11) 9216991; internet www.airports.co.za; f. 1993; owns and operates South Africa's nine principal airports, of which three (at Johannesburg, Cape Town and Durban) are classified as international airports; Chair. TOMMY OLIPHANT; Man. Dir MONHLA HLAHLA.

Civil Aviation Authority (CAA): Ikhaya Lokundiza, Bldg 16, Treur Close, Waterfall Park, Bekker St, Midrand; Private Bag X73, Halfway House 1685; tel. (11) 5451000; fax (12) 5451465; e-mail mail@caa.co.za; internet www.caa.co.za; Chair. COLIN JORDAAN.

Air Cape (Pty) Ltd: POB D. F. Malan Airport, Cape Town 7525; tel. (21) 9340344; fax (21) 9348379; scheduled internal passenger services and charters, engineering services and aerial surveys; Chair. Dr P. VAN ASWEGEN; Gen. Man. G. A. NORTJE.

Airlink Airline: POB 7529, Bonaero Park 1622; tel. (11) 9611700; fax (11) 3951076; internet www.saairlink.co.za; e-mail info@flyairlink.com; f. 1992; internal and external scheduled services and charters in Southern Africa; Man. Dirs RODGER FOSTER, BARRIE WEBB.

COMAIR Ltd: POB 7015, Bonaero Park 1622; tel. (11) 9210111; fax (11) 9733913; e-mail cr@comair.co.za; internet www.comair.co.za; f. 1946; scheduled domestic, regional and international services; Chair. D. NOVICK; Jt CEOs ERIK VENTER, GIDON NOVICK.

Safair (Pty) Ltd: POB 938, Kempton Park 1620; tel. 9280000; fax 3953060; e-mail marketing@safair.co.za; internet www.safair.co.za; f. 1965; subsidiary of Imperial Holdings Ltd; aircraft leasing, engineering and maintenance services; CEO CHRISTO KOK.

South African Airways (SAA): Airways Park, Jones Rd, Private Bag X13, Johannesburg 1627; tel. (11) 9781111; fax (11) 9781106; internet www.flysaa.com; f. 1934; state-owned; internal passenger services linking all the principal towns; international services to Africa, Europe, North and South America and Asia; Chair. JAKES GERWEL; CEO KHAYA NGQULA.

Tourism

Tourism is an important part of South Africa's economy. The chief attractions for visitors are the climate, scenery and wildlife reserves. In 2005 some 7.5m. tourists visited South Africa. In that year receipts from tourism receipts amounted to US $8,448m.

South African Tourism: Bojanala House, 90 Protea Rd, Chislehurston, Johannesburg 2196; Private Bag X10012, Sandton 2146; tel. (11) 8953000; fax (11) 8953001; internet www.southafrica.net; f. 1947; 11 overseas brs; CEO MOEKETSI MOSOLA.

SPAIN

Introductory Survey

Location, Climate, Language, Religion, Flag, Capital

The Kingdom of Spain, in south-western Europe, forms more than four-fifths of the Iberian peninsula. The country also includes the Balearic Islands in the Mediterranean Sea, the Canary Islands in the Atlantic Ocean and a few small enclaves in North Africa. Mainland Spain is bounded to the north by Andorra and France and to the west by Portugal. To the east is the Mediterranean Sea, and Morocco lies 30 km to the south. The climate is less temperate than in most of western Europe, with hot summers and, in the hilly interior, cold winters. The official national language is Spanish. Catalan, and its close relative Valencian, are widely spoken in the north-east, Basque in the north and Galician in the north-west; all have co-official status in their respective regions. The overwhelming majority of the population are Roman Catholics, but the 1978 Constitution laid down that Spain had no official state religion. The national flag (proportions 2 by 3) carries three horizontal stripes, of red, yellow (half the depth) and red. The state flag carries, in addition, the national coat of arms. The capital is Madrid.

Recent History

After winning the civil war of 1936–39, the Nationalist forces, led by Gen. Francisco Franco y Bahamonde, established an authoritarian rule which restricted individual liberties and severely repressed challenges to its power. In 1942 Gen. Franco revived the traditional legislative assembly, the Cortes (Courts), with limited powers. After keeping Spain neutral in the Second World War, Franco announced in 1947 that the monarchy (abolished in 1931) would be restored after his death or retirement. In 1967, in the first elections since the civil war, a portion of the Cortes was directly elected under a limited franchise. In July 1969 Franco nominated Prince Juan Carlos de Borbón (grandson of the last reigning monarch, King Alfonso XIII) as his successor, and in June 1973 relinquished the post of President of the Council of Ministers to Adm. Luis Carrero Blanco, who was killed in December. Responsibility for the assassination was claimed by Euskadi ta Askatasuna (ETA—Basque Homeland and Liberty), the Basque separatist organization. Carlos Arias Navarro became President of the Government (Prime Minister) in January 1974.

Franco died in November 1975. He was succeeded as Head of State by King Juan Carlos, and in December a more liberal Council of Ministers was formed. In 1976 restrictions on political activity were lifted. In July Arias Navarro resigned at the King's request, and was replaced by Adolfo Suárez González. The introduction of democratic government then proceeded rapidly, and an elected bicameral legislature was established. Most of the numerous de facto political parties were able to take part in the general elections for the Cortes, held in June 1977. An overall majority was won by the Unión de Centro Democrático (UCD), a coalition party headed by the Prime Minister. In December 1978 a new Constitution was endorsed by referendum and ratified by the King. It confirmed Spain as a parliamentary monarchy, with freedom for political parties, and guaranteed the right of Spain's 'nationalities and regions' to autonomy.

A general election was held in March 1979, resulting in little change in the distribution of seats in the Cortes. The new Government was again headed by Suárez. Basque and Catalan autonomous parliaments were established in March 1980 and, in elections to both parliaments, the UCD was heavily defeated by the moderate regionalist parties. Confidence in Suárez diminished and in January 1981 he resigned. Leopoldo Calvo-Sotelo Bustelo, hitherto the Deputy Prime Minister, succeeded him.

In February 1981 a group of armed civil guards, led by Lt-Col Antonio Tejero Molina, stormed into the Cortes, taking hostage 350 deputies. The military commander of Valencia, Lt-Gen. Jaime Milans del Bosch, declared a state of emergency in that region and sent tanks on to the streets of the city of Valencia. King Juan Carlos acted swiftly to secure the loyalty of other military commanders, and by the following morning had been able to persuade Milans himself to stand down. Tejero surrendered, and the deputies were released unharmed. More than 30 military officers were subsequently brought to trial, and both Tejero and Milans received lengthy prison sentences. Milans was released in 1990, and Tejero was released in 1996.

Immediately after the attempted coup, Calvo-Sotelo formed a new Council of Ministers, resisting pressure to establish a coalition government. The Prime Minister addressed various contentious issues during his term of office, including his decision to take Spain into the North Atlantic Treaty Organization (NATO, see p. 340). At the election for the first Galician Parliament, held in October 1981, the Alianza Popular (AP) won two seats more than the UCD. The overwhelming Socialist victory at the election for the Parliament of Andalucía (Andalusia) in May 1982 was a grave set-back for the central Government. Following Calvo-Sotelo's replacement as party leader by Landelino Lavilla Alsina in July, Suárez defected to found a rival party, the Centro Democrático y Social (CDS). Desertion from the UCD continued and by August the party no longer commanded a workable majority, and an early general election was called. In October, however, shortly before the election, a right-wing plot to stage a pre-emptive military coup was uncovered. Four colonels were arrested (three of whom were subsequently sentenced to prison terms), and Milans was also implicated. The election resulted in a decisive victory for the Partido Socialista Obrero Español (PSOE—Spanish Socialist Workers' Party), led by Felipe González Márquez, who formed a new Council of Ministers in December 1982.

One of the most serious problems facing the new Government was the continuing tension in the Basque region (see below). Moreover, in June 1985 hundreds of thousands of workers, motivated by the Unión General de Trabajadores (UGT) and supported by the Confederación Sindical de Comisiones Obreras (CCOO), protested against proposed reforms in the social security system and consequent reductions in pension rights. Following large-scale demonstrations against Spain's membership of NATO, in March 1986 a long-awaited referendum on the question of Spain's continued membership of the alliance was held. Contrary to expectations, the Spanish people voted to remain within NATO, following Prime Minister González's reversal on the issue and an extensive campaign by the Government.

In an early general election held in June 1986 the PSOE was returned to power, winning 184 of the 350 seats in the Congreso de los Diputados (Congress of Deputies), 18 fewer than at the 1982 election, while the conservative Coalición Popular (CP), which incorporated the AP, the Partido Demócrata Popular (subsequently Democracia Cristiana) and the Partido Liberal, won 105 seats. A new Council of Ministers was appointed in late July, again led by González. Following its defeat, the CP fell into disarray, and in December Manuel Fraga, the leader of the AP, resigned.

In June 1987 the results of the European Parliament, regional and municipal elections confirmed the continuing decline in support for the PSOE. The AP also sustained losses, while the centre-left CDS was able to strengthen its position. The growing rift between the Prime Minister and the UGT (a trade union traditionally allied to the PSOE) became increasingly evident, and in October Nicolás Redondo, the UGT leader, and a union colleague resigned from their seats as PSOE deputies in the Cortes, in protest against the Government's economic policies. The UGT and CCOO then combined forces to organize a new campaign of protests against the Government, which continued throughout 1988, culminating in December in a one-day general strike, which was supported by almost 8m. workers. Similar strikes in Madrid and elsewhere followed.

In January 1989 Fraga returned to the leadership of the AP, which was relaunched as the Partido Popular (PP) and which was subsequently joined by Democracia Cristiana and the Partido Liberal. The unity of the PSOE was undermined by the establishment of a dissident faction and by the defection to Izquierda Unida (IU—United Left, an alliance comprising the Partido Comunista de España (PCE) and other left-wing parties) of 100 PSOE members. Nevertheless, at the general election, held eight months early, in late October, the PSOE was returned to power on a provisional basis, pending investigations into allegations of polling irregularities. After several months of controversy, the PSOE's representation in the Congreso de los Diputados was reduced to 175 of the 350 seats, the PP holding 107 seats. The PSOE, however, was able to retain a majority by subsequently entering into a tactical alliance with the CDS, the Catalan nationalist Convergència i Unió (CiU) and the Euzko Alderdi Jeltzalea/Partido Nacionalista Vasco (EAJ/PNV—the Basque Nationalist Party).

Various corruption scandals involving both main parties were revealed over the course of the new legislative term. In April 1990 a number of PP officials and business executives were arrested in connection with allegations of bribery. In June 1991 Carlos Navarro, a senior PSOE treasurer, was obliged to resign, following the exposure of a scandal concerning alleged illicit donations to the ruling party. Public concern at apparent widespread corruption increased in February 1992 when the Governor of the central bank, the Banco de España, Mariano Rubio, was accused of irregularities relating to his personal investments. In early 1993 the PSOE's reputation was further damaged by new revelations concerning the party's financing. Having refused to permit inspection of its accounts, in late 1992 the PSOE headquarters had been forcibly searched on the orders of the judge investigating the allegations. The 'Filesa affair', as the principal scandal became known, was named after a Barcelona-based holding company which, it was claimed, had received illicit contributions on behalf of the party between 1989 and 1991. Following a Supreme Court inquiry into the affair, PSOE officials, business executives and bankers were charged, and in October 1997 Navarro and seven other defendants were sentenced to terms of imprisonment.

At the general election in June 1993 the PSOE failed to obtain an absolute majority in the Congreso de los Diputados, where its strength declined to 159 of the 350 seats. The PP increased its representation to 141 seats, while IU won 18 seats, CiU 17 and the EAJ/PNV five. The CDS lost all of its seats. The PSOE's negotiations with CiU and with the EAJ/PNV failed to result in the conclusion of a formal coalition agreement. In July, therefore, González commenced his fourth term as Prime Minister, at the head of a minority administration. With the Spanish economy in recession the Prime Minister appealed for support for drastic measures to address the economic crisis. In November, however, thousands of protesters demonstrated against the Government's economic policies. Controversial labour legislation, as amended to comply with CiU requests, was approved by the Congreso in March 1994.

In 1994–95 the Government came under increasing pressure over suggestions that it had been involved in the establishment of the Grupos Antiterroristas de la Liberación (GAL), a counter-terrorist grouping which had been formed in 1983 with the aim of combating ETA. It was alleged that members of the Ertzaintza (Basque Country police force) had given support to the organization, which was suspected of responsibility for the murders of numerous ETA members exiled in France. Investigations into the affair had begun in 1988, and in 1991 a senior police officer in Bilbao, José Amedo, and an accomplice, Michel Domínguez, were convicted of organizing the groups of mercenaries and imprisoned. In December 1994, following further questioning of the pair and the reopening of the case, Julián Sancristóbal, a former director-general of state security in the Ministry of the Interior, was arrested on suspicion of financing and assisting GAL. The Prime Minister denied that the Government had been connected in any way with the so-called 'dirty war' of the 1980s against ETA. In February 1995, however, the investigating judge Baltasar Garzón ordered the arrest of Rafael Vera, the former Secretary of State for Security, on suspicion of involvement in the kidnapping in 1983 of Segundo Marey, a French business executive mistaken for an ETA member, and of misuse of public funds. In March 1995 the remains of José Antonio Lasa and José Ignacio Zabala, two ETA members apparently tortured before being murdered by GAL in 1983, were identified by forensic scientists. An inquiry into their fate had been closed in 1988, ostensibly owing to lack of evidence. A new inquiry into their deaths was instigated. In April 1995, concluding that GAL had been established and financed by the Ministry of the Interior, Judge Garzón indicted a total of 14 former officials, including Vera and Sancristóbal, both of whom were subsequently released on bail. Garzón submitted a report of his investigations into the origins and financing of GAL to the Supreme Court in July. His findings implicated González along with the former Deputy Prime Minister and Minister of Defence, Narcís Serra, the Minister of the Interior during 1982–88, José Barrionuevo, the Basque socialist leader, Txiki Benegas, and other PSOE officials.

In September 1995 Judge Eduardo Móner was appointed by the Supreme Court to examine the allegations against the Prime Minister and the other senior politicians. Móner subsequently heard declarations from Sancristóbal that the abduction of Marey in 1983 had been approved by both Barrionuevo and Vera. In October 1995 José Luis Corcuera (who had succeeded Barrionuevo as Minister of the Interior), Sancristóbal and Vera were charged with misuse of public funds. In January 1996, his parliamentary immunity having been removed, Barrionuevo was indicted by the Supreme Court on three charges: illegal detention; misuse of public funds; and association with an armed group. In April Judge Móner reported that he had found no evidence linking González to the activities of the death squads, believed to be responsible for the murders of 27 ETA members, while Serra and Benegas were also exonerated; the case against all three was abandoned by the Supreme Court in November. In May, meanwhile, several members of the Civil Guard, including Gen. Enrique Rodríguez Galindo and two other senior generals, were detained in connection with the GAL inquiry. Charges included involvement in the murders of Lasa and Zabala. In June 1996 Vera was charged with concealing these two murders, while the former Governor of Guipúzcoa in the Basque Country (País Vasco or Euskadi), Julen Elgorriaga, was also imprisoned in connection with the case.

In April 1997 Judge Móner concluded his inquiry into the abduction of Marey. In September the Supreme Court confirmed that 12 defendants were to stand trial: Barrionuevo, former Minister of the Interior; Vera, former Secretary of State for Security; Sancristóbal, Amedo and Domínguez, the former civil guards; and seven others. The trial concluded in July 1998. Barrionuevo, Vera and Sancristóbal were found guilty of kidnapping and misappropriation of public funds, each receiving a prison sentence of 10 years. The sentences of the other nine defendants ranged from two to nine years. The 12 defendants were also ordered to pay 30m. pesetas in compensation to Marey. By the end of December, however, 11 of the prisoners had been set free, their sentences having been suspended, while the 12th was released in June 2000. A further trial began in September 2001, with González among some 100 witnesses called to testify. In January 2002 Barrionuevo and Corcuera were absolved of the charges of misappropriation of funds; however, Vera was sentenced to seven years' imprisonment and barred from holding public office for 18 years.

At the general election, held 15 months early, in March 1996, and in which 78% of the electorate participated, the PP took 156 of the 350 seats in the Congreso de los Diputados, thus falling short of an outright majority. The PSOE, its reputation severely damaged by the ongoing Marey affair, won 141 seats, IU 21 and CiU 16. In the Senado (Senate) the PP received 132 of the 256 seats (winning 111 by direct election), while the PSOE took 96 (81 by direct election). The King invited José María Aznar, the President of the PP, to form a government. After protracted negotiations, the PP and CiU reached agreement on a pact enabling Aznar to take office. Having also secured the support of the five EAJ/PNV deputies and of the four representatives of Coalición Canaria (CC), the new Prime Minister's investiture finally took place in early May. (The EAJ/PNV abandoned its pact with the Government in September 1997, however, withdrawing its support entirely in December 1999.)

One of the new administration's main priorities was the reduction of the budget deficit. Several aspects of the Government's policies, however, aroused intense opposition. In December 1996 civil servants took part in a 24-hour strike to protest against the Government's imposition of a pay 'freeze', while in February 1997 a two-week strike by truck drivers, in support of improved working conditions, caused severe disruption and led to the closure of the country's road borders. In early 1998 one miner died during violent protests in northern Spain, where the coal-miners of Asturias were demonstrating against proposed job losses (the Government having been obliged to plan decreases in coal output in order to comply with European Union (EU, see p. 244) directives regarding reductions in subsidies to state-owned industries). At the end of January, after a month-long strike that attracted much public sympathy, agreement was reached when the Government granted concessions on the terms of early retirement for miners.

At the PSOE congress in June 1997, after leading the party for 23 years, González unexpectedly announced his resignation as Secretary-General. Joaquín Almunia, hitherto the party's parliamentary spokesman and a loyal associate of González, was chosen to succeed him. In April 1998, in a new procedure that required the holding of primary elections in the contest for the selection of the PSOE's next prime ministerial candidate, Almunia was defeated by Josep Borrell, a former government minister. Almunia's offer of resignation from the party leadership was rejected. In November, in a bid to restore party unity, the PSOE designated Borrell as party leader and sole spokesman, while Almunia was to remain responsible for political affairs, at the head of the party's federal executive committee. However, in May 1999 Borrell resigned following the revelation of a financial scandal involving allegations of malpractice by two former colleagues during the 1980s. He was replaced in July by Almunia, who was selected unopposed as the party's prime ministerial candidate.

In April 1998, meanwhile, after an inquiry lasting three years, Judge Gómez de Liaño concluded his investigation into the fate of Lasa and Zabala, the two ETA activists allegedly killed by GAL members during the 'dirty war'. Criminal proceedings were instigated against seven suspects, including Vera, Elgorriaga and Gen. Rodríguez Galindo. In April 2000 Galindo and Elgorriaga were found guilty of involvement in the abduction and murder in 1983 of Lasa and Zabala. Both were sentenced to 71 years' imprisonment.

The ruling party's strong performance at the legislative election held on 12 March 2000 was largely attributed to the Government's record of economic success (in particular its reduction of the unemployment rate). In the lower house the PP won 183 of the 350 seats, thus unexpectedly securing an absolute majority. The PSOE's representation was reduced to 125 seats, while IU, which had conducted a joint campaign with the PSOE, suffered a sharp decline in support, losing 13 of its 21 seats in the Congreso de los Diputados. The moderate regional parties, CiU and the EAJ/PNV, took 15 and seven seats, respectively. In the Senado the PP increased its strength to 127 of the 208 directly elected seats, whereas the PSOE's representation decreased to 61 seats. The level of voter participation was less than 70%. Almunia immediately conceded defeat and resigned as leader of the PSOE. At the party congress in July José Luis Rodríguez Zapatero, a lawyer, was unexpectedly elected to the leadership of the PSOE. Zapatero, who excluded left-wingers from the new national executive committee, declared his intention to modernize the party in order to form an effective opposition.

At the end of April 2000, with the support of the 15 CiU and four CC deputies, Aznar, who expressed a desire to govern largely by consensus, was sworn in for a second term of office. The Prime Minister announced the composition of the new Council of Ministers on the following day. Mariano Rajoy, hitherto Minister of Education, was appointed Deputy Prime Minister and Minister of the Presidency. Rodrigo Rato also remained a Deputy Prime Minister, retaining the economy portfolio, while that of finance was allocated to Cristóbal Montoro. Josep Piqué i Camps became Minister of Foreign Affairs. The incoming Government's programme included the reduction of taxes, reforms in the financing of the Autonomous Communities and improvements in the judicial system.

In February 2001 Jaime Mayor resigned as Minister of the Interior to run as the PP candidate for Lehendakari (President of the Basque Government) in the Basque regional election. He was replaced by Rajoy, who was in turn replaced by Juan José Lucas.

During 2001 the Government suffered from the alleged involvement of several PP members in corruption cases. In mid-June the Supreme Court decided to proceed with an investigation into the role of the Minister of Foreign Affairs, Josep Piqué, in the fraudulent sale of Ertoil, a subsidiary of the Spanish fuel company Ercros, of whose board Piqué was a member, to the French company Elf Aquitaine. Aznar announced that he would wait for the results of the investigation before reviewing Piqué's position in the Council of Ministers. In mid-2001 the Government's reputation was undermined by the collapse of the Antonio Camacho Gescartera stockbroking company, as a result of which several prominent charities and organizations lost significant sums of money. In September the President of the National Securities and Exchange Commission (Comisión Nacional del Mercado de Valores—CNMV), Pilar Valiente, was remanded in custody following the publication of her personal diaries, in which it was revealed that she had long been aware of discrepancies in the stockbroker's accounts. Since Valiente had been appointed by the Deputy Prime Minister and Minister of the Economy, Rodrigo Rato, his position also came under scrutiny and a full reorganization of the CNMV was ordered in early 2002, following the implication of several more of its members in the case. In November 2002 a €2.1m. fine was imposed on the Spanish arm of the British HSBC bank, for its role in 'laundering' Gescartera funds worth some €100m. in 138 numbered accounts.

In January 2002 the PP re-elected Aznar as its President, but he made clear his intention not to seek a third term as Prime Minister in 2004. In May 2002, after the trial of Arnaldo Otegi of Batasuna (the political wing of ETA—see below) was dismissed by the Supreme Court, a request by Aznar for reconsideration was strongly criticized by the judiciary as misplaced government intervention. Also in May, as a result of the failure of negotiations between the Government, trade unions and employers' representatives over proposed reforms to employment law, the CCOO and the UGT announced plans to hold the first general strike since 1988; the following day the Government approved the imposition of reforms to unemployment subsidies by decree. The general strike proceeded in mid-June 2002, with the UGT claiming a rate of participation of 80%. In June disagreements between Aznar and Jordi Pujol i Soley, the President of CiU and of the Generalitat (the autonomous administration of Catalonia—Cataluña or Catalunya), in which Aznar accused the latter of disloyalty to the Government and support for the general strike, led to a freezing of relations between the PP and CiU for a 'period of reflection'. As a result of the strike the Minister of Labour, Juan Carlos Aparicio, resigned; he was replaced in mid-July by Eduardo Zaplana. Piqué was transferred to the Ministry of Science and Technology and was replaced as Minister of Foreign Affairs by Ana Palacio, while Rajoy was promoted from the position of Minister of the Interior to that of Deputy Prime Minister and was succeeded by Angel Acebes. Revised legislation on labour reform, which annulled the main provisions of the controversial decree, was approved by the Congreso de los Diputados in October.

In mid-November 2002 the Aznar Government was faced with a serious crisis following the sinking of the Liberian-registered, Greek-owned oil tanker Prestige 240 km off the coast of Galicia. The vessel, which had reported to the authorities that its hull had ruptured and that it was leaking oil, had been refused landfall and had been towed out to sea, where it split in two and sank six days later. An estimated 12,000 metric tons of the vessel's 77,000-ton capacity was believed to have been released into the sea in the first slick, around one-half of which soon reached the Galician coast, requiring the imposition of a prohibition of fishing in that area. It was subsequently revealed that the oil remaining in the wreck was still leaking (in early January 2003 the total amount of spillage was revised to 25,000 tons). Massive clean-up operations were launched, mostly by environmental groups and by the local population; a significant lack of aid from the Spanish military aroused widespread public discontent. Demonstrations were attended by some 150,000 people in Santiago de Compostela in December and by around 100,000 people in Vigo in January 2003, at which participants protested at the perceived mishandling of the disaster by both the regional and national PP authorities and demanded the resignation of Aznar. A local commission launched by the regional Government of Galicia met with obstruction from the central Government, which also delayed the setting up of a national investigation. Meanwhile, the oil slicks spread to the Basque region, and also reached the coastlines of France and Portugal. The total cost of the cleaning-up process to the Spanish Government was projected at more than €1,000m.

Amid the increasing likelihood of US-led military action against the Iraqi regime of Saddam Hussain in early 2003, Aznar was one of eight European leaders to sign a declaration at the end of January in support of US moves towards an ultimatum. Public opinion, however, already swayed against the PP by the Government's handling of the Prestige disaster, was, in general, strongly against military action, with 3m. people participating in anti-war demonstrations in mid-February, and opinion polls suggesting that at least 80% of the population was against the launching of armed conflict in Iraq. None the less, in late February Aznar expressed his support for US-led military action with a UN mandate. As the US intention to commence armed intervention with or without UN approval became clear, Aznar assured the Spanish people that Spain would not contribute to any military coalition. A summit meeting hosted in the Azores in March led to a joint declaration by Aznar, the British Prime Minister, Tony Blair, and the US President, George W. Bush, condemning the regime of Saddam Hussain and expressing support for necessary military actions. The subsequent announcement by the USA of its intention to act, if need be, without international ratification received the PP Government's concerted support. Although the PP Government strongly supported Aznar's policy on Iraq, by 1 April six parliamentary motions rejecting the war (which had commenced on 20 March) had been proposed by opposition parties, and on 29 March a number of non-governmental organizations filed charges against Aznar before the Supreme Court, accusing him of exceeding his authorities. Public demonstrations continued in March and April, with a march in Madrid on 6 April supported by a prominent judge, Baltasar Garzón, and another comprising up to 200,000 protesters in Barcelona on 12 April. In April seven diplomatic staff at the Iraqi embassy in Madrid were expelled at the request of the USA, ostensibly on the grounds of alleged espionage.

The scale of public protest against the Iraqi conflict prompted the drafting of legislation by the PP in April 2003 that would extend the jurisdiction of military courts to include trial (with a maximum sentence of six years) for acts of protest staged to discredit Spain's participation in international armed conflict; the proposed legislation, which was the first of its kind since the end of the Franco regime in 1975, was accused of constituting a threat to civil rights. In July, despite the level of popular feeling against the war and the dissent of all the opposition parties, the Government committed 1,300 troops to the peace-keeping force. In November seven Spanish intelligence officers were killed in Iraq, bringing the total number of Spaniards to have died as a direct result of the conflict to 10. Opinion polls reported that an estimated 90% of the Spanish population believed that the instigation of armed conflict in Iraq by the US-led coalition had been a mistake, and Zapatero, the leader of the PSOE, stated that if his party won the general election in March 2004, the Spanish troops would be withdrawn from Iraq. In September 2003 the Deputy Prime Minister, Rajoy, was appointed as the PP's prime ministerial candidate for the general election following his nomination by Aznar.

In opinion polls held before the general election of March 2004 it was widely predicted that the PP would win with a reduced majority. Aznar's popularity had suffered as a result of his policy towards Iraq and ongoing questions over the Government's handling of the *Prestige* disaster. Four days before the general election, on 11 March 2004, 10 bombs exploded in four commuter trains in Madrid, killing 191 people and injuring more than 1,500. The Minister of the Interior, Acebes, immediately indicated that ETA was the principal suspect; Batasuna, however, was swift to condemn the attacks. Campaigning for the election was suspended, and three days of national mourning were declared. On 12 March demonstrations against the atrocity were held throughout Spain, and more than 2m. people marched through the centre of Madrid. Despite the Government's initial supposition that the bombings had been carried out by ETA, suspicion increasingly came to rest on Islamist militants; in the days following the attacks three Moroccans suspected of having links to the al-Qa'ida (Base) organization of the Saudi-born militant Islamist Osama bin Laden and to the May 2003 suicide bombings in Casablanca, Morocco, were arrested.

The bombings became the central issue in the general election, which took place as scheduled on 14 March 2004. It was predicted that proof of ETA's involvement would help the cause of the PP, which had pursued an active anti-terrorism policy against the Basque separatists. Conversely, evidence that Islamist militants had been responsible would provide a connection between the bombings and the Government's already deeply unpopular involvement in Iraq. As evidence suggesting that Islamists had perpetrated the attacks was found, the Government was criticized for its premature response in blaming the Basque group and its unwillingness to consider other possibilities. In the event, the PSOE secured an unexpected victory in the elections to the lower house, winning 42.7% of the votes (164 seats), while the PP obtained 37.7% of the votes (148 seats). The PP retained its majority in the Senado, however, winning 102 of the directly elected seats, compared with the 93 directly elected seats secured by the PSOE. The PP held 126 seats in the final composition of the Senado, and the PSOE 111. The election turn-out, at 77.2%, was nine percentage points higher than in 2000. Immediately after his party's victory Zapatero reiterated his pledge to withdraw Spanish troops from Iraq if control in that country were not handed over by the US-led coalition authorities to the UN by 30 June. However, on assuming office he announced that the troops would be withdrawn as quickly as possible, and the Spanish withdrawal was completed by the end of May. Zapatero announced that he did not intend to form a coalition government; rather, the PSOE made pacts with smaller parties in the two legislative chambers, effectively isolating the PP. Having won a congressional vote of confidence, Zapatero and his new Council of Ministers were inaugurated on 17 April. Miguel Angel Moratinos assumed the position of Minister of Foreign Affairs and Co-operation, and José Antonio Alonso was appointed Minister of the Interior. Pedro Solbes, previously the EU Commissioner for Economic and Monetary Affairs, was appointed Second Deputy Prime Minister and Minister of the newly reunited departments of the economy and finance. The new Government's programme included constitutional reform, transforming the Senado into a more regionally representative body, fiscal reform, the implementation of a co-ordinated anti-terrorism policy and a focus on improving gender equality and reducing domestic violence.

On 2 April 2004, meanwhile, a bomb of the same type discovered on the trains involved in the earlier Madrid attacks was defused on the railway line between Madrid and Seville (Sevilla). The following day seven men who were suspected of involvement in the bombings apparently blew themselves up, killing one police officer, during a police raid on an apartment in Leganés, a suburb of Madrid; Abdelmajid Farkhet, the man suspected of organizing the 11 March attacks, was among the dead. In May a parliamentary commission of inquiry into the train bombings was established. Specifically, the commission was to investigate information on the attacks provided by the PP Government, that Government's anti-terrorist policy, and the trafficking of illegal arms in Spain. In late November the former Prime Minister, Aznar, was questioned by the commission. Aznar maintained that ETA was linked to the Islamist militants suspected of carrying out the bomb attacks. Zapatero, who subsequently appeared before the commission, alleged that the PP administration had deleted all government computer records relating to the train bombings before leaving office. In March 2005 the preliminary findings of the commission, supported by all the parliamentary groups except the PP, were published. Recommendations included an increase in the implementation of security measures; however, the commission was criticized by some observers for being overly political in its handling of the inquiry.

During its first two years in office Zapatero's Government relied less on support from the opposition in major policy areas than had the previous Government. In particular, the PP did not support the Government in its attempts to begin negotiations with ETA, or on the Catalan Statute of Autonomy (see below), and the Government passed its legislative agenda mainly with the support of Esquerra Republicana de Catalunya (ERC) and IU. In December 2004 the Government's budget was approved by the Congreso de los Diputados, despite having been vetoed in the PP-dominated Senado.

Despite opposition from leaders of the Roman Catholic church, legislation permitting marriage between couples of the same sex was adopted by the Senado in June 2005, following its approval by the Congreso de los Diputados in April. In November new defence legislation was passed that required any deployment of Spanish troops abroad to be approved by the Cortes, and limited the circumstances in which such a deployment might occur.

In February 2006 Spain's highest consultative body, the Council of State, voted to support the Government's proposed amendments to the Constitution. Among the changes anticipated were the alteration of the law of royal succession, removing the preference for a male heir, a restructuring of the Senado and an increase in the power of the Autonomous Communities in the upper house; also to be addressed was the contentious issue of whether the Autonomous Communities should be regarded as 'nations'. However, in May 2007 Zapatero announced that the Government was abandoning constitutional reform for the duration of the current legislature owing to lack of support from the PP.

In April 2006 Zapatero announced an unexpected reorganization of the Government, prompted by the resignation of the Minister of Defence, José Bono, who was replaced by Alonso, who was succeeded as Minister of the Interior by Alfredo Pérez Rubalcaba. Further cabinet changes occurred in early September after the Minister of Industry, Tourism and Trade, José Montilla, announced his intention to stand election as President of the Generalitat in the forthcoming Catalan elections; he was replaced by Joan Clos, hitherto Mayor of Barcelona. In February 2007 Juan Fernando López Aguilar relinquished the post of Minister of Justice to stand for the presidency of another regional government, that of the Canary Islands (Islas Canarias), and was replaced by the former Chief Prosecutor of Madrid, Mariano Fernández Bermejo.

The Government came under pressure in early 2007 over its handling of the situation in the Basque Country, following ETA's breach of its cease-fire and the subsequent collapse of nascent peace talks (see below). In early March the prison sentence of Iñaki de Juana Chaos, an ETA militant who had been on hunger strike for nearly four months in protest at his continued detention, was commuted to house arrest on humanitarian grounds. (De Juana's 18-year sentence had been due to end in 2004, but had been extended after he was convicted of making terrorist threats.) The Government had feared that de Juana would come to be regarded as a martyr for Basque nationalism if he were allowed to die in gaol. However, his release prompted protests from the opposition, which urged Zapatero to resign, while some 500,000 people participated in an anti-Government demonstration in Madrid, organized by the PP. However, following the declaration by ETA in early June that its cease-fire had ended, de Juana was returned to prison near Madrid. The Government attracted criticism again in late March, following the release of Arnaldo Otegi, the leader of Batasuna, who had been brought to trial in Madrid on charges of glorifying terrorism, after the prosecution withdrew the charges. Otega was re-arrested later in the year, when he began serving a 15-month prison sentence in relation to the same charges.

During 2007 a principal topic of political debate concerned proposals, presented personally by Zapatero as Prime Minister, to introduce a 'law on historic memory' that was intended to provide formal recognition to those who had lost their lives during and immediately before the civil war, and to those who had been the victims of political repression under the Franco regime. The draft legislation was subject to criticism from both the PP, which regarded the proposals contained within the law as potentially socially divisive and unwarranted, and from human rights groups and the Catalan nationalist allies of the Government, the ERC, which regarded the measures as insufficiently rigorous. None the less, the Congreso de los Diputados approved the legislation at the end of October. Public funds were to be provided to organizations involved in locating mass graves, and to identifying, exhuming and re-burying the dead. Trials on political charges conducted during the period of Franco's rule were to be declared illegitimate (sentences passed were not, however, to be repealed outright), while political rallies at Franco's place of burial were to be prohibited. Meanwhile, also in late October, tens of thousands of Spanish pilgrims paraded in the Vatican City, to commemorate the beatification by the Roman Catholic Church of some 498 priests and members of religious orders killed during the Civil War, principally by Republican forces.

Meanwhile, in September 2007 Zapatero announced that a general election was to be held on 9 March 2008. Campaigning for the election by the PSOE and PP was suspended one day early, following the assassination, seemingly by ETA, of a former PSOE candidate in local elections in Mondragon, the Basque Country. At the elections, both the PSOE and PP increased their share of the votes cast, and their representation in the Congreso de los Diputados, compared with the results of the 2004 election, to 43.6% and 169 seats, and 40.1% and 154 seats, respectively. The representation of IU and of the ERC decreased, to two and three seats, respectively, while CiU won 10 seats and the EAJ/PNV six seats. Four other parties, mostly representing regional interests, obtained representation in the chamber. As in the outgoing lower chamber, no party controlled an overall majority of seats, although it was anticipated that the PSOE would again form a minority government. In concurrent elections to the Senado, the PP remained the largest faction, with 98 of the directly elected seats, and (following the appointment, in the following month, of senators to represent the Autonomous Community of Andalusia, in which an election to the regional legislature had been held concurrently with the general election) a further 24 appointed seats. The PSOE obtained 79 directly elected seats, and held 14 appointees.

On 9 April 2008 Zapatero narrowly failed to obtain the requisite two-thirds' majority in the Congreso de los Diputados (176 deputies) to be confirmed as Prime Minister, although he succeeded in obtaining the simple majority required at a second vote held two days later. The appointment of a new Government, including the formation of two new ministries—of Equality and of Science and Innovation—was announced later in the month. Several principal positions remained unchanged from the outgoing administration: Moratinos retained his post as Minister of Foreign Affairs and Co-operation; Rubalcaba remained as Minister of the Interior; María Teresa Fernández de la Vega as First Deputy Prime Minister, Minister of the Presidency and Government Spokesperson; and Solbes as Second Deputy Prime Minister and Minister of the Economy and Finance. New appointments included Carme Chacón Piqueras as Minister of Defence, the first woman to assume that post in Spain. Indeed, excluding the premiership, women accounted for exactly one-half of the ministerial appointments.

Autonomous regional parliaments were established in the Basque Country and in Catalonia in 1980. The parliaments of Galicia and Andalucía were established in October 1981 and May 1982, respectively, and the remaining 13 Legislative Assemblies of the Autonomous Communities (Comunidades Autónomas) were elected in May 1983. In 2001 proposals were announced to complete the development process of the Autonomous Communities with a policy of co-operation between the communities, through meetings and conferences. The presidents of each Autonomous Community were to be incorporated into the Senado, thus making it more representative of Spain as a whole. (See Legislative Assemblies of the Autonomous Communities for details of the most recent elections to all regional parliaments.)

Prior to the regional elections in Catalonia in 2003, Jordi Pujol, who had been President of a CiU-led Government in Catalonia for 23 years, announced that he would retire. No party won an absolute majority in the Catalan regional elections held on 16 November, and the two leading parties, CiU and the Partit dels Socialistes de Catalunya (PSC), each entered negotiations to form a coalition with the separatist ERC, which, having almost doubled its representation to 23 seats, held the balance of power. A coalition was subsequently formed comprising the PSC, ERC and the ecologist Iniciativa per Catalunya-Verds (IC-V). The PSC candidate, Pasqual Maragall, was inaugurated as President of the Generalitat on 15 December.

In September 2005 the Catalan Parliament overwhelmingly approved the draft of a revised Statute of Autonomy, to replace the existing document which had been in force since 1979. The proposed statute provoked considerable controversy elsewhere in the country over its definition of Catalonia as a 'nation' and its provision for greater fiscal and judicial independence. In mid-January 2006 Lt-Gen. José Mena Aguado, the head of the army's ground forces, was dismissed and placed under house arrest after appearing to suggest that the military should intervene to preserve the unity of Spain, should the statute become law. Later that month Prime Minister Zapatero bypassed the PSC, traditionally allied to the national PSOE, and negotiated an agreement with the centre-right CiU to revise the proposed statute, significantly reducing the extent of financial independence that would be granted to Catalonia. In late March the Congreso de los Diputados approved the statute, despite the opposition of ERC, which favoured full independence, and the PP, which claimed that the statute violated the Constitution. In May Maragall dismissed the ERC members of the Catalan Government in response to the party's refusal to support the autonomy statute, and announced that early elections would take place following the referendum on the statute to be held on 18 June. At the referendum the new Statute of Autonomy was approved by 73.2% of voters in Catalonia; voter participation was 48.9%. The statute came into force in August. Meanwhile, in June Maragall declared that he would not be standing for the presidency of the Generalitat in the forthcoming elections; instead, the PSC's First Secretary, José Montilla, was elected as the party's candidate. At the elections, held on 1 November, CiU emerged as the largest party, with 48 parliamentary seats of a total of 135. However, the PSC, with 37 seats, was able to retain power by forming a left-wing coalition with ERC and IC-V, with Montilla as President of the Generalitat.

Several other autonomous communities, including Aragón, the Balearic Islands (Islas Baleares or Illes Balears), the Canary Islands, Castilla-La Mancha and Galicia, began proceedings to reform their statutes of autonomy in 2005 and 2006. In April 2006 a new statute for Valencia entered into force, which, *inter alia*, defined Valencia as an 'historic nationality' (a term traditionally applied to Catalonia, the Basque Country and Galicia), made Valencian an official language and increased judicial and tax-raising independence. A new statute for Andalucía, which also defined the region as an 'historic nationality', took effect in March 2007, after being approved by 87% of the participating electorate in a referendum in February.

In the Basque region, meanwhile, terrorist activity by the separatist organization, ETA, founded in 1959, continued. Having claimed its first victim in 1961, between 1978 and 1992 alone a total of 711 murders was attributed to the group. Despite bomb attacks in Bilbao in February 1983 and Madrid in July 1986, the central Government maintained its offer of social reintegration, instigated in mid-1984, to former ETA members. The explosion in June 1987 of a bomb beneath a crowded Barcelona supermarket, which killed 21 and injured 45, was the most devastating attack committed by the organization, prompting Herri Batasuna (HB), ETA's political wing, to issue its first condemnation of a terrorist attack. Co-operation with the authorities of France and Algeria (where numerous ETA members were discovered to be living) was strengthened, and in October the French police arrested 67 Basque suspects. In December five children were among the 12 killed in a bomb attack on the married quarters of a Civil Guard barracks in Zaragoza, which provoked a further public outcry and prompted the Government to break off negotiations with ETA early in the following year. In January 1988, after protracted negotiations, six Basque parties (excluding HB) signed the Ajuria Enea Pact, rejecting terrorism as a means of determining the region's future. In January 1989 ETA declared a unilateral truce in an effort to reopen negotiations with the Government. Secret discussions between representatives of the Government and of ETA subsequently commenced in Algeria, but collapsed in April. Violent action recommenced, resulting in reprisals by GAL in which an HB deputy-elect was murdered. In February 1990 a resolution declaring the right of the Basque people to self-determination was approved by the Basque Parliament.

During the early and mid-1990s the authorities achieved considerable success in their counter-terrorist activities against ETA, particularly with increased co-operation from France. The continuing arrests and convictions of members of ETA, including a number of the organization's senior leaders, put considerable pressure on ETA, prompting internal tensions over whether to negotiate with the Government, but did not halt the campaign of violence. In July 1992 ETA's offer of a truce (to coincide with the forthcoming Olympic Games in Barcelona), in return for the reopening of dialogue, was rebuffed by the Government, which continued to insist upon the group's permanent renunciation of violence. Moreover, between then and February 1993 (when a major arsenal was discovered in France and ETA's operational head was captured) more than 500 ETA suspects were arrested. However, hopes of thereby forcibly and judicially ending ETA's campaign of violence were ended in June by two car bomb explosions (one of which killed seven people) in Madrid.

The Basque people's growing revulsion at ETA's actions, demonstrated by HB's loss of two of its four seats in the Congreso de los Diputados at the 1993 general election, was intensified by the kidnapping of a Spanish industrialist, which led to a resurgence of the peace movement within the region. (The industrialist was released in October, reportedly upon the payment of a large ransom.) In August there were violent clashes in San Sebastián and Bilbao between peace demonstrators and supporters of ETA. In September there was renewed unrest in the Basque Country, following the deaths in custody of two ETA suspects and the disclosure of medical evidence suggesting violent treatment of a third detainee. Detentions in Spain of terrorist suspects totalled 127 in 1993. At the end of August 1994 the ETA leadership ordered its imprisoned members to embark upon a hunger strike, in an attempt to reassert its authority and to obstruct the process of rehabilitation.

The results of the election to the Basque Parliament in October 1994 demonstrated the continuing decline in support for HB. Several senior ETA leaders were captured in late 1994 and in mid-1995, but attacks on police officers continued. In January 1995 Gregorio Ordóñez, a member of the Basque Parliament and the PP candidate for the mayoralty of San Sebastián at the forthcoming municipal elections, was shot dead, the first politician since 1992 to be murdered by ETA. Thousands of Basque citizens took to the streets of San Sebastián and Bilbao to protest against the assassination. In April 1995 Aznar, leader of the opposition PP, narrowly survived a car-bomb attempt on his life in Madrid, which injured 19 others. In August the authorities announced that a plot to assassinate King Juan Carlos had been foiled. Successive murders of politicians in early 1996 provoked a public outcry. Some 1m. citizens, including Prime Minister González and many other political leaders, attended an anti-ETA march in Madrid. As the general election approached, Jon Idígoras, the veteran HB leader, was arrested, amid controversy arising from a campaign video that apparently supported the activities of ETA.

In July 1996, following a brief truce and the new PP Government's conditional offer of dialogue in the previous month, ETA renewed its bombing campaign, this time targeting the tourism industry. However, the authorities continued to arrest and convict ETA activists. A resurgence of violence in 1997 culminated in the abduction in July of Miguel Angel Blanco, a young PP councillor in the Basque town of Ermua. ETA issued an ultimatum that prisoners belonging to the separatist organization be transferred to gaols in the Basque Country. Despite numerous appeals, including a message from the Pope, Blanco was duly shot upon the expiry of ETA's 48-hour deadline. His death provoked an unprecedented display of public outrage. In the largest demonstration since the attempted military coup of 1981, millions of Spaniards took to the streets, including Prime Minister Aznar, who led a protest march in Madrid. The Prime Minister vowed to intensify the Government's campaign against ETA, while urging (along with the moderate Basque parties) the isolation of HB. However, in September 1997 the Government confirmed that it had uncovered a major extortion enterprise by ETA in the Navarra (Navarre) autonomy that neighbours the Basque Country. Later that month a large arsenal was discovered and a group of 12 suspected ETA collaborators arrested following the death of two alleged senior ETA leaders in an exchange of gunfire with the Civil Guard in Bilbao. In October an attempt to plant remote-controlled grenades outside the new Guggenheim Museum in Bilbao, which was due to be inaugurated by the King, was thwarted by the police, but resulted in the death of one officer.

In December 1997 the 23 members of the collective leadership of HB were each sentenced to seven years' imprisonment for collaborating with an armed group. In a significant development, for the first time the direct relationship between ETA and HB, which continued to claim to be independent of the terrorist organization, was recognized by the judiciary. The members of the collective leadership were released in July 1999, when their imprisonment was ruled unconstitutional. Meanwhile, in early 1998 a new HB leadership was elected, pledging to continue with the policies of its predecessors. ETA's campaign of targeting PP councillors continued, extending beyond the Basque region for the first time in January, when a councillor and his wife were murdered in Seville. The following month official efforts against ETA activity were distracted by the revelation that national police forces had been deployed in the Basque Country without the knowledge of the Basque regional Government. The disclosure of the clandestine deployment provoked a dispute between the Lehendakari and the central Government. Meanwhile, deadly violence by ETA continued into 1998. The capture of several ETA activists in San Sebastián, as they prepared to launch mortar bombs at a police barracks, resulted in the discovery of another plot to assassinate King Juan Carlos. In July Judge Garzón, who was investigating ETA's fund-raising activities, ordered the closure of *Egin*, a radical Basque newspaper, and that of an associated radio station, on the grounds of their connections to ETA.

Following a dispute regarding a proposal to oblige all members of the Basque Parliament to accord formal recognition to the Spanish Constitution, in June 1998 the Partido Socialista de Euskadi-Euskadiko Ezkerra (PSE-EE) withdrew from the Basque coalition Government after 12 years of co-operation. In early September, apparently attempting to pre-empt any ban on its activities and while still declining to renounce the use of violence, HB announced that it was to contest the forthcoming elections as the newly formed Euskal Herritarrok (EH). In mid-September both the PP and the opposition PSOE expressed reservations at the conclusion of an agreement (the 'Lizarra Pact') by the EAJ/PNV, Eusko Alkartasuna (EA), HB and IU on proposals for unconditional discussions with ETA. Nevertheless, following several months of secret talks between representatives of the EAJ/PNV and HB, on 16 September ETA declared an indefinite truce. In a conciliatory gesture, the Prime Minister indicated his willingness to transfer a number of ETA convicts to prisons in the Basque Country.

At the Basque elections held in October 1998, the EAJ/PNV again received the greatest support, while the PP supplanted the PSE-EE as the party with the second largest representation in the regional parliament. At the end of October it was announced that the State was to assume responsibility for compensation of the victims of ETA, the total sum in question now estimated at 60,000m. pesetas. However, the Government refused to compensate members of GAL. The Prime Minister also stated that, while being required to renounce the use of violence, ETA would not be obliged to relinquish all its weapons. In November the central Government announced the inauguration of direct contact with representatives of ETA, which reaffirmed its commitment to the cease-fire. In December, with the support of EH, an entirely nationalist Basque Government was established; the coalition was headed by Juan José Ibarretxe of the EAJ/PNV. In the same month, as transfers of ETA convicts to prisons located in the Basque Country continued, the Prime Minister invited EH to join discussions on the region's future. In January 1999, however, EH refused to attend the inauguration ceremony of the Basque Country's new Lehendakari, while thousands of Basques participated in a march to demonstrate support for the transfer of ETA inmates to prisons nearer their homes.

In February 1999, in France, the first arrest since the cease-fire of an ETA suspect was made. In March the police arrested six ETA activists, including the alleged head of ETA's military wing (who was convicted in April 2002). However, in May the Spanish Government announced that 304 (of an estimated 550) exiles, who had been obliged to leave Spain on account of their alleged connections to ETA, were to be permitted to return to their homeland. In June the Prime Minister admitted that direct talks between government representatives and members of ETA had taken place in the previous month, the first such official acknowledgement since 1989. In late June a newly elected deputy to the parliament of Navarra and member of ETA was sentenced to 60 years' imprisonment, along with an accomplice, upon conviction for the 1988 murder in Seville of a PP councillor and his wife.

In July 1999, for the first time, EH joined other Basque parties in signing a declaration rejecting the use of violence. In August ETA stated that dialogue with the Government was being suspended, owing to the latter's perceived attempt to gain political advantage from the peace process. In early September, as the first anniversary of the truce approached, it was revealed that a total of 180 ETA prisoners had been released within the last year. However, official monitoring of ETA activity continued and at the end of September three ETA suspects were arrested in France. In October ETA's proposals for the resumption of direct peace talks were rejected by the central Government on the grounds that the release of hundreds of ETA prisoners, as urged by the organization, was not negotiable. At the end of October ETA members exiled overseas were reported to be returning to Europe and regrouping in France. On 28 November, on the eve of the opening in Paris of the trial of 13 ETA defendants, the terrorist organization announced the end of the 14-month cease-fire. Thousands of citizens took to the streets to urge that the truce be maintained. Hours before the expiry of the truce on 3 December, the EAJ/PNV, along with other signatories of the Lizarra Pact, invited EH to sign a document demanding full sovereignty for the Basque Country and criticizing the policies of both the Spanish and French Governments.

Despite successful official action against ETA activities, in January 2000 the organization successfully exploded two car-bombs in Madrid, one of which killed an army officer. More than 1m. people, led by the Prime Minister, participated in a protest march in the capital. At the end of the month it was reported that ETA's international network, responsible for the co-ordination of financial and logistical support, had been dismantled. In February, in Vitoria, a Basque socialist politician and his bodyguard died in a bomb attack, prompting Ibarretxe to sever all links with EH, which subsequently announced that it was withdrawing from the Basque Parliament.

In early May 2000 the central Government excluded the possibility of renewed contact with ETA unless a cease-fire was reinstated. Also in May the Spanish and French Governments determined to intensify collaboration to combat terrorism. In June a PP politician was assassinated, resulting in the abolition of local government pacts between the EAJ/PNV and EH. In July the interior ministries of the central Government and the Basque Country established a joint co-ordinating committee to share and assess intelligence regarding ETA. Attacks in July and August claimed the lives of six people. In September 20 financial and political organizers of EKIN, ETA's fund-raising wing, were arrested. Seven of these were convicted in April 2001, on the same day that Judge Garzón pronounced EKIN illegal, owing to its associations with ETA. Meanwhile, on 15 September 2000 the French authorities arrested the suspected former leader of ETA, Ignacio Gracia Arregui ('Iñaki de Rentería') on charges of terrorism and attempting to assassinate the King in 1995. In December he was sentenced to five years' imprisonment, added to a previous sentence of 11 years. Subsequently, a PP politician was assassinated in Barcelona. On the following day some 100,000 people, led by Prime Minister Aznar, demonstrated in Barcelona.

In September 2000 EH abandoned the ruling coalition, leaving the EAJ/PNV without a majority in the Basque Government. In October Ibon Muñoa, a former HB politician, was convicted of providing ETA with information to aid the 1997 murder of Miguel Ángel Blanco. In the same month a public prosecutor in Andalucía and a senior military officer were assassinated, and five people were killed by car-bombs. Demonstrations were held in Madrid and in the Basque Country. In November a former health minister, Ernest Lluch, was assassinated in Barcelona, and in the following month a PP politician, Francisco Cano Consuegra, was killed in a car-bomb. During 2000 some 100 members or collaborators of ETA were detained following covert Civil Guard operations; six command units were dismantled; and 12 members of ETA were successfully extradited. However, street disturbances in Basque cities continued to escalate, many caused by Haika (Rise Up), the youth wing of ETA, and there were 23 fatalities resultant from ETA attacks. The violence continued into 2001, as did arrests of ETA suspects by the Spanish and French authorities.

On 20 February 2001 Ibarretxe announced that Basque regional elections would be held early, on 13 May. The PP and PSOE had proposed an all-party anti-terrorist pact to follow the elections, and a co-ordinating committee was established to form anti-terrorist policy. In March 16 people who were believed to be leaders of Haika were arrested and in May Judge Garzón pronounced Haika illegal. Following retaliatory attacks throughout March, ETA warned that it was to target holiday resorts. Elections to the Basque Parliament took place on 13 May. The EAJ/PNV-EA electoral coalition, led by Ibarretxe, retained power, taking 33 of the 75 seats. The PP obtained 19 seats, while the PSE-EE won 13, EH seven and IU-EB three seats. The EAJ/PNV and the EA now controlled more seats than the combined forces of the PP and the PSOE. Following its losses in the elections, HB elected new members to its leadership and declared that, henceforth, it wished to be known as Batasuna (Unity).

Violence continued through mid-2001, with the assassination of the financial director of the *El Diario Vasco* newspaper and various attempted bombings, including a parcel bomb in Madrid, which killed one person. In July Spain secured an agreement with Mexico for the extradition of 20 suspected ETA members and further co-operation against ETA. Less than two weeks later, however, the inauguration of Ibarretxe as Lehendakari was accompanied by ETA action in Tolosa, where a member of the Ertzaintza was assassinated, and in Leitxa, Navarra, where a local councillor was killed in a bomb attack. Two days later 50,000 people demonstrated in Pamplona to protest at the violence. In late July it became apparent that ETA had planned a series of bomb attacks on Spain's holiday resorts to coincide with the summer tourist season. A car-bomb at Málaga airport was defused on 26 July and a series of co-ordinated bomb attacks took place in towns across the Basque Country. The following day, a bomb injured three people in Barcelona. On 30 July two former leading ETA members were sentenced to 1,128 years' imprisonment for various crimes, including 46 counts of murder. ETA's campaign of violence and bombing continued throughout August, while at the end of the month it was estimated that, so far in 2001, some 51 arrests of alleged ETA members had been made.

There was a brief interlude in violence during September 2001. Nevertheless, the Minister of the Interior reported that month that police had discovered a list, compiled by ETA, of potential targets, which included more than 2,000 politicians, police and military personnel. In late September police in France captured the alleged chief of ETA logistics and four other suspects. In October Ibarretxe warned that he was determined to hold a referendum on self-determination for the Basque Country, should the Government in Madrid continue to reject dialogue and ETA continue its campaign of violence. However, Prime Minister Aznar condemned the proposal as unconstitutional, and the violence resumed with the bombing of a courthouse in Vitoria. On 12 October a car-bomb exploded in Madrid, injuring 17 people. It was later reported that the bomb had been intended to be detonated at a military parade earlier in the day, at which members of the royal family were present, to commemorate the National Day.

On 17 November 2001 some 35,000 people marched through Bilbao to demand the right for self-determination for the Basque region. This followed two high-profile bomb attacks on Madrid earlier that month, of which one took place during the city's 'rush hour' and injured 95 people. On the same day, two ETA gunmen assassinated a judge who had presided over the regional court of Vizcaya. Members of the Ertzaintza again became the targets of ETA when two were shot dead in Guipúzcoa province on 23 November. In December seven people were arrested in connection with the summer bombing campaign on tourist resorts.

Basque groups took advantage of the beginning of Spain's presidency of the EU in January 2002 to demand greater representation in the European Parliament. The central Government, however, welcomed the introduction of an EU-wide arrest warrant, due to come into effect in 2004, which it hoped would help capture ETA suspects. ETA claimed responsibility for several attacks in March. In the following month a demand from independent, left-wing Basque parties for a cease-fire was denounced by Batasuna and ETA. A total of 122 arrests of ETA members were carried out during 2002. In May the trial of Arnaldo Otegi of Batasuna for vocal support of ETA was dismissed by the Supreme Court, to the consternation of the Government which attempted to intervene. After a number of ETA actions during the EU summit in Seville in June, however, the Senado approved measures to outlaw political parties deemed to support terrorist organizations. The legislation was widely seen as targeting Batasuna, and, indeed, in August a parliamentary vote outlawed the party, while a separate Supreme Court order enforced the closure of party offices and a three-year suspension of party activities. Subsequently, in March 2003, the Supreme Court officially outlawed Batasuna. (The party was banned for a further two years in early 2006.) Meanwhile, ETA declared its intention to attack the political offices of the PP and PSOE, and a number of violent actions were attempted in late 2002, including a thwarted attack on shopping centres in Madrid in late December. During the last months of the year three senior ETA leaders were captured and Judge Garzón accused 20 Batasuna leaders of membership of ETA. In December an attempt to circumvent the delegalization of Batasuna led the party to establish another organization, Sozialista Abertzaleak (Patriotic Socialists), in the hope of contesting regional elections in May 2003.

In late December 2002 a silent rally in Bilbao organized by Ibarretxe, who had put forward a set of proposals for the establishment of an independent Basque state in October, protested against ETA's use of violence. In January 2003 the national legislature approved anti-terrorist legislation, extending the maximum sentence for terrorist activities from 30 to 40 years, and in February the Basque-language newspaper *Euskaldunon Egunkaria* was shut down on the grounds of its alleged links with ETA. Prime Minister Aznar's hope for external support in the eradication of ETA was widely believed to have been one of the reasons for his backing of US-led military action in Iraq during 2003 (see above). Prior to regional and municipal elections in May, the central Government banned some 1,500 candidates from standing on the grounds of their alleged links with ETA. In response, ETA urged the lodging of protest votes in support of the banned politicians. In July two members of ETA were given terms of imprisonment of 790 years and six months for the 1987 bombing of a supermarket in Barcelona, in which 21 people had died.

In September 2003 Ibarretxe presented to the regional legislature his plan for shared sovereignty over the Basque Country, which proposed the 'free association' of the Basque Country with Spain, the creation of a separate judiciary and education system and the right of the Basque Country to conduct international relations. The proposals—known as the Ibarretxe plan—were not widely supported in the region, and were strongly criticized by Madrid-based politicians and media, including Aznar, who accused Ibarretxe of treason. In early October 34 suspected ETA members were arrested as part of a joint Franco-Spanish operation, and in mid-November a further 12 suspected leaders of the illegal body were taken into custody. The following month four others, including Gorka Palacios Alday, the alleged military leader of ETA, were arrested in France. In December Spanish police foiled a planned attack by suspected ETA terrorists on a railway station in Madrid, and in February 2004, in the run-up to the general election in March, two men were captured driving towards Madrid with 500 kg of explosives. In the same month letters purporting to be from ETA were sent to businesses in the Spanish tourism sector warning that, as had been the case in 2003, tourists would be targeted during the summer season. At the same time ETA declared a cease-fire in Catalonia.

In January 2004 the Constitutional Court rejected Batasuna's appeal for legalization. Immediately following the PSOE's victory in the general election in March, ETA expressed a desire to begin a dialogue with the new Government; this was rejected, however, by the incoming administration of premier Zapatero. Responsibility for a series of bombs in seaside towns in mid-2004 was claimed by ETA. In late 2004, following the establishment of a Franco-Spanish anti-terrorism police force in September, a series of arrests of suspected members of ETA took place in France and Spain, including the capture in October of the alleged leader of the organization, Mikel 'Antza' Albizu Iriarte, in France. Subsequently Batasuna announced that it was prepared to negotiate. However, in December and January 2005 a series of bombs were detonated around Spain, and in early February ETA exploded a car bomb, injuring over 40 people, at a conference centre in Madrid, which was due to be visited by the King and President Vicente Fox of Mexico. In 2004 a total of 135 suspected members of ETA were arrested, 74 in Spain and the others in France and Belgium. In December Judge Garzón published a report stating that in the previous 10 years ETA had been responsible for the deaths of more than 800 people, and had caused some €8,000m. of damage; however, 2004 was notable for being the first year since the early 1970s in which ETA had not been responsible for any deaths.

In December 2004 the Basque Parliament voted in favour of the Ibarretxe plan, with the last-minute support of Sozialista Abertzaleak, the perceived successor to Batasuna, and thus the new political wing of ETA. In early February 2005 the plan was debated by the Congreso de los Diputados and rejected by an overwhelming majority, although Zapatero declared that he was prepared to enter into negotiations on the status of the Basque Country within Spain. Ibarretxe responded by bringing the date of the Basque regional elections forward to 17 April, and declaring that he would go ahead with plans for a referendum on the Ibarretxe plan, despite claims by the central Government that this was unconstitutional. The election was seen as a gauge of the popularity of the Ibarretxe plan. Prior to the poll, Aukera Guztiak, a nationalist party, was banned on the grounds of being close to ETA. In the event, Ibarretxe's EAJ/PNV-EA coalition won a reduced majority of 29 seats, equivalent to 38.7% of votes cast.

In May 2005 the Congreso de los Diputados approved government plans to open negotiations with ETA, should the group consent to disarm. An estimated 300,000 demonstrators opposed to talks with ETA marched in Madrid in early June. In October Harriet Aguirre, an alleged senior leader of ETA, was arrested in France, and in November, in the largest ever such prosecution, the trial commenced of 56 people suspected of belonging to, or aiding, ETA. Nevertheless, ETA continued its bombing campaign around Spain during 2005 and early 2006, although no fatalities were caused. However, on 22 March 2006 ETA declared a 'permanent cease-fire', the first time in its history that it had taken such a step. It was speculated that the cease-fire had been prompted by the arrest of many of the organization's leaders. Zapatero responded to ETA's unilateral declaration by stating in May that the Government intended to enter into peace talks with the group; in June the Prime Minister confirmed that negotiations would, eventually, take place. Despite these advances, during late 2006 ETA issued a number of statements indicating that it was not prepared to abandon violence or relinquish its weapons until the Basque Country became independent of Spain. In October the theft of 360 pistols from an arms depot near Nîmes, France, was attributed to ETA by the French and Spanish authorities, casting further doubt on the future of the peace process. On 30 December, less than two weeks after the Government held its first formal meeting with ETA officials, a car bomb exploded at Barajas airport in Madrid, killing two people. Although ETA claimed responsibility for the attack, it claimed that its permanent cease-fire remained intact; none the less, Zapatero suspended talks in the wake of the bombing.

In the approach to the municipal elections of 27 May 2007, a number of separatist political parties were prevented from standing because of suspected links with Batasuna. Following a failed attempt by Batasuna members in late March to register a party called Abertzale Sozialisten Batasuna (Patriotic Socialist Union) with the Ministry of Interior, in April Acción Nacionalista Vasca (ANV), a legal political party founded in 1930 as an offshoot of the EAJ/PNV but whose activity had become very limited, fielded candidates in municipalities throughout the Basque Country and Navarra. Concurrently, an electoral list bearing the name Abertzale Sozialistak (AS) stood for election in 232 municipalities. After it emerged that large numbers of candidates for both ANV and AS were members of Batasuna, in early May the Constitutional Court annulled all the AS lists and 133 (around one-half) of those fielded by ANV; however, it stopped short of recommending that ANV be banned entirely. Both AS and ANV were also prevented from standing in the elections to the parliament of Navarra, held on 27 May.

On 5 June 2007 ETA announced an immediate end to its cease-fire, issuing a statement accusing the Government of 'pursuing detentions, torture and persecution' of its members. Several days later Otegi was re-arrested and began serving a 15-month prison sentence on charges of glorifying terrorism. Later in the month 100 kg of explosives and other bomb-making equipment believed to belong to ETA was discovered in a car near the Spanish–Portuguese frontier. In late August an explosion in Durango, the Basque Country, in which two police officers were injured, was reported to constitute the first attack by ETA since the expiry of its cease-fire. Another car bomb later in the month resulted in no injuries. In early September, in a joint French-Spanish operation, four suspected members of ETA, who were believed to have been responsible for the attack at the airport in Madrid in December 2006 were arrested, and 350 kg of explosives were seized.

In early September 2007, in response to a request by Judge Garzón, some 23 senior members of Batasuna were arrested during a clandestine meeting of the organization in Segura. Batasuna described the arrests as constituting a 'declaration of war' by the Spanish authorities; the EAJ/PNV were also critical of the arrests. In early December two Spanish civil guards were shot by suspected members of ETA in Southern France; one of the officers was killed and the other left in a coma. The killing was believed to constitute the first killing perpetrated by ETA in France for some 30 years. Further bomb attacks against court buildings in the Basque country occurred in mid-December and in early February 2008, but in both instances no-one was injured. At the beginning of February another senior member of Batasuna, Pernando Barrena, was arrested. Later in the month, in response to a further request by Garzón, the High Court suspended the operations, for a period of three years, of two political parties that favoured the independence of the Basque Country from Spain. Garzón declared that the parties—the ANV and the Partido Comunista de la Tierra Vasca (PCTV—Communist Party of the Basque Lands)—were linked to Batasuna.

Catalan and Galician nationalist extremists pursued a limited terrorist campaign in the 1980s and 1990s. The Catalan organization, Terra Lliure (Free Land), claimed its first victim in 1987, and the Galician Exército Guerrilheiro do Povo Galego Ceive (EGPGC—Free Galician People's Guerrilla Army) carried out its only murder, of a civil guard, in early 1989. In mid-1989 the Catalan Government was reported to be negotiating with Terra Lliure, and in July 1991 the group's dissolution was announced, following its renunciation of the use of violence. In mid-1992, however, a dissident faction planted several bombs. The trial of 24 alleged members of Terra Lliure concluded in July 1995, 18 being found guilty; 15 were pardoned in June 1996. The EGPGC's campaign continued intermittently. In September 1991 the alleged leader of the group was apprehended by the authorities and, upon the arrest in November of eight suspected EGPGC members, it was believed that the organization had been dissolved. In June 1994 six EGPGC activists received prison sentences, while two others were acquitted.

Following the suicide attacks in the USA on 11 September 2001, it was reported that 16 Islamist activists had been arrested in Spain in late 2001. They were accused of belonging to al-Qa'ida, which was held principally responsible for the attacks, and charged with terrorist activities. Further arrests were made during April and June 2002. In January 2003 16 North Africans, mostly from Algeria, were arrested near Barcelona and Girona following the discovery of a cache of chemicals and explosives, which were purportedly intended to be used in attacks around Europe. In September five men of Syrian origin were arrested in Spain on suspicion of having links with al-Qa'ida. Baltasar Garzón issued an arrest warrant for Osama bin Laden, and a further 34 individuals were charged with belonging to a terrorist organization. The trial of 24 alleged members of al-Qa'ida, some of whom were charged with organizing the 11 September attacks, commenced in Madrid in April 2005. In September 18 of the defendants were found guilty of being members of al-Qa'ida; Syrian-born Imad Yarkas was sentenced to 27 years' imprisonment for involvement in the 11 September attacks, while the others received prison sentences of between six and 11 years for a range of terrorism offences.

In late March 2004 international arrest warrants were issued for six suspected terrorists with Moroccan connections, including Abdelmajid Farkhet, a Tunisian, who was suspected of having masterminded the 11 March train bombings in Madrid (see above) and who was known to have been preaching *jihad* (Islamic holy war) in the capital since mid-2003. Throughout the rest of 2004 and in early 2005 further arrests were made in Spain and in other European countries in connection with the Madrid train bombings; by early April 2005 a total of 24 people, mainly North Africans, had been charged on counts of terrorism and murder. In October and November 2004 some 33 suspected Islamist militants, reportedly with links to Moroccan fundamentalist groups, were arrested in connection with an alleged plot to detonate explosive devices in the high court and other public buildings in Madrid. In March 2006 32 people were charged in connection with the plot.

The first trial in connection with the train bombings was held in November 2004, and a 16-year-old Spaniard received a prison sentence of six years for trafficking explosives that were subsequently used in the attacks. In December Rabei Osman as-Sayed, one of the suspected leaders of the plot to blow up the trains in Madrid, was extradited from Italy, and in the same month Hassan al-Haski, who was alleged to be a leader of the Moroccan Islamist group, Groupe islamique combattant Marocain (GICM), was arrested and charged with 191 counts of murder. The GICM was reportedly connected to the May 2003 suicide bombings in Casablanca, Morocco. In November and December 2005 17 people were arrested on suspicion of providing logistical and financial assistance to an Algerian-based Islamist militant group, the Groupe salafiste pour la prédication et le combat. It was reported that a total of around 90 suspected Islamist militants were arrested in Spain during 2005, some of whom were alleged to have been involved in recruiting other radicals to join the insurgency in Iraq. In April 2006 29 people, mostly Moroccan nationals, but including three Spanish citizens (who had supplied the explosives used in the bombings), were charged with involvement in the Madrid train bombings. The trial of the suspects began in February 2007 and, at the end of October, 21 of the suspects were convicted of the attacks, while seven were acquitted, including an Egyptian citizen who had been accused of organizing the attacks. (Charges had been dropped against the remaining person charged, on grounds of lack of evidence.) Three defendants were sentenced to the equivalent of the maximum permissible prison term of 40 years, having been found guilty of murdering 191 people, procuring two involuntary abortions (as two of the people killed in the attacks were pregnant women) and conspiring to cause the deaths of the 1,856 people injured in the attacks. A further principal suspect in the attacks was arrested in January 2008 in Morocco, where he was to be brought to trial.

In the late 1990s there was growing concern over the increasing number of illegal immigrants entering Spain, mostly from Latin America and North Africa. In 2000 some 14,893 people were apprehended, compared with 3,569 in the previous year. The influx of illegal immigrants had resulted in social unrest in some areas, with anti-immigration protests and violent attacks against the immigrant population. Despite intense opposition from the other parties in the Congreso de los Diputados, in July 2000 the Government announced proposals for the reform of the immigration law (adopted by the Congreso in December 1999), introducing severe penalties for illegal immigrants, and for traffickers and employers of illegal immigrants. Those entering the country illegally could be deported within 48 hours. Illegal workers would be deprived of the right to strike and to join a trade union, and their use of public services would be limited. They would gain the right to remain in the country only after five years of employment, rather than the two years previously specified. The reforms entered into force in January 2001, at which time there were an estimated 200,000 illegal immigrants in Spain. Demonstrations against the reforms were staged across the country, and in Barcelona 300 illegal immigrants locked themselves into the Santa María del Pi Church and declared a hunger strike. In June the Government agreed to grant the protesters legal status. Despite criticism from the opposition, amendments to the electoral legislation received parliamentary approval in late July: these specified modalities whereby immigrants who could prove that they had been working in Spain since January 2001 could obtain residency.

In January 2003 changes to immigration legislation, allowing South Americans of Spanish ancestry to apply for Spanish citizenship, were expected to lead to some 1m. applications. At the same time, greater strictures were placed on applications from other non-EU countries.

In February 2005 an amnesty was granted to the estimated 800,000 illegal immigrants in Spain, the terms of which required employers to register illegal immigrants, thereby allowing them to receive working permits. Immigration was becoming an increasingly important factor in the Spanish economy, with the number of registered immigrants living in Spain rising from 900,000 in 2000 to 3.7m. in 2005, equivalent to 8.4% of the resident population. In March 2006 the Spanish Government announced its intention to open the Spanish labour market from May to citizens of the eight central and eastern European countries that joined the EU in May 2004, removing restrictions that had been imposed at that time. Meanwhile, large numbers of Africans continued to attempt to enter Spain, often by highly dangerous routes. In October 2005 hundreds of would-be immigrants attempted to climb the barriers separating Morocco from the Spanish exclaves of Ceuta and Melilla, while in March 2006 it was estimated that some 1,200 Africans had died in the previous four months attempting to sail from Mauritania to the Canary Islands. Spain and Mauritania subsequently agreed to tighten their borders in an effort to deter African migrants from trying to enter Europe. Nevertheless, large numbers of immigrants landed in the Canary Islands between May and September 2006—many of whom were repatriated by the Spanish authorities—and in the latter month it was reported that 27,000 immigrants had arrived in the islands so far that year, five times as many as in 2005.

In December 1988 Spain and the USA renewed their bilateral defence agreement, permitting the USA's use of bases in Spain for a further eight years from May 1989. In late 1996 the accord was extended until May 1998. In November 1999 the US Administration requested permission to establish their principal base in southern Europe in Cádiz. Spain was admitted to Western European Union (WEU, see p. 426) in November 1988. In November 1992 Spain dispatched a substantial contingent of troops to Bosnia and Herzegovina, the first Spanish soldiers to serve in a UN peace-keeping operation. Continuing to assume a greater international role, Spain contributed troops to the multinational force deployed in Albania in April 1997, and again in April 1999 during the NATO offensive against Yugoslavia (Serbia and Montenegro). Spain committed 1,200 ground troops to the international peace-keeping force deployed in the Serbian Province of Kosovo in June 1999. In mid-2003, despite widespread public opposition, Spain sent 1,300 peace-keeping troops to Iraq to join the US-led coalition forces, and in October of that year pledged €250m. to the reconstruction process in Iraq. Following the election of the PSOE Government in March 2004, however, the withdrawal of the Spanish troops was completed by the end of May. In June 2007 US Secretary of State Condoleezza Rice visited Madrid, becoming the first senior official of the US Administration to visit Spain since the PSOE Government took office. In early 2007 Spain was contributing to a number of international peace-keeping missions, including the United Nations Interim Force in Lebanon, in which some 1,100 Spanish troops were serving and the International Security Assistance Force in Afghanistan, in which some 742 Spanish troops were serving.

From 1998, under Spanish law persons accused of crimes against humanity, no matter where they had taken place, could be tried in a Spanish court. In the late 1990s criminal proceedings continued in Spain against former Argentine and Chilean officials of the military dictatorships of Argentina (1976–83) and of Chile (1979–90), during which numerous Spanish citizens had been killed. In November 1999 the investigating judge, Garzón, issued international arrest warrants for 98 citizens of Argentina. In January 2000, however, the judge's request for the extradition of 48 Argentines, accused of various atrocities, was refused. In August 2003 Ricardo Cavallo, an Argentine former naval officer, was extradited from Mexico on charges of human rights abuses. In November 1998, following the arrest in the United Kingdom of Gen. Augusto Pinochet and the instigation by Garzón of extradition proceedings against the former Chilean President, Chile's ambassador to Madrid was recalled for consultations. In October 1999 a British judge ruled that the former Chilean President could be extradited to Spain to answer 35 charges of torture and conspiracy. In March 2000, however, Pinochet was permitted to return to Chile from the United Kingdom, where he had remained under house arrest, extradition proceedings having been abandoned on medical grounds. In early 2005, following an indictment by Garzón, Adolfo Scilingo, an Argentine former army officer, was given a prison sentence of 640 years for crimes against humanity under the military rule in Argentina during 1976–83.

The PSOE Government elected in 2004 implemented a shift in foreign relations emphasis from the USA to Europe, and accords were signed on the creation of a joint anti-terrorism police force with France, and on increased military co-operation between EU member states, including the creation of a European rapid-reaction force. In late 2005 tensions arose with the USA over a Spanish agreement to sell military equipment to Venezuela. In April 2006 the foreign affairs committee of the Congreso de los Diputados requested that the Government compile a detailed report on alleged flights by the USA's Central Intelligence Agency (CIA) via Spain. This followed reports that the CIA had used European airports to transport suspected Islamist militants to third countries for interrogation.

Spanish ratification of the Treaty on European Union (the Maastricht Treaty) was completed in November 1992. A dispute between Spain and the United Kingdom over the sovereignty of the neighbouring British dependency of Gibraltar remained unresolved. Relations deteriorated in 1995 upon Spain's announcement that, in protest at the apparent inadequacy of British efforts, it was to implement stricter border controls to combat the problem of drugs- and tobacco-smuggling from Gibraltar. In May 1996, upon the election of a new Government in the territory, border controls were further strengthened by the Spanish authorities leading to renewed protests from the British Government. In 1997 the United Kingdom rejected Spanish initiatives entailing joint sovereignty for up to 100 years prior to an eventual transfer of power to Spain. In December Spanish proposals that, following a period of joint sovereignty, Gibraltar became an Autonomous Community were similarly rebuffed by the British Government. In 1998 tension was renewed over the issue of access to fishing grounds. The seizure of a Spanish fishing vessel in early 1999 led to a serious escalation of the dispute and the imposition of new border controls and travel restrictions by Spain. In April 2000 Spain and the United Kingdom signed an agreement relating to the administrative status of Gibraltar. The territory's identity cards would henceforth be accepted by Spain as valid for travel within the EU. Furthermore, the agreement permitted the implementation of numerous EU directives, long obstructed by Spain, which had refused to recognize the Government of Gibraltar as a 'competent authority' in EU affairs. It was also agreed that Spain and Gibraltar would communicate indirectly through a facility, based in London, provided by the British authorities. In March 2001 Spain condemned plans by the political parties of Gibraltar to request reforms to the 1969 Constitution, allowing self-determination, and to hold a referendum on decolonization. Following a meeting between Spanish and British officials in Brussels in mid-2001, the Minister of Foreign Affairs, Josep Piqué, and his British counterpart, Jack Straw, held discussions in October, at which they agreed to work towards solving the dispute by December 2002. The issue of the right of Gibraltarians to vote on any agreement reached by the two Governments continued to impede the progress of the discussions, Piqué warning the British Government that Spain would not accept the results of such a referendum. At further talks in November, however, Piqué announced plans to increase the number of telephone lines available to Gibraltar, from 35,000 to 100,000, and provide access to Spanish health care for the inhabitants of the territory. The deadline for achieving a solution was also brought forward to September 2002. In January 2002 it was reported that the Spanish Government had agreed to modify its demand for outright sovereignty over the territory and reconsider the option of sharing sovereignty over the territory with the United Kingdom for an indefinite period. In an open letter published in the Gibraltarian press, Piqué attempted to persuade the citizens of Gibraltar of the advantages of Spanish sovereignty and urged its Chief Minister, Peter Caruana, to join the discussions; Caruana had hitherto boycotted the negotiations. During May, however, Aznar announced that Spain would never withdraw its territorial claim to the British exclave. Negotiations progressed in mid-2002, although a stalemate emerged when Spain disagreed with the British conditions for joint sovereignty—that it be permanent, that the military base would remain under British control, and that all changes be approved by a referendum put to the people of Gibraltar. In a referendum organized by the local administration of Gibraltar in November, which was not, however, recognized by the Spanish or British Governments, the electorate voted overwhelmingly (by 99%, of a turn-out of 87.9%) against joint sovereignty with Spain. Relations were further strained in November 2003 when the Spanish Government ordered that the frontier with Gibraltar be closed for the first time since 1985. The Spanish authorities maintained that this action was taken as a precautionary measure when a cruise-ship carrying passengers suffering from a virulent stomach virus was docked in Gibraltar. Following informal talks between Spanish and Gibraltarian officials in September, Spain lifted its ban on cruise ships from outside the EU visiting both Gibraltar and Spain and announced that it would be seeking to reopen negotiations with the United Kingdom. In December the first of what was to be an annual tripartite meeting between the United Kingdom, Spain and Gibraltar was held in the United Kingdom, and it was subsequently announced that henceforth decisions on the territory's future must be agreed by all three parties. In early 2006 Spain opposed the inclusion of references to the right to self-determination of Gibraltarians in a proposed new constitution for Gibraltar. However, in March Straw assured the Spanish Government that the draft constitution would not change the current international status or sovereignty of the territory, nor affect Spanish rights over Gibraltar under the Treaty of Utrecht, which would constrain the right to self-determination, in the view of the British Government, and that independence would therefore only be a future option for Gibraltar with Spain's consent. The Constitution was subsequently approved in a referendum in the territory in December. Meanwhile, in September 2006 a meeting was held in Córdoba between the Spanish Minister of Foreign Affairs and Co-operation, Moratinos, the British Minister of State for Europe, Geoff Hoon, and Caruana, the first ever meeting between members of all three Governments. An agreement was signed which, *inter alia*, envisaged the expansion of Gibraltar Airport, with a new terminal building straddling the border, and allowed Spain to open a branch of the Spanish cultural organization, the Instituto Cervantes, in Gibraltar, over which the Spanish flag would fly.

A national referendum on the EU Treaty establishing a Constitution for Europe took place in Spain on 20 February 2005, with 76.2% of the votes cast being in favour of ratifying the treaty. The turn-out, however, was equivalent to only 42.3% of the electorate.

Relations with Morocco have been dominated by the issues of sovereignty of the Spanish exclaves of Ceuta and Melilla, illegal immigration and drugs-trafficking, and by disputes over fishing rights. By early 2000 the problems of illegal immigration (not only via Spanish North Africa but increasingly via the Canary Islands) had become a major political issue. In May, during a visit to Morocco, the Spanish Prime Minister confirmed that the recently implemented immigration law, one of the most liberal within the EU, was to be reformed (see above). Since its entry into force earlier in the year, the new legislation had encouraged more than 82,000 illegal migrants to apply for Spanish residency permits. Protests against the reforms were staged in Spanish North Africa as well as in mainland Spain. Negotiations on the renewal of the fishing agreement between Morocco and the EU, permitting Spanish vessels access to Moroccan waters, commenced in September 1999. The agreement expired in November and Morocco indicated that it would not be renewed. In October 2001 Morocco recalled its ambassador to Spain, declaring that it was dissatisfied with the level of bilateral relations following the failure of the EU negotiations. In the following month a Spanish fishing vessel was apprehended by the Moroccan authorities and charged with fishing without a licence. In early April 2002, however, it was reported that the two Governments were preparing to reinstate their respective ambassadors. Relations were threatened again in July, following the occupation of a small uninhabited islet near Ceuta, the Isla de Perejil (Laila), by 12 Moroccan soldiers. Spain lodged a formal protest against this action on 12 July, but Morocco refused to withdraw its men, claiming that Perejil had been a part of Morocco since independence in 1956. Spanish soldiers reoccupied the island on 17 July, and a subsequent US-mediated agreement between Spain and Morocco left the island unoccupied. Issues over the sovereignty of Ceuta and Melilla continued to be problematic, however, and in September Morocco accused Spain of repeated violations of its airspace and territorial waters and reasserted its claims over the exclaves before the UN. Relations improved somewhat in November, however, when Morocco offered the temporary use of its territorial waters to 64 Spanish fishing boats after the *Prestige* oil disaster. Meetings in December 2002 and January 2003 contributed to the re-establishment of diplomatic relations between the two countries in February 2003. During an official visit by Aznar to Morocco in December 2003 Spain and Morocco agreed to instigate a feasibility survey for a tunnel linking the two countries. A decision on whether to construct the tunnel was expected to be made in 2008.

Government

Under the Constitution approved in 1978, Spain is an hereditary monarchy, with the King as Head of State. He appoints the President of the Government (Prime Minister) and, on the latter's recommendation, other members of the Council of Ministers. Legislation is initiated for discussion in the Cortes (national assembly) in Madrid, in the Parliaments of the Autonomous Communities, or by popular petition. The King's actions in state affairs must receive the prior approval of the Cortes, to which the Government is responsible. The Council of State is the supreme consultative organ of the Government.

Legislative power is vested in the Cortes Generales, comprising two Houses, elected by direct universal adult suffrage for four years (subject to dissolution). The Congreso de los Diputados (Congress of Deputies) has 350 members, elected by proportional representation, and the Senado (Senate) has 208 directly elected members, plus 51 regional representatives, elected by the autonomous parliaments. A party can gain representation only if it obtains at least 3% of the votes.

Regional self-government was established in the 1978 Constitution. In October 1979 the statutes of the first of 17 Autonomous Communities were approved by referendum. The first Legislative Assemblies (Basque and Catalan) were elected in March 1980. The Galician Legislative Assembly was elected in October 1981 and that of Andalucía in May 1982. The remaining 13 were constituted in May 1983, thus completing the process of devolution. The regions possess varying degrees of autonomy. Each Legislative Assembly is elected for four years.

Spain comprises 50 provinces, each with its own Council (Diputación Provincial). The system of Civil Governors was replaced (by royal decree) in April 1997: a government sub-delegate is appointed by each Autonomous Community's government delegate.

Defence

Plans for the gradual abolition of military service and for the establishment of professional armed forces were announced in early 1996; conscription was abolished in 2000, while the final stages of professionalization were completed in 2003. Legislation to permit the entry of women to all sections of the armed forces took effect in early 1989. As assessed at November 2007, the total strength of the armed forces was 149,150, comprising: army 95,600, navy 23,200 (including 5,300 marines), air force 20,900, and 9,450 in joint service. The paramilitary Guardia Civil (Civil Guard) numbered 73,360. Spain became a member of the North Atlantic Treaty Organization (NATO, see p. 340) in May 1982. In December 1997 Spain's full integration into the military structure of NATO (with effect from January 1999) was approved by the alliance. Spain joined Western European Union (WEU, see p. 426) in November 1988. The US military presence in Spain comprised a naval force of 282 in August 2005. In September 2004 an agreement on the establishment of a *gendarmerie* comprising 3,000 troops was signed by Spain, France, Italy, Portugal and the Netherlands. In the same year Spain pledged some 2,000 troops to a European rapid reaction force, which was intended to be fully established by 2007. The 2006 draft budget for defence was €7,123.4m., equivalent to 2.6% of total expenditure.

Economic Affairs

In 2006, according to estimates by the World Bank, Spain's gross national income (GNI), measured at average 2004–06 prices, was US $1,200,704m., equivalent to $27,570 per head (or $28,030 per head on an international purchasing-power parity basis). During 1996–2006, it was estimated, the population increased at an average annual rate of 1.0%, while gross domestic product (GDP) per head increased, in real terms, by an average of 2.8% per year. Overall GDP increased, in real terms, at an average annual rate of 3.8% in 1996–2006, according to official estimates; growth was 3.9% in 2006.

Agriculture (including forestry and fishing) contributed an estimated 2.9% of GDP in 2006 and engaged 4.8% of the employed labour force in the same year. The principal crops are barley, wheat, sugar beet, vegetables, citrus fruits, grapes and olives; wine and olive oil are important products. Agricultural GDP grew at an average annual rate of 0.5% in 1996–2006, according to official estimates; it declined by 8.6% in 2005, mainly owing to severe drought, but increased by 2.3% in 2006. The fishing industry is significant. The Spanish fishing fleet is one of the largest in the world. In November 2002 the oil-tanker *Prestige* sank off the Galician coast, polluting an estimated 3,000 km of coastline. Catches of shellfish and inshore fish were reported to have declined by 80% in the period immediately following the tanker's sinking.

Industry (including mining, manufacturing, power and construction) contributed an estimated 30.4% of GDP in 2006, and engaged 29.5% of the employed labour force in the same year. According to the World Bank, industrial GDP increased at an average annual rate of 3.8% in 1996–2005; it increased by 2.5% in 2005.

The mining and quarrying industry provided less than 1.0% of GDP in 2004 and engaged 0.3% of the employed labour force in 2006. Hard coal and brown coal are the principal minerals extracted, although production fell in the late 1990s owing to environmental standards imposed by the European Union (EU, see p. 244). In 2005, according to the Energy Information Administration (a section of the US Department of Energy), proven oil reserves amounted to 158m. barrels.

Manufacturing contributed an estimated 15.2% of GDP in 2006 and engaged 15.7% of the employed labour force in the same year. In 2005 Spain was the world's fifth largest exporter of passenger cars. In that year exports of passenger vehicles numbered 2.25m. units. Other important industries are shipbuilding, chemicals, steel, textiles and footwear; some of these sectors underwent a process of rationalization in the 1980s. Investment is being made in new manufacturing industries, such as information technology and telecommunications equipment. Manufacturing GDP increased at an average annual rate of 3.3% in 1996–2006, according to official estimates; the rate of growth was 0.4% in 2004.

Energy (comprising mining and power) contributed an estimated 3.1% of GDP in 2006, and employed 0.9% of the labour force in the same year. Energy is derived principally from petroleum, most of which is imported. In 2004 imports of mineral fuels and petroleum products accounted for 11.2% of total import costs. Natural gas became an increasingly important fuel source in the late 1990s. Some natural gas requirements are obtained from the Bay of Biscay, the remainder being imported by pipeline from Algeria. Coal provided 23.0% of total electricity production in 2004, while nuclear energy provided 29% and hydroelectric power 11.4%. In 2004 wind power provided the equivalent of 6% of total electricity demand. According to official estimates, energy GDP increased by 2.3% annually in 1996–2006; energy GDP grew by 1.4% in 2006.

In 2006 the services sector accounted for an estimated 66.7% of GDP, while it engaged 65.7% of the employed labour force in the same year. The tourism industry makes an important contribution to the Spanish economy. In 2006 the number of tourist arrivals was estimated at 58.5m. (27.7% from the United Kingdom), and receipts from tourism reached €48,227m. Remittances from emigrants are also significant. In 2004 remittances amounted to €4.2m. According to official estimates, the GDP of the services sector increased at an average annual rate of 3.8% in 1996–2006; services GDP increased by 4.1% in 2006.

In 2006 Spain recorded a visible trade deficit of US $100,729m. and there was a deficit of $106,344m. on the current account of the balance of payments. In 2006 the principal sources of imports were Germany (14.2%) and France (12.8%). France was the main export market in that year, purchasing 18.7%, followed by Germany (10.9%). Italy, the United Kingdom and other EU countries are also important trading partners. The principal imports in 2004 were machinery and transport equipment, chemical products, mineral fuels and petroleum products, and food and live animals. The main exports were machinery and transport equipment, food and live animals (particularly fruit and vegetables), and chemical products.

In 2007 an overall budget deficit of €40,872m. (equivalent to 3.9% of projected GDP) was estimated. The annual rate of inflation averaged 2.6% in 1995–2000 and 3.1% in 2002–07; consumer prices increased by an average of 2.8% in 2007. The unemployment rate fell for the first time since 2001 in 2004, to 10.8%, and declined further, to 8.7% in 2005 and to 8.5% in 2006.

Spain became a member of the EU in January 1986, and joined the exchange rate mechanism of the European Monetary System in June 1989. According to the draft budget for 2006, in that year Spain was due to receive €16,705m. from the EU, while contributing €10,946m. Spain is also a member of the Organisation for Economic Co-operation and Development (OECD, see p. 347).

The PSOE Government that took office in April 2004 pledged to continue the fiscal policies of the previous administration, which had taken Spain into the single European currency (introduced in 1999) and had predicted annual budgetary surpluses for 2004–07. Membership of the euro had contributed to a sudden rise in inflation, but also encouraged GDP growth. In early 2005 a plan to generate economic growth by developing infrastructure and increasing competition was announced, and the IMF recommended reform of the pensions system, the phasing out of tax deductions for home owners and the limiting of government spending. The budget for 2006, approved by parliament in December 2005, provided for an increase of 11.3% in central transfers to the regional governments, in line with the Government's policy of increasing autonomy. Notably, the Government had decentralized health-care provision, although funding proved problematic. A public sector budget surplus equivalent to 1.8% of GDP was recorded in 2006, the highest for 30 years. This surplus was primarily used to retire public debt and build a reserve fund to pay future pensions. Unemployment fell to almost 8% as almost 700,000 jobs were created in 2006 (almost one-half the overall figure for the EU), encouraging immigrant workers and other new entrants to the job market, although there were fears that much of this job creation remained in low-wage, low-productivity parts of the economy. By the time the PSOE had won a second term in early 2008, Spain appeared to be entering a period of economic downturn, prompted in part by a decline in the previously buoyant housing sector. Although the government budget surplus of 2.3% recorded in 2007 was predicted to become a deficit of 0.7% in 2008, in April the newly installed Government approved measures valued at €10,000m. to increase investment in public infrastructure and provide tax rebates. In January 2008 the standard rate for corporate tax was reduced from 32.5% to 30%, finalizing an earlier programme of tax changes, and the Government also approved the abolition of the wealth tax. Inflation accelerated rapidly in late 2007 and early 2008 to reach a 12-year high of 4.5% in the year to March 2008. GDP growth of 3.8% was recorded in 2007. The Spanish Government estimated that the rate of growth would decline to 2.3% in 2008, although the IMF speculated that the actual figure could be significantly lower, at 1.8%. According to the IMF, two significant dangers facing the Spanish economy's growth prospects were the high levels of indebtedness in the private sector and the related size of the current account deficit, which was estimated at 9.1% of GDP in 2007.

Education

In 2005/06 some 1.48m. children were attending pre-school institutions. In that year 2.48m. children were enrolled at primary schools and a total of 2.99m. were enrolled in secondary education. Under reforms implemented in 1991, basic education is compulsory, and available free of charge, from the ages of six to 16 years. It comprises primary education, which begins at six years of age and lasts for six years, and secondary education, composed of two two-year cycles, followed between the ages of 12 and 16. Thereafter, students may take either a vocational training course, lasting one or two years, or the two-year *Bachillerato* course, in preparation for university entrance. Private schools, many of which are administered by the Roman Catholic Church, are responsible for the education of more than 30% of Spanish children. In the Autonomous Communities the teaching of languages other than Spanish (such as Catalan) is regulated by decree. In 2002/03 enrolment at primary schools included 100% of children (males 100%; females 99%) in the relevant age-group, while enrolment at secondary schools in that year included 96% of children (males 94%; females 98%) in the appropriate age-group. In 2004 the Government announced a reform of the education system, part of which included the designation of religious education as an optional, rather than compulsory, subject.

Some 1.44m. students were attending university in 2005/06. In that year there were 72 universities, including the open university (UNED, established in 1972). There are three cycles within university education. The first cycle lasts for three years and leads to the degree of *Diplomatura*. The second cycle lasts for two or three years and leads to the degree of *Licenciatura*. The degree of Doctor is awarded upon completion of the two-year third cycle and the writing of a thesis. Higher technical studies in engineering and architecture are followed at Escuelas Técnicas de Grado Medio and Escuelas Técnicas de Grado Superior. The 2006 draft budget allocated €1,888.2m. (0.7% of total expenditure) to education.

SPAIN

Public Holidays

2008: 1 January (New Year's Day), 6 January (Epiphany), 20 March (Maundy Thursday), 21 March (Good Friday), 1 May (Labour Day), 15 August (Assumption), 12 October (National Day, anniversary of the discovery of America), 1 November (All Saints' Day), 6 December (Constitution Day), 8 December (Immaculate Conception), 25 December (Christmas Day).

2009: 1 January (New Year's Day), 6 January (Epiphany), 9 April (Maundy Thursday), 10 April (Good Friday), 1 May (Labour Day), 15 August (Assumption), 12 October (National Day, anniversary of the discovery of America), 1 November (All Saints' Day), 6 November (Constitution Day), 8 December (Immaculate Conception), 25 December (St Stephen's Day).

Some of the above holidays are not observed in all the Autonomous Communities. In addition, various local holidays are established by regional and municipal authorities, giving an annual total of 14 public holidays.

Weights and Measures

The metric system is in force.

Statistical Survey

Source (unless otherwise stated): Instituto Nacional de Estadística, Paseo de la Castellana 183, 28071 Madrid; tel. (91) 5839100; fax (91) 5839158; internet www.ine.es.

Area and Population

AREA, POPULATION AND DENSITY*

Area (sq km)	505,988†
Population (census results)	
1 March 1991	38,872,268
1 November 2001	
Males	20,021,850
Females	20,825,521
Total	40,847,371
Population (official estimates at 1 July)	
2005	43,398,190
2006	44,068,244
2007	44,873,567
Density (per sq km) at 1 July 2007	88.7

* Including the Spanish External Territories (Spanish North Africa—area 33 sq km), an integral part of Spain. Ceuta had a population of 71,797 on 1 July 2006, while Melilla's population was 68,392.
† 195,363 sq miles.

PROVINCES
(population at 1 July 2007)*†

Alava	304,277	Lugo		347,486
Albacete	390,066	Madrid		6,112,078
Alacant (Alicante)	1,808,457	Málaga		1,509,026
Almería	655,690	Murcia		1,392,368
Avila	167,157	Navarra		600,646
Badajoz	669,703	Ourense		329,632
Illes Balears (Balearic Is)	1,028,635	Oviedo (Principado de Asturias)		1,058,743
Barcelona	5,303,733	Palencia		171,198
Burgos	361,165	Las Palmas		1,042,389
Cáceres	406,992	Pontevedra		935,002
Cádiz	1,190,105	Salamanca		346,842
Castellón (Castelló) de la Plana	565,372	Santa Cruz de Tenerife		976,910
Ciudad Real	507,575	Santander (Cantabria)		567,088
Córdoba	781,176	Segovia		158,312
A Coruña (La Coruña)	1,116,652	Sevilla		1,818,648
Cuenca	211,110	Soria		92,397
Girona (Gerona)	695,162	Tarragona		751,131
Granada	888,865	Teruel		143,394
Guadalajara	220,315	Toledo		622,322
Guipúzcoa	689,271	Valencia		2,450,739
Huelva	492,344	Valladolid		516,205
Huesca	218,980	Vizcaya		1,136,827
Jaén	653,159	Zamora		194,903
La Rioja	309,360	Zaragoza		923,911
León	483,855			
Lleida (Lérida)	416,005	**Total**		**44,733,378**

* Excluding the Spanish External Territories (Spanish North Africa).
† Including residents temporarily abroad.

PRINCIPAL TOWNS*
(population at 1 January 2005)

Madrid (capital)	3,155,359	Vitoria-Gasteiz	226,490
Barcelona	1,593,075	Santa Cruz de Tenerife	221,567
Valencia	796,549	Badalona	218,553
Sevilla	704,154	Elche	215,137
Zaragoza	647,373	Oviedo	212,174
Málaga	558,287	Mósteles	204,463
Murcia	409,810	Cartagena	203,945
Las Palmas de Gran Canaria	378,628	Alcalá de Henares	197,804
Palma de Mallorca	375,773	Sabadell	196,971
Bilbao	353,173	Jerez de la Frontera	196,275
Córdoba	321,164	Fuenlabrada	195,131
Valladolid	321,001	Terrassa	194,947
Alacant (Alicante)	319,380	Pamplona	193,328
Vigo	293,725	Santander	183,955
Gijón	273,931	Donostia-San Sebastián	182,930
Hospitalet de Llobregat	252,884	Almería	181,702
A Coruña (La Coruña)	243,349	Leganés	181,284
Granada	236,982	Burgos	172,421

* Population figures refer to *municipios*, each of which may contain some rural area as well as the urban centre.

BIRTHS, MARRIAGES AND DEATHS

	Registered live births		Registered marriages		Registered deaths	
	Number	Rate (per 1,000)	Number	Rate (per 1,000)	Number	Rate (per 1,000)
1999	380,130	9.5	208,129	5.2	371,102	9.3
2000	397,632	9.9	216,451	5.4	360,391	9.0
2001	406,380	10.1	208,057	5.1	360,131	8.9
2002	418,846	10.1	211,522	5.1	368,618	8.9
2003	441,881	10.5	212,300	5.0	384,828	9.2
2004	454,591	10.7	216,149	5.1	371,934	8.7
2005	465,616	10.8	209,125	4.8	387,019	8.9
2006	482,957	11.0	203,453	4.6	371,478	8.4

Expectation of life (years at birth, WHO estimates): 80.3 (males 76.9; females 83.6) in 2005 (Source: WHO, *World Health Statistics*).

SPAIN

ECONOMICALLY ACTIVE POPULATION
('000 persons aged 16 years and over)

	2004	2005	2006
Agriculture, hunting and forestry	868.1	940.6	893.0
Fishing	51.6	60.1	51.3
Mining and quarrying	57.7	60.4	66.4
Manufacturing	2,936.8	3,113.0	3,106.9
Electricity, gas and water supply	103.7	106.6	118.8
Construction	2,058.7	2,357.2	2,542.9
Wholesale and retail trade; repair of motor vehicles, motorcycles and personal and household goods	2,747.1	2,886.8	2,983.5
Hotels and restaurants	1,076.7	1,291.1	1,402.7
Transport, storage and communications	1,033.6	1,117.2	1,158.2
Financial intermediation	398.4	457.3	472.5
Real estate, renting and business activities	1,481.9	1,678.4	1,857.4
Public administration and defence; compulsory social security	1,137.4	1,196.7	1,221.6
Education	996.3	1,090.5	1,108.8
Health and social work	1,016.4	1,134.6	1,180.8
Other community, social and personal service activities	696.5	793.7	815.3
Private households with employed persons	454.6	682.8	760.6
Extra-territorial organizations and bodies	1.1	6.1	7.0
Total employed	17,116.6	18,973.2	19,747.7
Total unemployed	2,073.8	1,912.5	1,837.1
Total labour force	19,190.3	20,885.7	21,584.8
Males	11,300.6	12,251.7	12,534.1
Females	7,889.8	8,634.1	9,050.7

Health and Welfare

KEY INDICATORS

Total fertility rate (children per woman, 2005)	1.3
Under-5 mortality rate (per 1,000 live births, 2005)	5
HIV/AIDS (% of persons aged 15–49, 2005)	0.6
Physicians (per 1,000 head, 2004)	3.3
Hospital beds (per 1,000 head, 2004)	3.7
Health expenditure (2004): US $ per head (PPP)	2,099.2
Health expenditure (2004): % of GDP	8.1
Health expenditure (2004): public (% of total)	70.9
Human Development Index (2005): ranking	13
Human Development Index (2005): value	0.949

For sources and definitions, see explanatory note on p. vi.

Agriculture

PRINCIPAL CROPS
('000 metric tons)

	2004	2005	2006
Wheat	7,097	4,027	5,576
Rice (paddy)	883	824	746
Barley	10,640	4,626	8,318
Maize	4,831	4,120	3,461
Oats	1,043	542	918
Potatoes	2,774	2,563	2,502
Sugar cane	67	43	55*
Sugar beet	7,175	7,291	6,045
Olives	5,200	4,022	5,032
Sunflower seed	821	381	607
Lettuce	1,048	993	1,070
Tomatoes	4,383	4,810	3,679
Chillies and green peppers	1,077	1,064	1,074

—continued	2004	2005	2006
Dry onions	1,030	1,006	1,151
Oranges	2,767	2,376	3,211
Tangerines, mandarins, clementines and satsumas	2,460	1,957	2,000*
Lemons and limes	810	945	868
Apples	691	774	661
Pears	609	640	590
Peaches and nectarines	988	1,231	1,256
Grapes	7,064	6,054	6,401
Watermelons	816	720	718
Cantaloupes and other melons	1,071	1,087	1,042

* FAO estimate.

Aggregate production ('000 metric tons, may include official, semi-official or estimated data): Total cereals 24,809 in 2004, 14,364 in 2005, 19,353 in 2006; Total roots and tubers 2,805 in 2004, 2,595 in 2005, 2,537 in 2006; Total vegetables (incl. melons) 13,383 in 2004, 13,356 in 2005, 12,513 in 2006; Total fruits (excl. melons) 16,920 in 2004, 15,537 in 2005, 16,514 in 2006.

Source: FAO.

LIVESTOCK
('000 head, year ending September)

	2004	2005	2006
Horses	238	240	245
Asses, mules or hinnies	250	252	256
Cattle	6,653	6,463	6,464
Pigs	24,895	24,884	25,131
Sheep	22,910	22,749	22,514
Goats	2,833	2,905	2,835
Chickens	129,000	130,000	135,000

Source: FAO.

LIVESTOCK PRODUCTS
('000 metric tons)

	2004	2005	2006
Cattle meat	714	715	671
Sheep meat	231	224	227
Goat meat	13	17	12
Pig meat	3,076	3,168	3,230
Horse meat	5	5	6
Rabbit meat	72	75	72
Chicken meat	1,083	1,048	1,048
Cows' milk	6,576	6,553	6,553
Sheep's milk	424	423	403
Goats' milk	494	423	423
Hen eggs	852	828	850
Honey	37	27	30
Wool (greasy)	22	22	22

* FAO estimate.

Source: FAO.

Forestry

ROUNDWOOD REMOVALS
('000 cubic metres, excl. bark)

	2004	2005	2006
Sawlogs, veneer logs and logs for sleepers	7,795	7,343	5,860
Pulpwood	5,520	5,207	7,544
Other industrial wood	920	801	705
Fuel wood	2,055	2,180	1,607
Total	16,290	15,532	15,716

Source: FAO.

SPAIN

SAWNWOOD PRODUCTION
('000 cubic metres, incl. railway sleepers)

	2004	2005	2006
Coniferous (softwood)	2,730	2,750	2,860
Broadleaved (hardwood)	1,000	910	946
Total	3,730	3,660	3,806

Source: FAO.

Fishing

('000 metric tons, live weight)

	2003	2004	2005
Capture*	896.7	805.5	849.3
European pilchard (sardine)	55.8	64.4	66.0
Skipjack tuna	155.4	118.5	137.6
Yellowfin tuna	108.3	106.4	92.3
Jack and horse mackerels	37.0	39.9	38.5
Aquaculture	272.8	298.9	221.9
Blue mussel	205.6	231.6	158.1
Total catch*	1,169.5	1,104.3	1,071.2

* FAO estimates.

Note: Figures exclude Sardinia coral (metric tons): 9 in 2003; 8 in 2004; 7 in 2005.

Source: FAO.

Mining

('000 metric tons, unless otherwise indicated, estimates)

	2003	2004	2005
Anthracite	3,863	3,692	3,889
Lignite	8,795	8,147	7,587
Crude petroleum ('000 barrels)	2,404	1,913	1,261
Natural gas (million cubic metres)	550.0	370.0	330.0
Copper*	0.6	1.4	0.9
Lead*	1.8	n.a.	n.a.
Zinc (metric tons)*	15.1	n.a.	n.a.
Kaolin	450.0	438.0	450.0
Potash salts (crude)	594.4	590.0	575.0
Sepiolite	690.4	851.6	800.0
Dolomite	12,000	14,489	15,000
Fluorspar†	139.7	145.7	144.0
Salt (unrefined)	3,963	3,993	3,950
Gypsum (crude)	11,500	12,534	13,000

* Figures refer to the metal content of ores.
† Figures refer to total CaF_2 content (acid and metallurgical grades).

Source: US Geological Survey.

Industry

SELECTED PRODUCTS
('000 metric tons, unless otherwise indicated)

	2000	2001	2002
Fish (tinned)	342.9	347.9	368.9
Wheat flour	2,673	2,811	2,932
Vinegar	820	938	947
Distilled alcohol ('000 hectolitres)	1,605	1,863	2,907
Wine ('000 hectolitres)	n.a.	n.a.	27,891
Beer ('000 hectolitres)	26,388	26,802	28,631
Soft drinks ('000 hectolitres)	45,355	47,305	48,424
Cigarettes (million units)	74,799	n.a.	n.a.
Caustic soda	707	704	n.a.
Washing powders and detergents	2,073.9	2,122.9	2,306.8
Aluminium (primary)*	365.7	376.4	380.1
Refined copper (primary)*	316.0	290.7	308.2
Pig-iron†	4,059	4,219	4,021
Cement (Portland)*	38,154	40,512	42,500
Motorcycles ('000)	89	117	74
Passenger cars ('000)	2,619	2,406	2,518
Merchant ships launched ('000 gross tons)	527	263	141
Electricity (million kWh)	224,472	236,043	244,963

* Data from the US Geological Survey.
† Data from International Iron and Steel Institute.

Source: mainly UN, *Industrial Commodity Statistics Yearbook*.

2003 ('000 metric tons unless otherwise stated): Ham and other prepared meats 746.8; Tuna, bonito and other tinned fish 208.9; Olive oil 828.0; Wheat flour 2,950.1; Wine ('000 hectolitres) 8,523.8; Beer ('000 hectolitres) 31,028.4; Mineral water 4,664.6; Soft drinks ('000 litres) 4,243.6; Cement (Portland) 42,162.9; Concrete 182,768.5; Pig iron 4,000; Refined copper (primary) 290.3; Aluminium (primary) 389.1.

2004 ('000 metric tons unless otherwise stated): Ham and other prepared meats 880.6; Tuna, bonito and other tinned fish 224.1; Olive oil 1,109.0; Wheat flour 2,965.0; Wine ('000 hectolitres) 8,909.8; Beer ('000 hectolitres) 31,466.9; Mineral water 4,880.0; Soft drinks ('000 litres) 5,911.8; Cement (Portland) 42,256.7; Concrete 185,508.7; Pig iron 4,000; Refined copper (primary) 243.2; Aluminium (primary) 397.5.

2005 ('000 metric tons unless otherwise stated): Ham and other prepared meats 848.9; Tuna, bonito and other tinned fish 197.8; Olive oil 1,060.4; Wheat flour 3,073.0; Wine ('000 hectolitres) 9,788.9; Beer ('000 hectolitres) 31,156.0; Mineral water 5,161.5; Soft drinks ('000 litres) 4,773.8; Cement (Portland) 45,952.5; Concrete 185,162.2.

2006 ('000 metric tons unless otherwise stated): Ham and other prepared meats 858.9; Tuna, bonito and other tinned fish 212.1; Olive oil 979.3; Wheat flour 3,035.6; Wine ('000 hectolitres) 9,415.7; Beer ('000 hectolitres) 34,031.7; Mineral water 5,363.1; Soft drinks ('000 litres) 4,579.1; Cement (Portland) 49,301.5; Concrete 201,253.

Finance

CURRENCY AND EXCHANGE RATES

Monetary Units
  100 cent = 1 euro (€).

Sterling and Dollar Equivalents (31 December 2007)
  £1 sterling = 1.3609 euros;
  US $1 = 0.6793 euros;
  €10 = £7.35 = $14.72.

Average Exchange Rate (euros per US $)
  2005   0.8041
  2006   0.7971
  2007   0.7306

Note: The national currency was formerly the peseta. From the introduction of the euro, with Spanish participation, on 1 January 1999, a fixed exchange rate of €1 = 166.386 pesetas was in operation. Euro notes and coins were introduced on 1 January 2002. The euro and local currency circulated alongside each other until 28 February, after which the euro became the sole legal tender.

SPAIN

BUDGET
(€ million)

Revenue	2005	2006	2007
Current operations	116,097	127,078	144,840
Direct taxation	63,689	72,036	83,925
Indirect taxation	43,051	45,032	50,740
Rates and other revenue	2,237	2,298	2,486
Current transfers	5,353	5,605	5,757
Estate taxes	1,767	1,837	1,933
Capital operations	1,494	1,513	1,707
Transfer of real investments	94	98	109
Capital transfers	1,400	1,415	1,598
Financial assets	706	955	998
Total	118,297	129,546	147,545

Expenditure*	2005	2006	2007
Current	106,209	113,605	120,288
Social security	4,822	5,243	n.a.
Autonomous communities	29,620	32,668	35,977
State foundations	40	41	n.a.
State enterprises	2,125	2,832	n.a.
Autonomous organs	2,680	3,070	n.a.
Local corporations	11,078	12,769	13,730
Private companies	181	421	n.a.
Foreign contributions	10,435	11,300	n.a.
Families	2,585	2,625	n.a.
Personnel	20,447	22,124	23,686
Purchase of goods and services	2,905	3,069	3,431
Interest	19,293	17,443	15,946
Contingency fund	2,491	2,873	3,391
Capital	15,827	17,473	19,247
Investment	8,841	9,338	9,956
Capital transfers	6,986	8,134	9,257
Financial assets	7,782	9,677	12,112
Financial liabilities	30,070	31,348	33,378
Total	162,379	174,976	188,417

* Calculated according to recognized obligations rather than payments made.

Source: Ministerio de Economía y Hacienda, Madrid.

INTERNATIONAL RESERVES
(US $ million at 31 December)

	2004	2005	2006
Gold*	7,370	7,550	8,518
IMF special drawing rights	332	332	335
Reserve position in IMF	1,575	752	399
Foreign exchange*	10,481	8,594	10,088
Total	19,758	17,228	19,340

* Figures for gold and foreign exchange exclude deposits made with the European Monetary Institute (now the European Central Bank). Gold is valued at market-related prices.

Source: IMF, *International Financial Statistics*.

MONEY SUPPLY
(€ '000 million at 31 December)

	2004	2005	2006
Currency issued*	52.70	59.36	65.93
Demand deposits at banking institutions	214.72	433.70	493.26

* Currency put into circulation by the Banco de España was €74,200m. in 2004, €83,020m. in 2005 and €90,040m. in 2006.

Source: IMF, *International Financial Statistics*.

COST OF LIVING
(Consumer Price Index; base: 2006 = 100)

	2004	2005	2007
Food (excl. alcoholic beverages and tobacco)	93.1	96.1	103.7
Alcohol and tobacco	93.5	98.2	107.0
Household expenses	95.5	97.5	102.6
Clothing (incl. footwear)	97.4	98.8	101.1
Rent	89.1	93.9	103.7
Transport	90.0	95.7	102.1
All items (incl. others)	93.5	96.6	102.8

NATIONAL ACCOUNTS
(€ million at current prices)

National Income and Product

	2004*	2005*	2006†
Compensation of employees	400,953	427,225	455,772
Gross operating surplus and mixed income	352,121	381,903	415,644
Gross domestic product (GDP) at factor cost	753,074	809,128	871,416
Taxes, less subsidies on production and imports	91,633	101,812	111,477
GDP in market prices	844,707	910,940	982,893
Primary incomes (net)	−14,862	−15,235	−18,649
Gross national income	829,845	895,705	964,244
Less Consumption of fixed capital	125,004	138,692	152,355
Net national income	704,841	757,013	811,889
Current transfers (net)	−4,685	−6,940	−9,364
Gross national disposable income	700,156	750,073	802,525

* Preliminary.
† Estimates.

Expenditure on the Gross Domestic Product

	2004*	2005*	2006†
Final consumption expenditure	636,835	688,611	741,194
Households	479,820	516,818	554,495
Non-profit institutions serving households	7,259	8,053	8,721
General government	149,756	163,740	177,978
Gross capital formation	237,806	267,938	300,036
Gross fixed capital formation	235,805	266,624	298,189
Changes in inventories	2,001	1,314	1,847
Total domestic expenditure	874,641	956,549	1,041,230
Exports of goods and services	218,201	233,460	255,315
Less Imports of goods and services	251,800	281,559	315,591
GDP in market prices	841,042	908,450	980,954

* Preliminary.
† Estimates.

Gross Domestic Product by Economic Activity

	2004*	2005*	2006†
Agriculture, hunting, forestry and fishing	27,365	25,877	25,114
Mining and quarrying; electricity, gas and water supply‡	21,090	25,352	26,775
Manufacturing	119,293	124,568	132,419
Construction	80,480	94,042	106,361
Private sector service industries	399,094	425,776	455,643
Public sector service industries	109,347	117,819	127,391
Gross value added in basic prices	756,669	813,434	873,703
Import duties, value-added tax and other taxes, less subsidies on products	84,373	95,016	107,251
GDP in market prices	841,042	908,450	980,954

* Preliminary.
† Estimates.
‡ Including refinery products.

SPAIN

BALANCE OF PAYMENTS
(US $ million)

	2004	2005	2006
Exports of goods f.o.b.	185,209	196,580	216,483
Imports of goods f.o.b.	−251,939	−281,784	−317,212
Trade balance	−66,730	−85,204	−100,729
Exports of services	86,078	94,663	106,278
Imports of services	−59,188	−67,129	−78,315
Balance on goods and services	−39,841	−57,669	−72,766
Other income received	33,948	39,445	49,143
Other income paid	−48,986	−60,701	−75,597
Balance on goods, services and income	−54,879	−78,925	−99,220
Current transfers received	20,366	20,194	21,465
Current transfers paid	−20,353	−24,656	−28,590
Current balance	−54,865	−83,388	−106,344
Capital account (net)	10,450	10,107	7,831
Direct investment abroad	−61,504	−41,922	−88,726
Direct investment from abroad	24,792	24,573	20,167
Portfolio investment assets	−39,651	−119,356	−9,978
Portfolio investment liabilities	141,686	172,713	240,716
Financial derivatives liabilities	74	273	2,586
Other investment assets	−52,659	−42,198	−101,955
Other investment liabilities	24,226	79,803	39,771
Net errors and omissions	1,039	−2,524	−3,490
Overall balance	−6,412	−1,920	578

Source: IMF, *International Financial Statistics*.

External Trade

PRINCIPAL COMMODITIES
(distribution by SITC, US $ million)

Imports c.i.f.	2002	2003	2004
Food and live animals	13,326.7	16,303.6	18,890.2
Fish, crustaceans and molluscs, and products thereof	3,986.1	5,031.6	5,288.6
Vegetables and fruit	1,985.5	2,591.0	3,350.1
Beverages	1,243.8	1,693.5	1,967.0
Tobacco	1,147.5	1,530.6	1,942.1
Mineral products	17,956.2	21,546.3	29,032.2
Products of the chemical industries and related industries	20,834.0	26,495.5	30,971.8
Medicinal and pharmaceutical products	5,725.3	7,293.6	8,349.2
Organic chemicals	4,662.6	6,015.6	7,032.7
Paper, paperboard and related products	3,178.9	3,814.1	4,391.2
Plastics and related manufactures	4,000.7	5,031.8	6,116.5
Textiles and their manufactures	3,524.8	4,183.7	4,571.4
Iron and steel	4,697.6	6,711.5	9,068.4
Machinery and transport equipment	63,062.8	81,843.6	101,645.9
Total (incl. others)	165,918.5	210,860.4	259,264.6

Exports f.o.b.	2002	2003	2004
Food and live animals	15,292.2	19,316.4	21,179.8
Vegetables and fruit	8,554.2	10,801.4	11,508.6
Beverages and tobacco	2,017.2	2,540.0	2,817.0
Mineral products	3,281.1	4,925.1	6,917.5
Products of the chemical industries and related industries	13,798.9	17,431.4	19,893.1
Plastic materials, etc.	3,158.1	3,912.7	4,745.3
Paper, paperboard and related products	2,177.4	2,649.4	3,012.5
Textiles and their manufactures	3,223.9	3,695.0	3,948.3
Ceramic products	1,979.2	2,245.1	2,497.6
Iron and steel	3,505.9	4,429.7	6,335.4
Machinery and transport equipment	50,666.3	65,256.7	75,631.4
Total (incl. others)	125,872.2	158,213.1	182,727.2

Source: UN, *International Trade Statistics Yearbook*.

2005 (€ million): *Imports:* Consumer goods 66,987.5 (Food, beverages and tobacco 14,029.5; Motor vehicles 18,491.7); Intermediate goods 137,083.2 (Industrial products 100,808.1); Capital goods 27,300.9 (Machinery, etc. 16,061.4; Transport equipment 7,568.3); Total 231,371.6. *Exports:* Consumer goods 59,596.0 (Food, beverages and tobacco 18,678.0; Motor vehicles 19,346.5); Intermediate goods 79,107.3 (Industrial products 73,109.8); Capital goods 14,855.6 (Machinery, etc. 6,297.5; Transport equipment 7,540.3); Total 153,559.0.

2006 (€ million): *Imports:* Consumer goods 77,750.7 (Food, beverages and tobacco 14,562.4; Motor vehicles 19,277.6); Intermediate goods 159,068.1 (Industrial products 114,547.1); Capital goods 27,740.3 (Machinery, etc. 17,797.5; Transport equipment 6,085.8); Total 259,559.0. *Exports:* Consumer goods 64,688.0 (Food, beverages and tobacco 19,892.9; Motor vehicles 19,558.4); Intermediate goods 88,126.7 (Industrial products 81,496.4); Capital goods 17,057.1 (Machinery, etc. 7,048.2; Transport equipment 8,944.1); Total 169,871.9.

PRINCIPAL TRADING PARTNERS*
(US $ million)

Imports c.i.f.	2002	2003	2004
Algeria	2,804.3	3,082.8	3,599.7
Belgium	5,292.5	6,423.3	7,992.5
China, People's Republic	5,463.0	7,518.4	10,613.2
France (incl. Monaco)	27,251.3	34,079.9	39,610.4
Germany	26,779.2	34,551.5	41,508.0
Italy	15,025.0	19,348.5	23,584.3
Japan	4,031.3	5,507.5	7,152.9
Netherlands	6,524.0	8,525.6	10,602.5
Portugal	5,158.0	6,778.3	8,456.3
Russia	2,565.4	3,225.6	4,541.4
Sweden	2,166.2	3,212.8	3,363.2
United Kingdom	10,823.8	13,719.8	15,915.7
USA	6,819.8	7,639.5	9,323.6
Total (incl. others)	165,916.5	210,860.4	259,264.6

Exports f.o.b.	2002	2003	2004
Belgium	3,333.9	4,756.2	5,531.9
France (incl. Monaco)	23,945.6	30,394.1	35,431.8
Germany	14,466.8	19,008.0	21,246.2
Greece	1,479.7	1,898.5	2,237.5
Italy	11,863.6	15,486.4	16,521.4
Mexico	2,211.0	2,508.1	2,844.2
Morocco	1,601.2	2,133.4	2,719.3
Netherlands	4,075.3	5,318.5	6,087.1
Turkey	1,373.3	1,989.8	3,232.8
United Kingdom	12,150.4	14,644.8	16,500.2
USA	5,468.0	6,478.9	7,218.3
Total (incl. others)	125,872.2	158,213.1	182,727.2

* Imports by country of production; exports by country of last consignment. For exports the distribution by country excludes stores and bunkers for ships and aircraft.

Source: UN, *International Trade Statistics Yearbook*.

2005 (selected major trading partners, € million): *Imports:* Algeria 4,063.0; Australia 660.7; Canada 997.4; China, People's Republic 11,640.1; France 32,740.2; Germany 33,810.1; Italy 19,864.0; Japan 5,871.0; Morocco 2,101.6; Portugal 7,433.2; United Kingdom 13,196.3; USA 7,825.2; Total (incl. others) 231,371.6. *Exports:* Algeria 1,228.1; Australia 737.3; Canada 706.1; China, People's Republic 1,498.7; France 29,552.8; Germany 17,532.0; Italy 12,869.3; Japan 1,154.6; Morocco 2,230.1; Portugal 14,655.1; United Kingdom 13,026.3; USA 6,103.2; Total (incl. others) 153,651.7.

2006 (selected major trading partners, € million): *Imports:* Algeria 4,490.5; Australia 827.2; Canada 762.8; China, People's Republic 14,301.9; France 33,163.3; Germany 36,928.8; Italy 21,205.6; Japan 5,840.7; Morocco 2,432.2; Portugal 8,730.2; United Kingdom 12,753.8; USA 8,475.9; Total (incl. others) 259,559.0. *Exports:* Algeria 1,061.5; Australia 789.5; Canada 705.9; China, People's Republic 1,670.7; France 31,754.2; Germany 18,486.4; Italy 14,483.5; Japan 1,346.7; Morocco 2,562.5; Portugal 14,972.4; United Kingdom 13,414.5; USA 7,498.1; Total (incl. others) 169,872.0.

Transport

RAILWAYS
(RENFE only)

	2002	2003	2004
Number of passengers ('000)	484,460	490,440	484,461
Passenger-kilometres (million)	19,480	19,309	19,017
Freight ('000 metric tons)	26,359	26,929	26,806
Freight ton-kilometres (million)	11,660	11,866	11,927

Source: Red Nacional de los Ferrocarriles Españoles (RENFE), Madrid.

ROAD TRAFFIC
('000 motor vehicles in use at 31 December)

	2002	2003	2004
Passenger cars	18,732.6	18,688.3	19,541.9
Buses	57.0	56.0	57.0
Lorries	4,091.9	4,188.9	4,418.0
Motorcycles	1,517.2	1,513.5	1,612.1
Tractors	167.0	174.5	185.4
Other vehicles	500.1	548.2	618.3

SHIPPING
Merchant Fleet
(registered at 31 December)

	2004	2005	2006
Number of vessels	1,611	1,612	1,638
Displacement (grt)	2,869,127	2,361,683	3,004,626

Source: Lloyd's Register-Fairplay, *World Fleet Statistics*.

International Sea-borne Freight Traffic

	2002	2003	2004
Goods loaded ('000 metric tons)	63,045	68,227	74,576
Goods unloaded ('000 metric tons)	213,995	221,455	236,199
Passengers embarked ('000)	1,952	2,227	2,094
Passengers disembarked ('000)	2,156	2,351	2,034

Source: partly Puertos del Estado, Ministerio de Fomento, Madrid.

CIVIL AVIATION
(domestic and international traffic on scheduled services)

	2004	2005	2006
Passengers carried ('000)	163,889	179,047	191,125
Goods carried ('000 metric tons)	629,396	610,145	582,876

Source: Dirección General de Aviación Civil, Ministerio de Fomento, Madrid.

Tourism

FOREIGN TOURIST ARRIVALS
('000 persons, incl. Spaniards resident abroad)

Country of residence	2004	2005	2006
Belgium	1,743	1,734	1,903
France	7,499	8,765	9,152
Germany	10,022	9,928	10,146
Ireland	1,489	1,367	1,510
Italy	2,610	3,004	3,359
Netherlands	2,294	2,495	2,528
Portugal	2,006	2,041	2,200
Switzerland	1,080	1,146	1,390
United Kingdom	16,383	16,109	16,179
USA	934	882	930
Total (incl. others)	53,599	55,576	58,451

Receipts from tourism (€ million): 44,166 in 2004; 46,060 in 2005; 48,227 in 2006.

Source: Instituto de Estudios Turísticos, Madrid.

Communications Media

	2004	2005	2006
Telephones ('000 main lines in use)	17,934.5	18,004.0	18,384.7
Mobile cellular telephones ('000 subscribers)	38,622.8	42,694.1	46,152.0
Personal computers ('000 in use)	10,957	12,000	n.a.
Internet users ('000)	15,140	17,233	18,578
Broadband subscribers ('000)	3,401.4	5,035.2	6,654.9

Facsimile machines (1996): 700,000 in use (estimate).

Radio receivers ('000 in use, 1997): 13,100.

Book production (2003): titles ('000) 72.0; copies (million) 238.7.

Daily newspapers (2004): 151 (with combined average circulation of 6,183,000 copies per issue).

Non-daily newspapers (1999): 11 (with combined average circulation of 5,371,000).

Sources: partly UN, *Statistical Yearbook*; UNESCO Institute for Statistics; UNESCO, *Statistical Yearbook*; and International Telecommunication Union.

Education

(2007/08 forecasts unless otherwise indicated)

	Institutions*	Teachers	Students
Pre-primary	3,985	19,237†	1,620,505
Primary	9,805‡	117,753†	2,603,175
Special education	486	6,396†	29,555
Secondary: general	4,569‡	216,361†§	1,826,825
Secondary: vocational and university entrance			1,125,820
Universities, etc.	72	107,905	1,381,749

* 2005/06 figures.
† 2003/04 figure.
‡ Excluding institutions providing primary education and the first cycle of secondary education (2,475), or institutions providing both primary and secondary education (1,268).
§ Excluding personnel teaching at institutions that provide both primary and secondary education (147,300).

Source: Ministerio de Educación y Ciencia, Madrid.

Directory

The Constitution

The Constitution of the Kingdom of Spain was approved by popular referendum on 6 December 1978, and promulgated on 29 December 1978.

According to the final provisions, all the fundamental laws of the Franco regime are repealed, together with all measures incompatible with the Constitution.

The following is a summary of the main provisions:

PRELIMINARY PROVISIONS

Spain is a social and democratic State whose supreme values are freedom, justice, equality and political pluralism. National sovereignty and power reside with the Spanish people, the political form of the State being a parliamentary Monarchy.

The Constitution is based on the indissoluble unity of the Spanish nation, and recognizes and guarantees the right to autonomy of the nationalities and regions.

FUNDAMENTAL RIGHTS, DUTIES AND FREEDOMS

Standards concerning fundamental rights and freedoms recognized in the Constitution are to be interpreted in accordance with the Universal Declaration of Human Rights and other international treaties and agreements of a similar nature ratified by Spain.

All Spaniards are equal under the law and no Spaniard by birth may be deprived of his nationality. The age of majority is 18, suffrage is free and universal and every person has a right to public service.

The main freedoms listed are described below, bearing in mind that the Constitution contains the proviso that no person, group or action pose a threat to public order and safety. Free entry to and exit from Spain, freedom of thought, belief and expression are guaranteed, as is the right of access to state and public communications media by significant social and political groups and to administrative archives and registers by individuals, except in matters concerning state security and defence, and the private life and home of the individual, which are inviolable.

There is no state religion, but the state will maintain co-operation with the Roman Catholic Church and other religious groups.

Freedom of association is guaranteed, except for criminal, paramilitary and secret associations, all associations being bound to inscribe themselves in a public register; the right to form trade unions and to strike is also guaranteed, military personnel being subject to special laws in these cases.

Every person has a right to work for a just remuneration, under conditions of safety, hygiene and a healthy environment. The State is to be run on the principles of a market economy. Social security payments are provided for and it is stipulated that special care be taken of the handicapped and the elderly.

In criminal matters, the death penalty is abolished except under military criminal law in time of war. Extradition functions on the principle of reciprocity but the terms do not apply to political crimes, acts of terrorism, however, not being considered as such. All persons are presumed innocent before trial, and a habeas corpus clause provides for a detainee to be freed within 72 hours of arrest or to be brought before a court.

THE CROWN

The King is the Head of State, the symbol of its unity and permanence, and the highest representative of the Spanish State in international relations. His decisions and acts must be approved by the Government, and responsibility for the King's actions is borne by those who approve them. The Crown is hereditary descending to the sons of the Sovereign in order of seniority or, if there are no sons, to the daughters. Persons marrying against the wishes of the King or Cortes (national assembly) are excluded from the succession. The Constitution lays down the procedure for establishing the Regency.

The King's duties are as follows:

to approve and promulgate laws;

to convene and dissolve the Cortes Generales and to call elections and referendums (according to the Constitution);

to propose a candidate for the presidency of the Government and dismiss him;

to appoint the members of the Government on the proposal of the President;

to issue decrees approved by the Council of Ministers, and to confer civil and military posts and grant honours and distinctions in accordance with the laws;

to be informed of the affairs of State, and to preside over the Council of Ministers when he deems it necessary on the request of the President of the Government;

to command the Armed Forces;

to grant mercy according to the law (which may not authorize general pardons);

to accredit ambassadors and other diplomatic representatives;

to express the State's assent to bind itself to international treaties;

to declare war and peace on the prior authorization of the Cortes.

THE CORTES GENERALES

The Cortes represent the Spanish people and comprise the Congreso de los Diputados (Congress of Deputies—lower house) and the Senado (Senate—upper house).

The Congreso has a minimum of 300 deputies and a maximum of 400, elected by universal, free, equal, direct and secret suffrage. Each province forms one constituency, the number of deputies in each one being determined according to population and elected by proportional representation for four years, Ceuta and Melilla having one deputy each. Elections must be held between 30 and 60 days after the end of each parliamentary mandate, and the Congreso convened within 25 days of the elections.

The Senado is based on territorial representation. Each province elects four senators for four years. Each island or group of islands forms one constituency. Gran Canaria, Mallorca and Tenerife return three senators each, the others one each. The Autonomous Communities return, in addition, one senator, plus one more for each million inhabitants, appointed by the legislative assembly of the community.

Each House lays down its own rules of procedure and elects its own president and governing body. Each year there are two ordinary sessions of the Cortes, of four and five months each, and a standing committee of 21 members in each House looks after affairs while the Cortes are in recess or during electoral periods. Measures are adopted by a majority in both Houses providing that a majority of the members is present. If agreement is not reached between the Congreso and the Senado, a joint committee must attempt to solve the differences by drawing up a text to be voted on again by both Houses. In the case of further non-agreement, the issue is decided by an absolute majority vote in the Congreso.

LEGISLATION

Laws may not be retroactive.

Organic laws concern the development of fundamental rights and public freedoms, the approval of statutes of autonomy, the general electoral system, and other matters specified in the Constitution. Any approval, modification or repeal of these laws requires an absolute majority in the Congreso. The Cortes may delegate the power to issue measures called Legislative Decrees with the status of law to a governmental legislative body. In urgent cases the Government may issue provisional measures in the form of Decree-Laws not affecting the fundamental laws and rights of the nation, which must be voted upon by the Cortes within 30 days.

All laws must be sanctioned by the King within 15 days of their approval by the Cortes.

Provision is made for the popular presentation of bills if they are supported by 500,000 reputable signatures.

THE GOVERNMENT

The Government is the executive power and is composed of a President proposed by the King on the Cortes' approval and voted into office by the Congreso by absolute majority. If no President is elected within two months, the King will dissolve the Cortes and convene new elections with the approval of the President of the Congreso. The President of the Government designates the Ministers.

The Council of State is the supreme consultative organ of the Government. (An organic law will regulate its composition.)

Further articles provide for the procedure for declaring a state of alarm, emergency or siege.

THE JUDICIARY

Justice derives from the people and is administered in the name of the King by judges and magistrates subject only to the law. The principle of jurisdictional unity is the basis of the organization and functioning of the Courts, which are established in an organic law of judicial power.

The Judiciary is governed by the General Council of Judicial Power), presided over by the President of the Supreme Court and made up of 20 members appointed by the King for five years, of whom 12 are judges or magistrates, four are nominated by the Congreso and four by the Senado, these eight being elected by a three-fifths' majority from lawyers and jurists of more than 15 years' professional service.

The Attorney-General is appointed by the King on the Government's approval.

TERRITORIAL ORGANIZATION

The State is organized into municipalities, provinces and Autonomous Communities, all of which have local autonomy.

THE AUTONOMOUS COMMUNITIES

The peripheral provinces, with their own historical, cultural and economic characteristics, are entitled to accede to self-government, but the Constitution states that in no case will the federation of the Autonomous Communities be permitted.

The matters in which the Communities may assume competence include: land use and building, public works and transport, ports, agriculture, environment, minerals, economic development, culture, tourism, social aid, health and local policing, all within the framework of national laws and policy and as long as nothing outside the regional boundaries is involved. In the specific case of financial autonomy, revenue proceeds from the State and from each Autonomous Community's own taxes, and a State Compensation Fund acts to correct any imbalances between the Communities. State competence will always prevail over regional competence should conflict arise over matters not under the exclusive control of the Autonomous Communities.

The State may pass laws by absolute majority to establish the principles for the harmonization of measures taken by the Autonomous Communities, even concerning matters directly under their authority.

THE CONSTITUTIONAL COURT

This court monitors observance of the Constitution and comprises 12 members appointed by the King, of whom four are elected by the Congreso and four by the Senado by three-fifths' majority, two on the proposal of the Government and two on the proposal of the General Council of Judicial Power. They are appointed for nine years, with three members resigning every three years.

The Government

HEAD OF STATE

King of Spain, Head of State, Commander-in-Chief of the Armed Forces and Head of the Supreme Council of Defence: HM King JUAN CARLOS I (succeeded to the throne 22 November 1975).

COUNCIL OF MINISTERS
(April 2008)

President of the Government (Prime Minister): JOSÉ LUIS RODRÍGUEZ ZAPATERO.

First Deputy Prime Minister, Minister of the Presidency and Government Spokesperson: MARÍA TERESA FERNÁNDEZ DE LA VEGA SANZ.

Second Deputy Prime Minister and Minister of the Economy and Finance: PEDRO SOLBES MIRA.

Minister of Foreign Affairs and Co-operation: MIGUEL ÁNGEL MORATINOS CUYAUBÉ.

Minister of Justice: MARIANO FERNÁNDEZ BERMEJO.

Minister of Defence: CARME CHACÓN PIQUERAS.

Minister of the Interior: ALFREDO PÉREZ RUBALCABA.

Minister of Development: MAGDALENA ÁLVAREZ ARZA.

Minister of Education, Social Policy and Sport: MERCEDES CABRERA CALVO-SOTELO.

Minister of Labour and Immigration: CELESTINO CORBACHO CHAVES.

Minister of Industry, Tourism and Trade: MIGUEL SEBASTIÁN GASCÓN.

Minister of the Environment, Agriculture and the Marine: ELENA ESPINOSA MANGANA.

Minister of Public Administration: ELENA SALGADO MÉNDEZ.

Minister of Culture: CÉSAR ANTONIO MOLINA SÁNCHEZ.

Minister of Health and Consumer Affairs: BERNAT SORIA ESCOMS.

Minister of Housing: BEATRIZ CORREDOR SIERRA.

Minister of Science and Innovation: CRISTINA GARMENDIA MÉNDIZABAL.

Minister for Equality: BIBIANA AÍDO ALMAGRO.

MINISTRIES

Office of the President of the Government: Complejo de la Moncloa, Avda de Puerta de Hierro s/n, 28071 Madrid; fax (91) 3900217; e-mail jlrzapatero@presidencia.gob.es; internet www.la-moncloa.es.

Ministry of Culture: Plaza del Rey 1, 28071 Madrid; tel. (91) 7017000; fax (91) 7017352; e-mail contacte@mcu.es; internet www.mcu.es.

Ministry of Defence: Paseo de la Castellana 109, 28071 Madrid; tel. (91) 3955000; e-mail infodefensa@mde.es; internet www.mde.es.

Ministry of Development: Paseo de la Castellana 67, 28071 Madrid; tel. (91) 5978787; fax (91) 5978573; e-mail fomento@fomento.es; internet www.fomento.es.

Ministry of the Economy and Finance: Alcalá 9, 28014 Madrid; tel. (91) 5958348; fax (91) 5958486; e-mail informacion.alcala@meh.es; internet www.meh.es.

Ministry of Education, Social Policy and Sport: Alcalá 36, 28071 Madrid; tel. (91) 7018000; fax (91) 7018648; internet www.mec.es.

Ministry of the Environment, Agriculture and the Marine: Paseo Infanta Isabel 1, 28071 Madrid; tel. (91) 3475368; fax (91) 4675854; e-mail sministr@mapa.es; internet www.mapa.es.

Ministry of Equality: Madrid.

SPAIN

Ministry of Foreign Affairs and Co-operation: Plaza de la Provincia 1, 28012 Madrid; tel. (91) 3799700; e-mail informae@mae.es; internet www.mae.es.

Ministry of Health and Consumer Affairs: Paseo del Prado 18–20, 28014 Madrid; tel. 901 400100; fax (91) 5964480; e-mail oiac@msc.es; internet www.msc.es.

Ministry of Housing: Paseo de la Castellana 112, 28071 Madrid; tel. (91) 7284004; fax (91) 7284861; e-mail portal.vivienda@mviv.es; internet www.mviv.es.

Ministry of Industry, Tourism and Trade: Paseo de la Castellana 160, 28071 Madrid; tel. 902 446006; fax (91) 4578066; e-mail info@mityc.es; internet www.mityc.es.

Ministry of the Interior: Paseo de la Castellana 5, 28046 Madrid; tel. (91) 5371111; fax (91) 5371003; e-mail estafeta@mir.es; internet www.mir.es.

Ministry of Justice: San Bernardo 45, 28015 Madrid; tel. (91) 3904500; internet www.mju.es.

Ministry of Labour and Immigration: Nuevos Ministerios, Agustín de Bethencourt 4, 28071 Madrid; tel. (91) 3630000; e-mail gprensa@mtas.es; internet www.mtas.es.

Ministry of the Presidency: Complejo de la Moncloa, Avda de Puerta de Hierro s/n, 28071 Madrid; tel. (91) 3214000; e-mail sec@mpr.es; internet www.mpr.es.

Ministry of Public Administration: Paseo de la Castellana 3, 28071 Madrid; tel. (91) 2731029; fax (91) 2731012; e-mail portal@map.es; internet www.map.es.

Ministry of Science and Innovation: Madrid.

COUNCIL OF STATE

Consejo de Estado: Mayor 79, 28013 Madrid; tel. (91) 5166262; fax (91) 5166244; e-mail tramitaciones@consejo-estado.es; internet www.consejo-estado.es.

President: Francisco Rubio Llorente.

Legislature

LAS CORTES GENERALES

Congreso de los Diputados
(Congress of Deputies)

Carrera de San Jerónimo s/n, 28071 Madrid; tel. (91) 3906000; fax (91) 4298707; e-mail servicio.informacion@sgral.congreso.es; internet www.congreso.es.

President: José Bono Martínez (PSOE).

First Vice-President: Teresa Cunillera (PSOE).

General Election, 9 March 2008*

	%	Seats
Partido Socialista Obrero Español (PSOE)	43.64	169
Partido Popular (PP)	40.11	154
Convergència i Unió (CiU)	3.05	10
Euzko Alderdi Jeltzalea/Partido Nacionalista Vasco (EAJ/PNV)	1.20	6
Esquerra Republicana de Catalunya (ERC)	1.17	3
Izquierda Unida (IU)	3.80	2
Bloque Nacionalista Galego (BNG)	0.82	2
Coalición Canaria—Partido Nacionalista Canario (CC-PNC)	0.65	2
Union Progreso y Democracia (UPyD)	1.20	1
Nafarroa Bai (Na-Bai)	0.24	1
Total (incl. others)	100.00	350

* Provisional results.

Senado
(Senate)

Plaza de la Marina Española 8, 28071 Madrid; tel. (91) 5381000; fax (91) 5381003; e-mail webmaster@senado.es; internet www.senado.es.

President: Francisco Javier Rojo García (PSE-EE).

First Vice-President: Isidre Molas i Batllori (PSC-PSOE).

The Senate comprises 264 members, 208 of whom are directly elected for a term of four years. The remaining 56 regional representatives are chosen by the assemblies of the autonomous regions and are renewed following legislative elections in those regions. Following the general election held on 9 March 2008, and the appointment, in the following month, of seven senators to represent the Autonomous Community of Andalusia, the strength of the parties was as follows:

	Seats		
Grouping	Directly elected*	Appointed	Total
Partido Popular (PP)	98	24	122
Partido Socialista Obrero Español (PSOE)	79	14	93
Entesa Catalana de Progrés†	12	4	16
Partido Socialista de Euskaid-Euskadiko Ezkerra	6	1	7
Convergència i Unió (CiU)	4	3	7
Euzko Alderdi Jeltzalea/Partido Nacionalista Vasco (EAJ/PNV)	2	2	4
Unión del Pueblo de Navarra	3	—	3
Partido dos Socialistas de Galicia-PSOE	2	1	3
Coalición Canaria (CC)	1	1	2
Independent	1	1	2
Bloque Nacionalista Galego (BNG)	—	1	1
Partido Aragonés (PAR)	—	1	1
Partit Socialista de Mallorca-Entesa Nacionalista	—	1	1
Total	208	54	262

* According to provisional results of the general election of 9 March 2008.

† An alliance of the Esquerra Republicana de Catalunya, the Esquerra Unida i Alternativa, the Iniciativa per Catalunya Verds and the Partit dels Socialistes de Catalunya.

Legislative Assemblies of the Autonomous Communities

(For full names of political parties, see Political Organizations)

ANDALUCÍA (ANDALUSIA)

President of the Government (Junta): Manuel Chaves González (PSOE).

President of the Parliament: María del Mar Moreno (PSOE).

Election, 9 March 2008

	Seats
PSOE	56
PP	47
IU-LV-CA*	6
Total	109

* Convocatoria por Andalucía.

ARAGÓN

President of the Government: Marcelino Iglesias Ricou (PSOE).

President of the Parliament (Cortes): Francisco Pina Cuenca (PSOE).

Election, 27 May 2007

	Seats
PSOE	30
PP	23
PAR	9
ChA	4
IU	1
Total	67

ASTURIAS

President: Vicente Álvarez Areces (PSOE).

President of the Parliament (Junta General del Principado): María Jesús Álvarez González (PSOE).

SPAIN

Election, 27 May 2007

	Seats
PSOE	21
PP	20
IU	4
Total	45

BALEARIC ISLANDS (SEE ISLAS BALEARES)

BASQUE COUNTRY (SEE PAÍS VASCO)

CANARIAS (CANARY ISLANDS)

President of the Government: Paulino Rivero Baute (CC).
President of the Parliament: Antonio A. Castro Cordobez (CC).

Election, 27 May 2007

	Seats
PSOE	26
CC-PNC	17
PP	15
CC-AHI	2
Total	60

CANTABRIA

President: Miguel Ángel Revilla Roiz (PRC).
President of the Parliament: Miguel Ángel Palacio García (PSOE).

Election, 27 May 2007

	Seats
PP	17
PSOE	10
PRC	12
Total	39

CASTILLA Y LEÓN (CASTILE AND LEON)

President of the Government (Junta): Juan Vicente Herrera Campo (PP).
President of the Parliament (Cortes): José Manuel Fernández Santiago (PP).

Election, 27 May 2007

	Seats
PP	48
PSOE	33
UPL	2
Total	83

CASTILLA-LA MANCHA (CASTILE-LA MANCHA)

President of the Government (Junta de Comunidades): José María Barreda Fontes (PSOE).
President of the Parliament (Cortes): Francisco José Pardo Piqueras (PSOE).

Election, 27 May 2007

	Seats
PSOE	26
PP	21
Total	47

CATALUÑA/CATALUNYA (CATALONIA)

President of the Government (Generalitat): José Montilla Aguilera (PSC).
President of the Parliament: Ernest Benach i Pascual (ERC).

Election, 1 November 2006

	Seats
CiU	48
PSC-PSOE	37
ERC	21
PP	14
ICV-EUiA*	12
Ciutadans	3
Total	135

*Coalition of Iniciativa per Catalunya-Verds (ICV) and Esquerra Unida i Alternativa (EUiA).

COMUNIDAD VALENCIANA/COMUNITAT VALENCIANA (VALENCIA)

President of the Government (Generalitat): Francisco Enrique Camps Ortiz (PP).
President of the Parliament (Corts): María Milagrosa Martínez Navarro (PP).

Election, 27 May 2007

	Seats
PP	55
PSPV-PSOE	37
Compromís pel País Valencià*	7
Total	99

*A coalition of EUPV, Bloc Nacionalista Valenciana and Els Verds del País Valencià.

EXTREMADURA

President of the Government (Junta): Guillermo Fernández Vara (PSOE).
President of the Parliament (Asamblea): Juan Ramón Ferreira Díaz (PSOE).

Election, 27 May 2007

	Seats
PSOE	38
PP	27
Total	65

GALICIA

President of the Government (Xunta): Emilio Pérez Touriño (PS de G-PSOE).
President of the Parliament: Dolores Villarino Santiago (PS de G-PSOE).

Election, 19 June 2005

	Seats
PP	37
PS de G-PSOE	25
BNG	13
Total	75

ISLAS BALEARES/ILLES BALEARS (BALEARIC ISLANDS)

President of the Government: Francesc Antich i Oliver (PSOE).
President of the Parliament: Maria Antònia Munar i Riutort (UM).

Election, 27 May 2007

	Seats
PP	28
PSOE	16
PSOE-ExC	6
PSM-Bloc per Mallorca*	4
UM	3
PSM-Els Verds de Menorca	1
AIPF†	1
Total	59

*An alliance of PSM, Alternativa Esquerra Unida-Els Verds and ERC.
†Agrupació Independent Popular de Formentera.

SPAIN

MADRID

President: ESPERANZA AGUIRRE GIL DE BIEDMA (PP).
President of the Parliament (Asamblea): ELVIRA RODRÍGUEZ HERRER (PP).
Election, 27 May 2007

	Seats
PP	67
PSOE	42
IU	11
Total	120

MURCIA

President of the Government: RAMÓN LUIS VALCÁRCEL SISO (PP).
President of the Parliament (Asamblea Regional): FRANCISCO CELDRÁN VIDAL (PP).
Election, 27 May 2007

	Seats
PP	29
PSOE	15
IU-LV	1
Total	45

NAVARRA (NAVARRE)

President of the Government: MIGUEL SANZ SESMA (UPN).
President of the Parliament: MARÍA ELENA TORRES MIRANDA (PSN-PSOE).
Election, 27 May 2007

	Seats
UPN	22
Nafarroa Bai	12
PSN-PSOE	12
CDN	2
IU/NEB*	2
Total	50

*Nafarroako Ezker Batua.

PAÍS VASCO/EUSKADI (BASQUE COUNTRY)

Lehendakari (President): JUAN JOSÉ IBARRETXE MARKUARTU (PNV).
President of the Parliament: IZASKUN BÍLBAO BARANDÍKA (PNV).
Election, 17 April 2005

	Seats
PNV-EAJ/EA	29
PSE-EE	18
PP	15
PCTV-EHAK*	9
IU-EB†	3
Aralar	1
Total	75

*Partido Comunista de las Tierras Vascas-Euskal Herrialdeetako Alderdi Komunista.
†Ezker Batua.

LA RIOJA

President of the Government: PEDRO MARÍA SANZ ALONSO (PP).
President of the Parliament: JOSÉ IGNACIO CENICEROS GONZÁLEZ (PP).
Election, 27 May 2007

	Seats
PP	17
PSOE	14
PR	2
Total	33

VALENCIA (SEE COMUNIDAD VALENCIANA)

Political Organizations

In 2005 around 500 political parties were officially registered.

PRINCIPAL NATIONAL PARTIES

Izquierda Unida (IU) (United Left): Olimpo 35, 28043 Madrid; tel. (91) 7227500; fax (91) 3880405; e-mail org.federal@izquierda-unida.es; internet www.izquierda-unida.es; f. 1986 as coalition of Partido Comunista de España and other left-wing parties; Co-ordinator-Gen. GASPAR LLAMAZARES TRIGO.

Partido Comunista de España (PCE) (Communist Party of Spain): Olimpo 35, 28043 Madrid; tel. (91) 3004969; fax (91) 3004744; e-mail webmasterpce@pce.es; internet www.pce.es; f. 1922; Euro-communist; absorbed Partido Comunista Obrero Español (PCOE) in 1986, and most of Partido Comunista de los Pueblos de España (PCPE) in Jan. 1989; Sec.-Gen. FRANCISCO FRUTOS GRAS.

Partido Popular (PP) (People's Party): Génova 13, 28004 Madrid; tel. (91) 5577300; fax (91) 3122322; e-mail partidopopular@pp.es; internet www.pp.es; f. 1976; fmrly Alianza Popular, name changed Jan. 1989; absorbed Democracia Cristiana (fmrly Partido Demócrata Popular) and Partido Liberal in early 1989; centre-right, Christian Democrat; 600,000 mems (Feb. 2000); Pres. MARIANO RAJOY BREY; Sec.-Gen. (vacant).

Partido Socialista Obrero Español (PSOE) (Spanish Socialist Workers' Party): Ferraz 68 y 70, 28008 Madrid; tel. (91) 5820444; fax (91) 5820422; e-mail infopsoe@psoe.es; internet www.psoe.es; f. 1879; affiliated to the Socialist International; merged with the Partido Socialista Popular in 1978; joined by Partido de los Trabajadores de España-Unidad Comunista (PTE-UC) in 1991 and Partido de Nueva Izquierda (PDNI) in 2001; Pres. MANUEL CHAVES GONZÁLEZ; Sec.-Gen. JOSÉ LUIS RODRÍGUEZ ZAPATERO; 551,469 mems (2006).

Los Verdes (LV) (The Greens): Navellos 9, 2°, 46003 Valencia; tel. (96) 2817581; fax (96) 3921314; e-mail losverdes@verdes.es; internet www.verdes.es; f. 1984; confederation of various regional environmentalist parties; mems include Els Verds del País Valencià, Els Verds de Mallorca and Els Verds de Menorca.

REGIONAL PARTIES

There are branches of the main national parties in most autonomous communities, some of which bear alternative or additional names. There are also numerous regional parties, including the following:

Andalucía
(Andalusia)

Partido Andalucista (PA): Vidrio 32, 41003 Sevilla; tel. (95) 4502157; fax (95) 4210446; e-mail prensa@partidoandalucista.org; internet www.partidoandalucista.org; f. 1965; Sec.-Gen. JULIÁN ÁLVAREZ ORTEGA.

Aragón

Chunta Aragonesista (ChA): Conde de Aranda 14–16, 1°, 50003 Zaragoza; tel. (976) 284242; fax (976) 281311; e-mail sedenacional@chunta.com; internet www.chunta.com; f. 1986; left-wing; Pres. BIZÉN FUSTER SANTALIESTRA.

Partido Aragonés (PAR): Coso 87, 50001 Zaragoza; tel. (976) 200616; e-mail sugerencias@partidoaragones.es; internet www.partidoaragones.es; f. 1977; fmrly Partido Aragonés Regionalista; centre-right; Pres. JOSÉ ANGEL BIEL; Sec.-Gen. ALFREDO BONÉ PUEYO.

Asturias

Unión Renovadora Asturiana (URAS): Menéndez Valdés 2, 1°, 33201 Gijón; tel. (98) 5353245; internet www.uras.org; f. 1998 following split in PP of Asturias; in 2004 formed coalition, Unión Asturianista, with Partíu Asturianista (PAS); Pres. SERGIO MARQUÉS FERNÁNDEZ; Sec.-Gen. MARTA AURORA PRIETO BUSTO.

Canarias
(Canary Islands)

Agrupación Herreña Independiente (AHI): La Constitución 4, 38900 Valverde, El Hierro, Santa Cruz de Tenerife; tel. (922) 551134; fax (922) 551224; party of El Hierro island; Pres. TOMÁS PADRÓN HERNÁNDEZ.

Coalición Canaria (CC): Buenos Aires 24, 35001 Las Palmas, Gran Canaria; tel. (928) 363142; internet www.coalicioncanaria.org; f. 1993 as coalition of Canary Islands parties incl. Agrupaciones Independientes de Canarias, Centro Canario Nacionalista, Iniciativa Canaria and Asamblea Majorera; united as a single party in 2005; Pres. PAULINO RIVERO BAUTE.

Partido Nacionalista Canario (PNC): Sagasta 92, 35008 Las Palmas de Gran Canaria; tel. and fax (928) 221736; e-mail pnc@partidonacionalistacanario.com; internet www.narias.com/pnc; f. 1977; National Pres. JUAN MANUEL GARCÍA RAMOS; National Sec.-Gen. GUSTAVO DAVILA DE LEÓN.

Cantabria

Partido Regionalista de Cantabria (PRC): Amós de Escalante 2, 2°D, 39002 Santander; tel. (942) 229177; fax (942) 362337; e-mail prc@prc.es; internet www.prc.es; f. 1978; centre-right; Sec.-Gen. MIGUEL ÁNGEL REVILLA ROIZ.

Castilla y León
(Castile and Leon)

Unión del Pueblo Leonés (UPL): Avda República Argentina 13, 1°, 24004 León; tel. (987) 263309; fax (987) 204499; internet www.uniondelpuebloleones.com; f. 1986 as Unión Leonesista; advocates autonomy for León region; 4,000 mems; Pres. MELCHOR MORENO DE LA TORRE; Sec.-Gen. JOAQUÍN OTERO PEREIRA.

Cataluña/Catalunya
(Catalonia)

Ciutadans-Partit de la Ciutadania/Ciudadanos-Partido de la Ciudadanía (Citizens-Citizenship Party): Vilamarí 86–88, 08015 Barcelona; tel. (93) 3429436; e-mail sede@ciutadans-ciudadanos.com; internet www.ciutadans-ciudadanos.net; f. 2006; opposes Catalan nationalism; Pres. ALBERT RIVERA; Sec.-Gen. ANTONIO ROBLES.

Convergència i Unió (CiU): Còrsega 331, 08037 Barcelona; tel. (93) 2363100; e-mail ciu@ciu.info; internet www.ciu.info; f. 1978 as an electoral alliance; became confederation of parties in March 2001; Catalan nationalist, conservative; Pres. ARTUR MAS I GAVARRÓ; Sec.-Gen. JOSEP ANTONI DURAN I LLEIDA; an alliance of the following two parties:

Convergència Democràtica de Catalunya (CDC): Còrsega 331–333, 08037 Barcelona; tel. (93) 2363100; fax (93) 2363115; e-mail cdc@convergencia.org; internet www.convergencia.org; f. 1974; Catalan nationalist, centrist; 45,523 mems (2000); Pres. JORDI PUJOL I SOLEY; Sec.-Gen. ARTUR MAS I GAVARRÓ.

Unió Democràtica de Catalunya (UDC): Travessera de Gràcia 17–21, àtic, 08021 Barcelona; tel. (93) 2402200; fax (93) 2402201; e-mail info@unio.org; internet www.unio.org; f. 1931; Christian democrat; 34,255 mems (1998); Pres. JOSEP ANTONI DURAN I LLEIDA; Sec.-Gen. JOSEP MARIA PELEGRÍ I AIXUT.

Esquerra Republicana de Catalunya (ERC) (Republican Left of Catalonia): Calàbria 166, 08015 Barcelona; tel. (93) 4536005; fax (93) 3237122; e-mail info@esquerra.org; internet www.esquerra.cat; f. 1931; advocates independence for Catalonia within European context, a just society and national solidarity of Catalan people; Pres. JOSEP-LLUÍS CAROD-ROVIRA; Sec.-Gen. JOAN PUIGCERCÓS.

Esquerra Unida i Alternativa (EUiA): Doctor Aiguader 10, 08003 Barcelona; tel. (93) 3170034; fax (93) 3179251; e-mail euia@euia.cat; internet www.euia.cat; federation of five communist and left-wing parties in Catalonia; republican; affiliated to Izquierda Unida; Co-ordinator-Gen. JORDI MIRALLES I CONTE.

Iniciativa per Catalunya Verds (ICV): Ciutat 7, 08002 Barcelona; tel. (93) 3010612; fax (93) 4124252; e-mail iniciativa@iniciativa.cat; internet www.iniciativa.cat; f. 1987 as Iniciativa per Catalunya, a federation of left-wing parties; adopted current name in 1998 following alliance with Els Verds (Confederació Ecologista de Catalunya); Pres. JOAN SAURA LAPORTA.

Partit dels Socialistes de Catalunya (PSC-PSOE): Nicaragua 75, 08029 Barcelona; tel. (93) 4955400; fax (93) 4955435; e-mail info@socialistes.org; internet www.socialistes.cat; f. 1978 by merger of various Catalan parties of socialist ideology; allied to PSOE; Pres. JOSÉ MONTILLA AGUILERA.

Comunidad Valenciana/Comunitat Valenciana
(Valencia)
(see also Cataluña)

Bloc Nacionalista Valencià: Sant Jacint 28, entresòl, 46008 Valencia; tel. (96) 3826606; fax (96) 3826276; e-mail bloc@bloc.ws; internet www.bloc.ws; f. 1998 as federation of Unitat del Poble Valencià (f. 1982), Partit Valencià Nacionalista (f. 1990) and Nacionalistes d'Alcoi (f. 1994); progressive Valencian nationalist party; Pres. JOSEP MARIA PAÑELLA ALCACER; Sec. Gen. ENRIC XAVIER MORERA CATALÀ.

Esquerra Unida del País Valencià (EUPV): Gran Via Ramón i Cajál 55, 2°, 46007 Valencia; e-mail eu.pvalencia@izquierda-unida.es; tel. (963) 841888; fax (963) 847678; e-mail eupv@eupv.org; internet www.eupv.org; left-wing; affiliated to Izquierda Unida; Co-ordinator GLÒRIA MARCOS I MARTÍ.

Esquerra Valenciana (EV): 13129-4621994 Valencia; e-mail esquerravalenciana@ono.com; internet www.esquerravalenciana.org; f. 1934 as part of Front Popular; Pres. ROBERTO MORO; Sec.-Gen. VÍCTOR BAETA SUBIAS.

Partido Socialista del País Valenciano (PSPV-PSOE) (Valencian Socialist Party): Palau de les Corts Valencianes, Plaza San Lorenzo 4, 46003 Valencia; internet www.pspv-psoe.org; affiliated to PSOE; Pres. DIEGO MACÍA ANTÓN; Sec.-Gen. (vacant).

Galicia

Bloque Nacionalista Galego (BNG): Avda Rodríguez de Viguri 16, baixo, 15703 Santiago de Compostela; tel. (981) 555850; fax (981) 555851; e-mail sedenacional@bng-galiza.org; internet www.bng-galiza.org; f. 1982; Galician nationalist; Leader ANXO QUINTANA GONZÁLEZ.

Partido dos Socialistas de Galicia (PS de G-PSOE) (Galician Socialist Party): Rua do Pino 1–9, 15704 Santiago de Compostela; tel. (981) 552030; fax (981) 588708; e-mail ceng@psdeg-psoe.org; internet www.psdeg-psoe.org; Galician branch of the PSOE; Sec.-Gen. EMILIO PÉREZ TOURIÑO.

Islas Baleares/Illes Balears
(Balearic Islands)
(see also Cataluña)

Alternativa Esquerra Unida-Els Verds: Sindicat 74, 1r 2a, 07001 Palma de Mallorca; tel. (971) 724488; fax (971) 971711836; internet www.alternativa-euev.cat; alliance of Esquerra Unida de les Illes Balears (affiliated to Izquierda Unida) and Els Verds de Mallorca; Spokespersons EBERHARD GROSSKE, MIQUEL ÀNGEL LLAUGER.

Eivissa pel Canvi (ExC) (Ibiza for Change): Apdo Correos 40, Santa Gertrudis, Santa Eulària des Riu, Eivissa; internet www.eivissapelcanvi.org; f. 2006; opposes municipal corruption.

PSM-Entesa Nacionalista (PSM-EN): Isidoro Antillón 9, baixos, 07006 Palma de Mallorca; tel. (971) 775252; fax (971) 774848; e-mail federacio@psm-entesa.cat; internet www.psm-entesa.org; f. 1989 as Federació de l'Esquerra Nacionalista de les Illes Balears (FENIB); federation of PSM-Entesa Nacionalista de Mallorca (f. 1976 as Partit Socialista de les Illes, renamed Partit Socialista de Mallorca—PSM in 1977), PSM-Entesa Nacionalista de Menorca (f. 1977 as Partit Socialista de Menorca), Entesa Nacionalista i Ecologista d'Eivissa (f. 1989) and other groups; Socialist, Catalan nationalist, environmentalist; Sec.-Gen. BARTOLOMEU CARRIÓ TRUJILLANO.

Unió Mallorquina (UM): Sindicat 21, 07001 Palma de Mallorca; tel. (971) 726336; fax (971) 728116; e-mail um@unio-mallorquina.com; internet www.unio-mallorquina.com; f. 1982 as continuation of Unión de Centro Democrático in Mallorca; liberal, centrist; Pres. MARIA ANTÒNIA MUNAR I RIUTORT.

Navarra
(Navarre)
(see also País Vasco)

Aralar: Aduanaren txokoa 16-18, behea, 31001 Pamplona; tel. (948) 206362; fax (948) 206003; e-mail nafarroa@aralar.net; internet www.aralar.net; f. 1990; Basque separatist, left-wing; rejects violence; Co-ordinator-Gen. PATXI ZABALETA.

Batzarre (Assembly): Navarrería 15, 1°C, 31001 Pamplona; tel. (948) 224757; fax (948) 210063; e-mail batzarre@batzarre.org; internet www.batzarre.org; f. 1987; left-wing Basque nationalist party of Navarre.

Convergencia de Demócratas de Navarra (CDN): Avda Carlos III 7, 1°, 31002 Pamplona; tel. (948) 228185; fax (948) 227336; e-mail cdn@cdn.es; internet www.cdn.es; f. 1995; progressive centrist party; promotes Navarrese identity and opposes integration with Basque Country; Pres. JUAN CRUZ ALLI ARANGUREN; Sec. CARLOS PÉREZ-NIEVAS LÓPEZ DE GOICOECHEA.

Nafarroa Bai (Na Bai) (Navarre Yes): Plaza del Castillo 32, 1° izqda, 31001 Pamplona; tel. (948) 203033; fax (948) 203034; e-mail nafarroabai@nafarroabai.net; internet www.nafarroabai.net; coalition of Basque nationalist parties in Navarre: Aralar, Batzarre, Eusko Alkartasuna and EAJ-PNV; Leader PATXI ZABALETA.

Partido Socialista de Navarra (PSN): Paseo de Sarasate 15, 2°, 31002 Pamplona; tel. (948) 225003; fax (948) 221534; e-mail info@psn-psoe.org; internet www.psn-psoe.org; Navarrese branch of PSOE; Sec.-Gen. CARLOS CHIVITE CORNAGO.

Unión del Pueblo Navarro (UPN): Plaza Príncipe de Viana 1, 4° dcha, 31002 Pamplona; tel. (948) 223402; fax (948) 210810; e-mail info@upn.org; internet www.upn.org; f. 1979; allied to Partido Popular; centre-right; opposes closer ties between Navarre and Basque Country; Pres. MIGUEL SANZ SESMA; Sec.-Gen. ALBERTO CATALÁN HIGUERAS.

SPAIN

País Vasco/Euskadi
(Basque Country)

Aralar: see Navarra above.

Eusko Abertzale Ekintza-Acción Nacionalista Vasca (EAE-ANV): Sta Maria 2, 48920 Portugalete (Vizcaya); tel. (944) 955899; e-mail info@eae-anv.org; internet www.eae-anv.org; f. 1930 by a faction of Partido Nacionalista Vasco; left-wing, republican, Basque separatist; barred from standing in 2008 general election; Sec.-Gen. ANTXON GÓMEZ.

Eusko Alkartasuna (EA) (Basque Solidarity): Camino de Portuetxe 23, 1°, 20018 San Sebastián; tel. (943) 020130; fax (943) 020131; e-mail gipuzkoa@euskoalkartasuna.org; internet www.euskoalkartasuna.org; f. 1985 (as Eusko Abertzaleak—Basque Nationalists) by dissident group of progressive PNV mems; Pres. BEGOÑA ERRAZTI ESNAL; Sec.-Gen. UNAI ZIARRETA BILBAO.

Euzko Alderdi Jeltzalea-Partido Nacionalista Vasco (EAJ-PNV): Sabin Etxea, Ibáñez de Bilbao 16, 48001 Bilbao; tel. (94) 4039400; fax (94) 4039413; e-mail prentsa@eaj-pnv.com; internet www.eaj-pnv.com; f. 1895; Basque nationalist; seeks to achieve autonomy through peaceful means; 32,000 mems; Pres. IÑIGO URKULLU RENTERIA; Sec. JOSUNE ARIZTONDO AKARREGI.

Partido Comunista de las Tierras Vascas-Euskal Herrialdeetako Alderdi Komunista (PCTV): communist, Basque separatist; stood in 2005 elections to Basque Parliament adopting programme of the banned party Aukera Guztiak.

Partido Socialista de Euskadi-Euskadiko Ezkerra (PSE-EE) (Basque Socialist Party-Basque Left): Alameda de Recalde 27, 4°, 48009 Bilbao; tel. (94) 4242142; fax (94) 4238904; e-mail info@socialistasvascos.com; internet www.socialistasvascos.com; f. 1993 by merger of PSE-PSOE (Basque branch of PSOE) and Euskadiko Ezkerra; affiliated to PSOE; Pres. JESÚS EGUIGUREN; Sec.-Gen. PATXI LÓPEZ.

La Rioja

Partido Riojano (PR): Portales 17, 1°, 26001 Logroño; tel. (941) 238199; fax (941) 254396; e-mail partidoriojano@partidoriojano.es; internet www.partidoriojano.es; Pres. MIGUEL GONZÁLEZ DE LEGARRA; Sec.-Gen. JAVIER SÁENZ TORRE MERINO.

ILLEGAL ORGANIZATIONS

Illegal terrorist organizations include the Basque separatist Euskadi ta Askatasuna (ETA, Basque Homeland and Liberty, f. 1959) and the extreme left-wing Grupos de Resistencia Antifascista Primero de Octubre (GRAPO, First of October Anti-Fascist Resistance Groups, f. 1975). It was reported in June 2007 that the latter had been put out of action following a successful police operation. After the Madrid train bombings in March 2004 it was revealed that fundamentalist Islamist groups, thought to be connected to the Moroccan Groupe islamique combattant Marocain (GICM), were operating in Spain. A 2002 law facilitated the banning of political parties deemed to support violence or terrorism. The legislation was employed against a number of parties in the Basque Country, most notably Batasuna (f. 1978 as Herri Batasuna), a separatist party led by Arnaldo Otegi Mondragón, which was banned by the Supreme Court in March 2003 due to its links to ETA. A number of parties and lists deemed to be alternatives to Batasuna have also been prevented from standing for election.

Election Commission

Junta Electoral Central: Congreso de los Diputados, Floridablanca, 28071 Madrid; tel. (91) 3906367; fax (91) 3906991; internet www.juntaelectoralcentral.es; independent; Pres. JOSÉ MARÍA RUIZ-JARABO FERRÁN.

Diplomatic Representation

EMBASSIES IN SPAIN

Afghanistan: Umbría 8, 28043 Madrid; tel. (91) 7218581; fax (91) 7216832; e-mail embajadadeafganistanenmadrid@gmail.com; Chargé d'affaires GUL AHMAD SHERZADA.

Albania: María de Molina 64, 5°B, 28006 Madrid; tel. (91) 5612118; fax (91) 5613775; e-mail embassy.madrid@mfa.gov.al; Ambassador ANILA BITRI LANI.

Algeria: General Oráa 12, 28006 Madrid; tel. (91) 5629705; fax (91) 5629877; e-mail embargel@tsai.es; Ambassador MOHAMMED HANECHE.

Andorra: Alcalá 73, 28009 Madrid; tel. (91) 4317453; fax (91) 5776341; e-mail embajada@embajadaandorra.es; Ambassador XAVIER ESPOT MIRÓ.

Angola: Serrano 64, 3°, 28001 Madrid; tel. (91) 4356430; fax (91) 5779010; e-mail gabinete@embajadadeangola.com; internet www.embajadadeangola.com; Ambassador ARMANDO DA CRUZ NETO.

Argentina: Pedro de Valdivia 21, 28006 Madrid; tel. (91) 7710519; fax (91) 7710526; e-mail embajada@portalargentino.net; internet www.portalargentino.net; Ambassador CARLOS ANTONIO BETTINI.

Australia: Plaza del Descubridor Diego de Ordás 3, 28003 Madrid; tel. (91) 3536600; fax (91) 3536692; e-mail pilar.sanchez@dfat.gov.au; internet www.spain.embassy.gov.au; Ambassador NOEL CAMPBELL.

Austria: Paseo de la Castellana 91, 9°, 28046 Madrid; tel. (91) 5565315; fax (91) 5973579; e-mail madrid-ob@bmeia.gv.at; internet www.bmeia.gv.at/madrid; Ambassador Dr ULRIKE TILLY.

Azerbaijan: Ronda de la Avutarda 38, 28043 Madrid; tel. (91) 7596010; fax (91) 7597056; Ambassador MAMMAD NOVRUZ OĞLU ALIYEV.

Bangladesh: Diego de León 69, 2°D, 28006 Madrid; tel. (91) 4019932; fax (91) 4029564; e-mail chancery@bdoot-mad.e.telefonica.net; Ambassador SAIFUL AMIN KHAN.

Belgium: Paseo de la Castellana 18, 6°, 28046 Madrid; tel. (91) 5776300; fax (91) 4318166; e-mail madrid@diplobel.org; internet www.diplobel.org/spain; Ambassador CLAUDE RIJMENANS.

Bolivia: Velázquez 26, 3°, 28001 Madrid; tel. (91) 5780835; fax (91) 5773946; e-mail embajada@embajadadebolivia.es; internet www.embajadadebolivia.es; Ambassador MARÍA DEL CARMEN ALMENDRAS CAMARGO.

Bosnia and Herzegovina: Lagasca 24, 2°, 28001 Madrid; tel. (91) 5750870; fax (91) 4355056; e-mail ambasada@ctv.es; Ambassador JOSIP BRKIĆ.

Brazil: Fernando el Santo 6, 28010 Madrid; tel. (91) 7004650; fax (91) 7004660; e-mail adm@embajadadebrasil.es; internet www.brasil.es; Ambassador JOSÉ VIEGAS FILHO.

Bulgaria: Santa María Magdalena 15, 28016 Madrid; tel. (91) 3455761; fax (91) 3591201; e-mail embulmad@tyahoo.es; Ambassador IVAN YANKOV HRISTOV.

Cameroon: Rosario Pino 3, 28020 Madrid; tel. (91) 5711160; fax (91) 5712504; e-mail ambcammadrid@telefonica.net; Ambassador (vacant).

Canada: Núñez de Balboa 35, 28001 Madrid; tel. (91) 4233250; fax (91) 4233251; e-mail madrid@international.gc.ca; internet www.canada-es.org; Ambassador MALCOLM McKECHNIE.

Chile: Lagasca 88, 6°, 28001 Madrid; tel. (91) 4319160; fax (91) 5775560; e-mail echilees@tsai.es; Ambassador OSVALDO PUCCIO HUIDOBRO.

China, People's Republic: Arturo Soria 113, 28043 Madrid; tel. (91) 5194242; fax (91) 5192035; e-mail embajadachina@embajadachina.es; internet www.embajadachina.es; Ambassador QIU XIAOQI.

Colombia: General Martínez Campos 48, 28010 Madrid; tel. (91) 7004770; fax (91) 3102869; e-mail emadrid@cancilleria.gov.co; Chargé d'affaires a.i. LUIS ARMANDO SOTO BOUTIN.

Congo, Democratic Republic: Paseo de la Castellana 255, 1°, 28046 Madrid; tel. (91) 7332647; fax (91) 3231575; e-mail ambardcmadrid@hotmail.com; Ambassador (vacant).

Costa Rica: Paseo de la Castellana 164, 17°, 28046 Madrid; tel. (91) 3459622; fax (91) 3533709; e-mail embajada@embcr.org; Ambassador MELVIN ALFREDO SÁENZ BIOLLEY.

Côte d'Ivoire: Serrano 154, 28006 Madrid; tel. (91) 5626916; fax (91) 5622193; e-mail costamarfil@ic1.inycom.es; Ambassador JEANNE GUEHE MOULOT.

Croatia: Claudio Coello 78, 2°, 28001 Madrid; tel. (91) 5776881; fax (91) 5776905; e-mail croemb.madrid@mvp.hr; internet es.mvp.hr; Ambassador FILIP VUČAK.

Cuba: Paseo de la Habana 194, 28036 Madrid; tel. (91) 3592500; fax (91) 3596145; e-mail secreembajada@ecubamad.com; internet emba.cubaminrex.cu/espana; Ambassador ALBERTO VELAZCO SAN JOSÉ.

Cyprus: Paseo de la Castellana 45, 4–5°, 28046 Madrid; tel. (91) 5783114; fax (91) 5782189; e-mail embajadachipre@telefonica.net; internet www.mfa.gov.cy/embassymadrid; Ambassador REA YIORDAMLIS.

Czech Republic: Avda Pío XII 22–24, 28016 Madrid; tel. (91) 3531880; fax (91) 3531885; e-mail madrid@embassy.mzv.cz; internet www.mfa.cz/madrid; Ambassador MARTIN KOŠATKA.

Denmark: Serrano 26, 7°, 28001 Madrid; tel. (91) 4318445; fax (91) 4319168; e-mail madamb@um.dk; internet www.embajadadinamarca.es; Ambassador NIELS PULTZ.

Dominican Republic: Paseo de la Castellana 30, 28046 Madrid; tel. (91) 4315395; fax (91) 4358139; e-mail embajada@embajadadominicana.es; internet www.embajadadominicana.es; Ambassador ALEJANDRO GONZÁLEZ PONS.

Ecuador: Velázquez 114, 2°, 28006 Madrid; tel. (91) 5627215; fax (91) 7450244; e-mail embajada@mecuador.es; Ambassador NICOLÁS ISSA OBANDO.

Egypt: Velázquez 69, 28006 Madrid; tel. (91) 5776308; fax (91) 5781732; Ambassador YASSER MORAD HOSSNY.

El Salvador: General Oraá 9, 28006 Madrid; tel. (91) 5628002; fax (91) 5630584; e-mail madrid@embasalva.com; Ambassador Dr ENRIQUE BORGO BUSTAMANTE.

Equatorial Guinea: Avda Pio XII 14, 28016 Madrid; tel. (91) 3532169; fax (91) 3532165; Ambassador IGNACIO MILAN TANG.

Estonia: Claudio Coello 91, 28006 Madrid; tel. (91) 4261671; fax (91) 4261672; e-mail embassy.madrid@mfa.ee; internet www.estemb.es; Ambassador ANDRES RUNDU.

Finland: Paseo de la Castellana 15, 28046 Madrid; tel. (91) 3196172; fax (91) 3083901; e-mail sanomat.mad@formin.fi; internet www.finlandia.es; Ambassador MAIJA LAHTEENMAKI.

France: Salustiano Olózaga 9, 28001 Madrid; tel. (91) 4238900; fax (91) 4238908; e-mail chancellerie@ctv.es; internet www.ambafrance-es.org; Ambassador BRUNO DELAYE.

Gabon: Francisco Alcántara 3A, 28002 Madrid; tel. (91) 4138211; fax (91) 4131153; e-mail emb-gabon-es@nemo.es; Ambassador CARLOS VICTOR BOUNGOU.

Georgia: Felipe IV 10, 28014 Madrid; tel. (91) 4293329; fax (91) 4296883; e-mail embassymadrid@mfa.gov.ge; internet www.spain.mfa.gov.ge; Ambassador ZURAB POLOLIKASHVILI.

Germany: Fortuny 8, 28010 Madrid; tel. (91) 5579000; fax (91) 3102104; e-mail zreg@madri.auswaertiges-amt.de; internet www.madrid.diplo.de; Ambassador WOLF-RUTHART BORN.

Ghana: Capitán Haya 38, 10°A, 28020 Madrid; tel. (91) 5670390; fax (91) 5670393; e-mail mission@ghanaembassyspain.com; Ambassador FRANCIS TSEGAH.

Greece: Avda Dr Arce 24, 28002 Madrid; tel. (91) 5644653; fax (91) 5644668; e-mail embajadadegrecia@telefonica.net; internet www.embagrec.org; Ambassador GEÓRGIOS GABRIELIDES.

Guatemala: Rafael Salgado 3, 10° dcha, 28036 Madrid; tel. (91) 3441722; fax (91) 4587894; e-mail informacion@embajadaguatemala.es; internet www.embajadaguatemala.es; Ambassador (vacant).

Haiti: Marques del Duero 3, 1°, 28001 Madrid; tel. (91) 5752624; fax (91) 4314600; e-mail ambhaities@yahoo.es; Ambassador YOLETTE AZOR CHARLES.

Holy See: Avda de Pío XII 46, 28016 Madrid; tel. (91) 7668311; fax (91) 7667085; e-mail nunap@planalfa.es; Apostolic Nuncio Most Rev. MANUEL MONTEIRO DE CASTRO (Titular Archbishop of Benevento).

Honduras: Rafael Calvo 15, 6°D, 28010 Madrid; tel. (91) 7025157; fax (91) 7025158; e-mail info@embahonduras.es; internet www.embahonduras.es; Ambassador JOSÉ EDUARDO MARTELL MEJÍA.

Hungary: Fortuny 6, 4°, 28010 Madrid; tel. (91) 4137011; fax (91) 4134138; e-mail info@embajada-hungria.org; internet www.mfa.gov.hu/emb/madrid; Ambassador GÁBOR TÓTH.

India: Avda Pío XII 30–32, 28016 Madrid; tel. (91) 1315114; fax (91) 3451112; internet www.embajadaindia.com; Ambassador SURYA-KANTHI TRIPATTHI.

Indonesia: Agastia 65, 28043 Madrid; tel. (91) 4130294; fax (91) 4138994; e-mail kbri@embajadadeindonesia.es; internet www.embajadadeindonesia.es; Ambassador SLAMET SANTOSO MUSTAFA.

Iran: Jerez 5, Villa El Altozano, Chamartín, 28016 Madrid; tel. (91) 3450112; fax (91) 3451190; e-mail embiran@hotmail.com; Ambassador SEYED DAVOUD MOHSENI SALEHI MONFARED.

Iraq: Ronda de Sobradiel 67, 28043 Madrid; tel. (91) 7591282; fax (91) 7593180; e-mail mdremb@iraqmofamail.net; Ambassador TALAL H. AL-KHUDAIRI.

Ireland: Paseo de la Castellana 46, 4°, 28046 Madrid; tel. (91) 4364093; fax (91) 4351677; internet www.dfa.ie/home/index.aspx?id=33979; Ambassador PETER GUNNING.

Israel: Velázquez 150, 7°, 28002 Madrid; tel. (91) 7829500; fax (91) 7829555; e-mail embajada@embajada-israel.es; internet www.embajada-israel.es; Ambassador RAPHAEL SCHUTZ.

Italy: Lagasca 98, 28006 Madrid; tel. (91) 4233300; fax (91) 5757776; e-mail archivio.ambmadrid@esteri.it; internet www.ambmadrid.esteri.it; Ambassador PASQUALE TERRACCIANO.

Japan: Serrano 109, 28006 Madrid; tel. (91) 5907600; fax (91) 5901321; internet www.es.emb-japan.go.jp; Ambassador MOTOHIDE YOSHIKAWA.

Jordan: General Martínez Campos 41, 28010 Madrid; tel. (91) 3191100; fax (91) 3082536; e-mail jordania@telefonica.net; internet www.embjordaniaes.org; Ambassador ZAID M. AL-LOZI.

Kazakhstan: Cascanueces 25, 28043 Madrid; tel. (91) 7216290; fax (91) 7219374; e-mail embajada@kazesp.org; internet www.kazesp.org; Ambassador NURLAN DANENOV.

Korea, Republic: González Amigó 15, 28033 Madrid; tel. (91) 3532000; fax (91) 3532001; e-mail embspain.adm@mofa.go.kr; Ambassador CHUN-SEUN LEE.

Kuwait: Paseo de la Castellana 141, 16°, 28046 Madrid; tel. (91) 5792467; fax (91) 5702109; Ambassador ADIL HAMAD M. AL-AYYAR.

Latvia: Alfonso XII 52, 1°, 28014 Madrid; tel. (91) 3691362; fax (91) 3690020; e-mail lespan@telefonica.net; Ambassador MĀRTIŅŠ PERTS.

Lebanon: Paseo de la Castellana 178, 3° izqda, 28046 Madrid; tel. (91) 3451368; fax (91) 3455631; e-mail leem-e@teleline.es; Chargé d'affaires a.i. CHOUCRI FATHALLA ABBOUD.

Libya: Pisuerga 12, 28002 Madrid; tel. (91) 5635753; fax (91) 5643986; e-mail oficinapopularlibia-madrid@hotmail.com; Ambassador ABDULWAHED R. GAMMUDI.

Lithuania: Pisuerga 5, 28002 Madrid; tel. (91) 7022116; fax (91) 3104018; e-mail amb.es@urm.lt; internet es.mfa.lt; Ambassador MEČYS LAURINKUS.

Luxembourg: Claudio Coello 78, 1°, 28001 Madrid; tel. (91) 4359164; fax (91) 5774826; e-mail madrid.amb@mae.etat.lu; internet www.mae.lu/espagne; Ambassador JEAN-PAUL SENNINGER.

Macedonia, former Yugoslav republic: Don Ramón de la Cruz 107, 2°B, 28006 Madrid; tel. (91) 5717298; fax (91) 5713481; e-mail emb.mkd.madrid@gmail.com; Chargé d'affaires a.i. DANICA RUZIN.

Malaysia: Paseo de la Castellana 91, Edif. Centro 23, 10°, 28046 Madrid; tel. (91) 5550684; fax (91) 5555208; e-mail mwmadrid@adv.es; Ambassador NAIMUN ASHAKLI.

Malta: Paseo de la Castellana 45, 6° dcha, 28046 Madrid; tel. (91) 3913061; fax (91) 3913066; e-mail maltaembassy.madrid@gov.mt; Ambassador GAETAN A. NAUDI.

Mauritania: Velázquez 90, 3°, 28006 Madrid; tel. (91) 5757006; fax (91) 4359531; Ambassador SALEM OULD MEMMOU.

Mexico: Carrera de San Jerónimo 46, 28014 Madrid; tel. (91) 3692814; fax (91) 4202292; e-mail embamex@embamex.es; internet www.embamex.es; Ambassador JORGE ZERMEÑO INFANTE.

Monaco: Villanueva 12, 28001 Madrid; tel. (91) 5782048; fax (91) 4357132; e-mail ambmonacomad@hotmail.com; Ambassador JOSÉ BADIA.

Morocco: Serrano 179, 28002 Madrid; tel. (91) 5631090; fax (91) 5617887; e-mail correo@embajada-marruecos.es; internet www.embajada-marruecos.es; Ambassador OMAR AZZIMAN.

Mozambique: Goya 67, 1° izqda, 28001 Madrid; tel. (91) 5776382; fax (91) 5776705; e-mail embamocmadrid@worldonline.es; Ambassador ALVARO MANUEL T. DA SILVA.

Netherlands: Avda del Comandante Franco 32, 28016 Madrid; tel. (91) 3537500; fax (91) 3537565; e-mail nlgovmad@telefonica.net; internet spanje.nlambassade.org; Ambassador COMO VAN HELLENBERG HUBAR.

New Zealand: Pinar 7, 3°, 28006 Madrid; tel. (91) 5230226; fax (91) 5230171; e-mail embnuevazelanda@telefonica.net; internet www.nzembassy.com/spain; Ambassador GEOFFREY KENYON WARD.

Nicaragua: Paseo de la Castellana 127, 1°B, 28046 Madrid; tel. (91) 5555510; fax (91) 4555737; e-mail augusto.zamora@orange.es; Ambassador AUGUSTO C. ZAMORA RODRÍGUEZ.

Nigeria: Segre 28, 28002 Madrid; tel. (91) 5630911; fax (91) 5636320; e-mail nigerian-emb-sp@jet.es; internet www.nigeriainspain.org; Ambassador Dr KINGSLEY SUNNY EBENYI.

Norway: Serrano 26, 28001 Madrid; tel. (91) 4363840; fax (91) 3190969; e-mail emb.madrid@mfa.no; internet www.noruega.es; Ambassador PER LUDVIG MAGNUS.

Oman: Mirasierra Suite Hotel, hab. 416–17, Alfredo Marquerie 43, 28034 Madrid; tel. (91) 7277932; fax (91) 7277933; Ambassador HILAL B. MARHOON SALIM ALMAMARY.

Pakistan: Avda de Pio XII 11, 28016 Madrid; tel. (91) 3458995; fax (91) 3458158; e-mail cancilleria@embajada-pakistan.org; internet www.embajada-pakistan.org; Ambassador (vacant).

Panama: Claudio Coello 86, 1° dcha, 28006 Madrid; tel. (91) 5765001; fax (91) 5767161; Ambassador HUMBERTO LÓPEZ TIRONE.

Paraguay: Doctor Fleming 3, 1°, 28036 Madrid; tel. (91) 3082746; fax (91) 3085319; e-mail embapar@arrakis.es; Ambassador OSCAR J. CABELLO SARUBBI.

Peru: Príncipe de Vergara 36, 5° dcha, 28001 Madrid; tel. (91) 4314242; fax (91) 5776861; e-mail lepru@embajadaperu.es; Ambassador JOSÉ LUIS PÉREZ SÁNCHEZ-CERRO.

Philippines: Eresma 2, 28002 Madrid; tel. (91) 7823830; fax (91) 4116606; e-mail madridpe@terra.es; internet www.philmadrid.com; Ambassador JOSEPH DELANO BERNARDO Y MEDINA.

SPAIN

Poland: Guisando 23 bis, 28035 Madrid; tel. (91) 3736605; fax (91) 3736624; e-mail embajada@polonia.es; internet www.madrid.polemb.net; Chargé d'affaires a.i. BARBARA SOŚNICKA.

Portugal: Pinar 1, 28006 Madrid; tel. (91) 7824960; fax (91) 7824972; e-mail embmadrid@emb-portugal.es; internet www.embajadaportugal-madrid.org; Ambassador JOSÉ FILIPE MORAES CABRAL.

Qatar: Paseo de la Castellana 92, Hotel Villamagna, 28046 Madrid; tel. (91) 3106926; fax (91) 3104851; Ambassador Sheikh FAHAD BIN AWIDA ATH-THANI.

Romania: Avda Alfonso XIII 157, 28016 Madrid; tel. (91) 3501881; fax (91) 3452917; e-mail secretariat@embajadaderumania.es; internet madrid.mae.ro; Ambassador MARIA LIGOR.

Russia: Velázquez 155, 28002 Madrid; tel. (91) 4110807; fax (91) 5629712; e-mail embrues@infonegocio.com; internet www.spain.mid.ru; Ambassador ALEKSANDR I. KUZNETSOV.

San Marino: Padre de Jesús Ordóñez 18, 3°, 28002 Madrid; tel. (91) 5639000; fax (91) 5631931; e-mail sm_madrid@accessnet.es; Ambassador ENRICO MARIA PASQUINI.

Saudi Arabia: Dr Alvarez Sierra 3, 28033 Madrid; tel. (91) 3834300; fax (91) 3021145; e-mail info@arabiasaudi.org; internet www.arabiasaudi.org; Ambassador Prince SA'UD BIN NAIF BIN ABD AL-AZIZ AS-SA'UD.

Serbia: Velázquez 162, 28002 Madrid; tel. (91) 5635045; fax (91) 5630440; e-mail office@embajada-serbia.es; internet www.embajada-serbia.es; Ambassador JELA BAĆOVIĆ.

Slovakia: Pinar 20, 28006 Madrid; tel. (91) 5903861; fax (91) 5903868; e-mail mail@embajadaeslovaquia.es; Ambassador JÁN VALKO.

Slovenia: Hermanos Bécquer 7, 2°, 28006 Madrid; tel. (91) 4116893; fax (91) 5646057; e-mail vma@gov.si; Ambassador PETER REBERC.

South Africa: Claudio Coello 91, 28006 Madrid; tel. (91) 4363780; fax (91) 5777414; e-mail embassy@sudafrica.com; internet www.sudafrica.com; Ambassador VUSI BRUCE KOLOANE.

Sudan: Paseo de la Castellana 115, 11° izqda, 28046 Madrid; tel. (91) 4174903; fax (91) 5972516; e-mail sudani49@hotmail.com; Ambassador ELUZAI MOGA YOKWE.

Sweden: Caracas 25, 28010 Madrid; tel. (91) 7022000; fax (91) 7022040; e-mail ambassaden.madrid@foreign.ministry.se; internet www.swedenabroad.com/Start_9935.aspx; Ambassador ANDERS RÖNQUIST.

Switzerland: Núñez de Balboa 35A, 7°, 28001 Madrid; tel. (91) 4363960; fax (91) 4363980; e-mail vertretung@mad.rep.admin.ch; internet www.eda.admin.ch/madrid; Ambassador ARMIN RITZ.

Syria: Plaza de Platerías Martínez 1, 1°, 28014 Madrid; tel. (91) 4203946; fax (91) 4202681; Ambassador MAKRAM OBEID.

Thailand: Joaquín Costa 29, 28002 Madrid; tel. (91) 5632903; fax (91) 5640033; e-mail madthai@temb.e.telefonica.net; Ambassador BUSBA BUNNAG.

Tunisia: Avda Alfonso XIII 64–68, 28016 Madrid; tel. (91) 4473508; fax (91) 5938416; Ambassador HABIB M'BAREK.

Turkey: Rafael Calvo 18, 2°, 28010 Madrid; tel. (91) 3198111; fax (91) 3086602; e-mail info@tcmadridbe.org; internet www.tcmadridbe.org; Ambassador ENDER ARAT.

Ukraine: Ronda de la Abubilla 52, 28043 Madrid; tel. (91) 7489360; fax (91) 3887178; e-mail emb_es@mfa.gov.ua; Ambassador ANATOLIY A. SHCHERBA.

United Arab Emirates: Capitán Haya 40, 28020 Madrid; tel. (91) 5701003; fax (91) 5715176; e-mail ambassadormadrid@uae.e.telefonica.net; Ambassador Sultan MUHAMMAD AL-QORTASI AN-NOAIMI.

United Kingdom: Fernando el Santo 16, 28010 Madrid; tel. (91) 7008200; fax (91) 7008210; e-mail enquiries.madrid@fco.gov.uk; internet www.ukinspain.com; Ambassador DENISE MARY HOLT.

USA: Serrano 75, 28006 Madrid; tel. (91) 5872200; fax (91) 5872303; internet www.embusa.es; Ambassador EDUARDO AGUIRRE, Jr.

Uruguay: Paseo del Pintor Rosales 32, 1°, 28008 Madrid; tel. (91) 7580475; fax (91) 5428177; e-mail urumatri@urumatri.com; Ambassador RICARDO GONZÁLEZ ARENAS.

Uzbekistan: Madrid.

Venezuela: Avda Capitán Haya 1, 13°, Edif. Eurocentro, 28020 Madrid; tel. (91) 5981200; fax (91) 5971583; e-mail embajada@espana.gob.ve; internet espana.gob.ve; Ambassador ALFREDO TORO HARDY.

Viet Nam: Arturo Soria 201, 1°A, 28043 Madrid; tel. (91) 5102867; fax (91) 4157067; e-mail claudiomes@yahoo.com; internet www.embavietnam-madrid.org; Ambassador NGUYEN XUAN PHONG.

Yemen: Paseo de la Castellana 117, 8°, 28046 Madrid; tel. (91) 4119950; fax (91) 5623865; e-mail secretaria@embajadayemen.es; internet www.embajadayemen.es; Chargé d'affaires a.i. ABDULRAHMAN KAMARAMI.

Judicial System

Consejo General del Poder Judicial (CGPJ)
(General Council of Judicial Power)
Marqués de la Ensenada 8, 28071 Madrid; tel. (91) 7006100; fax (91) 7006358; e-mail webmaster@cgpj.es; internet www.poderjudicial.es.

The highest governing body of the judiciary; comprises a President, 20 members elected by the Cortes and appointed by the King for a five-year term (10 by the Congress of Deputies and 10 by the Senate); supervises the judicial system; independent of the Ministry of Justice; Pres. FRANCISCO JOSÉ HERNANDO SANTIAGO

General Prosecutor: CÁNDIDO CONDE-PUMPIDO.

CONSTITUTIONAL COURT

Tribunal Constitucional: Domenico Scarlatti 6, 28003 Madrid; tel. (91) 5508000; fax (91) 5449268; e-mail buzon@tribunalconstitucional.es; internet www.tribunalconstitucional.es; Pres. MARÍA EMILIA CASAS BAAMONDE.

SUPREME COURT

Tribunal Supremo: Palacio de Justicia, Plaza de la Villa de París s/n, 28071 Madrid; tel. (91) 3971200; internet www.poderjudicial.es; Composed of five courts: civil; criminal; litigation; company; and military, each with its president and its respective judges; Pres. FRANCISCO JOSÉ HERNANDO SANTIAGO.

HIGH COURTS

Audiencia Nacional (National Court): García Gutiérrez 1, 28004 Madrid; tel. (91) 3973339; fax (91) 3973306; established in 1977; consists of three divisions: Penal; Social; and Contencioso-Administrativo, each with its president and respective judges; attached to Second Court of Supreme Court; deals primarily with crimes associated with a modern industrial society, such as corruption, forgery, drugs-trafficking and also terrorism; Pres. CARLOS DÍVAR.

OTHER COURTS

The Higher Courts of Justice in the Autonomous Communities comprise civil, criminal, administrative and labour divisions, while Provincial Courts hear proceedings for prosecutions of offences by lengthy prison terms, and appeals against the rulings of lower courts. The lower courts are the Criminal, Administrative, Labour, Juvenile and Prison Supervisory Courts of First Instance and Trial Courts. In municipalities where there are no Courts of First Instance and Trial, there is a Magistrates' Court.

Religion

CHRISTIANITY

About 90% of Spain's inhabitants profess adherence to Roman Catholicism, and the country contains some 61,000 churches, with about 500 persons in each parish. Opus Dei, which seeks to integrate religious faith and professional work, plays an important role in Spanish society. There are some 30,000 Protestants in Spain.

The Roman Catholic Church

For ecclesiastical purposes, Spain (including Spanish North Africa) comprises 14 metropolitan archdioceses and 55 dioceses. At 31 December 2005 there were an estimated 41.0m. adherents, equivalent to 91.5% of the population.

Bishops' Conference

Conferencia Episcopal Española, Añastro 1, 28033 Madrid; tel. (91) 3439600; fax (91) 3439616; e-mail conferenciaepiscopal@planalfa.es; internet www.conferenciaepiscopal.es.

f. 1977; Pres. Mons. RICARDO BLÁSQUEZ PÉREZ (Bishop of Bilbao); Sec.-Gen. JUAN ANTONIO MARTÍNEZ CAMINO.

Archbishop of Barcelona: Cardinal LLUÍS MARTÍNEZ SISTACH.

Archbishop of Burgos: Most Rev. FRANCISCO GIL HELLÍN.

Archbishop of Granada: Most Rev. FRANCISCO JAVIER MARTÍNEZ FERNÁNDEZ.

Archbishop of Madrid: Cardinal ANTONIO MARÍA ROUCO VARELA.

Archbishop of Mérida-Badajoz: Most Rev. SANTIAGO GARCÍA ARACIL.

Archbishop of Oviedo: Most Rev. CARLOS OSORO SIERRA.

Archbishop of Pamplona and Tudela: Most Rev. Francisco Pérez González.
Archbishop of Santiago de Compostela: Most Rev. Julián Barrio Barrio.
Archbishop of Seville (Sevilla): Cardinal Carlos Amigo Vallejo.
Archbishop of Tarragona: Most Rev. Jaume Pujol Balcells.
Archbishop of Toledo: Cardinal Antonio Cañizares Llovera.
Archbishop of Valencia: Cardinal Agustín García-Gasco Vicente.
Archbishop of Valladolid: Most Rev. Braulio Rodríguez Plaza.
Archbishop of Zaragoza: Most Rev. Manuel Ureña Pastor.

Other Christian Churches

Iglesia Española Reformada Episcopal (IERE) (Spanish Reformed Episcopal Church): Beneficencia 18, 28004 Madrid; tel. (91) 4452560; fax (91) 5944572; e-mail eclesiae@arrakis.es; internet www.anglicanos.org; f. 1860; mem. of the Anglican Communion; 17 congregations (2004); Bishop Rt Rev. Carlos López Lozano.

Unión Evangélica Bautista Española (UEBE) (Baptist Evangelical Union of Spain): San Jacinto 26, 3°, 46008 Valencia; tel. (963) 591633; fax (963) 134581; e-mail secretaria@uebe.org; internet www.uebe.org; f. 1922; Pres. Rev. Roberto Velert; Gen. Sec. Rev. Manuel Sarrias.

ISLAM

It is estimated that there are some 1m. Muslims in Spain, many of whom are Moroccan migrant workers.

Comisión Islámica de España: Anastasio Herrero 5, 28020 Madrid; tel. (91) 5714040; fax (91) 5708889; e-mail cie@teleline.es; umbrella org.; negotiates with Govt on Islamic affairs; Sec.-Gen. Riay Tatary Bakry.

Federación Española de Entidades Religiosas Islámicas (FEERI): Madrid; f. 1989; 57 mem. groups; Pres. Félix Angel Herrero.

Unión de Comunidades Islámicas de España (UCIDE): Anastasio Herrero 5, Madrid 28020; tel. (91) 5714040; e-mail webmaster@islamhispania.org; internet www.islamhispania.org; Pres. Riay Tatary Bakry.

Comunidad Ahmadía del Islam en España: La Mezquita Basharat, 14630 Pedro Abad (Córdoba); tel. (957) 186203; fax (957) 186300; e-mail spain@alislam.org; internet www.alislam.org; Pres. Mubarik Ahmad Khan.

JUDAISM

There are an estimated 48,000 Jews in Spain.

Federación de Comunidades Israelitas de España (Federation of Jewish Communities of Spain): Balmes 3, 28010 Madrid; tel. (91) 7001600; fax (91) 3915717; e-mail fcje@fcje.org; internet www.fcje.org; 30 communities; Pres. Jacobo Israel Garzón.

The Press

The most widely read newspapers are *ABC*, *El Mundo*, *El País* and *La Razón*, published in Madrid, and *La Vanguardia*, published in Barcelona. Important regional newspapers include *El Periódico de Catalunya* (Barcelona), *El Correo* (Bilbao) and *La Voz de Galicia* (A Coruña). Sporting dailies, notably *Marca* and *As*, enjoy very high circulation figures. Much of the Spanish media is owned by large corporations, of which the most prominent are Grupo PRISA (*El País*) and Vocento (*ABC* and various regional titles).

PRINCIPAL DAILIES
(arranged by province)

Albacete

La Tribuna de Albacete: Paseo de la Cuba 14, 02005 Albacete; tel. (967) 191000; fax (967) 240386; e-mail redaccion@latribunadealbacete.es; internet www.latribunadealbacete.es; Propr Promecal; Dir Francisco Javier Martínez García.

Alicante

Información: Avda Dr Rico 17, Apdo 214, 03005 Alicante; tel. (96) 5989100; fax (96) 5989165; e-mail redaccion@epi.es; internet www.diarioinformacion.com; f. 1940; Propr Editorial Prensa Ibérica; Dir Juan R. Gil; circ. 32,303.

Almería

La Voz de Almería: Avda Mediterráneo 159, 1°, Edif. Cadena Ser, 04007 Almería; tel. (950) 280036; fax (950) 256458; e-mail lavoz@lavozdealmeria.com; internet www.lavozdealmeria.com; morning; Dir Pedro Manuel de la Cruz Alonso; circ. 10,575.

Asturias

El Comercio: Diario El Comercio 1, 33207 Gijón; tel. (98) 5179800; fax (98) 5340955; e-mail elcomercio@elcomerciodigital.es; internet www.elcomerciodigital.com; f. 1878; Propr Vocento; Dir Íñigo Noriega Gómez; circ. 26,102.

La Nueva España: Calvo Sotelo 7, Edif. Sedes, 33007 Oviedo; tel. (98) 5279700; fax (98) 5279711; e-mail pam@lne.es; internet www.lne.es; f. 1937; Propr Editorial Prensa Ibérica; Dir Isidoro Nicieza; circ. 60.469.

El Periódico—La Voz de Asturias: La Lila 6, bajo, 33002 Oviedo; tel. (98) 5101500; fax (98) 5101505; e-mail vozredaccion@elperiodico.com; internet www.lavozdeasturias.es; f. 1923; Propr Grupo Zeta; Dir Luis Mugueta San Martín; circ. 10,077.

Badajoz

Hoy—Diario de Extremadura: Carretera Madrid–Lisboa 22, 06008 Badajoz; tel. (924) 252511; fax (924) 205297; e-mail hoyredaccion@hoy.es; internet www.hoy.es; f. 1933; Catholic; Badajoz and Cáceres editions; Propr Vocento; Dir Julián Quirós; circ. 23,365.

Barcelona

Avui: Enric Granados 84, entresòl, 08008 Barcelona; tel. (93) 3163900; fax (93) 3163936; e-mail info@avui.cat; internet www.avui.cat; f. 1976; Catalan; Exec. Pres. Antoni Cambredó; Dir Xavier Bosch; circ. 28,591.

Mundo Deportivo: Avda Diagonal 577, 5°, 08036 Barcelona; tel. (93) 3444100; fax (93) 3444250; e-mail contacto@elmundodeportivo.es; internet www.elmundodeportivo.es; f. 1906; sport; Propr Grupo Godó; Dir Santi Nolla Zayas; circ. 96,561.

El Periódico de Catalunya: Consell de Cent 425–427, 08009 Barcelona; tel. (93) 2655353; fax (93) 4846512; e-mail atencion.lector@elperiodico.com; internet www.elperiodico.com; daily; f. 1978; parallel edns in Spanish and Catalan; Propr Grupo Zeta; Dir Rafael Nadal; circ. 177,830.

Sport: Consell de Cent 425–427, 6°, 08009 Barcelona; tel. (93) 2279400; fax (93) 2279410; e-mail redaccion@diariosport.com; internet www.sport.es; Propr Grupo Zeta; Dir Joan Vehils; circ. 104,987.

La Vanguardia: Avda Diagonal 477, 08036 Barcelona; tel. (93) 4812200; fax (93) 3185587; e-mail lavanguardia@lavanguardia.es; internet www.lavanguardia.es; f. 1881; Propr Grupo Godó; Dir José Antich; circ. 209,735.

Burgos

Diario de Burgos: Avda Castilla y León 62–64, 09006 Burgos; tel. (947) 268375; fax (947) 268003; e-mail redaccion@diariodeburgos.es; internet www.diariodeburgos.es; f. 1891; Catholic; Propr Promecal; Dir Antonio José Mencía Gullón; circ. 14,266.

Cáceres

El Periódico Extremadura: Doctor Marañón 2, Local 7, 10002 Cáceres; tel. (927) 620600; fax (927) 620626; e-mail avillar@elperiodico.com; internet www.elperiodicoextremadura.com; f. 1926; Propr Grupo Zeta; Dir Antonio Tinoco Ardila; circ. 7,654.

Cádiz

Diario de Cádiz: Edif. Fénix, Avda de El Puerto 2, 11007 Cádiz; tel. (956) 297900; fax (956) 261460; e-mail redaccion@diariodecadiz.es; internet www.diariodecadiz.es; f. 1867; Propr Grupo Joly; Dir José Joaquín León; circ. 26,073.

Diario de Jerez: Patricio Garvey s/n, Apdo 316, 11402 Jerez de la Frontera; tel. (956) 321411; fax (956) 349904; e-mail redaccion@diariojerez.es; internet www.diariodejerez.com; f. 1984; Propr Grupo Joly; Dir Rafael Navas Renedo; circ. 8,695.

Cantabria

Alerta—el Diario de Cantabria: 1 de Mayo s/n, Barrio San Martín, 39011 Peñacastillo; tel. (942) 320033; fax (942) 322046; e-mail director@eldiarioalerta.com; internet www.eldiarioalerta.com; f. 1937; independent; Dir Ciriaco Díaz Porras; circ. 30,619.

El Diario Montañés: La Prensa s/n, La Albericia, 39012 Santander; tel. (942) 354000; fax (942) 341806; e-mail redaccion.dm@eldiariomontanes.es; internet www.eldiariomontanes.es; f. 1902; Propr Vocento; Dir Manuel Angel Castañeda Pérez; circ. 39,901.

SPAIN   Directory

Castellón

El Periódico Mediterráneo: Carretera de Almassora s/n, 12005 Castellón de la Plana; tel. (964) 349500; fax (964) 349505; e-mail mediterraneo@elperiodico.com; internet www.elperiodicomediterraneo.com; f. 1938; Propr Grupo Zeta; Dir JOSÉ LUIS VALENCIA; circ. 10,810.

Ciudad Real

El Día de Ciudad Real: Plaza Cervantes 6, 13001 Ciudad Real; tel. (926) 223033; fax (926) 227185; e-mail redaccion@eldiadeciudadreal.com; internet www.eldiadeciudadreal.com; f. 2002; independent; Dir SANTIAGO MATEO SAHUQUILLO; circ. 4,500.

La Tribuna de Ciudad Real: Pedro Muñoz 3, 13005 Ciudad Real; tel. (926) 215301; fax (926) 215306; e-mail ciudadreal@diariolatribuna.com; internet www.diariolatribuna.com; Propr Promecal; Dir OSCAR GÁLVEZ MATÉ; circ. 3,976.

Córdoba

Córdoba: Ing. Juan de la Cierva 18 (Polígono Torrecilla), Apdo 2, 14013 Córdoba; tel. (957) 420302; fax (957) 204648; e-mail cordoba1@elperiodico.es; internet www.diariocordoba.com; f. 1941; Propr Grupo Zeta; Dir FRANCISCO LUIS CÓRDOBA BERJILLOS; circ. 15,503.

A Coruña

El Correo Gallego: Preguntoiro 29, 15704 Santiago de Compostela; tel. (981) 543700; fax (981) 543701; e-mail grupocorreogallego@elcorreogallego.es; internet www.elcorreogallego.es; f. 1878; Propr Grupo Correo Gallego; Dir JOSÉ MANUEL REY NÓVOA; circ. 18,238.

Galicia Hoxe: Preguntoiro 29, 15704 Santiago de Compostela; tel. (981) 543700; fax (981) 543701; e-mail info@galiciahoxe.com; internet www.galicia-hoxe.com; f. 1994 as *O Correo Galego*; refounded under current name 2003; Galician; Propr Grupo Correo Gallego; Dir JOSÉ MANUEL REY NÓVOA.

El Ideal Gallego: Polígono de Pocomaco, C12, 15190 Mesoiro; tel. (981) 173040; fax (981) 299327; e-mail elidealgallego@elidealgallego.com; internet www.elidealgallego.com; f. 1917; independent; Dir JUAN RAMÓN DÍAZ GARCÍA; circ. 15,500 (Sun. 20,000).

La Voz de Galicia: Avda de la Prensa 84–85, Polígono de Sabón, 15142 Arteixo; tel. (981) 180180; fax (981) 180410; e-mail redac@lavoz.com; internet www.lavozdegalicia.com; f. 1882; Propr Grupo Voz; Dir XOSÉ LUIS VILELA CONDE; circ. 103,702.

Girona

Diari de Girona: Passeig General Mendoza 2, 17002 Girona; tel. (972) 202066; fax (972) 202005; e-mail diaridegirona@epi.es; internet www.diaridegirona.cat; f. 1891; Catalan; Propr Editorial Prensa Ibérica; Dir JORDI XARGAYO I TEIXIDOR; circ. 7,961.

El Punt: Santa Eugènia 42, 17005 Girona; tel. (972) 186400; fax (972) 186420; e-mail elpunt@elpunt.com; internet www.vilaweb.cat; f. 1979; Catalan; various regional edns; also publishes weekly edns covering Valencia and Perpignan, France; Dir EMILI GISPERT; circ. 25,531.

Granada

Ideal: Huelva 2, Polígono de Asegra, 18210 Peligros; tel. (958) 809809; fax (958) 402480; e-mail cartasdirector@ideal.es; internet www.ideal.es; f. 1932; Propr Vocento; Dir EDUARDO PERALTA DE ANA; circ. 32,887; edns in Granada, Jaén and Almería.

Guipúzcoa

El Diario Vasco: Camino de Portuetxe 2, Barrio de Ibaeta, Apdo 201, 20018 San Sebastián; tel. (943) 410700; fax (943) 410814; e-mail redacción@diariovasco.com; internet www.diariovasco.com; f. 1934; Propr Vocento; Dir JOSÉ GABRIEL MUJIKA; circ. 98,700 (Sat./Sun. 121,000).

Gara: Camino Portuetxe 23, 2°, 20018 San Sebastián; tel. (943) 316999; fax (943) 316998; internet www.gara.net; f. 1999; Basque and Spanish; left-wing Basque nationalist; independent; Dir JOSU JUARISTI.

Illes Balears

Diari de Balears: Paseo Mallorca, 9°A, 07011 Palma de Mallorca; tel. (971) 788300; fax (971) 455740; e-mail master@diaridebalears.com; internet www.diaridebalears.com; f. 1939 as *Baleares*; refounded as Catalan daily in 1996; Propr Grupo Serra; Dir MIQUEL SERRA MAGRANER.

Diario de Ibiza: Avda de la Paz, 07800 Ibiza; tel. (971) 190000; fax (971) 190322; e-mail diariodeibiza@epi.es; internet www.diariodeibiza.es; Propr Editorial Prensa Ibérica; Dir JOAN SERRA TUR; circ. 7,615.

Diario de Mallorca: Puerto Rico 15, Polígono de Levante, 07006 Palma de Mallorca; tel. (971) 170300; fax (971) 170301; e-mail secretaria.diariodemallorca@epi.es; internet www.diariodemallorca.es; f. 1953; Propr Editorial Prensa Ibérica; Dir JOSÉ EDUARDO IGLESIAS BARCA; circ. 22,350.

Menorca, Diario Insular: Cap de Cavalleria 5, 07714 Mahón, Menorca; tel. (971) 351600; fax (971) 351983; e-mail redaccion@menorca.info; internet www.menorca.info; f. 1941; Dir JOAN BOSCO MARQUÈS BOSCH; circ. 6,609.

Última Hora: Paseo Mallorca 9A, 07011 Palma de Mallorca; tel. (971) 788333; fax (971) 454190; internet www.ultimahora.es; f. 1893; Propr Grupo Serra; Dir PEDRO COMAS BARCELÓ; circ. 36,487.

León

Diario de León: Carretera León–Astorga, Km 4,5, 24010 León; tel. (987) 840300; fax (987) 840340; e-mail web@diariodeleon.com; internet www.diariodeleon.es; Dir FERNANDO ALLER GONZÁLEZ; circ. 16,100.

Lleida (Lérida)

Segre: Riu 6, Apdo 543, 25007 Lérida; tel. (973) 248000; fax (973) 246031; e-mail redaccio@diarisegre.com; internet www.diarisegre.com; f. 1982; Catalan and Spanish edns; independent; Dir JUAN CAL SÁNCHEZ; circ. 13,184.

Lugo

El Progreso: Ribadeo s/n, 27002 Lugo; tel. (982) 298100; fax (982) 298102; e-mail correo@elprogreso.es; internet www.elprogreso.es; f. 1908; Dir LUIS RODRÍGUEZ GARCÍA; Editor-in-Chief BLANCA GARCÍA MONTENEGRO; circ. 15,509.

Madrid

ABC: Juan Ignacio Luca de Tena 7, 28027 Madrid; tel. (91) 3399000; fax (91) 3203680; e-mail cartas@abc.es; internet www.abc.es; f. 1905; conservative, monarchist; various regional edns; Propr Vocento; Dir JOSÉ ANTONIO ZARZALEJOS; circ. 230,422.

As: Albasanz 14, 4°, 28037 Madrid; tel. (91) 3752500; fax (91) 3752558; e-mail diarioas@diarioas.es; internet www.as.com; f. 1967; sport; Propr Grupo PRISA; Dir ALFREDO RELAÑO ESTAPÉ; circ. 225,670.

Cinco Días: Gran Vía 32, 2°, 28013 Madrid; tel. (91) 3537900; fax (91) 3537991; e-mail redaccion@5dias.com; internet www.cincodias.es; f. 1978; economic; Propr Grupo PRISA; Dir JORGE RIVERA; circ. 37,945.

El Economista: Condesa de Venadito 1, 3°, 28027 Madrid; tel. (91) 3246700; fax (91) 3246727; e-mail comunicacion@eleconomista.es; internet www.eleconomista.es; f. 2006; originally f. 1886 as weekly; daily; Pres. ALFONSO DE SALAS; Dir AMADOR G. AYORA; circ. 22,516.

Expansión: Paseo de la Castellana 66, 28046 Madrid; tel. (91) 3373220; fax (91) 3373266; e-mail expansion@recoletos.es; internet www.expansion.com; economic; Propr Unidad Editorial, SA; Dir JESÚS MARTÍNEZ DE RIOJA VÁZQUEZ; circ. 50,394.

La Gaceta de los Negocios: Pantoja 14, 28002 Madrid; tel. (91) 4327600; fax (91) 4327733; e-mail jpv@negocios.com; internet www.negocios.com; f. 1989; daily; business and finance; Dir JOSÉ MARÍA GARCÍA HOZ; circ. 37,902.

Marca: Paseo de la Castellana 66, 2°, 28046 Madrid; tel. (91) 3373220; fax (91) 3373276; e-mail marca.com@unidadeditorial.es; internet www.marca.com; f. 1938 as weekly in San Sebastián, 1942 as daily in Madrid; sport; Propr Unidad Editorial, SA; Dir RAFAEL ALIQUE; circ. 310,793.

Metro Directo: Serrano 90, 6°, 28006 Madrid; e-mail redaccion@metrospain.com; internet www.metrodirecto.com; edns in Alicante, Aragón, Canarias, Castellón, Castilla-La Mancha, Galicia, Madrid, País Vasco, Sevilla and Valencia; Propr Metro International SA; distributed free of charge; Dir RAMÓN PEDRÓS.

El Mundo (del Siglo Veintiuno): Pradillo 42, 28002 Madrid; tel. (91) 5864800; fax (91) 5864848; internet www.elmundo.es; f. 1989; centre-right; various regional edns; Propr Unidad Editorial, SA; Pres. CARMEN IGLESIAS; Dir PEDRO J. RAMÍREZ CODINA; circ. 337,172.

El País: Miguel Yuste 40, 28037 Madrid; tel. (91) 3378200; fax (91) 3377758; e-mail redaccion@elpais.com; internet www.elpais.com; f. 1976; centre-left; regional edns in Andalusia, Basque Country, Catalonia, Galicia and Valencia; Propr Grupo PRISA; Pres. IGNACIO POLANCO MORENO; Dir JAVIER MORENO BARBER; circ. 425,927.

Qué!: Orense 81, 3°, 28020 Madrid; tel. (91) 5726200; fax (91) 5710085; e-mail redaccion@quediario.com; internet www.quediario.com; f. 2005; free; 15 local edns; Propr Vocento; Dir ANA I. PEREDA; circ. 959,283.

La Razón: Josefa Valcárcel 42, 28027 Madrid; tel. (91) 3247000; fax (91) 7423604; e-mail sugerencias@larazon.es; internet www.larazon

.es; f. 1998; conservative; Pres. MAURICIO CASALS; Dir JOSÉ ALEJANDRO VARA; circ. 149,559.

20 Minutos: Condesa de Venadito 1, 1°, 28027 Madrid; tel. (91) 7015600; fax (91) 7015660; e-mail nosevende@20minutos; internet www.20minutos.es; f. 2000; free; 15 regional edns; Dir ARSENIO ESCOLAR; circ. 850,000.

Málaga

La Opinión de Málaga: Granada 42, 29015 Málaga; tel. (95) 2126200; fax (95) 2126255; e-mail secretaria@epi.es; internet www.laopiniondemalaga.es; f. 1999; Propr Editorial Prensa Ibérica; Dir JOAQUÍN MARÍN ALARCÓN; circ. 7,589.

Sur: Avda Dr Marañón 48, 29009 Málaga; tel. (95) 2649600; fax (95) 2279508; e-mail redaccion.su@diariosur.es; internet www.diariosur.es; f. 1937; Propr Vocento; Dir JOSÉ ANTONIO FRÍAS RUIZ; circ. 60,000; also publishes free English weekly; circ. 32,293.

Murcia

La Verdad: Camino Viejo de Monteagudo s/n, 30160 Murcia; tel. (968) 369100; fax (968) 369147; e-mail lectores@laverdad.es; internet www.laverdad.es; f. 1903; local edns published in Albacete and Alicante; propr Vocento; Dir JOSÉ MARÍA ESTEBAN IBÁÑEZ; circ. 29,794.

Navarra

Diario de Navarra: Carretera Zaragoza s/n, 31191 Cordovilla (Navarra); tel. (948) 236050; fax (948) 150320; internet www.diariodenavarra.es; f. 1903; conservative; independent; Dir INÉS ARTAJO AYESA; circ. 57,893.

Diario de Noticias: Altzutzate 8, Polígono Areta, 31620 Huarte; tel. (948) 332533; fax (948) 332518; e-mail redacción@noticiasdenavarra.com; internet www.noticiasdenavarra.com; f. 1994; independent; Dir PABLO MUÑOZ PEÑA; circ. 18,135.

Ourense

La Región: Polígono Industrial de San Cibrao das Viñas C4, 32091 Ourense; tel. (988) 600102; e-mail info@laregion.es; internet www.lrilaregion.es; f. 1910; independent; Pres. JOSÉ LUIS OUTEIRIÑO RODRÍGUEZ; Dir ALFONSO SÁNCHEZ IZQUIERDO; circ. 11,405.

Las Palmas (Gran Canaria)

Canarias 7: Profesor Lozano 7, Urbanización El Sebadal, 35008 Las Palmas; tel. (928) 301300; fax (928) 301434; e-mail infocan@canarias7.es; internet www.canarias7.es; f. 1982; Dir FRANCISCO SUÁREZ ÁLAMO; circ. 30,544.

La Provincia—Diario de las Palmas: Alcalde Ramírez Bethencourt 8, 35003 Las Palmas; tel. (928) 479410; fax (928) 479401; e-mail laprovincia@epi.es; internet www.laprovincia.es; *La Provincia* f. 1911, *Diario de las Palmas* f. 1895; Propr Editorial Prensa Ibérica; Dir ÁNGEL TRISTÁN PIMIENTA; circ. 30,990.

Pontevedra

Faro de Vigo: Factoría de Chapela, 36320 Redondela; tel. (986) 814600; fax (986) 814615; e-mail redaccion@farodevigo.es; internet www.farodevigo.es; f. 1853; Propr Editorial Prensa Ibérica; Dir JUAN CARLOS DA SILVA; circ. 40,263.

La Rioja

La Rioja: Vara del Rey 74, Apdo 28, 26002 Logroño; tel. (941) 279107; fax (941) 279106; e-mail redaccion@larioja.com; internet www.diariolarioja.com; f. 1889; Propr Vocento; Dir RAMÓN ALONSO; circ. 16,780.

Salamanca

La Gaceta Regional de Salamanca: Avda de los Cipreses 81, 37004 Salamanca; tel. (923) 252020; fax (923) 256155; e-mail admon@lagacetadesalamanca.com; internet www.lagacetadesalamanca.es; f. 1920; independent; Dir IÑIGO DOMÍNGUEZ DE CALATAYUD; circ. 14,985.

Santa Cruz de Tenerife

El Día: Avda de Buenos Aires 71, Apdo 97, 38005 Santa Cruz; tel. (922) 238300; fax (922) 214247; e-mail redaccioneldia@eldia.es; internet www.eldia.es; f. 1910; Dir JOSÉ E. RODRÍGUEZ RAMÍREZ; circ. 24,352.

Diario de Avisos: Salamanca 5, 38006 Santa Cruz; tel. (922) 272350; fax (922) 241039; e-mail redaccion@diariodeavisos.com; internet www.diariodeavisos.com; f. 1890; refounded 1976; Dir LEOPOLDO FERNÁNDEZ CABEZA DE VACA; circ. 12,293.

La Opinión de Tenerife: Plaza Santa Cruz de la Sierra 2, 38003 Santa Cruz; tel. (922) 471800; fax (922) 471801; internet www.laopinion.es; Propr Editorial Prensa Ibérica; Dir CARMEN RUANO; circ. 6,317.

Sevilla

El Correo de Andalucía: Américo Vespucio 39, Isla de la Cartuja. 41092 Sevilla; tel. (95) 4999251; fax (95) 4517635; e-mail redaccion@correoandalucia.es; internet www.correoandalucia.es; f. 1899; independent; Pres. JOSÉ RODRÍGUEZ DE LA BORBOLLA CAMOYÁN; Dir ANTONIO HERNÁNDEZ-RODICIO; circ. 15,470.

Diario de Sevilla: Rioja 14, 41001 Sevilla; tel. (95) 4506200; fax (95) 4506222; e-mail secretaria@diariodesevilla.es; internet www.diariodesevilla.es; f. 1999; Propr Grupo Joly; Dir MANUEL JESÚS FLORENCIO; circ. 22,378.

Tarragona

Diari de Tarragona: Domènech Guansé 2, 43005 Tarragona; tel. (977) 299700; fax (977) 223013; e-mail diari@diaridetarragona.com; internet www.diaridetarragona.com; f. 1808; Spanish and Catalan; Dir RAMON PEDRÓS; circ. 14,082.

Valencia

Levante—El Mercantil Valenciano: Traginers 7, 46014 Valencia; tel. (96) 3992200; fax (96) 3992276; e-mail levante-emv@epi.es; internet www.levante-emv.es; f. 1872; Propr Editorial Prensa Ibérica; Dir PEDRO MUELAS NAVARRETE; circ. 44,345.

Mini Diario: Jesús 40, 1°, 46007 Valencia; tel. (96) 3462624; fax (96) 3462620; e-mail redaccion@minidiario.com; internet www.minidiario.com; f. 1992; free; edns in Valencia and Alicante; Dir JUAN PÉREZ; circ. 56,360.

Las Provincias: Polígono Industrial Vara de Quart, Gremis 1, 46014 Valencia; tel. (96) 3502211; fax (96) 3590188; e-mail lasprovincias@lasprovincias.es; internet www.lasprovincias.es; f. 1866; rightist; Propr Vocento; Dir PEDRO ORTIZ SIMARRO; circ. 41,487.

Valladolid

El Día de Valladolid: Edif. Promecal, Los Astros s/n, 47009 Valladolid; tel. (983) 325045; fax (983) 325047; e-mail redaccion@diavalladolid.es; internet www.eldiadevalladolid.com; f. 2000; Propr Promecal; Pres ANTONIO MÉNDEZ POZO.

El Norte de Castilla: Vázquez de Menchaca 10 (Polígono de Argales), 47008 Valladolid; tel. (983) 412100; fax (983) 412111; e-mail redaccion.nc@nortecastilla.es; internet www.nortecastilla.es; f. 1854; Propr Vocento; Dir CARLOS ROLDÁN SAN JUAN; circ. 36,422.

Vizcaya

El Correo: Pintor Losada 7, Apdo 205, 48004 Bilbao; tel. (94) 4870100; fax (94) 4870111; e-mail info@diario-elcorreo.es; internet www.elcorreodigital.com; f. 1910; edns in Vizcaya and Álava; Propr Vocento; Dir ÁNGEL ARNEDO GIL; circ. 119,601.

Deia: Carretera Bilbao Galdácano 8 (Bolueta), 48004 Bilbao; tel. (94) 4599100; fax (94) 4599120; e-mail cartas@deia.com; internet www.deia.com; f. 1997; Basque nationalist, associated with the PNV; publishes weekly satirical supplement, *Caduca Hoy*; circ. 21,179.

Zaragoza

Heraldo de Aragón: Paseo de la Independencia 29, Apdo 175, 50001 Zaragoza; tel. (976) 765000; fax (976) 765001; e-mail redaccion@heraldo.es; internet www.heraldo.es; f. 1895; independent; also publishes edn in Huesca; Dir GUILLERMO FATÁS CABEZA; circ. 53,865.

El Periódico de Aragón: Hernán Cortés 37, bajo, 50005 Zaragoza; tel. (976) 700400; fax (976) 700458; e-mail eparagon@elperiodico.es; internet www.elperiodicodearagon.com; f. 1990; Propr Grupo Zeta; Dir JAIME ARMENGOL; circ. 12,481.

SELECTED PERIODICALS

The Arts

Arquitectura y Diseño: RBA Revistas, SA, Pérez Galdós 36 bis, 08012 Barcelona; internet www.rba.es; monthly; architecture and design; Dir-Gen. ARIADNA HERNÁNDEZ; circ. 47,741 (June 2007).

Claves de Razón Práctica: Julián Camarillo 29B, 1°, 28004 Madrid; tel. (91) 5386104; fax (91) 5222291; e-mail claves@progresa.es; internet claves.progresa.es/claves; f. 1990; monthly; books and culture; Dirs JAVIER PRADERA, FERNANDO SAVATER; circ. 4,500.

El Croquis: Avda de los Reyes Católicos 9, El Escorial, 28280 Madrid; tel. (91) 8969414; fax (91) 8969415; e-mail elcroquis@elcroquis.es; internet www.elcroquis.es; six a year; architecture, in Spanish and English; Dirs FERNANDO MÁRQUEZ CECILIA, RICHARD LEVENE; circ. 17,837 (June 2007).

Experimenta: Churruca 27, 4° ext. dcha, 28004 Madrid; tel. (91) 5214049; fax (91) 5213212; e-mail info@experimenta.es; internet www.experimenta.es; design; Dir PIERLUIGI CATTERMOLE FIORAVANTI.

Insula: Complejo Atica, Edif. 4, Vía de las Dos Castillas 33, 28224 Pozuelo de Alarcón, Madrid; tel. (91) 7848200; fax (91) 3589505; internet www.insula.es; f. 1946; monthly; literature and social sciences; Editor ARANTXA GÓMEZ SANCHO; circ. 6,000.

Letra Internacional: Monte Esquinza 30, 3° dcha, 28010 Madrid; tel. (91) 3104313; fax (91) 3194585; e-mail editorial@fpi.es; internet www.fpabloiglesias.es; f. 1986; quarterly; culture; Dir SALVADOR CLOTAS I CIERCO.

Magisterio: Javier Ferrero 2, 28002 Madrid; tel. (91) 5199131; fax (91) 4151124; e-mail informacion@magisnet.com; internet www.magisnet.com; f. 1866; Wed.; education; Dir JOSÉ MARÍA DE MOYA ANEGÓN; circ. 24,200.

Matador: Alameda 9, 28014 Madrid; tel. (91) 3601320; fax (91) 3601322; e-mail matador@lafabrica.com; internet www.lafabrica.com; f. 1995; annual; art; Dir ALBERTO ANAUT; Editor-in-Chief CAMINO BRASA; circ. 7,000.

Ritmo: Isabel Colbrand 10, Oficina 87, 28050 Madrid; tel. (91) 3588774; fax (91) 3588944; e-mail correo@ritmo.com; internet www.ritmo.com; monthly; classical music; Dir ANTONIO RODRÍGUEZ MORENO.

Qué Leer: Gran Vía de les Corts Catalanes 133, 2°, 08014 Barcelona; tel. (93) 2232136; fax (93) 4322907; e-mail queleer@hachette.es; internet www.que-leer.com; f. 1996; monthly; book news, etc.; Dir JORGE DE COMINGES; circ. 26,608.

Current Affairs, History, Religion, etc.

A Nosa Terra: Rúa Príncipe 22, 36202 Vigo; tel. (986) 222405; fax (986) 223101; e-mail info@anosaterra.com; internet www.anosaterra.com; f. 1907; weekly; Galician; Dir AFONSO EIRÉ LÓPEZ.

Aceprensa: Núñez de Balboa 125, 6°, 28006 Madrid; tel. (91) 5158975; fax (91) 5631243; e-mail redaccion@aceprensa.com; internet www.aceprensa.com; f. 1973; weekly; news and features; Editorial Dir IGNACIO ARÉCHAGA DUQUE; circ. 4,000.

Boletín Oficial del Estado (BOE): Avda de Manoteras 54, 28050 Madrid; tel. (902) 365303; fax (91) 3841555; internet www.boe.es; f. 1936; successor of *Gaceta de Madrid*, f. 1661; daily except Sun.; laws, decrees, orders, etc.; Dir-Gen. JULIO SEAGE MARIÑO; circ. 60,000.

Cambio 16: Arroyo de Fontarrón 51, 28030 Madrid; tel. (91) 4201199; fax (91) 3601302; e-mail cambio16@cambio16.info; internet www.cambio16.info; f. 1972; weekly, Wed.; general; Pres., Editorial Bd MANUEL DOMÍNGUEZ MORENO.

El Ciervo: Calvet 56, 08021 Barcelona; tel. (93) 2005145; fax (93) 2011015; e-mail redaccion@elciervo.es; internet www.elciervo.es; f. 1951; monthly; politics and culture; Dir ROSARIO BOFILL; circ. 5,000.

Ciudad Nueva: José Picón 28, 28028 Madrid; tel. (91) 7259530; fax (91) 7130452; e-mail revista@ciudadnueva.com; internet www.ciudadnueva.com; f. 1958; monthly; Dir JAVIER RUBIO; circ. 7,000.

La Clave: Avda de Argón 336, 28022 Madrid; tel. (91) 8373131; fax (91) 8373136; e-mail redaccion@laclave.com; internet www.laclave.com; f. 2001; weekly; news magazine; Dir JOSÉ LUIS BALBIN; circ. 60,000.

Clío: Gran Vía de les Corts Catalanes 133, 2°, 08014 Barcelona; tel. (93) 2232136; fax (93) 4322907; e-mail clio@hachette.es; internet www.cliorevista.com; f. 2001; monthly; history; Dir JOSEP A BORRELL; circ. 36,401.

Ecclesia: Alfonso XI 4, 28014 Madrid; tel. (91) 5315400; fax (91) 5225561; e-mail ecclesia@planalfa.es; f. 1941; weekly; religious information; Dir JESÚS DE LAS HERAS MUELA; Editor-in-Chief MIGUEL DE SANTIAGO; Propr Conferencia Episcopal Española; circ. 24,000.

Época: Paseo de la Castellana 36–38, 28046 Madrid; tel. (91) 5109100; fax (91) 5109149; e-mail epoca@epoca.es; internet www.epoca.es; weekly; Dir ALFONSO BASALLO FUENTES.

Historia 16: Rufino González 13,1°, 28037 Madrid; tel. (91) 3271171; fax (91) 3271220; e-mail h16redaccion@telefonica.net; f. 1976; monthly; history; Dir MARÍA ALDAVE; circ. 25,000.

El Jueves: Avda Diagonal 468, 5°, 08006 Barcelona; tel. (93) 2922217; fax (93) 2375824; e-mail redaccion@eljueves.es; internet www.eljueves.es; f. 1977; weekly, Wed.; satirical; Dir MANEL FONTDEVILA; circ. 73,454 (2006).

Mundo Cristiano: Paseo de la Castellana 210, 2°B, 28046 Madrid; tel. (91) 3507739; fax (91) 3590230; e-mail mundoc@edicionespalabra.es; f. 1963; monthly; Dir DARIO CHIMENO CANO; Editor-in-Chief JOSÉ M. NAVALPOTRO; circ. 12,747 (June 2007).

Nueva Revista: Javier Ferrero 2, 28002 Madrid; tel. (91) 5199756; fax (91) 4151254; e-mail nuevarevista@tst.es; internet www.nuevarevista.net; f. 1990; six a year; politics, culture, art; Pres. ANTONIO FONTÁN PÉREZ.

Política—Revista Republicana: Ríos Rosas 10, 1° B, 28003 Madrid; tel. (902) 158935; fax (91) 4411165; e-mail ir@bitmailer.net; internet www.izquierdarepublicana.com; f. 1935; bimonthly; organ of Izquierda Republicana; Dir ISABELO HERREROS.

Revista de Estudios Políticos: Plaza de la Marina Española 9, 28071 Madrid; tel. (91) 4228925; fax (91) 5419574; e-mail publicrev@cepc.es; internet www.cepc.es; f. 1941; quarterly; Dirs PEDRO DE VEGA, JUAN J. SOLOZÁBAL; publ. by Centro de Estudios Políticos y Constitucionales; circ. 1,000.

El Socialista: Gobelas 31, 28023 Madrid; tel. (91) 5820044; fax (91) 5820045; e-mail elsocialista@elsocialista.es; internet www.elsocialista.es; f. 1866; monthly; general information; Dir JOAQUÍN TAGAR; circ. 185,000.

El Temps: Octubre, Centre de Cultura Contemporània, Sant Ferran 12, 46001 Valencia; tel. (96) 3535100; fax (96) 3534569; e-mail eltemps@eltemps.net; internet www.eltemps.net; f. 1984; weekly; general information; in Catalan; Dir JORDI FORTUNY I BATALLA; circ. 25,000.

Tiempo de Hoy: O' Donnell 12, 3°, 28009 Madrid; tel. (91) 5863300; fax (91) 5863346; e-mail contacta.tiempo@zetadigital.es; internet www.tiempodehoy.es; weekly; Dir JESÚS RIVASÉS; circ. 43,408 (June 2007).

Treball: Ciutat 7, 08002 Barcelona; tel. (93) 3010612; fax (93) 4124252; e-mail treball@iniciativa.cat; internet www.iniciativa.cat; f. 1991; 6 a year; organ of Iniciativa per Catalunya Verds; Dir MARC RIUS; circ. 6,000.

Vida Nueva: Impresores 15, Urbanización Prado del Espino, 28660 Boadilla del Monte, Madrid; tel. (91) 4226255; fax (91) 4226118; e-mail juan.antonio.rubio@ppc-editorial.com; f. 1958; weekly; society and religion; Dir JUAN RUBIO; circ. 20,000.

Finance

Actualidad Económica: Paseo de la Castellana 66, 3°, 28046 Madrid; tel. (91) 3370346; fax (91) 5628415; e-mail aeconomica@recoletos.es; internet www.actualidad-economica.com; f. 1958; weekly, Mon.; Dir MIGUEL ÁNGEL BELLOSO; circ. 46,000.

Capital: Albasanz 15, Edif. A, 28037 Madrid; tel. (91) 4369800; fax (91) 5767881; e-mail mmoreno@gyj.es; internet www.capital.es; f. 2000; monthly; business and economics; publ. by Grupo G+J; Dir JOSÉ LUIS GÓMEZ; circ. 35,088 (June 2007).

Dinero: Pantoja 14, 28002 Madrid; tel. (91) 4327600; fax (91) 4327765; e-mail srodriguez@negocios.com; weekly; business and finance; Dir MIGUEL ORMAETXEA ARROYO; circ. 11,586 (June 2007).

El Empresario: Diego de León 50, 3°, 28006 Madrid; tel. (91) 4116161; fax (91) 5645269; e-mail elempresario@cepyme.es; internet www.cepyme.es; monthly; economics and business; circ. 15,000.

Información Comercial Española—Revista de Economía: Paseo de la Castellana 162, 5°, 28046 Madrid; tel. (91) 3493627; fax (91) 3493634; 8 a year; published by Ministry of the Economy; Dir ANTONIO HERNÁNDEZ GARCÍA.

Mi Cartera de Inversión: José Abascal 56, 7°, 28003 Madrid; tel. (91) 4563320; fax (91) 4563328; e-mail r.rubio@inverca.com; internet www.hoyinversion.com; Dir RAFAEL RUBIO GÓMEZ-CAMINERO; circ. 16,788 (Dec. 2006).

El Mundo Financiero: Peña Sacra 1, 28260 Madrid; tel. and fax (91) 8583547; e-mail mundofinanciero@ya.com; internet www.elmundofinanciero.com; f. 1946; monthly; Dir JOSÉ LUIS BARCELÓ MEZQUITA; circ. 15,000.

El Nuevo Lunes de la Economía y la Sociedad: Ferrocarril 37, dpdo, 28045 Madrid; tel. (91) 5160803; fax (91) 5160819; e-mail nuevolunes@elnuevolunes.com; internet www.elnuevolunes.es; weekly; Pres. JOSÉ GARCÍA ABAD.

Home, Fashion and General

Casa Diez: Avda Cardenal Herrera Oria 3, 28034 Madrid; tel. (91) 7287000; fax (91) 7289144; e-mail malvarez@hachette.es; internet www.casadiez.orange.es; monthly; home decoration; Dir MILAGROS ÁLVAREZ GORTARI; circ. 172,360 (June 2007).

Clara: Muntaner 40–42, 08011 Barcelona; tel. (93) 5087000; fax (93) 4545949; e-mail clara@hymsa.com; internet www.clara.es; f. 1992; monthly; Dir HORTÈNSIA GALÍ PÉREZ; circ. 133,388 (June 2007).

Cosmopolitan: Albasanz 15, Edif. A, 28037 Madrid; tel. (91) 4369820; fax (91) 4358701; e-mail cosmopolitan@gyj.es; internet www.cosmohispano.com; f. 1990; monthly; Dir SARAH GLATTSTEIN FRANCO; circ. 197,792 (June 2007).

Diez Minutos: Avda Cardenal Herrera Oria 3, 28034 Madrid; tel. (91) 7287000; fax (91) 7289279; e-mail diezminutos@hachette.es; internet www.diezminutos.es; f. 1951; weekly; celebrity gossip; Dir CRISTINA ACEBAL; circ. 376,797 (June 2007).

SPAIN

Elle: Avda Cardenal Herrera Oria 3, 28034 Madrid; tel. (91) 7287000; fax (91) 7289135; e-mail elle@hachette.es; internet www.elle.es; f. 1986; monthly; Dir SUSANA MARTÍNEZ VIDAL; circ. 221,425 (June 2007).

Elle Deco: Avda Cardenal Herrera Oria 3, 28034 Madrid; tel. (91) 7287000; fax (91) 7289144; e-mail elledeco@hachette.es; internet www.elledeco.es; f. 1989; 5 a year; Dir MILAGROS ALVAREZ GORTARI.

Gaceta Internacional: Alonso Cano 66, 1°, 28003 Madrid; tel. (91) 5547354; fax (91) 5539395; e-mail info@aphis.org; internet www.aphis.org; monthly; international magazine produced by the Asociación de la Prensa Hispanamerica; Dir ARMANDO RESTREPO BRETÓN; Editor-in-Chief YOLANDA ARRATIA GARCÍA; circ. 16,500 in Spain; 150,000 internationally.

GEO: Albasanz 15, Edif. A, 28037 Madrid; tel. (91) 4369800; fax (91) 4369781; e-mail geo@gyj.es; internet www.georevista.es; f. 1987; monthly; geography, nature, people, photo-journalism, travel; Dir DAVID CORRAL; circ. 36,858 (June 2007).

GQ: Paseo de la Castellana 9–11, 28046 Madrid; tel. (91) 7004170; fax (91) 3199325; e-mail gq@condenast.es; internet www.revistagq.com; monthly; men's magazine; Dir JAVIER FERNÁNDEZ DE ANGULO; circ. 39,130 (June 2007).

¡Hola!: Miguel Angel 1, 4°, 28010 Madrid; tel. (91) 7021300; fax (91) 3196444; internet www.hola.com; f. 1944; weekly; general illustrated; Dir EDUARDO SÁNCHEZ JUNCO; circ. 540,902 (June 2007).

Interviú: O'Donnell 12, 5°, 28009 Madrid; tel. (91) 5863300; fax (91) 5863555; e-mail interviu@grupozeta.es; internet www.interviu.es; f. 1976; weekly; Dir TERESA VIEJO; circ. 98,500 (June 2007).

Labores del Hogar: Muntaner 40–42, 08011 Barcelona; tel. (93) 5087000; fax (93) 4540551; e-mail labores@hymsa.com; f. 1926; monthly; home textile crafts; Dir EULÀLIA UBACH; circ. 59,695 (June 2007).

Lecturas: Muntaner 40–42, 08011 Barcelona; tel. (93) 5087000; fax (93) 4541322; e-mail lecturas@hymsa.com; f. 1921; weekly, Fri.; Dir JAVIER DE MONTINI; circ. 208,149 (June 2007).

Man: Consejo de Ciento 425, 5°, 08009 Barcelona; tel. (93) 4846600; fax (93) 2324542; internet www.revistaman.es; monthly; men's fashion, etc.; Dir JUAN CARLOS DE LA IGLESIA GONZÁLEZ; circ. 54,865 (June 2007).

Marie Claire: Albasanz 15, Edif. A, 28037 Madrid; tel. (91) 4369800; fax (91) 5767881; e-mail cplanchuelo@gyj.es; internet www.marie-claire.es; f. 1987; monthly; Dir JOANA BONET CAMPRUBÍ; circ. 112,825 (June 2007).

Mía: Albasanz 15, Edif. A, 28037 Madrid; tel. (91) 4369889; fax (91) 5758880; e-mail mia@gyj.es; internet www.miarevista.es; f. 1986; weekly; Dir KETTY RICO OLIVER; circ. 169,686 (June 2007).

Nuevo Estilo: Avda Cardenal Herrera Oria 3, 28034 Madrid; tel. (91) 7287000; fax (91) 7289338; e-mail nuevoestilo@hachette.es; internet www.nuevo-estilo.es; f. 1977; monthly; home decoration; Dir MARTA RIOPÉREZ; circ. 60,259 (June 2007).

Nuevo Vale: Gran Vía de Carlos III 124, 5°, 08034 Barcelona; tel. (93) 2061540; fax (93) 2805555; e-mail buzon@publicacionesheres.com; weekly; Dir ESTHER GIRALT; circ. 104,445 (June 2007).

Pronto: Gran Vía de Carlos III 124, 5°, 08034 Barcelona; tel. (93) 2061540; fax (93) 2805555; e-mail pronto@publicacionesheres.com; f. 1972; weekly; general information; Dir ANTONIO GÓMEZ ABAD; circ. 976,892 (June 2007).

Semana: Cuesta de San Vicente 28, 28008 Madrid; tel. (91) 5472300; fax (91) 5414488; e-mail redaccion@semana.es; internet www.semana.es; f. 1942; weekly; general, illustrated; Dir CHARO CARRACEDO ARMADA; circ. 206,349 (June 2007).

Ser Padres Hoy: Albasanz 15, Edif. A, 28037 Madrid; tel. (91) 4369800; fax (91) 5767881; e-mail publicidad@gyj.es; internet www.serpadres.es; f. 1974; monthly; for parents; Dir JAVIER J. GARCÍA GONZÁLEZ; circ. 44,885 (June 2007).

Súper Pop: Gran Vía Carlos III 124, 1°, 08034 Barcelona; tel. (93) 2521452; fax (93) 2521450; e-mail info@superpop.es; f. 1976; fortnightly; teenage magazine; Dir SILVIA ALEMÁN; circ. 196,207 (June 2007).

Telva: Paseo de la Castellana 66, 28046 Madrid; tel. (91) 3373220; fax (91) 3373143; e-mail telva@recoletos.es; internet www.telva.com; f. 1963; beauty, fashion, weddings, interviews, cookery and fitness; monthly; Dir NIEVES FONTANA LÍBANO; circ. 175,964 (June 2007).

Tu Bebé: Muntaner 40–42, 08011 Barcelona; tel. (93) 5087000; fax (93) 4541322; e-mail tu_bebe@hymsa.com; f. 1993; monthly; for parents; Dir PEDRO RIAÑO MARTÍNEZ; circ. 60,000.

Vogue España: Paseo de la Castellana 9–11, 28046 Madrid; tel. (91) 7004170; fax (91) 3199325; e-mail vogue@condenast.es; internet www.vogue.es; f. 1988; monthly; Dir YOLANDA SACRISTÁN; circ. 123,696 (June 2007).

Woman: Bailén 84, 2°, 08009 Barcelona; tel. (93) 4846600; fax (93) 2324630; e-mail woman@grupozeta.es; internet www.woman.es; f. 1992; monthly; Dir EMPAR PRIETO; circ. 142,308 (June 2007).

Leisure Interests and Sport

Automóvil: Ancora 40, 28045 Madrid; tel. (91) 3470100; fax (91) 3470135; e-mail automovil@mpib.es; internet www.motorpress-iberica.es; monthly; motoring; Dir FERNANDO GÓMEZ BLANCO; circ. 234,849 (June 2007).

Autopista: Ancora 40, 28045 Madrid; tel. (91) 3470100; fax (91) 3470135; e-mail autopista@mpib.es; internet www.motorpress-iberica.es; weekly; motoring; Editor ARANCHA PATO; circ. 29,291 (June 2007).

Cinemanía: Progresa (Grupo Prisa), Julián Camarillo 29B, 1°, 28037 Madrid; tel. (91) 5386104; fax (91) 5222291; e-mail cinemania@progresa.es; internet www.progresa.es; f. 1995; monthly; films; Dir LUIS MARTÍNEZ; circ. 48,311 (June 2007).

Coche Actual: Ancora 40, 28045 Madrid; tel. (91) 3470100; fax (91) 3470119; e-mail cocheactual@mpib.es; internet www.motorpress-iberica.es; weekly; cars; Dir ANTONIO RONCERO FERNÁNDEZ; circ. 26,343 (June 2007).

Don Balón: Avda Diagonal 435, 1–2°, 08036 Barcelona; tel. (93) 2092000; fax (93) 2412358; e-mail info@donbalon.org; internet www.donbalon.com; f. 1975; weekly; sport; Editor-in-Chief ANTONIO CASALS; circ. 10,480 (June 2006).

Fotogramas: Gran Vía de les Corts Catalanes 133, 2°, 08014 Barcelona; tel. (93) 2232790; fax (93) 4322907; e-mail fotogramas@hachette.es; internet www.fotogramas.es; f. 1946; monthly; cinema; Dir TONI ULLED NADAL; circ. 107,598.

Guía del Ocio—La Semana de Barcelona: Muntaner 492, bajos, 08022 Barcelona; tel. (93) 4185005; fax (93) 4179471; e-mail redaccion@guiadelociobcn.com; internet www.guiadelociobcn.com; f. 1977; weekly, Friday; listings and reviews of events; Dir XAVIER MUNIESA CALDERÓ; circ. 50,000.

Guía del Ocio—La Semana de Madrid: Alcalá 106, 2°, 28009 Madrid; tel. (91) 4316080; fax (91) 5769307; e-mail guiadelocio@guiadelociomad.com; internet www.guiadelocio.com; weekly, Fri.; listings and reviews of events; Dir-Gen. JUAN MIGUEL ALONSO SECO.

Motociclismo: Ancora 40, 28045 Madrid; tel. (91) 3470100; fax (91) 3470152; e-mail motociclismo@mpib.es; internet www.motociclismo.es; f. 1951; weekly; motorcycling; Dir and Editor AUGUSTO MORENO DE CARLOS; circ. 35,147 (June 2007).

Sport Life: Ancora 40, 28045 Madrid; tel. (91) 3470100; fax (91) 3470236; e-mail sportlife@mpib.es; internet www.motorpress-iberica.es; monthly; Editor FRANCISCO JESÚS CHICO; circ. 55,412 (June 2007).

Supertele: Avda Cardenal Herrera Oria 3, 28034 Madrid; tel. (91) 7287000; fax (91) 7289129; e-mail supertele@hachette.es; internet www.supertele.es; f. 1992; weekly; TV magazine; Dir PURIFICACIÓN BLANCO PAÍNO; circ. 80,673 (June 2007).

Tele Digital: Vallehermoso 32, 28015 Madrid; tel. (91) 4451950; fax (91) 4450621; internet www.sateliteinfos.com; Dir JOSÉ DA CUNHA.

Tele Indiscreta: Avda Cardenal Herrera Oria 3, 28034 Madrid; tel. (91) 7287000; fax (91) 3581348; e-mail teleindiscreta@hachette.es; internet www.teleindiscreta.es; weekly; popular illustrated; TV programmes; Dir PURIFICACIÓN BLANCO PAÍNO; circ. 31,852 (June 2007).

Telenovela: Avda Cardenal Herrera Oria 3, 28034 Madrid; tel. (91) 7287051; fax (91) 3581348; e-mail telenovela@hachette.es; internet www.tele-novela.orange.es; f. 1993; TV series; Dir AGUSTÍN DE TENA; circ. 64,946 (June 2007).

TP Teleprograma: Avda Cardenal Herrera Oria 3, 28034 Madrid; tel. (91) 7287000; fax (91) 7289129; e-mail tp@hachette.es; internet www.t-p.es; f. 1966; weekly; TV, cinema and video; Dir PURIFICACIÓN BLANCO PAÍNO; circ. 156,280 (June 2007).

Viajar: O'Donnell 12, 3°, 28009 Madrid; tel. (91) 5863630; fax (91) 5863411; e-mail mlopez.viajar@grupozeta.es; internet www.revistaviajar.es; f. 1978; monthly; travel; Dir MARIANO LÓPEZ; circ. 75,000.

Vinos de España: Islas Marquesas 28B, 28035 Madrid; tel. (91) 3865152; fax (91) 3860265; e-mail vinos@mundonatura.es; f. 1996; wines and viniculture; bimonthly; also trimonthly in German; Dir ALBERTO HUERTA; circ. 30,000.

Medicine, Science and Technology

Arbor: Vitruvio 8, 28006 Madrid; tel. (91) 5616651; fax (91) 5855326; e-mail arbor@csic.es; internet www.csic.es/arbor; f. 1944; monthly; science, thought and culture; publ. by Consejo Superior de Investigaciones Científicas (CSIC); Dir PEDRO GARCÍA BARRENO.

SPAIN

Avión Revue: Ancora 40, 28045 Madrid; tel. (91) 3470100; fax (91) 3470174; e-mail avionrevue@mpib.es; f. 1982; monthly; aeroplanes; Dir José María Parés; circ. 14,081 (June 2007; f.).

Computerworld: Fortuny 18, 4°, 28010 Madrid; tel. (91) 3496600; fax (91) 3196104; e-mail computerworld@idg.es; internet www.idg.es/computerworld; f. 1981; weekly; also available: PC World Digital, PC World PRO, CIO, Comunicaciones World, MacWorld, Dealer World, iWorld; Editor-in-Chief María José Marzal; circ. 10,327.

El Ecologista: Marqués de Laganés 12, 28004 Madrid; tel. (91) 5312389; fax (91) 5312611; e-mail comunicacion@ecologistasenaccion.org; internet www.ecologistasenaccion.org; f. 1979; quarterly; ecological issues; Dir José Luis García Cano; circ. 13,000.

Gaceta Médica de Bilbao: Lersundi 9, Apdo 5073, 48009 Bilbao; tel. (94) 4233768; fax (94) 4232161; e-mail gacetamedica@telefonica.net; f. 1894; quarterly; official publication of the Academia de Ciencias Médicas de Bilbao/Bilboko Sendalarintz Jakindia; Dir Dr Juan Ignacio Goiria Ormazabal; circ. 5,000.

Investigación y Ciencia: Muntaner 339, Pral 1°, 08021 Barcelona; tel. (93) 4143344; fax (93) 4145413; e-mail precisa@investigacionyciencia.es; internet www.investigacionyciencia.es; f. 1976; quarterly; Dir José María Vaderas Gallardo; circ. 20,866 (Dec. 2006).

Mundo Científico: Pérez Galdós 36, 08012 Barcelona; tel. (93) 4157374; fax (93) 2177378; monthly; Dir Jorge Alcalde.

Muy Interesante: Marqués de Villamagna 4, 28001 Madrid; tel. (91) 4369800; fax (91) 5759128; e-mail publicidad@gyj.es; internet www.muyinteresante.es; f. 1981; monthly; history, medicine, nature, science; Dir José Pardina Cancer; circ. 241,680 (June 2007).

Natura: Islas Marquesas 28B, 28035 Madrid; tel. (91) 3865152; fax (91) 3860265; e-mail redaccion@mundonatura.es; f. 1983; bimonthly; wildlife, archaeology, research, travel, food; Dir Jesús Iniesta; circ. 69,913.

PC Actual: López de Hoyos 141, 5°, 28002 Madrid; tel. (91) 5106600; fax (91) 5194813; e-mail javier-perez@rba.es; internet www.pc-actual.com; monthly; Dir Javier Pérez Cortijo.

Tiempos Médicos: Editores Médicos, SA, Alsasua 16, 28023 Madrid; tel. (91) 3768140; fax (91) 3739907; e-mail edimsa@edimsa.es; internet www.edimsa.es; 10 issues per year; Dir Dr A. Chicharro Papiri; circ. 10,000.

NEWS AGENCIES

Agencia EFE, SA: Espronceda 32, 28003 Madrid; tel. (91) 3467100; fax (91) 3467134; e-mail efe@efe.es; internet www.efe.es; f. 1939; national and international news; 140 bureaux and correspondents abroad; sports, features, radio and television, and photographic branches; Pres. and Dir-Gen. Álex Grijelmo.

Colpisa: José Abascal 56, 1°, 28003 Madrid; tel. (91) 4564600; fax (91) 4564701; f. 1972; Pres. José María Bergareche; Dir Rogelio Rodríguez.

Europa Press Noticias: Paseo de la Castellana 210, 3°, 28046 Madrid; tel. (91) 3592600; fax (91) 3503251; e-mail noticias@europapress.es; internet www.europapress.es; Dir Angel Expósito Mora.

Iberia Press: Velázquez 46, 1°, 28001 Madrid; tel. and fax (91) 8155319; e-mail press-bulletin@jet.es; f. 1977; Dir José Ramón Alonso.

PRESS ASSOCIATIONS

National Organizations

Asociación de Corresponsales de Prensa Extranjera (ACPE): Monte Esquinza 41, 1°, 28010 Madrid; tel. (91) 3101433; fax (91) 3080950; e-mail acpe.corresponsales@wanadoo.es; f. 1923; foreign correspondents' asscn; Pres. Luis Castro Obregón; Sec.-Gen. Karla Castillas; 150 mems.

Asociación de Editores de Diarios Españoles (AEDE): Orense 69, 2°, 28020 Madrid; tel. (91) 4251085; fax (91) 5796020; e-mail maribel@aede.es; internet www.aede.es; f. 1978; 33 mems, representing 95 daily newspapers (2008); Pres. Pilar de Yarza; Dir-Gen. Ignacio M. Benito García.

Asociación de Revistas Culturales en España (ARCE): Hortaleza 75, 28004 Madrid; tel. (91) 3086066; fax (91) 3199267; e-mail info@arce.es; internet www.arce.es; f. 1983.

Federación de Asociaciones de la Prensa de España (FAPE): Juan Bravo 6, 28006 Madrid; tel. and fax (91) 5850038; e-mail fape@fape.es; internet www.fape.es; f. 1922; Pres. Fernando González Urbaneja; Sec.-Gen. Carlos Sanz Establés; 46 mem. asscns.

Unión de Escritores y Periodistas Españoles: Madrid; f. 1978; journalists' asscn; Pres. Antonio Arias Piqueras; Sec.-Gen. Eloy S. Castañares; 4,000 mems.

Provincial Organizations

Barcelona

Centre Internacional de Premsa de Barcelona: Rambla de Catalunya 10, 1°, 08007 Barcelona; tel. (93) 4121111; fax (93) 3178386; e-mail cipb@periodistes.org; internet www.periodistes.org; f. 1988; facilities and services for journalists; Pres. Xavier Batalla García; Dir Mónica Viñas.

Bilbao

Asociación de Periodistas de Bizkaia (Bizkaiko Kazetarien Elkartea): Dr Achucarro 10, 1°, 48011 Bilbao; tel. and fax (94) 4168748; e-mail asociacion@periodistasvascos.com; internet www.periodistasvascos.com; Pres. José Manuel Alonso; Sec. Blanca García-Egocheaga.

Madrid

Asociación de la Prensa de Madrid: Juan Bravo 6, 28006 Madrid; tel. (91) 5850010; fax (91) 5850050; e-mail apm@apmadrid.es; internet www.apmadrid.es; f. 1895; Pres. Fernando González Urbaneja; Sec.-Gen. José María Lorente Toribio; 5,518 mems.

Centro de Prensa de Madrid: Claudio Coello 98, 28006 Madrid; tel. (91) 5850010; fax (91) 5850050; Sec.-Gen. José María Lorente Toribio.

Sevilla

Asociación de la Prensa de Sevilla: Plaza de San Francisco 9, 1°, 41004 Sevilla; tel. (95) 4500468; fax (95) 4225299; e-mail aps@asociacionprensa.org; internet www.asociacionprensa.org; f. 1909; Pres. Santiago Sánchez Traver; Sec.-Gen. Juan Teruel Salmerón.

Zaragoza

Centro de Prensa de Zaragoza: Cinco de Marzo 9, 50004 Zaragoza; tel. (976) 223210; fax (976) 222963; e-mail aparagon@aparagon.es; Pres. Ramón J. Buetas Coronas; Sec. Roberto García Bermejo.

Publishers

Alianza Editorial: Juan Ignacio Luca de Tena 15, 28027 Madrid; tel. (91) 3938888; fax (91) 7414343; e-mail alianza@anaya.es; internet www.alianzaeditorial.es; f. 1959; advanced textbooks, fiction, general non-fiction, reference, paperbacks; imprint of Grupo Anaya; Gen. Man. Valeria Ciompi.

Barcino Editorial: Montseny 9, 08012 Barcelona; tel. and fax (93) 2186888; e-mail info@editorialbarcino.com; internet www.editorialbarcino.com; f. 1924; Catalan classics, general; Dir Carles Duarte Montserrat.

Carroggio, SA de Ediciones: Pelai 28–30, 08001 Barcelona; tel. (93) 4949922; fax (93) 4949923; e-mail carroggio@carroggio.com; internet www.carroggio.com; f. 1911; art, literature, reference books, multimedia; Man. Dir Santiago Carroggio Guerim.

Columna Edicions: Peu de la Creu 4, 08001 Barcelona; tel. (93) 4437100; fax (93) 4417130; e-mail info@columnaedicions.cat; internet www.columnaedicions.cat; f. 1985; imprint of Grup 62; fiction and non-fiction in Catalan.

Durvan, SA de ediciones: Colón de Larreátegui 13, 3°, 48001 Bilbao; tel. (94) 4230777; fax (94) 4243832; e-mail editorial@durvan.com; internet www.durvan.com; f. 1960; Dir Javier Pereda Prado.

EDHASA (Editora y Distribuidora Hispano-Americana, SA): Avda Diagonal 519–521, 2°, 08029 Barcelona; tel. (93) 4949720; fax (93) 4194584; e-mail info@edhasa.es; internet www.edhasa.com; f. 1946; contemporary fiction, non-fiction, pocket books, historical fiction and non-fiction, crime, philosophy; Editorial Dir and Man. Daniel Fernández.

Ediciones Cátedra: Juan Ignacio Luca de Tena 15, 28027 Madrid; tel. (91) 3938787; fax (91) 7412118; e-mail catedra@catedra.com; internet www.catedra.com; f. 1973; imprint of Grupo Anaya; literature, literary criticism, history, humanities, linguistics, arts, cinema, music, feminism; Pres. José Manuel Gómez.

Ediciones de Cultura Hispánica: General Pardiñas 55, 28006 Madrid; tel. (91) 37999494; fax (91) 5838311; internet www.aeci.es; f. 1943; arts, law, history, economics for circulation in Latin America; Literary and Artistic Dir Antonio Papell.

Ediciones Destino: Provenza 260, 5°, 08008 Barcelona; tel. (93) 4967001; fax (93) 4967002; e-mail edicionesdestino@stl.logicontrol.es; internet www.edestino.es; f. 1942; imprint of Grupo Planeta; general fiction, history, art, children's books.

Ediciones Deusto: Alameda Recalde 27, 7°, 48009 Bilbao; tel. (94) 4356161; fax (94) 4356166; e-mail deustomail@ediciones-deusto.es;

internet www.ediciones-deusto.es; f. 1960; f. www.ediciones-deusto.es; management and law; Man. Dir ENRIQUE IGLESIAS MONTEJO.

Ediciones Encuentro: Ramírez de Arellano 17, 10°, 28043 Madrid; tel. (91) 5322607; fax (91) 5322346; e-mail encuentro@ediciones-encuentro.es; internet www.ediciones-encuentro.es; f. 1978; theology, philosophy, art, history, biography, society, politics, literature.

Ediciones Morata, SL: Mejía Lequerica 12, 28004 Madrid; tel. (91) 4480926; fax (91) 4480925; e-mail morata@edmorata.es; internet www.edmorata.es; f. 1920; psychology, psychiatry, pedagogics, sociology; Dir FLORA MORATA.

Ediciones Mensajero, SAU: Sancho de Azpeitia 2, 48014 Bilbao; tel. (94) 4470358; fax (94) 4472630; e-mail mensajero@mensajero.com; internet www.mensajero.com; f. 1915; arts, biography, theology, psychology, pedagogy, social science and paperbacks; Dir ANGEL ANTONIO PÉREZ GÓMEZ.

Ediciones Obelisco: Pedro IV 78, 3 y 5°, 08005 Barcelona; tel. (93) 3098525; fax (93) 3098523; e-mail info@edicionesobelisco.com; internet www.edicionesobelisco.com; f. 1981; general fiction and non-fiction; Dir JULI PERADEJORDI.

Ediciones Omega: Platón 26, 08006 Barcelona; tel. (93) 2010599; fax (93) 2097362; e-mail omega@ediciones-omega.es; internet www.ediciones-omega.es; f. 1948; biology, field guides, geography, geology, agriculture, photography; Chair. ANTONIO PARICIO.

Ediciones Pirámide: Juan Ignacio Luca de Tena 15, 28027 Madrid; tel. (91) 3938989; fax (91) 7423661; e-mail piramide@anaya.es; internet www.edicionespiramide.es; f. 1973; scientific and technical books, business, economics, psychology; imprint of Grupo Anaya; Man. Dir MARIANO JOSÉ NORTE.

Ediciones Polígrafa: Balmes 52, 08009 Barcelona; tel. (93) 4882381; fax (93) 4877392; e-mail info@edicionespoligrafa.com; internet www.edicionespoligrafa.com; f. 1960; arts, leisure; Man. Dir JUAN DE MUGA DÒRIA; Editor-in-Chief FRANCISCO REI.

Ediciones Siruela: Almagro 25, 28010 Madrid; tel. (91) 3555720; fax (91) 3552201; e-mail atencionlector@siruela.com; internet www.siruela.com; f. 1982; history, literature, art, children's books, translations; Dir JACOBO FITZ-JAMES STUART.

Ediciones Universidad de Navarra (EUNSA): Plaza de los Sauces 1 y 2, 31010 Barañain (Navarra); tel. (948) 256850; fax (948) 256854; e-mail info@eunsa.es; internet www.eunsa.es; f. 1967; architecture, natural sciences, law, history, social sciences, theology, philosophy, medical, engineering, journalism, education, economics and business administration, biology, literature, library science, paperbacks, etc.; Chair. GUIDO STEIN.

Edicións Xerais de Galicia: Doutor Marañón 12, 36211 Vigo; tel. (986) 214888; fax (986) 201366; e-mail xerais@xerais.es; internet www.xerais.es; f. 1979; imprint of Grupo Anaya; literature, education, history and reference books in Galician.

Editorial Anagrama: Pedró de la Creu 58, 08034 Barcelona; tel. (93) 2037652; fax (93) 2037738; e-mail anagrama@anagrama-ed.es; internet www.anagrama-ed.es; f. 1969; fiction, essays, foreign literature in translation; Editor and Dir JORGE HERRALDE.

Editorial Bosch: Comte d'Urgell 51 bis, Apdo 928, 08011 Barcelona; tel. (93) 4521050; fax (93) 4521057; e-mail bosch@bosch.es; internet www.bosch.es; f. 1934; law, social science, classics; Man. ALBERT FERRÉ.

Editorial Castalia: Zurbano 39, 28010 Madrid; tel. (91) 3195857; fax (91) 3102442; e-mail castalia@castalia.es; internet www.castalia.es; f. 1945; classics, literature; Pres. AMPARO SOLER GIMENO.

Editorial CEAC: Perú 164, 08020 Barcelona; tel. (93) 2660247; fax (93) 3084392; e-mail info@ceacedit.com; internet www.editorialceac.com; f. 1947; imprint of Grupo Planeta; textbooks, education, leisure; Man. JAIME PINTANEL.

Editorial Desclée de Brouwer: Henao 6, 3° dcha, 48009 Bilbao; tel. (94) 4246843; fax (94) 4237594; e-mail info@edesclee.com; internet www.edesclee.com; f. 1945; general non-fiction in Spanish and Basque; Pres. JAVIER GOGEASKOETXEA.

Editorial Edaf: Jorge Juan 30, 1°, 28001 Madrid; tel. (91) 4358260; fax (91) 4315281; e-mail edaf@edaf.net; internet www.edaf.net; f. 1967; literature, dictionaries, occult, natural health, paperbacks; Dir-Gen. JOSÉ ANTONIO FOSSATI SEDDON.

Editorial Everest: Carretera León–Coruña, Km 5, Apdo 339, 24080 León; tel. (987) 844200; fax (987) 844202; e-mail marketing@everest.es; internet www.everest.es; f. 1957; general; Dir-Gen. JOSÉ ANTONIO LÓPEZ MARTÍNEZ.

Editorial Galaxia: Avenida de Madrid 44, 36204 Vigo (Pontevedra); tel. (986) 432100; fax (986) 223205; e-mail galaxia@editorialgalaxia.es; internet www.editorialgalaxia.es; f. 1950; literary works, reviews, popular, children's, Galician literature; Dir VÍCTOR F. FREIXANES.

Editorial Gredos: Sánchez Pacheco 85, 28002 Madrid; tel. (91) 7444920; fax (91) 5192033; e-mail comercial@editorialgredos.com; internet www.editorialgredos.com; f. 1944; linguistics, philology, humanities, art, literature, dictionaries; Dir MANUEL OLIVEIRA CALVET.

Editorial Gustavo Gili: Rosselló 87–89, 08029 Barcelona; tel. (93) 3228161; fax (93) 3229205; e-mail info@ggili.com; internet www.ggili.com; f. 1902; photography, art, architecture, design, fashion; Dirs GABRIEL GILI, MÓNICA GILI.

Editorial Hispano-Europea: Bori y Fontestá 6, 08021 Barcelona; tel. (93) 2018500; fax (93) 4142635; e-mail hispanoeuropea@hispanoeuropea.com; internet www.hispanoeuropea.com; f. 1954; technical, scientific, sport, pets and reference; Propr and Man. Dir JORGE J. PRAT ROSAL.

Editorial Juventud: Provença 101, 08029 Barcelona; tel. (93) 4441800; fax (93) 4398383; e-mail info@editorialjuventud.es; internet www.editorialjuventud.es; f. 1923; general fiction, biography, history, art, music, reference, dictionaries, travel books, children's books, paperbacks, in Catalan and Spanish; Dir LUIS ZENDRERA.

Editorial Marfil: San Eloy 17, 03804 Alcoy; tel. (96) 5523311; fax (96) 5523496; e-mail editorialmarfil@editorial.marfil.com; internet www.editorialmarfil.com; f. 1947; textbooks, psychology, pedagogy, university texts, literature; Man. VERÓNICA CANTÓ DOMÉNECH.

Editorial Nerea: San Bartolomé 2, 5° dcha, 20007 San Sebastián; tel. (943) 432227; fax (943) 433379; e-mail nerea@nerea.net; internet www.nerea.net; f. 1987; architecture, art, history. photography.

Editorial Reus, SA: Preciados 23, 2°, 28013 Madrid; tel. (91) 5213619; fax (91) 5312408; e-mail reus@editorialreus.es; internet www.editorialreus.es; f. 1852; law; Pres. JESÚS M. PINTO VARELA.

Editorial Seix Barral: Avda Diagonal 662–664, 7°, 08034 Barcelona; tel. (93) 4967003; fax (93) 4967004; e-mail editorial@seix-barral.es; internet www.seix-barral.es; f. 1911; literary fiction.

Editorial Reverté: Loreto 13–15, Local B, 08029 Barcelona; tel. (93) 4193336; fax (93) 4195189; e-mail reverte@reverte.com; internet www.reverte.com; f. 1947; scientific and technical; Dir JAVIER REVERTÉ MASCÓ.

Editorial Tecnos: Juan Ignacio Luca de Tena 15, 28027 Madrid; tel. (91) 3938550; fax (91) 7426631; e-mail foro_tecnos@anaya.es; internet www.tecnos.es; f. 1947; law, social and political science, philosophy and economics; imprint of Grupo Anaya; Man. MANUEL GONZÁLEZ MORENO.

Editorial Teide: Viladomat 291, 08029 Barcelona; tel. 902 233030; fax (93) 3212640; e-mail info@editorialteide.com; internet www.editorialteide.es; f. 1942; educational, scientific, technical and art; Man. Dir FEDERICO RAHOLA.

Espasa: Complejo Ática, Edif. 4, Vía de las Dos Castillas 33, 28224 Pozuelo de Alárcon (Madrid); tel. (91) 7848200; fax (91) 3525020; e-mail surgerencias@espasa.es; internet www.espasa.com; f. 1860; encyclopaedias, history, dictionaries, literature, biographies, paperbacks, etc.; CEO EDUARDO BOFILL.

La Esfera de los Libros: Avda de Alfonso XIII 1, bajos, 28002 Madrid; tel. (91) 2960200; fax (91) 2960206; e-mail laesfera@esferalibros.com; internet www.esferalibros.com; history, journalism, biography; Dir JOSÉ MARÍA CALVÍN.

Fondo de Cultura Económica de España, SL (FCE España): Librería Juan Rulfo México, Fernando el Católico 86, 28015 Madrid; tel. (91) 7632800; e-mail fondoculturae@terra.es; internet www.fcede.es; f. 1974; psciences, literature, children's books, history, academic; Dir JUAN GUILLERMO LÓPEZ.

Galaxia Gutenberg: Travessera de Gràcia 47–49, 08021 Barcelona; tel. (93) 3660100; fax (93) 3660104; e-mail galaxiagutenberg@circulo.es; internet www.galaxiagutenberg.com; f. 1995; literary fiction, poetry, economics.

Grup 62: Peu de la Creu 4, 08001 Barcelona; tel. (93) 4437100; fax (93) 4437130; e-mail correu@grup62.com; internet www.grup62.com; f. 1962; 18 imprints publishing titles in Catalan and Spanish, including Art 62, Edicions 62, Editorial Empúries, Editorial Selecta, Ediciones Península, El Aleph Editores, Enciclopèdia Catalana, Luciérnaga, Nous Negocis, Planeta, Pòrtic i Mina, Proa, Salsa Books; Pres. J. M. MARTOS.

Grupo Anaya: Juan Ignacio Luca de Tena 15, 28027 Madrid; tel. (91) 3554405; fax (91) 3933937; e-mail administrador@anaya.es; internet www.anaya.es; f. 1959; imprints include Algaida, Alianza Editorial, Anaya, Barçanova, Clé Internacional, Del Prado, Ediciones Cátedra, Ediciones Pirámide, Edicións Xerais de Galicia, Editorial Tecnos, Eudema, Larousse and Oberon; reference, sciences, arts, literature, education; Pres. JOSÉ MANUEL GÓMEZ.

Grupo Edebé: Paseo San Juan Bosco 62, 08017 Barcelona; tel. (93) 2037408; fax (93) 2054670; e-mail informacion@edebe.net; internet www.edebe.com; f. 1968; imprints include Giltza, Rodeira, Marjal and Guadiel; children's and educational publications; Man. JOSÉ ALDUNATE JURÍO.

SPAIN
Directory

Grupo Editorial Bruño: Maestro Alonso 21, 28028 Madrid; tel. (91) 7244800; fax (91) 3613133; e-mail informacion@editorial-bruno.es; internet www.editorial-bruno.es; f. 1898; education, children's books; Dir-Gen. José Antonio Camacho.

Grupo Editorial Luis Vives: Xaudaró 25, 28034 Madrid; tel. (91) 3344883; fax (91) 3344882; e-mail dediciones@edelvivies.es; internet www.grupoeditorialluisvives.com; f. 1890; imprints include Edelvives, Baula (Catalan), Alhucema, Ibaizabal (Basque) and Tambre (Galician); children's books, textbooks, reference under the imprints.

Grupo Editorial Santillana: Torrelaguna 60, 28043 Madrid; tel. (91) 7449060; fax (91) 7449019; e-mail grupo@santillana.es; internet www.gruposantillana.com; f. 1960; part of Grupo PRISA; imprints include Aguilar, Alfarguara, Altea, Richmond Publishing and Taurus; Pres. Emiliano Martínez.

Grupo Océano: Milanesado 21–23, 08017 Barcelona; tel. (93) 2802020; fax (93) 2041073; e-mail info@oceano.com; internet www.oceano.com; f. 1950; imprints include Circe, Instituto Gallach de Librería y Ediciones and Oceano; general; Chair. José Lluis Monreal.

Grupo Planeta: Avda Diagonal 662–664, 08034 Barcelona; tel. (93) 4928000; fax (93) 4928565; internet www.planeta.es; f. 1949; imprints include Ediciones Destino, Ediciones Deusto, Ediciones Minotauro, Ediciones Temas de Hoy, Editorial CEAC, Editorial Crítica, Editorial Planeta, Emcé Editores, GeoPlaneta, MR Ediciones, Timun Mas; Pres. José Manuel Lara Bosch.

Herder Editorial, SA: Provença 388, 08025 Barcelona; tel. (93) 4762626; fax (93) 2073448; e-mail herder@herdereditorial.com; internet www.herdereditorial.com; f. 1944; literature, language, theology, sociology, psychology.

Iberoamericana de Libros y Ediciones, SL: Amor de Dios 1, 28014 Madrid; tel. (91) 4293522; fax (91) 4295397; e-mail info@iberoamericanalibros.com; internet www.ibero-americana.net; f. 1996; owned by Verveut Verlagsgesellschaft (Germany); academic books.

Larousse Editorial: Mallorca, 45, 3°, 08029 Barcelona; tel. (93) 2413505; fax (93) 241351; e-mail larousse@larousse.es; internet www.larousse.es; f. 1912; encyclopaedias, dictionaries, atlases, linguistics.

Marcombo, SA de Boixareu Editores: Gran Vía de les Corts Catalanes 594, 08007 Barcelona; tel. (93) 3180079; fax (93) 3189339; e-mail info@marcombo.com; internet www.marcombo.com; f. 1945; reference, sciences, textbooks; Pres. and Man. Dir Josep M. Boixareu Vilaplana.

Montagud Editores: Ausiàs Marc 25, 1°, 08010 Barcelona; tel. (93) 3182082; fax (93) 3025083; e-mail montagud@montagud.com; internet www.montagud.com; f. 1906; business; Chair. Francisco Antoja Giralt.

MR Ediciones, SA: Recoletos 4, 3°, 28001 Madrid; tel. (91) 4230314; fax (91) 4230306; e-mail info@ediciones-martinez-roca.es; internet www.edicionesmartinezroca.com; f. 1965; fmrly Ediciones Martínez Roca; fiction, New Age, spirituality, sport, 'how-to' books, psychology, psychiatry; Dir Laura Falcó.

Narcea, SA de Ediciones: Avda Dr Federico Rubio y Galí 9, 28039 Madrid; tel. (91) 5546484; fax (91) 5546487; e-mail narcea@narceaediciones.es; internet www.narceaediciones.es; f. 1968; humanities, pedagogy, psychology, textbooks; Man. Dir Ana María de Miguel Carro.

Nivola Libros y Ediciones, SL: Sector Islas 12, Local 3B, Tres Cantos, 28760 Madrid; tel. (91) 8045817; fax (91) 8041482; e-mail nivola@nivola.com; internet www.nivola.com; science.

Noguer y Caralt Editores: Santa Amèlia 22, bajos, 08034 Barcelona; tel. (93) 2801399; fax (93) 2801993; e-mail contact@noguercaralt.com; internet www.noguercaralt.com; f. 1993; dictionaries, children's, philosophy, art; Man. Emilio Ardévol.

Plaza y Janés: Travessera de Gràcia 47–49, 08021 Barcelona; tel. (93) 3660300; fax (93) 2002219; internet www.plaza.es; f. 1959; fiction and non-fiction, reference; imprint of Random House Mondadori; Dir-Gen. Juan Pascual.

Random House Mondadori: Travessera de Gràcia 47–49, 08021 Barcelona; tel. (93) 3660300; fax (93) 3660449; internet www.randomhousemondadori.es; f. 2001; imprints include Areté, Beascoa, Debate, Electa, Lumen, Montena, Plaza y Janés, Rosa dels Vents, and co listed below; Gen. Man. Ricardo Cavallero.

Siglo XXI de España, Editores: Menéndez Pidal 3 bis, 28036 Madrid; tel. (91) 5617748; fax (91) 5615819; e-mail sigloxxi@sigloxxieditores.com; internet www.sigloxxieditores.com; f. 1967; pocket collections, reference, history, social sciences; Pres. Pablo García-Arenal.

SM Grupo: Impresores 2, Urbanización Prado del Espino, 28660 Boadilla del Monte, Madrid; tel. (91) 4228800; fax (91) 5089927; e-mail clientes@grupo-sm.com; internet www.grupo-sm.com; f. 1940; textbooks, children's, reference, travel, literature; Pres. Juan de Isasa González Ubieta; Man. Dir Javier Cortés Soriano.

Thomson-Aranzadi: Camino de Galar 15, 31190 Cizur Menor, Navarra; tel. (948) 297297; fax (948) 297200; e-mail clientes@aranzadi.es; internet www.aranzadi.es; f. 1929; fmrly Editorial Aranzadi; law; Dir Juan Carlos Franquet.

Tusquets Editores: Cesare Cantú 8, 08023 Barcelona; tel. (93) 2530400; fax (93) 4176703; internet www.tusquets-editores.es; art, general fiction and non-fiction.

Vicens Vives: Polígono Industrial Pratense, 111, parcela 16, El Prat de Llobregat, 08820 Barcelona; tel. (93) 4782755; fax (93) 4783659; e-mail e@vicensvives.es; internet www.vicensvives.es; f. 1961; school and university, educational; Dir Rosario Rahola de Espona.

PUBLISHERS' ASSOCIATIONS

Asociación de Editoriales Universitarias Españolas (AEUE): Plaza de las Cortes 2, 7°, 28014 Madrid; tel. (91) 3600698; fax (91) 3601201; e-mail secretariatecnica@une.es; internet www.aeue.es; Pres. Magda Polo Pujadas; Sec. Isabel Terroba Pascual.

Associació d'Editors en Llengua Catalana (Association of Publishers in Catalan Language): València 279, 1°, 08009 Barcelona; tel. (93) 2155091; fax (93) 2155273; e-mail info@editorsencatala.org; internet www.catalanpublishers.org; f. 1978; Pres. Manuel Sanglas Muchart; Sec.-Gen. Segimon Borràs.

Federación de Gremios de Editores de España (Federation of Publishers' Associations of Spain): Cea Bermúdez 44, 2° dcha, 28003 Madrid; tel. (91) 5345195; fax (91) 5352625; e-mail fgee@fge.es; internet www.federacioneditores.org; f. 1978; Pres. Jordi Úbeda i Bauló; Exec. Dir Antonio María Avila.

Gremi d'Editors de Catalunya: València 279, 1°, 08009 Barcelona; tel. (93) 2155091; fax (93) 2155273; e-mail info@gremieditorscat.es; internet www.gremieditorscat.es; Pres. Josep M. Puig de la Bellacasa; Sec.-Gen. Segimon Borràs.

Gremio de Editores de Euskadi/Euskadiko Editoreen Elkartea: Lehendakari Aguirre 11, 3°, 48014 Bilbao; tel. (94) 4764313; fax (94) 4761980; internet www.editores-euskadi.com; Pres. Javier Gogeascoechea Arrien; Man. Dir Andrés Fernández Seco.

Gremio de Editores de Madrid: Santiago Rusiñol 8, 28040 Madrid; tel. (91) 5544745; fax (91) 5532553; e-mail editoresmadrid@editoresmadrid.org; internet www.editoresmadrid.org; f. 1977; Pres. Emiliano Martínez Rodríguez; Sec.-Gen. Amalia Martín Pereda.

Broadcasting and Communications
TELECOMMUNICATIONS

The telecommunications market was fully deregulated in December 1998.

BT España: Edif. Herre, Salvador de Madariaga 1, 28027 Madrid; tel. (91) 270800; fax (91) 2708888; internet www.btglobalservices.com/business/es/es/index.html; Dir-Gen. Jacinto Cavestany Vallejo.

Euphony: Plaza de la Independencia 10, 28001 Madrid; tel. (91) 5239577; e-mail serviciocliente.es@euphony.com; internet www.euphony.es; fixed-line and mobile cellular telecommunications services, internet service provider; Chief Exec. Giles Redpath.

Jazztel: Avda de Europa 14, La Moraleja, 28108 Alcobendas, Madrid; tel. (91) 2917200; fax (91) 2917201; e-mail contact@jazztel.com; internet www.jazztel.com; Pres. Leopoldo Fernández Pujals.

ONO: Basauri 7 y 9, 28023 Madrid; tel. (91) 1809300; internet www.ono.es; f. 1998; broadband internet, telephone and television; owns Grupo Auna; Pres. Eugenio Galdón; CEO Richard Alden.

Orange: Parque Empresarial La Finca, Paseo del Club Deportivo 1, Edif. 8, 28223 Pozuelo de Alarcón (Madrid); internet www.orange.es; owned by France Telecom España; fmrly Uni2 and Amena.

Telefónica: Gran Vía 28, 28013 Madrid; tel. (91) 7406918; e-mail prensa@telefonica.es; internet www.telefonica.es; f. 1924; privatized in 1997; monopoly on telephone services removed in 1998; incl. mobile network Telefónica Móviles; provides services in 41 countries (2007); Pres. César Alierta; CEO Julio Linares.

Vodafone España: Avda Europa 1 (Central), Parque Empresarial La Moraleja, 28108 Alcobendas, Madrid; tel. 607 133333; internet www.vodafone.es; f. 1998; fmrly Airtel; mobile services; Pres. José Manuel Entrecanales; CEO Francisco Román.

Xfera Moviles: Avda de la Vega 15, Alcobendas, 28100 Madrid; tel. (91) 1315200; fax (91) 1315202; e-mail prensa@yoigo.com; internet www.yoigo.com; f. 2006; 76.6% owned by TeliaSonera (Sweden); provides mobile cellular communications services under the brand name 'Yoigo'.

SPAIN

Regulatory Authorities

Comisión del Mercado de las Telecomunicaciones (CMT): Alcalá 37, 28014 Madrid; tel. (91) 3724300; fax (91) 3724205; e-mail cmt@cmt.es; internet www.cmt.es; f. 1996; Pres. REINALDO RODRÍGUEZ ILLERA.

Secretaría de Estado de Telecommunicaciones y para la Sociedad de la Información: Ministerio de Industria, Turismo y Comercio, Capitán Haya 41, 2°, 28071 Madrid; tel. (91) 3461583; fax (91) 3461520; internet www.setsi.mityc.es.

BROADCASTING

Corporación Radio Televisión Española (RTVE): Edif. Prado del Rey, 28223 Pozuelo de Alarcón, Madrid; tel. (91) 5815461; fax (91) 5815454; e-mail direccion.comunicacion@rtve.es; internet www.rtve.es; state-owned company; controls and co-ordinates radio and television; incorporates: Televisión Española, Televisión Española Internacional, Televisión Española Temática, Radio Nacional de España, Instituto Oficial de Radio y Televisión and the Orquesta Sinfónica y Coro; formerly Ente Público Radio Televisión Española; renamed and reformed in 2007 to become independent of govt influence; Pres. LUIS FERNÁNDEZ.

Independent Companies

Compañía de Radio y Televisión de Galicia (CRTVG): Bando-San Marcos, 15820 Santiago de Compostela (A Coruña); tel. (981) 540640; fax (981) 540829; internet www.crtvg.es; f. 1985; Galician language station; Dir-Gen. BENIGNO SÁNCHEZ GARCÍA.

Corporació Catalana de Ràdio i Televisió (CCRTV): Ganduxer 117, 08022 Barcelona; tel. (93) 4444800; fax (93) 4444824; e-mail comunicacio@ccrtv.es; internet www.ccrtv.es; f. 1983; Catalan language station; three television channels and four radio stations; Dir-Gen. VICENÇ VILLATORIO I LAMOLLA; Sec.-Gen. JOSEP BADIA I SÁNCHEZ.

Euskal Irrati Telebista (EITB)/Radiotelevisión Vasca: 48215 Iurreta (Vizcaya); tel. (94) 6031000; fax (94) 6031095; e-mail info@eitb.com; internet www.eitb.com; f. 1982; Basque station; two television channels, two international television channels and five radio stations; Dir-Gen. ANDONI ORTUZAR ARRUABARRENA.

Onda Regional de Murcia: Avda Libertad 6, bajo, 30009 Murcia; tel. (968) 200000; fax (968) 230850; e-mail ondaregional.or@carm.es; internet www.ondaregionalmurcia.es; Dir-Gen. JUAN MANUEL MÁIQUEZ ESTÉVEZ.

Ràdiotelevisió Valenciana (RTVV): Polígono Accés Ademús s/n, 46100 Burjassot (Valencia); tel. (96) 3183000; fax (96) 3183001; e-mail dgen@rtvv.es; internet www.rtvv.es; f. 1984; Dir-Gen. PEDRO GARCÍA GIMENO.

Radio Televisión de Andalucía (RTVA): Sede Central RTVA, Pabellón de Canal Sur (Antigua Pabellón de Andalucía), José de Gálvez s/n, 41092 Isla de la Cartuja (Sevilla); tel. (95) 5054600; fax (95) 5054937; e-mail comunicacion@rtva.es; internet www.rtva.es; Dir-Gen. RAFAEL CAMACHO.

Radio Televisión Madrid (RTVM): Paseo del Príncipe 3, Ciudad de la Imagen, 28223 Pozuelo de Alarcón (Madrid); tel. (91) 5128200; fax (91) 5128300; internet www.telemadrid.es; Dir-Gen. FRANCISCO GIMÉNEZ-ALEMÁN.

Radiotelevisión Canaria (RTVC): Avda Bravo Murillo 5, Edif. Mapfre, 1°, 38003 Santa Cruz de Tenerife; tel. (922) 470200; fax (922) 273173; internet www.tvcanaria.tv; f. 1997; broadcasts in the Canaries; Dir-Gen. FRANCISCO MORENO GARCÍA.

Radiotelevisión Castilla-La Mancha (RTVCM): Río Alberche s/n, Edif. RTVCM, Polígono Santa María de Benquerencia, 45007 Toledo; tel. (925) 288600; fax (925) 287883; e-mail comunicacion@rtvcm.es; internet www.rtvcm.es; Dir-Gen. JORDI GARCÍA CANDAU.

Federation

Federación de Asociaciones de Radio y Televisión de España: Evaristo San Miguel 8, 28008 Madrid; tel. (91) 5481222; fax (91) 5593630; e-mail artv@jazzfree.com; Pres. FEDERICO SÁNCHEZ AGUILAR; Sec.-Gen. JOSÉ ESTEBAN VERDES.

RADIO

Radio Nacional de España (RNE): Casa de la Radio, Prado del Rey, 28223 Pozuelo de Alarcón (Madrid); tel. (91) 5817000; fax (91) 5183240; e-mail secretario_general.rne@rtve.es; internet www.rne.es; broadcasts Radio 1, Radio Clásica, Radio 3, Radio 4, Radio 5 Todo Noticias; 17 regional stations; Dir-Gen. JAVIER ARENAS; Sec.-Gen. EDUARDO HERNÁNDEZ.

Radio Exterior de España (REE): Apdo 156.202, 28080 Madrid; tel. (91) 3461081; fax (91) 3461815; e-mail dir_radioexterior.rne@rtve.es; overseas service of RNE; broadcasts in 10 languages; includes a world service in Spanish; Dir FRANCISCO JAVIER GARRIGÓS.

Independent Stations

Ambiente Musical: Paseo de la Castellana 210, 10°, 28046 Madrid; tel. (91) 3454000; fax (91) 3591321; e-mail estudio@musicam.net; Dir-Gen. MANEL SALLÉS CARCELLER.

Cadena 100: Alfonso XI 4, 28014 Madrid; tel. (91) 5951244; fax (91) 5225454; e-mail jllano@cadena100.es; internet www.cadena100.es; Dir JAVIER LLANO ABRIL.

Cadena M80: Gran Vía 32, 8°, 28013 Madrid; tel. (91) 3470700; fax (91) 5228693; e-mail programas@m80radio.com; internet www.m80radio.com; Dir MANUEL DÁVILA MORENO.

Cadena Dial: Gran Vía 32, 8°, 28013 Madrid; tel. (91) 3470700; fax (91) 5211753; internet www.cadenadial.com; Dir FRANCISCO HERRERA.

Cadena Ona Catalana: Aragón 390–394, 2°, 08013 Barcelona; tel. (93) 2449990; fax (93) 2459459; e-mail onacatalana@onacatalana.com; internet www.onacatalana.com; Dir-Gen. JOSEP PUIGBÓ.

Cadena Ondacero Radio Voz Galicia: Ronda de Outeiro 1, bajo, 15009 A Coruña; tel. (981) 180600; fax (981) 180477; e-mail mantilla@radiovoz.com; internet www.radiovoz.com; Man. Dir MANUEL MANTILLA FERNÁNDEZ.

Cadena de Ondas Populares Españolas/Radio Popular, SA (COPE): Alfonso XI 4, 3°, 28014 Madrid; tel. (91) 5951200; fax (91) 5322008; e-mail comunicacion@cope.es; internet www.cope.es; f. 1959; controlled by Roman Catholic Church; numerous medium-wave and FM stations; Pres. and CEO ALFONSO CORONEL DE PALMA.

Cadena Radio España/Radio España Madrid: Manuel Silvela 9, 28010 Madrid; tel. (91) 4475300; fax (91) 5938413; Pres. and Dir-Gen. JOSÉ ANTONIO SÁNCHEZ.

Cadena Radio Estudio: Pasaje de la Radio 1, Alcobendas, 28100 Madrid; tel. (91) 6531199; fax (91) 6533072; e-mail radioestudio@futurnet.es; Dir-Gen. ROMÁN BEITIA ALONSO.

Cadena Radiolé: Gran Vía 32, 7°, 28013 Madrid; tel. (91) 3470740; Dir JUAN CARLOS CHAVES.

Cadena TOP Radio España: Manuel Silvela 9, 28010 Madrid; tel. (91) 4475300; fax (91) 4477026; internet www.topradio.es; Pres. JOSÉ ANTONIO SÁNCHEZ.

Catalunya Ràdio, SRG, SA: Avda Diagonal 614–616, 08021 Barcelona; tel. (93) 3069200; fax (93) 3069201; e-mail correo@catradio.cat; internet www.catradio.cat; f. 1983; run by Catalan autonomous govt; four channels: Catalunya Ràdio, Catalunya Música, Catalunya Informació, iCat; three internet channels; Dir OLEGUER SARSANEDAS PICAS.

COMRàdio: Pavelló Cambó, Recinte de la Maternitat, Travessera de les Corts 131–159, 08028 Barcelona; tel. (93) 5080600; fax (93) 5080810; e-mail comradio@comradio.com; internet www.comradio.com; Dir-Gen. JORDI LLONCH MASSANÉS.

EITB Radio: Miramón Pasealekua 172, 20014 San Sebastián; tel. (943) 012300; fax (943) 012295; e-mail info@eitb.com; internet www.eitb.com; run by Basque autonomous govt; broadcasts on FM and MW as Euskadi Irratia, Radio Euskadi (Bilbao), Radio Vitoria (Vitoria-Gasteiz) and EITB Irratia; Dir JULIAN BELOKI GERRA.

Europa FM: Bueso Pineda 7, 28043 Madrid; tel. (91) 4134361; fax (91) 4137175; e-mail europafm@europafm.com; internet europafm.com; Pres. FRANCISCO GAYA GONZÁLEZ.

Grupo Pavesa Comunicación, SL—Radio Ondas Riojanas: Sabto Domingo 5, 26580 Arnedo; tel. (941) 383350; fax (941) 383383; e-mail ondarioja@ondarioja.com; internet www.ondarioja.com; Pres. PEDRO VEGA FERNÁNDEZ.

Los 40 Principales: Gran Vía 32, 8°, 28013 Madrid; tel. (91) 3470705; fax (91) 5317370; internet www.los40.com; Dir JAUME BARÓ GARRIGA.

Muinmo, SL: Apolonio Morales 6–10, 28036 Madrid; tel. (91) 3536017; fax (91) 3536019; Dir-Gen. MIGUEL ANGEL MONTERO QUEVEDO.

Onda Cero Radio (OCR): José Ortega y Gasset 22–24, 28006 Madrid; tel. (91) 436400; fax (91) 436101; e-mail ondacero@ondacero.es; internet www.ondacero.es; owned by Telefónica; Dir-Gen. JOSÉ LUIS OROSA ROLDAN.

Radio Autonomía Madrid, SA: Paseo del Príncipe 3, Ciudad de la Imagen, 28223 Pozuelo de Alarcón (Madrid); tel. (91) 51286749; fax (91) 5123752; e-mail ondamadrid@ondamadrid.com; internet www.ondamadrid.es; f. 1985; Dir MIGUEL PÉREZ-PLA DE VIU.

Ràdio Autonomia Valenciana, SA/Ràdio Nou: Avda Blasco Ibáñez 136, 46022 Valencia; tel. (96) 3183600; fax (96) 3183602; internet www.radionou.com; Dir JESÚS WOLLSTEIN ALCARAZ.

Radio ECCA: Avda Escaleritas 64, 1°, 35011 Las Palmas de Gran Canaria; tel. (928) 257400; fax (928) 207395; e-mail info@radioecca.org; internet www.radioecca.org; adult education; Dir-Gen. LUCAS LÓPEZ PÉREZ.

Radio Galega (RG): San Marcos, 15780 Santiago de Compostela; tel. (981) 540940; fax (981) 540919; e-mail radiogalega@crtvg.es;

internet www.crtvg.es; f. 1985; run by Galician autonomous govt; Man. Dir VIRGILIO COSTAS PUMAR.

Radio Surco-Castilla La Mancha: Concordia 14, Bajo C, 13700 Tomelloso (Ciudad Real); tel. (926) 505959; fax (926) 505961; e-mail r.surco@retemail.es; internet www.radiosurco.es; Dir FRANCISCO CASTELLANOS CUELLAR.

Punto Radio: e-mail info@puntoradio.com; internet www.puntoradio.com; f. 2005; Pres. JOSÉ MARÍA BERGARECHE.

Sociedad Española de Radiodifusión (Cadena SER): Gran Vía 32, 28013 Madrid; tel. (91) 3477700; fax (91) 3470709; internet www.cadenaser.com; f. 1924; 235 regional stations; owned by Grupo PRISA; Dir-Gen. RAÚL RODRÍGUEZ.

Digital Radio

In March 1999 two digital radio licences were awarded for the frequencies MF-1 and MF-2. MF-1 was controlled by Cope, Intereconomía, Recoletos and El Mundo, while MF-2 was controlled by SER, Onda Rambla-Planeta, Onda Cero, Radio España, Onda Digital and Prensa Española. MF-1 began broadcasting in Madrid and Barcelona in July 2000.

Radio Association

Asociación Española de Radiodifusión Comercial (AERC): Plaza Independencia 2, 4° dcha, 28001 Madrid; tel. (91) 4357072; fax (91) 4356196; e-mail aerc@retemail.es; groups nearly all commercial radio stations; Pres. RAFAEL PÉREZ DEL PUERTO; Sec.-Gen. ALFONSO RUÍZ DE ASSIN.

TELEVISION

Legislation relating to the ending of TVE's monopoly and the regulation of private TV stations was approved in April 1988. In 2005–06 the existing private terrestrial broadcasters—Antena 3, Telecinco and Canal+—were joined by Cuatro (operated by Sogecable, SA) and La Sexta. It was envisaged that analogue broadcasts would cease in 2010.

Televisión Española (TVE): Edif. Prado del Rey, 28223 Pozuelo de Alarcón, Madrid; tel. (91) 3464968; fax (91) 3463055; e-mail consultas@rtve.es; internet www.tve.es; broadcasts on TVE-1 and La 2; production centres in Barcelona and Las Palmas de Gran Canaria and 15 regional centres; broadcasts to Europe and the Americas on Canal Internacional; Dir JAVIER PONS.

Independent Stations

Antena 3 Televisión: Avda de Isla Graciosa s/n, 28700 San Sebastián de los Reyes, Madrid; tel. (91) 6230500; fax (91) 6230994; e-mail antena3tv@antena3tv.com; internet www.antena3tv.com; f. 1989; owned by Grupo Planeta; Pres. JOSÉ MANUEL LARA BOSCH.

Canal 9—Televisió Autonómica Valenciana (TVV): Polígon Accés Ademús, 46100 Burjassot (Valencia); tel. (96) 3183000; fax (96) 3183001; e-mail wmaster@rtvv.es; internet www.rtvv.es; f. 1989; second channel commenced operations in 1997; Dir GENOVEVA REIG.

Canal Sur Televisión: Carretera San Juan de Aznalfarache, Apdo 132, 41920 San Juan de Aznalfarache, Sevilla; tel. (95) 5607600; fax (95) 5054740; e-mail csalinas@cica.es; internet www.canalsur.es; f. 1989; regional station for Andalucía; Dir-Gen. RAFAEL CAMACHO.

Euskal Telebista—ETB (TV Vasca): 48215 Iurreta (Vizcaya); tel. (94) 6031000; fax (94) 6031095; e-mail info@eitb.com; internet www.eitb.com; f. 1982; 2 channels broadcasting to Basque Country, one in Basque, one in Spanish; Dir BINGEN ZUPIRIA GOROSTIDI.

Popular TV: Alfonso XI 4, 28014 Madrid; tel. (91) 3096669; e-mail populartv@populartv.net; internet www.populartv.net; broadcasts on a local and national level; Pres. BERNARDO HERRÁEZ RUBIO; Dir-Gen. ALEJANDRO SAMANES PRAT.

Sogecable: Avda de los Artesanos 6, 28760 Tres Cantos (Madrid); tel. (91) 7367000; internet www.sogecable.es; f. 1989; satellite and digital television, internet services; operates Cuatro (national terrestrial channel), Digital+, (digital provider), Canal Satélite Digital, CNN+, Compañía Independiente de Televisión, Gestsport, Sogecine; 43.2% owned by Grupo PRISA, 16.7% by Telefónica; Pres. RODOLFO MARTÍN VILLA.

Grupo Telecinco: Carretera de Irún, Km 11,700, 28049 Madrid; tel. (91) 155555; e-mail oinf@telecinco.es; internet www.telecinco.es; f. 1990; private commercial national network; owned by Grupo Mediaset (Italy), Grupo Correo de Comunicación, Ice Finance (The Netherlands); Pres. ALEJANDRO ECHEVARRÍA.

Televisió de Catalunya: Carrer de la TV3, s/n, 08970 Sant Joan Despi, Barcelona; tel. (93) 4999333; fax (93) 4730671; internet www.tv3.cat; f. 1983; broadcasts in Catalan; Dir FRANCESC ESCRIBANO.

Televisión de Galicia (TVG): San Marcos, Apdo 707, 15820 Santiago de Compostela; tel. (981) 540640; fax (981) 540719; e-mail crtvg@crtvg.es; internet www.crtvg.es; f. 1985; broadcasts in Galician; Man. Dir ANGEL QUINTANILLA LOUZAO.

Televisión Autonomía Madrid, SA (Telemadrid): Paseo del Príncipe de España 1, 28223 Pozuelo de Alarcón (Madrid); tel. (91) 5128200; fax (91) 5128300; e-mail correo@telemadrid.com; internet www.telemadrid.es; commenced transmissions in 1989; controlled by RTVM; cultural channel, laOtra, commenced transmission in March 2001; Dir-Gen. FRANCISCO GIMÉNEZ ALEMÁN; Man. Dir FERNANDO JEREZ.

Other Satellite, Cable and Digital Television

By 2000 more than 2m. Spanish homes and businesses were served by cable telecommunications and some 900,000 received digital television, at which time there were more than 100 satellite, cable and digital television broadcasters in Spain. Many of these were operated by existing broadcasting companies. Others include:

Chello Multicanal: Saturno 1, Pozuelo de Alarcón, 28224 Madrid; tel. (91) 7141080; fax (91) 3516873; e-mail lineadirecta@chellomulticanal.com; internet www.chellomulticanal.com/es; f. 1996; cable; operates nine channels; Dir-Gen. EDUARDO ZULUETA.

Grupo Auna: Avda Diagonal 579–585, 08014 Barcelona; internet www.auna.es; part of ONO; telecommunications, internet and cable TV; operates the cable telecommunications providers Aragón de Cable, Cabletelca, Cable i Televisió de Catalunya, Madritel, Supercable de Andalucía, Supercable Sevilla and Supercable Almería.

Euskaltel: Parque Tecnológico Edificio 809, 48160 Derio (Vizcaya); internet www.euskaltel.es; cable.

Hispasat: Gobelas 41, 28023 Madrid; tel. (91) 7102540; fax (91) 3729000; e-mail comunicacion@hispasat.es; internet www.hispasat.com; satellite; Pres. PETRA MATEOS.

Telecable de Asturias: Marqués de Pidal 11, bajo, 33004 Oviedo, Asturias; tel. (985) 081111; fax (985) 081112; e-mail info@telecable.es; internet www.telecable.es; cable; f. 1995; operator for Asturias.

Telefónica Cable: Calle Virgilio 2, Edif. 2, 2°, 28223 Pozuelo de Alarcón (Madrid); tel. (91) 5129510; e-mail cac@tcable.es; internet www.telefonica-cable.com; f. 1997; cable.

Veo TV: Plaza de la Castellana 40, 28046 Madrid; internet www.veo.es; f. 2001; digital; Dir EDUARDO SÁNCHEZ ILLANA.

Associations

Agrupación de Operadores de Cable (AOC): Obenque 4, 28042 Madrid; f. 1998; by CYC Madrid, Retecal, Telecable and Grupo Cable; group of cable telecommunications operators; Dir JESÚS PELEGRÍN.

Promoción e Identificación de Servicios Emergentes de Telecomunicaciones Avanzadas (PISTA): Secretaría de Estado de Telecomunicaciones y para la Sociedad de la Información, Capitán Haya 41, 28071 Madrid; tel. (91) 3462820; fax (91) 3461567; e-mail jmontalban@mityc.es; part of Ministry of Industry, Tourism and Trade; initiative for the promotion and identification of emerging advanced telecommunications.

Unión de Televisiones Comerciales Asociadas (UTECA): Maldonado 4, bajo C, 28006 Madrid; tel. (91) 5759778; fax (91) 5776754; e-mail uteca@uteca.com; internet www.uteca.com; f. 1998; represents commercial television interests; Pres. JOSÉ MANUEL LARA BOSCH; Sec.-Gen. JORGE DEL CORRAL Y DÍEZ DEL CORRAL.

Finance

(cap. = capital, res = reserves, dep. = deposits, brs = branches, m. = million, amounts in euros)

BANKING

Central Bank

Banco de España: Alcalá 48, 28014 Madrid; tel. (91) 3386063; fax (91) 3385884; e-mail bde@bde.es; internet www.bde.es; f. 1782; granted exclusive right of issue in 1874; nationalized 1962; granted a degree of autonomy in 1994; cap. 1,000.0m., res 5,793.6m., dep. 38,344.6m. (Dec. 2006); Gov. MIGUEL ÁNGEL FERNÁNDEZ ORDÓÑEZ; 22 brs.

Principal Commercial and Development Banks

Banca March: Avda Alejandro Rosselló 8, 07002 Palma de Mallorca; tel. (971) 779100; fax (971) 779187; e-mail divinter@bancamarch.es; internet www.bancamarch.es; f. 1926; cap. 29.2m., res 1,576.6m., dep. 7,573.4m. (Dec. 2006); Pres. JOSÉ CARLOS MARCH DELGADO; Man. Dir FRANCISCO VERDÚ PONS; 271 brs.

Banco de Andalucía: Fernández y González 4, 41001 Sevilla; tel. (95) 4594700; fax (95) 4594802; internet www.bancoandalucia.es; f. 1844; cap. 16.3m., res 839.3m., dep. 9,883.3m. (Dec. 2006); Pres.

SPAIN

MIGUEL DE SOLÍS Y MARTÍNEZ CAMPOS; Gen. Man. FRANCISCO PARDO MARTÍNEZ; 298 brs.

Banco Bilbao Vizcaya Argentaria (BBVA): Paseo de la Castellana 81, 28046 Madrid; tel. (91) 4876000; fax (91) 4876417; internet www.bbva.es; f. 2000 by merger; cap. 1,740.5m., res 16,436.7m., dep. 366,230.4m. (Dec. 2006); Pres. JOSÉ IGNACIO GOIRIGOLZARRI TELLAECHE; Chair. and Chief Exec. FRANCISCO GONZÁLEZ RODRÍGUEZ; 3,375 brs.

Banco Caixa Geral: Juan Ignacio Luca de Tena 1, 28027 Madrid; tel. (91) 3099000; fax (91) 3209275; e-mail extranjero@bancaixageral.es; internet www.bancocaixageral.es; f. 1969; present name adopted 2006; 99.6% owned by Caixa Geral de Depósitos (Portugal); cap. 360.3m., res −45.4m., dep. 3,750.7m. (Dec. 2006); Pres. FRANCISCO BANDEIRA; Chief Exec. MANUEL LÓPEZ FÍGUERDA.

Banco de Castilla: Plaza de los Bandos 10, 37002 Salamanca; tel. (923) 290000; fax (923) 211902; internet www.bancocastilla.es; f. 1915; 95.2% owned by Grupo Banco Popular; cap. 26.0m., res 404.2m., dep. 4,272.8m. (Dec. 2006); Pres. GABRIEL GANCEDO DE SERAS; Gen. Man. JOSÉ BRAVO JIMÉNEZ; 199 brs.

Banco Cooperativo Español: Virgen de los Peligros 6, 28013 Madrid; tel. (91) 5956700; fax (91) 5956800; internet www.cajarural.com; f. 1990; cap. 72.9m., res 115.0m., dep. 8,853.0m. (Dec. 2006); Chair. JOSÉ LUIS GARCÍA PALACIOS; Gen. Man. JAVIER PETIT ASUMENDI; 4,100 brs.

Banco Español de Crédito (Banesto): Gran Vía de Hortaleza 3, 28043 Madrid; tel. (91) 3383100; fax (91) 3381883; e-mail uninternac@banesto.es; internet www.banesto.es; f. 1902; cap. 548.5m., res 2,631.2m., dep. 96,240.2m. (Dec. 2006); Chair. ANA PATRICIA BOTÍN-SANZ DE SAUTUOLA Y O'SHEA; CEO JOSÉ A. GARCÍA CANTERA; 1,703 brs.

Banco de Galicia: Policarpo Sanz 23, Pontevedra, 36202 Vigo; tel. (986) 822100; fax (986) 822101; internet www.bancogalicia.es; f. 1918; part of Grupo Banco Popular Español; cap. 9.1m., res 337.7m., dep. 3,624.3m. (Dec. 2006); Pres. JESÚS PLATERO; Gen. Man. JOSÉ FERNANDO MARTÍNEZ ISACH; 141 brs.

Banco Gallego: Avda Linares Rivas 30, 15005 A Coruña; tel. (981) 127950; fax (981) 126582; e-mail interventiongeneral@bancgellego.com; internet www.bancogallego.es; f. 1847; cap. 83.4m., res 62.5m., dep. 3,337.9m. (Dec. 2006); Pres. JUAN MANUEL URGOITI LÓPEZ-OCAÑA; Gen. Man. JOSÉ LUIS LOSADA RODRÍGUEZ; 163 brs.

Banco Guipuzcoano: Avda de la Libertad 21, 20004 San Sebastián; tel. (943) 418100; fax (943) 418337; e-mail bgintnal@bancogui.com; internet www.bancogui.es; f. 1899; cap. 34.3m., res 403.0m., dep. 8,279.5m. (Dec. 2006); Pres. JOSÉ MARÍA AGUIRRE GONZÁLEZ; Gen. Man. JUAN LUIS ARRIETA; 248 brs.

Banco Pastor: Cantón Pequeño 1, Edif. Pastor, 15003 La Coruña; tel. (981) 127600; fax (981) 210301; internet www.bancopastor.es; f. 1776; cap. 86.4m., res 1,068.2m., dep. 21,604.3m. (Dec. 2006); Chair. JOSÉ MARÍA ARIAS MOSQUERA; Chief Exec. JORGE GOST GIJÓN; 555 brs.

Banco Popular Español: Velázquez 34, 28001 Madrid; tel. (91) 5207000; fax (91) 5783274; internet www.bancopopular.es; f. 1926; cap. 121.5m., dep. 69,732.0m. (Dec. 2005); Pres. ÁNGEL CARLOS RON GÜIMIL; Chief Exec. FRANCISCO FERNÁNDEZ DOPICO; 2,224 brs.

Banco de Sabadell: POB 1, Plaza Sant Roc 20, Sabadell, 08201 Barcelona; tel. (93) 7289289; fax (93) 7270606; e-mail info@bancsabadell.com; internet www.bancsabadell.com; f. 1881; cap. 153.0m., res 3,232.8m., dep. 63,643.6m. (Dec. 2006); Chair. JOSEP OLIU; 1,069 brs.

Banco Santander: Plaza de Canalejas 1, 28014 Madrid; tel. (91) 5581111; internet www.gruposantander.com; f. 1857; cap. 3,127.1m., res 35,465.7m., dep. 745,204.4m. (Dec. 2006); Chair. EMILIO BOTÍN-SANZ DE SAUTUOLA Y GARCÍA DE LOS RÍOS; Man. Dir JUAN BOTÍN; 8,848 brs.

Banco Urquijo, SA: Príncipe de Vergara 131, 28002 Madrid; tel. (91) 3372000; fax (91) 3372096; internet www.bancourquijo.es; f. 1870; part of Grupo Banco de Sabadell; cap. 92.7m., res 148.7m., dep. 3,675.0m. (Dec. 2004); Pres. FERDINAND VERDONCK; CEO ALFONSO TOLCHEFF; 60 brs.

Banco de Valencia: Pintor Sorolla 2–4, 46002 Valencia; tel. (96) 3984500; fax (96) 3984570; e-mail division.internacional@bancodevalencia.es; internet www.bancodevalencia.es; f. 1900; cap. 102.9m., res 747.7m., dep. 14,550.4m. (Dec. 2006); Pres. JOSÉ LUIS OLIVAS MARTÍNEZ; Gen. Man. DOMINGO PARRA SORIA; 428 brs.

Banco de Vasconia: Plaza del Castillo 39, 31001 Pamplona; tel. (948) 179600; fax (948) 179665; e-mail servicioscentrales@bancovasconia.es; internet www.bancovasconia.es; f. 1901; 96.9% owned by Banco Popular Español; cap. 9.6m., res 173.5m., dep. 3,351.4m. (Dec. 2005); Pres. JOSÉ R. RODRÍGUEZ GARCÍA; Gen. Man. MIGUEL MOZO LOBATO; 121 brs.

Bankinter: Paseo de la Castellana 29, 28046 Madrid; tel. (91) 3397500; fax (91) 3397556; e-mail international@bankinter.es; internet www.ebankinter.com; f. 1965; finances industrial and business dealings with medium- and long-term loans and investments; cap. 116.9m., res 1,211.7m., dep. 37,975.4m. (Dec. 2005); Chair. JUAN ARENA DE LA MORA; CEO JAIME ECHEGOYEN; 253 brs.

Barclays Bank SA: Plaza de Colón 1, 28046 Madrid; tel. (91) 3361000; fax (91) 3361134; internet www.barclays.es; f. 1974; cap. 157.8m., res 666.5m., dep. 19,251.6m. (Dec. 2005); 99.7% owned by Barclays Bank PLC (United Kingdom); Chair. C. MARTÍNEZ DE CAMPOS; 163 brs.

Savings Banks

Bilbao Bizkaia Kutxa (Caja de Ahorros Municipal de Bilbao) (Caja de Ahorros Vizcaina): Gran Vía 30–32, 48009 Bilbao; tel. (94) 4017000; fax (94) 4017800; e-mail bbktelefono@bbk.es; internet www.bbk.es; f. 1907; cap. 0.0m., res 3,437.8m., dep. 20,345.6m. (Dec. 2006); Chair. and Chief Exec. XABIER DE IRALA; 330 brs.

CAIXANOVA (Caixa de Aforros de Vigo, Ourense e Pontevedra): Avda García Barbon 1–3, 36201 Vigo; tel. (986) 828200; fax (986) 828238; e-mail internacionalcx@caixanova.com; internet www.caixanova.com; f. 1929; present name adopted 2000; cap. 0.0m., res 1,048.8m., dep. 16,026.7m. (Dec. 2005); Pres. and Chair. JULIO FERNÁNDEZ GAYOSO; Gen. Man. JOSÉ LUIS PEGO ALONSO; 629 brs.

Caixa d'Estalvis de Catalunya (Caixa Catalunya): Plaza Antonio Maura 6, 08003 Barcelona; tel. (93) 4845000; fax (93) 4845141; e-mail international.services@caixacatalunya.es; internet www.caixacatalunya.es; f. 1926; res 2,664.8m., dep. 60,631.4m., total assets 67,551.4m. (Dec. 2006); Pres. NARCÍS SERRA; Gen. Man. JOSEP ADOLF TODÓ; 936 brs.

Caixa d'Estalvis de Sabadell (Caixa Sabadell): Gràcia 17, Sabadell, 08201 Barcelona; tel. (93) 7286700; fax (93) 7286555; e-mail info@caixasabadell.es; internet www.caixasabadell.com; f. 1859; res 482.3m., dep. 6,919.3m., total assets 8,676.2m. (Dec. 2005); Pres. LLUÍS BRUNET BERCH; Gen. Man. JORDI MESTRE GONZÁLEZ; 319 brs.

Caixa d'Estalvis de Tarragona (Caixa Tarragona): Plaza Imperial Tàrraco 6, 43005 Tarragona; tel. (977) 299200; fax (977) 299250; e-mail liniapreferent@caixatarragona.es; internet www.caixatarragona.es; f. 1952; res 405.6m., dep. 5,100.6m., total assets 5,659.5m. (Dec. 2005); Pres. GABRIEL FERRATÉ PASCUAL; Gen. Man. RAFAEL JENÉ VILLAGRASA; 289 brs.

Caixa d'Estalvis de Terrassa (Caixaterrassa): Ramble d'Ègara 350, 08221 Terrasa; tel. (93) 7397700; fax (93) 7397777; e-mail ct.0560.3@caixaterrassa.es; internet www.caixaterrassa.es; f. 1877; res 507.3m., dep. 6,066.3m., total assets 8,197.4m. (Dec. 2005); Pres. FRANCES ASTALS COMA; Gen. Man. ENRIC MATA TARRAGÓ; 164 brs.

Caja de Ahorros de Asturias (CAJASTUR): Plaza de la Escandalera 2, 33003 Oviedo; tel. (98) 5102222; fax (98) 5215649; e-mail extranjero@cajastur.es; internet www.cajastur.es; f. 1945; res 1,319.6m., dep. 7,474.0m., total assets 9,280.2m. (Dec. 2005); Pres. and CEO MANUEL MENÉNDEZ MENÉNDEZ; 250 brs.

Caja de Ahorros de Castilla la Mancha (CCM): Parque San Julián 20, 16002 Cuenca; tel. (969) 177314; fax (969) 177606; e-mail webmaster@ccm.es; internet www.ccm.es; f. 1992; cap. 0.0m., res 997.2m., dep. 17,174.4m. (Dec. 2005); Pres. JUAN PEDRO HERNÁNDEZ MOLTÓ; 390 brs.

Caja de Ahorros de Galicia (Caixa Galicia): Rúa Nueva 30, 15003 A Coruña; tel. (981) 188000; fax (981) 188001; internet www.caixagalicia.es; f. 1978; cap. 0.0m., res 2,211.3m., dep. 38,790.8m. (Dec. 2006); Pres. MAURO VARELA PÉREZ; Gen. Man. JOSÉ LUIS MÉNDEZ LÓPEZ; 703 brs.

Caja de Ahorros de la Inmaculada de Aragón (CAI): Paseo Independencia 10, 50004 Zaragoza; tel. (976) 718100; fax (976) 718377; e-mail info.corporativa@cai.es; internet www.cai.es; f. 1905; res 687.4m., dep. 7,865.4m., total assets 8,743.9m. (Dec. 2006); Pres. RAFAEL ALCÁZAR CREVILLÉN; 238 brs.

Caja de Ahorros del Mediterráneo (CAM): San Fernando 40, 03001 Alicante; tel. (96) 5905000; fax (96) 5905044; e-mail cam@cam.es; internet www.cam.es; f. 1875; cap. 0.0m., res 2,779m., dep. 54,960.6m. (Dec. 2006); Chair. VICENTE SALA BELLÓ; Gen. Man. ROBERTO LÓPEZ ABAD.

Caja de Ahorros y Monte de Piedad de las Baleares 'Sa Nostra': Ramón Llull 2, 07001 Palma de Mallorca; tel. (971) 171717; fax (971) 171797; e-mail sanostra@sanostra.es; internet www.sanostra.es; res 543.7m., dep. 8,693.8m., total assets 10,099.2m. (Dec. 2006); Chair. FERNANDO ALZAMORA CARBONELL; Gen. Man. PEDRO BATLE MAYO; 229 brs.

Caja de Ahorros y Monte de Piedad del Círculo Católico de Obreros de Burgos (CajaCírculo): Avda de los Reyes Católicos 1, 09005 Burgos; tel. (947) 288200; fax (947) 288210; internet www.cajacirculo.es; f. 1909; res 471.1m., dep. 3,902.2m., total assets 4,547.4m. (Dec. 2006); Chair. JOSÉ IGNACIO MIJANGOS LINAZA; Gen. Man. SANTIAGO RUIZ DIEZ; 176 brs.

Caja de Ahorros y Monte de Piedad de Gipuzkoa y San Sebastián (Gipuzkoa eta Donstiako Aurrezki Kutxa): Garibai 15, Apdo 1389, 20004 San Sebastián; tel. (943) 001000; fax (943) 001045;

e-mail infokutxa@kutxa.es; internet www.kutxa.es; f. 1896; cap. 180.3m., res 2,042.9m., dep. 16,090.7m. (Dec. 2006); Pres. and Chair. Carlos Etxepare Zugasti; 289 brs.

Caja de Ahorros y Monte de Piedad de Madrid (Caja Madrid): Plaza de Celenque 2, 28013 Madrid; tel. (91) 3792000; fax (91) 5216980; e-mail bvegasga@cajamadrid.es; internet www.cajamadrid.es; f. 1869; cap. 0.0m., res 8,451.5m., dep. 123,757.1m. (Dec. 2006); Pres. Miguel Blesa de la Parra; 1,914 brs.

Caja de Ahorros y Monte de Piedad de Navarra (Caja Navarra): Avda de Carlos III 8, 31002 Pamplona; tel. (948) 222333; fax (948) 208269; e-mail sac@can.es; internet www.can.es; f. 1921; cap. 0.0m., res 766.6m., dep. 11,554.7m. (Dec. 2006); Pres. Miguel Sanz Sesma; Gen. Man. Enrique Goñi Beltrán de Garizurieta; 323 brs.

Caja de Ahorros y Monte de Piedad de Zaragoza, Aragón y Rioja (IBERCAJA): Plaza del Paraíso 2, 50008 Zaragoza; tel. (976) 767676; fax (976) 214417; internet www.ibercaja.es; f. 1876; res 1,995.5m., dep. 32,420.1m., total assets 35,237.2m. (Dec. 2006); Chair. Amado Franco Lahoz; Gen. Man. José Luis Aguirre Loaso; 1,008 brs.

Caja de Ahorros de Murcia (Cajamurcia): Gran Vía Escultor Salzillo 23, 30005 Murcia; tel. (968) 361600; fax (968) 306160; internet www.cajamurcia.es; f. 1965; cap. 0.0m., res 1,248.7m., dep. 14,649.8m., total assets 16,719.6m. (Dec. 2006); Pres. Juan Roca Guillamón; Gen. Man. Carlos Egea Krauel; 380 brs.

Caja de Ahorros y Pensiones de Barcelona (La Caixa): Avda Diagonal 621–629, 08028 Barcelona; tel. (93) 4046000; fax (93) 3395703; e-mail estudis@lacaixa.es; internet www.lacaixa.es; f. 1990; res 11,186.1m., dep. 172,754.9m., total assets 209,123.2m. (Dec. 2006); Chair. Ricardo Fornesa; Pres. and Chief Exec. Isidro Fainé; 4,524 brs.

Caja de Ahorros de Valencia, Castellón y Alicante (BANCAJA) (Caixa d'Estalvis de València, Castelló i Alacant): Pintor Sorolla, 8, 46002 Valencia; tel. (96) 3875500; fax (96) 3527550; internet www.bancaja.es; f. 1878; res 2,714.6m., dep. 71,054.8m., total assets 79,577.2m. (Dec. 2006); Chair. José Luis Olivas Martínez; Gen. Man. José Fernando García Checa; 1,055 brs.

Caja Duero (Caja de Ahorros de Salamanca y Soria): Plaza de los Bandos 15–17, 37002 Salamanca; tel. (923) 279300; fax (923) 270680; internet www.cajaduero.es; f. 1881; res 1,092.3m., dep. 14,843.6m., total assets 16,774.3m. (Dec. 2006); Pres. and Chair. Julio Fermoso; Gen. Man. Lucas Hernández; 563 brs.

Caja España (Caja España de Inversiones, Caja de Ahorros y Monte de Piedad): Ordoño II 17, 24001 León; tel. (987) 218683; fax (987) 218067; e-mail buzon@cajaespana.es; internet www.cajaespana.es; f. 1900; res 950.6m., dep. 16,273.5m., total assets 18,053.0m. (Dec. 2005); Chair. Victorino González Ochoa; Gen. Man. José Ignacio Lagartos Rodríguez; 538 brs.

Caja Insular de Ahorros de Canarias (La Caja de Canarias): Triana 20, 35002 Las Palmas; tel. (928) 442254; fax (928) 442599; e-mail ciac@lacajadecanarias.es; internet www.lacajadecanarias.es; f. 1939; res 304.4m., dep. 5,376.4m., total assets 5,843.8m. (Dec. 2005); Pres. Antonio Marrero Hernández.

Caja Laboral Popular Coop. de Crédito (Caja Laboral): Paseo José María Arizmendiarrieta s/n, Guipúzcoa, 20500 Mondragón; tel. (943) 719500; fax (943) 719778; e-mail cajalaboral.net@cajalaboral.es; internet www.cajalaboral.es; f. 1959; cap. 384.6m., res 978.1m., dep. 15,660.5m. (Dec. 2006); Pres. Juan M. Otaegui Murua; Gen. Man. Elias Atucha Aresti; 377 brs.

Confederación Española de Cajas de Ahorros (CECA): Alcalá 27, 28014 Madrid; tel. (91) 5965000; fax (91) 5965742; e-mail admin@ceca.es; internet www.ceca.es; f. 1928; national asscn of savings banks; cap. 30.1m., res 538.0m., dep. 13,083.1m. (Dec. 2006); Pres. and Dir-Gen. Juan Ramón Quintás Seoane; 22,445 brs.

Deutsche Bank SAE: Avda Diagonal 446, 08006 Barcelona; tel. (93) 3673788; fax (93) 3673311; internet www.deutsche-bank.es; f. 1950; present name adopted 1994; 99.7% owned by Deutsche Bank AG (Germany); cap. 67.4m., res 561.4m., dep. 13,025.4m.; Chair. Hermann-Josef Lambertu.

Montes de Piedad y Caja de Ahorros de Ronda, Cádiz, Almería, Málaga y Antequera (Unicaja): Avda Andalucía 10–12, 29007 Málaga; tel. (952) 138000; fax (952) 138130; e-mail info@personal.unicaja.es; internet www.unicaja.es; f. 1991; cap. 0.0m., res 1,820.0m., dep. 19,478.1m. (Dec. 2005); Pres. Braulio Medel Camará; Gen. Man. Miguel Angel Cabello Jurado; 870 brs.

Banking Associations

Asociación Española de Banca (AEB): Velázquez 64–66, 28001 Madrid; tel. (91) 7891311; fax (91) 7891310; f. 1977; Pres. Miguel Martín; Sec.-Gen. Pedro Pablo Villasante.

Fondo de Garantía de Depósitos (FGD): José Ortega y Gasset 22, 28006 Madrid; tel. (91) 4316645; fax (91) 5755728; e-mail fogade@fgd.es; internet www.fgd.es; f. 1977; deposit guarantee fund; Pres. José María Viñals Iñiguez.

STOCK EXCHANGES

Bolsas y Mercados Españoles (BME): Palacio de la Bolsa, Plaza de la Lealtad 1, 28014 Madrid; tel. (91) 7095000; fax (91) 5326816; e-mail accionista@bolsasymercados.es; internet www.bolsasymercados.es; integrates cos that manage securities market and financial system; Pres. Antonio Zoido Martínez.

Bolsa de Barcelona: Paseo de Gracia 19, 08007 Barcelona; tel. (93) 4013555; fax (93) 4013650; e-mail informacion@borsabcn.es; internet www.borsabcn.es; f. 1915; Pres. Joan Hortalà i Arau.

Bolsa de Bilbao: José M. Olabarri 1, 48001 Bilbao; tel. (94) 4034400; fax (94) 4034430; e-mail bolsabilbao@bolsabilbao.es; internet www.bolsabilbao.es; f. 1890; CEO José Luis Damborenea.

Bolsa de Madrid: Plaza de la Lealtad 1, 28014 Madrid; tel. (91) 5891161; fax (91) 5312290; e-mail internacional@bolsamadrid.es; internet www.bolsamadrid.es; f. 1831; 49 mems; Chair. and CEO Antonio Zoido Martínez.

Bolsa de Valores de Valencia: Libreros 2 y 4, 46002 Valencia; tel. (96) 3870100; fax (96) 3870133; e-mail webmaster@bolsavalencia.es; internet www.bolsavalencia.es; f. 1980; Vice-Pres. and CEO Manuel Escámez Sánchez.

Regulatory Authority

Comisión Nacional del Mercado de Valores (CNMV): Paseo de la Castellana 19, 28046 Madrid; tel. (91) 5851500; fax (91) 3193373; e-mail inversores@cnmv.es; internet www.cnmv.es; f. 1988; national securities and exchange commission; Pres. Julio Segura Sánchez.

INSURANCE

Aegon Unión Aseguradora: Príncipe de Vergara 156, 28002 Madrid; tel. (91) 5636222; fax (91) 5639715; internet www.aegon.es; f. 1944; owned by Aegon NV (The Netherlands); life, property, health and personal insurance and reinsurance; Chair. Alejandro Royo-Villanova Payá; CEO Jesús Quintanal San Emeterio.

Allianz, Compañía de Seguros y Reaseguros: Paseo de la Castellana 39, 28046 Madrid; tel. (91) 5960400; fax (91) 5578702; internet www.allianz.es; f. 1999; total premiums 2,292m. (2004); Pres. Detlev Bremkamp; CEO Vicente Tardío.

Ascat Vida: Provença 398–404, 08025 Barcelona; tel. (93) 484600; tel. (93) 4846002; e-mail info_ascat@caixacatalunya.es; internet www.ascat.es; f. 1986; subsidiary of Caixa Catalunya.

Asistencia Sanitaria Interprovincial de Seguros (ASISA): Caracas 12, 28010 Madrid; tel. (91) 3190191; fax (91) 4103836; e-mail asisa.informacion@asisa.es; internet www.asisa.es; Pres. Francisco Carreño Castilla.

Axa: Paseo de la Castellana 79, 28046 Madrid; tel. (91) 5388200; fax (91) 5553197; internet www.axa.es; Pres. Eduardo de Aguirre Alonso-Allende.

Banco Vitalicio de España, Compañía Anónima de Seguros: Paseo de Gracia 11, 08007 Barcelona; tel. (93) 4840100; fax (93) 4840239; internet www.vitalicio.es; f. 1880; total premiums 1,221.2m. (2004); Pres. José María Amusátegui de la Cierva.

BBVA Seguros: Alcalá 17, 28014 Madrid; tel. (91) 5379231; fax (91) 3747266; e-mail servicioatencioncliente@grupobbva.com; internet www.bbvaseguros.com.

Bilbao, Cía Anónima de Seguros y Reaseguros (Seguros Bilbao): Paseo del Puerto 20, 48990 Neguri-Getxo (Vizcaya); tel. (94) 4898100; fax (94) 4898263; internet www.segurosbilbao.com; f. 1918; gen. insurance, represented throughout Spain; part of Grupo Catalana Occidente; Pres. Francisco José Arregui; Man. Dir Iñaki Alvares.

Caja de Seguros Reunidos, Cía de Seguros y Reaseguros (Caser Seguros): Plaza de la Lealtad 4, 28014 Madrid; tel. (91) 5955000; fax (91) 5955018; e-mail informacion@caser.es; internet www.caser.es; f. 1942; represented throughout Spain; total premiums 1,587.9m. (2005); Dir-Gen. Ignacio Eyries García de Vinuesa.

Crédito y Caución (Compañía Española de Seguros y Reaseguros): Paseo de la Castellana 4, 28046 Madrid; tel. (91) 4326300; fax (91) 4326506; e-mail sac@creditoycaucion.es; internet www.creditoycaucion.com; f. 1929; total premiums 361m. (2005); Pres. Jesús Serra Farré; CEO Isidro Unda Urzaiz.

Estrella Seguros: Orense 2, 28020 Madrid; tel. (91) 5905656; fax (91) 5907674; e-mail clientes@laestrella.es; internet www.laestrella.es; f. 1901; all classes of insurance and reinsurance; total premiums 1,007.3m. (2005); Pres. Duque Carlos Zurita Delgado; CEO Mónica Mondardini.

Grupo Catalana Occidente: Avda Alcalde Barnils 63, 08174 Sant Cugat del Vallés (Barcelona); tel. (93) 5820500; fax (93) 5820560; internet www.catalanaoccidente.com; insurance and reinsurance; Pres. José María Serra Farré.

SPAIN

Mapfre Mutualidad (Mapfre Mutualidad de Seguros y Reaseguros): Carretera de Pozuelo a Majadahonda, Km 3800, 28820 Majadahonda, Madrid; tel. (91) 6262100; fax (91) 6262308; internet www.mapfre.com; f. 1933; car insurance; Pres. José A. Rebuelta García.

Mapfre Seguros Generales: Paseo de Recoletos 23, 28004 Madrid; tel. (91) 5816300; fax (91) 5815252; internet www.mapfre.com; Pres. Rafael Galarraga Solores.

Mapfre Vida: Avda General Perón 40, 28020 Madrid; tel. (91) 5811400; fax (91) 5811592; internet www.mapfre.com; life; Man. Dir Sebastián Homet Dupra.

Mutua General de Seguros (MGS): Avda Diagonal 543, 08029 Barcelona; tel. (93) 3221212; fax (93) 3220971; e-mail mutua@mgs.es; internet www.mgs.es; f. 1907; Pres. Jorge Luque Vico.

Mutua Madrileña: Paseo de la Castellana 33, 28046 Madrid; tel. (902) 555555, (91) 5578200; fax (91) 3105223; internet www.mutua-mad.es; f. 1930; Pres. Ignacio Garralda Ruíz de Velasco.

Ocaso, SA, Compañía de Seguros y Reaseguros: Princesa 23, 28008 Madrid; tel. (91) 5380100; fax (91) 5418509; e-mail ocaso@ocaso.es; internet www.ocaso.es; f. 1920; total premiums 513m., cap. 100m. (2002); 370 brs in Spain, 1 in London, 1 in Puerto Rico; Pres. Isabel Castelo d'Ortega; Dir-Gen. D. Antonio Domínguez Cuerdo.

Sanitas de Seguros: Ribera del Loira 52, 28042 Madrid; tel. 902 230220; fax (91) 5852516; e-mail iferrando@sanitas.es; internet www.sanitas.es; health; Pres. Juan José López-Ibor.

SantaLucía Seguros: Plaza de España 15, 28008 Madrid; tel. (91) 5419387; fax (91) 5410133; e-mail atencion@santalucia.es; internet www.santalucia.es; f. 1922; Pres. Carlos J. Alvarez Navarro.

Vidacaixa: General Almirante 6, 08014 Barcelona; tel. (93) 2278700; fax (93) 3324441; internet www.vidacaixa.es; subsidiary of Grupo CaiFor; Pres. Tomás Muniesa Arantegui.

Zurich: Vía Augusta 192–200, 08021 Barcelona; tel. (93) 2099111; fax (93) 2014849; internet www.zurichspain.com.

Regulatory Authority

Dirección General de Seguros y Fondos de Pensiones: Paseo de la Castellana 44, 28046 Madrid; tel. (91) 3397000; fax (91) 3397113; e-mail dirseguros@meh.es; internet www.dgsfp.meh.es; supervisory body; part of Ministry of the Economy and Finance; Dir-Gen. Ricardo Lozano Aragüés.

Insurance Association

Unión Española de Entidades Aseguradoras y Reaseguradoras (UNESPA): Núñez de Balboa 101, 28006 Madrid; tel. (91) 7451530; fax (91) 7451531; internet www.unespa.es; f. 1977; Pres. Pilar González de Frutos; Sec.-Gen. Mirenchu del Valle; c. 300 mem. cos.

Trade and Industry

GOVERNMENT AGENCIES

Comisión Nacional de la Competencia (CNC): Barquillo 5, 28004 Madrid; tel. (91) 5680510; fax (91) 5680590; e-mail informacion@cncompetencia.es; internet www.cncompetencia.es; f. 2007 by merger of the Servicio de Defensa de la Competencia and the Tribunal de Defensa de la Competencia; investigates anti-competitive practices and enforces competition law; Pres Luis Berenguer Fuster.

Instituto Español de Comercio Exterior (ICEX): Paseo de la Castellana 14, 28046 Madrid; tel. (91) 3496100; fax (91) 4316128; internet www.icex.es; f. 1982; institute for foreign trade; Pres. María Elena Pisonero Ruiz.

Secretaría General de Comercio Exterior: Secretaría de Estado de Comercio y Turismo, Paseo de la Castellana 160, 28046 Madrid; tel. 902 446006; fax (91) 4578066; part of Ministry of Industry, Tourism and Trade; Sec.-Gen. Alfredo Bonet Baiget.

DEVELOPMENT ORGANIZATIONS

Instituto Andaluz de la Reforma Agraria (IARA): Tabladilla s/n, 41013 Sevilla; tel. (95) 5032271; fax (95) 5032149; empowered to expropriate land under the agricultural reform programme; Pres. Juan Angel Fernández Batanero.

Instituto Galego de Promoción Económica (IGAPE): Complejo Administrativo Barrio de San Lázaro s/n, 15703 Santiago de Compostela (A Coruña); tel. (981) 541147; fax (981) 558844; e-mail igape@igape.es; internet www.igape.es; promotes devt in Galicia; overseas brs in P.R. China, Germany, Japan, Poland and USA; Dir-Gen. Álvaro Álvarez-Blázquez Fernández; Sec.-Gen. Rosa María Pedrosa Pedrosa.

Instituto Madrileño de Desarrollo (IMADE): José Abascal 57, 28003 Madrid; tel. (91) 3997400; e-mail informacion@imade.es; internet www.imade.es; f. 1984; public devt institution for Madrid region; Dir Aurelio García de Sola y Arriaga.

Sociedad de Desarrollo de Navarra (SODENA): Avda Carlos III el Noble 36, 1° dcha, 31003 Pamplona; tel. (848) 421942; fax (848) 421943; e-mail info@sodena.com; internet www.sodena.com; promotes devt in Navarra; Pres. José Roig Aldasoro.

Sociedad para el Desarrollo Económico de Canarias (Sodecan): Villalba Hervás 4, 6°, 38002 Santa Cruz de Tenerife; tel. (922) 298020; fax (922) 298131; e-mail sodecantf@sodecan.es; internet www.sodecan.es; promotes devt in the Canary Islands; Pres. Eusebio Bautista Vizcaino.

Sociedad para el Desarrollo Industrial de Castilla y León (SODICAL): Doctrinos 6, 4°, 47001 Valladolid; tel. (983) 343811; fax (983) 330702; e-mail sodical@sodical.es; internet www.sodical.es; f. 1982; promotes devt in Castile and Leon; Dir-Gen. Manuel Fernández Díez.

Sociedad para el Desarrollo Industrial de Extremadura (Sodiex): Avda Virgen de Guadalupe, 10001 Cáceres; tel. (927) 224878; fax (927) 243304; e-mail sodiex@sodiex.es; internet www.sodiex.es; f. 1977; promotes industrial devt in Extremadura.

Sociedad para el Desarrollo Industrial de Galicia (SODIGA): Orense 6, La Rosaleda, 15701 Santiago de Compostela; tel. (981) 541621; fax (981) 566183; promotes industrial devt in Galicia.

CHAMBERS OF COMMERCE

Cámara de Comercio Internacional (International Chamber of Commerce): Avda Diagonal 452–4, 08006 Barcelona; tel. (93) 4169300; fax (93) 4169301; e-mail iccspain@cambrabcn.es; internet www.iccspain.org; f. 1922; Pres. Guillermo de la Dehesa; Sec.-Gen. Luis Solá Vilardell.

Confederación Española de Comercio (CEC): Orense 25, 2°C, 28020 Madrid; tel. (91) 5981050; fax (91) 5520967; e-mail cec@confespacomercio.com; internet www.confespacomercio.com; Pres. Pere Llorens Lorente; Sec.-Gen. Miquel Ángel Fraile Villagrasa; 400,000 mems.

Consejo Superior de Cámaras Oficiales de Comercio, Industria y Navegación de España (High Council of Official Chambers of Commerce, Industry, and Navigation of Spain): Ribera del Loira 12, 28042 Madrid; tel. (91) 5906900; fax (91) 5906913; e-mail info@cscamaras.es; internet www.camaras.org; f. 1922; Pres. Javier Gómez-Navarro; Dir-Gen. Fernando Gómez Aviles-Casco; comprises 85 Chambers throughout Spain, incl. the following:

Cámara de Comercio de Bilbao/Bilboko Merkataritza Ganbera: Gran Vía 13, 48001 Bilbao; tel. (94) 4706500; fax (94) 4436171; e-mail atencionalcliente@camarabilbao.com; internet www.camarabilbao.com; Pres. Ignacio María Echeberria Monteberria; Dir-Gen. Juan Luis Laskurain Argarate.

Cámara Oficial de Comercio e Industria de Madrid: Ribera del Loira 56–58, 28042 Madrid; tel. (91) 5383500; fax (91) 5383677; e-mail camara@camaramadrid.es; internet www.camaramadrid.es; f. 1887; Pres. Gerardo Díaz Ferrán; Dir-Gen. Manuel Garrido de la Cierva; 370,000 mems.

Cámara Oficial de Comercio, Industria y Navegación de Sevilla: Plaza de la Contratación 8, 41004 Sevilla; tel. (954) 211005; fax (954) 225619; e-mail ccinsevilla@camaradesevilla.com; internet www.camaradesevilla.com; f. 1886.

Cámara Oficial de Comercio, Industria y Navegación de Valencia: Poeta Querol 15, 46002 Valencia; tel. (96) 3103900; fax (96) 3531742; e-mail info@camaravalencia.com; internet www.camaravalencia.com; f. 1886; Pres. Arturo Virosque Ruíz; Dir Fernando Zárraga Quintana.

Cambra de Comerç de Barcelona: Avda Diagonal 452–454, 08006 Barcelona; tel. (90) 2448448; fax (93) 4169301; internet www.cambrabcn.es; f. 1886; Pres. Miquel Valls Maseda; Dir Xavier Carbonell i Roura.

INDUSTRIAL AND TRADE ASSOCIATIONS

Agrupación de Exportadores del Centro de España (AGRECE) (Group of Exporters of Central Spain): Ribera del Loira 56–58, 28042 Madrid; tel. (91) 5383500; fax (91) 5383718; e-mail cex2@camaramadrid.es; internet www.camaramadrid.es; part of Cámara Oficial de Comercio e Industria de Madrid; exporters.

Agrupación de Fabricantes de Cemento de España (OFICEMEN): José Abascal 53, 28003 Madrid; tel. (91) 4411688; fax (91) 4423817; e-mail direccion@oficemen.com; internet www.oficemen.com; cement manufacturers; Pres. Ignacio Madridejos; Dir-Gen. Aniceto Zaragoza.

Asociación de Comercio de Cereales y Oleaginosas de España (ACCOE) (Spanish Association of Oilseeds and Cereals Traders): Doctor Fleming 56, 3°D, 28036 Madrid; tel. (91) 3504305; fax (91)

SPAIN

Directory

3455009; e-mail info@accoe.org; internet www.accoe.org; f. 1977; cereal traders; Pres. Pelayo Moreno Sánchez; Sec.-Gen. José M. Alvarez Blasco.

Asociación de Criadores Exportadores de Sherry (ACES): Eguiluz 2, 11402 Jerez de la Frontera (Cádiz); tel. (956) 341046; fax (956) 346081; sherry exporters; Pres. Francisco Valencia Jaén.

Asociación de Empresas de Electrónica, Tecnologías de la Información y Telecomunicaciones de España (AETIC): Príncipe de Vergara 74, 4°, 28006 Madrid; tel. (91) 5902300; e-mail aetic@aetic.es; internet www.aetic.es; f. 1984; electronic, information and telecommunication industries; Pres. Jesús Banegas Núñez; Dir-Gen. Gonzalo Caro Santa Cruz; c. 1,000 mem. cos.

Asociación Española de Comercio Exterior de Cereales y Productos Análogos (AECEC): Orense 85, Edif. Lexington, 28020 Madrid; tel. (91) 678400; fax (91) 5714244; e-mail aecec@arrakis.es; cereal exporters; Pres. J. Cornejo; Sec.-Gen. Guillermo Lorenzo Zamorano.

Asociación Española de Exportadores de Electrónica e Informática (SECARTYS): Gran Vía de les Corts Catalanes 774, 4°, 08013 Barcelona; tel. (93) 2478560; fax (93) 2478561; e-mail secartys@secartys.org; internet www.secartys.org; f. 1968; electronics exporters; Pres. José Beltrán; Dir-Gen. Ignacio Tormo Marxuach.

Asociación Española de Fabricantes de Automóviles y Camiones (ANFAC): Fray Bernardino Sahagún 24, 28036 Madrid; tel. (91) 3431343; fax (91) 3450377; e-mail prensa@anfac.com; internet www.anfac.es; car and lorry manufacturers; Pres. Juan Antonio Fernández de Sevilla.

Asociación Española de Fabricantes de Equipos y Componentes para Automoción (SERNAUTO): Castelló 120, 28006 Madrid; tel. (91) 5621041; e-mail sernauto@sernauto.es; internet www.sernauto.es; f. 1967; asscn of manufacturers of equipment and components for automobile industry; Pres. José María Pujol Artigas; Dir-Gen. José Antonio Jiménez Saceda.

Asociación Española de la Industria y Comercio Exportador de Aceite de Oliva (ASOLIVA): José Abascal 40, 2°, 28003 Madrid; tel. (91) 4468812; fax (91) 5931918; e-mail asoliva@asoliva.es; internet www.asoliva.es; f. 1928; olive oil exporters; Pres. José Pont Amenos.

Asociación Española de Productoras de Fibras Químicas (PROFIBRA): Via Laietana 46, 2°, 08003 Barcelona; tel. and fax (93) 3196534; e-mail profibra@profibra.com; f. 1977; chemical fibre producers; Pres. Rafael Español Navarro; Sec.-Gen. Guillermo Graell Deniel.

Asociación de Exportadores de Pescado y Cefalopodos Congelados (AEPYCC): Diego de León 44, 28006 Madrid; tel. (91) 4112407; fax (91) 5618178; fish exporters; Pres. Ramón Maso; Sec. Ignacio Montenegro González.

Asociación Industrial Textil de Proceso Algodonero (AITPA): Gran Vía de les Corts Catalanes 670, 08010 Barcelona; tel. (93) 3189200; fax (93) 3026235; e-mail aitpa@aitpa.es; internet www.aitpa.es; cotton textile industry; Pres. Adria Serra.

Asociación Nacional Española de Fabricantes de Hormigón Preparado (ANEFHOP): Bretón de los Herreros 43, bajo, 28003 Madrid; tel. (91) 4416634; fax (91) 3993497; e-mail info@anefhop.es; internet www.anefhop.com; f. 1968; concrete manufacturers; Pres. Manuel A. Sobral Cruz; Dir-Gen. Francisco Javier Martínez de Eulate.

Asociación Nacional de Fabricantes de Pastas Papeleras, Papel y Cartón (ASPAPEL): Avda de Baviera 15, 28028 Madrid; tel. (91) 5763003; fax (91) 5774710; e-mail aspapel@aspapel.es; internet www.aspapel.es; f. 1977; paper and cardboard manufacturers; Pres. Juan Vila; Dir-Gen. Carlos Reinoso Torres.

Comité de Gestión de Cítricos (CGC): Monjas de Santa Catalina 8, 4°, 46002 Valencia; tel. (96) 3521102; fax (96) 3510718; e-mail comite@citricos.org; internet www.citricos.org; citrus fruit exporters; Pres. Vicente Bordils Ramón; Dir José Martínez Serrano.

Confederación de Cooperativas Agrarias de España (CCAE) (Confederation of Spanish Agrarian Co-operatives): Agustín de Bethencourt 17, 4°, 28003 Madrid; tel. (91) 5351035; fax (91) 5540047; e-mail ccae@ccae.es; internet www.ccae.es; Pres. Ricardo Martín Gutiérrez; Dir-Gen. Eduardo Baamonde Noche.

Confederación Española de Organizaciones Empresariales del Metal (CONFEMETAL): Príncipe de Vergara 74, 5°, 28006 Madrid; tel. (91) 5625590; fax (91) 5635758; e-mail informacion@confemetal.es; internet www.confemetal.es; metal asscns; Pres. Carlos Pérez de Bricio Olariaga; Sec.-Gen. Andrés Sánchez de Apellániz.

Confederación Nacional de la Construcción (CNC): Diego de León 50, 2°, 28006 Madrid; tel. (91) 5619715; fax (91) 5615269; e-mail cnc@cnc.es; internet www.cnc.es; f. 1977; construction industry; Pres. Juan Francisco Lazcano Acedo.

Consejo Intertextil Español (CIE): Gran Via de les Corts Catalanes 670, 08010 Barcelona; tel. (93) 3189200; fax (93) 3026235; e-mail cie@consejointertextil.com; internet www.consejointertextil.com; textile industry; Pres. Josep Casas; Sec.-Gen. Jordi Font; 7 mem. asscns.

Federación Empresarial de la Industria Química Española (FEIQUE): Hermosilla 31, 1°, 28001 Madrid; tel. (91) 4317964; fax (91) 5763381; e-mail info@feique.org; internet www.feique.org; chemical industry; Pres. Fernando Iturrieta; Dir-Gen. Fernando Galbis.

Federación Española de Asociaciones de Productores y Exportadores de Frutas, Hortalizas, Flores y Planta Vivas (FEPEX): Miguel Angel 13, 4A, 28010 Madrid; tel. (91) 3191050; fax (91) 3103812; e-mail fepex@fepex.es; internet www.fepex.es; fruit and vegetable producers and exporters; Pres. Andrés Cuartero Ruiz; Dir José María Pozancos; 26 mem. asscns.

Federación Española de Exportadores de Frutos Cítricos (FECIT): Hernan Cones 4E, 46004 Valencia; tel. (96) 3521284; fax (96) 3513187; citrus fruit exporters; Pres. Antonio Pelufo; Sec. Luis Ribera Peris.

Federación Española de Industrias de la Alimentación y Bebidas (FIAB): Diego de León 44, 1° izqda, 28006 Madrid; tel. (91) 4117211; fax (91) 4117344; e-mail fiab@fiab.es; internet www.fiab.es; f. 1977; food and drink industries; Pres. Arturo Gil Pérez Andujar; Sec.-Gen. Jorge Jordana Butticaz de Pozas.

Federación de Industrias del Calzado Español (FICE): Núñez de Balboa 116, 3°, 28006 Madrid; tel. (91) 5627003; fax (91) 5620094; e-mail info@fice.es; internet www.fice.es; f. 1977; footwear; Pres. Rafael Calvo Rodríguez.

Fundación Cotec: Marqués de Salamanca 11, 2° izqda, 28006 Madrid; tel. (91) 4364774; fax (91) 4311239; internet www.cotec.es; f. 1990; promotes technological innovation and understanding; Pres. José Ángel Sánchez Asiaín; Dir Juan Mulet.

Sociedad Estatal de Participaciones Industriales (SEPI): Velásquez 134, 28006 Madrid; tel. (91) 3961000; fax (91) 5628789; e-mail informacion@sepi.es; internet www.sepi.es; f. 1996; asscn of state-owned cos; Pres. Enrique Martínez Robles; Sec.-Gen. Fernando Sequeira Fuentes; 36 mems.

Unión de Empresas Siderúrgicas (UNESID): Castelló 128, 3°, 28006 Madrid; tel. (91) 5624010; fax (91) 5626584; e-mail unesid@unesid.org; internet www.unesid.org; f. 1968; asscn of Spanish producers of steel; Chair. Gonzalo Urquijo; Dir-Gen. Juan I. Bartolomé.

EMPLOYERS' ORGANIZATIONS

Círculo de Empresarios: Paseo de la Castellana 15, 6°, 28001 Madrid; tel. (91) 5781472; fax (91) 5774871; e-mail asociacion@circulodeempresarios.org; internet www.circulodeempresarios.org; f. 1977; comprises CEOs of more than 180 major cos; Pres. Claudio Boada Pallerés; Sec.-Gen. Pedro Morenés Eulate.

Confederación Española de Organizaciones Empresariales (CEOE) (Spanish Confederation of Employers' Organizations): Diego de León 50, 28006 Madrid; tel. (91) 5663400; fax (91) 5622562; e-mail ceoe@ceoe.es; internet www.ceoe.es; f. 1977; covers industry, agriculture, commerce and service sectors; comprises 210 orgs; Pres. Gerardo Díaz Ferrán; Vice-Pres. and Sec.-Gen. Juan Jiménez de Aguilar.

Confederación Empresarial de Madrid (CEIM): Diego de León 50, 1°, 28006 Madrid; tel. (91) 4115317; fax (91) 5627537; internet info@ceim.es; internet www.ceim.es; small, medium and large businesses; Pres. Gerardo Diaz Ferrán; Sec. Alejandro Couceiro.

Confederación Empresarial Valenciana (CEV): Plaza Conde de Carlet 3, 46003 Valencia; tel. (96) 3155720; fax (96) 3923199; e-mail cev@cev.es; internet www.cev.es; f. 1977; Pres. José Vicente Goutálet; Sec.-Gen. Enrique Soto.

Confederación Empresarial Vasca/Euskal Entrepresarien Konfederakuntza (CONFEBASK): Gran Vía 45, 2°, 48011 Bilbao; tel. (94) 4021331; fax (94) 4021333; e-mail confebask@confebask.es; internet www.confebask.es; f. 1983; Pres. Miguel Lazpiur; Sec.-Gen. José Guillermo Zubía Guinea.

Confederación Española de la Pequeña y Mediana Empresa (CEPYME): Diego de León 50, 3°, 28006 Madrid; tel. (91) 4116161; fax (91) 5645269; e-mail cepyme@cepyme.es; internet www.cepyme.es; small and medium businesses; Pres. Antonio Masa Godoy; Sec.-Gen. Elías Aparicio Bravo.

Fomento del Trabajo Nacional/Foment del Treball Nacional—Confederación Empresarial de Catalunya: Vía Laietana 32, 08003 Barcelona; tel. (93) 4841200; fax (93) 4841230; e-mail foment@foment.com; internet www.foment.com; f. 1771 as Real Compañia de Hilados de Algodón del Principado de Catalunya; devt of national labour; Pres. Joan Rosell Lastortras; Sec.-Gen. Juan Pujol Segarra.

UTILITIES

Secretaría General de Energía: Paseo de la Castellana 160, 28071 Madrid; tel. (91) 3494819; fax (91) 4587704; e-mail secgenenergia@mityc; part of Ministry of Industry, Tourism and Trade; Sec.-Gen. PEDRO MARÍN URIBE.

Comisión Nacional de Energía (CNE): Alcalá 47, 28014 Madrid; tel. (91) 4329600; fax (91) 5776218; e-mail dre@cne.es; internet www.cne.es; f. 1999; part of Ministry of Industry, Tourism and Trade; regulates energy systems; Pres. MARÍA TERESA COSTA CAMPI.

Instituto para la Diversificación y Ahorro de la Energía (IDAE): Madera 8, 28004 Madrid; tel. (91) 4564900; fax (91) 5230414; e-mail comunicacion@idae.es; internet www.idae.es; f. 1974 as Centro de Estudios de la Energía; under control of General Secretariat of Energy (Ministry of Industry, Tourism and Trade); Dir-Gen. ENRIQUE JIMÉNEZ LARREA.

Electricity

Asociación Española de la Industria Eléctrica (UNESA): Francisco Gervás 3, 28020 Madrid; tel. (91) 5674800; fax (91) 5674987; e-mail info@unesa.es; internet www.unesa.es; f. 1944; groups principal electricity cos; Pres. IÑIGO DE ORIOL; Dir-Gen. PEDRO RIVERO.

Operador del Mercado Ibérico de Energía—Polo Español (OMEL): Alfonso XI 6, 4° y 5°, 28014 Madrid; e-mail info@omel.es; internet www.omel.es; f. 2003; Spanish branch of the Iberian Energy Market; Pres. and CEO MARÍA LUISA HUIDOBRO Y ARREBA.

Red Eléctrica de España (REE): Paseo del Conde de los Gaitanes 177, 28109 La Moraleja (Madrid); tel. (91) 6508500; fax (91) 6504542; e-mail redelectrica@ree.es; internet www.ree.es; manages and operates the national grid; Pres. LUIS ATIENZA SERNA.

Principal Electricity Companies

Endesa: Ribera del Loira 60, Campo de las Naciones, 28042 Madrid; tel. (91) 2131000; fax (91) 5638181; internet www.endesa.es; f. 1983; generator, distributor and vendor of electricity; also provides gas; 67% owned by Enel (Italy); Pres. JOSÉ MANUEL ENTRECANALES DOMECQ.

Enel Viesgo: Medio 12, 39003 Santander; tel. (942) 246000; fax (942) 246034; internet www.viesgo.es; f. 1906; 100% owned by Enel (Italy); distributor; CEO MIGUEL ANTOÑANZAS.

HC Energía: Plaza de la Gesta 2, 33007 Oviedo (Asturias); tel. (98) 5230300; e-mail hcenergia@hcenergia.com; internet www.hcenergia.com; f. 1919; fmrly Hidroeléctrica del Cantábrico; generator, distributor and vendor of electricity; also provides gas; owned by Electricidade de Portugal; Pres. MANUEL MENÉNDEZ MENÉNDEZ.

Iberdrola: Cardenal Gardoqui 8, 48008 Bilbao; tel. (944) 151411; fax (944) 663194; e-mail informacion@iberdrola.es; internet www.iberdrola.com; generator, distributor and vendor of electricity; supplies mainly hydroelectric power; also provides gas; Pres. and CEO JOSÉ IGNACIO SÁNCHEZ GALÁN.

Unión Fenosa: Avda San Luis 77, 28033 Madrid; tel. (91) 5676000; fax (91) 5676658; e-mail unionfenosa@unionfenosa.es; internet www.unionfenosa.es; generator, distributor and vendor of electricity; also provides gas; Chair. PEDRO LÓPEZ JIMÉNEZ; CEO HONORATO LÓPEZ ISLA.

Gas

Enagás: Paseo de los Olmos 19, 28005 Madrid; tel. (902) 443700; e-mail contacta@enagas.es; internet www.enagas.es; operates gas transportation network; f. 1972; Pres. ANTONI LLARDÉN.

Endesa Gas: Aznar Molina 2, 50002 Zaragoza; tel. (976) 760000; fax (976) 760044; internet www.endesa.es; distributor of gas; comprises five subsidiaries; also provides electricity; subsidiary of Endesa; Pres. AMADO FRANCO LAHOZ; Dir-Gen. FERNANDO CORTINA GONZÁLEZ.

Gas Natural SDG: Avda Portal de l'Angel 22, 08002 Barcelona; tel. (93) 4025100; fax (93) 4029317; internet www.gasnatural.com; distributor of gas; also provides electricity and communications; comprises regional distribution cos; Pres. SALVADOR GABARRÓ SERRA; CEO RAFAEL VILLASECA MARCO.

NaturGas Energía: Plaza Pío Baroja 3, 2°, 48001 Bilbao; tel. (94) 4035700; fax (94) 4249733; e-mail webnaturgas@naturgas.es; internet www.naturgas.es; f. 1982; 56.2% owned by HC Energía; distributor of gas and electricity; Pres. MANUEL MENÉNDEZ.

Water

Dirección General del Agua: Plaza de San Juan de la Cruz s/n, 28071 Madrid; tel. (91) 5976660; part of Ministry of the Environment, Agriculture and the Marine; co-ordinates water policy and supervises water management; Dir-Gen. JAIME PALOP PIQUERAS.

Grupo Agbar: Torre Agbar, Avda Diagonal 211, 08018 Barcelona; tel. (93) 3422000; fax (93) 3422662; e-mail comunicacion@agbar.es; internet www.agbar.es; treatment of water and waste liquid; provision of sanitation and certification services; Pres. JORGE MERCADER MIRÓ; Dir-Gen. ANGEL SIMÓN.

Grupo Aguas de Valencia: Gran Vía Marqués del Turia 19, 46005 Valencia; tel. (96) 3860600; internet www.aguasdevalencia.es; water and sewerage services; Chair. V. BOLUDA FOS.

TRADE UNIONS

Central Sindical Independiente y de Funcionarios (CSI-CSIF): Fernando el Santo 17, 1°, 28010 Madrid; tel. (91) 2735900; fax (91) 2735991; e-mail s.presidencia@csi-csif.es; internet www.csi-csif.es; Pres. DOMINGO FERNÁNDEZ VEIGUELA; Sec.-Gen. LOURDES BLANCO AMILLATEGUI.

Confederación General de Trabajo (CGT) (General Confederation of Labour): Sagunto 15, 28010 Madrid; tel. (91) 4475769; fax (91) 4453132; e-mail sp-comunicacion@cgt.es; internet www.cgt.es; Sec.-Gen. ELADIO VILLANUEVA SARAVIA.

Confederación Intersindical Galega (CIG): Rua Miguel Ferro Caaveiro 10, 3°, 15073 Santiago de Compostela; tel. (981) 564300; fax (981) 571082; e-mail secretarioxeral@galizacig.net; internet www.galizacig.com; Galician confederation; Sec.-Gen. XÉSUS E. SEIXO FERNÁNDEZ.

Confederación Nacional del Trabajo (CNT) (National Confederation of Labour): Secretariado Permanente del Comité Nacional, Imagen 8, 5°B, 41003 Sevilla; tel. (945) 562395; e-mail sp_cn@cnt.es; internet www.cnt.es; Sec.-Gen. RAFAEL CORRALES.

Confederación Sindical de Comisiones Obreras (CCOO) (Workers' Commissions): Fernández de la Hoz 12, 28010 Madrid; tel. (91) 7028000; fax (91) 3104804; e-mail ccoo@ccoo.es; internet www.ccoo.es; f. 1956; independent left-wing; Sec.-Gen. JOSÉ MARÍA FIDALGO VELILLA; 1,050,000 mems (2005).

Eusko Langilleen Alkartasuna/Solidaridad de Trabajadores Vascos (ELA—Euskal Sindikatua) (Basque Workers' Solidarity): Barrainkua 13, 48009 Bilbao; tel. (94) 4037700; fax (94) 4037777; e-mail naziorte@elasind.org; internet www.ela-sindikatua.org; f. 1911; legally recognized 1977; independent; Sec.-Gen. JOSÉ ELORRIETA AURREKOETXEA; 106,000 mems (2006).

Unión General de Trabajadores (UGT) (General Union of Workers): Hortaleza 88, 28004 Madrid; tel. (91) 5897601; fax (91) 5897603; e-mail info@cec.ugt.org; internet www.ugt.es; f. 1888; eight affiliated federations; Sec.-Gen. CÁNDIDO MÉNDEZ RODRÍGUEZ.

Unión Sindical Obrera (USO) (Workers' Trade Union): Príncipe de Vergara 13, 7°, 28001 Madrid; tel. (91) 5774113; fax (91) 5772959; e-mail uso@uso.es; internet www.uso.es; f. 1960; independent; Sec.-Gen. JULIO SALAZAR MORENO; 105,000 mems.

Transport

RAILWAYS

In August 2000 it was announced that rail transport was to be liberalized by 2008, with private operators using the state rail infrastructure. In January 2001 Spain and Portugal agreed on the route of a high-speed train to be built, linking the two countries. The infrastructure was to be completed by 2008. A high-speed link from Madrid to the French border, via Barcelona, was scheduled to be completed in 2009. There were also plans for a high-speed link between Madrid and Valencia, and a new railway between Valencia and the Basque Country. From January 2005 the state railway company, RENFE, was divided into an operating and a management division, and the goods transport sector was open to competition. RENFE's monopoly on passenger transport was to end in 2010. In 2005 the total rail network was 12,624.5 km, 483.7 km of which was high-speed track.

Administrador de Infraestructuras Ferroviarias (Adif): Paseo del Rey 30, 28008 Madrid; tel. (91) 3008080; e-mail vialia@adif.es; internet www.adif.es; f. 2005; state-owned; fmrly part of state-owned railway co, Red Nacional de los Ferrocarriles Españoles (RENFE); manages railway infrastructure; Pres. ANTONIO GONZÁLEZ MARÍN; Sec.-Gen. MARÍA ROSA SANZ CEREZO.

RENFE Operadora: Avda Pío XII 110, 28036 Madrid; tel. (91) 3006600; e-mail comunicacion@renfe.es; internet www.renfe.es; f. 2005 following liberalization of railway sector; fmrly Red Nacional de los Ferrocarriles Españoles (RENFE); state-owned; Pres. JOSÉ SALGUEIRO CARMONA; Sec.-Gen. JOSÉ L. MARROQUÍN MOCHALES.

Eusko Trenbideak—Ferrocarriles Vascos (ET/FV) (EuskoTren): Atxuri 6, 48006 Bilbao; tel. (94) 4019700; fax (94) 4019901; e-mail attcliente@euskotren.es; internet www.euskotren.es; f. 1982;

controlled by the Basque Govt; 188 km of 1,000 mm gauge; 25.6m. passengers carried (1995); Dir-Gen. José Miguel Múgica Peral.

Ferrocarriles de Vía Estrecha (Feve) (Narrow Gauge Railways): Plaza de los Ferroviarios, 33012 Oviedo; tel. (98) 5297656; fax (98) 5281708; e-mail info@feve.es; internet www.feve.es; f. 1965 by integration of private cos; operates mainly in suburban areas of northern cities; 1,194 km (2006) of narrow-gauge track (of which 317 km were electrified); Pres. Dimas Sañudo Aja; Dir-Gen. Juan Carlos Albizuri Higuera.

Ferrocarrils de la Generalitat de Catalunya (FGC): Pau Casals 24, 8°, 08021 Barcelona; tel. (93) 3663000; fax (93) 3663350; e-mail rrpp@fgc.net; internet www.fgc.net; f. 1979; 290 km, of which 161 km are electrified; Pres. Joan Torres i Carol.

Ferrocarrils de la Generalitat de Valencia (FGV): Partida de Xirivelleta, 46014 Valencia; tel. (96) 3976565; fax (96) 3976580; e-mail webmaster_fgv@gva.es; internet www.fgv.es; f. 1986; 237 km of track; also operates Valencia Metro, with four lines and 143 km of line, and Tram Alicante (93 km); Pres. Mario Flores; Dir-Gen. Marisa Gracia Giménez.

Metro de Bilbao: Navarra 2, 48001 Bilbao; tel. (94) 4254000; e-mail info@metrobilbao.net; internet www.metrobilbao.com; f. 1995; 38.9 km; 2 lines and 36 stations; Dir-Gen. Rafael Sarria Ansoleaga.

Metro de Madrid: Cavanilles 58, 28007 Madrid; tel. 902 444403; fax (91) 7212957; e-mail prensa@metromadrid.es; internet www.metromadrid.es; 283 km, 13 lines, 231 stations, also light railway network (Metro Ligero) of 28 km, 3 lines, 38 stations; Pres. Manuel Melis Maynar; Dir Ildefonso de Matías Jiménez.

Transports Metropolitans de Barcelona (TMB): Carrer 60, 21–31, Sector A. Polígono industrial Zona Franca, 08040 Barcelona; tel. (93) 2987000; e-mail tmb@tmb.net; internet www.tmb.net; 85.8 km, 6 lines, 104 stations (2008); CEO Constantí Serralonga Tintoré.

ROADS

The total road network at December 2003 was 666,292 km, including 12,609 km of motorway and 24,858 km of main roads.

Dirección General de Carreteras: Paseo de la Castellana 67, 28071 Madrid; tel. (91) 5977000; fax (91) 5978535; part of Ministry of Development; Dir-Gen. Juan Francisco Lazcano Acedo.

SHIPPING

Spain has many ports. Among the most important are Algeciras, Barcelona, Valencia, Tarragona, Bilbao, Cartagena, Gijón, Huelva and Santa Cruz de Tenerife. The 1,638 ships of the merchant fleet totalled 3,004,626 grt in December 2006.

Asociación de Navieros Españoles (ANAVE): Dr Fleming 11, 1° dcha, 28036 Madrid; tel. (91) 4580040; fax (91) 4579780; e-mail anave@anave.es; internet www.anave.es; shipowners' asscn; Pres. Juan Riva Francos; Dir Manuel Carlier de Lavalle.

Dirección General de la Marina Mercante: Ruíz de Alarcón 1, 28014 Madrid; tel. (91) 5979118; fax (91) 5979120; part of Ministry of Development; Dir-Gen. Felipe Martínez Martínez.

Puertos del Estado: Avda del Partenón 10, 28042 Madrid; tel. (91) 5245500; fax (91) 5245501; e-mail webmaster@puertos.es; internet www.puertos.es; Pres. Mariano Navas Gutiérrez.

Principal Shipping Companies

Acciona Trasmediterránea: Avda de Europa 10, Parque Empresarial La Moraleja, 28018 Alcobendas (Madrid); tel. (91) 4238500; fax (91) 4238555; e-mail info@trasmediterranea.es; internet www.trasmediterranea.es; f. 1917; Spanish ports, Balearic and Canary Is and Spanish North African, Algerian and Moroccan ports; Pres. Miguel Angel Fernández Villamandos; Dir-Gen. José Manuel Fernández Villamandos.

Agencia Marítima Española Evge: Avda Francesc Cambó 17, 08003 Barcelona; tel. (93) 3905800; fax (93) 2681750; e-mail evge@evgebcn.com; internet www.evgebcn.com; f. 1959; international shipping agents; Man. Dir Ramón Oliete Cossio.

Auximar, SL (Marítima del Norte): Miño 4, 28002 Madrid; tel. (91) 7454300; fax (91) 7454303; e-mail central@auximar.es; internet www.auximar.es; f. 1957; ship management, refrigerated cargo vessels, liquefied gas tankers; Dirs Iñigo de Sendagorta, Javier de Sendagorta.

Compañía Remolcadores Ibaizabal: Muelle de Tomás Olabarri 4, 5°, 48930 Las Arenas (Vizcaya); tel. (94) 4645133; fax (94) 4645565; e-mail ibaizabal@ibaizabal.org; internet www.remolcadoresibaizabal.com; f. 1906; ocean-going, coastal, harbour, salvage; Pres. Alejandro Aznar Sainz.

Compañía Trasatlántica Española: José Abascal 58, 3°, 28003 Madrid; tel. (91) 4514244; fax (91) 3993736; internet www.trasatlantica.com; f. 1850; freight services to Europe, North Africa, Caribbean, South America; Man. Dir Javier Villasante.

Empresa Naviera Elcano: José Abascal, 4°, 28003 Madrid; tel. (91) 5369800; fax (91) 4451234; e-mail elcano@elcano.sa.es; Pres. José Silvera.

Ership: Lagasca 88, 28001 Madrid; tel. (91) 4263400; fax (91) 5750883; e-mail chart@ership.com; internet www.ership.com; fmrly TAC; CEO Gonzalo Alvargonzález.

Naviera Pinillos: Capitán Haya 21, 28020 Madrid; tel. (91) 5556711; fax (91) 5569777; e-mail pinillos@pinillos.com; internet www.pinillos.com; f. 1840; part of Grupo Boluda; services between Canary Is and other Spanish ports; Pres. Vicente Boluda; Dir Angel Mato.

Nenufar Shipping: Manuel Ferreo 13, 28036 Madrid; tel. (91) 3158393; fax (91) 3158384; e-mail nenufar@nenufar.com; internet www.nenufar.com; f. 1983; part of Grupo Boluda; services to Spanish ports, Canary Is, Italy, Portugal, the United Kingdom, Morocco and Mauritania.

Repsol Naviera Vizcaina: Juan de Aguriaguerra 35, 2°, 48009 Bilbao; tel. (94) 4251100; fax (94) 4251143; f. 1956; world-wide, but particularly Mediterranean, Near East and Persian (Arabian) Gulf to Spain and transatlantic trade; Man. Dir Javier González Juliá.

CIVIL AVIATION

In 2008 there were more than 50 airports, almost all of which were equipped to receive international flights.

Dirección General de Aviación Civil: Paseo de la Castellana 67, 28071 Madrid; tel. (91) 5975356; fax (91) 5975357; internet www.fomento.es/aviacioncivil; Dir-Gen. Manuel Bautista Pérez.

Aeropuertos Españoles y Navegación Aérea (AENA): Arturo Soria 109, 28043 Madrid; tel. (91) 3211000; fax (91) 3212571; internet www.aena.es; f. 1990; network of airports in Spain; Pres. Manuel Azuaga Moreno.

Principal Airlines

In mid-2006 a total of 30 Spanish airlines were registered with the Ministry of Development.

Air Europa Líneas Aéreas: Centro Empresarial Globalia. Apdo. Correos-132, 07620 Llucmajor; tel. (971) 178190; fax (971) 178353; internet www.air-europa.com; f. 1986; charter and scheduled services to Canary and Balearic Is, North Africa, Central, Southern and Eastern Europe; also Mexico, Cuba and Dominican Republic; Pres. Juan José Hidalgo Acera; Dir-Gen. Manuel Panadero.

Binter Canarias: Aeropuerto de Gran Canaria, Parcela 9, del ZIMA Apdo 50, Gran Canaria; tel. (928) 579601; fax (928) 579603; e-mail info@bintercanarias.es; internet www.bintercanarias.com; f. 1988; scheduled services within Canary Islands and to Madeira, Morocco, Western Sahara and Mauritania; subsidiary of Grupo Iberia; Pres. Pedro Agustín del Castillo; CEO Rodolfo Núñez Ruano.

Clickair: Solsones 2, Esc. B., 3° 1, Parc de Negocis Mas Blau, Prat de Llobregat, 08820 Barcelona; tel. (93) 3784400; e-mail info@clickair.com; internet www.clickair.com; f. 2006; low-cost airline; flights from Barcelona to other Spanish destinations (incl. Canary Islands), and to destinations in Europe, Israel, Russia and North Africa; Dir-Gen. Alex Cruz de Llano.

Grupo Iberia: Velázquez 130, 28006 Madrid; tel. (91) 5877462; fax (91) 5877949; e-mail prensaintl@iberia.es; internet www.iberia.com; f. 1927; domestic and international passenger and freight services to 101 destinations in 40 countries; partner in airline alliance OneWorld; Chair. and CEO Fernando Conte García.

Iberworld Airlines: Gran Vía Asima 23, Polígono Son Castelló, 07009 Palma de Mallorca; tel. (91) 229144; fax (91) 713184; e-mail iberworld@iberworld.com; internet www.iberworld.com; domestic, international and intercontinental charter flights.

LTE International Airways: Carrer del Ter 27, Polígono Son Fuster, 07009 Palma de Mallorca; tel. (971) 475700; fax (971) 478874; e-mail info@lte.es; internet www.lte.es; f. 1987; charter flights between Spanish islands, metropolitan Spain and Italy; Pres. José M. Goya; Dir Casimiro Bermúdez.

Spanair: Edif. Spanair, 07611 Palma de Mallorca; tel. (971) 745020; fax (971) 492100; e-mail spanair@spanair.es; internet www.spanair.com; f. 1986; passenger scheduled and charter services within Spain, incl. Canary and Balearic Islands and within Europe, and to Algeria and The Gambia; 100% owned by SAS Group (Denmark/Norway/Sweden); Pres. Gonzalo Pascual; Dir-Gen. Lars Nygaard.

Vueling Airlines: Edif. Muntadas, Berguedà 1, Parque de Negocios Mas Blau, El Prat de Llobregat, 08820 Barcelona; tel. (93) 3787878;

fax (93) 3787879; e-mail clients@vueling.com; internet www.vueling.com; f. 2004; low-cost airline; domestic and international flights; Pres. JOSEP PIQUÉ; CEO LARS NYGAARD.

Tourism

Spain's tourist attractions include its climate, beaches and historic cities. Tourism makes an important contribution to the country's economy. In 2006 58.5m. foreign tourists visited Spain. Receipts from tourism totalled €48,227m. in that year.

Instituto de Turismo de España (Turespaña): José Lázaro Galdiano 6, 28071 Madrid; tel. (91) 3433500; e-mail infosmile@tourspain.es; internet www.tourspain.es; promotes tourism; offices in Spain and abroad; Dir-Gen. AMPARO FERNÁNDEZ GONZÁLEZ.

Secretaría de Estado de Comercio y Turismo: Paseo de la Castellana 160, 28071 Madrid; fax (91) 4578066; internet www.comercio.es; Sec. PEDRO MEJÍA GÓMEZ.

SPANISH EXTERNAL TERRITORIES

The Spanish External Territories comprise mainly Ceuta and Melilla, two enclaves within Moroccan territory on the north African coast. Attached to Melilla, for administrative purposes, are Peñón de Vélez de la Gomera, a small fort on the Mediterranean coast, and two groups of islands, Peñón de Alhucemas and the Chafarinas. Ceuta and Melilla are seen as integral parts of Spain by the Spanish Government and have the status of autonomous cities, although Morocco has put forward a claim to both. Sovereignty over the uninhabited island of Perejil (known as Laila to the Moroccans) is disputed between Spain and Morocco.

CEUTA

Introductory Survey

Location, Climate, Language, Religion

Ceuta, one of the two main enclaves of Spanish North Africa, is situated on the north African coast opposite Gibraltar, the Strait here being about 25 km wide. The average temperature is 17°C. Spanish and Arabic are spoken. The majority of Europeans are Roman Catholic, most North Africans being Muslim. There are small Hindu and Jewish communities.

Recent History

The population of the enclave is mostly Spanish. The proportion of Arab residents, however, has increased, owing to the large number of immigrants from Morocco. Those born in the territory are Spanish citizens and subjects. An ancient port and walled city, Ceuta was retained by Spain upon Moroccan independence from France in 1956. Having developed as a military and administrative centre for the former Spanish Protectorate in Morocco, Ceuta now functions as a bunkering and fishing port. In 1974 the town became the seat of the Capitanía General de Africa. Two-thirds of Ceuta's land area are used exclusively for military purposes.

In November 1978 King Hassan of Morocco stated his country's claim to Ceuta and the other main Spanish enclave in North Africa, Melilla, a claim that was reiterated following the opening of the Spanish frontier with Gibraltar in early 1985. In October 1981 Spain declared before the UN that Ceuta and Melilla were integral parts of Spanish territory. Spain rejects any comparison between the two enclaves and Gibraltar. From 1984 there was increasing unease over Spanish North Africa's future, following rioting in Morocco in January and the signing of the treaty of union between Libya and Morocco in August. In July 1985 the joint Libyan-Moroccan assembly passed a resolution calling for the 'liberation' of Ceuta and Melilla.

Details of Ceuta and Melilla's new draft statutes, envisaging the establishment of two local assemblies, with jurisdiction over such matters as public works, agriculture, tourism, culture and internal trade, were approved by the central Government in December 1985. Unlike Spain's other regional assemblies, however, those of Ceuta and Melilla were not to be vested with legislative powers. After negotiations with representatives of the Muslim community, in May 1986 the central Government agreed to grant Spanish nationality to more than 2,400 Muslims resident in the enclaves. At the general election held in June the ruling Partido Socialista Obrero Español (PSOE) was successful in Ceuta.

In February 1988 it was announced that, in accordance with regulations of the European Community (EC, now European Union—EU, see p. 244), to which Spain had acceded in 1986, Moroccan citizens would in due course require visas to enter Spain. Entry to Spanish North Africa, however, was to be exempt from the new ruling.

In March 1988, after several months of negotiations, the central Government and principal opposition parties in Madrid reached a broad consensus on draft autonomy statutes for Spanish North Africa. Although it was envisaged that Spain would retain the territories, the possibility of a negotiated settlement with Morocco was not discounted. In July, seven years after the enclaves' first official request for autonomy, the central Government announced that the implementation of the territories' autonomy statutes was to be accelerated. Meanwhile, in October Morocco's Minister of Foreign Affairs formally presented his country's claim to Ceuta and Melilla to the UN General Assembly. In 1989 Spain and Morocco agreed to hold annual summit meetings in an effort to improve relations. At the general election held in October 1989 the ruling PSOE retained its Ceuta seats, despite allegations by the opposition Partido Popular (PP) that many names on the electoral register were duplicated.

In April 1990 the Spanish Government presented the autonomy statutes for discussion in the territories. It was confirmed that the enclaves were to remain an integral part of Spain, and that they were to be granted self-government at municipal, rather than regional, level. Moroccan political parties were united in their denunciation of what they considered an attempt to legalize Spanish possession of the territories. The draft autonomy statutes of Ceuta and Melilla were submitted to the Congreso de los Diputados (Congress of Deputies) in Madrid for discussion in October 1991. In November thousands of demonstrators, many of whom had travelled from the enclaves, attended a protest march in Madrid (organized by the Governments of Ceuta and Melilla), in support of demands for full autonomy for the territories. In early 1992, however, the central Government confirmed that the assemblies of Ceuta and Melilla were not to be granted full legislative powers. At the general election of June 1993 the PSOE of Ceuta lost its one seat in the Congreso and its two seats in the Senado (Senate) to the PP.

The final statutes of autonomy were approved by the Spanish Government in September 1994, in preparation for their presentation to the Cortes (parliament). The statutes provided for 25-member local assemblies with powers similar to those of the municipal councils of mainland Spain. Each assembly would elect from among its members a city president. The proposals for limited self-government were not well received in Ceuta where, in October, a general strike received widespread support, while demonstrations subsequently took place in both Ceuta and Madrid. Following their approval by the Congreso de los Diputados in December, the autonomy statutes were ratified by the Senado in February 1995. Approval of the statutes by the Spanish Cortes was denounced by Morocco, which declared that the recovery of Ceuta and Melilla was to be one of its major objectives.

Elections for the new local assemblies were held in May 1995. In Ceuta the PP won nine of the 25 seats, Progreso y Futuro de Ceuta (PFC) six, the nationalist Ceuta Unida (CEU) four and the PSOE three. Basilio Fernández López of the PFC was re-elected Mayor/President, heading a coalition with CEU and the PSOE. Mustafa Mizziam Ammar, leader of the Partido Democrático y Social de Ceuta (PDSC), became the first Muslim candidate ever to be elected in the territory.

In February 1996 the Spanish and Moroccan Prime Ministers met in Rabat, Morocco, for their first summit meeting since December 1993. At the general election held in March 1996 the three PP delegates to the Cortes in Madrid were re-elected. In July Mayor/President Fernández López resigned after seven months at the head of a minority administration, and was replaced by Jesús Fortes Ramos of the PP, who urged that the enclave be considered a fully autonomous region.

In mid-1996 attention focused once again on the issue of illegal immigration from Africa. Both Ceuta and Melilla appealed to the EU for financial assistance to counter the problems arising from the enclaves' attractive location as an entry point to Europe and from the recent implementation of the EU's Schengen Agreement permitting the free movement of persons among the accord's signatory countries. Negotiations in Madrid in October between the Spanish Minister of the Interior and his Moroccan counterpart resulted in an agreement on the establishment of two joint commissions to address the specific problems of illegal immigration and drugs-trafficking. At further discussions in December, for the first time since the signing of a joint accord in 1992, Morocco agreed to the readmission of illegal immigrants held in the Spanish enclaves. In September the Secretary-General of the North Atlantic Treaty Organization (NATO) confirmed that Ceuta and Melilla would remain outside the alliance's sphere of protection if Spain were to be fully integrated into NATO's military structure.

At the elections of June 1999 the most successful party was the Grupo Independiente Liberal (GIL), which secured 12 of the 25 seats in the Assembly. Antonio Sampietro Casarramona of the GIL replaced Jesús Fortes Ramos of the PP as Mayor/President in August, following the latter's removal from office by a motion of censure supported by a rebel PSOE deputy, Susana Bermúdez. The defection to the GIL of the socialist deputy was ostensibly due to the PSOE's apparent refusal to allocate her the education and culture portfolio, as desired. The authorities subsequently announced that a judicial inquiry into the defection of Bermúdez was to be conducted. Both the PSOE and the PP accused the GIL of having bribed the deputy to transfer her allegiance. In March 2000 Sampietro and Bermúdez were charged with bribery. At the general election held on 12 March Ceuta's three PP representatives in Madrid, one deputy and two senators, all secured re-election.

In early 1999 it was conceded that the security barrier along Ceuta's border with Morocco was proving inadequate. The EU-funded project had been initiated five years previously but remained unfinished. Between January and July alone a total of 21,411 illegal immigrants were apprehended on Ceuta's frontier and returned to Morocco. In November border security was reinforced by the army. Further improvements to the barrier were completed in February 2000. The implementation in that month of new legislation relating to immigrants' rights obliged the border post at Ceuta to provide legal assistance to those being denied entry to Spain by the police. In May the Government of Ceuta estimated that more than 25,000 potential immigrants, mainly Moroccans, were concentrated on the north African coast, awaiting an opportunity to travel to southern Spain. It was also revealed that during 1999 a total of 700,000 illegal immigrants had been refused admission to Spanish North Africa.

In Morocco, meanwhile, King Hassan died in July 1999. In January 2000 Prime Minister José María Aznar visited Ceuta and Melilla (although in his capacity as President of the PP, rather than President of the Government), describing the enclaves as constant parts of Spain's future. Morocco subsequently cancelled a scheduled official visit of the Spanish Minister of Foreign Affairs (although the official reason given by the Moroccan authorities for the cancellation was that King Muhammad was on holiday). In May Aznar declared that the controversial immigration law, which had taken effect in February, would need to be reviewed, as, since its entry into force, more than 82,000 immigrants had applied for Spanish residency permits. Large numbers of immigrants continued to enter the two enclaves illegally throughout 2000, and further clashes between migrants and the security forces were reported. The immigration law reforms, which entered into force in January 2001, intended to assist those seeking asylum but offered severe penalties to illegal immigrants and to traffickers in and employers of illegal immigrants. Protests against the reforms were staged in Spanish North Africa, as in Spain.

In September 2000, following a ruling in the Spanish courts that Ceuta and Melilla could not be considered to be autonomous communities, the ruling GIL proposed in the Ceuta Assembly that the Spanish Government grant Ceuta greater autonomy. Discussions on the proposal, which proved highly emotive, led to disturbances within the Assembly. However, the motion was subsequently carried by a majority vote.

In January 2001 five Ceuta councillors resigned their posts and announced their departure from the GIL, thus depriving the party of its majority in the Assembly. Former PSOE deputy Bermúdez subsequently withdrew her support for the GIL, which had previously enabled the party to assume office. A motion of censure against Sampietro, proposed by the PP, the PSOE, the PDSC and one of the former GIL councillors, was carried in February, with the support of 17 of the 25 deputies, and Juan Jesús Vivas Lara of the PP was appointed Mayor/President. A new Council was subsequently announced, including the five 'rebel' councillors (now members of the Grupo Mixto). The Vice-President of the Council, Jesús Simarro Marín, resigned in July; Cristina Bernal Durán was appointed to replace him.

The Government announced in September 2001 that the identification papers of Moroccans wishing to enter Ceuta and Melilla would be examined more closely and increased the police presence at the frontiers. In August the human rights organization Amnesty International had accused the Spanish Government of the systematic abuse of the rights of homeless children from Morocco and Algeria, citing Melilla and Ceuta as regions where the worst offences occurred.

Relations with Morocco remained tense in late 2001, especially following that country's abrupt withdrawal of its ambassador from Madrid in October. A confrontation developed between Moroccan and Spanish police in December when the Spanish authorities attempted to seize a vessel, allegedly laden with narcotics, which the Moroccans had already been pursuing through their own waters. Relations were threatened again in July 2002, after the occupation of Perejil, a small islet near Ceuta, by 12 Moroccan soldiers. Madrid made a formal protest to Rabat on 12 July, but Morocco refused to withdraw its men, claiming that Perejil (known as Laila to the Moroccans) had been a part of Morocco since independence in 1956. Four Spanish gunboats were dispatched to patrol the locality and Spanish soldiers reoccupied the island on 17 July. A subsequent US-mediated arrangement resulted in agreement by both countries to leave the islet unoccupied. However, in September Morocco reasserted its claims to Ceuta and Melilla at the UN. Later in the month Morocco additionally accused Spain of violating its airspace and territorial waters more than 90 times since July, and cancelled a scheduled meeting with Spain in protest against the alleged landing of a Spanish military helicopter on Perejil; Spain denied the claim. In response to several border incidents and in an attempt to halt illegal immigration, Spain ordered the permanent closure of the border with Morocco at Benzu in October.

A bilateral immigration accord signed by Spain and Morocco in February 2003 proposed the repatriation to Morocco of 200 illegal immigrant minors from Ceuta and Melilla in March. Early 2003 saw an increase in measures to strengthen border security. Moreover, a series of suicide bombings launched against Western targets in Casablanca in May, killing up to 45 people, resulted in a further tightening of border security. It was believed that one of the leaders of the militant Islamist group thought to be responsible for the attacks was a resident of Ceuta, and that others involved in the bombings had subsequently fled to mainland Spain via Ceuta. In June the Spanish Government's delegate in Ceuta initiated a request to the Ministry of Foreign Affairs in Madrid to withdraw citizenship from any dual-nationals in the enclave who were proven criminals, members of fundamentalist groups or pro-Moroccan. At the regional elections held in May 2003 the PP achieved an absolute majority in Ceuta for the first time, winning 19 out of 25 seats, while the Unión Demócrata Ceutí (UDCE), which represented the Muslim population, secured three. Juan Jesús Vivas Lara remained as Mayor/President.

In September 2003 Aznar visited Morocco for bilateral discussions, although the issue of sovereignty over Spain's North African possessions was reportedly avoided. In 2003 it was estimated that around 3,000 immigrants passed through Ceuta, and the enclave received more than 1,400 asylum requests, compared with 372 in 2002 and 82 in 2001. Official figures stated that 18% of the requests processed in 2003 were successful. In December 2003 Morocco and Spain made progress towards reaching an accord on the repatriation of illegal immigrant minors; however, a final agreement was not signed. Human rights groups criticized the two centres provided by the Spanish Government for immigrants as inadequate.

At the general election held on 14 March 2004 the PP retained the deputy and senators elected by Ceuta. In September the Mayor/President, Vivas Lara, met with the newly elected Spanish Prime Minister, José Luis Rodríguez Zapatero, to discuss the possible change in status of Ceuta from Ciudad Autónoma (Autonomous City) to Comunidad Autónoma (Autonomous Community), in line with other areas of Spain. In that year the height of the barrier separating Ceuta and Morocco reached 6 m. In November the central Government unveiled plans to build reception centres for immigrants on the mainland, to which illegal immigrants arrested in Ceuta and Melilla would be transported.

In 2005 potential immigrants continued to attempt to gain access to Europe through Ceuta and Melilla, with a succession of groups of would-be immigrants attempting to scale the walls separating the enclaves from Morocco. In September five would-be immigrants were killed by security forces during an attempt by some 600 people to climb the wall into Ceuta. It was announced at a Spanish-Moroccan summit held in late September in Seville, Spain, that security on both sides of the border would be increased following the attempts; however, the waves of immigration continued in early October, and more deaths resulted. Concern arose that immigrants captured by Moroccan security forces were being abandoned in Morocco's south-western desert. In October the Spanish Government authorized €3m. to improve facilities for immigrants in the enclaves. Heightened security reduced the number of attempts being made to climb the walls, but it appeared that immigrants were looking for new (and potentially more dangerous) routes to Europe via the Canary Islands.

In October 2005 the Congreso de los Diputados in Madrid re-affirmed the integral Spanish nature of the enclaves. In early 2006 Zapatero made the first official visit by a Prime Minister to the enclaves in over 25 years. His visit was condemned by the Moroccan authorities as a provocation, despite the fact that relations between Spain and Morocco had been favourable during the first two years of Zapatero's administration, with increasing co-operation on immigration issues. In May the Councillor of Development, Elena Sánchez, died suddenly. She was replaced by Juan António Rodríguez Ferrón, hitherto Councillor of the Interior. In the same month the Government Delegate in Ceuta, Jerónimo Nieto, was replaced by José Jenaro García-Arreciado Batanero.

In February 2007 the Spanish Government reached an agreement with the Governments of Ceuta and Melilla to abandon plans to change the cities' status to that of Autonomous Communities. In return, more powers would be devolved to the cities in the areas of employment and social services, and their budgets would be increased. At elections held on 27 May the PP retained its absolute majority in the Assembly, again winning 19 of the 25 seats; the UDCE, in alliance with the left-wing Izquierda Unida, secured four seats, while the PSOE won two. Vivas Lara resumed office as Mayor/President. The entire regional executive of the PSOE, headed by Secretary-General Antonia Palomo, resigned as a result of the party's poor performance in the elections. A temporary management committee was appointed pending the organization of a congress to elect a new Secretary-General, but in October ongoing divisions within the local branch of the PSOE led to its dissolution. The national leadership of the party delegated a commission to assume temporary responsibility for PSOE activities in Ceuta.

In early November 2007 a two-day visit to Ceuta and Melilla by King Juan Carlos, his first since acceding to the throne in 1975, was warmly welcomed by residents, but provoked considerable anger in Morocco. The Moroccan Government recalled its ambassador from Madrid for consultations ahead of the visit, which it deemed regrettable and provocative. The Spanish Prime Minister sought to defuse tensions, insisting that relations with Morocco, which had improved in recent years, remained strong. However, Morocco's King Muhammad VI noted that Spain risked jeopardizing bilateral relations, and urged Spain to engage in dialogue with Morocco over the disputed enclaves. Later in November the Moroccan Government postponed a planned visit to Rabat by the Spanish Minister of Development. The Moroccan ambassador to Spain returned to Madrid in January 2008, following a visit to Rabat by the Spanish Minister of Foreign Affairs and Co-operation, Miguel Ángel Moratinos, who delivered a conciliatory letter from Prime Minister Zapatero to King Muhammad.

At the general election held on 9 March 2008 the PP retained Ceuta's one seat in the Congreso de los Diputados and its two seats in the Senado. In April the Government of Ceuta opposed plans to reorganize the Spanish armed forces, amid fears that they would result in a substantial reduction in the number of troops stationed in the city. However, the central Government rejected this suggestion, insisting that the composition of the forces deployed in its North African territories would change, but that it did not intend to reduce overall numbers.

Government

Following the adoption of statutes of autonomy and the establishment of local assemblies in 1995, Ceuta and Melilla remain integral parts of Spain, but have greater jurisdiction over matters such as public works, internal trade and tourism. Each enclave has its own Mayor/President. Ceuta, Melilla and the island dependencies are known as *plazas de soberanía*, fortified enclaves over which Spain has full sovereign rights. In both Ceuta and Melilla civil authority is vested in an official (Delegado del Gobierno) directly responsible to the Ministry of the Interior in Madrid. This official is usually assisted by a government sub-delegate. There is also one delegate from each of the Ministries in Madrid.

Defence

Military authority is vested in a commandant-general. The enclaves are attached to the military region of Seville. Spain had 8,100 troops deployed in its North African territories in August 2003.

Economic Affairs

In 2005 the gross domestic product (GDP) of Ceuta was equivalent to €18,860 per head, ranking 12th (in terms of GDP per head) in a list of the 19 Spanish autonomous regions. According to preliminary official estimates, total GDP was €1,578.1m. in 2007. The population of Ceuta and Melilla together increased by an annual average of 0.5% in 1996–2006, while GDP for Ceuta alone grew by 3.5% during 2000–07; GDP increased, in real terms, by an estimated 3.9% in 2007.

Agricultural activity in Ceuta is negligible; according to preliminary estimates, the sector contributed just 0.3% of GDP in 2007. Agricultural GDP decreased, in real terms, by an annual average of 3.0% during 2000–07; the sector's GDP increased by an estimated 0.9% in 2007. In the first quarter of 2006 the economically active population totalled 32,100, of whom 2,700 were employed in industry (including 1,800 in construction) and 20,700 were engaged in employment in the services sector; 8,600 were unemployed.

Industry is on a limited scale (although there is a local brewery), but the sector contributed 15.0% of GDP in 2007, and 11.5% of the employed population were engaged in the sector, on average, during the first quarter of 2008. Manufacturing GDP increased, in real terms, by an annual average of 1.8% during 2000–07; the GDP of the manufacturing sector increased by 3.2% in 2007.

Services contributed an estimated 84.8% of GDP in 2007, and some 88.9% of the employed population were engaged in the sector, on average, in the first quarter of 2008. Services GDP increased, in real terms, by an annual average of 3.2% during 2000–07; the sector's GDP increased by 4.4% in 2007.

Most of the population's food is imported, with the exception of fish, which is obtained locally (sardines and anchovies are among the most significant catches). A large proportion of the tinned fish is sold outside Spain. More important to the economies of Ceuta and Melilla is the port activity; most of their exports take the form of fuel supplied—at very competitive rates—to ships. Most of the fuel comes from the Spanish refinery in Tenerife. Ceuta's port received a total of 8,506 ships in 2005. The main exports are frozen and preserved fish, foodstuffs and beer. Most trade is conducted with other parts of Spain. In 2004 Ceuta's trade deficit was €25,087m. Tourism makes a significant contribution to the territory's economy. In 2004 68,205 tourists visited Ceuta, attracted by duty-free goods. In 2006 604,838 overnight stays were recorded by visitors to Ceuta and Melilla. In 2004 there was an estimated budget surplus of €750,000, equivalent to 0.1% of GDP. The annual rate of inflation averaged 2.9% in 2002–07; the rate was 1.9% in 2007. According to provisional estimates, on average, some 16.8% of the labour force were unemployed during the first quarter of 2008.

Upon the accession in January 1986 of Spain to the European Community (EC, now European Union—EU, see p. 244), Ceuta was considered a Spanish city and therefore as European territory, and joined the organization as part of Spain. It retained its status as a free port. The statute of autonomy, adopted in early 1995, envisaged the continuation of the territory's fiscal benefits. Euro notes and coins became the sole legal tender on 28 February 2002.

Sustained Spanish economic growth in the 2000s and successive enlargements of the EU that took place during that decade limited Spain's access to EU aid, with the result that, although income in the enclave had not improved significantly, subsidies for Ceuta would be progressively reduced during the period 2007–13, with a view to their eventual withdrawal. The city's consolidated budget for 2007 included current and capital transfers from the Spanish state of €57.8m and €22.7m., respectively. Ceuta's economy relies heavily on a transient Moroccan work-force; unofficial estimates of unemployment among Ceuta's permanent residents suggest a rate of some 35%, the highest in Spain.

Education

The education system is similar to that of mainland Spain; however, there are also teachers of the Islamic religion in the city.

Statistical Survey

Sources (unless otherwise stated): Administración General del Estado, Beatriz de Silva 4, 51001 Ceuta; tel. (956) 512616; fax (956) 511893; Instituto Nacional de Estadística, Paseo de la Castellana 183, 28071 Madrid; tel. (91) 5839100; fax (91) 5839158; internet www.ine.es; *Memoria Socioeconómico y Laboral de 2004:* Consejo Económico y Social, Edif. La Tahoma, Esquina Salud Tejero y Dueñas, Ceuta; tel. (956) 519131; fax (956) 519146; e-mail ces-ceuta@ceuta.es.

AREA AND POPULATION

Area: 19.7 sq km (7.6 sq miles).

Population (census results): 67,615 at 1 March 1991; 71,505 at 1 November 2001 (males 35,991, females 35,514). *2008* (official estimate at 1 January): 71,989 (males 36,008, females 35,981).

Density (1 January 2008): 3,654 per sq km.

Births, Marriages and Deaths (2006): Live births 1,041 (birth rate 14.6 per 1,000); Marriages 325 (marriage rate 4.5 per 1,000); Deaths 479 (death rate 6.7 per 1,000).

Expectation of Life (years at birth): Total 78.6 (males 75.7; females 81.6) in 2005.

Immigration and Emigration (2006): Immigrants 640; Emigrants 113.

Economically Active Population ('000 persons aged 16 years and over, January–March 2008, estimates): Agriculture, hunting, forestry and fishing 0.0; Construction 1.9; Other industry 1.0; Services 22.4; *Total employed* 25.2; Unemployed 5.1; *Total labour force* 30.3.

AGRICULTURE, ETC.

Livestock (animals slaughtered, 2004): Sheep 1,025; Goats 108.

Fishing (metric tons, live weight of catch): 304.1 in 2002; 310.8 in 2003; 236.8 in 2004.

FINANCE

Currency and Exchange Rates: 100 cent = 1 euro (€). *Sterling and Dollar Equivalents* (31 December 2007): £1 Sterling = 1.3609 euros; US $1 = 0.6793 euros; 10 euros = £7.35 = $14.72. *Average Exchange Rate* (euros per US $): 0.8041 in 2005; 0.7971 in 2006; 0.7306 in 2007. Note: The local currency was formerly the Spanish peseta. From the introduction of the euro, with Spanish participation, on 1 January 1999, a fixed exchange rate of €1 = 166.386 pesetas was in effect. Euro notes and coins were introduced on 1 January 2002. The euro and local currency circulated alongside each other until 28 February, after which the euro became the sole legal tender.

Budget (€ '000, 2004): *Revenue:* Current operations 170,621.8 (Direct taxation 6,397.6, Indirect taxation 90,247.4, Rates and other revenue 14,342.8, Current transfers 54,106.2, Estate taxes 5,527.7); Capital operations 49,002.7 (Capital transfers 31,715.2, Transfers of

SPANISH EXTERNAL TERRITORIES

real investments 3,073.4, Assets 704.3, Liabilities 13,509.7); Total 219,624.5. *Expenditure:* Current operations 153,214.7 (Wages and salaries 74,948.9, Goods and services 55,016.6, Financial 3,561.4, Current transfers 19,687.8); Capital operations 65,659.8 (Real investments 53,365.5, Capital transfers 0.0, Assets 1,705.0, Liabilities 10,589.2); Total 218,874.5.

Cost of Living (Consumer Price Index; base: 2006 = 100): All items 94.5 in 2004; 96.9 in 2005; 101.9 in 2007.

Gross Domestic Product (€ million, provisional): 1,356.5 in 2005; 1,469.6 in 2006; 1,578.1 in 2007.

Gross Domestic Product by Economic Activity (€ million, 2007, provisional): Agriculture, hunting, forestry and fishing 3.7; Energy 60.0; Construction 114.9; Other industry 37.0; Services 1,198.6; *Subtotal* 1,414.2; Net taxes on products 163.9; *GDP at market prices* 1,578.1.

EXTERNAL TRADE

Principal Commodities (€ '000, 2004): *Imports:* Fuel, lubricants, etc. 29,859; Milk and dairy products 29,797; Textile and clothing 34,706; Transport vehicles 10,023; Total (incl. others) 191,145. *Exports:* Machines 21; Transport vehicles 4; Total 166,058.

Principal Trading Partners: *Imports* (percentage of total imports, 2000): People's Republic of China 22.1; Germany 5.5; Indonesia 4.5; Italy 14.0; Netherlands 10.1; Russia 4.4; Republic of Korea 13.4; United Kingdom 3.7. *Exports:* In 2001 the most important export partners were the Republic of Korea, Morocco, Japan, China and Argentina.

TRANSPORT

Road Traffic (Ceuta and Melilla, 2005): Vehicles registered 97,174 (Passenger cars 71,575, Buses, etc. 119, Lorries 14,435, Motorcycles 9,466, Tractors 180, Other 1,399).

Shipping (2005): Vessels entered 8,506 (48,044,942 grt); Goods handled 1,543,459 metric tons; Passenger movements 2,154,632.

Civil Aviation (2006, preliminary): Journeys made 2,343; Passengers carried ('000) 21; Goods transported 3 metric tons.

TOURISM

Visitor Arrivals (by country of residence, 2002): France 2,653; Germany 700; Italy 1,076; Portugal 1,062; Spain 41,593; United Kingdom 1,430; USA 2,939; Total (incl. others) 61,356. *2004:* Foreign visitors 17,243; Spanish visitors 50,962; Total visitors 68,205. *2006* (Ceuta and Melilla): 604,838 overnight stays.

COMMUNICATIONS MEDIA

Telephones (main lines in use, 2004): 24,849.

EDUCATION
(2005/06)

Pre-primary: 24 schools; 149 teachers; 2,961 students.

Primary: 22 schools; 411 teachers (excl. 42 engaged in both pre-primary and primary teaching); 5,948 students.

Secondary: First Cycle: 16 schools (of which 6 schools also provided second-cycle education and 5 provided vocational education, see below); 209 teachers (excl. 34 engaged in both secondary and primary teaching and 234 engaged in more than one cycle of secondary); 3,874 students.

Secondary: Second Cycle: 34 teachers; 1,298 students.

Secondary: Vocational: 83 teachers; 970 students.

Source: Ministry of Education and Science, Madrid.

Directory

Government

Government Delegate in Ceuta: JOSÉ JENARO GARCÍA-ARRECIADO BATANERO.

Deputy elected to the Congress in Madrid: FRANCISCO ANTONIO GONZÁLEZ PÉREZ (PP).

Representatives to the Senate in Madrid: NICOLÁS FERNÁNDEZ CUCURULL (PP), LUZ ELENA SANÍN NARANJO (PP).

COUNCIL OF GOVERNMENT
(April 2008)

Mayor/President: JUAN JESÚS VIVAS LARA.

Vice-President and Councillor of the Presidency: PEDRO GORDILLO DURÁN.

Councillor of Development: JUAN MANUEL DONCEL DONCEL.

Councillor of the Economy and Employment: GUILLERMO MARTÍNEZ ARCAS.

Councillor of Education, Culture and Women: MARÍA ISABEL DEU DEL OLMO.

Councillor of the Environment and Urban Services: YOLANDA BEL BLANCA.

Councillor of Health and Consumer Affairs: ADELA MARÍA NIETO SÁNCHEZ.

Councillor of the Interior: JOSÉ ANTONIO RODRÍGUEZ GÓMEZ.

Councillor of Finance: FRANCISCO MÁRQUEZ DE LA RUBIA.

Councillor of Social Affairs: CAROLINA PÉREZ GÓMEZ.

Councillor of Youth, Sports and New Technology: KISSY CHANDIRAMANI RAMESH.

GOVERNMENT OFFICES

Delegación del Gobierno: Beatriz de Silva 4, 51001 Ceuta; tel. (956) 984400; fax (956) 513671; e-mail roberto@ceuta.map.es.

Office of the Mayor/President: Plaza de Africa s/n, Asamblea, 1°, 51001 Ceuta; tel. and fax (956) 528309; e-mail presidencia@ceuta.es; internet www.ceuta.es.

Council of Development: Plaza de Africa s/n, Asamblea, 3°, 51001 Ceuta; tel. and fax (956) 528240; e-mail fomento@ceuta.es.

Council of the Economy and Employment: Edif. Ceuta Center, 1°, 51001 Ceuta; tel. and fax (956) 528262; e-mail economia@ceuta.es.

Council of Education, Culture and Women: Plaza de Africa s/n, Asamblea, 2°, 51001 Ceuta; tel. and fax (956) 528166; e-mail educacion@ceuta.es.

Council of the Environment and Urban Services: Plaza de Africa s/n, Asamblea, 3°, 51001 Ceuta; tel. and fax (956) 528164; e-mail medioambiente@ceuta.es; internet www.ceuta.es/medioambiente.

Council of Finance: Edif. Ceuta Center, 51001 Ceuta; e-mail hacienda@ceuta.es.

Council of Health and Consumer Affairs: Carretera San Amaro 12, Ceuta; tel. and fax (856) 200680; fax (856) 200723; e-mail sanidad@ceuta.es; internet www.ceuta.es:8080/sanidad.

Council of the Interior: Edif. Polifuncional, Avda España, 51001 Ceuta; tel. (956) 528076.

Council of Social Affairs: Carretera San Amaro 12, Ceuta; tel. (856) 200680; fax (856) 200723.

Council of Youth, Sports and New Technologies: Avda de Africa s/n, Ceuta; tel. (956) 518844; fax (956) 510295.

Assembly

Election, 27 May 2007

	Seats
Partido Popular (PP)	19
Unión Demócrata Ceutí (UDCE)-Izquierda Unida (IU)	4
Partido Socialista Obrero Español (PSOE)	2
Total	**25**

Election Commission

Junta Electoral de Zona y Provincial de Ceuta: Ceuta; Sec. FRANCISCO JAVIER IZQUIERDO CARBONERO.

Political Organizations

Izquierda Unida (IU): General Yaque, 4-1°, 11701 Ceuta; tel. and fax (956) 513558; e-mail izquierdaunidaceuta@hotmail.com; internet www.izquierda-unida.es; alliance of left-wing parties; Leader MOHAMMED HADDU MUSA.

Partido Democrático y Social de Ceuta (PDSC): Bolivia 35, 51001 Ceuta; Muslim party; Leader MUSTAFA MIZZIAM AMMAR.

Partido Popular (PP): Teniente Arrabal 4, Edif. Ainara, Bajo, 51001 Ceuta; tel. (956) 518139; fax (956) 513218; e-mail ceutapp@ceutapp.com; internet www.ceutapp.com; fmrly Alianza Popular; national-level, centre-right party; Pres. Pedro Gordillo Durán; Sec.-Gen. María Dolores Pastilla.

Partido Socialista Obrero Español (PSOE): Daóiz 1, 51001 Ceuta; tel. (956) 515553; internet www.ceuta.psoe.es; national-level, left-wing party; in Oct. 2007 the federal executive of the PSOE dissolved the local branch of the party and delegated a commission to assume temporary responsibility for its activities in Ceuta; Pres. of the Delegate Commission of the Federal Executive Salvador de la Encina.

Partido Socialista del Pueblo de Ceuta (PSPC): Echegarray 1, Local 1D, 51001 Ceuta; tel. and fax (956) 518869; e-mail pspc@pspc.info; internet www.pspc.es; f. 1986 by dissident members of PSOE and others; Sec.-Gen. Iván Chaves.

Unión Demócrata Ceutí (UDCE): Avda Teniente-Coronel Gautier 22, 2° dcha, Ceuta; Muslim party; Leader Muhammad Alí.

There are also various civic associations.

Judicial System

Tribunal Superior de Justicia de Andalucía, Ceuta y Melilla: Plaza Nueva, 10, Palacio de la Real Chancillería, 18071 Granada, Spain; tel. (958) 002600; fax (958) 002720; e-mail webmaster.ius@juntadeandalucia.es; internet www.juntadeandalucia.es; Pres. Augusto Méndez de Lugo y López de Ayala.

Religion

CHRISTIANITY

The Roman Catholic Church

Bishop of Cádiz and Ceuta: Antonio Ceballos Atienza (resident in Cádiz), Vicar-General Francisco Correro Tocón, Obispado de Ceuta, Plaza de Nuestra Señora de Africa, 51001 Ceuta; tel. (956) 517732; fax (956) 513208; e-mail obispadoceuta@planalfa.es; internet www.obispadodecadizyceuta.org.

OTHER RELIGIONS

Ceuta has a large Muslim population (estimated at around 30,000), as well as Jewish and Hindu communities.

The Press

El Faro de Ceuta: Sargento Mena 8, 51001 Ceuta; tel. (956) 524148; fax (956) 524147; e-mail ceuta@grupofaro.es; internet www.elfaroceutamelilla.es; f. 1934; morning; Pres. Rafael Montero Palacios; Editors-in-Chief José M. Gallardo, Tamara Crespo; circ. 5,000.

El Pueblo de Ceuta: Independencia 11, 1°, 51001 Ceuta; tel. (956) 514367; fax (956) 517650; e-mail elpuebloredaccion@telefonica.net; internet www.elpueblodeceuta.es; f. 1995; daily; Dir and Editor-in-Chief Salvador Vivancos Canales.

NEWS AGENCY

Agencia EFE: Milán Astray 1, 1°, Of. 8, 51001 Ceuta; tel. (956) 517550; fax (956) 516639; e-mail ceuta@agenciaefe.net; Correspondent Rafael Peña Soler.

PRESS ASSOCIATION

Asociación de la Prensa: Beatriz de Silva 14, 1° E, 51001 Ceuta; fax (956) 528205; Pres. Francisco Ruiz Jiménez Carmona.

Broadcasting

RADIO

Onda Cero Radio Ceuta: Delgado Serrano 1, 1° dcha, 51001 Ceuta; tel. (956) 200068; fax (956) 200179; internet www.ondacero.es; Dir Rafael Romaguera Mena.

Radio Televisión Ceuta: Real 90, Portón 4, 1° dcha, 51001 Ceuta; tel. (956) 511820; fax (956) 516820; internet www.rtvce.es; f. 1934; commercial; owned by Sociedad Española de Radiodifusión; Dir Antonio Rosa Guerrero.

Radio Nacional de España: Real 90, 51001 Ceuta; tel. (956) 524688; fax (956) 519067; internet www.rtve.es; Dir Eduardo Sánchez Dorado.

Radio Popular de Ceuta/COPE: Sargento Mena 8, 1°, 11701 Ceuta; tel. (956) 524200; fax (956) 524202; Dir Daniel Oliva.

TELEVISION

Radio Televisión Ceuta: Real 90, Portón 4, 1° dcha, 51001 Ceuta; tel. (956) 511820; fax (956) 516820; internet www.rtvce.es; Dir Manuel González Bolorino.

Finance

BANKING

In 2007 there were nine banks operating in Ceuta, all of which were based in mainland Spain.

Banco Bilbao Vizcaya Argentaria (BBVA): Plaza de los Reyes s/n, 51001 Ceuta; tel. (956) 510415; internet www.bbva.es; 4 brs.

Banco de España: Plaza de España 2, 51001 Ceuta; tel. (956) 513253; fax (956) 513108; internet www.bde.es.

Banco Español de Crédito (Banesto): Camoens 5, 51001 Ceuta; tel. (956) 524028; internet www.banesto.es.

Banco Popular Español: Paseo del Revellín 1, 51001 Ceuta; tel. (956) 515340; fax (956) 512970; internet www.bancopopular.es.

Banco Santander Central Hispano (BSCH): Paseo del Revellín 17–19, 51001 Ceuta; tel. (956) 511371; internet www.gruposantander.es; 2 brs.

Caja de Ahorros y Pensiones de Barcelona (La Caixa): Gran Vía s/n, 51001 Ceuta; tel. (956) 515886; fax (956) 513972; internet www.lacaixa.es; 4 brs.

Caja Duero: Sargento Coriat 5, 51001 Ceuta; tel. (956) 518040; fax (956) 517019; tel. www.cajaduero.es; 1 br.

Caja Madrid: Plaza de los Reyes s/n, 51001 Ceuta; tel. (956) 524016; fax (956) 524017; internet www.cajamadrid.es; 6 brs.

Montes de Piedad y Caja de Ahorros de Ronda, Cádiz, Almería, Málaga y Antequera (Unicaja): Paseo Revellín 21, 51001 Ceuta; tel. (956) 518340; fax (956) 519561; internet www.unicaja.es; 2 brs.

INSURANCE

MAPFRE: Paseo Marina Española 92, Edif. Patio Paramo, 51001 Ceuta; tel. (956) 519638; fax (956) 513916; e-mail balfaro@mapfre.com; internet www.mapfre.com; Commercial Man. Borja Alfaro Infante; 3 offices.

Trade and Industry

Cámara Oficial de Comercio, Industria y Navegación: Dueñas 2, 51001 Ceuta; tel. (956) 509590; fax (956) 509589; e-mail camerceuta@camaras.org; internet www.camaraceuta.org; chamber of commerce; Pres. Luis Moreno Naranjo; Sec.-Gen. María del Rosario Espinosa Suárez.

Confederación de Empresarios de Ceuta: Paseo de las Palmeras, Edif. Corona 26–28, 51001 Ceuta; tel. (856) 200038; e-mail administracion@confeceuta.es; internet www.confeceuta.es; employers' confed.; Pres. Rafael Montero Avalos; Sec.-Gen. Josefa Guerrero Ríos.

UTILITIES

Aguas de Ceuta Empresa Municipal, SA (ACEMSA): Solis 1, Edif. San Luis, Ceuta; tel. (956) 524619; e-mail aguasdeceuta@acemsa.es; internet www.acemsa.es; Pres. Yolanda Bel Blanco; Dir-Gen. Manuel Gómez Hoyos.

Empresa de Alumbrado Eléctrico de Ceuta SA: Beatriz de Silva 2, Ceuta; tel. (956) 511901; e-mail info@electricadeceuta.com; internet www.electricadeceuta.com; generates and transmits electricity; Rep. Alberto Ramón Gaitán Rodríguez.

TRADE UNION

Confederación Sindical de Comisiones Obreras (CCOO): Alcalde Fructuoso Miaja 1, 51001 Ceuta; tel. (956) 516243; fax (956) 517991; e-mail ccoo.ce@ceuta.ccoo.es; internet www.ccoo.es; 3,214 mems (2004); Sec.-Gen. José Luis Aróstegui Ruiz.

Transport

Much of the traffic between Spain and Morocco passes through Ceuta; there are ferry services to Algeciras, Melilla, Málaga and Almería. Plans for an airport are under consideration. Helicopter services to Málaga are provided by Helisureste. There were 28 km of paved roads in Ceuta in 2006. Construction of a highway between the Port of Ceuta and the Moroccan border was due to begin in 2008, with completion planned for 2010. The Port of Ceuta is one of the most important in the Mediterranean. In 2005 1.5m. metric tons of goods, 2.2m. passengers and 8,506 boats passed through the port.

SPANISH EXTERNAL TERRITORIES

Port of Ceuta: Autoridad Portuaria de Ceuta, Muelle de España s/n, 51001 Ceuta; tel. (956) 527000; fax (956) 527001; e-mail apceuta@puertodeceuta.com; internet www.puertodeceuta.com; Pres. JOSÉ FRANCISCO TORRADO LÓPEZ.

Acciona Trasmediterránea: Muelle Cañorero Dato 6, 51001 Ceuta; tel. (956) 505390; fax (956) 504714; e-mail info@trasmediterranea.es; internet www.trasmediterranea.es; f. 1917; services between Algeciras and Ceuta.

Euroferrys: Muelle Cañorero Dato, 51001 Ceuta; tel. (956) 507070; fax (956) 505588; e-mail clientes@euroferrys.com; internet www.euroferrys.com; f. 1998; owned by Acciona Trasmediterránea; passenger and cargo services between Algeciras and Ceuta; Pres. JOAQUÍN GONZÁLEZ SANJUÁN.

Tourism

Visitors are attracted by the historical monuments, the Parque Marítimo and the museums, as well as by the Shrine of Our Lady of Africa. There were 68,205 visitors to Ceuta in 2004, of whom 50,962 were from mainland Spain. In that year Ceuta had five hotels.

Viceconsejería de Turismo de Ceuta: Baluarte de los Mallorquines, Edrissis s/n, 51001 Ceuta; tel. (856) 200560; fax (856) 200565; e-mail turismo@ceuta.es; internet www.ceuta.es.

Patronato Municipal de Turismo: Estación Marítima, Avda Muelle Cañonero Dato s/n, 51001 Ceuta; tel. (956) 506275.

MELILLA

Introductory Survey

Location, Climate, Language, Religion

Melilla is situated on a small peninsula jutting into the Mediterranean Sea. The average temperature is 17°C. Spanish and Arabic are spoken. The majority of Europeans are Roman Catholic, most North Africans being Muslim.

Recent History

The population of Melilla is mostly Spanish. The proportion of Arab residents, however, has greatly increased, owing to the large number of immigrants from Morocco. Those born in the territory are Spanish citizens and subjects. Melilla was the first Spanish town to rise against the Government of the Popular Front in July 1936, at the beginning of the Spanish Civil War. Like Ceuta, Melilla was retained by Spain when Morocco became independent in 1956. In addition to its function as a port, Melilla now serves as a military base, more than one-half of the enclave's land area being used solely for military purposes. In October 1978 King Hassan of Morocco attempted to link the question of the sovereignty of Melilla to that of the return of the British dependent territory of Gibraltar to Spain. (See the chapter on Ceuta for details on Morocco's relationship with Spain and the North African enclaves.)

After negotiations with representatives of the Muslim community, in May 1986 the central Government in Madrid agreed to grant Spanish nationality to more than 2,400 Muslims resident in Melilla and Ceuta, under the terms of legislation introduced in July 1985 requiring all foreigners resident in Spain to register with the authorities. At that time only some 7,000 of the estimated 27,000-strong Muslim community in Melilla held Spanish nationality. In response to protests, particularly in Melilla, the central Government had given assurances that it would assist the full integration into Spanish society of Muslims in the enclaves. By mid-1986, however, the number of Muslims applying for Spanish nationality in Melilla had reached several thousand. As a result of delays in the processing of the applications, Aomar Muhammadi Dudú, the leader of the newly founded Muslim Partido de los Demócratas de Melilla (PDM), accused the Government of failing to fulfil its pledge to the Muslim residents.

At the general election of June 1986 the ruling Partido Socialista Obrero Español (PSOE) was defeated by the centre-right Coalición Popular (CP) in Melilla, the result indicating the strong opposition of the Spanish community to the Government's plan to integrate the Muslim population. Tight security surrounded the elections, and 'parallel elections', resulting in a vote of confidence in the PDM leader, were held by the Muslim community. Polling was accompanied by several days of unrest. Talks in Madrid between representatives of the main political parties in Melilla and the Ministry of the Interior resulted in concessions to the enclave. In September Dudú agreed to accept a senior post in the Ministry, with responsibility for relations with the Muslim communities of Spain. In November, however, Muslim leaders in Melilla announced that they wished to establish their own administration in the enclave, in view of the Madrid Government's failure to fulfil its promise of Spanish citizenship for Muslim residents. The Spanish Minister of the Interior reiterated assurances of the Government's commitment to integrating the Muslim community. Later in the month thousands of Muslims took part in a peaceful demonstration in support of Dudú, who had resigned his Madrid post after only two months in office. (He subsequently went into exile in Morocco and lost the support of Melilla's Muslim community.)

In February 1987 police reinforcements were dispatched from Spain, in response to a serious escalation of inter-racial tensions in Melilla. Numerous demonstrators were detained, and several prominent Muslims were charged with sedition and briefly held in custody. King Hassan reaffirmed his support for the Muslims of the Spanish enclaves.

In March 1988, after several months of negotiations, the central Government and main opposition parties in Madrid reached a broad consensus on draft autonomy statutes for the Spanish External Territories. (See the chapter on Ceuta for details of the statutes.)

At the general election held in October 1989 the election results were declared invalid, following the discovery of serious irregularities. At the repeated ballot, in March 1990, both seats in the Senado (Senate) and the one seat in the Congreso de los Diputados (Congress of Deputies) were won by the Partido Popular (PP), the latter result depriving the PSOE of its overall majority in the Madrid lower chamber. By 1990 almost all residents were in possession of an identity card.

At elections to the municipal council held in May 1991, the PP secured 12 of the 25 seats and Ignacio Velázquez Rivera of the right-wing Partido Nacionalista de Melilla (PNM) was elected Mayor of the enclave, replacing the previous PSOE mayor. At the general election of June 1993 the PSOE candidate defeated the incumbent PP member in the Congreso de los Diputados; the PP also lost one of its two seats in the Senado.

The final statutes of autonomy for Ceuta and Melilla were approved by the Spanish Government in September 1994, in preparation for their presentation to the Cortes (parliament—see the chapter on Ceuta). At elections for the new local assembly, held in May 1995, the level of participation was less than 62%. The PP won 14 of the 25 seats, the PSOE five seats, the Coalición por Melilla (CpM), a new Muslim grouping, four seats and the right-wing Unión del Pueblo Melillense (UPM) two seats. Ignacio Velázquez (PP/PNM) returned to the position of Mayor/President.

At the general election held in March 1996, the PSOE lost its seat in the lower house to the PP, which also took both seats in the Senado. In the same month thousands of Muslims took part in a demonstration, organized by the CpM, to protest against their position on the margins of society.

In March 1997 a motion of censure against Ignacio Velázquez resulted in the Mayor/President's defeat, owing to the defection to the opposition of two PP councillors, Enrique Palacios and Abdelmalik Tahar. The opposition then declared Palacios to be Mayor/President, although the central Government continued to recognize Velázquez as the rightful incumbent. In May, for the first time, the Mayor/Presidents of both Ceuta and Melilla attended a conference of the autonomous regions' presidents, held in Madrid. Despite the attempted 'coup' in Melilla, the territory was represented by Ignacio Velázquez. In November, from Tenerife, Abdelmalik Tahar accused Velázquez and five associates of having subjected him to blackmail and threats, as a result of which he had relinquished his seat on the Council, thereby permitting the PP to replace him and to regain its majority. In December Tahar, who was now under police protection, declared to the investigating judge that he had been offered 50m. pesetas (of which he had received 3m.) and a monthly sum of 200,000 pesetas. Following a judicial ruling leading to the successful revival of the motion of censure against Velázquez in February 1998, Palacios took office as Mayor/President of Melilla, accusing his predecessor of serious financial mismanagement. A new motion of censure, presented by the PP urging that (despite the bribery charges against him) Velázquez be restored to office, was deemed to be illegal and therefore rejected in a decree issued by Palacios, who also ordered the temporary closure of the local assembly. In July Palacios accused the PP of having employed public funds, amounting to more than 200m. pesetas, to secure the votes of some 2,500 Muslims at the 1995 local elections. The allegations were denied by the PP.

During 1997 there was increased concern regarding the numbers of illegal immigrants. In June police reinforcements were drafted into Melilla, following renewed disturbances in which one immigrant died. More than 100 illegal immigrants were immediately returned to Morocco as part of a special security operation, and on the same day a total of 873 Moroccans were denied entry to Melilla. (More than 10,000 Moroccans continued to cross the border legally each day, in order to work in the enclave.) In August the Spanish General Prosecutor demanded emergency measures to address the immigration crisis, having urged the Ministry of the Interior in June to find an immediate solution. In the same month various non-governmental organizations condemned the rudimentary conditions in which more than 900 illegal immigrants, mainly from sub-Saharan Africa and Algeria, were being held in Melilla. In December the Spanish Government announced that 1,206 sub-Saharan Africans were to be transferred from Ceuta and Melilla to the mainland.

In January 1999, after 12 years' exile in Morocco, Aomar Muhammadi Dudú, the former Muslim leader, returned to Melilla, in preparation for the local elections to be held in June. At the elections the Grupo Independiente Liberal (GIL), recently founded by Jesús Gil, the controversial Mayor of Marbella, Spain, secured seven of the 25 seats in the assembly of Melilla. In July the two newly elected PSOE councillors defied a central directive to vote with the five PP delegates (in order to obstruct the accession of the GIL to the city presidency), and instead gave their support to Mustafa Aberchán Hamed of the CpM, which had won five seats. The Muslim Aberchán was thus elected to replace Enrique Palacios as Mayor/President of Melilla. In mid-July Aberchán and the GIL agreed to form a minority Government. The two rebel PSOE councillors subsequently relinquished their seats. In October, following a disagreement between the CpM and the GIL, Aberchán was able to reach a broad agreement with members of the PP and UPM, enabling him to remain in office. In November the Melilla branch of the GIL announced that henceforth it was to operate independently of the mainland party. In the same month, a new agreement between Aberchán and the GIL having been concluded, the latter grouping declared its intention to renew its participation in the Government of Melilla. As a result, the socialist councillors withdrew from the administration.

In December 1999 the Mayor/President announced the composition of a new coalition Government, the post of First Vice-President being allocated to Crispin Lozano, the local leader of the GIL, while Enrique Palacios of the newly founded Partido Independiente de Melilla (PIM) became Second Vice-President. In the same month Ignacio Velázquez, the former PP Mayor/President, was barred from public office for six years, having been found guilty of neglecting his duty during his tenure of office. The conviction was in respect of an incident in 1992 when Velázquez had convened a session of the Council, which was scheduled to vote on a motion of censure against him, in full knowledge of the fact that at least one member was due to be in Madrid that day, thus rendering any vote invalid. However, he was acquitted of charges of misappropriation of public funds. In May 2000, following the defection to the opposition of two GIL deputies and one UPM representative, Aberchán declared that, despite the Government's loss of its majority, he would not resign. The opposition subsequently announced that they would request a vote of 'no confidence' in Aberchán's Government at the earliest opportunity. Later in the month the national leadership of the PP and the PSOE met in Madrid in an attempt to negotiate a solution to the political crisis in Melilla. The two parties agreed that, if Aberchán's Government were removed from office, they would form a coalition government in partnership with the UPM, whose leader, Juan José Imbroda Ortiz, would be nominated Mayor/President. In early July the remaining five GIL members left the Government and joined the opposition. The opposition subsequently introduced a motion of censure against Aberchán, whom they accused of nepotism, a lack of transparency and of harassment of the opposition. Aberchán, who described the accusations as being racially motivated, announced that the CpM was to withdraw from the legislature. In mid-July some 2,000 Muslim citizens of Melilla demonstrated in support of Aberchán. At the same time Palacios suspended the motion of censure by decree, reportedly without having consulted Aberchán. (Palacios was subsequently barred from public office for seven years, having been found guilty of perversion of the course of justice.) The opposition later successfully overturned the decree in the courts, and the vote on the motion of censure against Aberchán was therefore able to proceed. The motion was adopted in September, with the support of 16 of the 25 deputies, and Imbroda was elected as Mayor/President. In late 2000 four members of the GIL announced their departure from the party. In January 2002 Velázquez resigned as Councillor of the Presidency, after the Supreme Court upheld his 1999 conviction.

At the regional elections held in May 2003 a coalition of the PP and the UPM won 15 seats, with the CpM taking seven. The incumbent Mayor/President, Juan José Imbroda Ortiz, remained in power. The PP's success was, in part, the result of a concerted effort to prevent the perpetuation of unstable government that had characterized the previous four years under the GIL. A rising fear of immigration was another likely factor.

In May 2004 the Government of Melilla announced plans to improve security along the border with Morocco; however, in August, in the first mass entry for three years, approximately 450 people attempted to enter Melilla illegally by climbing the security fence. It was believed that up to 40 people succeeded in entering the territory. At the general election held on 14 March 2004, meanwhile, the PP retained Melilla. In September Juan José Imbroda met the recently elected Spanish Prime Minister, José Luis Rodríguez Zapatero, to discuss the possibility that Melilla would become a 'Comunidad Autónoma' (Autonomous Community), a move that would give legislative powers to the government of the territory. However, in February 2007 the plan was abandoned owing to disagreement over the content of the proposed statute of autonomy; instead, the Spanish Government agreed to devolve more powers to Ceuta and Melilla in the areas of education and social services.

During August–October 2005 increasing numbers of would-be immigrants attempted to scale the security barriers separating Melilla from Morocco, leading to the deaths of a number of people. In early October six potential immigrants were reportedly shot in clashes with Moroccan security forces. It was announced that one barrier would be doubled in height, and that border security would be increased; plans to build a third barrier were unveiled in that month. Meanwhile, the Spanish Government announced funding of €17m. for security in Melilla.

At the local election held on 27 May 2007 the PP (which had absorbed its coalition partner, the UPM) obtained 15 seats in the Assembly, the same number as previously, thereby retaining its overall majority; the CpM and the PSOE each won five seats. The constitution of the Assembly was delayed until early July owing to an appeal against the election result levied by the CpM, which alleged that the PP had engaged in acts of electoral fraud, including the falsification of postal ballots. The appeal was rejected by the Supreme Court of Justice of Andalusia, which ruled that the evidence presented by the CpM was not sufficient to indicate irregularity. Imbroda was subsequently re-elected as Mayor/President.

A two-day visit to Melilla and Ceuta by King Juan Carlos and Queen Sofía in early November 2007 was strongly condemned by the Moroccan authorities (see the chapter on Ceuta). Several thousand Moroccans, including politicians and trade union representatives, took part in a demonstration at the border with Melilla to protest against the presence of the Spanish King. The Government of Melilla issued a statement accusing the Moroccan Government of interfering in Spanish domestic affairs by criticizing the visit.

At the general election held on 9 March 2008 the PP retained Melilla's one seat in the Congreso de los Diputados, although only by a narrow margin, as well as its two seats in the Senado. Later that month Esther Donoso García-Sacristán was appointed as Councillor of Contracting and Heritage to replace María del Carmen Dueñas Martínez, who had been elected to the Senado. In April the Government of Melilla urged the Spanish Ministry of Defence to suspend plans to restructure the armed forces, claiming that they would entail a reduction in the number of troops stationed in the city. However, the central Government maintained that although there would be changes in the composition of the forces deployed in Melilla, overall numbers would not be reduced.

Two suspected Islamist militants were detained in Melilla at the beginning of April 2008, in accordance with international arrest warrants issued by the Moroccan Government over their alleged involvement in terrorist activities, including a series of suicide bombings launched against Western targets in Casablanca in May 2003, in which 45 people died.

Government

See the chapter on Ceuta.

Defence

See the chapter on Ceuta.

Economic Affairs

In 2005 the gross domestic product (GDP) of Melilla was equivalent to €18,304 per head, ranking 14th (in terms of GDP per head) in a list of the 19 Spanish autonomous regions. In 2007, according to preliminary figures, GDP totalled €1,441.4m. The population of Ceuta and Melilla together increased by an annual average of 0.5% in 1996–2006, while in Melilla alone GDP grew by an average of 3.4% per year, in real terms, during 2000–07; real GDP increased by an estimated 3.7% in 2007.

Agricultural activity in Melilla is negligible; according to preliminary estimates, the sector contributed just 0.7% of GDP in 2007. Agricultural GDP decreased, in real terms, by an annual average of 0.8% during 2000–07; however, the sector's GDP increased by an estimated 3.0% in 2007.

Although industry is on a limited scale, the sector contributed 14.3% of GDP in 2007, and 10.9% of the employed population were engaged in the sector, on average, during the first quarter of 2008. Manufacturing GDP increased, in real terms, by an annual average of 1.7% during 2000–07; the GDP of the manufacturing sector increased by 3.5% in 2007.

Services contributed an estimated 85.0% of GDP in 2007, and some 89.1% of the employed population were engaged in the sector, on average, in the first quarter of 2008. Services GDP increased, in real terms, by an annual average of 1.0% during 2000–07; the sector's GDP increased by 4.0% in 2007.

Most of the population's food is imported, with the exception of fish, which is obtained locally (sardines and anchovies are among the most significant catches). A large proportion of the tinned fish is sold outside Spain. More important to the economies of Melilla and Ceuta is the port activity; most of their exports take the form of fuel supplied—at very competitive rates—to ships. Most of the fuel comes from the Spanish refinery in Tenerife. Apart from the ferries from Málaga and Almería in mainland Spain, Melilla's port is not busy—a total of 1,077 vessels entered in 2005—and its exports are correspondingly low. Most trade is conducted with other parts of Spain. Tourism makes a significant contribution to the territory's economy. In 2006 604,838 overnight stays were recorded by visitors to Ceuta and Melilla. The annual rate of inflation averaged 3.5% in 2002–07; the rate was 2.7% in 2007. On average, some 22.6% of the labour force were unemployed during the first quarter of 2008.

Upon the accession in January 1986 of Spain to the European Community (EC, now European Union—EU, see p. 244), Melilla was considered a Spanish city and European territory, and joined the organization as part of Spain. It retained its status as a free port. The statute of autonomy, adopted in early 1995, envisaged the continuation of the territory's fiscal benefits. Euro notes and coins became the sole legal tender on 28 February 2002.

In June 1994 the EU announced substantial regional aid: between 1995 and 1999 Melilla was to receive a total of ECU 45m., of which ECU 18m. was to be in the form of direct aid. However, successive enlargements of the EU and sustained Spanish economic growth during the 2000s limited Spain's access to EU aid, with the result that, although income in the enclave had not improved significantly, subsidies for Melilla would be progressively reduced during the period 2007–13, with a view to their eventual withdrawal. The city's consolidated budget for 2007 included current and capital transfers from the Spanish state of €68.3m and €12.5m., respectively.

Education

The education system is similar to that of mainland Spain. In addition to the conventional Spanish facilities, the Moroccan Government finances a school for 600 Muslim children, the languages of instruction being Arabic and Spanish. The curriculum includes Koranic studies. In 1982 only 12% of Muslim children were attending school, but by 1990 the authorities had succeeded in achieving an attendance level of virtually 100%. The open university (Universidad Nacional de Educación a Distancia—UNED) maintains a branch.

The Peñón de Vélez de la Gomera, Peñón de Alhucemas and Chafarinas Islands

These rocky islets, situated, respectively, just west and east of al-Hocima (Alhucemas) and east of Melilla off the north coast of Morocco, are administered with Melilla. The three Chafarinas Islands lie about 3.5 km off Ras el-Ma (Cabo de Agua). The Peñón de Alhucemas is situated about 300 m from the coast. The Peñón de Vélez de la Gomera is situated about 80 km further west, lying 85 m from the Moroccan shore, to which it is joined by a narrow strip of sand. A small military base is maintained on the Peñón de Vélez, while a military garrison of fewer than 100 men is stationed on the Peñón de Alhucemas, and a garrison of about 100 Spanish soldiers is maintained on the Isla del Congreso, the most westerly of the Chafarinas Islands. A supply ship calls at the various islands every two weeks. Prospective visitors must obtain the necessary military permit in Ceuta or Melilla.

Statistical Survey

Source (unless otherwise stated): Instituto Nacional de Estadística, Paseo de la Castellana 183, 28071 Madrid; tel. (91) 5839100; fax (91) 5839158; internet www.ine.es.

AREA AND POPULATION

Area: 12.5 sq km (4.8 sq miles).

Population (census results): 56,600 at 1 March 1991; 66,411 at 1 November 2001 (males 33,224, females 33,187). *2008* (official estimate at 1 January): 69,699 (males 34,396, females 35,303).

Density (1 January 2008): 5,576 per sq km.

Births, Marriages and Deaths (2006): Live births 1,122 (birth rate 16.7 per 1,000); Marriages 400 (marriage rate 6.0 per 1,000); Deaths 454 (death rate 6.8 per 1,000).

Expectation of Life (years at birth): Total 79.3 (males 76.7; females 81.9) in 2005.

Immigration and Emigration (2006): Immigrants 2,111; Emigrants 164.

Economically Active Population ('000 persons aged 16 years and over, January–March 2008, estimates): Agriculture, hunting, forestry and fishing 0.0; Construction 1.5; Other industry 0.9; Services 19.7; *Total employed* 22.1; Unemployed 6.5; *Total labour force* 28.7.

FINANCE

Currency and Exchange Rates: 100 cent = 1 euro (€). *Sterling and Dollar Equivalents* (31 December 2007): £1 Sterling = 1.3609 euros; US $1 = 0.6793 euros; 10 euros = £7.35 = $14.72. *Average Exchange Rate* (euros per US $): 0.8041 in 2005; 0.7971 in 2006; 0.7306 in 2007. Note: The local currency was formerly the Spanish peseta. From the introduction of the euro, with Spanish participation, on 1 January 1999, a fixed exchange rate of €1 = 166.386 pesetas was in effect. Euro notes and coins were introduced on 1 January 2002. The euro and local currency circulated alongside each other until 28 February, after which the euro became the sole legal tender.

Cost of Living (Consumer Price Index, annual averages; base: 2006 = 100): All items 93.0 in 2004; 95.8 in 2005; 102.7 in 2007.

Gross Domestic Product (€ million, provisional): 1,237.6 in 2005; 1,341.4 in 2006; 1,441.4 in 2007.

Gross Domestic Product by Economic Activity (€ million, 2007, provisional): Agriculture, hunting, forestry and fishing 9.5; Energy 27.4; Construction 127.5; Other industry 29.8; Services 1,097.5; *Subtotal* 1,291.7; Net taxes on products 149.7; *GDP at market prices* 1,441.4.

EXTERNAL TRADE

Melilla is a duty-free port. Most imports are from Spain, but over 90% of exports go to non-Spanish territories. The chief export is fish.

TRANSPORT

Road Traffic (Ceuta and Melilla, 2005): Vehicles registered 97,174 (Passenger cars 71,575, Buses, etc. 119, Lorries 14,435, Motorcycles 9,466, Tractors 180, Other 1,399).

International Shipping (2005): Vessels entered 1,077 (9,531,589 grt); Goods handled 801,291 metric tons; Passenger movements 397,744.

Civil Aviation (2006, preliminary): Journeys made 9,742; Passengers transported ('000) 305; Goods transported 430 metric tons.

TOURISM

Tourist Arrivals (by country of residence, 2002): France 476; Germany 432; Italy 331; Netherlands 425; Spain 23,648; Total (incl. others) 31,812. *2006* (Ceuta and Melilla): 604,838 overnight stays.

EDUCATION

(2005/06)

Pre-primary: 20 schools; 159 teachers, 3,237 students.

Primary: 15 schools; 422 teachers (excl. 20 engaged in both pre-primary and primary teaching); 5,996 students.

Secondary: First Cycle: 9 schools (of which 4 schools also provided second-cycle education and 5 provided vocational education); 255 teachers (excl. 10 engaged in both primary and secondary teaching, and 198 engaged in more than one secondary cycle, and excl. 33 specialists); 3,923 students.

Secondary: Second Cycle: 53 teachers; 1,339 students.

Secondary: Vocational: 703 students; 65 teachers.

Source: Ministry of Education and Science, Madrid.

Directory

Government

Government Delegate in Melilla: José Fernández Chacón.

Deputy elected to the Congress in Madrid: Antonio Gutiérrez Molina (PP).

Representatives to the Senate in Madrid: María del Carmen Dueñas Martínez (PP), Juan José Imbroda Ortiz (PP).

SPANISH EXTERNAL TERRITORIES   Melilla

COUNCIL OF GOVERNMENT
(April 2008)

Mayor/President of Melilla: Juan José Imbroda Ortiz.
First Vice-President and Councillor of Public Administration: Miguel Marín Cobos.
Second Vice-President and Councillor of the Presidency and Civic Participation: Abdelmalik el-Barkani Abdelkader.
Councillor of Finance and Budgeting: Guillermo Frías Barerra.
Councillor of the Economy, Employment and Tourism: Daniel Conesa Mínguez.
Councillor of Development: Rafael Ricardo Marín Fernández.
Councillor of Social Welfare and Health: María Antonia Garbín Espigares.
Councillor of the Environment: Ramón Gavilán Aragón.
Councillor of Culture: Simi Chocrón Chocrón.
Councillor of Civic Security: Ramón Antón Mota.
Councillor of Education and Voluntary Organizations: Antonio Miranda Montilla.
Councillor of Contracting and Heritage: Esther Donoso García-Sacristán.
Councillor of Youth and Sport: Francisco Robles Ferrón.

GOVERNMENT OFFICES

Delegación del Gobierno: Avda de la Marina Española 3, 52001 Melilla; tel. (95) 2675840; fax (95) 2672657; e-mail puri@melilla.map.es.

Office of the Mayor/President: Palacio de la Asamblea, Plaza de España, 52001 Melilla; tel. (95) 2699100; fax (95) 2679230; e-mail presidencia@melilla.es; internet www.melilla.es.

Council of Civic Security: Jefatura Policía Local, General Astilleros 25, Melilla; tel. (95) 2698110; fax (95) 2698121; e-mail policialocal@melilla.es.

Council of Contracting and Heritage: Palacio de la Asamblea, Plaza de España, 52001 Melilla; tel. (95) 2699157; fax (95) 2699160; e-mail consejeriacontratacion@melilla.es.

Council of Culture: Palacio de la Asamblea, Plaza de España, 52001 Melilla; tel. (95) 2699193; fax (95) 2699158; e-mail consejeriacultura@melilla.es.

Council of Development: Antiguo Edif. Mantelete, Duque de Ahumada s/n, Melilla 52071; tel. (95) 2699223; fax (95) 2699224; e-mail consejeriafomento@melilla.es.

Council of the Economy, Employment and Tourism: Justo Sancho Miñano 2, 52801 Melilla; tel. (95) 2690381; fax (95) 2690036; e-mail consejeriaeconomia@melilla.es.

Council of Education and Voluntary Organizations: Querol 7, 52001 Melilla; tel. (95) 2699214; fax (95) 2699279; e-mail educacionmelilla@melilla.es.

Council of the Environment: Palacio de la Asamblea, Plaza de España, 52001 Melilla; tel. (95) 2699134; fax (95) 2699161; e-mail consejeriamedioambiente@melilla.es.

Council of Finance and Budgeting: Palacio de la Asamblea, Plaza de España, 52001 Melilla; tel. (95) 2699157; fax (95) 2699160; e-mail conserjeriahacienda@melilla.es.

Council of the Presidency and Civic Participation: Palacio de la Asamblea, Plaza de España, 52001 Melilla; tel. (95) 2699207; fax (95) 2699137; e-mail consejeriapresidencia@melilla.es.

Council of Public Administration: Palacio de la Asamblea, Plaza de España, 52001 Melilla; tel. (95) 2699102; fax (95) 2699103; e-mail cap@melilla.es.

Council of Social Welfare and Health: Carlos Ramírez de Arellano 10, Melilla; tel. (95) 2699301; fax (95) 2699302; e-mail consejeriabienstarsocial@melilla.es.

Council of Youth and Sport: Palacio de la Asamblea, Plaza de España, 52001 Melilla; tel. (95) 2699225; fax (95) 2699208; e-mail juventud@melilla.es.

Assembly

Election, 27 May 2007

	Seats
Partido Popular (PP)	15
Coalición por Melilla (CpM)	5
Partido Socialista Obrero Español (PSOE)	5
Total	**25**

Election Commission

Junta Electoral de Zona y Provincial de Melilla: Melilla; Sec. Ruperto Manuel García Hernández.

Political Organizations

Coalición por Melilla (CpM): Ejército Español 21, 1° dcha, 52001 Melilla; tel. (95) 2969188; fax (95) 2699247; internet www.coalicionpormelilla.es; f. 1995 by merger of Partido del Trabajo y Progreso de Melilla and Partido Hispano Bereber; Pres. Mustafa Hamed Mo Aberchán; Sec.-Gen. Juan Molina Peña Fiel.

Partido Popular (PP): Roberto Cano 2, 1° izqda, POB 384, 52001 Melilla; tel. (95) 2681095; fax (95) 2684477; e-mail melilla@pp.es; internet melilla.pp.es; national-level, centre-right party; absorbed the Unión del Pueblo Melillense in 2007; Pres. Arturo Esteban Albert; Sec. Gen. María Carmen Dueñas Martínez.

Partido Socialista de Melilla-Partido Socialista Obrero Español (PSME-PSOE): Doctor García Martínez 3, 52006 Melilla; tel. (95) 2677807; fax (95) 2679857; internet www.psoe.es; national-level, left-wing party; Pres. Andrés Visiedo Segura; Sec.-Gen. Dionisio Muñoz Pérez.

There are also various civic associations in Melilla.

Religion

As in Ceuta, most Europeans are Roman Catholics. The registered Muslim community numbered 20,800 in 1990. The Jewish community numbered 1,300. There is also a Hindu community.

ISLAM

Comisión Islámica de Melilla (CIM): García Cabrelles 13, Melilla; Sec.-Gen. Abderramán Benyahya.

CHRISTIANITY

The Roman Catholic Church

Melilla is part of the Spanish diocese of Málaga.

The Press

El Faro de Melilla: Castelar 5, 1°, Melilla; tel. (95) 2690029; fax (95) 2683992; e-mail melilla@grupofaro.es; internet www.elfaroceutamelilla.es; Pres. Rafael Montero Palacios; Editor-in-Chief Angela M. Perazzi.

Melilla Hoy: Polígono Industrial SEPES, La Espiga, Naves A-1/A-2, 52006 Melilla; tel. (95) 2690000; fax (95) 2675725; e-mail redaccion@melillahoy.es; internet www.melillahoy.es; f. 1985; Pres. Enrique Bohórquez López-Dóriga; Editor-in-Chief Mustafa Hamed; circ. 2,000.

Sur: Músico Granados 2, 52001 Melilla; tel. (95) 2691283; fax (95) 2673674; e-mail surmelilla@rusadirmedia.com; internet www.diariosur.es; local edn of Málaga daily; Perm. Rep. Avelino Gutiérrez Pérez.

El Telegrama de Melilla: Polígono La Espiga, Nave A-8, 52006 Melilla; tel. (95) 2691443; fax (95) 2691469; e-mail telegramademelilla@yahoo.es; internet www.eltelegrama.com; Dir Juan Carlos Heredia.

NEWS AGENCY

Agencia EFE: Cándido Lobera 4, 1° izqda, 52001 Melilla; tel. (95) 2685235; fax (95) 2680043; e-mail melilla@efe.es; Correspondent (vacant).

PRESS ASSOCIATION

Asociación de la Prensa: Apartado de Correos 574, 52001 Melilla; tel. (95) 2681854; fax (95) 2675725; Pres. Miguel Gómez Bernardi.

Broadcasting

RADIO

Cadena Dial Melilla: Muelle Ribera 18b, 52005 Melilla; tel. (95) 2682328; fax (95) 2681573; e-mail radiomelilla@unionradio.es; internet www.cadenadial.com; Rep. Rocío González Justo.

Onda Cero Radio Melilla: Músico Granados 2, 52004 Melilla; tel. (95) 2691283; e-mail ondaceromelilla@ondaceromelilla.net; internet www.ondaceromelilla.net; Dir José Jesús Navajas Trobat.

Radio Melilla: Muelle Ribera s/n, 52005 Melilla; tel. (95) 2681708; fax (95) 2681573; e-mail radiomelilla@unionradio.es; internet www.cadenaser.com; commercial; owned by Sociedad Española de Radiodifusión; Dir Antonia Ramos Peláez.

Radio Nacional de España (RNE): Duque de Ahumada 5, 52001, Melilla; tel. (95) 2681907; fax (95) 2683108; internet www.rtve.es/me; state-controlled; Rep. MONTSERRAT COBOS RUANO.

TELEVISION

A fibre optic cable linking Melilla with Almería was laid in 1990. From March 1991 Melilla residents were able to receive three private TV channels from mainland Spain: Antena 3, Canal+ and Tele 5.

Antena 3: Edif. Melilla, Urbanización Rusadir, 29805 Melilla; tel. (95) 2688840; internet www.antena3.com.

Finance

BANKING

There were seven banks operating in Melilla in 2007, all of which were based in mainland Spain.

Banco Bilbao Vizcaya Argentaria (BBVA): Teniente Aguilar De Mera 3 52001 Melilla; tel. (952) 686414; internet www.bbva.es; 5 brs.

Banco de España: Plaza de España 3, 52001 Melilla; tel. (95) 2683940; internet www.bde.es.

Banco Español de Crédito (Banesto): Avda Juan Carlos I 12, 52001 Melilla; tel. (95) 2684348; internet www.banesto.es; 2 brs.

Banco Popular Español: Avda Juan Carlos I 14, 52001 Melilla; tel. (95) 2684847; fax (95) 2676844; internet www.bancopopular.es.

Banco Santander Central Hispano (BSCH): Ejército Español 1, 52001 Melilla; tel. (95) 2681422; internet www.gruposantander.es; 3 brs.

Caja de Ahorros y Pensiones de Barcelona (La Caixa): Avda Juan Carlos I 28, 52001 Melilla; tel. (95) 2685760; fax (95) 2960276; internet www.lacaixa.es; 2 brs.

Montes de Piedad y Caja de Ahorros de Ronda, Cádiz, Almería, Málaga y Antequera (Unicaja): Ejército Español 9, 52001 Melilla; tel. (952) 682595; fax (952) 683684; internet www.unicaja.es; 4 brs.

INSURANCE

MAPFRE: Avda Democracia 9, 52004 Melilla; tel. (95) 2673189; fax (95) 2674977; e-mail maberna@mapfre.com; internet www.mapfre.com; Commercial Man. BERNABE ESCOZ; 2 offices.

Trade and Industry

Cámara Oficial de Comercio, Industria y Navegación: Cervantes 7, 52001 Melilla; tel. (95) 2684840; fax (95) 2683119; f. 1906; chamber of commerce; Pres. MARGARITA LÓPEZ ALMENDÁRIZ; Sec.-Gen. MARGARITA CEREZO FERNÁNDEZ.

Confederación de Empresarios de Melilla (CEME): Plaza 1 de Mayo, Bajo Dcha, 52003 Melilla; tel. (95) 2673696; fax (95) 2676175; e-mail ceme@cemelilla.org; internet www.cemelilla.org; f. 1979; employers' confed.; Pres. MARGARITA LÓPEZ ALMENDÁRIZ; Sec.-Gen. JERÓNIMO PÉREZ HERNÁNDEZ.

UTILITIES

The Spanish electricity company Endesa operates an oil-fired power station in Melilla. In 2007 a new 12.6-MW generator was installed, increasing capacity by 22%.

TRADE UNION

Confederación Sindical de Comisiones Obreras (CCOO): Plaza 1º de Mayo s/n, 3º, 29803 Melilla; tel. (95) 2676535; fax (95) 2672571; e-mail orga.melilla@melilla.ccoo.es; internet www.ccoo.es; Sec.-Gen. ANGEL GUTIÉRREZ GÓMEZ.

Transport

There is a daily ferry service to Málaga and a service to Almería. Melilla airport, situated 4 km from the town, is served by daily flights to various destinations on the Spanish mainland, operated by Iberia Regional/Air Nostrum. There were 30 km of paved roads in Melilla in 2006. The Port of Melilla handled 801,291 metric tons of goods and 397,744 passengers in 2005; in that year 1,077 boats passed through the port.

Port of Melilla: Autoridad Portuaria de Melilla, Avda de la Marina Española 4, 52001 Melilla; tel. (95) 2673600; fax (95) 2674838; e-mail puertodemelilla@puertomelilla.es; internet www.puertomelilla.es; Pres. ARTURO ESTEBAN; Dir JOSÉ LUIS ALMAZÁN.

Acciona Trasmediterránea: Avda General Marina 1, 52001 Melilla; tel. (95) 2681635; fax (95) 2682685; e-mail correom@trasmediterranea.es; internet www.trasmediterranea.es; operates ferry service between Melilla and Almería and Málaga, in mainland Spain.

Tourism

There is much of historic interest to the visitor, while Melilla is also celebrated for its modernist architecture. Several new hotels, including a luxury development, were constructed in the 1990s. In 2002 tourist arrivals, including visitors from mainland Spain, numbered 31,812.

Oficina Provincial de Turismo: Pintor Fortuny 21, 52004 Melilla; tel. (95) 2675444; fax (95) 2679616; e-mail info@melillaturismo.com; internet www.melillaturismo.com.

SRI LANKA

Introductory Survey

Location, Climate, Language, Religion, Flag, Capital

The Democratic Socialist Republic of Sri Lanka lies in southern Asia. It comprises one large island and several much smaller ones, situated in the Indian Ocean, about 80 km (50 miles) east of the southern tip of India. The climate is tropical, with an average annual temperature of about 27°C (81°F) in Colombo. There is very little seasonal variation in temperature: the monthly average in Colombo ranges from 25°C (77°F) to 28°C (82°F). The south-western part of the island receives rain from both the south-west and the north-east monsoons: average annual rainfall in Colombo is 2,365 mm (93 ins). Sinhala and Tamil are recognized national languages. One of the official languages, Sinhala, is spoken by more than 70% of the population. Tamil was made the country's second official language in 1988. According to the 2001 census, in 18 out of 25 districts 76.7% of the population are Buddhist, 8.5% are Muslim, 7.9% are Hindu and 6.1% are Roman Catholic. The census results did not cover the Tamil-dominated (and therefore mainly Hindu) northern and eastern districts. The national flag (proportions 1 by 2) consists mainly of a dark crimson rectangular panel, with a yellow border, in the fly. In the centre of the panel is a gold lion, carrying a sword, while in each corner (also in gold) there is a leaf of the bo (bodhi) tree, which is sacred to Buddhists. At the hoist are two vertical stripes, also edged in yellow, to represent Sri Lanka's minorities: one of green (for Muslims) and one of orange (for Tamils). The commercial capital is Colombo. In 1982 the ancient capital of Sri Jayawardenepura (Kotte) became the administrative capital.

Recent History

Sri Lanka, known as Ceylon until 1972, gained its independence from the United Kingdom in February 1948. From then until 1956, for a brief period in 1960 and from 1965 to 1970 the country was ruled, latterly in coalition, by the United National Party (UNP), which was concerned to protect the rights of the Tamils, Hindu members of an ethnic minority (closely linked with the inhabitants of the southern Indian state of Tamil Nadu), who are concentrated in the north (and, to a lesser extent, in the east) of the main island. The socialist Sri Lanka Freedom Party (SLFP), formed in 1951 by Solomon Bandaranaike, emphasized the national heritage, winning the support of groups that advocated the recognition of Sinhala as the official language and the establishment of Buddhism as the predominant religion. The SLFP won the 1956 elections decisively and remained in power, except for a three-month interruption in 1960, until 1965, having formed a coalition Government with the Lanka Sama Samaj Party (LSSP), a Trotskyist group, in 1964. Following the assassination of Solomon Bandaranaike in 1959, his widow, Sirimavo Bandaranaike, assumed the leadership of the SLFP. At the 1970 elections the SLFP became the leading partner of a United Front coalition Government with the LSSP and the Communist Party of Sri Lanka. In 1971 the United Front Government suppressed an uprising led by the left-wing Janatha Vimukthi Peramuna (JVP—People's Liberation Front). A state of emergency was declared, and the party was banned.

In 1976 the main Tamil party, the Federal Party, and other Tamil groups formed the Tamil United Liberation Front (TULF), demanding a separate Tamil state ('Eelam') in the northern and eastern parts of the country. In December of that year the communists supported strikes of transport unions, which were initiated by the UNP and the LSSP (the latter had been expelled from the coalition in 1975). The strikes ended in January 1977, and in February Sirimavo Bandaranaike prorogued the National State Assembly until May. Several members of the SLFP resigned, and seven members of the Communist Party left the coalition Government, forming an independent group within the opposition. In February the state of emergency, which had been imposed in 1971, was lifted and the JVP was legalized again. A general election was held in July 1977, accompanied by widespread violence. The UNP won the election, with an overwhelming majority, and the party's leader, Junius Richard Jayewardene, became Prime Minister. In August riots broke out between the Sinhalese majority and the Tamil minority. The TULF, which had become the main opposition party, increased its demands for an independent Tamil state. In October a constitutional amendment was passed to establish a presidential system of government, and in February 1978 Jayewardene became the country's first executive President.

Continued violence and pressure from the Tamils during 1978 led the Government to make some concessions, such as the recognition of the Tamil language, in the new Constitution of the Democratic Socialist Republic of Sri Lanka, which came into force in September. In view of this, the Ceylon Workers' Congress (CWC) joined the Government, but the TULF remained undecided, mainly for fear of reprisals by Tamil extremists. Further violence prompted the declaration of a state of emergency in July 1979 in the northern district of Jaffna, where the Tamils are in a majority. At the same time, stringent anti-terrorist legislation was passed in Parliament (as the National State Assembly had been renamed in 1978), and a presidential commission was established to study the Tamil issue.

In June 1980 a general strike, called by left-wing trade unions seeking higher wages, led to the declaration of a state of emergency between July and August, and more than 40,000 government workers lost their jobs. In August the TULF agreed to the establishment of District Development Councils, providing for a wide measure of regional autonomy. Elections to these, held in June 1981, were boycotted by the SLFP, the LSSP and the Communist Party, and the UNP won control of 18 of the 24 Councils. Subsequent communal disturbances between Sinhalese and Tamils led to the imposition of a state of emergency in the north for five days in June, and throughout the country from August 1981 to January 1982. Tamil MPs proposed a motion of no confidence in the Government and subsequently boycotted Parliament until November 1981, when a peace initiative to ease racial tension was proposed by the Government.

Meanwhile, in October 1980 the former Prime Minister, Sirimavo Bandaranaike, was found guilty of having abused power by a special presidential commission, which deprived her of all civic rights and effectively prevented her from standing in the next elections.

In August 1982 Parliament approved an amendment to the 1978 Constitution which enabled President Jayewardene to call a presidential election before his term of office expired, i.e. after four years instead of six. Sri Lanka's first presidential election was held in October 1982, and Jayewardene was returned to office with 53% of the votes cast. The SLFP candidate, Hector Kobbekaduwa, polled 39%, despite his party's disarray and Sirimavo Bandaranaike's loss of civic rights.

Following this success, the President announced, with the approval of Parliament and the Supreme Court, that, instead of a general election, a referendum would be held to decide whether to prolong the life of Parliament for a further six years after the session ended in July 1983. A state of emergency was in force between October 1982 and January 1983, and all opposition newspapers were closed by the Government. Sirimavo Bandaranaike was allowed to campaign in the referendum, which took place in December 1982 and resulted in approval of the proposal to prolong Parliament until 1989. On a 71% turn-out, 55% (3.1m.) voted in favour, with the dissenting minority of 2.6m. being concentrated mainly in and around Jaffna.

A state of emergency was declared in May 1983 to combat mounting terrorism, and in June Tamil terrorist activity led to army reprisals and the worst outbreak of violence for many years, with more than 400 deaths and particularly severe rioting in Jaffna and Colombo. A curfew and press censorship were imposed, and three left-wing parties (including the JVP) were banned. In July the 16 TULF MPs resigned in protest at the extension of Parliament, as approved by the referendum. In August Parliament passed a 'no-separation' amendment to the Constitution, depriving those espousing Tamil separatism of their civic rights. In October the TULF MPs were found to have forfeited their seats because of their parliamentary boycott. After much discussion and with the informal mediation of India, an All-Party Conference (APC) began in January 1984. The APC comprised representatives of the Buddhist, Christian and Muslim faiths as well as political leaders from the Sinhalese and Tamil communities. The Government proposed to establish provincial councils, with some regional autonomy, throughout the country. The TULF, however, demanded regional devolution that would enable the northern province, with its Tamil majority, to amalgamate with the eastern province where the Tamils were in a minority and thus create a Tamil state within the framework of a united Sri Lanka. The Sinhalese and the Muslims were implacably opposed to this proposal. The APC was finally abandoned in December, without agreement on the crucial question of the extent of regional autonomy.

Further violent outbursts in the northern part of the island in November and December 1984 led to the proclamation of another state of emergency. There were widespread accusations of gross military indiscipline, along with condemnation of government-sponsored settlement of Sinhalese in Tamil areas in the eastern province. A restricted zone was established between Mannar and Mullaitivu, to prevent contact with the Indian state of Tamil Nadu, where many of the Tamil militants were based.

In February 1986 there was a resurgence of violence in the northern and eastern provinces. In May a series of explosions in Colombo was widely believed to have been carried out by Tamil terrorists. The Government intensified its campaign against the insurgents by increasing defence expenditure and by launching an offensive against the militant Tamils in the Jaffna peninsula. This offensive made little headway, but the government cause was helped by internecine fighting between two of the principal Tamil militant groups, the Tamil Eelam Liberation Organization (TELO) and the Liberation Tigers of Tamil Eelam (LTTE—also known as the Tamil Tigers), which, over the year, emerged as the dominant Tamil separatist group under the leadership of Velupillai Prabhakaran. In May Tamil terrorists renewed their attacks on Sinhalese villagers who had been settled by the Government in Tamil-dominated areas in the eastern province. In June the Government presented fresh devolution proposals to a newly convened APC, in which the TULF was not invited to participate, while the SLFP boycotted the talks. The proposals again envisaged the formation of provincial councils, but did not satisfy the Tamils' demand for amalgamation of the northern and eastern provinces. The proposals were also rejected by the SLFP, on the grounds that they conceded too much to the Tamils.

In January 1987, in response to an announcement by the LTTE that they intended to seize control of the civil administration of Jaffna, the Government suspended, indefinitely, the distribution of all petroleum products to the peninsula. In the same month all the powers previously vested in the Prime Minister, Ranasinghe Premadasa, as Minister of Emergency Civil Administration were transferred to a new Ministry of National Security, directly supervised by the President. In February the Government launched an offensive against the terrorists in the Batticaloa district of the eastern province. The situation worsened in April, when the LTTE, having rejected an offer of a cease-fire by the Sri Lankan Government, carried out a series of outrages against the civilian population, including a bomb explosion in Colombo's main bus station, which killed more than 100 people. In response, the Government attempted to regain control of the Jaffna peninsula, the stronghold of the LTTE. During the resultant struggle between the LTTE and government forces, India demonstrated its support for the Tamils by violating Sri Lankan airspace to drop food and medical supplies in Jaffna. On 29 July, however, an important breakthrough was made when President Jayewardene and the Indian Prime Minister, Rajiv Gandhi, signed an accord regarding an attempted settlement of the country's ethnic crisis. The main points were: the provision of an Indian Peace-Keeping Force (IPKF) to oversee its proper implementation; a complete cessation of hostilities, and the surrender of all weapons held by the Tamil militants; the amalgamation of the northern and eastern provinces into one administrative unit, with an elected provincial council (together with the creation of provincial councils in the seven other provinces); the holding of a referendum in the eastern province at a date to be decided by the Sri Lankan President, to determine whether the mixed population of Tamils, Sinhalese and Muslims supported an official merger with the northern province into a single Tamil-dominated north-east province; a general amnesty for all Tamil militants; the repatriation of some 130,000 Tamil refugees from India to Sri Lanka (by early 1991 the number of Tamil refugees in India had risen to an estimated 210,000, and in early 1992 the Indian Government began to repatriate them, allegedly on a voluntary basis); the prevention of the use of Indian territory by Tamil militants for military or propaganda purposes; the prevention of the military use of Sri Lankan ports by any country in a manner prejudicial to Indian interests; and the provision that Tamil and English should have equal status with Sinhala as official languages. The accord encountered widespread disapproval among the Sinhalese population and from the SLFP, which claimed that it granted too much power to the Tamil minority.

In July and August 1987 more than 7,000 Indian troops were dispatched to Sri Lanka. After a promising start in August, the surrender of arms by the Tamil militant groups became more sporadic in September, and the implementation of the peace accord was impeded by further bitter internecine fighting among the Tamil militias (involving the LTTE in particular), which necessitated direct intervention by the IPKF. Under arrangements reported to have been negotiated in September with the Indian authorities, the LTTE were to be allocated a majority of seats on an interim council, which was to administer the northern and eastern provinces, pending the holding of elections. Despite this concession, the surrender of arms by the LTTE had virtually ceased by early October; the group had resumed its terrorist attacks on Sinhalese citizens, and had declared itself to be firmly opposed to the peace accord. In response to the resurgence in violence, the IPKF launched an offensive against the LTTE stronghold in the Jaffna peninsula in October. The Indian troops encountered fierce and prolonged resistance from the Tamil militants, which necessitated the deployment of thousands of reinforcements. By the end of the month, however, the IPKF had gained control of Jaffna city, while most of the LTTE militants had escaped to establish a new base for guerrilla operations, in the Batticaloa district of the eastern province. Both sides had suffered heavy casualties.

Because of the continuing violence, the Sri Lankan Government abandoned its plan to create an interim administrative council for the northern and eastern provinces. However, in November 1987, despite strong opposition from the SLFP (which vehemently opposed the proposed merger of the northern and eastern provinces), Parliament adopted the legislation establishing provincial councils.

Another major threat to the successful implementation of the peace accord was the re-emergence in 1987 of the outlawed Sinhalese group, the JVP, which had been officially banned in August 1983 and which was based mainly in the south of the island. This group claimed that the accord conceded too much power to the Tamils. As part of its anti-accord campaign, the JVP was widely believed to have been responsible for an assassination attempt on President Jayewardene in August, in which one MP was killed and several cabinet ministers were seriously wounded, and to have murdered more than 200 UNP supporters by February 1988, including the Chairman of the UNP, Harsha Abeywardene, and the leader of the left-wing Sri Lanka Mahajana (People's) Party (SLMP), Vijaya Kumaratunga, who supported the accord. In May 1988 the Government revoked the five-year ban on the JVP in return for an agreement by the party to end its campaign of violence, but JVP leaders disowned the agreement as a hoax.

In February 1988 a new opposition force emerged when an alliance, named the United Socialist Alliance (USA), was formed between the SLMP, the LSSP, the Communist Party of Sri Lanka, the Nava Sama Samaja Party, and (most notably) the Tamil rights group entitled the Eelam People's Revolutionary Liberation Front (EPRLF). Although the USA group, led by Chandrika Bandaranaike Kumaratunga (the widow of the SLMP leader and the daughter of Sirimavo Bandaranaike), comprised opposition parties, it expressed support for the peace accord.

Elections to seven of the new provincial councils were held in April and June 1988 (in defiance of the JVP's threats and violence); elections in the northern and eastern provinces were postponed indefinitely. The UNP won a majority and effective control in all seven, while the USA emerged as the main opposition group. The SLFP boycotted the elections, in protest at the continuing presence of the IPKF (which now numbered about 50,000) in Sri Lanka. In September President Jayewardene officially authorized the merger of the northern and eastern provinces into a single north-eastern province, prior to provincial council elections there. The JVP reacted violently, and was widely believed to have been responsible for the murder of the Minister of Rehabilitation and Reconstruction at the end of the month. In protest against the proposed elections in the new north-eastern province and the presidential election (due to be held in December), the JVP organized a series of disruptive strikes and violent demonstrations in the central, western and southern provinces in October. In an effort to curb the increasing violence, the Government applied extensive emergency regulations, imposed curfews in areas of unrest, and deployed armed riot police. Despite boycotts and threats by both the JVP and the LTTE, elections to the new north-eastern provincial council took place in November. The moderate and pro-accord Tamil groups, the EPRLF and the Eelam National Democratic Liberation Front (ENDLF), together with the Sri Lanka Muslim Congress (SLMC), were successful in the elections, while the UNP won only one seat. In early December Parliament unanimously approved a Constitution Amendment Bill to make Tamil one of the country's two official languages (with Sinhala), thus fulfilling one of the major commitments envisaged in the peace accord. On 19 December the presidential election took place, in circumstances of unprecedented disruption, and was boycotted by the LTTE and the JVP. None the less, about 55% of the total electorate was estimated to have voted. The Prime Minister, Ranasinghe Premadasa (the UNP's candidate), won by a narrow margin, with 50.4% of the total votes, while Sirimavo Bandaranaike, the President of the SLFP (whose civil rights had been restored in January 1986), received 44.9%. On the following day, as promised earlier in the month by the Government, Parliament was dissolved in preparation for a general election.

In early January 1989 Premadasa was sworn in as Sri Lanka's new President, and an interim Cabinet was appointed. In the same month, the Government repealed the state of emergency, which had been in force since May 1983, and abolished the Ministry of National Security. Concurrently, however, special security measures were invoked in an attempt to arrest the escalating violence. Shortly after his inauguration, Premadasa offered to confer with the extremists and invited all groups to take part in the electoral process. The JVP and the LTTE, however, intensified their campaigns of violence in protest at the forthcoming general election. In early February 1989 the moderate, pro-accord Tamil groups, the EPRLF, the ENDLF and the TELO, formed a loose alliance, under the leadership of the TULF, to contest the general election. In the election, which was held on 15 February and which was, again, marred by widespread violence, the UNP won 125 of the 225 contested seats. The new system of proportional representation, which was introduced at this election, was especially advantageous to the SLFP, which became the major opposition force in Parliament, with 67 seats. The comparatively low electoral participation of 64% confirmed, again, that intimidatory tactics, employed by the LTTE and the JVP, had had an effect on the voters. A few days later, President Premadasa installed a new Cabinet, and in March he appointed the Minister of Finance, Dingiri Banda Wijetunga, as the country's new Prime Minister. Although both the LTTE and the JVP rejected a conciliatory offer made by the President in April, in a surprising development, representatives of the LTTE began discussions with government officials in Colombo in the following month.

Between January and April 1989 five battalions of the IPKF left Sri Lanka, and in May the Sri Lankan Government announced that it wanted all Indian troops to have left Sri Lanka by the end of July. In response, Rajiv Gandhi stressed that the timetable for a complete withdrawal would have to be decided mutually, and that, before the Indian forces left, he wanted to ensure the security of the Tamils and the devolution of real power to the elected local government in the north-eastern province. In protest against the continued presence of the IPKF in Sri Lanka, the JVP organized a series of demonstrations and strikes. As a result of the escalating unrest, the Government reimposed a state of emergency on 20 June. In the same month, shortly after the murders of several prominent Tamil leaders, the peace negotiations between the Sri Lankan Government and the LTTE were temporarily discontinued. In September the Governments of Sri Lanka and India signed an agreement in Colombo, under which India promised to make 'all efforts' to withdraw its remaining 45,000 troops from Sri Lanka by the end of the year, and the IPKF was to declare an immediate unilateral cease-fire. In turn, the Sri Lankan Government pledged immediately to establish a peace committee for the north-eastern province in an attempt to reconcile the various Tamil groups and to incorporate members of the LTTE into the peaceful administration of the province.

The JVP suffered a very serious set-back when its leader, Rohana Wijeweera, and his principal deputy were shot dead by the security forces in November 1989. In the following month the leader of the military wing of the JVP, Saman Piyasiri Fernando, was killed in an exchange of gunfire in Colombo. Between September 1989 and the end of January 1990 the Sri Lankan security forces effectively destroyed the JVP as a political force, thus substantially transforming the country's political scene. All but one member of the JVP's political bureau and most leaders at district level had been killed. It was estimated, however, that the number of civilians killed in the lengthy struggle between the JVP and the Government might have been as high as 25,000–50,000.

As the Indian troops increased the speed of their withdrawal from Sri Lanka in the latter half of 1989, the LTTE initiated a campaign of violence against its arch-rivals, the more moderate Indian-supported EPRLF, which was mustering a so-called Tamil National Army, with Indian help, in the north-eastern province, to resist the LTTE. The LTTE accused the EPRLF and its allies of forcibly conscripting thousands of Tamil youths into the Tamil army. Following months of peace talks with the Government, however, the political wing of the LTTE was recognized as a political party by the commissioner of elections in December. The LTTE leaders then proclaimed that the newly recognized party would take part in the democratic process (it demanded immediate fresh elections in the north-eastern province) under the new name of the People's Front of the Liberation Tigers (PFLT). By the end of 1989 the inexperienced and undisciplined Tamil National Army had been virtually destroyed by the LTTE, who now appeared to have the tacit support of the central Government and had taken control of much of the territory in the north-eastern province.

Following further talks between the Governments of Sri Lanka and India, the completion date for the withdrawal of the IPKF was postponed until the end of March 1990. In early March the EPRLF-dominated north-eastern provincial council, under the leadership of Annamalai Varadharajah Perumal, renamed itself the 'National Assembly of the Free and Sovereign Democratic Republic of Eelam' and gave the central Government a one-year ultimatum to fulfil a charter of demands. Two weeks later, however, Perumal was reported to have fled to southern India. The last remaining IPKF troops left Sri Lanka on 24 March, a week ahead of schedule. In the next month the Government eased emergency regulations (including the ban on political rallies) in an effort to restore a degree of normality to the country after years of violence. At the same time, Sri Lanka's security forces, encouraged by the relative lull in violence, halted all military operations against the now much-weakened JVP and the Tamil militant groups. A fragile peace was maintained until June, when the LTTE abandoned their negotiations with the Government and renewed hostilities with surprise attacks on military and police installations in the north and north-east. Consequently, the Sri Lankan security forces were compelled to launch a counter-offensive. In mid-June the Government dissolved the north-eastern provincial council (despite protests by the EPRLF), and the holding of fresh elections in the province was postponed indefinitely pending the LTTE's agreement to participate in them (as earlier promised). In August the LTTE intensified their campaign of violence in the eastern province against the Muslim population, which retaliated with counter-attacks. At the end of August the Government launched a major offensive against the Tamil strongholds in the Jaffna peninsula. In March 1991 it was widely suspected that the LTTE were responsible for the assassination of a senior Sri Lankan cabinet member, the Minister of Plantation Industries and Minister of State for Defence, Ranjan Wijeratne (who had been in charge of both the government forces' successful offensive against the JVP, several years earlier, and the ongoing offensive against the LTTE), and for the bomb attack on an armed-forces building in Colombo in June. More significantly, for its regional implications, the LTTE were believed to have been responsible for the assassination of the former Indian Prime Minister, Rajiv Gandhi, near Madras (now known as Chennai), the state capital of Tamil Nadu, in May. In early 1992 the Indian Government proscribed the LTTE in India and banned their activities on Indian territory.

In May 1991 President Premadasa consolidated his political position when the UNP won a decisive victory in the local government elections. In August, however, the opposition, with the support of a number of UNP parliamentary members, began proceedings for the impeachment of the President. The impeachment motion listed 24 instances of alleged abuse of power and constituted a serious challenge to the authority of Premadasa and to the stability of his Government. However, it was rejected in October by the Speaker of Parliament on the grounds that some of the signatures on the resolution were invalid. Eight erstwhile UNP parliamentary members, including two former cabinet members, Lalith Athulathmudali and Gamini Dissanayake, who were expelled from the party (thus losing their parliamentary seats as well) by Premadasa for supporting the impeachment motion, formed a new party in December, called the Democratic United National Front (DUNF), to which they hoped to attract dissident members of the UNP.

The security forces suffered a serious reversal in August 1992, when 10 senior officers, including the northern military commander and the Jaffna peninsula commander, were killed in a land-mine explosion near Jaffna. Tension between the Muslim and Tamil populations in the north-eastern district of Polonnaruwa drastically increased following the massacre of more than 170 Muslim villagers by suspected LTTE guerrillas in October. In the next month the LTTE were also widely believed to have been responsible for the murder of the naval commander, Vice-Admiral Clancy Fernando, in Colombo. The LTTE themselves lost one of their most senior leaders when Velupillai Prabhakaran's chief deputy was killed at sea in January 1993.

In late April 1993 the opposition DUNF accused Premadasa's Government of having been responsible for the assassination of the party's leader, Lalith Athulathmudali. In response, Premadasa alleged that the perpetrators of the murder had been LTTE terrorists; the LTTE, however, denied any responsibility for the killing. The country was thrown into greater political turmoil on 1 May, when President Premadasa was assassinated in a bomb explosion in Colombo. The LTTE were officially blamed for the murder, although, again, they strenuously denied any involvement. A few days later Parliament unanimously elected the incumbent Prime Minister, Dingiri Banda Wijetunga, to serve the remaining presidential term (expiring in December 1994), and the erstwhile Minister of Industries, Science and Technology, Ranil Wickremasinghe, was appointed to replace him in the premiership. In provincial elections held in mid-May 1993 the UNP won control of four of the seven councils; no polling was carried out in the area covered by the now defunct north-eastern province (the province was officially declared invalid by the Supreme Court in October 2006). Although the ruling party received 47% of the votes, it was the first time since 1977 that its percentage of total votes had fallen below 50%, an indication of an erosion of its support base that became more pronounced in the early part of 1994.

The Sri Lankan forces achieved considerable success in their fight against ethnic violence in the eastern province in 1993, but were forced to abandon a massive military offensive in the Jaffna peninsula in October owing to the ferocity of the LTTE resistance. In the following month both sides suffered heavy casualties in the course of the battle over the military base at Pooneryn on the Jaffna lagoon. As a result of this military débâcle, in which, according to official figures, more than 600 army and naval personnel were either killed or captured, the Government established a new combined security forces command for the Jaffna and Kilinochchi districts to counter the LTTE threat.

Despite the continuing violence, provincial elections were held in the eastern province and in the northern town of Vavuniya in early March 1994; the UNP secured the greatest number of seats, while independent Tamil groups also performed well. The LTTE and the TULF boycotted the poll. The ruling party suffered its first major electoral reverse for 17 years at the end of the month, however, when an opposition grouping known as the People's Alliance (PA, of which the main constituents were the SLFP and the traditional Marxist left and which was headed by the former leader of the USA group, Chandrika Kumaratunga) won a clear majority in elections to the southern provincial council. On 24 June, in an apparent attempt to catch the opposition by surprise, the President dissolved Parliament and announced that early legislative elections were to be held on 16 August, ahead of the presidential election. Wijetunga's ploy failed, however: the PA obtained 48.9% of the votes, thus securing a narrow victory over the UNP, which received 44% of the poll. Under the prevailing system of proportional representation, this translated to 105 seats for the PA and 94 for the UNP in the 225-seat Parliament. The 17-year rule of the UNP had thus come to an end. On 18 August President Wijetunga abandoned hope of forming a UNP minority Government and appointed Kumaratunga as Prime Minister, the PA having secured the support of the SLMC, the TULF, the Democratic People's Liberation Front and a small, regional independent group. A new Cabinet was appointed on the following day, almost all members of which belonged to the SLFP. In line with her electoral pledge to abolish the executive presidency and to establish a parliamentary system in its place, the Prime Minister removed the finance portfolio from the President and assumed responsibility for it herself. Although Wijetunga retained the title of Minister of Defence, actual control of the ministry was expected to be exercised by the Deputy Minister of Defence. The Prime Minister's mother, Sirimavo Bandaranaike, was appointed as Minister without Portfolio. With regard to the Tamil question, overtures were made between the new Government and the LTTE concerning unconditional peace talks (these commenced in mid-October) and at the end of August, as a gesture of goodwill, the Government partially lifted the economic blockade on LTTE-occupied territory. In addition, the Prime Minister created a new Ministry of Ethnic Affairs and National Integration and assumed the portfolio herself, thus revealing her determination to seek an early solution to the civil strife.

In September 1994 Kumaratunga was unanimously elected by the PA as its candidate for the forthcoming presidential poll, while Gamini Dissanayake, the leader of the opposition (who had left the DUNF and returned to the UNP in 1993), was chosen as the UNP's candidate. The election campaign was thrown into confusion, however, on 24 October 1994, when Dissanayake was assassinated by a suspected LTTE suicide bomber in a suburb of Colombo; more than 50 other people, including the General Secretary of the UNP, Gamini Wijesekara, and the leader of the SLMP, Ossie Abeyagoonasekera, were killed in the blast. The Government declared a state of emergency and suspended the ongoing peace talks with the LTTE. Dissanayake had been an outspoken critic of these talks and had been one of the architects of the 1987 Indo-Sri Lankan accord. His widow, Srima Dissanayake, was chosen by the UNP to replace him as the party's presidential candidate. The state of emergency was revoked on 7 November (with the exception of the troubled areas in the north and east) to facilitate the fair and proper conduct of the presidential election, which was held on 9 November. Kumaratunga won the election, with 62.3% of the votes, while Srima Dissanayake obtained 35.9%. The Government viewed the victory as a clear mandate for the peace process initiated earlier that year. Sirimavo Bandaranaike was subsequently appointed Prime Minister, for the third time. The new President pledged to abolish the executive presidency before mid-July 1995, on the grounds that she believed that the post vested too much power in one individual, and promised to initiate a programme of social, economic and constitutional change.

The Government and the LTTE resumed peace talks in early January 1995, which resulted in the drawing up of a preliminary agreement on the cessation of hostilities as a prelude to political negotiations. This important development constituted the first formal truce since fighting was renewed in the north-east in June 1990. In April 1995, however, following several rounds of deadlocked negotiations, with both sides accusing each other of making unreasonable demands and proposals, the LTTE unilaterally ended the truce, withdrew from the peace talks and resumed hostilities against the government forces. In response, the Government cancelled all the concessions made to the guerrillas during the peace negotiations and placed the security forces on alert. A disturbing escalation in the violence was demonstrated at the end of the month by the LTTE's deployment, for the first time, of surface-to-air missiles.

In July 1995 the Government launched another major offensive in the Jaffna peninsula. As the offensive was intensified in mid-October, tens of thousands of civilians were compelled by the LTTE to flee the area. In retaliation against the army's attack, rather than actively confronting the troops, the LTTE detonated explosives on the country's two largest oil storage facilities near Colombo, which received virtually all of Sri Lanka's imported petroleum. As a result, about 20% of the island's petroleum supply was destroyed. In November two LTTE suicide bombers caused 18 deaths and more than 50 injuries in Colombo. In early December, however, the Sri Lankan army achieved a major victory in capturing the city of Jaffna and subsequently much of the Jaffna peninsula. Although the LTTE's military strength and morale were undermined, the rebels, as expected, reverted to guerrilla warfare and further terrorist activity. The day after the armed forces had raised the national flag above Jaffna, the LTTE rejected the President's offer of an amnesty in exchange for disarmament and announced a new recruitment drive. The Government's short-term strategy with regard to the Jaffna peninsula was to attempt to persuade the tens of thousands of civilians now living in refugee camps to return there and to establish a fully functional civil administration in the region. As widely feared, there was an escalation in LTTE-organized terrorist activity following the recapture of Jaffna; at the end of January 1996 more than 100 people were killed and about 1,400 were injured as a result of a suicide bomb attack on the Central Bank in Colombo. This devastating attack appeared to be the LTTE's response to the Government's release of the legal draft of devolution proposals earlier that month. Against a background of continuing conflict between the Tamil militants and the government forces in the north and east of the country, the President extended the state of emergency to cover the whole country in April (since coming to power in November 1994, the PA administration had restricted the emergency provisions to the troubled northern and eastern regions and Colombo). In mid-May 1996 the army announced that it now controlled the whole of the Jaffna peninsula and claimed that, of the 300,000 Tamil civilians who had been displaced by the ethnic violence, about 250,000 had returned to the government-held areas. Despite the army's controlling presence in the Jaffna peninsula, the LTTE were by no means a spent force. In mid-July the Tamil militants attacked and overran the isolated military base at Mullaitivu on the north-eastern coast of Sri Lanka, inflicting very heavy casualties on the army (according to the LTTE, at least 1,200 government soldiers were killed; according to official figures, the army death toll was about 300). About one week later the LTTE were suspected of planting a bomb on a crowded suburban train near Colombo, which left more than 70 people dead. In September the army seized control of the northern town of Kilinochchi, which had served as the LTTE's new headquarters since April. In the following month Prabhakaran and nine other militants were charged with more than 700 criminal acts of terrorism, including the bombing of the Central Bank in January. This constituted the first occasion that the Government had taken legal action against the LTTE leader. Fierce fighting between the Tamil militants and government troops continued into 1997, both in the north and east of the country; in early March it was estimated that more than 50,000 people had died and about one million people had been displaced as a result of the 14-year civil war.

The Government was given a considerable boost in March 1997, following its overwhelming success in local elections, in which it won more than 80% of the contested bodies (voting did not take place in the troubled northern and eastern provinces). However, although the Government secured control over a majority of the local bodies, its share of the total vote decreased to 48%, compared with the 62% it achieved in the presidential election of November 1994. The UNP obtained nearly 42% of the poll. None the less, the Government viewed the election results as a mandate to continue preparing its devolution plans offering limited autonomy to the Tamil secessionists (plans that had, so far, been blocked by the UNP). In May the Government launched a fresh military offensive against the LTTE, with the aim of gaining control of the 75-km stretch of the A9 highway between Vavuniya and Elephant Pass, which is the point of entry to the Jaffna peninsula. In late August the Government announced that it would submit its devolution proposals for parliamentary debate in October. In mid-October, however, 18 people were killed and more than 100 injured (including about 35 foreigners) when a bomb exploded in the car park of a Colombo hotel. It was widely believed that the LTTE deliberately targeted foreigners in this attack following the US Government's decision a few days earlier to place the organization on its official proscribed list of international terrorist groups. At the end of the month, despite protests from the UNP, the draft of the proposed constitutional amendments was presented to Parliament. The prospect of peace, however, appeared increasingly remote in late January 1998, when 16 people were killed in a suspected LTTE suicide bombing in Kandy at Sri Lanka's most sacred Buddhist temple, the Dalada Maligawa ('Temple of the Tooth'). The following day the Government retaliated by formally outlawing the LTTE, thus apparently ruling out the prospect of further peace negotiations in the near future and focusing instead on a military solution. (In October 2003 two Tamils were sentenced to death for carrying out the bombing; a third defendant was sentenced *in absentia* to 20 years' imprisonment. Death sentences were normally commuted to life imprisonment in Sri Lanka.) The Government suffered another set-back in late January 1998 when the UNP effectively rejected the proposed devolution package. The UNP disagreed with the Government's proposal to devolve wide-ranging powers to regional councils—including a Tamil-administered area—and favoured the concept of power-sharing at the centre. Also at the end of January, polls were conducted in Jaffna for the first time in 15 years. The local authority elections, which were monitored by tens of thousands of troops, were contested by a number of moderate Tamil political parties but were, not surprisingly, boycotted by the LTTE. The largest number of seats was won by the Eelam People's Democratic Party, but the turn-out was a mere 28%, owing to LTTE threats to disrupt the voting.

In mid-May 1998 the recently elected mayor of Jaffna (the first person to hold that position in 14 years), Sarojini Yogeswaran, who was a member of the moderate TULF, was assassinated by two suspected LTTE gunmen after refusing demands by Tamil militants to resign. In September Yogeswaran's replacement, Ponnuthurai Sivapalan, who was also a leading member of the TULF, was killed, along with 19 others, in a suspected LTTE bomb explosion in Jaffna city hall.

In early June 1998 the Government imposed an indefinite 'total ban' on news coverage (both local and foreign) of the ongoing civil war. In late September hundreds of troops on both sides were killed when the LTTE recaptured Kilinochchi and the army seized Mankulam, the last major town held by the guerrillas on the vital northern highway. By the end of the year, despite fierce fighting and large numbers of casualties on both sides, the army had still failed to capture completely the northern highway, which, if opened, would provide the military with a vital land route to the Jaffna peninsula (hitherto during the civil war, all government troops and supplies had had to be transported by sea or air). In early December the Government announced its decision to cancel the operation to capture the highway, which, since it was launched in May 1997, had cost the lives of more than 3,000 government troops. There were also indications that the army had a serious manpower problem (it needed to recruit 20,000 fresh troops), caused partly by desertions and growing numbers of casualties.

In late January 1999 the ruling PA won the elections to the north-western provincial council by a significant margin, but amid allegations of widespread electoral fraud and violence against opposition activists. A few days later the Supreme Court in Colombo overruled an order made by President Kumaratunga in August 1998 postponing elections to five other provincial councils. The Court stated that the presidency had no constitutional right to postpone the elections through the declaration of a state of emergency, as it had done, and asked the election commission to hold the polls within the next three months and to hold all five of them on a single day. In the provincial elections, which were eventually held in early April, the PA won control in four provinces and retained power in the fifth—the polls were very keenly contested, however, with the PA achieving about 43% of the total votes and the UNP obtaining around 41%. Elections to the southern province, which were held in May, also resulted in a PA-led administration. One noteworthy feature of this series of provincial polls was the resurgence of the JVP as a credible political force (it won 8% of the vote in all of the contested provincial councils, and, specifically, as much as 20% in the Hambantota district of the southern province).

Meanwhile, in March 1999 the army launched another offensive against the LTTE in the northern province, the objective of which was to reduce the area under the effective control of the Tamil guerrillas. In mid-June, in an unprecedented order, the President temporarily dissolved the powerful National Security Council and divested the Chief of Defence Staff of sweeping powers. Prospects of achieving a peace settlement in Sri Lanka appeared even more distant in late July, following the assassination by a suspected LTTE suicide bomber in Colombo of the TULF Vice-President, Neelan Tiruchelvam, who was a leading peace campaigner and human rights activist. In the same month Kumaratunga promoted 15 PA members to the position of deputy minister, in a move that was widely interpreted as an attempt to ensure that politicians remained loyal to the Alliance prior to and during the forthcoming general election. The promotions were heavily criticized by the opposition as financially profligate.

In October 1999 President Kumaratunga announced the holding of an early presidential election in December (about 11 months ahead of schedule), prompting the opposition to claim that her decision was aimed at bolstering the foundering ruling coalition prior to the legislative elections, which were due to be held in October 2000. In November 1999, however, the Government suffered a debilitating set-back following a rapid series of LTTE victories in the north-eastern Wanni region, thus reversing more than two years of territorial gains by the military. Following these demoralizing defeats and amid reports of large-scale desertions and mutiny in the army ranks, the Government announced a tightening of existing military censorship on domestic news coverage in an attempt to stem adverse publicity and reorganized the northern military command.

A few days before the presidential election, which was held on 21 December 1999, Kumaratunga survived an assassination attempt by a suspected LTTE suicide bomber in Colombo; the explosion killed more than 20 people and injured more than 100, while the President sustained wounds to her right eye. The election, which was contested by 13 candidates and attracted a 73% turn-out of the electorate, was marred by widespread allegations of vote-rigging, intimidation and violence. Kumaratunga was returned to power by a narrow majority (possibly having garnered a considerable sympathy vote), winning 51% of the total votes, while her main rival, Ranil Wickremasinghe of the UNP, secured 43%.

At the end of January 2000, in a dramatic reversal of policy, Wickremasinghe announced that, in spite of reservations, the UNP would henceforth offer legislative support to the Government's proposed constitutional amendments regarding devolution (first unveiled in 1995), which were designed to prepare the ground for peace talks with the LTTE; the opposition party, however, later appeared to vacillate with regard to its support, following indications that Kumaratunga intended to retain the executive presidency for a further six years. In early 2000 the Government confirmed that, at Kumaratunga's request, the Norwegian Government had agreed to play an intermediary role in any peace negotiations. The Norwegian Minister of Foreign Affairs, Knut Vollebæk, arrived in Colombo in February to discuss with Kumaratunga and Wickremasinghe the modalities for commencing direct peace talks between the Sri Lankan Government and the LTTE. Earlier that month Vollebæk had met a senior LTTE official in London, United Kingdom, to assess the separatists' opinions regarding peace negotiations. According to commentators, the preconditions of both sides (respectively, the withdrawal of all government troops from Tamil areas and the abandonment by the LTTE of their demand for an independent state) were the most serious obstacles to the commencement of talks.

Despite the steps being taken towards the instigation of peace talks, heavy fighting continued between the army and the LTTE in the north. In April 2000, having made several significant gains, the LTTE announced that they had captured the large military base at Elephant Pass at the strategic entrance point to the peninsula (the garrison had been under government control since the IPKF's withdrawal in 1990). In early May President Kumaratunga came under intense pressure from various quarters to seek Indian assistance in an attempt to halt the rapid LTTE march to recapture Jaffna; the Indian Government firmly ruled out military intervention, but offered to provide humanitarian aid (including mediation and the evacuation of troops). India also announced that it was extending its ban on the outlawed LTTE for a further two years. In response to the escalating military crisis, the Government imposed draconian security measures, banning all activities perceived as a threat to national security and giving extensive powers to the armed forces and police, and renewed press censorship on the foreign media. By mid-May the LTTE claimed to be only 1 km from the administrative centre of Jaffna, and thousands of terrified civilians were reported to be fleeing from the embattled city. In late May, as the army and the LTTE continued to struggle for control of the peninsula, the Government appealed for new army recruits, and Norway launched a fresh diplomatic initiative to find a peaceful solution to the ethnic crisis. In early June the Minister of Industrial Development, Clement V. Gunaratna, and more than 20 others were killed by a suspected LTTE suicide bomber in Colombo. At the end of the month President Kumaratunga and the leader of the opposition UNP, Ranil Wickremasinghe, began discussions on the draft of the new Constitution designed to resolve the conflict with the LTTE. The LTTE, however, immediately denounced the proposals. At the same time, the Supreme Court ruled that the recently renewed press censorship was illegal as the appointment of the official censor had not been approved by Parliament. Nevertheless, the President reimposed a series of restrictions on the local and foreign press and reappointed the official censor under the same emergency regulations employed in May. The Government and UNP then agreed on a draft constitution, which recommended converting the country into a *de facto* federal state through the establishment of eight semi-autonomous regional councils. However, the Tamil parliamentary parties, the TULF, PLOTE and Eelam People's Democratic Party (EPDP), rejected the proposals as providing inadequate autonomy to the Tamil regions of the country. Senior Buddhist monks rejected the reforms, owing to fears that devolution would threaten the Sinhalese-dominated population and prominence of Buddhism in Sri Lanka. In late July the UNP withdrew its support for the reforms. Street demonstrations were held in protest at the proposals. In August the President indefinitely postponed a parliamentary vote on the issue, and hence any further discussion of the reform programme, once it became clear that the Government would not obtain the two-thirds' majority required to secure the passage of the requisite legislation. The LTTE intensified attacks on security forces. On 10 August Sirimavo Bandaranaike announced her resignation as Prime Minister, owing to ill health. She was replaced by Ratnisiri Wickremanayake, the erstwhile Minister of Public Administration, Home Affairs and Plantation Industries. Parliament was dissolved in preparation for a general election.

Meanwhile, a report issued by the University Teachers for Human Rights in mid-July 2000 claimed that there had been a dramatic increase in the number of child soldiers forcibly recruited by the LTTE, in preparation for a major assault on Jaffna city. In September heavy fighting between the LTTE and Sri Lankan army continued; the army reclaimed a naval base and Jaffna's second largest town, Chavakachcheri. By the end of September, however, the LTTE had managed to regain some territory. In the same month the Minister of Shipping and Shipping Development, Mohammad H. M. Ashraff, and the President of the SLMC, along with 14 others, were killed in a helicopter crash in Kegalle District. A high-level investigation into the incident was ordered; there was widespread speculation that the aircraft had been shot down by LTTE guerrillas.

The parliamentary elections of 10 October 2000 were marred by allegations of electoral malpractice and by systematic violence and intimidation (particularly on the part of the incumbent PA). Nevertheless, the elections attracted a turn-out of 75% of the electorate. Despite the electoral irregularities, neither the PA nor the UNP won an absolute majority (taking 107 and 89 of the 225 parliamentary seats, respectively), but, having gained the support of the EPDP and National Unity Alliance (NUA—primarily a constituent of the SLMC), the PA was able to form a new, expanded coalition under the premiership of Wickremanayake. The former Prime Minister, Sirimavo Bandaranaike, died shortly after casting her vote. On 18 October Parliament elected Anura Bandaranaike, a member of the UNP and the President's estranged brother, as parliamentary Speaker; this was the first time in 40 years that the position had been held by a member of the opposition. This development was followed by an agreement between the PA and UNP to preserve the stability of the new Government for the next two years. On 19 October a new Cabinet was announced. In exchange for its support, the NUA established a 100-day deadline for the President to introduce a new constitution and to open negotiations with the LTTE. At the end of the month the JVP announced its willingness to support the Government in order to prevent the NUA from wielding excessive influence.

In late October 2000 negotiations between the leader of the LTTE, Velupillai Prabhakaran, and the Norwegian peace envoy, Erik Solheim, commenced. Discussions between Solheim and the President were also initiated. In early November Prabhakaran proposed direct peace negotiations with the Government, without any preconditions, but demanded a reduction in fighting and the lifting of an economic embargo on areas controlled by the LTTE to create a suitable atmosphere for talks. The Government did not immediately respond to the offer, although it had made it clear that it was willing to attempt to reach a peace accord. The Prime Minister ruled out an imminent cease-fire, declaring that the army would continue to fight LTTE guerrillas. In mid-December the Government announced that it was prepared to enter immediate peace negotiations, but would not scale down its offensive or lift the embargo until talks were under way. The LTTE rejected peace talks without the prior implementation of a cease-fire and later declared a unilateral one-month cease-fire, to begin from 24 December, as a 'goodwill gesture' to assist the peace process. Shortly afterwards, however, government troops launched an offensive in the Jaffna peninsula, and violence continued. The Government rejected the cease-fire, dismissing it as a strategic manoeuvre, and insisted that it would not discuss a cease-fire until the two parties entered peace negotiations.

On 23 January 2001, and at regular intervals thereafter, the LTTE extended the cease-fire by one month. The Government refused to reciprocate with a cease-fire. Nevertheless, dialogue between Solheim and representatives of the LTTE and Government, respectively, resumed in late January. In early March both sides appeared to react positively to Solheim's efforts to broker peace; however, in mid-March violence escalated and continued into April. Meanwhile, the United Kingdom banned the LTTE under its anti-terrorism legislation. At the end of April Solheim held negotiations with the President. Talks between Solheim and the Government and the LTTE, respectively, in mid-May ended inconclusively.

In early June 2001 a motion for the impeachment of Chief Justice Sarath Silva, accusing him of misconduct, was submitted to Parliament. Later that month the President dismissed the leader of the SLMC, Abdul Rauf Hakeem, from his position as Minister of Internal and International Trade, Commerce, Muslim Religious Affairs and Shipping Development, later accusing him of making anti-Government statements and refusing to support government policies. The President's strategy foundered, however, when Hakeem and six other members of the SLMC withdrew their support for the ruling PA, thereby reducing the coalition Government to a minority in Parliament. Immediately afterwards, opposition parties challenged the Government with a no-confidence motion. In order to prevent the motion from being debated in Parliament in mid-July, the President suspended the legislature on 10 July until 7 September, and announced that a referendum on a new constitution would take place on 21 August. The rulings, which were undemocratic and unconstitutional, respectively, caused a constitutional crisis. The UNP-led opposition organized a series of demonstrations against the President's decision to prorogue Parliament. The President also faced opposition within the Cabinet, particularly to the referendum. As a result, Kumaratunga announced in early August that the referendum would be postponed until mid-October.

In the mean time, in early June 2001 the Norwegian Minister of Foreign Affairs, Thorbjørn Jagland, arrived in Colombo, at the request of the President, in an attempt to bolster the peace initiative. The LTTE, however, protested against this development, claiming that it was an effort to reduce in importance Solheim's position. In early July President Kumaratunga circumvented Parliament and reimposed a state of emergency under anti-terrorist regulations. The President also extended a ban on the LTTE. On 24 July, the 18th anniversary of the start of the LTTE's separatist campaign, Tamil militants attacked the capital's international airport and an adjacent airbase. Several hours of shooting between Tamil militants and the army ended with all 13 guerrillas and seven soldiers killed. The LTTE had destroyed eight military aircraft and three civilian aircraft, and damaged others. The attack on the country's only international airport, renowned for its impenetrable security, adversely affected the tourist industry and, thus, the economy, and raised questions about the air force and airport's defence system. Following the incident, the army launched a retaliatory air attack on LTTE bases; violence between the army and guerrillas escalated. At the end of August the LTTE rejected the Government's offer of a cease-fire, dismissing it as a strategic manoeuvre.

In an attempt to resolve the political crisis, the Prime Minister and senior cabinet members conducted negotiations with the UNP on the possible establishment of a coalition government. The UNP, however, opted to form a UNP-led coalition with other opposition parties. Consequently, the President entered into negotiations with the left-wing, radical JVP. On 5 September 2001 the JVP formally agreed to support the minority Government for one year (but not to join the administration), in return for a set of conditions laid out in a 28-point memorandum of understanding. The JVP's 10 seats in Parliament raised the Government's share to a majority of 119 out of 225 seats. The President had already granted the JVP two of its demands by cancelling the referendum and announcing that Parliament would be reconvened one day earlier. In addition, the President agreed to suspend negotiations with the LTTE for one year and to postpone the privatization programme. According to the JVP's demands, in mid-September the size of the Cabinet was halved to 22 members. However, three senior cabinet members resigned, refusing to participate in an administration supported by the left-wing party. Several members of the PA criticized the pact and doubted its longevity. Later that month Parliament approved an item of legislation to establish a Constitutional Council, which would be responsible for removing political influence from major institutions and appointing independent commissions for public service, the judiciary, the police and elections. At the end of September a motion of no confidence in the Government was resubmitted to Parliament. On 8 October the SLFP removed its General Secretary, S. B. Dissanayake. (In December 2004 Dissanayake was sentenced to a two-year prison term, having been convicted of making 'defamatory comments' about the judges of the Supreme Court during his tenure as General Secretary.) Two days later 13 members of the PA, including several ministers, defected to the opposition, reducing the coalition to a minority. In order to forestall defeat in the vote of no confidence due to take place the next day, President Kumaratunga dissolved Parliament. The opposition condemned the decision, although the dissolution was constitutional (one year had passed since the previous legislative elections).

The general election on 5 December 2001, reportedly one of the most violent in Sri Lanka's history, was marred by incidents of vote-rigging and other electoral malpractices. Some tens of thousands of Tamil voters were barred from voting after the army prevented them from leaving LTTE-controlled areas to cast their vote. The outgoing Government claimed that the UNP had signed a secret pact with the LTTE, an allegation strongly denied by the opposition. Nevertheless, 72% of the electorate voted. The UNP won 109 of the 225 seats (45.6% of the vote) and the PA received 77 seats (37.2%). The JVP secured 16 seats (9.1%) and the Tamil Nationalist Alliance (TNA—a Tamil opposition alliance comprising the TULF, TELO, EPRLF and All Ceylon Tamil Congress formed prior to the election) won 15 seats (3.9%). The UNP leader, Ranil Wickremasinghe, formed the United National Front (UNF) with the SLMC to ensure a majority of 114 seats in Parliament, and on 9 December he was sworn in as Prime Minister. For the first time since 1984, the Prime Minister and the President were from two opposing parties. The President was at first reluctant to relinquish her defence and finance portfolios, which she eventually gave up in return for full control over the élite Presidential Security Division that was deployed for her personal protection, and refused initially to allow members of her former administration who had defected to the UNP to join the Government. After long negotiations, a new coalition Government, including the TNA and 12 members of the former PA administration, was sworn in on 12 December. In 2002 the right of the President to dissolve Parliament after one year from the date of the last election loomed over the new Government. In an attempt to curb the President's powers and to ensure stability for the peace process (see below), the Government recommended that parliamentary resolutions determine future elections; however, the President refused to support this suggestion. In September the Government introduced to Parliament a constitutional amendment which would restrict the right of the President to dissolve the legislature when the governing party has a majority in Parliament. In October, however, the Supreme Court ruled that the proposed statute required not only a two-thirds' majority in the legislature, but also endorsement by a national referendum.

The UNP's victory was largely attributed to the party's keenness to resume negotiations with the LTTE; on his accession, the Prime Minister reiterated this willingness. Significantly, the TNA was a member of the coalition Government. Although the LTTE launched major attacks against army troops and the police, during which 26 were killed, to mark the inauguration of the new Cabinet, on 19 December the Tamil extremists announced a unilateral one-month cease-fire from 25 December. On 21 December the Government responded with the declaration of a cease-fire as a 'gesture of goodwill'. The Prime Minister also announced that the free movement of food, medicine and other non-military supplies into the Tamil-controlled areas would be allowed; a concession refused, hitherto, by the President. In early January 2002 the Government announced the reduction of economic sanctions on the northern areas controlled by the LTTE. One week later a delegation of Norwegian diplomats, led by Norway's Deputy Minister of Foreign Affairs, Vidar Helgesen, arrived in Colombo to conduct negotiations with the Prime Minister and President, and eventually to facilitate peace talks between the Government and the LTTE. At the end of January both sides extended the cease-fire by one month. At the same time, the LTTE released 10 army and civilian prisoners. As a further confidence-building measure, the Government restored the electricity supply to part of the northern Tamil-controlled Vavuniya district.

On 22 February 2002 the Government and LTTE signed an agreement on an internationally monitored indefinite cease-fire to take effect the following day. Norway was requested to monitor the cease-fire. It was hoped that this breakthrough would lead to peace negotiations and end years of fighting in which more than 60,000 people had been killed. However, in mid-February there were several reports that the LTTE was continuing forcibly to recruit Tamil children.

In mid-March 2002 Prime Minister Wickremasinghe visited Jaffna, the first premier to do so since 1982. In early April the Government lifted a six-year ban on domestic flights and allowed commercial airlines to resume flights to Jaffna. A week later an important road linking the Jaffna peninsula with the rest of the country was opened for the first time in 12 years. On 10 April Prabhakaran addressed an international press conference for the first time in more than 10 years. He demanded the lifting of the ban on the LTTE as a prerequisite to negotiations and declared his commitment to peace and full support of the cease-fire. A few days later he signed a pact with the SLMC, allowing the largest Muslim party in Sri Lanka to participate in proposed negotiations with the Government. It was also agreed that nearly 100,000 Muslims expelled from the north by the LTTE about 10 years ago would be allowed to return to their homes. At the end of April the Prime Minister rejected the LTTE's demand for an independent Tamil state, or 'eelam', raising doubts about resolving the ethnic conflict. Meanwhile, Kumaratunga, who had reportedly criticized the Government for making too many concessions to the Tamil militants, expressed her support in late April for a public demonstration against the proposal to grant legal status to the LTTE.

In May 2002 a Tamil-owned trawler, reported to have been illegally importing weapons, was destroyed by the Sri Lankan navy in an exchange of gunfire off the coast of the eastern Batticaloa district—the first major violation of the cease-fire to have occurred. The LTTE refuted allegations that they had been smuggling arms and accused the army of attacking a civilian fishing boat in an effort to undermine the cease-fire. Later in the month the Norwegian-led Sri Lanka Monitoring Mission (SLMM) issued a statement conveying concern over the increasing number of cases of civilians being harassed by the LTTE. In June incidents of violence between Hindu Tamils and Muslims in eastern Sri Lanka resulted in eight deaths and several injuries.

Meanwhile, also in May 2002 the first direct talks for seven years between the Government and the LTTE took place on the Jaffna peninsula. Although the August deadline for the commencement of formal peace negotiations was not achieved, the cease-fire was upheld. According to the office of the UN High Commissioner for Refugees (UNHCR, see p. 66), by mid-August 103,000 displaced families had returned to their homes since the beginning of the cease-fire in February. On 4 September the Government lifted the official ban on the LTTE, a prerequisite to negotiations set by the LTTE. (The President, however, firmly opposed the removal of the ban until the talks were under way.) The first round of negotiations took place on 16–18 September in Thailand. The minister G. L. Peiris was chief negotiator for the Government; Anton Balasingham led negotiations on behalf of the LTTE. The talks were successful: both sides agreed to establish a joint committee to deal with security issues, and a joint task force to concentrate on the reconstruction of areas destroyed by war, the clearing of land-mines and the resettling of 800,000 internally displaced people to high-security zones. On the last day of negotiations Balasingham unexpectedly renounced the LTTE's long-standing demand for independence, instead agreeing to consider regional autonomy and self-government.

In early October 2002 four people were killed and 15 injured in clashes between government and LTTE forces in Ampara district, in one of the most serious violations of the cease-fire to date. On 31 October a Sri Lankan court convicted *in absentia* Prabhakaran for his role in a 1996 truck bombing in Colombo and sentenced him to 200 years' imprisonment. The sentencing did not have an effect on the second round of negotiations, which began on 31 October in Thailand. The four-day talks concentrated mainly on humanitarian issues, but concluded in a breakthrough, with both sides agreeing to create a subcommittee to examine a political solution to the conflict. Balasingham announced that the LTTE were willing to participate in the democratic process, would allow other political parties to operate in the areas under their control and would cease the recruitment of child soldiers. The LTTE also abandoned their demand for an interim government in the north-east. Both sides agreed to establish subcommittees to deal with rehabilitation and military de-escalation. However, while the talks progressed, a curfew was imposed in large parts of Colombo after three days of rioting between the majority Sinhalese and members of the Muslim community. Meanwhile, Sinhalese nationalists opposed to the peace process questioned the sincerity of the LTTE, dismissing the progress at the negotiations as an attempt to win publicity and international favour. Nevertheless, the peace process gained momentum in late November when Balasingham arrived in Norway to enter negotiations with the Prime Minister on the eve of a one-day international donor conference in support of the peace process. A few days later Prabhakaran confirmed in his annual address that the LTTE were prepared to accept regional autonomy rather than an independent state, but warned that violence would resume if negotiations collapsed.

In December 2002, at the third round of peace talks in Oslo, Norway, the two sides agreed on 'internal self-determination' based on a federal system of government within a united Sri Lanka. Peiris and Balasingham described the developments as unprecedented and historic. However, in order to achieve the two-thirds' majority required in Parliament to pass a constitutional amendment, the Government needed to secure the support of the President. Although Kumaratunga welcomed the peace agreement, she had repeatedly criticized the Government for making too many concessions during the peace process. In mid-December a close adviser of the President stated that the PA would not support a political solution unless the LTTE disarmed. However, at the fourth round of negotiations, held in early January 2003 in Thailand, Balasingham refused to yield to pressure to disarm the Tamil guerrillas prior to a political settlement and rejected Kumaratunga's demand that the LTTE's squad of suicide bombers disband. The talks concluded with an agreement to accelerate the rate of return and resettlement of up to 250,000 displaced people. Meanwhile, despite Tamil promises to halt the involuntary recruitment of children, the SLMM reported that the LTTE had enlisted hundreds of child soldiers since the beginning of the cease-fire. In late January the President ordered police and military chiefs to curb the recruitment of child soldiers within one week. Representatives of UNICEF conducted training sessions with the Sri Lankan military and talks with the LTTE on the recruitment of child soldiers, as well as issues of child protection and rehabilitation. The fifth round of negotiations, held in Germany in early February, was overshadowed by a serious violation of the cease-fire. On 7 February three LTTE guerrillas committed suicide by setting fire to their trawler after the Sri Lankan navy intercepted the vessel and Norwegian peace monitors discovered arms on board. The two-day negotiations focused on human rights issues; it was agreed that UNICEF would monitor a joint programme to rehabilitate child soldiers.

Meanwhile, the SLMC split in early December 2002 after two members of the party mounted a challenge to Hakeem's leadership. In early February 2003 President Kumaratunga censured the Prime Minister for granting a licence to the LTTE radio station, Voice of Tigers, amid rising tension in the 'cohabitation Government'. On 7 February the PA and JVP began negotiations to form a joint front against the UNF Government. The JVP strongly opposed the LTTE and attempted to persuade the President to dismiss the governing coalition. Prabhakaran failed to attend a meeting with Norwegian peace mediators in mid-March, reportedly owing to the sinking of a civilian Tamil ship by the Sri Lankan navy several days earlier. The LTTE declared that they were considering abandoning the peace talks as a result of the incident. Furthermore, the sixth round of negotiations on 18–21 March, held in Japan, ended without agreement, amid reports of renewed violence in Sri Lanka (some progress had been made, however, including an agreement by the LTTE to permit other Tamil parties to function in LTTE-controlled areas). Both sides reaffirmed their commitment to the cease-fire after a Chinese fishing trawler was attacked by suspected LTTE guerrillas off the coast of Sri Lanka. An international donor meeting in Washington, DC, USA, to consider aid for Sri Lanka's reconstruction in preparation for a major donor conference to be held in Japan in June, took place in mid-April. The LTTE, however, were not invited: the USA had not yet lifted its ban on the Tamil organization; neither had India, one of the attendees at the meeting. On 21 April the LTTE announced that they were temporarily withdrawing from the peace negotiations and that they would not attend the donor conference in Japan in June because they were excluded from the aid conference in the USA. They were also dissatisfied with the manner in which the cease-fire had been implemented (government troops remained stationed in many parts of the Tamil-controlled areas in a clear violation of the cease-fire) and the way in which the Government was carrying out rehabilitation and relief measures. Following the LTTE announcement, the President placed the security forces on high alert; however, the LTTE intended to uphold the cease-fire and there were no signs of renewed tension.

Efforts to revive the peace process suffered a set-back in May 2003. In a letter to the Prime Minister, Balasingham demanded that the Government establish an interim administration for the north-east of the country. The Government refused to agree, offering instead a 'development-orientated' structure for the area, with greater financial authority for the LTTE. The LTTE rejected this proposal as not extensive enough, and attempts to resume the peace negotiations failed. Informal talks, however, continued to take place. In mid-June a senior leader of the Varadharajah faction of the Eelam People's Revolutionary Front, Subathran, was shot dead. Subathran was the most senior of 30 politicians from rival Tamil parties and suspected army informants to have been assassinated since the beginning of the cease-fire; the LTTE were believed to have been responsible for the attack, creating serious doubts over the Tamil organization's commitment to multi-party politics. At the same time, an LTTE oil tanker exploded and sank during a confrontation with a Sri Lankan navy patrol. The LTTE and Government offered conflicting versions of the incident: military officials reported that the ship was smuggling weapons and that Tamil militants aboard the vessel refused to stop despite several warnings and caused the explosion to avoid being caught; the LTTE denied the charges, claiming that the Sri Lankan navy fired at the ship after capturing the crew. At the end of the month the LTTE organized a demonstration to demand the return of thousands of homes on the Jaffna peninsula occupied by the Sri Lankan army as high-security zones since the 1980s; some 150,000 people attended the rally. Although the Government was committed to vacating these zones, the army believed a sudden withdrawal would give the LTTE the opportunity to seize complete control of the Jaffna peninsula. Meanwhile, in early June an international donor Conference on the Reconstruction and Development of Sri Lanka took place in Tokyo, Japan, despite the refusal of the LTTE to attend. The international community agreed to give Sri Lanka US $4,500m. in aid over four years as long as the stalled peace process was revived.

In July 2003 the Government requested Norwegian peace envoy Jon Westbørg to inform the LTTE of the Government's new proposals for an interim administration, which reportedly included greater financial and political powers for the LTTE. The JVP opposed government plans to share power with Tamil militants in the north-east of the country and announced that it would organize public demonstrations in protest against the proposal. The LTTE agreed to consider the offer. In the same month the Sri Lankan administration decided to grant Sri Lankan citizenship to more than 160,000 Tamils of Indian origin who had been unable to return home since the beginning of the civil war. In August the SLMM reported that the Tamil militants had failed to comply with the terms of the cease-fire agreement by refusing to dismantle a camp in the north-eastern district of Trincomalee. Following talks with Norwegian monitors, and under pressure from the international community, the LTTE agreed to reconsider their position. However, at the end of August the Tamil rebels refused to dismantle the camp, insisting that it had existed before the cease-fire agreement was reached and should, therefore, be allowed to remain. This claim was rejected by the security forces and independent truce monitors. Controversy over the issue continued with allegations by the military and opposition that the LTTE had established 13 new camps since the beginning of the cease-fire; the Tamil militants denied the charges. The matter had also become a source of contention between the Prime Minister and President. Wickremasinghe censured the President for discussing security issues publicly, while President Kumaratunga continued to criticize the Government's conduct in the peace process. Meanwhile, the Kumaratunga-led PA and left-wing JVP failed to form an alliance owing to differences over their approach to the peace process and devolution of power.

Despite the political wrangling and the LTTE's increasingly rigid stance, the Prime Minister remained optimistic in late September 2003 that the stalled peace process would resume. However, on 9 October the Minister of Defence accused the LTTE of having increased their military strength two-fold and of having continued to conscript child soldiers since the beginning of the truce in February 2002. In late October 2003 the LTTE revealed a detailed plan for an Interim Self-Governing Authority (ISGA) to administer north-eastern Sri Lanka. The LTTE demanded an authority with a guaranteed Tamil majority and full control over regional administration for five years pending the achievement and implementation of a final settlement. The Government reacted cautiously to the plan; nevertheless, the Government announced that it would request Norwegian mediators to facilitate the resumption of talks. President Kumaratunga, however, condemned the offer, claiming that it was the first step towards a separate state.

On 4 November 2003 the country was plunged into a constitutional crisis when Kumaratunga took advantage of the Prime Minister's absence (he was attending trade negotiations in the USA) and suspended the legislature for a period of two weeks, dismissed the Minister of Interior and Christian Affairs, the Minister of Defence and of Transport, Highways and Aviation, and the Minister of Mass Communication, assuming the important portfolios herself, and deployed troops to key positions in the capital, Colombo, in the stated interest of preserving national security. It was reported that Kumaratunga had declared a state of emergency on 5 November, but withdrew the decree two days later on Wickremasinghe's return from the USA. The President claimed that the Prime Minister had made too many concessions to the LTTE during peace negotiations. Kumaratunga and Wickremasinghe held two meetings in an attempt to resolve the crisis, with little success: Wickremasinghe rejected the offer to form a government of national unity and suggested that, since the President had assumed the defence portfolio, Kumaratunga should lead the peace negotiations. However, the two leaders agreed to appoint a committee to establish by mid-December new power-sharing arrangements. In the mean time, in mid-November the Norwegian peace negotiators announced that they would withdraw from the peace process until it was made clear who held power and authority in Sri Lanka.

In mid-January 2004 the crisis worsened when Kumaratunga declared that she had held an undisclosed swearing-in ceremony in 2000 to give herself another year in office, thereby extending her term to December 2006. Analysts debated whether the action was constitutional. Later in January the Kumaratunga-led SLFP and the JVP formed the United People's Freedom Alliance (UPFA). The UPFA was joined by four more left-wing parties, which were members of the erstwhile PA, in early February. On 7 February Kumaratunga dissolved Parliament and called a general election for 2 April, almost four years ahead of schedule. Hours before the dissolution, the President created two new cabinet appointments for her supporters; the existing Cabinet was to operate in an acting capacity prior to the general election. Both the Cabinet and the LTTE condemned the decision, amid fears that the election would further undermine the peace process with the LTTE. The LTTE, however, pledged to maintain the cease-fire. Meanwhile, it was reported in late January that a Christian church at Mattegoda, near Colombo, had been attacked. The incident was the latest of at least 30 attacks on Christian churches since November 2003, which had allegedly been encouraged by hardline Buddhist clergy. Christians had been accused of sympathizing with the LTTE and carrying out unethical conversions. President Kumaratunga warned that anyone guilty of promoting religious tension would be severely punished.

In early March 2004 a rift within the LTTE appeared after a senior Tamil eastern regional commander declared his independence from the rest of the group. V. Muralitharan (commonly known as Col Karuna) withdrew his 6,000 fighters from the 15,000-strong LTTE in a dispute with the northern-based LTTE leader, Prabhakaran. Karuna, who accused northern Tamil groups of ignoring and discriminating against eastern groups, made it clear that he would not resume violence. However, he would not recognize the cease-fire agreement between the Government and Prabhakaran, and instead demanded a separate truce agreement with the Sri Lankan administration. Analysts feared that the schism might escalate into factional war; the split also raised questions about Prabhakaran's control over the LTTE and undermined the Tamil militants' claims that the main obstacle in the peace process was political divisions among Sinhalese political parties. The rift also adversely affected Norway's fresh attempt to revive the peace initiative. In late March the LTTE vowed to remove Karuna from Sri Lanka. The Tamil political candidate and supporter of Karuna, Rajan Sathyamoorthy, was shot dead by suspected Tamil militants in the eastern town of Batticaloa, raising fears of factional fighting. Although the LTTE denied any involvement in the killing, government troops were deployed to Batticaloa to maintain law and order. On 9 April fighting between the two factions broke out. The conflict ended on 13 April with Karuna reported to have fled from his base and gone into hiding, his forces having dispersed and the LTTE assuming full control of the eastern areas.

At the general election, which took place on 2 April 2004, the UPFA won 105 of the 225 seats, having taken 45.6% of the votes cast; Wickremasinghe's UNP retained 82 seats (with 37.8% of the votes), while the TNA won 22 seats (with 7%). In an unexpected development, the Buddhist Jathika Hela Urumaya (JHU—National Heritage Party) won nine seats. The LTTE had openly supported the TNA during the election campaign and described the large number of seats won by the alliance as an endorsement and recognition of the LTTE as 'the sole representative' of the Tamil population. Participation at the election was reported to have reached 75% of eligible voters. The poll concluded peacefully. However, there were claims of voter intimidation and electoral malpractice, particularly in the north and east of the country. The UPFA, which had not secured an outright majority of seats in Parliament, undertook negotiations with a view to forming a coalition administration. Meanwhile, Mahinda Rajapakse, a senior member of the UPFA and former fisheries minister, was sworn in as Prime Minister on 6 April. By 10 April the UPFA still needed the support of at least eight legislators to achieve an absolute majority in Parliament; nevertheless, a 31-member Cabinet was sworn in. While Kumaratunga retained the defence portfolio, Lakshman Kadirgamar was appointed Minister of Foreign Affairs. In late April, having resolved a dispute with the UPFA, four members of the JVP were also sworn in as ministers.

Meanwhile, the LTTE responded to the election result with a threat to return to violence if their demands for self-rule were not met. They later requested the Government to open negotiations on the basis of the proposed ISGA that they had submitted in late October 2003. President Kumaratunga had already agreed to abide by the cease-fire and pledged to resume negotiations with the LTTE; however, it was widely acknowledged that she would not be willing to grant the degree of devolution that was desired by the Tamil organization. The JVP was also hostile towards the LTTE's campaign for regional autonomy.

From June 2004 onwards the cease-fire between the LTTE and the Government came under increasing pressure. During discussions with Hagrup Haukland, leader of the Norwegian team monitoring the ongoing peace process, the LTTE accused the Sri Lankan armed forces of sheltering Col Karuna and of assisting him in waging a campaign against them. The armed forces initially denied that they had helped Karuna to escape following the April conflict; however, later in that month the Minister of Ports and Aviation and of Information and Media, Mangala Samaraweera, admitted that the army had helped Karuna to escape, while insisting that the plan had been carried out without government knowledge. Fears that the cease-fire was close to collapse were heightened when a suicide bomber blew herself up during questioning at a police station in Colombo in early July, having first attempted to meet the Tamil Secretary-General of the EPDP, Douglas Devananda, who was a long-standing opponent of the LTTE. Although the LTTE denied any involvement in the attack, they were widely believed to have been responsible both for the bombing, and for the assassination of an EPDP politician in Ampara district later in that month. Meanwhile, clashes continued to occur between the LTTE and members of the faction that had broken away under the leadership of Karuna. At the end of July Norway's Deputy Minister of Foreign Affairs, Vidar Helgesen, arrived in Sri Lanka to attempt to restart peace talks, accusing both the Government and the LTTE of complacency. The opposition UNP subsequently offered to support the Government in any parliamentary vote on the resumption of talks. However, in September it was reported that Norwegian envoy Erik Solheim had failed in his attempts to instigate new peace talks.

In September 2004 the UPFA Government achieved a legislative majority for the first time since its formation in April when the CWC, which had eight seats in Parliament, announced that it would join the ruling coalition. Muttu Sivalingam of the CWC was subsequently appointed Minister of Community Development and Estate Infrastructure. In the following month three members of the opposition SLMC defected to the UPFA, further strengthening the Government.

In December 2004 the LTTE formally rejected a new proposal by the Government that the two sides restart peace negotiations. The LTTE attributed their decision to the fact that the JVP, one of the members of the coalition Government, opposed their condition that any negotiations should be based upon their proposed ISGA. The LTTE had warned in November that they would return to their violent struggle for self-rule unless the Government agreed to discuss the ISGA. Concerns were raised by several prominent donor countries that the JVP's stance was undermining the peace process.

Sri Lanka was one of the countries most seriously affected by the devastating tsunami caused by a massive earthquake in the Indian Ocean on 26 December 2004. More than 31,000 Sri Lankans were killed in the disaster, which also left thousands homeless and without livelihoods. The tourism industry was badly affected by the catastrophe, with many hotels and resorts being damaged or destroyed. It was initially hoped that the scale of the disaster would serve to ease tensions between the Government and the LTTE, particularly as the Tamil areas of the island were amongst those worst hit. However, conflicts soon surfaced over the distribution of aid; the LTTE claimed that the Government was restricting the flow of international aid into Tamil-controlled areas and demanded that it be delivered directly to them. Talks intended to resolve the dispute held at the end of January ended without agreement. The situation deteriorated further in the following month, when it was revealed that around 70% of the survivors of the tsunami disaster had yet to receive any government relief, apparently owing to a combination of bureaucratic incompetence and corruption. The Tamil Relief Organization (TRO), controlled by the LTTE, alleged that only one-third of the aid was reaching the Tamil-controlled northern and eastern areas, despite government claims that two-thirds of the aid was destined for these areas.

Meanwhile, in February 2005 the Government announced that it was prepared to resume peace negotiations with the LTTE, based on the ISGA, prompting the JVP to threaten its withdrawal from the UPFA. Earlier in that month a senior LTTE leader, E. Kaushalyan, was murdered in his car near the town of Batticaloa. The police blamed the LTTE faction led by Col Karuna; however, the LTTE accused the armed forces of collaborating with Karuna's faction to fight against them. Karuna's faction continued to clash with the LTTE sporadically during the following months, and was suspected to be responsible for the assassination of a prominent Tamil journalist in April.

In June 2005 the Government finally signed an agreement—entitled the Post-Tsunami Operational Management Structure (P-TOMS)—that would allow the LTTE to participate in the distribution of aid for the reconstruction effort. The agreement had been reached only following the withdrawal from the ruling coalition of the JVP, which had remained stringently opposed to any deal with the LTTE. The JVP's withdrawal left the Government with a minority in the legislature, although the opposition UNP had assured the Government of its support for the aid-sharing mechanism. In the following month, however, in response to a petition from the JVP and the JHU, the Supreme Court suspended the implementation of the P-TOMS, ruling that several of its clauses were illegal. Meanwhile, increasing tensions between the LTTE and government forces, complicated by the former's ongoing clashes with the rebel Karuna faction, led to an upsurge in violence that prompted international donors to warn the two sides that the ongoing cease-fire was under threat. At the end of May the chief of military intelligence in Colombo, Maj. Nizam Muthalif, had become the most senior official to have been assassinated by the LTTE since the agreement of the cease-fire in February 2002.

In August 2005 the peace process between the Government and the LTTE was jeopardized when the Minister of Foreign Affairs, Lakshman Kadirgamar, was assassinated by unidentified gunmen at his home in Colombo. Although they denied responsibility, the LTTE were held responsible for the attack. In the aftermath of the murder, President Kumaratunga declared a state of emergency, granting the security forces broad powers of detention. Amid widespread fears that the cease-fire would collapse, both sides announced their commitment to its maintenance, and the LTTE agreed to meet with the Government to review the truce agreement. Later in August Kumaratunga announced the appointment of her brother, Anura Bandaranaike, the incumbent Minister of Tourism, as Kadirgamar's successor. Bandaranaike retained the tourism portfolio. In September the LTTE declined a Norwegian proposal that the talks should be held at the international airport near Colombo, while the Government rejected the LTTE's suggestion that they be held in Kilinochchi, the political centre of LTTE-controlled northern Sri Lanka. Later in the same month the European Union (EU) issued a statement banning LTTE delegations from visiting any of its member states. Sporadic violence continued throughout the following months.

Meanwhile, there was controversy over the schedule for the next presidential election. While, under the terms of the Constitution, the next election was due to be held in December 2005, President Kumaratunga claimed that the holding of an undisclosed swearing-in ceremony in 2000 (see above) had actually extended her second term until December 2006. In July the SLFP announced that its presidential candidate would be Prime Minister Mahinda Rajapakse. In August the Supreme Court brought an end to the controversy, ruling that the election should be held by 22 November 2005. In September it was announced that the election would take place on 17 November. Former Prime Minister Ranil Wickremasinghe subsequently declared that he would stand as the candidate of the UNP. The JVP offered its support to Rajapakse, on the condition that were he to secure victory he would commit his government to the retention of a unitary state, renegotiate the ongoing cease-fire with the LTTE and end the privatization of state assets. Rajapakse concluded a similar agreement with the JHU.

On 17 November 2005 14 candidates contested the presidential election. Rajapakse secured a narrow victory over his closest rival, Wickremasinghe, winning 50.3% of the vote, compared with 48.4% for Wickremasinghe. The election was notable for the low turn-out amongst the country's Tamil population, particularly in the LTTE-controlled northern and eastern areas; this was thought to have played a significant part in Wickremasinghe's defeat, as he had stressed his commitment to the ongoing cease-fire agreement during the electoral campaign. While the LTTE had stated that they would not prevent people from voting, there was widespread evidence that they had done so. Rajapakse subsequently nominated Minister of Agriculture, Public Security, Law and Order and of Buddha Sasana, Ratnasiri Wickremanayake, as Prime Minister. In the new Cabinet, announced shortly afterwards, Minister of Ports and Aviation Mangala Samaraweera was additionally allocated the foreign affairs portfolio, while Bandaranaike continued as Minister of Tourism. Neither the JVP nor the JHU were awarded any cabinet portfolios.

In December 2005 violence in the country escalated. At least 60 people died over the course of the month as a result of various attacks believed to have been co-ordinated by the LTTE. At the end of that month President Rajapakse stated that he was ready to hold talks with the LTTE. Shortly before his announcement, Norwegian peace envoy Erik Solheim had urged both sides to enter into new peace talks, stressing that the cease-fire was in imminent danger of collapse. In early January 2006 a suicide bomb attack on a naval patrol vessel resulted in the deaths of 13 sailors, constituting the largest loss of military life since the cease-fire began. A further nine sailors were killed in a land-mine explosion later in that month, as the number of violent incidents continued to increase. In February negotiators representing the LTTE and the Government convened in Geneva, Switzerland, to hold talks on how to control the recent upsurge in violence. A joint statement issued following the conclusion of the talks committed both sides to uphold the cease-fire. The LTTE agreed to attempt to prevent further attacks on the security forces, while the Government pledged to try to disarm the Karuna faction of the LTTE, which was believed to have been acting on behalf of the armed forces against its erstwhile colleagues. However, prior to the second round of talks, scheduled to take place in Geneva in mid-April, the violence intensified once again. Several days before the talks were due to commence, the LTTE requested that they be postponed, in order that members of their delegation could first meet with LTTE commanders. Later that month the LTTE stated that it would not attend talks, alleging that government forces had carried out attacks on Tamil civilians and that the Sri Lankan navy had prevented the LTTE commanders in the east of the country from meeting the LTTE political leaders in the north. In late April a suicide bombing believed to have been perpetrated by the LTTE at the army headquarters in Colombo killed at least 11 people and seriously injured the Chief of Staff of the Army, Lt-Gen. Sarath Fonseka. The Government subsequently ordered a number of air strikes on alleged LTTE bases near Trincomalee, which, according to the LTTE, caused the displacement of approximately 15,000 people. The violence continued, further jeopardizing the ongoing cease-fire: in May Maj.-Gen. (retd) Ulf Henricsson of the SLMM acknowledged that a 'low intensity war' was taking place. At the end of the month the EU classified the LTTE as a terrorist organization, which entailed a suspension of LTTE fund-raising in EU member states, a 'freeze' on the organization's assets and a ban on travel to the EU. The LTTE responded by demanding the withdrawal of EU members of the SLMM, resulting in the departure of Danish, Finnish and Swedish monitors in July and August. Amid escalating violence the LTTE withdrew from peace talks planned for June. In mid-June fears about the intensification of the conflict were realized when landmine explosions killed some 64 civilians, including several children, on a crowded bus in Kebithigollewa. Despite the LTTE's condemnation of the attack, the Government retaliated by launching air attacks on Kilinochchi. A new front in the fighting opened up over access to the Maavil-Aru waterway, which became the scene of a number of air and ground offensives in July. The violence spread to the town of Muttur, north of the waterway, forcing thousands of inhabitants, many of them Muslims, to flee in August. Clashes between LTTE fighters and army troops continued in the north and east of the country, with rising death tolls of civilians, rebels and government forces. At the end of September the SLMM estimated that the resumption of hostilities had resulted in the displacement of some 200,000 people. In October, following a suicide bombing near Habarana that killed approximately 100 naval officers, it was feared that relatively unaffected areas of the country would be drawn into the conflict when the LTTE attacked a naval base in the southern town of Galle. Little progress was made at peace talks held in Geneva at the end of October, although both sides agreed to uphold the terms of the cease-fire agreement. In November it was reported that an army attack on a Tamil refugee camp in LTTE-held territory had resulted in at least 65 civilian fatalities. Shortly afterwards a TNA member of Parliament was assassinated in Colombo, with no group immediately claiming responsibility. At his annual speech, given at the end of November, Prabhakaran declared the cease-fire to be 'defunct' and blamed the Government for failing to find a solution. In early December the Government amended existing laws to extend the powers of security officials and support anti-terrorist operations. Anton Balasingham, the chief LTTE negotiator, died in mid-December. In the same month Col. Karuna's forces were reported to have killed around 35 LTTE fighters in eastern Sri Lanka, while 24 children were kidnapped and later released by the LTTE, supposedly in error.

The violence continued into 2007, with government forces reportedly securing the eastern town of Vakarai in January after a series of battles and the displacement of an estimated 30,000 people. According to SLMM estimates published in February, the conflict had resulted in almost 4,000 fatalities over the preceding 15 months. In late February the ambassadors of Italy and the USA were injured in mortar fire during a visit to Batticaloa; the attack was blamed on the LTTE. In March there was a renewal of hostilities in eastern areas, reportedly as part of a larger government drive to secure the east of the country, as concerns mounted for the estimated 155,000 civilians left homeless by the fighting. In late March the strengthened capability of LTTE forces was demonstrated by an air attack on the government airbase at Katunayake, which was followed in late April by air bombings of fuel depots in the Colombo area.

Meanwhile, at the end of June 2006 Rajapakse was elected unopposed to replace Kumaratunga as President of the SLFP. In January 2007 more than 20 dissident politicians from the opposition parties joined the Government, thus giving it a parliamentary majority. This, in turn, precipitated a cabinet reshuffle in which UNP defectors and SLMC members were allocated several portfolios. Shortly after the defections from the UNP the party reportedly indicated that the memorandum of understanding signed between the UNP and the SLFP in October of the previous year to ensure co-operation on several issues of national importance, including the LTTE conflict, had been invalidated. Appointments to the new Cabinet, which now numbered more than 50 ministers, included the former Deputy Leader of the UNP, Karu Jayasuriya, as Minister of Public Administration and Home Affairs, and Rohitha Bogollagama as Minister of Foreign Affairs. Further ministerial changes were reported in the following month, when Minister of Ports and Aviation Mangala Samaraweera, Minister of National Heritage Anura Bandaranaike and Minister of Port Development Sripathi Sooriyarachchi were dismissed (Bandaranaike was, however, later reinstated). In June Samaraweera and Sooriyarachchi founded a new political party, the Sri Lanka Freedom Party—Mahajana Wing (SLFP—M), in reaction to the 'path of extremism' they believed the SLFP to be taking. In the following month the UNP and the SLFP—M signed an agreement, pledging to resolve the civil conflict within nine months should they come to power. (Sooriyarachchi was killed in a car accident in February 2008.) In December 2007 the SLMC withdrew its support for the governing coalition, and the party's leader, Abdul Rauf Hakeem, resigned from his position as Minister of Posts and Telecommunication. However, the Government retained sufficient support to obtain parliamentary approval for its budget later that month.

As fighting continued in the north and east of the country, it became increasingly difficult to determine accurate death tolls from the varying statements of the military and the LTTE; however, in mid-2007 it was estimated that the resumption of hostilities had resulted in approximately 5,000 fatalities since 2005. There were frequent reports of human rights violations on both sides. In June 2007 hundreds of Tamils were apparently forced to leave Colombo by the police, and accounts of abductions and disappearances were commonplace. The LTTE, in turn, was criticized for allegedly continuing to recruit child soldiers. During a visit to Sri Lanka in October, the UN High Commissioner for Human Rights, Louise Arbour, concluded that 'in the context of the armed conflict and of the emergency measures taken against terrorism, the weakness of the rule of law and prevalence of impunity [was] alarming', and highlighted the necessity of objective reporting on human rights issues. At the same time, Arbour expressed concern over the LTTE's 'recruitment of children, forced recruitment and abduction of adults, and political killings' and human rights violations committed by the Tamileela Makkal Viduthalai Pulikal (Tamileela People's Liberation Tigers—TMVP), a political group led by Col Karuna. However, the Government declined Arbour's offer to establish an office in the country.

In July 2007 the army claimed that its operations in the eastern province had resulted in a decisive victory over the LTTE and had led to its recapture of the region, prompting the Government to announce a development package worth Rs 6,500m. Government spending on defence had increased as the conflict escalated, resulting in reduced funding elsewhere. The front line shifted as fighting intensified in the north of the country. Both sides suffered set-backs in late 2007 and early 2008. In October 2007 the LTTE conducted an aerial and land attack on the Anuradhapura airbase, reportedly killing tens of military officers and destroying eight aircraft. S. P. Thamilselvan, the head of the LTTE's political wing and a leading member of its negotiating team, was killed in an aerial bombardment by the military in the following month. In early January 2008 a senior LTTE intelligence official was reportedly killed in a landmine explosion; his death was followed within days by that of D. M. Dassanayake, the Minister of Nation Building, in a bomb attack. The Government had given notice of its intention to withdraw from the cease-fire agreement, an action that was formalized on 16 January and that appeared to confirm the Government's preference for a military solution to the conflict. As a result, the SLMM announced the end of its activities in Sri Lanka. Also in January, Col Karuna, who had been apprehended while attempting to enter the United Kingdom on a false passport in late 2007, was sentenced to nine months' imprisonment by a British court. Speculation had arisen over the links between Karuna's faction and the Sri Lankan Government, and the role that this alleged alliance had played in the Government wresting control of the eastern province from the LTTE.

Following the collapse of the cease-fire agreement in January 2008, the All Party Representatives' Committee (APRC), which had been established in 2006 to work towards finding a political solution to the conflict, urged Rajapakse to create provincial councils as part of a devolution process in the affected regions. Observers noted that the APRC had excluded the TNA from its proceedings and lacked the support of certain sections of the opposition. The Government subsequently announced the formation of a Temporary Interim Advisory Council in the northern province, which, it was claimed, would have a diverse composition and address minority issues. In March 2008 local elections were conducted in the Batticaloa district of the eastern province, at which the TMVP, campaigning under the UPFA banner, secured victory. However, the TMVP was criticized for alleged violence and intimidation in the run-up to the elections, and the poll was boycotted by the UNP and the TNA. Full provincial council elections were held in May; the UPFA, with the support of the TMVP, secured a majority in the provincial council, although some observers claimed that the election was not free and fair. Meanwhile, the violence continued unabated; in early April the Minister of Highways and Road Development, Jeyaraj Fernandopulle, (together with at least 14 other people) was killed in a suspected LTTE suicide bombing carried out near Colombo and a suicide attack in the centre of the capital itself in mid-May left around 10 people dead. According to estimates published by the British Broadcasting Corporation (BBC) that month, the civil conflict had caused more than 70,000 deaths since 1983.

In foreign policy, Sri Lanka has adopted a non-aligned role. Sri Lanka is a founder member of the South Asian Association for Regional Co-operation (SAARC, see p. 384), formally established in 1985.

Government

A presidential form of government was adopted in October 1977 and confirmed in the Constitution of September 1978. The Constitution provides for a unicameral Parliament as the supreme legislative body, its members being elected by a system of modified proportional representation. Executive powers are vested in the President, who is Head of State. The President is directly elected for a term of six years and is not accountable to Parliament. The President has the power to appoint or dismiss the Prime Minister and members of the Cabinet; may assume any portfolio; and is empowered to dismiss Parliament. In 1982 the Constitution was amended, allowing the President to call a presidential election before his/her first term of office was completed. In 1983 the Constitution was further amended to include a 'no-separation' clause, making any division of Sri Lanka illegal, and any advocates of separatism liable to lose their civic rights.

Sri Lanka comprises nine provinces and 25 administrative districts, each with an appointed Governor and elected Development Council. A network of 68 Pradeshiya Sabhas (district councils) was inaugurated throughout the country in January 1988.

Defence

As assessed at November 2007, the armed forces totalled 150,900 (including recalled reservists): army 117,900, navy 15,000, air force 18,000. There were also paramilitary forces of around 88,600 (including 13,000 Home Guard, an estimated 15,000 National Guard and a 3,000-strong anti-guerrilla unit). Defence expenditure for 2007 was budgeted at Rs 139,000m. Military service is voluntary.

Economic Affairs

In 2006, according to estimates by the World Bank, Sri Lanka's gross national income (GNI), measured at average 2004–06 prices, was US $25,732m., equivalent to $1,300 per head (or $5,010 per head on an international purchasing-power parity basis). During 1996–2006, it was estimated, the population increased at an average annual rate of 0.8%, while gross domestic product (GDP) per head grew, in real terms, by an average of 4.1% per year. Overall GDP increased, in real terms, at an average annual rate of 4.8% in 1996–2006. According to official figures, real GDP rose by 7.7% in 2006 and by an estimated 6.8% in 2007.

In 2007 agriculture (including hunting, forestry and fishing) contributed an estimated 11.7% of GDP, while 32.2% of the employed labour force were engaged in the sector in 2006. The principal cash crops are tea (which accounted for 13.3% of total export earnings in 2006), rubber and coconuts. In 2004 Sri Lanka was the world's second largest tea exporter, having been overtaken by Kenya in that year. Rice production is also important. Cattle, buffaloes, goats and poultry are the principal livestock. During 1996–2006 agricultural GDP increased at an average annual rate of 1.7%. According to official figures, agricultural GDP expanded by 6.3% in 2006 and by an estimated 3.3% in 2007.

Industry (including mining and quarrying, manufacturing, construction and power) contributed an estimated 29.9% of GDP in 2007, and engaged 26.6% of the employed labour force (excluding inhabitants of the districts of Vavuniya, Mullaitivu and Kilinochchi) in 2006. During 1996–2006 industrial GDP increased at an average annual rate of 4.7%. According to official figures, industrial GDP rose by 8.1% in 2006 and by an estimated 7.6% in 2007.

Mining and quarrying contributed an estimated 2.1% of GDP in 2007, and, according to the Asian Development Bank (ADB), engaged 1.8% of the employed labour force in 2001. Gemstones are the major mineral export (accounting for 1.8% of total export earnings in 2006). Another commercially important mineral in Sri Lanka is graphite, and there are also deposits of iron ore, monazite, uranium, ilmenite sands, limestone and clay. During 2002–07 sectoral GDP increased at an average annual rate of 16.5%, according to official figures. Mining GDP increased by 24.2% in 2005 and by an estimated 19.2% in 2007.

Manufacturing contributed 18.5% of GDP in 2007, and engaged 19.2% of the employed labour force in 2006. The principal branches of manufacturing include wearing apparel (excluding footwear), textiles, food products, and also petroleum and coal products. The garment industry is Sri Lanka's largest earner of foreign exchange, with sales of garments and textiles providing an estimated 44.1% of total export earnings in 2006. During 1996–2006 manufacturing GDP increased by an average of 4.8% per year. The GDP of the manufacturing sector rose by 5.5% in 2006 and by an estimated 6.4% in 2007, according to official figures.

Energy is derived principally from petroleum, which accounted for 63.2% of electricity production in 2004. In the same year hydroelectric power accounted for 36.8% of electricity produced. In 2007 construction of a coal-fired electricity plant commenced; once operational, the plant was expected to alter significantly the structure of the energy sector. Imports of mineral fuels and lubricants comprised 16.7% of the value of total imports in 2006.

The services sector, which is dominated by tourism, contributed an estimated 58.4% of GDP in 2007, and engaged 41.2% of the employed labour force (excluding inhabitants of the districts of Vavuniya, Mullaitivu and Kilinochchi) in 2006. During 1996–2006 services GDP increased at an average annual rate of 5.3%. The sector's GDP grew by 7.7% in 2006 and by an estimated 7.1% in 2007, according to official figures.

In 2006 Sri Lanka recorded a visible trade deficit of US $2,345m. and there was a deficit of $1,434m. on the current account of the balance of payments. In 2006 the principal source of imports (18.5%) was India, while the USA was the principal market for exports (28.2%). Other major trading partners were the People's Republic of China, Singapore and the United Kingdom. The principal exports in 2006 were basic manufactures, including clothing, and tea. The principal imports were basic manufactures, machinery and transport equipment, and mineral fuels, lubricants, etc.

The budgetary deficit, before grants, for 2006 totalled Rs 235,813m. (equivalent to 8.4% of GDP). Sri Lanka's total external debt was US $11,444m. at the end of 2005, of which $9,812m. was long-term public debt. In that year the cost of debt-servicing was equivalent to 4.5% of earnings from the exports of goods and services. During 1997–2007 the average annual rate of inflation was 10.0%; the rate was 13.7% in 2006 and 17.5% in 2007. According to the ADB, an estimated 6.7% of the labour force were unemployed in 2006.

Sri Lanka is a member of the Asian Development Bank (ADB, see p. 182), a founder member of the South Asian Association for Regional Co-operation (SAARC, see p. 384), which seeks to improve regional co-operation, particularly in economic development, a founder member of the Colombo Plan (see p. 411), which seeks to promote economic and social development in Asia and the Pacific, and a member of the UN Economic and Social Commission for Asia and the Pacific (ESCAP, see p. 35).

Unemployment, a persistent fiscal deficit and inflation, together with the economic dislocation resulting from the ethnic conflict, are among the country's main economic problems. Following the declaration of a cease-fire between the Government and the Liberation Tigers of Tamil Eelam (LTTE) in February 2002, the economy showed clear signs of recovery. The export sector improved, and tourist arrivals increased. A privatization programme was also under way: the insurance, utilities, petroleum and telecommunications sectors were opened to private investment. In 2003 substantial progress was also made in public enterprise reform: several key public corporations were privatized and the electricity sector was opened to private investment. Donors at an international conference in June of that year pledged US $4,500m. in aid over the next five years to help rebuild the country's economy and infrastructure. The prerequisites to the assistance were a serious commitment from the Government to a restructuring programme and a permanent peace agreement between the LTTE and the Government. Progress in economic reform was constrained by weak governance, which, in turn, helped to precipitate a delay in the peace process; however, growth was sustained in 2004. The reconstruction effort necessitated by the devastating effect upon much of Sri Lanka's coastline of the massive tsunami in late December of that year impeded the country's economic performance to an extent in 2005. The fisheries and tourism sectors sustained extensive damage, resulting in the loss of many livelihoods. However, the more commercial areas in the west of the country were unaffected, limiting the economic impact of the disaster. Furthermore, the provision of substantial aid from the international community (notably the estimated $3,000m. pledged during a forum on post-tsunami reconstruction in May) generated a strong momentum in the rehabilitation effort and real GDP consequently rose by 5.7% in 2005. The 2006 budget focused on reducing poverty through the introduction of decreases in taxation and new allowances for the poor and increasing investment in rural industries. The persistent fiscal deficit remained a considerable obstacle to Sri Lanka's development, however, rising from 8.2% of GDP in 2004 to 8.7% in 2005. The Government increasingly relied on external creditors to finance this deficit, thus contributing to escalating levels of public debt and higher rates of inflation. More prudent budgetary operations led to a reduction in the deficit in 2006 (see above) and it was hoped that the authorities' decision to remove costly petrol subsidies would strengthen the fiscal position in the medium to long term. According to the ADB, a fiscal deficit equivalent to 7.7% of GDP was realized in 2007, owing largely to the broadening of Sri Lanka's tax base. However, in March 2008 the IMF warned that, despite improving fiscal conditions, rising inflation required the continued use of firm monetary policies and therefore discouraged the printing of further money. Moreover, escalating security problems and the official lifting of the cease-fire in early 2008 (see Recent History) were expected to engender additional expenditure on defence and to deter foreign investment. In the long term, the achievement of a durable solution to the conflict with the LTTE and the Government's ability to implement structural reforms and to manage the country's considerable level of debt are central to Sri Lanka's economic performance. The ADB projected GDP growth of 4% for 2008, on the condition that the security issues did not escalate beyond the level realized in 2007. A contraction in external demand (attributed mainly to the slowing US economy) was expected to temper the performance of Sri Lanka's garment exports, while the planned repeal of electricity subsidies (coupled with rising international prices for food and petroleum) was forecast to keep inflation at a high level in 2008.

Education

Education is officially compulsory for 11 years between five and 15 years of age, and it is available free of charge from lower kindergarten to university age. There are three types of school: state-controlled schools (mostly co-educational), denominational schools and Pirivenas (for Buddhist clergy and lay students). Primary education begins at the age of five and lasts for five years. Secondary education, beginning at 10 years of age, lasts for up to eight years, comprising a first cycle of six years and a second of two years. In 2003/04 the total enrolment at primary and secondary schools was equivalent to an estimated 88.1% of the school-age population (boys 88%; girls 90%). Primary enrolment in that year included an estimated 97.1% of children in the relevant age-group, while secondary enrolment was equivalent to an estimated 82.5% (boys 82%; girls 83%) of pupils. There are 26 teacher-training colleges, 12 universities, 13 polytechnic institutes, eight junior technical colleges and an open university. Budgeted expenditure on education by the central Government in 2005 was Rs 63,360m. (11.2% of total government spending).

Public Holidays

2008: 15 January (Tamil Thai Pongal Day), 4 February (Independence Commemoration Day), 6 March (Maha Shivaratri), 20 March (Milad un-Nabi, Birth of the Prophet), 12 April (Sinhala and Tamil New Year's Eve), 14 April (Sinhala and Tamil New Year's Day), 25 April (Good Friday), 1 May (May Day), 1 October (Id al-Fitr, Ramazan Festival Day), 27 October (Diwali—Festival of Lights), 9 December (Id al-Adha, Hadji Festival Day), 25 December (Christmas Day).

2009: 15 January (Tamil Thai Pongal Day), 4 February (Independence Commemoration Day), 23 February (Maha Shivaratri), 9 March (Milad un-Nabi, Birth of the Prophet), April (Sinhala and Tamil New Year's Eve), April (Sinhala and Tamil New Year's Day), 10 April (Good Friday), 1 May (May Day), 20 September (Id al-Fitr, Ramazan Festival Day), 17 October

SRI LANKA

(Diwali—Festival of Lights), 27 November (Id al-Adha, Hadji Festival Day), 25 December (Christmas Day).

Note: A number of Hindu, Muslim and Buddhist holidays depend on lunar sightings. There is a holiday every lunar month on the day of the full moon.

Weights and Measures

Legislation passed in 1974 provided for the introduction of the metric system, but imperial units are still used for some purposes.

Statistical Survey

Source (unless otherwise stated): Department of Census and Statistics, 15/12 Maitland Crescent, POB 563, Colombo 7; tel. (11) 2682176; fax (11) 2697594; e-mail dcensus@lanka.com.lk; internet www.statistics.gov.lk.

Area and Population

AREA, POPULATION AND DENSITY

Area (sq km)	65,525*
Population (census results)	
17 March 1981	14,846,750
17 July 2001 (provisional)†	
Males	8,343,964
Females	8,520,580
Total	16,864,544
Population (official estimates at mid-year)	
2004	19,462,000
2005	19,668,000
2006	19,886,000
Density (per sq km) at mid-2006	303.5

* 25,299 sq miles. This figure includes inland water (3,189 sq km).

† Figures refer to 18 out of 25 districts where enumeration was carried out completely. Enumeration was only partially conducted in Mannar, Vavuniya, Batticaloa and Trincomalee districts, owing to security concerns; data from these districts brought the total enumerated population to approximately 17,560,000. The census was not conducted in the districts of Jaffna, Mullaitivu and Kilinochchi, also owing to security concerns. The total estimated population for the entire country at July 2001 was 18,732,255.

ETHNIC GROUPS
(census results)

	1981	2001*†
Sinhalese	10,979,561	13,810,664
Sri Lankan Tamil	1,886,872	736,484
Indian Tamil	818,656	855,888
Sri Lankan Moors	1,046,926	1,349,845
Others	114,735	111,663
Total	14,846,750	16,864,544

* Provisional.
† Figures refer to 18 out of 25 districts.

DISTRICTS
(population estimates at mid-2006)

	Area (sq km, excl. inland water)*	Population ('000)	Density (persons per sq km)
Colombo	676	2,421	3,581
Gampaha	1,341	2,125	1,585
Kalutara	1,576	1,102	699
Kandy	1,917	1,361	710
Matale	1,952	471	241
Nuwara Eliya	1,706	735	431
Galle	1,617	1,040	643
Matara	1,270	804	633
Hambantota	2,496	547	219
Jaffna	929	595	640
Mannar	1,880	100	53
Vavuniya	1,861	164	88
Mullaitivu	2,415	145	60
Kilinochchi	1,205	142	118
Batticaloa	2,610	556	213
Ampara	4,222	627	149

—continued	Area (sq km, excl. inland water)*	Population ('000)	Density (persons per sq km)
Trincomalee	2,529	395	156
Kurunegala	4,624	1,511	327
Puttalam	2,882	745	259
Anuradhapura	6,664	791	119
Polonnaruwa	3,077	382	124
Badulla	2,827	837	296
Moneragala	5,508	420	76
Ratnapura	3,236	1,073	332
Kegalle	1,685	797	473
Total	62,705	19,886	317

* As at 1988; revised total land area is 62,336 sq km.

PRINCIPAL TOWNS
(provisional, population at 2001 census)

Colombo (Kolamba)*	642,020	Sri Jayawardenepura (Kotte)†	115,826
Dehiwala-Mount Lavinia	209,787	Kandy (Maha Nuwara)	110,049
Moratuwa	177,190	Kalmunai (Galmune)	94,457
Jaffna (Yapanaya)	145,600‡	Galle (Galla)	90,934
Negombo (Migamuwa)	121,933		

* Commercial capital.
† Administrative capital.
‡ Estimated population at mid-1997 (Source: Provincial Councils, Department of Elections).

Source: Thomas Brinkhoff, *City Population* (internet www.citypopulation.de).

BIRTHS, MARRIAGES AND DEATHS
(year of registration, provisional)

	Registered live births		Registered marriages	Registered deaths	
	Number	Rate (per 1,000)	Number	Number	Rate (per 1,000)
1999	329,521	18.1	169,634	114,472	6.3
2000	340,144	18.4	186,548	112,569	6.1
2001	354,101	18.9	186,698	111,100	5.9
2002	363,549	19.1	190,832	110,637	5.8
2003	363,343	18.9	193,387	114,310	5.9
2004	360,220	18.5	191,985	112,568	5.8
2005	370,424	18.8	n.a.	129,822	6.6
2006	371,264	18.7	n.a.	115,424	5.8

Expectation of life (years at birth, WHO estimates): 71.2 (males 67.9; females 75.1) in 2005 (Source: WHO, *World Health Statistics*).

SRI LANKA

EMPLOYMENT

('000 persons aged 10 years and over, excluding northern and eastern provinces)

	2004	2005	2006
Agriculture, hunting, forestry and fishing	2,215.3	2,059.3	2,287.3
Manufacturing	1,226.0	1,292.9	1,363.1
Mining and quarrying Electricity, gas and water Construction	349.7	417.2	526.9
Wholesale and retail trade, repair of motor vehicles, motorcycles and personal household goods	818.1	817.1	955.0
Restaurants and hotels	114.3	115.0	129.4
Transport, storage and communications	379.7	448.4	430.3
Financing, insurance, real estate and business services	165.9	226.1	221.1
Public administration and defence	477.4	465.4	400.5
Education	237.1	254.4	276.8
Health and social work	92.7	120.9	109.7
Other community, social and personal services	109.7	113.0	123.9
Private households with employed persons	67.5	48.3	80.2
Activities not adequately defined	450.5	410.2	201.2
Total employed	**6,704.0**	**6,788.1**	**7,105.3**

Health and Welfare

KEY INDICATORS

Total fertility rate (children per woman, 2005)	1.9
Under-5 mortality rate (per 1,000 live births, 2005)	14
HIV/AIDS (% of persons aged 15–49, 2005)	<0.1
Physicians (per 1,000 head, 2004)	0.55
Hospital beds (per 1,000 head, 2001)	3.0
Health expenditure (2004): US $ per head (PPP)	162.6
Health expenditure (2004): % of GDP	4.3
Health expenditure (2004): public (% of total)	45.6
Access to water (% of persons, 2004)	79
Access to sanitation (% of persons, 2004)	91
Human Development Index (2005): ranking	99
Human Development Index (2005): value	0.743

For sources and definitions, see explanatory note on p. vi.

Agriculture

PRINCIPAL CROPS

('000 metric tons)

	2004	2005	2006
Rice (paddy)	2,628	3,246	3,342
Maize	35	42	48
Potatoes	81	79	78
Sweet potatoes	40	41	42
Cassava (Manioc)	221	223	226
Sugar cane	990	992	1,137
Dry beans	8	9	8
Dry cow-peas	9	11	10
Coconuts	881	890	913
Copra*	60	67	65
Cabbages	61	64	59
Tomatoes	54	57	61
Pumpkins, squash and gourds	74	87	82
Cucumbers and gherkins	23	27	25
Aubergines (Eggplants)	80	84	88
Chillies and green peppers	53	67	67
Dry onions	77	109	134
Green beans	40	41	41

—continued	2004	2005	2006
Carrots	34	37	36
Plantains	540	545	504
Lemons and limes	5	5	5
Guavas, mangoes and mangosteens	92	93	85
Pineapples	58	58	57
Coffee (green)	8	7	7
Tea (made)	308	317	311
Pepper	19	18	19
Cinnamon	13	13	13
Natural rubber	95	104	109

* Unofficial figures.

Aggregate production ('000 metric tons, may include official, semi-official or estimated data): Total cereals 2,668 in 2004, 3,295 in 2005, 3,396 in 2006; Total roots and tubers 342 in 2004, 344 in 2005, 346 in 2006; Total vegetables (incl. melons) 561 in 2004, 640 in 2005, 660 in 2006; Total fruits (excl. melons) 757 in 2004, 768 in 2005, 718 in 2006.

Source: FAO.

LIVESTOCK

('000 head, year ending September)

	2004	2005	2006
Buffaloes	302	308	314
Cattle	1,161	1,185	1,125
Sheep	11	10	14
Goats	405	395	382
Pigs	79	85	92
Chickens	11,042	11,636	13,313

Source: FAO.

LIVESTOCK PRODUCTS

('000 metric tons)

	2004	2005	2006
Cattle meat	28.2	29.3	26.3
Buffalo meat*	3.5	4.0	4.0
Goat meat	1.4	1.5	1.5
Pig meat	2.1	2.2	2.3
Chicken meat	94.7	97.3	78.8
Cows' milk	134.9	136.7	139.3
Buffaloes' milk	25.8	26.1	26.7
Goats' milk*	4.9	5.1	5.1
Hen eggs	49.6	49.0	51.1

* FAO estimates.

Source: FAO.

Forestry

ROUNDWOOD REMOVALS

('000 cubic metres, excl. bark, FAO estimates)

	2003	2004	2005
Sawlogs, veneer logs and logs for sleepers	117	117	117
Other industrial wood	577	577	577
Fuel wood	5,710	5,646	5,584
Total	**6,404**	**6,340**	**6,278**

2006: Figures assumed unchanged from 2005 (FAO estimates).

Source: FAO.

SRI LANKA

SAWNWOOD PRODUCTION
('000 cubic metres, incl. railway sleepers)

	1999*	2000	2001
Coniferous (softwood)	—	—	30
Broadleaved (hardwood)	5	29	31
Total	5	29	61

* FAO estimates.

2002–06: Production assumed to be unchanged from 2001 (FAO estimates).

Source: FAO.

Fishing
('000 metric tons, live weight)

	2003	2004	2005
Capture	282.2	284.4	162.5
Tilapias	17.9	22.2	21.6
Demersal percomorphs	20.0	17.5	10.6
Clupeoids	56.4	54.4	24.9
Skipjack tuna	42.8	43.8	28.0
Carangids	14.9	13.6	6.0
Mackerels	17.8	18.4	9.7
Sharks, rays, skates etc.	17.6	16.4	5.3
Aquaculture	3.5	2.5	1.7
Total catch	285.6	286.9	164.2

Source: FAO.

Mining
('000 metric tons, unless otherwise indicated, estimates)

	2004	2005	2006
Natural graphite (metric tons)	3,400	3,000	3,200
Salt—unrefined	79	80	81
Kaolin	9	9	10
Phosphate rock (gross weight)	42	43	44

Ilmenite concentrates ('000 metric tons): 34.1 in 1998.

Zirconium concentrates ('000 metric tons): 13 in 1999.

Sources: US Geological Survey; UN, *Industrial Commodity Statistics Yearbook*.

Industry

SELECTED PRODUCTS
('000 barrels, unless otherwise indicated)

	2004	2005	2006
Raw sugar ('000 metric tons)	21	14	19
Cigarettes (million units)	5,003	n.a.	n.a.
Jet fuel*	650	650	700
Motor gasoline—petrol*	2,100	2,200	2,200
Kerosene*	1,500	1,500	1,500
Distillate fuel oil*	5,100	5,200	5,300
Residual fuel oil*	5,100	5,100	5,000
Cement ('000 metric tons)*	1,400	1,500	1,600
Plywood ('000 cu m)†	14	14	14
Electric energy (million kWh)	8,043	8,769	9,389

* Estimates.
† FAO estimates.

Naptha ('000 metric tons): 112 in 2002, 99 in 2003, 103 in 2004.

Sources: US Geological Survey; Asian Development Bank, *Key Indicators of Developing Asian and Pacific Countries*; FAO; UN, *Industrial Commodity Statistics Yearbook*.

Finance

CURRENCY AND EXCHANGE RATES

Monetary Units
100 cents = 1 Sri Lanka rupee (R).

Sterling, Dollar and Euro Equivalents (31 December 2007)
£1 sterling = Rs 217.808;
US $1 = Rs 108.719;
€1 = Rs 160.045;
1,000 Sri Lanka rupees = £4.59 = $9.20 = €6.25.

Average Exchange Rate (rupees per US $)
2005   100.498
2006   103.914
2007   110.626

BUDGET
(Rs million)

Revenue	2003	2004	2005*
Taxation	231,648	281,552	351,119
Taxes on income	39,397	41,372	55,361
Taxes on goods and services	97,230	120,382	142,690
Excise levy	50,972	65,790	76,865
Taxes on property	3,662	4,489	5,253
Taxes on international trade	39,667	48,655	66,243
Non-tax revenue	44,868	29,921	38,373
Property income	24,750	15,493	19,985
Other	15,618	7,981	11,934
Total	276,516	311,473	389,492

Expenditure	2003	2004	2005*
General public services	91,564	102,634	121,870
National security and defence	61,983	73,452	84,980
Social services	124,002	166,845	183,643
Education	39,116	42,340	63,360
Health	27,476	34,419	39,636
Economic services	77,559	83,545	123,753
Agriculture-related	15,422	17,083	27,023
Energy and water supply	23,810	22,395	24,386
Transport and communication	24,852	30,758	46,204
Interest payments	125,126	119,782	128,000
Other purposes	8,254	14,504	6,162
Total expenditure and net lending	426,505	487,310	563,428

* Forecasts.

Source: IMF, *Sri Lanka: Selected Issues and Statistical Appendix* (September 2005).

INTERNATIONAL RESERVES
(excluding gold, US $ million at 31 December)

	2004	2005	2006
IMF special drawing rights	—	2	3
Reserve position in IMF	74	68	72
Foreign exchange	2,058	2,581	2,762
Total	2,132	2,651	2,837

Source: IMF, *International Financial Statistics*.

MONEY SUPPLY
(Rs million at 31 December)

	2003	2004	2005
Currency outside banks	85,601	99,669	114,070
Demand deposits at commercial banks	76,014	88,777	116,620
Total money (incl. others)	162,640	189,339	231,621

Source: IMF, *International Financial Statistics*.

SRI LANKA

COST OF LIVING
(Consumer Price Index for Colombo; base: 2000 = 100)

	2004	2005	2006
Food (incl. beverages)	145.5	163.0	184.6
Fuel and light	157.0	178.1	228.3
Clothing (excl. footwear)	112.7	117.6	122.2
Rent	100.0	100.0	100.0
All items (incl. others)	143.0	159.7	181.5

Source: ILO.

NATIONAL ACCOUNTS
(Rs million at current prices)

Expenditure on the Gross Domestic Product

	2005	2006	2007*
Government final consumption expenditure	321,037	451,438	546,545
Private final consumption expenditure	1,692,765	1,988,378	2,403,167
Increase in stocks	84,756	91,306	112,012
Gross fixed capital formation	573,263	730,910	884,688
Total domestic expenditure	2,671,821	3,262,032	3,946,412
Exports of goods and services	793,153	885,381	1,046,075
Less Imports of goods and services	1,012,192	1,208,757	1,414,100
GDP at market prices	2,452,782	2,938,656	3,578,386
GDP at factor cost, at constant 2002 prices	1,941,671	2,090,548	2,232,387

* Provisional.

Gross Domestic Product by Economic Activity

	2005	2006	2007*
Agriculture, hunting, forestry and fishing	289,906	333,114	417,353
Mining and quarrying	35,932	46,202	56,645
Manufacturing	478,611	564,987	661,983
Construction	167,999	216,833	264,104
Electricity, gas and water	57,908	72,457	87,951
Transport, storage and communications	287,491	344,909	423,820
Wholesale and retail trade	569,255	659,597	790,628
Hotels and restaurants	14,218	16,646	18,367
Finance, real estate and	205,322	266,972	328,158
Ownership of dwellings	88,759	103,201	126,212
Public administration	206,497	257,837	334,261
Private services	50,886	55,902	68,905
GDP at market prices	2,452,782	2,938,656	3,578,386

* Provisional.

BALANCE OF PAYMENTS
(US $ million)

	2004	2005	2006
Exports of goods f.o.b.	5,757	6,347	6,883
Imports of goods f.o.b.	−7,200	−7,977	−9,228
Trade balance	−1,443	−1,630	−2,345
Exports of services	1,527	1,540	1,625
Imports of services	−1,908	−2,089	−2,394
Balance on goods and services	−1,824	−2,179	−3,114
Other income received	157	76	312
Other income paid	−360	−375	−700
Balance on goods, services and income	−2,027	−2,478	−3,502
Current transfers received	1,564	1,968	2,326
Current transfers paid	−214	−233	−258

—continued	2004	2005	2006
Current balance	−677	−743	−1,434
Capital account (net)	64	250	291
Direct investment abroad	−6	−38	−29
Direct investment from abroad	233	272	480
Portfolio investment assets	111	276	355
Portfolio investment liabilities	−100	−216	−304
Other investment assets	−354	−223	297
Other investment liabilities	−17	−4	−111
Net errors and omissions	−189	−73	−261
Overall balance	−935	−498	−717

Source: IMF, *International Financial Statistics*.

OFFICIAL DEVELOPMENT ASSISTANCE
(US $ million)

	1998	1999	2000
Bilateral donors	296.7	219.9	251.1
Multilateral donors	210.3	43.7	25.2
Total	507.0	263.6	276.3
Grants	195.6	198.4	187.2
Loans	311.4	65.2	89.1
Per caput assistance (US $)	28.3	14.5	15.0

Source: UN, *Statistical Yearbook for Asia and the Pacific*.

External Trade

PRINCIPAL COMMODITIES
(distribution by SITC, Rs million)

Imports c.i.f.	2004	2005	2006
Food and live animals	78,364	77,262	98,726
Beverages and tobacco	5,919	6,856	5,374
Crude materials (inedible), excluding fuels	12,014	17,935	23,538
Mineral fuels, lubricants, etc.	115,036	112,157	169,401
Animal, vegetable oil and fats	8,025	15,690	16,668
Chemicals	88,435	101,498	121,970
Basic manufactures	250,417	265,180	284,520
Machinery and transport equipment	163,984	172,344	225,525
Miscellaneous manufactured articles	30,736	30,139	30,712
Total (incl. others)	796,086	835,108	1,015,136

Exports f.o.b.	2004	2005	2006
Food and live animals	103,527	114,240	135,682
Tea	74,897	81,481	91,667
Machinery and transport equipment	34,694	28,172	37,147
Basic and miscellaneous manufactures	331,609	346,131	375,096
Garments	268,573	276,144	303,263
Total (incl. others)	583,967	638,276	687,181

Source: Asian Development Bank, *Key Indicators of Developing Asian and Pacific Countries*.

SRI LANKA

PRINCIPAL TRADING PARTNERS
(US $ million)

Imports c.i.f.	2004	2005	2006
China, People's Republic	454.0	630.6	1,218.2
Hong Kong	619.4	648.2	486.7
India	1,439.2	1,835.4	2,153.4
Iran	418.7	523.9	658.6
Japan	411.7	379.7	463.0
Korea, Republic	245.9	210.3	246.8
Malaysia	329.2	393.5	587.5
Singapore	698.5	736.9	1,013.8
United Arab Emirates	202.7	296.3	372.5
United Kingdom	312.1	276.5	212.2
Total (incl. others)	7,999.8	8,863.2	11,609.3

Exports f.o.b.	2004	2005	2006
France	102.3	121.4	110.6
Germany	274.1	271.8	299.8
India	391.5	566.4	664.5
Italy	152.9	199.6	248.7
Japan	157.6	144.6	183.1
Russia	151.0	157.7	181.9
United Arab Emirates	137.8	170.3	210.2
United Kingdom	779.2	777.3	850.3
USA	1,869.3	1,988.1	2,074.8
Total (incl. others)	5,757.2	6,383.7	7,361.7

Source: Asian Development Bank, *Key Indicators of Developing Asian and Pacific Countries*.

Transport

RAILWAYS

	2004	2005	2006
Passengers (million)	114.9	114.4	105.4
Freight carried ('000 metric tons)*	1,602	1,502	1,551

* Excluding livestock.

Source: Sri Lanka Railways.

ROAD TRAFFIC
(motor vehicles in use at 31 December)

	2000	2001	2002
Passenger cars	233,018	241,444	253,447
Buses and coaches	64,963	66,273	67,702
Lorries and vans	300,712	312,495	328,913
Road tractors	133,092	138,879	146,043
Motorcycles and mopeds	834,586	868,705	923,467
Total	1,566,371	1,627,796	1,719,572

Source: International Road Federation, *World Road Statistics*.

SHIPPING

Merchant Fleet
(registered at 31 December)

	2004	2005	2006
Number of vessels	77	82	81
Displacement ('000 grt)	156.6	177.8	174.1

Source: Lloyd's Register-Fairplay, *World Fleet Statistics*.

International Sea-borne Shipping
(freight traffic, '000 metric tons, Colombo, Trincomalee and Galle only)

	2003	2004	2005
Goods loaded	10,541.5	11,893.4	13,155.7
Goods unloaded	19,958.4	22,069.1	24,144.9

CIVIL AVIATION
(traffic on scheduled services)

	2001	2002	2003
Kilometres flown (million)	34	29	34
Passengers carried ('000)	1,719	1,741	1,958
Passenger-km (million)	6,641	6,327	6,910
Total ton-km (million)	822	778	864

Source: UN, *Statistical Yearbook*.

Tourism

FOREIGN TOURIST ARRIVALS*

Country of residence	2004	2005	2006
Australia	24,471	25,836	21,665
Belgium	5,718	3,891	6,373
Canada	14,974	21,335	14,863
France	30,422	26,641	22,703
Germany	58,932	46,320	47,296
India	104,390	113,023	128,520
Italy	17,984	10,147	12,353
Japan	19,747	17,163	16,217
Maldives	15,201	24,396	24,505
Netherlands	21,487	15,252	19,460
Pakistan	9,629	11,056	11,165
Switzerland	10,687	8,339	7,729
United Kingdom	107,042	92,929	88,531
USA	15,680	25,392	20,825
Total (incl. others)	566,202	549,308	559,603

* Excluding Sri Lanka nationals residing abroad.

Tourism receipts (US $ million, incl. passenger transport): 709 in 2003; 808 in 2004; 729 in 2005.

Sources: Ceylon Tourist Board; World Tourism Organization.

THE CABINET
(May 2008)

Prime Minister and Minister of Internal Administration: Ratnasiri Wickremanayake.
Minister of Foreign Affairs: Rohitha Bogollagama.
Minister of Defence, of Public Security, Law and Order, of Religious Affairs, of Finance and Planning, and of Nation Building: Mahinda Rajapakse.
Minister of Tourism: Milinda Moragoda.
Minister of Posts and Telecommunication, and of Special Projects: Mahinda Wijesekera.
Minister of Justice: Amarasiri Dodangoda.
Minister of Healthcare and Nutrition: Nimal Siripala de Silva.
Minister of Transport: Dullas Alahaperuma.
Minister of Trade, Marketing Development, Co-operatives and Consumer Affairs: Bandula Gunawardena.
Minister of Agricultural Development and Agrarian Services Development: Maithripala Sirisena.
Minister of Power and Energy: John Seneviratna.
Minister of Child Development and Women's Affairs: Sumedha G. Jayasena.
Minister of Mass Media and Information: Anura Priyadarshana Yapa.
Minister of Urban Development and Sacred Area Development: Dinesh Gunawardena.
Minister of Social Services and Social Welfare: Douglas Devananda.
Minister of Public Administration and Home Affairs: Karu Jayasuriya.
Minister of Housing and Common Amenities: Ferial Ashraff.
Minister of Education: Susil Premajayantha.
Minister of Labour Relations and Manpower: Athauda Seneviratne.
Minister of Rural Industries and Self-Employment Promotion: R. M. S. B. Navinne.
Minister of Vocational and Technical Training: Piyasena Gamage.
Minister of Local Government and Provincial Councils: Janaka Bandara Thenakoon.
Minister of Fisheries and Aquatic Resources: Felix Perera.
Minister of Science and Technology: Prof. Tissa Vitharana.
Minister of Enterprise Development and Investment Promotion: Dr Sarath Amunugama.
Minister of Constitutional Affairs and National Integration: D. E. W. Gunasekera.
Minister of Disaster Management and Human Rights: Mahinda Samarasinghe.
Minister of Plantation Industries: D. M. Jayaratne.
Minister of Petroleum and Petroleum Resources Development: A. H. M. Fowzie.
Minister of Highways and Road Development: (vacant).
Minister of Youth Empowerment and Socio-Economic Development: Arumugan Thondaman.
Minister of Community Development and Social Inequity Eradication: P. Chandrasekeran.
Minister of Water Supply and Drainage: A. L. M. Athaullah.
Minister of Resettlement and Disaster Relief Services: Abdul Risath Bathiyutheen.
Minister of Plan Implementation: P. Dayaratne.
Minister of Supplementary Crops Development: R. M. Dharmadasa Banda.
Minister of Parliamentary Affairs: M. H. Mohomed.
Minister of Export Development and International Trade: Prof. G. L. Peiris.
Minister of Public Estate Management and Development: Milroy Fernando.
Minister of Land and Land Development: Jeewan Kumaranatunga.
Minister of Youth Affairs: Pavithra Wanniarachchi.
Minister of Indigenous Medicine: Tissa Karaliyadde.
Minister of Sports and Public Recreation: Gamini Lokuge.
Minister of Construction and Engineering Services: Rajitha Senaratne.
Minister of Foreign Employment Promotion and Welfare: Keheliya Rambukwelle.
Minister of Livestock Development: R. M. C. B. Rathnayake.
Minister of Cultural Affairs: Mahinda Yapa Abeywardena.
Minister of Higher Education: Prof. Wiswa Warnapala.
Minister of Irrigation and Water Management, and of Ports and Aviation: Chamal Rajapaksa.
Minister of Industrial Development: Kumara Welgama.
Minister of Environment and Natural Resources: Champika Ranawaka.

MINISTRIES

President's Secretariat: Republic Sq., Colombo 1; tel. (11) 2324801; fax (11) 2331246; e-mail gosl@presidentsl.org; internet www.presidentsl.org.
Prime Minister's Office: 58 Sir Ernest de Silva Mawatha, Colombo 7; tel. (11) 2575317; fax (11) 2575454; internet www.pmoffice.gov.lk.
Ministry of Agrarian Services and Development of Farmer Communities: 'Govijana Mandiraya', 80/5 Rajamalwatta Rd, Battaramulla, Colombo; tel. (11) 2887439.
Ministry of Agricultural Development and Agrarian Services: 'Govijana Mandiraya', 80/5 Rajamalwatta Rd, Battaramulla, Colombo; tel. (11) 2869553; fax (11) 2868919; e-mail agmin@sltnet.lk; internet www.mimrd.gov.lk.
Ministry of Agriculture, Irrigation, Animal Production, Youth Affairs, Agrarian Services and Fisheries: POB 65, Gatambe, Peradeniya; tel. (81) 2388336; fax (81) 2389860; e-mail info@minagricp.lk; internet www.minagricp.lk.
Ministry of Child Development and Women's Empowerment: 177 Nawala Rd, Narahenpita, Colombo 5; tel. (11) 2505584; fax (11) 2369294; e-mail mwa@sltnet.lk.
Ministry of Community Development and Social Inequity Eradication: 35/A Dr N. M. Perera Mawatha, Colombo 8.
Ministry of Constitutional Affairs and National Integration: 310 Galle Rd, Colombo 3; tel. (11) 2375178; fax (11) 2375181; e-mail consas@constitution.gov.lk; internet www.constitution.gov.lk.
Ministry of Construction and Engineering Services: 'Sethsiripaya', 2nd Floor, Battaramulla, Colombo.
Ministry of Cultural Affairs: 'Sethsiripaya', 8th Floor, Battaramulla, Colombo; tel. (11) 2872001; fax (11) 2872021; e-mail mcasec@sltnet.lk.
Ministry of Defence, Public Security, Law and Order: 15/5 Baladaksha Mawatha, POB 572, Colombo 3; tel. (11) 2430860; fax (11) 2446300; e-mail secretary@defence.lk; internet www.defence.lk.
Ministry of Disaster Management and Human Rights: 2 Wijerama Mawatha, Colombo 7; tel. (11) 2695013; fax (11) 2681980; e-mail info@dmhr.gov.lk; internet www.dmhr.gov.lk.
Ministry of Education: 'Isurupaya', Pelawatte, Battaramulla, Colombo; tel. (11) 2785141; fax (11) 2785162; e-mail minedu@moe.gov.lk; internet www.moe.gov.lk.
Ministry of Enterprise Development and Investment Promotion: World Trade Centre, West Tower, 25th Level, Echelon Sq, Colombo 1; tel. (11) 2394951; fax (11) 2424960; e-mail secedip@sltnet.lk.
Ministry of Environment and Natural Resources: 82 Sampath Paya, Rajamalwatte Rd, Battaramulla, Colombo; tel. (11) 2882112; fax (11) 2863652; e-mail promotion@menr.lk; internet www.menr.lk.
Ministry of Export Development and International Trade: 'Rakshana Mandiraya', 21 Vauxhall St, Colombo 2.
Ministry of Finance and Planning: Galle Face Secretariat, Colombo 1; tel. (11) 2484500; fax (11) 2449823; e-mail mfsa@sltnet.lk; internet www.treasury.gov.lk.
Ministry of Fisheries and Aquatic Resources: Maligawatta, Colombo 10; tel. (11) 2446183; fax (11) 2541184; e-mail secretary@fisheries.gov.lk; internet www.fisheries.gov.lk.
Ministry of Foreign Affairs: Republic Bldg, Colombo 1; tel. (11) 2325371; fax (11) 2446091; e-mail publicity@formin.gov.lk; internet www.slmfa.gov.lk.
Ministry of Foreign Employment Promotion and Welfare: Level 33, West Tower, World Trade Centre, Colombo 1; tel. (11) 2438734; fax (11) 2438736; e-mail fep_gov@sltnet.lk; internet www.minfep.gov.lk.
Ministry of Healthcare and Nutrition: 'Suwasiripaya', 385 Wimalawansha Himi Mawatha, Colombo 10; tel. (11) 2694033; fax (11) 2692694; e-mail dhi@health.gov.lk; internet www.health.gov.lk.
Ministry of Higher Education: 18 Ward Place, Colombo 7; tel. (11) 2694486; fax (11) 2697239; e-mail mioh.hied@sltnet.lk; internet www.mohe.gov.lk.
Ministry of Highways and Road Development: Sethsiripaya Office Complex, 'C' Wing, 9th Floor, POB 53, Battaramulla, Colombo;

Communications Media

	1999	2000	2001
Television receivers ('000 in use)	1,900	2,100	2,200
Telephones ('000 main lines in use)	669.1	767.4	822.1
Mobile cellular telephones ('000 subscribers)	256.7	430.2	667.7
Personal computers ('000 in use)	105	135	175
Internet users ('000)	65.0	121.5	150.0
Newspapers	174	180	189
Books published: titles	4,655	1,818	n.a.
Books published: copies ('000)	n.a.	25,459.3	7,439.1

Facsimile machines (number in use, estimate): 11,000 in 1994.

Radio receivers ('000 in use): 3,850 in 1997.

2002 ('000): Telephones (main lines in use) 881.4; Mobile cellular telephones (subscribers) 931.6; Personal computers (number in use) 250; Internet users 200.0.

2003 ('000): Telephones (main lines in use) 939.0; Mobile cellular telephones (subscribers) 1,393.4; Personal computers (number in use) 325; Internet users 280.0; Broadband subscribers 3.4.

2004 ('000): Telephones (main lines in use) 993.4; Mobile cellular telephones (subscribers) 2,213.6; Personal computers (number in use) 530; Internet users 280.0; Broadband subscribers 20.4.

2005 ('000): Telephones (main lines in use) 1,244.0; Mobile cellular telephones (subscribers) 3,361.8; Personal computers (number in use) 530; Internet users 350.0; Broadband subscribers 26.1.

2006 ('000): Telephones (main lines in use) 1,884.1; Mobile cellular telephones (subscribers) 5,412.5; Internet users 428.0; Broadband subscribers 29.1.

Sources: UN, *Statistical Yearbook*; UNESCO, *Statistical Yearbook*; Telecommunications Regulatory Commission of Sri Lanka and International Telecommunication Union.

Education

(1995)

	Institutions	Teachers	Students
Primary	9,657	70,537	1,962,498
Secondary	5,771*	103,572	2,314,054
Universities and equivalent	n.a.	2,344	40,035
Distance learning	n.a.	206	20,601

* 1992 figure.

1996: Primary: 9,554 institutions, 66,339 teachers, 1,843,848 students.

1997: Primary: 60,832 teachers, 1,807,751 students; Secondary: 2,313,511 students.

1998: Primary: 1,798,162 students.

2001: Universities: 12 institutions, 2,999 teachers, 48,899 students.

2002: Universities: 12 institutions, 3,225 teachers (excl. open university), 48,667 students (excl. open university).

2003 (provisional): Universities: 12 institutions, 3,386 teachers (excl. open university), 59,734 students (excl. open university).

Sources: UNESCO, *Statistical Yearbook*; Ministry of Education, Colombo.

Adult literacy rate (UNESCO estimates): 90.7% (males 92.3%; females 89.1%) in 2001 (Source: UNESCO Institute for Statistics).

Directory

The Constitution

The Constitution of the Democratic Socialist Republic of Sri Lanka was approved by the National State Assembly (renamed Parliament) on 17 August 1978, and promulgated on 7 September 1978. The following is a summary of its main provisions:

FUNDAMENTAL RIGHTS

The Constitution guarantees the fundamental rights and freedoms of all citizens, including freedom of thought, conscience and worship and equal entitlement before the law.

THE PRESIDENT

The President is Head of State, and exercises all executive powers, including defence of the Republic. The President is directly elected by the people for a term of six years, and is eligible for re-election. The President's powers include the right to:

(i) choose to hold any portfolio in the Cabinet;

(ii) appoint or dismiss the Prime Minister or any other minister;

(iii) preside at ceremonial sittings of Parliament;

(iv) dismiss Parliament at will; and

(v) submit to a national referendum any Bill or matter of national importance which has been rejected by Parliament.

LEGISLATURE

The Parliament is the legislative power of the people. It consists of such number of representatives of the people as a Delimitation Commission shall determine. The members of Parliament are directly elected by a system of modified proportional representation. By-elections are abolished, successors to members of Parliament being appointed by the head of the party which nominated the outgoing member at the previous election. Parliament exercises the judicial power of the people through courts, tribunals and institutions created and established or recognized by the Constitution or established by law. Parliament has control over public finance.

OTHER PROVISIONS

Religion

Buddhism has the foremost place among religions and it is the duty of the State to protect and foster Buddhism, while assuring every citizen the freedom to adopt the religion of their choice.

Language

The Constitution recognizes two official languages, Sinhala and Tamil. Either of the national languages may be used by all citizens in transactions with government institutions.

Amendments

Amendments to the Constitution require endorsement by a two-thirds' majority in Parliament. In February 1979 the Constitution was amended by allowing members of Parliament who resigned or were expelled from their party to retain their seats, in certain circumstances. In January 1981 Parliament amended the Constitution to increase its membership from 168 to 169. An amendment enabling the President to seek re-election after four years was approved in August 1982. In February 1983 an amendment providing for by-elections to fill vacant seats in Parliament was approved. An amendment banning parties that advocate separatism was approved by Parliament in August 1983. In November 1987 Parliament adopted an amendment providing for the creation of eight provincial councils (the northern and eastern provinces were to be merged as one administrative unit); although the northern and eastern provinces were subsequently merged, the Supreme Court announced the merger to be officially invalid in October 2006. In December 1988 Parliament adopted an amendment affording Tamil the same status as Sinhala, as one of the country's two official languages.

The Government

HEAD OF STATE

President: Mahinda Rajapakse (sworn in 19 November 2005).

SRI LANKA

www.virakesari.lk; f. 1969; Tamil; Man. Dir Kumar Nadesan; Editor V. Thevaraj; circ. 29,000.

Silumina: Lake House, 35 D. R. Wijewardene Mawatha, Colombo 10; tel. (11) 2324772; fax (11) 2449069; e-mail editor@silumina.lk; internet www.silumina.lk; f. 1930; Sinhala; Editor Niwal Horana; circ. 264,000.

Sunday Island: 223 Bloemendhal Rd, POB 133, Colombo 13; tel. (11) 2421599; fax (74) 609198; e-mail manik@unl.upali.lk; f. 1981; English; Editor Manik de Silva; circ. 40,000.

The Sunday Leader: Colombo Commercial Bldg, 1st Floor, 121 Sir James Peiris Mawatha, Colombo 2; tel. (75) 2365892; fax (75) 2365891; e-mail editor@thesundayleader.lk; internet www.thesundayleader.lk; English; Editor Lasantha Wickramatunga.

Sunday Observer: D. R. Wijewardene Mawatha, POB 248, Colombo 10; tel. (11) 2429231; fax (11) 2429230; e-mail editor@sundayobserver.lk; internet www.sundayobserver.lk; f. 1923; English; Editor Jayatilleke de Silva; circ. 125,000.

Sunday Thinakkural: 68 Ellie House Rd, Colombo 15; internet www.thinakkural.com/sundaythinakkural; Tamil; also publ. from Jaffna; Editor A. Siyanesachelvan.

The Sunday Times: 8 Hunupitiya Cross Rd, Colombo 2; tel. (11) 2326247; fax (11) 2423922; e-mail editor@sundaytimes.wnl.lk; internet www.sundaytimes.lk; f. 1986; English and Sinhala; Editor Singha Ratnatunga; circ. 116,000.

Thinakaran Vaara Manjari: Lake House, 35 D. R. Wijewardene Mawatha, Colombo 10; tel. (11) 2221181; f. 1948; Tamil; Editor R. Srikanthan; circ. 35,000.

Virakesari Weekly: 185 Grandpass Rd, Colombo 14; tel. (11) 2320881; fax (11) 2448205; e-mail webmaster@virakesari.lk; internet www.virakesari.lk; f. 1931; Tamil and English; Man. Dir Kumar Nadesan; Editor Murugesampillai Subramaniam; circ. 110,000.

PERIODICALS
(weekly unless otherwise stated)

Athavan: Colombo; Tamil.

Aththa: 91 Dr N. M. Perera Mawatha, Colombo 8; tel. (11) 2691450; fax (11) 2691610; e-mail dew128@dialogsl.net; f. 1964; Sinhala; publ. by the Communist Party of Sri Lanka; Editor Gunasena Vithana; circ. 28,000.

Business Lanka: Trade Information Service, Sri Lanka Export Development Board, Level 7, 42 Navam Mawatha, POB 1872, Colombo 2; tel. (11) 2300677; fax (11) 2300715; e-mail tisinfo@tradenetsl.lk; f. 1981; quarterly; information for visiting business executives, etc.; Editor S. D. Isaac.

Ceylon Commerce: National Chamber of Commerce of Sri Lanka, NCCSL Bldg, 450 D. R. Wijewardene Mawatha, POB 1375, Colombo 10; tel. (11) 2689597; fax (11) 2689596; e-mail nccsl@slt.lk; internet www.nationalchamberlk.org; monthly.

Ceylon Medical Journal: 6 Wijerama Mawatha, Colombo 7; tel. (11) 2693324; fax (11) 2698802; e-mail slma@eureka.lk; internet www.medinet.lk/cmj; f. 1887; quarterly; Editors Prof. Colvin Goonaratna, Prof. H. Janaka de Silva.

The Economic Times: 130/C/8 Jothikarama Mawatha, Pannipitiya; tel. (11) 2796134; fax (11) 4305787; f. 1970; Editor Thimsy Fahim.

The Financial Times: 323 Union Place, POB 330, Colombo 2; tel. (11) 2226181; quarterly; commercial and economic affairs; Man. Editor Cyril Gardiner.

Gnanarthapradeepaya: Colombo Catholic Press, 2 Gnanarthapradeepaya Mawatha, Borella, Colombo 8; tel. (11) 2695984; fax (11) 2692586; e-mail pradeepaya@sltnet.lk; f. 1866; Sinhala; Roman Catholic; Chief Editor Rev. Fr Cyril Gamini Fernando; Exec. Dir Rev. Fr Rohan de Alwis; circ. 26,000.

Irudina: Lithira Publications (Pvt) Ltd, 98 Ward Place, Colombo 7; tel. (11) 5344202; fax (11) 5344200; e-mail editor@irudina.lk; internet www.irudina.lk; f. 2004; Sinhala; Editor Mohan Lal Piyadasa.

Janakavi: 47 Jayantha Weerasekera Mawatha, Colombo 10; fortnightly; Sinhala; Assoc. Editor Karunaratne Amerasinghe.

Manasa: 150 Dutugemunu St, Dehiwala, Colombo; tel. (11) 2553994; f. 1978; Sinhala; monthly; science of the mind; Editor Sumanadasa Samarasinghe; circ. 6,000.

Mihira: Lake House, 35 D. R. Wijewardene Mawatha, Colombo 10; tel. (11) 2419583; f. 1964; Sinhala children's magazine; Editor M. Newton Pinto; circ. 145,000.

Morning Star: 39 Fussels Lane, Colombo 6; tel. (11) 2511233; fax (11) 2584836; e-mail jdcsiacm@panlanka.net; f. 1841; English and Tamil; publ. by the Jaffna diocese of the Church of South India.

Nava Yugaya: Lake House, 35 D. R. Wijewardene Mawatha, Colombo 10; tel. (11) 2419581; f. 1956; literary fortnightly; Sinhala; Editor S. N. Senanayake; circ. 57,000.

Navaliya: 223 Bloemendhal Rd, Colombo 13; tel. (11) 2324001; fax (11) 2448103; internet www.navaliya.com; Sinhala; women's interest; Editor Chandani Wijetunge; circ. 148,260.

Pathukavalan: POB 2, Jaffna; tel. (21) 22280; f. 1876; Tamil; publ. by St Joseph's Catholic Press; Editor Rev. Fr Ruban Mariampillai; circ. 7,000.

Puthiya Ulaham: 115 4th Cross St, Jaffna; tel. (21) 22627; f. 1976; Tamil; six a year; publ. by Centre for Better Society; Editor Rev. Dr S. J. Emmanuel; circ. 1,500.

Ravaya: Colombo; Sinhala; Editor Victor Ivan.

Samajawadhaya: 91 Dr N. M. Perera Mawatha, Colombo 8; tel. (11) 2595328; monthly; theoretical; publ. by the Communist Party of Sri Lanka.

Sarasaviya: Lake House, 35 D. R. Wijewardene Mawatha, Colombo 10; tel. (11) 2429586; f. 1963; Sinhala; films; Editor Granville Silva; circ. 56,000.

Sinhala Bauddhaya: Maha Bodhi Mandira, 130 Rev. Hikkaduwe Sri Sumangala Nahimi Mawatha, Colombo 10; tel. and fax (11) 1677626; e-mail mahabodhi@asia.com; f. 1906; publ. by The Maha Bodi Society of Ceylon; Hon. Sec. Kirthi Kalahe; circ. 25,000.

Sirikatha: 8 Hunupitiya Cross Rd, Colombo 2; tel. (11) 2314714; fax (11) 2449504; Sinhala women's magazine; Editor Siri Ranasinghe.

Sri Lanka Government Gazette: Government Press, POB 507, Colombo; tel. (11) 2293611; f. 1802; Sinhala and Tamil; official govt bulletin; circ. 54,000.

Sri Lanka News: Lake House, 35 D. R. Wijewardene Mawatha, Colombo 10; tel. (11) 2429429; fax (11) 2449069; f. 1938; digest of news and features; printing temporarily suspended from March 2002; Editor Ruwan Godage.

Sri Lanka Today: Government Dept of Information, 7 Sir Baron Jayatilaka Mawatha, Colombo 1; tel. (11) 2228376; English; quarterly; Editor Manel Abhayaratne.

Subasetha: Lake House, 35 D. R. Wijewardene Mawatha, Colombo 10; tel. (11) 2221181; f. 1967; Sinhala; astrology, the occult and indigenous medicine; Editor Capt. K. Chandra Sri Kularatne; circ. 100,000.

Tharunee: Lake House, 35 D. R. Wijewardene Mawatha, Colombo 10; tel. (11) 2429588; fax (11) 2449069; f. 1969; Sinhala; women's journal; Editor Sumana Sapramadu; circ. 95,000.

Vidusara: 223 Bloemendhal Rd, Colombo 13; tel. (11) 2324001; fax (11) 2448103; internet www.vidusara.com; Sinhala; Editor Anura Siriwardena; circ. 103,992.

NEWS AGENCIES

Lankapuvath (National News Agency of Sri Lanka): Transworks House, Lower Chatham St, Colombo 1; tel. (11) 2673483; fax (11) 2673011; f. 1978; Chair. D. E. W. Gunasekara; Editor G. L. W. Wijesinha.

TamilNet: e-mail tamilnet@tamilnet.com; internet www.tamilnet.com; f. 1997; reports on Tamil affairs.

PRESS ASSOCIATIONS

Foreign Correspondents' Association of Sri Lanka: 20 1/1 Regent Flats, Sir Chittampalan Gardiner Mawatha, Colombo; tel. (11) 2231224.

Sri Lanka Press Association: Colombo; Pres. B. H. S. Jayewardene.

Publishers

W. E. Bastian and Co (Pvt) Ltd: 23 Canal Row, Fort, Colombo 1; tel. (11) 2432752; f. 1904; art, literature, technical; Dirs H. A. Munideva, K. Hewage, N. Munideva, G. C. Bastian.

Buddhist Publication Society: 54 Sangharaja Mawatha, POB 61, Kandy; tel. (81) 2237283; fax (81) 2223679; e-mail bps@sltnet.lk; internet www.bps.lk; f. 1958; philosophy, religion and theology; Pres. Bhikkhu Bodhi.

Colombo Catholic Press: 2 Gnanarthapradeepaya Mawatha, Borella, Colombo 8; tel. (11) 2678106; fax (11) 2692586; e-mail catholic@eureka.lk; f. 1865; religious; publrs of *The Messenger*, *Gnanarthapradeepaya*, *The Weekly*; Exec. Dir Rev. Fr Bertram Dabrera.

M. D. Gunasena and Co Ltd: 217 Olcott Mawatha, POB 246, Colombo 11; tel. (11) 2323981; fax (11) 2323336; e-mail mdgunasena@mail.ewisl.net; internet www.mdgunasena.com; f. 1913; educational and general; Chair M. D. Percy Gunasena; Man. Dir M. D. Ananda Gunasena.

Lake House Printers and Publishers Ltd: 41 W. A. D. Ramanayake Mawatha, POB 1458, Colombo 2; tel. (11) 2433271; fax (11)

2449504; e-mail wnl@wijeya.lk; f. 1965; Chair. R. S. Wijewardene; Sec. D. P. Anura Nishantha Kumara.

Pradeepa Publishers: 34/34 Lawyers' Office Complex, Colombo 12; tel. (11) 2435074; fax (11) 2863261; e-mail kjaytie@slt.lk; academic and fictional; Propr K. Jayatilake.

Saman Publishers Ltd: 49/16 Iceland Bldg, Colombo 3; tel. (11) 2223058; fax (11) 2447972.

Sarexpo International Ltd: Caves Bookshop, 81 Sir Baron Jayatilleke Mawatha, POB 25, Colombo 1; tel. (11) 2422676; fax (11) 2447854; e-mail sarexpo@eureka.lk; f. 1876; history, arts, law, medicine, technical, educational; Man. Dir C. J. S. Fernando.

K. V. G. de Silva and Sons (Colombo) Ltd: Shop No. 5, Liberty Plaza, Colombo 3; tel. (11) 7455646; fax (11) 7555543; e-mail photowave@sltnet.lk; f. 1898; art, philosophy, scientific, technical, academic, 'Ceyloniana', fiction; Man. Frederick Jayaratnam.

PUBLISHERS' ASSOCIATION

Sri Lanka Association of Publishers: 112 S. Mahinda Mawatha, Maradana, Colombo 10; tel. (11) 2695773; fax (11) 2696653; e-mail dayawansajay@hotmail.com; Pres. Dayawansa Jayakody; Sec.-Gen. Gamini Wijesuriya.

Broadcasting and Communications

TELECOMMUNICATIONS

Lanka Communication Services (Pvt) Ltd: 65c Dharmapala Mawatha, Colombo 7; tel. (11) 2437545; fax (11) 2537547; e-mail webmaster@lankacom.net; internet www.lankacom.net; f. 1991; subsidiary of Singapore Telecom International; Man. Dir Rohith Udalagama.

MTN Networks (Pvt) Ltd: 528 R. A. De Mel Mawatha, Colombo 3; tel. (11) 2678678; fax (11) 2678692; e-mail dialog@dialog.lk; internet www.dialog.lk; wholly owned subsidiary of Telekom Malaysia; operates Dialog GSM, Sri Lanka's largest mobile phone network; Chief Exec. Dr Shridhir Sariputta Hansa Wijayasuriya.

Sri Lanka Telecom Ltd: Telecom Headquarters, 7th Floor, Lotus Rd, POB 503, Colombo 1; tel. (11) 2329711; fax (11) 2440000; e-mail pr@slt.lk; internet www.slt.lk; 35% owned by Nippon Telegraph and Telephone Corpn (Japan), 49.5% by Govt of Sri Lanka and 3.5% by employees; Chair. P. Asoka Weerasinghe De Silva; CEO Shoji Takahashi.

Regulatory Authority

Telecommunications Regulatory Commission of Sri Lanka: 276 Elvitigala Mawatha, Manning Town, Colombo 8; tel. (11) 2689345; fax (11) 2689341; e-mail dgtsl@trc.gov.lk; internet www.trc.gov.lk; f. 1996; Chair. Lalith Weerathunga; Dir-Gen. Priyantha Kariyapperuma.

RADIO

Sri Lanka Broadcasting Corpn: Independence Sq., POB 574, Colombo 7; tel. (11) 2697491; fax (11) 2691568; e-mail chmnslbc@sltnet.lk; internet www.slbc.lk; f. 1967; under Ministry of Information and Media; controls all broadcasting in Sri Lanka; regional stations at Anuradhapura, Kandy and Matara; transmitting stations at Ambewela, Amparai, Anuradhapura, Diyagama, Ekala, Galle, Kanthalai, Mahiyangana, Maho, Matara, Puttalam, Ratnapura, Seeduwa, Senkadagala, Weeraketiya; home service in Sinhala, Tamil and English; foreign service also in Tamil, English, Sinhala, Hindi, Kannada, Malayalam, Nepali and Telugu; 893 broadcasting hours per week: 686 on domestic services, 182 on external services and 126 on education; Chair. Anusha Palpita; Dir-Gen. Samantha Weliweriya.

Asura FM: No. 52, 5th Lane, Colombo 3; tel. (11) 2575000; fax (11) 2301082; internet www.asurafm.com; broadcasts 24 hrs daily in Sinhala; Chair. Niraj Wickremesinghe.

Colombo Communications (Pvt) Ltd: 2/9 2nd Floor, Liberty Plaza, 250 R. A. de Mel Mawatha, Colombo 3; tel. (11) 2577924; fax (11) 2577929; commercial station; three channels broadcast 24 hrs daily in English, Sinhala and Tamil.

Lite FM: No. 52, 5th Lane, Colombo 3; tel. (11) 2575000; fax (11) 2301082; e-mail info@tnlradio.com; internet www.tnlradio.com; commercial station; broadcasts 24 hrs daily in English; Chair. Niraj Wickremesinghe.

MBC Networks (Pvt) Ltd: 7 Braybrooke Place, Colombo 2; tel. (11) 5340111; fax (11) 5340124; internet www.maharaja.lk; commercial station comprising four channels; broadcasts 24 hrs daily in English, Sinhala and Tamil.

TNL Radio: No. 52, 5th Lane, Colombo 3; tel. (11) 2575000; fax (11) 2301082; e-mail info@tnlradio.com; internet www.tnlradio.com; f. 1993; commercial station; broadcasts 24 hrs daily in English; Chair. Niraj Wickremesinghe.

Trans World Radio: 125/3 3rd Lane, Subadrarama Rd, POB 123, Nugegoda; tel. (5) 559321; fax (11) 2817749; e-mail rkoch@twr.org; internet www.twr.org; f. 1978; religious station; broadcasts two hrs every morning Monday–Friday, three hrs Saturday and Sunday morning, and six and a half hrs each evening to Indian subcontinent; Dir (Finance/Administration) Roger Koch; Eng. P. Velmurugan.

Voice of Tigers: Vanni; internet www.eelam.com/vot; f. 1990 by the LTTE; banned until 2003; broadcasts eight and a half hrs daily in Tamil and Sinhala.

TELEVISION

Sri Lanka Rupavahini Corpn (SLRC): Independence Sq., POB 2204, Colombo 7; tel. (11) 2599506; fax (11) 2580929; e-mail ict@rupavahini.lk; internet www.rupavahini.lk; f. 1982; studio at Colombo; transmitting stations at nine locations; broadcasts 18 hrs daily on Channel I, 15 hrs daily on Channel II; Dir-Gen. Nishantha Ranatunga; Chair. M. M. Zuhair.

Independent Television Network (ITN): Wickremasinghepura, Battaramulla; tel. (11) 2775494; fax (11) 2774591; e-mail itn@slt.lk; internet www.itn.lk; broadcasts about 19 hrs daily; operates Lakhanda Radio (24 hrs; daily); Chair. Anura Siriwardena; Gen. Man. W. P. A. M. Wijesinghe.

EAP Network (Pvt) Ltd: 676 Galle Rd, Colombo 3; tel. (11) 2503819; fax (11) 2503788; e-mail eapnet@slt.lk; Chair. Soma Edirisinghe; Man. Dir Jeevaka Edirisinghe.

MTV Channel (Pvt) Ltd: Araliya Uyana, Depanama, Pannipitiya; tel. (11) 5340111; e-mail info@media.maharaja.lk; f. 1992; broadcasts on three channels in English, Sinhala and Tamil.

National Television of Tamil Eelam (NTT): e-mail ntt_news@yahoo.com; f. 2005; broadcasts for two hrs daily.

Telshan Network (Pvt) Ltd (TNL): 9D Tower Bldg, 25 Station Rd, Colombo 4; tel. (11) 2596241; fax (11) 2706125; e-mail tnltvr@slt.lk; Chair. and Man. Dir Shantilal Nilkant Wickremesinghe.

Finance

(cap. = capital; res = reserves; dep. = deposits; m. = million; brs = branches; amounts in Sri Lanka rupees, unless otherwise indicated)

BANKING
Central Bank

Central Bank of Sri Lanka: 30 Janadhipathi Mawatha, POB 590, Colombo 1; tel. (11) 2477000; fax (11) 2477712; e-mail cbslgen@cbsl.lk; internet www.cbsl.gov.lk; f. 1950; sole bank of issue; cap. 15m., res 83,367m., dep. 126,803m. (Dec. 2005); Gov. and Chair. of the Monetary Board Ajith Nivard Cabraal; Dep. Govs Dr Ranee Jayamaha, W. A. Wijewardena; 3 regional offices.

Commercial Banks

Bank of Ceylon: 4 Bank of Ceylon Mawatha, POB 241, Colombo 1; tel. (11) 2446811; fax (11) 2447171; e-mail boc@boc.lk; internet www.boc.lk; f. 1939; 100% state-owned; cap. 4,000m., res 3,614m., dep. 262,676m. (Dec. 2006); Chair. Dr Gamini Wickramasinghe; Gen. Man. B. A. C. Fernando; 303 brs in Sri Lanka, 3 brs abroad.

Commercial Bank of Ceylon Ltd: Commercial House, 21 Bristol St, POB 856, Colombo 1; tel. (11) 2430416; fax (11) 2449889; e-mail e-mail@combank.net; internet www.combank.net; f. 1969; 29.77% owned by DFCC Bank, 29.91% by govt corpns and 40.32% by public; cap. 2,428.2m., res 13,414.7m., dep. 171,964.1m. (Dec. 2006); Chair. M. J. C. Amarasuriya; Man. Dir A. L. Gooneratne; 136 brs.

Hatton National Bank Ltd: 479 T. B. Jayah Mawatha, POB 837, Colombo 10; tel. (11) 2664664; fax (11) 2446523; e-mail moreinfo@hnb.net; internet www.hnb.net; f. 1970; 27.1% owned by individuals, 72.9% by institutions; cap. 1,177.6m., res 10,015.8m., dep. 155,808.8m. (Dec. 2006); Chair. Rienzie T. Wijetilleke; Man. Dir and CEO Rajendra Theagarajah; 160 brs.

Nations Trust Bank Ltd: 242 Union Place, Colombo 2; tel. (11) 4313131; fax (11) 2307854; e-mail info@nationstrust.com; internet www.nationstrust.com; f. 1999; privately owned; acquired Mercantile Leasing Ltd by merger to form Nations Leasing business; cap. 1,257.9m., res 1,265.2m., dep. 22,308.9m. (Dec. 2006); Chair. Ajit Gunewardene; CEO Zulfiqar Zavahir.

Pan Asia Banking Corpn Ltd: 450 Galle Rd, Colombo 3; tel. (11) 2565556; fax (11) 2565558; e-mail pabc@pabcbank.com; internet www.pabcbank.com; f. 1995; 100% privately-owned (82.9% owned by local shareholders, 17.1% by foreign shareholders); cap. 1,106.4m., res 128.7m., dep. 10,082.5m. (Dec. 2006); Chair. A. G. Weerasinghe; Man. Dir, Gen. Man. and CEO R. Nadarajah; 18 brs.

People's Bank: 75 Sir Chittampalam A. Gardiner Mawatha, POB 728, Colombo 2; tel. (11) 2327841; fax (11) 2433127; e-mail info@peoplesbank.lk; internet www.peoplesbank.lk; f. 1961; 92% owned by Govt, 8% by co-operatives; cap. 4,202.0m. (incl. special lending rights 4,152.0m. capital pending allotment), res 6,254.4m., dep. 269,947.2m. (Dec. 2006); Chair. W. Karunajeewa; CEO and Gen. Man. Asoka de Silva; 324 brs.

Sampath Bank Ltd: Sampath Centre Bldg, 110 Sir James Peiris Mawatha, POB 997, Colombo 2; tel. (11) 2303050; fax (11) 2303085; e-mail info@sampath.lk; internet www.sampath.lk; f. 1987; cap. 688.9m., res 5,936.4m., dep. 86,134.9m. (Dec. 2006); Chair. Edgar Gunatunga; Man. Dir/CEO Anil Amarasuriya; 100 brs.

Seylan Bank Ltd: Ceylinco Seylan Towers, 90 Galle Rd, POB 400, Colombo 3; tel. (11) 2456789; fax (11) 2456456; e-mail info@seylan.lk; internet www.eseylan.com; f. 1988; cap. 1,705.1m., res 4,648.8m., dep. 104,383.2m. (Dec. 2006); Chair. and Man. Dir J. L. B. Kotelawala; Gen. Man., Dir and CEO Ajita Pasqual; 116 brs.

Union Bank of Colombo Ltd: 15A Alfred Place, Colombo 3; tel. (11) 2370870; fax (11) 2370692; e-mail ubc@unionb.com; internet www.unionb.com; f. 1995; cap. 1,060.0m., res 9.8m., dep. 7,807.1m. (Dec. 2006); Chair. Ajita de Zoysa; CEO and Dir Mahendra Fernando.

Development Banks

Agricultural and Industrial Credit Corpn of Ceylon: POB 20, Colombo 3; tel. (11) 2223783; f. 1943; loan cap. 30m.; Chair. V. P. Vittachi; Gen. Man. H. S. F. Goonewardena.

DFCC Bank: 73/5 Galle Rd, POB 1397, Colombo 3; tel. (11) 2442442; fax (11) 2440376; e-mail info@dfccbank.com; internet www.dfccbank.com; f. 1956 as Development Finance Corpn of Ceylon; name changed as above 1997; provides long- and medium-term credit, investment banking and consultancy services; cap. 856.6m., res 8,628.6m., dep. 13,572.6m. (March 2007); Chair. Rajan Brito; Gen. Man. and CEO Nihal Fonseka; 3 brs.

National Development Bank Ltd: DHPL Bldg, 42 Nawam Mawatha, POB 1825, Colombo 2; tel. (11) 2314640; fax (11) 2314642; e-mail contact@ndbbank.com; internet www.ndbbank.com; f. 1979 by an Act of Parliament as National Development Bank of Sri Lanka; subsequently privatized and name changed as above in June 2005; provides long-term finance for projects, equity financing and merchant banking services; cap. 818.6m., res 7,736.2m., dep. 27,183.1 (Dec. 2006); Chair. P. M. Nagahawatte; CEO Nihal Welikala.

State Mortgage and Investment Bank: 269 Galle Road, POB 156, Colombo 3; tel. (11) 2573561; fax (11) 2573346; e-mail agmit@smib.lk; internet www.smib.lk; f. 1979; Chair. Chandima Weerakkody; Gen. Man. Ajith Weerasinhe.

Merchant Banks

Merchant Bank of Sri Lanka Ltd: Bank of Ceylon Merchant Tower, 28 St Michael's Rd, POB 1987, Colombo 3; tel. (11) 4711711; fax (11) 2565666; e-mail mbslbank@mbslbank.com; internet www.mbslbank.com; f. 1982; 53.8% owned by Bank of Ceylon; public ltd liability co; cap. p.u. 2,500m., total assets 2,128m. (2003); Chair. Janaka Ratnayake; CEO Gamini Karunathileka; 3 brs.

People's Merchant Bank Ltd: Hemas House, Level 4, 75 Braybrooke Place, Colombo 2; tel. (11) 2300191; fax (11) 2300190; e-mail pmbank@sltnet.lk; f. 1984 as a subsidiary of People's Bank; total assets 610m. (1999); Chair. Dr G. Fernando.

Financial Association

The Finance Houses' Association of Sri Lanka: 181/1A Dharmapala Mawatha, Colombo 7; tel. (11) 2665865; fax (11) 2665864; e-mail finass@sltnet.lk; internet www.fha.lk; f. 1958; represents the finance cos registered and licensed by the Central Bank of Sri Lanka; Chair. Shiley Perera; Sec.-Gen. Dennis Viswasam.

STOCK EXCHANGES

Securities and Exchange Commission of Sri Lanka: 11–01 East Tower, 28th and 29th Floors, World Trade Centre, Echelon Sq., Colombo 1; tel. (11) 2439144; fax (11) 2439149; e-mail mail@sec.gov.lk; internet www.sec.gov.lk; f. 1987; Dir-Gen. Channa de Silva; Chair. Gamini Wickramasinghe.

Colombo Stock Exchange: 04–01, West Block, World Trade Centre, Echelon Sq., Colombo 1; tel. (11) 2446581; fax (11) 2445279; e-mail cse@cse.lk; internet www.cse.lk; f. 1896; stock market; 20 mem. firms and 236 listed cos; Chair. A. N. Fonseka; Dir-Gen. Hiran Mendis.

INSURANCE

Ceylinco Insurance Co Ltd: Ceylinco House, 4th Floor, 69 Janadhipathi Mawatha, Colombo 1; tel. (11) 2485757; fax (11) 2485769; e-mail jagath@lanka.com.lk; internet www.ceylinco-insurance.com; f. 1987; general and life insurance; Chair. and Man. Dir J. L. B. Kotelawala.

Eagle Insurance Co Ltd: 'Eagle House', 75 Kumaran Ratnam Rd, Colombo 2; tel. (11) 2437090; fax (11) 2447620; e-mail info@eagle.com.lk; internet www.eagle.com.lk; f. 1988 as CTC Eagle Insurance Co Ltd; general and life insurance; mem. of Aviva International Holdings Ltd; Man. Dir Deepal Sooriyaarachchi.

Hayleys Ltd: Hayley Bldg, 400 Deans Rd, Colombo 10; internet www.hayleys.com; f. 1952; Chair. Sunil Mendis; Dep. Chair. R. Yatawara.

National Insurance Corpn Ltd: 47 Muttiah Rd, POB 2202, Colombo 2; tel. (11) 2445738; fax (11) 2445733; e-mail nicopl@slt.lk; general; Chair. T. M. S. Nanayakkara; Sec. A. C. J. de Alwis.

Sri Lanka Insurance Corporation Ltd: 'Rakshana Mandiraya', 21 Vauxhall St, POB 1337, Colombo 2; tel. (11) 2357537; fax (11) 2447742; e-mail slic@srilankainsurance.com; internet www.srilankainsurance.com; f. 1961; privatized in 2003; all classes of insurance; Chair. D. H. S. Jayawardene; CEO Nalaka Godahewa.

Union Assurance Ltd: Union Assurance Centre, 20 St Michael's Rd, Colombo 3; tel. (11) 2428428; fax (11) 2343065; e-mail unionassurance@ualink.lk; internet www.ualink.lk; f. 1987; general and life insurance; Chair. Ajit Gunewardene; CEO Marina Tharmaratnam.

Trade and Industry

GOVERNMENT AGENCIES

Board of Investment of Sri Lanka: World Trade Centre, West Tower, 26th Floor, Echelon Sq., Colombo 1; tel. (11) 2435027; fax (11) 2422407; e-mail infoboi@boi.lk; internet www.boi.lk; f. 1978 as the Greater Colombo Economic Commission; promotes foreign direct investment and administers the eight Export Processing Zones at Katunayake, Biyagama, Koggala, Mirigama, Malwatta, Horana, Mawathagama and Polgahawela; also administers industrial township at Watupitiwala and industrial parks at Seetawaka and Kandy; Chair. and Dir-Gen. Dhammika Perera.

Public Enterprises Reform Commission (PERC): World Trade Centre, West Tower, 11th Floor, Colombo 1; tel. (11) 2346831; fax (11) 2326116; e-mail info@perc.gov.lk; internet www.perc.gov.lk; f. 1995 to advise Govt on privatization and restructuring of loss-making state-sector enterprises and to promote national economic development; Chair. W. M. Bandusena; Dir-Gen. Leel Wickremarachchi.

Sri Lanka Gem and Jewellery Exchange: World Trade Centre, East Low Block, Levels 4 and 5, Echelon Sq., Colombo 1; e-mail slgje@sltnet.lk; internet www.slgemexchange.com; f. 1990; testing and certification of gems, trading booths; Dir-Gen. M. Wijesekera; Sen. Man. (Export Promotion) Ajith Perera.

National Gem and Jewellery Authority: 25 Galle Face Terrace, Colombo 3; tel. and fax (11) 2390650; fax (11) 2329352; e-mail chngja@sltnet.lk; internet www.srilankagemautho.com; f. 1971 as State Gem Corpn; Chair. W. Hasitha Tillekeratne; Dir-Gen. S. J. S. Chandraguptha.

Trade Information Service: Sri Lanka Export Development Board, Level 7, 42 Navam Mawatha, POB 1872, Colombo 2; tel. (11) 2300675; fax (11) 2300676; e-mail tisinfo@edb.tradenetsl.lk; internet www.srilankabusiness.com; f. 1981 to collect and disseminate commercial information and to provide advisory services to trade circles; Dir W. M. D. S. Weerakoon.

DEVELOPMENT ORGANIZATIONS

Coconut Development Authority: 11 Duke St, POB 386, Colombo 1; tel. (11) 2421027; fax (11) 2447602; e-mail cocoauth@panlanka.net; internet www.cda.lk; f. 1972; state body; promotes the coconut industry through financial assistance for mfrs of coconut products, market information, consultancy services and quality assurance; Chair. H. A. Tillekeratne.

Industrial Development Board of Ceylon (IDB): 615 Galle Rd, Katubedda, POB 09, Moratuwa; tel. (11) 2605326; fax (11) 2607002; e-mail idb@sltnet.lk; internet www.idb.lk; f. 1969; under Ministry of Rural Industries and Self Employment Promotion; promotes industrial development through provincial network; Chair. Gamini Senanayake; Gen. Man. G. R. Jayathilake.

Centre for Entrepreneurship Development and Consultancy Services: 615 Galle Rd, Katubedda, POB 09, Moratuwa; tel. (11) 2632156; f. 1989; Dir T. M. Kularathne (acting).

Centre for Industrial and Technology Information Services (CITIS): 615 Galle Rd, Katubedda, POB 09, Moratuwa 10400; tel. (11) 2605372; fax (11) 2607002; e-mail idb@sltnet.lk; internet www.idb.lk; f. 1989; disseminates information to small and medium-sized enterprises; Dir G. J. K. Ariyadasa.

SRI LANKA

Information and Communication Technology Association of Sri Lanka (ICTA): 160/24 Kirimandala Mawatha, Colombo 5; tel. (11) 2369099; fax (11) 2369091; e-mail info@icta.lk; internet www.icta.lk; f. 2003; govt-owned; responsible for development of information communication technology in Sri Lanka; COO RESHAN DEWAPURA.

Janatha Estates Development Board: 55/75 Vauxhall St, Colombo 2; tel. (11) 2320901; fax (11) 2446577; f. 1975; manages 18 tea and spice plantations; 10,164 employees; 1 regional office.

Sri Lanka Export Development Board: Trade Information Service, Level 7, 42 Navam Mawatha, Colombo 2; tel. (11) 2300705; fax (11) 2300715; e-mail tisinfo@edb.tradenetsl.lk; internet www.tradenetsl.lk/edb; f. 1979; Chair. ROHANTHA ATHUKORALA.

CHAMBERS OF COMMERCE

Federation of Chambers of Commerce and Industry of Sri Lanka: 53 Vauxhall Lane, 3rd Floor, Colombo 2; tel. (11) 2304253; fax (11) 2304255; e-mail fccisl@fccisl.lk; internet www.fccisl.lk; f. 1973; a central org. of 53 chambers of commerce and industry and trade asscns representing 12,500 cos throughout Sri Lanka; Pres. NAWAZ RAJABDEEN; Sec.-Gen. SAMANTHA ABEYWICKRAMA.

All Ceylon Trade Chamber: 212/45 1/3 Bodhiraja Mawatha, Colombo 11; tel. (11) 2432428; Pres. MUDLIYAR N. W. J. MUDALIGE; Gen. Sec. Y. P. MUTHUKUMARANA.

Ceylon Chamber of Commerce: 50 Navam Mawatha, POB 274, Colombo 2; tel. (11) 2421745; fax (11) 2449352; e-mail info@chamber.lk; internet www.chamber.lk; f. 1839; 517 mems; Chair. MAHENDRA DAYANANDA; Sec.-Gen. and CEO PREMA COORAY.

Ceylon National Chamber of Industries: Galle Face Court 2, Rm 20, 1st Floor, POB 1775, Colombo 3; tel. (11) 2423734; fax (11) 2331443; e-mail info@cnci.biz; internet www.cnci.biz; f. 1960; 325 mems; Chair. A. K. RATNARAJAH; Sec.-Gen. and CEO UPALI SAMARASINGHE.

International Chamber of Commerce Sri Lanka: 141/7 Vauxhall St, POB 1733, Colombo 2; tel. (11) 2307825; fax (11) 2307841; e-mail iccsl@sltnet.lk; internet www.iccsl.lk; f. 1955; Chair. TARIQ M. RANGOONWALA; CEO GAMINI PEIRIS.

National Chamber of Commerce of Sri Lanka: NCCSL Bldg, 450 D. R. Wijewardena Mawatha, POB 1375, Colombo 10; tel. (11) 2689600; fax (11) 2689596; e-mail sg@nccsl.lk; internet www.nccsl.lk; f. 1948; Pres. D. EASSUWEREN; Hon. Sec. SUNIL G. WIJESINHA.

INDUSTRIAL AND TRADE ASSOCIATIONS

Association of Computer Training Organizations: 5 Clifford Ave, Colombo 3; tel. (11) 2565193; fax (11) 2713821; e-mail infotel@sri.lanka.net; f. 1991; 29 mems; Pres. KITHSIRI MANCHANAYAKE.

Ceylon Coir Fibre Exporters' Association: c/o Volanka Ltd, 193 Minuwangoda Rd, Kotugoda; tel. (11) 2232475; fax (11) 2232477; e-mail com@volanka.com; internet www.slcfa.lk; Chair. INDRAJITH PIYASENA.

Ceylon Hardware Merchants' Association: 159 1/5 Mahavidyalaya Mawatha, Colombo 10; tel. (11) 2433085; fax (11) 2423342; 191 mems; Pres. S. THILLAINATHAN.

Ceylon Planters' Society: 40/1 Sri Dhammadara Mawatha, Ratmalana; tel. (11) 2715656; fax (11) 2716758; e-mail plansoty@yahoo.com; f. 1936; 1,133 mems (plantation mans); 25 brs and nine regional organizations; Pres. NISSANKA SENEVIRATHE; Sec. D. N. R. WIJEWARDENA.

Coconut Products Traders' Association: c/o Ceylon Chamber of Commerce, 50 Navam Mawatha, POB 274, Colombo 2; tel. (11) 2421745; fax (11) 2449352; e-mail info@chamber.lk; internet www.chamber.lk; f. 1925; Chair. SANJAY PROROA; Sec. E. P. A. COORAY.

Colombo Rubber Traders' Association: c/o Ceylon Chamber of Commerce, 50 Navam Mawatha, POB 274, Colombo 2; tel. (11) 2421745; fax (11) 2449352; e-mail info@chamber.lk; internet www.chamber.lk; f. 1918; Chair. A. L. WEERASINGHE; Sec. E. P. A. COORAY.

Colombo Tea Traders' Association: c/o Ceylon Chamber of Commerce, 50 Navam Mawatha, POB 274, Colombo 2; tel. (11) 2421745; fax (11) 2449352; e-mail info@chamber.lk; internet www.chamber.lk; f. 1894; 203 mems; Chair. TYEAB AKBARALLY; Sec. E. P. A. COORAY.

Free Trade Zone Manufacturers' Association: Plaza Complex, Unit 6 (Upper Floor), IPZ, Katunayake; tel. (11) 2252813; Chair. AJITH DIAS.

Joint Apparel Association Forum (JAAF): 16 De Fonseka Rd, Colombo 5; tel. (11) 4528494; fax (11) 2501753; e-mail info@jaafsl.com; internet www.jaafsl.com; f. 2002; co-ordinates and develops apparel industry; Chair. AJITH DIAS; Sec.-Gen. T. G. ARIYARATNE.

Sea Food Exporters' Association: c/o Andriesz & Co Ltd, 39 Nuge Rd, Peliyagoda; tel. 530021.

Software Exporters' Association: c/o Ceylon Chamber of Commerce, 50 Navam Mawatha, Colombo 2; tel. (11) 2343702; fax (11) 2449352; e-mail rukshika@chamber.lk; internet www.softwaresrilanka.com; f. 1999; 52 mems; Chair. JAYANTHA DE SILVA.

Sri Lanka Apparel Exporters' Association: 45 Rosmead Place, Colombo 7; tel. (11) 2670778; fax (11) 2683118; e-mail srilanka-apparel@eureka.lk; internet www.srilanka-apparel.com; f. 1982; Chair. RANJAN CASIE CHETTY; Sec. HEMAMALI SIRISENA.

Sri Lanka Association of Manufacturers and Exporters of Rubber Products (SLAMERP): 425 Thimbirigasyaya Rd, Colombo 5; tel. (11) 2521200; fax (11) 2521222; e-mail slamerp@panlanka.net; f. 1984; Chair. ANANDA CALDERA; Sec.-Gen. C. DIAS BANDARANAYAKE.

Sri Lanka Association of Printers: 290 D. R. Wijewardena Mawatha, Colombo 10; tel. (11) 2472315; fax (11) 2386716; e-mail slap@sltnet.lk; internet www.lankaprint.org; f. 1956; 390 mems; publishes quarterly magazine *Printceylon*; Pres. KOSALA TILLEKERATNE; Sec. SHAMAL JAYATHILLEKE.

Sri Lanka Chamber of the Pharmaceutical Industry: 15 Tichbourne Passage, Colombo 10; tel. (11) 2694823; fax (11) 2671877; e-mail nimjay@sltnet.lk; Pres. N. DIAS JAYASINHA; Sec. NAUSHAD ISMAIL.

Sri Lanka Fruit and Vegetables Producers, Processors and Exporters' Association: c/o Sri Lanka Export Development Board, 42 Navam Mawatha, Colombo 2; tel. (11) 2300705; fax (11) 2304879; e-mail harz47@edb.tradenetsl.lk; internet www.tradenetsl.lk; Sec. M. A. JUNAID.

Sri Lanka Importers, Exporters and Manufacturers' Association (SLIEMA): POB 12, Colombo; tel. (11) 2696321; fax (11) 2684480; e-mail tradelink@slt.lk; f. 1955; Pres. WILLIAM JOHN TERRENCE PERERA.

Sri Lanka Jewellery Manufacturing Exporters' Association: Colombo; tel. (11) 2445141; fax (11) 2445105; Pres. IFTHIKHAR AZIZ; Sec. CHANAKA ELLAWELA.

Sri Lanka Shippers' Council: c/o Ceylon Chamber of Commerce, 50 Nawam Mawatha, POB 274, Colombo 2; tel. (11) 2422156; internet www.slsc.ws.

Sri Lanka Tea Board: 574 Galle Rd, POB 1750, Colombo 3; tel. (11) 2508991; fax (11) 2589132; e-mail teaboard@pureceylontea.com; internet www.pureceylontea.com; f. 1976 for development of tea industry through quality control and promotion in Sri Lanka and in world markets; Chair. NIRAJ DE MEL; Dir-Gen. H. D. HEMARATNE.

Sri Lanka Wooden Furniture and Wood Products Manufacturers' and Exporters' Association: c/o E. H. Cooray & Sons Ltd, 411 Galle Rd, Colombo 3; tel. (11) 2509227; fax (11) 2575198; Pres. PATRICK AMARASINGHE; Sec. PINSIRI FERNANDO.

Sugar Importers' Association of Sri Lanka: c/o C. W. Mackie & Co Ltd, 36 D. R. Wijewardena Mawatha, POB 89, Colombo 10; tel. (11) 2423554; fax (11) 2438069; e-mail nalin@export.cwmackie.com; Pres. M. THAVAYOGARAJAH; Sec. C. KAPUWATTA.

EMPLOYERS' ORGANIZATION

Employers' Federation of Ceylon: 385 J3 Old Kotte Rd, Rajagiriya, Colombo; tel. (11) 2867966; fax (11) 2867942; e-mail efc@empfed.lk; internet www.empfed.lk; f. 1929; mem. of International Organization of Employers and Confederation of Asia Pacific Employers; 510 mems; Chair. H. D. S. AMARASURIYA; Dir-Gen. R. L. P. PEIRIS.

UTILITIES

Electricity

Ceylon Electricity Board: 50 Sir Chittampalam A. Gardiner Mawatha, POB 540, Colombo 2; tel. (11) 2324471; fax (11) 2323935; e-mail admin@ceb.lk; internet www.ceb.lk; f. 1969; Chair. UDAYASRI KARIYAWASAM.

Water

National Water Supply and Drainage Board (NWSDB): Galle Rd, Ratmalana, Colombo; tel. (11) 2638999; fax (11) 2636449; e-mail gm@waterboard.lk; internet waterboard.lk; f. 1975; govt corpn; Chair. S. C. AMARASINGHE.

CO-OPERATIVES

In 2000 there were an estimated 11,793 co-operative societies in Sri Lanka, with membership totalling 17,235,000.

TRADE UNIONS

At the end of 2000 there were 1,588 trade unions functioning in Sri Lanka.

All Ceylon Federation of Free Trade Unions (ACFFTU): 94-1/6 York Bldg, York St, Colombo 1; tel. (11) 2431847; fax (11) 2470874;

e-mail nwc@itmin.com; 10 affiliated unions; 84,000 mems; Pres. MARCELL C. RAJAHMONEY; Sec.-Gen. ANTON LODWICK.

Ceylon Federation of Labour (CFL): 457 Union Place, Colombo 2; tel. (11) 2694273; f. 1957; 16 affiliated unions, 155,969 mems; Pres. Dr COLVIN R. DE SILVA; Gen. Sec. S. S. SIRIWARDANE.

Ceylon Mercantile, Industrial and General Workers' Union (CMU): 3 22nd Lane, Colombo 3; tel. (11) 2328157; fax (11) 2434025; e-mail cgscmu@sltnet.lk; Gen. Sec. BALA TAMPOE.

Ceylon Trade Union Federation (CTUF): Colombo; tel. (11) 2220365; f. 1941; 24 affiliated unions; 35,271 mems; Sec.-Gen. L. W. PANDITHA.

Ceylon Workers' Congress (CWC): 'Savumia Bhavan', 72 Ananda Coomarasamy Mawatha, POB 1294, Colombo 7; tel. (11) 2301359; fax (11) 2301355; e-mail cwconline@sltnet.lk; f. 1939; political entity; represents mainly plantation workers of recent Indian origin; 50 district offices and seven regional offices; 250,000 mems; Pres. and Gen. Sec. S. ARUMUGAN THONDAMAN.

Democratic Workers' Congress (DWC): 70 Bankshall St, POB 1009, Colombo 11; tel. (11) 2423746; fax (11) 2435961; f. 1939; 201,382 mems (1994); Pres. MANO GANESHAN; Gen. Sec. R. KITNAN.

Government Workers' Trade Union Federation (GWTUF): 457 Union Place, Colombo 2; tel. (11) 2295066; 52 affiliated unions; 100,000 mems; Leader P. D. SARANAPALA.

Jathika Sevaka Sangamaya (JSS) (National Employees' Union): 416 Kotte Rd, Pitakotte, Colombo; tel. (11) 2565432; f. 1959; 357,000 mems; represents over 70% of unionized manual and clerical workers of Sri Lanka; Pres. W. A. NEVILLE PERERA; Sec. SIRINAL DE MEL.

Lanka Jathika Estate Workers' Union (LJEWU): 60 Bandaranayakepura, Sri Jayawardenepura Mawatha, Welikada, POB 1918, Rajagiriya; tel. (11) 2865138; fax (11) 2862262; e-mail ctucljeu@sri.lanka.net; f. 1958; 350,000 mems; Pres. RAJAH SENEVIRATNE; Gen. Sec. K. VELAYUDAM.

Public Service Workers' Trade Union Federation (PSWTUF): 35/5, 19–20 Main St, Colombo 11; tel. (11) 2231125; 100 affiliated unions; 100,000 mems.

Sri Lanka Nidahas Sewaka Sangamaya (Sri Lanka Free Workers' Union): 301 T. B. Jayah Mawatha, POB 1241, Colombo 10; tel. and fax (11) 2694074; f. 1960; 478 br. unions; 193,011 mems; Gen. Sec. LESLIE DEVENDRA.

Trade Union Confederation: Colombo; f. 2008; 40 affiliated unions; Pres. K. S. WEERASEKERA; Sec. H. M. NAWARATNE BANDARA.

Transport

RAILWAYS

Sri Lanka Railways Authority (SLRA): Colombo; f. 2003; responsible for running of national railway network; Gen. Man. T. LALITHASIRI GUNARUWAH.

Sri Lanka Railways (SLR): Olcott Mawatha, POB 335, Colombo 10; tel. (11) 2431177; fax (11) 2446490; e-mail slrail@itmin.com; internet www.scienceland.lk/railway; f. 1864; under Ministry of Transport; operates 1,447 track-km; there are nine railway lines across the country and 164 stations, with 134 sub-stations (1997); Gen. Man. W. K. B. WERAGAMA.

ROADS

In 1999 there were an estimated 96,695 km of roads in Sri Lanka, of which 11,462 km were main roads, while in 2003 the road network was estimated to have expanded to 97,286 km, of which 81% was paved. In April 2002 a major highway linking the Jaffna peninsula with the rest of the country was opened for the first time in 12 years. Delayed construction of a four-lane Southern Expressway, extending from Colombo to Matara and jointly funded by the Asian Development Bank (ADB) and Japanese Bank for International Co-operation, was in progress in 2006 at a revised cost of US $175.2m. Completion was tentatively scheduled for 2010. The ADB agreed a $150m. loan to Sri Lanka for the widening and rehabilitation of 350 km of national highways in December 2006.

Ministry of Transport: 1 D. R. Wijewardene Mawatha, POB 588, Colombo 10; tel. (11) 2687212; fax (11) 2687284; e-mail transplan@eol.lk; internet www.transport.gov.lk; maintains 11,661 km of national highways and 4,429 bridges through the Road Development Authority.

Department of Motor Traffic: 581-341 Elvitigala Mawatha, POB 533, Colombo 5; tel. (11) 2694331; fax (11) 2694338; e-mail dmtsl@sltnet.lk.

Sri Lanka Transport Board: 200 Kirula Rd, Narahenpita, POB 1435, Colombo 5; tel. (11) 2581120; fax (11) 2368921; e-mail chairmanctb@sltnet.lk; f. 1958; nationalized organization responsible for road passenger transport services consisting of a central transport board, 11 Cluster Bus Cos and one regional transport board; fleet of 8,900 buses (2001); Chair. TUDER CAYARATNE; Sec. D. P. W. DE LIVERA.

SHIPPING

Colombo is one of the most important ports in Asia and is situated at the junction of the main trade routes. The other main ports of Sri Lanka are Trincomalee, Galle and Jaffna. Trincomalee is the main port for handling tea exports.

Ceylon Association of Ships' Agents (CASA): 56 Ward Place, Colombo 7; tel. (11) 2696227; fax (11) 2698648; e-mail casa@sltnet.lk; internet www.casa.lk; f. 1944; primarily a consultative organization; represents mems in dealings with govt authorities; 120 mems; Chair. Capt. AJITH PEIRIS; Sec.-Gen. DHAMMIKA WALGAMPAYA.

Sri Lanka Ports Authority: 19 Chaithya Rd, POB 595, Colombo 1; tel. (11) 2421201; fax (11) 2440651; e-mail info@slpa.lk; internet www.slpa.lk; f. 1979; responsible for all cargo handling operations and harbour development and maintenance in the ports of Colombo, Galle, Kankasanthurai, Trincomalee, Oluvil and Point Pedro; Chair. SALIYA WICKRAMASURIRYA; Man. Dir W. G. SAMARATUNGA.

Shipping Companies

Ceylon Ocean Lines Ltd: 'Sayuru Sevana', 46/12 Nawam Mawatha, Colombo 2; tel. (11) 2434928; fax (11) 2439245; e-mail oceanlines@col.lk; f. 1956; shipping agents, freight forwarders, charterers, container freight station operators and bunkers; Dirs Capt. L. P. WEINMAN, Capt. A. V. RAJENDRA.

Ceylon Shipping Corpn Ltd: 6 Sir Baron Jayatilaka Mawatha, POB 1718, Colombo 1; tel. (11) 2328772; fax (11) 2447547; e-mail cscemail@sri.lanka.net; f. 1971 as govt corpn; became govt-owned limited liability co in 1992; operates fully-containerized service to Europe, the Far East, the Mediterranean, USA and Canada (East Coast); Chair. SUNDRA JAYAWARDHANA; Gen. Man. M. S. P. GUNAWARDENA.

Ceylon Shipping Lines Ltd: 450 D. R. Wijewardena Mawatha, POB 891, Colombo 10; tel. (11) 2689500; fax (11) 2689510; shipping agents, travel agents, off dock terminal operators; Chair. E. A. WIRASINHA; Man. Dir T. D. V. GUNARATNE.

Ceyoceanic Ltd: 80 Reclamation Rd, POB 795, Colombo 11; tel. (11) 2236071; Dir M. T. G. ANAAM.

Colombo Dockyard Ltd: Port of Colombo, Graving Docks, POB 906, Colombo 15; tel. (11) 2429000; fax (11) 2446441; e-mail coldock@cdl.lk; internet www.cdl.lk; f. 1974; 51% owned by Onomichi Dockyard Co Ltd, Japan, and 49% by Sri Lankan public and government institutions; four dry-docks, seven repair berths (1,200 m), repair of ships up to 125,000 dwt, and builders of steel/aluminium vessels of up to 3,000 dwt; Chair. S. TATEBE; Man. Dir and CEO M. P. B. YAPA.

Mercantile Shipping Co Ltd: Bohen House, 108 Aluthmawatha Rd, Colombo 15; tel. (11) 2331792; fax (11) 2331799.

Sri Lanka Shipping Co Ltd: 46/5 Navam Mawatha, POB 1125, Colombo 2; tel. (11) 2336853; fax (11) 2437420; e-mail lankaship@slsc.lk; internet www.srilankashipping.com; f. 1956.

INLAND WATERWAYS

There are more than 160 km of canals open for traffic.

CIVIL AVIATION

Civil aviation is controlled by the Government's Department of Civil Aviation. There are airports at Batticaloa, Colombo (Bandaranaike for external flights and Ratmalana for internal), Gal Oya, Palali, Jaffna and Trincomalee. In April 2002 the Government lifted a six-year ban on domestic flights and permitted commercial airlines to resume services to Jaffna.

Civil Aviation Authority of Sri Lanka: Supreme Bldg, 64 Galle Rd, Colombo 3; tel. (11) 2433213; fax (11) 2440231; e-mail slcaa@sltnet.lk; internet www.caa.lk; f. 2002; under the supervision of the Ministry of Ports and Aviation; Chair. Air Vice-Marshal P. H. MENDIS; CEO and Dir-Gen. Civil Aviation PARAKRAMA DISSANAYAKE.

SriLankan Airlines Ltd: World Trade Centre, East Tower, 22nd Floor, Echelon Sq., Colombo 1; tel. (11) 97335555; fax (11) 97335122; e-mail ulweb@srilankan.aero; internet www.srilankan.aero; f. 1979 as Air Lanka Ltd, name changed as above in 1999; international services to Europe, the Middle East, South Asia and the Far East; Chair. Dr P. B. JAYASUNDERA; CEO MANOJ GUNAWARDENA.

Helitours: Air Headquarters, POB 594, Colombo 2; tel. (11) 2508927; fax (11) 220541; e-mail slafgops@slk.lk; commercial wing of Sri Lankan Air Force; charter services to major tourist destinations.

Lionair (Pvt) Ltd: Asian Aviation Centre, Colombo Airport, Ratmalana, Colombo; tel. (11) 2622622; fax (11) 2611540; e-mail citadeld@sierra.lk; f. 1994; scheduled and charter services to eight domestic destinations; Chair. CHANDRAN RUTNAM; Man. Dir ASOKA PERERA.

Mihin Lanka: 4-109, Bandaranaike Memorial International Conference Hall, Bauddhaloka Mawatha, Colombo 7; tel. (11) 2699305; fax (11) 2697525; e-mail info@mihinlanka.com; internet www.mihinlanka.com; f. 2007; govt-owned; international services to India, the Maldives, United Arab Emirates, Thailand and Singapore; Chair. SAJIN VAS GUNAWARDENA.

Tourism

As a stopping place for luxury cruises and by virtue of the spectacle of its Buddhist festivals, ancient monuments and natural scenery, Sri Lanka is one of Asia's most important tourist centres. Good motor roads connect Colombo to the main places of interest.

Owing to the continuing intercommunal violence, tourist arrivals decreased from 403,101 in 1995 to 302,265 in 1996 and tourism receipts fell from US $224m. to $168m. The tourism sector, however, recovered well in the latter half of the 1990s, with tourist arrivals reaching 436,440 in 1999. At the end of 2000 the industry appeared to be improving, although arrivals decreased to 400,414 in that year. However, the LTTE attack on Colombo's international airport in July 2001 caused severe damage to the tourist industry. As a result, the number of tourist arrivals in 2001 decreased to 336,794 and tourist receipts fell from $250.8m. to $211.1m. In 2002 the industry recovered; total arrivals reached 393,171 and tourist receipts increased to stand at an estimated $595.0m. Tourist arrivals rose by 27.3% in 2003 to reach 500,642; in the same year tourist receipts totalled an estimated $709.0m. In 2004 tourist arrivals continued to increase, to 566,202, with tourist receipts amounting to $808.0m. In 2005, however, arrivals declined to 549,308; they recovered slightly to reach a total of 559,603 in 2006. Following a deterioration in the security situation, in 2007, according to figures from the Sri Lanka Tourism Development Authority, tourist arrivals decreased to 494,008 and tourist receipts fell to $385m.

Sri Lanka Tourism Promotion Bureau: 80 Galle Rd, Colombo 3; tel. (11) 2437059; fax (11) 2440001; e-mail info@srilanka.travel; internet www.srilanka.travel; f. 1966; Chair. RENTON DE ALWIS; Man. Dir DILEEP MUDADENIYA.

SUDAN

Introductory Survey

Location, Climate, Language, Religion, Flag, Capital

The Republic of Sudan lies in north-eastern Africa. It is bordered by Egypt to the north, by the Red Sea, Eritrea and Ethiopia to the east, by the Central African Republic, Chad and Libya to the west, and by Kenya, Uganda and the Democratic Republic of the Congo (formerly Zaire) to the south. The climate shows a marked transition from the desert of the north to the rainy equatorial south. Temperatures vary with altitude and latitude. The annual average for the whole country is about 21°C (70°F). Arabic is the official language, although other languages are spoken and English is widely understood. Most northern Sudanese are Muslims, while in the south most of the inhabitants are animists or Christians. The national flag (proportions 1 by 2) has three equal horizontal stripes, of red, white and black, with a green triangle at the hoist. The capital is Khartoum.

Recent History

The Sudan (as the country was known before 1975) achieved independence as a parliamentary republic on 1 January 1956. After a military coup in November 1958, a Supreme Council of the Armed Forces was established and ruled until October 1964, when it was overthrown in a civilian revolution. In May 1969 power was seized by a group of officers, led by Col Gaafar Muhammad Nimeri. All existing political institutions and organizations were abolished, and the 'Democratic Republic of the Sudan' was proclaimed, with supreme authority in the hands of the Revolutionary Command Council (RCC). In October 1971 a referendum confirmed Nimeri's nomination as President. A new Government was formed, the RCC was dissolved, and the Sudanese Socialist Union (SSU) was recognized as the only political party.

An early problem facing the Nimeri Government concerned the disputed status of the three southern provinces (Bahr al-Ghazal, Equatoria and Upper Nile), whose inhabitants are racially and culturally distinct from most of the country's population. Rebellion against rule from the north had first broken out in 1955, and fighting continued until March 1972, when an agreement to give the three provinces a degree of autonomy was concluded between members of the Government and representatives of the South Sudan Liberation Movement. A High Executive Council (HEC) for the Southern Region was established in April 1972, and Sudan's permanent Constitution was endorsed in April 1973. Elections to the Regional People's Assembly for southern Sudan took place in November 1973, followed by elections to the National People's Assembly in April 1974.

In October 1981 the National People's Assembly was dissolved. When new elections were held in December, its membership had been reduced from 366 to 151, as many powers had been devolved to the regions. At the same time, the southern HEC was dissolved. The entire Sudanese Government was dismissed in November, although many individuals were later reinstated. In April 1982 a new Southern Region People's Assembly was elected.

In April 1983 President Nimeri was re-elected for a third six-year term. During that year Sudan's north–south conflict escalated, and in June Nimeri finally decided to redivide the south into three smaller regions, each with its own assembly, in an effort to quell the unrest. In September Nimeri suddenly announced the imposition of strict Islamic law (the *Shari'a*), provoking anger in the largely non-Muslim south, and in April 1984 Nimeri proclaimed a state of emergency. The stringent application of *Shari'a* law aggravated tensions within the country and strained relations between Sudan and its allies, Egypt and the USA.

In May 1984 Nimeri replaced his Council of Ministers with a 64-member Presidential Council, in accordance with the '*Shoura*' (consultation) principle of *Shari'a* law. In July, however, the National People's Assembly rejected his proposed constitutional amendments to make Sudan a formal Islamic state. In October Nimeri ended the state of emergency and offered to revoke the redivision of the south, if a majority of southerners desired it. The situation in the south continued to deteriorate, with the emergence of the Sudan People's Liberation Movement (SPLM), whose armed forces, the Sudan People's Liberation Army (SPLA), rapidly gained military control over large areas of the provinces of Bahr al-Ghazal and Upper Nile.

On 6 April 1985, while Nimeri was visiting the USA, he was deposed in a bloodless military coup. The country's new leader, Gen. Abdel-Rahman Swar ad-Dahab (who had recently been made Minister of Defence and Commander-in-Chief of the army by Nimeri), appointed a Transitional Military Council (TMC) to govern the country, but he pledged a return to civilian rule after a one-year transitional period. The SSU and the National People's Assembly were dissolved, and hundreds of Nimeri's officials were arrested; Nimeri went into exile in Cairo, Egypt. A transitional Constitution was introduced in October 1985 that allowed new political groupings to emerge in preparation for a general election, and in December the name of the country was officially changed to 'the Republic of Sudan'.

In a general election in April 1986 the Umma Party (UP), led by Sadiq al-Mahdi, won 99 of the 264 seats in the new National Assembly, followed by the Democratic Unionist Party (DUP), with 63 seats. A coalition Government was formed by the UP and DUP, with four portfolios in the Council of Ministers allocated to southern parties. Al-Mahdi became Prime Minister and Minister of Defence, and a six-member Supreme Council assumed the functions of Head of State. With these appointments, the TMC was dissolved, signifying a return to civilian rule.

In response to the April 1985 coup, the SPLM initially declared a cease-fire, but presented the new regime with a series of demands concerning the southern region. Despite Swar ad-Dahab's offer of various concessions to the south, the SPLM refused to negotiate with the TMC, and fighting resumed. In May 1987, following increasing instability in the south, a temporary Council for the Southern Sudan (CSS) was established. Its influence on the army and the SPLM, the two contending de facto ruling powers that now existed in the south, was, however, negligible. In June al-Mahdi announced that the coalition parties had agreed on guidelines for the conduct of government policy and that laws based on a 'Sudanese legal heritage' would replace those unacceptable to non-Muslims, who would be exempted from Islamic taxation and special penalties. However, the SPLM continued to demand a total abrogation of Islamic law as a precondition for peace negotiations, while the National Islamic Front (NIF) demanded that the Islamic code be imposed on the whole country. On 25 July the Government imposed a 12-month state of emergency, aimed at bringing under control the worsening economic situation.

In May 1988 a new Government of National Unity, comprising members of the UP, the DUP, the NIF and some southern Sudanese political parties, was formed. In November representatives of the SPLM met senior members of the DUP and reached agreement on proposals to end the civil war. A statement issued by the two sides stipulated that, prior to the convening of a national constitutional conference, the Islamic legal code should be suspended, that military agreements between Sudan and other countries should be abandoned, and that the state of emergency be lifted and a cease-fire implemented in the south. In December, however, a state of emergency was again declared amid reports of an attempted military coup, and the DUP withdrew from the Government.

In February 1989 Dr Hassan at-Turabi, the leader of the NIF, was appointed Deputy Prime Minister. Although the peace agreement concluded by the DUP and the SPLM in November had been widely endorsed, the NIF opposed its provision for the suspension of Islamic laws as a prelude to the negotiation of a peace settlement. The NIF was consequently excluded from a new Government formed in March. Peace negotiations between a government delegation and the SPLM commenced in Ethiopia in April, and at the beginning of May the SPLM leader, Col John Garang, proclaimed a one-month cease-fire (subsequently extended to 30 June), renewing hopes for peace and aiding the work of famine relief. The negotiations culminated in an agreement to suspend Islamic laws, pending the proposed convening, in September, of a constitutional conference.

On 30 June 1989 a bloodless coup, led by Brig. (later Lt-Gen.) Omar Hassan Ahmad al-Bashir, removed al-Mahdi's Government. Al-Bashir formed a 15-member Revolutionary Command Council for National Salvation (RCC), which declared its primary aim to be the resolution of the southern conflict. Al-Bashir, who became Head of State, Chairman of the RCC, Prime Minister and Minister of Defence, and Commander-in-Chief of the armed forces, abolished the Constitution, the National Assembly and all political parties and trade unions, and declared a state of emergency.

The SPLM's response to the coup was cautious. In July 1989 Lt-Gen. al-Bashir declared a one-month unilateral cease-fire and offered amnesty to those opposing the Government 'for political reasons'. By August the SPLM's terms for a negotiated settlement to the conflict included the immediate resignation of the RCC, prior to the establishment of an interim government, in which the SPLM, the banned political parties and other groupings would be represented. However, the new regime's proximity to the NIF had become apparent, and the negotiations collapsed immediately over the issue of Islamic law. Hostilities, which had been in abeyance since the beginning of May, resumed at the end of October.

In February 1991 the RCC enacted a decree instituting a new, federal system of government. Sudan was divided into nine states, each of which had its own governor, deputy governor and cabinet of ministers, and assumed responsibility for local administration and the collection of some taxes. The central Government retained control over foreign policy, military affairs, the economy and the other principal areas of administration. At the beginning of February it had been announced that a new penal code, based on *Shari'a* law, would take effect in March, but would not apply in the three southern states, pending the establishment there of elected assemblies to resolve the issue. The SPLM nevertheless regarded the application of Islamic law in the northern states as unacceptable, citing the large numbers of non-Muslims resident there.

The overthrow, in May 1991, of the Ethiopian Government, led by Mengistu Haile Mariam, had implications for the SPLA forces, who had previously enjoyed Ethiopian support. In late May armed clashes were reported within Ethiopia between SPLA forces and those of the new Ethiopian Government, and the Sudanese Government declared its recognition of, and support for, the new Ethiopian regime. In October Sudan and Ethiopia signed a treaty of friendship and co-operation.

In February 1992 al-Bashir appointed all 300 members of a new transitional National Assembly, which included the entire RCC, all government ministers and the governors of Sudan's nine states. The Assembly was accorded legislative authority, with the power to examine all decrees issued by the RCC, and responsibility for preparing the country for parliamentary elections.

In early 1993 the NIF was reported to be opposed to the continued military character of the Government, and to favour the dissolution of the RCC. In January al-Bashir effected an extensive reorganization of the Cabinet, but stated that the RCC would not be dissolved. Rather, in 1994 the gradual transfer of power to the regional councils would begin. Talks between the Government and the SPLA ended inconclusively in January 1993. By this time the SPLA was reported to have split into three factions.

In July 1993 Garang's faction of the SPLA launched a major offensive after attacks by government troops, aided by rival SPLA factions. Renewed fighting between government troops and the SPLA in July caused the influx of some 100,000 starving people into the area around the southern provincial capital of Malakal.

In mid-October 1993 al-Bashir announced political reforms in preparation for presidential and legislative elections in 1994 and 1995, respectively. The RCC was dissolved after it had appointed al-Bashir as President and as head of a new civilian Government. Cabinet ministers were requested to remain in office until elections took place. Later in October al-Bashir appointed a new Minister of Defence—a portfolio that he had formerly held himself—and a new Vice-President.

In January 1994 the two principal rival factions of the SPLA were reported to have agreed on a cease-fire. In February Sudan was redivided into 26 states instead of the nine that had formed the basis of administration since 1991. The executive and legislative powers of each state government were to be expanded, and southern states were to be exempted from *Shari'a* law. In March delegations representing the Government and two factions of the SPLA participated in peace talks held in Nairobi, Kenya, under the auspices of the Intergovernmental Authority on Drought and Development (IGADD—superseded in 1996 by the Intergovernmental Authority on Development—IGAD, see p. 311), which in September 1993 had formed a committee on the Sudanese conflict comprising the Heads of State of Kenya, Ethiopia, Uganda and Eritrea. All parties to the talks agreed to allow the free passage of relief supplies to southern Sudan. In April 1994 the Government adopted legislation providing for the appointment, by the President, of an independent commission to supervise legislative elections scheduled to take place in the second half of 1994, and for a constitutional referendum.

A further round of IGADD-sponsored peace negotiations was held in Nairobi on 18–28 July 1994. On 23 July the Government announced a unilateral cease-fire, to which Garang's faction of the SPLA reportedly responded on 28 July with a cease-fire of its own. However, when the negotiations resumed in early September, divergent positions on the issues of the governance of the south and the role of religion in government quickly led to deadlock. The severing, in December, of diplomatic relations between Sudan and Eritrea led Sudan to inform the IGADD in early 1995 that it no longer considered Eritrea to be a suitable intermediary in the Sudanese conflict. A cabinet reshuffle in February suggested a reinforcement of the Islamic character of the Government.

In mid-March 1995 Garang announced that his faction of the SPLA was to mount a new northern offensive in collaboration with other northern rebels. The New Sudan Brigade aimed to unite other insurgent groups against the Government, but did not appear to gain the support of rival SPLA factions. In late March it was reported that former US President Jimmy Carter had persuaded the Government to declare a unilateral cease-fire for a period of two months, and to offer rebel groups an amnesty if they surrendered their weapons. The SPLA and the South Sudan Independence Movement (SSIM) responded by also declaring cease-fires. In late May the Government extended its cease-fire for two months. However, it soon became apparent that the army was continuing to conduct military operations. In June a conference of groups and parties opposed to the Sudanese Government commenced in Asmara, Eritrea. The conference, hosted by the Eritrean People's Front for Democracy and Justice and organized by the Asmara-based National Democratic Alliance (NDA), was attended, among others, by representatives of the DUP, the UP and the Sudanese Communist Party. It was agreed that, once the al-Bashir regime had been ousted, religion would be separated from politics and that a referendum would be held regarding the secession of the southern provinces. The conference was also reported to have achieved a rapprochement between the SPLA and other opposition groups.

In August 1995 a reshuffle of the Cabinet was announced. The DUP claimed that those ministers who had been dismissed had been involved in the attempted assassination of President Mubarak of Egypt in June (see below). Later in August President al-Bashir announced that legislative and presidential elections would be held in 1996. At the end of January 1996 the USA announced the withdrawal of its diplomatic personnel from Sudan, owing to doubts about the Government's ability to guarantee their safety. Prior to their withdrawal, the UN Security Council had unanimously adopted Resolution 1044, which accused Sudan of supporting terrorism and condemned its role in the attempted assassination of Mubarak. The resolution also demanded that Sudan immediately extradite three individuals implicated in the attempted assassination.

Legislative and presidential elections took place in March 1996. Some 5.5m. of Sudan's 10m. eligible voters were reported to have participated in the election of 275 deputies to a new, 400-seat National Assembly. The remaining 125 deputies had been appointed at a national conference in January. Representatives of opposition groups and parties alleged that electoral malpractice had been widespread. In the presidential election al-Bashir (who was reportedly opposed only by token candidates) obtained 75.7% of the total votes cast, and formally commenced a five-year term of office on 1 April. On the same day Dr Hassan at-Turabi, the Secretary-General of the NIF, was unanimously elected President of the National Assembly.

Rumours of an attempted *coup d'état* in late March 1996 prejudiced the newly constituted regime's claim that the elections signified the beginning of a new period of stability and reconciliation, as did reports of serious unrest in Khartoum in early April and the decision not to appoint a new Cabinet until it became clear whether the UN would impose sanctions on Sudan for its failure to comply with the terms of UN Security Council Resolution 1044. On 10 April a 'political charter for peace' was signed by the Government, the SSIM and the SPLA-United, pledging to preserve Sudan's national unity and to take joint action to develop those areas of the country that had been affected by the civil war. The charter also provided for the holding of a referendum as 'a means of realizing the aspirations of southern citizens' and affirmed that Islamic law would be the basis of future legislation. On 17 April Sudan's First Vice-President was reported to have invited Garang to sign the charter on behalf of his faction of the SPLA, prompting speculation that this was part of an ongoing attempt to form a new government of national unity. However, the new Cabinet, announced on 21 April, retained the military, Islamist cast of its predecessor. On 28 April the UN Security Council imposed diplomatic sanctions on Sudan for failing to comply with the terms of Resolution 1044. In October al-Bashir appointed eight deputies to the National Assembly to represent constituencies in the south where, owing to the civil war, it had not been possible to hold elections in March.

In April 1997 a peace accord, covering major issues such as power-sharing and *Shari'a* law, and promising a referendum on southern secession after a four-year transition period, was signed by six rebel groups. Both the NDA and the SPLA, however, rejected the agreement. In August, in accordance with the terms of the agreement, the Southern States Co-ordination Council (SSCC) was established; Dr Riek Mashar Teny-Dhurgon, the leader of the Southern Sudan Defence Force (SSDF), was sworn in as its Chairman. At the beginning of September the SPLA-United declared a cease-fire, and its commander, Dr Lam Akol, returned to Khartoum in the following month.

In March 1998 al-Bashir announced a government reorganization in which a number of former rebel leaders were appointed to the Cabinet, including Akol as Minister of Transport. In April a new Constitution was approved by the National Assembly and endorsed by 96.7% of voters in a referendum held between 1 and 20 May. Under its terms, executive power would be vested in the Council of Ministers, which would be appointed by the President but responsible to the National Assembly. Legislative power was to be vested in the National Assembly. The Constitution also guaranteed freedom of thought and religion, and the right to lawful political association. New legislation approved in November 1998 provided for the establishment of an independent election commission and of a Constitutional Court, and for the legalization of political associations. Registration of political parties began in January 1999.

In May 1999 former President Nimeri returned to Sudan after 14 years in exile in Egypt. His return was welcomed by the Government, although opposition parties demanded his prosecution for crimes he had allegedly committed while President. In the same month at-Turabi held talks in Switzerland with Sadiq al-Mahdi, with the aim of initiating a process of reconciliation. At the end of May a meeting took place in Kampala, Uganda, between al-Mahdi, Garang and Mubarak al-Mahdi (of the NDA), to discuss several issues regarding their conflict with the Sudanese Government.

In August 1999 the Government accepted a Libyan peace initiative, which envisaged a cease-fire, an end to media propaganda, direct talks through a conference of national dialogue and the establishment of a preparatory committee. The peace effort was to be co-ordinated jointly by Egypt and Libya. The Government did, however, express reservations over a number of conditions proposed by the NDA, which included the suspension of articles in the Constitution that restricted public liberty and the release of political prisoners. In September the SPLA stated that it supported the Egyptian-Libyan peace initiative 'in principle', although after a meeting with the US Secretary of State in October (see below) Garang discounted the Egyptian-Libyan initiative in favour of the IGAD-sponsored peace process.

At a conference, held in Cairo in October 1999, the leaders of the NDA decided to examine ways of combining the peace initiative sponsored by IGAD and the Egyptian-Libyan initiative, in order to unite the parties of the NDA, a number of whom opposed the pursuit of two parallel initiatives. At the end of November Djibouti hosted a regional IGAD summit meeting, attended by Kenya, Ethiopia and Sudan, to discuss issues related to development and stability in the region. While in Djibouti, President al-Bashir met the UP leader, al-Mahdi, following which the Sudanese Government and the UP signed a declaration of principles, which envisaged a federal system of government and the holding of a referendum within four years to allow southerners to choose between the division of the country or unity with decentralized powers. The agreement was welcomed by many parties; however, the NDA responded by stating that it would escalate the war in the south, not end it. Garang later condemned and disavowed the Djibouti agreement.

During 1999 there were increasing reports of rivalry between al-Bashir and at-Turabi, particularly following the introduction of a bill in the National Assembly that sought to remove the President's power to appoint and dismiss state governors. Consideration of the draft legislation was repeatedly delayed, but a vote was scheduled to be held in mid-December in which the National Assembly was widely expected to approve it. However, on 12 December al-Bashir dissolved the National Assembly and imposed a three-month state of emergency, claiming that he had taken these measures in order to end the 'duality' in the administration. An emergency order suspended some articles of the Constitution, although provincial councils and governors were to continue working. At-Turabi accused al-Bashir of having carried out a *coup d'état*, although a legal challenge, mounted against the measures, was later rejected by the Constitutional Court.

IGAD-sponsored talks held in Nairobi in January 2000 made some progress on the issue of a referendum. At the end of January al-Bashir appointed a new Cabinet and state governors. An emergency development programme, formulated by the SSCC, for the southern states was approved by the Government in February. Teny-Dhurgon resigned as Chairman of the SSCC in February in protest at the Government's failure to implement the terms of the peace accords and at al-Bashir's disregard for the Constitution. In mid-February Teny-Dhurgon claimed a major victory over government forces and announced the establishment of the Sudan People's Defence Force (SPDF).

In March 2000 the Government extended the state of emergency until the end of the year, and approved a law allowing the formation of political parties (superseding the 1998 law), although this was rejected by the opposition, as it still incorporated provisions to suspend the activities of any party. In the same month the UP announced its decision to suspend its membership of the NDA during a meeting in Asmara. In April 2000 it was reported that a presidential election was planned for October; the ruling National Congress (NC) had nominated al-Bashir as its candidate in October 1999. However, most opposition parties, including the UP, indicated that they would not participate in any elections prior to the convening of a national conference to discuss the problems in Sudan.

A meeting between the leaders of Egypt, Sudan and Libya was held in Cairo in April 2000 to discuss the Egyptian-Libyan peace initiative. At that time al-Bashir revealed that discussions were under way for the return of al-Mahdi to Sudan. In May al-Bashir announced the suspension of the secretariat of the NC, including the activities of at-Turabi and his deputies, and affirmed his intention to restructure the party.

IGAD-sponsored peace talks, held in April 2000, ended inconclusively, and in May the SPLM suspended its participation in protest at the Government's alleged continued bombing of civilian targets. It reaffirmed its commitment to the unification of the IGAD process and the Egyptian-Libyan initiative, but did not indicate on what conditions it would resume talks. The next round of IGAD-sponsored talks had been scheduled to begin on 17 May. In June the SPLM announced it would rejoin the peace talks, and in that month al-Bashir declared a general amnesty for all opponents of the Government; however, it was rejected by a number of opposition groups, including the SPLM. Later that month at-Turabi announced the formation of a new political party, the Popular National Congress (PNC), whose registration was formally approved in August.

In September 2000 al-Mahdi confirmed the withdrawal of the UP from the NDA alliance. Later that month al-Bashir visited Asmara, where he met with an NDA delegation. The two parties discussed possible political settlements to the situation in Sudan and agreed to meet for further direct talks, although no date for such discussions was set. In October it was reported that al-Bashir had dismissed Maj.-Gen. George Kongor Arop from the post of Second Vice-President. The following month al-Mahdi returned to Sudan from his four-year self-imposed exile in Eritrea and Egypt, but announced that he would not participate in the forthcoming elections.

Presidential and legislative elections were held concurrently over a 10-day period in mid-December 2000, although they were boycotted by the main opposition parties. As expected, al-Bashir was re-elected President, with 86.5% of the votes cast, comfortably defeating his nearest rival, former President Nimeri, who obtained 9.6% of the vote. Voting did not take place in the three southern states. The NC secured 355 seats in the new 360-member National Assembly; the remaining five seats were won by small opposition parties. On 3 January 2001 al-Bashir extended the state of emergency for a further year.

On 21 February 2001 at-Turabi was arrested at his home in Khartoum after it was announced that the PNC and the SPLM had signed a memorandum of understanding in Switzerland, which urged the Sudanese people to participate in 'peaceful popular resistance' against the al-Bashir regime. In early March at-Turabi and several other members of the PNC's leadership council were reported to have been charged with criminal conspiracy, undermining the constitutional order, waging war on the state and calling for violent opposition to public authority. (In late May at-Turabi was released from prison and placed under house arrest.) Meanwhile, the day after at-Turabi's arrest, al-Bashir implemented a major reorganization of the Cabinet and replaced many of the country's state governors. Several new ministries were created, and, although the new, 32-member Cabinet was dominated by NC members, al-Bashir incorporated four members of two minor opposition parties into the Government. Two members of the UDSF retained their positions in the Cabinet, but the UP, despite earlier indications to the contrary, refused to participate in the new administration and officially stated that it would not accept ministerial posts before the holding of free and fair elections in the south of the country and the resolution of the armed conflict in that region.

In early July 2001 it was reported that the Sudanese Government and the NDA had both provisionally accepted a renewed Libyan-Egyptian peace initiative, which provided for an immediate cease-fire, the establishment of a transitional government and a number of constitutional reforms. Later that month the leadership council of the NC approved the Libyan-Egyptian plan. However, al-Bashir maintained that he would not support any proposals that involved the separation of state and religion or the partition of the country, thus endangering the success of the initiative, as the NDA concurrently reiterated its demand for the right of the southern states to be granted self-determination.

In late September 2001 the UN Security Council voted to remove the sanctions imposed on Sudan in 1996 (see above) and praised the country's recent efforts to combat terrorism. Notably, the USA, which had previously used its vote to veto the lifting of sanctions, abstained, enabling the motion to be carried. In mid-December the state of emergency was again extended for a further 12 months. In January 2002 Teny-Dhurgon and Garang announced the merger of the SPDF and the SPLA. Teny-Dhurgon had defected from the SPLM/SPLA in 1991 and had signed a peace accord with the Government in 1997 (as leader of the SSDF); however, this agreement had collapsed in early 2001.

In mid-January 2002 talks sponsored jointly by the USA and Switzerland commenced in Buergenstock, Switzerland. Following six days of intensive discussions, the Sudanese Government and the SPLA agreed to observe a six-month cease-fire, to be supervised by a joint military commission, in the central Nuba region in order to facilitate the delivery of vital aid supplies to the area. However, the following month the SPLA announced that it had suspended discussions with the Sudanese Government, after two separate incidents earlier that month in which Sudanese air force planes had bombed civilians collecting food supplies in the Bahr al-Ghazal province. In the second incident at least 24 civilians were killed when a UN World Food Programme (WFP) relief centre came under fire. Although the Government insisted that the earlier incident was accidental, the US Department of State declared that discussions would not recommence until it had received a full explanation for the attacks from the Sudanese Government. The Sudanese Minister of External Relations subsequently issued an apology for the attack and in mid-March the USA brokered an agreement between the SPLA and the Sudanese Government, which aimed to guarantee the protection of civilians from military attacks; the agreement was to be monitored by two teams of international observers. In early July the cease-fire was extended for a further six months, and in late December it was agreed that it would continue until July 2003.

In May 2002 the Minister of Finance, Adb ar-Rahim Muhammad Hamdi, reportedly resigned owing to ill health. There was, however, speculation that he had been dismissed by al-Bashir following the implementation of several unpopular economic measures. Hamdi was subsequently replaced by Muhammad al-Hasan az-Zubayr. In June three members of the NC, including Akol, resigned from the party in protest at the increasing dominance of al-Bashir. In mid-August al-Bashir renewed the detention order that had been placed on at-Turabi the previous year for a further 12 months, and in September at-Turabi was transferred to prison. In the previous month al-Bashir had effected a minor reorganization of the Council of Ministers, and in September Akol was dismissed as Minister of Transport; Akol was one of a number of former NC members who had, earlier that month, established a new political party, the Justice Party. In November al-Bashir carried out a further reshuffle of the Council of Ministers and created two new ministries. In December the state of emergency was once again extended for a further 12 months.

Meanwhile, in mid-June 2002 a new round of IGAD-sponsored peace talks between the Government and the SPLM opened in Machakos, Kenya. Despite the ongoing discussions, fighting between the two sides continued, and there were numerous reports of heavy civilian casualties following bombing raids on southern towns by government forces. Nevertheless, a major breakthrough in the conflict was achieved on 20 July, when delegations from the SPLM and the Government signed an accord, known as the Machakos Protocol, which provided for a six-year period of autonomy for the south, to be followed by an internationally monitored referendum on self-determination. The Protocol also stated that Sudan's Constitution would be rewritten to ensure that *Shari'a* law would not be applied to non-Muslim southerners. Government and SPLM delegations reconvened in Machakos in mid-August for talks. However, further outbreaks of fighting between the two sides were reported, and in early September, in response to the SPLA's capture of Torit, the Government announced that it had suspended talks with the SPLM and launched an offensive to try and reclaim the town. Despite agreeing to cease hostilities and resume peace talks, government forces recaptured Torit in early October. Later that month the two sides reconvened in Machakos and signed a cease-fire agreement for the duration of the ongoing discussions. Both sides subsequently accused each other of breaking the cease-fire, and it was reported that some 300 government troops had been killed by rebel forces just hours after the signing of the accord. Negotiations between the Government and the SPLM were halted in mid-November, after no agreement could be reached on the number of government and civil service posts to be allocated to southerners and the distribution of petroleum revenues. Disputes also remained over control of the Abeyi, Blue Nile and Nuba Mountains provinces in central Sudan and the religious status of Khartoum. The two sides did, however, agree to extend the cease-fire until the end of March 2003.

Talks resumed in Nairobi in mid-January 2003, and the following month a memorandum of understanding was signed under which the Government and the SPLM agreed to allow international observers to monitor the cease-fire. In April al-Bashir and Garang met for only the second time in 20 years and announced that they anticipated that the peace talks would be concluded by the end of June; they also reaffirmed their commitment to the Machakos Protocol and pledged to facilitate unrestricted delivery of humanitarian assistance to those in the south of the country. However, in May it became apparent that the talks would not be concluded as expected, after negotiations between the Government and the SPLM ended with a number of key issues, including wealth- and power-sharing, still unresolved. In July the government delegation rejected a document presented by the IGAD mediators, providing for a separate army and an independent central bank for the south, as it maintained that this was in conflict with the Machakos Protocol, which had enshrined the unity of Sudan. In mid-August talks between the Government and the SPLM recommenced in the Kenyan town of Nanyuki, and later that month the discussions were extended until mid-September in order to give both sides additional time to resolve their outstanding differences.

In mid-September 2003 the SPLA and the Sudanese Government agreed to extend their cease-fire for a further two months, and days later the two sides signed a landmark security agreement. Under the terms of the arrangement, two separate armed forces were to be created, as well as a number of integrated units, comprising both government and SPLA troops. Both sides agreed to contribute 12,000 soldiers to a joint force to be deployed in southern Sudan, and a further 6,000 soldiers from each side were to be dispatched to the disputed Nuba Mountains and Blue Nile provinces. Furthermore, 80% of the government forces in southern Sudan would be withdrawn to the north no later than two and a half years after the signing of a comprehensive peace agreement. It was also agreed that both sides' forces would be reduced at a later, unspecified date and that they would be placed under the command of a joint defence board composed of SPLM and government officials. In October the US Secretary of State, Colin Powell, secured assurances from the Sudanese Government and the SPLM that a comprehensive settlement would be reached by the end of the year. Nevertheless, later in October US sanctions on Sudan (see below) were extended for a further 12 months. Also in October at-Turabi was released from detention, and all restrictions on the NPC's activities were lifted. In late March 2004 the Sudanese security forces arrested some 27 people, among them at-Turabi, five other members of the PNC and 10 military officers, on suspicion of plotting to overthrow the Government. In January 2005 a number of those apprehended were released; however, at-Turabi remained in detention along with some 12 other PNC members. Meanwhile, in October 2004 al-Bashir dismissed the Assistant President, Mubarak al-Fadil al-Mahdi, who was reportedly not replaced.

In early December 2003 SPLM delegates visited Khartoum for the first time since the escalation of the north–south conflict in 1983, prior to convening for further talks with the Government in Naivasha, Kenya. Later that month the Government and the SPLM agreed 'in principle' to divide petroleum revenues equally between the north and the south, and it was reported that they had also reached preliminary agreement on the distribution of tax revenues and the role of the new central bank. Nevertheless, no final agreement was concluded by the end of the month, and talks recommenced in early January 2004. On 7 January the two sides signed an accord on wealth- and revenue-sharing, which also provided for the establishment of two separate banking systems for the north and the south, as well as a new national currency on the signing of a final peace settlement. Although talks resumed in Kenya in mid-February, progress on other matters remained stalled, and by mid-May, despite intense international pressure, the two sides had still not concluded a definitive peace agreement. Furthermore, in mid-April the UN announced it had been forced to suspend aid operations in southern Sudan, owing to renewed violence, and that some 50,000 people had fled their homes in the region during the previous month.

The Government and the SPLM signed three protocols on 26 May 2004, which removed the remaining obstacles to the conclusion of a comprehensive peace accord. Specifically, the protocols stated that the SPLM and other southern groups would hold 30% of government seats in the north, while holding 70% of seats in the south; that the contested regions of the Blue Nile and the Nuba Mountains would be governed by an administration in which 55% of the seats would be taken by government officials and 45% by the SPLM, while the petroleum-rich region of Abeyi would be granted special status and be governed by the presidential office; and that Khartoum would remain under Islamic law with certain protections for non-Muslims. The final round of the IGAD-sponsored talks began in Naivasha in late June with the stated aim of finalizing and implementing a comprehensive cease-fire and it was announced that the two sides hoped to conclude a definitive agreement by August. Progress was delayed, however, by the Sudanese authorities' attempts to involve other pro-government southern militias in the talks. On 31 August the cease-fire was extended for a further three months and in early October the Naivasha talks recommenced. In early November the UN Security Council met in Nairobi in an attempt to prompt a definitive conclusion to proceedings, and it was announced that the Government and the SPLM had agreed to finalize a peace agreement by the end of the year.

On 31 December 2004, at a ceremony in Naivasha, a permanent cease-fire was agreed by the Sudanese Government and the SPLM. On 9 January 2005 Garang and Vice-President Ali Osman Muhammad Taha signed the Comprehensive Peace Agreement (CPA) in Nairobi in the presence of Powell and representatives from the UN, the EU, the African Union—AU (see p. 164) and IGAD, thus formally bringing an end to more than 20 years of civil conflict between the SPLA and successive governments. Under the agreement Garang was to assume the position of Sudanese Vice-President in late February and would act as President of southern Sudan during the six-year period of autonomy, after which a referendum on secession would be held. However, by mid-April Garang had yet to take up either position and it was announced that the commission charged with formulating a new constitution would not be appointed until later that month. Meanwhile, in mid-January the Government signed a peace accord with the NDA in Cairo, Egypt, which allowed for the return of NDA leaders to Sudan and granted them the right to conduct their political activities in the country.

In late January 2005 it was announced that the administrative capital of southern Sudan would be established at Rumbek, a town with limited electricity and running water, which had been extensively damaged by bombing during the civil conflict. The UN appealed for the international community to assist with the reconstruction of southern Sudan's infrastructure. On 25 January the UN announced that it had restored diplomatic ties with Sudan and would contribute some €50m. in aid, to be divided equally between the north and the south, and in early February the UN Secretary-General, Kofi Annan, announced plans to deploy some 10,000 peace-keeping troops to Sudan to monitor the cease-fire and assist with the disarmament process. In mid-February it was announced that the SPLM intended to release some 750 prisoners of war. In mid-March the Government launched its six-year recovery and development plan, the main priority of which was to rebuild the country's infrastructure, predicted to cost US $8,000m. over two years. In late March the UN Security Council unanimously approved Resolution 1590, which provided for the establishment of the UN Mission in Sudan (UNMIS), comprising up to 10,000 peace-keeping troops and 715 civilian personnel and to be deployed in southern Sudan for an initial period of six months; a contingent of Nepalese soldiers duly commenced duties at the end of the month. Talks began in early May between the Government, the SPLM and opposition parties regarding an interim constitution which was to incorporate the provisions of the CPA into law and to enable the formation of a government of national unity. However, the UP refused to enter the talks and demanded greater representation for opposition parties.

In early June 2005 the UP, the PNC and 14 smaller opposition parties signed an agreement to form a new coalition, styled the National Forces Coalition. At a meeting held in Cairo in mid-June Taha and the NDA leaders signed an agreement for the NDA to join a power-sharing administration and the NDA subsequently nominated 27 of its members to the commission charged with drafting the new interim Constitution. In late June al-Bashir announced the release of 'all political detainees', among them at-Turabi. Earlier that month the President had lifted the ban prohibiting all political activity by the PNC. On 6 July the National Assembly ratified the new interim Constitution (see below) and on 9 July Garang was appointed First Vice-President of the new presidential council, replacing Taha who took the role of Vice-President, and as President of Southern Sudan. In mid-July Government troops withdrew from Juba and the surrounding area in accordance with the CPA, which stipulated that 17% of Government troops be redeployed within six months of signing the agreement, and Garang named the SPLM deputy leader, Commdr Salva Kiir Mayardit, as Vice-President of the new southern administration. Interim governors were also appointed to each of the 10 states in southern Sudan.

On 1 August 2005 it was announced that Garang had been killed in a helicopter crash as he travelled to Rumbek from Kampala, Uganda. During 1–4 August at least 130 people were killed in Khartoum during violent clashes between protesters angry at Garang's death and the security forces. Salva Kiir succeeded Garang as leader of the SPLA/SPLM, and in early August was appointed as First Vice-President of Sudan and President of Southern Sudan. Also in early August al-Bashir announced the formation of a committee to investigate the circumstances surrounding Garang's death.

During August 2005 differences regarding wealth-sharing and the allocation of the energy portfolio continued to obstruct the formation of a government of national unity. However, in late September an agreement was reached and the list of government ministers was announced, in which 16 portfolios (including those of defence, interior, finance and energy and mining) were awarded to members of the NC, nine to the SPLM and four to members of smaller opposition parties. In late January 2006, at the sixth AU summit, which took place in Khartoum, the emergence of al-Bashir as the leading candidate for the chairmanship of the organization provoked widespread criticism from the international community and proved unacceptable to representatives from a number of AU member states. Following two days of negotiations, it was agreed that the President of the Republic of Congo, Gen. Denis Sassou-Nguesso, would assume the chairmanship in 2006, to be succeeded by al-Bashir in 2007. Faced with unanimous opposition, in January 2007 al-Bashir withdrew his candidacy and the President of Ghana, John Kufuor, assumed the role of Chairman.

Meanwhile, in February 2003 a new area of conflict emerged in the Darfur region of western Sudan. The Sudan Liberation Movement (SLM) announced the commencement of an armed campaign to end Darfur's political and economic marginalization and to combat the Government's 'ethnic cleansing' activities in the region. The SLM, which was reported to have some 1,500 troops and received support from Eritrea, subsequently attacked the provincial capital, Al-Fasher, and claimed to have killed more than 70 government soldiers. In an attempt to suppress the revolt the Sudanese authorities armed pro-Government ethnic Arab militias, known as the *Janjaweed*, who systematically razed entire villages to the ground and carried out indiscriminate killings. In April the Sudanese authorities refused offers of talks with the rebels, dismissed senior security officials in the region, and deployed additional forces to Darfur to retake most of the territory that had been lost to the SLM. Fighting continued in the area until early September, when, following mediation from the Chadian Government, a cease-fire was agreed between the Sudanese Government and the SLM. Under the accord, the Government agreed to release more than 50 suspected SLM members from detention. However, there were reports of ongoing incidents in Darfur during late 2003, with large numbers of Sudanese, fleeing alleged human rights abuses, crossing the border into Chad to seek refuge. In December aid agencies maintained that the Sudanese Government was preventing food and medical supplies from reaching the Darfur region, and in January 2004 Sudanese planes reportedly bombed a number of villages in the border area, just weeks after the rebels claimed to have killed some 700 government troops. Talks, again with Chadian mediation, broke down without making any progress, and by March it was estimated that more than 130,000 Sudanese had entered Chad and as many as 900,000 people had been displaced as a result of the ongoing conflict and the rapidly deteriorating humanitarian situation. At the end of that month indirect peace talks between the Government, the SLM and the Sudan Justice and Equality Movement (SJEM), attended by international observers, commenced in Chad, and on 8 April a 45-day humanitarian cease-fire was signed by representatives of the three parties. There were reports of serious human rights violations by government troops in the Darfur region and in early May a series of clashes occurred between Sudanese militiamen pursuing Sudanese rebels across the border and Chadian troops. By early June it was estimated that as a result of the violence in Darfur more than 30,000 people had been killed and a further 1m. people had been displaced, with 350,000 of those at risk from starvation and disease. The UN and the international human rights organization Amnesty International, along with the US and British Governments, placed renewed pressure on the Government to address the situation.

Following visits from Annan and Powell to refugee camps in Darfur in late June 2004 and the threat of the imposition of UN sanctions on the *Janjaweed*, in early July the Sudanese authorities committed to a series of actions, including the more aggressive use of the security forces to deal with the militia, the easing of travel restrictions for aid workers and the deployment of AU troops in Darfur. There followed a marginal improvement in access granted to humanitarian aid agencies but the security situation remained precarious as militias continued to attack civilian populations. In mid-July AU-sponsored peace talks between the Sudanese Government and the rebels opened in Addis Ababa, Ethiopia. The talks swiftly collapsed after the Government rejected the preconditions set out by the SLM and the SJEM for further negotiations, which included the disarmament of the *Janjaweed* and the removal of those *Janjaweed* fighters absorbed by the police and army; the observation of the April cease-fire agreement; the prosecution of the perpetrators of crimes and an inquiry into allegations of genocide; unimpeded humanitarian access for aid agencies; the release of prisoners of war; and a 'neutral' venue for future talks. In late July the US House of Representatives approved a resolution declaring the human rights abuses in Darfur a 'genocide' and on 30 July the UN Security Council adopted a resolution (No. 1556), that called on the Sudanese Government to end the conflict in Darfur, to facilitate the delivery of humanitarian aid, and to grant AU peace monitors access to the region. The resolution was rejected by the Sudanese Government and the armed forces spokesman, Gen. Muhammad Bashir Suleiman, described it as a 'declaration of war'.

In early August 2004 the UN Special Envoy to Sudan, Jan Pronk, agreed a number of measures with the Sudanese Government, aimed at averting the imposition of sanctions if certain conditions were fulfilled. However, in mid-August aid workers continued to report government-imposed travel restrictions and incidences of government-assisted violence occurring across the Darfur region. On 20 August the Sudanese Government admitted to the UN that it had control over certain *Janjaweed* members and stated that it would divulge the names of those fighters it was aware of. On 25 August the Government agreed to allow further foreign troops into Darfur. However, as the UN Security Council resolution expired at the end of the month, observers of the cease-fire reported that the government forces had launched attacks on civilians in Darfur only one week previously and Annan announced that the Sudanese authorities had failed to meet the requirements set out by the UN.

In mid-September 2004 the UN Security Council approved a second resolution (No. 1564), stating that it would consider imposing sanctions affecting Sudan's petroleum industry should it fail to take steps to disarm the *Janjaweed* and protect civilians from further attacks. The UN was also to establish a commission to investigate claims that the human rights abuses in Darfur amounted to genocide, while the AU planned to increase the size of its monitoring force in the region (the African Union Mission in Sudan—AMIS) from 350 to some 3,500. Further peace talks held days earlier between the Government, the SLA and the SJEM in Abuja, Nigeria, ended without agreement. In early October 2004 the British Prime Minister, Anthony (Tony) Blair, arrived in Sudan for talks with President al-Bashir in an attempt to resolve the Darfur issue. A five-point peace plan, proposed by Blair, was accepted by the President. In agreeing to the plan, the Sudanese Government pledged to allow an increase in the number of AU troops in the country; to identify its forces in Darfur to enable the effective monitoring of the cease-fire; to commit to a cessation of hostilities in Darfur within three months and to negotiate a comprehensive agreement to the ongoing conflict in southern Sudan (see above) by the end of 2004; and to assist with the distribution of humanitarian aid.

Further peace talks between the Government and the Darfur rebel groups commenced in Abuja in October 2004 and in mid-November an agreement was signed according to which the two sides pledged to end hostilities, with the Government also agreeing to establish a 'no-fly' zone over the Darfur region (the rebels had accused government forces of using aircraft to support *Janjaweed* attacks). During late 2004, however, aid workers reported attacks on refugee camps by Sudanese police and several aid agencies were forced to temporarily withdraw their staff from the region. In mid-December AU cease-fire monitors reported that they had witnessed large quantities of arms and ammunition being delivered to government forces in Darfur. Days later, following the expiry of a deadline imposed by the AU for both sides to cease all hostilities, the Sudanese authorities agreed to end military operations in Darfur on the condition that the rebels also refrained from acts of violence. By that time it was estimated that some 70,000 people had been killed and 2m. people had been displaced since the start of the conflict. Despite the agreement, the AU reported later in December that government forces had attacked the village of Labado in the south of the Darfur region.

Continued attacks were reported and in early February 2005 a UN commission of inquiry revealed that although serious crimes against humanity had taken place, these did not amount to genocide. It did, however, identify 51 suspected war criminals and recommended that they be tried by the International Criminal Court—(ICC, see p. 314). In late March the UN Security Council adopted Resolution 1593, demanding that the Sudanese Government and all other parties to the Darfur conflict co-operate fully with the ICC, which was to undertake preparatory analysis of the situation prior to deciding whether to commence a full investigation into allegations of war crimes committed in Darfur. The decision prompted the Government to organize a mass demonstration in Khartoum. For his part, al-Bashir pledged not to send any Sudanese nationals abroad for trial, but the Minister of External Relations, Dr Mustafa Osman Ismail, subsequently offered to hold any future ICC trial in Sudan. In late April the AU confirmed that a new round of talks between the Government and rebel groups would begin in Abuja in May, and it was also announced that 3,320 additional AU peace-keeping troops would arrive in Darfur by the end of September, increasing the number of AMIS troops to 7,731.

In mid-May 2005 the SLM and the SJEM agreed to maintain a cease-fire and to engage in further talks with the Government. However, according to the UN there was an increase in the number of reported instances of rape and kidnapping in the region during the month of April and attacks on civilians by *Janjaweed* fighters continued. In late May a conference for international donor countries was held in Addis Ababa and US $200m. was pledged to fund the enlarged AU peace-keeping operation in Darfur. NATO had previously announced that it would provide training, logistics and technical support to the mission. In early June the ICC commenced an investigation into allegations that the Sudanese Government and the *Janjaweed* had committed crimes against humanity in the Darfur region. Talks between rebels and the Government resumed in Abuja in mid-June, and following four weeks of negotiations, the two sides signed a declaration of principles. Meanwhile, in mid-June the Government established a court at which 162 people accused of committing crimes against humanity in the Darfur region were to be tried, and referred to the institution as 'an alternative' to the ICC. The court was rejected by rebel groups in Darfur, who claimed that Sudanese officials would escape trial, and Pronk dismissed the notion that the court could replace the ICC. In mid-July the SLM and SJEM signed an agreement to end their dispute and to normalize relations following a meeting in Tripoli, Libya. However, talks between the Government and the two rebel groups, scheduled to be held in Abuja during late August, were postponed for one month. Despite the absence of an SLM faction, talks resumed in mid-September amid reports of increasing violence in Darfur. In early October a rebel faction captured 18 AU peace-keeping staff close to the border with Chad, although most were released after one day. Also in early October four AU peace-keepers were killed in southern Darfur and in mid-October concerns over escalating violence prompted the UN to withdraw all non-essential staff from Darfur. In late November Annan reported a further increase in violence against civilians in the region and the AU called for an end to the killing of civilians as peace talks resumed in Abuja. The human rights organization Human Rights Watch (HRW) released a report in mid-December, which accused al-Bashir, Taha and several other senior Government officials of involvement in crimes against humanity committed in Darfur. The report also called for them to be investigated by the ICC and added to a UN list of suspects eligible for sanctions. Later in December ICC investigators were refused permission by the Government to visit Darfur to gather evidence of alleged crimes against humanity.

In mid-January 2006 Annan called upon the USA and European countries to contribute logistical support and troops for a planned UN peace-keeping mission in Darfur. The AU had earlier warned that a lack of funds would lead to the eventual withdrawal of AMIS from the region. Sudan declared its vehement opposition to the proposal and al-Bashir reportedly stated that Darfur would become a 'graveyard' for any foreign troops deployed in the region. In late January the SLM and the SJEM announced the formation of the Alliance of Revolutionary Forces in West Sudan, in a move intended to strengthen the rebels' position in the Abuja negotiations. In early March the AU voted to extend the mandate of AMIS until September, when a UN force was expected to assume peace-keeping duties. However, Arab League heads of state, meeting in Khartoum in late March, agreed to provide funds for the AU force to remain and voted to support Sudanese opposition to the deployment of non-African peace-keeping troops. In late April the UN Security Council approved Resolution 1672, imposing sanctions on four individuals suspected of involvement in crimes committed in the Darfur region: Maj.-Gen. Gaafar Muhammad el-Hassan, Commander of the Western Military Region for the Sudanese Air Force; the Commander of the SLA, Adam Yacub Shant; the Field Commander of the rebel National Movement for Reform and Development, Gabril Abdulkareem Badri; and Sheikh Musa Hilal of the *Janjaweed* militia were banned from travelling outside of Sudan and any assets they held abroad were to be 'frozen'. Also in late April the Government agreed to accept an AU peace agreement. However, the 30 April deadline was twice extended by two days, and officials from the USA and United Kingdom arrived in Abuja to aid the negotiations.

On 4 May 2006 the SJEM and the SLM faction led by Abd al-Wahid Muhammad an-Nur rejected the agreement. Nevertheless, the faction led by Minni Minawi announced that it had accepted the proposals, despite reservations regarding certain conditions, and the Darfur Peace Agreement (DPA) was signed on 5 May. The measures stipulated in the document included, *inter alia*, a Government undertaking to disarm completely the *Janjaweed* by mid-October; the establishment of buffer zones around refugee camps and access routes for humanitarian aid organizations; the integration of rebel forces into the Sudanese armed forces and police; the allocation of eight seats in the National Assembly to Minawi's group; and the transfer of US $300m. to a reconstruction and development fund for Darfur, and further annual transfers of $200m. for two years thereafter. The agreement also proposed that a referendum be held in 2008 to decide upon the issue of Darfur being recognized as a region rather than as three separate states. In mid-May 2006 the deadline for the two remaining rebel groups to accept the DPA was extended until the end of May and negotiations continued. However, the deadline passed and the two remaining factions maintained their opposition to the DPA. It was believed that an-Nur was beginning to gain popular support among the refugees, many of whom believed that the peace agreement was being forced upon them, strengthening the Government's position and that of the perceived minority. It was also reported that rebel factions were beginning to recruit new members from within the refugee camps.

In June 2006 a joint AU-UN delegation arrived in Darfur to assess the needs of AMIS and the feasibility of its replacement by a UN force. In July, at an AU Summit in Banjul, The Gambia, the UN Secretary-General announced that President al-Bashir had refused to allow UN troops to take over from AMIS. It was also announced that the AU would withdraw its peace-keeping force from the region at the end of September. A conference convened in mid-July under the auspices of the UN also failed to convince the Sudanese Government to accept a UN peace-keeping force, although participating countries pledged some US $200m. in funds, the majority of which would be used to assist the increasingly overwhelmed AU troops. Concerns began to emerge that UN peace-keepers would eventually be deployed but under a weaker mandate, thus limiting the force's scope to protect civilians. Minawi repeatedly called for UN forces to be sent to the troubled region and in mid-June he threatened to withdraw from the peace agreement, claiming that the deal would collapse without the immediate support of the international community. In July the two signatories of the DPA, the Government and Minawi's faction of the SLM, launched violent attacks on the rebel groups who had rejected the peace agreement. New factions had begun to emerge to challenge Minawi's increasing power in the north of Darfur, joining forces to form the National Redemption Front (NRF). Fighting subsequently spread from northern Darfur towards the west of the region.

On 31 August 2006 the UN Security Council adopted a resolution (No. 1706), which provided for some 17,300 additional military personnel and 3,300 civilian police to be dispatched to Sudan to support UNMIS, and for its mandate to be extended to assume the responsibilities of AMIS in Darfur. Violence in the region had escalated during that month and the UN, the AU and humanitarian agencies alleged that Minawi's troops had joined Government forces and the *Janjaweed* militia in fighting the rebel groups. By early September the Sudanese Government continued to refuse to allow UN forces into Darfur and demanded that AU troops leave the country. (This demand was later withdrawn.) Sudanese reinforcements were deployed to the region and AU forces remaining in the area reported that Government troops had bombed rebel-held villages, threatening the delivery of aid supplies and demonstrating the Government's intent to use force to end the conflict. In response the AU increased the number of peace-keeping personnel and stated that AMIS would remain in Darfur until the end of the year.

On 27 September 2006 President al-Bashir issued a decree establishing an interim authority in Darfur, in accordance with the terms of the DPA. The authority was to be headed by Minawi, in his capacity as senior assistant to the President, a position to which he was appointed following the signing of the CPA. He was to be supported by a group of advisers, including the Governors of the three states in Darfur.

In an unprecedented move to deter the deployment of UN troops Sudan allegedly issued a warning to neighbouring countries in October 2006 that any offer to provide peace-keeping personnel would be considered a 'hostile act'. The Government denied this claim, but maintained that it would only accept UN assistance given under the auspices of the AU, despite the AU's continued warnings that it was unable to cope under the pressure of limited funding and resources. Also that month bombs were detonated in Juba, southern Sudan; intelligence officers suspected that Government forces were behind the attacks, which followed threats by the Sudanese Government that it would withdraw from the DPA if UN troops were deployed. Rebel groups in Darfur stated that they were obliged to take appropriate action to defend themselves since the Government had refused to allow UN troops into the region to protect civilians. A spokesman for the NRF claimed that the new rebel force was not bound by any previous cease-fire agreement and the conflict continued.

Following a meeting of the Council of Ministers in October 2006, the Government issued a statement that a plan had been devised to fulfil the commitments of the DPA, including the disarmament of the Arab militia group. The plan was submitted to the AU and was to be implemented over a two-month period, extending the original deadline for disarming the militia group by two months. The following month, Minawi alleged that the Government was rearming and mobilizing the *Janjaweed* and called for the international community to act swiftly to find a resolution to the conflict. Also in October the Government accused Pronk of abusing his position, after he reported two defeats of military forces by rebel troops and other sensitive details of the conflict, and ordered him to leave Sudan. Pronk retained his position until his contract ended in December 2006 when Jan Eliasson, hitherto the Swedish Minister for Foreign Affairs, was appointed as his replacement.

In November 2006 discussions took place in Addis Ababa on measures to reinforce the AMIS forces, which had thus far failed to halt the violence in Darfur. Proposals were made for a hybrid AU-UN force with a greater role to be assumed by the UN troops. Sudan again reiterated its opposition to the presence of UN troops; however, later that month Sudan announced that it accepted, in principle, the proposal of a hybrid force, but requested further discussions on key issues before any changes could be implemented. Meanwhile, the AU agreed to extend the mandate of AMIS until mid-2007 as the UN temporarily withdrew non-essential staff from the capital of Northern Darfur state amid fears of escalating violence between rebel fighters and the *Janjaweed*.

The UN Security Council continued with efforts to persuade Sudan to accept a joint AU-UN mission in Darfur, and in late December 2006 al-Bashir accepted the proposals, stating that UN plans required immediate implementation. However, it was stipulated that the AU was to remain in command of the hybrid force. A three-part UN plan was initiated: the first phase included reinforcing the much-weakened AU force with UN troops and supplies, to be followed by further support packages. The third phase required the overhaul of the size and command of the force, in favour of a greater UN role, to which Sudan remained resolutely opposed. Nevertheless, by 31 December the AU had secured a tentative cease-fire agreement from rebel groups in northern Darfur.

Peace efforts were undermined in January 2007 when the day after the cease-fire was agreed insurgent-held positions were bombed. A Government spokesman initially denied any involvement in the attacks; however, al-Bashir subsequently admitted that Government troops had bombed rebel forces, but claimed that this did not breach the cease-fire agreement since they were defending themselves from rebel attacks. The Government appeared to relent and agreed to measures to restore peace, including a 60-day cease-fire and an AU-UN-sponsored peace summit, to be held in Ethiopia later that month. Journalists were once more permitted to enter the region after a two-month ban. In late January the ICC dispatched a team of officials to Khartoum to investigate crimes committed during the conflict in Darfur and in late February the ICC indicted the former Minister of State for the Interior, Ahmad Muhammad Harun, and the leader of the *Janjaweed* militia, Ali Muhammad Ali Abd al-Rahman, on multiple charges of war crimes and crimes against humanity. The following month the Sudanese authorities announced that they had suspended all co-operation with the ICC. In May that body issued arrest warrants for Harun and al-Rahman, who was reported to be in Sudanese custody. Meanwhile, a further shift in the stance of the Sudanese Government was reported in early February when al-Bashir appointed two members of rebel factions to executive positions in the Council of Ministers and in the Darfur administration.

With increasingly widespread acceptance that the DPA signed in May 2006 had broken down, rebel factions agreed upon a need to collaborate in order to challenge the power of the ruling NC. By the end of December an alliance had formed, uniting many of the rebel groups that had refused to sign the DPA, styled the Non-Signatory Factions (NSF). A conference of NSF and remaining NRF commanders was due to be held in early 2007 to renegotiate the terms of the failed peace agreement. However, in the months prior to the meeting, government forces carried out a series of bomb attacks in the area where the conference was to take place, forcing its postponement. Divisions also remained between the groups and an-Nur's faction of the SLM, fearful of being overpowered by the NSF, joined with remaining non-signatories to threaten the credibility of the impending conference. The conference was postponed indefinitely after several rebel groups refused to attend. Many resumed hostilities, causing further divisions between the factions with no single leader to unite them. The conference eventually commenced in February 2007.

Meanwhile, in January 2006 the National Assembly adopted controversial legislation governing the registration of political parties. The legislation prohibited any member of the armed forces (excluding al-Bashir and the First Vice-President Salva Kiir), the police, the security forces or the SPLA, and judges, judicial advisers, diplomats and high-ranking civil servants from joining any political party. The new law also made provisions for any party to be dissolved, or prevented from participating in elections, if it was believed to be undertaking activities that breached the CPA. The legislation was proposed by the SPLM and approved by the NC. Claiming that this contravened the Constitution and defied democratic rule, the NDA withdrew from the National Assembly in protest.

As the conflict in western Sudan continued, the people of eastern Sudan, including the Rashaida and the Beja communities, expressed their increasing resentment towards the Government. The eastern regions had been severely affected by drought and famine and, encouraged by the success of the SPLA in forcing negotiations with the Government, some of the Beja launched an armed struggle, supported by NDA and SPLA forces. The Beja Congress, which emerged during the 1960s, was joined during the 1990s by the Rashaida Free Lions group, and in 2005 the two groups merged to form the Eastern Front (EF). Although their forces were much smaller than those rebel groups fighting in Darfur, they occupied strategic points, launching attacks on the road and rail routes that provided access to the only port on the coast of Sudan, and threatened to destabilize the country's economy. Military offensives by government forces failed to prevent the EF from launching more attacks on eastern Sudan's transport and economic infrastructure and in 2006 the Government agreed to negotiate with the group. In June 2006 talks were held in Asmara, presided over by the Eritrean authorities, and on 19 June the Government and the EF signed an agreement on a set of principles for developing a peace agreement; a cease-fire was also implemented, to be monitored by Eritrean military officials. Peace talks resumed in July and, after lengthy negotiations, a power-sharing agreement was signed on 9 October. The following day the positions of presidential assistant and presidential adviser were assigned to members of the rebel group, along with other positions in the Government at both national and regional level. The peace deal was ratified by the Sudanese authorities on 18 October, ending several years of conflict between the Government and the EF.

Meanwhile, concerns were raised in late 2005 that the ongoing conflict in Darfur could spread into neighbouring Chad. In late November Sudan accused the Chadian air force of violating Sudanese airspace by flying over the Darfur region and claimed that Chadian armed forces had crossed the border into Darfur to steal cattle. Chad responded with accusations that Sudan had provided weapons to a group of soldiers who had deserted the Chadian army and were planning to overthrow the President of Chad, Gen. Idriss Deby. In mid-December Chadian rebels based in Darfur attacked the town of Adre, near the border between Chad and Sudan and the Chadian Government declared 'a state of belligerence' with Sudan, which it held ultimately responsible for the assault. In February 2006 HRW reported that the *Janjaweed* had regularly crossed the border into Chad from Darfur and had carried out similar crimes to those it was accused of committing in Darfur. Later that month the two countries held talks in Libya aimed at preventing further escalation in the dispute and agreement was reached to restore diplomatic relations and to prevent rebels from using territory to launch cross-border raids. However, in March Deby publicly questioned Sudan's commitment to the accord following a series of attacks on villages in Chad by the *Janjaweed*, allegedly with Sudanese 'material and financial' assistance. In mid-April Deby expelled the Sudanese ambassador to Chad and ordered the closure of the land border between the two countries following an attack on the Chadian capital, N'djamena, by rebel forces. However, a threat to forcibly return Sudanese refugees was subsequently withdrawn. In early August, at a meeting convened in N'Djamena the two countries agreed to restore diplomatic relations and reopen border crossings and embassies. In October it was reported that the *Janjaweed* had once again instigated a series of attacks on villages in Chad housing Sudanese refugees. By November it had become apparent that the conflict in Darfur had spread into the Central African Republic (CAR). In the north of that country, groups of rebel fighters had begun to form, forming allegiances with Chadian factions and providing a route through to Chad for the Sudanese rebels. As the conflict spread many aid workers began to withdraw, leaving the inhabitants of eastern Chad facing a potential health crisis. In February 2007 a summit was held under the auspices of French President Jacques Chirac, during which the CAR, Chad and Sudan agreed that they would cease support for rebel fighters in either of the three countries. In early May, following mediation by Saudi Arabia's King Abdallah, Presidents al-Bashir and Deby agreed to co-operate with the AU and the UN in their attempts to stabilize the Chad–Sudan border. Both countries approved the formation of a joint border force, and pledged to cease training and funding rebel groups and to stop all cross-border attacks.

Also in April 2007 the UN Security Council approved the extension of the mandate the mandate of UNMIS until October. In mid-June 2007, following further discussions in Addis Ababa, the Government of Sudan agreed to accept a joint AU-UN peace-keeping force, comprising up to 20,000 troops. However, shortly after issuing a statement accepting the deployment of peace-keeping personnel, the Government began to delay the process, questioning the command structure of the operation. Nevertheless, the following month the UN Security Council adopted Resolution 1769 establishing UNAMID, the UN-AU hybrid operation in Darfur, with an initial mandate of 12 months. Further disagreements threatened to disrupt the process when, in August, the AU announced that UNAMID peace-keeping forces would comprise only African personnel, safe-guarding the AU's lead role in Sudan. UNAMID assumed peace-keeping operations on 31 December but was severely under-resourced with less than one-half of the pledged 20,000 troops deployed. Progress towards restoring peace was limited and government-led attacks on civilians and peace-keepers in Darfur continued. However, in February 2008 a legal framework was agreed, which would allow UNAMID peace-keepers to move freely within the country without fear of attacks by government forces. Nevertheless, violence in the region continued and thousands more civilians were reported to have crossed the border into Chad to escape the conflict.

Meanwhile, Salva Kiir effected a minor ministerial reshuffle of the Government of Southern Sudan (GOSS) in July 2007 in an attempt to consolidate his cabinet's power, suggesting that the SPLM planned to take a firmer approach to dealing with the ruling NC. In September Salva Kiir accused the Government in Khartoum of undermining the CPA by failing to withdraw troops from the southern oilfields and refusing to pay Southern Sudan its due revenues.

In September 2007 the UN Secretary General, Ban Ki-Moon, announced that a further round of peace talks on Darfur had been scheduled for the following month, to take place in Tripoli. The Government later agreed to comply with the terms of a cease-fire agreement, to be enforced during the peace negotiations. Al-Bashir also urged rebel leaders to attend the talks, although it was not immediately apparent which of the rebel groups had agreed to participate. In late September 10 AU peace-keepers in Darfur were killed in an attack believed to have been carried out by a breakaway rebel faction, while further attacks were reported in other parts of the country. As delegates arrived in Libya for the conference, rebel factions launched attacks on an oilfield in Kordofan province in central Sudan. Talks commenced in Tripoli on 27 October; however, in response to continued attacks by government forces, many rebel groups declined to attend the meeting and instead held separate talks in Juba, convened by the Government of Southern Sudan. The Tripoli talks had been further hindered by the collapse of the coalition Government in Khartoum earlier that month. In mid-October the SPLM withdrew from the Government in protest against delays in implementing the CPA. Al-Bashir subsequently reorganized the Council of Ministers, naming SPLM members Deng Alor Kol as Minister of Foreign Affairs and Mansur Khaled as Minister of Foreign Trade among the new appointments. Salva Kiir also effected changes to the GOSS in which two ministers were dismissed and two new presidential advisers were appointed. Additional governmental changes were implemented in December when seven SPLM members were appointed to the central Government. Akol, who had been demoted from the position of Minister of Foreign Affairs to Minister of Cabinet Affairs in the October reshuffle, was dismissed from the cabinet and replaced by Pagan Amum of the SPLM. Akol had been accused by fellow SPLM members of developing close ties with the NC. Al-Bashir carried out a further minor reorganization of the Government in mid-February 2008.

In addition to civil war and economic crisis, Sudan has experienced drought and famine, and the problem has been compounded by a very large number of refugees in the southern provinces, mainly from Ethiopia and Chad. At the end of 2006, according to estimates from the office of the UN High Commissioner for Refugees (UNHCR), there were some 550,337 Sudanese refugees abroad, of whom 221,525 were in Chad, 171,565 in Uganda, 73,004 in Kenya, and 66,980 in Ethiopia. Sudan was also host to some 129,758 refugees at that time, of whom 108,120 were originally from Eritrea. During 1997 there had been large-scale refugee repatriation, particularly to Ethiopia and the DRC, but in 1998 a further 37,000 refugees arrived in Sudan, including 10,300 from Kenya and 9,500 from Uganda. During 2000 more than 94,000 Eritrean refugees fleeing the border war with Ethiopia entered Sudanese territory; by the end of that year, however, some 68,000 had been repatriated. In early 2003 the US Committee for Refugees stated that Sudan possessed the largest internally displaced population in the world, officially estimated at 4m. people. By late 2004, as a result of the Darfur conflict, it was estimated by UNHCR that some 1.6m. people were displaced within Darfur and that some 200,000 people had fled to neighbouring Chad. In December 2002 the refugee status of Eritreans living in Sudan expired, and in the following month UNHCR convoys, which would return Eritreans to their country, recommenced. It was reported that since May 2001 more than 100,000 Eritreans had been repatriated. In 2002 some 18,000 Sudanese were repatriated from Kenya. In late December 2005 UNHCR announced that some 500,000 refugees were to be repatriated to southern Sudan from neighbouring countries. The process commenced earlier that month when 90,000 Sudanese refugees left northern Kenya. However, in mid-March 2006 a UNHCR compound in the town of Yei was attacked by armed men, and UNHCR operations in southern Sudan were subsequently suspended for two weeks.

In June 1997 the Government banned relief flights to the south—an act that caused concern to aid agencies; the UN Children's Fund stated that thousands of children were at risk and announced that there had been a rise in the infant mortality rate in that area. By April 1998 many aid agencies were warning of widespread famine in the south if immediate action was not taken. The Government initially refused to act, as it claimed that aid would fall into rebel hands. However, in May the Government agreed to reopen all relief corridors in the worst affected areas and to allow the aid agencies to operate a total of 22 food distribution sites. It also agreed to increase the frequency of relief flights and to provide some food aid from that year's surplus in the north. Relief operations continued throughout mid-1998. In October, however, the Government banned aid agency flights in the country. In November, following two days of negotiations in Rome, Italy, the Government and the rebels signed an agreement to guarantee the safety of aid workers and to facilitate access to the worst affected areas, despite the continuing fighting. In March 1999 further warnings were issued of impending famine. Hostilities again escalated in the south in August 2000, and the Sudanese Government was accused of deliberately bombing relief facilities in that region. In response, the UN announced the suspension of all aid flights under the Operation Lifeline Sudan programme. However, later that month, following personal assurances from al-Bashir that measures were being taken to ensure the safety of all humanitarian workers in the region, the UN agreed to resume relief flights. In February 2001 WFP launched an appeal for US $135m. of food aid, required to feed the estimated 2.9m. people in Sudan under threat of starvation as a result of the ongoing civil war and severe drought. Appeals for significant humanitarian assistance were repeated in May, as conditions in Sudan reached critical levels. However, in that month the International Committee of the Red Cross temporarily suspended all aid deliveries, after the co-pilot of one of its planes was killed while flying over southern Sudan. Aid flights were subsequently resumed later that month. In mid-April 2005 donors from the international community, including the USA, the European Commission and the United Kingdom, pledged $4,500m. in aid which was to go directly to southern Sudan. By March 2006, however, the UN Special Envoy to Sudan, Jan Pronk, acknowledged that only a small portion of the money pledged had thus far been spent.

Following an unsuccessful coup attempt in 1976, Sudan severed diplomatic relations with Libya and established a mutual defence pact with Egypt. Diplomatic links between Sudan and Libya were restored in 1978, but relations became strained in 1981, during Libya's occupation of Chad, and President Nimeri frequently accused Libya of supporting plots against him. After the 1985 coup, Libya was the first country to recognize the new regime, and relations between the two countries improved significantly. Although Libya's military involvement in Chad declined, some Libyan forces remained in north-western Sudan, despite repeated Sudanese demands for their withdrawal. The regime that took power in Sudan in 1985 adopted a foreign policy of non-alignment, in contrast to Nimeri's strongly pro-Western attitude, and sought improved relations with Ethiopia and the USSR, to the concern of Sudan's former allies, Egypt and the USA. In 1990, after Lt-Gen. al-Bashir had visited Col Qaddafi, the Libyan leader, in Tripoli, Sudan and Libya signed a 'declaration of integration' that envisaged the complete union of the two countries within four years. In 1995 Sudan, Libya and Chad were reported to be discussing integration after eventual legislative elections in Chad. Tension subsequently arose between Libya and Sudan as a result of Libya's expulsion of Sudanese expatriate workers, but did not, apparently, detract from the two countries' commitment to integration, reiterated in 1996.

In September 1995 Ethiopia accused Sudan of harbouring terrorists implicated in the attempted assassination of President Mubarak in June and, in response, announced the closure of some Sudanese diplomatic facilities in the country and of non-governmental organizations connected with Sudan. In April 1996 Sudan claimed that Ethiopian government forces had collaborated with the SPLA in attacks on two towns in south-eastern Sudan, while in June Ethiopia accused Sudan of attempting to destabilize the region. In January 1997 relations deteriorated further when, following alleged attacks on Sudan, President al-Bashir declared a *jihad* (holy war) against Ethiopian aggression and ordered a general mobilization. Ethiopia, however, denied any involvement in the attacks. An improvement in relations was reported during 1998, although in December the Ethiopian Minister of Foreign Affairs stated that relations between the two countries would not improve until Sudan handed over those responsible for the attempted assassination of the Egyptian President. One of the suspects was extradited in 1999 (see below), and in November, on his return from a visit to Ethiopia, al-Bashir stated that relations with that country were fully normalized. The common border was reopened in early 2000, and in March the Sudanese and Ethiopian Governments signed a number of agreements, which provided for increased co-operation in political, cultural, commercial and transport sectors. Further agreements regarding border security were signed in the following month. Relations between the two countries were temporarily strained in late April 2001 after an internal Ethiopian flight was hijacked and diverted to Khartoum. Although the incident was brought to a swift conclusion, and all passengers on board the aircraft were released unharmed, the Sudanese authorities refused Ethiopia's request for the hijackers to be extradited to Ethiopia for trial.

Sudan's relations with Eritrea deteriorated after 1991, and in December 1994 Eritrea severed diplomatic relations with Sudan. Eritrea has sponsored meetings of the principal groups opposed to the Sudanese regime, which it accuses of lending support to the insurgent Eritrean Islamic Jihad. In December 1994 Eritrea sponsored a meeting between various Sudanese opposition groups, which resulted in a 'Declaration of Political Agreement'. The signatories included the SPLA, the UP and the DUP. In January 1995 Sudan demanded that Eritrea withdraw from the IGADD peace committee (see above), which also included Ethiopia, Kenya and Uganda. A further deterioration in relations occurred after a conference of the Sudanese opposition, organized by the NDA, was held in Asmara in June (see above). In July 1996 Sudanese government forces claimed that attacks had been launched against them from within Eritrea. In April 1997 Sudan protested to the UN over Eritrean aggression on its territory. In June Sudan denied Eritrean accusations that the Sudanese Government had masterminded a plot to assassinate the Eritrean President. At the end of the month Sudan closed the border with Eritrea and mobilized its forces to maximum levels for fear of a military strike against Sudan. The border was again closed in February 1998 in order to prevent Eritrean troops entering the country following reported border clashes between the two countries. Further attacks were reported in the border area by both Eritrea and Sudan throughout 1998. Following talks held in November 1998, in Qatar, the two sides signed an agreement for the open discussion of bilateral issues. A further meeting, held in May 1999, resulted in an accord, signed by the Presidents of Sudan and Eritrea, in which they agreed to restore diplomatic relations, to refrain from hostile propaganda and to establish joint committees, both to implement the terms of the accord and to study any further issues that might arise between the two countries. However, tensions between the two countries remained, and in June Sudan accused Eritrea of violating the Doha agreement, following an NDA conference in Asmara. At that time the two countries established joint committees in accordance with the terms of the Doha agreement. In August it was reported that Eritrea had ordered the Sudanese opposition to cease political activity and to leave the Sudanese embassy, which it had occupied since December 1994. A further agreement was signed in Asmara in January 2000, providing for the immediate reopening of the two countries' borders and embassies and the resumption of flights between their airports. In February the Presidents of Eritrea and Sudan held talks in Khartoum, and it was agreed to issue passports to residents in the border area. Furthermore, they declared that they would not allow opposition groups located in their respective countries to launch cross-border raids. However, relations between the two countries deteriorated in July, when the Sudanese Government accused Eritrea of assisting the NDA with a planned offensive in eastern Sudan. In October President Afewerki visited Khartoum, where he held talks with al-Bashir, during which both sides expressed their desire for a fresh beginning to their bilateral relations and agreed to take measures to settle differences between the two countries in a peaceful manner. In July 2001 Eritrea and Sudan signed an agreement on border security, which aimed to eradicate smuggling and illegal infiltration, as well as ensure the safe passage of people and goods. Relations between the two countries deteriorated again in mid-2002, and in October the Sudanese authorities closed the common border, claiming that Eritrea had been involved in an NDA offensive in eastern Sudan. Following a meeting with the Yemeni President, Ali Abdullah Saleh, and the Ethiopian Prime Minister, Meles Zenawi, in December 2003, President al-Bashir accused Eritrea of arming and training rebels in the Darfur region of Sudan and maintained that Eritrea was a destabilizing force in the region. Eritrea refuted the allegations. In mid-January 2004 Eritrea claimed that the Sudanese authorities had arrested several Eritreans and closed community centres used by Eritreans in Khartoum. In late May the Eritrean authorities accused Sudan of carrying out a bomb attack which killed seven people in Barentu, Eritrea. Sudan vehemently denied any involvement in the incident and stated that the explosion had been the work of Eritrean opposition forces. In mid-October Eritrea accused Sudan of complicity in an attempt to assassinate President Afewerki, while Sudan maintained that Eritrea had provided rebels with arms in an attempt to destabilize the Sudanese Government. In mid-March 2005 it was announced that talks between the NDA and Sudanese authorities would take place in a further attempt to normalize relations. Relations between the two countries were again strained in late June when Sudan accused Eritrea of providing assistance to rebel forces who had attacked Sudanese government troops in eastern Sudan earlier that month. However, at a meeting in Khartoum in October Akol, who had earlier been appointed Minister of Foreign Affairs, signed an agreement with his Eritrean acting counterpart to work towards normalizing relations between Sudan and Eritrea. In August 2006 Second Vice-President Taha received a ministerial delegation from Eritrea; the two parties discussed the possibility of joint co-operation in fields such as agriculture and economics.

Sudan and Uganda have accused each other of supporting groups opposed to their respective regimes, and in 1995 Uganda broke off diplomatic relations with Sudan. A further deterioration in relations in December brought the two countries to the brink of open war. In 1996, following mediation by President Rafsanjani of Iran, Sudan and Uganda agreed to restore diplomatic relations, provided that each side undertook to cease its support for rebel factions operating from the other's territory, and to participate in an international committee to monitor the agreement. In February 1997, in response to protests about its deployment of troops on the Sudan–Uganda border, Uganda denied accusations that it intended to invade Sudan. In late April Sudan denied allegations that its forces had invaded northern Uganda and, at the end of the month Dr Riek Mashar Teny-Dhurgon, the Chairman of the SSCC, visited Uganda to discuss relations between the two countries prior to the forthcoming IGAD summit meeting. Talks held in Kenya in May achieved little progress in easing tension, and the planned IGAD summit meeting was later cancelled, owing to a concurrent meeting of leaders of the Organization of African Unity (OAU, now the AU). In August President Mandela of South Africa hosted talks between the two countries. Mandela later said that the talks had been successful, although he did not reveal what progress had been made. At the end of the year there were reports of Ugandan attacks in the border area; Uganda, however, denied the reports and said that the attacks had been made by the SPLA and had been wrongly attributed to Uganda. Relations with Uganda improved during 1999, and in December, following a meeting in Nairobi, mediated by former US President Jimmy Carter, the two countries signed an accord in which they agreed to restore diplomatic relations and to end support to each other's rebel groups; shortly afterwards it was announced that eight leaders of the Lord's Resistance Army (LRA) were to be relocated from Sudan to a country of their choice in accordance with the agreement. In February 2000, however, Uganda expressed its dissatisfaction with Sudan's implementation of the accord and called for Sudan to disarm the LRA and to disband all LRA camps within Sudan. Sudan reaffirmed its commitment to the agreement. In October it was agreed that Egyptian and Libyan observers would be deployed on the Uganda–Sudan border to prevent any further violations by the SPLA and the LRA. In mid-May 2001 President al-Bashir attended the inauguration of the Ugandan President, Yoweri Museveni, in Kampala, and in the following month the two countries exchanged diplomats. In August the Ugandan embassy in Khartoum reopened, and a chargé d'affaires was appointed. In March 2002 the two countries signed an agreement whereby Sudan temporarily authorized Ugandan troops to pursue LRA rebels within Sudan, and later that month the Ugandan Government announced that its troops had captured all four main bases in Sudan belonging to the LRA. In late November the Sudanese authorities agreed to extend permission for Ugandan troops to remain on its territory for as long as Uganda deemed necessary. Meanwhile, the two countries upgraded relations to ambassadorial level.

President Nimeri was one of very few Arab leaders to support President Sadat of Egypt's initiative for peace with Israel in 1978. Sudan's close relations with Egypt were consolidated in 1982, when a 'charter of integration' was signed. The first session of the joint 'Nile Valley Parliament', created by the charter, was convened in 1983 with 60 Sudanese and 60 Egyptian members. After the 1985 coup, the leaders of the two countries reaffirmed links between Khartoum and Cairo, despite the change of government in Sudan. Relations with Egypt deteriorated in 1991, as a result of the Sudanese Government's support for Iraq during the Gulf crisis. Egypt also expressed concern at the perceived growth of Islamic 'fundamentalism' in Sudan. The two countries are involved in a dispute over the Halaib border area, and in early 1992 relations deteriorated sharply following the announcement that Sudan had awarded a Canadian company a concession to explore for petroleum there. Relations deteriorated further, as Egypt repeatedly accused Sudan of supporting illegal Islamic fundamentalist groups in Egypt, while Sudan alleged that Egypt was supporting the SPLA. In August the Sudanese Government sought international arbitration on the Halaib issue, claiming that Egypt had been settling families in the area in an effort to bring it under Egyptian control. In January 1993 Sudan complained to the UN Security Council that Egyptian troops had infringed Sudan's territorial integrity. In March Egypt announced the construction of a new road link to Halaib. Sudan retaliated by appropriating the Khartoum campus of the University of Cairo. In June Sudan announced that it was closing two Egyptian consulates in Sudan and two of its own consulates in Egypt. A meeting between Lt-Gen. al-Bashir and President Mubarak of Egypt, during a summit session of the OAU at the end of June appeared, however, to ease tensions between the two countries, and was followed by a meeting of their respective Ministers of Foreign Affairs at the end of July. In May 1994 Sudan accused Egypt of establishing military posts on Sudanese territory, and at the end of the month the Sudanese Ministry of Foreign Affairs announced that Sudan wished to refer its dispute with Egypt to the International Court of Justice (ICJ) in The Hague, Netherlands, for arbitration. In January 1995 Egypt rejected a request by Sudan to refer the dispute over the Halaib border area to a meeting of the OAU's council of Ministers of Foreign Affairs in Addis Ababa. On 26 June relations suffered a further, serious setback after the attempted assassination of President Mubarak of Egypt on his arrival in Addis Ababa to attend the annual conference of the OAU. The Egyptian Government immediately accused Sudan of complicity in the attack, and the OAU made the same allegation in September. In January 1996 the UN Security Council condemned Sudan's role in the attempted assassination and adopted Resolution 1044 seeking the extradition of three individuals implicated in the attack. Relations between Sudan and Egypt appeared to improve in 1997; in December talks were held between President al-Bashir and senior Egyptian officials, and in January 1998 it was agreed that a joint chamber of commerce would be established. In May a joint Sudanese-Egyptian technical committee met in Khartoum to finalize details for the return of several institutions in Sudan to Egyptian control. Both sides agreed that the institutions should be returned, although differences remained over the time period for this operation. In October Sudan and Egypt agreed on a plan to hasten the normalization of relations, and a further meeting was held in Cairo in January 1999 to discuss bilateral relations. In June it was announced that diplomatic relations between the two countries were to be upgraded. Relations improved further in July when it was announced that Sudan had extradited one of the three suspects implicated in the attempted assassination of Mubarak. In December the two countries agreed to normalize their relations and to resolve their dispute over the Halaib issue amicably. In March 2000 it was announced that the University of Cairo in Khartoum was to be reopened, and later that month Egypt appointed an ambassador to Sudan for the first time since the assassination attempt on Mubarak. In September the Sudanese and Egyptian ministers responsible for foreign affairs held the first session of the Egyptian-Sudanese Commission for 10 years, at which the two countries expressed their commitment to further bilateral economic development. In May 2003 Mubarak visited Khartoum for the first time since the attempted assassination and held talks with al-Bashir, during which the two leaders reaffirmed their commitment to improving relations between Egypt and Sudan.

The USA has been one of the severest critics of the present Sudanese Government, frequently expressing concern about Sudan's links with Iran. Allegations of Sudanese involvement in terrorism resulted in the detention in the USA, in 1993, of five Sudanese residents suspected of plotting to blow up buildings and road tunnels in New York, and to assassinate President Mubarak of Egypt on a visit to the USA; the USA subsequently added Sudan to its list of countries accused of sponsoring terrorism. In August 1997 the USA imposed economic sanctions against Sudan, owing to its alleged continued support for terrorism. In late August 1998 the USA launched a missile attack on what it claimed was a chemical weapons factory in Khartoum. Immediately after the attack, however, the Sudanese Government denied these claims and stated that it was, in fact, a private pharmaceuticals plant. Sudan recalled its ambassador to the USA and refused permission for US aircraft to use its airspace; its requests for a UN inquiry into the attack were unanimously refused by the Security Council, despite backing from the League of Arab States (see p. 332) and the Organization of the Islamic Conference (see p. 369). By February 1999 it had become evident that the US intelligence on which the attack had been based was fundamentally flawed. In May Sudan requested compensation for the damage caused by the bomb attack, and in July 2000 the proprietor of the factory announced his intention to sue the US Government for damages. Meanwhile, in April 1999 the USA had announced its decision to ease sanctions on the export of food and medicine to Sudan, and at the end of May Sudan fulfilled one of the conditions set by the USA for a review of the sanctions regime by signing a treaty banning chemical weapons. In November, however, the USA enacted controversial legislation allowing food aid to be delivered directly to the Sudanese rebels. An improvement in relations was evident in March 2000 following a visit to Sudan by a US diplomat to discuss the possibility of reopening the US embassy in Khartoum; in mid-April the embassy was duly reopened. However, relations once again deteriorated in December, when Sudan lodged an official complaint with the UN after the US Assistant Secretary of State, Susan Rice, visited rebel-held areas of southern Sudan in November, without the permission of the Sudanese Government. Following the election of a new US Administration, under the leadership of President George W. Bush, in January 2001, there was some uncertainty regarding the USA's policy towards Sudan. In July the Bush administration outlined its three main policy objectives for Sudan: to deal with the humanitarian crisis, to end Sudan's role as a sanctuary for terrorism, and to promote a just peace by bringing the warring parties together. In September Bush appointed a former senator, John Danforth, as his special envoy to Sudan.

Following the September 2001 suicide attacks on New York and Washington, DC, Sudan agreed to assist the USA with its search for terrorist suspects, and by late September the Sudanese authorities had arrested some 30 individuals resident in Sudan who were suspected of having links to Osama bin Laden, a Saudi-born Islamist activist exiled in Afghanistan, and the al-Qa'ida (Base) organization, which the USA held responsible for the attacks. Nevertheless, US sanctions remained in place, and Sudan continued to be listed by the US Department of State as a sponsor of terrorism. Furthermore, two Sudanese banks were among numerous institutions under US investigation as possible sources of financial support for bin Laden. Sudan expressed criticism of the US-led military strikes on Afghanistan, which commenced in November, and later that month the USA extended sanctions until November 2002. In October 2002 Bush approved legislation that allowed the USA to impose further sanctions, including the suspension of multilateral loans, on the Sudanese Government, should it fail to negotiate in good faith with the southern rebels or interfere with humanitarian efforts in the south of the country. The USA also froze the financial assets of 12 Sudanese companies, including the National Broadcasting Corporation. Under the Sudan Peace Act, conditions in Sudan would be evaluated every six months, although the law also made provision for the expenditure of US $100m. a year by the USA until 2005 in areas of Sudan not under the Sudanese Government's control. In October 2003 the US Agency for International Development pledged a further $40m. to finance initiatives to assist Sudan to recover from the civil war. However, Natsios warned that the additional aid was conditional on the implementation of a comprehensive peace agreement. In mid-November the US embassy in Khartoum was temporarily closed in response to a 'specific threat' to US interests in Sudan. The conflict in Darfur (see above) resulted in the deterioration of relations between Sudan and the USA and in September 2004 the US Administration accused the Sudanese Government of committing genocide. The USA subsequently proposed a draft UN resolution, which threatened to impose sanctions on Sudan's petroleum industry if the Sudanese authorities did not act to end the violence in the region. In late July 2005 the US Secretary of State, Condoleezza Rice, met with al-Bashir in Khartoum and also visited the Abu Shouk refugee camp in the Darfur region, and called for 'actions, not words' from the Sudanese administration to resolve the conflict in Darfur. During the visit, Rice also indicated that the USA was to send an ambassador to Khartoum for the first time since 1997. In early August 2005, two US envoys arrived in Sudan tasked with assisting the reinforcement of the Comprehensive Peace Agreement following the death of Garang. In mid-October 2006 President Bush approved the Darfur Peace and Accountability Act of 2006, which provided for the imposition of sanctions against those responsible for genocide, war crimes, and crimes against humanity, and supports humanitarian efforts and measures to secure peace in the region of Darfur. He also issued an executive order freezing the assets and property of the Sudanese Government and prohibiting financial transactions with that body. The USA threatened to impose economic sanctions on state-controlled companies in Sudan in April 2007 unless the Government agreed to co-operate in restoring peace to the Darfur region. The following month President Bush implemented measures to exclude Sudanese companies from the US financial system.

Sudan's relations with the United Kingdom deteriorated in May 1998, following a statement made by the British Secretary of State for International Development in which she accused Sudan of using food aid as a weapon in Bahr al-Ghazal. The Sudanese Government vehemently denied this and accused the United Kingdom of having a negative attitude towards forthcoming peace negotiations. The British Government played an active role in attempting to end the violence in Darfur—the British Secretary of State for Foreign and Commonwealth Affairs, Jack Straw, visited the region in August 2004, and Prime Minister Blair visited Khartoum in October to increase diplomatic pressure on the Sudanese Government. In December 2006 Prime Minister Blair announced his intention to support plans to impose a 'no-fly zone' and stated that he would seek UN approval for the measure, which was to be enforced by US and British troops.

Government

In October 1993 the Revolutionary Command Council for National Salvation, which had assumed power after the military coup of 30 June 1989, was dissolved after appointing Lt-Gen. al-Bashir as President and head of a new civilian Government. In April 1998 a new Constitution was endorsed by the National Assembly, and was presented to President al-Bashir. The document was endorsed by 96.7% of voters in a national referendum held in May. Under its terms, executive power is vested in the Council of Ministers, which is appointed by the President, but is responsible to the National Assembly. Legislative power is vested in the National Assembly. The 360-member National Assembly serves a term of four years. Of its 360 members, 270 are directly elected in single seat constituencies, 35 members represent women, 26 represent university graduates and 29 represent trade unions.

In February 1994 Sudan was redivided into 26 states (rather than the nine that had formed the basis of administration since 1991). A governor assumed responsibility for each state, assisted by five—in the case of the southern states six—state ministers.

In early July 2005 the National Assembly approved an interim Constitution as part of the Comprehensive Peace Agreement signed in January between the Sudanese Government and the Sudan People's Liberation Movement (SPLM). The interim Constitution provided for the establishment of a Government of National Unity, representation in which was to be divided between northerners and southerners, with the former holding 70% of the posts and the latter 30%. The interim Constitution also stipulated that, pending legislative elections, which were to be held no later than the end of the fourth year of the interim period, the National Assembly shall be composed of 450 members who shall be appointed by the President of the Republic in consultation with the First Vice-President, according to the 70%:30% north and south ratio.

Provision was also made in the interim Constitution for the election of the President of the Government of Southern Sudan and the establishment of a transitional Southern Sudan Assembly. The President of Government of Southern Sudan shall be elected directly by the people of southern Sudan for a five-year mandate, renewable only once. The transitional Southern Sudan Assembly shall be an inclusive, constituent legislature composed of 170 appointed members with 70% representing the SPLM; 15% representing the National Congress; and 15% representing the other southern Sudanese political forces.

Defence

As assessed at November 2007, the armed forces comprised: army an estimated 105,000, navy an estimated 1,300, air force 3,000. A paramilitary Popular Defence Force included 17,500 active members and 85,000 reserves. Budgeted defence expenditure in 2007 was an estimated US $579m. Military service is compulsory for males aged 18–30 years and lasts for up to two years.

Economic Affairs

In 2006, according to estimates by the World Bank, Sudan's gross national income (GNI), measured at average 2004–06 prices, was US $29,892m., equivalent to $810 per head (or $2,160 on an international purchasing-power parity basis). During 1996–2006, it was estimated, the population increased at an average annual rate of 2.1%, while gross domestic product (GDP) per head increased, in real terms, by an average of 4.8% per year. Overall GDP increased, in real terms, at an average annual rate of 7.0% in 1996–2006; growth in 2007 was 11.2%, according to the African Development Bank (ADB).

According to the World Bank, agriculture (including forestry and fishing) contributed 30.8% of GDP in 2006 and employed about 56.5% of the labour force in mid-2005. The principal cash crop is sesame seed (including oilcake), which accounted for 3.0% of total export earnings in 2003. The principal subsistence crops are sorghum, millet and wheat. The GDP of the agricultural sector increased by an average of 7.5% per year in 1996–2006, according to the ADB. Agricultural GDP increased by 5.0% in 2006.

Industry (including mining, manufacturing, construction and power) contributed 35.0% of GDP in 2006, according to the World Bank, and employed 7.9% of the labour force in 1983. In 1996–

2006 industrial GDP increased at an average annual rate of 8.3%, according to the ADB. Industrial GDP increased by 15.0% in 2006.

Mining accounted for only 0.1% of employment in 1983 and an estimated 0.9% of GDP in 1999. Sudan has reserves of petroleum (estimated at 563m. barrels in July 2005), chromite, gypsum, gold, iron ore and wollastonite. Sudan began to develop its petroleum reserves in the mid-1990s; proven reserves totalled 6,400m. barrels at the end of 2006, sufficient to sustain production at current levels for more than 46 years. In that year Sudan was the sixth largest producer of petroleum in Africa. In 2003 petroleum and petroleum products accounted for 78.1% of total export earnings. The GDP of the mining sector increased by 22.5% in 2001.

According to the World Bank, manufacturing contributed 6.4% of GDP in 2006. The most important branch of the sector is food-processing, especially sugar-refining, while the textile industry, cement production and petroleum-refining are also significant. Some 4.6% of the labour force were employed in manufacturing in 1983. According to the ADB, in 1996–2006 manufacturing GDP declined at an average annual rate of 0.2%. However, manufacturing GDP increased by 3.0% in both 2005 and 2006.

Energy is derived from petroleum (which contributed 72.8% of total output in 2004) and hydroelectric power (27.2%). In May 2004 the Government announced plans to provide 90% of the country with electricity over the following five years by harnessing more of the hydro-electric potential of the Nile. Sudan is a net exporter of fuels, with imports of refined petroleum products comprising an estimated 2.9% of the total value of imports in 2004.

Services contributed 34.1% of GDP in 2006, according to the World Bank, and employed 18.8% of the labour force in 1983. During 1995–2002, according to the ADB, the GDP of the services sector increased at an average annual rate of 5.5%. In 2006 the GDP of the services sector rose by 16.6%.

In 2006 Sudan recorded a visible trade deficit of US $1,448.1m., and there was a deficit of $5,109.6m. on the current account of the balance of payments. In 2005 the principal sources of imports were the People's Republic of China (accounting for 20.5% of the total), Saudi Arabia, the United Arab Emirates and Japan. In that year the principal market for Sudanese exports was also the People's Republic of China (taking 71.0%); Japan was the other major purchaser. The principal exports in 2003 were petroleum and petroleum products, and live animals. The principal imports in that year were machinery and transport equipment, basic manufactures, food and live animals, and chemicals and related products.

In 2005 Sudan recorded an overall budget deficit of 121m. Sudanese dinars. At the end of 2005 Sudan's total external debt was US $18,455m., of which $11,163m. was long-term public debt. In that year the cost of debt-servicing was equivalent to 6.5% of the total value of exports of goods and services. In 2000–06 the average annual rate of inflation was 7.7%. Consumer prices increased by an average of 7.1% in 2006.

Sudan is a member of the ADB (see p. 162), the Arab Bank for Economic Development in Africa (see p. 333), the Council of Arab Economic Unity (see p. 222) and the Islamic Development Bank (see p. 329). In 1997 Sudan's membership of both the Arab Fund for Economic and Social Development (AFESD, see p. 174) and the Arab Monetary Fund (see p. 175) was suspended. Membership of the AFESD was restored in April 2000.

Sudan's formidable economic problems can be traced back to the 1970s, when the country's agricultural potential was neglected and the Government began to borrow heavily. The problems were compounded by civil conflict in the south, which, in addition to depressing economic activity in the areas where it was waged, caused a massive waste of state resources. Sudan began exporting petroleum in late 1999 and further discoveries of petroleum in 2001 led to a vast increase in export revenues; however, much of these earnings were used by the Government to fund the war against the rebels in the south, which was estimated to cost US $1m. per day, and the country's reliance on petroleum has caused some concern in recent years. Much of Sudan's proven reserves of oil are located in the south of the country and following the Comprehensive Peace Agreement (CPA) signed by the Government and the SPLM in January 2005, levels of foreign investment were expected to increase as well as growth, thus providing capital for reconstruction programmes in the regions affected by the civil war. However, in recent years international financial institutions have been reluctant to provide funding and the donor community remained deeply concerned by the ongoing conflict and humanitarian crisis in the Darfur region. Significantly, while many companies from Europe and North America have been reluctant to invest in Sudan, due in part to events in Darfur, companies from the People's Republic of China, India and Malaysia have acquired major stakes in a number of Sudanese oil concessions. In February 2007 China and Sudan signed a US $1,150m. agreement to construct a new railway linking Khartoum and Port Sudan in the east of the country (where there are significant gold and natural gas reserves). Uganda and Sudan, meanwhile, opened a new trading centre in Juba, which was expected to facilitate a large increase in commerce between southern Sudan and Uganda. Juba has emerged as a major distribution centre for the south of the country since the signing of the CPA and significant investment has been made in improving air links to the region. GDP growth of 11.2% was recorded in 2007, although the IMF forecast that this rate would decline to 7.6% in 2008.

Education

The Government provides free primary education from the ages of six to 12 years. Secondary education begins at 13 years of age and lasts for up to five years. In 2000/01 enrolment at primary schools included 49% of children in the relevant age-group (boys 54%; girls 45%), according to UNESCO estimates, while in 1998/99 enrolment at secondary schools was equivalent to 30% of children in the relevant age-group (boys 31%; girls 29%). There are 26 public universities in Sudan.

Public Holidays

2008: 1 January (Independence Day), 10 January*† (Muharram, Islamic New Year), 20 March* (Mouloud, Birth of the Prophet), 6 April (Uprising Day, anniversary of the 1985 coup), 28 April (Sham an-Nassim, Coptic Easter Monday), 30 June (Revolution Day), 1 October* (Id al-Fitr, end of Ramadan), 9 December* (Id al-Adha, Feast of the Sacrifice), 25 December (Christmas), 29 December*† (Muharram, Islamic New Year).

2009: 1 January (Independence Day), 9 March* (Mouloud, Birth of the Prophet), 6 April (Uprising Day, anniversary of 1985 coup), 20 April (Sham an-Nassim, Coptic Easter Monday), 30 June (Revolution Day), 20 September* (Id al-Fitr, end of Ramadan), 27 November* (Id al-Adha, Feast of the Sacrifice), 18 December* (Muharram, Islamic New Year), 25 December (Christmas).

* The dates of Islamic holidays are determined by sightings of the moon, and may be slightly different from those given above.

† This festival occurs twice (marking the start of the Islamic years AH 1429 and 1430) within the same Gregorian year.

Weights and Measures

The metric system is gradually replacing traditional weights and measures.

Statistical Survey

Source (unless otherwise stated): Department of Statistics, Ministry of Finance and National Economy, POB 735, Khartoum; tel. (183) 777563; fax (183) 775630; e-mail info@mof-sudan.net; internet www.mof-sudan.net.

Area and Population

AREA, POPULATION AND DENSITY

Area (sq km)	2,505,813*
Population (census results)†	
1 February 1983	20,594,197
15 April 1993‡	
Males	12,518,638
Females	12,422,045
Total	24,940,683
Population (UN estimates at mid-year)§	
2005	36,900,000
2006	37,707,000
2007	38,560,000
Density (per sq km) at mid-2007	15.4

* 967,500 sq miles.
† Excluding adjustments for underenumeration, estimated to have been 6.7% in 1993.
‡ Provisional result.
§ Source: UN, *World Population Prospects: The 2006 Revision*.

PROVINCES
(1983 census, provisional)*

	Area (sq miles)	Population	Density (per sq mile)
Northern	134,736	433,391	3.2
Nile	49,205	649,633	13.2
Kassala	44,109	1,512,335	34.3
Red Sea	84,977	695,874	8.2
Blue Nile	24,009	1,056,313	44.0
Gezira	13,546	2,023,094	149.3
White Nile	16,161	933,136	57.7
Northern Kordofan	85,744	1,805,769	21.1
Southern Kordofan	61,188	1,287,525	21.0
Northern Darfur	133,754	1,327,947	9.9
Southern Darfur	62,801	1,765,752	28.1
Khartoum	10,883	1,802,299	165.6
Eastern Equatoria	46,073	1,047,125	22.7
Western Equatoria	30,422	359,056	11.8
Bahr al-Ghazal	52,000	1,492,597	28.7
Al-Buhayrat	25,625	772,913	30.2
Sobat	45,266	802,354	17.7
Jonglei	47,003	797,251	17.0
Total	**967,500**	**20,564,364**	**21.3**

* In 1991 a federal system of government was inaugurated, whereby Sudan was divided into nine states, which were sub-divided into 66 provinces and 281 local government areas. A constitutional decree, issued in February 1994, redivided the country into 26 states.

PRINCIPAL TOWNS
(population at 1993 census)

Omdurman	1,271,403	Nyala	227,183
Khartoum (capital)	947,483	El-Gezira	211,362
Khartoum North	700,887	Gedaref	191,164
Port Sudan	308,195	Kosti	173,599
Kassala	234,622	El-Fasher	141,884
El-Obeid	229,425	Juba	114,980

Source: UN, *Demographic Yearbook*.

Mid-2007 ('000, including suburbs, UN estimate): Khartoum 4,754 (Source: UN, *World Urbanization Prospects: The 2007 Revision*).

Births and Deaths
(annual averages, UN estimates)

	1990–95	1995–2000	2000–05
Birth rate (per 1,000)	40.0	37.9	34.4
Death rate (per 1,000)	13.1	11.9	11.2

Source: UN, *World Population Prospects: The 2006 Revision*.

Expectation of life (years at birth, WHO estimates): 59.1 (males 56.7; females 61.6) in 2005 (Source: WHO, *World Health Statistics*).

ECONOMICALLY ACTIVE POPULATION*
(persons aged 10 years and over, 1983 census, provisional)

	Males	Females	Total
Agriculture, hunting, forestry and fishing	2,638,294	1,390,411	4,028,705
Mining and quarrying	5,861	673	6,534
Manufacturing	205,247	61,446	266,693
Electricity, gas and water	42,110	1,618	43,728
Construction	130,977	8,305	139,282
Trade, restaurants and hotels	268,382	25,720	294,102
Transport, storage and communications	209,776	5,698	215,474
Financing, insurance, real estate and business services	17,414	3,160	20,574
Community, social and personal services	451,193	99,216	550,409
Activities not adequately defined	142,691	42,030	184,721
Unemployed persons not previously employed	387,615	205,144	592,759
Total	**4,499,560**	**1,843,421**	**6,342,981**

* Excluding nomads, homeless persons and members of institutional households.

Mid-2005 (estimates in '000): Agriculture, etc. 8,220; Total 14,558 (Source: FAO).

Health and Welfare

KEY INDICATORS

Total fertility rate (children per woman, 2005)	4.2
Under-5 mortality rate (per 1,000 live births, 2005)	90
HIV/AIDS (% of persons aged 15–49, 2005)	1.6
Physicians (per 1,000 head, 2004)	0.22
Hospital beds (per 1,000 head, 2004)	0.70
Health expenditure (2004): US $ per head (PPP)	54.0
Health expenditure (2004): % of GDP	4.1
Health expenditure (2004): public (% of total)	35.4
Access to water (% of persons, 2004)	70
Access to sanitation (% of persons, 2004)	34
Human Development Index (2005): ranking	148
Human Development Index (2005): value	0.526

For sources and definitions, see explanatory note on p. vi.

Agriculture

PRINCIPAL CROPS
('000 metric tons)

	2004	2005	2006
Wheat*	435	415	642
Rice (paddy)	36	20	20†
Maize†	46	60	60
Millet*	281	745	792
Sorghum (Durra)*	2,704	4,275	5,203
Potatoes	336	385	260*
Cassava (Manioc)†	11	11	11
Yams†	142	145	145
Sugar cane†	6,984	7,186	7,186
Dry beans	14	15	23†
Dry broad beans	173	112	138†
Groundnuts (in shell)	790	520	540*
Sunflower seed	7	12	14*
Sesame seed	399	277	200*
Melonseed†	46	46	46
Cottonseed	155	202	202†
Tomatoes	556	484	484†
Pumpkins, squash and gourds†	71	72	72
Aubergines (Eggplants)†	255	272	272
Dry onions†	59	59	59
Garlic†	18	19	19
Melons†	29	30	30
Watermelons†	152	157	157
Dates	336	328	328†
Oranges†	19	19	19
Lemons and limes†	64	66	66
Grapefruits and pomelos†	70	71	71
Guavas, mangoes and mangosteens†	213	225	225
Bananas†	76	78	78

* Unofficial figure(s).
† FAO estimate(s).

Aggregate production ('000 metric tons, may include official, semi-official or estimated data): Total cereals 3,502 in 2004, 5,515 in 2005, 6,717 in 2006; Total roots and tubers 498 in 2004, 551 in 2005, 426 in 2006; Total vegetables (incl. melons) 2,201 in 2004, 2,098 in 2005, 2,098 in 2006; Total fruits (excl. melons) 1,192 in 2004, 1,200 in 2005, 1,200 in 2006.

Source: FAO.

LIVESTOCK
('000 head, year ending September)

	2004	2005	2006
Horses*	26	26	26
Asses and mules*	751	751	751
Cattle	39,760	40,468	40,468
Camels	3,724	3,908	3,908
Sheep	48,910	49,797	49,797
Goats	42,179	42,526	42,526
Poultry*	37,000	37,000	37,000

* Estimates.
Source: FAO.

LIVESTOCK PRODUCTS
('000 metric tons)

	2004	2005	2006*
Sheep meat*	n.a.	n.a.	148
Goat meat	139	186	186
Chicken meat*	29	29	29
Other meat*	717	769	583
Cows' milk	5,384	5,480	5,480
Sheep's milk	475	487	487
Goats' milk	1,500	1,519	1,519
Hen eggs*	47	47	47
Wool: greasy*	46	46	46

* Estimates.
Source: FAO.

Forestry

ROUNDWOOD REMOVALS
('000 cubic metres, FAO estimates)

	2004	2005	2006
Sawlogs, veneer logs and logs for sleepers	123	123	123
Other industrial wood	2,050	2,050	2,050
Fuel wood	17,482	17,698	17,901
Total	19,655	19,871	20,074

Source: FAO.

Gum arabic ('000 metric tons, year ending 30 June): 24 in 1993/94; 27 in 1994/95; 25 in 1995/96 (Source: IMF, *Sudan—Recent Economic Developments*, March 1997).

Fishing

('000 metric tons, live weight, FAO estimates)

	2003	2004	2005
Capture	59.0	57.0	62.0
Nile tilapia	20.0	20.0	21.5
Other freshwater fishes	34.0	34.0	35.0
Marine fishes	4.9	4.9	5.4
Aquaculture	1.6	1.6	1.6
Total catch	60.6	58.6	63.6

Source: FAO.

Mining

('000 metric tons, unless otherwise stated)

	2004	2005*	2006
Crude petroleum ('000 barrels)	111,000	126,000	158,000*
Salt (unrefined)*	63.0	65.0	68.0
Chromite	26.0	21.7	22.0*
Gold ore (kilograms)†	5,000	3,625	3,158

* Estimated figure(s).
† Figures refer to the metal content of ores.
Source: US Geological Survey.

Industry

PETROLEUM PRODUCTS
(metric tons)

	2004	2005	2006
Motor spirit (petrol)	8,109	7,827	9,717
Naphtha	248	248	216
Jet fuels	1,562	1,596	1,445
Kerosene	294	340	320
Gas-diesel (distillate fuel) oils	9,708	9,965	13,554
Residual fuel oils	2,444	2,589	2,566

Source: US Geological Survey.

SUDAN

SELECTED OTHER PRODUCTS
('000 metric tons)

	2002	2003	2004
Wheat flour	840	890	870
Raw sugar	732	686	n.a.
Cement	190*	272	280

* Estimate.

2002 ('000 metric tons): Refined sugar 674; Vegetable oils ('000 metric tons) 63.

Source: UN, *Industrial Commodity Statistics Yearbook*.

Finance

CURRENCY AND EXCHANGE RATES

Monetary Units
100 piastres = 1 Sudanese dinar.

Sterling, Dollar and Euro Equivalents (31 October 2007)
£1 sterling = 4.220 dinars;
US $1 = 2.035 dinars;
€1 = 2.940 dinars;
1,000 Sudanese dinars = £2.37 = $4.91 = €3.40.

Average Exchange Rate (Sudanese dinars per US $)
2005   2.4362
2006   2.1715
2007   2.0161

Note: On 1 March 1999 the Sudanese pound (£S) was replaced by the Sudanese dinar, equivalent to £S10. The pound was withdrawn from circulation on 31 July 1999. A new Sudanese pound, equivalent to 100 dinars (and 1,000 old pounds) was introduced on 10 January 2007. The new currency was to circulate along with previous currencies (the old pound had continued to circulate in some regions) for a transitional period, but was to become the sole legal tender on 1 July 2007.

CENTRAL GOVERNMENT BUDGET
('000 million Sudanese dinars)

Revenue	2003	2004	2005*
Tax revenue	270.0	420.5	472.1
Direct taxes	52.3	74.7	92.2
Indirect taxes	217.7	345.8	379.9
Non-tax revenue	471.9	684.0	1,000.8
Departmental fees	10.7	14.1	15.3
National revenues	461.2	669.9	985.5
Non-petroleum revenues	38.7	90.6	84.5
Petroleum revenues	422.6	579.3	901.0
Total	741.9	1,104.5	1,472.9

Expenditure	2003	2004	2005*
Current expenditure	563.8	762.5	1,382.7
Wages, salaries and pensions	191.1	273.8	301.1
Other current spending	321.3	404.6	651.0
Debt service paid	73.0	81.1	86.2
Goods and services	54.5	71.0	72.4
General reserve	104.0	144.3	123.3
Other obligations	89.8	108.1	369.1
Transfers to states	51.4	84.2	430.7
Capital expenditure	135.2	277.2	227.6
Locally financed	112.8	227.5	178.1
Foreign financed	22.4	49.7	49.5
Statistical discrepancy	9.3	−20.2	−16.4
Total	708.4	1,019.5	1,593.9

* Preliminary figures.

Source: IMF, *Sudan: 2006 Article IV Consultation and Staff-Monitored Program—Staff Report; Staff Statement; Public Information Notice on the Executive Board Discussion; and Statement by the Executive Director for Sudan* (May 2006).

INTERNATIONAL RESERVES
(US $ million at 31 December)

	2004	2005	2006
IMF special drawing rights	—	0.1	—
Foreign exchange	1,338.0	1,868.5	1,659.9
Total	1,338.0	1,868.6	1,659.9

Source: IMF, *International Financial Statistics*.

MONEY SUPPLY
('000 million Sudanese dinars at 31 December)

	2004	2005	2006
Currency outside banks	304.90	376.13	535.53
Demand deposits at deposit money banks	279.46	393.72	481.39
Total money (incl. others)	604.37	813.01	1,052.41

Source: IMF, *International Financial Statistics*.

COST OF LIVING
(Consumer Price Index; base: 1992 = 100)

	1998	1999	2000
Food, beverages and tobacco	3,930.8	4,670.3	4,883.3
Clothing and footwear	3,615.7	4,010.5	3,985.6
Housing	3,826.8	5,257.2	6,192.9
Household operations	3,677.7	3,899.3	3,706.4
Health care	5,277.9	6,313.5	6,984.7
Transport and communications	7,107.7	8,661.7	9,082.8
Entertainment	2,261.2	3,046.0	4,149.7
Education	5,947.8	7,057.0	8,048.7
All items (incl. others)	4,299.8	5,077.0	5,451.9

Source: Bank of Sudan.

All items (Consumer Price Index; base: 2000 = 100): 134.0 in 2004; 145.5 in 2005; 155.9 in 2006 (Source: IMF, *International Financial Statistics*).

NATIONAL ACCOUNTS

Expenditure on the Gross Domestic Product
(US $ million at current prices)

	2005	2006	2007
Government final consumption expenditure	4,675.05	6,089.25	6,613.65
Private final consumption expenditure	19,839.60	27,190.75	32,720.23
Gross fixed capital formation	6,109.09	8,226.54	10,013.87
Total domestic expenditure	30,623.74	41,506.54	49,347.75
Exports of goods and services	4,972.80	6,052.25	6,847.82
Less Imports of goods and services	7,701.14	9,994.69	10,470.14
GDP in purchasers' values	27,895.39	37,564.10	45,725.43
GDP at constant 2000 prices	16,219.32	18,133.20	20,164.12

Source: African Development Bank.

Gross Domestic Product by Economic Activity
('000 million Sudanese dinars at current prices, estimates)

	1997	1998	1999
Agriculture and forestry	745.7	841.6	1,040.3
Mining and quarrying	4.2	5.5	20.9
Manufacturing and handicrafts	100.7	177.4	217.3
Electricity and water	14.3	16.1	19.0
Construction	73.1	132.5	156.8
Trade, restaurants and hotels	260.5	405.9	492.0
Transport and communications	150.5	116.3	142.3
Other services	266.0	290.8	354.1
GDP at factor cost	1,615.1	1,986.0	2,442.7
Indirect taxes, *less* subsidies	61.9	76.1	93.6
GDP in purchasers' values	1,677.0	2,062.1	2,536.3

Source: IMF, *Sudan—Statistical Appendix* (July 2000).

SUDAN

BALANCE OF PAYMENTS
(US $ million)

	2004	2005	2006
Exports of goods f.o.b.	3,777.8	4,824.3	5,656.6
Imports of goods f.o.b.	−3,586.2	−5,946.0	−7,104.7
Trade balance	191.6	−1,121.7	−1,448.1
Exports of services	44.1	113.9	205.6
Imports of services	−1,064.5	−1,844.4	−2,789.5
Balance on goods and services	−828.8	−2,852.2	−4,032.0
Other income received	21.8	44.1	89.3
Other income paid	−1,134.5	−1,405.9	−2,103.3
Balance on goods, services and income	−1,941.5	−4,214.0	−6,046.0
Current transfers received	1,580.2	1,680.5	1,877.1
Current transfers paid	−509.6	−479.6	−940.7
Current balance	−870.9	−3,013.1	−5,109.6
Direct investment from abroad	1,511.1	2,304.6	3,534.1
Portfolio investment assets	19.9	50.6	−0.1
Portfolio investment liabilities	—	—	−35.3
Other investment assets	598.8	1,134.7	208.2
Investment liabilities	−702.0	−605.3	1,031.7
Net errors and omissions	225.5	743.0	−219.9
Overall balance	782.4	614.5	−590.6

Source: IMF, *International Financial Statistics*.

External Trade

PRINCIPAL COMMODITIES
(US $ million)

Imports c.i.f.	2001	2002	2003
Food and live animals	328.3	411.6	402.7
Cereals and cereal preparations	187.3	242.8	214.3
Unmilled durum wheat	133.4	203.3	186.2
Mineral fuels, lubricants, etc.	43.1	120.1	88.9
Refined petroleum products	39.5	117.5	85.1
Chemicals and related products	221.6	261.5	302.6
Medicinal and pharmaceutical products	57.9	73.2	85.1
Basic manufactures	382.6	495.0	641.7
Textiles and textile products (excl. clothing)	77.7	90.1	123.0
Cement	50.6	91.8	103.7
Iron and steel	83.8	113.0	185.1
Machinery and transport equipment	772.1	945.0	1,112.4
Power generating machinery and equipment	90.3	122.3	107.7
Machinery specialized for particular industries	123.5	166.9	197.7
Miscellaneous industrial machinery	94.2	112.8	125.7
Telecommunication and recording equipment	72.8	73.2	125.1
Road vehicles	267.5	285.0	353.3
Passenger vehicles (excl. buses)	76.4	91.1	102.1
Lorries and special purpose vehicles	88.5	96.9	112.9
Miscellaneous manufactured articles	136.3	172.3	242.2
Total (incl. others)	1,958.0	2,492.8	2,898.1

Exports f.o.b.	2001	2002	2003
Food and live animals	57.7	193.8	168.6
Live animals	1.5	124.6	97.7
Sheep and goats	—	122.2	85.3
Sheep	—	121.0	83.5
Crude materials (inedible) except fuels	194.5	172.9	248.5
Oil seeds and oleaginous fruit	121.9	82.4	89.8
Sesame seeds	97.8	68.8	74.3
Cotton	47.3	55.2	106.4
Mineral fuels, lubricants, etc.	1,480.0	1,118.0	1,969.5
Petroleum and petroleum products	1,458.1	1,100.0	1,938.3
Crude petroleum and bituminous oils	—	128.8	—
Refined petroleum products	1,458.1	971.2	1,938.3
Other commodities and transactions	48.6	73.4	55.5
Non-monetary gold, unwrought	48.6	72.7	55.5
Total (incl. others)	1,812.1	1,616.6	2,480.6

Source: UN, *International Trade Statistics Yearbook*.

PRINCIPAL TRADING PARTNERS
(US $ million)

Imports c.i.f.	2003	2004	2005
Brazil	6.3	23.9	54.3
China, People's Repub.	229.1	529.6	1,383.0
France (incl. Monaco)	50.9	72.8	220.7
Germany	142.6	185.1	81.2
India	115.9	197.1	317.8
Italy	52.4	118.5	257.6
Japan	85.0	165.1	341.8
Jordan	33.2	35.1	45.3
Korea, Repub.	51.1	89.3	149.8
Netherlands	40.5	60.1	93.4
Russia	17.1	19.0	57.5
Saudi Arabia	723.9	471.5	627.5
Sweden	27.2	46.6	82.0
United Arab Emirates	180.0	239.2	394.8
United Kingdom	125.6	151.3	221.9
USA	11.1	34.0	129.7
Total (incl. others)	2,882.0	4,075.2	6,756.8

Exports f.o.b.	2003	2004	2005
Bangladesh	17.3	14.4	19.7
China, People's Repub.	1,761.9	2,527.0	3,427.1
France	12.0	23.8	26.1
Germany	18.7	34.3	27.3
Italy	11.3	14.3	19.1
Japan	167.7	402.2	577.5
Korea, Repub.	18.3	23.5	7.9
Saudi Arabia	114.8	164.2	136.4
Syria	12.1	15.8	12.7
United Arab Emirates	83.0	90.2	90.0
United Kingdom	66.4	56.1	21.8
USA	2.7	2.9	12.4
Yemen	3.7	3.5	10.8
Total (incl. others)	2,542.2	3,777.8	4,824.3

Source: Bank of Sudan.

Transport

RAILWAY TRAFFIC*

	1991	1992	1993
Freight ton-km (million)	2,030	2,120	2,240
Passenger-km (million)	1,020	1,130	1,183

*Estimates.

Source: UN Economic Commission for Africa, *African Statistical Yearbook*.

2000 (passengers carried): 258,000 (Source: Sudan Railways).

ROAD TRAFFIC
(motor vehicles in use)

	2000	2001	2002
Passenger cars	46,000	46,400	47,300
Commercial vehicles	60,500	61,800	62,500

Source: UN, *Statistical Yearbook*.

SHIPPING
Merchant Fleet
(registered at 31 December)

	2004	2005	2006
Number of vessels	17	17	19
Displacement (grt)	15,650	15,650	25,904

Source: Lloyd's Register-Fairplay, *World Fleet Statistics*.

International Sea-borne Freight Traffic
(estimates, '000 metric tons)

	1991	1992	1993
Goods loaded	1,290	1,387	1,543
Goods unloaded	3,800	4,200	4,300

Source: UN Economic Commission for Africa, *African Statistical Yearbook*.

CIVIL AVIATION
(traffic on scheduled services)

	2001	2002	2003
Kilometres flown (million)	6	6	7
Passengers carried ('000)	415	409	420
Passenger-km (million)	761	767	786
Total ton-km (million)	98	98	103

Source: UN, *Statistical Yearbook*.

Tourism

	2002	2003	2004
Tourist arrivals	52,000	52,291	60,577
Tourism receipts (US $ million, excl. passenger transport)	108	118	n.a.

Source: World Tourism Organization.

Communications Media

	2004	2005	2006
Telephones ('000 main lines in use)	1,028.9	570.0	636.9
Mobile cellular telephones ('000 subscribers)	1,049	1,828	4,683
Personal computers ('000 in use)	606	3,250	n.a.
Internet users ('000)	1,140	2,800	3,500
Broadband subscribers	800	1,300	2,100

Source: International Telecommunication Union.

1996: Daily newspapers 5 (average circulation 737,000 copies) (Source: UNESCO, *Statistical Yearbook*).

1997: Radio receivers ('000 in use) 7,550 (Source: UNESCO, *Statistical Yearbook*).

1998: Non-daily newspapers 11 (average circulation 5,644,000); Periodicals 54 (average circulation 68,000 copies) (Source: UN, *Statistical Yearbook*).

2000: Television receivers ('000 in use) 8,500 (Source: International Telecommunication Union).

Education

(2004/05, unless otherwise stated)

	Institutions*	Teachers	Students
Pre-primary	5,984	17,105	498,248
Primary	11,982	113,094	3,278,090
Secondary	3,512	63,682	1,369,735
Universities, etc.	n.a.	4,486†	200,538†

* Figures refer to 1998.
† Estimates for 2000.

Source: UNESCO Institute for Statistics.

1999/2000: Primary: 11,923 schools. Secondary: 1,694 schools (Source: Ministry of Education).

Adult literacy rate (UNESCO estimates): 60.9% (males 71.1%; females 51.8%) in 2000 (Source: UNESCO Institute for Statistics).

Directory

The Constitution

Following the coup of 6 April 1985, the Constitution of April 1973 was abrogated. A transitional Constitution, which entered into force in October 1985, was suspended following the military coup of 30 June 1989. In April 1998 a new Constitution was approved by the National Assembly, and presented to President al-Bashir. At a referendum held in June, the new Constitution was endorsed by 96.7% of voters. This Constitution, which entered into force on 1 July 1998, vests executive power in the Council of Ministers, which is appointed by the President but responsible to the National Assembly. Legislative power is vested in the National Assembly. The Constitution guarantees freedom of thought and religion, and the right to political association, provided that such activity complies with the law.

On 9 July 2005 the National Assembly approved an interim Constitution, as part of the Comprehensive Peace Agreement signed in January between the Sudanese Government and the Sudan People's Liberation Movement (SPLM). The Interim National Constitution provided for the establishment of a Government of National Unity (GONU), representation in which was to be divided between northerners and southerners, with the former holding 70% and the latter 30% of the posts. In the GONU, the National Congress shall be represented by 52% (49% northerners and 3% southerners); the SPLM shall be represented by 28% (21% southerners and 7% northerners); other northern political forces shall be represented by 14%; and other southern political forces shall be represented by 6%.

The Interim National Constitution also stipulated that, pending legislative elections, which were to be held by no later than the end of the fourth year of the interim period, the National Assembly shall be composed of 450 members who shall be appointed by the President of the Republic in consultation with the First Vice-President, according to the 70%:30% north-south ratio.

Provision was also made in the Interim National Constitution for the election of the President of the Government of Southern Sudan and for the establishment of a transitional Southern Sudan Assembly. The President of Government of Southern Sudan shall be elected directly by the people of Southern Sudan for a five-year mandate, renewable only once. The transitional Southern Sudan Assembly shall be an inclusive, constituent legislature composed of 170 appointed members with 70% representing the SPLM, 15% representing the National Congress, and 15% representing the other southern Sudanese political forces.

The Government

HEAD OF STATE

President: Lt-Gen. OMAR HASSAN AHMAD AL-BASHIR (took power as Chairman of the Revolutionary Command Council for National Salvation (RCC) on 30 June 1989; appointed President by the RCC on 16 October 1993; elected President in March 1996; re-elected in December 2000).

First Vice-President: Commdr SALVA KIIR MAYARDIT.

Second Vice-President: ALI OSMAN MUHAMMAD TAHA.

COUNCIL OF MINISTERS
(March 2008)

Prime Minister: Lt-Gen. OMAR HASSAN AHMAD AL-BASHIR (National Congress).

Minister of Foreign Affairs: DENG ALOR KOL (SPLM).

Minister of the Interior: IBRAHIM MOHAMMED HAMED.

Minister of the Presidency: Maj. Gen. BAKRI HASSAN SALEH (National Congress).

Minister of Cabinet Affairs: PAGAN AMUM (SPLM).

Minister of Defence: Maj.-Gen. Eng. ABD AR-RAHIM MUHAMMAD HUSSEIN (National Congress).

Minister of Justice: ABD AL-BASIT SALEH SABDARAT (National Congress).

Minister of Information and Communication: ZAHAWI IBRAHIM MALEK (UP).

Minister of Federal Government: Lt-Gen. ADB AL-RAHMAN SAID (NDA).

Minister of Finance and National Economy: Dr AWAD AHMAD AL-JAZ (National Congress).

Minister of Foreign Trade: JAMES KOCK RONA (SPLM).

Minister of International Co-operation: AT-TIJANI SALEH FEDAIL (National Congress).

Minister of Industry: JALAL YUSUF MUHAMMAD AD-DUQAYR (DUP).

Minister of Investment: KOSTI MANYEBI (SPLM).

Minister of Agriculture and Forestry: Prof. ZUBEIR BESHIR TAHA (National Congress).

Minister of Animal Resources: MOHAMMED AHMED TAHER ABU KALABISH (National Congress).

Minister of Irrigation and Water Resources: Eng. KAMAL ALI MUHAMMAD (National Congress).

Minister of Energy and Mining: AZ-ZOBEIR AHMED HASSAN (National Congress).

Minister of Transport, Roads and Bridges: PHILIP THON (SPLM).

Minister of Culture, Youth and Sport: MUHAMMAD YUSSUF ABDALLAH (National Congress).

Minister of Tourism and Wildlife: JOSEF MALWAL (UDSF).

Minister of Scientific Research and Technology: IBRAHIM MUHAMAD OMAR (NC).

Minister of Education: HAMID MUHAMAD IBRAHIM (NDA).

Minister of Labour, Public Services and Development of Human Resources: Maj.-Gen. (retd) ALISON MANANI MAGAYA (National Congress).

Minister of Health: Dr TABITA SOKAYA (SPLM).

Minister of Humanitarian Affairs: JAMES HARUN RUN LUAL (SPLM).

Minister of Religious Affairs and Waqf: AZHARI AT-TIGANI AWAD AS-SID (National Congress).

Minister of Welfare and Social Development: SAMIA AHMAD MUHAMMAD.

Minister of the Environment and Urban Development Construction: AHMED BABKIR NAHAR (National Congress).

Minister of Parliamentary Affairs: JOSEPH OKELLO (USAP).

In addition, there is one presidential adviser and 39 Ministers of State. The President also has 14 special advisers who are considered part of the Government.

GOVERNMENT OF SOUTHERN SUDAN
(March 2008)

President: Commdr SALVA KIIR MAYARDIT.

Vice-President and Minister for Housing, Lands and Public Service: Dr RIEK MACHAR.

Minister for Presidential Affairs: Dr JUSTIN YAAC AROP.

Minister of Parliamentary Affairs: Dr MARTIN ALIA.

Minister for Police and Security: DANIEL AWET.

Minister of Finance and Economic Planning: ARTHA AKWIN CHUOL.

Minister of Regional Co-operation: Dr BARNABA MARIAL BENJAMIN.

Minister for Legal Affairs and Constitutional Development: MICHAEL MAKUEI.

Minister for Education, Science and Technology: Prof. JOB DHORUAI.

Minister for Health: Dr THEOPHILUS OCHAN.

Minister for Industry and Mining: Dr JOHN LUK JOK.

Minister for Trade and Supplies: ANTHONY LINO MAKANA.

Minister for Information, Broadcasting and Television: GABRIEL CHANGSON.

Minister for Communication and Postal Services: GEER CHAN.

Minister for Transport and Roads: REBECCA NYAN DENG DE MABIOR.

Minister for Environment, Protection of Wildlife and Tourism: AGNES LUKUDU.

Minister for Agriculture and Forestry: Dr SAMSON KWAJE.

Minister for Public Services and Human Resource Development: DAVID DENG ATHORBI.

Minister for Animal Resources and Fisheries: MUHAMMAD AHMAD ABU-KALABISH.

Minister for Culture, Youth and Sports: Maj.-Gen. (Retd) ALBINO AKOL.

Minister for Diversity and Social and Religious Affairs: MARY KIDEN.

Minister for Water and Irrigation: JOSEPH DWER.

In addition, there are nine presidential advisers.

MINISTRIES

Ministry of Agriculture and Forestry: POB 285, al-Gamaa Ave, Khartoum; tel. (183) 780951; e-mail moafcc@sudanmail.net.

Ministry of Animal Resources: Khartoum.

Ministry of Cabinet Affairs: Khartoum.

Ministry of Culture, Youth and Sport: Khartoum.

Ministry of Defence: POB 371, Khartoum; tel. (183) 774910.

Ministry of Education: Khartoum; tel. (183) 772808; e-mail moe-sd@moe-sd.com; internet www.moe-sd.com.

Ministry of Energy and Mining: POB 2087, Khartoum; tel. (183) 775595; fax (183) 775428.

Ministry of the Environment and Urban Development Construction: POB 300, Khartoum; tel. (183) 462604.

Ministry of Federal Government: Khartoum.

Ministry of Finance and National Economy: POB 735, Khartoum; tel. (183) 777563; fax (183) 775630; e-mail info@mof-sudan.net; internet mof-sudan.com.

Ministry of Foreign Affairs: POB 873, Khartoum; tel. (183) 773101; fax (183) 772941; e-mail ministry@mfa.gov.sd; internet www.sudanmfa.com.

Ministry of Foreign Trade: Khartoum; tel. (183) 772793; fax (183) 773950.

Ministry of Health: POB 303, Khartoum; tel. (183) 773000; e-mail inhsd@sudanet.net; internet www.fmoh.gov.sd.

Ministry of Higher Education and Scientific Research: POB 2081, Khartoum; tel. (183) 779312; e-mail mhesr@sudanmail.net.

Ministry of Humanitarian Affairs: POB 1976, Khartoum; tel. (183) 780675; e-mail human@mha.gov.sd; internet www.mha.gov.sd.

Ministry of Industry: POB 2184, Khartoum; tel. (183) 777830.

Ministry of Information and Communication: Khartoum.

Ministry of the Interior: POB 2793, Khartoum; tel. (183) 776554.

Ministry of International Co-operation: POB 2092, Khartoum; tel. (183) 772169; fax (183) 780115; e-mail info@micsudan.com; internet www.micsudan.com.

Ministry of Investment: POB 6286, Khartoum; tel. (183) 787194; fax (183) 787199; internet www.sudaninvest.gov.sd.

Ministry of Irrigation and Water Resources: POB 878, Khartoum; tel. (183) 783221; fax (183) 773388; e-mail oehamad@hotmail.com.

Ministry of Justice: POB 302, an-Nil Ave, Khartoum; tel. (183) 774842; fax (183) 771479.

Ministry of Labour, Public Services and Development of Human Resources: Khartoum.

Ministry of Parliamentary Affairs: Khartoum.

Ministry of Religious Affairs and Waqf: Khartoum.

Ministry of Tourism and Wildlife: POB 2424, Khartoum; tel. (183) 471329; fax (183) 471437; e-mail admin@sudan-tourism.com.

Ministry of Transport, Roads and Bridges: POB 300, Khartoum; tel. (183) 781629; fax (183) 780507.

Ministry of Welfare and Social Development: Khartoum.

STATE GOVERNORS
(March 2008)

Al-Buhayrat: Lt-Gen. Daniel Wet Akot.
Bahr al-Jabal: Maj.-Gen. Clement Wani Konga.
Blue Nile: Abdallah Uthman al-Haj.
Eastern Equatoria: Aloysio Amor.
Gadarif: Abd ar-Rahman Ahmed al-Khadr.
Gezira: Lt-Gen. (retd) Abd ar-Rahman Sir al-Khatim.
Jonglei: Phillip Thon Leek.
Kassala: Lt-Gen. Faruq Hasan Muhammad Nur.
Khartoum: Dr Abd-al-Halim Ismail al-Muta'afi.
Northern: Maj.-Gen. (retd) al-Hadi Bushra Hassan.
Northern Bahr al-Ghazal: Maryang Akoi Ago.
Northern Darfur: Osman Muhammad Yusuf Kibir.
Northern Kordofan: Ghulam ad-Din Uthman.
Red Sea: Maj.-Gen. (retd) Hatim al-Wasil Ash-Shaykh as-Sammani.
River Nile: Dr Bdella Masar.
Sennar: Ahmed Abbas.
Southern Darfur: Adam Hamid Musa.
Southern Kordofan: Somi Zaydan Attiyah.
Upper Nile: Dr Dak Dok Bishok.
Wahdah: Brig. Taban Deng Gai.
Warab: Anthony Bol Madut.
Western Bahr al-Ghazal: Mark Nabibosh Obong.
Western Darfur: Staff Maj.-Gen. (retd) Sulayman Abdallah Adam.
Western Equatoria: Commdr Samuel Abu John Kabashi.
Western Kordofan: Maj.-Gen. at-Tayib Abd ar-Rahman Mukhtar.
White Nile: Majdhub Yusuf Babikir.

President

PRESIDENT
Election, 13–22 December 2000

Candidate	% of total votes cast
Omar Hassan Ahmad al-Bashir (National Congress)	86.5
Gaafar Muhammad Nimeri (Alliance of the People's Working Forces)	9.6
Malik Hussain	1.6
as-Samawi'it Husayn Osman Mansur (Independent Democrats)	1.0
Mahmoud Ahmad Juna	1.0

Legislature

MAJLIS WATANI
(National Assembly)

Speaker: Ahmad Ibrahim at-Tahir.
Deputy Speakers: Angelo Beda, Abdallah al-Hardello.

Election, 13–22 December 2000

	Seats
National Congress	355
Others	5
Total	360*

*Of the 360 members, 270 are directly elected in single seat constituencies, 35 members represent women, 26 represent university graduates and 29 represent trade unions.

According to the interim Constitution approved by the National Assembly in July 2005, the National Assembly shall be composed of 450 members who shall be appointed by the President of the Republic in consultation with the First Vice-President. Legislative elections were to be held by no later than the end of the fourth year of the interim period.

Election Commission

General Election Commission (GEC): PO 14416, Omdurman; tel. (15) 558537; fax (15) 560950; e-mail info@sudan-parliament.org; comprises of a chairman and two mems appointed for the election period only; mems appointed by the President, subject to the approval of the National Assembly; responsible for the election of the President, provincial magistrates, and national, provincial and local assembly mems; Chairman Abd al-Mun'im al-Zayn al-Nahhas.

Political Organizations

National Congress: Khartoum; successor to National Islamic Front; Pres. Lt-Gen. Omar Hassan Ahmad al-Bashir; Sec.-Gen. Prof. Ibrahim Ahmad Umar.

The right to political association, subject to compliance with the law, was guaranteed in the Constitution approved by referendum in June 1998. (All political organizations had been banned following the military coup of 30 June 1989.) The registration of parties began in January 1999. The following parties are among the most active:

Alliance of the People's Working Forces: Khartoum; Head Gaafar Muhammad Nimeri; Acting Sec.-Gen. Kamal ad-Din Muhammad Abdullah.

Democratic Unionist Party (DUP): Khartoum; Leader Osman al-Mirghani; participates in National Democratic Alliance (see below).

Free Sudanese National Party (FSNP): Khartoum; Chair. Fr Philip Abbas Ghabbush.

Independent Democrats: Khartoum; Leader as-Samawi't Husayn Osman Mansur.

Islamic-Christian Solidarity: Khartoum; Founder Hatim Abdullah az-Zaki Husayn.

Islamic Revival Movement: Khartoum; Founder Siddiq al-Haj as-Siddiq.

Islamic Socialist Party: Khartoum; Leader Salah al-Musbah.

Islamic Ummah Party: Khartoum; Chair. Wali ad-Din al-Hadi al-Mahdi.

Justice Party: Khartoum; f. 2002 by fmr members of the National Congress.

Moderate Trend Party: Khartoum; Leader Mahmud Jiha.

Muslim Brotherhood: Khartoum; Islamic fundamentalist; Leader Dr Habir Nur ad-Din.

National Democratic Party: Khartoum; f. 2002 following merger of the Union of Nationalistic Forces, the Communist Party and the National Solidarity Party.

Nile Valley Conference: Khartoum; Founder Lt-Gen. (retd) Umar Zaruq.

Popular Masses' Alliance: Khartoum; Founder Faysal Muhmad Husayn.

Popular National Congress (PNC): Khartoum; f. 2000; Founder Hassan at-Turabi.

Socialist Popular Party: Khartoum; Founder Sayyid Khalifah Idris Habbani.

Sudan Green Party: Khartoum; Founder Prof. Zakaraia Bashir Imam.

Sudan People's Liberation Movement (SPLM): e-mail webmaster@splmtoday.com; internet www.splmtoday.com; Leader Commdr Salva Kiir Mayardit; Sec.-Gen. Pagan Amum.

Sudanese Central Movement: Khartoum; Founder Dr Muhammad Abu al-Qasim Haj Hamad.

Sudanese Initiative Party: Khartoum; Leader J'afar Karar.

Sudanese National Party (SNP): Khartoum; Leader HASAN AL-MAHI; participates in the National Democratic Alliance (see below).

Umma Party (UP): internet www.umma.org; f. 1945; Mahdist party based on the Koran and Islamic traditions; Chair. Dr UMAR NUR AD-DA'IM; Leader SADIQ AL-MAHDI; withdrew from the National Democratic Alliance (see below) in March 2000.

Union of Sudan African Parties (USAP): f. 1987; Chair. JOSEPH OKELLO; Sec.-Gen. Prof. AJANG BIOR.

United Democratic Salvation Front (UDSF): Khartoum; political wing of the Sudan People's Defence Force; Chair. Dr RIEK MASHAR TENY-DHURGON.

A number of opposition movements are grouped together in the Asmara-based **National Democratic Alliance (NDA)** (Chair. OSMAN AL-MIRGHANI; Sec.-Gen. JOSEPH OKELU). These include the **Beja Congress** (Sec.-Gen. Amna Dirar), the **Legitimate Command (LC)**, the **Sudan Alliance Forces (SAF)** (f. 1994; Commdr-in-Chief Brig. ABD EL-AZIZ KHALID OSMAN), the **Sudan Federal Democratic Alliance (SFDA)** (f. 1994; advocates a decentralized, federal structure for Sudan; Chair. AHMAD DREIGE).

In 2003 two rebel groups, the **Sudan Liberation Movement (SLM)** (Leader MINNI ARKUA MINAWI) and the **Sudan Justice and Equality Movement (SJEM)**, began an armed rebellion in the Darfur region of western Sudan.

At a meeting convened in Asmara in 2006 the **National Redemption Front (NRF)** was formed by the leader of the SJEM, Dr KHALIL IBRAHIM MOHAMED, his counterpart, AHMAD DREIGE of the SFDA, and KHAMIS ABDALLA ABAKAR, the former Deputy Chairman of Abd al-Wahid Muhammad an-Nur's faction of the SLM, and leader of the **Group of 19 (G-19)**. The G-19 emerged as the principal faction of the NRF, originally formed as a group of commanders who defected from an-Nur's faction during the Abuja negotiations. In December 2006 a group of Arab rebels, opposed to the Sudanese army and the *Janjaweed*, formed an alliance called the **Popular Forces Troops (PFT)**.

Diplomatic Representation

EMBASSIES IN SUDAN

Afghanistan: Madinatol Riyadh, Shareol Moshtal Sq. 10, House No. 81, Khartoum; tel. (183) 221852; fax (183) 222059; e-mail afembsudan@hotmail.com; Chargé d'affaires a.i. KHALILURRAHMAN HANANI.

Algeria: Blvd El-Mechtel Eriad, POB 80, Khartoum; tel. (183) 234773; fax (183) 224190; Ambassador SALIH BEN KOBBI.

Bulgaria: St 31, House No. 9, Block 10, al-Amarat, POB 1690, 11111 Khartoum; tel. (183) 560106; fax (183) 560107; e-mail bgembsdn@yahoo.co.uk; Chargé d'affaires a.i. SVILEN BOZHANOV.

Chad: St 57, al-Amarat, Khartoum; tel. (183) 471612; Ambassador MOUSSA MAHAMAT SEID MEDELA.

China, People's Republic: POB 1425, Khartoum; tel. (183) 272730; fax (183) 271138; e-mail ssddssgg@yahoo.com.cn; Ambassador LI CHENGWEN.

Congo, Democratic Republic: St 13, Block 12 CE, New Extension, 23, POB 4195, Khartoum; tel. (183) 471125; Chargé d'affaires a.i. BAWAN MUZURI.

Egypt: University St, POB 1126, Khartoum; tel. (183) 777646; fax (183) 778741; e-mail sphinx-egysud@yahoo.com; Ambassador MOHAMED ABDEL MONEIM EL SHAZLY.

Eritrea: St 39, House No. 26, POB 1618, Khartoum 2; tel. (183) 483834; fax (183) 483835; e-mail erena@sudanet.net; Ambassador Gen. ISSA AHMED ISSA.

Ethiopia: Plot No. 4, Block 384BC, POB 844, Khartoum; tel. (183) 471379; fax (183) 471141; e-mail eekrt@hotmail.com; Ambassador Dr KADAFO MOHAMMED HANFARE.

France: al-Amarat, St 13, Plot No. 11, Block 12, POB 377, 11111 Khartoum; tel. (183) 471082; fax (183) 465928; e-mail cad.khartoum@diplomatie.gouv.fr; internet www.ambafrance-sd.org; Ambassador CHRISTINE ROBICHON.

Germany: 53 Baladia St, Block No. 8D, Plot 2, POB 970, Khartoum; tel. (183) 777990; fax (183) 777622; e-mail reg1@khar.auswaertiges-amt.de; internet www.khartum.diplo.de; Ambassador Dr STEPHAN KELLER.

Greece: Sharia al-Gamhouria, Block 5, No. 30, POB 1182, Khartoum; tel. (183) 765902; fax (183) 765901; e-mail grembkrt@mfa.gr; Ambassador GEORGIOS VEIS.

Holy See: Kafouri Belgravia, POB 623, Khartoum (Apostolic Nunciature); tel. (183) 330037; fax (183) 330692; e-mail kanuap@yahoo.it; Apostolic Nuncio Most Rev. LEO BOCCARDI (Titular Archbishop of Bitettum).

India: 61 Africa Rd, POB 707, Khartoum II; tel. (183) 574001; fax (183) 574050; e-mail ambassador.office@indembsdn.com; internet www.indembsdn.com; Ambassador DEEPAK VOHRA.

Indonesia: St 60, 84, Block 12, ar-Riyadh, POB 13374, Khartoum; tel. (183) 225106; fax (183) 225528; e-mail kbri_khartoum@sudanmail.com; Ambassador SYAMSUDIN YAHYA.

Iran: Sq. 15, House No. 4, Mogran, POB 10229, Khartoum; tel. (183) 781490; fax (183) 778668; e-mail iranemb_khartoum@mfa.gov.ir; Ambassador REZA AMERI.

Iraq: Sharia ash-Shareef al-Hindi, POB 1969, Khartoum; tel. (183) 271867; fax (183) 271855; e-mail krtemb@iraqmofamail.net; Ambassador SAMIR KHAIREE ALNEEMA.

Italy: St 39, Block 61, POB 793, Khartoum; tel. (183) 471615; fax (183) 471217; e-mail ambasciata.khartoum@esteri.it; internet www.ambkhartoum.esteri.it; Ambassador LORENZO ANGELONI.

Japan: St 43, House No. 67, POB 1649, Khartoum; tel. (183) 471601; fax (183) 471600; Ambassador YUICHI ISHII.

Jordan: St 33, House No. 13, POB 1379, Khartoum; tel. (183) 483125; fax (183) 471038; Ambassador MUNTHER QUBAAH.

Kenya: St 3, POB 8242, Khartoum; tel. (183) 265163; fax (183) 281233; Ambassador Col (Retd) ELIJAH MALEKYA MATIBO.

Korea, Republic: House No. 2, St 1, New Extension, POB 2414, Khartoum; tel. (183) 451136; fax (183) 452822; e-mail ssudan@mofat.go.kr; Ambassador DONG EOK KIM.

Kuwait: Africa Ave, near the Tennis Club, POB 1457, Khartoum; tel. (183) 781525; Ambassador MUNTHIR BADR SALMAN.

Lebanon: Khartoum; Ambassador AHMAD SHAMMATT.

Libya: 50 Africa Rd, POB 2091, Khartoum; Secretary of People's Bureau GUMMA AL-FAZANI.

Malaysia: St 3, Block 2, al-Amarat, POB 11668, Khartoum; tel. (183) 482763; fax (183) 482762; e-mail mwktoum@kln.gov.my; Ambassador HAJI ZAINAL HAMZAH.

Morocco: St 19, 32, New Extension, POB 2042, Khartoum; tel. (183) 473068; fax (183) 471053; e-mail sifmasoud@sudan.mail.net; Ambassador MUHAMMAD MAA EL-AININE.

Netherlands: St 47, House No. 76, POB 391, Khartoum; tel. (183) 471200; fax (183) 471204; e-mail nlgovkha@mail.com; internet www.mfa.nl/kha; Ambassador J. H. M. WOLFS.

Nigeria: St 17, Sharia al-Mek Nimr, POB 1538, Khartoum; tel. (183) 779120; Ambassador IBRAHIM KARLI.

Norway: St 49, House No. 63, POB 13096, Khartoum; tel. (183) 578336; fax (183) 577180; e-mail emb.khartoum@mfa.no; internet www.norway-sudan.org; Ambassador FRIDTJOV THORKILDSEN.

Oman: St 1, New Extension, POB 2839, Khartoum; tel. (183) 471606; fax (183) 471017; Ambassador SALIM BIN FANKHAR AL-SHANFARI.

Pakistan: Dr Mehmood Sharif St, House No. 13, Block 35, POB 1178, Khartoum; tel. (183) 265599; fax (183) 273777; e-mail parepkhartoum@yahoo.com; Ambassador KHALID HUSSAIN YOUSFANI.

Qatar: Elmanshia Block 92H, POB 223, Khartoum; tel. (183) 261113; fax (183) 261116; e-mail qatarembkht@yahoo.com; Ambassador ALI HASSAN ABDULLAH AL-HAMADI.

Romania: Kassala Rd, Plot No. 172–173, Kafouri Area, POB 1494, Khartoum North; tel. (185) 338114; fax (185) 341497; e-mail ambro_khartoum@hotmail.com; Ambassador Dr EMIL GHITULESCU.

Russia: A10 St, B1, New Extension, POB 1161, Khartoum; tel. (183) 471042; fax (183) 471239; e-mail rfsudan@hotmail.com; Ambassador VALERII Y. SUKHIN.

Saudi Arabia: St 11, New Extension, Khartoum; tel. (183) 741938; Ambassador SAYED MOHAMMED SIBRI SULIMAN.

Somalia: St 23–25, New Extension, POB 1857, Khartoum; tel. (183) 744800; Ambassador Prof. MAHDI ABUKAR.

South Africa: St 11, House No. 16, Block B9, al-Amarat, POB 12137, Khartoum; tel. (183) 585301; fax (183) 585082; e-mail khartoum@foreign.gov.za; Ambassador Dr MANELISI GENGE.

Switzerland: St 15, House No. 7, Amarat, POB 1707, Khartoum; tel. (183) 471010; fax (183) 471115; e-mail vertretung@kha.rep.admin.ch; Ambassador ANDREJ MOTYL.

Syria: St 3, New Extension, POB 1139, Khartoum; tel. (183) 471152; fax (183) 471066; Ambassador MOHAMMED AL-MAHAMEED.

Tunisia: St 15, 35, al-Amarat, Khartoum; tel. (183) 487947; fax (183) 487950; e-mail at_khartoum@yahoo.fr; Ambassador ABDESSALEM BOUAÏCHA.

Turkey: St 29, 31, New Extension, POB 771, Khartoum; tel. (183) 794215; fax (183) 794218; e-mail trembkh@sudanmail.net; Ambassador Dr ALI ENGIN OBA.

Uganda: POB 2676, Khartoum; tel. (183) 158571; fax (183) 797868; e-mail ugembkht@hotmail.com; Ambassador MULL KATENDE.

United Arab Emirates: St 3, New Extension, POB 1225, Khartoum; tel. (183) 744476; Ambassador ISA ABDULLAH AL-BASHAR.
United Kingdom: St 10, off Baladia St, POB 801, Khartoum; tel. (183) 777105; fax (183) 776457; e-mail Media.Khartoum@fco.gov.uk; internet www.britishembassy.gov.uk/sudan; Ambassador IAN CLIFF.
USA: Ali Abd al-Latif St, POB 699, Khartoum; tel. (183) 774701; internet khartoum.usembassy.gov; Chargé d'affaires ALBERTO M. FERNANDEZ.
Yemen: St 11, New Extension, POB 1010, Khartoum; tel. (183) 743918; Ambassador ABDOULJALIL AZZOUZ.

Judicial System

Until September 1983 the judicial system was divided into two sections, civil and Islamic, the latter dealing only with personal and family matters. In September 1983 President Nimeri replaced all existing laws with Islamic (*Shari'a*) law. Following the coup in April 1985, the *Shari'a* courts were abolished, and it was announced that the previous system of criminal courts was to be revived. In June 1986 the Prime Minister, Sadiq al-Mahdi, reaffirmed that the *Shari'a* law was to be abolished. It was announced in June 1987 that a new legal code, based on a 'Sudanese legal heritage', was to be introduced. In July 1989 the military Government established special courts to investigate violations of emergency laws concerning corruption. It was announced in June 1991 that these courts were to be incorporated in the general court administration. Islamic law was reintroduced in March 1991, but was not applied in the southern states of Equatoria, Bahr al-Ghazal and Upper Nile.

Chief Justice: GALAL ED-DIN MUHAMMAD OSMAN.

Religion

The majority of the northern Sudanese population are Muslims, while in the south the population are principally Christians or animists.

ISLAM

Islam is the state religion. Sudanese Islam has a strong Sufi element, and is estimated to have more than 15m. adherents.

CHRISTIANITY

Sudan Council of Churches: Inter-Church House, St 35, New Extension, POB 469, Khartoum; tel. (183) 742859; f. 1967; 12 mem. churches; Chair. Most Rev. PAOLINO LUKUDU LORO (Roman Catholic Archbishop of Juba); Gen. Sec. Rev. CLEMENT H. JANDA.

Roman Catholic Church

Latin Rite

Sudan comprises two archdioceses and seven dioceses. At 31 December 2005 there were an estimated 4,886,496 adherents, representing about 10.6% of the total population.

Sudan Catholic Bishops' Conference

General Secretariat, POB 6011, Khartoum; tel. (183) 225075. f. 1971; Pres. Most Rev. PAOLINO LUKUDU LORO (Archbishop of Juba); Sec.-Gen. JOHN DINGI MARTIN.

Archbishop of Juba: Most Rev. PAOLINO LUKUDU LORO, Catholic Church, POB 32, Juba, Equatoria State; tel. 820303; fax 820755; e-mail archbishopofjuba@hotmail.com.

Archbishop of Khartoum: Cardinal GABRIEL ZUBEIR WAKO, Catholic Church, POB 49, Khartoum; tel. (183) 782174; fax (183) 783518; e-mail ayuong@yahoo.com.

Maronite Rite

Maronite Church in Sudan: POB 244, Khartoum; Rev. Fr YOUSEPH NEAMA.

Melkite Rite

Patriarchal Vicariate of Egypt and Sudan: Greek Melkite Catholic Patriarchate, 16 Sharia Daher, 11271 Cairo, Egypt; tel. (2) 5905790; fax (2) 5935398; e-mail grecmelkitecath_egy@hotmail.com; General Patriarchal Vicar in Egypt and Sudan Mgr (JOSEPH) JULES ZEREY (Titular Archbishop of Damietta); Patriarchal Vicar in Sudan Mgr Exarkhos GEORGE BANNA; POB 766, Khartoum; tel. (183) 777910.

Syrian Rite

Syrian Church in Sudan: Under the jurisdiction of the Patriarch of Antioch; Protosyncellus Rt Rev. JOSEPH-CLÉMENT HANNOUCHE (Bishop of Cairo).

Orthodox Churches

Coptic Orthodox Church

Metropolitan of Khartoum, Southern Sudan and Uganda: Rt Rev. ANBA DANIAL, POB 4, Khartoum; tel. (183) 770646; fax (183) 785646; e-mail metaous@email-sudan.net.

Bishop of Atbara, Omdurman and Northern Sudan: Rt Rev. ANBA SARABAMON, POB 628, Omdurman; tel. (183) 550423; fax (183) 556973.

Greek Orthodox Church

Metropolitan of Nubia: POB 47, Khartoum; tel. (183) 772973; Archbishop DIONYSSIOS HADZIVASSILIOU.

The Ethiopian Orthodox Church is also active.

The Anglican Communion

Anglicans are adherents of the (Episcopal) Church of the Province of the Sudan. The Province, with 24 dioceses and about 1m. adherents, was established in 1976.

Archbishop in Sudan: Most Rev. JOSEPH BIRINGI HASSAN MARONA, POB 110, Juba; tel. (183) 20065.

Other Christian Churches

Evangelical Church: POB 57, Khartoum; c. 1,500 mems; administers schools, literature centre and training centre; Chair. Rev. RADI ELIAS.

Presbyterian Church: POB 40, Malakal; autonomous since 1956; 67,000 mems (1985); Gen. Sec. Rev. THOMAS MALUIT.

The Africa Inland Church, the Sudan Interior Church and the Sudanese Church of Christ are also active.

The Press

DAILIES

Press censorship was imposed following the 1989 coup.

Abbar al-Youm: Khartoum; tel. (183) 779396; daily; Editor AHMED AL-BALAL AT-TAYEB.

Al-Anbaa: Khartoum; tel. (183) 466523; f. 1998; Editor-in-Chief NAJIB ADAM QAMAR AD-DIN.

Al-Wan: Khartoum; tel. (183) 775036; e-mail alwaan@cybergates .net; daily; independent; pro-Govt; Editor HOUSSEN KHOGALI.

An-Nasr: Khartoum; tel. (183) 772494; Editor Col YOUNIS MAHMOUD.

Ar-Rai al-Akhar: Khartoum; tel. (183) 777934; daily; Editor MOHI AD-DIN TITTAWI.

Ar-Rai al-Amm: Khartoum; tel. (183) 778182; fax (183) 772176; e-mail info@rayaam.net; internet www.rayaam.net; daily; Editor SALAH MUHAMMAD IBRAHIM.

Khartoum Monitor: St 61, New Extension, Khartoum; e-mail Khartoummonitor@hotmail.com; Chair. and Editor ALFRED TABAN; Man. Editor WILLIAM EZEKIEL.

Sudan Mirror: POB 59163, 00200 Nairobi, Kenya; tel. and fax (20) 3876439; e-mail info@sdt.co.ke; e-mail daneiffe@gmail.com; internet www.sudanmirror.com; f. 2003; Dir DANIEL EIFFE.

Sudan Standard: Ministry of Information and Communication, Khartoum; daily; English.

PERIODICALS

Al-Guwwat al-Musallaha (The Armed Forces): Khartoum; f. 1969; publs a weekly newspaper and monthly magazine for the armed forces; Editor-in-Chief Maj. MAHMOUD GALANDER; circ. 7,500.

New Horizon: POB 2651, Khartoum; tel. (183) 777913; f. 1976; publ. by the Sudan House for Printing and Publishing; weekly; English; political and economic affairs, devt, home and international news; Editor AS-SIR HASSAN FADL; circ. 7,000.

Sudanow: POB 2651, Khartoum; tel. (183) 777913; f. 1976; publ. by the Sudan House for Printing and Publishing; monthly; English; political and economic affairs, arts, social affairs and diversions; Editor-in-Chief AHMED KAMAL ED-DIN; circ. 10,000.

NEWS AGENCIES

Sudan News Agency (SUNA): Sharia al-Gamhouria, POB 1506, Khartoum; tel. (183) 775770; e-mail suna@sudanet.net; internet www.suna-sd.net; Dir-Gen. ALI ABD AR-RAHMAN AN-NUMAYRI.

Sudanese Press Agency: Khartoum; f. 1985; owned by journalists.

Publishers

Ahmad Abd ar-Rahman at-Tikeine: POB 299, Port Sudan.

Al-Ayyam Press Co Ltd: Aboulela Bldg, POB 363, United Nations Sq., Khartoum; f. 1953; general fiction and non-fiction, arts, poetry, reference, newspapers, magazines; Man. Dir BESHIR MUHAMMAD SAID.

As-Sahafa Publishing and Printing House: POB 1228, Khartoum; f. 1961; newspapers, pamphlets, fiction and govt publs.

As-Salam Co Ltd: POB 944, Khartoum.

Claudios S. Fellas: POB 641, Khartoum.

Khartoum University Press: POB 321, Khartoum; tel. (183) 776653; f. 1964; academic, general and educational in Arabic and English; Man. Dir ALI EL-MAK.

GOVERNMENT PUBLISHING HOUSE

El-Asma Printing Press: POB 38, Khartoum.

Broadcasting and Communications

TELECOMMUNICATIONS

A mobile cellular telephone network for Khartoum State was inaugurated in 1997.

Ministry of Information and Communication: Khartoum; regulatory body; Sec.-Gen. Eng. AWAD E. WIDAA.

MTN-Sudan: 264 Garden City, POB 34611111, Khartoum; tel. (92) 1111111; internet www.mtn.sd; f. 2005; mobile cellular telephone provider; CEO IMAD KREIDIEH; 1.4m. subscribers (2007).

Posts and Telegraphs Public Corpn: Khartoum; tel. (183) 770000; fax (183) 772888; e-mail sudanpost@maktoob.com; regulatory body; Dir-Gen. AHMAD AT-TIJANI ALALLIM.

Sudan Telecom Co (SUDATEL): Sudatel Tower, POB 11155, Khartoum; tel. (183) 797400; fax (183) 782322; e-mail info@sudatel.net; internet www.sudatel.net; f. 1993; service provider for Sudan; Chair. Dr AHMAD MAGZOUB; Gen. Man. EMAD ALDIN HUSSAIN AHMAD.

BROADCASTING

Radio

Sudan Radio: POB 572, Omdurman; tel. (187) 559315; fax (187) 560566; e-mail info@sudanradio.info; internet www.sudanradio.info; f. 1940; state-controlled service broadcasting daily in Arabic, English, French and Swahili; Dir-Gen. MUTASIM FADUL USUD.

Voice of Sudan: active since 1995; run by the National Democratic Alliance; Arabic and English.

Television

An earth satellite station operated on 36 channels at Umm Haraz has much improved Sudan's telecommunications links. A nation-wide satellite network is being established with 14 earth stations in the provinces. There are regional stations at Geziera (Central Region) and Atbara (Northern Region).

Sudan Television: POB 1094, Omdurman; tel. (15) 550022; internet www.sudantv.net; f. 1962; state-controlled; 60 hours of programmes per week; Head of Directorate HADID AS-SIRA.

Finance

(cap. = capital; res = reserves; dep. = deposits; m. = million; brs = branches; amounts in Sudanese dinars, unless otherwise indicated)

BANKING

All domestic banks are controlled by the Bank of Sudan. Foreign banks were permitted to resume operations in 1976. In December 1985 the Government banned the establishment of any further banks. It was announced in December 1990 that Sudan's banking system was to be reorganized to accord with Islamic principles. In 2000 there were a total of 25 banks in Sudan. In May 2000 the Bank of Sudan issued new policy guidelines under which Sudan's banks were to merge into six banking groups to improve their financial strength and international competitiveness; the mergers were to be implemented during the period 2007–09.

Central Bank

Bank of Sudan: Gamaa Ave, POB 313, Khartoum; tel. (187) 056000; fax (183) 780273; e-mail sudanbank@sudanmail.net; internet www.bankofsudan.org; f. 1960; bank of issue; cap. 1,200.0m., res 7,474.9m., dep. 772,433.7m. (Dec. 2004); Gov. Dr SABIR MUHAMMAD HASSAN; 9 brs.

Commercial Banks

Al-Baraka Bank: Al-Baraka Tower, Zubeir Pasha St, POB 3583, Khartoum; tel. (183) 783927; fax (183) 778948; internet www.albarakasudan.com; f. 1984; 87.8% owned by Al-Baraka Banking Group (Bahrain); investment and export promotion; cap. 1,365.5m., res 3,748.7m., dep. 23,286.0m. (Dec. 2004); Chair. OSMAN AHMED SULIMAN; Gen. Man. ABDALLAH KHAIRY HAMID; 24 brs.

Ash-Shamal Islamic Bank: Ash-Shamal Islamic Tower, as-Sayid Abd ar-Rahman St, POB 10036, 11111 Khartoum; tel. (183) 779078; fax (183) 772661; e-mail info@alshamalbank.com; internet www.alshamalbank.com; f. 1990; total assets 18,258.0m. (Dec. 2003); Pres. GAFAAR OSMAN FAGIR; Gen. Man. ABDELMONEIM HASSAN SAYED (acting); 17 brs.

Bank of Khartoum Group: Intersection Gamhouria St and El-Gaser St, POB 1008, Khartoum; tel. (183) 772800; fax (183) 781120; e-mail admin@bankofkhartoum.net; internet www.bankofkhartoum.net; f. 1913; 55% owned by Dubai Islamic Bank PLC; absorbed National Export/Import Bank and Unity Bank in 1993; cap. 11,800m., res 450.1m., dep. 48,600m. (Dec. 2003); Chair. OSMAN ALHADI IBRAHIM; Gen. Man. MUHAMMAD SALAH ELDIN; 118 brs.

Blue Nile Mashreg Bank: Parliament St, POB 984, Khartoum; tel. (183) 784690; fax (183) 782562; e-mail info@bluemashreg.com; internet www.bluemashreg.com; cap. 1,531.8m., res 277.7m., dep. 13,076.4m. (Dec. 2004); Chair. MUHAMMAD ISMAIL MUHAMMAD; Gen. Man. ABDEL KHALIG ALSAMANI ABDEL RAZIG.

Farmers Commercial Bank: POB 11984, Al-Qasr Ave, Khartoum; tel. (183) 774960; fax (183) 773687; f. 1960 as Sudan Commercial Bank; name changed as above in 1999 following merger with Farmers Bank for Investment and Rural Development; cap. 3,001.0m., res 1,162.0m., dep. 19,466.9m. (Dec. 2004); Chair. ET-TAYB ELOBEID BADR; Gen. Man. SULIMAN HASHIM MUHAMMAD; 28 brs.

National Bank of Sudan: Kronfli Bldg, Zubeir Pasha St, POB 1183, Khartoum; tel. (183) 778153; fax (183) 779545; f. 1982; 70% owned by Bank Audi SAL, Lebanon; cap. 593.0m., res 313.6m., dep. 8,384.0m. (Dec. 2001); Chair. HASSAN IBRAHIM MALIK; Gen. Man. MUHAMMAD KHEIR ISMAIL; 13 brs in Sudan, 2 abroad.

Omdurman National Bank: Al-Qaser Ave, POB 11522, Khartoum; tel. (183) 770400; fax (183) 777219; e-mail info@omd-bank.com; internet www.omd-bank.com; f. 1993; cap. 6,096.3m., res 8,362.2m., dep. 342,391.2m. (Dec. 2005); Gen. Man. ABDEL RAHMAN HASSAN ABDEL RAHMAN; 19 brs; 890 employees.

Sudanese French Bank: Plot No. 6, Block A, Al-Qasr Ave, POB 2775, Khartoum; tel. (183) 771730; fax (183) 771740; e-mail sfbankb@sudanet.net; f. 1978 as Sudanese Investment Bank; name changed as above in 1993; cap. 5,067.3m., res 1,671.1m., dep. 48,598.9m. (Dec. 2006); Chair. Dr EZZELDEIN EBRAHIM; Gen. Man. MASSAD MOHAMMED AHMED; 11 brs.

Tadamon Islamic Bank: Baladia St, POB 3154, Khartoum; tel. (183) 771505; fax (183) 773840; e-mail info@tadamonbank-sd.com; internet www.tadamonbank-sd.com; f. 1981; cap. 6,775.5m., res 1,363.9m., dep. 66,768.0m. (Dec. 2006); Chair. Dr HASSAN OSMAN SAKOTA; Gen. Man. ABDALLAH NOGD ALLAH AHMAIDI; 18 brs.

Foreign Banks

Byblos Bank Africa Ltd: 21 Al-Amarat St, POB 8121, Khartoum; tel. (183) 566444; fax (183) 566454; internet www.byblosbank.com.lb; f. 2003; cap. 6,375m., res 207m., dep. 13,408m.; Chair. Dr FRANÇOIS S. BASSIL; Gen. Man. NADIM GHANTOUS.

Faisal Islamic Bank (Sudan) (Saudi Arabia): Faiha Bldg, Ali al-Latif St, POB 2415, Khartoum; tel. (183) 777920; fax (183) 780193; e-mail fibsudan@fibsudan.com; internet www.fibsudan.com; f. 1977; cap. 3,000.0m., res 834.4m., dep. 24,677.2m. (Dec. 2004); Chair. Prince MUHAMMAD AL-FAISAL AS-SAUD; Gen. Man. ALI OMAR IBRAHIM FARAH; 28 brs.

Habib Bank (Pakistan): Al-Qasr St, POB 8246, Khartoum; tel. (183) 782820; fax (183) 781497; internet www.habibbankltd.com; f. 1982; cap. and res 13.8m. Sudanese pounds, total assets 27.3m. (Dec. 1987); Gen. Man. BAZ MUHAMMAD KHAN.

National Bank of Abu Dhabi (United Arab Emirates): Taka Bldg, Atbara St, POB 2465, Khartoum; tel. (183) 787203; fax (183) 774892; e-mail nbadkh@sudanmail.net; internet www.nbad.com; f. 1976; cap. and res 16.9m. Sudanese pounds, total assets 12.5m. (Dec. 1987); Man. GAAFER OSMAN MUHAMMAD.

Saudi Sudanese Bank: Baladia St, POB 1773, Khartoum; tel. (183) 776700; fax (183) 781836; e-mail saudi-sud@saudisb.com; internet www.saudisb.com; f. 1986; Saudi Arabian shareholders have a 57.3% interest, Sudanese shareholders 42.7%; cap. 422.6m., res 2,630.5m., dep. 26,072.2m. (Dec. 2004); Chair. ABDEL GALIL EL-WASIA; Gen. Man. MUDATHIR ALI AL-BASHIR (acting); 13 brs.

Development Banks

Agricultural Bank of Sudan: Ghoumhoria Ave, POB 1263, Khartoum; tel. (183) 777432; fax (183) 778296; e-mail agribank@yahoo.com; f. 1957; cap. 5,200.0m., res 3,609.4m., dep. 18,864.9m. (Dec. 2003); provides finance for agricultural projects; Pres. As-Sayid Gaffar Muhammad al-Hassan; Gen. Man. As-Sayid al-Kindi Muhammad Osman; 40 brs.

Islamic Co-operative Development Bank (ICDB): Et-Tanmha Tower, Kolyat Eltib St, POB 62, Khartoum; tel. (183) 780223; fax (183) 777715; f. 1983; cap. and res 3,821.0m., total assets 28,250.4m. (Dec. 2003); Chair. El-Haj Atta el-Manan Idris; 6 brs.

El-Nilein Industrial Development Bank: United Nations Sq., POB 1722, Khartoum; tel. (183) 771117; fax (183) 771984; internet www.nidbg.com; f. 1993 by merger of El-Nilein Bank and Industrial Bank of Sudan; partially privatized in 2006; 40% govt-owned, 60% owned by Dubai-based Amlak Finance; provides tech. and financial assistance for private-sector industrial projects and acquires shares in industrial enterprises; cap. 3,096.9m., res 779.6m., dep. 33,713.8m. (Dec. 2003); Chair. Dr Sabir Muhammad el-Hassan; Man. Dir Wagie Alla El Naw; 43 brs.

NIMA Development and Investment Bank: Hashim Hago Bldg, As-Suk al-Arabi, POB 665, Khartoum; tel. (183) 779496; fax (183) 781854; f. 1982 as National Devt Bank; name changed as above 1998; 90%-owned by NIMA Groupe, 10% private shareholders; finances or co-finances economic and social devt projects; cap. 4,000m. Sudanese pounds, res 106m. (Dec. 1998); Dir-Gen. Salim el-Safi Hugir; 6 brs.

Sudanese Estates Bank: Baladia St, POB 309, Khartoum; tel. (183) 777917; fax (183) 779465; f. 1967; mortgage bank financing private-sector urban housing devt; cap. and res 1,700m. Sudanese pounds, total assets 9,500m. (Dec. 1994); Chair. Eng. Muhammad Ali el-Amin; 6 brs.

STOCK EXCHANGE

Sudanese Stock Exchange: Al-Baraka Tower, 5th Floor, POB 10835, Khartoum; tel. (183) 776235; fax (183) 776134; f. 1995; Chair. Hamza Muhammad Jenawi; 27 mems.

INSURANCE

African Insurance Co (Sudan) Ltd: New Abu Ella Bldg, Parliament Ave, Khartoum; tel. (183) 173402; fax (183) 177988; f. 1977; fire, accident, marine and motor; Gen. Man. An-Noman as-Sanusi.

Blue Nile Insurance Co (Sudan) Ltd: Al-Qasr Ave, Blue Nile Insurance Bldg, POB 2215, Khartoum; tel. (183) 170580; fax (183) 172405; internet www.blue-nile-insurance.com; f. 1965; Gen. Man. Muhammad al-Amin Mirghani.

Foja International Insurance Co Ltd: POB 879, Khartoum; tel. (183) 784470; fax (183) 783248; fire, accident, marine, motor and animal; Gen. Man. Mamoon Ibrahim Abd Alla.

General Insurance Co (Sudan) Ltd: El-Mek Nimr St, POB 1555, Khartoum; tel. (183) 780616; fax (183) 772122; f. 1961; Gen. Man. Elsamawl Elsayed Hafiz.

Islamic Insurance Co Ltd: Al-Faiha Commercial Bldg, Ali Abdullatif St, POB 2776, Khartoum; tel. (183) 772656; f. 1979; all classes; CEO Dr Othman Abdul Wahab.

Khartoum Insurance Co Ltd: Al-Taminat Bldg, Al-Jamhouriya St, POB 737, Khartoum; tel. (183) 778647; f. 1953; Chair. Mudawi M. Ahmad; Gen. Dir Yousif Khairy.

Juba Insurance Co Ltd: Al-Baladiya St, Sayen Osnam Al-Amin Bldg, 2nd Floor, POB 10043, Khartoum; tel. (183) 783245; fax (183) 781617; Gen. Man. Abdul Aal Eldawi Abdul Aal.

Middle East Insurance Co Ltd: Al-Qasr St, Kuronfuli Bldg, 1st Floor, POB 3070, Khartoum; tel. (183) 772202; fax (183) 779266; f. 1981; fire, marine, motor and general liability; Chair. Ahmad I. Malik; Gen. Dir Ali Muhammad Ahmed el-Fadl.

Sudanese Insurance and Reinsurance Co Ltd: Al-Gamhouria St, Nasr Sq., Middle Station Makati Bldg, 3rd Floor, POB 2332, Khartoum; tel. (183) 770812; f. 1967; CEO Hassan es-Sayed Muhammad Ali.

United Insurance Co (Sudan) Ltd: Makkawi Bldg, Al-Gamhouria St, POB 318, Khartoum; tel. (183) 776630; fax (183) 770783; e-mail abdin@unitedinsurance.ws; internet www.unitedinsurance.ws; f. 1968; Chair. Hashim el-Berier; Dir-Gen. Muhammad Abdeen Babiker.

Trade and Industry

GOVERNMENT AGENCIES

Agricultural Research Corpn: POB 126, Wadi Medani; tel. (5118) 42226; fax (5118) 43213; e-mail arcdg@sudanmail.net; f. 1967; Dir-Gen. Prof. Azhari Hamada.

Animal Production Public Corpn: POB 624, Khartoum; tel. (183) 778555; Gen. Man. Dr Fouad Ramadan Hamid.

General Petroleum Corpn: POB 2649, Khartoum; tel. (183) 777554; fax (183) 773663; e-mail secretarygeneral@spc.sd; f. 1976; Chair. Dr Awad Ahmed Al Jazz; Sec.-Gen. Dr AOmer Mohamed Kheir.

Gum Arabic Co Ltd: POB 857, Khartoum; tel. (183) 461061; fax (183) 471336; e-mail info@gum-arab.com; internet www.gum-arab.com; f. 1969; Chair. Abd el-Hamid Musa Kasha; Gen. Man. Hassan Saad Ahmed.

Industrial Production Corpn: POB 1034, Khartoum; tel. (183) 771278; f. 1976; Dir-Gen. Osman Tammam.

  Cement and Building Materials Sector Co-ordination Office: POB 2241, Khartoum; tel. (183) 774269; Dir T. M. Khogali.

  Food Industries Corpn: POB 2341, Khartoum; tel. (183) 775463; Dir Muhammad al-Ghali Suliman.

  Leather Industries Corpn: POB 1639, Khartoum; tel. (183) 778187; f. 1986; Man. Dir Ibrahim Salih Ali.

  Oil Corpn: POB 64, Khartoum North; tel. (183) 332044; Gen. Man. Bukhari Mahmoud Bukhari.

  Spinning and Weaving General Co Ltd: POB 765, Khartoum; tel. (183) 774306; f. 1975; Dir Muhammad Salih Muhammad Abdallah.

  Sudan Tea Co Ltd: POB 1219, Khartoum; tel. (183) 781261.

  Sudanese Mining Corpn: POB 1034, Khartoum; tel. (183) 770840; f. 1975; Dir Ibrahim Mudawi Babiker.

  Sugar and Distilling Industry Corpn: POB 511, Khartoum; tel. (183) 778417; Man. Mirghani Ahmad Babiker.

Mechanized Farming Corpn: POB 2482, Khartoum; Man. Dir Awad al-Karim al-Yass.

National Cotton and Trade Co Ltd: POB 1552, Khartoum; tel. (183) 80040; f. 1970; Chair. Abd el-Ati A. Mekki; Man. Dir Abd ar-Rahman A. Moniem; Gen. Man. Zubair Muhammad al-Bashir.

Port Sudan Cotton Trade Co Ltd: POB 590, Port Sudan; POB 590, Khartoum; Gen. Man. Saïd Muhammad Adam.

Public Agricultural Production Corpn: POB 538, Khartoum; Chair. and Man. Dir Abdallah Bayoumo; Sec. Saad ad-Din Muhammad Ali.

Public Corpn for Building and Construction: POB 2110, Khartoum; tel. (183) 774544; Dir Naim ad-Din.

Public Corpn for Irrigation and Excavation: POB 619, Khartoum; tel. (183) 780167; Gen. Sec. Osman an-Nur.

Public Corpn for Oil Products and Pipelines: POB 1704, Khartoum; tel. (183) 778290; Gen. Man. Abd ar-Rahman Suliman.

Rahad Corpn: POB 2523, Khartoum; tel. (183) 775175; financed by the World Bank, Kuwait and the USA; Man. Dir Hassan Saad Abdalla.

State Trading Corpn: POB 211, Khartoum; tel. (183) 778555; Chair. E. R. M. Tom.

  Automobile Corpn: POB 221, Khartoum; tel. (183) 778555; importer of vehicles and spare parts; Gen. Man. Dafalla Ahmad Siddiq.

  Captrade Engineering and Automobile Services Co Ltd: POB 97, Khartoum; tel. (183) 789265; fax (183) 775544; e-mail cap1@sudanmail.net; f. 1925; importers and distributors of engineering and automobile equipment; Gen. Man. Essam Mohd el-Hassan Kambal.

  Gezira Trade and Services Co: POB 17, Port Sudan; tel. (311) 825109; fax (311) 822029; e-mail gtsportsudan@hotmail.com; f. 1980; importer of agricultural machinery, spare parts, electrical and office equipment, foodstuffs, clothes and footwear; exporter of oilseeds, grains, hides and skins and livestock; provides shipping insurance and warehousing services; agents for Lloyds and P and I Club; Chair. Nasr ed-Din M. Omer.

  Khartoum Commercial and Shipping Co: POB 221, Khartoum; tel. (183) 778555; f. 1982; import, export and shipping services, insurance and manufacturing; Gen. Man. Idris M. Salih.

  Silos and Storage Corpn: POB 1183, Khartoum; stores and handles agricultural products; Gen. Man. Ahmad at-Taieb Harhoof.

Sudan Cotton Co Ltd: POB 1672, Khartoum; tel. (183) 771567; fax (183) 770703; e-mail sccl@sudanmail.net.sd; internet www.sudancottonco.com; f. 1970; exports and markets cotton; Chair. Abbas Abd al-Bagi Hammad; Dir-Gen. Dr Abdin Muhammad Ali.

Sudan Gezira Board: POB 884, HQ Barakat Wadi Medani, Gezira Province; tel. 2412; Sales Office, POB 884, Khartoum; tel. (183) 740145; f. 1950; responsible for Sudan's main cotton-producing area; the Gezira scheme is a partnership between the Govt, the tenants and the board. The Govt provides the land and is responsible for irrigation. Tenants pay a land and water charge and receive the work

SUDAN

Directory

proceeds. The Board provides agricultural services at cost, technical supervision and execution of govt agricultural policies relating to the scheme. Tenants pay a percentage of their proceeds to the Social Development Fund. The total potential cultivable area of the Gezira scheme is c. 850,000 ha and the total area under systematic irrigation is c. 730,000 ha. In addition to cotton, groundnuts, sorghum, wheat, rice, pulses and vegetables are grown for the benefit of tenant farmers; Man. Dir Prof. FATHI MUHAMMAD KHALIFA.

Sudan Oilseeds Co Ltd: Parliament Ave, POB 167, Khartoum; tel. (183) 780120; f. 1974; 58% state-owned; exporter of oilseeds (groundnuts, sesame seeds and castor beans); importer of foodstuffs and other goods; Chair. SADIQ KARAR AT-TAYEB; Gen. Man. KAMAL ABD AL-HALIM.

DEVELOPMENT CORPORATIONS

Sudan Development Corpn (SDC): 21 al-Amarat, POB 710, Khartoum; tel. (183) 472151; fax (183) 472148; f. 1974 to promote and co-finance devt projects with special emphasis on projects in the agricultural, agri-business, and industrial sectors; cap. p.u. US $200m.; Man. Dir ABDEL WAHAB AHMED HAMZA.

Sudan Rural Development Co Ltd (SRDC): POB 2190, Khartoum; tel. (183) 773855; fax (183) 773235; e-mail srdfc@hotmail.com; f. 1980; SDC has 27% shareholding; cap. p.u. US $20m.; Gen. Man. EL-AWAD ABDALLA H. HIJAZI (designate).

Sudan Rural Development Finance Co (SRDFC): POB 2190, Khartoum; tel. (183) 773855; fax (183) 773235; f. 1980; Gen. Man. OMRAN MUHAMMAD ALI.

CHAMBER OF COMMERCE

Union of Sudanese Chambers of Commerce: POB 81, Khartoum; tel. (183) 772346; fax (183) 780748; e-mail chamber@sudanchamber.org; internet www.sudanchamber.org; f. 1908; Pres. ELTAYEB AHMED OSMAN; Sec.-Gen. IBRAHIM MUHAMMAD OSMAN.

INDUSTRIAL ASSOCIATION

Sudanese Industries Association: Africa St, POB 2565, Khartoum; tel. (183) 773151; f. 1974; Chair. FATH AR-RAHMAN AL-BASHIR; Exec. Dir A. IZZ AL-ARAB YOUSUF.

UTILITIES

Public Electricity and Water Corpn: POB 1380, Khartoum; tel. (183) 81021; Dir Dr YASIN AL-HAJ ABDIN.

CO-OPERATIVE SOCIETIES

There are about 600 co-operative societies, of which 570 are officially registered.

Central Co-operative Union: POB 2492, Khartoum; tel. (183) 780624; largest co-operative union operating in 15 provinces.

TRADE UNIONS

All trade union activity was banned following the 1989 coup. The following organizations were active prior to that date.

Federations

Sudan Workers Trade Unions Federation (SWTUF): POB 2258, Khartoum; tel. (183) 777463; includes 42 trade unions representing c. 1.75m. public service and private sector workers; affiliated to the Int. Confed. of Arab Trade Unions and the Org. of African Trade Union Unity; Pres. MUHAMMAD OSMAN GAMA; Gen. Sec. YOUSUF ABU SHAMA HAMED.

Sudanese Federation of Employees and Professionals Trade Unions: POB 2398, Khartoum; tel. (183) 773818; f. 1975; includes 54 trade unions representing 250,000 mems; Pres. IBRAHIM AWADALLAH; Sec.-Gen. KAMAL AD-DIN MUHAMMAD ABDALLAH.

Transport

RAILWAYS

The total length of railway in operation in 2002 was 5,978 route-km. The main line runs from Wadi Halfa, on the Egyptian border, to al-Obeid, via Khartoum. Lines from Atbara and Sinnar connect with Port Sudan. There are lines from Sinnar to Damazin on the Blue Nile (227 km) and from Aradeiba to Nyala in the south-western province of Darfur (689 km), with a 445-km branch line from Babanousa to Wau in Bahr al-Ghazal province. In 2001 plans were announced for the construction of a rail link between Port Sudan and Moyale, Ethiopia.

Sudan Railways Corpn (SRC): POB 65, Atbara; tel. 2000; f. 1875; Gen. Man. OMAR MUHAMMAD NUR.

ROADS

Roads in northern Sudan, other than town roads, are only cleared tracks and often impassable immediately after rain. Motor traffic on roads in the former Upper Nile province is limited to the drier months of January–May. There are several good gravelled roads in Equatoria and Bahr al-Ghazal provinces which are passable all the year, but in these districts some of the minor roads become impassable after rain.

Over 48,000 km of tracks are classed as 'motorable'; there were 3,160 km of main roads and 739 km of secondary roads in 1985. A 1,190-km tarmac road linking the capital with Port Sudan was completed during 1980. In 1996, according to World Bank estimates, some 36.3% of Sudan's roads were paved. By 1997 a 270-km road linking Jaili with Atbara had been completed, as part of a scheme to provide an alternative route from Khartoum to the coast. A 484-km highway linking Khartoum, Haiya and Port Sudan was scheduled for completion in 2006.

National Transport Corpn: POB 723, Khartoum; Gen. Man. MOHI AD-DIN HASSAN MUHAMMAD NUR.

Public Corpn for Roads and Bridges: POB 756, Khartoum; tel. (183) 770794; f. 1976; Chair. ABD AR-RAHMAN HABOUD; Dir-Gen. ABDOU MUHAMMAD ABDOU.

INLAND WATERWAYS

The total length of navigable waterways served by passenger and freight services is 4,068 km, of which approximately 1,723 km is open all year. From the Egyptian border to Wadi Halfa and Khartoum navigation is limited by cataracts to short stretches, but the White Nile from Khartoum to Juba is almost always navigable.

River Transport Corpn (RTC): POB 284, Khartoum North; operates 2,500 route-km of steamers on the Nile; Chair. ALI AMIR TAHA.

River Navigation Corpn: Khartoum; f. 1970; jtly owned by Govts of Egypt and Sudan; operates services between Aswan and Wadi Halfa.

SHIPPING

Port Sudan, on the Red Sea, 784 km from Khartoum, and Suakin are the only commercial seaports.

Axis Trading Co Ltd: POB 1574, Khartoum; tel. (183) 775875; f. 1967; Chair. HASSAN A. M. SULIMAN.

Red Sea Shipping Corpn: POB 308, Khartoum; tel. (183) 777688; fax (183) 774220; e-mail redseaco@sudan.net; Gen. Man. OSMAN AMIN.

Sea Ports Corpn: Port Sudan; f. 1906; Gen. Man. MUHAMMAD TAHIR AILA.

Sudan Shipping Line Ltd: POB 426, Port Sudan; tel. 2655; POB 1731, Khartoum; tel. (183) 780017; f. 1960; 10 vessels totalling 54,277 dwt operating between the Red Sea and western Mediterranean, northern Europe and United Kingdom; Chair. ISMAIL BAKHEIT; Gen. Man. SALAH AD-DIN OMER AL-AZIZ.

United African Shipping Co: POB 339, Khartoum; tel. (183) 780967; Gen. Man. MUHAMMAD TAHA AL-GINDI.

CIVIL AVIATION

In June 2005 the Government announced that preliminary construction work had been completed for a new international airport at a site 40 km south-west of Khartoum. Work to build runways and two passenger terminals was scheduled to begin in 2007. The airport was expected to open in 2010.

Civil Aviation Authority: Sharia Sayed Abd ar-Rahman, Khartoum; tel. (183) 772264; Dir-Gen. ABOU BAKR GAAFAR AHMAD.

Air West Express: POB 10217, Khartoum; tel. (183) 452503; fax (183) 451703; f. 1992; passenger and freight services to destinations in Africa; Chair. SAIF M. S. OMER.

Azza Transport: POB 11586, Mak Nimir St, Khartoum; tel. (183) 783761; fax (183) 770408; e-mail sawasawa@sudanet.net; f. 1993; charter and dedicated freight to Africa and the Middle East; Man. Dir Dr GIBRIL I. MOHAMED.

Sudan Airways Co Ltd: POB 253, Sudan Airways Complex, 161 Obeid Khatim St, Riadh Nlock No. 10, Khartoum; tel. (183) 243708; fax (183) 243722; e-mail captidris@sudanair.com; internet www.sudanair.com; f. 1947; internal flights and international services to Africa, the Middle East and Europe; Man. Dir Capt. ABDALLA M. IDRIS (acting).

Sudanese Aeronautical Services (SASCO): POB 8260, al-Amarat, Khartoum; tel. (183) 7463362; fax (183) 4433362; fmrly Sasco Air Charter; chartered services; Chair. M. M. Nur.

Trans Arabian Air Transport (TAAT): POB 1461, Africa St, Khartoum; tel. (183) 451568; fax (183) 451544; e-mail ftaats@sudanmail.net; f. 1983; dedicated freight; services to Africa, Europe and Middle East; Man. Dir Capt. El-Fati Abdin.

United Arabian Airlines: POB 3687, Office No. 3, Elekhwa Bldg, Atbara St, Khartoum; tel. (183) 773025; fax (183) 784402; e-mail krthq@uaa.com; f. 1995; charter and dedicated freight services to Africa and the Middle East; Man. Dir M. Kordofani.

Tourism

Although tourism in Sudan remains relatively undeveloped, the eastern Red Sea coast and Nile tributaries offer opportunities for water sports. Other attractions include ancient Egyptian remains and the Al-Dinder National Tourist Park, a game reserve established in 1935. In 1991 Sudan's first Marine National Park opened on Sanganeb atoll. A total of 60,577 tourists visited Sudan in 2004.

Public Corpn of Tourism and Hotels: POB 7104, Khartoum; tel. (183) 781764; f. 1977; Dir-Gen. Maj.-Gen. El-Khatim Muhammad Fadl.

SURINAME

Introductory Survey

Location, Climate, Language, Religion, Flag, Capital

The Republic of Suriname lies on the north-east coast of South America. It is bordered by Guyana to the west, by French Guiana to the east, and by Brazil to the south. The climate is sub-tropical, with fairly heavy rainfall and average temperatures of between 21°C (70°F) and 30°C (86°F). Average annual rainfall varies from 3,720 mm (146 ins) in the north to 804 mm (32 ins) in the south. The official language is Dutch. The other main languages are Hindustani and Javanese. The majority of the people can speak the native language Sranang Tongo, a Creole language known as Negro English or taki-taki, while Chinese, English, French and Spanish are also used. The principal religions are Christianity (professed by about 48% of the population), Hinduism (24%) and Islam (16%). The national flag (proportions 2 by 3) has five horizontal stripes: a broad central band of red (with a five-pointed yellow star in the centre), edged with white, between bands of green. The capital is Paramaribo.

Recent History

Settlers from England landed in Suriname in the 1630s, and the territory was alternately a British and a Dutch colony until it was eventually awarded to the Netherlands by the Treaty of Vienna in 1815. The colony's economy depended on large sugar plantations, for which labour was provided by slaves of African origin. Following the abolition of slavery in 1863, immigration of labourers from India and the then Dutch East Indies was encouraged, and many of them settled permanently in Suriname. This history explains the country's current ethnic diversity: there are small communities of the original Amerindian population (mainly in the interior) and of ethnic Chinese and Europeans; a Creole population, largely of African descent, constitutes about one-third of the population, as do the Asian-descended 'East' Indians (known locally as Hindustanis); the Indonesian-descended 'Javanese' form about 15% of the population, and another Creole group, the 'boschnegers' or Bush Negroes, forms a further 10% (the Bush Negroes are the Dutch-speaking descendants of escaped slaves, long-established in the rainforest as a tribalized society of four clans). Under a Charter signed in December 1954, Suriname (also known as Dutch Guiana) became an equal partner in the Kingdom of the Netherlands, with the Netherlands Antilles and the Netherlands itself, and gained full autonomy in domestic affairs.

The Hindustani-dominated Government, in power since 1969 and led by Dr Jules Sedney, resigned in February 1973. General elections in November were won by an alliance of parties, the Nationale Partij Kambinatie (NPK), which favoured complete independence from the Netherlands, and in December Henck Arron, leader of the Nationale Partij Suriname (NPS—a predominantly Creole party), became Prime Minister. Suriname became independent on 25 November 1975. Dr Johan Ferrier, hitherto the Governor of Suriname, became the new republic's first President. Some 40,000 Surinamese emigrated to the Netherlands after independence, leaving Suriname with a severely underskilled work-force. Border disputes with French Guiana and Guyana also ensued. The general election of October 1977 resulted in a clear majority for the NPK, and Henck Arron continued as Prime Minister.

The Arron administration was overthrown in February 1980 by a group of soldiers, who formed a military council, the Nationale Militaire Raad (NMR). President Ferrier refused to agree to the retention of supreme power by the NMR, and in March he appointed a civilian administration led by Dr Henk Chin-A-Sen, a former leader of the Partij Nationalistische Republiek. In August the Army Chief of Staff, NMR member Sgt-Maj. (later Lt-Col) Désiré (Desi) Bouterse (subsequently Commander-in-Chief of the armed forces), led a coup. Ferrier was replaced by Chin-A-Sen; the legislature was dissolved, and a state of emergency declared. A Hindustani-inspired counter-coup, led by Sgt-Maj. Wilfred Hawker, failed in March 1981. In September the President announced details of a draft Constitution, which sought to limit the army to a supervisory role in government. The army responded with the formation of the Revolutionary People's Front, a comprehensive political alliance headed by Bouterse and two other members of the NMR, Maj. Roy Horb and Lt (later Commdr) Iwan Graanoogst, together with three leaders of workers' and students' organizations. In February 1982 the NMR, led by Bouterse, seized power from Chin-A-Sen and his civilian Government. The Vice-President of the Supreme Court, L. Fred Ramdat Misier, was appointed interim President. Hawker was executed after attempting a further coup in March. (Chin-A-Sen left for the Netherlands, where, in January 1983, he formed the Movement for the Liberation of Suriname, which aimed to remove Bouterse from power by peaceful means.)

A state of siege was declared, and martial law was imposed in December 1982. In order to prevent the Netherlands from suspending its aid, a 12-member Cabinet of Ministers with a civilian majority was appointed, and a moderate economist, Henry Neyhorst, became Prime Minister, although Bouterse remained effectively in control. Failure to effect promised social and economic changes lost Bouterse the support of left-wing groups and trade unions, which supported the business community in demanding a return to constitutional rule. In October the arrest of Cyriel Daal, the leader of Suriname's principal trade union (De Moederbond), prompted strikes and demonstrations. In order to avert a general strike, Bouterse agreed to arrange for the election of a constituent assembly to draft a new constitution by March 1983 (to be followed by the establishment of an elected government), but he later reneged on this commitment. In December 1982 members of the armed forces burned down several buildings used by the opposition. During the ensuing disturbances, 15 prominent citizens, including Daal, were killed, in what became known as the 'December Murders'. The Government resigned, the Netherlands and the USA halted all aid, and the country was placed under rule by decree; an interim, military-dominated Government was appointed. An attempted coup in January 1983, the sixth since February 1980, resulted in the dismissal of two-thirds of the officers of the armed forces and the death of Maj. Horb. In February 1983 Dr Errol Alibux, a former Minister of Social Affairs, was appointed Prime Minister. He formed a new Cabinet of Ministers, composed of members of two left-wing parties, the Progressieve Arbeiders en Landbouwers Unie (PALU) and the Revolutionaire Volkspartij. The new Government immediately ended the restrictions imposed in December 1982.

In January 1984, after a series of widely observed strikes in support of demands for the restoration of civilian rule and the organization of free elections, Bouterse dismissed the Cabinet of Ministers. Agreement was reached with the strike organizers, following the withdrawal of proposals to increase taxation rates. An interim Government, with Wim Udenhout, a former adviser to Bouterse, as Prime Minister, was created in February to formulate a timetable for the gradual restoration of constitutional rule. Nominees of the trade unions and business sector were also included in the new Government. Bouterse hoped to consolidate his position by securing a political base through Standvaste (the 25 February Movement), which he had founded in November 1983. In December 1984 plans for a nominated National Assembly (comprising representatives of Standvaste, the trade unions and the business community) were announced. The Netherlands Government, however, refused to consider the changes as a significant move towards democratic rule, deeming them insufficient to merit the resumption of aid. None the less, the National Assembly was inaugurated in January 1985. A new Cabinet of Ministers, based on the previous administration, was formed by Udenhout.

The tripartite administration collapsed in April 1985, after the withdrawal from the Cabinet of Ministers of three of the four trade union nominees. A reconstituted Cabinet, formed in June, contained new members with links to traditional political parties. In November the ban on political parties was revoked, and in the same month, former NPS Prime Minister Arron, together with Jaggernath Lachmon of the Hindustani-based Vooruitstrevende Hervormings Partij (VHP) and Willy Soemita of the Kaum-Tani Persuatan Indonesia (KTPI), accepted an invitation to join the NMR, renamed the Topberaad (Supreme Council). By

July 1986 only two military officers remained on the Topberaad. In that month Bouterse appointed a new Cabinet of Ministers, including representatives from industry, business, political parties, trade unions and Standvaste. Pretaap Radhakishun, a business executive and member of the VHP, was appointed Prime Minister. The Cabinet drafted a new Constitution, which was approved by a national referendum in September 1987.

From July 1986 anti-Government guerrillas began a series of attacks on military posts on the eastern border of the country. The guerrillas were led by Ronnie Brunswijk (a former presidential bodyguard). Mainly Bush Negroes, they claimed that government resettlement policies threatened the autonomy of their tribal society, as guaranteed by treaties, signed in 1760, with the former Dutch authorities. It was reported that financial support for the guerrillas (known as the Jungle Commando, or Surinamese Liberation Army—SLA) was being provided by Surinamese exiles in the Netherlands, in particular by members of the Movement for the Liberation of Suriname. By November most of the eastern district of Marowijne was under guerrilla control, and the rebels had also occupied the area near Zanderij (later renamed Johan Adolf Pengel) International Airport, south of Paramaribo. Rebel attacks on the mining town of Moengo forced the closure of the country's principal bauxite mines. The town was recaptured by the armed forces in December, but the mines remained closed. At the beginning of December a state of emergency was declared in eastern and southern Suriname, and a curfew was imposed. Reports that some 200 civilians had been massacred by government troops in the search for guerrillas led to protests by the Netherlands and US Governments.

In February 1987 five members of the Cabinet of Ministers, including Radhakishun, resigned. Jules Wijdenbosch, hitherto the Minister of Internal Affairs and a member of Standvaste, was appointed Prime Minister. The entire Cabinet resigned at the end of March 1987, and a new Cabinet, led by Wijdenbosch, was appointed by Bouterse in April.

In 1987, in preparation for the general election that was to be held in November, several political parties resumed their activities. Standvaste was reconstituted, under Wijdenbosch, as the Nationale Democratische Partij (NDP—National Democratic Party). Three major opposition parties, the NPS, the VHP and the KTPI (whose name was changed to the Kerukanan Tulodo Pranatan Ingil in October 1987), announced an electoral alliance, the Front voor Demokratie en Ontwikkeling (FDO—Front for Democracy and Development). Brunswijk's SLA observed a cease-fire for the duration of the voting.

The FDO won a decisive victory in elections to the 51-seat National Assembly held in November 1987. In January 1988 the National Assembly unanimously elected Ramsewak Shankar (a former Minister of Agriculture) as President of the Republic, and Henck Arron was elected Vice-President and thus (in accordance with the new Constitution) Prime Minister. In December 1987 Bouterse was appointed leader of a five-member Military Council, established under the new Constitution to 'guarantee a peaceful transition' to democracy. In July 1988 the Netherlands Government agreed to resume aid to Suriname, but under more restrictive conditions than hitherto. Aid was to be provided only on a project-by-project basis until the Suriname Government implemented the IMF's structural-adjustment programme, considered necessary to correct the economic crisis. However, relations remained tense, largely owing to the Dutch administration's mistrust of the intentions of the Surinamese army.

In July 1989 representatives of the Government and the SLA, meeting in French Guiana, signed an agreement at Kourou, which was ratified by the National Assembly in August. The main provisions of the Kourou Accord were: a general amnesty for those involved in the recent conflicts; the ending of the state of emergency; the incorporation of many members of the SLA into a special police unit for the interior of the country; and significant investment in the interior. The armed forces declared their opposition to the Accord, but took no direct action against continuing negotiations. However, at the end of August there was a further outbreak of guerrilla activity, in the west of the country, by an Amerindian group critical of some of the provisions of the Accord. The group, known as the Tucayana Amazonica, principally opposed the involvement of the SLA in the proposed police force for the interior; it also requested the restoration of the Bureau for Amerindian Affairs. Several of the group's demands were similar to those of the army command, and there were allegations that Tucayana were being armed and encouraged by the military, exploiting the traditional antipathy between the Amerindians and many of the Bush Negroes. In October, however, the Tucayana spokesmen were augmented by elected representatives of the Amerindian communities (the Commission of Eight) and the two groups met representatives of the National Assembly, who stated that the Government was prepared to supplement, but not rescind, the Kourou Accord.

Also in October 1989 Tucayana received the support of another new insurgent group, the Mandela Bush Negro Liberation Movement (BBM), which declared itself to be dissatisfied with the Kourou Accord. The BBM was formed by members of the most westerly (and, hitherto, least involved in the civil war) of the Bush Negro clans, the Matauriërs. In the same month, however, Brunswijk's SLA secured the support of another new insurgent group, the Union for Liberation and Democracy (UBD), which occupied the mining town of Moengo. Apparently composed of radical former members of the SLA, the UBD declared its support for the Accord.

On 22 December 1990 Bouterse resigned as Commander-in-Chief of the armed forces, after President Shankar failed to issue an official protest at the Netherlands' treatment of Bouterse, who was denied access to the country while in transit at Amsterdam's airport. Suspicions that Bouterse's resignation might portend a military coup were realized two days later, when the acting Commander-in-Chief of the armed forces, Graanoogst, seized power from the Government. The coup was immediately condemned by the Dutch Government, which suspended development aid to Suriname. Johan Kraag (honorary chairman of the NPS and a former Minister of Labour) was appointed provisional President on 29 December, and promptly invited Bouterse to resume command of the armed forces, thus substantiating speculation that Kraag was merely acting on behalf of Bouterse. A transitional Government (led by Jules Wijdenbosch) was sworn in on 7 January 1991, and it was announced that a general election would take place within 100 days, later extended to 150 days. In March Brunswijk and Bouterse (who had continued negotiations intermittently since 1989) signed a peace accord in the rebel stronghold of Drietabbetje. In April four rebel groups, the SLA, Tucayana, the BBM and Angula (or 'Defiance', led by Carlos Maassi), signed a further agreement with the Government, promising to respect the law and not to obstruct the conduct of free elections.

The elections, which were monitored by a delegation from the Organization of American States (OAS, see p. 360), were held in May 1991. The Nieuw Front (NF), an electoral alliance comprising the members of the former FDO and the Surinaamse Partij van de Arbeid, secured 30 seats in the National Assembly, while the NDP won 12. The remaining nine seats were won by a new coalition, Democratisch Alternatief 1991 (DA '91), mainly comprising former members of the FDO critical of the Government's failure to curb the political influence of the military. Despite the fact that it had not secured the two-thirds' majority in the Assembly necessary to elect automatically its presidential candidate, Runaldo R. Venetiaan, the NF refused to consider the possibility of any agreement involving the formation of a coalition government or the cession of ministerial posts or policy commitments to either the NDP or DA '91. When a series of meetings of the National Assembly in July failed to result in any one presidential candidate securing a majority, the Chairman of the Assembly, Jaggernath Lachman, in accordance with provisions incorporated in the Constitution, convened the Vereinigde Volksvergadering (United People's Assembly), a body comprising the members of the National Assembly and representatives of the municipal and district councils, in order to elect a President. On 7 September Venetiaan was elected with an overwhelming 79% of the votes. One of Venetiaan's first acts as President was to announce, in October, the reduction of the armed forces by two-thirds and a reduction in the defence budget of 50%. These measures were introduced as part of a government programme of 'socialization' of the armed forces. In addition, amendments to the Constitution, approved in March 1992, included measures to curb the political influence of the military, removing all its constitutional duties except those of national defence and the combating of organized subversion, and banning serving members of the security forces from holding representative public office. In April the Military Council, established under the 1987 Constitution, was abolished.

In August 1992 a peace agreement was signed by the Government and the SLA and the Tucayana; the BBM also committed itself to the agreement. Under the terms of the agreement, the amnesty law envisaged under the Kourou Accord of 1989, covering all civil conflicts since 1985 and amended to include insurgent groups formed since the ratification of the Kourou Accord, was to be implemented. All weapons were to be surrendered to the Government, under OAS supervision. Following disarmament, members of all the groups would be eligible for recruitment into a special police force for the interior of the country. In addition, the Government gave assurances that the interior would receive priority in its programmes for economic development and social welfare. However, in March 2005 former guerrillas claimed that the Government had not fulfilled its pledge to provide them with jobs and medical care.

In November 1992 Bouterse resigned as Commander-in-Chief of the armed forces, prompting public concern that the move might once again signal a coup. Venetiaan's appointment of Col (retd) Arthy Gorré as Bouterse's successor resulted in a confrontation between the Government and senior military officers in April 1993. (Gorré had supported the 1980 coup staged by Bouterse, but had resigned from the armed forces in 1987, following a disagreement with the latter.) Graanoogst, who had occupied the position of Commander-in-Chief on an interim basis since Bouterse's resignation, refused to concede the post to Gorré. He was supported by his fellow members of the military high command and by Bouterse, who, despite his resignation, remained effectively in control of the armed forces. Venetiaan subsequently deferred Gorré's appointment until May, when it was endorsed by a majority in the National Assembly, despite veiled threats of a military coup and an attack on the national television station, which had allegedly been instigated by Bouterse. All four members of the military high command subsequently acceded to a request by the National Assembly for their resignations. Three of them, including Graanoogst, later accepted posts as advisers to the Government, thus assuaging fears of an escalation of the conflict. Indications that the Netherlands might intervene to assist the Government were also considered influential in averting further military defiance of civilian rule.

At a general election conducted in May 1996 no single party secured a legislative majority, much less the two-thirds' majority necessary to elect its presidential candidate. The NF secured 24 seats, the NDP 16, DA '91 and Pendawa Lima four each and Alliantie the remaining three seats. Venetiaan, having rejected an offer from Bouterse to form a coalition government, began negotiations with the three other parties with representation in the legislature. However, the negotiations failed to produce agreement on a coalition. Neither Venetiaan nor the candidate of the NDP, former Prime Minister Jules Wijdenbosch, were able to command the two-thirds' majority in the National Assembly necessary to secure the presidency, and responsibility for electing the president consequently passed to the Vereinigde Volksvergadering. Wijdenbosch obtained the simply majority required to win and was inaugurated as President on 14 September. The KTPI and a dissident faction of the VHP, the Beweging voor Vernieuwing en Democratie (BVD), subsequently left the NF alliance, joining an NDP-led coalition. However, the support of the KTPI and the BVD was conditional upon Bouterse's exclusion from the new Government. The parties also stipulated that the portfolios of foreign affairs, finance, defence and internal affairs should not be allocated to the NDP. The new coalition Government, appointed in September, comprised members of the NDP, KTPI, BVD and the Hernieuwde Progressieve Partij (HPP).

In August 1997 the Government recalled its ambassador to the Netherlands for consultations, following the decision by the Dutch Government to seek an international arrest warrant for Bouterse on charges of illegal drugs-trafficking. Bouterse was reportedly in hiding following the issue of the warrant. Talks aimed at improving relations between the Governments of Suriname and the Netherlands were conducted, at ministerial level, in New York, USA, in April 1998. However, the fact that Bouterse was continuing to serve on the Council of State, as part of the Suriname Government, remained a serious source of dissatisfaction for the Netherlands' delegation, which resisted pressure from Suriname's police force to withdraw the warrant for Bouterse's arrest. In March 1999 the Dutch authorities began legal proceedings against Bouterse *in absentia*, on charges of corruption and drugs-trafficking. Similar *in absentia* court proceedings were initiated in the Netherlands against the guerrilla leader Ronnie Brunswijk (who was found guilty on charges of drugs-trafficking in April, and sentenced to eight years' imprisonment) and the President of the Central Bank of Suriname, Henk Goedschalk, who was accused of deliberate financial mismanagement. Despite the Suriname Government's refusal to accede to the demands of the Netherlands Government for the apprehension and extradition of Bouterse, in April President Wijdenbosch dismissed Bouterse from the Council of State, claiming that he represented a divisive force in Surinamese politics. In July Bouterse was convicted and sentenced, *in absentia*, to 16 years in prison (later reduced to 11 years) and fined US $2.3m. The Attorney-General of the Netherlands filed further charges (this time for torture resulting in death) against Bouterse in January 2000. The new charges concerned the 1982 December Murders and arose because of a complaint filed by relatives of the victims.

Dissatisfaction with the Government's management of the economy increased in 1998 and 1999. In June 1998 widespread industrial action brought chaos to the country for several days. There was further labour unrest in the agriculture and mining sectors later in the year. Following another national strike, which brought the country to a virtual standstill, the entire Cabinet resigned in May 1999. In June the National Assembly passed a vote of 'no confidence' in the President. However, the result fell short of the two-thirds' majority needed to force him from office and Wijdenbosch refused to tender his own resignation. Instead he called for early elections to be held by 25 May 2000 and asked the cabinet members to remain in office. However, in December the Government resubmitted its resignation after several of its members were implicated in financial and sexual scandals. President Wijdenbosch accepted several ministers' resignations, distributing their portfolios among the remaining ministers. Prior to the election, in an apparent attempt to distance himself from Bouterse, Wijdenbosch left the NDP and formed a new electoral coalition, Democratisch Nationaal Platform 2000 (DNP 2000).

Voting proceeded on 25 May 2000, when Venetiaan's NF (an electoral alliance comprising the NPS, the Pertajah Luhur, the Surinaamse Partij van de Arbeid, and the VHP) secured 33 of the 51 seats; the Millenium Combinatie (an alliance including the NDP) took 10, and DNP 2000 three. Having narrowly failed to secure the two-thirds' majority to appoint a new President directly, the NF entered into coalition negotiations with the smaller parties. On 4 August Venetiaan was elected to the presidency for the second time, winning 37 of the 51 votes cast in the National Assembly. On assuming office on 12 August, the new President pledged to fight corruption, accelerate economic development and reduce debt. In October the Dutch Government agreed to resume aid to Suriname, which had been suspended since 1998.

On 1 November 2000 the Suriname Court of Justice ruled that Bouterse must stand trial in Suriname in connection with the December Murders. In May 2001 a key witness in the case against Bouterse, the former activist and founder of the Labour Party, Fred Derby, died. In September the Dutch High Court ruled that Bouterse could not be prosecuted in the Netherlands under the UN's Convention on Torture, as the legislation had not been ratified in that country until 1989, seven years after the atrocities took place. However, in the following month it upheld Bouterse's 1999 conviction for drugs-trafficking and demanded he be extradited to serve his 11-year prison sentence—a measure that could not be enacted, as the Surinamese Constitution prohibited extradition of its citizens.

The arrival of a detachment of Dutch marines in June 2002 prompted speculation that the Dutch Government would attempt to arrest Bouterse; the Netherlands claimed that the troops were merely engaged in a joint military exercise. However, in the same month, the Dutch Government dispatched forensic specialists to assist Surinamese police officers investigating the December Murders. In December a judge presiding over the case ordered the exhumation of the remains of the 15 murder victims. As a result of a four-year investigation, a military court indicted Bouterse and 25 other suspects for the 1982 December Murders in December 2004. In mid-March 2007 Bouterse publicly apologized to the families of the 15 victims and advocated an amnesty for the suspects. At a preliminary hearing of the military tribunal on 30 November 2007, the judge rejected an appeal by Bouterse's lawyer that, as a former head of state, his client was entitled to stand trial in a civilian court. All other formal objections had been rejected by April 2008, when the hearings were adjourned until further notice. In August 2005 the OAS's Inter-American Court of Human Rights instructed the Government to investigate a massacre that occurred in the Maroon village of Moiwana in 1986, during Bouterse's presidency, and to pay US $13,000 compensation to the 130 survivors.

President Venetiaan formally apologized for the massacre at a ceremony in Moengo on 15 July 2006.

The illegal trafficking of drugs continued to be a problem in Suriname. The UN's Drug Control Programme estimated that some 22 metric tons of cocaine were transported annually to Europe via Suriname. In March 2002 three Surinamese, three Brazilians and one Colombian were sentenced to up to 14 years' imprisonment for attempting to bring 1,198 kg of cocaine into the country. The men had been arrested in March 2001 in what had been the largest ever seizure of illegal drugs by the Surinamese police. In October 2002 the Netherlands announced the provision of training and equipment to assist the Surinamese security forces' campaign against drugs-trafficking and funds for the construction of a new police headquarters in Paramaribo. Following negotiations held in January 2004 the two Governments agreed to co-operate on intelligence-gathering and sea patrols; it was also agreed that security would be increased on both passenger and cargo flights from Suriname. By 2008 the US Department of State's International Narcotics Control Strategy Report asserted that efforts to combat drugs-trafficking had yielded results during the previous year. The publication noted that in 2007 206 kg of cocaine were seized and 667 people were arrested for drugs-related offences. However, it identified a lack of resources, limited law enforcement capabilities and corruption in the judicial system as inhibitors in the Government's ongoing progress in addressing the problem.

Legislative elections were scheduled to be held on 25 May 2005. In March the NDP formally nominated Bouterse as its candidate in the indirect presidential election that was to follow the legislative ballot, in June. The USA reacted to the NDP's nomination by threatening to sever diplomatic links with Suriname in the event of Bouterse being re-elected President. The NDP accused the USA of political interference and lodged a formal complaint with the Caribbean Community and Common Market (CARICOM, see p. 196) and the OAS. The other main contenders for the presidency were the incumbent Venetiaan, who was seeking a third term in office, and former President Jules Wijdenbosch, representing the Volksalliantie Voor Vooruitgang (VVV—People's Alliance for Progress), an alliance comprising the DNP 2000, the BVD and the Democratisch Alternatief.

The ruling NF's popularity waned in the months preceding the election. Mounting political pressure regarding allegations of corruption led, in May 2005, to the resignation of Minister of Public Works Dewanand Balesar, pending an investigation into his alleged participation in a scheme that awarded contracts to fictitious contractors. (In September the National Assembly voted to remove Balesar's immunity from prosecution and in late March 2007 Balesar was brought to trial charged with defrauding the state.) Nevertheless, at the election the NF retained its position as the largest party in the National Assembly, attracting 39.4% of the votes cast and securing 23 of the 51 seats. The NDP also performed well, obtaining 22.2% of total votes and 15 seats, while the VVV secured just five seats (13.8%). Bouterse and former guerrilla leader Ronnie Brunswijk were both elected to the legislature.

Following the election the NF entered into negotiations with smaller parties in order to garner the two-thirds' parliamentary majority needed to re-elect Venetiaan to the presidency. As a result, on 13 July 2005 Venetiaan was nominated by a coalition of the NF, the DA '91 and the A-Combinatie (a coalition that included the Algemene Bevrijdings- en Ontwikkeling Partij—General Liberation and Development Party—led by Brunswijk). In an unexpected move, two days later the NDP presidential candidate Bouterse withdrew from the contest, nominating his former running mate Rabin Parmessar in his stead. The NDP and the VVV formed a coalition, nominating Wilfried Roseval, formerly Wijenbosch's running mate, for the vice-presidency. However, neither Venetiaan or Parmessar secured the requisite two-thirds' majority during the two rounds of voting held on 19 and 26 July. Responsibility for electing the new head of state subsequently passed to the 891-member Vereinigde Volksvergadering. With only a simple majority required, on 3 August Venetiaan secured the presidency with 560 votes, compared with 315 for Parmessar. At his inauguration on 12 August President Venetiaan pledged to combat criminal activity and to continue to pursue established financial policies and budgetary discipline to secure economic stability.

In an attempt to reduce the cost of imported petroleum, in July 2005 the Government signed the PetroCaribe energy accord with Venezuela, thereby gaining access to favourable energy concessions and the option of preferential terms should the price of petroleum exceed US $40 per barrel. However, the steep increases in the retail cost of petroleum products, and consequently of transportation, led to civil unrest in the latter half of 2005 and early 2006. Public transport was disrupted across the country in September 2005 as a result of industrial action by bus drivers and in January 2006 teachers, angry at the Government's failure to increase transport subsidies, staged demonstrations outside government buildings. Power shortages in the west of the country in February prompted further protests.

There were a number of cabinet changes in 2006 and early 2007. In January 2006 the Minister of Trade and Industry, Siegfried Gilds, resigned following accusations of money-laundering and membership of a criminal organization. Meanwhile, in mid-March 2006 the Surinamese ambassador to the Netherlands, Edgar Amanh, tendered his resignation following an incident at Schiphol Airport, Amsterdam, during which the Surinamese Minister of Transport, Communications and Tourism, Alice H. Amafo, was requested to undergo an unexpected security inspection. Amanh was reportedly held responsible for failing to inform the Government about the new Dutch security measures. Amafo tendered her own resignation in March 2007 following allegations of financial misconduct related to an official expenses claim for her birthday celebrations (totalling US $13,000). Her ministerial responsibilities were subsequently added to the portfolio of Minister of the Interior Maurits S. H. Hassankhan.

A number of international agreements were reached in 2007. In April the Surinamese Government acceded to the UN Development Assistance Framework agreement, under which US $40m. would be made available for social development initiatives in the country in 2008–11. Suriname also benefited from the assistance of the EU which, in July 2007, approved various contracts for the upgrade and development of the country's tourism and transport sectors, totalling allocations of €1.5m. and €3.2m., respectively.

Workers from four different sectors staged strikes in late 2007 and early 2008, causing disruption and drawing attention to their poor working conditions. In late November 2007 over 1,000 teachers left their positions, seeking higher wages and a fair system of benefits. The strike continued until the end of January 2008, when the Government agreed to increase wages by 10%, with further talks due to take place between the Government and union representatives later in the year to resolve outstanding issues. Airports had to operate a revised schedule during December 2007 when air traffic controllers initiated strike action to demand the implementation of measures agreed upon earlier in the year. Workers had expected to receive new equipment and to operate under improved safety standards, as well as receiving increased allowances. In mid-March 2008 the Jarikaba banana plant was forced to close for a week when workers protested at what they considered to be an unacceptable pay increase of 5%. In the following month bauxite workers went on strike in support of demands for a more substantial salary increase.

Suriname has a territorial dispute with Guyana over an estimated 15,000 sq km (6,000 sq miles) of land in the Corentije region, and another with French Guiana over land to the east of the Litani river. In April 1990, with the mediation of the UN High Commissioner for Refugees, France and Suriname agreed terms providing for the repatriation of an estimated 10,000 Surinamese refugees from French Guiana. In October French Guiana was reported to have begun forcible repatriation of Surinamese refugees. In April 1992, under a plan agreed between France, Suriname and the UN, some 6,000 Surinamese refugees were offered voluntary repatriation. In July the Suriname Government delivered an official protest to the French authorities concerning the alleged compulsory repatriation of refugees. By that time some 2,500 Surinamese refugees had returned to Suriname. Relations with France deteriorated in early 2007 when the French Government designated a 2m. ha region along the disputed border with French Guiana as a national park. Under its new protected status, the traditional hunting and fishing practices of the indigenous Surinamese communities were strictly prohibited in the park. The Organization of Indigenous People in Suriname (OIS) protested against the restrictions to the French Government in July, and in February 2008 it was reported that Suriname and France were due to resume talks, with France seeking to expand the maritime boundary by lodging a claim with the UN Convention on the Law of the Sea.

In 1995 Guyana and Suriname reached agreement on the establishment of a joint commission in order to seek a resolution of the countries' territorial dispute. In June 1998 Guyana granted the Canadian-based company, CGX Energy Inc, a concession to explore for petroleum and gas along the continental margin off Guyana, part of which lay within the disputed maritime area. In May 2000 Suriname formally claimed that Guyana had violated its territorial integrity, and invited Guyana to begin negotiations regarding the maritime boundary. In June the Surinamese Navy forced CGX to remove the drilling platform. In June 2001 the Ministers of Foreign Affairs of the two countries issued a declaration of their Governments' commitment to peace and co-operation. The Guyana–Suriname Bilateral Co-operation Council was revived in January 2002 and members agreed to investigate the possibility of a joint exploration for petroleum in the disputed territory. The two Governments also agreed to improve co-operation in trade, investments and joint ventures. However, relations again became strained in March 2003 when the Surinamese Government decreed that maps of the country circulated by diplomatic missions in Paramaribo must include the disputed territory. Guyana lodged a formal protest and sent a naval detachment to patrol the Corentijn River. Both countries subsequently strengthened their military presence in the area and in February 2004 two Surinamese gunboats expelled a Canadian company, exploring for oil with Guyana's permission, from the area. At the end of that month Guyana referred the maritime boundary dispute to arbitration at the UN's International Tribunal for the Law of the Sea, in Hamburg, Germany. Representatives of the two countries participated in negotiations in May. Guyana also requested a number of interim measures that would allow gas and oil exploration to continue. In September 2007 the Tribunal ruled in favour of Guyana, granting sovereignty over 33,152 sq km (12,800 sq miles) of coastal waters; Suriname was awarded 17,891 sq km (6,900 sq miles). Guyana's subsequent claims for compensation of US $34m. for damage arising from the expulsion of the oil rig were dismissed by the UN Permanent Court of Arbitration, which ruled that Suriname had not used armed force.

In March 2002 the Surinamese and Dutch Ministers of Foreign Affairs approved the establishment of a Returned Emigration Committee to oversee the voluntary repatriation of Surinamese with Dutch nationality without the loss of social benefits. In October 2004 customs officials in Suriname and the Netherlands reached an agreement to share information in an attempt to reduce tax evasion on imports from the Netherlands.

Government

Under the provisions of the 1987 Constitution, legislative power is held by the National Assembly, with 51 members, elected by universal adult suffrage for a five-year term. The Assembly elects the President and the Vice-President of the Republic. Executive power is vested in the President, who appoints the Cabinet of Ministers, led by the Vice-President, who is also the Prime Minister. The Cabinet is responsible to the National Assembly. A Council of State, comprising civilians and members of the armed forces, advises the President and the Cabinet of Ministers on policy, and has power of veto over legislation approved by the Assembly. Suriname comprises 10 administrative districts.

Defence

Suriname's armed forces numbered 1,840 men and women, as assessed at November 2007. There is an army of 1,400, a navy of 240, and an air force of about 200. Defence expenditure in 2007 was budgeted at US $22m.

Economic Affairs

In 2006, according to estimates by the World Bank, Suriname's gross national income (GNI), measured at average 2004–06 prices, was US $1,446m., equivalent to $3,200 per head (or $8,120 per head on an international purchasing-power parity basis). During 1996–2006, it was estimated, the population increased at an average annual rate of 0.8%, while gross domestic product (GDP) per head increased, in real terms, by an average of 3.0% per year over the same period. According to World Bank figures, overall GDP increased, in real terms, at an average annual rate of 3.8% in 1996–2006; growth was estimated at 5.8% in 2006.

Agriculture (including hunting, forestry and fishing) contributed an estimated 6.1% of GDP (excluding the informal sector) in 2006, and the sector engaged 8.0% of the employed population at the census conducted in the same year. The principal crop is rice, which supplies domestic demand and provided 1.3% of export earnings in 2004. Bananas are cultivated for export, together with plantains, sugar cane and citrus fruits, while Suriname also produces coconuts, maize and vegetables. In April 2002 the Government closed the state-run banana company Surland after it accumulated debt of some US $8m. However, the company was subsequently restructured with the aid of a US $6m. loan from the Inter-American Development Bank (IDB, see p. 308), and production and exports resumed in March 2004. In January 2005 some US $23m. was granted by the Dutch Government to assist the diversification of the agricultural sector and to improve rural roads and irrigation systems. Livestock is being developed, as are the extensive timber reserves (more than 80% of Suriname's total land area is covered by forest). Commercial fishing is important (exports of shrimp and fish providing an estimated 6.1% of total export revenue in 2005). In January 2007 it was announced that Japan was to fund construction of a US $8m. fisheries centre. According to the World Bank, agricultural GDP increased by 2.9% per year in 1996–2005; the sector grew by 1.4% in 2005.

Industry (including mining, manufacturing, public utilities and construction) contributed 42.2% of GDP (excluding the informal sector) in 2006, and the sector engaged some 22.9% of the employed labour force at the 2004 census. The principal activity is the bauxite industry, which dominates both the mining and manufacturing sectors. In early 2005 Alcoa World Alumina and Chemicals (AWAC) completed a project to increase production at the refinery in Paranam by 250,000 metric tons, to 2.2m. tons per year. In the early 2000s there were plans to build an industrial development zone near to Johan Adolf Pengel International Airport at Zanderij. According to the World Bank, industrial GDP increased by an annual average of 4.4% in 1996–2005; the sector increased by 8.6% in 2005.

Mining and quarrying contributed an estimated 15.4% of GDP (excluding the informal sector) in 2006, and the sector engaged 5.9% of the employed labour force at the 2004 census. The principal product is bauxite (used in the manufacture of aluminium), of which Suriname is one of the world's leading producers (producing an estimated 4.1m. metric tons in 2004). In 2003 the US-based aluminium company Alcoa reached an accord with the Government to allow Alcoa to increase the capacity of its existing bauxite operations in the country. Alcoa was also granted permission for a joint venture with the Australian company BHP for an aluminium melting plant and hydroelectric dam in the Backhuis Mountains. In November 2004 Alcoa and BHP Billiton announced joint plans to invest in two new bauxite mines, which began operations in 2006. The large-scale exploitation of gold in central-eastern Suriname was postponed in the late 1990s, owing to falling gold prices; gold reserves at the Gross Rosebel mine, situated some 80 km south of Paramaribo, were estimated at 2.4m. oz. In late 2002 the Canadian gold-mining corporation Cambior began construction on new facilities at Gross Rosebel. Extraction began in January 2004, and in that year gold production reportedly reached a record 8,513 kg, rising to 10,619 kg in 2005. In 2005 gold contributed some 36.4% of total export revenue. Reserves of petroleum in Suriname are exploited at a rate of around 12,500 barrels per day. Some 40% of production is for export, but much is used domestically in the bauxite industry. Unproven reserves are also thought to exist in the Saramacca district. Suriname also has extensive deposits of iron ore and reserves of manganese, copper, nickel, platinum and kaolin. According to government estimates, the GDP of the mining sector increased by an average of 10.6% per year in 2000–04; sectoral GDP increased by a dramatic 31.3% in 2004.

Manufacturing contributed an estimated 16.8% of GDP (excluding the informal sector) in 2006, and the sector engaged an estimated 7.0% of the employed labour force in the same year, according to the 2004 census. Bauxite refining and smelting is the principal industry (alumina accounted for an estimated 48.1% of export revenue in 2005), but there are also important food-processing industries and manufacturers of cigarettes, beverages and chemical products. According to government figures, manufacturing GDP increased by an estimated average of 4.2% per year in 1996–2005; the sector expanded by 7.1% in 2005.

Energy is currently derived principally from hydrocarbon fuels, which are mainly imported; in 2004 fuels and lubricants accounted for 13.0% of total merchandise imports. The country has considerable potential for the development of hydroelectric power; there is a hydroelectric station for the aluminium industry. In April 2004 the Government announced plans to install a major power line from the Afobakka hydroelectric dam to

SURINAME

Paramaribo. The three-year project would be undertaken by two companies based in India and financed by a loan from the Indian Government. In 2001 Suriname produced 1,921m. kWh of electricity, derived mostly from hydroelectric power.

The services sector contributed some 51.7% of GDP (excluding the informal sector) in 2006, and the sector engaged an estimated 64.3% of the employed labour force at the 2004 census. The GDP of the services sector increased by an estimated average of 3.3% per year in 1996–2005; sectoral growth was 4.3% in 2005.

In 2006 Suriname recorded a visible trade surplus of US $161.0m., and there was a deficit of $110.4m. on the current account of the balance of payments. The principal source of imports in 2005 was the USA (providing 24.4% of the value of total imports); other significant suppliers in that year were the Netherlands, Trinidad and Tobago and Japan. The principal markets for exports in 2005 were Norway (an estimated 23.9% of the value of total exports), the USA and France. The principal imports in 2004 were machinery and transport equipment, manufactured goods, mineral fuels and lubricants and food and live animals. The principal exports the same year were alumina, gold, and shrimp and fish.

In 2006 there was an estimated budgetary surplus of 5.2m. Surinamese dollars (equivalent to under 0.1% of GDP, excluding the contributions of the informal sector). At the end of 2002 the total external public debt stood at an estimated US $319.8m., of which $161.9m. was long-term public debt. By the end of December 2004 total external public debt had declined to US $235.6m. According to the IMF, the annual rate of inflation averaged 26.7% in 1996–2006. According to official figures, consumer prices increased by an average of 11.3% in 2006. According to official sources, the rate of unemployment was 9.5% in 2004. It was estimated that the informal sector contributed an estimated 15.3% of GDP in 2006.

In February 1995 Suriname was granted full membership of the Caribbean Community and Common Market (CARICOM, see p. 196). It was also one of the six founder members of CARICOM's Caribbean Single Market and Economy (CSME), established on 1 January 2006. The CSME was intended to enshrine the free movement of goods, services and labour throughout the CARICOM region. Forecasts in January 2007 indicated that the CSME would be fully operational by 31 December 2008.

On assuming office in September 2000, the Government of Runaldo Venetiaan discovered that most of the country's gold reserves had been converted into US dollars. With the country nearing bankruptcy, in October the new President announced a series of measures intended to stabilize the exchange rate and the domestic inflation rate. The official exchange rate was devalued by 89% and tariffs on utilities were raised. As a result, the annual inflation rate fell to 38.6% in 2001 and to 15.5% in 2002. The stricter fiscal regime implemented by Venetiaan's administration contributed to a stable economic outlook. However, in 2004–05 rising international oil prices and concomitant government fuel subsidies contributed to a widening of the fiscal deficit, which reached an estimated 4.0% of GDP in 2005. The annual rate of growth in consumer prices, which stood at 9.5% in 2005, rose to 11.3% in 2006, partly owing to the steep increase in the price of fuel. Economic activity is relatively diversified in range, but the dominant sector is the bauxite industry. In 2005 the IMF highlighted Suriname's dependence on a non-renewable resource and recommended that the Government establish a revenue stabilization fund in preparation for the eventual depletion of bauxite deposits. An IMF report published the following year further advised the Government to endeavour to strengthen the competitiveness of non-mining sectors and to reduce the public sector. The IMF estimated economic growth at 5.8% in 2007, in part due to a €1.5m. grant from the EU increasing capacity in the tourism sector. GDP growth was forecast to increase to 6.8% over 2008, although a subsequent rise in inflation towards 8.0% was also anticipated.

Education

Primary education is compulsory for children between seven and 12 years of age. Primary education begins at six years of age and lasts for six years. Secondary education comprises a first cycle of four years and a second cycle of three years. All education in government and denominational schools is provided free of charge. In 2004/05 the total enrolment in primary education was equivalent to 94.2% of children in the relevant age-group, while the total enrolment in secondary education was equivalent to 74.7% of children in the relevant age-group. The traditional educational system, inherited from the Dutch, was amended after the 1980 revolution to place greater emphasis on serving the needs of Suriname's population. This included a literacy campaign and programmes of adult education. Higher education is provided by technical and vocational schools and by the University of Suriname at Paramaribo, which has faculties of law, economics, medicine, social sciences and technology. Of total expenditure by the Central Government in 1996, an estimated Sf 3,480.5m (3.2%) was for education. In March 2003 the Inter-American Development Bank (IDB, see p. 308) approved a US $12.5m. loan to fund the reform of the basic education system into a single 10-year cycle. It was also intended to provide for a modernized curriculum with redesigned text books and a reform of the examination system. It was hoped that the funds would result in a 10% increase in the number of pupils who finished sixth grade and a 20% reduction in drop-out and repetition rates. A further $13m. grant for the sector was approved by the Dutch Government in January 2005.

Public Holidays

2008: 1 January (New Year's Day), March* (Phagwa), 21–24 March (Easter), 1 May (Labour Day), 1 July (National Union Day), 1 October (Id al-Fitr, end of Ramadan), 25 November (Independence Day), 25–26 December (Christmas).

2009: 1 January (New Year's Day), March* (Phagwa), 10–13 April (Easter), 1 May (Labour Day), 1 July (National Union Day), 20 September (Id al-Fitr, end of Ramadan), 25 November (Independence Day), 25–26 December (Christmas).

* Exact date dependent upon sightings of the moon.

Weights and Measures

The metric system is in force.

Statistical Survey

Sources (unless otherwise stated): Algemeen Bureau voor de Statistiek, Kromme Elleboogstraat 10, POB 244, Paramaribo; tel. 473927; fax 425004; e-mail info@statistics-suriname.org; internet www.statistics-suriname.org; Ministry of Trade and Industry, Havenlaan 3, POB 9354, Paramaribo; tel. 402080; fax 402602.

AREA AND POPULATION

Area: 163,820 sq km (63,251 sq miles).

Population: 355,240 (males 175,814, females 179,426) at census of 1 July 1980; 492,829 (males 247,846, females 244,618, not known 365) at census of 2 August 2004. *Mid-2007* (estimate): 458,000 (Source: UN, *World Population Prospects: The 2006 R*).

Density (at mid-2007): 2.8 per sq km.

Ethnic Groups (1980 census, percentage): Creole 34.70; Hindustani 33.49; Javanese 16.33; Bush Negro 9.55; Amerindian 3.10; Chinese 1.55; European 0.44; Others 0.84.

Administrative Districts (population at census of 2 August 2004): Paramaribo 242,946; Wanica 85,986; Nickerie 36,639; Coronie 2,887; Saramacca 15,980; Commewijne 24,649; Marowijne 16,642; Para 18,749; Brokopondo 14,215; Sipaliwini 34,136; *Total* 492,829.

Principal Towns (census of 2 August 2004): Paramaribo (capital) 205,000; Lelydorp 15,600; Nieuw Nickerie 11,100. Source: Thomas Brinkoff, *City Population* (internet www.citypopulation.de).

Births, Marriages and Deaths (2004): Registered live births 9,062 (birth rate 18.6 per 1,000); Marriages 1,951 (4.0 per 1,000); Registered deaths 3,319 (death rate 6.8 per 1,000). Source: UN, *Demographic Yearbook*.

Expectation of Life (years at birth, WHO estimates): 68.5 (males 66.2; females 70.8) in 2005. Source: WHO, *World Health Statistics*.

Economically Active Population ('000 persons aged 15–64 years, census of 2004): Agriculture, hunting, forestry and fishing 12,593;

SURINAME

Mining and quarrying 9,308; Manufacturing 10,971; Utilities 1,659; Construction 14,031; Trade 25,012; Hotels, restaurants and bars 4,833; Transport, storage and communication 8,711; Financial intermediation 2,723; Real estate, renting and business activities 6,350; Public administration and defence 27,995; Education 8,355; Health and social work 6,797; Other community, social and personal service activities 9,911; Unknown 7,456; *Total employed* 156,705 (males 101,919, females 54,768, unknown 18); Unemployed 16,425; *Total labour force* 173,130.

HEALTH AND WELFARE
Key Indicators

Total Fertility Rate (children per woman, 2005): 2.5.

Under-5 Mortality Rate (per 1,000 live births, 2005): 39.

HIV/AIDS (% of persons aged 15–49, 2005): 1.9.

Physicians (per 1,000 head, 2000): 0.45.

Hospital Beds (per 1,000 head, 2004): 3.1.

Health Expenditure (2004): US $ per head (PPP): 376.

Health Expenditure (2004): % of GDP: 7.8.

Health Expenditure (2004): public (% of total): 46.0.

Access to Water (% of persons, 2004): 92.

Access to Sanitation (% of persons, 2004): 94.

Human Development Index (2005): ranking: 85.

Human Development Index (2005): value: 0.774.

For sources and definitions, see explanatory note on p. vi.

AGRICULTURE, ETC.

Principal Crops ('000 metric tons, 2006, FAO estimates): Rice (paddy) 195.0; Roots and tubers 6; Sugar cane 112; Coconuts 9; Vegetables 19; Bananas 17; Plantains 11; Oranges 10; Other citrus fruit 4.

Livestock ('000 head, 2006, FAO estimates): Cattle 137; Sheep 8; Goats 7; Pigs 25; Chickens 3,800.

Livestock Products ('000 metric tons, 2006, FAO estimates): Cattle meat 2; Pig meat 1; Chicken meat 2; Cows' milk 7; Hen eggs 3.

Forestry ('000 cu metres, 2006, FAO estimates): *Roundwood Removals:* Sawlogs, veneer logs and logs for sleepers 191; Other industrial wood 3; Fuel wood 45; Total 239. *Sawnwood Production:* Total (incl. railway sleepers) 69.

Fishing ('000 metric tons, 2005, FAO estimates): Capture 39.9 (Marine fishes 17.4; Penaeus shrimps 1.7; Atlantic seabob 20.6); Aquaculture 0.2; *Total catch* 40.2.

Source: FAO.

MINING

Selected Products (2005, estimates): Crude petroleum ('000 barrels) 4,380; Bauxite ('000 metric tons) 4,757; Gold (Au content, kg) 10,619. Source: US Geological Survey.

INDUSTRY

Selected Products ('000 metric tons unless otherwise indicated, 2002 unless otherwise indicated): Gold-bearing ores 300 (kg, 2003); Gravel and crushed stone 85; Distillate fuel oil 40; Residual fuel oils 334; Cement 65 (2005, estimate); Alumina 1,944 (2005, estimate); Beer of barley 16 (2001); Coconut oil 0.82 (2001); Palm oil 0.22 (2001); Cigarettes 483 (million, 1996); Plywood 1 ('000 cubic metres, 2005); Electricity 1,921 (million kWh). Sources: mainly UN, *Industrial Commodity Statistics Yearbook* and FAO.

FINANCE

Currency and Exchange Rates: 100 cents = 1 Surinamese dollar. *Sterling, Dollar and Euro Equivalents* (31 December 2007): £1 sterling = 5.499 Surinamese dollars; US $1 = 2.745 Surinamese dollars; €1 = 4.041 Surinamese dollars; 100 Surinamese dollars = £18.19 = US $36.43 = €27.08. *Average Exchange Rate* (Surinamese dollars per US $): 2.732 in 2005; 2.744 in 2006; 2.745 in 2007. *Note:* Between 1971 and 1993 the official market rate was US $1 = 1.785 guilders. A new free market rate was introduced in June 1993, and a unified, market-determined rate took effect in July 1994. A mid-point rate of US $1 = 401.0 guilders was in effect between September 1996 and January 1999. A new currency, the Surinamese dollar, was introduced on 1 January 2004, and was equivalent to 1,000 old guilders. Some data in this survey are still presented in terms of the former currency.

Budget (million Surinamese dollars, 2006, preliminary): *Revenue:* Direct taxation 610.4; Indirect taxation 674.7 (Domestic taxes on goods and services 282.0, Taxes on international trade 388.4, Other taxes (incl. bauxite levy) 4.3); Non-tax revenue 299.6; Total 1,584.7 (excl. grants 81.1). *Expenditure:* Wages and salaries 607.7; Subsidies and transfers 216.3; Goods and services 520.3; Interest payments 106.7; Capital 197.2; Total 1,648.2 (excl. net lending 12.4). Source: IMF, *Suriname: Statistical Appendix* (May 2007).

International Reserves (US $ million at 31 December 2007): Gold (national valuation) 32.77; IMF special drawing rights 0.89; Reserve position in IMF 9.68; Foreign exchange 390.36; Total 433.70. Source: IMF, *International Financial Statistics*.

Money Supply ('000 Surinamese dollars at 31 December 2007): Currency outside banks 409,242; Demand deposits at deposit money banks 696,343; Total money (incl. others) 1,145,554. Source: IMF, *International Financial Statistics*.

Cost of Living (Consumer Price Index for Paramaribo area; base: October–December 2000 = 100): 162.0 in 2004; 177.4 in 2005; 197.4 in 2006.

Gross Domestic Product ('000 Surinamese dollars at constant 1990 prices, preliminary figures): 4,529 in 2002; 4,773 in 2003; 5,145 in 2004.

Expenditure on the Gross Domestic Product ('000 Surinamese dollars at current prices, 2004, preliminary figures): Public consumption 1,015,201; Private consumption 2,105,154; Public investment 146,514; Private investment 764,342; Exports of goods and non-factor services 1,059,242; *Less* Imports of goods and non-factor services 1,952,281; *GDP in purchasers' values* 3,138,172. Source: IMF, *Suriname: Statistical Appendix* (February 2006).

Gross Domestic Product by Economic Activity ('000 Surinamese dollars at current prices, 2006, preliminary figures): Agriculture, hunting, forestry and fishing 272,799; Mining and quarrying 687,804; Manufacturing 749,826; Electricity, gas and water 274,092; Construction 176,858; Wholesale and retail trade 548,222; Hotels and restaurants 84,872; Transport, storage and communications 459,316; Financial intermediation 304,069; Real estate, renting and business activities 296,137; Public administration 326,875; Education 199,405; Health and social work 27,529; Other community, social and personal services 66,952; Informal sector 808,561; *Subtotal* 5,283,317; *Less* Imputed bank service charge 124,776; *Gross value added in basic prices* 5,158,541; Taxes on products, less subsidies 643,924; *GDP at market prices* 5,802,465. Source: IMF, *Suriname: Statistical Appendix* (May 2007).

Balance of Payments (US $ million, 2006): Exports of goods f.o.b. 1,174.4; Imports of goods f.o.b. −1,013.4; *Trade balance* 161.0; Exports of services 233.6; Imports of services −268.5; *Balance on goods and services* 126.1; Other income received 28.0; Other income paid −79.6; *Balance on goods, services and income* 74.5; Current transfers received 73.5; Current transfers paid −37.6; *Current balance* 110.4; Capital account (net) 19.3; Direct investment from abroad −163.4; Portfolio investment liabilities −0.3; Other investment assets 8.4; Other investment liabilities −25.2; Net errors and omissions 144.9; *Overall balance* 94.1. Source: IMF, *International Financial Statistics*.

EXTERNAL TRADE

Principal Commodities (US $ million, 2005): *Imports c.i.f.:* Food and live animals 99.7; Mineral fuels, lubricants, etc. 171.4; Chemicals 76.2; Manufactured goods 150.4; Machinery and transport equipment 295.0; Total (incl. others, excl. re-exports) 1,099.9. *Exports:* Alumina 446.6.; Gold 338.1; Shrimp and fish 56.8; Crude oil 53.6; Rice 14.0; Total (incl. others) 929.1. Source: IMF, *Suriname: Statistical Appendix* (May 2007).

Principal Trading Partners (US $ million, 2005): *Imports:* Belgium 23.6; Brazil 39.3; Canada 10.1; China, People's Repub. 59.5; Germany 23.9; Japan 47.5; Netherlands 160.0; Trinidad and Tobago 116.0; United Kingdom 18.3; USA 267.9; Total (incl. others) 1,099.9. *Exports:* Barbados 6.6; France 74.8; Iceland 26.9; Japan 10.7; Netherlands 24.2; Norway 222.4; Trinidad and Tobago 20.7; USA 155.6; Total (incl. others) 929.1. Source: IMF, *Suriname: Statistical Appendix* (May 2007).

TRANSPORT

Road Traffic (registered motor vehicles, 2000 estimates): Passenger cars 61,365; Buses and coaches 2,393; Lorries and vans 20,827; Motorcycles and mopeds 30,598.

Shipping: *International Sea-borne Freight Traffic* (estimates, '000 metric tons, 2001): Goods loaded 2,306; Goods unloaded 1,212. *Merchant Fleet* (registered at 31 December 2005): Number of vessels 13; Total displacement 5,229 grt. Source: Lloyd's Register-Fairplay, *World Fleet Statistics*.

SURINAME

Civil Aviation (traffic on scheduled services, 2003): Kilometres flown (million) 4; Passengers carried ('000) 253; Passenger-km (million) 1,469; Total ton-km (million) 183. Source: UN, *Statistical Yearbook*.

TOURISM

Tourist Arrivals (number of non-resident arrivals at national borders, '000): 137.8 in 2004; 160.0 in 2005.
Tourism Receipts (US $ million, excl. passenger transport): 18 in 2003; 52 in 2004; 96 in 2005.

Source: World Tourism Organization.

COMMUNICATIONS MEDIA

Radio Receivers (1997): 300,000 in use.
Television Receivers (2000): 110,000 in use.
Telephones (2006): 81,500 main lines in use.
Facsimile Machines (1996): 800 in use.
Mobile Cellular Telephones (2006): 320,000 subscribers.
Personal Computers (2001): 20,000 in use.
Internet Users (2006): 32,000.
Broadband Subscribers (2006): 2,700.
Daily Newspapers (2005): 4.
Non-daily Newspapers (2000): 10.

Sources: mainly UNESCO, *Statistical Yearbook*; UN, *Statistical Yearbook*; International Telecommunication Union.

EDUCATION

Pre-primary (2004/05): 717 teachers; 16,090 pupils.
Primary (2004/05 unless otherwise stated, incl. special education): 308 schools (2001/02); 3,520 teachers; 65,527 pupils.
Secondary (2004/05 unless otherwise stated, incl. teacher-training): 141 schools (2001/02); 3,296 teachers; 45,818 pupils.
University (2001/02): 1 institution; 350 teachers; 3,250 students.
Other Higher (2001/02): 3 institutions; 200 teachers; 1,936 students.
Adult Literacy Rate (UNESCO estimates): 89.6% (males 92.0%; females 87.2%) in 2004.

Source: mainly UNESCO Institute for Statistics.

Directory

The Constitution

The 1987 Constitution was approved by the National Assembly on 31 March and by 93% of voters in a national referendum in September.

THE LEGISLATURE

Legislative power is exercised jointly by the National Assembly and the Government. The National Assembly comprises 51 members, elected for a five-year term by universal adult suffrage. The Assembly elects a President and a Vice-President and has the right of amendment in any proposal of law by the Government. The approval of a majority of at least two-thirds of the number of members of the National Assembly is required for the amendment of the Constitution, the election of the President or the Vice-President, the decision to organize a plebiscite and a People's Congress and for the amendment of electoral law. If it is unable to obtain a two-thirds' majority following two rounds of voting, the Assembly may convene a United People's Assembly (Vereinigde Volksvergadering) and supplement its numbers with members of local councils. The approval by a simple majority is sufficient in the United People's Assembly.

THE EXECUTIVE

Executive authority is vested in the President, who is elected for a term of five years as Head of State, Head of Government, Head of the Armed Forces, Chairman of the Council of State, the Cabinet of Ministers and the Security Council.

The Government comprises the President, the Vice-President and the Cabinet of Ministers. The Cabinet of Ministers is appointed by the President from among the members of the National Assembly. The Vice-President is the Prime Minister and leader of the Cabinet, and is responsible to the President.

In the event of war, a state of siege, or exceptional circumstances to be determined by law, a Security Council assumes all government functions.

THE COUNCIL OF STATE

The Council of State comprises the President (its Chairman) and 14 additional members, composed of two representatives of the combined trade unions, one representative of the associations of employers, one representative of the National Army and 10 representatives of the political parties in the National Assembly. Its duties are to advise the President and the legislature and to supervise the correct execution by the Government of the decisions of the National Assembly. The Council may present proposals of law or of general administrative measures to the Government. The Council has the authority to suspend any legislation approved by the National Assembly which, in the opinion of the Council, is in violation of the Constitution. In this event, the President must decide within one month whether or not to ratify the Council's decision.

The Government

HEAD OF STATE

President: RUNALDO RONALD VENETIAAN (assumed office 12 August 2000; re-elected by vote of the United People's Assembly 3 August 2005).

Council of State: Chair. RUNALDO RONALD VENETIAAN (President of the Republic); 14 mems; 10 to represent the political parties in the National Assembly, one for the Armed Forces, two for the trade unions and one for employers.

CABINET OF MINISTERS
(April 2008)

Vice-President: RAMDIEN SARDJOE (VHP).
Minister of Finance: HUMPHREY HILDENBERG (NPS).
Minister of Foreign Affairs: LYGIA L. KRAAG-KETELDIJK (NPS).
Minster of Defence: IVAN C. FERNALD (NPS).
Minister of Home Affairs: MAURITS S. H. HASSANKHAN (VHP).
Minister of Justice and the Police: CHANDRIKAPERSAD SANTOKHI (VHP).
Minister of Planning and Foreign Aid: RICARDO OTTO VAN RAVENSWAAY (DA'91).
Minister of Agriculture, Animal Husbandry and Fisheries: KERMECHEND STANLEY RAGHOEBARSING (VHP).
Minister of Transport, Communications and Tourism: RICHEL APENSA (AC).
Minister of Public Works: GANESHKOEMAR KANDHAI (VHP).
Minister of Social Affairs and Housing: HENDRIK SOERAT SETROWIDJOJO (PL).
Minister of Trade and Industry: CLIFFORD MARICA (SPA).
Minister of Regional Development: MICHEL FELISIE (AC).
Minister of Education and Community Development: EDWIN TOEKIDJAN WOLF (PL).
Minister of Health: CELCIUS WALDO WATERBERG (AC).
Minister of Labour, Technological Development and the Environment: JOYCE AMARELLO-WILLIAMS (SPA).
Minister of Natural Resources: GREGORY ALLAN RUSLAND (NPS).
Minister of Physical Planning and of Land and Forestry Management: MICHAEL JONG TJIEN FA (PL).

MINISTRIES

Ministry of Agriculture, Animal Husbandry and Fisheries: Letitia Vriesdelaan 7, Paramaribo; tel. 477698; fax 470301; e-mail minlvvv@sr.net.

Ministry of Defence: Kwattaweg 29, Paramaribo; tel. 474244; fax 420055; e-mail defensie@sr.net.

SURINAME

Ministry of Education and Community Development: Dr Samuel Kafiludistraat 117–123, Paramaribo; tel. 498383; fax 495083; e-mail minond@sr.net.

Ministry of Finance: Tamarindelaan 3, Paramaribo; tel. 472610; fax 476314; e-mail financien@sr.net; internet www.minfin.sr.

Ministry of Foreign Affairs: Lim A Postraat 25, POB 25, Paramaribo; tel. 471209; fax 410411; e-mail buza@sr.net.

Ministry of Health: Henck Arronstraat 64, POB 201, Paramaribo; tel. 410441; fax 473923; e-mail info@volksgezondheid.gov.sr; internet www.volksgezondheid.gov.sr.

Ministry of Home Affairs: Wilhelminastraat 3, Paramaribo; tel. 476461; fax 421170; e-mail gensur@sr.net.

Ministry of Justice and the Police: Henck Arronstraat 1, Paramaribo; tel. 475805; fax 412109; e-mail ipoffsur@sr.net.

Ministry of Labour, Technological Development and the Environment: Wageswegstraat 22, POB 911, Paramaribo; tel. 477045; fax 410465; e-mail arbeid@sr.net.

Ministry of Land and Forestry Management: Paramaribo.

Ministry of Natural Resources: Dr J. C. de Mirandastraat 11–13, Paramaribo; tel. 410160; fax 472911; e-mail minnh@sr.net.

Ministry of Physical Planning: Cornelis Jongbawstraat 10–12, Paramaribo; tel. 470728; fax 473316; e-mail mpjong@datsunsuriname.com.

Ministry of Planning and Foreign Aid: Dr S. Redmondstraat 118, Paramaribo; tel. 471108; fax 421056; e-mail plos@sr.net; internet www.plos.sr.

Ministry of Public Works: Verlengde Jagernath Lachmonstraat 167, Paramaribo; tel. 462500; fax 464901; e-mail minow@sr.net.

Ministry of Regional Development: Van Rooseveltkade 2, Paramaribo; tel. 471269; fax 424333; e-mail regon@sr.net.

Ministry of Social Affairs and Housing: Waterkant 30–32, Paramaribo; tel. 472340; fax 470516; e-mail soza@sr.net.

Ministry of Trade and Industry: Havenlaan 3, POB 9354, Paramaribo; tel. 402886; fax 402602; e-mail dhisur@yahoo.com.

Ministry of Transport, Communications and Tourism: Prins Hendrikstraat 24–26, Paramaribo; tel. 420905; fax 420425; e-mail odc@mintct.sr; internet www.mintct.sr.

Legislature

NATIONAL ASSEMBLY

Chairman: PAUL SALAM SOMOHARDJO.

General Election, 25 May 2005

Party	Seats	% of votes cast
Nieuwe Front*	23	39.37
Nationale Democratische Partij	15	22.20
Volksalliantie Voor Vooruitgang†	5	13.79
A-Combinatie‡	5	7.21
A1§	3	5.86
Unie van Progressieve Surinamers/Partij voor Democratie en Ontwikkeling in Eenheid	—	4.67
Nieuw Suriname	—	1.57
Progressieve Arbeiders en Landbouwers Unie	—	0.89
Progressieve Politieke Partij	—	0.17
Total	51	100.00‖

* An alliance of the Nationale Partij Suriname (NPS), the Pertajah Luhur (PL), the Surinaamse Partij van de Arbeid (SPA) and the Vooruitstrevende Hervormingspartij (VHP).
† An alliance of the Democratisch Nationaal Platform 2000 (DNP 2000), the Basispartij voor Vernieuwing en Democratie (BVD), the Kerukanan Tulodo Pranatan Ingigil (KTPI) and the Democratisch Alternatief.
‡ Including candidates of the Algemene Bevrijdings- en Ontwikkelingspartij (ABOP) and the Broederschap en Eenheid in Politiek (BEP).
§ Including candidates from the Democratisch Alternatief 1991 (DA '91), the Democraten van de 21 (D21) and the Politieke Vleugel van de FAL (PVF).
‖ Including invalid votes.

Election Commission

Centraal Hoofdstembureau (CHS) (Central Polling Authority): Wilhelminastraat 3, Paramaribo; tel. 410362; independent; Chair. LOTHAR BOKSTEEN.

Political Organizations

Algemene Bevrijdings- en Ontwikkelingspartij (ABOP) (General Liberation and Development Party): Jaguarstraat 15, Paramaribo; f. 1986; contested the 2005 election as part of the A-Combinatie (AC) electoral list; Pres. RONNIE BRUNSWIJK.

Alternatief Forum (AF) (Alternative Forum): Gladiolenstraat 26–28, Paramaribo; tel. 432342; Chair. GERARD BRUNINGS.

Amazone Partij Suriname (APS) (Suriname Amazon Party): Wilhelminastraat 91, Paramaribo; tel. 452081; Pres. KENNETH VAN GENDEREN.

Broederschap en Eenheid in Politiek (BEP): Ariestraat BR 34, S. O. B. Projekt, Paramaribo; tel. 494466; f. 1986; contested the 2005 election as part of the A-Combinatie (AC) electoral list; Chair. CAPRINO ALLENDY.

Democraten van de 21 (D21) (Democrats of the 21st Century): Goudstraat 22, Paramaribo; f. 1986; contested the 2005 election as part of the A1 electoral list; Chair. SOEWARTO MUSTADJA.

Democratisch Alternatief 1991 (DA '91) (Democratic Alternative 1991): POB 91, Paramaribo; tel. 470276; fax 493121; e-mail info@da91.sr; f. 1991; contested the 2005 election as part of the A1 electoral list; social-democratic; Chair. W. JESSERUN.

Hernieuwde Progressieve Partij (HPP) (Renewed Progressive Party): Tourtonnelaan 51, Paramaribo; tel. 426965; e-mail hpp@cq-link.sr; f. 1986; Chair. HARRY KISOENSINGH.

Nationale Democratische Partij (NDP) (National Democratic Party): Dr H. D. Benjaminstraat 38, Paramaribo; tel. 499183; fax 432174; e-mail ndpsur@sr.net; internet www.ndp.sr; f. 1987 by Standvaste (the 25 February Movt); army-supported; Pres. DESIRÉ (DESI) BOUTERSE.

Nationale Partij Voor Leiderschap en Ontwikkeling (NPLO) (National Party for Leaderhip and Development): Tropicaweg 1, Paramaribo; tel. 551252; f. 1986; Chair. OESMAN WANGSABESARIE.

Naya Kadam (New Choice): Naarstraat 5, Paramaribo; tel. 482014; fax 481012; e-mail itsvof@sr.net; Chair. INDRA DJWALAPERSAD; Sec. WALDO RAMDIHAL.

Nieuw Front (NF) (New Front): Paramaribo; f. 1987 as Front voor Demokratie en Ontwikkeling (FDO—Front for Democracy and Devt); name changed as above in 1991; Pres. RUNALDO R. VENETIAAN; an alliance comprising:

Nationale Partij Suriname (NPS) (Suriname National Party): Wanicastraat 77, Paramaribo; tel. 477302; fax 475796; e-mail nps@sr.net; internet www.nps-suriname.com; f. 1946; predominantly Creole; Sec. OTMAR ROEL RODGERS.

Pertijajah Luhur (PL) (Full Confidence Party): Hoek Gemenlandsweg-Daniel Coutinhostraat, Paramaribo; tel. 401087; fax 420394; Pres. PAUL SALAM SOMOHARDJO.

Surinaamse Partij van de Arbeid (SPA) (Suriname Labour Party): Rust en Vredestraat 64, Paramaribo; tel. 425912; fax 420394; f. 1987; affiliated with C-47 trade union; social democratic party; joined NF in 1991; Leader SIEGFRIED F. GILDS.

Vooruitstrevende Hervormings Partij (VHP) (Progressive Reformation Party): Jagernath Lachmonstraat 130, Paramaribo; tel. 425912; fax 420394; internet www.parbo.com/vhp; f. 1949 as Verenigde Hindostaanse Partij (United Indian Party); name changed as above in 1973; leading left-wing party; predominantly Indian; Leader R. SARDJOE.

Nieuw Suriname (NS) (New Suriname): Paramaribo; contested the 2005 election.

Partij voor Demokratie en Ontwikkeling in Eenheid (DOE) (Party for Democracy through Unity and Development): Kamperfoeliestraat 23, Paramaribo; internet www.angelfire.com/nv/DOE; f. 1999.

Pendawa Lima: Bonistraat 115, Geyersvlij, Paramaribo; tel. 551802; f. 1975; predominantly Indonesian; Chair. RAYMOND SAPOEN.

Politieke Vleugel van de FAL (PVF): Keizerstraat 150, Paramaribo; political wing of farmers' org. Federatie van Agrariërs en Landarbeiders; contested the 2005 election as part of the A1 electoral list; Chair. JIWAN SITAL.

Progressieve Arbeiders en Landbouwers Unie (PALU) (Progressive Workers' and Farm Labourers' Union): Dr S. Kafiluddistraat 27, Paramaribo; tel. 400115; e-mail palu@sr.net; socialist party; Chair. JIM K. HOK; Vice-Chair. HENK RAMNANDANLAL.

Progressieve Bosneger Partij (PBP): f. 1968; resumed political activities 1987; represents members of the Bush Negro (Boschneger) ethnic group; associated with the Pendawa Lima (see above).

Progressieve Politieke Partij (PPP) (Progressive Political Party): Paramaribo; contested the 2005 election; Chair. SURINDER MUNGRA.

SURINAME

Progressieve Surinaamse Volkspartij (PSV) (Suriname Progressive People's Party): Keizerstraat 122, Paramaribo; tel. 472979; f. 1946; resumed political activities 1987; Christian democratic party.

Seeka: Paramaribo; contested the 2005 election as part of the A-Combinatie (AC) electoral list; Chair. PAUL ABENA.

Unie van Progressieve Surinamers/Partij voor Democratie en Ontwikkeling in Eenheid (UPS/DOE): Paramaribo; contested the 2005 election.

Volksalliantie Voor Vooruitgang (People's Alliance for Progress): Paramaribo; contested the 2005 election; Leader JULES WIJDENBOSCH; alliance comprising:

Basispartij voor Vernieuwing en Democratie (BVD) (Base Party for Renewal and Democracy): Hoogestraat 28–30, Paramaribo; tel. 422231; e-mail info@bvdsuriname.org; internet www.bvdsuriname.org; Chair. TJAN GOBARDHAN.

Democratisch Alternatief (Democratic Alternative): Jadnanansinghlaan 5, Paramaribo.

Democratisch Nationaal Platform 2000 (DNP 2000) (National Democratic Platform 2000): Gemenlandsweg 83, Paramaribo; f. 2000; Pres. JULES WIJDENBOSCH.

Kerukunan Tulodo Pranatan Inggil (KTPI) (Party for National Unity and Solidarity): Bonistraat 64, Geyersvlijt, Paramaribo; tel. 456116; f. 1947 as the KaumTani Persuatan Indonesia; largely Indonesian; Leader WILLY SOEMITA.

Partij Pembangunan Rakat Suriname (PPRS): Paramaribo; Chair. R. KAAIMAN.

Diplomatic Representation

EMBASSIES IN SURINAME

Brazil: Maratakkastraat 2, POB 925, Paramaribo; tel. 400200; fax 420774; e-mail brasemb@sr.net; internet www2.mre.gov.br/suriname/index.asp; Ambassador RICARDO LUIZ VIANA DE CARVALHO.

China, People's Republic: Anton Dragtenweg 154, POB 3042 Paramaribo; tel. 451570; fax 452540; e-mail chinaemb_sr@mfa.gov.cn; internet sr.chineseembassy.org; Ambassador SU GE.

Cuba: Brokopondolaan 4, Paramaribo; tel. 434917; fax 432626; e-mail embacubasuriname@gmail.com; internet embacu.cubaminrex.cu/surinaming; Ambassador ANDRÉS MARCELO GONZÁLEZ GARRIDO.

France: Henck Arronstraat 5–7 boven, POB 2648, Paramaribo; tel. 476455; fax 471208; e-mail ambafrance.paramaribo@diplomatie.gouv.fr; internet www.ambafrance-sr.org; Ambassador RICHARD BARBEYRON.

Guyana: Gravenstraat 82, POB 785, Paramaribo; tel. 477895; fax 472679; e-mail guyembassy@sr.net; Ambassador KARSHANJE ARJUN.

India: Rode Kruislaan 10, POB 1329, Paramaribo; tel. 498344; fax 491106; e-mail india@sr.net; internet www.indembassysuriname.com; Ambassador ASHOK KUMAR SHARMA.

Indonesia: Van Brussellaan 3, Uitvlugt, POB 157, Paramaribo; tel. 431230; fax 498234; e-mail indonemb@sr.net; Ambassador SUPRIJANTO MUHADI.

Japan: Henck Arronstraat 23–25, POB 2921, Paramaribo; tel. 474860; fax 412208; e-mail eojparbo@sr.net; Ambassador YASUO MATSUI (resident in Venezuela).

Netherlands: Van Roseveltkade 5, POB 1877, Paramaribo; tel. 477211; fax 477792; e-mail prm@minbuza.nl; Ambassador TANYA VAN GOOL.

Russia: Anton Dragtenweg 7, POB 8127, Paramaribo; tel. and fax 472387; Ambassador PAVEL SERGIEV.

USA: Dr Sophie Redmondstraat 129, POB 1821, Paramaribo; tel. 472900; fax 425690; e-mail embuscen@sr.net; internet paramaribo.usembassy.gov; Ambassador LISA BOBBIE SCHREIBER HUGHES.

Venezuela: Henck Arronstraat 23–25, POB 3001, Paramaribo; tel. 475401; fax 475602; e-mail embajador@suriname.gob.ve; internet www.suriname.gob.ve; Ambassador FRANCISCO DE JESÚS SIMANCAS.

Judicial System

The administration of justice is entrusted to a Court of Justice, the six members of which are nominated for life, and three Cantonal Courts. Suriname recognized the Caribbean Court of Justice (CCJ) on matters of original jurisdiction pertaining to international trade. The CCJ was inaugurated in Port of Spain, Trinidad and Tobago, on 16 April 2005.

President of the Court of Justice: JOHN VON NIESEWAND.
Attorney-General: SUBHAAS PUNWASI.

Religion

Many religions are represented in Suriname. According to the census at August 2004, Christians represented approximately 48.3% of the population, Hindus 23.6% and Muslims 16.0%. The Bahá'í faith is also represented.

CHRISTIANITY

Committee of Christian Churches: Paramaribo; Chair. Rev. JOHN KENT (Praeses of the Moravian Church).

The Roman Catholic Church

For ecclesiastical purposes, Suriname comprises the single diocese of Paramaribo, suffragan to the archdiocese of Port of Spain (Trinidad and Tobago). The Bishop participates in the Antilles Episcopal Conference (currently based in Port of Spain, Trinidad and Tobago). At 31 December 2005 adherents to the Roman Catholic faith represented some 28% of the population.

Bishop of Paramaribo: WILHELMUS ADRIANUS JOSEPHUS MARIA DE BEKKER, Bisschopshuis, Henck Arronstraat 12, POB 1230, Paramaribo; tel. 425918; fax 471602; e-mail cabisdom@sr.net.

The Anglican Communion

Within the Church in the Province of the West Indies, Suriname forms part of the diocese of Guyana. The Episcopal Church is also represented.

Anglican Church: St Bridget's, Hoogestraat 44, Paramaribo.

Protestant Churches

Evangelisch-Lutherse Kerk in Suriname: Waterkant 102, POB 585, Paramaribo; tel. 425503; fax 481856; e-mail elks@sr.net; Pres. WIM LOOR; 4,000 mems.

Moravian Church in Suriname (Evangelische Broeder Gemeente): Maagdenstraat 50, POB 1811, Paramaribo; tel. 473073; fax 475794; e-mail ebgs@sr.net; f. 1735; Praeses MAARTEN MINGOEN; 40,000 mems (2004).

Adherents to the Moravian Church consitute some 15% of the population. Also represented are the Christian Reformed Church, the Dutch Reformed Church, the Baptist Church, the Evangelical Methodist Church, Pentecostal Missions, the Seventh-day Adventists and the Wesleyan Methodist Congregation.

HINDUISM

Arya Dewaker: Johan Adolf Pengelstraat 210, Paramaribo; tel. 400706; e-mail aryadewaker@sr.net; members preach the Vedic Dharma; disciples of Maha Rishi Swami Dayanand Sarswati, the founder of the Arya Samaj in India; f. 1929; Chair. INDERDATH TILAKDHARIE.

Sanatan Dharm: Koningstraat 31–33, POB 760, Paramaribo; tel. 404190; f. 1930; Pres. Dr R. M. NANNAN PANDAY; over 150,000 mems.

ISLAM

Federatie Islamitische Gemeenten in Suriname: Paramaribo; Indonesian Islamic org.; Chair. K. KAAIMAN.

Stichting der Islamitische Gemeenten Suriname: Verlengde Mahonielaan 39, Paramaribo; Indonesian Islamic org.

Surinaamse Islamitische Organisatie (SIO): Watermolenstraat 10, POB 278, Paramaribo; tel. 475220; f. 1978; Pres. Dr I. JAMALUDIN; Sec. Dr K. MOENNE; 6 brs.

Surinaamse Moeslim Associatie: Kankantriestraat 55–57, Paramaribo; Javanese Islamic org.

JUDAISM

The Dutch Jewish Congregation and the Dutch Portuguese-Jewish Congregation are represented in Suriname.

Jewish Community: The Synagogue Neve Shalom, Keizerstraat, POB 1834, Paramaribo; tel. 400236; fax 402380; e-mail rene-fernandes@cq-link.sr; internet www.ujcl.org; f. 1854; mem. of Union of Jewish Congregations of Latin America and the Caribbean (UJCL); Officiant JACQUES VAN NIEL; 300 mems (2005).

The Press

DAILIES

Dagblad Suriname: Zwartenhovenbrugstraat 154, POB 975, Paramaribo; tel. 426336; fax 471718; e-mail general@dbsuriname.com; internet www.dbsuriname.com; f. 2002; Dir FARIED PIERKHAN; Editor LAL MAHOMED JAMES.

De Ware Tijd: Malebatrumstraat 9, POB 1200, Paramaribo; tel. 472833; fax 411169; e-mail infodwt@dwt.net; internet www.dwtonline.com; f. 1957; morning; Dutch; independent/liberal; Dir STEVE JONG TJIEN FA; Editor-in-Chief RICARDO CARROT.

De West: Dr J. C. de Mirandastraat 2–6, POB 176, Paramaribo; tel. 473327; fax 470322; e-mail dewest@cq-link.sr; internet www.dewestonline.cq-link.sr; f. 1909; midday; Dutch; liberal; Editor GEORGE D. C. FINDLAY; circ. 15,000–18,000.

PERIODICALS

Advertentieblad van de Republiek Suriname: Henck Arronstraat 120, POB 56, Paramaribo; tel. 473501; fax 454782; f. 1871; 2 a week; Dutch; govt and official information bulletin; Editor E. D. FINDLAY; circ. 1,000.

CLO Bulletin: Gemenelandsweg 95, Paramaribo; f. 1973; irreg.; Dutch; labour information publ. by civil servants' union.

Kerkbode: Burenstraat 17–19, POB 219, Paramaribo; tel. 473079; fax 475635; e-mail stadje@sr.net; f. 1906; weekly; religious; circ. 2,000.

Omhoog: Henck Arronstraat 21, POB 1802, Paramaribo; tel. 425992; fax 426782; e-mail rkomhoog@sr.net; f. 1952; Dutch; weekly; Catholic bulletin; Editor S. MULDER; circ. 5,000.

Xtreme Magazine: Uranusstraat 49, Paramaribo; tel. 456969.

Publishers

Afaka International NV: Residastraat 23, Paramaribo; tel. and fax 530640; e-mail info@afaka.biz; internet www.afaka.biz; f. 1996; Dir GERRIT BARRON.

Educatieve Uitgeverij Sorava NV: Latourweg 10, POB 8382, Paramaribo; tel. and fax 480808.

IMWO, Universiteit van Suriname: Universiteitscomplex, Leysweg 1, POB 9212, Paramaribo; tel. 465558; fax 462291; e-mail bmhango@yahoo.com.

Ministerie van Onderwijs en Volksontwikkeling (Ministry of Education and Community Development): Dr Samuel Kafilludistraat 117–123, Paramaribo; tel. 498850; fax 495083.

Okopipi Publ. (Publishing Services Suriname): Van Idsingastraat 133, Paramaribo; tel. 472746; e-mail pssmoniz@sr.net; fmrly I. Krishnadath.

Papaya Media: Plutostraat 30, POB 8304, Paramaribo; tel. and fax 454530; e-mail roy_bhikharie@sr.net; f. 2002; Man. Dir ROY BHIKHARIE.

Stichting Wetenschappelijke Informatie (Foundation for Information and Development): Prins Hendrikstraat 38, Paramaribo; tel. 475232; fax 422195; e-mail swin@sr.net; f. 1977.

Tabiki Productions: Weidestraat 34, Paramaribo; tel. 478525; fax 478526; e-mail insightsuriname@yahoo.com.

VACO, NV: Domineestraat 26, POB 1841, Paramaribo; tel. 472545; fax 410563; f. 1952; Dir EDUARD HOGENBOOM.

PUBLISHERS' ASSOCIATION

Publishers' Association Suriname: Domineestraat 32, POB 1841, Paramaribo; tel. 472545; fax 410563.

Broadcasting and Communications

TELECOMMUNICATIONS

Regulatory Authority

Telecommunications Authority Suriname (TAS): Heerenstraat 13–15, 1°, Paramaribo; tel. 421463; fax 421465; e-mail tasur@sr.net; f. April 2006 under new Telecommunication Provisions Act; regulatory authority; Dir JETTIE OLFF.

Major Service Providers

Digicel Suriname: Henck Arronstraat 27–29, POB 1848, Paramaribo; tel. 473169; fax 551533; mobile operating licence granted in Aug. 2006; operations commenced Dec. 2007; Dir MITCHELL TJIN A DJIE; Country Man. PHILIP VAN DALSEN.

International Telecommunication Suriname NV (IntelSur NV): Paramaribo; mobile operating licence granted in August 2006 formalized in April 2007; CEO ERIC LELIENHOF.

Telecommunication Corporation Suriname (Telesur): Heiligenweg 1, POB 1839, Paramaribo; tel. 473944; fax 404800; internet www.telesur.sr; liberalization of the telecommunications sector ended Telesur's monopoly in April 2007; supervisory function of Telesur assumed by new regulatory body, Telecommunication Authority Suriname (q.v.); Man. Dir DIRK M. R. CURRIE.

BROADCASTING
Radio

ABC Radio (Ampie's Broadcasting Corporation): Maystraat 57, Paramaribo; tel. 464609; fax 464680; e-mail info@abcsuriname.com; internet www.abcsuriname.com; f. 1975; re-opened in 1993; commercial; Dutch and some local languages.

Radio Apintie: Verlengde Gemenelandsweg 37, POB 595, Paramaribo; tel. 498855; fax 400684; e-mail apintie@sr.net; internet www.apintie.sr; f. 1958; commercial; Dutch and some local languages; Gen. Man. CHARLES VERVUURT.

Radio Bersama: Bonniestraat 115, Paramaribo; tel. 551804; fax 551803; f. 1997; Dir AJOEB MOENTARI.

Radio Boskopou: Roseveltkade 1, Paramaribo; tel. 410300; govt-owned; Sranang Tongo and Dutch; Head Mr VAN VARSEVELD.

Radio Garuda: Goudstraat 14–16, Paramaribo; tel. 422422; Dir TOMMY RADJI.

Radio Nickerie (RANI): Waterloostraat 3, Nieuw Nickerie; tel. 231462; commercial; Hindi and Dutch.

Radio Paramaribo (Rapar): Verlengde Jagernath Lachmonstraat 34, POB 975, Paramaribo; tel. 499995; fax 493121; e-mail rapar@sr.net; f. 1957; commercial; Dutch and some local languages; Dir RASHIED PIERKHAN.

Radio Radika: Indira Gandhiweg 165, Paramaribo; tel. 482800; fax 482910; e-mail radika@sr.net; re-opened in 1989; Dutch and Hindi; Dir ROSHNI RADHAKISHUN.

Radio Sangeet Mala: Indira Gandhiweg 73, Paramaribo; tel. 485893; Dutch and Hindi; Dirs RADJEN SOEKHRADJ, SOEDESH RAMSARAN.

Radio SRS (Stichting Radio Omroep Suriname): Jacques van Eerstraat 20, POB 271, Paramaribo; tel. 498115; fax 498116; e-mail radiosrs@sr.net; f. 1965; commercial; govt-owned; Dutch and some local languages; Dir LEOPOLD DARTHUIZEN.

Radio Ten: Letitia Vriesdelaan 5, Paramaribo; tel. 410881; fax 410885; e-mail radio10@cq-link.sr; internet www.radio10.cq-link.sr.

Other stations include: Radio KBC, Radio Koyeba, Radio Pertjaya, Radio Shalom, Radio Zon, Ramasha Radio, Rasonic Radio and Trishul Radio.

Television

ABC Televisie (Ampie's Broadcasting Corporation): Maystraat 57, Paramaribo; tel. 464555; fax 464680; e-mail info@abcsuriname.com; internet www.abcsuriname.com; Channel 4.

Algemene Televisie Verzorging (ATV): Adrianusstraat 55, POB 2995, Paramaribo; tel. 404611; fax 402660; e-mail info@atv.sr; internet www.atv.sr; f. 1985; govt-owned; commercial; Dutch, English, Portuguese, Spanish and some local languages; Channel 12; Man. GUNO COOMAN.

STVS (Surinaamse Televisie Stichting): Letitia Vriesdelaan 5, POB 535, Paramaribo; tel. 473031; fax 477216; e-mail adm@stvs.info.sr; internet www.parbo.com/stvs; f. 1965; govt-owned; commercial; local languages, Dutch and English; Channel 8; Dir KENNETH OOSTBURG.

Finance

(cap. = capital; res = reserves; dep. = deposits; m. = million; brs = branches; amounts in Suriname guilders)

BANKING
Central Bank

Centrale Bank van Suriname: 18–20 Waterkant, POB 1801, Paramaribo; tel. 473741; fax 476444; e-mail info@cbvs.sr; internet www.cbvs.sr; f. 1957; Gov. ANDRÉ E. TELTING.

Commercial Banks

Finabank NV: Dr Sophie Redmondstraat 59–61, Paramaribo; tel. 472266; fax 422672; e-mail finabank@sr.net; internet www.finabanknv.com; f. 1991; Gen. Man. MERLEEN ATMODIKROMO.

Handels-Krediet- en Industriebank (Hakrinbank NV): Dr Sophie Redmondstraat 11–13, POB 1813, Paramaribo; tel. 477722; fax 472066; e-mail hakrindp@sr.net; internet www.hakrinbank.com; f. 1936; cap. 0.1m., res 33.2m., dep. 552.5m. (Dec. 2006); Pres. and Chair. A. K. R. SHYAMNARAIN; Man. Dirs M. TJON-A-TEN, J. D. BOUSAID; 6 brs.

Landbouwbank NV: FHR Lim A Postraat 34, POB 929, Paramaribo; tel. 475945; fax 411965; e-mail lbbank@sr.net; f. 1972; govt-owned; agricultural bank; Chair. D. FERRIER; Pres. R. MERHAI; 5 brs.

RBTT Bank NV: Kerkplein 1, Paramaribo; tel. 471555; fax 411325.

De Surinaamsche Bank NV: Henck Arronstraat 26–30, POB 1806, Paramaribo; tel. 471100; fax 411750; e-mail info@dsbbank.sr;

SURINAME

internet www.dsbbank.sr; f. 1865; cap. 0.2m., res 73.1m., dep. 921.8m. (Dec. 2006); Chair. S. SMIT; 8 brs.

Surinaamse Postspaarbank: Knuffelsgracht 10–14, POB 1879, Paramaribo; tel. 472256; fax 472952; e-mail spsbdir@sr.net; f. 1904; savings and commercial bank; cap. and res 1,044m., dep. 66,533m. (Dec. 2004); Man. ALWIN R. BAARH (acting); 2 brs.

Surinaamse Volkscredietbank: Waterkant 104, POB 1804, Paramaribo; tel. 472616; fax 473257; e-mail btlsvcb@sr.net; f. 1949; cap. and res 170.3m. (Dec. 1997); Man. Dir THAKOERDIEN RAMLAKHAN; 3 brs.

Development Bank

Nationale Ontwikkelingsbank van Suriname NV: Jagernath Lachmonstraat 160–162, POB 677, Paramaribo; tel. 465000; fax 497192; f. 1963; govt-supported; cap. and res 34m. (Dec. 1992).

INSURANCE

Assuria NV: Grote Combeweg 37, POB 1501, Paramaribo; tel. 477955; fax 472390; e-mail assuria@sr.net; internet www.assuria.sr; f. 1961; life and indemnity insurance; Man. Dir Dr S. SMIT.

Assuria Schadeverzekering NV: Henck Arronstraat 5–7, POB 1030, Paramaribo; tel. 473400; fax 476669; e-mail assuria@sr.net; internet www.assuria.sr; Chair. J. J. HEALY; Man. Dir Dr S. SMIT.

CLICO Life Insurance Company Ltd: Klipstenenstraat 29, POB 3026, Paramaribo; tel. 472525; fax 476777; e-mail clicosur@sr.net; internet www.clico.com/suriname; CEO CLAUDIUS DACON; Dir KAREN-ANN GARDIER.

Fatum Levensverzekering NV: Noorderkerkstraat 5–7, Paramaribo; tel. 471541; fax 410067; e-mail fatum@sr.net; internet www.fatum-suriname.com.

Hennep Verzorgende Verzekering NV: Dr Sophie Redmondstraat 246, Paramaribo; tel. 425205; fax 425209; e-mail hennep@sr.net; internet www.uitvaarthennep.com; f. 1896; Man. Dir H. J. HENNEP.

Parsasco NV: Henck Arronstraat 117, Paramaribo; tel. 421212; fax 421325; e-mail parsasco@sr.net; internet www.parsasco.com; Dir L. KHEDOE.

Self Reliance: Herenstraat 22, Paramaribo; tel. 472582; fax 472475; e-mail self-reliance@sr.net; internet www.self-reliance.sr; life insurance; Dir N. J. VEIRA.

Trade and Industry

DEVELOPMENT ORGANIZATIONS

Centre for Industry and Export Development: Rust en Vredestraat 79–81, POB 1275, Paramaribo; tel. 474830; fax 476311; f. 1981; Man. R. A. LETER.

Stichting Planbureau Suriname (National Planning Office of Suriname): Dr Sophie Redmondstraat 118, POB 172, Paramaribo; tel. 447408; fax 475001; e-mail dirsps@sr.net; internet www.planbureau.net; f. 1951; responsible for regional and socio-economic long- and short-term planning; Man. Dir LILIAN J. M. MONSELS-THOMPSON.

CHAMBER OF COMMERCE

Kamer van Koophandel en Fabrieken (Chamber of Commerce and Industry): Dr J. C. de Mirandastraat 10, POB 149, Paramaribo; tel. 474536; fax 474779; e-mail chamber@sr.net; f. 1910; Pres. R. L. A. AMEERALI; 16,109 mems.

Surinaams–Nederlandse Kamer voor Handel en Industrie (Suriname–Netherlands Chamber of Commerce and Industry): Jagernath Lachmonstraat 158, Paramaribo; tel. and fax 476909.

INDUSTRIAL AND TRADE ASSOCIATIONS

Associatie van Surinaamse Fabrikanten (ASFA) (Suriname Manufacturers' Assen): Jaggernath Lachmonstraat 187, POB 3046, Paramaribo; tel. 439797; fax 439798; e-mail asfa@sr.net; Chair. KATHLEEN LIEUW KIE SONG; 317 mems.

Vereniging Surinaams Bedrijfsleven (Suriname Trade and Industry Association): Prins Hendrikstraat 18, POB 111, Paramaribo; tel. 475286; fax 475287; e-mail info@vsbstia.org; internet www.vsbstia.org; Pres. MARCEL A. MEYER; 290 mems.

UTILITIES

Electricity

Staatsolie Maatschappij Suriname: Dr Ir Adhinstraat 21, POB 4069, Paramaribo; tel. 499649; fax 491105; e-mail mailstaatsolie@staatsolie.com; internet www.staatsolie.com; state-owned electricity supplier; Man. Dir M. C. H. WAALDIJK.

TRADE UNIONS

Council of the Surinamese Federation of Trade Unions (RAVAKSUR): f. 1987; Sec. FREDDY WATERBERG; comprises:

Algemeen Verbond van Vakverenigingen in Suriname 'De Moederbond' (AVVS) (General Confederation of Trade Unions): Verlengde Jagernath Lachmonstraat 134, POB 2951, Paramaribo; tel. 463501; fax 465116; e-mail avvsmoederbonds51@hotmail.com; right-wing; Pres. IMRO GREP; Gen. Sec. ALESSANDRO SPRONG; 15,000 mems.

Centrale Landsdienaren Organisatie (CLO) (Central Organization for Civil Service Employees): Gemenelandsweg 743, Paramaribo; tel. 499839; Pres. RONALD HOOGHART; 13,000 mems.

Organisatie van Samenwerkende Autonome Vakbonden (OSAV): Noorderkerkstraat 2–10, Paramaribo; Pres. SONNY CHOTKAN; Gen. Sec. HAROLD CODRINGTON.

Progressieve Werknemers Organisatie (PWO) (Progressive Workers' Organization): Limesgracht 80, POB 406, Paramaribo; tel. 475840; f. 1948; covers the commercial, hotel and banking sectors; Pres. ANDRE KOORNAAR; Sec. EDWARD MENT; 4,000 mems.

Progressive Trade Union Federation (C-47): Wanicastraat 230, Paramaribo; tel. 494365; fax 401149; Pres. ROBBY BERENSTEIN.

Federation of Civil Servants Organization (CLO): Verlengde Gemenelandsweg 74, Paramaribo; tel. 464200; fax 493918; Pres. RONALD HOOGHART; Gen. Sec. DOROTHY TELTING.

Federation of Farmers and Agrarians (FAL): Keizerstraat 150, Paramaribo; tel. 464200; fax 499839; Pres. JIWAN SITAL; Gen. Sec. ANAND DWARKA.

Nickerie Banana Workers' Union (BABN): Paramaribo; f. 2008; Pres. DAYANAND DWARKA.

Transport

RAILWAYS

There are no public railways operating in Suriname.

ROADS

In 2003 Suriname had an estimated 4,304 km (2,674 miles) of roads, of which 26.3% were paved. The principal east–west road, 390 km in length, links Albina, on the eastern border, with Nieuw Nickerie, in the west.

SHIPPING

Suriname is served by many shipping companies and has about 1,500 km (930 miles) of navigable rivers and canals. A number of shipping companies conduct regular international services (principally for freight) to and from Paramaribo including EWL, Fyffesgroup, the Alcoa Steamship Co, Marli Marine Lines, Bic Line, Nedlloyd Line, Maersk Lines and Tecmarine Lines (in addition to those listed below). There are also two ferry services linking Suriname with Guyana, across the Corentijn river, and with French Guiana, across the Marowijne river.

Maritieme Autoriteit Suriname (Suriname Maritime Authority): Cornelis Jongbawstraat 2, POB 888, Paramaribo; tel. 476769; fax 472940; e-mail info@mas.sr; fmrly Dienst voor de Scheepvaart; govt authority supervising and controlling shipping in Surinamese waters; Man. of Nautical Affairs M. HARRIS.

Scheepvaart Maatschappij Suriname NV (SMS) (Suriname Shipping Line Ltd): Waterkant 44, POB 1824, Paramaribo; tel. 472447; fax 474814; e-mail surinam_line@sr.net; f. 1936; state-owned; passenger services in the interior; Chair. A. T. EDENBURG.

Suriname Coast Traders NV: Flocislaan 4, Industrieterrein Flora, POB 9216, Paramaribo; tel. 463040; fax 463831; internet www.pasonsgroup.com; f. 1981; subsidiary of Pasons Group.

NV VSH United Suriname Shipping Company: Van het Hogerhuysstraat 9–11, POB 1860, Paramaribo; tel. 402558; fax 403515; e-mail sales@vshunited.com; internet www.vshunited.com/shipping.html; shipping agents and freight carriers; Man. RICHARD STEENLAND.

CIVIL AVIATION

The main airport is Johan Adolf Pengel International Airport (formerly Zanderij International Airport), 45 km from Paramaribo. Domestic flights operate from Zorg-en-Hoop Airport, located in a suburb of Paramaribo. There are 35 airstrips throughout the country.

Surinaamse Luchtvaart Maatschappij NV (SLM) (Suriname Airways): Mr Jagernath Lachmonstraat 136, POB 2029, Paramaribo; tel. 465700; fax 491213; e-mail publicrelations@slm.firm.sr; internet www.surinamairways.net; f. 1962; services to Amsterdam (Netherlands) and to destinations in North America, South America and the Caribbean; Vice-Pres. CLYDE CAIRO.

Gonini Air Service Ltd: Doekhiweg 1, Zorg-en-Hoop Airport, POB 1614, Paramaribo; tel. 499098; fax 498363; f. 1976; privately owned; licensed for scheduled and unscheduled national and international services (charters, lease, etc.); Man. Dir GERARD BRUNINGS.

Gum Air NV: Doekhieweg 3, Zorg en Hoop Airfield, Paramaribo; tel. 498888; fax 497670; e-mail info@gumair.com; internet www.gumair.com; privately owned; unscheduled domestic and regional flights; Man. HENK GUMMELS.

Tourism

Efforts were made to promote the previously undeveloped tourism sector in the 1990s. Attractions include the varied cultural activities, a number of historical sites and an unspoiled interior with many varieties of plants, birds and animals. There are 13 nature reserves and one nature park. There were a total of 160,000 foreign tourist arrivals in 2005, of which a majority came from the Netherlands. In 2005 tourism receipts totalled US $96m.

Suriname Tourism Foundation: Dr J. F. Nassylaan 2, Paramaribo; tel. 424878; fax 477786; e-mail info@suriname-tourism.org; internet www.suriname-tourism.org; f. 1996; Exec. Dir ARMAND LI-A-YOUNG.

SWAZILAND

Introductory Survey

Location, Climate, Language, Religion, Flag, Capital

The Kingdom of Swaziland is a land-locked country in southern Africa, bordered by South Africa to the north, west, south and south-east, and by Mozambique to the east. The average annual temperature is about 16°C (61°F) on the Highveld, and about 22°C (72°F) in the sub-humid Lowveld, while annual rainfall ranges from 1,000 mm (40 ins) to 2,280 mm (90 ins) on the Highveld, and from 500 mm (20 ins) to 890 mm (35 ins) in the Lowveld. English and siSwati are the official languages. About 60% of the population profess Christianity, while most of the remainder adhere to traditional beliefs. The national flag (proportions 2 by 3) is blue, with a yellow-edged horizontal crimson stripe (one-half of the depth) in the centre. On this stripe is a black and white Swazi shield, superimposed on two spears and a staff, all lying horizontally. The capital is Mbabane.

Recent History

Swaziland, which was previously under the joint rule of the United Kingdom and the South African (Transvaal) Republic, became a British protectorate in 1903, and one of the High Commission Territories in 1907, the others being the colony of Basutoland (now the Kingdom of Lesotho) and the protectorate of Bechuanaland (now the Republic of Botswana). The British Act of Parliament that established the Union of South Africa in 1910 also provided for the inclusion in South Africa of the three High Commission Territories, subject to consultation with the local inhabitants.

Swaziland's first Constitution, which was introduced by the British Government, entered into force in January 1964. The Paramount Chief (iNgwenyama—the Lion), King Sobhuza II, subsequently established a traditionalist political party, the Imbokodvo National Movement (INM), which secured all of the seats in the new Legislative Council at elections in June of that year. In 1965, in response to continued pressure from the INM, the British Government established a committee to draft proposed constitutional amendments. A new Constitution, which was promulgated in 1966 and came into effect in April 1967, provided for the introduction of internal self-government pending the attainment of full independence by the end of 1969. Executive power was vested in King Sobhuza as the hereditary monarch and constitutional Head of State. The Legislative Council was dissolved in March 1967, and elections to the new bicameral Parliament took place in April. The INM secured all 24 elective seats in the House of Assembly, although the Ngwane National Liberatory Congress (NNLC) received 20% of the votes cast. In May King Sobhuza formed Swaziland's first Cabinet, appointing the leader of the INM, Prince Makhosini Dlamini, as Prime Minister. On 6 September 1968 Swaziland was granted full independence within the Commonwealth, and a new Constitution (based on the existing Constitution) was adopted.

At elections to the House of Assembly in May 1972, the INM secured 21 seats, while the NNLC won the remaining three elective seats. In April 1973, in accordance with a parliamentary resolution, King Sobhuza repealed the Constitution, imposed a state of emergency under which all political activity was suspended, introduced legislation providing for detention without trial for a period of 60 days, and announced the formation of a national army. A new Constitution, promulgated on 13 October 1978, confirmed the King's control of executive and legislative decisions. The functions of the bicameral parliament, comprising a House of Assembly and a Senate, were confined to debating government proposals and advising the King. The existing 40 traditional local councils (Tinkhundla—singular: Inkhundla) were each to nominate two members to an 80-member electoral college, which was, in turn, to elect 40 deputies to the House of Assembly. Members of the House of Assembly were to select 10 members of the Senate, while the King was to nominate a further 10 members to each chamber. All political parties (including the INM) were prohibited. Legislative elections took place later that year, and the parliament was inaugurated in January 1979. In June 1982 the Swaziland National Council, an advisory body on matters of Swazi tradition, comprising members of the royal family, was redesignated as the Supreme Council of State (Liqoqo).

King Sobhuza died in August 1982. In accordance with Swazi tradition, the powers of Head of State devolved upon the Queen Mother (Ndlovukazi—Great She Elephant) Dzeliwe, who was authorized to act as Regent until King Sobhuza's designated successor, Prince Makhosetive (born in 1968), attained the age of 21. Shortly afterwards Queen Regent Dzeliwe appointed the Liqoqo, which was to advise her in all affairs of State. Competition to secure supreme executive power subsequently emerged between the Prime Minister, Prince Mabandla N. F. Dlamini, and several prominent members, led by Prince Mfanasibili Dlamini, of the Liqoqo. In March 1983 Prince Mabandla was replaced as Prime Minister by a traditionalist, Prince Bhekimpi Dlamini. In August, under the powers of the 'Authorized Person' (an important hereditary post, held by Prince Sozisa Dlamini, the Chairman of the Liqoqo), Queen Regent Dzeliwe was deposed, apparently as a result of her reluctance to dismiss Prince Mabandla. Following an attempt by Queen Regent Dzeliwe to appeal against her deposition, Prince Mfanasibili and his followers obtained an official declaration that the High Court had no jurisdiction in matters concerning Swazi custom and tradition. Widespread opposition to the deposition of Queen Regent Dzeliwe was suppressed, and in September Queen Ntombi, the mother of Prince Makhosetive, was officially invested as Regent. In November elections to the Libandla took place, and a new Cabinet was appointed, in which only Prince Bhekimpi and the Minister of Foreign Affairs, Richard Dlamini, were retained.

In October 1985, following protests by prominent members of the royal family at the Liqoqo's monopoly of power, Queen Regent Ntombi dismissed Prince Mfanasibili. It was subsequently announced that the Liqoqo was to be reconstituted in its former capacity as an advisory body on matters pertaining to traditional law and custom. In December all those convicted of conspiracy in late 1984 were pardoned and released. In January 1986 it was announced that Prince Makhosetive was to be crowned in April, three years earlier than expected, in order to end the competition for power among vying royal factions.

Prince Makhosetive was crowned on 25 April 1986, and assumed the title of King Mswati III. In May King Mswati dissolved the Liqoqo, thereby consolidating his power. In July the King reorganized the Cabinet, and in October he appointed a former senior member of the security forces, Sotsha Dlamini, as Prime Minister. In May 1987 12 prominent officials, including Prince Bhekimpi and Prince Mfanasibili, were charged with sedition and treason, in connection with the removal from power of Queen Regent Dzeliwe in 1983. In November King Mswati established a special tribunal to preside over all cases involving alleged offences against the King or the Queen Regent; defendants appearing before the tribunal were not to be granted the right to legal representation or appeal. In March 1988 10 of those accused of involvement in the deposition of Queen Regent Dzeliwe were convicted of treason by the special tribunal, and received custodial sentences; two defendants were acquitted. In July, however, it was reported that the 10 convicted in March had been released.

In November 1987 elections to the legislature took place, one year earlier than scheduled. In July 1998 King Mswati dismissed Sotsha Dlamini for alleged disobedience, replacing him with Obed Dlamini, a former leader of the Swaziland Federation of Trade Unions (SFTU).

In early 1990 the People's United Democratic Movement (PUDEMO), which had been established in 1983, distributed tracts questioning the legitimacy of the monarchy in its existing form and demanding constitutional reform. Security forces subsequently arrested a number of suspected members of PUDEMO, who were variously charged with treason, sedition or conspiring to form a political party. All the defendants were acquitted of the principal charges, although five were convicted of illegally attending a political gathering (the sentences of two of the five were annulled on appeal in October 1991). In November King Mswati dismissed the reformist Minister of Justice, Reginald Dhladhla, reportedly on the advice of the Swaziland National Council (which had been reconstituted from the former Liqoqo), prompting public concern that it continued to exert undue influence on government policies. Later in November five members of PUDEMO (who had previously been acquitted of all charges) were arrested under legislation enabling the detention of suspects without trial. In March 1991 the prisoners were released, as a result of international pressure. In an attempt to advance its objectives through legal bodies, PUDEMO subsequently established a number of affiliated organizations, including the Human Rights Association of Swaziland (HUMARAS) and the Swaziland Youth Congress (SWAYOCO), but these were not accorded official recognition.

In September and October 1991 a committee, termed Vusela (Greetings), conducted a series of public forums throughout the country to elicit popular opinion on political reforms. Widespread demands for the abolition of the existing electoral system were reported, while there was substantial criticism of the composition of the Vusela committee itself. In subsequent months several peaceful demonstrations, organized by SWAYOCO to demand the establishment of a democratic system of government, were suppressed by security forces. In October King Mswati announced an extensive reorganization of the Cabinet. In February 1992 PUDEMO declared itself a legal opposition party (in contravention of the prohibition on political association), rejected King Mswati's efforts to institute political reform, and demanded a constitutional referendum. Two further opposition movements, the Swaziland United Front (SUF) and the Swaziland National Front (SWANAFRO), subsequently re-emerged. In February King Mswati appointed a second committee (Vusela 2), which was to present recommendations for consideration by the King, based on the conclusions of the first committee.

In October 1992 King Mswati approved several proposals submitted by Vusela 2. The House of Assembly (redesignated the National Assembly) was to be expanded to 65 deputies (of whom 55 were to be directly elected by secret ballot from candidates nominated by the Tinkhundla, and 10 appointed by the King), and the Senate to 30 members (10 selected by the National Assembly and 20 appointed by the King); in addition, the legislation providing for detention without trial was to be abrogated, and a new constitution, incorporating the amendments, enshrining an hereditary monarchy and confirming the fundamental rights of the individual and the independence of the judiciary, was to be drafted. However, opposition groups protested at the committee's failure to recommend the immediate restoration of a multi-party political system: the issue was to be postponed until the forthcoming elections, in order to determine the extent of public support. PUDEMO announced its opposition to the electoral reforms, and demanded that the Government organize a national convention to determine the country's constitutional future. King Mswati subsequently dissolved parliament, and announced that he was to rule by decree, with the assistance of the Council of Ministers (as the Cabinet had been restyled), pending the adoption of a new constitution and the holding of parliamentary elections. Later in October King Mswati announced that elections to the National Assembly would take place in the first half of 1993. At a series of public meetings doubts were expressed as to the viability of the reformed electoral system; in early 1993, in response to public concern, it was announced that legislation preventing the heads of the Tinkhundla from exerting undue influence in the nomination of candidates had been introduced.

The first round of elections to the expanded National Assembly took place on 25 September 1993. The second round of parliamentary elections, on 11 October, was contested by the three candidates in each Inkhundla who had obtained the highest number of votes in the first poll; the majority of members of the former Council of Ministers (which had been dissolved in late September), including Obed Dlamini, failed to secure seats in the Assembly. Later in October King Mswati nominated a further 10 deputies to the National Assembly, which elected 10 of its members to the Senate; King Mswati subsequently appointed the remaining 20 senators, among them Obed Dlamini and Prince Bhekimpi. In November the former Minister of Works and Construction, Prince Jameson Mbilini Dlamini, considered a traditionalist, was appointed Prime Minister, and a new Council of Ministers was formed.

In February 1994, following a report by the US Department of State that stated that the parliamentary elections had been 'undemocratic', the Government claimed that the majority of the Swazi people were opposed to the establishment of a multi-party political system. It was announced, however, that King Mswati was to appoint a 15-member commission, comprising representatives of organs of State and non-governmental organizations, to draft a new constitution, and a national policy council, which was to prepare a manifesto of the Swazi people. Elections to the Tinkhundla (which had been postponed from March) finally took place, although a high rate of abstention by voters was reported. (The heads of the Tinkhundla had previously been appointed by the King.)

In March 1995 the SFTU undertook a two-day general strike in support of a set of 27 demands (first presented in January 1994) that included the repeal of the 1973 decree banning all political activity. The unions subsequently suspended further strike action after the Government established an independent committee to consider the SFTU's demands. In August the Senate approved a motion supporting a statement made by King Mswati to the effect that the Swazi population was not in favour of a multi-party system.

In January 1996 PUDEMO announced a campaign of protests and civil disobedience, owing to the Government's failure to respond to demands for the installation of a multi-party system and for the adoption of a constitution restricting the monarch to a largely ceremonial role. Security forces intervened to suppress demonstrations by SFTU members, and violent clashes ensued, in which three people were reported to have been killed. The SFTU refused to enter into negotiations with the Government, stipulating that the 1973 decree and restrictions on trade unions be revoked prior to discussions. Meanwhile, it was reported that some members of the Government, including Obed Dlamini, also favoured political reform. King Mswati accused the trade unions of attempting to overthrow the monarchy, and threatened to order his traditional warriors to suppress the strike. The SFTU subsequently suspended strike action to allow negotiations to proceed with the Government (which continued to reject the unions' preconditions for discussions). In February 1996 King Mswati announced that the process of drafting a new constitution would be initiated later that year, and that the ban on political activity would also be reviewed. In May King Mswati indicated that a 'People's Parliament', comprising a series of consultative meetings between citizens and government leaders, had been initiated to solicit public opinion regarding constitutional reform. At the same time King Mswati dismissed Prince Mbilini as Prime Minister, and announced that he would appoint his successor in consultation with the Swaziland National Council.

In late July 1996, following an emergency meeting (attended by the Heads of State of Mozambique, Botswana, Zimbabwe and South Africa) to discuss Swaziland's political situation, King Mswati appointed a Constitutional Review Commission, comprising chiefs, political activists and trade unionists, to collate submissions from the Swazi people and subsequently draft proposals for a new constitution. (The Commission received substantial funds from international donors.) At the same time, Dr Barnabas Sibusiso Dlamini, an IMF Executive Director and former Minister of Finance, was appointed Prime Minister.

In December 1996 the Prime Minister announced that a 'task force', composed of workers, employers and government representatives, had discussed the SFTU's demands made in March 1995, and that the implementation of the recommendations outlined in the resulting report was to be overseen by the Labour Advisory Board. In January 1997, however, the SFTU claimed that there had been no response to its demands for democratic reform, and resolved to begin indefinite strike action from February. Meanwhile, the PUDEMO President, Mario Masuku, declared that Swaziland's leaders were not committed to change, and withdrew from the Constitutional Review Commission. At the end of January the four main leaders of the SFTU were arrested and subsequently charged with intimidating bus owners into joining the forthcoming strike. The strike, pronounced illegal by the Government, proceeded, and was apparently observed by approximately one-half of the labour force. On the ninth day of industrial action six strikers were seriously injured in violent clashes with the security forces. The SFTU leaders declined the Government's offer to release them on condition that they end the strike; their trial was dismissed in February, owing to lack of evidence. At the beginning of March the Congress of South African Trade Unions (COSATU), which had asserted its support for the SFTU throughout the strike, initiated a one-day blockade of the Swazi border. The SFTU decided to suspend the strike shortly afterwards, as the Government had agreed to commence negotiations, but resolved to continue industrial action on the first two days of each month until its 27 demands had been met. In April 1997 the SFTU postponed a further blockade indefinitely, in order to allow the Government adequate time to review the situation.

In October 1997 the SFTU called a nation-wide strike in support of its ongoing demands for democratic reform, after talks with the Government failed to produce any agreement, although support for the strike was low. Teachers none the less resolved to continue with separate industrial action in support of pay demands. Meanwhile, SFTU and other protesters demanded the recall from Swaziland of the British High Commissioner, whom they accused of colluding with the King and interfering in domestic affairs.

In August 1998 King Mswati dissolved the National Assembly, in preparation for elections scheduled for October. Opposition groups urged voters to boycott the polls, in the absence of the immediate legalization of political parties. Some 350 candidates were nominated by the Tinkhundla to contest the 55 elective seats in the Assembly. Voting took place on 16 and 24 October; turn-out was reportedly low. A new Cabinet, with Sibusiso Dlamini as Prime Minister, was appointed in mid-November, and a new Senate and Swaziland National Council were formed.

In April 1999 the NNLC, PUDEMO and the SFTU united to form the Swaziland Democratic Alliance (SDA). The NNLC leader, Obed Dlamini, was elected Chairman. The formal launch of the SDA was scheduled for 11 April, to coincide with the end of the Southern African Development Community (SADC, see p. 386) labour conference in Mbabane. However, following warnings from the police that the proposed inauguration, which had been rescheduled for 19 April, was illegal and would not be permitted to take place, the executive of the SDA met and cancelled the event.

A judicial crisis developed in late 2002 when, with reference to decrees issued by the King in connection with the evictions of some 200 people from their homes in October 2000, the six South African judges of the Swaziland Court of Appeal resigned in protest at the Government's refusal to accept two rulings that the King had no power to overrule the National Assembly. The judges of the High Court subsequently announced that they would refuse to sit or set dates for hearings, and a strike by members of the legal profession ensued. In April 2003 a report by the International Bar Association attributed the judicial crisis to the lack of clearly defined roles for the executive, legislature and judiciary. In May the Government withdrew a statement in which it had accused the judges of being under external influence. In mid-September 2004 the Government reversed its position on the rulings which had provoked the crisis. Hearings were scheduled to resume at the Court of Appeal in November on condition that those evicted were allowed to return to their villages.

Meanwhile, in June 2001 King Mswati provoked international criticism by promulgating a decree that, it was claimed, effectively amounted to the declaration of a state of emergency; the legislation ensured that no person or body, including the courts, had the authority to challenge the King, prevented newspapers from challenging publishing bans, allowed the King to appoint judges and traditional chiefs personally, and made ridiculing or impersonating the King a criminal offence. Opposition groups in Swaziland condemned the decree as reinforcing tyrannical rule, and criticized the international community's lack of interest in the country's political situation. The King revoked the decree in July, in response to international diplomatic pressure, notably a threat by the USA to impose economic sanctions. However, at the same time the King issued a new decree that retained certain sections of the original decree, including a provision allowing the detention of Swazi citizens without the option of bail for some offences.

In August 2001 the Constitutional Review Commission submitted its report, which recommended that the King's powers be extended and political parties remain outlawed, but stated that the introduction of a bill of rights that was not in conflict with Swazi laws and customs was a possibility. The SFTU and PUDEMO rejected the Commission's proposals. In February 2002 a 15-member committee, appointed by the King, began drafting a new constitution; PUDEMO criticized the Government for allegedly manipulating the Commission's report and selecting members of the drafting committee who were sympathetic to government policy. In May Prince David, the King's brother, and Chairman of the constitution-drafting committee, announced a new draft constitution, which, inter alia, envisaged the retention of the Tinkhundla system for forthcoming elections to the National Assembly.

King Mswati introduced the Internal Security Bill in June 2002, intended to suppress political dissent. It provided variously for fines and prison sentences for those found guilty of carrying or wearing banners or flags of banned political formations, or of participating in mass strikes or boycotts. Training abroad to commit acts of insurgency in Swaziland would be punishable by up to 20 years' imprisonment. The bill was severely criticized by the SFTU, PUDEMO and various foreign governments, which considered it to be inconsistent with the bill of rights and the proposed constitutional reform.

In October 2002 the King was the subject of a legal challenge from the mother of a girl chosen to be his 10th wife; the woman alleged that her daughter had been abducted by two of the King's emissaries. However, she withdrew the case in early November, when her daughter stated that she had no objection to becoming a queen. Further controversy arose over the King's order for a private aircraft costing around US $45m. The National Assembly voted against the purchase of the aircraft in November, after it was revealed that development funds from international donors had been diverted to pay for it, but the vote was overruled by the Council of Ministers. The European Union (EU) had previously suspended financial aid to the country over the issue in September 2002. In August 2003 the Prime Minister denied newspaper reports that claimed that the aircraft had been purchased. In January 2004 the King's request for funds to construct a new palace for each of his wives provoked further controversy.

In April 2003 a cabinet reorganization was effected; nine portfolios were redistributed, and the Minister of Public Works and Transport, Titus Mlangeni, was dismissed on suspicion of fraud. On 31 May King Mswati announced the dissolution of the National Assembly. Pending elections to a new Assembly, scheduled for October, a council, styled the King's Order-in-Council, was charged with debating and enacting legislation in collaboration with the King. The elections to the National Assembly, duly held in October, were reportedly marked by a very low turn-out, many voters having apparently heeded an appeal by pro-democracy groups for a boycott of the polls. Although several members of proscribed political organizations stood as independent candidates, a Commonwealth monitoring team subsequently declared that the elections had been largely meaningless, in view of the lack of basic democratic freedoms that prevailed in Swaziland. In November the King appointed Themba Dlamini, a former incumbent on various parastatal bodies and a close associate of the royal family, as the new Prime Minister. At the same time, the King accepted a new draft constitution that, observers noted, safeguarded many of the monarchy's existing prerogatives. Among the provisions of the proposed new basic law was that the King should remain the head of the executive and retain responsibility for appointing the Prime Minister. He would, furthermore, retain a power of veto over any bill that received parliamentary approval. However, the draft Constitution did propose the removal of the King's power to rule by decree and provided for the replacement of the Court of Appeal by a new Supreme Court as Swaziland's highest judicial body.

Meanwhile, in March 2004 Marwick Khumalo resigned as Speaker of the National Assembly and was replaced, in May, by Charles S'gayoyo Magongo. Khumalo claimed that he had been forced to resign, owing to his opposition to government attempts to purchase a private aircraft for the King. In May the National Assembly voted to suspend itself in protest at the Government's stated intention to review the Industrial Court's ruling that the Clerk of Parliament had been illegally dismissed by the previous Prime Minister and should be reinstated. Also in May the National Constituent Assembly (NCA—a pressure group composed of churches, political parties, labour and human rights organizations) announced a legal challenge to what it claimed was the King's intention of promulgating the proposed new Constitution by decree. In mid-June the NCA petitioned the High Court, demanding that the constitution-drafting committee should be required to hold public hearings and receive submissions from interested parties. The High Court agreed that it would hear the petition in August, although no date was fixed.

In January 2005 the SFTU commenced a two-day general strike in protest at the proposed constitutional reform, which it maintained entrenched the power of the monarchy. The new Constitution was finally approved by a joint sitting of the Senate and the National Assembly in early June. It was ratified by King

Mswati on 26 July and came into effect on 7 February 2006. The Constitution was viewed as being socially progressive, according greater rights to women—legally recognized as adults for the first time—and guaranteeing the right to primary education, but politically conservative: executive power was concentrated in the King and the Tinkhundla remained as the basis of the parliamentary system; the King would also continue to appoint the Prime Minister and the Cabinet, Chiefs and High Court judges and could dissolve the legislature. A bill of rights guaranteed freedom of assembly and speech; however, these rights could be suspended by the King if he considered it to be in the public interest. Furthermore, while there existed provision for the judiciary to interpret the Constitution, ultimate authority was vested with the King. There also remained considerable ambiguity regarding the legality of political parties, although the Constitution stated that the 'people of Swaziland have a right to be heard through and represented by their own freely chosen representatives in the government of the country'. In February 2006 the President of the Swaziland Law Society instigated legal proceedings at the High Court to clarify the issue.

In late February 2006 the King effected a reshuffle of the Cabinet. Moses Mathendele Dlamini was appointed Minister of Foreign Affairs and Trade, replacing Mabili Dlamini, who assumed the housing and urban development portfolio vacated by Dumsile Sukati. Sukati was appointed Minister of Natural Resources and Energy, replacing Mfomfo Nkambule, who took over the health and social welfare portfolio from Chief Sipho Shongwe. A minor government reshuffle was carried out in May in which Nkambule was replaced by Njabulo Mabuza.

Swaziland has been severely affected by the HIV/AIDS pandemic. The Government has been criticized for its reluctance to confront the problem directly; proposed measures have included sterilizing or branding those infected with HIV. In an attempt to prevent the spread of the disease, in September 2001 the Government ordered women aged 18 years or younger to remain celibate and avoid shaking hands with men for a period of five years. In February 2004 the Prime Minister declared a national disaster, brought about by Swaziland's high incidence of HIV infection in combination with drought, land degradation and rising poverty. Following a visit to the country, in mid-March 2006 the UN Secretary-General's special envoy reported that 42.6% of the adult population (aged between 15 and 49 years) was infected with HIV; a recent survey of pregnant women between the ages of 25 and 29 had indicated a prevalence rate of 56.3%. It was anticipated that by 2010 orphaned children would represent between 10% and 15% of the population. New legislation was proposed in April 2006 to prohibit direct or indirect discrimination against employees; most notably, the bill contained a clause relating to discrimination against those infected with HIV. In August 2007 a new national health policy was launched, aimed at addressing the decline in the quality of health care services by 2015 and limiting the spread of HIV/AIDS. In January 2008 nurses voted to begin strike action in protest over the Government's failure to address poor working conditions and delayed payment of salaries. Meanwhile, in September 2007 it was announced that a new, decentralized strategy for combating HIV/AIDS was to be implemented, affording communities the responsibility of determining the action required in that area. Basic centres were to be established, from which a secretary, heading an HIV/AIDS committee elected from the community, would identify those in need of specific medical care and co-ordinate aid response from non-governmental organizations.

In September 2006 the Deputy Prime Minister, Albert Shabangu, collapsed and died at his private residence in Mhlosheni, in the south of the country. He was accorded a state funeral in early October, having served the Government as a cabinet minister for over 15 years. Later that month it was announced that Constance Simelane, hitherto the Minister of Education, had been appointed as the new Deputy Prime Minister. Themba Msibi assumed responsibility for the education portfolio, while Magongo replaced him as Minister of Public Service and Information.

During the apartheid era Swaziland pursued a policy of dialogue and co-operation with South Africa. In 1982 the two countries signed a secret non-aggression pact; several members of the African National Congress of South Africa (ANC), which had increasingly used Swaziland as a base for guerrilla attacks into South Africa, were subsequently arrested and expelled from Swaziland. The signing, in March 1984, of the Nkomati accord between South Africa and Mozambique (which banned both countries from harbouring dissidents) led many ANC members to flee from Mozambique to neighbouring Swaziland. Following the murder, in 1984, of the deputy chief of the Swazi security police, the Government initiated a campaign to arrest all ANC fugitives remaining in the country (the ANC denied involvement in the killing). In 1986 leading Swazi politicians expressed opposition to the imposition of economic sanctions against South Africa, owing to the dependence of Swaziland's own economy on that country. Detentions and deportations of ANC members by the Swazi Government continued, while several suspected ANC members were abducted by South African security forces or killed in Swaziland by gunmen who were widely assumed to be South African. Following the legalization of the ANC in 1990, the Swazi Prime Minister, Obed Dlamini, pledged to conduct an inquiry (which, however, he failed to initiate) into state operations against ANC members. Formal diplomatic relations were established in 1993. From the late 1990s prominent South African organizations, including the ANC and COSATU, expressed support for the SFTU's demands for political reform, prompting the Swazi Government to protest of interference in its domestic affairs. In April 1995 the South African Government announced that it had rejected a long-standing claim by Swaziland to a region in the Mpumalanga province (formerly Eastern Transvaal). However, King Mswati declared in a letter to South African President, Thabo Mbeki, in early 2001 that he had not abandoned his intention to reincorporate parts of Mpumalanga and KwaZulu/Natal provinces into Swaziland. In 2003 the Chairperson of the Swaziland Border Adjustment Committee, Prince Khuzulwandle, criticized Mbeki for declining to discuss realignments of the border. During pro-democracy protests in April 2007 at five crossing points on the border with South Africa, at least six PUDEMO members were arrested.

Following the ratification of the October 1992 peace accord in Mozambique (q.v.), an agreement signed by the Governments of Swaziland and Mozambique and the office of the UN High Commissioner for Refugees in August 1993 provided for the repatriation of some 24,000 Mozambican nationals from Swaziland. In December the number of Swazi troops deployed at the border with Mozambique was increased, following clashes between Swazi and Mozambican forces in the region. Mozambique subsequently protested at alleged border incursions by members of the Swazi armed forces. In early 1994 discussions took place between Swazi and Mozambican officials to seek mutually satisfactory arrangements for the joint patrol of the border, and in 1995 it was announced that the Mhlumeni border post, closed since the 1970s, would reopen as the second official transit point between the two countries. In September 1997, during the first visit to Swaziland made by a Mozambican Prime Minister, a bilateral extradition agreement was signed, with the aim of reducing cross-border crime. In December 1999 the Swazi authorities expelled some 500 Mozambican citizens who had been declared illegal immigrants. In the following month a campaign began to encourage Mozambicans living in Swaziland to register for military service there.

Government

The Constitution of 7 February 2006 vests supreme executive power in the hereditary King, who is the Head of State, and provides for a bicameral legislature, comprising a House of Assembly and a Senate. The functions of the legislature are confined to debating government proposals and advising the King. Executive power is exercised through the Cabinet, which is appointed by the King.

The Parliament of Swaziland consists of the Senate, comprising not more than 31 members (of whom 20 are appointed by the King—at least eight of these are women—and 10 elected by the House of Assembly, one-half of which are women) and the House of Assembly, which comprises not more than 76 members. Of these, 60 are directly elected from candidates nominated by traditional local councils, known as Tinkhundla, and 10 are appointed by the King, one-half of which are women. Additionally one women is selected from each of the four regions of Swaziland and the Attorney-General is also an ex officio member.

The King appoints the Prime Minister and the Cabinet and has the power to dissolve the bicameral legislature. The Swazi National Council (Sibaya) constitutes the highest policy and advisory council of the nation and functions as the annual general meeting of the nation. A Council of Chiefs, composed of 12 chiefs drawn from the four regions of Swaziland advises the King on customary issues and any matter relating to chieftancy.

SWAZILAND

Defence

The Umbutfo Swaziland Defence Force, created in 1973, totalled 2,657 regular troops in November 1983. Swaziland also has a paramilitary police force. Military service is compulsory and lasts for two years. Of total current expenditure by the central Government in 2001/02, E 168m. (6.6%) was allocated to defence.

Economic Affairs

In 2006, according to estimates by the World Bank, Swaziland's gross national income (GNI), measured at average 2004–06 prices, was US $2,737m., equivalent to $2,430 per head (or $5,170 per head on an international purchasing-power parity basis). During 1996–2006, it was estimated, the population increased at an average annual rate of 1.9%, while gross domestic product (GDP) per head increased, in real terms, by an average of 0.7% per year. Overall GDP increased, in real terms, at an average annual rate of 2.7% in 1996–2006; growth in 2006 was 2.1%.

Agriculture (including forestry) contributed 7.9% of GDP in 2006. About 31.6% of the labour force were employed in the agricultural sector in mid-2005 (including subsistence farming), according to FAO. However, according to IMF estimates, at June 2005 only 20.8% of those in paid employment were engaged in agriculture. The principal cash crops are sugar cane (sugar accounted for 5.9% of domestic export earnings in 2002), cotton, citrus fruits, pineapples and maize. Tobacco and rice are also cultivated. Livestock-rearing is traditionally important. Poor harvests in 2001 and 2002 necessitated the imports of basic foods in those years and substantial food imports were required in 2004, owing to low cereal production caused by drought. An estimated 70% of the maize crop was destroyed by drought in February 2005. At that time the UN World Food Programme was supplying food aid to some 260,000 people. Commercial forestry (which employs a significant proportion of the population) provides wood for the manufacture of pulp. During 1996–2006, according to the World Bank, agricultural GDP increased by an average of 0.4% per year. Agricultural GDP increased by 2.3% in 2006.

Industry (including mining, manufacturing, construction and power) contributed 45.3% of GDP in 2006, and engaged 28.8% of those in paid employment in June 2005. During 1996–2006, according to the World Bank, industrial GDP increased at an average annual rate of 2.5%. Industrial GDP increased by 2.3% in 2006.

Mining contributed 0.4% of GDP in 2006 and engaged 1.3% of those in paid employment in June 2005. Swaziland has extensive reserves of coal, much of which is exported. Asbestos is also an important mineral export. In addition, Swaziland has reserves of tin, kaolin, talc, iron ore, pyrophyllite and silica. During 2000–04, according to the IMF, mining GDP declined by an average of 5.0% per year; mining GDP declined by 20.2% in 2003 but increased by 9.0% in 2004.

Manufacturing contributed 39.9% of GDP in 2006, and in June 2005 engaged 21.2% of those in paid employment. Manufacturing is mainly based on the processing of agricultural, livestock and forestry products. During 1996–2006, according to the World Bank, manufacturing GDP increased at an average annual rate of 2.1%. Manufacturing GDP increased by 2.4% in 2006.

Swaziland imports most of its energy requirements from South Africa. The Swazi Government aimed to increase domestic energy output to cover approximately 50% of the country's needs, following the construction of a hydroelectric power station on the Maguga Dam, which began operations in 2002. However, in 2005 80.7% of total electrical energy generated and imported was obtained from South Africa and Mozambique, compared with 77.1% in 2002. Mineral fuels and lubricants accounted for an estimated 10.9% of imports in 2006. In November 2004 plans were being discussed for the construction of a 100-MW thermal power station in the Lowveld using bagasse, the waste left from processing sugar cane.

The services sector contributed 46.7% of GDP in 2006 and engaged 50.3% of those in paid employment in June 2005. According to the World Bank, the GDP of the services sector increased by an average of 3.2% per year in 1996–2006. Services GDP increased by 1.7% in 2006.

In 2006, according to the IMF, Swaziland recorded a visible trade surplus of US $15.0m., while there was a surplus of $98.1m. on the current account of the balance of payments. In 2002 the principal source of imports was South Africa (84.6%) which was also the principal market for exports (67.5%); the USA and Mozambique were also important markets. The principal imports in 2006 were machinery and transport equipment, basic manufactures, food and live animals, and chemicals and chemical products; the principal exports in 2004 were edible concentrates, cotton yarn and other textiles, sugar and wood pulp.

In the financial year ending 31 March 2007 there was an overall budgetary deficit of E 1,969.6m. Swaziland's external debt totalled US $532.1m. at the end of 2005, of which $450.5m. was long-term public debt. In that year the cost of debt-servicing was equivalent to 1.9% of the value of exports of goods and services. In 2000–05 annual inflation averaged 6.9%; consumer prices increased by an average of 4.8% in 2005. It was estimated that 40% of the labour force were unemployed in 1995.

Swaziland is a member of the Common Market for Eastern and Southern Africa (see p. 205), of the Southern African Development Community (SADC, see p. 386) and of the Southern African Customs Union (SACU), which also includes Botswana, Lesotho, Namibia and South Africa.

Swaziland's economy is vulnerable to fluctuations in international prices for some major exports, including sugar, as well as to the effects of unfavourable weather conditions. In addition, prevailing economic conditions in neighbouring South Africa have a pronounced impact on the Swazi economy: although Swaziland may determine the exchange rate of its currency, the lilangeni, this has remained at par with the South African rand. At the beginning of 2004 the new Prime Minister, Themba Dlamini, made a number of proposals for the improvement of Swaziland's economic prospects, including a review of government spending, the encouragement of foreign investment and the promotion of small businesses; however, any progress was expected to be slow. The removal in January 2005 of World Trade Organization quotas for textile exports to the USA brought Swaziland into direct competition with exporters based in Asia, while the EU's proposals to reduce the price at which it purchased sugar from Swaziland by some 36% by 2007 was expected to cost the industry some E 370m. during 2007–10. The EU did, however, allocate €100m. to assist Swazi farmers in diversifying into alternative crops, such as cotton, while the Government continued to encourage farmers to grow geraniums for their essential oils. Furthermore, in early 2008 the European Commission granted Swazi sugar producers €15m. to protect them from the lowering in prices for that commodity. The significant decline in export revenues, owing to the strength of the currency, the decline in textile production and the lowering of sugar prices slowed GDP growth in 2005. However, exports of soft drink concentrate rose significantly in 2007 (despite strike action taken by sugar refinery staff in mid-2007 over the monarchy's resistance to multi-party elections), contributing to a lowering of the current account deficit. GDP growth averaged only some 2% per year in 2000–06, and the poor performance has been compounded by lack of investment and slow implementation of economic reforms, which have done little to reduce unemployment and poverty levels. Inflation has also risen since 2006 as a result of high food and petroleum prices. The medium-term prospects of the Swazi economy were also seriously threatened by the extremely high rate of HIV/AIDS infection among the labour force, while the securing of significant amounts of much-needed foreign investment in Swaziland remained dependent on a satisfactory political settlement. The IMF forecast GDP growth of 2.4% in 2007 and of 2.0% in 2008.

Education

Education is neither free nor compulsory in Swaziland. Primary education begins at six years of age and lasts for seven years; the Government announced in the 2001 budget that it hoped to provide free primary education in the future. Secondary education begins at 13 years of age and lasts for up to five years, comprising a first cycle of three years and a second of two years. According to UNESCO estimates, in 2002/03 77% of children in the relevant age-group (males 76%; females 77%) were enrolled at primary schools, while in that year secondary enrolment included 29% of children in the appropriate age-group (males 26%; females 32%). In 2003/04 4,198 students were enrolled at the University of Swaziland, which has campuses at Luyengo and Kwaluseni; there are also a number of other institutions of higher education. According to the IMF, of total expenditure by the central Government in the financial year 2004/05, E 27.9m. (5.0%) was for education.

Public Holidays

2008: 1 January (New Year's Day), 21–24 March (Easter), 19 April (Birthday of King Mswati), 25 April (National Flag Day), 1 May (Workers' Day), 1 May (Ascension Day), 22 July

SWAZILAND

Statistical Survey

(Birthday of the late King Sobhuza), 6 September (Somhlolo—Independence—Day), 24 October (UN Day), 25–26 December (Christmas and Boxing Day).
2009: 1 January (New Year's Day), 10–13 April (Easter), 19 April (Birthday of King Mswati), 25 April (National Flag Day), 1 May (Workers' Day), 21 May (Ascension Day), 22 July (Birthday of the late King Sobhuza), 6 September (Somhlolo—Independence—Day), 24 October (UN Day), 25–26 December (Christmas and Boxing Day).

The Incwala and Umhlanga Ceremonies are held in December or January, and August or September (respectively), but the exact dates are variable each year.

Statistical Survey

Source (unless otherwise stated): Central Statistical Office, POB 456, Mbabane; internet www.gov.sz/home.asp?pid=75.

Area and Population

AREA, POPULATION AND DENSITY

Area (sq km)	17,363*
Population (census results)†	
25 August 1986	681,059
11–12 May 1997	929,718
Population (UN estimates at mid-year)‡	
2005	1,125,000
2006	1,134,000
2007	1,141,000
Density (per sq km) at mid-2007	65.7

* 6,704 sq miles.
† Excluding absentee workers.
‡ Source: UN, *World Population Prospects: The 2006 Revision*.

ETHNIC GROUPS
(census of August 1986)

Swazi	661,646
Other Africans	14,468
European	1,825
Asiatic	228
Other non-Africans	412
Mixed	2,403
Unknown	77
Total	681,059

REGIONS
(population at census of May 1997; provisional figures, excluding absentee workers)

	Area (sq km)	Population	Density (per sq km)
Hhohho	3,569	247,539	69.4
Manzini	5,945	276,636	46.5
Shiselweni	4,070	198,084	48.7
Lebombo	3,779	190,617	50.4
Total	17,363	912,876	52.6

PRINCIPAL TOWNS
(population at census of May 1997)

Mbabane (capital)	57,992		Manzini	25,571

Mid-2007 (incl. suburbs, UN estimate): Mbabane 78,000 (Source: UN, *World Urbanization Prospects: The 2007 Revision*).

BIRTHS AND DEATHS
(annual averages, UN estimates)

	1990–1995	1995–2000	2000–05
Birth rate (per 1,000)	38.7	33.3	30.4
Death rate (per 1,000)	9.7	11.2	17.2

Source: UN, *World Population Prospects: The 2006 Revision*.

Expectation of life (years at birth, WHO estimates): 37.6 (males 38.2; females 37.1) in 2005 (Source: WHO, *World Health Statistics*).

EMPLOYMENT
(persons in paid employment at June)

	2003	2004	2005
Agriculture, hunting, forestry and fishing	21,491	20,804	19,955
Mining and quarrying	1,153	1,407	1,283
Manufacturing	19,485	19,874	20,272
Electricity, gas and water	1,418	1,389	859
Construction	4,824	5,293	5,115
Distribution	9,021	9,988	11,454
Transportation	2,491	2,265	3,007
Finance	6,422	5,202	6,430
Social services	26,758	27,247	27,228
Total employed	93,063	93,469	95,603

Source: IMF, *Kingdom of Swaziland: Selected Issues and Statistical Appendix* (March 2008).

Mid-2005 (estimates in '000): Agriculture, etc. 115; Total labour force 370 (Source: FAO).

Health and Welfare

KEY INDICATORS

Total fertility rate (children per woman, 2005)	3.7
Under-5 mortality rate (per 1,000 live births, 2005)	160
HIV/AIDS (% of persons aged 15–49, 2005)	33.4
Physicians (per 1,000 head, 2004)	0.16
Health expenditure (2004): US $ per head (PPP)	367.2
Health expenditure (2004): % of GDP	6.3
Health expenditure (2004): public (% of total)	63.8
Access to water (% of persons, 2004)	62
Access to sanitation (% of persons, 2004)	48
Human Development Index (2005): ranking	141
Human Development Index (2005): value	0.547

For sources and definitions, see explanatory note on p. vi.

SWAZILAND

Agriculture

PRINCIPAL CROPS
('000 metric tons)

	2004	2005	2006
Maize	68.1	74.5	26.2
Potatoes*	6	6	6
Sweet potatoes*	2.5	2.6	2.6
Sugar cane*	n.a.	5,200	5,000
Groundnuts (in shell)*	4.6	4.8	4.8
Cottonseed*	3.4	2.8	2.8
Cotton (lint)*	2	2	2
Tomatoes*	3.3	3.2	3.2
Oranges*	36	36	36
Grapefruit and pomelos*	35	34	34
Pineapples*	16	9	9

* FAO estimates.

Aggregate production ('000 metric tons, may include official, semi-official or estimated data): Total cereals 68 in 2004, 75 in 2005, 27 in 2006; Total roots and tubers 55 in 2004, 55 in 2005, 55 in 2006; Total vegetables (incl. melons) 11 in 2004, 10 in 2005, 10 in 2006; Total fruits (excl. melons) 95 in 2004, 87 in 2005, 87 in 2006.

Source: FAO.

LIVESTOCK
('000 head, year ending September, FAO estimates)

	2004	2005	2006
Horses	1.4	1.4	1.4
Asses, mules or hinnies	14.9	14.9	14.9
Cattle	580	580	580
Pigs	30	30	30
Sheep	27	27	27
Goats	274.0	274.0	275.0
Chickens	3,200	3,200	3,200

Source: FAO.

LIVESTOCK PRODUCTS
('000 metric tons, FAO estimates)

	2004	2005	2006
Cattle meat	12.5	12.5	12.5
Goat meat	1.9	1.9	1.9
Pig meat	1.2	1.2	1.2
Chicken meat	6.1	6.7	5.0
Cows' milk	37.5	37.5	37.5

Source: FAO.

Forestry

ROUNDWOOD REMOVALS
('000 cubic metres, excl. bark, FAO estimates)

	2004	2005	2006
Sawlogs, veneer logs and logs for sleepers	260	260	260
Other industrial wood	70	70	70
Fuel wood	560	560	996
Total	890	890	1,326

Source: FAO.

SAWNWOOD PRODUCTION
('000 cubic metres, incl. railway sleepers, FAO estimates)

	1995	1996	1997
Total (all coniferous)	90	100	102

1998–2006: Production assumed to be unchanged from 1997 (FAO estimates).

Source: FAO.

Fishing

(metric tons, live weight)

	1999	2000*	2001*
Capture	70*	70	70
Aquaculture	61	69	72
Common carp	18	20	20
Mozambique tilapia	20	25	25
Redbreast tilapia	12	13	15
North African catfish	5	6	6
Red claw crayfish	6	5	6
Total catch	131*	139	142

* FAO estimate(s).

2002–05 (metric tons, live weight, FAO estimate): Capture 70.
Source: FAO.

Mining

(metric tons, unless otherwise indicated)

	2003	2004	2005
Coal	448,664	488,314	221,701
Ferrovanadium	1,011	1,150	345
Quarrystone ('000 cu m)	324	230	567

Source: US Geological Survey.

Industry

SELECTED PRODUCTS
('000 metric tons, unless otherwise indicated)

	2001	2002	2003
Raw sugar	334	406	616
Wood pulp	191	191	191
Electrical energy (million kWh)*	475	475	475

* Estimates.

Source: UN, *Industrial Commodity Statistics Yearbook*.

Electrical energy (million kWh, excl. self-generated power of some industrial units): 203.7 in 2002; 123.0 in 2003; 103.5 in 2004.

Sources: Swaziland Electricity Board and IMF, *Kingdom of Swaziland: Statistical Appendix* (March 2006).

Finance

CURRENCY AND EXCHANGE RATES

Monetary Units
  100 cents = 1 lilangeni (plural: emalangeni).

Sterling, Dollar and Euro Equivalents (31 December 2007)
  £1 sterling = 13.6432 emalangeni;
  US $1 = 6.8100 emalangeni;
  €1 = 10.0250 emalangeni;
  100 emalangeni = £7.33 = $14.68 = €9.98.

Average Exchange Rate (emalangeni per US $)
  2005 6.359
  2006 6.772
  2007 7.045

Note: The lilangeni is at par with the South African rand.

SWAZILAND

Statistical Survey

BUDGET
(million emalangeni, year ending 31 March)

Revenue*	2004/05	2005/06	2006/07
Tax revenue	4,627.8	5,189.5	7,683.3
Taxes on net income and profits	1,164.0	1,267.4	1,534.0
Companies	324.0	472.5	598.0
Individuals	742.0	761.7	891.9
Non-resident dividends and interest	98.0	33.3	44.1
Taxes on property	12.0	13.3	17.4
Taxes on goods, services, and international trade	3,445.8	3,894.4	6,118.7
Receipts from Southern African Customs Union	2,772.8	3,101.1	5,321.8
Levies on sugar exports	22.0	21.1	33.1
Hotel and gaming taxes	5.0	7.8	9.6
Sales tax	549.0	734.9	620.1
Licences and other taxes	97.0	29.4	134.0
Other taxes	6.0	14.4	13.3
Other current revenue	98.0	137.3	172.1
Property income	46.0	53.4	88.6
Fees, fines, and non-industrial sales	52.0	83.9	83.5
Total	4,725.8	5,326.8	7,855.4

Expenditure†	2004/05	2005/06	2006/07
Current expenditure	4,295.0	4,416.3	4,661.8
Wages and salaries	1,964.0	2,443.0	2,621.8
Other purchases of goods and services	1,421.0	995.8	1,051.6
Interest payments	168.0	194.4	163.4
Domestic	49.0	31.6	35.3
Foreign	119.0	162.9	128.1
Subsidies and other current transfers	742.0	783.1	824.9
Capital expenditure	1,259.0	1,409.7	1,411.8
Health	82.6	47.8	95.4
Education	27.9	18.9	32.9
Agriculture	104.5	171.6	122.7
Transport and communications	347.6	387.0	381.1
Other	696.4	784.4	779.7
Total	5,554.0	5,826.0	6,073.7

* Excluding grants received (million emalangeni): 116.0 in 2004/05; 172.2 in 2005/06; 165.6 in 2006/07.
† Excluding net lending (million emalangeni): 3.0 in 2004/05; −68.3 in 2005/06; −21.6 in 2006/07.

Source: IMF, *Kingdom of Swaziland: Statistical Appendix* (March 2008).

INTERNATIONAL RESERVES
(excl. gold, US $ million at 31 December)

	2005	2006	2007
IMF special drawing rights	3.55	3.74	9.96
Reserve position in IMF	9.38	9.87	10.37
Foreign exchange	230.97	358.91	748.32
Total	243.90	372.52	768.65

Source: IMF, *International Financial Statistics*.

MONEY SUPPLY
(million emalangeni at 31 December)

	2005	2006	2007
Currency outside banks	242.08	250.51	248.64
Demand deposits at deposit money banks	1,046.03	1,106.01	1,417.33
Total (incl. others)	1,294.76	1,358.14	1,666.78

COST OF LIVING
(Consumer Price Index; base: 2000 = 100)

	2003	2004	2005
Food	145.7	155.7	169.2
Fuel	114.0	119.2	123.9
Clothing	114.4	115.2	116.9
Housing	105.7	117.5	119.6
All items (incl. others)	129.0	133.5	139.9

Source: ILO.

NATIONAL ACCOUNTS
(million emalangeni at current prices)

Expenditure on the Gross Domestic Product

	2004	2005	2006
Government final consumption expenditure	3,422.6	3,449.1	3,683.9
Private final consumption expenditure	9,496.4	11,665.3	11,397.0
Gross fixed capital formation	2,831.6	2,983.3	2,986.4
Change in inventories	—	—	1.0
Total domestic expenditure	15,750.6	18,097.7	18,068.3
Exports of goods and services	13,279.8	12,062.8	12,009.8
Less Imports of goods and services	13,677.1	13,543.8	13,461.5
Statistical discrepancy	—	—	2,237.5
GDP in purchasers' values	15,353.4	16,616.6	18,854.1
GDP in constant 2000 prices	9,729.4	9,958.7	10,240.2

Gross Domestic Product by Economic Activity

	2004	2005	2006
Agriculture and forestry	1,083.7	1,139.1	1,151.7
Mining	57.0	44.2	56.6
Manufacturing	4,820.2	5,042.0	5,798.3
Electricity and water	124.6	132.1	138.9
Construction	655.8	568.3	588.2
Wholesale and retail trade	813.5	919.9	1,048.6
Hotels and restaurants	206.9	211.4	264.2
Transport and communications	1,004.4	1,086.8	1,131.9
Banking, finance and insurance	382.4	443.6	491.6
Real estate	559.3	597.6	637.3
Government services	2,222.5	2,434.3	2,711.8
Other services	226.5	242.0	251.4
Owner-occupied dwellings	232.7	239.4	248.6
Sub total	12,389.5	13,100.7	14,519.1
Less Imputed bank service charge	258.4	299.7	332.1
GDP at factor cost	12,131.1	12,800.7	14,186.8
Indirect taxes / *Less* Subsidies	3,222.3	3,816.0	4,667.2
GDP at purchasers' values	15,353.4	16,616.6	18,854.1

Source: IMF, *Kingdom of Swaziland: Statistical Appendix* (March 2008).

SWAZILAND

BALANCE OF PAYMENTS
(US $ million)

	2004	2005	2006
Exports of goods f.o.b.	1,806.2	1,965.5	1,975.7
Imports of goods f.o.b.	−1,715.3	−1,949.4	−1,960.7
Trade balance	90.9	16.1	15.0
Exports of services	249.6	284.4	282.9
Imports of services	−402.0	−407.1	−368.5
Balance on goods and services	−61.5	−106.6	−70.6
Other income received	132.3	158.4	167.6
Other income paid	−124.9	−96.0	−166.7
Balance on goods, services and income	−54.1	−44.2	−69.6
Current transfers received	370.8	412.3	457.4
Current transfers paid	−265.0	−281.7	−289.7
Current balance	51.7	86.4	98.1
Capital account (net)	−0.6	−0.2	52.9
Direct investment abroad	1.4	24.3	−2.4
Direct investment from abroad	70.6	−49.6	36.3
Portfolio investment assets	−0.9	3.7	0.3
Portfolio investment liabilities	−0.3	0.8	—
Other investment assets	−216.7	−121.7	−39.9
Other investment liabilities	−44.0	66.9	23.6
Net errors and omissions	96.5	−12.5	−27.7
Overall balance	−42.3	−1.9	141.4

Source: IMF, *International Financial Statistics*.

External Trade

PRINCIPAL COMMODITIES
(US $ million)

Imports c.i.f.	2004	2005	2006
Food and live animals	176	237	239
Beverages and tobacco	41	54	55
Crude materials (inedible)	43	58	58
Minerals, fuels and lubricants	133	191	206
Chemicals and chemical products	171	230	233
Basic manufactures	249	335	338
Machinery and transport equipment	316	424	428
Miscellaneous manufactures	128	172	174
Total (incl. others)	1,387	1,877	1,895

Exports f.o.b. (incl. re-exports)	2002	2003	2004
Sugar	64	118	124
Wood pulp	69	178	81
Edible concentrates	276	762	639
Cotton yarn and other textiles	163	—	267
Other food products	37	—	51
Total (incl. others)	1,387	1,809	1,612

Source: IMF, *Kingdom of Swaziland: Selected Issues and Statistical Appendix* (March 2008).

PRINCIPAL TRADING PARTNERS
(US $ million)

Imports c.i.f.	2000	2001	2002
China, People's Repub.	4.2	3.9	12.9
Hong Kong	11.9	8.2	19.6
Japan	8.1	7.5	8.1
South Africa	1,023.4	786.5	675.3
Total (incl. others)	1,098.6	832.0	797.8

Exports f.o.b.	2000	2001	2002
Angola	5.8	10.0	7.5
Mozambique	55.5	31.4	52.2
South Africa	531.5	528.6	657.5
Tanzania	27.1	9.4	13.3
United Kingdom	33.0	7.2	12.3
USA	78.8	26.8	78.3
Zimbabwe	33.4	7.3	28.2
Total (incl. others)	890.8	677.8	974.1

Source: UN, *International Trade Statistics Yearbook*.

Transport

RAILWAYS
(traffic)

	2002	2003	2004
Net total ton-km (million)	728	726	710

Source: UN, *Statistical Yearbook*.

ROAD TRAFFIC
(motor vehicles in use at 31 December 2003)

Passenger cars	44,113
Buses and coaches	6,424
Lorries and vans	42,576
Motorcycles and mopeds	3,184

Source: International Road Federation, *World Road Statistics*.

CIVIL AVIATION
(traffic on scheduled services)

	1998	1999	2000
Kilometres flown (million)	1	1	2
Passengers carried ('000)	41	12	90
Passenger-km (million)	43	13	68
Total ton-km (million)	4	1	6

Source: UN, *Statistical Yearbook*.

Tourism

TOURIST ARRIVALS
(at hotels)

Country of residence	2003	2004	2005
Australia	701	1,725	1,527
Mozambique	11,642	17,619	15,597
Portugal	8,666	828	733
South Africa	85,899	112,027	99,176
United Kingdom	13,702	17,776	15,737
Total (incl. others)	218,813	352,040	311,656

Tourism receipts (US $ million, incl. passenger transport): 113.0 in 2003; 54.1 in 2004; 69.3 in 2005.

Source: World Tourism Organization.

SWAZILAND

Communications Media

	2004	2005	2006
Telephones ('000 main lines in use)	44.5	35.0	44.0
Mobile cellular telephones ('000 subscribers)	145.0	200.0	250.0
Personal computers ('000 in use)	36	n.a.	n.a.
Internet users ('000)		36.0	41.6	n.a.

Source: International Telecommunication Union.

Radio receivers (year ending 31 March 1998): 155,000 in use (Source: UN, *Statistical Yearbook*).

Television receivers (2002): 32,000 in use (Source: International Telecommunication Union).

Daily newspapers (2004): 2 (estimated circulation 27,000) (Source: UNESCO Institute for Statistics).

Education

(2004/05, unless otherwise indicated)

	Institutions	Teachers	Students
Pre-primary	n.a.	451	9,523*
Primary	541†	6,625	214,054
Secondary	182†	3,754	67,849
University‡	1§	432	5,897

* Figure for 2003/04.
† Figure for 2001/02.
‡ Figures exclude vocational, technical and teacher-training colleges. In 2000, there were 1,822 students enrolled at these institutions, which numbered 10 in 2003.
§ Figure for 2000.

Source: UNESCO Institute for Statistics.

Adult literacy rate (UNESCO estimates): 79.6% (males 80.9%; females 78.3%) in 2000 (Source: UNESCO Institute for Statistics).

Directory

The Constitution

A new Constitution entered into force on 7 February 2006, replacing that of October 1978. It vests supreme executive power in the hereditary King (iNgwenyama—the Lion) and succession is governed by traditional law and custom. In the event of the death of the King, the powers of Head of State are transferred to the constitutional dual monarch, the Queen Mother (Ndlovukazi—Great She Elephant), who is authorized to act as Regent until the designated successor, the Crown Prince (Umntfwana), attains the age of 21.

The Parliament of Swaziland consists of the Senate, comprising not more than 31 members of whom 20 are appointed by the King—at least eight of these are women—and 10 elected by the House of Assembly, one-half of which are women, and the House of Assembly, which comprises not more than 76 members. Of these, 60 are directly elected from candidates nominated by traditional local councils, known as Tinkhundla, and 10 are appointed by the King, one-half of which are women. Additionally one woman is selected from each of the four regions of Swaziland and the Attorney-General is also an ex officio member.

The King appoints the Prime Minister and the Cabinet and has the power to dissolve the bicameral legislature. The Swazi National Council (Sibaya) constitutes the highest policy and advisory council of the nation and functions as the annual general meeting of the nation. A Council of Chiefs, composed of 12 chiefs drawn from the four regions of Swaziland, advises the King on customary issues and any matter relating to chieftancy.

The Constitution affirms the fundamental human rights and freedoms of the individual.

The Government

HEAD OF STATE

King: HM King MSWATI III (succeeded to the throne 25 April 1986).

COUNCIL OF MINISTERS
(March 2008)

Prime Minister: ABSALOM THEMBA DLAMINI.
Deputy Prime Minister: CONSTANCE SIMELANE.
Minister of Justice and Constitutional Affairs: Prince DAVID.
Minister of Finance: MAJOZI SITHOLE.
Minister of Home Affairs: Prince GABHENI.
Minister of Foreign Affairs and Trade: MOSES MATHENDELE DLAMINI.
Minister of Education: THEMBA MSIBI.
Minister of Regional Development and Youth Affairs: Chief SIPHO SHONGWE.
Minister of Agriculture and Co-operatives: MTITI FAKUDZE.
Minister of Enterprise and Employment: LUTFO DLAMINI.
Minister of Economic Planning and Development: Rev. ABSALOM DLAMINI.
Minister of Health and Social Welfare: NJABULO MABUZA.
Minister of Public Service and Information: CHARLES S'GAYOYO MAGONGO.
Minister of Public Works and Transport: ELIJAH SHONGWE.
Minister of Natural Resources and Energy: DUMSILE SUKATI.
Minister of Tourism, the Environment and Communication: THANDI SHONGWE.
Minister of Housing and Urban Development: MABILI DLAMINI.

MINISTRIES

Office of the Prime Minister: POB 433, Swazi Plaza, Mbabane; tel. 4042251; fax 4043943; internet www.gov.sz.

Office of the Deputy Prime Minister: POB 433, Swazi Plaza, Mbabane; tel. 4042723; fax 4044085.

Ministry of Agriculture and Co-operatives: POB 162, Mbabane; tel. 4042731; fax 4044700.

Ministry of Economic Planning and Development: POB 602, Mbabane; tel. 4043765; fax 4042157.

Ministry of Education: POB 39, Mbabane; tel. 4042491; fax 4043880.

Ministry of Enterprise and Employment: POB 451, Mbabane; tel. 4043201; fax 4044711; e-mail sglabour@realnet.co.sz.

Ministry of Finance: POB 443, Mbabane; tel. 4048148; fax 4043187.

Ministry of Foreign Affairs and Trade: POB 518, Mbabane; tel. 4042661; fax 4042669.

Ministry of Health and Social Welfare: POB 5, Mbabane; tel. 4042431; fax 4042092.

Ministry of Home Affairs: POB 432, Mbabane; tel. 4042941; fax 4044303.

Ministry of Housing and Urban Development: POB 1832, Mbabane; tel. 4041739; fax 4045290.

Ministry of Justice and Constitutional Affairs: POB 924, Mbabane; tel. 4046010; fax 4043533; e-mail ps@justice.gov.sz.

Ministry of Natural Resources and Energy: POB 57, Mbabane; tel. 4046244; fax 4042436; e-mail nergyswa@realnet.co.sz.

Ministry of Public Service and Information: POB 338, Mbabane; tel. 4042761; fax 4042774.

Ministry of Public Works and Transport: POB 58, Mbabane; tel. 4042321; fax 4042364.

Ministry of Regional Development and Youth Affairs: Phutfumani Bldg, Warner St, Mbabane; POB 125, Mbabane H100.

Ministry of Tourism, the Environment and Communication: POB 2652, Mbabane; tel. 4046556; fax 4045415; internet www.mintour.gov.sz.

Legislature

SENATE

The Senate comprises not more than 31 members, of whom 20 are appointed by the King—at least eight of these are women—and 10 elected by the House of Assembly, one-half of which are women.

President: MUNTU MSAWANE.

HOUSE OF ASSEMBLY

The House of Assembly comprises not more than 76 members. Of these, 60 are directly elected from candidates nominated by traditional local councils, known as Tinkhundla, and 10 are appointed by the King, one-half of which are women. Additionally one woman is selected from each of the four regions of Swaziland and the Attorney-General is also an ex officio member. The latest elections to the National Assembly took place on 18 October 2003.

Speaker: PRINCE GUDUZA.

Election Commission

National Elections Office: POB 4842, Mbabane; tel. 4162813; fax 4161970; Chief Electoral Officer ROBERT TWALA.

Political Organizations

Party political activity was banned by royal proclamation in April 1973, and formally prohibited under the 1978 Constitution. Since 1991, following indications that the Constitution was to be revised, a number of political associations have re-emerged. Following the introduction of the new Constitution in February 2006, the legal status of party political activity remained unclear.

Imbokodvo National Movement (INM): f. 1964 by King Sobhuza II; traditionalist movement, which also advocates policies of devt and the elimination of illiteracy; Leader (vacant).

Ngwane National Liberatory Congress (NNLC): Ilanga Centre, Martin St, Manzini; tel. 5053935; f. 1962 by fmr mems of the SPP; advocates democratic freedoms and universal suffrage, and seeks abolition of the Tinkhundla electoral system; Pres. OBED DLAMINI; Sec.-Gen. DUMISA DLAMINI.

People's United Democratic Movement (PUDEMO): POB 4588, Manzini; tel. and fax 5054181; internet www.members.nbci.com/pudemo; f. 1983; seeks constitutional limitation of the powers of the monarchy; affiliated orgs include the Human Rights Asscn of Swaziland and the Swaziland Youth Congress (SWAYOCO—Pres. ALEX LANGWENYA; Sec.-Gen. KENNETH KUNENE); Pres. MARIO BONGANI MASUKU; Sec. SIKHUMBUZO PHAKATHI.

Swaziland National Front (SWANAFRO): Mbabane; Pres. ELMOND SHONGWE; Sec.-Gen. GLENROSE DLAMINI.

Swaziland Progressive Party (SPP): POB 6, Mbabane; tel. 2022648; f. 1929; Pres. J. J. NQUKU.

Swaziland United Front (SUF): POB 14, Kwaluseni; f. 1962 by fmr mems of the SPP; Leader MATSAPA SHONGWE.

Diplomatic Representation

EMBASSIES IN SWAZILAND

China (Taiwan): Makhosikhosi St, Mbabane; tel. 4044739; fax 4046688; e-mail rocembassy@africaonline.co.sz; Ambassador LEONARD CHAO.

Mozambique: Princess Dr., POB 1212, Mbabane; tel. 4043700; fax 4048402; Ambassador AMOUR ZACARIAS KAPELA.

South Africa: The New Mall, 2nd Floor, Dr Sishayi Rd, POB 2507, Mbabane; tel. 4044651; fax 4044335; e-mail sahc@africaonline.co.sz; High Commissioner Dr MZOLISI MABUDE.

USA: 2350 Mbabane Pl., Mbabane; tel. 4046441; fax 4045959; internet mbabane.usembassy.gov; Ambassador MAURICE S. PARKER.

Judicial System

Following the introduction of the new Constitution, the Swaziland Superior Court of Judicature comprised the Supreme Court and the High Court, which replaced the existing Court of Appeal and the High Court. The Supreme Court is headed by the Chief Justice and consists of not less than four other Justices of the Supreme Court, and is the final Court of Appeal. The High Court consists of the Chief Justice and not less than four Justices of the High Court, and has unlimited original jurisdiction in civil and criminal matters.

Religion

About 60% of the adult Swazi population profess Christianity. Under the new Constitution, which came into effect on 7 February 2006, Christianity ceased to be recognized as the country's official religion. At mid-2005 there was a growing Muslim population, reported to number some 10,000 adherents. Most of the remainder of the population hold traditional beliefs.

CHRISTIANITY

At mid-2000 there were an estimated 153,000 Protestants and 466,000 adherents professing other forms of Christianity.

Council of Swaziland Churches: Mandlenkosi Ecumenical House, 142 Esser St, Manzini; POB 1095, Manzini; tel. 5053697; fax 5055841; e-mail c.o.c@africaonline.co.sz; f. 1976; Chair. Bishop NCAMISO LOUIS NDLOVU; Gen. Sec. KHANGEZILE I. DLAMINI; 10 mem. churches incl. Roman Catholic, Anglican, Kukhany'okusha Zion Church and Lutheran.

League of African Churches: POB 230, Lobamba; asscn of 48 independent churches; Chair. SAMSON HLATJWAKO.

Swaziland Conference of Churches: 175 Ngwane St, POB 1157, Manzini; tel. and fax 5055253; e-mail scc@africaonline.co.sz; internet www.swazilandcc.org; f. 1929; Pres. Rev. JOHANNES V. MAZIBUKO; Gen. Sec. Rev. S. F. DLAMINI.

The Anglican Communion

Swaziland comprises a single diocese within the Church of the Province of Southern Africa. The Metropolitan of the Province is the Archbishop of Cape Town, South Africa. The Church had some 40,000 members at mid-2000.

Bishop of Swaziland: Rt Rev. MESHACK BOY MABUZA, Bishop's House, Muir St, POB 118 Mbabane; tel. 4043624; fax 4046759; e-mail anglicanchurch@africaonline.co.sz.

The Roman Catholic Church

The Roman Catholic Church was established in Swaziland in 1913. For ecclesiastical purposes, Swaziland comprises the single diocese of Manzini, suffragan to the archdiocese of Pretoria, South Africa. At 31 December 2005 there were an estimated 55,500 adherents in Swaziland (some 5.1% of the total population). The Bishop participates in the Southern African Catholic Bishops' Conference (based in Pretoria, South Africa).

Bishop of Manzini: Rt Rev. LOUIS NCAMISO NDLOVU, Bishop's House, Sandlane St, POB 19, Manzini; tel. 5056900; fax 5056762; e-mail bishop@africaonline.co.sz.

Other Christian Churches

Church of the Nazarene: POB 1460, Manzini; tel. 5054732; f. 1910; 7,649 adherents (1994).

The Evangelical Lutheran Church in Southern Africa: POB 117, Mbabane; tel. 4046453; f. 1902; Bishop M. D. BIYELA; 2,800 adherents in Swaziland (1994).

Mennonite Central Committee: POB 329, Mbabane; tel. 4042805; fax 4044732; f. 1971; Co-ordinator HLOB'SILE NXUMALO.

The Methodist Church in Southern Africa: POB 218, Mbabane; tel. 4042658; f. 1880; 2,578 adherents (1992).

United Christian Church of Africa: POB 1345, Nhlangano; tel. 2022648; f. 1944; Pres. Rev. WELLINGTON B. MKHALIPHI; Founder and Gen. Sec. Dr J. J. NQUKU.

The National Baptist Church, the Christian Apostolic Holy Spirit Church in Zion and the Religious Society of Friends (Quakers) are also active.

BAHÁ'Í FAITH

National Spiritual Assembly: POB 298, Mbabane; tel. 5052689; f. 1960; mems resident in 153 localities.

ISLAM

Ezulwini Islamic Institute: Al Islam Dawah Movement of Swaziland, POB 133, Ezulwini; c. 3,000 adherents (1994).

The Press

PRINCIPAL NEWSPAPERS

The Guardian of Swaziland: POB 4747, Mbabane; tel. 404838; f. 2001; daily newspaper; publ. suspended May 2001, resumed Sept. 2001; Editor THULANI MTHETHWA.

The Swazi News: Sheffield Rd, POB 156, Mbabane; tel. 4042520; fax 4042438; e-mail swazinews@times.co.sz; internet www.times.co.sz; f. 1983; weekly; English; owned by *The Times of Swaziland*; Editor THULANI THWALA; circ. 24,000.

Swazi Observer: Observer House, 3 West St, POB A385, Swazi Plaza, Mbabane; tel. 4049600; fax 4045503; e-mail info@observer.org.sz; internet www.observer.org.sz; f. 1981; owned by Tibiyo Taka Ngwane; Mon.–Sat.; *Weekend Observer* (Sun.); publ. suspended Feb. 2000, resumed March 2001; CEO S. MYZO MAGAGULA; Editor-in-Chief MUSA NDLANGAMANDLA.

Swaziland Today: POB 395, Mbabane; tel. 4041432; fax 4043493; weekly; govt newsletter.

The Times of Swaziland: Sheffield Rd, POB 156, Mbabane; tel. 4042211; fax 4042438; e-mail editor@times.co.sz; internet www.times.co.sz; f. 1897; Mon.–Fri., Sun.; also monthly edn; English; other publs incl. *What's Happening* (tourist interest); Editor MARTIN DLAMINI; circ. 18,000.

PRINCIPAL PERIODICALS

Farming in Swaziland: POB 592, Mbabane; tel. and fax 4041839; e-mail cft@realnet.co.sz; quarterly; Editor CHRISTINA FORSYTH-THOMPSON; circ. 3,000.

The Nation: Mbabane House, 3rd Floor, Warner St, POB 4547, Mbabane; tel. and fax 4046611; e-mail thenation@realnet.co.sz; f. 1997; monthly; independent news magazine; publ. suspended briefly May 2001; Editor BHEKI MAKHUBU.

Swaziview: Mbabane; tel. 4042716; monthly magazine; general interest; circ. 3,500.

UNISWA Journal of Agriculture: Faculty of Agriculture, University of Swaziland, Luyengo Campus, PO Luyengo M205; tel. and fax 5283021; e-mail mwendera@agric.uniswa.sz; annually; Editor-in-Chief Prof. EMMANUEL J. MWENDERA.

UNISWA Research Journal of Agriculture, Science and Technology: Private Bag 4, Kwaluseni; tel. 5184011; fax 5185276; e-mail research@uniswa.sz; internet www.uniswa.sz; 2 a year; publ. of the Faculties of Agriculture, Health Sciences and Science of the Univ. of Swaziland; Chair. Prof. E. M. OSSOM.

Publishers

Apollo Services (Pty) Ltd: POB 35, Mbabane; tel. 4042711.

GBS Printing and Publishing (Pty) Ltd: POB 1384, Mbabane; tel. 5052779.

Jubilee Printers: POB 1619, Matsaka; tel. 5184557; fax 5184558.

Longman Swaziland (Pty) Ltd: POB 2207, Manzini; tel. 5053891.

Macmillan Boleswa Publishers (Pty) Ltd: POB 1235, Manzini; tel. 5184533; fax 5185247; e-mail macmillan@africaonline.co.sz; f. 1978; textbooks and general; CEO DUSANKA STOJAKOVIC.

Swaziland Printing & Publishing Co Ltd: POB 28, Mbabane; tel. 4042716; fax 4042710.

Whydah Media Publishers Ltd: Mbabane; tel. 4042716; f. 1978.

Broadcasting and Communications

TELECOMMUNICATIONS

MTN Swaziland: Smuts St, POB 5050, H100 Mbabane; tel. 4060000; fax 4046217; e-mail yellohelp@mtn.co.sz; internet www.mtn.co.sz; f. 1998; jt venture btwn MTN Group, South Africa, and Swaziland Posts and Telecommunications Corpn; operates mobile cellular telephone network; 213,000 subscribers (2005); CEO THEMBA KHUMALO.

Swaziland Posts and Telecommunications Corpn (SPTC): Phutfumani Bldg, Mahlokohla St, POB 125, H100 Mbabane; tel. 4052000; fax 4052001; e-mail info@sptc.co.sz; internet www.sptc.co.sz; f. 1983; Chair. SABELO MASUKU; Man. Dir E. NATHI DLAMINI.

BROADCASTING

Radio

Swaziland Broadcasting and Information Service: POB 338, Mbabane; tel. 4042763; fax 4046953; e-mail sbisnews@africaonline.co.sz; f. 1966; broadcasts in English and siSwati; Dir STAN MOTSA.

Swaziland Commercial Radio (Pty) Ltd: POB 1586, Alberton 1450, South Africa; tel. (11) 4344333; fax (11) 4344777; privately owned commercial service; broadcasts to southern Africa in English and Portuguese; music and religious programmes; Man. Dir A. DE ANDRADE.

Trans World Radio: POB 64, Manzini; tel. 5052781; fax 5055333; internet www.twr.org; f. 1974; religious broadcasts from five transmitters in 30 languages to southern, central and eastern Africa and to the Far East.

Television

Swaziland Television Authority (Swazi TV): POB A146, Swazi Plaza, Mbabane; tel. 4043036; fax 4042093; e-mail swazitv.eng@africaonline.co.sz; f. 1978; state-owned; broadcasts seven hours daily in English; colour transmissions; CEO VUKANI MAZIYA.

Finance

(cap. = capital; res = reserves; dep. = deposits; m. = million; brs = branches; amounts in emalangeni)

BANKING

Central Bank

Central Bank of Swaziland: POB 546, Mahlokohla St, Mbabane; tel. 4082000; fax 4042636; e-mail info@centralbank.org.sz; internet www.centralbank.org.sz; f. 1974; bank of issue; cap. 21.8m., res 31.4m., dep. 303.7m. (March 2006); Gov. MARTIN G. DLAMINI; Dep. Gov. S. G. MDLULI.

Commercial Banks

First National Bank of Swaziland Ltd: Sales House Bldg, 2nd Floor, POB 261, Mbabane; tel. 4045401; fax 4044735; e-mail hnsibande@fnb.co.za; f. 1988; fmrly Meridien Bank Swaziland Ltd; cap. and res 61.5m., dep. 484.5m. (June 2002); Chair. Dr D. M. J. VON WISSEL; Man. Dir I. J. M. LEYENAAR; 7 brs and 1 agency.

Nedbank (Swaziland) Ltd: Nebank House, Dr Sishayi and Sozisa Rds, Swazi Plaza, POB 68, Mbabane; tel. 4081000; fax 4044060; e-mail info@nedbank.co.sz; internet www.nedbank.co.sz; f. 1974; fmrly Standard Chartered Bank Swaziland Ltd; 23.1% state-owned; cap. 11.9m., res 84.3m., dep. 711.3m. (Dec. 2005); Chair. ZACHEUS M. NKOSI; Man. Dir AMBROSE DLAMINI; 6 brs and 1 agency.

Development Banks

Standard Bank Swaziland Ltd: Standard House, 1st Floor, Swazi Plaza, POB A294, Mbabane; tel. 4046930; fax 4045899; internet www.standardbank.co.sz; f. 1988; fmrly Stanbic Bank Swaziland, present name adopted 1997; merged with Barclays Bank of Swaziland in Jan. 1998; 10% state-owned; cap. 14.6m., res 89.3m., dep. 1,454.3m. (Dec. 2005); Chair. R. J. ROSSOUW (acting); Man. Dir MERVYN LUBBE; 10 brs, 1 agency.

Swaziland Development and Savings Bank (SwaziBank—Libhange LeSive): Engungwini Bldg, Gwamile St, POB 336, Mbabane; tel. 4042551; fax 4042550; internet www.swazibank.sz; f. 1965; state-owned; taken over by central bank in 1995; under independent management since 2000; cap. and res 143.0m., total assets 557.9m. (Mar. 2002); Chair NOKUKHANYA GAMEDZE; Man. Dir STANLEY M. N. MATSEBULA; 8 brs.

Financial Institution

Swaziland National Provident Fund: POB 1857, Manzini; tel. 5082000; fax 5082001; internet www.snpf.co.sz; f. 1974; provides benefits for employed persons on retirement from regular employment or in the event of becoming incapacitated; employers are required by law to pay a contribution for every eligible staff member; total assets 290m. (June 1996); CEO Prince LONKHOKHELA DLAMINI.

STOCK EXCHANGE

Swaziland Stock Exchange: Capital Markets Development Unit, Infumbe Bldg, 1st Floor, Warner St, POB 546, Mbabane; tel. 4082164; fax 4049493; e-mail info@ssx.org.sz; internet www.ssx.org.sz; f. 1990 as Swaziland Stock Market (SSM); state-owned; Chair. MARTIN G. DLAMINI.

INSURANCE

Between 1974 and 1999 the state-controlled Swaziland Royal Insurance Corpn (SRIC) operated as the country's sole authorized insurance company, although cover in a number of areas not served by SRIC was available from several specialized insurers. In 1999 it was proposed that legislation would be enacted to end SRIC's monopoly and provide for the company's transfer to private sector ownership. The legislation was passed as the Insurance Act in 2005.

SWAZILAND

Insurance Company

Swaziland Royal Insurance Corpn (SRIC): SRIC House, Somhlolo Rd, Gilfillan St, POB 917, H100 Mbabane; tel. 4043231; fax 4046415; e-mail sric@sric.sz; internet www.sric.sz; f. 1974; 41% state-owned; 59% owned by Munich-Reinsurance Co of Africa Ltd, Mutual and Fed. Insurance Co of South Africa Ltd, Swiss Re Southern Africa Ltd, S.A. Eagle Insurance Co Ltd, Old Mutual, and Mutual and Federal; Chair. Dr E. T. GINA; Gen. Man. ZOMBODZE R. MAGAGULA.

Insurance Association

Insurance Brokers' Association of Swaziland (IBAS): POB 1072, Mbabane H100; tel. 4043394; fax 4045035; f. 1983; Chair. KEITH P. DUKES; 4 mems.

Trade and Industry

GOVERNMENT AGENCY

Small Enterprise Development Co (SEDCO): POB A186, Swazi Plaza, Mbabane; tel. 4042811; fax 4040723; e-mail business@sedco.co.sz; internet www.sedco.biz; f. 1970; devt agency; supplies workshop space, training and expertise for 165 local entrepreneurs at eight sites throughout the country; CEO DORRINGTON MATIWANE.

Swaziland Investment Promotion Authority (SIPA): Mbandzeni House, 7th Floor, Church St, POB 4194, Mbabane; tel. 4040472; fax 4043374; e-mail e.nathi@sipa.org.sz; internet www.sipa.org.sz; f. 1998; Gen. Man. JOHN W. CREAMER (acting).

DEVELOPMENT ORGANIZATIONS

National Industrial Development Corpn of Swaziland (NIDCS): POB 866, Mbabane; tel. 4043391; fax 4045619; f. 1971; state-owned; administered by Swaziland Industrial Devt Co; Admin. Dir P. K. THAMM.

Swaziland Coalition of Concerned Civic Organisations (SCCCO): Smithco Industrial Centre, Mswati III Ave, 11th St, Matsapha; POB 4173, Mbabane; tel. and fax 5187688; e-mail webmaster@swazicoalition.org.sz; internet www.swazicoalition.org.sz; f. 2003; promotes constitutional democracy, poverty alleviation, fiscal discipline, economic stability, competitive regional and international trade, social justice, and the rule of law; Sec.-Gen. MUSA HLOPE; 9 mems:

Coordinating Assembly of Non-Governmental Organisations (CANGO): POB A67, Swazi Plaza, Mbabane; tel. 4044721; fax 4045532; e-mail director@cango.org.sz; internet www.cango.org.sz; f. 1983; Exec. Dir EMMANUEL NDLANGAMANDLA; over 70 mem. orgs.

Federation of Swaziland Employers and Chamber of Commerce (FSECC): POB 72, Mbabane; tel. 4040768; fax 4090051; e-mail fsecc@business-swaziland.com; internet www.business-swaziland.com; f. 2003 by merger of Fed. of Swaziland Employers (f. 1964) and Swaziland Chamber of Commerce (f. 1916); CEO ZODWA MABUZA; c. 500 mems (2005).

Association of the Swazi Business Community.

Federation of the Swazi Business Community.

Swaziland Association of Teachers.

Swaziland Federation of Labour.

Swaziland Federation of Trade Unions.

Swaziland Law Society.

Women and Law Southern Africa.

Swaziland Industrial Development Co (SIDC): Dhlan'Ubeka House, 5th Floor, cnr Tin and Walker Sts, POB 866, Mbabane; tel. 4044010; fax 4045619; e-mail info@sidc.co.sz; internet www.sidc.co.sz; f. 1986; 34.9% state-owned; finances private-sector projects and promotes local and foreign investment; cap. E 24.1m., total assets E 178.4m. (June 1999); Chair. TIM ZWANE; Man. Dir TAMBO GINA.

Swaki (Pty) Ltd: Liqhaga Bldg, 4th Floor, Nkoseluhlaza St, POB 1839, Manzini; tel. 5052693; fax 5052001; e-mail info@swaki.co.sz; jtly owned by SIDC and Kirsh Holdings; comprises a number of cos involved in manufacturing, services and the production and distribution of food.

Tibiyo Taka Ngwane (Bowels of the Swazi Nation): POB 181, Kwaluseni, Manzini; tel. 5184306; fax 5184399; internet www.tibiyo.com; f. 1968; national devt agency, with investment interests in all sectors of the economy; participates in domestic and foreign jt investment ventures; total assets: E 604m. (1999); Chair. Prince MANGALISO; Man. Dir NDUMISO MAMBA.

Swaziland Solidarity Network (SSN): c/o COSATU House, 3rd Floor, 1–5 Leyds St, Braamfontein, South Africa; POB 1027, Johannesburg 2000; tel. (11) 3393621; fax (11) 3394244; e-mail ssnnetwork@gmail.org.za; internet www.swazisolidarity.org; f. 1997; umbrella org. promoting democracy; incorporates mems from Swaziland and abroad incl. PUDEMO, SWAYOCO, and the Swaziland Democratic Alliance (f. 1999); also incl., from South Africa, the ANC, SACP and COSATU.

CHAMBERS OF COMMERCE

Sibakho Chamber of Commerce: POB 2016, Manzini; tel. and fax 5057347.

Swaziland Chamber of Commerce and Industry: see Fed. of Swaziland Employers and Chamber of Commerce.

INDUSTRIAL AND TRADE ASSOCIATIONS

National Agricultural Marketing Board: POB 4261, Manzini; tel. 5055314; fax 5054072; internet www.namboard.co.sz; Chair. Dr MICAH B. MASUKU; CEO OBED HLONGWANE.

National Maize Corpn: POB 158, Manzini; tel. 5187432; fax 5184461; f. 1985.

Swaziland Citrus Board: Sokhamila Bldg, cnr Dzeliwe and Mdada Sts, POB 343, Mbabane H100; tel. 4044266; fax 4043548; e-mail citrus@realnet.co.sz; f. 1969; Chair. H. C. NODDEBOE.

Swaziland Commercial Board: POB 509, Mbabane; tel. 4042930; Man. Dir J. M. D. FAKUDZE.

Swaziland Cotton Board: POB 220, Manzini; tel. and fax 5052775; e-mail dlaminiaa@gov.sz; f. 1967; CEO TOM JELE.

Swaziland Dairy Board: Enguleni Bldg, 3rd Floor, 287 Mahleka St., POB 2975, Manzini; tel. 5058262; fax 5058260; e-mail ceo-swazidairy@africaonline.co.sz; internet swazidairy.org; f. 1971; Gen. Man. N. T. GUMEDE.

Swaziland Sugar Association: 4th Floor, cnr Dzeliwe and Msakato Sts, POB 445, Mbabane; tel. 4042646; fax 4045005; e-mail info@ssa.co.sz; internet www.ssa.co.sz; CEO Dr MICHAEL MATSEBULA.

EMPLOYERS' ORGANIZATIONS

Building Contractors' Association of Swaziland: POB 518, Mbabane; tel. 4040071; fax 4044258; e-mail soconswad@realnet.co.sz.

Swaziland Association of Architects, Engineers and Surveyors: Swazi Plaza, POB A387, Mbabane; tel. 4042309.

Swaziland Institute of Personnel and Training Managers: c/o UNISWA, Private Bag, Kwaluseni; tel. 5184011; fax 5185276.

UTILITIES

Electricity

Swaziland Electricity Board: Mhlambanyatsi Rd, Eluvatsini House, POB 258, Mbabane; tel. 4042521; fax 4042335; internet www.seb.co.sz; statutory body; f. 1963; Man. Dir (vacant).

Water

Swaziland Water Services Corpn: Dhlan'Ubeka House, 6th and 7th Floor, POB 20, Mbabane; tel. 4043161; fax 4045585; internet www.swsc.co.sz; state authority; Chair. ESAU N. ZWANE; CEO PETER N. BHEMBE.

CO-OPERATIVE ASSOCIATIONS

Swaziland Central Co-operatives Union: POB 551, Manzini; tel. 5052787; fax 5052964.

There are more than 123 co-operative associations, of which the most important is:

Swaziland Co-operative Rice Co Ltd: handles rice grown in Mbabane and Manzini areas.

TRADE UNIONS

At mid-2005 there were 55 organizations recognized by the Department of Labour. Only non-managerial workers may belong to a union.

Trade Union Federations

Swaziland Amalgamated Trade Unions (SATU): POB 7138, Manzini; tel. 5059544; fax 5052684; f. 2003 by merger of five industrial unions; affiliated to the Int. Metalworkers' Fed.; Sec.-Gen. FRANK NKULULEKO MNCINA; 3,500 mems (2005).

Swaziland Federation of Labour (SFL): Swazi Plaza, POB 1173, Mbabane; tel. 4045216; fax 4044261; e-mail sufiaw@realnet.co.sz; affiliated to the Int. Trade Union Confed.; Sec.-Gen. VINCENT V. NCONGWANE; 4,000 mems (2002).

Swaziland Federation of Trade Unions (SFTU): POB 1158, Manzini; tel. and fax 5056575; internet www.cosatu.org.za/sftu; f. 1973; affiliated to the Int. Trade Union Confed.; prin. trade union org. since mid-1980s; represents workers in the agricultural, private and public sectors; Pres. RICHARD NXUMALO; Sec.-Gen. JAN SITHOLE; 83,000 mems.

21 affiliated mem. unions incl.:

Swaziland Agriculture and Plantation Workers' Union (SAPWU): POB 2010, Manzini; tel. 4526010; fax 4526106.

Swaziland Communications Workers' Union (SCWU): c/o Swaziland Post and Telecommunications Corpn, POB 125, Mbabane; fax 4042093; fmrly Swaziland Post and Telecommunications Workers' Union; present name adopted in 2006; Pres. KENNEDY DLAMINI; Sec.-Gen. MANDLA MDLULI.

Swaziland Manufacturing and Allied Workers' Union (SMAWU): Agora Shopping Complex, King Mswati III Ave, Matsapha, POB 2379, Manzini; tel. 5186503; fax 5187028; e-mail smawu@realnet.co.sz; affiliated to the Int. Textile, Garment and Leather Workers' Fed.; Gen. Sec. SIPHO PETERSON MAMBA; 7,000 mems (2004).

Swaziland National Association of Civil Service (SNACS): POB 2811, Manzini M200; tel. 557882; fax 557887; e-mail snacs@swazi.net; f. 1980; reportedly suspended from the SFTU in 2006; affiliated to the Public Services Int.; Pres. CHARLES KHUMALO; Gen. Sec. ABSOLOM DLAMINI; 3,855 mems (2002).

Swaziland Nurses Association (Swaziland National Association of Nurses): POB 6191, Manzini; tel. and fax 5058070; f. 1965; affiliated to the Public Services Int.; Pres. PATRICK MASITSELA MHLANGA; Gen. Sec. JULIA JABULILE ZIYANÉ.

Swaziland Transport and Allied Workers' Union (STAWU): POB 3362, Manzini; affiliated to the Int. Transport Workers' Fed.

Other unions affiliated to the SFTU include the Building and Construction Workers' Union of Swaziland; the Swaziland Commercial and Allied Workers' Union; the Swaziland Conservation Workers' Union; the Swaziland Electricity Supply, Maintenance and Allied Workers' Union; the Swaziland Hotel, Catering and Allied Workers' Union; the Swaziland Manufacturing and Allied Workers' Union; the Swaziland Media and Publications Workers' Union; the Swaziland Mining, Quarrying and Allied Workers' Union; the Swaziland Motor Engineering Allied Workers' Union; the Swaziland Union of High Learning Institutions; the Workers' Union of Swaziland Security Guards; the Workers' Union of Town Councils; and the Swaziland Water and Co-operation Workers' Union.

Swaziland National Association for Teachers (SNAT): POB 1575, M200 Manzini; tel. 5052603; fax 5060386; e-mail snatcentre@africaonline.co.sz; affiliated to Education Int.; Pres. SIMON BRIAN MAKHANYA; Sec.-Gen. DOMINIC NXUMALO; 6,000 mems.

Swaziland Union of Financial Institutions and Allied Workers (SUFIAW): 100 Johnson St, Mbabane; tel. 4044261; fax 4045216; e-mail sufiaw@realnet.co.sz; Pres. VINCENT V. NCONGWANE.

Other registered unions include the Association of Lecturers and Academic Personnel of the University of Swaziland; the University of Swaziland Workers' Union; and the Workers' Union of Swaziland Security Guards.

Staff Associations

Three staff associations exist for employees whose status lies between that of worker and that of management: the Nyoni Yami Irrigation Scheme Staff Association, the Swazican Staff Association and the Swaziland Electricity Board Staff Association.

Transport

Buses are the principal means of transport for many Swazis. Bus services are provided by private operators who are required to obtain annual permits for each route from the Road Transportation Board, which also regulates fares.

RAILWAYS

The rail network, which totalled 297 km in 1998–99, provides a major transport link for imports and exports. Railway lines connect with the dry port at Matsapha, the South African ports of Richards Bay and Durban in the south, the South African town of Komatipoort in the north and the Mozambican port of Maputo in the east. Goods traffic is mainly in wood pulp, sugar, molasses, coal, citrus fruit and canned fruit. In June 1998 the Trans Lebombo rail service was launched to carry passengers from Durban to Maputo via Swaziland. The service was terminated in May 2000, owing to insufficient demand. In August 2004 the Government announced plans to privatize Swaziland Railways.

Swaziland Railways: Swaziland Railway Bldg, cnr Johnston and Walker Sts, POB 475, Mbabane; tel. 4047211; fax 4047210; internet www.swazirail.co.sz; f. 1962; Chair. B. A. G. FITZPATRICK; CEO GIDEON J. MAHLALELA.

ROADS

In 2002 there were an estimated 3,594 km of roads, including 1,465 km of main roads and 2,129 km of secondary roads. About 28.2% of the road network was paved in 1994. The rehabilitation of about 700 km of main and 600 km of district gravel-surfaced roads began in 1985, financed by World Bank and US loans totalling some E 18m. In 1991 work commenced on the reconstruction of Swaziland's main road artery, connecting Mbabane to Manzini, via Matsapha, and in 2001 the Government announced the construction of two main roads in the north of the country, financed by Japanese loans.

Roads Department: Ministry of Public Works and Transport, POB 58, Mbabane; tel. 4042321; fax 4045825; Chief Roads Engineer T. M. TSHABALALA.

SHIPPING

Royal Swazi National Shipping Corpn Ltd: POB 1915, Manzini; tel. 5053788; fax 5053820; f. 1980 to succeed Royal Swaziland Maritime Co; 76% owned by Tibiyo Taka Ngwane; owns no ships, acting only as a freight agent; Gen. Man. M. S. DLAMINI.

CIVIL AVIATION

Swaziland's only airport is at Matsapha, near Manzini, about 40 km from Mbabane. In mid-1997 the Government initiated a three-year programme to upgrade the airport. In early 2003 construction began of an international airport at Sikhupe, in eastern Swaziland. In March 2006 Swaziland Airlink was one of 92 airlines banned from landing at European Union airports owing to safety concerns.

Swaziland Airlink: POB 939, Matsapha Airport, Manzini; tel. 5186155; fax 5186148; f. 1999; fmrly Royal Swazi Nat. Airways Corpn; jt venture between SA Airlink, South Africa (40%) and the Govt of Swaziland; scheduled passenger services from Manzini to Johannesburg, South Africa; Chair. LINDIWE KHUMALO-MATSE.

Tourism

Swaziland's attractions for tourists include game reserves (at Malolotja, Hawane, Mlawula and Mantenga) and magnificent mountain scenery. In 2005 tourist arrivals declined to 311,656 from 352,040 in 2004; receipts from tourism amounted to US $69.3m. in 2005.

Hotel and Tourism Association of Swaziland: Oribi Court, 1st Floor, Gwamile St, 462, Mbabane; tel. 4042218; fax 4044516; e-mail aliand@realnet.co.sz; internet www.visitswazi.com/tourismassoc; f. 1979.

Swaziland National Trust Commission (SNTC): POB 100, Lobamba; tel. 4161516; fax 4161875; e-mail director@sntc.org.sz (parks and wildlife); e-mail curator@sntc.org.sz (museums and monuments); internet www.sntc.org.sz; f. 1972; parastatal org. responsible for conservation of nature and cultural heritage (national parks, museums and monuments); CEO S. MAMBA.

Swaziland Tourism Authority: POB A1030, Swazi Plaza, Mbabane; tel. 4049693; fax 4049683; e-mail secretary@tourismauthority.org.sz; internet www.welcometoswaziland.com; f. 2001; CEO ERIC SIPHO MASEKO.

SWEDEN

Introductory Survey

Location, Climate, Language, Religion, Flag, Capital

The Kingdom of Sweden lies in north-western Europe, occupying about two-thirds of the Scandinavian peninsula. It is bordered by Finland to the north-east, and by Norway to the north-west and west. About 15% of Sweden's area lies north of the Arctic Circle. The Baltic Sea and the Gulf of Bothnia are to the east, the Skagerrak and Kattegat channels to the south-west. The country is relatively flat and is characterized by thousands of inland lakes and small coastal islands. There is a mountain range, the Kjølen mountains, in the north-west. Winters are cold and summers mild. In Stockholm the mean summer temperature is 18°C (64°F) and the mean winter temperature −3°C (27°F). The national language is Swedish, but there are Finnish and Lapp (Sámi) minorities (the latter numbering between 17,000 and 20,000), retaining their own languages. A majority of the inhabitants profess Christianity, and about 78% are adherents of the Evangelical Lutheran Church of Sweden. The national flag (proportions 5 by 8) is light blue with a yellow cross, the upright of the cross being to the left of centre. The capital is Stockholm.

Recent History

Sweden has been a constitutional monarchy, traditionally neutral, since the early 19th century. During this time the country has not participated in any war or entered any military alliance. Norway, formerly united with Sweden, became independent in 1905. Sweden adopted parliamentary government in 1917, and universal adult suffrage was introduced in 1921. From 1932 until 1976, except for a short break in 1936, Sweden was governed by the Socialdemokratiska Arbetareparti (SAP—Social Democratic Labour Party), either alone or as the senior partner in coalitions (1936–45 and 1951–57). During those 44 years the country had only three Prime Ministers, all Social Democrats. Since the Second World War Sweden has become an active member of many international organizations, including the UN (to which it has given military support), the Council of Europe (see p. 225) and, from 1995, the European Community (EC, now European Union—EU, see p. 244).

Olof Palme succeeded Dr Tage Erlander as Prime Minister and leader of the SAP in October 1969. After a general election in September 1970, Palme formed a minority Government. Under a constitutional reform, the Riksdag (Parliament) was reconstituted from January 1971, its two chambers being replaced by a unicameral assembly. King Gustaf VI Adolf, who had reigned since 1950, died in September 1973 and was succeeded by his grandson, Carl XVI Gustaf. A revised Constitution, effective from January 1975, ended the monarch's prerogative to appoint the Prime Minister: the Speaker of the Riksdag was to have this responsibility in future.

At the September 1976 election, dissatisfaction with high rates of taxation, necessary to maintain the advanced social welfare system that Sweden had developed, brought about the defeat of the SAP. Thorbjörn Fälldin, leader of the Centerpartiet (CP—Centre Party), formed a centre-right coalition in October. The wish of the CP to abandon Sweden's nuclear power programme caused serious controversy in June 1978, when an independent commission recommended its continuation. This view was endorsed by the Folkpartiet (FP—Liberals) and Moderata Samlingspartiet (MS—Moderates), whose rejection of a proposal by Fälldin to submit the nuclear issue to a national referendum precipitated the Government's resignation in October 1978. The FP formed a minority Government, led by Ola Ullsten. Following a general election in September 1979, Fälldin returned as Prime Minister of a coalition comprising members of the CP, the MS and the FP, with an overall parliamentary majority of only one seat. A referendum on the future of nuclear power was held in March 1980, at which a narrow majority of the electorate approved a limited programme of nuclear reactor development, to be progressively eliminated by 2010 and replaced by alternative energy resources.

During 1980 the Government's economic policies came under attack, mainly because of the rising rate of inflation, and there was severe industrial unrest. The MS, who disagreed with proposed tax reforms, left the coalition in May 1981. At the next general election, held in September 1982, the SAP was returned to power, winning 45.6% of the votes cast (securing 166 of the 349 seats in the Riksdag), but gaining an overall majority over the three non-socialist parties. In October Palme formed a minority Government, following an undertaking by the Vänsterpartiet—Kommunisterna (VpK—Left Party—Communists), which held 20 seats, to support the SAP. Palme's Government was returned to power in September 1985, with the support of the VpK. The SAP and the VpK together won 50.0% of the votes cast (178 seats), while the three main non-socialist parties won 48.0% (171 seats). The FP increased its share of seats in the legislature from 21 to 51, attracting voters from all of the other main parties. Palme undertook to continue to follow his 'third way' economic policy, seeking to combat inflation and recession while avoiding both excessively high levels of public spending and reductions in social welfare benefits.

In February 1986 Palme was murdered by an unknown assailant in Stockholm. In March the Deputy Prime Minister, Ingvar Carlsson, took office as Prime Minister and was also appointed acting Chairman of the SAP, pending ratification by the National Congress in 1987. Carlsson retained Palme's Cabinet and declared that he would continue the policies of his predecessor. During 1986–87 little progress was made towards discovering the identity of Palme's assassin, and considerable controversy surrounded the case, as disputes increased between the police and successive public prosecutors. In December 1988 Christer Pettersson, a man with a history of mental illness and violent crime, was arrested, and in mid-1989 he was tried for the murder of Palme. He was convicted amid some controversy, only to be acquitted on appeal in October. In December 1997 the public prosecutor's office petitioned the Supreme Court to re-examine the case against Pettersson in the light of the discovery of new, allegedly incriminating, evidence. In May 1998, however, the Supreme Court ruled that there was insufficient new evidence to conduct a retrial.

Meanwhile, ecological concerns were heightened in 1988 by two disasters affecting the marine environment along Sweden's coast, both of which were attributed to the effects of pollutants. At the general election in September the environmentalist Miljöpartiet de Gröna (MP—Green Party) gained parliamentary representation for the first time, but the SAP remained in power with the continued support of the VpK. The MS remained the second largest party in the Riksdag. In February 1990 the VpK (subsequently restyled the Vänsterpartiet—VP—Left Party) and the MP refused to support the Government's proposed austerity measures. Carlsson resigned, but, having secured support for a more moderate set of proposals, he formed another minority Government.

During 1990 the Swedish economy entered into recession, and in December the Riksdag approved a new programme of austerity measures, intended to reduce inflation and to restore confidence in the economy. The Government was forced to abandon the long-held belief that the commitment to full employment and the defence of the welfare state (supported by high levels of taxation and of public expenditure) should be overriding priorities.

However, the popularity of the SAP continued to decline, and in the general election of September 1991 the party did not win enough seats to form a government, although it remained the largest party in the Riksdag, with 138 seats. The MS increased their representation to 80 seats, while the Kristdemokratiska Samhällspartiet (KdS—Christian Democrats) and a recently formed right-wing party, Ny demokrati (ND—New Democracy), won 26 and 25 seats respectively, at the expense of the FP and the CP; the MP failed to secure 4% of the total votes cast, and thereby lost its seats. Carlsson resigned as Prime Minister for the second time, and in early October Carl Bildt, the leader of the MS (the largest non-socialist party in the legislature), formed a coalition government comprising members of four non-socialist parties—the MS, the CP, the FP and the KdS. Since these four parties, even in combination, still formed a minority in the Riksdag, they were obliged to rely on the ND for support in securing approval for legislation. Without delay, the new Government began to accelerate the deregulation of the economy already undertaken by its predecessor.

During 1992 the recession continued in Sweden. Although the Government's austerity measures succeeded in reducing inflation, the high level of the budgetary deficit was a cause of concern. In September speculation on the international currency markets caused a rapid outflow of capital, and in November a fresh outflow of capital, following the SAP's refusal to approve reductions in public expenditure, forced the Government to allow the krona to 'float' in relation to other currencies, thereby effectively devaluing it by some 10%. In March 1993 the Government was defeated in the Riksdag when the ND refused to support budgetary proposals, but later in the same month the Government won a parliamentary vote of confidence (the ND abstained from voting).

At the general election in September 1994 the SAP secured 45.3% of the votes cast, increasing its representation to 161 seats. The VP won 22 seats (compared with 16 in 1991) and the MP won 18 seats. Although the MS maintained the level of support they gained at the previous election, the other parties in the incumbent coalition Government fared badly. Bildt resigned as Prime Minister, and in October 1994 Carlsson formed a minority SAP Government. The results appeared to indicate a trend of increased support for parties opposed to Sweden's joining the EU (as the EC had become). Despite opposition to EU membership within the SAP, Carlsson declared that a major objective of his Government would be to secure a mandate for Sweden to join the EU in the forthcoming national referendum (see below). He also emphasized the need for stringent economic measures to reduce unemployment, stabilize the budgetary deficit and safeguard welfare provisions.

In March 1996 Carlsson relinquished his dual posts as Prime Minister and leader of the SAP, in order to retire from political life. Göran Persson, hitherto Minister of Finance, was elected unopposed as Prime Minister and leader of the SAP. Persson immediately initiated a broad cabinet reorganization.

In October 1996 Persson urged that the process to enlarge the EU be accelerated in order to strengthen European security. In November an independent study group, which had been commissioned by the Government to consider Sweden's proposed participation in Economic and Monetary Union (EMU, see p. 288), recommended that Sweden should not join EMU until the unemployment rate had been significantly reduced. In February 1997, however, the central bank advocated membership of EMU from its inception in 1999. Nevertheless, in June 1997 the Government announced that Sweden would not be participating in the first wave of EMU, citing a lack of public support for the project. The Government reiterated this stance in October, when it was also announced that Sweden had no intention of participating in the European Exchange Rate Mechanism (ERM).

In August 1997 details of a national programme of enforced sterilization conducted during 1935–75 against some 60,000 individuals assessed to be of inferior intellectual or physical capabilities, reported in the Swedish daily newspaper *Dagens Nyheter*, provoked national outrage and prompted the Government to announce the creation of a comprehensive public inquiry into the country's post-First World War eugenics programme. It was subsequently revealed that minimal compensation had been paid to just 16 victims of the programme during the previous 10 years. In March 1999 the Ministry of Health and Social Affairs announced that compensation amounting to a maximum of 175,000 kronor would be paid to each surviving victim of the programme. In August 2001 the State Sterilization Compensation Board stated that some 2,000 people had sought financial reparation, and that, of these, about 1,500 had received compensation, the total amount paid out being approximately 256m. kronor.

In March 1991 the Swedish and Danish Governments agreed to construct a 16-km combined bridge and tunnel for road and rail traffic, across the Öresund strait, between Malmö and Copenhagen (to be known as the Öresund Link). The plan aroused opposition in Sweden, on the grounds that the link might hinder the flow of water into the Baltic Sea, as well as increasing pollution by emissions from vehicles. In May 1994 a Swedish marine commission concluded that plans for the link did not provide sufficient guarantees to protect the flow of water into the Baltic. In the following month, however, the Swedish Government approved construction plans, prompting the resignation from the Government of the Minister of the Environment and leader of the CP, Olof Johansson. The link was opened in July 2000.

Prior to Sweden's membership of the EU (see below), trade with EU countries was conducted by means of a free-trade area, the European Economic Area (EEA), created in 1994 under the aegis of the European Free Trade Association (EFTA, see p. 412). Negotiations on admission to the EU began in February 1993, when the Bildt Government declared that the country's tradition of neutrality would not prevent Sweden from participating fully in the common foreign and security policy of the EU. The negotiations were concluded in March 1994. Sweden obtained safeguards for its traditional policy of freedom of official information, and for its strict environmental standards, and won concessions on the maintenance of subsidies for agriculture in remote areas. A national referendum on membership was held on 13 November, producing a 52.2% majority in favour of joining the EU. The Riksdag formally ratified membership in December, and Sweden's accession to the EU took effect from 1 January 1995 (whereupon Sweden withdrew from EFTA). It was widely held that concern about the possible effects on the domestic economy of remaining outside the EU, together with fears regarding Sweden's ability to influence international affairs, such as the maintenance of effective environmental controls, had been major factors in the outcome of the referendum. Following the vote, the Carlsson Government reiterated that Sweden would retain its non-aligned policy within the EU and therefore remain outside the North Atlantic Treaty Organization (NATO, see p. 340), although it would apply for observer status within Western European Union (WEU, see p. 426).

At the general election held in September 1998 the SAP maintained its position as the largest party in the Riksdag (winning 131 seats), despite a substantial reduction in its parliamentary representation compared with 1994. This was the SAP's worst electoral performance for some 70 years, and the party required the support of the VP and the MP to remain in government. The MS retained the position of second largest party in the Riksdag, obtaining 82 seats. Like the CP and the Kristdemokraterna (Kd, as the KdS had been renamed), the MS indicated their unwillingness to support the SAP in government. At about 81%, the participation rate at the election was the lowest for some 50 years. Post-electoral analysis identified the SAP's pursuit of financial regularity at the perceived expense of socialist policies as the probable cause of its poor performance: many voters had transferred their allegiance from the SAP to the VP. It was reported that, in return for its support, the VP would seek to persuade the Government to increase expenditure on social welfare and employment, and would encourage the slower repayment of Sweden's national debt, higher taxes, the complete decommissioning of Sweden's nuclear power stations, and a less stringent programme of privatization. Both the VP and the MP remained strongly opposed to any future participation by Sweden in EMU. In early October a new Cabinet was announced. At the same time the Government presented its statement of policy, which envisaged a more active role in Europe for Sweden. The Government would also seek to achieve sustainable economic growth in order to increase labour-force participation to a targeted 80% by 2004. This aim was reflected in the reconstitution of the Ministry of Industry, with additional responsibility for labour, energy, information technology and infrastructure. In April 1999 the Minister of Finance, Erik Asbrink, resigned following a reported disagreement with Persson over the content of the forthcoming budget; he was replaced by Bosse Ringholme. Following the announcement of former premier Bildt's retirement from party politics, in August Bo Lundgren was elected to succeed him as leader of the MS.

In late 1999 it was reported that public spending on defence equipment was to be reduced drastically. Additionally, proposed reform of the national defence system was likely to result in the loss of some 10,000 military and civilian jobs. Earlier in the year the military high command had indicated that the Government's programme of defence rationalization would lead to an eventual halving of the strength of the armed forces, in terms of both personnel and hardware, prompting speculation that Sweden might be about to reconsider its non-aligned status with regard to regional security. In November 2000 Persson announced proposals to that effect. He asserted that neutrality was no longer relevant after the end of the Cold War, and that it did not cover all aspects of Sweden's security policy, such as disarmament, the non-proliferation of nuclear weapons and stability in Europe. However, Persson ruled out any move to join NATO, asserting that it was essential for the stability of northern Europe that Sweden remain non-aligned.

At the general election held on 15 September 2002 the SAP maintained its position as the largest party in the Riksdag, winning 39.8% of the votes cast and securing 144 of the 349 seats. Persson formed a minority SAP Government with the parliamentary support of the MP and the VP. In return for their support, the MP and the VP required the Government to espouse some of their policies, including, among others, a reduction of 6,000m. kronor in defence expenditure over five years and a moratorium on cod-fishing in the Baltic Sea from 1 January 2003, with compensation for the fishing industry.

In March 2000 a national congress of the SAP endorsed the adoption of future EMU entry as official party policy, despite a significant degree of opposition. Following the 2002 general election, Persson announced that a referendum would be held on the adoption of the euro in September 2003. In December 2002 opinion polls reported equal proportions in favour of and against adopting the euro, but by May 2003 the proportion of those opposing the euro had increased to 47%, while the proportion of those in favour had fallen to 40% and the number of undecided voters had increased to 13%. Meanwhile, the SAP remained sharply divided on the issue. Five of the party's 22 cabinet ministers were opposed to joining EMU, among them the Deputy Prime Minister, Margareta Winberg. The MS and other parties of the centre-right supported Sweden's entry into EMU. The campaign for the adoption of the euro was supported by the national media and the business community, whereas opposition to the new currency was focused in the trade unions, the MP and the VP. Most Swedes, and especially those in rural and northern areas or in public-sector employment, wanted to keep their generous social welfare provisions, which were funded through high taxation, and opponents of EMU feared that membership would force Sweden to reduce public spending so as not to breach the 3% budget deficit limit imposed by the EU's Stability and Growth Pact.

In September 2003, four days prior to the referendum on entry into EMU, the Minister for Foreign Affairs, Anna Lindh, was stabbed in central Stockholm; she died of her injuries the following day. Prior to her death, she had been one of the Government's most effective campaigners for entry into EMU, and was widely seen as a potential future SAP leader. The referendum was held as planned on 14 September, and speculation that support for the euro would be enhanced as a result of sympathy following Lindh's death, thereby undermining the legitimacy of the decision, proved unfounded, as voters decisively rejected the adoption of the euro. The result of the referendum, for which turn-out was 82.6%, was 42.0% in favour, 55.9% against and 2.1% blank. Only in Stockholm did the proposal to adopt the euro receive a majority of votes cast.

Mijail Mijailović, a Swede of Serbian origin, was arrested in September 2003 on suspicion of Lindh's murder. He initially denied any involvement in the killing but later confessed to police during his interrogation. Mijailović, who had a history of mental illness and claimed there was no political motive for the attack, was tried in January 2004, and was convicted of murder and sentenced to life imprisonment. Mijailović appealed against his conviction, and in July the Court of Appeal in Stockholm ruled that he should be sent to a psychiatric institution rather than serving a prison sentence. The Lindh family challenged the decision in the Supreme Court, which in December confirmed Mijailović's sentence of life imprisonment.

With the prospect of the enlargement of the EU from 15 to 25 countries on 1 May 2004, concerns arose that the Swedish welfare system would be unduly burdened by an influx of workers from the new member states. In March of that year, following similar action by other EU member countries, the Government introduced legislation in the Riksdag proposing welfare and labour restrictions for migrant workers from the 10 accession countries for at least two years. However, the Riksdag rejected the bill at the end of April by 187 votes to 137. This defeat was seen as a major reverse for the Government, and meant that Sweden was one of the few EU countries without any restrictions limiting access to jobs or social security to citizens of the new member states.

The perceived failure of the main political parties adequately to address the strong current of EU scepticism expressed in Sweden's rejection of the euro led to the formation, in February 2004, of a new political grouping, the Junilistan (June List), which opposed further integration with the EU, but did not advocate withdrawal. The grouping stressed that it was not itself a political party, and went as far as appending its candidates' usual party affiliation to their names on the ballots for the forthcoming elections to the European Parliament. Thus voters would be able to support the June List on the issue of the EU while not altogether abandoning their usual party. This strategy proved successful, allowing the June List to draw support from across the political spectrum. At the elections, held on 13 June, the June List won 14.4% of the votes cast and three of Sweden's 19 seats in the European Parliament. The SAP, in contrast, suffered its worst electoral result since 1912, obtaining just 24.7% (five seats), while the MS won 18.2% (four seats). The VP and FP each won two seats, and the CP, MP and Kd one apiece. It was widely believed that the June List's success in the European elections might increase pressure on the Government to consider holding a national referendum on the ratification of the EU constitutional treaty, which had finally been approved by the Council of the EU in June 2004. However, the Government chose to present the treaty for approval (or otherwise) in the Riksdag: legislation was to be presented by September 2005, with a view to adoption in December of that year. However, following the rejection of the treaty at national referendums in France and the Netherlands in mid-2005, Sweden was one of several member states to decide to delay the ratification process indefinitely. At a meeting of the European Council in Brussels in June 2007, a preliminary agreement was reached to replace the rejected constitutional treaty. On December 13 EU leaders met in Lisbon, Portugal, to sign the new Reform Treaty, which was to amend existing treaties. The Treaty of Lisbon, as it was subsequently known, was approved by the House of Representatives in February 2008, and was due to be ratified by all member states by the end of that year.

Meanwhile, in mid-September 2004 Lars Engqvist was replaced at the Ministry of Health and Social Affairs by Ylva Johansson, and in late October Persson implemented a wider government reorganization. Pär Nuder, previously Minister for Policy Co-ordination, was appointed Minister for Finance, in place of Bosse Ringholm (who became Deputy Prime Minister). Thomas Östros, hitherto Minister for Education and Science, replaced Leif Pagrotsky as Minister for Industry and Trade, while Pagrotsky became head of a reorganized Ministry of Education, Research and Culture (which also included Ibrahim Baylan as Minister for Schools). The reorganization was widely viewed as an attempt by Persson (following the SAP's poor performance in the European parliamentary elections) to renew, and revive support for, his administration in advance of the general election scheduled for 2006.

In May 2005 the UN Committee against Torture ruled that Sweden had violated the 1984 UN Convention against Torture and Other Cruel, Inhuman or Degrading Treatment or Punishment in December 2001 by returning an asylum seeker to Egypt, where he had been convicted *in absentia* of membership of a terrorist group; the Committee stated that the Swedish authorities should have known at the time of the expulsion that Egypt used torture against detainees. Human rights groups had earlier expressed concern at the treatment of the asylum seeker and another Egyptian national deported at the same time; the two men had controversially been flown to Egypt in a US-leased aircraft, having been handed over to US security officials by the Swedish authorities. In November 2005 the Swedish Government ordered the Civil Aviation Authority to investigate media reports that aircraft used by the US Central Intelligence Agency (CIA) had landed at Swedish airports while transporting suspected terrorists to third countries for interrogation. In the following month the Authority, which examined the period from January 2002, reported that it could not substantiate the claims.

In September 2005 the Riksdag rejected a proposed amnesty for illegal immigrants living in Sweden, despite considerable public support for such a measure. Following the vote, a number of protests took place and 150,000 signatures were collected in favour of an amnesty. In November the Riksdag approved legislation allowing failed asylum seekers to reapply for a residence permit before the end of March 2006. It was estimated that 20,000 asylum seekers whose deportation orders had not been carried out owing to conditions in their home countries, or who had gone into hiding after having their original applications refused, would be eligible to submit new applications under the law.

In February 2006 the Government announced its intention for Sweden to overcome its dependency on petroleum within 15 years, without constructing any further nuclear power stations. A committee of industrialists, academics, farmers, vehicle manufacturers, civil servants and others was charged with devising a plan to achieve this, and was to report to the Riksdag later that year. The Government hoped to protect Sweden from the adverse economic effects of climate change and from fluctuations in the price of petroleum, which had increased substantially in recent years.

In March 2006 Laila Freivalds resigned as Minister for Foreign Affairs, following criticism of her ministry's involvement in forcing the temporary closure, in February, of the website of *SD-Kuriren*—the newspaper of the far-right Sverigedemokraterna (SD, Swedish Democrats)—which had asked readers to submit cartoons of the Prophet Muhammad. (The publication of caricatures depicting the Prophet in a Danish newspaper in late 2005, and in a number of other European newspapers in early 2006, had led to world-wide protests by Muslims—see the chapter on Denmark.) Freivalds had initially denied responsibility for the decision to intervene, which Persson had denounced as being contrary to the freedom of the press. She had already come under pressure to resign in December 2005 after an independent commission held her partly responsible for the Government's slow response to the tsunamis in South-East Asia on 26 December 2004 (which killed more than 500 Swedes). Jan Eliasson, the President of the UN General Assembly, was appointed as the new Minister for Foreign Affairs; he was to hold both positions until the expiry of his UN term in September 2006.

At the general election, held on 17 September 2006, the centre-right Alliance for Sweden, comprising the MS, the FP, the CP and the Kd, emerged as the largest group in the Riksdag, the four parties together winning 178 seats. Of those, the MS, led by Fredrik Reinfeldt, won 97 seats (compared with 55 seats in the 2002 elections), the CP 29, the FP 28 and the Kd 24. The four main non-socialist parties had presented a joint programme for government, which included plans to reduce welfare dependency and increase the labour supply by means of tax cuts for the lower paid and reductions in the levels of unemployment benefit, to reduce the role of the state in the economy through the privatization of state-owned companies and to introduce private sector competition in health care and education. In contrast to its partners in the Alliance, the FP suffered a significant decline in support, recording a loss of 20 seats, compared with the 2002 elections. The revelation of a scandal regarding a group of FP activists, who, during the election campaign, had gained illegal access to the computer network of the SAP and distributed information they had obtained to fellow activists in the FP, was considered to have been a decisive factor in the party's poor electoral performance. The SAP, despite remaining the largest party in the Riksdag (with 130 seats), recorded its worst electoral result since 1914. Persson immediately resigned as Prime Minister and announced that he would relinquish the leadership of the SAP in March 2007. As the leader of the largest party in the Alliance, Reinfeldt assumed the role of Prime Minister.

Reinfeldt's appointments to the new coalition Government in October 2006 included Maud Olofsson, of the CP, as Deputy Prime Minister and Minister for Enterprise and Energy, and the former Prime Minister, Bildt, as Minister for Foreign Affairs. The appointment of Nyamko Sabuni, a former refugee from Zaire (now the Democratic Republic of the Congo), as Minister for Integration and Gender Equality in the new Cabinet was controversial, with Muslim groups organizing a petition calling for her resignation. Her outspoken views on integration, including a proposal for a ban on the wearing of the *hijab* (Islamic headscarf) by girls under the age of 15 years, compulsory checks for genital mutilation and the termination of state funding for religious schools, provoked criticism from immigrant communities. Shortly after assuming office the Minister for Culture, Cecilia Stegö Chilò, and the Minister for Foreign Trade, Maria Borelius, both of the MS, were forced to resign following allegations of irregularities in their personal finances. Stegö Chilò attracted particularly intense criticism after it was revealed that she had not paid her television licence fee for 16 years; as Minister for Culture, she was ultimately responsible for the state broadcasting corporation, which was financed by the licence fee. Lena Adelsohn Liljeroth and Sten Tolgfors, both of the MS, assumed the culture and foreign trade portfolios, respectively.

At the SAP party conference in mid-March 2007, Mona Sahlin was elected to succeed Persson as party leader. The trial of six people on charges relating to the illegal accessing of SAP computer data by FP activists, commenced in early April. Later that month three of the defendants were convicted and received substantial fines, while three members of the FP, including a former party secretary, were acquitted. None the less, the reputation of the party had been severely damaged. In that month, Lars Leijonborg, the Minister for Education and Research, whose leadership of the FP had been the subject of criticism for several months, announced that he would resign as leader of the FP following the party conference, scheduled for September, as he could no longer command sufficient support within the party to remain in his post.

A Swedish artist, Lars Vilks, provoked anger among Muslim communities in August 2007, when he depicted the head of the Prophet Muhammad on a dog's body. The satirical image was deemed particularly offensive, not only for infringing Islamic tradition (which prohibits the representation of the Prophet) but because dogs are widely considered to be unclean in Islamic culture. The decision by Swedish newspaper *Nerikes Allehanda* to print the caricature resulted in formal protests by Egypt, Iran and Pakistan. In September Reinfeldt met with diplomats from a number of Muslim countries in an effort to defuse the tension. He apologized for any offence the image may have caused, but defended the right of Swedish citizens to freedom of expression. Vilks was subsequently placed under police protection, following reports that the head of al-Qa'ida in Iraq, Abu Omar al-Baghdadi, had offered a US $100,000 reward for his murder.

A minor government reorganization took place in September 2007. Sten Tolgfors, the Minister for Foreign Trade, was appointed Minister for Defence, following Mikael Odenberg's decision to resign from the post over government proposals to reduce the defence budget by up to 4,000m. kronor by 2010. Ewa Björling succeeded Tolgfors as the Minister for Foreign Trade. In November Ulrica Schenström resigned from her position as State Secretary to the Prime Minister, following revelations that she had consumed a significant quantity of alcohol with a journalist, while officially on call for the Government's emergency response unit. Hans Gustaf Wessberg was appointed as her successor.

Six people were arrested in Sweden and Norway in February 2008, on suspicion of financing militant organizations and planning terrorist acts. Three of the suspects, who were reported to be Swedish citizens, were apprehended at separate locations in Stockholm. The arrests were part of a co-ordinated action by the Swedish and Norwegian security forces.

The Swedish Government expressed its opposition to the US-led military operation against the regime of Saddam Hussain in Iraq from early 2003. In October of that year, however, Sweden pledged 250m. kronor towards the reconstruction of Iraq (in addition to a substantial amount of humanitarian aid).

Government

Sweden is a constitutional monarchy. The hereditary monarch is Head of State but has very limited formal prerogatives. Executive power rests with the Cabinet (Regeringen), which is responsible to the legislature (Riksdag). The unicameral Riksdag was introduced in January 1971. It has 349 members, elected by universal adult suffrage for four years, on the basis of proportional representation. The Prime Minister is nominated by the Speaker of the Riksdag and later confirmed in office by the whole House. The country is divided into 21 counties (Län) and 288 municipal districts (Kommun). Both counties and municipalities have popularly elected councils.

Defence

Proposals for a significant reduction in defence spending and resources were announced during 1999 (see Recent History). As assessed at November 2006, Sweden maintained total armed forces of 27,600, compared with 53,100 in 1999. The army consisted of 13,800 men, of whom 8,600 were conscripts; the navy 7,900 men, including 2,000 conscripts, and the air force 5,900 men, including 1,500 conscripts. In addition, there were voluntary defence reservists totalling 262,000, compared with 570,000 in 1999. Military service for males (aged between 19 and 47) lasts between seven and 15 months in the army and navy, and between eight and 12 months in the air force. Basic training for women is voluntary. In 2007 defence was allocated 46,900m. kronor in the budget. In November 2004 the European Union (EU, see p. 244) ministers responsible for defence agreed to create 13 'battlegroups' (each numbering about 1,500 men), which could be deployed at short notice to crisis areas around the world. The EU battlegroups, two of which were to be ready for deployment at any one time, following a rotational schedule, reached full operational capacity from 1 January 2007. In May 2006 Sweden, Finland, Norway and Estonia signed a co-operation agreement with regard to the establishment of a joint Nordic battle group. Sweden was to contribute 2,000 troops,

Finland 200, Norway 150 and Estonia 50. In April 2007 Ireland's participation in the Nordic group was approved by its legislature.

Economic Affairs

In 2006, according to estimates by the World Bank, Sweden's gross national income (GNI), measured at average 2004–06 prices, was US $394,207m., equivalent to $43,580 per head (or $35,070 on an international purchasing-power parity basis). During 1996–2006, it was estimated, the population grew at an average annual rate of 0.2%, while gross domestic product (GDP) per head increased, in real terms, by an average of 2.8% per year. Sweden's overall GDP increased, in real terms, by an average of 3.0% per year in 1996–2006. According to official figures, GDP increased by 4.4% in 2006.

Agriculture (including hunting, forestry and fishing) contributed 1.4% of GDP and employed 2.0% of the working population in 2006. The main agricultural products are dairy produce, meat, cereals and potatoes, primarily for domestic consumption. In 2006 forestry products (wood, pulp and paper) accounted for 10.6% of total merchandise exports. Agricultural GDP decreased by an average of 0.1% per year during 1996–2005; it contracted by 8.8% in 2005.

Industry (including mining, manufacturing, construction and power) provided 29.0% of GDP and employed 22.1% of the working population in 2006. Industrial GDP increased by an average of 4.6% per year in 1996–2005. Industrial GDP grew by 8.6% in 2004 and by 3.2% in 2005.

Mining contributed 0.5% of GDP and employed 0.2% of the working population in 2006. The principal product is iron ore, but there are also large reserves of uranium (some 15% of the world's total known reserves), copper, lead and zinc. The GDP of the mining and quarrying sector grew, in real terms, by an average of 4.5% per year in 2001–06, according to Statistics Sweden; it increased by 6.5% in 2005 and by 1.0% in 2006.

Manufacturing contributed 20.4% of GDP and employed 15.1% of the working population in 2006. Sweden's principal manufactures were paper and paper products, motor vehicles, chemicals, basic iron and steel, television and radio transmitters and other communications apparatus and general purpose machinery. Manufacturing GDP increased, in real terms, by an average of 5.9% per year in 2001–06, according to Statistics Sweden; it rose by 5.7% in 2006.

Energy is derived principally from nuclear power, which provided some 51.1% of electricity generated in 2004, and hydroelectric power, which provided 39.6% of electricity generated in the same year. Sweden has 10 nuclear reactors. Alternative sources of energy are being developed, because of strict environmental legislation, the lack of potential for further hydroelectric projects and, primarily, the Riksdag's resolution to phase out nuclear power. In February 2006 the Government announced its intention for Sweden to overcome its dependency on petroleum within 15 years, without constructing any further nuclear power stations. Imports of petroleum and petroleum products accounted for 10.5% of total imports in 2006.

The services sector contributed 69.5% of GDP and engaged 75.9% of the employed population in 2006. The GDP of the services sector increased, in real terms, at an average annual rate of 2.4% during 1996–2005; it grew by 2.7% in 2005.

In 2006 Sweden recorded a visible trade surplus of US $21,415m., and there was a surplus of $28,413m. on the current account of the balance of payments. The European Union (EU, see p. 244) dominates Swedish trade: in 2006 it provided 70.5% of imports and took 60.0% of exports. The European Free Trade Association (EFTA, see p. 412) is also an important trading partner. In 2006 the principal single source of imports was Germany (contributing 18.0% of total imports); other major suppliers were Denmark (9.7%), Norway (8.5%), the Netherlands (6.3%), the United Kingdom (6.3%) and Finland (5.9%). Germany was also the principal market for exports in that year (accounting for 9.9% of total exports); other major purchasers were the USA (9.3%), Norway (9.1%), the United Kingdom (7.2%), Denmark (also 7.2%) and Finland (6.3%). The principal exports in 2006 were machinery and transport equipment, basic manufactured goods and chemicals. The principal imports in 2006 were machinery and transport equipment, and basic and other manufactures.

In 2006 there was a budget surplus of 18,373m. kronor, equivalent to 0.6% of GDP. In that year the central Government's total debt was 1,269,950m. kronor, equivalent to 44.7% of GDP. The annual rate of inflation averaged 1.0% in 1996–2006. Consumer prices increased by an average of 2.2% in 2007. The unemployment rate averaged 5.4% in 2006.

Sweden is a member of the Nordic Council (see p. 424) and the Nordic Council of Ministers (see p. 424). In January 1995 Sweden became a full member of the EU.

Sweden's economy is more diversified than is usual for a country of its size. Alongside traditional industries based on iron ore and wood (Sweden's most significant raw materials), the engineering industry and high-technology sectors have become increasingly important. Unlike many relatively small countries, Sweden has significant domestic aviation and nuclear power industries, as well as automotive manufacturers, an advanced arms industry, a world-leading telecommunications industry and major pharmaceutical and medical research capabilities. In the late 1990s, following the country's most serious economic recession in some 60 years (triggered by high inflation and public sector salary bills), Sweden experienced a considerable economic recovery. Expansion in the high-technology sector fuelled exports and helped to achieve robust GDP growth. In 2002–03 Sweden's economy compared favourably with the members of the euro area, arguably influencing its rejection of participation in European Economic and Monetary Union (EMU, see p. 288) in a national referendum held in September 2003. While strong growth in 2004 was largely export-driven, domestic demand and investment became the main impetus for growth in 2005, when GDP increased by an estimated 2.7%. A new centre-right coalition Government took office in September 2006. The 2007 budget aimed to reduce welfare dependency and increase the labour supply, through cuts in income taxes for low- and medium-income groups and a reduction in unemployment benefits. In late 2007 it was announced that both wealth and property taxes would be abolished early in 2008. The new Government also announced its intention to sell stakes in many state-owned companies, which would contribute to a reduction in the level of public debt. By March 2008, however, the scheduling for the Government's privatization programme was under threat as a result of the low-income mortgage crisis in the USA and the ensuing crisis in investor confidence. In April 2008 the Government lowered its growth forecast for the year from 3.2% to 2.1%, blaming uncertainty in the financial market. Economic growth was 2.5% in 2007.

Education

Basic education, which is compulsory, extends for nine years, starting at the age of six or seven years, and is received at the comprehensive school (grundskolan). At the end of this period a pupil may enter the integrated upper secondary school (gymnasieskolan). In accordance with legislation implemented in 1992–95, courses at upper secondary schools last three years, and are organized into 16 nationally defined study programmes, comprising two university entrance programmes and 14 vocational programmes. All publicly funded schools follow a national curriculum. However, most schools are operated by municipal authorities, which have some autonomy over the profile of each school. In addition, parents have the right to send their children to independent schools, which are publicly funded and must share the same objectives as municipally-run schools, but may differ in character and methods. Enrolment at pre-primary level included 80% of children in the relevant age-group in 2003/04. Enrolment at primary schools in that year included 99% of children (100% of boys; 99% of girls) in the relevant age-group, while the comparable ratio for secondary enrolment was 98% (98% of boys; 99% of girls). There are some 39 higher education institutions in Sweden, including 10 that are privately owned. Slightly more than 30% of young people in Sweden proceed to higher education within five years of completing their upper secondary schooling. In 2003/04 enrolment in higher education was equivalent to 82% of people in the relevant age-group (males 65%; females 100%). The budget for 2007 allocated 44,200m. kronor (5.7% of total expenditure) to education and university research.

Public Holidays*

2008: 1 January (New Year's Day), 6 January (Epiphany), 21 March (Good Friday), 23 March (Easter), 24 March (Easter Monday), 1 May (May Day and Ascension Day), 11 May (Whit Sunday), 6 June (National Day), 21 June (Midsummer Holiday), 1 November (All Saints' Day), 25 December (Christmas), 26 December (St Stephen's Day).

2009: 1 January (New Year's Day), 6 January (Epiphany), 10 April (Good Friday), 12 April (Easter), 13 April (Easter Monday), 1 May (May Day), 21 May (Ascension Day), 31 May (Whit Sunday), 6 June (National Day), 20 June (Midsummer

SWEDEN

Statistical Survey

Holiday), 1 November (All Saints' Day), 25 December (Christmas), 26 December (St Stephen's Day).

*The eve of a holiday is as important or more so than the holiday itself. Most Swedes have the day off, including those working in the civil service, banks, public transport, hospitals, shops and the media. Others have at least a half-day. This applies especially to Midsummer's Eve, All Saints' Day Eve and Christmas Eve. The eve of May Day is sometimes called Valborg Eve or St Walpurgis. When a holiday falls on a Thursday many Swedes have the following Friday off in addition. When a holiday falls on a Saturday or Sunday it is not taken on the following Monday.

Weights and Measures

The metric system is in force.

Statistical Survey

Sources (unless otherwise stated): Statistics Sweden, Klostergatan 23, 701 89 Örebro; tel. (19) 17-60-00; fax (19) 17-70-80; e-mail information@scb.se; internet www.scb.se; Nordic Statistical Secretariat (Copenhagen), *Yearbook of Nordic Statistics*.

Area and Population

AREA, POPULATION AND DENSITY

Area (sq km)	
Land	410,335
Inland waters	39,960
Total	450,295*
Population (census results)†	
1 November 1985	8,360,178
1 November 1990	
Males	4,242,351
Females	4,345,002
Total	8,587,353
Population (official estimates at 31 December)†	
2005	9,047,752
2006	9,113,257
2007	9,182,927
Density (per sq km) at 31 December 2007	22.4‡

* 173,859 sq miles.
† Population is *de jure*.
‡ Density refers to land area only.

COUNTIES
(31 December 2007)

	Land area (sq km)*	Population	Density (per sq km)
Stockholms län	6,519.3	1,949,516	299.0
Uppsala län	7,036.7	323,270	45.9
Södermanlands län	6,103.1	265,190	43.5
Östergötlands län	10,604.6	420,809	39.7
Jönköpings län	10,495.4	333,610	31.8
Kronobergs län	8,467.3	180,787	21.4
Kalmar län	11,219.1	233,834	20.8
Gotlands län	3,151.4	57,122	18.1
Blekinge län	2,946.7	151,900	51.5
Skåne län	11,035.4	1,199,357	108.7
Hallands län	5,461.6	291,393	53.4
Västra Götalands län	23,956.1	1,547,298	64.6
Värmlands län	17,591.3	273,826	15.6
Örebro län	8,546.3	276,067	32.3
Västmanlands län	6,317.9	249,193	39.4
Dalarnus län	28,195.6	275,618	9.8
Gävleborgs län	18,200.1	275,556	15.1
Västernorrlands län	21,684.5	243,449	11.2
Jämtlands län	49,343.1	126,937	2.6
Västerbottens län	55,189.7	257,593	4.7
Norrbottens län	98,249.0	250,602	2.6
Total†	410,335.4	9,182,927	22.4

* According to new estimates for land area.
† Including area of 21.2 sq km outside of existing county boundaries.

PRINCIPAL TOWNS
(estimated population of municipalities at 31 December 2007)*

Stockholm (capital)	795,163	Örebro	130,429
Göteborg (Gothenburg)	493,502	Norrköping	126,680
Malmö	280,801	Helsingborg	124,986
Uppsala	187,541	Jönköping	123,709
Linköping	140,367	Umeå	111,771
Västerås	133,728	Lund	105,286

* According to the administrative subdivisions of 1 January 2006.

BIRTHS, MARRIAGES AND DEATHS

	Registered live births		Registered marriages		Registered deaths	
	Number	Rate (per 1,000)	Number	Rate (per 1,000)	Number	Rate (per 1,000)
1999	88,173	9.9	35,628	4.0	94,726	10.7
2000	90,441	10.2	39,895	4.5	93,461	10.5
2001	91,446	10.3	35,778	4.0	93,752	10.5
2002	95,815	10.7	38,012	4.3	95,009	10.6
2003	99,157	11.0	39,041	4.3	92,961	10.4
2004	100,928	11.2	43,088	4.8	90,532	10.0
2005	101,346	11.2	44,381	n.a.	91,710	10.1
2006	105,913	11.6	45,551	n.a.	91,177	10.0

Expectation of life (years at birth, WHO estimates): 80.9 (males 78.7; females 83.0) in 2005 (Source: WHO, *World Health Statistics*).

IMMIGRATION AND EMIGRATION

	2005	2006	2007
Immigrants	65,229	95,750	99,485
Emigrants	38,118	44,908	45,418

ECONOMICALLY ACTIVE POPULATION
(sample surveys, '000 persons aged 16 to 64 years)

	2004	2005	2006
Agriculture, hunting and forestry	89	84	84
Fishing	1	2	2
Mining and quarrying	6	7	8
Manufacturing	679	652	653
Electricity, gas and water supply	27	27	25
Construction	242	253	270
Wholesale and retail trade, repair of motor vehicles, motorcycles and personal and household goods	529	535	536
Hotels and restaurants	124	117	128
Transport, storage and communications	265	269	274
Financial intermediation	87	81	84
Real estate, renting and business activities	545	582	603

SWEDEN

—continued	2004	2005	2006
Public administration and defence, compulsory social security, extra-territorial organizations and bodies	246	238	249
Education	472	472	480
Health and social work	683	707	701
Other community, social and personal service activities, private households with employed persons	214	228	233
Activities not adequately defined	3	10	9
Total employed	4,213	4,263	4,341
Unemployed	246	270	246
Total labour force	4,459	4,533	4,587
Males	2,323	2,373	2,404
Females	2,136	2,161	2,181

Note: From 2005, data reflect revised methodology, and are therefore not strictly comparable with data for 2004.

Source: ILO.

Health and Welfare

KEY INDICATORS

Total fertility rate (children per woman, 2004)	1.7
Under-5 mortality rate (per 1,000 live births, 2005)	4
HIV/AIDS (% of persons aged 15–49, 2005)	0.2
Physicians (per 1,000 head, 2002)	3.28
Hospital beds (per 1,000 head, 1997)	5.2
Health expenditure (2004): US $ per head (PPP)	2,827.9
Health expenditure (2004): % of GDP	9.1
Health expenditure (2004): public (% of total)	84.9
Human Development Index (2005): ranking	6
Human Development Index (2005): value	0.956

For sources and definitions, see explanatory note on p. vi.

Agriculture

PRINCIPAL CROPS
('000 metric tons; holdings of more than 2 ha of arable land)

	2004	2005	2006
Wheat	2,412.3	2,246.8	2,001.4
Rye	133.4	112.3	117.8
Barley	1,691.9	1,592.9	1,112.4
Oats	925.3	746.3	635.0
Triticale (wheat-rye hybrid)	270.2	271.5	263.2
Potatoes	979.1	947.3	772.6
Rapeseed	227.5	198.2	221.0
Sugar beets	2,287.1	2,381.2	2,381.2

Aggregate production ('000 metric tons, may include official, semi-official or estimated data): Total cereals 5,507.8 in 2004, 5,050.6 in 2005, 4,173.8 in 2006; Total roots and tubers 979.1 in 2004, 947.3 in 2005, 772.6 in 2006; Total vegetables (incl. melons) 326.5 in 2004, 327.1 in 2005, 323.2 in 2006; Total fruits (excl. melons) 34.1 in 2004, 32.6 in 2005, 32.9 in 2006.

Source: FAO.

LIVESTOCK
('000 head, year ending September; holdings of more than 2 ha of arable land, or with large numbers of livestock)

	2004	2005	2006
Cattle	1,628.5	1,604.9	1,590.4
Sheep	451	456	480
Pigs	1,818.0	1,811.2	1,680.5
Horses	95.7	95.7*	95.7*
Chickens	6,620	6,762	6,762
Turkeys*	200	200	200

* FAO estimate(s).

Source: FAO.

LIVESTOCK PRODUCTS
('000 metric tons)

	2003	2004	2005
Cattle meat	140.4	143.0	135.0
Horse meat	1.4	1.4	1.0
Sheep meat	3.7	3.8	4.1
Pig meat	287.5	294.5	275.1
Chicken meat	97.9	91.2	107.5*
Game meat	18.5	18.5*	18.5*
Cows' milk	3,253.0	3,275.0	3,206.0
Hen eggs	92.3	102.0†	101.0†

* FAO estimate.
† Unofficial figure.

2006: Production assumed to be unchanged from 2005 (FAO estimates).

Source: FAO.

Forestry

ROUNDWOOD REMOVALS
('000 cubic metres)

	2004	2005	2006
Sawlogs, veneer logs and logs for sleepers	35,400	56,500	28,300
Pulpwood	25,500	35,300	27,300
Fuel wood*	5,900	5,900	5,900
Other industrial wood*	500	500	500
Total	67,300	98,200	62,000

* FAO estimates.

Source: FAO.

SAWNWOOD PRODUCTION
('000 cubic metres, incl. railway sleepers)

	2004	2005	2006
Coniferous (softwood)	16,740	17,440	17,840
Broadleaved (hardwood)*	160	160	160
Total	16,900	17,600	18,000

* FAO estimates.

Source: FAO.

Fishing

('000 metric tons, live weight)

	2003	2004	2005
Capture	286.9	269.9	256.4
Atlantic cod	16.3	16.4	11.7
Blue whiting (Poutassou)	65.5	20.0	4.4
Sandeels (Sandlances)	22.0	34.6	8.8
Atlantic herring	86.6	89.0	105.6
European sprat	76.7	90.7	109.4
Aquaculture	6.3	6.0	5.9
Total catch	293.2	275.9	262.2

Note: Figures exclude aquatic mammals, recorded by number rather than by weight. The number of harbour porpoises caught was: 5 in 2003; 1 in 2004; nil in 2005.

Source: FAO.

Mining

('000 metric tons, unless otherwise indicated)

	2003	2004	2005
Iron ore*	14,100	14,700	15,300
Copper ore	96.0	90.6	97.8
Gold (kilograms)	4,300	5,200	4,400
Silver (metric tons)	306.8	292.6	267.2
Zinc ore	185.9	197.0	214.6
Lead ore	51.0	54.3	58.7

* Estimates.

Note: Figures relate to the metal content of ores.

Source: US Geological Survey.

Industry

SELECTED PRODUCTS
('000 metric tons, unless otherwise indicated)

	2003	2004	2005
Pig-iron and sponge-iron*†	3,700	3,600	3,500
Crude steel*	5,707	5,949	6,000
Aluminium*‡	131.2	130.4	132.6
Copper (refined)*†‡	214	235	222
Lead (refined)*†‡	76.2	82.2	80.0
Mechanical wood pulp§	3,222.6	3,397.0	3,445.0
Chemical wood pulp§	8,236	8,417	8,365
Newsprint§	2,548.0	2,649.0	2,572.0
Printing and writing paper§	2,817.0	3,033.0†	3,119.0
Other paper and paperboard†§	5,696.6	5,907.0	6,084.0
Cement (hydraulic)*†	2,650	2,700	2,800
Dwellings completed (number)	19,986	25,283	23,068
Electricity (million kWh)	132,535	148,824	154,982

* Source: US Geological Survey.
† Estimate(s).
‡ Primary and secondary metals.
§ Source: FAO.

2006 ('000 metric tons, unless otherwise indicated): Mechanical wood pulp 3,489; Chemical wood pulp 8,292; Newsprint 2,541; Printing and writing paper 3,414; Other paper and paperboard 6,111; Electricity (million kWh) 140,307 (Source: mainly FAO).

Finance

CURRENCY AND EXCHANGE RATES

Monetary Units
100 öre = 1 Swedish krona (plural: kronor).

Sterling, Dollar and Euro Equivalents (31 December 2007)
£1 sterling = 12.849 kronor;
US $1 = 6.414 kronor;
€1 = 9.441 kronor;
100 Swedish kronor = £7.78 = $15.59 = €10.59.

Average Exchange Rate (kronor per US $)
2005   7.4731
2006   7.3783
2007   6.7588

STATE BUDGET
(million kronor)

Revenue	2005	2006	2007*
Tax revenue	682,268	744,461	751,444
Other current revenue	33,185	43,450	64,227
Capital revenue	6,689	56	18,024
Loan repayment	2,303	2,144	2,044
Computed revenue	8,788	7,763	8,113
Contributions from the European Union	12,592	12,441	13,347
Total	745,825	810,315	857,200

Expenditure	2005	2006	2007*
Justice	27,025	28,505	30,248
Defence	43,591	43,771	46,242
Health	38,473	42,176	45,473
Social insurance for the sick and disabled	127,049	125,683	121,219
Social insurance for the elderly	46,120	45,019	43,900
Social insurance for families and children	55,467	60,066	61,267
Social insurance for the unemployed / Employment	70,721	69,496	62,244
Education and university research	43,695	46,495	43,481
Community planning and housing	8,737	8,742	6,219
Communications	31,833	31,133	34,960
Agriculture, forestry and fisheries	17,408	20,985	17,181
General grants to municipalities	57,325	60,246	73,059
Interest on central government debt	32,657	49,472	41,195
Contributions to the European Union	25,635	25,920	25,515
Total (incl. others)	731,771	791,942	768,604

* Forecasts.

INTERNATIONAL RESERVES
(US $ million at 31 December)

	2004	2005	2006
Gold	2,617	2,800	3,245
IMF special drawing rights	209	176	386
Reserve position in IMF	1,308	532	318
Foreign exchange	20,640	21,382	24,074
Total	24,774	24,890	28,023

Source: IMF, *International Financial Statistics*.

MONEY SUPPLY
(million kronor at 31 December)*

	2004	2005	2006
Currency outside banks	108,890	100,370	100,770
Demand deposits	839,340	973,110	1,103,460
Total money	948,230	1,073,480	1,204,230

* Figures are rounded to the nearest 10m. kronor.

Source: IMF, *International Financial Statistics*.

SWEDEN

Statistical Survey

COST OF LIVING
(Consumer Price Index; base: 1980 = 100)

	2005	2006	2007
Food and non-alcoholic beverages	238.1	239.9	244.8
Alcoholic beverages and tobacco	351.6	356.4	382.6
Clothing and footwear	159.6	164.7	168.7
Housing, water, electricity and fuels	327.3	338.8	352.4
Furniture and household goods	226.0	220.3	221.3
Health	748.8	752.3	772.7
Transport	362.2	368.0	372.1
Communication	201.3	188.1	181.9
Recreation and culture	191.1	188.5	187.8
Restaurants and hotels	397.5	407.2	420.2
Miscellaneous goods and services	305.0	317.4	327.1
All items	**280.4**	**284.2**	**290.5**

NATIONAL ACCOUNTS
(million kronor at current prices)

National Income and Product
(preliminary)

	2004	2005	2006
Compensation of employees	1,450,708	1,500,028	1,567,654
Net operating surplus / Net mixed income	457,289	490,457	547,432
Domestic factor incomes	1,907,997	1,990,485	2,115,086
Consumption of fixed capital	322,829	336,152	351,960
Gross domestic product (GDP) at factor cost	2,230,826	2,326,637	2,467,046
Taxes, less subsidies, on production and imports	394,138	408,581	432,607
GDP in market prices	2,624,964	2,735,218	2,899,653
Primary incomes received from abroad (net)	−5,753	−4,123	12,718
Gross national income	2,619,211	2,731,095	2,912,371
Less Consumption of fixed capital	322,829	336,152	351,960
Net national income	2,296,382	2,394,943	2,560,411
Other current transfers from abroad (net)	−33,075	−40,406	−40,071
Net national disposable income	2,263,307	2,354,537	2,520,340

Expenditure on the Gross Domestic Product

	2004	2005	2006
Final consumption expenditure	1,943,035	2,009,126	2,097,587
Households / Non-profit institutions serving households	1,239,816	1,284,965	1,338,695
General government	703,001	723,914	758,892
Gross capital formation	417,316	457,666	508,603
Gross fixed capital formation	417,601	460,250	508,831
Changes in inventories	−769	−2,948	−497
Acquisitions, less disposals, of valuables	484	364	269
Total domestic expenditure	2,360,351	2,466,792	2,606,190
Exports of goods and services	1,184,533	1,300,587	1,455,877
Less Imports of goods and services	979,828	1,096,832	1,223,655
GDP in market prices	2,565,056	2,670,547	2,838,412
GDP at constant 2000 prices	2,420,347	2,490,615	2,600,932

Gross Domestic Product by Economic Activity

	2004	2005	2006
Agriculture, forestry and fishing	39,519	27,969	35,595
Mining and quarrying	7,615	10,377	13,619
Manufacturing	443,093	465,847	505,503
Electricity, gas and water	67,859	70,186	76,811
Construction	101,767	111,110	124,750
Wholesale and retail trade	240,286	256,919	273,167
Hotels and restaurants	33,153	35,113	37,373
Transport, storage and communications	162,274	167,035	173,855
Financial intermediation	101,223	88,352	86,912
Real estate and business services*	430,219	457,874	482,306
Government services	478,910	492,627	515,221
Education, health and social services	58,611	61,819	66,800
Other community, social and personal services	48,557	49,947	53,731
Other services†	34,218	35,065	36,494
Gross value added in basic prices	2,247,304	2,330,240	2,482,137
Taxes on products	333,393	351,657	368,251
Less Subsidies on products	15,641	11,350	11,976
GDP in market prices	2,565,056	2,670,547	2,838,412

* Including imputed rents of owner-occupied dwellings.
† Domestic services and non-profit institutions serving households.

Note: Financial intermediation services indirectly measured data are distributed to production sectors.

BALANCE OF PAYMENTS
(US $ million)

	2004	2005	2006
Exports of goods f.o.b.	123,187	131,319	148,756
Imports of goods f.o.b.	−100,217	−111,971	−127,341
Trade balance	22,970	19,349	21,415
Exports of services	39,023	42,946	50,374
Imports of services	−33,138	−35,273	−39,774
Balance on goods and services	28,855	27,022	32,014
Other income received	31,332	38,490	45,310
Other income paid	−31,310	−35,708	−44,215
Balance on goods, services and income	28,876	29,804	33,109
Current transfers received	4,067	5,027	4,894
Current transfers paid	−8,817	−9,600	−9,590
Current balance	24,127	25,230	28,413
Capital account (net)	34	308	−2,585
Direct investment abroad	−21,318	−26,968	−23,754
Direct investment from abroad	10,957	10,252	27,299
Portfolio investment assets	−24,768	−12,913	−36,489
Portfolio investment liabilities	1,586	17,955	14,175
Financial derivatives assets	27,730	29,417	54,071
Financial derivatives liabilities	−27,969	−30,347	−53,935
Other investment assets	−19,845	−13,363	−49,730
Other investment liabilities	27,617	1,717	35,481
Net errors and omissions	750	−1,038	8,343
Overall balance	−1,100	250	1,289

Source: IMF, *International Financial Statistics*.

OFFICIAL ASSISTANCE TO DEVELOPING COUNTRIES
(million kronor)

	2002	2003	2004
Bilateral assistance	12,581	14,374	15,249
Multilateral assistance	7,212	5,014	4,747
Total	19,793	19,388	19,996

External Trade

PRINCIPAL COMMODITIES
(distribution by SITC, million kronor)

Imports c.i.f.	2004	2005	2006
Food and live animals	46,673	52,766	59,738
Fresh fruit and vegetables	12,419	13,511	14,984
Crude materials (inedible) except fuels	26,013	27,076	31,605
Mineral fuels, lubricants, etc.	71,880	98,335	116,058
Petroleum, petroleum products, etc.	59,947	85,692	98,169
Chemicals and related products	79,295	88,589	97,857
Organic chemicals	14,071	15,174	17,146
Medical and pharmaceutical preparations	18,356	20,665	23,721
Unprocessed plastics	12,688	15,116	17,373
Basic manufactures	112,013	126,134	143,161
Iron and steel	33,457	38,409	39,386
Machinery and transport equipment	298,752	328,631	364,508
Power-generating machinery and equipment	21,325	24,839	25,298
General industrial machinery, equipment and parts	37,749	41,434	48,477
Office machines and automatic data-processing equipment	30,672	35,096	39,415
Telecommunications and sound equipment	44,692	48,454	52,116
Other electrical machinery, apparatus, etc.	50,675	51,428	58,318
Road vehicles and parts*	80,800	90,561	100,565
Miscellaneous manufactured articles	94,538	101,400	111,433
Clothing and accessories (excl. footwear)	21,238	22,272	24,113
Other miscellaneous manufactured articles	30,084	33,595	36,169
Total (incl. others)	739,203	832,640	935,675

Exports f.o.b.	2004	2005	2006
Crude materials (inedible) except fuels	48,479	54,538	63,698
Wood, lumber and cork	22,009	24,078	27,137
Pulp and waste paper	14,870	14,356	15,084
Mineral fuels, lubricants, etc.	37,491	52,437	65,218
Petroleum, petroleum products, etc.	31,956	45,074	58,987
Chemicals and related products	103,580	109,049	124,759
Medical and pharmaceutical preparations	52,961	54,001	64,393
Basic manufactures	185,623	198,527	218,300
Paper, paperboard and manufactures	66,686	69,164	72,837
Iron and steel	51,644	57,825	61,777

Exports f.o.b.—continued	2004	2005	2006
Manufactures of metals	26,340	27,384	31,085
Machinery and transport equipment	415,671	435,574	477,060
Power-generating machinery and equipment	34,579	34,235	38,900
Machinery specialized for particular industries	37,496	41,834	46,711
General industrial machinery, equipment and parts	58,699	63,284	71,992
Telecommunications and sound equipment	84,514	92,600	91,255
Other electrical machinery, apparatus, etc.	43,035	42,679	49,131
Road vehicles and parts*	128,950	133,577	146,346
Miscellaneous manufactured articles	80,919	83,465	94,232
Total (incl. others)	904,532	970,815	1,085,287

* Data on parts exclude tyres, engines and electrical parts.

PRINCIPAL TRADING PARTNERS
(million kronor)

Imports c.i.f.	2004	2005	2006
Austria	8,221	8,984	9,884
Belgium	29,776	33,360	39,204
China, People's Repub.	17,565	22,495	28,991
Denmark	68,020	79,027	90,375
Finland	47,346	50,009	55,338
France	41,195	42,623	44,340
Germany	138,294	151,262	168,752
Hong Kong	6,914	7,907	8,745
Ireland	10,352	11,490	12,316
Italy	25,352	27,436	31,734
Japan	15,527	17,465	18,143
Netherlands	49,917	54,932	59,348
Norway	56,174	68,084	79,937
Poland	18,612	20,341	25,497
Russia	16,103	24,730	32,135
Spain	11,796	13,510	14,428
Switzerland	8,599	8,527	9,291
United Kingdom	55,056	57,722	58,626
USA	25,562	28,182	31,493
Total (incl. others)	739,203	832,640	935,675

Exports f.o.b.	2004	2005	2006
Australia	9,708	11,183	14,388
Austria	9,507	9,108	10,434
Belgium	40,906	41,652	49,892
Canada	10,242	10,535	11,404
China, People's Repub.	19,024	18,863	20,776
Denmark	60,320	66,838	78,079
Finland	51,628	58,870	68,491
France	43,283	46,841	53,951
Germany	92,055	100,703	107,966
Italy	33,447	32,744	36,772
Japan	16,682	14,847	16,859
Netherlands	43,176	44,101	52,430
Norway	78,137	83,655	99,128
Poland	15,939	17,416	22,646
Russia	13,623	15,987	17,849
Spain	26,517	27,777	33,577
Switzerland	9,821	9,216	9,680
United Kingdom	70,581	75,607	78,663
USA	96,594	102,732	100,755
Total (incl. others)	904,532	970,815	1,085,287

SWEDEN   *Statistical Survey*

Transport

RAILWAYS
(traffic)

	2003	2004	2005
Passengers (million)	145	147	150
Passenger-km (million)	8,834	8,658	8,936
Freight (million metric tons)	58	60	63
Freight ton-km (million)	20,170	20,856	21,675

Freight ton-km (million): 20,856 in 2004.

ROAD TRAFFIC
('000 motor vehicles in use at 31 December)

	2004	2005	2006
Passenger cars	4,113	4,154	4,202
Buses and coaches	13	13	14
Lorries and vans	440	461	480
Motorcycles	235	250	269

SHIPPING

Merchant Fleet
(registered at 31 December)

	2004	2005	2006
Number of vessels	579	567	564
Total displacement ('000 grt)	3,666.9	3,765.7	3,876.5

Source: Lloyd's Register-Fairplay, *World Fleet Statistics*.

International Sea-borne Freight Traffic

	2004	2005	2006
Vessels entered ('000 grt)	106,690	115,715	119,917
Vessels cleared ('000 grt)	102,311	110,059	115,788
Goods loaded ('000 metric tons)	65,547	69,275	74,494
Goods unloaded ('000 metric tons)	79,088	82,641	83,267

CIVIL AVIATION
(traffic on scheduled services)*

	2001	2002	2003
Kilometres flown (million)	167	130	129
Passengers carried ('000)	13,123	12,421	11,873
Passenger-kilometres (million)	11,277	11,663	11,638
Total ton-kilometres (million)	1,384	1,427	1,410

*Including an apportionment (3/7) of the international services of Scandinavian Airlines System (SAS), operated jointly with Denmark and Norway.

Source: UN, *Statistical Yearbook*.

Tourism*

VISITORS BY ORIGIN
('000 nights in all types of tourist accommodation)†

	2003	2004	2005
Denmark	686.5	680.4	694.5
Finland	323.0	308.8	349.6
France	162.0	175.1	188.4
Germany	844.7	844.6	935.3
Italy	156.3	215.4	221.0
Japan	109.6	118.2	114.9
Netherlands	202.2	237.6	223.4
Norway	1,076.5	968.6	1,003.0
Russia	113.1	132.0	132.5
United Kingdom	533.7	565.8	610.3
USA	364.8	383.2	420.9
Total (incl. others)	6,038.3	6,233.5	6,596.0

*Since the introduction of the Scandinavian Passport Control Area, there are no figures available for total arrivals in Sweden.
†Excluding nights at campsites (million, all nationalities, incl. Swedish): 17.1 in 2003; 15.6 in 2004; 16.4 in 2005.

Tourism receipts (US $ million, incl. passenger transport): 6,548 in 2003; 7,649 in 2004; 8,584 in 2005 (Source: World Tourism Organization).

Communications Media

	2004	2005	2006
Telephones ('000 main lines in use)	5,484.8	5,458.0	5,398.8
Mobile cellular telephones ('000 subscribers)	8,785	9,104	9,607
Personal computers ('000 in use)	6,861	n.a.	n.a.
Internet users ('000)	6,800.0	6,890.0	6,981.2
Broadband subscribers ('000)	1,410.0	1,918.0	2,346.3
Daily newspapers:			
titles	165	168	166
average net circulation ('000 copies)	4,000	3,998	3,928
Weekly newspapers and periodicals:			
titles	417	423	443
average net circulation ('000 copies)	22,668	22,800	21,950
Book production (titles)	17,683	21,413	21,765

Television receivers ('000 in use, 2001): 8,600.

Radio receivers ('000 in use, 1997): 8,250.

Facsimile machines (estimated '000 in use, 1996): 450.

Sources: mainly International Telecommunication Union, UN, *Statistical Yearbook*, and UNESCO, *Statistical Yearbook*.

Education

(2004/05, unless otherwise indicated)

	Institutions	Teachers[1]	Students
Primary: grades 1–6	} 4,963	} 108,233	650,342
Secondary: grades 7–9			373,292
Integrated upper secondary schools	641[2]	37,640	347,713[3]
Higher education	64	20,000[4]	397,679[5]
People's colleges	147[2]	n.a.	108,742[6]
Municipal adult education	400[7]	6,593	226,851[5]

[1] Full-time and part-time teachers and teachers on leave.
[2] 1996/97.
[3] At 15 October 2004.
[4] 1994/95.
[5] 2003/04.
[6] Autumn term.
[7] 1993/94.

Directory

The Constitution

The Swedish Constitution is based on four fundamental laws and the Riksdag Act. The four fundamental laws are the Instrument of Government (originally dating from 6 June 1809), the Act of Succession (1810), the Freedom of the Press Act (1949) and the Fundamental Law on Freedom of Expression (1992). Following partial reforms in 1968 and 1969, a new Instrument of Government and a new Riksdag Act were adopted in 1973 and 1974, and the revised Constitution, summarized below, came into force on 1 January 1975. The Riksdag Act, which contains detailed rules as to the functioning of the Riksdag (parliament), was formerly a fundamental law, but has occupied an intermediate position between that of a fundamental law and that of an ordinary law since 1974.

GOVERNMENT

The Cabinet governs Sweden and is responsible to the Riksdag (parliament). The Constitution of 1975 formalized the position of the Monarch relative to the Cabinet and the Riksdag, and laid down rules on the selection and resignation of the Cabinet. In 1978 the Riksdag amended the constitutional law of succession to allow the first-born royal child, whether male or female, to be heir to the throne, with effect from 1980.

As Head of State, the Monarch has representative and ceremonial duties only. The Monarch does not participate in the government of the country, which is conducted rather by the Cabinet at meetings not attended by the Monarch. Decisions of government do not require the Monarch's signature, and it is the Speaker of the Riksdag, and not the Monarch, who leads the procedure resulting in the formation of a new Government. Following consultations within the Riksdag, the Speaker nominates a candidate for Prime Minister. If not more than one-half of the total number of members of the Riksdag vote against the proposed candidate, he or she is approved. Failing this approval, the procedure has to be repeated. After four unsuccessful attempts to secure Riksdag approval of a candidate for the premiership, a new election to the Riksdag must be held within three months. A candidate for the premiership approved by the Riksdag nominates the other members of the Government.

The Prime Minister can be dismissed at his or her own request, by the Speaker of the Riksdag, or in the event of a vote of 'no confidence' in the Riksdag. Other ministers can be dismissed at their own request, by the Prime Minister or by a vote of no confidence. If the Prime Minister should resign or die, all of the ministers in the Cabinet must resign. A Cabinet that is due to resign shall, however, remain in power until a new Prime Minister has been appointed.

A demand for a vote of 'no confidence' will be considered only if it is supported by 10% of the members of the Riksdag. A vote of 'no confidence' requires the support of more than one-half of the Riksdag members. If the Riksdag decides upon a vote of no confidence, the Cabinet can avoid resigning if it calls for an extra general election within one week. The Riksdag may continue its business, or be summoned to convene, even after a decision has been made to hold new elections. A Riksdag session may, however, be terminated by a special decision of the Cabinet. Existing terms of office do not expire until the new terms of office have begun.

LEGISLATURE

The Riksdag is the prime representative of the Swedish people. It enacts laws, decides the amount and use of taxation and examines the Government's actions. The Riksdag contains 349 members, elected for four years.

In accordance with tradition, the work of the Swedish Riksdag is, to a great extent, carried on in a non-partisan atmosphere. This is largely the result of the thorough attention given to all questions by numerous standing committees elected by the Riksdag on a basis of proportional representation. Besides the Utrikesnämnden (Advisory Council on Foreign Affairs) and Special Committees, every Riksdag appoints from within the assembly a Constitution Committee, a Finance Committee, a Taxation Committee and at least 12 other committees.

The Constitution Committee examines the minutes of the Cabinet and deals with or initiates proposals concerning alterations of the fundamental laws and of laws regulating local government.

ELECTORAL SYSTEM

In order that local and national government terms of office should coincide, the Constitution calls for local and general elections to be held on the same day. In both cases the term of office for the elected candidate is four years. Proportional representation was introduced in Sweden between the years 1906 and 1909, universal and equal suffrage by 1921. Under the provisions of legislation passed in 1976, all aliens resident in the country for three years are permitted to vote in local elections. The minimum voting age is 18 years. In allocating the 349 seats in the Riksdag, the seats are divided into two groups. The first group of 310 'constituency seats' is distributed among the constituencies according to the number of eligible voters, and within each constituency among the parties. The remaining 39 seats are distributed as 'adjustment seats'. First, it is calculated how many seats each party would have obtained if the whole country had been treated as a single constituency and if the distribution of seats had taken place according to a modified Sainte-Laguë method. From this figure is subtracted the number of 'constituency seats' received, the result being the number of 'compensatory seats' to be allocated to each party. These seats are filled by candidates nominated in the constituencies. There is a check to the emergence of small parties in that only parties that have received at least 4% of the total votes cast are entitled to a seat. However, any party that receives 12% or more of the votes in any constituency will be allowed to compete for a permanent seat in that constituency.

The Government

HEAD OF STATE

Monarch: HM King CARL XVI GUSTAF (succeeded to the throne 15 September 1973).

THE CABINET
(April 2008)

A coalition of the Moderata Samlingspartiet (MS), the Centerpartiet (CP), the Folkpartiet liberalerna (FP) and the Kristdemokraterna (Kd).

Prime Minister: FREDRIK REINFELDT (MS).

Deputy Prime Minister and Minister for Enterprise and Energy: MAUD OLOFSSON (CP).

Minister for Finance: ANDERS BORG (MS).

Minister for the Environment: ANDREAS CARLGREN (CP).

Minister for Justice: BEATRICE ASK (MS).

Minister for Foreign Affairs: CARL BILDT (MS).

Minister for EU Affairs: CECILIA MALMSTRÖM (FP).

Minister for Social Security: CRISTINA HUSMARK PEHRSSON (MS).

Minister for Agriculture: ESKIL ERLANDSSON (CP).

Minister for International Development Co-operation: GUNILLA CARLSSON (MS).

Minister for Health and Social Affairs: GÖRAN HÄGGLUND (KD).

Minister for Education: JAN BJÖRKLUND (FP).

Minister for Higher Education and Research: LARS LEIJONBORG (FP).

Minister for Culture: LENA ADELSOHN LILJEROTH (MS).

Minister for Elderly Care and Public Health: MARIA LARSSON (KD).

Minister for Local Government and Financial Markets: MATS ODELL (KD).

Minister for Defence: STEN TOLGFORS (MS).

Minister for Integration and Gender Equality: NYAMKO SABUNI (FP).

Minister for Foreign Trade: EWA BJÖRLING (MS).

Minister for Employment: SVEN OTTO LITTORIN (MS).

Minister for Migration and Asylum Policy: TOBIAS BILLSTRÖM (MS).

Minister for Communications: ÅSA TORSTENSSON (CP).

MINISTRIES

Prime Minister's Office: Rosenbad 4, 103 33 Stockholm; tel. (8) 405-10-00; fax (8) 723-11-71; e-mail registrator@primeminister.ministry.se.

Ministry of Agriculture: Fredsgt. 8, 103 33 Stockholm; tel. (8) 405-10-00; fax (8) 20-64-96; e-mail registrator@agriculture.ministry.se; internet jordbruk.regeringen.se.

Ministry of Culture: Drottninggt. 16, 103 33 Stockholm; tel. (8) 405-10-00; fax (8) 21-68-13; e-mail registrator@culture.ministry.se; internet kultur.regeringen.se.

Ministry of Defence: Jakobsgt. 9, 103 33 Stockholm; tel. (8) 405-10-00; fax (8) 723-11-89; e-mail registrator@defence.ministry.se; internet forsvar.regeringen.se.

SWEDEN

Ministry of Education and Research: Drottninggt. 16, 103 33 Stockholm; tel. (8) 405-10-00; fax (8) 723-11-92; e-mail registrator@educcult.ministry.se; internet utbildning.regeringen.se.

Ministry of Employment: Jakobsgt. 26, 103 33 Stockholm; tel. (8) 405-10-00; fax (8) 411-36-16.

Ministry of Enterprise, Energy and Communications: Jakobsgt. 26, 103 33 Stockholm; tel. (8) 405-10-00; fax (8) 411-36-16; e-mail registrator@industry.ministry.se; internet naring.regeringen.se.

Ministry of the Environment: Tegelbacken 2, 103 33 Stockholm; tel. (8) 405-10-00; fax (8) 24-16-29; e-mail registrator@environment.ministry.se; internet miljo.regeringen.se.

Ministry of Finance: Drottninggt. 21, 103 33 Stockholm; tel. (8) 405-10-00; fax (8) 21-73-86; e-mail registrator@finance.ministry.se; internet finans.regeringen.se.

Ministry for Foreign Affairs: Gustav Adolfs torg 1, 103 39 Stockholm; tel. (8) 405-10-00; fax (8) 723-11-76; e-mail registrator@foreign.ministry.se; internet utrikes.regeringen.se.

Ministry of Health and Social Affairs: Fredsgt. 8, 103 33 Stockholm; tel. (8) 405-10-00; fax (8) 723-11-91; e-mail registrator@social.ministry.se; internet social.regeringen.se.

Ministry of Integration and Gender Equality: Fredsgt. 8, 103 33 Stockholm; tel. (8) 405-10-00; fax (8) 543-560-39; e-mail registrator@integration.ministry.se.

Ministry of Justice: Rosenbad 4, 103 33 Stockholm; tel. (8) 405-10-00; fax (8) 20-27-34; e-mail registrator@justice.ministry.se; internet justitie.regeringen.se.

Office of Administrative Affairs: Fredsgt. 8, 103 33 Stockholm; tel. (8) 405-10-00; fax (8) 24-46-31.

Legislature

SVERIGES RIKSDAG

100 12 Stockholm; tel. (8) 786-40-00; e-mail riksdagsinformation@riksdagen.se; internet www.riksdagen.se.

Speaker: PER WESTERBERG (MS).

General Election, 17 September 2006

Party	Votes	% of votes	Seats
Sveriges Socialdemokratiska Arbetareparti (SAP)	1,942,625	34.99	130
Moderata Samlingspartiet (MS)*	1,456,014	26.23	97
Centerpartiet (CP)*	437,389	7.88	29
Folkpartiet liberalerna (FP)*	418,395	7.54	28
Kristdemokraterna (Kd)*	365,889	6.59	24
Vänsterpartiet (VP)	324,722	5.85	22
Miljöpartiet de Gröna (MP)	291,121	5.24	19
Others	315,014	5.67	—
Total	**5,551,278**	**100.00**	**349**

*Contested the elections as the Alliance for Sweden.

Election Commission

Valmyndigheten (Election Authority): Solna Strandväg 78, POB 4210, 171 04 Solna; tel. (8) 635-69-00; fax (8) 635-69-20; e-mail valet@val.se; internet www.val.se; independent; Dir GUNNAR SKARELL.

Political Organizations

Centerpartiet (CP) (Centre Party): Stora Nygt. 4, POB 2200, 103 15 Stockholm; tel. (8) 617-38-00; fax (8) 617-38-10; e-mail info@centerpartiet.se; internet www.centerpartiet.se; f. 1910 as an agrarian party; aims at social, environmental and progressive development and decentralization; Leader MAUD OLOFSSON; 69,000 mems.

Feministiskt initiativ (F!) (Feminist Initiative): POB 498, 101 29 Stockholm; tel. (0) 706-100-190; e-mail info@feministisktinitiativ.se; internet www.feministisktinitiativ.se; f. 2005; Principal Speakers STINA SUNDBERG, GERD GUDRUN MARIA SCHYMAN.

Folkpartiet liberalerna (FP) (Liberal Party): POB 2253, Stora Nygt. 2A, 103 16 Stockholm; tel. (8) 410-242-00; fax (8) 509-116-60; e-mail info@liberal.se; internet www.folkpartiet.se; f. 1902; advocates market-orientated economy and social welfare system; Chair. JAN BJÖRKLUND.

Junilistan (June List): Vasagt. 40, 111 20 Stockholm; tel. and fax (8) 23-01-11; e-mail info@junilistan.se; internet www.junilistan.se; f. 2004 to contest elections to the European Parliament; opposes further powers for EU; Leader NILS LUNDGREN.

Kristdemokraterna (Kd) (Christian Democratic Party): POB 2373, Munkbron 1, 103 18 Stockholm; tel. (8) 723-25-00; fax (8) 723-25-10; e-mail info@kristdemokraterna.se; internet www.kristdemokraterna.se; f. 1964 as Kristdemokratiska Samhällspartiet (KdS); promotes emphasis on Christian values in political life; Chair. GÖRAN HÄGGLUND; 24,000 mems.

Miljöpartiet de Gröna (MP) (Green Party): International Secretary, Swedish Parliament, 100 12 Stockholm; tel. (8) 786-57-44; fax (8) 786-53-75; internet www.mp.se; f. 1981; Principal Speakers MARIA WETTERSTRAND, PETER ERIKSSON; c. 9,000 mems.

Moderata Samlingspartiet (MS) (Moderate Party): POB 2080, Stora Nygt. 30, 103 12 Stockholm; tel. (8) 676-80-00; fax (8) 21-61-23; e-mail info@moderat.se; internet www.moderat.se; f. 1904; advocates liberal-conservative market-orientated economy; Chair. FREDRIK REINFELDT; 100,000 mems.

Piratpartiet (Pirate Party): POB 307, 101 26 Stockholm; tel. (8) 720-04-00; e-mail info@piratpartiet.se; internet www.piratpartiet.se; f. 2006; advocates the citizen's right to complete and exclusive control of information pertaining to his or her private life and the abolition of copyright on all material for non-commercial use; Chair. RICKARD FALKVINGE.

Sverigedemokraterna (SD) (Sweden Democrats): POB 200 85, 104 60 Stockholm; tel. (8) 50-00-00-50; fax (8) 643-92-60; e-mail info@sverigedemokraterna.se; internet www.sverigedemokraterna.se; f. 1988; nationalist, anti-immigration; currently unrepresented in the Riksdag, but has won representation at local level; Leader JIMMIE ÅKESSON.

Sveriges Socialdemokratiska Arbetareparti (SAP) (Swedish Social Democratic Party): Sveavägen 68, 105 60 Stockholm; tel. (8) 700-26-00; fax (8) 20-42-57; e-mail info@sap.se; internet www.socialdemokraterna.se; f. 1889; egalitarian; Chair. MONA SAHLIN; Sec.-Gen. MARITA ULVSKOG; 143,000 mems.

Vänsterpartiet (VP) (Left Party): Kungsgt. 84, POB 12660, 112 93 Stockholm; tel. (8) 654-08-20; fax (8) 653-23-85; e-mail partikansliet@vansterpartiet.se; internet www.vansterpartiet.se; f. 1917 as Left Social Democratic Party of Sweden; affiliated to the Communists International 1919; renamed the Communist Party in 1921; renamed Left Party—Communists in 1967; renamed Left Party in 1990; policies based on the principles of Marxism, feminism and other theories; Chair. LARS OHLY.

Diplomatic Representation

EMBASSIES IN SWEDEN

Albania: Capellavägen 7, 181 32 Lidingö; tel. (8) 731-09-20; fax (8) 767-65-57; Ambassador RUHI HADO (designate).

Algeria: Danderydsgt. 3–5, POB 26027, 100 41 Stockholm; tel. (8) 679-91-30; fax (8) 611-49-57; e-mail embassy.algeria@telia.com; internet www.embalgeria.se; Ambassador MERZAK BEDJAOUI.

Angola: Skeppsbron 8, POB 3199, 103 64 Stockholm; tel. (8) 24-28-90; fax (8) 34-31-27; e-mail info@angolaemb.se; internet www.angolaemb.se; Ambassador DOMINGOS CULOLO.

Argentina: POB 14039, 104 40 Stockholm; Narvavägen 32, 3rd Floor, Apartment 3, 115 22 Stockholm; tel. (8) 663-19-65; fax (8) 661-00-09; e-mail cancilleria@argemb.se; Ambassador HERNÁN MASSINI EZCURRA.

Australia: Sergels Torg 12, POB 7003, 103 86 Stockholm; tel. (8) 613-29-00; fax (8) 613-29-82; e-mail reception@austemb.se; internet www.sweden.embassy.gov.au; Ambassador HOWARD CRAIG BROWN.

Austria: Kommendörsgt. 35, 5th Floor, 114 58 Stockholm; tel. (8) 665-17-70; fax (8) 662-69-28; e-mail stockholm-ob@bmeia.gv.at; internet www.aussenministerium.at/stockholm; Ambassador STEPHAN TOTH.

Azerbaijan: Stockholm; e-mail azerembassy@gmail.com; Ambassador RAFAEL IBRAHIMOV.

Bangladesh: Anderstorpsvägen 12, 1st Floor, 171 54 Solna; tel. (8) 730-58-50; fax (8) 730-58-70; e-mail banijya@bangladeshembassy.se; Ambassador MUHAMMAD AZIZUL HAQUE.

Belarus: Herserudsvägen 5, 4th Floor, 181 34 Lidingö; tel. (8) 731-57-45; fax (8) 767-07-46; e-mail sweden@belembassy.org; internet www.belembassy.org/sweden; Ambassador ANDREI M. GRINKEVICH.

Belgium: POB 1040, 101 38 Stockholm; Kungsbroplan 2, 2nd Floor, 112 27 Stockholm; tel. (8) 534-802-00; fax (8) 534-802-07; e-mail stockholm@diplobel.org; internet www.diplomatie.be/stockholm; Ambassador MARC BAPTIST.

SWEDEN — Directory

Bolivia: Södra Kungsvägen 60, 181 32 Lidingö; tel. (8) 731-58-30; fax (8) 767-63-11; e-mail embolivia-estocolmo@telia.com; Chargé d'affaires a.i. María Elena García de Baccino.

Bosnia and Herzegovina: Birger Jarlsgt. 55, POB 7102, 103 87 Stockholm; tel. (8) 440-05-40; fax (8) 24-98-30; e-mail amb.bih.sto@telia.com; Ambassador Jakov Skočibušić.

Botswana: Tyrgt. 11, POB 26024, 100 41 Stockholm; tel. (8) 545-258-00; fax (8) 723-00-87; Ambassador Bernadette Sebage Rathedi.

Brazil: Odengt. 3, 114 24 Stockholm; tel. (8) 545-163-00; fax (8) 545-163-14; e-mail stockholm@brazilianembassy.se; internet www.brazilianembassy.se; Ambassador Antonino Lisboa Mena Gonçalves.

Bulgaria: Karlavägen 29, 114 31 Stockholm; tel. (8) 723-09-38; fax (8) 21-45-03; e-mail bg.embassy@telia.com; internet www.bulgarien.se; Ambassador Goran Yonov.

Canada: Tegelbacken 4, 7th Floor, POB 16129, 103 23 Stockholm; tel. (8) 453-30-00; fax (8) 453-30-16; e-mail stkhm@international.gc.ca; internet www.canadaemb.se; Ambassador Alexandra Volkoff.

Chile: Sturegt. 8, 3rd Floor, 114 35 Stockholm; tel. (8) 679-82-80; fax (8) 679-85-40; e-mail echilese@embassyofchile.se; internet www.embassyofchile.se; Ambassador Ovid Harasich.

China, People's Republic: Lidovägen 8, 115 25 Stockholm; tel. (8) 579-364-37; fax (8) 579-364-54; e-mail protocol@chinaembassy.se; internet www.chinaembassy.se; Ambassador Chen Mingming.

Colombia: Östermalmsgt. 46, 3rd Floor, POB 5627, 114 86 Stockholm; tel. (8) 21-43-20; fax (8) 21-84-90; e-mail embcol@telia.com; Ambassador Fernando Alzate Donoso.

Congo, Democratic Republic: Stockholmsvägen 33, 4th Floor, POB 1171, 181 23 Lidingö; tel. (8) 765-83-80; fax (8) 765-85-91; e-mail rdcongo6@hotmail.com; Chargé d'affaires a.i. Henri Mbayahe Ndungo.

Croatia: Birger Jarlsgt. 13, 1st Floor, 111 45 Stockholm; tel. (8) 678-42-20; fax (8) 678-83-20; e-mail croemb.stockholm@mvpei.hr; Ambassador Dr Svjetlan Berković.

Cuba: Sturevägen 9, 182 73 Stocksund; tel. (8) 545-83-277; fax (8) 545-83-270; e-mail primero.enero59@swipnet.se; internet home.swipnet.se/embacubasuecia; Ambassador Ernesto Mélendez Bachs.

Cyprus: Birger Jarlsgt. 37, 4th Floor, POB 7649, 103 94 Stockholm; tel. (8) 24-50-08; fax (8) 24-45-18; e-mail info@cyprusemb.se; internet www.cyprusemb.se; Ambassador Pavlos Anastasiades.

Czech Republic: Villagt. 21, POB 26156, 100 41 Stockholm; tel. (8) 440-42-10; fax (8) 440-42-11; e-mail stockholm@embassy.mzv.cz; internet www.mzv.cz/stockholm; Ambassador Jan Kára.

Denmark: Jakobs Torg 1, POB 16119, 103 23 Stockholm; tel. (8) 406-75-00; fax (8) 791-72-20; e-mail stoamb@um.dk; internet www.ambstockholm.um.dk; Ambassador Tom Risdahl Jensen.

Dominican Republic: Sibyllegt. 13, 4th Floor, POB 5584, 114 85 Stockholm; tel. (8) 667-46-11; fax (8) 667-51-05; e-mail stockholm@domemb.se; Ambassador Marina Isabel Cacres de Estvez.

Ecuador: Engelbrektsgt. 13, 114 32 Stockholm; tel. (8) 679-60-43; fax (8) 611-55-93; e-mail suecia@embajada-ecuador.se; internet www.embajada-ecuador.se; Ambassador Roberto Betancourt Ruales.

Egypt: Strandvägen 35, POB 14230, 104 40 Stockholm; tel. (8) 459-98-60; fax (8) 661-26-64; e-mail egypt.embassy@chello.se; Ambassador Samah Muhammad Sotouhi.

El Salvador: Herserudsvägen 5A, 5th Floor, 181 34 Lidingö; tel. (8) 765-86-21; fax (8) 731-72-42; e-mail embassy@elsalvador.se; internet www.elsalvador.se; Ambassador Martin Rivera Gómez.

Eritrea: Stjärnvägen 2B, 4th Floor, POB 1164, 181 23 Lidingö; tel. (8) 441-71-70; fax (8) 446-73-40; e-mail info@eritrean-embassy.se; internet www.eritrean-embassy.se; Chargé d'affaires a.i. Yonas Manna Bairu.

Estonia: Tyrgt. 3, 114 27 Stockholm; POB 26076, 100 41 Stockholm; tel. (8) 545-122-80; fax (8) 545-122-99; e-mail info@estemb.se; internet www.estemb.se; Ambassador Alar Streimann.

Ethiopia: Löjtnantsgt. 17, POB 10148, 100 55 Stockholm; tel. (8) 665-60-30; fax (8) 660-81-77; e-mail ethio.all@telia.com; internet www.ethemb.se; Ambassador Dina Mufti.

Finland: Gärdesgt. 11, POB 24285, 104 51 Stockholm; tel. (8) 676-67-00; fax (8) 20-74-97; e-mail info@finland.se; internet www.finland.se; Ambassador Alec Aalto.

France: Kommendörsgt. 13, POB 5135, 102 43 Stockholm; tel. (8) 459-53-00; fax (8) 459-53-41; e-mail presse@ambafrance-se.org; internet www.ambafrance-se.org; Ambassador Joël De Zorzi.

Georgia: Humlegårdsgt. 19, 1st Floor, 114 46 Stockholm; tel. (8) 678-02-60; fax 678-02-64; e-mail geoemb.sweden@telia.com; internet www.sweden.mfa.gov.ge; Ambassador Amiran Kavadze.

Germany: Artillerigt. 64, POB 27832, 115 93 Stockholm; tel. (8) 670-15-00; fax (8) 670-15-72; e-mail zreg@stoc.diplo.de; internet www.stockholm.diplo.de; Ambassador Wolfgang Trautwein.

Greece: Kommendörsgt. 16, POB 55565, 102 04 Stockholm; tel. (8) 545-660-10; fax (8) 660-54-70; e-mail grembstockholm@greekembassy.se; internet www.greekembassy.se; Ambassador Evangelos Carokis.

Guatemala: Munkbron 3, 111 28 Stockholm; tel. (8) 660-52-29; fax (8) 660-42-29; e-mail embassy@guatemala.se; internet www.guatemala.se; Ambassador Susana Barrios Beltranena.

Holy See: Svalnäsvägen 10, 182 63 Djursholm; tel. (8) 446-51-10; fax (8) 622-51-10; e-mail nunciature@telia.com; Charge d'affaires a.i. Rev. Dagoberto Campos Salas.

Honduras: Stjärnvägen 2, 7th Floor, 181 34 Lidingö; tel. (8) 731-50-84; fax (8) 636-99-83; e-mail hondurasembassy@telia.com; internet www.hondurasembassy.se; Chargé d'affaires a.i. Iliana Waleska Pastor Melghem.

Hungary: Dag Hammarskjölds Väg 10, POB 24125, 104 51 Stockholm; tel. (8) 661-67-62; fax (8) 660-29-59; e-mail embassy.stockholm@kum.hu; internet www.mfa.gov.hu/kulkepviselet/se; Ambassador Gábor Iklódy.

Iceland: Kommendörsgt. 35, 114 58 Stockholm; tel. (8) 442-83-00; fax (8) 660-74-23; e-mail icemb.stock@utn.strj.is; internet www.iceland.org/se; Ambassador Guðmundur Árni Stefánsson.

India: Adolf Fredriks Kyrkogt. 12, POB 1340, 111 83 Stockholm; tel. (8) 10-70-08; fax (8) 24-85-05; e-mail information@indianembassy.se; internet www.indianembassy.se; Ambassador Deepa Gopalan Wadhwa.

Indonesia: Sysslomansgt. 18/I, POB 12520, 102 29 Stockholm; tel. (8) 545-55-880; fax (8) 650-87-50; e-mail kbri@indonesiskaambassaden.se; internet www.indonesiskaambassaden.se; Ambassador Linggawaty Hakim.

Iran: Västra Yttringe Gård, Elfviksvägen, POB 6031, 181 06 Lidingö; tel. (8) 636-36-77; fax (8) 636-36-13; internet www.iran.se; Ambassador Hassan Ghashghavi.

Iraq: Baldersgt. 6A, POB 26031, 100 41 Stockholm; tel. (8) 411-44-43; fax (8) 796-53-66; Ambassador Ahmad A. Bamarni.

Ireland: Östermalmsgt. 97, POB 10326, 100 55 Stockholm; tel. (8) 661-80-05; fax (8) 660-13-53; e-mail stockholmembassy@dfa.ie; Ambassador Barrie Robinson.

Israel: Storgt. 31, POB 14006, 104 40 Stockholm; tel. (8) 528-065-00; fax (8) 528-065-55; e-mail info@stockholm.mfa.gov.il; internet stockholm.mfa.gov.il; Ambassador Eviatar Manor.

Italy: Oakhill, Djurgården, 115 21 Stockholm; tel. (8) 545-671-00; fax (8) 660-05-05; e-mail info.stockholm@esteri.se; internet www.ambstoccolma.esteri.it; Ambassador Anna Della Croce Brigante Colonna.

Japan: Gärdesgt. 10, 115 27 Stockholm; tel. (8) 579-353-00; fax (8) 661-88-20; e-mail protocol@japansamb.se; internet www.se.emb-japan.go.jp; Ambassador Akira Nakajima.

Kenya: Birger Jarlsgt. 37, 2nd Floor, POB 7694, 103 95 Stockholm; tel. (8) 21-83-04; fax (8) 20-92-61; e-mail kenya.embassy@telia.com; Ambassador Purity W. Muhindi.

Korea, Democratic People's Republic: Norra Kungsvägen 39, 181 31 Lidingö; tel. (8) 767-38-36; fax (8) 767-38-35; e-mail koscom@telia.com; Ambassador Jon In Chan.

Korea, Republic: Laboratoriegt. 10, POB 27237, 102 53 Stockholm; tel. (8) 545-894-00; fax (8) 660-28-18; e-mail koremb.sweden@mofat.go.kr; internet www.mofat.go.kr/sweden; Ambassador Lee Joon-Hee.

Kuwait: Banérgt. 37, POB 10030, 100 55 Stockholm; tel. (8) 450-99-80; fax (8) 450-99-55; e-mail kuwaitambassad@telia.com; Ambassador Sami Muhammad al-Sulaiman.

Laos: Badstrandsvägen 11, POB 34050, 112 65 Stockholm; tel. (8) 618-20-10; fax (8) 618-20-01; e-mail info@laoembassy.se; internet www.laoembassy.se; Ambassador Done Somvorachit (designate).

Latvia: Odengt. 5, POB 19167, 104 32 Stockholm; tel. (8) 700-63-00; fax (8) 14-01-51; e-mail embassy.sweden@mfa.gov.lv; internet www.stockholm.mfa.gov.lv; Ambassador Elita Kuzma.

Lebanon: Kommendörsgt. 35, POB 5360, 102 49 Stockholm; tel. (8) 665-19-65; fax (8) 662-68-24; Ambassador Nasrat al-Assad Bassile.

Libya (People's Bureau): Valhallavägen 74, POB 10133, 100 55 Stockholm; tel. (8) 14-34-35; fax (8) 10-43-80; e-mail libyanembassy06@hotmail.com; Chargé d'affaires a.i. Hagi Dhan.

Lithuania: Grevgt. 5, 114 53 Stockholm; tel. (8) 667-54-55; fax (8) 667-54-56; e-mail info@litemb.se; internet www.litemb.se; Ambassador Remigijus Motuzas.

Macedonia, former Yugoslav republic: Riddargt. 35, POB 10128, 100 55 Stockholm; tel. (8) 661-18-30; fax (8) 661-03-25; e-mail macedonian.embassy@telia.com; Ambassador Agon Demjaha.

Malaysia: Karlavägen 37, POB 26053, 100 41 Stockholm; tel. (8) 791-76-90; fax (8) 791-87-60; e-mail mwstholm@algohotellet.se; Ambassador Dato' Kamarudin Mustafa.

Mexico: Grevgt. 3, 114 53 Stockholm; tel. (8) 663-51-70; fax (8) 663-24-20; e-mail suecia.embamex@telia.com; internet www.sre.gob.mx/suecia; Ambassador Norma Bertha Pensado Moreno.

Moldova: Engelbrektsgt. 10, 114 32 Stockholm; tel. (8) 411-40-64; fax (8) 411-40-74; e-mail stockholm@moldovaembassy.se; internet www.moldovaembassy.se; Ambassador Natalia Gherman.

Morocco: Kungsholmstorg 16, 112 21 Stockholm; tel. (8) 545-511-30; fax (8) 545-511-39; e-mail sifamastock@stockholm.mail.telia.com; internet www.marockosambassad.com; Ambassador Zohour Alaoui.

Mozambique: Sturegt. 46, 4th Floor, POB 5801, 102 48 Stockholm; tel. (8) 666-03-50; fax (8) 663-67-29; e-mail info@embassymozambique.se; internet www.embassymozambique.se; Ambassador Pedro Comissário Afonso.

Namibia: Luntmakargt. 86–88, POB 19151, 104 32 Stockholm; tel. (8) 442-98-00; fax (8) 612-66-55; e-mail info@embassyofnamibia.se; internet www.embassyofnamibia.se; Ambassador Theresia Samaria.

Netherlands: Götgt. 16A, POB 15048, 104 65 Stockholm; tel. (8) 556-933-00; fax (8) 556-933-11; e-mail sto@minbuza.nl; internet www.nlemb.se; Ambassador Antoine François van Dongen.

Nicaragua: Sandhamnsgt. 40, 6th Floor, 115 28 Stockholm; tel. (8) 667-18-57; fax (8) 662-41-60; e-mail embajada.nicaragua@swipnet.se; Chargé d'affaires a.i. Alvaro Baca Rodríguez.

Nigeria: Tyrgt. 8, POB 628, 101 32 Stockholm; tel. (8) 246-39-05; fax (8) 24-63-98; e-mail nigerian.embassy@swipnet.se; Ambassador Funmilayo A. Adebo-Kiencke.

Norway: Skarpögt. 4, POB 27829, 115 27 Stockholm; tel. (8) 665-63-40; fax (8) 782-98-99; e-mail emb.stockholm@mfa.no; internet www.norge.se; Ambassador Odd Lauritz Fosseidbråten.

Pakistan: Karlavägen 65, 1st Floor, POB 5872, 102 40 Stockholm; tel. (8) 20-33-00; fax (8) 24-92-33; e-mail info@pakistanembassy.se; internet www.pakistanembassy.se; Ambassador Shaheen Amin Gilani.

Panama: Östermalmsgt. 59, POB 55547, 102 04 Stockholm; tel. (8) 662-65-35; fax (8) 662-89-91; Ambassador (vacant).

Peru: Brunnsgt. 21B, 2nd Floor, 111 38 Stockholm; tel. (8) 440-87-40; fax (8) 20-55-92; e-mail info@peruembassy.se; internet www.peruembassy.se; Chargé d'affaires a.i. Jorge Arturo Jarama Alvan.

Philippines: Skeppsbron 20, 1st Floor, POB 2219, 103 15 Stockholm; tel. (8) 23-56-65; fax (8) 14-07-14; e-mail stockholm@philembassy.se; internet www.philembassy.se; Ambassador Maria Zeneida Angara Collinson.

Poland: Karlavägen 35, 114 31 Stockholm; tel. (8) 505-750-00; fax (8) 505-750-86; e-mail info.polen@tele2.se; internet www.sztokholm.polemb.net; Ambassador Michał Czyż.

Portugal: Narvavägen 32, 2nd Floor, POB 10194, 100 55 Stockholm; tel. (8) 545-670-60; fax (8) 662-53-29; e-mail portugal@embassyportugal.se; internet www.embassyportugal.se; Ambassador José Carlos Júlio da Cruz Almeida.

Romania: Östermalmsgt. 36, POB 26043, 100 41 Stockholm; tel. (8) 10-86-03; fax (8) 10-28-52; e-mail info@romanianembassy.se; internet stockholm.mae.ro; Ambassador Victoria Popescu.

Russia: Gjörwellsgt. 31, 112 60 Stockholm; tel. (8) 13-04-41; fax (8) 618-27-03; e-mail rusembassy@telia.com; internet www.ryssland.se; Ambassador Aleksandr M. Kadakin.

Saudi Arabia: Sköldungagt. 5, POB 26073, 100 41 Stockholm; tel. (8) 23-88-00; fax (8) 796-99-56; Chargé d'affaires a.i. Mogbel as-Suraihi.

Senegal: Birger Jarlsgt. 37, 3 tr., POB 7384, 111 45 Stockholm; tel. (8) 411-71-60; fax (8) 411-71-68; e-mail senegalembassy@telia.com; Ambassador Henri-Antoine Turpin.

Serbia: Valhallavägen 70, POB 26209, 100 41 Stockholm; tel. (8) 21-84-36; fax (8) 21-84-95; e-mail serbiaemb@telia.com; Ambassador Prof. Dr Ninoslav D. Stojadinović.

Slovakia: Arsenalsgt. 2, 3rd Floor, POB 7183, 103 88 Stockholm; tel. (8) 545-039-60; fax (8) 545-039-69; e-mail slovakembassy@stockholm.mfa.sk; internet www.stockholm.mfa.sk; Ambassador Peter Kmec.

Slovenia: Styrmansgt. 4, 1st Floor, 114 54 Stockholm; tel. (8) 545-65-885; fax (8) 662-92-74; e-mail vst@mzz-dkp.gov.si; Ambassador Vojislav Šuc.

South Africa: Flemingt. 20, 4th Floor, 112 26 Stockholm; tel. (8) 24-39-50; fax (8) 660-71-36; e-mail saemb.swe@telia.com; internet www.southafricanemb.se; Ambassador Sophonia Raphulane Makgetla.

Spain: Djurgårdsvägen 21, Djurgården, POB 10295, 100 55 Stockholm; tel. (8) 667-94-30; fax (8) 663-79-65; e-mail emb.estocolmo@mae.es; internet www.mae.es/embajadas/estocolmo; Ambassador Enrique Viguera Rubio.

Sri Lanka: Strandvägen 39, POB 24055, 104 50 Stockholm; tel. (8) 663-65-23; fax (8) 660-00-89; e-mail slembassy@comhem.se; internet www.slembassy.se; Ambassador Ranjith Pemsiri Jayasooriya.

Sudan: POB 26142, 100 41 Stockholm; Stockholmsvägen 33, 181 33 Lidingö; tel. (8) 611-77-80; fax (8) 611-77-82; e-mail sudanembassy@telia.com; Ambassador Moses Mojwok Akol.

Switzerland: Valhallavägen 64, POB 26143, 100 41 Stockholm; tel. (8) 676-79-00; fax (8) 21-15-04; e-mail sto.vertretung@eda.admin.ch; internet www.eda.admin.ch/stockholm; Ambassador Robert Reich.

Syria: Narvavägen 32, POB 24262, 104 51 Stockholm; tel. (8) 660-88-10; fax (8) 660-88-05; internet www.syrianembassy.se; Ambassador Muhammad Bassam Hatem Imadi.

Tanzania: Näsby Allé 6, 183 55 Täby; tel. (8) 732-24-30; fax (8) 732-24-32; e-mail mailbox@tanemb.se; internet www.tanemb.se; Ambassador Dr Ben Gwai Moses.

Thailand: Floragt. 3, POB 26220, 100 40 Stockholm; tel. (8) 791-73-40; fax (8) 791-73-51; e-mail info@thaiembassy.se; internet www.thaiembassy.se; Ambassador Apichart Chinwanno.

Tunisia: Narvavägen 32, 1st Floor, POB 24030, 104 50 Stockholm; tel. (8) 545-855-20; fax (8) 662-19-75; e-mail at.stockholm@swipnet.se; Chargé d'affaires a.i. Ammar Amari.

Turkey: Dag Hammarskjölds Väg 20, POB 24105, 104 51 Stockholm; tel. (8) 23-08-40; fax (8) 663-55-14; e-mail turkbe@turkemb.se; internet www.turkemb.se; Ambassador Necip Egüz.

Ukraine: Stjärnvägen 2A, 181 34 Lidingö; tel. (8) 731-76-90; fax (8) 731-56-90; e-mail ukraina.embassy@ukrainaemb.se; internet www.mfa.gov.ua/sweden; Ambassador Anatolii Ponomarenko.

United Arab Emirates: Norrlandsgt. 20, POB 7485, 103 92 Stockholm; tel. (8) 411-12-44; fax (8) 411-12-45; Chargé d'affaires a.i. Saeed Rashid O. Saif az-Zaabi.

United Kingdom: Skarpögt. 6–8, POB 27819, 115 93 Stockholm; tel. (8) 671-30-00; fax (8) 671-31-04; e-mail info@britishembassy.se; internet www.britishembassy.se; Ambassador Andrew J. Mitchell.

USA: Dag Hammarskjölds Väg 31, 115 89 Stockholm; tel. (8) 783-53-00; fax (8) 661-19-64; e-mail stockholmweb@state.gov; internet www.usemb.se; Ambassador Michael M. Wood.

Uruguay: Kommendörsgt. 35, POB 10114, 100 55 Stockholm; tel. (8) 660-31-96; fax (8) 665-31-66; e-mail urustoc@uruemb.se; Chargé d'affaires a.i. Mercedes Corominas Galloso.

Venezuela: Engelbrektsgt. 35B, POB 26012, 100 41 Stockholm; tel. (8) 411-09-96; fax (8) 21-31-00; e-mail venezuela.embassy@chello.se; Ambassador Horacio Arteaga Acosta.

Viet Nam: Örby Slottsvägen 26, 125 71 Älvsjö; tel. (8) 556-210-70; fax (8) 556-210-80; e-mail info@vietnamemb.se; internet www.vietnamemb.se; Ambassador Trinh Quang Thanh.

Zambia: Gårdsvägen 18, 3rd Floor, POB 3056, 169 03 Solna; tel. (8) 679-90-40; fax (8) 679-68-50; e-mail info@zambiaembassy.se; internet www.zambiaembassy.se; Ambassador Joyce Musenge.

Zimbabwe: Herserudsvägen 5A, 7th Floor, 181 34 Lidingö; POB 3253, 103 65 Stockholm; tel. (8) 765-53-80; fax (8) 21-91-32; e-mail mbuya@stockholm.mail.telia.com; Ambassador Mary Sibusisiwe Mubi.

Judicial System

The judiciary and the executive are separate. Judges are appointed by the Government. A judge can be removed by an authority other than a court, but may, in such an event, request a judicial trial of the decision.

To supervise the courts in administrative matters, there is a central authority, the Domstolsverket, in Jönköping. This authority has no control over the judicial process, in which the court is independent even of the legislature and Government.

There are state officers who exercise control over the judiciary as well as the administrative authorities. The Justitiekansler (Chancellor of Justice or Attorney-General) and the four Justitieombudsmän supervise the courts and the general administration including the armed forces. The Justitiekansler performs his functions on behalf of the Government. The Justitieombudsmän are appointed by and act on behalf of the legislature.

Attorney-General (Justitiekansler): Göran Lambertz.

SUPREME COURT

Högsta domstolen (Supreme Court in Stockholm): Riddarhustorget 8, POB 2066, 103 12 Stockholm; tel. (8) 617-64-00; fax (8) 617-65-21; e-mail hogsta.domstolen@dom.se; internet www.hogstadomstolen.se; the Supreme Court in Stockholm, consisting of a minimum of 14 members, is the Court of Highest Instance. The

SWEDEN

Court works in three chambers, each of which is duly constituted of five members. Certain cases are decided by full session of the Court. There are also special divisions with three members (or, in simple cases, one member) which decide whether the Court is to consider a case.

Chairman of the Supreme Court: JOHAN MUNCK.

Justices: GERTRUD LENNANDER, LEIF THORSSON, STEFAN LINDSKOG, DAG VICTOR, SEVERIN BLOMSTRAND, TORGNY HÅSTAD, MARIANNE LUNDIUS, LARS DAHLLÖF, ANN-CHRISTINE LINDEBLAD, ELLA NYSTRÖM, KERSTIN CALISSENDORFF, PER VIRDESTEN, ANNA SKARHED, GUDMUND TOIJER, LENA MOORE.

APPELLATE COURTS

The Court of Appeal, the Court of Second Instance, consists of a president, judges of appeal and associate judges of appeal. The work is apportioned between various divisions, each of which has five or six members. In criminal cases the bench consists of three professional judges and two lay assessors; in petty and civil cases there are three professional judges only. There are six Courts of Appeal (hovrätt).

President of the Court of Appeal (Stockholm): JOHAN HIRSCHFELDT.

President of the Court of Appeal (Jönköping): LARS ÅHLÉN.

President of the Court of Appeal (Malmö): LARS-GÖRAN ENGSTRÖM.

President of the Court of Appeal (Göteborg): O. LINDH.

President of the Court of Appeal (Sundsvall): BARBRO HEGRELIUS JONSON.

President of the Court of Appeal (Umeå): ANDERS IACOBÆUS.

DISTRICT COURTS

The District Court acts as a Court of First Instance in both civil and criminal cases. At mid-2007 there were 68 District Courts (tingsrätt). In criminal cases the court is composed of a presiding professional judge and three or, in serious cases, five lay assessors; in petty cases the court consists of the professional judge only. In civil cases the court is ordinarily composed of three professional judges; however, preparatory sessions are conducted by one professional judge. In family law cases, the court is composed of a professional judge and three lay assessors. The lay assessors are elected for a period of four years (during which they are on duty for about 10 days a year). They act as members of the bench and should consequently be distinguished from the jurors of other countries. In certain types of case technical experts may sit alongside the judges.

ADMINISTRATIVE COURTS

In each of the 23 administrative districts of the country there is a County Administrative Court (länsrätten). This Court handles appeal cases concerning the assessment of social security and welfare. The bench ordinarily consists of a professional judge and three lay assessors, although in simple cases a professional judge may preside alone.

Appeals against decisions by the County Administrative Courts may be made to Administrative Courts of Appeal (kammarrätter) consisting of a president, judges of appeal and associate judges of appeal. The courts work in divisions, each of which normally has six members. The bench consists of at least three and not more than four judges. In certain cases there are, however, three professional judges and two lay assessors. There are four Administrative Courts of Appeal.

The Supreme Administrative Court of Sweden (Regeringsrätten) in Stockholm, consisting of 14 members, is the Court of Highest Instance in Administrative cases. The composition of the Court is governed by rules very similar to those that apply to the Supreme Court.

Chairman of the Supreme Administrative Court: GUNNAR BJÖRNE.

President of the Administrative Court of Appeal (Stockholm): STEN HECKSCHER.

President of the Administrative Court of Appeal (Göteborg): ELISABETH PALM.

President of the Administrative Court of Appeal (Sundsvall): BJÖRN ORRHEDE.

President of the Administrative Court of Appeal (Jönköping): MARGARETA ÅBERG.

SPECIAL COURTS

Special courts exist for certain categories of cases, e.g. fastighetsdomstolar (real estate courts) for cases concerning real estate.

OMBUDSMEN

The post of Justitieombudsman was created in 1800 to supervise the manner in which judges, government officials and other civil servants observe the laws, and to prosecute those who act illegally, misuse their position or neglect their duties. The Ombudsman is allowed access to all documents and information and has the right to be present at the considerations of the courts and other authorities. Government ministers in Sweden are not subject to supervision by the Ombudsman. The term of office is four years.

Ombudsmen: CLAES EKLUNDH, SUSANNE KNÖÖS, JAN PENNLÖV, RUNE LAVIN.

Religion

CHRISTIANITY

About 78% of the population are members of the Svenska Kyrkan (Church of Sweden). Since the constitutional link between the Church and the State was severed in 2000 a significant number of people have left the Church each year (68,145 in 2004).

Sveriges Kristna Råd (Christian Council of Sweden): Ekumeniska Centret, Starrbäcksgt. 11, 172 99 Sundbyberg; tel. (8) 453-68-00; fax (8) 453-68-29; e-mail info@skr.org; internet www.skr.org; f. 1993; 27 mem. churches; Chair. Most Rev. ANDERS WEJRYD; Gen. Sec. SVEN-BERNHARD FAST.

Church of Sweden

Svenska kyrkan

Kyrkans Hus, Sysslomansgt. 4, 751 70 Uppsala; tel. (18) 16-95-00; fax (18) 16-96-07; e-mail info@svenskakyrkan.se; internet www.svenskakyrkan.se.

Evangelical Lutheran; 13 dioceses, 2,200 parishes, 3,300 active clergy (including missionaries in the mission fields); the Archbishop of Uppsala is head of the Church.

Archbishop of Uppsala: Most Rev. ANDERS WEJRYD, 751 70 Uppsala; tel. (18) 16-95-00; fax (18) 16-96-25.

Evangeliska Fosterlands-Stiftelsen (Swedish Evangelical Mission): Sysslomansgt. 4, 751 70 Uppsala; tel. (18) 16-98-00; fax (18) 16-98-01; e-mail efs@efs.svenskakyrkan.se; internet www.efs.nu; f. 1856; an independent mission org. within the Church of Sweden; 17,994 mems; Chair. RAY RAWALL; Mission Dir ANDERS SJÖBERG.

Other Protestant Churches

Eesti Evangeeliumi Luteri Usu Kirik (Estonian Evangelical Lutheran Church): POB 450 74, 104 30 Stockholm 45; tel. (8) 20-69-78; e-mail ingo.jaagu@bredband.net; 12,000 mems; Dean INGO TIIT JAAGU; Gen. Sec. IVAR NIPPAK.

Metodistkyrkan i Sverige (United Methodist Church): Danska vägen 20, 412 66 Göteborg; tel. (31) 733-78-40; fax (31) 733-87-49; e-mail info@metodistkyrkan.se; internet www.metodistkyrkan.se; f. 1868; 3,565 mems; Bishop ØYSTEIN OLSEN; Pres. of Conference Board ANDERS SVENSSON.

Sjundedags Adventistsamfundet (Seventh-day Adventists): POB 536, 101 30 Stockholm; tel. (8) 545-297-70; fax (8) 20-48-68; e-mail info@adventist.se; internet www.adventist.se; f. 1880; 2,800 mems; Pres. BOBBY SJÖLANDER; Sec. AUDREY ANDERSSON.

Svenska Baptistsamfundet (Baptist Union of Sweden): Starrbäcksgt. 11, 172 99 Sundbyberg; tel. (8) 564-827-00; fax (8) 564-827-27; e-mail info@baptist.se; internet www.baptist.se; f. 1848; 223 churches, 17,195 mems (2007); mem. European Baptist Fed., Baptist World Alliance and Christian Council of Sweden (Sveriges Kristna Råd); Pres. Rev. KARIN WIBORN; Gen. Sec. LARS DALESJÖ.

Svenska Missionskyrkan (Mission Covenant Church of Sweden): Tegnérgt. 8, POB 6302, 113 81 Stockholm; tel. (8) 674-07-00; fax (8) 674-07-93; e-mail info@missionskyrkan.se; internet www.missionskyrkan.se; f. 1878; 61,769 mems; Pres. GÖRAN ZETTERGREN; Chair. of Board ULF HÅLLMARKER.

The Roman Catholic Church

For ecclesiastical purposes, Sweden comprises the single diocese of Stockholm, directly responsible to the Holy See. At 31 December 2006 there were 140,000 adherents in the country, representing 1.5% of the total population.

Scandinavian Bishops' Conference

POB 135, 421 22 Västra Frölunda; tel. (31) 709-57-15; fax (31) 49-21-70; e-mail nbk@bishopsoffice.org; internet www.nordiskabiskopskonferensen.org.

f. 1960; new statutes approved 2000; covers Sweden, Norway, Denmark, Finland and Iceland; Pres. Rt Rev. ANDERS ARBORELIUS; Sec.-Gen. Rt Rev. GEORG MÜLLER.

Bishop of Stockholm: Rt Rev. ANDERS ARBORELIUS, Götgt. 68, POB 4114, 102 62 Stockholm; tel. (8) 462-66-00; fax (8) 702-05-55; e-mail biskop@katolskakyrkan.se; internet www.katolskakyrkan.se.

Other Denominations

Other Christian Churches include the Pentecostal Movement (with an estimated 90,000 mems in 2004), the Orthodox Churches of the Greeks, Romanians, Russians, Serbians and Finnish (together numbering about 100,000 mems in 2004), the Church of Jesus Christ of Latter-day Saints (Mormons—9,000 mems in 2004), the Swedish Alliance Missionary Society (12,895 mems in 1997), the Jehovah's Witnesses (23,000 mems in 2004) and the Salvation Army (25,531 mems in 1997).

ISLAM

In 2004 there were approximately 300,000 to 350,000 Muslims in Sweden, of whom around 100,000 were believed to be religiously active. Muslim affiliations represented among immigrant groups are predominantly with the Shi'a and Sunni branches of Islam.

Islamiska Radet i Sverige (Islamic Council of Sweden—IRIS): POB 3053, 14503 Norsborg; tel. (8) 531-707-95; fax (8) 531-706-65; f. 1986.

Islamiska Kulturcenterunionen i Sverige (Union of the Islamic Cultural Centres in Sweden—IKUS): POB 3053, 145 03 Norsborg; tel. (8) 531-707-95; fax (8) 531-706-65; f. 1984.

Sveriges Muslimska Förbund (SMUF): Stockholms Moske, Kapellgränd 10, 116 25 Stockholm; tel. and fax (8) 643-10-04; e-mail aldebe@arabia.com.

JUDAISM

In 2004 the total number of Jews living in Sweden was estimated to be approximately 18,500–20,000; however, the Jewish community estimated 10,000 active, or practising, members. There are Orthodox, Conservative and Reform Jewish synagogues. The largest Jewish community is in Stockholm.

Jewish Community in Stockholm: Wahrendorffsgt. 3B, POB 7427, 103 91 Stockholm; tel. (8) 587-858-00; fax (8) 587-858-58; e-mail info@jfst.se; internet www.jfst.se; c. 4,500 mems; Exec. Dir THOMAS BAB.

BAHÁ'Í FAITH

Svenska Bahá'í-samfundet (Swedish Bahá'í Community): Solhagavägen 11, 163 52 Spånga; tel. (8) 21-51-90; fax (8) 21-51-91; e-mail secretariat@bahai.se; internet www.bahai.se; f. 1962; Gen. Sec. ÖRJAN WIDEGREN.

OTHER RELIGIONS

In 2004 there were approximately 3,000–4,000 Buddhists and a similar number of Hindus in Sweden.

The Press

Press freedom in Sweden dates from a law of 1766. The 1949 Freedom of the Press Act, a fundamental law embodying the whole of the press legislation in the Constitution, guarantees the Press's right to print and disseminate ideas; protects those supplying information by forbidding editors to disclose sources under any circumstances; authorizes all public documents to be publicly available, official secrets being the only exception; and contains provision for defamation. Press offences are to be referred to common law, and all cases against the Press must be heard by jury.

In 1916 the Press Council was founded by press organizations to monitor ethical matters within the Press. Lacking judicial status, it has powers to rehabilitate persons wronged by the Press who refuse to apply to courts of law. Its judgments are widely published and highly respected.

In 1969 the office of Press Ombudsman was established to supervise adherence to ethical standards. Public complaints shall be directed to the Press Ombudsman, who is also entitled to act on his own initiative. He may dismiss a complaint if unfounded, or if the newspaper agrees to publish a retraction or rectification acceptable to the complainant. When he finds that the grievance is of a more serious nature, he will file a complaint with the Press Council, which will then publish a statement acquitting or criticizing the newspaper. The findings of the Council are published in the newspaper concerned.

The dominating influence of the few major dailies is largely confined to Stockholm, the provinces having a strong Press of their own. The major dailies are: *Aftonbladet, Dagens Nyheter, Expressen, Svenska Dagbladet, Dagens Industri* (all Stockholm), *Göteborgs-Posten* (Gothenburg), *Sydsvenskan* (Malmö). In 2004 there were an estimated 165 daily newspapers with a combined circulation of 4.0m.

The two principal magazine publishers in Sweden are the Bonnier group (also a large book publisher and the majority shareholder in the newspapers *Dagens Nyheter, Expressen* and *Sydsvenskan*) and the Aller company. Four other companies produce most of the remainder of Sweden's magazine circulation. The most popular weekly periodicals include the family magazines *Året Runt, Hemmets Veckotidning, Allers* and *Hemmets Journal*, and the home and household magazine *ICAKuriren*. *Vi* caters for serious cultural and political discussion and *Bonniers Litterära Magasin* specializes in literary topics.

PRINCIPAL NEWSPAPERS

Newspapers with a circulation exceeding 15,000 are listed below.

Ängelholm

Nordvästra Skånes Tidningar: 262 83 Ängelholm; tel. (431) 84-000; fax (431) 26-177; f. 1847; daily; Conservative; Editor-in-Chief BENNIE OHLSSON; circ. 42,400 (1996).

Borås

Borås Tidning: 501 85 Borås; tel. (33) 700-07-00; fax (33) 10-14-36; f. 1826; morning; Conservative; Editor JAN ÖJMERTZ; circ. 53,000 (2001).

Eksjö

Smålands-Tidningen: POB 261, 575 23 Eksjö; tel. (381) 13-200; fax (381) 17-145; f. 1899; morning; independent; Editor BENGT WENDLE; circ. 18,700 (1996).

Eskilstuna

Eskilstuna-Kuriren Strengnäs Tidning: POB 120, 631 02 Eskilstuna; tel. (16) 15-60-00; fax (16) 51-63-04; e-mail ek@ekuriren.se; internet www.ekuriren.se; f. 1890; morning; Liberal; Editor PEO WÄRRING; circ. 33,000 (2006).

Falkenberg

Hallands Nyheter: 311 81 Falkenberg; tel. (346) 29-000; fax (346) 29-115; e-mail redaktionen@hn.se; internet www.hn.se; f. 1905; morning; Centre; Editor ANNA KARIN LITH; circ. 31,000 (2001).

Falun

Dala-Demokraten: POB 825, Stigaregat. 17, 791 29 Falun; tel. (23) 47-500; fax (23) 20-668; e-mail redaktionen@deladem.se; internet www.dalademokraten.se; f. 1917; morning; Social Democrat; Editor GÖRAN GREIDER; circ. 24,400 (1996).

Falu-Kuriren: POB 265, 791 26 Falun; tel. (23) 93-500; fax (23) 12-073; e-mail red@falukuriren.se; internet www.falukuriren.se; f. 1894; morning; Liberal; Editor CHRISTER GRUHS; circ. 29,400 (1996).

Gävle

Arbetarbladet: POB 287, 801 04 Gävle; tel. (26) 15-93-00; fax (26) 12-14-06; f. 1902; morning; Social Democrat; Editor KENNET LUTTI; circ. 29,100 (1996).

Gefle Dagblad: POB 367, 801 05 Gävle; tel. (26) 15-95-00; fax (26) 15-97-00; f. 1895; morning; Liberal; Editor ROBERT ROSÉN; circ. 30,800 (1996).

Göteborg
(Gothenburg)

Göteborgs-Posten: Polhemsplatsen 5, 405 02 Göteborg; tel. (31) 62-40-00; fax (31) 62-45-85; e-mail redaktion@gp.se; internet www.gp.se; f. 1858; morning; Liberal; Editor-in-Chief PETER HJORNE; circ. 245,600 (2006).

Halmstad

Hallandsposten: 301 81 Halmstad; tel. (35) 14-75-00; fax (35) 14-76-88; e-mail redaktionen@hallandsposten.se; internet www.hallandsposten.se; f. 1850; morning; Liberal; Editor SVERKER EMANUELSSON; circ. 32,200 (1996).

Hässleholm

Norra Skåne: 281 81 Hässleholm; tel. (451) 74-50-00; fax (451) 74-50-32; e-mail chefred@nsk.se; internet www.nsk.se; f. 1899; morning; Centre; Editor BILLY BENGTSSON; circ. 21,800 (2001).

Helsingborg

Helsingborgs Dagblad: Vasatorpsvägen 1, 251 83 Helsingborg; tel. (20) 23–24–00; e-mail redaktionen@hd.se; internet hd.se; f. 1867; morning; independent; Editor-in-Chief ANNA BERGENSTRÖM; circ. 49,500 (1996).

SD-Kuriren: POB 130 45, 250 13 Helsingborg; tel. (73) 62-60-661; fax (455) 151-33; e-mail redaktion@sdkuriren.se; internet www.sdkuriren.se; f. 1988; organ of the Sverigedemokraterna; Editor-in-Chief RICHARD JOMSHOF; circ. 30,000.

Hudiksvall

Hudiksvalls Tidning: POB 1201, 824 15 Hudiksvall; tel. (650) 355-00; fax (650) 355-60; e-mail redaktion@ht.se; internet www.ht.se; f. 1909; includes Hälsinglands Tidning; morning; Centre; Man. Dir RUBEN JACOBSSON; Editor JÖRGEN BENGTSON; circ. 17,600 (1998).

Jönköping

Jönköpings-Posten/Smålands Allehanda: 551 80 Jönköping; tel. (36) 30-40-50; fax (36) 12-61-11; f. 1865; morning; independent; Editor STIG FREDRIKSSON; circ. 42,900 (1996).

Kalmar

Barometern med Oskarshamns-Tidningen: 391 88 Kalmar; tel. (480) 59-100; fax (480) 59-131; f. 1841; morning; Conservative; Editor GUNILLA ANDREASSON; circ. 47,400 (1999).

Karlskrona

Blekinge Läns Tidning: 371 89 Karlskrona; tel. (455) 77-000; fax (455) 82-170; e-mail kudcenter@blt.se; internet www.blt.se; f. 1869; morning; Liberal; Editor-in-Chief KERSTIN JOHANSSON; circ. 36,800 (2003).

Sydöstra Sveriges Dagblad: Landbrogt. 17, 371 88 Karlskrona; tel. (455) 19-000; fax (455) 82-237; f. 1903; morning; Social Democrat; Editor ANDERS HAGQUIST; circ. 18,000 (1998).

Karlstad

Nya Wermlands-Tidningen: POB 28, 651 02 Karlstad; tel. (54) 19-90-00; fax (54) 19-96-00; e-mail redaktion@nwt.se; internet www.nwt.se; f. 1836; morning; Conservative; Editor STAFFAN ANDER; circ. 59,500 (1996).

Värmlands Folkblad: POB 67, 651 03 Karlstad; tel. (54) 17-55-06; fax (54) 15-16-59; e-mail kundtjanst@vf.se; internet www.vf.se; f. 1918; morning; Social Democrat; Editor PETER FRANKE; circ. 25,300 (1996).

Kristianstad

Kristianstadsbladet: 291 84 Kristianstad; tel. (44) 18-55-00; fax (44) 21-17-01; e-mail kb@kristianstadsbladet.se; internet www.kristianstadsbladet.se; f. 1856; morning; Liberal; Man. Dir BO WIGERNÄS; Editor HAKAN BENGTSSON; circ. 31,900 (2004).

Lidköping

Nya Läns-Tidningen: 531 81 Lidköping; tel. (510) 89-700; fax (510) 89-796; e-mail post@nlt.se; f. 1903; morning; 3 a week; Liberal; Editor LENNART HÖRLING; circ. 26,300.

Linköping

Östgöta Correspondenten: 581 89 Linköping; tel. (13) 28-00-00; fax (13) 28-03-24; e-mail nyhet@corren.se; internet www.corren.se; f. 1838; morning; Liberal; Editor OLA SIGVARDSSON; circ. 59,300 (2006).

Luleå

Norrbottens-Kuriren: 971 81 Luleå; tel. (920) 37-500; fax (920) 67-107; f. 1861; morning; Conservative; Editor (vacant); circ. 30,700 (1996).

Norrländska Socialdemokraten: 971 83 Luleå; tel. (920) 36-000; fax (920) 36-279; f. 1919; morning; Social Democrat; Editor LENNART HÅKANSSON; circ. 39,600 (1996).

Malmö

Kvällsposten: 205 26 Malmö; tel. (40) 28-16-00; fax (40) 93-92-24; f. 1990; evening; Liberal; Editor LARS KLINT; circ. 62,900.

Skånska Dagbladet: Östergt. 11, POB 165, 201 21 Malmö; tel. (40) 660-55-00; fax (40) 97-47-70; f. 1888; morning; Centre; Editor JAN A. JOHANSSON; circ. 29,400 (1996).

Sydsvenskan: 205 05 Malmö; tel. (40) 28-12-00; fax (40) 93-54-75; e-mail sydsvenskan@sydsvenskan.se; internet sydsvenskan.se; f. 1848; morning; Liberal independent; Editors JONAS GRUVÖ, HEIDI AVELLAN; circ. 136,400 (2003).

Norrköping

Norrköpings Tidningar: 601 83 Norrköping; tel. (11) 20-00-00; fax (11) 20-02-40; e-mail redaktionen@nt.se; internet www.nt.se; f. 1758; morning; Conservative; Editor KARL-ÅKE BREDENBERG; circ. 49,900 (2000).

Nyköping

Södermanlands Nyheter: 611 79 Nyköping; tel. (155) 76-700; fax (155) 26-88-01; e-mail redaktionen@sn.se; internet www.sn.se; f. 1893; morning; Editor GÖRAN CARLSTORP; circ. 25,300 (2006).

Örebro

Nerikes Allehanda: 701 92 Örebro; tel. (19) 15-50-00; fax (19) 12-03-83; e-mail redaktionen@na.se; internet www.na.se; f. 1843; morning; Liberal; Editor KRISTER LINNER; circ. 68,000 (1999).

Örnsköldsvik

Örnsköldsviks Allehanda: POB 110, 891 23 Örnsköldsvik; tel. (660) 29-50-00; fax (660) 15-064; e-mail lars.nordstrom@allehanda.se; f. 1843; morning; Liberal; Editor LARS NORDSTRÖM; circ. 20,800 (2001).

Östersund

Länstidningen: 831 89 Östersund; tel. (63) 15-55-00; fax (63) 15-55-95; f. 1924; morning; Social Democrat; Editors PETER SWEDENMARK, CHRISTER SJÖSTRÖM; circ. 17,000 (2003).

Östersunds-Posten: POB 720, 831 28 Östersund; tel. (63) 16-16-00; fax (63) 10-58-02; f. 1877; morning; Centre; Editors BOSSE SVENSSON, HÅKAN LARSSON; circ. 27,100 (1996).

Piteå

Piteå-Tidningen: POB 193, 941 24 Piteå; tel. (911) 64-500; fax (911) 64-650; f. 1915; morning; Social Democrat; Editor OLOV CARLSSON; circ. 17,600 (1996).

Skara

Skaraborgs Läns Tidning: POB 214, 532 23 Skara; tel. (511) 13-010; fax (511) 18-815; f. 1884; morning; Liberal; Editor HANS OLOFSSON; circ. 17,100 (1995).

Skellefteå

Norra Västerbotten: POB 58, 931 21 Skellefteå; tel. (910) 57-700; fax (910) 57-875; e-mail redaktionsavderlning@norran.se; internet www.norran.se; f. 1910; morning; 6 days a week; Liberal; Editor OLA THEANDER; circ. 30,500 (2000).

Skövde

Skaraborgs Allehanda: POB 407, 541 28 Skövde; tel. (500) 46-75-00; fax (500) 48-05-82; e-mail redaktion@sla.se; internet www.sla.se; f. 1884; morning; Conservative; Editor MÅNS JOHNSON; circ. 23,700 (1997).

Södertälje

Länstidningen: 151 82 Södertälje; tel. (8) 550-921-00; fax (8) 550-877-72; e-mail redaktion@lt.se; f. 1861; morning; 6 a week; Centre; Editor TORSTEN CARLSSON; circ. 17,600 (2002).

Stockholm

Aftonbladet: 105 18 Stockholm; tel. (8) 725-20-00; fax (8) 600-01-70; e-mail redaktion@aftonbladet.se; internet www.aftonbladet.se; f. 1830; evening; Social Democrat independent; Editor-in-Chief KALLE JUNGKVIST; circ. 381,200 (1996).

Dagen: 105 36 Stockholm; tel. (8) 619-24-00; fax (8) 619-60-51; e-mail info@dagen.se; f. 1945; morning; 4 a week; Christian independent; Editor DANIEL GRAHN; circ. 20,200 (2003).

Dagens Industri: 113 90 Stockholm; tel. (8) 736-50-00; fax (8) 31-19-06; internet di.se; f. 1976; 6 a week; business news; Editor LINUS PAULSSON; circ. 110,200 (1998).

Dagens Nyheter: 105 15 Stockholm; tel. (8) 738-10-00; fax (8) 738-21-80; e-mail info@dn.se; internet www.dn.se; f. 1864; morning; independent; Editor-in-Chief THORBJÖRN LARSSON; CEO LENA HERRMANN; circ. 368,000 (2003).

Expressen: Gjörwellsgt. 30, 105 16 Stockholm; tel. (8) 738-30-00; fax (8) 738-33-40; e-mail redaktionen@expressen.se; internet www.expressen.se; f. 1945; evening; Liberal; Editor OTTO SJÖBERG; circ. 353,000 (2003).

Svenska Dagbladet: 105 17 Stockholm; tel. (8) 13-50-00; fax (8) 13-56-80; e-mail svd@svd.se; internet www.svd.se; f. 1884; morning; Conservative; Editor-in-Chief LENA K. SAMUELSSON; circ. 170,000 (2000).

Sundsvall

Sundsvalls Tidning: 851 72 Sundsvall; tel. (60) 19-70-00; fax (60) 15-44-33; e-mail redaktion@st.nu; internet www.st.nu; f. 1841; morning; Liberal; Editor KJELL CARNBRO; circ. 35,700 (2005).

SWEDEN

Trollhättan

Trollhättans Tidning: POB 54, 461 22 Trollhättan; tel. (520) 49-42-00; fax (520) 49-43-19; f. 1906; morning; 5 a week; independent; Editor TORBJÖRN HÅKANSSON; circ. 17,300 (1996).

Uddevalla

Bohusläningen med Dals Dagblad: 451 83 Uddevalla; tel. (522) 99-000; fax (522) 51-18-88; f. 1878; morning; Liberal; Editor ULF JOHANSSON; circ. 32,400 (1996).

Umeå

Västerbottens-Kuriren: 901 70 Umeå; tel. (90) 15-10-00; fax (90) 77-00-53; e-mail info@vk.se; internet www.vk.se; f. 1900; morning; Liberal; circ. 41,500 (1998).

Uppsala

Upsala Nya Tidning: POB 36, Danmarksgt. 28, 751 03 Uppsala; tel. (18) 478-00-00; fax (18) 12-95-07; e-mail hakan.holmberg@unt.se; internet www.unt.se; f. 1890; morning; Liberal; Editor-in-Chief LARS NILSSON; circ. 62,800 (2002).

Värnamo

Värnamo Nyheter: 331 84 Värnamo; tel. (370) 30-19-56; fax (370) 493-95; e-mail redaktion@varnamonyheter.se; internet www.varnamonyheter.se; f. 1917; morning; independent; Editor STIG-ERIC EINARSSON; circ. 23,000 (2000).

Västerås

Vestmanlands Läns Tidning: POB 3, 721 03 Västerås; tel. (21) 19-90-00; fax (21) 19-90-60; e-mail nyheter@vlt.se; internet www.vlt.se; f. 1831; morning; Liberal; Editor ELISABETH BÄCK; circ. 48,000 (2003).

Växjö

Smålandsposten: 351 70 Växjö; tel. (470) 77-05-00; fax (470) 209-49; f. 1866; morning; Conservative; Editor CLAES-GÖRAN HEGNELL; circ. 41,500 (1996).

Ystad

Ystads Allehanda: 271 81 Ystad; tel. (411) 55-78-00; fax (411) 13-955; e-mail nyheter@ystadsallehanda.se; internet www.ystadsallehanda.se; f. 1873; morning; Liberal; Man. Dir BO WIGERNÄS; Editor MARGARETHA ENGSTRÖM; circ. 26,100 (2004).

POPULAR PERIODICALS

Allas Veckotidning: Allers Förlag, 205 35 Malmö; tel. (40) 38-59-00; fax (40) 38-59-64; e-mail allas@aller.se; f. 1931; weekly; family; Editor-in-Chief TINA JANSSON; circ. 138,400.

Allers: 251 85 Helsingborg; tel. (42) 17-35-00; fax (42) 17-35-68; e-mail redaktionen@allers.aller.se; f. 1877; weekly; family; Editor-in-Chief ÅSA TENGVALL; circ. 247,400.

Allt om Mat: Sveavägen 53, 105 44 Stockholm; tel. (8) 736-53-00; fax (8) 34-00-88; e-mail red@aom.bonnier.se; internet www.alltommat.se; f. 1970; 18 a year; food specialities; Editor-in-Chief JAN HOLMSTRÖM; circ. 125,800.

Antik och Auktion: Landskronåvagen 23, 251 85 Helsingborg; tel. (42) 12-35-00; fax (42) 17-37-40; e-mail carin.stentorp@aller.se; internet www.antikochauktion.se; f. 1978; monthly; antiques; Editor CARIN STENTORP; circ. 57,900.

Året Runt: 105 44 Stockholm; tel. (8) 736-52-00; fax (8) 30-49-00; f. 1946; weekly; family; Editor LILLIAN EHRENHOLM-DAUN; circ. 243,500.

Bilsport: POB 529, 371 23 Karlskrona; tel. (455) 33-53-25; fax (455) 291-75; e-mail bilsport@fabas.se; internet www.bilsport.se; f. 1962; fortnightly; motor-sport, cars; Editor-in-Chief FREDRIK SJÖQVIST; circ. 67,300.

Damernas Värld: 105 44 Stockholm; tel. (8) 736-53-00; fax (8) 24-46-46; e-mail red@dv.bonnier.se; f. 1940; monthly; women's interest; Editor MONA JOHANSSON; circ. 118,800.

Elle: St Eriksplan 2, 113 93 Stockholm; tel. (8) 457-80-00; fax (8) 457-80-80; e-mail ellered@hachette.se; internet www.elle.se; f. 1988; monthly; women's interest; Editor KRISTINA ADOLFSSON; circ. 81,900.

Femina Månadens Magasin: 251 85 Helsingborg; tel. (42) 17-35-00; fax (42) 17-36-82; e-mail femina@aller.se; f. 1981; monthly; women's interest; Editor LISBETH LUNDAHL; circ. 118,500.

Frida: Hammarby Kajväg 14, 120 30 Stockholm; tel. (8) 587-481-00; fax (8) 587-481-07; e-mail frida@frida.forlag.se; internet www.frida.se; fortnightly; for teenage girls; Editor-in-Chief KAROLINA OLOVSSON; circ. 67,000.

Hänt Extra: POB 27704, 115 91 Stockholm; tel. (8) 679-46-00; fax (8) 679-46-77; f. 1986; weekly; family; Editors-in-Chief JAN BARD, THORD SKÖLDEKRANS; circ. 113,300.

Hänt i Veckan: POB 27704, 115 91 Stockholm; tel. (8) 679-46-00; fax (8) 679-46-33; f. 1964; weekly; family; Editor-in-Chief STEN HEDMAN; circ. 132,300.

Hemmets Journal: Egmont Tidskrifter AB, 205 07 Malmö; tel. (40) 38-52-00; fax (40) 38-53-98; e-mail red.hj@egmont.se; internet www.hj.egmont.se; f. 1920; weekly; family; Editor-in-Chief JANNE WALLES; circ. 231,800.

Hemmets Veckotidning: Allers Förlag AB, 205 35 Malmö; tel. (40) 38-59-00; fax (40) 38-59-14; f. 1929; weekly; family; Editor ULLA COCKE; circ. 215,300.

Hus & Hem: ICA Förlaget AB, POB 6630, 113 84 Stockholm; tel. (8) 728-23-00; fax (8) 34-56-37; e-mail kundtjanst.husohem@formapg.se; internet www.husohem.se; 12 a year; for house-owners; Editor ANNA LILJEBERG; circ. 153,000.

ICA Kuriren: POB 6630, 113 84 Stockholm; tel. (8) 728-23-00; fax (8) 728-23-50; e-mail red.kuriren@forlaget.ica.se; internet www.icakuriren.se; f. 1942; weekly; home and household; Editor (vacant); circ. 364,300.

Kalle Anka & Co: 205 08 Malmö; tel. (40) 693-94-00; fax (40) 693-94-95; e-mail kalle.anka@egmont.se; internet www.ankeborg.egmont.se; f. 1948; weekly; comics; Editor TORD JÖNSSON; circ. 138,000.

Kvällsstunden: Tidningshuset Kvällsstunden AB, POB 1080, 721 27 Västerås; tel. (21) 19-04-00; fax (21) 13-62-62; e-mail info@tidningshuset.com; internet www.tidningshuset.com; weekly; family magazine; Editor ÅKE LINDBERG; circ. 54,300.

Må Bra: POB 27780, 115 93 Stockholm; tel. (8) 679-46-00; fax (8) 667-34-39; f. 1978; monthly; health and nutrition; Editor-in-Chief INGER RIDSTRÖM; circ. 97,900.

OKEJ: Egmont Kärnan AB, Ö Förstadsgt. 34, 205 08 Malmö; tel. (40) 693-94-00; fax (40) 693-94-94; e-mail okej@egmont.se; internet www.okej.se; f. 1980; monthly; pop-music magazine; Editor ANDERS TENGNER; circ. 44,400.

Premium Motor: POB 6019, 175 06 Järfälla; tel. (8) 761-09-50; fax (8) 761-09-49; motoring; Editor STAFFAN SWEDENBORG; circ. 44,615.

Privata Affärer: Sveavägen 53, 105 44 Stockholm; tel. (8) 736-53-00; fax (8) 31-25-60; e-mail pren@privataaffarer.se; internet www.privataaffarer.se; f. 1978; monthly; personal money management; Editor-in-Chief HANS BOLANDER; circ. 111,200.

Röster i Radio/TV: POB 27704, 115 91 Stockholm; tel. (8) 679-46-00; fax (8) 679-46-33; f. 1934; weekly; family magazine and programme guide to radio and television; Editor-in-Chief EDGAR ANTONSSON; circ. 140,000.

Sköna hem: 105 44 Stockholm; tel. (8) 736-52-00; fax (8) 33-74-11; e-mail skonahem@skh.bonnier.se; internet www.skonahem.se; f. 1979 (Sköna Hem), 1956 (Allt i Hemmet), merged 1992; monthly; interior decoration; Editor-in-Chief EVA ABRAHAMSSON; circ. 98,800.

Svensk Damtidning: POB 27710, 115 91 Stockholm; tel. (8) 679-46-00; fax (8) 679-47-50; f. 1891; weekly; women's interest; Editor-in-Chief KARIN LENMOR; circ. 132,400.

Teknikens Värld: 105 44 Stockholm; tel. (8) 736-52-00; fax (8) 736-00-11; internet www.teknikensvarld.com; f. 1947; fortnightly; motoring; Editor-in-Chief DANIEL FRODIN; circ. 58,500.

Vår bostad: POB 12651, 112 93 Stockholm; tel. (8) 692-02-00; fax (8) 650-06-41; e-mail info@varbostad.se; internet www.varbostad.se; f. 1924; 11 a year; house and home; Editor ULRICA AMBJÖRN; circ. 928,700.

Vecko-Revyn: Kungsgt. 34, 105 44 Stockholm; tel. (8) 736-52-00; fax (8) 24-16-02; e-mail ebba@veckorevyn.com; internet veckorevyn.net; f. 1935; weekly; young women's interest; Editor EBBA VON SYDOW; circ. 91,100.

Vi Bilägare: POB 23800, 104 35 Stockholm; tel. (8) 736-12-00; fax (8) 736-12-49; e-mail redaktionen@vibilagare.se; internet www.vibilagare.se; f. 1930; fortnightly; auto and travel; Editor NILS-ERIC FRENDIN; circ. 170,000.

Vi Föräldrar: 105 44 Stockholm; tel. (8) 736-53-00; fax (8) 34-00-43; e-mail red@vf.bonnier.se; internet www.viforaldrar.se; f. 1968; monthly; parents' magazine; Editor-in-Chief HELENA RÖNNBERG; circ. 59,500.

SPECIALIST PERIODICALS

Aktuellt i Politiken: Sveavägen 68, 105 60 Stockholm; tel. (8) 700-26-00; fax (8) 11-65-42; weekly; social, political and cultural affairs; organ of Social Democratic Labour Party; circ. 55,000.

Allt om Jakt & Vapen: POB 3263, 103 65 Stockholm; tel. (8) 30-16-30; fax (8) 28-59-74; e-mail jaktochvapen@pressdata.se; internet www.jaktovapen.com; 11 a year; hunting; Editor ERIK WALLIN; circ. 41,500.

Arbetsledaren: POB 12069, 102 22 Stockholm; tel. (8) 652-01-20; fax (8) 653-99-68; f. 1908; 10 a year; journal for foremen and supervisors; Editor INGRID ASKEBERG; circ. 87,400.

Barn: 107 88 Stockholm; tel. (8) 698-90-00; fax (8) 698-90-14; e-mail barn@rb.se; internet www.rb.se/barn; owned by Rädda Barnen (Save the Children Sweden); 6 a year; children's rights; Editor-in-Chief SOFIE ARNÖ; circ. 125,700.

Båtliv: POB 8097, 371 38 Karlskrona; tel. (445) 297-80; fax (455) 36-97-99; e-mail info@batliv.se; internet www.batliv.se; 5 a year; for boat-owners and boat-club members; Editor LARS-ÅKE REDÉEN; circ. 126,300.

Byggnadsarbetaren: 106 32 Stockholm; tel. (8) 728-49-00; fax (8) 728-49-80; e-mail kenneth.petterson@byggnadsarbetaren.se; internet www.byggnadsarbetaren.se; f. 1949; 18 a year; building; Editor KENNETH PETTERSSON; circ. 130,700 (2006).

Dina Pengar: Konsument Göteborg, POB 11364, 404 28 Göteborg; tel. (8) 573-650-60; e-mail redaktionen@dinarpengar.se; internet www.di.se; 9 a year; finance; Editor BJÖRN HEDENSJÖ; circ. 83,000.

Du&jobbet: Maria Skolgt. 83, POB 17550, 118 91 Stockholm; tel. (8) 442-46-00; fax (8) 442-46-07; e-mail redaktionen@duochjobbet.com; internet www.duochjobbet.com; monthly; working environment; circ. 105,000.

Handelsnytt: POB 1146, 111 81 Stockholm; tel. (8) 412-68-00; fax (8) 21-43-33; e-mail handelsnytt@handels.se; internet www.handelsnytt.se; f. 1906; 11 a year; organ of the Union of Commercial Employees; circ. 71,300.

Hundsport: POB 11141, 100 61 Stockholm; tel. (8) 642-37-20; fax (8) 641-00-62; monthly; for dog-owners; Editor TORSTEN WIDHOLM; circ. 101,300.

Jaktmarker och Fiskevatten: Västra Torggt. 18, 652 24 Karlstad; tel. (54) 10-03-70; fax (54) 10-09-83; 11 a year; hunting and fishing; circ. 48,100.

Kommunalarbetaren: POB 19034, 104 32 Stockholm; tel. (8) 728-28-00; fax (8) 30-61-42; e-mail kommunalarbetaren@kommunal.se; internet www.ka.se; 22 a year; organ of the Union of Municipal Workers; Editor LIV BECKSTRÖM; circ. 605,000.

Kyrkans Tidning: POB 15412, 104 65 Stockholm; tel. (8) 462-28-00; fax (8) 644-76-71; e-mail redaktionen@kyrkanstidning.com; internet www.kyrkanstidning.com; f. 1982; weekly; organ of the Church of Sweden; Man. Dir THOMAS GRAHL; Editor DAG TUVELIUS; circ. 46,700.

LAND-Familjetidningen: Gävlegt. 22, 113 92 Stockholm; tel. (8) 588-365-10; fax (8) 588-369-59; e-mail land@lrfmedia.lrf.se; internet www.tidningenland.com; f. 1971; weekly; organ of the farmers' asscn; circ. 234,000 (2006).

LAND Lantbruk: Gävlegt. 22, 113 92 Stockholm; tel. (8) 787-51-00; fax (8) 787-55-02; e-mail internetredaktionen@lantbruk.com; internet www.lantbruk.com; f. 1971; weekly; organ of the farmers' asscn; agriculture, forestry; circ. 121,800.

Lärarförbundet: Segelbåtsvägen 15, POB 12229, 102 26 Stockholm; tel. (8) 737-65-00; e-mail sten.svensson@lararforbundet.se; internet www.lararforbundet.se; 22 a year; for teachers; Editor-in-Chief STEN SVENSSON; circ. 225,000.

Lön & Jobb: POB 30102, 104 25 Stockholm; tel. (8) 737-80-00; fax (8) 618-67-22; e-mail lonjobb@htf.se; internet www.lon-jobb.nu; 18 a year; organ of the Union of Commercial Salaried Employees; Editor-in-Chief CARL VON SCHÉELE; circ. 147,300.

Metallarbetaren: Olof Palmesgt. 11, 105 52 Stockholm; tel. (8) 10-68-30; fax (8) 11-13-02; f. 1888; weekly; organ of Swedish Metal Workers' Union; Editor PER AHLSTRÖM; circ. 415,400.

Motor: POB 23142, 104 35 Stockholm; tel. (8) 690-38-00; fax (8) 690-38-22; monthly; cars and motoring; circ. 141,700.

Motorföraren: Heliosgt. 11, 120 30 Stockholm; tel. (8) 555-765-55; fax (8) 555-765-95; e-mail motorforaren@mhf.se; internet www.mhf.se; f. 1927; 8 a year; motoring and tourism; Editor SÖREN SEHLBERG; circ. 41,300.

Musiktidningen Musikomanen: POB 6903, 102 39 Stockholm; tel. (8) 31-00-07; e-mail alexander.scarlat@chello.se; f. 1964; 4 a year; classical and modern music; circ. 90,000; Senior Editor ALEXANDER SCARLAT.

Ny Teknik: Mäster Samuelsgt. 56, 106 12 Stockholm; tel. (8) 796-66-00; fax (8) 613-30-28; e-mail redaktion@nyteknik.se; internet www.nyteknik.se; f. 1967; weekly; technical publication owned by the two largest engineering societies of Sweden; Editor-in-Chief LARS NILSSON; circ. 150,500.

PRO-Pensionären: POB 3274, 103 65 Stockholm; tel. (8) 701-67-00; fax (8) 20-33-58; e-mail info@pro.se; internet www.pro.se; f. 1942; 10 a year; magazine for pensioners; Editor AGNETA BERG-WAHLSTEDT; circ. 293,900.

SEKO-magasinet: Barnhusgt. 10, POB 1102, 111 81 Stockholm; tel. (8) 791-41-00; fax (8) 21-16-94; f. 1955; 11 a year; organ of the National Union of Services and Communications Employees; Editor-in-Chief JESPER BENGTSSON; circ. 154,700.

SIA-Skogsindustriarbetaren: Olof Palmesgt. 31, POB 1138, 111 81 Stockholm; tel. (8) 701-77-90; fax (8) 411-27-42; e-mail sia@skogstrafacket.org; monthly; forestry; circ. 69,100.

SIF-Tidningen: SIF-huset, Olof Palmesgt. 17, 105 32 Stockholm; tel. (8) 508-970-00; fax (8) 508-970-12; e-mail bjorn.oijer@sif.se; internet www.siftidn.sif.se; 19 a year; organ of the Union of Clerical and Technical Employees; Editor-in-Chief BJORN OIJER; circ. 331,800.

Skog & Såg: Sag i Syd, POB 37, 551 12 Jönköping; tel. (36) 34-30-00; fax (36) 12-86-10; f. 1966; 4 a year; sawmills and forestry; Editor HENRIK ASPLUND; circ. 75,000.

SKTF-Tidningen: POB 7825, 103 97 Stockholm; tel. (8) 789-63-00; fax (8) 789-64-79; e-mail sktftidningen@sktf.se; internet www.sktftidningen.nu; 20 a year; organ of the Union of Municipal Employees; Editor KENT KÄLLQVIST; circ. 182,800.

Sunt Förnuft: 114 95 Stockholm; tel. (8) 613-17-00; fax (8) 21-38-58; 8 a year; tax-payers' magazine; circ. 175,100.

Svensk Bokhandel (Journal of the Swedish Book Trade): Birkagt. 16c, POB 6888, 113 86 Stockholm; tel. (8) 545-417-70; fax (8) 545-417-75; e-mail redaktion@svb.se; internet www.svb.se; co-publ. by Swedish Publrs' Asscn and Swedish Booksellers' Asscn, for booksellers, publishers, antiquarians and librarians; Editor LARS WINKLER; circ. 4,400.

Svensk Golf: POB 84, 182 11 Danderyd; tel. (8) 622-15-00; fax (8) 622-69-30; e-mail info@golf.se; internet www.golf.se; monthly; golf; Editor TOBIAS BERGMAN; circ. 353,000.

Svensk Jakt: Skedhults Säteri, 575 96 Eksjö; tel. (381) 371-80; fax (381) 371-85; e-mail svenskjakt@telia.com; internet www.jagareforbundet.se/svenskjakt; f. 1862; 11 a year; for hunters and dog-breeders; circ. 157,800 (2004).

Sveriges Natur: POB 4625, 116 91 Stockholm; tel. (8) 702-65-00; fax (8) 702-27-02; e-mail sveriges.natur@snf.se; internet www2.snf.se/sveriges-natur; f. 1909; 5 a year; organ of Swedish Society for Nature Conservation; Editor CARL-AXEL FALL; circ. 120,000.

Tidningen C: POB 2200, 103 15 Stockholm; tel. (8) 617-38-30; fax (8) 617-38-10; e-mail c.redaktionen@centrepartiet.se; f. 1929; 10 a year; organ of the Centre Party; Editor EVA-KANN LIND; circ. 68,000.

Transportarbetaren: POB 714, 101 33 Stockholm; tel. (8) 723-77-00; fax (8) 723-00-76; 11 a year; organ of the Swedish Transport Workers' Union; Editor JAN LINDKVIST; circ. 72,000.

Turist: 101 20 Stockholm; tel. (8) 463-21-00; 6 a year; tourism and travel; Editor MONIKA TROZELL; circ. 215,000.

NEWS AGENCIES

Svenska Nyhetsbyrån (Swedish Conservative Press Agency): POB 3553, 103 69 Stockholm; tel. (8) 14-07-50; fax (8) 10-10-48; e-mail red@snb.se; internet www.snb.se; Pres. FREDRIK HAAGE; Editor-in-Chief and Dir PER SELSTAM.

Svensk-Internationella Pressbyrån AB (SIP) (Swedish-International Press Bureau): Stymansgt. 4, 114 54 Stockholm; tel. (8) 528-088-10; fax (8) 528-088-30; e-mail ld@publicitet.com; internet www.publicitet.se; f. 1927; Editor-in-Chief CHRISTER LIEDHOLM.

Tidningarnas Telegrambyrå (Swedish News Agency): Kungsholmsgt. 5, 105 12 Stockholm; tel. (8) 692-26-00; fax (8) 651-53-77; e-mail redaktionen@tt.se; internet www.tt.se; f. 1921; co-operative news agency, working in conjunction with Reuters, AFP, the 'Groupe 39' agencies, dpa and other telegraph agencies; Chair. GUNNAR STRÖMBLAD; Gen. Man. and Editor-in-Chief EBBA LINDSÖ.

PRESS ASSOCIATIONS

Pre Cent (Centre Party's Press Agency): POB 2033, 103 11 Stockholm; tel. (8) 786-48-84; fax (8) 24-30-04; e-mail red@precent.se; f. 1987; Editor-in-Chief JIMMY DOMINIUS; 33 mems.

Svenska Journalistförbundet (Swedish Union of Journalists): POB 1116, 111 81 Stockholm; tel. (8) 613-75-00; fax (8) 21-26-80; e-mail kansliet@sjf.se; internet www.sjf.se; f. 1901; Pres. ANITA VAHLBERG; 19,000 mems.

Svenska Tidningsutgivareföreningen (Swedish Newspaper Publishers' Asscn): Kungsholmstorg 5, POB 22500, 104 22 Stockholm; tel. (8) 692-46-00; fax (8) 692-46-38; e-mail info@tu.se; internet www.tu.se; f. 1898; Man. Dir PÄR FAGERSTRÖM; 200 mems.

Sveriges Tidskrifter (Swedish Magazine Publishers' Asscn): Vasagt. 50, 111 20 Stockholm; tel. (8) 545-298-90; fax (8) 14-98-65; e-mail info@sverigestidskrifter.se; internet www.sverigestidskrifter.se; f. 1943; Man. Dir LARS STRANDBERG.

Sveriges Vänsterpressförening (Liberal Press Asscn): 901 70 Umeå; tel. (90) 15-10-00; fax (90) 77-46-47; f. 1905; Pres. OLOF KLEBERG; Sec. MATS OLOFSSON; c. 130 mems.

SWEDEN

Publishers

Alfabeta Bokförlag AB: POB 4284, 102 66 Stockholm; tel. (8) 714-36-30; fax (8) 643-24-31; e-mail info@alfamedia.se; internet www.alfamedia.se; fiction, psychology, biography, cinema, art, music, travel guides, children's books; Man. Dir DAG HERNRIED.

Bokförlaget Atlantis AB: Sturegt. 24, 114 36 Stockholm; tel. (8) 545-660-70; fax (8) 545-660-71; e-mail mail@atlantisbok.se; internet www.atlantisbok.se; f. 1977; fiction, non-fiction, art; Man. Dir PETER LUTHERSSON.

Berghs Förlag AB: Observatoriegt. 10, POB 45084, 104 30 Stockholm; tel. (8) 31-65-59; fax (8) 32-77-45; f. 1954; non-fiction for adults and children, picture books and fiction for children, craft books, popular science, 'New Age' literature; Man. Dir CARL HAFSTRÖM.

Bonnier Carlsen Bokförlag AB: POB 3159, 103 63 Stockholm; tel. (8) 696-89-30; fax (8) 696-89-31; e-mail info@carlsen.bonnier.se; internet www.bonniercarlsen.se; picture books, juvenile books, non-fiction, board books, comics; Man. Dir ANNA BORNÉ MINBERGER.

Bonnierförlagen AB: Sveavägen 56, POB 3159, 103 63 Stockholm; tel. (8) 696-80-00; fax (8) 696-80-46; e-mail info@bok.bonnier.se; internet www.bok.bonnier.se; f. 1837; fiction, non-fiction, encyclopaedias, reference books, quality paperbacks; includes Albert Bonniers Förlag AB, Bonnier Utbildning AB, Bokförlaget Forum AB, AB Wahlström & Widstrand, Autumn Publishing, Bonnier Audio, Bonnier Carlsen, Bokförlaget Rebus, Bokförlaget Max Ström; Chair. JACOB DALBORG; Man. Dir CHRISTIAN BUJÁN.

Bokförlaget Bra Böcker: POB 892, 201 80 Malmö; tel. (40) 665-46-00; f. 1965; Man. Dir JOHAN MÖLLER.

Brombergs Bokförlag AB: Hantverkargt. 26, POB 12886, 112 98 Stockholm; tel. (8) 562-620-80; fax (8) 562-620-85; e-mail info@brombergs.se; internet www.brombergs.se; quality fiction, non-fiction; Man. Dir DOROTEA BROMBERG.

Brutus Östlings Bokförlag Symposion: POB 148, 241 22 Eslöv; tel. (413) 609-90; e-mail order.symposion@swipnet.se.

Carlsson Bokförlag AB: Stora Nygt. 31, 111 27 Stockholm; tel. (8) 411-23-49; fax (8) 796-84-57; art, photography, ethnology, history, politics; Man. Dir TRYGVE CARLSSON.

Bokförlaget DN: POB 703 21, 107 23 Stockholm; tel. (8) 696-87-90; fax (8) 696-83-67; e-mail ma; internet www.bokforlagetdn.se; publishing division of Dagens Nyheter newspaper; Publr and Pres. ALBERT BONNDER.

Eriksson & Lindgren Bokförlag AB: St Eriksgt. 14, POB 12085, 102 23 Stockholm; tel. (8) 652-32-26; fax (8) 652-32-23; e-mail info@eriksson-lindgren.se; internet www.eriksson-lindgren.se; f. 1990; Man. Dir GUNILLA HALKJÆR OLOFSSON.

Bokförlaget T. Fischer & Co: Näs Gård, 762 93 Rimbo; tel. (175) 620-52; fax (175) 620-54; e-mail bokforlaget@fischer-co.se; internet www.fischer-co.se; non-fiction; Man. Dir KIM MODIN.

Forum Publishers: POB 70321, 107 23 Stockholm; tel. (8) 696-84-40; fax (8) 696-83-67; internet www.forum.se; f. 1943; general fiction, non-fiction; Man. Dir MAGNUS NYTELL.

Gedins Förlag: Tystagt. 10, 115 20 Stockholm; tel. (8) 662-15-51; fax (8) 663-70-73; fiction, non-fiction, poetry, food, psychology, politics; Man. Dir PER I. GEDIN.

Gehrmans Musikförlag AB: POB 42026, 126 12 Stockholm; tel. (8) 610-06-00; fax (8) 610-06-27; e-mail info@gehrmans.se; internet www.gehrmans.se; f. 1893; orchestral and choral music; general music publishing; Pres. JOE LINDSTRÖM; CEO KETTIL SKARBY.

ICA-förlaget AB: 721 85 Västerås; tel. (21) 19-40-00; fax (21) 19-42-83; e-mail bok@publ.ica.se; internet www.publ.ica.se; f. 1945; non-fiction, cookery, handicrafts, gardening, natural history, popular psychology, health, domestic animals, sports; Publr GÖRAN SUNEHAG; Man. Dir HANS RINKEBORN.

Informationsförlaget: Sveavägen 61, POB 6884, 113 86 Stockholm; tel. (8) 545-560-50; fax (8) 31-39-03; f. 1979; publishers of books for cos and orgs on demand; reference, encyclopaedias, gastronomy, illustrated books; Man. Dir ULF HEIMDAHL.

Liber AB: 113 98 Stockholm; tel. (8) 690-90-00; fax (8) 690-94-70; e-mail export@liber.se; internet www.liber.se; general and educational publishing; Man. Dir JERKER NILSSON.

Liber Hermods AB: Råsundavägen 18, 113 98 Stockholm; tel. (8) 690-94-00; e-mail helena.holmstrom@liber.se; f. 1993; Man. Dir HELENA HOLMSTRÖM.

J. A. Lindblads Bokförlags AB: Warfvingesvägen 30, POB 30195, 104 25 Stockholm; tel. (8) 618-78-98; e-mail bertil.wahlstrom@lindblads.se; internet www.lindblads.se; fiction, non-fiction, juvenile, paperbacks; Man. Dir BERTIL WAHLSTRÖM.

Abraham Lundquist AB Musikförlag: POB 93, 182 11 Danderyd; tel. (8) 732-92-35; fax (8) 732-92-38; e-mail info@abrahamlundquist.se; internet www.abrahamlundquist.se; f. 1838; music; Man. Dir (vacant).

Directory

Bokförlaget Natur och Kultur: Karlavägen 31, POB 27323, 102 54 Stockholm; tel. (8) 453-86-00; fax (8) 453-87-90; e-mail info@nok.se; internet www.nok.se; f. 1922; textbooks, general literature, fiction; Man. Dir GUNN JOHANSSON.

Norstedts Förlag AB: Tryckerigt. 4, POB 2052, 103 12 Stockholm; tel. (8) 769-87-50; fax (8) 769-87-64; e-mail info@norstedts.se; internet www.norstedts.se; f. 1823; fiction, non-fiction; Man. Dir SVANTE WEYLER.

Norstedts Juridik AB: 106 47 Stockholm; tel. (8) 690-90-90; fax (8) 690-91-91; e-mail info.fritzes@nj.se; internet www.nj.se; f. 1837; owned by Wolters Kluwer NV (Netherlands); fmrly C. E. Fritzes AB; CEO PATRIK HOGBERG.

Bokförlaget Opal AB: Tegelbergsvägen 31, POB 20113, 161 02 Bromma; tel. (8) 28-21-79; fax (8) 29-66-23; e-mail opal@opal.se; internet www.opal.se; f. 1973; Man. Dir BENGT CHRISTELL.

Ordfront Förlag AB: Bellmansgt. 30, POB 17506, 118 91 Stockholm; tel. (8) 462-44-00; fax (8) 462-44-90; e-mail info@ordfront.se; internet www.ordfront.se; fiction, history, politics; Man. Dir JAN-ERIK PETTERSSON.

Prisma Bokförlaget: Tryckerigt. 4, POB 2052, 103 12 Stockholm; tel. (8) 769-89-00; fax (8) 769-89-13; e-mail info@prismabok.se; internet www.prismabok.se; f. 1963; Dir VIVECA EKELUND.

Rabén & Sjögren Bokförlag: Tryckerigt. 4, POB 2052, 103 12 Stockholm; tel. (8) 789-30-00; fax (8) 789-30-52; e-mail raben-sjogren@raben.se; internet www.raben.se; f. 1942; general, juvenile; Dir SUZANNE ÖHMAN-SUNDEN.

Bokförlaget Semic: Landsvägen 57, POB 1243, 172 25 Sundbyberg; tel. (8) 799-30-50; fax (8) 799-30-64; e-mail info@semic.se; internet www.semic.se; handbooks, calendars, comic magazines, juvenile; Pres. RICKARD EKSTRÖM.

Stenströms Bokförlag AB: Linnégt. 98, POB 24086, 104 50 Stockholm; tel. (8) 663-76-01; fax (8) 663-22-01; f. 1983; Man. Dir BENGT STENSTRÖM.

Streiffert Förlag AB: Skeppargt. 27, POB 5334, 102 47 Stockholm; tel. (8) 661-58-80; fax (8) 783-04-33; e-mail info@streiffert.se; internet www.streiffert.se; f. 1990; Man. Dir BO STREIFFERT.

Svenska Förlaget liv & ledarskap AB: POB 3313, 103 66 Stockholm; e-mail kundservice@svenskaforlaget.com; internet www.svenskaforlaget.com; non-fiction.

Timbro/SFN: POB 5234, 102 45 Stockholm; tel. (8) 587-898-00; fax (8) 587-898-55; e-mail info@timbro.se; internet www.timbro.com; economics, political science; Pres. MARIA RANKKA.

Verbum Förlag AB: St Paulsgt. 2, POB 15169, 104 65 Stockholm; tel. (8) 743-65-00; fax (8) 641-45-85; e-mail info.forlag@verbum.se; internet www.verbum.se; f. 1911; theology, fiction, juvenile, music; Man. Dir CLAES-GÖRAN GUNNARSSON.

AB Wahlström & Widstrand: Sturegt. 32, POB 5587, 114 85 Stockholm; tel. (8) 696-84-80; fax (8) 696-83-80; f. 1884; fiction, non-fiction, biography, history, science, paperbacks; Man. Dir UNN PALM.

PUBLISHERS' ASSOCIATIONS

Föreningen Svenska Läromedelsproducenter (Swedish Asscn of Educational Publishers): Drottninggt. 97, 113 60 Stockholm; tel. (8) 736-19-40; fax (8) 736-19-44; e-mail fsl@forlagskansli.se; f. 1973; Dir JERKER FRANKSSON; 25 mems.

Svenska Förläggareföreningen (Swedish Publishers' Asscn): Drottninggt. 97, 113 60 Stockholm; tel. (8) 736-19-40; fax (8) 736-19-44; e-mail info@forlaggare.se; internet www.forlaggare.se; f. 1843; Chair. LARS GRAHN; Dir KJELL BOHLUND; 68 mems.

Broadcasting and Communications

TELECOMMUNICATIONS

Regulatory Authority

Post-och Telestyrelsen (PTS): POB 5398, Birger Jarlsgt. 16, 102 49 Stockholm; tel. (8) 678-55-00; fax (8) 678-55-05; e-mail pts@pts.se; internet www.pts.se; Dir-Gen. MARIANNE TRESCHOW.

Major Service Providers

Tele 2 AB: Skeppsbron 18, POB 2094, 103 13 Stockholm; tel. (85) 562-000-60; fax (85) 562-000-40; e-mail press.relations@tele2.com; internet www.tele2.com; f. 1993; Pres. and CEO LARS-JOHAN JARNHEIMER.

Telefonaktiebolaget LM Ericsson: Torshamngt. 23, 164 83 Stockholm; tel. (8) 719-00-00; fax (8) 719-19-76; e-mail investor.relations.se@ericsson.com; internet www.ericsson.com; parent co of the Ericsson group; mobile and fixed network provider; represented in

SWEDEN
Directory

140 countries; Chair. MICHAEL TRESCHOW; CEO CARL-HENRIC SVANBERG.

TeliaSonera AB: Sturegt. 1, 106 63 Stockholm; tel. (8) 504-550-00; fax (8) 504-550-01; e-mail teliasonera@teliasonera.se; internet www.teliasonera.se; f. by merger of Telia AB (Sweden) with Sonera Ltd (Finland); 37.3% owned by Govt of Sweden, 13.7% by Govt of Finland, 49.0% by individual and institutional investors; Chair. TOM VON WEYMARN; Pres. and CEO LARS NYBERG.

Telenor Sverige AB: Campus Gräsvik 12, 371 80 Karlskrona; tel. (4) 553-310-00; fax (4) 553-312-22; internet www.telenor.se; fmrly Vodafone Sverige AB; provides mobile cellular communications under brand name *Djuice*, as well as broadband internet access and digital television services; acquired by Telenor AS (Norway) in 2005; Man. Dir JOHAN LINDGREN.

Teracom AB: Esplanaden 9, POB 1366, 172 27 Sundbyberg; tel. (8) 555-420-00; fax (8) 555-420-01; e-mail webmaster@teracom.se; internet www.teracom.se; provides digital television and radio services, fixed-line telephony and broadband internet access; Pres. HÅKAN TIDLUND; Dir CRISTER FRITZSON.

BROADCASTING

Until the end of 1992 public service radio and television were organized within the state broadcasting corporation, Sveriges Radio AB, a public service organization financed by licence fees; this operated two national television channels and three national radio channels, together with 24 local radio stations. On 1 January 1993 the state corporation was replaced by three companies, Sveriges Radio AB, Sveriges Television AB, and Sveriges Utbildningsradio AB, responsible for radio, television, and educational radio and television, respectively. The operations of these companies are regulated by law and by agreements with the Government. From 1 January 1994 the three companies came into the ownership of three foundations.

Radio

There are four public service radio channels, as well as neighbourhood radio stations and private local radio stations (financed by advertising).

IBRA Radio AB: POB Regulatorvägen 11, Flemingsberg, 141 99 Stockholm; tel. (8) 608-96-00; fax (8) 608-96-50; e-mail info@ibra.se; internet www.ibra.se; non-commercial private Christian co broadcasting to all continents; Pres. JACK-TOMMY ARDENFORS; Dir HANS OLOFSSON.

Sveriges Radio AB (SR): Oxenstiernsgt. 20, 105 10 Stockholm; tel. (8) 784-50-00; fax (8) 784-15-00; e-mail mikael.nilsson@sr.se; internet www.sr.se; f. 1993; independent co responsible for national radio broadcasting; Man. Dir KERSTIN BRUNNBERG.

Sveriges Utbildningsradio AB: 113 95 Stockholm; tel. (8) 784-40-00; fax (8) 784-43-91; e-mail Kundtjanst@ur.se; internet www.ur.se; f. 1978; public service co responsible for educational broadcasting on radio and television; CEO CHRISTINA BJÖRK.

Television

There are two public service television channels (SVT 1 and SVT 2). The broadcasts are financed by licence fees. In 1991 the Government awarded the licence for a third terrestrial nation-wide television channel to TV 4 (which is financed by advertising). Television channels transmitted by satellite and cable, and directed at the Swedish audience, include: TV 3, Kanal 5, TV 6, Kanal 9, Z-TV, and the film channels TV 1000, FilmMax, Filmnet Plus and Filmnet Movie.

Kanal 5: Rådmansgt. 42, 114 99 Stockholm; tel. (8) 674-15-00; fax (8) 612-05-95; e-mail info@kanal5.se; internet kanal5.se; commercial satellite channel; owned by ProSiebenSat1 (Germany); Dir-Gen. JONAS SJÖGREN.

Sveriges Television AB (SVT): TH T2, Oxenstiernsgt. 26-34, 105 10 Stockholm; tel. (8) 784-00-00; fax (8) 784-15-00; e-mail eva.hamilton@svt.se; internet www.svt.se; f. 1956; independent; operates seven channels: SVT1, SVT2, SVT24, SVT Barnkanalen, Kunskapskanalen, SVT Europa and SVT HD; Dir-Gen. EVA HAMILTON.

Sveriges Utbildningsradio AB: see Radio.

TV 3: Stockholm; tel. (8) 562-023-00; fax (8) 562-023-30; e-mail info@tv3.se; internet www.tv3.se; commercial satellite channel.

TV 4: Tegeluddsvägen 3–5, 115 79 Stockholm; tel. (8) 459-40-00; fax (8) 459-44-44; internet www.tv4.se; commercial terrestrial channel; Man. Dir TORSTEN LARSSON.

Finance
(cap. = capital; res = reserves; dep. = deposits; m. = million; brs = branches; amounts in kronor unless otherwise stated)

SUPERVISORY BODY

Finansinspektionen (Financial Supervisory Authority): POB 7821, Brunnsgt. 3, 103 97 Stockholm; tel. (8) 787-80-00; fax (8) 24-13-35; e-mail finansinspektionen@fi.se; internet www.fi.se; f. 1991 by merger of Bankinspektionen (Bank Inspection Board, f. 1907) and Försäkringsinspektionen (Private Insurance Supervisory Service, f. 1904), for the supervision of commercial and savings banks, financial companies, insurance companies, insurance brokers, friendly societies, mortgage institutions, securities firms and unit trusts, the stock exchange and clearing functions, the securities registry centre and the information registry centre; Chair. BENGT WESTERBERG; Dir-Gen. INGRID BONDE.

BANKING

In 2005 there were 124 banks in Sweden, with total assets of 4,539,904m. kronor.

Central Bank

Sveriges Riksbank: Brunkebergstorg 11, 103 37 Stockholm; tel. (8) 787-00-00; fax (8) 21-05-31; e-mail registratorn@riksbank.se; internet www.riksbank.se; f. 1668; bank of issue; led by an executive board of six members (including a Governor), appointed by a General Council of 11 members, all of whom are, in turn, appointed by the Riksdag; cap. 1,000m., res 53,769m., dep. 14,093m. (Dec. 2006); Chair., Gen. Council JOHAN GERNANDT; Gov. STEFAN INGVES; 10 brs.

Commercial Banks

Danske Bank i Sverige: Norrmalmstorg 1, POB 7523, 103 92 Stockholm; tel. (8) 524-800-00; internet www.danskebank.se; f. 1837 as Östgöta Enskilda Bank; subsidiary of Den Danske Bank (Denmark); Chair. PETER STRAARUP; Pres. and CEO ULF LUNDAHL; 30 brs.

Nordea Bank AB: Smålandsgt. 17, 105 71 Stockholm; tel. (8) 614-78-00; fax (8) 20-08-46; internet www.nordea.com; f. 1974 as Post- och Kreditbanken; present name adopted 2001; part of Nordea Group; 19.9% owned by Swedish Govt; cap. €1,072m., res €4,055m., dep. €145,340m. (Dec. 2005); Chair. HANS DALBORG; CEO CHRISTIAN CLAUSEN; 252 brs in Sweden.

Skandinaviska Enskilda Banken AB (SEB): Kungsträdgårdsgt. 8, 106 40 Stockholm; tel. (8) 763-80-00; fax (8) 763-83-89; internet www.seb.se; f. 1972; cap. 6,872m., res 30,979m., dep. 1,600m. (Dec. 2006); Chair. MARCUS WALLENBERG; Pres. and Group CEO ANNIKA FALKENGREN; 260 brs.

Svenska Handelsbanken AB: Kungsträdgårdsgt. 2, 106 70 Stockholm; tel. (8) 701-10-00; fax (8) 701-24-37; e-mail info@handelsbanken.se; internet www.handelsbanken.se; f. 1871 as A. B. Stockholms Handelsbank; present name adopted 1956; cap. 2,888m., res 50,210m., dep. 1,630,212m. (Dec. 2006); Pres. and CEO PÄR BOMAN; 459 brs in Sweden.

Swedbank AB: Brunkebergstorg 8, 105 34 Stockholm; tel. (8) 585-900-00; fax (8) 796-80-92; internet www.swedbank.se; f. 1997 by merger of Föreningsbanken and Sparbanken Sverige; present name adopted 2006; cap. 10,823m., res 6,489m., dep. 635,810m. (Dec. 2006); Chair. CARL ERIC STÅLBERG; Pres. and CEO JAN LIDÉN; 470 brs in Sweden.

Banking Organization

Svenska Bankföreningen (Swedish Bankers' Asscn): Regeringsgt. 38, POB 7603, 103 94 Stockholm; tel. (8) 453-44-00; fax (8) 796-93-95; e-mail info@bankforeningen.se; internet www.bankforeningen.se; f. 1880; Pres. JAN LIDÉN; Man. Dir ULLA LUNDQUIST; 29 mems.

STOCK EXCHANGE

NASDAQ OMX Nordic Exchange Stockholm: Tullvaktsvägen 15, 105 78 Stockholm; tel. (8) 405-60-00; fax (8) 405-60-01; internet www.nasdaqomx.com; f. 1863 under govt charter; automated trading system introduced by 1990; Stockholmsbörsen merged with OMX AB in 1998; acquired by NASDAQ Stock Market, Inc (USA) in 2008; part of OMX Nordic Exchange with the Copenhagen (Denmark), Helsinki (Finland) and Reykjavík (Iceland) exchanges; Group CEO ROBERT GREIFELD; Group Pres. MAGNUS BÖCKER.

INSURANCE

The total assets of Swedish insurance companies in 2005 was 440,147m. kronor.

SWEDEN

Principal Insurance Companies

Folksam: Bohusgt. 14, 106 60 Stockholm; tel. (8) 772-60-00; fax (8) 702-99-22; e-mail info@floksam.se; internet www.folksam.se; f. 1908; all branches of life and non-life insurance; Pres. and CEO ANDERS SUNDSTRÖM.

Skandia Insurance Co Ltd: Sveavägen 44, 103 50 Stockholm; tel. (8) 788-10-00; fax (8) 788-30-80; e-mail contact@oldmutual.com; internet www.skandia.com; f. 1855; owned by Old Mutual PLC (United Kingdom); all branches of life insurance; Chair. LARS OTTERBECK; Pres. and CEO JULIAN ROBERTS.

Trygg-Hansa: Flemminggt. 18, 106 26 Stockholm; tel. (8) 693-10-00; fax (8) 650-93-67; internet www.trygghansa.se; f. 1828; all branches of non-life insurance; owned by Codan Forsikring A/S (Denmark); CEO RICKARD GUSTAFSON.

Insurance Associations

Konsumernternas försäkringsbyrå (Swedish Consumers' Insurance Bureau): Karlavägen 108, 104 51 Stockholm; tel. (8) 22-58-00; fax (8) 24-88-91; e-mail angela.olsson@konsumenternas.se; internet www.konsumenternas.se; f. 1979; provides free advice to consumers on various insurance matters; principles are the Konsumentverket (Swedish Consumer Agency), the Finansinpektionen (Financial Supervisory Authority) and the Sveriges Försäkringsförbund (Swedish Insurance Fed.); Chair. GUNNAR OLSSON.

Svenska Försäkringsföreningen (Swedish Insurance Society): Karlavägen 108, POB 24213, 104 51 Stockholm; tel. (8) 522-789-00; fax (8) 522-789-95; e-mail info@forsakringsforeningen.se; internet www.forsakringsforeningen.se; f. 1875; promotes sound development of the Swedish insurance business; Chair. LARS ROSÉN; Sec. SARA RÅSMAR.

Sveriges Försäkringsförbund (Swedish Insurance Federation): Karlavägen 108, POB 24043, 104 50 Stockholm; tel. (8) 522-785-00; fax (8) 522-785-15; e-mail info@forsakringsforbundet.com; internet www.forsakringsforbundet.com; Chair. TORBJÖRN MAGNUSSON; Man. Dir ANDERS BESKOW (acting).

Trade and Industry

GOVERNMENT AGENCIES

Arbetsmarknadsstyrelsen (AMS) (Labour Market Board): 171 99 Solna, Stockholm; tel. (8) 730-60-00; fax (8) 27-83-68; e-mail ams-infocenter@ams.amv.se; internet www.ams.se; f. 1948; central authority within the National Labour Market Administration (Arbetsmarknadsverket—AMV); autonomous public agency, responsible for administration of Sweden's labour market; main aims: to provide social means for easing structural change in the economy, to organize labour market by balancing requirements of workers and employers, and to uphold commitment to concept of full employment; board mems appointed by Govt, employers and trades unions; Dir-Gen. ANDERS L. JOHANSSON.

Exportrådet (Swedish Trade Council): POB 240, 101 24 Stockholm; tel. (8) 588-660-00; fax (8) 588-661-90; e-mail infocenter@swedishtrade.se; internet www.swedishtrade.se; f. 1972; Chair. ANDERS NARVINGER; Man. Dir ULF BERG.

Nutek (Swedish Agency for Economic and Regional Growth): Götgatan 74, 116 21 Stockholm; tel. (8) 681-91-00; fax (8) 19-68-26; e-mail nutek@nutek.se; internet www.nutek.se; Dir Gen. SUNE HALVARSSON (acting).

CHAMBERS OF COMMERCE

Handelskammaren i Jönköpings Län: Elmiavägen 11, 554 54 Jönköping; tel. (36) 30-14-30; fax (36) 12-95-79; e-mail info@jonkoping.cci.se; f. 1975; Pres. JOHAN SVEDBERG; Man. Dir GÖRAN KINNANDER; 450 mems.

Handelskammaren Mälardalen: POB 8044, 700 08 Örebro; tel. (19) 16-61-60; fax (19) 11-77-50; e-mail info@malardalen.cci.se; internet www.malardalen.cci.se; f. 1907; Pres. EGON LINDEROTH; Sec. SVEN SVENSSON.

Handelskammaren Mittsverige (Mid-Sweden Chamber of Commerce): Kyrkogt. 26, 852 32 Sundsvall; tel. (60) 17-18-80; fax (60) 61-86-40; e-mail sdl@midchamber.se; internet www.midchamber.se; f. 1913; Chair. ROLF JOHANNESSON; Man. Dir DICK JANSSON; 400 mems.

Handelskammaren Värmland: Södra Kyrkogt. 6, 652 24 Karlstad; tel. (54) 22-14-80; fax (54) 22-14-90; e-mail info@handelskammarenvarmland.se; internet www.handelskammarenvarmland.se; f. 1912; Pres. JOHAN ENGSTRÖM; Sec. ULF LJUNGDAHL; 1,200 mems.

Mellansvenska Handelskammaren: POB 296, 801 04 Gävle; tel. (26) 66-20-80; fax (26) 66-20-99; e-mail chamber@mhk.cci.se; internet www.mhk.cci.se; f. 1907; Pres. OVE ANONSEN; Man. Dir ANDERS FRANCK; 465 mems.

Norrbottens Handelskammare: Storgt. 9, 972 38 Luleå; tel. (920) 122-10; fax (920) 94-857; e-mail lundgren@north.cci.se; internet www.north.cci.se; f. 1904; Chair. INGA-LILL HOLMGREN; Dir STURE LUNDGREN.

Östsvenska Handelskammaren: Nya Rådstugugt. 3, 602 24 Norrköping; tel. (11) 28-50-30; fax (11) 13-77-19; e-mail info@east.cci.se; internet www.east.cci.se; f. 1913; covers Östergötland, Södermanland and Gotland; c. 600 mem. cos; Man. Dir LARS ERICHS.

Stockholms Handelskammare: V. Trädgårdsgt. 9, POB 16050, 103 21 Stockholm; tel. (8) 555-100-00; fax (8) 566-316-20; e-mail info@chamber.se; internet www.chamber.se; f. 1902; Pres. MARGARETA BOSVED; Dir PETER EGARDT.

Sydsvenska Handelskammaren (Chamber of Commerce and Industry of Southern Sweden): Skeppsbron 2, 211 20 Malmö; tel. (40) 73-550; fax (40) 611-86-09; e-mail info@handelskammaren.com; f. 1905; Pres. HANS CAVALLI-BJÖRKMAN; Man. Dir STEPHAN MÜCHLER; 3,050 mems.

Västsvenska Industri- och Handelskammaren: POB 5253, 402 25 Göteborg; tel. (31) 83-59-00; fax (31) 83-59-36; e-mail info@handelskammaren.net; internet www.handelskammaren.net; f. 1661; Man. Dir ANDERS KÄLLSTRÖM; c. 2,600 mems.

INDUSTRIAL AND TRADE ASSOCIATIONS

Svenskt Näringsliv (Confederation of Swedish Enterprise): Storgt. 19, 114 82 Stockholm; tel. (8) 553-430-00; fax (8) 553-430-99; e-mail info@svensktnaringsliv.se; internet www.svensktnaringsliv.se; f. 2001 by merger of Sveriges Industriförbund (f. 1910) and Svenska Arbetsgivareföreningen (f. 1902); central org. representing Swedish business and industry; Pres. SÖREN GYLL; Vice-Pres BJÖRN ANDERSSON, SIGRUN HJELMQUIST, MICHAEL TRESCHOW; Dir-Gen. GÖRAN TUNHAMMAR; consists of 50 mem. asscns, representing c. 54,000 cos.

Företagarnas Riksorganisation (Federation of Private Enterprises): 106 67 Stockholm; tel. (8) 406-17-00; fax (8) 24-55-26; e-mail info@foretagarna.se; internet www.foretagarna.se; f. 1990; Chair. JAN CARLZON; Man. Dir ANNA-STINA NORDMARK; 55,000 mems.

Grafiska Företagens Förbund (Graphic Companies' Federation): Karlavägen 108, POB 24184, 104 51 Stockholm; tel. (8) 762-68-00; fax (8) 611-08-28; e-mail info@grafiska.se; internet www.grafiska.se; Chair. LARS FREDRIKSON; Man. Dir LARS JOSEFSSON.

Järnverksföreningen (Swedish Steel Producers' and Distributors' Asscn): Kungsträdgårdsgt. 10, POB 1721, 111 87 Stockholm; f. 1889; Pres. BENGT LINDAHL; Sec. MATHIAS TERNELL; 35 mems.

Jernkontoret (Steel Producers' Asscn): Kungsträdgårdsgt. 10, POB 1721, 111 87 Stockholm; tel. (8) 679-17-00; fax (8) 611-20-89; e-mail office@jernkontoret.se; internet www.jernkontoret.se; f. 1747; Man. Dir ELISABETH NILSSON.

Lantbrukarnas Riksförbund (LRF) (Federation of Swedish Farmers): Klara Östra Kyrkogt. 12, 105 33 Stockholm; tel. (0) 771-573-573; e-mail info@lrf.se; internet www.lrf.se; 163,000 mems.

Plast- & Kemiföretagen (Swedish Plastics and Chemicals Asscn): Storgt. 19, POB 5501, 114 85 Stockholm; tel. (8) 783-86-00; fax (8) 663-63-23; e-mail info@plastkemiforetagen.se; internet www.plastkemiforetagen.se; f. 1917; Pres. TORD SVEDBERG; Man. Dir OWE FREDHOLM; 265 mems.

Skogsindustrierna (Swedish Forest Industries' Federation): POB 55525, 102 04 Stockholm; tel. (8) 762-72-60; fax (8) 611-71-22; e-mail terese.sundberg@skogsindustrierna.org; internet www.forestindustries.se; Chair. CHRISTER AGREN; Dir-Gen. MARIE S. ARWIDSON.

SveMin (Föreningen för gruvor, mineral- och metallproducenter i Sverige) (Swedish Asscn of Mines, Mineral and Metal Producers): POB 1721, 111 87 Stockholm; tel. (8) 762-67-35; fax 8) 611-62-64; e-mail info@svemin.se; internet www.svemin.se; f. 2004; Pres. MARTIN IVERT; Man. Dir BENGT HULDL; 20 mem. cos.

Svensk Handel (Swedish Federation of Trade): 103 29 Stockholm; tel. (8) 762-77-00; fax (8) 762-77-77; e-mail info@svenskhandel.se; internet www.svenskhandel.se; Chair. KENNETH BENGTSSON; Man. Dir DAG KLACKENBERG; 13,000 mems.

Svensk Industriförening (Swedish Industry Asscn): Klara Norra Kyrkogt. 31, POB 22307, 104 22 Stockholm; tel. (8) 440-11-70; fax (8) 440-11-71; e-mail info@sinf.se; internet www.sinf.se; f. 1941; Man. Dir ANDERS EKDAHL; 1,500 mems.

Svenska Garveriidkareföreningen (Swedish Tanners' Asscn): c/o Elmo Leather AB, 512 81 Svenljunga; tel. (325) 66-14-00; fax (325) 61-10-04; f. 1901; Chair. BJÖRN JOHANSSON; Man. Dir C. LENNARTSON; 5 mems.

Svenska Glasbruksföreningen (Swedish Crystal Manufacturers' Asscn): POB 5501, 114 85 Stockholm; tel. (8) 783-86-00; fax (8) 663-63-23; e-mail jan.eriksson@plastkemiforetagen.se; internet www.plastkemiforetagen.se; Chair. GEORG WERGEMAN.

Svenska Skofabrikantföreningen (Swedish Shoe Manufacturers' Asscn): c/o Arbesko-Gruppen AB, POB 1642, 701 16 Örebro; tel. (19) 30-66-00; fax (19) 30-66-50; f. 1910.

TEKO (Textile and Clothing Industries' Asscn): Storgt. 5, POB 5510, 114 85 Stockholm; tel. (8) 762-68-80; fax (8) 762-68-87; e-mail teko@teko.se; internet www.teko.se; f. 1907; Chair. LARS. KARLSSON; Man. Dirs OLE TOFTEGAARD, KARL OLOF STENQVIST; 263 mems.

EMPLOYERS' ORGANIZATIONS

ALMEGA: Sturegat. 11, POB 55545, 102 04 Stockholm; tel. (8) 762-69-00; fax (8) 762-69-48; e-mail almega.epost@almega.se; internet www.almega.se; f. 1921; Chair. HÅKAN BRYNGELSON; Dir-Gen. JONAS MILTON; 8,900 mems.

ARBIO (Swedish Federation of Wood and Furniture Industry): Södra Blasieholmshamnen 4A, POB 16006, 103 21 Stockholm; tel. (8) 762-72-00; fax (8) 762-72-14; internet www.traindustrierna.org; Chair. BJÖRN HÄGGLUND; Man. Dir KARL-EWERT LIDMAN; 5,000 mems.

Biltrafikens Arbetsgivareförbund (Road Transport Employers): Blasieholmsgt. 4A, 111 48 Stockholm; tel. (8) 762-60-00; fax (8) 611-46-99; Chair. REINHOLD ÖHMAN; Man. Dir GÖRAN LJUNGSTRÖM; 5,330 mem. cos.

Byggnadsämnesförbundet (Building Material Manufacturers Employers): POB 16347, 103 26 Stockholm; tel. (8) 762-65-07; fax (8) 762-65-12; Chair. GULL-BRITT JONASSON; Man. Dir GUNNAR GÖTHBERG; 278 mem. cos.

Elektriska Installatörsorganisationen EIO (The Swedish Electrical Contractors' Association): POB 17537, 118 91 Stockholm; tel. (8) 762-75-00; fax (8) 668-86-17; e-mail info@eio.se; internet www.eio.se; Chair. GÖSTA ALLTHIN; Man. Dir HANS ENSTRÖM; 2,500 mem. cos.

Försäkringsbranschens Arbetsgivareorganisation (Insurance Employers): POB 24168, 104 51 Stockholm; tel. (8) 522-786-00; fax (8) 522-786-70; e-mail info@fao.se; internet www.fao.se; Chair. TOMMY PERSSON; Man. Dir ANNIKA LUNDIUS; 115 mem. cos.

Livsmedelsbranschens Arbetsgivareförbund (Food Producers): POB 16105, 103 22 Stockholm; tel. (8) 762-69-00; fax (8) 762-69-48; Chair. SUNE SIGVARDSSON; Man. Dir GUNNAR GÖTHBERG; 385 mem. cos.

Maskinentreprenörerna (Earth-Moving Contractors): POB 1609, 111 86 Stockholm; tel. (8) 762-70-65; fax (8) 611-85-41; Chair. ROLF GUNNARSSON; Man. Dir SVEN-OLA NILSSON; 3,703 mem. cos.

Medie- och Informationsarbetsgivarna (Media and Information Employers' Association): POB 16383, 103 27 Stockholm; tel. (8) 762-70-30; fax (8) 611-41-47; e-mail info@mediearbetsgivarna.org; internet www.mediearbetsgivarna.org; Chair. LENNART WIKLUND; Man. Dir CHARLOTT RICHARDSON; 400 mem. cos.

Motorbranschens Arbetsgivareförbund (Motor Trade Employers): Blasieholmsgt. 4A, POB 1621, 111 86 Stockholm; tel. (8) 762-71-00; fax (8) 611-46-99; e-mail info@transportgruppen.se; internet www.transportsgruppen.se; Chair. PER OLAV PERSSON; Dir PETER JEPPSSON; 2,138 mem. cos.

Petroleumbranschens Arbetsgivareförbund (Petroleum Industry Employers): Blasieholmsgt. 4A, POB 1621, 111 86 Stockholm; tel. (8) 762-60-00; fax (8) 611-46-99; f. 1936; Chair. HANS VON UTHMANN; Man. Dir GÖRAN LJUNGSTRÖM; 53 mem. cos.

Plåtslageriernas Riksförbund (Platers): Rosenlundsgt. 40, POB 17536, 118 91 Stockholm; tel. (8) 762-75-85; fax (8) 616-00-72; e-mail info@plr.se; internet www.plr.se; Chair. LARS SJÖBLOM; Man. Dir ROBERT KIEJSTUT; 808 mem. cos.

Samhallförbundet (Samhall Employers' Association): POB 16105, 103 22 Stockholm; tel. (8) 762-69-00; fax (8) 762-69-48; Chair. HÅKAN ANDERSSON; Man. Dir JOHAN RIMMERFELDT; 3 mem. cos.

Stål och Metall Arbetsgivareförbundet (Steel and Metal Industry Employers): Kungsträdgårdsgt. 10, POB 1721, 111 87 Stockholm; tel. (8) 762-67-35; fax (8) 611-62-64; e-mail info@metallgruppen.se; internet www.stalometall.se; f. 1906; Pres. PETER GOSSAS; Man. Dir BENGT HULDT; 200 mems with 44,000 employees.

SVEMEK (Welding Engineering): POB 1721, 111 87 Stockholm; tel. (8) 762-67-35; fax (8) 611-62-64; e-mail info@metallgruppen.se; internet www.svemek.se; fmrly Svets Mekaniska Arbetsgivareförbundet; Pres. GUNNAR SKÖLD; Man. Dir BENGT HULDT; 414 mems with 4,629 employees.

Sveriges Bageriförbund (Bakery and Confectionery Employers): POB 16141, 103 23 Stockholm; tel. (8) 762-60-00; fax (8) 678-66-64; e-mail kansli@bageri.se; internet www.bageri.se; f. 1900; Chair. MATS ROSÉU; Man. Dir BJÖRN HELLWAU; 570 mems.

Sveriges Byggindustrier (Swedish Construction Federation): Storgt. 19, POB 5054, 102 42 Stockholm; tel. (8) 698-58-00; fax (8) 698-59-00; e-mail info@bygg.org; internet www.bygg.org; Pres. BO ANTONI; 2,800 mem. cos.

Sveriges Hamnar (Ports): POB 1621, 111 86 Stockholm; tel. (8) 762-71-00; fax (8) 611-12-18; e-mail ports@transportgruppen.se; internet www.transportgruppen.se/sweports; f. 1906; Vice-Pres. MARIAV NYGREN; 53 mem. cos.

Teknikföretagen (Asscn of Swedish Engineering Industries): Storgt. 5, POB 5510, 114 85 Stockholm; tel. (8) 782-08-00; fax (8) 782-09-00; e-mail info@teknikforetagen.se; internet www.teknikforetagen.se; f. 1896 as VI Sveriges Verkstadsindustrier; Pres. LENNART NILSSON; Man. Dir ANDERS NARVINGER; 3,000 mem. cos.

Trä- och Möbelindustriförbundet (Swedish Wood Products Industry Employers' Asscn): POB 16006, 103 21 Stockholm; tel. (8) 762-72-00; fax (8) 611-60-25; e-mail info@traindustrin.org; Chair. LARS-ERIK SANDSTRÖM; Man. Dir KARL-EWERT LIDMAN; 700 mem. cos.

VVS företagen (Heating, Plumbing, Refrigeration and Insulation Employers): POB 47160, Mejerivägen 3, 100 74 Stockholm; tel. (8) 762-75-00; fax (8) 669-41-19; e-mail info@vvsforetagen.se; internet www.vvsforetagen.se; f. 1918; Chair. OSTEN LINDGREN; Man. Dir ROINE KRISTIANSON; 1,360 mems.

UTILITIES

Regulatory Authority

Energimyndigheten (Swedish Energy Agency): Kungsgt. 43, POB 310, 631 04 Eskilstuna; tel. (16) 544-20-00; fax (16) 544-20-99; e-mail registrator@energimyndigheten.se; internet www.energimyndigheten.se; f. 1998; monitors and advises electricity and natural gas cos, also undertakes research into renewable energy; Dir-Gen. THOMAS KORSFELDT.

Major Service Providers

Ängelholms Energi AB: Energigt. 1, 262 73 Ängelholm; tel. (431) 878-00.

Billeberga Kraft & Energi AB: Industrivägen 5, POB 53, 260 21 Billeberga; tel. (418) 45-08-50.

E.ON Sverige AB: Carl Gustafs väg 1, 205 09 Malmö; tel. (40) 25-50-00; e-mail info@eon.se; internet www.eon.se; f. 2001; frmly Sydkraft AB; part of E.ON Group (Germany); generation, distribution and supply of electricity and natural gas; Pres. and CEO LARS FRITHIOF.

Fortum AB: Hangövägen 19, 115 77 Stockholm; tel. (8) 671-70-00; fax (8) 671-77-77; e-mail ann.lindell.saeby@fortum.com; internet www.fortum.se; f. 1998 by merger of Imatran Voima and Neste Oyj (both Finland); mem. of Fortum Corpn (Finland), international energy co with core businesses in gas, power and heat; electricity production, distribution and supply; Chair. PETER FAGERNÄS; Dir-Gen. MIKAEL LILIUS.

Gullspång: Forsövägen 4, POB 33, 820 10 Arbrå; tel. (278) 277-00.

Helsingborg Energi: V. Sandgt. 4, POB 642, 251 06 Helsingborg; tel. (42) 490-32-70; fax (42) 490-32-56.

Höganäs Energi AB: Stadshuset, 253 82 Höganäs; tel. (42) 33-71-00.

KREAB Energi AB: Ljungbygt. 22, 260 70 Lyungbyhed; tel. (20) 41-00-10.

Norrlands Energi Försäljning AB: Kyrkogt. 12, POB 736, 851 21 Sundsvall; tel. (60) 19-59-00.

NVSH Energi AB: Verkstadsgt. 1, POB 505, 267 25 Bjuv; tel. (42) 856-00.

Skövde Elnät: Badhusgt. 22, 541 83 Skövde; tel. (500) 46-82-14.

Sollefteå Energi: Sollefteå; tel. (620) 68-20-00; internet www.solleftea.se.

Vattenfall AB: 162 87 Stockholm; tel. (8) 739-50-00; fax (8) 739-51-29; e-mail info@vattenfall.se; internet www.vattenfall.se; f. 1909; became limited liability co in 1992; state-owned; power generation and distribution; some 90 directly or indirectly owned operational subsidiaries; interests in Germany, Poland, Finland and Denmark; Pres. and CEO LARS G. JOSEFSSON.

Vinninga Elektriska Förening Ek. för.: Vallmovägen, POB 3052, 531 03 Vinninga; tel. (510) 500-60.

TRADE UNIONS

The three principal trade union bodies are the Swedish Trade Union Confederation (LO), the Confederation of Professional Employees (TCO) and the Confederation of Professional Associations (SACO).

Landsorganisationen i Sverige (LO) (Swedish Trade Union Confederation): Barnhusgt. 18, 105 53 Stockholm; tel. (8) 796-25-00; fax (8) 796-28-00; e-mail mailbox@lo.se; internet www.lo.se; f. 1898; affiliated to ITUC; Pres. WANJA LUNDBY-WEDIN.

Fifteen affiliated unions, with a total membership of 1,586,729 (June 2007):

Byggnads (Building Workers): Hagagt. 2, 106 32 Stockholm; tel. (8) 728-48-00; fax (8) 34-50-51; e-mail forbundet@byggnads.se; internet www.byggnads.se; Pres. HANS TILLY; 117,000 mems.

SWEDEN

Fastighetsanställdas Förbund (Building Maintenance Workers): Upplandsgt. 4, 2nd Floor, POB 70446, 107 25 Stockholm; tel. (8) 696-11-50; fax (8) 24-46-90; e-mail info.fk@fastighets.se; internet www.fastighets.se; f. 1936; Pres. Hans Öhlund; 39,243 mems (Dec 2005).

Grafiska Fackförbundet—Mediafacket (Graphic and Media Workers): Barnhusgt. 20, 3rd Floor, POB 1101, 111 81 Stockholm; tel. (8) 791-16-00; fax (8) 411-41-01; e-mail gf@gf.se; internet www.gf.se; f. 1973; Pres. Tommy Andersson; 23,000 mems (Dec. 2005).

Handelsanställdas Förbund (Commercial Employees): Upplandsgt. 5, POB 1146, 111 81 Stockholm; tel. (8) 412-68-00; fax (8) 10-00-62; e-mail handels@handels.se; internet www.handels.se; f. 1906; Pres. Lars-Anders Häggström; 172,000 mems (Dec. 2005).

Hotell- och Restaurang Facket (Hotel and Restaurant Workers): Olof Palmesgt. 31, 3rd Floor, POB 1143, 111 81 Stockholm; tel. (0) 771-57-58-59; fax (8) 411-71-18; internet www.hrf.net; f. 1918; Pres. Ella Niia; 60,000 mems (Dec. 2005).

IF Metall: Olof Palmesgt. 11, 105 52 Stockholm; tel. (8) 786-80-00; fax (8) 240-86-74; e-mail postbox.fk@ifmetall.se; internet www.ifmetall.se; f. 2006 by merger of Industrifacket and Svenska Metallindustriarbetareförbundet; Pres. Stefan Löfven; c. 415,000 mems.

Kommunal—Svenska Kommunalarbetareförbundet (Swedish Municipal Workers' Union): Hagagt. 2, 1st Floor, POB 19039, 104 32 Stockholm; tel. (8) 728-28-00; fax (8) 31-87-45; e-mail kommunal.forbundet@kommunal.se; internet www.kommunal.se; Pres. Ylva Thörn; 573,600 mems.

SEKO—Facket för Service och Kommunikation (Services and Communications Employees): Barnhusgt. 6–10, POB 1105, 111 81 Stockholm; tel. (8) 791-41-00; fax (8) 21-89-53; e-mail seko@seko.se; internet www.seko.se; f. 1970; present name since 1995; Pres. Janne Rudén; c. 153,000 mems.

Skogs- och Träfacket (Swedish Forest and Wood Trade Union): Olof Palmesgt. 31, 5th Floor, POB 1152, 111 81 Stockholm; tel. (8) 701-77-00; fax (8) 20-79-04; e-mail postbox.fk@skogstrafacket.org; internet www.skogstrafacket.org; f. 1998 by merger of Svenska Skogsarbetareförbundet and Svenska Träindustriarbetareförbundet; Chair. and Pres. Kjell Dahlström; 55,000 mems.

Svenska Elektrikerförbundet (Electricians): Upplandsgt. 14, 1st Floor, POB 1123, 111 81 Stockholm; tel. (8) 412-82-82; fax (8) 412-82-01; e-mail postbox.fk@sef.com; internet www.sef.com; f. 1906; Pres. Stig Larsson; 26,000 mems.

Svenska Livsmedelsarbetareförbundet (Food Workers): Upplandsgt. 3, POB 1156, 111 81 Stockholm; tel. (8) 769-29-00; fax (8) 796-29-03; e-mail info@livs.se; internet www.livs.se; f. 1896; Pres. Hans-Olof Nilsson; 48,285 mems (Dec. 2005).

Svenska Målareförbundet (Painters): Olof Palmesgt. 31, POB 1113, 111 81 Stockholm; tel. (8) 587-274-00; fax (8) 587-274-99; e-mail post@malareforbundet.se; internet www.malareforbundet.se; f. 1887; Chair. Lars-Åke Lundin; 15,900 mems.

Svenska Musikerförbundet (Musicians): Alströmergt. 25B, POB 49144, 101 29 Stockholm; tel. (8) 587-060-00; fax (8) 16-80-20; e-mail info@musikerforbundet.se; internet www.musikerforbundet.se; f. 1907; Pres. Jan Granvik; 3,700 mems (Dec. 2001).

Svenska Pappersindustriarbetareförbundet (Swedish Paperworkers' Union): Olof Palmesgt. 11, 5th Floor, POB 1127, 111 81 Stockholm; tel. (8) 796-61-00; fax (8) 411-41-79; e-mail info@pappers.se; internet www.pappers.se; f. 1920; Pres. Jan-Henrik Sandberg; 25,090 mems (2002).

Svenska Transportarbetareförbundet (Transport Workers): Olof Palmesgt. 29, 6th Floor, POB 714, 101 33 Stockholm; tel. (10) 480-30-00; fax (8) 24-03-91; e-mail transport.fk@transport.se; internet www.transport.se; f. 1897; Chair. Per Winberg; c. 73,000 mems.

SACO (Confederation of Professional Asscns): POB 2206, Lilla Nygt. 14, 103 15 Stockholm; tel. (8) 613-48-00; fax (8) 24-77-01; e-mail kansli@saco.se; internet www.saco.se; f. 1947; affiliated to ITUC; Chair. Anna Ekström; 421,500 mems (June 2007).

There are 24 affiliated unions and professional orgs, of which the following are the largest:

Jusek: Nybrogt. 30, POB 5167, 102 44 Stockholm; tel. (8) 665-29-00; fax (8) 662-79-23; e-mail vaxel@jusek.se; internet www.jusek.se; asscn of graduates in law, business administration and economics, computer and systems science, personnel management and social science; Pres. Göran Arrius; 65,000 mems.

Lärarnas riksförbund (National Union of Teachers in Sweden): Sveavägen 50, POB 3529, 103 69 Stockholm; tel. (8) 613-27-00; fax (8) 21-91-36; e-mail lr@lr.se; internet www.lr.se; f. 1884; Pres. Metta Fjelkner; 80,000 mems.

Sveriges Ingenjörer (Swedish Asscn of Graduate Engineers): Malmskillnadsgt. 48, POB 1419, 111 84 Stockholm; tel. (8) 613-80-00; fax (8) 796-71-02; e-mail info@sverigesingenjorer.se; internet www.sverigesingenjorer.se; Pres. Ulf Bengtsson; 120,000 mems.

Tjänstemännens Centralorganisation (TCO) (Confederation of Professional Employees): Linnégt. 14, 114 94 Stockholm; tel. (8) 782-91-00; fax (8) 663-75-20; e-mail info@tco.se; internet www.tco.se; f. 1944; affiliated to ITUC, European Trade Union Confed. and Council of Nordic Trade Unions; Pres. Sture Nordh.

17 affiliated unions with total membership of 1,026,000 (June 2007), of which the following are the largest:

Fackförbundet ST (Civil Servants): Sturegt. 15, POB 5308, 102 47 Stockholm; tel. (8) 790-51-00; fax (8) 24-29-24; e-mail st@st.org; internet www.st.org; fmrly Statstjänstemannaförbundet; Pres. Annette Carnhede; 100,000 mems.

Finansförbundet (Bank Employees): Olof Palmesgt. 17, POB 720, 101 34 Stockholm; tel. (8) 614-03-00; fax (8) 611-38-98; e-mail finansforbundet.se; internet www.finansforbundet.se; Pres. Lillemor Smedenvall; 39,000 mems.

Lärarförbundet (Teachers): Segelbåtsvägen 15, POB 12229, 102 26 Stockholm; tel. (8) 737-65-00; fax (8) 656-94-15; e-mail kansli@lararforbundet.se; internet www.lararforbundet.se; Pres. Eva-Lis Preisz; 227,000 mems.

Ledarna—Sveriges chefsorganisation (Professional and Managerial Staff): St Eriksgt. 26, POB 12069, 102 22 Stockholm; tel. (8) 598-990-00; fax (8) 598-990-10; e-mail ledarna@ledarna.se; internet www.ledarna.se; f. 1905; Pres. Annika Elias; 70,000 mems.

Sif (Clerical and Technical Employees in Industry): Olof Palmesgt. 17, 105 32 Stockholm; tel. (8) 508-970-00; fax (8) 508-970-01; e-mail koc@sif.se; internet www.sif.se; f. 1920 as Sveriges Verkstäders Tjänstemannaförening, restyled Svenska Industritjänstemannaförbundet 1932; present name adopted 2000; Pres. Mari-Ann Krantz; 350,000 mems.

SKTF—Sveriges Kommunaltjänstemannaförbund (Local Government Officers): Kungsgt. 28A, POB 7825, 103 97 Stockholm; tel. (8) 789-63-00; fax (8) 789-64-81; e-mail sktf@sktf.se; internet www.sktf.se; Pres. Eva Nordmark; 170,000 mems.

Tjänstemannaförbundet HTF (Commercial Salaried Employees): Franzéngt. 5, POB 30102, 104 25 Stockholm; tel. (8) 737-80-00; fax (8) 618-77-19; e-mail htf@htf.se; internet www.htf.se; f. 1937; fmrly Handelstjänstemannaförbundet; Pres. Bengt Olsson; 158,436 mems (Feb. 2004).

Vårdförbundet (Swedish Asscn of Health Professionals): Adolf Fredriks Kyrkogt. 11, POB 3260, 103 65 Stockholm; tel. (8) 14-77-00; fax (8) 411-42-29; e-mail info@vardforbundet.se; internet www.vardforbundet.se; fmrly Svenska Hälso- och Sjukvårdens Tjänstemannaförbund; Pres. Anna-Karin Eklund; 108,480 mems (June 2007).

Transport

RAILWAYS

In March 2007 there were 11,904 km of standard- and narrow-gauge railways, of which 9,683 km of track was electrified. A railway line linking Stockholm and Arlanda international airport opened in September 1999. In mid-2007 a railway line extending 190 km, connecting Nyland and Umeå on the north-eastern coast of Sweden, was under construction and was scheduled to be completed by late 2010.

SJ AB (Statens Järnvägar): 105 50 Stockholm; tel. (10) 751-50-00; fax (10) 751-54-24; e-mail sjinfo@sj.se; internet www.sj.se; f. 1856; state-owned; runs passenger traffic on all state-owned railway track; CEO Jan Forsberg.

Banverket: Jussi Björlings väg 2, 781 85 Borlänge; tel. (243) 44-50-00; e-mail banverket@banverket.se; internet www.banverket.se; primarily govt funded; manages Sweden's state-owned railway infrastructure; Dir-Gen. Minoo Akhtarzand.

Malmö-Limhamns Järnvägs AB: POB 30022, 200 61 Limhamn; tel. (40) 36-15-04; fax (40) 15-86-24; 5 km of 1,435-mm gauge; Dir Uwe Johnson; Traffic Man. K. Holmberg.

TGOJ Trafik AB: Gredbyvägen 3–5, 632 21 Eskilstuna; tel. (16) 17-26-61; fax (16) 17-26-66; e-mail info@tgojtrafik.se; internet www.tgojtrafik.se; f. 1877; 300 km of 1,435-mm gauge electrified railways; Chair. Jan Sundling; Pres. Bengt Fors.

ROADS

At 31 December 2004 there were an estimated 424,597 km of roads, of which 1,591 km were motorways, 15,385 km were main or national roads and 82,883 km of secondary or regional roads. In 2001 a road-rail link between Malmö and Copenhagen (Denmark), across the 16-km Öresund strait, was opened. A bridge linking Sweden and Norway, at Svinesund, was opened in 2005.

SHIPPING

The principal ports in terms of cargo handled are Göteborg (Gothenberg), Brofjorden, Trelleborg, Luleå and Malmö. Stockholm is also an important port.

Principal Shipping Companies

B & N & Nordsjöfrakt AB: POB 32, 471 21 Skärhamn; tel. (304) 67-47-00; fax (304) 67-47-70; e-mail bn@bn.se; Man. Dir FOLKE PATRIKSSON.

Broström Ship Management AB: POB 39, 471 21 Skärhamn; tel. (304) 67-67-00; fax (304) 67-11-10; e-mail info@brostrom.se; internet www.brostrom.se; management co, operating specialized tanker services; Man. Dir LENART SIMONSSON.

Broström Tankers AB: 403 30 Göteborg; tel. (31) 61-60-00; fax (31) 61-60-12; e-mail brotank@brostrom.se; internet www.brostrom.se; f. 1990; specializes in transporting petroleum products, in north-west Europe and world-wide; Man. Dir TORE ANGERVALL.

EffJohn International: Stockholm; tel. (8) 666-34-00; f. 1990 following merger of Effoa Finland Steamship Co and Johnson Line (Sweden); passenger ferry operations; EffJohn Group covers operations in the Baltic: Silja Line, SeaWind Line, Wasa Ferries, Sally Line, JBT, Svea Management; elsewhere in Europe: Sally Line UK; in USA: Commodore Cruise Line, Crown Cruise Line; Pres. HANS H. CHRISTNER.

N&T Argonaut AB: Skeppsbron 34, POB 1215, 111 82 Stockholm; tel. (8) 613-19-00; fax (8) 21-31-37; e-mail nt@ntargonaut.com; internet nt.argonaut.se; f. 1983; Pres. BJORN ERSMAN.

Nordström & Thulin AB: Skeppsbron 34–36, POB 1215, 111 82 Stockholm; tel. (8) 613-19-00; fax (8) 21-22-28; f. 1850; Man. Dir ANDERS BERG.

Stena AB: 405 19 Göteborg; tel. (31) 85-80-00; fax (31) 12-06-51; f. 1939; Stena Line ferry service since 1962; in 1990 acquired Sealink (United Kingdom); Man. Dir DAN STEN OLSSON.

Wallenius Lines AB/Wallenius Rederierna AB: Swedenborgsgt. 19, POB 17086, 104 62 Stockholm; tel. (8) 772-05-00; fax (8) 640-68-54; e-mail info@walleniuslines.com; internet www.walleniuslines.com; f. 1934; car and truck carriers; Pres. LONE FØNSS SCHRØDER.

Associations

Föreningen Sveriges Sjöfart och Sjöförsvar (Swedish Maritime League): Kastellet, Kastellholmen, 111 49 Stockholm; tel. (8) 611-74-81; fax (8) 611-74-76; e-mail fsss@algonet.se; f. 1983 by merger of Swedish General Shipping Asscn and Swedish Navy League; Pres. CLAES TORNBERG; Gen. Sec. STEN GÖTHBERG; 2,000 mems.

Sveriges Redareförening (Swedish Shipowners' Asscn): POB 330, 401 25 Göteborg; tel. (31) 62-95-25; fax (31) 15-23-13; e-mail srf@sweship.se; internet www.sweship.se; f. 1906; Pres. CHRISTER OLSSON; Man. Dir LARS HØGLAND; mems. 156 shipping cos with 259 ships (1996).

CIVIL AVIATION

The main international airport is at Arlanda, connected by bus service to Stockholm, 42 km away. There are other international airports at Landvetter, 25 km from Göteborg (Gothenburg), and at Sturup, 28 km from Malmö. There are regular flights between the main cities in Sweden. Many domestic flights operate from Bromma (Stockholm's city airport).

Luftfartsstyrelsen (Swedish Civil Aviation Authority): Vikboplan 7, 601 73 Norrköping; tel. (11) 415-20-00; e-mail luftfartsstyrelsen@luftfartsstyrelsen.se; internet www.luftfartsstyrelsen.se; f. 1923 as Luftfartsverket; present name adopted 2005; state body; central govt authority for matters concerning civil aviation; Dir-Gen. NILS GUNNAR BILLINGER.

Scandinavian Airlines System (SAS): Frösundavik Allé 1, Solna, 195 87 Stockholm; tel. (8) 797-00-00; fax (8) 797-15-15; internet www.sas.se; f. 1946; the national carrier of Denmark, Norway and Sweden. It is a consortium owned two-sevenths by SAS Danmark A/S, two-sevenths by SAS Norge ASA and three-sevenths by SAS Sverige AB. Each parent org. is a limited co owned 50% by Govt and 50% by private shareholders. The SAS group includes the consortium and the subsidiaries in which the consortium has a majority or otherwise controlling interest; the Board consists of two members from each of the parent cos and the chairmanship rotates among the three national chairmen on an annual basis. SAS absorbed Linjeflyg AB (domestic passenger, newspaper and postal services in Sweden) in 1993; strategic alliance with Lufthansa (Germany) formed in 1995; Chair. FRITZ H. SCHUR; Pres. and CEO MATS JANSSON.

Nordic East Airways: POB 79, 190 45 Stockholm; tel. (8) 594-906-00; fax (8) 593-614-44; f. 1991; charter services; Chair. and CEO GUNNAR OHLSSON.

Swedair AB: 195 87 Stockholm; tel. (8) 797-00-00; fax (8) 85-96-38; f. 1975 as result of merger of Svensk Flygtjanst and Crownair; passenger services to destinations within Scandinavia; Pres. BENNY ZAKRISSON.

Transwede Airways AB: POB 2011, 438 11 Landvetter; tel. (31) 94-79-80; fax (31) 94-79-90; e-mail trygve.gjertsen@transwede.com; internet www.transwede.se; f. 1985 as Aerocenter Trafikflyg AB; current name adopted 1986; relaunched 2005; operates charter passenger services within Scandinavia; Pres. TRYGVE GJERTSEN.

West Air Sweden: POB 5433, 402 29 Göteborg; tel. (31) 703-04-50; fax (31) 703-04-55; e-mail info@westair.se; internet www.westair.se; f. 1963; present name since 1993; Pres. GUSTAF THUREBORN.

Tourism

Sweden offers a variety of landscape, from the mountains of the 'Midnight Sun', north of the Arctic Circle, to the white sandy beaches of the south. There are many lakes, waterfalls and forests, and Stockholm is famed for its beautiful situation and modern architecture. Most tourists come from the other Scandinavian countries, Germany and the United Kingdom. In 2005 tourism receipts totalled an estimated US $8,548m.

Svenska Turistföreningen (Swedish Touring Club): Ameralitetsbacken 1, POB 25, 101 20 Stockholm; tel. (8) 463-21-00; fax (8) 678-19-58; e-mail info@stfturist.se; internet www.stfturist.se; f. 1885; 300,000 mems; owns and operates mountain hotels and youth hostels; co-ordinates nature and cultural activities in local clubs; Pres. TORGNY HÅSTAD; Sec.-Gen. YVONNE ARENTOFT.

Turistdelegationen: POB 4044, 102 61 Stockholm; tel. (8) 681-90-00; e-mail nutek@nutek.se; internet www.nutek.se/turistnaringen; f. 1995; Swedish Tourist Authority became part of Nutek, the Swedish Agency for Economic and Regional Growth, in January 2006; state-owned; promotes enterprise and entrepreneurship in the tourist industry in Sweden and produces and disseminates tourism information; Dir DENNIS BEDEROFF.

SWITZERLAND

Introductory Survey

Location, Climate, Language, Religion, Flag, Capital

The Swiss Confederation lies in central Europe, bounded to the north by Germany, to the east by Austria and Liechtenstein, to the south by Italy and to the west by France. The climate is generally temperate, but varies considerably with altitude and aspect. In Zürich the average temperature ranges from −1°C (30°F) in winter to 16°C (61°F) in summer. There are four national languages—German, French, Italian and Romansh (Rumantsch), spoken by 72.5%, 21.0%, 4.3% and 0.6% of resident Swiss nationals, respectively, in 2000. Other languages are spoken by the remaining 1.6% of the population. Including resident aliens, the linguistic proportions in 2000 were: German 63.7%, French 20.4%, Italian 6.5%, Romansh 0.5% and other languages 9.0%. Most Swiss citizens profess Christianity: in 2000 42.7% were Protestants and 41.2% Roman Catholics. Of the total resident population in 2000, 35.3% were Protestants and 41.8% Roman Catholics. The Federal flag, which is square, consists of a white upright cross in the centre of a red ground. The capital is Bern (Berne).

Recent History

Switzerland, whose origins date back to 1291, has occupied its present area since its borders were fixed by treaty in 1815. At the same time, it was internationally recognized as a neutral country. Despite the strategic importance of Switzerland, its 'permanent neutrality' has never since been violated. The country has not entered any military alliances, and it avoided participation in both World Wars. Executive authority is exercised on a collegial basis by the Federal Council (cabinet), with a President who serves, for only one year at a time, as 'the first among equals'. Owing to the restricted powers of the Federal Council, initiatives and referendums form the core of the political process. Switzerland is a confederation of 20 cantons and six half-cantons. In 1979 the mainly French-speaking region of Jura seceded from the predominantly German-speaking canton of Bern, becoming the first new canton to be established since 1815.

Despite the fact that Switzerland has long been the headquarters of many international organizations, the country did not join the UN until 2002, owing to concerns that it would conflict with the country's traditional neutrality. Switzerland was a founder member of the European Free Trade Association (EFTA, see p. 412) in 1960 and joined the Council of Europe (see p. 225) in 1963.

Since 1959 government posts have been divided between the members of the Social Democratic Party, the Radical Democratic Party, the Christian Democratic People's Party and the Swiss People's Party. This coalition holds more than 80% of the seats in the National Council (the lower house of the Federal Assembly), and all but three of the 46 seats in the Council of States (the upper house). The ruling coalition dominated the National Council at elections held between 1975 and 1995, although it lost some support to the Green Party of Switzerland, which grew to become the fifth largest party as public concern regarding ecological issues increased.

Switzerland began to emerge from its traditional isolation in the early 1990s. This was largely due to economic pressures resulting from the world recession and the further integration of the European Community (EC, now European Union—EU, see p. 244). In May 1992 the Government's proposal for Switzerland to join the IMF and the World Bank was approved in a referendum. On the following day, the Federal Council announced that it was to apply for membership of the EC. In a referendum on 6 December, however, the Swiss electorate voted against ratification of an agreement, signed in May, to create a free-trade zone encompassing both EC and EFTA member states. (The European Economic Area was established, without Switzerland, in January 1994.) Despite this set-back, the Government declared its intention to continue to pursue its application for membership of the EC. During 1993 Switzerland confined itself to seeking bilateral negotiations with the EC on issues of particular national interest, including transport and involvement in EC research programmes. Agreement was reached in December 1996 to phase out Swiss work permits for citizens of EU member states over a period of six years. At the beginning of December 1998 Switzerland and the EU concluded a bilateral trade agreement, having settled a lengthy dispute over the imposition of tolls on road freight traffic through Switzerland. By February 2000 the Government had negotiated seven bilateral free-trade agreements with the EU. The accords included the gradual elimination of immigration controls between Switzerland and the EU over a period of 12 years. Although the Government insisted that Swiss sovereignty was not affected by the trade agreements, opponents of Swiss membership of the EU submitted a petition, thereby forcing a referendum on the agreements. At the referendum, which was held in May, 67.2% of those who voted approved the agreements. Following the submission of a petition by pro-EU lobbyists, a referendum was held in March 2001 on whether to begin 'fast-track' accession negotiations with the EU; the ballot attracted an unusually high participation rate and the motion was rejected by 77% of the voters. The result was believed to have been influenced in part by a letter from the European Commission in February, widely perceived as coercive, which urged the acceleration of negotiations with the EU regarding co-operation against customs fraud and tax evasion. The Government insisted that the vote did not represent a rejection of the EU, but rather reflected the desire to move towards accession at a slower pace, and that its plans for eventual membership of the EU remained unchanged.

The enfranchisement of women in federal elections was approved at a referendum in February 1971. However, the half-cantons of Appenzell Ausserrhoden and Appenzell Innerrhoden introduced female suffrage only in 1989 and 1990, respectively. In October 1984 the Federal Assembly elected Switzerland's first female cabinet minister, Dr Elisabeth Kopp of the Radical Democratic Party, who became Head of the Federal Department of Justice and Police. In December 1988 the Assembly elected Kopp, by a large majority, to be Vice-President of the Swiss Confederation for 1989, concurrently with her other duties in the Federal Council. In the same month, however, she announced her resignation from her post as Head of the Federal Department of Justice and Police, following allegations that she had violated regulations concerning official secrecy. In February 1989, following an official investigation of the case, Kopp was replaced as Vice-President; in February 1990, however, she was acquitted by the Federal Supreme Court.

In January 1993 the Head of the Federal Department of Foreign Affairs, René Felber, resigned. Under the terms of the coalition, Felber was to be replaced by another francophone member of the Social Democratic Party. In March the party's official candidate, Christiane Brunner, a trade union leader, was rejected by other members of the coalition in favour of a male candidate, Francis Matthey, who, however, following pressure from within the party, refused to accept his election. The Social Democratic Party subsequently reconfirmed Brunner's candidacy but presented another female candidate in addition, Ruth Dreifuss, also a trade union activist. Following three rounds of voting, Dreifuss became the second woman to be elected to a ministerial position in Switzerland. In December 1998 the Federal Assembly elected Dreifuss (by then Head of the Federal Department of Home Affairs) as President of the Confederation for 1999. A female Christian Democratic People's Party candidate, Ruth Metzler, was elected Head of the Federal Department of Justice and Police in March 1999. In the following month 59.2% of voters in a national referendum approved a revised draft Constitution that included new provision for the right to undertake strike action by the labour force.

The commission that had investigated the allegations against Kopp during 1989 subsequently revealed that the office of the Federal Public Prosecutor held about 900,000 secret files on some 200,000 Swiss citizens and foreigners. In March 1990 about 30,000 people demonstrated in Bern in protest at the existence of such files; the demonstration ended in rioting. The Government subsequently announced that it would commission a report on the activities of the security services and introduce new laws regulating state security; it also opened most of the files to public scrutiny. The completed report, which was published in June

1993, found that security service observation had been largely restricted to left-wing groups since 1945 and that security service personnel had at times behaved in an unprofessional manner.

Meanwhile, during 1986 the Government introduced legislation that aimed to restrict the number of refugees who were to be granted political asylum in Switzerland. However, the new legislation was criticized by socialist, religious and humanitarian groups, and in April 1987 a national referendum on the issue was held. Of the 41.8% of the electorate who voted at the referendum, a substantial majority was in favour of the new restrictions. In March 1994, in an attempt to control increasing drugs-related crime (following allegations that immigrants trading in illicit drugs were exploiting the asylum laws to avoid extradition), the Government approved legislation restricting the rights of asylum seekers and immigrants, which included provisions for their arrest and detention without trial for failure to possess the requisite identification documents; further stringent measures against foreigners suspected of trafficking in illegal drugs were approved by national referendum in December. Civil rights groups accused the Government of yielding to popular xenophobic sentiment in an effort to divert attention from its failure to overcome the drugs problem. In December 1996 a proposal sponsored by the Swiss People's Party to confiscate the earnings of asylum seekers in Switzerland and to expel automatically all those without sufficient documentation was narrowly rejected in a national referendum. In a referendum held in September 2000 63.7% of voters rejected a motion to reduce the number of foreigners allowed to settle in Switzerland from 20% of the total population to 18%. At a referendum held in November 2002, 51.1% of voters rejected proposals, drawn up by the Swiss People's Party, under which would-be refugees arriving in Switzerland via any country free of political persecution (in practice, all neighbouring countries) would automatically be denied refugee status and returned to that country.

The results of elections to the National Council and the Council of States, held in October 1999, challenged, initially at least, some of the assumptions generally made about the Swiss political process. They were characterized, above all, by the strong performance of the Swiss People's Party, which, in terms of votes gained, became the country's largest party. In the National Council the Swiss People's Party overtook both the Radical Democrats and the Christian Democratic People's Party to become the second largest party after the Social Democrats. Seats in the National Council are allotted in proportion to votes gained. However, the complex, 'cantonal' nature of the electoral system ensured ultimate victory for the Social Democratic Party. In the Council of States, the Swiss People's Party obtained a total of seven seats, thereby becoming the third largest party (after the Radical Democrats and the Christian Democrats).

In the early years of the 21st century the stability of the 'grand coalition' that had governed Switzerland since 1959 was increasingly threatened by the growing influence of the Swiss People's Party. Under the so-called 'magic formula' traditionally used to determine the distribution of government seats among the coalition partners, the Social Democratic Party, the Radical Democratic Party and the Christian Democratic People's Party each received two seats and the Swiss People's Party received only one. However, at the general election held on 19 October 2003 the Swiss People's Party received the largest share of the votes cast and thus for the first time became the largest party in the National Council, with 55 seats. The party demanded a second seat on the Federal Council to reflect this (to be taken by Christoph Blocher), and threatened to withdraw from the coalition, effectively ending the era of consensus politics, if its demand was not met. (Traditionally, Swiss ministers are reappointed at each election, and keep their seats until such time as they resign.) When the Federal Assembly elected the Federal Council on 10 December, however, Blocher contested the seat held by Metzler and, after three ballots, won with a majority of just five votes. This was the first ministerial deselection for 130 years, and the first time the composition of the governing coalition had been changed in 44 years. When the new Federal Council took office on 1 January 2004, Blocher became Head of the Federal Department of Justice and Police, which carried with it responsibility not only for policy on immigration and asylum but also for negotiating with the EU on Swiss membership of the Schengen Agreement (which binds signatories to the abolition of border controls) and the Dublin Convention on Asylum (relating to common formal arrangements on asylum).

In December 2004 the Federal Assembly approved a second set of bilateral agreements with the EU, which had been signed in October. Under the agreements Switzerland was to introduce (incrementally between 1 July 2005 and 2011) a withholding tax of 35% on the income of EU citizens' savings held in Switzerland, with banking secrecy to be retained. The agreements also provided for co-operation against customs fraud and for Switzerland's associate membership of the Schengen Agreement and Dublin Convention, as well as for the extension of the first set of bilateral agreements (see above) to the 10 states (mostly in Central and Eastern Europe) that had acceded to full membership of the EU earlier in the year. The National Council voted against submitting the agreement on the Schengen/Dublin accords to an obligatory referendum. However, the Swiss People's Party gathered sufficient signatures to force a referendum on the issue. At the referendum, held on 5 June 2005, 54.6% of participating voters (56.6% of the electorate) supported Switzerland's adherence to the Schengen/Dublin accords. (Switzerland was expected to implement the Schengen/Dublin accords in November 2008.) The extension of existing bilateral agreements to the new EU member states was approved by 56.0% of voters at a referendum held on 25 September 2005; a participation rate of 54.5% was recorded.

In June 2004 the National Council approved a two-tier immigration policy whereby priority was to be given to EU and EFTA nationals, with immigration otherwise restricted to only highly skilled workers in the agricultural, construction, health and tourism sectors. A national referendum held in September rejected proposals to relax the country's laws on citizenship: a government plan to ease citizenship procedures for Swiss-born second-generation immigrants was opposed by 56.8% of those who participated, while a plan to grant automatic citizenship to third-generation immigrants was rejected by 51.6%. (Foreigners comprise approximately 20% of Switzerland's population.) In November 66.4% of voters in a referendum approved legislation allowing scientists to experiment on cells taken from human embryos (known as stem cell research), which was henceforth to be regulated by federal law. Voters also approved a programme of fiscal reform for the redistribution of funds between the Federal Government and the cantons, and a federal resolution that extended the Government's power to levy direct federal and value-added taxes to 2020 (this mandate had been due to expire in 2006).

A referendum on the registration of same-sex partnerships was held on 5 June 2005 (concurrently with the referendum on the Schengen/Dublin accords—see above), at which 58.0% of voters supported proposals to grant registered same-sex couples similar legal rights to married couples in areas such as taxation and pensions (although they would not be allowed to adopt children, nor would they be eligible for fertility treatment). The participation rate was 56.5%.

In April 2006 Josef Deiss, of the Christian Democratic People's Party, unexpectedly announced his resignation as Head of the Federal Department for Economic Affairs. He was replaced in June by party colleague Doris Leuthard. At a national referendum, held on 24 September, 67.8% of the valid votes cast were in favour of a proposal, supported by the Swiss People's Party, further to curtail the rights of asylum seekers and foreign migrants to Switzerland. Under the proposals, refugees would be required to present valid identification documents to the authorities within two days of their arrival in Switzerland and the issuance of work permits to non-skilled individuals from non-EU and -EFTA countries would effectively be ended. A concurrent proposal by left-wing groups, which was opposed by the Government, to use some of the annual profits of the Swiss National Bank to alleviate a deficit in the state-run pension scheme was overwhelmingly rejected. In December Micheline Calmy-Rey of the Social Democratic Party was appointed as President for 2007.

Campaigning for a general election, scheduled for late October 2007, was characterized by the increased polarization of the electorate. In mid-September controversy arose following accusations of racism against the Swiss People's Party by a UN official in Switzerland, which followed that party's use of images deemed to be xenophobic in its campaign posters. In early October the campaign was marred by violent clashes in the capital between police and left-wing activists who had attempted to disrupt a rally held by the Swiss People's Party.

At the election, which was held on 21 October 2007, the Swiss People's Party strengthened its position as the largest party, winning 62 seats in the National Council. The Social Democratic

Party performed poorly, taking just 43 seats, while the Radical Democratic Party and the Christian Democratic People's Party won 31 seats apiece. The Green Party increased its representation, winning 20 seats. Opposition to the Swiss People's Party centred increasingly on Blocher, who was due to become Vice-President of the Confederation for 2008. A large number of Federal Assembly members opposed Blocher's re-election to the Federal Council, in particular the Green Party, which announced its intention to propose its own candidate. However, prior to the vote, which took place on 12 December 2007, the Green Party withdrew its candidate in favour of a moderate member of the Swiss People's Party, Eveline Widmer-Schlumpf, who eventually defeated Blocher after two rounds of voting. In defiance of the party leadership, Widmer-Schlumpf announced that she would accept a role in the Federal Council. The Swiss People's Party subsequently announced the withdrawal of its support for the Government, in protest at Blocher's deselection. On 1 January 2008 Widmer-Schlumpf took office as Head of the Federal Department of Justice and Police, while Pascal Couchepin of the Radical Democratic Party was appointed as President for 2008; Hans-Rudolf Merz, also of the Radical Democratic Party, assumed the vice-presidency.

In September 1995 the Swiss Bankers' Association (SBA) announced the introduction of measures that would enable relatives to trace and recover the assets deposited in Swiss bank accounts by victims of the Nazi massacre of Jews in the Second World War. To assist in this process an accord was signed in May 1996 by the SBA and the World Jewish Congress establishing an Independent Committee of Eminent Persons (ICEP), chaired by Paul Volcker, a former Chairman of the Board of Governors of the US Federal Reserve, which was to be responsible for auditing all dormant Swiss bank accounts. In September controversial documents were released from British and US archives, claiming that gold valued at several thousand million dollars, at current prices, had been deposited in Swiss banks during the Second World War. Much of it was suspected to have belonged to Jews killed in the Holocaust. The Swiss Federal Assembly subsequently approved legislation establishing an independent panel to investigate the ownership of these assets, and legislation ordering banks to release all records that might pertain to dealings with the Nazi regime in Germany or its victims. In December the Federal Government appointed an international commission to conduct a broad historical investigation of Switzerland's role as a financial centre during the Second World War.

Meanwhile, the issue of 'Nazi gold' had received much coverage in the international press. Jewish organizations threatened to boycott Swiss financial institutions, claiming that insufficient efforts were being made to recover their assets and expressing outrage at what they regarded as antagonistic comments made by Jean-Pascal Delamuraz (President of the Confederation in 1996) and by Carlo Jagmetti (who subsequently resigned as Switzerland's ambassador to the USA). In March 1997 three of Switzerland's most prominent banks, Crédit Suisse, Swiss Bank Corporation and Union Bank of Switzerland, established a special humanitarian fund for impoverished survivors of the Holocaust, under the administration of the Federal Government; the first payments from the fund were made in November. In December Swiss banks issued the first payments to claimants of funds from dormant accounts that had been opened prior to and during the Second World War.

In March 1998 senior US public finance officials, threatening an imminent boycott of Swiss banks and industrial interests, placed the former under increasing pressure to agree to a swift 'global settlement' of the issue of Holocaust victims' accounts, involving the establishment of a victims' fund and a timetable for payment; soon afterwards (against the wishes of the Swiss Government, which believed the ICEP to be making adequate progress in assessing claims) Swiss Bank Corporation and Union Bank of Switzerland, which subsequently merged to form UBS, and Crédit Suisse announced their intention to negotiate such a settlement. In August UBS and Crédit Suisse agreed to pay US $1,250m. to the World Jewish Congress as compensation for the role of Swiss financial institutions in retaining dormant Jewish assets, handling gold deposited by the Nazis and lending money during the Second World War to German companies that had utilized Jewish slave labour. In return, all threats of boycotts and legal action against Swiss concerns were withdrawn.

In December 1999 the ICEP reported that its audit of all dormant Swiss bank accounts had shown that some 54,000 of these might have belonged to Jews murdered in the Holocaust (although the figure was subsequently reduced to 36,000). The Committee recommended that details of 25,000 of the 54,000 accounts should be publicized in order to alert survivors of the Holocaust or their heirs to their existence, and it criticized some Swiss banks for their insensitivity and for their obstruction of legitimate claims. The Committee did not attempt to value the funds held in the accounts, but stated that the total would probably not exceed the US $1,250m. already committed by UBS and Crédit Suisse to the World Jewish Congress. The publication of the ICEP report was followed, almost immediately, by that of the international historical commission appointed in December 1996. The commission concluded that, by closing its border to an estimated 24,500 fugitive Jews from 1942, Switzerland bore partial responsibility for their deaths at the hands of the Nazis. Following the release of the historical commission's report, the Government formally apologized for Switzerland's role in the Second World War. Further details emerged in August 2001, which indicated that several of Switzerland's largest companies, including Nestlé, had ignored reports of Nazi atrocities and had continued to trade with Germany during the Second World War, thereby contributing to the German war effort. Moreover, it was revealed that, despite Switzerland's neutrality, the Government had issued Germany and Italy with credits to buy Swiss-made machinery and weapons. In December a further report indicated that Switzerland had harboured substantial amounts of Nazi funds and assets, and even concealed entire German companies, during the Second World War. The report also stated that Switzerland had provided a refuge for several prominent Nazi war criminals following the end of hostilities.

In May 2000 UBS and Crédit Suisse agreed to allow researchers to examine records of more than 2m. bank accounts in order to verify or reject claims by Holocaust survivors. The proposed settlement of US $1,250m. to end the threat of litigation by Holocaust survivors against Swiss banks was approved by a judge in the USA in July. The two banks formally agreed the settlement in August; four Swiss insurers added a further $50m. in response to claims that the insurance policies of Holocaust survivors had not been honoured. Swiss companies that had used forced labour during the Second World War were also required to contribute. In February 2001, in preparation for the beginning of payments, Swiss banks published lists of dormant bank accounts, thought to be linked to the Holocaust, to be claimed by the account-holders or their heirs.

In January 2004 legislation entered into force pardoning many Swiss citizens who were condemned and punished for illegally helping refugees during the Second World War. Although almost 30,000 Jews took refuge in Switzerland during the war, more than 20,000 were turned away, many of whom later died in Nazi concentration camps. Many Swiss citizens who helped refugees across the border or hid them after their arrival were prosecuted and imprisoned and, in most cases, their criminal records were allowed to stand. The new legislation allowed those prosecuted, or their relatives and other organizations, to apply for a pardon via a parliamentary commission. There was, however, no provision for compensation.

In November 1989 64.4% of voters in a referendum rejected a proposal to abolish the armed forces by 2000. The referendum, which had been instigated by the Group for Switzerland Without an Army (an alliance of socialist, pacifist, youth and ecological organizations), attracted an unusually high level of participation, almost 70% of the electorate. Following the referendum, the Federal Military (Defence) Department established a working party to examine proposals for reforms in the armed forces; consequently, the strength of the armed forces was considerably reduced during the early 1990s. In June 1993 the Federal Assembly approved legislation that sought permission for Swiss forces to be included in future UN peace-keeping operations. However, at a referendum on the issue, which took place in June 1994, 57.3% of voters rejected the proposal. Switzerland did subsequently join the 'Partnership for Peace' (see p. 342) programme of the North Atlantic Treaty Organization (NATO) in 1996. Swiss peace-keepers have participated in operations in Bosnia and Herzegovina, while Swiss truce-verifiers have worked in Kosovo under the Organization for Security and Co-operation in Europe (OSCE, see p. 354). In November 2000 a referendum was held on proposals to reduce the military budget by one-third; the motion was rejected by 62.4% of voters. A further proposal to abolish the armed forces was rejected by 78.1% of voters in a referendum held in December 2001; 76.8% of voters also rejected a replacement civilian force.

Following the accident in April 1986 at the Chornobyl (Chernobyl) nuclear power station, in Ukraine, public concern about nuclear safety became a national issue in Switzerland. In June a large-scale anti-nuclear demonstration took place at Gösgen, the site of the largest of Switzerland's five nuclear power stations, and in the same month the Social Democratic Party initiated a campaign to collect signatures for a referendum on the nuclear issue, advocating the progressive elimination of the country's existing reactors and the cancellation of any future nuclear projects. In March 1989 the Federal Assembly, after protracted debate, approved legislation to cancel the projected construction of a sixth nuclear power station, at Kaiseraugst (near Basel), and to provide compensation for the construction consortium. The decision followed increasing public disapproval of the project. In a referendum held in September 1990, a majority of voters rejected proposals to abandon the use of nuclear power, but approved a proposal for a 10-year moratorium on the construction of further nuclear power stations in Switzerland. The Federal Council announced in October 1998 that the five existing nuclear plants would eventually be closed on environmental grounds; it did not, however, propose a timescale for the withdrawal from nuclear energy. At a referendum held in May 2003, 66.3% of those that voted rejected a proposal to end nuclear energy production in Switzerland, while in a concurrent plebiscite 58.4% of voters rejected an extension to the moratorium on the construction of nuclear plants. In early 2007 the Federal Council announce its intention to continue nuclear energy production in Switzerland, while refusing to rule out the construction of additional nuclear plants. In response to criticism of the plans by environmental campaigners, the Head of the Federal Department of the Environment, Transport, Energy and Communications, Moritz Leuenberger, cited the need to maintain domestic electricity production in response to increased demand.

In the late 1990s a series of high-profile money-laundering cases threatened to damage Switzerland's reputation as a stable financial centre. Most notably, these included the freezing of assets and accounts linked to Gen. Sani Abacha and Slobodan Milošević, the former leaders of Nigeria and Yugoslavia respectively, and the former head of the Peruvian secret service, Vladimiro Montesinos. Suspect funds found in Swiss bank accounts were linked to missing IMF aid paid to Russia and also to the former leader of the Philippines, Ferdinand Marcos. The total value of suspect funds under investigation in Switzerland increased from 333m. Swiss francs in 1999 (representing 160 cases) to 1,543m. Swiss francs (representing 370 cases) in 2000. Swiss laws denying foreign investigators access to information about bank accounts unless local laws are broken attracted criticism, as did Switzerland's continued (although diminished) use of anonymous bank accounts.

In August 2003 Switzerland declared itself willing to co-operate with Nigeria's efforts to recover funds stolen by Abacha. The Nigerian Government estimated that Abacha had embezzled some US $2,000m., of which about $700m. was believed to have been deposited in Switzerland. The Swiss Government announced in April 2006 that it had returned all of the funds to the Nigerian Government. Appeals from the Abacha family for ownership of the money had been rejected. According to an agreement reached between Switzerland and Nigeria, the World Bank was to ensure the returned funds were used for development projects in health, education and basic infrastructure. In April 2005 Switzerland secured the extradition from Germany of Abacha's son, Abba Abacha; he was subsequently charged with money-laundering, fraud, forgery and participation in a criminal organization.

In 2006 the Federal Supreme Court ruled that indefinite freezes imposed by the Government on privately-held assets in Swiss banks were unconstitutional. Non-governmental organizations expressed fears that the ruling could lead to the release of further assets whose provenance was suspected to be illegal, including an estimated 10m. Swiss francs believed to have been deposited by former President Mobutu Sese Seko of Zaire (now Democratic Republic of Congo).

Until 2002, although Switzerland maintained a permanent observer at the UN and had joined the organization's non-political specialized agencies, it was not a full member of the UN. At a referendum in 1986, although the Government campaigned in its favour, some 75.7% of voters had rejected full membership of the UN. The proportion of the electorate voting in the referendum, at 50.2%, represented a higher than average level of participation in the Swiss system of direct democracy. In March 2000 a petition favouring membership of the UN forced a further future referendum on the issue, to take place in 2002. In September 2001 the Federal Assembly approved proposals for Switzerland to join the UN. At the referendum, which was held on 3 March 2002, the proposals required not only the support of the majority of voters, but also the approval of at least one-half of the cantons in order to be adopted. In the event, 54.6% of voters and 12 (of 23) cantons supported the proposals; the participation rate at the referendum was 57.8%. Switzerland was formally admitted as a member of the UN in September of that year.

At a national referendum held in February 2003 70.3% of voters cast their ballots in favour of two proposed reforms whereby voters would be given the automatic right to challenge treaties signed between Switzerland and other countries (although, in practice, all important agreements are already subject to a referendum), and petitions with the requisite number of signatures could be used to introduce legislation, rather than solely constitutional amendments as was already the case. The rate of participation in the referendum, however, was markedly low, at only 28%.

Government

The Swiss Confederation, composed of 20 cantons and six half-cantons, has a republican federal Constitution. Legislative power is held by the bicameral Federal Assembly: the Council of States, with 46 members representing the cantons (two for each canton and one for each half-canton), elected for three to four years; and the National Council, with 200 members directly elected by universal adult suffrage for four years, on the basis of proportional representation. Executive power is held by the Federal Council, which has seven members elected for four years by a joint session of the Federal Assembly. The Assembly also elects one of the Federal Councillors to be President of the Confederation (Head of State) for one year at a time.

National policy is the prerogative of the Federal Government, but considerable power is vested in the cantons. Under the Constitution, the autonomous cantons hold all powers not specifically delegated to the federal authorities. The Swiss citizen shares three distinct allegiances—communal, cantonal and national. Direct participation is very important in communal government, and all adult Swiss residents may take part in the communal assemblies or referendums, which decide upon local affairs. Each canton has its own written constitution, government and legislative assembly. The referendum, which can be on a communal, cantonal or national scale, further ensures the possibility of direct public participation in decision-making.

Defence

National defence is based on compulsory military service. Switzerland maintains no standing army except for a small permanent personnel of commissioned and non-commissioned officers primarily concerned with training. Military service consists of 18 weeks' compulsory recruit training for males at the age of 19–20 years, followed by seven three-week 'refresher' training courses between the ages of 20 and 30 years. Each soldier keeps his equipment in his own home, and receives compulsory marksmanship training between periods of service. As assessed at November 2007, the total strength of the armed forces, when mobilized, was 240,800, comprising an active force of 22,600 and reserves of 218,200 (army 161,400; air force 31,300; command support organization 14,000; and logistics organization 11,500). In addition, there is a paramilitary force numbering 105,000 reservists. The Confederation belongs to no international defence organizations, and the strategy of the army and air force is defensive. In December 1996 Switzerland signed the 'Partnership for Peace' (see p. 342) framework document of the North Atlantic Treaty Organization (NATO). Defence expenditure for 2008 was budgeted at 3,902m. Swiss francs.

Economic Affairs

In 2006, according to estimates by the World Bank, Switzerland's gross national income (GNI), measured at average 2004–06 prices, was US $425,890m., equivalent to $57,230 per head (or $40,930 per head on an international purchasing-power parity basis). During 1996–2006, it was estimated, the population grew by an average of 0.5% per year, while gross domestic product (GDP) per head increased, in real terms, at an average annual rate of 1.2%. Overall GDP increased, in real terms, by an average of 1.7% per year in 1996–2006; real GDP increased by 2.7% in 2006.

Agriculture (including forestry and fishing) contributed an estimated 1.2% of GDP in 2006, and engaged 3.7% of the employed labour force in the same year. The principal cash crops are sugar beet, potatoes and wheat. Dairy products, notably cheese, are also important. At a national referendum held in November 2005, 55.7% of voters approved a five-year ban on the use of genetically modified crops. According to FAO, agricultural production declined at an average annual rate of 0.2% in 1995–2004; it decreased by 1.5% in 2003, and remained static in 2004.

Industry (including mining and quarrying, manufacturing, power and construction) contributed an estimated 27.5% of GDP in 2006, and engaged 23.8% of the employed labour force in the same year. Industrial GDP increased by 0.8% in 2002, and declined by 0.1% in 2003.

Switzerland is not richly endowed with mineral deposits, and only rock salt and building materials are mined or quarried in significant quantities. In 2006 only 0.1% of the working population were employed in mining and quarrying. The sector contributed just 0.2% of GDP in 2003.

The manufacturing sector, which contributed an estimated 18.5% of GDP in 2003, engaged 16.0% of the employed labour force in 2006. The most important branches are precision engineering (in particular clocks and watches, which provided 7.6% of export revenue in 2005), heavy engineering, machine-building, textiles, chocolate, chemicals and pharmaceuticals.

Of total electricity output in 2004, 53.1% was provided by hydroelectric power and 42.4% by nuclear power (from five reactors with a total generating capacity of 3,077 MW). In 1998 Switzerland imported 82% of the energy that it consumed, mainly in the form of petroleum and related products (which accounted for 61.2% of final energy consumption in that year). Imports of mineral fuels comprised 7.1% of the value of total imports in 2005. Switzerland is a net exporter of electricity.

The services sector contributed 71.2% of GDP in 2006, and engaged 72.4% of the employed labour force in the same year. Switzerland plays an important role as a centre of international finance, and Swiss markets account for a significant share of international financial transactions. The insurance sector is also highly developed, and Swiss companies are represented throughout the world. The reputation of the banking sector abroad was adversely affected in the 1990s by revelations concerning the ignoble role played by Swiss banks in respect of funds deposited by Jewish victims of the Nazi Holocaust (see Recent History). The resolution of this issue in 2001 was overshadowed by a series of high-profile money-laundering scandals. Switzerland draws considerable revenue from tourism; receipts from tourism totalled 13,334m. Swiss francs in 2006. The tourism sector was anticipated to grow in 2008 due to Switzerland co-hosting the European Football Championships in June–July, with over 1m. visitors expected.

In 2006 Switzerland recorded a visible trade surplus of US $4,663m., and there was a surplus of $63,494m. on the current account of the balance of payments. The European Union (EU, see p. 244) accounted for the majority of Switzerland's trade, providing 78.6% of the country's imports and taking 61.6% of exports in 2006. In that year the principal source of imports was Germany (providing 33.3% of total imports), followed by Italy (11.1%), France (10.3%) and the USA (5.0%). Germany was also the principal market for exports (accounting for 20.2% of total exports), followed by the USA (10.3%), Italy (9.0%) and France (8.6%). The principal exports in 2006 were chemicals, pharmaceutical products, machinery and clocks and watches. The main imports in that year were chemicals, machinery, pharmaceutical products and agricultural and forestry products.

Switzerland recorded a consolidated budgetary deficit of 947m. Swiss francs (equivalent to 0.2% of GDP) in 2006. Total government debt was 123,600m. Swiss francs in 2006, equivalent to 25.4% of GDP. The annual rate of inflation averaged 0.8% in 1996–2006; consumer prices increased by 0.7% in 2007. The rate of unemployment averaged 3.3% in 2006. Of all the major European countries, Switzerland has the highest percentage of foreign workers (25.6% of the working population in 2006).

Switzerland is a founder member of the European Free Trade Association (EFTA, see p. 412).

Switzerland is a prosperous country, despite its small size, with a high level of income per head. Its economic success, built around financial services and a modern industrial sector, is in large part due to a highly educated labour force and a flexible labour market. Although Switzerland is not a member of the EU, it is nevertheless largely dependent on the euro area for economic growth and enjoys privileged access to the EU's internal market through numerous bilateral agreements. Inflation and unemployment in Switzerland are low as a result of sound monetary and fiscal policies. In 2004–05 the emphasis of Switzerland's economic policy shifted to improving the country's business environment through structural measures. The economy recovered in 2005–06, partly due to the growth of private banking, which benefited from inflows of new money, notably from Asia. A robust insurance sector also contributed to growth in 2006, together with increased consumer spending and capital investment. Despite the strength of the economy, the Swiss franc remained weak against the euro, which benefited exports in 2005–06. Eight interest rate rises were introduced between December 2005 and September 2007, successfully curbing inflationary pressures but exerting little effect on the value of the Swiss franc against the euro. Internationally, market turbulence in the financial sector from late 2007, related to the availability of credit, was expected to impact upon the Swiss economy. Towards the end of that year the country's largest bank, UBS, announced that it would make a loss of 4,400m. Swiss francs for the year, primarily due to investments in high-risk US mortgages. Some 4,000m. Swiss francs were written off from the value of US mortgage-related holdings held by the bank. Moreover, concerns remained that further write-offs of debt might become necessary in the banking sector during 2008. GDP growth remained strong at 3.1% in 2007, underpinned by exports and private consumption. The crisis in the financial sector was a principal factor in leading the Swiss Government to forecast a lower rate of growth, of some 1.9%, for 2008.

Education

Primary and secondary education are controlled by the cantons, with the result that there are 26 different systems in operation. Responsibility for higher education is shared between the cantons and the Federal Government. Education is compulsory for children between the ages of seven and 16 years. Primary education, which commences at the age of six or seven, lasts for up to six years. The duration and system of secondary education depends on individual cantonal policy. Some 20% of 17-year-olds continue their studies at a higher secondary school (Gymnasium/Collège), and a leaving certificate (Matura/Maturité) from one of these is a prerequisite for entry to academic higher education. About 70% proceed to vocational training (trade and technical) for a period of three to four years. There are 10 cantonal universities, two Federal Institutes of Technology (of university standing) and one Academic Institute (a teacher-training college of university standing), as well as seven universities of applied sciences. Numerous private schools exist, as well as one private university of applied sciences. In 2004/05 enrolment at pre-primary level included 72% of children in the relevant age-group; the comparable ratios for primary and secondary education were 89% and 82% (males 84%; females 80%), respectively. Enrolment at tertiary level in that year was equivalent to 46% of those in the relevant age-group (males 48%; females 43%). In 2005 federal, cantonal and communal expenditure on education amounted to 27,415m. Swiss francs (19.6% of total public expenditure).

Public Holidays

2008: 1 January (New Year's Day), 21 March (Good Friday), 24 March (Easter Monday), 1 May (Labour Day and Ascension Day), 12 May (Whit Monday), 1 August (National Day), 24 December (Christmas Eve)*, 25 December (Christmas), 26 December (St Stephen's Day), 31 December (New Year's Eve)*.

2009: 1 January (New Year's Day), 10 April (Good Friday), 13 April (Easter Monday), 1 May (Labour Day), 21 May (Ascension Day), 1 June (Whit Monday), 1 August (National Day), 24 December (Christmas Eve)*, 25 December (Christmas), 26 December (St Stephen's Day), 31 December (New Year's Eve)*.

In addition, various cantonal and local holidays are observed.

* Half day only.

Weights and Measures

The metric system is in force.

Statistical Survey

Source (unless otherwise stated): Federal Statistical Office, Information Service, 10 Espace de l'Europe, 2010 Neuchâtel; tel. 327136011; fax 327136012; e-mail info@bfs.admin.ch; internet www.bfs.admin.ch.

Area and Population

AREA, POPULATION AND DENSITY

Area (sq km)	41,284*
Population (census results)	
4 December 1990	6,873,687
5 December 2000	
Males	3,567,567
Females	3,720,443
Total	7,288,010
Population (official estimates at 31 December)†	
2005	7,459,128
2006	7,508,739
2007	7,591,400
Density (per sq km) at 31 December 2007	183.9

* 15,940 sq miles.
† Figures refer to permanent resident population, and have not been adjusted to take the results of the 2000 census into account.

LANGUAGES
(Swiss nationals, %)

	1980	1990	2000
German	73.5	73.4	72.5
French	20.1	20.5	21.0
Italian	4.5	4.1	4.3
Rumantsch	0.9	0.7	0.6
Others	1.0	1.3	1.6

REGIONS AND CANTONS

Region/Canton	Area (sq km)*	Population (2006†) Total	Per sq km	Capital (with population, 2000‡)
Région lémanique	8,718.7	1,389,988	159.4	—
Genève	282.4	433,235	1,534.1	Genève (177,964)
Valais	5,224.4	294,608	56.4	Sion (27,171)
Vaud	3,211.9	662,145	206.2	Lausanne (124,914)
Espace Mittelland	10,062.0	1,703,966	169.3	—
Bern	5,959.3	958,897	160.9	Bern (128,634)
Fribourg	1,670.6	258,252	154.6	Fribourg (35,547)
Jura	838.5	69,292	82.6	Delémont (11,353)
Neuchâtel	802.9	168,912	210.4	Neuchâtel (32,914)
Solothurn	790.7	248,613	314.4	Solothurn (15,489)
Nordwestschweiz	1,958.2	1,026,801	524.4	—
Aargau	1,403.6	574,813	409.5	Aarau (15,470)
Basel-Stadt	37.0	184,822	4,995.2	Basel (166,558)
Basel-Landschaft	517.6	267,166	516.2	Liestal (12,930)
Zürich	1,728.9	1,284,052	742.7	Zürich (363,273)
Ostschweiz	11,521.1	1,065,253	92.5	—
Appenzell Ausserrhoden	242.8	52,509	216.3	Herisau (15,882)
Appenzell Innerrhoden	172.5	15,300	88.7	Appenzell (5,447)
Glarus	685.1	38,084	55.6	Glarus (5,556)
Graubünden	7,105.5	187,920	26.4	Chur (32,989)
St Gallen	2,025.7	461,810	228.0	St Gallen (72,626)
Schaffhausen	298.5	73,866	247.5	Schaffhausen (33,628)
Thurgau	991.0	235,764	237.9	Frauenfeld (21,954)
Zentralschweiz	4,483.6	713,828	159.2	—
Luzern	1,493.5	359,110	240.4	Luzern (59,496)
Nidwalden	275.9	40,012	145.0	Stans (6,983)
Obwalden	490.6	33,755	68.8	Sarnen (9,145)
Schwyz	908.2	138,832	152.9	Schwyz (13,802)
Uri	1,076.7	34,948	32.5	Altdorf (8,541)
Zug	238.7	107,171	449.0	Zug (22,973)
Ticino	2,812.2	324,851	115.5	Bellinzona (16,463)
Total	**41,284.2**	**7,508,739**	**181.9**	—

* Figures exclude lakes larger than 5 sq km (total area 1,289.5 sq km). Also excluded are special territories (total area 7.2 sq km).
† Estimated permanent resident population at 31 December.
‡ Census figures.

PRINCIPAL TOWNS
(estimated population at 31 December 2005)

Zürich (Zurich)	347,517	Biel (Bienne)	48,735
Genève (Genf or Geneva)	178,722	Thun (Thoune)	41,138
Basel (Bâle)	163,930	Köniz	37,250
Bern (Berne, capital)	122,178	La Chaux-de-Fonds	36,809
Lausanne	117,388	Schaffhausen (Schaffhouse)	33,569
Winterthur (Winterthour)	93,546	Fribourg (Freiburg)	33,008
St Gallen (Saint-Gall)	70,316	Chur (Coire)	32,409
Luzern (Lucerne)	57,533	Neuchâtel (Neuenburg)	32,117

BIRTHS, MARRIAGES AND DEATHS

	Registered live births		Registered marriages		Registered deaths	
	Number	Rate (per 1,000)	Number	Rate (per 1,000)	Number	Rate (per 1,000)
1999	78,408	11.0	40,646	5.7	62,503	8.7
2000	78,458	10.9	39,758	5.5	62,528	8.7
2001	73,509	10.2	35,987	5.0	61,287	8.5
2002	72,372	9.9	40,213	5.5	61,768	8.5
2003	71,848	9.8	40,056	5.4	63,070	8.6
2004	73,082	9.9	39,460	5.3	60,180	8.1
2005	72,903	9.8	40,139	5.4	61,124	8.2
2006	73,371	9.8	39,817	5.3	60,283	8.1

Expectation of life (years at birth, WHO estimates): 81.4 (males 78.7; females 83.8) in 2005 (Source: WHO, *World Health Statistics*).

SWITZERLAND

EMPLOYMENT*
(April–June, '000 persons aged 15 years and over)

	2004	2005	2006
Agriculture, hunting, forestry and fishing	159	161	160
Mining and quarrying	5	5	5
Manufacturing	665	668	685
Electricity, gas and water supply	26	25	25
Construction	288	295	302
Wholesale and retail trade; repair of motor vehicles, motorcycles and personal and household goods	654	647	647
Hotels and restaurants	244	237	248
Transport, storage and communications	275	271	277
Financial intermediation	219	214	217
Real estate, renting and business activities	489	494	513
Public administration and defence; compulsory social security	170	176	176
Education	274	274	279
Health and social work	479	484	494
Other community, social and personal service activities	180	184	190
Private households with employed persons	58	52	53
Total employed	**4,176**	**4,185**	**4,272**
Males	2,322	2,320	2,366
Females	1,854	1,864	1,905

* Refers to workers who are employed for at least one hour per week, and includes foreign workers ('000): 1,061 in 2004; 1,058 in 2005; 1,093 in 2006.

Health and Welfare

KEY INDICATORS

Total fertility rate (children per woman, 2005)	1.4
Under-5 mortality rate (per 1,000 live births, 2005)	5
HIV/AIDS (% of persons aged 15–49, 2005)	0.4
Physicians (per 1,000 head, 2002)	3.61
Hospital beds (per 1,000 head, 2004)	5.7
Health expenditure (2004): US $ per head (PPP)	4,011.3
Health expenditure (2004): % of GDP	11.5
Health expenditure (2004): public (% of total)	58.5
Human Development Index (2005): ranking	7
Human Development Index (2005): value	0.955

For sources and definitions, see explanatory note on p. vi.

Agriculture

PRINCIPAL CROPS
('000 metric tons)

	2004	2005	2006
Wheat	539.3	531.2	540.7
Barley	257.4	231.2	229.4
Maize	180.9	198.9	151.1
Rye	11.3	9.4	8.6
Oats	15.7	15.3	12.0
Triticale (wheat-rye hybrid)	82.9	68.4	64.5
Potatoes	526.7	485.0	392.0
Sugar beet	1,455.8	1,409.4	1,242.7
Rapeseed	59.1	58.8	56.3
Cabbages	39.1	34.4	28.5
Lettuce and chicory	65.6	65.0	57.0
Tomatoes	29.6	27.1	26.9
Green onions and shallots	2.2	1.7	1.8
Carrots	57.6	59.0	53.0
Apples	284.6	204.8	266.3
Pears	72.0	64.6	83.0
Grapes	146.9	126.9	128.1

Aggregate production ('000 metric tons, may include official, semi-official or estimated data): Total cereals 1,089 in 2004, 1,057 in 2005, 1,008 in 2006; Total roots and tubers 527 in 2004, 485 in 2005, 392 in 2006; Total vegetables (incl. melons) 329 in 2004, 313 in 2005, 288 in 2006; Total fruits (excl. melons) 551 in 2004, 432 in 2005, 517 in 2006.

Source: FAO.

LIVESTOCK
('000 head, year ending September)

	2004	2005	2006
Cattle	1,570.2	1,544.5	1,554.7
Horses	53.7	55.1	56.3
Pigs	1,537.5	1,609.5	1,652.0
Sheep	440.5	446.4	449.3
Goats	67.4	74.0	76.9
Chickens	7,913	8,117	7,805

Source: FAO.

LIVESTOCK PRODUCTS
('000 metric tons)

	2004	2005	2006
Cattle meat	133.9	132.3	134.9
Sheep meat	6.6	6.2	5.8
Pig meat	227.1	236.3	243.5
Poultry meat	59.7	58.0	51.7
Cows' milk	3,914.0	3,933.8	3,922.5
Goats' milk	19.0	20.0	21.0
Hen eggs	38.4	38.9	38.8

Source: FAO.

Forestry

ROUNDWOOD REMOVALS
('000 cubic metres, excluding bark)

	2004	2005	2006
Sawlogs, veneer logs and logs for sleepers	3,424	3,421	3,630
Pulpwood	560	584	634
Other industrial wood	—	29	20
Fuel wood	1,148	1,251	1,417
Total	**5,132**	**5,285**	**5,701**

Source: FAO.

SWITZERLAND

SAWNWOOD PRODUCTION
('000 cubic metres, including railway sleepers)

	2004	2005	2006
Coniferous (softwood)	1,410	1,500	1,580
Broadleaved (hardwood)	95	91	88
Total	1,505	1,591	1,668

Source: FAO.

Fishing
(metric tons, live weight)

	2003	2004	2005
Capture	1,815	1,602	1,475
Roach	162	167	163
European perch	485	359	281
Whitefishes	986	912	865
Aquaculture	1,100	1,205	1,214
Rainbow trout	1,100	1,110	1,107
Total catch	2,915	2,807	2,689

Source: FAO.

Industry

SELECTED PRODUCTS
('000 metric tons, unless otherwise indicated)

	2002	2003	2004
Cement*	3,771	3,613	3,851
Cigars (million)	167	166	n.a.
Cigarettes (million)	37,160	38,140	39,059
Aluminium (unwrought, primary)*†	40.0	43.5	44.5
Flour (wheat)	395	395	395
Chocolate and chocolate products	142.2	139.7	148.2
Motor spirit (petrol, '000 barrels)*	9,928	9,089	10,000
Distillate fuel oils ('000 barrels)*	15,002	14,126	14,000
Residual fuel oil ('000 barrels)*	4,782	4,891	5,000
Electric energy (million kWh)‡	66,649	67,166	65,299

* Source: US Geological Survey.
† Source: World Metal Statistics, London.
‡ Including Liechtenstein.

Source (unless otherwise indicated): UN, *Industrial Commodity Statistics Yearbook*.

Watches ('000 exported): 17,840 in 1984; 25,137 in 1985; 28,075 in 1986.

New dwellings (units completed): 35,961 in 1997; 33,734 in 1998; 33,108 in 1999.

2005 ('000 barrels, unless otherwise indicated): Cement 4,022,000 metric tons; Aluminium (primary, unwrought) 44,800 metric tons; Motor spirit (petrol) 10,000; Distillate fuel oils 14,000; Residual fuel oil 5,000 (Source: US Geological Survey).

2006 ('000 barrels, unless otherwise indicated): Cement 4,000,000 metric tons; Aluminium (primary, unwrought) 12,000 metric tons; Motor spirit (petrol) 10,000; Distillate fuel oils 14,000; Residual fuel oil 5,000 (Source: US Geological Survey).

Finance

CURRENCY AND EXCHANGE RATES

Monetary Units
100 Rappen (centimes) = 1 Schweizer Franken (franc suisse) or Swiss franc.

Sterling, Dollar and Euro Equivalents (31 December 2007)
£1 sterling = 2.2548 francs;
US $1 = 1.2255 francs;
€1 = 1.6568 francs;
100 Swiss francs = £44.35 = $88.85 = €60.36.

Average Exchange Rates (Swiss francs per US $)
2005 1.2452
2006 1.2538
2007 1.2004

BUDGET
(million Swiss francs)*

Revenue†	2002	2003	2004
Taxes	95,697	94,568	97,643
Taxes on income and wealth	64,935	63,418	65,412
Income and wealth tax	45,591	45,986	46,590
Corporation and capital gains tax	12,615	12,118	12,218
Pre-paid tax	2,628	1,641	2,628
Other taxes on income and wealth	4,101	3,673	3,976
Stamp duty	2,819	2,624	2,755
Taxes on property and goods	1,895	1,937	1,960
Taxes on motor vehicles	1,774	1,820	1,851
Taxes on consumption	23,735	24,204	25,052
Value-added tax	16,857	17,156	17,666
Taxes on traffic	1,067	999	993
Customs duty	1,091	1,090	1,054
Agricultural duty	3	3	4
Duty from drivers	86	105	124
Duty from casinos	65	189	291
Other revenue	38,913	35,246	36,581
Total	134,610	129,814	134,224

Expenditure	2002	2003	2004
General administration	8,818	9,204	8,855
Public order and safety	7,514	7,872	7,970
Defence	5,162	5,066	4,979
Foreign relations	2,373	2,365	2,427
Education	25,786	26,560	27,684
Culture and leisure activities	4,187	4,212	4,249
Health	18,047	18,839	19,326
Social welfare	25,411	26,481	27,742
Transport and administration	14,671	14,024	14,411
Environment	4,909	4,897	4,907
National economy	7,058	6,466	6,344
Finances and taxes	10,317	9,825	9,486
Total	134,253	135,811	138,379

* Incorporates federal, cantonal and communal budgets, but excludes social security obligations. The consolidated accounts (including social security obligations) were (million Swiss francs): *Revenue:* 162,213 in 2002; 161,932 in 2003; 165,097 in 2004. *Expenditure:* 163,687 in 2002; 167,981 in 2003; 170,738 in 2004.
† Not including parish taxes.

2005 (million Swiss francs, excluding social security obligations): Total revenue 135,536; Total expenditure 141,977 (Source: Swiss National Bank).

Consolidated accounts (million Swiss francs, incl. social security obligations): *Revenue:* 173,641 in 2005; 173,270 in 2006*. *Expenditure:* 173,215 in 2005; 174,217 in 2006*.

* Budget proposals.

SWITZERLAND

INTERNATIONAL RESERVES
(US $ million at 31 December)

	2004	2005	2006
Gold (national valuation)	19,123	21,342	26,404
IMF special drawing rights	71	60	275
Reserve position in IMF	1,792	816	455
Foreign exchange	53,634	35,421	37,364
Total	74,620	57,639	64,498

Source: IMF, *International Financial Statistics*.

MONEY SUPPLY
('000 million Swiss francs at 31 December)

	2004	2005	2006
Currency outside banks	42.14	43.83	45.71
Demand deposits at deposit money banks	181.92	194.73	186.90
Total money	224.06	238.56	232.61

Source: IMF, *International Financial Statistics*.

COST OF LIVING
(Consumer Price Index; annual averages; base: December 2005 = 100)

	2004	2005	2006
Foodstuffs	102.0	101.3	100.6
Alcoholic beverages and tobacco	94.6	99.0	100.3
Clothing and footwear	92.4	92.3	102.0
Housing and energy	95.8	98.7	101.8
Household equipment, etc.	100.4	100.4	100.8
Health	99.5	100.1	99.8
Transport	95.5	98.8	100.2
Communication	112.0	105.6	97.8
Education	97.9	99.0	101.7
Recreation and culture	100.3	99.7	99.2
Restaurants and hotels	98.9	100.0	100.9
Other goods and services	99.0	99.9	100.7
All items	98.3	99.4	100.6

NATIONAL ACCOUNTS
(million Swiss francs at current prices)

National Income and Product

	2004	2005*	2006*
Compensation of employees	277,085	286,518	302,093
Operating surplus	79,333	79,320	82,154
Domestic factor incomes	356,418	365,838	384,247
Consumption of fixed capital	81,093	83,190	86,164
Gross domestic product (GDP) at factor cost	437,511	449,028	470,411
Indirect taxes	32,336	33,437	34,976
Less Subsidies	18,468	18,792	19,209
GDP in purchasers' values	451,379	463,673	486,178
Factor income received from abroad	89,220	127,373	132,395
Less Factor income paid abroad	57,017	83,726	87,592
Gross national product	483,583	507,321	530,981
Less Consumption of fixed capital	81,093	83,190	86,164
National income in market prices	402,490	424,131	444,817

* Provisional figures.

Expenditure on the Gross Domestic Product

	2004	2005*	2006*
Final consumption expenditure	325,359	333,438	341,847
Households and non-profit institutions serving households	272,333	279,571	287,885
General government	53,026	53,868	53,962
Gross capital formation	94,922	100,054	107,635
Gross fixed capital formation	93,946	98,198	103,749
Changes in inventories	411	−580	−111
Acquisitions, less disposals, of valuables	565	2,436	3,997
Total domestic expenditure	420,281	433,492	449,482
Exports of goods and services	209,119	226,336	255,019
Less Imports of goods and services	178,021	196,155	218,323
GDP in market prices	451,379	463,673	486,178

* Provisional figures.

Gross Domestic Product by Economic Activity

	2004	2005*	2006*
Agriculture, hunting, forestry and fishing	5,934	5,478	5,502
Industry (incl. electricity and water)	89,428	93,293	100,273
Construction	23,821	24,912	25,737
Wholesale and retail trade; hotels and restaurants; transport; storage and communications	95,849	97,695	101,291
Financial intermediation; insurance, real estate and business activities	95,966	98,521	105,104
Public administration; education; health and social work; other community, social and personal service activities	113,753	116,500	119,494
Sub-total	424,751	436,400	457,402
Taxes on products	29,929	30,425	31,841
Less Subsidies on products	3,302	3,152	3,065
GDP in market prices	451,379	463,673	486,178

* Provisional figures.

BALANCE OF PAYMENTS
(US $ million)

	2004	2005	2006
Exports of goods f.o.b.	141,874	151,309	166,987
Imports of goods f.o.b.	−126,083	−145,422	−162,324
Trade balance	15,791	5,886	4,663
Exports of services	43,085	47,106	51,955
Imports of services	−24,401	−26,242	−28,963
Balance on goods and services	34,475	26,750	27,655
Other income received	72,418	106,711	116,369
Other income paid	−44,260	−63,512	−73,579
Balance on goods, services and income	62,633	69,950	70,444
Current transfers received	14,272	14,926	17,448
Current transfers paid	−20,218	−23,903	−24,398
Current balance	56,688	60,973	63,494
Capital account (net)	−1,400	−783	−759
Direct investment abroad	−26,073	−54,069	−81,556
Direct investment from abroad	2,296	−600	25,975
Portfolio investment assets	−42,412	−53,263	−41,702
Portfolio investment liabilities	2,858	5,636	71
Other investment assets	−27,882	−71,373	−48,487
Other investment liabilities	28,129	81,785	61,564
Net errors and omissions	9,414	14,002	21,771
Overall balance	1,618	−17,691	371

Source: IMF, *International Financial Statistics*.

SWITZERLAND

Statistical Survey

External Trade

Note: Swiss customs territory includes the Principality of Liechtenstein, the German enclave of Büssingen and the Italian commune of Campione, but excludes the free zone of the Samnaun Valley.

PRINCIPAL COMMODITIES
(million Swiss francs)

Imports c.i.f.	2003	2004	2005
Agricultural and forestry products	10,368.7	10,505.2	10,997.4
Mineral fuels	6,905.7	7,767.7	11,194.4
Textiles and items of clothing	8,611.5	8,699.3	8,846.2
Clothing (excl. footwear)	5,384.9	5,435.2	5,655.5
Paper, paperboard and graphics	4,478.2	4,901.0	5,049.5
Leather, rubber and plastic products	4,453.1	4,835.9	5,198.8
Chemical products	27,489.4	29,606.7	32,796.5
Chemical elements and unmoulded plastics	6,603.4	7,499.4	8,933.6
Pharmaceutical products	16,104.3	17,411.5	19,166.4
Metal products	9,789.9	11,571.9	12,367.2
Machinery (incl. electrical)	26,009.6	27,659.7	29,972.3
Industrial machinery	9,105.2	9,631.8	10,548.6
Office machines	5,929.2	5,796.3	6,019.7
Electronics	7,439.9	8,375.8	9,311.0
Passenger cars	7,639.0	7,761.6	7,790.3
Precision instruments	4,463.3	4,882.4	5,373.6
Precious metals and gemstones	5,202.9	5,698.2	6,499.6
Total (incl. others)	134,986.7	143,996.2	157,544.5

Exports f.o.b.	2003	2004	2005
Agricultural and forestry products	4,427.0	4,863.4	5,192.2
Chemical products	45,193.6	49,601.9	54,838.0
Chemical elements and unmoulded plastics	5,815.7	6,331.8	6,425.0
Pharmaceutical products	30,947.8	34,819.8	39,792.5
Metals and metal products	9,976.0	11,112.5	11,663.7
Machinery (incl. electrical)	31,183.3	33,839.3	35,172.0
Industrial machinery	20,047.7	21,650.8	21,803.8
Electronics	8,488.6	9,513.1	10,715.1
Precision instruments	9,757.6	10,204.6	11,500.2
Clocks and watches	10,216.9	11,157.9	12,390.3
Precious metals and gemstones	4,521.9	5,085.2	4,791.1
Total (incl. others)	141,157.5	152,756.5	162,991.1

2006 (million Swiss francs): *Imports:* Machinery, equipment and electronics 32,018; Precision instruments, watches and jewellery 12,171; Chemicals 35,785; Textiles, clothing and footwear 9,392; Motor vehicles 15,495; Total (incl. others) 165,410. *Exports:* Machinery, equipment and electronics 38,630; Precision instruments 12,925; Watches 13,743; Chemicals 62,975; Textiles, clothing and footwear 4,405; Metals 13,424; Total (incl. others) 177,475 (Source: Swiss National Bank).

PRINCIPAL TRADING PARTNERS
(million Swiss francs)*

Imports c.i.f.	2003	2004	2005
Austria	5,662.6	6,085.7	7,219.9
Belgium	4,031.0	4,249.5	4,793.7
China, People's Republic	2,423.0	2,840.9	3,378.4
France	15,297.8	15,107.2	15,804.4
Germany	42,738.3	46,341.9	49,732.2
Ireland	4,796.1	4,692.5	5,652.4
Italy	14,076.4	15,848.3	16,530.1
Japan	2,845.8	3,046.6	2,918.1
Netherlands	6,555.6	6,989.6	7,551.5
Russia	1,202.8	1,042.0	1,023.1
Spain	3,193.5	3,440.1	3,980.4
Sweden	1,675.3	1,676.1	1,484.5
United Kingdom	5,609.8	5,842.1	6,951.0
USA	7,356.6	7,253.6	8,328.0
Total (incl. others)	134,986.7	143,996.2	157,544.5

Exports f.o.b.	2003	2004	2005
Austria	4,660.6	4,901.2	5,169.1
Belgium	2,757.8	2,855.9	2,932.5
Canada	1,437.6	1,994.2	2,268.6
China, People's Republic	2,485.1	3,107.0	3,466.8
France	12,416.9	13,511.7	14,136.3
Germany	29,224.1	30,922.2	31,691.8
Hong Kong	4,144.4	4,237.0	4,011.8
Israel	710.1	746.5	776.6
Italy	12,782.6	13,712.0	14,816.2
Japan	5,408.9	5,722.3	5,892.1
Netherlands	4,484.6	4,462.8	5,548.2
Singapore	1,365.3	1,500.7	1,633.1
Spain	4,903.8	5,975.9	6,595.2
Sweden	1,628.6	1,651.0	1,605.8
Turkey	1,692.7	1,997.1	2,054.4
United Kingdom	6,768.2	7,676.8	8,803.2
USA	15,442.4	15,780.0	17,513.2
Total (incl. others)	141,157.5	152,756.5	162,991.1

* Imports by country of production; exports by country of consumption.

2006 (million Swiss francs): *Imports:* Austria 7,496.6; Belgium 5,093.3; China, People's Republic 3,918.6; France 17,096.7; Germany 55,099.8; Ireland 4,613.1; Italy 18,426.0; Netherlands 8,267.0; Spain 4,038.4; United Kingdom 6,006.6; USA 8,308.4; Total (incl others) 165,410.3. *Exports:* Austria 5,829.1; China, People's Republic 3,753.0; France 15,224.8; Germany 35,827.6; Hong Kong 3,562.0; Italy 15,913.8; Japan 6,361.0; Netherlands 6,034.1; Spain 6,880.7; United Kingdom 8,343.1; USA 18,255.0; Total (incl others) 177,474.8 (Source: Swiss National Bank).

Transport

RAILWAY TRAFFIC

	2002	2003	2004
Passengers carried (million)*	319	327	336
Passenger-kilometres (million)	14,147	14,509	14,914
Freight carried (million metric tons)	60.9	62.4	69.3
Freight ton-kilometres (million)†	10,746	10,598	11,489

* Excluding multiple journeys.
† Net ton-kilometres (excl. weight of containers, etc.): 9,639 in 2002; 9,534 in 2003; 10,245 in 2004.

ROAD TRAFFIC
(motor vehicles in use at 30 September)

	2004	2005	2006
Passenger cars	3,811,351	3,863,807	3,899,917
Buses and coaches	44,784	45,785	46,445
Lorries and vans	298,193	307,264	314,020
Agricultural vehicles	180,898	182,093	185,450
Other industrial vehicles	50,957	51,860	53,437
Motorcycles	583,010	592,194	608,648

INLAND WATERWAYS
(freight traffic at port of Basel, '000 metric tons)

	1996	1997	1998
Goods loaded	876.9	837.5	688.4
Goods unloaded	6,283.4	7,002.4	7,420.3

Source: Federal Department of Transport.

SHIPPING

Merchant Fleet
(at 31 December)

	2004	2005	2006
Number of vessels	23	26	29
Displacement ('000 grt)	487.5	479.6	510.0

Source: Lloyds Register-Fairplay, *World Fleet Statistics*.

SWITZERLAND

CIVIL AVIATION
(traffic on scheduled services)

	2001	2002	2004
Kilometres flown (million)	304	256	218
Passengers carried ('000)	16,915	13,292	10,118
Passenger-kilometres (million)	33,470	26,704	23,295
Total ton-kilometres (million)	4,970	3,720	3,617

Source: UN, *Statistical Yearbook*.

Tourism

FOREIGN TOURIST ARRIVALS
(at hotels, and similar establishments)

Country of residence	2001	2002	2003
Belgium	208,505	197,957	191,463
France	502,797	488,817	488,468
Germany	2,179,224	1,952,214	1,881,932
Italy	438,736	429,436	434,515
Japan	522,674	416,306	320,593
Netherlands	312,080	289,118	284,982
Spain	156,045	146,149	137,904
United Kingdom	661,497	619,313	612,435
USA	827,155	688,820	598,046
Total (incl. others)	7,454,855	6,867,696	6,530,112

2005: Total foreign tourist arrivals (at hotels, '000) 7,229.

2006: Total foreign tourist arrivals (at hotels, '000) 7,863.

Tourism receipts (million Swiss francs): 12,549 in 2005; 13,334 in 2006.

Communications Media

	2004	2005	2006
Telephones ('000 main lines in use)	5,262.6	5,149.7	5,039.6
Mobile cellular telephones ('000 subscribers)	6,275.0	6,834.0	7,418.0
Personal computers ('000 in use)	6,105	6,430	n.a.
Internet users ('000)	3,500	3,800	4,360
Broadband subscribers ('000)	1,227.4	1,657.8	2,140.3
Books published (titles)	11,061	10,128	11,875
Newspapers:			
number	210	216	n.a.
circulation ('000)	2,365.2	2,290.5	n.a.

Source: mainly International Telecommunication Union.

Television receivers ('000 in use): 4,000 in 2001.

Facsimile machines ('000 in use, 1996): 207.

Radio licences ('000, 1996): 2,805.

Education

(2005)

	Institutions	Teachers	Students
Pre-primary	4,982	13,700	156,129
Compulsory primary*	} 5,954	{ 42,800	} 806,905
Compulsory secondary*		{ 34,000	
Upper secondary	982	11,500	
General	n.a.	11,500	} 317,417
Vocational	n.a.	n.a.	
Higher	344	76,547	
Vocational	n.a.	n.a.	
Universities of applied sciences†	n.a.	21,136‡	} 206,404
Universities	n.a.	44,321‡	

* Excluding schools with special curriculums.

† Excluding teacher-training colleges and other institutions offering courses of study at a similar level that are not integrated within the seven technical colleges.

‡ Including teaching assistants and administrative and technical personnel.

Directory

The Constitution

The Constitution (summarized below) was adopted on 29 May 1874. A revised version of the Constitution, which included new provision for the right to undertake strike action by the labour force, was approved by 59.2% of voters at a federal referendum on 18 April 1999 and entered into force in January 2000.

Switzerland is divided into federated cantons, which have sovereign authority except where the Constitution defines limits to their powers or accords responsibility to the Federal authority. After a referendum in September 1978, the Constitution was amended to allow for the formation of the canton of Jura, increasing the number of cantons to 26.

Principally, the Federal authority is responsible for civil, penal and commercial law, legislation concerning marriage, residence and settlement, export and import duties, defence, postal and telecommunications services, the mint, forestry, hunting and fishing, hydroelectric power, the economy, railways, important roads and bridges, social insurance, and international affairs. Administration is largely in the hands of the cantons, and in the combined management of Federal authorities and cantons. The cantons derive their revenue from direct taxation. The Federal authority draws its revenue from direct and indirect taxation. The profits from Federal enterprises and customs duties are received by the Federal authorities.

COMMUNES

Each of the more than 3,000 communes of Switzerland has local autonomy over such matters as public utilities and roads, and grants primary citizenship. Decisions are made by communal assemblies. The smallest communes have fewer than 20 inhabitants, the largest, Zürich, around 370,000.

CANTONS

The 26 cantons of the Swiss Confederation each have their own constitution and their own method of choosing the members of the cantonal assembly and cantonal government and the States Councillors who represent them at the federal level. Two cantons, Glarus and Appenzell Innerrhoden, retain the Landsgemeinde, an annual assembly open to all citizens of the canton of voting age, as their supreme decision-making authority. Elsewhere, democracy is less direct, the secret ballot and the referendum having replaced the mass assembly.

FEDERAL ASSEMBLY

The Federal Assembly (Bundesversammlung/Assemblée Fédérale) is the supreme governing body of the Confederation. It is composed of two bodies, the National Council (Nationalrat/Conseil National) and the Council of States (Ständerat/Conseil des Etats), which deliberate separately. The 200 members of the National Council are elected directly, by proportional representation, every four years. The minimum age for voting and eligibility for election in the Confederation is 18 years. Women gained full political rights at federal level and in almost all of the cantons in 1971; female suffrage had been introduced in all 26 cantons by late 1990. The Council of States is composed of representatives of the cantons, elected by the people in various ways, according to the cantonal constitutions. The six half-cantons of Appenzell Ausserrhoden, Appenzell Innerrhoden, Nidwalden, Obwalden, Basel-Landschaft and Basel-Stadt each send one member and the remaining cantons each send two. Legislative and

SWITZERLAND

fiscal measures must be accepted by both houses in order to be adopted. The Federal Assembly supervises the army, the civil service and the application of the law, exercises the right of pardon and elects the Federal Supreme Court, the General who commands the army in times of crisis, and the Federal Council.

FEDERAL COUNCIL

Executive authority is vested in the Federal Council, whose members are each in charge of a Federal Department. Each year the Federal Assembly appoints the President and Vice-President of the Confederation from among the Federal Councillors. Generally, the Councillors are chosen from the members of the Federal Assembly for four years after every general election.

REFERENDUMS AND INITIATIVES

Referendums are held on both cantonal and federal levels. In many cantons all legislation has to be accepted by a majority of the voters, and in some cantons major financial matters have to be submitted to the popular vote. In federal affairs the consent of a majority of the voters and of the cantons must be obtained for amendments to the Federal Constitution, for extraconstitutional emergency legislation and for the decision to join collective security organizations or international bodies, but referendums are optional for other legislation. A petition from 50,000 voters, or of eight cantons, is needed to bring about a national referendum, which can accept or reject any legislation that has been passed by Parliament. The initiative gives voters in many cantons the right to propose a constitutional or legislative amendment and to demand a popular vote on it. A petition by 100,000 voters is needed to initiate a vote on an amendment to the Federal Constitution, but as federal laws cannot be proposed by means of an initiative, some constitutional amendments introduced in this manner concern relatively unimportant matters and participation of the voters is, on average, 30% to 45%. The initiative is also used by the political opposition to effect changes in government policy.

The Government

FEDERAL COUNCIL
(April 2008)

President of the Swiss Confederation for 2008 and Head of the Federal Department of Home Affairs: PASCAL COUCHEPIN (Radical Democratic Party).

Vice-President and Head of the Federal Department of Finance: HANS-RUDOLF MERZ (Radical Democratic Party).

Head of the Federal Department of Foreign Affairs: MICHELINE CALMY-REY (Social Democratic Party).

Head of the Federal Department of Justice and Police: EVELINE WIDMER-SCHLUMPF (Swiss People's Party).

Head of the Federal Department of Defence, Civil Protection and Sports: SAMUEL SCHMID (Swiss People's Party).

Head of the Federal Department of Economic Affairs: DORIS LEUTHARD (Christian Democratic People's Party).

Head of the Federal Department of the Environment, Transport, Energy and Communications: MORITZ LEUENBERGER (Social Democratic Party).

Chancellor of the Swiss Confederation: CORINA CASANOVA (Christian Democratic People's Party).

FEDERAL DEPARTMENTS

Federal Chancellery: Bundeshaus West, 3003 Bern; tel. 313223791; fax 313223706; e-mail webmaster@admin.ch; internet www.bk.admin.ch.

Federal Department of Defence, Civil Protection and Sports: Bundeshaus Ost, 3003 Bern; tel. 313245058; fax 313245104; e-mail postmaster.vbs@gs-vbs.admin.ch; internet www.vbs.admin.ch.

Federal Department of Economic Affairs: Bundeshaus Ost, 3003 Bern; tel. 313222007; fax 313222194; e-mail info@gs-evd.admin.ch; internet www.evd.admin.ch.

Federal Department of the Environment, Transport, Energy and Communications: Bundeshaus Nord, Kochergasse 10, 3003 Bern; tel. 313222111; fax 313222692; e-mail info@gs-uvek.admin.ch; internet www.uvek.admin.ch.

Federal Department of Finance: Bernerhof, Bundesgasse 3, 3003 Bern; tel. 313226033; fax 313233852; e-mail info@gs-efd.admin.ch; internet www.efd.admin.ch.

Federal Department of Foreign Affairs: Bundeshaus West, 3003 Bern; tel. 313222111; fax 313234001; e-mail info@eda.admin.ch; internet www.eda.admin.ch.

Federal Department of Home Affairs: Bundeshaus, Inselgasse 1, 3003 Bern; tel. 313228041; fax 313227901; internet www.edi.admin.ch.

Federal Department of Justice and Police: Bundeshaus West, 3003 Bern; tel. 313222111; fax 313227832; internet www.ejpd.admin.ch:

Legislature

BUNDESVERSAMMLUNG/ASSEMBLÉE FÉDÉRALE
(Federal Assembly)

Nationalrat/Conseil National
(National Council)

Parlamentsgebäude, 3003 Bern; tel. 313228790; e-mail information@pd.admin.ch.

President: ANDRÉ BUGNON (2007/08).

General Election, 21 October 2007

	Seats
Swiss People's Party	62
Social Democratic Party	43
Radical Democratic Party	31
Christian Democratic People's Party	31
Green Party	20
Liberal Party	4
Green Liberal Party	3
Evangelical People's Party	2
Workers' Party	1
Union of Federal Democrats	1
Ticino League	1
Christian Socialist Party	1
Total	**200**

Ständerat/Conseil des Etats
(Council of States)

Parlamentsgebäude, 3003 Bern; tel. 313228790; e-mail information@pd.admin.ch.

President: CHRISTOFFEL BRÄNDLI (2007/08).

Elections, 2007

	Seats
Christian Democratic People's Party	15
Radical Democratic Party	12
Social Democratic Party	9
Swiss People's Party	7
Green Party	2
Green Liberal Party	1
Total	**46**

Note: Members are elected by canton; method and period of election differs from canton to canton.

Political Organizations

Christlichdemokratische Volkspartei der Schweiz—Parti démocrate-chrétien suisse (Christian Democratic People's Party): Klaraweg 6, Postfach 5835, 3001 Bern; tel. 313573333; fax 313522430; e-mail info@cvp.ch; internet www.cvp.ch; f. 1912; advocates a Christian outlook on world affairs, federalism and Christian social reform by means of professional asscns; non-sectarian; Pres. CHRISTOPHE DARBELLAY; Gen. Sec. RETO NAUSE; Leader of Parliamentary Group URS SCHWALLER.

Christlichsoziale Partei—Parti chrétien-social (Christian Social Party): Eichenstr. 79, 3184 Wünnewil; tel. 264963074; e-mail info@csp-pcs.ch; internet www.csp-pcs.ch; f. 1997; Pres. MONIKA BLOCH SÜSS; Sec. MARLIES SCHAFER-JUNGO.

Demokratisch-Soziale Partei Basel-Stadt (Democratic Social Party Basel-City): Rheinsprung 22, Postfach, 4001 Basel; tel. 612612117; fax 612612137; e-mail geschaeftsstelle@dsp-bs.ch; internet www.dsp-bs.ch; f. 1982 by breakaway faction of Social Democratic Party; sister party in Graubünden; Pres. DANIEL REICKE.

Eidgenössisch-Demokratische Union—Union Démocratique Fédérale (Federal Democratic Union): Frutigenstr. 8, Postfach 2144, 3601 Thun; tel. 332223637; fax 332223744; e-mail info@edu-schweiz.ch; internet www.edu-schweiz.ch; Pres. HANS MOSER.

Evangelische Volkspartei der Schweiz—Parti évangélique suisse (Evangelical People's Party): Josefstr. 32, Postfach 7334,

8023 Zürich; tel. 442727100; fax 442721437; e-mail info@evppev.ch; internet www.evppev.ch; f. 1919; Pres. Heiner Studer; Gen. Sec. Joel Blunier.

Freiheits-Partei der Schweiz (Freedom Party of Switzerland): Eigasse 13, Postfach, 4622 Egerkingen; tel. 623983838; fax 623984848; e-mail zs@freiheits-partei.ch; internet www.freiheits-partei.ch; f. 1985 as the Automobile Party (Die Auto-Partei) to support motorists' rights; subsequently campaigned for restricted immigration; Pres. Peter Commarmot; Sec. Walter Müller.

Freisinnig-Demokratische Partei der Schweiz—Parti radical-démocratique suisse (Radical Democratic Party): Neuengasse 20, Postfach 6136, 3001 Bern; tel. 313203535; fax 313203500; e-mail info@fdp.ch; internet www.fdp.ch; led the movement that gave rise to the Federative State and the Constitution of 1848; promotes a strong Fed. Govt, while respecting the legitimate rights of the cantons and all the minorities; liberal democratic principles; Pres. Dr Fulvio Pelli; Leader of Parliamentary Group Gabi Huber; Gen. Sec. Stefan Brupbacher.

Grüne Partei der Schweiz—Parti écologiste suisse (Green Party of Switzerland): Waisenhauspl. 21, 3011 Bern; tel. 313126660; fax 313126662; e-mail gruene@gruene.ch; internet www.gruene.ch; f. 1983; Pres. Ueli Leuenberger; Gen. Sec. Hubert Zurkinden; Leader of Parliamentary Group Therese Frösch.

Grünliberale Partei Schweiz (Green Liberal Party of Switzerland): Postfach, 8613 Uster; tel. 447012400; e-mail schweiz@grunliberale.ch; internet www.schweiz.grunliberale.ch; f. 2007 to contest federal elections; represented in Federal Assembly and Zürich cantonal council; Pres. Martin Bäumle.

Lega dei Ticinesi (Ticino League): via Monte Boglia 7, CP 2311, 6901 Lugano; tel. 919731048; fax 919731040; internet www.legaticinesi.ch; f. 1991; Pres. Giuliano Bignasca; Sec. Mauro Malandra.

Liberal-Demokratische Partei Basel-Stadt (Die Liberalen) (Liberal-Democratic Party Basel-City): Postfach, 4010 Basel; tel. 612721236; fax 612721743; e-mail info@ldp.ch; internet www.ldp.ch; Pres. Christoph Bürgenmeier.

Liberale Partei der Schweiz—Parti libéral suisse (Liberal Party): Spitalgasse 32, Postfach 7107, 3001 Bern; tel. 313116404; fax 313125474; e-mail info@liberal.ch; internet www.liberal.ch; Pres. Pierre Weiss; Sec. Christophe Berdat.

Mouvement Citoyens Genevois (Geneva Citizens' Movement): CP 340, 1211 Geneva 17; tel. 228497333; fax 223214507; e-mail info@mcge.ch; internet www.mcge.ch; f. 2005; Pres. Georges Jost.

Partei der Arbeit der Schweiz—Parti suisse du travail (Parti ouvrier et populaire) (Workers' Party): Postfach 533, 3000 Bern 22; tel. 794146494; e-mail secret-pst-pda@gouvernement.ch; internet www.gouvernement.ch/pst; f. 1944; Pres. Nelly Buntschu.

Schweizer Demokraten—Démocrates suisses (Swiss Democrats): Postfach 8116, 3001 Bern; tel. 319742010; fax 319742011; e-mail sd-ds@bluewin.ch; internet www.schweizer-demokraten.ch; f. 1961 as Nationale Aktion gegen die Überfremdung von Volk und Heimat—Action nationale; present name adopted 1990; 6,000 mems; main objectives are preservation of the country's political independence and of individual freedom, protection of the environment, and restriction of immigration; Pres. Bernhard Hess; Gen. Sec. Roland Schöni.

Schweizerische Volkspartei—Union démocratique du centre (Swiss People's Party—SPP): Brückfeldstr. 18, 3000 Bern 26; tel. 313005858; fax 313005859; e-mail gs@svp.ch; internet www.svp.ch; f. 1971; Pres. Ueli Maurer; Gen. Sec. Yves Bichel; Leader of Parliamentary Group Caspar Baader.

Sozialdemokratische Partei der Schweiz—Parti socialiste suisse (Social Democratic Party): Spitalgasse 34, 3001 Bern; tel. 313296969; fax 313296970; e-mail info@spschweiz.ch; internet www.spschweiz.ch; f. 1888; bases its policy on democratic socialism; mem. of Socialist International and assoc. mem. of Party of European Socialists; c. 40,000 mems; Pres. Christian Levrat; Sec.-Gen. Thomas Christen; Leader of Parliamentary Group Ursula Wyss.

> **Partito Socialista, sezione ticinese del PSS** (Socialist Party): piazza Governo 4, 6500 Bellinzona; tel. 918259462; fax 918259601; e-mail segreteria@ps-ticino.ch; internet www.ps-ticino.ch; f. 1992; fmrly the Partito Socialista Unitario; Pres. Manuele Bertoli.

Diplomatic Representation

EMBASSIES IN SWITZERLAND

Afghanistan: 63 rue de Lausanne, 1202 Geneva; tel. 227311616; fax 227314510; e-mail mission.afghanistan@bluewin.ch; internet www.mission-afghanistan.ch; Ambassador Nanguyulai Tarzi.

Albania: Pourtalèsstr. 45A, 3074 Muri bei Bern; tel. 319526010; fax 319526012; e-mail emalb.ch@bluewin.ch; Ambassador Mehmet Elezaj.

Algeria: Willadingweg 74, 3000 Bern 15; tel. 313501050; fax 313501059; e-mail ambalg.berne@bluewin.ch; Ambassador Kamel Houhou.

Angola: Laubegstr. 18, 3006 Bern; tel. 313518585; fax 313518586; e-mail berna@ambassadeangola.ch; internet www.ambassadeangola.ch; Ambassador Apolinario Jorge Correia.

Argentina: Jungfraustr. 1, 3005 Bern; tel. 313564343; fax 313564340; e-mail esuiz@mrecic.gov.ar; internet www.embargentina-suiza.org; Chargé d'affaires a.i. Fernando Raúl Lerena.

Armenia: 28 ave du Mail, 1205 Geneva; tel. 223201100; fax 223206148; e-mail arm.mission@deckpoint.ch; Ambassador Zohrab Mnatsakanian.

Austria: Kirchenfeldstr. 77–79, 3005 Bern; tel. 313565252; fax 313515664; e-mail bern-ob@bmeia.gv.at; internet www.aussenministerium.at/bern; Ambassador Hans Peter Manz.

Azerbaijan: Dalmaziquai 27, 3005 Bern; tel. 313505040; fax 313505041; e-mail bern@mission.mfa.gov.az; internet www.azembassy.ch; Ambassador Elchin Amirbayov.

Belarus: Quartierweg 6, CP 438, 3074 Muri bei Bern; tel. 319527914; fax 319527616; e-mail swiss@belembassy.org; Chargé d'affaires a.i. Alyaksandr Ganevich.

Belgium: Jubiläumstr. 41, 3005 Bern; tel. 313500150; fax 313500165; e-mail bern@diplobel.org; internet www.diplomatie.be/bern; Ambassador Régine De Clercq.

Bosnia and Herzegovina: Thorackerstr. 3, 3074 Muri bei Bern; tel. 313511052; fax 313511079; e-mail emb-ch-brn@vtxmail.ch; Ambassador Jasmina Pašalić.

Brazil: Monbijoustr. 68, 3007 Bern; tel. 313718515; fax 313710525; e-mail info@brasbern.ch; internet www.brasbern.ch; Ambassador Eduardo dos Santos.

Bulgaria: Bernastr. 2–4, 3005 Bern; tel. 313511455; fax 313510064; e-mail bulembassy@bluewin.ch; internet www.bulembassy.ch; Ambassador Atanas Pavlov.

Cameroon: Brunnadernrain 29, 3006 Bern; tel. 313524734; fax 313524736; e-mail ambacam.berne@yahoo.fr; Ambassador Jean Simplice Ndjemba Endezoumou.

Canada: Kirchenfeldstr. 88, 3005 Bern; tel. 313573200; fax 313573210; e-mail bern@international.gc.ca; internet www.canada-ambassade.ch; Ambassador Robert Collette.

Chile: Eigerpl. 5, 12th Floor, 3007 Bern; tel. 313700058; fax 313720025; e-mail embajada@embachile.ch; Ambassador María Carolina Rosetti Gallardo.

China, People's Republic: Kalcheggweg 10, 3006 Bern; tel. 313527333; fax 313514573; e-mail chinaemb_ch@mfa.gov.cn; internet www.china-embassy.ch; Ambassador Dong Jinyi.

Colombia: Dufourstr. 47, 3005 Bern; tel. 313511700; fax 313527072; e-mail colombie@iprolink.ch; internet www.emcol.ch; Ambassador Claudia Elena Jiménez Jaramillo.

Congo, Democratic Republic: Sulgenheimweg 21, 3007 Bern; tel. 313713538; fax 313727466; e-mail rdcambassy@bluewin.ch; Ambassador Kesia-Mbe Mindua.

Costa Rica: Schwarztorstr. 11, 3007 Bern; tel. 313727887; fax 313727834; e-mail costarica@bluewin.ch; Ambassador Edgar Mohs Villalta.

Côte d'Ivoire: Thormannstr. 51, 3005 Bern; tel. 313508080; fax 313508081; e-mail acibe-1@acibe.org; internet www.acibe.org; Ambassador Mamadou Diarrassouba.

Croatia: Thunstr. 45, 3005 Bern; tel. 313520275; fax 313520373; e-mail croemb.bern@mvpei.hr; Ambassador Jakša Muljačić.

Cuba: Gesellschaftsstr. 8, CP 5275, 3012 Bern; tel. 313022111; fax 313029830; e-mail embacuba.berna@bluewin.ch; internet emba.cubaminrex.cu/suiza; Ambassador Ana María Rovira Ingidua.

Czech Republic: Muristr. 53, Postfach 537, 3000 Bern 31; tel. 313504070; fax 313504098; e-mail bern@embassy.mzv.cz; internet www.mfa.cz/bern; Ambassador Dr Boris Lazar.

Denmark: Thunstr. 95, 3006 Bern; tel. 313505454; fax 313505464; e-mail brnamb@um.dk; internet www.ambbern.um.dk; Ambassador Lars Møller.

Dominican Republic: Wettposstr. 4, Postfach 22, 3000 Bern 15; tel. 313511585; fax 313511587; e-mail embaj.rep-dom@freesurf.ch; Ambassador José Tomás Ares Germán.

Ecuador: Kramgasse 54, 3011 Bern; tel. 313516254; fax 313512771; e-mail embecusuiza@bluewin.ch; Ambassador Jaime Marchan Romero.

Egypt: Elfenauweg 61, 3006 Bern; tel. 313528012; fax 313520625; Ambassador Nihad Zikry.

SWITZERLAND

Finland: Weltpoststr. 4, Postfach 11, 3015 Bern; tel. 313504100; fax 313504107; e-mail sanomat.brn@formin.fi; internet www.finlandia.ch; Ambassador PEKKA OJANEN.

France: Schosshaldenstr. 46, 3006 Bern; tel. 313592111; fax 313592191; e-mail scac@ambafrance-ch.org; internet www.ambafrance-ch.org; Ambassador JEAN-DIDIER ROISIN.

Georgia: 1 rue Richard Wagner, 1202 Geneva; tel. 229191010; fax 227339033; e-mail geomission.geneva@bluewin.com; internet www.switzerland.mfa.gov.ge; Chargé d'affaires a.i. TEIMURAZ BAKRADZE.

Germany: Willadingweg 83, Postfach 250, 3000 Bern 15; tel. 313594111; fax 313594444; e-mail vw-pfb1@bern.diplo.de; internet www.bern.diplo.de; Ambassador ANDREAS VON STECHOW.

Ghana: Belpstr. 11, Postfach, 3001 Bern; tel. 313817852; fax 313814941; e-mail ghanaemb@tcnet.ch; internet www.ghanaembassy.ch; Ambassador KWABENA BAAH-DUODU.

Greece: Weltpostr. 4, 3015 Bern; tel. 313561414; fax 313681272; e-mail gremb.brn@mfa.gr; internet www.greekembassy.ch; Ambassador CONSTANTINE TRITARIS.

Holy See: Thunstr. 60, 3006 Bern (Apostolic Nunciature); tel. 313526040; fax 313525064; e-mail nunziaturach@yahoo.com; Apostolic Nuncio Most Rev. FRANCESCO CANALINI (Titular Archbishop of Valeria).

Hungary: Muristr. 31, Postfach 216, 3000 Bern 15; tel. 313528572; fax 313512001; e-mail huembbrn@bluemail.ch; internet www.mfa.gov.hu/emb/bern; Ambassador JENŐ BOROS.

India: Kirchenfeldstr. 28, 3006 Bern; tel. 313511110; fax 313511557; e-mail india@spectraweb.ch; internet www.indembassybern.ch; Chargé d'affaires a.i. AJANEESH KUMAR.

Indonesia: Elfenauweg 51, 3006 Bern; tel. 313520983; fax 313516765; e-mail kbribern@bgb.ch; internet www.indonesia-bern.org; Ambassador LUCIA HELWINDA RUSTAM.

Iran: Thunstr. 68, 3006 Bern; tel. 313510801; fax 313515652; e-mail secretariat@iranembassy.ch; internet www.iranembassy.ch; Ambassador KEYVAN IMANI.

Iraq: Elfenstr. 6, 3006 Bern; tel. 313514043; fax 313518312; e-mail bernemb@iraqmofamail.net; Chargé d'affaires a.i. AHMED KHALIL AHMED AL-ANI.

Ireland: Kirchenfeldstr. 68, 3005 Bern; tel. 313521442; fax 313521455; e-mail berneembassy@dfa.ie; Ambassador JAMES STARKEY.

Israel: Alpenstr. 32, 3006 Bern; tel. 313563500; fax 313563556; e-mail info@bern.mfa.gov.il; internet bern.mfa.gov.il; Ambassador ILAN ELGAR.

Italy: Elfenstr. 14, 3000 Bern 16; tel. 313500777; fax 313500711; e-mail ambasciata.berna@esteri.it; internet www.ambberna.esteri.it; Ambassador GIUSEPPE DEODATO.

Japan: Engestr. 53, 3000 Bern 9; tel. 313002222; fax 313002255; e-mail eojs@bluewin.ch; internet www.ch.emb-japan.go.jp; Ambassador NOBUYASU ABE.

Jordan: Belpstr. 11, 3007 Bern; tel. 313840404; fax 313840405; e-mail jordanie@bluewin.ch; internet www.jordanie.ch; Ambassador SHEHAB AD-DIN MADI.

Kazakhstan: Alleeweg 15, 3006 Bern; tel. 313517972; fax 313517975; e-mail kasachische.botschaft@freesurf.ch; Ambassador AMANZHOL ZHANKULIYEV.

Korea, Democratic People's Republic: Pourtalèsstr. 43, 3074 Muri bei Bern; tel. 319516621; fax 319515704; e-mail dprk.embassy@bluewin.ch; Ambassador RI CHOL.

Korea, Republic: Kalcheggweg 38, 3006 Bern; tel. 313562444; fax 313562450; e-mail swiss@mofat.go.kr; internet www.mofat.go.kr/switzerland; Ambassador CHANG CHUL-KYOON.

Kuwait: Brunadernrain 19, 3006 Bern; tel. 313567000; fax 313567001; internet www.kuwaitembassy.ch; Ambassador SUHAIL KHALIL YOUSEF SHUHAIBER.

Lebanon: Thunstr. 10, 3074 Muri bei Bern; tel. 319506565; fax 319506566; e-mail ambalibch@hotmail.com; Chargé d'affaires a.i. HUSSEIN RAMMAL.

Libya: Tavelweg 2, 3006 Bern; tel. 313513076; fax 313511325; Chargé d'affaires a.i. IBRAHIM AD-DREDI.

Liechtenstein: Willadingweg 65, Postfach, 3000 Bern 15; tel. 313576411; fax 313576415; e-mail info@bbrn.liv.li; internet www.bern.liechtenstein.li; Ambassador HUBERT FERDINAND BÜCHEL.

Lithuania: Kramgasse 12, 3011 Bern; tel. 313525291; fax 313525292; e-mail amb.ch@urm.lt; internet ch.mfa.lt; Ambassador VYTAUTAS PLEČKAITIS.

Luxembourg: Kramgasse 45, 3000 Bern 8; tel. 313114732; fax 313110019; e-mail berne.am@mae.etat.lu; Ambassador GÉRARD PHILIPPS.

Macedonia, former Yugoslav republic: Kirchenfeldstr. 30, 3005 Bern; tel. 313520002; fax 313520037; e-mail makedamb@bluewin.ch; Chargé d'affaires a.i. KENAN RAMADANI.

Malaysia: Jungfraustr. 1, 3005 Bern; tel. 313504700; fax 313504702; e-mail malberne@greenmail.ch; Ambassador Dato' MOHD YUSOF BIN AHMAD.

Mexico: Bernastr. 57, 3005 Bern; tel. 313574747; fax 313574748; e-mail embamex1@swissonline.ch; internet www.sre.gob.mx/suiza; Ambassador LUCIANO JOUBLANC MONTANO.

Monaco: Hallwylstr. 34, 3005 Bern; tel. 313562858; fax 313562855; e-mail ambassademonaco@bluewin.ch; Ambassador ROBERT FILLON.

Morocco: Helvetiastr. 42, 3005 Bern; tel. 313510362; fax 313510364; e-mail sifamaberne2@bluewin.ch; internet www.amb-maroc.ch; Ambassador MUHAMMAD GUEDIRA.

Netherlands: Seftigenstr. 7, 3007 Bern; tel. 313508700; fax 313508710; e-mail ben@minbuza.nl; internet www.nlembassy.ch; Ambassador EDO HOFLAND.

Nigeria: Zieglerstr. 45, Postfach 574, 3007 Bern; tel. 313842600; fax 313842626; e-mail info@nigerianbern.org; internet www.nigerianbern.org; Ambassador Dr MARTIN I. UHOMOIBHI.

Norway: Bubenbergpl. 10, Postfach 5264, 3011 Bern; tel. 313105555; fax 313105550; e-mail emb.bern@mfa.no; internet www.amb-norwegen.ch; Ambassador LARS PETTER FORBERG.

Pakistan: Bernstr. 47, 3005 Bern; tel. 313501790; fax 313501799; e-mail parepberne@bluewin.ch; Ambassador AYESHA RIYAZ.

Paraguay: Kramgasse 58, Postfach 523, 3000 Bern 8; tel. 313123222; fax 313123432; e-mail embapar@embapar.ch; Chargé d'affaires RAÚL ALBERTO FLORENTÍN ANTOLA.

Peru: Thunstr. 36, 3005 Bern; tel. 313518555; fax 313518570; e-mail infoperu@bluewin.ch; Ambassador ELIZABETH ASTETE RODRÍGUEZ.

Philippines: Kirchenfeldstr. 73–75, 3005 Bern; tel. 313501717; fax 313522602; e-mail berne_pe@bluewin.ch; Ambassador MINERVA JEAN FALCON.

Poland: Elfenstr. 20A, 3000 Bern 15; tel. 313580202; fax 313580216; e-mail polishemb@dial.eunet.ch; internet www.berno.polemb.net; Chargé d'affaires a.i. JERZY WIECZOREK.

Portugal: Weltpoststr. 20, 3015 Bern; tel. 313528602; fax 313514432; e-mail embpt.berna@scber.dgaccp.pt; Ambassador EURICO JORGE HENRIQUES PAES.

Romania: Kirchenfeldstr. 78, 3005 Bern; tel. 313523522; fax 313526455; e-mail roumanie.amb@befree.ch; internet berna.mae.ro; Ambassador IONEL NICU SAVA.

Russia: Brunnadernrain 37, 3006 Bern; tel. 313520566; fax 313525595; e-mail rusbotschaft@bluewin.ch; internet www.switzerland.mid.ru; Ambassador IGOR B. BRATCHIKOV.

Saudi Arabia: Kramburgstr. 12, 3006 Bern; tel. 313521555; fax 313514581; e-mail chemb@mofa.gov.sa; Chargé d'affaires a.i. SAUD ABDULLAH HASSAN KATIB.

Serbia: Seminarstr. 5, 3006 Bern; tel. 313526353; fax 313514474; e-mail info@ambasadasrbije.ch; internet www.ambasadasrbije.ch; Ambassador DRAGAN MARŠIĆANIN.

Slovakia: Thunstr. 99, 3006 Bern 1; tel. 313563930; fax 313563933; e-mail slovak@spectraweb.ch; internet www.bern.mfa.sk; Ambassador ŠTEFAN SCHILL.

Slovenia: Schwanengasse 9, 3011 Bern; tel. 313109000; fax 313124414; e-mail vbe@gov.si; internet bern.embassy.si; Chargé d'affaires a.i. BRANKO ZUPANC.

South Africa: Alpenstr. 29, Postfach, 3000 Bern 6; tel. 313501313; fax 313501310; e-mail political@southafrica.ch; internet www.southafrica.ch; Ambassador KONJI SEBATI.

Spain: Kalcheggweg 24, Postfach 99, 3000 Bern 15; tel. 313505252; fax 313505255; e-mail emb.berna@mae.es; internet www.mae.es/embajadas/berna/es/home; Ambassador FERNANDO RIQUELME LIDÓN.

Sweden: Bundesgasse 26, Postfach, 3001 Bern; tel. 313287000; fax 313287001; e-mail ambassaden.bern@foreign.ministry.se; internet www.swedenabroad.com/bern; Ambassador PER THÖRESSON.

Thailand: Kirchstr. 56, 3097 Liebefeld-Bern; tel. 319703030; fax 319703035; e-mail thai.bern@bluewin.ch; Ambassador CHAIYONG SATJIPANON.

Tunisia: Kirchenfeldstr. 63, 3005 Bern; tel. 313528226; fax 313510445; e-mail at.berne@bluewin.ch; Chargé d'affaires a.i. MUHAMMAD FAWZI BLOUT.

Turkey: Lombachweg 33, 3006 Bern; tel. 313597070; fax 313528819; e-mail tcbern@tr-botschaft.ch; internet www.tr-botschaft.ch; Ambassador ALEV KILIÇ.

Ukraine: Feldeggweg 5, 3005 Bern; tel. 313522316; fax 313516416; e-mail emb_ch@mfa.gov.ua; internet www.ukremb.ch; Chargé d'affaires a.i. YAN OMELCHENKO.

SWITZERLAND

United Kingdom: Thunstr. 50, 3000 Bern 15; tel. 313597700; fax 313597701; e-mail info@britain-in-switzerland.ch; internet www.britishembassy.ch; Ambassador SIMON FEATHERSTONE.

USA: Jubiläumsstr. 93, 3005 Bern; tel. 313577011; fax 313577320; internet bern.usembassy.gov; Ambassador PETER R. CONEWAY.

Uruguay: Kramgasse 63, 3011 Bern; tel. 313122226; fax 313112747; e-mail uruhelve@bluewin.ch; Ambassador CARLOS BRUGNINI GARCÍA LAGOS.

Venezuela: Schosshaldenstr. 1, Postfach 1005, 3000 Bern 23; tel. 313505757; fax 313505758; e-mail embavenez@greenmail.ch; internet www.embavenez-suiza.com; Chargé d'affaires a.i. FÁTIMA MAJZOUB EL-MAJZOUB.

Viet Nam: Schlösslistr. 26, 3008 Bern; tel. 313887878; fax 313887879; e-mail info@vietnam-embassy.ch; internet www.vietnam-embassy.ch; Ambassador NGUYEN NGOC SON.

Judicial System

Switzerland has possessed a common Civil Code since 1912, but the Penal Code was only unified in 1942. Under the Code capital punishment was abolished by the few cantons that still retained it. The individual cantons continue to elect and maintain their own magistracy, and retain certain variations in procedure. The canton of Zürich, for example, has justices of the peace (Friedensrichter—normally one for each commune), District Courts (Bezirksgerichte), Labour Courts (Arbeitsgerichte), Courts for Tenancy Matters, an Appeal Court (Obergericht) with various specialized benches, a Cassation Court (Kassationsgericht), and, for the more important cases under penal law, a Jury Court (Geschworenengericht).

At the federal level, the Federal Supreme Court has, in principle, jurisdiction over judicial matters. However, federal appeals commissions adjudicate appeals against rulings by the federal authority. From 1997 a revision of the federal judicial system was undertaken that saw the establishment of two new judicial bodies of first instance, in order to alleviate the burden on the Federal Supreme Court. These were the Federal Criminal Court in Bellinzona (from April 2004) and the Federal Administrative Court (from January 2007). In January 2007 the competences of the Federal Insurance Court were merged with the Federal Supreme Court. There are also military courts at the federal level.

Most disputes relating to the application of federal administrative law are first judged by the Federal Administrative Court. In January 2007 the Federal Administrative Court replaced some 30 federal appeals commissions as well as the current departmental appeals services.

FEDERAL SUPREME COURT

Schweizerisches Bundesgericht—Tribunal fédéral
Schweizerhofquai 6, 6004 Lucerne; 29 ave du Tribunal fédéral, 1000 Lausanne 14; tel. 213189111; fax 213233700; e-mail direktion@bger.admin.ch; internet www.bger.ch.

Composed of 30 judges elected for a six-year term by the Federal Assembly. According to the Constitution any citizen eligible for election to the National Council can theoretically be elected Justice to the Court, but in practice only lawyers are considered for this office. All three official Swiss languages must be represented in the Court. The President of the Federal Supreme Court is elected by the Federal Assembly for a two-year term, with no possibility of re-election, from among the senior judges of the Court. The Court is divided into six permanent branches or chambers, each of which has jurisdiction over cases pertaining to a specific subject, namely: (a) two 'Public', i.e. Constitutional and Administrative Law Divisions, being composed of seven and six judges, respectively; (b) two Civil or Private Law Divisions of six judges each, which serve mainly as Courts of Appeal in civil matters; (c) the Debt Execution and Bankruptcy Law Chamber of three judges (members of the Second Civil Law Division); (d) the Criminal Law Division, the so-called Court of Cassation, which is composed of five judges and which hears mainly appeals in criminal law matters. There are also four non-permanent divisions hearing exclusively cases that involve certain crimes against the Confederation, certain forms of terrorism, and other offences related to treason.

President: Dr ARTHUR AESCHLIMANN.
Vice-President: Dr SUZANNE LEUZINGER-NAEF.

FEDERAL CRIMINAL COURT

Bundesstrafgericht—Tribunal pénal fédéral
CP 2720, 6501 Bellinzona; Viale Stefano Franscini 3, 6500 Bellinzona; tel. 918226262; fax 918226242; e-mail info@bstger.admin.ch; internet www.bstger.ch.

f. 2004; composed of 13 judges elected by the Federal Assembly; court of first instance for criminal cases assigned to federal jurisdiction; in particular, may adjudicate offences such as crimes and misdemeanours against the Confederation's interests, offences committed using explosives, economic crime, organized crime or money-laundering beyond the internal or external borders of Switzerland.

President: ALEX STAUB.
Vice-President: ANDREAS J. KELLER.

FEDERAL ADMINISTRATIVE COURT

Bundesverwaltungsgericht—Tribunal administratif fédéral
3000 Bern 14; tel. 587052626; fax 587052980; e-mail info@bvger.admin.ch; internet www.bvger.ch.

Composed of 72 judges elected by the Federal Assembly, for a renewable period of six years; court of first instance for cases arising from administrative decisions at the federal level; appeals in some cases relating to civil and public law matters may be heard in the Federal Supreme Court.

President: CHRISTOPH BANDLI.

Religion

According to the 2000 census, the religious adherence of the total resident population was as follows: Roman Catholic 41.8%, Protestant 35.3%, Orthodox Church 1.8%, Old Catholic 0.2%, Muslim 4.3%, Jewish 0.2%, other religions (including Buddhist and Hindu) 0.8% and those without religion 11.1%.

CHRISTIANITY

The Roman Catholic Church

For ecclesiastical purposes, Switzerland comprises six dioceses and two territorial abbacies. All of the dioceses and abbacies are directly responsible to the Holy See. At 31 December 2005 there were an estimated 3,176,292 adherents (some 44.7% of the total population).

Bishops' Conference

Secrétariat de la Conférence des Evêques Suisses, 21 ave du Moléson, CP 122, 1706 Fribourg; tel. 263224794; fax 263224993; e-mail sbk-ces@gmx.ch; internet www.kath.ch/sbk-ces-cvs.

f. 1863; Pres. Rt Rev. KURT KOCH (Bishop of Basel); Sec.-Gen. Abbé FELIX GMÜR.

Bishop of Basel: Rt Rev. Dr KURT KOCH, Bischöfliches Ordinariat, Baselstr. 58, Postfach 216, 4501 Solothurn; tel. 326255825; fax 326255845; e-mail generalvikariat@bistum-basel.ch; internet www.bistum-basel.ch.

Bishop of Chur: Rt Rev. VITUS HUONDER, Bischöfliches Ordinariat, Hof 19, Postfach 133, 7002 Chur; tel. 812586000; fax 812586001; e-mail kanzlei@bistum-chur.ch; internet www.bistum-chur.ch.

Bishop of Lausanne, Geneva and Fribourg: Rt Rev. BERNARD GENOUD, 86 rue de Lausanne, CP, 1701 Fribourg; tel. 263474850; fax 263474851; e-mail chancellerie@diocese-lgf.ch; internet www.diocese-lgf.ch.

Bishop of Lugano: Rt Rev. PIER GIACOMO GRAMPA, CP 5382, Via Borghetto 6, 6901 Lugano; tel. 919138989; fax 919138990; e-mail curialugano@catt.ch; internet www.catt.ch.

Bishop of Sankt Gallen: Rt Rev. MARKUS BÜCHEL, Bischöfliches Ordinariat, Klosterhof 6B, Postfach 263, 9001 Sankt Gallen; tel. 712273340; fax 712273341; e-mail kanzlei@bistum-stgallen.ch; internet www.bistum-stgallen.ch.

Bishop of Sion: Rt Rev. NORBERT BRUNNER, 12 rue de la Tour, CP 2124, 1950 Sion 2; tel. 273291818; fax 273291836; e-mail diocese.sion@cath-vs.ch; internet www.cath-vs.ch.

Protestant Churches

Federation of Swiss Protestant Churches (Schweizerischer Evangelischer Kirchenbund—Fédération des Eglises protestantes de Suisse): Sulgenauweg 26, Postfach, 3000 Bern 23; tel. 313702525; fax 313702580; e-mail info@sek-feps.ch; internet www.sek-feps.ch; f. 1920; comprises the 26 reformed cantonal churches of Aargau, Appenzell (incl. Appenzell Ausserrhoden and Appenzell Innerrhoden), Basel-Stadt, Basel-Landschaft, Bern-Jura-Solothurn, Fribourg, Geneva, Glarus, Graubünden, Luzern, Neuchâtel, Nidwalden, St Gallen, Schaffhausen, Schwyz, Solothurn, Ticino, Thurgau, Unterwalden, Uri, Valais, Vaud, Zug, Zürich, the Eglise évangélique libre de Genève and the United Methodist Church; the exec. organ is the Council of the Federation (Rat des Schweizerischen Evangelischen Kirchenbundes, Conseil de la Fédération); Pres. Rev. THOMAS WIPF.

SWITZERLAND

ISLAM

According to the 2000 census there were 310,807 Muslims recorded in Switzerland, making Islam the second largest religion in the country. There are two major mosques, one in Zürich and one in Geneva, and approximately 200 Muslim centres located throughout the country.

Föderation Islamischer Gemeinschaften in der Schweiz: Hohlstrasse 615A, 8050 Zürich; tel. 443013151.

League of Muslims in Switzerland: CP 1861, 2002 Neuchâtel; tel. 319314595.

Musulmans, Musulmanes de Suisse (MMS): Postfach 7303, 3001 Bern; tel. 313229780; fax 313222235; e-mail info@islam.ch; internet www.islam.ch.

JUDAISM

According to the 2000 census there were 17,900 Jews in Switzerland.

Schweizerischer Israelitischer Gemeindebund—Fédération suisse des communautés israélites: Gotthardstr. 65, Postfach 2105, 8027 Zürich; tel. 433050777; fax 433050766; e-mail info@swissjews.org; internet www.swissjews.org; f. 1904; Pres. Prof. Dr ALFRED DONATH; Gen. Sec. DENNIS L. RHEIN.

The Press

Freedom of the Press in Switzerland is guaranteed by Article 55 of the amended 1874 Constitution, and the only formal restrictions on the press are the legal restraints concerned with abuses of this freedom.

Switzerland's federal constitutional structure and the coexistence of diverse languages and religions have tended to produce a decentralized press, fragmented into numerous local papers, often with very low circulations. In 2001 there were 72 daily newspapers with a combined circulation of 2,871,100. The majority of newspapers are regional, even such high circulation ones as *Tages-Anzeiger* and *Berner Zeitung* and national dailies such as *Neue Zürcher Zeitung*. About 67% of newspapers are printed in German, 27% in French, 4% in Italian and less than 1% in Romansh. Some 100,000 copies of French, German, Italian and Spanish newspapers are imported daily.

PRINCIPAL DAILIES

Baden

Aargauer Zeitung: Stadtturmstr. 19, 5400 Baden; tel. 582005858; fax 582005859; e-mail azredaktion@azag.ch; internet www.aargauerzeitung.ch; f. 1996 by merger of *Aargauer Tagblatt* and *Badener Tagblatt*; Editor-in-Chief PETER BURI; circ. 129,321 (2007).

Basel/Bâle

Basler Zeitung: Aeschenpl. 7, 4002 Basel; tel. 616391111; fax 616381582; e-mail redaktion@baz.ch; internet www.baz.ch; f. 1976; liberal; Editor-in-Chief MATTHIAS GEERING; circ. 94,084 (2007).

Bellinzona

La Regione Ticino: Via Ghiringhelli 9, 6500 Bellinzona; tel. 918211121; fax 918211122; e-mail info@laregione.ch; internet www.laregione.ch; f. 1992; Editor GIACOMO SALVIONI; circ. 33,308 (2007).

Bern/Berne

Berner Zeitung: Nordring/Dammweg 9, 3001 Bern; tel. 3133003111; fax 313327724; e-mail redaktion@bernerzeitung.ch; internet www.bzonline.ch; f. 1844; independent; Editors-in-Chief MARKUS EISENHUT, MICHAEL HUG; circ. 213,544 (2007).

Der Bund: Bubenbergpl. 8, 3001 Bern; tel. 313851111; fax 313851112; e-mail redaktion@derbund.ch; internet www.ebund.ch; f. 1850; liberal; Editor-in-Chief ARTUR K. VOGEL; circ. 60,500 (2005).

Biel/Bienne

Bieler Tagblatt: Robert-Walser-Pl. 7, 2502 Biel; tel. 323219111; fax 323219119; e-mail btredaktion@bielertagblatt.ch; internet www.bielertagblatt.ch; independent; Editor-in-Chief CATHERINE DUTTWEILER; circ. 27,576 (2007).

Brig

Walliser Bote: Furkastr. 21, 3900 Brig; tel. 279229988; fax 279229989; e-mail info@walliserbote.ch; internet www.walliserbote.ch; Catholic; Editor-in-Chief PIUS RIEDER; circ. 26,727 (2007).

La Chaux-de-Fonds

L'impartial: 14 rue Neuve, 2300 La Chaux-de-Fonds; tel. 329102000; fax 329102009; e-mail redaction@limpartial.ch; internet www.limpartial.ch; f. 1880; independent; Editor-in-Chief NICOLAS WILLEMIN; circ. 15,182 (2007).

Chur/Coire

Bündner Tagblatt: Comercialstr. 22, 7007 Chur; tel. 812555000; fax 812555123; e-mail redaktion-bt@suedostschweiz.ch; internet www.suedostschweiz.ch/medien/bt; f. 1852; independent; Editor-in-Chief CHRISTIAN BUXHOFER.

La Quotidiana: Via Centrala 4, 7130 Glion; tel. 819200710; fax 819200715; e-mail redaktion-lq@suedostschweiz.ch; f. 1997; in Romansh; Publr Südostschweiz Presse AG; Editor-in-Chief MARTIN CABALZAR.

Die Südostschweiz: Comercialstr. 22, 7007 Chur; tel. 812255050; fax 812255102; e-mail zentralredaktion@suedostschweiz.ch; internet www.suedostschweiz.ch; publ. regional editions for Gaster und See and Glarus; independent; Publr Südostschweiz Presse AG; Editor-in-Chief ANDREA MASÜGER; circ. 126,697 (2007).

Delémont

Le Quotidien Jurassien: 6 route de Courroux, 2800 Delémont; tel. 324211818; fax 324211890; e-mail lqj@lqj.ch; internet www.lqj.ch; f. 1993; independent; Editor-in-Chief PIERRE-ANDRÉ CHAPATTE; circ. 21,246 (2007).

Dielsdorf

Zürcher Unterländer: Schulstr. 12, 8157 Dielsdorf; tel. 18548282; fax 18530690; e-mail redaktion@zuonline.ch; internet www.zuonline.ch; Editor-in-Chief CHRISTINE FIVIAN; circ. 22,544 (2007).

Frauenfeld

Thurgauer Zeitung: Promenadenstr. 16, 8501 Frauenfeld; tel. 527235757; fax 527235707; e-mail redaktion@thurgauerzeitung.ch; internet www.thurgauerzeitung.ch; f. 1798; independent; Publrs Huber & Co AG; Editor-in-Chief URSULA FRAEFEL; circ. 39,406 (2007).

Freiburg/Fribourg

La Liberté: 42 blvd de Pérolles, 1705 Fribourg; tel. 264264411; fax 264264444; e-mail redaction@laliberte.ch; internet www.laliberte.ch; Editor-in-Chief LOUIS RUFFIEUX; circ. 38,735 (2007).

Genève
(Geneva)

Le Temps: 3 pl. de Cornavin, CP 2570, 1211 Geneva 2; tel. 227995858; fax 227995859; e-mail info@letemps.ch; internet www.letemps.ch; f. 1998; Dir and Editor-in-Chief JEAN-JACQUES ROTH; circ. 45,103 (2007).

Tribune de Genève: CP 5115, 11 rue des Rois, 1211 Geneva 11; tel. 223224000; fax 227810107; e-mail alain.giroud@edipresse.ch; internet www.tdg.ch; f. 1879; independent; morning; Editor-in-Chief PIERRE RUETSCHI; circ. 62,003 (2007).

Herisau

Appenzeller Zeitung: Kasernenstr. 64, 9100 Herisau; tel. 713546474; fax 713546475; e-mail redaktion@appon.ch; internet www.appenzellerzeitung.ch; radical democratic; f. 1828; Publrs Appenzeller Medienhaus Schläpfer AG; Editor-in-Chief MONIKA EGLI.

Lausanne

Le Matin: 33 ave de la Gare, 1001 Lausanne; tel. 213494949; fax 21494929; internet www.lematin.ch; f. 1862; independent; Editor-in-Chief PETER ROTHENBÜHLER; circ. 70,012 (2007).

24 heures: 33 ave de la Gare, 1001 Lausanne; tel. 213494444; fax 213494419; internet www.24heures.ch; f. 1762; independent; Editor-in-Chief THIERRY MAYER; circ. 89,102 (2007).

Lugano

Corriere del Ticino: Via Industria, 6933 Muzzano; tel. 919603131; fax 919682779; e-mail cdt@cdt.ch; internet www.cdt.ch; f. 1891; independent; Dir GIANCARLO DILLENA; circ. 38,108 (2007).

Giornale del Popolo: Via San Gottardo 50, 6900 Lugano; tel. 919223800; fax 919223805; e-mail redazione@gdp.ch; internet www.gdp.ch; f. 1926; independent; Pres. PIER GIACOMO GRAMPA; circ. 18,057 (2007).

SWITZERLAND

Luzern/Lucerne

Neue Luzerner Zeitung: Maihofstr. 76, 6006 Lucerne; tel. 414295252; fax 414295181; e-mail redaktion@neue-lz.ch; internet www.zisch.ch; f. 1996; Editor-in-Chief THOMAS BORNHAUSER; circ. 130,213 (2007).

Neuchâtel/Neuenburg

L'Express: 39 rue de la Pierre-à-Mazel, 2000 Neuchâtel; tel. 327235300; fax 327235209; e-mail redaction@lexpress.ch; internet www.lexpress.ch; f. 1738; independent; Editor-in-Chief NICOLAS WILLEMIN; circ. 23,344 (2007).

Sankt Gallen/Saint-Gall

St Galler Tagblatt: Fürstenlandstr. 122, 9001 St Gallen; tel. 712727711; fax 712727476; e-mail zentralredaktion@tagblatt.ch; internet www.tagblatt.ch; f. 1839; liberal; Editor-in-Chief GOTTLIEB F. HÖPLI; circ. 101,732 (2007).

Schaffhausen/Schaffhouse

Schaffhauser Nachrichten: Vordergasse 58, 8201 Schaffhausen; tel. 526333111; fax 526333401; e-mail redaktion@shn.ch; internet www.shn.ch; f. 1861; liberal; Editor-in-Chief NORBERT NEININGER; circ. 24,657 (2007).

Sion

Le Nouvelliste: 13 rue de l'Industrie, 1950 Sion; tel. 273297511; fax 273297578; e-mail redaction@nouvelliste.ch; internet www.lenouvelliste.ch; Catholic; Editor-in-Chief JEAN-FRANÇOIS FOURNIER; circ. 42,671 (2007).

Stäfa

Zürichsee-Zeitung: Seestr. 86, 8712 Stäfa; tel. 19285555; fax 19285550; e-mail redstaefa@zsz.ch; internet www.zsz.ch; f. 1845; radical democratic; Editor-in-Chief BENJAMIN GEIGER; circ. 45,519 (2007).

Thun/Thoune

Berner Oberländer: Rampenstr. 1, 3602 Thun; tel. 332251515; fax 332251505; e-mail redaktion-bo@bom.ch; internet www.berneroberlaender.ch; f. 1898; independent; Publrs Berner Oberland Medien AG; Editor-in-Chief RENÉ E. GYGAX; circ. 23,500 (2005).

Thuner Tagblatt: Rampenstr. 1, 3602 Thun; tel. 332251515; fax 332251505; e-mail redaktion-tt@bom.ch; internet www.thunertagblatt.ch; independent; publ. by Berner Oberland Medien AG; Editor-in-Chief RENÉ E. GYGAX; circ. 24,000 (2005).

Wetzikon

Zürcher Oberländer: Rapperswilerstr. 1, 8620 Wetzikon; tel. 19333333; fax 19323232; e-mail redaktion@zol.ch; internet www.zo-medien.ch; f. 1852; liberal; Editor-in-Chief CHRISTOPH VOLLENWEIDER; circ. 38,663 (2007).

Winterthur/Winterthour

Der Landbote: Garnmarkt 1–10, Postfach, 8401 Winterthur; tel. 522669901; fax 522669911; e-mail redaktion@landbote.ch; internet www.landbote.ch; f. 1836; independent; morning; Editor-in-Chief COLETTE GRADWOHL; circ. 35,898 (2007).

Zofingen

Zofinger Tagblatt: Vordere Hauptgasse 33, 4800 Zofingen; tel. 627459350; fax 627459419; e-mail ztredaktion@ztonline.ch; internet www.zofingertagblatt.ch; f. 1873; liberal; Editor BEAT KIRCHHOFER.

Zürich

Blick: Dufourstr. 23, 8008 Zürich; tel. 442596262; fax 442596665; e-mail redaktion@blick.ch; internet www.blick.ch; independent; Editor-in-Chief BERNHARD WEISSBERG; circ. 240,066 (2007).

Neue Zürcher Zeitung: Falkenstr. 11, Postfach, 8021 Zürich; tel. 442581111; fax 442521329; e-mail redaktion@nzz.ch; internet www.nzz.ch; f. 1780; independent-liberal; Editor-in-Chief MARKUS SPILLMANN; circ. 143,875 (2007).

Tages-Anzeiger: Werdstr. 21, 8021 Zürich; tel. 442484411; fax 442484471; e-mail redaktion@tages-anzeiger.ch; internet www.tagesanzeiger.ch; f. 1893; independent; Editor-in-Chief PETER HARTMEIER; circ. 216,411 (2007).

20 Minuten: Werdstr. 21, Postfach, 8021 Zürich; tel. 442486820; fax 442486821; e-mail redaktion@20minuten.ch; internet www.20min.ch; f. 1999; distributed free of charge; six regional editions: Bern/Basel, Geneva, Luzern, Région, St Gallen and Zürich; Editor-in-Chief MARCO BOSELLI; circ. 435,460 (2007).

PERIODICALS AND JOURNALS

Allgemeine Schweizerische Militärzeitschrift: Verlag Huber & Co AG, Postfach, 8501 Frauenfeld; tel. 527235622; fax 527235632; e-mail redaktion@asmz.ch; internet www.asmz.ch; f. 1834; 11 a year; Editor-in-Chief LOUIS GEIGER; circ. 21,000.

Die Alpen: Monbijoustr. 61, Postfach, 3000 Bern 23; tel. 313701885; fax 313701890; e-mail alpen@sac-cas.ch; internet www.sac-cas.ch; monthly; publ. by Schweizer Alpen-Club; circ. 90,000.

Annabelle création: Baslerstr. 30, 8048 Zürich; tel. 444046333; fax 444046218; e-mail redaktion@an-creation.ch; f. 1998; creative lifestyle and living magazine; monthly; circ. 102,866.

Auto & Lifestyle (ACS Clubmagazin): Wasserwerkgasse 39, 3000 Bern 13; tel. 313283111; fax 313110310; e-mail acszv@acs.ch; internet www.acs.ch; publ. by the Automobile Club of Switzerland; 10 a year; circ. 63,200.

Automobil Revue: Dammweg 9, 3001 Bern; tel. 313303034; fax 313303032; e-mail office@automobilrevue.ch; internet www.automobilrevue.ch; f. 1906; weekly publ. in German and French (*Revue automobile*); Editor PETER RUCH; circ. 67,412.

Beobachter: Förrlibuckstr. 70, 8021 Zürich; tel. 434445252; fax 434445353; e-mail redaktion@beobachter.ch; internet www.beobachter.ch; f. 1927; 2 a month; circ. 315,081.

Bilanz: Förrlibuckstr. 70, 8021 Zürich; tel. 434445520; fax 434445521; internet www.bilanz.ch; f. 1977; review of business in Switzerland; circ. 57,548.

Courrier neuchâtelois: 2013 Colombier; tel. 328417250; fax 328411521; e-mail administration@editionsduchateau.ch; weekly; Editor RENÉ GESSLER; circ. 88,087.

Du—Zeitschrift für Kultur: Du Verlags AG, Holbeinstr. 8, 8008 Zürich; tel. 432434600; fax 432434611; e-mail redaktion@dumag.ch; internet www.dumag.ch; f. 1941; monthly art review; Editor ANDREAS KLÄUI; circ. 31,915.

Echo Magazine: 12 rue de Meyrin, CP 80, 1211 Geneva 7; tel. 225930303; fax 225930319; e-mail abo.echo.magazine@saripress.ch; internet www.echomagazine.ch; f. 1929; weekly; circ. 22,000; Editor-in-Chief BERNARD LITZLER.

L'Eco dello Sport: Via Industria, 6933 Muzzano; tel. 919603131; fax 91575750; circ. 44,000.

Finanz und Wirtschaft: Hallwylstr. 71, Postfach, 8021 Zürich; tel. 442983535; fax 442983500; e-mail verlag@fuw.ch; internet www.finanzinfo.ch; f. 1928; 2 a week; finance and economics; circ. 44,308.

Freisinn: Postfach 6136, 3001 Bern; tel. 313203535; fax 313203500; e-mail zila@fdp.ch; internet www.fdp.ch; f. 1979; monthly; politics; Editor-in-Chief NICO ZILA; circ. 71,160.

Glücks-Post: Dufourstr. 49, 8008 Zürich; tel. 442596912; fax 442596930; e-mail gluec kspost@ringier.ch; internet www.gluec kspost.ch; women's interest; f. 1977; weekly; Editor-in-Chief HELMUT-MARIA GLOGGER; circ. 148,737.

Graphis: Dufourstr. 107, 8008 Zürich; tel. 443838211; fax 443831643; f. 1944; bi-monthly; graphic art and applied arts; publ. by Graphis Press Corpn; Editor B. MARTIN PEDERSEN; circ. 29,000.

Handels Zeitung: Seestr. 37, 8027 Zürich; tel. 442883555; fax 442883575; e-mail redaktion@handelszeitung.ch; internet www.handelszeitung.ch; f. 1862; financial, commercial and industrial weekly; Publr RALPH BÜCHI; Chief Editor MARTIN SPIELER; circ. 33,044.

L'Hebdo: Pont Bessières 3, POB 6682, 1002 Lausanne; tel. 213317600; fax 213317601; e-mail courrier.hebdo@ringier.ch; internet www.hebdo.ch; f. 1981; weekly; news magazine; Editor-in-Chief ALAIN JEANNET; circ. 48,451 (2007).

L'Illustré: 3 Pont Bessières, POB 6505, 1002 Lausanne; tel. 213317500; fax 213317501; e-mail illustre@ringier.ch; internet www.illustre.ch; f. 1921; weekly; Chief Editor FREDERICO CAMPOMODO; circ. 97,974.

Museum Helveticum: Steinentorstr. 13, 4010 Basel; tel. 612789565; fax 612789566; e-mail verlag@schwabe.ch; internet www.schwabe.ch; f. 1944; quarterly; Swiss journal for classical philology, ancient history and classical archaeology; Editors Prof. M. BILLERBECK, Prof. A. GIOVANNINI, Prof. TH. GELZER, Prof. H. HARICH-SCHWARZBAUER; publ. by Schwabe AG.

Music Scene: 5401 Baden; tel. 562032200; fax 562032299; e-mail info@music-scene.ch; internet www.music-scene.ch; f. 1924; young people's fortnightly; circ. 50,000.

Nebelspalter: Bahnhofstr. 17, 9326 Horn; tel. 718468876; fax 718468879; e-mail redaktion@nebelspalter.ch; internet www.nebelspalter.ch; f. 1875; 10 a year; satirical; Editor-in-Chief MARCO RATSCHILLER; publ. by Engeli & Partner Verlag; circ. 12,600.

PRO: Im Morgental 8, 8126 Zumikou; tel. 19182728; f. 1951; monthly; Editor ANNEMARIE FREY.

Revue médicale suisse: Editions Médecine et Hygiène, 46 chemin de la Mousse, POB 475, 1225 Chêne-Bourg 4; tel. 227029311; fax

SWITZERLAND

227029366; e-mail redac@revmed.ch; internet www.revmed.ch; f. 2005 to replace Revue médicale de la suisse romande and Médecine et Hygiène; monthly; circ. 5,600.

Revue militaire suisse: 3 ave de Florimont, 1006 Lausanne; tel. 213114817; fax 213119709; e-mail info@jcrc.ch; internet www.revuemilitairesuisse.ch; f. 1856; 8 a year; Editor-in-Chief Maj. ALEXANDRE VAUTRAVERS.

Revue suisse de zoologie: Muséum d'Histoire Naturelle, CP 6434, 1211 Geneva 6; tel. 224186300; fax 224186301; e-mail danielle.decrouez@mhn.ville-ge.ch; f. 1893; quarterly; Dir DANIELLE DECROUEZ.

Schweizer Archiv für Neurologie und Psychiatrie (Archives Suisses de Neurologie et de Psychiatrie): Schwabe AG Verlag, Steinentorstr. 13, 4010 Basel; tel. 612789565; fax 612789566; internet www.schwabe.ch; f. 1917; 8 a year.

Schweizer Familie: Werdstr. 21, Postfach, 8021 Zürich; tel. 442486106; fax 444248096; internet www.schweizerfamilie.ch; f. 1893; weekly; Editor ANDREAS DURISCH; Man. Dir JOSEF BURCH; circ. 205,529.

Schweizer Illustrierte: Dufourstr. 23, 8008 Zürich; tel. 442596363; fax 442620442; internet www.schweizer-illustrierte.ch; f. 1911; illustrated weekly; circ. 232,519; Chief Editor DOMINIC GEISSELER.

Schweizer Monatshefte: Vogelsangstr. 52, 8006 Zürich; tel. 443612606; fax 443637005; e-mail info@schweizermonatshefte.ch; internet www.schweizermonatshefte.ch; f. 1921; political, economic and cultural monthly; Editors ROBERT NEF, SUZANN RENNINGER; circ. 2,500.

Schweizerisches Handelsamtsblatt (Feuille officielle suisse du commerce): Effingerstr. 1, Postfach 8164, 3001 Bern; tel. 313240992; fax 313240961; e-mail info@shab.ch; internet www.shab.ch; f. 1883; commercial daily; publ. by Federal Dept of Foreign Trade; circ. 10,000.

Snowactive: Strike Media Schweiz AG, Gösgerstr. 15, 5012 Schönenwerd; tel. 326247685; fax 326247251; e-mail j.weibel@snowactive.ch; internet www.snowactive.ch; f. 1968; 7 a year; German and French/Italian editions; Editor JOSEPH WEIBEL; circ. 85,000.

Sport: Förrlibuckstr. 10, 8021 Zürich; tel. 444487373; fax 444487673; f. 1920; weekly; Chief Editor PETER ZWICKY; circ. 55,477.

Swiss Engineering (STZ): Les Cerisiers, 1585 Bellerive; tel. 266773270; fax 266773269; e-mail mediakom@bluewin.ch; internet www.swissengineering-stz.ch; 1 a year; technical journal in German; Editor-in-Chief HANNES GYSLING; circ. 20,000.

Swiss Journal of Psychology/ Schweizerische Zeitschrift für Psychologie/ Revue suisse de psychologie: Unitobler, Muesmattstr. 45, 3000 Bern 9; e-mail margit.oswald@psy.unibe.ch; internet www.verlag-hanshuber.com/zeitschriften/journal.php?abbrev=sjp; f. 1942; quarterly; Editor-in-Chief Prof. Dr FRIEDRICH WILKENING.

Swiss Medical Weekly: EMH Swiss Medical Publrs Ltd, Steinentorstr. 13, 4010 Basel; tel. 614678555; fax 614678556; e-mail red@smw.ch; internet www.smw.ch; f. 1871; fortnightly; Man. Editor Dr NATALIE MARTY.

TCS-Zürich: Geissbüelstr. 24–26, 8604 Volketswil; tel. 442868613; fax 442868637; official organ of the Zürich Touring Club; monthly; Chief Editor RETO CAVEGN; circ. 200,000.

Tele: Dufourstr. 23, 8008 Zürich; tel. 442596111; fax 442598697; e-mail telesekr@ringier.ch; internet www.tele.ch; f. 1967; television, cinema and multimedia; weekly; Editor KLAUS KRIESEL; circ. 214,214.

Touring: Maulbeerstr. 10, 3001 Bern; tel. 313805000; fax 313805006; f. 1935; fortnightly; German, French and Italian editions; Chief Editor STEFAN SENN; circ. 1,306,000.

TV 8: 3 Pont Bessières, 1005 Lausanne; tel. 213317700; fax 213317701; e-mail tv8@ringier.ch; weekly; circ. 52,720.

Vox Romanica: Centre de dialectologie, Université de Neuchâtel, 6 ave DuPeyrou, 2000 Neuchâtel; tel. 327181720; fax 327181721; e-mail vox.romanica@unine.ch; internet www.unine.ch/dialectologie/vox/vox.html; f. 1936; annual review of Romance linguistics and medieval literature; publ. by Collegium Romanicum (Swiss Association of Romanists); Editors Prof. Dr RITA FRANCESCHINI, Prof. ANDRES KRISTOL.

Weltwoche: Förrlibuckstr. 70, 8021 Zürich; tel. 434445111; fax 434445669; e-mail redaktion@weltwoche.ch; internet www.weltwoche.ch; f. 1933; weekly; independent; Editor-in-Chief ROGER KÖPPEL; circ. 92,337.

Werk, Bauen + Wohnen: Talstr. 39, 8001 Zürich; tel. 442181430; fax 442181434; e-mail wbw.zh@bluewin.ch; internet www.werkbauenundwohnen.ch; f. 1913; monthly; architecture; circ. 8,000.

NEWS AGENCY

Schweizerische Depeschenagentur AG/ Agence Télégraphique Suisse SA (SDA/ATS) (Swiss News Agency): Länggassstr. 7, 3001 Bern; tel. 313093333; fax 313018538; f. 1894; agency for political and general news; Chief Editor BERNARD REIST.

PRESS ASSOCIATIONS

Association Presse Suisse/ Verband Schweizer Presse: Baumackerstr. 42, Postfach, 8050 Zürich; tel. 3186464; fax 3186462; e-mail contact@schweizerpresse.ch; internet www.schweizerpresse.ch; f. 1899; Pres. HANSPETER LEBRUMENT; 180 mems.

Impressum—Die Schweizer Journalistinnen/ Les journalistes suisses/ I giornalisti svizzeri: Grand'Places 14A, 1701 Fribourg; tel. 263471500; fax 263471509; e-mail info@impressum.ch; internet www.impressum.ch; Pres ANTOINE GESSLER, STEFAN ROHRBACH.

Publishers

FRENCH-LANGUAGE PUBLISHING HOUSES

Academic Press Fribourg: 42 blvd de Pérolles, CP 176, 1705 Fribourg; tel. 264264311; fax 264264300; e-mail info@paulusedition.ch; internet www.paulusedition.ch; Dir FELIX C. FURRER.

Editions 24 heures: 33 ave de la Gare, 1001 Lausanne; tel. 213495013; fax 213495029; Dir J.-P. MÉROT.

Editions l'Age d'Homme SA: 10 rue de Genève, BP B2, 1003 Lausanne 9; tel. 213120095; fax 213208440; e-mail info@agedhomme.com; internet www.agedhomme.com; f. 1966; fiction, biography, music, art, social science, science fiction, literary criticism; Man. Dir VLADIMIR DIMITRIJEVIC.

Editions de l'Aire SA: 15 rue de l'Union, BP 57, 1800 Vevey; tel. 219236836; fax 219236823; e-mail editionaire@bluewin.ch; internet www.editions-aire.ch; f. 1978; literature, history, philosophy, religion; Man. MICHEL MORET.

La Bibliothèque des Arts: 55 ave de Rumine, 1005 Lausanne; tel. 213123667; fax 213123615; e-mail webmaster@bibliotheque-des-arts.com; internet www.bibliotheque-des-arts.com; f. 1952; art, culture; Dir OLIVIER DAULTE.

Librairie Droz SA: 11 rue Firmin-Massot, 1211 Geneva 12; tel. 223466666; fax 223472391; e-mail droz@droz.org; internet www.droz.org; f. 1924; history, medieval literature, French literature, linguistics, social sciences, economics, archaeology; Dir MAX ENGAMMARE.

Edipresse Publications SA: 33 ave de la Gare, 1001 Lausanne; tel. 213494545; fax 213494110; e-mail epsa.info@edipresse.ch; internet www.edipresse.com; f. 1988; newspapers, magazines; Pres. PIERRE LAMUNIÈRE.

Editions Eiselé SA: 42 Confrérie, CP 128, 1008 Prilly; tel. 21623650; fax 216236359; e-mail jleisele@worldcom.ch; internet www.eisele.ch; arts, education, popular science, textbooks.

Editions d'En Bas: 12 rue du Tunnel, 1005 Lausanne; tel. 213233918; fax 213123240; e-mail enbas@bluewin.ch; internet www.enbas.ch; literature, politics, memoirs, travel, poetry; Dir JEAN RICHARD.

Françoise Gonin Editions d'Art: 1 chemin du Grand-Praz, 1012 Lausanne; tel. 217285948; fax 217285948; internet www.gonin.org/editions; f. 1926; art books.

Editions du Grand-Pont: 2 place Bel-Air, 1003 Lausanne; tel. 213124466; fax 213113222; f. 1971; general, art books and literature; Dir JEAN-PIERRE LAUBSCHER.

Editions du Griffon: 17 Faubourg du Lac, 2000 Neuchâtel; tel. 327252204; f. 1944; science, arts.

Editions Ides et Calendes: Évole 19, 2001 Neuchâtel; tel. 327253861; fax 327255880; e-mail info@idesetcalendes.com; internet www.idesetcalendes.com; f. 1941; art, photography, literature; Dir ALAIN BOURET.

La Joie de Lire SA: 2 bis rue Saint-Léger, 1205 Geneva; tel. 228073399; fax 228073392; e-mail info@lajoiedelire.ch; internet www.lajoiedelire.ch; f. 1987; juvenile; Dir FRANCINE BOUCHET.

Editions Labor & Fides SA: 1 rue Beauregard, 1204 Geneva; tel. 223113290; fax 227813051; e-mail contact@laboretfides.com; internet www.laboretfides.com; f. 1924; theological and religious publs; Dir GABRIEL DE MONTMOLLIN.

Loisirs et Pédagogie SA (LEP): en Budron B4A, 1052 Le Mont-sur-Lausanne; tel. 216512570; fax 216535751; e-mail contact@editionslep.ch; internet www.editionslep.ch; Dir PHILIPPE BURDEL.

Médecine et Hygiène: 78 ave de la Roseraie, CP 456, 1211 Geneva 4; tel. 227029311; fax 227029355; e-mail librairie@medecinehygiene.ch; internet www.medhyg.ch; f. 1943; medicine, psychology, general science, university textbooks; Man. Dirs Bertrand Kiefer, Jacqueline Monnier.

Editions Mondo SA: 7 passage St-Antoine, 1800 Vevey; tel. 219241450; fax 219244662; e-mail info@mondo.ch; internet www.mondo.ch; Dir Arslan Alamir.

Noir sur Blanc SA: Le Mottâ, 1147 Montricher; tel. 218645931; fax 218644026; e-mail noirsurblanc@bluewin.ch; f. 1986; literature.

Olizane: 11 rue des Vieux-Grenadiers, 1205 Geneva; tel. 223285252; fax 223285796; e-mail guides@olizane.ch; internet www.olizane.ch; f. 1981; travel, tourism, orientalism, photography; Dir Matthias Huber.

Editions Payot Lausanne: Nadir SA, 18 ave de la Gare, CP 529, 1001 Lausanne; tel. 213290264; fax 213290266; f. 1875; technical, textbooks, medicine, law, popular science, art books, tourism, history, music, general non-fiction, academic pubs; Dir Jacques Scherrer.

Presses Polytechniques et Universitaires Romandes: EPFL, Centre-Midi, CP 119, 1015 Lausanne-Ecublens; tel. 216934131; fax 216934027; e-mail ppur@epfl.ch; internet www.ppur.org; f. 1980; technical and scientific; also publishes in English as EPFL Press; Man. Dir Olivier Babel.

Editions Pro Schola: 3 pl. Chauderon, 1003 Lausanne; tel. 213236655; fax 213236777; e-mail jbenedict@benedictinternational.com; internet www.benedict-international.com; f. 1928; education, language textbooks, audio-visual material; Dir Jean Benedict.

Editions Scriptar SA: 25 chemin du Creux-de-Corsy, 1093 Geneva; tel. 217960096; fax 217914084; e-mail info@jsh.ch; internet www.jsh.ch; f. 1946; watches and jewellery, gemmology; Dir. F. Mugnier.

Slatkine Reprints: 5 rue des Chaudronniers, CP 3625, 1211 Geneva 3; tel. 227762551; fax 227763527; e-mail slatkine@slatkine.com; internet www.slatkine.com; Dir M.-E. Slatkine.

Editions du Tricorne: 14 rue Lissignol, 1201 Geneva; tel. 227388366; fax 227319749; e-mail tricorne@tricorne.org; internet www.tricorne.org; f. 1976; philosophy, human sciences, art, religion, psychology, mathematics; Dir Serge Kaplun.

Institut Universitaire d'Etudes du Développement: 20 rue Rothschild, CP 136, 1211 Geneva 21; tel. 229065940; fax 229065947; e-mail iued@unige.ch; internet www.iued.unige.ch; f. 1961; educational, health and development; Dir Michel Carton.

Editions Zoé: 11 rue des Moraines, 1227 Carouge-Geneva; tel. 223093606; fax 223093603; e-mail info@editionszoe.ch; internet www.editionszoe.ch; literature, criticism, fiction, essays, theatre, art, music, cookery; Dir Marlyse Pietri-Bachmann.

GERMAN-LANGUAGE PUBLISHING HOUSES

Arche Literatur Verlag AG: Niederdorfstr. 90, 8001 Zürich; tel. 442522410; fax 442611115; internet www.arche-verlag.com; f. 1944; literature; Dirs Elisabeth Raabe, Regina Vitali.

Benteli Verlags AG: Seftigenstr. 310, 3084 Wabern-Bern; tel. 319608484; fax 319617414; e-mail info@benteliverlag.ch; internet www.benteliverlag.ch; f. 1898; fine arts, photography, non-fiction, philology; Dir Till Schaap.

Birkhäuser Verlag AG: Viaduktstr. 42, Postfach 133, 4010 Basel; tel. 612050707; fax 612050799; e-mail info@birkhauser.ch; internet www.birkhauser.ch; scientific and technical books, architecture, periodicals; Man. Dir Sven Fund.

Cosmos Verlag AG: Kräyigenweg 2, 3074 Muri bei Bern; tel. 319506464; fax 319506460; e-mail info@cosmosverlag.ch; internet www.cosmosverlag.ch; f. 1923; literature, local history, reference, children's, tax management; Dir Reto M. Aeberli.

Diogenes Verlag AG: Sprecherstr. 8, 8032 Zürich; tel. 442548511; fax 442528407; e-mail info@diogenes.ch; internet www.diogenes.ch; f. 1952; belles-lettres, fiction, graphic arts, children's; Publrs Daniel Keel, Rudolf C. Bettschart.

Europa Verlag AG: Rämistr. 5, 8024 Zürich; tel. 442611629; fax 442516081; e-mail info@europa-verlag.ch; internet www.europa-verlag.ch; f. 1933; politics, philosophy, history, biography, sociology, fiction; Dir Marlys Moser.

Hallwag Kümmerly+Frey AG: Grubenstr. 109, 3322 Schönbühl; tel. 318503131; fax 318503100; e-mail info@swisstravelcenter.ch; internet www.swisstravelcenter.ch; f. 1912; maps and guides, road maps, atlases, travel guides; CEO Peter Niederhauser.

H. E. P. Verlag AG: Brunngasse 36, Postfach, 3000 Bern 7; tel. 313183135; fax 313183135; e-mail info@hep-verlag.ch; internet www.hep-verlag.ch; imprints Baufachverlag and Ott Verlag; educational and training material; Dir Peter Egger.

Huber & Co AG: Promenadenstr. 16, Postfach 382, 8501 Frauenfeld; tel. 527235511; fax 527235530; e-mail info@huber.ch; internet www.huber.ch; f. 1809; art, history, politics, marketing/communications, philology, military, textbooks; Gen. Man. Hansrudolf Frey.

S. Karger AG: Allschwilerstr. 10, Postfach, 4009 Basel; tel. 613061111; fax 613061234; e-mail karger@karger.ch; internet www.karger.com; f. 1890 in Berlin, 1937 in Basel; international medical journals, books on medicine, chemistry, psychology; Pres. Dr Thomas Karger; CEO Steven Karger.

Peter Lang AG: Moosstr. 1, Postfach 350, 2542 Pieterlen; tel. 323761717; fax 323761727; e-mail info@peterlang.com; internet www.peterlang.com; f. 1977; humanities, social sciences, German language and literature, Romance literatures and languages, linguistics, music, art, theatre, ethnology; CEO Tony Albalá.

Müller Rüschlikon Verlags AG: Gewerbestr. 10, 6330 Cham; tel. 417403040; fax 417417115; e-mail info@bucheli-verlag.ch; f. 1936; non-fiction; Dir Heinz Jansen.

Nagel & Kimche AG, Verlag: Nordstr. 9, Postfach, 8035 Zürich; tel. 443666680; fax 443666688; e-mail info@nagel-kimche.ch; internet www.nagel-kimche.ch; f. 1983; belles-lettres, juvenile; Dir Dr Dirk Vaihinger.

Neptun Verlag AG: Erlenstr. 2, 8280 Kreuzlingen; tel. 716779655; fax 716779650; e-mail neptun@bluewin.ch; internet www.neptunart.ch; f. 1946; travel books, children's, contemporary history; Dir H. Berchtold-Mühlemann.

Neue Zürcher Zeitung, Buchverlag: Postfach, 8021 Zürich; tel. 442581505; fax 442581399; e-mail buch.verlag@nzz.ch; internet www.nzz-libro.ch; Man. Hans-Peter Thür.

Verlag Niggli AG: Steinackerstr. 8, Postfach 135, 8583 Sulgen; tel. 716449111; fax 716449190; e-mail info@niggli.ch; internet www.niggli.ch; f. 1950; art, architecture, design, typography; Gen. Man. Dr J. Christoph Bürkle.

Novalis Verlag AG: Felsstr. 3, Postfach 1021, 8212 Neuhausen; tel. 526258764; fax 526258766; e-mail verlag@novalis.ch; internet www.novalis.ch; f. 1974; the arts, cultural and social sciences, education; Dir Dr M. Frensch.

Orell Füssli Verlag: Dietzingerstr. 3, Postfach, 8036 Zürich; tel. 444667711; fax 444667412; e-mail info@ofv.ch; internet www.ofv.ch; f. 1519; management, history, law, schoolbooks, trade directories; Gen. Man. Manfred Hiefner-Hug.

Verlag Pro Juventute/Atlantis Kinderbücher: Seehofstr. 15, 8032 Zürich; tel. 442567717; fax 442567778; e-mail info@projuventute.ch; internet www.projuventute.ch; social science, children's, families; Man. Urs Gysling.

Friedrich Reinhardt Verlag: Missionsstr. 36, Postfach 393, 4012 Basel; tel. 612646464; e-mail verlag@reinhardt.ch; internet www.reinhardt.ch; f. 1900; belles-lettres, theology, periodicals; Dir Alfred Rüdisühli.

Rex-Verlag: Arsenalstr. 24, 6011 Kreins; tel. 414194719; fax 414194711; e-mail info@rex-verlag.ch; internet www.rex-verlag.ch; f. 1931; theology, pedagogics, fiction, juvenile; Dir Markus Kappeler.

Ringier AG: Dufourstr. 23, 8008 Zürich; tel. 442596111; fax 442598635; e-mail info@ringier.ch; internet www.ringier.ch; f. 1831; newspapers, magazines, online services, television, print; CEO Martin Werfeli.

Sauerländer Verlage AG: Ausserfeldstr. 9, 5036 Oberentfelden; tel. 628368626; fax 628268620; e-mail verlag@sauerlaender.ch; internet www.sauerlaender.ch; f. 1807; juvenile, school books, textbooks, history, chemistry, periodicals (professional, trade, science); Dir Klaus Willberg.

Schulthess Juristische Medien AG: Zwinglipl. 2, 8022 Zürich; tel. 442002999; fax 442002998; e-mail werbung@schulthess.com; internet www.schulthess.com; f. 1791; legal, social science, university textbooks; Man. Dir Werner Stocker.

Schwabe AG: Steinentorstr. 13, 4010 Basel; tel. 612789565; fax 612789566; e-mail verlag@schwabe.ch; internet www.schwabe.ch; f. 1488; medicine, art, history, philosophy; Dirs R. Bienz, Dr U. Breitenstein.

Schweizer Spiegel Verlag: Zürich; tel. 444221666; f. 1925; art, philosophy, psychology, poetry, education, general; Dir Dr P. Huggler.

Stämpfli Verlag AG: Wölflistr. 1, Postfach 8326, 3001 Bern; tel. 313006311; fax 313006688; e-mail verlag@staempfli.com; internet www.staempfliverlag.com; f. 1799; law, economics, history, art; Man. Dir Dr Rudolf Stämpfli.

Tobler Verlag AG: Trogenerstr. 80, Postfach 642, 9450 Altstätten; tel. 717556060; fax 717551254; e-mail books@tobler-verlag.ch; internet www.tobler-verlag.ch; f. 1995.

TVZ Theologischer Verlag Zürich AG: Badenerstr. 73, Postfach, 8026 Zürich; tel. 442993355; fax 442993358; e-mail tvz@ref.ch; internet www.tvz-verlag.ch; f. 1934; religion, theology; Dir Marianne Stauffacher.

Ch. Walter Verlag AG: Dorfstr. 81, Postfach 121, 8706 Meilen; e-mail info@walter-verlag.ch; internet www.walter-verlag.ch; f. 1992; children's books, history, literature; Pres. Dr Chlaus Walter.

SWITZERLAND

Wepf & Co AG Verlag: Eisengasse 5, 4001 Basel; tel. 612698515; fax 612630244; e-mail wepf@dial.eunet.ch; internet www.wepf.ch; f. 1755; architecture, engineering, ethnology, geography, geology, mineralogy; Dir H. HERRMANN.

PUBLISHERS' ASSOCIATIONS

Association Suisse des Editeurs de Langue Française: 2 ave Agassiz, CP 1215, 1001 Lausanne; tel. 213197111; fax 213197910; e-mail aself@centrepatronal.ch; f. 1975; asscn of French-speaking publrs; Pres. FRANCINE BOUCHET; Vice-Pres. OLIVIER BABEL; Sec.-Gen. FRANÇOIS PERRET; 75 mems.

Schweizer Buchhändler- und Verleger-Verband (SBVV): Alderstr. 40, Postfach, 8034 Zürich; tel. 444212800; fax 444212818; e-mail sbvv@swissbooks.ch; internet www.swissbooks.ch; f. 1849; asscn of German-speaking Swiss booksellers and publrs; Central Pres. MEN HAUPT; Dir Dr MARTIN JANN; 550 mem. and affiliated firms.

Broadcasting and Communications

TELECOMMUNICATIONS

Orange Communications SA: World Trade Center, 2 ave Gratta-Paille, CP 455, 1000 Lausanne; tel. 212161010; fax 212161515; internet www.orange.ch; f. 1999; mobile cellular communications and broadband internet access; owned by Orange SA (France); CEO ANDREAS S. WETTER; 1.4m. subscribers (June 2007).

Sunrise Communications AG: Hagenholzstr. 20–22, Postfach, 8050 Zürich; tel. 587777777; fax 587777778; internet www.sunrise.ch; f. 1997; mobile cellular and fixed-line telecommunications and internet access; owned by TDC A/S (Denmark); CEO CHRISTOPH BRAND; 2.2m. subscribers (2006).

Swisscom AG: Alte Tiefenaustr. 6, 3048 Worblaufen; tel. 313421111; fax 313422549; e-mail swisscom@swisscom.com; internet www.swisscom.com; fmrly Swiss Telecom PTT; 58.41% owned by Government; full privatization proposed Nov. 2005; Chair. ANTON SCHERRER; CEO CARSTEN SCHLOTER.

BROADCASTING

The Swiss Broadcasting Corporation (SBC) is a private non-profit-making company, which fulfils a public duty on the basis of a licence granted to it by the Federal Government. The SBC uses the electrical and radio-electrical installations of Swisscom AG for public broadcasting of radio and television programmes. Swisscom is responsible for all technical aspects of transmission. Some 75.1% of the receiver licence fee is allocated to the SBC, while Swisscom takes 24.2% and the remainder is distributed among local radio and television stations.

SRG SSR idée suisse (Swiss Broadcasting Co—SBC): Belpstr. 38, 3000 Bern 14; tel. 313509111; fax 313509256; e-mail info@srgssrideesuisse.ch; internet www.srgssrideesuisse.ch; f. 1931; Pres. JEAN-BERNARD MÜNCH; Dir-Gen. ARMIN WALPEN; Deputy Dir-Gen. DANIEL ECKMANN; SRG SSR idée suisse is composed of the following regional companies:

Cuminanza Rumantscha Radio e Televisiun (CRR): Via da Masans 2, 7002 Chur; tel. 812557575; fax 812557500; internet www.rtr.ch; Pres. DURI BEZZOLA.

Radio-Télévision suisse romande (RTSR): 40 ave du Temple, 1010 Lausanne; tel. 213186975; fax 213181976; e-mail info@rtsr.ch; internet www.rtsr.ch; Pres. JEAN CAVADINI.

Società cooperativa per la radiotelevisione Svizzera di lingua italiana (CORSI): Segreteria CORSI, via Canevascini 5, 6903 Lugano; tel. 918036325; fax 918036337; Pres. CLAUDIO GENERALI.

SRG Idée suisse DEUTSCHSCHWEIZ (Radio- und Fernsehgesellschaft DRS): Fernsehstr. 1–4, Postfach, 8052 Zürich; tel. 443056611; fax 443056710; e-mail info@srgdeutschschweiz.ch; internet www.srgdeutschschweiz.ch; formerly Radio- und Fernsehgesellschaft der Deutschen und der Rätoromanischen Schweiz (RDRS); Pres. HANS FÜNFSCHILLING.

Radio

Digital audio broadcasting (DAB) began in 1999 in Bern, Biel, Interlaken and Solothurn in 1999 and had expanded to cover most of the German-speaking cantons, the Italian-speaking canton of Ticino, Geneva and Lausanne by 2007. DAB programmes were received by approximately 80% of the population in 2007 and will be available throughout Switzerland by 2009. SRG SSR idée suisse is the sole DAB operator, providing 11 channels in the German-speaking regions, 10 in the French-speaking regions and nine in the Italian-speaking regions.

Radio Rumantsch (RR): Via da Masans 2, 7002 Chur; tel. 812557575; fax 812557500; e-mail contact@rtr.ch; internet www.rtr.ch; operated by Radio e Televisiun Rumantscha (RTR); 24-hour programming in Romansh; Dir BERNARD CATHOMAS.

Radio suisse romande (RSR): 40 ave du Temple, 1010 Lausanne; tel. 213181111; fax 216523719; e-mail webmaster@rsr.ch; internet www.rsr.ch; offers four stations: **La Première** news and background reports, stories, entertainment and music; **Espace 2** classical and contemporary music, jazz and folk, with features on the arts, history and society, radio plays and concert broadcasts; **Couleur 3** youth station playing rock and pop, with current affairs features; **Option Musique** music station with news bulletins, traffic reports and weather forecasts; Dir GÉRARD TSCHOPP; Dir of Programmes ISABELLE BINGGELI; Dir of Information PATRICK NUSSBAUM.

Radio svizzera di lingua italiana (RSI): CP, 6903 Lugano; tel. 918035111; fax 918035355; e-mail info@rtsi.ch; internet www.rtsi.ch; operated by Radiotelevisione svizzera di lingua italiana (RTSI); operates three Italian-language stations: **Rete Uno** current affairs and reportage, also general entertainment programmes and public service broadcasts, **Rete Due** educational and general interest programmes, music and news, **Rete Tre** rock and pop music; Dir of Radio JACKY MARTI.

Schweizer Radio DRS (SR DRS): Brunnenhofstr. 22, 8042 Zürich; tel. 443661111; e-mail kommunikation@srdrs.ch; internet www.drs.ch; SR DRS is the Swiss national radio programme for the German part of Switzerland with three main studios in Zürich, Basel and Bern from which it operates six radio stations; **DRS 1** current affairs, traffic and weather reports and entertainment, six regional news magazines report regularly from around Switzerland; **DRS 2** classical music, jazz, culture, science, economics, politics and philosophy; **DRS 3** pop music and information, specializes in live concert broadcasts; **DRS 4 News** non-stop news; **DRS Musikwelle** traditional music of all genres, with news and DRS 1 programmes; **DRS Virus** youth and multimedia; Dir WALTER RÜEGG.

Swiss Satellite Radio (SsatR): Giacomettistr. 1, 3000 Bern 15; tel. 313509333; fax 313509663; three Swiss Satellite Radio music channels, broadcast via the internet, cable and satellite; **Radio Swiss Pop** music-only service; **Radio Swiss Classic** classical music service with minimal presentation; **Radio Swiss Jazz** music service playing jazz, blues and soul; Dir PIETRO RIBI.

Swissinfo—Schweizer Radio International (SRI): Giacomettistr. 1, 3000 Bern 15; tel. 313509222; fax 313500544; e-mail contact_swissinfo@swissinfo.ch; internet www.swissinfo.org; f. 1935; news and information programmes about Switzerland in English, French, German, Italian, Spanish, Portuguese, Japanese, Chinese and Arabic; Dir BEAT WITSCHI.

There are also 48 local and regional radio stations active in Switzerland.

Television

A complete television programme service for each linguistic region and regular broadcasts in Romansh are provided on the 1st (VHF) channel. The 2nd and 3rd (UHF) channels are used in each linguistic region for transmitting programmes of the other two linguistic regions. Limited direct advertising is allowed.

Digital Video Broadcasting (DVB) began in 2005, with analogue broadcasting to be discontinued in 2015.

Schweizer Fernsehen (SF): Fernsehstr. 1–4, Postfach, 8052 Zürich; tel. 443056611; fax 443055660; e-mail sf@sf.tv; internet www.sf.tv; operates **SF1**, **SF2** and a third channel, **SF info**, which repeats current affairs programmes from SF1, SF2 and **Presse TV** in hourly and half-hourly blocks; Dir INGRID DELTENRE.

Télévision suisse romande (TSR): 20 quai Ernest-Ansermet, CP 234, 1211 Geneva 8; tel. 227082020; fax 223204813; e-mail tsr@tsr.ch; internet www.tsr.ch; operates **TSR1** and **TSR2**; Dir GILLES MARCHAND.

Televisione svizzera di lingua italiana (TSI): CP, 6903 Lugano; tel. 918035111; fax 918035355; e-mail info@rtsi.ch; internet www.rtsi.ch; operated by Radiotelevisione svizzera di lingua italiana (RTSI); two Italian-language channels: **TSI1** full-service channel aimed at a broad audience, **TSI2** complementary channel with sport, children's programmes and repeats of news programmes from TSI1; Dir of TV RENIGIO RATTI.

Televisiun Rumantscha (TvR): Via da Masans 2, 7002 Chur; tel. 812557575; fax 812557500; e-mail contact@rtr.ch; internet www.rtr.ch; operated by Radio e Televisiun Rumantscha (RTR); provides programming in Romansh (*Telesguard* and *Cuntrasts*) which is broadcast on SF1; Dir BERNARD CATHOMAS.

There are also 83 local and regional television stations, 18 of which have high transmission activity.

Finance

(cap. = capital; res = reserves; dep. = deposits; m. = million; brs = branches; all values are in Swiss francs)

BANKING

Switzerland's banks have a long-standing reputation as a secure repository for foreign capital. The Swiss Banking Law of 1934 declared it a penal offence for a bank to provide information about its clients without their explicit authorization, unless a court had ordered otherwise. When foreign authorities wish to investigate Swiss accounts, criminal charges must have been made in a foreign court and accepted as valid by Switzerland. The system of numbered accounts has also shielded depositors' shares from investigation. However, the abuse of bank secrecy by organized crime led Switzerland and the USA to sign a treaty in May 1973, whereby banking secrecy rules may be waived in the case of common-law crime (although not for non-criminal tax evasion and anti-trust law infringements). Further amendments to banking secrecy legislation were introduced in 1990 and 1998.

In June 1977 the Swiss banks agreed a code of practice which required the introduction of stricter controls over the handling of foreign funds. The opening of numbered accounts was subjected to closer scrutiny and the practice of actively encouraging the flow of foreign money into the country was checked. The agreement was modified in 1982. In 1987, following the withdrawal from the agreement of the Swiss National Bank, the code was adapted by the Swiss Bankers' Association into rules of professional conduct; further modifications to the code were introduced in 1992. In 1978, in view of the steady increase in Swiss banks' international business, the Federal Banking Commission was given greater supervisory powers. Banks were required for the first time to submit consolidated balance sheets to the Commission and new consolidation requirements forced banks to raise capital to between 6% and 8% of total liabilities. The capital requirement is now one of the highest in the world.

At the end of 2007 there were 337 banks operating in Switzerland.

The 24 canton banks are mostly financed and controlled by the cantons, and their activities are co-ordinated by the Association of Swiss Cantonal Banks. In 2006 they had 808 branches and controlled more than one-third of Switzerland's savings deposits.

Central Bank

Schweizerische Nationalbank/ Banque nationale suisse (Swiss National Bank): Börsenstr. 15, Postfach 2800, 8022 Zürich; tel. 446313111; fax 446313911; e-mail snb@snb.ch; internet www.snb.ch; f. 1907; conducts the country's monetary policy as an independent central bank; obliged by the Constitution and statute to act in accordance with the interests of the country as a whole; primary goal is to ensure price stability, while taking due account of economic developments; Dept I handles international affairs, economic affairs, legal and administrative affairs, human resources and communications; Dept II handles cash, finance and controlling, financial stability and oversight, and security; Dept III handles financial markets, asset management, risk management, banking operations and information technology; cap. 25m., res 16,473m., dep. 8,359m. (Dec. 2006); Chair. of Governing Bd Dr JEAN-PIERRE ROTH.

Canton Banks

There are 24 cantonal banks, of which the following are the largest:

Aargauische Kantonalbank: Bahnhofstr. 58, 5001 Aarau; tel. 628357777; fax 628357925; e-mail akb@akb.ch; internet www.akb.ch; f. 1913; cap. 200m., res 293m., dep. and bonds 14,167m. (Dec. 2006); Pres. ARTHUR ZELLER; CEO RUDOLF DELLENBACH; 28 brs.

Banca dello Stato del Cantone Ticino: Viale H. Guisan 5, 6501 Bellinzona; tel. 918037111; fax 918037170; e-mail contatto@bsct.ch; internet www.bancastato.ch; f. 1915; cap. 100m., res 125m., dep. and bonds 6,277m. (Dec. 2006); Chair. FULVIO PELLI; Pres., Exec. Bd DONATO BARBUSCIA; 3 brs.

Banque Cantonale de Fribourg: 1 blvd de Pérolles, 1701 Fribourg; tel. 848223223; fax 263507709; e-mail info@bcf.ch; internet www.bcf.ch; f. 1892 as Banque de l'Etat de Fribourg; present name adopted 1996; cap. 70m., res 350m., dep. and bonds 8,097m. (Dec. 2006); Chair. GILBERT MONNERON; CEO ALBERT MICHEL; 25 brs.

Banque Cantonale de Genève: 17 quai de l'Ile, CP 2251, 1211 Geneva; tel. 223172727; fax 223172737; e-mail info@bcge.ch; internet www.bcge.ch; f. 1994; cap. 360m., res 333m., dep. and bonds 11,609m. (Dec. 2006); Chair. MICHEL MATTACCHINI; CEO BLAISE GOETSCHIN; 25 brs.

Banque Cantonale du Jura: 10 rue de la Chaumont, CP 278, 2900 Porrentruy; tel. 324651301; fax 324651495; e-mail bcj@bcj.ch; internet www.bcj.ch; f. 1979; cap. 45m., res 57m., dep. and bonds 1,571m. (Dec. 2006); Chair. Dr PAUL-ANDRÉ SANGLARD; Gen. Man. BERTRAND VALLEY; 13 brs.

Banque Cantonale du Valais: 8 pl. des Cèdres, CP 133, 1951 Sion; tel. 273246111; fax 273246666; e-mail info@bcvs.ch; internet www.bcvs.ch; f. 1917; cap. 150m., res 254m., dep. and bonds 7,388m. (Dec. 2006); Chair. MAURICE DE PREUX; CEO JEAN-DANIEL PAPILLOUD; 6 brs.

Banque Cantonale Neuchâteloise: 4 pl. Pury, 2001 Neuchâtel; tel. 327236111; fax 327236236; e-mail info@bcn.ch; internet www.bcn.ch; f. 1883; cap. 125m., res 145m., dep. 4,345m. (Dec. 2006); Pres. JEAN-PIERRE GHELFI; Gen. Man. JEAN-NOËL DUC; 1 br.

Banque Cantonale Vaudoise: 14 pl. St François, CP 300, 1003 Lausanne; tel. 212121000; fax 212121596; e-mail info@bcv.ch; internet www.bcv.ch; f. 1845; cap. 997m., res 1,887m., dep. and bonds 27,211m. (Dec. 2006); Chair. OLIVIER STEIMER; CEO ALEXANDRE ZELLER; 66 brs.

Basellandschaftliche Kantonalbank: Rheinstr. 7, 4410 Liestal; tel. 619259494; fax 619259674; e-mail info@blkb.ch; internet www.blkb.ch; f. 1864; cap. 240m., res 536m., dep. and bonds 12,895m. (Dec. 2006); Pres. WERNER DEGEN; CEO Dr BEAT OBERLIN; 8 brs.

Basler Kantonalbank: Spiegelgasse 2, 4002 Basel; tel. 612662121; fax 612618434; e-mail bkb@bkb.ch; internet www.bkb.ch; f. 1899; cap. 269m., res 378m., dep. and bonds 12,269m. (Dec. 2006); Chair. Dr WILLI GERSTER; CEO HANS-RUDOLF MATTER; 22 brs.

BEKB/BCBE (Berner Kantonalbank/ Banque Cantonale Bernoise): Bundespl. 8, 3001 Bern; tel. 316661111; fax 316666040; e-mail bekb@bekb.ch; internet www.bekb.ch; f. 1834 as Banque Cantonale de Berne; present name adopted 1991; cap. 326m., res 701m., dep. and bonds 18,197m. (Dec. 2006); Pres. PETER W. KAPPELER; CEO JEAN-CLAUDE NOBILI; 78 brs.

Graubündner Kantonalbank: Postfach, 7002 Chur; tel. 812569111; fax 812526729; e-mail info@gkb.ch; internet www.gkb.ch; f. 1870; cap. 250m., res 204m., dep. and bonds 11,668m. (Dec. 2006); Pres. Dr HANS HATZ; CEO ALOIS VINZENS; 9 brs.

Luzerner Kantonalbank: Pilatusstr. 12, 6002 Lucerne; tel. 412062222; fax 412062200; e-mail info@lukb.ch; internet www.lukb.ch; f. 1850; cap. 357m., res 603m., dep. and bonds 16,381m. (Dec. 2006); Chair. FRITZ STUDER; 26 brs.

Schwyzer Kantonalbank (SKZB): Bahnhofstr. 3, 6431 Schwyz; tel. 418194111; fax 418117355; e-mail kundenzentrum@szkb.ch; internet www.szkb.ch; f. 1889 as Kantonalbank Schwyz, present name adopted 1997; cap. 120m., res 224m., dep. and bonds 8,955m. (Dec. 2006); Pres. ALOIS CAMENZIND; CEO GOTTFRIED WEBER; 27 brs.

St Galler Kantonalbank: St Leonhardstr. 25, Postfach 2063, 9001 St Gallen; tel. 712313131; fax 712313196; e-mail info@sgkb.ch; internet www.sgkb.ch; f. 1868; cap. 557m., res 871m., dep. and bonds 17,623m. (Dec. 2006); Chair. Dr FRANZ-PETER OESCH; Pres., Exec. Bd ROLAND LEDERGERBER; 37 brs.

Thurgauer Kantonalbank: Bankpl. 1, Postfach 160, 8570 Weinfelden; tel. 848111444; fax 848111445; e-mail info@tkb.ch; internet www.tkb.ch; f. 1871; cap. 400m., res 194m., dep. and bonds 13,226m. (Dec. 2006); Chair. HANSPETER STRICKLER; CEO HANSPETER HERGER; 15 brs.

Urner Kantonalbank: Bahnhofstr. 1, 6460 Altdorf; tel. 418756000; fax 418756313; e-mail info@urkb.ch; internet www.urkb.ch; f. 1915; cap. 30m., res 47m., dep. and bonds 1,609m. (Dec. 2006); Pres. Dr HANSRUEDI STADLER; Man. PETER ZGRAGGEN; 9 brs.

Zuger Kantonalbank: Baarerstr. 37, 6301 Zug; tel. 417091111; fax 417091555; e-mail service@zugerkb.ch; internet www.zugerkb.ch; f. 1892; cap. 144m., res 254m., dep. and bonds 5,862m. (Dec. 2006); Chair. and Pres. B. BERNET; Gen. Man. T. LUGINBÜHL; 10 brs.

Zürcher Kantonalbank: Bahnhofstr. 9, 8010 Zürich; tel. 442939393; fax 442923802; e-mail info@zkb.ch; internet www.zkb.ch; f. 1870; cap. 1,925m., res 3,981m., dep. and bonds 79,106m. (Dec. 2006); Chair. Dr URS OBERHOLZER; 83 brs.

Commercial Banks (Selected List)

Baloise Bank SoBa: Amthauspl. 4, 4502 Solothurn; tel. 326260202; fax 326233692; e-mail bank@baloise.ch; internet www.baloise.ch; f. 1994; cap. 50m., res 252m., dep. 4,842m. (Dec. 2003); Chair. Dr ROLF SCHÄUBLE; CEO ALOIS MÜLLER.

Banca del Gottardo: Viale S. Franscini 8, CP 2811, 6901 Lugano; tel. 918081111; fax 919239487; e-mail info@gottardo.ch; internet www.gottardo.ch; f. 1957; cap. 70m., res 675m., dep. and bonds 10,705m. (Dec. 2006); Chair. FELIX R. EHRAT; CEO R. W. AEBERLI; 6 brs.

Bank Julius Baer & Co Ltd: Bahnhofstr. 36, 8010 Zürich; tel. 588881111; fax 588881122; internet www.juliusbaer.com; f. 1890; cap. 575m., res 2,559m., dep. 25,111m. (Dec. 2006); Chair. RAYMOND J. BAER; Pres., Exec. Bd and CEO JOHANNES A. DE GIER; 4 brs.

Banque Thaler SA: 3 rue Pierre-Fatio, 1211 Geneva 3; tel. 227070909; fax 227070910; e-mail info@banquethaler.ch; internet www.banquethaler.ch; f. 1982 as KBC Bank (Suisse) SA; present name adopted 2000; cap. 20m., res 6m., dep. 36m. (Dec. 2006); Pres. ROBERT CUYPERS; Gen. Man. DIRK EELBODE.

SWITZERLAND

Directory

BNP Paribas (Suisse) SA: 2 pl. de Hollande, 1204 Geneva; tel. 582122111; fax 582122222; internet www.bnpparibas.com; f. 1961 as United Overseas Bank SA; present name adopted 2001; cap. 320m., res 1,619m., dep. and bonds 34,860m. (Dec. 2006); Chair. GEORGE CHODRON DE COURCEL; Pres. and CEO LOUIS BAZIRE; 5 brs.

BSI SA: Via Magatti 2, 6900 Lugano; tel. 918093111; fax 918093678; e-mail info@bsi.ch; internet www.bsi.com; f. 1873 as Banca della Svizzera italiana; present name adopted 1998; cap. 440m., res 392m., dep. and bonds 10,270m. (Dec. 2006); Chair. Dr GIORGIO GHIRINGHELLI; CEO Dr ALFREDO GYSI; 6 brs.

Clariden Leu AG: Bahnhofstr. 32, 8001 Zürich; tel. 442191111; fax 442193797; e-mail info@claridenleu.com; internet www.claridenleu.com; f. 2007 by merger of Bank Hofmann, Bank Leu, BGP Banca di Gestione Patrimoniale, Clariden Bank and Crédit Suisse Fides; Pres. and CEO F. BERNARD STALDER.

Coutts Bank von Ernst Ltd: Stauffacherstr. 1, 8022 Zürich; tel. 432455111; fax 432455396; internet www.coutts.com; f. 1930; current name adopted 2004; cap. 110m., res 834m., dep. 15,644m. (Dec. 2006); Chair. DAVID DOUGLAS-HOME, Earl of Home; 5 brs.

Crédit Suisse Group: Crédit Suisse: Paradepl. 8, 8001 Zürich, Postfach 100, 8070 Zürich; tel. 442121616; fax 443332587; internet www.credit-suisse.ch; f. 1856; cap. 607m., res 15,318m., dep. 1,077,017m. (Dec. 2006); Group CEO BRADY W. DOUGAN; CEO (Switzerland) ULRICH KÖRNER; 290 brs.

Hyposwiss Private Bank AG: Schützengasse 4, 8021 Zürich; tel. 442143111; fax 442115223; e-mail info@hyposwiss.ch; internet www.hyposwiss.ch; f. 1889 as Schweizerische Hypothekenbank; present name adopted 2002; cap. 26m., res 78m., dep. 448m. (Dec. 2007); Chair. ROLAND LEDERGERBER; Exec. Pres. THEODOR HORAT.

Migrosbank AG: Seidengasse 12, 8023 Zürich; tel. 442298111; fax 442298715; e-mail info@migros.ch; internet www.migrosbank.ch; f. 1958; cap. 700m., res 1,360m., dep. 26,014m. (Dec. 2006); Chair. HERBERT BOLLIGER; Pres., Exec. Bd Dr HARALD NEDWED; 44 brs.

Neue Aargauer Bank: Bahnhofstr. 49, 5001 Aarau; tel. and fax 628388080; e-mail webmaster@nab.ch; internet www.nab.ch; f. 1989; 98.6% owned by Crédit Suisse Group AG; cap. 137m., res 592m., dep. 16,578m. (Dec. 2006); Pres. JOSEF BÜRGE; CEO HANS-MATHIAS KÄPPELI; 42 brs.

Raiffeisen Schweiz Genossenschaft/ Raiffeisen Switzerland Cooperative: Raffeisenpl., 9001 St Gallen; tel. 712258888; fax 712258887; e-mail direct@raiffeisen.ch; internet www.raiffeisen.ch; f. 1902; cap. 428m., res 5,603m., dep. 105,126m. (Dec. 2006); Chair., Bd of Dirs FRANZ MARTY; Chair., Exec. Bd Dr PIERIN VINCENZ; 395 associated banks.

Swissquote Bank: 16 route des Avouillons, 1196 Gland; tel. 229999411; fax 229999495; e-mail info@bank.swissquote.ch; internet www.swissquote.ch; f. 2000; cap. 25m., dep. 180m. (Dec. 2002); Chair. MARIO FONTANA; CEO and Gen. Man. MARC BÜRKI.

UBS AG: Bahnhofstr. 45, 8021 Zürich; tel. 442341111; fax 442399111; e-mail info@ubs.com; internet www.ubs.com; f. 1998 by merger of Union Bank of Switzerland (f. 1912) and Swiss Bank Corpn (f. 1872); cap. 211m., res 324m., dep. 2,065,815m. (Dec. 2006); Chair. PETER KURER; Group CEO MARCEL ROHNER; 357 brs.

Union Bancaire Privée: 96–98 rue du Rhône, CP 1320, 1211 Geneva 1; tel. 228192111; fax 228192200; e-mail ubp@ubp.ch; internet www.ubp.ch; f. 1990 by merger of TDB American Express Bank (f. 1956) and Compagnie de Banque et d'Investissements (f. 1969); cap. 300m., res 961m., dep. and bonds 14,961m. (Dec. 2006); Chair. EDGAR DE PICCIOTTO; Pres. and CEO GUY DE PICCIOTTO; 6 brs.

Valiant Bank: Bundespl. 4, Postfach 5333, 3001 Bern; tel. 313209111; fax 313209112; internet www.valiant.ch; f. 2001 by merger of Spar- und Leihkasse in Bern, Gewerbekasse in Bern, bank in Langnau, BB Bank Belp and Ersparniskasse Murten; cap. 110m., res 965m., dep. and bonds 14,935m. (Dec. 2006); Chair. Prof. Dr ROLAND VON BÜREN; CEO MIKE HOBMEIER.

Private Banks

Switzerland's private banking sector is the largest, in terms of assets, in the world. In 2006 there were 14 privately owned banks in Switzerland, of which the following are among the most important:

Banque Privée Edmond de Rothschild SA: 18 rue de Hesse, 1204 Geneva; tel. 228189111; fax 228189121; internet www.lcf-rothschild.ch; f. 1924; cap. 45m., res 450m., dep. and bonds 1,014m. (Dec. 2006); Chair. Baron BENJAMIN DE ROTHSCHILD; Gen. Man. CLAUDE MESSULAM; 2 brs.

EFG Bank: Bahnhofstr. 16, Postfach 2255, 8022 Zürich; tel. 442261717; fax 442261726; internet www.efgbank.com; f. 1997 as EFG Private Bank SA; present name adopted 2005; cap. 62m., res 247m., dep. 9,228m. (Dec. 2006); Chair. JEAN-PIERRE CUONI; CEO MARKUS CADUFF.

HSBC Private Bank (Suisse) SA: 2 quai Général Guisan, CP 3580, 1211 Geneva 3; tel. 587055555; fax 587055151; internet www.hsbcprivatebank.com; f. 1988 as Republic National Bank New York (Suisse) SA; present name adopted 2004; cap. 683m., res 1,834m., dep. 53,248m. (Dec. 2006); Chair. PETER WIDMER; CEO PETER F. BRAUNWALDER; 3 brs.

Lombard Odier Darier Hentsch & Cie: 11 rue de la Corraterie, 1211 Geneva 11; tel. 227092111; fax 227092911; e-mail contact@lodh.com; internet www.lodh.com; f. 2002 by merger of Lombard Odier & Cie (f. 1798) and Darier Hentsch & Cie (f. 1991); Snr Partners PIERRE DARIER, THIERRY LOMBARD; Man. Partners JEAN A. BONNA, PATRICK ODIER, JEAN PASTRÉ, BERNARD DROUX, ANNE-MARIE DE WECK, CHRISTOPHE HENTSCH, HUBERT KELLER.

Pictet & Cie Banquiers: 60 route des Acacias, 1211 Geneva 73; tel. 583232323; fax 583232324; e-mail info@pictet.com; internet www.pictet.com; f. 1805; Snr Partner IVAN PICTET; Partners CLAUDE DEMOLE, JACQUES DE SAUSSURE, NICOLAS PICTET, PHILIPPE BERTHERAT, JEAN-FRANÇOIS DEMOLE, RENAUD DE PLANTA, RÉMY BEST.

Central Co-operative Credit Institution

Bank Coop AG: Aeschenpl. 3, 4002 Basel; tel. 612862121; fax 612714595; e-mail netteam@bankcoop.ch; internet www.bankcoop.ch; f. 1927 as Co-operative Central Bank; present name adopted 2001; cap. 338m., res 319m., dep. 10,416m. (Dec. 2006); Chair. WILLI GERSTER; Pres., Exec. Bd ANDREAS WÄSPI; 32 brs.

Regulatory Authorities

Eidgenössische Bankenkommission (Federal Banking Commission): Sekretariat, Schwanengasse 12, 3001 Bern; tel. 313226911; fax 313226926; e-mail info@ebk.admin.ch; internet www.ebk.admin.ch; Pres. Dr EUGEN HALTINER; Dir DANIEL ZUBERBÜHLER.

Swiss Banking Ombudsman: Bahnhofpl. 9, Postfach 1818, 8021 Zürich; tel. 432661414; fax 432661415; internet www.bankingombudsman.ch; Ombudsman HANSPETER HÄNI.

Bankers' Organizations

Association of Foreign Banks in Switzerland: Löwenstr. 51, Postfach 1211, 8021 Zurich; tel. 442244070; fax 442210029; e-mail info@foreignbanks.ch; internet www.foreignbanks.ch; f. 1972; 144 mems (Dec. 2007); Chair. Dr ALFREDO GYSI; Sec. Gen. Dr MARTIN MAURER.

Association Suisse des Banquiers/ Schweizerische Bankiervereinigung (Swiss Bankers' Assen): Aeschenpl. 7, Postfach 4182, 4002 Basel; tel. 612959393; fax 612725382; e-mail office@sba.ch; internet www.swissbanking.org; f. 1912; 768 mems; Chair. PIERRE MIRABAUD; CEO Dr URS P. ROTH.

Verband Schweizerischer Kantonalbanken/ Union des Banques Cantonales Suisses (Assen of Swiss Cantonal Banks): Wallstr. 8, 4002 Basel; tel. 612066666; fax 612066667; e-mail vskb@vskb.ch; internet www.kantonalbank.ch; f. 1907; perm. office est. 1971; Chair. PAUL NYFFELER; Dir HANSPETER HESS.

STOCK EXCHANGES

BX Berne eXchange (Berner Börsenverein): Aarbergergasse 36, 3011 Bern; tel. 313114042; fax 313115309; e-mail office@berne-x.com; internet www.bernerboerse.ch; f. 1884; 9 mems, 5 assoc. mems; Dir JÜRG NIEDERHÄUSER.

SWX Swiss Exchange: Selnaustr. 30, 8021 Zürich; tel. 588545454; fax 588545455; e-mail swx@swx.com; internet www.swx.com; f. 1873; 51 mems; Pres. Prof. Dr PETER GOMEZ; CEO Dr HEINRICH HENCKEL.

INSURANCE

In 2006 there were 262 insurance companies in Switzerland.

Allianz Suisse: Bleicherweg 19, Postfach, 8022 Zürich; tel. 442095111; fax 442095120; e-mail contact@allianz-suisse.ch; internet www.allianz-suisse.ch; subsidiaries: Allianz Suisse Versicherungen, Allianz Suisse Leben, Allianz Suisse Personal Financial Services; Pres. Dr MANFRED KNOF.

AXA Winterthur: Gen. Guisan-Str. 40, Postfach 357, 8401 Winterthur; tel. 522611111; fax 522136620; e-mail communication@axa-winterthur.ch; internet www.axa-winterthur.ch; f. 1875; fmrly Winterthur Schweizerische Versicherungs-Gesellschaft; owned by AXA Group; Pres. ALFRED BOUCKAERT; CEO PHILIPPE EGGER.

Basler Versicherungen: Aeschengraben 21, Postfach 2275, 4002 Basel; tel. 612858585; fax 612857070; e-mail insurance@baloise.ch; internet www.baloise.ch; f. 1864; all classes; Chair. Dr ROLF SCHÄUBLE; Vice-Chair. WALTER FREHNER.

Converium: General Guisan-Quai 26, Postfach, 8022 Zürich; tel. 446399393; fax 446399090; internet www.converium.ch; Chair. MARKUS DENNLER; CEO INGA BEALE.

Generali Schweiz Versicherungen: Soodmattenstr. 10, 8134 Adliswil 1; tel. 447124040; fax 447124425; e-mail info@generali.ch; internet www.generali.ch; part of Generali Group (Italy); Group Chair. ANTOINE BERNHEIM.

SWITZERLAND

Helvetia Versicherungen: St Alban-Anlage 26, 4002 Basel; tel. 582801000; internet www.helvetia.ch; f. 1861; owned by Helvetia Holding; life, fire, burglary, accident liability, motor; Chair. Dr ERICH WALSER; CEO STEFAN LOACHER.

Schweizerische Mobiliar Versicherungsgesellschaft: Bundesgasse 35, 3001 Bern; tel. 313896111; fax 313896852; e-mail info@mobi.ch; internet www.mobi.ch; f. 1826; accident, sickness, fire and damage by the elements, theft, valuables, damage by water, glass breakage, machines, construction work, interruption of business, epidemics, warranty, guarantee, third-party liability, motor vehicles, travel, transport; Pres. of Exec. Bd URS BERGER.

Schweizerische National-Versicherungs-Gesellschaft: Steinengraben 41, 4003 Basel; tel. 612752111; fax 612752656; internet www.nationalesuisse.ch.

Swiss Life: General Guisan-Quai 40, POB 2831, 8022 Zürich; tel. 432843311; fax 432846311; e-mail info.com@swisslife.ch; internet www.swisslife.com; f. 1857; specializes in international employee benefit and pension plans; brs in France, Germany, Liechtenstein and Luxembourg; CEO ROLF DÖRIG.

Swiss Re (Schweizerische Rückversicherungs-Gesellschaft) (Swiss Reinsurance Co): Mythenquai 50/60, 8022 Zürich; tel. 442852121; fax 442852999; e-mail contact@swissre.com; internet www.swissre.com; f. 1863; world-wide reinsurance; Chair. Prof. Dr PETER FORSTMOSER; CEO JACQUES AIGRAIN.

Vaudoise Versicherungen: Pl. de Milan, 1001 Lausanne; internet www.vaudoise.ch; f. 1895; subsidiaries: Vaudoise Leben (life), Vaudoise Allgemeine (non-life); Pres. ROLF MEHR.

Zürich Versicherungs-Gesellschaft: Postfach, Talackerstr. 1, 8085 Zürich; tel. 446282828; fax 446288444; e-mail kontakt@zurich.ch; internet www.zurich.ch; f. 1922; part of Zurich Financial Services group; life; CEO MARKUS HONGLER.

Insurance Organization

Schweizerischer Versicherungsverband—Association suisse d'assurances (SVV—ASA) (Swiss Insurance Asscn): C. F. Meyer-Str. 14, Postfach 4288, 8022 Zürich; tel. 442082828; fax 442082801; e-mail info@svv.ch; internet www.svv.ch; f. 1901; Pres. ALBERT LAUPER; Dir LUCIUS DÜRR; 80 mems.

Trade and Industry

GOVERNMENT AGENCIES

Osec Business Network Switzerland: Stampfenbachstr. 85, Postfach 492, 8035 Zürich; tel. 443655151; fax 443655221; e-mail info.zurich@osec.ch; internet www.osec.ch; promotes trade; CEO BALZ HÖSLY.

Staatssekretariat für Wirtschaft—SECO/Secrétariat d'Etat à l'économie—SECO/ State Secretariat for Economic Affairs: Effingerstr. 31, 3003 Bern; tel. 313230710; fax 313248600; e-mail invest@seco.admin.ch; internet www.locationswitzerland.ch; promotes investment in Switzerland.

PRINCIPAL CHAMBERS OF COMMERCE

Aargauische Industrie- und Handelskammer: Entfelderstr. 11, 5001 Aarau; tel. 628371818; fax 628371819; Pres. H. P. ZEHNDER.

Berner Handelskammer: Gutenbergstr. 1, 3001 Bern; tel. 313821711; fax 313821715; Pres. WALTER LEUENBERGER.

Bündner Handels- und Industrieverein: Poststr. 43, 7002 Chur; tel. 812526306; fax 812520449; Pres. OTTO BECK.

Camera di commercio dell'industria e dell'artigianato del Cantone Ticino: Corso Elvezia 16, 6901 Lugano; tel. 919115111; fax 919115112; e-mail cciati@cci.ch; internet www.cciati.ch; f. 1917; Pres. FRANCO AMBROSETTI; Dir CLAUDIO CAMPONOVO; 900 mems.

Chambre fribourgeoise du commerce, de l'industrie et des services: 37 route du Jura, 17061 Fribourg; tel. 263471220; fax 263471239; e-mail info@cfcis.ch; internet www.cfcis.ch; f. 1917; Pres. CHARLES PHILLOT; Dir VIVIANE COLLAUD (acting).

Chambre de commerce et d'industrie de Genève: 4 blvd du Théâtre, 1211 Geneva 11; tel. 228199111; fax 228199100; e-mail ccig@cci.ch; internet www.ccig.ch; f. 1865; Pres. MICHEL BALESTRA; Dir JACQUES JEANNERAT; 1,500 mems.

Chambre de commerce et d'industrie du Jura: 23 rue de l'Avenir, CP 274, 2800 Delémont 1; tel. 324214545; fax 324214540; e-mail ccjura@cci.ch; internet www.ccij.ch; Pres. JEAN-PAUL RENGGLI; Dir JEAN-FRÉDÉRIC GERBER.

Chambre neuchâteloise du commerce et de l'industrie: 4 rue de la Serre, 2001 Neuchâtel; tel. 327257541; fax 327247092; Pres. YANN RICHTER; Dir CLAUDE BERNOULLI.

Directory

Chambre valaisanne de commerce et d'industrie: 6 rue Pré-Fleuri, CP 288, 1951 Sion; tel. 273273535; fax 273273536; Pres. JACQUES-ROLAND COUDRAY; Dir THOMAS GSPONER; 492 mems.

Chambre vaudoise du commerce et de l'industrie: 47 ave d'Ouchy, CP 315, 1001 Lausanne; tel. 216133535; fax 216133505; e-mail cvci@cvci.ch; internet www.cvci.ch; Pres. HUBERT BARDE; Dir JEAN-LUC STROHM; 2,100 mems.

Glarner Handelskammer: Spielhof 14A, 8750 Glarus; tel. 556401173; fax 556403639; e-mail glhk@landolt-partner.ch; Pres. ANDERS HOLTE; Sec. Dr KARLJÖRG LANDOLT.

Handelskammer beider Basel: Aeschenvorstadt 67, Postfach, 4010 Basel; tel. 612706060; fax 612706005; e-mail hkbb@hkbb.ch; internet www.hkbb.ch; Pres. THOMAS STAEHELIN; 800 mems.

Handelskammer und Arbeitgebervereinigung Winterthur (HAW): Neumarkt 15, 8401 Winterthur; tel. 522137352; Pres. Dr VIKTOR BEGLINGER.

Industrie- und Handelskammer St Gallen-Appenzell: Gallusstr. 16, Postfach, 9001 St Gallen; tel. 712241010; fax 712241060; e-mail sekretariat@ihk.ch; internet www.ihk.ch; f. 1466; Pres. Dr KONRAD HUMMLER.

Industrie- und Handelskammer Thurgau: Schmidstr. 9, Postfach, 8570 Weinfelden; tel. 716221919; fax 716226257; e-mail info@ihk-thurgau.ch; internet www.ihk-thurgau.ch; Pres. P. A. SCHIFFERLE.

Junior Chamber Switzerland: c/o Unirevisa AG, Spielhof 14A, 8750 Glarus; tel. 556407252; fax 556407435; e-mail zs@juniorchamber.ch; internet www.juniorchamber.ch; Sec. F. DÄLLENBACH.

Schweizerische Zentrale für Handelsförderung/ Office suisse d'expansion commerciale (OSEC): Stampfenbachstr. 85, 8035 Zürich; and 4 ave de l'Avant-Poste, 1001 Lausanne; tel. 443655151; fax 443655221; e-mail info.zurich@osec.ch; tel. 213203231; fax 213207337; f. 1927; Pres. PHILIPPE LÉVY; Dir MARTIN MONSCH; 2,000 mems.

Solothurner Handelskammer: Grabackerstr. 6, Postfach 1554, 4502 Solothurn; tel. 326262424; fax 326262426; e-mail info@sohk.ch; internet www.sohk.ch; f. 1874; Pres. KURT HOOSLI; Dir Dr HANS-RUDOLF MEYER.

Zentralschweizerische Handelskammer: Kapellpl. 2, 6002 Lucerne; tel. 414106865; fax 414105288; e-mail info@hkz.ch; internet www.hkz.ch; f. 1889; Pres. Dr WERNER STEINEGGER; Dir ALEX BRUCKERT; 500 mems.

Zürcher Handelskammer: Bleicherweg 5, Postfach 3058, 8022 Zürich; tel. 442174050; fax 442174051; e-mail direktion@zurichcci.ch; internet www.zurichcci.ch; f. 1873; Pres. PETER QUADRI; CEO Dr LUKAS BRINER; 1,800 mems.

INDUSTRIAL AND TRADE ASSOCIATIONS

Associazione Industrie Ticinesi: Corso Elvezia 16, 6901 Lugano; tel. 919235041; fax 919234636; Pres. GIANCARLO BORDONI.

Basler Volkswirtschaftsbund: Aeschenvorstadt 71, Postfach 4010 Basel; tel. 612059600; fax 612059609; e-mail bvb@bvb.ch; internet www.bvb.ch; Pres. MARC R. JAQUET; Dir BARBARA GUTZWILLER-HOLLIGER; 9,000 mems.

Chocosuisse—Verband Schweizerischer Schokoladefabrikanten: Münzgraben 6, 3000 Bern 7; tel. 313100990; fax 313100999; e-mail info@chocosuisse.ch; internet www.chocosuisse.ch; f. 1901; asscn of chocolate mfrs; Dir Dr F. U. SCHMID; 21 mems.

Economiesuisse (Swiss Business Federation): Hegibachstr. 47, Postfach 1072, 8032 Zürich; tel. 444213535; fax 444213434; e-mail info@economiesuisse.ch; internet www.economiesuisse.ch; f. 1870; as Schweizerischer Handels- und Industrie-Verein, present name adopted 2000; Pres. GEROLD BÜHRER; Exec. Dir Dr PASCAL GENTINETTA; 163 mems.

Fédération de l'Industrie Horlogère Suisse (FH): 6 rue d'Argent, 2501 Bienne; tel. 323280828; fax 323280880; e-mail info@fhs.ch; internet www.fhs.ch; f. 1876; watch industry; Pres. J. D. PASCHE; 542 mems.

Föderation der Schweizerischen Nahrungsmittel-Industrien: Thunstr. 82, 3000 Bern 16; Münzgraben 6, 3000 Bern 7; and Elfenstrasse 19, 3000 Bern 16; tel. 313562121; fax 313510065; e-mail info@advo-emmenegger.ch; foodstuffs; Secs B. HODLER, G. EMMENEGGER, Dr F. U. SCHMID; 216 mems.

Schweizerischer Baumeisterverband (SBV): Weinbergstr. 49, Postfach, 8035 Zürich; tel. 442588111; fax 442588335; e-mail verband@baumeister.ch; internet www.baumeister.ch; f. 1897; building contractors; Pres. W. MESSMER; 3,000 mems.

Schweizerischer Elektrotechnischer Verein (SEV): Luppmenstr. 1, 8320 Fehraltorf; tel. 19561111; fax 19561122; electronics; Pres. ANDREAS BELLWALD.

SWITZERLAND

Schweizerischer Gewerbeverband (SGV) (Swiss Union of Small and Medium Enterprises): Schwarztorstr. 26, 3007 Bern; tel. 313801414; fax 313801415; e-mail info@sgv-usam.ch; internet www.sgv-usam.ch; f. 1879; Pres. EDI ENGELBERGER; 284 sections.

Schweizerischer Verband für visuelle Kommunikation (Viscom): Alderstr. 40, Postfach, 8034 Zürich; tel. 414212828; fax 414212829; e-mail info@viscom.ch; internet www.viscom.ch; f. 1869; printing industry; Pres. PETER EDELMANN; Dir THOMAS GSPONER; 900 mems.

Schweizerischer Versicherungsverband: (see under Insurance).

SGCI Chemie Pharma Schweiz (Swiss Society of Chemical Industries): Nordstr. 15, Postfach, 8021 Zürich; tel. 443681711; fax 443681770; e-mail mailbox@sgci.ch; internet www.sgci.ch; f. 1882; chemical and pharmaceutical industry; Pres. Dr R. WEHRLI; Dir Dr B. MOSER; 180 mems.

Swiss Cigarette: 15 route des Arsenaux, CP 137, 1705 Fribourg; tel. 264255050; fax 264255055; e-mail office@cisc.ch; internet www.swiss-cigarette.ch; f. 1933; formerly Communauté de l'industrie suisse de la cigarette; cigarette mfrs; Pres. (vacant); Sec.-Gen. CHANTAL AEBY PÜRRO.

Swiss Retail Federation: Marktgasse 50, 3000 Bern 7; tel. 313124040; fax 313124041; e-mail info@swiss-retail.ch; internet www.swiss-retail.ch; formerly Verband der Schweizerischen Waren- und Kaufhäuser; Pres. Dr KLAUS HUG.

Textilverband Schweiz: Beethovenstr. 20, Postfach 2900, 8022 Zürich; tel. 442897979; fax 442897980; e-mail contact@tvs.ch; internet www.swisstextiles.ch; f. 1874; textiles and fashion; Pres. THOMAS ISLER; Dir Dr TH. SCHWEIZER; 230 mems.

Verband der Schweizerischen Gasindustrie: Grütlistr. 44, Postfach, 8027 Zürich; tel. 412883131; fax 412021834; f. 1920; Pres. J. CAVADINI.

Verband Schweizerischer Kreditbanken und Finanzierungsinstitute (VSKF): Toblerstr. 97/Neuhausstr. 4, 8044 Zürich; tel. 442504340; fax 442504349; e-mail office@gigersimmen.ch; internet www.vskf.org; asscn of credit banks and finance institutes; Sec. Dr ROBERT SIMMEN.

Verband Schweizerische Ziegelindustrie: c/o Herrn RA Dr Peter R. Burkhalter, Advokatbüro Hodler & Emmenegger, Elfenstr. 19, Postfach, 3000 Bern 16; tel. 313521188; fax 313521185; e-mail info@chziegel.ch; internet www.chziegel.ch; f. 1874; heavy clay; Sec.-Gen. Dr PETER R. BURKHALTER.

EMPLOYERS' ORGANIZATIONS
Central Organizations

Schweizerischer Arbeitgeberverband (Confed. of Swiss Employers): Hegibachstr. 47, Postfach, 8032 Zürich; tel. 444211717; fax 444211718; e-mail verband@arbeitgeber.ch; internet www.arbeitgeber.ch; f. 1908; Pres. Dr RUDOLF STAEMPFLI; Vice-Pres. WOLFGANG MARTZ; Dir THOMAS DAUM; 74 mems.

Schweizerischer Bauernverband (Union Suisse des Paysans, Lega svizzera dei contadini, Swiss Farmers' Union): Laurstr. 10, 5201 Brugg; tel. 564625111; fax 564415348; e-mail info@sbv-usp.ch; internet www.bauernverband.ch; f. 1897; Pres. H. J. WALTER; Dir JACQUES BOURGEOIS.

Principal Regional Organizations

Fédération des entreprises romandes: 98 rue de Saint-Jean, CP 5278, 1211 Geneva 11; tel. 227153111; fax 227153213; e-mail info@fer-ge.ch; internet www.fer-ge.ch; Pres. DANIEL DELAY; Sec.-Gen. BLAISE MATTHEY.

Luzerner Industrie-Vereinigung: Kapellpl. 2, Postfach 3142, 6002 Lucerne; tel. 4106889; e-mail info@hkz.ch; internet www.hkz.ch; Pres. ANTON LAUBER; Dir ALEX BRUCKERT.

Union des associations patronales genevoises: 98 rue de Saint-Jean, 1211 Geneva 11; tel. 227153241; fax 227380434; e-mail uapg@uapg.ch; union of employers' asscns in Geneva; Pres. ANDRÉ GALIOTTO.

Union des industriels valaisans: CP 2106, 1905 Sion; tel. 273232992; fax 273232288; Pres. JURG HEROLD.

Verband der Arbeitgeber Region Bern (VAB): Kapellenstr. 14, Postfach 6916, 3001 Bern; tel. 313902581; fax 313902582; f. 1919; employers' asscn for the Bern region; Pres. Dr RUDOLF STÄMPFLI.

Vereinigung Zürcherischer Arbeitgeberorganisationen: Selnaustr. 30, 8021 Zürich; tel. 588542827; fax 588542833; e-mail dieter.sigrist@swx.com; f. 1947; asscn of Zürich employers' orgs; Pres. THOMAS ISLER; Sec. DIETER SIGRIST.

Sectional Organizations

Arbeitgeberverband Schweizerischer Papier-Industrieller: Bergstr. 110, 8032 Zürich; tel. 442669921; fax 442669949; e-mail zpk@zpk.ch; internet www.zpk.ch; paper mfrs; Pres. FRANK RUEPP; Dir M. FRITZ; 11 mems.

Convention Patronale de l'Industrie Horlogère Suisse: 65 ave Léopold-Robert, 2301 La Chaux-de-Fonds; tel. 329100383; fax 329100384; e-mail info@cpih.ch; internet www.cpih.ch; f. 1937; watch mfrs; Pres. ELISABETH ZÖLCH; Gen. Sec. FRANÇOIS MATILE; seven mems.

Swissmem (ASM and VSM) (Swiss Mechanical and Electrical Engineering Industries): Kirchenweg 4, Postfach, 8032 Zürich; tel. 443844111; fax 443844242; e-mail info@swissmem.ch; internet www.swissmem.ch; f. 1905; Pres. J. N. SCHNEIDER-AMMANN; Dir THOMAS DAUM; c. 930 mems.

UTILITIES
Electricity

Verband Schweizerischer Elektrizitätsunternehmen: Hintere Bahnhofstr. 10, Postfach, 5001 Aarau; tel. 628252525; fax 628252526; e-mail info@strom.ch; internet www.strom.ch; electricity producers' asscn; f. 1895; Pres. Dr R. STEINER; Dir A. BUCHER.

Gas

Verband der Schweizerischer Gasindustrie: Grütlistr. 44, 8002 Zürich; tel. 442883131; fax 442021834; e-mail vsg@erdgas.ch; internet www.erdgas.ch; gas industry asscn.

Water

The cantons are responsible for the supply of water, but delegate to the municipalities and communes. As a result Switzerland has some 3,000 water companies. Water is usually supplied by a public company or co-operative, such as the municipal water suppliers for Winterthur, Basel and Zürich (Städische Werke Winterthur, Industrielle Werke Basel, Wasserversorgung Zürich).

TRADE UNIONS

Schweizerischer Gewerkschaftsbund (Swiss Fed. of Trade Unions): Monbijoustr. 61, 3007 Bern; tel. 313770101; fax 313770102; e-mail info@sgb.ch; internet www.sgb.ch; f. 1880; main trade union org.; affiliated to ITUC; Pres. PAUL RECHSTEINER.

Sixteen affiliated unions with a total membership of 380,000, of which the principal unions are:

Comedia (Media): Monbijoustr. 33, Postfach 6336, 3001 Bern; tel. 313906611; fax 313906691; e-mail info@comedia.ch; internet www.comedia.ch; f. 1858; Pres DANIÈLE LENZIN, ROLAND KREUZER; 15,000 mems.

Gewerkschaft Kommunikation (Communications Union): Looslistr. 15, Postfach 370, 3027 Bern; tel. 319395211; fax 319395262; e-mail zentralsekretariat@syndicom.ch; internet www.gewerkschaftkom.ch; f. 1999; Pres. CHRISTIAN LEVRAT; 37,000 mems.

Schweizerischer Eisenbahn- und Verkehrspersonal-Verband (SEV) (Railway Workers): Steinerstr. 35, Postfach, 3000 Bern 6; tel. 313575757; fax 313575858; internet www.sev-online.ch; f. 1919; Pres. PIERRE-ALAIN GENTIL; 48,000 mems.

Schweizerischer Verband des Personals öffentlicher Dienste (Public Services): Birmensdorferstr. 67, Postfach 8279, 8036 Zürich; tel. 442665252; fax 442665253; e-mail vpod@vpod-ssp.ch; internet www.vpod-ssp.ch; f. 1905; Pres. CHRISTINE GOLL; Gen. Sec. STEFAN GIGER; 35,000 mems.

Unia: Weltpoststr. 20, Postfach, 3000 Bern 15; tel. 313502111; fax 313502211; e-mail info@unia.ch; internet www.unia.ch; f. 2004 by merger of Gewerkschaft Bau und Industrie (GBI), Gewerkschaft Industrie, Gewerbe, Dienstleistungen (SMUV), Gewerkschaft Verkauf, Handel, Transport, Lebensmittel (VHTL) and Gewerkschaft unia; represents construction and engineering industries as well as employees in the retail and catering sectors; Pres RENZO AMBROSETTI, ANDREAS RIEGER; 200,000 mems (Dec. 2006).

Travail.Suisse: Hopfenweg 21, Postfach 5775, 3001 Bern; tel. 313702111; fax 313702109; e-mail info@travailsuisse.ch; internet www.travailsuisse.ch; f. 2002 by merger of Confédération des Syndicats Chrétiens de Suisse and Fédération des Sociétés Suisses d'Employés; Pres. HUGO FASEL; 170,000 mems.

Eleven affiliated unions, including:

Syna (Syndicat Interprofessionnel, Sindicato Interprofessionale): Josefstr. 59, 8031 Zürich; tel. 442797171; fax 442797172; e-mail zuer@syna.ch; internet www.syna.ch; f. 1998 to replace Landesverband freier Schweizer Arbeitnehmer (f. 1919); Pres. KURT REGOTZ; 65,000 mems.

Transport

RAILWAYS

Construction of the 35-km Lötschberg rail tunnel was completed in June 2007, shortening travel time between Germany and the Italian city of Milan by about one hour. Excavation of a further 57-km rail tunnel, the Gotthard Base Tunnel, was scheduled for completion in 2016. The Saint Gotthard rail tunnel was opened in 1982.

Schweizerische Bundesbahnen (SBB) (Chemins de fer fédéraux suisses): Hochschulstr. 6, 3000 Bern 65; tel. 512201111; fax 512204265; e-mail railinfo@sbb.ch; internet www.sbb.ch; f. 1902; 3,034 km in 2007 (of which 1,707 km were multiple track); Chair. THIERRY LALIVE D'EPINAY; CEO ANDREAS MEYER.

Small private companies control private railways in Switzerland, chiefly along short mountain routes, with a total length of around 2,032 km. The following are among the principal private railways:

BLS Loetschbergbahn Ltd: Genfergasse 11, Postfach, 3001 Bern; tel. 313272727; fax 313272910; e-mail info@bls.ch; internet www.bls.ch; f. 1906; 245 km; 11 passenger routes; cargo services on Lötschberg–Simplon route; direct car-train connection from Bern to the Valais and Italy; boat services on Lakes Thun and Brienz; 5 commuter rail services in Bern; Man. Dr M. TROMP.

Centovalli Railway: Via Franzoni 1, CP 146, 6601 Locarno; tel. 917560400; fax 917560499; e-mail fart@centovalli.ch; internet www.centovalli.ch; f. 1909; 19 km; Locarno–Camedo; Dir DIRK MEYER.

Matterhorn Gotthard Bahn AG: Nordstr. 20, 3900 Brig; tel. 279277777; fax 279277779; e-mail info@mgbahn.ch; internet www.mgbahn.ch; f. 2003; merger between BVZ Zermatt-Bahn AG and Furka Oberalp Bahn AG; 25% state-owned, 75% owned by BVZ Holding AG; Zermatt–Brig–Disentis and Andermatt–Göschenen; 144 km; Chair. DANIEL LAUBER; Dir HANS MOOSER.

Matterhorn Gotthard Bahn Verkehrs AG: Nordstr. 20, 3900 Brig; tel. 279277777; fax 279277779; e-mail info@mgbahn.ch; internet www.mgbahn.ch; 75% owned by BVZ Holding AG, 25% state-owned; controls all railway operation, incl. rolling stock, depots and related maintenance; Pres. DANIEL LAUBER.

Matterhorn Gotthard Bahn Infrastruktur AG: Nordstr. 20, 3900 Brig; tel. 279277777; fax 279277779; e-mail info@mgbahn.ch; internet www.mgbahn.ch; 100% state-owned; responsible for track, overhead catenary equipment, operating control centres, station bldgs and workshops; Pres. ROLF ESCHER.

Montreux-Oberland Bernois: CP 1426, 1820 Montreux; tel. 219898181; fax 219898100; e-mail mob@mob.ch; internet www.mob.ch; f. 1899; 75 km; Montreux–Château d'Oex–Gstaad–Zweisimmen–Lenk i/S; operates tour services incl. GoldenPass Panoramic, Belle Epoque, Rochers-de-Naye, Les Pléiades and the Chocolate Train; operates funicular railways on Vevey–Chardonne–Mont-Pèlerin and Les Avants–Sonloup routes; Dir R. KUMMROW.

Rhaetian Railway: Bahnhofstr. 25, 7002 Chur; tel. 812549100; fax 812549118; e-mail info@rhaetische-bahn.ch; internet www.rhaetische-bahn.ch; f. 1889; 375 km; the most extensive of the privately run railways; Dir S. FASCIATI.

Südostbahn AG: Bahnhofplatz 1A, 9001 St Gallen; tel. 712282323; fax 712282333; e-mail info@sob.ch; internet www.sob.ch; f. 1889; founded by a merger between Schweizerische Südostbahn and Bodensee–Toggenburg-Bahn in 2001; 119km; Pres. GEORG HESS.

ROADS

In 2004 Switzerland had 71,214 km of roads, including 1,728 km of motorways and expressways and 18,048 km of other main roads. The construction of a national network of approximately 1,857 km of motorways is scheduled for completion by 2010. The 17-km road tunnel through the Saint Gotthard Pass, a European road link of paramount importance, was opened in 1980.

Swiss Federal Roads Office (Bundesamt für Strassen/Office fédéral des routes): Mühlestr. 2, Ittigen, 3003 Bern; tel. 313229411; fax 313232303; e-mail info@astra.admin.ch; internet www.astra.admin.ch; Dir RUDOLF DIETERLE.

INLAND WATERWAYS

Inland navigation legislation is the responsibility of the Confederation, but sovereignty over the waterways rests with the Cantons. This means, in practice, that the Confederation limits its activities to the supervision of the licensed shipping companies (passenger ships and the related infrastructure, such as landing stages) and pilots; the Cantons supervise pleasure-boat navigation (sports boats, i.e. sail and motor boats, etc.) and the non-licensed passenger vessels and goods shipping on the lakes and rivers.

SHIPPING

In 2006 Switzerland's registered merchant fleet comprised 29 vessels, with an aggregate displacement of 510,000 grt. The principal shipping companies in Switzerland are:

Keller Shipping Ltd: Holbeinstr. 68, Postfach 3479, 4002 Basel; tel. 612818686; fax 612818679; Pres. A. R. KELLER.

Mediterranean Shipping Co SA: 40 ave Eugène-Pittard, 1206 Geneva; tel. 227038888; fax 227038787; Dir G. APONTE.

Natural van Dam AG: Westquaistr. 62, 4019 Basel; tel. 616399233; fax 616399250; e-mail naturalvandam@nvd.ch; internet www.nvd.ch; shipping management; Dir HEINZ AMACKER.

Navirom AG: St Alban-Anlage 64, 4052 Basel; tel. 613135816; fax 613135805.

Schweizerische Reederei & Neptun AG: Wiesendamm 4, 4019 Basel; tel. 616393333; fax 616393466; e-mail info@srn.ch; internet www.srn.ch; Dir H. SCHMITT.

Stolt-Nielsen AG: Uferstr. 90, Postfach, 4057 Basel; tel. 616388200; fax 616388211.

Suisse-Atlantique, Société de Navigation Maritime SA: 7 ave des Baumettes, CP 48, 1020 Renens 1; tel. 216372201; fax 216372202; e-mail activity@suisse-atlantique.ch; world-wide tramping services; Pres. E. ANDRE; Dir C. DIDAY; mans of:

Navemar SA: 1 Grand' Places, 1700 Fribourg.

Van Ommeren (Schweiz) AG: Hafenstr. 87–89, Postfach, 4127 Birsfelden.

Vinalmar SA: 7 rue du Mont-Blanc, 1211 Genève 1; tel. 229060431; fax 227386467.

CIVIL AVIATION

Switzerland's principal airports are situated at Zürich and Geneva. A major airport at Basel-Mulhouse-Freiburg (EuroAirport) serves northern Switzerland, but is situated across the border in France.

Darwin Airline: Lugano Airport, 6982 Agno; tel. 916124500; fax 916124520; e-mail info@darwinairline.com; internet www.darwinairline.com; f. 2003; low-cost airline; flights from four Swiss airports to destinations in Italy and Spain; Pres. SERGIO ERMOTTI; CEO FABIO PARINI.

Swiss (Swiss International Air Lines): Postfach, 4002 Basel; tel. 615820000; fax 615823333; e-mail communications@swiss.com; internet www.swiss.com; f. 1979 as Crossair, took over operations from Swissair and adopted current name in 2002; national carrier operating routes to 76 destinations in 42 countries; subsidiary of Deutsche Lufthansa AG (Germany); CEO CHRISTOPH FRANZ.

Tourism

Switzerland's principal attractions are the lakes and lake resorts and the mountains. Walking, mountaineering and winter sports are among the chief pastimes. Foreign tourist arrivals at hotels and similar establishments totalled 7.9m. in 2006. Receipts from tourism in that year were 13,334m. Swiss francs.

Switzerland Tourism: Tödistr. 7, 8027 Zürich; tel. 442881111; fax 442881205; e-mail info@myswitzerland.com; internet www.myswitzerland.com; f. 1917; Dir JÜRG SCHMID.

SYRIA

Introductory Survey

Location, Climate, Language, Religion, Flag, Capital

The Syrian Arab Republic lies in western Asia, with Turkey to the north, Iraq to the east and Jordan to the south. Lebanon and Israel are to the south-west. Syria has a coastline on the eastern shore of the Mediterranean Sea. Much of the country is mountainous and semi-desert. The coastal climate is one of hot summers and mild winters. The inland plateau and plains are dry but cold in winter. Average temperatures in Dimashq (Damascus) range from 2°C to 12°C (36°F to 54°F) in January and from 18°C to 37°C (64°F to 99°F) in August. The national language is Arabic, with Kurdish a minority language. According to the UN Relief and Works Agency for Palestine Refugees in the Near East (UNRWA), at December 2007 there were 451,467 Palestinian refugees registered in Syria. More than 80% of the population are Muslims (mostly Sunnis), but there is a substantial Christian minority of various sects. The national flag (proportions 2 by 3) has three equal horizontal stripes, of red, white and black, with two five-pointed green stars in the centre of the white stripe. The capital is Damascus.

Recent History

Syria was formerly part of Turkey's Ottoman Empire. Turkish forces were defeated in the First World War (1914–18) and Syria was occupied in 1920 by France, in accordance with a League of Nations mandate. Syrian nationalists proclaimed an independent republic in September 1941. French powers were transferred in January 1944, and full independence was achieved on 17 April 1946. In December 1949 Syria came under a military dictatorship, led by Brig. Adib Shishekly. He was elected President in July 1953, but was overthrown by another army coup in February 1954.

In February 1958 Syria merged with Egypt to form the United Arab Republic (UAR). In September 1961, following a military coup in Damascus, Syria seceded and formed the independent Syrian Arab Republic. In 1963 Maj.-Gen. Amin al-Hafiz formed a Government in which members of the Arab Socialist Renaissance (Baath) Party were predominant. In February 1966 the army deposed the Government of President al-Hafiz, replacing him with Dr Nur ed-Din al-Atasi. However, in November 1970, after a bloodless coup, the military (moderate) wing of the Baath Party seized power, led by Lt-Gen. Hafiz al-Assad, who was elected President in March 1971. In March 1972 the National Progressive Front (NPF), a grouping of the five main political parties (including the Baath Party), was formed under the leadership of President Assad.

Increasing border tension between Syria and Israel was a major influence leading to the Six-Day War of June 1967, when Israel attacked its Arab neighbours in reprisal for the closure of the Strait of Tiran by the UAR (Egypt). Israeli forces made swift territorial gains, including the Golan Heights region of Syria, which remains under Israeli occupation. An uneasy truce lasted until October 1973, when Egyptian and Syrian forces launched simultaneous attacks on Israeli-held territory. On the Syrian front, there was fierce fighting in the Golan Heights until a cease-fire was agreed after 18 days. In May 1974 the US Secretary of State, Henry Kissinger, secured an agreement for the disengagement of forces. Israel's formal annexation of the Golan Heights in December 1981 effectively impeded the prospect of a negotiated Middle East settlement at this time.

Syria disapproved of the second interim Egyptian-Israeli Disengagement Agreement, signed in September 1975, but agreed to acknowledge it as a *fait accompli* in return for Egypt's acceptance of Syria's role in Lebanon. Syria had progressively intervened in the Lebanese civil war during 1976, finally providing the bulk of the 30,000-strong Arab Deterrent Force (ADF). Syria condemned the Egyptian President, Anwar Sadat, for Egypt's peace initiative with Israel in November and December 1977, the Camp David agreements signed by Egypt and Israel in September 1978, and the subsequent peace treaty concluded between them.

From 1977 frequent assassinations of Alawites (the minority Islamic sect to which Assad belonged) indicated sectarian tension within Syrian society. Assad attributed much of the opposition to the Muslim Brotherhood, a conservative Islamist group, and he ordered the brutal suppression of an uprising in Hamah (Hama), led by the outlawed Brotherhood, in February 1982. From November 1983, after Assad suffered a heart attack, rivals to the succession—including Col Rifaat al-Assad, the President's brother—vied for pre-eminence. In March 1984, following Assad's recovery, the appointment of three Vice-Presidents had the effect of equally distributing power among the President's potential successors and giving none the ascendancy. Assad was also able to rely on a cadre of loyal officers who ensured the army's continued support for the President.

The ADF, based in northern Lebanon, was unable to act when Israel invaded southern Lebanon in June 1982 and surrounded Beirut, trapping Syrian troops and fighters of the Palestine Liberation Organization (PLO). The Syrian and Palestinian forces in Beirut were evacuated in August, under the supervision of a multinational peace-keeping force, and some 50,000 Syrian troops, deployed in the Beka'a valley and northern Lebanon, faced 25,000 Israelis in the south of the country, even though the ADF's mandate had expired. Syria rejected the May 1983 Israel-Lebanon peace agreement, formulated by US Secretary of State George Shultz, refusing to withdraw its forces from Lebanon and continuing to supply the militias of the Lebanese Druze and Shi'ite factions in their fight against the Lebanese Government and the Christian Phalangists. From May 1983 Syria supported a revolt against Yasser Arafat and the leadership of Fatah (the Palestine National Liberation Movement) and by November Syrian and rebel PLO forces had cornered Arafat, the PLO Chairman, in the Lebanese port of Tarabulus (Tripoli). Arafat and some 4,000 of his supporters were eventually evacuated, under UN protection, in December.

In March 1984 President Amin Gemayel of Lebanon capitulated to Syria's influence over Lebanese affairs, and abrogated the May 1983 agreement with Israel. In April President Assad approved Gemayel's plans for a Lebanese government of national unity, giving equal representation to Muslims and Christians. In September Syria arranged a truce to end fighting in Tripoli between the pro-Syrian Arab Democratic Party and the Sunni Tawhid Islami (Islamic Unification Movement). The Lebanese army entered the city in late 1984, under the terms of a Syrian-backed extended security plan, to assert the authority of the Lebanese Government. Syria also authorized Lebanon's participation in talks with Israel to co-ordinate the departure of the Israeli Defence Force (IDF) from southern Lebanon (with that of other security forces), in order to prevent an outbreak of civil violence. After the final stage of the Israeli withdrawal in June 1985, several hundred Israeli troops and advisers remained in Lebanon to assist the Israeli-backed 'South Lebanon Army' (SLA) in policing a narrow buffer zone along the Lebanese side of the international border. Syria removed 10,000–12,000 troops from the Beka'a valley in July, leaving some 25,000 in position.

President Assad was re-elected for a third seven-year term of office in February 1985, and in early 1985 Syria involved itself in seeking to resolve Lebanon's sectarian unrest. Through its proxy, Amal, Syria sought to prevent Yasser Arafat from re-establishing a power base in Beirut, and around 650 people died in the fighting before a cease-fire was agreed in Damascus in June. In December the three main Lebanese militias—the Druze, Amal and Lebanese Forces (LF) Christian militia—met in Damascus to sign a Syrian-brokered accord outlining a politico-military settlement of the civil war. However, the Shi'ite Hezbollah and Sunni Murabitoun militias were not party to the accord and President Gemayel, who had not been consulted during the drafting of the agreement, refused to endorse it. Opposition to the accord was further manifested following Samir Gaegea's promotion to the leadership of the LF in January 1986. Syria brokered another cease-fire in June, this time in the Palestinian refugee camps around Beirut (where fighting between Palestinian guerrillas and Shi'ite Amal militiamen had recently escalated); this proved to be the first stage in a Syrian-sponsored peace plan for Muslim west Beirut. The co-operation of the Amal, Druze and Sunni militias was dependent upon the deployment of uniformed Syrian troops in Beirut for the first time since 1982. Though the activities of the militias in west Beirut were temporarily curbed, the plan was strongly opposed in Christian east Beirut and was not extended to the predominantly Shi'ite southern suburbs, where most of the city's Palestinian refugees lived. By early 1987 heavy fighting had resumed in west Beirut, between Amal forces and an alliance of Druze, Murabitoun and Communist Party militias. Syrian troops (soon numbering some 7,500) succeeded in enforcing a cease-fire in the central and northern areas of west Beirut, but were not deployed in the southern suburbs.

At a general election held in February 1986 the Baath Party and other members of the NPF (excluding the Communist Party, which contested the poll independently) obtained 151 of the 195 seats in the People's Assembly. The communists won nine seats, and independents 35. In November 1987, following the resignation of Abd ar-Rauf al-Kassem as Prime Minister, Mahmoud az-Zoubi, the Speaker of the Assembly, was appointed premier. In May 1988 Syria's interest in the Lebanese presidential election, scheduled to be held in August of that year, prompted an intense period of fighting between Amal and Hezbollah in Beirut's southern suburbs. Overt Syrian support for the candidacy of Sulayman Franjiya (President of Lebanon during 1970–76), and later for Mikhail ad-Daher (after the first postponement of the election), aroused the opposition of Lebanese Christian leaders, who objected to candidates imposed by foreign powers. Consequently, Syria refused to recognize the interim military administration appointed by President Gemayel shortly before his term of office expired. From March 1989 Christian forces, commanded by Gen. Michel Awn (the head of the interim Lebanese Government), attempted to expel Syrian forces from Lebanon, thereby provoking one of the most violent confrontations of the entire civil war.

In October 1989, under the auspices of the League of Arab States (the Arab League, see p. 332), the Lebanese National Assembly endorsed a charter of national reconciliation (the Ta'if agreement). The Lebanese authorities envisaged a continuing role for the Syrian army in Lebanon by stipulating that it should assist in the implementation of two security plans incorporated in the accord, which also included the constitutional amendments that Syria had long sought to effect in Lebanon. (For further details concerning the Ta'if agreement, see the chapter on Lebanon.) In May 1991 Syria and Lebanon signed a treaty of 'fraternity, co-operation and co-ordination', which was immediately denounced by Israel as a further step towards the formal transformation of Lebanon into a Syrian protectorate. Israel responded by deploying armed forces inside the buffer zone in southern Lebanon, and any likelihood of Israel's compliance with UN Security Council Resolution 425 (adopted in March 1978), which demanded the withdrawal of Israeli armed forces from southern Lebanon, diminished. Syria was the only Arab state which refused to recognize the independent Palestinian state (proclaimed by the Palestine National Council in November 1988), in accordance with its long-standing policy of preventing any other force in Lebanon from acquiring sufficient power to challenge Syrian interests. Meanwhile, Syria persistently denied claims, principally by the USA, that it was sponsoring international terrorism, and refused to restrict the activities of Palestinian groups on its territory. Following a series of bomb attacks in Europe in 1985–86, in November 1986 members of the European Community (EC, now European Union—EU, see p. 244), excluding Greece, imposed limited diplomatic and economic sanctions against Syria, as did the USA and Canada. However, the EC (with the exception of the United Kingdom) ended its ban on ministerial contacts with Syria in July 1987; financial aid was resumed in September, although a ban on the sale of weapons to Syria remained in force.

At elections to the People's Assembly (now expanded to 250 seats) in May 1990, the Baath Party won 134 seats and other parties 32, while 84 seats were reserved for independent candidates. In December 1991 it was announced that 2,864 political prisoners were to be released; this was regarded as the first indication of President Assad's intention to liberalize Syria's political system. In March 1992 Assad indicated that new political parties might in future be established, but he rejected the implementation of foreign democratic frameworks as unsuited to the country's level of economic development. In January 1994 Basel al-Assad, President Assad's eldest son and presumed successor, was killed in a road accident; the President's second son, Bashar, was reportedly instructed to assume the role of his late brother in order to avoid a power struggle. In August senior government officials, including the Commander of the Special Forces, were removed from office in an apparent attempt by Assad to consolidate his position and improve Syria's international standing.

The ruling Baath Party and its NPF allies reinforced their dominance of Syrian affairs at elections to the People's Assembly in August 1994, winning 167 of the 250 seats. In November 1995—the 25th anniversary of President Assad's seizure of power—some 1,200 political prisoners, including members of the banned Muslim Brotherhood, were released under an amnesty, while a number of the Brotherhood's leaders were allowed to return from exile. During 1996 there were reports of several explosions in Damascus, in addition to a number of attacks on Syrian targets in Lebanon. In January 1997 the Syrian-based Islamic Movement for Change claimed responsibility for a bomb attack in central Damascus in December 1996, in which 11 people died.

In February 1998 President Assad unexpectedly dismissed his brother, Col Rifaat al-Assad, as Vice-President (a post he had held since 1984, although he had spent much of the intervening period overseas). In July President Assad appointed new chiefs of both the Syrian army and the intelligence service, prompting speculation that he was seeking to extend the political influence of his second son, Bashar.

Elections to the People's Assembly were held on 30 November and 1 December 1998, at which the NPF, led by the ruling Baath Party, again won 167 of the 250 seats. On 11 February 1999 a national referendum ratified the incoming Assembly's decision to nominate President Assad for a fifth term of office. It was widely speculated that Bashar would be promoted to the vice-presidency in a new administration, having already been promoted to the rank of army colonel in January, and reportedly granted new powers over important domestic matters. In June the Syrian authorities were said to be undertaking an 'unprecedented' campaign, led by Bashar al-Assad, to counter corruption in public office. Several leading officials and businessmen were subsequently incarcerated, and in October, following a nine-month trial, a former director of Syria's intelligence service received a lengthy prison sentence for alleged corruption and embezzlement of public funds. Details emerged in September of large-scale arrests (involving 1,000 people, according to some reports) by security forces in Damascus and Al-Ladhiqiyah (Latakia) against supporters and relatives of Rifaat al-Assad. Subsequent closures of Rifaat's interests (including port facilities in Latakia) provoked several days of violent clashes between his supporters and the security forces, in which, according to reports rejected by the Government, hundreds of people were killed or injured.

In July 1999 President Assad ordered a general amnesty for prisoners convicted of certain economic crimes, and for army deserters and those who had evaded military service. The amnesty was to affect hundreds (some reports claimed thousands) of prisoners, including a number of Muslim Brotherhood activists. In February 2000, however, a report by the British-based Amnesty International alleged that in recent months several hundred Syrians (including many Islamists) opposed to a future peace accord with Israel had been arrested. Meanwhile, it was reported that Syria's military intelligence chief, Gen. Ali Duba, had been removed from his post, owing to alleged 'administrative offences', and replaced by his deputy, Maj.-Gen. Hassan Khalil.

Having accepted the resignation of Mahmoud az-Zoubi and his administration in March 2000, President Assad named Muhammad Mustafa Mero, formerly governor of Halab (Aleppo), as Prime Minister. A new Cabinet was subsequently inaugurated, with a programme to accelerate social and economic reforms, to strengthen anti-corruption measures, and to resume peace negotiations with Israel. In all, 22 new ministers were appointed (including a number of younger technocrats and supporters of Bashar al-Assad), although the foreign affairs, defence and interior portfolios remained unchanged. In May az-Zoubi was expelled from the Baath Party for alleged 'irregularities and abuses' during his period in office. His assets were subsequently seized, and he was expected to stand trial on corruption charges. However, in late May official sources reported that az-Zoubi had committed suicide.

President Assad died on 10 June 2000. Shortly after his death the People's Assembly amended the Constitution, lowering the minimum age required of a president from 40 to 34 years, thus enabling Bashar al-Assad to assume the presidency. Bashar al-Assad was also nominated as Commander-in-Chief of the Armed

Forces, and his military rank was upgraded to that of Lieutenant-General. Following approval of Bashar's nomination for the presidency by the People's Assembly in late June (the Baath Party having already endorsed his candidacy), a nation-wide referendum on the succession was scheduled for July; the First Vice-President, Abd al-Halim Khaddam, assumed the role of acting President. In mid-June Bashar al-Assad was elected Secretary-General of the Baath Party. Rifaat al-Assad claimed that the assumed succession by Bashar was unconstitutional, and declared that he would challenge his nephew for the presidency. (The Syrian authorities reportedly issued a warrant for Rifaat's arrest should he attempt to enter the country from exile.) At the national referendum held on 10 July, Bashar al-Assad (the sole presidential candidate) received the endorsement of a reported 97.29% of voters. In his inaugural address to the People's Assembly on 17 July, President Assad emphasized as priorities for his administration economic reform, the elimination of official corruption and the conclusion of a peace treaty with Israel.

In July 2000 the new President released a significant number of political prisoners, the majority of whom were communists and members of the Muslim Brotherhood. Nevertheless, in September a statement by 99 Syrian intellectuals, published in the Lebanese press, demanded increased democracy and freedom of expression, an end to the state of emergency (in force since 1963) and the release of political detainees. In November the army deployed tanks and armoured vehicles in the southern region of As-Suweida, in order to quell three days of violent clashes between members of the Sunni bedouin and Druze communities; 20 people died in the fighting, and some 200 were injured. On the 30th anniversary of his father's seizure of power, commemorated in mid-November, President Bashar al-Assad declared an amnesty for about 600 political detainees, as well as a general amnesty for several non-political offences. The decision to free as many as 100 Lebanese prisoners was widely viewed as a gesture of 'goodwill' at a time when influential elements within Lebanon were demanding a lessening of Syrian influence in Lebanese political life.

In January 2001 a group of at least 1,000 intellectuals, among them a prominent businessman and deputy, Riad Seif, urged the Syrian regime to approve political reforms. They demanded the suspension of martial law, the holding of free elections, a free press, the release of political prisoners and an end to discrimination against women. Later that month a new 'liberal' political organization, the Movement for Social Peace, was reportedly established under Seif's leadership; there were, however, reports that it had subsequently been disbanded. Meanwhile, following a decision by the Baath Party in November 2000 to permit the other political parties in the NPF to issue their own newspapers, it was announced in early 2001 that the first non-state-controlled newspaper for several decades was to be published by the Communist Party. Syria's first privately owned newspaper for almost 40 years was also issued from February, while the launch was announced of the official newspaper of the Syrian Arab Socialist Union.

Reports emerged in February 2001 that the Baath Party was to restrict the activities of civic discussion forums being held by Syrian intellectuals by requiring that groups should henceforth apply for permission several days in advance of convening meetings. In April the Deputy Prime Minister and Minister of Defence, Maj.-Gen. Mustafa Tlass, accused Syrian intellectuals of being agents of the US Central Intelligence Agency. Later that month another civil rights document was issued, defining for President Assad a list of the principles on which reforms should be based. Also in April a report published by the UN Human Rights Committee expressed concerns regarding violations of human rights in Syria, including unfair trials and the torture of prisoners, the practice of extra-judicial executions and the continued imposition of martial law.

A series of actions by the authorities against influential opposition activists in August–September 2001 revived speculation that, contrary to early impressions, the President was less than willing to tolerate dissent. In August an independent deputy, Mamoun al-Homsi, was detained after starting a hunger strike in protest at official corruption and the Government's failure to end martial law. In September the leader of the Communist Party, Riad at-Turk, was taken into custody on charges of defaming the presidency (he had reportedly criticized the system of 'hereditary succession'). A few days later Riad Seif, who had held an 'illegal' discussion forum on political reform, was arrested. Trial proceedings began in October against al-Homsi and Seif, and in March 2002 al-Homsi was convicted of 'attempting to change the Constitution by illegal means' and sentenced to a five-year custodial term. Seif also received a five-year gaol sentence in April, having been convicted on similar charges; he was released from prison in January 2006. In June 2002 at-Turk was sentenced to two-and-a-half years' imprisonment, although he was freed by President Assad in November, reportedly on 'humanitarian grounds'. Meanwhile, in November 2001 some 120 political prisoners were released under a general amnesty. In January 2002 legislation relating to private broadcasting was relaxed.

President Assad effected an extensive reorganization of the Government in December 2001. Prime Minister Mero retained his post, as did the Ministers of Defence and Foreign Affairs (the long-serving Minister of Foreign Affairs, Farouk ash-Shara', additionally became the fourth Deputy Prime Minister), although a new Minister of the Interior, Maj.-Gen. Ali Hammoud (former head of the intelligence service), was named. However, several 'pro-reform' ministers were appointed to strategic portfolios relating to the economy, among them Muhammad al-Atrash as Minister of Finance. In January 2002 Maj.-Gen. Hasan at-Turkmani replaced Maj.-Gen. Ali Aslan as the new Chief of Staff of the Armed Forces. In February Assad reportedly accepted the resignation of the Deputy Prime Minister and Minister of Defence, Maj.-Gen. Mustafa Tlass, effective from July; however, there were further reports in May that Tlass had been ordered by the President to remain in office for a further two years.

Elections to the People's Assembly were held on 2 and 3 March 2003, at which the NPF, led by the ruling Baath Party, again won 167 of the 250 seats, with the remaining 83 going to independents. Electoral turn-out was estimated to be 63.5%. Opposition parties, under an umbrella grouping called the National Democratic Rally, boycotted the election on the grounds that it was undemocratic. On 9 March the newly reconvened legislature elected the Deputy Prime Minister in charge of Public Services, Muhammad Naji al-Otari, as the new Speaker of the People's Assembly. Al-Otari was replaced as Deputy Prime Minister by Muhammad Safi Abu Wdan in late March.

The Government reacted to the outbreak of conflict in Iraq in March 2003 (see below) by authorizing large anti-war demonstrations in Damascus and other major cities. However, this new-found tolerance of public demonstrations had not been extended to protests by Syrian Kurds earlier in February, when hundreds of members of one of Syria's outlawed Kurdish parties had protested outside the People's Assembly, leading to the arrest of the party's leadership.

In July 2003 it was reported that President Bashar al-Assad had passed a decree effectively ending the Baath Party's monopoly on government, military and public sector positions. In September Prime Minister Mero resigned, along with his Cabinet, apparently as a result of his failure to accelerate the process of political reform. Al-Otari was appointed as the new Prime Minister, and his first Cabinet was announced at the end of the month. Notable new appointments included Dr Muhammad al-Hussain, a former Deputy Prime Minister, as Minister of Finance, and Ahmad al-Hassan as Minister of Information. Soon afterwards at least 16 government officials were dismissed as part of a new anti-corruption campaign. In September assets belonging to the former Minister of Industry in the Government of Prime Minister Mero, Dr Issam az-Zaim, were seized in connection with alleged corruption at a state-owned textile plant in Latakia. In May 2004 Maj.-Gen. Mustafa Tlass retired from the posts of Minister of Defence and Deputy Commander-in-Chief of the Armed Forces; he was succeeded in both posts by armed forces Chief of Staff Hasan at-Turkmani, who was in turn replaced by Gen. Ali Habib (hitherto Special Forces Commander).

Issues of civil rights came to the fore in early 2004. In February a prominent lawyer and human rights activist, Haitham Malih, was prevented from travelling to the United Arab Emirates; the Syrian Human Rights Association claimed that Malih was being punished for having criticized the ongoing state of emergency (in force since 1963) in a speech he made to the German Bundestag (Federal Assembly) two months earlier. At the same time the Lebanese newspaper An-Nahar published a petition signed by 1,500 Syrian intellectuals, democratic activists and lawyers urging the Government to instigate radical reforms, including the lifting of the state of emergency and the release of political prisoners. At the end of the month foreigners were banned from studying at the 20 Islamic schools licensed by the Ministry of

Labour and Social Affairs; they would henceforth only be allowed to study Islamic law at Damascus University. Although the official reason given was that the degrees awarded by the schools were not yet officially recognized, the decision was widely regarded as a crackdown by the secular regime on foreign Islamists who were using their studies as a cover for militant, fund-raising or recruitment activities.

There was a widespread outbreak of violent, predominantly Kurdish, protest in March 2004. The unrest started in the north-eastern town of Al-Qamishli, close to the border with Turkey, when fighting at a football match escalated into large-scale anti-Government protests and fighting between the Arab majority and Kurdish minority; a number of deaths were reported. Minister of the Interior Hammoud travelled to the region to oversee the quelling of the violence, and the Government accused Kurdish political groups of deliberately inciting the riots. However, the unrest quickly spread to the town of Al-Hasakah, and Kurdish émigrés in many European countries staged demonstrations of solidarity with the Kurds outside Syrian embassies. There were also outbreaks of violence at commemorations of the anniversary of a chemical attack by the former Iraqi regime of Saddam Hussain on the Kurdish town of Halabja, in northern Iraq, in 1988, and at least seven Kurds were reported to have been killed in Aleppo and Afrin. By April 2004 it appeared that hundreds of Kurds were still being detained by the authorities in connection with the previous month's clashes, and Amnesty International called for an independent inquiry into the unrest and for any remaining detainees to be either charged or released. In connection with the violence, in June it was alleged that Syrian military intelligence had announced to three senior Kurdish leaders the end of state tolerance of the actitivities of unlicensed Kurdish parties; hundreds of Kurds allegedly remained in custody, having been arrested on suspicion of involvement in the March incident. Meanwhile, in April 2004 a car bomb exploded outside the former offices of the UN Disengagement Observer Force in Damascus; an exchange of fire between police and four people fleeing the scene resulted in the deaths of two assailants, a police officer and a bystander; the other two attackers were arrested by the authorities.

In July and August 2004, as part of an amnesty declared by President Assad, 251 political prisoners were freed, including members of the Muslim Brotherhood and Imad Shiash, who had been serving a prison sentence since 1975 for his membership of the proscribed Arab Communist Organization. In October Assad announced a significant reorganization of the Council of Ministers, dismissing eight ministers from their posts. Prominent appointees included Maj.-Gen. Ghazi Kanaan, a former head of Syrian military intelligence in Lebanon, who assumed the interior portfolio from Hammoud, and Mahdi Dakhlallah, a well-known journalist, who was appointed Minister of Information. In February 2005 it was reported that Maj.-Gen. Khalil had reached retirement age, and had been replaced as military intelligence chief by Brig.-Gen. Asef Shawkat. (For further details regarding internal political developments, see below.)

In July 1991, following a meeting with the US Secretary of State, James Baker, President Assad agreed for the first time to participate in direct negotiations with Israel at a regional peace conference, for which the terms of reference would be a comprehensive settlement based on UN Security Council Resolutions 242 (of 1967) and 338 (1973). In August 1991 the Israeli Cabinet formally agreed to attend a peace conference on terms proposed by the USA and the USSR. An initial, 'symbolic' session of the conference was held in Madrid, Spain, in October, and attended by Israeli, Syrian, Egyptian, Lebanese and Palestinian-Jordanian delegations. Syria's principal aim was to recover the Golan Heights, occupied by Israel since 1967. However, it emphasized that it was not prepared to achieve national goals at the expense of a comprehensive Middle East peace settlement. Syria regarded the Declaration of Principles on Palestinian Self-Rule in the Occupied Territories—the basis of a peace settlement signed by Israel and the PLO in September 1993—as deeply flawed. Furthermore, President Assad viewed the secret negotiations between Israel and the PLO prior to the Declaration of Principles as having undermined the united Arab position in the peace process, and Syria gave no indication that it would cease to support those Palestinian factions, such as the Damascus-based Popular Front for the Liberation of Palestine—General Command (PFLP—GC), which actively opposed the accord.

President Assad met US President Bill Clinton in Geneva, Switzerland, in January 1994—his first such meeting with a US leader since 1977—in an attempt to give fresh impetus to the Syrian track of the peace process. In June Syria reacted warily to the signing by Jordan and Israel of 'sub-agendas' for future bilateral discussions, and continued to adhere to the principle of a united Arab approach to negotiation with Israel. In September Israel published details of a plan for the partial withdrawal of its armed forces from the Golan Heights; Syria rejected the proposals, although President Assad continued to affirm his willingness to achieve peace with Israel. Clinton visited Damascus in October for talks with Assad (the first visit by a US President to Syria for some 20 years), in a further attempt to facilitate the resumption of dialogue between Syria and Israel. However, it was not until March 1995 that bilateral negotiations finally resumed.

In May 1995 Israel and Syria concluded a 'framework understanding on security arrangements', in order to facilitate the participation in the discussions of the two countries' military Chiefs of Staff. Israel stated publicly that it had proposed a four-year timetable for the withdrawal of its armed forces from the Golan Heights, but that Syria had insisted on one of 18 months. In June the Israeli and Syrian Chiefs of Staff held talks in Washington, DC. Negotiations became deadlocked once again, however, and the situation was aggravated by political turmoil in Israel following the assassination of the Prime Minister, Itzhak Rabin, in November. The acting Israeli Prime Minister, Shimon Peres, indicated that no further discussions would take place until after the Israeli general election in May, owing to Syria's refusal to condemn the violence in Israel and to take firmer action against terrorism generally. Following the election to the Israeli premiership of Likud leader Binyamin Netanyahu, an emergency Arab League summit meeting, held in Cairo, Egypt, in June, urged the new right-wing Government in Israel not to abandon the principle of negotiating 'land-for-peace', and demanded the removal of all Israeli settlements in the Golan Heights and their return to Syria. Netanyahu rejected the 'land-for-peace' policies of his Labour predecessor and also insisted that continued Israeli sovereignty over the Golan Heights must be the basis of any peace settlement with Syria. The redeployment, in September, of Syrian armed forces in Lebanon to positions in the Beka'a valley gave rise to speculation in Israel that Syria, frustrated at the lack of progress in the peace process, might be preparing an attack on Israeli forces.

The Israeli-Syrian peace initiative was further interrupted by the construction of a controversial new Jewish settlement at Jabal Abu Ghunaim (Har Homa) in Arab East Jerusalem in March 1997. Prospects of a resumption in negotiations were further frustrated after the Israeli Knesset approved a preliminary reading of proposed legislation stipulating that the return of land to Syria would require the approval of at least two-thirds of deputies. In March 1998 Syria accused Israel of attempting to sabotage its relationship with Lebanon after the Israeli Prime Minister offered to withdraw from southern Lebanon in exchange for a security arrangement before reaching a formal agreement with Syria regarding the Golan Heights. Both Syria and Lebanon reiterated that any withdrawal must be unconditional, in compliance with UN Security Council Resolution 425. Syria was sceptical regarding the likely success of the US-brokered Wye Memorandum, signed in October by Israel and the Palestinian (National) Authority (PA), towards achieving a lasting peace in the Middle East, and President Assad again demanded a resumption of 'land-for-peace' negotiations.

Syria welcomed the success of Ehud Barak and his Labour-led One Israel coalition in the Israeli elections of May 1999. Barak reportedly proposed a five-phase plan to negotiate peace with Syria and to effect an Israeli withdrawal from southern Lebanon. Syria responded with the demand that Barak uphold his pre-election pledge to withdraw from Lebanon within one year of his election, and to resume peace talks from their point of deadlock in 1996. At the inauguration of the new Israeli Cabinet in early July 1999, Barak promised to negotiate a bilateral peace with Syria, based on UN Security Council Resolutions 242 and 338, thus apparently signalling to the Assad regime his intention to return most of the occupied Golan Heights to Syria in exchange for peace and normalized relations. In mid-July, prior to a meeting in Washington, DC, between Barak and President Clinton, Syria was reported to have warned dissidents of Damascus-based Palestinian organizations to cease their military operations against Israel, and to have interrupted the supply of Iranian weapons to Hezbollah guerrillas in southern Lebanon. Moreover, in late July Syria reported a 'cease-fire' with Israel, although mutual disagreements remained, most notably over the point at which previous negotiations had been suspended. In

September, as Israel and the PA signed the Sharm esh-Sheikh Memorandum (or Wye Two—see the chapter on Israel) in Egypt, US Secretary of State Albright held talks with President Assad in Damascus.

In early December 1999 Israel and Syria agreed to resume negotiations from the point at which they had stalled in 1996 (this was following mediation by Clinton). The first round of discussions between the Syrian Minister of Foreign Affairs, Farouk ash-Shara', and the Israeli premier, Ehud Barak, was opened by the US President in mid-December 1999 in Washington, DC. Both sides agreed to resume discussions in the following month, and in late December Syria and Israel were reported to have agreed an informal 'cease-fire' in order to limit the conflict in Lebanon. A second round of talks between ash-Shara' and Barak proceeded in early January 2000 (with the involvement of Clinton) in Shepherdstown, West Virginia. Syria and Israel had agreed meanwhile on the establishment of committees to discuss simultaneously the issues of borders, security, normalization of relations, and water sharing. However, in mid-January the peace talks were postponed indefinitely. Syria declared that it required a 'written' commitment from Israel to withdraw from the Golan Heights prior to a resumption of talks, while Israel demanded the personal involvement of President Assad in the negotiating process, and that Syria take action to restrain Hezbollah in southern Lebanon. In March the Israeli Cabinet voted unanimously to withdraw its forces from Lebanon by July, even in the absence of a peace settlement with Syria, while the Knesset voted to change the majority required in the event of an Israeli withdrawal from the Golan from 50% of participating voters to 50% of the registered electorate.

In May 2000 ash-Shara' hosted discussions in Palmyra with his Egyptian and Saudi Arabian counterparts in an effort to co-ordinate a united Arab position towards the USA and Israel prior to the planned Israeli withdrawal from southern Lebanon. Reports following the talks suggested that Saudi Arabia and Egypt had pledged military support to Syria in the event of Israeli aggression. The accelerated withdrawal of Israeli armed forces from southern Lebanon was completed on 24 May, several weeks ahead of the original Israeli deadline. Following the death, in June, of President Assad, and the succession of his second son, Bashar al-Assad, in July, the Israeli-Syrian track of the Middle East peace process remained stalled. Nevertheless, Bashar indicated a desire to resume negotiations in the near future, although he emphasized that Syrian policy on the Golan Heights remained unchanged. The escalation of the Palestinian al-Aqsa *intifada* from September strained Syria's relations with Israel and, as tensions increased throughout the Middle East, Israel accused Syria of involvement in the abduction of Israeli military personnel by Hezbollah in the disputed Shebaa Farms area of southern Lebanon. (Shebaa Farms has been designated by the UN as being part of Syria, and thus subject to the Syrian track of the peace process.) During an emergency summit meeting of the Arab League held in Cairo in October, Farouk ash-Shara' urged all Arab countries to sever diplomatic ties with Israel.

Following the election of Likud leader Ariel Sharon to the Israeli premiership in February 2001, President Assad again reiterated Syria's position: namely that negotiations would only be resumed upon a full Israeli withdrawal from the Golan Heights. Tensions between the two sides increased in April following an attack by Israeli forces on a Syrian radar station in eastern Lebanon, in which at least one Syrian soldier died. In December, following talks in Damascus between Egypt's President Hosni Mubarak and President Assad, Egypt and Syria issued a joint statement condemning Israeli military actions in the West Bank and Gaza, and called on the international community to put pressure on Israel to halt its 'aggression'. In January 2003 a Syrian soldier was killed during a rare exchange of gunfire between Israeli and Syrian forces in the Golan Heights. In November 2004 Assad announced that he was willing to resume peace talks with Israel unconditionally (although it was unclear whether the Syrian President intended for negotiations to resume from where they had collapsed in 2000—see above); however, Israel refused to conduct talks with Syria until it closed the headquarters of Hamas and Islamic Jihad, and Assad rejected Israel's setting of conditions as unacceptable.

In April 2003 US President George W. Bush handed to the Israeli and Palestinian leaderships the so-called 'roadmap' peace plan, which had been drawn up by the Quartet group (comprising the USA, the UN, Russia and the EU). The plan envisaged an end to the Arab–Israeli conflict and the creation of a sovereign Palestinian state by 2005–06 (for full details of the roadmap, see the chapter on Israel). A fully negotiated peace settlement between Israel and Syria was one of the objectives of the roadmap, but Syria was keen to emphasize that the new plan must run in tandem with the Syrian track of negotiations on the Golan Heights issue; however, in May 2003 President Assad reportedly assured Javier Solana, the EU's High Representative for the Common Foreign and Security Policy, that Syria would unconditionally accept the roadmap. An offer from Syria to resume peace talks with Israel in July was firmly rejected by Israeli Prime Minister Ariel Sharon as 'insincere'. In the following month Israel accused Syria of masterminding an attack by Hezbollah in Shebaa Farms. In October Israel launched an air attack against an alleged Palestinian militant training camp inside Syria. Israel claimed that the camp at Ain Saheb near Damascus was being used by Hamas and Islamic Jihad, which the latter group denied, while another Palestinian militant group, the Popular Front for the Liberation of Palestine (PFLP), stated that the facility at Ain Saheb was in fact not in use. Israel insisted that the attack was not directed against Syria, but was in retaliation for a suicide bomb attack in Haifa, Israel, in which 19 Israelis were killed. In January 2004 President Assad rejected Israeli offers to resume peace negotiations, describing them as a 'media manouevre'. Following an Israeli warning of military action against Syria for its presumed involvement in suicide attacks in Israel that killed 16 people in August, a senior Hamas official was assassinated in Damascus in September, provoking an angry response from Syrian officials.

There was increasing agitation in Lebanon for a cessation of Syrian influence on Lebanese political affairs after the inauguration of a new Syrian President and the Israeli withdrawal from southern Lebanon. In July 2000 Maronite Christian leaders in Lebanon requested that President Assad release all Lebanese political prisoners held in Syria, and in the following month a coalition of Christian political parties in Lebanon urged voters there to boycott the forthcoming parliamentary elections, on the grounds that Syria would predetermine the outcome of the poll. The results of the elections, at which former premier Rafik Hariri resoundingly defeated the Syrian-sponsored Government of Selim al-Hoss, served to intensify speculation about Syria's future role in Lebanese affairs. Syrian officials reacted angrily when the Lebanese Druze leader and traditional ally of Syria, Walid Joumblatt, demanded a 're-evaluation' of Syria's role in Lebanon. In December 46 Lebanese prisoners (many of whom were Christians detained by Syrian troops during the civil war) were released from Syrian detention; hitherto Syria had never confirmed that it was holding Lebanese political prisoners.

In June 2001 Syria withdrew some 6,000–10,000 of its armed forces from predominantly Christian districts of east and south Beirut, and from Mount Lebanon; some of the troops were redeployed in the Beka'a valley. However, Syria retained a number of military bases in strategic areas of the Lebanese capital. President Assad's discussions with President Emile Lahoud in March 2002 reportedly centred on the forthcoming Arab League conference in Beirut, at which Saudi Arabia's Crown Prince Abdullah was formally to submit his proposals for a Middle East peace settlement (for further details, see the chapter on Lebanon). The two leaders reportedly demanded that any peace deal should include the right of return for Palestinian refugees. Redeployments of Syrian troops from central Lebanon took place in April 2002, and from northern Lebanon in February 2003. The new Lebanese Government formed under Hariri in April was widely considered to be the most pro-Syrian administration in Lebanon for more than a decade. In June unidentified assailants fired rockets at the studios of Hariri's Future Television in central Beirut. Syria was blamed for having organized the attack, chiefly as a warning to the Lebanese Prime Minister following remarks he made on a state visit to Brazil in which Hariri appeared to call for an improvement in Arab–Israeli relations. Moreover, the attack coincided with a further redeployment of Syrian troops from Lebanon.

Syrian influence on Lebanese political affairs continued during 2004: following meetings with Syrian officials, Lebanon decided not to effect any government changes in response to a strike in the southern suburbs of Beirut in late May, and Prime Minister Hariri, also following meetings with Syrian officials, withdrew his objection to the extension, in August, of President Lahoud's mandate by three years. However, international pressure on Syria increased following the adoption in early September of UN Security Council Resolution 1559, which, without referring to Syria explicitly, demanded that Lebanon's sovereignty be respected and that all foreign forces leave the country.

(See the chapter on Lebanon for further details of Lebanese domestic affairs and of the UN resolution.) The Syrian army subsequently redeployed about 3,000 special forces from positions south of Beirut, and further troops were withdrawn in December from the northern town of Batrun and from Beirut's southern suburbs and airport to the Beka'a valley. However, the new Lebanese Government approved by the legislature in November (in which Rafik Hariri had been replaced as Prime Minister by Omar Karami) was regarded as being even more favourable than its predecessor to continued Syrian influence in Lebanese affairs. In December a number of Lebanese political parties issued a joint statement demanding the cessation of foreign interference in the country.

Former Lebanese Prime Minister Rafik Hariri was killed in a car bombing in Beirut on 14 February 2005. Although President Assad condemned the attack, the USA, without accusing Syria of involvement in the incident, withdrew its ambassador to Syria for consultations, and later demanded the complete withdrawal of Syrian troops from Lebanon and a thorough and transparent investigation into the attack. Meanwhile, Syria and Iran agreed to form a 'united front' against foreign threats to their states. Syria declared later in the month that it would redeploy all of its troops in Lebanon to the Beka'a valley. Mass protests against Syria's influence on Lebanese affairs, and against the Syrian military presence in Lebanon, followed, and in late February President Bush demanded that Syria: withdraw all troops and security service personnel from Lebanon; stop using its territory to support militant groups; support free and fair elections in Lebanon; and adhere to UN Security Council Resolution 1559 (see above). The UN Secretary-General, Kofi Annan, called on Syria to withdraw its troops from Lebanon by April.

In late February 2005 Karami announced the resignation of his administration, but, under President Lahoud's request, he and his ministers remained in office pending the appointment of a new government. Opposition groups continued to demand that Syrian army and intelligence personnel withdraw from Lebanon, and that senior Lebanese security officials resign. In early March the US Secretary of State, Condoleezza Rice, reiterated Bush's demands and warned Syria that it was threatening peace and preventing change in the Middle East. She also stated that there was evidence of the involvement of Islamic Jihad in a bombing in Tel-Aviv, Israel, in February. Meanwhile, Presidents Assad and Lahoud agreed at a summit meeting to the withdrawal of Syrian troops to the Beka'a valley by the end of March; Syria later promised to withdraw all troops before Lebanon's general election in May, and to provide the UN with a timetable for the withdrawal. Rice praised the decision, but urged the two countries to accelerate the process. Syria reportedly withdrew 4,000–6,000 of its troops from Lebanon to Syria in mid-March, removing Syrian soldiers and intelligence agents from their barracks and offices around Tripoli and Beirut; 8,000–10,000 troops reportedly remained in the Beka'a valley. A UN report released in late March blamed Syria for allowing political tension in Lebanon to mount before the murder of Hariri; it also criticized Lebanon's initial attempts to investigate the incident. In early April the UN Security Council approved Resolution 1595, which established an International Independent Investigation Commission (UNIIIC) to investigate Hariri's murder. The German prosecutor Detlev Mehlis was appointed to head the commission. The formation of a new Lebanese administration, headed by newly appointed Prime Minister Najib Mikati, was announced in mid-April. Later in the month Syria declared that it had withdrawn all of its troops and security forces from Lebanon, and in early May a UN team dispatched to Lebanon to confirm the withdrawal announced that thus far it had not found a single Syrian soldier in areas that it had inspected.

Legislative elections were held in Lebanon in four rounds between 29 May and 19 June 2005 (see the chapter on Lebanon). A broad anti-Syrian alliance, led by Rafik Hariri's son, Saad ed-Din al-Hariri, secured the highest number of seats in the National Assembly (72 of 128 seats). A pro-Syrian bloc that included Hezbollah and Amal secured 35 seats, and a bloc led by a former Commander-in-Chief of the Lebanese army, Gen. Michel Awn, who had allied himself with pro-Syrian factions immediately prior to the elections, won 21 seats. Pro-Syrian Nabih Berri was re-elected as President of the National Assembly in late June, and Fouad Siniora, a close ally of Rafik Hariri, was appointed as Prime Minister. A new Cabinet was installed in July. Syrian President Assad and Prime Minister Otari met Fouad Siniora in Syria in August. The two states reportedly agreed to improve relations based on mutual respect, and Siniora emphasized Lebanon's support of Syria and its commitment to bilateral agreements. Various prominent Lebanese figures opposed to Syrian influence in Lebanon were killed or injured in bomb attacks during mid- to late 2005, including the former Secretary-General of the Parti communiste libanais (Lebanese Communist Party), who was killed in a car bombing in Beirut in June.

At the 10th national congress of the Baath Party in June 2005, President Assad was re-elected as Secretary-General. Vice-President and member of the party leadership Abd al-Halim Khaddam reportedly asked to be relieved of all of his duties, citing a wish to allow more young people to be represented in the party and state leadership. Although there was no confirmation that Khaddam's resignation as Vice-President had been accepted, it was announced that he had not been re-elected to the party leadership. The political committee of the Baath Party endorsed proposals to relax laws relating to the state of emergency, and to produce legislation allowing the formation of independent parties and increased freedom of the press; however, by 2007 the proposed reforms did not appear to have received the required parliamentary approval. In late December 2005 Khaddam, who had been living in exile in Paris since his resignation, held an interview with the Dubai-based satellite television station *Al-Arabia* in which he accused Assad of having personally threatened Rafik Hariri a few months prior to his assassination. Khaddam subsequently declared that, in his view, Assad had ordered Hariri's killing, although he awaited the final decision of the investigating commission. He declared that the current Syrian regime could not be reformed, and called on opposition groups in Syria to co-operate to defeat it. In early January 2006 the Baath Party announced that it had formally expelled Khaddam, accusing him of treachery against the party, his country and the Arab nation for his accusations against the Syrian President. Meanwhile, in December 2005 the People's Assembly unanimously approved a motion calling for Khaddam to be brought to trial on charges of treason and corruption. In January 2006 the Syrian Government froze Khaddam's assets, and in April a military court formally charged the former Vice-President with a series of offences, including inciting a foreign attack on Syrian soil and plotting to seize political and civil power.

In response to reports that Syrian intelligence agents might not have completely withdrawn from Lebanon, the UN announced in early June 2005 that it was considering sending a commission to the country to investigate the claims. (Syria continued to assert that it had removed all of its security personnel.) UNIIIC began its inquiry into Rafik Hariri's assassination in mid-June, with a three-month mandate. In August UNIIIC arrested three former Lebanese security officials with close ties to Syria, who had tendered their resignations in April, for questioning regarding the assassination. A fourth security chief, who had retained his post after Hariri's murder, subsequently handed himself in to the organization. A former, pro-Syrian parliamentary deputy was also detained. In mid-October, shortly before UNIIIC issued its first report on the investigation, the official Syrian Arab News Agency announced the death, by suicide, of the Minister of the Interior, Maj.-Gen. Ghazi Kanaan; a formal investigation subsequently confirmed the cause of death. Shortly before his apparent suicide, Kanaan had issued a statement to a Lebanese radio station defending Syria's role in Lebanon and announcing that he had been questioned by UNIIIC, but had not given any evidence against Syria. Some analysts noted that Kanaan, a potential alternative to the Syrian President who had opposed the decision to extend Lebanese President Lahoud's tenure by three years in 2004 (see above), had been seen as a threat to Assad.

According to its first report, issued in late October 2005, UNIIIC had found evidence that Lebanese and Syrian intelligence and security services were directly involved in the assassination of Rafik Hariri. Moreover, the report reasoned, the act was too complex and too well planned to have taken place without the approval of senior Syrian security officials and their Lebanese counterparts. UNIIIC expressed its extreme concern at the lack of co-operation of the Syrian authorities. Lebanon and Syria both rejected the report, criticizing the investigation's findings as politically motivated, and Syria announced that it had established a special judicial commission to deal with all matters relating to UNIIIC's mission. The commission was granted an extension to its mandate to mid-December. The UN Security Council reacted to the report by adopting Resolution 1636 at the end of October 2005, establishing measures against suspects in the assassination, including prohibitions on travel and the freezing of assets, and urging Syria to co-operate fully with the investigation commission and to detain suspects identified by the inquiry as suspects in Hariri's assassination, threatening unspecified 'further action' should Syria not fulfil the resolution's demands. The Security Council gave Syria until 15 December to comply with the resolution, which was sponsored by the USA, France and the United Kingdom. Syria reported in early November that it had arrested six government officials for questioning. Meanwhile, in late October 2005, the UN Special Envoy, Terje Roed-Larsen, published his report on compliance with UN Security Council Resolution 1559, in which he lauded Syria's withdrawal of its troops from Lebanon, but criticized Lebanon for not complying with the resolution's demands.

In his second report to the UN Security Council, issued in mid-December 2005, Mehlis noted that Syria had presented five officials suspected of involvement in the murder of Hariri to UNIIIC for interrogation in Vienna, Austria. However, the report again accused Syria of reluctance to co-operate with the investigating body and of hindering the investigation. UNIIIC had found further evidence of the involvement of the Lebanese and Syrian intelligence and security services in the assassination, and Mehlis identified 19 suspects, six of whom were Syrian (of which five were those currently under interrogation in Vienna). Mehlis resigned as head of UNIIIC shortly after he presented the report, citing personal and professional reasons; he was replaced by Serge Brammertz. UNIIIC's mandate was extended to 15 June 2006.

In early January 2006, after Abd al-Halim Khaddam accused President Assad of having personally threatened Hariri (see above), UNIIIC investigators declared that they wished to question the Syrian President and Minister of Foreign Affairs ash-Shara'. However, the following day the Minister of Information, Mahdi Dakhlallah, declared that Syria would not permit UNIIIC to interview Assad. Brammetz met ash-Shara' and other unspecified Syrian officials in late February. Ash-Shara' announced in early March that he had reached an agreement with UNIIIC providing for full Syrian co-operation with the investigation, while maintaining the country's 'sovereignty and dignity'. (Khaddam reiterated his claims that Assad was ultimately responsible for Hariri's assassination throughout 2006, and called for a popular revolt to effect the President's removal from office.)

The distribution and reprinting in both Western and Muslim-majority countries of caricatures of the Prophet Muhammad originally published in a Danish newspaper in September 2005 provoked considerable anger among Muslim communities worldwide in early 2006 (see the chapter on Denmark). Depiction of the Prophet is forbidden by Islamic tradition, and the cartoons in question were considered to be particularly offensive. Violent protests against the publication of the caricatures took place in a number of Muslim countries, and in early February the Danish and Norwegian embassies in Damascus (as well as in the capitals of other majority-Muslim countries) were attacked and forced to close temporarily due to a perceived threat to their security.

President Assad effected a comprehensive reorganization of the Council of Ministers in mid-February 2006. Ash-Shara' was appointed as Vice-President to replace Khaddam, and given additional responsibility for Foreign Affairs and Information; he was replaced as Minister of Foreign Affairs by Walid Mouallem. In late March Dr Najah al-Attar was also named as a Vice-President.

In May 2006 274 Lebanese and Syrian intellectuals and activists signed the Beirut-Damascus Declaration, a petition urging the Syrian Government to reassess its policy on Lebanon, to respect the sovereign independence of that country and to establish normal diplomatic relations; many of those who signed the Declaration were subsequently arrested. The Government appeared to have intensified its efforts against the signatories in early 2007. In April Anwar al-Bunni, a well-known advocate for democratic reform in Syria, was convicted on charges of disseminating false information and thereby damaging national morale, and was sentenced to five years' imprisonment. Four other prominent Syrian activists, all of whom, like al-Bunni, had signed the Declaration, were convicted on similar charges in the following month; two received three-year prison sentences, while the other two (convicted *in absentia*) were sentenced to 10 years' imprisonment. Human rights groups quickly denounced the convictions, which they claimed were a violation of the right of free speech and part of an ongoing process of intimidation by means of which the Syrian Government hoped to silence dissidents.

Meanwhile, the third and fourth UNIIIC reports on the assassination of Hariri were published in March and June 2006, respectively. Recent Syrian co-operation was described as 'generally satisfactory', and the investigators claimed to have made considerable progress with regard to their understanding both of the circumstances surrounding the murder and of the links between the planners and the perpetrators of the killing. However, the report acknowledged that more thorough investigation was required into alleged links between Hariri's assassination and 14 other attacks against anti-Syrian figures in Lebanon since October 2004. In mid-June 2006 UNIIIC's mandate was extended for another year. The fifth UNIIIC report was released by Brammertz in September, and again described Syrian co-operation with the investigation as 'general satisfactory'.

Syria was forced to deny accusations that it had orchestrated the assassination of Pierre Gemayel, the Lebanese Minister of Industry, renowned for his anti-Syrian disposition, who was shot dead in his car on the outskirts of Beirut in November 2006 (see the chapter on Lebanon). Among those quick to apportion the blame firmly on Syria was Saad ed-Din Hariri, the son of Rafik. The US ambassador to the UN, John Bolton, while refraining from making any explicit accusations, also suggested that Syria might logically be considered a likely suspect in Gemayel's killing.

In preparation for legislative elections scheduled to take place in April 2007, in January President Assad approved amendments to electoral legislation, which included the introduction of stricter regulations on the financing of campaigns. No changes were made to the quota system by which 167 of the 250 seats were reserved for the NPF, despite widespread calls for its abolition from reformists. Ten days before the polls the Government announced that the number of seats reserved for the NPF would actually be increased to 170, thus reducing the number of seats set aside for independent candidates to just 80. At the elections to the People's Assembly on 22–23 April, voter turn-out was officially reported at 56.1% of the registered electorate, yet opponents of the Government claimed that the true rate of participation was, at most, 10%–20%. Speaking at an official press conference on 26 April, the Minister of the Interior announced that the NPF had secured 172 seats, two more than its recently allocated share and five more than its original two-thirds' quota; the number of independents thus fell to 78. The opposition, which had boycotted the polls, called upon the international community to condemn the elections and to acknowledge the illegitimacy of the newly installed legislature, and both domestic and external human rights groups (as well as even government-controlled newspapers) denounced the elections as undemocratic.

In mid-May 2007 the legislature unanimously approved the Baath Party's nomination of Bashar al-Assad for a second term as President, a national referendum on which was duly held on 27 May. Assad was endorsed for another seven-year term of office by a reported 97.6% of votes; turn-out was officially declared to have been more than 95.8%. However, the opposition dismissed the referendum as merely another means of perpetuating the undemocratic nature of the Syrian leadership. In mid-December, amid an intensification of repressive measures taken by the authorities against Syrian dissidents, at least 30 opposition activists were reported to have been detained. Some of the dissidents had recently established a new National Council of the Damascus Declaration, which intended to press the regime to implement radical political reforms. Riad Seif, head of the Declaration's Secretariat, was among those arrested in the latest clampdown against opponents of the regime, his arrest being reported at the end of January 2008. Although several of those detained were charged with undermining the state, others were released in subsequent weeks. Meanwhile, in early December 2007 President Assad effected a minor reorganization of the Council of Ministers, in which new Ministers of Communications and Technology and of Awqaf (Islamic Endowments) were appointed.

The Syrian Government condemned the massive suicide attacks carried out against US citizens in New York and Washington, DC, on 11 September 2001. However, Syria was openly critical of the decision of the US Administration of George W. Bush—as part of its world-wide 'war on terror'—to launch a military campaign against targets in Afghanistan linked to the Taliban regime and to the militant Islamist organization held principally responsible for the attacks, the al-Qa'ida (Base) network of Osama bin Laden. In October the British Prime Minister, Tony Blair, undertook an official visit to Syria, to garner Arab support for the US-led campaign in Afghanistan, and asked the Syrian leadership to end its support for militant groups such as Hezbollah and the PFLP. However, President Assad condemned the West's bombing of Afghan civilians and stated that organizations engaged in fighting the Israeli occupation were 'legitimate'. In December 2002 President Bashar al-Assad became the first Syrian leader to visit the United Kingdom, where he expressed his opposition to a US-led military campaign to bring about 'regime change' in Iraq, and rejected Blair's demand to curb militant Palestinian groups operating in Syria. In April of that year US Secretary of Defense Donald Rumsfeld had accused Syria, Iran and Iraq of involvement in terrorism against Israeli civilians. Relations between Syria and the USA deteriorated further during late 2002 and early 2003. Several members of the US Administration proposed the imposition of economic sanctions against Syria as punishment for its continued support for militant Palestinian organizations such as Islamic Jihad, Hamas and the PFLP. US officials also accused Syria of involvement in the illegal purchase of oil from Iraq. In November 2002 the Syrian leadership refused US demands that it close the Damascus office of Islamic Jihad, following a renewed campaign by that organization against targets in Israel.

As the US-led coalition forces launched a military campaign to oust the regime of Saddam Hussain in Iraq in March 2003, the USA also increasingly hinted that Syria might be the next target for a US-imposed 'regime change'. Damascus referred to the campaign in Iraq as an 'illegal invasion'. Moreover, Syrians were angered in late March when a bus close to the border with Iraq was hit by a stray US missile, killing five Syrian civilians. Damascus strongly denied claims by the Bush Administration that it was providing military equipment to Iraq during the conflict. The USA alleged that Syria had assisted leading members of the Iraqi Baath Party to flee the country after the collapse of Saddam Hussain's regime and that Iraqi weapons of mass destruction might have been transported to cross the border into Syria. However, in April President Bush declared that Syria was co-operating with the US-led coalition, having recently sealed its border with Iraq. Nevertheless, US officials from the Department of the Treasury estimated that US $3,000m. of Iraqi money was being held by Syrian-controlled banks in Damascus and Lebanon, in contravention of a UN resolution calling on all Iraqi funds held abroad to be handed over to the US-controlled Iraqi Fund for Development.

In December 2003 US President Bush signed the Syria Accountability Act, which allowed him to impose a range of sanctions on Syria unless the country met a series of conditions (including ending its support for terrorist groups). The sanctions were eventually put in place on 11 May 2004; they included a ban on all US exports to Syria other than food or medicine, and a halt to flights between the two countries. Syria rejected the sanctions, asserting that they would not affect the country or its economy, and in October Syria signed a bilateral agreement with the EU for greater economic co-operation, with Syria agreeing to renounce proliferation of nuclear weapons. In December it was reported that evidence had been found that Syria was permitting the training on its territory of militants to be used as insurgent fighters in Iraq, as well as allowing insurgents across the border between the two countries; Syria denied the claims. In May 2005, following reports that Iraqi militants had planned recent bombings at a meeting in Syria, the USA and Iraq urged Syria to prevent foreign fighters from crossing the border into Iraq.

In March 2007 Syria called for a 'serious dialogue' with the USA on a wide range of concerns pertaining to the Middle East. In the following month Nancy Pelosi, Speaker of the US House of Representatives (the third highest ranking elected official in the USA after the President and Vice-President), visited Damascus as part of a wider tour of the region, thus becoming the most senior US official to visit Syria since 2003. Pelosi's unauthorized visit drew strong criticism from President Bush, who, stung by the challenge to his Administration's policy of isolation towards the Syrian Government, accused Pelosi of usurping executive powers and of sending 'mixed signals' to a 'state sponsor of terrorism'. Pelosi, of the Democratic Party, dismissed such censure, pointing out that three Republican congressmen had also visited Syria very recently without attracting any disapproval from the Bush Administration. The Syrian ambassador to the USA, Imad Moustapha, described Pelosi's overture as a 'positive step', but one that offered little likelihood of a change in US policy. However, in May 2007 US Secretary of State Condoleezza Rice held landmark talks with Syrian Minister of Foreign Affairs Mouallem on the sidelines of a major summit meeting held in Egypt, intended to address the situation in Iraq. The sideline negotiations represented the first official high-level talks between the two countries since the murder of Rafik Hariri. During the talks Rice urged the Syrian leadership to take further action to prevent foreign fighters from crossing into Iraq from Syria in order to participate in the anti-US insurgency.

It was hoped that Syrian–US tensions would be eased in late November 2007, when Syria agreed to send a low-level delegation to the international peace meeting held under US auspices in Annapolis, Maryland, USA, with the aim of relaunching the Middle East peace process. However, such optimism proved to be shortlived. In mid-February 2008 President Bush approved an expanded range of sanctions against the Syrian regime, which he accused of destabilizing both Iraq and Lebanon. The new sanctions included a freeze on the assets of prominent Syrian officials or businessmen deemed to have benefited from corrupt practices. In early March the US Administration also announced that maritime vessels docking in US ports that had previously visited Syrian ports would henceforth be placed on a Port Security Advisory List, amid US concerns regarding Syrian links with international terrorist networks. The Bush Administration extended sanctions further against Syria in early May, imposing an embargo on exports of certain goods to the country. This tighter sanctions regime was imposed following allegations by US intelligence agencies that there existed a covert nuclear co-operation between Syria and the Democratic People's Republic of Korea (North Korea—see below).

During 2007 the Syrian leadership continued to oppose demands by the international community, including the US Administration, that an international tribunal be established in order to try suspects in Hariri's murder. In response to the adoption by the UN Security Council, on 31 May, of Resolution 1757 establishing a special tribunal for this purpose, Syria emphasized its position that the tribunal represented a violation of Lebanese sovereignty, and that it would refuse to hand over any Syrian suspects to the new body. In March 2007 it was reported that Iran and Syria had, during a visit to the Syrian capital by the Iranian Minister of Defence and Armed Forces Logistics, signed a further memorandum of understanding with regard to defence co-operation, and in July President Mahmoud Ahmadinejad also undertook a high-profile visit to Damascus.

The EU had resumed a formal dialogue with Syria in March 2007, when Javier Solana, the Secretary-General of the Council of the European Union and High Representative for the Common Foreign and Security Policy, met with Mouallem and President Assad. However, President Nicolas Sarkozy of France announced at the end of December that his Government would cease all diplomatic contacts with Syria until the regime demonstrated that it was committed to enabling the Lebanese National Assembly to elect a successor to President Lahoud (see the chapter on Lebanon). Syrian officials were swift to deny claims by many Western governments that they were preventing the presidential vote from taking place and were seeking to bring about the collapse of Lebanon's Western-backed Government by providing military assistance to Hezbollah and its allies. A summit meeting of Arab League member states, held in Damascus at the end of March 2008, was boycotted by several leading officials, amid ongoing disputes among Arab governments with regard to the political crisis in Lebanon. Notable absentees were Egypt's President Mubarak and Saudi Arabia's King Abdullah, both of whom blamed Syria and Iran for contributing to the crisis through their support for the Hezbollah-led opposition in Lebanon. At the Damascus summit Arab states agreed to review the 'land-for-peace' initiative for a Middle East settlement originally proposed in 2002.

In August 1999 a diplomatic crisis developed between Syria and the Palestinian authorities after the Syrian Deputy Prime Minister and Minister of Defence, Maj.-Gen. Mustafa Tlass, publicly accused Yasser Arafat of having 'sold Jerusalem and the Arab nation' in peace agreements concluded with Israel since 1993, and made other personal insults against the Palestinian leader. The PA demanded that Tlass resign (and Fatah reportedly issued a death warrant against Tlass), while President Assad was apparently angered by the minister's remarks. Arafat attended the funeral of President Hafiz al-Assad, and in mid-2000 the PA renewed its demand that Syria free all remaining Palestinian prisoners from its gaols; seven Palestinians were released into Lebanese custody in December. Amid Syrian efforts to support the Palestinians in their escalating conflict with the Israelis, and following talks between Assad and Arafat during the summit meeting of Arab League states in Jordan in March 2001, the two leaders declared that they had achieved a reconciliation. In December 2004 PLO leader Mahmud Abbas made the first official Palestinian visit to Damascus since 1996. Abbas, the Palestinian Prime Minister, Ahmad Quray, the Minister of Foreign Affairs, Dr Nasser al-Kidwa, and President Assad discussed the current situation in the Palestinian territories and preparations for the presidential election scheduled to be held there in January 2005. Assad emphasized Syria's support for the Palestinian people and their struggle for national unity, while Abbas stressed the importance of co-operation between Syria and the PA.

In October 1998 the Jordanian Government demanded 'immediate answers' from Syria concerning a list of 239 Jordanians allegedly missing in Syria, and a further 190 who it claimed were being held in Syrian prisons. The Syrian authorities agreed to investigate the matter, but stated that most of those listed were in fact members of Palestinian organizations linked with Jordan and had violated Syrian laws. In February 1999 President Assad unexpectedly attended the funeral of King Hussein of Jordan, and reportedly held a private meeting with the new monarch. Syria had welcomed the succession of King Abdullah, and the new Jordanian King made his first official visit to Syria in April. The two leaders urged a resumption of the peace process and increased bilateral co-operation; Syria agreed to supply Jordan with water during 1999, as the latter was undergoing a drought, and both sides agreed to hold future discussions regarding the Jordanian prisoners in Syria. King Abdullah made an unscheduled visit to Syria in July, at a time when Jordan was concerned that any separate peace settlement between Syria and Israel might undermine the Palestinian position in future negotiations. The joint Syrian-Jordanian Higher Committee met in August in Amman, under the chairmanship of both countries' premiers—the first time in almost a decade that a senior Syrian delegation had visited Jordan's capital. Meanwhile, the Syrian Government stated that many of the Jordanian prisoners held in Syria had been released under a general amnesty granted in July (see above) and that the 'very few' who remained in Syrian gaols were non-political detainees. Later in August Syria ended a 10-year ban on the free circulation of Jordanian newspapers and publications in the country. A further 17 Jordanian prisoners were reportedly released from Syrian gaols in March 2000. Following the death of President Assad in June, King Abdullah visited Damascus in July for talks with Syria's new President, Bashar al-Assad; Syria again agreed to supply Jordan with water during that summer. It was reported in November that Syria had upgraded its diplomatic representation in Jordan to ambassadorial level. In January 2001 Syrian officials reportedly gave assurances to Jordan that all Jordanian political prisoners would soon be released. In February 2004 Syria and Jordan launched the Wahdah Dam project on Jordan's River Yarmuk. The project, which was completed in September 2006, aimed to provide Jordan with water and Syria with electricity.

Relations between Syria and Iraq had been strained since the early 1970s due to a rivalry between the respective factions of the Baath Party in Damascus and Baghdad. Notably, Syria supported Iran in its war with Iraq in 1980–88. Although an extraordinary summit meeting of the Arab League in November 1987 produced a unanimous statement expressing solidarity with Iraq and condemning Iran for prolonging the war and for its occupation of Arab territory, Syria announced subsequently that a reconciliation with Iraq had not taken place, and that Syrian relations with Iran remained fundamentally unchanged. Syria also used its veto to prevent the adoption of an Iraqi proposal to readmit Egypt to the Arab League, but it could not prevent the inclusion in the final communiqué of a clause permitting individual member nations to re-establish diplomatic relations with Egypt. However, Egypt's recognition of the newly proclaimed Palestinian state in November 1988 gave fresh impetus to attempts to achieve a reconciliation between Egypt and Syria. These culminated in the restoration of bilateral relations in December 1989, and in the visit of Egypt's President Hosni Mubarak to Damascus.

Syria appeared keen to take advantage of the diplomatic opportunities arising from Iraq's invasion of Kuwait in August 1990, and in particular to improve its relations with the USA. Syria endorsed Egypt's efforts to co-ordinate an Arab response to the invasion, and agreed to send troops to Saudi Arabia as part of a pan-Arab deterrent force, supporting the US-led effort to deter an Iraqi invasion of Saudi Arabia; Syria also committed itself to the demand for an unconditional Iraqi withdrawal from Kuwait. Indications that Syria's participation in the multinational force was transforming its relations with the West were confirmed in November when diplomatic ties were restored with the United Kingdom. Iraq's overwhelming military defeat by the US-led multinational force in February 1991 strengthened Syria's position with regard to virtually all its major regional concerns. In March the Ministers of Foreign Affairs of the members of the Co-operation Council for the Arab States of the Gulf (Gulf Co-operation Council, see p. 219) met their Egyptian and Syrian counterparts in Damascus to discuss regional security. The formation of an Arab peace-keeping force, comprising mainly Egyptian and Syrian troops, was subsequently announced. (In May, however, Egypt declared its intention to withdraw its forces from the Gulf region within three months, thus casting doubt on the future of joint Syrian-Egyptian security arrangements.) Moreover, Syria's decision to ally itself, in opposition to Iraq, with the Western powers and the 'moderate' Arab states led the USA to realize that it could no longer seek to exclude Syria from any role in the resolution of the Arab–Israeli conflict. A shift in Syria's relations with the USSR, a major source of military assistance but whose programmes of political liberalization President Assad had recently criticized, provided another reason for its realignment with the West.

After Iraq's defeat by the multinational force in February 1991, Syria became a centre for elements of the Iraqi opposition. However, it remains committed to the territorial integrity of Iraq, fearing that disintegration might encourage minorities within Syria (particularly the Kurds) to pursue their own autonomy. Three crossing points on the Syria–Iraq border were reopened in June 1997 to facilitate bilateral trade (Syria closed its border with Iraq in 1980), and in September 1998 Iraq, Iran and Syria agreed to establish a joint forum for foreign policy co-ordination (particularly with regard to the USA). In the same month Syria and Iraq reopened commercial centres in one another's capitals, and in April 1999 a series of mutual agreements were signed, as part of the process of normalizing relations. Throughout 1998–2002 the Syrian Government criticized US and British air-strikes against Iraqi air defence targets, as well as the maintenance of UN sanctions against Iraq.

In August 2000 a rail link between Aleppo and the Iraqi capital was reopened after an interval of some 20 years, and in December the Syrian authorities reportedly removed all restrictions on Iraqi citizens travelling to Syria. In November, furthermore, Iraq was reported to have begun transporting crude petroleum to Syria via a pipeline not used since the early 1980s. When the US Secretary of State, Colin Powell, visited Damascus in February 2001, his discussions with the Syrian President apparently centred on Syria's alleged violation of UN sanctions regarding the supply of petroleum from Iraq; in January 2002 British officials publicly accused Syria of sanctions violations. In August 2001 the Syrian Prime Minister, leading a ministerial and commercial delegation, became the most senior Syrian official to visit Iraq for two decades. Syria was particularly concerned (as was Turkey) by the potential ascendance of Iraqi Kurdish groups should the incumbent regime in Baghdad be overthrown, although, visiting these countries in March 2002, the PUK leader, Jalal Talabani, gave assurances that Iraq's Kurdish groups had no intention of establishing their own state. There were reports in mid-2002 that Syria was involved in mediation efforts between Iraq and Kuwait. (In October 2001 Syria had been elected as a non-permanent member of the UN Security Council for 2002–03.) Despite its unexpected support for UN Security Council Resolution 1441, approved in November, which imposed strict terms according to which Iraq must disarm or else face probable military action, Syria expressed its firm opposition to the US-led military campaign against the Iraqi regime which began in March 2003 (see the chapter on Iraq). However, Syrian officials asserted that the resolution did not give the USA the right to use force against the Iraqi regime.

In February 2006 Syria and Iraq announced that they were to restore full diplomatic relations and exchange ambassadors as soon as a new government was installed in Iraq. Relations were formally restored in November, ending a hiatus of more than 20 years, and the two sides also agreed to co-operate on security issues. It was hoped that the renewal of diplomatic ties would facilitate the policing of the shared border, across which a large number of militants were still reported to be entering Iraq. In

February 2007 a spokesman for the Iraqi Government claimed that 50% of those who had committed suicide bomb attacks in Iraq had entered the country from Syria, although this was staunchly denied by the Syrian Government.

Meanwhile, in the context of a long-standing commitment to establish a regional common market under the auspices of the Council of Arab Economic Unity (see p. 222), plans for a quadripartite free trade zone encompassing Iraq, Egypt, Libya and Syria were advanced following a meeting of the Council held in the Iraqi capital in June 2001.

Relations between Syria and Turkey became increasingly strained in the 1990s, owing to disagreements over the sharing of water from the Euphrates river. No permanent agreement on this resource has been concluded, and both Syria and Iraq are concerned that new dams in Turkey will reduce their share of water from the Euphrates. Syria's relations with Turkey deteriorated sharply in April 1996 after it was revealed that Turkey and Israel had concluded a military co-operation agreement earlier in the year. In August 1997 Syria condemned the decision by the USA, Israel and Turkey to conduct joint naval manoeuvres, although the three countries claimed that the exercises (carried out in January 1998) were solely for humanitarian purposes. Tension between Syria and Turkey increased considerably in October 1998, when Turkey threatened to invade Syria if its demands for an end to alleged Syrian support for the separatist Kurdistan Workers' Party (Partiya Karkeren Kurdistan—PKK) were not met. The Turkish authorities also demanded the extradition of the PKK leader, Abdullah Öcalan (who, they claimed, was directing PKK operations from Damascus), and insisted that Syria renounce its historic claim on the Turkish province of Hatay. Turkey's aggressive stance was viewed by Syria as evidence of a Turkish-Israeli military and political alliance, and as a result both Syria and Turkey ordered troops to be deployed along their joint border. Diplomatic efforts to defuse the crisis by Egypt, Iran and the UN, and Syrian assurances that Öcalan was not residing in Syria, allowed a degree of normalization in bilateral relations. In late October, following two days of negotiations in southern Turkey, representatives of the two countries signed an agreement whereby the PKK was to be banned from entering Syrian territory, while the organization's active bases in Syria and Lebanon's Beka'a valley were to be closed. Turkey and Syria also agreed mutual security guarantees, and resolved to invite Lebanon to participate in further discussions regarding the issue of PKK activity.

Despite persistent Syrian concerns regarding the close nature of Turkish-Israeli relations, it was reported in March 2000 that Syrian and Turkish officials were holding discussions in Damascus on a memorandum of principles, intended to establish a new framework for future bilateral relations. In September Syria and Turkey signed a co-operation agreement relating to countering terrorism and organized crime, and in June 2002 they signed two military co-operation accords. Moreover, reports in February that the Turkish army was to begin the clearance of landmines along its border with Syria were seen as evidence of a steady improvement in bilateral relations. In December 2003 relations were strengthened by Syria's decision to hand over 22 suspects sought by the Turkish authorities in connection with four suicide bomb attacks in Istanbul in November, in which at least 60 people were killed. In early January 2004 President Assad made the first ever visit by a Syrian Head of State to Turkey. Turkey's membership of NATO, and hence its relatively close relationship with the USA, as well as shared concerns about a possible 'ripple-effect' of increased Kurdish autonomy in northern Iraq following the removal of the regime of Saddam Hussain, were believed to be among the principal reasons for Syria's initiative to improve its relations with Turkey. In December Syria and Turkey agreed to create a bilateral free trade zone, and the agreement took effect in January 2007.

In November 1998 Syria and Russia signed a military agreement, whereby Russia would assist in the modernization of Syria's defence systems and provide training to military personnel. However, in January 1999 Syria denied Western reports that it was receiving assistance from Russia in the development of chemical weapons. President Assad visited Moscow in July for talks with President Boris Yeltsin and the then Russian premier, Sergei Stepashin. During the discussions Russia reiterated its support for Syria's demand for a complete Israeli withdrawal from the Golan Heights and southern Lebanon, and that Israeli-Syrian peace negotiations be resumed from their point of suspension in 1996. In May 2000 it was reported that a major arms deal had been concluded whereby Russia would supply Syria with defensive weaponry worth some US $2,000m. In mid-January 2005 reports that Russia was to sell missiles to Syria that could be used against targets in Israel provoked anger in that country. In late January Assad held official talks in Russia with the Russian President, Vladimir Putin, and other senior officials; the two Presidents reportedly signed an agreement relating to greater co-operation. Russia confirmed its intention to sell missiles to Syria in February, asserting that the weapons could only be used for defence purposes.

In December 2006 Israeli Prime Minister Ehud Olmert rejected an appeal from President Assad for a resumption of formal peace negotiations with Syria. Olmert accused Assad of merely trying to curry international favour at a time when Syria was under intense scrutiny for its alleged complicity in the assassinations in Lebanon of Rafik Hariri and Pierre Gemayel (see above). In the previous month a diplomatic initiative proposed by the British Prime Minister, Tony Blair, urging Syria to reopen Middle East peace negotiations, had met with a cool reception from the Israeli Government. Vice-Premier Shimon Peres stated that Israel would welcome negotiations with Syria, but only when that country had ceased its support of militant organizations such as Hamas and Hezbollah. In January 2007 a former Israeli diplomat claimed that Israel and Syria had in fact conducted secret negotiations concerning a possible peace deal between September 2004 and July 2006, in which month the outbreak of the conflict between Israel and Hezbollah (see the chapters on Israel and Lebanon) had abruptly brought the proceedings to a close. (According to reports in the Israeli media, prior to the collapse of talks, mutual understandings had been reached with regard to an Israeli withdrawal from the Golan Heights and other issues of contention.) The diplomat's claims were strongly denied by the Syrian Government; however, Israeli officials acknowledged that meetings might have been held between non-governmental representatives from the two countries. In March 2007 President Assad was reported to have confirmed that in fact secret talks had taken place between 'non-official' channels.

In June 2007, amid reports that Olmert had established a ministerial committee whose task would be to examine Israel's military preparedness for a potential conflict with Syria, the Israeli premier was said to have declared that he was ready to engage in direct negotiations with the Syrian regime, without preconditions first being met. The Israeli media commented that Olmert had relayed to Syria, through Turkish and German officials, the proposal that Israel withdraw from the Golan Heights in exchange for Syria's undertaking to 'gradually dissolve' its links with Iran and militant organizations in Lebanon and the Palestinian territories. Tensions between Israel and Syria worsened in early September, after Israel carried out an air-strike on a military installation 'deep within' Syrian territory. The motivation for the military strike was not immediately evident, although there was initial speculation in the Israeli media that the target had been a shipment of Iranian-supplied weapons en route to Lebanon for use by Hezbollah fighters. In early October President Assad stated that the Israeli strike had hit a military building that was under construction and denied media reports speculating that it might have been a concealed nuclear reactor. In late April 2008 US intelligence officials reportedly presented evidence that the target of the Israeli air-strike was in fact a nuclear facility that was being constructed with assistance from North Korea; the Syrian authorities again strongly rejected the claims. Official Israeli and Syrian sources confirmed in late May that peace negotiations brokered by Turkey were expected to begin shortly, with both sides declaring a mutual commitment to reaching a comprehensive peace between their two nations.

Government

Under the 1973 Constitution (as subsequently amended), legislative power is vested in the unicameral People's Assembly, with 250 members elected by universal adult suffrage to serve a four-year term. Executive power is vested in the President, elected by direct popular vote for a seven-year term. (Following the death of President Hafiz al-Assad on 10 June 2003, the Constitution was amended to allow his son, Lt-Gen. Bashar al-Assad, to accede to the presidency). He governs with the assistance of an appointed Council of Ministers, led by the Prime Minister. Syria has 14 administrative districts (*mohafazat*).

Defence

National service, which normally lasts for 30 months, is compulsory for men. As assessed at November 2007, the regular armed forces totalled 292,600 men: an army of 215,000 (including conscripts), an air defence command of 40,000, a navy of 7,600 and an air force of 30,000. In addition, Syria had 314,000-strong reserve forces (army 280,000; air force 10,000; air defence 20,000; navy 4,000). Paramilitary forces included a gendarmerie (connected to the Ministry of the Interior) of 8,000 and a Baath Party Workers' Militia of an estimated 100,000. Some 8,000–10,000 Syrian troops were deployed in Lebanon in March 2005; however, in April Syria claimed to have withdrawn all of its forces from that country (see the chapter on Lebanon). Defence expenditure for 2007 was budgeted at £S74,900m.

Economic Affairs

In 2006 according to estimates by the World Bank, Syria's gross national income (GNI), measured at average 2004–06 prices, was US $30,699m., equivalent to $1,570 per head (or $3,930 per head on an international purchasing-power parity basis). During 1996–2006, it was estimated, the population increased at an average annual rate of 2.6%, while gross domestic product (GDP) per head increased, in real terms, by an average of 0.7% per year. Overall GDP increased, in real terms, at an average annual rate of 3.2% in 1996–2006; growth was 5.1% in 2006.

Agriculture (including forestry and fishing) contributed 20.1% of GDP in 2006, and engaged 26.2% of the employed labour force (excluding foreign workers) in 2003. The principal cash crops are cotton (which accounted for about 2.4% of export earnings in 2003) and fruit and vegetables. Agricultural GDP increased at an average annual rate of 4.3% in 1995–2005; the sector's GDP increased by 10.2% in 2006.

Industry (comprising mining, manufacturing, construction and utilities) provided 29.7% of GDP in 2006, and engaged 24.8% of the employed labour force (excluding foreign workers) in 2003. The GDP of the industrial sector increased by a negligible annual average during 1995–2005; however, industrial GDP decreased by 1.6% in 2006.

Mining contributed an estimated 19.7% of GDP in 2003, and employed 0.3% of the working population (excluding foreign workers) in 1999. Crude petroleum is the major mineral export, accounting for 58.5% of total export earnings in 2003, and phosphates are also exported. Syria also has reserves of natural gas and iron ore. At the end of 2006 Syria had proven oil reserves of 3,000m. barrels, and estimated average oil production was 417,000 barrels per day (b/d), having declined from 596,000 b/d in 1995. Syria was estimated to have 290,000m. cu m of proven natural gas reserves at the end of 2006, and in that year production of natural gas reached an estimated daily average of 5,500m. cu m. In 2001 Syria and Lebanon signed an agreement under which Syria was to supply gas to northern Lebanon. However, although the pipeline intended to supply the natural gas was completed in 2005, the two countries did not implement the agreement owing to political differences.

Manufacturing contributed an estimated 7.3% of GDP in 2004, and employed 12.7% of the working population in 1999. The principal branches of manufacturing, measured by gross value of output, are: food products, beverages and tobacco; chemicals, petroleum, coal, rubber and plastic products; textiles, clothing, leather products and footwear; metal products, machinery, transport equipment and appliances; and non-metallic mineral products. The GDP of the manufacturing sector increased by an average of 6.5% per year during 1995–2004; manufacturing GDP increased by 2.5% in 2004.

Energy is derived principally from petroleum (providing 45.6% of total electricity production in 2004), and also natural gas (41.2%) and hydroelectric power (13.2%). Imports of mineral fuels and lubricants comprised 27.1% of the value of total imports in 2006.

Services accounted for 50.1% of GDP in 2006, and engaged 49.0% of the employed labour force (excluding foreign workers) in 2003. The GDP of the services sector increased at an average rate of 3.9% per year in 1995–2005; growth of the sector was 4.7% in 2006.

In 2006 Syria recorded a visible trade surplus of US $886m., and there was a surplus of $890m. on the current account of the balance of payments. In 2005 the principal source of imports (5.9%) was the People's Republic of China; other important suppliers were Saudi Arabia, Turkey, Italy, Egypt and the USA. Italy was the primary market for exports in that year (21.0%); other major purchasers were France, Saudi Arabia, Spain and Turkey. The principal exports in 2006 were mineral fuels and lubricants, food and live animals, basic manufactures and chemicals, while the principal imports were mineral fuels and lubricants, machinery and transport equipment, basic manufactures, chemicals, and food and live animals.

A budget deficit of £S58,800m. was projected for 2006. At the end of 2005 Syria's total external debt was US $6,508m., of which $5,640m. was long-term public debt. The cost of debt-servicing in that year was equivalent to 1.9% of the total value of exports of goods and services. Annual inflation averaged 2.9% in 1996–2006. Consumer prices increased by 9.4% in 2006. According to a study published by the Central Bureau of Statistics and the UN Development Programme in mid-2005, 8.2% of the labour force were unemployed; however, other sources estimated unemployment to be more than double this rate.

Syria is a member of the UN Economic and Social Commission for Western Asia (ESCWA, see p. 43), the Arab Fund for Economic and Social Development (AFESD, see p. 174), the Arab Monetary Fund (see p. 175), the Council of Arab Economic Unity (see p. 222), the Islamic Development Bank (see p. 329) and the Organization of Arab Petroleum Exporting Countries (OAPEC, see p. 366).

Since July 2000 the regime under President Bashar al-Assad has implemented a bolder programme of economic reforms than his predecessor, Hafiz al-Assad, although progress has remained slow. The Syrian economy suffered from the temporary loss of trade with Iraq, as a result of the US-led military campaign to oust the regime of Saddam Hussain in early 2003. Moreover, the USA levied trade sanctions on Syria in May 2004 (see Recent History). However, the economy recovered to a limited extent in 2004–06, largely owing to an increase in exports (particularly tourism) and private investment. A decline in petroleum production limited economic growth, and it was considered likely that Syria would become a net importer of petroleum by as early as 2010, and that its supplies would be exhausted by 2030, making a reduction of the economy's dependence on revenue from petroleum essential to ensuring long-term growth. Nevertheless, in May 2006 Marathon Oil Corpn of the USA signed a production-sharing agreement worth US $125m. with the Syrian Gas Co covering the exploration and development of oilfields in the Palmyra area over a 25-year period. Despite the recent high international oil prices and, in the short term, the large petroleum revenues being collected by the Syrian Government, dwindling reserves have necessitated a number of medium- to long-term economic reforms, including liberalization of the financial system and encouragement of private entrepreneurship. The authorities' economic plan for 2006–10 focuses on improving the country's financial and business climate, liberalizing trade and stimulating GDP growth. In late 2005 Syria announced that it intended to secure $6,000m. of annual investment in all sectors of the economy, and to increase the number of tourists to 15m. per year by 2015. Other planned reforms included the introduction, with IMF assistance, of a value-added tax by 2008 (subsequently delayed until 2009), and the phasing out of petroleum price subsidies. Meanwhile, unemployment remained high, at over 20% according to some sources. Moreover, the population was growing rapidly and was expected to increase by 50% by 2020: the Government reportedly needed to invest some $100,000m. to create sufficient employment opportunities for the greatly expanding labour force. In February 2006 Prime Minister Muhammad Naji al-Otari issued a decree ordering that all government and private sector foreign currency transactions be carried out in euros rather than dollars, reportedly in order to make foreign assets more secure and to strengthen Syria's ability to counter political pressure from the USA. The US Administration tightened the trade sanctions in place against the Syrian regime in May 2008 (see Recent History). By early 2008 the country's first two Islamic banks were operational, with a further six having received licenses. The Syrian International Islamic Bank, which opened in September 2007, claimed to have taken deposits totalling some $160m. through its branches in Damascus and Aleppo. As the banking sector continues to grow, the first Islamic venture in the market, Cham Bank, suggested that Islamic companies could eventually account for 40% of banking in Syria. The country's economic performance in 2007 was influenced by the presence of more than 1m. refugees from Iraq, with the consequent increased levels of demand and rise in inflation. Consumer prices increased by an estimated 10.0% in 2007, although the IMF forecast a decline in the inflation rate towards 7.0% during 2008. According to the Central Bank of Syria, GDP growth averaged 6.0% in 2007, with expansion increasingly supported by the non-petroleum sector. The IMF anticipated growth of 4.0% in 2008. For the immediate future, further improvements to Syria's economic situation are expected

SYRIA

to be dependent upon both domestic restructuring and reform, as well as the conclusion of a comprehensive peace agreement with Israel.

Education

Primary education, which begins at six years of age and lasts for six years, is officially compulsory. In 2004/05 total enrolment at primary and secondary level was equivalent to 86.8% of children in the relevant age-group. In 2001/02 primary enrolment included 94.5% of children in the appropriate age-group. Secondary education, beginning at 12 years of age, lasts for a further six years, comprising two cycles of three years each. In 2004/05 enrolment at secondary schools included 62.0% of children in the relevant age-group. There are agricultural and technical schools for vocational training, and five state-run universities. In 2003 the decision was made to end the state monopoly on education, imposed by the Baath Party in 1963. By 2006/07 there were eight private universities and numerous private schools; in that year there were 380,000 students enrolled in Syrian universities: 250,000 at state institutions, 6,000 at private institutions and a further 2,500 at the Syrian Virtual University (established in 2002, and which offers degree courses via the internet). Expenditure on education by all levels of government in 1999 was estimated at £S26,324m. (10.3% of total government expenditure).

The UN Relief and Works Agency (UNRWA) provides education for Palestinian refugees in Syria. During the academic year 2006/07 UNWRA operated 119 elementary and preparatory schools in Syria, with a total enrolment of 66,187 pupils.

Public Holidays

2008: 1 January (New Year's Day), 10 January*† (Muharram, Islamic New Year), 8 March (Revolution Day), 20 March* (Mouloud/Yum an-Nabi, Birth of Muhammad), 21 March (Mother's Day), 17 April (Independence Day), 25–28 April (Greek Orthodox Easter), 1 May (Labour Day), 6 May (Martyrs' Day), 30 July* (Leilat al-Meiraj, Ascension of Muhammad), 1 October* (Id al-Fitr, end of Ramadan), 6 October (Anniversary of October War), 9 December* (Id al-Adha, Feast of the Sacrifice), 25 December (Christmas Day), 29 December*† (Muharram, Islamic New Year).

2009: 1 January (New Year's Day), 8 March (Revolution Day), 9 March* (Mouloud/Yum an-Nabi, Birth of Muhammad), 21 March (Mother's Day), 17 April (Independence Day), 17–20 April (Greek Orthodox Easter), 1 May (Labour Day), 6 May (Martyrs' Day), 19 July* (Leilat al-Meiraj, Ascension of Muhammad), 20 September* (Id al-Fitr, end of Ramadan), 6 October (Anniversary of October War), 27 November* (Id al-Adha, Feast of the Sacrifice), 18 December* (Muharram, Islamic New Year), 25 December (Christmas Day).

* These holidays are dependent on the Islamic lunar calendar and may vary by one or two days from the dates given.

† This festival occurs twice (marking the start of the Islamic years AH 1429 and 1430) within the same Gregorian year.

Weights and Measures

The metric system is in force.

Statistical Survey

Source (unless otherwise stated): Central Bureau of Statistics, rue Abd al-Malek bin Marwah, Malki Quarter, Damascus; tel. (11) 3335830; fax (11) 3322292; e-mail cbs@mail.sy; internet www.cbssyr.org.

Area and Population

AREA, POPULATION AND DENSITY

Area (sq km)	
Land	184,050
Inland water	1,130
Total	185,180*
Population (census results)†	
8 September 1981	9,052,628
3 September 1994	
Males	7,048,906
Females	6,733,409
Total	13,782,315
Population (official estimates at 31 December)	
2004	17,921,000
2005	18,269,000
2006‡	18,717,000
Density (per sq km) at 31 December 2006	101.1

* 71,498 sq miles.
† Official estimates at mid-year, including Palestinian refugees. According to the United Nations Relief and Works Agency for Palestine Refugees in the Near East (UNRWA), there were 451,467 Palestinian refugees in Syria at 31 December 2007.
‡ Preliminary figure.

PRINCIPAL TOWNS
(population at census of 3 September 1994)

Halab (Aleppo)	1,582,930	Ar-Raqqah (Rakka)	165,195	
Dimashq (Damascus, capital)	1,394,322	Al-Qamishli	144,286	
Hims (Homs)	540,133	Deir ez-Zor	140,459	
Al-Ladhiqiyah (Latakia)	311,784	Al-Hasakah	119,798	
Hamah (Hama)	264,348			

Source: UN, *Demographic Yearbook*.

Mid-2007 ('000, incl. suburbs, UN estimates): Aleppo 2,738; Damascus 2,466; Homs 1,005 (Source: UN, *World Urbanization Prospects: The 2007 Revision*).

BIRTHS, MARRIAGES AND DEATHS
(excl. nomad population and Palestinian refugees, estimates)

	Registered live births — Number	Rate (per 1,000)	Registered marriages	Registered deaths
1997	496,140	32.9	128,146	53,366
1998	505,008	32.4	130,835	57,893
1999	503,473	31.3	136,157	56,564
2000	505,484	31.0	139,843	57,759
2001	524,212	31.4	153,842	60,814
2002	471,970	27.6	174,449	53,252
2003	492,639	28.1	n.a.	53,778
2004	491,476	n.a.	178,166	57,855

Source: UN, *Demographic Yearbook*.

Expectation of life (years at birth, WHO estimates): 72.2 (males 69.9; females 74.6) in 2005 (Source: WHO, *World Health Statistics*).

ECONOMICALLY ACTIVE POPULATION
(labour force sample survey, persons aged 15 years and over, 2003)*

	Males	Females	Total
Agriculture, hunting, forestry and fishing	816,598	352,145	1,168,743
Mining and quarrying; manufacturing; and electricity, gas and water	558,324	50,381	608,705
Construction	492,657	7,727	500,384
Trade, restaurants and hotels	650,835	26,394	677,229
Transport, storage and communications	258,541	6,946	265,487
Financing, insurance, real estate and business services	78,585	11,162	89,747
Community, social and personal services	851,357	306,922	1,158,279
Total employed	3,706,897	761,677	4,468,574
Unemployed	334,066	214,372	548,438
Total labour force	4,040,963	976,049	5,017,012

* Figures refer to Syrians only, excluding armed forces.

SYRIA

Health and Welfare

KEY INDICATORS

Total fertility rate (children per woman, 2005)	3.3
Under-5 mortality rate (per 1,000 live births, 2005)	15
HIV/AIDS (% of persons aged 15–49, 2003)	<0.1
Physicians (per 1,000 head, 2001)	1.4
Hospital beds (per 1,000 head, 2003)	1.30
Health expenditure (2004): US $ per head (PPP)	108.8
Health expenditure (2004): % of GDP	4.7
Health expenditure (2004): public (% of total)	47.4
Access to water (% of persons, 2004)	93
Access to sanitation (% of persons, 2004)	90
Human Development Index (2005): ranking	108
Human Development Index (2005): value	0.724

For sources and definitions, see explanatory note on p. vi.

Agriculture

PRINCIPAL CROPS
('000 metric tons)

	2004	2005	2006
Wheat	4,537.5	4,668.8	4,668.8*
Barley	527.2	767.4	700.0
Maize	210.2	187.2	215.2*
Potatoes	541.7	608.4	608.4*
Sugar beet	1,217.7	1,096.3	1,096.3*
Chick-peas	45.3	65.2	65.2*
Lentils	125.3	153.7	165.0
Almonds*	119.9	119.6	119.6
Olives	875.0	501.0	501.0*
Cabbages	37.4	39.5	39.5*
Lettuce	52.4	51.7	51.7*
Tomatoes	920.0*	945.5	945.5*
Cauliflowers	28.0*	45.5	45.5*
Pumpkins, squash and gourds*	103.0	99.6	99.6
Cucumbers and gherkins	149.1	146.7	146.7*
Aubergines (Eggplants)	157.9	154.4	154.4*
Chillies and green peppers*	41.5	41.8	41.8
Green onions and shallots	46.0	47.6	47.6*
Dry onions	116.6	125.1	125.1*
Oranges*	472.1	503.0	503.0
Lemons and limes*	84.0	85.0	85.0
Apples*	299.8	312.5	312.5
Apricots*	100.0	101.0	101.0
Sweet cherries*	39.7	39.7	39.7
Peaches and nectarines	36.0*	51.6	51.6*
Grapes*	300.0	310.0	310.0
Watermelons	812.1	588.3	588.3*
Cantaloupes and other melons	100.0*	105.9	105.9*
Figs	43.4*	49.8	49.8*

*FAO estimate(s).

Aggregate production ('000 metric tons, may include official, semi-official or estimated data): Total cereals 5,279 in 2004, 5,631 in 2005, 5,592 in 2006; Total roots and tubers 542 in 2004, 608 in 2005, 608 in 2006; Total oilcrops 2,594 in 2004, 2,239 in 2005, 2,239 in 2006; Total vegetables (incl. melons) 2,858 in 2004, 2,783 in 2005, 2,783 in 2006; Total fruits (excl. melons) 1,798 in 2004, 1,888 in 2005, 1,888 in 2006.

Source: FAO.

LIVESTOCK
('000 head, year ending September)

	2003	2004	2005
Horses	17.0*	15.0	15.0
Asses, mules or hinnies	137.0*	123.0	118.0
Cattle	937.0	1,024.0	1,082.6
Camels	15.2	20.4	23.4
Sheep	15,292.7	17,565.0	19,651.1
Goats	1,017.3	1,130.0	1,295.7
Chickens	29,000*	28,861	23,795

*FAO estimate.

2006: Figures assumed to be unchanged from 2005 (FAO estimates).

Source: FAO.

LIVESTOCK PRODUCTS
('000 metric tons)

	2004	2005	2006
Cattle meat	47.4	55.2	55.2*
Sheep meat	207.0*	179.9	200.0*
Chicken meat*	128.2	132.5	132.5
Cows' milk*	1,250.0	1,250.0	1,250.0
Sheep's milk*	604.2	604.2	604.2
Goats' milk*	62.1	62.1	62.1
Hen eggs*	167.0	167.0	167.0
Wool: greasy*	33.6	33.7	33.7

*FAO estimate(s).

Source: FAO.

Forestry

ROUNDWOOD REMOVALS
('000 cubic metres, excl. bark)

	2004	2005	2006
Sawlogs, veneer logs and logs for sleepers	16	16	16
Other industrial wood	24	24	24
Fuel wood	15	15	20
Total	55	55	60

*FAO estimate.

Sawnwood production ('000 cubic metres): *1980*: Coniferous (softwood) 6.6; Broadleaved (hardwood) 2.4; Total 9.0. *1981–2006:* Production as in 1980 (FAO estimates).

Source: FAO.

Fishing

(metric tons, live weight)

	2003	2004	2005
Capture	8,911	8,528	8,447
Freshwater fishes	5,851	5,451	4,770
Aquaculture	7,217	8,682	8,533
Common carp	2,937	4,245	3,920
Tilapias	3,439	3,650	3,363
Total catch	16,128	17,210	16,980

Source: FAO.

Mining

('000 metric tons, unless otherwise indicated)

	2003	2004	2005*
Phosphate rock	2,414	2,883	3,850
Salt (unrefined)	128	141	140
Gypsum	377	432	440
Natural gas (million cu m)	9,401	9,700	9,700
Crude petroleum ('000 42-gallon barrels)*	205,130	193,085	171,185

*Estimates.

Source: US Geological Survey.

Industry

SELECTED PRODUCTS
(metric tons, unless otherwise indicated)

	2001	2002	2003
Cotton yarn (pure and mixed)*	83,000	90,600	98,400
Silk textiles	10	20	n.a.
Cotton textiles	21,559	23,477	n.a.
Wool yarn (pure and mixed)*	2,700	2,700	2,400
Plywood (cu m)	34,458	43,401	44,615
Cement ('000 metric tons)	5,399	5,224	5,098
Glass and pottery products	70,265	69,937	73,449
Soap	17,563	18,834	16,492
Refined sugar ('000 metric tons)	121	214	123
Olive oil	95,384	194,599	103,947
Vegetable oil	106,506	114,454	111,917
Cottonseed cake ('000 metric tons)	328	1,122	1,129
Manufactured tobacco	12,007	12,863	13,412
Refrigerators	83,658	80,655	81,230
Washing machines	62,105	84,997	85,260
Television receivers*	139,000	164,000	148,000
Electricity (million kWh)	25,544	26,896	28,264

* Source: UN, *Industrial Commodity Statistics Yearbook*.

Finance

CURRENCY AND EXCHANGE RATES

Monetary Units
100 piastres = 1 Syrian pound (£S).

Sterling, Dollar and Euro Equivalents (31 December 2007)
£1 sterling = £S22.488;
US $1 = £S11.225;
€1 = £S16.524;
£S1,000 = £44.47 sterling = $89.09 = €60.52.

Exchange Rate: Between April 1976 and December 1987 the official mid-point rate was fixed at US $1 = £S3.925. On 1 January 1988 a new rate of $1 = £S11.225 was introduced. In addition to the official exchange rate, there is a promotion rate (applicable to most travel and tourism transactions) and a flexible rate.

BUDGET
(£S '000 million)

Revenue	2003	2004	2005
Oil-related proceeds	152.5	141.2	98.9
Non-oil tax revenue	120.2	145.4	160.3
Income and profits	39.8	59.1	59.3
International Trade	24.4	31.3	30.7
Excises	18.6	3.4	4.5
Other	37.4	51.6	65.8
Non-oil non-tax revenue	45.8	55.9	97.1
Total	318.5	342.5	356.3

Expenditure	2003	2004	2005
Current expenditure	209.0	248.5	277.0
Wages and salaries	113.6	144.1	157.0
Goods and services	21.9	19.3	21.5
Interest payments	29.6	21.3	29.0
Subsidies and transfers	43.8	63.8	69.5
Development expenditure	147.7	156.6	154.4
Social	40.7	53.7	60.3
Agriculture	20.3	17.9	15.5
Extractive industries	11.5	8.5	8.1
Manufacturing industries	17.6	7.8	8.4
Utilities	22.8	36.4	34.6
Construction	0.7	0.4	0.4
Trade	2.5	2.4	1.8
Transport and communications	26.9	26.0	21.3
Finance	1.9	1.9	2.4
Other	2.9	1.6	1.5
Total	356.7	405.1	431.4

2006 (£S '000 million, preliminary figures): Total revenue 434.9; Total expenditure 493.7.

Source: Ministry of Finance, Damascus.

CENTRAL BANK RESERVES
(US $ million at 31 December)

	1986	1987	1988
Gold*	29	29	29
Foreign exchange	144	223	193
Total	173	252	222

* Valued at $35 per troy ounce.

1989–2006 (US $ million, national valuation): Gold 29.

Source: IMF, *International Financial Statistics*.

MONEY SUPPLY
(£S million at 31 December)

	2004	2005	2006
Currency outside banks	333,055	384,719	399,093
Demand deposits at commercial banks	246,260	287,637	241,543
Total money (incl. others)	602,131	688,276	660,804

Source: IMF, *International Financial Statistics*.

COST OF LIVING
(Consumer Price Index; base: 2000 = 100)

	2001	2002	2003
Food and beverages	100.2	99.6	107.3
Electricity, gas and other fuels (incl. water)	100.0	111.2	119.5
Clothing and footwear	100.5	96.5	102.9
Rent	100.7	102.9	124.0
All items (incl. others)	100.4	101.4	109.3

2004: Food and beverages 112.8; All items (incl. others) 114.1.
2005: Food and beverages 122.4; All items (incl. others) 122.6.
2006: Food and beverages 138.0; All items (incl. others) 134.1.
Source: ILO.

NATIONAL ACCOUNTS
(£S million at current prices)

Expenditure on the Gross Domestic Product

	2004	2005*	2006
Government final consumption expenditure	197,909	206,631	218,796
Private final consumption expenditure	810,037	993,118	1,127,397
Gross fixed capital formation	301,010	359,909	365,701
Changes in stocks	−81,075	−98,262	−66,322
Total domestic expenditure	1,227,881	1,461,396	1,645,572
Exports of goods and services	512,445	618,278	684,560
Less Imports of goods and services	477,186	588,876	621,383
GDP in market prices	1,263,140	1,490,798	1,708,749
GDP at constant 2000 prices	1,085,992	1,134,861	1,192,740

SYRIA

Gross Domestic Product by Economic Activity

	2004	2005*	2006
Agriculture, hunting, forestry and fishing	281,177	305,351	347,361
Mining and quarrying			
Manufacturing	331,959	418,503	466,859
Electricity, gas and water			
Construction	36,162	40,320	45,450
Wholesale and retail trade	221,393	300,022	349,380
Transport and communications	141,599	160,851	192,504
Finance and insurance	53,329	73,969	103,359
Government services	154,044	159,460	175,762
Other community, social and personal services	31,421	37,162	42,511
Non-profit private services	706	795	908
Sub-total	1,251,790	1,496,433	1,724,094
Import duties	22,572	22,904	17,200
Less Imputed bank service charges	−11,223	−28,539	−32,549
GDP in market prices	1,263,139	1,490,798	1,708,745

* Preliminary figures.

BALANCE OF PAYMENTS
(US $ million)

	2004	2005	2006
Exports of goods f.o.b.	7,220	8,602	10,245
Imports of goods f.o.b.	−6,957	−8,742	−9,359
Trade balance	263	−140	886
Exports of services	2,613	2,910	2,924
Imports of services	−2,235	−2,359	−2,520
Balance on goods and services	642	411	1,290
Other income received	385	395	428
Other income paid	−1,114	−1,258	−1,363
Balance on goods, services and income	−88	−452	355
Current transfers received	690	763	770
Current transfers paid	−16	−16	−235
Current balance	587	295	890
Capital account (net)	18	18	18
Direct investment from abroad	275	500	600
Other investment assets	−237	−524	−733
Other investment liabilities	−135	−138	−919
Net errors and omissions	−256	−137	−588
Overall balance	251	14	−732

Source: IMF, *International Financial Statistics*.

External Trade

PRINCIPAL COMMODITIES
(distribution by SITC major group, £S million)

Imports	2004	2005	2006
Food and live animals	45,816	54,709	56,856
Beverages and tobacco	3,009	2,746	4,694
Crude materials, inedible, except fuels	18,974	22,236	21,376
Mineral fuels and lubricants	24,219	123,650	143,926
Animal and vegetable oils and fats	3,333	3,788	3,754
Chemicals and related products	49,000	59,061	59,677
Basic manufactures	89,841	106,775	111,669
Machinery and transport equipment	83,437	99,593	112,685
Total (incl. others)	389,006	502,368	531,324

Exports	2004	2005	2006
Food and live animals	32,566	31,899	75,470
Beverages and tobacco	2,686	3,096	3,166
Crude materials, inedible, except fuels	11,812	13,754	15,256
Mineral fuels and lubricants	168,380	211,775	203,756
Animal and vegetable oils and fats	1,878	5,001	9,120
Chemicals and related products	4,024	9,288	24,765
Basic manufactures	16,502	18,111	56,217
Machinery and transport equipment	2,639	3,785	23,861
Total (incl. others)	346,166	424,300	505,012

PRINCIPAL TRADING PARTNERS
(£S million)

Imports c.i.f.	2003	2004	2005
Belgium	3,470	2,577	3,907
China, People's Republic	13,913	22,909	29,414
Egypt	4,629	9,283	12,963
France	6,133	6,486	8,499
Germany	8,523	9,686	10,870
India	9,328	6,605	8,689
Italy	9,978	12,790	13,871
Japan	7,552	7,613	11,556
Lebanon	3,742	5,934	8,292
Netherlands	3,737	3,111	3,427
Romania	4,432	5,148	4,207
Russia	6,025	15,885	13,765
Saudi Arabia	9,396	15,278	15,903
Spain	2,955	2,921	3,550
Sweden	2,650	2,793	4,588
Turkey	13,501	13,923	15,564
United Kingdom	2,930	4,257	3,052
USA	11,826	13,869	11,824
Total (incl. others)	236,769	389,006	502,369

Exports f.o.b.	2003	2004	2005
Belgium	1,460	820	773
Egypt	3,831	5,136	6,731
France	38,077	47,743	52,424
Germany	1,410	1,307	4,675
Italy	87,887	60,007	89,031
Jordan	6,522	7,050	7,036
Kuwait	2,012	2,611	2,555
Lebanon	10,676	9,221	8,778
Netherlands	1,322	5,869	13,054
Russia	617	404	444
Saudi Arabia	15,687	16,493	17,120
Spain	10,383	9,494	14,163
Turkey	19,918	17,047	13,414
United Kingdom	5,523	4,425	12,017
USA	9,817	8,392	14,164
Total (incl. others)	265,039	301,553	424,300

Transport

RAILWAYS
(traffic)

	2002	2003	2004
Passenger-km ('000)	384,321	525,357	691,916
Freight ('000 metric tons)	5,927	6,414	7,232

SYRIA

ROAD TRAFFIC
(motor vehicles in use)

	2002	2003	2004
Passenger cars	175,918	200,933	227,639
Buses	4,758	4,767	4,758
Lorries, trucks, etc.	362,392	376,543	388,716
Motorcycles	99,009	104,732	122,323

SHIPPING

Merchant Fleet
(registered at 31 December)

	2004	2005	2006
Number of vessels	173	162	151
Total displacement ('000 grt)	446.7	412.5	388.7

Source: Lloyd's Register-Fairplay, *World Fleet Statistics*.

International Sea-borne Traffic

	1996	1997	1998
Vessels entered ('000 net reg. tons)	2,901*	2,640	2,622
Cargo unloaded ('000 metric tons)	4,560	4,788	5,112
Cargo loaded ('000 metric tons)	1,788	2,412	2,136

* Excluding Banias.

Vessels entered ('000 net registered tons): 2,928 in 1999; 2,798 in 2000; 2,827 in 2001.

Source: mainly UN, *Monthly Bulletin of Statistics* and *Statistical Yearbook*.

CIVIL AVIATION
(traffic on scheduled services)

	2001	2002	2003
Kilometres flown (million)	15	16	9
Passengers carried ('000)	761	824	940
Passenger-km (million)	1,465	1,609	744
Total ton-km (million)	153	169	173

Source: UN, *Statistical Yearbook*.

Tourism

FOREIGN VISITOR ARRIVALS
(incl. excursionists)*

Country of nationality	2003	2004	2005
Iran	213,931	196,699	247,662
Iraq	253,120	804,131	913,266
Jordan	752,935	851,095	940,413
Kuwait	72,693	105,715	103,474
Lebanon	1,654,001	2,262,733	1,681,158
Saudi Arabia	361,758	461,035	469,118
Turkey	470,900	658,581	688,978
Total (incl. others)	4,388,119	6,153,653	5,837,980

* Figures exclude Syrian nationals resident abroad.

Tourism receipts (US $ million, incl. passenger transport): 877 in 2003; 1,888 in 2004; 2,283 in 2005.

Source: World Tourism Organization.

Communications Media

	2004	2005	2006
Telephones ('000 main lines in use)	2,666	2,903	3,243
Mobile cellular telephones ('000 in use)	2,345	2,950	4,675
Personal computers ('000 in use)	600	800	n.a.
Internet users ('000)	800	1,100	1,500
Broadband subscribers ('000)	0.6	1.2	5.6

1992: Book production 598 titles.
1996: Daily newspapers 8 (average circulation 287,000 copies).
1997 ('000 in use): Radio receivers 4,150.
1998 ('000 in use): Facsimile machines 22.
2000 ('000 in use): Television receivers 1,080.

Sources: UNESCO, *Statistical Yearbook*; UN, *Statistical Yearbook*; International Telecommunication Union.

Education

(2004/05, unless otherwise indicated)

	Institutions*	Teachers	Males	Females	Total
Pre-primary	1,431	6,818	79,879	69,932	149,811
Primary		124,665†	1,176,405	1,075,740	2,252,145
Secondary: general	1,140	26,273*	1,187,846	1,079,181	2,267,027
Secondary: vocational	595	17,368†	70,038	52,318	122,356
Higher*	4	8,702	106,975	94,714	201,689

* 2002/03 figure(s).
† 2003/04 figure.

Source: mainly UNESCO Institute for Statistics.

Adult literacy rate (UNESCO estimates): 80.8% (males 87.8%; females 73.6%) in 2004 (Source: UNESCO Institute for Statistics).

Directory

The Constitution

A new and permanent Constitution was endorsed by 97.6% of voters in a national referendum held on 12 March 1973. The 157-article Constitution defines Syria as a 'Socialist popular democracy' with a 'pre-planned Socialist economy'. Under the new Constitution, Lt-Gen. Hafiz al-Assad remained President, with the power to appoint and dismiss his Vice-President, Premier and government ministers, and also became Commander-in-Chief of the Armed Forces, Secretary-General of the Baath Socialist Party and President of the National Progressive Front. According to the Constitution, the President is elected by direct popular vote for a seven-year term. Legislative power is vested in the People's Assembly, with 250 members elected for a four-year term by universal adult suffrage.

Following the death of President Hafiz al-Assad on 10 June 2000, the Constitution was amended to allow his son, Lt-Gen. Bashar al-

SYRIA

Assad, to accede to the presidency. Bashar al-Assad also became Commander-in-Chief of the armed forces, Secretary-General of the Baath Socialist Party and President of the National Progressive Front.

The Government

HEAD OF STATE

President: Lt-Gen. BASHAR AL-ASSAD (assumed office 17 July 2000).
Vice-President, responsible for Foreign Affairs and Information: FAROUK ASH-SHARA'.
Vice-President: Dr NAJAH AL-ATTAR.

COUNCIL OF MINISTERS
(April 2008)

Prime Minister: MUHAMMAD NAJI AL-OTARI.
Deputy Prime Minister, responsible for Economic Affairs: ABDULLAH AD-DARDARI.
Minister of Defence: Lt-Gen. HASSAN AT-TURKMANI.
Minister of Foreign Affairs: WALID MOUALLEM.
Minister of Information: MOHSEN BILAL.
Minister of the Interior: Brig.-Gen. BASSAM ABD AL-MAJID.
Minister of Local Administration and Environment: HILAL AL-ATRASH.
Minister of Education: ALI SA'D.
Minister of Higher Education: GHIATH BARAKAT.
Minister of Electricity: AHMAD KHALED AL-ALI.
Minister of Culture: RIYAD NA'ASAN AGHA.
Minister of Transport: YAAROB SULEIMAN BADR.
Minister of Petroleum and Mineral Resources: SUFIAN ALLAW.
Minister of Industry: FOUAD ISSA JONI.
Minister of Finance: Dr MUHAMMAD AL-HUSSEIN.
Minister of Housing and Construction: HAMOUD AL-HUSSEIN.
Minister of Justice: MUHAMMAD AL-GAFRI.
Minister of Agriculture and Agrarian Reform: Dr ADEL SAFAR.
Minister of Irrigation: NADER AL-BUNI.
Minister of Communications and Technology: IMAD ABD AL-GHANI SABOUNI.
Minister of Health: Dr MAHER HUSSAMI.
Minister of Awqaf (Islamic Endowments): MUHAMMAD ABD AS-SATTAR AS-SAYYID.
Minister of Labour and Social Affairs: DIALA HAJ-AREF.
Minister of Tourism: Dr SAADALLAH AGHA AL-QALLA.
Minister of Presidential Affairs: GHASSAN AL-LAHHAM.
Minister of Expatriates: BOUTAINA SHA'BAN.
Ministers of State: YOUSUF SULEIMAN AL-AHMAD, BASHAR ASH-SH'AR, HUSSEIN MAHMOUD FARZAT, JOSEPH SWEID, HASSAN AS-SARRI, GHIATH JARAATLY.

MINISTRIES

Office of the President: Damascus.
Office of the Prime Minister: rue Chahbandar, Damascus; tel. (11) 2226000.
Ministry of Agriculture and Agrarian Reform: rue Jabri, place Hedjaz, Damascus; tel. (11) 2213613; fax (11) 2216627; e-mail agre-min@syriatel.net; internet www.syrian-agriculture.org.
Ministry of Awqaf (Islamic Endowments): Rukeneddin, Damascus; tel. (11) 4419079; fax (11) 419969.
Ministry of Communications and Technology: rue Abed, Damascus; tel. (11) 3320807; fax (11) 2246403; e-mail admin@moct.gov.sy; internet www.moct.gov.sy.
Ministry of Construction: rue Sa'dallah al-Jaberi, Damascus; tel. (11) 2223595.
Ministry of Culture: rue George Haddad, Rawda, Damascus; tel. (11) 3331556; fax (11) 3320804.
Ministry of Defence: place Omayad, Damascus; tel. (11) 7770700; fax (11) 2237842.
Ministry of Economy and Trade: rue Maysaloun, Damascus; tel. (11) 2213514; fax (11) 2225695; e-mail econ-min@net.sy; internet www.syrecon.org.
Ministry of Education: rue Shahbander, al-Masraa, Damascus; tel. (11) 4444703; fax (11) 4420435; e-mail mudhar@syrianeducation.org.sy; internet www.syrianeducation.org.sy.
Ministry of Electricity: BP 4900, rue al-Kouatly, Damascus; tel. (11) 2223086; fax (11) 2223686.
Ministry of Expatriates: Damascus; tel. (11) 3134302; fax (11) 3134301; e-mail webmaster@moex.gov.sy; internet ministryofexpatriates.gov.sy.
Ministry of Finance: BP 13136, rue Jule Jammal, Damascus; tel. (11) 2239624; fax (11) 2224701; e-mail mof@net.sy; internet www.syrianfinance.org.
Ministry of Foreign Affairs: rue ar-Rashid, Damascus; tel. (11) 3331200; fax (11) 3327620.
Ministry of Health: rue Majlis ash-Sha'ab, Damascus; tel. (11) 3311020; fax (11) 3311114; e-mail health-min@net.sy; internet www.moh.gov.sy.
Ministry of Higher Education: BP 9251, place Mezzeh Gamarik, Damascus; tel. (11) 2119865; fax (11) 2128919; e-mail mhe@shem.net; internet www.mhe.gov.sy.
Ministry of Housing and Construction: place Yousuf al-Azmeh, as-Salheyeh, Damascus; tel. (11) 2217571; fax (11) 2217570; e-mail mhu@net.sy.
Ministry of Industry: BP 12835, rue Maysaloun, Damascus; tel. (11) 2231834; fax (11) 2231096; e-mail min-industry@syriatel.net; internet www.syrianindustry.org.
Ministry of Information: Immeuble Dar al-Baath, Autostrade Mezzeh, Damascus; tel. and fax (11) 6664681; e-mail info@moi.gov.sy; internet www.moi.gov.sy.
Ministry of the Interior: rue al-Bahsah, al-Marjeh, Damascus; tel. (11) 2313471; fax (11) 2324835; e-mail admin@civilaffair-moi.gov.sy; internet www.civilaffair-moi.gov.sy.
Ministry of Irrigation: BP 4451, rue Fardoss; tel. (11) 2212741; fax (11) 3320691.
Ministry of Justice: rue an-Nasr, Damascus; tel. (11) 2214105; fax (11) 2246250.
Ministry of Labour and Social Affairs: place Yousuf al-Azmeh, as-Salheyeh, Damascus; tel. (11) 2210355; fax (11) 2247499.
Ministry of Local Administration and Environment: Damascus; e-mail webmaster@mlae-sy.org; internet www.mlae-sy.org.
Ministry of Petroleum and Mineral Resources: BP 40, al-Adawi, Insha'at, Damascus; tel. (11) 4451624; fax (11) 4463942; e-mail mopmr@net.sy.
Ministry of Tourism: BP 6642, rue Barada, Damascus; tel. (11) 2210122; fax (11) 2242636; e-mail min-tourism@mail.sy; internet www.syriatourism.org.
Ministry of Transport: BP 33999, rue al-Jala'a, Damascus; tel. (11) 3316840; fax (11) 3323317; e-mail min-trans@net.sy; internet www.mot.gov.sy.

Legislature

MAJLIS ASH-SHA'AB
(People's Assembly)

Speaker: MAHMOUD AREF AL-ABRASH.
Election, 22 and 23 April 2007

Party	Seats
National Progressive Front*	172
Independents	78
Total	**250**

*The National Progressive Front reportedly comprised 10 political parties, headed by the Baath Arab Socialist Party.

Political Organizations

The **National Progressive Front (NPF—Al-Jabha al-Wataniyah at-Taqadumiyah)**, headed by the late President Hafiz al-Assad, was formed in March 1972 as a coalition of five political parties. The Syrian Constitution defines the Baath Arab Socialist Party as 'the leading party in the society and the state'. At mid-2007 the NPF consisted of 10 parties:

Arab Socialist Party: Damascus; a breakaway socialist party; contested the 1994 election to the People's Assembly as two factions; Leader ABD AL-GHANI KANNOUT.

Arab Socialist Union (al-Ittihad al-Ishtiraki al-'Arabi): Damascus; f. 1973, following the separation of the Syrian branch from the international Arab Socialist Union; Nasserite; supportive of the policies of the Baath Arab Socialist Party; Leader SAFWAN AL-QUDSI.

Baath Arab Socialist Party (al-Hizb al-Ba'th al-'Arabi al-Ishtiraki): National Command, BP 9389, Autostrade Mezzeh, Damascus; tel. (11) 6622142; fax (11) 6622099; e-mail baath@baath-party.org; internet www.baath-party.org; Arab nationalist socialist party; f. 1947, as a result of merger between the Arab Revival (Baath) Movement (f. 1940) and the Arab Socialist Party (f. 1940); in power since 1963; supports creation of a unified Arab socialist society; approx. 1m. mems in Syria; brs in most Arab countries; Sec.-Gen. Lt-Gen. BASHAR AL-ASSAD.

Democratic Arab Unionist Party (Hizb al-Ittihad ad-Dimuqrati al-'Arabi): f. 1981, following split from the Arab Socialist Union; considers the concerns of the Arab world in general as secondary to those of Syria itself in the pursuit of pan-Arab goals; Chair. GHASSAN AHMAD OSMAN.

Democratic Socialist Unionist Party (al-Hizb al-Wahdawi al-Ishtiraki ad-Dimuqrati): f. 1974, following split from the Arab Socialist Union; Chair. FADLALLAH NASR AD-DIN.

Socialist Unionists (Al-Wahdawiyyun al-Ishtirakiyyun): f. 1961, through split from the Baath Arab Socialist Party following that organization's acceptance of Syria's decision to secede from the United Arab Republic; Nasserite; aims for Arab unity, particularly a new union with Egypt; produces weekly periodical *Al-Wehdawi*; Chair. FAYEZ ISMAIL.

Syrian Arab Socialist Union Party: Damascus; tel. (11) 239305; Nasserite; Sec.-Gen. SAFWAN KOUDSI.

Syrian Communist Party (Bakdash) (al-Hizb ash-shuyu'i as-suri): Damascus; f. 1924 by Fouad Shamal in Lebanon and Khalid Bakdash (died 1995); until 1943 part of joint Communist Party of Syria and Lebanon; party split into two factions under separate leaders, Bakdash and Faisal (q.v.), in 1986; Marxist-Leninist; publishes fortnightly periodical *Sawt ash-Shaab*; Sec.-Gen. WISSAL FARHA BAKDASH.

Syrian Communist Party (Faisal) (al-Hizb ash-shuyu'i as-suri): Damascus; f. 1986, following split of Syrian Communist Party into two factions under separate leaders, Faisal and Bakdash (q.v.); aims to end domination of Baath Arab Socialist Party and the advantages given to mems of that party at all levels; advocates the lifting of the state of emergency and the release of all political prisoners; publishes weekly periodical *An-Nour*; Sec.-Gen. YOUSUF RASHID FAISAL.

Syrian Social Nationalist Party (Centralist Wing) (al-Hizb as-Suri al-Qawmi al-Ijtima'i): e-mail administrator@snp.com; internet www.ssnp.com; f. 1932 in Beirut, Lebanon; joined the NPF in 2005; also known as Parti populaire syrien; seeks creation of a 'Greater Syrian' state, incl. Syria, Lebanon, Jordan, the Palestinian territories, Iraq, Kuwait, Cyprus and parts of Egypt, Iran and Turkey; advocates separation of church and state, the redistribution of wealth, and a strong military; supports Syrian involvement in Lebanese affairs; has brs world-wide, and approx. 90,000 mems in Syria; Chair. ISSAM MAHAYIRI.

The **Syrian Democratic People's Party** (al-Hizb ash-Sha'ab as-Suri ad-Dimuqrati—leader ABULLAH HOSHA) was founded in 1973 as the Syrian Communist Party (Political Bureau), following the decision by founder Riad at-Turk to split from that party after its leader, Khalid Bakdash, decided to allow the organization to join the NPF. The party adopted its current name in 2005.

There is also a **Marxist-Leninist Communist Action Party**, which regards itself as independent of all Arab regimes.

An illegal Syrian-based organization, the **Islamic Movement for Change (IMC)**, claimed responsibility for a bomb attack in Damascus in December 1996.

Diplomatic Representation

EMBASSIES IN SYRIA

Afghanistan: BP 12217, ave Secretariat, Mezzeh Ouest, Damascus; tel. (11) 6112910; fax (11) 6133595; Ambassador MUHAMMADULLAH HAIDARI.

Algeria: Immeuble Noss, Raouda, Damascus; tel. (11) 3331446; fax (11) 3334698; Ambassador LAHSAN ABU FARIS.

Argentina: BP 116, Damascus; tel. (11) 3334167; fax (11) 3327326; e-mail easir@net.sy; Ambassador HERNÁN ROBERTO PLORUTTI.

Armenia: BP 33241, Ibrahim Hanono St, Malki, Damascus; tel. (11) 6133560; fax (11) 6130952; e-mail am309@net.sy; Ambassador ARCHAD BOLADIAN.

Austria: BP 5634, Immeuble Mohamed Naim ad-Deker, 1 rue Farabi, Mezzeh Est, Damascus; tel. (11) 6116730; fax (11) 6116734; e-mail damaskus-ob@bmaa.gv.at; Ambassador Dr Iur. KARL SHRAMEK.

Bahrain: BP 36225, Damascus; tel. (11) 6132314; fax (11) 6130502; e-mail bed@net.sy; Ambassador WAHID MUBARAK SAYYAR.

Belarus: BP 16239, 27 rue Qurtaja, Mezzeh Est, Damascus; tel. (11) 6118097; fax (11) 6132802; e-mail syria@belembassy.org; Ambassador VLADIMIR N. LOPATO-ZAGORSKII.

Belgium: 3 rue Salaam, Bâtiment 101, 2e–3e étage, Mezzeh Est, Damascus; tel. (11) 61399931; fax (11) 61399977; e-mail damascus@diplobel.org; internet www.diplomatie.be/damascus; Ambassador DERRICK LUNCK.

Brazil: BP 2219, 39 rue Al-Farabi, Mezzeh Est, Damascus; tel. (11) 6124551; fax (11) 6124553; e-mail braemsyr@net.sy; Ambassador EDUARDO MONTEIRO DE BARROS ROXO.

Bulgaria: BP 2732, 8 rue Pakistan, place Arnous, Damascus; tel. (11) 3318445; fax (11) 4419854; e-mail bul-emb@scs-net.org; Ambassador GEORGI YANKOV.

Canada: BP 3394, Damascus; tel. (11) 6116692; fax (11) 6114000; e-mail dmcus@dfait-maeci.gc.ca; internet www.dfait-maeci.gc.ca/syria; Ambassador MARK BAILEY.

Chile: 6 rue Ziad Bin Abi Soufian, Rawda, Damascus; tel. (11) 3338443; fax (11) 3331563; e-mail echilesy@scs-net.org; Ambassador RICARDO FIEGELIST.

China, People's Republic: BP 2455, 83 rue Ata Ayoubi, Damascus; tel. (11) 3339594; fax (11) 3338067; e-mail chinaemb_sy@mfa.gov.cn; internet sy.chineseembassy.org; Ambassador LI HUAXIN.

Cuba: Immeuble Istouani and Charbati, 40 rue ar-Rachid, Damascus; tel. (11) 3339624; fax (11) 3333802; e-mail embacubasy@net.sy; Ambassador LUIS MAIRISI VIGIRDO.

Cyprus: BP 9269, 278G rue Malek bin Rabia, Mezzeh Ouest, Damascus; tel. (11) 6130812; fax (11) 6130814; e-mail syriapio@scs-net.org; Ambassador EFSTATHIOS ORPHANIDES.

Czech Republic: BP 2249, place Abou al-Ala'a al-Maari, Damascus; tel. (11) 3331383; fax (11) 3338268; e-mail damascus@embassy.mzv.cz; internet www.mzv.cz/damascus; Ambassador TOMÁŠ ULIČNÝ.

Denmark: BP 2244, Fatmeh Idriss 6, rue al-Ghazzawi, Mezzeh Ouest, Damascus; tel. (11) 61909000; fax (11) 61909033; e-mail damamb@um.dk; internet www.ambdamaskus.um.dk; Ambassador OLE EGBERG MIKKELSEN.

Egypt: BP 12443, rue al-Gala'a, Abou Roumaneh, Damascus; tel. (11) 3330756; fax (11) 3337961; fax egyemb@syria.net; Ambassador SHAWKI ISMAIL ALI SOLIMAN.

Eritrea: BP 12846, Autostrade Al-Mazen West, 82 rue Akram Mosque, Damascus; tel. (11) 6112357; fax (11) 6112358; Chargé d'affaires a.i. HUMMED MOHAMED SAEED KULU.

Finland: BP 3893, Immeuble 164A, rue Doha, Area 3, Mezzeh Est, Damascus; tel. (11) 6127570; fax (11) 6119777; Ambassador PERTTI HARVOLA.

France: BP 769, rue Ata al-Ayoubi, al-Afif, Damascus; tel. (11) 3390200; fax (11) 3390221; e-mail ambafr@net.sy; Ambassador MICHEL DUCLOS.

Germany: BP 2237, 16 rue Abd al-Mun'im Riyad, al-Malki, Damascus; tel. (11) 37900000; fax (11) 3323812; e-mail germemb@scs-net.org; internet www.damaskus.diplo.de; Ambassador VOLKMAR KARL WENZEL.

Greece: BP 30319, Immeuble Pharaon, 11 rue Farabi, Mezzeh Est, Damascus; tel. (11) 6113035; fax (11) 6114920; e-mail gremb.dam@mfa.gr; Ambassador KONSTANTINA ZAGORIANOU-PRIFTI.

Holy See: BP 2271, 1 place Ma'raket Ajnadin, al-Malki, Damascus (Apostolic Nunciature); tel. (11) 3332601; fax (11) 3327550; e-mail noncesy@mail.sy; Apostolic Nuncio Most Rev. MORANDINI GIOVANNI BATTISTA (Titular Archbishop of Grado).

Hungary: BP 2607, 12 rue as-Salam, Mezzeh Est, Damascus; tel. (11) 6117966; fax (11) 6117917; e-mail mission.dam@kum.hu; internet www.mfa.gov.hu/kulkepviselet/sy; Ambassador Prof. PÉTER MEDGYES.

India: BP 685, Immeuble Yassin Noueilati, 40/46 ave Adnan al-Malki, Damascus; tel. (11) 3739082; fax (11) 3326231; e-mail indemcom@scs-net.org; Ambassador GOTAM MOKOBAD HAYA.

Indonesia: BP 3530, Immeuble 26, Bloc 270A, 132 rue Al-Madina al-Munawar, Mezzeh Est, Damascus; tel. (11) 6119630; fax (11) 6119632; e-mail kbridams@net.sy; internet kbri-damascus.go.id; Ambassador MUHAMMAD BASYOUNI.

Iran: BP 2691, Autostrade Mezzeh, nr ar-Razi Hospital, Damascus; tel. (11) 6117675; fax (11) 6110997; e-mail iran-dam@net.sy; Ambassador SAYED AHMAD MOUSSAVI.

Iraq: Damascus; tel. (11) 3341290; fax (11) 3341291; e-mail dmkemb@iraqmofamail.net; Ambassador SABAH ABD AL-WAHAB AL-IMAM.

Italy: BP 2216, rue al-Ayoubi, Damascus; tel. (11) 3338338; fax (11) 3320325; e-mail ambasciata.damasco@esteri.it; internet www.ambdamasco.esteri.it; Ambassador AKELLI FRANCO LUIGI AMIRIO.

Japan: BP 3366, 3537 Sharkasiya, rue al-Jala'a, Abou Roumaneh, Damascus; tel. (11) 3338273; fax (11) 3339920; Ambassador MASAKI KUNEIDA.

SYRIA — Directory

Jordan: rue Abou Roumaneh, Damascus; tel. (11) 3334642; fax (11) 3336741; Ambassador Dr HASHEM MUHAMMAD TALEB ASH-SHABBOUL.

Korea, Democratic People's Republic: rue Fares al-Khouri-Jisr Tora, Damascus; Ambassador KIM PYONG-NAM.

Kuwait: rue Ibrahim Hanano, Damascus; Ambassador FAHED AHMAD AL-AWADHI.

Libya: Abou Roumaneh, Damascus; Head of People's Bureau AHMAD ABD AS-SALAM BIN KHAYAL.

Malaysia: Immeuble 15, Abd al-Kader al-Jazairy St, Abou Roumaneh, Damascus; tel. (11) 3343388; fax (11) 3341002; e-mail mwsyria@scs-net.org; Ambassador ZEIN EDDIN YEHYA.

Mauritania: ave al-Jala'a, rue Karameh, Damascus; Ambassador (vacant).

Morocco: 35 rue Abu Bakr Al Karkhi-Villas, Mezzeh Ouest, Damascus; tel. (11) 6110451; fax (11) 6117885; e-mail sifmar@scs-net.org; Ambassador ABDELOUAHAB BELLOUKI.

Netherlands: BP 702, Immeuble Tello, rue al-Jala'a, Abou Roumaneh, Damascus; tel. (11) 3336871; fax (11) 3339369; e-mail dmc@minbuza.nl; Ambassador DÉSIRÉE BONIS.

Norway: BP 7703, Immeuble 2, rue Shafei, Mezzeh Est, Damascus; tel. (11) 6122941; fax (11) 6131159; e-mail emb.damascus@mfa.no; internet www.norway.org.sy; Ambassador HANS WILHELM LONGVA.

Oman: BP 9635, rue Ghazzawi, Mezzeh Ouest, Damascus; tel. (11) 6110408; fax (11) 6110944; Ambassador MUHAMMAD BIN SALEM BIN SAID ASH-SHANFARI.

Pakistan: BP 9284, rue al-Farabi, Mezzeh Est, Damascus; tel. (11) 6132694; fax (11) 6132662; e-mail parepdam@scs-net.org; Ambassador MUNZER SHAFIQ.

Panama: BP 2548, Apt 7, Immeuble az-Zein, rue al-Bizm, Malki, Damascus; tel. (11) 224743; Chargé d'affaires CARLOS A. DE GRACIA.

Poland: BP 501, rue Baha Eddin Aita, Abou Roumaneh, Damascus; tel. (11) 3333010; fax (11) 3315318; e-mail damapol@scs-net.org; internet www.damaszek.polemb.net; Ambassador JACEK CHODOROWICZ.

Qatar: BP 4188, rue Ahmed Shouki, Abou Roumaneh, Damascus; e-mail damascus@mofa.gov.qa; tel. (11) 3336717; fax (11) 3342455; Ambassador MAJED GHANEM AL-ALI AL-MAADEED.

Romania: BP 4454, 8 rue Ibrahim Hanano, Damascus; tel. (11) 3327570; fax (11) 3327572; e-mail ro.dam@net.sy; Ambassador DANTOS FLORIN SANDOVETCH.

Russia: rue Umar bin al-Khattab, ad-Dawi, Damascus; tel. (11) 4423155; fax (11) 4423182; e-mail rusemb@scs-net.org; Ambassador SERGEI KIRPICHENKO.

Saudi Arabia: rue al-Jala'a, Abou Roumaneh, Damascus; tel. (11) 3334914; fax (11) 3337383; e-mail syemb@mofa.gov.sa; Ambassador (vacant).

Serbia: BP 739, 18 rue al-Jala'a, Abou Roumaneh, Damascus; tel. (11) 3336222; fax (11) 3333690; e-mail ambasada@srbija-damask.org; internet www.srbija-damask.org; Chargé d'affaires Dr GORDANA ANIČIĆ.

Slovakia: BP 33115, 158 rue ash-Shafei, Mezzeh Est, Damascus; tel. (11) 6132114; fax (11) 6132598; e-mail slovemb@scs-net.org; internet www.damascus.mfa.sk; Ambassador OLDRICH HLAVÁČEK.

Somalia: ave Ata Ayoubi, al-Afif, Damascus; Ambassador (vacant).

South Africa: BP 9141, rue al-Ghazaoui, 7 Jadet Kouraish, Mezzeh Ouest, Damascus; tel. (11) 61351520; fax (11) 6111714; e-mail saembdam@ses-net.org; Ambassador MUHAMMAD DANGOR.

Spain: BP 392, rue ash-Shafi, Mezzeh Est, Damascus; tel. (11) 6132900; fax (11) 6132941; e-mail spainemda@net.sy; Ambassador JUAN RAMÓN SERRAT CUENCA-ROMERO.

Sudan: Damascus; tel. (11) 6111036; fax (11) 6112904; e-mail sud-emb@net.sy; Ambassador ABD AR-RAHMAN DERAR.

Sweden: BP 4266, Immeuble du Patriarcat Catholique, rue Chakib Arslan, Abou Roumaneh, Damascus; tel. (11) 33400700; fax (11) 3327749; e-mail ambassaden.damaskus@foreign.ministry.se; internet www.swedenabroad.com/damascus; Ambassador CATHARINA KIPP.

Switzerland: BP 234, 2 rue ash-Shafi, Mezzeh Est, Damascus; tel. (11) 6111972; fax (11) 6111976; e-mail dam.vertretung@eda.admin.ch; internet www.eda.admin.ch/damascus; Ambassador JACQUES DE WATTEVILLE.

Tunisia: BP 4114, 6 rue ash-Shafi, blvd Fahim, Mezzeh, Damascus; tel. (11) 6132700; fax (11) 6132704; e-mail at.damas@net.sy; Ambassador HEDI BEN NASR.

Turkmenistan: Miset, 4097 Ruki ed-Din, 2e étage, Damascus; tel. (11) 2241834; fax (11) 3320905.

Turkey: BP 3738, 56–58 ave Ziad bin Abou Soufian, Damascus; tel. (11) 33501930; fax (11) 3339243; e-mail sambe@mfa.gov.tr; Ambassador KHALED CEVIK.

Ukraine: BP 33944, 14 rue as-Salam, Mezzeh Est, Damascus; tel. (11) 6113016; fax (11) 6121355; e-mail emb_sy@mfa.gov.ua; internet www.mfa.gov.ua/syria; Chargé d'affaires a.i. MYKOLA KRAVCHENKO.

United Arab Emirates: Immeuble Housami, 62 rue Raouda, Damascus; Ambassador YOUSUF MUHAMMAD HUSSEIN AL-MADFA'AI.

United Kingdom: BP 37, Immeuble Kotob, 11 rue Muhammad Kurd Ali, Malki, Damascus; tel. (11) 3739241; fax (11) 3921873; e-mail british.embassy.damascus@fco.gov.uk; internet www.britishembassy.gov.uk/syria; Ambassador SIMON COLLIS.

USA: BP 29, 2 rue al-Mansour, Abou Roumaneh, Damascus; tel. (11) 33914444; fax (11) 33913999; e-mail damasweb-query@state.gov; internet syria.usembassy.gov; Chargé d'affaires MICHAEL CORBIN.

Venezuela: BP 2403, Immeuble at-Tabbah, 5 rue Lisaneddin bin al-Khateb, place Rauda, Damascus; tel. (11) 3335356; fax (11) 3333203; e-mail embavenez@net.sy; Ambassador DIA NADER AL-ANDARI.

Yemen: Abou Roumaneh, Charkassieh, Damascus; Ambassador SALAH ALI AHEMD AL-ANSI.

Note: Syria and Lebanon have very close relations but do not exchange formal ambassadors.

Judicial System

The Courts of Law in Syria are principally divided into two juridical court systems: Courts of General Jurisdiction and Administrative Courts. Since 1973 the Supreme Constitutional Court has been established as the paramount body of the Syrian judicial structure.

THE SUPREME CONSTITUTIONAL COURT

This is the highest court in Syria. It has specific jurisdiction over: (i) judicial review of the constitutionality of laws and legislative decrees; (ii) investigation of charges relating to the legality of the election of members of the Majlis ash-Sha'ab (People's Assembly); (iii) trial of infractions committed by the President of the Republic in the exercise of his functions; (iv) resolution of positive and negative jurisdictional conflicts and determination of the competent court between the different juridical court systems, as well as other bodies exercising judicial competence. The Supreme Constitutional Court is composed of a Chief Justice and four Justices. They are appointed by decree of the President of the Republic for a renewable period of four years.

Chief Justice of the Supreme Court: NASRAT MOUNLA-HAYDAR, Damascus; tel. (11) 3331902.

COURTS OF GENERAL JURISDICTION

The Courts of General Jurisdiction in Syria are divided into six categories: (i) The Court of Cassation; (ii) The Courts of Appeal; (iii) The Tribunals of First Instance; (iv) The Tribunals of Peace; (v) The Personal Status Courts; (vi) The Courts for Minors. Each of the above categories (except the Personal Status Courts) is divided into Civil, Penal and Criminal Chambers.

(i) The Court of Cassation: This is the highest court of general jurisdiction. Final judgments rendered by Courts of Appeal in penal and civil litigations may be petitioned to the Court of Cassation by the Defendant or the Public Prosecutor in penal and criminal litigations, and by any of the parties in interest in civil litigations, on grounds of defective application or interpretation of the law as stated in the challenged judgment, on grounds of irregularity of form or procedure, or violation of due process, and on grounds of defective reasoning of judgment rendered. The Court of Cassation is composed of a President, seven Vice-Presidents and 31 other Justices (Councillors).

(ii) The Courts of Appeal: Each court has geographical jurisdiction over one governorate (Mouhafazat). Each court is divided into Penal and Civil Chambers. There are Criminal Chambers which try felonies only. The Civil Chambers hear appeals filed against judgments rendered by the Tribunals of First Instance and the Tribunals of Peace. Each Court of Appeal is composed of a President and sufficient numbers of Vice-Presidents (Presidents of Chambers) and Superior Judges (Councillors). There are 54 Courts of Appeal.

(iii) The Tribunals of First Instance: In each governorate there are one or more Tribunals of First Instance, each of which is divided into several Chambers for penal and civil litigations. Each Chamber is composed of one judge. There are 72 Tribunals of First Instance.

(iv) The Tribunals of Peace: In the administrative centre of each governorate, and in each district, there are one or more Tribunals of Peace, which have jurisdiction over minor civil and penal litigations. There are 227 Tribunals of Peace.

(v) Personal Status Courts: These courts deal with marriage, divorce, etc. For Muslims each court consists of one judge, the 'Qadi Shari'i'. For Druzes there is one court consisting of one judge, the 'Qadi Mazhabi'. For non-Muslim communities there are courts for Roman Catholics, Orthodox believers, Protestants and Jews.

(vi) Courts for Minors: The constitution, officers, sessions, jurisdiction and competence of these courts are determined by a special law.

PUBLIC PROSECUTION

Public prosecution is headed by the Attorney-General, assisted by a number of Senior Deputy and Deputy Attorneys-General, and a sufficient number of chief prosecutors, prosecutors and assistant prosecutors. Public prosecution is represented at all levels of the Courts of General Jurisdiction in all criminal and penal litigations and also in certain civil litigations as required by the law. Public prosecution controls and supervises enforcement of penal judgments.

ADMINISTRATIVE COURTS SYSTEM

The Administrative Courts have jurisdiction over litigations involving the state or any of its governmental agencies. The Administrative Courts system is divided into two courts: the Administrative Courts and the Judicial Administrative Courts, of which the paramount body is the High Administrative Court.

MILITARY COURTS

The Military Courts deal with criminal litigations against military personnel of all ranks and penal litigations against officers only. There are two military courts: one in Damascus, the other in Aleppo. Each court is composed of three military judges. There are other military courts, consisting of one judge, in every governorate, which deal with penal litigations against military personnel below the rank of officer. The different military judgments can be petitioned to the Court of Cassation.

Religion

The majority of Syrians follow a form of Islamic Sunni orthodoxy. There are also a considerable number of religious minorities: Shi'a Muslims; Isma'ili Muslims; the Isma'ili of the Salamiya district, whose spiritual head is the Aga Khan; a large number of Druzes, the Nusairis or Alawites of the Jebel Ansariyeh (a schism of the Shi'ite branch of Islam, to which about 11% of the population, including President Assad, belongs) and the Yezidis of the Jebel Sinjar; and a minority of Christians.

The Constitution states only that 'Islam shall be the religion of the head of the state'. The original draft of the 1973 Constitution made no reference to Islam at all, and this clause was inserted only as a compromise after public protest. The Syrian Constitution is thus unique among the constitutions of Arab states (excluding Lebanon) with a clear Muslim majority in not enshrining Islam as the religion of the state itself.

ISLAM

Grand Mufti: Sheikh AHMAD BADER ED-DIN HASSOUN, POB 7410, Damascus; tel. (11) 2688601; fax (11) 2637650; e-mail info@drhassoun.com; internet www.drhassoun.com.

CHRISTIANITY

Orthodox Churches

Greek Orthodox Patriarchate of Antioch and all the East: BP 9, Damascus; tel. (11) 5424400; fax (11) 5424404; e-mail info@antiochpat.org; internet www.antiochpat.org; Patriarch of Antioch and all the East His Beatitude IGNATIUS HAZIM; has jurisdiction over Syria, Lebanon, Iran and Iraq.

Syrian Orthodox Patriarchate of Antioch and all the East: BP 22260, Bab Touma, Damascus; tel. (11) 54498989; e-mail patriarch-z-iwas@scs-net.org; Patriarch of Antioch and all the East His Holiness IGNATIUS ZAKKA I IWAS; the Syrian Orthodox Church includes one Catholicose (of India), 37 Metropolitans and one Bishop, and has an estimated 4m. adherents throughout the world.

The Armenian Apostolic Church is also represented in Syria.

The Roman Catholic Church

Armenian Rite

Patriarchal Exarchate of Syria: Exarchat Patriarcal Arménien Catholique, BP 22281, Bab Touma, Damascus; tel. (11) 5413820; fax (11) 5419431; f. 1985; represents the Patriarch of Cilicia (resident in Beirut, Lebanon); 4,500 adherents (31 December 2007); Exarch Patriarchal Bishop JOSEPH ARNAOUTIAN.

Archdiocese of Aleppo: Archevêché Arménien Catholique, BP 97, 33 at-Tilal, Aleppo; tel. (21) 2119307; fax (21) 2119308; e-mail armen.cath@mail.sy; 17,000 adherents (31 December 2005); Archbishop BOUTROS MARAYATI.

Diocese of Kamichlié: Evêché Arménien Catholique, BP 17, Al-Qamishli; tel. (53) 424211; fax (53) 426211; 4,000 adherents (31 December 2005); Bishop (vacant).

Chaldean Rite

Diocese of Aleppo: Evêché Chaldéen Catholique, BP 4643, 1 rue Patriarche Elias IV Mouawwad, Soulémaniyé, Aleppo; tel. (21) 4441660; fax (21) 4600800; e-mail chalalep@mail.sy; 15,000 adherents (31 December 2005); Bishop ANTOINE AUDO.

Latin Rite

Apostolic Vicariate of Aleppo: BP 327, 19 rue Antaki, Aleppo; tel. (21) 2210204; fax (21) 2219031; e-mail vicariatlatin@mail.sy; f. 1762; 12,000 adherents (31 December 2005); Vicar Apostolic GIUSEPPE NAZZARO (Titular Bishop of Forma).

Maronite Rite

Archdiocese of Aleppo: Archevêché Maronite, BP 203, 57 rue Fares-El-Khoury, Aleppo; tel. and fax (21) 2248048; fax (21) 2243048; e-mail maronite-aleppo@net.sy; 4,000 adherents (31 December 2005); Archbishop YOUSSEF ANIS ABI-AAD.

Archdiocese of Damascus: Archevêché Maronite, BP 2179, 6 rue ad-Deir, Bab Touma, Damascus; tel. (11) 5412888; fax (11) 54499272; e-mail psamirn@cyberia.net.lb; 14,000 adherents (31 December 2006); Archbishop SAMIR NASSAR.

Diocese of Latakia: Evêché Maronite, BP 161, rue Hamrat, Tartous; tel. (43) 223433; fax (43) 322939; 33,000 adherents (31 December 2005); Bishop YOUSSEF-MASSOUD MASSOUD.

Melkite Rite

Melkite Greek Catholic Patriarchate of Antioch: Patriarcat Grec-Melkite Catholique, BP 22249, Damascus; tel. (11) 5441030; fax (11) 5418966; e-mail gcp@pcg-lb.org; or BP 70071, Antélias, Lebanon; tel. (4) 413111; fax (4) 418113; f. 1724; jurisdiction over 1.5m. Melkites throughout the world (including 290,000 in Syria); Patriarch of Antioch and all the East, of Alexandria and of Jerusalem His Beatitude GRÉGOIRE III LAHAM; the Melkite Church includes the patriarchal sees of Damascus, Cairo and Jerusalem and four other archdioceses in Syria; seven archdioceses in Lebanon; one in Jordan; one in Israel; and six eparchies (in the USA, Brazil, Canada, Australia, Venezuela, Argentina and Mexico).

Archdiocese of Aleppo: Archevêché Grec-Catholique, BP 146, 9 place Farhat, Aleppo; tel. (21) 2213218; fax (21) 2223106; e-mail gr.melkcath@mail.sy; 17,000 adherents (31 December 2005); Archbishop JEAN-CLÉMENT JEANBART.

Archdiocese of Busra and Hauran: Archevêché Grec-Catholique, Khabab, Hauran; tel. (15) 855012; e-mail derbosra@hotmail.com; 27,000 adherents (31 December 2005); Archbishop BOULOS NASSIF BORKHOCHE.

Archdiocese of Homs: Archevêché Grec-Catholique, BP 1525, rue El-Mo'tazila, Boustan ad-Diwan, Homs; tel. (31) 2482587; fax (31) 2464587; e-mail isidore_battikha@yahoo.fr; 30,000 adherents (31 December 2005); Archbishop ABRAHAM NEHMÉ.

Archdiocese of Latakia: Archevêché Grec-Catholique, BP 151, rue al-Moutannabi, Latakia; tel. (41) 460777; fax (41) 467002; e-mail saouafnicolas@yahoo.fr; 10,000 adherents (31 December 2005); Archbishop NICOLAS SAWAF.

Syrian Rite

Archdiocese of Aleppo: Archevêché Syrien Catholique, place Mère Teresa de Calcutta, Azizié, Aleppo; tel. (21) 2126750; fax (21) 2126752; 8,000 adherents (31 December 2005); Archbishop ANTOINE CHAHDA.

Archdiocese of Damascus: Archevêché Syrien Catholique, BP 2129, 157 rue Al-Mustaqeem, Bab Charki, Damascus; tel. and fax (11) 5445343; e-mail psamirm@cyberia.met.lb; 14,000 adherents (31 December 2006); Archbishop SAMIR NASSAR.

Archdiocese of Hassaké-Nisibi: Archevêché Syrien Catholique, BP 6, Hassaké; tel. (52) 320812; 5,630 adherents (31 December 2005); Archbishop JACQUES BEHNAN HINDO.

Archdiocese of Homs: Archevêché Syrien Catholique, BP 368, rue Hamidieh, Homs; tel. (31) 221575; fax (21) 224350; 10,000 adherents (31 December 2005); Archbishop THÉOPHILE GEORGES KASSAB.

The Anglican Communion

Within the Episcopal Church in Jerusalem and the Middle East, Syria forms part of the diocese of Jerusalem (see the chapter on Israel).

SYRIA

Other Christian Groups

Protestants in Syria are largely adherents of either the National Evangelical Synod of Syria and Lebanon or the Union of Armenian Evangelical Churches in the Near East (for details of both organizations, see the chapter on Lebanon).

The Press

Since the Baath Arab Socialist Party came to power, the structure of the press has been modified according to socialist patterns. Most publications are issued by political, religious or professional associations (such as trade unions), and several are published by government ministries. Anyone wishing to establish a new paper or periodical must apply for a licence.

The major dailies are *Al-Baath* (the organ of the party), *Tishreen* and *Ath-Thawra* in Damascus, *Al-Jamahir* in Aleppo and *Al-Fida'* in Hama.

PRINCIPAL DAILIES

Al-Baath (Renaissance): BP 9389, Autostrade Mezzeh, Damascus; tel. (11) 6622142; fax (11) 6622099; e-mail baath@baath-party.org; internet www.baath-party.org; f. 1946; morning; Arabic; organ of the Baath Arab Socialist Party; Editor ILYAS MURAD; circ. 45,000.

Barq ash-Shimal (The Syrian Telegraph): rue Aziziyah, Aleppo; morning; Arabic; Editor MAURICE DJANDJI; circ. 6,400.

Champress: Immeuble Arnos, place Arnos, Damascus; tel. (11) 44681199; fax (11) 44681190; e-mail mail@champress.com; internet www.champress.com; privately owned; political; online only; Arabic; Dir ALI JAMALO.

Al-Fida' (Redemption): Hama; Al-Wihdat Press, Printing and Publishing Organization, BP 2448, Dawar Kafr Soussat, Damascus; tel. (11) 225219; e-mail fedaa@thawra.com; internet fedaa.alwehda.gov.sy; morning; Arabic; political; Editor A. AULWANI; circ. 4,000.

Al-Horubat: Homs; Al-Wihdat Press, Printing and Publishing Organization, BP 2448, Dawar Kafr Soussat, Damascus; tel. (11) 225219; morning; Arabic; circ. 5,000.

Al-Jamahir (The People): Aleppo; Al-Wihdat Press, Printing and Publishing Organization, BP 2448, Dawar Kafr Soussat, Damascus; tel. (21) 214309; fax (21) 214308; Arabic; political; Chief Editor MORTADA BAKACH; circ. 10,000.

Syria Times: BP 5452, Medan, Damascus; tel. (11) 2247359; fax (11) 2231374; e-mail syriatimes@teshreen.com; internet syriatimes.tishreen.info; English; publ. by Tishreen Foundation for Press and Publishing; Editor FOUAD MARDOUD; circ. 15,000.

Ath-Thawra (Revolution): Al-Wihdat Press, Printing and Publishing Organization, BP 2448, Dawar Kafr Soussat, Damascus; tel. (11) 2210850; fax (11) 2216851; e-mail admin@thawra.com; internet thawra.alwehda.gov.sy/thakafi.asp; f. 1963; morning; Arabic; political; circ. 40,000.

Tishreen (October): BP 5452, Medan, Damascus; tel. (11) 2131100; fax (11) 2246860; e-mail tnp@mail.sy; internet www.tishreen.info; Arabic; publ. by the Tishreen Foundation for Press and Publishing; Chief Editor KHALAF AL-JARAAD; circ. 50,000.

Al-Wihdat (Unity): Latakia; Al-Wihdat Press, Printing and Publishing Organization, BP 2448, Dawar Kafr Soussat, Damascus; Arabic.

WEEKLIES AND FORTNIGHTLIES

Abyad wa Aswad (White and Black): internet www.awaonline.net; f. 2002; weekly; Arabic; political; privately owned; Editor AYMAN AD-DAQUQ.

Al-Ajoua' (The Air): Compagnie de l'Aviation Arabe Syrienne, BP 417, Damascus; fortnightly; Arabic; aviation; Editor AHMAD ALLOUCHE.

Al-Esbou ar-Riadi (The Sports Week): Immeuble Tibi, ave Fardoss, Damascus; weekly; Arabic; sports; Asst Dir and Editor HASRAN AL-BOUNNI; circ. 14,250.

Al-Fursan (The Cavalry): Damascus; Arabic; political magazine; Editor RIFAAT AL-ASSAD.

Al-Iqtisadiya: f. 2001; weekly; Arabic; economic; privately owned; Editor WADDAH ABD AR-RABBO.

Kifah al-Oummal al-Ishtiraki (The Socialist Workers' Struggle): Fédération Générale des Syndicats des Ouvriers, rue Qanawat, Damascus; weekly; Arabic; labour; publ. by General Federation of Labour Unions; Editor SAID AL-HAMAMI.

Al-Maukef ar-Riadi (Sport Stance): Al-Wihdat Press, Printing and Publishing Organization, BP 2448, Dawar Kafr Soussat, Damascus; tel. (11) 225219; e-mail riadi@thawra.com; internet riadi.alwehda.gov.sy; weekly; Arabic; sports; circ. 50,000.

An-Nas (The People): BP 926, Aleppo; f. 1953; weekly; Arabic; Publr VICTOR KALOUS.

Nidal al-Fellahin (Peasants' Struggle): Fédération Générale des Laboureurs, BP 9389, Autostrade Mezzeh, Damascus; weekly; Arabic; Editor MANSOUR ABU AL-HOSN; circ. 8,100.

Ar-Riada (Sport): BP 292, nr Electricity Institute, Damascus; weekly; Arabic; sports; Dir NOUREDDINE RIAL; Publr and Editor OURFANE UBARI.

As-Sakafat al-Usbouiya (Weekly Culture): BP 2570, Soukak as-Sakr, Damascus; weekly; Arabic; cultural; Publr, Dir and Editor MADHAT AKKACHE.

Sawt ash-Shaab (Voice of the People): Damascus; f. 1937, but publ. suspended in 1939, 1941, 1947 and 1958; relaunched in 2001; fortnightly; Arabic; organ of the Syrian Communist Party (Bakdash).

Al-Yanbu al-Jadid (New Spring): Immeuble Al-Awkaf, Homs; weekly; Arabic; literary; Publr, Dir and Editor MAMDOU AL-KOUSSEIR.

OTHER PERIODICALS

Al-Arabieh (The Arab Lady): Syrian Women's Association, BP 3207, Damascus; tel. (11) 3316560; monthly; Editor S. BAKOUR.

Ad-Dad: rue Tital, Wakf al-Moiriné Bldg, Aleppo; monthly; Arabic; literary; Dir RIAD HALLAK; Publr and Editor ABDULLAH YARKI HALLAK.

Al-Fikr al-Askari (The Military Idea): BP 4259, blvd Palestine, Damascus; fax (11) 2125280; f. 1950; 6 a year; Arabic; official military review publ. by the Political Administration Press.

Al-Ghad (Tomorrow): Association of Red Cross and Crescent, BP 6095, rue Maysat, Damascus; tel. (11) 2242552; fax (11) 7777040; monthly; environmental health; Editor K. ABED-RABOU.

Al-Irshad az-Zirai (Agricultural Information): Ministry of Agriculture, rue Jabri, Damascus; tel. (11) 2213613; fax (11) 2216627; 6 a year; Arabic; agriculture.

Jaysh ash-Sha'ab (The People's Army): Ministry of Defence, BP 3320, blvd Palestine, Damascus; fax (11) 2125280; f. 1946; monthly; Arabic; army magazine; publ. by the Political Department of the Syrian Army.

Al-Kalima (The Word): Al-Kalima Association, Aleppo; monthly; Arabic; religious; Publr and Editor FATHALLA SAKAL.

Al-Kanoun (The Law): Ministry of Justice, rue an-Nasr, Damascus; tel. (11) 2214105; fax (11) 2246250; monthly; Arabic; juridical.

Al-Maaloumatieh (Information): National Information Centre, BP 11323, Damascus; tel. (11) 2127551; fax (11) 2127648; e-mail nice@net.sy; f. 1994; quarterly; computer magazine; Editor ABD AL-MAJID AR-RIFAI; circ. 10,000.

Al-Ma'arifa (Knowledge): Ministry of Culture, rue ar-Rouda, Damascus; tel. (11) 3336963; f. 1962; monthly; Arabic; literary; Editor ABD AL-KARIM NASIF; circ. 7,500.

Al-Majalla al-Batriarquia (The Magazine of the Patriarchate): Syrian Orthodox Patriarchate, BP 914, Damascus; tel. (11) 4447036; f. 1962; monthly; Arabic; religious; Editor SAMIR ABDOH; circ. 15,000.

Al-Majalla at-Tibbiya al-Arabiyya (Arab Medical Magazine): rue al-Jala'a, Damascus; monthly; Arabic; publ. by Arab Medical Commission; Dir Dr Y. SAKA; Editor Prof. ADNAN TAKRITI.

Majallat Majma' al-Lughat al-Arabiyya bi-Dimashq (Magazine of the Arab Language Academy of Damascus): Arab Academy of Damascus, BP 327, Damascus; tel. (11) 3713145; fax (11) 3733363; e-mail mla@net.sy; f. 1921; quarterly; Arabic; Islamic culture and Arabic literature, Arabic scientific and cultural terminology; Chief Editor Dr SHAKER FAHAM; circ. 1,600.

Al-Mawkif al-Arabi (The Arab Situation): Ittihab al-Kuttab al-Arab, rue Murshid Khatir, Damascus; monthly; Arabic; literary.

Monthly Survey of Arab Economics: BP 2306, Damascus; BP 6068, Beirut; f. 1958; monthly; English and French editions; published by Centre d'Etudes et de Documentation Economiques, Financières et Sociales; Dir Dr CHAFIC AKHRAS.

Al-Mouallem al-Arabi (The Arab Teacher): National Union of Teachers, BP 2842-3034, Damascus; tel. (11) 225219; f. 1948; monthly; Arabic; educational and cultural.

Al-Mouhandis al-Arabi (The Arab Engineer): Order of Syrian Engineers and Architects, BP 2336, Immeuble Dar al-Mouhandisen, place Azme, Damascus; tel. (11) 2214916; fax (11) 2216948; e-mail lbosea@net.sy; f. 1961; 4 a year; Arabic; scientific and cultural; Dir Eng. M. FAYEZ MAHFOUZ; Chief Editor Dr Eng. AHMAD AL-GHAFARI; circ. 50,000.

Al-Munadel (The Militant): c/o BP 11512, Damascus; fax (11) 2126935; f. 1965; monthly; Arabic; magazine of Baath Arab Socialist Party; Dir Dr FAWWAZ SAYYAGH; circ. 100,000.

An-Nashra al-Iktissad (Economic Bulletin): Damascus Chamber of Commerce; tel. (11) 2218339; fax (11) 2225874; e-mail dcc@net.sy; f. 1922; quarterly; finance and investment; Editor GHASSAN KALLA; circ. 3,000.

SYRIA

Risalat al-Kimia (Chemistry Report): BP 669, Immeuble al-Abid, Damascus; monthly; Arabic; scientific; Publr, Dir and Editor HASSAN AS-SAKA.

Saut al-Forat: Deir ez-Zor; monthly; Arabic; literary; Publr, Dir and Editor ABD AL-KADER AYACHE.

Ash-Shourta (The Police): Directorate of Public Affairs and Moral Guidance, Damascus; monthly; Arabic; juridical.

As-Sinaa (Industry): Damascus Chamber of Commerce, BP 1305, rue Mou'awiah, Harika, Damascus; tel. (11) 2222205; fax (11) 2245981; monthly; commerce, industry and management; Editor Y. HINDI.

Souriya al-Arabiyya (Arab Syria): Ministry of Information, Immeuble Dar al-Baath, Autostrade Mezzeh, Damascus; tel. (11) 6622141; fax (11) 6617665; monthly; publicity; in four languages.

Syria Today: Baramkeh, Free Zone, Damascus; tel. (11) 88270310; fax (11) 2137343; e-mail mail@syria-today.com; internet www.syria-today.com; monthly; English; economic and social development; Chair. LOUMA TARABINE; Man. Editor FRANCESCA DE CHÂTEL.

At-Tamaddon al-Islami (Islamic Civilization Society): Darwichiyah, Damascus; tel. (11) 2240562; fax (11) 3733563; e-mail isltmddn@hotmail.com; f. 1932; monthly; Arabic; religious; published by At-Tamaddon al-Islami Association; Pres. of Asscn AHMAD MOUAZ AL-KHATIB.

At-Taqa Wattanmiya (Energy and Expansion): BP 7748, rue al-Moutanabbi, Damascus; tel. (11) 233529; monthly; Arabic; publ. by the Syrian Petroleum Co.

Al-Yakza (The Awakening): Al-Yakza Association, BP 6677, rue Sisi, Aleppo; f. 1935; monthly; Arabic; literary social review of charitable institution; Dir HUSNI ABD AL-MASSIH; circ. 12,000.

Az-Zira'a (Agriculture): Ministry of Agriculture and Agrarian Reform, rue Jabri, Damascus; tel. (11) 2213613; fax (11) 2244023; f. 1985; monthly; Arabic; agriculture; circ. 12,000.

NEWS AGENCY

Syrian Arab News Agency (SANA): BP 2661, Baramka, Damascus; tel. (11) 2129702; fax (11) 2228265; e-mail public-relation@sana.sy; internet www.sana.sy; f. 1966; supplies bulletins on Syrian news to foreign news agencies; 16 offices abroad; 16 foreign correspondents; Dir-Gen. Dr ADNAN MAHMOUD.

Publishers

Arab Advertising Organization: BP 2842-3034, 28 rue Moutanabbi, Damascus; tel. (11) 2225219; fax (11) 2220754; e-mail sy-adv@net.sy; f. 1963; exclusive govt establishment responsible for advertising; publishes Directory of Commerce and Industry, Damascus International Fair Guide, Daily Bulletin of Official Tenders; Dir-Gen. MONA F. FABAH.

Damascus University Press: Damascus; tel. (11) 2215100; fax (11) 2236010; f. 1946; 12 journals; medicine, engineering, social sciences, agriculture, arts; Dir HUSSEIN OMRAN.

Institut Français du Proche-Orient: BP 344, Damascus; tel. (11) 3330214; fax (11) 3327887; e-mail secretariat@ifporient.org; internet www.ifporient.org; f. 1922; sociology, anthropology, Islamic studies, archaeology, history, language and literature, arts, philosophy, geography, religion; Dir JEAN-YVES L'HÔPITAL.

OFA-Business Consulting Center—Documents Service: BP 3550, 3 place Chahbandar, Damascus; tel. (11) 3318237; fax (11) 4426021; e-mail ofa1@net.sy; internet www.ofa-bcc.com; f. 1964; numerous periodicals, monographs and surveys on political and economic affairs; Dir-Gen. SAMIR A. DARWICH; has one affiliated branch, OFA-Business Consulting Centre (foreign co representation and services).

The Political Administration Press: BP 3320, blvd Palestine, Damascus; fax (11) 2125280; publishes Al-Fikr al-Askari (6 a year) and Jaysh ash-Sha'ab (monthly).

Syrian Documentation Papers: BP 2712, Damascus; f. 1968; publishers of Bibliography of the Middle East (annual), General Directory of the Press and Periodicals in the Arab World (annual), and numerous publications on political, economic, literary and social affairs, as well as legislative texts concerning Syria and the Arab world; Dir-Gen. LOUIS FARÈS.

Tishreen Foundation for Press and Publishing: BP 5452, Medan, Damascus; tel. (11) 2131100; fax (11) 2246860; publishes Syria Times and Tishreen (dailies).

Al-Wihdat Press, Printing and Publishing Organization (Institut al-Ouedha pour l'impression, édition et distribution): BP 2448, Dawar Kafr Soussat, Damascus; tel. (11) 225219; publishes Al-Fida', Al-Horubat, Al-Jamahir, Ath-Thawra and Al-Wihdat (dailies).

Al-Maukef ar-Riadi (weekly) and other commercial publications; Dir-Gen. FAHD DIYAB.

Broadcasting and Communications

TELECOMMUNICATIONS

Syrian Telecommunications Establishment (STE—Syrian Telecom): BP 11774, Autostrade Mezzeh, Damascus; tel. (11) 2240000; fax (11) 6110000; e-mail ste-gm@net.sy; internet www.ste.gov.sy; f. 1975; Dir.-Gen. Dr HAITHAM CHEDYAK.

Syriatel: Immeuble STE, 6e étage, rue Thawra, Damascus; tel. (11) 3341910; fax (11) 3341917; e-mail info@syriatel.com.sy; internet www.syriatel.com; f. 2000; provider of mobile telephone services; Chair. RAMI MAKHLOUF; CEO NADER KALAI; 2.35m. subscribers (2006).

MTN Syria: BP 34474, Immeuble Al-Mohandis al-Arabi, Autostrade Mezzeh, Damascus; fax (11) 6667483; e-mail customercare@mtn.com.sy; internet www.mtnsyria.com; f. 2001 as Spacetel Syria; name changed to Areeba Syria in 2004; present name adopted in 2007 following the acquisition of a 75% stake by MTN Group (South Africa); provider of mobile telephone services; Chair. JAMAL RAMADAN; CEO ISMAIL JAROUDI; 2.59m. subscribers (2007).

BROADCASTING

Radio and Television

General Organization of Radio and Television: place Omayyad, Damascus; tel. (11) 720700; internet www.rtv.gov.sy.

Organisme de la Radio-Télévision Arabe Syrienne (ORTAS): place Omayyad, Damascus; tel. (11) 720700; fax (11) 2234930; radio broadcasts started in 1945, television broadcasts in 1960; Dir-Gen. FAYEZ AS-SAYEGH; Dirs NAIF HAMMOUD (Radio), Dr FOUAD SHERBAJI (Television).

Finance

(cap. = capital; res = reserves; dep. = deposits; m.= million; brs = branches; amounts in £S unless otherwise indicated)

BANKING

Central Bank

Central Bank of Syria: place du 17 avril, Damascus; tel. (11) 2212642; fax (11) 2248329; e-mail info@bcs.gov.sy; internet www.banquecentrale.gov.sy; f. 1956; cap. and res 117.595m., dep. 375,169m. (Dec. 2005); Gov. Dr ADIB MAYALEH; 12 brs.

Other Banks

Agricultural Co-operative Bank: BP 4325, rue at-Tajehiz, Damascus; tel. and fax (11) 2213461; fax (11) 2241261; e-mail info@agrobank.org; internet www.agrobank.org; f. 1888; cap. 10,000m., res 671m., dep. 12,000m. (Dec. 2001); Chair. and Dir-Gen. YASSER AS-SAMOR; 106 brs.

Arab Bank Syria (ABS): BP 38, rue Al-Mahdi bin Barakeh, Abou Roumaneh, Damascus; tel. (11) 3348130; fax (11) 3349844; e-mail ali.zatar@arabbank-syria.com; internet www.arabbank.com; f. 2005; jt venture between Syrian investors (51%) and Arab Bank (Jordan—49%); private commercial bank; cap. 1,500.0m., res −20.7m., dep. 7,574.5m. (Dec. 2006); Gen. Man. ALI ZATAR; 4 brs.

Bank Audi Syria: Damascus; f. 2005; 47% owned by Audi Saradar Group (Lebanon), 26% by Syrian investors, 2% by a Saudi investor; remaining 25% oversubscribed in an initial public offering in Aug. 2005; private commercial bank; cap. 2,500.0m., res −38.2m., dep. 15,094.6m. (Dec. 2006); Dep. Chair. and Gen. Man. BASSEL HAMWI.

Bank of Syria and Overseas: BP 3103, Harika-Bab Barid, Lawyers' Syndicate Bldg, nr Chamber of Commerce, Damascus; tel. (11) 2460560; fax (11) 2460555; e-mail bsomail@bso.com.sy; internet www.bso.com.sy; f. 2004; jt venture between Banque du Liban et d'Outre Mer (BLOM, Lebanon—39%), the World Bank's International Finance Corporation (10%) and Syrian investors (51%); private commercial bank; cap. 3,000.0m., dep. 21,088.5m., total assets 25,949.9m. (Dec. 2005); Pres. Dr RATEB SHALLAH; Man. SAMEER BASSOUS; 11 brs.

Banque BEMO Saudi Fransi SA (BBSF): 39 rue Ayyar, Salhiah, Damascus; tel. (11) 2317778; fax (11) 2318778; e-mail bbsf@mail.sy; internet www.bbsfbank.com; f. 2004; jt venture between Syrian investors (51%), Banque Saudi Fransi (Saudi Arabia—27%) and Banque Européenne pour le Moyen-Orient (Lebanon—22%); private commercial bank; cap. 1,750m., res −75m., dep. 37,129m. (Dec. 2005);

Chair. ABD AR-RAHMAN JAWA; Vice-Chair. and CEO RIAD OBEGI; 10 brs.

Byblos Bank Syria: POB 5424, Al-Chaalan, rue Amin Loutfi Hafez, Damascus; tel. (11) 3348240; fax (11) 3348207; e-mail byblosbanksyria@byblosbank.com; internet www.byblosbank.com.lb/aboutbbkgroup/bbk_sa/board/index.shtml; f. 2005; 41.5% owned by Byblos Bank SAL (Lebanon), 51% by Syrian investors and 7.5% by the Organization of Petroleum Exporting Companies Fund for International Development; private commercial bank; cap. US $40m.; Chair. SEMAAN BASSIL; Dep. Gen. Man. WALID ABD AN-NOUR; 6 brs.

Commercial Bank of Syria: BP 933, place Yousuf al-Azmeh, Damascus; tel. (11) 2218890; fax (11) 2216975; e-mail tec.cbs@mail.sy; internet www.cbs-bank.com; f. 1967; govt-owned bank; cap. 70,000m., res 17,451m., dep. 473,667m. (Dec. 2006); Chair. and Gen. Man. Dr DOURAID AHMAD DERGHAM; 53 brs.

Industrial Bank: BP 7578, Immeuble Dar al-Mohandessin, rue Maysaloon, Damascus; tel. (11) 2228200; fax (11) 2228412; e-mail ind-bank@mail.sy; f. 1959; nationalized bank providing finance for industry; cap. 257m., total assets 8,131m. (Dec. 2001); Chair. and Gen. Man. MUHAMMAD ABU AN-NASSER; 13 brs.

The International Bank for Trade and Finance: place Hejazz, Damascus; tel. (11) 2460500; fax (11) 2460505; e-mail info@ibtf.com; internet www.ibtf.com.sy; f. 2004; 49% owned by Housing Bank for Trade and Finance (Jordan), 51% by Syrian investors; dep. 14,580.0m., total assets 16,843.7m. (Dec. 2005); private commercial bank; Chair. ABD AL-LATIF AL-KIP; Gen. Man. SULTAN AZ-ZU'BI; 16 brs.

Popular Credit Bank: BP 2841, 6e étage, Immeuble Dar al-Mohandessin, rue Maysaloon, Damascus; tel. (11) 2227604; fax (11) 2211291; f. 1967; govt-owned bank; provides loans to the services sector and is sole authorized issuer of savings certificates; Pres. and Gen. Man. MUHAMMAD HASSAN AL-HOUJJEIRI; 50 brs.

Real Estate Bank: BP 2337, place Yousuf al-Azmeh, Damascus; tel. (11) 2218602; fax (11) 2233107; e-mail realestate@realestate-sy.com; internet www.realestatebank-sy.com; f. 1966; govt-owned bank; provides loans and grants for housing, schools, hospitals and hotel construction; cap. 1,000m. (Dec. 2001); Chair. and Gen. Man. MUHAMMAD AHMAD MAKHLOUF; 15 brs.

Syrian Lebanese Commercial Bank SAL (SLCB): c/o Commercial Bank of Syria, BP 933, Immeuble G.M., 6e étage, place Youssef Azmeh, Damascus; tel. (11) 2225206; fax (11) 2243224; e-mail hamra@slcbk.com; internet www.slcb.com.lb; f. 1974; head office is in Beirut, Lebanon; Pres., Chair. and Gen. Man. Dr DOURAID AHMAD DERGHAM.

INSURANCE

Syrian General Organization for Insurance (Syrian Insurance Co): BP 2279, 29 rue Ayyar, Damascus; tel. (11) 2218430; fax (11) 2220494; e-mail chairman@syrian-insurance.com; internet www.syrian-insurance.com; f. 1953; auth. cap. 1,000m.; nationalized co; operates throughout Syria; Chair. and Gen. Man. GHASSAN BAROUDIT; Assistant Gen. Man. and Admin. Dir SULAYMAN AL-HASSAN.

Trade and Industry

STATE ENTERPRISES

Syrian industry is almost entirely under state control. There are national organizations responsible to the appropriate ministry for the operation of all sectors of industry, of which the following are examples:

Cotton Marketing Organization: BP 729, rue Bab al-Faraj, Aleppo; tel. (21) 2238486; fax (21) 2218617; f. 1965; governmental authority for purchase of seed cotton, ginning and sales of cotton lint; Pres. and Dir-Gen. Dr AHMAD SOUHAD GEBBARA.

General Company for Phosphate and Mines (GECOPHAM): BP 288, Homs; tel. (31) 420405; fax (31) 412961; e-mail gecopham@net.sy; f. 1970; production and export of phosphate rock; Gen. Dir Eng. FARHAN AL-HUHSSIN.

General Organization for Engineering Industries: POB 3120, Damascus; tel. (11) 2122650; fax (11) 2123375; e-mail g.o.eng.ind@net.sy; 13 subsidiary cos.

General Organization for the Exploitation and Development of the Euphrates Basin (GOEDEB): Rakka; Dir-Gen. Dr Eng. AHMAD SOUHAD GEBBARA.

General Organization for Food Industries (GOFI): BP 105, rue al-Fardous, Damascus; tel. (11) 2457008; fax (11) 2457021; e-mail foodindustry@mail.sy; internet www.syriafoods.net; f. 1975; food-processing and marketing; Chair. and Gen. Dir KHALIL JAWAD.

General Organization for the Textile Industries: BP 620, rue al-Fardoss, Bawabet As-Salhieh, Damascus; tel. (11) 2216200; fax (11) 2216201; e-mail syr-textile@mail.syr; internet textile.org.sy; f. 1975; control and planning of the textile industry and supervision of textile manufacture; 27 subsidiary cos; Dir-Gen. Dr JAMAL ALOMAR.

Syrian Petroleum Company (SPC): BP 2849, rue al-Moutanabbi, Damascus; tel. (11) 2228298; fax (11) 2225648; e-mail spcgenman@net.sy; internet www.spc-sy.com; f. 1958; state agency; holds the oil and gas concession for all Syria; exploits the Suweidiya, Karatchouk, Rumelan and Jbeisseh oilfields; also organizes exploring, production and marketing of oil and gas nationally; Gen. Man. Dr Eng. MUHAMMAD KHADDOUR.

    Al-Furat Petroleum Company: BP 7660, Damascus; tel. (11) 6183333; fax (11) 6184444; e-mail afpc@afpc.net.sy; internet www.afpc-sy.com; f. 1985; owned 50% by SPC and 50% by a foreign consortium of Syria Shell Petroleum Development B.V. and Deminex Syria GmbH; exploits oilfields in the Euphrates river area; Chair. SAID HUNEDI; Gen. Man. CAMPBELL KEIR.

DEVELOPMENT ORGANIZATIONS

State Planning Commission: Rukeneddin, Damascus; tel. (11) 5161015; fax (11) 5161010; e-mail info@planning.gov.sy; internet www.planning.gov.sy; Head ABDALLAH DARDARI.

Syrian Consulting Bureau for Development and Investment: BP 12574, 2nd Floor, Bldg 1, cnr Zuheir Ben Abi Sulma St and Ibin al-Khateeb St, Rawda, Damascus; tel. (11) 3345757; fax (11) 3340711; e-mail scb@scbdi.com; internet www.scbdi.com; f. 1991; independent; Man. Dir NABIL SUKKAR.

CHAMBERS OF COMMERCE AND INDUSTRY

Federation of Syrian Chambers of Commerce: BP 5909, rue Mousa Ben Nousair, Damascus; tel. (11) 3337344; fax (11) 3331127; e-mail syr-trade@mail.sy; internet www.fedcommsyr.org; f. 1975; Pres. Dr RATEB ASH-SHALLAH; Sec.-Gen. BASHAR NOURI.

Aleppo Chamber of Commerce: BP 1261, Aleppo; tel. (21) 2238236; fax (21) 2213493; e-mail alepchmb@mail.sy; internet www.aleppochamber.org; f. 1885; Pres. MUHAMMAD SALEH AL-MALLAH; Gen. Sec. MUHAMMAD MANSOUR.

Aleppo Chamber of Industry: BP 1859, rue al-Moutanabbi, Aleppo; tel. (21) 3620601; fax (21) 3620040; e-mail info@aleppo-coi.org; internet www.aleppo-coi.org; f. 1935; Pres. GHASSAN KRAYEM; Gen. Man. MUHAMMAD GHREWATI; 7,705 mems.

Alkalamoun Chamber of Commerce: BP 2507, rue Bucher A. Mawla, Damascus; fax (11) 778394; Pres. M. SOUFAN.

Damascus Chamber of Commerce: BP 1040, rue Mou'awiah, Damascus; tel. (11) 2211339; fax (11) 2225874; e-mail dcc@net.sy; internet www.dcc-sy.com; f. 1890; Pres. Dr RATEB ASH-SHALLAH; Gen. Sec. BASHAR NOURI; 11,500 mems.

Damascus Chamber of Industry: BP 1305, rue Harika Mou'awiah, Damascus; tel. (11) 2215042; fax (11) 2245981; e-mail dci@mail.sy; internet www.dci-syria.org; Pres. Eng. IMAD GHRIWATI; Sec. Eng. AYIMEN MAOULAWI.

Hama Chamber of Commerce and Industry: BP 147, rue al-Kouatly, Hama; tel. (33) 525203; fax (33) 517701; e-mail hamacham@scs-nct.org; f. 1934; Pres. HAMZEH KASSAB BASHI; Dir ABD AR-RAZZAK AL-HAIT.

Homs Chamber of Commerce and Industry: BP 440, rue Abou al-Of, Homs; tel. (31) 471000; fax (31) 464247; e-mail homschamber@homschamber.org; f. 1928; Pres. Dr Eng. ADEL TAYYARA; Dir M. FARES AL-HUSSAMY.

Latakia Chamber of Commerce and Industry: 8 rue Attar, Latakia; tel. (41) 479531; fax (41) 478526; e-mail lattakia@chamberlattakia.com; internet www.chamberlattakia.com; Pres. KAMAL ISMAIL AL-ASSAD.

Tartous Chamber of Commerce and Industry: POB 403, Tartous; tel. (43) 329852; fax (43) 329728; e-mail contact@souria.com; Pres. WAHIB KAMEL MERI; Vice-Pres. ABD AL-KADR SABRA.

EMPLOYERS' ORGANIZATIONS

Fédération Générale à Damas: Damascus; f. 1951; Dir TALAT TAGLUBI.

Fédération de Damas: Damascus; f. 1949.

Fédération des Patrons et Industriels à Lattaquié: Latakia; f. 1953.

Order of Syrian Engineers and Architects: BP 2336, Immeuble Al Mohandessin, place Azmeh, Damascus; tel. (11) 2214916; fax (11) 2216948; e-mail osea@net.sy; Pres. M. FAYEZ MAHFOUZ.

UTILITIES

Electricity

Public Establishment for Electricity Generation and Transmission (PEEGT): BP 3386, rue Nessan 17, Damascus; tel. (11)

SYRIA — Directory

2229654; fax (11) 2229062; e-mail peegt@net.sy; f. 1965; renamed 1994; state-owned; operates 11 power stations through subsidiary companies; Dir-Gen. Dr AHMAD AL-ALI.

TRADE UNIONS

General Federation of Labour Unions (Ittihad Naqabat al-'Ummal al-'Am fi Suriya): BP 2351, rue Qanawat, Damascus; f. 1948; Chair. 'Izz AD-DIN NASIR; Sec. MAHMOUD FAHURI.

Transport

RAILWAYS

In 2004 the railway system totalled 2,460 km of track.

Syrian Railways: Ministry of Transport, BP 182, Aleppo; tel. (21) 2294602; fax (21) 2283162; e-mail info@cfssyria.org; internet www.cfssyria.org; f. 1897; Pres. and Dir-Gen. Eng. MUHAMMAD IYAD GHAZAL.

General Organization of the Hedjaz-Syrian Railway: BP 2978, rue Hedjaz, Damascus; tel. (11) 3331625; f. 1908; the Hedjaz Railway has 347 km of track (gauge 1,050 mm) in Syria; services operate between Damascus and Amman, on a branch line of about 24 km from Damascus to Katana, and there is a further line of 64 km from Damascus to Serghaya; Dir-Gen. S. AHMED.

ROADS

Arterial roads run across the country linking the north to the south and the Mediterranean to the eastern frontier. In 2004 Syria's total road network was 48,767 km, including 36,412 km of highways, main or national roads and 9,711 km of secondary roads. In the late 1990s work was scheduled to commence on the first stage of a project costing £S1,800m. to improve the road linking Rakka with Deir ez-Zor. In 2001 the Syrian Government awarded a contract for the construction of a 100-km, four-lane highway, connecting the eastern port town of Latakia with Ariba in the northern governorate of Aleppo, at an estimated cost of US $207m. The project was to be financed by loans from the Kuwaiti-based Arab Fund for Economic and Social Development and the Kuwait Fund for Arab Economic Development.

General Co for Roads: BP 3143, Aleppo; tel. (21) 555406; f. 1975; Gen. Man. Eng. M. WALID EL-AJLANI.

PIPELINES

The oil pipelines that cross Syrian territory are of great importance to the national economy, representing a considerable source of foreign exchange. In the early 2000s a number of gas pipelines, linking gas fields in the Palmyra area to Aleppo and Lebanon, were under construction.

Syrian Co for Oil Transport (SCOT): BP 13, Banias; tel. (43) 711300; fax (43) 710418; f. 1972; Gen. Man. JIHAD HAMZEH.

SHIPPING

Latakia is the principal port; the other major ports are at Banias and Tartous.

General Directorate of Syrian Ports: BP 505, Latakia; tel. (41) 473333; fax (41) 475805; e-mail danco@net.sy; internet www.syrianports.com; Dir-Gen. Rear-Adm. MOHSEN HASSAN.

Syrian General Authorities for Maritime Transport (SYRIA-MAR): BP 730, 2 rue Argentina, Damascus; tel. (11) 3316418.

Abdulkader, Abu Bakr: Arwad, Latakia; operates a fleet of 5 general cargo vessels.

Delta Marine Transport: POB 1908, rue de Baghdad, Latakia; tel. (41) 222426; fax (41) 226047.

Ismail, A. M., Shipping Agency Ltd: BP 74, rue al-Mina, Tartous; tel. (43) 221987; fax (43) 318949; operates 8 general cargo vessels; Man. Dir MAHMOUD ISMAIL.

Latakia Port Authority: BP 220, rue Baghdad, Latakia; tel. (41) 476452; fax (41) 475760; e-mail lattakiaport@lattakiaport.com; internet www.lattakiaport.gov.sy; Gen. Man. SULEIMAN A. BALOUCH.

Muhieddine Shipping Co: BP 779, rue al-Mina, Tartous; tel. (43) 323090; fax (43) 317139; operates 7 general cargo ships.

Riamar Shipping Co Ltd: Al Kornish ash-Sharki, BP 284, Immeuble Tarwin, rue du Port, Tartous; tel. (43) 314999; fax (43) 212616; e-mail tarekg@scs-net.org; operates 6 general cargo vessels; Chair. and Man. Dir ABD AL-KADER SABRA.

Samin Shipping Co Ltd: BP 62, rue al-Mina, Tartous; tel. (43) 318835; fax (43) 318834; operates 10 general cargo ships.

Syro-Jordanian Shipping Co: BP 148, rue Port Said, Latakia; tel. (41) 471635; fax (41) 470250; e-mail syjomar@net.sy; f. 1976; operates 2 general cargo ships; transported 70,551 metric tons of goods in 1992; Chair. OSMAN LEBBADY; Tech. Man. M. CHOUMAN.

Tartous Port Authority: BP 86, Tartous; tel. (43) 225150; fax (43) 315602; e-mail ta-pco@mail.sy; internet www.tartousport.com.

CIVIL AVIATION

There are international airports at Damascus and Aleppo. The upgrading of Damascus airport to accommodate 28 aircraft and handle 3m. passengers per year, is planned, while Aleppo airport is to be upgraded to accommodate 12 aircraft and 1.5m. passengers per year.

Directorate-General of Civil Aviation: BP 6257, place Nejmeh, Damascus; tel. (11) 3331306; fax (11) 2232201.

Syrian Arab Airlines (Syrianair): BP 417, 5th Floor, Social Insurance Bldg, Youssef al-Azmeh Sq., Damascus; tel. (11) 2220700; fax (11) 224923; e-mail syr-air@syriatel.net; internet www.syriaair.com; f. 1946; refounded 1961 to succeed Syrian Airways, after revocation of merger with Misrair (Egypt); domestic passenger and cargo services (from Damascus, Aleppo, Latakia and Deir ez-Zor) and routes to Europe, the Middle East, North Africa and the Far East; Chair. and Man. Dir NACHAAT NUMIR.

Tourism

Syria's tourist attractions include a pleasant Mediterranean coastline, the mountains, town bazaars and antiquities of Damascus and Palmyra, as well as hundreds of deserted ancient villages in the north-west of the country. In 2005 some 5.8m. tourists visited Syria, and tourism receipts totalled US $2,283m.

Ministry of Tourism: BP 6642, rue Barada, Damascus; tel. (11) 2210122; fax (11) 2242636; e-mail min-tourism@mail.sy; internet www.syriatourism.org; f. 1972; Counsellor to the Minister SAWSAN JOUZY; Dir of Tourism Promotion and Marketing NIDAL MACHFEJ.

Middle East Tourism: BP 201, rue Fardoss, Damascus; tel. (11) 3325655; fax (11) 2246545; e-mail daadouche@net.sy; internet www.daadouche.com; f. 1952; Pres. MAHER DAADOUCHE; 7 brs.

Syrian Arab Co for Hotels and Tourism (SACHA): BP 5549, Mezzeh, Damascus; tel. (11) 2223286; fax (11) 2219415; f. 1977; Chair. DIRAR JUMA'A; Gen. Man. ELIAS ABOUTARA.

TAJIKISTAN

Introductory Survey

Location, Climate, Language, Religion, Flag, Capital

The Republic of Tajikistan is situated in the south-east of Central Asia. To the north and west it borders Uzbekistan, to the north-east Kyrgyzstan, to the east the People's Republic of China and to the south Afghanistan. The climate varies considerably according to altitude. The average temperature in January in Khujand (lowland) is −0.9°C (30.4°F); in July the average is 27.4°C (81.3°F). In the southern lowlands the temperature variation is somewhat more extreme. Rainfall is low in the valleys, in the range of 150–250 mm (6–10 ins) per year. In mountain areas winter temperatures can fall below −45°C (−51°F); the average January temperature in Murgab, in the mountains of south-east Kuhistoni Badakhshon, is −19.6°C (−3.3°F). Levels of rainfall are very low in mountain regions, seldom exceeding 60–80 mm (2–3 ins) per year. The official language is Tajik, an Iranian language; the Constitution grants Russian the status of a language of inter-ethnic communication, and all ethnic groups are guaranteed the right to use their native languages freely. The major religion is Islam. Most Tajiks and ethnic Uzbek residents follow the Sunni tradition, but the Pamiris are mostly Isma'ilis, a Shi'ite sect. The national flag (proportions 1 by 2) consists of three horizontal stripes from top to bottom of red, white and green, with a stylized gold crown surmounted by seven gold stars arranged in a semicircle in the centre of the white stripe. The capital is Dushanbe.

Recent History

In 1918 northern Tajikistan (which had been part of the Russian Empire since the 19th century) was conquered by the Bolsheviks, and the territory was incorporated into the Turkestan Autonomous Soviet Socialist Republic (ASSR). However, Dushanbe and the other southern regions of Tajikistan (which were subject to the Emirate of Bukhara) did not come under the control of the Bolsheviks until 1921. Opposition to Soviet rule was led by the *basmachis* (local guerrilla fighters) and foreign interventionists. In 1924 the Tajik ASSR was established as a part of the Uzbek Soviet Socialist Republic (SSR), and in January 1925 the south-east of Tajikistan was designated a Special Pamir Region (later renamed the Kuhistoni Badakhshon—Gornyi Badakhshan Autonomous Viloyat) within the Tajik ASSR. On 16 October 1929 the Tajik ASSR became a full Union Republic of the USSR and was slightly enlarged by the addition of the Khujand district from the Uzbek SSR. Soviet rule brought economic and social benefits to Tajikistan, but living standards remained low, and cattle-breeding, the main occupation in the uplands, was severely disrupted by collectivization. During the repressions of the 1930s almost all ethnic Tajiks in the republican Government were replaced by Russians.

During the 1970s increased Islamic influence was reported, as was violence towards non-indigenous nationalities. In 1978 there were reports of an anti-Russian riot, involving some 13,000 people, and after 1979 there were arrests of some activists opposed to Soviet intervention in Afghanistan. As in other Central Asian republics of the USSR, the first manifestation of the policies of Mikhail Gorbachev, who came to power as Soviet leader in 1985, was a campaign against corruption. Rakhmon Nabiyev, who had been First Secretary of the Communist Party of Tajikistan (CPT) since 1982, was replaced in late 1985 by Kakhar Makhkamov, who accused his predecessor of tolerating nepotism and corruption. Censorship was relaxed, and there was increased debate in the media of perceived injustices—such as alleged discrimination against Tajiks in Uzbekistan, and the legitimacy of the Uzbekistani–Tajikistani boundary. Greater freedom of expression encouraged interest in Tajik (and Iranian) culture and in 1989 Tajik was declared the state language.

In February 1990, following reports that Armenian refugees from the conflict in Nagornyi Karabakh (see the chapter on Azerbaijan) were to be settled in the capital, Dushanbe, violence broke out at a protest rally, when about 3,000 demonstrators clashed with police. A state of emergency was declared, and more than 5,000 troops suppressed the demonstrations; 22 people were reported dead and 565 injured. The unrest prompted a more inflexible attitude towards political pluralism by the republic's leadership. Two nascent opposition parties, Rebirth (Rastokhez), which had been involved in the February demonstrations, and the Democratic Party of Tajikistan (DPT), were refused official registration, and the Islamic Rebirth Party (IRP) was denied permission to hold a founding congress. Opposition politicians were barred from contesting the elections to the republic's Supreme Soviet (Supreme Council—legislature), held in March; 94% of the deputies elected were members of the CPT. None the less, in an apparent concession to growing Tajik nationalism the Supreme Soviet adopted a declaration of sovereignty on 25 August. In November Makhkamov was elected to the new post of executive President of the Republic by the Supreme Soviet; his only opponent was Nabiyev.

The Tajikistani Government, possibly anxious about increased Turkic dominance in Central Asia, displayed enthusiasm for a new Union Treaty (effectively preserving the USSR), and 90.2% of eligible voters in the republic were reported to have voted for the preservation of the USSR in the all-Union referendum in March 1991. In August, however, before the Treaty could be signed, conservative communists staged a coup in the Soviet and Russian capital, Moscow. Makhkamov did not oppose the coup, and on 31 August, after it had collapsed, he resigned as President, following demonstrations, which continued throughout much of September. On 9 September, following the declarations of independence by neighbouring Uzbekistan and Kyrgyzstan, the Tajikistani Supreme Soviet voted to proclaim an independent state, the Republic of Tajikistan. Kadriddin Aslonov, the Chairman of the Supreme Council and acting President, issued a decree that banned the CPT and nationalized its assets. In response, the communist majority in the Supreme Council demanded Aslonov's resignation, declared a state of emergency in the republic and rescinded the prohibition of the CPT. Aslonov resigned, and was replaced by Nabiyev. Nabiyev was, however, rapidly obliged to make substantial concessions to the opposition, and in early October the Supreme Council rescinded the state of emergency, suspended the CPT and legalized the IRP. Shortly afterwards he resigned as acting President, in advance of the presidential election.

Seven candidates contested the direct presidential election, which took place on 24 November 1991. Attracting strong support in rural areas, Nabiyev won 57% of the votes cast, compared with 30% for the candidate favoured by the main opposition parties, Davlat Khudonazarov. Nabiyev took office in December. In late December Tajikistan signed the declaration establishing the Commonwealth of Independent States (CIS, see p. 215), the successor body to the USSR. In January 1992 a new Prime Minister, Akbar Mirzoyev, was appointed.

Anti-Government demonstrations began in Dushanbe in March 1992, initially prompted by Nabiyev's dismissal of Mamadayez Navzhuvanov, a prominent Badakhshoni, from the post of Minister of Internal Affairs. Protests against his dismissal were led by the group Lale Badakhshon, which advocated greater autonomy for the Pamiri peoples of the southern Kuhistoni Badakhshon Autonomous Viloyat. It was joined by Rebirth, the IRP and the DPT. Protesters demanding the resignation of Nabiyev and the Government remained encamped in the centre of Dushanbe for nearly two months; in response, the Government organized rival demonstrations, bringing supporters to the capital from the southern region of Kulob (Kulyab) and from Leninabad (later Khujand), in the north—the traditional areas of support for the CPT. In April members of the newly formed national guard loyal to Nabiyev opened fire on the demonstrators, killing at least eight people. In the following month the National Security Committee (NSC—the successor to the Soviet Committee for State Security—KGB) allegedly distributed weapons to pro-communist supporters, and the ensuing violent clashes escalated into civil war. Fighting in Dushanbe ended after Nabiyev negotiated a truce with opposition leaders and formed a new 'Government of National Reconciliation' led by Mirzoyev, in which eight of the 24 ministers were members of opposition parties. However, violent clashes erupted in Kulob Viloyat between pro-communist Kulobi forces, who opposed the President's compromise with the opposition, and members of

Islamist and democratic groups. In late May the conflict spread into Qurgonteppa Viloyat (the main base of support for the Islamist and democratic groups), where a Kulobi militia, the Tajik People's Front (TPF), led by Sangak Safarov, attempted to suppress the local forces of the informal Islamist-democratic coalition. The Kulobis alleged that their opponents were receiving weapons and assistance from Islamist groups in Afghanistan, and there were reports that Gulbuddin Hekmatyar, the leader of the Afghan *mujahidin* group, Hizb-i Islami, had established training camps in Afghanistan for Tajikistani fighters. The Islamist-democratic alliance, for its part, claimed that the ex-Soviet (Russian) garrisons were arming the pro-Government militias.

In August 1992 several members of the DPT and Lale Badakhshon were killed by Kulobi militia forces in Qurgonteppa. A violent conflict ensued between local members of the opposition and Kulobis, in which several hundred people were reportedly killed. Meanwhile, in Dushanbe anti-Government demonstrations resumed, and at the end of August demonstrators entered the presidential palace and took 30 officials hostage. In September Nabiyev was seized by opposition forces at Dushanbe airport, and was forced to announce his resignation. Akbarsho Iskandarov, the Chairman of the Supreme Council, temporarily assumed the responsibilities of Head of State. Mirzoyev also resigned, and Abdumalik Abdullojonov, a communist from Leninabad (later Soghd) Viloyat, was appointed acting Prime Minister. Iskandarov's administration, which had the support of all the main Islamist and democratic groups, had little influence, however, outside Dushanbe; much of the south of the country was under the control of the TPF militia, and some leaders of Leninabad Viloyat (which had a large Uzbek community) threatened to secede from Tajikistan if there was any attempt to introduce an Islamic state. In October the Islamist-democratic alliance's control of Dushanbe was threatened when forces led by Safarali Kenjayev, a former Chairman of the Supreme Soviet and a supporter of Nabiyev, entered the capital and attempted to seize power. Kenjayev briefly proclaimed himself Head of State, but his troops were forced to retreat by forces loyal to the regime. During the ensuing two months, however, Kenjayev's militias effectively enforced an economic blockade of the capital.

In November 1992, having failed to end the civil war, Iskandarov and the Government resigned. The legislature abolished the office of President, and Emomali Rakhmonov, a collective-farm chairman from Kulob Viloyat, was appointed Chairman of the Supreme Council (equivalent to Head of State). The legislature appointed a new Government, in which Abdullojonov retained the post of Prime Minister. However, all members of the opposition parties lost their portfolios, and the majority of the new ministers were Kulobis or supporters of Nabiyev. The Supreme Council also voted to combine Qurgonteppa and Kulob Viloyats into one unit, based in Qurgonteppa, and to be known as Khatlon Viloyat, in an apparent attempt to ensure control of the south of the country by pro-communist Kulobi forces.

In December 1992 forces loyal to the new Government, the TPF and Kulobi militias, captured Dushanbe, hitherto under the control of the Popular Democratic Army (PDA), a recently formed military coalition of Islamist and democratic groups. Between December 1992 and January 1993 some 60,000 Tajikistanis fled to Afghanistan, after alleged reprisals against supporters of the democratic and Islamist forces. Among those who fled was the influential *qazi* (Islamic judge) of Tajikistan, Akbar Turajonzoda, a senior member of the IRP, who was accused by the new Government of attempting to establish an Islamist state. In February he was replaced as spiritual leader of Tajikistan's Muslims by Fatkhullo Sharifzoda, who was given the title of *mufti*.

In February 1993 insurgents in the central region of Garm attempted to declare an 'autonomous Islamic republic', but the Government had secured control of most of the country by March. The Government estimated that 30,000 people had been killed and some 800,000 people displaced during the civil war; however, other sources claimed that as many as 100,000 people had died. Although the civil war effectively ended in early 1993, the continued insurgency of Islamist-democratic forces, notably from across the Afghan border, continued to destabilize the country. Rebel resistance near Garm was ended in March. In June the Supreme Court formally proscribed the IRP, Lale Badakhshon, Rebirth and the DPT, leaving the CPT as the only legal party. Two new parties established later in the year—the Party of Economic Freedom and the People's Democratic Party of Tajikistan (PDPT)—were founded or sponsored by members of the Government or its associates.

In December 1993 Abdullojonov resigned as premier; he was replaced by Abdujalil Samadov. From the end of 1993 Rakhmonov, who secured for his own office responsibility for the powerful Ministries of Defence and Internal Affairs, as well as for the NSC (and, in February 1994, operational supervision of the broadcast media), began to show signs of compromise. In March he announced his willingness to negotiate with the Islamist-democratic opposition, and talks began in April in Moscow, under the auspices of the UN and in the presence of representatives from Iran, Pakistan, Russia and the USA. The negotiations resulted in a protocol on the establishment of a joint commission on refugees. However, reconciliation was far from having been achieved: from March border incursions from Afghanistan intensified, resulting in clashes with the CIS troops stationed on the frontier (see below), and there was renewed insurgency in Kuhistoni Badakhshon. The continuing conflict along the Tajikistani–Afghan border was interpreted by some observers as being partly a battle for control of drugs-smuggling routes: since securing independence Tajikistan had become a major conduit for illicit drugs (chiefly opium) from Pakistan, Iran and Afghanistan to Russia and western Europe.

In August 1994 the forthcoming presidential election was postponed, to allow time for opposition candidates to be included in the poll, and in September a temporary cease-fire was agreed, but did not come into effect until the following month after rebel forces launched a large-scale offensive in Tavil Dara, which was repelled by government troops. In December the UN Security Council authorized the deployment of a Mission of Observers in Tajikistan (UNMOT). When the election eventually took place on 6 November, the only two candidates were Rakhmonov and Abdullojonov. Some 85% of eligible voters were reported to have participated in the election, which was won by Rakhmonov, with some 58% of the votes cast; Abdullojonov received about 35% of the votes. The result reflected regional loyalties; Rakhmonov (a Kulobi) secured most of his support in the south, and Abdullojonov received a large proportion of the votes in Khujand and in Kuhistoni Badakhshon. In a concurrent referendum, some 90% of voters approved a new constitution. In December Jamshed Karimov was appointed as Chairman of the Council of Ministers.

In February 1995 renewed peace talks opened in Almaty, Kazakhstan, but little progress was achieved. Also in February the newly formed Party of Popular Unity and Accord (PPUA—led by Abdullojonov) announced that it would not contest the legislative elections scheduled to take place later that month, after Abdullojonov's candidature had been disallowed by the electoral authorities. The Organization for Security and Co-operation in Europe (OSCE, see p. 354) refused to send observers to the elections, claiming that the electoral law was severely flawed. Despite the opposition boycott, elections to the new Majlisi Oli (Supreme Assembly) took place on 26 February, with the participation of an estimated 84% of the electorate. In some 40% of constituencies there was only one candidate, and most of those elected were reported to be state officials loyal to the President, largely without party affiliation. A second round of voting was held on 12 March to decide 19 seats that had not been filled.

In March 1995 the opposition announced a unilateral, 50-day extension of the cease-fire, but later that month there were further attacks on border posts on the Tajikistani–Afghan frontier. In early April there was a serious escalation of the conflict in the region, and 34 border guards and 170 rebel troops were reportedly killed during one week of fighting. The opposition forces (comprising the IRP and Lale Badakhshon) claimed that they were responding to a large deployment of Tajikistani government troops and Russian border guards in Kuhistoni Badakhshon, in violation of the cease-fire agreement. The cease-fire was extended in late April, and again, for three months, in May. An exchange of prisoners was agreed at further talks in May. In July Rakhmonov met the leader of the IRP, Sayed Abdullo Nuri, and other opposition leaders for talks in Tehran, Iran, and in August the cease-fire was extended for six months. During the second half of 1995 conflict continued in the south of the country and on the border with Afghanistan. In September fighting was reported in Qurgonteppa between two military units, both formerly loyal to the Government. By the end of that month, when government forces regained control of the town, some 300 people had reportedly died. Further peace negotiations were convened, under UN auspices, in Aşgabat, Turkmenistan, in November. However, the opposition withdrew, in response to the Government's refusal to accede to its demand for the formation of a national reconciliation council to govern the country alongside Rakhmonov during a two-year transition period.

In January 1996 Sharifzoda was killed by gunmen. Although the Government accused the IRP of responsibility for his death, the opposition denied any involvement. At the end of January opposition forces began a major offensive in the Tavil Dara region of Kuhistoni Badakhshon, and military commanders of the government troops initiated rebellions in two towns. The western town of Tursunzoda was taken by forces under Ibodullo Boitmatov, and Makhmoud Khudoberdiyev took control of Qurgonteppa. The commanders (both ethnic Uzbeks) demanded changes to the Government, notably the removal of several Kulobi ministers. In early February Khudoberdiyev's troops approached Dushanbe, but retreated when they encountered government forces. Following negotiations, Rakhmonov agreed to the commanders' demands; Karimov was replaced as premier by Yakhyo Azimov.

Despite the announcement of an indefinite extension of the cease-fire, fighting intensified in March and April 1996 near Tavil Dara, where it was reported that Russian border guards and aircraft were supporting Tajikistani government troops in attacks on rebel forces; in May opposition forces captured the town of Tavil Dara. Talks resumed in Aşgabat in July. A cease-fire was brokered in Tavil Dara, and agreement was reached on the conduct of further peace negotiations and on a gradual exchange of prisoners of war. However, large-scale hostilities resumed around Tavil Dara and opposition forces regained control of the town in mid-August; meanwhile, government and rebel troops fought for command of the strategic central region of Tajikistan. A further cease-fire agreement was reached, but was almost immediately violated as fierce fighting continued around Garm. However, later that month, in Moscow, Rakhmonov and Nuri agreed to form a National Reconciliation Council (NRC), to be headed by a representative of what had come to be known as the United Tajik Opposition (UTO), comprising both Islamists and supporters of democracy. The NRC was to have extensive executive powers to revise legislation on elections, political parties and the media, to debate constitutional amendments and to monitor the implementation of the peace agreement. A general amnesty was agreed, as were terms for an exchange of prisoners and the repatriation of refugees.

Negotiations were held in Tehran in January 1997 to determine the structure and composition of the NRC, and at further UN-mediated peace talks held in Mashhad, Iran, in February, it was agreed that the NRC was to comprise 26 seats divided equally between the Government and the UTO. Negotiations on the reintegration of opposition forces into Tajikistan's military structures, the exchange of prisoners and the legalization of opposition parties were held in Moscow and Tehran throughout March and April. In April Rakhmonov was wounded in an assassination attempt in Khujand. The UTO denied any involvement and condemned the attack. Following talks held in Tehran later that month, a protocol was signed by government and UTO representatives, which guaranteed the provisions of the December 1996 peace agreement. These were confirmed in the General Agreement on Peace and National Accord in Tajikistan, signed by Rakhmonov and Nuri in Moscow on 27 June 1997, which formally ended the five-year civil conflict. In July Nuri was elected Chairman of the NRC, at its inaugural session; a policy of 'mutual forgiveness' was concluded, as well as an amnesty to allow UTO fighters to return to Tajikistan.

In September 1997, for the first time in five years, Nuri arrived in Dushanbe, to participate in the NRC. Some 200 UTO fighters were deployed in the capital to guard members of the NRC, sessions of which formally commenced in mid-September. Meanwhile, opposition to the agreement led to a series of minor bomb explosions in Dushanbe in early September. In October an attack on the barracks of the presidential guard, attributed to Makhmoud Khudoberdiyev, resulted in the deaths of at least 14 servicemen.

By mid-November 1997 some 10,000 Tajikistani refugees had been repatriated from Afghanistan. Meanwhile, negotiations were held between Nuri and Rakhmonov to determine the allocation of portfolios in the new government (under the terms of the peace agreement, the UTO was to receive one-third of posts in both the central and regional administrations). In January 1998 the UTO delegation to the NRC temporarily suspended its participation in the Council, claiming that the Government had failed to implement the terms of the peace agreement. In February, however, three portfolios, including those of Labour and Employment and of the Economy and Foreign Economic Relations, were formally allocated to UTO members. Turajonzoda, the deputy leader of the UTO, who had been living in exile in Iran, made his return to Tajikistan conditional on his appointment to the Government as a Deputy Chairman; he arrived in Tajikistan in late February, and was appointed First Deputy Chairman, with responsibility for relations with CIS countries.

In March 1998 several people, including the brother of the former Prime Minister, Abdullojonov, were sentenced to death for their part in the attempted assassination of Rakhmonov in April 1997. An upsurge in fighting between government and opposition forces, in the vicinity of Dushanbe, resulted in many civilian deaths. In April 1998 Rakhmonov, who had joined the PDPT in March, was elected Chairman of the party. In May a cease-fire was agreed, following the outbreak of fighting between government and opposition forces close to Dushanbe. In August Rakhmonov confirmed the appointment of several UTO members to government posts. However, other opposition appointments were rejected by the President, bringing the number of UTO members in the Government to 11, rather than the 14 agreed under the terms of the peace accord. At the end of August five local officials in western Tajikistan were killed; the Government reportedly blamed supporters of Khudoberdiyev. In September the trial of four men, said to be associates of Khudoberdiyev, accused of attempting to overthrow the Government in August 1997, began in Dushanbe. In late September 1998 a senior opposition member, Otakhon Latifi, was assassinated in the capital. Meanwhile, accusations by the Government of opposition involvement in the deaths of the four UNMOT workers in July prompted the UTO to announce its withdrawal from the Government and the NRC at the end of September. The crisis was defused after intensive talks between Rakhmonov and UTO representatives resulted in agreement on a 10-point programme (which included measures to ensure the safety of opposition groups and the formation of a joint commission to investigate Latifi's death) to accelerate the peace process. (In June 2000 a militant was imprisoned, having been found guilty of Latifi's murder.)

In October 1998 an operation by government forces against two rebel factions in Dushanbe resulted in some 13 deaths and the detention of six rebels. Heavy fighting was reported around Khujand in early November, in what was regarded as the most violent uprising since the 1997 peace agreement, following the seizure by Khudoberdiyev's forces of police and security headquarters and a nearby airport. An estimated 100–300 people were killed; some 500 were injured and a number of police-officers were taken hostage. Khudoberdiyev's forces were reportedly defeated after five days of fighting. President Rakhmonov accused Abdullojonov of having instigated the rebellion. Criminal proceedings were initiated against the former premier shortly afterwards, as well as against Khudoberdiyev and two other prominent figures.

In mid-November 1998 the Majlisi Oli endorsed the appointment of several UTO members to the Council of Ministers, including Zokir Vazirov as a Deputy Chairman and Davlat Usmon as Minister of the Economy and Foreign Economic Relations. In December 1998 Nuri announced that the UTO would disband its armed forces in early 1999. In March 1999 the re-registration of political parties was effected by the Ministry of Justice: of the eight parties previously registered, only five received new licences. Criminal charges against leading opposition party members, including Nuri and Turajonzoda, were abandoned, in accordance with the 1997 amnesty; 360 UTO members were thus granted immunity from prosecution. At the end of the month the Supreme Court sentenced seven supporters of Khudoberdiyev to 10–14 years' imprisonment, following their conviction on charges of involvement in the attack on government forces in October 1997.

The Majlisi Oli adopted a resolution in mid-May 1999 whereby the estimated 5,500 opposition fighters registered were to receive a general amnesty. In late May the UTO leadership withdrew from the NRC: among its demands were the holding of elections to the Majlisi Oli in 1999, in advance of the presidential election scheduled for November, and further UTO appointments to government posts (so that it held one-third of all government positions, as specified by the 1997 peace agreement). In June 1999 President Rakhmonov and Nuri signed an agreement outlining a timetable for the implementation of the provisions of the peace agreement; furthermore, four UTO members were appointed to government posts. In July Rakhmonov appointed another five UTO representatives to government positions. In the same month the President reportedly announced that 21 of the 69 local government posts would be offered to opposition members. In August the UTO leadership announced that the integration of its fighters into the regular armed forces had been completed. Rakhmonov responded later that month by lifting a ban on opposition parties and their media that had been imposed in 1993.

At a referendum held on 26 September 1999, some 72% of the votes cast by an estimated 92% of the electorate gave their endorsement to amendments to the Constitution, proposed by President Rakhmonov, which included: the formation of a bilateral legislature; the extension of the presidential mandate from five to seven years; and the legalization of religious-based political parties. The IRP was subsequently permitted to register as a political party. In October the UTO again temporarily withdrew from the NRC, alleging that pledges made by the Government had not been met and sought a postponement of the forthcoming presidential election, owing to the fact that three of its candidates had been prevented from contesting the presidency. Meanwhile, it was reported in mid-October that the First Deputy Prime Minister and deputy leader of the UTO, Turajonzada, had been expelled from the organization and its largest constituent party, the IRP, after dissenting from party policy.

In the presidential election, held on 6 November 1999, Rakhmonov received some 97.0% of the total votes cast, according to official sources, defeating his only opponent, Usmon. The rate of participation by the electorate was reported to be almost 99%. However, the opposition demanded that the election be declared invalid, owing to alleged electoral malpractice; the OSCE had again refused to send any monitors to the election. Following the inauguration of President Rakhmonov on 16 November, the Government tendered its resignation, although ministers remained in office until the formation of a new Government in late December. Akil Akilov was appointed Chairman of the Council of Ministers (Prime Minister).

In December 1999 the legislature approved the reorganization of the Majlisi Oli as a bicameral parliament. Although six political parties were registered to participate in forthcoming elections to the upper and lower chambers, it was reported that a number of opposition parties had been barred from contesting the poll. (The further re-registration of parties was carried out during the month.) In the elections to the new Majlisi Namoyandagon (Assembly of Representatives), the lower chamber of the Majlisi Oli, held on 27 February 2000, Rakhmonov's PDPT (with its allies) was reported to have won 64.5% of the total votes cast and secured 45 of the 63 seats. The CPT won around 20.6% of the votes (13 seats), while the IRP secured about 7.5% (two seats). According to official sources, some 93% of eligible voters participated in the election. There were claims by the OSCE and opposition parties that electoral malpractice had been widespread. Following the elections, Nuri made a formal complaint to Rakhmonov, the UN and the OSCE, alleging that the President had reneged on pledges made to him in November 1999 regarding electoral procedures. A second round of voting took place on 12 March 2000 for 11 constituencies in which the requisite quorum of 50% had not been achieved. Results in a further three constituencies had been declared invalid at the first round of voting; re-elections for two seats took place in April and December, respectively. Meanwhile, on 23 March indirect elections to the Majlisi Milliy (National Assembly), the legislative upper chamber, were held for the first time (25 members of the chamber were elected by regional deputies, with eight further members appointed by the President of the Republic). At the end of the month the NRC was dissolved. In May UNMOT announced the cessation of its peace-keeping activities and withdrew from the country. On 1 June it was succeeded, with the authorization of the UN Security Council, by the UN Tajikistan Office of Peacebuilding (UNTOP). In October a new currency, the somoni, was introduced, replacing the Tajik rouble, which had been in use since May 1995.

In December 2000 the Supreme Court suspended the activities of the Justice (Adolatkhoh) Party for six months; the party claimed that the ruling was a consequence of its opposition to the President during the legislative elections. In August 2001 the party was banned, after it failed to re-register its members during its period of suspension. Meanwhile, in April several bomb attacks took place, which killed at least four people. In June state security forces launched an attack against a group of militants, led by a former UTO field commander, Rakhmon Sanginov, near Dushanbe; it was reported that some 36 rebels were killed. In August Sanginov was killed by security forces, and at the end of the month officials claimed that only about 10 of his supporters remained at large.

In September 2001 the Minister of Culture, Press and Information, Abdurakhim Rakhimov, was assassinated; Karomatullo Olimov was appointed as his successor in October. It was reported in December that 10 men had been sentenced to between eight and 25 years' imprisonment on charges of treason, terrorism and sedition, relating to the November 1998 insurrection in Khujand. In January 2002 two new ministries were created—the Ministries of Industry and of State Revenues and Tax Collection. In March a public accord agreement, signed in 1996 by pro-Government political parties and non-governmental organizations to express support for the peace process, and renewed in 1999, was extended indefinitely; the accord was signed by a representative of the IRP for the first time.

Drugs-smuggling remained a significant problem in Tajikistan, at times apparently involving government officials as well as Islamist militants. In August 2002 the former Deputy Minister of Defence, Col Nikolai Kim, was sentenced to 13 years' imprisonment for drugs-trafficking and embezzlement while in office in 1998. Organized crime also remained a problem: in October 2002 a senior police official was sentenced to 25 years' imprisonment on charges of murder, fraud and extortion. Also in October two men were sentenced to death, and a further six were reported to have received terms of imprisonment of between two and 25 years, after being found guilty of belonging to an armed grouping loyal to Khudoberdiyev. It was reported that almost 75 supporters of Khudoberdiyev had been convicted since 1999.

In January 2003 President Rakhmonov carried out a major reorganization of the Council of Ministers and other government structures. On 22 June an estimated 96% of the electorate participated in a referendum on proposed amendments to the Constitution, which were approved by 93% of the votes cast. The amendments approved included: an extension of judges' terms of office from five to 10 years; the removal from the Constitution of references to religious parties; and the abolition of the right to both free health care and higher education. Significantly, Rakhmonov would also be permitted to stand for two further seven-year terms of office upon the expiry of his existing mandate in 2006.

A Deputy Chairman of the IRP, Shamsiddin Shamsiddinov, was arrested in May 2003, and in October he became the first person to be tried on charges relating to the period of civil conflict. Shamsiddinov's detention and trial was widely interpreted as a new initiative by the Government to suppress Islamist groups by accusing them of war crimes. Following a closed trial, in January 2004 Shamsiddinov was sentenced to 16 years' imprisonment. Meanwhile, in October 2003 the former commander of the interior ministry rapid-reaction forces, Maj. Shodi Alimadov, was sentenced to eight years in prison, after being convicted on charges of corruption, extortion and abuse of office. In December and in January 2004 Rakhmonov effected a number of high-level government changes. Notably, Jurabek Nurmakhmadov was appointed as Minister of Energy, in place of Abdullo Yorov.

In September 2004 20 members of the banned transnational militant Islamist group Hizb-ut-Tahrir al-Islami (Party of Islamic Liberation—Hizb-ut-Tahrir) were sentenced to prison terms ranging from six months to 15 years. (According to the Office of the Prosecutor-General, between 2000 and July 2005 209 people were convicted of membership of Hizb-ut-Tahrir; no person arrested on suspicion of belonging to the organization had been acquitted. In January 2006 it was reported that 99 suspected members of the movement had been detained in 2005, of whom 40 had been tried and sentenced.)

In January 2005 Rakhmonov removed Kozidavlat Koimdodov from the post of Deputy Prime Minister, appointing him ambassador to Turkmenistan. Zokir Vazirov was dismissed as Deputy Prime Minister in February, and appointed Minister of Labour, Employment and Social Welfare. Meanwhile, in January the Chairman of the DPT, Makhmadruzi Iskandarov, was denied permission to register as a candidate in the parliamentary elections scheduled for 27 February, owing to criminal charges; Iskandarov had been arrested in Moscow in December 2004, accused of corruption and involvement in an attack on the Tajikabad region Ministry of Internal Affairs and prosecutor's offices in August; the DPT asserted that the arrest was politically motivated. Sulton Kuvvatov, the leader of the Union and Development Party (which had been denied registration in March 2004), was also detained and refused permission to register as a candidate in the elections, having been accused of insulting

Rakhmonov and inciting ethnic hatred. In January 2005 a car bomb explosion outside the Ministry of Emergency Situations and Civil Defence in Dushanbe killed the driver of the vehicle and injured several others. A further bomb outside the same ministry in June injured four people. In January 2006 the Minister of Internal Affairs, Khomiddin Sharipov, announced the completion of an investigation into the two bombings. At least two people suspected of organizing the attacks were still to be apprehended, but a number of others, believed to be members of the militant Islamist group, the Islamic Movement of Uzbekistan (IMU), had been imprisoned; one of the suspected IMU members was reported to have committed suicide while in detention.

Six political parties participated in the elections to the Majlisi Namoyandagon held on 27 February and 13 March 2005. Rakhmonov's PDPT reportedly won 74% of the votes cast nation-wide to decide the allocation of seats on the basis of party lists, securing a total of 52 of the 63 seats in the chamber. The CPT won 13% of the national vote on the basis of party lists (four seats in total), while the IRP secured 8% (two seats). A reported 92.6% of the electorate participated in the poll. The OSCE (and opposition parties) claimed that electoral malpractice was widespread and that amendments to the constitutional law on elections adopted in July 2004 had not been fully implemented. Several members of the IRP and other opposition parties received prison sentences, widely believed to be politically motivated, after being found guilty of charges of hooliganism, defamation and embezzlement. The first session of the newly elected Majlisi Namoyandagon was held on 17 March 2005. Indirect elections to the Majlisi Milliy took place on 24 March, and the eight presidential nominees were announced the following day. The first session of the new upper chamber convened on 15 April.

In late April 2005 it was reported that a former Minister of the Interior, Yakub Salimov, who had been extradited from Russia in February 2004, had been sentenced to 15 years' imprisonment for treason, after a five-month closed trial. Meanwhile, in early April 2005 the Russian authorities released Iskandarov, owing to a lack of evidence, after refusing a request by Tajikistan for his extradition. However, Iskandarov was arrested in Dushanbe later that month; he claimed to have been kidnapped in Russia and brought to Tajikistan by unknown individuals. After the Russian and Tajikistani authorities failed to clarify the details of Iskandarov's transfer to Tajikistan, the DPT announced in May its temporary withdrawal from the Public Council (a body established in 1994 by Rakhmonov, and usually comprising social and cultural organizations and five of Tajikistan's six officially registered parties); in addition, the DPT criticized alleged malpractice during the legislative elections. The IRP and CPT subsequently also announced their withdrawal from the Public Council, in protest at the conduct of the elections.

In June 2005 the deputy leader of the Union and Development Party was found guilty of provoking ethnic discord and insulting President Rakhmonov, whom he had accused of genocide: he was sentenced to almost six years' imprisonment. In October the Supreme Court sentenced Iskandarov to 23 years' imprisonment, after he was found guilty of charges of terrorism, embezzlement and the possession of illegal weapons. Iskandarov vehemently denied the charges, but in January 2006 the verdict was upheld by the court of appeal. In March the Chairman of the opposition Social Democratic Party of Tajikistan (SDPT), Rakhmatullo Zoyirov, declared that there were some 1,000 political prisoners in Tajikistan. Also in March the European Union (EU, see p. 244) released a statement in which it expressed concern at the unclear circumstances surrounding Iskandarov's transfer from Russia to Tajikistan, and at allegations that he was mistreated prior to his trial.

There was considerable concern regarding the freedom of the media in 2005. Media representatives accused state officials of withholding information from and threatening journalists, and no independent newspapers or magazines were registered. The authorities reportedly prevented several independent newspapers and printing houses from publishing, and in April a privately owned television station was closed, ostensibly for failing to submit the requisite documentation. Meanwhile, in November two new political parties were registered: the Party of Economic Reforms and the Agrarian Party of Tajikistan. Zoyirov asserted that the organizations were instruments of the Government. In August 2006 the former commander of the presidential guard, Lt-Gen. Gaffor Mirzoyev, was sentenced to life imprisonment, following his conviction, by a closed trial, on charges of terrorism and of conspiring to overthrow the Government. Also in August Nuri died, and in the following month Muhiddin Kabiri was elected as Chairman of the IRP in his stead

A presidential election, which was contested by five candidates, took place on 6 November 2006; Rakhmonov was re-elected to office, with 79.3% of the votes cast, while Olimjon Boboyev of the Party of Economic Reforms, with only 6.2% of votes cast, was the second-placed candidate. The OSCE declared that the elections failed to meet international standards. A new Council of Ministers was announced by presidential decree on 1 December and approved by the Majlisi Oliy on 16 December; additionally, 10 ministries and government agencies were either dissolved or merged with other ministries and agencies. Ministers who retained their portfolios from the previous Government included Prime Minister Akilov (who was also appointed Minister of Construction), Deputy Prime Minister Asadullo Ghulomov and Minister of Defence Maj.-Gen. Sherali Khayrulloyev. Notable changes included the appointment of Hamrokhon Zaripov, former Tajikistani ambassador to the USA, as Minister of Foreign Affairs, and that of Mahmadnazar Solehov as Minister of Internal Affairs, succeeding Sharipov. Izbillo Khojayev became Chairman of the Constitutional Court, and was replaced as Chairman of the Supreme Court by Nasratullo Abdulloyev. In January 2007 a new Agency for State Financial Control and Suppression of Corruption was established by presidential decree; Sherkhon Salimov, a representative of the PDPT in the Majlisi Namoyandagon, was chosen to head the new agency.

In mid-January 2007 Procurator-General Bobojon Bobokhonov announced that 10 opposition and Islamist organizations had been banned, owing to their alleged extremist disposition. In early February the DPT was refused registration by the Ministry of Justice, on the grounds of apparently inconsistent statements within the party's founding statute. The DPT immediately declared that it would appeal against the decision. At the same time a reorganization of the Ministry of Internal Affairs, including the foundation of a new Migration Service, was announced.

In mid-March 2007 the Ministry of Justice requested that the SDPT submit papers regarding its financing; in mid-April the Ministry reported that it had not received the requested documentation and announced that it would be filing a complaint with the Supreme Court to suspend the activities of the SDPT. However, the legal challenge was withdrawn in late April since, according to the Ministry of Justice, the SDPT had rectified the discrepancies in registration. Meanwhile, in March President Rakhmonov announced that he was to abandon the Russian-style '-ov' suffix from his surname and that henceforth he wished to be known as Emomali Rakhmon, on the grounds that it was more 'Tajik'. Minister of Foreign Affairs Zaripov made a similar declaration in April, stating that he wished to be known as Hamrokhon Zarifi, and parents were encouraged to follow this example when naming their children. Other presidential decrees issued at this time were aimed primarily at schools, including the introduction of a new dress-code (reinforcing, *inter alia*, a prohibition on women wearing headscarves that had been introduced in 2005) and the abolition of Soviet-era holidays. In July the mandate of UNTOP was officially concluded. In November it was reported that the central government offices complex in Dushanbe had been damaged in a bomb explosion, in which one civilian had been killed; the perpetrators of the attack remained unknown. In January 2008 President Rakhmon removed three ministers in a government reorganization and also replaced serval public senior state officials, after criticizing their failure to address increasing energy shortages. By February a critical humanitarian situation had developed in the country, as a result of severe weather conditions, together with continuing energy shortages, necessitating substantial humanitarian assistance. In April the authorities ordered the closure of an independent radio station, Radio Imruz (Today), purportedly on technical grounds; Radio Imruz, having reported on public discontent, and social and economic difficulties since it commenced broadcasting in Dushanbe in the previous year, had been perceived as unusually critical of the authorities.

After the dissolution of the USSR, Russian troops remained in Tajikistan, officially adopting a neutral stance during the civil war. However, following the communist victory in Dushanbe in December 1992, they openly assisted pro-communist troops in quelling the opposition forces, and the Tajikistani Government became increasingly dependent on Russia, both militarily and economically. In January 1993 Russia, Kazakhstan, Kyrgyzstan and Uzbekistan committed themselves to the defence of Tajikistan's southern frontiers, thus supporting the Government in the continuing conflict on the Tajikistani–Afghan border. In practice, mainly Russian troops were responsible for repelling rebel fighters entering Tajikistan, with Russia defending the southern CIS border as if it were its own. In August Russia and the Central Asian states (excluding Turkmenistan) signed an agreement establishing a CIS peace-keeping force to police Tajikistan's border with Afghanistan.

Despite Russia's involvement in the civil conflict in Tajikistan, it also sought to mediate between the Government and the opposition leadership in exile. During 1994–95 relations between the Russian authorities and the Rakhmonov regime deteriorated. However, in 1996 and 1997 Russia hosted several rounds of the UN-sponsored negotiations for a political settlement in Tajikistan, which culminated in the signature of the peace agreement in Moscow in June 1997. In April 1999 Russia and Tajikistan signed an agreement on the establishment of a Russian military base in Tajikistan; in the same month nine major bilateral agreements were signed, including a Treaty of Alliance and Co-operation. In October 2004 Russia officially opened a military base in Tajikistan and took formal control of the Nurek space monitoring centre, after a meeting between the Russian President, Vladimir Putin, and President Rakhmonov; in return, Russia agreed to cancel US $242m. of Tajikistan's $300m. debt to Russia.

During the civil conflict in Tajikistan, the leadership of Uzbekistan provided military and political support to the Rakhmonov administration. In October 1994 Tajikistan and Uzbekistan signed a Co-operation Agreement envisaging greater bilateral co-ordination, especially in foreign policy and security. However, the Uzbekistani Government reportedly criticized the treatment of the Uzbek ethnic minority in Tajikistan, alleging that many ethnic Uzbeks had been replaced in their posts by Kulobis. None the less, Uzbekistan continued to provide considerable technical and military support for the Tajikistani administration. Following the signature of the peace agreement in June 1997, the Uzbekistani leadership expressed renewed concern at the possible Islamicization of Tajikistan. Further tensions arose in August 1999, when northern Tajikistan came under attack by unidentified aircraft, which, according to the Tajikistani leadership, belonged to Uzbekistani forces, which were assisting Kyrgyzstan in repelling a group of Islamist militants in that country's nearby Osh region, in the Farg'ona valley. (The Uzbekistani Government subsequently admitted that its forces might accidentally have bombed the territory.) In April 2000 Tajikistan was strongly criticized by the Uzbekistani and Kyrgyzstani Governments for failing to expel the leader of a group of Uzbek anti-Government Islamist rebels, who had allegedly established a permanent base in Tajikistan. Armed incursions into those two countries by insurgents commenced in August. By the end of 2000 hostilities had subsided, although occasional violent incidents continued to be reported. In March 2001, in response to a claim by the Kyrgyzstani Government that Tajikistan harboured some 2,500 international terrorists, the Tajikistani Government declared there to be no members of any rebel organization on its territory, and invited the Kyrgyzstani Government to examine its borders. Uzbekistan, which had begun laying landmines along its border with Tajikistan from mid-2000, in an effort to prevent cross-border incursions by Islamist insurgents, officially informed Tajikistan of its actions only in May 2001. At the end of the month a Tajikistani border official accused Uzbekistan of violating international law by planting mines along the Tajikistani–Uzbekistani border, which had not been delineated in mountainous areas; it was further observed that, thus far, all of the casualties had been Tajikistani and Uzbekistani citizens. However, bilateral relations subsequently improved. President Rakhmonov visited President Karimov of Uzbekistan in December; it was announced that a crossing between the Penjakent region of Tajikistan and Uzbekistan's Samarqand region was to reopen, and the two leaders also agreed to collaborate to combat terrorism, crime and drugs-trafficking. In February 2002, at a meeting of the Tajikistani and Uzbekistani premiers, an agreement on border-crossing procedures was reached. In October a border agreement was signed by Presidents Rakhmonov and Karimov, although four areas in the northern Soghd Viloyat remained in dispute. None the less, landmines on the border with Uzbekistan continued to kill civilians and border guards in the mid-2000s, and the Government was co-operating with international organizations to remove the devices.

Tajikistan had begun to develop relations outside the USSR before its dissolution in 1991, notably with Iran, with which the Tajiks have strong ethnic and linguistic ties. However, the effective collapse of central authority in Tajikistan in 1992 severely hindered further development of foreign relations, although several states attempted to influence the progress of the country's civil war. Anti-Islamist groups in Tajikistan asserted that Iran was supplying armaments and other goods to Islamist elements in Tajikistan, but the Iranian authorities insisted that they were providing only cultural and humanitarian assistance. In July 1995 President Rakhmonov visited Tehran, where a number of agreements on cultural and economic co-operation were signed. Further agreements were signed in late 1996, providing for Iranian investment in Tajikistan's industrial and agricultural sectors, followed by economic, cultural and defence accords in late 1998. UN-sponsored peace negotiations between Tajikistani government and opposition representatives were held in Tehran in 1996 and 1997. In April 2002 Tajikistan and Iran signed nine protocols on co-operation in economic, political and social affairs. In April 2005 the two countries signed a memorandum of understanding on enhanced co-operation in defence matters, and for the provision, *inter alia*, of equipment and training for Tajikistani military personnel. Iran explained the agreement as an attempt to prevent 'external powers' from increasing their military presence in the region and threatening Iranian national security, widely interpreted as an intention to prevent the USA from securing control of additional military bases in Central Asia.

Relations with Afghanistan were strained by the apparent inability of the Afghan Government to prevent *mujahidin* fighters and consignments of weapons from crossing the frontier into Tajikistan. The election of the largely pro-communist Tajikistani Government in late 1992 further strained bilateral relations, and in April 1993 the Tajikistani Government protested to the Afghan authorities about alleged incursions across the border by Afghans, apparently to assist rebel troops. In December the Afghan President, Burhanuddin Rabbani, made an official visit to Tajikistan, which resulted in the signature of a bilateral friendship and co-operation treaty, as well as agreements on economic co-operation and border security. A tripartite agreement was signed, together with the office of the UN High Commissioner for Refugees, on the safety of refugees returning to Tajikistan. In April 1995 Afghanistan protested strongly against alleged Russian attacks on rebel bases within Afghanistan, and continued to deny any official support of rebel Tajik factions within the country. The widespread victory of Taliban forces in Afghanistan in that year threatened to destabilize the fragile situation in Tajikistan and, as the Taliban increased their territorial gains in northern Afghanistan, there was increasing concern in Tajikistan and neighbouring countries, which feared an influx of large numbers of refugees. In July 1998, while heavy fighting occurred close to Tajikistan's border with Afghanistan, the frontier was reinforced by Russian troops. As fighting escalated in Afghanistan in September 2000, the Tajikistani Government closed its border with that country.

Following the suicide attacks on the USA of 11 September 2001, attributed to the al-Qa'ida (Base) organization of the Saudi Arabian-born Islamist militant Osama bin Laden, Russian troops along the Tajikistani–Afghan border were placed on a state of alert, in anticipation of military strikes against Afghanistan by the USA and allied countries. Although Rakhmonov announced his willingness to co-operate with the USA, both Tajikistan and Russia initially dismissed the possibility of Tajikistani territory being used as a base for any US-led military action; however, US specialists were granted entry to the country to oversee the distribution of humanitarian aid to Afghanistan. The Tajikistani Government declared its support for the aerial bombardment of Taliban and al-Qa'ida targets in Afghanistan, which commenced on 7 October, and in early November it was confirmed that Tajikistan had permitted US troops and forces of the North Atlantic Treaty Organization (NATO, see p. 340) to utilize three of its airbases. In January 2002 it was announced that US restrictions on the transfer of defence equipment to Tajikistan, imposed in 1993, had been lifted. In February 2002 Tajikistan joined NATO's 'Partnership for Peace' programme of military co-operation. In October 2004 the Secretary-General of NATO, Jaap de Hoop Scheffer, signed a bilateral transit agreement with Rakhmonov in support of NATO's International Security Assistance Force in Afghanistan. In December Russia began to transfer military control of the Pamir stretch of the Tajikistani–Afghan border to the Tajikistani authorities. The transfer was completed in September 2005; however, a Russian task force was to remain in Tajikistan, and

Russia was to continue to train Tajikistan's border guards. Throughout the transfer, concern had been expressed at a possible increase in the cross-border smuggling of drugs from Afghanistan, and later in September international donors signed an agreement with Tajikistan on the security of the Tajikistani–Afghan border, according to which Tajikistan was to be provided with installations, equipment and training to help manage its borders. In early October the Majlisi Namoyandagon ratified a bilateral security agreement with Afghanistan on co-operation in countering terrorism, extremism and transnational organized crime. In August 2007 the Presidents of Tajikistan and Afghanistan inaugurated a bridge across the river Pyanzh at the border between the two countries; construction of the 680m-long bridge, which had cost US $37m., was funded principally by the US authorities.

In the mid-1990s Tajikistan sought to develop relations with other Asian states, in particular the People's Republic of China. In April 1996 Tajikistan signed (together with Russia, Kazakhstan and Kyrgyzstan) a wide-ranging border agreement with China. This was supplemented by a further border accord, signed in August 1999. In January 2002 Tajikistan signed a further treaty with China, resolving contentious issues regarding the two countries' joint border on the edge of Kuhistoni Badakhshon, and in mid-May Tajikistan signed a border agreement, conceding 1,000 sq km of disputed territory to China. Meanwhile, in April 1997 an agreement on confidence-building measures in the military sphere was concluded. Members of the Shanghai Co-operation Organization (SCO, see p. 425), comprising China, Kazakhstan, Kyrgyzstan, Russia, Tajikistan and Uzbekistan, signed the Shanghai Convention on Combating Terrorism, Separatism and Extremism in mid-2001. At an emergency meeting in October of that year, the members agreed to establish an anti-terrorism centre. In September 2004 members of the SCO, meeting in Bishkek, Kyrgyzstan, agreed to increase co-operation in trade, science, technology, and humanitarian projects, as well as to improve anti-terrorism measures.

In March 2000 joint military exercises were conducted in southern Tajikistan by Kazakhstan, Kyrgyzstan, Tajikistan, Uzbekistan and Russia, as part of a joint commitment to combat international terrorism in the region. In May 2001 the signatory countries of the Collective Security Treaty—Armenia, Belarus, Kazakhstan, Kyrgyzstan, Russia and Tajikistan—formed a Rapid Reaction Force to combat Islamist militancy in Central Asia; in January 2002 it was announced that the force was ready to undertake combat missions. In March the Central Asian Economic Community, which Tajikistan joined in March 1998, was superseded by the Central Asian Co-operation Organization (CACO). In April 2003 the signatories of the Collective Security Treaty inaugurated a successor organization, known as the Collective Security Treaty Organization (CSTO). In April 1998 Tajikistan joined a customs union, already comprising Russia, Belarus, Kazakhstan and Kyrgyzstan. In October 2000 a new economic body, the Eurasian Economic Community (EURASEC, see p. 412), was established to supersede the customs union, and this organization merged with CACO in January 2006. In October 2007 EURASEC held a meeting in Dushanbe, when Tajikistan assumed the rotational chairmanship of the organization. EURASEC leaders approved the legal basis for the establishment of a new customs union that was initially to comprise Belarus, Kazakhstan and Russia, with Kyrgyzstan, Tajikistan and Uzbekistan expected to join by 2011.

Government

Under the Constitution of November 1994 (to which a number of amendments were passed in September 1999 and June 2003), Tajikistan has a presidential system of government. The President is Head of State and also heads the executive branch of power. The President appoints a Prime Minister (or Chairman) to head the Government (Council of Ministers). Legislative power is vested in the 63-member lower chamber, the Majlisi Namoyandagon (Assembly of Representatives), and the upper chamber, the Majlisi Milliy (National Assembly), which has a minimum of 33 members. For administrative purposes, the country is divided into three viloyats (regions or oblasts): Soghd (known as Leninabad in 1936–92, and subsequently Khujand, until 2000), in the north; Khatlon (formerly the two viloyats of Kulob and Kurgan-Tyube), in the south; and the nominally autonomous viloyat of Kuhistoni Badakhshon. These regions are further subdivided into districts and towns. The city of Dushanbe has a separate status. Three cities and 10 districts of central Tajikistan are not incorporated into any of the viloyats, and are known as the Regions of Republican Subordination.

Defence

Following the dissolution of the USSR in December 1991, Tajikistan became a member of the Commonwealth of Independent States (CIS, see p. 215) and its Collective Security Treaty. In April 2003 the Collective Security Treaty Organization (CSTO) was inaugurated as the successor to the CIS collective security system, with the participation of Armenia, Belarus, Kazakhstan, Kyrgyzstan, Russia and Tajikistan. A Ministry of Defence was established in September 1992; in December it was announced that Tajikistan's national armed forces were to be formed on the basis of the Tajik People's Front and other paramilitary units supporting the Government. Integration of United Tajik Opposition (UTO) force members into the Tajikistani armed forces took place from 1998. Military service lasts for 24 months (12 months for those with higher-education degrees). As assessed at November 2007, the armed forces numbered 8,800, comprising an army of 7,300 and an air force of 1,500. Some 7,500 paramilitary border guards were attached to the Ministry of Internal Affairs. There were plans to form an Air Force squadron. The budget for 2007 allocated an estimated 300m. somoni to defence. Tajikistan became a member of the North Atlantic Treaty Organization's 'Partnership for Peace' (see p. 342) programme of military co-operation in February 2002.

Economic Affairs

In 2006, according to estimates by the World Bank, Tajikistan's gross national income (GNI), measured at average 2004–06 prices, was US $2,572m., equivalent to $390 per head (or $1,410 per head on an international purchasing-power parity basis). During 1996–2006, it was estimated, the population increased by an annual average of 1.3%, while gross domestic product (GDP) per head increased by an annual average of 5.9%, in real terms. Overall GDP increased, in real terms, by an average of 7.2% per year during 1996–2006. According to the Asian Development Bank (ADB, see p. 182), GDP increased by 7.8% in 2007.

Despite the fact that only 7% of Tajikistan's land is arable (the remainder being largely mountainous), the Tajikistani economy has traditionally been predominantly agricultural: agriculture contributed 24.2% of GDP in 2006, and provided 67.2% of employment in the same year. According to IMF estimates, the rural population accounted for some 72.4% of the total in 2000–03. The principal crop is grain, followed in importance by cotton, vegetables and fruit. Approximately 95% of the country's arable land is irrigated. Agricultural production was severely disrupted by the civil war. In 1996 proposals were announced to transfer collective and state farms to private ownership. However, although in mid-1998 legislation was passed to establish a centre to aid farm privatization, agricultural reform has proceeded slowly. The IMF estimated that 51% of Tajikistan's arable land was privately owned at the end of 2001. During 1996–2006 agricultural GDP increased, in real terms, by an average of 8.1% annually. Real agricultural GDP increased by 8.0% in 2006.

Industry (comprising manufacturing, mining, utilities and construction) contributed 26.6% of GDP in 2006, and provided 8.5% of employment in the same year. There is little heavy industry, except for mineral extraction, aluminium production and power generation. Light industry concentrates on food-processing, textiles and carpet-making. Industrial GDP increased, in real terms, by an annual average of 8.8% in 1996–2006. Sectoral GDP increased by 8.0% in 2005.

Tajikistan has considerable mineral deposits, including gold, antimony, silver, aluminium, iron, lead, mercury and tin. There are deposits of coal as well as reserves of petroleum and natural gas. Mineral extraction is hampered by the mountainous terrain.

The GDP of the manufacturing sector increased, in real terms, by an annual average of 8.2% in 1996–2006. Real manufacturing GDP increased by 8.0% in 2006.

Although imports of fuel and energy comprised 29.5% of the value of merchandise imports in 2001 (mainly supplied by Turkmenistan, Uzbekistan, Kazakhstan and Russia), Tajikistan is believed to have sufficient unexploited reserves of petroleum and natural gas to meet its requirements. The mountain river system is widely used for hydroelectric power generation, and Tajikistan is one of the largest producers of hydroelectric power world-wide. In 2004 hydroelectricity accounted for 97.7% of energy production. In January 2005 Tajikistan signed a protocol with Russia and Iran on the construction of two hydroelectric power plants, Sangtuda-1 (originally conceived in the 1980s, but work on which had been suspended owing to lack of funding) and Sangtuda-2. At the end of March Tajikistan also signed an agreement with Pakistan on the construction of a 700-km transmission line to transport electricity from Tajikistan's Roghun plant to Pakistan, from 2009. Construction work on Sangtuda-2 commenced in February 2006; both power stations were scheduled for completion in 2009. The completion of Sangtuda-1 was to be fully funded by Russia, and Iran was to provide significant funding for the construction of the Sangtuda-2 plant, ownership of which was to be secured by Tajikistan in 2018. Tajikistan imports some 90% of its gas requirements, principally from Uzbekistan. However, in February 2006 Uzbekistan announced that it was to reduce natural gas exports to Tajikistan by some 25%, because of the accumulation of arrears by Tojikgaz, the state-owned natural gas company.

The services sector contributed 49.3% of GDP in 2006, and provided 24.3% of employment in the same year. The GDP of the services sector increased, in real terms, by an annual average of 5.2% in 1996–2006; real services GDP increased by 8.0% in 2006.

In 2006, according to the IMF, Tajikistan recorded a visible trade deficit of US $442.8m., and there was a deficit of $21.4m. on the current account of the balance of payments. In 2006 the principal source of imports was Russia (accounting for 20.9% of the total); other important suppliers were Uzbekistan (10.4%), Kazakhstan (11.4%) and Azerbaijan (7.8%) The major market for exports in 2005 was the USA (accounting for 23.2% of the total); the Netherlands (15.5%), Turkey (10.9%) and Uzbekistan (8.1%) were also significant purchasers. The principal exports in 2002 were non-precious metals and mineral products; the principal imports were mineral products and chemicals.

According to the IMF, the planned budget for 2006 provided for an overall deficit of 380m. somoni, equivalent to 4.1% of GDP. Tajikistan's total external debt was US $1,022m. at the end of 2005, of which $785m. was long-term public debt. The cost of debt-servicing in that year was equivalent to 4.5% of the value of exports of goods and services. The average annual rate of inflation was 303.4% in 1990–2000. The rate of inflation was 12.5% in 2001 and 14.5% in 2002. According to the ADB, the rate of inflation was 13.1% in 2007. Figures from the ADB indicated that the rate of unemployment was 2.6% in 2007; however, other sources estimated the rate to be much higher.

In 1992 Tajikistan joined the Economic Co-operation Organization (ECO, see p. 238) and the European Bank for Reconstruction and Development (EBRD, see p. 239), as a 'Country of Operations'; it became a member of the IMF and the World Bank in 1993. In November 1996 Tajikistan joined the Islamic Development Bank (see p. 329) and it became a member of the ADB in 1998. In 2001 Tajikistan was granted observer status at the World Trade Organization (WTO, see p. 396).

Formerly the poorest of the republics of the former USSR, the Tajikistani economy was severely affected by the civil war that broke out in 1992. Following the conclusion of a peace agreement in 1997, international financial organizations allocated credit to assist in rebuilding the country's infrastructure. The country's economic performance improved significantly from 2000, although poverty remained widespread. According to a World Bank report published in October 2005, 74% of the population were living on less than US $2.15 per day in 2003, and it was estimated that some 900,000 Tajikistani citizens travelled to Russia each year to seek employment; remittances from abroad were estimated to account for some 20% of annual GDP. (In 2007 the National Bank of Tajikistan estimated the total value of remittances from abroad at $1,800m.) By 2005 some progress had been made in implementing structural reform, particularly in the banking and energy sectors. Moreover, Tajikistan had managed significantly to reduce its total debt stocks, expressed as a proportion of GNI, from 109.5% at the end of 2000 to 46.0% at the end of 2005. Inflation was a concern in 2007, recording an average rate of 13.1% that year, owing largely to increases in the price of wheat, which rose by approximately 80% in 2007, and in energy prices, which were affected by an increase of 45% in the rates charged by neighbouring Uzbekistan for supplies of natural gas. Cotton production, a central component of the domestic economy, declined by 4% in 2007, according to the ADB. Electricity shortages were also a problem in 2007, affecting the important aluminium sector: despite possessing significant hydroelectric power resources, Tajikistan suffers from a winter power deficit of 3,000m.–3,500m. kWh. In early 2008 severe winter conditions, exacerbated by reduced energy supplies from Uzbekistan and Turkmenistan, caused critical energy shortages and had a strongly detrimental impact on agricultural production. In February the UN announced that 260,000 people were in need of emergency food assistance, and issued an appeal for international aid. In March the IMF declared that the Central Bank had supplied the Fund with misleading financial information, in violation of the terms of a poverty reduction agreement, and demanded that the Government repay some US $47m. However, in April a visiting IMF delegation pledged to recommend support for a new aid programme for Tajikistan. The ADB recorded GDP growth of 7.8% in 2007, with growth of 8.0% projected for 2008.

Education

Education is controlled by the Ministry of Education. Education is officially compulsory for nine years, to be undertaken between seven and 17 years of age. Primary education begins at seven years of age and lasts for four years. Secondary education, beginning at the age of 11, lasts for up to seven years, comprising a first cycle of five years and a second of two years. In 1998/99 total enrolment at primary schools was equivalent to 94% of the relevant age-group (males 97%; females 91%). In the 2002/03 academic year, according to UN estimates, total enrolment at secondary schools was equivalent to 83% of the relevant age-group (males 90%; females 76%). Since independence, greater emphasis has been placed in the curriculum on Tajik language and literature, including classical Persian literature. In 2003 President Emomali Rakhmonov announced that the compulsory teaching of Russian was to be reintroduced. Constitutional amendments approved in June 2003 provided for the withdrawal of free higher education. In 2002/03 some 96,583 students were enrolled at 33 institutes of higher education. In 2005 expenditure on education by all levels of government was 250m. somoni (equivalent to 15.9% of government expenditure), according to preliminary figures. Spending was expected to be increased to 336m. somoni in 2006 (17.3% of anticipated expenditure).

Public Holidays

2008: 1 January (New Year's Day), 8 March (International Women's Day), 20–22 March (Navrus, Spring Holiday), 1 May (International Labour Day), 9 May (Victory Day), 27 June (National Accord Day), 9 September (Independence Day), 1 October* (Id-al-Fitr, end of Ramadan), 6 November (Constitution Day), 8 December* (Id-al-Adha, Feast of the Sacrifice).

2009: 1 January (New Year's Day), 8 March (International Women's Day), 20–22 March (Navrus, Spring Holiday), 1 May (International Labour Day), 9 May (Victory Day), 27 June (National Accord Day), 9 September (Independence Day), 20 September* (Id-al-Fitr, end of Ramadan), 6 November (Constitution Day), 27 November* (Id-al-Adha, Feast of the Sacrifice).

* These holidays are dependent on the Islamic lunar calendar and may vary by one or two days from the dates given.

Weights and Measures

The metric system is in force.

TAJIKISTAN

Statistical Survey

Source (unless otherwise indicated): State Committee for Statistics, 734001 Dushanbe, Kuchai Boxtar 17; tel. (372) 23-25-53; fax (372) 21-43-75; e-mail stat@tojikiston.com; internet www.stat.tj.

Area and Population

AREA, POPULATION AND DENSITY

Area (sq km)	143,100*
Population (census results)†	
12 January 1989	5,092,603
20 January 2000	
Males	3,069,100
Females	3,058,393
Total	6,127,493
Population (official estimates at 1 January)	
2004	6,780,400
2005	6,920,300
2006	7,063,800
Density (per sq km) at 1 January 2006	49.4

* 55,251 sq miles.
† Figures refer to *de jure* population. The *de facto* total at the 1989 census was 5,108,576.

POPULATION BY ETHNIC GROUP
(2000 census)

	Number ('000 persons)	%
Tajik	4,898.4	79.9
Uzbek	936.7	15.3
Russian	68.2	1.1
Kyrgyz	65.5	1.1
Others	158.7	2.6
Total	6,127.5	100.0

ADMINISTRATIVE DIVISIONS
(1 January 2005, official estimates)

	Area (sq km)	Population	Density (per sq km)	Capital city
Viloyats				
Khatlon	24,800	2,463,300	99.3	Qurgonteppa
Soghd	25,400	2,060,900	81.1	Khujand
Autonomous Viloyat				
Kuhistoni Badakhshon	64,200	218,400	3.4	Khorog
Capital City				
Dushanbe	100	646,400	6,464.0	—
Regions of Republican Subordination *	28,600	1,531,300	53.5	—
Total	143,100	6,920,300	48.4	

* The Regions of Republican Subordination comprise 3 cities (Gissar; Kofarnikhon; Rogun) and 10 raions or districts (Faizabad; Garm; Gissar; Darban; Jirgital; Lenin; Shakhrinav; Tajikabad; Tavildara; and Varzov) in central Tajikistan where there is no higher tier of local government.

PRINCIPAL TOWNS
(population at 1 January 2002)

Dushanbe (capital)	575,900	Kanibadam	45,100
Khujand*	147,400	Kofarnihon‡	45,100
Kulob	79,500	Tursunzade	38,100
Qurgonteppa	61,200	Isfara	37,300
Istravshan†	51,700	Panjakent	33,200

* Known as Leninabad between 1936 and 1992.
† Also known as Urateppa (Ura-Tyube).
‡ Formerly Ordzhonikidzeabad.

Mid-2007 (incl. suburbs, UN estimate): Dushanbe 553,000 (Source: UN, *World Urbanization Prospects: The 2007 Revision*).

BIRTHS, MARRIAGES AND DEATHS

	Registered live births		Registered marriages		Registered deaths	
	Number	Rate (per 1,000)	Number	Rate (per 1,000)	Number	Rate (per 1,000)
1999	180,888	29.8	22,536	3.9	25,384	4.2
2000	167,246	27.0	26,257	4.2	29,387	4.7
2001	171,623	27.2	28,827	4.6	32,015	5.1
2002*	175,600	27.3	32,299	5.0	31,100	4.8
2003*	177,900	27.1	39,102	6.0	33,200	5.0
2004*	179,600	26.8	47,320	7.1	29,700	4.4
2005*	180,800	26.4	52,352	7.6	31,500	4.6
2006*	186,500	26.7	57,278	8.6	n.a.	n.a.

* From 2002 onwards, figures for registered births and deaths are rounded to the nearest 100.

Expectation of life (years at birth, WHO estimates): 64.9 (males 63.8; females 66.0) in 2005 (Source: WHO, *World Health Statistics*).

IMMIGRATION AND EMIGRATION

	2004	2005	2006
Immigrants	15,244	17,962	19,646
Emigrants	24,663	27,311	30,554

ECONOMICALLY ACTIVE POPULATION
(annual averages, '000 persons)

	2004	2005	2006
Activities of the material sphere	1,750	1,770	1,790
Agriculture*	1,391	1,424	1,432
Industry†	118	121	118
Construction	68	62	64
Trade and catering‡	109	101	110
Transport and communications	64	62	66
Activities of the non-material sphere	338	342	341
Housing and municipal services	28	33	33
Health care, social security, physical culture and sports	80	72	74
Education, culture and arts	183	186	186
Science, research and development	4	4	4
Government and finance	29	31	34
Other non-material	14	16	10
Statistical discrepancy	—	—	6
Total employed	2,088	2,112	2,137
Unemployed	42	42	48
Total labour force	2,132	2,154	2,185

* Including forestry.
† Comprising manufacturing (except printing and publishing), mining and quarrying, electricity, gas, water, logging and fishing.
‡ Including material and technical supply.

TAJIKISTAN

Health and Welfare

KEY INDICATORS

Total fertility rate (children per woman, 2005)	3.6
Under-5 mortality rate (per 1,000 live births, 2005)	71
HIV/AIDS (% of persons aged 15–49, 2005)	0.1
Physicians (per 1,000 head, 2004)	2.03
Hospital beds (per 1,000 head, 2005)	6.2
Health expenditure (2004): US $ per head (PPP)	53.9
Health expenditure (2004): % of GDP	4.4
Health expenditure (2004): public (% of total)	21.6
Human Development Index (2005): ranking	122
Human Development Index (2005): value	0.673

For sources and definitions, see explanatory note on p. vi.

Agriculture

PRINCIPAL CROPS
('000 metric tons)

	2004	2005	2006
Wheat	631	611	571
Rice (paddy)	51	62	60*
Barley	63	65	62
Maize	113	156	150*
Potatoes	527	555	574
Cottonseed	330†	289	290*
Cabbages	44†	47*	50*
Tomatoes	199†	209†	221*
Dry onions	180†	188†	199*
Carrots†	111	117	124
Watermelons	150	170	218
Apples	85†	85*	115*
Apricots	25†	28*	42*
Peaches and nectarines	20†	21*	32*
Grapes	93	91	108
Cotton (lint)	172†	151	145*
Tobacco (leaves)	3	n.a.	n.a.

* FAO estimate.
† Unofficial figure(s).

Aggregate production ('000 metric tons, may include official, semi-official or estimated data): Total cereals 860 in 2004, 895 in 2005, 844 in 2006; Total roots and tubers 527 in 2004, 555 in 2005, 574 in 2006; Total vegetables (incl. melons) 832 in 2004, 889 in 2005, 978 in 2006; Total fruits (excl. melons) 241 in 2004, 242 in 2005, 319 in 2006.

Source: FAO.

LIVESTOCK
('000 head at 1 January)

	2004	2005	2006
Horses	74	77	75
Asses, mules or hinnies	147	156	160*
Cattle	1,219	1,303	1,377
Camels*	40	40	42
Sheep	1,672	1,782	1,893
Goats	920	975	1,160
Poultry	1,888	n.a.	n.a.

* FAO estimate(s).
Source: FAO.

LIVESTOCK PRODUCTS
('000 metric tons)

	2004	2005	2006
Cattle meat	21.8	24.3	25.3
Sheep meat	23.8	26.5	27.7
Chicken meat*	2.3	2.7	2.8
Cows' milk	450.0†	488.0*	494.0*
Goats' milk*	39.8	45.0	50.9
Cheese*	11.2	n.a.	n.a.
Wool: greasy	3.9	4.0*	n.a.

* FAO estimate(s).
† Unofficial figure.
Source: FAO.

Fishing
(metric tons, live weight)

	2002	2003	2004
Capture	181	158	184
Freshwater bream	25	24	28
Common carp	51	52	45
Crucial carp	17	11	8
Silver carp	16	12	14
Sichel	4	2	10
Asp	5	3	9
Other cyprinids	27	23	32
Wels (Som) catfish	12	9	18
Pike-perch	24	22	20
Aquaculture	143	167	26
Common carp	17	47	12
Grass carp (White amur)	29	30	3
Silver carp	95	88	7
Total catch	324	325	210

2005: Production assumed to be unchanged from 2004 (FAO estimates).
Source: FAO.

Mining
(metric tons, unless otherwise indicated)

	2002	2003	2004
Coal	30,000	46,500	92,200
Crude petroleum	16,000	17,700	18,600
Natural gas (million cu m)	30.0	32.8	35.6
Lead concentrate*†	800	800	800
Antimony ore*†	3,000	1,800	2,000
Mercury*†	20	30	30
Silver (kilograms)†	5,000	5,000	5,000
Gold (kilograms)*†	2,700	2,700	3,000
Gypsum (crude)*	40,000	45,000	50,000

* Estimated production.
† Figures refer to the metal content of ores and concentrates.

Source: US Geological Survey.

2005 ('000 metric tons, unless otherwise indicated): Coal 91; Crude petroleum 21; Natural gas (million cu m) 27 (Source: Asian Development Bank, *Key Indicators of Developing Asian and Pacific Countries*).

2006 ('000 metric tons, unless otherwise indicated): Coal 102; Crude petroleum 22; Natural gas (million cu m) 18 (Source: Asian Development Bank, *Key Indicators of Developing Asian and Pacific Countries*).

TAJIKISTAN

Industry

SELECTED PRODUCTS
('000 metric tons, unless otherwise indicated)

	2000	2001	2002
Cottonseed oil (refined)*	23	26	31
Wheat flour	307	315	304
Ethyl alcohol ('000 hectolitres)	23	25	18
Wine ('000 hectolitres)	39	56	63
Beer ('000 hectolitres)	4	8	9
Soft drinks ('000 hectolitres)	58	127	134
Cigarettes (million)	667	1,155	585
Wool yarn (pure and mixed)	0.5	0.6	0.7
Cotton yarn (pure and mixed)	15.0	14.9	8.5
Woven cotton fabrics (million sq metres)	11	14	20
Woven silk fabrics ('000 sq metres)	253	248	136
Footwear, excl. rubber ('000 pairs)	110	100	84
Caustic soda (Sodium hydroxide)	4	3	3
Clay building bricks (million)	30	24	29
Cement	55	69	89
Aluminium (unwrought): primary‡	269.2	289.0	307.6
Electric energy (million kWh)†	14,247	14,382	15,302

* Unofficial figure(s) from FAO.
† Source: Asian Development Bank, *Key Indicators of Developing Asian and Pacific Countries*.
‡ Source: US Geological Survey.

2003 ('000 metric tons, unless otherwise indicated): Cottonseed oil (refined) 34*; Wheat flour 399†; Cement 166†; Electric energy (million kWh) 16,509; Aluminium (unwrought): primary 319.4†.

2004 ('000 metric tons, unless otherwise indicated): Wheat flour 458†; Cement 194†; Electric energy (million kWh) 16,491: Aluminium (unwrought): primary 358.1†.

2005 ('000 metric tons, unless otherwise indicated): Cement 253†; Electric energy (million kWh) 17,086; Wheat flour 464†.

2006 ('000 metric tons, unless otherwise indicated): Cement 282†; Electric energy (million kWh) 16,924; Wheat flour 457†.

Source (unless otherwise indicated): UN, *Industrial Commodity Statistics Yearbook*.

Finance

CURRENCY AND EXCHANGE RATES

Monetary Units
100 diram = 1 somoni.

Sterling, Dollar and Euro Equivalents (31 October 2007)
£1 sterling = 7.147 somoni;
US $1 = 3.447 somoni;
€1 = 4.979 somoni;
100 somoni = £13.99 = $29.01 = €20.08.

Average Exchange Rate (somoni per US $)
2004   2.9705
2005   3.1166
2006   3.2984

Note: The Tajikistani rouble was introduced in May 1995, replacing the Russian (formerly Soviet) rouble at the rate of 1 Tajikistani rouble = 100 Russian roubles. A new currency, the somoni (equivalent to 1,000 Tajikistani roubles), was introduced in October 2000.

Statistical Survey

BUDGET
(million somoni)*

Revenue†	2004	2005‡	2006§
Tax revenue	934	1,169	1,374
Income and profit tax	105	142	156
Payroll taxes	120	146	172
Property taxes	34	51	66
Internal taxes on goods and services	482	625	728
International trade and operations tax	185	205	252
Non-tax revenue	129	143	154
Total	1,063	1,312	1,528

Expenditure‖	2004	2005‡	2006§
General administrative services	117	157	185
Protection services	134	194	239
Social services	438	664	805
Education	161	250	336
Health	62	91	106
Social security and welfare	153	228	238
Other	61	95	125
Economic services	119	148	167
Interest payments	43	56	57
Other purposes	211	144	156
External financing of public investment programme (PIP)	189	284	336
Total	1,250	1,648	1,944

* Figures refer to the consolidated operations of the State Budget, comprising the budgets of the central (republican) Government and local authorities, and the Social Security Fund.
† Excluding grants received (million somoni): 41 in 2004; 38 in 2005 (preliminary); 38 in 2006 (budget proposal).
‡ Preliminary figures.
§ Budget proposals.
‖ Including lending minus repayments (million somoni): 3 in 2004; 2 in 2005 (preliminary); 2 in 2006 (budget proposal).

Source: IMF, *Republic of Tajikistan: Sixth Review Under the Poverty Reduction and Growth Facility—Staff Report; Staff Statement; Press Release on the Executive Board Discussion; and Statement by the Executive Director for the Republic of Tajikistan* (January 2006).

INTERNATIONAL RESERVES
(US $ million at 31 December)

	2004	2005	2006
Gold (national valuation)	14.6	20.7	28.7
IMF special drawing rights	1.3	5.4	3.5
Foreign exchange	156.2	162.8	171.6
Total	172.1	188.9	203.8

Source: IMF, *International Financial Statistics*.

MONEY SUPPLY
(million somoni at 31 December)

	2004	2005	2006
Currency outside banks	175.4	155.3	166.4
Demand deposits	64.4	84.8	146.2
Total money (incl. others)	241.1	241.0	314.2

Source: IMF, *International Financial Statistics*.

COST OF LIVING
(Consumer Price Index; base: previous year = 100)

	2004	2005	2006
Food	105.0	108.9	113.6
Non-food	107.4	103.6	103.8
All items	106.8	107.8	111.9

Source: Asian Development Bank, *Key Indicators of Developing Asian and Pacific Countries*.

TAJIKISTAN

Statistical Survey

NATIONAL ACCOUNTS
(million somoni at current prices)

Expenditure on the Gross Domestic Product

	2003	2004	2005
Final consumption expenditure	4,319.4	5,292.8	6,899.4
Households Non-profit institutions serving households	3,739.3	4,566.0	5,847.1
General government	580.1	726.8	1,052.3
Gross capital formation	475.6	752.6	839.4
Gross fixed capital formation	382.6	640.0	801.3
Acquisitions, less disposals, of valuables Changes in inventories	93.0	112.6	38.1
Total domestic expenditure	4,795.0	6,045.4	7,738.8
Exports of goods and services	3,044.6	3,624.3	3,910.7
Less Imports of goods and services	3,511.4	4,293.1	5,245.0
Sub-total	4,328.2	5,376.6	6,404.5
Statistical discrepancy*	433.3	790.7	802.2
GDP in market prices	4,761.4	6,167.2	7,206.6

* Referring to the difference between the sum of the expenditure components and official estimates of GDP, compiled from the production approach.

Gross Domestic Product by Economic Activity

	2004	2005	2006
Agriculture	1,184.1	1,526.7	1,993.5
Mining, manufacturing and electricity, gas and water	1,644.4	1,645.1	1,706.1
Construction	262.3	327.1	482.2
Transport and communications	409.0	533.3	556.3
Trade	1,017.0	1,191.1	1,975.0
Others, including public administration and finance	970.7	1,152.1	1,528.4
GDP at factor cost	5,487.5	6,357.4	8,241.5
Indirect taxes, less subsidies	679.7	831.2	1,030.7
GDP in purchasers' values	6,167.2	7,206.6	9,272.2

Source: Asian Development Bank, *Key Indicators of Developing Asian and Pacific Countries*.

BALANCE OF PAYMENTS
(US $ million)

	2004	2005	2006
Exports of goods f.o.b.	1,096.9	1,108.1	1,511.8
Imports of goods c.i.f.	−1,232.4	−1,430.9	−1,954.6
Trade balance	−135.5	−322.8	−442.8
Exports of services	122.9	146.3	134.2
Imports of services	−212.5	−251.5	−394.5
Balance on goods and services	−225.1	−428.0	−703.1
Other income received	1.7	9.6	12.4
Other income paid	−59.2	−50.4	−76.4
Balance on goods, services and income	−282.7	−468.8	−767.0
Current transfers received	348.4	599.9	1,146.0
Current transfers paid	−122.8	−150.0	−400.4
Current balance	−57.0	−18.9	−21.4
Direct investment (net)	272.0	54.5	338.6
Portfolio investment (net)	5.3	—	n.a.
Other investment assets	−28.4	−71.3	−301.9
Other investment liabilities	−155.5	118.3	239.2
Net errors and omissions	−32.5	−76.3	−264.7
Overall balance	3.9	6.3	−10.1

Source: IMF, *International Financial Statistics*.

External Trade

PRINCIPAL COMMODITIES
(US $ million, excl. alumina and aluminium)

Imports c.i.f.*	2004	2005	2006
Natural gas	28	27	35
Petroleum products	107	126	191
Electricity	65	58	67
Grain and flour	48	76	77
Total (incl. others)	1,191	1,330	1,725

Exports f.o.b.†	2004	2005	2006
Cotton fibre	162	144	129
Electricity	58	53	49
Total (incl. others)	915	909	1,399

* These figures do not include separate data for imports of alumina, one of Tajikistan's principal import goods. The most recent data available were for 2001, when imports of alumina accounted for US $184m. of $688m. in total imports (c.i.f.).
† These figures do not include separate data for exports of aluminium, Tajikistan's principal export item. The most recent data available were for 2001, when imports of aluminium accounted for US $397m. of $909m. in total exports (f.o.b.).

PRINCIPAL TRADING PARTNERS
(US $ million)

Imports	2004	2005	2006
Azerbaijan	86.0	114.9	134.8
China, People's Rep.	57.0	92.5	336.3
Iran	26.3	33.0	n.a.
Italy	13.8	51.7	17.8
Kazakhstan	152.6	168.3	197.5
Romania	13.1	61.7	n.a.
Russia	240.8	256.5	360.0
Turkey	37.9	45.3	n.a.
Turkmenistan	33.7	53.8	63.1
Ukraine	53.8	82.0	96.2
USA	79.2	11.7	47.4
Uzbekistan	168.8	152.9	179.4
Total (incl. others)	1,191.3	1,329.8	1,725.0

Exports	2004	2005	2006
Hungary	22.1	—	1.6
Iran	29.6	36.7	45.3
Italy	11.4	15.6	46.9
Latvia	64.8	44.2	0.3
Netherlands	379.2	423.4	26.9
Norway	74.0	n.a.	n.a.
Russia	60.5	82.8	96.4
Switzerland	63.4	27.0	27.9
Turkey	139.7	143.4	107.6
USA	0.5	226.2	n.a.
Uzbekistan	65.9	66.5	78.0
Total (incl. others)	914.9	908.7	1,399.0

Source: Asian Development Bank, *Key Indicators of Developing Asian and Pacific Countries*.

Transport

RAILWAYS

	2003	2004	2005
Passengers (million journeys)	0.5	0.7	0.7
Freight carried ('000 metric tons)	11,720.5	12,268.3	12,114.2

Passenger-km (million): 32 in 2001.

Freight ton-km (million): 1,248 in 2001.

TAJIKISTAN

CIVIL AVIATION
(traffic on scheduled services)

	2003	2004	2005
Passengers carried ('000) . . .	400	600	500
Freight carried ('000 metric tons) .	3.8	4.1	3.7

Kilometres flown (million): 4 in 1999.

Passenger-km (million): 229 in 1999.

Freight ton-km (million): 23 in 1999.

Source: partly UN, *Statistical Yearbook*.

Communications Media

	2004	2005	2006
Telephones ('000 main lines in use)	245.2	280.2	280.2
Mobile cellular telephones ('000 subscribers)	240.0	265.0	265.0
Internet users ('000)	5.0	19.5	19.5

Television receivers ('000 in use): 2,000 in 2000.

Facsimile machines (number in use): 2,100 in 1999.

Books published (titles): 150 in 1997.

Books published (copies): 997,000 in 1996.

Daily newspapers (estimates): 2 titles and 120,000 copies (average circulation) in 1996.

Non-daily newspapers: 73 titles and 153,000 copies (average circulation) in 1996.

Other periodicals: 11 titles and 130,000 copies (average circulation) in 1996.

Radio receivers ('000 in use): 850 in 1997.

Sources: UNESCO, *Statistical Yearbook*; International Telecommunication Union.

Education

(2006/07, unless otherwise indicated)

	Students ('000)		
	Males	Females	Total
Pre-primary	32,800	28,400	61,200
Primary			
Secondary:			
Lower	n.a.	n.a.	1,672,800*
Upper			
Vocational	13,800	18,600	32,400
Professional technical†	17,955	7,013	24,968
Higher (incl. universities)	106,100	40,100	146,200

* Figures exclude 18,700 pupils at evening classes (including those conducted by correspondence).
† 2005/06 data.

Institutions (2006/07, unless otherwise indicated): Pre-primary 485; Primary 670; Secondary—Lower 826; Secondary—Upper 2,282; Secondary—Vocational 52; Professional Technical 71 (2005/06); Higher (incl. universities) 34. Figures exclude 11 schools for pupils with mental or physical disabilities and 41 evening schools.

Teachers (2006/07, unless otherwise stated): Pre-primary 6,615 (1996/97); Primary *and* Secondary—Lower, Upper *and* Vocational 99,900; Professional Technical n.a.; Higher (incl. universities) 6,100 (2001/02).

Directory

The Constitution

Tajikistan's Constitution entered into force on 6 November 1994, when it was approved by a majority of voters in a nation-wide plebiscite. It replaced the previous Soviet republican Constitution, adopted in 1978. The following is a summary of its main provisions (including amendments approved by referendum on 26 September 1999 and 22 June 2003).

PRINCIPLES OF THE CONSTITUTIONAL SYSTEM

The Republic of Tajikistan is a sovereign, democratic, law-governed, secular and unitary state. The state language is Tajik, but Russian is accorded the status of a language of communication between nationalities.

Recognition, observance and protection of human and civil rights and freedoms is the obligation of the State. The people of Tajikistan are the expression of sovereignty and the sole source of power of the State, which they express through their elected representatives.

Tajikistan consists of Kuhistoni Badakhshon Autonomous Viloyat (Region), viloyats, towns, districts, settlements and villages. The territory of the State is indivisible and inviolable. Agitation and actions aimed at the disunity of the State are prohibited.

No ideology, including religious ideology, may be granted the status of a state ideology.

The Constitution of Tajikistan has supreme legal authority and its norms have direct application. Laws and other legal acts which run counter to the Constitution have no legal validity. The State, its bodies and officials are bound to observe the provisions of the Constitution.

Tajikistan will implement a peaceful policy, respecting the sovereignty and independence of other states of the world, and will determine foreign relations on the basis of international norms. Agitation for war is prohibited.

The economy of Tajikistan is based on various forms of ownership. The State guarantees freedom of economic activity, entrepreneurship, equality of rights and the protection of all forms of ownership, including private ownership. Land and natural resources are under state ownership.

FUNDAMENTAL DUTIES OF INDIVIDUALS AND CITIZENS

The freedoms and rights of individuals are protected by the Constitution, the laws of the republic and international documents to which Tajikistan is a signatory. The State guarantees the rights and freedoms of every person, regardless of nationality, race, sex, language, religious beliefs, political persuasion, social status, knowledge and property. Men and women have the same rights. Every person has the right to life. No one may be subjected to torture, punishment or inhuman treatment. No one may be arrested, kept in custody or exiled without a legal basis, and no one is adjudged guilty of a crime except by the sentence of a court in accordance with the law. Every person has the right freely to choose their place of residence, to leave the republic and return to it. Every person has the right to profess any religion, individually or with others, or not to profess any, and to take part in religious ceremonies. Every citizen has the right to take part in political life and state administration; to elect and be elected from the age of 18; to join and leave political parties, trade unions and other associations; to take part in meetings, rallies or demonstrations. Every person is guaranteed freedom of speech. State censorship is prohibited.

Every person has the right: to ownership and inheritance; to work; to housing; to social security in old age, or in the event of sickness or disability. Basic general education is compulsory.

A state of emergency is declared as a temporary measure to ensure the security of citizens and of the State in the instance of a direct threat to the freedom of citizens, the State's independence, its territorial integrity, or natural disasters. The period of a state of emergency is up to three months; it can be prolonged by the President of the Republic.

MAJLISI OLI (SUPREME ASSEMBLY)

The Majlisi Oli (Supreme Assembly) is the highest representative and legislative body of the republic. It is a bicameral legislative body, comprising a 63-member lower chamber, the Majlisi Namoyandagon (Assembly of Representatives), and an upper chamber, the Majlisi Milliy (National Assembly). The members of the Majlisi Namoyandagon are elected for a five-year term, 22 by proportional representation and 41 in single-mandate constituencies. Twenty-five members of the Majlisi Milliy are indirectly elected for a term of five years by regional deputies. Eight members of the chamber are appointed by the President of the Republic. Additionally, former Heads of State of the Republic of Tajikistan are entitled to a seat in the chamber.

The powers of the Majlisi Oli include: enactment and amendment of laws, and their annulment; interpretation of the Constitution and laws; determination of the basic direction of domestic and foreign policy; ratification of presidential decrees on the appointment and dismissal of the Chairman of the National Bank, the Chairman and members of the Constitutional Court, the Supreme Court and the Supreme Economic Court; ratification of the state budget; determining and altering the structure of administrative territorial units; ratification and annulment of international treaties; ratification of presidential decrees on a state of war and a state of emergency.

Laws are adopted by a majority of the legislative deputies. If the President does not agree with the law, he may return it to the Majlisi Oli. If the legislature once again approves the law, with at least a two-thirds' majority, the President must sign it.

THE PRESIDENT OF THE REPUBLIC

The President of the Republic is the Head of State and the head of the executive. The President is elected by the citizens of Tajikistan on the basis of universal, direct and equal suffrage for a seven-year term. Any citizen who knows the state language and has lived on the territory of Tajikistan for the preceding 10 years may be nominated to the post of President of the Republic.

The President has the authority: to represent Tajikistan inside the country and in international relations; to establish or abolish ministries with the approval of the Majlisi Oli; to appoint or dismiss the Chairman (Prime Minister) and other members of the Council of Ministers and to propose them for approval to the Majlisi Oli; to appoint and dismiss chairmen of regions, towns and districts, and propose new appointments for approval to the relevant assemblies of people's deputies; to appoint and dismiss members of the Constitutional Court, the Supreme Court and the Supreme Economic Court (with the approval of the Majlisi Oli); to appoint and dismiss judges of lower courts; to sign laws; to lead the implementation of foreign policy and sign international treaties; to appoint diplomatic representatives abroad; to be Commander-in-Chief of the armed forces of Tajikistan; to declare a state of war or a state of emergency (with the approval of the Majlisi Oli).

In the event of the President's death, resignation, removal from office or inability to perform his duties, the duties of the President will be carried out by the Chairman of the Majlisi Oli until further presidential elections can be held. New elections must be held within three months of these circumstances. The President may be removed from office in the case of his committing a crime, by the decision of at least two-thirds of deputies of the Majlisi Oli, taking into account the decisions of the Constitutional Court.

THE COUNCIL OF MINISTERS

The Council of Ministers consists of the Chairman (Prime Minister), the First Deputy Chairman, Deputy Chairmen, Ministers and Chairmen of State Committees. The Council of Ministers is responsible for implementation of laws and decrees of the Majlisi Oli and decrees and orders of the President. The Council of Ministers leaves office when a new President is elected.

LOCAL GOVERNMENT

The local representative authority in regions, towns and districts is the assembly of people's deputies. Assemblies are elected for a five-year term. Local executive government is the responsibility of the President's representative: the chairman of the assembly of people's deputies, who is proposed by the President and approved by the relevant assembly. The Majlisi Oli may dissolve local representative bodies, if their actions do not conform to the Constitution and the law.

KUHISTONI BADAKHSHON AUTONOMOUS VILOYAT

Kuhistoni Badakhshon Autonomous Viloyat is an integral and indivisible part of Tajikistan, the territory of which cannot be changed without the consent of the regional assembly.

JUDICIARY

The judiciary is independent and protects the rights and freedoms of the individual, the interests of the State, organizations and institutions, and legality and justice. Judicial power is implemented by the Constitutional Court, the Supreme Court, the Supreme Economic Court, the Military Court, the Court of Kuhistoni Badakhshon Autonomous Viloyat, and courts of viloyats, the city of Dushanbe, towns and districts. The term of judges is 10 years. The creation of emergency courts is not permitted.

Judges are independent and are subordinate only to the Constitution and the law. Interference in their activity is not permitted.

THE OFFICE OF THE PROCURATOR-GENERAL

The Procurator-General and procurators subordinate to him ensure the control and observance of laws within the framework of their authority in the territory of Tajikistan. The Procurator-General is responsible to the Majlisi Oli and the President, and is elected for a five-year term.

PROCEDURES FOR INTRODUCING AMENDMENTS TO THE CONSTITUTION

Amendments and addenda to the Constitution are made by means of a referendum. A referendum takes place with the support of at least two-thirds of the people's deputies. The President, or at least one-third of the people's deputies, may submit amendments and addenda to the Constitution. The form of public administration, the territorial integrity and the democratic, law-governed and secular nature of the State are irrevocable.

The Government

HEAD OF STATE

President: EMOMALI RAKHMON (elected by popular vote 6 November 1994; re-elected 6 November 1999 and 6 November 2006).

COUNCIL OF MINISTERS
(April 2008)

Chairman (Prime Minister) and Minister of Construction: AKIL AKILOV.
Deputy Chairman, in charge of the Economy: MURODALI ALIMARDONOV.
Deputy Chairman: ASADULLO GHULOMOV.
Deputy Chairman: RUQIYA QURBONOVA.
Minister of Agriculture and the Protection of the Environment: QOSIM QOSIMOV.
Minister of Culture: MIRZOSHOHRUKH ASROROV.
Minister of Defence: Maj.-Gen. SHERALI KHAYRULLOYEV.
Minister of Economic Development and Trade: GHULOMJON BOBOYEV.
Minister of Education: ABDUJABBOR RAHMONOV.
Minister of Energy and Industry: SHERALI GULOV.
Minister of Finance: SAFARALI NAJMIDDINOV.
Minister of Foreign Affairs: HAMROKHON ZARIFI.
Minister of Health: NUSRATULLO SALIMOV.
Minister of Internal Affairs: MAHMADNAZAR SOLEHOV.
Minister of Justice: BAKHTIYOR KHUDOYOROV.
Minister of Labour and Social Welfare: SHUKURJON ZUHUROV.
Minister of Land Improvement and Water Resources: MASAID HOMIDOV.
Minister of Transport and Communications: ABDURAHIM ASHUROV.

Note: The Chairmen of State Committees are also members of the Council of Ministers.

MINISTRIES

Office of the President: 734023 Dushanbe, Xiyoboni Rudaki 80; tel. (372) 21-04-18; fax (372) 21-18-37; e-mail mail@president.tj; internet www.president.tj.

Secretariat of the Prime Minister: 734023 Dushanbe, Xiyoboni Rudaki 80; tel. (372) 21-18-71; fax (372) 21-51-10.

Ministry of Agriculture and the Protection of the Environment: 734025 Dushanbe, Xiyoboni Rudaki 14; tel. (372) 21-15-96; fax (372) 21-57-94.

Ministry of Culture: 734025 Dushanbe, Xiyoboni Rudaki 34; tel. (372) 21-03-05; fax (372) 21-47-01.

Ministry of Defence: 734025 Dushanbe, Kuchai Bokhtar 59; tel. (372) 23-18-97; fax (372) 23-19-37.

TAJIKISTAN

Ministry of Economic Development and Trade: 734002 Dushanbe, Kuchai Bokhtar 37; tel. (372) 27-34-34; fax (372) 21-04-04; e-mail sharipov_jamshed@hotmail.com; internet www.met.tj.

Ministry of Education: 734025 Dushanbe, Kuchai Chexov 13A; tel. (372) 21-46-05; fax (372) 21-70-41.

Ministry of Energy and Industry: 734025 Dushanbe, Kuchai Boxtar 10; tel. (37) 221-50-64; fax (37) 227-90-10; e-mail energo@rs.tj; internet www.minenergo.tj.

Ministry of Finance: 734067 Dushanbe, Nazarov 64/14; tel. (37) 881-25-79; e-mail nii_finance@mail.tj.

Ministry of Foreign Affairs: 734051 Dushanbe, Xiyoboni Rudaki 42; tel. (372) 21-18-08; fax (372) 21-02-59; e-mail dushanbe@mfaumo.td.silk.org; internet www.mid.tj.

Ministry of Health: 734025 Dushanbe, Kuchai Shevchenko 69; tel. (372) 21-30-64; fax (372) 21-48-71.

Ministry of Internal Affairs: 734025 Dushanbe, Kuchai Texron 29; tel. (372) 21-17-40; fax (372) 21-26-05.

Ministry of Justice: 734025 Dushanbe, pr. Rudaki 25; tel. (372) 21-44-05; fax (372) 21-80-66.

Ministry of Labour and Social Welfare: 734028 Dushanbe, Kuchai A. Navoi 52; tel. (372) 36-18-37; fax (372) 36-24-15.

Ministry of Land Improvement and Water Resources: 734001 Dushanbe, Xiyoboni Rudaki 78; tel. (372) 35-35-66.

Ministry of Transport and Communications: 734025 Dushanbe, Xiyoboni Rudaki 57; tel. (37) 221-22-84; fax (37) 221-29-53; e-mail info@mincom.tj; internet www.mincom.tj.

President

Presidential Election, 6 November 2006, provisional results

Candidates	%
Emomali Rakhmonov* (People's Democratic Party of Tajikistan)	79.3
Olimjon Boboyev (Party of Economic Reforms)	6.2
Amirkul Karakulov (Agrarian Party of Tajikistan)	5.3
Ismoil Talbakov (Communist Party of Tajikistan)	5.1
Abdukhalim Gafforov (Socialist Party of Tajikistan)	2.8
Total†	100.0

* Known as Emomali Rakhmon from 2007.
† Including invalid votes, equivalent to 1.3% of the total.

Legislature

Constitutional amendments approved by a referendum in September 1999 provided for the establishment of a bicameral legislative body, the Majlisi Oli (Supreme Assembly), comprising a 63-member lower chamber, the Majlisi Namoyandagon (Assembly of Representatives), and an upper chamber, the Majlisi Milliy (National Assembly), which has a minimum of 33 members.

Majlisi Milliy
(National Assembly)

734051 Dushanbe, Xiyoboni Rudaki 42; tel. (372) 23-19-33; fax (372) 21-51-10; e-mail mejparl@parliament.tojikiston.com.

President: MAKHMADSAID UBAYDULLOYEV.

The Majlisi Milliy has a minimum of 33 members, of whom 25 (five from each of the five administrative regions of Tajikistan) are indirectly elected for a term of five years by regional deputies. Eight members of the chamber, who also serve for a term of five years, are appointed by the President of the Republic. All former Presidents of Tajikistan are also entitled to a seat in the Majlisi Milliy. Elections to the Majlisi Milliy were held on 24 March 2005, and the eight presidential nominees were announced on 25 March. The new chamber convened on 15 April.

Majlisi Namoyandagon
(Assembly of Representatives)

734051 Dushanbe, Xiyoboni Rudaki 42; tel. (372) 21-23-66; fax (372) 21-92-81; e-mail mejparl@parliament.tojikiston.com.

President: SAIDULLO KHAIRULLAYEV.

Elections, 27 February and 13 March 2005*

	Party lists†		Single-mandate seats	Total seats
	% of votes	Resulting seats		
People's Democratic Party of Tajikistan (PDPT)	74	17	35	52
Communist Party of Tajikistan (CPT)	13	3	1	4
Islamic Rebirth Party of Tajikistan (IRP)	8	2	—	2
Independents	—	—	5	5
Total (incl. others)	100	22	41	63

* Final provisional results.
† Each party was required to obtain at least 5% of the total votes cast in order to win seats on the basis of party lists.

Election Commission

Central Commission for Elections and Referenda: 734051 Dushanbe, Xiyoboni Rudaki 42; tel. (372) 21-13-75; comprises Chair., Sec. and 13 mems, elected by the Majlisi Namoyandagon at the proposal of the President of the Republic; Chair. MIRZOALI BOLTUYEV; Sec. VERA NAIMOVA.

Political Organizations

In September 2006 there were eight registered parties in Tajikistan.

Agrarian Party of Tajikistan (Agrarnaya partiya Tadzhikistana): 734000 Dushanbe; f. 2005; supports creation of a civil society and aims to protect the interests of the agricultural sector and its workers; Chair. AMIRKUL KARAKULOV; 1,300 mems (2005).

Communist Party of Tajikistan (CPT) (Kommunisticheskaya partiya Tadzhikistana): 734002 Dushanbe, Kuchai F. Niyazi 37; tel. (372) 23-29-53; internet www.kpt.freenet.tj; f. 1924; sole registered party until 1991; Chair. SHODI D. SHABDOLOV; Sec. of Central Cttee ISMOIL TALBAKOV; 60,000 mems (Jan. 2005).

Democratic Party of Tajikistan (DPT) (Khizbi demokrati Tochikiston): 734000 Dushanbe, Kuchai Pushkin 64; tel. (372) 21-77-87; internet www.democrat-tj.org; f. 1990; banned in 1993; permitted to re-register 1996 and 1999; secular nationalist and pro-Western; Chair. SAIDJAFAR ISMONOV (acting) (Chair. of Vatan—Fatherland faction registered by the Ministry of Justice in Sept. 2006); Chair. (of unregistered faction) RAHMATULLO VALIEV; c. 4,500 mems (Jan. 2005).

Islamic Rebirth Party of Tajikistan (IRP): 734000 Dushanbe, pos. Kalinina, Kuchai Tukhagul 55; tel. (372) 27-25-30; fax (372) 27-53-93; f. 1990 by split from the All-Union Islamic Renaissance Party of the USSR; leadership formerly based in Tehran, Iran; registered in 1991; banned 1993–99; Chair. MUHIDDIN KABIRI; 20,000 mems (Jan. 2005).

Justice (Adolatkoh): 734000 Dushanbe, Kuchai S. Nosirov 41; tel. (372) 24-90-55; f. and regd 1996; campaigns for the establishment of social justice and construction of a state based on the rule of law; registration revoked 2001; Leader ABDURAKHMON KARIMOV.

Party of Economic Reforms (Partiya ekonomicheskikh reform): 734000 Dushanbe; f. 2005; supports establishment of a market economy on the basis of democratic principles; aims to reduce poverty, undertake privatization and increase foreign investment; Chair. OLIMJON BOBOYEV; c. 1,000 mems (2005).

Party of Popular Unity and Accord (PPUA): 734000 Dushanbe; f. 1994; represents interests of northern Tajikistan; banned 1998; Leader ABDUMALIK ABDULLOJONOV.

People's Democratic Party of Tajikistan (PDPT) (Xizbi Xalkii Demokratii Tojikston): 734000 Dushanbe, Xiyoboni Rudaki 107; tel. (372) 21-63-21; e-mail ndpt1994@yahoo.com; internet www.hhdt.tj; f. 1994; campaigns for a united and secular state; Chair. EMOMALI SH. RAKHMON; First Dep. Chair. DAVLATALI DAVLATOV; 70,000 mems (Jan. 2005).

Social Democratic Party of Tajikistan (SDPT/KhSDT): 734000 Dushanbe, Xiyoboni Rudaki 81/49; tel. (372) 23-47-40; internet www.hsdt-tj.org; f. 1998; regd fmrly Justice and Progress of Tajikistan; Chair. RAKHMATULLO KH. ZOYIROV; 5,000 mems (Dec. 2004).

Socialist Party of Tajikistan: 734000 Dushanbe, Xiyoboni Rudaki 137; tel. (372) 34-77-11 (officially registered faction led by A. Gafforov); tel. (372) 27-39-59 (unregistered faction led by M. Narziyev); f. 1996; split into two factions in 2003, only one of which was

TAJIKISTAN

registered by the Ministry of Justice; Chairmen ABDUKHALIM GAFFOROV (Chair. of faction registered by the Ministry of Justice), MIRKHUSEYN NARZIYEV (Chair. of unregistered faction); 15,000 mems (2003).

Union and Development Party (Xizb-i Ittihod va Taraqqiyot—Taraqqiyot): 734000 Dushanbe; f. 2000; unregistered; formerly a faction of the Democratic Party of Tajikistan; Chair. SULTON KUVVATOV; 3,000 mems (2001).

Unity Party (Hizb-i-Vahdat): 734000 Dushanbe; f. 2001; unregistered.

The transnational militant Islamist Hizb-ut-Tahrir al-Islami (Party of Islamic Liberation—Hizb-ut-Tahrir) was believed to be operative in Tajikistan. As in neighbouring states, the organization was banned in Tajikistan, and a number of people have received gaol sentences for their alleged membership of the group, despite its stated intention of using only peaceful means of pursuing its goals, notably the restoration of a caliphate.

Diplomatic Representation

EMBASSIES IN TAJIKISTAN

Afghanistan: 734000 Dushanbe, Kuchai Pushkin 34; tel. (372) 221-67-35; fax (372) 251-00-96; e-mail afghanemintj@yahoo.com; Ambassador SAYED MUHAMMAD KHAIRKHOH.

China, People's Republic: 734002 Dushanbe, Khiyoboni Rudaki 143; tel. (372) 224-20-07; fax (372) 251-00-24; e-mail chinaembassy@tajnet.com; internet tj.china-embassy.org; Ambassador ZUO XUELIANG.

France: 734025 Dushanbe, Kuchai Rakhimi 17; tel. (372) 21-78-55; fax (372) 51-00-82; e-mail ambassade.douchanbe@diplomatie.gouv.fr; Ambassador OLIVIER MAITLAND PELEN.

Germany: 734017 Dushanbe, Kuchai Varzov 16; tel. (372) 221-21-89; fax (372) 224-03-90; e-mail info@dusc.diplo.de; internet www.duschanbe.diplo.de; Ambassador RAINER MÜLLER.

India: 734000 Dushanbe, Kuchai Buxoro 45; tel. (372) 221-71-72; fax (372) 251-00-45; e-mail hocdushanbe@tojikiston.com; Ambassador AMAR SINHA.

Iran: 734000 Dushanbe, Kuchai Boxtar 18; tel. (372) 221-00-74; fax (372) 251-00-89; e-mail iran-embassy@tajnet.com; Chargé d'affaires AHMADI AJALLUYON.

Japan: 734000 Dushanbe, Kuchai X. Nazarov 80A; tel. (372) 21-39-70; fax (44) 600-54-78; e-mail embjpn@embjpn.tojikiston.com; Ambassador YUICHI KUSUMOTO.

Kazakhstan: 734000 Dushanbe, Kuchai Xuseinzoda 31/1; tel. (372) 221-11-08; fax (372) 251-01-08; e-mail dipmiskz7@tajnet.com; Ambassador YERLAN A. ABILDAYEV.

Kyrgyzstan: 734000 Dushanbe, Kuchai Studentcheskaya 67; tel. and fax (372) 224-26-11; e-mail kyremb@tajnet.com; Ambassador TURATBEK E. JUNUSHALIYEV.

Pakistan: 734000 Dushanbe, Kuchai Dostoyevski 1–3, POB 55; tel. (372) 24-68-39; fax (372) 21-17-29; e-mail pareptaj@rs.tj; Ambassador KHALID USMAN QAISER.

Russia: 734000 Dushanbe, Kuchai Abu Ali ibni Sino 29/31; tel. (372) 235-70-65; fax (372) 235-88-06; e-mail rambtadjik@rambler.ru; internet www.rusembassy.tajnet.com; Ambassador RAMAZAN G. ABDULATIPOV.

Turkey: 734019 Dushanbe, Khiyoboni Rudaki 17/2; tel. (372) 21-08-00; fax (372) 51-00-12; e-mail turemdus@tajik.net; Ambassador AKIF AYHAN.

Turkmenistan: 734000 Dushanbe, Kuchai Chexov 22; tel. and fax (372) 221-68-84; e-mail embturkm@tjinter.com; Ambassador AKHMED KURBANOV.

United Kingdom: 734002 Dushanbe, Kuchai M. Tursunzoda 65; tel. (372) 224-22-21; fax (372) 227-17-26; e-mail dushanbe.reception@fco.gov.uk; internet www.britishembassy.gov.uk/tajikistan; Ambassador GRAEME LOTEN.

USA: 734019 Dushanbe, Khiyoboni I. Somoni 109A; tel. (372) 229-20-00; fax (372) 229-20-50; e-mail usembassydushanbe@state.gov; internet dushanbe.usembassy.gov; Ambassador TRACEY ANN JACOBSON.

Uzbekistan: 734003 Dushanbe, Kuchai L. Sherali 15; tel. (372) 21-21-84; fax (372) 24-90-77; e-mail ruzintaj@rambler.ru; internet www.uzembassy-tadjik.mfa.uz; Ambassador SHOQOSIM I. SHOISLOMOV.

Judicial System

Chairman of the Constitutional Court: IZBILLO KHOJAYEV, 734025 Dushanbe, Kuchai Boxtar 48; tel. (372) 21-61-96.

Chairman of the Supreme Court: NASRATULLO ABDULLOYEV, 734000 Dushanbe, pr. N. Karabayeva 1; tel. (372) 73-40-18.

Procurator-General: BOBOJON BOBOKHONOV, 734000 Dushanbe, Kuchai Abu Ali ibni Sino 126; tel. (372) 35-19-72.

Higher Economic Court: 734000 Dushanbe, Kuchai F. Niyazi 37; tel. (372) 21-15-58; f. 1995; Chair. AMIRKHOJA GOIBNAZAROV.

Religion

ISLAM

The majority of Tajiks are adherents of Islam and are mainly Sunnis (Hanafi school). Many of the Pamiri peoples, however, are Ismaʻilis (followers of the Aga Khan), a Shiʻite sect. Under the Soviet regime the Muslims of Tajikistan were subject to the Muslim Board of Central Asia and a muftiate, both of which were based in Tashkent, Uzbekistan. The senior Muslim cleric in Tajikistan was the *qazi* (supreme judge). In 1992 the incumbent *qazi* fled to Afghanistan, and in 1993 the Government appointed an independent *mufti* (expert in Islamic law). The Tajikistani Government, however, abolished the post of *mufti* in 1996, following the murder of the incumbent, and established a Council of Islamic Scholars (or *ulema*), as the highest Islamic religious authority in the country.

Council of Islamic Scholars (Ulema): 734000 Dushanbe; Chair. QARI AMANULLOH NEMATZADE.

CHRISTIANITY

Most of the minority Christian population is Slav, the main denomination being the Russian Orthodox Church. There are some Protestant and other groups, notably a Baptist Church in Dushanbe.

Roman Catholic Church

The Church is represented in Tajikistan by a Mission, established in September 1997. There were an estimated 250 adherents at 31 December 2005.

Superior: Rev. CARLOS AVILA, 734006 Dushanbe, Xiyoboni Titova 21/10; tel. (372) 21-21-90; fax (372) 23-26-77; e-mail caranavi2000@msn.com; internet tajikistan.ive.org.

The Russian Orthodox Church (Moscow Patriarchate)

The Church in Tajikistan comes under the jurisdiction of the Eparchy of Tashkent and Central Asia, based in Uzbekistan and headed by the Metropolitan of Tashkent and Central Asia, VLADIMIR (IKIM).

JUDAISM

In the mid-2000s there were an estimated 350 Jews in Dushanbe. In 2003 the Government announced that it intended to demolish the only synagogue remaining in Tajikistan, purportedly in order to construct state buildings. Dismantlement of the synagogue began in February 2006. However, following international protests, in late March the Government reversed its decision and announced that the Jewish community was to be permitted to reconstruct the synagogue, which by that time had been partially destroyed, at their own expense.

Leader of the Dushanbe Synagogue: VALERII DAVYDOV, 734001 Dushanbe, Kuchai N. Xikmata 26; tel. (372) 21-76-58.

The Press

In 2000 there were four national newspapers. In 1996 two daily newspapers and 73 non-daily newspapers were published in Tajikistan. There were also 11 periodicals published in that year.

PRINCIPAL NEWSPAPERS

Adabiyet va sanat (Literature and Art): 734001 Dushanbe, Kuchai I. Somoni 8; tel. (372) 24-57-39; f. 1959; weekly; organ of Union of Writers of Tajikistan and Ministry of Culture; in Tajik; Editor GULNAZAR KELDI; circ. 4,000.

Adolat (Justice): 731000 Dushanbe; in Tajik; organ of the Democratic Party of Tajikistan; publication suspended by Ministry of Culture in Sept. 2006, and again in Oct. 2006; Editor-in-Chief RAJAB MIRZO; circ. 1,000 (2006).

Biznes i Politika (Business and Politics): 734025 Dushanbe, Kuchai M. Tursunzoda 30; tel. (372) 23-52-50; e-mail b_p@rambler.ru; f. 1992; weekly; in Russian; Editor-in-Chief U. RAHMON; circ. 10,000.

Charxi gardun (Wheel of Fortune): 734018 Dushanbe, Xiyoboni S. Sherozi 16; tel. (372) 33-56-72; e-mail gazeta@tojikiston.com; f. 1996; weekly; in Tajik; Editor-in-Chief KHABIBULLO YEROV.

TAJIKISTAN

Daijest press (Press Digest): 734018 Dushanbe, Xiyoboni S. Sherozi 16; tel. (372) 33-25-03; e-mail gazeta@tojikiston.com; f. 1994; weekly; in Russian; overview of world press; economics; popular culture; Editor-in-Chief MARKHABO ZUNUNOVA.

Djavononi Tochikiston (Youth of Tajikistan): 734000 Dushanbe, Kuchai F. Niyazi 32; tel. (372) 23-38-01; f. 1930; weekly; organ of the Union of Youth of Tajikistan; in Tajik; Editor DAVLAT NAZRIYEV; circ. 3,000.

Ittixod (Unity): 734000 Dushanbe, Xiyoboni Rudaki 137; tel. (372) 34-77-11; organ of the Socialist Party of Tajikistan.

Jumhuriyat (Republic): 734018 Dushanbe, Xiyoboni S. Sherozi 16; tel. (372) 33-08-11; e-mail jumhuriyat@tojikiston.com; f. 1925; organ of the Government and presidential administration; 3 a week; in Tajik; Editor-in-Chief KAMOL ABDURAHIMOV; circ. 8,000.

Kurer Tadzhikistana (Tajikistan Courier): 734018 Dushanbe, Xiyoboni S. Sherozi 16; tel. (372) 33-08-15; e-mail ttemirov@td.silk.org; weekly; independent; in Russian; Editor KH. YUSIPOV; circ. 40,000.

Millat (Nation): 734000 Dushanbe; f. 2005; in Tajik; independent; Editor ADOLAT UMAROVOI.

Minbari Xalk (People's Tribune): 734018 Dushanbe, Xiyoboni S. Sherozi 16; tel. (372) 33-72-10; organ of the People's Democratic Party of Tajikistan; Editor MANSUR SAIFIDDINOV.

Najot (Salvation): 734000 Dushanbe, Kuchai Toktogul 55; tel. (372) 31-47-38; organ of the Islamic Rebirth Party of Tajikistan; weekly; Editor-in-Chief SIDUMAR KHUSAINI.

Narodnaya Gazeta (People's Newspaper): 734018 Dushanbe, Xiyoboni S. Sherozi 16; tel. (372) 33-08-30; e-mail narodnaja2004@mail.ru; f. 1929; fmrly Kommunist Tadzhikistana (Tajik Communist); organ of the Govt; 1 a week; in Russian; Editor VLADIMIR VOROBIYEV; circ. 3,000.

Nerui Sukhan (Power of the Word): 734018 Dushanbe, Xiyoboni S. Sherozi 16; weekly; f. 2003; Editor-in-Chief MUKHTOR BOKIZODA.

Nidoi ranchbar (Call of the Workers): 734018 Dushanbe, Xiyoboni S. Sherozi 16; tel. (372) 33-38-50; f. 1992; weekly; organ of the Communist Party of Tajikistan; in Tajik; Editor-in-Chief KHABIBULLO YOROV; circ. 6,000.

Odamu olam (Person and World): 734000 Dushanbe; weekly; in Tajik; independent; socio-political; Editor-in-Chief MIRAHMAD AMIRSHO.

Oila: 734018 Dushanbe, Xiyoboni S. Sherozi 16; tel. (372) 33-32-51; weekly; independent; Editor-in-Chief FIRUZA SATTORI.

Omuzgor (Teacher): 734000 Dushanbe, Kuchai Aini 45; tel. (372) 21-63-36; f. 1932; weekly; organ of the Ministry of Education; in Tajik; Editor-in-Chief SAMIULLO SAIFULLOYEV; circ. 3,000.

Ruzi Nav (New Day): 734018 Dushanbe, Xiyoboni S. Sherozi 16; tel. (372) 33-14-40; f. 2003; weekly; independent; politics and government; Chief Editor RAJABI MIRZO.

Sadoi mardum (The Voice of the People): 734018 Dushanbe, Xiyoboni S. Sherozi 16; tel. (372) 22-42-47; f. 1991; 3 a week; organ of the legislature; in Tajik; Editor MURADULLO SHERALIYEV; circ. 8,000.

Tojikiston (Tajikistan): 734018 Dushanbe, Xiyoboni S. Sherozi 16; tel. (372) 34-94-11; e-mail nt@tajnet.com; f. 1938; weekly; social and political; in Tajik; Editor-in-Chief SHARIF KHAMDAMPUR; circ. (annual) 9,000.

Tojikiston ovozi/Golos Tadzhikistana (Voice of Tajikistan): 734018 Dushanbe, Xiyoboni S. Sherozi 16; tel. (372) 33-06-08; f. 1992; organ of the Central Committee of the Communist Party of Tajikistan; weekly; in Tajik and Russian; Editors SULAYMAN ERMATOV, INOM MUSOYEV; circ. 24,700.

Tribun.tj: 731000 Dushanbe, Xiyoboni Rudaki 107; tel. (372) 21-05-45; fax (372) 21-25-36; e-mail dustov@tribun.tj; internet www.tribun.tj; f. 2005; online only; in Russian; organ of the People's Democratic Party of Tajikistan; daily.

Vechernii Dushanbe (Dunshanbe Evening News): 734018 Dushanbe, Xiyoboni S. Sherozi 16; tel. (372) 33-08-15; fax (372) 33-30-25; e-mail anush@tajnet.com; f. 1968; weekly; social and political; in Russian; Editor-in-Chief SAIDALI SIDDIKOV.

Xalk ovozi (Voice of the People): 734018 Dushanbe, Xiyoboni S. Sherozi 16; tel. (372) 33-05-04; f. 1929; organ of the President; 3 a week; in Uzbek; Editor I. MUKHSINOV; circ. 8,600.

Zindagi (Life): 734000 Dushanbe; f. 2004; weekly; in Tajik; independent; politics; Editor-in-Chief KHURSHED ATOVULLO.

PRINCIPAL PERIODICALS

Monthly, unless otherwise indicated.

Adab: 734025 Dushanbe, Kuchai Chexov 13; tel. (372) 23-49-36; organ of the Ministry of Education; in Tajik; Editor SH. SHOKIRZODA; circ. (annual) 24,000.

Avitsenna: 734018 Dushanbe, Xiyoboni S. Sherozi 16; tel. (372) 34-34-44; in Russian; weekly; medicine, health, sport; Editor-in-Chief RUSTAM TURSUNOV.

Bunyod-i Adab (Culture Fund): 734000 Dushanbe; f. 1996 to foster cultural links among the country's Persian-speaking peoples; weekly; Editor ASKAR KHAKIM.

Djashma (Spring): 734018 Dushanbe, Xiyoboni S. Sherozi 16; tel. (372) 33-08-48; f. 1986; journal of the Ministry of Culture; for children; Editor KAMOL NASRULLO; circ. (annual) 10,000.

Farxang (Culture): 734003 Dushanbe, Xiyoboni Rudaki 124; tel. (372) 24-02-39; f. 1991; journal of the Culture Fund and Ministry of Culture; in Tajik; Editor-in-Chief J. AKOBIR; circ. 15,000.

Firuza: 734018 Dushanbe, Xiyoboni S. Sherozi 16; tel. (372) 33-89-10; f. 1932; organ of the Ministry of Culture; social and literary journal for women; Editor ZULFIYA ATOI; circ. (annual) 29,400.

Ilm va khayot (Science and Life): 734025 Dushanbe, Xiyoboni Rudaki 34; tel. (372) 27-48-61; f. 1989; organ of the Academy of Sciences; popular science; Editor T. BOIBOBO; circ. (annual) 12,000.

Istikbol: 734018 Dushanbe, Xiyoboni S. Sherozi 16; tel. (372) 33-14-52; f. 1952; organ of the Ministry of Culture; in Tajik; Chief Editor L. KENJAYEVA; circ. (annual) 10,000.

Marifat: 734024 Dushanbe, Kuchai Aini 45; tel. (372) 23-42-84; organ of the Ministry of Education; in Tajik; Editor O. BOZOROV; circ. (annual) 40,000.

Pamir: 734001 Dushanbe, Kuchai I. Somoni 8; tel. (372) 24-56-56; f. 1949; journal of the Union of Writers of Tajikistan; fiction; in Russian; Editor-in-Chief BORIS PSHENICHNYI.

Sadoi shark (Voice of the East): 734001 Dushanbe, Kuchai I. Somoni 8; tel. (372) 24-56-79; f. 1927; journal of the Union of Writers of Tajikistan; fiction; in Tajik; Editor URUN KUKHZOD; circ. 1,600.

NEWS AGENCIES

Asia-Plus TV-Radio Company: 734002 Dushanbe, Kuchai Boxtar 35/1, 8th Floor; tel. (372) 23-59-95; fax (372) 23-01-07; e-mail manager@asiaplus.tj; internet www.asiaplus.tj; f. 2002; independent; reports in Tajik and Russian; Gen. Dir UMED BABAKHANOV.

Avesta News Agency: 734025 Dushanbe, Xiyoboni Rudaki 21A; e-mail zafar@avesta.tj; internet www.avesta.tj; Dir ZAFAR ABDULLAYEV.

Khovar (East): 737025 Dushanbe, Xiyoboni Rudaki 40; tel. (372) 23-23-83; fax (372) 21-21-37; e-mail khovar@tojikiston.com; internet www.khovar.tj; f. 1925; govt information agency; Dir ZAFAR SAIDOV.

Mizon: 734000 Dushanbe; independent information agency; Dir ASATULLO VALIYOV.

Varorud: 735700 Soghd Viloyat, Khujand, Kuchai Ferdovsi 123; tel. and fax (342) 24-09-33; e-mail varorud@varorud.org; internet www.varorud.org; f. 2000; independent; Dir ILKHOM JAMOLOV.

PRESS ASSOCIATIONS

Internews Network—Tajikistan: 734025 Dushanbe, Kuchai Ak. Rajabov 7/1/4; tel. (372) 21-99-33; fax (372) 21-99-34; e-mail chuck@internews.tj; internet www.internews.tj; f. 1995; non-governmental org.; provides support and funding to media organizations, and in the training of journalists; Country Dir CHARLES RICE.

National Association of Independent Mass Media: 734025 Dushanbe, Kuchai Kuchai Xuseinzoda 34; tel. (372) 21-37-11; e-mail nansmit@tojikiston.com; internet www.nansmit.org; f. 1999; Chair. NURIDDIN KARSHIBOYEV.

Publishers

Adib (Writer): 734000 Dushanbe, Xiyoboni Rudaki 37; tel. (372) 23-08-92; fax (372) 23-37-94; state-owned; Tajik and Russian; fiction, incl. poetry, and non-fiction, incl. books on Tajikistani and Central Asian culture.

Donish (Knowledge): 734000 Dushanbe, Xiyoboni Akademiya Nauk 33; state-owned; Russian and Tajik; non-fiction, incl. geography, literature, history, and art; associated with the Academy of Sciences.

Irfon (Light of Knowledge) Publishing House: 734018 Dushanbe, Kuchai N. Karabayev 17; tel. (372) 33-39-06; f. 1925; politics, social sciences, economics, agriculture, medicine and technology; Dir J. SHARIFOV; Editor-in-Chief A. OLIMOV.

Maorif va Farxang (Education and Culture) Publishing House: 734018 Dushanbe, Kuchai N. Karabayev 17; tel. and fax (372) 33-93-97; e-mail najmidin@netrt.org; f. 1958; educational, academic; Gen. Dir NAJMIDDIN ZAYNIDDINOV.

Sarredaksiyai Ilmii Entsiklopediyai Millii Tajik (Tajik National Scientific Encyclopaedia) Publishing House:

TAJIKISTAN

731000 Dushanbe, Kuchai Aini 126; tel. (372) 25-81-55; e-mail encyclopedia@yahoo.com; f. 1969; Editor-in-Chief A. Qurbonov.

Sharki Ozod Publishing House: 734018 Dushanbe, Xiyoboni S. Sherozi 16; tel. (372) 34-94-11; e-mail tadjikis@tajnet.com; state-owned; Dir Manzurhon Dodohonov.

Surushan Publishing House: 734025 Dushanbe, Xiyoboni Rudaki 37; tel. and fax (372) 21-54-62; e-mail surushan@net.org; f. 1997; literary fiction, educational; Dir Nuriddin Zayniddinov.

Broadcasting and Communications

TELECOMMUNICATIONS

Babilon-Mobil (Babilon-M): 734001 Dushanbe, Kuchai I. Somoni 5; tel. (372) 24-20-21; e-mail babilon-m@tojikiston.com; internet www.babilon-m.com; f. 2002; mobile cellular telecommunications.

Indigo Tajikistan: 734000 Dushanbe, Kuchai M. Tursunzoda 23; tel. (372) 23-21-21; fax (372) 23-21-23; e-mail sales@indigo.tajnet.com; internet www.indigo.tj; f. 2001; mobile cellular telecommunications.

Tajiktelecom: 734025 Dushanbe, Xiyoboni Rudaki 57a; tel. (372) 21-31-78; fax (372) 23-21-19; e-mail ttelecom@rs.tj; internet www.tajiktelecom.tj; f. 1996; national telecommunications operator; Dir-Gen. Gulmahmad Kayumov.

BROADCASTING

In December 2001 there were some 20 independent television stations.

Regulatory Authority

State Committee for Broadcasting: 734000 Dushanbe; Chair. A. K. Rakhmonov.

Radio

State TV-Radio Broadcasting Co of Tajikistan: 734025 Dushanbe, Kuchai Chapayev 31; tel. (372) 27-75-27; fax (372) 21-34-95; e-mail soro@ctvrtj.td.silk.org; Chair. Abdodzhabbor Rakhmonov.

Asia-Plus Radio: 734000 Dushanbe, Kuchai Boxtar 35/1, 8th Floor; tel. (372) 23-59-95; fax (371) 23-01-07; e-mail radio@asiaplus.tajik.net; f. 2002; country's first independent radio station; broadcasts 19 hours per day in Russian and Tajik; Dir Umed Babakhanov.

Tajik Radio: 734025 Dushanbe, Kuchai Chapayev 31; tel. (372) 27-65-69; broadcasts in Russian, Tajik and Uzbek.

Tiroz: 735700 Soghd Viloyat, Khujand, Mikroraion 27; tel. (342) 25-66-89; e-mail trrktiroz@sugdien.com; internet www.tiroz.sugdien.com; Dir Khurshed Ulmasov.

Television

State TV-Radio Broadcasting Co of Tajikistan: 734025 Dushanbe, Kuchai Chapayev 31; tel. (372) 27-75-27; fax (372) 21-34-95; e-mail soro@ctvrtj.td.silk.org; Chair. Abdodzhabbor Rakhmonov.

Tajik Television (TTV): 734013 Dushanbe, Kuchai Behzod 7; tel. (372) 22-43-57.

Poitaxt: 734013 Dushanbe, Kuchai Azizbekov 20; tel. (372) 23-26-29; independent; Dir Rakhmon Ostonov.

Finance

(cap. = capital; res = reserves; dep. = deposits; brs = branches; m. = million; amounts in somoni, unless otherwise stated)

BANKING

Central Bank

National Bank of the Republic of Tajikistan (Bonki Millii Tochikiston): 734025 Dushanbe, Xiyoboni Rudaki 23/2; tel. (372) 21-26-28; fax (372) 51-00-68; e-mail info@natbank.tajnet.com; internet www.nbt.tj; f. 1991; cap. 0.8m., res 25.4m., dep. 604.8m. (Oct. 2003); Chair. Sharif Rahimzoda.

State Savings Bank

Amonatbonk: 734018 Dushanbe, Kuchai Loxuti 24; tel. (372) 221-70-81; fax (372) 223-14-16; e-mail info@amonatbonk.tj; internet www.amonatbonk.tj; f. 1991; fmrly br. of USSR Sberbank; licensed by presidential decree and not subject to the same controls as the commercial and trading banks; Chair. of Bd Maxmadamin B. Maxmadaminov; 58 brs, 480 sub-brs.

Other Banks

In June 2005 President Rakhmonov announced the removal of all restrictions on the activities of foreign banks in Tajikistan. There were reported to be 16 commercial banks in operation in Tajikistan in early 2005, including the following:

Agroinvestbank: 734018 Dushanbe, Xiyoboni S. Sherozi 21; tel. (372) 36-50-05; fax (372) 36-51-66; e-mail info@aib-tj.com; internet www.agroinvestbank.tj; f. 1992; fmrly Agroprombank; cap. 15.0m., res 11.0m., dep. 73.2m. (Jan. 2005); Chair. Niyozmurod M. Saidmurodov; 60 brs (Jan. 2005).

Orienbank: 734001 Dushanbe, Xiyoboni Rudaki 95/1; tel. (372) 21-09-20; fax (372) 21-18-77; e-mail info@orienbank.com; internet www.orienbank.com; f. 1922; cap. 8.0m., res 3.3m., dep. 61.9m. (Dec. 2003); commercial bank; Chair. of Bd Hasan Saduloev; Chair. of Bank Council Shermalik Malikov; 30 brs.

Tajbank: 734064 Dushanbe, Kuchai I. Somoni 59/1; tel. (372) 27-46-54.

Tajprombank (Tajik Joint-Stock Bank for Reconstruction and Development): 734025 Dushanbe, Kuchai X. Dexlavi 12/3; tel. (372) 21-27-20; e-mail tpb@tjinter.com; cap. US $1m., res $3m., dep. $4m.; Chair. Dzhamshed Ziyayev; 8 brs.

Tojiksodirotbonk (Bank for Foreign Economic Affairs of the Republic of Tajikistan): 734012 Dushanbe, Kuchai X. Dexlavi 4; tel. (372) 21-59-52; fax (372) 21-47-38; e-mail sham@sodirotbonk.com; fmrly br. of USSR Vneshekonombank; underwent restructuring in 1999; Chair. I. L. Lalbekov; 6 brs.

COMMODITY EXCHANGES

Tajik Republican Commodity Exchange (NAVRUZ): 734001 Dushanbe, Kuchai Orjonikidze 37; tel. (372) 23-48-74; fax (372) 27-03-91; f. 1991; Chair. Suleyman Chulebayev.

Vostok-Mercury Torgovyi Dom: 734000 Dushanbe; tel. and fax (372) 24-60-61; f. 1991; trades in a wide range of goods.

INSURANCE

Muin Insurance Co: 734025 Dushanbe, Kuchai Sh. Rustaveli 16/1; tel. (372) 21-32-80; fax (372) 21-72-09.

Orien Insurance: 734001 Dushanbe, Xiyoboni Rudaki 100; tel. and fax (372) 21-12-30; e-mail info@orieninsurance.tj; internet www.orieninsurance.tj; f. 2004; life and non-life; Dir Iskandar Kh. Sharipov.

Tojiksurguta State Insurance Co: 734025 Dushanbe, Kuchai Chexov 4a; tel. (372) 21-75-07.

Trud Insurance Co: 734000 Dushanbe, Kuchai Bekzod 70; tel. (372) 227-24-24; fax (372) 221-72-21; e-mail info@trud.tj; internet www.trud.tj; f. 2004; life and non-life.

Trade and Industry

GOVERNMENT AGENCIES

Presidential Agency for the Combat of Corruption and Economic Crime: 734000 Dushanbe.

Presidential Agency for Control of Narcotics: 734000 Dushanbe, Kuchai Karabayev 52; tel. (372) 34-81-30; fax (372) 34-81-29; e-mail dca@tojikiston.com; f. 1999; documents and curbs regional drugs-trafficking; receives financial and technical assistance from the UN Office on Drugs and Crime; Dir Col-Gen. Rustam Nazarov.

State Committee for Investment and the Management of State Property: 734000 Dushanbe; f. 2006; Chair. Sharif Rahimov.

CHAMBER OF COMMERCE

Chamber of Commerce and Industry of the Republic of Tajikistan: 734012 Dushanbe, Kuchai Valamatzade 21; tel. (372) 21-52-84; fax (372) 21-14-80; e-mail chamber@tpp.tj; internet www.tpp.tj; f. 1960; brs in Khujant, Qurgonteppa, Khorog, and Chamber of Services in Dushanbe; Chair. Sharif S. Saidov.

INDUSTRIAL ASSOCIATION

Tajikvneshtorg (Tajik External Trade) Industrial Asscn: 734035 Dushanbe, Xiyoboni Rudaki 25, POB 48; tel. (372) 23-29-03; fax (372) 22-81-20; f. 1988; co-ordinates trade with foreign countries in a wide range of goods; Pres. Abdurakhmon Mukhtashov.

EMPLOYERS' ORGANIZATION

National Asscn of Small and Medium-Sized Businesses of Tajikistan: 734000 Dushanbe, Kuchai Bofanda 9; tel. (372) 27-79-78; fax (372) 21-17-26; f. 1993 with govt support; independent org.; Chair. Matljuba Uljabaeva.

UTILITIES

Electricity

Barqi Tojik (Tajik Electricity): 734000 Dushanbe, Kuchai I. Somoni 64; tel. (372) 35-86-68; fax (372) 35-86-92; e-mail barkitojik@tajnet.com; Chair. BAHROM SIROJEV.

Pamir Energy Co (PamirEnergy): 736100 Kuhistoni Badakhshon, Khorog; e-mail daler.jumaev@pamirenergy.com; f. 2002; jt venture between Governments of Tajikistan and Switzerland, the Aga Khan Fund for Economic Development, the International Finance Corpn and the International Development Association to provide electricity to Kuhistoni Badakhshon; Gen. Dir DALER JUMAYEV.

Gas

Dushanbegaz: 734000 Dushanbe; tel. (372) 27-89-28; supplies gas to Dushanbe city.

Soghdgaz: 735700 Soghd Viloyat, Khujand, 20 Kvartal; tel. (342) 22-53-95; fax (342) 24-35-16; supplies gas to Soghd Viloyat.

Tojikgaz: 734012 Dushanbe, Xiyoboni Rudaki 6; tel. (372) 21-66-68; fax (372) 21-28-16; state-controlled gas utility co.; Dir FATXIDDIN MUXSIDDINOV.

TRADE UNIONS

Federation of Trade Unions: 734012 Dushanbe, Xiyoboni Rudaki 20; tel. (372) 23-17-79; fax (372) 23-25-06; f. 1926; present name adopted 1992; Chair. MURODALI S. SALIKHOV; 1.3m. mems.

Transport

RAILWAYS

There are few railways in Tajikistan. In 1999 the total length of the rail network was 482 km. Lines link the major centres of the country with the railway network of Uzbekistan, connecting Khujand to the Farg'ona (Fergana) valley lines, and the cotton-growing centre of Qurgonteppa to Termiz. A new line, between the town of Isfara, in Soghd Viloyat, and Xavast, in Uzbekistan, was opened in 1995 and in 1997 a passenger route between Dushanbe and Volgograd, Russia, was inaugurated. The first section of a new line between Qurgonteppa and Kulob, in the south-west of Tajikistan, was inaugurated in 1998. In October 2002 a route from Kulob to Astrakhan, Russia, was opened. The predominantly mountainous terrain makes the construction of a more extensive network unlikely.

Tajik Railways: 734012 Dushanbe, Kuchai Nazarshoyev 35; tel. (372) 21-88-54; fax (372) 21-83-34; e-mail belugin@railway.td.silk.glas.apc.org; Pres. AMONULLO KH. KHUKUMOV.

ROADS

In mid-2002 Tajikistan's road network totalled an estimated 30,000 km, including 13,747 km of highways. The principal highway links the northern city of Khujand, across the Anzob Pass (3,372 m), with the capital, Dushanbe, continuing to Khorog (Kuhistoni Badakhshon), before wending through the Pamir Mountains, to the east and north, to Osh, Kyrgyzstan, across the Akbaytal Pass (4,655 m). This arterial route exhibits problems common to much of the country's land transport: winter weather is likely to cause the road to be closed by snow for up to eight months of the year. In 2000 Tajikistan and the Asian Development Bank signed a memorandum of understanding for the rehabilitation of the road linking Dushanbe to the south-western cities of Qurgonteppa and Kulob. In the same year a road linking eastern Tajikistan with the People's Republic of China was completed, giving Tajikistan access to the Karakorum highway, which connects China and Pakistan.

CIVIL AVIATION

The main international airport is at Dushanbe, and there is also a major airport at Khujand. The country is linked to cities in Russia and other former Soviet republics, and to a growing number of destinations in Europe and Asia.

Tajikistan Airlines: 734006 Dushanbe, Kuchai Titova 32/1; tel. (372) 21-21-45; fax (372) 21-86-85; e-mail tt_gart@tajnet.com; internet www.tajikistan-airlines.com; f. 1990; fmrly Tajik Air; state-owned; operates flights to destinations in Afghanistan, the People's Republic of China (Xinjiang Uygur autonomous region), Germany, India, Iran, Kazakhstan, Kyrgyzstan, Pakistan, Russia, Turkey and the United Arab Emirates; Gen. Dir HOKIMSHO TILLOYEV.

Tourism

There was little tourism in Tajikistan even before the 1992–97 civil war. There is some spectacular mountain scenery, hitherto mainly visited by climbers, and, particularly in the Farg'ona (Fergana) valley, in the north of the country, there are sites of historical interest, notably the city of Khujand.

State Committee for Youth, Sports and Tourism: 734000 Dushanbe; f. 2006.

Tajikistan Republican Council of Tourism and Excursions: 734008 Dushanbe, Xiyoboni Rudaki 20; tel. (372) 27-27-51; fax (372) 51-01-40; f. 1960; Chair. MADZHID SOBIROV.

Sayoh State Unitary Tourism Company: 734025 Dushanbe, Kuchai Pushkin 14; tel. (372) 23-14-01; fax (372) 21-71-84; e-mail gafarov@cada.tajik.net; internet www.tajiktour.tajnet.com; Chair. KASIM GAFAROV.

TANZANIA

Introductory Survey

Location, Climate, Language, Religion, Flag, Capital

The United Republic of Tanzania consists of Tanganyika, on the African mainland, and the nearby islands of Zanzibar and Pemba. Tanganyika lies on the east coast of Africa, bordered by Uganda and Kenya to the north, by Rwanda, Burundi and the Democratic Republic of the Congo (formerly Zaire) to the west, and by Zambia, Malawi and Mozambique to the south. Zanzibar and Pemba are in the Indian Ocean, about 40 km (25 miles) off the coast of Tanganyika, north of Dar es Salaam. The climate varies with altitude, ranging from tropical in Zanzibar and on the coast and plains to semi-temperate in the highlands. The official languages are Swahili and English and there are numerous tribal languages. There are Muslim, Christian and Hindu communities. Many Africans follow traditional beliefs. The national flag (proportions 2 by 3) comprises two triangles, one of green (with its base at the hoist and its apex in the upper fly) and the other of blue (with its base in the fly and its apex at the lower hoist), separated by a broad, yellow-edged black diagonal stripe, from the lower hoist to the upper fly.

Recent History

Tanganyika became a German colony in 1884, and was later incorporated into German East Africa, which also included present-day Rwanda and Burundi. In 1918, at the end of the First World War, the German forces in the area surrendered, and Tanganyika was placed under a League of Nations mandate, with the United Kingdom as the administering power. In 1946 Tanganyika became a UN Trust Territory, still under British rule. At a general election in September 1960 the Tanganyika African National Union (TANU) won 70 of the 71 seats in the National Assembly, and the party's leader, Dr Julius Nyerere, became Chief Minister. Internal self-government was achieved in May 1961, when Nyerere became Prime Minister. Tanganyika became independent, within the Commonwealth, on 9 December 1961, but Nyerere resigned as Prime Minister in January 1962, in order to devote himself to the direction of TANU. He was succeeded as premier by Rashidi Kawawa. On 9 December 1962, following elections in November, Tanganyika became a republic, with Nyerere as the country's first President. Kawawa became Vice-President. Zanzibar (including the island of Pemba), a British protectorate since 1890, became an independent sultanate in December 1963. Following an armed uprising by the Afro-Shirazi Party (ASP) in January 1964, the Sultan was deposed and a republic proclaimed. The new Government signed an Act of Union with Tanganyika in April 1964, thus creating the United Republic. The union was named Tanzania in October 1964, and a new Constitution was introduced in July 1965, which provided for a one-party state (although, until 1977, TANU and the ASP remained the respective official parties of mainland Tanzania and Zanzibar, and co-operated in affairs of state). Nyerere was elected President of the United Republic in September 1965, and was subsequently re-elected in 1970, 1975 and 1980.

Despite its incorporation into Tanzania, Zanzibar retained a separate administration, which ruthlessly suppressed all opposition. A separate Constitution for Zanzibar was adopted in October 1979, providing for a popularly elected President and a House of Representatives elected by delegates of the ruling party. The first elections to the 40-member Zanzibar House of Representatives were held in January 1980. In June of that year a coup plot against Aboud Jumbe, Chairman of the ruling Revolutionary Council of Zanzibar and First Vice-President of the United Republic, was thwarted; Jumbe won an overwhelming majority at Zanzibar's first presidential election, held in October. However, mounting dissatisfaction among Zanzibaris concerning the union with Tanganyika culminated in the resignation, in January 1984, of Jumbe and three of his ministers. In April Ali Hassan Mwinyi, a former Zanzibari Minister of Natural Resources and Tourism, was elected unopposed as President of Zanzibar, winning 87.5% of the votes cast. A new Constitution for Zanzibar came into force in January 1985, providing for the House of Representatives to be directly elected by universal adult suffrage.

In February 1977 TANU and the ASP were amalgamated to form Chama Cha Mapinduzi (CCM), the Revolutionary Party of Tanzania. In April the National Assembly approved a permanent Constitution for Tanzania; this provided for the election to the National Assembly of representatives from Zanzibar, in addition to those from the Tanzanian mainland. At a general election in October 1980 about one-half of the elected members of the Assembly, including several ministers, failed to retain their seats. Major changes to the Constitution were approved by the National Assembly in October 1984, limiting the President's powers and increasing those of the National Assembly.

President Nyerere retired in November 1985, and was succeeded by Mwinyi, who, as the sole candidate, had won 96% of the votes cast at a presidential election in October. Elections to the National Assembly were held on the same day. Mwinyi appointed Joseph Warioba (previously Minister of Justice) as Prime Minister and First Vice-President. At presidential and legislative elections in Zanzibar, also held in October, Idris Abdul Wakil (formerly Speaker of the Zanzibar House of Representatives) was elected President of Zanzibar to replace Mwinyi; although the sole candidate, he received only 61% of the votes. Nyerere remained Chairman of the CCM until August 1990 when he resigned and Mwinyi was appointed in his place.

In early 1988 tension began to increase in Zanzibar, reflecting underlying rivalries between the inhabitants of the main island and those of the smaller island of Pemba, between Zanzibar's African and Arab populations, and between supporters and opponents of unity with Tanganyika. In January Wakil suspended the islands' Government, the Supreme Revolutionary Council, and assumed control of the armed forces from the office of his main rival, Chief Minister Seif Sharrif Hamad, following earlier claims by Wakil that a group of dissidents, including members of the Council, had been plotting the overthrow of his administration. Hamad was replaced later that month by Dr Omar Ali Juma and in May Hamad and six other officials were expelled from the CCM for allegedly opposing the party's aims and endangering Tanzanian unity.

In October 1990 concurrent parliamentary and presidential elections were held in Zanzibar. Wakil did not stand for re-election; the sole presidential candidate, Dr Salmin Amour, was elected as Wakil's successor by 97.7% of the votes cast. Amour subsequently reappointed Juma as Chief Minister of Zanzibar. At the end of October national parliamentary and presidential elections took place. Mwinyi, the sole candidate in the presidential election, was re-elected for a second term, taking 95.5% of the votes cast. In November Mwinyi replaced Warioba as Prime Minister with John Malecela, previously the Tanzanian High Commissioner to the United Kingdom. In December 1994 Mwinyi reorganized the Cabinet. Malecela was replaced as Prime Minister and First Vice-President by Cleopa Msuya, hitherto the Minister of Industry and Trade and previously Prime Minister in 1980–83.

Meanwhile, in December 1991 a presidential commission published recommendations for the establishment of a multi-party political system. In February 1992 proposed constitutional amendments to this effect were ratified by a special congress of the CCM, which stipulated that, in order to protect national unity, all new political organizations should command support in both Zanzibar and mainland Tanzania, and should be free of tribal, religious and racial bias. In May the Constitutions of both the United Republic and Zanzibar were amended to enshrine a multi-party system. Several political organizations were officially registered from mid-1992.

In October 1995 multi-party legislative elections were held for the first time, concurrently with presidential elections, both in Zanzibar and throughout the Tanzanian union. At elections on 22 October the CCM secured 26 of the 50 elective seats in the Zanzibari House of Representatives, while the Civic United Front (CUF, campaigning for increased Zanzibari autonomy) took 24 seats. Amour was re-elected President of the islands by 50.2% of the votes cast, only narrowly defeating Hamad, who represented the CUF. Amour appointed a new ruling council, with Dr Mohamed Gharib Bilali, formerly a government official, as Chief Minister. The CUF contested the election results, accusing the Zanzibari authorities of electoral malpractice and refusing to recognize the legitimacy of the new Amour administration, while party delegates initially declined to take up their seats in the House of Representatives. The Tanzanian national elections, on 29 October, were disrupted by a combination of apparent organizational chaos and further allegations by opposition parties of electoral fraud. Administrative inefficiency led to the cancellation of the election results in seven constituencies in Dar es Salaam; these polls were repeated in mid-November. The opposition parties, alleging that the CCM was manipulating the voting process, refused to re-run, withdrew their candidates from the presidential election, and unsuccessfully petitioned the High Court to declare all results null and void. The Government proceeded to publish the results, whereby the CCM won 186 of the 232 elective seats in the National Assembly, the CUF 24, the National Convention for Reconstruction and Reform (NCCR—Mageuzi) 16, and Chama Cha Democrasia na Maendeleo (Chadema) and the United Democratic Party (UDP) three seats each. Benjamin Mkapa, hitherto Minister of Science, Technology and Higher Education, was deemed to have been elected President, winning 61.8% of the votes cast. The former Minister of Home Affairs, Augustine Mrema, took 27.8% of the votes. President Mkapa was inaugurated in late November; Juma (hitherto Chief Minister of Zanzibar) was appointed Vice-President. Shortly afterwards Mkapa announced a new Cabinet, with Frederick Sumaye (formerly Minister of Agriculture) as Prime Minister.

In his election campaign Mkapa had pledged to tackle corruption in high public office, and in January 1996 he appointed a special presidential commission; in December the commission issued a report asserting that corruption was widespread in the public sector. At a special congress of the CCM in June, Mkapa was elected party Chairman. In September a parliamentary select committee investigating bribery allegations against the Minister of Finance, Simon Mbilinyi, published a report recommending that he be made accountable for having illegally granted tax exemptions. Mbilinyi subsequently resigned. Meanwhile, in October Mrema unexpectedly won a parliamentary by-election in a Dar es Salaam constituency for NCCR—Mageuzi, of which he had become Chairman following his dismissal from Government in 1995; although his campaign had focused on financial impropriety in government, Mrema had recently been accused of having presented false evidence to the parliamentary select committee on corruption in order to undermine the Government's credibility.

During 1996 external donors began to suspend aid disbursements to Zanzibar in view of the continuing political deadlock between the CUF and the islands' administration. There were signs of a rapprochement in January 1997, when representatives of the mainland branch of the CUF reportedly agreed to accept the legitimacy of the Amour Government. During December 1997 and early January 1998, however, 17 members of the CUF, including some delegates to the House of Representatives, were arrested on suspicion of conspiring to overthrow the Amour Government. From January CUF members refused to attend sessions of the House of Representatives in protest; consequently, in February all CUF deputies were officially suspended from the House for 10 days as a punitive measure. During January the Secretary-General of the Commonwealth, Chief Emeka Anyaoku, visited Zanzibar and presented proposals for a peaceful solution to the dispute, including a cessation of confrontational statements, the removal of restrictions on party political activity and a return to the House of Representatives by CUF delegates. Both the CUF and the Zanzibari section of the CCM contained elements that were strongly opposed to negotiating a compromise. Chief Anyaoku subsequently appointed a special envoy, Dr Moses Anafu, to continue mediation efforts, and in early May the UN Secretary-General, Kofi Annan, declared the full support of his organization for the Commonwealth's initiative. During that month a member of a CUF delegation that had been negotiating with Dr Anafu was arrested on suspicion of treason. Treason charges against the 18 CUF members who had been detained in 1997 and 1998 were finally presented in February 1999. The Zanzibari CCM came under considerable pressure from senior mainland CCM officials to reach an agreement with the CUF, while that party's leadership eventually resigned itself to accepting Amour's tenure of the presidency until the end of his term of office in 2000; a mutual accord was finally concluded in June 1999. In January 2000 45 deputies of the mainland CCM were reported to have petitioned the Zanzibari President to withdraw the charges against the 18 CUF members being tried for treason. By that time the court proceedings had already been adjourned several times, and two days prior to the deputies' appeal the Zanzibari Attorney-General had been dismissed after he had ordered the arrest of two more leading members of the CUF. Nevertheless, in February President Amour declared that the trial would not be abandoned. (The charges were dropped in November by Amani Abeid Karume following his election as President of Zanzibar—see below.) Later in February the National Executive Committee of the CCM rejected a proposal to amend the Zanzibari Constitution in order to allow President Amour to serve a third term of office.

In August 1998 a car bomb exploded outside the US embassy in Dar es Salaam (concurrently with a similar attack at the US mission in Nairobi, Kenya); 11 people were killed in Dar es Salaam and some 75 were injured. The attacks were believed to have been co-ordinated by international Islamist terrorists led by a Saudi-born dissident, Osama bin Laden, and the USA retaliated by launching air-strikes against targets in Afghanistan and Sudan. In the aftermath of the bomb attacks, Tanzanian investigators and US federal agents made extensive nation-wide inquiries. Four men were convicted of involvement in the bombings by a court in New York, USA, in May 2001 and were later sentenced to life imprisonment.

A committee was appointed by the Government in July 1998 to assess public opinion on constitutional reform. In September Mkapa reorganized the Cabinet, following the nullification of the election to the National Assembly, in 1995, of two ministers and the resignation in August of the Minister of State in the President's Office, Hassy Kitine, who was alleged to have used state funds to finance medical treatment abroad for his wife. In April 1999 Mrema and his faction of NCCR—Mageuzi defected to the Tanzania Labour Party (TLP). Mrema initially assumed the chairmanship of the TLP, but in May he was banned by the High Court from holding any official post in that party. There was speculation that the death in October of former President Nyerere might give rise to increased pressure for a restructuring of the United Republic of Tanzania. This was, to some extent, reinforced by the release in December of the report of the committee charged with assessing public opinion on constitutional reform. While it found that some 96.3% of Zanzibaris and 84.8% of mainland Tanzanians favoured a 'two-tier' government for the United Republic, the committee itself recommended the establishment of a 'three-tier' system. In so doing it was adjudged by President Mkapa to have exceeded its mandate. In February 2000 the National Assembly approved draft legislation to amend the Constitution in accordance with citizens' recommendations as reported by the committee. Among these recommendations was one that the President should henceforth be elected by a majority vote.

At a presidential election held on 29 October 2000 Benjamin Mkapa was re-elected as President, securing 71.7% of votes cast; Prof. Ibrahim Lipumba, the Chairman of the CUF, won 16.3% of the votes cast, Augustine Mrema 7.8% and John Cheyo 4.2%. The participation rate was 84%. In the following month the CUF and Chadema agreed to form a five-year alliance and field joint candidates for the presidential elections in both the United Republic of Tanzania and in Zanzibar. It was agreed that if either candidate (both from the CUF) won, the respective prime minister would be drawn from Chadema. Candidates from the TLP and NCCR—Mageuzi failed to secure the minimum 200 referees and thus were not allowed to stand for election. At legislative elections, held concurrently, the CCM secured 244 seats in the National Assembly. The largest opposition group to obtain representation was the CUF, with 15 seats; the three other opposition parties (Chadema, the TLP and the UDP) won four, three and two seats, respectively. The polls were declared by international observers to have been freely and fairly conducted. In November Mkapa appointed a new Cabinet, reappointing Frederick Sumaye as Prime Minister.

In marked contrast, presidential and legislative elections were also held in Zanzibar and Pemba on 29 October 2000, amid widespread accusations of electoral fraud. Voting in 16 of the islands' 50 constituencies was annulled owing to a lack of ballot papers and voter registration lists. The Zanzibar Electoral Commission (ZEC) announced that new polls would be held in the 16 constituencies (all areas where the CUF enjoyed strong support), and that counting for the presidential elections for both Zanzibar and the United Republic would be delayed until the new results were received. Opposition parties and Commonwealth electoral observers called for a full re-run of the elections, but this was rejected by the ZEC. Following a week of confusion and violent clashes between the police and opposition supporters, the repeated polls were held on 5 November. Accusations of electoral fraud persisted, and the participation rate was reported to be low. Following the poll, the CCM claimed that it had won 67% of the votes cast (thereby winning 34 seats in the House of Representatives). The CUF refused to recognize the results of the ballot. Despite the concerns of the opposition parties and international observers, the ZEC proclaimed Amani Abeid Karume of the CCM as President of Zanzibar. The CUF refused to recognize Karume as President and demanded that a repeat election be held within four months.

In February 2001 two prominent CUF leaders, including the Deputy Secretary-General, were arrested and charged with the murder of a police officer during the January demonstrations; the human rights organization Amnesty International criticized the charges as politically motivated. One of Karume's first acts as President had been to withdraw treason charges that the two, along with 16 other CUF members, had been facing since 1997 (see above). The Tanzania Court of Appeal had subsequently ruled that treason was not possible in Zanzibar because the isles were not a sovereign state.

In April 2001 an estimated 60,000 supporters of 12 opposition parties gathered peacefully in Dar es Salaam to demand that the Government hold fresh elections in Zanzibar, draft a new Constitution for the United Republic and establish independent electoral commissions. A similar, peaceful demonstration in Zanzibar later that month was attended by an estimated 60,000–85,000 protesters. President Karume, however, continued to reject the opposition's demands. In May 11 members of the Zanzibar House of Representatives and five members of the National Assembly were dismissed from their respective legislatures for having boycotted three successive sittings—their actions were part of the CUF's ongoing refusal to recognize the 2000 election results. The Attorney-General rejected subsequent demands from the CUF for their reinstatement. By-elections were held on 15 May 2003, at which the CUF won every seat it contested (amounting to 15 in the National Assembly and 11 in the Zanzibar House of Representatives). CUF candidates were disqualified from contesting six seats in the House of Representatives; these were won by CCM candidates.

In June 2001 it emerged that, following the violence of the 2000 elections, the CCM and the CUF had been holding a series of secret negotiations intended to resolve the political impasse in Zanzibar. The negotiations concluded with the signing of a *muafaka* (peace accord) between the two parties in Zanzibar in October 2001. Shortly afterwards the State withdrew all 109 legal cases related to the January demonstrations, including the murder charges against the two CUF leaders.

In accordance with the CCM-CUF accord signed in October 2001, amendments to the Zanzibari Constitution were approved by the House of Representatives in April 2002. The amendments provided for the restructuring of the electoral commission to include opposition representatives (duly appointed in October 2002), the creation of a permanent voters' register and the removal of legislation requiring a person to live in a particular area for five consecutive years in order to qualify as a voter. Also included were the introduction of the right to appeal against High Court decisions and the appointment of a separate director of public prosecutions for Zanzibar.

President Mkapa was re-elected Chairman of the CCM at the party's general convention, which was held in October 2002. Later that year 11 Tanzanian opposition parties (including Chadema, NCCR—Mageuzi and the CUF) agreed in principle to field a joint candidate to contest the 2005 presidential election; the proposal remained subject to approval by the parties' members. However, in July 2003 the CUF declared that it would not join the coalition, following its strong performance at May by-elections (see above).

In late 2003 and early 2004 political tension in Zanzibar intensified ahead of the elections due in late 2005. Supporters of the CUF were keen to avoid a repetition of the irregularities that had marred the elections of 1995 and 2000. Zanzibaris were reportedly particularly anxious as, according to the prevailing custom of the United Republic, they were to elect the next President. However, following remarks from President Mkapa that this custom was not guaranteed by law, many Zanzibaris feared that they were becoming marginalized. In November 2003 the CUF Chairman, Lipumba, threatened to obtain a court injunction blocking the 2005 elections unless the register of voters was completed in time, and in April 2004 the leader of the Democratic Party made a similar threat, stating his intention to sue the National Electoral Commission (NEC) and the ZEC unless both bodies were reformed to include members of parties other than the CCM and the CUF. Opposition supporters were also concerned that the Government's efforts to encourage mainlanders who had been living in Zanzibar for more than 10 years to register for Zanzibari citizenship (thus making them eligible to vote in Zanzibar) constituted an attempt to manipulate voter registration in favour of the CCM. The Government, in contrast, deplored the circulation of leaflets throughout Zanzibar urging mainlanders to leave and alleged intimidation of mainlanders.

In early 2004 Islamism appeared to be exerting an increasing influence on politics in Zanzibar. Members of religious groups from Pakistan and Afghanistan were reported to have entered Zanzibar in March 2003 and begun spreading 'seditious teachings'. Moderate Zanzibari Muslim leaders expressed concern about rising extremism, and in March 2004 the island's Mufti, Sheikh Harith bin Kalef, denounced a radical Islamic group, the Zanzibar Union for Awakening and Islamic Forums Community (also known as Uamsho), as a political organization that used religion to disguise its efforts to destabilize Zanzibar. Police banned a demonstration by Uamsho, which insisted that the Mufti should be elected by Muslims rather than appointed by the Government and, it was claimed, advocated killing secular leaders who refused to impose Islamic law in Zanzibar. The demonstration proceeded, but was dispersed by the security forces. A series of bomb attacks followed, targeting Zanzibari power-stations, schools, and other government and private property. In late March two bombs exploded in Stone Town, outside the residences of the Mufti and the Minister of Communications and Transport, Zubeir Ali Maulid, while a third bomb was defused in a bar. A number of Uamsho leaders were subsequently arrested in connection with the bombings.

In early 2004 the Supreme Revolutionary Council stated that from 2005 Zanzibar was to fly its own, separate flag at its interests abroad rather than that of the United Republic of Tanzania. All of Zanzibar's national symbols had been abolished on 26 April 1964 when it entered into union with Tanganyika. However, a separate Zanzibari flag was enshrined in the island's Constitution of 1985 and had been used within Zanzibar for some time.

It was reported in February 2004 that the Government was to prepare, for the first time in 10 years, a supplementary budget, in order to cover additional costs associated with the 2005 elections (including the introduction of identity cards and the establishment of a permanent register of voters), as well as to counteract the effects of drought. In August, amid growing tension in Zanzibar, the CUF petitioned the UN to dispatch observers to the 2005 elections. The CUF noted that a permanent voters' register had yet to be established, and that the reformed ZEC still lacked a director. Moreover, the Joint Presidential Supervisory Commission (JPSC), established to implement the 2001 *muafaka*, was being investigated following allegations of embezzlement. The JPSC was partly funded by international donors, who suspended their contributions following the allegations.

In February 2005 Lipumba declared his candidacy for the presidential election, at which he would represent the CUF. The CCM elected Jakaya Mrisho Kikwete as its presidential candidate at its national party congress in May. (Under the terms of the Constitution, Mkapa was prohibited from standing for re-election to the presidency.) There were sporadic outbreaks of civil unrest on Zanzibar during the voter registration period, where new legislation requiring voters to have lived in their constituencies for at least three years resulted in some 32,000 potential voters being disqualified. Hamad, the CUF's presidential candidate in Zanzibar, had initially been barred from registering (which would have disqualified him from standing in the election) but appealed successfully against the decision.

Following the death of a candidate, it was announced in October 2005 that the elections on the mainland would be delayed until December. The elections in Zanzibar proceeded as scheduled on 30 October 2005 at which Karume was elected President, securing 53.2% of the valid votes cast; Hamad received 46.1% and the four other candidates who contested the presidential election received negligible support. In the legislative elections the CCM won 31 seats in the House of Representatives, and the CUF 18. The ballot in the one remaining constituency was rerun on 14 December, although the result was not made available. The ZEC declared the poll to have been free and fair, while observers from the Commonwealth generally agreed, but recommended investigations into violence and irregularities in voting in Stone Town. There were reports of sporadic violence and numerous unsubstantiated claims of fraud. However, the extreme violence of previous elections was avoided. Karume was sworn in as President of Zanzibar on 2 November.

On mainland Tanzania the delayed presidential and legislative elections were held concurrently on 14 December 2005. Turn-out was officially recorded at 72% and voting proceeded without notable incident. Kikwete was elected President with 80.3% of the votes cast, while Lipumba received 11.7%. The CCM won 207 seats in the National Assembly, the CUF 18, Chadema five and the TLP and UDP one seat each. The CCM received a further 59 of the 75 seats reserved for women (of the remainder the CUF received 10 and Chadema six) and six of the 10 seats reserved for presidential nominees (four remained vacant). Of the five representatives sent from the Zanzibari legislature, three were from the CCM and two from the CUF. The Attorney-General was also a CCM member. Thus, the CCM's final strength in the National Assembly came to 276 seats and the CUF's 30; Chadema secured 11 seats and the TLP and UDP one each. At his inauguration, on 21 December, Kikwete stated that his main priority as President would be to resolve the tensions on Zanzibar, while he also pledged to continue Mkapa's free-market economic policies. On 4 January 2006 Kikwete unveiled his new Cabinet, appointing Edward Lowassa, hitherto the Minister of Water Livestock and Development, as Prime Minister. In late June Kikwete assumed the chairmanship of the CCM.

In September 2006 a commission issued its preliminary report into the alleged illegal distribution of land on Zanzibar. It was claimed that several government ministers and officials had assumed false names in order fraudulently to acquire plots of land. The Minister of Water, Works, Energy and Land, Mansour Yussuf Himid, had requested the investigation, following complaints from citizens who had previously been unsuccessful in their attempts to secure land. The commission noted that the owners of more than 300 plots did not appear in person during the process of its investigation.

In mid-October 2006 Kikwete effected a reshuffle in which 10 cabinet ministers were reassigned to new portfolios. Among those affected by the reorganization was the Minister of Home Affairs, Capt. John Zefania Chiligati, who was replaced by Joseph James Mungai, hitherto the Minister of Agriculture, Food Security and Co-operatives; Chiligati became the new Minister of Labour, Employment and Youth Development, replacing Prof. Jumanne Abdallah Maghembe. Further changes to the Cabinet were implemented in early January 2007, following the death of Juma Akukweti, the Minister of State in the Prime Minister's Office, responsible for Parliamentary Affairs; Dr Batilda Burian was named as his replacement. It was also announced that Dr Asha Rose Migiro had been appointed as Deputy Secretary-General of the UN. Bernard Kamillius Membe assumed her vacated foreign affairs and international co-operation portfolio.

In October 2007 it was announced that 3,000m. shillings was to be allocated to the construction of three dams in the Songwe River to control flooding and serve as a permanent demarcation of the border between Tanzania and Malawi.

Prime Minister Lowassa tendered his resignation in early February 2008 in response to the findings of a parliamentary investigation into his administration's awarding of a power-generation contract in 2006; the Minister of Energy and Minerals and the Minister of East African Co-operation also resigned as a result of their alleged role. President Kikwete named Mizengo Pinda, hitherto Minister of State in the Prime Minister's Office, as Lowassa's successor. Pinda subsequently named a new Cabinet, which included Membe as Minister of Foreign Affairs and International Co-operation and Mwinyi as Minister of Defence and National Service.

At a meeting of representatives from the ruling CCM and the CUF on Zanzibar in February 2008, a proposed power-sharing accord between the two parties was discussed. The CUF approved the arrangement in mid-March, while the CCM did not immediately issue a statement on the agreement; however, the CCM was due to hold a meeting later that month at which the proposal was expected to be adopted. Several issues were to be discussed at the meeting, including Zanzibar governance issues and the composition of the ZEC. However, despite earlier indications of acceptance of the deal, the CCM rejected the proposal, claiming that the issue of power-sharing should be decided at a referendum. In early April the CUF staged demonstrations in opposition to the proposed referendum in an attempt to exert pressure on the CCM to accept the power-sharing agreement.

Tanzania's relations with Uganda and Kenya were strained throughout the 1970s, particularly after the dissolution of the East African Community (EAC, see p. 412) in 1977. Uganda briefly annexed the Kagera salient from Tanzania in November 1978. In early 1979 Tanzanian troops supported the Uganda National Liberation Front in the overthrow of President Idi Amin Dada. In June 2000 Tanzania called on Uganda to pay 98,500m. shillings to cover the cost of the operation. President Mkapa later stated that the amount was to be regarded as a military debt and not, as some claimed, as compensation for those killed during the war. The Tanzania–Kenya border, closed since 1977, was reopened in November 1983, following an agreement on the distribution of the EAC's assets and liabilities. In the following month Tanzania and Kenya agreed to establish full diplomatic relations. The two countries reached agreement on a trade treaty and on the establishment of a joint co-operation commission in 1986. Tanzania pledged its support for the Government of Yoweri Museveni, which took power in Uganda in January of that year, and in November Tanzania began to send military instructors to Uganda to organize the training of Ugandan government troops. In November 1994, meeting in Arusha, the Presidents of Tanzania, Kenya and Uganda established a commission for co-operation; in March 1996 they met again in Nairobi, Kenya, to inaugurate formally the Secretariat of the Permanent Tripartite Commission for East African Co-operation, which aimed to revive the EAC. A treaty for the re-establishment of the EAC, providing for the creation of a free trade area (with the eventual introduction of a single currency), for the development of infrastructure, tourism and agriculture within the Community, and for the establishment of a regional legislative assembly and court, was formally ratified by the Tanzanian, Kenyan and Ugandan Heads of State in November 1999. The new East African Council of Ministers held its first meeting in Tanzania in January 2001. Talks on integrating the economies of the three EAC members followed, and in March 2004 Mkapa, Museveni, and President Mwai Kibaki of Kenya signed a protocol on the creation of a customs union, eliminating most duties on goods within the EAC, which came into force on 1 January 2005.

In August 1993, following a protracted mediation effort by the Mwinyi Government, a peace agreement was signed in Arusha by the Rwandan authorities and the rebel Front patriotique rwandais. In April 1994, however, following the assassination of the Rwandan President, Juvénal Habyarimana, hundreds of thousands of Rwandans fled to Tanzania to escape the atrocities being perpetrated in their homeland. In May the Tanzanian authorities appealed for international emergency aid to assist in the care of the refugees, many of whom were sheltering in makeshift camps in the border region. In March 1995 Tanzania banned the admission of further refugees from both Rwanda and Burundi (where violent unrest had erupted in late 1994); some 800,000 Rwandan and Burundian refugees were reportedly sheltering in Tanzania in September 1995. The International Criminal Tribunal for Rwanda, authorized by the UN to charge and try Rwandan nationals accused of direct involvement in the genocide perpetrated in that country during 1994, was inaugurated in June 1995 in Arusha. After the Tutsi-led military coup, which took place in Burundi in July 1996 (following the failure of peace talks mediated by former President Nyerere), the Mkapa administration imposed economic sanctions against the new regime of President Pierre Buyoya, in co-operation with other regional governments. Relations between Tanzania and Burundi remained strained, owing both to the presence of Burundian rebels in northern Tanzania, which the Buyoya regime accused the Mkapa administration of supporting, and to the increasing numbers of Burundians seeking refuge in Tanzania throughout 1996 and 1997. Talks between the Buyoya Government and opposition politicians, once again mediated by Nyerere, were convened in Arusha in 1998 and early 1999. The regional economic sanctions that were imposed against Burundi in 1996 were suspended in January 1999. In July 2002, following a meeting between President Mkapa and the Burundian Vice-President, Domitien Ndayizeye, the two countries stated that they were to normalize their relations. Peace negotiations between the Burundian transitional Government and rebel groups took place in Dar es Salaam in August and October of that year.

TANZANIA

In December 1996 some of the Rwandan refugees remaining in Tanzania were repatriated, following the threat of forcible repatriation by the Tanzanian Government; however, 200,000 refugees, unwilling to return to Rwanda, reportedly fled their camps. In March 1997 the Tanzanian Government appealed for further international assistance in coping with the remaining refugees (an estimated 200,000 Burundians and 250,000 Zaireans). In June 1997 it was agreed to repatriate some 100,000 refugees to the Democratic Republic of the Congo (DRC—formerly Zaire). At the end of December the office of the UN High Commissioner for Refugees (UNHCR) estimated that some 74,300 refugees from the DRC remained in Tanzania, while the number of Burundian refugees was believed to have increased to 459,400.

In February 2000 the Government announced that nine refugee camps in the Kigoma region of west Tanzania had become saturated. Instability in Burundi and the DRC recently led to further heavy influxes of refugees from those countries. At that time the number of officially registered refugees in west Tanzania reportedly totalled 468,000, but it was claimed that an additional 200,000 unregistered refugees were also present in the region. Burundians accounted for 70% of all refugees, and refugees from the DRC for 29%. In August 2000 a peace accord was signed in Arusha between the Burundian Government and various rebel groups; however, the main rebel groups refused to sign the agreement. Although the agreement neither stopped the fighting in Burundi, nor allowed the refugees to return home, it nevertheless resulted in a serious decline in the level of aid donations (for example, the UNHCR allocation for refugee camps in Tanzania was reduced by 55%). In May 2001 UNHCR and the Governments of Tanzania and Burundi signed an agreement to establish a tripartite commission for the voluntary repatriation of Burundian refugees in Tanzania, of whom there were an estimated 800,000 at that time. In August 2003 Burundi and Tanzania agreed to open additional border crossings to facilitate the return of refugees. An estimated 494,200 Burundian refugees remained in Tanzania in December of that year; by April 2004 a further 34,000 had returned to Burundi, and UNHCR aimed to repatriate a further 122,000 by the end of the year, in view of progress in the peace process and the improved security situation. At the end of 2006 there remained 352,640 Burundian refugees in Tanzania. In February 2004 the remaining Rwandan refugees in Tanzanian camps were repatriated. However, it was reported that an estimated 20,000 Rwandans were illegally resident in Tanzania at this time. At the end of 2006 there were some 127,973 refugees from the DRC in Tanzania. Remaining refugee camps were to close in January 2008; however, by April, it was estimated that some 100,000 Burundian refugees and more than 90,000 from the DRC remained in Tanzania.

Government

Under the provisions of the 1977 Constitution, with subsequent amendments, legislative power is held by the unicameral National Assembly, whose members serve for a term of five years. There is constitutional provision for both directly elected members (chosen by universal suffrage) and nominated members (including five members elected by and from the Zanzibar House of Representatives). The number of directly elected members exceeds the number of nominated members. The Electoral Commission may review and, if necessary, increase the number of constituencies before every general election. Executive power lies with the President, elected by popular vote for five years. The President must be at least 40 years of age and his mandate is limited to a maximum of two five-year terms. The President appoints a Vice-President, to assist him in carrying out his functions, and presides over the Cabinet, which is composed of a Prime Minister and other ministers who are appointed from among the members of the National Assembly.

Zanzibar has its own administration for internal affairs, and the amended Zanzibar Constitution, which came into force in January 1985, provides for the President, elected by universal adult suffrage, to hold office for a maximum of two five-year terms, and for the House of Representatives, of 45–55 members, to be directly elected by universal adult suffrage. The President of Zanzibar appoints the Chief Minister, and the two co-operate in choosing the other members of the Supreme Revolutionary Council, which has a maximum of 20 members.

In May 1992 the United Republic's Constitution was amended to legalize a multi-party political system.

Defence

As assessed at November 2007, the total active armed forces numbered an estimated 27,000, of whom about 23,000 were in the army, 1,000 in the navy and 3,000 in the air force. There are also paramilitary forces including a 1,400-strong Police Field Force and an 80,000-strong reservist Citizens' Militia. The estimated defence budget was 200,000m. shillings in 2007.

Economic Affairs

In 2006, according to estimates by the World Bank, mainland Tanzania's gross national income (GNI), measured at average 2004–06 prices, was US $13,404m., equivalent to $350 per head (or $740 per head on an international purchasing-power parity basis). During 1996–2006, it was estimated, the population of the country as a whole increased at an average annual rate of 2.5%, while gross domestic product (GDP) per head increased, in real terms, by an average of 2.8% per year. Overall GDP increased, in real terms, at an average annual rate of 5.4% in 1996–2006; growth was 5.9% in 2006.

Agriculture (including hunting, forestry and fishing) contributed an estimated 45.3% of GDP in 2006 and, according to FAO estimates, employed some 78.1% of the labour force in 2005. The principal cash crops are cashew nuts (which provided 4.7% of export revenues in 2004), coffee (3.4%), cotton (3.4%) and cloves (Zanzibar's most important export, cultivated on the island of Pemba—they provided 0.9% of export revenues in 2003/04). Other cash crops include tobacco, tea, sisal, pyrethrum, coconuts, sugar and cardamom. Exports of cut flowers (grown in the vicinity of Kilimanjaro Airport and freighted to Europe) commenced in the mid-1990s. Seaweed production is an important activity in Zanzibar. Farmers have been encouraged to produce essential food crops, most importantly cassava and maize. Cattle-rearing is also significant. A large proportion of agricultural output is produced by subsistence farmers. Tanzania's agricultural GDP increased at an average annual rate of 4.1% during 1996–2006, according to the World Bank; agricultural GDP increased by 3.8% in 2006.

Industry (including mining, manufacturing, construction and power) contributed an estimated 17.4% of GDP in 2006; the sector employed 2.6% of the working population in 2001. During 1996–2006 industrial GDP increased by an average of 8.5% per year, according to the World Bank; growth in 2006 was 8.6%.

Mining provided an estimated 2.7% of GDP in 2003. The sector employed 0.2% of the working population on mainland Tanganyika in 2001. Gold, diamonds, other gemstones (including rubies and sapphires), salt, phosphates, coal, gypsum, tin, kaolin, limestone and graphite are mined, and it is planned to exploit reserves of natural gas. Other mineral deposits include nickel, silver, cobalt, copper, soda ash, iron ore and uranium. In late 2003 three companies were bidding for licences to explore for petroleum in the Rufiji delta, Zanzibar, Mafia and the Mkuranga district on the mainland coast. Petroleum was discovered on Tanzania's coastal belt in the 1960s, but was only recently being considered seriously by companies searching for sources of petroleum outside the Middle East. In January 2004 it was announced that a Canadian company, the Barrick Gold Corpn, was to construct a new 526,000-oz gold mine in Tulawaka. According to the IMF, the GDP of the mining sector increased by an average of 12.9% per year in 1990–99; it grew by 9.1% in 1999.

Manufacturing contributed an estimated 6.9% of GDP in 2006. The sector employed 1.5% of the working population on mainland Tanganyika in 2001. The most important manufacturing activities are food-processing, textile production, cigarette production and brewing. Pulp and paper, fertilizers, cement, clothing, footwear, tyres, batteries, pharmaceuticals, paint, bricks and tiles and electrical goods are also produced, while other activities include oil-refining, metal-working, vehicle assembly and engineering. Tanzania's manufacturing GDP increased at an average annual rate of 6.7% in 1996–2006, according to the World Bank; it grew by 7.1% in 2006.

Energy is derived principally from hydroelectric power, which supplied 95.1% of Tanzania's electricity in 2004. Imports of petroleum and petroleum products accounted for 9.9% of the total value of imports in 2005.

The services sector contributed 37.3% of GDP in 2006; the sector employed 15.3% of the working population on mainland Tanganyika in 2001. Tourism is an important potential growth sector: tourism receipts were approximately US $836m. in 2005. According to the World Bank, the GDP of the services sector increased by an average of 5.6% per year in 1996–2006. Growth in the sector was 7.2% in 2006.

In 2006 Tanzania recorded a visible trade deficit of US $2,141.1m., and there was a deficit of $1,442.7m. on the current account of the balance of payments. In 2004 the principal sources of imports were South Africa (providing 13.1% of total imports), India, the United Arab Emirates, Japan, the People's Republic of China, Bahrain and Kenya. The main markets for exports were the United Kingdom (taking 32.3% of total exports), South Africa, India and Kenya. The principal exports in 2004 were gold, fish and fish products and manufactured goods. The principal imports were machinery and transport equipment, petroleum, basic manufactures, chemicals and related products and cereals and cereal preparations.

In the financial year ending 30 June 2006 there was a budgetary deficit of 426,100m. shillings. At the end of 2005 Tanzania's external debt totalled US $7,763m., of which $6,183m. was long-term public debt. In that year the cost of debt-servicing was equivalent to 4.3% of the value of exports of goods and services. On 14 January 2005 the British Chancellor of the Exchequer, Gordon Brown, signed a memorandum of understanding with the Government under which the United Kingdom would service 10% of the debt (both interest and capital repayments) owed by Tanzania to the World Bank, IMF and African Bank for Reconstruction. It was part of a wider move to ease the debt burden of heavily indebted poor countries, and it was hoped his move would persuade other rich nations to act similarly. However, the United Kingdom would cease to service Tanzanian debt if the Tanzanian Government breached undertakings on good governance and democracy. The annual rate of inflation for Tanganyika averaged 6.9% in 1996–2006; consumer prices there increased by 9.1% in 2006. The annual rate of inflation for Zanzibar averaged 7.2% in 1995–2005; consumer prices on the islands increased by 9.8% in 2005.

Tanzania is a member of the African Development Bank (see p. 162) and of the Southern African Development Community (see p. 386). Tanzania is a founder member (with Kenya and Uganda) of the restored East African Community (EAC, see p. 412).

By the mid-2000s Tanzania had become one of Africa's better-performing economies: since 2000 real GDP growth has averaged 6.4% a year, of which agriculture and services (mostly trade, tourism and hotels) each accounted for about one-third. Tourism has been particularly successful: between 1990 and 2005 the number of tourist arrivals more than quadrupled, from 150,000 to 613,000, and receipts rose dramatically, reaching US $836m. This was accompanied by strong productivity growth. However, this economic improvement was accompanied by only a modest reduction in poverty, and in terms of GNI per head, Tanzania remains one of the world's poorest countries. One of the country's greatest economic problems is the very high level of its external debt. The IMF approved two three-year loans in 2000 and 2003 equivalent to some $208.5m. for Tanzania, under its Poverty Reduction and Growth Facility (PRGF), and in November 2001 the country was granted enhanced debt relief, effectively halving its external debt. However, there was concern about Tanzania's continued dependence on foreign aid. The IMF's fifth review under the PRGF arrangement in April 2006 commended the sustained economic performance, leading to a further disbursement of $4.1m. The new President, Jakaya Kikwete, stated that he would continue the free-market policies of his predecessor; thus, it seemed likely that Tanzania's strong economic performance and good relations with donors would continue. However, there was a risk that drought or adverse commodity prices could depress growth. Concerns were also raised that increased government spending on education and training to counteract a lack of skills in the labour force could prove insufficient, and it was feared that HIV/AIDS could constrain productivity improvements. After estimated growth of 6.2% in 2007, the Government forecast GDP to expand by 7.3% in 2008, with agricultural output recovering from drought in the previous year. Employment in the tourism sector was anticipated to continue to increase, while growth in mining was also expected. Nevertheless, there remained no discernible improvement in the standard of living for the majority of the population.

Education

In 2004/05 enrolment at pre-pimary level was 23% (23% of both boys and girls). Education at primary level is officially compulsory and is provided free of charge. In secondary schools a government-stipulated fee is paid: from January 1995 this was 8,000 shillings per year for day pupils at state-owned schools and 50,000–60,000 shillings per year for day pupils at private schools. Villages and districts are encouraged to construct their own schools with government assistance. Almost all primary schools are government-owned. Primary education begins at seven years of age and lasts for seven years. According to UNESCO estimates, in 2004/05 enrolment at primary level included 91% of pupils in the appropriate age-group (92% of boys; 91% of girls). Secondary education, beginning at the age of 14, lasts for a further six years, comprising a first cycle of four years and a second of two years. Secondary enrolment in 1999/2000 included only 6% of children in the appropriate age-group (males 6%; females 5%), according to UNESCO estimates. In November 2001 it was announced that approximately 7m. children were to be enrolled in primary schools, under the Government's five-year plan to reintroduce universal primary education by 2005. Enrolment at tertiary level included just 1% of those in the relevant age-group in 2004/05 (males 2%; females 1%). There are 10 universities, including one on Zanzibar. Tanzania also has a number of vocational training centres and technical colleges. Education was allocated 23% of total recurrent budgetary expenditure by the central Government in 1994.

Public Holidays

2008: 1 January (New Year's Day), 10 January*† (Muharram, New Year), 12 January (Zanzibar Revolution Day), 5 February (Chama Cha Mapinduzi Day), 20 March* (Maulid, Birth of the Prophet), 21–24 March (Easter), 26 April (Union Day), 1 May (International Labour Day), 7 July (Saba Saba, Industry's Day), 8 August (Peasants' Day), 26 August (Sultan's Birthday)‡, 1 October* (Id El Fitr, end of Ramadan), 29 October (Naming Day), 9 December* (Id El Haji, Feast of the Sacrifice), 9 December (Independence Day), 25–26 December (Christmas), 29 December*† (Muharram, New Year).

2009: 1 January (New Year's Day), 12 January (Zanzibar Revolution Day), 5 February (Chama Cha Mapinduzi Day), 9 March* (Maulid, Birth of the Prophet), 10–13 April (Easter), 26 April (Union Day), 1 May (International Labour Day), 7 July (Saba Saba, Industry's Day), 8 August (Peasants' Day), 26 August (Sultan's Birthday)‡, 20 September* (Id El Fitr, end of Ramadan), 29 October (Naming Day), 27 November* (Id El Haji, Feast of the Sacrifice), 9 December (Independence Day), 18 December* (Muharram, New Year), 25–26 December (Christmas).

* These holidays are dependent on the Islamic lunar calendar and may vary by one or two days from the dates given.

† This festival occurs twice (marking the start of the Islamic years AH 1429 and 1430) within the same Gregorian year.

‡ Zanzibar only.

Weights and Measures

The metric system is in force.

TANZANIA

Statistical Survey

Source (unless otherwise stated): Economic and Research Policy Dept, Bank of Tanzania, POB 2939, Dar es Salaam; tel. (22) 2110946; fax (22) 2113325; e-mail info@hq.bot-tz.org; internet www.bot-tz.org.

Area and Population

AREA, POPULATION AND DENSITY

Area (sq km)	945,087*
Population (census results)	
28 August 1988	23,126,310
25 August 2002	
Males	16,910,321
Females	17,658,911
Total	34,569,232
Population (UN estimates at mid-year)†	
2005	38,478,000
2006	39,459,000
2007	40,454,000
Density (per sq km) at mid-2007	42.8

* 364,900 sq miles. Of this total, Tanzania mainland is 942,626 sq km (363,950 sq miles), and Zanzibar 2,461 sq km (950 sq miles).
† Source: UN, *World Population Prospects: The 2006 Revision*.

ETHNIC GROUPS
(private households, census of 26 August 1967)

African	11,481,595	Others	839
Asian	75,015	Not stated	159,042
Arabs	29,775	**Total**	11,763,150
European	16,884		

REGIONS
(at census of 25 August 2002)

Arusha	1,292,973	Mwanza	2,942,148
Dar es Salaam	2,497,940	Pwani	889,154
Dodoma	1,698,996	North Pemba†	186,013
Iringa	1,495,333	North Unguja†	136,953
Kagera	2,033,888	Rukwa	1,141,743
Kigoma	1,679,109	Ruvuma	1,117,166
Kilimanjaro	1,381,149	Shinyanga	2,805,580
Lindi	791,306	Singida	1,090,758
Manyara*	603,691	South Pemba†	176,153
Mara	1,368,602	South Unguja†	94,504
Mbeya	2,070,046	Urban West†	391,002
Morogoro	1,759,809	Tabora	1,717,908
Mtwara	1,128,523	Tanga	1,642,015

* Before the 2002 census Manyara was included in the region of Arusha.
† Part of the autonomous territory of Zanzibar.

PRINCIPAL TOWNS
(estimated population at mid-1988)

Dar es Salaam	1,360,850	Mbeya	152,844
Mwanza	223,013	Arusha	134,708
Dodoma	203,833	Morogoro	117,760
Tanga	187,455	Shinyanga	100,724
Zanzibar	157,634		

Source: UN, *Demographic Yearbook*.

Mid-2007 ('000, incl. suburbs, UN estimate): Dar es Salaam 2,930 (Source: UN, *World Urbanization Prospects: The 2007 Revision*).

BIRTHS AND DEATHS
(annual averages, UN estimates)

	1990–1995	1995–2000	2000–05
Birth rate (per 1,000)	42.4	41.5	42.1
Death rate (per 1,000)	14.8	15.4	14.6

Source: UN, *World Population Prospects: The 2006 Revision*.

Expectation of life (years at birth, WHO estimates): 49.1 (males 48.5; females 49.7) in 2005 (Source: WHO, *World Health Statistics*).

ECONOMICALLY ACTIVE POPULATION
(Mainland Tanganyika only, persons aged 10 years and over, at March 2001)

	Males	Females	Total
Agriculture, forestry, hunting and fishing	6,698.6	7,191.2	13,890.1
Mining and quarrying	15.5	13.8	29.2
Manufacturing	161.7	83.8	245.4
Electricity, gas and water supply	13.5	1.2	14.7
Construction	147.5	4.2	151.7
Wholesale and retail trade and restaurants and hotels	565.5	697.5	1,263.0
Transport, storage and communications	103.9	7.6	111.6
Financing, insurance, real estate and business services	22.2	4.3	26.5
Community, social and personal services	622.8	559.9	1,182.7
Total employed	8,351.3	8,563.5	16,914.8
Unemployed	388.4	524.4	912.8
Total labour force	8,739.7	9,087.9	17,827.6

Source: ILO.

Mid-2005 (estimates in '000): Agriculture, etc. 15,802; Total labour force 20,224 (Source: FAO).

Health and Welfare

KEY INDICATORS

Total fertility rate (children per woman, 2005)	4.8
Under-5 mortality rate (per 1,000 live births, 2005)	122
HIV/AIDS (% of persons aged 15–49, 2005)	6.5
Physicians (per 1,000 head, 2004)	0.02
Hospital beds (per 1,000 head, 1992)	0.89
Health expenditure (2004): US $ per head (PPP)	28.5
Health expenditure (2004): % of GDP	4.0
Health expenditure (2004): public (% of total)	43.6
Access to water (% of persons, 2004)	62
Access to sanitation (% of persons, 2004)	47
Human Development Index (2005): ranking	159
Human Development Index (2005): value	0.467

For sources and definitions, see explanatory note on p. vi.

Agriculture

PRINCIPAL CROPS
('000 metric tons)

	2004	2005	2006
Wheat	74.0	115.0	111.0
Rice (paddy)	586.0	957.0	784.0
Maize	3,232.0	3,288.0	3,373.0
Millet	215.0	155.0*	185.0†
Sorghum	820.1	890.0*	750.0†
Potatoes†	237.6	250.7	250.7
Sweet potatoes†	1,013.0	1,056.4	1,056.4
Cassava (Manioc)	6,152	7,000†	6,500†
Sugar cane	n.a.	n.a.	2,750.0†
Dry beans†	280.0	290.0	290.0
Cashew nuts	79.0	72.0	90.4
Groundnuts (in shell)*	54.0	54.0	54.0
Coconuts†	371.3	372.0	372.0
Oil palm fruit†	66.8	68.1	68.1
Seed cotton*	330.0	315.0	300.0
Tomatoes†	144.3	149.6	149.6

TANZANIA

Statistical Survey

—continued	2004	2005	2006
Onions (dry)†	55.0	55.0	55.0
Bananas	147.8	150.0†	150.0†
Plantains	591.2	600.0†	600.0†
Mangoes†	195.0	200.0	200.0
Pineapples†	77.5	78.0	78.0
Coffee (green)	32.5	54.0	34.3
Tea (made)	30.1	30.7	30.3
Cloves (whole and stems)†	12.1	12.3	12.3
Tobacco (leaves)	34.0	47.0	52.0
Cotton (lint)*	118.0	126.0	99.0

* Unofficial figure(s).
† FAO estimate(s).

Aggregate production ('000 metric tons, may include official, semi-official or estimated data): Total cereals 4,946.5 in 2004, 5,424.4 in 2005, 2,478.2 in 2006; Total roots and tubers 7,413.6 in 2004, 8,319.1 in 2005, 7,819.1 in 2006; Total vegetables (incl. melons) 1,245.7 in 2004, 1,251.3 in 2005, 1,251.3 in 2006; Total fruits (excl. melons) 1,321.8 in 2004, 1,338.5 in 2005, 1,338.5 in 2006.

Source: FAO.

LIVESTOCK
('000 head, year ending September)

	2003	2004	2005
Asses, mules or hinnies*	182.0	182.0	182.0
Cattle	17,704.0	17,472.1	17,719.1
Pigs	455.0	455.0	455.0
Sheep	3,521.2	3,521.0	3,521.0
Goats	12,556.2	12,550.0*	12,550.0*
Chickens*	30,000	30,000	30,000

* FAO estimate(s).

2006: Figures assumed to be unchanged from 2005 (FAO estimates).
Source: FAO.

LIVESTOCK PRODUCTS
('000 metric tons, FAO estimates)

	2003	2004	2005
Cattle meat	246.3	246.3	246.3
Sheep meat	10.3	10.3	10.3
Goat meat	30.6	30.6	30.6
Pig meat	13.0	13.0	13.0
Chicken meat	47.0	47.0	47.0
Cows' milk	840.0	840.0	840.0
Goats' milk	104.0	104.0	104.0
Hen eggs	35.1	35.1	35.1
Honey	27.0	27.0	27.0

2006: Production assumed to be unchanged from 2005 (FAO estimates).
Source: FAO.

Forestry

ROUNDWOOD REMOVALS
('000 cubic metres, excluding bark, FAO estimates)

	2004	2005	2006
Sawlogs, veneer logs and logs for sleepers	317	317	317
Pulpwood	153	153	153
Other industrial wood	1,844	1,844	1,844
Fuel wood	21,477	21,683	21,885
Total	23,791	23,997	24,199

Source: FAO.

SAWNWOOD PRODUCTION
('000 cubic metres, including railway sleepers, FAO estimates)

	1992	1993	1994
Coniferous (softwood)	26	21	13
Broadleaved (hardwood)	22	18	11
Total	48	39	24

1995–2006: Production assumed to be unchanged from 1994 (FAO estimates).
Source: FAO.

Fishing

('000 metric tons, live weight)

	2003	2004	2005*
Capture	351.1	347.8	348.1
Tilapias	50.0	51.7	51.7
Nile perch	98.5	98.5	98.5
Other freshwater fishes	98.8	97.0	97.0
Dagaas	43.5	40.0	40.0
Sardinellas	14.2	15.0	15.0
Aquaculture*	0.0	0.0	0.0
Total catch	351.1	347.8	348.1

* FAO estimates.

Note: Figures exclude aquatic plants ('000 metric tons): 9.5 (capture 2.5, aquaculture 7.0) in 2003; 6.2 (capture 0.2, aquaculture 6.0) in 2004; 6.2 (capture 0.2, aquaculture 6.0) in 2005. Also excluded are aquatic mammals, recorded by number rather than by weight. The number of Risso's dolphins caught was: 1 in 2003; 1 in 2004; nil in 2005. The number of Indo-Pacific hump-backed dolphins caught was: 4 in 2003; 1 in 2004; nil in 2005. The number of Bottlenose dolphins caught was: 16 in 2003; 6 in 2004; nil in 2005. The number of Spinner dolphins caught was: 10 in 2003; 3 in 2004; nil in 2005. The number of other spotted dolphins caught was: 2 in 2003; 1 in 2004; nil in 2005. The number of Nile crocodiles caught was: 1,469 in 2003; 1,560 in 2004; 1,467 in 2005.

Source: FAO.

Mining

('000 metric tons, unless otherwise indicated)

	2003	2004	2005
Coal (bituminous)	55	65	75
Diamonds ('000 carats)*	237	304	220
Gold (refined, kilograms)	48,018	48,178	52,236
Salt	59	57	135
Gypsum and anhydrite	33	59	63
Limestone, crushed	1,206	1,391	2,780
Pozzolanic materials	106	153	163
Sand	2,036	2,400†	2,800†

* Estimated at 85% gem-quality and 15% industrial-quality stones. Excluding smuggled artisanal production.
† Estimate.

Source: US Geological Survey.

TANZANIA

Industry

SELECTED PRODUCTS
('000 metric tons, unless otherwise indicated)

	2001	2002	2003*
Sugar	184.0	189.6	212.9
Cigarettes (million)	3.5	3.8	3.9
Beer (million litres)	175.7	175.9	194.1
Non-alcoholic beverages (million litres)	198.7	208.7	208.4
Textiles (million sq metres)	84.3	106.3	125.8
Cement	900.0	1,026.0	1,186.0
Rolled steel	16.1	25.4	39.6
Iron sheets	25.9	35.1	33.6
Aluminium	0.1	0.1	0.2
Sisal ropes	4.5	5.9	6.9
Paints (million litres)	9.0	13.6	16.8

* Provisional.

Source: IMF, *Tanzania—Selected Issues and Statistical Appendix* (September 2004).

Cement ('000 metric tons): 1,281 in 2004; 1,375 in 2005 (Source: US Geological Survey).

Finance

CURRENCY AND EXCHANGE RATES

Monetary Units
100 cents = 1 Tanzanian shilling.

Sterling, Dollar and Euro Equivalents (31 November 2007)
£1 sterling = 2,419.16 Tanzanian shillings;
US $1 = 1,170.71 Tanzanian shillings;
€1 = 1,728.08 Tanzanian shillings;
10,000 Tanzanian shillings = £4.13 = $8.54 = €5.79.

Average Exchange Rate (Tanzanian shillings per US $)
2004 1,089.33
2005 1,128.93
2006 1,251.90

BUDGET
('000 million shillings, year ending 30 June)*

Revenue†	2001/02	2002/03	2003/04‡
Tax revenue	938.5	1,105.7	1,325.1
Import duties	88.9	106.4	130.1
Value-added tax	352.3	424.3	494.8
Excises	177.6	187.3	216.6
Income tax	228.4	276.1	360.4
Other taxes	91.3	111.7	123.2
Non-tax revenue	104.5	111.8	122.3
Ministries and regions	68.0	78.0	85.4
Total	1,042.9	1,217.5	1,447.3

Expenditure	2001/02	2002/03	2003/04‡
Recurrent expenditure	1,171.4	1,488.6	1,887.1
Wages	342.0	397.8	464.1
Interest	121.1	99.8	121.7
Goods, services and transfers	708.3	991.1	1,301.4
Clearance of domestic payment arrears	59.1	—	—
Development expenditure and net lending	291.3	500.9	644.4
Local	50.2	95.7	136.1
Foreign	241.1	405.2	508.3
Total	1,521.9	1,989.5	2,531.5

* Figures refer to the Tanzania Government, excluding the revenue and expenditure of the separate Zanzibar Government.
† Excluding grants received.
‡ Provisional.

Source: IMF, *Tanzania—Selected Issues and Statistical Appendix* (September 2004).

2004/05: ('000 million shillings): Total revenue (including grants) 2,736.0; Total expenditure (including lending minus repayments) 3,275.6.

2005/06 ('000 million shillings): Total revenue (including grants) 3,474.7; Total expenditure (including lending minus repayments) 3,900.8 (Source: IMF, *International Financial Statistics*).

INTERNATIONAL RESERVES
(excl. gold, US $ million at 31 December)

	2005	2006	2007
IMF special drawing rights	0.7	0.1	0.2
Reserve position in IMF	14.3	15.0	15.8
Foreign exchange	2,033.8	2,244.2	2,870.4
Total	2,048.8	2,259.3	2,886.4

Source: IMF, *International Financial Statistics*.

MONEY SUPPLY
('000 million shillings at 31 December)

	2005	2006	2007
Currency outside banks	843.16	989.23	1,164.18
Demand deposits at commercial banks	915.65	961.10	1,397.96
Total money	1,758.81	1,950.33	2,562.14

Source: IMF, *International Financial Statistics*.

COST OF LIVING
(Consumer Price Index)

Tanganyika
(base: 2000 = 100)

	2003	2004	2005
Food (incl. beverages)	112.0	118.6	125.6
Fuel, light and water	107.7	112.9	107.6
Clothing (incl. footwear)	106.6	109.0	113.2
Rent	111.2	113.8	122.4
All items (incl. others)	109.8	114.5	119.4

2006 (base: 2000 = 100): All items 130.3.

Source: ILO.

Zanzibar
(base: 2001 = 100)

	2002	2003
Food (incl. beverages)	106.9	116.7
Fuel, light and water	100.0	106.0
Clothing (incl. footwear)	106.7	128.3
Rent	104.9	118.0
All items (incl. others)	105.2	114.7

2004: Food (incl. beverages) 128.6; All items (incl. others) 124.0.
2005: Food (incl. beverages) 143.7; All items (incl. others) 136.1.

Source: ILO.

TANZANIA

Statistical Survey

NATIONAL ACCOUNTS
(Tanzania mainland, current prices)

National Income and Product
(million shillings, provisional)

	1992	1993	1994
Compensation of employees	88,230	119,119	148,194
Operating surplus	906,923	1,132,774	1,462,193
Domestic factor incomes	995,153	1,251,894	1,610,387
Consumption of fixed capital	35,802	36,697	49,542
Gross domestic product (GDP) at factor cost	1,030,955	1,288,591	1,659,929
Indirect taxes	109,442	183,389	260,039
Less Subsidies	9,801	67,611	97,398
GDP in purchasers' values	1,130,596	1,404,369	1,822,570
Factor income received from abroad	2,563	7,934	8,648
Less Factor income paid abroad	72,969	67,842	78,173
Gross national product (GNP)	1,060,190	1,344,460	1,753,045
Less Consumption of fixed capital	35,802	36,697	49,542
National income in market prices	1,024,387	1,307,763	1,703,504
Other current transfers from abroad (net)	282,813	291,673	308,518
National disposable income	1,307,200	1,599,436	2,084,022

Expenditure on the Gross Domestic Product
(US $ million)

	2005	2006	2007
Government final consumption expenditure	2,484.23	2,512.09	2,848.14
Private final consumption expenditure	9,373.40	9,680.62	9,358.10
Gross fcapital formation	3,544.14	3,960.21	4,794.92
Total domestic expenditure	15,401.77	16,152.92	17,001.16
Exports of goods and services	2,944.76	3,136.60	3,795.18
Less Imports of goods and services	4,204.55	5,111.40	6,292.83
GDP at market prices	14,141.97	14,178.11	14,503.51

Source: African Development Bank.

Gross Domestic Product by Economic Activity
('000 million shillings)

	2001	2002	2003*
Agriculture, forestry, fishing and hunting	1,919.7	2,205.2	2,508.9
Mining and quarrying	120.5	153.0	191.2
Manufacturing	564.7	638.7	711.0
Electricity and water	124.8	145.8	157.0
Construction	335.9	389.7	454.2
Trade, restaurants and hotels	926.9	1,038.1	1,153.3
Transport and communications	361.6	404.9	454.0
Public administration	723.1	810.3	869.3
Financial and business services	421.5	494.8	564.3
Other services	73.9	82.7	86.9
Sub-total	5,572.4	6,363.1	7,150.0
Less Imputed bank service charge	157.8	168.8	182.3
Total monetary GDP	5,414.6	6,194.3	6,967.7
Non-monetary GDP	2,210.0	2,505.6	2,843.8
Agriculture, forestry, fishing and hunting	1,486.4	1,679.4	1,909.0
Construction	69.2	80.3	92.0
Owner-occupied dwellings	654.3	745.9	842.9
Total GDP at factor cost	7,624.6	8,699.9	9,811.6
Net taxes	650.0	745.6	880.9
Total GDP at market prices	8,274.6	9,445.5	10,692.4

* Provisional figures.

Source: IMF, *Tanzania—Selected Issues and Statistical Appendix* (September 2004).

BALANCE OF PAYMENTS
(US $ million)

	2004	2005	2006
Exports of goods f.o.b.	1,473.1	1,675.8	1,723.0
Imports of goods f.o.b.	−2,482.8	−2,997.6	−3,864.1
Trade balance	−1,009.8	−1,321.8	−2,141.1
Exports of services	1,133.6	1,269.2	1,483.2
Imports of services	−974.7	−1,207.3	−1,249.4
Balance on goods and services	−850.9	−1,260.0	−1,907.2
Other income received	81.8	80.9	80.2
Other income paid	−200.9	−198.0	−165.2
Balance on goods, services and income	−970.0	−1,377.0	−1,992.1
Current transfers received	651.7	563.0	615.6
Current transfers paid	−65.0	−66.5	−65.6
Current balance	−383.3	−880.6	−1,442.7
Capital account (net)	459.9	633.2	5,292.9
Direct investment from abroad	330.6	447.6	474.5
Other investment assets	−11.0	−61.5	−175.0
Portfolio investment liabilities	2.4	2.5	2.6
Other investment liabilities	−46.4	276.6	−4,589.3
Net errors and omissions	−148.4	−671.7	873.8
Overall balance	203.9	−253.8	437.4

Source: IMF, *International Financial Statistics*.

External Trade

PRINCIPAL COMMODITIES
(US $ million)

Imports c.i.f.	2002	2003	2004
Food and live animals	156.0	188.9	277.1
Cereals and cereal preparations	94.9	133.9	202.8
Wheat and meslin, unmilled	58.4	76.8	119.2
Mineral fuels, lubricants, etc.	197.6	405.8	417.4
Petroleum, petroleum products, etc.	195.5	401.7	409.4
Petroleum products, refined	188.6	394.4	400.7
Motor spirit, incl. aviation spirit	61.7	394.2	—
Gas oils	99.4	—	—
Animal and vegetable oils, fats and waxes	67.4	85.9	85.1
Fixed vegetable oils and fats	63.2	78.1	77.0
Palm oil	57.0	73.9	74.3
Chemicals and related products	219.4	265.8	354.7
Medicinal and pharmaceutical products	38.0	54.1	56.3
Artificial resins and plastic materials, cellulose esters, etc.	54.8	65.4	—
Basic manufactures	270.7	341.2	382.4
Iron and steel	57.1	81.5	98.7
Other metal manufactures	55.3	83.1	76.4
Machinery and transport equipment	601.7	698.6	775.4
Power generating machinery and equipment	25.3	45.6	43.9
Rotating electric plant, and parts thereof	14.0	20.4	23.8
Electric motors (incl. ac/dc motors), other than direct current	1.2	1.3	3.1
Machinery specialized for particular industries	138.0	141.4	166.9

TANZANIA

Imports c.i.f.—continued	2002	2003	2004
General industrial machinery, equipment and parts	68.5	85.4	108.2
Telecommunications, sound recording and reproducing equipment	49.4	60.8	59.7
Telecommunication equipment, parts and accessories	42.2	52.9	50.3
Other electrical machinery, apparatus and appliances, and parts	56.1	53.9	82.3
Road vehicles	198.1	213.4	223.5
Passenger motor vehicles, excl. buses	63.6	71.9	78.2
Lorries and special purpose motor vehicles	73.4	68.1	78.2
Vehicles for the transportation of goods or materials	67.8	64.4	72.6
Miscellaneous manufactured articles	117.9	139.2	172.7
Total (incl. others)	1,691.2	2,189.5	2,531.2

Exports f.o.b.	2002	2003	2004
Food and live animals	315.1	384.9	399.0
Fish, crustaceans, molluscs and preparations thereof	116.7	134.5	125.6
Fish, fresh, chilled or frozen	103.6	116.4	110.1
Fish fillets, fresh or chilled	43.3	69.9	75.7
Fish fillets, frozen	59.3	44.1	30.6
Cereals and cereal preparations	35.2	63.0	61.3
Vegetables and fruit	70.0	76.9	95.6
Fruit and nuts, fresh, dried	49.0	46.3	70.4
Cashew nuts, fresh or dried	47.2	43.5	68.7
Coffee, tea, cocoa, spices, and manufactures thereof	77.7	93.4	98.0
Coffee and coffee substitutes	36.0	49.9	50.1
Coffee, not roasted; coffee husks and skins	35.0	49.1	49.4
Beverages and tobacco	57.4	54.4	70.1
Tobacco and tobacco manufactures	56.2	51.6	66.1
Tobacco, wholly or partly stripped	25.8	33.5	55.4
Crude materials, inedible, except fuels	160.0	179.6	256.9
Textile fibres (not wool tops) and their wastes (not in yarn)	38.1	56.4	83.5
Raw cotton, excl. linters, not carded or combed	25.9	40.8	50.3
Metalliferous ores and metal scrap	75.8	64.4	107.3
Ores and concentrates of precious metals	75.2	61.0	105.5
Basic manufactures	72.1	89.0	121.3
Non-metallic mineral manufactures	53.7	53.4	58.5
Pearl, precious and semi-precious stones, unworked or worked	42.2	43.1	49.1
Diamonds cut or otherwise worked, but not mounted or set	21.2	24.3	23.4
Gold, non-monetary, unwrought or semi-manufactured	268.5	438.1	524.6
Total (incl. others)	901.4	1,218.4	1,465.8

Source: UN, *International Trade Statistics Yearbook*.

PRINCIPAL TRADING PARTNERS
(US $ million)

Imports c.i.f.	2002	2003	2004
Australia	73.2	54.7	75.2
Bahrain	79.8	116.1	171.7
Belgium	23.4	33.4	35.3
Canada	17.8	31.3	39.8
China, People's Repub.	79.8	116.1	171.7
Denmark	15.8	20.4	21.8
France	39.4	40.8	40.6
Germany	60.6	68.8	75.4
India	107.9	167.4	216.4
Indonesia	62.7	75.9	86.6

Imports c.i.f.—continued	2002	2003	2004
Italy	45.4	39.7	40.6
Japan	140.2	169.7	180.9
Kenya	96.2	116.2	130.3
Korea, Repub.	18.5	28.0	27.0
Malaysia	12.7	17.6	19.4
Netherlands	27.6	32.1	42.8
Saudi Arabia	47.8	51.3	55.5
South Africa	190.7	306.3	331.0
Sweden	22.2	38.5	23.7
Switzerland	23.0	22.9	18.8
Thailand	36.3	20.6	29.7
United Arab Emirates	98.0	146.5	184.9
United Kingdom	95.9	108.2	110.4
USA	92.1	69.5	78.2
Total (incl. others)	1,691.2	2,189.5	2,531.2

Exports f.o.b.	2002	2003	2004
Belgium	21.5	35.6	26.9
Congo, Democratic Repub.	16.0	36.5	41.6
France	156.2	79.5	12.3
Germany	27.9	30.9	34.3
Hong Kong	11.3	9.9	12.4
India	64.9	74.4	104.2
Ireland	14.2	0.0	0.1
Italy	24.7	23.4	28.3
Japan	97.3	88.7	65.0
Kenya	35.7	83.4	90.0
Malawi	18.0	13.1	22.8
Netherlands	54.5	67.8	60.5
Saudi Arabia	17.0	8.5	12.7
Singapore	4.0	13.3	15.6
South Africa	16.7	39.1	120.3
Switzerland	5.7	12.6	30.1
Uganda	5.5	48.1	55.6
United Arab Emirates	14.6	16.6	18.7
United Kingdom	159.2	386.9	473.2
USA	13.7	11.4	15.2
Zambia	17.6	24.9	16.3
Total (incl. others)	901.4	1,218.4	1,465.8

Source: UN, *International Trade Statistics Yearbook*.

Transport

RAILWAYS

	2003	2004	2005
Passengers ('000)	666	464	514
Freight ('000 metric tons)	1,443	1,002	1,169

Source: National Bureau of Statistics, *Tanzania in Figures 2005*.

ROAD TRAFFIC
(estimates, '000 motor vehicles in use)

	1994	1995	1996
Passenger cars	28.0	26.0	23.8
Buses and coaches	78.0	81.0	86.0
Lorries and vans	27.2	27.7	29.7
Road tractors	6.7	6.7	6.6

Source: IRF, *World Road Statistics*.

SHIPPING

Merchant fleet
(registered at 31 December)

	2004	2005	2006
Number of vessels	51	50	52
Displacement ('000 grt)	38.9	36.8	37.5

Source: Lloyd's Register-Fairplay, *World Fleet Statistics*.

TANZANIA

International sea-borne traffic

	2003	2004	2005
Vessels docked	2,350	2,898	3,895
Cargo ('000 metric tons)	5,346	4,179	4,307
Passengers ('000)	648	525	1,072

Source: National Bureau of Statistics, *Tanzania in Figures 2005*.

CIVIL AVIATION
(traffic on scheduled services)

	2001	2002	2003
Kilometres flown (million)	4	3	4
Passengers carried ('000)	175	134	150
Passenger-km (million)	181	136	151
Total ton-km (million)	21	14	16

Source: UN, *Statistical Yearbook*.

Tourism

FOREIGN VISITOR ARRIVALS
(by country of origin)

	2003	2004	2005
Burundi	11,907	3,157	5,767
Canada	10,354	10,613	10,922
Congo, Democratic Repub.	6,850	8,030	9,479
France	22,103	21,849	23,547
Germany	19,222	19,222	18,170
India	22,215	14,804	17,598
Italy	24,675	44,045	49,829
Kenya	119,406	124,967	112,766
Malawi	14,267	16,868	19,999
Netherlands	15,272	14,594	15,805
Rwanda	12,061	6,089	17,037
South Africa	35,071	25,849	28,922
Spain	9,565	11,168	11,709
Uganda	34,664	24,253	25,373
United Kingdom	43,656	59,547	52,442
USA	36,419	40,248	47,621
Zambia	10,670	25,405	29,120
Total (incl. others)	576,198	582,807	612,754

Tourism receipts (US $ million, incl. passenger transport): 654 in 2003; 762 in 2004; 836 in 2005.

Source: World Tourism Organization.

Communications Media

	2004	2005	2006
Telephones ('000 main lines in use)	148.4	154.4	157.3
Mobile cellular telephones ('000 subscribers)	1,942.0	3,389.8	5,766.6
Personal computers ('000 in use)	278	278	n.a.
Internet users ('000)	333	384	384

Source: International Telecommunication Union.

Television receivers ('000 in use, 2000): 700.

Radio receivers ('000 in use, estimate, 1997): 8,800 (Source: UNESCO, *Statistical Yearbook*).

Daily newspapers (2004): 14; average circulation ('000 copies, estimate) 60 (Source: UNESCO Institute for Statistics).

Education

(2005)

	Institutions	Teachers	Students
Primary (state)	14,053	132,409	1,853,000
Primary (private)	204	2,604	16,154
Secondary (state)	1,202	13,448	199,602
Secondary (private)	543	10,457	90,753
Higher (state)*	64	n.a.	15,384
Higher (private)†	31	n.a.	1,388

* Comprising 34 teacher training colleges, 4 technical colleges, 5 full universities, 3 constituent universities and 18 other higher institutions.
† Comprising 18 teacher training colleges and 13 universities.

Source: National Bureau for Statistics, *Tanzania in Figures 2005*.

Adult literacy rate (UNESCO estimates): 69.4% (males 77.5%; females 62.2%) in 2002 (Source: UNESCO Institute for Statistics).

Directory

The Constitution

The United Republic of Tanzania was established on 26 April 1964, when Tanganyika and Zanzibar, hitherto separate independent countries, merged. An interim Constitution of 1965 was replaced, on 25 April 1977, by a permanent Constitution for the United Republic. In October 1979 the Revolutionary Council of Zanzibar adopted a separate Constitution, governing Zanzibar's internal administration, with provisions for a popularly elected President and a legislative House of Representatives elected by delegates of the then ruling party. A new Constitution for Zanzibar, which came into force in January 1985, provided for direct elections to the Zanzibar House of Representatives. The provisions below relate to the 1977 Constitution of the United Republic, as subsequently amended.

GOVERNMENT

Legislative power is exercised by the Parliament of the United Republic, which is vested by the Constitution with complete sovereign power, and of which the present National Assembly is the legislative house. The Assembly also enacts all legislation concerning the mainland. Internal matters in Zanzibar are the exclusive jurisdiction of the Zanzibar executive, the Supreme Revolutionary Council of Zanzibar, and the Zanzibar legislature, the House of Representatives.

National Assembly

The National Assembly comprises both directly elected members (chosen by universal adult suffrage) and nominated members (including five members elected from the Zanzibar House of Representatives). The number of directly elected members exceeds the number of nominated members. The Electoral Commission may review and, if necessary, increase the number of electoral constituencies before every general election. The National Assembly has a term of five years.

President

The President is the Head of State, Head of the Government and Commander-in-Chief of the Armed Forces. The President has no power to legislate without recourse to Parliament. The assent of the President is required before any bill passed by the National Assembly becomes law. Should the President withhold his assent and the bill be repassed by the National Assembly by a two-thirds' majority, the President is required by law to give his assent within 21 days unless, before that time, he has dissolved the National Assembly, in which case he must stand for re-election.

The President appoints a Vice-President to assist him in carrying out his functions. The President presides over the Cabinet, which comprises a Prime Minister and other ministers who are appointed from among the members of the National Assembly.

JUDICIARY

The independence of the judges is secured by provisions which prevent their removal, except on account of misbehaviour or incapacity when they may be dismissed at the discretion of the President. The Constitution also makes provision for a Permanent Commission of Enquiry, which has wide powers to investigate any abuses of authority.

CONSTITUTIONAL AMENDMENTS

The Constitution can be amended by an act of the Parliament of the United Republic, when the proposed amendment is supported by the votes of not fewer than two-thirds of all the members of the Assembly.

The Government

HEAD OF STATE

President: Lt-Col (Retd) JAKAYA MRISHO KIKWETE (took office 21 December 2005).

Vice-President: Dr ALI MOHAMMED SHEIN.

CABINET
(March 2008)

President and Commander-in-Chief of the Armed Forces: Lt-Col (Retd) JAKAYA MRISHO KIKWETE.

Prime Minister: MIZENGO KAYANZA PETER PINDA.

Minister of Foreign Affairs and International Co-operation: BERNARD KAMILLIUS MEMBE.

Minister of East African Co-operation: Dr DIODORUS BUBERWA KAMALA.

Minister of Planning and Finance: MUSTAFA MKURO.

Minister of Industry, Trade and Marketing: Dr MARY MICHAELL NAGU.

Minister of Agriculture, Food Security and Co-operatives: Prof. PETER MAHMOUD MSOLLA.

Minister of Natural Resources and Tourism: SHAMSA MWANGUNGA.

Minister of Water and Irrigation: Prof. MARK JAMES MWANDOSYA.

Minister of Energy and Minerals: WILLIAM NGELEJE.

Minister of Infrastructure Development: ANDREW JOHN CHENGE.

Minister of Health and Social Welfare: Prof. DAVID HOMELI MWAKYUSA.

Minister of Education and Vocational Training: Prof. JUMANNE ABDALLAH MAGHEMBE.

Minister of Science, Technology and ICT Development: Dr SHUKURU JUMANNE KAWAMBWA.

Minister of Labour, Employment and Youth Development: Prof. JUMA ATHUMANI KAPUYA.

Minister of Land, Housing and Human Settlements Development: Capt. JOHN ZEFANIA CHILIGATI.

Minister of Information, Culture and Sports: GEORGE MKUCHIKA.

Minister of Defence and National Service: Dr HUSSEIN ALI MWINYI.

Minister of Home Affairs: LAWRENCE KEGO MASHA.

Minister of Justice and Constitutional Affairs: MATHIAS MEINRAD CHIKAWE.

Minister of Community Development, Gender and Children: MARGARETH SIMWANZA SITTA.

Minister of Livestock and Fisheries Development: JOHN POMBE JOSEPH MAGUFULI.

Ministers of State in the President's Office: HAWA ABDULRAHMAN GHASIA (Public Service Management), SOFIA MNYAMBI SIMBA (Good Governance).

Ministers of State in the Vice-President's Office: MUHAMMED SEIF KHATIB (Union Affairs), Dr BATILDA SALHA BURIAN (Environment).

Ministers of State in the Prime Minister's Office: STEPHEN MASATU WASSIRA (Regional Administration and Local Governments), PHILIP SANG'KA MARMO (Parliamentary Affairs).

MINISTRIES

Office of the President: State House, POB 9120, Dar es Salaam; tel. (22) 2116679; fax (22) 2113425; internet www.tanzania.go.tz/poffice.htm.

Office of the Vice-President: POB 5380, Dar es Salaam; tel. (22) 2113857; fax (22) 2113856; e-mail makamu@twiga.com; internet www.tanzania.go.tz/vpoffice.htm.

Office of the Prime Minister: POB 980, Dodoma; tel. (26) 233201; internet www.tanzania.go.tz/pmoffice.htm.

Ministry of Agriculture, Food Security and Co-operatives: Kilimo I Building, Temeke, POB 9192, Dar es Salaam; tel. (22) 2862480; fax (22) 2865951; e-mail psk@kilimo.go.tz; internet www.kilimo.go.tz.

Ministry of Community Development, Gender and Children: POB 3448, Dar es Salaam; tel. (22) 2111459; fax (22) 2110933; e-mail info_wic@uccmail.co.tz; internet www.mcdcg.go.tz.

Ministry of Defence and National Service: POB 9544, Dar es Salaam; tel. (22) 2117153; fax (22) 2116719.

Ministry of East African Co-operation: POB 9280, Dar es Salaam; tel. (22) 2126827; fax (22) 2126651; internet www.meac.go.tz.

Ministry of Education and Vocational Training: POB 9121, Dar es Salaam; tel. (22) 2120403; fax (22) 2113271; e-mail psmoevt@moe.go.tz; internet www.moe.go.tz.

Ministry of Energy and Minerals: POB 2000, Dar es Salaam; tel. (22) 2112791; fax (22) 2121606; e-mail madini@africaonline.co.tz; internet www.mem.go.tz.

Ministry of Foreign Affairs and International Co-operation: Kivukoni Front, POB 9000, Dar es Salaam; tel. (22) 2111906; fax (22) 2116600; e-mail nje@foreign.go.tz; internet www.mfaic.go.tz.

Ministry of Health and Social Welfare: POB 9083, Dar es Salaam; tel. (22) 2120261; fax (22) 2139951; e-mail moh@cats-net.com.

Ministry of Home Affairs: POB 9223, Dar es Salaam; tel. (22) 2119050; fax (22) 2119050; e-mail permsec@moha.go.tz; internet www.moha.go.tz.

Ministry of Industry, Trade and Marketing: POB 9503, Dar es Salaam; tel. (22) 2181397; fax (22) 2182481.

Ministry of Information, Culture and Sports: Dar es Salaam; internet www.hum.go.tz.

Ministry of Infrastructure Development: Pamba Rd, Tancot House, POB 9144, Dar es Salaam; tel. (22) 2137650; fax (22) 2112751; e-mail permsec@infrastructure.go.tz; internet www.infrastructure.go.tz.

Ministry of Justice and Constitutional Affairs: POB 9050, Dar es Salaam; tel. (22) 2117099.

Ministry of Labour, Employment and Youth Development: POB 1422, Dar es Salaam; tel. (22) 2120419; fax (22) 2113082.

Ministry of Lands, Housing and Human Settlements Development: POB 9132, Dar es Salaam; tel. (22) 2121241; fax (22) 2113224; internet www.ardhi.go.tz.

Ministry of Livestock and Fisheries Development: Dar es Salaam; internet www.mifugo.go.tz.

Ministry of Natural Resources and Tourism: POB 9372, Dar es Salaam; tel. (22) 2111061; fax (22) 2110600; e-mail nature.tourism@mnrt.org; internet www.mnrt.org.

Ministry of Planning and Finance: POB 9111, Dar es Salaam; tel. (22) 2111174; fax (22) 2110326; internet www.mof.go.tz.

Ministry of Science, Technology and ICT Development: POB 2645, Dar es Salaam; tel. (22) 2666376; fax (22) 2666097; e-mail msthe@msthe.go.tz.

Ministry of Water and Irrigation: POB 9153, Dar es Salaam; tel. (22) 2117153; fax (22) 37138; e-mail dppmaj@raha.com.

SUPREME REVOLUTIONARY COUNCIL OF ZANZIBAR
(March 2008)

President and Chairman and Minister of Finance and Economic Planning: AMANI ABEID KARUME.

Chief Minister: SHAMSI VUAI NAHODHA.

Deputy Chief Minister and Minister of Information, Culture and Sport: ALI JUMA SHAMHUNA.

Minister of Communication and Transport: ADAM MWAKANJUKI.

Minister of Education and Vocational Training: HAROUN ALI SULEIMAN.

Minister of Employment, Youth, Women and Children: ASHA ABDALLAH JUMA.

Minister of Agriculture, Livestock and Co-operatives: BURHANI SAADAT HAJI.

Minister of Water, Works, Energy and Land: MANSOUR YUSSUF HIMID.

Minister of Tourism, Trade and Investment: SAMIA SULUHU HASSAN.

Ministers of State in the President's Office: MWINYIAHJI MAKAME MWADINI (Finance and Economic Affairs), SULEIMAN OTHMAN NYANGA (Regional Administration, Local Government and Special Forces), RAMADHAN ABDALLAH SHAABAN (Constitutional Affairs and Good Governance).

Minister of State in the Chief Minister's Office: SALUM JUMA OTHMAN.

MINISTRIES

Office of the President: POB 776, Zanzibar; tel. (24) 2230814; fax (24) 2233722.

Office of the Chief Minister: POB 239, Zanzibar; tel. (24) 2311126; fax (24) 233788.

Ministry of Agriculture, Livestock and Co-operatives: Zanzibar; tel. (24) 232662.

Ministry of Communication and Transport: POB 266, Zanzibar; tel. (24) 2232841.

Ministry of Education and Vocational Training: POB 394, Zanzibar; tel. (24) 232827.

Ministry of Employment, Youth, Women and Children: POB 884, Zanzibar; tel. (24) 30808.

Ministry of Finance and Economic Planning: POB 1154, Zanzibar; tel. (24) 231169.

Ministry of Information, Culture and Sport: POB 236, Zanzibar; tel. (24) 232640.

Ministry of Tourism, Trade and Investment: POB 772, Zanzibar; tel. (24) 232321.

Ministry of Water, Works, Energy and Land: Zanzibar.

President and Legislature

PRESIDENT

Election, 14 December 2005

Candidate	Votes	% of votes
Lt-Col (Retd) Jakaya Mrisho Kikwete (CCM)	9,123,952	80.28
Prof. Ibrahim Haruna Lipumba (CUF)	1,327,125	11.68
Freeman Mbowe (Chadema)	668,756	5.88
Augustine Lyatonga Mrema (TLP)	84,901	0.75
Sengondo Mvungi (NCCR—Mageuzi)	55,819	0.49
Others	104,924	0.92
Total	11,365,477	100.00

NATIONAL ASSEMBLY

Speaker: SAMUEL SITTA.

Election, 14 December 2005

Party	Seats*
Chama Cha Mapinduzi (CCM)	266
Civic United Front (CUF)	28
Chama Cha Demokrasia na Maendeleo (Chadema)	11
Tanzania Labour Party (TLP)	1
United Democratic Party (UDP)	1
Total	307

*In addition to the 232 elective seats, 75 seats are reserved for women (included in the figures above). Furthermore, 10 seats are reserved for presidential nominees and five for members of the Zanzibar House of Representatives; the Attorney-General is also an ex officio member of the National Assembly.

ZANZIBAR PRESIDENT

Election, 30 October 2005

Candidate	Votes	% of votes
Amani Abeid Karume	239,832	53.18
Seif Sharif Hamad	207,733	46.06
Haji Mussa Kitole	2,110	0.47
Others	1,293	0.29
Total	450,968	100.00

ZANZIBAR HOUSE OF REPRESENTATIVES

Speaker: (vacant).

Election, 30 October 2005

Party	Seats*
Chama Cha Mapinduzi (CCM)	31
Civic United Front (CUF)	18
Total	49

*In addition to the 50 elective seats, five seats are reserved for regional commissioners, 10 for presidential nominees, 15 for women (on a party basis in proportion to the number of elective seats gained) and one for the Attorney-General. Results in one constituency were invalidated; a fresh ballot was held on 14 December 2005 for which results were yet to be released.

Election Commission

National Election Commission of Tanzania (NEC): Posta House, POB 10923, Ghana/Ohio St, 6th and 7th Floor, Dar es Salaam; tel. (22) 2114963; fax (22) 2116740; e-mail info@nec.go.tz; internet www.nec.go.tz; f. 1993; Chair. LEWIS M. MAKAME; Dir of Elections R. R. KIRAVU.

Political Organizations

Bismillah Party: Pemba; seeks a referendum on the terms of the 1964 union of Zanzibar with mainland Tanzania.

Chama Cha Amani na Demokrasia Tanzania (CHADETA): House No. 41, Sadan St Ilala, POB 15809, Dar es Salaam; tel. (744) 889453; granted temporary registration in 2003.

Chama Cha Demokrasia na Maendeleo (Chadema—Party for Democracy and Progress): House No. 170 Ufipa St, POB 31191, Dar es Salaam; tel. (22) 2182544; supports democracy and social development; Chair. FREEMAN MBOWE; Sec.-Gen. WILIBROD SLAA.

Chama Cha Haki na Usitawi (Chausta—Party for Justice and Development): Drive Inn Oysterbay, POB 5450, Dar es Salaam; tel. (741) 247266; f. 1998; officially regd 2001; Chair. JAMES MAPALALA.

Chama Cha Mapinduzi (CCM) (Revolutionary Party of Tanzania): Kuu St, POB 50, Dodoma; tel. 2180575; e-mail katibumkuu@ccmtz.org; internet www.ccmtz.org; f. 1977 by merger of the mainland-based Tanganyika African National Union (TANU) with the Afro-Shirazi Party, which operated on Zanzibar and Pemba; sole legal party 1977–92; socialist orientation; Chair. JAKAYA MRISHO KIKWETE; Vice-Chair. PIUS MSEKWA, AMANI A. KARUME; Sec.-Gen. YUSUF MAKAMBA.

Civic United Front (CUF): Mtendeni St at Malindi, POB 3637, Zanzibar; tel. (24) 2237446; fax (24) 2237445; e-mail headquarters@cuftz.org; internet www.cuftz.org; f. 1992 by merger of Zanzibar opposition party Kamahuru and the mainland-based Chama Cha Wananchi; commands substantial support in Zanzibar and Pemba, for which it demands increased autonomy; Chair. Prof. IBRAHIM HARUNA LIPUMBA; Sec.-Gen. SEIF SHARIF HAMAD.

Democratic Party (DP): Ilala Mchikichini, POB 63102, Dar es Salaam; tel. (741) 430516; e-mail dp_watanganyika@yahoo.com; f. 2002; Chair. Rev. CHRISTOPHER MTIKILA.

Demokrasia Makini (MAKINI): Kibo Ubungo, POB 75636, Dar es Salaam; tel. (744) 295670; officially regd 2001.

Forum for Restoration of Democracy (FORD): House No. 6, Rufiji St, Kariakoo, POB 15587, Dar es Salaam; tel. (741) 292271; f. 2002.

Movement for Democratic Alternative (MDA): Zanzibar; seeks to review the terms of the 1964 union of Zanzibar with mainland Tanzania; supports democratic institutions and opposes detention without trial and press censorship.

National Convention for Construction and Reform (NCCR—Mageuzi): Plot No. 2 Kilosa St, Ilala, POB 72444, Dar es Salaam; tel. (744) 318812; f. 1992; Chair. Dr KASSIM MAGUTU; Sec.-Gen. MABERE MARANDO.

National League for Democracy (NLD): Plot No. 7310 Sinza, POB 352, Dar es Salaam; f. 1993; Chair. EMMANUEL J. E. MAKAIDI; Sec.-Gen. MICHAEL E. A. MHINA.

National Reconstruction Alliance (NRA): Bububu St, Tandika Kilimahewa, POB 45197, Dar es Salaam; tel. (744) 496724; f. 1993; Chair. ULOTU ABUBAKAR ULOTU; Sec.-Gen. SALIM R. MATINGA.

TANZANIA

Popular National Party (PONA): Plot 104, Songea St, Ilala, POB 21561, Dar es Salaam; Chair. WILFREM R. MWAKITWANGE; Sec.-Gen. NICOLAUS MCHAINA.

Tanzania Democratic Alliance Party (TADEA): Buguruni Malapa, POB 482, Dar es Salaam; tel. (22) 2865244; f. 1993; Pres. JOHN D. LIFA-CHIPAKA; Sec.-Gen. CHARLES DOTTO LUBALA.

Progressive Party of Tanzania (PPT-Maendeleo): Wibu St, Kinondoni, POB 31932, Dar es Salaam; tel. (744) 300302; f. 2003; Leader PETER MZIRAY; Sec.-Gen. AHMED HAMAD.

Tanzania Labour Party (TLP): Argentina Manzese, POB 7273, Dar es Salaam; tel. (22) 2443237; f. 1993; Chair. AUGUSTINE MREMA.

Tanzania People's Party (TPP): Mbezi Juu, Kawe, POB 60847, Dar es Salaam; removed from register of political parties 2002; Chair. ALEC H. CHE-MPONDA; Sec.-Gen. GRAVEL LIMO.

United Democratic Party (UDP): Mbezi Juu, SLP 5918, Dar es Salaam; tel. (748) 613723; f. 1994; Leader JOHN MOMOSE CHEYO.

United People's Democratic Party (UPDP): Mtaa wa Shariff Muss, POB 3121, Zanzibar; tel. (744) 753075; f. 1993; Chair. KHALFANI ALI ABDULLAH; Sec.-Gen. AHMED M. RASHID.

Union for Multi-Party Democracy (UMD): House No. 84, Plot No. 630, Block No. 5, Kagera St. Magomeni, POB 2985, Dar es Salaam; tel. (744) 478153; f. 1993; Chair. ABDALLAH FUNDIKIRA.

Diplomatic Representation

EMBASSIES AND HIGH COMMISSIONS IN TANZANIA

Algeria: 34 Ali Hassan Mwinyi Rd, POB 2963, Dar es Salaam; tel. (22) 2117619; fax (22) 2117620; e-mail algemb@twiga.com; Ambassador ABDELMOUN'AAM AHRIZ.

Angola: Plot 78, Lugalo Rd, POB 20793, Dar es Salaam; tel. (22) 2117674; fax (22) 2132349; Ambassador (vacant).

Belgium: Ocean Rd, POB 9210, Dar es Salaam; tel. (22) 2112688; fax (22) 2117621; e-mail daressalaam@diplobel.be; internet www.diplomatie.be/dar-es-salaam; Ambassador PETER MADDENS.

Burundi: Plot 1007, Lugalo Rd, POB 2752, Upanga, Dar es Salaam; tel. (22) 238608; e-mail burundemb@raha.com; Ambassador LEANDRE AMURI BANGENGWANUBUSA.

Canada: 38 Mirambo St, Garden Ave, POB 1022, Dar es Salaam; tel. (22) 2163300; fax (22) 2116897; e-mail dslam@international.gc.ca; internet www.dfait-maeci.gc.ca/tanzania; High Commissioner JANET SIDDALL.

China, People's Republic: 2 Kajificheni Close at Toure Dr., POB 1649, Dar es Salaam; tel. (22) 2667212; Ambassador LIU XISHENG.

Congo, Democratic Republic: 438 Malik Rd, POB 975, Upanga, Dar es Salaam; tel. (22) 2150282; fax (22) 2153341; Chargé d'affaires a.i. NSINGI ZI LUBAKI.

Cuba: Plot 313, Lugalo Rd, POB 9282, Upanga, Dar es Salaam; tel. (22) 2115928; fax (22) 2115927; e-mail embacuba.tz@raha.com; Ambassador FELIPE RUIZ O'FARRILL.

Denmark: Ghana Ave, POB 9171, Dar es Salaam; tel. (22) 2113887; fax (22) 2116433; e-mail daramb@um.dk; internet www.ambdaressalaam.um.dk; Ambassador BJARNE HENNEBERG SØRENSEN.

Egypt: 24 Garden Ave, POB 1668, Dar es Salaam; tel. (22) 2117622; fax (22) 2112543; e-mail egypt.emb.tz@Cats-net.com; Ambassador SABRY MAGDY SABRY.

Finland: cnr Mirambo St and Garden Ave, POB 2455, Dar es Salaam; tel. (22) 2196565; fax (22) 2196573; e-mail sanomat.dar@formin.fi; internet www.finland.or.tz; Ambassador JUHANI TOIVONEN.

France: Ali Hassan Mwinyi Rd, POB 2349, Dar es Salaam; tel. (22) 2198800; fax (22) 2198815; e-mail ambfrance@africaonline.co.tz; internet www.ambafrance-tz.org; Ambassador JACQUES CHAMPAGNE DE LABRIOLLE.

Germany: Umoja House, Mirambo St/Garden Ave, 2nd Floor, POB 9541, Dar es Salaam; tel. (22) 2117409; fax (22) 2112944; e-mail german.embassy@bol.co.tz; internet www.daressalam.diplo.de; Ambassador WOLFGANG RINGE.

Holy See: Oyster Bay, Plot 146, Haile Selassie Rd, POB 480, Dar es Salaam (Apostolic Nunciature); tel. (22) 2666422; fax (22) 2668059; e-mail nunzio@cats-net.com; Apostolic Nuncio Most Rev. JOSEPH CHENNOTH (Titular Archbishop of Milevum).

Indonesia: 299 Ali Hassan Mwinyi Rd, POB 572, Dar es Salaam; tel. (22) 2119119; fax (22) 2115849; e-mail kbridsm@raha.com; Ambassador TRIJONO MARJONO.

Ireland: 353 Toure Dr., POB 9612, Oyster Bay, Dar es Salaam; tel. (22) 2602355; fax (22) 2602362; e-mail embassydaresalaam@dfa.ie; Ambassador ANNE BARRINGTON.

Italy: Plot 316, Lugalo Rd, POB 2106, Dar es Salaam; tel. (22) 2115935; fax (22) 2115938; e-mail segr.dar@esteri.it; internet www.ambdaressalaam.esteri.it; Ambassador FRANCESCO CATANIA.

Japan: 1018 Ali Hassan Mwinyi Rd, POB 2577, Dar es Salaam; tel. (22) 2115827; fax (22) 2115830; internet www.tz.emb-japan.go.jp; Ambassador MAKOTO ITO.

Kenya: Plot 127 Mafinga St, Kinondoni, POB 5231, Dar es Salaam; tel. (22) 2668285; fax (22) 2668213; e-mail info@kenyahighcom.tz.org; internet www.kenyahighcomtz.org; High Commissioner BOAZ KIDIGA MBAYA.

Korea, Democratic People's Republic: Plot 5, Ursino Estate, Kawawa Rd, Msasani, POB 2690, Dar es Salaam; tel. (22) 2775395; fax (22) 2700838; Ambassador SOON CHUN LEE.

Korea, Republic: Plot 97, Msese Rd, Kingsway, Kinondoni, POB 1154, Dar es Salaam; tel. (22) 2668788; fax (22) 2667509; e-mail embassy-tz@mofat.go.kr; internet tza.mofat.go.kr; Ambassador KIM YOUNG-JUN.

Libya: 386 Mtitu St, POB 9413, Dar es Salaam; tel. (22) 2150188; fax (22) 2150068; Secretary of People's Bureau Dr AHMED IBRAHIM EL-ASHHAB.

Malawi: Plot 38, Ali Hassan Mwinyi Rd, POB 7616, Dar es Salaam; tel. (22) 2666284; fax (22) 2668161; e-mail mhc@africaonline.co.tz; High Commissioner (vacant).

Mozambique: 25 Garden Ave, POB 9370, Dar es Salaam; tel. and fax (22) 2116502; High Commissioner ZACARIAS KUPELA.

Netherlands: Umoja House, 4th Floor, Garden Ave, POB 9534, Dar es Salaam; tel. (22) 2110000; fax (22) 2110044; e-mail dar@minbuza.nl; internet tanzania.nlembassy.org; Ambassador KAREL VAN KESTEREN.

Nigeria: 83 Haile Selassie Rd, POB 9214, Oyster Bay, Dar es Salaam; tel. (22) 2666000; fax (22) 2668947; e-mail nhc-dsm@raha.com; High Commissioner AHMED M. USMAN.

Norway: 160/50 Mirambo St, POB 2646, Dar es Salaam; tel. (22) 2113366; fax (22) 2116564; e-mail emb.daressalaam@mfa.no; internet www.norway.go.tz; Ambassador JON LOMØY.

Poland: 63 Alykhan Rd, Upanga, POB 2188, Dar es Salaam; tel. (22) 2115271; fax (22) 2115812; e-mail polamb@wingrouptz.com; Chargé d'affaires a.i. EUGENIUSZ RZEWUSKI.

Russia: Plot No. 73, Ali Hassan Mwinyi Rd, POB 1905, Dar es Salaam; tel. (22) 2666005; fax (22) 2666818; e-mail embruss@bol.co.tz; Ambassador LEONARD ALEKSEEVIC.

Rwanda: Plot 32, Ali Hassan Mwinyi Rd, POB 2918, Dar es Salaam; tel. (22) 2115889; fax (22) 2115888; e-mail ambadsm@minaffet.gov.rw; Ambassador ZEPHYR MUTANGUHA.

South Africa: Plot 1338/1339, Mwaya Rd, Msaski, POB 10723, Dar es Salaam; tel. (22) 2601800; fax (22) 2600684; e-mail highcomm@sahc-tz.com; High Commissioner S. G. MFENYANA.

Spain: 99B Kinondoni Rd, POB 842, Dar es Salaam; tel. (22) 2666936; fax (22) 2666938; e-mail embesptz@mail.mae.es; Ambassador GERMÁN ZURITA SÁENZ DE NAVARRETE.

Sudan: 'Albaraka', 64 Ali Hassan Mwinyi Rd, POB 2266, Dar es Salaam; tel. (22) 2117641; fax (22) 2115811; e-mail sudan.emb.dar@raha.com; Ambassador ELMUGHIRA ALI OMAR.

Sweden: Mirambo St and Garden Ave, POB 9274, Dar es Salaam; tel. (22) 2196500; fax (22) 2196503; e-mail ambassaden.dar-es-salaam@foreign.ministry.se; internet www.swedenabroad.se/daressalaam; Ambassador STAFFAN HERRSTROM.

Switzerland: 79 Kinondoni Rd/Mafinga St, POB 2454, Dar es Salaam; tel. (22) 2666008; fax (22) 2666736; e-mail dar.vertretung@eda.admin.ch; Ambassador EMMANUEL JENNI.

Syria: 246 Alykhan Rd, Upanga, POB 2442, Dar es Salaam; tel. (22) 2117656; fax (22) 2115860; Chargé d'affaires a.i. M. B. IMADI.

Uganda: Extelcom Bldg, 7th Floor, Samora Ave, POB 6237, Dar es Salaam; tel. (22) 2116754; fax (22) 2112974; High Commissioner IBRAHIM MUKIIBI.

United Kingdom: Umoja House, Garden Ave, POB 9200, Dar es Salaam; tel. (22) 2110101; fax (22) 2110102; e-mail bhc.dar@fco.gov.uk; internet www.britishhighcommission.gov.uk/tanzania; High Commissioner PHILIP PARHAM.

USA: 686 Old Bagamoyo Rd, Msasani, POB 9123, Dar es Salaam; tel. (22) 2668001; fax (22) 2668238; e-mail embassyd@state.gov; internet tanzania.usembassy.gov; Ambassador MARK GREEN.

Yemen: 353 United Nations Rd, POB 349, Dar es Salaam; tel. (22) 2117650; fax (22) 2115924; Chargé d'affaires a.i. MOHAMED ABDULLA ALMAS.

Zambia: 5–6 Ohio St/Sokoine Dr. Junction, POB 2525, Dar es Salaam; tel. and fax (22) 2112977; e-mail zhcd@raha.com; High Commissioner JOHN KASHONKA CHITAFU.

TANZANIA   *Directory*

Zimbabwe: 2097 East Upanga, off Ali Hassan Mwinyi Rd, POB 20762, Dar es Salaam; tel. (22) 2116789; fax (22) 2112913; e-mail zimdares@cats-net.com; Ambassador J. M. SHAVA.

Judicial System

Permanent Commission of Enquiry: POB 2643, Dar es Salaam; tel. (22) 2113690; fax (22) 2111533; Chair. and Official Ombudsman Prof. JOSEPH F. MBWILIZA; Sec. A. P. GUVETTE.

Court of Appeal
Consists of the Chief Justice and four Judges of Appeal.
Chief Justice of Tanzania: AUGUSTINO RAMADHANI.
Chief Justice of Zanzibar: HAMID MAHMOUD HAMID.
High Court: headquarters at Dar es Salaam, but regular sessions held in all Regions; consists of a Jaji Kiongozi and 29 Judges.
District Courts: situated in each district and presided over by either a Resident Magistrate or District Magistrate; limited jurisdiction, with a right of appeal to the High Court.
Primary Courts: established in every district and presided over by Primary Court Magistrates; limited jurisdiction, with a right of appeal to the District Courts and then to the High Court.
Attorney-General: ANDREW CHENGE.
Director of Public Prosecutions: KULWA MASSABA.
People's Courts were established in Zanzibar in 1970. Magistrates are elected by the people and have two assistants each. Under the Zanzibar Constitution, which came into force in January 1985, defence lawyers and the right of appeal, abolished in 1970, were reintroduced.

Religion

Religious surveys were eliminated from all government census reports after 1967. However, religious leaders and sociologists generally believe that the country's population is 30%–40% Christian and 30%–40% Muslim, with the remainder consisting of practitioners of other faiths, traditional indigenous religions and atheists. Foreign missionaries operate in the country, including Roman Catholics, Lutherans, Baptists, Seventh-day Adventists, Mormons, Anglicans and Muslims.

ISLAM
The Muslim population is most heavily concentrated on the Zanzibar archipelago and in the coastal areas of the mainland. There are also large Muslim minorities in inland urban areas. Some 99% of the population of Zanzibar is estimated to be Muslim. Between 80% and 90% of the country's Muslim population is Sunni; the remainder consists of several Shi'a groups, mostly of Asian descent. A large proportion of the Asian community is Isma'ili.

Ismalia Provincial Church: POB 460, Dar es Salaam.
National Muslim Council of Tanzania: POB 21422, Dar es Salaam; tel. (22) 234934; f. 1969; supervises Islamic affairs on the mainland only; Chair. Sheikh HEMED BIN JUMA BIN HEMED; Exec. Sec. Alhaj MUHAMMAD MTULIA.
Supreme Muslim Council: Zanzibar; f. 1991; supervises Islamic affairs in Zanzibar; Mufti Sheikh HARITH BIN KALEF.
Wakf and Trust Commission: POB 4092, Zanzibar; f. 1980; Islamic affairs; Exec. Sec. YUSUF ABDULRAHMAN MUHAMMAD.

CHRISTIANITY
The Christian population is composed of Roman Catholics, Protestants, Pentecostals, Seventh-day Adventists, members of the Church of Jesus Christ of Latter-day Saints (Mormons) and Jehovah's Witnesses.

Jumuiya ya Kikristo Tanzania (Christian Council of Tanzania): Church House, POB 1454, Dodoma; tel. (26) 2324445; fax (26) 2324352; f. 1934; Chair. Rt Rev. DONALD LEO MTETEMELA (Bishop of the Anglican Church); Gen. Sec. Rev. Dr LEONARD AMOS MTAITA.

The Anglican Communion
Anglicans are adherents of the Church of the Province of Tanzania, comprising 16 dioceses.

Archbishop of the Province of Tanzania and Bishop of Ruaha: Most Rev. DONALD LEO MTETEMELA, POB 1028, Iringa; fax (26) 2702479; e-mail ruaha@maf.or.tz.
Provincial Secretary: Dr R. MWITA AKIRI (acting), POB 899, Dodoma; tel. (26) 2321437; fax (26) 2324265; e-mail cpt@maf.org.

Greek Orthodox
Archbishop of East Africa: NICADEMUS OF IRINOUPOULIS (resident in Nairobi, Kenya); jurisdiction covers Kenya, Uganda and Tanzania.

Lutheran
Evangelical Lutheran Church in Tanzania: POB 3033, Arusha; tel. (57) 8855; fax (57) 8858; 1.5m. mems; Presiding Bishop Rt Rev. Dr SAMSON MUSHEMBA (acting); Exec. Sec. AMANI MWENEGOHA.

The Roman Catholic Church
Tanzania comprises five archdioceses and 25 dioceses. There were an estimated 11,102,193 adherents at 31 December 2005, equivalent to about 27.1% of the total population.

Tanzania Episcopal Conference
Catholic Secretariat, Mandela Rd, POB 2133, Dar es Salaam; tel. (22) 2851075; fax (22) 2851133; e-mail tec@cats-net.com; internet www.rc.net/tanzania/tec.
f. 1980; Pres. Mgr JUDE THADDAEUS RUWA'ICHI (Bishop of Dodoma).

Archbishop of Arusha: Most Rev. JOSAPHAT LOUIS LEBULU, Archbishop's House, POB 3044, Arusha; tel. (27) 2544361; fax (27) 2548004; e-mail angelo.arusha@habari.co.tz.
Archbishop of Dar es Salaam: Cardinal POLYCARP PENGO, Archbishop's House, POB 167, Dar es Salaam; tel. (22) 2113223; fax (22) 2125751; e-mail nyumba@cats-net.com.
Archbishop of Mwanza: Most Rev. ANTHONY MAYALA, Archbishop's House, POB 1421, Mwanza; tel. (28) 2500351; fax (28) 2501029; e-mail archmwz@mwanza-online.com.
Archbishop of Songea: Most Rev. NORBERT WENDELIN MTEGA, Archbishop's House, POB 152, Songea; tel. (25) 2602004; fax (25) 2602593; e-mail askofunw@yahoo.com.
Archbishop of Tabora: PAUL R. RUZOKA, Archbishop's House, Private Bag, PO Tabora; tel. (26) 2665608; fax (26) 2604000; e-mail archbishops-office@yahoo.co.uk.

Other Christian Churches
Baptist Mission of Tanzania: POB 9414, Dar es Salaam; tel. (22) 2170130; fax (22) 2170127; f. 1956; Admin. FRANK PEVEY.
Christian Missions in Many Lands (Tanzania): German Branch, POB 34, Tunduru, Ruvuma Region; f. 1957; Gen. Sec. THOMAS MÜHLING.
Moravian Church in Tanzania: POB 377, Mbeya; 113,656 mems; Gen. Sec. Rev. O. M. T. MPAYO.
Pentecostal Church: POB 34, Kahama.
Presbyterian Church: POB 2510, Dar es Salaam; tel. (22) 229075.

BAHÁ'Í FAITH
National Spiritual Assembly: POB 585, Dar es Salaam; tel. and fax (22) 2152766; e-mail bahaitz@africaonline.tz; mems resident in 2,301 localities.

OTHER RELIGIONS
Many people follow traditional beliefs. There are also some Hindu communities.

The Press
NEWSPAPERS
Daily

The African: Sinza Rd, POB 4793, Dar es Salaam; Editor-in-Chief JOHN KULEKANA.
Alasiri: POB 31042, Dar es Salaam; Swahili; Editor LUCAS MNUBI.
Daily News: POB 9033, Dar es Salaam; tel. (22) 2110165; fax (22) 2112881; f. 1972; govt-owned; Man. Editor SETHI KAMUHANDA; circ. 50,000.
The Democrat: Dar es Salaam; independent; Editor IDRISS LUGULU; circ. 15,000.
The Guardian: POB 31042, Dar es Salaam; tel. (22) 275250; fax (22) 273583; e-mail guardian@ipp.co.tz; internet www.ippmedia.com; f. 1994; English and Swahili; Man. Dir KIONDO MSHANA; Man. Editor PASCAL SHIJA.
Kipanga: POB 199, Zanzibar; Swahili; publ. by Information and Broadcasting Services.
Majira: POB 71439, Dar es Salaam; tel. (22) 238901; fax (22) 231104; independent; Swahili; Editor THEOPHIL MAKUNGA; circ. 15,000.
Nipashe: POB 31042, Dar es Salaam; Swahili; Editor HAMISI MZEE.

Uhuru: POB 9221, Dar es Salaam; tel. (22) 2182224; fax (22) 2185065; f. 1961; official publ. of CCM; Swahili; Man. Editor SAIDI NGUBA; circ. 100,000.

Weekly

Business Times: POB 71439, Dar es Salaam; tel. (22) 238901; fax (22) 231104; e-mail majira@bcsmedia.com; internet www.bcstimes.com; independent; English; Editor ALLI MWAMBOLA; circ. 15,000.

The Express: POB 20588, Dar es Salaam; tel. (22) 2180058; fax (22) 2182665; e-mail express@raha.com; internet www.theexpress.com; independent; English; Editor FAYAZ BHOJANI; circ. 20,000.

The Family Mirror: Faru/Nyamwezi St, Karikoo Area, POB 6804, Dar es Salaam; tel. (22) 181331; Editor ZEPHANIAH MUSENDO.

Gazette of the United Republic: POB 9142, Dar es Salaam; tel. (22) 231817; official announcements; Editor H. HAJI; circ. 6,000.

Government Gazette: POB 261, Zanzibar; f. 1964; official announcements.

Kasheshe: POB 31042, Dar es Salaam; Swahili; Editor VENANCE MLAY.

Leta Raha: POB 31042, Dar es Salaam; Swahili; Editor EDMOND MSANGI.

Mfanyakazi (The Worker): POB 15359, Dar es Salaam; tel. (22) 226111; Swahili; trade union publ; Editor NDUGU MTAWA; circ. 100,000.

Mzalendo: POB 9221, Dar es Salaam; tel. (22) 2182224; fax (22) 2185065; e-mail uhuru@udsm.ac.tz; f. 1972; publ. by CCM; Swahili; Man. Editor SAIDI NGABA; circ. 115,000.

Nipashe Jumapili: POB 31042, Dar es Salaam; Swahili.

Sunday News: POB 9033, Dar es Salaam; tel. (22) 2116072; fax (22) 2112881; f. 1954; govt-owned; Man. Editor SETHI KAMUCHANDA; circ. 50,000.

Sunday Observer: POB 31042, Dar es Salaam; e-mail guardian@ipp.co.tz; Man. Dir VUMI URASA; Man. Editor PETER MSUNGU.

Taifa Letu: POB 31042, Dar es Salaam; Swahili.

PERIODICALS

The African Review: POB 35042, Dar es Salaam; tel. (22) 2410130; e-mail mubakar@udsm.ac.tz; 2 a year; journal of African politics, development and international affairs; publ. by the Dept of Political Science, Univ. of Dar es Salaam; Chief Editor Dr MOHAMMED BAKARI; circ. 1,000.

Eastern African Law Review: POB 35093, Dar es Salaam; tel. (22) 243254; f. 1967; 2 a year; Chief Editor N. N. N. NDITI; circ. 1,000.

Elimu Haina Mwisho: POB 1986, Mwanza; monthly; circ. 45,000.

Habari za Washirika: POB 2567, Dar es Salaam; tel. (22) 223346; monthly; publ. by Co-operative Union of Tanzania; Editor H. V. N. CHIBULUNJE; circ. 40,000.

Jenga: POB 2669, Dar es Salaam; tel. (22) 2112893; fax (22) 2113618; journal of the National Development Corpn; circ. 2,000.

Kiongozi (The Leader): POB 9400, Dar es Salaam; tel. (22) 229505; f. 1950; fortnightly; Swahili; Roman Catholic; Editor ROBERT MFUGALE; circ. 33,500.

Kweupe: POB 222, Zanzibar; weekly; Swahili; publ. by Information and Broadcasting Services.

Mlezi (The Educator): POB 41, Peramiho; tel. 30; f. 1970; every 2 months; Editor Fr DOMINIC WEIS; circ. 8,000.

Mwenge (Firebrand): POB 1, Peramiho; tel. 30; f. 1937; monthly; Editor JOHN P. MBONDE; circ. 10,000.

Nchi Yetu (Our Country): POB 9142, Dar es Salaam; tel. (22) 2110200; f. 1964; govt publ; monthly; Swahili; circ. 50,000.

Nuru: POB 1893, Zanzibar; f. 1992; bi-monthly; official publ. of Zanzibar Govt; circ. 8,000.

Safina: POB 21422, Dar es Salaam; tel. (22) 234934; publ. by National Muslim Council of Tanzania; Editor YASSIN SADIK; circ. 10,000.

Sikiliza: POB 635, Morogoro; tel. and fax (23) 2604374; quarterly; Seventh-day Adventist; Editor MIKA D. MUSA; circ. 100,000.

Taamuli: POB 899, Dar es Salaam; tel. (22) 243500; 2 a year; journal of political science; publ. by the Dept of Political Science, Univ. of Dar es Salaam; circ. 1,000.

Tantravel: POB 2485, Dar es Salaam; tel. (22) 2111244; fax (22) 2116420; e-mail safari@ud.co.tz; internet www.tanzaniatouristboard.com; quarterly; publ. by Tanzania Tourist Board; Editor STEVE FISHER.

Tanzania Education Journal: POB 9121, Dar es Salaam; tel. (22) 227211; f. 1984; 3 a year; publ. by Institute of Education, Ministry of Education; circ. 8,000.

Tanzania Trade Currents: POB 5402, Dar es Salaam; tel. (22) 2851706; fax (22) 851700; e-mail betis@intafrica.com; bi-monthly; publ. by Board of External Trade; circ. 2,000.

Uhuru na Amani: POB 3033, Arusha; tel. (57) 8855; fax (57) 8858; quarterly; Swahili; publ. by Evangelical Lutheran Church in Tanzania; Editor ELIZABETH LOBULU; circ. 15,000.

Ukulima wa Kisasa (Modern Farming): Farmers' Education and Publicity Unit, POB 2308, Dar es Salaam; tel. (22) 2116496; fax (22) 2122923; e-mail fepu@twiga.com; f. 1955; bi-monthly; Swahili; publ. by Ministry of Food and Agriculture; Editor H. MLAKI; circ. 15,000.

Ushirika Wetu: POB 2567, Dar es Salaam; tel. (22) 2184081; e-mail ushirika@covision2000.com; monthly; publ. by Tanzania Federation of Co-operatives; Editor SIMON J. KERARYO; circ. 40,000.

Wela: POB 180, Dodoma; Swahili.

NEWS AGENCY

Press Services Tanzania (PST) Ltd: POB 31042, Dar es Salaam; tel. and fax (22) 2119195.

Publishers

Central Tanganyika Press: POB 1129, Dodoma; tel. (26) 2300012; fax (26) 324565; e-mail ctzpress@maf.or.tz; internet www.anglican.or.tz/ctp.htm; f. 1954; religious; Man. PETER MAKASSI MANGATI.

DUP (1996) Ltd: POB 7028, Dar es Salaam; tel. and fax (22) 2410137; e-mail director@dup.udsm.ac.tz; f. 1979; educational, academic and cultural texts in Swahili and English; Dir Dr N. G. MWITTA.

Eastern Africa Publications Ltd: POB 1002 Arusha; tel. (57) 3176; f. 1979; general and school textbooks; Gen. Man. ABDULLAH SAIWAAD.

Inland Publishers: POB 125, Mwanza; tel. (68) 40064; general non-fiction, religion, in Kiswahili and English; Dir Rev. S. M. MAGESA.

Oxford University Press: Maktaba Rd, POB 5299, Dar es Salaam; tel. (22) 229209; f. 1969; literature, literary criticism, essays, poetry; Man. SALIM SHAABAN SALIM.

Tanzania Publishing House: 47 Samora Machel Ave, POB 2138, Dar es Salaam; tel. (22) 2137402; e-mail tphhouse@yahoo.com; f. 1966; educational and general books in Swahili and English; Gen. Man. PRIMUS ISIDOR KARUGENDO.

GOVERNMENT PUBLISHING HOUSE

Government Printer: Office of the Prime Minister, POB 9124, Dar es Salaam; tel. (22) 2860900; fax (22) 2866955; e-mail gptz@pmo.go.tz; Dir KASSIAN C. CHIBOGOYO.

Broadcasting and Communications

TELECOMMUNICATIONS

Tanzania Communications Regulatory Authority (TCRA): POB 474, Dar es Salaam; tel. (22) 2118947; fax (22) 2116664; e-mail dg@tcra.go.tz; internet www.tcra.go.tz; f. 1993; licenses postal and telecommunications service operators; manages radio spectrum; acts as ombudsman; Dir-Gen. Prof. JOHN NKOMA.

Celtel Tanzania: Celtel House, Ali Hassan Mwinyi Rd, Dar es Salaam; tel. (22) 2748181; e-mail helpdesk@tz.celtel.com; internet www.tz.celtel.com; f. 2001; Man. Dir BASHAR ARAFEH.

MIC Tanzania Ltd: Lugoda St, POB 2929, Dar es Salaam; tel. (741) 800800; fax (741) 123064; e-mail mobitel@mobitel.co.tz; operates mobile cellular telecommunications services through Mobitel network.

Tanzania Telecommunications Co Ltd (TTCL): Extelcoms House, Samora Ave, POB 9070, Dar es Salaam; tel. (22) 2142000; fax (22) 2113232; e-mail ttcl@ttcl.co.tz; internet www.ttcl.co.tz; 35% sold to consortium of Detecon (Germany) and Mobile Systems International (Netherlands) in Feb. 2001; CEO BILL BECKMAN.

Vodacom (Tanzania) Ltd: 14th Floor PPF Towers, POB 2369, Dar es Salaam; tel. (754) 705000; fax (754) 704014; e-mail feedback@vodacom.co.tz; internet www.vodacom.co.tz; mobile cellular telephone operator.

Zanzibar Telecom (Zantel): POB 3459, Zanzibar; tel. (24) 2234823; fax (24) 2234850; e-mail customerservices@zantel.co.tz; internet www.zantel.co.tz; f. 1999; mobile cellular telephone operator for Zanzibar; Chair. SALEM AL SHARHAN; CEO NOEL HERRITY.

TANZANIA

BROADCASTING

Radio

Radio FM Zenj 96.8: Zanzibar; f. 2005; owned by Zanzibar Media Corpn; broadcasts to 60% of Zanzibar, to be extended to all of Zanzibar and mainland coast from southern Tanzania to Kenya; Gen. Man. AUSTIN MAKANI.

Radio Kwizera: N'Gara; tel. (28) 2223679; fax (28) 2223795; e-mail rkngara@jrstz.co.tz; f. 1995; station's objective is to educate, entertain and inform refugee and local communities, with the aim of bringing about peace and reconciliation; Dir DAMAS S. J. MISSANGA.

Radio One: POB 4374, Dar es Salaam; tel. (22) 275914; e-mail ipptech@ipp.co.tz; internet www.ippmedia.com.

Radio Tanzania Zanzibar: state-owned.

Radio Tumaini (Hope): 1 Bridge St, POB 167, Dar es Salaam; tel. (22) 2117307; fax (22) 2112594; e-mail tumaini@africaonline.co.tz; broadcasts in Swahili within Dar es Salaam; operated by the Roman Catholic Church; broadcasts on religious, social and economic issues; Dir Fr JEAN-FRANÇOIS GALTIER.

Sauti Ya Tanzania Zanzibar (The Voice of Tanzania Zanzibar): POB 1178, Zanzibar; f. 1951; state-owned; broadcasts in Swahili on three wavelengths; Dir SULEIMAN JUMA.

Tanzania Broadcasting Corporation (TBC): Broadcasting House, Nyerere Rd, POB 9191, Dar es Salaam; f. 2008; incorporates Radio Tanzania Dar es Salaam and the national TV network, Televisheni ya Taifa; Dir-Gen. DUNSTAN TIDO MHANDO.

> **Radio Tanzania Dar es Salaam (RTD):** POB 9191, Dar es Salaam; tel. (22) 2860760; fax (22) 2865577; f. 1951; state-owned; subsidiary of TBC; domestic services in Swahili; external services in English.

Television

Dar es Salaam Television (DTV): POB 21122, Dar es Salaam; tel. (22) 2116341; fax (22) 2113112; e-mail franco.dtv@raha.com; f. 1994; Man. Dir FRANCO TRAMONTANO.

Independent Television (ITV): Mikocheni Light Industrial Area, POB 4374, Dar es Salaam; tel. (22) 2775914; fax (22) 2775915; e-mail info@itv.co.tz; internet www.itv.co.tz; f. 1994; wholly owned by IPP Ltd; 62% of programmes are locally produced and in Kiswahili; Man. Dir JOYCE MHAVILLE.

Star TV: POB 1732, Mwanza,; tel. (28) 2503262; fax (28) 2500713; e-mail marketing@startvtz.com; internet www.startvtz.com; f. 2000.

Tanzania Broadcasting Corporation (TBC): see radio

> **Televisheni ya Taifa (TVT):** POB 31519, Dar es Salaam; tel. (22) 2700011; fax (22) 2700468; e-mail tvt-dg@africaonline.co.tz; f. 2000.

Television Zanzibar: POB 314, Zanzibar; tel. and fax (24) 22315951; e-mail karumehouse@tvz.co.tz; internet www.tvz.co.tz/; f. 1973; Dir JAMA SIMBA.

Finance

(cap. = capital; res = reserves; dep. = deposits; m. = million; brs = branches; amounts in Tanzanian shillings, unless otherwise indicated)

BANKING

Central Bank

Bank of Tanzania (Benki Kuu Ya Tanzania): 10 Mirambo St, POB 2939, Dar es Salaam; tel. (22) 2110946; fax (22) 2113325; e-mail info@hq.bot-tz.org; internet www.bot-tz.org; f. 1966; bank of issue; cap. 10,000m., res 343,825m., dep. 948,562m. (June 2005); Gov. and Chair. Prof. BENNO NDULU; 4 brs.

Principal Banks

African Banking Corpn (Tanzania) Ltd: Barclays House, 1st Floor, Ohio St, POB 31, Dar es Salaam; tel. (22) 2119303; fax (22) 2112402; e-mail abct@africanbankingcorp.com; internet www.africanbankingcorp.com; wholly owned by African Banking Corpn Holdings Ltd; cap. 5,404m. (Dec. 2003); Chair. Dr JONAS KIPOKOLA.

Akiba Commercial Bank Ltd: TDFL Bldg, Ali Hassan Mwinyi Rd, POB 669, Dar es Salaam; tel. (22) 2118340; fax (22) 2114173; e-mail akiba@cats-net.com; cap. 2,793m., res 115m., dep. 21,951m. (Dec. 2004); Chair. D. M. MOSHA; Man. Dir J. LYALE.

Azania Bancorp Ltd: POB 9271, Dar es Salaam; tel. (22) 2117997; fax (22) 2118010; e-mail info@azaniabank.co.tz; internet www.azaniabank.co.tz; 55% owned by National Social Security Fund, 31% owned by Parastatal Pension Fund, 9% owned by East African Development Bank, 5% owned by individuals; cap. 6,168m. (Dec. 2003); Chair. N. NSEMWA; CEO CHARLES SINGILI.

Barclays Bank (Tanzania) Ltd: Barclays House, Ohio St, POB 5137, Dar es Salaam; tel. (22) 2129381; fax (22) 2129757; e-mail karl.stumke@barclays.com; 99.9% owned by Barclays PLC (United Kingdom), 0.1% owned by Ebbgate Holdings Ltd; cap. 18,750m. (Dec. 2003); Chair. J. K. CHANDE; Man. Dir KARL STUMKE.

Capital Finance Ltd: TDFL Bldg, 5th Floor, 1008 Ohio St/Upanga Rd, POB 9032, Dar es Salaam; tel. (22) 2135152; fax (22) 2135150; e-mail mail@cfl.co.tz; wholly owned by Tanzania Development Finance Co Ltd; cap. 4,000m. (Dec. 2003); Chair. H. K. SENKORO; CEO J. H. McGUFFOG.

CF Union Bank Ltd: Jivan Hirji Bldg, Indira Gandhi/Mosque St, POB 1509, Dar es Salaam; tel. (22) 2110212; fax (22) 2118750; e-mail cfunionbank@raha.com; f. 2002 by merger of Furaha Finance Ltd and Crown Finance & Leasing Ltd; cap. 4m. (Dec. 2006); Chair. MUNIR ASGARALI BHARWANI; CEO SUBRAMANIAN GOPALAN.

Citibank Tanzania Ltd: Ali Hassan Mwinyi Rd, POB 71625, Dar es Salaam; tel. (22) 2117575; fax (22) 2113910; 99.98% owned by Citibank Overseas Investment Corpn; Chair. EMEKA EMUWA.

CRDB Bank: Azikiwe St, POB 268, Dar es Salaam; tel. (22) 2117442; fax (22) 2116714; e-mail crdb@crdb.com; internet www.crdb.com; f. as Co-operative and Rural Development Bank in 1947, transferred to private ownership and current name adopted 1996; 30% owned by DANIDA Investment; provides commercial banking services and loans for rural development; cap. 12,367m., res 13,730m., dep. 662,811m. (Dec. 2005); Chair JERRY SOLOMON; Man. Dir Dr CHARLES S. KIMEI; 34 brs.

Dar es Salaam Community Bank Ltd (DCB): Arnautoglu Bldg, Bibi Titi Mohamed St, POB 19798, Dar es Salaam; tel. (22) 2180253; fax (22) 2180239; e-mail dcb@africaonline.co.tz; f. 2001; cap. 1,796m. (Dec. 2003); Chair. PAUL MILVANGE RUPIA; Man. Dir EDMUND PANCRAS MKWAWA.

Diamond Trust Bank Tanzania Ltd: POB 115, cnr of Mosque St and Jamaat St, Dar es Salaam; tel. (22) 2114888; fax (22) 2114210; f. 1946 as Diamond Jubilee Investment Trust; converted to bank and adopted current name in 1996; 33.4% owned by Diamond Trust Bank Kenya Ltd, 31.2% owned by Aga Khan Fund for Economic Development SA (Switzerland); cap. 1,108m., res 222m., dep. 49,069m. (Dec. 2005); Chair. MAHMOOD MANJI; CEO SANJEEV KUMAR.

Eurafrican Bank (Tanzania) Ltd: NDC Development House, cnr Kivukoni Front and Ohio St, POB 3054, Dar es Salaam; tel. (22) 2111229; fax (22) 2113740; e-mail eab@eurafricanbank-tz.com; f. 1994; 78.8% owned by Belgolaise/Fortis Bank Group; other shareholders: FMO-Netherlands Development Co (9.83%), Tanzania Development Finance (9.41%), others (1.96%); cap. 6,478m. (Dec. 2002); Chair. FULGENCE M. KAZAURA; Man. Dir JUMA KISAAME.

EXIM Bank (Tanzania) Ltd: NIC Investment House, Samora Ave, POB 1431, Dar es Salaam; tel. (22) 2113091; fax (22) 2119737; e-mail enquiry@eximbank-tz.com; internet www.eximbank-tz.com; cap. 12,900m., res 31m., dep. 179,159m. (Dec. 2005); Chair. YOGESH MANEK; Man. Dir S. M. J. MWAMBENJA.

FBME Bank Ltd: POB 8298, Samora Ave, Dar es Salaam; tel. (22) 2126000; fax (22) 2126006; e-mail headoffice@fbme.com; internet www.fbme.com; f. 1982 in Cyprus as Federal Bank of the Middle East Ltd, subsidiary of Federal Bank of Lebanon SAL (Lebanon); changed country of incorporation to Cayman Islands in 1986, and to Tanzania in 2003; present name adopted 2005; cap. US $43m., res US $2m., dep. US $676m. (Dec. 2005); Chair. AYOUB-FARID M. SAAB, FADI M. SAAB; Gen. Man. (Tanzania) JAN VAN JAAREN.

Habib African Bank Ltd: India St, POB 70086, Dar es Salaam; tel. (22) 2111107; fax (22) 2111014; cap. 1,300m. (Dec. 2003); Chair. HABIB MOHAMMED D. HABIB; Man. Dir MANZAR A. KAZMI.

International Bank of Malaysia (Tanzania) Ltd: Upanga/Kisutu St, POB 9363, Dar es Salaam; tel. (22) 2110518; fax (22) 2110196; e-mail ibm@afsat.com; Chair. JOSEPHINE PREMLA SIVARETNAM; CEO M. RAHMAT.

Kenya Commercial Bank (Tanzania) Ltd: National Audit House, Samora/Ohio St, POB 804, Dar es Salaam; tel. (22) 2115386; fax (22) 2115391; internet www.kcb.co.ke; cap. 6,000m. (Dec. 2003); Chair. S. MUDHUME; Man. Dir BAZRA TABULO.

Kilimanjaro Co-operative Bank Ltd: Mawenzi Rd, POB 1760, Moshi; tel. (27) 54470; fax (27) 53570; Chair. A. P. KAVISHE; Gen. Man. J. KULAYA.

Mufindi Community Bank: POB 147, Mafinga; tel. and fax (26) 2772165; e-mail mucoba@africaonline.co.tz; cap. 100m. (Dec. 2003); Chair. J. J. MUNGAI; Gen. Man. DANY MPOGOLE.

Mwanga Community Bank: Mwanga Township, POB 333, Mwanga, Kilimanjaro; tel. and fax (27) 2754235; Man. Dir CHRIS HALIBUT.

National Microfinance Bank Ltd (NMB): Samora Ave, POB 9213, Dar es Salaam; tel. (22) 2124048; fax (22) 2110077; e-mail ceo@nmbtz.com; internet www.nmb.co.tz; f. 1997 following disbandment of The National Bank of Commerce; Chair. M. NGATUNGA; CEO JOHN R. GILES.

TANZANIA

NBC Ltd (National Bank of Commerce Ltd): NBC House, Sokoine Drive, POB 1863, Dar es Salaam; tel. (22) 2112082; fax (22) 2112887; e-mail nbcltd@nbctz.com; internet www.nbctz.com; f. 1997 following disbandment of National Bank of Commerce; 55% owned by ABSA Group Ltd (South Africa), 30% by Govt and 15% by International Finance Corpn; cap. 12,000m., res 26,349m., dep. 546,831m. (Dec. 2005); Chair. CHARLES M. NYIRABU; Man. Dir CHRISTO DE VRIES; 33 brs.

People's Bank of Zanzibar Ltd (PBZ): POB 1173, Stone Town, Zanzibar; tel. (24) 2231119; fax (24) 2231121; e-mail pbzltd@zanlik.com; f. 1966; controlled by Zanzibar Govt; cap. 16m. (June 1991); Chair. ABDUL RAHMAN M. JUMBE; Man. Dirs J. M. AMOUR, N. S. NASSOR; 3 brs.

Savings & Finance Ltd: Mission St/Samora Ave, POB 20268, Dar es Salaam; tel. (22) 2118625; fax (22) 2116733; Man. Dir SURANJAN GHOSH.

Stanbic Bank Tanzania Ltd: Sukari House, cnr Ohio St and Sokoine Drive, POB 72647, Dar es Salaam; tel. (22) 2112195; fax (22) 2113742; e-mail tanzaniainfo@stanbic.com; internet www.stanbic.co.tz; f. 1993; wholly owned by Standard Africa Holdings PLC; cap. 2,000m., res 871m., dep. 230,804m. (Dec. 2005); Chair ARNOLD B. S. KILEWO; Man. Dir BASHIR AWALEO; 4 brs.

Standard Chartered Bank Tanzania Ltd: International House, 1st Floor, cnr Shaaban Robert St and Garden Ave, POB 9011, Dar es Salaam; tel. (22) 2122160; fax (22) 2113770; f. 1992; wholly owned by Standard Chartered Holdings (Africa) BV, Netherlands; cap. 1,000m., res 20,613m., dep. 351,182m. (Dec. 2004); Man. Dir H. SHAH.

Tanzania Development Finance Co Ltd (TDFL): TDFL Bldg, Plot 1008, cnr Upanga Rd and Ohio St, POB 2478, Dar es Salaam; tel. (22) 2116417; fax (22) 2116418; e-mail mail@tdfl.co.tz; f. 1962; owned by Govt (32%), govt agencies of the Netherlands and Germany (5% and 26% respectively), the Commonwealth Development Corpn (26%) and the European Investment Bank (11%); cap. 3,303m. (Dec. 2001); Chair. H. K. SENKORO; CEO J. McGUFFOG.

Tanzania Investment Bank (TIB): cnr Zanaki St and Samora Machel Ave, POB 9373, Dar es Salaam; tel. (22) 2111708; fax (22) 2113438; e-mail md@tib.co.tz; internet www.tib.co.tz; f. 1970; provides finance, tech. assistance and consultancy, fund administration and loan guarantee for economic devt; 99% govt-owned; cap. 7,641m., res 838m., dep. 32,515m. (Dec. 2003); Man. Dir WILLIAM A. MLAKI.

Tanzania Postal Bank (TPB): Extelecoms Annex Bldg, Samora Ave, POB 9300, Dar es Salaam; tel. (22) 2112358; fax (22) 2114815; e-mail md@postalbank.co.tz; internet www.postalbank.co.tz; f. 1991; state-owned; cap. 1,041m. (Dec. 2003); Chair. PAUL JUSTIN MKANGA; Man. Dir and CEO ALPHONSE R. KIHWELE; 4 brs and 113 agencies.

Ulc (Tanzania) Ltd: POB 31, Dar es Salaam; tel. (22) 2119422; fax (22) 2112402; e-mail jmacharia@ulc.co.tz; cap. 2,204m. (Dec. 1999); Chair. Dr JONAS KIPOKOLA; CEO JAMES MACHARIA.

United Bank of Africa Ltd: PPF House, Ground/Mezzanine Floors, Samora Ave/Morogoro Rd, POB 9640, Dar es Salaam; tel. (22) 2130113; fax (22) 2130116; e-mail uba@cats-net.com; cap. 2,532m. (Dec. 2002); Chair. N. N. KITOMARI; Man. Dir I. J. MITCHELL.

STOCK EXCHANGE

Dar es Salaam Stock Exchange: Twigga Bldg, 4th Floor, Samora Ave, POB 70081, Dar es Salaam; tel. (22) 2133659; fax (22) 2122421; e-mail des@cats-net.com; internet www.darstockexchange.com; f. 1998; Chair. GABINUS MAGANGA; Chief Exec. Dr HAMISI S. KIBOLA.

INSURANCE

Jubilee Insurance Co of Tanzania Ltd (JICT): Dar es Salaam; 40% owned by Jubilee Insurance Kenya, 24% by local investors, 15% by the IFC, 15% by the Aga Khan Fund for Economic Devt, 6% by others; cap. US $2m.

National Insurance Corporation of Tanzania Ltd (NIC): POB 9264, Dar es Salaam; tel. (22) 2113823; fax (22) 2113403; e-mail info-nic@nictanzania.com; internet www.nictanzania.com; f. 1963; state-owned; all classes of insurance; Chair. Prof. J. L. KANYWANYI; Man. Dir OCTAVIAN W. TEMU; 30 brs.

Niko Insurance (Tanzania) Ltd: PPF House, 8th Floor, Morogoro Rd/Samora Ave, POB 21228, Dar es Salaam; tel. (22) 2120188; fax (22) 2120193; e-mail info@nikoinsurance.co.tz; internet www.nikoinsurance.co.tz; f. 1998; subsidiary of NICO Holdings Ltd (based in Malawi); Gen. Man. MANFRED Z. SIBANDE.

Trade and Industry

GOVERNMENT AGENCIES

Board of External Trade (BET): POB 5402, Dar es Salaam; tel. (22) 2851706; fax (22) 2851700; e-mail betis@intafrica.com; f. 1978; trade and export information and promotion, market research, marketing advisory and consultancy services; Dir-Gen. MBARUK K. MWANDORO.

Board of Internal Trade (BIT): POB 883, Dar es Salaam; tel. (22) 228301; f. 1967 as State Trading Corpn; reorg. 1973; state-owned; supervises seven national and 21 regional trading cos; distribution of general merchandise, agricultural and industrial machinery, pharmaceuticals, foodstuffs and textiles; shipping and other transport services; Dir-Gen. J. E. MAKOYE.

Parastatal Sector Reform Commission (PSRC): Sukari House, POB 9252, Dar es Salaam; tel. (22) 2115482; fax (22) 2113065; e-mail masalla@raha.com.

Tanzania Investment Centre (TIC): POB 938, Dar es Salaam; tel. (22) 2116328; fax (22) 2118253; e-mail information@tic.co.tz; internet www.tic.co.tz; f. 1997; promotes and facilitates investment in Tanzania; Exec. Dir SAMUEL SITTA.

CHAMBERS OF COMMERCE

Dar es Salaam Chamber of Commerce: Kelvin House, Samora Machel Ave, POB 41, Dar es Salaam; tel. (744) 270438; fax (22) 2112754; e-mail dcc1919@yahoo.com; f. 1919; Exec. Dir Y. P. MSEKWA.

Tanzania Chamber of Commerce, Industry and Agriculture: POB 9713, Dar es Salaam; tel. and fax (22) 2119437; e-mail tccia.info@cats-net.com; internet www.tccia.co.tz; f. 1988; Pres. E. MUSIBA.

Zanzibar Chamber of Commerce: POB 1407, Zanzibar; tel. (24) 2233083; fax (24) 2233349.

DEVELOPMENT CORPORATIONS

Capital Development Authority: POB 1, Dodoma; tel. (26) 2324053; f. 1973 to develop the new capital city of Dodoma; govt-controlled; Dir-Gen. EVARIST BABISI KEWBA.

Economic Development Commission: POB 9242, Dar es Salaam; tel. (22) 2112681; f. 1962 to plan national economic development; state-controlled.

National Development Corporation: Kivukoni Front, Ohio St, POB 2669, Dar es Salaam; tel. (22) 2112893; fax (22) 2113618; e-mail epztz@ndctz.com; internet www.ndctz.com; f. 1965; state-owned; cap. Ts. 30.0m.; promotes progress and expansion in production and investment.

Small Industries Development Organization (SIDO): Mfaume/Fire Rd, Upanga, POB 2476, Dar es Salaam; tel. (22) 2151946; fax (22) 2152070; e-mail dg@sido.go.tz; internet www.sido.go.tz; f. 1973; promotes and assists development of small-scale enterprises in public, co-operative and private sectors, aims to increase the involvement of women in small businesses; Chair. JAPHET S. MLAGALA; Dir-Gen. MIKE LAISOR.

Sugar Development Corporation: Dar es Salaam; tel. (22) 2112969; fax (22) 230598; Gen. Man. GEORGE G. MBATI.

Tanzania Petroleum Development Corporation (TPDC): POB 2774, Dar es Salaam; tel. (22) 2181407; fax (22) 2180047; f. 1969; state-owned; oversees petroleum exploration and undertakes autonomous exploration, imports crude petroleum and distributes refined products; Man. Dir YONA S. M. KILLAGANE.

There is also a development corporation for textiles.

INDUSTRIAL AND TRADE ASSOCIATIONS

Cashewnut Board of Tanzania: POB 533, Mtwara; tel. (59) 333445; fax (59) 333536; govt-owned; regulates the marketing, processing and export of cashews; Chair. GALUS ABEID; Dir-Gen. A. BENO MHAGAMA.

Confederation of Tanzania Industries (CTI): POB 71783, Dar es Salaam; tel. (22) 2123802; fax (22) 2115414; e-mail cti@cti.co.tz; f. 1991; Chair. REGINALD MENGI; Exec. Dir CHRISTINE KILINDU.

National Coconut Development Programme: POB 6226, Dar es Salaam; tel. (22) 2700552; fax (22) 275549; e-mail mari@mari.or.tz; f. 1979 to revive coconut industry; processing and marketing via research and devt in disease and pest control, agronomy and farming systems, breeding and post-harvest technology; based at Mikocheni Agricultural Research Inst; Dir Dr ALOIS K. KULLAYA.

Tanganyika Coffee Growers' Association Ltd: POB 102, Moshi.

Tanzania Horticultural Association (TAHA): Kanisa Rd, House No. 49, POB 3003, Arusha; tel. and fax (27) 2544568; e-mail taha@habari.co.tz; internet www.tanzaniahorticulture.com; f. 2004; Dir PHILLEMON KISAMO.

Tanzania Coffee Board (TCB): POB 732, Moshi; tel. (55) 52324; fax (55) 53033; e-mail coffee@eoltz.com; internet www.newafrica.com; Man. Dir LESLIE OMARI.

Tanzania Cotton Board: Pamba House, Garden Ave, POB 9161, Dar es Salaam; tel. (22) 2122564; fax (22) 2112894; e-mail tclb@tancotton.co.tz; internet www.tancotton.co.tz; f. 1984; regulates,

TANZANIA

develops and promotes the Tanzanian cotton industry; Dir Gen. Dr JOE KABISSA.

Tanzania Exporters' Association: Plot No. 139, Sembeti Rd, POB 1175, Dar es Salaam; tel. (22) 2781035; fax (22) 2112752; e-mail smutabuz@hotmail.com.

Tanzania Pyrethrum Board: POB 149, Iringa; f. 1960; Chair. Brig. LUHANGA; CEO P. B. G. HANGAYA.

Tanzania Sisal Authority: POB 277, Tanga; tel. (53) 44401; fax (53) 42759; Chair. W. H. SHELLUKINDO; Man. Dir S. SHAMTE.

Tanzania Tobacco Board: POB 227, Mazimbu Rd, Morogoro; tel. (23) 2603364; fax (23) 2604401; Chair. V. KAWAWA; CEO FRANK S. URIO.

Tanzania Wood Industry Corporation: POB 9160, Dar es Salaam; Gen. Man. E. M. MNZAVA.

Tea Association of Tanzania: POB 2177, Dar es Salaam; tel. (22) 2122033; e-mail trit@twiga.com; f. 1989; Chair. Dr NORMAN C. KELLY; Exec. Dir DAVID E. A. MGWASSA.

Tea Board of Tanzania: TETEX House, Pamba Rd, POB 2663, Dar es Salaam; tel. and fax (22) 2114400; Chair. ROSTAM AZIZI; Dir-Gen. MATHIAS ASSENGA BENEDICT.

Zanzibar State Trading Corporation: POB 26, Zanzibar; govt-controlled since 1964; sole exporter of cloves, clove stem oil, chillies, copra, copra cake, lime oil and lime juice; Gen. Man. ABDULRAHMAN RASHID.

UTILITIES

Electricity

Tanzania Electric Supply Co Ltd (TANESCO): POB 9024, Dar es Salaam; tel. (22) 2451130; fax (22) 2113836; e-mail info@tanesco.com; internet www.tanesco.com; state-owned; placed under private management in May 2002; privatization pending; Chair. FULGENCE M. KAZAURA; Man. Dir Dr IDRIS RASHIDI.

Gas

Enertan Corpn Ltd: POB 3746, Dar es Salaam.

Songas Ltd: POB 6342, Dar es Salaam; tel. (22) 2117313; fax (22) 2113614; internet www.songas.com; f. 1998; Gen. Man. JIM MCCARDLE.

Water

Dar es Salaam Water and Sanitation Authority: POB 1573, Dar es Salaam; e-mail dawasapiu@raha.com; privatization pending.

National Urban Water Authority: POB 5340, Dar es Salaam; tel. (22) 2667505.

CO-OPERATIVES

There are some 1,670 primary marketing societies under the aegis of about 20 regional co-operative unions. The Co-operative Union of Tanzania is the national organization to which all unions belong.

Tanzania Federation of Co-operatives Ltd: POB 2567, Dar es Salaam; tel. (22) 2184082; fax (22) 2184081; e-mail ushirika@ushirika.co.tz; internet www.ushirika.coop; f. 1962; Exec. Sec. GERALD P. MALIMA; 700,000 mems.

Department of Co-operative Societies: POB 1287, Zanzibar; f. 1952; promotes formation and development of co-operative societies in Zanzibar.

Principal Societies

Bukoba Co-operative Union Ltd: POB 5, Bukoba; 74 affiliated societies; 75,000 mems.

Kilimanjaro Native Co-operative Union (1984) Ltd: POB 3032, Moshi; tel. (27) 2752785; fax (27) 2754204; e-mail kncu@kilinet.co.tz; f. 1984; represents smallhold farmers and coffee-producers; 68 regd co-operative societies; Gen. Man. RAYMOND KIMARO.

Nyanza Co-operative Union Ltd: POB 9, Mwanza.

TRADE UNIONS

Union of Tanzania Workers (Juwata): POB 15359, Dar es Salaam; tel. (22) 226111; f. 1978; Sec.-Gen. JOSEPH C. RWEGASIRA; Dep. Secs-Gen. C. MANYANDA (mainland Tanzania), I. M. ISSA (Zanzibar).

Agricultural Workers: Sec. G. P. NYINDO.

Central and Local Government and Medical Workers: Sec. R. UTUKULU.

Communications and Transport Workers: POB 13920, Dar es Salaam; Sec. M. E. KALUWA.

Domestic, Hotels and General Workers: Sec. E. KAZOKA.

Industrial and Mines Workers: Sec. J. V. MWAMBUMA.

Railway Workers: Sec. C. SAMMANG' OMBE.

Teachers: Sec. W. MWENURA.

Principal Unaffiliated Unions

Organization of Tanzanian Trade Unions (OTTU): Dar es Salaam; Sec.-Gen. BRUNO MPANGAL.

Workers' Department of Chama Cha Mapinduzi: POB 389, Vikokotoni, Zanzibar; f. 1965.

Transport

RAILWAYS

Tanzania Railways Corporation (TRC): POB 468, Dar es Salaam; tel. and fax (22) 2110599; e-mail ccm_shamte@trctz.com; internet www.trctz.com; f. 1977 after dissolution of East African Railways; privatization pending; operates 2,600 km of lines within Tanzania; Chair. J. K. CHANDE; Dir-Gen. LINFORD MBOMA.

Tanzania-Zambia Railway Authority (Tazara): POB 2834, Dar es Salaam; tel. (22) 2862191; fax (22) 2862474; e-mail acistz@twiga.com; internet www.tazara.co.tz; jtly owned and administered by the Tanzanian and Zambian Govts; operates a 1,860-km railway link between Dar es Salaam and New Kapiri Mposhi, Zambia, of which 969 km are within Tanzania; Chair. SALIM MSOMA; Man. Dir K. MKANDAWIRE; Regional Man. (Tanzania) A. F. S. NALITOLELA.

ROADS

In 2004 Tanzania had an estimated 85,000 km of classified roads, of which some 5,169 km were paved. A 1,930-km main road links Zambia and Tanzania, and there is a road link with Rwanda. A 10-year Integrated Roads Programme, funded by international donors and co-ordinated by the World Bank, commenced in 1991. Its aim was to upgrade 70% of Tanzania's trunk roads and to construct 2,828 km of roads and 205 bridges, at an estimated cost of US $650m.

The island of Zanzibar has 619 km of roads, of which 442 km are bituminized, and Pemba has 363 km, of which 130 km are bituminized.

INLAND WATERWAYS

Steamers connect with Kenya, Uganda, the Democratic Republic of the Congo, Burundi, Zambia and Malawi. A joint shipping company was formed with Burundi in 1976 to operate services on Lake Tanganyika. A rail ferry service operates on Lake Victoria between Mwanza and Port Bell.

SHIPPING

Tanzania's major harbours are at Dar es Salaam (eight deep-water berths for general cargo, three berths for container ships, eight anchorages, lighter wharf, one oil jetty for small oil tankers up to 36,000 gross tons, offshore mooring for oil supertankers up to 100,000 tons, one 30,000-ton automated grain terminal) and Mtwara (two deep-water berths). There are also ports at Tanga (seven anchorages and lighterage quay), Bagamoyo, Zanzibar and Pemba. A programme to extend and deepen the harbour entrance at Dar es Salaam commenced in 1997.

Tanzania Ports Authority (TPA): POB 9184, Dar es Salaam; tel. (22) 2116258; fax (22) 232066; e-mail dp@tanzaniaports.com; internet www.tanzaniaports.com; f. 2005 to replace the Tanzania Harbours Authority, in preparation for privatization; Dir-Gen. EPHRAIM MGAWE.

Chinese-Tanzanian Joint Shipping Co: POB 696, Dar es Salaam; tel. (22) 2113389; fax (22) 2113388; f. 1967; services to People's Republic of China, South East Asia, Eastern and Southern Africa, Red Sea and Mediterranean ports.

National Shipping Agencies Co Ltd (NASACO): POB 9082, Dar es Salaam; f. 1973; state-owned shipping co; Man. Dir D. R. M. LWIMBO.

Tanzania Central Freight Bureau (TCFB): POB 3093, Dar es Salaam; tel. (22) 2114174; fax (22) 2116697; e-mail tcfb@cats-net.com.

Tanzania Coastal Shipping Line Ltd: POB 9461, Dar es Salaam; tel. (22) 237034; fax (22) 2116436; regular services to Tanzanian coastal ports; occasional special services to Zanzibar and Pemba; also tramp charter services to Kenya, Mozambique, the Persian (Arabian) Gulf, Indian Ocean islands and the Middle East; Gen. Man. RICHARD D. NZOWA.

CIVIL AVIATION

There are 53 airports and landing strips. The major international airport is at Dar es Salaam, 13 km from the city centre, and there are also international airports at Kilimanjaro, Mwanza and Zanzibar. The management of Kilimanjaro International Airport was priva-

TANZANIA

tized in 1998. In 2005 it was reported that privatization was to be extended to the management of airports at Dar es Salaam, Mtware and Mwanza.

Tanzania Civil Aviation Authority (TCAA): IPS Bldg, cnr Samora Machel Ave and Azikiwe St, POB 2819, Dar es Salaam; tel. (22) 2115079; fax (22) 2118905; e-mail tcaa@tcaa.go.tz; internet www.tcaa.go.tz; f. 2003; replaced Directorate of Civil Aviation (f. 1977); ensures aviation safety and security, provides air navigation services; Dir-Gen. MARGARET T. MUNYAGI.

Air Tanzania: ATC House, Ohio St/Garden Ave, POB 543, Dar es Salaam; tel. (22) 2197200; fax (22) 2125221; e-mail bookings@airtanzania.com; internet www.airtanzania.com; f. 1977; operates an 18-point domestic network and international services to Africa, the Middle East and Europe; Chair. MUSTAFA NYANG'ANYI; CEO DAVID MATTAKA.

Air Zanzibar: POB 1784, Zanzibar; f. 1990; operates scheduled and charter services between Zanzibar and destinations in Tanzania, Kenya and Uganda.

New ACS Ltd: Peugeot House, 36 Upanga Rd, POB 21236, Dar es Salaam; fax (22) 237017; operates domestic and regional services; Dir MOHSIN RAHEMTULLAH.

Precisionair: New Safari Hotel Bldg, Boma Rd, POB 1636, Arusha; tel. (27) 2502818; fax (27) 2508204; e-mail jgwaseko@precisionairtz.com; internet www.precisionairtz.com; f. 1993; operates scheduled and charter domestic and regional services.

Tanzanair: Julius Nyerere Int. Airport, POB 364, Dar es Salaam; tel. (22) 2843131; fax (22) 2844600; e-mail info@tanzanair.com; internet www.tanzanair.com; f. 1969; operates domestic and regional charter services, offers full engineering and maintenance services for general aviation aircraft; Dep. Man. Dir JOHN SAMARAS.

Tourism

Mount Kilimanjaro is a major tourist attraction. Tanzania has set aside about one-quarter of its land area for 12 national parks, 17 game reserves, 50 controlled game areas and a conservation area. Other attractions for tourists include beaches and coral reefs along the Indian Ocean coast, and the island of Zanzibar (which received 86,495 tourists in 1997 and is expanding and upgrading its tourism facilities). Visitor arrivals totalled 612,754 in 2005, and in that year revenue from tourism was US $836m.

Tanzania Tourist Board: IPS Bldg, 3rd Floor, POB 2485, Dar es Salaam; tel. (22) 2111244; fax (22) 2116420; e-mail safari@ud.co.tz; internet www.tanzaniatouristboard.com; state-owned; supervises the development and promotion of tourism; Man. Dir GEOFFREY E. TENGENEZA.

Tanzania Wildlife Co: POB 1144, Arusha; tel. (57) 8830; fax (57) 8239; e-mail info@tanzaniaquest.com; internet www.tanzaniaquest.com; f. 1974; organizes hunting, photographic, horseback and adventure safaris; also exports and deals in live animals, birds and game-skin products; Man. Dir LEON LAMPRECHT.

Zanzibar Tourist Corporation: POB 216, Zanzibar; tel. (24) 2238630; fax (24) 2233417; e-mail ztc@zanzinet.com; internet www.zanzibartouristcorporation.com; f. 1985; operates tours and hotel services; Gen. Man. SABAAH SALEH ALI.

THAILAND

Introductory Survey

Location, Climate, Language, Religion, Flag, Capital

The Kingdom of Thailand lies in South-East Asia. It is bordered to the west and north by Myanmar (Burma), to the north-east by Laos and to the south-east by Cambodia. Thailand extends southward, along the isthmus of Kra, to the Malay Peninsula, where it borders Malaysia. The isthmus, shared with Myanmar, gives Thailand a short coastline on the Indian Ocean, and the country also has a long Pacific coastline on the Gulf of Thailand. The climate is tropical and humid, with an average annual temperature of 29°C (85°F). There are three main seasons: hot, rainy and cool. Temperatures in Bangkok are generally between 20°C (68°F) and 35°C (95°F). The national language is Thai. There are small minorities of Chinese, Malays and indigenous hill peoples. The predominant religion is Buddhism, mainly of the Hinayana (Theravada) form. About 4% of the population, predominantly Malays, are Muslims, and there is also a Christian minority, mainly in Bangkok and the north. The national flag (proportions 2 by 3) has five horizontal stripes, of red, white, blue, white and red, the central blue stripe being twice as wide as each of the others. The capital is Bangkok.

Recent History

Formerly known as Siam, Thailand took its present name in 1939. Under the leadership of Marshal Phibul Songkhram, Thailand entered the Second World War as an ally of Japan. Phibul was deposed in 1944, but returned to power in 1947 after a military coup. His influence declined during the 1950s, and in 1957 he was overthrown in a bloodless coup, led by Field Marshal Sarit Thanarat. Elections took place, but in 1958 martial law was declared and all political parties were dissolved. Sarit died in 1963 and was succeeded as Prime Minister by Gen. (later Field Marshal) Thanom Kittikachorn, who had served as Deputy Prime Minister since 1959. Thanom continued the combination of military authoritarianism and economic development instituted by his predecessor. A Constitution was introduced in 1968, and elections to a National Assembly took place in 1969, but in November 1971, following an increase in communist insurgency and internal political unrest, Thanom annulled the Constitution, dissolved the National Assembly and imposed martial law.

During 1972 there were frequent student demonstrations against the military regime, and in October 1973 the Government was forced to resign, after the army refused to use force to disperse student protesters, and King Bhumibol withdrew his support from the administration. An interim Government was formed under Dr Sanya Dharmasakti, the President of the Privy Council. In October 1974 a new Constitution, legalizing political parties, was promulgated, and in January 1975 elections were held to the new House of Representatives. A coalition Government was formed in February by Seni Pramoj, the leader of the Democrat Party (DP), but it was defeated by a vote of no confidence in the following month.

A new right-wing coalition Government, headed by the leader of the Social Action Party (SAP), Kukrit Pramoj (brother of Seni), was unable to maintain its unity, and Kukrit resigned in January 1976. After further general elections in April, a four-party coalition Government was formed, with Seni as Prime Minister. However, following violent student demonstrations in October during which the security forces killed hundreds of demonstrators, the Seni Government was dissolved, and a right-wing military junta, the National Administrative Reform Council (NARC), seized power. Martial law was declared, the Constitution was annulled, political parties were banned and strict press censorship was imposed. A new Constitution was promulgated, and a new Cabinet was announced, with Thanin Kraivixien, a Supreme Court judge, as Prime Minister.

Under the Thanin Government there was considerable repression of students and political activists. In October 1977 the Government was overthrown in a bloodless coup by a Revolutionary Council (later known as the National Policy Council—NPC) of military leaders, most of whom had been members of the NARC. The 1976 Constitution was abrogated, and the Secretary-General of the NPC (who was also the Supreme Commander of the Armed Forces), Gen. Kriangsak Chomanan, became Prime Minister. Many detainees were released, censorship was partially relaxed and the King nominated a National Assembly on the advice of the NPC. In December 1978 the National Assembly approved a new Constitution, and elections to a new House of Representatives were held in April 1979. Members of the Senate, however, were all nominated by the Prime Minister, and were almost all military officers. Kriangsak remained Prime Minister and formed a new Council of Ministers, after which the NPC was dissolved. However, Kriangsak resigned in March 1980, and was replaced by Gen. Prem Tinsulanonda, the Commander-in-Chief of the Army and the Minister of Defence. A new coalition Government, composed largely of centre-right politicians acceptable to the armed forces, was formed.

Prem's administration survived an abortive coup attempt in April 1981. In December Prem effected a ministerial reorganization, reincorporating members of the SAP (who had been excluded from the Government in March), in order to repulse a challenge from the new National Democracy Party (NDP), established by Kriangsak. In April 1983 no single party won an overall majority in elections to the House of Representatives, and a coalition Government was formed by the SAP, Prachakorn Thai, the DP and the NDP, despite Chart Thai being the party with the largest number of seats. Prem was again appointed Prime Minister.

In September 1985 a group of military officers carried out a coup attempt in Bangkok. Troops loyal to the Government quickly suppressed the revolt, but at least five people were killed during the fighting. The leader of the revolt, Col Manoon Roopkachorn (who had also led the coup attempt in 1981), fled the country, but 40 others, including Kriangsak, were put on trial in October, accused of inciting sedition and rebellion. Gen. Arthit Kamlang-ek, the Supreme Commander of the Armed Forces and Commander-in-Chief of the Army (who was believed to have been sympathetic to the aims of the coup leaders), was replaced in his posts by Gen. Chavalit Yongchaiyudh, hitherto the army Chief of Staff.

In September 1985 and January 1986 there were extensive changes in the Government, including the replacement of all members of the SAP, following the resignation of Kukrit as the party's leader. In May 1986, following a parliamentary defeat for the Government over proposed vehicle taxation, the House of Representatives was dissolved. A general election for an enlarged legislature was held in July, when the DP won 100 of the 347 seats (compared with 56 of the 324 seats at the previous election). A coalition Government was formed, including members of the DP, Chart Thai, the SAP, Rassadorn and seven 'independent' ministers. Prem remained Prime Minister.

In April 1988 the rejection by dissident members of the DP of proposed legislation on copyright prompted 16 ministers belonging to the DP to resign for failing to maintain party unity. The King dissolved the House of Representatives, at Prem's request, and new elections were held in July. Internal disputes weakened support for the DP (25 dissidents had resigned in May), and Chart Thai won the largest number of seats (87). Gen. Chatichai Choonhavan, the leader of Chart Thai, was appointed Prime Minister in August, after Prem declined an invitation to remain in the post. A new Council of Ministers was formed, comprising members of Chart Thai, the DP, the SAP, Rassadorn, the United Democratic Party and the Muan Chon party. In April 1989 Ruam Thai, the Community Action Party, the Prachachon Party and the Progressive Party merged to form an opposition grouping called Ekkaparb (Solidarity). Nine members of the Prachachon Party subsequently defected to Chart Thai, giving the ruling coalition control of 229 of the 357 seats in the House of Representatives.

In March 1990 Chavalit resigned as acting Supreme Commander of the Armed Forces; he also resigned as Commander-in-Chief of the Army, in which post he was succeeded by Gen. Suchinda Kraprayoon, hitherto his deputy. In July, despite growing criticism of Chatichai's administration, following a number of corruption scandals and labour unrest, the House of Representatives overwhelmingly rejected an opposition motion of no confidence in the Government. In August, however,

Chatichai reorganized the Council of Ministers, incorporating Puangchon Chao Thai in the ruling coalition, and reducing the influence of the SAP, following the implication of many of its members in allegations of corruption.

In November 1990 Chatichai demoted the leader of the Muan Chon party, Chalerm Yoobamrung, an outspoken critic of the armed forces, from his position as Minister to the Prime Minister's Office. The leadership of the armed forces had demanded Chalerm's dismissal, threatening unspecified intervention if government changes did not take place. In early December Chatichai resigned as Prime Minister; he was reappointed on the next day and subsequently formed a coalition Government comprising Chart Thai, Rassadorn, Puangchon Chao Thai and former opposition parties Prachakorn Thai and Ekkaparb, which provided him with reduced support (227 of the 357 seats) in the House of Representatives.

On 23 February 1991 Chatichai's Government was ousted in a bloodless military coup. Gen. Sunthorn Kongsompong, the Supreme Commander of the Armed Forces, assumed administrative power as the Chairman of the newly created National Peace-keeping Council (NPC). The NPC was actually dominated by the effective head of the armed forces, Gen. Suchinda, who was appointed joint Deputy Chairman of the NPC together with the Commanders-in-Chief of the Air Force and Navy and the Director-General of the Police. The coup leaders cited government corruption and abuse of power to justify their action; however, the coup was also widely believed to have been organized in response to the recent erosion of military influence.

Under the NPC, the Constitution was abrogated, the House of Representatives, the Senate and the Council of Ministers were dissolved, and martial law was imposed. The NPC won unprecedented royal approval, and in March 1991 an interim Constitution, approved by the King, was published. Anand Panyarachun, a business executive and former diplomat, was appointed acting Prime Minister pending fresh elections. Anand appointed a predominantly civilian interim Cabinet, composed mainly of respected technocrats and former ministers. Chatichai and Arthit, who had been arrested at the time of the coup, were released after two weeks. The NPC appointed a 292-member National Legislative Assembly, which included 149 serving or former military personnel, as well as many civilians known to have connections with the armed forces.

In May 1991 martial law was repealed in most areas, and political activity was permitted to resume. The New Aspiration Party (NAP—formed in October 1990 by Gen. Chavalit) gathered support as the traditional parties were in disarray, largely owing to investigations of corruption by the newly created Assets Examination Committee. In June 1991 a new party, Samakkhi Tham, was created to compete with the NAP. It was sponsored by the Commander-in-Chief of the Air Force, Air Chief Marshal Kaset Rojananin, and led by Narong Wongwan, a former leader of Ekkaparb. In August Suchinda assumed, in addition to the post of Commander-in-Chief of the Army, the role of Supreme Commander of the Armed Forces.

In November 1991 the Constitution Scrutiny Committee, which had been effectively nominated by the NPC, presented a draft Constitution to the National Legislative Assembly. Following public criticism of the draft (including a demonstration by 50,000 protesters in Bangkok), the document was amended to reduce the number of nominated senators from 360 to 270, and to abolish provisions that allowed the Senate the right to participate in the selection of the Prime Minister. Opposition parties, including the NAP and Palang Dharma (led by the popular and influential Governor of Bangkok, Maj.-Gen. Chamlong Srimuang), continued to oppose the draft, claiming that it perpetuated the power of the NPC. The National Legislative Assembly approved the new Constitution in December, but campaigners continued to express concern over certain provisional clauses (which were to remain in effect for four years), under which the NPC was to appoint the Prime Minister and the Senate, and regarding the Senate's right to vote jointly with the elected House on motions of no confidence, thus enabling the Senate to dismiss a government with the support of only 46 elected representatives.

The general election took place on 22 March 1992, when 15 parties contested the 360 seats; 59.2% of the electorate voted. Despite the establishment of an independent organization, Poll Watch, to monitor the elections, the practice of 'vote-buying' persisted in the poorer northern and north-eastern regions. Samakkhi Tham and Chart Thai secured the largest number of seats, 79 and 74 respectively. The NAP secured 72 seats and Palang Dharma won 41 seats, 32 of which were in Bangkok. On the day of the election the NPC appointed the 270 members of the Senate, 154 of whom were officers of the armed forces or police.

In late March 1992 it was announced that Narong Wongwan would lead a coalition government comprising his own party (Samakkhi Tham), Chart Thai, Prachakorn Thai, the SAP and Rassadorn, which together controlled 195 seats in the House of Representatives. US allegations of Narong's involvement in illicit drugs-trafficking, however, caused the nomination to be rescinded. In early April 1992 Suchinda was named as Prime Minister, despite his assurances before the election that he would not accept the post. He was replaced as Supreme Commander of the Armed Forces by Kaset and as Commander-in-Chief of the Army by his brother-in-law, Gen. Issarapong Noonpakdi, hitherto his deputy. Suchinda's accession to the premiership prompted an immediate popular protest by more than 50,000 demonstrators against the appointment of an unelected Prime Minister. Later in April Suchinda appointed eight other unelected members to a new Cabinet, retaining several technocrats from Anand's interim Government. The 49-member Council of Ministers also included three ministers who had been found guilty of 'possessing unusual wealth' by the Assets Examination Committee.

In early May 1992 Chamlong announced, at a rally attended by 100,000 demonstrators, that he would fast until death unless Suchinda resigned. The demonstrations continued uninterrupted for one week until the government parties agreed to amend the Constitution to prevent an unelected Prime Minister (including the incumbent Suchinda, who would have to resign) from taking office, and to limit the power of the unelected Senate. Chamlong abandoned his hunger strike, and temporarily suspended the demonstration. However, violent anti-Government demonstrations erupted in Bangkok when it appeared that the Government might renege on its commitments. The Government declared a state of emergency in Bangkok and neighbouring provinces, introducing a curfew and banning any large gatherings. Chamlong was arrested and more than 3,000 people were detained by security forces in a brutal attempt to suppress the riots, which continued for several days.

Following unprecedented intervention by King Bhumibol, Suchinda ordered the release of Chamlong, announced a general amnesty for those involved in the protests and pledged to introduce amendments to the Constitution. On 24 May 1992 Suchinda resigned, after failing to retain the support of the five coalition parties. On 10 June the National Assembly approved constitutional amendments, whereby the Prime Minister was required to be a member of the House of Representatives, the authority of the Senate was restricted and the President of the House of Representatives was to be the President of the National Assembly. On the same day the King, contrary to expectations, named Anand as Prime Minister. Anand appointed a politically neutral, unelected Cabinet, which included many of the figures from his previous administrations, and dissolved the National Assembly in preparation for a general election.

At the end of June 1992 the four parties that had opposed the military Government (the DP, the NAP, Palang Dharma and Ekkaparb) formed an alliance, the National Democratic Front, to contest the forthcoming elections. In July, in an effort to dissociate himself from the traditional coalition parties that had supported the Suchinda regime, Chatichai declined the leadership of Chart Thai and formed a new party, Chart Pattana, which quickly gained widespread support.

During mid-1992 Anand introduced measures to curb the political power of the armed forces, reduce military control of state enterprises, and remove the authority of the armed forces to intervene in situations of social unrest. In August Kaset and Issarapong were dismissed from their positions at the head of the armed forces and demoted to inactive posts. A more extensive reallocation of military posts took place in September. The new Commander-in-Chief of the Army, Gen. Wimol Wongwanit, pledged that the army would not interfere in politics under his command.

The general election took place on 13 September 1992, when 12 parties contested the 360 seats in the House of Representatives; 62.1% of the electorate voted. Poll Watch reported that 'vote-buying' and violence persisted, especially in the north-eastern region. The DP won the largest number of seats (79), while Chart Thai and Chart Pattana secured 77 and 60 seats respectively. The DP was able to form a coalition with its electoral allies, the NAP, Palang Dharma and Ekkaparb, which commanded 185 of the 360 seats. Despite its participation in the previous administration, the SAP (with 22 seats) was also subsequently invited to join the Government. On 23 September Chuan Leekpai, the leader of the DP, was formally approved as Prime Minister. Chuan declared his intention to eradicate corrupt practices, to decentralize government, to enhance rural development and to reduce the powers of the Senate.

Although Chuan's integrity as Prime Minister remained unquestioned, widespread dissatisfaction with his style of leadership began to emerge in early 1993. The SAP was critical of Chuan's alleged indecisiveness and slow progress in the implementation of national policy. In June, however, two motions of no confidence in the Cabinet, introduced by Chart Pattana and Chart Thai, were rejected by a considerable margin. In September the SAP announced that it was to merge with four opposition parties, including Chart Pattana, under the leadership of Chatichai, while remaining in the ruling coalition. However, four days later the SAP was expelled from the Government and replaced by the Seritham Party.

In September 1994 Chamlong resumed the leadership of Palang Dharma in party elections, and subsequently persuaded the party executive committee to approve the replacement of all 11 of the party's cabinet members. Chamlong's nominations for inclusion in the Cabinet included Thaksin Shinawatra, a prominent business executive, and Vichit Surapongchai, a banking executive, as Minister of Foreign Affairs and Minister of Transport and Communications respectively. Despite some opposition to the selection of unelected candidates, the appointments were confirmed in a cabinet reorganization in October, when Chamlong was named a Deputy Prime Minister.

In December 1994 the NAP withdrew from the ruling coalition over a constitutional amendment providing for the future election of local government representatives, including village headmen. The NAP voted against the Government to protect the vested interests of incumbent local administrators who would control many votes at the next election. In order to secure a parliamentary majority, Chuan was obliged to include Chatichai's Chart Pattana in the governing coalition, although this severely compromised the Government's claims to represent honesty and reform.

In January 1995 Chuan finally obtained the approval of the National Assembly for a series of amendments to the Constitution to expand the country's democratic base. Attempts in the previous year had been obstructed by the opposition, with the support of the majority of senators (who were mostly appointees of the 1991 coup leaders). The reforms adopted in 1995 included a reduction in the size of the appointed Senate to two-thirds of that of the elective House of Representatives, the lowering of the eligible voting age from 20 years to 18, equality for women, the establishment of an administrative court, the introduction of parliamentary ombudsmen and the prohibition of senators and members of the Government from holding monopolistic concessions with government or state bodies. This last amendment necessitated the resignation of Thaksin as Minister of Foreign Affairs, owing to his extensive business interests.

In May 1995 the opposition tabled a motion of no confidence in the Government, in connection with a land reform scandal, which had prompted the resignation of the Minister of Agriculture and Co-operatives in December 1994. During a government investigation allegations that the land reform programme had been used to benefit wealthy landowners were substantiated. In April 1995, in what was regarded by the opposition as an inadequate response, land titles were removed from seven deed-holders and a senior official was dismissed from the land reform department. Following an announcement by Chamlong that Palang Dharma would not support the coalition in the no confidence vote, Chuan dissolved the House of Representatives on 19 May.

At elections to an enlarged House of Representatives, which took place on 2 July 1995, 12 political parties contested 391 seats; 62.0% of eligible voters participated in the election. Chart Thai won the largest number of seats (92), followed by the DP (86) and the NAP (57). Support for these parties was based on provincial patronage politics and allegations of 'vote-buying' were widespread. The leader of Chart Thai, Banharn Silapa-Archa (who was among those accused of 'possessing unusual wealth' by the military junta in 1991), formed a coalition Government comprising Chart Thai, the NAP, Palang Dharma, the SAP, Prachakorn Thai, Muan Chon and later Nam Thai (a business-orientated party formed in 1994 by Amnuay Viravan, a former minister). Thaksin (who had relinquished majority control of his company) had been elected to the leadership of Palang Dharma in May, following the resignation of Chamlong. Banharn appointed all the leaders of the coalition parties (except for the Muan Chon party) as Deputy Prime Ministers. The composition of Banharn's Cabinet was widely criticized, owing to the predominance of professional politicians (who were often subject to allegations of corruption and 'vote-buying'). There was also dissatisfaction at the appointment of the inexperienced Surakiart Sathirathai, a lawyer, as Minister of Finance while the country was undergoing a process of financial liberalization.

In March 1996 Banharn announced the composition of the new Senate, the first to be appointed by a democratically elected Prime Minister. In contrast to the previous Senate, only 39 active military officers were named as senators; other appointees included academics and business executives.

In May 1996 10 government ministers, including the Prime Minister, survived motions of no confidence, despite opposition revelations of financial irregularities at the Bangkok Bank of Commerce, including loans extended without collateral to members of the Thai Cabinet, notably the Deputy Minister of the Interior, Suchart Tancharoen, and the Deputy Minister of Finance, Newin Chidchob, both members of Chart Thai. Palang Dharma refused to support Suchart in the debate. In order to preempt the withdrawal of Palang Dharma from the ruling coalition, five members of Chart Thai, including Suchart and Newin, resigned from their government positions. Palang Dharma subsequently agreed to remain in the coalition but announced the resignation of all five of its ministers from the Cabinet. In the ensuing cabinet reorganization at the end of May Surakiart, who had failed to take action to prevent huge losses at the Bangkok Bank of Commerce, was replaced by a former official in the Ministry of Finance, Bodi Chunnananda, Amnuay was appointed Minister of Foreign Affairs and the Palang Dharma ministers all agreed to return to their positions in the Cabinet.

In July 1996 Vijit Supinit resigned from his position as Governor of the Bank of Thailand following a series of financial scandals. In August the Government suffered a set-back following the withdrawal of Palang Dharma from the ruling coalition. This defection, which was the apparent result of a cabinet dispute over alleged bribery in the awarding of bank licences, reduced the Government's legislative majority by 23 seats. In September Banharn was able to secure the support of his coalition partners in a scheduled motion of no confidence in his administration only by undertaking to resign from the premiership. However, the inability of the coalition partners to agree on the appointment of a new Prime Minister led to the dissolution of the House of Representatives on 27 September.

In the general election, which was held on 17 November 1996 and was marred by violence and alleged extensive ballot-rigging, the NAP won 125 of the 393 seats, while the DP secured 123 seats. The majority of NAP seats were gained through provincial patronage politics, while the more politically-aware electorate of Bangkok returned the DP to 29 of the city's 37 seats. Chavalit, the leader of the NAP, was appointed Prime Minister, heading a coalition that incorporated Chart Pattana, the SAP, Prachakorn Thai, Muan Chon and the Seritham Party. The ruling coalition thus held 221 seats in the House of Representatives. Chatichai was appointed as the Chairman of the Prime Minister's special advisory group on economic and foreign affairs, and the majority of the other influential cabinet posts were assigned to other members of Chart Pattana and the NAP. Thaksin resigned as leader of Palang Dharma following the party's failure to win more than one seat in the House of Representatives.

As evidence of Chavalit's avowed intention to revive the economy, he allocated the finance portfolio and the deputy premiership with responsibility for economic affairs to Amnuay, a respected technocrat. However, Chavalit subsequently failed to give Amnuay the necessary support to overcome the obstacles imposed by other coalition members anxious to prevent the implementation of austere fiscal policies. In June 1997 Amnuay resigned and was replaced by the little-known Thanong Bidaya, the President of the Thai Military Bank. The Government's indecisive handling of the economy contributed to a financial crisis in mid-1997, following a series of sustained assaults on the Thai baht by currency speculators, which led to the baht's effective devaluation in early July. At the end of July the Governor of the Central Bank, Rerngchai Marakanonda, also resigned, citing political interference. The deterioration in the state of the economy in 1997 was reflected in an increase in popular protests. The most significant of these was an encampment of about 15,000 representatives of the Assembly of the Poor (a non-governmental organization campaigning for the improvement of conditions for impoverished farmers and landless agricultural labourers) outside the Prime Minister's office in January. The protesters dispersed in May, following the establishment of a fund to compensate villagers for relocation and destruction caused by government infrastructure projects. The Government introduced measures in June to constrain media attacks on the authorities and to limit mass protests.

In August 1997 Chavalit implemented a cabinet reorganization in an attempt to regain public confidence. On the advice of former Prime Minister Prem, the former Minister of Finance, Virabongsa Ramangkura, an outspoken critic of the Government's handling of the economic crisis, was appointed Deputy Prime Minister with responsibility for economic affairs, while Thaksin joined the Cabinet as Deputy Prime Minister with responsibility for regional development and trade. Despite the announcement of strict austerity measures and the intervention of the IMF, the economic situation continued to deteriorate.

Meanwhile, in January 1997 an assembly of 99 members was elected by the legislature to draft a new constitution following the unanimous approval of a constitution amendment bill by the National Assembly in September 1996. The draft Constitution included provisions for: a directly elected Senate; the replacement in the House of Representatives of 393 deputies from multi-member constituencies by 400 deputies from single-member constituencies and 100 deputies elected by proportional representation; the resignation of cabinet ministers from the legislature; the establishment of a minimum educational requirement for members of the National Assembly; the formation of an Election Commission to supervise elections (in place of the Ministry of the Interior); the centralization of vote-counting; compulsory voting; and the guarantee of press freedom. Although the draft gained the support of opposition parties and the media, there was considerable opposition to the new charter from within the ruling administration. Chavalit himself reneged on his pledge to support the draft, but then finally gave it his endorsement following the application of pressure by both business representatives and the armed forces.

Chavalit ensured his survival of a no confidence motion tabled by the opposition by scheduling the censure debate prior to the vote on the draft Constitution. If defeated, Chavalit could thus dissolve the National Assembly rather than resign, delaying the vote on the draft Constitution and forcing fresh elections under the existing Constitution. In the event the Government won the no confidence vote and the draft Constitution was approved on 27 September 1997. The new Constitution was promulgated on 11 October.

In October 1997 Thanong resigned as Minister of Finance, citing obstruction of his attempts to implement the extensive economic reforms required. Following popular demonstrations demanding the resignation of Chavalit, a cabinet reorganization was announced at the end of October. The new appointments, however, which included that of the Executive Vice-President of Bangkok Bank and a former minister, Khosit Panpiamrat, as the Minister of Finance, failed to restore public or investor confidence in the Government, and the Thai currency continued to depreciate. At the beginning of November Chavalit's announcement that he would resign from the premiership on 6 November, following the adoption of important electoral and financial legislation, caused a slight recovery of the Thai baht. Both Prem and Chatichai rejected approaches by members of the ruling coalition to prevent its collapse by assuming the leadership. Finally, on 9 November Chuan, who maintained his reputation for integrity, assumed the premiership, following the formation of a coalition comprising Chuan's DP, Chart Thai, the SAP, Ekkaparb, the Seritham Party, Palang Dharma and the Thai Party (as well as 12 of the 18 members of Prachakorn Thai), which commanded the support of 210 of the 393 seats in the House of Representatives.

The transfer of power to Chuan, under the terms of the new Constitution, without the intervention of the armed forces or resort to a non-elected leader, received widespread approval and represented significant democratic progress. The new Cabinet included Tarrin Nimmanhaeminda as Minister of Finance (a post he had occupied in Chuan's previous administration) and the former Deputy Prime Minister, Supachai Panichpakdi, as Minister of Commerce. However, the baht continued to depreciate, causing intermittent social unrest. In March a vote of no confidence in Chuan's Government, which retained popular support, was defeated.

In May 1998 the Governor of the Central Bank, Chaiyawat Wibulsawadi, resigned, shortly before the publication of an independent report into the alleged mismanagement of the economy preceding the devaluation of the baht in July 1997 and the onset of the subsequent financial crisis. The report attributed much blame for the country's difficulties to the economic strategy followed by Chaiyawat, his predecessor, Rerngchai Marakanonda, the former Prime Minister, Chavalit, and the former Minister of Finance, Amnuay Viravan. Chaiyawat was replaced by Chatu Mongol Sonakul, a former permanent secretary of finance. Also in May new electoral legislation was approved, enabling polls to be held six months later. There were fears that, under the new legislation, the 12 members of the ruling coalition who had defected from Prachakorn Thai to help form the Government in November 1997 might lose their legal status as legislators. (The 12 were formally expelled from Prachakorn Thai in October 1998 but continued to form part of the coalition Government.) In July a new political party, Thai Rak Thai, was established by the former Deputy Prime Minister, Thaksin Shinawatra.

By August 1998 Thailand's economy appeared to have stabilized, and Chuan received rare public praise from Queen Sirikit. However, the Government was beset by allegations of corruption. In October Chuan reorganized his Government, bringing the Chart Pattana party into the ruling coalition and thereby increasing to 257 the number of seats held by the coalition in the House of Representatives. Five new ministers were appointed to the Cabinet, including the Secretary-General of Chart Pattana, Suwat Liptapanlop, who was assigned the industry portfolio; however, many of the most influential portfolios were retained by the DP. In December the opposition filed a motion to remove Chuan and Tarrin from office, on the grounds that they had allegedly acted in breach of the Constitution by submitting four Letters of Intent to the IMF without first securing the approval of the House of Representatives; the motion was unsuccessful.

In July 1999 the SAP withdrew from the governing coalition, reportedly as a result of intense disputes within the party concerning the allocation of cabinet positions, prompting a reorganization of the Cabinet. By August, however, public approval of the Government appeared to be in decline, and the coalition faced increasing demands from the opposition that the House of Representatives be dissolved and that elections be called. Thai Rak Thai intensified its recruitment campaign from mid-1999; a public debate on the alleged use of financial inducements by Thai Rak Thai to recruit members of other parties was initiated by members of the DP. In November Chavalit pledged his willingness to support Thai Rak Thai in the forthcoming general election in the event of his own NAP performing poorly at the polls.

In August 1999 a report on the state-owned Krung Thai Bank, which exposed the bank's dubious loan policies and other irregularities, was disclosed to the Senate and the press. The report led to criticism of the Government and to allegations of corruption being made against Tarrin, whose brother, Sirin Nimmanhaeminda, had been the President of Krung Thai Bank until his resignation in January. Although the Government was reported in October to have exonerated a number of senior Krung Thai executives, including Sirin, of allegations of inefficiency and dishonesty, the controversy surrounding the bank continued and constituted the main focus of a joint no confidence motion filed by three main opposition parties against the Government in December, in which the ruling coalition was accused of mismanagement of the economy and of condoning corruption. Although the Government survived the censure debate, the proceedings exposed divisions within the governing coalition (particularly between the DP and Chart Thai), and also proved particularly damaging to Tarrin and to the Deputy Prime Minister and Minister of the Interior, Maj.-Gen. (retd) Sanan Kajornprasart.

The DP fared badly in provincial elections held in February 2000, possibly owing to discontent among the rural population with the Government's refusal to subsidize crop prices. In late January, however, the opposition NAP had also suffered a serious reverse when as many as 40 of its members of the House of Representatives, led by the former NAP Secretary-General, Sano Thienthong, boycotted a gathering intended to reaffirm their allegiance to the party in the approach to the anticipated elections. Sano, who had been forcibly removed from the party leadership in March 1999, was subsequently reported to have claimed that the dissident legislators were seeking a merger with Thai Rak Thai, which was enjoying increasing public support. Allegations of corruption against the ruling coalition re-emerged in 2000. In March Sanan was accused by the National Anti-

Corruption Committee (NACC) of having falsified his assets declaration statement (recently required of all cabinet ministers). Although he denied the allegations, Sanan swiftly resigned from his ministerial positions and from his membership of the legislature, pending a ruling on the NACC's report by the Constitutional Court. (Sanan did, however, retain his position as Secretary-General of the DP.) Banyat Bantadtan was appointed to replace Sanan as Deputy Prime Minister and Minister of the Interior. In August Sanan was convicted of corruption by the Constitutional Court.

On 4 March 2000 elections to the new 200-member Senate were contested by more than 1,500 candidates. The level of voter participation was reported at 70%, with voting being compulsory for the first time. Although an increased focus on the suitability of the candidates themselves was reported, the widespread practice of 'vote-buying' persisted, and on 21 March the Election Commission disqualified 78 of the 200 winning candidates (including the wives of two cabinet ministers). A second round of polling was held in the 78 affected constituencies on 29 April, in which all but two of the disqualified contestants were permitted to stand again. However, there were further allegations of electoral fraud following the second round of voting, with 34 of the previously disqualified candidates being accused of various electoral violations. The Election Commission responded by declaring that a second re-run of the polls would be held in at least nine of the affected constituencies, rejecting appeals for the dismissal of the allegations of fraud in the interest of political continuity. (While the final results of the elections remained in dispute, none of the declared winners were able to assume their seats as they lacked the necessary quorum, resulting in a backlog of legislation and obliging the outgoing Senate to remain in office in an interim capacity.) Although in May it was reported that 22 senatorial candidates had been cleared of allegations of fraud by the Election Commission owing to lack of evidence, a third round of polling was scheduled to be held in June in a number of constituencies. The Election Commission also announced that a number of prominent individuals were likely to be prosecuted for their involvement in electoral misconduct. Further allegations of electoral fraud necessitated a fourth and fifth round of polling in June and July respectively. Despite the resignation of almost 100 NAP deputies from the House of Representatives in June and July in support of an early dissolution of the House, Chuan reiterated his intention to dissolve the House in October. The SAP also withdrew from the House of Representatives in July in a similar attempt to gain an early dissolution. On 1 August Thailand's first-ever democratically elected Senate was formally inaugurated.

In November 2000 it was announced that elections to the House of Representatives would be held in January 2001. In December 2000 the NACC recommended that Thaksin Shinawatra should be indicted for having violated the Constitution by concealing financial assets and seeking to avoid the payment of taxes. One notable feature of Thai Rak Thai's electoral campaign was its targeting of rural votes by pledging grants of 1m. baht for each of Thailand's 70,000 villages and offering a debt-relief scheme for farmers. At the legislative elections held on 6 January 2001 Thai Rak Thai won 248 of the 500 seats in the House of Representatives, thereby almost gaining an unprecedented absolute majority. However, the elections were marred by widespread allegations of malpractice; indeed, many domestic and international observers declared that, despite the vigilance of the Election Commission, they had been the most corrupt ever held in Thailand. In late January repolling was held in more than 60 constituencies where the Election Commission had found evidence of fraudulent practice. In February a new cabinet nominated by Thaksin was formally approved by the King. All but five of the appointees were members of Thai Rak Thai, with which the Seritham Party had merged since the election, thus affording Thai Rak Thai an absolute majority in the House of Representatives. With the support of its coalition partners, the NAP and Chart Thai, the incoming Thai Rak Thai administration controlled 339 of the 500 seats in the House.

In April 2001 the Constitutional Court formally commenced hearing charges of corruption brought against the Prime Minister, as recommended by the NACC. In the same month two bombs exploded in southern Thailand, killing a child and injuring 42 people. The involvement of a militant Islamist separatist organization, the Pattani United Liberation Organization (PULO), was suspected. The PULO belonged to Bersatu, an umbrella organization of three separatist movements, which, the Government claimed, was seeking to establish a Muslim state in southern Thailand.

On 30 June 2001 by-elections were held in seven constituencies to fill seats in the House of Representatives vacated by members disqualified for breaches of campaign rules after the January elections. However, the polls were again marred by allegations of corruption.

The Prime Minister was acquitted of the charges against him regarding concealment of his assets in August 2001. The judges ruled by a narrow eight-to-seven majority in his favour. His exoneration was welcomed by his many supporters, who had conducted a popular campaign that was thought to have exerted some influence over the court's verdict.

In October 2001 the Government introduced a plan to provide low-cost health care for the nation's poorest people, thus implementing one of the Prime Minister's election pledges. Doubts remained over the quality of the service provided. Later in the same month the limits to the Government's reform efforts were highlighted when army Sub-Lt Duangchalerm Yoobamrung, son of Chalerm Yoobamrung (the former leader of the Muan Chon party, now an influential NAP member of the House of Representatives), allegedly murdered a police officer during a fight in a night-club. Duangchalerm subsequently fled to Cambodia. As a result of his son's actions and subsequent popular criticism of the Government for its ineffectual attempts to bring him to justice, Chalerm was forced to resign from the deputy leadership of the NAP, although he retained an influential position within the Government. In May 2002 Duangchalerm surrendered himself to the Thai embassy in Malaysia, having entered the country illegally, and agreed to return home, where he entered a plea of not guilty to the charges against him. In March 2004 Duangchalerm was acquitted of all the charges against him, allegedly owing to insufficient evidence.

In November 2001 a panel of judges acting for the Public Prosecutor recommended that the former Governor of the Central Bank, Rerngchai Marakanonda, face a civil lawsuit for the part that he had played in precipitating the 1997 financial crisis. The hearing began in February 2002. In November 2003, however, the Administrative Court ruled in favour of a petition submitted by Rerngchai requesting that the civil lawsuit against him be dismissed. Meanwhile, in December 2002 King Bhumibol made a speech to mark his birthday in which he publicly criticized the Prime Minister, commenting that his Government's 'double standards' were effectively leading Thailand towards 'catastrophe'. His criticism was thought to be linked to his reported disapproval of the business relationship that existed between the Prime Minister and the King's son, Crown Prince Vajiralongkorn.

Prime Minister Thaksin's apparent sensitivity to criticism was reflected in his Government's increasingly repressive policies towards the media. In January 2002 an edition of the *Far Eastern Economic Review*, a Hong Kong-based publication, was banned for its inclusion of an article that suggested that tensions existed in the relationship between King Bhumibol and the Prime Minister. Meanwhile, it was reported that the Ministry of Defence had ordered the Nation Media Group to cease its provision of news programmes to a Bangkok radio station. The ban followed the broadcast of an interview with a senior opposition figure that was deemed to have been critical of the Prime Minister. The armed forces, which controlled all Thai radio frequencies, claimed that the decision had been taken for commercial reasons.

In January 2002 the NAP voted to merge with its coalition partner, Thai Rak Thai. Despite opposition from several NAP politicians, the party was legally dissolved in March. In the same month the Government was further strengthened when Chart Pattana joined the ruling coalition; a minor cabinet reorganization took place shortly afterwards in which Suwat Liptapanlop, Secretary-General of Chart Pattana, was allocated a ministerial position. Meanwhile, by-elections were held in 14 constituencies where the January 2001 general election results had been invalidated owing to electoral fraud and corruption. Thai Rak Thai lost five seats as a result, but retained its commanding majority in the National Assembly. Shortly afterwards six policemen died after gunmen attacked three security outposts—two in Pattani province and one in Yala province. The attacks were suspected to have been carried out by one of the militant Islamist separatist organizations known to exist in the area. Two bombs later exploded in Yala province, coinciding with a tour of the region by the Minister of the Interior. A Thai military official attributed the attacks to the Guragan Mujahideen Islam Pattani, a constituent group of Bersatu thought to be linked to the international terrorist network al-Qa'ida. In April the Constitutional Court formally granted the NAP's request that it be permitted to merge with Thai Rak Thai.

In May 2002 the Government succeeded in defeating no confidence motions that had been brought by the opposition against 15 of its ministers, including nine members of the Cabinet. In October Prime Minister Thaksin implemented an extensive cabinet reorganization, in which, among other changes, Chavalit Yongchaiyudh was replaced as Minister of Defence by Thammarak Isarangura, while former Minister of Transport Wan Muhamad Nor Matha became Minister of the Interior. Six ministers were also appointed to take responsibility for new ministries that had been created as part of the Government's ongoing bureaucratic reforms.

In February 2003 a further redistribution of cabinet portfolios took place. The Minister of Finance, Somkid Jatusripitak, and the Minister of Justice, Purachai Piemsomboon, were both appointed Deputy Prime Ministers; Somkid was replaced by his deputy, Suchart Jaovisidha, while Purachai was succeeded by former Minister of Energy Pongthep Thepkanjana. Deputy Prime Minister Prommin Lertsuridej was awarded the energy portfolio. Meanwhile, the Government announced the commencement of an intensive anti-drugs campaign intended to eliminate Thailand's drug problem within three months. As the campaign continued, the huge number of suspected drug dealers being killed prompted criticism from both local and international human rights groups, which claimed that the Thai authorities were operating an illegal 'shoot to kill' policy and effectively condoning extra-judicial violence. The Government rejected a request from the Office of the UN High Commissioner for Human Rights (OHCHR, see p. 49) that it be permitted to send a representative to the country to investigate the killings. In March Thaksin acknowledged that mistakes had been made during the campaign, but denied that the police had been responsible for any extra-judicial killings. However, later in that month Thaksin ordered that the campaign should henceforth be concentrated upon provinces along the border with Myanmar, where the majority of drugs-smuggling activity was believed to take place. By mid-April 2003, according to a statement issued by police, as a result of the campaign some 2,275 people had been killed, of whom the police admitted to shooting 51 fatally for reasons of self-defence. At the end of April Thaksin stated that the campaign had eradicated 'about 90%' of the country's drugs problem and, later in that year, declared it to have been a success. Meanwhile, two attacks on army bases in the south of the country were reportedly carried out by the PULO. In the following month, owing to the success of the anti-drugs offensive, Thaksin announced the commencement of a 'war on dark influences' intended to eradicate criminal networks operating in the country.

In April 2003 the DP elected Banyat Bantadtan as its new leader, following the retirement of Chuan Leekpai. In May, after a two-day no confidence debate in the House of Representatives, five cabinet ministers evaded censure, following the tabling of an opposition motion accusing them of corruption. In the following month Thai Rak Thai defeated the DP at a by-election in Si Sa Ket. Later in June three men were arrested on suspicion of being members of the regional terrorist organization Jemaah Islamiah; they later confessed to having plotted to attack embassies and tourist destinations in the country. A further suspect was arrested in July. In the following month, in response to the perceived terrorist threat to Thailand, the Cabinet approved two anti-terrorism laws by decree, circumventing the legislature owing to the reported gravity of the threat. Shortly afterwards, the alleged former operational head of Jemaah Islamiah, the Indonesian citizen Riduan Isamuddin, also known as Hambali, was apprehended in Thailand; he was later taken into custody by the USA. In September the four suspected members of Jemaah Islamiah arrested earlier in the year were officially charged with membership of the organization and with plotting terrorist attacks in Thailand. Those charged, together with a fifth man being detained in Singapore, pleaded not guilty to the charges against them. Their trials began in November.

In October 2003, following the conclusion of its anti-drugs offensive five months previously, the Government announced the commencement of a 60-day campaign intended to rid Thailand of 'social evils' such as drug addiction, poverty and organized crime. In November a cabinet reorganization took place, which resulted in the removal of Chart Pattana from the Government. In consequence, Deputy Prime Minister Korn Dabbaransi and Minister of Labour and Social Welfare Suwat Liptapanlop were ousted from the Cabinet; they were succeeded by, respectively, Bhokin Bhalakula and Uraiwan Thienthong.

In January 2004 an outbreak of violence in the south of the country, which resulted in the deaths of several members of the security forces and included arson attacks on several schools, prompted the Government to declare martial law in the predominantly Muslim provinces of Pattani, Yala and Narathiwat, on the border with Malaysia. The violence was suspected by the Government to have been perpetrated by Guragan Mujahideen Islam Pattani, although involvement by militants affiliated to Jemaah Islamiah was not discounted as a possibility. Two suspects arrested in January were believed to be members of Bersatu. The unrest continued into the following months, resulting in the temporary closure of approximately 1,000 schools in the area. Meanwhile, the Government responded by arresting local Islamic leaders and conducting army raids on *madrasahs* (Islamic religious schools), angering many members of the local Muslim population. In mid-February Prime Minister Thaksin proposed the construction of a security fence along the border, in order to prevent militants from taking refuge in Malaysia.

In March 2004 a further cabinet reorganization was implemented, in which the Ministers of Finance, Defence and the Interior—Suchart Jaovisidha, Thammarak Isarangura and Wan Muhamad Nor Matha—were replaced by, respectively, Somkid Jatusripitak, Chettha Thanajaro and Bhokin Bhalakula. Korn Dabbaransi returned to the Cabinet as Minister of Science and Technology. The changes were believed to have been made in response to the ongoing deterioration in the security situation in the south of the country, together with a decline in the performance of the Stock Exchange of Thailand and public protests at the Government's planned privatization of the Electricity Generating Authority of Thailand. Candidates supported by Thai Rak Thai performed well in local elections in mid-March, securing control of 47 of 74 newly created Provincial Administrative Organizations.

In mid-March 2004, following further arson attacks in the south, which had destroyed some 36 government buildings, Prime Minister Thaksin dismissed the national police chief and the army commander for the southern region. Later that month a bomb explosion in Sungai Kolok, in Narathiwat province, which injured 29 people, including 10 Malaysian tourists, prompted the Government to suspend a US $300m. development aid programme intended for Narathiwat, Pattani and Yala. Thaksin claimed that those responsible for the attack had crossed into Malaysia. A few days later a group of suspected militants stole a large quantity of explosives from a quarry in Yala province. In early April four police officers were arrested in connection with the recent disappearance of Somchai Neelapaijit, a prominent Muslim human rights lawyer who was defending the men charged in September 2003 with plotting attacks for Jemaah Islamiah.

The violence in the south escalated at the end of April 2004, when more than 100 suspected Islamic militants staged a series of raids on police and army bases. The security forces suppressed the attacks, killing 108 of the insurgents, including 32 who had taken refuge in a mosque in Pattani. Five security officials also died in the fighting. After the UN, human rights groups and some Muslim leaders had questioned the level of force used by the security forces to quash the attacks, in early May the Government established an independent commission to investigate the incident at the mosque. Meanwhile, a censure motion tabled by the DP against eight cabinet ministers on the grounds of alleged incompetence, corruption and abuse of power was rejected by the House of Representatives.

In late May 2004 the Government announced that it had established unofficial contact with the leader of Bersatu, Wan Kadir Che Man, with the aim of holding peace talks. Wan Kadir, who was living in exile in Malaysia, had recently stated that he was willing to abandon Bersatu's demand for a separate homeland in southern Thailand. None the less, religious tension in the south persisted, as the body of a Buddhist farmer was found decapitated and a Buddhist shrine in Pattani was ransacked. The proposed talks with Wan Kadir were indefinitely suspended at the end of the month, following strong opposition from Deputy Prime Minister Chavalit Yongchaiyudh, who feared the meeting could be regarded as formal recognition of Bersatu and its leader. In mid-June some 3,000 teachers attended a rally in Pattani in support of demands for improved security following the killing of a colleague. At the end of the month more than 4,000 teachers in Narathiwat commenced strike action after a further shooting, but returned to work after two days in response to assurances of increased protection from the security forces.

At the end of June 2004 Chart Pattana rejoined the Government when Suwat Liptapanlop was appointed as a Deputy Prime Minister, in what was regarded as an attempt by Thaksin to consolidate support ahead of the legislative elections due to be held in early 2005. A number of deputies from Chart Thai and the DP subsequently defected to Thai Rak Thai, and in August 2004 Chart Pattana merged into Thaksin's party. Meanwhile, several former senior members of the DP formed a new party, Mahachon. In early August, in its first report since its establishment in 2001, the National Human Rights Commission claimed that human rights violations had increased under Thaksin's administration, notably during the anti-drugs campaign in 2003, and accused the Government of becoming increasingly authoritarian. Thaksin rejected the report's criticisms, and declared a second anti-drugs offensive in October, which was to last for one year. The election of the DP candidate, Apirak Kosayodhin, as Governor of Bangkok in late August represented a set-back for Thaksin, who had favoured the candidacy of Paveena Hongsakul, the former Secretary-General of Chart Pattana, who had stood as an independent.

More than 300 suspected insurgents had surrendered to the authorities by mid-July 2004 in response to a government campaign; they were transferred to a detention facility at a military camp to undergo a re-education programme. Nevertheless, violent attacks and minor bomb explosions continued to occur in the southern provinces, with killings of public officials, police officers, Buddhist monks and civilians regularly reported. In early August the independent commission investigating the deaths at the mosque in April released its report, which criticized the security forces for using grenades and concluded that troops had used disproportionate force. The Government announced that unspecified compensation would be paid to the families of those killed. At the end of August Thaksin visited Narathiwat, Pattani and Yala provinces, one day after a bomb had exploded at a market in Sukhirin, in Narathiwat, killing one person and injuring 31. The Government conceded that it had failed to control the violence in the south, and pledged to develop new strategies to quell the unrest.

In October 2004 Thaksin effected a reorganization of the Cabinet, which included the replacement of the Minister of Defence and the Minister of Agriculture and Co-operatives in an apparent response to the ongoing crisis in the south and an outbreak of avian influenza. The violence in southern Thailand continued throughout late 2004. One of the most serious incidents occurred in late October when troops fired tear gas to disperse more than 2,000 Muslim protesters who were demonstrating in Tak Bai, in Narathiwat province, against the detention of six suspected militants. Seven of the protesters were killed in the ensuing clashes and 78 of 1,300 demonstrators who were arrested later died, many from suffocation, as they were transported in overcrowded trucks to an army barracks. Amid increasing international concern at events in southern Thailand and at the Government's response to the unrest, Prime Minister Thaksin ordered an independent inquiry into the deaths. Most of those detained in connection with the protests were later released. A few days later two people were killed and 20 injured in a bomb attack in Sungai Kolok. Shortly afterwards, as tensions continued to rise, a further 20 people, including 15 police officers, were injured in two bomb explosions in Yala province. The deteriorating security situation prompted rare interventions from the monarchy. King Bhumibol urged the Government to use more restraint in the southern provinces, and Queen Sirikit called for an end to the violence. In the first two weeks of November around 30 Buddhists were killed in apparent revenge attacks by suspected Islamic militants. The PULO had earlier vowed to retaliate in response to the deaths in Tak Bai. Later that month an alleged leader of Bersatu was killed in a gunfight with the security forces in Panare, in the province of Pattani.

In a campaign devised by Prime Minister Thaksin, an estimated 100m. paper origami birds, folded and inscribed with peace messages by people in northern Thailand, were dropped by military planes over the southern provinces of Narathiwat, Pattani and Yala in early December 2004. However, critics dismissed the gesture, urging the Government to address the underlying problems behind the violence in the south, where more than 500 people had died since the beginning of the year. Shortly afterwards suspected Islamic militants shot dead a former prosecutor in Pattani, and two bomb explosions in Narathiwat injured five soldiers. In mid-December four Islamic teachers, who were suspected of being leaders of the separatist group Barisan Revolusi Nasional (part of Bersatu), were charged with terrorism and treason. Meanwhile, the inquiry into the incident at Tak Bai in October, in which 85 protesters died, concluded that the deaths had not been caused deliberately, but that the dispersal of the crowd and the transport of the prisoners had been mishandled and that senior officials had been negligent; three army commanders were subsequently transferred to inactive posts. The Cabinet later approved compensation worth more than 30m. baht for families of the dead and those injured. In late December at least two people were killed and several injured after a bomb exploded in Sungai Kolok. Following the fatal shooting of two of their colleagues, thousands of teachers in the south went on indefinite strike, urging the authorities to do more to protect them from attacks by Muslim militants.

The west coast of Thailand, in particular the province of Phang Nga, was severely affected by a series of tsunamis caused by a massive earthquake in the Indian Ocean on 26 December 2004. More than 5,300 people, including at least 1,700 foreigners from some 36 countries, were killed, and a further 2,900 were reported missing. The Thai Government largely refused international relief aid, but did accept considerable technical assistance in identifying the dead, a task that was made more difficult by the large number of foreign victims.

Thai Rak Thai won an overwhelming victory in legislative elections held on 6 February 2005, securing a large majority with 377 of the 500 seats in the House of Representatives. Although 20 parties contested the elections, only three other parties secured representation: the DP took 96 seats, Chart Thai 25 and Mahachon only two. The rate of voter participation was reported at 72%. Thai Rak Thai's success, which enabled it to form a single-party government for the first time, was widely attributed to Thaksin's prompt response to the devastation caused by the tsunamis in December and the strong performance of the economy under his premiership. As in previous election campaigns, however, there were allegations of widespread 'vote-buying', and numerous complaints of electoral malpractice were made. The election results prompted the immediate resignation of Banyat Bantadtan as leader of the DP; Abhisit Vejjajiva was elected as his replacement in March. Prime Minister Thaksin began an unprecedented second consecutive term in office in March, following his formal re-election to the premiership by the House of Representatives. Somkid Jatusripitak retained his position as Minister of Finance in the new Cabinet, and was also appointed as a Deputy Prime Minister, while Kantathee Supamongkol, hitherto a trade representative, was allocated the foreign affairs portfolio, replacing Surakiart Sathirathai, who became a Deputy Prime Minister. Thammarak Isarangura, who had served as Minister of Defence during part of Thaksin's first term before being appointed as a Deputy Prime Minister, reassumed the defence portfolio.

The violence in southern Thailand continued unabated throughout early 2005, and by early March more than 690 people had died since January 2004. In February 2005 the Government approved the formation of a new 12,000-strong army regiment to be stationed in the south. The troops were to focus on development work, as well as on improving security. However, local Islamic leaders warned that an increased military presence in the region (where Thai Rak Thai had failed to secure a single seat in the recent elections) would only heighten disillusionment with the Government. During a three-day visit to the south in mid-February Thaksin announced controversial proposals to allocate development aid to villages in the region depending on the degree of violence found there. Some 1,580 villages had already been surveyed and categorized as red, yellow or green. The 358 villages where violent incidents were deemed to occur frequently were classified as 'red zones' and were to be deprived of funding. However, Thaksin later appeared to have abandoned the plans, which were widely criticized. As the Prime Minister's visit came to an end, a car bomb in Sungai Kolok killed six people and injured more than 40. In March Thaksin indicated that he was considering adopting a more moderate approach towards the insurgency in the south. He appointed former Prime Minister Anand Panyarachun to chair a 48-member National Reconciliation Commission (NRC), which was charged with restoring peace, and announced his intention to reduce the number of troops deployed in the region. None the less, in early April two people were killed and more than 60 injured in three bomb explosions in the southern province of Songkhla, the first major attacks to occur outside the provinces of Narathiwat, Pattani and

Yala. In early November Thaksin extended martial law, already in force in the three southernmost provinces (see above), to encompass the districts of Chana and Thepha in Songkhla province.

Meanwhile, in May 2005 a major corruption scandal was revealed concerning Minister of Transport Suriya Jungrungreangkit's alleged improprieties during the purchase of baggage-scanning equipment for the new Suvarnabhumi International Airport. While the details of the case remained unclear, Suriya was the subject of a no-confidence motion instigated by the DP, which, although easily defeated in the House of Representatives, caused considerable damage to the reputation of the ruling party. In a cabinet reorganization effected in August, Suriya was transferred to the less prominent position of Minister of Industry.

In June 2005 a delegation from the Organization of the Islamic Conference (OIC, see p. 369) was dispatched to Thailand on a fact-finding mission, at the invitation of Prime Minister Thaksin. In their subsequent report, the members of the delegation concluded, contrary to the claims of Islamic nations and rights groups, that religious issues were not the predominant factor in the ongoing militant attacks in the south of the country.

In late January 2006, in the largest corporate take-over in Thailand's history, Prime Minister Thaksin's family sold its 49.6% holding stake in national telecommunications firm Shin Corporation Public Co Ltd (Shin Corp) to Singapore's state investment wing, Temasek Holdings, at a price of 70,000m. baht (US $1,900m.). The transaction took place on the same day on which a new law raising the limit on foreign ownership in telecommunication firms from 25% to 49% came into effect. The sale provoked outrage within Thailand. Many Thais were angered by the massive tax-free gains made by the Shinawatra family; there were demands for the Prime Minister to donate to the state the 26,000m. baht that had been waived in tax, rather than to profit in this way and thus effectively condone tax evasion. Considerable suspicion was also aroused by the fact that Thaksin's son and daughter had purchased shares in Shin Corp from Ample Vision (an investment company established by the Prime Minister in the British Virgin Islands) at a cost of one baht per share and yet had been able to sell them, just three days later, at a price of 49.25 baht per share. Furthermore, there was widespread concern about the sale of a telecommunications firm to a foreign company on account of the potential threat to national security. Thaksin denied any wrongdoing.

In early February 2006 the Minister of Culture, Uraiwan Thienthong, tendered her resignation from the Cabinet, citing 'the decline in political morality' as the reason for her decision. Later that month, and without prior warning, Prime Minister Thaksin announced that the House of Representatives was being dissolved in preparation for an early election; it was subsequently declared that the poll was to be held in early April. While there was little doubt that the ruling Thai Rak Thai would win the election, the question of whether the party would attract a sufficient proportion of the vote to ease the pressure on Thaksin to resign was less certain. The premier's tactics were countered in an unexpected manner by the three main opposition parties—DP, Chart Thai and Mahachon—all of which announced that they were to boycott the proceedings. In an attempt to defuse the political tension, Thaksin offered to include the three parties within a national coalition government, regardless of whether or not they participated in the election; the offer was, however, rejected. Thaksin also declared his intention to resign if Thai Rak Thai failed to secure more than 50% of the votes cast. During the period prior to the election there were numerous protest rallies in the capital, with angry demonstrators demanding the removal from power of Thaksin. The political tension was accompanied by an intensification of violence in the southern regions. Hundreds of schools in Yala were closed temporarily following the killing of three Buddhist teachers, allegedly by Muslim militants. In March the Prime Minister's son, Phantongtae Shinawatra, was adjudged to have been guilty of securities violations relating to the sale of Shin Corp, and was fined 5.98m. baht (US $153,000), by the Securities and Exchange Commission (SEC); Phantongtae was deemed to have failed fully to disclose transactions pertaining to his stock-holdings.

On 2 April 2006 the legislative election was held and, as expected, Thai Rak Thai secured victory, winning approximately 57% of votes cast. Turn-out was an estimated 64.8% of registered voters. However, 33.1% of those who voted selected the 'no vote' option on ballot papers. Owing to the boycott of the poll by the three main opposition parties, the House of Representatives was unable to convene by the end of the month as a significant number of seats remained vacant, despite the holding of several by-elections. Soon after the election Thaksin announced that he would not seek to return to the office of Prime Minister on a permanent basis and appointed the Deputy Prime Minister, Gen. Chidchai Wannasathit, to the role in an acting capacity. In May the Constitutional Court annulled the results of the election, declaring that they were invalid as the poll had been organized too quickly following the dissolution of the House of Representatives. The Election Commission subsequently announced that a new legislative election would take place in October. At the end of May Thaksin confirmed that he was returning to the post of interim Prime Minister.

Mounting tension between Prime Minister Thaksin and King Bhumibol, who was becoming increasingly vocal on the subject of the country's troubled political situation, was temporarily alleviated in June 2006 by celebrations to commemorate the 60th anniversary of the King's accession to the throne. The festivities included a lavish ceremony in Bangkok, which was attended by members of 22 of the world's royal families and numerous other dignitaries. In stark contrast, in the same month militants carried out a series of co-ordinated attacks over a period of several days, detonating in excess of 50 bombs that targeted more than 30 locations across the three southernmost provinces; the attacks were reported to have killed at least four people and injured more than 20 others. In late August almost two dozen bank branches in the province of Yala were targeted in another spate of co-ordinated explosions, which killed two people and injured a further 28. Meanwhile, at the end of June a team of prosecutors from the Attorney-General's office urged the disbandment of various parties, including Thai Rak Thai and the DP, on charges related to the April election, the former being accused of funding token opposition candidates, while the latter was alleged to have instigated a boycott of the poll. In July the Chairman of the Election Commission and two commissioners were found guilty of election law contravention and sentenced to four years' imprisonment by the Criminal Court.

On 19 September 2006, while Thaksin Shinawatra was out of the country, the Government was ousted from power in a bloodless military coup led by the Commander-in-Chief of the Army, Gen. Sonthi Boonyaratglin. Gen. Sonthi, acting as part of the so-called Council for Democratic Reform, imposed martial law and suspended the Constitution, the Government and the legislature. In a statement to the media the Council claimed to have the support of King Bhumibol and ordered the cessation of activities by political parties, promising the imminent appointment of an interim Prime Minister with a mandate to oversee fresh elections. Within a week the Council had initiated an investigation into allegations of corruption within the Thaksin Government. At the beginning of October, following the signing of an interim Constitution by King Bhumibol, Gen. (retd) Surayud Chulanont was sworn in as Prime Minister by the military leadership, which had been renamed the Council for National Security and retained significant powers over the Government and the Constitution. Elections were projected for 2007, upon the drafting and approval of a new constitution. The Governor of the Bank of Thailand, Pridiyathorn Devakula, and the chairman of Bangkok Bank, Kosit Panpiemras, were appointed Deputy Prime Ministers in the Cabinet that was subsequently announced, taking additional charge of the finance and industry portfolios respectively. The National Legislative Assembly, comprising the Council's appointees, was approved by the King and convened in mid-October 2006. In November martial law was rescinded in approximately 40 provinces (although this did not take effect until January 2007). Meanwhile, Thaksin, who had remained overseas since the coup, announced his resignation from Thai Rak Thai in October 2006, following a large number of resignations from the party, which were said to have been prompted by the military leadership's assertion that those associated with political organizations guilty of election malpractice would be punished. In November Thaksin's son and daughter were ordered to pay tax on their share of the proceeds of the Shin Corp sale.

Hopes of a resolution to the ongoing insurgency in the south were raised by Gen. Sonthi's announcement in October 2006 that the military leadership was willing to engage in dialogue with certain groups. In the following month Prime Minister Surayud apologized for the deaths of the Muslim protesters in Tak Bai in 2004 (see above), and it was later announced that charges against several demonstrators would be rescinded. Despite the apparent progress towards reconciliation, however, the violence continued in 2007: by March it was estimated that the conflict had caused more than 2,100 fatalities, of which more than 400 had occurred since the coup. At the end of December 2006 a series of eight bomb explosions in Bangkok killed three people and injured several others, but the attacks were not immediately attributed to the insurgents; rather, it was implied by some sources that associates of Thaksin were responsible, a claim he subsequently denied. In January 2007 the Government suspended Thaksin's diplomatic passport and requested a media ban on his lawyer's statements. Thaksin's subsequent visit to Singapore and his meeting with the Singaporean Deputy Prime Minister, Shanmugam Jayakumar, provoked a negative reaction from the Thai Government. Surayud later affirmed that Thaksin would be permitted to return to Thailand on the condition that he did not engage in political activity. Doubts were expressed at the end of February about the stability of the Government after the Deputy Prime Minister and Minister of Finance, Pridiyathorn Devakula, resigned, citing internal discord among other reasons. The interim Government's economic policies, which were based on a principle of 'self-sufficiency' advocated by the King and had thus far included measures to restrict the movement of foreign capital and foreign ownership of Thai companies, had been widely criticized and had damaged investor confidence. In the cabinet reorganization that followed, Chalongphob Sussangkarn succeeded Pridiyathorn as Minister of Finance. Paiboon Wattanasiritham, while retaining the social development and human security portfolio, was promoted to the position of Deputy Prime Minister. At the end of March Thaksin's wife, Pojaman Shinawatra, was charged with tax evasion in relation to a 1997 share transaction of the company that later became known as Shin Corp. Meanwhile, Gen. Sonthi was reported to have requested the enforcement of emergency rule to address the alleged threat of instability posed by regular anti-coup demonstrations in Bangkok. Surayud denied the request and announced that elections would be held in December 2007, following a constitutional referendum which was to be conducted by September.

In late May 2007 the Constitutional Tribunal (which had replaced the Constitutional Court under the interim Constitution) found Thai Rak Thai guilty of violating electoral legislation prior to the April 2006 poll, but acquitted the DP of all charges of malpractice. The Tribunal ordered the dissolution of Thai Rak Thai and a ban on 111 party members, including Thaksin, from participating in politics for five years. Thai Rak Thai had been accused of funding minor opposition parties to field candidates in constituencies in which it would have been unlikely to achieve the 20% of the vote required to secure election in uncontested seats. A number of demonstrations by the party's supporters in Bangkok followed the verdict. The ban on activities by political organizations was removed in early June 2007 to allow parties to begin campaigning for the forthcoming legislative election. In mid-June the Assets Examination Committee 'froze' bank accounts held by Thaksin (some jointly with his wife, Pojaman) containing a total of 52,900m. baht; the Committee later ordered additional assets to be 'frozen' as investigations continued into the former Prime Minister, who remained in self-imposed exile. A week later corruption charges were filed against Thaksin and Pojaman in relation to Pojaman's purchase in 2003 of a plot of land in Bangkok from a state agency for a sum allegedly far lower than its true value. Thaksin was also accused of concealing his assets. Despite these difficulties, Thaksin's high-profile bid to acquire an English Premier League football team, Manchester City, was successful in the following month, prompting further speculation about his finances.

The Constitution Drafting Assembly (the members of which had effectively been appointed by the Council for National Security) approved the final draft of a new constitution in early July 2007. The proposed constitution was designed to curb the powers of the Prime Minister, who would be limited to serving two four-year terms and barred from owning large stakes in private companies. In addition, the threshold for initiating a debate on a motion of no confidence in the Prime Minister would be reduced from two-fifths of the members of the House of Representatives in favour to one-fifth (although such a motion would still require the support of more than one-half of deputies to be passed). The Senate would be transformed from a fully elected body of 200 senators to one in which 74 of its 150 senators would be selected by a seven-member committee of judges and other senior state officials (such as the President of the Constitutional Court and the Chairperson of the Election Commission), with the remainder directly elected in each province, while the number of deputies in the House of Representatives would be reduced from 500 to 480 (400 to be elected on a multi-member constituency basis and 80 on a proportional representation basis). Further notable provisions committed the state to the implementation of the 'sufficient economy philosophy' and guaranteed an amnesty for those involved in the coup of September 2006. Critics of the draft claimed that it was 'anti-Thaksin' and less democratic than the 1997 Constitution. However, while acknowledging its flaws, the DP and Chart Thai supported the draft in the interest of restoring democracy as swiftly as possible. The draft Constitution was endorsed by 57.8% of voters in a referendum on 19 August 2007. A relatively low turn-out, of 57.6%, was recorded. More detailed results suggested that the country remained politically divided, with the charter rejected by nearly 63% of voters in the rural north-east, a stronghold of the dissolved Thai Rak Thai, but approved by some 88% of voters in the south. After receiving royal assent, the new Constitution took effect on 24 August. Meanwhile, in late July a demonstration against military rule by several thousand people in Bangkok ended in violence, as protesters clashed with police after staging a rally outside the house of former Prime Minister Prem Tinsulanonda, now a senior royal adviser, whom they claimed had been involved in co-ordinating the coup. Nine alleged leaders of the demonstration, reported to be either allies of Thaksin or pro-democracy activists, were subsequently arrested and charged with illegal assembly and inciting violence.

In late July 2007 the National Legislative Assembly adopted legislation forbidding new political parties from using the same names, logos or acronyms as parties dissolved by the Constitutional Tribunal for a period of five years. Many former Thai Rak Thai deputies subsequently joined the little-known People's Power Party (PPP), while others participated in the formation of new parties, such as Puea Pandin and Ruam Jai Thai (the latter later merging with Chart Pattana); Samak Sundaravej, a right-wing political veteran and former Governor of Bangkok, was elected leader of the PPP in August. In mid-August the Supreme Court issued arrest warrants for Thaksin and Pojaman after they failed to answer a summons to appear before the Court to answer the corruption charges relating to the land purchase in 2003. Thaksin's lawyers had unsuccessfully sought a postponement of the case until after the forthcoming elections. Further arrest warrants were issued for the couple by a criminal court in Bangkok in early September 2007 in connection with a police inquiry into alleged violations of stock-trading legislation. In late August it was announced that elections to the House of Representatives would be held on 23 December. Meanwhile, the insurgency in the south continued unabated. A report released by the US-based Human Rights Watch stated that 2,463 people (including 2,196 civilians) had been killed in attacks between January 2004 and July 2007.

Gen. Sonthi was appointed Deputy Prime Minister in charge of Security in early October 2007, having retired as Commander-in-Chief of the Army and resigned as Chairman of the Council for National Security, prompting speculation that he intended to remain in political office beyond the elections scheduled for December. He was replaced as Chairman of the Council for National Security by Air Chief Marshal Chalit Pukpasuk, the Commander-in-Chief of the Air Force. Sonthi's appointment was part of a wider cabinet reorganization necessitated by the recent resignations of five ministers who were under investigation by the National Counter Corruption Commission for allegedly breaching a 5% limit on ministerial shareholdings in private companies. Prime Minister Surayud and Deputy Prime Minister and Minister of Industry, Kosit Panpiemras, assumed additional responsibility for the interior and information and communications technology portfolios, respectively. In late October the Cabinet ordered martial law to be revoked in 221 districts, but maintained in 179 districts in 31 provinces.

During the week preceding the election, amid protests outside the parliament building by students and civil society activists, the National Legislative Assembly adopted many new pieces of legislation, most notably a controversial act giving the Internal Security Operations Command, an agency comprising military and civilian representatives, wide-ranging powers to counter perceived threats to national security. These enhanced powers, which were strongly criticized by human rights groups, included the ability to order curfews, detain suspects without trial, restrict freedom of movement and override the authority of government officials.

Some 74.5% of registered voters participated in the legislative elections, which took place, as scheduled, on 23 December 2007.

Polls were repeated in the following month in a number of constituencies where the Election Commission had annulled results owing to 'vote-buying' and other irregularities. The PPP emerged as the largest party in the House of Representatives, securing 233 of the 480 seats, while the DP won 164, Chart Thai 34, Puea Pandin 24, Matchimathipataya 11, Ruam Jai Thai Chart Pattana nine and Pracharaj five. Essentially the successor to Thai Rak Thai, the PPP achieved greatest success in the north and north-east of the country, and its victory was regarded as a rejection of the 2006 coup and the outgoing military leadership. None the less, its failure to secure an outright majority of seats forced the PPP to negotiate with other parties to establish a coalition administration.

In mid-January 2008 the PPP leader, Samak Sundaravej, officially announced the formation of a six-party coalition controlling 316 of the 480 seats in the House of Representatives, leaving the DP as the sole opposition party in the legislature. The new House of Representatives was convened two days later, subsequently electing Yongyuth Tiyapairat, the deputy leader of the PPP, as its new Speaker and Samak as Prime Minister. Meanwhile, the Council for National Security was disbanded. Samak's new Cabinet was sworn in by King Bhumibol in early February. Many strategic posts in the new Government were allocated to personal allies of Thaksin. Samak assumed personal responsibility for the defence portfolio, while Surapong Suebwonglee, the Secretary-General of the PPP, was appointed Deputy Prime Minister and Minister of Finance. Noppadon Pattama, Thaksin's legal adviser, and Chalerm Yoobamrung, another close associate of the deposed Prime Minister, became Minister of Foreign Affairs and Minister of the Interior, respectively. Later that month the Government announced plans to resume several populist policies initiated by Thaksin and to commence a new anti-drugs campaign, similar to those conducted under the former Prime Minister (which had resulted in some 2,500 deaths). Amendments to the Constitution were also envisaged. Thaksin returned to Thailand in late February after 17 months in exile, insisting that he had retired from active politics. He was immediately taken to hear the corruption charges against him and was granted bail. In mid-March he pleaded not guilty before the Supreme Court to using his influence to assist his wife with her land purchase in 2003. Thaksin's wife, Pojaman, had already returned in January 2008, when she was also granted bail and denied the charges against her. Elections to fill 76 of the 150 seats in the Senate were held on 2 March, the remaining 74 members having been appointed in the previous month by the selection committee. Electoral turn-out was estimated at 55.9%. The appointed senators were considered to be closer to the outgoing military leadership, while many of the elected senators were reported to be allies of Thaksin. Prasobsuk Boondech, an appointed senator and former Chief Justice of the Court of Appeals, was elected Speaker of the Senate in mid-March.

Despite the restoration of civilian rule, political uncertainty persisted in early 2008. In late February the new administration suffered a set-back when the Election Commission voted in favour of disqualifying Speaker Yongyuth from office, concluding that he had bribed local officials in exchange for votes during the general election campaign, and referred the case to the Supreme Court. There was a possibility that the PPP might be disbanded by the Constitutional Court if the Supreme Court were to find Yongyuth guilty and judge that the party was aware of 'vote-buying'. Yongyuth stood down as Speaker pending the Supreme Court's verdict. Chart Thai and Matchimathipataya were also threatened with dissolution owing to allegations of electoral fraud by senior party officials. Furthermore, in April the Election Commission was investigating a complaint that the PPP and Thaksin had violated legislation governing political parties, the former by allegedly acting as a 'nominee' of Thai Rak Thai and the latter through his alleged involvement with the PPP, despite being barred from participating from politics. Meanwhile, the DP accused the coalition Government of self-interest in its plans to revise the Constitution, particularly its desire to amend the article allowing for an entire party to be held responsible for the wrongdoing of a single party executive. In April martial law was rescinded in all areas of the country except for the southern provinces of Narathiwat, Yala, Pattani and part of Songkhla, where the death toll in the ongoing insurgency had recently surpassed 3,000.

In foreign affairs Thailand is a member of the Association of South East Asian Nations (ASEAN, see p. 185) and generally maintains good relations with the other member states. Its former dependence on the USA has been greatly reduced by the increasing importance of regional trade and diplomatic relations. In the late 1980s Prime Minister Chatichai adopted a new business-orientated policy towards Cambodia, Laos, Viet Nam and Myanmar, encouraging investment in their developing economies; this was policy successfully pursued by subsequent premiers. In April 1995, following lengthy discussions with Viet Nam, Cambodia and Laos, the four countries established the Mekong River Commission (see p. 413) to promote the joint development of the Mekong's resources. Relations with the People's Republic of China also improved as Thailand became one of China's most significant trading partners. In October 1993 Thailand was accepted as a full member of the Non-aligned Movement (see p. 424).

In January 1993, despite its previous reluctance to do so, Thailand officially closed its border with Cambodia to trade with areas controlled by the communist Cambodian insurgent group, the Party of Democratic Kampuchea (known as the Khmers Rouges), in compliance with UN sanctions against the movement. Nevertheless, violations of the embargo (mainly exports of logs and gems from Cambodia through Thailand) were widely reported during 1993. Accusations by representatives of the Cambodian Government that Thai complicity with the Khmers Rouges was undermining Cambodian attempts to end the insurgency were substantiated by reports from UN peace-keeping troops that members of the Thai armed forces were providing transport, medical care and other support for the Khmers Rouges. Official Thai government policy was to support the elected Government of Cambodia, but the armed forces controlled the border and were unwilling to jeopardize their lucrative business relations with the Khmers Rouges.

In January 1994 Chuan Leekpai made an official visit to Cambodia (the first such visit by a Thai premier), following which more strenuous efforts were made to control illicit border trade and to prevent members of the armed forces from co-operating with the Khmers Rouges. However, clashes between Thai and Cambodian troops continued as a result of incursions into Thai territory by Cambodian government forces in pursuit of the Khmers Rouges. In September 1995 Thailand and Cambodia signed an agreement to establish a border co-ordination committee. At its first meeting in November three border checkpoints, which had been closed in April, were reopened. In the latter half of 1997 intense fighting in Cambodia between forces loyal to the First Prime Minister, Hun Sen, and those of the former Second Prime Minister, Prince Norodom Ranariddh, led to further incursions, across Thailand's eastern border with Cambodia, and resulted in an influx of refugees to Thailand. In May 1998 Hun Sen visited Bangkok to hold discussions with Prime Minister Chuan. In January 1997, meanwhile, the Thai Government adopted a potentially controversial resolution unilaterally to extend Thailand's maritime jurisdiction over waters that were also claimed by Cambodia and Viet Nam. The Thai Government, however, insisted that its decision was legal under international practice.

In January 2003 Thai-Cambodian relations were severely strained when the Thai embassy and several Thai businesses situated in the Cambodian capital, Phnom-Penh, were attacked by Cambodian demonstrators. Those who perpetrated the attacks were protesting against remarks, allegedly made by a Thai actress, claiming that the temples at Angkor Wat in Cambodia in fact belonged to Thailand. In response to the rioting, Prime Minister Thaksin downgraded diplomatic relations with Cambodia and announced plans to evacuate all Thai citizens from the country and to expel illegal Cambodian immigrants living in Thailand; the joint border was subsequently closed. The Cambodian Government issued a formal apology for the incident and promised compensation for those who had been affected by the violence. The Thai Government permitted a limited reopening of the border for commercial reasons in February. In early March Cambodia's Prime Minister, Hun Sen, ordered the border to be closed again, owing to alleged security concerns and in protest at the economic inequality between the two countries. However, later in that month the border was fully reopened and, in April, diplomatic relations were upgraded.

Following a military coup in Burma (now Myanmar) in September 1988, thousands of Burmese students fled to Thailand to avoid government repression. A prominent human rights group, Amnesty International, subsequently accused the Thai Government of coercing the students to return (resulting in their arrest and, in some cases, execution). In 1990 Myanma soldiers achieved unprecedented success in attacks on the strongholds of ethnic minorities on the Thai–Myanma border, since they were able to launch offensives from inside Thailand. The attacks resulted in a new influx of Myanma students and members of rebel ethnic groups seeking refuge in Thailand. The Thai Government refused to recognize those fleeing from Myanmar as refugees or to offer them aid. This refusal was motivated by its wish not to jeopardize the preferential treatment that it received from the Myanma Government, which had recently granted many licences to Thai businesses for the exploitation of Myanmar's natural resources.

In 1992 Myanma forces intensified their attacks on rebel bases near the Thai border. In March the Myanma Government warned Thai armed forces to withdraw from nearby border areas, but later in the month Thai troops clashed with Myanma forces which had entered Thailand to attack a nearby rebel base. In early December King Bhumibol appealed for a peaceful agreement to end the tension caused by the continued occupation by Myanma forces of Hill 491 in Chumphan province. In accordance with a bilateral agreement signed shortly afterwards, Myanma troops were withdrawn from the hill by late December. In February 1993 the two countries resolved to demarcate their common border. In April 1994 Thailand invited Myanmar to attend the annual ASEAN meeting of ministers responsible for foreign affairs, in Bangkok. In early 1995, however, relations with Myanmar were strained by the persistent border incursions into Thailand by forces of the Myanma Government during their offensive to capture the headquarters of the rebel Karen (Kayin) National Union (KNU) and subsequent attacks on disarmed Kayin refugees held in Thai camps along the border. In August Myanmar closed its land border with Thailand in protest at the alleged killing of a substantial number of Myanma seamen by Thai fishermen. A visit by Prime Minister Chavalit to Yangon, the capital of Myanmar, in September failed to resolve the situation and further discussions were held in November. In October 1996 the Thai Government approved the opening of three border checkpoints.

In late 1996 and early 1997 attacks allegedly carried out by breakaway Kayin rebels on Kayin refugee camps in Thailand resulted in a number of minor clashes between the Thai army and the rebels. In December 1997 the Thai and Myanma Governments agreed jointly to establish a panel to determine the legitimacy of an estimated 98,000 Kayin refugees sheltered along Thailand's border with Myanmar. In the same month, relief agencies operating along the border accused the Thai military authorities of using oppressive tactics to encourage the refugees to return to Myanmar, although the Thai military had earlier denied reports of its involvement in the forced repatriation of Kayin refugees. In March 1998 the Thai Government announced plans for the forced repatriation of several hundred thousand Myanma immigrants working illegally in Thailand, in response to the economic crisis afflicting the country. In the same month one of the largest Kayin refugee camps along the Thai–Myanma border was destroyed in a cross-border attack by the pro-Government grouping, the Democratic Karen (Kayin) Buddhist Organization.

Relations between Thailand and Myanmar were placed under some strain in late 1999 when a group of armed Myanma student activists seized control of the Myanma embassy in Bangkok in early October, taking 89 people hostage and demanding the release of all political prisoners in Myanmar and the opening of a dialogue between the military Government and the opposition. All the hostages were released by the gunmen within 24 hours, in exchange for the Thai Government's provision of helicopter transport to give the hostage-takers safe passage to the Thai–Myanma border. The Thai Government's release of the hostage-takers angered the ruling military junta in Myanmar, prompting the country to close its border with Thailand. In November, in a further indication of a deterioration in relations between the two countries, Thai forces expelled thousands of illegal Myanma migrant workers from the town of Mai Sot on the Thai–Myanma border, despite threats made by Myanma government troops to shoot the returnees. Although the border was reopened to commerce in late November, relations between the two countries remained fraught.

In January 2000 10 armed Myanma rebels took control of a hospital in Ratchaburi, Thailand, holding hundreds of people hostage. The hostage-takers, reported by some sources to be linked to the Kayin insurgent group, God's Army (a small breakaway faction of the KNU—the main KNU denied any connection with the gunmen), issued several demands, including that the shelling of their base on the Thai–Myanma border by the Thai military be halted, that co-operation between Thai and Myanma government forces against the Kayins should cease, and that their people be allowed to seek refuge in Thailand. However, in contrast to its peaceful handling of the siege of the Myanma embassy in Bangkok in October 1999, the response of the Thai Government to this second hostage crisis (which raised doubts about Thailand's national security and provoked further criticism from both the Thai political opposition and the general population of the Thai Government's relative tolerance of Myanma dissident activity in Thailand) was severe: government forces stormed the hospital, killing all 10 of the hostage-takers and releasing all of the hostages unharmed. This uncompromising resolution of the incident was praised by the military Government in Myanmar, and was regarded by many observers as the signal of a broader campaign by the Thai authorities against dissident activity by ethnic Myanma opposition groups operating in Thailand.

In February 2001 a border incident erupted between Thailand and Myanmar after Myanma forces pursued rebels belonging to the Shan State Army (SSA) into the northern Thai province of Chiang Rai, prompting reprisals by Thai troops. Despite the agreement of a cease-fire, Thailand sealed its border with Myanmar, and the situation was aggravated by Myanmar's assertion that Thailand was assisting the SSA. In April officials belonging to a non-governmental organization in Thailand claimed that the number of refugees of Myanma origin in Thailand had been underestimated and that, as of early April, they totalled almost 131,000. In May the Minister of Foreign Affairs, Surakiart Sathirathai, visited Myanmar in an effort to resolve the ongoing border tensions, but with little success. In the same month the United Wa State Army (UWSA), a Myanma ethnic militia, captured Hua Lone Hill near Chiang Mai; Thai troops recaptured the hill following a four-day battle in which at least 20 members of the UWSA were killed. The Government later lodged a formal protest with the Myanma Government after its forces allegedly bombed a Thai outpost situated near the hill. The Myanma Government responded by accusing the Thai armed forces of having launched air strikes into its territory. The problems were exacerbated when an article appeared in a Myanma newspaper that the Thai authorities claimed was insulting to the monarchy. In June 2001, after repeatedly denying reports that he intended to visit Myanmar, Thaksin Shinawatra became the first Thai Prime Minister to visit Yangon since 1997. While the subsequent discussions succeeded in defusing the immediate tensions, the two sides failed to come to any firm agreement as to how they would overcome the problems affecting bilateral relations. In July the Minister of Defence, Chavalit Yongchaiyudh, also visited Myanmar, and the two countries agreed to work together to expedite the repatriation of refugees on the common border. In September Gen. Khin Nyunt of Myanmar visited Thailand on a trip considered by many to constitute a starting point for a new era of improved relations. In January 2002 a joint Thai-Myanma commission met for the first time since 1999 to discuss plans to establish a task force that would aid in the repatriation of illegal Myanma immigrants. Further talks were held in February 2002, intended to facilitate bilateral co-operation in controlling the cross-border narcotics trade.

In March 2002 Thai-Myanma relations were placed under severe strain when Thai soldiers clashed with members of the UWSA in Chiang Mai. Following the incident, in which one Thai soldier and 12 UWSA guerrillas were killed, the Thai Government lodged a formal protest with Myanmar's ruling military junta. In April a bomb exploded on the so-called 'Friendship Bridge' linking the two countries, resulting in the deaths of at least seven people. Later in the same month the Vice-Chairman of Myanmar's ruling State Peace and Development Council (SPDC) visited Thailand to hold talks with the Government concerning drugs-smuggling and the continued border tensions. However, in May fresh fighting broke out along the joint border between Myanma government troops, together with their UWSA allies, and the SSA; subsequently, the SPDC again accused the Thai Government of supporting the SSA, following which it closed the shared border, owing to the deterioration of bilateral relations. Meanwhile, following the commencement of a Myanma military campaign on the border, intended to reclaim outposts and camps in the country's Shan State, Thai troops fired across the frontier when two Thai soldiers were allegedly injured by Myanma shells. The Government denied that it supported Myanma insurgent ethnic militias but admitted that it had allowed refugees from Myanmar to cross into Thailand. Shortly afterwards Thaksin claimed that bilateral relations had deteriorated to a new low point and that only an apology from Myanmar would improve the situation. In August the Thai Minister of Foreign Affairs stated that the two countries had agreed to hold talks in an effort to resolve the ongoing bilateral tensions; the joint border finally reopened in October. Relations continued to improve in 2003 and, in February, Thaksin paid a visit to Myanmar, during which the possibility of bilateral co-operation to address the problems posed by the cross-border narcotics trade and illegal immigration were discussed. In July the Thai Government announced plans to relocate all Myanma political refugees resident in Thailand to refugee camps near the joint border, where it was believed they could more easily be controlled and would thus present less of a threat to Thailand's relations with Myanmar. In early 2004 Myanmar announced that it was to award Thailand fishing concessions in its waters for one year. Fishing rights had been terminated in May 2001 following tensions on the joint border. In June 2004 Prime Minister Gen. Khin Nyunt of Myanmar visited Thailand and discussed various economic, development and border issues with Prime Minister Thaksin. In December Thaksin paid a visit to Myanmar, his first since the ousting of Khin Nyunt in October, and held talks with the new Prime Minister, Lt-Gen. Soe Win. In January 2005 Thailand increased security along the border with Myanmar, amid concerns that fighting between Myanma troops and insurgents might encroach upon Thai territory. At the end of March the Thai Government ordered the relocation of about 3,000 Myanma political refugees to camps near the joint border. Around 1,000 of the refugees failed to meet a deadline to register with the Thai authorities, however, and were to be detained and deported to Myanmar. In April Thailand again increased security along the border with Myanmar, in response to renewed fighting between rival Myanma ethnic rebel groups close to Thai territory. In December 2007 UNHCR reported that 124,300 Myanma refugees remained resident in nine camps in Thailand.

Relations with Malaysia were adversely affected in November 1995 by the killing of two Thai fishermen by a Malaysian patrol vessel. In December an understanding was reached on the issue and it was agreed to establish a joint committee to resolve a long-standing dispute over fishing rights. Relations were also strained in early 1996 by Thai opposition to the Malaysian construction of a wall along the countries' common border. In late 1996 and early 1997 Thailand co-operated with Malaysia to prevent illegal Bangladeshi workers from entering Malaysia. Relations between the two countries continued to improve during 1998: by April, Prime Minister Chuan and his Malaysian counterpart, Mahathir Mohamad, had met five times in as many months to discuss bilateral issues. In January the Malaysian authorities arrested, and transferred to the Thai authorities, three alleged Muslim separatist leaders wanted in Thailand in connection with terrorist activities in the southern provinces of the country. In February 1997 Malaysia and Thailand established the Kolok river as the border demarcation between the two countries. In April 2001 the two countries agreed to co-operate to find those responsible for two bomb attacks in southern Thailand. In the same month Prime Minister Thaksin paid an official visit to Malaysia, during which the two countries discussed border demarcation issues and agreed that the planned construction of a gas pipeline between Thailand and Malaysia would proceed as originally intended. Relations remained cordial and, in December 2002, the cabinets of the two countries held an historic joint meeting, during which trade and security issues were discussed. In early 2004 the Malaysian Government co-operated with Thailand in an attempt to bring an end to the escalating violence in the south of the country. In February the Thai Government mooted plans to construct a security fence along parts of the joint border, in the hope of preventing militants from seeking refuge in Malaysia. As unrest in southern Thailand continued, Prime Minister Thaksin visited Malaysia in April for talks with his counterpart, Abdullah Badawi, on security along the border and the economic development of the surrounding area. None the less, the Malaysian Government rejected suggestions that the suspected perpetrators of the violence in southern Thailand had escaped to Malaysia. Bilateral relations were strained in December, when the Thai Government claimed to have photographic evidence that militants in southern Thailand had received training in Malaysia. In January 2005 the Malaysian authorities arrested Abdul Rahman Ahmad, whom Thailand held responsible for organizing much of the separatist violence in the south. A diplomatic dispute arose between the two countries in October concerning the fate of 131 Muslim asylum-seekers, who had fled from the violence-stricken southern province of Narathiwat to neighbouring Malaysia (see the chapter on Malaysia). Although the issue was eventually resolved in February 2006 when the Thai Government announced that it was to allow the refugees to remain in Malaysia, relations between the two countries had by that stage descended to their lowest point in recent years. In November 2005 former Malaysian Prime Minister Mahathir Mohamad visited Thailand for discussions with Prime Minister Thaksin regarding the ongoing insurgency in southern Thailand. The negotiations made some progress towards easing the tension that had been caused by Thai security officials' accusations that the Malaysian authorities were failing to prevent insurgents from crossing the border into Thailand. Thaksin and Mahathir agreed that the two countries should cease their 'war of words' and Mahathir was to stop advocating autonomy for Thailand's southern regions. In December Manasae Saeloh, a suspected leader of PULO, was arrested in Malaysia and relinquished to the Thai authorities, by which he was wanted in connection with numerous bomb attacks and other acts of violence. Gen. (retd) Surayud Chulanont visited Malaysia soon after taking office as interim Prime Minister in October 2006, holding talks with Abdullah Badawi on the insurgency in Thailand's southern provinces. An official visit to Thailand by Abdullah Badawi in February 2007 was reciprocated by Surayud in August. In December the two Prime Ministers officially opened a new bridge across the Kolok river, which it was hoped would lead to a reduction in violence in the border region by improving economic prospects.

In November 1996 the Government approved a proposal for the establishment of a Joint Thai-Lao Border Committee. In December 1997 it was announced by the office of the UN High Commissioner for Refugees (UNHCR) that the review of the status of the last remaining group of Laotian refugees at the Ban Napho refugee camp in the Nakhan Phanom province of Thailand was scheduled to be completed by January 1998, after which the refugees were to be either allowed to settle in a third country or repatriated. In September 1999 282 Laotian refugees who had been residing at the camp were compulsorily repatriated by Thai officials and UNHCR after having been refused refugee status; a further 291 Laotian refugees were repatriated in December. In December 2003 the USA agreed to accept around 15,000 Laotian Hmong refugees living in refugee camps in Thailand. The first group of refugees was resettled in the USA in June 2004, under the aegis of the International Organization for Migration. Meanwhile, in August 2000 a border dispute arose between Thailand and Laos after Laos apparently attempted to assert sovereignty over all islands in the Mekong river, as it claimed was its right under the Siam-Franco treaty of 1926. The occupation by Laotian armed forces of the Mano I and Mano II islands took place during the demarcation of the river boundary (due to be completed by the end of 2000) between the two countries. In March 2002 a Thai court convicted 28 people, including 17 Laotian nationals, of charges relating to the dispute. Despite the existence of a bilateral extradition treaty, concluded in 2001, it was thought unlikely that Thailand would comply with a Lao Government request to extradite its citizens to Laos. In March 2004 the Thai and Laotian Governments held a joint cabinet meeting to discuss bilateral co-operation. In August 2006 the Ministries of Foreign Affairs of Thailand and of Laos indicated that the two countries would co-operate to find a solution to the Hmong refugee issue, although neither side claimed responsibility. Through a joint process, the two countries were later reported to be verifying the origin of the migrants. In January 2007 the Thai Government decided against the forcible repatriation to Laos of some 153 Hmong migrants who had been arrested in Bangkok in 2006, following offers of asylum from several Western countries. However, the group of Hmong, now numbering 149, and all recognized as refugees, remained in Thailand in early 2008, according to UNHCR, which urged the Thai authorities to release them so that they could take up the previous offers of asylum in other countries. In February 2008, following a visit to Laos, the Thai Minister of Foreign Affairs announced that the Thai authorities had almost completed the process of verifying the identity of the Hmong remaining in refugee camps in Phetchabun province (estimated at some 7,000). Later that month 10 Hmong were repatriated to Laos ahead of an official visit to that country by the new Thai Prime Minister, Samak Sundaravej. Meanwhile, the two countries agreed to finalize the

THAILAND

demarcation of their land border by the end of 2008, followed by that of the maritime border in 2010.

In February 1998 it was reported that, owing to the country's ongoing economic crisis, Thailand was to reduce financial aid to neighbouring countries, including Cambodia, Laos, Myanmar and Viet Nam. In October the Vietnamese President, Tran Duc Luong, paid an official visit to Thailand, the first visit to the country by a Vietnamese head of state since the establishment of diplomatic relations more than 20 years previously. At the 31st annual ASEAN ministerial meeting in July, Thailand's Minister of Foreign Affairs, Surin Pitsuwan, proposed the modification of ASEAN's long-standing policy of non-interference in the internal affairs of member countries in favour of a policy of 'flexible engagement'; however, the proposal met with a generally negative response from most other ASEAN members. In November 2004, ahead of a summit meeting of ASEAN leaders in Vientiane, Laos, Prime Minister Thaksin Shinawatra threatened to walk out of the summit if other members raised concerns over his Government's handling of the unrest in Thailand's southern provinces. In the event Thaksin held separate talks with the leaders of Malaysia and Indonesia on regional security co-operation.

In 1999 Thailand contributed 1,500 troops to the multinational peace-keeping force in the UN-administered territory of East Timor (now Timor-Leste), following the territory's vote for independence from Indonesia in a referendum held in August. The country also maintained a cordial bilateral relationship with Indonesia, affirmed when the Thai Prime Minister visited Jakarta in February 2002.

In December 2001 the Prime Minister paid an official visit to the USA. During his stay he held talks with US President George W. Bush and assured him that Thailand would remain a strong ally in the US-led 'war on terror' in the aftermath of the September terrorist attacks (see the chapter on the USA). In response, the US President praised the Thai Government for its consistent support throughout the campaign. In June 2003 Thaksin met with President Bush again in Washington, DC, to discuss counter-terrorism issues. In October President Bush attended a summit meeting of the Asia-Pacific Economic Co-operation (APEC, see p. 176) in Bangkok, having paid an official state visit to Thailand in the days preceding the summit. The two heads of state announced that they were to enter into formal negotiations with regard to the signing of a bilateral free trade agreement. The terms of the deal were expected to be comprehensive, including measures intended to liberalize trade in consumer goods, agricultural products, services and investment, as well as intellectual property rights. However, following the completion of the sixth round of talks between the two countries, held in January 2006, scant progress had been made. Furthermore, the political upheaval of 2006–07 led to further delays. Preliminary discussions on the resumption of formal free trade negotiations were held in March 2008, following the return to democratic rule in Thailand. In the previous month the USA had announced the ending of its suspension of military aid to Thailand, which had been imposed following the coup of September 2006.

Following the terrorist attack on the Indonesian island of Bali in October 2002 (see the chapter on Indonesia), the Thai Government increased security in the country owing to speculation that Thailand, and in particular the tourist resort of Phuket, might be the target of further regional terrorist activity. Evidence was discovered that suggested southern Thailand as one of the locations used by those responsible for planning the Bali attack. Meanwhile, several foreign governments issued advisory warnings against unnecessary travel to the country. However, the Thai Government expressed its concern that such warnings were excessive and urged that they be rescinded.

Government

In December 1991 a new Constitution was promulgated, which provided for a National Assembly (comprising an elected House of Representatives and an appointed Senate) and a Cabinet headed by a Prime Minister. In June 1992 the National Assembly approved a constitutional amendment requiring the Prime Minister to be a member of the House of Representatives. In January 1995 the National Assembly approved a constitutional charter, which provided for a number of amendments; these included lowering the voting age from 20 to 18 years and reducing the membership of the Senate to two-thirds of that of the House of Representatives.

A new draft Constitution was promulgated on 11 October 1997 (see Constitution, below); enabling legislation for the new Constitution was completed within 240 days. In September 2006, following the military coup (see Recent History, above), the Council for Democratic Reform (CDR) released an interim Constitution; this came into effect in the following month. A permanent Constitution was later drafted by a committee appointed by the CDR, and in August 2007 was put to a national referendum, wherein it was approved by 57.8% of voters, and duly became law.

The bicameral National Assembly of Thailand consists of the House of Representatives (Sapha Poothaen Rassadorn) and the Senate (Woothi Sapha). The House of Representatives has 480 members, of whom 400 are directly elected by constituency voting, while the remainder are elected by a party list system of proportional representation. Members are elected for a term of four years. The Senate consists of 150 members, of whom 76 are elected (one from each of Thailand's 76 provinces) and 74 are appointed by a selection committee. Senators serve six-year terms.

Defence

As assessed at November 2007, the Thai armed forces had a total strength of 306,600: 190,000 in the army, 70,600 in the navy and an estimated 46,000 in the air force. Military service is compulsory for two years between the ages of 21 and 30. Paramilitary forces, including a volunteer irregular force, numbered an estimated 113,700. The defence budget was 115,000m. baht for 2007.

Economic Affairs

In 2006, according to estimates by the World Bank, Thailand's gross national income (GNI), measured at average 2004–06 prices, was US $193,734m., equivalent to $2,990 per head (or $9,140 per head on an international purchasing-power parity basis). During 1996–2006, it was estimated, the population increased at an annual average rate of 0.9%, while gross domestic product (GDP) per head increased, in real terms, by an average of 1.7% per year. Overall GDP increased, in real terms, at an average annual rate of 2.6% in 1996–2006. According to the Asian Development Bank (ADB), GDP increased by 5.1% in 2006 and by 4.8% in 2007.

Agriculture (including forestry, hunting and fishing) contributed an estimated 11.4% of GDP in 2007. In 2006 42.1% of the employed labour force were engaged in the sector. Thailand's staple crop and principal agricultural export commodity is rice (Thailand became the world's largest exporter of rice in 1981). Rice exports accounted for 2.8% of the total value of exports in 2004. Other major crops include sugar cane, cassava (tapioca), oil palm fruit, maize, natural rubber, bananas, mangoes and pineapples. Fisheries products and livestock (mainly cattle, buffaloes, pigs and poultry) are also important. Thailand is one of the world's largest exporters of farmed shrimp. During 1997–2007 agricultural GDP increased by an estimated annual average of 2.7%. Agricultural GDP was estimated to have risen by 3.8% in 2006 and by 3.9% in 2007.

Industry (including mining, manufacturing, construction and utilities) provided an estimated 43.9% of GDP in 2007. In 2006 20.6% of the employed labour force were engaged in industrial activities. During 1997–2007 industrial GDP increased at an annual average rate of 4.3%. The GDP of the industrial sector increased by an estimated 5.7% in 2006 and by 5.4% in 2007.

Mining and quarrying contributed an estimated 3.3% of GDP in 2007 and engaged less than 0.2% of the employed labour force in 2006. Gemstones, notably diamonds, are the principal mineral export. Natural gas and, to a lesser extent, petroleum are also exploited, and production of these fuels increased substantially from the late 1990s. Tin, lignite, gypsum, tungsten, lead, antimony, manganese, gold, zinc, iron and fluorite are also mined. During 1997–2007 the GDP of the mining sector increased at an estimated average annual rate of 4.7%. Mining GDP increased by an estimated 4.2% in 2006 and by 3.5% in 2007.

Manufacturing provided an estimated 34.9% of GDP in 2007. In 2006 14.6% of the employed labour force were engaged in the sector. In 1999 manufacturing's contribution to export earnings was 80%. Textiles and garments and electronics and electrical goods (particularly semiconductors) constitute Thailand's principal branches of manufacturing. Other manufacturing activities include the production of cigarettes, chemicals, cement and beer, sugar and petroleum refining, motor vehicle production, rubber production and the production of iron and steel. During 1997–2007 manufacturing GDP increased by an estimated annual average of 5.0%. The GDP of the sector increased by an estimated 5.9% in 2006 and by 5.8% in 2007.

Energy is derived principally from hydrocarbons. In 2006 47.1m. barrels of crude petroleum and 27.5m. cu m of natural gas were produced. In 2006 petroleum accounted for 44.3% of total fuel consumption, natural gas for 27.5%, coal for 12.4% and hydroelectricity for 1.8%. Lignite is also exploited. In 2003 solar and wind energy accounted for about 1% of electric power. However, Thailand remains dependent on imported petroleum and electricity. In 2007 imports of mineral fuels comprised 18.5% of the value of merchandise imports.

Services (including transport and communications, commerce, banking and finance, public administration and other services) contributed an estimated 44.7% of GDP in 2007 and 37.2% of the employed labour force were engaged in the services sector in 2006. Tourism has become a major source of foreign exchange, and in the early 2000s was estimated to account for 6% of the country's GDP. The number of tourist arrivals totalled 11.6m. in 2005, and receipts reached US $12,629m. However, the tourism sector has been intermittently affected by the unrest in southern Thailand (see Recent History). During 1997–2007 the GDP of the services sector expanded by an estimated annual average of 2.4%. The GDP of the sector increased by 4.8% in 2006 and by 4.3% in 2007.

In 2006 Thailand recorded a visible trade surplus of US $13,936m.; in the same year there was a surplus of $2,175m. on the current account of the balance of payments. In 2007 the principal source of imports (20.3%) was Japan; other major suppliers in that year were the People's Republic of China (11.6%), the USA, Malaysia and the United Arab Emirates. The principal markets for exports in 2007 were the USA (12.6%), Japan (11.9%) and China (9.7%); other major purchasers were Singapore, Hong Kong and Malaysia. The principal imports in 2007 were machinery (36.2%), mineral fuels and lubricants, basic manufactures and chemical products. The principal exports were machinery (45.1%), basic manufactures, food and live animals, miscellaneous manufactured goods (including clothing and accessories) and chemicals and related products. The 2007/08 budget projected a deficit of 209,700m. baht, equivalent to an estimated 2.3% of GDP. According to the ADB, Thailand's external debt totalled US $61,486m. at the end of 2007; in that year the cost of debt-servicing was equivalent to 11.1% of the value of exports of goods and services. The annual rate of inflation averaged 2.8% in 1997–2007. Consumer prices increased by 2.3% in 2007. In 2006 1.4% of the labour force were unemployed.

Thailand is a member of the UN Economic and Social Commission for Asia and the Pacific (ESCAP, see p. 35), the Asian Development Bank (ADB, see p. 182), the Association of South East Asian Nations (ASEAN, see p. 185), the Colombo Plan (see p. 411) and Asia-Pacific Economic Co-operation (APEC, see p. 176). In January 1993 the establishment of the ASEAN Free Trade Area (AFTA) commenced; the reduction of tariffs to between 0% and 5% was originally to be implemented by 2008 but this was subsequently brought forward to 2002. The target date for zero tariffs was advanced from 2015 to 2010 in November 1999. AFTA was formally established on 1 January 2002.

Thailand's steady recovery from the regional economic crisis of the late 1990s was subsequently curbed by the deceleration of the global economy in the aftermath of the terrorist attacks on the USA in September 2001. The removal of the democratically elected Government in October 2006 (see Recent History) significantly weakened business confidence, but the installation of the new coalition Government in January 2008 raised hopes of the development of more favourable investment conditions. According to the ADB, foreign direct investment rose from US $7,978m. in 2006 to $8,285m. in 2007. Strengthening international demand for rice in 2007 had resulted in a substantial increase in price for this commodity, and it was hoped that additional revenues generated from rice exports would lessen the impact of weaker external demand in other areas during 2008. Contrary to the position adopted by other major rice-producing countries, and as global shortages of the commodity began to develop, in April 2008 Thailand indicated that it intended to fulfil its export targets for the financial year ending in September 2008. The continued economic growth of 2007 was largely due to the strong performance of Thailand's export sector (particularly sales of palm oil and natural rubber) and to sustained growth in the industrial sector. However, high international prices for food commodities and mineral fuels were expected to increase inflationary pressures. Substantial rises in consumer prices were expected during 2008, with GDP growth of about 5% being anticipated. Rapid currency appreciation had moderated inflation in 2007, but this had jeopardized Thailand's merchandise exports (which became more expensive as the baht gained in value). The central bank attributed currency appreciation to speculative foreign investment in the Thai stock market and imposed capital controls to deter this activity in December 2006. However, this strategy was not deemed successful, as the new regulations precipitated large outflows of foreign capital and a devaluation of bonds and shares. The central bank therefore repealed these measures in March 2008, and the Thai administration indicated that currency appreciation would be addressed henceforth by the refinancing of foreign currency debt and by facilitating outward foreign investment. Furthermore, there were indications in early 2008 that controversial proposals for amendments to the Foreign Business Act, whereby firms in Thailand would be required to reduce foreign ownership stakes to less than 50% within three years, were to be abandoned.

Education

From January 2003, education became officially compulsory for 10 years, to be undertaken between the ages of seven and 16 years. In October 2002 12 years of free basic education was granted to students throughout the country for the first time, and in May 2004 this was expanded to 14 years, with the two years of pre-primary schooling henceforth also being offered free to all. Primary education begins at six years of age and lasts for six years. In 2004/05 enrolment in pre-primary schools was equivalent to 90% of children from the relevant age-group (males 91%; females 89%). In the same year enrolment within primary education was equivalent to 97.1% of children in the relevant age group (males 100%; females 95%). Secondary education, beginning at 12 years of age, also lasts for six years, divided into two equal cycles. In 2004/05 total secondary enrolment was equivalent to 73.2% of children within the relevant age-group (males 72%; females 74%). There were 20 state universities (12 of which were in Bangkok) and 26 private universities and colleges in 1995. In 2003 a total of approximately 1.9m. students were enrolled within the tertiary education sector. Budgetary expenditure on education by the central Government was 279,600m. baht (19.6% of total spending and equivalent to about 3.6% of GDP) in the financial year ending 30 September 2006, according to preliminary figures.

Public Holidays

2008: 1 January (New Year's Day), 21 February* (Makhabuja), 7 April (for Chakri Day), 13–15 April (Songkran Festival), 1 May (Labour Day), 5 May (Coronation Day), 19 May* (Visakhabuja), 1 July (Half Year Bank Holiday), 17 July (Asalhabuja), 18 July* (Khao Phansa, beginning of Buddhist Lent), 12 August (Queen's Birthday), 23 October (Chulalongkorn Day), 5 December (King's Birthday), 10 December (Constitution Day), 31 December (New Year's Eve).

2009: 1 January (New Year's Day), February/March* (Makhabuja), 6 April (Chakri Day), 13–15 April (Songkran Festival), 1 May (Labour Day), 5 May (Coronation Day), May/June* (Visakhabuja), 1 July (Half Year Bank Holiday), July* (Khao Phansa, beginning of Buddhist Lent), July* (Asalhabuja), 12 August (Queen's Birthday), 23 October (Chulalongkorn Day), 5 December (King's Birthday), 10 December (Constitution Day), 31 December (New Year's Eve).

*Regulated by the Buddhist lunar calendar.

Weights and Measures

The metric system is in force, but a number of traditional measures are also used.

THAILAND

Statistical Survey

Source (unless otherwise stated): National Statistical Office, Thanon Larn Luang, Bangkok 10100; tel. (2) 281-0333; fax (2) 281-3815; e-mail onsoadm@nso.go.th; internet www.nso.go.th.

Area and Population

AREA, POPULATION AND DENSITY

Area (sq km)	513,120*
Population (census results)†	
1 April 1990	54,548,530
1 April 2000	
Males	29,844,870
Females	30,762,077
Total	60,606,947
Population (official estimates at mid-year)†	
2005	62,418,054
2006	62,828,706
2007	63,038,247
Density (per sq km) at mid-2007	122.9

* 198,117 sq miles.
† Excluding adjustment for underenumeration.

REGIONS
(estimates at mid-2007)

	Area (sq km)	Population ('000)	Density (per sq km)
Bangkok	1,568.7	5,716	3,643.9
Central Region	102,336.0	15,410	150.6
Northern Region	169,644.3	11,872	70.0
Northeastern Region	168,855.3	21,386	126.7
Southern Region	70,715.2	8,655	122.4
Total	513,119.5	63,038	122.9

PRINCIPAL TOWNS
(population at 2000 census)

Bangkok Metropolis*	6,320,174	Pak Kret		141,788
Samut Prakan	378,694	Si Racha		141,334
Nanthaburi	291,307	Khon Kaen		141,034
Udon Thani	220,493	Nakhon Pathom		120,657
Nakhon Ratchasima	204,391	Nakhon Si Thammarat		118,764
Hat Yai	185,557	Thanya Buri		113,818
Chon Buri	182,641	Surat Thani		111,276
Chiang Mai	167,776	Rayong		106,585
Phra Padaeng	166,828	Ubon Ratchathani		106,552
Lampang	147,812	Khlong Luang		103,282

* Formerly Bangkok and Thonburi.

Mid-2007 ('000, incl. suburbs, UN estimate): Bangkok 6,704 (Source: UN, *World Urbanization Prospects: The 2007 Revision*).

BIRTHS, MARRIAGES AND DEATHS*

	Registered live births		Registered marriages		Registered deaths	
	Number	Rate (per 1,000)	Number	Rate (per 1,000)	Number	Rate (per 1,000)
1998	897,495	14.7	324,262	5.3	317,793	5.2
1999	754,685	12.3	348,803	5.7	362,607	5.9
2000	773,009	12.5	339,443	5.4	365,741	5.9
2001	790,425	12.7	324,661	n.a.	369,493	6.0
2002	782,911	12.5	n.a.	n.a.	380,364	6.1
2003	742,183	11.8	328,356	n.a.	384,131	6.1
2004	813,069	13.0	365,721	n.a.	393,592	6.3
2005†	809,485	13.0	345,234	n.a.	395,374	6.4

* Registration is incomplete. According to UN estimates, the average annual rates in 1990–95 were: Births 18.4 per 1,000; Deaths 7.4 per 1,000; in 1995–2000: Births 17.0 per 1,000; Deaths 8.1 per 1,000; in 2000–05: Births 15.4 per 1,000; Deaths 8.6 per 1,000 (Source: UN, *World Population Prospects: The 2006 Revision*).
† Provisional.

Expectation of life (years at birth, WHO estimates): 70.3 (males 67.5; females 73.3) in 2005 (Source: WHO, *World Health Statistics*).

EMPLOYMENT*
('000 persons aged 13 years and over, July–September of each year)

	2004	2005	2006
Agriculture, hunting and forestry	14,719	15,008	14,887
Fishing	396	441	428
Mining and quarrying	35	40	55
Manufacturing	5,313	5,350	5,307
Electricity, gas and water	99	107	99
Construction	1,878	1,853	2,039
Wholesale and retail trade; repair of motor vehicles, motorcycles and personal and household goods	5,452	5,297	5,402
Hotels and restaurants	2,206	2,300	2,215
Transport, storage and communications	1,068	1,076	1,053
Financial intermediation	303	340	350
Real estate, renting and business activities	634	652	659
Public administration and defence; compulsory social security	1,015	1,096	1,170
Education	1,083	1,122	1,080
Health and social work	535	611	603
Other community, social and personal service activities	713	719	710
Private households with employed persons	239	242	222
Extra-territorial organizations and bodies	1	2	0
Activities not adequately defined	23	48	66
Total employed	35,712	36,302	36,345

* Excluding the armed forces.

Unemployed ('000 persons aged 13 years and over, July–September of each year): 549 in 2004; 496 in 2005; 450 in 2006.

Source: ILO.

THAILAND

Health and Welfare

KEY INDICATORS

Total fertility rate (children per woman, 2005)	1.9
Under-5 mortality rate (per 1,000 live births, 2005)	21
HIV/AIDS (% of persons aged 15–49, 2005)	1.4
Physicians (per 1,000 head, 2000)	0.37
Hospital beds (per 1,000 head, 2000)	2.20
Health expenditure (2004): US $ per head (PPP)	293.3
Health expenditure (2004): % of GDP	3.5
Health expenditure (2004): public (% of total)	64.7
Access to water (% of persons, 2004)	99
Access to sanitation (% of persons, 2004)	99
Human Development Index (2005): ranking	78
Human Development Index (2005): value	0.781

For sources and definitions, see explanatory note on p. vi.

Agriculture

PRINCIPAL CROPS
('000 metric tons)

	2004	2005	2006
Rice (paddy)	28,538	30,292	29,269
Maize	4,216	3,886	3,696
Sorghum	93	77	65
Cassava (Manioc, Tapioca)	21,440	16,938	22,584
Sugar cane	64,996	49,586	47,658
Dry beans	135	112	113
Soybeans (Soya beans)	218	226	225
Groundnuts (in shell)*	114	114	117
Coconuts	2,126	1,871	1,871†
Oil palm fruit	5,182	5,003	6,519
Cabbages†	260	265	265
Tomatoes	266	198	198
Pumpkins, squash, gourds†	220	219	219
Cucumbers and gherkins†	221	221	221
Dry onions	321	279	279†
Garlic	96	107	81
Green corn (maize)	305	273	273†
Watermelons†	420	432	432
Bananas†	1,859	1,865	1,865
Oranges†	339	339	339
Tangerines, mandarins, clementines, satsumas†	668	670	670
Mangoes†	1,700	1,800	1,800
Pineapples	2,101	2,183	2,705
Papayas†	125	131	131
Tobacco (leaves)	68	n.a.	70†
Natural rubber	3,008	2,980	3,157

* Unofficial figures.
† FAO estimate(s).

Aggregate production ('000 metric tons, may include official, semi-official or estimated data): Total cereals 32,958 in 2004, 34,371 in 2005, 33,146 in 2006; Total roots and tubers 21,661 in 2004, 17,192 in 2005, 22,842 in 2006; Total vegetables (incl. melons) 3,348 in 2004, 3,257 in 2005, 3,231 in 2006; Total fruits (excl. melons) 7,916 in 2004, 8,126 in 2005, 8,648 in 2006.

Source: FAO.

LIVESTOCK
('000 head, year ending September)

	2004	2005	2006
Horses	3	6	2
Cattle	5,297	5,610	6,004
Buffaloes	1,738	1,771	1,772
Pigs	7,726	8,023	8,187
Sheep	42	42	51
Goats	250	338	324
Chickens	250,956	187,371	203,201
Ducks	15,649	21,540	20,844
Geese*	270	270	270

* FAO estimates.
Source: FAO.

LIVESTOCK PRODUCTS
('000 metric tons)

	2004	2005	2006
Cattle meat	157.5	167.6	176.0
Buffalo meat*	60.2	n.a.	62.5
Pig meat	679.8*	687.0*	700.0
Chicken meat	878.5	950.0	1,100.0†
Duck meat	84.8	85.0*	85.0*
Cows' milk	842.6	888.2	826.5
Hen eggs	393.4†	468.7*	513.3
Other poultry eggs*	305	310	310

* FAO estimate(s).
† Unofficial figure.
Source: FAO.

Forestry

ROUNDWOOD REMOVALS
('000 cubic metres, excl. bark, FAO estimates)

	2004	2005	2006
Sawlogs, veneer logs and logs for sleepers	300	300	300
Pulpwood	2,900	2,900	2,900
Other industrial wood	5,500	5,500	5,500
Fuel wood	19,985	19,866	19,736
Total	28,685	28,566	28,436

Source: FAO.

SAWNWOOD PRODUCTION
('000 cubic metres, incl. railway sleepers)

	2000	2001	2002
Coniferous (softwood)	17	18	18*
Broadleaved (hardwood)	203	215	270
Total	220	233	288

* FAO estimate.

2003–06: Production assumed to be unchanged from 2002 (FAO estimates).
Source: FAO.

Fishing

('000 metric tons, live weight)

	2003	2004	2005
Capture	2,849.7	2,839.6	2,599.4
Bigeyes	104.0	136.6	105.3
Sardinellas	124.9	119.9	117.8
Anchovies, etc.	153.7	163.2	140.5
Indian mackerels	156.2	160.4	139.3
Aquaculture	1,064.4	1,260.0	1,144.0
Catfish (hybrid)	101.6	159.3	114.3
Whiteleg shrimp	132.4	251.7	299.0
Giant tiger prawn	194.9	106.9	75.0
Green mussel	263.9	261.7	249.6
Total catch	3,914.1	4,099.6	3,743.4

Source: FAO.

THAILAND
Statistical Survey

Mining

(production in metric tons, unless otherwise indicated)

	2004	2005	2006
Lignite ('000 metric tons)	20,038	21,429	19,056
Crude petroleum ('000 barrels)	31,299	41,570	47,067
Natural gas—gross production (million cu m)	24,963	25,363	27,466
Iron ore—gross weight	135,580	230,946	264,289
Iron ore—metal content	68,000	116,000	132,000
Zinc ore—metal content*	43,400	30,572	32,100
Tin concentrates—metal content	586	158*	190*
Manganese ore—metal content*	2,180	42,400	480
Tungsten concentrates—metal content*	180	430	380
Tantalum—metal and oxide powder	317	150	230
Antimony ore—metal content	52	356*	1,409
Silver (kilograms)	10,700	14,100	11,400
Gold (kilograms)	4,500	4,400	3,500
Marble—dimension stone ('000 cu m)	236.6	267.8	547.6
Granite—dimension stone ('000 cu m*)	10.0	9.5	10.0
Granite—industrial ('000 metric tons)*	3,500	3,000	3,200
Limestone ('000 metric tons)*	133,196	130,584	136,583
Dolomite ('000 metric tons)	992.9	795.5	899.5
Calcite ('000 metric tons)	436.6	692.9	626.0
Silica sand ('000 metric tons)	587.7	718.3	861.8
Ball clay ('000 metric tons)	610.2	393.9	1,003.3
Kaolin—marketable production ('000 metric tons)	430.4	580.4	675.9
Phosphate rock, crude	2,580	3,020	900
Fluorspar—metallurgical grade ('000 metric tons)	2,375	295	3,240
Feldspar	1,001.1	1,149.7*	1,067.7
Barite	211.3	4.0	4.5
Perlite*	6,000	5,500	6,000
Gypsum ('000 metric tons)	7,619	7,113	8,355
Gemstones ('000 carats)	911	699	81

* Estimate(s).

Source: US Geological Survey.

Industry

SELECTED PRODUCTS
('000 metric tons, unless otherwise indicated)

	2005	2006	2007
Raw sugar	5,028	5,719	7,344
Beer (million litres)	1,695	2,011	2,161
Spirits (million litres)	600	635	551
Synthetic fibre	809.0	725.4	674.6
Wood pulp	925.5	999.4	1,037.4
Petroleum products (million litres)	48,133	49,285	49,856
Cement	37,872	39,408	35,668
Galvanized iron sheets	283.6	297.7	247.2
Integrated circuits (million units)	11,378	13,954	14,334
Computer monitors ('000 units)	2,210	1,380	942
Computer keyboards ('000 units)	7,454	958	931
Hard disk drives ('000 units)	120,707	153,980	205,277
Printers ('000 units)	19,241	16,577	17,439

Source: Bank of Thailand, Bangkok.

Finance

CURRENCY AND EXCHANGE RATES

Monetary Units
100 satangs = 1 baht.

Sterling, Dollar and Euro Equivalents (31 December 2007)
£1 sterling = 67.609 baht;
US $1 = 33.747 baht;
€1 = 49.679 baht;
1,000 baht = £14.79 = $29.63 = €20.13.

Average Exchange Rate (baht per US $)
2005   40.220
2006   37.882
2007   34.523

Note: Figures refer to the average mid-point rate of exchange available from commercial banks. In July 1997 the Bank of Thailand began operating a managed 'float' of the baht. In addition, a two-tier market was introduced, creating separate exchange rates for purchasers of baht in domestic markets and those who buy the currency overseas.

GOVERNMENT FINANCE
(central government transactions, non-cash basis, '000 million baht, year ending 30 September)

Summary of Balances

	2003/04	2004/05*	2005/06*
Revenue	1,275.1	1,498.7	1,580.0
Less Expense	1,077.3	1,166.1	1,267.6
Net operating balance	197.8	332.6	312.4
Less Net acquisition of non-financial assets	124.6	155.6	161.3
Net lending/borrowing	73.2	177.0	151.1

Revenue

	2003/04	2004/05*	2005/06*
Taxes	1,032.9	1,223.0	1,317.3
Taxes on income, profits and capital gains	407.9	491.8	576.7
Taxes on goods and services	510.8	601.1	633.1
Social contributions	62.0	73.3	74.0
Grants	2.2	1.9	1.7
Other revenue	178.0	200.5	187.1
Total	1,275.1	1,498.7	1,580.0

Expense/Outlays

Expense by economic type	2003/04	2004/05*	2005/06*
Compensation of employees	357.9	403.3	505.6
Use of goods and services	229.0	253.1	264.2
Consumption of fixed capital	n.a.	34.5	35.4
Interest	85.1	90.8	112.8
Subsidies	67.7	88.9	26.8
Grants	121.0	173.0	194.6
Social benefits	141.1	93.5	113.1
Other expense	75.0	29.1	15.0
Total	1,077.3	1,166.1	1,267.6

THAILAND

Outlays by functions of government†	2003/04	2004/05*	2005/06*
General public services	194.0	220.7	342.0
Defence	81.2	83.5	89.7
Public order and safety	67.8	74.5	82.4
Economic affairs	301.1	397.3	286.2
Agriculture, forestry and fishing	76.3	71.8	71.2
Fuel and energy	49.1	73.5	17.2
Transport	64.7	69.0	56.6
Environmental protection	11.1	7.0	35.6
Housing and community amenities	10.9	28.6	38.8
Health	118.0	115.9	125.7
Recreation, culture and religion	7.5	9.1	16.6
Education	265.0	268.1	279.6
Pre-primary and primary	186.4	155.7	148.1
Secondary	0.3	23.7	24.0
Tertiary	35.2	42.5	41.9
Social protection	145.5	117.0	132.2
Total	**1,202.1**	**1,321.7**	**1,428.9**

* Preliminary figures.
† Including net acquisition of non-financial assets.
Source: IMF, *Government Finance Statistics Yearbook*.

INTERNATIONAL RESERVES
(US $ million at 31 December)

	2005	2006	2007
Gold*	1,374	1,693	2,234
IMF special drawing rights	1	1	—
Reserve position in IMF	188	143	111
Foreign exchange	50,502	65,147	85,100
Total	**52,065**	**66,984**	**87,445**

* Revalued annually on the basis of the London market price.
Source: IMF, *International Financial Statistics*.

MONEY SUPPLY
('000 million baht at 31 December)

	2005	2006	2007
Currency outside banks	603.4	621.6	685.8
Demand deposits at deposit money banks	256.2	254.9	275.5
Total money (incl. others)	**863.0**	**880.2**	**965.2**

Source: IMF, *International Financial Statistics*.

COST OF LIVING
(Consumer Price Index; base: 2002 = 100)

	2005	2006	2007
Food (incl. non-alcoholic beverages)	113.7	118.9	123.7
Fuel and light	135.6	156.0	159.7
Clothing (incl. footwear)	100.7	100.9	101.1
Rent	101.3	103.3	103.4
All items (incl. others)	**109.3**	**114.4**	**117.0**

Source: Bank of Thailand.

NATIONAL ACCOUNTS
(million baht at current prices)

National Income and Product

	2004	2005	2006*
Compensation of employees	1,927,134	2,073,106	2,245,146
Operating surplus	2,994,311	3,327,209	3,707,961
Domestic factor incomes	**4,921,445**	**5,400,315**	**5,953,107**
Consumption of fixed capital	868,249	927,391	994,839
Gross domestic product (GDP) at factor cost	**5,789,694**	**6,327,706**	**6,947,946**
Indirect taxes	777,210	857,811	922,019
Less Subsidies	77,428	89,898	39,636
GDP in market prices	**6,489,476**	**7,095,619**	**7,830,329**
Net factor income from abroad	−291,032	−344,014	−322,153
Gross national product	**6,198,444**	**6,751,605**	**7,508,176**

Expenditure on the Gross Domestic Product
(million baht)

	2005	2006*	2007*
Government final consumption expenditure	840,841	924,609	1,070,140
Private final consumption expenditure	4,053,376	4,375,478	4,538,390
Changes in inventories	180,344	26,998	3,929
Gross fixed capital formation	2,048,015	2,208,035	2,270,043
Total domestic expenditure	**7,122,576**	**7,535,120**	**7,882,502**
Exports of goods and services	5,211,230	5,751,585	6,209,513
Less Imports of goods and services	5,301,855	5,477,803	5,563,364
Statistical discrepancy	63,668	21,427	−43,451
GDP in market prices	**7,095,619**	**7,830,329**	**8,485,200**
GDP at constant 1988 prices	**3,855,111**	**4,052,006**	**4,244,607**

Gross Domestic Product by Economic Activity

	2005	2006*	2007*
Agriculture, hunting and forestry	623,872	727,426	847,943
Fishing	109,404	113,708	119,148
Mining and quarrying	222,618	256,750	276,148
Manufacturing	2,461,915	2,748,488	2,960,136
Electricity, gas and water	220,429	238,852	243,354
Construction	216,359	234,958	248,677
Wholesale and retail trade; repair of motor vehicles, motorcycles and personal and household goods	1,039,439	1,110,188	1,181,270
Hotels and restaurants	346,910	386,382	416,550
Transport, storage and communications	519,663	567,149	616,509
Financial intermediation	262,099	283,365	306,007
Real estate, renting and business activities	198,511	208,987	214,309
Public administration and defence; compulsory social security	325,936	350,060	383,567
Education	280,956	316,355	369,538
Health and social work	135,219	150,016	170,112
Other community, social and personal service activities	123,758	128,907	122,715
Private households with employed persons	8,531	8,738	9,217
GDP in market prices	**7,095,619**	**7,830,329**	**8,485,200**

* Preliminary figures.
Source: National Economic and Social Development Board, Bangkok.

THAILAND

BALANCE OF PAYMENTS
(US $ million)

	2004	2005	2006
Exports of goods f.o.b.	94,979	109,199	127,929
Imports of goods f.o.b.	−84,194	−105,995	−113,993
Trade balance	10,785	3,204	13,936
Exports of services	19,040	20,163	24,130
Imports of services	−23,077	−27,120	−32,415
Balance on goods and services	6,748	−3,753	5,651
Other income received	3,244	3,640	4,659
Other income paid	−9,364	−10,813	−11,502
Balance on goods, services and income	628	−10,926	−1,193
Current transfers received	2,479	3,351	3,764
Current transfers paid	−348	−348	−396
Current balance	2,759	−7,923	2,175
Direct investment abroad	−77	−501	−1,033
Direct investment from abroad	5,860	8,055	9,004
Portfolio investment assets	1,232	−1,522	−2,025
Portfolio investment liabilities	1,856	7,070	5,714
Financial derivatives assets	11	382	−270
Financial derivatives liabilities	−116	−908	623
Other investment assets	−1,695	−1,726	−10,005
Other investment liabilities	−3,410	232	3,641
Net errors and omissions	−710	2,257	4,845
Overall balance	5,710	5,417	12,669

Source: IMF, *International Financial Statistics*.

External Trade

PRINCIPAL COMMODITIES
(distribution by SITC, '000 million baht)

Imports c.i.f.	2005	2006	2007
Food	152.5	157.6	170.5
Crude materials (inedible) except fuels	161.5	145.9	160.4
Mineral fuels, lubricants, etc.	842.7	972.0	900.1
Chemicals and related products	483.9	503.8	535.6
Basic manufactures	801.0	829.4	852.5
Machinery	1,806.0	1,821.7	1,765.0
Total (incl. others)	4,754.0	4,942.9	4,872.0

Exports f.o.b.	2005	2006	2007
Food	495.5	534.4	583.4
Crude materials (inedible) except fuels	226.1	289.7	289.0
Mineral fuels and lubricants	192.0	247.2	235.2
Chemicals and related products	358.3	394.6	419.6
Basic manufactures	546.1	620.0	678.1
Machinery	1,990.8	2,203.7	2,371.1
Miscellaneous manufactured articles	537.1	543.0	558.2
Total (incl. others)	4,438.7	4,937.4	5,255.0

Source: Bank of Thailand, Bangkok.

PRINCIPAL TRADING PARTNERS
('000 million baht)

Imports c.i.f.	2005	2006	2007
Australia	130.6	130.7	132.2
China, People's Republic	448.9	521.5	564.6
France	75.4	56.2	45.2
Germany	128.7	125.9	136.4
Hong Kong	60.4	59.2	50.1
India	51.2	62.0	71.9
Indonesia	125.7	131.9	138.6
Italy	45.6	57.2	47.4
Japan	1,046.9	985.8	988.5
Korea, Republic	156.4	196.7	184.2

Imports c.i.f.—continued	2005	2006	2007
Malaysia	325.3	325.3	299.9
Philippines	75.7	81.3	74.6
Russia	64.4	49.0	53.6
Singapore	216.5	218.1	218.7
Switzerland	53.0	50.0	51.9
Taiwan	181.1	196.0	199.8
United Arab Emirates	229.2	272.4	237.8
United Kingdom	51.4	50.5	52.7
USA	349.4	367.1	330.7
Total (incl. others)	4,754.0	4,942.9	4,872.0

Exports f.o.b.	2005	2006	2007
Australia	127.1	165.2	197.5
Belgium	51.3	54.6	57.4
Canada	41.4	47.2	47.0
China, People's Republic	367.4	446.0	510.8
France	51.9	54.2	56.9
Germany	80.3	88.6	99.1
Hong Kong	247.0	272.8	299.0
Indonesia	158.9	126.2	164.2
Italy	49.8	56.8	63.7
Japan	602.9	623.9	625.1
Korea, Republic	90.6	101.6	102.3
Malaysia	232.9	252.0	268.6
Netherlands	111.0	123.1	131.1
Philippines	82.3	97.8	100.0
Singapore	308.0	318.6	328.2
Switzerland	27.1	35.0	48.9
Taiwan	108.9	128.1	114.8
United Arab Emirates	47.1	56.1	75.9
United Kingdom	112.1	129.4	122.5
USA	680.3	740.7	662.7
Viet Nam	94.8	116.9	130.9
Total (incl. others)	4,438.7	4,937.4	5,255.0

Source: Bank of Thailand, Bangkok.

Transport

RAILWAYS
(year ending 30 September)

	2003/04	2004/05	2005/06
Passengers carried ('000)	50,873	49,671	48,867
Passenger-kilometres (million)	9,332	9,052	8,824
Freight carried ('000 metric tons)	13,796	12,817	12,566
Freight ton-kilometres (million)	4,085	3,621	3,508

ROAD TRAFFIC
('000 motor vehicles in use at 31 December)

	2005	2006
Passenger cars	3,396.5	3,312.9
Buses and trucks	766.0	848.8
Vans and pick-ups	4,752.4	4,173.6
Motorcycles	15,501.0	15,650.3
Total (incl. others)	25,266.3	24,807.3

SHIPPING

Merchant Fleet
(registered at 31 December)

	2004	2005	2006
Number of vessels	751	789	789
Total displacement ('000 grt)	2,889.9	3,025.3	2,822.7

Source: Lloyd's Register-Fairplay, *World Fleet Statistics*.

THAILAND

International Sea-borne Freight Traffic
(Ports of Bangkok and Laem Chabang, year ending 30 September)

	2003/04	2004/05	2005/06
Goods loaded ('000 metric tons)	18,872	21,456	22,401
Goods unloaded ('000 metric tons)	28,834	30,071	32,951
Vessels entered	7,060	7,640	8,975

Source: Port Authority of Thailand.

CIVIL AVIATION
(traffic on scheduled services)

	2001	2002	2003
Kilometres flown (million)	182	194	204
Passengers carried ('000)	17,662	18,112	17,892
Passenger-km (million)	44,142	48,337	45,449
Total ton-km (million)	5,702	6,241	5,920

Sources: UN, *Statistical Yearbook*.

Tourism

FOREIGN TOURIST ARRIVALS BY COUNTRY OF RESIDENCE*

Country of origin	2003	2004	2005
Australia	284,749	396,959	423,825
China, People's Republic	624,923	780,050	762,388
France	220,659	252,458	261,672
Germany	389,293	449,765	445,155
Hong Kong	657,458	664,988	441,458
India	230,790	300,634	352,965
Japan	1,026,287	1,194,480	1,188,871
Korea, Republic	695,034	910,891	816,501
Malaysia	1,340,193	1,391,379	1,342,988
Singapore	633,805	737,677	797,782
Sweden	210,882	223,031	223,484
Taiwan	525,916	560,198	378,047
United Kingdom	550,087	634,750	685,077
USA	469,165	566,726	591,114
Total (incl. others)	10,082,109	11,737,413	11,567,341

* Includes Thai nationals resident abroad.

Receipts from tourism (US $ million, including passenger transport): 10,456 in 2003; 13,054 in 2004; 12,629 in 2005.

Source: World Tourism Organization.

Communications Media

	2004	2005	2006
Telephones ('000 main lines in use)	6,797.0	7,034.7	7,073.4
Mobile cellular telephones ('000 subscribers)	27,378.7	31,136.5	40,815.5
Personal computers ('000 in use)	3,716	n.a.	n.a.
Internet users ('000)	6,971.5	7,284.2	8,465.8
Broadband subscribers ('000)	75.0	105.0	n.a.

Radio receivers ('000 in use): 13,959 in 1997.

Television receivers ('000 in use): 18,400 in 2001.

Facsimile machines ('000 in use): 150 in 1997.

Book production (titles, excluding pamphlets): 8,142 in 1996.

Daily newspapers: 35 (with average circulation of 2,766,000 copies) in 1994; 35 (with average circulation of 2,700,000* copies) in 1995; 30 (with average circulation of 3,808,000 copies) in 1996.

Non-daily newspapers: 280 in 1995; 320 in 1996.
* Provisional.

Sources: International Telecommunication Union; UNESCO, *Statistical Yearbook*; UN, *Statistical Yearbook*.

Education

(2005, unless otherwise indicated)

	Institutions	Teachers	Students
Ministry of Education:			
Office of the Permanent Secretary	3,774	123,486	2,296,415
Office of the Basic Education Commission	32,340	420,965	8,697,983
Office of the Higher Education Commission	156	45,824	1,950,892
Office of Vocational Education Commission	408	16,731	615,548
Mahidol Wittayanusorn School	1	63	704
Mahamakut Buddhist University*	8	150	6,436
Mahachulalongkornrajavidyalaya University*	12	373	8,999
Bangkok Metropolitan Education Department	437	13,196	349,063
Royal Thai Police	192	2,082	29,985
Department of Local Administration	520	18,297	400,361
Ministry of Social Development and Human Security	3	38	407
Ministry of Public Health	39	2,971	17,750
Merchant Marine Training Centre	1	220	918
Civil Aviation Training Centre	1	37	1,052
National Bureau of Buddhism	404	3,188	51,414
Fine Arts Department	16	1,423	10,014
Office of Sports and Recreational Development	28	1,857	13,794
Armed Forces	11	1,400	7,476

* Figures for 2004.

Source: Ministry of Education.

Adult literacy rate (UNESCO estimates): 92.6% (males 94.9%; females 90.5%) in 2000 (Source: UNESCO Institute for Statistics).

Directory

The Constitution

On 19 September 2006 a military junta, which subsequently came to be known as the Council for National Security (CNS), ousted the Government of Thaksin Shinawatra and abolished the Constitution promulgated in October 1997. The CNS drafted a new, interim Constitution, which was endorsed by the King and promulgated on 1 October. It was to remain in place until the drafting of a permanent Constitution could take place, prior to legislative elections scheduled for late 2007. The interim Constitution granted overwhelming power to the executive branch and the CNS, with the chairman of the latter being given the power to remove the Prime Minister. A ban on political gatherings of more than five people and restrictions on press freedom, introduced in the immediate aftermath of the coup, were to remain in place. In August 2007 a referendum was held to ascertain the extent of public support for the draft Constitution; as a result of a majority vote in favour of the draft, and upon royal approval, the new Constitution came into effect later that month.

The Government

HEAD OF STATE

King: HM King BHUMIBOL ADULYADEJ (King Rama IX—succeeded to the throne June 1946).

PRIVY COUNCIL

Members: Gen. (retd) PREM TINSULANONDA (President), Dr CHAOVANA NASYLVANTA, THANIN KRAIVICHIEN, Rear-Adm. M. L. USNI PRAMOJ, Air Vice-Marshal KAMTHON SINDHAVANANDA, Air Chief Marshal SIDDHI SAVETSILA, CHULANOPE SNIDVONGS, Gen. PICHITR KULLAVANIJAVA, AMPOL SENARONG, CHAMRAS KEMACHARU, M. R. THEPKAMOL DEVAKULA, Prof. KASEM WATANACHAI, PALAKORN SUWANNARAT, SAWAT WATTANAYAKORN, SANTI THAKARAL, Adm. CHUMPOL PACHUSANONDA, ANTANITHI DITSAMANAJ, Gen. SURAYUD CHULANONT, SUPACHAI PHOO-NGAM, CHANCHAI LIKHITCHITTA.

CABINET
(April 2008)

Prime Minister and Minister of Defence: SAMAK SUNDARAVEJ.

Deputy Prime Minister and Minister of Education: SOMCHAI WONGSAWAT.

Deputy Prime Minister and Minister of Commerce: MINGKWAN SAENGSUWAN.

Deputy Prime Minister and Minister of Finance: SURAPONG SUEBWONGLEE.

Deputy Prime Ministers: SAHAS BANDITKUL, SANAN KACHORNPRASART.

Deputy Prime Minister and Minister of Industry: SUWIT KHUNKITTI.

Ministers in the Prime Minister's Office: CHAKRAPOB PENKAIR, CHOOSAK SIRININ.

Minister of Foreign Affairs: NOPPADON PATTAMA.

Minister of Tourism and Sports: WEERASAK KOHSURAT.

Minister of Social Development and Human Security: SUTHA CHANSAENG.

Minister of Agriculture and Co-operatives: SOMSAK PRISSANANANTAKUL.

Minister of Transport: SANTI PROMPHAT.

Minister of Natural Resources and Environment: ANONGWAN THEPSUTHIN.

Minister of Information and Communications Technology: MUN PATTANOTHAI.

Minister of Energy: POONPIROM LIPTAPANLOP.

Minister of the Interior: CHALERM YOOBAMRUNG.

Minister of Justice: SOMPONG AMORNWIWAT.

Minister of Labour: URAIWAN THIENTHONG.

Minister of Culture: ANUSORN WONGWAN.

Minister of Science and Technology: WUTTHIPONG CHAISANG.

Minister of Public Health: CHAIYA SASOMSAP.

MINISTRIES

Office of the Prime Minister: Government House, Thanon Nakhon Pathom, Bangkok 10300; tel. (2) 280-3526; fax (2) 282-8792; e-mail webmaster@opm.go.th; internet www.opm.go.th.

Ministry of Agriculture and Co-operatives: Thanon Ratchadamnoen Nok, Bangkok 10200; tel. (2) 281-5955; fax (2) 282-1425; e-mail webmaster@moac.go.th; internet www.moac.go.th.

Ministry of Commerce: 44/100 Thanon Nonthaburi 1, Amphur Muang, Nonthaburi, Bangkok 11000; tel. (2) 507-8000; fax (2) 507-7717; e-mail webmaster@moc.go.th; internet www.moc.go.th.

Ministry of Culture: Thanalongkorn Bldg, Thanon Boromrachanonnee, Bangplud, Bangkok 10700; tel. (2) 522-8888; e-mail webmaster@m-culture.go.th; internet www.m-culture.go.th.

Ministry of Defence: Thanon Sanamchai, Bangkok 10200; tel. (2) 222-1121; fax (2) 226-3117; internet www.mod.go.th.

Ministry of Education: Wang Chankasem, Thanon Ratchadamnoen Nok, Bangkok 10300; tel. (2) 281-9809; fax (2) 281-9241; e-mail website@emisc.moe.go.th; internet www.moe.go.th.

Ministry of Energy: 17 Kasatsuk Bridge, Thanon Rama I, Rong Mueng, Pathumwan, Bangkok 10330; tel. (2) 223-3344; fax (2) 222-3785; e-mail moen@energy.go.th; internet www.energy.go.th.

Ministry of Finance: Thanon Rama VI, Samsennai, Phaya Thai, Rajatevi, Bangkok 10400; tel. (2) 273-9021; fax (2) 273-9408; e-mail prinya@mof.go.th; internet www.mof.go.th.

Ministry of Foreign Affairs: Thanon Sri Ayudhya, Bangkok 10400; tel. (2) 643-5000; fax (2) 225-6155; e-mail information@mfa.go.th; internet www.mfa.go.th.

Ministry of Industry: 75/6 Thanon Rama VI, Ratchathewi, Bangkok 10400; tel. (2) 202-3000; fax (2) 202-3048; internet www.industry.go.th.

Ministry of Information and Communications Technology: Bangkok 10210; tel. (2) 238-5422; fax (2) 238-5423; e-mail pr@mict.go.th; internet www.mict.go.th.

Ministry of the Interior: Thanon Atsadang, Bangkok 10200; tel. (2) 222-1141; fax (2) 223-8851; e-mail webteam@moi.go.th; internet www.moi.go.th.

Ministry of Justice: Thanon Ratchadaphisek, Chatuchak, Bangkok 10900; tel. (2) 502-8051; fax (2) 502-8059; e-mail webmaster@moj.go.th; internet www.moj.go.th.

Ministry of Labour: Thanon Mitmaitri, Dindaeng, Huay Kwang, Bangkok 10400; tel. (2) 232-1421; fax (2) 246-1520; e-mail webmaster@mol.go.th; internet www.mol.go.th.

Ministry of Natural Resources and Environment: 92 Phaholyothin Soi 7, Samsen Nai, Bangkok 10400; tel. (2) 298-2754; fax (2) 298-2020; e-mail web@mnre.go.th; internet www.monre.go.th.

Ministry of Public Health: Thanon Tiwanon, Amphoe Muang, Nonthaburi 11000; tel. (2) 590-1000; fax (2) 591-8492; e-mail eng-webmaster@health.moph.go.th; internet www.moph.go.th.

Ministry of Science and Technology: Thanon Rama VI, Ratchathewi, Bangkok 10400; tel. (2) 246-0064; fax (2) 246-5146; internet www.most.go.th.

Ministry of Social Development and Human Security: Bangkok 10100; tel. (2) 659-6399; e-mail society@m-society.go.th; internet www.m-society.go.th.

Ministry of Tourism and Sports: Thanon Rama I, Pathumwan, Bangkok 10330; tel. (2) 283-1500; fax (2) 356-0746; e-mail webmaster@mots.go.th; internet www.mots.go.th.

Ministry of Transport: 38 Thanon Ratchadamnoen Nok, Khet Pom Prab Sattruphai, Bangkok 10100; tel. (2) 281-3871; fax (2) 283-3049; e-mail mot@mot.go.th; internet www.mot.go.th.

Legislature

RATHA SAPHA (NATIONAL ASSEMBLY)

Woothi Sapha (Senate)

The Senate consists of 150 members, of whom 76 members are elected to represent each of Thailand's 75 provinces and Bangkok, and the remainder are selected by a committee consisting primarily of judicial officials. Senators thus selected are drawn from lists of nominees made by organizations in various sectors.

Elections to the Senate were held on 2 March 2008.

Speaker of the Senate: PRASOBSUK BOONDECH.

THAILAND

Sapha Poothaen Rassadorn (House of Representatives)

Speaker of the House of Representatives and President of the National Assembly: CHAI CHIDCHOB.

Election, 23 December 2007

Party	Seats
People's Power Party	233
Democrat Party	164
Chart Thai	34
Puea Pandin	24
Matchimathipataya	11
Ruam Jai Thai Chart Pattana	9
Pracharaj	5
Total	**480***

*A total of 400 candidates were elected in multi-member constituencies and the remaining 80 through a party-list system.

Election Commission

Election Commission of Thailand (ECT): Srijullasup Bldg, 19th Floor, 44 Thanon Rama I, Pathumwan, Bangkok 10330; tel. (2) 613-7333; fax (2) 219-3411; e-mail dav@ect.go.th; internet www.ect.go.th; Chair. APHICHART SUKHATKHANON.

Political Organizations

Chart Thai (Thai Nation): 1 Thanon Pichai, Dusit, Bangkok 10300; tel. (2) 243-8070; fax (2) 243-8074; e-mail chartthai@chartthai.or.th; internet www.chartthai.or.th; f. 1981; right-wing; founded political reform policy; includes mems of fmr United Thai People's Party and fmr Samakkhi Tham (f. 1991); Leader BANHARN SILAPA-ARCHA; Sec.-Gen. PRAPAT PHOTHASUTHON.

Democrat Party (DP) (Prachatipat): 67 Thanon Setsiri, Samsen Nai, Phyathai, 10400 Bangkok; tel. (2) 270-0036; fax (2) 279-6086; e-mail admin@democrat.or.th; internet www.democrat.or.th; f. 1946; liberal; Leader ABHISIT VEJJAJIVA; Sec.-Gen. SUTHEP THUAGSUBAN.

Ekkaparb (Solidarity): 670/104 Soi Thepnimit, Thanon Jaransanitwong, Bangpaid, Bangkok 10700; tel. (2) 424-0291; fax (2) 424-8630; f. 1989; opposition merger by the Community Action Party, the Prachachon Party, the Progressive Party and Ruam Thai; Leader CHAIYOS SASOMSAP; Sec.-Gen. NEWIN CHIDCHOB.

Matchimathipataya (Neutral Democratic Party): 26/56, 10/F, TPI Tower, Thanon Chan Tat Mai, Thung Mahamek, Sathon, Bangkok 10110; e-mail webmaster@matchima.or.th; internet www.matchima .or.th; f. 2006; Leader PRACHAI LIEOWPHAIRAT; Sec.-Gen. ANONGWAN THEPSUTHIN.

Muan Chon (Mass Party): 630/182 Thanon Prapinklao, Bangkok 10700; tel. and fax (2) 424-0851; f. 1985; dissolved after defection of leader Capt. Chalerm Yoobamrung to New Aspiration Party (NAP); re-formed in 2002 following merger of NAP with Thai Rak Thai; Leader Gen. VORAVIT PIBOONSILP; Sec.-Gen. KAROON RAKSASUK.

People's Power Party (PPP) (Palang Prachachan): 1770 Thanon Petchaburi Tat Mai, Bang Gapi, Huay Kwang, Bangkok 10310; tel. (2) 686–7000; internet www.ppp.or.th; f. 2007; est. by fmr mems of Thai Rak Thai and supporters of deposed Prime Minister Thaksin Shinawatra; Thai Rak Thai dissolved in May 2007; Leader SAMAK SUNDARAVEJ; Sec.-Gen. SURAPONG SUEBWONGLEE.

Prachakorn Thai (Thai Citizens Party): 1213/323 Thanon Srivara, Bangkapi, Bangkok 10310; tel. (2) 559-0008; fax (2) 559-0016; internet www.prachakornthai.org; f. 1981; right-wing; monarchist; Leader SUMIT SUNDARAVEJ; Sec.-Gen. THIRAYUTH NIMSAKUL.

Pracharaj (Royal People Party): 18/F, TPI Tower, 26/56 Thanon Chan Tat Mai, Tungmahorn, Sathorn, Bangkok 10120; f. 2006 by breakaway faction of Thai Rak Thai; Leader SNOH THIENTHONG; Sec.-Gen. CHIENGCHUANG KANLAYANAMITH.

Puea Pandin (For the Land): 1 Thanon Wittayu, Lumphini, Pathumwan, Bangkok 10330; tel. (2) 253-0428; e-mail pueapandin@gmail.com; internet www.ppd.or.th; f. 2007; Leader SUWIT KUNKITTI; Sec.-Gen. WACHARA PHANCHET.

Ruam Jai Thai Chart Pattana (Thais United National Development): c/o House of Representatives, Bangkok; f. 2007; est. by merger of Chart Pattana and Thais United; Leader CHETTHA THANNAJARO.

Other parties that contested the 2007 election included Farmer Network of Thailand, For our Homeland, Free Thai, Prachamati, Rak Muang Thai and Artist Party.

Groupings in armed conflict with the Government include:

Barasan Revolusi Nasional (BRN) (National Revolutionary Front): Yala; f. 1963; was organized into three principal factions—the BRN Congress (its military wing); the BRN Co-ordinate (its political wing); and the BRN Uram (its religious wing)—in the 1980s; Muslim secessionists.

Gerakan Mujahideen Islami Pattani (GMIP): Pattani; f. 1986; dissolved in 1993 following internal disagreement, but re-formed in 1995; seeks the transformation of Pattani into an Islamic state; Leader KARIM KARUBANG.

Pattani United Liberation Organization (PULO): advocates secession of the five southern provinces (Satun, Narathiwat, Yala, Pattani and Songkhla); Pres. LUKMAN B. LIMA (acting).

Runda Kumpulan Kecil (RKK): Yala; f. 2005; splinter group of the BRN Congress; seeks the implementation of an independent Islamic state in Thailand's southern provinces; Leader USTAZ RORHING AHSONG.

Diplomatic Representation

EMBASSIES IN THAILAND

Argentina: 16th Floor, Suite 1601, Glas Haus Bldg, 1 Soi Sukhumvit 25, Klongtoey, Bangkok 10110; tel. (2) 259-0401; fax (2) 259-0402; e-mail embtail@mozart.inet.co.th; Ambassador FELIPE FRYDMAN.

Australia: 37 Thanon Sathorn Tai, Bangkok 10120; tel. (2) 344-6300; fax (2) 344-6593; e-mail austembassy.bangkok@dfat.gov.au; internet www.austembassy.or.th; Ambassador BILL PATERSON.

Austria: 14 Soi Nandha, off Thanon Sathorn Tai, Soi 1, Bangkok 10120; tel. (2) 303-6057; fax (2) 287-3925; e-mail bangkok-ob@bmaa .gv.at; Ambassador ARNO RIEDEL.

Bangladesh: 727 Soi Thonglor, Thanon Sukhumvit 55, Bangkok 10110; tel. (2) 392-9437; fax (2) 391-8070; e-mail bdoot@samart.co.th; Ambassador MUSTAFA KAMAL.

Belgium: 17th Floor, Sathorn City Tower, 175 Thanon Sathorn Tai, Tungmahamek, Sathorn, Bangkok 10120; tel. (2) 679-5454; fax (2) 679-5467; e-mail bangkok@diplobel.org; internet www.diplomatie .be/bangkok; Ambassador JAN MATTHYSEN.

Bhutan: 375/1 Soi Ratchadanivej, Thanon Pracha-Uthit, Huay Kwang, Bangkok 10320; tel. (2) 274-4740; fax (2) 274-4743; e-mail bht_emb_bkk@yahoo.com; Ambassador SINGYE DORJI.

Brazil: 34th Floor, Lumpini Tower, 1168/101 Thanon Rama IV, Sathorn, Bangkok 10120; tel. (2) 679-8567; fax (2) 679-8569; e-mail embrasbkk@inet.co.th; internet www.brazilembassy.th; Ambassador EDGARD TELLES RIBEIRO.

Brunei: 12 Soi Ekamai 2, Thanon Sukhumvit 63, Prakanong Nua, Wattana, Bangkok 10110; tel. (2) 714-7395; fax (2) 714-7383; Ambassador Pengiran Dato' Paduka Haji SHARIFUDDIN BIN Haji YUSSOF.

Bulgaria: 83/24 Soi Witthayu 1, Thanon Whitthayu, Lumpini, Pathumwan, Bangkok 10330; tel. (2) 627-3872; fax (2) 627-3874; e-mail bulgemth@csloxinfo.com; Chargé d'affaires MIMA DIMITROVA STOILOVA-NIKOLOVA.

Cambodia: 518/4, Thanon Pracha Uthit, Ramkhamhaeng Soi 39, Wangtonglang, Bangkok 10310; tel. (2) 957-5851; fax (2) 957-5850; e-mail recbkk@cscoms.com; Ambassador UNG SEAN.

Canada: Abdulrahim Bldg, 15th Floor, 990 Thanon Rama IV, Bangrak, Bangkok 10500; tel. (2) 636-0540; fax (2) 636-0565; e-mail bngkk@international.gc.ca; internet geo.international.gc.ca/asia/bangkok; Ambassador DAVID SPROULE.

Chile: 83/17 Witthayu Place, Soi Witthayu 1, Thanon Witthayu, Lumpini, Pathumwan, Bangkok 10330; tel. (2) 251-9470; fax (2) 2251-9475; e-mail embajada@chile-thai.com; internet www .chile-thai.com; Ambassador JOAQUÍN MONTES.

China, People's Republic: 57 Thanon Ratchadaphisek, Bangkok 10310; tel. (2) 245-7043; fax (2) 246-8247; e-mail chinaemb_th@mfa .gov.cn; internet www.chinaembassy.or.th/eng; Ambassador ZHANG JIUHUAN.

Cuba: Mela Mansion Apartment 3C, 5 Soi Sukhumvit 27, Klongtoey Nua, Wattana, Bangkok 10110; tel. (2) 665-2803; fax (2) 661-6560; e-mail cubaemb1@loxinfo.co.th; internet embacuba.cubaminrex.cu/tailandiaing; Ambassador MARÍA LUISA FERNÁNDEZ.

Czech Republic: 71/6 Soi Ruamrudi 2, Thanon Ploenchit, Bangkok 10330; tel. (2) 255-3027; fax (2) 253-7637; e-mail bangkok@embassy .mzv.cz; internet www.mfa.cz/bangkok; Ambassador IVAN HOTĚK.

Denmark: 10 Soi Attakarn Prasit, Thanon Sathorn Tai, Bangkok 10120; tel. (2) 343-1100; fax (2) 213-1752; e-mail bkkamb@um.dk; internet www.ambbangkok.um.dk; Ambassador MICHAEL STERNBERG.

Egypt: 6 Las Colinas Bldg, 42nd Floor, Sukhumvit 21, Wattana, Bangkok 10110; tel. (2) 661-7184; fax (2) 262-0235; e-mail egyptemb@

loxinfo.co.th; Ambassador Mohamed Ashraf Mohamed Kamal El Kholy.

Finland: Amarin Tower, 16th Floor, 500 Thanon Ploenchit, Bangkok 10330; tel. (2) 250-8801; fax (2) 250-8802; e-mail sanomat.ban@formin.fi; internet www.finland.or.th; Ambassador Lars Erik Backström.

France: 35 Soi Rong Phasi Kao, Thanon Charoenkrung, Bangkok 10500; tel. (2) 657-5100; fax (2) 657-5111; e-mail ambassade@ambafrance-th.org; internet www.ambafrance-th.org; Ambassador Laurent Aublin.

Germany: 9 Thanon Sathorn Tai, Bangkok 10120; tel. (2) 287-9000; fax (2) 287-1776; e-mail info@german-embassy.or.th; internet www.bangkok.diplo.de; Ambassador Dr Christoph Brümmer.

Greece: Unit 25/5-9, 9th Floor, BKI/YWCA Bldg, 25 Thanon Sathorn Tai, Bangkok 10120; tel. (2) 679-1462; fax (2) 679-1463; e-mail embgrbkk@ksc.th.com; Ambassador Ioannis Papadopoulos.

Holy See: 217/1 Thanon Sathorn Tai, POB 12-178, Bangkok 10120 (Apostolic Nunciature); tel. (2) 212-5853; fax (2) 212-0932; e-mail nuntiusth@csloxinfo.com; Apostolic Nuncio Most Rev. Salvatore Pennacchio (Titular Archbishop of Montemarano).

Hungary: Oak Tower, 20th Floor, President Park Condominium, 95 Sukhumvit Soi 24, Prakhanong, Bangkok 10110; tel. (2) 661-1150; fax (2) 661-1153; e-mail huembbgk@mozart.inet.co.th; internet www.mfa.gov.hu/kulkepviselet/TH/hu; Ambassador Dr Andras Balogh.

India: 46 Soi Prasarnmitr, 23 Thanon Sukhumvit, Bangkok 10110; tel. (2) 258-0300; fax (2) 258-4627; e-mail indiaemb@mozart.inet.co.th; internet indianembassy.gov.in/bangkok; Ambassador Vijaya Latha Reddy.

Indonesia: 600–602 Thanon Phetchaburi, Ratchathewi, Bangkok 10400; tel. (2) 252-3135; fax (2) 255-1267; e-mail kukbkk@ksc11.th.com; internet www.kbri-bangkok.com; Ambassador Ibrahim Yusuf.

Iran: 215 Thanon Sukhumvit, Soi 49, Klongtan Nua, Wattana, Bangkok 10110; tel. (2) 390-0871; fax (2) 390-0867; e-mail info@iranembassy.or.th; internet www.iranembassy.or.th; Ambassador Majid Bizmark (designate).

Israel: Ocean Tower II, 25th Floor, 75 Sukhumvit, Soi 19, Thanon Asoke, Bangkok 10110; tel. (2) 204-9200; fax (2) 204-9255; e-mail info@bangkok.mfa.gov.il; internet bangkok.nfa.gov.il; Ambassador Yael Rubinstein.

Italy: 399 Thanon Nang Linchee, Thungmahamek, Yannawa, Bangkok 10120; tel. (2) 285-4090; fax (2) 285-4793; e-mail ambasciata.bangkok@esteri.it; internet www.italian-embassy.org.ae/Ambasciata_Bangkok; Ambassador Ignazio Di Pace.

Kenya: 62 Thonglor Soi 5, Thanon Sukhumvit 55, Klongtan, Wattana, Bangkok 10110; tel. (2) 712-5721; fax (2) 712-5720; Ambassador Richard Titus Ekai.

Korea, Democratic People's Republic: 14 Mooban Suanlaemthong 2, Thanon Pattanakarn, Suan Luang, Bangkok 10250; tel. (2) 319-2686; fax (2) 318-6333; Ambassador O Yong Son.

Korea, Republic: 23 Thanon Thiam-Ruammit, Huay Kwang, Bangkok 10320; tel. (2) 247-7537; fax (2) 247-7535; e-mail korea_emb_th@yahoo.co.kr; Ambassador Han Tae-Kyu.

Kuwait: 100/44 Sathorn Nakhon Tower, 24th Floor, Thanon Sathorn Nua, Bangrak, Bangkok 10500; tel. (2) 636-6600; fax (2) 636-7360; e-mail kwembasy@inet.co.th; Ambassador Hafeez Mohammed Salem al-Ajmi.

Laos: 502/502/1–3 Soi Sahakarnpramoon, Thanon Pracha Uthit, Wangthonglang, Bangkok 10310; tel. (2) 539-6667; fax (2) 539-3827; e-mail sabaidee@bkklaoembassy.com; internet www.bkklaoembassy.com; Ambassador Ouan Phommachack.

Malaysia: 35 Thanon Sathorn Tai, Tungmahamek, Sathorn, Bangkok 10120; tel. (2) 679-2190; fax (2) 679-2208; e-mail malbangkok@kln.gov.my; internet www.kln.gov.my/mission/bangkok; Ambassador Dato' Sharaani bin Ibrahim.

Mexico: 20/60–62 Thai Wah Tower I, 20th Floor, Thanon Sathorn Tai, Bangkok 10120; tel. (2) 285-0995; fax (2) 285-0667; e-mail mexthai@loxinfo.co.th; internet www.sre.gob.mx/tailandia; Ambassador Luis Arturo Puente Ortega.

Mongolia: 100/3, Soi Ekamai 22, Thanon Sukhumvit 63, Prakanong Nua, Wattana, Bangkok 10110; tel. (2) 381-1400; fax (2) 392-1499; e-mail mongemb@loxinfo.co.th; internet www.mongolmissionbkk.com; Ambassador Yaichil Batsuuri.

Morocco: Sathorn City Tower, 12th Floor, 175 Thanon Sathorn Tai, Sathorn, Bangkok 10120; tel. (2) 679-5604; fax (2) 2679-5603; e-mail sifambkk@samarts.com; internet www.moroccoembassybangkok.org; Ambassador El Hassane Zahid.

Myanmar: 132 Thanon Sathorn Nua, Bangkok 10500; tel. (2) 233-2237; fax (2) 236-6898; Ambassador U Ye Win.

Nepal: 189 Soi 71, Thanon Sukhumvit, Prakanong, Bangkok 10110; tel. (2) 390-2280; fax (2) 381-2406; e-mail nepembkk@asiaaccess.net.th; Ambassador Navin Prakash Jung Shah.

Netherlands: 15 Soi Tonson, Thanon Ploenchit, Lumpini, Pathumwan, Bangkok 10330; tel. (2) 309-5200; fax (2) 309-5205; e-mail ban@minbuza.nl; internet www.mfa.nl/ban; Ambassador Pieter J. Th. Marres.

New Zealand: M Thai Tower, 14th Floor, All Seasons Place, 87 Thanon Witthayu, Lumpini, Pathumwan, Bangkok 10330; tel. (2) 254-2530; fax (2) 253-9045; e-mail nzembbkk@loxinfo.co.th; internet www.nzembassy.com/home.cfm?c=21; Ambassador Brook Barrington.

Nigeria: 412 Thanon Sukhumvit 71, Prakhanong, Wattana, Bangkok 10110; tel. (2) 711-3076; fax (2) 392-6398; e-mail info@embnigeriabkk.com; Ambassador Umaru A. Sulaiman (designate).

Norway: UBC II Bldg, 18th Floor, 591 Thanon Sukhumvit, Soi 33, Bangkok 10110; tel. (2) 204-6500; fax (2) 262-0218; e-mail emb.bangkok@mfa.no; internet www.emb-norway.or.th; Ambassador Merette Fjeld Brattested.

Oman: 82 Saeng Thong Thani Tower, 32nd Floor, Thanon Sathorn Nua, Bangkok 10500; tel. (2) 639-9380; fax (2) 639-9390; Ambassador Hafeedh Salim Mohamed Ba-Omar.

Pakistan: 31 Soi Nana Nua, Thanon Sukhumvit, Bangkok 10110; tel. (2) 253-0288; fax (2) 253-0290; e-mail parepbkk@ji-net.com; Ambassador Khateer Hassan Khan.

Panama: 1168/37 Lumpini Tower Bldg, 16th Floor, Tungmahamek, Sathorn, Bangkok 10120; tel. (2) 679-7988; fax (2) 679-7991; e-mail embajada@panathai.com; internet www.panathai.com; Ambassador David Guardia Varela.

Peru: Glas Haus Bldg, 16th Floor, 1 Soi Sukhumvit 25, Khet Wattana, Bangkok 10110; tel. (2) 260-6243; fax (2) 260-6244; e-mail peru@peruthai.or.th; internet www.peru.org.pe; Ambassador Carlos Manuel Velasco Mendiola.

Philippines: 760 Thanon Sukhumvit, cnr Soi 30/1, Klongtan, Klongtoey, Bangkok 10110; tel. (2) 259-0139; fax (2) 259-2809; e-mail inquiry@philembassy-bangkok.net; internet www.philembassy-bangkok.net; Ambassador Antonio V. Rodriguez.

Poland: 100/81-82, Vongvanij Bldg B, 25th Floor, Thanon Phra Ram IX, Huaykwang, Bangkok 10310; tel. (2) 645-0367; fax (2) 645-0365; e-mail polemb@loxinfo.co.th; internet www.polemb.or.th; Ambassador Bogdan Goralczyk.

Portugal: 26 Bush Lane, Thanon Charoenkrung, Bangkok 10500; tel. (2) 234-2123; fax (2) 238-4275; e-mail portemb@loxinfo.co.th; Ambassador António Felix Machado de Faria e Maya.

Qatar: Capital Tower, 14th Floor, All Seasons Place, 87/1 Thanon Witthayu, Lumpini, Pathumwan, Bangkok 10330; tel. (2) 660-1111; fax (2) 660-1122; e-mail info@qatarembassy.or.th; internet www.qatarembassy.or.th; Ambassador Abdalla Ibrahim Abdulrahman al-Hamar.

Romania: 20/1 Soi Rajakhru, Phaholyothin Soi 5, Thanon Phaholyothin, Phayathai, Bangkok 10400; tel. (2) 617-1551; fax (2) 617-1113; e-mail romembnk@ksc.th.com; Ambassador Radu Gabriel Mateescu.

Russia: 78 Thanon Sap, Bangrak, Bangkok 10500; tel. (2) 234-9824; fax (2) 237-8488; e-mail rusembbangkok@rambler.ru; internet www.thailand.mid.ru; Ambassador Yevgeny V. Afanasiev.

Saudi Arabia: 82 Saeng Song Thani Bldg, 23rd Floor, Thanon Sathorn Nua, Bangrak, Bangkok 10500; tel. (2) 639-2960; fax (2) 639-2950; Ambassador Nabil H. H. Ashri.

Singapore: 129 Thanon Sathorn Tai, Bangkok 10120; tel. (2) 286-2111; fax (2) 286-6966; e-mail singemb_bkk@sgmfa.gov.sg; internet www.mfa.gov.sg/bangkok; Ambassador Peter Chan.

Slovakia: 25/9-4, BKI/YWCA Bldg, 9th Floor, Thanon Sathorn Tai, Tungmahamek, Bangkok 10120; tel. (2) 677-3445; fax (2) 677-3447; e-mail slovakemb@actions.net; Ambassador Vasil Pytel.

South Africa: M-Thai Tower, Floor 12A, All Seasons Place, 87 Thanon Witthayu, Prathumwan, Lumpini, Bangkok 10330; tel. (2) 250-9012; fax (2) 685-3500; e-mail saembbkk@loxinfo.co.th; internet www.saembbangkok.com; Ambassador Douglas Harvey Monro Gibson.

Spain: Lake Rajada Office Complex, 23rd Floor, 193 Thanon Rajadapisek, Klongtoey, Bangkok 10110; tel. (2) 661-8284; fax (2) 661-9220; e-mail emb.bangkok@mae.es; internet www.mae.es/embajadas/bangkok/es/home; Ambassador Juan Manuel López Nadal.

Sri Lanka: Ocean Tower II, 13th Floor, 75/6–7 Sukhumvit, Soi 19, Bangkok 10110; tel. (2) 261-1934; fax (2) 261-1936; e-mail slemb@ksc.th.com; Ambassador Jayaratna Banda Disanayaka.

Sweden: First Pacific Place, 20th Floor, 140 Thanon Sukhumvit, Bangkok 10110; tel. (2) 263-7200; fax (2) 263-7260; e-mail ambassaden.bangkok@foreign.ministry.se; internet www.swedenabroad.com/bangkok; Ambassador Lennart Linnér.

Switzerland: 35 Thanon Witthayu, Lumpini, Pathumwan, Bangkok 10330; tel. (2) 253-0156; fax (2) 255-4481; e-mail ban

THAILAND

.vertretung@eda.admin.ch; internet www.eda.admin.ch/bangkok_emb; Ambassador RODOLPHE S. IMHOOF.

Turkey: 61/1 Soi Chatsan, Thanon Suthisarn, Huay Kwang, Bangkok 10310; tel. (2) 274-7262; fax (2) 274-7261; e-mail tcturkbe@mail.cscoms.com; Ambassador CINAR ALDEMIR.

Ukraine: 87 All Seasons Place, CRC Tower, 33rd Floor, Thanon Witthayu, Lumpini, Pathumwan, Bangkok 10330; tel. (2) 685-3216; fax (2) 685-3217; e-mail ukremb@thailand.truemail.co.th; internet www.ukremb.or.th; Chargé d'affaires a.i. ANDRIY BESHTA.

United Arab Emirates: 82 Saeng Thong Thani Bldg, 25th Floor, Thanon Sathorn Nua, Bangkok 10500; tel. (2) 639-9820; fax (2) 639-9818; Ambassador SALIM ISSA ALI AL-KATTAM AL-ZAABI.

United Kingdom: 14 Thanon Witthayu, Lumpini, Pathumwan, Bangkok 10330; tel. (2) 305-8333; fax (2) 255-8619; e-mail info.bangkok@fco.gov.uk; internet www.britishembassy.gov.uk/Thailand; Ambassador QUINTON MARK QUAYLE.

USA: 95 Thanon Witthayu, Lumpini, Pathumwan, Bangkok 10330; tel. (2) 205-4000; fax (2) 254-1171; e-mail acsbkk@state.gov; internet bangkok.usembassy.gov; Ambassador ERIC G. JOHN.

Viet Nam: 83/1 Thanon Witthayu, Lumpini, Pathumwan, Bangkok 10330; tel. (2) 251-3551; fax (2) 251-7203; e-mail vnembassy@bkk.a-net.net.th; Ambassador NGUYEN DUY HUNG.

Judicial System

SUPREME COURT

(Sarn Dika)

Thanon Ratchadamnoen Nai, Bangkok 10200; tel. (2) 221-3161; e-mail supremec@judiciary.go.th; internet www.supremecourt.or.th.

The final court of appeal in all civil, bankruptcy, labour, juvenile and criminal cases. Its quorum consists of three judges. However, the Court occasionally sits in plenary session to determine cases of exceptional importance or where there are reasons for reconsideration or overruling of its own precedents. The quorum, in such cases, is one-half of the total number of judges in the Supreme Court.

President (Chief Justice): WIRAT LIMWICHAI.

Vice-Presidents: PHICHIT KHAMFAENG, THEERARAT PHATTARANWAT, MONGKHOL THAPTHIENG, PANYA SUTHIBODI, WATTANCHAI CHOTICHUTRAKUL, RUNGROJ RUENRENGWONG.

COURT OF APPEALS

(Sarn Uthorn)

Thanon Ratchadaphisek, Chatuchak, Bangkok 10900; internet www.judiciary.go.th/appealc.

Appellate jurisdiction in all civil, bankruptcy, juvenile and criminal matters; appeals from all the Courts of First Instance throughout the country, except the Central Labour Court, come to this Court. Two judges form a quorum.

Chief Justice: KAIT CHATANIBAND.

Deputy Chief Justices: PORNCHAI SMATTAVET, CHATISAK THAMMASAKDI, SOMPOB CHOTIKAVANICH, SOMPHOL SATTAYA-APHITARN.

COURTS OF FIRST INSTANCE

Includes the categories of general courts (Civil Courts, Criminal Courts, Provincial Courts and Kwaeng Courts), juvenile and family courts, and specialized courts (Central Labour Court, Central Tax Court, Central Intellectual Property and International Trade Court, Central Bankruptcy Court).

Religion

Buddhism is the predominant religion, professed by more than 95% of Thailand's total population. About 4% of the population are Muslims, being ethnic Malays, mainly in the south. Most of the immigrant Chinese are Confucians. The Christians number about 352,000, mainly in Bangkok and northern Thailand. Brahmins, Hindus and Sikhs number about 85,000.

BUDDHISM

Sangha Supreme Council

The Religious Affairs Dept, Thanon Ratchadamnoen Nok, Bangkok 10300; tel. (2) 281-6080; fax (2) 281-5415.

Governing body of Thailand's 350,000 monks, novices and nuns.

Supreme Patriarch of Thailand: NYANASAMVARA SUVADDHANA.

The Buddhist Association of Thailand: 41 Thanon Phra Aditya, Bangkok 10200; tel. (2) 281-5693; fax (2) 281-9564; f. 1934; under royal patronage; 7,139 mems; Pres. NUTTAPASH INTUPUTI.

CHRISTIANITY

The Roman Catholic Church

For ecclesiastical purposes, Thailand comprises two archdioceses and eight dioceses. At 31 December 2005 there were an estimated 329,628 adherents in the country, representing about 0.5% of the population.

Catholic Bishops' Conference of Thailand

122/11 Soi Naksuwan, Thanon Nonsi, Yannawa, Bangkok 10120; tel. (2) 681-5365; fax (2) 681-5370; e-mail cbct_th@hotmail.com.

f. 1969; Pres. Cardinal MICHAEL MICHAI KITBUNCHU (Archbishop of Bangkok).

Archbishop of Bangkok: Cardinal MICHAEL MICHAI KITBUNCHU, Assumption Cathedral, 51 Thanon Oriental, Charoenkrung 40, Bangrak, Bangkok 10500; tel. (2) 237-1031; fax (2) 237-1033; e-mail arcdibkk@loxinfo.co.th.

Archbishop of Tharé and Nonseng: Bishop LOUIS CHAMNIERN SANTISUKNIRAN, POB 6, Amphoe Muang, Sakon Nakhon 47000; tel. (42) 711-272; fax (42) 712-023.

The Anglican Communion

Thailand is within the jurisdiction of the Anglican Bishop of Singapore (q.v.).

Other Christian Churches

Baptist Church Foundation (Foreign Mission Board): 90 Soi 2, Thanon Sukhumvit, Bangkok 10110; tel. (2) 252-7078; Mission Admin. TOM WILLIAMS (POB 832, Bangkok 10501).

Church of Christ in Thailand: 328 Thanon Phayathai, Khet Phayathai, Bangkok 10400; tel. (2) 214-6001; fax (2) 214-6010; e-mail webmaster_cct@cct.or.th; internet www.cct.or.th; f. 1934; c. 100,000 communicants; Moderator Rev. Dr BOONRATNA BOAYEN; Gen. Sec. Rev. Dr SINT KIMHACHANDRA.

ISLAM

Office of the Chularajmontri: 100 Soi Prom Pak, Thanon Sukhumvit, Bangkok 10110; Sheikh Al-Islam (Chularajmontri) Haji SAWASDI SUMALAYASAK.

BAHÁ'Í FAITH

National Spiritual Assembly: 1415 Sriwara Soi 94, Wangthonglang, Bangkapi, Bangkok 10310; tel. (2) 530-7417; fax (2) 935-6515; e-mail nsa@bahai.or.th; internet www.thai-bahais.org; mems resident in 76 provinces.

The Press

DAILIES

Thai Language

Baan Muang: 1 Soi Pluem-Manee, Thanon Vibhavadi Rangsit, Bangkok 10900; tel. (2) 513-3101; fax (2) 513-3106; internet www.banmuang.co.th; f. 1972; Editor MANA PRAEBHAND; circ. 200,000.

Daily News: 1/4 Thanon Vibhavadi Rangsit, Laksi, Bangkok 10210; tel. (2) 561-1456; fax (2) 940-9875; internet www.dailynews.co.th; f. 1964; Editor PRACHA HETRAKUL; circ. 800,000.

Khao Sod (Fresh News): 12 Thanon Tethsaban Naruaman, Prachanivate 1, Chatuchak, Bangkok 10900; tel. (2) 580-0021; fax (2) 580-2301; e-mail matisale@matichon.co.th; internet www.matichon.co.th/khaosod; Editor-in-Chief KIATICHAI PONGPANICH; circ. 650,000.

Kom Chad Luek (Sharp, Clear, Deep): 44 Moo 10, Thanon Bangna Trad, Km 4.5, Bang Na, Bangkok 10260; tel. (2) 325-5555; fax (2) 317-2071; internet www.komchadluek.com; Editor ADISAL LIMPRUNGPATAKIT.

Krungthep Turakij Daily: Nation Multimedia Group Public Co Ltd, 44 Moo 10, Thanon Bangna-Trad, Bangna, Prakanong, Bangkok 10260; tel. (2) 317-0042; fax (2) 317-1489; e-mail ktwebeditor@nationgroup.com; internet www.bangkokbiznews.com; f. 1987; Publr and Group Editor SUTHICHAI YOON; Editor DUANGKAMOL CHOTANA; circ. 75,882.

Manager Daily: Baan Phra Atit, 102/1 Thanon Phra Atit, Phra Nakorn, Bangkok; internet www.manager.co.th; f. 1990; Editor KHUNTHONG LORSERIVANICH.

Matichon: 12 Thanon Tethsaban Naruaman, Prachanivate 1, Chatuchak, Bangkok 10900; tel. (2) 580-0021; fax (2) 580-2301; e-mail

THAILAND

matisale@matichon.co.th; internet www.matichon.co.th; f. 1977; Man. Editor PRASONG LERTRATANAVISUTH; circ. 550,000.

Naew Na (Frontline): 96 Moo 3, Thanon Vibhavadi Rangsit, Talaat Bang Khen, Bangkok 10210; tel. (2) 973-4250; fax (2) 552-3800; e-mail naewna@naewna.com; internet www.naewna.com; Editor WANCHAI WONGMEECHAI; circ. 200,000.

Post Today: 136 Thanon Na Ranong, Sonthorn Kosa, Klongtoey, Bangkok 10110; tel. (2) 240-3700; fax (2) 671-3147; e-mail nhakranl@posttoday.com; internet www.posttoday.com; f. 2003; business news; Editor NA KAL LAOHAWILAI; circ. 100,000.

Siam Keela (Siam Sport): 66/26–29, Moo 12, Soi Ram Indra 40, Thanon Ram Indra, Klong Kum, Bueng Kum, Bangkok 10230; tel. (2) 508-8000; e-mail webmaster@siamsport.co.th; internet www.siamsport.co.th; f. 1973.

Siam Rath (Siam Nation): 12 Mansion 6, Thanon Rajdamnern, Bangkok 10200; tel. (2) 622-1810; fax (2) 224-1982; e-mail siamrath@siamrath.co.th; internet www.siamrath.co.th; f. 1950; Editor CHACHAWAN KHONGUDOM; circ. 120,000.

Thai Rath: 1 Thanon Vibhavadi Rangsit, Bangkok 10900; tel. (2) 272-1030; fax (2) 272-1324; e-mail feedback@thairath.co.th; internet www.thairath.co.th; f. 1948; Editor SORAWUT WACHARAPHOL; circ. 800,000.

Thai Post: 1852 Thanon Kasemrat, Klong Toei, Bangkok 10110; tel. (2) 240-2612; fax (2) 249-0295; internet www.thaipost.net; Editor ROJ NGAMMAEN.

Than Setakij (Economic Base): 222 Than Setakij Bldg, Thanon Vibhavadi Rangsit, Chatuchak, Bangkok 10900; tel. (2) 513-9896; e-mail webmaster@thannews.th.com; internet www.thannews.th.com.

English Language

Bangkok Post: Bangkok Post Bldg, 136 Soi Na Ranong, Klongtoey, Bangkok 10110; tel. (2) 240-3700; fax (2) 671-3174; e-mail edmger@bangkokpost.co.th; internet www.bangkokpost.net; f. 1946; morning; Editor-in-Chief PICHAI CHUENSUKSAWADI.

Business Day: Olympia Thai Tower, 22nd Floor, 444 Thanon Ratchadaphisek, Huay Kwang, Bangkok 10310; tel. (2) 512-3579; fax (2) 512-3565; e-mail info@bday.net; internet www.biz-day.com; f. 1994; business news; Man. Editor CHATCHAI YENBAMROONG.

The Nation: 44 Moo 10, Editorial Bldg, 6th Floor, Thanon Bangna Trad, Km 4.5, Bang Na, Phra Khanong, Bangkok 10260; tel. (2) 325-5555; fax (2) 751-4446; e-mail info@nationgroup.com; internet www.nationmultimedia.com; f. 1971; morning; Publr and Group Editor SUTHICHAI YOON; Editor TULSATHIT TAPTIM; circ. 55,000.

Chinese Language

Sing Sian Yit Pao Daily News: 267 Thanon Charoenkrung, Talad-Noi, Bangkok 10100; tel. (2) 222-6601; fax (2) 225-4663; e-mail info@singsian.com; internet www.singsian.com; f. 1950; Man. Dir NETRA RUTHAIYANONT; Editor TAWEE YODPETCH; circ. 70,000.

Tong Hua Daily News: 877/879 Thanon Charoenkrung, Talad-Noi, Bangkok 10100; tel. (2) 236-9172; fax (2) 238-5286; Editor CHART PAYONITHIKARN; circ. 85,000.

WEEKLIES
Thai Language

Bangkok Weekly: 533–539 Thanon Sri Ayuthaya, Bangkok 10400; tel. (2) 245-2546; fax (2) 247-3410; Editor VICHIT ROJANAPRABHA.

Mathichon Weekly Review: 12 Thanon Tethsaban Naruaman, Prachanivate 1, Chatuchak, Bangkok 10900; tel. (2) 580-0021; fax (2) 580-2301; e-mail weekly@matichon.co.th; internet www.matichon.co.th/weekly/; Editor RUANGCHAI SABNIRAND; circ. 300,000.

Siam Rath Weekly Review: 12 Mansion 6, Thanon Rajdamnern, Bangkok 10200; Editor PRACHUAB THONGURAI.

Sakul Thai: 58 Soi 36, Thanon Sukhumvit, Bangkok 10110; tel. (2) 258-5861; fax (2) 258-9130; internet www.sakulthai.com; Editor SANTI SONGSEMSAWAS.

English Language

Bangkok Post Weekly Review: U-Chuliang Bldg, 3rd Floor, 968 Thanon Phra Ram Si, Bangkok 10500; tel. (2) 233-8030; fax (2) 238-5430; f. 1989; Editor ANUSSORN THAVISIN; circ. 10,782.

FORTNIGHTLIES
Thai Language

Darathai: 9-9/1 Soi Sri Ak-Sorn, Thanon Chuapleung, Tungmahamek, Sathorn, Bangkok 10120; tel. (2) 249-1576; fax (2) 249-1575; f. 1954; television and entertainment; Editor USA BUKKAVESA; circ. 80,000.

Directory

Dichan: 1400 Thai Bldg, Thanon Phra Ram Si, Bangkok; tel. (2) 249-0351; fax (2) 249-9455; e-mail dichan@pacific.co.th; Man. Editor KHUNYING TIPYAVADI PRAMOJ NA AYUDHYA.

Praew: 65/101–103 Thanon Chaiyaphruk, Taling Chan, Bangkok; tel. (2) 422-9999; fax (2) 434-3555; e-mail chantana@amarin.co.th; internet www.praew.com; f. 1979; women and fashion; Editorial Dir SUPAWADEE KOMARADAT; Editor CHANTANA YUTDHANAPHUM; circ. 150,000.

MONTHLIES

Bangkok 30: 98/5–6 Thanon Phra Arthit, Bangkok 10200; tel. (2) 282-5467; fax (2) 280-1302; f. 1986; Thai; business; Publr SONCHAI LIMTHONGKUL; Editor BOONSIRI NAMBOONSRI; circ. 65,000.

Chao Krung: 12 Mansion 6, Thanon Rajdamnern, Bangkok 10200; Thai; Editor NOPPHORN BUNYARIT.

The Dharmachaksu (Dharma-vision): Foundation of Mahamakut Rajavidyalai, 241 Thanon Phra Sumeru, Bangkok 10200; tel. (2) 281-1085; fax (2) 629-4015; e-mail books@mahamakuta.inet.co.th; internet www.mahamakuta.inet.co.th; f. 1894; Thai; Buddhism and related subjects; Editor WASIN INDASARA; circ. 5,000.

Grand Prix: 4/299 Moo 5, Soi Ladplakhao 66, Thanon Ladplakhao, Bangkhen, Bangkok 10220; tel. (2) 971-6450; fax (2) 971-6469; e-mail pinyo@grandprixgroup.com; internet www.grandprixgroup.com/gpi/maggrandprix/grandprix.asp; f. 1970; Editor PINYO SILPASARTDUMRONG; circ. 80,000.

The Investor: Pansak Bldg, 4th Floor, 138/1 Thanon Phetchaburi, Ratchathawi, Bangkok 10400; tel. (2) 282-8166; f. 1968; English language; business, industry, finance and economics; Editor TOS PATUMSEN; circ. 6,000.

Kasikorn: Dept of Agriculture, Catuchak, Bangkok 10900; tel. (2) 561-4677; fax (2) 579-5369; e-mail pannee@doa.go.th; internet www.doa.go.th; f. 1928; Thai; agriculture and agricultural research; Editor-in-Chief SOPIDA HE-MAKOM; Editor PANNEE WICHACHOO.

Look: 1/54 Thanon Sukhumvit 30, Pra Khanong, Bangkok 10110; tel. (2) 258-1265; Editor KANOKWAN MILINDAVANIJ.

Look East: 52/38 Soi Saladaeng 2, Silom Condominium, 12th Floor, Thanon Silom, Bangkok 10500; tel. (2) 235-6185; fax (2) 236-6764; f. 1969; English; Editor ASHA SEHGAL; circ. 30,000.

Metro Magazine: 109 Moo 8, 7th Floor, Srithepthai Bldg, Thanon Bangna-Trad, Bangna, Bangkok 10260; tel. (2) 746-7250; fax (2) 746-7266; e-mail mon@bkkmetro.com; internet www.bkkmetro.com; f. 1996; English language; lifestyle, events listings and consumer-oriented articles; Publr and Editor-in-Chief MUNINTRA SAENGSUVIMOL; circ. 35,000.

Motorcycle Magazine: 4/299 Moo 5, Soi Ladplakhao 66, Thanon Ladplakhao, Bangkhan, Bangkok 10220; tel. (2) 522-1731; fax (2) 522-1730; e-mail motorcycle@grandprixgroup.com; internet www.grandprixgroup.com/gpi/magmotor/motorcycle.asp; Publr PRACHIN EAMLAMNOW; circ. 70,000.

Saen Sanuk: 50 Soi Saeng Chan, Thanon Sukhumvit 42, Bangkok 10110; tel. (2) 392-0052; fax (2) 391-1486; English; travel and tourist attractions in Thailand; Editor SOMTAWIN KONGSAWATKIAT; circ. 85,000.

Sarakadee Magazine: 28-30 Soi Parinayok, Bangkok 10200; tel. (2) 281-6110; fax (2) 282-7003; e-mail admin@sarakadee.com; internet www.sarakadee.com; Thai; events, culture and nature.

Satawa Liang: 689 Thanon Wang Burapa, Bangkok; Thai; Editor THAMRONGSAK SRICHAND.

Villa Wina Magazine: Chalerm Ketr Theatre Bldg, 3rd Floor, Bangkok; Thai; Editor BHONGSAKDI PIAMLAP.

NEWS AGENCY

Thai News Agency (TNA): 63/1 Thanon Phra Rama 9, Huaykwang, Bangkok 10320; operated by MCOT PLC, fmrly the Mass Communications Organization of Thailand; news service in Thai and English.

PRESS ASSOCIATIONS

Confederation of Thai Journalists: 299 Thanon Ratchasima, Dusit, Bangkok 10300; tel. (2) 668-9422; fax (2) 668-7505; internet www.ctj.in.th; Pres. CHATRI LIMCHAROON; Sec.-Gen. NATTAYA CHETCHOTIROS.

Press Association of Thailand: 299 Thanon Ratchasima, Dusit, Bangkok 10300; tel. (2) 537-3777; fax (2) 537-3888; e-mail webmaster@thaipressasso.com; internet www.thaipressasso.com; f. 1941; Pres. MANIT LUEPRAPHAI.

Thai Journalists' Assen: 538/1 Thanon Samsen, Dusit, Bangkok 10300; tel. (2) 668-9422; fax (2) 668-7505; e-mail reporter@inet.co.th; internet www.tja.or.th; Pres. ANANT NILMANON.

There are also regional press organizations and journalists' organizations.

THAILAND

Publishers

Advance Media: 1400 Rama IV Shopping Centre, Klongtoey, Bangkok 10110; tel. (2) 249-0358; Man. PRASERTSAK SIVASAHONG.

Amarin Printing and Publishing Public Co Ltd: 65/101–103 Moo 4 Thanon Chaiyaphruk, Taling Chan, Bangkok 10170; tel. (2) 422-9999; fax (2) 434-3555; e-mail info@amarin.co.th; internet www.amarin.com; f. 1976; general books and magazines; CEO METTA UTAKAPAN.

Bhannakij Trading: 34 Thanon Nakornsawan, Bangkok 10100; tel. (2) 282-5520; fax (2) 282-0076; Thai fiction, school textbooks; Man. SOMSAK TECHAKASHEM.

Chalermnit Publishing Co Ltd: 108 Thanon Sukhumvit, Soi 53, Bangkok 10110; tel. (2) 662-6264; fax (2) 662-6265; e-mail chalermnit@hotmail.com; internet www.chalermnit.com; f. 1937; dictionaries, history, literature, guides to Thai language, works on Thailand and South-East Asia; Man. Dir Dr PARICHART JUMSAI.

Dhamabuja: 5/1–2 Thanon Asadang, Bangkok; religious; Man. VIROCHANA SIRI-ATH.

Graphic Art Publishing: 105/19–2 Thanon Naret, Bangkok 10500; tel. (2) 233-0302; f. 1972; textbooks, science fiction, photography; CEO Mrs ANGKANA SAJJARAKTRAKUL.

Prae Pittaya Ltd: POB 914, 716–718 Wangburabha, Bangkok 10200; tel. (2) 221-4283; fax (2) 222-1286; general Thai books; Man. CHIT PRAEPANICH.

Praphansarn: 413/26 Thanon Aroon Amarin, Bangkok 10700; tel. (2) 434-1347; fax (2) 434-6812; e-mail editor@praphansarn.com; internet www.praphansarn.com; f. 1961; Thai pocket books; Man. Dir SUPHOL TAECHATADA.

Ruamsarn (1977): 864 Wangburabha, Thanon Panurangsri, Bangkok 10200; tel. (2) 221-6483; fax (2) 222-2036; f. 1951; fiction and history; Man. PITI TAWEWATANASARN.

Sermvitr Barnakarn: 222 Werng Nakorn Kasem, Bangkok 10100; general Thai books; Man. PRAVIT SAMMAVONG.

Silkworm Books: 6 Thanon Sukkasem, T. Suthep, Muang, Chiang Mai 50200; tel. (53) 226-161; fax (53) 226-643; e-mail info@silkwormbooks.com; internet www.silkwormbooks.com; f. 1991; South-East Asian studies; English language.

Suksapan Panit (Business Organization of Teachers' Institute): 128/1 Thanon Ratchasima, Bangkok 10300; tel. (2) 416-7403; internet www.suksapan.or.th; f. 1950; general, textbooks, children's, pocket books; Pres. PANOM KAW KAMNERD.

Suriyabarn Publishers: 14 Thanon Pramuan, Bangkok 10500; tel. (2) 234-7991; f. 1953; religion, literature, Thai culture; Man. Dir PRASIT SAETANG.

Thai Watana Panich: 905 Thanon Rama 3, Yannawa, Bangkok 10120; tel. (2) 683-3333; fax (2) 683-2000; e-mail webmaster@twp.co.th; internet www.twp.co.th; children's, school textbooks; Man. Dir INTIRA BUNNAG.

Watana Panit Printing and Publishing Co Ltd: 31/1–2 Soi Siripat, Thanon Mahachai, Samranrat, Pranakorn, Bangkok 10120; tel. (2) 222-1016; fax (2) 225-6556; school textbooks; Man. ROENGCHAI CHONGPIPATANASOOK.

White Lotus Co Ltd: 14 Soi Huay Yai Chin, Pattaya, Banglamung, Chonburi 20150; tel. (3) 823-9883; fax (3) 823-9885; e-mail ande@loxinfo.co.th; internet whitelotusbooks.com; f. 1972; regional interests, incl. art and culture, history, sociology and natural history; Publr DIETHARD ANDE.

PUBLISHERS' ASSOCIATION

Publishers' and Booksellers' Association of Thailand (PUBAT): 83/159 Moo 6, Thanon Ngam Wong Wan, Thung Song Hong, Lak Si, Bangkok 10210; tel. (2) 954-9560; fax (2) 954-9565; e-mail info@pubat.or.th; internet www.pubat.or.th; f. 1960; organizes national book fairs and provides promotional opportunities for publishers; Pres. THANACHAI SANTICHAIKUL; Gen. Sec. WORAPHAN LOKITSATHAPORN.

Broadcasting and Communications

TELECOMMUNICATIONS

National Telecommunications Commission (NTC): 87 Thanon Phaholyotin, Soi 8, Phayatai, Bangkok 10400; tel. (2) 271-3511; fax (2) 290-5240; e-mail prnews@ntc.or.th; internet www.ntc.or.th; f. 2004; responsible for regulation and administration of telecommunications industry; Chair. Gen. CHOOCHART PROMPRASITM; Sec.-Gen. SURANAN WONGVITHAYAKAMJORN.

Advanced Info Service Public Co Ltd: 414 Thanon Phaholyotin, Shinawatra Tower I, Phayathai, Bangkok 10400; tel. (2) 299-5000; fax (2) 299-5719; e-mail callcenter@ais.co.th; internet www.aisco.th; mobile telephone network operator providing 3G (third generation) cellular services; CEO VIKROM SRIPRATAKS; Chair. SOMPRASONG BOONYACHAI.

CAT Telecom Public Co Ltd: 99 Thanon Changwattana, Laksi, Bangkok 10210; tel. (2) 573-0099; fax (2) 574-6054; e-mail pr@cattelecom.com; internet www.cattelecom.com; f. 2003 following division of Communications Authority of Thailand (CAT); state-owned; telephone operator; privatized in 2004; Chair. KRAISORN PORNSUTEE.

Samart Corpn Public Co Ltd: 99/1 Moo 4, Software Park Bldg, 35th Floor, Thanon Chaengwattana, Klong Gluar, Pak-kred, Nonthaburi 11120; tel. (2) 502-6000; fax (2) 502-6043; e-mail nikhila@samartcorp.com; internet www.samartcorp.com; f. 1952; telecommunications installation and distribution; Hon. Chair. CHERDCHAI VILAILUCK; Chair. PICHAI VASANASONG.

Thai Telephone and Telecommunication Public Co Ltd (TT&T): 252/30 Muang Thai Phatra Complex Tower 1, 24th Floor, Thanon Ratchadaphisek, Huay Kwang, Bangkok 10320; tel. (2) 693-2100; fax (2) 693-2124; e-mail ir@ttt.co.th; internet www.ttt.co.th; f. 1992; distributors of telecommunications equipment and services; Chair. SONGRIT KUSOMROSANANAN; Pres. PRACHUAB TANTINONDA.

Thailand Post Co Ltd: 111 Moo 3, Thanon Chaengwattana, Thung Song Hong, Laksi, Bangkok 10210; tel. (2) 831-3131; fax (2) 831-3514; e-mail contact@thailandpost.co.th; internet www.thailandpost.com; f. 2003; Chair. PHAWORN PANICHAPHAN; Man. Dir ORMSIN CHEEWAPRUEK.

TOT Public Co Ltd: 89/2 Moo 3, Thanon Chaengwattana, Thungsonghong, Laksi, Bangkok 10210; tel. (2) 505-1000; e-mail prtot@tot.co.th; internet www.tot.co.th; state-owned; f. 2002; fmrly Telephone Organization of Thailand; name changed to TOT Corpn Public Co Ltd; name changed as above in 2005; telephone operator; de facto regulator; scheduled for transfer to private sector; Chair. Prof. THEERAYUT BUNYASOPORN; Pres. WARUT SUWAKORN (acting).

Total Access Communications Public Co Ltd: Chai Bldg, 19th Floor, 333/3 Moo 4, Thanon Vibhavadi Rangsit, Ladyao Chatuchak, Bangkok 10900; tel. (2) 202-87000; fax (2) 202-8102; e-mail feedback@dtac.co.th; internet www.dtac.co.th; f. 1989; mobile telephone network operator; 41.46% owned by United Communication Industry Public Co Ltd; 29.94% owned by Telenor Asia Pte Ltd; Chair. BOONCHAI BENCHARONGKUL; CEO SIGVE BREKKE.

True Corpn PCL: 18 True Tower, Thanon Ratchadaphisek, Huay Khwang, Bangkok 10310; tel. (2) 643-1111; fax (2) 643-9669; internet www.truecorp.co.th/eng/index.jsp; f. 1990 under the name Telecomasia Corpn PCL; name changed as above in 2004; telecommunications services; Chair. DHANIN CHEARAVANONT; Pres. and CEO SUPACHAI CHEARAVANONT.

True Move: 18 True Tower, Thanon Ratchadaphisek, Huai Khwang, Bangkok 10310; tel. (2) 647-5000; internet www.truemove.com; f. 2002; fmrly TA Orange Co Ltd; name changed as above in 2005; mobile telephone network operator; Chief Exec. SUPACHAI CHEARAVANONT; 2,800 employees.

United Communication Industry Public Co Ltd (UCOM): 333/3 Chai Bldg, 18th Floor, Thanon Vibhavadi Rangsit, Ladyao, Chatuchak, Bangkok 10900; tel. (2) 202-8000; fax (2) 202-8929; e-mail ir.ucom@dtac.co.th; internet www.ucom.co.th; telecommunications service provider; Chair. SRIBHUMI SUKHANETR; Pres. and Chief Exec. BOONCHAI BENCHARONGKUL.

BROADCASTING

Regulatory Authority

Radio and Television Executive Committee (RTEC): Programme, Administration and Law Section, Division of RTEC Works, Government Public Relations Dept, Thanon Ratchadamnoen Klang, Phra Nakhon Region, Bangkok 10200; constituted under the Broadcasting and TV Rule 1975, the committee consists of 17 representatives from 14 government agencies and controls the administrative, legal, technical and programming aspects of broadcasting in Thailand; regulatory functions were assumed by the National Broadcasting Commission; Dir-Gen. BOWON TECHAINDRA.

Radio

Radio Thailand (RTH): National Broadcasting Services of Thailand, Government Public Relations Dept, Soi Aree Sampan, Thanon Phra Ram VI, Khet Phayathai, Bangkok 10400; tel. (2) 618-2323; fax (2) 618-2340; internet www.prd.go.th/mcic/radio.htm; f. 1930; govt-controlled; educational, entertainment, cultural and news programmes; operates 109 stations throughout Thailand; Dir of Radio Thailand PAITOON SRIRAWD.

Home Service: 12 stations in Bangkok and 97 affiliated stations in 50 provinces; operates three programmes; Dir CHAIVICHIT ATISAB.

THAILAND

External Services: f. 1928; in Thai, English, French, Vietnamese, Khmer, Japanese, Burmese, Lao, Malay, Chinese (Mandarin), German and Bahasa Indonesia; Dir AMPORN SAMOSORN.

Ministry of Education Broadcasting Service: Centre for Innovation and Technology, Ministry of Education, Bangkok; tel. (2) 246-0026; f. 1954; morning programmes for schools (Mon.–Fri.); afternoon and evening programmes for general public (daily); Dir of Centre PISAN SIWAYABRAHM.

Pituksuntirad Radio Stations: stations at Bangkok, Nakorn Rachasima, Chiangmai, Pitsanuloke and Songkla; programmes in Thai; Dir-Gen. PAITOON WAIJANYA.

Radio Saranrom: Thanon Ratchadamnoen, POB 2-131, Bangkok 10200; tel. (2) 224-4904; fax (2) 226-1825; internet www.mfa.go.th/web/151.php; f. 1968 as Voice of Free Asia; name changed as above in 1998; operated by the Ministry of Foreign Affairs; broadcasts in Thai; Dir of Broadcasting PAIBOON KUSKUL.

Television

Bangkok Broadcasting & TV Co Ltd (Channel 7): 998/1 Soi Sirimitr, Phaholyothin, Talad Mawchid, POB 456, Bangkok 10900; tel. (2) 272-0201; fax (2) 272-0010; e-mail prdept@ch7.com; internet www.ch7.com; commercial.

Bangkok Entertainment Co Ltd (Channel 3): 3199 Maleenont Tower, Thanon Phra Ram IV, Klong Ton, Klongtoey, Bangkok 10110; tel. (2) 204-3333; fax (2) 204-1384; e-mail internet@thaitv3.com; internet www.thaitv3.com; Programme Dir PRAVIT MALEENONT.

The Mass Communication Organization of Thailand (Modernine TV): 222 Thanon Asoke-Dindaeng, Bangkok 10300; tel. (2) 201-6000; fax (2) 245-1855; e-mail webmaster@mcot.net; internet www.mcot.net; f. 1952 as Thai Television Co Ltd; colour service; also operates radio stations and news agency; Dir-Gen. WASANT PAILEEKLEE.

National Broadcasting of Thailand (NBT): Public Relations Dept, Fortune Town Bldg, 26th Floor, Thanon Ratchadaphisek, Huay Kwang, Bangkok 10310; tel. and fax (2) 248-1601; internet www.prd.go.th/p_link/pr_tv.php; f. 1985; fmrly Channel 11; Dir-Gen. SURIN PLAENGPRASOPCHOK.

The Royal Thai Army Television HSA-TV (Channel 5): 210 Thanon Phaholyothin, Sanam Pao, Bangkok 10400; tel. (2) 227-0060; fax (2) 271-0930; e-mail webadmin@tv5.co.th; internet www.tv5.co.th; f. 1958; operates channels nation-wide; Dir-Gen. Maj.-Gen. KITTITAT PANECHAPHAN.

Thai Public Broadcasting Service: 1010 Shinwatra Tower III, Thanon Vibhavadi Rangsit, Chatuchak, Bangkok 10900; tel. (2) 791-1000; fax (2) 791-1010; e-mail webmaster@thaipbs.or.th; internet www.thaipbs.or.th; f. 2008; succeeded the former iTV.

Thai TV Global Network: c/o Royal Thai Army HSA-TV, 210 Thanon Phaholyothin, Sanam Pao, Bangkok 10400; tel. (2) 278-1697; fax (2) 615-2066; e-mail tgn@tv5.co.th; internet www.thaitvglobal.com; established with the co-operation of all stations; distributes selected news, information and entertainment programmes from domestic stations for transmission to 170 countries world-wide via six satellite networks; Chair. Maj.-Gen. SOONTHORN SOPHONSIRI.

Finance

(cap. = capital; p.u. = paid up; res = reserves; dep. = deposits; m. = million; brs = branches; amounts in baht)

BANKING

Central Bank

Bank of Thailand: 273 Thanon Samsen, Bangkhunprom, Bangkok 10200; tel. (2) 283-5353; fax (2) 280-0449; e-mail webmaster@bot.or.th; internet www.bot.or.th; f. 1942; bank of issue; cap. 20m., res 7,688.0m., dep. 419,905m. (Dec. 2006); Gov. TARISA WATANAGASE; 4 brs.

Commercial Banks

Bangkok Bank Public Co Ltd: 333 Thanon Silom, Bangrak, Bangkok 10500; tel. (2) 231-4333; fax (2) 231-4742; e-mail info@bangkokbank.com; internet www.bangkokbank.com; f. 1944; cap. 19,088.4m., res 117,485.7m., dep. 1,276,984.2m. (Dec. 2005); 49% foreign-owned; Chair. CHARTRI SOPHONPANICH; Pres. CHARTSIRI SOPHONPANICH; 656 local brs, 22 overseas brs.

Bank of Ayudhya Public Co Ltd: 1222 Thanon Rama III, Bang Phongphang, Yan Nawa, Bangkok 10120; tel. (2) 296-2000; fax (2) 683-1484; e-mail webmaster@krungsri.com; internet www.krungsri.com; f. 1945; cap. 29,408.1m., res 11,010.0m., dep. 583,480.5m. (Dec. 2006); Pres. JAMLONG ATIKUL; Chair. KRIT RATANARAK; 384 local brs, 3 overseas brs.

BankThai Public Co Ltd: 44 Thanon Sathorn Nua, Silom, Bangrak, Bangkok 10500; tel. (2) 638-8000; fax (2) 633-9026; e-mail webmaster@bankthai.co.th; internet www.bankthai.co.th; f. 1998; cap. 14,935m., res −3,601m., dep. 252,913m. (Dec. 2005); Chair. TAWEE BUTSUNTORN; Pres. PHIRASILP SUBHAPHOLSIRI; 98 brs.

Kasikorn Bank Public Co Ltd: 1 Soi Kasikornthai, Thanon Ratburana, Bangkok 10140; tel. (2) 888-8800; fax (2) 888-8882; e-mail info@kasikornbank.com; internet www.kasikornbank.com; f. 1945; fmrly Thai Farmers Bank Public Co Ltd; name changed as above April 2003; cap. 23,821m., res 29,790m., dep. 776,929m. (Dec. 2006); 48.98% foreign-owned; Chair. BANYONG LAMSAM; CEO BANTHOON LAMSAM; Pres. Dr PRASARN TRAIRATVORAKUL; 508 local brs, 4 overseas brs.

Kiatnakin Bank Public Co Ltd: Amarin Tower, 12th Floor, 500 Thanon Ploenchit, Pathumwan, Bangkok 10330; tel. (2) 680-3333; fax (2) 256-9933; internet www.kiatnakinbank.com; f. 1971 under the name Kiatnakin Finance and Securities Co Ltd; name changed in 1999 to Kiatnakin Finance Public Co Ltd following separation of its finance and securities businesses; name changed as above in 2005; Chair. NAWAAPORN RYANSKUL; Pres. TAWATCHAI SUDTIKITPISAIN; 16 brs.

Krung Thai Bank Public Co Ltd (State Commercial Bank of Thailand): 35 Thanon Sukhumvit, Klongtoey, Bangkok 10110; tel. (2) 255-2222; fax (2) 255-9391; e-mail call@contactcenter.ktb.co.th; internet www.ktb.co.th; f. 1966; cap. 57,604.0m., res 6,629.5m., dep. 1,019,299.8m. (Dec. 2006); taken under the control of the central bank in 1998, pending transfer to private sector; merged with First Bangkok City Bank Public Co Ltd in 1999; Chair. SUPARUT KAWATKUL; Pres. APISAK TANTIVORAWONG; 511 local brs, 12 overseas brs.

Siam City Bank Public Co Ltd: 1101 Thanon Phetchaburi Tadmai, Bangkok 10400; tel. (2) 208-5000; fax (2) 253-1240; e-mail scibweb@scib.co.th; internet www.scib.co.th; f. 1941; cap. 21,128m., res 4,652m. (Dec. 2004), dep. 382,165m. (Dec. 2005); taken under the control of the central bank in Feb. 1998; merged with Bangkok Metropolitan Bank Public Co Ltd in April 2002; Chair. SOMPOL KIATPHAIBOOL; Pres. and CEO CHAIWAT UTAIWAN; 387 local brs, 1 overseas br.

Siam Commercial Bank Public Co Ltd: 9 Thanon Ratchadaphisek, Lardyao, Chatuchak, Bangkok 10900; tel. (2) 544-1000; fax (2) 937-7754; e-mail investor.relations@scb.co.th; internet www.scb.co.th; f. 1906; cap. and res 100,559.7m., dep. 792,081.4m. (Dec. 2006); Exec. Chair. Dr VICHIT SURAPHONGCHAI; Pres. and CEO KHUNYING JADA WATTANASIRITHAM; 477 local brs, 4 overseas brs.

Standard Chartered Bank (Thai) Public Co Ltd: 90 Thanon Sathorn Nua, Silom, Bangkok 10500; tel. (2) 724-4000; fax (2) 236-1968; internet www.standardchartered.co.th; f. 1933 as Wang Lee Bank Ltd, renamed 1985; cap. 11,386m., res 7,965m., dep. 102,022m. (July 2007); taken under the control of the central bank in July 1999, 75% share sold to Standard Chartered Bank (United Kingdom); name changed to Standard Chartered Nakornthon Bank PCL in 1999; name changed as above in 2005; Chair. KAIKHUSHRU SHIAVAX NORGALWALA; CEO MEE HAR FOO; 67 brs.

Thanachart Bank Public Co Ltd: 1st, 2nd, 14th and 15th Floors, Thonson Bldg, 900 Thanon Phoenchit, Lumpini, Patumwan, Bangkok 10330; tel. (2) 655-9000; fax (2) 655-9001; e-mail nfs_rb@nfs.co.th; f. 2002; Man. Dir SUVARNAPHA SUVARNAPRATHIP.

TMB Bank Public Co Ltd: 3000 Thanon Phahon Yothin, Ladyao, Chatuchak, Bangkok 10900; tel. (2) 299-1111; fax (2) 273-7121; e-mail ir@tmbbank.com; internet www.tmbbank.com; f. 1957; fmrly known as Thai Military Bank Public Co Ltd; name changed as above 2005; merged with DBS Thai Danu Bank Public Co Ltd and Industrial Finance Corpn of Thailand Sept. 2004; cap. 185,287.4m., res −77,767.2m., dep. 591,669.8m. (Dec. 2006); Chair. SOMCHAINUK ENGTRAKUL; Pres. and CEO SUBHAK SIWARAKSA; 367 local brs, 3 overseas brs.

United Overseas Bank (Thai) Public Co Ltd (UOBT): 191 Thanon Sathorn Tai, Bangkok 10120; tel. (2) 343-3000; fax (2) 287-2973; e-mail webmaster@uob.co.th; internet www.uob.co.th; f. 1998 as the result of the merger of Laem Thong Bank Ltd with Radanasin Bank; name changed to UOB Radanasin Bank Public Co Ltd in Nov. 1999; name changed as above in 2005 following merger with Bank of Asia Public Co Ltd; cap. 82,170.6m., res −24,071.9m., dep. 157,845.4m. (Dec. 2006); Chair. WEE CHO YAW; Pres. and CEO WONG KIM CHOONG; 154 brs.

Development Banks

Bank for Agriculture and Agricultural Co-operatives (BAAC): 469 Thanon Nakorn Sawan, Dusit, Bangkok 10300; tel. (2) 280-0180; fax (2) 280-0442; e-mail train@baac.or.th; internet www.baac.or.th; f. 1966 to provide credit for agriculture; cap. and res 49,911m., dep. 431,401m. (March 2006); Exec. Chair. VARATHEP RATANAKORN; Pres. TANGTHIRASUNAN THIRAPHONG; 491 brs.

THAILAND

Export-Import Bank of Thailand (EXIM THAILAND): EXIM Bldg, 1193 Thanon Phaholyothin, Phayathai, Bangkok 10400; tel. (2) 271-3700; fax (2) 271-3204; e-mail info@exim.go.th; internet www.exim.go.th; f. 1993; provides financial services to Thai exporters and Thai investors investing abroad; cap. 6,500m., res 1,877m., dep. 12,509m. (Dec. 2006); Chair. NARONGCHAI AKRASANEE; Pres. APICHAI BOONTHERAWARA; 9 brs.

Government Housing Bank: 63 Thanon Rama IX, Huay Kwang, Bangkok 10310; tel. (2) 645-9000; fax (2) 246-1789; e-mail crm@ghb.co.th; internet www.ghb.co.th; f. 1953 to provide housing finance; Chair. WISUDHI SRISUPHAN; Pres. KHAN PRACHUABMOH; 120 brs.

Small and Medium Enterprise Development Bank of Thailand: 9th Floor, Siripinyo Bldg, 475 Thanon Sri Ayudhaya, Rajtavee, Bangkok 10400; tel. (2) 201-3700; fax (2) 201-3723; e-mail sme@smebank.co.th; internet www.smebank.co.th; f. under above name in 2002; fmrly Small Industries Finance Office, which became Small Industrial Finance Co Ltd in 1991; Chair. NIMMANHAEMIN PIYABHAN.

Savings Bank

Government Savings Bank: 470 Thanon Phaholyothin, Phayathai, Bangkok 10400; tel. (2) 299-8000; fax (2) 299-8490; e-mail vicheal@gsb.or.th; internet www.gsb.or.th; f. 1913; cap. 0.1m., res 8,765m., dep. 538,823m. (Dec. 2005); Chair. SOMCHAINUK ENGTRAKUL; Dir-Gen. Dr CHARNCHAI MUSIGNISARKORN; 578 brs.

Bankers' Association

Thai Bankers' Association: Lake Rachada Office Complex, Bldg 2, 4th Floor, 195/5–7 Thanon Ratchadaphisek, Klongtoey, Bangkok 10110; tel. (2) 264-0883; fax (2) 264-0888; e-mail infodesk@tba.or.th; internet www.tba.or.th; f. 1958; Chair. APISAK TANTIVORAWONG.

STOCK EXCHANGE

Stock Exchange of Thailand (SET): The Stock Exchange of Thailand Bldg, 62 Thanon Ratchadaphisek, Klongtoey, Bangkok 10110; tel. (2) 229-2000; fax (2) 654-5649; e-mail infoproducts@set.or.th; internet www.set.or.th; f. 1975; 27 mems; Pres. PATAREEYA BENJAPOLCHAI; Chair. PAKORN MALAKUL NA AYUDHYA.

Securities and Exchange Commission: Diethelm Towers B, 10th/13th–16th Floors, 93/1 Thanon Witthayu, Lumpini, Patumwan, Bangkok 10330; tel. (2) 695-9999; fax (2) 256-7711; e-mail info@sec.or.th; internet www.sec.or.th; f. 1992; supervises new share issues and trading in existing shares; chaired by Minister of Finance; Sec.-Gen. THIRACHAI PHUVANAT NARANUBULA.

INSURANCE

In March 1997 the Government granted licences to 12 life assurance companies and 16 general insurance companies, bringing the total number of life insurance companies to 25 and non-life insurance companies to 83.

Selected Insurance Companies

Aioi Bangkok Insurance Co Ltd: 22nd Floor, Bangkok Insurance/YMCA Bldg, 25 Thanon Sathorn Tai, Thungmahamek, Sathorn, Bangkok 10120; tel. (2) 620-8000; fax (2) 677-3978-9; e-mail center@aioibkkins.co.th; f. 1951; fmrly known as Wilson Insurance Co Ltd; fire, marine, motor car, general; CEO YOSHIHIKO FUKASAWA; Pres. NOPADOL SANTIPAKORN.

American International Assurance Co Ltd: American International Tower, 181 Thanon Surawongse, Bangkok 10500; tel. (2) 634-8888; fax (2) 236-6452; e-mail bkk.group@aig.com; internet www.aia.co.th; f. 1983; ordinary and group life, group and personal accident, credit, life; Exec. Vice-Pres. and Gen. Man. DHADOL BUNNAG.

Ayudhya Insurance Public Co Ltd: Ploenchit Tower, 7th Floor, Thanon Ploenchit, Pathumwan, Bangkok 10300; tel. (2) 263-0335; fax (2) 263-0589; e-mail info@ayud.co.th; internet www.ayud.co.th; non-life; Chair. VERAPHAN TEEPSUWAN; Pres. ROWAN D'ARCY.

Bangkok Insurance Public Co Ltd: Bangkok Insurance Bldg, 25 Thanon Sathorn Tai, Bangkok 10120; tel. (2) 285-8888; fax (2) 677-3737; e-mail corp.comm1@bki.co.th; internet www.bki.co.th; f. 1947; non-life; Chair. and Pres. CHAI SOPHONPANICH.

Bangkok Union Insurance Public Co Ltd: 175–177 Bangkok Union Insurance Bldg, Thanon Surawongse, Bangrak, Bangkok 10500; tel. (2) 233-6920; fax (2) 237-1856; e-mail underwrite@bui.co.th; internet www.bui.co.th; f. 1929; non-life; Chair. MANU LIEWPAIROT.

China Insurance Co (Siam) Ltd: 36/68–69, 20th Floor, PS Tower, Thanon Asoke, Sukhumvit 21, Bangkok 10110; tel. (2) 259-3718; fax (2) 259-1402; f. 1948; non-life; Chair. JAMES C. CHENG; Man. Dir FANG RONG-CHENG.

Indara Insurance Public Co Ltd: 364/29 Thanon Si Ayutthaya, Ratchthewi, Bangkok 10400; tel. (2) 247-9261; fax (2) 247-9260; e-mail contact@indara.co.th; internet www.indara.co.th; f. 1949; non-life; Chair. PRATIP WONGNIRUND; Man. Dir SUCHART TRISIRIWETAWATTANA.

Mittare Insurance Co Ltd: 295 Thanon Si Phraya, Bangrak, Bangkok 10500; tel. (2) 237-4646; fax (2) 236-1376; internet www.mittare.com; f. 1947; life, fire, marine, health, personal accident, automobile and general; fmrly Thai Prasit Insurance Co Ltd; Chair. SURACHAN CHANSRICHAWLA; Man. Dir SUKHATHEP CHANSRICHAWLA.

Navakij Insurance Public Co Ltd: 90/4-6, 100/50-55 Sathorn Nakorn Tower, Thanon Sathorn Nua, Silom, Bangrak, Bangkok 10500; tel. (2) 636-7900; fax (2) 636-7997; internet www.navakij.co.th; f. 1933; Pres. NIPHON TANGJEERAWONGSA.

Ocean Life Insurance Co Ltd: 170/74–83 Ocean Tower I Bldg, Thanon Rachadapisek, Klongtoey, Bangkok 10110; tel. (2) 261-2300; fax (2) 261-3344; e-mail info@oli.co.th; internet www.oli.co.th; f. 1949; life; Chair. KIRATI ASSAKUL; Man. Dir DAYANA BUNNAG.

Paiboon Insurance Co Ltd: Thai Life Insurance Bldg, 19th–20th Floors, 123 Thanon Ratchadapisek, Bangkok 10310; tel. (2) 246-9635; fax (2) 246-9660; f. 1927; non-life; Chair. ANUTHRA ASSAWANONDA; Pres. VANICH CHAIYAWAN.

Prudential TS Life Assurance Public Co Ltd: Sengthong Thani Tower, 28th, 30th and 31st Floors, 82 Thanon Sathorn Nua, Bangkok 10500; tel. (2) 639-9500; fax (2) 639-9699; e-mail customer.service.ptsl@ibm.net; internet www.prudential.co.th; f. 1983; Chair. BURAPHA ATTHAKON; Man. Dir TED C. RIDGEWAY.

Siam Commercial New York Life Insurance Public Co Ltd: 4th Floor, SCB Bldg 1, 1060 Thanon Phetchaburi, SCB Chidlom, Ratchathewi, Bangkok 10400; tel. (2) 655-3000; fax (2) 256-1517; e-mail customerservice@scnyl.com; internet www.scnyl.com; f. 1976; life; Chair. and CEO KANNIKA CHALITAPHORN.

Southeast Insurance (2000) Co Ltd (Arkanay Prakan Pai Co Ltd): Southeast Insurance Bldg, 315G, 1–3 Thanon Silom, Bangrak, Bangkok 10500; tel. (2) 631-1331; internet www.seic2000.com; f. 1946; life and non-life; Chair. CHAYUT CHIRALERSPONG; Gen. Man. WICHAI INTARANUKULAKIJ.

Syn Mun Kong Insurance Public Co Ltd: 279 Thanon Srinakarin, Bangkapi, Bangkok 10240; tel. (2) 379-3140; fax (2) 731-6590; e-mail info@smk.co.th; internet www.smk.co.th; f. 1951; fire, marine, automobile and personal accident; Chair. RUENGWIT DUSADEESURAPOJ; Man. Dir RUENGDEJ DUSADEESURAPOJ.

Thai Health Insurance Co Ltd: 31st Floor, RS Tower, 121/89 Thanon Ratchadapisek, Din-Daeng, Bangkok 10400; tel. (2) 642-3100; fax (2) 642-3130; e-mail info@thaihealth.co.th; internet www.thaihealth.co.th; f. 1979; Chair. APIRAK THAIPATANAGUL; Man. Dir VARANG SRETHBHAKDI.

Thai Insurance Public Co Ltd: 34/3 Soi Lang Suan, Thanon Ploenchit, Lumpini, Pathumwan, Bangkok 10330; tel. (2) 613-0100; fax (2) 652-2870; e-mail tic@thaiins.com; internet www.thaiins.com; f. 1938; non-life; Chair. KAVI ANSVANANDA.

Thai Life Insurance Co Ltd: 123 Thanon Ratchadapisek, Din-Daeng, Bangkok 10400; tel. (2) 247-0247; fax (2) 246-9945; internet www.thailife.com; f. 1942; life; Chair. and CEO VANICH CHAIYAWAN.

ThaiSri Insurance Co Ltd: 126/2 Thanon Krunthonburi, Klongsam, Bangkok 10600; tel. (2) 878-7111; fax (2) 860-7365; e-mail info@thaisri.com; internet www.thaisri.com; f. 1997; personal accident, automobile, fire, marine; jt venture between Thai Metropole Insurance and Zurich Financial Services Group (Switzerland); Chair. SIRIN NIMMANAHAEMINDA; Pres. NATEE PANICHEWA.

Viriyah Insurance Co Ltd: RS Tower, 121/7 Thanon Ratchadapisek, Din-Daeng, Bangkok 10320; tel. (2) 239-1000; fax (2) 641-3902; e-mail info@viriyah.co.th; internet www.viriyah.co.th; f. 1947; Chair. JARE CHUTHARATTANAKUL; Man. Dir SUVAPORN THONGTHEW.

Associations

General Insurance Association: 223 Soi Ruamrudee, Thanon Witthayu, Bangkok 10330; tel. (2) 256-6032; fax (2) 256-6039; e-mail general@thaigia.com; internet www.thaigia.com; Pres. SUCHIN WANGLEE; Sec.-Gen. JEERAPHAN ASAWATHANAKUL; 71 mems.

Thai Life Assurance Association: 36/1 Soi Sapanku, Thanon Rama IV, Thungmahamek, Sathorn, Bangkok 10120; tel. (2) 287-4596; fax (2) 679-7100; e-mail tlaa@tlaa.org; internet www.tlaa.org; Pres. SARA LAMSAM; Sec.-Gen. PHERAPONG UNCHIT; 25 mems.

Trade and Industry

GOVERNMENT AGENCIES

Board of Investment (BOI): 555 Thanon Vibhavadi Rangsit, Chatuchak, Bangkok 10900; tel. (2) 537-8111; fax (2) 537-8177; e-mail head@boi.go.th; internet www.boi.go.th; f. 1958; formed to publicize investment potential and encourage economically and

THAILAND

socially beneficial investments and also to provide investment information; chaired by the Prime Minister; Sec.-Gen. SATIT CHANJAVANAKUL.

Board of Trade of Thailand: 150/2 Thanon Rajbopit, Bangkok 10200; tel. (2) 622-1860; fax (2) 225-3372; internet www.thaiechamber.com; f. 1955; mems: chambers of commerce, trade asscns, state enterprises and co-operative societies (large and medium-sized companies have associate membership); Chair. AIVA TAULANANDA.

Financial Sector Restructuring Authority (FSRA): 130–132 Tower 3, Thanon Witthayu, Patumwan, Bangkok 10330; tel. (2) 263-2620; fax (2) 650-9872; f. 1997 to oversee the restructuring of Thailand's financial system; Chair. KAMOL JUNTIMA; Sec.-Gen. MONTRI CHENVIDAYAKAM.

Forest Industry Organization: 76 Thanon Ratchadamnoen Nok, Bangkok 10100; tel. (2) 282-3243; fax (2) 282-5197; e-mail info@fio.co.th; internet www.fio.co.th; f. 1947; oversees all aspects of forestry and wood industries; Man. MANOONSAK TONTIWIWATTANA.

Office of the Cane and Sugar Board: Ministry of Industry, Thanon Phra Ram Hok, Bangkok 10400; tel. (2) 202-3291; fax (2) 202-3293; e-mail ocsb0601@ocsb.go.th; internet www.ocsb.go.th; Sec.-Gen. RATTANAPORN CHUENGSANGUANSIT.

Rubber Estate Organization: Nabon Station, Nakhon Si Thammarat Province 80220; tel. (75) 411554; e-mail reothai@reothai.co.th; internet www.reothai.co.th; Man. Dir CHAIROJ THAMMARATTANA (acting).

DEVELOPMENT AGENCIES

National Economic and Social Development Board: 962 Thanon Krung Kasem, Bangkok 10100; tel. (2) 282-8454; fax (2) 281-3938; e-mail mis@nesdb.go.th; internet www.nesdb.go.th; economic and social planning agency; Sec.-Gen. AMPON KITTI-AMPON.

Royal Developments Projects Board: Office of the Prime Minister, Government House, Thanon Nakhon Pathom, Bangkok 10300; tel. (2) 280-6193; e-mail webmaster@rdpb.go.th; internet www.rdpb.go.th; Sec.-Gen. SOMPOL PANMANEE.

CHAMBER OF COMMERCE

Thai Chamber of Commerce: 150 Thanon Rajbopit, Bangkok 10200; tel. (2) 622-1880; fax (2) 225-3372; e-mail tcc@thaiechamber.com; internet www.thaiechamber.com; f. 1946; 2,000 mems, 10 assoc. mems (1998); Chair. PRAMON SUTIVONG; Pres. VICHIEN TEJAPHAIBOON.

INDUSTRIAL AND TRADE ASSOCIATIONS

The Federation of Thai Industries: Queen Sirikit National Convention Center, Zone C, 4th Floor, 60 Thanon Ratchadaphisek Tadmai, Klongtoey, Bangkok 10110; tel. (2) 345-1000; fax (2) 345-1296; e-mail information@off.fti.or.th; internet www.fti.or.th; f. 1987; fmrly The Association of Thai Industries; 4,800 mems; Chair. SANTI WILATSAKDANON.

Mining Industry Council of Thailand: Soi 222/2, Thai Chamber of Commerce University, Thanon Vibhavadi Rangsit, Din-Daeng, Bangkok 10400; tel. (2) 275-7684; fax (2) 692-3321; e-mail miningthai@miningthai.org; internet www.miningthai.org; f. 1983; intermediary between govt organizations and private mining enterprises; Chair. YONGYOTH PETCHSUWAN; Sec.-Gen. ORANUCH RAMAKOMUT.

Rice Exporters' Association of Thailand: 37 Soi Ngamdupli, Thanon Phra Rama IV, Tungmahamek, Sathorn, Bangkok 10120; tel. (2) 287-2674; fax (2) 287-2678; e-mail contact@riceexporters.or.th; internet www.riceexporters.or.th; Pres. CHOOKIERT OPHASAWONG; Sec.-Gen. KORBSUK IEMSURI.

Sawmills Association: 101 Thanon Amnuaysongkhram, Dusit, Bangkok 10300; tel. (2) 243-4754; fax (2) 243-8629; e-mail info@thaisawmills.com; internet www.thaisawmills.com; Pres. SURASAK IEMDEENGAMLERT.

Thai Coffee Exporters Association: 1302–1306 Thanon Songwad, Samphantawong, Bangkok 10100; tel. (2) 221-1264; fax (2) 225-1962; e-mail cofexpo@cscoms.com.

Thai Contractors' Association: 110 Thanon Witthayu, Bangkok 10330; tel. (2) 251-0697; fax (2) 255-3990; e-mail webmaster@tca.or.th; internet www.tca.or.th; f. 1928 under the name The Engineering Association of Siam; name changed to The Engineering Contractors Asscn in 1967 and as above in 1983; Pres. POLPAT KARNASUTA; Sec.-Gen. ANGSURAS AREEKUL.

Thai Diamond Manufacturers Association: 87/139–40, Modern Town Bldg, 18/F, Soi Ekamai 3, Thanon Sukhumvit 63, Klong Ton Nua, Wattana, Bangkok 10110; tel. (2) 390-0341; fax (2) 711-4039; e-mail odtcbkk@loxinfo.co.th; internet www.thaidiamonds.org; 11-mem. board; Pres. CHIRAKITTI TANGKATHAC.

Thai Food Processors' Association: Tower 1, Ocean Bldg, 9th Floor, 170/21–22 Thanon Rajchadapisaktadmai, Klongtoey, Bangkok 10110; tel. (2) 261-2684; fax (2) 261-2996; e-mail thaifood@thaifood.org; internet www.thaifood.org; Pres. VILAI KIATSRICHART.

Thai Lac Association: 57/1 Soi Saphantia, Thanon Sipraya, Mahapreuktaram, Bangrak, Bangkok 10500; tel. (2) 233-4583; fax (2) 633-2913.

Thai Maize and Produce Traders' Association: Sathorn Thani II Bldg, 11th Floor, 92/26–27 Thanon Sathorn Nua, Bangrak, Bangkok 10500; tel. (2) 234-4387; fax (2) 236-8413.

Thai Pharmaceutical Manufacturers Association: 188/107 Thanon Charansanitwongs, Banchanglaw, Bangkoknoi, Bangkok 10700; tel. (2) 863-5106; fax (2) 863-5108; e-mail tpma@asiaaccess.net.th; f. 1969; Pres. CHERNPORN TENGAMNUAY.

Thai Rice Mills Association: 81–81/1 Trok Rongnamkheng, 24 Thanon Charoenkrung, Talat Noi, Sampanthawong, Bangkok 10100; internet www.thairicemillers.com; tel. (2) 235-7863; fax (2) 234-7286; Pres. WATTANA RATTANAWONG.

Thai Rubber Association: 45–47 Thanon Chotivithayakun 3, Hat Yai, Songkhla 90110; tel. (74) 429-011; fax (74) 429-312; e-mail webmaster@thainr.com; internet www.thainr.com; f. 1951; est. as Thai Rubber Traders' Asscn; Pres. LUKCHAI KITTIPHOL.

Thai Silk Association: Textile Industry Division, Soi Trimitr, Thanon Rama IV, Klongtoey, Bangkok 10110; tel. (2) 712-4328; fax (2) 258-8769; e-mail thsilkas@thaitextile.org; internet www.thaitextile.org/tsa; f. 1962; Pres. SETR VANIJVONGSE.

Thai Sugar Manufacturing Association: 78 Keatnakin Bldg, Captain Bush Lane, Thanon Charoenkrung, Bangkok 10500; tel. (2) 233-5858; fax (2) 233-4156; e-mail tsma2000@cscoms.com; internet www.thaisugar.org.

Thai Sugar Producers' Association: 8th Floor, Thai Ruam Toon Bldg, 794 Thanon Krung Kasem, Pomprap, Bangkok 10100; tel. (2) 282-0990; fax (2) 281-0342.

Thai Tapioca Trade Association: Sathorn Thani II Bldg, 20th Floor, 92/58 Thanon Sathorn Nua, Silom, Bangkok 10500; tel. (2) 234-4724; fax (2) 236-6084; e-mail ttta@loxinfo.co.th; internet www.ttta-tapioca.org; f. 1963; Pres. SUNAI SATHAPORN.

Thai Textile Manufacturing Association: 454–460 Thanon Sukhumvit, Klongton, Klongtoey, Bangkok 10110; tel. (2) 258-2023; fax (2) 260-1525; e-mail ttma@thaitextile.org; internet www.thaitextile.org/ttma; f. 1960; Pres. PHONGSAK ASSAKUL.

Union Textile Merchants' Association (Thai Textile Merchants' Association): 562 Espreme Bldg, 4th Floor, Thanon Rajchawong, Samphanthawong, Bangkok 10100; tel. (2) 622-6711; fax (2) 622-6714; e-mail tma@thaitextile.org; internet www.thaitextile.org/tma; Chair. THAVON TANTISIRIVIT.

UTILITIES

Electricity

Electricity Generating Authority of Thailand (EGAT): 53 Thanon Charan Sanit Wong, Bang Kruai, Nothaburi, Bangkok 11130; tel. (2) 436-0000; fax (2) 436-4723; e-mail webmaster@egat.co.th; internet www.egat.co.th; f. 1969; scheduled for transfer to the private sector in 2004; Gov. SOMBAT SANTIJAREE.

Electricity Generating Public Co Ltd (EGCO): EGCO Tower, 222 Moo 5, Thanon Vibhavadi Rangsit, Tungsonghong, Laksi, Bangkok 10210; tel. (2) 998-5999; fax (2) 955-0956; e-mail corp_com@egco.com; internet www.egco.com; a subsidiary of the Electricity Generating Authority of Thailand (EGAT); 59% transferred to the private sector in 1994–96; 14.9%-owned by China Light and Power Co (Hong Kong); Chair. PORNCHAI RUJIPRAPA; Pres. VISIT AKARAVINAK.

The Metropolitan Electricity Authority: 30 Soi Chidlom, Thanon Ploenchit, Lumpini, Pathumwan, Bangkok 10330; tel. (2) 254-9550; fax (2) 251-9586; internet www.mea.or.th; f. 1958; one of the two main power distribution agencies in Thailand; Gov. PORNTHAPE THUNYAPONGCHAI.

The Provincial Electricity Authority: 200 Thanon Ngam Wongwan, Chatuchak, Bangkok 10900; tel. (2) 589-0100; fax (2) 589-4850; e-mail webmaster@pea.co.th; internet www.pea.co.th; f. 1960; one of the two main power distribution agencies in Thailand; Gov. ADISORN KIERTICHOKWIWAT.

Water

Metropolitan Waterworks Authority: 18/137 Thanon Prachachuen, Don Muang, Bangkok 10210; tel. (2) 504-0123; fax (2) 503-9493; e-mail pubrela@mwa.co.th; internet www.mwa.co.th; f. 1967; state-owned; provides water supply systems in Bangkok; Gov. CHAROEN CHAIKITTISILPA.

Provincial Waterworks Authority: 72 Thanon Chaengwattana, Don Muang, Bangkok 10210; tel. (2) 551-1020; fax (2) 552-1547;

THAILAND

e-mail pr@pwa.co.th; internet www.pwa.co.th; f. 1979; provides water supply systems except in Bangkok Metropolis; Gov. CHAVALIT SARUN; Chair. SURA-AT THONGNIRAMOL.

CO-OPERATIVES

In January 2002 there were 5,617 co-operatives, with a combined membership in excess of 8m. people. Of the total number of co-operatives, 64% were in agriculture, 24% in thrift and credit, 8% in the consumer market and 4% in services.

TRADE UNIONS

Under the Labour Relations Act (1975), a minimum of 10 employees are required in order to form a union; by August 1997 there were an estimated 1,028 such unions.

Confederation of Thai Labour (CTL): 25/20 Thanon Sukhumvit, Viphavill Village, Tambol Paknam, Amphur Muang, Samutprakarn, Bangkok 10270; tel. (2) 756-5346; fax (2) 323-1074; internet www.ctl.or.th; represents 44 labour unions; Pres. MANAS PHOSORN.

Labour Congress of Thailand (LCT): 420/393–394 Thippavan Village 1, Thanon Teparak, Samrong-Nua, Muang, Samutprakarn, Bangkok 10270; tel. and fax (2) 384-6789; e-mail lct_org@hotmail.com; f. 1978; represents 224 labour unions, four labour federations and approx. 140,000 mems; Pres. PRATNENG SAENGSANK; Gen. Sec. SAMAM THOMYA.

National Congress of Private Employees of Thailand (NPET): 142/6 Thanon Phrathoonam Phrakanong, Phrakanong, Klongtoey, Bangkok 10110; tel. and fax (2) 392-9955; represents 31 labour unions; Pres. BANJONG PORNPATTANANIKOM.

National Congress of Thai Labour (NCTL): 1614/876 Samutprakarn Community Housing Project, Sukhumvit Highway Km 30, Tai Baan, Muang, Samutprakarn, Bangkok 10280; tel. (2) 389-5134; fax (2) 385-8975; represents 171 unions; Pres. PANAS THAILUAN.

National Free Labour Union Congress (NFLUC): 277 Moo 3, Thanon Ratburana, Bangkok 10140; tel. (2) 427-6506; fax (2) 428-4543; represents 51 unions; Pres. ANUSSAKDI BOONYAPRANAI.

National Labour Congress (NLC): 586/248–250 Moo 2, Mooban City Village, Thanon Sukhumvit, Bang Phu Mai, Mueng, Samutprakarn, Bangkok 10280; tel. and fax (2) 709-9426; represents 41 labour unions; Pres. CHIN THAPPHLI.

Thai Trade Union Congress (TTUC): 420/393–394 Thippavan Village 1, Thanon Teparak, Tambol Samrong-nua, Amphur Muang, Samutprakarn, Bangkok 10270; tel. and fax (2) 384-0438; f. 1983; represents 172 unions; Pres. PANIT CHAROENPHAO.

Thailand Council of Industrial Labour (TCIL): 99 Moo 4, Thanon Sukhaphibarn 2, Khannayao, Bungkum, Bangkok; tel. (2) 517-0022; fax (2) 517-0628; represents 23 labour unions; Pres. TAVEE DEEYING.

Transport

RAILWAYS

Thailand has a railway network of 4,429 km, connecting Bangkok with Chiang Mai, Nong Khai, Ubon Ratchathani, Nam Tok and towns on the isthmus.

State Railway of Thailand: 1 Thanon Rong Muang, Rong Muang, Pathumwan, Bangkok 10330; tel. (2) 220-4567; fax (2) 225-3801; e-mail info@railway.co.th; internet www.railway.co.th; f. 1897; 4,429 km of track in 2007; responsible for licensing a 4,044-km passenger and freight rail system, above ground; Chair. SIWA SAENGMANEE; Gov. BANCHA KONGNAKORN (acting).

Bangkok Mass Transit System Public Co Ltd: 1000 Thanon Phahonyothin, Lad Yao, Chatuchak, Bangkok 10900; tel. (2) 617-7300; fax (2) 617-7133; e-mail nuduan@bts.co.th; internet www.bts.co.th; f. 1992; responsible for the construction and management of the Skytrain, a two-line, 23.5-km elevated rail system, under the supervision of the Bangkok Metropolitan Area, the initial stage of which was opened in December 1999; Chair. KASAME CHATIKAVANIJ; Exec. Chair. and CEO KEEREE KANJANAPAS.

Mass Rapid Transit Authority of Thailand (MRTA): 175 Thanon Rama IX, Huay Kwang, Bangkok 10320; tel. (2) 612-2444; fax (2) 612-2436; e-mail pr@mrta.co.th; internet www.mrta.co.th; a 20-km subway system was opened in Bangkok in July 2004; as part of the planned extension of the mass rapid transit system to 291 km, was charged with the construction of three new lines, totalling 91 km in length: 27-km Blue Line (Hua Lamphong–Bang Khae; Bang Sue–Tha Phra); 24-km Orange Line (Bang Kapi–Bang Bumru); and 40-km Purple Line (Bang Yai–Rat Burana); Chair. KRIENGSAK LOHACHALA; Sec.-Gen. PRAPAT CHONGSANGUAN.

ROADS

The total length of the road network was an estimated 51,466 km in 2005. A network of toll roads has been introduced in Bangkok in an attempt to alleviate the city's severe congestion problems.

Bangkok Mass Transit Authority (BMTA): 131 Thanon Thiam Ruammit, Huay Kwang, Bangkok 10310; tel. (2) 246-0973; fax (2) 247-2189; e-mail cnai.bmta@motc.go.th; internet www.bmta.co.th; controls Bangkok's urban transport system; Chair. ATHIKHOM TONLES; Dir and Sec. SUKREE KHUMPHAN.

Department of Highways: Thanon Sri Ayudhaya, Ratchathevi, Bangkok 10400; tel. (2) 245-9912; e-mail doh9999@doh.go.th; internet www.doh.go.th; Dir-Gen. SONGSAK PHAECHAROEN.

Department of Land Transport: 1032 Thanon Phaholyothin, Chatuchak, Bangkok 10900; tel. (2) 272-5671; fax (2) 272-5680; e-mail admin@dlt.go.th; internet www.dlt.go.th; Dir-Gen. SILPACHAI CHARUKASEMRATTANA.

Department of Rural Roads: 218/1, Thanon Phra Ram VI, Phayathai, Bangkok 10400; tel. (2) 299-4591; fax (2) 299-4606; e-mail webmaster@dor.go.th; internet www.dor.go.th; f. 2002; Dir-Gen. RAPHIN CHARUTUL.

Expressway and Rapid Transit Authority of Thailand (ETA): 2380 Thanon Phaholyothin, Senanikhom, Chatuchak, Bangkok 10900; tel. (2) 579-5380; e-mail webmasters@eta.co.th; internet www.eta.co.th; f. 1972; Dir-Gen. PHACHOEN PHAIROJSAK.

SHIPPING

There is an extensive network of canals, providing transport for bulk goods. The port of Bangkok is an important shipping junction for South-East Asia, and consists of 37 berths for conventional and container vessels.

Marine Department: 1278 Thanon Yotha, Talardnoi, Samphanthawong, Bangkok 10100; tel. (2) 233-1311; fax (2) 236-7148; e-mail marine@md.go.th; internet www.md.go.th; Dir-Gen. TAWALYARAT ONSIRA.

Port Authority of Thailand: 444 Thanon Tarua, Klongtoey, Bangkok 10110; tel. (2) 269-3000; fax (2) 249-0885; e-mail patonline@port.co.th; internet www.port.co.th; 18 berths at Bangkok Port, 12 berths at Laem Chabang Port; originally scheduled for transfer to private sector in 1999, but plans have been repeatedly delayed; Chair. SATHIRAPAN KEYANONT; Dir-Gen. SUNIDA SAKULRATTANA.

Principal Shipping Companies

Jutha Maritime Public Co Ltd: Mano Tower, 2nd Floor, 153 Soi 39, Thanon Sukhumvit, Bangkok 10110; tel. (2) 260-0050; fax (2) 259-9825; e-mail office@jutha.co.th; internet www.jutha.co.th; services between Thailand, Malaysia, Korea, Japan and Viet Nam; Chair. Rear-Adm. CHANO CHENPENJATI; Man. Dir CHANET PHENJATI.

Precious Shipping Public Co Ltd: Cathay House, 7th Floor, 8/30 Thanon Sathorn Nua, Bangrak, Bangkok 10500; tel. (2) 696-8800; fax (2) 633-8460; e-mail psl@preciousshipping.com; internet www.preciousshipping.com; Chair. Adm. AMNARD CHANDANAMATTHA; Man. Dir HASHIM KHALID MOINUDDIN.

Regional Container Lines Public Co Ltd: Panjathani Tower, 30th Floor, 127/35 Thanon Ratchadaphisek, Chongnonsee Yannawa, Bangkok 10120; tel. (2) 296-1096; fax (2) 296-1098; e-mail rclbkk@rclgroup.com; internet www.rclgroup.com; Chair. KUA PHEK LONG; Pres. SUMATE TANTHUWANIT.

Thai International Maritime Enterprises Ltd: Sarasin Bldg, 5th Floor, 14 Thanon Surasak, Bangkok 10500; tel. (2) 236-8835; services from Bangkok to Japan; Chair. and Man. Dir SUN SUNDISAMRIT.

Thai Maritime Navigation Co Ltd: Manorom Bldg, 15th Floor, 51 Thanon Rama IV, Klongtoey, Bangkok 10110; tel. (2) 672-8690; fax (2) 249-0108; e-mail tmn@tmn.co.th; internet www.tmn.co.th; f. 1940; state-owned; services from Bangkok to Japan, the USA, Europe and ASEAN countries; Chair. NIPHON CHAKSUDUL; Sec.-Gen. SUWAPHAT SUVANNAKIJBORIHAN.

Thai Mercantile Marine Ltd: 599/1 Thanon Chua Phloeng, Klongtoey, Bangkok 10110; tel. (2) 240-2582; fax (2) 249-5656; e-mail tmmbkk@asiaaccess.net.th; f. 1967; services between Japan and Thailand; Chair. SUTHAM TANPHAIBUL; Man. Dir TANAN TANPHAIBUL.

Thoresen Thai Agencies Public Co Ltd: 26/26–27 Orakarn Bldg, 8th Floor, 26–27 Soi Chidlom, Thanon Ploenchit, Kwang Lumpinee, Khet Pathumwan, Bangkok 10330; tel. (2) 254-8437; fax (2) 655-5631; e-mail tta@thoresen.com; internet www.thoresen.com; shipowner, liner operator, shipping agent (in Thailand and Viet Nam), ship repairs, offshore and diving services; Chair. M. R. CHANDRAM S. CHANDRATAT; Man. Dir M. L. CHANDCHUTHA CHANDRATAT.

Unithai Group: 11th Floor, 25 Alma Link Bldg, Soi Chidlom, Thanon Ploenchit, Pathumwan, Bangkok 10330; tel. (2) 254-8400;

THAILAND

fax (2) 253-3093; e-mail info@unithai.com; internet www.unithai.com; regular containerized/break-bulk services to Europe, Africa and Far East; also bulk shipping/chartering; Chair. SIVAVONG CHANGKASIRI; CEO NARONG BOONYASAQUAN.

CIVIL AVIATION

Bangkok, Chiang Mai, Chiang Rai, Hat Yai, Phuket and Surat Thani airports are of international standard. U-Tapao is an alternative airport. In May 1991 plans were approved to build a new airport at Nong Ngu Hao, south-east of Bangkok, at an estimated cost of US $1,200m. Construction began in 1995, and the project was scheduled for completion in 2000. In January 1997, however, it was announced that, owing to the Government's financial problems, the Nong Ngu Hao project was to be suspended; priority was, instead, to be given to the existing airport at Don Muang in Bangkok. However, in December 2001 the project was revived when construction of the passenger terminal complex of Bangkok's second airport, Suvarnabhumi International Airport, which was ultimately to replace Don Muang Airport, commenced. The project was subject to various delays, but the new airport opened in September 2006. Constructed at an estimated cost of $4,000m., it would, when fully operational, have a capacity of 45m. passengers a year.

Airports of Thailand Public Co Ltd (AOT): 333 Thanon Cherdwutagard, Don Muang, Bangkok 10210; tel. (2) 535-1111; fax (2) 531-5559; e-mail aotpr@airportthai.co.th; internet www.airportthai.co.th; f. 1998; Chair. Gen. SAPRANG KALYANAMITRA.

Department of Civil Aviation: 71 Soi Ngarmduplee, Thanon Rama IV, Tung Mahamek, Sathorn District, Bangkok 10120; tel. (2) 287-0320; fax (2) 286-3373; e-mail dca@aviation.go.th; internet www.aviation.go.th; f. 1963; Dir-Gen. CHAISAK ANGKASUWAN.

Bangkok Airways: 99 Mu 14, Thanon Vibhavadirangsit, Chom Phon, Chatuchak, Bangkok 10900; tel. (2) 265-5678; fax (2) 265-5500; e-mail reservation@bangkokair.com; internet www.bangkokair.com; f. 1968 as Sahakol Air; name changed as above in 1989; privately owned; scheduled and charter passenger services to 20 regional and domestic destinations; Pres. and CEO Dr PRASERT PRASARTTONG-OSOTH.

Nok Air: 89 Thanon Vibhavadi Rangsit, Bangkok 10900; tel. (2) 513-0121; fax (2) 513-0203; e-mail public.info@thaiairways.co.th; internet www.nokair.com; f. 2004; 39%-owned by Thai Airways International Public Co Ltd; flights to six domestic destinations; CEO PATEE SARASIN.

One-Two-Go: 18 Thanon Ratchadaphisek, Klongtoey, Bangkok 10110; tel. (2) 229-4260; fax (2) 229-4278; e-mail info@orient-thai.com; internet www.fly12go.com; f. 2003; subsidiary of Orient Thai Airlines; low-cost domestic flights; Chair. UDOM TANTIPRASONGCHAI.

Orient Thai Airlines: 138/70 17th Floor, Jewellery Centre, Thanon Nares, Bangrak, Bangkok 10500; tel. (2) 267-2999; fax (2) 267-3217; e-mail info@orient-thai.com; internet www.orient-thai.com; f. 1993 as Orient Express Air; domestic and international flights; CEO and Man. Dir UDOM TANTIPRASONGCHAI.

PB Air: 17th Floor, UBC2 Bldg, 591 Sukhumvit 33, Watanna, Bangkok 10110; tel. (2) 261-0271; fax (2) 261-0229; e-mail admin@pbair.com; internet www.pbair.com; f. 1990; scheduled domestic passenger services; Exec. Chair. CHATRACHAI BUNYA-ANANTA; Chair. PIYA BHIROM BHAKDI.

Phuket Air: 1168/102, 34th Floor, Lumpini Tower Bldg, Thanon Rama IV, Thungmahamek, Bangkok 10120; tel. (62) 679-8999; fax (62) 679-8236; e-mail info@phuketairlines.com; internet www.phuketairlines.com; f. 1999; international charter services; Pres. VIKROM AISIRI.

SGA Airlines: 19/18-19 Royal City Ave Block A, Thanon Phra Ram 9, Bangkapi, Huay Kwang, Bangkok 10310; tel. (2) 641-4190; fax (2) 641-4807; internet www.sga.co.th; f. 2002; scheduled and chartered domestic services; Pres. JAIN CHARNNARONG.

SkyStar Airways: 18 SCB Park Plaza, 18th Floor, Tower 2, Thanon Ratchadaphisek, Chatuchak, Bangkok 10900; tel. (2) 937-5353; fax (2) 937-5356; e-mail info@skystarairways.com; internet www.skystarairways.com; f. 2005; scheduled and charter flights to the Republic of Korea; Pres. Gen. ARCHAVIN SVETASRENI.

Thai AirAsia Co Ltd: 89/170, 9/F, Juthamas Bldg, Thanon Vibhavadi Rangsit, Talad Bang Khen, Laksi, Bangkok; internet www.airasia.com; f. 2004; 50% owned by Asia Aviation, 49% owned by Air Asia Sdn Bhd (Malaysia); low-cost domestic flights; Chair. ARAK CHOLTANON; CEO TASSAPON BIJLEVELD.

Thai Airways International Public Co Ltd (THAI): 89 Thanon Vibhavadi Rangsit, Bangkok 10900; tel. (2) 545-1000; fax (2) 545-3322; e-mail public.info@thaiairways.co.th; internet www.thaiair.com; f. 1960; 51% owned by the Ministry of Finance; shares listed in July 1991, began trading in July 1992; merged with Thai Airways Co in 1988; domestic services from Bangkok to 20 cities; international services to over 50 destinations in Australasia, Europe, North America and Asia; Chair. Air Chief Marshal CHALIT PUKPASUK; Pres. APINAN SUMANASENI.

Tourism

Thailand is a popular tourist destination, noted for its temples, palaces, beaches and islands. In 2006 tourist arrivals rose to 13.8m., from 11.6m. in the previous year. Tourism is Thailand's largest single source of foreign exchange. Revenue from tourism (including passenger transport) was an estimated US $12,629m. in 2005.

Tourism Authority of Thailand (TAT): 1600 Thanon Phetchaburi Tat Mai, Makkasan, Ratchathewi, Bangkok 10400; tel. (2) 250-5500; fax (2) 250-5511; e-mail center@tat.or.th; internet www.tat.or.th; f. 1960; Gov. SIRI MANONAN.

TIMOR-LESTE
(EAST TIMOR)

Introductory Survey

Location, Climate, Language, Religion, Flag, Capital

The Democratic Republic of Timor-Leste, which is styled Timor Loro Sa'e (Timor of the rising sun) in the principal indigenous language, Tetum, occupies the eastern half of the island of Timor, which lies off the north coast of Western Australia. The western half of the island is Indonesian territory and constitutes part of the East Nusa Tenggara Province. In addition to the eastern half of Timor island, the territory also includes an enclave around Oecusse (Oekussi) Ambeno on the north-west coast of the island, and the islands of Ataúro (Pulo Cambing) and Jaco (Pulo Jako). Timor's climate is dominated by intense monsoon rain, succeeded by a pronounced dry season. The north coast of the island has a brief rainy season from December to February; the south coast a double rainy season from December to June, with a respite in March. The mountainous spine of the island has heavy rains that feed torrential floods. Tetum and Portuguese are the official languages. More than 30 languages are in use in Timor-Leste. The predominant religion is Christianity; 86% of the population were adherents of Roman Catholicism in 1997. Islam and animism are also practised. A national flag was officially adopted on 20 May 2002. The flag (proportions 1 by 2) displays a black triangle at the hoist (approximately one-third of the length of the flag) overlapping a yellow triangle (approximately one-half of the length of the flag) on a red background. The black triangle bears a five-pointed white star with one point aimed at the upper hoist corner. The capital is Dili.

Recent History

The Portuguese began trading in Timor in about 1520, principally for sandalwood, and they later established settlements and several ports on the island. They were forced to move to the north and east of the island by the Dutch, who had arrived in the early part of the 18th century and had established themselves at Kupana in the south-west. The division of the island between Portugal and the Netherlands was formalized in a treaty of 1859, although the boundaries were modified slightly in 1904. Portuguese Timor and Macao were administered as a single entity until 1896, when Portuguese Timor became a separate province. The eastern half remained a Portuguese overseas province when the Dutch recognized the western area as part of Indonesia in 1949.

The military coup in Portugal in April 1974 was followed by increased political activity in Portuguese Timor. In August 1975 the União Democrática Timorense (UDT—Timorese Democratic Union) demanded independence for Timor. The UDT allied with two other parties, the Associação Popular Democrática de Timor (APODETI—Popular Democratic Association of Timor) and the Klibur Oan Timor Asuwain (KOTA—Association of Timorese Heroes) against the alleged threat of a Communist regime being established by the Frente Revolucionária do Timor Leste Independente (Fretilin—Revolutionary Front for an Independent East Timor), and fighting broke out. The UDT forces were supported by the Indonesians. Gains on both sides were uneven, with Fretilin in control of Dili in mid-September. In the same month the Portuguese administration abandoned the capital and moved to the offshore island of Ataúro. A Portuguese attempt to arrange peace talks was rejected in October. The Indonesians intervened directly and by the beginning of December Indonesian troops controlled the capital. Portuguese-Indonesian peace talks in Rome in November were unsuccessful, and diplomatic relations were suspended after Indonesian military involvement. Two meetings of the UN Security Council voted for immediate withdrawal of Indonesian troops. Fretilin's unilateral declaration of independence in November was recognized in December by the People's Republic of China. In December the enclave of Oecusse (Oekussi) Ambeno in West Timor was declared part of Indonesian territory. In May 1976 the People's Representative Council of East Timor voted for integration with Indonesia. The UN did not recognize the composition of the Council as being representative, however, and by mid-1976 the Portuguese had not formally ceded the right to govern, although they had no remaining presence in the territory.

In July 1976 East Timor was declared the 27th province of Indonesia. Human rights organizations claimed that as many as 200,000 people, from a total population of 650,000, might have been killed by the Indonesian armed forces during the annexation. In February 1983 the UN Commission on Human Rights adopted a resolution affirming East Timor's right to independence and self-determination. In September, following a five-month cease-fire (during which government representatives negotiated with Fretilin), the armed forces launched a major new offensive. The rebels suffered a serious set-back in August 1985, when the Australian Government recognized Indonesia's incorporation of East Timor. In November 1988 Gen. Suharto, the President of Indonesia, visited East Timor, prior to announcing that travel restrictions (in force since the annexation in 1976) were to be withdrawn. The territory was opened to visitors in December. In October 1989 the Pope visited East Timor, as part of a tour of Indonesia, and made a plea to the Government to halt violations of human rights. In November 1990 the Government rejected proposals by the military commander of Fretilin, José Alexandre (Xanana) Gusmão, for unconditional peace negotiations aimed at ending the armed struggle in East Timor.

In 1991 tension in East Timor increased prior to a proposed visit by a Portuguese parliamentary delegation. Some Timorese alleged that the armed forces had initiated a campaign of intimidation to discourage demonstrations during the Portuguese visit. The mission, which was to have taken place in November, was postponed, owing to Indonesia's objection to the inclusion of an Australian journalist who was a prominent critic of Indonesia's policies in East Timor. In November the armed forces fired on a peaceful demonstration (believed to have been originally organized to coincide with the Portuguese visit) at the funeral of a separatist sympathizer in Dili. The Indonesian Armed Forces (ABRI), which admitted killing 20 civilians, claimed that the attack had been provoked by armed Fretilin activists. Independent observers and human rights groups refuted this and estimated the number of deaths at between 100 and 180. There were also subsequent allegations of the summary execution of as many as 100 witnesses. Under intense international pressure, Suharto established a National Investigation Commission. The impartiality of the Commission was challenged, however, on the grounds that it excluded non-governmental organizations, and Fretilin announced that it would boycott the investigation. Despite this, the Commission's findings received cautious foreign approbation, as they were mildly critical of ABRI and stated that 50 people had died, and 90 disappeared, in the massacre. The senior military officers in East Timor were replaced, and 14 members of the armed forces were tried by a military tribunal. The most severe penalty received by any of the soldiers involved was 18 months' imprisonment; this contrasted starkly with the sentences of convicted demonstrators, which ranged from five years' to life imprisonment.

In July 1992 Indonesia and Portugal agreed to resume discussions on East Timor under the auspices of the UN Secretary-General. In August the UN General Assembly adopted its first resolution condemning Indonesia's violations of fundamental human rights in East Timor. In September the appointment of Abílio Soares as Governor of East Timor provoked widespread criticism in the province; although Soares was a native of East Timor, he was a leading advocate of the Indonesian occupation. In October the US Congress suspended defence training aid to Indonesia, in protest at the killing of separatist demonstrators in November 1991. In October 1992, prior to the anniversary of the massacre, Amnesty International reported that hundreds of suspected supporters of independence had been arrested and tortured to prevent a commemorative demonstration.

In November 1992 Xanana Gusmão was arrested. He was subsequently taken to Jakarta, where he was to be tried in February 1993 on charges of subversion and illegal possession of firearms. Two weeks after his capture, Gusmão publicly recanted his opposition to Indonesian rule in East Timor and advised Fretilin members to surrender. It transpired, however, that he was only co-operating with the authorities in order to gain the opportunity to speak publicly at a later date. In May Gusmão was found guilty of rebellion, conspiracy, attempting to establish a separate state and illegal possession of weapons, and was condemned to life imprisonment. The sentence was commuted to 20 years by Suharto in August. During the same month it was announced that all government combat forces were to be withdrawn from East Timor, leaving only troops involved in development projects. In September, however, the acting leader of Fretilin, Konis Santana, declared that, contrary to announcements, the Indonesians were renewing their forces in East Timor and that killings and atrocities continued.

In December 1993 Xanana Gusmão managed to convey letters to the Portuguese Government and the International Commission of Jurists demanding an annulment of his trial, owing to the lack of impartiality of his defence lawyer. The Government subsequently banned Gusmão from receiving visitors. In January 1994 Indonesia announced to the UN Secretary-General's envoy that it would facilitate access to East Timor by human rights and UN organizations. In May, however, a privately organized human rights conference being held in the Philippines, entitled the Asia-Pacific Conference on East Timor, provoked diplomatic tension with the Indonesian Government, which had attempted to force the abandonment of the conference. The outcome of the conference was the establishment of an Asia-Pacific coalition on East Timor, which consisted mainly of non-governmental organizations active in the region.

In July 1994 the Indonesian authorities suppressed a demonstration in Dili, following weeks of increasing tension in the capital; at least three people were reportedly killed during the protest. In August it was reported that the armed forces had held talks with Xanana Gusmão, included in which was the discussion of the possibility of holding a referendum under the auspices of the UN to determine the future status of the disputed territory. The Indonesian Minister of Foreign Affairs, Ali Alatas, held discussions in October in New York, USA, with José Ramos Horta, the Secretary for International Relations of Fretilin, the first such talks to be officially recognized. At the beginning of November President Suharto agreed to hold talks with exiled East Timorese dissidents. The Government's increasingly conciliatory position on East Timor was, however, reported largely to be a superficial attempt to improve the country's human rights image prior to the holding of the Asia-Pacific Economic Co-operation (APEC, see p. 176) summit meeting in Bogor, 60 km south of Jakarta, in mid-November.

In January 1995 Alatas, the Portuguese Minister of Foreign Affairs and the UN Secretary-General met in Geneva, Switzerland, for the fifth round of talks on East Timor. Agreement was reached to convene a meeting between separatist and pro-integrationist Timorese activists under the auspices of the UN, called the All-Inclusive Intra-East Timorese Dialogue (AETD). The AETD, which was held in June 1995, March 1996 and October 1997, failed to achieve any conclusive progress. The sixth and seventh rounds of talks between the Portuguese and Indonesian ministers responsible for foreign affairs took place in July 1995 and January 1996, again with little progress.

In September 1995 the worst rioting that year took place in protest against Indonesian Muslim immigrants, following an Indonesian prison official's alleged insult to Roman Catholicism. Mosques and Muslim businesses were burned, and some Muslims were forced to flee the island. Further riots erupted in October, in which rival groups of separatists and integrationists clashed on the streets. The Roman Catholic Apostolic Administrator in Dili, the Rt Rev. Carlos Filipe Ximenes Belo, persuaded the rioters to return home following an agreement with ABRI; however, the agreement was subsequently broken by the armed forces, who arrested more than 250 alleged rioters.

From September 1995 East Timorese activists began forcing entry into foreign embassies in Jakarta and appealing for political asylum. They were granted asylum by the Portuguese, who were still officially recognized by the UN as the administrative power in East Timor. The Indonesian Government permitted the asylum-seekers to leave, but denied that there was any persecution in East Timor. The culmination of the successful campaign was the storming in December of the Dutch and Russian embassies by 58 and 47 activists respectively. The demonstrators, some of whom were non-Timorese and belonged to a radical group called the People's Democratic Union, demanded unsuccessfully a meeting with the UN High Commissioner for Human Rights, José Ayala Lasso, who was visiting Indonesia and who, following a brief visit to East Timor, confirmed the occurrence of severe violations of human rights in the province.

In February 1996 President Suharto and the Portuguese Prime Minister met in Bangkok, Thailand (the first meeting on East Timor by heads of government). During the negotiations Portugal offered to re-establish diplomatic links in return for the release of Xanana Gusmão and the guarantee of human rights in East Timor. International awareness of East Timor was heightened in October, when Belo and José Ramos Horta were jointly awarded the Nobel Prize for Peace. The Indonesian Government, displeased with the Nobel committee's choice, declared that there would be no change in its policy on East Timor. Four days after the announcement of the award, Suharto visited East Timor for the first time in eight years.

Following the announcement of the Nobel Peace Prize, Bishop Belo repeated demands that the Government conduct a referendum on the issue of autonomy for East Timor. In November 1996 he became involved in a controversy regarding an interview that he had given to a German periodical, Der Spiegel, which quoted several controversial remarks, allegedly made by Belo, about the treatment of the East Timorese people by the Indonesian Government and ABRI. Belo denied having made the remarks, but was requested to appear before a parliamentary commission in Jakarta to explain the matter. This controversy, and the temporary confiscation of Belo's passport by the Indonesian authorities (which threatened to prevent Belo's visit to Norway to receive the Nobel award), prompted five days of demonstrations in his support in Dili. The rallies were reportedly the largest since 1975, but were conducted peacefully.

The award of the Nobel Peace Prize to José Ramos Horta proved even more controversial. The Governor of East Timor accused Ramos Horta of ordering the torture and killing of East Timorese people. Ramos Horta himself declared that the award should have been made to Xanana Gusmão and invited the Indonesian Government to enter into serious negotiations on the future of East Timor. Ramos Horta was banned from visiting the Philippines for the duration of an APEC summit meeting which took place there in late 1996; this ban was subsequently extended.

In November 1996 the Indonesian Government withdrew permission for foreign journalists to visit East Timor, where they had planned to attend a press conference conducted by Belo. In December Ramos Horta and Belo attended the Nobel Prize ceremony in Oslo, Norway. Riots in Dili (following a gathering of Belo's supporters to welcome him upon his return) resulted in the death of a member of ABRI; it was reported later in the month that at least one East Timorese citizen had been killed by the Indonesian authorities in a raid to capture those believed to be responsible for the soldier's death. (It was, however, generally recognized by non-governmental organizations working in East Timor that the Indonesian authorities had become more lenient about allowing demonstrations in 1996.)

Following an increase in clashes between resistance forces and ABRI prior to the general election, in June 1997 a military commander of Fretilin, David Alex, was apprehended by the Indonesian armed forces. His subsequent death in custody was highly controversial; resistance groups rejected the official explanation that he had been fatally injured in a clash with security forces and claimed that he had been tortured to death. Guerrilla activity subsequently intensified and in September at least seven Indonesian soldiers were killed in a clash with resistance forces. Further fighting took place in November and December.

In November 1997 the Australia-East Timor Association released a report cataloguing human rights abuses perpetrated by members of the Indonesian armed forces against Timorese women; abuses cited in the report included enforced prostitution, rape and compulsory sterilization programmes. Also in November shots were fired when Indonesian troops stormed the campus of the University of East Timor in Dili, following a vigil held by students to commemorate the massacre in Dili in 1991. According to reports, at least one student was killed in the incident, a number of others were injured and many were arrested. Belo accused the Indonesian security forces of having used 'excessive force', and this was confirmed by a report made by the Indonesian National Commission on Human Rights in early December. Also in December the Commission demanded the abolition of the country's anti-subversion legislation. In the same month two

Timorese were sentenced to death under the legislation for their part in an ambush of election security officials earlier in the year, prompting threats of increased guerrilla activities by separatist forces, and a further four were sentenced to 12 years' imprisonment for taking part in armed resistance operations. Meanwhile, Abílio Soares, who had been re-elected as Governor of East Timor in September, ordered the arrest of the leaders of the recently formed Movement for the Reconciliation and Unity of the People of East Timor (MRUPT), which he declared to be a proscribed movement.

In January 1998 it was announced that a Timorese resistance congress that was due to be held in Portugal in March was to be replaced by a national convention to ensure the participation of the UDT. The convention, held in April, unanimously approved the 'Magna Carta' of East Timor, a charter intended to provide the basis for the constitution of future self-determination within the territory, and ratified plans for the establishment of the Conselho Nacional de Resistência Timorense (National Council of Timorese Resistance), a body intended to give the Timorese resistance movement a single national structure and to bring together representatives of the defunct National Council of Maubere Resistance (CNRM), Fretilin and the UDT. Xanana Gusmão was appointed President of the new Conselho Nacional de Resistência Timorense, and Ramos Horta was named as Vice-President. In March 1998, meanwhile, Konis Santana, the acting military leader of Fretilin, died following an accident; Taur Matan Ruak was appointed as his successor.

The accession of B. J. Habibie to the Indonesian presidency in May 1998 raised hopes that independence for East Timor might be granted in the near future. However, while President Habibie publicly suggested that the territory might be given a new 'special' status within Indonesia and that troops might be withdrawn, there was no initial indication that the Government was contemplating independence for the territory. While a number of prominent political prisoners were released soon after Habibie replaced Suharto as President, Xanana Gusmão's 20-year sentence was reduced by a mere four months. Following the killing of an East Timorese youth by Indonesian soldiers in June, the Government renewed efforts to demonstrate its conciliatory position and, in late July, effected a much-publicized withdrawal of a limited number of troops from the territory. However, opposition groups subsequently claimed that fresh troops were being sent by the Indonesian Government to replace those leaving (a claim denied by Indonesian military leaders).

In August 1998 it was announced that Indonesia and Portugal had agreed to hold discussions on the possibility of 'wide-ranging' autonomy for East Timor, and in early November the UN was reported to be opening discussions with the two countries regarding a UN plan for extensive autonomy for the territory. Following an outbreak of severe violence in the Alas region of East Timor later that month, in which 82 people were reported to have been killed, Portugal suspended its involvement in the talks; however, in January 1999 it was announced that the talks were to resume. During his visit to East Timor in December 1998, UN special envoy Jamsheed Marker held talks with both Xanana Gusmão and Belo; in the same month, Gusmão reportedly advocated that the Timorese people should consider the UN's proposal for autonomy, but only as a transitional stage prior to the holding of a referendum (the possibility of which, in December, was still ruled out by the Indonesian Government).

In January 1999 the Australian Government announced a significant change in its policy on East Timor, stating that it intended actively to promote 'self-determination' in the territory (although the precise intended meaning of 'self-determination' remained unclear). Later the same month, total independence for East Timor in the near future emerged as an apparent possibility when, in its boldest move to date to appease the East Timorese and the international community, the Indonesian Government suggested that a vote might be held in the national legislature, the Majelis Permusyawaratan Rakyat (MPR, People's Consultative Assembly), following the election to the House of Representatives (part of the MPR) scheduled for June, on the issue of Indonesia's granting independence to the territory. As a result of a request from the UN Secretary-General, Kofi Annan, the Government also announced that it was to allow Xanana Gusmão to serve the remainder of his 20-year prison sentence under house arrest in Jakarta. Following the Government's announcement regarding the possibility of independence for East Timor, a number of outbreaks of violence, attributed to supporters of the territory's integration with Indonesia, were reported to have occurred.

On 27 January 1999 the Indonesian Government unexpectedly announced that, if the East Timorese voted to reject Indonesia's proposals for autonomy, it would consider granting independence to the province. Although the Indonesian Government was initially opposed to a referendum on the issue of independence for East Timor, it signed an agreement with Portugal on 5 May, giving its assent to a process of 'popular consultation' taking the form of a UN-supervised poll to determine the future status of East Timor. The UN Mission in East Timor (UNAMET) was established by the UN Security Council in June to organize the poll in which the East Timorese could opt for a form of political autonomy or for independence. The 'popular consultation' was initially scheduled to be held on 8 August, and all East Timorese, including those living in exile, were to be allowed to participate in the ballot.

Following the announcement of the scheduled referendum, violence in the territory escalated. Anti-independence militia groups based within East Timor initiated a campaign of violence and intimidation in advance of the poll, which included summary killings, kidnappings, harassment and the forced recruitment of young East Timorese. The Indonesian military itself was discovered to be not only supporting but also recruiting, training and organizing many of the militias. Violence continued to escalate throughout the territory during April and May 1999. In one incident in April anti-independence militia members massacred 57 people in a churchyard in the town of Liquiça (Likisia); further massacres were reported to have occurred in other areas, including Dili. Also in April Xanana Gusmão (now under house arrest in Jakarta) responded to the increasing violence from anti-independence militias by reversing his previous position and urging guerrillas in Fretilin's military wing, the Forças Armadas Libertação Nacional de Timor Leste (Falintil), to resume their struggle. Although rival pro-independence and integrationist factions signed a peace accord in June supporting a cease-fire and disarmament in advance of the scheduled referendum, the violence continued unabated.

The escalating violence in the territory, together with logistical difficulties, led the UN to postpone the referendum to 21 August 1999 and then to 30 August. Although intimidation and violence by the militias continued, the referendum proceeded on 30 August. About 98.5% of those eligible to vote participated in the poll, which resulted in an overwhelming rejection, by 78.5% of voters, of the Indonesian Government's proposals for autonomy and in the endorsement of independence for East Timor. The announcement of the result of the referendum, however, precipitated a rapid descent into anarchy. Pro-Jakarta militias embarked upon a campaign of murder and destruction in which hundreds of civilians were killed; as many as 500,000 (according to the UN) were forced to flee their homes, and many buildings were destroyed in arson attacks. While many of those who were displaced from their homes sought refuge in the hills, about one-half were estimated by the UN to have left the territory (a large number having entered West Timor), some involuntarily. In one incident during the campaign of extreme violence that followed the announcement of the result of the referendum, anti-independence militia members stormed the residence of Bishop Belo, evicting at gunpoint some 6,000 refugees who had sought shelter in the compound; the home of the bishop was burned down and dozens of East Timorese were reported to have been killed in the attack. Bishop Belo was evacuated to Australia, while Xanana Gusmão (who was released from house arrest in Jakarta by the Indonesian Government on 7 September) took refuge in the British embassy in Jakarta. Thousands of civilians besieged the UN compound in Dili, the premises of other international agencies, churches and police stations, seeking protection from the indiscriminate attacks of the militias. On 7 September martial law was declared in the territory, and a curfew was imposed. The violence continued unabated, however, and in mid-September, following international condemnation of the situation and intense diplomatic pressure, the Indonesian Government reversed its earlier opposition to a proposal by the Australian Government and agreed to permit the deployment of a multinational peacekeeping force. As the massacre of civilians continued, thousands of refugees were airlifted to safety in northern Australia, along with the remaining employees of the UN (many local staff members of UNAMET were among the victims of the violence); shortly after the UN withdrew its staff, anti-independence militia members set fire to the UN compound in Dili. Meanwhile, aid agencies warned that as many as 300,000 East Timorese people would starve if humanitarian assistance were not urgently provided.

The first contingent of several thousand UN peace-keeping troops, forming the International Force for East Timor (Interfet), was deployed in the territory on 20 September 1999. Led by Australia, which committed 4,500 troops, the force gradually restored order. A week later the Indonesian armed forces formally relinquished responsibility for security to the multinational force. At the end of October, after 24 years as an occupying force, the last Indonesian soldiers left East Timor. In late September Indonesia and Portugal reiterated their agreement for the transfer of authority in East Timor to the UN. On 19 October the result of the referendum was ratified by the MPR, thus permitting East Timor's accession to independence to proceed. Shortly thereafter, on 25 October, the UN Security Council established the UN Transitional Administration in East Timor (UNTAET—subsequently the UN Mission of Support in East Timor—UNMISET) as an integrated peace-keeping operation fully responsible for the administration of East Timor during its transition to independence. UNTAET, with an initial mandate until 31 January 2001, was to exercise all judicial and executive authority in East Timor, to undertake the establishment and training of a new police force, and to assume responsibility for the co-ordination and provision of humanitarian assistance and emergency rehabilitation; the transfer of command of military operations in the territory from Interfet to the UNTAET peace-keeping force was completed on 23 February 2000. Meanwhile, the UN also began a large-scale emergency humanitarian relief effort; however, many displaced and homeless East Timorese remained without access to adequate food supplies, shelter and basic health care facilities.

Following reports that in mid-October 1999 Indonesian troops and militias had entered the isolated East Timorese enclave of Oecusse (situated within West Timor) and allegedly massacred around 50 people, Interfet troops were deployed in Oecusse; most of the enclave's population of 57,000 were believed to have been removed to refugee camps in West Timor, and by early November only 10,000 of its citizens had been accounted for. Following his popularly acclaimed return to Dili in October, Xanana Gusmão met with the UNTAET Transitional Administrator, Sérgio Vieira de Mello, in November, and reportedly communicated the concerns of local East Timorese organizations that they were being marginalized by UNTAET officials. In late November he visited Jakarta in order to establish relations with the Indonesian Government, and in early December he visited Australia, where he met with representatives of the Australian Government to discuss the Timor Gap Treaty. (The Treaty, which had been concluded between Australia and Indonesia in 1991, provided a framework for petroleum and gas exploration in the maritime zone between Australia and East Timor and for the division of any resulting royalties between Australia and Indonesia. Indonesia ceased to be party to the original Treaty when it relinquished control of East Timor in October 1999, however, and the transitional administration in East Timor subsequently expressed a desire to renegotiate the terms of the Treaty, which the UN considered to have no legal standing, as Indonesian sovereignty over East Timor had never been recognized by the international body. In February 2000 a memorandum of understanding (MOU) relating to the Treaty was signed by the Australian Government and East Timor's UN administrators, temporarily maintaining the arrangement for the division of royalties (although between Australia and East Timor rather than Australia and Indonesia). East Timor received its first payment of royalties from Australia under the MOU in October 2000. In the same month, however, the formal renegotiation of the Treaty began, with East Timor requesting the redrawing of the boundaries covered by the Treaty and a larger share of petroleum and gas royalties. Following independence in May 2002 both countries formally signed the Treaty. However, owing to prolonged negotiations over the division of royalties, Australia did not ratify the agreement until March 2003.)

On 1 December 1999 José Ramos Horta returned to East Timor after 24 years of exile. Ramos Horta, who commanded much popular support, urged the East Timorese people to show forgiveness towards their former oppressors and called for reconciliation between Indonesia and East Timor. On 11 December Vieira de Mello convened the first meeting of the National Consultative Council (NCC) in Dili; the 15-member Council, comprising members of the Conselho Nacional de Resistência Timorense and other East Timorese political representatives as well as UNTAET officials, was established in late 1999 to advise UNTAET.

A number of mass graves containing the bodies of suspected victims of the violence perpetrated by the anti-independence militias both before and after the holding of the referendum in August 1999 were discovered in East Timor (including two in the Oecusse enclave) in late 1999 and early 2000. In December 1999 Sonia Picado Sotela, the Chair of the International Commission of Inquiry in East Timor, confirmed that the team of UN investigators had discovered evidence of 'systematic killing'.

In January 2000 a panel appointed by the Indonesian Government to investigate human rights abuses in East Timor delivered its report to the Indonesian Attorney-General. The panel reportedly named 24 individuals whom it recommended should be prosecuted for their alleged involvement in violations of human rights in the territory. One of those named was the former Minister of Defence and Security and Commander-in-Chief of the Indonesian armed forces, Gen. Wiranto, who had since been appointed Co-ordinating Minister for Political, Legal and Security Affairs in the Indonesian Government; also named were a number of senior military officers, as well as leaders of the pro-Jakarta militias responsible for the extreme violence perpetrated during the period following the referendum. However, pro-independence leaders in East Timor strongly criticized the report as inadequate. In the same month the International Commission of Inquiry in East Timor recommended that the UN establish an independent international body to investigate allegations of human rights violations in East Timor, and an international tribunal to deal with the cases of those accused by the investigators. In February the recently appointed President of Indonesia, Abdurrahman Wahid, visited East Timor and publicly apologized for the atrocities committed by the Indonesian armed forces during the Republic's occupation of the territory. Wahid reaffirmed the commitment of the Indonesian Government to the prosecution of any individuals implicated in the violation of human rights in East Timor. In the same month Wahid suspended Gen. Wiranto from the Indonesian Government. (Wiranto subsequently resigned in May.) The UN Secretary-General, Kofi Annan, made an official visit to East Timor in mid-February, during which he pledged that investigations into violations of human rights in the territory would be carried out.

In April 2000 UNTAET signed an agreement with the Indonesian Government regarding the extradition to East Timor of Indonesian citizens facing charges relating to the violence of 1999, and in July 2000 a team from the Indonesian Attorney-General's Office visited East Timor to investigate a limited number of cases of human rights violations. However, relations between East Timor and Indonesia remained tense, and the introduction in August 2000 (in the closing stages of the annual session of the country's principal legislative body, the MPR) of an amendment to Indonesia's Constitution providing for the exclusion of military personnel from retroactive prosecution prompted fears among many international observers that the possibility of the prosecution of members of the Indonesian military believed responsible for recent human rights abuses in East Timor would be placed in serious jeopardy (despite the suggestions of senior Indonesian legislators that the amendment would probably not apply to crimes such as genocide, war crimes and terrorism). In September the Indonesian Attorney General's Office named 19 people whom it suspected of involvement in the violence of 1999. While human rights groups in both East Timor and Indonesia welcomed the publication of the list, which included the names of several former high-ranking members of the Indonesian armed forces, there was widespread disappointment that Gen. Wiranto was not among those named.

In June 2000 an agreement was reached between UNTAET and East Timorese leaders on the formation of a new transitional coalition Government, in which the two sides were to share political responsibility. The Cabinet of the new transitional Government, which was formally appointed in July, initially included four East Timorese cabinet ministers: João Carrascalão, President of the UDT and a Vice-President of the Conselho Nacional de Resistência Timorense, who was allocated responsibility for infrastructure; Mari Alkatiri, Secretary-General of Fretilin, who was appointed Minister for Economic Affairs; Father Filomeno Jacob, who was appointed to oversee social affairs; and Ana Pessôa, who was placed in charge of internal administration. The new Cabinet also included four international representatives. Mariano Lopes da Cruz, an East Timorese national, was appointed as Inspector-General. It was reported that Xanana Gusmão, while holding no formal position in the new Government, was to be consulted on an informal basis by Sérgio Vieira de Mello (who was to retain ultimate control over the approval of any draft legislation proposed to the Cabinet) with respect to all political decisions. In October the Cabinet was expanded to nine members, with the appointment of José Ramos Horta as Minister of Foreign Affairs.

In mid-July 2000 UNTAET approved the establishment of a 'National Council' to advise the new Cabinet. The East Timorese National Council, the membership of which was expanded from 33 to 36 in October, consisted of a selection of East Timorese representatives from the political, religious and private sectors. The new National Council was inaugurated on 23 October and replaced the 15-member NCC. In the same month Xanana Gusmão was elected to lead the National Council.

In August 2000, meanwhile, Xanana Gusmão retired as the Military Commander of Falintil, in order to concentrate on his political role in the process of guiding East Timor towards full independence, relinquishing control of the guerrilla army to his deputy, Taur Matan Ruak. Initially, Falintil faced an uncertain future, and the refusal of the UN to allow the active involvement of the unit in attempts to combat incursions by Indonesian paramilitaries into East Timor led Xanana Gusmão to voice indirect criticism of the international organization in his resignation speech. In February 2001, however, a new East Timorese Defence Force (ETDF) was established, consisting of an initial 650 recruits drawn exclusively from the ranks of Falintil, which was itself to be dissolved. The former Military Commander of the guerrilla army, Taur Matan Ruak, was promoted to the rank of Brigadier-General and appointed to command the new force. Meanwhile, a fund was established to finance the support and retraining of an estimated 1,000 Falintil veterans who were to be demobilized. Training of the new Defence Force was to be conducted by Portugal and Australia; its role was described as that of 'policing', with the defence of the territory remaining the responsibility of UNTAET peace-keeping troops.

In December 2000 four of the five East Timorese members of the transitional Cabinet threatened to resign, reportedly in protest at their treatment by the UN. The ministers, who allegedly claimed that they were merely 'puppet ministers' in the new coalition Government, demanded further clarification of the legal status of the Cabinet and of their authority as individual cabinet ministers, and called for the establishment of a more clearly defined relationship between UNTAET and the Cabinet. Further complaints about UNTAET's treatment of East Timorese officials were voiced at a donors' conference for East Timor held in the same month, and press reports suggested the existence of a level of public resentment of the UN's presence in East Timor. However, in January 2001 Ramos Horta warned that any attempt to scale down the UN's presence in East Timor would destabilize the territory's progression towards independence. In late January 2001 the UN Security Council extended UNTAET's mandate (which had initially been scheduled to expire on 31 January 2001) until 31 January 2002. It was acknowledged, however, that modifications of the mandate might be necessary to take into account developments in East Timor's progression towards full independence and, in January 2002, the mandate was extended until 20 May 2002, the date set for independence. From August 2000, meanwhile, in a move that allowed for greater formal East Timorese influence in the governing of the territory during the period preceding the territory's accession to full independence, a process commenced whereby the transitional Government began to be redefined as the East Timorese Transitional Administration (ETTA). Consisting of both UNTAET and East Timorese staff, ETTA was composed of the transitional Cabinet, the National Council and the judiciary. Final authority over ETTA rested with the Special Representative of the UN Secretary-General and Transitional Administrator, Sérgio Vieira de Mello.

In February 2001 legislation providing for an election to an 88-seat Constituent Assembly, to be conducted on 30 August, was approved. The single chamber was to comprise 75 deputies elected on a national basis, using proportional representation, and one elected delegate from each of East Timor's 13 districts, chosen on a 'first-past-the-post' basis. The members of the Constituent Assembly were to be responsible for the preparation and adoption of a constitution, which would require the endorsement of at least 60 members. Meanwhile, a National Constitutional Commission, comprising representatives of various groups, was to be established in order to facilitate consultation with the people of East Timor.

In March 2001 Xanana Gusmão tendered his resignation as Speaker of the National Council, having become disaffected by the stagnation of the political process. At the same time he announced that he would not stand for President in the forthcoming election for the post, despite commanding an overwhelming level of public support for his candidacy. In April UNTAET announced that José Ramos Horta would serve as Gusmão's replacement on the National Council, prompting his resignation as the Minister for Foreign Affairs (the two posts could not be held simultaneously). However, in the 9 April election for the post of Speaker, Manuel Carrascalão emerged victorious, defeating Ramos Horta, and criticized UNTAET for supporting his rival. Two weeks later José Ramos Horta resigned from the National Council and resumed his position in the transitional Cabinet. In June the Conselho Nacional de Resistência Timorense announced its dissolution, reportedly in order to enable the groups of which it was comprised to evolve into fully independent political parties, and, in August, Xanana Gusmão finally yielded to immense popular pressure and international encouragement and announced his intention to stand for the presidency in 2002.

On 30 August 2001 91.3% of the eligible populace turned out to vote in the country's first free parliamentary election. Fretilin secured 55 of the 88 seats available in the Constituent Assembly, commanding 57% of the votes cast. In second place, with seven seats, was the Partido Democrático (PD, Democratic Party). The Partido Social Democrata (PSD, Social Democrat Party) and the Associação Social-Democrata Timorense (ASDT, Timor Social Democratic Association) won six seats each. In September Sérgio Vieira de Mello swore in the members of the Constituent Assembly, and five days later the second transitional Government was appointed. Mari Alkatiri of Fretilin was appointed leader of the Cabinet and retained the economy portfolio. José Ramos Horta continued as Minister for Foreign Affairs. Of 20 available government positions, nine were allocated to Fretilin, two to the PD and the remaining nine to independents and various experts. In October the Constituent Assembly appointed a committee to oversee the drafting of the Constitution, taking into account the views of over 36,000 East Timorese summarized in reports presented by 13 Constitutional Commissions. In November 2001 the Assembly approved the structure of the draft Constitution.

In December 2000 UNTAET issued its first indictments for crimes committed against humanity in connection with the violence that had surrounded the referendum in 1999, charging 11 people (including an officer of the Indonesian special forces) with the murder of nine civilians in September 1999. In January 2001 an East Timor court sentenced a former pro-Jakarta militia member to 12 years' imprisonment for the murder of a village chief in September 1999, marking the first successful prosecution related to the violence of 1999. In September 2001 the UN filed 'extermination' charges against nine militiamen and two Indonesian soldiers accused of murdering 65 people two years previously. In October, in the first civil case of its kind, a US federal court awarded six East Timorese a total of US $66m. in damages after Indonesian Gen. Johny Lumintang was found to bear responsibility for human rights abuses. In December 2001 a UN tribunal took the first step in bringing those responsible for the atrocities committed in 1999 to justice. Of the 11 individuals indicted in December 2000, 10 were convicted of crimes against humanity and sentenced to prison terms of up to 33 years. However, the Jakarta authorities resisted the extradition of the indicted Indonesian Special Forces Officer to face trial.

In February 2000, meanwhile, the Australian Government announced that all 470 East Timorese refugees remaining in Australia were expected to be returned to East Timor by the end of the month. Also in February, however, the UN expressed its concern that very few of the estimated 90,000 East Timorese refugees remaining in camps across the border in West Timor were returning to East Timor; it had earlier been reported that pro-Jakarta militias had been intimidating the refugees in West Timor and preventing them from returning home. In September the UN temporarily suspended its relief work among East Timorese refugees in West Timor, following the murder by pro-Jakarta militias of three UN aid workers in the territory earlier in the month. The murders prompted international criticism of the Indonesian Government for its failure to control the militia groups operating in West Timor. In November Ramos Horta alleged that estimates of the number of East Timorese refugees residing in West Timor (reported by some sources to be as high as 130,000) were being deliberately exaggerated by the Indonesian Government, and estimated the actual number of refugees to be no higher than 60,000–70,000. In December 2000 and January 2001, in an attempt to dispel the fears of refugees remaining in West Timor about the security situation in East Timor, UNTAET arranged for a number of groups of refugees to visit their homeland. The visits resulted in a number of refugees opting to return permanently to East Timor.

In June 2001 refugees from East Timor participated in a process of registration through which they were permitted to decide whether or not they wished to return to the newly independent state. Of the 113,791 refugees who took part, 98% wished to remain in Indonesia. However, it was thought that intimidation by pro-Indonesia militias might have influenced the result and that the survey did not necessarily reflect the participants' long-term intentions. In the same month the six men accused of the murder of the three UN aid workers in September 2000 were found guilty of violence against people and property rather than murder and given light sentences. The UN criticized the verdicts and pressed for a review.

Following the formal declaration of the election results, the families of former East Timorese militiamen began returning to their homeland in mid-September 2001. In October the Indonesian authorities announced the imminent halting of aid to an estimated 80,000 East Timorese who remained in refugee camps in West Timor and in November Xanana Gusmão visited West Timor in an effort to promote reconciliation and encourage thousands of the remaining refugees to return home.

In October 2001 the newly elected Constituent Assembly requested that the UN formally grant East Timor independence on 20 May 2002. Xanana Gusmão reluctantly lent his support to the request, although he commented that the choice of date was too politically partisan as it commemorated the 28th anniversary of the founding of the country's first political party. However, the UN Security Council endorsed the Assembly's request, and agreed to maintain a peace-keeping presence in the region for between six months and two years after the granting of independence.

On 22 March 2002 the Constituent Assembly finally promulgated East Timor's first Constitution, which was to become effective upon independence on 20 May of that year. The document provided for the adoption of Tetum and Portuguese as the country's official languages.

On 14 April 2002 East Timor held its first presidential election, which resulted in an overwhelming victory for Xanana Gusmão, who secured almost 83% of the votes cast. The only other candidate was Francisco Xavier do Amaral. Later in the same month Madalena Brites Boavida was sworn in as Minister of Finance and Planning in the second transitional Government, following the resignation of Fernando Borges.

On 20 May 2002 East Timor celebrated its formal accession to independence, upon which it became known officially as the Democratic Republic of Timor-Leste. The tenure of the UN interim administration was officially terminated and UNTAET was replaced by a smaller mission, the UN Mission of Support in East Timor (UNMISET), which was to remain in the country for two years to support administrative development and to assist in the maintenance of law and order, while downsizing its military presence as rapidly as possible. Xanana Gusmão was officially inaugurated as President and swore in the country's first Government. The National Parliament, as the Constituent Assembly had become, then held its inaugural session. Prime Minister Alkatiri stressed that the new Government would give priority to spending on health and education. The President of Indonesia, Megawati Sukarnoputri, attended the independence day celebrations, despite criticism from several members of the Indonesian legislature. On the following day Sérgio Vieira de Mello left the country; he was succeeded by Kamalesh Sharma, the head of UNMISET. Tension developed between Gusmão and Alkatiri after the latter was seen to have used Fretilin's parliamentary majority to secure the passage of a new Constitution that rendered Gusmão a largely symbolic head of state. The ill feeling persisted and in November 2002 Gusmão called for the resignation of one of Alkatiri's firmest allies, Rogério Lobato, Minister for Internal Administration. However, Gusmão eventually retreated from his position, following which relations between the President and the Prime Minister appeared to improve somewhat.

In July 2002 President Gusmão visited Indonesia on his first official trip abroad since assuming the presidency. In September Timor-Leste became the 191st member of the UN. In the same month the Indonesian Government announced that the remaining refugee camps in West Timor would be closed at the end of 2002 and, in November, Gusmão visited the province in an effort to encourage the estimated 30,000 refugees who remained there to return to their homeland. In the following month the Government declared a state of alert in the country following an outbreak of rioting in Dili during which two people were killed. The protests had begun when a police officer allegedly shot at a student participating in a peaceful demonstration outside the police headquarters in the city. The violence was the worst to have occurred in the country since independence. In January 2003 further violence ensued when a group of armed men attacked villages near the town of Atsabe in the Ermera district, resulting in the deaths of five people. In the following month a bus travelling to Dili was ambushed by a group of armed men; two people subsequently died. It was feared that the violence reflected the possible establishment of several militias and insurgent groups intent on undermining the stability of the new nation.

In March 2003 Prime Minister Alkatiri announced the appointment of Ana Pessôa to the newly created post of Deputy Prime Minister. The justice portfolio, formerly held by Pessôa, was allocated to her deputy, Domingos Sarmento. In the following month, owing to the apparent increase of violence in Timor-Leste in the preceding months, the UN Security Council announced that UNMISET would no longer follow its original downsizing plan (under which the phased withdrawal of UN troops from the country would have commenced in July 2003) and would instead implement an alternative two-phase plan. Under the new strategy, UNMISET would retain primary responsibility for national security until December 2003, maintaining its peace-keeping force at its existing level, before preparing to hand over full responsibility for national defence to Falintil-ETDF (see Defence) on 20 May 2004. In May 2003 the UN Security Council formally extended the mandate of UNMISET until 20 May 2004. In October 2003 the Timorese authorities assumed responsibility for the administration of border crossings in the country from the UN. However, in February 2004 UN Secretary-General Kofi Annan recommended that the mandate of UNMISET be extended, in a modified form and with a considerably reduced military presence, for a further six months following its expiry in May, in order to allow for consolidation of the progress that had been made in the country. In May 2004 the UN Security Council voted unanimously to renew UNMISET's mandate for an additional period of six months, extending the mission until 20 May 2005. In March 2005 Annan recommended that UNMISET be deployed for an additional year, extending the mandate until 20 May 2006, a suggestion that both the USA and Australia opposed, insisting that peace-keeping forces were no longer required in the country.

From mid-2002, at a specially created court in Jakarta (the Ad Hoc Indonesian Human Rights Tribunal on East Timor), the trials took place of 18 officers, government officials and militiamen believed to have participated in the violence that had surrounded the referendum for independence in 1999. In August 2002 Abílio Soares, the former Governor of East Timor, was found guilty of two charges of 'gross rights violations'; he was sentenced to a three-year prison term. The sentence was widely criticized for its apparent leniency. In the same month the former chief of police in East Timor, Timbul Silaen, was acquitted of charges of failing to control his subordinates; five other Indonesian police and army officers were also acquitted shortly afterwards. In November former Indonesian militia leader Eurico Guterres was sentenced to 10 years in prison, having been convicted of crimes against humanity. In the following month the former military chief of Dili, Lt-Col Soedjarwo, was sentenced to a five-year prison term for his role in the violence. In March 2003 the court sentenced Brig.-Gen. Noer Muis, a former army chief in East Timor, to five years in prison for crimes against humanity. In August Indonesian armed forces officer Maj.-Gen. Adam Damiri, the last and most senior official to be tried by the tribunal, was convicted of having failed to prevent atrocities in East Timor and sentenced to three years in prison. The court was subjected to widespread international criticism, owing to the fact that only six of those tried were convicted of the charges against them. In April 2004, following an appeal, the Indonesian Supreme Court upheld the conviction of Abílio Soares. However, in July the Jakarta High Court overruled the guilty verdicts of Lt-Col Soedjarwo, Brig.-Gen. Muis, Maj.-Gen. Damiri and Col Gultom (a former Dili police chief), and also halved the sentence of Eurico Guterres to five years. The decision meant that all of the police and military officials indicted by the Tribunal had been released, leaving only the two civilians

(Soares and Guterres) serving sentences. The USA and the European Union (EU) denounced the acquittals as massive failings of justice. In November, moreover, Soares was cleared of the charges against him by Indonesia's Supreme Court, leaving only the conviction of Guterres standing. However, having reinstated his 10-year sentence in March 2006, the Supreme Court decided to rescind Guterres' conviction in April 2008, and he was released from prison.

In early 2003 a UN-sponsored Special Panel for Serious Crimes (SPSC) that had been established in Dili began to issue indictments for crimes against humanity against several military officials in relation to the violence surrounding the referendum in 1999, including the former chief of the Indonesian armed forces, Gen. Wiranto, who faced prosecution for the first time. Wiranto denied the charges against him. The Indonesian Government, however, stated that it would refuse to permit the extradition of those charged to face trial. In April 2003 the SPSC sentenced José Cardosa Fereira, an East Timorese militia leader, to a 12-year prison term following his conviction for crimes against humanity. In June Quelo Mauno, a former leader of a pro-Indonesia militia, was convicted of the murder of an independence supporter in Oecusse in 1999 and sentenced to seven years in prison. In the following month the Dili court found a further two former pro-Indonesia militia leaders guilty of crimes against humanity and, by February 2004, some 47 people had been convicted of crimes relating to the referendum period. Meanwhile, the total number of people indicted by the court had risen to approximately 350, many of whom were resident in Indonesia; the Indonesian Government continued to refuse to extradite those indicted to face trial. In May 2004 the SPSC finally issued an arrest warrant for Wiranto, who had been nominated in the previous month as a candidate for Indonesia's presidential election, the first round of which was scheduled for July. Fearing a breach in relations with Indonesia, President Gusmão and the Prosecutor-General, Longuinhos Monteiro, both moved to distance themselves from the warrant, insisting that a good rapport with neighbouring countries should take precedence over court proceedings to hold people accountable for crimes committed during the emergence of their nation. In December 2004 Timor-Leste and Indonesia agreed to establish the joint Commission of Truth and Friendship (CTF) to investigate the killings carried out during the period of the Timorese vote for independence, and this was formally approved by their respective Governments in March 2005. However, the CTF was rapidly dismissed by the international community; none of the crimes committed during Indonesian occupation prior to 1999 was to be investigated, and the CTF process was not intended to lead to prosecution. Furthermore, offenders who co-operated 'fully in revealing the truth' were to be guaranteed impunity, irrespective of the nature of their crimes. In August 2005, despite the overwhelmingly negative response to the Commission, the 10-member panel was formally sworn in. Meanwhile, in February of that year the UN established the Commission of Experts, which was to review the judicial processes of the Ad Hoc Indonesian Human Rights Tribunal on East Timor, as well as the Serious Crimes Investigation Unit and the SPSC in Timor-Leste.

In February 2004, as sporadic outbreaks of violence, reportedly perpetrated by rebel militias based in rural areas, continued to occur in Timor-Leste, Cristiano da Costa, the leader of the Conselho Popular pela Defesa da República Democrática de Timor Leste (CPD-RDTL, Popular Council for the Defence of the Democratic Republic of East Timor), announced that his organization intended to challenge the legitimacy of the established Government in Timor-Leste following the planned withdrawal of UNMISET in May 2004. However, UNMISET's mandate was subsequently extended for an additional year, although its presence was reduced to a mere 604 officers, while responsibility for law and order in the capital and for external security was transferred to the Government in advance of the formal full transfer of power. It was feared that the methods employed by the Government to suppress insurgents might result in further instability in the country. The use of the police to suppress political opposition was a particular cause for concern. In July 2004 the National Union of Resistance Staff and Veterans held a rally in Dili, demanding a cabinet reshuffle and the dismissal of the unpopular Rogério Lobato. Police officers were drafted in, and resorted to beatings and the use of tear gas to disperse the crowd; some witnesses also claimed that guns were fired. Dili was the scene of another disturbance in December of the same year, when a group of 20 armed soldiers attacked a police station, injuring two officers and causing damage to the premises. There were also numerous reported sightings of alleged ex-militia groups, especially within border areas. In January 2005, in an operation intended to verify the accuracy of one such reported sighting in the Bobonaro district, police encountered six armed men and, following the resultant exchange of gunfire, one of the group was arrested. Prime Minister Alkatiri was quick to assert that it should not be assumed that the men were necessarily acting at the behest of the Indonesian army.

In December 2004 the first local elections since Timorese independence were held in Bobonaro and in the enclave of Oecusse. In order to promote female participation, a minimum of three women were to be elected to each village council. There was a high turn-out, exceeding 90% in some areas, and voters were able to cast their ballots in a calm and orderly manner, free from intimidation. However, there were numerous logistical problems, including errors on the electoral roll, which prohibited some people from casting their vote and delayed the outcome of the elections from being determined. By October 2005 elections had been held in the remaining 11 districts. While local councils held extremely limited authority, the election results revealed a considerable decline in popular support for Fretilin. Timor-Leste's principal party still maintained a sizeable majority, but its share of the vote decreased to less than 50% in some regions, representing a marked decline from previous levels of support.

Meanwhile, on 20 May 2005 the mandate of UNMISET was officially concluded, and the last remaining UN troops were withdrawn from Timor-Leste in the following month. The UN Office in Timor-Leste (UNOTIL) was established to facilitate the transfer of complete power to the Timorese authorities; its mandate was due to be concluded on 19 May 2006.

In July 2005 Prime Minister Alkatiri effected a cabinet reorganization, providing for an enlarged government comprising 17 ministries, with 15 deputy ministers and 11 state secretaries. Four state secretary portfolios, including those of defence and of public works, were transformed into full ministries. Alkatiri relinquished the role of Minister of Development and assumed control of the natural resources, minerals and energy policy portfolio. Abel Ximenes was selected to be the new Minister of Development; Antoninho Bianco was appointed as the inaugural Minister of Defence; and Odete Victor became Minister for Public Works.

In early February 2006 an estimated 400 soldiers (approximately one-quarter of Timor-Leste's 1,600-strong army) staged a protest about living conditions in their barracks and about alleged discrimination against soldiers from western regions of the country; they claimed that army officers, who were predominantly from Timor-Leste's eastern regions, frequently passed over for promotion soldiers from western regions in favour of those from their own localities. Having deserted their duties, the protesting soldiers presented a petition to President Gusmão, who promised a government inquiry into their complaints and urged them to return to their barracks. However, the rebellion escalated in late February when more than 170 additional soldiers deserted their barracks. The military leadership issued an ultimatum, demanding that they return to duty or be dismissed; when they had failed to return by March, the Commander-in-Chief of the Army, Brig.-Gen. Taur Matan Ruak, sanctioned their dismissal. Ruak's action precipitated a series of large-scale protests, which escalated into violence at the end of April, when supporters of the dismissed soldiers clashed with the police. The demonstrations, said to involve gangs, developed into looting, the destruction of property and eventually ethnic violence between eastern and western Timorese, which had claimed at least 37 lives and caused the displacement of an estimated 100,000 people by the following month. Prime Minister Alkatiri was criticized over his Government's handling of the situation, and anti-Government sentiments were increasingly voiced among protesters, who demanded Alkatiri's resignation. The turmoil led to the resignation of the Minister for Development, Abel Ximenes, at the beginning of May. At a Fretilin congress in mid-May, José Luís Guterres, the Timorese ambassador to the USA and Permanent Representative to the UN, withdrew his leadership challenge against Alkatiri after it emerged that the vote was to be determined by a show of hands rather than a secret ballot. At the end of May, in response to a request from Alkatiri, Australia deployed troops to Timor-Leste as part of an international effort to restore stability; Malaysia and New Zealand also contributed troops, while Portugal dispatched a contingent of police officers. The Minister for Foreign Affairs and Co-operation, Ramos Horta, attributed the unrest in part to a 'failure of leadership'; it was reported that Ramos Horta had communicated with Maj. Alfredo Reinado, the leader of the protesting soldiers. President Gusmão subsequently acted to curb the violence by assuming emergency powers and control of the country's security from the Minister for Defence, Roque Rodrigues, and the Minister for Interior Affairs, Rogério Lobato, both of whom resigned. Gusmão later assigned their portfolios to Ramos Horta, who engaged in dialogue with leaders of the rebel troops. Alkatiri finally yielded to considerable pressure to resign from several quarters, including Gusmão and the protesters, at the end of June, following the resignation of Ramos Horta on the previous day. Ramos Horta was appointed Prime Minister, retaining the defence portfolio, in July, in advance of the swearing in of a new Cabinet comprising several ministers of the previous administration, including the Minister for Agriculture, Forestry and Fisheries, Estanislau Aleixo da Silva, as Deputy Prime Minister. Rui Maria de Araújo retained the health portfolio and was additionally promoted to the position of Deputy Prime Minister, while José Luís Guterres became Minister for Foreign Affairs and Co-operation. The new Government was to remain in power until parliamentary elections, scheduled for mid-2007, were held.

In an indication that the security situation had improved significantly, in July 2006 Australia began to reduce its deployment in Timor-Leste, although some 2,000 personnel were projected to remain; in September Malaysia withdrew its remaining forces. Maj. Reinado was apprehended at the end of July following the expiry of a weapons amnesty, but escaped from prison in August. In the same month UNOTIL was replaced by the UN Integrated Mission in Timor-Leste (UNMIT) for an initial period of six months. With an authorized strength of up to 1,608 police personnel and up to 34 military liaison and staff officers, supported by civilian staff, UNMIT aimed to maintain security and promote reconciliation and good governance. (UNMIT's mandate was later extended to February 2008.)

In October 2006 the UN Independent Special Commission of Inquiry for Timor-Leste released its report on the unrest: among other conclusions, it found that Rodrigues, Lobato and Ruak had unlawfully transferred weapons to civilians and that, although Alkatiri was not necessarily directly implicated in the transfer, he had failed to denounce it. The Commission consequently recommended further investigation into Alkatiri's involvement. The findings followed allegations that Alkatiri had formed a militia to consolidate his power base and to take action against opponents. Lobato's trial began in January 2007. In March he was found guilty of arming a group of civilians, led by Vicente da Conceição, a former Falintil guerrilla, and was sentenced to seven-and-a-half-years' imprisonment. (In October da Conceição was himself arrested and charged in connection with his role in the unrest.) Although stability had been largely restored, outbursts of violence continued, and the ongoing plight of refugees was highlighted by the Australian Minister of Defence, Dr Brendan Nelson, in November 2006; it was estimated that 70,000 internally displaced people remained in camps. Maj. Reinado continued to elude the security forces, despite the Government's attempts at negotiation, and at the beginning of March 2007 reports of an unsuccessful attempt to capture Reinado prompted protests in Dili.

In February 2007 Prime Minister Ramos Horta declared his candidacy for the forthcoming presidential election. In March President Gusmão indicated his desire to become Prime Minister and announced that he intended to join the Congresso Nacional da Reconstrução de Timor-Leste (CNRT—National Congress for the Reconstruction of Timor-Leste), a new political party, following the expiry of his presidential term. The first stage of the presidential election, held on 9 April, was contested by eight candidates. Francisco Guterres, the President of Fretilin, secured 27.9% of the votes cast, followed by Ramos Horta, who was favoured by Gusmão, with 21.8%, and Fernando de Araújo, President of the PD, with 19.2%. An official appeal against the results, lodged by three of the losing candidates, including de Araújo, on the grounds of alleged widespread manipulation of the vote and other serious irregularities, was dismissed. The National Electoral Commission had earlier rejected demands from five of the candidates for a recount of the votes.

As no candidate achieved the requisite overall majority, the two leading contenders proceeded to a second round of voting, which was conducted on 9 May 2007: Ramos Horta received 69.2% of the votes cast. Francisco Guterres duly conceded defeat, promising to support the new President for the sake of the country's development. Unlike the first round, which had been marred by widespread violence and intimidation, the second stage of polling was conducted peacefully with no reports of any serious irregularities. Turn-out was high in both the first and second rounds, at 81.8% and 81.0%, respectively. The election victory of José Ramos Horta, who formally took office on 20 May, was attributed to the support of the five non-Fretilin candidates who had been defeated in the first round of voting. Shortly after the inauguration ceremony one man was killed and several others injured in clashes in Dili between supporters of rival political parties. Meanwhile, Estanislau Aleixo da Silva, hitherto the Deputy Prime Minister, assumed the role of Prime Minister in an interim capacity. Among the incoming President's priorities were plans for radical reform of the police force and judiciary. He also intended to address the issue of the nearly 600 so-called 'petitioner soldiers' who had abandoned their barracks in February 2006 in protest at low pay and discrimination (see above).

The legislative election held on 30 June 2007 was contested by 14 political organizations and alliances. The number of seats in the National Parliament was reduced from 88 to 65. International observers declared their satisfaction with the conduct of the polls, in which 80.5% of the electorate participated. The electoral campaign had been generally peaceful, with the notable exception of the killing of two CNRT supporters in early June and a few minor clashes between rival supporters. Fretilin remained the largest party in the legislature following the elections, winning 21 seats, although its share of the vote declined to 29% compared with 57% at the 2001 election. The CNRT came a close second, with 24% of the vote and 18 seats, while an alliance of the ASDT and the PSD took 11 seats and the PD eight. Fretilin's relatively poor performance was attributed to public disillusion with the pace of reform since independence.

As none of the parties had secured sufficient seats to govern alone, talks aimed at forming a coalition government ensued. On 6 July 2007 the CNRT, the ASDT-PSD alliance and the PD announced their intention to establish a coalition. However, Fretilin insisted on its right, as the largest parliamentary party, to participate in government, initially suggesting that it could form a minority administration and later proposing the creation of a 'government of national unity'. After weeks of deadlock, on 6 August Ramos Horta invited the CNRT-led coalition to form a government. The President's decision was denounced as unconstitutional by Fretilin and prompted violent protests by supporters of the party. Nevertheless, Gusmão was inaugurated as Prime Minister on 8 August; his new Cabinet included José Luís Guterres as Deputy Prime Minister. Gusmão pledged to improve security, to combat corruption and to facilitate the return to their homes of the thousands of refugees who remained in camps following their displacement during the unrest of April–May 2006. Meanwhile, Fernando de Araújo was elected Speaker of the National Parliament at its first session at the end of July.

President Ramos Horta held a meeting with Alfredo Reinado in mid-August 2007, under the mediation of the Swiss-based Centre for Humanitarian Dialogue. However, Reinado subsequently rejected attempts by the Timorese Government to initiate further talks aimed at achieving a negotiated settlement. In mid-November another leader of the 'petitioner soldiers', former Lt Gastão Salsinha, announced that the dismissed troops would not engage in dialogue with the Government until they were reinstated into the armed forces. A week later Reinado reiterated this demand for reintegration into the military, threatening to mount further attacks in Dili if the Government did not comply. He also demanded the withdrawal of foreign troops and judges from Timor-Leste. Four former soldiers were convicted of murder and sentenced to up to 12 years' imprisonment in late November for shooting dead eight unarmed police officers in April 2006. Reinado's trial on charges of murder, attempted murder and revolt commenced *in absentia* in early December 2007, after he refused to surrender to the authorities. Nonetheless, the Government persisted in its efforts to maintain contact with the rebel soldiers.

The UN Secretary-General, Ban Ki-Moon, visited Timor-Leste in mid-December 2007, pledging continued UN assistance for the reform of the security forces and the judiciary. The process of gradually transferring authority from UNMIT to the national police commenced in early February 2008, when local officers assumed control of three police posts in Dili, although they were to remain under UN supervision.

On 11 February 2008 President Ramos Horta was shot by renegade soldiers in an attack on his residence in Dili, during which Reinado and another rebel were killed by presidential guards. Seriously injured, the President was evacuated to Darwin, Australia, for medical treatment. Prime Minister Gusmão, who had been targeted shortly afterwards in a separate assault reportedly led by Gastão Salsinha, but was unharmed, announced a 48-hour state of emergency in response to what he described as an attempted coup, imposing a night-time curfew in Dili and a ban on public gatherings and protests. Australia swiftly dispatched around 200 additional troops to Timor-Leste following the apparent assassination attempts, amid fears of renewed conflict, although no further violent incidents were reported in the days that followed. Speaker Fernando de Araújo replaced his deputy, Vicente Guterres, as acting President on 13 February after returning from overseas. On the same day arrest warrants were issued for several people suspected of involvement in the shootings, including Salsinha, and a 10-day extension of the state of emergency was approved by the National Parliament. Salsinha subsequently announced that he had assumed the leadership of the group of 'petitioner soldiers' and denied that they had attempted to murder Ramos Horta and Gusmão. Several days later Angela Pires, reported to be Reinado's legal adviser and alleged to have been with the rebel leader in the hours before the attacks, was arrested on suspicion of conspiracy, but was released on bail. Prime Minister Gusmão ordered the Timorese military and police forces temporarily to form a joint command to boost efforts to apprehend the perpetrators of the shootings. Meanwhile, the Prosecutor-General, Longuinhos Monteiro, stated that the authorities now believed that the rebels had intended to kidnap the President and Prime Minister rather than kill them. Three officers from the US Federal Bureau of Investigation were assisting Monteiro with his investigations.

The National Parliament voted to prolong the state of emergency for a further 30 days on 22 February 2008, and later that month UNMIT's mandate was extended for a further year. By late February most of the 'petitioner soldiers' had agreed to hold talks with the Government aimed at resolving their situation and were being held in a camp in Dili. In early March Amaro da Costa, a senior rebel leader, was the first of a number of suspects to surrender to the joint command that month, although several others, including Salsinha and Marcelo Caetano, whom Ramos Horta had apparently identified as the gunman who had shot him, remained at large. Having undergone a series of operations in Australia, on 17 April Ramos Horta returned to Dili, where he was welcomed by several thousand supporters, and resumed office immediately, urging Salsinha and his followers to surrender. Three former Timorese soldiers suspected of involvement in the shootings were detained in Indonesia on the following day and later extradited to Timor-Leste. In late April, following several days of negotiations with security officials, Salsinha, Caetano and 10 other rebels surrendered, relinquishing their weapons at a formal ceremony in Dili attended by Ramos Horta and Deputy Prime Minister José Luís Guterres. It was hoped that an end to the insurrection would encourage the estimated 100,000 displaced people who remained in camps to return to their homes. Meanwhile, the Australian Government announced the withdrawal of the additional troops that had been deployed to Timor-Leste in February. None the less, some 750 troops from Australia and 170 from New Zealand remained in the country to support UNMIT in its efforts to maintain security.

In the conduct of its foreign affairs, Timor-Leste accorded high priority to the development of cordial relations with Indonesia. In June 2003 Prime Minister Alkatiri paid his first official visit to Indonesia, holding talks with President Megawati Sukarnoputri. However, despite an agreement between the two countries to co-operate in resolving outstanding border demarcation issues, in early 2004 Indonesia caused tensions by announcing that it planned to deploy security forces on the disputed islet of Sinai, located off Oecusse. The Government had previously protested when Indonesia had conducted military exercises on the islet in late 2003. In June 2004 the Timorese Minister for Foreign Affairs, José Ramos Horta, and his Indonesian counterpart, Hassan Wirayuda, signed an agreement that resolved 90% of the border demarcation question. The remaining nine disputed land segments included territory in the Oecusse enclave; however, six of the nine segments were subsequently agreed upon in October, leaving merely three areas still to be resolved. A formal border agreement between the two countries was signed by the respective heads of state during a visit by Indonesian President Susilo Bambang Yudhoyono to Dili in April 2005. During his stay Yudhoyono paid his respects at the cemetery in which victims from the 1991 Dili massacre (see above) were buried. It was hoped that the visit would facilitate the forging of closer relations. In October, however, tensions arose between the two countries after clashes in the Oecusse enclave, allegedly involving gangs that were supported by Indonesian troops. Both the Timorese and the Indonesian Ministers of Foreign Affairs dismissed the violence as mere civilian land disputes arising from confusion over the delineation of the border. Relations were further sullied by a report published in January 2006 by the Commission for Reception, Truth and Reconciliation (a national body created in 2002, charged with investigating alleged human rights violations during Indonesia's occupation of Timor-Leste). The report documented a catalogue of abuses allegedly carried out by Indonesian security forces in Timor-Leste between April 1974 and October 1999, claiming that as many as 180,000 Timorese civilians had died as a result of the Indonesian army's alleged deliberate policy of starvation. Later that month a scheduled meeting between Presidents Gusmão and Yudhoyono was cancelled; no official reason was given for the decision, but it was widely perceived to be as a result of Yudhoyono's displeasure with the findings of the report. In February 2007 the CTF (Commission of Truth and Friendship—see above), jointly formed by Indonesia and Timor-Leste in 2004 to establish the truth about the events of 1999, held its first hearing. The CTF held five sessions of hearings between February and September 2007, before retiring to prepare its recommendations. Prominent figures who appeared before the Commission included Gen. Wiranto, Gusmão and Brig.-Gen. Ruak. In July the UN prohibited its officials from testifying, owing to the decision to grant amnesty to perpetrators of serious crimes, while human rights organizations continued to criticize the process, claiming that insufficient numbers of victims had been summoned to give evidence. Meanwhile, in early June, some two weeks after taking office as President of Timor-Leste, José Ramos Horta visited Indonesia. Ramos Horta and Indonesian President Yudhoyono reaffirmed their commitment to the CTF, extending its mandate by six months, and emphasized the importance of further improving bilateral relations. The presentation of the CTF's final report to the Presidents of Indonesia and Timor-Leste was to have taken place by the end of March 2008, but was delayed pending Ramos Horta's full recovery from injuries sustained when he was shot in February.

In September 2007 President José Ramos Horta announced that he had established a task force to prepare for Timor-Leste's eventual accession to the Association of South East Asian Nations (ASEAN, see p. 185), with a view to securing membership within around five years.

Meanwhile, Timor-Leste's relations with Australia were strained by ongoing discussions relating to the Timor Sea Treaty. In November 2003 bilateral negotiations began concerning the demarcation of the maritime boundary between the two countries, an important issue owing to its ramifications for the allocation of revenues from petroleum and gas fields in the Timor Sea. Australia refused to recognize the boundary delineated by the UN Convention on the Law of the Sea. Prime Minister Alkatiri accused Australia of deliberately attempting to stall the negotiations, following its refusal to agree to the holding of monthly discussions in order to bring about a more rapid resolution to the boundary issues. Months of acrimonious dispute ensued, during which numerous aid agencies, including the British-based Oxfam, accused Australia of pushing Timor-Leste to the point of ruin; Oxfam declared that if a maritime boundary were established between the two countries under international law, 'most, if not all' of the petroleum reserves would be allocated to Timor-Leste. In September 2004 the two countries appeared finally to have agreed upon a revenue-sharing arrangement, which over a period of 30 years would afford Timor-Leste $A5,000m. in tax and royalty payments from the natural gas project in the Timor Sea. However, the negotiations again broke down, principally owing to the two countries' failure to agree on the contentious boundary issues. In February 2005 further acrimony ensued when the Australian Government agreed to a mid-point boundary with New Zealand but still refused to consider a similar arrangement with Timor-Leste, provoking widespread accusations of blatant hypocrisy. Instead, Australia proposed that the decision with Timor-Leste be deferred for up to 100 years while the major petroleum and gas deposits were exhausted, dismissing Timor-Leste's bid for a mid-point boundary as an 'ambit claim'. In November a deal was finally reached, with both countries agreeing to share equally the oil and gas revenues from the disputed region, which included the Greater Sunrise Project; a final decision on the contentious issue of the delineation of a maritime boundary was deferred for 50 years in order to allow petroleum and gas projects to proceed. The agreement was formally signed in the Australian city of Sydney in January 2006 and entered into force in February 2007, following ratification by Timor-Leste's National Parliament. Despite these tensions, the Australian Government remained a major source of financial assistance for Timor-Leste, and announced a $A240m. four-year aid programme in August. The new Prime Minister of Australia, Kevin Rudd, visited Dili soon after taking office in December, pledging continued support for Timor-Leste in the area of security. Timorese President Ramos Horta and Prime Minister Gusmão had both urged Rudd to maintain Australian troops in Timor-Leste until at least the end of 2008. Rudd returned to Timor-Leste shortly after the attacks on Ramos Horta and Gusmão in February 2008. Australia had dispatched additional troops to the country following the shootings (see above). In April Ramos Horta requested Australian assistance in investigating the source of a large sum of money that the President claimed had been deposited in an Australian bank account held jointly by Alfredo Reinado and his associate, Angela Pires, as well as a series of telephone calls to Australia apparently made by Reinado. The Australian Minister for Foreign Affairs, Stephen Smith, subsequently rejected Timorese suggestions that Australia was delaying the investigation into the shooting, stating that telecommunications records had already been provided and urging the Timorese authorities to follow the appropriate procedures to gain access to financial records.

Government

In March 2002 the Constituent Assembly promulgated East Timor's first Constitution and, on 14 April, the territory held its first presidential election. The President serves a five-year term. Upon the territory's accession to independence in May of that year, the Constituent Assembly transformed itself into the National Parliament. (The number of seats in the National Parliament was reduced from 88 to 65 at the 2007 election.) In 2002 the UN Transitional Administration in East Timor (UNTAET) formally relinquished its responsibility for the administration of the country and was succeeded by the UN Mission of Support in East Timor (UNMISET), which remained in the country, in a supporting role, ultimately for three years. UNMISET was replaced in May 2005 by the UN Office in Timor-Leste (UNOTIL), which was superseded by the UN Integrated Mission in Timor-Leste (UNMIT) in August 2006.

Defence

Following the official completion of the mandate of the UN Mission of Support in East Timor (UNMISET), the last remaining UN peace-keeping troops withdrew from Timor-Leste in mid-2005. As assessed at November 2007, according to Western estimates, the East Timorese Defence Force (Falintil-ETDF) comprised 1,250 army personnel, including 30 women and a naval element of 36.

Economic Affairs

In 2006, according to estimates by the World Bank, Timor-Leste's gross national income (GNI), measured at average 2004–06 prices, was US $865m., equivalent to $840 per head. During 1996–2006, it was estimated, the population increased at an average annual rate of 3.0%, while gross domestic product (GDP) per head, in real terms, declined by 1.5% in 1999–2006. Overall GDP decreased, in real terms, at an average annual rate of 2.5% during 1999–2006. According to the Asian Development Bank (ADB), GDP decreased by 5.8% in 2006, before increasing by 7.8% in 2007.

The economy of Timor-Leste is based principally on the agricultural sector, which, according to FAO, in mid-2005 engaged some 81% of the Timorese labour force. In 2006 the agricultural sector (including forestry and fishing) contributed an estimated 32.2% of non-oil GDP. Coffee is a significant export commodity. According to IMF estimates, revenue from coffee exports, which constituted some 75% of total non-oil export receipts in 2006, reached US $6m. in that year, compared with $8m. in 2005. The coffee sector remained extremely susceptible to climatic conditions, which, combined with poor irrigation systems, were primarily responsible for significant fluctuations in annual output. There are small plantations of coconut, cloves and cinnamon. Subsistence crops include rice, maize and cassava. Livestock raised includes cattle and water buffalo. There is some small-scale fishing, and the forestry sector may yield as yet undeveloped potential. According to World Bank estimates, the GDP of the agricultural sector increased, in real terms, at an average annual rate of 1.5% in 1999–2006. Real growth in the sector's GDP was estimated by the ADB at 6.3% in 2005, but no growth was recorded in 2006.

The industrial sector (including mining and quarrying, manufacturing, utilities and construction) contributed an estimated 12.8% of non-oil GDP in 2006. According to figures from the World Bank, industrial GDP declined at an average annual rate of 1.8% in 1999–2006. According to the ADB, the industrial sector's GDP increased, in real terms, by 10.6% in 2005, before declining significantly, by 16.3%, in 2006.

In the 1990s sizeable natural gas fields were discovered in and around the Timor Gap zone, and petroleum reserves in the region were estimated by some sources to total a potential 500m. barrels. Although detailed data for the contribution made to GDP by petroleum and gas activities were not available, the IMF estimated that these sectors generated incomes of US $342m. in 2005 and $492m. in 2006 (equivalent to 138% of the value of non-oil GDP in the latter year). The mining sector, excluding petroleum and gas, was estimated to have contributed only 0.6% of GDP in 2006. In addition to offshore petroleum and gas, mineral resources include high-grade marble. According to the IMF, the GDP of the non-oil mining sector was estimated to have decreased at an average annual rate of 11.7% in 2000–06. The sector's GDP decreased by 33.3% in 2006.

There is a small manufacturing sector, which is mainly concerned with the production of textiles, the bottling of water and coffee processing. In 2006 the manufacturing sector provided an estimated 2.6% of non-oil GDP. In May of that year one of the world's largest wet-processing coffee factories was opened in Estado, which, together with expanded production at the existing Maubisse factory, was expected to increase significantly Timor-Leste's annual coffee output. According to World Bank estimates, manufacturing GDP expanded, in real terms, at an average annual rate of 0.9% in 1999–2006. The GDP of the manufacturing sector decreased by 25.0% in 2006.

The construction sector contributed an estimated 8.4% of non-oil GDP in 2006. According to IMF estimates, the construction sector's GDP declined by an average annual rate of 7.4% in 2000–06. In 2005 the GDP of the sector increased by 13.7%, but in 2006 it contracted by 13.6%.

In 2002 the Government elected to transfer control of the national power authority, Electricidade de Timor-Leste (EDTL), to external management. Although the rehabilitation of the rural power infrastructure was largely complete by 2003, supplies of electricity subsequently remained intermittent. According to figures from the IMF, the GDP of the utilities sector rose at an average annual rate of 8.9% in 2000–06; the sector's GDP was estimated to have increased by 20.5% in 2005, but contracted by an estimated 4.3% in 2006.

The services sector (including UN contributions) was responsible for an estimated 55.1% of non-oil GDP in 2006. According to World Bank estimates, the services sector's GDP rose at an average annual rate of 4.0% in 1999–2006. According to the ADB, the sector's GDP, in real terms, declined by 2.0% in 2005, but increased by 1.6% in 2006. In 2006 public administration and defence accounted for an estimated 23.3% of non-oil GDP. Tourism remained negligible, owing to a lack of basic infrastructure, as well as to prohibitively high air fares from Indonesia and Australia.

In 2006 Timor-Leste recorded a visible trade deficit of US $133m., while there was a surplus of $411m. on the current account of the balance of payments (largely owing to the allocation of oil and gas export revenues to the income and transfers accounts). Reliable data for exports of oil and gas were not available (see above), but these, together with coffee, constituted the most significant merchandise exports in 2006.

In 2008 the Ministry of Finance envisaged budgetary expenditure of US $319.2m. Total government revenue was projected to rise from $711.7m. in 2007 to $1,379.3m. in 2008, when a fiscal surplus of $667.6m. was anticipated. According to the IMF, consumer prices increased by an average annual rate of 3.6% in 2000–07; the inflation rate increased to 10.3% in 2007. In 2001 the rate of unemployment was estimated by the ADB at 5.3%. According to the census of 2004, those recorded as unemployed, or deterred from seeking work, accounted for one-half of Dili residents aged between 15 and 24 years.

TIMOR-LESTE

Following independence in May 2002, Timor-Leste became a member of the Asian Development Bank (ADB, see p. 182), the Comunidade dos Países de Língua Portuguesa (Community of Portuguese-Speaking Countries, see p. 423) and the UN Economic and Social Commission for Asia and the Pacific (ESCAP, see p. 35). The country was also granted observer status at the Association of South East Asian Nations (ASEAN, see p. 185). Timor-Leste attended the third Summit of the African, Caribbean and Pacific group of states (ACP), held in Fiji in July 2002, as an observer.

Upon independence in 2002 Timor-Leste's first National Development Plan (NDP) was implemented, its principal objectives, over an 18-year period, including the reduction of poverty. The Plan proposed the introduction of a phased programme of development, under which priority would be given in the short term to the creation of a legislative framework, the enlargement of institutional capacity and further infrastructural growth. External aid remained of vital importance to the Timorese economy. The Timor Sea Arrangement, relating to the sharing of petroleum and gas royalties with Australia (see Recent History), was signed in 2002. In 2003 a US company was granted permission to develop the Bayu-Undan liquefied natural gas (LNG) field in the Timor Sea. The agreement signed by Timor-Leste and Australia in January 2006 regarding the allocation of revenue from the Greater Sunrise gas project (see Recent History) was another significant development. Timor-Leste's natural gas resources thus appeared to offer the greatest hopes of long-term economic self-sufficiency. In June 2005 the Government approved the creation of a Petroleum Fund, which was to serve as a long-term repository for all petroleum revenues. Following the contraction of the economy in 2006, primarily owing to the deterioration in the security situation, a good recovery was achieved in 2007. Timor-Leste was forecast by the ADB to record a second consecutive year of strong growth in 2008, with GDP being expected to expand by 6.5%. The growth of 7.8% (excluding the offshore petroleum and gas sector, as well as UN operations) in 2007 was achieved despite an estimated contraction of at least 2% in the agricultural sector, in which the majority of the workforce was engaged. Adverse weather conditions and seed shortages, concomitant with low stocks of food, exacerbated the intermittent shortages of foodstuffs, the situation being compounded by the high rate of population growth. The World Food Programme was reported to be supporting nearly 30% of the Timorese population. Substantial increases in food costs were recorded in 2007 and, as global prices for basic commodities such as rice continued to rise in early 2008, the rate of inflation was expected to accelerate. Meanwhile, however, Timor-Leste continued to benefit from the strength of international oil prices. Higher petroleum revenues thus permitted a consolidation of the country's fiscal position.

Education

The education system was badly disrupted by the civil conflict of 1999. It was estimated that 75%–80% of primary and secondary schools were either partially or completely destroyed. However, a total of 240,000 students registered for the 2000/01 academic year, a much higher number than anticipated. In 2004/05 enrolment within primary education included 68% (males 70%, females 67%) of pupils in the relevant age-group. In the same year, enrolment within secondary education was equivalent to 53% (males 53%, females 53%) of pupils in the relevant age group. Literacy rates were reported to have reached only 41% by 1998, with lower rates recorded for women than for men, although this had increased moderately to 58.6% by 2004. In January 2001 the reopening of the university improved the country's tertiary education facilities, enabling the enrolment of 4,500 students on degree courses and 3,000 on bridging programmes. In 2001/02 enrolment in tertiary education was equivalent to 10% (males 9%, females 11%) of students in the relevant age group. Following Timor-Leste's accession to nationhood in May 2002, the Government accorded priority to the development of education. In June 2002 the Emergency Schools Readiness Project, funded by the Trust Fund for East Timor (TFET), was completed, having effected the renovation of 535 schools and 2,780 classrooms since August 2000. It was succeeded by the Fundamental School Quality Project, under which 65 primary schools were to be constructed during 2002/03. The budget of the Central Fund for East Timor (CFET) allocated an estimated US $17.1m. to the education sector in 2002/03, 24.2% of total expenditure.

Public Holidays

2008: 1 January (New Year's Day), 21 March (Good Friday), 1 May (Labour Day), 20 May (Independence Day), 15 August (Assumption), 30 August (Constitution Day), 20 September (Liberation Day), 1 November (All Saints' Day), 12 November (Santa Cruz Day), 8 December (Immaculate Conception), 25 December (Christmas Day).

2009: 1 January (New Year's Day), 10 April (Good Friday), 1 May (Labour Day), 20 May (Independence Day), 15 August (Assumption), 30 August (Constitution Day), 20 September (Liberation Day), 1 November (All Saints' Day), 12 November (Santa Cruz Day), 8 December (Immaculate Conception), 25 December (Christmas Day).

Weights and Measures

The metric system is in force.

Statistical Survey

Area and Population

AREA, POPULATION AND DENSITY

Area (sq km)	14,609*
Population (census results)	
31 October 1990	747,750
31 July 2004	
Males	467,757
Females	456,885
Total	924,642
Population (UN estimates at mid-year)†	
2005	1,067,000
2006	1,114,000
2007	1,155,000
Density (per sq km) at mid-2007	79.1

* 5,641 sq miles.
† Source: UN, *World Population Prospects: The 2006 Revision*.

PRINCIPAL TOWNS
(population at 2000)

Dili (capital)	48,200	Maliana	12,300
Dare	17,100	Ermera	12,000
Baucau	14,200		

Source: Stefan Helders, *World Gazetteer* (internet www.world-gazetteer.com).

Mid-2007 (incl. suburbs, UN estimate): Dili 159,000 (Source: UN, *World Urbanization Prospects: The 2007 Revision*).

BIRTHS AND DEATHS
(annual averages, UN estimates)

	1990–95	1995–2000	2000–05
Birth rate (per 1,000)	43.0	45.7	41.7
Death rate (per 1,000)	15.4	12.6	10.2

Source: UN, *World Population Prospects: The 2006 Revision*.

Expectation of life (years at birth, WHO estimates): 65.5 (males 63.1; females 68.4) in 2005 (Source: WHO, *World Health Statistics*).

TIMOR-LESTE

Health and Welfare

KEY INDICATORS

Total fertility rate (children per woman, 2005)	7.8
Under-5 mortality rate (per 1,000 live births, 2005)	61
Physicians (per 1,000 head, 2004)	0.10
Health expenditure (2004): US $ per head	142.5
Health expenditure (2004): % of GDP	11.2
Health expenditure (2004): public (% of total)	78.9
Access to water (% of persons, 2004)	58
Access to sanitation (% of persons, 2004)	36
Human development index (2005): ranking	150
Human development index (2005): value	0.514

For sources and definitions, see explanatory note on p. vi.

Agriculture

PRINCIPAL CROPS
('000 metric tons)

	2003	2004	2005
Maize	70.2*	91.0†	80.0†
Cassava (Manioc)	41.5*	46.6†	47.2†
Rice (paddy)	65.4*	65.0†	65.0†
Sweet potatoes†	26.0	26.4	26.9
Dry beans†	4.5	4.5	4.5
Groundnuts (in shell)†	4.0	4.5	4.8
Coconuts†	14.0	13.9	14.0
Copra†	2.0	2.0	2.0
Bananas†	2.0	2.0	2.0
Guavas, mangoes and mangosteens†	3.0	3.4	3.7
Coffee (green)†	14.0	14.8	15.4

* Unofficial figure.
† FAO estimate(s).

Maize ('000 metric tons, FAO estimate) 90 in 2006.

Rice (paddy) ('000 metric tons, FAO estimate) 65 in 2006.

Aggregate production ('000 metric tons, may include official, semi-official or estimated data): Total cereals 156 in 2004, 145 in 2005, 155 in 2006; Total roots and tubers 117 in 2004, 118 in 2005, 118 in 2006; Total vegetables (incl. melons) 18 in 2004, 18 in 2005, 18 in 2006; Total fruits (excl. melons) 6 in 2004, 6 in 2005, 6 in 2006.

Source: FAO.

LIVESTOCK
('000 head, FAO estimates unless otherwise stated)

	2003	2004	2005
Cattle	170	170	171
Buffaloes	107	108	110
Pigs	340	346	346
Horses	48	48	48
Goats	80	80	80
Sheep	25	25	25
Chickens	1,300	2,100	2,200*

* Official figure.

Note: Data were not available for 2006.
Source: FAO.

LIVESTOCK PRODUCTS
('000 metric tons, FAO estimates)

	2003	2004	2005
Cattle meat	1.2	1.1	1.1
Pig meat	8.0	7.6	7.4
Chicken meat	1.4	1.4	1.4
Hen eggs	1.6	1.6	1.6

Note: No data were available for 2006.
Source: FAO.

Fishing

(metric tons, live weight, FAO estimates)

	2003	2004	2005
Total catch	350	350	350

Source: FAO.

Finance

CURRENCY AND EXCHANGE RATES (US currency is used)

Monetary Units
100 cents (centavos) = 1 United States dollar ($).

Sterling and Euro Equivalents (31 December 2007)
£1 sterling = US $2.0034;
€1 = $1.4721;
US $100 = £49.92 = €67.93.

BUDGET
(US $ million, calculated on cash basis)

Revenue	2004/05	2005/06*	2006/07†
Domestic revenue	36.9	33.4	39.1
Direct taxes	10.7	8.5	7.9
Indirect taxes	19.0	15.9	21.4
Non-tax revenues and other	7.1	9.1	9.8
Oil and gas revenues	265.6	451.3	683.5
Tax revenues	209.4	362.8	557.9
Royalties and interest	56.2	88.5	125.5
Grants	34.2	—	10.0
Total	336.7	485.0	732.9

Expenditure	2004/05	2005/06*	2006/07†
Recurrent expenditure	56.4	66.3	172.2
Salaries and wages	25.1	25.7	47.4
Goods and services	26.0	33.0	93.6
Subsidies to agencies	5.3	7.5	12.9
Capital expenditure	2.8	15.7	137.0
Carried over from previous year	12.2	11.0	—
Total	71.4	93.0	309.2

* Estimates.
† Budget forecasts.

Source: IMF, *Timor-Leste: Selected Issues and Statistical Appendix* (February 2007).

2007 (general government budget, US $ million, estimates): *Revenue:* Domestic revenue 14.4 (Direct taxes 4.1, Indirect taxes 5.0, Non-tax revenues and other 5.3); Oil and gas revenues 697.3 (Taxes and royalties 634.1, Petroleum fund interest 63.2); Total 711.7. *Expenditure:* Salaries and wages 19.1; Goods and services 57.5; Minor capital 3.0; Capital and development 0.1; Public transfer payments 12.1; Total 91.8.

2008 (general government budget, US $ million, estimates): *Revenue:* Domestic revenue 20.7 (Direct taxes 3.2, Indirect taxes 8.3, Non-tax revenues and other 9.2); Oil and gas revenues 1,358.6 (Taxes and royalties 1,249.7, Petroleum fund interest 108.7, Other petroleum revenue 0.2); Total 1,379.3. *Expenditure:* Salaries and wages 46.7; Goods and services 124.4; Minor capital 23.8; Capital and development 60.5; Public transfer payments 63.9; Total 319.2.

MONEY SUPPLY
(US $ million at 31 December)

	2005	2006	2007
Currency outside banks	1.790	1.811	2.273
Demand deposits	37.391	51.304	72.663
Total	39.181	53.115	74.935

Source: IMF, *International Financial Statistics*.

TIMOR-LESTE

COST OF LIVING
(Consumer Price Index; base: 2000 = 100)

	2005	2006	2007
All items	111.9	116.3	128.2

Source: IMF, *International Financial Statistics*.

NATIONAL ACCOUNTS
(US $ million at current prices)
Expenditure on Non-oil Gross Domestic Product

	2004	2005	2006*
Government final consumption expenditure	183.4	172.1	178.2
Private final consumption expenditure	244.9	238.3	243.5
Change in stocks	6.0	6.8	6.8
Gross fixed capital formation	58.7	60.2	60.8
Total domestic non-oil expenditure	493.0	477.4	489.3
Exports of goods and services	8.3	9.2	7.9
Less Imports of goods and services	162.7	136.6	141.3
Non-oil GDP in purchasers' values	338.6	349.9	355.7
Non-oil GDP at constant 2000 prices	323.7	331.1	325.8

Non-oil Gross Domestic Product by Economic Activity

	2004	2005	2006*
Agriculture, forestry and fishing	103.7	111.3	114.6
Mining and quarrying (non-oil)	2.7	2.9	2.0
Manufacturing	11.6	11.8	9.1
Electricity, gas and water	4.1	5.0	4.4
Construction	29.0	33.4	29.9
Wholesale and retail trade	24.5	24.9	23.4
Transport and communications	31.9	33.8	29.2
Finance, rents and business services	27.7	28.3	25.4
Public administration and defence	74.1	80.5	82.8
United Nations	29.3	18.0	35.1
Non-oil GDP in purchaser's values	338.6	349.9	355.7

* Estimates.

Source: IMF, *Timor-Leste: Selected Issues and Statistical Appendix* (February 2007).

BALANCE OF PAYMENTS
(US $ million, estimates)

	2004	2005	2006
Exports of goods f.o.b.	8	9	8
Imports of goods f.o.b.	−163	−137	−141
Trade balance	−154	−127	−133
Services (net)	−32	−27	−33
Balance on goods and services	−186	−154	−166
Income (net)	43	83	117
Balance on goods, services and income	−143	−71	−49
Current transfers (net)	246	363	460
Current balance	103	292	411
Capital transfers	41	41	44
Other capital flows (net)	−23	8	27
Overall balance	121	341	482

Source: IMF, *Timor-Leste: Selected Issues and Statistical Appendix* (February 2007).

External Trade

SELECTED COMMODITIES
(US $ '000)

Imports c.i.f	2004	2005
Cereals	8,111	4,690
Preparations of cereals, flour, starch or milk; pastry cooks' products	2,113	2,162
Beverages, spirits and vinegar	1,739	2,229
Mineral fuels, mineral oils and products of their distillation; bituminous substances; mineral waxes	36,757	35,136
Nuclear reactors, boilers, machinery and mechanical appliances; parts thereof	4,651	7,847
Vehicles, other than railway or tramway rolling stock, and parts thereof	14,735	7,018
Electrical machinery and equipment and parts thereof; sound recorders and reproducers; televisions, etc.	9,821	5,470
Pharmaceutical products	2,652	2,636
Iron or steel articles	1,391	2,629
Plastics and articles thereof	1,287	2,362
Total (incl. others)	113,489	101,619

Exports f.o.b (excl. oil and gas)	2004	2005
Coffee	6,899	7,630
Total (incl. others)	6,972	8,093

Re-exports (US $ '000): 98,682 in 2004; 35,358 in 2005. Note: the significance of re-exports may appear overstated owing to the inclusion of data connected with the outflow of foreign personnel and equipment as peace-keeping operations were scaled down.

2005 (US $ '000, revised figures): Total imports 109,109; Total domestic exports (excl. oil and gas) 8,086; Re-exports 35,364.

2006 (US $ '000): Total imports 100,803; Total domestic exports (excl. oil and gas) 8,445; Re-exports 52,241.

Source: Ministério do Plano e das Finanças, Dili.

PRINCIPAL TRADING PARTNERS
(US $ '000)

Imports c.i.f.	2004	2005
Australia	20,051	14,145
China, People's Republic	1,149	1,684
Indonesia	60,200	47,769
Japan	1,269	10,535
Korea, Republic	1	878
Malaysia	709	788
Portugal	1,686	1,656
Singapore	15,154	14,796
Thailand	1,306	1,122
Viet Nam	5,242	4,534
Total (incl. others)	113,489	101,619

Exports f.o.b. (excl. oil and gas)	2004	2005
Australia	511	445
Canada	—	44
Germany	441	1,672
Indonesia	1,277	406
Japan	80	100
New Zealand	48	24
Norway	71	71
Portugal	579	968
Singapore	158	91
Taiwan	93	196
Thailand	—	48
USA	3,551	3,978
Total (incl. others)	6,972	8,093

Source: Ministério do Plano e das Finanças, Dili.

Tourism

TOURIST ARRIVALS
('000 foreign visitors, excl. Indonesians, at classified hotels*)

	1996	1997	1998
Total	0.8	1.0	0.3

*Arrivals at non-classified hotels: 204 in 1996; 245 in 1997; 41 in 1998.

Communications Media

	2004	2005	2006
Internet users	—	1,000	1,200
Telephones ('000 main lines in use)	2.1	2.3	2.5
Mobile cellular telephones ('000 subscribers)	50.1	33.1	49.1

Daily newspapers: 2 in 2004.

Non-daily newspapers: 3 in 2004.

Source: UNESCO Institute for Statistics and International Telecommunication Union.

Education

(2004/05, unless otherwise indicated)

	Teachers	Students
Pre-primary	237	n.a.
Primary	5,211	177,970
Lower Secondary	1,810	50,014
Upper Secondary	1,350	24,808
Tertiary*	123	6,349

*2001/02 estimates.

Source: UNESCO Institute for Statistics.

Adult literacy rate (UNESCO estimate): 58.6% in 2003 (Source: UN Development Programme, *Human Development Report*).

Directory

The Constitution

The Constitution of the Democratic Republic of East Timor was promulgated by the Constituent Assembly on 22 March 2002 and became effective on 20 May 2002, when the nation formalized its independence. (From this date the country elected to be known by its official name, the Democratic Republic of Timor-Leste.) The main provisions of the Constitution are summarized below:

FUNDAMENTAL PRINCIPLES

The Democratic Republic of East Timor is a democratic, sovereign, independent and unitary state. Its territory comprises the historically defined eastern part of Timor island, the enclave of Oecussi, the island of Atauro and the islet of Jaco. Oecussi Ambeno and Atauro shall receive special administrative and economic treatment.

The fundamental objectives of the State include the following: to safeguard national sovereignty; to guarantee fundamental rights and freedoms; to defend political democracy; to promote the building of a society based on social justice; and to guarantee the effective equality of opportunities between women and men.

Sovereignty is vested in the people. The people shall exercise political power through universal, free, equal, direct, secret and periodic suffrage and through other forms stated in the Constitution.

In matters of international relations, the Democratic Republic of East Timor shall establish relations of friendship and co-operation with all other peoples. It shall maintain privileged ties with countries whose official language is Portuguese.

The State shall recognize and respect the different religious denominations, which are free in their organization. Tetum and Portuguese shall be the official languages.

FUNDAMENTAL RIGHTS, DUTIES, LIBERTIES AND GUARANTEES

All citizens are equal before the law and no one shall be discriminated against on grounds of colour, race, marital status, gender, ethnic origin, language, social or economic status, political or ideological convictions, religion, education and physical or mental condition. Women and men shall have the same rights and duties in family, political, economic, social and cultural life. Rights, freedoms and safeguards are upheld by the State and include the following: the right to life; to personal freedom, security and integrity; to habeas corpus; to the inviolability of the home and of correspondence; to freedom of expression and conscience; to freedom of movement, assembly and association; and to participate in political life. Freedom of the press is guaranteed.

Rights and duties of citizens include the following: the right and the duty to work; the right to vote (at over 17 years of age); the right to petition; the right and duty to contribute towards the defence of sovereignty; the freedom to form trade unions and the right to strike; consumer rights; the right to private property; the duty to pay taxes; the right to health and medical care; the right to education and culture.

ORGANIZATION OF POLITICAL POWER

Political power lies with the people. The organs of sovereignty shall be the President of the Republic, the National Parliament, the Government and the Courts. They shall observe the principle of separation and interdependence of powers. There shall be free, direct, secret, personal and regular universal suffrage. No one shall hold political office for life.

PRESIDENT OF THE REPUBLIC

The President of the Republic is the Head of State and the Supreme Commander of the Defence Force. The President symbolizes and guarantees national independence and unity and the effective functioning of democratic institutions. The President of the Republic shall be elected by universal, free, direct, secret and personal suffrage. The candidate who receives more than one-half of the valid votes shall be elected President. Candidates shall be original citizens of the Democratic Republic of East Timor, at least 35 years of age, in possession of his/her full faculties and have been proposed by a minimum of 5,000 voters. The President shall hold office for five years. The President may not be re-elected for a third consecutive term of office.

The duties of the President include the following: to preside over the Supreme Council of Defence and Security and the Council of State; to set dates for elections; to convene extraordinary sessions of the National Parliament; to dissolve the National Parliament; to promulgate laws; to exercise the functions of the Supreme Commander of the Defence Force; to veto laws; to appoint and dismiss the Prime Minister and other government members; to apply to the Supreme Court of Justice; to submit relevant issues of national interest to a referendum; to declare a State of Emergency following the authorization of the National Parliament; to appoint and dismiss diplomatic representatives; to accredit foreign diplomatic representatives; to declare war and make peace with the prior approval of the National Parliament.

COUNCIL OF STATE

The Council of State is the political advisory body of the President of the Republic. It is presided over by the President of the Republic and comprises former Presidents of the Republic who were not removed from office, the Speaker of the National Parliament, the Prime Minister, five citizens elected by the National Parliament and five citizens nominated by the President of the Republic.

TIMOR-LESTE

NATIONAL PARLIAMENT

The National Parliament represents all Timorese citizens, and shall have a minimum of 52 and a maximum of 65 members, elected by universal, free, direct, equal, secret and personal suffrage for a term of five years. The duties of the National Parliament include the following: to enact legislation; to confer legislative authority on the Government; to approve plans and the Budget and monitor their execution; to ratify international treaties and conventions; to approve revisions of the Constitution; to propose to the President of the Republic that issues of national interest be submitted to a referendum. The legislative term shall comprise five legislative sessions, and each legislative session shall have the duration of one year.

GOVERNMENT

The Government is the supreme organ of public administration and is responsible for the formulation and execution of general policy. It shall comprise the Prime Minister, the Ministers and the Secretaries of State, and may include one or more Deputy Prime Ministers and Deputy Ministers. The Council of Ministers shall comprise the Prime Minister, the Deputy Prime Ministers, if any, and the Ministers. It shall be convened and presided over by the Prime Minister. The Prime Minister shall be appointed by the President of the Republic. Other members of the Government shall be appointed by the President at the proposal of the Prime Minister. The Government shall be responsible to the President and the National Parliament. The Government's programme shall be submitted to the National Parliament for consideration within 30 days of the appointment of the Government.

JUDICIARY

The Courts are independent organs of sovereignty with competence to administer justice. There shall be the Supreme Court of Justice and other courts of law, the High Administrative, Tax and Audit Court, other administrative courts of first instance and military courts. There may also be maritime courts and courts of arbitration.

It is the duty of the Public Prosecutors to represent the State. The Office of the Prosecutor-General shall be the highest authority in public prosecution and shall be presided over by the Prosecutor-General, who is appointed and dismissed by the President of the Republic. The Prosecutor-General shall serve for a term of six years.

ECONOMIC AND FINANCIAL ORGANIZATION

The economic organization of East Timor shall be based on the co-existence of the public, private, co-operative and social sectors of ownership, and on the combination of community forms with free initiative and business management. The State shall promote national investment. The State Budget shall be prepared by the Government and approved by the National Parliament. Its execution shall be monitored by the High Administrative, Tax and Audit Court and by the National Parliament.

NATIONAL DEFENCE AND SECURITY

The East Timor defence force—Falintil-ETDF—is composed exclusively of national citizens and shall be responsible for the provision of military defence to the Democratic Republic of East Timor. There shall be a single system of organization for the whole national territory. Falintil-ETDF shall act as a guarantor of national independence, territorial integrity and the freedom and security of the population against any external threat or aggression. The police shall guarantee the internal security of the citizens.

The Superior Council for Defence and Security is the consultative organ of the President of the Republic on matters relating to defence and security. It shall be presided over by the President of the Republic and shall include a higher number of civilian than military entities.

GUARANTEE AND REVISION OF THE CONSTITUTION

Declaration of unconstitutionality may be requested by: the President of the Republic; the Speaker of the National Parliament; the Prosecutor-General; the Prime Minister; one-fifth of the Members of the National Parliament; the Ombudsman.

Changes to the Constitution shall be approved by a majority of two-thirds of Members of Parliament and the President shall not refuse to promulgate a revision statute.

FINAL AND TRANSITIONAL PROVISIONS

Confirmation, accession and ratification of bilateral and multilateral conventions, treaties, agreements or alliances that took place before the Constitution entered into force shall be decided by the respective bodies concerned; the Democratic Republic of East Timor shall not be bound by any treaty, agreement or alliance not thus ratified. Any acts or contracts concerning natural resources entered into prior to the entry into force of the Constitution and not subsequently confirmed by the competent bodies shall not be recognized.

Indonesian and English shall be working languages, together with the official languages, for as long as is deemed necessary.

Acts committed between 25 April 1974 and 31 December 1999 that can be considered to be crimes of humanity, of genocide or of war shall be liable to criminal proceedings within the national or international courts.

The Government

HEAD OF STATE

President: José Ramos Horta (took office 20 May 2007).

CABINET
(April 2008)

Prime Minister, Minister for Defence and Security and Minister for Natural Resources: José Alexandre (Xanana) Gusmão.

Deputy Prime Minister: José Luís Guterres.

Minister for State Administration: Arcângelo Leite Pinto.

Minister for Foreign Affairs and Co-operation: Zacarias da Costa.

Minister for Justice: Lúcia Lobato.

Minister for Health: Nélson Martins.

Minister for Planning and Finance: Maria Madalena Emília Pires.

Minister for Education: João Câncio.

Minister for Economy and Development: João Gonçalves.

Minister for Agriculture, Forestry and Fisheries: Mariano Sabino Lopes.

Minister for Social Solidarity: Maria Domingas Alves.

Minister for Tourism, Commerce and Industry: Gil da Costa Alves.

Minister for Infrastructure: Pedro Lay.

MINISTRIES

Office of the President: Palácio das Cinzas, Kaikoli, Dili; tel. 3339011.

Office of the Prime Minister: Palácio do Governo, Av. Presidente Nicolau Lobato, Dili; tel. 7243559; fax 3339503; e-mail mail@primeministerandcabinet.gov.tp; internet www.pm.gov.tp.

Ministry of Agriculture, Forestry and Fisheries: Dili; e-mail agriculture@gov.east-timor.org; internet www.maf.gov.tl.

Ministry of Defence: Palácio do Governo 3, Edif. 4, Av. Presidente Nicolau Lobato, Dili; tel. 3310478; e-mail sed-tl@easttimor.minihub.org; internet www.timor-leste.gov.tl/mindef.

Ministry of Economy and Development: Dili.

Ministry of Education, Culture, Youth and Sport: Dili; e-mail education@gov.east-timor.org.

Ministry of Finance: Palácio do Governo, Edif. 5, Av. Presidente Nicolau Lobato, Dili; tel. 3339546; e-mail info@mof.gov.tl; internet www.mof.gov.tl.

Ministry of Foreign Affairs and Co-operation: Edif. GPA 1, Ground Floor, Av. Presidente Nicolau Lobato, POB 6, Dili; tel. 3339600; fax 3339025; e-mail administration@mnec.gov-tl.net; internet www.mfac.gov.tp.

Ministry of Health: Edif. dos Serviços Centrais do Ministério da Saúde, Rua de Caicoli, POB 374, Dili; tel. 3322467; fax 3325189; e-mail ministerforhealthtl@yahoo.com; internet www.minsau.gov.tl.

Ministry of Justice: Av. Jacinto Candido, Dili; tel. 3331160; e-mail mj@mj.gov.tl; internet www.mj.gov.tl.

Ministry of Natural Resources, Minerals and Energy Policy: Dili.

Ministry of Transport, Communications and Public Works: Av. Bispo de Madeiros, Dili; tel. 3339354; fax 3339350; e-mail info@mtcop.gov.tl; internet www.timor-leste.gov.tl/MTC.

TIMOR-LESTE

President and Legislature

PRESIDENT

Presidential Election, First Ballot, 9 April 2007

Candidate	Votes	% of votes
Francisco Guterres (Fretilin)	112,666	27.89
José Ramos Horta (Independent)	88,102	21.81
Fernando de Araújo (PD)	77,459	19.18
Francisco Xavier do Amaral (ASDT)	58,125	14.39
Lucia Maria B. F. Lobato	35,789	8.86
Manuel Tilman (KOTA)	16,534	4.09
Avelino Coelho da Silva (PST)	8,338	2.06
João Viegas Carrascalão (UDT)	6,928	1.72
Total	**403,941**	**100.00**

Presidential Election, Second Ballot, 9 May 2007

Candidate	Votes	%
José Ramos Horta	285,835	69.18
Francisco Guterres	127,342	30.82
Total	**413,177**	**100.00**

NATIONAL PARLIAMENT

A single-chamber Constituent Assembly was elected by popular vote on 30 August 2001. Its 88 members included 75 deputies elected under a national system of proportional representation and one representative from each of Timor-Leste's 13 districts, elected under a 'first-past-the-post' system. Upon independence on 20 May 2002 the Constituent Assembly became the National Parliament; it held its inaugural session on the same day. At the election of June 2007 the number of members was reduced from 88 to 65.

Speaker: FERNANDO DE ARAÚJO.

General Election, 30 June 2007

	Seats
Frente Revolucionária do Timor Leste Independente (Fretilin)	21
Congresso Nacional da Reconstrução de Timor-Leste	18
Associação Social-Democrata Timorense-Partido Social Democrata Timor Lorosae (ASDT-PSD)	11
Partido Democrático (PD)	8
Partido Unidade Nacional (PUN)	3
Aliança Democrática Klibur Oan Timor Asuwain-Partido do Povo de Timor (AD KOTA-PPT)	2
Partido Unidade Nacional Democrática da Resistência Timorense (UNDERTIM)	2
Total	**65**

Election Commission

National Electoral Commission (CNE): Av. Bispo Medeiros-Kintal, Dili; tel. 3310082; f. 2004; govt body; Chair. Dr FAUSTINO CARDOSO.

Political Organizations

Associação Popular Democrática de Timor Pro Referendo (Apodeti Pro Referendo) (Pro-Referendum Popular Democratic Association of Timor): c/o Frederico Almeida Santos Costa, CNRT Office, Balide, Dili; tel. 3324994; f. 1974 as Apodeti; adopted present name in August 2000; fmrly supported autonomous integration with Indonesia; Pres. FREDERICO ALMEIDA SANTOS COSTA.

Associação Social-Democrata Timorense (ASDT) (Timor Social Democratic Association): Av. Direitos Humanos Lecidere, Dili; tel. 3983331; f. 2001; Pres. FRANCISCO XAVIER DO AMARAL.

Barisan Rakyat Timor Timur (BRTT) (East Timor People's Front): fmrly supported autonomous integration with Indonesia; Pres. FRANCISCO LOPES DA CRUZ.

Congresso Nacional da Reconstrução de Timor-Leste (CNRT) (National Congress for the Reconstruction of Timor-Leste): Rua Nu Laran, Bairro dos Grilos, Dili; tel. 7358696; internet www.cnrt-timor.org; f. 2007; Pres. JOSÉ ALEXANDRE 'XANANA' GUSMÃO.

Conselho Popular pela Defesa da República Democrática de Timor Leste (CPD-RDTL) (Popular Council for the Defence of the Democratic Republic of East Timor): opp. the Church, Balide, Dili; tel. 3481462; f. 1999; promotes adoption of 1975 Constitution of Democratic Republic of East Timor; Spokesperson CRISTIANO DA COSTA.

Frente Revolucionária do Timor Leste Independente (Fretilin) (Revolutionary Front for an Independent East Timor): Rua dos Mártires da Pátria, Dili; tel. 3321409; internet fretilin-rdtl.blogspot.com; f. 1974 to seek full independence for East Timor; entered into alliance with the UDT in 1986; Pres. FRANCISCO GUTERRES.

Klibur Oan Timor Asuwain (KOTA) (Association of Timorese Heroes): Rua dos Mártires da Pátria, Fatuhada, Dili; tel. 3324661; e-mail clementinoamaral@hotmail.com; f. 1974 as pro-integration party; supported independence with Timorese traditions; Pres. MANUEL TILMAN.

Movement for the Reconciliation and Unity of the People of East Timor (MRUPT): f. 1997; Chair. MANUEL VIEGAS CARRASCALÃO.

Partai Democratik Maubere (PDM) (Maubere Democratic Party): Blk B II, 16 Surikmas Lama Kraik, Fatumeta, Dili; tel. 3184508; e-mail pdm_party@hotmail.com; f. 2000; Pres. PAOLO PINTO.

Partai Liberal (PL) (Liberal Party): Talbessi Sentral, Dili; tel. 3786448; Pres. ARMANDO JOSÉ DOURADO DA SILVA.

Partido Democrata Cristão (PDC) (Christian Democrat Party): Former Escola Cartilha, Rua Quintal Kiik, Bairro Economico, Dili; tel. 3324683; e-mail arlindom@octa4.net.au; f. 2000; Pres. ANTÓNIO XIMENES.

Partido Democrático (PD) (Democratic Party): 1 Rua Democracia, Pantai Kelapa, Dili; tel. 3608421; e-mail flazama@hotmail.com; Pres. FERNANDO DE ARAÚJO.

Partido Nacionalista Timorense (PNT) (Nationalist Party of Timor): Dili; tel. 3323518; internet pnt-timor-leste.planetaclix.pt; Pres. Dr ABÍLIO ARAÚJO.

Partido do Povo de Timor (PPT) (Timorese People's Party): Dili; tel. 3568325; f. 2000; pro-integration; supported candidacy of Xanana Gusmão for presidency of East Timor; Pres. Dr JACOB XAVIER.

Partido Republika National Timor Leste (PARENTIL) (National Republic Party of East Timor): Perumnar Bairopite Bob Madey Ran, Fahan Jalam, Ailobu Laran RTK; tel. 3361393; Pres. FLAVIANO PEREIRA LOPEZ.

Partido Social Democrata Timor Lorosae (PSD) (Social Democrat Party of East Timor): Apartado 312, Correios de Dili, Dili; tel. 3357027; e-mail psdtimor@hotmail.com; f. 2000; Pres. MÁRIO VIEGAS CARRASCALÃO.

Partido Socialista de Timor (PST) (Socialist Party of Timor): Rua Colegio das Madras, Balide, Dili; tel. 3560246; e-mail kaynaga@hotmail.com; Marxist-Leninist Fretilin splinter group; Pres. AVELINO COELHO DA SILVA.

Partido Trabalhista Timorense (PTT) (Timor Labour Party): 2B Rua Travessa de Befonte, 2 Bairro Formosa, Dili; tel. 3322807; f. 1974; Pres. PAULO FREITAS DA SILVA.

Partido Unidade Nacional (PUN) (United National Party): c/o National Parliament, Dili; f. 2005; Pres. FERNANDA BORGES.

Partido Unidade Nacional Democrática da Resistência Timorense (UNDERTIM): c/o National Parliament, Dili; Pres. CORNELIO GAMA.

União Democrata-Cristão de Timor (UDC/PDC) (Christian Democratic Union of Timor): 62 Rua Almirante Américo Thomás, Mandarin, Dili; tel. 3325042; f. 1998; Pres. VINCENTE DA SILVA GUTERRES.

União Democrática Timorense (UDT) (Timorese Democratic Union): Palapagoa Rua da India, Dili; tel. 3881453; e-mail joaocarrascalao@email.msn.com; internet fitini.net/udttimor; f. 1974; allied itself with Fretilin in 1986; Pres. JOÃO CARRASCALÃO; Sec.-Gen. DOMINGOS OLIVEIRA.

Diplomatic Representation

EMBASSIES IN TIMOR-LESTE

Australia: Av. dos Mártires da Pátria, Dili; tel. 3322111; fax 3322247; e-mail austemb_dili@dfat.gov.au; internet www.easttimor.embassy.gov.au; Ambassador PETER HEYWARD.

Brazil: Av. Governador Serpa Rosa, POB 157, Farol, Dili; tel. 3324203; fax 3324620; e-mail esctimor@office.net.au; Ambassador EDSON MARINHO DUARTE MONTEIRO.

China, People's Republic: Av. Governador Serpa Rosa, Farol, Dili; tel. 3325168; fax 3325166; e-mail chinaemb_tp@mfa.gov.cn; Ambassador SU JIAN.

TIMOR-LESTE

Indonesia: Farol, Palapaco, POB 207, Dili; tel. 3317107; fax 3312332; e-mail kukridil@hotmail.com; internet www.kbridili.org; Ambassador AHMED BEY SOFWAN.

Japan: Pertamina 6, Dili; tel. 3323131; fax 3323130; e-mail japrepet@yahoo.co.jp; Ambassador KENJI SHIMIZU.

Korea, Republic: Av. de Portugal, Motael, Dili; tel. 3321635; fax 3323636; e-mail koreadili@mofat.go.kr; Ambassador RYU JIN-KYU.

Malaysia: Rua Almirante Américo Thomás, Mandarin, Dili; tel. 3311141; fax 3321805; e-mail mwdili@mail.timortelecom.tp; internet www.kln.gov.my/perwakilan/dili; Chargé d'affaires a. i. AZRI MAT YACOB.

New Zealand: Rua Alferes Duarte Arbiro, Lighthouse Area, Farol, Dili; fax 3324982; e-mail dili@mfat.gov.nz; Ambassador RUTH NUTTALL.

Philippines: Rooms 8–10, Hotel Turismo, Rua Direitos Humanos, Bidau Lecidere, Dili; tel. 33310408; fax 3310407; e-mail dilipe@dfa.gov.ph; Ambassador FARITA A. AGUILUCHO-ONG.

Portugal: Edif. ACAIT, Av. Presidente Nicolau Lobato, Dili; tel. 3312533; fax 3312526; e-mail embaixada.portugal@embpor.tp; internet www.embpor.tp; Ambassador JOÃO RAMOS PINTO.

Thailand: Av. de Portugal, Motael, Dili; tel. 3310609; fax 3322179; e-mail thaidli@mfa.go.th; Ambassador WIWAT KUNTHONTHIEN.

USA: Av. de Portugal, Praia dos Coqueiros, Dili; tel. 3324684; fax 3313206; e-mail larsonta@state.gov; Ambassador HANS G. KLEMM.

Judicial System

Until independence was granted on 20 May 2002 all legislative and executive authority with respect to the administration of the judiciary in East Timor was vested in UNTAET. During the transitional period of administration a two-tier court structure was established, consisting of District Courts and a Court of Appeal. The Constitution, promulgated in March 2002, specified that Timor-Leste should have three categories of courts: the Supreme Court of Justice and other law courts; the High Administrative, Tax and Audit Court and other administrative courts of first instance; and military courts. The judiciary would be regulated by the Superior Council of the Judiciary, the function of which would be to oversee the judicial sector and, in particular, to control the appointment, promotion, discipline and dismissal of judges. The effectiveness of the newly established judicial system was severely impaired by Timor-Leste's lack of human and material resources. In July 2002 there were only 22 judges in Timor-Leste, none of whom possessed more than two years of legal experience. In July 2003 the Court of Appeal was reconstituted. However, in the same month a ruling by its President that Timor-Leste's law should be based on that of Portugal and not Indonesia (as was currently the case) threatened to have serious consequences for the legal system.

Court of Appeal: Dili; Pres. CLAUDIO XIMENES.

Office of the Prosecutor-General: Dili; Prosecutor-General LONGUINHOS MONTEIRO; Dep. Prosecutor-General AMANDIO BENEVIDES.

Religion

In 2004 it was estimated that about 93.5% of the total population were Roman Catholic.

CHRISTIANITY

The Roman Catholic Church

Timor-Leste comprises the dioceses of Dili and Baucau, directly responsible to the Holy See. In December 2005 there were an estimated 916,541 Roman Catholics.

Bishop of Baucau: Most Rev. BASILIO DO NASCIMENTO, Largo da Catedral, Baucau 88810; tel. 4121209; fax 4121380.

Bishop of Dili: Most Rev. ALBERTO RICARDO DA SILVA, Av. dos Direitos Humanos, Bidau Lecidere, CP 4, Dili 88010; tel. 3324850; fax 3321177.

Protestant Church

Igreja Protestante iha Timor Lorosa'e: Jl. Raya Comoro, POB 1186, Dili 88110; tel. and fax 3323128; f. 1988 as Gereja Kristen Timor Timur (GKTT); adopted present name 2000; Moderator Rev. FRANCISCO DE VASCONCELOS; 30,000 mems.

The Press

The Constitution promulgated in March 2002 guarantees freedom of the press in Timor-Leste.

Lalenok (Mirror): Rua Gov. Celestino da Silva, Farol, Dili; tel. 3321607; e-mail lalenok@hotmail.com; f. 2000; publ. by Kamelin Media Group; Tetum; 3 a week; Dir-Gen. and Chief Editor VIRGÍLIO DA SILVA GUTERRES; Editor JOSÉ MARIA POMPELA; circ. 300.

Lian Maubere: Dili; f. 1999; weekly.

The Official Gazette of East Timor: Dili; f. 1999 by UNTAET; forum for publication of all govt regulations and directives, acts of organs or institutions of East Timor and other acts of public interest requiring general notification; published in English, Portuguese and Tetum, with translations in Bahasa Indonesia available on request.

Suara Timor Lorosae: 7 Av. Martinez da Patria, Dili; tel. 322823; fax 322821; e-mail redaksi@suaratimorlorosae.com; internet www.suaratimorlorosae.com; f. 2000; daily; Editor-in-Chief and Publr SALVADOR J. XIMENES SOARES.

Tais Timor: Dili; f. 2000; fmrly published by the Office of Communication and Public Information (OCPI) of the UN; Tetum, English, Portuguese and Bahasa Indonesia; every fortnight; distributed free of charge; circ. 75,000.

Timor Post: Rua Dom Aleixo Corte-Real No. 6, Dili; f. 2000; managed by editors and staff of the fmr Suara Timor Timur; Bahasa Indonesia, Tetum, Portuguese and English; daily; Man. Editor OTELIO OTE; Chief Editor and Dir ADERITO HUGO DA COSTA; circ. 600.

PRESS ASSOCIATION

Sindicato dos Jornalistas de Timor-Leste (SJTL): Rua Dom Aleixo Corte-Real, Bebora, Dili; tel. 7248549; e-mail sjti@yahoo.com; f. 2001; Pres. RODOLFO DE SOUSA.

Timor Lorosae Journalists' Association (TLJA): Rua de Caicoli, Dili; tel. 3324047; fax 3327505; e-mail ajtl_tlja@hotmail.com; f. 1999; Co-ordinator OTELIO OTE; Pres. VIRGÍLIO DA SILVA GUTERRES.

Broadcasting and Communications

TELECOMMUNICATIONS

In July 2002 the Government granted a consortium led by Portugal Telecom a 15-year concession permitting it to establish and operate Timor-Leste's telecommunications systems. Under the terms of the concession the consortium agreed to provide every district in Timor-Leste with telecommunications services at the most inexpensive tariffs viable within 15 months. At the expiry of the concession in 2017 the telecommunications system was to be transferred to government control.

Timor-Leste Telecom (TT): Sala No. 7, Hotel Timor, Av. dos Mártires da Pátria, POB 135, Dili; tel. 3303000; fax 3303209; e-mail info@timortelecom.tp; internet www.timortelecom.tp; f. 2002; jt venture mainly operated by Portugal Telecom; provides telecommunications services in Timor-Leste; CEO JOSÉ BRANDÃO DE SOUSA; 114 employees.

BROADCASTING

Following independence UNMISET transferred control of public television and radio in Timor-Leste to the new Government. In 2003 a Public Broadcasting Service was established, controlled by an independent board of directors.

Radio

There are 18 radio stations operating in Timor-Leste, including community radio stations for each of the country's 13 districts. In addition to the public service, Ratio Timor-Leste, the Roman Catholic Church operates a radio station, Radio Kamanak, while a third populist station, Voz Esperança, broadcasts in Dili. A fourth radio station, Radio Falintil FM, also operates in Dili and, in October 2003, the Christian station Voice FM was established. In 2000 the US radio station, Voice of America, began broadcasting to Timor-Leste seven days a week in English, Portuguese and Bahasa Indonesia.

Radio Timor-Leste (RTL): Rua de Caicoli, Dili; tel. 3321826; e-mail radio@rttl.org; internet www.rttl.org; fmrly Radio UNTAET; name changed as above in 2002; broadcasts mainly in Bahasa Indonesia, but also in English, Portuguese and Tetum, to an estimated 90% of Timor-Leste's population; Man. PAULA RODRIGES.

Television

TV Timor-Leste (TVTL): Rua de Caicoli, Dili; tel. 3321825; e-mail tv@rttl.org; internet www.rttl.org; f. 2000 as Televisaun Timor Lorosa'e by UNTAET; adopted present name in May 2002; broadcasts in Tetum and Portuguese; Gen. Man. ANTONIO DIAZ.

TIMOR-LESTE

Finance

(cap. = capital; res = reserves; dep. = deposits)

BANKING

In February 2001 the East Timor Central Payments Office was officially opened. This was succeeded in November of that year by the Banking and Payments Authority, which was intended to function as a precursor to a central bank.

Banking and Payments Authority (BPA): Av. Bispo Medeiros, POB 59, Dili; tel. 3313712; fax 3313713; e-mail info@bancocentral.tl; internet www.bancocentral.tl; inaugurated Nov. 2001; regulates and supervises Timor-Leste's financial system, formulates and implements payments system policies, provides banking services to Timor-Leste's administration and foreign official institutions, manages fiscal reserves; fmrly Central Payments Office; cap. US $18.2m., res $1.9m., dep. $117.9m. (March 2006); Chair. and Gen. Man. ABRAÃO F. DE VASCONSELOS; Dep. Gen. Mans MARIA JOSÉ DE JESUS SARMENTO, NUR AINI DJAFAR ALKATIRI.

Foreign Banks

Australia and New Zealand Banking Group Ltd (ANZ) (Australia): Cnr Av. Presidente Nicolau Lobato and Rua Belarmino Lobo, Bidau Lecidere, POB 264, Dili; tel. 3324800; fax 3324822; e-mail anzeasttimor@anz.com; internet www.anz.com/TimorLeste; retail and commercial banking services; Gen. Man. PETER BOUTCHER; Group CEO JOHN MCFARLANE.

Banco Nacional Ultramarino (Portugal): Edif. BNU, 12–13 Av. Presidente Nicolau Lobato, Dili; tel. 3323385; fax 3323678; e-mail cgd.timor@mail.timortelecom.tp; internet www.cgd.pt/english/international_network/timor.htm; Gen. Man. Dr CORREIA PINTO; 9 brs.

PT Bank Mandiri (Persero) (Indonesia): 12 Av. Presidente Nicolau Lobato, Colmera, Dili; tel. 3317777; fax 3317444; e-mail dili_timorleste@bankmandiri.co.id; internet www.bankmandiri.co.id; Group Chair. EDWIN GERUNGAN.

Trade and Industry

GOVERNMENT AGENCIES

Direcção Nacional de Petróleo e Gas: 1st Floor, Fomento Bldg, Mandarin, POB 171, Dili; tel. and fax 3317143; e-mail amandiogusmao@yahoo.com; internet www.timor-leste.gov.tl/EMRD/index.asp; controlled by the Ministry of Natural Resources, Minerals and Energy Policy; Dir AMANDIO GUSMÃO SOARES.

The Timor Sea Designated Authority (TSDA): 5 Av. de Portugal, POB 113, Farol, Dili; tel. 3324098; fax 3324082; e-mail dilioffice@timorseada.org; internet www.timorseada.org; f. 2003; responsible for regulating all petroleum activities and for securing new exploration and production contracts within the Joint Petroleum Development Area, on behalf of the respective govts of Timor-Leste and Australia; also has an office in Darwin, Australia; Exec. Sec. MARIA PIRES.

TradeInvest Timor-Leste: Memorial Hall, Av. Praia dos Coqueros Farol, Dili 8000; tel. 3331084; fax 3331087; e-mail tradeinvest_tl@yahoo.com; internet www.timor-leste.gov.tl/TradeInvest; f. 2005; est. to encourage devt of entrepreneurship within Timor-Leste.

UTILITIES

In the early 2000s Timor-Leste's total generating capacity amounted to some 40 MW. As a result of the civil conflict in 1999, some 13–23 power stations were reported to require repairs ranging from moderate maintenance to almost complete rehabilitation. The rehabilitation of the power sector was ongoing in 2006, with funding largely provided by foreign donors. By July 2003 31 generators had been restored, supplying electricity to Dili, as well as to 12 districts and 33 subdistricts.

Electricidade de Timor-Leste (EDTL): EDTL Bldg, Rua Estrada de Balide, Caicoli, Dili; tel. 3339254; fax 7230095; e-mail virgiliofguterres@hotmail.com; govt dept; responsible for power generation, distribution and financial management of power sector in Timor-Leste; transferred to external management in 2002; Dir VIRGILIO GUTERRES.

CO-OPERATIVE

Cooperativa Café Timor (CCT): 16 Rua Barros Gomes, Dili; f. 2000 under the Timor Economic Rehabilitation and Development Project; produces, markets and distributes organic coffee; also provides information and advisory services for member farmers; Operational Dir SISTO MONIZ PIEDADE; 19,000 mems.

TRADE UNIONS

Konfederasaun Sindikatu Timor-Leste (KSTL) (Trade Union Confederation of Timor-Leste): Rua Sebastiao da Costa, Colmera, Dili; f. 2001; represents nine unions, comprising approximately 4,700 workers within the press, teaching, nursing, and the construction, agricultural, maritime and transport sectors; Pres. JOSÉ DA CONCEIÇÃO DA COSTA.

Labour Advocacy Institute of East Timor (LAIFET): Rua Abílio Monteiro Palapaso, Dili; tel. 3317243; Dir DOMINGOS BAPTISTA DE ARAÚJO.

Serikat Buruh Socialis Timor (SBST) (Timor Socialist Workers' Union): Dili; controlled by Partido Socialista de Timor; Dir Dr LUCIANO DA SILVA.

Transport

ROADS

The road network in Timor-Leste is poorly designed and has suffered from long-term neglect. In December 1999 the World Bank reported that some 57% of the country's 1,414 km of paved roads were in poor or damaged condition. Many gravel roads are rough and potholed and are inaccessible to most vehicles. Some repair and maintenance work on the road network was carried out in 2005, using funding supplied by external donors.

SHIPPING

Timor-Leste's maritime infrastructure includes ports at Dili, Carabela and Com, smaller wharves at Oecusse (Oekussi) and Liquiça (Likisia), and slip-landing structures in Oecusse, Batugade and Suai. In November 2001, following its reconstruction, the management of the port at Dili was transferred to the Government. The port was expected to be a significant source of revenue.

Port Authority of Timor-Leste (APORTIL): 2 Rua Almirante Américo Thomás, Dili; f. 2003.

Principal Shipping Companies

Everise Freight Forwarding Inc: 2 Rua Belarminolobo, Dili; tel. 3324844; fax 3312856; e-mail everisedili@yahoo.com.

SDV Logistics (East Timor): Av. Presidente Nicolau Lobato, Bairro dos Grilos, POB 398, Dili; tel. 3322818; fax 3324077; e-mail dili@sdv.com; internet www.sdveasttimor.com; f. 1999; freight forwarder, shipping agent and customs broker; Man. Dir ERIC MANCINI.

CIVIL AVIATION

Timor-Leste has two international airports and eight grass runways. At mid-2000 operators of international flights to East Timor included Qantas Airways and Air North of Australia. In June 2001 Dili Express Pte was the first Timor-based company to begin international flights, with a service to Singapore. In 2005 Timor-Leste's first national carrier, Kakoak Air, commenced operations.

Civil Aviation Division (CAD): Dili; tel. 3317110; fax 3317111; e-mail henriques_sabino@yahoo.com; internet www.timor-leste.gov.tl/CAA/index.html; arm of the Ministry of Transport, Communications and Public Works; responsible for overall planning, implementation and operation of aviation services in Timor-Leste; Dir JULIAO X. CARLOS.

Kakoak Air: Dili; internet www.kakoakair.tp; f. 2005; operates twice-weekly passenger service between Dili and Kupang, Indonesia; Gen. Dir JORGE SERANNO.

Tourism

The tourism sector remains undeveloped. The country's first national park was established in 2007. Nino Konis Santana National Park, which encompasses more than 123,600 ha, aims to protect a number of endangered species, including 25 endemic birds. The park also incorporates a marine area of 55,600 ha, which contains a globally important biodiversity of coral and reef fish.

Turismo de Timor-Leste: Apartado 194, Dili; tel. 3339015; fax 3339016; e-mail info@turismotimorleste.com; internet www.turismotimorleste.com; f. 2002; Dir MIGUEL LOBATO.

TOGO

Introductory Survey

Location, Climate, Language, Religion, Flag, Capital

The Togolese Republic lies in West Africa, forming a narrow strip stretching north from a coastline of about 50 km (30 miles) on the Gulf of Guinea. It is bordered by Ghana to the west, by Benin to the east, and by Burkina Faso to the north. The climate in the coastal area is hot and humid, with an average annual temperature of 27°C (81°F); rainfall in this zone averages 875 mm (34.4 ins) per year, and is heaviest during May–October. Precipitation in the central region is heaviest in May–June and in October, and in the north, where the average annual temperature is 30°C (86°F), there is a rainy season from July–September. The official languages are French, Kabiye and Ewe. About one-half of the population follows animist beliefs, while about 35% are Christians and 15% Muslims. The national flag (approximate proportions 3 by 5) has five equal horizontal stripes, alternately green and yellow, with a square red canton, containing a five-pointed white star, in the upper hoist. The capital is Lomé.

Recent History

Togoland, of which modern Togo was formerly a part, became a German colony in 1894. Shortly after the outbreak of the First World War, the colony was occupied by French and British forces. After the war, a League of Nations mandate divided Togoland into two administrative zones, with France controlling the larger eastern section, while the United Kingdom governed the west. The partition of Togoland split the homeland of the Ewe people, who inhabit the southern part of the territory, and this has been a continuing source of friction. After the Second World War, French and British Togoland became UN Trust Territories. In May 1956 a UN-supervised plebiscite in British Togoland produced, despite Ewe opposition, majority support for a merger with the neighbouring territory of the Gold Coast, then a British colony, in an independent state. The region accordingly became part of Ghana in the following year. In October 1956, in another plebiscite, French Togoland voted to become an autonomous republic, with internal self-government, within the French Community. Togo's foremost political parties at that time were the Comité de l'unité togolaise (usually known as the Unité togolaise—UT), led by Sylvanus Olympio, and the Parti togolais du progrès (PTP), led by Nicolas Grunitzky, Olympio's brother-in-law. In 1956 Grunitzky became Prime Minister in the first autonomous Government, but in April 1958 a UN-supervised election was won by the UT. Olympio became Prime Minister and led Togo to full independence on 27 April 1960.

At elections in April 1961 Olympio became Togo's first President, while the UT was elected (unopposed) to all 51 seats in the Assemblée nationale. At the same time a referendum approved a new Constitution. On 13 January 1963 the UT regime was overthrown by a military revolt, in which Olympio was killed. Grunitzky subsequently assumed the presidency on a provisional basis. A referendum in May approved another Constitution, confirmed Grunitzky as President and elected a new legislature from a single list of candidates, giving equal representation to the four main political parties.

President Grunitzky was deposed by a bloodless military coup, led by Lt-Col (later Gen.) Etienne (Gnassingbé) Eyadéma, the Army Chief of Staff, on 13 January 1967. Eyadéma, a member of the Kabiye ethnic group, who had taken a prominent part in the 1963 rising and was reputedly Olympio's assassin, assumed the office of President in April. Political parties were banned, and the President ruled by decree. In November 1969 a new ruling party, the Rassemblement du peuple togolais (RPT), was founded, led by Eyadéma. Comprehensive government changes in January 1977 left Eyadéma as the sole representative of the armed forces in the Council of Ministers.

In Togo's first elections for 16 years, held on 30 December 1979, Eyadéma (the sole candidate) was confirmed as President of the Republic for a seven-year term. At the same time a new Constitution was overwhelmingly endorsed, while the list of 67 candidates for a single-party Assemblée nationale was approved by 96% of votes cast. On 13 January 1980 Eyadéma proclaimed the 'Third Republic'. In December 1986 President Eyadéma was re-elected, unopposed, for a further seven-year term.

In March 1990 some 230 candidates, all loyal to the RPT, contested elections to the Assemblée nationale's 77 seats. In October a commission was established to draft a new constitution, to be submitted to a national referendum in late 1991. In December 1990 the constitutional commission presented a draft document, which envisaged, *inter alia*, a plurality of political parties. Meanwhile, several recently formed, unofficial opposition movements formed a co-ordinating organization, the Front des associations pour le renouveau (FAR), led by Yawovi Agboyibo, to campaign for the immediate introduction of a multi-party political system. Eyadéma subsequently agreed to implement a general amnesty for political dissidents and to permit the legalization of political organizations. Following instances of violent unrest in April 1991, Eyadéma, fearing a civil conflict between the Kabiye and Ewe ethnic groups (the Government and armed forces were composed overwhelmingly of members of the first group, while opposition groups for the most part represented the Ewe people), announced that a new constitution would be introduced within one year, and that multi-party legislative elections would be organized. At the end of the month it was announced that the FAR was to be disbanded. Agboyibo subsequently formed his own party, the Comité d'action pour le renouveau (CAR), which in May became one of 10 parties to enter into a Front de l'opposition démocratique (FOD, later renamed the Coalition de l'opposition démocratique—COD).

Following the organization of a general strike by the FOD, the Government agreed, in June 1991, that a 'national conference' would be held, with the power to choose a transitional Prime Minister and to establish a transitional legislative body. The conference opened in July, however, when it adopted resolutions suspending the Constitution, dissolving the Assemblée nationale and giving the conference sovereign power, government representatives withdrew. Subsequently the conference resolved to 'freeze' the assets of the RPT, to transfer most of the powers of the President to a Prime Minister, and to prevent Eyadéma from contesting future elections. In defiance of a decree issued by Eyadéma temporarily suspending proceedings, the conference elected a Prime Minister, Joseph Kokou Koffigoh (a senior lawyer and prominent human rights activist), announced the dissolution of the RPT and the formation of a transitional legislature, the Haut Conseil de la République (HCR). Eyadéma capitulated, signing a decree that proclaimed Koffigoh as transitional Prime Minister. In September Koffigoh formed a transitional Government, most of whose members had not previously held office: he himself assumed the defence portfolio.

In October 1991 members of the armed forces seized control of the national broadcasting station, demanding that full executive powers be restored to Eyadéma. They returned to barracks on Eyadéma's orders. Koffigoh confirmed that a constitutional referendum and elections would be held in 1992. In November 1991, following the adoption of legislation by the HCR confirming the dissolution of the RPT, troops seized the broadcasting headquarters and surrounded the Prime Minister's residence, demanding that Eyadéma nominate a new government and that the HCR be abolished. At least 20 people were killed in the fighting that ensued. In December troops captured Koffigoh during an attack on his residence, killing several of his guards. Koffigoh agreed to form a new government. At the end of December the reconvened HCR restored legal status to the RPT and announced the formation of a transitional 'Government of National Union', which comprised many of the members of the previous transitional administration, but also two close associates of Eyadéma.

In January 1992 an electoral schedule was announced; the constitutional referendum and local, legislative and presidential elections were to be held by June of that year. In May the attempted assassination of Gilchrist Olympio, the son of the former President, who was regarded as a potential presidential candidate, and the murder of another prominent member of the opposition provoked renewed unrest. In late May the Council of Ministers abandoned the electoral timetable. In July the HCR adopted the draft Constitution and an electoral code, and the constitutional referendum was scheduled for August, although it was subsequently postponed. Meanwhile, a report published by the International Federation of Human Rights concluded that members of the armed forces had been responsible for the attempted murder of Olympio, implicating Eyadéma's son, Capt. Ernest Gnassingbé (a military officer). Later in July Tavio Ayao Amorin, a member of the HCR regarded as a radical was shot and fatally wounded. In response, the recently formed Collectif de l'opposition démocratique (COD-2), an alliance of some 25 political organizations and trade unions, called a general strike, which was widely observed. In August agreement was reached on opposition access to the state-controlled media, and on the extension until 31 December of the transition period. In late August the HCR restored to Eyadéma the power to preside over the Council of Ministers, and to represent Togo abroad; furthermore, his agreement would henceforth be necessary in the appointment of members of the Government. The draft Constitution was amended so that members of the armed forces would no longer be obliged to resign their commissions before seeking election to public office.

The transitional Government was dissolved on 1 September 1992. Later that month a new transitional Government, led by Koffigoh, was appointed, including representatives of 10 parties; the most influential ministries were allocated to members of the RPT. On 27 September the new Constitution was approved in a referendum by 98.1% of the votes cast. At the end of the month, however, it was announced that the local, legislative and presidential elections were to be further postponed. In October eight opposition parties announced the formation of a 'Patriotic Front', to be led by the leader of the Union togolaise pour la démocratie (UTD), Edem Kodjo, and Agboyibo. In November Koffigoh dismissed two ministers (both adherents of the RPT) for their conduct during an attack on the HCR by members of the armed forces in October, but Eyadéma overruled this decision.

In January 1993 Eyadéma dissolved the Government, reappointing Koffigoh as Prime Minister, and stated that he would appoint a new government of national unity to organize elections. His action provoked protests by the opposition parties, who claimed that, according to the Constitution, the HCR should appoint a Prime Minister since the transition period had now expired. In the same month two ministers representing the French and German Governments visited Togo to offer mediation in the political crisis. During their visit at least 20 people were killed when police opened fire on anti-Government protesters. Thousands of Togolese subsequently fled from Lomé, many seeking refuge in Benin or Ghana. In February inter-Togolese discussions organized by the French and German Governments in France failed when the presidential delegation withdrew after one day. In that month the French, German and US Governments suspended their programmes of aid to Togo. A new Government, in which supporters of Eyadéma retained the principal posts, was formed in February. In March COD-2 member parties stated that they now regarded Koffigoh as an obstacle to democratization, and nominated a 'parallel' Prime Minister, Jean-Lucien Savi de Tové.

In April 1993 a new electoral schedule was announced, envisaging elections to the presidency and the legislature in July and August, respectively. The RPT designated Eyadéma as its presidential candidate. In May the COD-2 declared that it would boycott the elections, alleging that they would not be fairly conducted, and that opposition politicians had no guarantee of their safety. In July, however, the Togolese Government and the COD-2 signed an agreement establishing 25 August as the date for the first round of presidential voting. The agreement stipulated that the Togolese armed forces should be confined to barracks during the election period, and that international military observers should be present to confirm this, while international civilian observers should also be present for the election. An independent, nine-member Commission électorale nationale (CEN) was to be established, to include three members nominated by the opposition parties. Later in July the COD-2 nominated Kodjo as its presidential candidate; however, in the same month two other candidates—Agboyibo and Abou Djobo Boukari—were nominated by parties affiliated to the COD-2. Three candidates eventually contested the presidential election held on 25 August at which Eyadéma was reported to have obtained 96.49% of the votes cast. French election observers concluded that the poll had not been satisfactorily conducted; observers from the USA and Germany had withdrawn from Togo shortly before the elections took place.

In the legislative elections, finally held, on 6 and 20 February 1994, some 347 candidates contested 81 seats. Despite the murder of an elected CAR representative after the first round, and violent incidents at polling stations during the second round, international observers expressed themselves satisfied with the conduct of the elections. The opposition won a narrow victory in the polls, with the CAR winning 36 seats and the UTD seven; the RPT obtained 35 seats and two other smaller pro-Eyadéma parties won three. During March Eyadéma consulted the main opposition parties on the formation of a new government. In late March the CAR and the UTD reached an agreement on the terms of their alliance and jointly proposed the candidacy of Agboyibo for Prime Minister. In March and April the Supreme Court declared the results of the legislative elections invalid in three constituencies (in which the CAR had won two seats and the UTD one) and ordered by-elections. In April Eyadéma nominated Kodjo as Prime Minister. The CAR subsequently declared that it would not participate in an administration formed by Kodjo. Kodjo took office on 25 April; his Government, formed in May, comprised eight members of the RPT and other pro-Eyadéma parties, three members of the UTD, and eight independents.

At the by-elections, conducted on 4 and 18 August 1996 in the presence of 22 international observers, the RPT won control of all three constituencies. Consequently, the RPT and its allies were able to command a majority in the legislature, thus precipitating the resignation of the Kodjo administration. On 20 August Eyadéma appointed Kwassi Klutse, hitherto Minister of Planning and Territorial Development, as Prime Minister, and the new Council of Ministers, appointed in late August, comprised almost exclusively supporters of Eyadéma. In November the Union pour la justice et la démocratie, which held two seats in the legislature, announced that it was officially to merge with the RPT, thus giving the RPT an overall majority, with 41 seats.

In September 1997 a new electoral code was approved, providing for a CEN comprising nine members, chaired by the President of the Court of Appeal and including four members appointed by the opposition. The CAR, however, boycotted the legislative session in protest at the Government's refusal to reveal the findings of a report by a mission of the European Union (EU, see p. 244) on the country's electoral process. Later that month opposition parties, led by the CAR and the Union des forces de changement (UFC), organized a demonstration in Lomé in protest at the new electoral law and condemned as fraudulent the Government's preparations for the forthcoming presidential election.

During campaigning for the presidential election, scheduled for 21 June 1998, Eyadéma permitted rival candidates to make brief campaign speeches on state television. Shortly before the election, however, the Government refused to permit the presence of 500 national observers trained by the EU. The election proceeded amid accusations of electoral malpractice, and on the following day counting of votes was halted without explanation, reportedly when the early returns showed Eyadéma to be in second place. Four members of the CEN resigned the same day, alleging intimidation. The Minister of the Interior and Security, Gen. Seyi Memene, announced that he assumed responsibility for the ballot count, and that Eyadéma had been re-elected President with 52.1% of the valid votes cast. Gilchrist Olympio, who had contested the election from exile in Ghana, was officially stated to have won 34.1%. Following the announcement of the result, violent protests erupted throughout Lomé. The USA condemned the conduct of the election, and called on the Government to respect its own laws and electoral code, while the EU decided not to recognize the result, which was, none the less, confirmed by the Constitutional Court.

In September 1998 Klutse announced his new Council of Ministers. Despite Eyadéma's stated intention to form a government of national unity, no opposition figures were willing to be included. Among the few new appointments was Koffigoh, as Minister of State, responsible for Foreign Affairs and Co-operation. In November the Government survived a legislative vote of censure tabled by the CAR and the UTD.

Elections to the Assemblée nationale took place on 21 March 1999, contested only by the RPT and by two small parties loyal to Eyadéma, including Koffigoh's Coordination nationale des forces nouvelles, as well as by 12 independent candidates. (The principal opposition parties had boycotted the polling.) The Constitutional Court ruled that the RPT had won 77 seats, and that independent candidates had taken two seats. By-elections were to take place in two constituencies in which voting had been invalidated. (Both of these seats were subsequently won by the RPT.) Despite international criticism, Eyadéma rejected demands for fresh elections, declaring that the opposition had been afforded ample opportunity to participate. In April Klutse tendered his Government's resignation; in May Eugene Koffi Adogboli was appointed Prime Minister.

In May 1999 Amnesty International published a report detailing numerous abuses of human rights committed by Togolese security forces, alleging that hundreds of political opponents of Eyadéma had been killed following the 1998 presidential election. In late July 1999 Eyadéma (who rejected the validity of the report) urged the UN and the Organization of African Unity (OAU, now the African Union—AU, see p. 164) to assist in the establishment of an international commission of inquiry into the allegations; such a commission was established in June 2000.

Discussions between the Government and opposition began in Lomé in July 1999, with the assistance of four international facilitators, representing France, Germany, the EU and La Francophonie. Eyadéma's announcement that he would not stand for re-election in 2003 and that new legislative elections would be held, was widely credited with breaking the deadlock in negotiations, and, after the opposition had agreed to accept Eyadéma's victory in the presidential election, an accord was signed on 29 July 1999 by all the parties involved in negotiations. The accord made provision for the creation of an independent electoral body and for the creation of a code of conduct to regulate political activity.

The first meeting took place in August 1999 of the 24-member Comité paritaire de suivi (CPS) responsible for the implementation of the accord, composed of an equal number of opposition and pro-Eyadéma representatives, and also including intermediaries from the EU. Harry Octavianus Olympio, the Minister for the Promotion of Democracy and the Rule of Law (and a cousin of Gilchrist Olympio), was appointed to head the CPS. Despite the reservations of the UFC, a compromise agreement on announcing election results was reached in September, and in December agreement was reached on a revised electoral code, providing for the establishment of an independent electoral commission. In April 2000 Eyadéma obliged the Assemblée nationale to accept the new electoral code. The EU subsequently offered to provide financial support for the elections, which were scheduled to be held later in 2000. The 20 members of the new Commission électorale nationale indépendante (CENI) were named in June, and in July Arthème Ahoomey-Zounou of the Convergence patriotique panafricaine (CPP—formed in 1999 by the amalgamation of the UTD and three smaller parties, and headed by Edem Kodjo) was elected as president of the CENI.

In August 2000 Adogboli was overwhelmingly defeated in a legislative vote of no confidence; he therefore presented his resignation and that of his Government to Eyadéma. In late August Eyadéma appointed Agbéyomè Kodjo, hitherto the President of the Assemblée nationale, and regarded as a close ally of the President, as Prime Minister. A government reshuffle was effected in October. In January 2001 the CENI announced that the legislative elections would be held in two rounds, on 14 and 28 October 2001, and that the disputed electoral registers from the 1998 presidential election would be used in these polls.

In August 2001 Agboyibo was jailed for six months and fined 100,000 francs CFA, having been convicted of libelling Prime Minister Agbéyomè Kodjo. Several opposition groups withdrew from the CPS in protest at Agboyibo's detention, and two protest marches in support of his release were prohibited by the authorities. In late August Kodjo announced that the legislative elections would be further postponed until 2002, and declared his support for a proposed constitutional change that would allow Eyadéma to contest a further term of office as President. In late November 2001 Eyadéma implied that he would be prepared to offer a pardon to Agboyibo, should he request one. Agboyibo, however, launched an appeal against his conviction. Although the appeals court found in favour of Agboyibo in mid-January 2002, he was immediately rearrested on charges of conspiring to commit violence during the 1998 presidential election campaign; Agboyibo was finally released from prison in mid-March 2002, on the orders of Eyadéma, who stated that the release was intended to facilitate national reconciliation; the charges against Agboyibo of conspiring to commit violence were also withdrawn.

In February 2002 the Assemblée nationale approved amendments to electoral legislation and to the remit and constitution of the CENI; notably, henceforth all candidates for legislative elections were required to have been continuously resident in Togo for six months prior to elections, with presidential candidates to have been resident for a continuous 12 months. The CENI was also to be reduced in size from 20 to 10 members, and decisions were to be taken by a two-thirds' majority, instead of the four-fifths' majority required hitherto; these amendments led to a further postponement of the elections, which had been scheduled to take place in March. These measures attracted international disapproval, notably prompting the EU to suspend aid intended to finance the legislative elections. In mid-February five opposition parties issued a joint communiqué accusing the Government of having broken the conditions of the accord signed in July 1999, and in early March 2002 they rejected an invitation by Kodjo to nominate representatives to the CENI. The Government consequently announced that no date for the legislative elections could be announced until a complete electoral commission had been formed. In late March 10 opposition parties, which had not been party to the accord signed in 1999 and were therefore excluded from the CPS, announced the formation of a Coordination des partis de l'opposition constructive, headed by Harry Octavianus Olympio, who had also assumed the leadership of the Rassemblement pour le soutien de la démocratie et du développement (RSDD). In mid-May 2002 a committee of seven judges (the Comité de sept magistrats—C-7), charged with monitoring the electoral process at the proposed legislative elections, was appointed. At the end of May the EU announced that it would not renew funding for the three facilitators it supported in Togo, in view of the continued lack of progress towards democracy.

In late June 2002 Eyadéma dismissed Kodjo as Prime Minister and appointed Koffi Sama, the Secretary-General of the RPT, as Prime Minister; a new Government, which included several principal members of the former administration, was appointed in early July. Kodjo subsequently issued a statement criticizing the 'monarchic, despotic' regime of Eyadéma, and (in contrast to his former stated position) called for measures to ensure that Eyadéma would be unable to amend the Constitution to stand for a further term of office. The state prosecutor filed a suit against Kodjo on charges of disseminating false information and demeaning the honour of the President; Kodjo was expelled from the RPT and subsequently left Togo, taking up residence in France.

Meanwhile, in early August 2002 four parties, including the CAR, announced the formation of an opposition alliance, the Front uni de l'opposition (Le Front), headed by Agboyibo. In late August renewed concern about the freedom of the press in Togo arose, following the approval by the Council of Ministers of a draft text of modifications to the press code; notably, journalists convicted of insulting the President could be sentenced to five years' imprisonment under the new proposed legislation.

In early October 2002 the Assemblée nationale was dissolved, pending fresh elections on 27 October. In late October nine opposition parties that had declined to participate in the elections announced the formation of a new alliance, the Coalition des forces démocrates (CFD); members of the grouping included the CAR, the CPP and the UFC, in addition to a faction of 'renovators' within the RPT (which subsequently became the Pacte socialiste pour le renouveau—PSR, led by Maurice Dahuku Pere). Meanwhile, a group of 'constructive opposition' parties (including the RSDD), which were prepared to participate in the electoral process and form alliances with the RPT, formed the Coordination des partis politiques de l'opposition constructive (CPOC). The 81 seats of the Assemblée nationale were contested by 126 candidates, comprising 118 candidates nominated by 15 parties and eight independent candidates, although the RPT was the sole party to contest every seat. The RPT won 72 seats (in 46 of which they had been unopposed) and the RSDD three, while three other parties won a total of five seats, and one independent candidate was elected. The C-7, which now comprised six judges (following the resignation of one member of the committee on the day before the elections), estimated electoral turn-out at 67.4%, although the CFD claimed that only 10% of the electorate had voted. Eyadéma reappointed Sama as Prime Minister in mid-November; a new Government was formed in early December. All ministers were members of the RPT, with the exception of Harry Octavianus Olympio, who was appointed Minister responsible for Relations with Parliament.

In December 2002 the Assemblée nationale approved several constitutional amendments regarding the eligibility of presidential candidates. The restriction that had limited the President to serving two terms of office was to be removed, and the age of eligibility was to be reduced from 45 to 35 years. (It was widely believed that these measures were intended to permit Eyadéma to serve a further term of office, and also to permit the possible presidential candidacy of Eyadéma's son, Faure Gnassingbé.) Candidates were henceforth to be required to hold solely Togolese citizenship. In February 2003 the UFC, having opposed the constitutional amendments, announced its withdrawal from the CFD, after other parties within the grouping agreed to appoint representatives to the CENI prior to the holding of a presidential election later in the year. In late April Eyadéma confirmed that he was to seek re-election; however, in May the CENI rejected the candidacy of Gilchrist Olympio, who had recently returned to Togo. (This rejection was confirmed by the Constitutional Court later in the month.) By mid-May six opposition candidates (including four representatives of the constituent parties of the CFD) had emerged. Emmanuel Bob Akitani, the First Vice-President of the UFC, was announced as his party's candidate, following Olympio's debarment.

Eyadéma was returned to office in the presidential election held on 1 June 2003, receiving 57.79% of the votes cast. His nearest rival was Bob Akitani, with 33.69% of votes. Several of the defeated candidates declared that the election had been conducted fraudulently, although observers from the Economic Community of West African States (ECOWAS), the AU and the Conseil de l'Entente refuted these claims. Eyadéma was inaugurated for a further term of office on 20 June. Sama resigned as Prime Minister later in the month, but was reappointed as premier on 1 July, apparently with instructions from Eyadéma to form a government of national unity. However, most opposition parties reportedly declined representation in the administration, and the new Government, formed on 29 July, included only two representatives of the 'constructive opposition'. Faure Gnassingbé received his first ministerial posting, as Minister of Equipment, Mines, Posts and Telecommunications. In December Dama Dramani was elected as Secretary-General of the RPT, replacing Sama.

Talks between the EU and the Government on the conditions for a resumption of economic co-operation commenced in April 2004 in Brussels, Belgium; the government delegation, led by Sama, pledged to implement 22 measures such as introducing more transparent conditions for fair elections, revising the press code and guaranteeing political parties the freedom to conduct their activities without fear of harassment. Under pressure from the EU to strengthen democracy, President Eyadéma officially opened talks between the Government and opposition parties in May, despite a boycott of the ceremony by the CAR, the UFC and the Convention démocratique des peuples africains—Branche Togolaise (CDPA—BT), which criticized the lack of preparations prior to the discussions; the UFC also deplored the exclusion of Gilchrist Olympio, who, it claimed, had been denied entry into Togo. In early June an EU mission charged with assessing Togo's progress in implementing democratic reforms held meetings with the Government, political and religious leaders and human rights organizations. The CAR, the UFC and the CDPA—BT refused to participate in a multi-party commission established in mid-July to consider the revision of the electoral code and the funding of political parties. In early August it was reported that Gilchrist Olympio had been provided with a Togolese passport. Later that month the Assemblée nationale adopted amendments to the press code, notably abolishing prison sentences for offences such as defamation and repealing the powers of the Ministry of the Interior, Security and Decentralization to order the closure or seizure of newspapers.

In November 2004 the EU announced that it was to resume partial economic co-operation with Togo, in view of progress towards fulfilment of the 22 conditions established in April. It was emphasized, however, that the full resumption of development aid was dependent on the holding of free and fair elections within six months. In December Eyadéma announced that legislative elections would be held during the first half of 2005. In anticipation of the proposed elections, in January 2005 the Assemblée nationale adopted legislation introducing several amendments to the electoral code in accordance with the demands of the EU, notably strengthening the powers of the CENI and increasing its membership to 13, to include two representatives of civil society.

On 5 February 2005 Prime Minister Sama announced that President Eyadéma had died while being transported out of the country for medical treatment. The Togolese military closed the country's borders, thus preventing Natchaba, the President of the Assemblée nationale, who according to the Constitution was to assume the functions of head of state pending elections to be held within 60 days, from returning to Togo from a visit to Europe. Hours later it was announced that the Constitution had been suspended and that the armed forces had pledged their allegiance to Eyadéma's son, Faure Gnassingbé, as the new head of state. The following day an extraordinary session of the Assemblée nationale was convened, at which deputies voted to remove Natchaba from his post as President of the legislature and appoint Gnassingbé in his place. The Assemblée also approved a constitutional amendment authorizing an interim president to serve the remainder of the deceased predecessor's term, rather than arranging elections within 60 days (Eyadéma's term was due to expire in June 2008).

Gnassingbé was formally sworn in as President of Togo on 7 February 2005. The circumstances of his succession provoked domestic and international condemnation: the inauguration ceremony was boycotted by diplomats from Nigeria, the EU, the USA and the UN, while the AU and ECOWAS demanded that Gnassingbé stand down to allow fair and democratic elections to be held. Meanwhile, the Togolese opposition called a two-day strike for 8 and 9 February, in protest at the perceived *coup d'état*; however, the strike was only partially observed. Subsequent protests, concentrated in the Lomé suburb of Bè, reportedly a stronghold of opposition support, resulted in at least four deaths and several injuries from clashes with security forces, who allegedly used tear gas and live ammunition to disperse protesters.

Following intense diplomatic pressure from ECOWAS, and from Nigeria in particular, Gnassingbé announced on 18 February 2005 that elections would be held within 60 days—however, he declined to stand down before that time. Following this announcement, on 21 February the Assemblée nationale voted to reverse the constitutional amendments adopted on 6 February. Judging these concessions to be insufficient, ECOWAS imposed an arms embargo on Togo and travel restrictions on members of the Government, while the ambassadors of ECOWAS states were withdrawn from Lomé. The AU declared its support for the imposition of sanctions, while the USA announced that it would terminate all military assistance to Togo unless Gnassingbé stood down. On 25 February it was revealed that Gnassingbé had been appointed President of the RPT, and endorsed as the party's candidate in the forthcoming presidential election. Later that day, Gnassingbé announced that he was resigning from the post of President of the Assemblée nationale, and hence from the position of interim President, stating that he did not wish to compromise the transparency and fairness of the election. Abbas Bonfoh, Vice-President of the Assemblée nationale, became the acting head of state. The announcement was welcomed by ECOWAS, whose sanctions were immediately lifted; opposition groups, however, continued to demand that Natchaba (who returned to Togo in early March) should assume the post of interim President, and sporadic protests continued, concentrated once more in Bè.

The date of the election was subsequently set for 24 April 2005; ECOWAS approved the date, although the opposition protested that it would be impossible to organize fair and transparent elections in such a brief period of time. (The EU also expressed doubts that fair elections could be held so promptly, and declined to send electoral observers.) Nevertheless, the radical opposition, which had grouped itself into a coalition of six parties (including, in addition to the four parties of the Front uni de l'opposition, the PSR and the UFC), subsequently announced that it would present a single candidate, Bob Akitani, to stand against Gnassingbé. Two members of the 'constructive opposition'—Harry Octavianus Olympio and the leader of the Parti du renouveau et de la rédemption, Nicolas Lawson—announced their candidacies; Gnassingbé's candidature was supported by five small parties of the 'constructive opposition' as well as by the RPT.

On 11 April 2005 a peaceful demonstration in the capital was reported to have been attended by several thousand supporters of the opposition, who protested against what was described as the 'repression' exercised by the authorities, and demanded that polling be postponed. On 16 April at least seven people were reported to have been killed, and some 150 injured, in clashes between supporters of the opposition and supporters of the youth wing of the RPT in Lomé. Bob Akitani refused to attend a meeting in Niamey, Niger on 20 April convened by the Nigerien President, Mamadou Tandja under the auspices of ECOWAS, to discuss the recent political violence in Togo, although Gnassingbé and the two candidates of the 'constructive opposition' attended. On 22 April Bonfoh dismissed the Minister of the

Interior, Security and Decentralization, Maj. François Akila Esso Boko, after Boko had called for the presidential election to be postponed and for the appointment of a temporary premier from the opposition, citing the risk of civil war if the elections went ahead; following his dismissal, Esso Boko sought asylum in the German embassy in Lomé. On 23 April Lawson announced the withdrawal of his candidacy, in protest at Esso Boko's dismissal.

The Presidential elections were held, as scheduled, on 24 April 2005, amid ongoing tensions. Although widespread violence was not reported on polling day, the seizure of ballot boxes, following the closure of polls, in areas of Lomé in which the opposition was known to have considerable support, and in other areas of the interior, was reported. Preliminary results, issued by the CENI on 26 April, indicated that Gnassingbé had been elected as President by a significant majority. Although Gnassingbé announced that he envisaged the establishment of a government of national unity, the announcement of his victory precipitated widespread rioting, particularly in Lomé and in southern regions, with some reports suggesting that as many as 100 people had died in the violence. (According to official figures, 22 people were killed in the rioting.) Meanwhile, Gilchrist Olympio, who had returned to Togo in March, declared that Bob Akitini had been the legitimate winner of polling, claiming that the opposition candidate had received more than 70% of the votes cast. However, on 27 April ECOWAS observers issued a report on the elections, stating that the irregularities in the conduct of the election had not been such as to invalidate or draw into question the declared results. By early May more than 20,000 Togolese were reported to have fled the country for either Benin or Ghana. On 3 May the Constitutional Court announced the final results of the elections, which were not substantially different from the preliminary figures declared by the CENI; Gnassingbé was attributed 60.16% of the votes cast, compared with the 38.25% awarded to Bob Akitani; Lawson (despite the formal withdrawal of his candidacy) and Harry Octavianus Olympio each received around 1%. Some 63% of the electorate were reported to have voted. Gnassingbé was inaugurated as President on 4 May. Although the European Parliament adopted a resolution criticizing the conduct of the election, the election result was generally accepted by the international community.

On 19 May 2005 President Olusegun Obasanjo of Nigeria chaired a reconciliation summit in Abuja, the Nigerian capital, under the aegis of ECOWAS and the AU, which was attended by Gnassingbé, Gilchrist Olympio and other opposition leaders, as well as the Heads of State of Benin, Burkina Faso, Gabon, Ghana and Niger. (Bob Akitani was unable to participate owing to ill health.) The talks ended without agreement, however, as the radical opposition continued to reject the legitimacy of Gnassingbé's victory and demanded a full investigation of alleged election irregularities as a precondition for entering into any power-sharing arrangement. None the less, Gnassingbé subsequently held meetings with a number of opposition leaders to discuss the formation of what he termed a government of national unity. While the UFC upheld its refusal to participate in negotiations, most of the other opposition parties decided to join the talks. In late May the AU removed sanctions against Togo, declaring that it considered conditions in Togo to be constitutional. Meanwhile, refugees continued to flee Togo, amid reports that opposition supporters were being arrested or kidnapped by the security forces, and by late May 34,416 Togolese refugees (19,272 in Benin and 15,144 in Ghana) had been registered by the office of the UN High Commissioner for Refugees (UNHCR). It was estimated that a further 10,000 people had been internally displaced within Togo. Several thousand more people were reported to have fled Togo in subsequent months.

On 8 June 2005 Gnassingbé announced the appointment of former premier Edem Kodjo, regarded as a member of the moderate opposition, as Prime Minister. Negotiations between the President and five 'radical' opposition parties had been unsuccessful, as Gnassingbé refused to accede to several principal opposition demands, including the scheduling of fresh presidential elections and the transfer of some presidential powers to the Prime Minister. Later in June the formation of a 30-member Council of Ministers, dominated by the RPT, but also including several representatives of the opposition and of civil society, was announced. Notably, Tchessa Abi of the PSR, was appointed as Keeper of the Seals, Minister of Justice; the other five members of the six-party coalition refused to participate and later condemned Abi's acceptance of a ministerial position, deciding to expel the PSR from the coalition. (The Minister of Culture, Tourism and Leisure, Gabriel Sassouvi Dosseh-Anyroh was expelled from the UFC, following his acceptance of a post in the administration.) Zarifou Ayéva, the leader of the moderate opposition Parti pour la démocratie et le renouveau (which was absorbed into the RPT later in the year), was appointed as Minister of State, Minister of Foreign Affairs and African Integration, while an elder brother of the President, Kpatcha Gnassingbé, became Minister-delegate at the Presidency of the Republic, responsible for Defence and Veterans.

The return of the refugees was discussed by Gnassingbé and Gilchrist Olympio at a meeting in Rome, Italy, in July 2005, at which the two men also condemned violence and agreed that political prisoners arrested during the electoral process should be released. (Another meeting between the two men was held in Rome in November.) In August Gnassingbé ordered the release from custody of 14 men, including a former member of the élite presidential guard, who had been suspected of plotting a *coup d'état* in 2003, while 42 supporters of the opposition, who had been detained after the 2005 election, were also released. In late September Gnassingbé announced that the holding of legislative elections was to be expedited (although no date was specified), and that, in a measure intended to promote national unity, the country's first President, Sylvanius Olympio, was to be officially rehabilitated. In early November, as a further gesture of reconciliation, some 460 political prisoners were released from gaol in Lomé; the release of political prisoners was also expected to take place in other cities and regions.

In mid-March 2006 the Government announced, that, to encourage Togolese refugees to return to their country (at least 19,000 were believed to be resident in Benin at the end of 2005) no legal proceedings were to be taken against opposition activists suspected of involvement in the unrest in 2005, excepting those involved in 'bloody crimes'; moreover, President Gnassingbé called for a formal resumption of the national dialogue between the authorities and the opposition. The inter-Togolese national dialogue, which had broken down following the death of Eyadéma, finally resumed in Lomé in April 2006, with the participation of six political parties (the CAR, the CDPA—BT, the CPP, the Parti pour la démocratie et le renouveau, the RPT and the UFC), as well as two civil society organizations and the Government.

On 20 August 2006, following negotiations chaired by the President of Burkina Faso, Blaise Compaoré, the Government signed a comprehensive political accord with the main opposition parties in Lomé that provided for the establishment of a transitional government, which would include members of opposition parties. It also called for the re-establishment of the CENI, which would organize and supervise transparent and democratic elections. (In January 2007 the CENI was approved as the official decision-making body for national elections.) Agboyibo replaced Kodjo as Prime Minister in September 2006 and tasked with forming a government of national unity and organizing elections for 2007. He announced the formation of his new Council of Ministers later that month. In June 2007 the EU agreed to provide funding to support the forthcoming elections (initially scheduled to take place that month but subsequently postponed until August). Meanwhile, in March Adji Ayassour replaced Payadowa Boukpessi as Minister of Finance, the Budget and Privatization. The Minister of Youth and Sports, Richard Attipoé, was killed in a helicopter crash in Sierra Leone in June. His successor was not immediately appointed.

After further delays, legislative elections finally took place on 14 October 2007; the RPT secured 50 of the available 81 seats, the UFC took 27 seats and the CAR four. Voter turn-out was estimated at 95% and international observers declared the election to have been largely free and fair, despite allegations by opposition parties of procedural irregularities. In November Agboyibo, having completed his task of leading the country through legitimate legislative elections, submitted his resignation; Komlan Mally, hitherto Minister of Towns and Town Planning, was appointed Prime Minister in early December and named a new 21-member Council of Ministers, including Léopold Messan Gnininvi as Minister of State, Minister of Foreign Affairs and Regional Integration. Notable dismissals included that of Minister of Defence and Veterans Kpatcha Gnassingbé; responsibility for his portfolio was assumed by the presidency. The EU had announced in November its resumption of full co-operation with Togo and granted the country €123m. in development aid.

Relations with neighbouring Ghana have frequently become strained, as the common border with Togo has periodically been closed in an effort to combat smuggling and to curb political activity by exiles on both sides. In March 1993 and January 1994 the Togolese Government accused Ghana of supporting armed attacks on Eyadéma's residence, reflecting earlier accusations of Ghanaian involvement in unrest in Togo in early 1991. Full diplomatic relations between the two countries, suspended since 1982, were formally resumed in November 1994, and various joint commissions were subsequently reactivated. The newly elected President of Ghana, John Kufuor, visited Togo to mark the celebrations for Liberation Day on 13 January 2001, and a rapprochement in relations between the two countries was subsequently reported.

Relations with fellow ECOWAS members were jeopardized by the perceived *coup d'état* by which Gnassingbé assumed power following the death of his father Eyadéma (see above). Relations with Nigeria, in particular, were further compromised when the Togolese authorities refused to grant an aeroplane carrying the advance delegation of President Olusegun Obasanjo permission to land in Lomé. Nigeria withdrew its ambassador to Togo and imposed restrictions on visits of Togolese officials to Nigeria following the incident, anticipating the sanctions imposed by ECOWAS after Gnassingbé initially declined to stand down as interim President in advance of presidential elections. Following Gnassingbé's resignation on 25 February 2005, Nigeria and the other ECOWAS member states lifted their sanctions, returned their ambassadors to Lomé and resumed co-operation with Togo, approving the 24 April date for the presidential election and pledging to provide assistance to ensure the fairness and transparency of the poll. In February 2007 Benin, Nigeria and Togo signed a security agreement to promote stability and development within the three countries. An early warning system was to be established and the ECOWAS policy of free movement of goods and persons would be implemented.

Government

Under the terms of the Constitution that was approved in a national referendum on 27 September 1993, and subsequently modified, executive power is vested in the President of the Republic, who is directly elected, by universal adult suffrage, for a period of five years. The legislature is the unicameral Assemblée nationale, whose 81 members are also elected, by universal suffrage, for a five-year period. The Prime Minister is appointed by the President from among the majority in the legislature, and the Prime Minister, in consultation with the President, nominates other ministers. For administrative purposes, the country is divided into five regions. It is further divided into 30 prefectures and sub-prefectures.

Defence

As assessed at November 2007, Togo's armed forces officially numbered about 8,550 (army around 8,100, air force 250, navy 200). Paramilitary forces comprised a 750-strong gendarmerie. Military service is by selective conscription and lasts for two years. Togo receives assistance with training and equipment from France. The defence budget was estimated at 20,000m. francs CFA in 2007.

Economic Affairs

In 2006, according to estimates by the World Bank, Togo's gross national income (GNI), measured at average 2004–06 prices, was US $2,229m., equivalent to $350 per head (or $1,490 on an international purchasing-power parity basis). During 1996–2006, it was estimated, the population increased at an average annual rate of 3.1%, while gross domestic product (GDP) per head increased by an average of 0.5% per year. Overall GDP increased, in real terms, at an average annual rate of 2.5% in 1996–2006. Real GDP increased by 1.5% in 2006.

Agriculture (including forestry and fishing) contributed 40.9% of GDP in 2006; in the previous year 56.7% of the working population were employed in the sector. The principal cash crops are cotton (which contributed 15.3% of earnings from merchandise exports in 2004), coffee and cocoa. Togo has generally been self-sufficient in basic foodstuffs: the principal subsistence crops are cassava, yams, maize, millet and sorghum. Imports of livestock products and fish are necessary to satisfy domestic needs. During 1996–2006, according to the World Bank, agricultural GDP increased at an average annual rate of 2.0%; agricultural GDP increased by 3.7% in 2006.

Industry (including mining, manufacturing, construction and power) contributed 17.7% of GDP in 2006, and employed 10.1% of the working population in 1990. During 1995–2005, according to the World Bank, industrial GDP increased by an average of 3.9% per year; industrial GDP increased by 6.5% in 2005.

Mining and quarrying contributed 2.9% of GDP in 2006. Togo has the world's richest reserves of first-grade calcium phosphates. Concerns regarding the high cadmium content of Togolese phosphate rock have prompted interest in the development of lower-grade carbon phosphates, which have a less significant cadmium content; exports of crude fertilizers and crude minerals provided 16.6% of earnings from merchandise exports in 2002. Limestone and marble are also exploited. There are, in addition, smaller deposits of iron ore, gold, diamonds, zinc, rutile and platinum. In 1998 marine exploration revealed petroleum and gas deposits within Togo's territorial waters. In October 2002 the Togolese Government, the Hunt Oil Co of the USA and Petronas Carigali of Malaysia signed a joint-venture oil-production agreement, providing for the first offshore drilling in Togolese territorial waters. The GDP of the mining sector was estimated to have declined at an average annual rate of 3.2% in 1991–95.

Manufacturing contributed 7.9% of GDP in 2006. About 6.6% of the labour force were employed in the sector in 1990. Major companies are engaged notably in agro-industrial activities, the processing of phosphates, steel-rolling and in the production of cement. An industrial 'free zone' was inaugurated in Lomé in 1990, with the aim of attracting investment by local and foreign interests by offering certain (notably fiscal) advantages in return for guarantees regarding export levels and employment; a second 'free zone' has since opened, and provision has been made for 'free zone' terms to apply to certain businesses operating outside the regions. According to the World Bank, manufacturing GDP increased by an average of 5.6% per year in 1995–2005; manufacturing GDP increased by 7.2% in 2005.

Togo's dependence on imports of electrical energy from Ghana was reduced following the completion, in 1988, of a 65-MW hydroelectric installation (constructed in co-operation with Benin) at Nangbeto, on the Mono river. In early 2004 the Togolese and Beninois authorities announced that the Adjarralla hydroelectric installation, also on the Mono river, was to be modernized, and its production capacity increased markedly. In 2004 some 61.1% of electricity produced in Togo was generated from hydroelectric sources; the remaining 38.9% was generated from petroleum. In 2005 fuel imports constituted 29.0% of all merchandise imports by value. It was planned to connect the electricity grids of Togo and Benin, and to construct further power stations in both countries. A pipeline to supply natural gas from Nigeria to Togo (and also to Benin and Ghana) was expected to come on stream in early 2008.

The services sector contributed 41.4% of GDP in 2006, and engaged 24.4% of the employed labour force in 1990. Lomé has been of considerable importance as an entrepôt for the foreign trade of land-locked countries of the region. However, political instability in the early 1990s and in 2005 resulted in the diversion of a large part of this activity to neighbouring Benin and undermined the tourism industry (previously an important source of foreign exchange). According to the World Bank, the GDP of the services sector increased by an average of 3.3% per year in 1995–2005; services GDP increased by 0.5% in 2003, but declined by 0.2% in 2005.

In 2006 Togo recorded a visible trade deficit of US $224.0m., while there was a estimated deficit of $70.1m. on the current account of the balance of payments. In 2004 the principal source of imports was France (19.5%); other major suppliers were the People's Republic of China and Côte d'Ivoire. The principal market for exports in that year was Burkina Faso (which took 13.1% of Togo's exports); other significant purchasers were Benin and Ghana. The principal exports in 2004 were food and live animals, cement, cotton, crude fertilizers and crude minerals, and iron and steel. The principal imports in that year were refined petroleum products, iron and steel, road vehicles, cement and cereals and cereal preparations.

Togo's overall budget deficit for 2006 was 32,300m. francs CFA (equivalent to 2.8% of GDP). Togo's total external debt was US $1,708m. at the end of 2005, of which $1,469m. was long-term public debt. In 2004 the cost of debt-servicing was equivalent to 2.2% of the value of exports of goods and services. Annual inflation averaged 2.6% in 1990–93. Following the devaluation of the CFA franc in January 1994, inflation in that year averaged 39.2%. Consumer prices increased by an annual average of 2.3% in 1996–2006. Consumer prices increased by 0.9% in 2007.

Togo is a member of the Economic Community of West African States (see p. 232), of the West African organs of the Franc Zone (see p. 307), of the International Cocoa Organization (see p. 408), of the International Coffee Organization (see p. 408) and of the Conseil de l'Entente (see p. 412). Togo was admitted to the Islamic Development Bank (see p. 329) in 1998.

From the late 1990s the Togolese economy was adversely affected by a number of economic and political factors. A sharp and sustained decline in the output of phosphates, historically one of Togo's major sources of export earnings, persistently low international prices for another of Togo's principal exports, cotton, and high international prices for a principal import, petroleum, had a negative impact on the trade balance. The European Union (EU) suspended development aid to Togo in 1993, citing the lack of a functioning democratic system within the country, while further external sources of aid were suspended in the wake of the internationally criticized presidential election of 1998. Although repeatedly delayed legislative elections were held in October 2002, both the USA and the EU declared themselves dissatisfied with the conduct of the polls, and therefore much international aid remained suspended. Many sources of economic assistance were further jeopardized by the accession to the presidency of Faure Gnassingbé in early 2005, widely denounced as a *coup d'état* and the consequent unrest, that resulted in more than 30,000 Togolese citizens fleeing the country (see above). However, following the holding of free and fair legislative elections in October 2007 the EU agreed to resume development aid to Togo. In late 2006 the IMF had recommended that the Government restrict expenditure to budgeted activities, with particular emphasis on health and education outlays, and that further efforts be made to privatize state-owned enterprises. The Fund agreed to resume aid to Togo in early 2008, after withdrawing support in 1994 citing the Government's poor management of public funds. A loan of US $108.4m. was approved to support the Government's economic policies in 2008–09. The 2008 budget was approved in January, with an estimated deficit of 42,450m. francs CFA. Expenditure of 307,620m. francs CFA was primarily focused on the social sector, with provisions for increased civil servant salaries and the recruitment of more than 1,000 public sector employees. Meanwhile, the Minister of Economy and Finance signed a memorandum in April 2008 with the African Development Bank, ensuring the cancellation of Togo's $24.1m. debt to the institution. The IMF forecast GDP growth of 3.0% in 2008.

Education

Primary education, which begins at six years of age and lasts for six years, is (in theory) compulsory. Secondary education, beginning at the age of 12, lasts for a further seven years, comprising a first cycle of four years and a second of three years. According to UNESCO estimates, in 2003/04 enrolment at primary schools included 79% of children in the relevant age-group (85% of boys; 72% of girls), while in 1999/2000 secondary enrolment was equivalent to 22% of the relevant age group (boys 30%; girls 14%). Proficiency in the two national languages, Ewe and Kabiye, is compulsory. Mission schools are important, educating almost one-half of all pupils. In 1998 15,028 students were enrolled in institutions providing higher education. The Université du Lomé (formerly the University du Bénin) had about 14,000 students in the early 2000s, and scholarships to French universities are available. A second university opened in Kara, in the north of Togo, in early 2004. Current expenditure on education was an estimated 23,800m. francs CFA in 1995 (16.2% of total expenditure by the central Government), and a further 3,700m. francs CFA was allocated to scholarships and training (2.5% of total expenditure).

Public Holidays

2008: 1 January (New Year's Day), 13 January (Liberation Day, anniversary of the 1967 coup), 24 January (Day of Victory, anniversary of the failed attack at Sarakawa), 24 March (Easter Monday), 24 April (Day of Victory), 27 April (Independence Day), 1 May (Labour Day and Ascension Day), 12 May (Whit Monday), 15 August (Assumption), 23 September (anniversary of the failed attack on Lomé), 1 October* (Id al-Fitr, end of Ramadan), 1 November (All Saints' Day), 9 December* (Tabaski, Feast of the Sacrifice), 25 December (Christmas).

2009: 1 January (New Year's Day), 13 January (Liberation Day, anniversary of the 1967 coup), 24 January (Day of Victory, anniversary of the failed attack at Sarakawa), 13 April (Easter Monday), 24 April (Day of Victory), 27 April (Independence Day), 1 May (Labour Day), 21 May (Ascension Day), 1 June (Whit Monday), 15 August (Assumption), 20 September* (Id al-Fitr, end of Ramadan), 23 September (anniversary of the failed attack on Lomé), 1 November (All Saints' Day), 27 November* (Tabaski, Feast of the Sacrifice), 25 December (Christmas).

* These holidays are dependent on the Islamic lunar calendar and may vary by one or two days from the dates given.

Weights and Measures

The metric system is in force.

Statistical Survey

Source (except where otherwise indicated): Direction de la Statistique, BP 118, Lomé; tel. 221-62-24; fax 221-27-75; e-mail dgscn_tg@yahoo.fr; internet www.stat-togo.org.

Area and Population

AREA, POPULATION AND DENSITY

Area (sq km)	56,600*
Population (census results)	
1 March–30 April 1970	1,997,109
22 November 1981	2,703,250
Population (UN estimates at mid-year)†	
2005	6,239,000
2006	6,410,000
2007	6,585,000
Density (per sq km) at mid-2007	116.3

* 21,853 sq miles.
† Source: UN, *World Population Prospects: The 2006 Revision*.

Ethnic Groups (percentage of total, 1995): Kabré 23.7; Ewe 21.9; Kabiyé 12.9; Watchi 10.1; Guin 6.0; Tem 6.0; Mobamba 4.9; Gourmantché 3.9; Lamba 3.2; Ncam 2.4; Fon 1.2; Adja 0.9; Others 2.9 (Source: La Francophonie).

ADMINISTRATIVE DIVISIONS
(2003, official estimates)

Region	Area (sq km)	Population ('000)	Density (per sq km)	Principal city
Centrale	13,317	478	35.9	Sokodé
Kara	11,738	647	55.1	Kara
Maritime	6,100	2,113	346.4	Lomé
Plateaux	16,975	1,142	67.3	Atakpamé
Savanes	8,470	590	69.7	Dapaoug
Total	56,600	4,970	87.8	

PRINCIPAL TOWNS
(2003, official estimates)

Lomé (capital)	839,000	Atakpamé	68,000
Golfe Urbain	355,000	Kpalimé	68,000
Sokodé	101,000	Dapaong	49,000
Kara	95,000	Tsevie	44,300

Mid-2007 (incl. suburbs, UN estimate): Lomé 1,452,000 (Source: UN, *World Urbanization Prospects: The 2007 Revision*).

TOGO

BIRTHS AND DEATHS
(annual averages, UN estimates)

	1990–95	1995–2000	2000–05
Birth rate (per 1,000)	43.1	41.3	39.6
Death rate (per 1,000)	11.2	10.7	10.8

Source: UN, *World Population Prospects: The 2006 Revision*.

Expectation of life (years at birth, WHO estimates): 53.8 (males 52.0; females 55.6) in 2005 (Source: WHO, *World Health Statistics*).

ECONOMICALLY ACTIVE POPULATION
(census of 22 November 1981)

	Males	Females	Total
Agriculture, hunting, forestry and fishing	324,870	254,491	579,361
Mining and quarrying	2,781	91	2,872
Manufacturing	29,307	25,065	54,372
Electricity, gas and water	2,107	96	2,203
Construction	20,847	301	21,148
Trade, restaurants and hotels	17,427	87,415	104,842
Transport, storage and communications	20,337	529	20,866
Financing, insurance, real estate and business services	1,650	413	2,063
Community, social and personal services	50,750	12,859	63,609
Activities not adequately defined	14,607	6,346	20,953
Total employed	484,683	387,606	872,289
Unemployed	21,666	7,588	29,254
Total labour force	506,349	395,194	901,543

Mid-2005 (estimates in '000): Agriculture, etc. 1,485; Total labour force 2,621 (Source: FAO).

Health and Welfare

KEY INDICATORS

Total fertility rate (children per woman, 2005)	5.1
Under-5 mortality rate (per 1,000 live births, 2005)	139
HIV/AIDS (% of persons aged 15–49, 2005)	3.2
Physicians (per 1,000 head, 2004)	0.04
Hospital beds (per 1,000 head, 2005)	0.90
Health expenditure (2004): US $ per head (PPP)	62.6
Health expenditure (2004): % of GDP	5.5
Health expenditure (2004): public (% of total)	20.7
Access to water (% of persons, 2004)	52
Access to sanitation (% of persons, 2004)	35
Human Development Index (2005): ranking	152
Human Development Index (2005): value	0.512

For sources and definitions, see explanatory note on p. vi.

Agriculture

PRINCIPAL CROPS
('000 metric tons)

	2004	2005	2006*
Rice (paddy)	68.5	72.9	76.3
Maize	523.7	509.5	543.3
Millet	35.0	42.2	43.7
Sorghum	169.8	206.0	224.6
Cassava (Manioc)	679.1	678.2	767.4
Taro (Coco Yam)	17.8	12.9	13.4
Yams	636.3	585.4	621.1
Dry beans	49.4	67.4	52.8
Groundnuts (in shell)	34.9	33.4	39.3
Coconuts*	14.5	14.5	14.5
Oil palm fruit*	115	115	120
Cottonseed†	87	86	64
Bananas*	17	17	19
Oranges*	12.1	12.1	12.5
Cotton (lint)†	71	69	52
Coffee (green)†	13.5	8.4	10.2
Cocoa beans†	21.7	59.0	73.0

* FAO estimates.
† Unofficial figures.

Aggregate production ('000 metric tons, may include official, semi-official or estimated data): Total cereals 799 in 2004, 833 in 2005, 889 in 2006; Total roots and tubers 1,334 in 2004, 1,280 in 2005, 1,405 in 2006; Total vegetables (incl. melons) 135 in 2004, 134 in 2005, 140 in 2006; Total fruits (excl. melons) 50 in 2004, 50 in 2005, 51 in 2006.

Source: FAO.

LIVESTOCK
('000 head, year ending September, FAO estimates)

	2003	2004	2005
Cattle	279	279	280
Sheep	1,800	1,850	1,850
Pigs	310	320	320
Goats	1,470	1,480	1,480
Horses	2	2	2
Asses, mules or hinnies	3	3	3
Poultry	8,500	9,000	9,000

2006: Figures assumed to be unchanged from 2005 (FAO estimates).
Source: FAO.

LIVESTOCK PRODUCTS
('000 metric tons, FAO estimates)

	2004	2005	2006
Cattle meat	5.7	5.7	5.7
Sheep meat	4.1	4.1	4.2
Goat meat	3.7	3.7	3.8
Pig meat	4.2	4.0	5.1
Chicken meat	10.9	11.2	11.6
Game meat	4.5	4.5	4.5
Cows' milk	9.2	9.3	9.5
Hen eggs	6.4	6.4	7.3

Source: FAO.

Forestry

ROUNDWOOD REMOVALS
('000 cubic metres, excluding bark)

	2004	2005	2006*
Sawlogs, veneer logs and logs for sleepers	44	86	86
Other industrial wood	210	80	80
Fuel wood	4,424	5,762	5,816
Total	4,678	5,928	5,982

* FAO estimates.
Source: FAO.

TOGO

Fishing

('000 metric tons, live weight)

	2003	2004	2005
Capture	27.5	28.0	27.7
Tilapias	3.5	3.5	3.5
Other freshwater fishes	1.5	1.5	1.5
West African ilisha	0.5	2.2	1.2
Bigeye grunt	0.4	1.5	0.8
Round sardinella	4.0	4.7	9.4
European anchovy	11.5	6.9	6.5
Atlantic bonito	1.7	1.4	1.2
Marlins, sailfishes	0.9	0.1	0.0
Jack and horse mackerels	0.6	0.9	0.5
Jacks, crevalles	0.7	1.2	1.0
Other mackerels	1.9	2.0	n.a.
Aquaculture	1.2	1.5*	1.5
Total catch	**28.7**	**29.5**	**29.3**

*FAO estimate.
Source: FAO.

Mining

('000 metric tons)

	2003	2004	2005
Limestone*	2,400	2,400	2,400
Phosphate rock (gross weight)	1,471	1,115	1,021
Phosphate content	530*	418	368*

*Estimate(s).
Source: US Geological Survey.

Industry

SELECTED PRODUCTS
('000 metric tons, unless otherwise indicated)

	2002	2003	2004
Palm oil	7.0	7.0	7.0
Cement	800	800	800
Electric energy (million kWh)	234	291	262

Sources: FAO; US Geological Survey; UN, *Industrial Commodity Statistics Yearbook*.

Finance

CURRENCY AND EXCHANGE RATES

Monetary Units
100 centimes = 1 franc de la Communauté financière africaine (CFA).

Sterling, Dollar and Euro Equivalents (31 December 2007)
£1 sterling = 892.702 francs CFA;
US $1 = 445.593 francs CFA;
€1 = 655.957 francs CFA;
10,000 francs CFA = £11.20 = $22.44 = €15.24.

Average Exchange Rate (francs CFA per US $)
2005 527.47
2006 522.89
2007 479.27

Note: An exchange rate of 1 French franc = 50 francs CFA, established in 1948, remained in force until January 1994, when the CFA franc was devalued by 50%, with the exchange rate adjusted to 1 French franc = 100 francs CFA. This relationship to French currency remained in effect with the introduction of the euro on 1 January 1999. From that date, accordingly, a fixed exchange rate of €1 = 655.957 francs CFA has been in operation.

BUDGET
('000 million francs CFA)

Revenue*	2004	2005	2006
Tax revenue	161.0	162.1	179.1
Direct tax revenue	50.0	43.5	46.9
Indirect tax revenue	110.0	118.5	132.3
Taxes on international trade	68.9	81.0	92.3
Other current revenue	10.7	12.8	16.8
Total	**171.7**	**174.9**	**195.9**

Expenditure†	2004	2005	2006
Current expenditure	153.9	184.1	202.5
Salaries and wages	51.7	49.2	59.3
Other operational expenses	20.8	35.9	9.6
Interest payments on public debt	4.9	0.7	0.5
External	13.0	10.9	10.0
Capital expenditure	15.8	30.9	41.6
Externally financed	12.8	17.3	18.2
Total†	**169.8**	**215.0**	**244.2**

* Excluding grants received ('000 million francs CFA): 7.9 in 2004; 13.1 in 2005; 16.0 in 2006.
† Including lending minus repayments.

Source: IMF, *Togo: Statistical Appendix* (June 2007).

INTERNATIONAL RESERVES
(excluding gold, US $ million at 31 December)

	2005	2006	2007
IMF special drawing rights	—	0.1	0.1
Reserve position in IMF	0.5	0.5	0.5
Foreign exchange	194.1	373.9	437.5
Total	**194.6**	**374.5**	**438.1**

Source: IMF, *International Financial Statistics*.

MONEY SUPPLY
('000 million francs CFA at 31 December)

	2005	2006	2007
Currency outside banks	63.3	100.4	122.0
Demand deposits at deposit money banks	121.5	145.3	150.7
Total money (incl. others)	**186.7**	**248.4**	**278.4**

Source: IMF, *International Financial Statistics*.

COST OF LIVING
(Consumer Price Index for Lomé; base: 1996 = 100)

	2004	2005	2006
Food, beverages and tobacco	101.9	113.0	111.7
Clothing	114.9	116.0	115.3
Housing, water, electricity and gas	109.1	112.4	120.5
All items (incl. others)	**115.3**	**123.1**	**125.8**

Source: IMF, *Togo: Statistical Appendix* (June 2007).

All items (base: 2000 = 100)): 113.7 in 2005; 116.3 in 2006; 117.4 in 2007. (Source: IMF, *International Financial Statistics*).

TOGO

NATIONAL ACCOUNTS
('000 million francs CFA at current prices)

Expenditure on the Gross Domestic Product

	2004	2005	2006
Final consumption expenditure	1,063.4	1,168.7	1,234.7
Households	} 958.8	1,028.5	1,094.0
Non-profit institutions serving households			
General government	104.6	140.2	140.7
Gross capital formation	113.5	131.8	151.2
Gross fixed capital formation	125.1	126.6	151.2
Changes in inventories	} −11.6	5.2	0.0
Acquisitions, less disposals, of valuables			
Total domestic expenditure	1,176.9	1,300.5	1,385.9
Exports of goods and services	421.1	448.4	468.9
Less Imports of goods and services	574.7	636.2	696.0
GDP at market prices	1,023.3	1,112.7	1,158.8
GDP at constant 2000 prices	966.5	978.5	998.1

Gross Domestic Product by Economic Activity

	2004	2005	2006
Agriculture, hunting, forestry and fishing	370.8	436.7	432.4
Mining and quarrying	29.9	33.0	31.0
Manufacturing	83.9	95.3	83.6
Electricity, gas and water	35.7	36.1	36.0
Construction	26.0	27.3	36.5
Trade, restaurants and hotels	126.8	124.2	156.4
Transport, storage and communications	57.9	56.8	69.1
Banking and insurance	21.6	23.1	24.6
Non-market services	103.4	99.1	98.7
Other services	77.1	80.6	89.2
Sub-total	933.1	1,012.3	1,057.4
Import duties and taxes	90.2	100.3	101.4
GDP in purchasers' values	1,023.3	1,112.7	1,158.8

Source: IMF, *Togo: Statistical Appendix* (June 2007).

BALANCE OF PAYMENTS
('000 million francs CFA at current prices)

	2004	2005	2006
Exports of goods f.o.b.	317.5	314.2	319.8
Imports of goods f.o.b.	−450.8	−497.0	−543.8
Trade balance	−133.3	−182.8	−224.0
Exports of services	103.6	134.2	149.1
Imports of services	−123.9	−139.2	−152.1
Balance on goods and services	−153.6	−187.8	−227.0
Other income (net)	−17.7	−9.4	−13.2
Balance on goods, services and income	−171.3	−197.2	−240.2
Current transfers (net)	141.1	138.3	170.2
Current balance	−30.2	−58.9	−70.1
Direct investment abroad (net)	38.0	24.2	39.8
Portfolio investment assets (net)	15.7	12.7	33.7
Other investment assets net)	−21.9	−29.3	27.7
Overall balance	1.6	−51.3	31.1

Source: IMF, *Togo: Statistical Appendix* (June 2007).

External Trade

PRINCIPAL COMMODITIES
(US $ million)

Imports c.i.f.	2002	2003	2004
Food and live animals	65.4	65.2	53.1
Fish, crustaceans and molluscs and preparations thereof	6.9	7.6	4.9
Fish, fresh, chilled or frozen	6.0	6.7	4.0
Fish, frozen, excl. fillets	5.8	6.6	3.9
Cereals and cereal preparations	38.3	35.5	26.7
Wheat and meslin, unmilled	29.2	25.6	16.7
Mineral fuels, lubricants, etc.	61.0	106.9	125.9
Petroleum products, refined	60.3	106.3	124.9
Animal and vegetable oils, fats and waxes	12.6	13.6	14.3
Chemicals and related products	42.6	59.1	52.9
Medicinal and pharmaceutical products	15.4	20.8	23.6
Basic manufactures	99.5	135.4	141.8
Textile yarn, fabrics, made-up articles and related products	14.4	18.7	27.5
Cotton fabrics, woven*	9.4	8.9	11.3
Other woven fabrics, 85% plus of cotton, bleached, etc., finished	8.2	7.7	10.1
Non-metallic mineral manufactures	33.8	43.2	45.6
Lime, cement and fabricated construction materials	30.3	36.4	40.5
Cement	29.0	34.4	38.8
Iron and steel	31.0	44.1	44.6
Iron and steel bars, rods, shapes and sections	15.6	27.6	24.9
Iron and steel bars, rods, shapes and sections, of other than high carbon or alloy steel	14.9	26.7	23.3
Machinery and transport equipment	79.8	126.8	75.9
Telecommunications, sound recording and reproducing equipment	9.2	7.7	6.7
Telecommunication equipment, parts and accessories	8.6	5.8	3.4
Road vehicles	33.1	36.0	35.1
Passenger motor vehicles (excl. buses)	11.0	13.2	11.6
Miscellaneous manufactured articles	22.5	29.0	38.5
Total (incl. others)	405.3	568.4	548.1

TOGO   Statistical Survey

Exports f.o.b.	2002	2003	2004
Food and live animals	41.7	45.3	73.6
Cereals and cereal preparations	11.6	10.6	8.9
Coffee, tea, cocoa, spices, and manufactures thereof	10.5	12.9	27.7
Coffee, not roasted; coffee husks and skins	2.9	1.1	2.7
Crude materials, inedible, except fuels	86.6	114.2	111.2
Textile fibres and their waste†	40.0	70.2	59.6
Cotton	39.9	69.5	58.8
Raw cotton, excl. linters, not carded or combed	26.4	53.4	48.4
Cotton, carded or combed	13.4	16.0	10.3
Crude fertilizers and crude minerals	41.7	37.9	47.6
Crude fertilizers and crude minerals (unground)	41.4	35.0	47.5
Basic manufactures	93.1	166.0	148.8
Non-metallic mineral manufactures	66.8	124.2	97.8
Cement	66.3	73.2	66.4
Iron and steel	18.5	28.1	40.7
Iron and steel bars, rods, shapes and sections	8.4	12.6	27.3
Machinery and transport equipment	5.9	111.8	5.0
Total (incl. others)	250.6	494.6	384.4

* Excluding narrow or special fabrics.
† Excluding wool tops and wastes in yarn.

Source: UN, *International Trade Statistics Yearbook*.

PRINCIPAL TRADING PARTNERS
(US $ million)

Imports c.i.f.	2002	2003	2004
Belgium	20.5	21.9	26.5
Canada	23.6	9.9	7.3
China, People's Repub.	11.7	23.4	45.7
Côte d'Ivoire	25.5	33.0	33.2
France (incl. Monaco)	82.4	118.7	106.8
Germany	20.4	25.7	18.0
Ghana	8.1	13.5	9.6
Hong Kong	7.3	10.1	14.0
India	4.8	8.2	9.6
Indonesia	7.8	10.5	11.3
Italy	14.6	25.1	20.5
Japan	7.8	8.2	8.9
Mauritania	4.5	4.2	3.2
Netherlands	13.0	68.3	18.4
Russia	6.1	4.6	6.0
Senegal	5.5	8.1	4.8
South Africa	8.1	23.6	7.9
Spain	10.7	17.2	15.7
Ukraine	12.9	17.2	12.2
United Kingdom	6.8	5.2	11.2
USA	18.6	6.5	13.3
Total (incl. others)	405.3	568.4	548.1

Exports f.o.b.	2002	2003	2004
Australia	9.2	4.5	6.4
Belgium	1.2	1.5	10.4
Benin	33.1	46.2	46.8
Brazil	0.6	3.3	4.2
Burkina Faso	32.6	72.3	50.2
France (incl. Monaco)	2.3	5.1	15.3
Ghana	53.8	68.0	45.6
India	5.0	10.4	15.4
Indonesia	2.9	8.2	7.9
Italy	4.5	4.5	3.3
Malaysia	5.0	5.4	2.4
Morocco	2.7	4.1	2.9
Netherlands	4.9	99.6	15.2
New Zealand	8.5	5.5	7.4
Niger	11.6	19.2	12.9
Nigeria	5.0	6.1	7.2
Poland	5.9	0.8	1.3
South Africa	5.9	3.8	5.2
Thailand	4.3	2.7	3.6
USA	0.9	10.4	1.5
Total (incl. others)	250.6	494.6	384.4

Source: UN, *International Trade Statistics Yearbook*.

Transport

RAILWAYS
(traffic)

	1997	1998	1999
Passengers carried ('000)	152.0	35.0	4.4
Freight carried ('000 metric tons)	250	759	1,090
Passenger-km (million)	12.7	3.4	0.4
Freight ton-km (million)	28.8	70.6	92.4

Source: Société Nationale des Chemins de Fer du Togo, Lomé.

ROAD TRAFFIC
(motor vehicles registered at 31 December)

	1994	1995	1996*
Passenger cars	67,936	74,662	79,200
Buses and coaches	529	547	580
Goods vehicles	31,457	32,514	33,660
Tractors (road)	1,466	1,544	1,620
Motorcycles and scooters	39,019	52,902	59,000

* Estimates.

Source: IRF, *World Road Statistics*.

SHIPPING

Merchant Fleet
(registered at 31 December)

	2004	2005	2006
Number of vessels	26	27	26
Total displacement ('000 grt)	19.5	20.6	18.5

Source: Lloyd's Register-Fairplay, *World Fleet Statistics*.

International Sea-borne Freight Traffic
('000 metric tons)

Port Lomé	1997	1998	1999
Goods loaded	432.4	794.6	1,021.4
Goods unloaded	1,913.9	1,912.9	1,812.4

Source: Port Autonome de Lomé.

TOGO

CIVIL AVIATION
(traffic on scheduled services)*

	1999	2000	2001
Kilometres flown (million)	3	3	1
Passengers carried ('000)	84	77	46
Passenger-km (million)	235	216	130
Total ton-km (million)	36	32	19

*Including an apportionment of the traffic of Air Afrique.

Source: UN, *Statistical Yearbook*.

Tourism

FOREIGN TOURIST ARRIVALS*

	2003	2004	2005
Belgium, Luxembourg and the Netherlands	509	1,024	3,517
Benin	5,111	7,434	5,909
Burkina Faso, Mali and Niger	5,953	8,132	8,069
Côte d'Ivoire	4,134	5,860	5,916
France	14,154	17,674	16,511
Germany	830	879	1,092
Ghana	1,585	2,161	1,880
Italy	570	960	674
Nigeria	3,152	3,572	3,356
United Kingdom	655	879	619
USA	1,384	2,097	2,141
Total (incl. others)	60,592	82,686	80,763

*Arrivals at hotels and similar establishments, by country of residence.

Receipts from tourism (US $ million, incl. passenger transport): 26 in 2003; 25 in 2004; n.a. in 2005.

Source: World Tourism Organization.

Communications Media

	2004	2005	2006
Telephones ('000 main lines in use)	65.9	62.8	82.1
Mobile cellular telephones ('000 subscribers)	332.6	443.6	708.0
Personal computers ('000 in use)	171	185	n.a.
Internet users ('000)	221	300	320

Television receivers ('000 in use): 150 in 2000.

Radio receivers ('000 in use): 940 in 1997.

Facsimile machines ('000 in use): 17 in 1997.

Daily newspapers: 1 (average circulation 10,000 copies) in 1999; 1 (average circulation 10,000 copies) in 2000.

Book production (number of titles): 5 in 1998.

Sources: International Telecommunication Union; UNESCO, *Statistical Yearbook*, UNESCO Institute for Statistics; UN, *Statistical Yearbook*.

Education

(2004/05, unless otherwise indicated)

	Institutions*	Teachers	Males	Females	Total
Pre-primary†	319	707	6,580	6,465	13,045
Primary	4,701	22,210†	538,792	457,915	996,707
Secondary	n.a.	11,029†	264,707	134,331	399,038
Tertiary	n.a.	388*	15,336‡	3,119‡	18,455‡

* 1999/2000.
† 2003/04.
‡ 2000/01.

Source: UNESCO Institute for Statistics.

Adult literacy rate (UNESCO estimates): 53.2% (males 68.7%; females 38.5%) in 2000 (Source: UNESCO Institute for Statistics).

Directory

The Constitution

The Constitution that was approved in a national referendum on 27 September 1992, and subsequently amended, defines the rights, freedoms and obligations of Togolese citizens, and defines the separation of powers among the executive, legislative and judicial organs of state.

Executive power is vested in the President of the Republic, who is elected, by direct universal adult suffrage, with a five-year mandate. The legislature, the Assemblée nationale, is similarly elected for a period of five years, its 81 members being directly elected by universal suffrage. The President of the Republic appoints a Prime Minister who is able to command a majority in the legislature, and the Prime Minister, in consultation with the President, appoints other government ministers. A Constitutional Court is designated as the highest court of jurisdiction in constitutional matters.

Constitutional amendments, approved by the Assemblée nationale in late December 2002, removed the previous restriction limiting the President to serving two terms of office; reduced the minimum age for presidential candidates from 45 to 35 years; and required presidential candidates holding dual or multiple citizenships to renounce their non-Togolese nationality or nationalities.

An amendment authorizing an interim President to serve the remainder of a deceased predecessor's term was approved by the Assemblée nationale in February 2005; later that month, however, the amendment was reversed.

The Government

HEAD OF STATE

President: FAURE GNASSINGBÉ (inaugurated 4 May 2005).

COUNCIL OF MINISTERS
(March 2008)

Prime Minister: KOMLAN MALLY.

Minister of State, Minister of Health: CHARLES KONDI AGBA.

Minister of State, Minister of Foreign Affairs and Regional Integration: LÉOPOLD MESSAN GNININVI.

Minister of State, Minister of Territorial Administration, Decentralization and Local Communities, Spokesperson for the Government: PASCAL BODJONA.

Minister of the Environment, Tourism and Forest Resources: ISSIFOU OKOULOU-KANTCHATI.

Minister of the Economy and Finance: ADJI AYASSOR.

Minister of the Civil Service, Administrative Reform and Relations with the Institutions of the Republic: KATARI FOLI-BAZI.

Minister of Trade, Industry, Crafts and Small and Medium-sized Enterprises: YANDJA YENTCHABRÉ.

Minister of Co-operation, Development and Land Settlement: GILBERT BAWARA.

Minister of Security and Civil Protection: Col ATCHA TITIKPINA.

Keeper of the Seals, Minister of Justice: KOKOU TOZOUN.

Minister of Social Affairs, the Promotion of Women, the Protection of Children and the Elderly: MÉMOUNATOU IBRAHIMA.

Minister of Primary and Secondary Education, Technical Education, Professional Training and Literacy: YVES NAGOU MADOW.

Minister of Higher Education and Research: MESSAN ADIMADO ADUAYOM.

Minister of Post, Telecommunications and Technological Innovations: KOKOUVI DOGBÉ.

TOGO

Minister of Human Rights and Democracy: Célestine Akouavi Aïdam.

Minister of Public Works, Transport, Town Planning and Housing: Célestin Talaki.

Minister of Communication, Culture and Civil Training: Cornélius Aïdam.

Minister of Mines, Energy and Water: Noupokou Dammipi.

Minister of Agriculture, Stockbreeding and Fisheries: Kossi Messan Ewovor.

Minister of Youth, Sport and Leisure: Antoine Folly.

Minister of Labour and Social Security: Octave Nicoué Broohm.

MINISTRIES

Office of the President: Palais Présidentiel, ave de la Marina, Lomé; tel. 221-27-01; fax 221-18-97; e-mail presidence@republicoftogo.com; internet www.republicoftogo.com.

Office of the Prime Minister: Palais de la Primature, BP 1161, Lomé; tel. 221-15-64; fax 221-37-53; internet www.gouvernement.tg.

Ministry of Agriculture, Stockbreeding and Fisheries: 5 ave de Duisburg, BP 385, Lomé; tel. 220-40-20; fax 220-44-99.

Ministry of the Civil Service, Administrative Reform and Relations with the Institutions of the Republic: angle ave de la Marina et rue Kpalimé, BP 372, Lomé; tel. 221-41-83; fax 222-56-85.

Ministry of Communication, Culture and Civic Training: BP 40, Lomé; tel. 221-29-30; fax 221-43-80; e-mail info@republicoftogo.com.

Ministry of Co-operation, Development and Land Settlement: Lomé.

Ministry of the Economy and Finance: CASEF, ave Sarakawa, BP 387, Lomé; tel. 221-00-37; fax 221-25-48; e-mail eco@republicoftogo.com.

Ministry of the Environment, Tourism and Forest Resources: Lomé; tel. 221-56-58; fax 221-03-33.

Ministry of Foreign Affairs and Regional Integration: place du Monument aux Morts, BP 900, Lomé; tel. 221-36-01; fax 221-39-74; e-mail diplo@republicoftogo.com.

Ministry of Health: rue Branly, BP 386, Lomé; tel. 221-35-24; fax 222-20-73.

Ministry of Higher Education and Research: rue Colonel de Roux, BP 12175, Lomé; tel. 222-09-83; fax 222-07-83.

Ministry of Human Rights and Democracy: BP 1325, Lomé; tel. 222-60-63; fax 220-07-74; e-mail mdhdcab@yahoo.fr.

Ministry of Justice: ave de la Marina, rue Colonel de Roux, Lomé; tel. 221-26-53; fax 222-29-06.

Ministry of Labour and Social Security: Lomé.

Ministry of Mines, Energy and Water: Lomé.

Ministry of Post, Telecommunication and Technological Innovations: ave de Sarakawa, BP 389, Lomé; tel. 223-14-00; fax 221-68-12; e-mail eco@republicoftogo.com.

Ministry of Primary and Secondary Education, Technical Education, Professional Training and Literacy: BP 398, Lomé; tel. 221-20-97; fax 221-89-34.

Ministry of Public Works, Transport, Town Planning and Housing: Lomé.

Ministry of Security and Civil Protection: rue Albert Sarraut, Lomé; tel. 222-57-12; fax 222-61-50; e-mail info@republicoftogo.com.

Ministry of Social Affairs, the Promotion of Women, the Protection of Children and the Elderly: Lomé.

Ministry of Territorial Administration, Decentralization and Local Communities: Lomé.

Ministry of Trade, Industry, Crafts and Small and Medium-sized Enterprises: 1 ave de Sarakawa, face au Monument aux Morts, BP 383, Lomé; tel. 221-20-25; fax 221-05-72; e-mail eco@republicoftogo.com.

Ministry of Youth, Sport and Leisure: BP 40, Lomé; tel. 221-22-47; fax 222-42-28.

President and Legislature

PRESIDENT

Presidential Election, 24 April 2005

Candidate	Votes	% of votes
Faure Gnassingbé (RPT)	1,323,622	60.16
Emmanuel Bob Akitani (UFC)	841,642	38.25
Nicolas Lawson (PRR)	22,979	1.04
Harry Octavianus Olympio (RSDD)	12,033	0.55
Total	**2,200,276**	**100.00**

LEGISLATURE

Assemblée nationale

Palais des Congrès, BP 327, Lomé; tel. 222-57-91; fax 222-11-68; e-mail assemblee.nationale@syfed.tg.refer.org.

President: El Hadj Abass Bonfoh.

General Election, 14 October 2007

Party	Votes	% of votes	Seats
Rassemblement du peuple togolais (RPT)	922,636	32.71	50
Union des forces de changement (UFC)	867,507	30.75	27
Comité d'action pour le renouveau (CAR)	192,218	6.81	4
Others	838,484	29.72	—
Total	**2,820,845**	**100.00**	**81**

Election Commission

Commission électorale nationale indépendante (CENI): rue des Echis, BP 7005, Lomé; tel. 222-29-51; fax 222-39-61; e-mail info@cenitogo.tg; internet www.cenitogo.tg; 19 mems; Pres. Tozim Potopere.

Political Organizations

In mid-2007 there were 68 registered political parties, of which the following were among the most influential:

Alliance démocratique pour la Patrie (ADP): Lomé; f. 2006; opposed to regime of Pres. Faure Gnassingbé; Leaders Agbeyome Kodjo, Maurice Dahuku Pere.

Coalition des forces démocrates (CFD): Lomé; f. Oct. 2002 by nine parties that boycotted legislative elections held in that month; opposed the administration of fmr Pres. Eyadéma; the UFC left the coalition in Feb. 2003; Chair. Edem Kodjo (acting).

Constituent parties and groupings include:

Convergence patriotique panafricaine (CPP): BP 12703, Lomé; tel. 221-58-43; f. 1999 by merger of the Parti d'action pour la démocratie (PAD), the Parti des démocrates pour l'unité (PDU), the Union pour la démocratie et la solidarité (UDS) and the Union togolaise pour la démocratie (UTD); did not participate in legislative elections in 2002; Pres. Edem Kodjo; First Vice-Pres. Jean-Lucien Savi de Tové.

Front uni de l'opposition (Le Front): Lomé; f. 2002; Coordinator Me Yawovi Agboyibo.

Alliance des démocrates pour le développement intégral (ADDI): Lomé; tel. 221-47-90; Leader Dr Nagbandja Kampatibe.

Comité d'action pour le renouveau (CAR): 58 ave du 24 janvier, BP06, Lomé; tel. 222-05-66; fax 221-62-54; e-mail yagboyibo@bibway.com; moderately conservative; Leader Me Yawovi Agboyibo; Sec.-Gen. Dodji Apevon; 251,349 mems (Dec. 1999).

Convention démocratique des peuples africains—Branche togolaise (CDPA—BT): 2 rue des Cheminots, BP 13963, Lomé; tel. 221-71-75; fax 226-46-55; e-mail cdpa-bt@cdpa-bt.org; internet www.cdpa-bt.org; f. 1991; socialist; Gen.-Sec. Léopold Gnininvi; First Sec. Prof. Emmanuel Y. Gu-Konu.

Union pour la démocratie et la solidarité—Togo (UDS—Togo): 276 blvd Circulaire, BP 8580, Lomé; tel. 222-55-64; fax 221-81-95; e-mail uds-togo@wanadoo.fr; Leader Antoine Folly.

Pacte socialiste pour le renouveau (PSR): Lomé; f. 2003 by fmr 'renovationist' mems of RPT; Leader Tchessa Abi.

TOGO — Directory

Coordination des partis politiques de l'opposition constructive (CPOC): Lomé; f. 2002; alliance of 'constructive opposition' parties that favoured working with the regime of fmr Pres. Eyadéma

In mid-2003 members included:

Juvento—Mouvement de la jeunesse togolaise: Lomé; f. 2001; nationalist youth movement; Pres. ABALO FIRMIN.

Mouvement des croyants pour l'égalité et la paix (MOCEP): Lomé; Leader COMLANGAN MAWUTOÈ D'ALMEIDA.

Union pour la démocratie et le progrès social (UDPS): Lomé; Sec.-Gen. SEKODONA SEGO.

Coordination nationale des forces nouvelles (CFN): Lomé; f. 1993; centrist; Pres. Me JOSEPH KOKOU KOFFIGOH.

Parti démocratique togolais (PDT): Lomé; Leader M'BA KABASSÉMA.

Parti du renouveau et de la rédemption (PRR): Lomé; Pres. NICOLAS LAWSON.

Parti des travailleurs (PT): 49 ave de Calais, BP 13974, Nyékonakpoé, Lomé; tel. 913-65-54; socialist; Co-ordinating Sec. CLAUDE AMEGANVI.

Rassemblement du peuple togolais (RPT): pl. de l'Indépendance, BP 1208, Lomé; tel. 226-93-83; e-mail rpttogo@yahoo.fr; f. 1969; sole legal party 1969–91; Pres. FAURE GNASSINGBÉ; Sec.-Gen. SOLITOKI ESSO.

Rassemblement pour le soutien de la démocratie et du développement (RSDD): Lomé; tel. 222-38-80; expelled from the CPOC (q.v.) in August 2003; Leader HARRY OCTAVIANUS OLYMPIO.

Union des forces de changement (UFC): 59 rue Koudadzé, Lom-Nava, BP 62168 Lomé; tel. and fax 221-33-32; e-mail contact-togo@ufctogo.com; internet www.ufctogo.com; f. 1992; social-democratic; First Vice-Pres. Emmanuel Bob Akitani contested presidential election in June 2003 under the designation Parti des forces de changement—Union des forces de changement; Pres. GILCHRIST OLYMPIO; First Vice-Pres. EMMANUEL BOB AKITANI; Sec.-Gen. JEAN-PIERRE FABRE.

Union des libéraux indépendants (ULI): f. 1993 to succeed Union des démocrates pour le renouveau; Leader KWAMI MENSAN JACQUES AMOUZOU.

Diplomatic Representation

EMBASSIES IN TOGO

China, People's Republic: 1381 rue de l'Entente, BP 2690, Lomé; tel. 222-38-56; fax 221-40-75; e-mail chinaemb_tg@mfa.gov.cn; Ambassador YANG MIN.

Congo, Democratic Republic: Lomé; tel. 221-51-55; Ambassador LOKOKA IKUKELE BOMOLO.

Egypt: 1163 rue de l'OCAM, BP 8, Lomé; tel. 221-24-43; fax 221-10-22; Ambassador ADEL MOSTAFA AHMED EL-SALASY.

France: rue de la Marina, BP 7485, Lomé; tel. 223-46-40; fax 223-46-56; e-mail Eric.BOSC@diplomatie.fr; internet www.ambafrance-tg.org; Ambassador ALAIN HOLLEVILLE.

Gabon: Lomé; tel. 222-18-93; fax 222-18-92; Ambassador (vacant).

Germany: blvd de la République, BP 1175, Lomé; tel. 221-23-70; fax 222-18-88; e-mail amballtogo@cafe.tg; Ambassador HELMUT KOLB.

Ghana: 8 rue Paulin Eklou, Tokoin-Ouest, BP 92, Lomé; tel. 221-31-94; fax 221-77-36; e-mail ghmfa01@cafe.tg; Ambassador KWABENA MENSA-BONSU.

Guinea: Lomé; tel. 221-74-98; fax 221-81-16.

Korea, Democratic People's Republic: Lomé; Ambassador KIM PYONG GI.

Libya: Cite OUA, BP 4872, Lomé; tel. 261-47-08; fax 261-47-10; Chargé d'affaires a.i. AHMED M. ABDULKAFI.

Nigeria: 311 blvd du 13 janvier, BP 1189, Lomé; tel. and fax 221-59-76; Ambassador BABA GANA ZANNA.

USA: rue Kouenou, angle rue 15 Beniglato, BP 852, Lomé; tel. 221-29-94; fax 221-79-52; e-mail RobertsonJJ2@state.gov; internet togo.usembassy.gov; Ambassador DAVID BERNARD DUNN.

Judicial System

Justice is administered by the Constitutional Court, the Supreme Court, two Appeal Courts and the Tribunaux de première instance, which hear civil, commercial and criminal cases. There is a labour tribunal and a tribunal for children's rights. In addition, there are two exceptional courts, the Cour de sûreté de l'Etat, which judges crimes against internal and external state security, and the Tribunal spécial chargé de la répression des détournements de deniers publics, which deals with cases of misuse of public funds.

Constitutional Court: 32 ave Augustino de Souza, Lomé; tel. 221-72-98; fax 221-07-40; f. 1997; seven mems; Pres. ATSU KOFFI AMEGA.

Supreme Court: BP 906, Lomé; tel. 221-22-58; f. 1961; consists of three chambers (judicial, administrative and auditing); Chair. FESSOU LAWSON; Attorney-General KOUAMI AMADOS-DJOKO.

State Attorney: ATARA NDAKENA.

Religion

It is estimated that about 50% of the population follow traditional animist beliefs, some 35% are Christians and 15% are Muslims.

CHRISTIANITY

The Roman Catholic Church

Togo comprises one archdiocese and six dioceses. At 31 December 2005 there were an estimated 1,525,419 adherents in the country, representing about 24.4% of the total population.

Bishops' Conference

Conférence Episcopale du Togo, 561 rue Aniko Palako, BP 348, Lomé; tel. 221-22-72; fax 222-48-08.

Statutes approved 1979; Pres. Most Rev. AMBROISE KOTAMBA DJOLIBA (Archbishop of Sokodé).

Archbishop of Lomé: Most Rev. PHILIPPE FANOKO KOSSI KPODZRO, Archevêché, 561 rue Aniko Palako, BP 348, Lomé; tel. 221-46-12; fax 221-02-46; e-mail archlome@lome.ocicnet.net.

Protestant Churches

There are about 250 mission stations, with a personnel of some 250, affiliated to European and US societies and administered by a Conseil Synodal, presided over by a moderator.

Directorate of Protestant Churches: 1 rue Maréchal Foch, BP 378, Lomé; Moderator Pastor AWUME (acting).

Eglise Evangélique Presbytérienne du Togo: 1 rue Tokmake, BP 2, Lomé; tel. 221-46-69; fax 222-23-63; Moderator Rev. Dr KODJO BESSA.

Fédération des Evangéliques du Togo: Lomé; Co-ordinator HAPPY AZIADEKEY.

BAHÁ'Í FAITH

Assemblée spirituelle nationale: BP 1659, Lomé; tel. 221-21-99; e-mail asnbaha@yahoo.fr; Sec. ALLADOUM NGOMNA; 19,002 adherents (2006).

The Press

DAILY

Togo-Presse: BP 891, Lomé; tel. 221-53-95; fax 222-37-66; f. 1961; official govt publ; French, Kabiye and Ewe; political, economic and cultural; circ. 8,000.

PERIODICALS

L'Aurore: Lomé; tel. 222-65-41; fax 222-65-89; e-mail aurore37@caramail.com; weekly; independent; Editor-in-Chief ANKOU SALVADOR; circ. 2,500.

Carrefour: 596 rue Ablogame, BP 6125, Lomé; tel. 944-45-43; e-mail carrefour1@caramail.com; f. 1991; pro-opposition; weekly; Dir HOLONOU HOUKPATI; circ. 3,000 (2000).

Cité Magazine: 50 ave Pas de Souza, BP 6275, Lomé; tel. and fax 222-67-40; e-mail citemag@cafe.tg; internet www.cafe.tg/citemag; monthly; Editor-in-Chief GAËTAN K. GNATCHIKO.

Le Citoyen: Lomé; tel. 221-73-44; independent.

La Colombe: Lomé; f. 2001; weekly.

Le Combat du Peuple: 62 rue Blagogee, BP 4682, Lomé; tel. 904-53-83; fax 222-65-89; e-mail combat@webmails.com; f. 1994; pro-opposition weekly; Editor LUCIEN DJOSSOU MESSAN; circ. 3,500 (2000).

Le Courrier du Golfe: rue de l'OCAM, angle rue Sotomarcy, BP 660, Lomé; tel. 221-67-92.

Crocodile: 299 rue Kuévidjin, no 27 Bé-Château, BP 60087, Lomé; tel. 221-38-21; fax 226-13-70; e-mail crocodile@caramail.com; f. 1993; pro-opposition; weekly; Dir VIGNO KOFFI HOUNKANLY; Editor FRANCIS-PEDRO AMAZUN; circ. 3,500 (2000).

Le Débat: BP 8737, Lomé; tel. 222-42-84; f. 1991; 2 a month; Dir PROSPER ETEH.

TOGO

La Dépêche: BP 20039, Lomé; tel. and fax 221-09-32; e-mail ladepeche@hotmail.com; f. 1993; 2 a week; Editor Esso-We Appolinaire Mèwènamèssè; circ. 3,000.

L'Etoile du matin: S/C Maison du journalisme, Casier no 50, Lomé; e-mail wielfridsewa18@hotmail.com; f. 2000; weekly; Dir Wielfrid Séwa Tchoukouli.

Etudes Togolaises: Institut National de la Recherche Scientifique, BP 2240, Lomé; tel. 221-57-39; f. 1965; quarterly; scientific review, mainly anthropology.

L'Eveil du Peuple: Lomé; weekly; re-established in 2002, having ceased publication in 1999.

L'Evénement: 44–50 rue Douka, Kotokoucondji, BP 1800, Lomé; tel. 222-65-89; f. 1999; independent; weekly; Dir Mensah Koudjodji; circ. 3,000 (2000).

L'Exilé: Maison du journalisme, Casier no 28, Lomé; e-mail jexil@hotmail.com; f. 2000; weekly; independent; Editor Hippolyte Agboh.

Game su/Tev Fema: 125 ave de la Nouvelle Marché, BP 1247, Lomé; tel. 221-28-44; f. 1997; monthly; Ewe and Kabiye; govt publ. for the newly literate; circ. 3,000.

Hébdo-forum: 60 rue Tamakloe, BP 3681, Lomé; weekly.

Journal Officiel de la République du Togo (JORT): BP 891, Lomé; tel. 221-37-18; fax 222-14-89; government acts, laws, decrees and decisions.

Kpakpa Désenchanté: BP 8917, Lomé; tel. 221-37-39; weekly; independent; satirical.

Kyrielle: BP 81213, Lomé; e-mail noel@journaliste.org; f. 1999; monthly; culture, sport; Dir Credo Tetteh; circ. 3,000 (2000).

Libre Togovi: BP 81190, Lomé; tel. 904-43-36; e-mail libretogovi@mail.com; 2 a week; pro-democracy, opposed to Govt of fmr Pres. Eyadéma; distributed by the Comité presse et communication de la concertation nationale de la société civile.

La Matinée: Tokoin Nkafu, rue Kpoguédé, BP 30368, Lomé; tel. 226-69-02; f. 1999; monthly; Dir Kasséré Pierre Sabi.

Le Miroir du Peuple: 48 rue Defale, BP 81231, Lomé; tel. 946-60-24; e-mail nouveau90@hotmail.com; f. 1998; fmrly Le Nouveau Combat; weekly; independent; Dir Elias Edoh Hounkanly; circ. 1,000 (2000).

Motion d'Information: Lomé; f. 1997; weekly; pro-opposition.

Nouvel Echo: BP 3681, Lomé; tel. 947-72-40; f. 1997; pro-opposition; weekly; Dir Alphonse Nevame Klu; Editor Julien Ayih.

Nouvel Eclat: Lomé; tel. 945-55-42; e-mail nouvel.eclat@caramail.com; f. 2000; weekly; Dir Charles Passou; circ. 2,500 (2000).

Nouvel Horizon: Maison du journalisme, Casier no 38, BP 81213, Lomé; tel. 222-09-55; f. 2000; weekly; Dir Donnas A. Amozougan; circ. 3,000 (2000).

La Nouvelle République: Lomé; tel. 945-55-43; e-mail nouvelle.republique@caramail.com; f. 1999; Dir Wielfrid Séwa Tchoukouli; circ. 2,500 (2000).

La Parole: Lomé; tel. 221-55-90.

Politicos: Lomé; tel. 945-32-66; fax 226-13-70; e-mail politicos@hotmail.com; f. 1993; weekly; Editor Elvis A. Kao; circ. 1,500 (2000).

Le Regard: BP 81213, Lomé; tel. 222-65-89; fax 226-13-70; e-mail leregard@webmails.com; f. 1996; weekly; pro-opposition; supports promotion of human rights; Editor Abass Mikaïla Saibou; circ. 3,000 (2000).

Le Reporter des Temps Nouveaux: Maison du journalisme, Casier no 22, BP 1800, Lomé; tel. 945-40-45; fax 226-18-22; e-mail le_reporter@hotmail.com; f. 1998; weekly; independent; political criticism and analysis; Man. Editor Romain Attiso Koudjodji; circ. 3,000 (2000).

Le Scorpion—Akéklé: S/C Maison du journalisme, BP 81213, Lomé; tel. 944-43-80; fax 226-13-70; e-mail lescorpion@webmails.com; f. 1998; opposition weekly; Dir Didier Agbleto; circ. 3,500 (2000).

Le Secteur Privé: angle ave de la Présidence, BP 360, Lomé; tel. 221-70-65; fax 221-47-30; monthly; publ. by Chambre de Commerce et d'Industrie du Togo.

Le Soleil: Lomé; tel. 944-41-97; e-mail joel12@dromadaire.com; f. 1999; weekly; Dir Aristo Gaba; circ. 2,000 (2000).

Témoin de la Nation: Maison du journalisme, Casier no 48, BP 434, Lomé; tel. 221-24-92; f. 2000; weekly; Dir Elias Eboh.

Tingo Tingo: 44–50 rue Douka, Kotokoucondji, BP 80419, Lomé; tel. 222-17-53; e-mail jtingo-tingo@yahoo.fr; f. 1996; weekly; independent; Editor Augustin Asionbo; circ. 3,500 (2000).

Togo-Images: BP 4869, Lomé; tel. 221-56-80; f. 1962; monthly series of wall posters depicting recent political, economic and cultural events in Togo; publ. by govt information service; Dir Akobi Bedou; circ. 5,000.

Togo-Presse: BP 891, Lomé; tel. 221-53-95; fax 22-37-66; f. 1962; publ. by Govt in French, Ewe and Kabre; political, economic and cultural affairs; Dir Wiyao Dadja Pouwi; circ. 5,000 (2000).

La Tribune du Peuple: BP 1756, Lomé; tel. 222-65-89; e-mail novapress.tg@assala.com; weekly; pro-opposition; Dir Kodjo Afatsao Siliadin.

PRESS ASSOCIATION

Union des Journalistes Indépendants du Togo: BP 81213, Lomé; tel. 226-13-00; fax 221-38-21; e-mail maison-du-journalisme@ids.tg; also operates Maison de Presse; Sec.-Gen. Gabriel Ayité Baglo.

NEWS AGENCY

Agence Togolaise de Presse (ATOP): 35 rue des Medias, BP 891, Lomé; tel. 221-53-95; fax 222-37-66; f. 1975; Dir-Gen. Seedem Abassa.

Publishers

Centre Togolais de Communication Evangélique—Editions Haho (CTCE—Editions Haho): 1 rue de Commerce, BP 378, Lomé; tel. 221-45-82; fax 221-29-67; e-mail ctcte@cafe.tg; f. 1983; general literature, popular science, poetry, school textbooks, Christian interest; Dir Kodjo Mawuli Etsé.

Editions Akpagnon: BP 3531, Lomé; tel. and fax 222-02-44; e-mail yedogbe@yahoo.fr; f. 1978; general literature and non-fiction; Man. Dir Yves-Emmanuel Dogbé.

Editions de la Rose Bleue: BP 12452, Lomé; tel. 222-93-39; fax 222-96-69; e-mail dorkenoo_ephrem@yahoo.fr; general literature, poetry; Dir Ephrem Seth Dorkenoo.

Les Nouvelles Editions Africaines du Togo (NEA-TOGO): 239 blvd du 13 janvier, BP 4862, Lomé; tel. and fax 222-10-19; e-mail neatogo@yahoo.fr; general fiction, non-fiction and textbooks; Dir-Gen. Kokou A. Kalipe; Editorial Dir Tchotcho Christiane Ekue.

Les Presses de l'Université du Lomé: BP 1515, Lomé; tel. 225-48-44; fax 225-87-84.

Société Nationale des Editions du Togo (EDITOGO): BP 891, Lomé; tel. 221-61-06; f. 1961; govt-owned; general and educational; Pres. Biossey Kokou Tozoun; Man. Dir Wiyao Dadja Pouwi.

Broadcasting and Communications

TELECOMMUNICATIONS

Télécel Togo: Cité Maman N'Danida, route de Kpalimé, BP 14511, Lomé; tel. 225-82-50; fax 225-82-51; e-mail telecel@telecel.tg; internet www.telecel.tg; operates mobile cellular telecommunications network in Lomé and six other towns.

Togo Télécom: ave N. Grunitzky, BP 333, Lomé; tel. 221-44-01; fax 221-03-73; e-mail togotelecom@togotel.net.tg; internet www.togotel.net.tg; Dir-Gen. Kossivi Paul Ayikoe.

Togo Cellulaire—Togocel: Lomé; tel. 004-05-06; e-mail togocel@togocel.tg; internet www.togocel.tg; f. 2001; provides mobile cellular communications services to more than 70% of the territory of Togo.

BROADCASTING

Radio

Legislation providing for the liberalization of radio broadcasting was ratified in November 1990. However, no definitive licences for radio stations had been issued by mid-2002, when 11 private stations were, nevertheless, in operation.

Radiodiffusion du Togo (Internationale)—Radio Lomé: BP 434, Lomé; tel. 221-24-93; fax 221-24-92; e-mail radiolome@yahoo.fr; f. 1953; state-controlled; radio programmes in French, English and vernacular languages; Dir Amévi Dabla.

Radiodiffusion du Togo (Nationale): BP 21, Kara; tel. 660-60-60; f. 1974 as Radiodiffusion Kara (Togo); state-controlled; radio programmes in French and vernacular languages; Dir M'Ba Kpenougou.

Radio Avenir: BP 20183, 76 blvd de la Kara, Doumassessé, Lomé; tel. 221-20-88; fax 221-03-01; f. 1998; broadcasts in French, English, Ewe and Kotokoli; Dir Kpéle-Koffi Ahoomey-Zunu.

Radio Carré Jeunes: BP 2550, Adidogomé, Lomé; tel. 225-77-44; e-mail carrejeunes@yahoo.fr; f. 1999; community radio stn; popular education, cultural information; broadcasts in French, Ewe, Kabyè and other local languages; Dir Foly Alodé Glidjito Amagli.

Radio de l'Evangile-Jésus Vous Aime (JVA): Klikamé, Bretelle Atikoumé, BP 2313, Lomé; tel. 225-44-95; fax 225-92-81; e-mail radio.jva@fatad.org; f. 1995; owned by the West Africa Advanced School of Theology (Assemblies of God); Christian; education and development; broadcasts on FM frequencies in Lomé and Agou in French, English and 12 local languages; Dir Pastor Douti Lallebili Flindja.

Radio Galaxy: BP 20822, 253 rue 48, Doumassessé, Lomé; tel. and fax 221-63-18; e-mail radiogalaxy@yahoo.fr; f. 1996; broadcasts in French, English, Ewe and Kabyè; Dir Paul S. Tchassoua.

Radio Kanal FM: Immeuble Decor, blvd du 13 janvier, BP 61554, Lomé; tel. 221-33-74; fax 220-19-68; e-mail kanalfm@cafe.tg; f. 1997; broadcasts in French and Mina; independent; Dir Modeste Messavussua-Kue.

Radio Maria Togo: BP 30162, 155 de la rue 158, Hédzranawoé, Lomé; tel. 226-11-31; fax 226-35-00; e-mail info.tog@radiomaria.org; internet www.radiomaria.tg; f. 1997; Roman Catholic; broadcasts in French, English and six local languages; Dir Yigbe Faustin.

Radio Metropolys: 157 rue Missahoé, Tokoin Hôpital, derrière Pharmacie Ave Marie, Lomé; tel. 222-86-81; e-mail metropolys.lome@voila.fr; f. 2000; secular and apolitical broadcasts in French only; Dir Noëlie Assogbavi.

Radio Nana FM: BP 6035, Immeuble du Grand Marché du Lomé, Lomé; tel. 220-12-02; e-mail nanafm@woezon.com; f. 1999; broadcasts in French and Mina; community stn; political, economic and cultural information; Dir Peter Dogbé.

Radio Nostalgie: 14 ave de la Victoire, Quartier Tokoin-Hôpital, BP 13836, Lomé; tel. 222-25-41; fax 221-07-82; e-mail nostalgietogo@yahoo.fr; internet www.nostalgie.tg; f. 1995; broadcasts in French, Ewe and Mina; Pres. and Dir-Gen. Flavien Johnson.

Radio Tropik FM: BP 2276, Quartier Wuiti, Lomé; tel. 226-11-11; e-mail tropikfm@nomade.fr; f. 1995; broadcasts in French, Kabyè and Tem; Dir Blaise Yao Amedodji.

Radio Zion: BP 13853, Kpalimé, Lomé; tel. 441-09-15; f. 1999; religious; broadcasts in French, Ewe and Kabyè; Dir Emmanuel Kounougna.

Television

Télévision Togolaise: BP 3286, Lomé; tel. 221-53-57; fax 221-57-86; e-mail televisiontogolaise@yahoo.fr; internet www.tvt.tg; f. 1973; state-controlled; three stations; programmes in French and vernacular languages; Dir Kuessan Yovodevi.

Broadcasting Association

Organisation Togolaise des Radios et Télévisions Indépendantes (ORTI): Lomé; tel. 221-33-74; e-mail kawokou@syfed.tg.refer.org; Pres. Raymond Awokou Koukou.

Finance

(cap. = capital; res = reserves; dep. = deposits; m. = million; br(s). = branch(es); amounts in francs CFA, unless otherwise indicated)

BANKING

Central Bank

Banque centrale des états de l'Afrique de l'ouest (BCEAO): rue Branly, BP 120, Lomé; tel. 221-25-12; fax 221-76-02; e-mail ocourrier@lome.bceao.int; internet www.bceao.int; HQ in Dakar, Senegal; f. 1962; bank of issue for the mem. states of the Union économique et monétaire ouest-africaine (UEMOA, comprising Benin, Burkina Faso, Côte d'Ivoire, Guinea-Bissau, Mali, Niger, Senegal and Togo); cap. and res 859,313m., total assets 5,671,675m. (Dec. 2002); Gov. Damo Justin Baro (acting); Dir in Togo Ayéwanou Agetoho Gbeasor; br. at Kara.

Commercial Banks

Banque Internationale pour l'Afrique au Togo (BIA—Togo): 13 rue de Commerce, BP 346, Lomé; tel. 221-32-86; fax 221-10-19; e-mail bia-togo@cafe.tg; f. 1965; fmrly Meridien BIAO—Togo; 57.5% owned by Banque Belgolaise (Belgium); cap. and res 567m., total assets 51,793m. (Dec. 2003); Pres. Komla Alipui; Dir-Gen. Jean-Paul Le Calm; 7 brs.

Banque Togolaise pour le Commerce et l'Industrie (BTCI): 169 blvd du 13 janvier, BP 363, Lomé; tel. 223-55-00; fax 221-32-65; e-mail btci@btci.tg; f. 1974; 48.5% owned by Groupe BNP Paribas (France) 24.8% owned by Société Financière pour les Pays d'Outre-mer; cap. 1,700m. (Dec. 2006); Pres. Barry Moussa Barqué; Dir-Gen. Yao Patrice Kanekatoua; 9 brs.

Ecobank Togo (Ecobank-T): 20 ave Sylvanus Olympio, BP 3302, Lomé; tel. 221-72-14; fax 221-42-37; internet www.ecobank.com; f. 1988; 80.7% owned by Ecobank Transnational Inc (operating under the auspices of the Economic Community of West African States), 14.0% by Togolese private investors; cap. and res 6,031.7m., total assets 80,556.0m. (Dec. 2004); Dir-Gen. Roger Daha Chinamon; 2 brs.

Ecobank Transnational Inc: 2 ave Sylvanus Olympio, BP 3261, Lomé; tel. 221-03-03; fax 221-51-19; e-mail info@ecobank.com; internet www.ecobank.com; f. 1985; holding co for banking cos in Benin, Burkina Faso, Cameroon, Côte d'Ivoire, Ghana, Guinea, Liberia, Mali, Niger, Nigeria, Senegal and Togo, Ecobank Development Corpn and EIC Bourse; cap. and res US \$105.5m., total assets \$1,523.1m. (Dec. 2003); Pres. and Dir-Gen. Philip C. Asiodu.

Financial Bank Togo: 11 ave du 24 janvier, Lomé; tel. 271-32-71; fax 271-48-51; e-mail jean-yves.le-paulmier@financial-bank.com; f. 2004; cap. 1,500m. (2004); Pres. Mensavi Lulu Mensah.

Société Interafricaine de Banque (SIAB): 14 rue de Commerce, BP 4874, Lomé; tel. 221-28-30; fax 221-58-29; e-mail info@siab-togo.com; internet www.siab-togo.com; f. 1975; fmrly Banque Arabe Libyenne-Togolaise du Commerce Extérieur; 86% owned by Libyan Arab Foreign Bank, 14% state-owned; cap. and res 181m., total assets 6,999m. (Dec. 2003); Pres. Ayawovi Demba Tignokpa; CEO Khalifa Achour Ettalua.

Union Togolaise de Banque (UTB): blvd du 13 janvier, Nyékonakpoé, BP 359, Lomé; tel. 221-64-11; fax 221-22-06; e-mail utbsg@cafe.tg; f. 1964; 100% state-owned; transfer to majority private ownership proposed; cap. and res −12.3m., total assets 49.0m. (Dec. 2003); Pres. Essowédéou Agba; Dir-Gen. Yaovi Attigbé Itou; 11 brs.

Development Banks

Banque Ouest-Africaine de Développement (BOAD): 68 ave de la Libération, BP 1172, Lomé; tel. 221-42-44; fax 221-72-69; e-mail boadsiege@boad.org; internet www.boad.org; f. 1973; promotes West African economic development and integration; cap. 682,100m., total assets 849,993m. (Dec. 2004); Interim Pres. Issa Coulibaly.

Banque Togolaise de Développement (BTD): ave des Nîmes, angle ave N. Grunitzky, BP 65, Lomé; tel. 221-36-41; fax 221-44-56; e-mail togo_devbank@bibway.com; f. 1966; 43% state-owned, 20% owned by BCEAO, 13% by BOAD; transfer to majority private ownership pending; cap. and res 10,111m., total assets 33,418m. (Dec. 2003); Pres. Esso Kandja; Dir-Gen. Zakari Darou-Salim; 8 brs.

Société Nationale d'Investissement et Fonds Annexes (SNI & FA): 11 ave du 24 janvier, BP 2682, Lomé; tel. 221-62-21; fax 221-62-25; e-mail sni@ids.tg; f. 1971; 23% state-owned; cap. 2,600m., total assets 13,219m. (Dec. 2001); Pres. Palouki Massina; Dir-Gen. Richard K. Attipoe.

Savings Bank

Caisse d'Epargne du Togo (CET): 23 ave de Kléber Dadjo, Lomé; tel. 221-20-60; fax 221-85-83; e-mail cet@ids.tg; internet www.cet.tg; state-owned; privatization proposed; cap. and res 544m., total assets 27,988m. (Dec. 2006); Pres. Djossou Semondji.

Credit Institution

Société Togolaise de Crédit Automobile (STOCA): 3 rue du Mono, BP 899, Lomé; tel. 221-37-59; fax 221-08-28; e-mail stoca@ids.tg; f. 1962; 93.3% owned by SAFCA; cap. and res −112m., total assets 1,677m. (Dec. 2003); Pres. Diack Diawar; Dir-Gen. Délali Agbale.

Bankers' Association

Association Professionnelle des Banques et Etablissements Financiers du Togo: Lomé; tel. 221-24-84; fax 221-85-83.

STOCK EXCHANGE

Bourse Régionale des Valeurs Mobilières (BRVM): BP 3263, Lomé; tel. 221-23-05; fax 221-23-41; e-mail brvm@brvm.org; internet www.brvm.org; f. 1998; national branch of BRVM (regional stock exchange based in Abidjan, Côte d'Ivoire, serving the member states of UEMOA); Man. in Togo Nathalie Bitho Atcholi.

INSURANCE

Colina Togo: 10 rue du Commerce, BP 1349, Lomé; tel. 222-93-65; fax 221-73-58; e-mail togo@groupecolina.com; internet www.colina-sa.com; affiliated to Colina SA (Côte d'Ivoire); Dir-Gen. Marcus Laban.

Compagnie Commune de Réassurance des Etats Membres de la CICA (CICA—RE): 43, ave du 24 janvier, BP 12410, Lomé; tel. 221-62-69; fax 221-49-64; e-mail cica-re@cica-re.com; internet www.cica-re.com; f. 1981; reinsurance co operating in 12 west and central African states; Chair. Léon-Paul N'Goulakia; Gen. Man. Digbeu Kipre.

Groupement Togolais d'Assurances (GTA): route d'Atakpamé, BP 3298, Lomé; tel. 225-60-75; fax 225-26-78; e-mail gta@laposte.tg; f. 1974; 62.9% state-owned; all classes of insurance and reinsurance;

Pres. Minister of the Economy, Finance and Privatization; Man. Dir Kossi Nambea.

Sicar Gras Savoye Togo: 140 blvd du 13 janvier, BP 2932, Lomé; tel. 221-35-38; fax 221-82-11; e-mail sicargs@sicargs.tg; internet www.grassavoye.com; affiliated to Gras Savoye (France); Dir Guy Bihannic.

UAT: Immeuble BICI, 169 blvd du 13 janvier, BP 495, Lomé; tel. 221-10-34; fax 221-87-24.

Trade and Industry

ECONOMIC AND SOCIAL COUNCIL

Conseil Economique et Social: Lomé; tel. 221-53-01; f. 1967; advisory body of 25 mems, comprising five trade unionists, five reps of industry and commerce, five reps of agriculture, five economists and sociologists, and five technologists; Pres. Koffi Gbodzidi Djondo.

GOVERNMENT AGENCIES

Direction Générale des Mines et de la Géologie: BP 356, Lomé; tel. 221-30-01; fax 221-31-93; organization and administration of mining in Togo; Dir-Gen. Ankoume P. Aregba.

EPZ Promotion Board: BP 3250, Lomé; tel. 221-13-74; fax 221-52-31; promotes the Export Processing Zone at Lomé internationally.

Société d'Administration des Zones Franches (SAZOF): BP 2748, Lomé; tel. 221-07-44; fax 221-43-05; administers and promotes free zones; Dir Gen. Yazaz Egbaré.

Société Nationale de Commerce (SONACOM): 29 blvd Circulaire, BP 3009, Lomé; tel. 221-31-18; f. 1972; cap. 2,000m. francs CFA; importer of staple foods; Dir-Gen. Jean Ladoux.

DEVELOPMENT ORGANIZATIONS

Agricultural development is under the supervision of five regional development authorities, the Sociétés régionales d'aménagement et de développement.

Agence Française de Développement (AFD): 437 ave de Sarakawa, BP 33, Lomé; tel. 221-04-98; fax 221-79-32; e-mail afdlome@groupe-afd.org; internet www.afd.fr; Country Dir Geneviève Javaloyes.

Association Française des Volontaires du Progrès (AFVP): BP 1511, Lomé; tel. 221-09-45; fax 221-85-04; e-mail afvp@togo-imet.com; internet www.afvp.org; f. 1965; Nat. Del. Marc Lescaudron.

Association Villages Entreprises: BP 23, Kpalimé; tel. and fax 441-00-62; e-mail averafp@hotmail.com; Dir Komi Afelete Julien Nyuiadzi.

Office de Développement et d'Exploitation des Forêts (ODEF): 59 QAD rue de la Kozah, BP 334, Lomé; tel. 221-79-86; fax 221-34-91; f. 1971; develops and manages forest resources; Man. Dir Badékéné K. Kommongou.

Recherche, Appui et Formation aux Initiatives d'Autodéveloppement (RAFIA): BP 43, Dapaong; tel. 770-80-89; fax 770-82-37; f. 1992; Dir Noigue Tambila Lenne.

Service de Coopération et d'Action Culturelle: BP 91, Lomé; tel. 221-21-26; fax 221-21-28; e-mail scac-lome@tg.refer.org; administers bilateral aid from the French Ministry of Foreign Affairs; Dir Henri-Luc Thibault.

Société d'Appui a la Filière Café-Cacao-Coton (SAFICC): Lomé; f. 1992; development of coffee, cocoa and cotton production.

CHAMBER OF COMMERCE

Chambre de Commerce et d'Industrie du Togo (CCIT): ave de la Présidence, angle ave Georges Pompidou, BP 360, Lomé; tel. 221-70-65; fax 221-47-30; e-mail ccit@ccit.tg; internet www.ccit.tg; f. 1921; Pres. Alexis Lamseh Looky; Sec.-Gen. Djahlin Broohm (acting); br. at Kara.

EMPLOYERS' ORGANIZATIONS

Conseil National du Patronat: 55 ave N. Grunitzky, BP 12429, Lomé; tel. and fax 221-08-30; f. 1989; Pres. A. J. Koudoyor.

Groupement Interprofessionnel des Entreprises du Togo (GITO): BP 345, Lomé; Pres. Clarence Olympio.

Syndicat des Commerçants Importateurs et Exportateurs du Togo (SCIMPEXTO): BP 1166, Lomé; tel. 222-59-86; Pres. C. Sitterlin.

Syndicat des Entrepreneurs de Travaux Publics, Bâtiments et Mines du Togo: BP 12429, Lomé; tel. 221-19-06; fax 221-08-30; Pres. Josèphe Naku.

UTILITIES

Electricity

Communauté Electrique du Bénin: ave de la Kozah, BP 1368, Lomé; tel. 221-61-32; fax 221-37-64; e-mail dg@cebnet.org; f. 1968 as a jt venture between Togo and Benin to exploit the energy resources in the two countries; Chairs Koffi Djeri, Z. Marius Hounkpatin; Man. Cyr M'po Kouagou.

Togo Electricité: 426 ave du Golfe, BP 42, Lomé; tel. 221-27-43; fax 221-64-98; e-mail m.ducommun@ids.tg; internet www.togoelectricite.com; f. 2000; to replace Compagnie Energie Electrique du Togo; production, transportation and distribution of electricity; Man. Dir Marc Ducommun-Ricoux.

Gas

Société Togolaise de Gaz SA (Togogaz): BP 1082, Lomé; tel. 221-44-31; fax 221-55-30; 71% privatization pending; Dir-Gen. Joël Pompa.

Water

Société Togolaise des Eaux (STE): 53 ave de la Libération, BP 1301, Lomé; tel. 221-34-81; fax 221-46-13; f. 2003 to replace Régie Nationale des Eaux du Togo; production and distribution of drinking water.

TRADE UNIONS

Collectif des Syndicats Indépendants (CSI): Lomé; f. 1992 as co-ordinating org. for three trade union confederations.

Confédération Nationale des Travailleurs du Togo (CNTT): Bourse du Travail, BP 163, 160 blvd du 13 janvier, Lomé; tel. 222-02-55; fax 221-48-33; f. 1973; Sec.-Gen. Douevi Tchiviakou.

Confédération Syndicale des Travailleurs du Togo (CSTT): 14 rue Van Lare, BP 3058, Lomé; tel. 222-11-17; fax 222-44-41; e-mail cstt-tg@cstt-togo.org; f. 1949, dissolved 1972, re-established 1991; comprises 36 unions and 7 professional federations (Agro-Alimentation, Education, General Employees, Industry, Public Services, Transport, Woodwork and Construction); Sec.-Gen. Beliki Adrien Akouete; 50,000 mems.

Union Nationale des Syndicats Indépendants du Togo (UNSIT): Tokoin-Wuiti, BP 30082, Lomé; tel. 221-32-88; fax 221-95-66; e-mail unsit@netcom.tg; f. 1991; Sec.-Gen. Norbert Gbikpi-Benissan; 17 affiliated unions.

Transport

RAILWAYS

Société Nationale des Chemins de Fer du Togo (SNCT): BP 340, Lomé; tel. 221-43-01; fax 221-22-19; e-mail togorail@yahoo.com; f. 1900; owned by West African Cement (Wacem) since Jan. 2003; total length 519 km, incl. lines running inland from Lomé to Atakpamé and Blitta (276 km), Lomé to Tabligbo (77 km); a coastal line, running through Lomé and Aného, was closed to passenger traffic in 1987 (a service from Lomé to Kpalimé—119 km—has also been suspended); passengers carried (1999): 4,400 (compared with 628,200 in 1990); freight handled (2007): 631,798 metric tons; Gen. Man. M. M. Reddy.

ROADS

In 1996 there were an estimated 7,520 km of roads, of which 2,376 km were paved. The rehabilitation of the 675-km axis road that links the port of Lomé with Burkina Faso, and thus provides an important transport corridor for land-locked West African countries, was considered essential to Togo's economic competitiveness; in 1997 the World Bank provided a credit of US $50m. for the rehabilitation of a severely deteriorated 105-km section of the road between Atakpamé and Blitta. In 1998 Kuwait awarded Togo a loan of 6,000m. francs CFA francs to improve the Notse-Atakpamé highway. Other principal roads run from Lomé to the borders of Ghana, Nigeria and Benin.

Africa Route International (ARI—La Gazelle): Lomé; tel. 225-27-32; f. 1991 to succeed Société Nationale de Transports Routiers; Pres. and Man. Dir Bawa S. Mankoubi.

SHIPPING

The major port, at Lomé, generally handles a substantial volume of transit trade for the land-locked countries of Mali, Niger and Burkina Faso, although political unrest in Togo, in the early 1990s, resulted in the diversion of much of this trade to neighbouring Benin. In 1995 the Banque ouest-africaine de développement approved a loan of 5,000m. francs CFA to help finance the rehabilitation of the infrastructure at Lomé port. The project aimed to re-establish Lomé as one of the principal transit ports on the west coast of Africa, and further upgrading of the port's facilities, including the computerization of port operations and the construction of a new container terminal, was implemented in the late 1990s, with private-sector funding. By 1999 freight traffic had recovered to 2.8m. metric tons, compared with only 1.1m. tons in 1993. There is another port at Kpémé for the export of phosphates.

Port Autonome de Lomé: BP 1225, Lomé; tel. 227-47-42; fax 227-08-18; e-mail togoport@togoport.tg; internet www.togoport.tg; f. 1968; transferred to private management in Jan. 2002; Pres. ASSIBA AMOUSSOU-GUENOU; Man. Dir Adm. ADEGNON KODJO FOGAN; 1,600 employees (2003).

Conseil National des Chargeurs Togolais (CNCT): BP 2991, Lomé; tel. 223-71-00; fax 227-08-37; e-mail cnct@cnct.tg; internet www.cnct.tg; f. 1980; restructured 2001; Dir-Gen. MAGUÉNANI KOMOU.

Ecomarine International (Togo): Immeuble Ecomarine, Zone Portuaire, BP 6014, Lomé; tel. 227-48-04; fax 227-48-06; e-mail ecomarine@ecomarineint.com; f. 2001 to develop container-handling facility at Lomé Port; operates maritime transport between Togo, Senegal and Angola; Chair. Alhaji BAMANGA TUKUR.

Société Ouest-Africaine d'Entreprises Maritimes Togo (SOAEM—Togo): Zone Industrielle Portuaire, BP 3285, Lomé; tel. 221-07-20; fax 221-34-17; f. 1959; forwarding agents, warehousing, sea and road freight transport; Pres. JEAN FABRY; Man. Dir JOHN M. AQUEREBURU.

Société Togolaise de Navigation Maritime (SOTONAM): pl. des Quatre Etoiles, rond-point du Port, BP 4086, Lomé; tel. 221-51-73; fax 227-69-38; state-owned; privatization pending; Man. PAKOUM KPEMA.

SOCOPAO—Togo: 18 rue du Commerce, BP 821, Lomé; tel. 221-55-88; fax 221-73-17; f. 1959; freight transport, shipping agents; Pres. GUY MIRABAUD; Man. Dir HENRI CHAULIER.

SORINCO—Marine: 110 rue de l'OCAM, BP 2806, Lomé; tel. 221-56-94; freight transport, forwarding agents, warehousing, etc.; Man. AHMED EDGAR COLLINGWOOD WILLIAMS.

Togolaise d'Armements et d'Agence de Lignes SA (TAAL): 21 blvd du Mono, BP 9089, Lomé; tel. 222-02-43; fax 221-06-09; f. 1992; shipping agents, haulage management, crewing agency, forwarding agents; Pres. and Man. Dir LAURENT GBATI TAKASSI-KIKPA.

CIVIL AVIATION

There are international airports at Tokoin, near Lomé (Gnassingbé Eyadéma International Airport), and at Niamtougou. In addition, there are smaller airfields at Sokodé, Sansanné-Mango, Dapaong and Atakpamé.

Air Togo—Compagnie Aérienne Togolaise: Aéroport International de Lomé-Tokoin, BP 20393, Lomé; tel. 226-22-11; fax 226-22-30; e-mail airtogo@airtogo.net; internet www.airtogo.net; f. 1963; cap. 5m. francs CFA; scheduled internal services; Man. Dir AMADOU ISAAC ADE.

Peace Air Togo (PAT): Lomé; tel. and fax 222-71-40; internal services and services to Burkina Faso, Côte d'Ivoire and Ghana; Man. Dir PELSSEY NORMAN.

Société aéroportuaire de Lomé-Tokoin (SALT): Aéroport International de Lomé-Tokoin, BP 10112, Lomé; tel. 223-60-60; fax 226-88-95; e-mail salt@cafe.tg; Dir-Gen. Dr AKRIMA KOGOE.

Transtel Togo: Lomé; f. 2001; flights between Togo and France and Belgium; Gen. Man. M. MOROU.

Tourism

Togo's tourist industry declined precipitously in the wake of the political instability of the early 1990s; occupancy rates in the capital's hotels dropped from 33% in 1990 to 10% in 1993. The tourist industry did, however, recover in the late 1990s. Some 80,763 foreign tourist arrivals were reported in 2005. In 2004 receipts from tourism totalled US $25m.

Office National Togolais du Tourisme (ONTT): BP 1289, Lomé; tel. 221-43-13; fax 221-89-27; internet www.togo.tourisme.com; f. 1963; Dir FOLEY DAHLEN (acting).

TONGA

Introductory Survey

Location, Climate, Language, Religion, Flag, Capital

The Kingdom of Tonga comprises 170 islands in the south-western Pacific Ocean, about 650 km (400 miles) east of Fiji. The Tonga (or Friendly) Islands are divided into three main groups: Vava'u, Ha'apai and Tongatapu. Only 36 of the islands are permanently inhabited. The climate is mild (16°–21°C or 61°–71°F) for most of the year, though usually hotter (27°C or 81°F) in December and January. The languages are Tongan, which is a Polynesian language, and English. Tongans are predominantly Christians of the Wesleyan faith, although there are some Roman Catholics and Anglicans. The national flag (proportions 1 by 2) is red, with a rectangular white canton, containing a red cross, in the upper hoist. The capital is Nuku'alofa, on Tongatapu Island.

Recent History

The basis of the constitutional monarchy was established in the 19th century. The kingdom was neutral until 1900, when it became a British Protected State. The treaty establishing the Protectorate was revised in 1958 and 1967, giving Tonga increasing control over its affairs. Prince Tupouto'a Tungi, who had been Prime Minister since 1949, succeeded to the throne as King Taufa'ahau Tupou IV in December 1965 and appointed his brother, Prince Fatafehi Tu'ipelehake, as Prime Minister. Tonga achieved full independence, within the Commonwealth, on 4 June 1970.

Elections to the Legislative Assembly held in May 1981 resulted unexpectedly in the new Assembly becoming dominated by traditionalist conservatives. In March 1982 the Minister of Finance, Mahe Tupouniua, resigned at the King's request after refusing to grant him extrabudgetary travel funds. Further elections to the Legislative Assembly took place in May 1984. In September 1985 the King declared his support for the French Government's programme of testing nuclear weapons in the South Pacific, on the grounds that it was in the broader interests of the Western alliance. However, he upheld his former statement of opposition to the tests in French Polynesia.

Elections were held in February 1987 to the nine commoner seats in the Legislative Assembly; among the six newcomers to the legislature were reported to be some of the Government's harshest critics. In July 1988 the Supreme Court awarded 26,500 pa'anga in damages to 'Akilisi Pohiva, the editor of a local independent journal and an elected member of the Legislative Assembly, after the Government had been found guilty of unfairly dismissing him from his post in the Ministry of Education in 1985, because he had reported on controversial issues. The court ruling intensified opposition demands for the abolition of perceived feudal aspects within Tongan society.

In September 1989 the commoner members of the Legislative Assembly boycotted the Assembly, leaving it without a quorum, in protest at the absence of the Minister of Finance, whom they had wanted to question about the proceeds of the Government's sale of Tongan passports to foreign nationals, a process that had begun in 1983 as a means of acquiring revenue. Upon resuming their seats in the Assembly later in the month, the commoners introduced a motion demanding the reform of the Assembly to make it more accountable to the people. The motion proposed the creation of a more balanced legislature by increasing elected representation from nine to 15 seats and reducing noble representation to three seats (the Cabinet's 12 members also sit in the Assembly). In March 1990 a group of Tongan conservatives submitted an electoral petition, alleging bribery and corruption by Pohiva, the leader of the pro-reform commoners, and his colleagues, who had been re-elected by substantial majorities in the February general election. (In July 1988 the King had indicated his opposition to majority rule, claiming that the monarchical Government reacted more quickly to the needs of the people than the Government of a parliamentary democracy.)

In October 1990 Pohiva initiated a court case against the Government, claiming that its controversial sale of passports to foreign citizens was unconstitutional and illegal. The passports were sold mainly in Hong Kong, for as much as US $30,000 each, allowing the purchasers, in theory, to avoid travel restrictions imposed on Chinese passport-holders. However, in February 1991 a constitutional amendment to legalize the naturalization of the new passport-holders was adopted at an emergency session of the Legislative Assembly, and the case was therefore dismissed. In March a large demonstration was held in protest at the Government's actions, and a petition urging the King to invalidate the 426 passports in question and to dismiss the Minister of Police (who was responsible for their sale), was presented by prominent commoners and church leaders. In the following month the Government admitted that the former President of the Philippines, Ferdinand Marcos, and his family had been given Tongan passports as gifts, after his removal from power in 1986. The events that ensued from the sale of passports were widely viewed as indicative of the growing support for reform and for greater accountability in the government of the country. By 1996 most of the 6,600 passports sold under the scheme had expired.

In August 1991 the Prime Minister, Prince Fatafehi Tu'ipelehake, retired from office, owing to ill health (the Prince died in April 1999), and was succeeded by the King's cousin, Baron Vaea of Houma, who had previously held the position of Minister of Labour, Commerce and Industries.

Plans by campaigners for democratic reform to establish a formal political organization were realized in November 1992, when the Pro-Democracy Movement was founded. The group, led by Fr Seluini 'Akau'ola (a Roman Catholic priest), organized a constitutional convention in the same month, at which options for the introduction of democratic reform were discussed. However, the Government refused to recognize or to participate in the convention, prohibiting any publicity of the event and denying visas to invited speakers from abroad. Nevertheless, the pro-democracy reformists appeared to be attracting increased public support, and, at elections in February 1993, won six of the nine elective seats in the Legislative Assembly. Pohiva's position was undermined when, in December 1993 and February 1994, he lost two defamation cases in the Supreme Court, following the publication of allegations of fraudulent practice in his journal, *Kele'a*. In August 1994 Tonga's first political party was formed when the Pro-Democracy Movement (which had been recognized in 1992, the group having been formed in the early 1970s as the Human Rights and Democracy Movement in Tonga) launched its People's Party, under the chairmanship of a local businessman, Huliki Watab.

In May 1995 the Minister of Finance, Cecil Cocker, resigned from the Cabinet following allegations that he had sexually harassed three women while attending a regional conference in Auckland. Cocker received an official reprimand for his conduct from New Zealand's acting Prime Minister, Don McKinnon.

Elections took place on 24 January 1996, at which pro-democracy candidates retained six seats in the Legislative Assembly. In March three journalists, including the editor of *The Times of Tonga*, were arrested and imprisoned in connection with an article in the newspaper that criticized the newly appointed Minister of Police, Fire Services and Prisons, Clive Edwards, for unfavourable remarks that he had made regarding the People's Party. All three were subsequently released, but were found guilty in April under a law against angering a civil servant.

In July 1996 the Legislative Assembly voted to resume the sale of Tongan passports to Hong Kong Chinese, despite the controversy caused by the similar scheme operated in the early 1990s (see above). As many as 7,000 citizenships were to be made available for between 10,000 and 20,000 pa'anga, granting purchasers all the rights of Tongan nationality, except ownership of land.

In September 1996 a motion to impeach the Minister of Justice and Attorney-General, Tevita Topou, was proposed in the Legislative Assembly. The motion alleged that Topou had continued to receive his daily parliamentary allowance during an unauthorized absence from the Assembly. Moreover, the publication of details of the impeachment motion, which had been reported to *The Times of Tonga* by Pohiva, before it had been submitted to the Legislative Assembly, resulted in the imprisonment of Pohiva and of the newspaper's editor, Kalafi Moala, and also the deputy editor, Filakalafi Akau'ola, for contempt of parliament. The three were subsequently released, although in October Moala was found guilty on a further charge of contempt. In the same month the King closed the Assembly (which had been expected to sit until mid-November) until further notice. He denied that he had taken this decision in order to prevent further impeachment proceedings against Topou. Furthermore, in February 1997 the Speaker of the Legislative Assembly was found guilty of contempt of court for criticizing the Chief Justice's decision to release the three journalists imprisoned in September of the previous year. The Government rejected accusations made in early 1997 by journalists in Tonga and media organizations throughout the region that it was attempting to force the closure of *The Times of Tonga*, despite forbidding Moala (who was resident in New Zealand) to enter Tonga without written permission from the Government, banning all government-funded advertising in the publication and forbidding all government employees to give interviews to its journalists.

Parliament reopened in late May 1997. In June Akau'ola was arrested once again and charged with sedition for publishing a letter in *The Times of Tonga* that questioned government policy. However, in the same month the Government suffered a significant reverse when the Court of Appeal ruled that the imprisonment of Pohiva and the two journalists in late 1996 had been unlawful. In August the Prime Minister of New Zealand, Jim Bolger, paid an official visit to Tonga. Following the visit, Pohiva, who had unsuccessfully sought a meeting with Bolger, criticized New Zealand's relationship with Tonga, claiming that financial assistance from the country hindered democratic reform.

In September 1997, following a formal apology from Topou, the Legislative Assembly voted to abandon impeachment proceedings against him. In October Pohiva announced that he was helping to prepare a proposed draft Constitution for presentation to the Legislative Assembly; the document's principal recommendation was to be the direct election of all 30 members of the Assembly.

In March 1998 Fakafanua, a former Minister of Lands, Survey and Natural Resources, was arrested and remanded on bail in connection with charges of fraud, extortion and accepting bribes. He was released by the Supreme Court later in the month after he accused the police of unlawful imprisonment. One police officer was convicted of this charge in April, while five other men, including Edwards, were acquitted.

In mid-September 1998 the King closed the Legislative Assembly in response to a petition, signed by more than 1,000 people, that sought the removal from office of the Speaker, Eseta Fusitu'a. A parliamentary committee was forced to conduct an inquiry into the activities of Fusitu'a, who was accused of misappropriating public funds and of abusing his position. Pohiva and other pro-democracy activists commended the king for his decisive action in response to the petition. Draft legislation presented later that month, which proposed that in future the Legislative Assembly should appoint cabinet ministers (a responsibility hitherto reserved for the King), was regarded as further evidence of the increasing influence of the pro-democracy lobby in the political life of the country.

At the general election held on 11 March 1999 five members of the reformist Tonga Human Rights and Democracy Movement (formerly the Pro-Democracy Movement/People's Party) were returned to the Legislative Assembly, compared with six at the previous election. In April Veikune was appointed as Speaker and Chairman of the Legislative Assembly, replacing Eseta Fusitu'a, who had lost her seat at the general election. In late 1999 the former Minister for Lands, Survey and Natural Resources, Fakafanua, appeared in court on charges of forgery and bribery.

In January 2000 the King appointed his youngest son, Prince 'Ulukalala-Lavaka-Ata, as Prime Minister, replacing Baron Vaea who had in 1995 announced his desire to retire. It had been expected that Crown Prince Tupouto'a would take up the position, but his support for constitutional reform in Tonga (notably the abolition of life-time terms for the Prime Minister and ministers) contrasted with the King's more conservative approach. In March of that year a report published by the US State Department claimed that Tonga's system of Government, whereby the Legislative Assembly is not directly elected, was in breach of UN and Commonwealth human rights guide-lines. The report was welcomed by the leader of the Tonga Human Rights and Democracy Movement, 'Akilisi Pohiva, who reiterated the party's demands for greater democracy, set out in a draft constitution completed in late 1999.

In January 2001 the Prime Minister announced a reallocation of cabinet positions in which he assumed responsibility for the newly created telecommunications portfolio. In the same month claims in a newspaper report that members of the pro-democracy movement had been involved in a plot to assist an escape from prison, to seize weapons from the army and to assassinate a cabinet minister were vehemently denied by representatives of the group. Meanwhile, ongoing concerns for the freedom of the media in Tonga were renewed following the arrest of the deputy editor of *The Times of Tonga* on charges of criminal libel.

In February 2001 the Tonga Human Rights and Democracy Movement launched a public petition to amend Tonga's Nationality Act to allow Tongans who had taken up citizenship in other countries to retain their Tongan citizenship. Their stated objective in undertaking the petition was to acknowledge Tonga's dependence on remittances from Tongans living overseas.

In September 2000, meanwhile, protests took place in Nuku'alofa, prompted by concerns that Chinese immigrant businesses, encouraged by the Government to establish themselves in Tonga, were creating unfavourable economic conditions for Tongan enterprises. The Tonga Human Rights and Democracy Movement appealed to the Government to cease issuing work permits to foreign (predominantly Chinese) business people and to end the sale of Tongan passports. In order to protect this money from his ministers, who he feared would squander it on unsuitable public works projects should it enter Tonga, the King requested that the funds be placed in the Tonga Trust Fund, held in a Californian cheque account, at the San Francisco branch of the Bank of America. In June 1999 Jesse Bogdonoff, a Bank of America employee, successfully sought royal approval to invest the money in a company in Nevada called Millennium Asset Management, where Bogdonoff was named as the Fund's Advising Officer. Bogdonoff later claimed that he had made a profit of about US $11m., which so impressed the King that he appointed Bogdonoff as Court Jester. The balance of the Fund and the interest it had accrued (totalling some $40m.) was due to be returned to Tonga on 6 June 2001; instead the money appeared to have vanished, along with Millennium Asset Management, which had ceased to exist. In September Princess Pilolevu, acting as Regent in the absence of the King and the Crown Prince, dismissed Kinikinilau Tutoatasi Fakafanua, currently Minister of Education but who at the time of the incident had been Minister of Finance, along with the Deputy Prime Minister and Minister of Justice, Tevita Tupou, both of whom were trustees of the fund. She appointed the Minister of Police, Fire Services and Prisons, Clive Edwards, as Acting Deputy Prime Minister. Parliament created a committee to investigate the crime and tabled a motion to impeach Fakafanua and Tupou. There were no apparent reprisals, or legal action, against Bogdonoff, who claimed that he had been deliberately misled as to the value of the funds. In October the Acting Deputy Prime Minister denied that the Privy Council had directed the transfers from the Fund or that any ministers were implicated. He stressed that at least $2.1m. of the fund, invested in Tongan banks, was duly accounted for. However, in June 2002 the Government admitted that about $26m. had been lost as a result of Bogdonoff's actions and that legal proceedings had been initiated in the USA. It was announced in February 2003 that the case would be heard in December of that year; also in February the Legislative Assembly began impeachment proceedings against the ministers implicated in the matter. In February 2004 it was reported that the Government had agreed to settle out of court with Bogdonoff, who was to pay just $1m. in compensation to the Tongan authorities.

In January 2002 Pohiva published allegations that the King held a secret 'offshore' bank account containing US $350m., some of which was believed to be the proceeds of gold recovered from an 18th century shipwreck. He claimed to possess a letter written to the King from within the palace referring to the account. The Government dismissed the letter as a forgery. Nevertheless, Pohiva was briefly held in custody in February, while police searched the offices of the Tonga Human Rights and Democracy Movement and confiscated computer equipment, in an attempt to find the source material of the allegations. Later that month New Zealand's Minister of Foreign Affairs and Trade condemned Tonga as being endemically corrupt, implying that New Zealand's annual aid of $NZ6m. profited the élite rather than the Tongan people as a whole. In February the King admitted that he did possess an overseas account, with the Bank of Hawaii, but claimed that it contained the profits of vanilla sales from his own plantation. Nevertheless, Pohiva was formally charged with the use and publication of a forged document. In May 2002 he was acquitted of charges of sedition.

A general election was held on 6–7 March 2002, at which 52 candidates competed for the nine commoners' seats in the Legislative Assembly. The Tonga Human Rights and Democracy Movement won seven seats. In September, having repeatedly failed since 1998 to secure government approval for the group's registration under this name, the organization once again became known as the Human Rights and Democracy Movement in Tonga (HRDMT). However, in November 2005 the Government gave approval for a licence to be granted under the Incorporated Societies Act as Friendly Islands Human Rights and Democracy Movement Inc (FIHRDM Inc).

In July 2002 it was reported that Pohiva, Moala and Akau'ola were seeking damages from the Tongan Government for wrongful imprisonment, following their incarceration in 1996 on charges of contempt of parliament. Concerns for the freedom of the media re-emerged in February 2003 when the Government declared *The Times of Tonga*, the twice-weekly newspaper printed in New Zealand, to be a 'prohibited import', describing it as a foreign publication with a political agenda. The ban was challenged, and in April Tonga's Chief Justice, Gordon Ward, ruled that it was both illegal and unconstitutional. However, within hours of the ruling the Government ordered a new ban under different legislation. Ward overruled the ban in the following month, describing it as 'an ill-disguised attempt to restrict the freedom of the press', but on arrival from New Zealand 2,000 copies of the paper were seized by the Tongan customs authorities. Moreover, a few days later legislation was proposed that aimed to limit the power of the Supreme Court by excluding laws and ordinances approved by the Legislative Assembly and the Privy Council from judicial review. In early June the Supreme Court granted an injunction to *The Times of Tonga* ordering the Government to allow its distribution. The Government once again defied the order, stating that it would appeal. In mid-June the newspaper (which had been banned in Tonga since February) was finally allowed to go on sale within the country, after Gordon Ward had threatened each individual member of the Cabinet with contempt of court if they did not permit its distribution.

One of the most vocal critics of the affair was the King's nephew, Prince 'Uluvalu Tu'ipelehake, who in June 2003 expressed concern that the attempts to legislate against the freedom of the press and to restrict the right to seek judicial review would bring Tonga into disrepute. In mid-July it was reported that the Government had abandoned its proposals to limit the powers of the Supreme Court, as a result of strong opposition to the plans. However, later that month the Legislative Assembly approved the Media Operators' Bill, which introduced restrictions on the involvement of foreign nationals in Tonga's media. The legislation was widely viewed as a further attempt to ban *The Times of Tonga*, the editor of which resided in New Zealand. In early October Tonga's Roman Catholic bishop led a march by some 8,600 people to the government buildings in Nuku'alofa. The demonstration, which was the largest of its kind in Tonga's history, aimed to persuade the Government not to introduce any further restrictions on media freedom in the country. However, a few days later the Legislative Assembly voted in favour of a constitutional amendment allowing for greater control of the media, and shortly afterwards introduced the Newspaper Act, which gave the Government increased powers to regulate the content of newspapers in the country. It was reported that the legislation had been approved by 16 parliamentary votes to 11, with virtually all of the elected members voting against the proposals and virtually all of the appointed members voting in favour.

The introduction of legislation restricting media freedom in the country in late 2003 threatened to jeopardize Tonga's international relations, and in November the New Zealand Government announced that it was to review its relationship with Tonga. The Tongan Government summoned New Zealand's ambassador to the islands to register its displeasure. However, in January 2004 Prince 'Uluvalu Tu'ipelehake appealed to Australia's Minister for Foreign Affairs, Alexander Downer, to encourage political reform and to support attempts to increase democratic representation in Tonga.

In February 2004 the King of Tonga's second son, Ma'atu Fatafehi Alaivahamama'o Tuku'aho, died of a heart attack at 48 years of age. Some 6,000 people attended his funeral and the King and Queen announced that they would undertake a period of mourning lasting 100 nights.

Serious financial problems at the national carrier, Royal Tongan Airlines, culminated in April 2004 in the grounding and repossession of the company's passenger jet in Auckland, New Zealand, and the consequent suspension of all international flights. Domestic flights continued to be operated by the airline, but in the following month the entire company ceased all operations when its last remaining domestic aircraft broke down and it was announced that no funds were available to repair it. The failure of the airline caused considerable disquiet throughout Tonga, particularly among those involved in the islands' increasingly important tourist industry. At the opening session of the Legislative Assembly in late May seven of the nine elected representatives staged a boycott, demanding the resignation of the Prime Minister, who they claimed had allowed millions of pa'anga to be wasted during his tenure as chairman of the airline.

A legal challenge to the constitutional amendments governing media freedom, introduced by the Government in 2003, was begun in the Supreme Court in August 2004. Shortly before the legal hearing began the Prime Minister announced the dismissal of three cabinet ministers, including the Minister of Police, Fire Services and Prisons, Clive Edwards, who had been one of the principal proponents of the constitutional amendments. In November the Prime Minister announced that four new cabinet ministers would be appointed from among the elected members of the Legislative Assembly (two from the Nobles and two from the People's Representatives) following the elections in March 2005. The announcement, which represented a departure from the usual procedure whereby ministers were selected from outside parliament, was seen by many, including members of the pro-democracy movement, as a welcome concession towards democratic reform. However, Clive Edwards criticized the proposals, claiming that they were anti-democratic, as they required two members of the Legislative Assembly, elected by the people, to relinquish their seats in order to assume the new positions from which they could be dismissed at the discretion of the King.

Elections for the nine Nobles' seats took place on 16 March and for the nine commoners' seats on 17 March 2005. The latter were contested by a record number of 60 candidates. Two newly elected members from each group were appointed to positions in the Cabinet, and a by-election for the four vacated seats took place on 3–5 May. The Minister of Defence, 'Aloua Fetu'utolu Tupou, died suddenly in mid-April. One of the new representatives elected at the subsequent by-election was the former cabinet minister and member of the newly formed People's Democratic Party (PDP), Clive Edwards. The PDP had been launched in April by a breakaway group from the HRDMT, which had stated its intention to pursue political reform in a more aggressive manner. The new organization was registered in early July, despite fears that this might be deemed illegal, as no provision existed in the Constitution for the establishment of political parties.

In late May 2005 some 8,000 people marched to Tonga's Royal Palace in one of the largest demonstrations of its kind to take place in the country. The protesters presented a petition to the King expressing discontent at high electricity prices charged by the Shoreline Power Group and the excessive salaries reportedly paid to the company's executives. Demonstrators urged the Government to renationalize the generation and distribution of power supply in Tonga.

In July 2005 public servants voted to approve the first national strike in Tonga's history, following the Government's rejection of a request by the Public Service Association (PSA) to reconsider large disparities in salary increases awarded to public sector workers in the recent budget. Almost all of the country's teachers, numerous health care workers and employees from many other public services, initially totalling some 3,000 workers, joined the strike. Accusations of government attempts to restrict the PSA's access to the media were made when the power supply of a private television station was cut shortly before a statement by the PSA was due to be broadcast. During the third week of the strike some 10,000 people marched to the Royal Palace in support of the PSA. Striking public servants expressed the hope that the King might overrule the Cabinet, which had hitherto rejected their demands. Subsequent reports of vandalism against school property and government vehicles were received, and an attempt had apparently been made to burn down the house of a senior executive of the Shoreline Power

Group. Moreover, an unoccupied house belonging to the King on the island of Tongatapu was destroyed by fire in an incident believed by some to be related to recent events in the country. A range of measures, including a new salary scale, subsequently proposed by the Government, was again rejected by the PSA. However, the strike ended in early September when the two sides signed an agreement allowing for salary increases of between 60% and 80%. More significantly, the agreement also provided for the establishment of a commission to review the country's Constitution and to examine possibilities for a more democratic form of government. This represented a major victory for the PSA, which had maintained throughout the dispute that the basic cause of its grievances lay in Tonga's political system. Shortly afterwards a further demonstration by more than 10,000 people took place, appealing to the King to dismiss the entire Government and to conduct a constitutional review within 12 months. Protesters also reiterated their demands for the renationalization of government assets, particularly power generation, but also Tonga's orbital satellite positions and its internet domain address. In October the King agreed to the establishment of a parliamentary committee to examine the issue of constitutional reform.

In February 2006, following the Cabinet's consideration of measures to permit a significant reduction in the number of public servants, the PSA threatened further strike action, stating that the Government's proposals breached the agreement signed in September 2005. Also in February 2006, Prime Minister 'Ulukalala-Lavaka-Ata resigned from office, relinquishing all his portfolios. People's Representative Dr Feleti (Fred) Sevele, a commoner and advocate of constitutional reform, was appointed acting Prime Minister. Sevele also assumed temporary responsibility for the Prince's other ministerial portfolios (including civil aviation, telecommunications, marine and ports). Prince 'Ulukalala had faced increasing demands for his resignation, amid accusations of incompetence and inefficiency. In view of his pro-democracy stance, the appointment of Sevele was widely welcomed. He was expected to be influential in the establishment of democratic government in Tonga, partly owing to his close relationship with the progressive Crown Prince.

In March 2006 the proposals relating to the reduction in the number of government departments were hastily approved by the Cabinet in order to meet final deadlines for submission. It was agreed that most ministries would remain in place, although some were to merge, thereby reducing the existing 16 ministries to 14. Following his confirmation in the position of Prime Minister at the end of March, Dr Feleti Sevele retained responsibility for the portfolios of labour, commerce, industries, disaster relief and communications in a reallocation of cabinet portfolios in mid-May. Other changes included the replacement of Cecil Cocker as Deputy Prime Minister by Dr Viliami Tangi and the appointment of 'Alisi Taumoepeau, the country's first female minister, who became Attorney-General and Minister of Justice. During the course of his first official visit to New Zealand, Prime Minister Feleti Sevele confirmed that about one-quarter of posts in the civil service were to be abolished, as part of the Government's commitment to the reduction of budgetary expenditure. The National Committee for Political Reform (NCPR) was due to present its findings in August, but in July its Chairman, Prince 'Uluvalu Tu'ipelehake, was killed in a car accident in the USA.

On 11 September 2006, after a protracted illness, King Taufa'ahau Tupou IV died in New Zealand, prompting a month of national mourning. Among those present at the King's funeral were the New Zealand Prime Minister, Helen Clark, and Crown Prince Naruhito of Japan. Crown Prince Tupouto'a succeeded to the throne as King George Tupou V. Two new ministers were later appointed to the Cabinet: Afu'olo Matoto became Minister of Public Enterprises, while Lisiate 'Akolo was named Minister of Labour, Commerce and Small Industries. In October the NCPR's report on political reform, which had been submitted to King Tupou IV in late August, was discussed at length by members of the Legislative Assembly. The report envisaged a 26-member legislature, comprising 17 representatives elected by the people and nine representatives elected by nobles; the King would nominate a Prime Minister from the legislature, who would in turn select his cabinet from the elected representatives. Prime Minister Sevele subsequently stated that the Cabinet had proposed the establishment of a new parliamentary tripartite committee composed of cabinet members and nobles' and people's representatives, which would deliberate on the political reform process and present its conclusions in the following year.

As part of its 'roadmap for political reform' the Cabinet made the following recommendations: that the Legislative Assembly should comprise between 23 and 28 representatives, nine of whom would be nobles' representatives and 14 people's representatives, elected according to constituency; the Cabinet should comprise between 12 and 14 members, including two Governors, with at least two-thirds being elected representatives of the Legislative Assembly; the King should appoint two-thirds of the Cabinet on the advice of the Prime Minister and the remaining one-third independently; the Prime Minister should be an elected representative of the Legislative Assembly, appointed by the King on the advice of the Legislative Assembly, and with responsibility for portfolio assignment.

In mid-November 2006 demonstrations in Nuku'alofa against the slow pace of democratic reform developed into riots, with protesters engaging in widespread looting and destruction. According to reports, approximately 80% of the buildings in the business area of the city were burned down, and police later verified that at least six bodies had been found in the ruins. Responding to Sevele's appeal, security forces from Australia and New Zealand arrived to help restore stability. In the aftermath of the violence hundreds of people were arrested. Apparently in response to the unrest, it was announced that a new, modified programme of reform had been approved, envisaging a 30-member legislature made up of 21 people's representatives and nine nobles' representatives. The Prime Minister, it was agreed, would be elected by the legislature. It was revealed that King Tupou V had in fact endorsed the reforms in the previous month, but the final decision had been delayed pending the conclusions of the tripartite committee. Soon after, King Tupou V, in an address to the Legislative Assembly prior to its recess, highlighted the reconstruction efforts necessary after the 'shame' of the unrest, and reiterated the importance of democratic reform that was 'appropriate' for Tonga.

In early 2007 five pro-reform people's representatives were detained on charges that included sedition, in connection with their alleged involvement in the riots of November 2006. In September other charges against the representatives, who included Clive Edwards, were abandoned; however, each representative still faced a charge of sedition. Several others were convicted in February 2008 of various offences related to the riots, while the emergency measures proclaimed following the unrest remained in effect. In June 2007 the Minister of Agriculture, Forestry and Fisheries, Peauafi Haukinima, resigned; Prime Minister Sevele assumed responsibility for his portfolios in an acting capacity. Sevele also took charge of finance following the departure of Siosiua 'Utoikamanu in February 2008, but later transferred the portfolio to Afu'alo Matoto, who became Minister of Finance, National Planning, Public Enterprises and Information. From March Fineasi Funaki, the Minister of Tourism, was reportedly forfeiting three months' salary because of his appropriation of funds provided by the Chinese embassy. In early 2008 it was reported that an independent anti-corruption commission would be established by the end of the year. The formation of the Paati Langafonua Tu'uola (PLT), a new political organization, was announced by its president, Sione Fonua, in August 2007.

On 23 April 2008 29 nobles elected nine representatives to the Assembly, and on the following day elections were held to determine the nine commoners' seats. Approximately 48% of the electorate voted in the latter election, in which 71 candidates participated. Pro-democracy candidates, including several awaiting trial on sedition charges, secured a majority of the commoners' seats, indicating continuing popular support for the reform movement. Although the elections were described as the last to be held under the prevailing system (with constitutional changes expected to increase dramatically the proportions of democratically elected seats, as well as reducing the number of ministers nominated by the King, scheduled to be introduced in 2010) reformists urged the King to formalize the process at his coronation, which was scheduled for August 2008. In early May the King named Tu'ilakepa as the new Speaker of the Assembly.

A friendship treaty that Tonga signed with the USA in July 1988 provided for the safe transit within Tongan waters of US ships capable of carrying nuclear weapons. Tonga was virtually alone in the region in failing to condemn the French Government for its decision to resume nuclear-weapons tests in the South Pacific in mid-1995. However, in May 1996 it was announced that Tonga was finally to accede to the South Pacific Nuclear-Free Zone Treaty (see p. 381).

In September 1990 Tongasat, a Tongan telecommunications company founded earlier that year by Tongan citizens jointly with a US entrepreneur, laid claim to the last 16 satellite positions remaining in the earth's orbit that were suitable for trans-Pacific communications. Despite the protests of leading member nations of Intelsat (the international consortium responsible for most of the world's satellite services), the International Telecommunication Union (see p. 135), was obliged to approve the claim, and Tongasat was subsequently granted six positions. A dispute with Indonesia, concerning that country's use of satellite positions reserved by Tonga in 1990, was resolved by the signing of an agreement in December 1993. In May of the following year the two countries established diplomatic relations at ambassadorial level.

In November 1998 Tonga announced that it had decided to terminate its diplomatic links with Taiwan and to establish relations with the People's Republic of China. Tonga opened a consulate in China in May 2005. Several Chinese businesses were targeted in the Nuku'alofa riots of November 2006, prompting China to evacuate hundreds of its citizens.

In January 2002, in the Red Sea, Israeli commandos seized a ship that was allegedly transporting weapons to Palestinians. The ship was flying a Tongan 'flag of convenience' and had been registered in the Kingdom. The reformist politician 'Akilisi Pohiva criticized Tonga's policy of international ship registration, which generated income through sales of flags of convenience. (The issue of international shipping registration had never been debated in Parliament.) Following the seizure, the registration system was closed in June. However, in September another Tongan-registered ship was seized off the coast of Italy and its crew arrested on suspicion of plotting an al-Qa'ida-sponsored terrorist attack in Europe. Furthermore, it was reported in early October that the Greek businessman in charge of the Tongan International Registry of Ships, Pelopidas Papadopoulos, had absconded with the proceeds of the operation owed to the Tongan Government, totalling some US $0.3m.

Government

Tonga is a hereditary monarchy. The King is Head of State and Head of Government. He appoints, and presides over, the Privy Council which acts as the national Cabinet. Apart from the King, the Council includes 14 ministers (increased from 10 in 2005), appointed for life and led by the Prime Minister, and the Governors of Ha'apai and Vava'u. The unicameral Legislative Assembly comprises the King and 33 members: the Privy Council, nine hereditary nobles (chosen by their peers) and nine representatives elected by all adult Tongan citizens. Elected members hold office for three years. There are no official political parties, although opposition groupings continue to campaign for democratic reform.

Defence

Tonga has its own defence force, consisting of both regular and reserve units. Projected government expenditure on defence in the financial year 1999/2000 was 3.3m. pa'anga (5.0% of total budgetary expenditure); in the same year estimated expenditure on law and order was 4.6m. pa'anga (6.9% of total current expenditure).

Economic Affairs

In 2006, according to estimates by the World Bank, Tonga's gross national income (GNI), measured at average 2004–06 prices, was US $223m., equivalent to $2,170 per head (or $8,580 per head on an international purchasing-power parity basis). During 1996–2006, it was estimated, the population increased at an average annual rate of 0.5%, while gross domestic product (GDP) per head increased, in real terms, by an average of 1.7% per year. Overall GDP increased, in real terms, at an average annual rate of 2.2% in 1996–2006. GDP was estimated by the Asian Development Bank (ADB) to have increased by 1.9% in 2006, before the economy contracted by 3.5% in 2007.

Agriculture (including forestry and fishing) contributed 25.1% of GDP in 2006, and engaged about 32% of the employed labour force in 2005. According to the World Bank, agricultural GDP increased at an average annual rate of 0.4% in 1996–2005. The principal cash crops are coconuts, vanilla and squash (pumpkin), which normally form the major part of Tonga's exports. In 2005 squash accounted for 42.1% of export earnings. Vanilla acquired greater significance in the 1990s, but production subsequently declined, and vanilla beans accounted for only 1.7% of total export earnings in 2005. Yams, taro, sweet potatoes, watermelons, tomatoes, cassava, lemons and limes, oranges, groundnuts and breadfruit are also cultivated as food crops, while the islanders keep pigs, goats, poultry and cattle. The importance of the fishing industry increased from the 1990s. Exports of fish reached 11.3m. pa'anga in 2003, when they contributed 37.2% of total export earnings. The value of sales declined in subsequent years, and in 2006 fish accounted for 20.4% of export receipts. The ADB estimated that agricultural GDP decreased by 0.5% in 2006 and by 1.2% in 2007.

Industry (including mining, manufacturing, construction and utilities) provided 13.5% of GDP in 2006 and engaged 26.4% of the employed labour force in 1996. According to the World Bank, industrial GDP expanded at an average annual rate of 1.6% in 1996–2005. Compared with the previous year, industrial GDP was calculated by the ADB to have expanded by 9.7% in 2005, before contracting by 2.2% in 2006 and by 1.1% in 2007. Manufacturing contributed 3.1% of GDP in 2006, and (with mining) employed 22.8% of the labour force in 1996. Output of food products and beverages dominates the manufacturing sector. other manufacturing activities include the production of concrete blocks, small excavators, furniture, handicrafts, textiles, leather goods, sports equipment (including small boats), brewing and coconut oil. There is also a factory for processing sandalwood.

In an attempt to reduce fuel imports, a 2-MW wave-energy power plant was constructed in the early 1990s and would, it was hoped, supply one-third of the islands' total electricity requirements when in full operation. A project to provide all the outer islands with solar power by 2000 was begun in 1996. Imports of mineral products accounted for almost 26.5% of total import costs in 2007.

Service industries contributed 61.3% of GDP in 2006 and engaged 39.5% of the employed labour force in 1996. According to the World Bank, the GDP of the services sector increased at an average annual rate of 3.4% in 1996–2005. The ADB estimated that the GDP of the services sector expanded by 2.0% in 2006 before declining by 5.2% in 2007. Tourism makes a significant contribution to the economy. Tourism receipts decreased from US $15m. in 2004 to $11m. in 2005. Visitor arrivals were reported to have risen from 39,451 in 2006 to 46,040 in 2007.

In 2007, according to the ADB, Tonga recorded a visible trade deficit of US $95m., and a deficit of $25m. on the current account of the balance of payments. The latter was equivalent to 10.1% of GDP in 2007. In 2007 the principal sources of imports were New Zealand (33.7%), Fiji (13.3%) and Australia (11.7%), while New Zealand and the USA were the principal markets for exports (purchasing 35.6% and 29.1% respectively). The principal exports in that year were foodstuffs. Squash, vanilla and fish are important export items. The principal imports were foodstuffs, mineral products, machinery and transport equipment and basic manufactures.

According to the ADB, in the financial year ending 30 June 2006 there was a budgetary deficit of 15.7m. pa'anga. An overall budgetary surplus, estimated at the equivalent of 1.4% of GDP, was anticipated in 2006/07. Tonga's total external debt reached US $83m. in 2007, compared with $82m. in 2006. In the latter year the cost of debt-servicing was equivalent to 10.5% of the total revenue from exports of goods and services. In 2007/08 official development assistance from Australia was projected at $A15.7m., while aid from New Zealand in the same year amounted to $NZ11.5m. The annual rate of inflation averaged 7.3% in 1996–2006. According to ADB figures, consumer prices increased by an average of 7.2% in 2006 and 5.1% in 2007. Some 5.5% of the labour force were unemployed in 2003, according to the ADB.

Tonga is a member of the Pacific Community (see p. 377), the Pacific Islands Forum (see p. 380), the Asian Development Bank (ADB, see p. 182) and the UN Economic and Social Commission for Asia and the Pacific (ESCAP, see p. 35). The country is a signatory of the Lomé Conventions and the successor Cotonou Agreement (see p. 301) with the European Union (EU). Tonga was formally admitted to the World Trade Organization (WTO, see p. 396) in July 2007.

The constraints on Tonga's economic development have included inflationary pressures, large-scale emigration and over-reliance on the agricultural sector, in particular sales of squash to the international market. The relatively low rate of growth recorded in 2006 was, in part, attributable to the decline in prices on the world market for Tonga's principal export product, squash; the squash industry remained depressed in 2007. Budgetary and inflationary pressures were expected to rise following the implementation of increases of 60%–80% in public

TONGA

sector salaries. The salary increases envisaged for 2007 and 2008 were expected to reach the equivalent of 11.0% and 7.8% respectively of GDP. Remittances from Tongans resident overseas have remained an important source of income, although such remittances were reported to have declined in 2007. In 2005 Tonga renewed a bilateral trade agreement with the People's Republic of China. An agreement on technical and economic co-operation between China and Tonga was signed in May 2007. A value-added tax was introduced in 2005. As the country's dependence on revenue from trade taxes was decreased, Tonga's admission to the WTO in mid-2007 was expected to provide further momentum in the area of trade liberalization. Meanwhile, riots in the capital of Nuku'alofa in November 2006 (see Recent History), had an adverse impact on the economy, with reconstruction costs estimated at more than 50m. pa'anga. With rebuilding work thus progressing, and recovery in the tourist sector anticipated, the ADB forecast GDP growth of 1.0% in 2008, following the contraction of 2007. However, the steady rise in the country's debt service ratio had continued to cause some concern, which was intensified in late 2007 when Tonga accepted a loan of US $50m. from China for the purposes of financing reconstruction work. Nevertheless, the Government's management of the economy was praised in an IMF report released in April 2008.

Education

Free state education is compulsory for children between five and 14 years of age, while the Government and other Commonwealth countries offer scholarship schemes enabling students to go abroad for higher education. In 1999 there were 117 primary schools, with a total of 17,032 pupils in 2005. There were a total of 14,505 pupils in secondary education in 2005 and secondary schools numbered 69 in 1999. In 2000 enrolment at pre-primary schools included 22% of pupils from the relevant age-group. In 2005 enrolment at primary school level included 95.4% of children in the relevant age-group while in 2004 enrolment in secondary schools included 67.7% of children. There were also four technical and vocational colleges in 2001, with a total of 467 students, and one teacher-training college, with 288 students. In 1990 there were 230 Tongans studying overseas. Some degree courses are offered at the university division of 'Atenisi Institute. A new establishment offering higher education, the 'Unuaki 'o Tonga Royal Institute (UTRI), opened in 2004. Recurrent government expenditure on education in 1999/2000 was an estimated 10.9m. pa'anga (equivalent to 16.5% of total recurrent budgetary expenditure).

Public Holidays

2008: 1 January (New Year's Day), 21–24 March (Easter), 25 April (ANZAC Day), 4 June (Independence Day), 12 July (Birthday of the Heir to the Crown of Tonga), 1 August (Coronation Day and Official Birthday of King Tupou V), 4 November (Tonga National Day), 4 December (Tupou I Day), 25–26 December (Christmas Day and Boxing Day).

2009: 1 January (New Year's Day), 10–13 April (Easter), 25 April (ANZAC Day), 4 June (Independence Day), 12 July (Birthday of the Heir to the Crown of Tonga), 1 August (Official Birthday of King Tupou V), 4 November (Tonga National Day), 4 December (Tupou I Day), 25–26 December (Christmas Day and Boxing Day).

Weights and Measures

In 1980 Tonga adopted the metric system of weights and measures in place of the imperial system.

Statistical Survey

Source (unless otherwise indicated): Tonga Government Department of Statistics, POB 149, Nuku'alofa; tel. (676) 23300; fax (676) 24303; e-mail dept@stats.gov.to; internet http://www.spc.int/prism/country/to/stats.

AREA AND POPULATION

Area: 748 sq km (289 sq miles).

Population: 97,784 at census of 30 November 1996; 101,991 (males 51,772, females 50,219) at census of 30 November 2006. *By Island Group* (2006 census, provisional): Tongatapu 71,260; Vava'u 15,485; Ha'apai 7,572; 'Eua 5,165; Niuas 1,652; Total 101,134.

Density (census 2006): 136.4 per sq km.

Principal Towns (population at 2006 census, provisional): Nuku'alofa (capital) 23,438; Neiafu 4,108; Haveluloto 3,384; Tofoa-Koloua 3,193; Vaini 3,076 (Source: Thomas Brinkhoff, *City Population*—internet www.citypopulation.de). *Mid-2007* (incl. suburbs, UN estimate): Nuku'alofa 25,000 (Source: UN, *World Urbanization Prospects: The 2007 Revision*).

Births, Marriages and Deaths (2002): Registered live births 2,662 (birth rate 26.4 per 1,000); Registered marriages 750 (marriage rate 7.4 per 1,000); Registered deaths 591 (death rate 5.9 per 1,000). *Live Births:* 2,781 in 2003; 2,628 in 2004. *Deaths:* 617 in 2003; 559 in 2004. Source: mainly UN, *Demographic Yearbook* and *Population and Vital Statistics Report*.

Expectation of Life (years at birth, WHO estimates): 70.9 (males 71.7; females 70.2) in 2005. Source: WHO, *World Health Statistics*.

Economically Active Population (persons aged 15 years and over, 1996): Agriculture, forestry and fishing 9,953; Mining and quarrying 43; Manufacturing 6,710; Electricity, gas and water 504; Construction 500; Trade, restaurants and hotels 2,506; Transport, storage and communications 1,209; Financing, insurance, real estate and business services 657; Public administration and defence 3,701; Education 1,721; Health and social work 510; Other community, social and personal services 1,320; Extra-territorial organizations 72; *Total employed* 29,406 (males 18,402, females 11,004); Unemployed 4,502 (males 3,293, females 1,209); *Total labour force* 33,908 (males 21,695, females 12,213). *Mid-2005* (estimates): Agriculture, etc. 12,000; Total labour force 38,000 (Source: FAO).

HEALTH AND WELFARE

Key Indicators

Total Fertility Rate (children per woman, 2005): 3.3.

Under-5 Mortality Rate (per 1,000 live births, 2005): 24.

Physicians (per 1,000 head, 2001): 0.34.

Hospital Beds (per 1,000 head, 2004): 2.9.

Health Expenditure (2004): US $ per head (PPP): 315.9.

Health Expenditure (2004): % of GDP: 6.3.

Health Expenditure (2004): public (% of total): 79.5.

Access to Sanitation (% of persons, 2004): 96.

Human Development Index (2005): ranking 55.

Human Development Index (2005): value 0.819.

For sources and definitions, see explanatory note on p. vi.

AGRICULTURE, ETC.

Principal Crops ('000 metric tons, 2006, FAO estimates): Sweet potatoes 6.7; Cassava 4.8; Taro 3.7; Yams 2.0; Other roots and tubers 2.0; Coconuts 69.2; Pumpkins, squash and gourds 18.4; Other vegetables and melons 6.0; Bananas 0.5; Plantains 1.9; Oranges 0.7; Lemons and limes 2.4; Other fruits 2.6.

Livestock ('000 head, year ending September 2006, FAO estimates): Pigs 81; Horses 11; Cattle 11; Goats 13; Chickens 300.

Livestock Products (metric tons, 2006, FAO estimates): Pig meat 1,484; Other meat 725; Hen eggs 28; Honey 10; Cows' milk 370.

Forestry ('000 cu m, 1999): *Roundwood Removals* (excl. bark): 2; *Sawnwood Production:* 2 (FAO estimate). *2000–06* (FAO estimates): Annual output as in 1999.

Fishing (metric tons, live weight, 2005): Marine fishes 1,500 (Snappers and jobfishes 171; Albacore 283; Bigeye tuna 125; Yellowfin tuna 219); Marine crustaceans 350 (FAO estimate); Total catch (incl. others) 1,901 (excl. aquatic plants 887).

Source: FAO.

INDUSTRY

Production (2006): Electric energy 54 million kWh. Source: Asian Development Bank, *Key Indicators of Developing Asian and Pacific Countries*.

TONGA

FINANCE

Currency and Exchange Rates: 100 seniti (cents) = 1 pa'anga (Tongan dollar or $T). *Sterling, US Dollar and Euro Equivalents* (28 September 2007): £1 sterling = $T3.9728; US $1 = $T1.9558; €1 = $T3.6060; $T100 = £25.17 = US $51.13 = €36.06. *Average Exchange Rate* (pa'anga per US $): 1.9716 in 2004; 1.9430 in 2005; 2.0259 in 2006.

Budget (million pa'anga, year ending 30 June 2005): *Revenue:* Taxation 98.4; Non-taxation 17.6; Capital receipts 0.0; Total 116.0 (excl. grants received from abroad 5.4). *Expenditure:* Current expenditure 104.7; Capital expenditure 7.6; Total 112.4 (excl. net lending –1.1). Source: Asian Development Bank, *Key Indicators of Developing Asian and Pacific Countries*.

International Reserves (US $ million at 31 December 2007): IMF special drawing rights 0.65; Reserve position in the IMF 2.70; Foreign exchange 61.88; Total 65.24. Source: IMF, *International Financial Statistics*.

Money Supply ('000 pa'anga at 31 December 2006): Currency outside banks 21,504; Demand deposits at deposit money banks 48,358; Total money 69,862. Source: IMF, *International Financial Statistics*.

Cost of Living (Consumer Price Index, excl. rent; base: November 2002 = 100): All items 125.2 in 2005; 170.7 in 2006; 146.2 in 2007. Source: IMF, *International Financial Statistics*.

Gross Domestic Product (million pa'anga at constant 2000/01 prices, year ending 30 June): 304.7 in 2003/04; 298.0 in 2004/05; 307.5 in 2005/06. Source: Asian Development Bank, *Key Indicators of Developing Asian and Pacific Countries*.

Gross Domestic Product by Economic Activity (million pa'anga at current prices, year ending 30 June 2006): Agriculture, forestry and fishing 100.6; Mining and quarrying 1.7; Manufacturing 12.5; Electricity, gas and water 9.7; Construction 30.4; Trade, restaurants and hotels 59.7; Transport, storage and communications 21.5; Finance and real estate 49.9; Public administration 75.3; Other services 39.4; *Sub-total* 400.8; *Less* Imputed bank service charges 12.4; *Gross value added in basic prices* 388.4; Indirect taxes, *less* subsidies 90.2; *GDP at market prices* 478.5. Source: Asian Development Bank, *Key Indicators of Developing Asian and Pacific Countries*.

Balance of Payments (US $ million, 2006): Exports of goods f.o.b. 9.6; Imports of goods f.o.b. –86.4; *Trade balance* –76.9; Exports of services and income 31.3; Imports of services –58.2; *Balance on goods and services* –103.8; Other income received 11.3; Other income paid –3.1; *Balance on goods, services and income* –95.6; Current transfers received 92.7; Current transfers paid –12.5; *Current balance* –15.4; Capital account (net) 7.0; Direct investment abroad 11.6; Direct investment from abroad –1.5; Other investment assets 7.9; Other investment liabilities –6.3; Net errors and omissions –4.3; *Overall balance* –1.1. Source: IMF, *International Financial Statistics*.

EXTERNAL TRADE

Principal Commodities ('000 pa'anga, 2007): *Imports:* Animals and animal products 30,142; Vegetable products 8,745; Prepared foodstuffs 43,192; Mineral products 74,392; Chemical products 10,833; Wood and wood products 8,720; Wood pulp, paper and paperboard 8,741; Base metals and articles thereof 13,875; Machinery, mechanical appliances and electrical equipment 30,372; Transportation equipment 12,918; Miscellaneous manufactured articles 6,393; Works of art, collectors' pieces and antiques 15,099; Total (incl. others) 281,032. *Exports* (including re-exports): Animal and animal products 5,621; Vegetable products 8,598; Chemical products 744; Wood and wood products 437; Machinery, mechanical appliances and electrical equipment 537; Total (incl. others) 16,716.

Principal Trading Partners ('000 pa'anga, 2007): *Imports:* Australia 32,924; China, People's Republic 17,501; Fiji 37,372; Indonesia 4,208; Japan 7,320; New Zealand 94,766; Singapore 47,942; USA (incl. Hawaii) 28,545; Total (incl. others) 281,032. *Exports:* American Samoa 599; Australia 1,155; Japan 2,063; Korea, Republic 304; New Zealand 5,949; Samoa 757; Taiwan 353; USA (incl. Hawaii) 4,858; Total (incl. others) 16,716.

TRANSPORT

Road Traffic (registered motor vehicles, 2004): Passenger cars 6,580; Light goods vehicles 5,183; Heavy goods vehicles 2,698; Buses 114; Taxis 845; Total (incl. others) 16,748.

Shipping: *International Traffic* ('000 metric tons, 1998 unless otherwise indicated): Goods loaded 13.8; Goods unloaded 80.4. Vessels entered ('000 net registered tons) 1,950 in 1991 (Source: UN, *Statistical Yearbook*). *Merchant Fleet* (registered at 31 December 2006): Vessels 52; Total displacement ('000 grt) 79.0 (Source: Lloyd's Register-Fairplay, *World Fleet Statistics*).

Civil Aviation (traffic on scheduled services, 2002): Kilometres flown 1 million; Passengers carried 61,000; Passenger-km 15 million; Total ton-km 1 million. Source: UN, *Statistical Yearbook*.

TOURISM

Foreign Tourist Arrivals (excl. cruise-ship passengers): 40,110 in 2003; 41,208 in 2004; 41,862 in 2005.

Tourist Arrivals by Country (2005): Australia 8,854; Fiji 1,535; Germany 868; Japan 661; New Zealand 17,495; United Kingdom 943; USA 7,861; Total (incl. others) 41,862.

Tourism Receipts (US $ million, excl. passenger transport): 14 in 2003; 15 in 2004; 11 in 2005.

Source: World Tourism Organization.

COMMUNICATIONS MEDIA

Radio Receivers (1997): 61,000 in use.

Television Receivers (1997): 2,000 in use.

Telephones ('000 main lines, 2006): 13.7 in use.

Mobile Cellular Telephones (2006): 29,900 subscribers.

Personal Computers (2002): 2,000.

Internet Users (2006): 3,100.

Broadband Subscribers (2006): 400.

Facsimile Machines (1996): 250 in use.

Daily Newspapers (1996): 1; estimated circulation 7,000.

Non-daily Newspapers (2001): 2; estimated circulation 13,000.

Sources: UNESCO, *Statistical Yearbook*; UN, *Statistical Yearbook*; Audit Bureau of Circulations, Australia; and International Telecommunication Union.

EDUCATION

Primary (2004, unless otherwise indicated): 117 schools (1999); 759 teachers; 17,105 pupils.

General Secondary (2004, unless otherwise indicated): 39 schools (1999); 1,041 teachers; 13,586 pupils.

Technical and Vocational: 4 colleges (2001); 45 teachers (1990); 467 students (1999).

Teacher-training (1999, unless otherwise indicated): 1 college; 22 teachers (1994); 288 students.

Universities, etc. (1985): 17 teachers; 85 students.

Other Higher Education: 36 teachers (1980); 620 students (1985); in 1990 230 students were studying overseas on government scholarships.

Directory

The Constitution

The Constitution of Tonga is based on that granted in 1875 by King George Tupou I. It provides for a government consisting of the Sovereign; a Privy Council, which is appointed by the Sovereign and consists of the Sovereign and the Cabinet; the Cabinet, which consists of a Prime Minister, a Deputy Prime Minister, several other ministers (formerly eight but increased to 12 in 2005) and the Governors of Ha'apai and Vava'u; a Legislative Assembly and a Judiciary. Limited law-making power is vested in the Privy Council and any legislation passed by the Executive is subject to review by the Legislative Assembly. The unicameral Legislative Assembly comprises the King, the Cabinet, nine hereditary nobles (chosen by their peers) and nine representatives elected by all adult Tongan citizens. Elected members hold office for three years.

TONGA
Directory

The Government

HEAD OF STATE

The Sovereign: HM King GEORGE TUPOU V (succeeded to the throne 11 September 2006).

CABINET
(April 2008)

Prime Minister and Acting Minister of Food, Agriculture, Forestry and Fisheries: Dr FELETI (FRED) SEVELE.

Deputy Prime Minister and Minister of Health: Dr VILIAMI TANGI.

Minister of Foreign Affairs, Acting Minister of Defence and Acting Governor of Vava'u: TU'A TAUMOEPEAU TUPOU.

Minister of Finance, National Planning, Public Enterprises and Information: AFU'ALO MATOTO.

Minister of Education, Women's Affairs and Culture: Dr TEVITA HALA PALEFAU.

Governor of Ha'apai: MALUPO.

Minister of Labour, Commerce and Industries: LISIATE 'AKOLO.

Minister of Lands, Survey, Natural Resources and Environment: TUITA.

Minister of Police, Fire Services and Prisons: SIAOSI TAIMANI 'AHO.

Minister of Training, Employment, Youth and Sports: TU'IVAKANO.

Minister of Works: NUKU.

Attorney-General and Minister of Justice: MALIA VIVIENA 'ALISI NUMIA AFEAKI TAUMOEPEAU.

Minister of Civil Aviation, Marine and Ports: PAUL KARALUS.

Minister of Tourism: FINEASI FUNAKI.

GOVERNMENT MINISTRIES AND OFFICES

Office of the Prime Minister: POB 62, Taufa'ahau Rd, Kolofo'ou, Nuku'alofa; tel. 24644; fax 23888; e-mail fttuita@pmo.gov.to; internet www.pmo.gov.to.

Palace Office: Salote Rd, Kolofo'ou, Nuku'alofa; tel. 21000; fax 24102; internet www.palaceoffice.gov.to.

Ministry of Agriculture, Food, Forestry and Fisheries: Administration Office, Vuna Rd, Kolofo'ou, Nuku'alofa; tel. 23038; fax 23039; e-mail pvea@kalianet.to.

Ministry of Civil Aviation: POB 845, Salote Rd, Nuku'alofa; tel. 24144; fax 24145; e-mail info@mca.gov.to; internet www.mca.gov.to.

Ministry of Education: POB 61, Vuna Rd, Kolofo'ou, Nuku'alofa; tel. 23511; fax 23596; e-mail moe@kalianet.to.

Ministry of Finance and National Planning: Treasury Bldg, POB 87, Vuna Rd, Kolofo'ou, Nuku'alofa; tel. 23066; fax 21010; e-mail info@finance.gov.to; internet www.finance.gov.to.

Ministry of Foreign Affairs: National Reserve Bank Bldg, Salote Rd, Kolofo'ou, Nuku'alofa; tel. 23600; fax 23360; e-mail secfo@candw.to.

Ministry of Health: POB 59, Taufa'ahau Rd, Tofoa, Nuku'alofa; tel. 23200; fax 24921; internet www.health.gov.to.

Ministry of Internal Affairs: POB 110, Salote Rd, Fasi-moe-afi, Nuku'alofa; tel. 23688; fax 23880.

Ministry of Justice: POB 130, Railway Rd, Kolofo'ou, Nuku'alofa; tel. 21055; fax 23098; internet www.justice.gov.to.

Ministry of Labour, Commerce and Industries: POB 110, Nuku'alofa; tel. 23688; fax 23887; e-mail info@mlci.gov.to; internet www.mlci.gov.to.

Ministry of Lands, Survey and Natural Resources: POB 5, Vuna Rd, Kolofo'ou, Nuku'alofa; tel. 23611; fax 23216; internet www.lands.gov.to.

Ministry of Marine and Ports: POB 397, Vuna Rd, Ma'ufanga, Nuku'alofa; tel. 22555; fax 26234; e-mail marine@kalianet.to.

Ministry of Police, Fire Services and Prisons: Mauikisikisi Rd, Longolongo; tel. 23233; fax 23226.

Ministry of Public Enterprises and Information: Nuku'alofa; tel. 28144; fax 24598.

Ministry of Works and Disaster Relief Activities: 'Alaivahamama'o Rd, Vaololoa, Nuku'alofa; tel. 23100; fax 25440; e-mail mowtonga@kalianet.to.

Legislative Assembly

The Legislative Assembly consists of the Speaker, the members of the Cabinet, nine nobles chosen by the 33 Nobles of Tonga, and nine representatives elected by all Tongans over 21 years of age. There are elections every three years, and the Assembly is required to meet at least once every year. The most recent election was held on 23–24 April 2008, when pro-democracy candidates won a majority of the nine seats.

Speaker and Chairman of the Legislative Assembly: TU'ILAKEPA.

Political Organizations

Although the Constitution of Tonga does not provide for the official establishment of political parties, the following groups have been active:

Friendly Islands Human Rights and Democracy Movement Inc (FIHRDM Inc): POB 843, Nuku'alofa; tel. 25501; fax 26330; e-mail demo@kalianet.to; internet fihrdm.org; f. late 1970s; est. and recognized in 1992 as the Pro-Democracy Movement; application in 1998 for incorporation under new name of Tonga Human Rights and Democracy Movement refused by the Govt; reverted to the name of Human Rights and Democracy Movement in Tonga (HRDMT) in 2002; assumed present name in Nov. 2005; campaigns for democratic reform and increased parliamentary representation for the Tongan people; Sec. 'AKILISI POHIVA.

Kotoa Movement: f. 2001; campaigns in support of monarchy; Sec. SEMISI KAILAHI.

Paati Langafonua Tu'uloa (PLT): f. 2007; Pres. SIONE FONUA.

People's Democratic Party: Nuku'alofa; f. 2005; breakaway group from HRDMT; Pres. SIONE TEISINA FUKO; Vice-Pres. SIONE TU'ALAU MANGISI; Sec. SEMISI TAPUELUELU.

Diplomatic Representation

EMBASSY AND HIGH COMMISSIONS IN TONGA

Australia: Salote Rd, Private Bag 35, Nuku'alofa; tel. 23244; fax 23243; e-mail ahctonga@kalianet.to; internet www.tonga.embassy.gov.au; High Commissioner BRUCE HUNT.

China, People's Republic: Vuna Rd, POB 877, Nuku'alofa; tel. 24554; fax 24595; e-mail chinaemb_to@mfa.gov.cn; Ambassador HU YESHUN.

New Zealand: cnr Taufa'ahau and Salote Rds, POB 830, Nuku'alofa; tel. 23122; fax 23487; e-mail nzhcnuk@kalianet.to; High Commissioner CHRISTINE BOGLE.

Judicial System

There are eight Magistrates' Courts, the Land Court, the Supreme Court and the Court of Appeal.

Appeal from the Magistrates' Courts is to the Supreme Court, and from the Supreme Court and Land Court to the Court of Appeal (except in certain matters relating to hereditary estates, where appeal lies to the Privy Council). The Chief Justice and Puisne Judge are resident in Tonga and are judges of the Supreme Court and Land Court. The Court of Appeal is presided over by the Chief Justice and consists of three judges from other Commonwealth countries. In the Supreme Court the accused in criminal cases, and either party in civil suits, may elect trial by jury. In the Land Court the judge sits with a Tongan assessor. Proceedings in the Magistrates' Courts are in Tongan, and in the Supreme Court and Court of Appeal in Tongan and English.

Supreme Court

POB 11, Nuku'alofa; tel. 23599; fax 22380; e-mail cj_tonga@kalianet.to.

Chief Justice: ANTHONY FORD.

Puisne Judge: ROBERT SHUSTER.

Chief Registrar: MANAKOVI PAHULU.

Religion

The Tongans are almost all Christians, and about 36% of the population belong to Methodist (Wesleyan) communities. There are also significant numbers of Roman Catholics (15%) and Latter-day Saints (Mormons—15%). Anglicans (1%) and Seventh-day

TONGA

Adventists (5%) are also represented. Fourteen churches are represented in total.

CHRISTIANITY

Kosilio 'ae Ngaahi Siasi 'i Tonga (Tonga National Council of Churches): POB 1205, Nuku'alofa; tel. 23291; fax 27506; e-mail tncc@kalianet.to; f. 1973; three mem. churches (Free Wesleyan, Roman Catholic and Anglican); Chair. Rt Rev. SOANE LILO FOLIAKI; Gen. Sec. Rev. SIKETI TONGA.

The Anglican Communion

Tonga lies within the diocese of Polynesia, part of the Church of the Province of New Zealand. The Bishop of Polynesia is resident in Fiji.

Archdeacon of Tonga and Samoa: The Ven. SAM KOY, The Vicarage, POB 31, Nuku'alofa; tel. 22136.

The Roman Catholic Church

The diocese of Tonga, directly responsible to the Holy See, comprises Tonga and the New Zealand dependency of Niue. At 31 December 2005 there were an estimated 14,566 adherents in the diocese. The Bishop participates in the Catholic Bishops' Conference of the Pacific, based in Fiji.

Bishop of Tonga: SOANE PATITA MAFI, Toutaimana Catholic Centre, POB 1, Nuku'alofa; tel. 23822; fax 23854; e-mail cathbish@kalianet.to.

Other Churches

Church of Jesus Christ of Latter-day Saints (Mormon): Mission Centre, POB 58, Nuku'alofa; tel. 26007; fax 23763; 53,000 mems; Pres. LYNN C. MCMURRAY.

Church of Tonga: Nuku'alofa; f. 1928; a branch of Methodism; 6,912 mems; Pres. Rev. FINAU KATOANGA.

Free Constitutional Church of Tonga: POB 23, Nuku'alofa; tel. 23966; fax 24458; f. 1885; 15,941 mems (1996); Pres. Rev. SEMISI FONUA; brs in Australia, New Zealand and USA.

Free Wesleyan Church of Tonga (Koe Siasi Uesiliana Tau'ataina 'o Tonga): POB 57, Nuku'alofa; tel. 23522; fax 24020; e-mail fwc@kalianet.to; internet www.fwc.to; f. 1826; 36,500 mems; Pres. Rev. Dr 'ALIFALETI MONE.

Tokaikolo Christian Fellowship: Nuku'alofa; f. 1978; breakaway group from Free Wesleyan Church; 5,000 mems.

BAHÁ'Í FAITH

National Spiritual Assembly: POB 133, Nuku'alofa; tel. 21568; fax 23120; e-mail nsatonga@patco.to; mems resident in 142 localities.

The Press

Eva, Your Guide to Tonga: POB 958, Nuku'alofa; tel. 25779; fax 24749; e-mail vapress@matangitonga.to; internet www.matangitonga.to; f. 1989; 4 a year; publication suspended under media restrictions in Jan. 2004; Editor PESI FONUA; circ. 4,500.

Ko e Kele'a (Conch Shell): POB 1567, Nuku'alofa; tel. 25501; fax 26330; internet www.planet-tonga.com/tongatimes/kelea; f. 1986; monthly; activist-orientated publication, economic and political; Editor 'AKILISI POHIVA; circ. 3,500.

Lali: Nuku'alofa; f. 1994; monthly; English; national business magazine; Publr KALAFI MOALA.

Lao and Hia: POB 2808, Nuku'alofa; tel. 14105; weekly; Tongan; legal newspaper; Editor SIONE HAFOKA.

Matangi Tonga: POB 958, Nuku'alofa; tel. 25779; fax 24749; e-mail vapress@matangitonga.to; internet www.matangitonga.to; f. 1986; monthly; national news magazine ceased publication following suspension of licence in Jan. 2004 and subsequently published solely on internet; Man. Editor MARY FONUA.

'Ofa ki Tonga: c/o Tokaikolo Fellowship, POB 2055, Nuku'alofa; tel. 24190; monthly; newspaper of Tokaikolo Christian Fellowship; Editor Rev. LIUFAU VAILEA SAULALA.

Taumu'a Lelei: POB 1, Nuku'alofa; tel. 27161; fax 23854; e-mail tmlcath@kalianet.to; f. 1931; monthly; Roman Catholic; Editor Dr SOANE LILO FOLIAKI.

The Times of Tonga/Koe Taimi'o Tonga: POB 880, Nuku'alofa; tel. 23177; fax 23292; e-mail times@kalianet.to; internet timesoftonga.com; f. 1989; twice-weekly; English edition covers Pacific and world news, Tongan edition concentrates on local news; licence suspended in Feb. 2004; Publr KALAFI MOALA; Editor MATENI TAPUELUELU; circ. 8,000.

Tohi Fanongonongo: POB 57, Nuku'alofa; tel. 26533; fax 24020; e-mail fwctf@kalianet.to; monthly; Wesleyan; Editor Rev. TEVITA PAUKAMEA TIUETI.

Tonga Chronicle/Kalonikali Tonga: POB 197, Nuku'alofa; tel. 23302; fax 23336; e-mail chroni@kalianet.to; internet www.netstorage.com/kami/tonga/news; f. 1964; govt-sponsored; weekly; Tongan and English; Man. 'ALIFELETI TU'IHALAMAKA; circ. 3,000.

Publisher

Vava'u Press Ltd: POB 958, Nuku'alofa; tel. 25779; fax 24749; e-mail vapress@matangitonga.to; internet www.matangitonga.to; f. 1980; books and magazines; Pres. PESI FONUA.

Broadcasting and Communications

TELECOMMUNICATIONS

Tonga Communications Corporation: Private Bag 4, Nuku'alofa; tel. 20000; fax 26701; internet www.tcc.to; f. 2000; responsible for domestic and international telecommunications services; Man. Dir STEPHEN TUSLER.

Tongasat—Friendly Islands Satellite Communications Ltd: POB 2921, Nuku'alofa; tel. 24160; fax 23322; e-mail panuve@tongasat.com; internet www.tongasat.com; 80% Tongan-owned; private co but co-operates with Govt in management and leasing of orbital satellite positions; Chair. Princess PILOLEVU TUITA; Man. Dir SEMISI PANUVE; Sec. CLIVE EDWARDS.

BROADCASTING

Radio

Tonga Broadcasting Commission: POB 36, Tungi Rd, Fasi-moe-afi, Nuku'alofa; tel. 23550; fax 28921; internet www.tonga-broadcasting.com; independent statutory board; commercially operated; manages two stations, A3Z Radio Tonga 1 and Radio Tonga 2, with programmes in Tongan and English; Gen. Man. ELENOA AMANAKI.

93FM: Pacific Partners Trust, POB 478, Nuku'alofa; tel. 23076; fax 24970; broadcasts in English, Tongan, German, Mandarin and Hindi.

A3V The Millennium Radio 2000: POB 838, Nuku'alofa; tel. 25891; fax 24195; e-mail a3v@tongatapu.net.to; broadcasts on FM; musical programmes; Gen. Man. SAM VEA.

Tonga News Association: Nuku'alofa; Pres. PESI FONUA.

Television

Oceania Broadcasting Inc started relaying US television programmes in 1991. The Tonga Broadcasting Commission launched the country's first television service in July 2000. The studios and broadcasting facilities are located near Nuku'alofa, providing local news and sport.

Oceania Broadcasting Network: POB 91, Nuku'alofa; tel. 23314; fax 23658.

Television Tonga: Fasi-moe-afi, Nuku'alofa; f. 2000; 60% of programmes in English; 40% of programmes in Tongan; Man. KATALINA TOHI.

Tonfön TV: POB 895 Nuku'alofa; e-mail stekiteki@tonfon.to; internet www.tonfon.to; part of Shoreline Group of cos; operates 5 channels.

Finance

(cap. = capital; res = reserves; dep. = deposits; m. = million; amounts in Tongan dollars)

BANKING

Australia and New Zealand Banking Group Ltd: cnr of Salote and Railway Rds, POB 910, Nuku'alofa; tel. 24944; fax 23870; e-mail anztonga@anz.com; internet www.anz.com/Tonga; Gen. Man. PAUL PELZER.

Bank of Tonga: POB 924, Nuku'alofa; tel. 23933; fax 23634; f. 1974; owned by Govt of Tonga (40%) and Westpac Banking Corpn (60%); cap. 3.0m., res 10.6m., dep. 88.6m. (Sept. 2003); Chair. ALAN WALTER; Gen. Man. MISKA TUIFA; 4 brs.

MBf Bank Ltd: POB 3118, Nuku'alofa; tel. 24600; fax 24662; e-mail info@mbfbank.to; internet www.mbfbank.to; f. 1993; 93.35% owned by MBf Asia Capital Corpn Holdings Ltd, 4.75% owned hitherto by King George Tupou V, 0.95% owned by Tonga Investments Ltd,

TONGA

0.95% owned by Tonga Co-operative Federation Society; Gen. Man. H. K. YEOH.

National Reserve Bank of Tonga: POB 25, Post Office, Nuku'alofa; tel. 24057; fax 24201; e-mail nrbt@reservebank.to; internet www.reservebank.to; f. 1989; to assume central bank functions of Bank of Tonga; issues currency; manages exchange rates and international reserves; cap. 2.0m., res 5.1m., dep. 75.0m. (June 2005); Gov. JOYCE MAFI; Chair. Crown Prince TUPOUTO'A LAVAKA.

Tonga Development Bank: Fatafehi Rd, POB 126, Nuku'alofa; tel. 23333; fax 23775; e-mail tdevbank@tdb.to; internet www.tdb.to; f. 1977; to provide credit for developmental purposes, mainly in agriculture, fishery, tourism and housing; cap. 10.5m., res 9.9m. (Dec. 2007); Man. Dir SIMIONE SEFANAIA; 5 brs.

Westpac Bank of Tonga: POB 924, Nuku'alofa; tel. 23933; fax 25889; f. 1973 as Bank of Tonga; name changed as above in 2002; 60% owned by Westpac Banking Corpn, 40% owned by Govt of Tonga; cap. 3.0m., res 10.6m., dep. 121.9m. (Sept. 2005); Gen. Man. MISHKA TU'IFUA.

Trade and Industry

DEVELOPMENT ORGANIZATIONS

Tonga Investments Ltd: POB 27, Nuku'alofa; tel. 24388; fax 24313; f. 1992; to replace Commodities Board; govt-owned; manages five subsidiary companies; Chair. Baron VAEA OF HOUMA; Man. Dir ANTHONY WAYNE MADDEN.

Tonga Association of Small Businesses: Nuku'alofa; f. 1990; to cater for the needs of small businesses; Chair. SIMI SILAPELU.

CHAMBER OF COMMERCE

Tonga Chamber of Commerce and Industry: Tungi Arcade, POB 1704, Nuku'alofa; tel. 25168; fax 26039; e-mail chamber@kalianet.to; internet www.tongachamber.org; Pres. TAPU PANUVE.

TRADE ASSOCIATIONS

Tonga Kava Council: Nuku'alofa; to promote the development of the industry both locally and abroad; Chair. TO'IMOANA TAKATAKA.

Tonga Squash Council: Nuku'alofa; promotes the development of the industry; introduced a quota system for exports in 2004; Pres. TSUTOMU NAKAO; Sec. STEVEN EDWARDS.

UTILITIES

Shoreline Power Group: POB 47, Taufa'ahau Rd, Kolofo'ou, Nuku'alofa; tel. 23311; fax 23632; provides electricity via diesel motor generation, took over operations from the Tonga Electric Power Board in 2004; CEO SOANE RAMANLAL.

Tonga Water Board: POB 92, Taufa'ahau Rd, Kolofo'ou, Nuku'alofa; tel. 23298; fax 23518; operates four urban water systems, serving about 25% of the population; Man. SAIMONE P. HELU.

CO-OPERATIVES

In April 1990 there were 78 registered co-operative societies, including the first co-operative registered under the Agricultural Organization Act.

Tonga Co-operative Federation Society: Tungi Arcade, Nuku'alofa.

TRADE UNIONS

Association of Tongatapu Squash Pumpkin Growers: Nuku'alofa; f. 1998.

Public Service Association (PSA): Nuku'alofa; Pres. FINAU TUTONE; Gen. Sec. (vacant).

Tonga Nurses' Association and Friendly Islands Teachers' Association (TNA/FITA): POB 859, Nuku'alofa; tel. and fax 23972; e-mail fita@candw.to; Pres. FINAU TUTONE; Gen. Sec. TOKANKAMEA PULEIKU.

Transport

ROADS

Total road length was estimated at 680 km in 1999, of which some 27% were all-weather paved roads. Most of the network comprises fair-weather-only dirt or coral roads.

SHIPPING

The chief ports are Nuku'alofa, on Tongatapu, and Neiafu, on Vava'u, with two smaller ports at Pangai and Niuatoputapu.

Shipping Corporation of Polynesia Ltd: Queen Salote Wharf, Vuna Rd, POB 453, Nuku'alofa; tel. 23853; fax 23250; e-mail info@olovaha.com; internet www.olovaha.com; govt-owned; regular inter-islands passenger and cargo services; Chair. 'ALISI TAUMOEPEAU; CEO JOHN JONESSE.

Uata Shipping Lines: 'Uliti Uata, POB 100, Nuku'alofa; tel. 23855; fax 23860.

Warner Pacific Line: POB 93, Nuku'alofa; tel. 21088; services to Samoa, American Samoa, Australia and New Zealand; Man. Dir MA'AKE FAKA'OSIFOLAU.

CIVIL AVIATION

Tonga is served by Fua'amotu International Airport, 22 km from Nuku'alofa, and airstrips at Vava'u, Ha'apai, Niuatoputapu, Niuafo'ou and 'Eua. Following financial failure of the country's international airline, Royal Tongan Airlines, in May 2004, a new domestic carrier, Air Peau 'o Vava'u, was established in June, to provide limited internal air services. Air New Zealand provides a regular service to Australia and New Zealand and a regional carrier, Reef Air, operates between Tonga, Niue and Fiji. The New Zealand-based low-cost airline, Pacific Blue, began two direct flights per week between Sydney and Tonga and three per week between Auckland and Tonga in 2005. In the same month the monopoly of Air Peau 'o Vava'u was ended. Following a review, Tonga's 'single airline' policy was officially terminated in April 2006 when a second carrier, Airlines Tonga, a joint venture between Air Fiji and Teta Tours (a Tongan travel company), was permitted to continue its operations on a long-term basis. In September 2006 it was announced that a government-owned agency, Tonga Airports Ltd (TAL), was to assume responsibility for the management of all airports with effect from January 2007. In November 2006 Air Peau 'o Vava'u ceased operations, and the Government sought a foreign carrier to replace it. Chathams Pacific, owned by Air Chathams of New Zealand, became Tonga's second carrier in April 2008.

Airlines Tonga: c/o Teta Tours, cnr of Railway St and Wellington St, Nuku'alofa; tel. 23690; fax 23238; e-mail tetatour@kalianet.to; internet www.airfiji.com.fj/pages.cfm/home/airlines-tonga.html; f. 2006; jt venture between Teta Tours of Tonga and Air Fiji Ltd; sole operator of domestic services in Tonga from Nov. 2006; Man SITAFOOTI 'AHO.

Chathams Pacific (The Friendly Islands Airline): POB 907, Nuku'alofa; tel. 28000; fax 23447; e-mail sales@chathamspacific.com; internet www.chathamspacific.com; f. 2008; owned by Air Chathams (New Zealand); Gen. Man. RUSSELL JENKINS.

Tourism

Tonga's attractions include scenic beauty and a pleasant climate. Visitor arrivals increased from an estimated 39,451 in 2006 to 46,040 in 2007. In 2005 revenue from the industry totalled US $11m. The majority of tourists were from New Zealand, the USA and Australia.

Tonga Tourist Association: POB 74, Nuku'alofa; tel. 23344; fax 23833; e-mail royale@kalianet.to; Pres. PAPILOA FOLIAKI; Sec. KOLOLIANA NAUFAHU.

Tonga Visitors' Bureau: Vuna Rd, POB 37, Nuku'alofa; tel. 25334; fax 23507; e-mail tvb@kalianet.to; internet www.tongaholiday.com; f. 1978; Dir VA'INGA PALU.

TRINIDAD AND TOBAGO

Introductory Survey

Location, Climate, Language, Religion, Flag, Capital

The Republic of Trinidad and Tobago consists of Trinidad, the southernmost of the Caribbean islands, and Tobago, which is 32 km (20 miles) to the north-east. Trinidad, which accounts for 94% of the total area, lies just off the north coast of Venezuela, on the South American mainland, while the country's nearest neighbour to the north is Grenada. The climate is tropical, with a dry season from January to May. Rainfall averages 1,561 mm (61.5 ins) per year. Annual average daytime temperatures range between 32°C (90°F) and 21°C (70°F). The official and main language is English, but French, Spanish, Hindi and Chinese are also spoken. In 2000 some 55% of the population were Christians, mainly Roman Catholics (30%) and Anglicans (25%), while 23% were Hindus and 6% Muslims. The national flag (proportions 3 by 5) is deep red, divided by a white-edged black diagonal stripe from upper hoist to lower fly. The capital is Port of Spain, on the island of Trinidad.

Recent History

Trinidad was first colonized by the Spanish in 1532, but was ceded to the British in 1802. Africans were transported to the island to work as slaves, but slavery was abolished in 1834. Shortage of labour led to the arrival of large numbers of Indian and Chinese immigrants, as indentured labourers, during the second half of the 19th century. In 1888 the island of Tobago, which had finally been ceded to the British in 1814, was joined with Trinidad as one political and administrative unit, and the territory remained a British colony until its independence on 31 August 1962.

Modern politics emerged in the 1930s with the formation of a trade union movement. The first political party, the People's National Movement (PNM), was founded in 1956 by Dr Eric Williams. It campaigned successfully at the elections to the Legislative Council in September 1956, and Williams became the colony's first Chief Minister in October. In 1958 the territory became a member of the newly established Federation of the West Indies, and in the following year achieved full internal self-government, with Williams as Premier. The Federation collapsed in 1961, however, following the secession of Jamaica and, subsequently, Trinidad and Tobago. After independence, in 1962, Williams was restyled Prime Minister, and the Governor became Governor-General. In 1967 Trinidad and Tobago became the first member of the Commonwealth (see p. 206) to join the Organization of American States (OAS, see p. 360).

In April 1970 the Government declared a state of emergency, following violent demonstrations, lasting several weeks, by supporters of 'Black Power', protesting against foreign influence in the country's economy and demanding solutions to the problem of unemployment, which was particularly severe among Trinidadians of African descent. On the day that the emergency was proclaimed, part of the Trinidad and Tobago Regiment (the country's army) mutinied. The mutiny collapsed after only three days, and some officers and soldiers who participated were subsequently imprisoned. At a general election in May 1971, the PNM won all 36 seats in the House of Representatives.

A new Constitution came into effect on 1 August 1976, whereby Trinidad and Tobago became a republic, within the Commonwealth. The first parliamentary elections of the republic were held in September, when the PNM won 24 of the 36 seats in the House of Representatives. The United Labour Front (ULF), a newly formed party led by trade unionists, won 10 seats, while the Democratic Action Congress (DAC) won the two Tobago seats. The former Governor-General, Ellis Clarke, was sworn in as the country's first President in December 1976. A parliamentary resolution in 1977 to grant Tobago self-rule resulted, after long resistance from the Government, in the formation in 1980 of a Tobago House of Assembly, giving the island limited autonomy. Tobago was granted full internal self-government in January 1987.

Williams died in March 1981, having consistently refused to nominate a successor. The President selected George Chambers, a deputy leader of the PNM and Minister of Agriculture, to assume the leadership on an interim basis. He was formally adopted as party leader in May and confirmed as Prime Minister. The PNM increased its majority in the House of Representatives in a general election in November. The ULF, the DAC and the Tapia House Movement, campaigning jointly as the Trinidad and Tobago National Alliance, succeeded in retaining only 10 seats. The newly formed Organization for National Reconstruction (ONR), led by a former PNM minister, Karl Hudson-Phillips, secured 22% of the total vote but no seats.

Co-operation between the four opposition parties increased, and, at local elections in August 1983, they successfully combined to inflict electoral defeat on the PNM. In August 1984 the National Alliance and the ONR established a common front, to be known as the National Alliance for Reconstruction (NAR). At elections to the Tobago House of Assembly in November 1984, the DAC achieved a convincing victory, reducing the PNM's representation to one seat. In September 1985 Arthur Napoleon Raymond (A. N. R.) Robinson, leader of the DAC and a former Deputy Prime Minister in the PNM Government, was elected leader of the NAR. In February 1986 the four parties merged to form one opposition party, still known as the NAR.

The stringent economic policies of the PNM Government undermined its public support and provoked labour unrest over wage restraint, notably in a bitter strike at Trinidad's petroleum refineries during May 1984. The next general election, held in December 1986, resulted in a decisive victory for the NAR. Robinson was appointed Prime Minister. Chambers was among those members of the PNM who lost their seats, and in January 1987 Patrick Manning, the former Minister of Energy, was appointed leader of the parliamentary opposition. In March Noor Mohammed Hassanali, formerly a senior judge, took office as President, following the retirement of Ellis Clarke.

The NAR experienced internal difficulties during 1987 and 1988. In June 1987 former members of the Tapia House Movement announced that they were to leave the NAR. In February 1988 more than 100 NAR members met to discuss the leadership of the alliance and the direction of its policies. Two cabinet ministers (including Basdeo Panday, the Minister of External Affairs) and one junior minister were subsequently dismissed from the Government. All three were former members of the ULF, which derived most of its support from the 'East' Indian community. Despite their accusations of racism against the NAR leadership, they were expelled from the party in October. In April 1989 Panday and the other dissidents announced the formation of a left-wing opposition party, the United National Congress (UNC). In July 1990 Panday was elected leader of the UNC at the party's first national assembly. In September President Hassanali confirmed Panday as the leader of the parliamentary opposition, replacing Manning. The UNC, with six seats in the House of Representatives, replaced the PNM, with only three seats, as the principal opposition party.

In July 1990 members of the Jamaat al Muslimeen, a small Muslim group led by Yasin Abu Bakr, attempted to seize power. The rebels destroyed the capital's police headquarters and took control of the parliament building and the state television station. Some 45 people were taken hostage, among them Robinson and several cabinet ministers. The rebels demanded Robinson's resignation, elections within 90 days and an amnesty for those taking part in the attempted coup. On 28 July a state of emergency was declared and a curfew was imposed: police preoccupation with the political crisis had resulted in widespread looting in the capital. On 31 July the Prime Minister, who had sustained gunshot wounds, was released from captivity by the rebels. On 1 August the attempted coup, in which some 30 people were killed and another 500 injured, ended after the rebels surrendered unconditionally. An amnesty pardoning them, signed by the President of the Senate, Joseph Emmanuel Carter, in his capacity as acting Head of State, was proclaimed invalid, on the grounds that it had been signed under duress. In mid-August Bakr and his followers were charged with treason, a capital offence.

In November 1991 the imprisoned Jamaat al Muslimeen rebels won an appeal to the Judicial Committee of the Privy Council in the United Kingdom (the final court of appeal for

Trinidad and Tobago), which ruled that the validity of the presidential pardon issued during the attempted coup in July 1990 should be determined before the rebels were brought to trial, and that an application for their release should be heard by the High Court of Trinidad and Tobago immediately. On 30 June 1992 the High Court ruled that the pardon was valid, and ordered the immediate release of the 114 defendants. The Government announced that it would pursue all legal means of appeal against the decision, which it deemed to be of great constitutional significance. In March 1993 delays in the payment of compensation to the rebels, for what the High Court ruled was their wrongful imprisonment, led Bakr to threaten 'action' against the Government. In October the Court of Appeal ruled to uphold the decision of the High Court. In October 1994 the Privy Council ruled to overturn the decisions of the High Court and the Court of Appeal, declaring the pardon invalid. As a result, the Jamaat al Muslimeen would be unable to claim compensation for wrongful imprisonment. However, it was also ruled that to rearrest the rebels and try them for offences committed during the insurrection would constitute an abuse of the legal process. However, the Jamaat al Muslimeen was subsequently awarded some TT $2.1m. in compensation for the destruction of its buildings following the coup attempt.

A general election, held in December 1991, resulted in a decisive victory for the PNM. The implementation of unpopular austerity measures was widely acknowledged as the main cause of the defeat of the NAR, and Robinson resigned as leader. A notable feature of the elections was the re-emergence of ethnic voting, with the vast majority of the votes divided between the Afro-Trinidadian-orientated PNM and the largely Indo-Trinidadian UNC, which secured 13 seats in the House of Representatives. Patrick Manning was sworn in as Prime Minister the day after the ballot. A promise made by the PNM in its election manifesto to settle a public sector claim for salaries and allowances withheld during the austerity programme of the outgoing NAR Government was honoured in the budget submitted to Parliament in January 1992. However, the Government's continued failure to effect a settlement led to escalating industrial unrest. In February 1993 several thousand public sector employees joined protests against the delay in payments and at the Government's plans to restructure inefficient state enterprises, involving some 2,600 redundancies. In early 1994 a government offer of a settlement of the public sector claim was rejected by the majority of employees. In mid-1995 the Government introduced a new plan to settle the claim, involving the issue of bonds with tax credits, which was accepted by the Trinidad and Tobago Unified Teachers' Association. However, industrial action resumed in September, when some 25,000 public sector employees observed a 24-hour strike in support of demands for a more favourable settlement. In March 1996, following a further 48-hour stoppage, agreement was finally reached on a settlement involving the issue, over a period of four years, of bonds worth TT $1,000m. Meanwhile, industrial unrest persisted in opposition to continuing government plans for the rationalization and privatization of unproductive public utilities.

The NAR retained control of the Tobago House of Assembly following elections in December 1992. In July 1993 the Government and the Tobago House of Assembly agreed to begin discussions concerning the upgrading of Tobago's constitutional status. Measures subsequently submitted for consideration by the legislature included the establishment of an executive council on Tobago and the appointment of an independent senator to represent the island.

Appeals for the restoration of capital punishment, prompted by growing public concern at the increasing rate of murder and violent crime in Trinidad and Tobago, gained considerable impetus in August 1993 following the murder of the country's Prison Commissioner. Warrants issued shortly afterwards for the execution of two convicted murderers were suspended following protests by human rights organization Amnesty International. In July 1994 Trinidad and Tobago conducted its first execution since 1979. However, the convicted murderer, Glen Ashby, was hanged only minutes before a facsimile transmission from the Privy Council in the United Kingdom was sent to the Court of Appeal in Trinidad granting a stay of execution. Reportedly, an undertaking had been given by the Attorney-General, Keith Sobion, that the execution would not be conducted until all applications for a stay had been exhausted. In July 1994 the Privy Council issued a conservatory order whereby, in the case of two men due to be heard by the Trinidad Court of Appeal, should their execution be ordered, it could not be conducted until the case had been heard by the Privy Council itself. This decision provoked protest from the Chief Justice of Trinidad and Tobago, who accused the Privy Council of preempting the Court of Appeal's exercise of its jurisdiction. Subsequently, the Government announced its intention to introduce legislation establishing the Court of Appeal as the final appeal court for criminal cases, pending regional agreement on a Caribbean appeal court. In March 1995 an international jurists' inquiry found that the execution of Ashby was illegal and that sufficient evidence existed to cite Sobion for contempt of court. However, the report was non-binding, and no action was taken.

In July 1995 the Speaker of the House of Representatives, Occah Seapaul, was accused by the Government of bringing her office into disrepute; an unsuccessful attempt by Seapaul to sue a former business partner, Victor Jattan, had led the court to question the veracity of her testimony. Seapaul refused to accede to demands for her resignation. Lacking the necessary two-thirds' majority in the legislature to unseat Seapaul, the Government introduced draft legislation to amend the Constitution in order to allow the removal of the Speaker by means of a simple majority. The proposal was approved by the Senate, but debate of the bill was obstructed in the House of Representatives by Seapaul, who adjourned the session and ordered the suspension of the leader of the House, Ken Valley, for six months, on a charge of contempt. In August acting President Joseph Emmanuel Carter declared a limited state of emergency in the capital, thus empowering the Government to place Seapaul under house arrest and facilitating the prompt approval in the House of Representatives of the constitutional amendment. The state of emergency was ended after four days, and Seapaul was released from detention, having agreed to vacate her position pending a High Court ruling on constitutional motions filed by her against the Government.

A general election was held in November 1995. The PNM and the UNC each secured 17 seats, while the NAR won the remaining two. Following discussions between the leader of the UNC, Basdeo Panday, and Robinson, who had resumed the leadership of the NAR in October, a coalition Government was established, with Panday as Prime Minister. The Cabinet included Robinson as Minister Extraordinaire and Adviser to the Cabinet, with special responsibility for Tobago. It was widely understood that the NAR's support for the UNC in forming the Government had been dependent on undertakings concerning the prompt upgrading of Tobago's constitutional status.

The NAR secured 10 of the 12 elective seats in elections to the Tobago House of Assembly in December 1996; the PNM obtained one seat, and the remaining seat was won by an independent candidate.

In mid-February 1997 Robinson was elected President to replace Noor Mohammed Hassanali on his retirement from the position in March. However, the appointment (by an electoral college comprising the members of the Senate and the House of Representatives) was, for the first time, contested: traditionally, all parties support the nominee of the Government for the presidency, which is a ceremonial position only. On this occasion, however, the PNM objected to the Government's nomination of Robinson, owing to his status as an active politician with party affiliation.

In March 1998 militia of the Jamaat al Muslimeen prevented employees of the Ministry of Works and Transport from establishing a barrier around land inhabited by the Jamaat al Muslimeen, in order to halt further expansion of settlements. Bakr denounced the Government for attempting to provoke a violent reaction from the militants. A fence was eventually constructed after Government employees resumed their task, under the protection of the police force. In December 1999 the Jamaat al Muslimeen repeated their warning that they would not permit building work to take place adjacent to their headquarters.

In January 2000 Hanraj Sumairsingh, a member of the UNC, was found murdered. It was subsequently reported that Sumairsingh had written to the Prime Minister several times regarding threats by the Minister of Local Government, Dhanraj Singh, following Sumairsingh's revelation of alleged corruption in the unemployment relief programme administered by Singh's ministry. In October Singh was dismissed from his government post and replaced by Carlos John. Singh was charged with the murder of Sumairsingh, but in October 2003 he was found not guilty of ordering the killing.

In October 1997 it was announced that the Government had approved a proposal by the Attorney-General to expedite executions of persons convicted of murder, whereby the Government would allow only 18 months for completion of a hearing before the UN Human Rights Committee (UNHRC) and the Inter-American Commission on Human Rights (IACHR), in the event of the Privy Council rejecting an appeal. The Government hoped, by imposing a time limit on the UNHRC and the IACHR, to complete the appeals process within the five years allowed by the Privy Council as the maximum length of time between sentencing and execution. In April 1998 the Government refused to grant leave for the hearing of appeals against the death penalty made by nine men convicted of murder (the so-called 'Chadee gang'). The nine subsequently appealed to the UNHRC. In May 1998 the Government announced that it was withdrawing from the UNHRC and the IACHR, as neither body had been able to guarantee to hear appeals within the 18 months requested by the Government. Many Caribbean states expressed their support for Trinidad and Tobago, although the opposition PNM criticized the withdrawals as damaging the islands' international reputation, while the Roman Catholic Church and Amnesty International also criticized the move on humanitarian grounds. In June 1998 the IACHR ordered Trinidad and Tobago not to execute five people whose cases it had been scheduled to review; however, the authorities announced that the IACHR no longer had any jurisdiction over the cases, and that the executions would be carried out.

In October 1998, in what was considered a landmark case, the Privy Council rejected the appeals of two convicted murderers, who had claimed that their constitutional rights had been infringed by the conditions in which they had been imprisoned. In January 1999, in a further landmark judgment, the Privy Council ruled that, even though Trinidad and Tobago had withdrawn from the IACHR, two convicted killers could not be executed while their appeals were being considered by the Commission, since the appeals had been made prior to the withdrawal. In April the Privy Council ordered the release of three prisoners who had spent almost four years awaiting execution.

In May 1999 the Privy Council rejected an appeal for clemency made by the nine members of the Chadee gang, who had claimed that they were being held in cruel and degrading conditions. However, the Privy Council granted a stay of execution on the grounds that the Court of Appeal in Trinidad and Tobago had been hurried into a decision by the Government, in order to allow time to consider the legality of hanging as a means of administering the death penalty. At the end of May the Privy Council ruled that Trinidad and Tobago could legally proceed with the nine executions, which, despite international protests, were carried out in early June.

In April 2000 the Government announced that it was to withdraw from the first optional protocol to the International Covenant on Civil and Political Rights, following a judgment from the UNHRC that Trinidad and Tobago could not continue to adhere to the resolution while differing on the subject of the death sentence. The announcement attracted widespread international condemnation. The Government, however, stated that the withdrawal was intended purely to prevent condemned murderers from addressing lengthy appeals to the UNHRC. The Government also announced the introduction of a constitutional amendment, which would allow executions to proceed before the IACHR and the UNHRC had ruled on the cases. On 14 February 2001, at a Caribbean Community and Common Market (CARICOM, see p. 196) summit in Barbados, the leaders of 11 Caribbean states signed an agreement to establish the Caribbean Court of Justice (CCJ). The Court was to replace the Privy Council as the final court of appeal, and was to be based in Trinidad and Tobago. The CCJ would be financed by a US $100m. trust fund raised by the Caribbean Development Bank. In February Parliament voted to accept the authority of the new Court to settle CARICOM matters. The Court was eventually inaugurated on 16 April 2005. However, owing to UNC opposition to adopting the appellate jurisdiction of the CCJ, the new Court was only to have jurisdiction over CARICOM matters.

At a general election in December 2000 the UNC secured 19 of the 36 seats in the House of Representatives, while the PNM won 16 seats and the NAR secured one. Panday was inaugurated as Prime Minister for the second time. At elections to the Tobago House of Assembly, held on 29 January 2001, the PNM secured eight of the 12 elective seats, ending the traditional domination of the House by the NAR, which obtained the remaining four seats.

The Government was beset by allegations of corruption in mid-2001 regarding the receipt of payments in exchange for supporting tenders for contracts with the state-owned oil company, Petrotin, and irregularities in the accounts of the North West Regional Health Authority (NWRHA). Minister of Communications and Information Technology Ralph Maraj threatened to resign if Panday did not act to curb corruption. Panday responded by relieving Maraj and Panday's party rival, Attorney-General Ramesh Maharaj, of some of their responsibilities. Maharaj, with Maraj and two other cabinet members, formed a faction within the UNC. This faction, which was known as Team Unity, subsequently gained control of the party's national executive. Despite attempts by Team Unity to prevent UNC constituent elections from taking place on 9 September, supporters of Panday were victorious in 30 of the 34 constituencies.

In October 2001 it was confirmed that Maharaj and the Minister of Food Production and Marine Resources, Trevor Sudama, had been dismissed from their government posts for their continued criticism of the Prime Minister. Maraj later also resigned from his position. The Government's legislative majority was effectively lost when the three ministers subsequently formed a coalition with the PNM and the NAR and obstructed attempts by Panday to approve the budget. Amid increasing pressure from the opposition for his resignation and threats of a vote of 'no confidence' in his Government, on 10 October Panday asked President Robinson to dissolve Parliament in preparation for a general election, to be held on 10 December.

Meanwhile, in September 2001 an independently published report into the allegations of corruption at the NWRHA recommended the dismissal of four senior executives. In November Dr Tim Gopeesingh, the former Chairman of the NWRHA, admitted to charges of fraud in relation to a cheque for US $50,000 issued to Panday by Gopeesingh in his capacity as leader of UNC's Northwest Liaison Office, at the time of the 2000 elections. In December Panday and other government ministers were implicated in alleged instances of misconduct relating to contracts given to the US-owned power company Inncogen Ltd to supply electricity to four new factories in Trinidad, which had failed to be built.

In the general election of 10 December 2001 the UNC and the PNM secured an equal number (18) of seats in the House of Representatives. The two party leaders reached an agreement on political collaboration in government, although not a coalition arrangement, that would allow the President to appoint the Prime Minister and Speaker in the House of Representatives and to reform the electoral process. However, following the appointment of Manning as Prime Minister and PNM nominee Max Richards as Speaker of the House of Representatives, the UNC withdrew from the post-election agreement.

Panday's refusal to be sworn in as leader of the opposition and to agree to elect a Speaker in the House of Representatives (Richards had withdrawn from the position after his impartiality was questioned) prevented the convening of the new Parliament in early January 2002. Panday announced the UNC's intention to prevent Parliament from sitting for the next six months, thereby forcing Manning to call a new election, according to the provisions of the Constitution. Following concern expressed by the business community at the effect of the political impasse on the country's economy, at the end of January Manning and Panday met for discussions. However, neither these meetings, nor negotiations mediated by CARICOM leaders in February, provided a solution to the dispute. Later in February Manning agreed to put the UNC's proposals for an executive comprising equal numbers of PNM and UNC representatives to the PNM party council. The UNC accused the Prime Minister of deliberately delaying the process. In the following month controversy also arose over Robinson's continued occupation of the position of President. His tenure expired on 18 March, but, as the legislature had not been convened, Robinson obtained Manning's permission to remain in office. The first session of the new House of Representatives was reconvened in early April; however, owing to the failure of the two parties to elect a Speaker, proceedings were adjourned.

Meanwhile, in March 2002 Panday's former finance minister, Brian Kuei Tung, and several senior government officials and prominent businessmen were arrested on charges of fraud and misbehaviour in public office with regard to the construction of a new terminal at Piarco Airport. Manning ordered a Commission of Inquiry into the project. In July the Commission of Inquiry accused two more UNC members of parliament of criminal activity. Former Minister of Works and Transport Carlos John was accused of ignoring tender procedures during his time in office and in the same month cocaine worth US $246,000 and two missiles were apparently found at the home of the former housing minister Sadiq Baksh. Panday was also questioned by the authorities regarding his failure to declare a joint bank account held with his wife in the United Kingdom, and in September he was officially charged with fraud. In April 2006 Panday was found guilty of failing fully to declare his income while Prime Minister. He was sentenced to two years' imprisonment.

A report by the Commission of Inquiry into the Elections and Boundaries Commission in June 2002 documented countless flaws in its practices and recommended that all its members should resign. However, its members failed to relinquish their posts, despite Manning's pledge to implement the recommended reforms. In July Manning announced that if Parliament failed to elect a Speaker by 31 October, further elections would be held. Manning made a final attempt to convene Parliament in August; however, the members again failed to elect a Speaker, some UNC representatives resorting deliberately to voting against their own candidate. Manning subsequently dissolved Parliament and announced that elections would take place on 7 October. In September a new political party, the Citizens' Alliance, was formed. It was led by a former PNM finance minister, Wendell Mottley, and aimed to prevent another tied election.

In elections held in October 2002 the PNM won 20 seats in the House of Representatives, while the UNC secured 16 seats. Manning again acceded to the office of Prime Minister, stating his intention to seek solutions to issues that divided the nation's political and racial communities. He appointed a new Cabinet, which included most of the members of the previous administration in their former positions. One of the new Government's first acts was the proposal of legislation aimed at preventing abduction and acts of terrorism, in addition to a planned increase in penalties for acts of corruption committed by holders of public office.

The Government's preferred candidate, Maxwell Richards, was elected President on 14 February 2003. In August the Government inaugurated a Committee on Race Relations to promote understanding and mutual respect among the various sectors of the population. In November Manning carried out a cabinet reorganization; notable among the reallocation of portfolios was the appointment of Howard Lee Chin, hitherto Minister of National Security, to the newly established tourism portfolio. The new ministry had been created in an attempt to increase growth in the sector.

Despite government efforts, in 2003 and 2004 there were increasing concerns over the continuing rise in crime rates, particularly kidnapping and murder. The number of kidnappings for ransom totalled 51 in 2004, compared with 27 in 2002, while the number of murders rose from 172 in 2002 to 260 in 2004. In June 2003 the Senate approved legislation imposing a minimum 25-year prison sentence on those convicted of kidnap. In an effort to address the rising levels of violent crime, in February 2004 the Government initiated a joint military-police unit. Manning pledged to invest in new technology to increase intelligence and surveillance capabilities.

In a landmark ruling, in November 2003 the Privy Council ruled that Trinidad and Tobago's mandatory death sentence for convicted murderers was unconstitutional and inconsistent with the country's international obligations. The ruling followed an appeal brought by Balkissoon Roodal, who had been sentenced to death in July 1999. However, in July 2004 the Privy Council overturned its earlier ruling. A panel of nine judges, rather than the customary five, decreed that the Trinidadian Constitution did not allow outside intervention to abolish the mandatory death penalty. However, the judges further ruled that this would not apply to the estimated 100 prisoners who had benefited from the November judgment.

In October 2004 Manning announced that the Integrity Commission would investigate allegations that the Minister of Housing, Dr Keith Rowley, had used materials designated for a state hospital for a private sector project. However, the Prime Minister dismissed opposition demands that Rowley resign and in February 2008 the Commission ruled that it had found no evidence to pursue the allegations. In April 2005 a parliamentary inquiry cleared Rowley of assaulting a UNC member of parliament in the tearoom of the legislature in the previous September. However, the UNC criticized the inquiry and urged members not to sign the report exonerating Rowley. Two UNC deputies, Gillian Lucky and Fuad Khan, responded by declaring themselves to be independent members of parliament. In April it was disclosed that an independent tribunal was to investigate allegations that Chief Justice Satnarine Sharma had sought to pervert the course of justice. The Attorney-General and the Director of Public Prosecutions claimed that Sharma had attempted to prevent a doctor being charged with the murder of his wife. Sharma subsequently filed for a judicial review of Manning's actions, claiming that the Prime Minister's recommendation for an investigation into the allegations was biased.

Despite continuing concerns about the rise in criminal activity and allegations of government corruption, at an election to the Tobago House of Assembly in January 2005 the governing PNM increased its majority from eight to 11 of the 12 seats, while the NAR, which had campaigned on a pro-devolution platform, secured just one legislative seat.

Allegations of political corruption persisted throughout 2005. In May corruption charges were filed against Panday, his wife, and the former UNC Minister of Works and Transport, Carlos John, in relation to the construction project at Piarco Airport. In November former Minister of Works and Transport Franklin Khan was charged with six counts of corruption, while in January 2006 Minister of Energy and Energy Industries Eric Williams was charged with accepting bribes from a potential contractor. Both Williams and Khan denied the charges. Williams stepped down from government and responsibility for energy and energy industries was subsequently added to the portfolio of the Minister of Public Administration and Information, Dr Lenny Saith. However, seven charges of misconduct against Williams were dismissed in December 2007, while the case against Khan was proceeding through the courts in mid-2008.

In July–October 2005 five bombs exploded in Port of Spain, injuring at least 30 people. The bombs were believed to be criminal, rather than terrorist, attacks; police suggested that they may have been planted to distract attention from drugs-related activities. Following the fourth explosion five people, including Yasin Abu Bakr, were arrested, but were subsequently released without being charged. The Jamaat al Muslimeen denied responsibility for the attacks. The authorities' perceived failure to find the perpetrators prompted widespread anger throughout the country. Mounting public pressure on the Government to curb the deterioration in law and order culminated on 22 October in a demonstration in the capital, attended by thousands of protesters.

In September 2005 Manning pledged to reduce unemployment, which, he claimed, was a major cause of the high crime rate. He also announced that he had invited the British Metropolitan Police Service and the USA's Federal Bureau of Investigation to establish specialist units in Trinidad and Tobago. (Some 39 police officers from the United Kingdom arrived in April 2006. They were expected to be incorporated into the Special Anti-Crime Unit for at least two years.) In October 2005 the Minister of National Security, Martin Joseph, admitted that the murder rate and the rate of detection were unacceptable. He declared that the increase in drugs- and arms-trafficking was largely responsible for the rise in kidnappings and killings. The total number of murders in 2005 rose to 389, while the rate of detection declined from 44% in 2002 to 21% in mid-2005. Some 80% of murders were committed with illegal guns. The number of murders in 2006 stood at 368.

In November 2005 the Government announced a number of initiatives aimed at stemming the rise in violent crime. Proposed reforms to the police force increased Parliament's role in selecting members of the Police Service Commission and the Police Commissioner, while removing the Prime Minister's right to veto the appointment of the latter. The reforms also conferred on the Commissioner of Police greater powers of discipline and management. Another proposal was the establishment of a court expressly for hearing cases involving gun-related crime and kidnapping. Furthermore, legislation would prevent kidnappers and alleged perpetrators of more than three violent crimes from securing bail, and allow suspected kidnappers to be held for up to 60 days before being charged.

In November 2005 Yasin Abu Bakr was rearrested and charged with seditious speech, incitement and terrorism, after allegedly preaching a sermon that called for a war on affluent Muslims who refused to pay *zakat*, a tithe for the poor, to his organization. In February 2006 the Attorney-General sought high court authorization for the state to confiscate 12 properties from members of the Jamaat al Muslimeen in compensation for damage caused during the attempted coup in 1990.

In July 2006 Chief Justice Satnarine Sharma was again accused of seeking to pervert the course of justice; on this occasion as a result of allegations by Chief Magistrate Sherman McNicolls that Sharma had attempted to influence his verdict in the trial of Basdeo Panday earlier that year (see above). Despite Sharma's protestations that the allegations were politically motivated, the Privy Council ruled that he be arrested and prosecuted. However, at the trial in March 2007 McNicolls declined to testify in court and consequently the case was dismissed. Sharma resumed his duties later the same month. However, in May a three-member tribunal was established to consider the permanent removal of Sharma, who in June was once again suspended from his duties. At the end of December the tribunal cleared the Chief Justice of any wrongdoing. Sharma retired from the role in January 2008.

In September 2006 Winston Dookeran announced his resignation as political leader of the UNC to launch a new political organization, to be known as Congress of the People (COP). Some 20,000 people attended the launch rally; however, it remained to be seen whether the new party would present a serious challenge to the UNC and PPM at the forthcoming legislative elections.

At a general election held on 5 November 2007 the PNM secured 45.9% of the votes cast and 26 seats in the enlarged 41-seat House of Assembly. The main opposition party, now known as the United National Congress—Alliance (UNC—A), won the remaining 15 seats and 29.8% of votes. Despite securing 22.6% of votes, the COP failed to secure a seat in the legislature. Some 66% of the registered electorate participated in the ballot. However, the PNM did not gain the two-thirds' parliamentary majority necessary in order to gain legislative approval for proposed constitutional reforms, including the creation of an executive president. Manning continued as Prime Minister but relinquished the finance portfolio, assigning it to Karen Nunez-Tesheira. He introduced 12 other new ministers, including Paula Gopee-Scoon as Minister of Foreign Affairs, and appointed Brigid Annisette-George as Attorney-General. Manning committed his administration to diversifying the economy, aiding growth in the commodities, information technology and tourism sectors, in order for Trinidad and Tobago to achieve Developed Nation status by 2020. He was also faced with the problem of increasing public concern over the level of crime; the number of murders in 2007 was subsequently recorded as the highest on record at 395. After the election defeat, Basdeo Panday replaced Kamla Persad-Bissessar as leader of the UNC—A. In February 2008 Maxwell Richards was re-elected unopposed for a second term as President.

Investigations into allegations of corruption involving Panday continued in 2007 and 2008. In December 2007 Panday, his wife, Carlos John and businessman Ishwar Galbaransingh were committed to stand trial over charges relating to the construction project at Piarco Airport. Panday was accused of receiving a £25,000 bribe from John and Galbaransingh in return for awarding the contract to the latter's construction company. In early April 2008 the Privy Council ruled that Panday must face a retrial regarding false financial declarations between 1997 and 1999. Panday had claimed that the magistrate involved in the original proceedings had been biased; the Court of Appeal overturned the convictions and ordered a retrial although Panday had appealed the decision at the Privy Council.

In late April 2008 Manning dismissed Dr Keith Rowley as Minister of Trade and Industry, owing to his 'unacceptable behaviour' at a meeting of the Urban Development Corporation of Trinidad and Tobago. However, Rowley claimed that the action had been taken because of his suggestion of possible corruption in the Corporation's financial operations. He was replaced by Dr Lenny Saith.

In July 1991 Trinidad and Tobago ratified with Venezuela a joint declaration on maritime boundaries, under which Trinidad and Tobago's maritime boundary was to be extended from 200 nautical miles (370 km) to 350 nautical miles (648 km). Relations with Venezuela deteriorated in late 1996 and early 1997 owing to a series of incidents involving Trinidadian fishing vessels. In May 1997 a two-year fishing agreement was completed for approval by both Governments. However, tensions were revived later in the month after 15 Trinidadian fishermen were arrested by Venezuelan coast-guards. The Trinidadian Government referred the issue to the OAS and, in response, Venezuela briefly withdrew its ambassador from the country. A revised two-year treaty was endorsed in December, permitting an unlimited number of vessels from each country into a shared fishing area. A joint fisheries commission was also re-established. In October 1998 it was agreed that the two countries would negotiate treaties on free trade and on co-operation against drugs-trafficking. In August 2003 the two countries signed a memorandum of understanding on the joint exploitation of cross-border oil and gas fields. Negotiations recommenced in January 2006. The discussions stalled temporarily following Trinidad and Tobago's refusal to sign Venezuela's PetroCaribe energy accord, launched the previous year, which offered oil concessions and favourable financing terms to Caribbean nations. The accord was expected adversely to affect, at least initially, Trinidad and Tobago's energy sector. However, negotiations resumed in March, and in February 2007 an agreement was reached on the division of the cross-border Loran natural gas field, which apportioned some 75% of the gas to Venezuela.

In July 2000 talks were held to find a solution to the maritime border dispute between Trinidad and Barbados. Despite further talks being held over the next two years, little progress was made. In January 2004 the Prime Minister of Trinidad and Tobago indicated he would refer the matter to CARICOM. Bilateral relations deteriorated in February after several Barbadian fishermen were arrested in Trinidad and Tobago's waters; Barbados subsequently imposed economic sanctions on imports from Trinidad and Tobago, which they were later ordered to lift by CARICOM's Council for Trade and Economic Development. Meanwhile, in February Barbados announced plans to seek UN arbitration under the UN Convention on the Law of the Sea. This move was criticized by the Trinidad and Tobago Government, which claimed it undermined the proposed CCJ. None the less, hearings on the boundary dispute commenced in October 2005 at the International Dispute Resolution Centre and in April 2006 a decision was handed down establishing a median line between the two exclusive economic zones. The Centre rejected Trinidad and Tobago's claim to a large area to the south-east of Barbados and instructed the two countries to negotiate a fishing agreement for a large disputed area to the north of Tobago, which would remain in Trinidad and Tobago's possession. Progress on the agreement stalled in mid-2008 pending a study by the Food and Agriculture Organization but the Prime Ministers of the two countries expressed their commitment to achieve a resolution by the end of that year.

Government

Legislative power is vested in the bicameral Parliament, consisting of the Senate, with 31 members, and the House of Representatives, with 41 members. Representatives are elected for a five-year term by universal adult suffrage. The President is a constitutional Head of State, chosen by an electoral college of members of both the Senate and the House of Representatives. Members of the Senate are nominated by the President in consultation with, and on the advice of, the Prime Minister and the Leader of the Opposition. The Cabinet has effective control of the Government and is responsible to Parliament. Tobago Island was granted its own House of Assembly in 1980 and given full internal self-government in January 1987. The Tobago House of Assembly has 15 members, of whom 12 are elected; the remaining three members are selected by the majority party.

Defence

As assessed at November 2007, the defence forces consisted of an army estimated at 2,000 men, and a coastguard of 700, with 25 patrol craft. Included in the coastguard is an air force of 50. The defence budget for 2007 was an estimated TT $350m. (US $56m.).

Economic Affairs

In 2006, according to estimates by the World Bank, Trinidad and Tobago's gross national income (GNI), measured at average 2004–06 prices, was US $17,461m., equivalent to US $13,340 per head (or US $16,260 on an international purchasing-power parity basis). During 1996–2006, it was estimated, the population increased at an average annual rate of 0.3%, while gross domestic product (GDP) per head increased, in real terms, by an average of 6.9% per year. Overall GDP increased, in real terms, at an average annual rate of 7.3% in 1996–2006; according to the World Bank, economic growth was 12.5% in 2006.

Agriculture (including forestry, hunting and fishing) contributed 0.6% of GDP in 2006, and employed 4.4% (excluding unclassified activities) of the working population in the same year. The principal cash crops are sugar cane, coffee, cocoa and citrus fruits. The fishing sector is small-scale, but is an important local source of food. During 1995–2005, according to the World

TRINIDAD AND TOBAGO

Bank, agricultural GDP declined by an average of 1.4% per year. The sector contracted by 21.0% in 2004 and by 0.6% in 2005.

Industry (including mining and quarrying, manufacturing, construction and power) provided 59.8% of GDP in 2006, and employed 30.9% (excluding undefined activities) of the working population in the same year. During 1995–2005, according to the World Bank, industrial GDP increased at an average annual rate of 8.5%. Industrial GDP increased by 10.0% in 2005.

The petroleum sector provided an estimated 45.0% of GDP in 2006. In that year the mining and quarrying sector (including petroleum production) employed some 3.5% of the working population (excluding activities undefined). The petroleum industry is the principal sector of Trinidad and Tobago's economy. According to the IMF, the GDP of the petroleum sector increased at an estimated annual average rate of 15.0% during 2001–05; the sector grew by 8.2% in 2005. Trinidad has the world's largest deposits of natural asphalt, and substantial reserves of natural gas. In 2006 Trinidad and Tobago was the world's second largest producer (after Chile) of methanol, a by-product of natural gas. Cement, limestone and sulphur are also mined.

Manufacturing contributed an estimated 5.7% of GDP in 2006 and employed 9.5% (excluding undefined activities) of the working population in the same year. During 1995–2005 manufacturing GDP increased at an average annual rate of 7.2%. Manufacturing GDP increased by 8.6% in 2005.

Almost all of the country's energy is derived from natural gas (it provided 99.5% of total electricity production in 2004). Natural gas is also used as fuel for the country's two petroleum refineries and several manufacturing plants. Imports of fuel products comprised 34.8% of the value of merchandise imports in 2005. In the previous year exports of gas accounted for an estimated 31.7% of total exports, while exports of petroleum and petroleum products accounted for an estimated 26.3%. Mineral fuels and lubricants together contributed 70.2% of export earnings in 2005.

The services sector contributed an estimated 39.6% of GDP in 2006 and employed some 64.7% (excluding unclassified activities) of the working population in the same year. Tourism is a major source of foreign exchange; in 2005 receipts from tourism totalled US $661m. and some 463,191 foreign tourists visited the islands. However, there were fears that the increasing rates of violent crime would adversely affect tourism revenues. In February 2004 Prime Minister Manning announced a series of initiatives to promote leisure and 'eco-tourism' in Tobago and business tourism in Trinidad. According to the World Bank, the GDP of the services sector increased at an average annual rate of 4.3% in 1995–2005. Sectoral GDP increased by 2.9% in 2005.

In 2007 Trinidad and Tobago recorded a visible trade surplus of a projected US $4,399m., and there was a surplus of US $1,200m. on the current account of the balance of payments. In 2005 the principal source of imports was the USA (28.7%); other major suppliers were Brazil and Venezuela. The USA was also the principal market for exports (58.3%) in that year; other significant purchasers were Jamaica and Barbados. The principal exports in 2005 were mineral fuels and lubricants (70.2%), chemicals (19.0%) and basic manufactures (4.2%). The principal imports were mineral fuels and lubricants (34.8%), machinery and transport equipment (26.4%) and basic manufactures (12.6%).

In 2005/06 there was an estimated budgetary surplus of TT $7,426.7m., equivalent to 6.5% of GDP. At the end of 2004 Trinidad and Tobago's total external debt was US $2,652m., of which US $1,197m. was long-term public debt. In 2004 the cost of debt-servicing was equivalent to 5.4% of the value of exports of goods and services. The annual rate of inflation averaged 4.5% in 1996–2006. Consumer prices increased by an estimated average of 7.9% in 2007. An estimated 6.2% of the labour force was unemployed in 2006.

Trinidad and Tobago is a member of the Caribbean Community and Common Market (CARICOM, see p. 196), the Inter-American Development Bank (IDB, see p. 308), the Latin American Economic System (SELA, see p. 413), and the Association of Caribbean States (ACS, see p. 411). In November 2005 a bilateral free trade agreement was signed with Costa Rica, enabling duty-free access to markets for more than 90% of goods. Trinidad and Tobago was one of the six founder members of CARICOM's Caribbean Single Market and Economy (CSME), which was inaugurated on 1 January 2006. It was anticipated that the CSME would facilitate the free movement of goods, services and labour throughout most of the CARICOM region. The CSME was scheduled to be fully operational by 31 December 2008.

The discovery of significant petroleum and natural gas deposits in the 1990s, combined with substantial foreign investment, meant that by the early 21st century the energy sector was a major contributor to Trinidad and Tobago's economy. The development of a major liquefied natural gas (LNG) plant at Point Fortin from 2001 would eventually make Trinidad and Tobago one of the world's leading suppliers of LNG. In April 2003 Atlantic LNG's third train was commissioned and a fourth train, the largest single gas train in the world, with an annual capacity of 5.2m. metric tons, began operations in December 2005. In September 2003 BP Energy Company of Trinidad and Tobago (formerly BP Amoco) announced the discovery of the country's largest ever natural gas deposit. Substantial foreign investment allowed increased industrialization, which, combined with high international fuel prices, contributed to rapid economic expansion and a substantial trade surplus between 2002–06. However, the strong economic performance of the energy sector was not representative of the economy as a whole. In early 2007 a planned US $1,500m. aluminum smelter project (to be run by US company Alcoa) was cancelled by the Government amid environmental fears. If the project had proceeded, it was expected to create some 800 jobs and produce on average 375 metric tons of aluminium annually. Meanwhile, concerns about rising crime rates damaged investor confidence, increased security costs for businesses and threatened the tourism industry. Furthermore, there was concern over the standard of public services and infrastructure, as well as the increasing public sector debt. The economy has shown signs of diversifying, with the energy sector growing at a slower rate than the non-energy sector in 2007. This was predominantly due to expansion in manufacturing, finance and real estate as a result of continued construction growth. The President stated in early 2008 that diversification must continue with a particular focus on social growth, education and a more highly skilled labour force. After reaching 12.0% in 2006, GDP growth decreased to an estimated 7.0% in 2007, with forecasts anticipating the decline to continue during 2008 with a projected growth rate of 5.7%. The decline in economic growth was accompanied by a concomitant fall in the rate of inflation, from 9.1% in 2006 to 7.6% in 2007 and a projected 6.8% in 2008.

Education

Primary and secondary education is provided free of charge. Attendance at school is officially compulsory for children between five and 12 years of age. Primary education begins at the age of five and lasts for seven years. Secondary education, beginning at 12 years of age, lasts for up to five years, comprising a first cycle of three years and a second of two years. Entrance to secondary schools is determined by the Common Entrance Examination. Many schools are administered jointly by the state and religious bodies. In 2005 enrolment at primary schools included 89.7% of children in the relevant age-group (males 89.9%; females 89.5%), while enrolment at secondary schools was equivalent to 69.0% of children in the relevant age-group (males 67.8%; females 70.2%). In 2000 the Government announced an education reform programme to improve access to, and levels of, education. A school-to-work apprenticeship programme was also to be established.

The Trinidad campus of the University of the West Indies (UWI), at St Augustine, offers undergraduate and postgraduate programmes. The UWI Institute of Business offers postgraduate courses, and develops programmes for local companies. Other institutions of higher education are the Eric Williams Medical Sciences complex, the Polytechnic Institute and the East Caribbean Farm Institute. The country has one teacher training college and three government-controlled technical institutes and vocational centres, including the Trinidad and Tobago Hotel School. In the late 1990s the Government established the Trinidad and Tobago Institute of Technology, and the College of Science, Technology and Applied Arts of Trinidad and Tobago. In March 2004 a Steering Committee was appointed to conduct a strategic review of tertiary education, and distance and lifelong learning, in an attempt to improve consistency within the tertiary sector and in relation to the education system as a whole. Budgeted expenditure on education by the central Government in 2005 was TT $3,140.3m., equivalent to 11.2% of total government expenditure.

Public Holidays

2008: 1 January (New Year's Day), 21–24 March (Easter), 31 March (for Spiritual Baptist Shouters' Liberation Day), 22 May (Corpus Christi), 30 May (Indian Arrival Day),

19 June (Labour Day), 1 August (Emancipation Day), 1 September (for Independence Day), 24 September (Republic Day), 1 October* (Id al-Fitr, end of Ramadan), 28 October† (Diwali), 25–26 December (Christmas).

2009: 1 January (New Year's Day), 30 March (Spiritual Baptist Shouters' Liberation Day), 10–13 April (Easter), 30 May (Indian Arrival Day), 11 June (Corpus Christi), 19 June (Labour Day), 1 August (Emancipation Day), 31 August (Independence Day), 20 September* (Id al-Fitr, end of Ramadan), 24 September (Republic Day), 17 October† (Diwali), 25–26 December (Christmas).

* These holidays are dependent on the Islamic lunar calendar and may vary by one or two days from the dates given.

† Dependent on lunar sightings.

Weights and Measures

The metric system is replacing the imperial system of weights and measures.

Statistical Survey

Sources (unless otherwise stated): Central Statistical Office, National Statistics Bldg, 80 Independence Sq., POB 98, Port of Spain; tel. 623-6945; fax 625-3802; e-mail info@cso.gov.tt; internet www.cso.gov.tt; Central Bank of Trinidad and Tobago, POB 1250, Port of Spain; tel. 625-4835; fax 627-4696; e-mail info@central-bank.org.tt; internet www.central-bank.org.tt.

Area and Population

AREA, POPULATION AND DENSITY

Area (sq km)	5,128*
Population (census results)	
2 May 1990	1,213,733
15 May 2000	
Males	633,051
Females	629,315
Total	1,262,366
Population (official estimates at mid-year)	
2004	1,290,600
2005	1,294,500
2006	1,297,900
Density (per sq km) at mid-2006	253.1

* 1,980 sq miles. Of the total area, Trinidad is 4,828 sq km (1,864 sq miles) and Tobago 300 sq km (116 sq miles).

POPULATION BY ETHNIC GROUP
(1990 census*)

	Males	Females	Total	%
African	223,561	221,883	445,444	39.59
Chinese	2,317	1,997	4,314	0.38
'East' Indian	226,967	226,102	453,069	40.27
Lebanese	493	441	934	0.08
Mixed	100,842	106,716	207,558	18.45
White	3,483	3,771	7,254	0.64
Other	886	838	1,724	0.15
Unknown	2,385	2,446	4,831	0.43
Total	560,934	564,194	1,125,128	100.00

* Excludes some institutional population and members of unenumerated households, totalling 44,444.

ADMINISTRATIVE DIVISIONS
(population at 2000 census)

	Population	Capital
Trinidad	1,208,282	Port of Spain
Port of Spain (city, capital)	49,031	—
San Fernando (city)	55,419	—
Arima (borough)	32,278	Arima
Chaguanas (borough)	67,433	Chaguanas
Point Fortin (borough)	19,056	Point Fortin
Diego Martin	105,720	Petit Valley
San Juan/Laventille	157,295	Laventille
Tunapuna/Piarco	203,975	Tunapuna
Couva/Tabaquite/Talparo	162,779	Couva
Mayaro/Rio Claro	33,480	Rio Claro
Sangre Grande	64,343	Sangre Grande
Princes Town	91,947	Princes Town
Penal/Debe	83,609	Penal
Siparia	81,917	Siparia
Tobago	54,084	Scarborough

BIRTHS AND DEATHS
(annual averages, UN estimates)

	1990–95	1995–2000	2000–05
Birth rate (per 1,000)	18.1	15.0	14.5
Death rate (per 1,000)	6.8	7.1	7.9

Source: UN, *World Population Prospects: The 2006 Revision*.

Expectation of life (years at birth, WHO estimates): 70.7 (males 67.3; females 74.4) in 2005 (Source: WHO, *World Health Statistics*).

ECONOMICALLY ACTIVE POPULATION
('000 persons aged 15 years and over)

	2003	2004	2005
Agriculture, forestry, hunting and fishing	31.4	26.0	24.8
Mining and quarrying	16.9	20.1	20.4
Manufacturing	55.0	58.7	55.6
Electricity, gas and water	7.4	7.3	6.9
Construction	72.6	83.8	94.8
Wholesale and retail trade, restaurants and hotels	99.0	101.2	103.5
Transport, storage and communication	41.5	41.6	41.8
Finance, insurance, real estate and business services	45.0	46.3	45.0
Community, social and personal services	163.2	175.3	178.5
Other services	1.9	1.8	2.5
Total employed	534.1	562.2	574.0
Unemployed	62.4	51.1	49.7
Total labour force	596.6	613.3	623.7
Males	360.4	365.3	364.9
Females	236.1	248.0	258.8

Source: ILO.

2006 ('000 persons aged 15 and over): Agriculture 25.7; Petroleum and gas (incl. mining and quarrying) 20.4; Manufacturing 55.5; Construction (incl. utilities) 104.5; Transport, storage and communications 42.7; Wholesale and retail trade 106.6; Community, social and personal services 181.0; Finance, insurance and real estate 48.1; Not classified 1.6; Total employed 586.2; Unemployed 39.0; Total labour force 625.2.

TRINIDAD AND TOBAGO

Health and Welfare

KEY INDICATORS

Total fertility rate (children per woman, 2005)	1.6
Under-5 mortality rate (per 1,000 live births, 2005)	19
HIV/AIDS (% of persons, aged 15–49, 2005)	2.6
Physicians (per 1,000 head, 1997)	0.79
Hospital beds (per 1,000 head, 2003)	3.3
Health expenditure (2004): US $ per head (PPP)	522.6
Health expenditure (2004): % of GDP	3.5
Health expenditure (2004): public (% of total)	38.9
Access to water (% of persons, 2004)	91
Human Development Index (2005): ranking	59
Human Development Index (2005): value	0.814

For sources and definitions, see explanatory note on p. vi.

Agriculture

PRINCIPAL CROPS
('000 metric tons)

	2004	2005	2006*
Rice (paddy)	1.7	2.1	2.1
Maize	3.0	3.1*	3.1
Taro (coco yam)	4.8	4.9*	4.9
Sugar cane	680.0	n.a.	420.0
Pigeon peas	1.5	1.0	1.0
Coconuts*	13.6	10.6	10.6
Cabbages	1.6	1.1*	1.1
Lettuce	1.4*	1.5*	1.5
Tomatoes	1.7	1.6	1.6
Pumpkins, squash and gourds	4.9	2.2	2.2
Cucumbers and gherkins	1.9	2.0*	2.0
Aubergines	3.0	3.0*	3.0
Watermelons*	1.2	1.2	1.2
Bananas*	6.8	7.0	7.0
Plantains*	4.5	4.7	4.7
Oranges*	5.1	5.3	5.3
Lemons and limes*	1.5	1.7	1.7
Grapefruit and pomelo*	2.7	2.8	2.8
Pineapples*	4.2	4.5	4.5
Coffee (green)	0.1	0.4*	0.4
Cocoa beans	1.3	1.4*	1.4

* FAO estimate(s).

Aggregate production ('000 metric tons, may include official, semi-official or estimated data): Total cereals 5 in 2004, 5 in 2005, 5 in 2006; Total roots and tubers 9 in 2004, 9 in 2005, 9 in 2006; Sugarcrops 535 in 2004, 420 in 2005, 420 in 2006; Total vegetables (incl. melons) 21 in 2004, 19 in 2005, 19 in 2006; Total fruits (excl. melons) 67 in 2004, 69 in 2005, 69 in 2006.

Source: FAO.

LIVESTOCK
('000 head, year ending September)

	2003	2004	2005*
Horses*	1.2	1.2	1.3
Asses, mules or hinnies*	4.0	4.1	4.1
Cattle	29.0	29.0	29.0
Buffaloes*	5.7	5.7	5.7
Pigs	41.4	42.5*	43.0
Chickens*	27,500	28,200	28,200
Sheep*	3.4	3.4	3.4
Goats*	58.6	59.0	59.3

* FAO estimate(s).
2006: Figures assumed to be unchanged from 2005 (FAO estimates).
Source: FAO.

LIVESTOCK PRODUCTS
('000 metric tons)

	2003	2004	2005*
Cattle meat	0.8	0.8*	0.8
Pig meat	2.8	2.5*	2.3
Chicken meat	56.5	57.6	56.9
Cows' milk	8.9	10.0*	10.5
Hen eggs	3.6†	3.8†	3.8

* FAO estimate(s).
† Unofficial figure.
2006: Production assumed to be unchanged from 2005 (FAO estimates).
Source: FAO.

Forestry

ROUNDWOOD REMOVALS
('000 cubic metres, excl. bark)

	2004	2005	2006
Sawlogs, veneer logs and logs for sleepers	51.0	65.0	65.0
Fuel wood*	34.9	34.5	34.1
Total	85.9	99.5	99.1

* FAO estimates.
Source: FAO.

SAWNWOOD PRODUCTION
('000 cubic metres, incl. railway sleepers)

	2004	2005	2006
Total (all broadleaved)	32	41	41

Source: FAO.

Fishing

('000 metric tons, live weight of capture)

	2003	2004	2005
Demersal percomorphs	2.6	2.4	3.8
Atlantic bonito	0.2	0.3	0.1
King mackerel	0.8	0.6	0.7
Serra Spanish mackerel	1.9	2.1	2.7
Frigate and bullet tunas	n.a.	0.4	n.a.
Tuna-like fishes	0.2	0.0	0.5
Sharks, rays, skates, etc.	1.0	1.3	2.2
Other marine fishes	1.8	1.5	2.3
Penaeus shrimps	0.7	0.6	0.7
Total catch (incl. others)	9.9*	10.0	13.4

* FAO estimate.
Source: FAO.

Mining

('000 barrels, unless otherwise indicated)

	2003*	2004*	2005
Crude petroleum	49,117	44,985	52,740
Natural gas liquids	10,500	10,687	9,889
Natural gas (million cu m)†	26,810	30,273	33,270

* Estimated production.
† Figures refer to the gross volume of output; marketed production (in million cu m) was: 26,046 in 2003; 29,456 in 2004; 31,348 in 2005.
Source: US Geological Survey.

TRINIDAD AND TOBAGO

Industry

SELECTED PRODUCTS
('000 metric tons, unless otherwise indicated)

	2003	2004	2005
Raw sugar	68	43	33
Crude oil ('000 barrels)	49,117	44,985	52,740
Natural gas liquids ('000 barrels)	10,505	10,687	9,889
Fertilizers	4,965	5,336	5,936
Methanol	2,846	3,418	4,695
Cement	766	768	686
Iron (direct reduced)	2,275	2,337	2,055
Steel:			
billets	896	790	712
wire rods	641	616	472

Electric energy: (million kWh) 5,460 in 2001; 5,643 in 2002. Source: UN Economic Commission for Latin America and the Caribbean, *Statistical Yearbook*.

Finance

CURRENCY AND EXCHANGE RATES

Monetary Units
100 cents = 1 Trinidad and Tobago dollar (TT $).

Sterling, US Dollar and Euro Equivalents (31 December 2007)
£1 sterling = TT $12.6522
US $1 = TT $6.3154;
€1 = TT $9.2969;
TT $100 = £7.90 = US $15.83 = €10.76.

Average Exchange Rate (TT $ per US $)
2005   6.2996
2006   6.3080
2007   6.3256

CENTRAL GOVERNMENT BUDGET
(TT $ million)

Revenue	2003/04	2004/05	2005/06
Energy sector	7,641.7	14,044.1	21,385.3
Corporation tax	5,428.3	10,805.6	17,620.3
Withholding tax (oil)	200.7	429.2	614.4
Royalties	1,094.5	1,228.5	1,679.3
Unemployment levy	294.2	903.2	1,275.0
Oil impost	36.8	42.7	65.9
Excise duties	587.2	634.8	130.4
Non-energy sector	12,983.9	15,594.6	17,094.3
Taxes	11,735.6	13,795.4	15,343.9
Taxes on income	6,304.5	8,058.4	7,959.5
Taxes on property	85.4	62.7	64.2
Taxes on goods and services	4,103.0	4,200.8	5,487.7
Value-added tax	3,021.2	2,962.6	4,084.2
Other	505.3	584.8	711.7
Taxes on international trade	1,242.7	1,473.5	1,832.5
Non-tax revenue of non-oil sector	1,248.1	1,799.1	1,750.4
Capital revenue and grants	4.2	9.1	9.0
Total	20,629.7	29,647.9	38,488.6

Expenditure	2003/04	2004/05	2005/06
Current expenditure	17,498.5	21,842.4	26,530.3
Wages and salaries	4,849.2	5,309.2	5,458.4
Goods and services	2,374.5	3,170.1	3,754.4
Interest payments	2,364.3	2,541.5	2,496.9
Domestic	1,638.2	1,875.5	1,837.3
External	726.1	666.0	659.6
Transfers and subsidies	7,910.6	10,821.6	14,820.6
Households	2,173.0	2,601.2	4,336.8
Loans and grants to statutory boards and state enterprises	2,448.7	2,481.6	3,805.5
Capital expenditure and net lending	1,621.1	2,798.6	4,531.6
Total	19,119.6	24,641.0	31,061.9

INTERNATIONAL RESERVES
(US $ million at 31 December)

	2004	2005	2006
Gold (national valuation)	26.8	31.4	39.0
IMF special drawing rights	2.7	3.7	3.0
Reserve position in IMF	172.5	71.3	51.8
Foreign exchange	2,993.0	4,781.4	6,514.7
Total	3,195.0	4,887.8	6,608.5

Source: IMF, *International Financial Statistics*.

MONEY SUPPLY
(TT $ million at 31 December)

	2004	2005	2006
Currency outside banks	1,957.4	2,425.4	2,654.4
Demand deposits at commercial banks	5,795.3	9,358.6	10,219.2
Total money (incl. others)	8,375.4	13,292.6	14,994.5

Source: IMF, *International Financial Statistics*.

COST OF LIVING
(Consumer Price Index; base: January 2003 = 100)

	2005	2006	2007
Food	150.5	185.4	217.6
Clothing	91.8	91.3	93.3
Transport	108.3	110.1	114.4
Housing	105.8	108.9	113.5
All items (incl. others)	112.9	122.3	132.0

NATIONAL ACCOUNTS
(TT $ million at current prices)
National Income and Product

	1998	1999	2000
Compensation of employees	17,864.3	19,087.3	20,004.0
Operating surplus	11,918.8	13,569.3	24,233.0
Domestic factor incomes	29,783.1	32,656.6	44,237.0
Consumption of fixed capital	4,562.8	4,787.0	6,063.0
Gross domestic product (GDP) at factor cost	34,345.9	37,443.6	50,300.0
Indirect taxes	4,070.4	3,989.3	1,379.0*
Less Subsidies	379.6	398.9	807.0
GDP in purchasers' values	38,036.7	41,034.0	50,872.0
Net factor income	−2,527.0	−2,518.0	−3,953.0
Gross national income (GNI)	35,509.7	38,516.0	46,919.0
Less Consumption of fixed capital	4,410.0	5,177.0	6,063.0
National income at market prices	31,099.7	33,339.0	40,856.0

*Figure obtained as a residual.

Source: UN, Economic Commission for Latin America and the Caribbean, *Statistical Yearbook*.

Expenditure on the Gross Domestic Product

	2004	2005	2006*
Government final consumption expenditure	9,584.5	11,884.7	13,054.6
Private final consumption expenditure	43,869.3	48,431.5	50,822.9
Gross capital formation	13,906.3	14,748.7	15,859.9
Total domestic expenditure	67,360.1	75,064.9	79,737.4
Exports of goods and services	45,480.7	61,315.3	79,226.7
Less Imports of goods and services	33,014.7	41,323.2	44,489.7
GDP in purchasers' values	79,826.1	95,057.0	114,474.4

*Estimated figures.

TRINIDAD AND TOBAGO

Gross Domestic Product by Economic Activity

	2004	2005	2006
Agriculture, hunting, forestry and fishing	729	627	705
Petroleum	29,849	39,813	51,600
Manufacturing	5,331	5,956	6,492
Electricity and water	925	892	867
Construction and quarrying	6,184	7,731	9,586
Transport, storage and communication	5,780	5,708	5,955
Distribution and restaurants	10,624	12,212	13,427
Hotels	310	357	375
Finance, insurance and real estate	10,539	11,709	13,310
Government	5,964	6,523	8,147
Education	2,166	2,558	2,982
Personal services	1,145	1,214	1,261
Sub-total	79,544	95,298	114,706
Less Imputed bank service charges	2,889	3,190	3,537
Value-added tax	3,171	2,948	3,305
GDP in purchaser's values	79,826	95,057	114,474

BALANCE OF PAYMENTS
(US $ million)

	2005*	2006†	2007‡
Exports of goods f.o.b.	9,672	12,100	12,436
Imports of goods f.o.b.	−5,725	−6,843	−8,037
Trade balance	3,947	5,257	4,399
Services (net)	356	286	275
Balance on goods and services	4,303	5,543	4,674
Other income (net)	−760	−936	−857
Balance on goods, services and income	3,543	4,607	3,817
Current transfers (net)	50	47	67
Current balance	3,594	4,654	3,884
Portfolio investment	−81	−157	−55
Direct investment	599	513	1,332
Heritage and stabilization fund	−419	−525	−272
Commercial banks	98	−845	−385
Other private sector capital	−2,315	−2,522	−3,304
Overall balance	1,476	1,119	1,200

* Preliminary figures.
† Estimates.
‡ Projected figures.

External Trade

PRINCIPAL COMMODITIES
(TT $ million)

Imports c.i.f.	2004	2005
Food and live animals	2,208.5	2,723.8
Beverages and tobacco	177.7	264.5
Crude materials except fuels	715.0	1,665.5
Mineral fuels and lubricants	7,407.2	12,482.6
Animal and vegetable oils and fats	104.8	112.8
Chemicals	2,130.0	2,633.9
Manufactured goods	5,075.1	4,502.3
Machinery and transport equipment	11,262.6	9,484.4
Miscellaneous manufactured articles	1,490.1	1,958.3
Miscellaneous transactions and commodities	29.3	41.0
Total	30,600.3	35,869.1

Exports f.o.b.	2004	2005
Food and live animals	884.2	1,048.9
Beverages and tobacco	520.9	800.7
Crude materials except fuels	97.7	255.6
Mineral fuels and lubricants	24,209.5	42,503.2
Animal and vegetable oils and fats	45.6	49.3
Chemicals	9,543.2	11,518.3
Manufactured goods	3,607.2	2,980.3
Machinery and transport equipment	813.6	875.8
Miscellaneous manufactured articles	418.6	514.6
Miscellaneous transactions and commodities	3.9	1.8
Total	40,144.4	60,548.5

PRINCIPAL TRADING PARTNERS
(TT $ million)

Imports c.i.f.	2003	2004	2005
Barbados	139.0	141.9	179.5
Brazil	2,207.8	3,204.5	4,859.1
Canada	731.9	675.5	770.7
European Free Trade Association (EFTA)	247.7	229.9	425.8
European Union (EU)	3,907.1	6,312.9	3,266.1
Guyana	140.4	163.0	137.7
Jamaica	105.0	88.8	93.3
USA	7,388.6	10,375.4	10,295.7
Venezuela	1,656.5	962.1	2,164.6
Total (incl. others)	24,501.4	30,600.3	35,869.1

Exports f.o.b.	2003	2004	2005
Barbados	1,225.6	1,228.4	2,541.9
Canada	597.4	506.4	654.3
Central and South America	2,165.5	1,765.7	3,814.2
European Union (EU)	1,005.7	1,207.7	1,063.0
Guyana	914.6	669.1	1,671.6
Jamaica	2,195.0	1,467.0	4,496.9
USA	17,444.6	27,626.0	34,888.9
Total (incl. others)	31,882.1	39,893.2	59,861.5

Transport

ROAD TRAFFIC
(motor vehicles in use)

	1997	1998	1999
Passenger cars	194,300	213,400	229,400
Commercial vehicles	47,700	51,100	53,900

Source: UN, *Statistical Yearbook*.

Total number of registered vehicles: 292,908 in 1999; 316,163 in 2000; 331,595 in 2001 (provisional figure).

SHIPPING

Merchant Fleet
(registered at 31 December)

	2004	2005	2006
Number of vessels	95	102	104
Total displacement ('000 grt)	33.5	39.0	38.8

Source: Lloyd's Register-Fairplay, *World Fleet Statistics*.

International Sea-borne Freight Traffic
(estimates, '000 metric tons)

	1988	1989	1990
Goods loaded	7,736	7,992	9,622
Goods unloaded	4,076	4,091	10,961

Source: UN, *Monthly Bulletin of Statistics*.

1998: Port of Spain handled 3.3m. metric tons of cargo.

TRINIDAD AND TOBAGO

CIVIL AVIATION
(traffic on scheduled services)

	2001	2002	2003
Kilometres flown (million)	29	28	31
Passengers carried ('000)	1,388	1,269	1,084
Passenger-km (million)	2,723	2,875	2,671
Total ton-km (million)	288	295	276

Source: UN, *Statistical Yearbook*.

Tourism

FOREIGN TOURIST ARRIVALS

Country of origin	2003	2004	2005
Barbados	37,320	35,456	35,319
Canada	43,036	43,565	47,702
Germany	7,491	8,178	8,666
Grenada	19,220	19,575	19,501
Guyana	22,783	22,328	22,208
Saint Lucia	7,423	8,192	8,823
Saint Vincent and Grenadines	11,041	11,747	12,658
United Kingdom	57,566	66,090	63,523
USA	138,935	159,467	167,985
Venezuela	10,273	10,528	10,191
Total (incl. others)	409,069	442,596	463,191

Tourism receipts (US $ million, incl. passenger transport): 437 in 2003; 568 in 2004; 661 in 2005.

Sources: World Tourism Organization.

Communications Media

	2004	2005	2006
Telephones ('000 main lines in use)	321.3	323.5	325.5
Mobile cellular telephones ('000 subscribers)	647.9	800.0	1,654.9
Personal computers ('000 in use)	160	160	n.a.
Internet users ('000)	160.0	163.0	163.0
Broadband subscribers ('000)	4.2	10.8	20.6

Radio receivers (1997, '000 in use): 680.

Facsimile machines (1998, number in use): 5,024.

Daily newspapers: 4 in 1997 (average circulation: 191,000 in 2001).

Non-daily newspapers: 5 in 1997 (average circulation 167,000 in 2001).

Television receivers ('000 in use): 449 in 2001.

Sources: International Telecommunication Union; UN, *Statistical Yearbook*; UNESCO, *Statistical Yearbook*.

Education

(2004/05, unless otherwise indicated)

	Institutions	Teachers	Males	Females	Total
Pre-primary	50*	2,186	12,370	11,943	24,313
Primary	480†	7,839	66,654	63,049	129,703
Secondary	101†	5,896	48,148	48,932	97,080
University and equivalent	3‡	1,800	7,515	9,405	16,920

* Government schools and assisted schools only, in 1992/93.
† 2001/02.
‡ 2003/04.

Source: UNESCO.

Adult literacy rate (UNESCO estimates): 98.4% (males 98.2%; females 97.8%) in 2004 (Source: UNESCO Institute for Statistics).

Directory

The Constitution

Trinidad and Tobago became a republic, within the Commonwealth, under a new Constitution on 1 August 1976. The Constitution provides for a President and a bicameral Parliament comprising a Senate and a House of Representatives. The President is elected by an Electoral College of members of both the Senate and the House of Representatives. The Senate consists of 31 members appointed by the President: 16 on the advice of the Prime Minister, six on the advice of the Leader of the Opposition and nine at the President's own discretion from among outstanding persons from economic, social or community organizations. The House of Representatives consists of 41 members who are elected by universal adult suffrage. The duration of a Parliament is five years. The Cabinet, presided over by the Prime Minister, is responsible for the general direction and control of the Government. It is collectively responsible to Parliament.

The Government

HEAD OF STATE

President: Prof. GEORGE MAXWELL RICHARDS (took office 17 March 2003; re-elected by vote of the Electoral College of the Parliament 11 February 2008).

THE CABINET
(April 2008)

Prime Minister: PATRICK MANNING.
Attorney-General: BRIGID ANNISETTE-GEORGE.
Minister of Agriculture, Land and Marine Resources: ARNOLD PIGGOTT.
Minister of Community Development, Culture and Gender Affairs: MARLENE MCDONALD.
Minister of Education: ESTHER LE GENDRE.
Minister of Energy and Energy Industries: CONRAD ENIL.
Minister of Finance: KAREN NUNEZ-TESHEIRA.
Minister of Foreign Affairs: PAULA GOPEE-SCOON.
Minister of Health: JERRY NARACE.
Minister of Information: NEIL PARSANLAL.
Minister of Labour and Small and Micro Enterprise Development: RENNIE DUMAS.
Minister of Legal Affairs: PETER TAYLOR.
Minister of Local Government: HAZEL ANNE MARIE MANNING.
Minister of National Security: MARTIN JOSEPH.
Minister of Planning, Housing and the Environment: Dr EMILY GAYNOR DICK-FORDE.
Minister of Public Administration: KENNEDY SWARATSINGH.
Minister of Public Utilities: MUSTAPHA ABDUL-HAMID.
Minister of Science, Technology and Tertiary Education: CHRISTINE KANGALOO.
Minister of Social Development: Dr AMERY BROWNE.
Minister of Sport and Youth Affairs: GARY HUNT.
Minister of Tourism: JOSEPH ROSS.
Minister of Trade and Industry: Dr LENNY SAITH.
Minister of Works and Transport: COLM IMBERT.
Minister in the Ministry of Finance: MARIANO BROWNE.

Minister of State in the Ministry of Community Development, Culture and Gender Affairs: DONNA COX.
Minister of State in the Ministry of Planning, Housing and the Environment: TINA GRONLUND-NUNEZ.
Minister of State in the Ministry of Science, Technology and Tertiary Education: FITZGERALD JEFFREY.
Minister of State in the Ministry of Social Development: ALICIA HOSPEDALES.
Minister of State in the Office of the Prime Minister: STANFORD CALLENDER.

MINISTRIES

Office of the President: President's House, Circular Rd, St Ann's, Port of Spain; tel. 624-1261; fax 625-7950; e-mail presoftt@carib-link.net.

Office of the Prime Minister: Whitehall, 29 Maraval Rd, Port of Spain; tel. 622-1625; fax 622-0055; e-mail permsec@opm.gov.tt; internet www.opm.gov.tt.

Ministry of Agriculture, Land and Marine Resources: St Clair Circle, St Clair, Port of Spain; tel. 622-1221; fax 622-8202; e-mail apdmalmr@trinidad.net; internet www.agriculture.gov.tt.

Ministry of the Attorney-General: Cabildo Chambers, 23–27 St Vincent St, Port of Spain; tel. 623-7010; fax 625-0470; e-mail ag@ag.gov.tt.

Ministry of Community Development, Culture and Gender Affairs: ALGICO Bldg, Jerningham Ave, Belmont, Port of Spain; tel. 625-3012; fax 625-3278; e-mail cdcga@tstt.net.tt; internet www.cdcga.gov.tt.

Ministry of Education: 18 Alexandra St, St Clair; tel. 622-2181; fax 622-4892; e-mail mined@tstt.net.tt; internet www.moe.gov.tt.

Ministry of Energy and Energy Industries: Level 9, Riverside Plaza, Cnr Besson and Piccadilly Sts, Port of Spain; tel. 623-6708; fax 623-0306; e-mail info@energy.gov.tt; internet www.energy.gov.tt.

Ministry of Finance: Level 8, Eric Williams Finance Bldg, Independence Sq., Port of Spain; tel. 627-9700; fax 627-5882; e-mail comm.finance@gov.tt; internet www.finance.gov.tt.

Ministry of Foreign Affairs: Knowsley Bldg, 1 Queen's Park West, Port of Spain; tel. 623-4116; fax 624-4220; e-mail press@foreign.gov.tt; internet www.foreign.gov.tt.

Ministry of Health: Cnr Park and Edwards Sts, Port of Spain; tel. 627-0012; fax 623-9528; e-mail sandra.jones@health.gov.tt; internet www.healthsectorreform.gov.tt.

Ministry of Information: Level 5, NALIS Bldg, Abercromby St, Port of Spain.

Ministry of Labour and Small and Micro Enterprise Development: Level 11, Riverside Plaza, Cnr Besson and Piccadilly Sts, Port of Spain; tel. 623-4241; fax 624-4091; e-mail rplan@tstt.net.tt; internet www.labour.gov.tt.

Ministry of Legal Affairs: Registration House, Huggins Bldg, South Quay, Port of Spain; tel. 623-7163; fax 625-9803; e-mail mlalr@tstt.net.tt.

Ministry of Local Government: Kent House, Maraval Rd, Port of Spain; tel. 622-1669; fax 622-4783; e-mail molg2@carib-link.net; internet www.localgov.gov.tt.

Ministry of National Security: Temple Court, 31–33 Abercromby St, Port of Spain; tel. 623-2441; fax 627-8044; e-mail info@mns.gov.tt; internet www.nationalsecurity.gov.tt.

Ministry of Planning, Housing and the Environment: NHA Bldg, 44–46 South Quay, Port of Spain; tel. 623-4663; fax 625-2793; e-mail info@housing.gov.tt; internet www.planning.gov.tt.

Ministry of Public Administration: Level 7, National Library Bldg, Cnr Hart and Abercromby Sts, Port of Spain; tel. 623-8578; fax 623-6027.

Ministry of Public Utilities: Sacred Heart Bldg, 16–18 Sackville St, Port of Spain; tel. 623-4853; fax 625-7003.

Ministry of Science, Technology and Tertiary Education: Level 3, Nahous Bldg, Cnr Agra and Patna Sts, St James; tel. 622-9922; fax 622-7640; e-mail stte@stte.gov.tt; internet www.stte.gov.tt.

Ministry of Social Development: Ansa McAl Bldg, 69 Independence Sq., Port of Spain; tel. and fax 627-4853; e-mail infor@msd.gov.tt; internet www.socialservices.gov.tt.

Ministry of Sport and Youth Affairs: ISSA Nicholas Bldg, Cnr Frederick and Duke Sts, Port of Spain; tel. 625-8874; fax 623-5006.

Ministry of Tourism: Clarence House, 127–129 Duke Street, Port of Spain; tel. 624-1403; fax 625-0437; e-mail mintourism@tourism.gov.tt.

Ministry of Trade and Industry: Levels 11–17, Nicholas Tower, 63-65 Independence Sq., Port of Spain; tel. 623-2931; fax 627-8488; e-mail info@tradeind.gov.tt; internet www.tradeind.gov.tt.

Ministry of Works and Transport: Level 6, Administrative Bldg, Cnr Richmond and London Sts, Port of Spain; tel. 625-1225; fax 625-8070; internet www.mowt.gov.tt.

Legislature

PARLIAMENT

Senate

President: Dr LINDA BABOOLAL.

House of Representatives

Speaker: BARENDRA SINANAN.
Election, 5 November 2007, preliminary results

Party	Seats
People's National Movement	26
United National Congress	15
Total	41

TOBAGO HOUSE OF ASSEMBLY

The House is elected for a four-year term of office and consists of 12 elected members and three members selected by the majority party.

Chief Secretary: ORVILLE LONDON.
Election, 17 January 2005

Party	Seats
People's National Movement	11
Democratic Action Congress	1
Total	12

Election Commission

Elections and Boundaries Commission (EBC): Scott House, 134–138 Frederick St, Port of Spain; tel. 623-4622; fax 627-7881; Chair. Dr NORBERT MASSON.

Political Organizations

Congress of the People: Pasea Rd, Tunapuna; tel. 662-1067; e-mail headoffice@coptnt.com; internet www.coptnt.com; f. 2006; Leader WINSTON DOOKERAN; Chair. ROY AUGUSTUS.

Democratic Action Congress: Scarborough; f. Jan. 2003 by faction of National Alliance for Reconstruction (q.v.); only active in Tobago; Leader HOCHOY CHARLES.

Democratic National Assembly (DNA): Port of Spain; f. March 2006; Chair. Dr KIRK MEIGHOO.

Democratic Party of Trinidad and Tobago (DPTT): Port of Spain; f. March 2002; joined the United National Congress—Alliance (UNC—A) in July 2007; Leader STEVE ALVAREZ.

National Alliance for Reconstruction (NAR): 71 Dundonald St, Port of Spain; tel. 627-6163; f. 1983 as a coalition of moderate opposition parties; reorganized as a single party in 1986; joined the United National Congress—Alliance (UNC—A) in July 2007; Leader CARSON CHARLES; Chair. CHRISTO GIFT.

National Democratic Party (NDP): Port of Spain; f. 2005; joined the United National Congress—Alliance (UNC—A) in July 2007; Leader MICHAEL SIMS.

National Transformation Movement (NTM): Port of Spain; f. 2006; Leader LLOYD ELCOCK.

People's National Movement (PNM): Balisier House, 1 Tranquility St, Port of Spain; tel. 625-1533; e-mail pnm@carib-link.net; internet www.pnm.org.tt; f. 1956; moderate nationalist party; Leader PATRICK MANNING; Chair. FRANKLIN KHAN; Gen. Sec. MARTIN JOSEPH.

United National Congress—Alliance (UNC—A): Rienzi Complex, 78–81 Southern Main Rd, Couva; tel. 636-8145; e-mail info@unc.org.tt; internet www.unc.org.tt; f. 1989 as the United National Congress; formed an alliance with the Democratic Party of Trinidad and Tobago (DPTT), the National Alliance for Reconstruction (NAR) and the National Democratic Party (NDP) to contest the 2007 general election and adopted the above name; social democratic; Leader BASDEO PANDAY; CEO TIM GOPEESINGH.

Diplomatic Representation

EMBASSIES AND HIGH COMMISSIONS IN TRINIDAD AND TOBAGO

Argentina: TATIL Bldg, 4th Floor, 11 Maraval Rd, POB 162; Port of Spain; tel. 628-7557; fax 628-7544; e-mail etrin@mrecic.gov.ar; internet www.trinidadytobago.embajada-argentina.gov.ar; Ambassador JOSÉ LUIS VIGNOLO.

Brazil: 18 Sweet Briar Rd, St Clair, POB 382, Port of Spain; tel. 622-5779; fax 622-4323; e-mail embassyofbrazil@tstt.net.tt; internet www.brazilembtt.org; Ambassador LUIZ FERNANDO DE ATHAYDE.

Canada: Maple House, 3–3A Sweet Briar Rd, St Clair, POB 1246, Port of Spain; tel. 622-6232; fax 628-1830; e-mail pspan@international.gc.ca; internet www.portofspain.gc.ca; High Commissioner HOWARD STRAUSS.

China, People's Republic: 39 Alexandra St, St Clair, Port of Spain; tel. 622-6976; fax 622-7613; e-mail tian@wow.net; internet tt.chineseembassy.org; Ambassador HUANG XING.

Cuba: Furness Bldg, 2nd Floor, 90 Independence Sq., Port of Spain; tel. 627-1306; fax 627-3515; e-mail embajador@tstt.net.tt; Ambassador SERGIO OLIVA GUERRA.

Dominican Republic: Suite 8, 1 Dere St, Queen's Park West, Port of Spain; tel. 624-7930; fax 623-7779; e-mail embdomtrinidadytobago@serex.gov.do; Ambassador JOSÉ MANUEL CASTILLO BETANCES.

El Salvador: 29 Long Circular Rd, St James, Port of Spain; tel. 628-4454; fax 622-8314; Ambassador CARLOS MAURICIO PINEDA.

France: TATIL Bldg, 6th Floor, 11 Maraval Rd, Port of Spain; tel. 622-7447; fax 628-2632; e-mail francett@wow.net; internet www.ambafrance-tt.org; Ambassador CHARLEY CAUSERET.

Germany: 7–9 Marli St, Newtown, POB 828, Port of Spain; tel. 628-1630; fax 628-5278; e-mail germanembassy@tstt.net.tt; internet www.port-of-spain.diplo.de; Ambassador Dr ERNST MARTENS.

Holy See: 11 Mary St, St Clair, POB 854, Port of Spain; tel. 622-5009; fax 628-5457; e-mail apnun@tstt.net.tt; Apostolic Nuncio Most Rev. THOMAS EDWARD GULLICKSON (Titular Archbishop of Bomarzo).

India: 6 Victoria Ave, POB 530, Port of Spain; tel. 627-7480; fax 627-6985; e-mail hcipos@tstt.net.tt; High Commissioner JAGJIT SINGH SAPRA.

Jamaica: 2 Newbold St, St Clair, Port of Spain; tel. 622-4995; fax 628-9043; e-mail jhctnt@tstt.net.tt; High Commissioner PETER BLACK.

Japan: 5 Hayes St, St Clair, POB 1039, Port of Spain; tel. 628-5991; fax 622-0858; e-mail embassyofjapan@tstt.net.tt; internet www.tt.emb-japan.go.jp; Ambassador KOICHIRO SEKI.

Mexico: 12 Hayes St, St Clair, Port of Spain; tel. 622-1422; fax 628-8488; e-mail info@mexico.tt; Ambassador RICARDO VILLANUEVA HALLAL.

Netherlands: Life of Barbados Bldg, 3rd Floor, 69–71 Edward St, POB 870, Port of Spain; tel. 625-1210; fax 625-1704; e-mail info@holland.tt; internet www.holland.tt; Ambassador H. P. P. M. HORBACH.

Nigeria: 3 Maxwell-Phillip St, St Clair, Port of Spain; tel. 622-4002; fax 622-7162; e-mail nigerianpos@tstt.net.tt; High Commissioner EDWARD AGBE.

Panama: Suite 6, 1A Dere St, Port of Spain; tel. 623-3435; fax 623-3440; e-mail embapatt@wow.net; Ambassador GERARDO MALONEY.

Suriname: Tatil Bldg, 5th Floor, 11 Maraval Rd, Port of Spain; tel. 628-0704; fax 628-0086; e-mail surinameembassy@tstt.net.tt; Ambassador FIDELIA GRAAND-GALON.

United Kingdom: 19 St Clair Circle, St Clair, POB 778, Port of Spain; tel. 622-2748; fax 622-4555; e-mail csbhc@tstt.net.tt; internet www.britishhighcommission.gov.uk/trinidadandtobago; High Commissioner ERIC JENKINSON.

USA: 15 Queen's Park West, POB 752, Port of Spain; tel. 622-6371; fax 625-5462; e-mail usispos@trinidad.net; internet trinidad.usembassy.gov; Ambassador Dr ROY L. AUSTIN.

Venezuela: 16 Victoria Ave, POB 1300, Port of Spain; tel. 627-9821; fax 624-2508; e-mail embaveneztt@carib-link.net; Ambassador VINICIO ROMERO MARTÍNEZ.

Judicial System

The Chief Justice, who has overall responsibility for the administration of justice in Trinidad and Tobago, is appointed by the President after consultation with the Prime Minister and the Leader of the Opposition. The President appoints and promotes judges on the advice of the Judicial and Legal Service Commission. The Judicial and Legal Service Commission, which comprises the Chief Justice as chairman, the chairman of the Public Service Commission, two former judges and a senior member of the bar, appoints all judicial and legal officers. The Judiciary comprises the higher judiciary (the Supreme Court) and the lower judiciary (the Magistracy). In February 2005 Parliament voted to accept the authority of the Caribbean Court of Justice (CCJ) to settle international trade disputes. The Court was formally inaugurated in Port of Spain on 16 April 2005.

Chief Justice: IVOR ARCHIE.

Supreme Court of Judicature: Knox St, Port of Spain; tel. 623-2417; fax 627-5477; e-mail ttlaw@wow.net; internet www.ttlawcourts.org; the Supreme Court consists of the High Court of Justice and the Court of Appeal. The Supreme Court is housed in three locations: Port of Spain, San Fernando and Tobago. There are 23 Supreme Court Puisne Judges who sit in criminal, civil, and matrimonial divisions; Registrar EVELYN ANN PETERSEN.

Court of Appeal: The Court of Appeal hears appeals against decisions of the Magistracy and the High Court. Further appeals are directed to the Judicial Committee of the Privy Council of the United Kingdom, sometimes as of right and sometimes with leave of the Court. The Court of Appeal consists of the Chief Justice, who is President, and six other Justices of Appeal.

The Magistracy and High Court of Justice

The Magistracy and the High Court exercise original jurisdiction in civil and criminal matters. The High Court hears indictable criminal matters, family matters where the parties are married, and civil matters involving sums over the petty civil court limit. High Court judges are referred to as either Judges of the High Court or Puisne Judges. The Masters of the High Court, of which there are four, have the jurisdiction of judges in civil chamber courts. The Magistracy (in its petty civil division) deals with civil matters involving sums of less than TT $15,000. It exercises summary jurisdiction in criminal matters and hears preliminary inquiries in indictable matters. The Magistracy, which is divided into 13 districts, consists of a Chief Magistrate, a Deputy Chief Magistrate, 13 Senior Magistrates and 29 Magistrates.

Chief Magistrate: SHERMAN MCNICHOLLS, Magistrates' Court, St Vincent St, Port of Spain; tel. 625-2781.

Director of Public Prosecutions: GEOFFREY HENDERSON.

Religion

In 2000 it was estimated that one half the population practised Christianity, including Anglican (7.8%), Pentecostal (6.8%), Seventh-day Adventist (4%) and Presbyterian (3.3%), while some 22.5% of the population was Hindu, 5.8% Muslim and 5.4% Shouter Baptist.

CHRISTIANITY

Caribbean Conference of Churches: POB 876, Curepe; tel. 662-2979; fax 662-1303; e-mail cchq@tstt.net.tt; internet www.ccc-caribe.org; f. 1973; Pres. Rev. Dr LESLEY G. ANDERSON; Gen. Sec. GERARD A. J. GRANADO.

Christian Council of Trinidad and Tobago: Hayes Court, 21 Maraval Rd, Port of Spain; tel. 637-9329; f. 1967; church unity org. formed by the Roman Catholic, Anglican, Presbyterian, Methodist, African Methodist, Spiritual Baptist and Moravian Churches, the Church of Scotland and the Salvation Army, with the Ethiopian Orthodox Church and the Baptist Union as observers; Pres. The Rt Rev. CALVIN WENDELL BESS (Anglican Bishop of Trinidad and Tobago); Sec. GRACE STEELE.

The Anglican Communion

Anglicans are adherents of the Church in the Province of the West Indies, comprising eight dioceses. The Archbishop of the West Indies is the Bishop of Nassau and the Bahamas.

Bishop of Trinidad and Tobago: The Rt Rev. CALVIN WENDELL BESS, Hayes Court, 21 Maraval Rd, Port of Spain; tel. 622-7387; fax 628-1319; e-mail bessc@tstt.net.tt; internet www.trinidad.anglican.org.

Protestant Churches

Baptist Union of Trinidad and Tobago: 104 High St, Princes Town; tel. 655-2291; e-mail baptuni@tstt.net.tt; f. 1816; Pres. Rev. EDWIN H. LEWIS; Gen. Sec. Rev. JOHN S. C. BRAMBLE; 24 churches, 3,300 mems.

Presbyterian Church in Trinidad and Tobago: POB 187, Paradise Hill, San Fernando; tel. and fax 652-4829; e-mail pctt@tstt.net.tt; f. 1868; Moderator Rt Rev. ELVIS ELAHIE; Gen. Sec. ALVIN SEEREERAM; 40,000 mems.

TRINIDAD AND TOBAGO

Directory

The Roman Catholic Church

For ecclesiastical purposes, Trinidad and Tobago comprises the single archdiocese of Port of Spain. At 31 December 2005 there were some 335,000 adherents in the country, representing about 26% of the total population.

Antilles Episcopal Conference: 9A Gray St, Port of Spain; tel. 622-2932; fax 628-3688; e-mail aec@carib-link.net; internet www.catholiccaribbean.org; f. 1975; 21 mems from the Caribbean and Central American regions; Pres. Most Rev. LAWRENCE ALOYSIUS BURKE (Archbishop of Kingston, Jamaica); Gen. Sec. Rev. GERARD E. FARFAN.

Archbishop of Port of Spain: EDWARD JOSEPH GILBERT, 27 Maraval Rd, Port of Spain; tel. 622-1103; fax 622-1165; e-mail abishop@carib-link.net.

HINDUISM

Hindu immigrants from India first arrived in Trinidad and Tobago in 1845. The vast majority of migrants, who were generally from Uttar Pradesh, were Vishnavite Hindus, who belonged to sects such as the Ramanandi, the Kabir and the Sieunaraini. The majority of Hindus currently subscribe to the doctrine of Sanathan Dharma, which evolved from Ramanandi teaching.

Arya Pratinidhi Sabha of Trinidad Inc (Arya Samaj): Seereeram Memorial Vedic School, Old Southern Main Rd, Montrose Village, Chaguanas; tel. 663-1721; e-mail president@trinidadaryasamaj.org; Pres. LAKHRAM VIJAY BACHAN.

Pandits' Parishad (Council of Pandits): Maha Sabha Headquarters, Eastern Main Rd, St Augustine; tel. 645-3240; works towards the co-ordination of temple activities and the standardization of ritual procedure; affiliated to the Maha Sabha; 200 mems.

Sanathan Dharma Maha Sabha of Trinidad and Tobago Inc: Maha Sabha Headquarters, Eastern Main Rd, St Augustine; tel. 645-3240; e-mail mahasabha@ttemail.com; f. 1952; Hindu pressure group and public org.; organizes the provision of Hindu education; Pres. Dr D. OMAH MAHARAJH; Sec. Gen. SATNARAYAN MAHARAJ.

The Press

DAILIES

Newsday: 19–21 Chacon St, Port of Spain; tel. 623-2459; fax 657-5008; internet www.newsday.co.tt; f. 1993; CEO and Editor-in-Chief THERESE MILLS; circ. 2,200,000.

Trinidad Guardian: 22 St Vincent St, POB 122, Port of Spain; tel. 623-8871; fax 625-5702; e-mail letters@ttol.co.tt; internet www.guardian.co.tt; f. 1917; morning; independent; Editor-in-Chief DOMINIC KALIPERSAD; circ. 52,617.

Trinidad and Tobago Express: 35 Independence Sq., Port of Spain; tel. 623-1711; fax 627-1451; e-mail express@trinidadexpress.com; internet www.trinidadexpress.com; f. 1967; morning; CEO KEN GORDON; Editor ALAN GEERE; circ. 55,000.

PERIODICALS

The Boca: Crews Inn Marina and Boatyard, Village Sq., Chaguaramas; tel. 634-2055; fax 634-2056; e-mail enquiry@boatersenterprise.com; internet www.boatersenterprise.com/boca; monthly; magazine of the sailing and boating community; Man. Dir JACK DAUSEND.

The Bomb: Southern Main Rd, Curepe; tel. 645-2744; weekly.

Caribbean Beat Magazine: 6 Prospect Ave, Maraval, Port of Spain; tel. 622-3821; fax 628-0639; e-mail info@meppublishers.com; internet www.caribbean-beat.com; f. 1991; 6 a year; distributed by Caribbean Airlines; Publr JEREMY TAYLOR; Man. HELEN SHAIR-SINGH.

Catholic News: 31 Independence Sq., Port of Spain; tel. 623-6093; fax 623-9468; e-mail cathnews@trinidad.net; internet www.catholicnews-tt.net; f. 1892; weekly; Editor JUNE JOHNSTON; circ. 16,000.

Economic Bulletin: Eric Williams Plaza, Independence Sq., POB 1250, Port of Spain; tel. 625-4835; fax 627-4696; e-mail info@central-bank.org.tt; internet www.central-bank.org.tt; f. 1950; issued 3 times a year by the Central Bank; Information Man. KAREN CAMPBELL.

Energy Caribbean: 6 Prospect Ave, Maraval, Port of Spain; tel. 622-3821; fax 628-0639; e-mail dchin@meppublishers.com; internet www.meppublishers.com; f. 2002; bimonthly; Editor DAVID RENWICK.

Showtime: Cnr 9th St and 9th Ave, Barataria; tel. 674-1692; fax 674-3228; circ. 30,000.

Sunday Express: 35 Independence Sq., Port of Spain; tel. 623-1711; fax 627-1451; e-mail express@trinidadexpress.com; internet www.trinidadexpress.com; f. 1967; circ. 51,405.

Sunday Guardian: 22 St Vincent St, POB 122, Port of Spain; tel. 623-8870; fax 625-7211; e-mail esunday@ttol.co.tt; internet www.guardian.co.tt; f. 1917; independent; morning; Editor-in-Chief DOMINIC KALIPERSAD; circ. 48,324.

Sunday Punch: Cnr 9th St and 9th Ave, Barataria; tel. 674-1692; fax 674-3228; internet www.tntmirror.com; weekly; Editor ANTHONY ALEXIS; circ. 40,000.

Tobago News: Milford Rd, Scarborough; tel. 639-5565; fax 625-4480; e-mail ccngroupc@tstt.net.tt; internet www.thetobagonews.com; f. 1985; weekly; Editor COMPTON DELPH.

Trinidad and Tobago Gazette: 2–4 Victoria Ave, Port of Spain; tel. 625-4139; weekly; official govt paper; circ. 3,300.

Trinidad and Tobago Mirror: Cnr 9th St and 9th Ave, Barataria; tel. 674-1692; fax 674-3228; internet www.tntmirror.com; 2 a week; Editors KEN ALI, KEITH SHEPHERD; circ. 35,000.

Tropical Agriculture: Faculty of Agriculture and Natural Sciences, University of the West Indies, St Augustine; tel. and fax 645-3640; e-mail tropicalagri@fans.uwi.tt; f. 1924; journal of the School of Agriculture (fmrly Imperial College of Tropical Agriculture); quarterly; Editor-in-Chief Prof. FRANK A. GUMBS.

Weekend Heat: Southern Main Rd, Curepe; tel. 625-4583; weekly; Editor STAN MORA.

Publishers

Caribbean Children's Press: 7 Coronation St, St James; tel. and fax 628-4248; e-mail caripres@tstt.net.tt; f. 1987; educational publishers for primary schools.

Caribbean Educational Publishers: Gulf View Link Rd, La Romaine; tel. 657-9613; fax 652-5620; e-mail mbscep@tstt.net.tt; Pres. TEDDY MOHAMMED.

Charran Publishing House Ltd: Wrightson Road, POB 126, Port of Spain; tel. 625-9821; fax 623-6597; e-mail charran_pub@yahoo.com; internet www.charranpublishers.com; Man. Dir REGINALD CHARRAN.

Lexicon Trinidad Ltd: 48 Boundary Rd, San Juan; tel. 675-3395; fax 675-3360; e-mail lexicon@tstt.net.tt; Dir KEN JAIKARANSINGH.

Morton Publishing: 97 Saddle Rd, Maraval; tel. 348-37777; fax 762-9923; e-mail morton@morton-pub.com; internet www.morton-pub.com; f. 1977; educational books; Pres. DOUG MORTON; Dir JULIE MORTON.

Prospect Press (Media and Editorial Projects Ltd—MEP): 6 Prospect Ave, Maraval, Port of Spain; tel. 622-3821; fax 628-0639; e-mail prospectpress@meppublishers.com; internet www.meppublishers.com; f. 1991; Caribbean interest magazine and book publishing; Publr JEREMY TAYLOR.

Royards Publishing Co: 7A Macoya Industrial Estate, Macoya; tel. 663-6002; fax 663-6316; e-mail royards@aol.com; internet www.royards.com; f. 1984; educational publishers; Dirs CLIFFORD NARINESINGH, DWIGHT NARINESINGH.

Trinidad Publishing Co Ltd: 22–24 St Vincent St, Port of Spain; tel. 623-8870; fax 625-7211; e-mail business@ttol.co.tt; internet www.guardian.co.tt; f. 1917; Man. Dir GRENFELL KISSOON.

Broadcasting and Communications

TELECOMMUNICATIONS

Regulatory Body

Telecommunications Authority of Trinidad and Tobago (TATT): Suites 3–5, BEN Court, 76 Boundary Rd, San Juan; tel. 675-8288; fax 674-1055; e-mail info@tatt.org.tt; internet www.tatt.org.tt; f. 2001 to oversee the liberalization of the telecommunications sector; Chair. Dr KHALID HASSANALI.

Major Companies

bmobile: 114 Frederick St, Port of Spain; fax 625-5807; e-mail service@tstt.co.tt; internet www.bmobile.co.tt; f. 1991 as TSTT Cellnet; name changed as above 2006; 51% state-owned, 49% by Cable & Wireless (United Kingdom); mobile cellular telephone operator; Vice-Pres. GARY BARROW.

Columbus Communications Trinidad Ltd (CCTL): Port of Spain; fax 624-9584; e-mail residentialsales@columbustrinidad.com; internet www.flowtrinidad.com; f. 2005; digital cable television, internet and local telephone service providers; mobile cellular telephone licence granted in 2006; Pres. and CEO JOHN REID; 250 employees (2007).

Digicel Trinidad and Tobago: 11–13 Victoria Ave, Port of Spain; tel. 628-7000; fax 622-0887; e-mail tt.customer.care@digicelgroup

TRINIDAD AND TOBAGO

.com; internet www.digiceltrinidadandtobago.com; owned by an Irish consortium; mobile cellular telephone licence granted in 2005; Chair. Denis O'Brien; CEO Niall Dorrian.

LaqTel Ltd: 38–40 Sackville St, Port of Spain; tel. and fax 625-6001; fax 623-0587; e-mail learnmore@laqtel.com; internet www.laqtel.net; f. 2002; privately owned; awarded mobile cellular telephone licence in 2005; CEO Michael Barrow.

One Caribbean Media Ltd (OCM): 35 Independence Sq., Port of Spain; tel. 623-1711; fax 625-5712; e-mail tjohnson@trinidadexpress.com; internet www.onecaribbeanmedia.net; f. 2006 by merger of Caribbean Communications Network (CCN) and The Nation Corpn (Barbados); Chair. Sir Fred Gollop; CEO Craig Reynald.

Open Telecom Ltd: 88 Edward St, Port of Spain; tel. 622-6736; e-mail sales@opentelecom.com; internet wwww.gillettegroup.com/opentelecom/index.htm; Chair. Peter Gillette.

Telecommunication Services of Trinidad and Tobago (TSTT) Ltd: 1 Edward St, POB 3, Port of Spain; tel. 625-4431; fax 627-0856; e-mail tsttceo@tstt.net.tt; internet www.tstt.co.tt; 51% state-owned, 49% by Cable & Wireless (United Kingdom); 51% privatization pending; CEO Roberto Peón.

BROADCASTING

Radio

Homeviewtnt.com: Port of Spain; e-mail customerservice@homeviewtnt.com; internet www.homeviewtnt.com; operates 6 commercial radio stations: Radio 90.5 FM; Sangeet 106 FM; 103 FM; Ebony 104 FM; Vibe CT105 FM; Radio Trinbago 94.7 FM.

Hott 93 FM: Cumulus Broadcasting Inc, 3A Queens Park West, Port of Spain; tel. 623-4688; fax 624-3234; e-mail studio@hott93.com.

Love 94.1 and Power 102 FM: 88–90 Abercromby St, Port of Spain; tel. 627-6937; fax 624-8223; internet www.power102fm.com; CEO Lennox Toussaint; Gen. Man. Rueben Mohammed.

Music Radio 97 FM: Long Circular Rd, St James; tel. 622-9797; fax 624-3234.

National Broadcasting Network Ltd (FM 100, Yes 98.9 FM, Swar Milan 91.1, Radio 610): 11A Maraval Rd, Port of Spain; tel. 662-4141; fax 622-0344; e-mail bdesilva@nbn.co.tt; f. 1957; AM and FM transmitters at Chaguanas, Cumberland Hill, Hospedales and French Fort, Tobago; govt-owned; CEO Dominic Beaubrun; Man. Brenda de Silva; est. regular audience 105,000.

Trinidad Broadcasting Co Ltd (Radio Trinidad, Radio Nine Five): Broadcasting House, 11B Maraval Rd, POB 716, Port of Spain; tel. 622-1151; fax 622-2380; commercial.

Trinidad Broadcasting Company (Radio Trinidad 730 AM, Rhythm Radio, Caribbean Tempo and WEFM 96.1 FM): 22 St Vincent St, Port of Spain; tel. 623-9202; fax 622-2380; f. 1947; commercial; four programmes; Man. Dir Grenfell Kissoon.

Trinidad and Tobago Radio Network: 35 Independence Sq., Port of Spain; tel. 624-7078.

Television

National Broadcasting Network Ltd: 11A Maraval Rd, POB 665, Port of Spain; tel. 622-4141; fax 622-0344; e-mail bdesilva@nbn.co.tt; f. 1962; state-owned commercial station; operates channels 2, 4, 13, 16, TIC and The Information Channel; CEO Dominic Beaubrun.

TV6: 35 Express House, Independence Sq., Port of Spain; tel. 627-8806; fax 627-1451; e-mail tjohnson@trinidadexpress.com; internet www.onecaribbeanmedia.net; f. 1991; operates channels 6 and 18; owned by One Caribbean Media Ltd (OCM); Chair. Sir Fred Gollop; CEO Craig Reynald.

Finance

(cap. = capital; dep. = deposits; res = reserves; m. = million; brs = branches; amounts in TT $ unless otherwise stated)

BANKING

Central Bank

Central Bank of Trinidad and Tobago: Eric Williams Plaza, Brian Lara Promenade, POB 1250, Port of Spain; tel. 625-4835; fax 627-4696; e-mail info@central-bank.org.tt; internet www.central-bank.org.tt; f. 1964; cap. 100.0m., res 100.0m., dep. 29,044.2m. (Sept. 2006); Gov. Ewart S. Williams.

Commercial Banks

Citibank (Trinidad and Tobago) Ltd: 12 Queen's Park East, POB 1249, Port of Spain; tel. 625-1046; fax 624-8131; internet www.citicorp.com; f. 1983; fmrly The United Bank of Trinidad and Tobago Ltd; name changed as above 1989; owned by Citicorp Merchant Bank Ltd; cap. 30.0m., res 14.7m., dep. 455.5m. (Dec. 1996); Chair. Ian E. Dasent; Man. Dir Steve Bideshi; 2 brs.

Citicorp Merchant Bank Ltd: 12 Queen's Park East, POB 1249, Port of Spain; tel. 623-3344; fax 624-8131; cap. 57.1m., res 28.5m., dep. 473.6m. (Dec. 2002); owned by Citibank Overseas Investment Corpn; Chair. Ian E. Dasent; Man. Dir Karen Darbasie.

First Citizens Bank Ltd: 9 Queen's Park East, Port of Spain; tel. 624-3178; fax 627-4548; e-mail enquiries@simplyfirst.net; internet www.firstcitizenstt.com; f. 1993 following merger of National Commercial Bank of Trinidad and Tobago Ltd, Trinidad Co-operative Bank Ltd and Workers' Bank of Trinidad and Tobago; state-owned; cap. 340.0m., res 253.4m., dep. 8,472.1m. (Sept. 2006); Chair. Samuel A. Martin; CEO Larry Howai; 22 brs.

RBTT Ltd: Royal Court, 19–21 Park St, POB 287, Port of Spain; tel. 623-1322; fax 625-3764; e-mail royalinfo@rbtt.co.tt; internet www.rbtt.com; f. 1972 as Royal Bank of Trinidad and Tobago to take over local brs of Royal Bank of Canada; present name adopted April 2002; bought by Royal Bank of Canada in 2007; cap. 404.0m., res 215.4m., dep. 10,083.1m. (March 2006); Chair. Peter J. July; CEO Suresh Sookoo; 21 brs.

Republic Bank Ltd: 9–17 Park St, POB 1153, Port of Spain; tel. 623-1056; fax 624-1323; e-mail email@republictt.com; internet www.republictt.com; f. 1837 as Colonial Bank; became Barclays Bank in 1972; name changed as above 1981; merged with Bank of Commerce Trinidad and Tobago Ltd 1997; cap. 537.1m., res 951.8m., dep. 28,549.4m. (Sept. 2006); Chair. Ronald F. Harford; Man. Dir David Dulal-Whiteway; 34 brs.

Republic Finance & Merchant Bank Ltd: 9–17 Park St, POB 1153, Port of Spain; tel. 623-1056; fax 624-1323; e-mail email@republictt.com; internet www.republictt.com; f. 1965; owned by Republic Bank Ltd (q.v.); cap. 30.0m., res 44.5m., dep. 1,836.5m. (Sept. 2004); Chair. Ronald F. Harford; Man. Dir Cheryl F. Greaves.

Scotiabank Trinidad and Tobago Ltd: 56–58 Richmond St, POB 621, Port of Spain; tel. 625-3566; fax 627-5278; e-mail scotiamain@tstt.net.tt; internet www.scotiabank15.com; cap. 167.6m., res 277.4m., dep. 7,543.7m. (Oct. 2006); Chair. Robert H. Pitfield; Man. Dir Richard P. Young; 23 brs.

Development Banks

Agricultural Development Bank of Trinidad and Tobago: 87 Henry St, POB 154, Port of Spain; tel. 623-6261; fax 624-3087; e-mail adbceo@tstt.net.tt; f. 1968; provides long-, medium- and short-term loans to farmers and the agri-business sector; Chair. Hubert Alleyne; CEO Jacqueline Rawlins.

DFL Caribbean: 10 Cipriani Blvd, POB 187, Port of Spain; tel. 623-4665; fax 624-3563; e-mail df@dflcaribbean.com; internet www.dflcaribbean.com; provides short- and long-term finance, and equity financing for projects in manufacturing, agro-processing, tourism, industrial and commercial enterprises; total assets US $84.2m. (Dec. 1998); Chair. Audley Walker; Man. Dir Gerard M. Pemberton.

Credit Unions

Co-operative Credit Union League of Trinidad and Tobago Ltd: 32–34 Maraval Rd, St Clair; tel. 622-3100; fax 622-4800; e-mail culeague@tstt.net.tt; internet www.ccultt.org; Chair. Gary Cross.

Hindu Credit Union Co-operative Society Ltd: Ramlals Bldg, Main Rd, Chaguanas; tel. 671-3718; e-mail e-mail@hinducreditunion.com; internet www.hinducreditunion.com/hcu.html; Pres. Harry Harnarine.

STOCK EXCHANGE

Trinidad and Tobago Stock Exchange Ltd: Nicholas Tower, 10th Floor, 63–65 Independence Sq., Port of Spain; tel. 625-5107; fax 623-0089; e-mail ttstockx@tstt.net.tt; internet www.stockex.co.tt; f. 1981; 39 cos listed (2006); electronic depository system came into operation in 2003; Chair. Andrew McEachrane; CEO Hugh Edwards.

INSURANCE

American Life and General Insurance Co (Trinidad and Tobago) Ltd: ALGICO Plaza, 91–93 St Vincent St, POB 943, Port of Spain; tel. 625-4425; fax 623-6218; e-mail algico@wow.net; Man. Dir Gordon Deane.

Bankers Insurance Co of Trinidad and Tobago Ltd: 177 Tragarete Rd, Port of Spain; tel. 622-4613; fax 628-6808; e-mail bankersinsurance@hcu.co.tt; internet www.hinducreditunion.com; subsidiary of Hindu Credit Union.

Barbados Mutual Life Assurance Society: The Mutual Centre, 16 Queen's Park West, POB 356, Port of Spain; tel. 628-1636; Gen. Man. Hugh Mazely.

TRINIDAD AND TOBAGO

Directory

Capital Insurance Ltd: 38–42 Cipero St, San Fernando; tel. 657-8077; fax 652-7306; f. 1958; motor and fire insurance; total assets $65m.; 10 brs and 9 agencies.

Colonial Fire & General Insurance Co Ltd (COLFIRE): e-mail info@colfire.com; internet www.colfire.com; f. 1995; mem. of C. L. Financial Group; Chair. ROBERT NG CHOW; Man. Dir WILLARD P. HARRIS.

Colonial Life Insurance Co (Trinidad) Ltd: Colonial Life Bldg, 29 St Vincent St, POB 443, Port of Spain; tel. 623-1421; fax 627-3821; e-mail info@clico.com; internet www.clico.com; f. 1936; Chair. LAWRENCE A. DUPREY; CEO CLAUDIUS DACON.

CUNA Caribbean Insurance Society Ltd: 37 Wrightson Rd, POB 193, Port of Spain; tel. 623-7963; fax 623-6251; e-mail cunains@trinidad.net; internet www.cunacaribbean.com; f. 1991; marine aviation and transport; motor vehicle, personal accident, property; Gen. Man. ANTHONY HALL; 3 brs.

Furness Anchorage General Insurance Ltd: 11–13 Milling Ave, Sea Lots, POB 283, Port of Spain; tel. 623-0868; fax 625-1243; e-mail furness@wow.net; internet www.furnessgroup.com; f. 1979; general; Chair. IGNATIUS SEVEIRANO FERREIRA; Exec. Chair. WILLIAM A. FERREIRA.

GTM Fire Insurance Co Ltd: 95–97 Queen St, Port of Spain; tel. 623-1525; e-mail gtmis@tstt.net.tt.

Guardian General Insurance Ltd: Princes Court, Keate St, Port of Spain; tel. 623-4741; fax 623-4320; e-mail info@guardiangenerallimited.com; internet www.guardiangenerallimited.com; founded by merger of NEMWIL and Caribbean Home; Chair. HENRY PETER GANTEAUME; CEO RICHARD ESPINET.

Guardian Life of the Caribbean: 1 Guardian Dr., West Moorings, Port of Spain; tel. 625-5433; internet www.guardianlife.co.tt; Chair. ARTHUR LOK JACK; Pres. and CEO DOUGLAS CAMACHO.

Gulf Insurance Ltd: 1 Gray St, St Clair, Port of Spain; tel. 622-5878; fax 628-0272; e-mail info@gulfinsuranceltd.com; internet www.gulfinsuranceltd.com; f. 1974; general; Exec. Chair. GERRARD LEE-INNISS.

Maritime Financial Group: Maritime Centre, 10th Ave, POB 710, Barataria; tel. 674-0130; fax 638-6663; f. 1978; property and casualty; CEO JOHN SMITH.

Motor and General Insurance Co Ltd: 1–3 Havelock St, St Clair, Port of Spain; tel. 622-2637; fax 622-5345.

New India Assurance Co (T & T) Ltd: 22 St Vincent St, Port of Spain; tel. 623-1326; fax 625-0670; e-mail newindia@wow.net; tel. www.newindia.co.in.

Presidential Insurance Co Ltd: 54 Richmond St, Port of Spain; tel. 625-4788; e-mail pic101@tstt.net.tt.

Trinidad and Tobago Export Credit Insurance Co Ltd: 30 Queen's Park West, Port of Spain; tel. and fax 628-2762; e-mail eximbank@wow.net; internet www.eximbankt.com; state-owned; CEO BRIAN AWANG; Gen. Man. JOSEPHINE IBLE.

Trinidad and Tobago Insurance Ltd (TATIL): 11 Maraval Rd, POB 1004, Port of Spain; tel. 622-5351; fax 628-0035; e-mail info@tatil.co.tt; internet www.tatil.co.tt; acquired by ANSA McAL in 2004; Chair. JOHN JARDIM; CEO RELNA VIRE.

United Insurance Co: 30 O'Connor St, Woodbrook, Port of Spain; tel. 628-8343; fax 628-6575; e-mail trinidad@unitedinsure.com; internet unitedinsure.com; 95.0% owned by Barbados Shipping and Trading Co; Gen. Man. DENNIS BENISAR.

INSURANCE ORGANIZATIONS

Association of Trinidad and Tobago Insurance Companies: 28 Sackville St, Port of Spain; tel. 624-2817; fax 625-5132; e-mail jsc-attic@trinidad.net; internet www.attic.org.tt; Chair. INEZ SINANAN.

National Insurance Board: Cipriani Pl., 2A Cipriani Blvd, Port of Spain; tel. 625-2171-8; fax 627-1787; e-mail nib@nibtt.co.tt; internet www.nibtt.co.tt; f. 1971; statutory corporation; Chair. CALDER HART; Exec. Dir JEFFREY MC FARLANE.

Trade and Industry

GOVERNMENT AGENCIES

Cocoa and Coffee Industry Board: 27 Frederick St, POB 1, Port of Spain; tel. 625-0298; fax 627-4172; e-mail ccib@tstt.net.tt; f. 1962; marketing of coffee and cocoa beans, regulation of cocoa and coffee industry; Man. BARRY JOEFIELD.

Export-Import Bank of Trinidad and Tobago Ltd (EXIM-BANK): 30 Queen's Park West, Port of Spain; tel. 628-2762; fax 622-3545; e-mail eximbank@wow.net; internet www.eximbankt.com; Chair. CLARRY BENN; CEO BRIAN AWANG.

Trinidad and Tobago Forest Products Ltd (TANTEAK): Connector Rd, Carlsen Field, Chaguanas; tel. 665-0078; fax 665-6645; f. 1975; harvesting, processing and marketing of state plantation-grown teak and pine; privatization pending; Chair. RUSKIN PUNCH; Man. Dir CLARENCE BACCHUS.

DEVELOPMENT ORGANIZATIONS

National Energy Corporation of Trinidad and Tobago Ltd: PLIPDECO House, Orinoco Dr., POB 191, Point Lisas, Couva; tel. 636-4662; fax 679-2384; e-mail infocent@carib-link.net; internet www.ngc.co.tt; owned by the Nat. Gas Co of Trinidad and Tobago Ltd (q.v.); f. 1979; Chair. KENNETH BIRCHWOOD; Pres. FRANK LOOK KIN.

National Housing Authority: 44–46 South Quay, POB 555, Port of Spain; tel. 627-1703; fax 625-3963; e-mail info@housing.gov.tt; internet www.housing.gov.tt; f. 1962; Chair. ANDRE MONYEIL; CEO NOEL GARCIA.

Point Lisas Industrial Port Development Corporation Ltd (PLIPDECO): PLIPDECO House, Orinoco Dr., POB 191, Point Lisas, Couva; tel. 636-2201; fax 636-4008; e-mail plipdeco@plipdeco.com; internet www.plipdeco.com; f. 1966; privatized in the late 1990s; deep-water port handling general cargo, liquid and dry bulk, to serve adjacent industrial estate, which now includes iron and steel complex, methanol, ammonia, urea and related downstream industries; Chair. Commdr KAYAM MOHAMMED; CEO Capt. RAWLE BADDALOO.

CHAMBERS OF COMMERCE

South Trinidad Chamber of Industry and Commerce: Suite 313, Cross Crossing Shopping Centre, Lady Hailes Ave, San Fernando; tel. 652-5613; fax 653-4983; e-mail execoffice@stcic.org; internet www.stcic.org; f. 1956; Pres. RAMPERSAD MOTILAL; CEO Dr THACKWRAY DRIVER.

Trinidad and Tobago Chamber of Industry and Commerce (Inc): Chamber Bldg, Columbus Circle, Westmoorings, POB 499, Port of Spain; tel. 637-6966; fax 637-7425; e-mail chamber@chamber.org.tt; internet www.chamber.org.tt; f. 1891; Pres. IAN WELCH; CEO JOAN FERREIRA; 600 mems.

INDUSTRIAL AND TRADE ASSOCIATIONS

Agricultural Society of Trinidad and Tobago: 1st Floor, Henry St, Port of Spain; tel. 623-7797; fax 623-3087; e-mail agrisoc@tstt.net.tt.

Coconut Growers' Association (CGA) Ltd: Eastern Main Rd, POB 229, Laventille, Port of Spain; tel. 623-5207; fax 623-2359; e-mail cgaltd@tstt.net.tt; f. 1936; 354 mems; Exec. Chair. PHILIPPE AGOSTINI.

Co-operative Citrus Growers' Association of Trinidad and Tobago Ltd: Eastern Main Rd, POB 174, Laventille, Port of Spain; tel. 623-2255; fax 623-2487; e-mail ccga@wow.net; internet www.ccga.co.tt; f. 1932; Pres. FELIX CLARK; Gen. Man. KENNETH DEBIQUE; 437 mems.

Pan Trinbago Inc: Victoria Park Suites, 14–17 Park St, Port of Spain; tel. 623-4486; fax 625-6715; e-mail admin@pantrinbago.co.tt; internet www.pantrinbago.co.tt; f. 1971; official body for Trinidad and Tobago steelbands; Pres. PATRICK LOUIS ARNOLD; Sec. RICHARD FORTEAU.

Shipping Association of Trinidad and Tobago: 15 Scott Bushe St, Port of Spain; tel. 623-3355; fax 623-8540; e-mail gm@shipping.co.tt; internet www.shipping.co.tt; f. 1938; Pres. HAYDN JONES; Gen. Man. E. JOANNE EDWARDS-ALLEYNE.

Sugar Association of the Caribbean: Brechin Castle, Couva; tel. 636-2449; fax 636-2847; f. 1942; promotes and protects sugar industry in the Caribbean; Chair. IAN MCDONALD; Sec. A. MOHAMMED; 6 mem. asscns.

Trinidad and Tobago Contractors' Association: Morequito Ave, Valsayn Park, Valsayn; tel. 637-2967; fax 637-2963; e-mail sec@ttca.com; internet www.ttca.com; f. 1968; represents contractors and manufacturers and suppliers to the sector; Pres. HUGH SCHAMBER.

Trinidad and Tobago Manufacturers' Association: 1TTMA Bldg, 42 Tenth Ave, Barataria; tel. 675-8862; fax 675-9000; e-mail info@ttma.com; internet www.ttma.com; f. 1956; Pres. KAREN DE MONTBRUN; 260 mems.

EMPLOYERS' ORGANIZATION

Employers' Consultative Association of Trinidad and Tobago (ECA): 23 Chacon St, Port of Spain; tel. 625-4723; fax 625-4891; e-mail ecatt@tstt.net.tt; internet www.ecatt.org; f. 1959; Chair. CLARENCE RAMBHARAT; CEO LINDA BESSON; 500 mems.

STATE HYDROCARBONS COMPANIES

National Gas Co of Trinidad and Tobago Ltd (NGC): Orinoco Dr., Point Lisas Industrial Estate, POB 1127, Port of Spain; tel. 636-

TRINIDAD AND TOBAGO

4662; fax 679-2384; e-mail ngc@ngc.co.tt; internet www.ngc.co.tt; f. 1975; purchases, sells, compresses, transmits and distributes natural gas to consumers; Chair. KEITH AWONG; Pres. FRANK LOOK KIN.

Petroleum Co of Trinidad and Tobago Ltd (Petrotrin): Petrotrin Administration Bldg, Cnr Queen's Park West and Cipriani Blvd, Port of Spain; tel. 625-5240; fax 624-4661; e-mail kharnanan@petrotrin.com; internet www.petrotrin.com; f. 1993 following merger between Trinidad and Tobago Oil Co Ltd (Trintoc) and Trinidad and Tobago Petroleum Co Ltd (Trintopec); govt-owned; petroleum and gas exploration and production; operates refineries and a manufacturing complex, producing a variety of petroleum and petrochemical products; Chair. MALCOLM JONES; Pres. WAYNE BERTRAND; Gen. Man. KAIN LOOK YEE.

Petrotrin Trinmar Operations: Petrotrin Administration Bldg, Point Fortin; tel. 648-2127; fax 648-2519; f. 1962; owned by Petrotrin; marine petroleum and natural gas co; Gen. Man. ALLAN RUSSELL; 705 employees.

Trintomar Ltd: Petrotrin Administration Bldg, Pointe-à-Pierre; tel. 647-8861; fax 647-3193; e-mail lisle.ramyad@petrotrin.com; f. 1988; 80% owned by EOG Resources, 20% owned by NGC; develops offshore petroleum sector; Man. LISLE RAMYAD.

UTILITIES

Regulatory Authority

Regulated Industries Commission: 90 Independence Sq., Port of Spain; tel. 627-0821; fax 624-2027; e-mail ricoffice@ric.org.tt; internet www.ric.org.tt; Chair. DENNIS PANTIN; Exec. Dir HARJINDER S. ATWAL.

Electricity

Power Generation Co of Trinidad and Tobago (PowerGen): 6A Queen's Park West, Port of Spain; tel. 624-0383; fax 625-3759; 51% owned by Trinidad and Tobago Electricity Commission; 39% owned by Mirant (USA); 10% owned by BP; operates 3 generation plants in Point Lisas, Port of Spain and Penal; Gen. Man. GARTH CHATOOR.

Trinidad and Tobago Electricity Commission (T&TEC): 63 Frederick St, POB 121, Port of Spain; tel. 623-2611; fax 623-3759; e-mail ttecisd@trinidad.net; internet www.ttec.co.tt; state-owned electricity transmission and distribution co; Chair. DEVANAND RAMLAL; Gen. Man. INDARJIT SINGH (acting).

Trinity Power Ltd: Railway Rd, Dow Village, Couva; tel. 679-4542; fax 679-4463; e-mail gthompson@trinitypm.com; jt venture by Power Management Co (51.1%) and Centennial Energy; fmrly Inncogen Ltd; Gen. Man. CELIA LOUGHEIDE.

Gas

National Gas Co of Trinidad and Tobago Ltd: see State Hydrocarbons Companies.

Water

Water and Sewerage Authority (WASA): Farm Rd, St Joseph; tel. 662-9272; fax 652-1253; internet www.wasa.gov.tt; Chair. Dr ROLLIN BERTRAND; CEO ERROL GRIMES.

TRADE UNIONS

Federation of Independent Trade Unions and NGOs (FITUN): Paramount Bldg, 99A Circular Rd, San Fernando; tel. 652-2701; fax 652-7170; e-mail fitun_tt@yahoo.com; f. 2003; Pres. DAVID ABDULLAH; Gen. Sec. MORTON MITCHELL.

National Trade Union Centre (NATUC): 16 New St, Port of Spain; tel. 625-3023; fax 627-7588; e-mail natuc@carib-link.net; f. 1991 as umbrella org. unifying entire trade-union movt, incl. former Trinidad and Tobago Labour Congress and Council of Progressive Trade Unions; Pres. ROBERT GIUSEPPI; Gen. Sec. VINCENT CARBERA.

Principal Affiliates

Airline Superintendents' Association: c/o Data Centre Bldg, Piarco International Airport, Port of Spain; tel. 664-3401; fax 664-3303; Pres. JEFFERSON JOSEPH; Gen. Sec. THEO OLIVER.

All-Trinidad Sugar and General Workers' Trade Union (ATSGWTU): Rienzi Complex, Exchange Village, Southern Main Rd, Couva; tel. 636-2354; fax 636-3372; e-mail atsgwtu@tstt.net.tt; f. 1937; Pres. RUDRANATH INDARSINGH; Gen. Sec. SYLVESTER MARAJH; 2,000 mems.

Amalgamated Workers' Union: 16 New St, Port of Spain; tel. 627-6717; fax 627-8993; f. 1953; Pres.-Gen. CYRIL LOPEZ; Sec. FLAVIUS NURSE; c. 7,000 mems.

Directory

Association of Technical, Administrative and Supervisory Staff: Brechin Castle, Couva; Pres. Dr WALLY DES VIGNES; Gen. Sec. ISAAC BEEPATH.

Aviation, Communication and Allied Workers' Union: Aero Services Bldg, Orange Grove Rd, Tacarigua; tel. and fax 640-6518; f. 1982; Pres. CHRISTOPHER ABRAHAM; Gen. Sec. SIEUNARINE BALROOP.

Banking, Insurance and General Workers' Union: 85 Eight Street, Barataria, Port of Spain; tel. 675-9135; fax 675-4664; e-mail union@bigwu.org; internet www.bigwu.org; f. 1974 as Bank and General Workers' Union; name changed as above following merger with Bank Employees' Union in 2003; Pres. VINCENT CABRERA; Gen. Sec. TREVOR JOHNSON.

Communication, Transport and General Workers' Trade Union: Aero Services Credit Union Bldg, Orange Grove Rd, Tacarigua; tel. and fax 640-8785; e-mail cattu@tstt.net.tt; Pres. JAGDEO JAGROOP; Gen. Sec. RAYMOND SMALL.

Communication Workers' Union: 146 Henry St, Port of Spain; tel. 623-5588; fax 625-3308; e-mail cwutdad@tstt.net.tt; f. 1953; Pres. PATRICK HALL; Gen. Sec. LYLE TOWNSEND; c. 2,100 mems.

Contractors' and General Workers' Trade Union (CGWTU): 37 Rushworth St, San Fernando; tel. 657-8072; fax 657-6834; Pres. OWEN HINDS; Gen. Sec. AINSLEY MATTHEWS.

Customs and Excise Extra Guard Association: Nicholas Court, Abercromby St, Port of Spain; tel. 625-3311; Pres. ALEXANDER BABB; Gen. Sec. NATHAN HERBERT.

Fire Services Association (FSA): 52 Lewis St, Woodbrook, Port of Spain; tel. 628-1033; Pres. LENNOX LONDON; Vice-Pres. MICHAEL SPENCER.

National General Workers' Union: c/o 143 Charlotte St, Port of Spain; tel. 623-0694; Pres. JIMMY SINGH; Gen. Sec. CHRISTOPHER ABRAHAM.

National Union of Domestic Employees (NUDE): 53 Wattley Circular Rd, Mount Pleasant Rd, Arima; tel. 667-5247; fax 664-0546; e-mail domestic@tstt.net.tt; f. 1982; Gen. Sec. IDA LE BLANC.

National Union of Government and Federated Workers: 145–147 Henry St, Port of Spain; tel. 623-4591; fax 625-7756; e-mail headoffice@nugfw.org.tt; internet nugfw.org.tt; f. 1937; Pres. Gen. ROBERT GUISEPPI; Gen. Sec. JACQUELINE JACK; c. 20,000 mems.

Oilfield Workers' Trade Union (OWTU): Paramount Bldg, 99A Circular Rd, San Fernando; tel. 652-2701; fax 652-7170; e-mail owtu@owtu.org; internet www.owtu.org; f. 1937; Pres. ERROL MCLEOD; Gen. Sec. WENDY JOY WHITE; 9,000 mems.

Public Services Association: 89–91 Abercromby St, POB 353, Port of Spain; tel. 623-7987; fax 627-2980; e-mail psa@tstt.net.tt; f. 1938; Pres. JENNIFER BAPTISTE-PRIMUS; Sec. KAREN FERREIRA; c. 15,000 mems.

Seamen and Waterfront Workers' Trade Union: 1D Wrightson Rd, Port of Spain; tel. 625-1351; fax 625-1182; e-mail swwtu@tstt.net.tt; f. 1937; Pres.-Gen. MICHAEL ANNISETTE; Sec.-Gen. ROSS ALEXANDER; c. 3,000 mems.

Steel Workers' Union of Trinidad and Tobago: c/o ISPAT, Point Lisas, Couva; tel. 679-4666; fax 679-4175; e-mail swutt@tstt.net.tt; Pres. LEX LOVELL; Gen. Sec. PHILIP SANCHO.

Transport and Industrial Workers' Union: 114 Eastern Main Rd, Laventille, Port of Spain; tel. 623-4943; fax 623-2361; e-mail tiwu@tstt.net.tt; f. 1962; Pres. ROLAND SUTHERLAND; Gen. Sec. JUDY CHARLES; c. 5,000 mems.

Trinidad and Tobago Airline Pilots' Association (TTALPA): 35A Brunton Rd, St James; tel. 628-6556; fax 628-2418; e-mail info@ttalpa.org; internet www.ttalpa.org; Chair. Capt. ANTHONY WIGHT; Man. CHRISTINE DAVIS.

Trinidad and Tobago Postal Workers' Union: c/o General Post Office, Wrightson Rd, POB 692, Port of Spain; tel. 625-2121; fax 642-4303; Pres. (vacant); Gen. Sec. EVERALD SAMUEL.

Trinidad and Tobago Unified Teachers' Association: Cnr Fowler and Southern Main Rd, Curepe; tel. 645-2134; fax 662-1813; e-mail ttuta@trinidad.net; Pres. CLYDE PERMELL; Gen. Sec. DAVID LEWIS.

Union of Commercial and Industrial Workers: TIWU Bldg, 114 Eastern Main Rd, POB 460, Port of Spain; tel. and fax 626-2285; f. 1951; Pres. KELVIN GONZALES; Gen. Sec. ROSALIE FRASER; c. 1,500 mems.

Transport

RAILWAYS

In 2005 the Ministry of Works and Transport announced plans to reintroduce a railway service, which had been discontinued in 1968. The design phase of the project began in 2008 and construction was expected to take 10–15 years, costing an estimated TT $15,000m.

Services on the first section of railway line, connecting Port of Spain, St Joseph and Chaguanas, were expected to commence in 2009.

ROADS

In 1999 there were 8,320 km (5,170 miles) of roads in Trinidad and Tobago, of which 51.1% were paved. In 2005 the Ministry of Works and Transport announced plans to invest some TT $140m. in building a 40 km highway to connect Princes Town to Mayaro. In the same year the US Agency for International Development allocated US $3.2m. to fund the repair of roads damaged by 'Hurricane Ivan' in 2004.

Public Transport Service Corporation: Railway Bldgs, South Quay, POB 391, Port of Spain; tel. 623-2341; fax 625-6502; f. 1965; national bus services, operates a fleet of buses; CEO EDISON ISAAC.

SHIPPING

The chief ports are Port of Spain, Pointe-à-Pierre and Point Lisas in Trinidad and Scarborough in Tobago. Port of Spain handles 85% of all container traffic, and all international cruise arrivals. In 1998 Port of Spain handled 3.3m. metric tons of cargo. Port of Spain and Scarborough each have a deep-water wharf. Port of Spain possesses a dedicated container terminal, with two large overhead cranes. Plans were put in place in 2002 for an expansion of operations, through the purchase of an additional crane, the computerization of operations, and the deepening of the harbour (from 9.75 m to 12 m).

Caribbean Drydock Ltd: Port Chaguaramas, Western Main Rd, Chaguaramas; tel. 634-4226; fax 625-1215; ship repair, marine transport, barge and boat construction.

Point Lisas Industrial Port Development Corporation Ltd (PLIPDECO): see Trade and Industry—Development Organizations.

Port Authority of Trinidad and Tobago: Dock Rd, POB 549, Port of Spain; tel. 623-2901; fax 627-2666; e-mail vilmal@patnt.com; internet www.patnt.com; f. 1962; Chair. DEREK HUDSON; CEO CHRISTOPHER MENDEZ.

Shipping Association of Trinidad and Tobago: 15 Scott Bushe St, Port of Spain; tel. 623-3355; fax 623-8570; e-mail satt@wow.net; internet shipping.co.tt; Pres. STEWART SANKAR; Gen. Man. JENNIFER GONZÁLEZ.

CIVIL AVIATION

Piarco International Airport is situated 25.7 km (16 miles) south-east of Port of Spain and is used by numerous airlines. The airport was expanded and a new terminal was constructed in 2001. Piarco remains the principal air transportation facility in Trinidad and Tobago. However, following extensive aerodrome development at Crown Point Airport (located 13 km from Scarborough) in 1992 the airport was opened to jet aircraft. It is now officially named Crown Point International Airport. There is a domestic service between Trinidad and Tobago.

Airports Authority of Trinidad and Tobago (AATT): Airport Administration Centre, Piarco International Airport; tel. 669-8047; fax 669-2319; e-mail airport@tntairports.com; internet www.airporttnt.com; administers Piarco and Crown Point International Airports; Chair. LINUS ROGERS.

Caribbean Airlines: Sunjet House, 30 Edward St, Port of Spain; tel. 625-7200; e-mail mail@caribbean-airlines.com; internet www.caribbean-airlines.com; f. 2007 as successor to BWIA (f. 1940); operates scheduled passenger and cargo services linking destinations in the Caribbean region, South America, North America and Europe; CEO PHILIP SAUNDERS; Chair. ARTHUR LOK JACK.

Tourism

The climate and coastline attract visitors to Trinidad and Tobago. The latter island is generally believed to be the more beautiful and is less developed. The annual pre-Lenten carnival is a major attraction. In 2005 there were 463,191 foreign visitors, excluding cruise-ship passengers. Tourism receipts were estimated at US $661m. in that year. In 2000 there were an estimated 104,061 cruise-ship passenger arrivals. However, this declined to 67,196 by 2005. There were 5,943 hotel rooms in Trinidad and Tobago in 2003, of which 57.5% were on Tobago.

Tourism Development Co of Trinidad and Tobago (TDC): Maritime Centre, Level 1, 29 Tenth Ave, Barataria; tel. 675-7034; fax 675-7722; e-mail info@tdc.co.tt; internet www.tdc.co.tt; f. 1993 as Tourism and Industrial Devt Co of Trinidad and Tobago; restructured and renamed as above in 2005; Chair. DAVID LEWIS; Pres. JAMES HEPPLE.

Trinidad Hotels, Restaurants and Tourism Association (THRTA): c/o Trinidad & Tobago Hospitality and Tourism Institute, Airway Rd, Chaguaramas; tel. 634-1174; fax 634-1176; e-mail info@tnthotels.com; internet www.tnthotels.com; Pres. BARRY BIDAISEE; Exec. Dir GREER ASSAM.

> **Tobago Hotel and Tourism Association:** Apt 1, Lambeau Credit Union Bldg, Auchenskeoch, Carnbee; tel. and fax 639-9543; e-mail tthtatob@tstt.net.tt; Pres. CAROL ANN BIRCHWOOD-JAMES.

TUNISIA

Introductory Survey

Location, Climate, Language, Religion, Flag, Capital

The Republic of Tunisia lies in north Africa, bordered by Algeria to the west and by Libya to the south-east. To the north and east, Tunisia has a coastline on the Mediterranean Sea. The climate is temperate on the coast, with winter rain, but hot and dry inland. Temperatures in Tunis are generally between 6°C (43°F) and 33°C (91°F). The country's highest recorded temperature is 55°C. Average annual rainfall is up to 1,500 mm in the north, but less than 200 mm in the southern desert. The official language is Arabic, and there is a small Berber Tamazight-speaking minority. French is widely used as a second language. Islam is the state religion, and almost all of the inhabitants are Muslims. There are small minorities of Christians and Jews. The national flag (proportions 2 by 3) is red, with a white disc, containing a red crescent moon and a five-pointed red star, in the centre. The capital is Tunis.

Recent History

Formerly a French protectorate, Tunisia was granted internal self-government by France in September 1955 and full independence on 20 March 1956. Five days later elections were held for a Constitutional Assembly, which met in April and appointed Habib Bourguiba as Prime Minister in a Government dominated by members of his Néo-Destour (New Constitution) Party. In July 1957 a republic was established, with Bourguiba as Head of State, and a new Constitution was promulgated in June 1959. At elections held in November Bourguiba was elected unopposed to the new office of President, and the Néo-Destour Party won all 90 seats in the new National Assembly.

By 1964 the Néo-Destour Party had become the only legal political organization and in November of that year it was renamed the Parti socialiste destourien (PSD). A moderate socialist economic programme was introduced, which began with the expropriation of foreign-owned lands. However, attempts to introduce agricultural collectivization in 1964–69, under the direction of Ahmad Ben Salah, Minister of Finance and Planning, were abandoned in September 1969 because of resistance from the rural population. Ben Salah was dismissed, arrested and subsequently sentenced to 10 years' hard labour. He escaped in 1973 and fled to Europe, from where he organized the radical Mouvement de l'unité populaire (MUP). In 1970 Hédi Nouira, hitherto Governor of the Banque Centrale de Tunisie, was appointed Prime Minister. He began to reverse Ben Salah's socialist economic policies, with the introduction of liberal economic reforms in the sectors of industry and agriculture.

Liberalization of the economy was not accompanied by political reform, and the extensive powers of Nouira and Bourguiba were increasingly challenged by younger PSD members in the early 1970s. However, at the 1974 PSD Congress, Bourguiba was elected President-for-Life of the PSD and Nouira was confirmed as Secretary-General. In March 1975, after approving the necessary amendments to the Constitution, the National Assembly elected Bourguiba President-for-Life of Tunisia. Political differences emerged concerning economic policy, and the previously loyal trade union movement, the Union Générale Tunisienne du Travail (UGTT), led by Habib Achour, began to assert its independence from the PSD. In January 1978, for the first time since independence, a 24-hour general strike took place, organized by the UGTT. In violent clashes between troops and strikers, at least 50 people were killed and many trade union leaders, including Achour, were arrested. Subsequently Achour was sentenced to 10 years' hard labour and a new Secretary-General of the UGTT, Tijani Abid, declared the willingness of trade unions to co-operate with the Government.

In April 1980 Nouira resigned, owing to ill health, and was succeeded as Prime Minister and Secretary-General of the PSD by Muhammad Mzali. Under Mzali, signs of greater political tolerance became apparent. The one-party system ended in mid-1981, when the Parti communiste tunisien (PCT), which had been proscribed in 1963, was granted legal status. The Government announced that any political group that gained more than 5% of the votes cast in the forthcoming legislative elections would also be officially recognized. Many of the UGTT leaders imprisoned after the 1978 disturbances were pardoned, and Achour was reappointed Secretary-General of the UGTT. At elections to the National Assembly in November 1981 the PSD and the UGTT formed an electoral alliance, the Front national, which received 94.6% of the total votes cast and won all 126 seats in the new Assembly.

In July 1986 Mzali was replaced as Prime Minister by Rachid Sfar (hitherto Minister of Finance), and was dismissed as Secretary-General of the PSD. Mzali subsequently fled to Algeria, and was sentenced *in absentia* to terms of imprisonment and hard labour for defamatory comments against Tunisian leaders and mismanagement of public funds. Elections to the National Assembly in November were boycotted by the opposition parties, with the result that the PSD, opposed only by 15 independent candidates, won all 125 seats.

During late 1987 President Bourguiba's behaviour became increasingly erratic. In October he revoked several of his recent appointments of leading state officials, and dismissed Sfar from the premiership. Zine al-Abidine Ben Ali was appointed Prime Minister and Secretary-General of the PSD; he retained the interior portfolio, which he had held since 1986. In early November 1987 a disagreement between Bourguiba and Ben Ali was reported, apparently concerning the recent trial of 90 Islamists accused of plotting against the Government. On 7 November seven doctors declared that President Bourguiba was unfit to govern, owing to senility and ill health. In accordance with the Constitution, Ben Ali was sworn in as President. Hédi Baccouche (previously Minister of Social Affairs) was appointed Prime Minister, and a new Council of Ministers was formed, which excluded several close associates of Bourguiba. Ben Ali announced plans to reform the Constitution and to permit greater political freedom. In the same month the Government permitted the publication of previously suspended opposition newspapers, and by early 1988 some 3,000 political and non-political detainees had been released. In February the PSD was renamed the Rassemblement constitutionnel démocratique (RCD), in order to reflect the new administration's commitment to democratic reform.

In April 1988 legislation was enacted by the National Assembly to institute a multi-party political system, and in July the Assembly approved a series of proposals to reform the Constitution. The office of President-for-Life was abolished, and the President was, henceforth, to be elected by universal suffrage every five years and limited to two consecutive terms of office. In the same month there was a significant reorganization of the Government, notably affecting ministers who had served under Bourguiba. In September two further opposition parties, the left-wing Rassemblement socialiste progressiste and the liberal Parti social pour le progrès (renamed the Parti social libéral—PSL—in 1993) were legalized. In November the Government claimed that there were no longer any political prisoners in Tunisia, a total of 8,000 people having been released during the first year of Ben Ali's regime.

Ben Ali was nominated as the sole candidate (supported by all the officially recognized parties) for the presidential election of 2 April 1989, and was duly elected President, receiving 99.3% of the votes cast. In legislative elections the RCD won all 141 seats in the National Assembly, with some 80% of the votes cast. The fundamentalist Hizb an-Nahdah or the Parti de la renaissance (whose candidates contested the election as independents, since the party was not officially recognized), won some 13% of the votes cast, but failed to win any seats under an electoral system that favoured the ruling party. In September Ben Ali dismissed Prime Minister Baccouche, following a disagreement concerning the Government's economic policy, and appointed Hamed Karoui, the former Minister of Justice, in his place.

In May 1990 the National Assembly approved a reformed electoral code, introducing a system of partial proportional representation for forthcoming municipal elections. The winning party was to receive 50% of the seats, while the remainder were to be distributed among all the parties, according to the number of votes received by each one. However, the six legal opposition parties boycotted the elections, held in June, arguing that they were neither free nor fair. Consequently, the RCD won control of all but one of the 245 municipal councils.

Ben Ali stated in December 1991 that changes to the electoral system, to be formulated in consultation with opposition parties, would be implemented during 1992, with the aim of ensuring greater representation at the national level for parties other than the RCD. In December 1992 Ben Ali announced a revision of the electoral code, to include the introduction of partial proportional representation at legislative elections scheduled for March 1994. However, this apparent willingness to co-operate with the legalized opposition was accompanied by further repression of the Islamist movement, with increased censorship of publications sympathetic to their cause, and the harassment of suspected activists.

In March 1992 the human rights organization Amnesty International published a report which detailed the arrests of some 8,000 suspected an-Nahdah members over an 18-month period, and cited 200 cases of the torture and ill-treatment of detainees. It also claimed that at least seven Islamists had died while in custody. The Government initially denied the allegations, but later conceded that some violations of human rights had occurred. In mid-March it was announced that human rights 'units' were to be established within the Ministries of Foreign Affairs, Justice and the Interior, although new restrictions were imposed on the activities of unofficial, quasi-political groups such as the Ligue tunisienne des droits de l'homme (LTDH). In the same month an amnesty was granted to more than 1,000 detainees. In July and August the trials were held in Tunis of 171 alleged members of an-Nahdah, and of 108 alleged members of the organization's military wing, who were all accused of conspiring to overthrow the Government; 46 of the defendants were sentenced to life imprisonment, 16, including Rachid Ghannouchi, the leader of an-Nahdah, *in absentia*. (In 1993 Ghannouchi was granted political asylum in the United Kingdom.) Prison sentences of between one and 24 years were imposed on the remainder. In October appeals on behalf of 265 of those convicted were rejected, and another 20 an-Nahdah sympathizers were reportedly arrested and quantities of weapons and explosives seized in police raids.

There were indications in 1993 of a revival of political activity, and in April a new political organization, the Mouvement du renouveau (MR—Ettajdid, now known as the Mouvement ettajdid), held its first Congress. In November Ben Ali announced that presidential and legislative elections were to take place in March 1994. His candidacy for the presidency was supported not only by the RCD, but also by most of the legal opposition parties. In January 1994 the National Assembly adopted reforms to the electoral code: thenceforth 19 of the 163 seats in the enlarged Assembly were to be allocated to opposition parties in proportion to their overall national vote. At the presidential election, which took place concurrently with the legislative elections on 20 March 1994, Ben Ali was re-elected President, receiving 99.9% of the votes cast. The RCD received 97.7% of the total votes cast in the legislative elections, securing all 144 seats that were contested under a simple majority system. Of the 19 seats reserved for opposition candidates, the Mouvement des démocrates socialistes (MDS) secured 10, the MR four, the Union démocratique unioniste (UDU) three and the Parti de l'unité populaire (PUP) two.

In October 1995 Muhammad Mouada, the MDS Secretary-General, was arrested and accused of having received money from an unnamed foreign country. The previous day Mouada had, in an open letter to the President, criticized the lack of political freedom in Tunisia; however, government officials denied any connection between the letter and Mouada's arrest. In late October the Tunisian authorities prevented Khemais Chamari, an MDS member of the National Assembly, from travelling to Malta to attend an international conference on human rights. In the following month Chamari's parliamentary immunity was withdrawn, in order to allow judicial charges (relating to Mouada's trial) to be brought against him. Meanwhile, in an apparently conciliatory gesture towards the opposition, Ben Ali pardoned the leader of the Parti communiste des ouvriers tunisiens (PCOT), Hamma Hammami, who had been imprisoned in April 1994, and his associate Muhammad Kilani, the former editor of the PCOT journal. (Nevertheless, Hammami apparently remained the object of official harassment, and in July 1999 he was given a nine-year prison sentence *in absentia* for belonging to an illegal organization. However, having commenced a hunger strike to protest against his subsequent imprisonment in 2002, Hammami was released on health grounds in September of that year.) Meanwhile, in February 1996 Mouada was sentenced to two years' imprisonment for 'illegal detention of currency'. Although a court of appeal subsequently reduced his term by one year, at the end of the month Mouada was sentenced to 11 years' imprisonment for maintaining links with and receiving money from Libya. In July Chamari was sentenced to five years' imprisonment for breaching security proceedings relating to Mouada's trial. Human rights organizations protested at the severity of the sentence and appealed to the Tunisian authorities to release all political detainees. In December Mouada and Chamari were released conditionally on humanitarian grounds.

In December 1996 Ben Ali announced plans to amend the electoral law, which, *inter alia*, would lower the minimum eligible age of candidates for the National Assembly (from 25 to 23 years) and increase the representation of legal opposition parties in the Assembly and in municipal councils. Political parties would not be permitted to be based on religion, language, race or region, nor to have foreign links. The scope of referendums was also to be widened. In December 1997 the Council of Ministers reached consensus on draft legislation to amend the electoral law.

In January 1999 draft legislation was presented to the National Assembly to introduce extraordinary provisions to the Constitution which would allow pluralism in the presidential election scheduled for that year. The amendments, which were approved in March, allowed for the leaders of all political parties to contest the presidency provided that they had held their current leadership position for at least five consecutive years, and that their party was represented by one or more deputies in the legislature. (Hitherto opposition parties had been unable to present candidates, owing to the requirement that they be supported by at least 30 deputies in the Assembly.) Despite the new provisions, only two leaders of opposition parties were eligible to contest the presidency, namely Abderrahmane Tlili (UDU) and Muhammad Belhadj Amor (PUP). Ben Ali had himself been re-elected Chairman of the RCD at a party congress in July 1998, when he had been formally nominated as the party's presidential candidate.

The first contested presidential election since independence was held on 24 October 1999. As expected, Ben Ali comprehensively defeated his two rivals, securing 99.5% of the vote. Voter participation was officially estimated at 91.4%. At concurrent elections to the National Assembly the RCD won all of the 148 seats contested under a simple majority system. Of the 34 seats reserved for opposition candidates, 13 were won by the MDS, the UDU and the PUP both took seven seats, the MR won five and the PSL two. Some 91.5% of the electorate voted, according to official sources. In November the President effected a major government reorganization: Hamed Karoui was replaced as Prime Minister by Muhammad Ghannouchi (previously Minister of International Co-operation and Foreign Investment) and Abdallah Kallel succeeded Ali Chaouch as Minister of the Interior. At municipal elections held in May 2000 the RCD won more than 94% of the 4,128 seats being contested, and maintained control over all local councils.

In June 2000 the President of the Conseil national pour les libertés en Tunisie (CNLT), Moncef Marzouki, visited London, United Kingdom, where he declared that a national democratic conference was to be held later in the year. Marzouki reportedly held talks with the leader of an-Nahdah, Rachid Ghannouchi, and proposed future co-operation between secular and Islamist factions of the Tunisian opposition. In December Marzouki received a one-year prison sentence, having been convicted of belonging to an illegal group and of disseminating false information. His sentence was suspended in September 2001 by the court of appeal, although his civil rights were not restored. Marzouki, who had been prevented from travelling abroad on several occasions during 2001, finally had the ban on him leaving Tunisia lifted in early December; he departed for France later that month.

Meanwhile, in November 2000 President Ben Ali announced a number of initiatives aimed at furthering the democratization process and promoting human rights in Tunisia. The measures included: state compensation for detainees held in police custody without reasonable grounds; the transfer of responsibility for the prison system from the Ministry of the Interior to the Ministry of Justice; new legislation to improve conditions in prisons and to reduce censorship of the press; and an increase, by 50%, in government subsidies allocated for other political parties and their publications.

At the fifth congress of the LTDH, held in October 2000, a new executive board was elected, with Mokhtar Trifi, an outspoken critic of the Ben Ali regime, as President. Four former members of the board subsequently filed a suit against the new leadership, claiming that, owing to procedural irregularities, it was invalid, and in November a court imposed a moratorium on the activities of the LTDH. The Tunisian Government denied having ordered the ruling, but was strongly criticized by international and local human rights groups for its perceived role in the affair. Trial proceedings against the LTDH began in January 2001, and in the following month a judgment was issued that the results of the October congress should be invalidated. In March Trifi was charged with dissemination of false information and violation of the recent court ruling; however, in June the court of appeal ruled that the LTDH could resume its activities and ordered it to hold another congress within a year.

In March 2001 more than 250 human rights activists in Tunisia produced a petition that demanded wide-ranging democratic reforms in the country prior to the presidential and legislative elections scheduled for 2004. In the same month some 100 moderate figures in civil society signed a separate petition accusing Ben Ali of corruption and nepotism and denouncing his plans to amend the Constitution so as to permit him to seek a fourth term in office. In April an-Nahdah released a joint communiqué with Mouada's faction of the MDS, proposing the formation of an opposition coalition to unite Islamists and liberals against the Ben Ali regime. Later that month the President instructed the Ministry of the Interior to investigate all alleged abuses by the security forces against Tunisian citizens and to ensure that those found guilty were punished. In May he made a series of conciliatory gestures, including the release of a number of political prisoners; however, the detention and imprisonment of several leading opponents of the regime continued. Meanwhile, in late April the National Assembly approved revisions to the press code under which the offence of 'defamation of public order' was abolished. The amendments also removed the threat of prison sentences for certain violations of the code. The changes were, however, condemned as inadequate by the Association des journalistes tunisiens.

The central committee of the ruling RCD announced in September 2001 that it would formally propose changes to the country's Constitution in order to enable Ben Ali to seek a fourth presidential term. In April 2002 members of the National Assembly overwhelmingly approved a constitutional reform bill, and at a referendum held on 26 May, according to official figures, the constitutional changes were approved by 99.5% of voters; the rate of voter participation was officially recorded at 95.6%. The amendments raised the age limit for presidential candidates from 70 to 75 years, and removed the limit on the number of terms that could be served by a President. In August 2003 the changes were promulgated and Ben Ali formally announced his intention to stand for a fourth term at elections scheduled for late 2004. Provision was also made for the creation of a second legislative chamber, to be called the Chamber of Advisers, for the establishment of a two-round presidential election system and for a number of measures that would improve civil liberties and public freedoms.

In early April 2002 a tanker lorry exploded outside a synagogue on the island of Djerba, causing the deaths of 21 people, most of whom were German tourists. The driver of the lorry was among those killed. The Tunisian authorities initially claimed that the explosion had been an accident, but a spokesman for the Israeli Ministry of Foreign Affairs insisted that it was an anti-Semitic terrorist attack. The Tunisian authorities subsequently confirmed that the explosion had been a 'premeditated criminal act'. A number of Arabic newspapers immediately carried claims that the al-Qa'ida (Base) organization of Osama bin Laden—the principal suspect in the September 2001 attacks on New York and Washington, DC—was responsible. In June 2002 the Qatar-based satellite television station Al-Jazeera broadcast a statement by a spokesman for al-Qa'ida, asserting that the attack had been perpetrated in the name of al-Qa'ida in protest against Israel's recent military offensive against Palestinian-controlled areas of the West Bank. In November eight people were arrested in Lyon, France, in connection with the explosion, while in early 2003 several arrests took place in Spain, France and Saudi Arabia. In May 2007 two men were sentenced to five years' imprisonment each by a court in Madrid, Spain, for their role in the financing of the attack; in June the uncle of the lorry driver was sentenced to 20 years in gaol by a court in Tunis for helping to prepare the explosion.

In January 2003 Ben Ali announced the merger of a number of ministries, reducing them in number from 29 to 25, in an attempt to improve efficiency in government operations. The most notable changes were the creation of a Ministry of Justice and Human Rights and of a Ministry of Employment. Ben Ali carried out a further minor reshuffle of the Council of Ministers in January 2004. Among other changes, the Minister of Finance, Taofik Baccar, was appointed Governor of the Banque Centrale de Tunisie and his vacated ministerial portfolio was assumed by Munir Jeidan, hitherto Secretary of State to the Minister of Finance, in charge of the Budget. Another limited reorganization of the Government took place in March, with Muhammad Rachid Kechiche being appointed Minister of Finance in place of Jeidan, who assumed Kechiche's previous post of Government Secretary-General in charge of Relations with the Chamber of Deputies and the Chamber of Advisers.

During 2003–04 the Tunisian authorities continued to take stern action against opponents of the Ben Ali regime. In July 2003 Abdallah Zouari, an Islamist journalist who had been released from detention in June 2002, having served an 11-year sentence for 'belonging to an illegal organization', was sentenced to four months' imprisonment for libel; in August 2003 Zouari received a further nine-month term for 'failing to obey an administrative order'. Between October and December Radhia Nasraoui, a prominent Tunisian human rights lawyer, went on a hunger strike in protest against her alleged harassment by the authorities, claiming that she had been targeted because she had defended political prisoners and had accused the Government of using torture against opposition activists.

In the months prior to the 2004 presidential election, a group of opposition figures, including Moncef Marzouki, now the leader of the Congrès pour la République, urged President Ben Ali to step down and the Constitution to be amended so as to prevent the President from remaining in office indefinitely. Ben Ali responded by addressing members of the RCD in July 2004 and assuring them that the elections would be held 'within a context of transparency and the respect of law', while requesting that foreign observers be present at the elections. By mid-September four candidates had officially registered to run for President—namely Ben Ali, Muhammad Bouchiha of the PUP, Mounir Béji of the PSL and Muhammad Ali Halouani of the MR. The Parti démocrate progressiste (PDP) announced in mid-October that it was withdrawing its candidates for the legislative elections in protest at what it considered an illegitimate electoral process in which it was denied access to the media and faced serious delays in having its manifesto approved. The presidential election took place on 24 October; Ben Ali received 94.49% of the votes cast, while Bouchiha secured 3.78%, Halouani 0.95% and Béji 0.79%. Voter turn-out was officially estimated at 91.5%. At the legislative elections, which took place concurrently, the RCD won all of the 152 seats contested under a simple majority system, 25% of which would be occupied by women under new legislation, while of the 37 reserved for the opposition, the MDS won 14 seats, the PUP 11, the UDU seven, and the MR and PSL three and two seats, respectively. In November Ben Ali announced a major reshuffle of the Council of Ministers, appointing new Ministers of National Defence, of Foreign Affairs and of the Interior and Local Development, and creating new Ministries of Transport and of Environment and Land Planning.

In 2004–05 there was increased concern on the part of international human rights organizations regarding the holding of political prisoners and claims of abuse in Tunisian gaols. In April 2004 eight young people were arrested and sentenced to between 19 and 26 years' imprisonment for using the internet to plan terrorist activities, although six of the prisoners subsequently had their sentences reduced to 13 years. In June the leader of the UDU, Abderrahmane Tlili, was imprisoned for nine years after being convicted of abusing his position while he was head of the Office de l'Aviation Civile et des Aéroports. A report published in July by the organization Human Rights Watch criticized the Government's handling of political prisoners, many of whom, it claimed, had spent several years in solitary confinement, and urged the Tunisian authorities to allow domestic and international monitors to inspect prison standards. In November President Ben Ali pardoned 80 Islamist prisoners. A further 20 Islamist convicts were freed in July 2007 as part of an amnesty to mark the 50th anniversary of the Tunisian republic, including three former leaders of the banned an-Nahdah party.

At a meeting of the Central Committee of the RCD in February 2005, Ben Ali announced plans to create a national electoral observatory in time for the forthcoming municipal elections. He also reiterated his determination to see women occupying at least 25% of the electoral lists for these elections. At the municipal elections, held on 8 May, the RCD won 4,098 of the 4,366 council seats contested. In July elections were first held to the new Chamber of Advisers, as provided for by the constitutional amendments of 2002. The new second chamber was composed of 126 members, of whom 43 were indirectly elected by municipal councillors and parliamentary deputies (as representatives of the regions) and 42 by the main professional federations and trade unions; the remaining 41 members were appointed by the President. All 43 regional representatives elected were RCD candidates. The Chamber of Advisers held its inaugural session in October and Abdullah Kallel was elected as Speaker; however, 14 seats remained vacant after the UGTT refused to elect its members to the new chamber. Meanwhile, in August Ben Ali effected a major reshuffle of the Council of Ministers: Abdelwahab Abdallah, a former principal adviser to the President, was appointed Minister of Foreign Affairs and Kamel Morjane received the defence portfolio. Ali Chaouch, the former interior minister, assumed the post of Minister of Social Affairs, Solidarity and Tunisians Abroad and was succeeded as Secretary-General of the RCD by Morjane's predecessor, Hédi M'henni. A further reorganization was announced by Ben Ali in September 2007, which included the appointment of Mondher Zenaïdi as Minister of Public Health and Sarra Kanoun Jarraya as Minister of Women's, Family, Children's and Elderly Affairs.

In September and October 2006 the Tunisian authorities increasingly began to take action against the wearing of the Islamic headscarf, following public comments by Ben Ali and other senior politicians that it was a 'sectarian' form of dress that was not native to the country. There were reports that the ban on headscarves in schools and government offices, introduced by President Bourguiba in 1981, was being enforced more rigorously, and that the police were stopping women in the street and asking them to uncover their hair. Also in October 2006 Tunisia closed its embassy in Qatar in protest at an interview with Moncef Marzouki broadcast by Al-Jazeera, in which he spoke against the Government's human rights record and advocated a campaign of civil resistance. In January 2007 the Minister of the Interior and Local Development, Rafik Belhaj Kacem, confirmed that police had shot dead 14 members of a suspected militant Islamist organization and arrested a number of others in Soliman, near Tunis. Two members of the security forces were killed during the operation. Kacem reported that the group, which had been assembled by six militants who had entered the country from Algeria and which was suspected of having links to the Algerian Groupe salafiste pour la prédication et le combat (which in that month restyled itself as 'al-Qa'ida in the Islamic Maghreb'—AQIM, see the chapter on Algeria), had been in possession of explosives and details of foreign embassies and diplomatic staff in Tunis. In January 2008 a court in Tunisia issued its judgment on the suspected militants: two of the defendants were handed down death penalties, eight were sentenced to life imprisonment, and a further 20 received prison terms ranging from five to 30 years. The LTDH subsequently issued a statement concluding that, while violence was unacceptable as a means of political expression, the proceedings had lacked the 'minimum conditions' necessary for a fair trial.

In September 2007 two leading members of the PDP went on a hunger strike to protest against legal efforts to evict the party and its official weekly newspaper, Al-Mawkif, from their premises for alleged violation of the lease agreement. PDP Secretary-General Maya Jribi and Al-Mawkif Managing Director Ahmed Néjib Chebbi ended their hunger strike a month later, when the owner of the party offices abandoned a lawsuit against the party and sanctioned a new lease agreement. The outcome was hailed by Jribi as a victory for the Tunisian people in their 'struggle for freedom'. None the less, it was reported in April 2008 that the distribution of Al-Mawkif was being prevented by the authorities; with some sources claiming that this apparent official censorship of the newspaper was linked to Chebbi's declared intention to contest the presidential election scheduled for 2009. Al-Mawkif's Editor-in-Chief, Rachid Khechana, and its Publications Director, Monji Ellouze, also went on a hunger strike later that month to protest against these alleged restrictions on the publication and distribution of the newspaper. However, they suspended their strike after two weeks following a return to normal patterns of distribution for Al-Mawkif.

Meanwhile, in November 2007 Ben Ali made a speech in front of a large audience in Radès to mark the 20th anniversary of his accession to power. The Tunisian President used the occasion to propose a reduction in the voting age, from 20 to 18 years, and an amendment of the electoral law to preclude any single party from holding more than 75% of seats in municipal councils. Nine imprisoned members of the banned an-Nahdah party were also reportedly pardoned to mark the anniversary. During the speech Ben Ali announced a range of measures designed to promote democracy and human rights in the country; these included increasing the level of funding allocated to opposition parties and their press. None the less, in May 2008 the recently founded Syndicat National des Journalistes Tunisiens (SNJT—which replaced the pro-Government Association des Journalistes Tunisiens) made renewed calls for a review of media regulations in line with international standards of press freedom. This followed the publication of an SNJT report which detailed the various alleged violations of journalists' rights that had occurred in the previous year.

In February 2008 two Austrian tourists went missing, apparently while in southern Tunisia. In the days following their disappearance a spokesmen for a branch of AQIM claimed that the couple had been kidnapped by the militant group, and demanded the release of prisoners in Algeria and Tunisia, as well as a ransom payment of €5m., in exchange for their safe return. (There were subsequent reports that the Austrians might in fact have been kidnapped after having crossed the Algerian border, and that their captors had moved them to Mali.) The deadline set by the al-Qa'ida affiliate for the pardoning of the prisoners passed and was extended several times in the ensuing weeks. Despite extensive search operations by the Tunisian authorities, the pair were still missing in April, and it was unclear whether further demands would be issued by their captors.

Relations with the other countries of the Maghreb improved considerably in the 1980s. A meeting between President Bourguiba and President Ben Djedid Chadli of Algeria in March 1983 led to the drafting of the Maghreb Fraternity and Co-operation Treaty, which envisaged the eventual creation of a Greater Maghreb Union, and was signed by Mauritania in December. In January 1988 Tunisia and Algeria held further discussions on the establishment of a greater Arab Maghreb, and in April border restrictions between Tunisia and Libya were removed. In February 1989, at a meeting of North African heads of state in Morocco, a treaty was concluded that proclaimed the Union of the Arab Maghreb (Union du Maghreb arabe—UMA, see p. 414), comprising Algeria, Libya, Mauritania, Morocco and Tunisia. The treaty envisaged: the establishment of a council of heads of state; regular meetings of ministers responsible for foreign affairs; and, eventually, the free movement of goods, people, services and capital throughout the countries of the region.

In 1982 President Bourguiba permitted the Palestine Liberation Organization (PLO) to establish its headquarters near Tunis. In October 1985 Israeli aircraft attacked the PLO headquarters, causing the deaths of some 72 people, including 12 Tunisians. US support for the right of Israel to retaliate (the attack was a reprisal for the murder of three Israeli citizens in Cyprus) severely strained relations between Tunisia and the USA. In April 1988 Abu Jihad, the military commander of the PLO, was assassinated at his home in Tunis. The Tunisian Government blamed Israel for the murder, and complained to the UN Security Council. The PLO transferred its offices to Gaza in mid-1994, following the signing of the PLO-Israeli Cairo Agreement on implementing Palestinian self-rule in the Gaza Strip and Jericho.

In January 1988 the Tunisian Government announced that diplomatic relations with Egypt, which had been severed in 1979, would be resumed. In March 1990 Ben Ali made the first visit to Cairo by a Tunisian President since 1965, and signed several agreements on bilateral co-operation. In September 1990 a majority of members of the League of Arab States (the Arab League, see p. 332) resolved to move the League's headquarters from Tunis (where it had been established 'temporarily' in 1979) to its original site in Cairo: the Tunisian Government protested at the decision.

Tunisia assumed the annual presidency of the UMA in January 1993. The Government made clear its determination to reactivate the process of Maghreb union, as well as dialogue with the European Community (now European Union—EU, see p. 244). In April 1994 the UMA ratified 11 agreements designed to improve co-operation and trade within the Maghreb. However, tensions between the UMA's member states subsequently undermined the activities of the Union. In March 1999 Ben Ali made his first official visit to Morocco, during which he pledged to strengthen relations with that country, and to revive the UMA. A summit meeting of ministers responsible for foreign affairs of the five UMA member states was arranged, and proceeded in the Algerian capital in March 2001. However, the meeting, which was to have made preparations for the first summit meeting of UMA heads of state since 1995, quickly broke down following disagreements between Moroccan and Algerian representatives. There were several further unsuccessful attempts to co-ordinate a summit meeting before it eventually took place in Tangier, Morocco, in April 2008. In spite of some residual tension between Moroccan and Algerian officials, the summit ended peacefully with renewed calls for regional collaboration.

Relations with Algeria improved appreciably after the second round of Algerian elections, at which the fundamentalist Front islamique du salut (FIS) had been expected to secure victory, was suspended in January 1992, and Tunisia welcomed the appointment of Muhammad Boudiaf as Chairman of the High Council of State, as well as the suppression of the FIS. During a visit to Tunis in February 1993, Boudiaf's successor, Ali Kafi, exchanged letters with Ben Ali to ratify the official demarcation of the 1,000-km border between Tunisia and Algeria, which had been the subject of dispute since Algerian independence. Ben Ali and Kafi also pledged to co-operate in countering the threat of terrorism in the region. In early 1995 six Tunisian border guards were killed in an attack perpetrated by Algerian Islamists in protest at the Tunisian authorities' alleged support for the Algerian security forces. Another serious incident occurred at the joint border in May 2000, when Tunisian security forces responded to an attack by Algerian Islamists; three of the Islamists were killed and two Tunisian soldiers wounded. The attack followed the signing of a bilateral customs agreement aimed at ending cross-border smuggling, considered by the Algerian Government to facilitate the activities of Islamist groups in Algeria. A number of bilateral agreements were signed during a visit to Algeria by Ben Ali in February 2002; most notably, the two countries pledged to formalize delineation of their maritime border.

In December 2003 Tunisia hosted the '5+5 Dialogue Summit', attended by the heads of state of the five UMA countries and Portugal, Spain, Italy, France and Malta, at which discussions focused on political stability, economic co-operation, immigration and the continued crisis between the Israelis and the Palestinians. At the conclusion of the summit the 10 countries issued a declaration, which provided a working blueprint for future economic, political and cultural co-operation within the Euro-Mediterranean region.

In October 1994 Tunisia and Israel signalled the beginning of the normalization of bilateral relations with the announcement of plans to establish interests offices in the Belgian embassies in Tunis and Tel-Aviv. The offices opened in April and May 1996, respectively. Relations between the two countries were strained in early 1997, following Tunisia's criticism of Israel's alleged failure to implement agreements concluded with the PLO; although the two countries' respective interests offices remained open, Tunisia suspended the process of normalizing relations with Israel. The Tunisian Government installed a liaison office in the Gaza Strip in April 1995; a second office was planned for Jericho. In February 2000 a senior-level delegation from Tunisia visited Israel, where it was agreed, *inter alia*, that the two countries would establish a joint committee for advancing trade and tourism. However, in October, in response to the escalating Israeli–Palestinian crisis and what the Tunisian authorities deemed to be Israeli aggression, Tunisia announced that it had severed all diplomatic ties with Israel. In November 2003 it was reported that representatives from the Tunisian and Israeli Ministries of Foreign Affairs had held talks in Tunis with regard to the possible reopening of the interests offices in Tel-Aviv and Tunis. In March 2004 Tunisia postponed a summit meeting of the Arab League, scheduled to be held in Tunis, citing differences among member states concerning an agenda for the talks (reportedly to include an appropriate Arab response to US pressure for political reform in the Middle East and to recent Israeli actions in the Palestinian territories). The summit eventually commenced in Tunis in May; however, conflicts over the summit's agenda remained and no agreement was reached on an Arab-Israeli peace initiative.

In June 1993 President Ben Ali, addressing the European Parliament in Strasbourg, advocated the establishment of a Euro-Maghreb Development Bank, which, by stimulating economic growth in North Africa, would alleviate illegal immigration into Europe. In July 1995 Tunisia concluded an association agreement with the EU, designed to foster closer commercial and political co-operation. In October the new French President, Jacques Chirac, made an official visit to Tunisia. Chirac and Ben Ali agreed that henceforth they would meet annually, in order to consolidate bilateral relations. Ben Ali made an official visit to France in October 1997, during which he countered criticisms regarding his country's record on human rights by claiming that there were currently no political prisoners in Tunisia. Several Tunisian deputies demanded a suspension of the association agreement in June 2000, after EU member states (particularly France) criticized the Tunisian authorities' failure to protect human rights. Relations between France and Tunisia deteriorated further during 2001 when the French Government again criticized the growing use of violence against human rights activists and voiced its concern at gaol sentences imposed upon prominent opposition figures. Relations improved, however, during 2002–04 and in December 2003 Chirac again visited Tunisia. The two countries signed a number of co-operation agreements relating to tourism and bilateral social security arrangements. In November 2005 the EU made an official complaint to the Tunisian Government days before the UN-sponsored World Summit on the Information Society was scheduled to begin in Tunis. Tunisian security forces had prevented a group of international delegates, including the German ambassador to the UN and representatives of international human rights bodies and non-governmental organizations, from entering the German cultural institute in the Tunisian capital. In April 2008 the French President, Nicolas Sarkozy, made his first state visit to Tunisia since taking office in May 2007. During the visit Sarkozy and Ben Ali supervised the signing of several agreements designed to increase nuclear and aviation co-operation between the two countries. Ben Ali also expressed his support for Sarkozy's Mediterranean Union project (a proposed community of EU member states and countries bordering the Mediterranean Sea), due to be officially launched at a summit meeting of European and Mediterranean leaders in July.

In December 2003 the US Secretary of State, Colin Powell, visited Tunisia for talks with President Ben Ali and the Tunisian Minister of Foreign Affairs, Habib Ben Yahia. Powell praised the excellent relations between the two countries and Tunisia's contribution to the 'war on terror'; however, he urged the Tunisian Government to pursue further political and economic reforms. In February 2004 Ben Ali visited Washington, DC, where he met with the US President, George W. Bush, to discuss a number of trade-related issues. During the talks Bush also stressed that, while the USA applauded Tunisia's efforts to liberalize its society, it remained critical of the country's poor human rights record and the continued oppression of the Tunisian media.

Government

Under the 1959 Constitution (with subsequent amendments), legislative power is held by the unicameral National Assembly, with 189 members who are elected by universal adult suffrage for a five-year term. (Of the 189 members, 152 are elected under a simple majority system, while 37 seats are reserved for the opposition, allotted according to the proportion of votes received nationally by each party.) In 1988 a multi-party system was officially permitted by law. Executive power is held by the President, elected for five years by popular vote at the same time as the Assembly. The President, who is Head of State and Head of Government, appoints a Council of Ministers, led by a Prime Minister, which is responsible to him. Constitutional amendments relating to the presidency and legislature were approved at a national referendum in May 2002 (see Recent History). For local administration the country is divided into 24 governorates.

Defence

As assessed at November 2007, total armed forces numbered an estimated 35,800 (including some 22,700 conscripts), consisting of an army of 27,000, a navy of about 4,800 and an air force of 4,000. Paramilitary forces included a 12,000-strong national guard. From 2003 women were required to complete military service. Officer-training is undertaken in the USA and France, as well as in Tunisia. The defence budget for 2007 totalled an estimated TD 625m.

Economic Affairs

In 2006, according to estimates by the World Bank, Tunisia's gross national income (GNI), measured at average 2004–06 prices, was US $30,091m., equivalent to $2,970 per head (or $8,490 per head on an international purchasing-power parity basis). During 1996–2006, it was estimated, the population increased at an average annual rate of 1.1%, while gross domestic product (GDP) per head increased, in real terms, by an average of 3.7%. Overall GDP increased, in real terms, at an average annual rate of 4.9% per year in 1996–2006; it grew by 5.2% in 2006.

Agriculture (including forestry and fishing) contributed 11.3% of GDP and employed 18.5% of the working population in 2007. The principal crops are wheat, barley, potatoes, olives, tomatoes and watermelons. However, Tunisia imports large quantities of cereals, dairy produce, meat and sugar. The country's main agricultural export is olive oil; olives, citrus fruit and dates are also grown for export. During 1996–2006, according to the World Bank, agricultural GDP increased at an average annual rate of 2.5%. Agricultural GDP decreased by 5.0% in 2005, but increased by 3.0% in 2006.

Industry (including mining, manufacturing, construction and power) contributed 33.2% of GDP and engaged 32.5% of the employed labour force in 2007. According to the World Bank, industrial GDP increased by an average of 4.2% per year during 1996–2006, and by 3.7% in 2006.

Mining (excluding hydrocarbons) contributed 0.6% of GDP in 2007. In 1994 mining (with gas, electricity and water) employed 1.6% of the working population. In 2000 the principal mineral export was petroleum (which accounted for 10.4% of total export earnings). Tunisia's proven published oil reserves at the end of 2006 were estimated at 700m. barrels, sufficient to maintain production (at 2006 levels—averaging an estimated 69,000 barrels per day) for 27.5 years. Iron, zinc, lead, barite, gypsum, phosphate, fluorspar and sea salt are also mined. In addition, Tunisia possesses large reserves of natural gas. The GDP of the mining sector (excluding hydrocarbons) decreased by 1.1% in 2007.

Manufacturing (excluding hydrocarbons) contributed 18.4% of GDP in 2007, and employed 19.6% of the working population in 1994. Manufacturing is based on the processing of the country's principal agricultural and mineral products. Other important sectors include textiles, construction materials, machinery, chemicals, and paper and wood. In 1996–2006, according to the World Bank, manufacturing GDP increased at an average annual rate of 4.4%. Manufacturing GDP grew by 4.2% in 2006.

Energy is derived principally from gas (which contributed 90.2% of total electricity output in 2004) and petroleum (8.3%), although Tunisia also has several hydroelectric plants. Imports of energy and lubricants comprised 13.3% of the value of total imports in 2005. In the mid-2000s the Tunisian electricity grid was interconnected with that of Libya.

The services sector accounted for 55.5% of GDP and employed 49.0% of the working population in 2007. Tourism represents an important source of revenue: receipts from tourism in 2005 totalled US $2,782m., and there were 6.5m. tourist arrivals in 2006. The GDP of the services sector increased by an average of 5.7% per year in 1996–2006, according to the World Bank. Growth in the sector's GDP was recorded at 6.3% in 2006.

In 2006 Tunisia recorded a visible trade deficit of US $2,527m., and a deficit of $634m. on the current account of the balance of payments. In 2005 the principal sources of imports were France (accounting for 23.5% of the total), Italy (20.9%), Germany and Spain. The principal markets for Tunisian exports in that year were also France (taking 32.9%), Italy (24.0%), Germany and Spain. The member states of the European Union (EU, see p. 244) accounted for 80.5% of Tunisia's exports and 71.4% of its imports in 1999. Tunisia's principal exports in 2007 were textiles, manufactured garments and leather products; machinery, electrical products and transport equipment; energy and lubricants; and agricultural and food products. The principal imports in 2005 were machinery, electrical products and transport equipment; textiles, manufactured garments and leather products; miscellaneous manufactured articles; and energy and lubricants.

In 2006 there was an estimated budgetary deficit of TD 705m. (excluding receipts from privatization). The 2007 budget forecast a deficit of TD 1,289m. (excluding receipts from privatization). At the end of 2005 Tunisia's total external debt was US $17,789m., of which $12,982m. was long-term public debt. In that year the cost of debt-servicing was equivalent to 13.0% of the value of exports of goods and services. The average annual rate of inflation was 3.0% in 1996–2006; consumer prices increased by 4.5% in 2006. A reported 14.1% of the labour force were unemployed in 2007, with university graduates accounting for some 60% of those without jobs.

Tunisia is a member of the Arab Fund for Economic and Social Development (AFESD, see p. 174), the Arab Monetary Fund (see p. 175) and the Union of the Arab Maghreb (Union du Maghreb arabe—UMA, see p. 414).

From the mid-1990s Tunisia experienced strong economic growth, low inflation and declining poverty as a result of sound macroeconomic policies and improvements to the country's regulatory framework. The Government remained committed to the privatization of state-owned enterprises, and the sale of 33.5% of the Banque du Sud was completed in November 2005, raising revenue of some US $80m. Tunisia's tourism industry, which provides an estimated 7% of total GDP, was adversely affected by the recession in global travel following the suicide attacks against the USA in September 2001, as well as the terrorist attack at Djerba in April 2002 (see Recent History). However, by mid-2003 the industry had begun to recover, with visitor numbers to Tunisia increasing once again and reaching 6.5m. in 2006. The Government proceeded apace with its ambitious programme to develop the tourism sector, which aimed to increase the number of visitors to the country to 10m. by 2010. Meanwhile, the Tunisian economy continued to become more closely integrated with those of the EU member states, and in January 2008 all trade barriers between Tunisia and the EU were lifted when the country formally entered into a free trade zone agreement. Unemployment remained a serious issue in Tunisia: in 2007 some 14.1% of the population were unemployed, and levels were particularly high among the country's youth. One of the principal aims of the Government's 11th development plan (for 2007–11), approved in July 2007, was the reduction of unemployment to 13.4% by 2011. The Government also aimed to increase growth to 6.1% from 4.8% over the previous decade. In order to achieve these objectives, it outlined plans to reduce public debt, which stood at 59.8% of total debt in 2006, to increase private investment and to reform the education system. Tunisia has welcomed foreign investment, with increasing numbers of French information technology firms choosing Tunisia as a location in order to take advantage of low cost overheads and a well-educated pool of youthful labour.

Education

Education is compulsory in Tunisia for a period of nine years between the ages of six and 16. Primary education begins at six years of age and normally lasts for six years. Secondary education begins at the age of 12 and lasts for seven years, comprising a first cycle of three years and a second cycle of four years. In 2004/05, according to UNESCO estimates, the total enrolment at primary schools included 96.8% of the relevant age-group. Enrolment at secondary schools included 65.0% of the appropriate age-group in 2002/03. Arabic is the first language of instruction in primary and secondary schools, but French is also used. The University of Tunis was divided in 1988 to form separate institutions, one for the arts, the other for the sciences, and two new universities were opened in 1986, at Monastir and Sfax. In 2006/07 the number enrolled at the 178 higher educational establishments in Tunisia was equivalent to 326,185 full-time students. Public expenditure on education was equivalent to 18.2% of total government spending in 2001/02.

Public Holidays

2008: 1 January (New Year's Day), 20 March (Independence Day), 21 March (Youth Day), 9 April (Martyrs' Day), 1 May (Labour Day), 25 July (Republic Day), 13 August (Women's Day), 1 October* (Aid es-Seghir—Id al-Fitr, end of Ramadan), 15 October (Evacuation of Bizerta), 7 November (accession of President Ben Ali), 9 December* (Aid el-Kebir—Id al-Adha, Feast of the Sacrifice).

2009: 1 January (New Year's Day), 20 March (Independence Day), 21 March (Youth Day), 9 April (Martyrs' Day), 1 May (Labour Day), 25 July (Republic Day), 13 August (Women's Day), 20 September* (Aid es-Seghir—Id al-Fitr, end of Ramadan), 15 October (Evacuation of Bizerta), 7 November (accession of President Ben Ali), 27 November* (Aid el-Kebir—Id al-Adha, Feast of the Sacrifice).

* These holidays are dependent on the Islamic lunar calendar and may differ by one or two days from the dates given.

Weights and Measures

The metric system is in force.

TUNISIA

Statistical Survey

Source (unless otherwise stated): Institut National de la Statistique, Ministère du Développement Economique, 70 rue al-Cham, 1002 Tunis; tel. (71) 891-002; fax (71) 792-559; e-mail ins@e-mail.ati.tn; internet www.ins.nat.tn.

Area and Population

AREA, POPULATION AND DENSITY

Area (sq km)	
Land	154,530
Inland waters	9,080
Total	163,610*
Population (census results)	
20 April 1994	8,785,364
28 April 2004	
Males	4,965,435
Females	4,945,437
Total	9,910,872
Population (official estimate at 1 July)	
2005	10,029,000
2006	10,128,100
2007	10,225,400
Density (per sq km) at 1 July 2007	66.2†

* 63,170 sq miles.
† Land area only.

GOVERNORATES
(at 1 July 2007)

	Area (sq km)*	Population (estimates)	Density (per sq km)
Tunis	346	990,100	2,861.6
Ariana	498	459,200	922.1
Ben Arous	761	542,700	713.1
Manouba	1,060	352,400	332.5
Nabeul	2,788	723,800	259.6
Zaghouan	2,768	168,100	60.7
Bizerte	3,685	536,200	145.5
Béja	3,558	303,200	85.2
Jendouba	3,102	420,400	135.5
Le Kef	4,965	257,300	51.8
Siliana	4,631	233,300	50.4
Kairouan	6,712	551,900	82.2
Kasserine	8,066	422,900	52.4
Sidi Bouzid	6,994	403,500	57.7
Sousse	2,621	579,200	221.0
Monastir	1,019	484,400	475.4
Mahdia	2,966	386,600	130.3
Sfax	7,545	894,200	118.5
Gafsa	8,990	329,800	36.7
Tozeur	4,719	100,300	21.3
Kébili	22,084	146,500	6.6
Gabès	7,175	351,500	49.0
Médenine	8,588	443,700	51.7
Tataouine	38,889	144,200	3.7
Total	**163,610**	**10,225,400**	**62.5**

* Including inland water.

Note: Total for population may not be equal to the sum of components, owing to rounding.

PRINCIPAL TOWNS
(2004, census results)

Tunis (capital)	728,453	Ettadhamen	118,487
Sfax (Safaqis)	265,131	Kairouan (Qairawan)	117,930
Ariana	240,749	Gabès	116,323
Sousse	173,047	Bizerta (Bizerte)	114,371

Source: Thomas Brinkhoff, *City Population* (internet www.citypopulation.de).

Births, Marriages and Deaths

	Registered live births		Registered marriages		Registered deaths	
	Number	Rate (per 1,000)	Number	Rate (per 1,000)	Number	Rate (per 1,000)
1990	205,345	25.4	55,612	6.8	45,700	5.6
1991	207,455	25.2	59,010	7.1	46,500	5.6
1992	211,649	25.2	64,700	7.6	46,300	5.5
1993	207,786	24.1	54,120	6.3	49,400	5.7
1994	200,223	22.7	52,431	5.9	50,300	5.7
1995	186,416	20.8	53,726	6.0	52,000	5.8
1996	178,801	19.7	56,349	6.2	40,817	5.5
1997	173,757	18.9	57,861	6.3	42,426	5.6

Birth rate (per 1,000): 16.8 in 2004; 17.1 in 2005; 17.1 in 2006.
Death rate (per 1,000): 6.0 in 2004; 5.9 in 2005; 5.6 in 2006.
Expectation of life (years at birth, WHO estimates): 72.2 (males 70.0; females 74.6) in 2005 (Source: WHO, *World Health Statistics*).

EMPLOYMENT
('000 persons aged 15 years and over at 20 April 1994)

	Males	Females	Total
Agriculture, forestry and fishing	393.7	107.3	501.0
Manufacturing	244.7	211.0	455.7
Electricity, gas and water*	34.4	2.4	36.8
Construction	302.6	3.2	305.8
Trade, restaurants and hotels†	277.8	37.8	315.6
Community, social and personal services‡	503.9	163.2	667.1
Activities not adequately defined	28.6	10.0	38.6
Total employed	**1,785.7**	**534.9**	**2,320.6**

* Including mining and quarrying.
† Including financing, insurance, real estate and business services.
‡ Including transport, storage and communications.

Total labour force ('000 persons aged over 15 years): 3,414.6 in 2005; 3,506.2 in 2006; 3,593.2 in 2007.

Health and Welfare

KEY INDICATORS

Total fertility rate (children per woman, 2005)	1.9
Under-5 mortality rate (per 1,000 live births, 2005)	24
HIV/AIDS (% of persons aged 15–49, 2005)	0.1
Physicians (per 1,000 head, 2004)	1.34
Hospital beds (per 1,000 head, 2004)	1.80
Health expenditure (2004): US $ per head (PPP)	502.3
Health expenditure (2004): % of GDP	6.2
Health expenditure (2004): public (% of total)	52.1
Access to water (% of persons, 2004)	93
Access to sanitation (% of persons, 2004)	85
Human Development Index (2005): ranking	91
Human Development Index (2005): value	0.766

For sources and definitions, see explanatory note on p. vi.

Agriculture

PRINCIPAL CROPS
('000 metric tons)

	2004	2005	2006
Wheat	1,722*	1,627	1,251
Barley	395	465	354
Potatoes	375	310	370
Broad beans (dry)	46	45	47
Almonds	44	57	50
Olives	650	600	1,000
Artichokes	12	12	15
Tomatoes	1,118	960	850
Pumpkins, squash and gourds†	31	28	28
Cucumbers and gherkins†	32	32	32
Chillies and green peppers	255	256	260
Green onions and shallots	105*	138*	140
Dry onions	85*	117*	120
Green peas	15*	15†	15†
Carrots and turnips	52*	52†	52†
Watermelons	351*	350	350†
Oranges	101	101	101†
Tangerines, mandarins, clementines and satsumas	25	33	33†
Lemons and limes	28	27†	27†
Grapefruit and pomelos†	68	67	67
Apples	135	130	120
Pears	62	65	60
Apricots	27	35	30
Peaches and nectarines†	90	92	92
Grapes	127	135	135
Figs	27*	25	25†
Dates	122	125	125

* Unofficial figure.
† FAO estimate(s).

Aggregate production ('000 metric tons, may include official, semi-official or estimated data): Total cereals 2,161 in 2004, 2,133 in 2005, 1,646 in 2006; Total roots and tubers 745 in 2004, 310 in 2005, 370 in 2006; Total pulses 87 in 2004, 89 in 2005, 106 in 2006; Total vegetables (incl. melons) 2,320 in 2004, 2,221 in 2005, 2,123 in 2006; Total fruits (excl. melons) 1,060 in 2004, 1,098 in 2005, 1,083 in 2006.

Source: FAO.

LIVESTOCK
('000 head, year ending September)

	2003	2004	2005
Horses*	57	57	57
Asses, mules or hinnies*	311	311	311
Cattle	679	657	686
Camels*	231	231	231
Sheep	6,613	6,949	7,213
Goats	1,379	1,412	1,427
Chickens*	62,000	64,000	64,000
Turkeys*	4,400	4,400	4,400

* FAO estimates.

2006: Figures assumed to be unchanged from 2005 (FAO estimates).
Source: FAO.

LIVESTOCK PRODUCTS
('000 metric tons)

	2003	2004	2005
Cattle meat	57.5	53.4	55.0*
Sheep meat	51.4	52.0	55.0*
Chicken meat	90.0	95.6	100.6
Cows' milk	941.0	864.0	930.0
Sheep's milk*	17.3	17.3	17.3
Goats' milk*	12.2	12.2	12.2
Hen eggs*	78.0	83.0	83.0
Wool: greasy*	8.8	8.8	8.8

* FAO estimate(s).

2006: Figures assumed to be unchanged from 2005 (FAO estimates).
Source: FAO.

Forestry

ROUNDWOOD REMOVALS
('000 cu m, excl. bark, FAO estimates)

	2004	2005	2006
Sawlogs, veneer logs and logs for sleepers	20	25	25
Pulpwood	61	75	75
Other industrial wood	118	118	118
Fuel wood	2,138	2,149	2,156
Total	2,337	2,367	2,374

Source: FAO.

SAWNWOOD PRODUCTION
('000 cu m, incl. sleepers)

	1992	1993	1994
Coniferous (softwood)	2.2	5.8	6.8
Broadleaved (hardwood)	4.0	13.6	13.6
Total	6.2	19.4	20.4

1995–2006: Production as in 1994 (FAO estimates).
Source: FAO.

Fishing

('000 metric tons, live weight)

	2003	2004	2005
Capture	90.3	111.6	109.2
Mullets	3.2	2.6	2.5
Common pandora	2.8	2.9	2.8
Sargo breams	0.4	0.4	0.4
Bogue	3.4	3.0	2.8
Jack and horse mackerels	4.1	7.0	5.5
Sardinellas	11.8	13.5	12.8
European pilchard	12.1	14.3	18.6
Chub mackerel	4.5	9.4	9.0
Common cuttlefish	7.2	6.0	6.2
Aquaculture	2.1	2.5	2.7
Total catch (incl. others)	92.4	114.1	111.8

Source: FAO.

Mining

('000 metric tons, unless otherwise indicated)

	2003	2004	2005*
Crude petroleum ('000 barrels)	24,300	25,700	26,200
Natural gas (million cu m)	2,167	2,530	2,585
Iron ore: gross weight	164	256	206
Iron ore: metal content	97	134	108
Lead concentrates (metric tons)†	5,000	5,470	8,708
Zinc concentrates (metric tons)†	36,000	29,011	15,889
Phosphate rock‡	7,890	8,051	8,220
Barite (Barytes) (metric tons)	3,000	1,813	—
Salt (marine)	700	1,117	1,132
Gypsum (crude)§	110	108	113

* Preliminary figures.
† Figures refer to metal content of concentrates.
‡ Figures refer to gross weight. The estimated phosphoric acid content (in '000 metric tons) was: 1,164 in 2003; 1,241 in 2004; 1,217 in 2005 (preliminary).
§ Estimated production.
Source: US Geological Survey.

TUNISIA

Industry

SELECTED PRODUCTS
('000 metric tons, unless otherwise indicated)

	2002	2003	2004
Superphosphates	796	875	868
Cement	6,022	6,038	6,662
Beer ('000 hectolitres)	1,100	997	n.a.
Wine ('000 hectolitres)	271	246	n.a.
Olive oil	30	70	n.a.
Flour	753	785	n.a.
Refined sugar	126	131	n.a.
Crude steel	200	86	70*
Quicklime	471	446	476
Motor gasoline ('000 barrels)	3,380	3,600	3,450
Kerosene ('000 barrels)	1,590	1,270	1,310
Diesel oil ('000 barrels)	3,500	3,780	3,220
Residual fuel oil ('000 barrels)	4,020	4,050	3,960
Electric energy (million kWh)	11,281	11,829	13,067

* Preliminary figure.

2005 ('000 metric tons unless otherwise indicated): Superphosphates 848; Cement 6,691; Crude steel 66; Quicklime 424; Motor gasoline ('000 barrels) 1,880; Kerosene ('000 barrels) 1,770; Diesel oil ('000 barrels) 3,630; Residual fuel oil ('000 barrels) 4,030.

Sources: partly UN, *Industrial Commodity Statistics Yearbook*; US Geological Survey.

Finance

CURRENCY AND EXCHANGE RATES

Monetary Units
1,000 millimes = 1 Tunisian dinar (TD).

Sterling, Dollar and Euro Equivalents (31 December 2007)
£1 sterling = 2.446 dinars;
US $1 = 1.221 dinars;
€1 = 1.797 dinars;
100 Tunisian dinars = £40.89 = $81.92 = €55.65.

Average Exchange Rate (dinars per US $)
2005 1.2974
2006 1.3310
2007 1.2814

BUDGET
(million dinars)*

Revenue†	2005	2006‡	2007§
Tax revenue	7,904	8,470	8,892
Direct taxes	2,886	3,107	3,427
Trade taxes	506	490	425
Value-added tax (VAT)	2,301	2,466	2,714
Excise	1,212	1,255	1,295
Other taxes	999	1,152	1,031
Non-tax revenue	996	1,314	1,319
Capital revenue	6	6	2
Total	8,906	9,789	10,213

Expenditure‖	2005	2006‡	2007§
Current expenditure	7,693	8,317	8,804
Wages and salaries	4,560	4,901	5,378
Goods and services	713	744	719
Interest payments	1,062	1,130	1,120
Domestic	473	499	520
External	589	631	600
Transfers and subsidies	1,359	1,542	1,527
Non-allocated	—	—	60
Capital expenditure	2,409	2,548	2,698
Direct investment	1,259	1,422	1,448
Capital transfers and equity	1,150	1,127	1,120
Non-allocated	—	—	131
Total	10,103	10,865	11,502

* Figures refer to the consolidated accounts of the central Government, including administrative agencies and social security funds. The data exclude the operations of economic and social agencies with their own budgets.
† Excluding grants from abroad (million dinars): 70 in 2005; 483 in 2006 (estimate); 100 in 2007 (projected). Also excluded are receipts from privatization (million dinars): 170 in 2005; 3,000 in 2006 (estimate); 50 in 2007 (projected).
‡ Estimated figures.
§ Projected figures.
‖ Excluding net lending (million dinars): 16 in 2005; 112 in 2006 (estimate); 10 in 2007 (projected).

Source: IMF, *Tunisia: 2007 Article IV Consultation—Staff Report; Public Information Notice on the Executive Board Discussion; and Statement by the Executive Director for Tunisia* (August 2007).

CENTRAL BANK RESERVES
(US $ million at 31 December)

	2005	2006	2007
Gold (national valuation)	3.2	3.4	3.6
IMF special drawing rights	2.2	1.3	2.0
Reserve position in IMF	28.9	30.5	32.0
Foreign exchange	4,405.6	6,741.4	7,816.8
Total	4,439.9	6,776.6	7,854.4

Source: IMF, *International Financial Statistics*.

MONEY SUPPLY
(million dinars at 31 December)

	2005	2006	2007
Currency outside banks	3,478	3,873	4,100
Demand deposits at commercial banks	5,088	5,856	6,748
Total money (incl. others)	9,140	10,339	11,583

Source: IMF, *International Financial Statistics*.

COST OF LIVING
(Consumer Price Index; base: 2000 = 100)

	2004	2005	2006
Food	115.1	115.2	121.4
Electricity, gas and other fuels	113.3	120.6	129.3
Clothing	105.8	108.9	111.9
Rent	114.7	118.3	121.9
All items (incl. others)	111.5	113.8	118.9

Source: ILO.

TUNISIA

Statistical Survey

NATIONAL ACCOUNTS

Expenditure on the Gross Domestic Product
(US $ million at current prices)

	2004	2005	2006
Government final consumption expenditure	4,339.73	4,449.18	4,626.40
Private final consumption expenditure	17,820.66	18,280.52	19,239.80
Gross capital formation	6,886.80	6,702.33	7,186.22
Total domestic expenditure	29,047.19	29,432.03	31,052.42
Exports of goods and services	13,199.43	13,761.05	14,564.40
Less Imports of goods and services	14,025.95	14,519.70	15,371.33
GDP in purchasers' values	28,220.67	28,673.38	30,245.50
GDP at constant 2000 prices	23,213.48	24,194.19	25,598.95

Source: African Development Bank.

Gross Domestic Product by Economic Activity
(million dinars at current prices)

	2005	2006	2007
Agriculture and fishing	4,089.7	4,320.8	4,754.2
Mining (excluding hydrocarbons)	230.7	232.4	244.1
Manufacturing (excluding hydrocarbons)	6,455.3	7,002.4	7,723.5
Hydrocarbons, electricity and water	2,177.4	2,565.3	3,455.4
Construction and public works	2,073.0	2,319.0	2,501.3
Transport and telecommunications	3,879.6	4,424.2	5,025.8
Hotels and restaurants	2,228.5	2,377.5	2,475.8
Trade, finance, etc.	8,197.7	8,881.2	9,835.3
Non-market services	5,122.1	5,544.4	5,930.1
Sub-total	34,454.0	37,667.2	41,945.5
Less Imputed bank service charges	924.6	1,019.0	1,287.3
Statistical discrepancy	—	−10.0	—
GDP at factor cost	33,529.4	36,638.2	40,658.3
Indirect taxes, *less* subsidies	4,175.2	4,456.1	4,374.5
Statistical discrepancy	−18.0	10.0	—
GDP in purchasers' values	37,686.6	41,104.3	45,032.5

BALANCE OF PAYMENTS
(US $ million)

	2004	2005	2006
Exports of goods f.o.b.	9,679	10,488	11,507
Imports of goods f.o.b.	−12,110	−12,456	−14,035
Trade balance	−2,430	−1,968	−2,527
Exports of services	3,629	4,021	4,295
Imports of services	−1,986	−2,191	−2,454
Balance on goods and services	−787	−138	−687
Other income received	114	118	160
Other income paid	−1,412	−1,786	−1,746
Balance on goods, services and income	−2,084	−1,805	−2,273
Current transfers received	1,564	1,537	1,676
Current transfers paid	−31	−36	−37
Current balance	−551	−304	−634
Capital account (net)	108	127	145
Direct investment abroad	−2	−10	−30
Direct investment from abroad	593	723	3,270
Portfolio investment liabilities	24	12	65
Other investment assets	−205	17	19
Other investment liabilities	1,028	394	−729
Net errors and omissions	−18	−23	−24
Overall balance	977	936	2,082

Source: IMF, *International Financial Statistics*.

External Trade

PRINCIPAL COMMODITIES
(million dinars)

Imports c.i.f.	2003	2004	2005
Agricultural and food products	1,261.6	1,526.6	1,626.7
Energy, lubricants, etc.	1,456.2	1,658.0	2,267.7
Minerals, phosphates and related products	318.7	369.5	421.1
Textiles, manufactured garments, leather and leather products	3,409.6	3,326.6	3,303.5
Machinery, electrical products and transport equipment	5,404.7	6,528.5	6,641.1
Transport equipment	998.8	1,210.5	1,265.7
Other industrial machinery, equipment and parts	2,716.9	3,310.6	3,306.4
Electrical machinery, apparatus, etc.	1,689.0	2,007.5	2,068.9
Miscellaneous manufactured articles	2,188.1	2,551.1	2,841.5
Total	14,038.9	15,960.3	17,101.5

Exports f.o.b.	2003	2004	2005
Agricultural and food products	749.9	1,368.9	1,452.6
Energy, lubricants, etc.	1,032.6	1,151.0	1,757.3
Minerals, phosphates and related products	685.9	864.9	953.5
Textiles, manufactured garments, leather and leather products	4,880.6	5,111.8	5,133.1
Machinery, electrical products and transport equipment	2,149.7	2,597.9	3,141.7
Transport equipment	221.4	284.7	351.9
Other industrial machinery, equipment and parts	730.2	806.0	869.0
Electrical machinery, apparatus, etc.	1,198.2	1,507.1	1,920.8
Miscellaneous manufactured articles	843.8	960.5	1,169.4
Total	10,342.6	12,054.9	13,607.7

2006 (million dinars): *Imports:* Total 19,766.1. *Exports:* Agricultural and food products 1,868.0; Energy, lubricants, etc. 2,017.6; Minerals, phosphates and related products 1,033.6; Textiles, manufactured garments, leather and leather products 5,150.6; Machinery, electrical products and transport equipment 3,861.4; Other industrial manufactures 1,385.2; Total 15,316.3.

2007 (million dinars): *Imports:* Total 24,279.8. *Exports:* Agricultural and food products 1,882.7; Energy, lubricants, etc. 3,138.5; Minerals, phosphates and related products 1,348.7; Textiles, manufactured garments, leather and leather products 5,984.6; Machinery, electrical products and transport equipment 5,197.3; Other industrial manufactures 1,682.8; Total 19,234.8.

PRINCIPAL TRADING PARTNERS
(million dinars)*

Imports c.i.f.	2003	2004	2005
Algeria	167.5	93.5	175.7
Belgium	413.8	444.9	449.4
China, People's Republic	238.7	362.5	494.6
France	3,653.0	3,978.1	4,015.8
Germany	1,267.8	1,339.3	1,402.8
Italy	2,804.7	3,011.1	3,578.7
Japan	255.9	317.6	276.4
Libya	460.4	526.9	661.9
Netherlands	285.3	284.3	318.2
Spain	748.8	839.1	879.3
Sweden	166.1	226.5	130.7
Switzerland	165.0	175.8	185.3
United Kingdom	314.1	345.5	376.2
USA	345.4	445.7	424.7
Total (incl. others)	14,038.9	15,960.3	17,101.5

TUNISIA

Exports f.o.b.	2003	2004	2005
Algeria	133.4	135.6	237.2
Belgium	405.9	358.9	373.8
France	3,365.5	3,986.7	4,474.8
Germany	1,105.6	1,105.2	1,148.2
India	59.7	106.9	126.7
Italy	2,281.4	3,051.4	3,260.6
Libya	453.8	432.6	612.9
Netherlands	239.1	265.7	292.8
Spain	481.8	729.4	747.0
Switzerland	218.2	49.0	62.6
United Kingdom	337.3	346.6	362.2
Total (incl. others)	10,342.6	12,054.9	13,607.7

* Imports by country of production; exports by country of last destination.

2006 (million dinars): *Imports:* Total 19,766.1. *Exports:* Total 15,316.3.

2007 (million dinars): *Imports:* Total 24,279.8. *Exports:* Total 19,234.8.

Transport

RAILWAYS
(traffic)

	2003	2004	2005
Passengers carried ('000)	35,706.0	36,329.0	36,790.0
Passenger-kilometres (million)	1,239.0	1,294.0	1,317.0
Freight carried ('000 metric tons)	11,569.3	11,035.0	10,800.8
Freight net ton-kilometres (million)	2,172.9	2,082.6	2,068.2

ROAD TRAFFIC
(estimates, motor vehicles in use at 31 December)

	2000	2001	2002
Passenger cars	516,525	552,897	585,194
Buses and coaches	11,143	11,973	12,181
Lorries and vans	240,421	253,760	266,499
Road tractors	8,307	9,165	9,605

Source: International Road Federation, *World Road Statistics*.

2004: Passenger cars 825,990; Buses and coaches 12,181; Lorries and vans 106,883; Motorcycles 6,057.

SHIPPING
Merchant Fleet
(vessels registered at 31 December)

	2004	2005	2006
Number of vessels	73	75	75
Total displacement ('000 grt)	175.3	169.3	168.1

Source: Lloyd's Register-Fairplay, *World Fleet Statistics*.

International Sea-borne Freight Traffic
('000 metric tons)

	2003	2004	2005
Goods loaded*	6,720	6,976	7,227
Goods unloaded	13,882	14,032	14,454

* Excluding Algerian crude petroleum loaded at La Skhirra.

CIVIL AVIATION
(traffic on scheduled services)

	2001	2002	2003
Kilometres flown (million)	26	24	25
Passengers carried ('000)	1,926	1,789	1,720
Passenger-km (million)	2,696	2,511	2,459
Total ton-km (million)	283	266	261

Source: UN, *Statistical Yearbook*.

Tourism

FOREIGN TOURIST ARRIVALS BY NATIONALITY
('000)

	2003	2004	2005
Algeria	811.5	914.1	930.7
Austria	70.1	84.4	86.4
Belgium	132.6	140.8	155.1
France	834.0	1,020.8	1,170.1
Germany	488.5	569.5	571.9
Italy	379.8	448.3	472.8
Libya	1,325.7	1,435.8	1,404.0
Switzerland	85.8	99.1	92.8
United Kingdom	223.2	300.8	327.5
Total (incl. others)	5,114.3	5,997.9	6,378.4

2006: Total arrivals 6,549.

Receipts from tourism (US $ million, incl. passenger transport): 1,935 in 2003; 2,432 in 2004; 2,782 in 2005.

Source: mainly World Tourism Organization.

Communications Media

	2004	2005	2006
Telephones ('000 main lines in use)	1,203.5	1,257.5	1,268.5
Mobile cellular telephones ('000 subscribers)	3,735.7	5,680.7	7,339.0
Personal computers ('000 in use)	472	568	n.a.
Internet users ('000)	835.0	953.8	1,294.9
Broadband subscribers ('000)	2.8	17.6	n.a.

Radio receivers ('000 in use): 2,060 in 1997.

Facsimile machines (number in use): 31,000 in 1997.

Book production (titles): 1,260 in 1999.

Daily newspapers: 7 (average circulation 180,000) in 2000; 10 in 2004.

Non-daily newspapers: 39 (average circulation 963,861) in 2001.

Periodicals (titles): 182 in 2000 (average circulation 525,000).

Television receivers ('000 in use): 1,900 in 2000.

Sources: UNESCO, *Statistical Yearbook*; UNESCO Institute for Statistics; UN, *Statistical Yearbook*; and International Telecommunication Union.

Education

(2006/07, unless otherwise indicated)

	Institutions	Teachers	Students
Primary (public)	4,504	57,739	1,053,416
Secondary	698	68,147	1,088,816
Higher	190	18,117*	326,185*

* Full-time equivalent.

Adult literacy rate (UNESCO estimates): 74.3% (males 83.4%; females 65.3%) in 2004 (Source: UNESCO Institute for Statistics).

Directory

The Constitution

A new Constitution for the Republic of Tunisia was promulgated on 1 June 1959 and amended on 12 July 1988; further amendments were approved by national referendum on 26 May 2002. Its main provisions are summarized below:

NATIONAL ASSEMBLY

Legislative power is exercised by a bicameral parliament: the Chamber of Deputies and the Chamber of Advisers, which was established by the constitutional amendments approved in May 2002. Every citizen who has had Tunisian nationality for at least five years and who has attained 20 years of age has the right to vote. The Chamber of Deputies, which is elected (at the same time as the President) every five years, shall hold two sessions every year, each session lasting not more than three months. Additional meetings may be held at the demand of the President or of a majority of the deputies. The Chamber of Advisers currently consists of 126 members; while this number is revised every six years, it must never exceed two-thirds of the number of members of the Chamber of Deputies. One-third of the members of the Chamber of Advisers is composed of representatives of the main professional unions and federations, one-third by representatives of the 24 governorates (one or two from each governorate, depending on the size of its population), and the remainder are appointed by the President. The members of the Chamber of Advisers serve a six-year term; one-half of its members are replaced every three years.

HEAD OF STATE

The President of the Republic is both Head of State and Head of the Executive. He must be not less than 40 years of age and not more than 75 (not more than 70, prior to the May 2002 amendments). The President is elected by universal suffrage for a five-year term. The amendments approved in May 2002 removed restrictions on the renewal of the presidential mandate (previously, this was renewable twice consecutively). The President is also the Commander-in-Chief of the army and makes both civil and military appointments. The Government may be censured by the National Assembly, in which case the President may dismiss the Assembly and hold fresh elections. If censured by the new Assembly thus elected, the Government must resign. Should the presidency fall vacant for any reason before the end of a President's term of office, the President of the National Assembly shall take charge of affairs of the state for a period of 45 to 60 days. At the end of this period a presidential election shall be organized. The President of the National Assembly shall not be eligible as a presidential candidate.

COUNCIL OF STATE

Comprises two judicial bodies: an administrative body dealing with legal disputes between individuals and state or public bodies, and an audit office to verify the accounts of the state and submit reports.

ECONOMIC AND SOCIAL COUNCIL

Deals with economic and social planning and studies projects submitted by the National Assembly. Members are grouped in seven categories representing various sections of the community.

The Government

HEAD OF STATE

President: ZINE AL-ABIDINE BEN ALI (took office on 7 November 1987; elected 2 April 1989; re-elected 20 March 1994, 24 October 1999 and 24 October 2004).

COUNCIL OF MINISTERS
(April 2008)

Prime Minister: MUHAMMAD GHANNOUCHI.
Minister of State, Special Adviser to the President and Spokesman for the Presidency: ABDELAZIZ BEN DHIA.
Minister of Foreign Affairs: ABDELWAHAB ABDALLAH.
Minister of the Interior and Local Development: RAFIK BELHAJ KACEM.
Minister of National Defence: KAMEL MORJANE.
Minister of Justice and Human Rights: BÉCHIR TEKKARI.
Minister of Religious Affairs: BOUBAKER AL-AKHZOURI.
Minister Director of the Presidential Office: AHMAD IYADH OUEDERNI.
Minister of Women's, Family, Children's and Elderly Affairs: SARRA KANOUN JARRAYA.
Minister of Social Affairs, Solidarity and Tunisians Abroad: ALI CHAOUCH.
Minister of Education and Training: SADOK KORBI.
Minister of the Environment and Sustainable Development: NADHIR HAMADA.
Minister of Culture and Heritage Preservation: MUHAMMAD AL-AZIZ BEN ACHOUR.
Minister of Public Health: MONDHER ZENAÏDI.
Minister of Youth, Sports and Physical Education: ABDALLAH KAÂBI.
Minister of Employment and Professional Integration of Youth: CHADLI LAROUSSI.
Minister of Finance: MUHAMMAD RACHID KECHICHE.
Minister of Communication Technologies: HAJ KLAÏ.
Minister of Agriculture and Water Resources: MUHAMMAD HABIB HADDAD.
Minister of Transport: ABDERRAHIM ZOUARI.
Minister of Tourism: KHELIL LAJIMI.
Minister of Trade and Handicrafts: RIDHA TOUITI.
Minister of Equipment, Housing and Territorial Development: SAMIRA KHAYACH BELHAJ.
Minister of Development and International Co-operation: MUHAMMAD NOURI JOUINI.
Minister of State Property and Land Affairs: RIDHA GRIRA.
Minister of Communications and Relations with Parliament: RAFAÂ DEKHIL.
Minister of Higher Education, Scientific Research and Technology: LAZHAR BOUOUNI.
Minister of Industry, Energy and Small and Medium Enterprises: AFIF CHELBI.
Minister-delegate to the Prime Minister, in charge of Civil Service and Administrative Development: ZOUHAIR MDHAFFER.
Government Secretary-General in charge of Relations with the Chamber of Deputies and the Chamber of Councillors: ABD AL-HAKIM BOURAOUI.

There are, in addition, 17 Secretaries of State. The Governor of the Central Bank also has full ministerial status.

MINISTRIES

Office of the President: Palais de Carthage, 2016 Carthage; internet www.carthage.tn.
Office of the Prime Minister: place du Gouvernement, La Kasbah, 1008 Tunis; tel. (71) 565-400; e-mail prm@ministeres.tn; internet www.ministeres.tn.
Ministry of Agriculture and Water Resources: 30 rue Alain Savary, 1002 Tunis; tel. (71) 786-833; e-mail mag@ministeres.tn.
Ministry of Communication Technologies: 3 bis rue d'Angleterre, 1000 Tunis; tel. (71) 359-000; fax (71) 352-353; e-mail info@infocom.tn; internet www.infocom.tn.
Ministry of Culture and Heritage Preservation: 8 rue 2 Mars 1934, la Kasbah, 1006 Tunis; tel. (71) 562-661; fax (71) 574-580; e-mail mcu@ministeres.tn; internet www.culture.tn.
Ministry of Development and International Co-operation: place Ali Zouaoui, 1069 Tunis; tel. (71) 240-133; fax (71) 799-069; e-mail boc@mdci.gov.tn; internet www.investissement.tn.
Ministry of Education and Training: ave Bab Benat, 1030 Tunis; tel. (71) 568-768; e-mail med@ministeres.tn; internet www.education.tn.
Ministry of Employment and Professional Integration of Youth: 10 ave Ouled Haffouz, 1006 Tunis; tel. (71) 792-432; fax (71) 794-615; e-mail webmaster@email.ati.tn; internet www.info-emploi.tn.
Ministry of the Environment and Sustainable Development: Centre Urbain Nord, Ariana, 2080 Tunis; tel. (70) 728-455; fax (70) 728-655; e-mail boc@mineat.gov.tn; internet www.environnement.nat.tn.
Ministry of Equipment, Housing and Territorial Development: 10 blvd Habib Chrita, Cité Jardin, 1002 Tunis; tel. (71) 842-244; fax (71) 780-397; e-mail meh@ministeres.tn.
Ministry of Finance: place du Gouvernement, La Kasbah, 1008 Tunis; tel. (71) 571-888; fax (71) 572-390; e-mail mfi@ministeres.tn; internet www.portail.finances.gov.tn.
Ministry of Foreign Affairs: ave de la Ligue des états arabes, Tunis; tel. (71) 847-500; e-mail mae@ministeres.tn; internet www.diplomatie.gov.tn.

TUNISIA

Ministry of Higher Education, Scientific Research and Technology: ave Ouled Haffouz, 1030 Tunis; tel. (71) 786-300; fax (71) 786-701; e-mail mes@mes.rnu.tn; internet www.mes.tn.

Ministry of Industry, Energy and Small and Medium Enterprises: Immeuble Beya, 40 rue 8011, Montplaisir, 1002 Tunis; tel. (71) 791-132; fax (71) 782-742; e-mail webmaster@industrie.gov.tn; internet www.industrie.gov.tn.

Ministry of the Interior and Local Development: ave Habib Bourguiba, 1000 Tunis; tel. (71) 333-000; fax (71) 340-888; e-mail mint@ministeres.tn.

Ministry of Justice and Human Rights: 31 ave Bab Benat, 1006 Tunis; tel. (71) 561-440; fax (71) 586-106; e-mail mju@ministeres.tn.

Ministry of National Defence: blvd Bab Menara, 1030 Tunis; tel. (71) 560-240; fax (71) 561-804; e-mail defnat@defense.tn; internet www.defense.tn.

Ministry of Public Health: Bab Saâdoun, 1006 Tunis; tel. (71) 560-545; fax (71) 567-100; e-mail msp@ministeres.tn.

Ministry of Religious Affairs: 176 ave Bab Benat, 1009 Tunis; tel. (71) 570-147; fax (71) 570-123; e-mail mar@ministeres.tn; internet www.affaires-religeuses.tn.

Ministry of Social Affairs, Solidarity and Tunisians Abroad: 25 ave Bab Benat, 1006 Tunis; tel. (71) 567-502; fax (71) 568-722; e-mail mas@ministeres.tn; internet www.social.tn.

Ministry of State Property and Land Affairs: 19 ave de Paris, 1000 Tunis; tel. (71) 341-644; fax (71) 342-410; e-mail mdeaf@ministeres.tn; internet www.cpf.gov.tn.

Ministry of Tourism: 1 ave Muhammad V, 1001 Tunis; tel. (71) 341-077; fax (71) 332-070; e-mail mta@ministeres.tn.

Ministry of Trade and Handicrafts: 37 ave Kheireddine Pacha, 1002 Tunis; tel. (71) 890-070; fax (71) 781-324; e-mail mcmr@ministeres.tn; internet www.commerce.gov.tn.

Ministry of Transport: blvd 7 Novembre 1987, 2035 Tunis; tel. (71) 772-110; e-mail mtr@ministeres.tn.

Ministry of Women's, Family, Children's and Elderly Affairs: 2 rue d'Alger, 1001 Tunis; tel. (71) 252-514; fax (71) 349-900; e-mail maffepa@email.ati.tn; internet www.femmes.tn.

Ministry of Youth, Sports and Physical Education: Avenue Med Ali Akid, Cité El Khadhra, 1003 Tunis; tel. (71) 841-433; e-mail Portail.sport@sport.tn; internet www.sport.tn.

President and Legislature

PRESIDENT
Presidential Election, 24 October 2004

Candidate	Votes	% of votes
Zine al-Abidine Ben Ali	4,204,292	94.49
Muhammad Bouchiha	167,986	3.78
Muhammad Ali Halouani	42,213	0.95
Mounir Béji	35,067	0.79
Total*	4,449,558	100.00

* Excluding 14,779 invalid votes.

LEGISLATURE
Majlis an-Nuab
(Chamber of Deputies)

President: FOUAD MEBAZAÂ.
Election, 24 October 2004

Party	Votes	%	Seats
Rassemblement constitutionnel démocratique	3,678,645	87.62	152
Mouvement des démocrates socialistes	194,829	4.64	14
Parti de l'unité populaire	152,987	3.64	11
Union démocratique unioniste	92,708	2.21	7
Mouvement du renouveau	43,268	1.03	3
Parti social libéral	25,261	0.60	2
Others	10,473	0.25	0
Total*	4,198,171	100.00	189†

* Excluding 15,305 spoilt ballot papers.
† Under the terms of an amendment to the electoral code adopted by the National Assembly in 1998, 20% of the seats in the National Assembly (and thus 37 in the current legislature) were reserved for candidates of opposition parties. These were allotted according to the proportion of votes received nationally by each party.

Majlis al-Mustasharin
(Chamber of Advisers)

Speaker: ABDULLAH KALLEL.
Election, 3 July 2005

	Seats*
Representatives of the main professional unions and federations	42
Representatives of the governorates†	43
Appointed by the President‡	41
Total	126

* Members of the Chamber of Advisers serve a six-year term; one-half of its members are replaced every three years.
† One or two members are elected from each of the 24 governorates, depending on the size of its population.
‡ Appointed on 1 August 2005.

Political Organizations

Congrès pour la République: Tunis; e-mail cprtunisie@yahoo.fr; internet www.cprtunisie.net; f. 2001; Leader MONCEF MARZOUKI.

Forum démocratique pour le travail et les libertés (FDTL): Tunis; internet www.fdtl.org; f. 2002; Leader Dr MUSTAPHA BEN JAFAÂR.

Mouvement des démocrates socialistes (MDS): Tunis; in favour of a pluralist political system; participated in 1981 election and was officially recognized in Nov. 1983; Political Bureau of 11 mems, National Council of 60 mems, normally elected by the party Congress; Sec.-Gen. ISMAIL BOULAHYA.

Mouvement ettajdid: 6 rue Métouia, 1000 Tunis; tel. (71) 256-400; fax (71) 240-981; internet ettajdid.attariq.org; f. 1993 as Mouvement du renouveau, successor to Parti communiste tunisien; legal; Sec.-Gen. AHMED BRAHIM; Pres. of Nat. Council MUHAMMAD ALI HALOUANI.

Mouvement de l'unité populaire (MUP): Tunis; supports radical reform; split into two factions, one led by Ahmed Ben Salah living in exile until 1988; the other became the Parti de l'unité populaire (see below); Co-ordinator BRAHIM HAYDER.

Parti démocrate progressiste (PDP): Tunis; e-mail admin@pdpinfo.org; internet www.pdpinfo.org; f. 1983 as Rassemblement socialiste progressiste; officially recognized in Sept. 1988; name changed as above in 2001; leftist; Sec.-Gen. MAYA JRIBI.

Parti de la renaissance—Hizb an-Nahdah: Tunis; e-mail nahdha@ezzeitouna.org; fmrly Mouvement de la tendance islamique (banned in 1981); Leader RACHID GHANOUCHI; Sec.-Gen. Sheikh ABD AL-FATHA MOUROU.

Parti communiste des ouvriers tunisiens (PCOT): Tunis; e-mail pcot@albadil.org; internet www.albadil.org; illegal; Leader HAMMA HAMMAMI.

Parti social libéral (PSL): 42 ave Hédi Chaker, 1002 Tunis; tel. and fax (71) 789-089; fax (71) 789-060; e-mail mondherthabet@gnet.tn; f. 1988; officially recognized in Sept. 1988 as the Parti social pour le progrès; adopted present name in 1993; liberal; Pres. Dr MONDHER THABET.

Parti de l'unité populaire (PUP): 7 rue d'Autriche, 1002 Tunis; tel. (71) 289-678; fax (71) 796-031; internet www.elwahda.org.tn; split from MUP (see above); officially recognized in Nov. 1983; Leader MUHAMMAD BOUCHIHA.

Parti des verts pour le progrès (PVP): f. 2006; seeks to promote awareness of the environment; Sec.-Gen. MONGI KHAMASSI.

Rassemblement constitutionnel démocratique (RCD): blvd 9 avril 1938, Tunis; e-mail info@rcd.tn; internet www.rcd.tn; f. 1934 as the Néo-Destour Party, following a split in the Destour (Constitution) Party; renamed Parti socialiste destourien in 1964; adopted present name in Feb. 1988; moderate left-wing republican party, which achieved Tunisian independence; Political Bureau of nine mems, and a Cen. Cttee of 200, elected by the party Congress; Chair. ZINE AL-ABIDINE BEN ALI; First Vice-Chair. HAMED KAROUI; Second Vice-Chair. MUHAMMAD GHANNOUCHI; Sec.-Gen. HÉDI M'HENNI.

Union démocratique unioniste (UDU): Tunis; officially recognized in Nov. 1988; supports Arab unity; Sec.-Gen. AHMED INOUBLI.

Diplomatic Representation

EMBASSIES IN TUNISIA

Algeria: 18 rue de Niger, 1002 Tunis; tel. (71) 783-166; fax (71) 788-804; Ambassador ABDELAZIZ MAOUI.

TUNISIA

Directory

Argentina: 10 rue al-Hassan et Houssaine, BP 9, al-Menzah IV, 1002 Tunis; tel. (71) 231-222; fax (71) 750-058; e-mail etune@emb_argentina.intl.tn; Ambassador Jesús Fernando Taboada.

Austria: 16 rue ibn Hamdiss, BP 23, al-Menzah, 1004 Tunis; tel. (71) 751-091; fax (71) 767-824; e-mail tunis-ob@bmeia.gv.at; Ambassador Dr Johann Fröhlich.

Bahrain: 72 rue Mouaouia ibn Soufiane, BP 79, al-Menzah VIII, 2019 Tunis; tel. (71) 750-865; fax (71) 766-549; e-mail tunis.mission@mofa.gov.bh; Ambassador Abd ar-Rahman Mubarak as-Sulaiti.

Belgium: 47 rue du 1er juin, BP 24, 1002 Tunis; tel. (71) 781-655; fax (71) 792-797; e-mail tunis@diplobel.org; internet www.diplomatie.be/tunis; Ambassador Michel Carlier.

Brazil: 5 rue Sufétula, BP 83, 1002 Tunis; tel. (71) 893-569; fax (71) 846-995; e-mail brasemb.tunis@gnet.tn; internet www.ambassadedubresil.com; Ambassador Marilia Sardenberg Zelner Gonçalves.

Bulgaria: 5 rue Ryhane, BP 6, Cité Mahragène, 1082 Tunis; tel. (71) 798-962; fax (71) 791-667; e-mail bgtunis.amb@planet.tn; Ambassador (vacant).

Canada: 3 rue du Sénégal, place d'Afrique, BP 31, Belvédère, 1002 Tunis; tel. (71) 104-000; fax (71) 104-190; e-mail tunis@international.gc.ca; internet www.dfait-maeci.gc.ca/tunisia; Ambassador Bruno Picard.

China, People's Republic: 22 rue Dr Burnet, 1002 Tunis; tel. (71) 780-064; fax (71) 792-631; e-mail ambassade.chine@ati.tn; Ambassador Liu Yuhe.

Congo, Democratic Republic: 11 rue Tertullien, Notre Dame, Tunis; tel. (71) 281-833; Ambassador Mboladinga Katako.

Côte d'Ivoire: 17 rue el-Mansoura, BP 21, Belvédère, 1002 Tunis; tel. (71) 755-911; fax (71) 755-901; e-mail acitn@ambaci-tunis.org; Ambassador Yapo Atchapo Thomas.

Cuba: 1 rue Amilcar, al-Menzah VIII, 1004 Tunis; tel. (71) 767-235; fax (71) 755-922; e-mail embajador-tunez@topnet.tn; internet emba.cubaminrex.cu/tunezar; Ambassador Rolando González Téllez.

Czech Republic: 98 rue de Palestine, BP 53, Belvédère, 1002 Tunis; tel. (71) 780-456; fax (71) 793-228; e-mail tunis@embassy.mzv.cz; internet www.mzv.cz/tunis; Ambassador Jaromír Přívratský.

Egypt: ave Muhammad V, Quartier Montplaisir, rue 8007, Tunis; tel. (71) 792-233; fax (71) 794-389; e-mail egyembassy.tunis@planet.tn; Ambassador Shadia Hussein Farraq.

Finland: Dar Nordique, rue du Lac Neuchâtel, Les Berges du Lac, 1053 Tunis; tel. (71) 861-777; fax (71) 961-080; e-mail sanomat.tun@formin.fi; internet www.finlandtunis.org; Ambassador Laura Reinilä.

France: 2 place de l'Indépendance, 1000 Tunis; tel. (71) 105-111; fax (71) 105-100; e-mail courrier@ambassadefrance-tn.org; internet www.ambassadefrance-tn.org; Ambassador Serge Degallaix.

Germany: 1 rue al-Hamra, BP 35, Mutuelleville, 1002 Tunis-Mutuelleville; tel. (71) 786-455; fax (71) 788-242; e-mail reg1@tunis.diplo.de; internet www.tunis.diplo.de; Ambassador Dr Horst-Wolfram Kerll.

Greece: 6 rue Saint Fulgence, Notre Dame, 1082 Tunis; tel. (71) 288-411; fax (71) 789-518; e-mail gremb.tun@mfa.gr; Ambassador Dimitrios Karatidis.

Hungary: 12 rue Achtart, 1082 Nord Hilton, BP 572, Tunis; tel. (71) 780-544; fax (71) 781-264; e-mail huembtun@planet.tn; internet www.mfa.gov.hu/emb/tunis; Ambassador Dr Pál Pataki.

India: 4 place Didon, Notre Dame, 1002 Tunis; tel. (71) 787-819; fax (71) 783-394; e-mail embassy.india@email.ati.tn; Ambassador Basant K. Gupta.

Indonesia: BP 63, al-Menzah, 1004 Tunis; tel. (71) 860-377; fax (71) 861-758; e-mail kbritun@gnet.tn; Ambassador Hertomo Reksodiputro.

Iran: 10 rue de Docteur Burnet, Belvédère, 1002 Tunis; tel. (71) 790-084; fax (71) 793-177; Ambassador Muhammad Taghi Moayed.

Iraq: ave Tahar B. Achour, route X2 m 10, Mutuelleville, Tunis; tel. (71) 962-480; fax (71) 963-737; e-mail tunemb@iraqmofamail.net; Ambassador Ghazi Tahir Khalid.

Italy: 37 rue Jamal Abdelnaceur, 1000 Tunis; tel. (71) 321-811; fax (71) 324-155; e-mail ambitalia.tunisi@esteri.it; internet www.ambtunis.esteri.it; Ambassador Antonio D'Andria.

Japan: 9 rue Apollo XI, BP 163, Cité Mahrajène, 1082 Tunis; tel. (71) 791-251; fax (71) 786-625; internet www.tn.emb-japan.go.jp; Ambassador Shigeru Endo.

Jordan: 10 Nahj ash-Shankiti, 1002 Tunis; tel. (71) 785-829; fax (71) 786-461; e-mail emb.jordan@planet.tn; Ambassador Samir Mustapha Khalifa.

Korea, Republic: 16 rue Caracalla, BP 297, Notre Dame, 1082 Tunis; tel. (71) 799-905; fax (71) 791-923; e-mail tunisie@mofat.go.kr; Ambassador Son Se-Joo.

Kuwait: 40 route Ariane, al-Menzah, Tunis; tel. (71) 236-811; Ambassador (vacant).

Lebanon: Nahj 7037, no 3, al-Menzah, Tunis; tel. (71) 754-011; fax (71) 750-724; Ambassador Farid Abboud.

Libya: 48 bis rue du 1er juin, Mutuelle ville, 1002 Tunis; tel. (71) 780-866; fax (71) 795-338.

Mali: 117 ave Jugurtha Matuelleville, BP 54, Nouvelle Ariana, 1002 Tunis; tel. (71) 792-589; fax (71) 791453; e-mail ambamali@wanadoo.tn; Ambassador Arafa M'Barakou Askia Touré.

Mauritania: 17 rue Fatma Ennechi, BP 62, al-Menzah, Tunis; tel. (71) 234-935; Ambassador Ahmed S. Ould Saleck.

Morocco: 39 ave du 1er juin, 1002 Tunis; tel. (71) 782-775; fax (71) 787-103; e-mail ambamaroc@sifamatunis.net; Ambassador Najib Zerouali el-Ouariti.

Netherlands: 6–8 rue Meycen, BP 47, Belvédère, 1082 Tunis; tel. (71) 797-724; fax (71) 785-557; e-mail tun@minbuza.nl; internet www.hollandembassy-tunisia.com; Ambassador Rita Dulci Rahman.

Norway: BP 124, Les Berges du Lac, 1053 Tunis; tel. (71) 861-777; fax (71) 961-080; e-mail emb.tunis@mfa.no; internet www.norvege-tunisie.org; Ambassador Per Kristian Pedersen.

Pakistan: 35 rue Ali Ayari, al-Menzah IX, Tunis; tel. (71) 871-330; fax (71) 871-410; e-mail pareptunis@yahoo.com; Ambassador Faiz Muhammad Khoso.

Poland: 5 Impasse no. 1, rue de Cordoue, El Manar I, Tunis; tel. (71) 873-837; fax (71) 872-987; e-mail amb.pologne@wanadoo.tn; internet www.tunis-polemb.net; Chargé d'affaires a.i. Dariusz Szewczyk.

Portugal: 2 rue Sufétula, Belvédère, 1002 Tunis; tel. (71) 893-981; fax (71) 791-008; e-mail embportunes@embport.intl.tn; Ambassador Maria Rita da Franca Sousa e Ferro Levy Gomes.

Qatar: rue Alhadi Krai, Northern al-Omran Quarter, 1082 Tunis; tel. (71) 849-600; fax (71) 749-073; e-mail tunis@mofa.gov.qa; Ambassador Saad bin Nasser al-Humaidi.

Romania: 18 ave d'Afrique, BP 57, al-Menzah V, 1004 Tunis; tel. (71) 766-926; fax (71) 767-695; e-mail amb.roumanie@planet.tn; internet www.ambassade-roumanie.intl.tn; Ambassador Sorin-Mihail Tănăsescu.

Russia: 4 rue Bergamotes, BP 48, El Manar I, 2092 Tunis; tel. (71) 882-446; fax (71) 882-478; e-mail ambrustn@mail.ru; internet www.tunisie.mid.ru; Ambassador Andrei Polyakov.

Saudi Arabia: blvd du 7 Novembre, Centre Urbain-Nord C, Mahrajène, 1080 Tunis; tel. (70) 728-666; fax (70) 728-440; Ambassador Ibrahim as-Saad al-Brahim.

Senegal: 122 ave de la Liberté, Belvédère, Tunis; tel. (71) 802-397; fax (71) 780-770; internet www.ambasenegal.intl.tn; Ambassador Abdourahmane Sow.

Serbia: 4 rue de Libéria, Belvédère, 1002 Tunis; tel. (71) 783-057; fax (71) 796-482; e-mail amb.serbia@gnet.tn; Ambassador Milorad Jovanović.

Somalia: 6 rue Hadramout, Mutuelleville, Tunis; tel. (71) 289-505; Ambassador Ahmad Abdallah Muhammad.

South Africa: 7 rue Achtart, Nord Hilton, 1082 Tunis; tel. (71) 800-311; fax (71) 796-742; e-mail sa@emb-safrica.intl.tn; internet www.southafrica.intl.tn; Ambassador Daniel Nicholaas Meyer.

Spain: 22–24 ave Dr Ernest Conseil, Cité Jardin, 1002 Tunis; tel. (71) 782-217; fax (71) 786-267; e-mail emb.tunez@mae.es; Ambassador Juan Manuel Cabrera Hernández.

Sudan: 37 rue d'Afrique, al-Menzah V, 1008 Tunis; tel. (71) 231-322; fax (71) 751-756; e-mail contact@soudanembassy-tn.com; internet www.sudanembassy-tn.com; Ambassador Ismail Ahmed Ismail.

Switzerland: BP 56, Les Berges du Lac, 1053 Tunis; tel. (71) 962-997; fax (71) 965-796; e-mail vertretung@tun.rep.admin.ch; Ambassador Christian Faessler.

Syria: 119 Azzouz Ribai-Almanar 3, Tunis; tel. (71) 888-188; Ambassador Dr Sami Glaiel.

Turkey: 30 ave d'Afrique, BP 134, al-Menzah V, Tunis; tel. (71) 750-668; fax (71) 767-045; e-mail tunus.be@planet.tn; Ambassador Hüseyin Naci Akinci.

Ukraine: 7 rue Saint Fulgence, Notre Dame, 1002 Tunis; tel. (71) 845-861; fax (71) 840-866; e-mail ambassade.ukraine@planet.tn; Ambassador Valeriy Rylach.

United Arab Emirates: 9 rue Achtart, Nord Hilton, Belvédère, 1002 Tunis; tel. (71) 788-888; fax (71) 788-777; e-mail emirates.embassy@planet.tn; Ambassador Muhammad Hamad Omrane.

United Kingdom: rue du Lac Windermere, Les Berges du Lac, 1053 Tunis; tel. (71) 108-700; fax (71) 108-769; e-mail british.emb@planet.tn; internet www.britishembassy.gov.uk/tunisia; Ambassador Alan Goulty.

USA: Les Berges du Lac, 1053 Tunis; tel. (71) 107-000; fax (71) 107-090; e-mail tuniswebsitecontact@state.gov; internet tunis.usembassy.gov; Ambassador Robert F. Godec.

TUNISIA

Yemen: rue Mouaouia ibn Soufiane, al-Menzah VI, Tunis; tel. (71) 237-933; Ambassador ABD AL-MALEK MANSOUR HASSAN.

Judicial System

The Cour de Cassation in Tunis has three civil and one criminal sections. There are three **Cours d'Appel** at Tunis, Sousse and Sfax, and 13 **Cours de Première Instance**, each having three chambers, except the **Cour de Première Instance** at Tunis, which has eight chambers. **Justices Cantonales** exist in 51 areas.

Religion

The Constitution of 1956 recognizes Islam as the state religion, with the introduction of certain reforms, such as the abolition of polygamy. An estimated 99% of the population are Muslims. Minority religions include Judaism (an estimated 2,000 adherents in 1993) and Christianity. The Christian population comprises Roman Catholics, Greek Orthodox, and French and English Protestants.

ISLAM

Grand Mufti of Tunisia: Sheikh KAMAL AD-DIN JA'EIT.

CHRISTIANITY

The Roman Catholic Church

There were an estimated 20,035 adherents in Tunisia in December 2005.

Bishop of Tunis: Most Rev. MAROUN E. LAHHAM, Evêché, 4 rue d'Alger, 1000 Tunis; tel. (71) 335-831; fax (71) 335-832; e-mail eveche.tunisie@evechetunisie.org; internet www.diocesetunisie.org.

The Protestant Church

Reformed Church of Tunisia: 36 rue Charles de Gaulle, 1000 Tunis; tel. (71) 327-886; e-mail eglisereformee@yahoo.fr; f. 1880; c.220 mems; Pastor WILLIAM BROWN.

The Press

DAILIES

Ach-Chourouk (Sunrise): 25 rue Jean Jaurès, BP 36619, Tunis; tel. (71) 331-000; fax (71) 253-024; e-mail directiongenerale@alchourouk.com; internet www.alchourouk.com; Arabic; Dir SLAHEDDINE AL-AMRI; Editor-in-Chief ABD AL-HAMID RIAHI; circ. 70,000.

Al-Horria: 8 rue de Rome, 1000 Tunis; tel. (71) 351-578; fax (71) 350-721; e-mail alhorria@email.ati.tn; internet www.alhorria.info.tn; Arabic; organ of the RCD; Dir ABDESSALEM TOUMI; circ. 50,000.

La Presse de Tunisie: 6 rue Ali Bach-Hamba, 1000 Tunis; tel. (71) 341-066; fax (71) 349-720; e-mail contact@lapresse.tn; internet www.lapresse.tn; f. 1936; French; Pres. and Dir-Gen. MUHAMMAD GONTARA; circ. 40,000.

Le Quotidien: 25 rue Jean Jaurès, 1000 Tunis; tel. (71) 331-000; fax (71) 235-024; e-mail directiongenerale@lequotidien-tn.com; internet www.lequotidien-tn.com; f. 2001; French; Dir SLAHEDDINE AL-AMRI; Editor-in-Chief CHOUKRY BAKOUCHE; circ. 20,000.

Le Renouveau: 8 rue de Rome, 1000 Tunis; tel. (71) 352-498; fax (71) 351-927; e-mail lerenouveau@lerenouveau.com.tn; internet www.tunisieinfo.com/LeRenouveau; f. 1988; French; organ of the RCD; Dir and Editor-in-Chief NEJIB OUERGHI.

As-Sabah (The Morning): ave du 7 novembre 1987, BP 441, al-Menzah, 1004 Tunis; tel. (71) 238-222; fax (71) 232-761; e-mail info@assabah.com.tn; internet www.assabah.com.tn; f. 1951; Arabic; Dir RAOUF CHEIKHROUHOU; circ. 50,000.

As-Sahafa: 6 rue Ali Bach-Hamba, 1000 Tunis; tel. (71) 341-066; fax (71) 349-720; e-mail contact@essahafa.info.tn; internet www.essahafa.info.tn; f. 1936; Arabic; Dir SAHRAOUI GAMOUN.

Le Temps: ave 7 novembre 1987, BP 441, al-Menzah, 1004 Tunis; tel. (71) 238-222; fax (71) 719-927; e-mail letemps@gnet.tn; internet www.letemps.com.tn; f. 1975; French; Dir RAOUF CHEIKHROUHOU; circ. 42,000.

PERIODICALS

Afrique Economie: 16 rue de Rome, BP 61, 1015 Tunis; tel. (71) 347-441; fax (71) 353-172; e-mail iea@planet.tn; f. 1970; monthly; Dir MUHAMMAD ZERZERI.

Al-Akhbar (The News): 1 passage d'al-Houdaybiyah, 1000 Tunis; tel. (71) 344-100; fax (71) 355-079; internet www.akhbar.tn; f. 1984; weekly; Arabic; general; Dir MUHAMMAD BEN YOUSUF; circ. 75,000.

Les Annonces: 6 rue de Sparte, BP 1343, Tunis; tel. (71) 350-177; fax (71) 347-184; f. 1978; 2 a week; French and Arabic; Dir MUHAMMAD NEJIB AZOUZ; circ. 170,000.

Al-Anouar at-Tounissia (Tunisian Lights): 25 rue ach-Cham, 5000 Tunis; tel. (71) 331-000; fax (71) 253-024; internet www.alanouar.com; Arabic; Dir SLAHEDDINE AL-AMRI; circ. 165,000.

L'Avenir: 26 rue Gamal Abd an-Nasser, BP 1200, Tunis; tel. (71) 258-941; f. 1980; weekly; organ of the Mouvement des démocrates socialistes (MDS).

Al-Bayan (The Manifesto): 61 rue Abderrazek, Chraîbi, 1001 Tunis; tel. (71) 339-633; fax (71) 338-533; e-mail darelbayane@gnet.tn; f. 1976; weekly; general; organ of the Union tunisienne de l'industrie, du commerce et de l'artisanat; Dir HÉDI DJILANI; circ. 100,000.

Al-Biladi (My Country): 15 rue 2 mars 1934, Tunis; f. 1974; Arabic; political and general weekly for Tunisian workers abroad; Dir HÉDI AL-GHALI; circ. 90,000.

Bulletin Mensuel de Statistiques: Institut National de la Statistique, 70 rue al-Cham, BP 265, 1080 Tunis; tel. (71) 891-002; fax (71) 792-559; e-mail ins@mdci.gov.tn; internet www.ins.nat.tn; monthly.

Conjoncture: 37 ave Kheireddine Pacha, 1002 Tunis; tel. (71) 891-826; fax (71) 200-706; e-mail conjoncture2003@yahoo.fr; f. 1974; monthly; economic and financial surveys; Dir HABIB BEDHIAFI; circ. 5,000.

Démocratie: Tunis; f. 1978; monthly; French; organ of the MDS; Dir HASSIB BEN AMMAR; circ. 5,000.

Dialogue: 15 rue 2 mars 1934, Tunis; tel. (71) 264-899; f. 1974; weekly; French; cultural and political organ of the RCD; Dir NACEUR BECHEKH; circ. 30,000.

L'Economiste Maghrébin: 3 rue el-Kewekibi, 1002 Tunis; tel. (71) 790-773; fax (71) 793-707; e-mail leconomiste@planet.tn; internet www.leconomiste.com.tn; f. 1990; bi-weekly; Wed; French; Dir HÉDI MÉCHRI; circ. 30,000.

Etudiant Tunisien: Tunis; f. 1953; French and Arabic; Chief Editor FAOUZI AOUAM.

Al-Fajr (Dawn): Tunis; f. 1990; weekly; Arabic; organ of the Parti de la renaissance—Hizb an-Nahdah.

Al-Falah: rue Alain Savary, al-Khadra, 1003 Tunis; tel. (71) 806-800; fax (71) 809-074; e-mail elfalah@u_t_a_p.com; weekly; organ of the Union tunisienne de l'agriculture et de la pêche (UTAP); Dir MABROUK BAHRI; Editor GHARBI HAMOUDA; circ. 7,000.

Al-Fikr (Thought): Tunis; f. 1955; monthly; Arabic; cultural review.

L'Hebdo Touristique: rue 8601, 40, Zone Industrielle, La Charguia 2, 2035 Tunis; tel. (71) 786-866; fax (71) 794-891; e-mail haddad.tijani@planet.tn; f. 1971; weekly; French; tourism; Dir TIJANI HADDAD; circ. 5,000.

IBLA: Institut des Belles Lettres Arabes, 12 rue Jemaâ el-Haoua, 1008 Tunis; tel. (71) 560-133; fax (71) 572-683; e-mail ibla@gnet.tn; internet www.iblatunis.org; 2 a year; French, Arabic and English; social and cultural review on Maghreb and Muslim-Arab affairs; Dirs J. FONTAINE, K'MAR BENDANA; circ. 800.

Al-Idhaa wa Talvaza (Radio and Television): 71 ave de la Liberté, Tunis; tel. (71) 782-700; fax (71) 796-691; e-mail revue@ertt.nat.tn; f. 1956; fortnightly; Arabic language broadcasting magazine; Dir MUSTAPHA KHAMMARI; Editor JAMEL KARMAOUI.

Irfane (Children): 6 rue Muhammad Ali, 1000 Tunis; tel. (71) 256-877; fax (71) 351-521; f. 1965; monthly; Arabic; Dir-Gen. RIDHA EL OUADI; circ. 100,000.

Jeunesse Magazine: 6 rue Muhammad Ali, 1000 Tunis; tel. (71) 256-877; fax (71) 351-521; f. 1980; monthly; Arabic; Dir-Gen. RIDHA EL OUADI; circ. 30,000.

Journal Officiel de la République Tunisienne: ave Farhat Hached, 2040 Radès; tel. (71) 299-914; fax (71) 297-234; f. 1860; the official gazette; French and Arabic editions publ. twice weekly by the Imprimerie Officielle (The State Press); Pres. and Dir-Gen. ROMDHANE BEN MIMOUN; circ. 20,000.

Al-Mawkif: 10 rue Eve Nohelle, 1001 Tunis; tel. (71) 332-271; fax (71) 332-194; e-mail mawkef_21@yahoo.fr; f. 1984; weekly; organ of the Parti démocrate progressiste; Dir AHMED NÉJIB CHEBBI; Editor-in-Chief RACHID KHECHANA.

Al-Maraa (The Woman): 56 blvd Bab Benat, 1006 Tunis; tel. (71) 567-845; fax (71) 567-131; e-mail unft@email.a.t.i.tn; f. 1961; monthly; Arabic/French; political, economic and social affairs; issued by the Union nationale de la femme tunisienne; Pres. AZIZA HABIRA; circ. 10,000.

Le Mensuel: Tunis; f. 1984; monthly; economic, social and cultural affairs.

Al-Moussawar: 10 rue ach-Cham, Tunis; tel. (71) 289-000; fax (71) 289-357; internet www.almoussawar.com; weekly; circ. 75,000.

Outrouhat: Tunis; monthly; scientific; Dir LOTFI BEN AÏSSA.

TUNISIA

Ar-Rai (Opinion): Tunis; f. 1977 by the MDS; weekly; opposition newspaper; Dir HASSIB BEN AMMAR; circ. 20,000.

Réalités: 6–7 rue de Cameroun, 1002 Tunis; tel. (71) 788-313; fax (71) 787-160; e-mail redaction@realites.com.tn; internet www.realites.com.tn; f. 1979; weekly; French/Arabic; Dir TAÏEB ZAHAR; circ. 25,000.

At-Tariq al-Jadid (New Road): 6 rue Metouia, 1069 Tunis; tel. (71) 256-400; fax (71) 240-981; f. 1981; weekly; Arabic; organ of the Mouvement ettajdid; Dir MUHAMMAD HARMEL; Editor-in-Chief HICHAM SKIK.

Tounes al-Khadra: 6 rue Alain Savary, al-Khadra, 1003 Tunis; tel. (71) 800-800; fax (71) 798-598; e-mail utap@gnet.tn; f. 1976; bi-monthly; agricultural, scientific and technical; organ of the UTAP; Dir MABROUK BAHRI; Editor GHARBI HAMOUDA; circ. 5,000.

Tunis Hebdo: 1 passage d'al-Houdaybiyah, 1000 Tunis; tel. (71) 344-100; fax (71) 355-079; e-mail tunishebdo@tunishebdo.com.tn; internet www.tunishebdo.com.tn; f. 1973; weekly; French; general and sport; Dir MUHAMMAD BEN YOUSUF; circ. 35,000.

Tunisia News: rue 8601, 40, Zone Industrielle, La Charguia 1, 2035 Tunis; tel. (71) 786-866; fax (71) 794-891; e-mail haddad.tijani@planet.tn; f. 1993; weekly; English; Dir TIJANI HADDAD; circ. 5,000.

NEWS AGENCY

Tunis Afrique Presse (TAP): 7 ave Slimane Ben Slimane, al-Manar, 2092 Tunis; tel. (71) 889-000; fax (71) 883-500; e-mail desk.intern@email.ati.tn; internet www.tap.info.tn; f. 1961; Arabic, French and English; offices in Algiers, Rabat, Paris and New York; daily news services; Chair. and Gen. Man. MUHAMMAD BEN EZZEDDINE.

Publishers

Ad-Dar al-Arabia Lil Kitab: 4 ave Mohieddine el-Klibi, al-Manar, BP 32, al-Manar 2, 2092 Tunis; tel. (71) 888-255; fax (71) 888-365; e-mail mal@gnet.tn; f. 1975; general literature, children's books, non-fiction; Dir-Gen. MUSTAPHA ATTIA.

Centre de Publications Universitaires: Campus Universitaire, BP 255, 1080 Tunis; tel. (71) 874-000; fax (71) 871-677; e-mail cpu@cpu.rnu.tn; internet www.mes.tn/cpu; educational books, journals.

Cérès Editions: 6 rue Alain Savary, Belvédère, 1002 Tunis; tel. (71) 280-505; fax (71) 287-216; e-mail info@ceres-editions.com; internet www.ceres-editions.com; f. 1964; social sciences, art books, literature, novels; Pres. MUHAMMAD BEN SMAIL.

Dar Cheraït: Centre Culturel et Touristique Dar Cheraït, Route Touristique, 2200 Tozeur; tel. (76) 452-100; fax (76) 452-329; e-mail darcherait@planet.tn; internet www.darcherait.com.tn.

Dar al-Kitab: 5 ave Bourguiba, 4000 Sousse; tel. (73) 25097; f. 1950; literature, children's books, legal studies, foreign books; Pres. TAÏEB KACEM; Dir FAYÇAL KACEM.

Dar as-Sabah: ave 7 Novembre 1987, BP 441, al-Menzah, 1004 Tunis; tel. (71) 717-222; fax (71) 232-761; f. 1951; 200 mems; publishes daily and weekly papers which circulate throughout Tunisia, North Africa, France, Belgium, Luxembourg and Germany; Dir-Gen. RAOUF CHEIKHROUHOU.

Editions Apollonia: 4 rue Claude Bernard, 1002 Tunis; tel. (71) 786-381; fax (71) 799-190; e-mail sales@apollonia.com.tn; internet www.apollonia.com.tn; art, literature, essays, poetry.

Editions Bouslama: 15 ave de France, 1000 Tunis; tel. (71) 243-745; fax (71) 381-100; f. 1960; history, children's books; Man. Dir ALI BOUSLAMA.

Institut National de la Statistique: 70 rue al-Cham, BP 265, 1080 Tunis; tel. (71) 891-002; fax (71) 792-559; e-mail ins@mdci.gov.tn; internet www.ins.nat.tn; publishes a variety of annuals, periodicals and papers concerned with the economic policy and devt of Tunisia.

Librairie al-Manar: 60 ave Bab Djedid, BP 179, 1008 Tunis; tel. (71) 253-224; fax (71) 336-565; e-mail librairie.almanar@planet.tn; f. 1938; general, educational, Islam; Man. Dir HABIB M'HAMDI.

Maison Tunisienne d'Edition: Tunis; f. 1966; all kinds of books, magazines, etc.; Dir ABDELAZIZ ACHOURI.

Société d'Arts Graphiques, d'Edition et de Presse: 15 rue 2 mars 1934, La Kasbah, Tunis; tel. (71) 264-988; fax (71) 569-736; f. 1974; prints and publishes daily papers, magazines, books, etc.; Chair. and Man. Dir HASSAN FERJANI.

Sud Editions: 79 rue de Palestine, 1002 Tunis; tel. (71) 785-179; fax (71) 792-905; f. 1976; Arab literature, art and art history, history, sociology, religion; Man. Dir M. MASMOUDI.

GOVERNMENT PUBLISHING HOUSE

Imprimerie Officielle de la République Tunisienne: ave Farhat Hached, 2040 Radès; tel. (71) 434-211; fax (71) 434-234; f. 1860; Man. Dir ROMDHANE BEN MIMOUN.

Broadcasting and Communications

TELECOMMUNICATIONS

Société Tunisienne d'Entreprises des Télécommunications (SOTETEL): rue des Entrepreneurs, Zone Industrielle, BP 640, La Charguia 2, 1080 Tunis; tel. (71) 941-100; fax (71) 940-584; e-mail sotetel@email.ati.tn; internet www.sotetel.com.tn; transferred to private ownership in 1998; Dir-Gen. HÉDI FRIOUI.

Orascom Telecom Tunisia: 11 rue 8607, Zone Industrielle, La Charguia 1, 2035 Tunis; internet www.tunisiana.com; Chair. and CEO NAGUIB SAWIRIS.

Tunisie Télécom: Cité Ennassim, ave du Japon, Montplaisir, 1073 Tunis; tel. (71) 901-717; fax (71) 900-777; e-mail actel.virtuelle@ttnet.tn; internet www.tunisietelecom.tn; 65% state-owned, 35% owned by Tecom-Dig (Dubai, United Arab Emirates); Pres. and Gen. Man. AHMED MAHJOUB.

BROADCASTING
Radio

Etablissement de la Radiodiffusion-Télévision Tunisienne (ERTT): 71 ave de la Liberté, 1002 Tunis; tel. (71) 847-300; fax (71) 781-058; e-mail info@radiotunis.com; internet www.radiotunis.com; govt service; broadcasts in Arabic, French, German, Italian, Spanish and English; radio stations at Gafsa, El-Kef, Monastir, Sfax, Tataouine and Tunis (three); television stations Tunis 7 and Canal 21; Pres. MUSTAPHA KHAMMARI.

Radio Mosaïque: Tunis; tel. (71) 287-246; e-mail dg@mosaiquefm.net; internet www.mosaiquefm.net; f. 2003; first privately owned radio station when launched in 2003; broadcasts in Arabic and French to Tunis and the north-east of the country; Dir-Gen. NOUREDDINE BOUTAR.

Television

Television was introduced in northern and central Tunisia in January 1966, and by 1972 transmission covered the country. A relay station to link up with European transmissions was built at al-Haouaria in 1967, and a second channel was introduced in 1983.

Etablissement de la Radiodiffusion-Télévision Tunisienne: see Radio.

Office National de la Télédiffusion (ONT) (National Broadcasting Corporation of Tunisia): Cite Ennasim, 1 Borjel, BP 399, 1080 Tunis; tel. (71) 801-177; fax (71) 781-927; e-mail ont@telediffusion.net.tn; internet www.telediffusion.net.tn; f. 1993.

Finance

(cap. = capital; dep. = deposits; res = reserves; m. = million; brs = branches; amounts in dinars unless otherwise stated)

BANKING
Central Bank

Banque Centrale de Tunisie (BCT): 25 rue Hédi Nouira, BP 777, 1080 Tunis; tel. (71) 340-588; fax (71) 354-214; e-mail boc@bct.gov.tn; internet www.bct.gov.tn; f. 1958; cap. 6.0m., res 81.4m., dep. 3,025.9m., total assets 7,347.6m. (Dec. 2005); Gov. TAOUFIK BACCAR; 10 brs.

Commercial Banks

Amen Bank: ave Muhammad V, 1002 Tunis; tel. (71) 835-500; fax (71) 833-517; e-mail amen.bank@amenbank.com.tn; internet www.amenbank.com.tn; f. 1967 as Crédit Foncier et Commercial de Tunisie; name changed as above in 1995; cap. 70.0m., res 134.6m., dep. 1,965.2m. (Dec. 2006); Chair. and Pres. RACHID BEN YEDDER; Gen. Man. AHMAD EL-KARM; 81 brs.

Arab Banking Corpn Tunisie: ABC Building, rue du Lac d'Annecy, Les Berges du Lac, 1053 Tunis; tel. (71) 861-861; fax (71) 860-921; e-mail abc.tunis@arabbanking.com; internet www.arabbanking.com; f. 2000; cap. 40m., res −25.2m., dep. 164.4m. (Dec. 2006); Chair. AGELI ABDESSALEM BRENI; Country Man. SADDEK EL-KABER; Gen. Man. SADOK ATTIA; 4 brs.

Arab Tunisian Bank: 9 rue Hédi Nouira, POB 520, 1001 Tunis; tel. (71) 351-155; fax (71) 342-852; e-mail atbbank@atb.com.tn; internet www.atb.com.tn; f. 1982; 64.2% owned by Arab Bank PLC (Jordan);

TUNISIA

Directory

cap. 60m., res 100.4m., dep. 1,952.8m. (Dec. 2006); Pres. Farouk El-Kharouf; Gen. Man. Muhammad Ferid Ben Tanfous; 62 brs.

Attijari Bank: 95 ave de la Liberté, 1002 Tunis; tel. (71) 141-400; fax (71) 782-663; e-mail courrier@attijaribank.com.tn; internet www.attijaribank.com.tn; f. 1968 as Banque du Sud; present name adopted 2006; cap. 150.0m., res 126.4m., dep. 1,976.3m. (Dec. 2006); shareholders include Attijariwafa Bank, Morocco (37.11%) and Banco Santander, Spain (17.46%); Pres. Moncef Chaffar; Gen. Man Hassan Bertal; 93 brs.

Banque de l'Habitat: 21 ave Kheireddine Pacha, BP 242, 1002 Tunis; tel. (71) 785-277; fax (71) 784-417; e-mail banquehabitat@bh.fin.tn; internet www.bh.com.tn; f. 1984; 32.62% govt-owned; cap. 75m., res 130.1m., dep. 2,615.3m. (Dec. 2005); Pres. and Chair. Abou Hafs Amor Najï; 79 brs.

Banque Internationale Arabe de Tunisie (BIAT): 70–72 ave Habib Bourguiba, BP 520, 1080 Tunis; tel. (71) 340-733; fax (71) 346-454; e-mail correspondent.banking@biat.com.tn; internet www.biat.com.tn; f. 1976; cap. 170.0m., res 225.7m., dep. 3,464.3m. (Dec. 2006); Gen. Man Slaheddine Ladjimi; 110 brs.

Banque Nationale Agricole: rue Hédi Nouira, 1001 Tunis; tel. (71) 831-000; fax (71) 832-807; e-mail bna@bna.com.tn; internet www.bna.com.tn; f. 1989 by merger of the Banque Nationale du Développement Agricole and the Banque Nationale de Tunisie; cap. 100.0m., res 249.5m., dep. 3,964.0m. (Dec. 2006); Pres. and Gen. Man. Moncef Dakhli; 147 brs.

Banque de Tunisie SA: 2 rue de Turquie, BP 289, 1001 Tunis; tel. (71) 332-188; fax (71) 349-401; e-mail finance@bt.com.tn; f. 1884; cap. 75.0m., res 201.5m., dep. 1,453.9m. (Dec. 2006); Chair. and Man. Dir Faouzi Bel Kahia; 83 agencies.

Banque Tuniso-Koweïtienne: 10 bis ave Muhammad V, BP 49, 1001 Tunis; tel. (71) 340-000; fax (71) 343-106; e-mail contact.btkd@planet.tn; internet www.btknet.com; f. 1981 as Banque Tuniso-Koweïtienne de Développement; present name adopted 2007; cap. 100m., res 74.9m. (Dec. 2000); Chair. Motlaq Mubarak as-Sanaa; Dir-Gen. Abdelghaffar Ezzeddine.

Société Tunisienne de Banque (STB): rue Hédi Nouira, BP 638, 1001 Tunis; tel. (71) 340-477; fax (71) 348-400; e-mail stb@stb.com.tn; internet www.stb.com.tn; f. 1957; 24.81% govt-owned; merged with Banque Nationale de Développement Touristique and Banque de Développement Economique de Tunisie in 2000; cap. 124.2m., res 267.3m., dep. 2,842.6m. (Dec. 2005); Pres. and Dir-Gen. Laroussi Bayoudh; 116 brs.

Union Bancaire pour le Commerce et l'Industrie: 139 ave de la Liberté, Belvédère, 1002 Tunis; tel. (71) 842-000; fax (71) 346-737; e-mail saber.mensi@bnpparibas.com; internet www.ubcinet.net; f. 1961; cap. 50.0m., res 92.0m., dep. 1,022.0m. (Dec. 2005); affiliated to and 50% owned by BNP Paribas (France); Pres. and Gen. Man. Slaheddine Bougerra; 87 brs.

Union Internationale de Banques SA: 65 ave Habib Bourguiba, BP 109, 1000 Tunis; tel. (71) 347-000; fax (71) 353-090; e-mail lilia.meddeb@uib.fin.tn; internet www.uib.com.tn; f. 1963 as a merging of Tunisian interests by the Société Franco-Tunisienne de Banque et de Crédit with Crédit Lyonnais (France) and other foreign banks, including Banca Commerciale Italiana; 52.3% owned by Société Générale (France); cap. 106.0m., res 59.6m., dep. 1,479.0m. (Dec. 2005); Pres. Alia Abdallah; Gen. Man. Philippe Amestoy; 94 brs.

Merchant Banks

Banque d'Affaires de Tunisie (BAT): 32 rue Hédi Karray, 1082 Tunis; tel. (71) 703-175; fax (71) 703-604; e-mail bat@bat.com.tn; internet www.bat-tunisie.com; f. 1997; cap. 4.5m.; Gen. Man. Habib Karaoul.

International Maghreb Merchant Bank (IM Bank): Immeuble Maghrebia, Bloc B, 3ème étage, Les Berges du Lac, 2045 Tunis; tel. (71) 860-816; fax (71) 860-057; e-mail imbank@imbank.com.tn; internet www.imbank.com.tn; f. 1995; Pres. Olivier Pastré; CEO Kacem Bousnina.

Development Banks

Banque de Tunisie et des Emirats (BTE): 5 bis blvd Muhammad Badra, 1002 Tunis; tel. (71) 783-600; fax (71) 287-409; e-mail imed.cherif@bte.com.tn; f. 1982 as Banque de Tunisie et des Emirats d'Investissement; name changed as above in 2005; cap. 90.0m., res 38.4m., dep. 53.6m. (Dec. 2006); Chair. Salam Rachid al-Mohannadi; Gen. Man. Chedli Aissa.

Banque Tunisienne de Solidarité (BTS): 56 ave Muhammad V, 1002 Tunis; tel. (71) 844-040; fax (71) 845-537; e-mail bts@email.ati.tn; internet www.bts.com.tn; f. 1997; provides medium- and short-term finance for small-scale projects; cap. 40m.; Pres. Naïja Ahmed; 25 brs.

Banque Tuniso-Libyenne: 25 ave Kheireddine Pacha, BP 102, Belvédère, 1002 Tunis; tel. (71) 781-500; fax (71) 782-818; f. 1983 as Banque Arabe Tuniso-Libyenne de Développement et de Commerce; name changed as above in 2005; promotes trade and devt projects between Tunisia and Libya, and provides funds for investment in poorer areas; cap. 70.0m., res 2.5m., dep. 123.5m. (Dec. 2005); Pres. and Man. Dir Saïd M'Rabet.

Société Tuniso-Séoudienne d'Investissement et de Développement (STUSID): 32 rue Hédi Karray, BP 20, 1082 Tunis; tel. (71) 718-233; fax (71) 719-233; e-mail commercial@stusid.com.tn; internet www.stusid.com.tn; f. 1981; provides long-term finance for devt projects; cap. 100.0m., res 84.4m., dep. 10.5m. (Dec. 2002); Chair. Dr Abd al-Aziz A. an-Nasrallah; Pres. and Dir-Gen. Abd al-Waheb Nachi.

'Offshore' Banks

Alubaf International Bank: 8007 rue Montplaisir, BP 51, Belvédère, 1002 Tunis; tel. (71) 783-500; fax (71) 793-905; e-mail alub.tn@gnet.tn; f. 1985; 100% owned by Libyan Arab Foreign Bank; cap. US $25.0m., res $6.0m., dep. $126.3m. (Dec. 2006); Chair. Dr Ahmad Mneissi; Gen. Man. Muhammad Lahmar.

Beit Ettamwil Saudi Tounsi (BEST): 88 ave Hédi Chaker, 1002 Tunis; tel. (71) 790-000; fax (71) 780-235; e-mail bestbank@planet.tn; f. 1983; Islamic bank; Pres. Dr Salah Jemil Malaika.

North Africa International Bank: ave Kheireddine Pacha, BP 485, 1002 Tunis; tel. (71) 950-800; fax (71) 950-840; e-mail naib@naibank.com; f. 1984; cap. US $30.0m., res $16.5m., dep. $129.8m. (Dec. 2004); Chair. and Gen. Man. Giuma M. Waheba; 1 br.

Tunis International Bank: 18 ave des Etats-Unis d'Amérique, BP 81, 1002 Tunis; tel. (71) 782-411; fax (71) 782-223; e-mail tib1.tib@planet.tn; internet www.tib.com.tn; f. 1982; 86.6% owned by United Gulf Bank (Bahrain); cap. US $25.0m., res $13.3m., dep. $271.8m. (Dec. 2004); Chair. Masoud J. Hayat; Dep. Chair. and Man. Dir Muhammad Fekih; 3 brs.

STOCK EXCHANGE

Bourse des Valeurs Mobilières de Tunis (Bourse de Tunis): Tour Babel, Escalier E, Cité Montplaisir, 1073 Tunis; tel. (71) 780-288; fax (71) 789-189; e-mail info@bvmt.com.tn; internet www.bvmt.com.tn; f. 1969; Chair. Yousuf Kortobi.

INSURANCE

BEST Reinsurance (BEST Re): Rue du Lac de Côme, Les Berges du lac, BP 484, 1080 Tunis; tel. (71) 860-355; fax (71) 861-011; e-mail general@bestre.com.tn; internet www.best-re.com; f. 1985; operates according to Islamic principles; cap. US $100m.; Dir-Gen. Riadh Karray.

Caisse Tunisienne d'Assurances Mutuelles Agricoles—Mutuelle Générale d'Assurances (CTAMA—MGA): 6 ave Habib Thameur, 1069 Tunis; tel. (71) 340-933; fax (71) 332-276; e-mail ctama@planet.tn; internet www.ctamamga.com; f. 1912; Pres. Moktar Bellagha; Dir-Gen. Mezri Jelizi.

Cie d'Assurances Tous Risques et de Réassurance (ASTREE): 45 ave Kheireddine Pacha, BP 780, 1002 Tunis; tel. (71) 792-211; fax (71) 794-723; e-mail courrier@astree.com.tn; internet www.astree.com.tn; f. 1949; cap. 4m.; Pres. and Dir-Gen. Muhammad Habib Ben Saad.

Cie Tunisienne pour l'Assurance du Commerce Extérieur (COTUNACE): ave Muhammad V, Montplaisir I, rue 8006, 1002 Tunis; tel. (71) 783-000; fax (71) 782-539; e-mail cotunace.ddc@planet.tn; internet www.cotunace.com.tn; f. 1984; cap. 5m.; 65 mem. cos; Pres. and Dir-Gen. Moncef Zouari.

Société Tunisienne d'Assurance et de Réassurance (STAR): ave de Paris, Tunis; tel. (71) 340-866; fax (71) 340-835; e-mail star@star.com.tn; internet www.star.com.tn; f. 1958; Pres. and Dir-Gen. Abdelkrim Merdassi.

Tunis-Ré (Société Tunisienne de Réassurance): ave Muhammad V, Montplaisir 1, BP 29, 1073 Tunis; tel. (71) 844-011; fax (71) 787-573; e-mail tunisre@tunisre.com.tn; internet www.tunisre.com.tn; f. 1981; various kinds of reinsurance; cap. 35m.(2006); Chair. and Gen. Man. Muhammad Dkhili.

Trade and Industry

GOVERNMENT AGENCIES

Centre de Promotion des Exportations (CEPEX): Centre Urbain, BP 225, 1080 Tunis; tel. (71) 234-200; fax (71) 237-325; e-mail info@cepex.nat.tn; internet www.cepex.nat.tn; f. 1973; state export promotion org.; Pres. and Dir-Gen. Youssef Neji.

Foreign Investment Promotion Agency (FIPA): rue Slaheddine al-Ammami, Centre Urbain Nord, 1004 Tunis; tel. (71) 752-540; fax (71) 231-400; e-mail boc.fipa@mci.gov.tn; internet www.investintunisia.tn; f. 1995; Dir-Gen. Abdessalem Mansour.

TUNISIA

Office du Commerce de la Tunisie (OCT): 65 rue de Syrie, 1002 Tunis; tel. (71) 800-040; fax (71) 788-974; e-mail OCT@Email.ati.tn; f. 1962; CEO Belgacem Nafti; Sec.-Gen. Mustapha Debbabi.

CHAMBERS OF COMMERCE AND INDUSTRY

Chambre de Commerce et d'Industrie de Tunis: 31 ave de Paris, 1000 Tunis; tel. (71) 247-322; fax (71) 354-744; e-mail ccitunis@planet.tn; internet www.ccitunis.org.tn; f. 1885; 30 mems; Pres. Mounir Mouakhar.

Chambre de Commerce et d'Industrie du Centre: rue Chadli Khaznadar, 4000 Sousse; tel. (73) 225-044; fax (73) 224-227; e-mail ccis.sousse@planet.tn; internet www.ccicentre.org.tn; f. 1895; 30 mems; Pres. Kaboudi Moncef; Dir Faten Basly.

Chambre de Commerce et d'Industrie du Nord-Est: Tom Bereaux Bizerte Center, angle rues 1er mai, Med Ali, 7000 Bizerte; tel. (72) 431-044; fax (72) 431-922; e-mail ccine.biz@gnet.tn; internet www.ccibizerte.org.tn; f. 1902; 30 mems; Pres. Faouzi Ben Aissa; Dir Moufida Chakroun.

Chambre de Commerce et d'Industrie de Sfax: Rue du Lieutenant Hammadi Tej, BP 794, 3000 Sfax; tel. (74) 296-120; fax (74) 296-121; e-mail ccis@ccis.org.tn; internet www.ccis.org.tn; f. 1895; 35,000 mems; Pres. Abdessalem Ben Ayed; Dir Sofiene Sallemi.

INDUSTRIAL AND TRADE ASSOCIATIONS

Agence de Promotion de l'Industrie (API): 63 rue de Syrie, 1002 Tunis; tel. (71) 792-144; fax (71) 782-482; e-mail api@api.com.tn; internet www.tunisieindustrie.nat.tn; f. 1987 by merger; co-ordinates industrial policy, undertakes feasibility studies, organizes industrial training and establishes industrial zones; overseas offices in Belgium, France, Germany, Italy, the United Kingdom, Sweden and the USA; 24 regional offices; Gen. Man. Muhammad Ben Abdallah.

Centre Technique du Textile (CETTEX): ave des Industries, Zone Industrielle, Bir el-Kassaâ, BP 279, Ben Arous, 2013 Tunis; tel. (71) 381-133; fax (71) 382-558; e-mail cettex@cettex.com.tn; internet www.textiletunisia.com.tn; f. 1991; responsible for the textile industry; Dir Khaled Touibi.

Cie des Phosphates de Gafsa (CPG): Cité Bayech, 2100 Gafsa; tel. (76) 226-022; fax (76) 224-132; e-mail cpg@cpg.com.tn; internet www.cpg.com.tn; f. 1897; production and marketing of phosphates; Pres. Kaïs Daly.

Entreprise Tunisienne d'Activités Pétrolières (ETAP): 27 ave Kheireddine Pacha, BP 367, 1073 Tunis; tel. (71) 782-288; fax (71) 786-141; e-mail dexprom@etap.com.tn; internet www.etap.com.tn; responsible for exploration and investment in hydrocarbons.

Office des Céréales: Ministry of Agriculture and Water Resources, 30 rue Alain Savary, 1002 Tunis; tel. (71) 790-351; fax (71) 789-573; f. 1962; responsible for the cereals industry; Chair. and Dir-Gen. A. Saddem.

Office National des Mines: 24 rue 8601, BP 215, 1080 Tunis; tel. (71) 788-242; fax (71) 794-016; e-mail contact@ontm.nat.tn; internet www.ontm.nat.tn; f. 1963; mining of iron ores; research and study of mineral wealth; Chair. and CEO Mohammed Fadhel Zerelli.

Office National des Pêches (ONP): Le Port, La Goulette, Tunis; tel. (71) 275-093; marine and fishing authority; Dir-Gen. L. Halab.

Office des Terres Domaniales (OTD): 30 rue Alain Savary, 1002 Tunis; tel. (71) 800-322; fax (71) 795-026; e-mail otd@email.ati.tn; f. 1961; responsible for agricultural production and the management of state-owned lands; Dir Béchir Ben Smaïl.

UTILITIES

Electricity and Gas

Société Tunisienne de l'Electricité et du Gaz (STEG): 38 rue Kemal Atatürk, BP 190, 1080 Tunis; tel. (71) 341-311; fax (71) 349-981; e-mail dpsc@steg.com.tn; internet www.steg.com.tn; f. 1962; responsible for generation and distribution of electricity and for production of natural gas; Pres. and Dir-Gen. Othman Ben Arfa; 35 brs.

Water

Société Nationale d'Exploitation et de Distribution des Eaux (SONEDE): ave Slimane ben Slimane, el-Manar 2, 2092 Tunis; tel. (71) 887-000; fax (71) 871-000; e-mail sonede@sonede.com.tn; internet www.sonede.com.tn; f. 1968; production and supply of drinking water; Chair. and Man. Dir Muhammad Ali Khouaja.

TRADE AND OTHER UNIONS

Union Générale des Etudiants de Tunisie (UGET): 11 rue d'Espagne, Tunis; f. 1953; 600 mems; Pres. Mekki Fitouri.

Union Générale Tunisienne du Travail (UGTT): 29 place Muhammad Ali, 1000 Tunis; tel. (71) 332-400; fax (71) 332-439; e-mail ugtt.tunis@email.ati.tn; internet www.ugtt.org.tn; f. 1946 by Farhat Hached; affiliated to ICFTU; 360,000 mems in 24 affiliated unions; 18-mem. exec. bureau; Sec.-Gen. Abdessalem Jerad.

Union Nationale des Agriculteurs (UNA): 6 ave Habib Thameur, 1000 Tunis; tel. (71) 246-920; fax (71) 349-843; f. 1955; Pres. Bacha Abd al-Baki.

Union Nationale de la Femme Tunisienne (UNFT): 56 blvd Bab Benat, 1008 Tunis; tel. (71) 560-178; fax (71) 567-131; e-mail unft@email.ati.tn; internet www.unft.org.tn; f. 1956; promotes the rights of women; 150,000 mems; 28 regional delegations, 199 professional training centres, 13 professional alliances; Pres. Aziza Hatira; Vice-Pres. Faïza Azouz; 23 brs abroad.

Union Tunisienne de l'Industrie, du Commerce et de l'Artisanat (UTICA): 103 ave de la Liberté, Belvédère, 1002 Tunis; tel. (71) 780-366; fax (71) 782-143; internet www.utica.org.tn; f. 1946; mems: 15 national federations and 170 syndical chambers at national levels; Pres. Hédi Jilani.

Transport

RAILWAYS

In 2004 the total length of railways was 2,153 km; 36.3m. passengers travelled by rail in Tunisia in that year. Plans for an expansion of the public transport system were in progress in the mid-2000s.

Société Nationale des Chemins de Fer Tunisiens (SNCFT): Gare de Tunis ville, pl. Barcelone, 1001 Tunis; tel. (71) 345-188; fax (71) 254-320; e-mail sncft@sncft.com.tn; internet www.sncft.com.tn; f. 1956; state org. controlling all Tunisian railways; Pres. and Dir-Gen. Abd al-Aziz Chabane.

Société des Transports de Tunis (TRANSTU): 1 ave Habib Bourgiba, BP 660, 1025 Tunis; tel. (71) 259-422; fax (71) 342-727; e-mail contact@snt.com.tn; internet www.snt.com.tn; f. 2003 following merger of the Société Nationale des Transports and the Société du Métro Léger de Tunis; operates 5 light train routes with 136 trains, and 206 local bus routes with 1,050 buses; also operates in the suburbs of Tunis-Goulette-Marsa, with 18 trains; plans approved in 2006 for expansion of the light rail system, with five new express lines; Chair. and Man. Dir Chedly Hajri.

ROADS

In 2004 there were 262 km of motorways, 4,080 km of main roads and 6,520 km of secondary roads. The total length of the road network was 19,232 km, of which 65.8% was paved.

Société Nationale de Transport Interurbain (SNTRI): ave Muhammad V, BP 40, Belvédère, 1002 Tunis; tel. (71) 784-433; fax (71) 786-605; e-mail drn@sntri.com.tn; internet www.sntri.com.tn; f. 1981; Dir-Gen. Sassi Yahia.

Société des Transports de Tunis: see above.

There are 12 **Sociétés Régionales des Transports**, responsible for road transport, operating in different regions in Tunisia.

SHIPPING

Tunisia has seven major ports: Tunis-La Goulette, Radès, Bizerta, Sousse, Sfax, Gabès and Zarzis. There is a special petroleum port at La Skhirra. A new deep-water port at Enfidha was expected to be operational in 2008.

Office de la Marine Marchande et des Ports: Bâtiment Administratif, Port de la Goulette, 2060 La Goulette; tel. (71) 735-300; fax (71) 735-812; e-mail ommp@ommp.nat.tn; internet www.ommp.nat.tn; maritime port administration; Pres. and Dir-Gen. Ali Labiedh.

Cie Générale Maritime: Résidence Alain Savary, Bloc D7, Apt 74, 1003 Tunis; tel. and fax (71) 860-430; e-mail logwan.girgen@gnet.tn; Chair. Elias Maherzi.

Cie Méditerranéenne de Navigation: Tunis; tel. (71) 331-544; fax (71) 332-124.

Cie Tunisienne de Navigation SA (CTN): 5 ave Dag Hammarskjööld, BP 40, 1001 Tunis; tel. (71) 341-777; fax (71) 345-736; e-mail cotunav@ctn.com.tn; internet www.ctn.com.tn; f. 1959; state-owned; brs at Bizerta, La Goulette, Sfax and Sousse; Chair. M. Yonsaâ.

Gabès Marine Tankers: Immeuble SETCAR, route de Sousse, km 13, 2034 Tunis; tel. (71) 454-644; fax (71) 450-350; e-mail gabesmarine@gmt.com.tn; internet www.setcar-group.com; f. 1994; part of the Setcar Group; Chair. Férid Abbès.

Gas Marine: Immeuble SETCAR, route de Sousse, km 13, 2034 ez-Zahra; tel. (71) 454-644; fax (71) 454-650; Chair. Hammadi Abbès.

Hannibal Marine Tankers: 2ème Etage, Residence Lakeo, rue du Lac Michigan, Les Berges du Lac, 1053 Tunis; tel. (71) 960-037; fax (71) 960-243; e-mail hannibal.tankers@gnet.tn; Gen. Man. Ameur Mahjoub.

Société Tunisienne de Navigation Petrolière (PETRONAV): Residence Raoudha, Les Berges du Lac, 1053 Tunis; tel. (71) 861-965; fax (71) 861-780; Chair. HICHEM KHATTECH.

SONOTRAK: 179 ave Muhammad Hédi Khefacha, Gare Maritime de Kerkenna, 3000 Sfax; tel. (74) 498-216; fax (74) 497-496; e-mail jabeur.m@planet.tn; Chair. TAOUFI JRAD.

Tunisian Shipping Agency: Zone Industrielle, Radès 2040, BP 166, Tunis; tel. (71) 448-379; fax (71) 448-410; e-mail tsa.rades@planet.tn; Chair. MUHAMMAD BEN SEDRINE.

CIVIL AVIATION

There are international airports at Tunis-Carthage, Sfax, Djerba, Monastir, Tabarka, Gafsa and Tozeur. Construction of a new airport at Enfidha, 100 km south of Tunis, commenced in March 2005 and was scheduled to be completed by 2009.

Office de l'Aviation Civile et des Aéroports: BP 137 and 147, Aéroport International de Tunis-Carthage, 1080 Tunis; tel. (71) 755-000; fax (71) 755-133; e-mail relations.exterieures@oaca.nat.tn; internet www.oaca.nat.tn; f. 1970; civil aviation and airport authority; Pres. and Dir-Gen. MUHAMMAD CHERIF.

Nouvelair Tunisie: Zone Touristique Dkhila, 5065 Monastir; tel. (73) 520-600; fax (73) 520-666; e-mail info@nouvelair.com.tn; internet www.nouvelair.com; f. 1989 as Air Liberté Tunisie; name changed as above in 1996; Tunisian charter co; flights from Tunis, Djerba and Monastir airports to Scandinavia and other European countries; Chair. AZIZ MILAD; Gen. Man. KAMEL OUERGHEMNI.

Tuninter: Immeuble Securas, Zone Industrielle, BP 1080, La Charguia 11, 1080 Tunis; tel. (71) 701-717; fax (71) 712-193; e-mail tuninter@mail.gnet.tn; f. 1992; Tunisian charter co; Man. Dir ABD AL-KARIM OUERTANI.

TunisAir (Société Tunisienne de l'Air): blvd du 7 novembre 1987, 2035 Tunis; tel. (71) 700-100; fax (71) 700-897; e-mail mail@tunisair.com.tn; internet www.tunisair.com; f. 1948; 45.2% govt-owned; 20% of assets privatized in 1995; flights to Africa, Europe and the Middle East; Pres. and Dir-Gen. NABIL CHETTAOUI.

Tunisavia (Société de Transports, Services et Travaux Aériens): blvd du leader Yasser Arafat, 2035 Tunis-Carthage International Airport, Tunis; tel. (71) 280-555; fax (71) 281-333; e-mail siege@tunisavia.com.tn; internet www.tunisavia.com.tn; f. 1974; helicopter and charter operator; Pres. AZIZ MILAD; Gen. Man MOHSEN NASRA.

Tourism

The main tourist attractions are the magnificent sandy beaches, Moorish architecture and remains of the Roman Empire. Tunisia contains the site of the ancient Phoenician city of Carthage. Tourism, a principal source of foreign exchange, has expanded rapidly, following extensive government investment in hotels, improved roads and other facilities. The number of hotel beds increased from 71,529 in 1980 to 188,600 in 1999. There were 6.5m. foreign tourist arrivals in 2006 (compared with 4.7m. in 1998), and receipts from tourism totalled US $2,782m. in 2005.

Office National du Tourisme Tunisien: 1 ave Muhammad V, 1001 Tunis; tel. (71) 341-077; fax (71) 350-997; e-mail ontt@email.ati.tn; internet www.bonjour-tunisie.com; f. 1958; Dir-Gen. KHALED CHEIKH.

TURKEY

Introductory Survey

Location, Climate, Language, Religion, Flag, Capital

The Republic of Turkey lies partly in south-eastern Europe and partly in western Asia. The European and Asian portions of the country (known, respectively, as Thrace and Anatolia) are separated by the Sea of Marmara, linking the Black Sea and the Aegean Sea. Turkey has an extensive coastline: on the Black Sea, to the north; on the Mediterranean Sea, to the south; and on the Aegean Sea, to the west. Most of Turkey lies in Asia, the vast Anatolian peninsula being bordered to the east by Armenia, Georgia, the Nakhichevan Autonomous Republic (part of Azerbaijan) and Iran, and to the south by Iraq and Syria. The smaller European part of the country is bordered to the west by Greece and Bulgaria. In the Asian interior the climate is one of great extremes, with hot dry summers and cold, snowy winters on the plateau. Temperatures in Ankara are generally between $-4°C$ ($25°F$) and $30°C$ ($86°F$). On the Mediterranean coast it is more equable, with mild winters and warm summers. The principal language is Turkish, spoken by 90% of the population. About 7% speak Kurdish, mainly in the south-east. In 1928 the Arabic characters of the written Turkish language were superseded by Western-style script. Islam is the religion of 99% of the population. The national flag (proportions 2 by 3) is red, with a white crescent and a five-pointed white star to the left of centre. The capital is Ankara.

Recent History

Turkey was formerly a monarchy, ruled by a Sultan, with his capital in Constantinople (now İstanbul). At its zenith, the Turkish Empire, under the Osmanlı (Ottoman) dynasty, extended from the Persian (Arabian) Gulf to Morocco, including most Arab regions and south-eastern Europe. Following the dissolution of the Ottoman Empire after the First World War, political control of Turkey itself passed to the nationalist movement led by Mustafa Kemal, a distinguished army officer. On 23 April 1920, in defiance of the Sultan, a newly elected assembly established a provisional Government, led by Kemal, in Ankara, then a minor provincial town. Kemal's forces waged war against the Greek army in 1920–22, forcing the Greeks to evacuate Smyrna (İzmir) and eastern Thrace (the European portion of Turkey). The new regime abolished the sultanate in November 1922 and declared Turkey a republic, with Ankara as its capital and Kemal as its first President, on 29 October 1923. The Ottoman caliphate (the former monarch's position as Islamic religious leader) was abolished in March 1924.

Kemal remained President of Turkey, with extensive dictatorial powers, until his death in 1938. He pursued a radical programme of far-reaching reform and modernization, including the: secularization of the state (in 1928); abolition of Islamic courts and religious instruction in schools; emancipation of women (enfranchised in 1934); banning of polygamy; development of industry; introduction of a Latin alphabet; adoption of the Gregorian (in place of the Islamic) calendar; and encouragement of European culture and technology. Another Westernizing reform was the introduction of surnames in 1934: Kemal assumed the name Atatürk ('Father of the Turks'). His autocratic regime attempted, with considerable success, to replace the country's Islamic traditions by the principles of republicanism, nationalism, populism and state control.

Following Atatürk's death, his Cumhuriyet Halk Partisi (CHP—Republican People's Party), the only authorized political grouping, remained in power under his close associate, İsmet İnönü, who had been Prime Minister in 1923–24 and 1925–37. İnönü was President from 1938 to 1950, and maintained Turkey's neutrality during most of the Second World War (Turkey declared war on Germany in February 1945). After the war İnönü introduced some liberalization of the regime. The one-party system was ended in 1946, when opposition leaders, including Celâl Bayar and Adnan Menderes, registered the Demokratik Parti (DP—Democratic Party); numerous other parties were subsequently formed. The DP won Turkey's first free election in 1950, and ruled for the next decade. Bayar became President, with Menderes as Prime Minister.

In May 1960 the Government was overthrown by a military coup, led by Gen. Cemal Gürsel, who assumed the presidency, claiming that the DP regime had betrayed Atatürk's principle of secularism. A series of coalition governments, mostly led by İnönü, held office from November 1961 until October 1965, when an election was won by the conservative Adalet Partisi (Justice Party), led by Süleyman Demirel, which appealed to supporters of the former DP. The Demirel Government remained in power until March 1971, when escalating student and labour unrest caused the armed forces to demand its resignation. 'Guided democracy', under military supervision, continued until October 1973, with a succession of right-wing 'non-party' administrations, martial law and the rigorous suppression of all left-wing activities.

The return to civilian rule began in April 1973, when the Turkish Grand National Assembly (TGNA—the legislative body established in 1961) chose Adm. Fahri Korutürk as President, in preference to a candidate supported by the armed forces. Military participation in government was ended by an election in October 1973. No single party received sufficient support to form a government, and it was not until January 1974 when Bülent Ecevit, leader of the CHP (which had become a left-of-centre party), took office as Prime Minister, having negotiated a coalition with the Milli Selamet Partisi (MSP—National Salvation Party), a pro-Islamic right-wing group. Deteriorating relations with Greece were exacerbated by the Greek-backed coup in Cyprus (q.v.) in July 1974, when Turkey responded by dispatching troops, and occupying the northern part of the island, to protect the Turkish Cypriot population. Despite the failure of the coup, Turkish forces retained control of northern Cyprus, and the island remained effectively partitioned.

A long period of political instability was fostered by a succession of unsuccessful coalitions, headed by either Ecevit or Demirel, and prompted an escalation in political violence, mainly involving clashes between left-wing and right-wing groups. On 12 September 1980, as the violence neared the scale of a civil war, the armed forces, led by Gen. Kenan Evren, Chief of the General Staff, seized power in a bloodless coup; a five-member National Security Council (NSC) was formed, which appointed a mainly civilian Cabinet. Martial law was declared throughout the country. In December the NSC published a decree endowing the military regime with unlimited powers. During 1981–83 a campaign to eradicate all possible sources of political violence was undertaken. In April 1981 former politicians were banned from future political activity, and in October all political parties were disbanded.

The new Government succeeded in reducing the level of political violence in Turkey and in restoring law and order. However, that this had been achieved at the expense of respect for human rights caused concern among Western governments: Turkey was banned from the Parliamentary Assembly of the Council of Europe (see p. 225), aid from the European Community (EC, now European Union—EU, see p. 244) was suspended, and fellow members of NATO urged Turkey to return to democratic rule as soon as possible. In October 1981 a Consultative Assembly was established to draft a new constitution, which was approved by referendum in November 1982; objections were widely expressed that the President was to be accorded excessive powers while judicial powers and the rights of trade unions and the press were to be curtailed. An appended 'temporary article' installed Evren as President for a seven-year term.

In May 1983 the NSC revoked the ban on political organizations, permitting the formation of parties, subject to strict rules, in preparation for the first election to be held under the new Constitution. All the former political parties remained proscribed, and 723 former members of the TGNA and leading party officials were banned from political activity for up to 10 years. Followers of the former parties thus regrouped under new names and with new leaders. Of the 15 new parties, however, only three were allowed to take part in the election: the Milliyetçi Demokrasi Partisi (MDP—Nationalist Democracy Party) and the Halkçı Partisi (HP—Populist Party), both of which had the tacit support of the NSC, and the conservative Anavatan Partisi

(ANAVATAN—Motherland Party), led by Turgut Özal. In the November election ANAVATAN won 211 of the 400 seats in the unicameral legislature, and Özal was appointed Prime Minister in December. This result, which was followed by the holding of local government elections in March 1984, suggested a decisive rejection of military rule.

In November 1985 the HP and the Sosyal Demokrasi Partisi (Social Democratic Party), respectively the main opposition parties within and outside the National Assembly, merged to form the Sosyal Demokrat Halkçı Parti (SHP—Social Democratic Populist Party). However, the left-wing opposition was split as a result of the immediate formation of the Demokratik Sol Parti (DSP—Democratic Left Party), which drew support from the former CHP. The MDP voted to disband in May 1986.

At a national referendum in September 1987 a narrow majority approved the repeal of the ban on participation in political affairs imposed on more than 200 politicians in 1981. This enabled Ecevit to assume the leadership of the DSP, while Demirel was elected as leader of the Doğru Yol Partisi (DYP—True Path Party). In a general election conducted in November 1987 ANAVATAN obtained 292 of the 450 seats in the enlarged TGNA, while the SHP won 99 seats and the DYP 59.

Özal succeeded Evren as President in November 1989, having secured the support of the simple majority required in a third round of voting by the TGNA in October. Yıldırım Akbulut, the Speaker of the TGNA and a former Minister of the Interior, was subsequently appointed Prime Minister. However, having been defeated by former Minister of Foreign Affairs Mesut Yılmaz in a contest for the ANAVATAN leadership in June 1991, Akbulut subsequently resigned as premier. In accordance with the Constitution, President Özal invited Yılmaz, the leader of the party's liberal faction, to head a new administration.

In a general election held on 20 October 1991 the DYP, under Demirel's leadership, received an estimated 27.3% of the votes cast, narrowly defeating ANAVATAN (with 23.9%) and the SHP (20.6%). Demirel formed a coalition administration with the SHP (who with the DYP accounted for 266 of the 450 newly elected deputies in the TGNA), with Erdal İnönü, the SHP leader, as deputy premier. The coalition outlined a programme for political and economic reform, and international observers were impressed by Demirel's apparent commitment to human rights. The implementation of amendments designed to discourage torture were, however, impeded by a lack of consensus within the Government, and the problems were exacerbated during 1992 by a succession of political defections from the SHP, which by September had reduced the representation of the coalition parties in the TGNA to 229. Although the DYP and the SHP performed well at municipal elections in June, the reactivation of the CHP in September (following a relaxation of guide-lines for the formation of political parties) threatened to undermine left-wing support for the Government.

At a special ANAVATAN party conference in December 1992, concern was expressed that right-wing extremism had become the dominant force behind the party leadership, prompting the emergence of a dissident, more conservative faction of the party. Subsequently some 70 deputies announced their intention to leave ANAVATAN in order to form a new party headed by President Özal. In April 1993, however, Özal died of heart failure. In May Süleyman Demirel was elected to the presidency, with a simple majority in a third round of voting by the TGNA. Minister of State Tansu Çiller was elected to the DYP party leadership in June and promptly assumed the premiership. Çiller (Turkey's first female Prime Minister) formed a new Cabinet, retaining the 12 SHP members of the previous Government but replacing 17 former DYP ministers, notably several Demirel loyalists. The Prime Minister's personal support was consolidated in December, when five DYP ministers were replaced.

The new administration was strained by a sharp escalation of violence on the part of the outlawed Partiya Karkeren Kurdistan (PKK—Kurdistan Workers' Party). Plans to extend cultural and educational rights to the Kurds were abandoned following strong opposition from Demirel, right-wing members of the DYP and military leaders, who, in October, effectively resisted a proposal to discuss the establishment of local autonomy for the Kurdish population in the south-east of the country.

In early 1994 Çiller's political standing was damaged by a devaluation of the Turkish lira, following a loss of confidence in the currency on the part of international credit agencies. The DYP performed unexpectedly well in municipal elections in March, however; Çiller was thus able to pursue her programme of economic austerity, although in July the Constitutional Court halted her accelerated privatization plans. In February 1995 a special conference of the SHP voted to merge with the CHP, consequently increasing the Government's parliamentary majority but forcing a renegotiation of the conditions of the coalition. Agreement was reached by Çiller and Hikmet Çetin, the CHP leader, in March, and an extensive reorganization of the Government was undertaken in order to accommodate the party. Çetin became Deputy Prime Minister and Minister of State; İsmet İnönü assumed the foreign affairs portfolio. In June the DYP obtained 39% of votes cast in municipal elections, a result that Çiller claimed to be a vindication of her personal standing as leader and of her Government's policies, in particular the pursuit of closer relations with the EU. However, efforts by the Prime Minister to extend democratic rights within the Constitution encountered considerable opposition, both from conservative elements within her own party and from the fundamentalist Islamist Refah Partisi (RP—Welfare Party). Certain constitutional reforms, including the removal of restrictions on political associations and trade unions, the lowering of the age of eligibility to vote from 21 to 18 years and the expansion of the TGNA by 100 parliamentary seats to 550, were finally approved in July. Yet Çiller failed to obtain sufficient support for the amendment of the 'anti-terrorism' legislation, which was expected to be crucial in securing the European Parliament's ratification of the EU-Turkish customs union (see below).

Deniz Baykal was elected leader of the CHP in September 1995. All CHP ministers subsequently resigned their cabinet positions, and ensuing coalition negotiations with Çiller failed as it became apparent that the political differences between the two leaders were insurmountable. Later in September Demirel was forced to accept the Prime Minister's resignation, but Çiller was immediately invited to form a new government. A significant obstacle to a new DYP-CHP agreement was removed when Çiller conceded the necessity of holding an early general election. A DYP-CHP Government, headed by Çiller, with Baykal as Deputy Prime Minister and Minister of Foreign Affairs, took office in November.

At the general election held in December 1995, the RP, which had campaigned to strengthen political and economic relations with other Islamic countries, to withdraw from NATO and the EU customs union, and to increase state involvement in the economy, secured the largest number of parliamentary seats (158), with 21.4% of the votes cast. The DYP won 135 seats, with 19.2% of the votes, while ANAVATAN took 132, with 19.7% of the votes. Since no party had an absolute majority, the two other parties securing parliamentary representation, the DSP and the CHP, were expected to have considerable political leverage in the new parliament. (Under the new electoral arrangements, eight other parties secured no seats in the legislature, having failed to reach the minimum requirement of 10% of support.) In January 1996 President Demirel invited RP leader Necmettin Erbakan to attempt to form a government. However, despite Erbakan's declared willingness to negotiate an agreement with any of the four main parties, no coalition partner could be found. Subsequent efforts by Çiller to form a government through an agreement with ANAVATAN also failed, and in February Demirel invited Mesut Yılmaz, of ANAVATAN, to establish a new administration. Following protracted negotiations, Yılmaz and Çiller reached a coalition agreement, which was signed and approved by Demirel in March; Çiller conceded the premiership to Yılmaz, under a rotating arrangement. The new Government secured a parliamentary vote of confidence, but was soon strained by tensions between the two leaders, and allegations of corruption against Çiller. In April and May ANAVATAN deputies failed to support Çiller, following votes in the TGNA to establish commissions to investigate her alleged illegal involvement in the sale of the TEDAŞ state electricity company and of a Turkish car manufacturer. Members of the DYP accused Yılmaz of further undermining Çiller's position by passing information to the media detailing evidence of the misappropriation of secret security funds under her premiership, in order to force her resignation before her scheduled assumption of the office of Prime Minister in 1997. Meanwhile, opposition parties questioned the credibility of the Government after the Constitutional Court annulled the March 1996 vote of confidence. At the end of May Çiller announced the withdrawal of her party's support for the Government and publicly called for Yılmaz's resignation. Political tensions were heightened in that month by an assassination attempt on President Demirel.

In June 1996, having won 34% of the votes cast in municipal elections, the RP renewed its demands for a general election and secured the DYP's support for a censure motion against the Government to be considered in the TGNA. This was withdrawn when Yılmaz announced the resignation of his Government, following the official publication of the Constitutional Court's ruling. Necmettin Erbakan was subsequently invited to form a government, and at the end of June the RP concluded an agreement with the DYP; Erbakan was to lead the new coalition administration, with Çiller assuming the deputy premiership and foreign affairs portfolio. The leaders asserted that the objective of the new Government was to secure political and economic stability, and they guaranteed that Turkey would adhere to its existing international and strategic agreements. Eight DYP deputies in the TGNA resigned from the party in protest at the coalition with the RP, and a further 15 DYP deputies failed to endorse the new administration in a parliamentary vote of confidence conducted in July. Although the Government secured a narrow majority, it was immediately confronted by local demonstrations and mounting international concern regarding several hundred left-wing prisoners who had initiated a hunger strike in May, in protest at their treatment and conditions of confinement. At the end of July, following the deaths of 12 protesters and widespread unrest within many prisons, the Government concluded an agreement with the prisoners to end their action in return for guarantees that included the transfer of 102 activists from a high-security prison in Anatolya and greater access to medical care.

The contradictions inherent in the new RP-DYP administration became evident in many aspects of government policy. In foreign affairs, the Government attempted to reassure its Western allies of its continued support. At the end of July 1996 the mandate for the use of Turkish airbases by allied forces engaged in 'Operation Provide Comfort' (see below) was extended, and in August a new military co-operation agreement was signed with Israel, expanding on an accord concluded in February. In addition, there was evidence of the military's asserting its authority by dismissing 13 officers in August on disciplinary charges relating to Islamist practices (50 officers had been dismissed on similar grounds in December 1995). At the same time, however, Prime Minister Erbakan embarked on a tour of Asian and Middle Eastern Muslim countries in order to strengthen bilateral relations and co-operation. In August Turkey and Iran finalized an economic agreement, shortly after legislation had been ratified in the USA that threatened punitive measures against countries undertaking investments in Iran. Censure motions brought against Erbakan's administration by three opposition parties were defeated in a single vote in the TGNA. In January 1997 the TGNA cleared Çiller of the final corruption charges against her. In the same month Hüsamettin Cindoruk, who had been expelled from the DYP in October 1995, established a new breakaway party, the Demokrat Türkiye Partisi (DTP—Democratic Turkey Party).

There were civil disturbances in February 1997, following an Islamist rally in the Sincan district of Ankara, at which Iran's ambassador to Turkey criticized Turkey's relations with Israel and its NATO allies and advocated the introduction of *Shari'a* law. At the same time pressure from the military and DYP members of the Government forced the RP to withdraw proposals to extend Muslim education and to allow religious garments to be worn by public workers. In late February the Government defeated a censure motion in the TGNA, proposed by the DSP and CHP in protest at the Government's alleged undermining of the secular state. At a meeting of the NSC held at the end of February, the military leadership presented an 18-point memorandum which set out to ensure the protection of Turkish secular state traditions, including greater supervision of Islamic financial and media operations, the removal of Islamists from public administration and closure of all unauthorized Islamic groupings; the military warned of punitive action if the proposals were not implemented. Political tension was defused when Erbakan, who had initially criticized the NSC for attempting to impose laws on the Government, signed a memorandum endorsing the NSC measures and declared that the leaders of all the main political parties were unanimous in their view that the Constitution must be upheld. The Council of Ministers agreed in March to implement the NSC proposals, but concern subsequently arose over the failure of the Government to act on the measures. Two dissident DYP government ministers resigned in protest at Erbakan's leadership, and demanded an early election on the grounds that their party leader, Çiller, had failed to restrain the Islamist tendencies of the RP. At a meeting of the NSC held in April, however, Erbakan agreed to pursue the military's demands, including restrictions on Islamic education. Although the Government defeated an opposition attempt in that month to pursue a censure motion in the TGNA, the political situation remained critical, and charges from the military, opposition parties and dissident members of the DYP that the Government was undermining the modern secular tradition were reinforced when the country's chief prosecutor initiated legal proceedings to ban the RP (on the grounds that the party had violated the Constitution). By June the coalition had lost its majority in the TGNA as a result of defections principally from the DYP. Erbakan announced that he would seek an early election, but the military continued to exert pressure on the Government, and the Prime Minister finally resigned. President Demirel asked the ANAVATAN leader, Mesut Yılmaz, to form a new administration, and a coalition with the DSP and the DTP was inaugurated in July; the coalition controlled only a minority of seats in the TGNA, and was dependent on the support of the CHP. The tripartite Government pledged to improve law and order, implement previously proposed changes to the education system, and vigorously pursue EU membership. Defections from the DYP continued, and by the end of July its representation in the TGNA had been reduced from 135 to 93.

In August 1997 the TGNA approved legislation extending compulsory education from five to eight years. This was intended to raise the entry age to Islamic schools from 11 to 14, thus reducing attendance at such schools and lessening Islamic influence. The RP organized popular demonstrations in protest against the legislation (which constituted a principal demand of the military). A further 73 members of the armed forces were expelled, owing to suspected affiliation to Islamist organizations, while further public demonstrations were prompted by the military's insistence on the strict enforcement of the ban on wearing Islamic dress in public buildings, notably educational establishments. In early March 1998 the University of Istanbul temporarily annulled the ban and the Government stated that it would not be strictly enforced. In mid-March the Government survived its third censure motion, which was presented against the Minister for Education for his handling of the issue of Islamic dress. A few days later 20 members of a proscribed Islamist organization were arrested for inciting the demonstrations. At the end of the month the NSC criticized the Government for advocating a relaxation of the enforcement of anti-Islamic legislation; the Government subsequently proposed further measures to curb Islamist radicalism, and the universities announced their decision to enforce the dress code.

Meanwhile, Çiller's participation in the coalition with the RP and her opposition to a possible ban on the party had caused offence to the secular establishment, causing a deterioration in the previously good relations between Çiller and the armed forces. In March 1998 the Court of Appeals ruled that Çiller could not be prosecuted in connection with a particular allegation that she had misused government funds during her premiership, owing to the threat to national security interests. However, in April her loss of support in the TGNA led to a vote in favour of the commencement of an investigation into alleged irregularities in Çiller's accumulation of wealth between 1991 and 1996. In October 1997 Çiller's husband, Ozer Çiller, had been charged with forgery.

In January 1998 the Constitutional Court ordered the dissolution of the RP on the grounds that it was responsible for undermining the secular regime, and banned seven of its members, including Erbakan, from holding political office for five years. Many former RP deputies joined the Fazilet Partisi (FP—Virtue Party), which had been established in December 1997. By March 1998 the FP's representation in the TGNA had risen to 140 seats, making it the largest parliamentary party (ANAVATAN controlled 139 seats). In April the mayor of Istanbul, Reçep Tayyip Erdoğan, who was expected to assume the leadership of the FP, was sentenced to 10 months' imprisonment for inciting hatred; he was released pending an appeal. Erdoğan's conviction, the January ruling and the investigation of hundreds of public officials for their alleged support of Islamist organizations was widely criticized.

The stability of Yılmaz's minority Government was threatened by the demands of the CHP for an early general election. The CHP demonstrated its power in April 1998 by voting with the opposition in favour of an investigation into allegations of corruption against the Prime Minister. Following an agreement signed by Yılmaz and CHP leader Deniz Baykal, the Prime

Minister announced in June 1998 that he was to resign at the end of the year; he was to be succeeded by an interim government that would call early elections for April 1999.

In May 1998 Çiller's husband was found guilty of misleading a parliamentary commission; his sentence, of five months' imprisonment, was later commuted to a fine. In August 12 former RP politicians, including Erbakan and FP leader Recai Kutan, were charged with illegally diverting funds from the party prior to its dissolution. An investigation into Çiller's assets was begun in September. Further investigations were launched in that month into Çiller and the former Minister of Finance for financial irregularities, and the immunity of the former TGNA Speaker was revoked, to allow an investigation, at his request, into his conduct following corruption allegations. Meanwhile, the Court of Appeal upheld the prison sentence on the mayor of Istanbul. As a result of his conviction, Erdoğan was deprived of his position of mayor; he also resigned from the FP. In December new charges were filed against him for insulting the judiciary in a speech following his sentencing. In November 1998 corruption charges against Çiller were dismissed by a parliamentary commission, owing to insufficient evidence, while Erbakan was acquitted on charges of slandering the judiciary, and Minister of State Güneş Taner was removed from office, following a parliamentary censure motion arising from corruption allegations. In December Ozer Çiller was acquitted on charges of falsifying documents.

The Government resigned in November 1998, after the TGNA approved a motion of no confidence submitted by the CHP in response to accusations of corruption against Yılmaz. In January 1999, following protracted political manoeuvring, Bülent Ecevit of the DSP formed a Government, comprising DSP and independent deputies, which was to hold office until the elections in April. Also in January a motion was filed for the dissolution of the pro-Kurdish nationalist Halkın Demokrasi Partisi (HADEP—People's Democracy Party), owing to its alleged links with the Kurdish separatist PKK (see below); however, in March the Constitutional Court ruled that HADEP was to be allowed to contest the elections.

In February 1999 the trial began of 79 alleged Islamists, including Erbakan. Hasan Celal Güzel, the leader of the Yeniden Doğuş Partisi (YDP—Rebirth Party), was sentenced to one year's imprisonment in that month for inciting hatred in a speech at a meeting in Kayseri province; he received a further one-year sentence in May for insulting the President, and was imprisoned for five months from December for incitement to vengeance and hostility. Meanwhile, the High Election Council ruled that former RP deputies would not be allowed to take part in the forthcoming elections as independent candidates.

Despite pressure to postpone the elections, voting proceeded as scheduled on 18 April 1999. No party secured an outright majority in the TGNA; the DSP won 136 of the 550 seats, and subsequently formed a coalition with the Milliyetçi Hareket Partisi (MHP—Nationalist Movement Party), which had won 129 seats, and ANAVATAN, with 86 seats. The remaining seats in the TGNA were won by the FP (111) and the DYP (85), with three seats won by independent candidates. HADEP performed strongly in the south-east, but failed to secure the 10% of the national vote necessary for a seat in the TGNA. The CHP leader, Deniz Baykal, resigned following the poor performance of his party. The new Government, led by Bülent Ecevit, won a parliamentary vote of confidence in June.

In August 1999 some 17,100 people were killed in an earthquake measuring 7.8 on the Richter scale, which struck near Izmit, in north-west Turkey. Both the Government and the armed forces were criticized for the lack of co-ordination and for the slowness of their response to the crisis. A second earthquake, measuring 7.2 on the Richter scale, resulted in a further 800 deaths in the same region in November. In that month Turkey enacted legislation to allow conscripts to pay to shorten their military service in order to raise funds for reconstruction after the earthquake.

Several articles of a political parties act relating to the closure of parties were approved in August 1999: no party would be permitted to reform, even under a different name, party officials would be prohibited from active politics for five years and would be forbidden from standing as candidates for the party, although they would be permitted to stand as independent candidates. In September the FP submitted its preliminary defence against the motion to ban it. In October the assets of Erbakan and nine other former RP officials were frozen as part of the continuing trial of a case brought by the Treasury demanding the repayment of aid given to the RP in 1997, as well as the repayment of allegedly unregistered party funds. In March 2000 Erbakan was sentenced to one year in prison and a lifetime ban from politics for provoking animosity and hatred in a speech made in 1994; his conviction was upheld by an appeals court in July. (In January 2001, however, his sentence was suspended, under penal legislation allowing conditional release for certain convictions. Moreover, in July 2006 the European Court of Human Rights—ECHR—ruled that Erbakan had not received a fair trial.) In December 1999, meanwhile, 300 people were detained following protests over the ban on wearing headscarves in universities; the Court of Appeals ruled that the prerogative to wear Islamic headscarves was not a democratic right.

In January 2000, following a lack of agreement within the TGNA on a suitable presidential candidate (Demirel's term of office was to end in May), Ecevit announced plans for a constitutional amendment that would allow Demirel to renew his term. Despite the agreement of the governing coalition for the proposal, a vote in the TGNA failed to achieve the necessary level of support for the amendment to be carried. In April the parties of the governing coalition agreed to nominate the Chairman of the Constitutional Court, Ahmet Necdet Sezer, as their joint candidate for the presidency; he was elected in a third round of voting.

In June 2000 the TGNA rejected a recommendation to indict former Prime Minister Mesut Yılmaz on corruption charges related to the sale of state-owned land. The rejection came after Yılmaz indicated that ANAVATAN could be forced to withdraw its support from the governing coalition, and thereby cause the collapse of the Government. In July, as part of a minor reorganization, Yılmaz joined the Government as Minister of State, also replacing Cumhur Ersümer, the Minister of Energy and Natural Resources, as Deputy Prime Minister. At HADEP's national conference in November Murat Bozlak was elected unopposed as leader, replacing Ahmet Turan Demir. Deniz Baykal was re-elected leader of the CHP in the same month.

Under the relative stability of the Ecevit Government, the Turkish economy appeared to be making significant improvements during 2000, with the implementation of structural reform measures. In November, however, a severe banking crisis was provoked by an investigation by the Banking and Supervision Agency into 10 failed banks. The investigation exposed the vulnerability of the banking sector and the lack of confidence of foreign investors in the Turkish economy, as a result of a widening current account deficit and delays to the structural reform programme. The IMF and the World Bank agreed to emergency loans in order to support the programme. In February 2001 a second economic crisis was precipitated following a dispute between the President and Prime Minister: Sezer had accused Ecevit of not responding adequately to allegations of government corruption. Opposition parties and the business community had demanded the dismissal of Deputy Prime Minister Hüsamettin Özkan, the Minister of Energy and Natural Resources, Cumhur Ersümer, and the Minister of Public Works, Koray Aydın, and the initiation of a parliamentary investigation into the affairs of Ersümer and Aydın. The precarious balance of power within the governing coalition was, however, thought to have dissuaded Ecevit from undertaking any action against the alleged corruption. Later in February Turkey, with the support of the IMF, abandoned its exchange rate controls and allowed the lira to float, while empowering the Central Bank to pursue a rigorous monetary policy to control inflation.

Following the crisis, in March 2001 Ecevit replaced the Minister of Finance, Reçep Onal, with Kemal Derviş, a senior economist at the World Bank, in an attempt to salvage Turkey's economic reforms and restore confidence in the financial markets. He also replaced the Governor of the Central Bank, Gazi Erçel, with Süreyya Serdegeçti. Following Derviş's appointment, the head of the Banking and Supervision Agency resigned. Derviş announced an emergency plan for economic stabilization, which included the restructuring of three state-owned banks under one supervisory board, and succeeded in securing the financial support of the IMF and the World Bank. Yet the political implications of the financial crisis continued to be felt in April, as anti-Government demonstrations involving tens of thousands of people degenerated into riots in Ankara and İzmir, which were dispersed by security forces. Ecevit, however, rejected demands for his Government to resign. Later in the month it was announced that 15 officials and business executives were to be tried on conspiracy and bribery charges, following a high-profile investigation into corruption in the state energy sector. The testimonies of the defendants resulted in the resignation of Ersümer, who was succeeded as head of the energy portfolio by Zeki Cakan of the ANAVATAN in early May.

In May 2001 the TGNA approved legislation designed to meet conditions demanded by the IMF before the latter was to release US $10,000m. in financial aid. A major condition was the privatization of Turkey's telecommunications sector, which was widely opposed by TGNA members. At the end of the month the Minister of State for Privatization, Yuksel Yalova, resigned, owing to disagreements within the Government over the liberalization of the tobacco industry stipulated by the IMF. Prime Minister Ecevit attempted to replace Yalova with the Minister of the Interior, Sadettin Tantan, but the latter refused the transfer and resigned from his cabinet and ANAVATAN posts in June, following disagreements with Mesut Yılmaz. Tantan was succeeded as Minister of the Interior by Rüştü Kazim Yücelen, hitherto State Minister in charge of human rights. In July the Minister of Communications, Enis Öksüz, resigned, owing to his opposition to the planned IMF-imposed reforms in the telecommunications sector. In September the Minister of Public Works and Housing, Koray Aydin, also resigned from his government post and from the TGNA, after corruption charges were brought against him with regard to his alleged receipt of funds from contracts relating to reconstruction in the aftermath of the 1999 earthquake damage.

In June 2001 the Constitutional Court banned the FP, on the grounds that it was essentially a continuation of the banned Islamist RP and was thus regarded as seeking to undermine the secular system. The Court expelled two FP members from the TGNA; however, it refrained from ordering the mass expulsions of the 100 remaining FP members from the legislature, who were allowed to remain in place as independents or join two planned successor parties. The ban was, nevertheless, opposed by most TGNA members, who were reportedly concerned that it would lead to more political instability. In July the ECHR upheld the Government's 1998 decision to ban the RP. In July 2001 former FP leader Recai Kutan established a new Islamist party, Saadet Partisi (SP—Felicity Party), incorporating about one-half of the former members of the FP (mainly from the conservative wing); the new party pledged to defend religious rights without challenging the secular state. It was believed that, as with the FP, Erbakan was the main force in the party. In August the remaining members of the FP joined the new reformist Islamist Adalet ve Kalkınma (AKP—Justice and Development Party), established by the former mayor of İstanbul, Reçep Tayyip Erdoğan, and FP member Gül as an alternative to the SP. Shortly afterwards Erdoğan came under investigation for comments he had reportedly made in 1994 that allegedly insulted the Turkish state.

The TGNA in October 2001 overwhelmingly approved a number of constitutional amendments designed to facilitate Turkey's admission to the EU. The changes largely pertained to political freedoms and civil liberties, including minority rights (notably regarding the use of the Kurdish language); however, amendments to articles concerning the death penalty refrained from abolishing capital punishment outright. Significantly, the number of civilians on the powerful NSC would rise from five to nine, thereby lessening the power of the military (which would retain five members). Improved rights for women were approved in November.

In January 2002 the Constitutional Court imposed restrictions on the political activities of AKP leader Erdoğan, owing to his earlier allegedly seditious activities. The Court banned him from contesting the elections to the TGNA, and ordered his party to remove him from its leadership within six months. In March Ankara's Higher Criminal Court sentenced Erbakan to two years and four months in prison for embezzling party funds. (In December 2003 the Court of Appeals in Ankara upheld this sentence, although it was deferred for one year on medical grounds.)

In February 2002 the TGNA approved additional laws on freedom of thought and expression by means of a 'mini-reform' programme designed to satisfy EU standards. In subsequent weeks the ruling coalition experienced increasing disagreement over the possible execution of PKK leader Abdullah Öcalan, and on broadcasting and education in the Kurdish language, with the MHP taking an uncompromising stance on these issues in opposition to ANAVATAN. In July Prime Minister Ecevit was forced to call early elections to the TGNA for November, after several of his ministers and numerous DSP party legislators resigned, thereby denying the ruling coalition a majority in the TGNA. The MHP had earlier that month publicly called for an early election. Notable resignations included those of Deputy Prime Minister and Minister of State Hüsamettin Özkan and Minister of Foreign Affairs İsmail Cem. Cem formed a new party, the Yeni Türkiye Partisi (YTP—New Turkey Party), with 62 defectors from the DSP, whose representation in the TGNA had fallen from 128 seats to 65 seats. Ecevit appointed DSP member Şükrü Sina Gürel as Deputy Prime Minister and Minister of State, and concurrently Minister of Foreign Affairs. In early August the Minister of Finance, Kemal Derviş, resigned, and subsequently agreed to co-operate with the CHP. At the end of the month the notably pro-EU and strongly secularist commander of the army's ground forces, Gen. Hilmi Özkök, was appointed to the powerful position of Chief of the General Staff for a four-year term.

In September 2002 the AKP, which was leading in opinion polls, underwent a reverse, when Turkey's highest election board confirmed the Constitutional Court's decision to ban Erdoğan from holding public office. Although he had publicly professed secular and pro-European views, Erdoğan retained the distrust of the secularist military and judiciary, and in October the chief prosecutor sought to obtain an outright ban on the AKP, although this was not implemented. Attempts by several political parties to delay the election also failed.

The elections to the TGNA, held on 3 November 2002, significantly transformed the Turkish political landscape. With voter participation of 79.0%, the AKP won 34.3% of the votes cast, securing 363 seats in the TGNA. Only one other party, the CHP, achieved the 10% of the vote required for representation in the TGNA, winning 19.4% of the votes cast and securing 178 seats. Following the election, President Sezer appointed AKP deputy leader Abdullah Gül as Prime Minister, since Erdoğan was ineligible for the position. (None the less, Erdoğan acted as de facto Prime Minister, exerting a strong influence on the new Government and making a number of official foreign visits.) The new Council of Ministers largely consisted of technocrats from the AKP. Three Deputy Prime Ministers were appointed, while Ali Babacan became Minister of State with responsibility for the Economy and Kemal Unakıtan acquired the finance portfolio. Mehmet Vecdi Gönül was appointed Minister of National Defence. Owing to the fact that AKP's representation in the TGNA was only four seats less than the two-thirds' majority needed to amend the Constitution, and the party commanded the support of several independents, in December the legislature approved constitutional reforms allowing Erdoğan to contest a forthcoming by-election. Initially vetoed by Sezer, these changes were subsequently re-endorsed by the TGNA, forcing the President to accept them.

In January 2003 Erdoğan was re-elected leader of the AKP and immediately announced plans to contest the by-election for the TGNA, membership of which would allow him to become Prime Minister. In February the electoral commission endorsed his candidacy, and Erdoğan was elected to the TGNA on 9 March. Two days later President Sezer appointed Erdoğan as Prime Minister. Erdoğan appointed a new Council of Ministers, which retained most ministers from the incumbent Government. Gül replaced Yalçınbayır as Deputy Prime Minister and also assumed the foreign affairs portfolio. In June the TGNA adopted a further series of human rights reforms, including additional legislation to permit education and broadcasting in Kurdish and other minority languages, and to amend the existing legal definition of terrorism, in order to qualify for accession negotiations with the EU. At the end of that month Sezer vetoed one of the amendments, under which peaceful advocacy of an independent Kurdish state would no longer be illegal. However, the TGNA utilized its power to overrule the veto by returning the legislation to the President without amendment. Further reforms approved by the TGNA (in accordance with EU requirements) in July included the reconstitution of the predominantly military NSC as an entirely advisory body and the offer of a qualified amnesty to supporters of KADEK (the Congress for Freedom and Democracy in Kurdistan—see below), with the specific exclusion of those believed to have committed acts of violence; these measures were formally approved by Sezer in August. In September a decision by the Court of the Appeals over the November 2002 elections confirming the disqualification of DEHAP (as HADEP had become reconstituted in March 2003—see below) for malpractice prompted concern that the results would be annulled, thereby ending the majority of the AKP. However, on 4 October 2003 the High Electoral Council upheld the election results. In the same month an independent parliamentary deputy joined the Liberal Demokratik Parti, which consequently secured one seat in the TGNA.

Some 25 people were killed and about 300 injured in suicide bombings outside two of İstanbul's largest synagogues on 15 November 2003. On 20 November a further two suicide bombs exploded outside the Hong Kong and Shanghai Banking Corporation and the British consulate in İstanbul, killing more than 31 people (including the Consul-General) and injuring more than 450. Although several extremist Turkish Islamist groups, including the Great Eastern Islamic Raiders' Front (IBDA-C), claimed responsibility for the attacks, the involvement of the militant Islamist al-Qa'ida (Base) network led by Osama bin Laden was immediately suspected. Erdoğan condemned all acts of terrorism in a national statement, and demonstrations were staged in Turkey against the bombings, although popular sentiment also attributed blame to the US-led military action in Iraq. By the end of that month a total of 62 had been killed in the four bomb attacks, and 159 had been arrested on suspicion of involvement, of whom a number had been charged. The Turkish authorities announced that the bombings had been organized by a cell of Turkish nationals connected to al-Qa'ida, all of whom had been trained outside Turkey; one principal suspect was repatriated from Syria, while another was arrested on Turkey's south-eastern border with Iran.

Local government elections, which were held on 28 March 2004, resulted in a strong increase in support for the AKP, which secured 42% of the votes cast and 58 of the country's 81 provinces. The CHP, having become subject to internal factional divisions, won only 18% of the votes. In May, as part of the series of reforms intended to bring Turkey into conformity with EU human rights and democratic standards, the TGNA adopted draft constitutional amendments to: abolish the death penalty and anti-terrorist state security courts; guarantee equality for women; and establish full parliamentary control over the budget of the armed forces. The approval in that month of new education legislation, ending restrictions on university entrance for those trained in religious schools, was viewed with concern by defendants of Turkey's official secularism. Consequently, the Government's decision at the beginning of June, following a veto by President Sezer, to suspend the introduction of the legislation was generally welcomed. Security concerns shortly before a NATO summit, attended by US President George Bush, in June were heightened by further explosions in İstanbul, including a suicide bombing, in which four people were killed. In the same month Turkey's stated commitment to new human rights standards, in compliance with EU requirements, was demonstrated by the Supreme Court's decision to order the release of the four Kurdish former parliamentary deputies, who had been sentenced to 15 years' imprisonment in 1994 for supporting the PKK. Following their release, a court in July 2004 overturned their convictions and ordered retrials. The most celebrated of the four, Leyla Zana, after her release, urged the organization to reinstate the cease-fire ended by the organization in September 2003 (see below). In a further significant measure, the TGNA in July 2004 authorized the prosecution for corruption of former Prime Minister Mesut Yılmaz and three other former ministers. In August a further three bombs exploded at hotels in İstanbul, killing two people, and were again attributed by the authorities to Kurdish militants.

In January 2005, following the provisional offer by the EU in December 2004 to commence accession negotiations, Islamist party leaders criticized the conditions imposed and demanded that the Government organize a referendum on EU membership; protests were organized in İstanbul and in İzmit. In February 2005 the Chairman of the Human Rights Consultative Council tendered his resignation, citing continuing impediments posed by the Government (which had rejected a previous critical report of the Council over the stance on human rights). Turkey's new penal code, adopted as a precondition for the commencement of EU accession talks (see below), entered into force at the beginning of June, after a two-month postponement. Sezer subsequently vetoed an amendment reducing the penalties for anti-secular teaching in illegal religious schools. However, at the end of June the TGNA overruled the President's veto, which was supported by the ruling AKP.

The Government's announcement in late 2005 that the renowned Turkish writer, Orhan Pamuk, had been charged with denigrating the Turkish state, after he made a reference in an interview to a Swiss newspaper to the massacre of some 1.5m. Armenians by Turks between 1915 and 1923, prompted international criticism. Pamuk's trial began, amid nationalist protests, in December 2005 but was immediately adjourned, after the municipal court in İstanbul ruled that, under the terms of the unrevised penal code, the Ministry of Justice should decide whether or not it proceed. In January 2006 the charges against Pamuk were abandoned, after the Minister of Justice referred the case back to the court, which refused to uphold it. (It was reported, however, that some 60 journalists were on trial at that time on charges of insulting the Turkish state.) Pamuk was awarded the Nobel Prize for Literature in October.

In February 2006 the trial began of five prominent journalists, including the editor of a principal Armenian newspaper, who had been charged with denigrating the judiciary, after criticizing a September 2005 court decision to prohibit a university conference in İstanbul on the massacre of Armenians in 1915–23. The murder of a prominent Armenian-Turkish journalist and human rights campaigner, Hrant Dink, in İstanbul in January 2007 provoked considerable outrage among the population. Eight suspects, some with close links to nationalist organizations, were arrested following Dink's killing, while several local police officers were suspended from duty for allegedly having failed to offer sufficient protection to the journalist after he had received death threats, or for apparently having shown support to the incarcerated principal suspect. A teenage youth suspected of having links with extreme right-wing nationalist organizations had reportedly confessed to Dink's murder. Trial proceedings against the alleged murderer, together with 17 other suspects, commenced in the Turkish capital in July.

Meanwhile, in February 2006 Erdoğan criticized the decision of the Council of State to refuse to allow the promotion of a teacher who had worn a headscarf on her way to work. In May an extremist Islamist lawyer angered at the ruling entered the Council of State building and assassinated a senior judge. Large demonstrations followed in Ankara, supported by the judiciary and the Chief of the General Staff, Gen. Hilmi Özkök; protesters demanded the protection of secularization in Turkey. (The Islamist lawyer was given two terms of life imprisonment by an Ankara court in February 2008, having been one of four defendants convicted of involvement in the murder.) In August Gen. Yaşar Büyükanıt succeeded Özkök as Chief of the General Staff. In April 2006, meanwhile, after controversially rejecting the Government's selected appointee to the post of Governor of the Central Bank, Sezer approved the nomination of Durmuş Yılmaz, a long-standing director of the bank; Yılmaz pledged commitment to the IMF-supported policy of monetary restraint. In the same month the trial of two Syrian nationals, including a suspected member of al-Qa'ida, was merged with that of 71 defendants charged with involvement in the bombings in İstanbul in November 2003. (In February 2007 seven people—six Turks and a Syrian—were sentenced to life imprisonment for their involvement in the attacks; 41 were given prison terms of between four and 18 years, while 26 were acquitted.) In March 2006 three people were killed when a bomb exploded near the Governor's office in the south-eastern town of Van, and in April a further bomb attack was staged at the offices of the AKP in İstanbul. A number of suspected al-Qa'ida militants were detained in south-eastern Turkey in January 2008, on suspicion of plotting large-scale attacks within the country.

In mid-April 2007, as the TGNA began preparations to elect a successor to President Sezer (whose term of office was to end on 16 May), some 300,000 people held a demonstration in Ankara to demand that Turkey remain a secular state. The protest was organized amid strong speculation that Prime Minister Erdoğan was intending to stand for the presidency; many feared that Erdoğan would pursue an Islamist agenda if he became President. However, on 24 April, the day before the deadline for the registration of candidates, the Prime Minister declared that the Minister of Foreign Affairs, Abdullah Gül, had been chosen as the ruling AKP's candidate. Gül immediately pledged to retain Turkey's secular status should he be elected to the presidency, although there was considerable scepticism about the likelihood of this since Gül's wife chooses to wear the Islamic headscarf. The initial round of voting in the TGNA on 27 April was boycotted by the CHP and other opposition parties, who complained that they had not been consulted about Gül's application; they lodged an appeal with the Constitutional Court for the voting process to be cancelled. Since Gül secured only 357 out of 550 votes at the first round—10 fewer than the requisite number—it was announced on 30 April that the Constitutional Court had annulled the initial vote. Prime Minister Erdoğan subsequently asked the legislature to approve proposals initiated by his party to endorse a constitutional amendment enabling the President henceforth to be directly elected for a five-year term and that a general election (scheduled for November) be brought forward to 24 June in order to resolve the political crisis. The Higher Council of Elections ruled on 3 May that an election should be held on 22 July. Meanwhile, the AKP's legislation was approved by the TGNA, but subsequently vetoed by President Sezer, initially in May 2007.

At the legislative elections on 22 July 2007, the ruling AKP of Prime Minister Erdoğan obtained 46.66% of the votes and 341 seats, against the CHP's 20.85% and 112 seats. The MHP came third, with 14.29% and 71 seats; however, one of the party's elected representatives died on 26 July, resulting in one seat remaining vacant. Pro-Kurdish deputies entered the TGNA as independents—the first time that there had been Kurdish representation in the legislature for 13 years. In early August Köksal Toptan of the AKP was elected Speaker of the Assembly, in succession to Bülent Arınç. Shortly afterwards Abdullah Gül signalled his desire to remain a candidate for the presidency, and he was endorsed unanimously by his party. The first round of the presidential vote was held on 20 August; Gül failed to secure the required two-thirds' majority to be elected at this stage. However, by the third round of voting on 28 August, when a simple majority was all that was needed, Gül was chosen as Turkey's 11th President, securing 339 votes. At his inauguration the new President again pledged his commitment to secularism, pluralism and freedom of belief. A new Council of Ministers was approved by President Gül on 29 August. Among the principal appointees were Ali Babacan as Minister of Foreign Affairs and Chief Negotiator of Turkey for European Union Affairs, and Dr Beşir Atalay as Minister of Internal Affairs. The new Government's programme, which won a vote of confidence in early September, included proposals to reform and modernize the Turkish Constitution, and measures aimed at increasing economic prosperity. Concerns were raised in mid-September, when the Prime Minister recommended an amendment to the Constitution specifically to overturn the ban on women wearing the Islamic headscarf in Turkish universities.

At the nation-wide referendum held on 21 October 2007, a reported 68.95% of eligible voters approved the constitutional reforms regarding the direct election of future Turkish presidents. The serving term of a president was also reduced from seven to five years (renewable once), while those of TGNA deputies were reduced from five to four years. At the end of January 2008 the AKP and the MHP together submitted a motion to the TGNA which would lift the ban on women wearing the Islamic headscarf at universities. The two constitutional amendments were passed into law by President Gül in late February, having received parliamentary approval. The development provoked anger among Turkish secularists, who protested against the decision in Ankara and elsewhere.

Although Turkey was readmitted to the Parliamentary Assembly of the Council of Europe in May 1984, the Assembly continued to advocate the establishment of full democracy and political freedom in the country. In July 1987 all martial law decrees were repealed when martial law was replaced with a state of emergency in several provinces. The Government's signing, in January 1988, of UN and Council of Europe agreements denouncing torture, however, met with a cynical response from both the domestic and international media. Turkey's human rights record has continued to be a focus of international scrutiny.

In July 1999 the ECHR found Turkey guilty of 13 counts of violating rights of free speech and ordered it to pay some 110,000m. lira in damages. In August amnesty legislation was approved by the TGNA to ease the extreme overcrowding in Turkish prisons, with the release of some 26,500 prisoners (of a total prison population of 69,000) and the reduction in sentence for a further 32,000. Although the legislation was initially intended to encourage Kurdish rebels to surrender, it was subsequently altered so that prisoners serving sentences for terrorism would not benefit from the law. However, the bill received widespread criticism and was vetoed by President Demirel in September. Unrest broke out in that month in prisons across the country as a result of the poor conditions and overcrowding; 10 prisoners were killed and a number of guards were taken hostage. The Minister of Justice later announced that a special force was to be established to ensure prison security. In September some 100 people were arrested in İstanbul while trying to issue a press release on the prison incidents. Prison unrest continued, and in February 2000 a protocol was signed providing for the education of prison inmates.

The ECHR in December 1999 found Turkey guilty of breaking the European Convention on Human Rights by its closure of the pro-Kurdish Demokrasi Partisi (DEP—Democracy Party, see below) and ordered it to pay compensation of 70,000 French francs. It was also announced that a human rights consultation committee was to be established to provide information and to act on any complaints received. A report published by the Turkish Human Rights Foundation in June 2000 asserted that as many as 1m. people had been victims of torture over the preceding decade. The report criticized the fact that perpetrators of torture were not subjected to due investigation.

In November 2000 hundreds of political prisoners throughout Turkey (mainly members of left-wing organizations) embarked on a hunger strike, in protest against plans to transfer them to high-security prisons where they would be held in isolation cells. Following attempts to force-feed the prisoners, in violation of international medical ethics, confrontations ensued between the prisoners and the authorities. In December Turkish security forces raided some 20 prisons in an attempt to end the hunger strikes. The three-day action resulted in the deaths of 30 prisoners and two soldiers. After the authorities regained control of the prisons, over 1,000 prisoners were transferred to the isolation cells. There were widespread allegations, supported by human rights organizations Human Rights Watch and Amnesty International, that many prisoners had been subjected to torture both before and after their transfer to these cells, where many prisoners resumed their hunger strike. Also in December the TGNA approved legislation granting an amnesty to as many as 35,000 prisoners by reducing their sentences by 10 years; the legislation was, however, rejected by President Sezer on the grounds that it was divisive and would not serve the cause of justice. By the end of April the number of deaths resulting from the hunger strike had reached 20, with some 30 more seriously ill. The Government refused to open negotiations with the prisoners, although the Minister of Justice announced an initiative to improve prison inspections. In May EU officials warned that failure to resolve the issue could jeopardize Turkey's candidacy for the EU. During the remainder of 2001 many of the strikers were released or hospitalized; of these, some subsequently ended their strike. In November police stormed the houses of some of the released strikers in an attempt forcibly to end the strikes; four protesters reportedly died of self-immolation during the police operation. By January 2003 104 people had died as a result of the ongoing hunger strikes, but no compromise had been reached on the issue of prison accommodation.

Meanwhile, during 2001 the TGNA introduced new legislation, including constitutional amendments, designed to improve the country's human rights and civil liberties in preparation for eventual EU accession (see above). In March the Government had announced a new programme aimed at facilitating EU membership that entailed, *inter alia*, the eventual abolition of the death penalty and ending restrictions on freedom of expression, as well as improving the rights of minorities, but EU officials criticized the programme for its lack of specifics. Despite such plans, the TGNA approved a four-month extension of the state of emergency in the predominantly Kurdish south-east of the country, and in May the Turkish Radio and Television Supreme Council ordered the closure of 89 radio and television stations for broadcasting separatist and disruptive programmes. In October the TGNA approved wide-ranging constitutional amendments embracing improvements in civil liberties and human rights; further liberalizing reforms were approved in February 2002 (see above). Meanwhile, in November women were granted new rights, including equal status to men in several key areas.

In June 2002 the Government proposed additional reforms that abolished the death penalty and removed a ban on broadcasting and education in the Kurdish language. In August the TGNA formally abolished the death penalty in peacetime; in September, however, Amnesty International released a report alleging the widespread use of torture by police, citing testimony from more than 60 individuals during the first half of 2002. In October a court in İstanbul sentenced 10 police officers to prison terms ranging from five to 10 years for beating, torturing and sexually abusing 15 teenage suspects in 1995. The police officers had been acquitted on two previous occasions, resulting in strong condemnation by human rights groups. The officers launched an appeal against their verdict, but in April 2003 the Court of Appeals upheld the sentences. Following his appointment as Prime Minister in March, Erdoğan immediately pledged to bring about major improvements in Turkey's human rights record and to eliminate the use of torture. A series of reforms, approved by the TGNA in July (see above), included provisions for the prompt investigation of allegations of torture and for prohibiting the trial of civilians in military courts in peacetime. In May 2004 the TGNA approved a number of constitutional amendments, in accordance with EU requirements, which included the removal of references to the death penalty and the abolition of the country's system of State Security Courts (used to try dissidents). However, Turkey's perceived failure to maintain the pace of its reforms led, by November 2006, to the suspension of some parts of its accession negotiations (see below).

The Government's position on the Kurdish situation remained a major element of its human rights policy. In January 2002 the Government acted against a campaign to allow the Kurdish language to be taught in schools and universities by arresting hundreds of activists. In February an İstanbul court acquitted a publisher, Fatih Tas, for disseminating 'separatist' articles, written by US academic and linguist Noam Chomsky, which criticized US support for Turkish military operations aimed at suppressing Kurdish nationalism. Chomsky himself attended the trial in support of Tas. In March clashes between security forces and Kurds at a HADEP-organized Kurdish new year celebration in Mersin resulted in the deaths of two policemen and one demonstrator. The decision by the AKP Government in November to permit a maximum of 30 minutes per day of Kurdish language programmes on state television and a maximum of 45 minutes on state radio was greeted with disappointment by Kurdish groups, who had long sought unlimited broadcasting of Kurdish programmes on commercial and local radio and television stations. In March 2003 a ruling by Turkey's Constitutional Court banned HADEP from political activity on the grounds that it had been aiding the PKK (a charge denied by the party). Some 46 members of the party were also subjected to a five-year ban. Shortly afterwards HADEP became reconstituted as the Democratik Halkın Partisi (DEHAP—Democratic People's Party).

A significant increase in outbreaks of urban terrorism in early 1990, together with a perceived increase in the influence of fundamentalist thought, led to widespread fears of a return to the extremist violence of the late 1970s. The increase in terrorist attacks by Islamist and left-wing groups, especially the Dev-Sol (Revolutionary Left), was exacerbated by the Government's stance in the Gulf crisis of 1990–91 (see below), and both factions unleashed a series of attacks against Western targets in Turkey, including US civilians, diplomatic missions and offices of several national airlines and banks in İstanbul and Ankara. The leader of Dev-Sol, Dursun Karatas, was detained in France in September 1994, and diplomatic efforts began to ensure his extradition. Two weeks later a former Minister of Justice, Mehmet Topaç, was shot dead by Dev-Sol members in Ankara. In August 1995 several bombs exploded in İstanbul (killing two civilians), at least one of which was reported to have been placed by a previously unknown Islamist group. In January 1996 a left-wing faction of Dev-Sol, Devrimci Halk Kurtuluş Partisi—Cephesi (DHKP—C, the Revolutionary People's Liberation Party—Front), claimed responsibility for the murder of two leading Turkish business executives in İstanbul. At the end of the year it was reported that Dev-Sol had been subsumed by the DHKP—C.

In January 2000 the Government launched a major operation against the fundamentalist guerrilla group Hezbollah (apparently sponsored by fundamentalist elements in Iran, but unrelated to the Lebanese group of the same name). An armed confrontation between police and Hezbollah members resulted in the death of its leader, Hüseyin Velioğlu, and the capture of two of his closest associates; information provided by these associates led to the discovery of the bodies of nine men, believed to have been abducted by the group in İstanbul. In early 2000 the operation succeeded in detaining some 690 suspected Hezbollah members and the bodies of more than 50 people, believed to have been victims of the group, were discovered. At that time the Government denied that it had tolerated the activities of Hezbollah, owing to its anti-PKK activities, and the office of the Chief of the General Staff strongly denied allegations of links between Hezbollah and the army. In February Çiller denied that the state had supplied weapons to Hezbollah during her time as Prime Minister, and in March two regional FP staff were arrested on suspicion of membership of Hezbollah. In October Turkish security forces captured Mehmet Sudan, Velioğlu's successor, and the Ministry of the Interior reported that since January some 1,600 people with ties to Hezbollah had been arrested.

In December 2000 two police officers were killed following an attack on a police bus in İstanbul. In January 2001 the DHKP—C claimed responsibility for a suicide bomb attack on a police building, which killed two people. In April Sahil Izzet Erdis, the leader of the outlawed IBDA—C, was sentenced to death on charges of seeking to overthrow the secular state. In September a suicide bomber, believed to be acting on behalf of the DHKP—C, killed two policemen and a foreign tourist in central İstanbul. In May 2002 the EU designated the DHKP—C as a terrorist organization. Security forces arrested several members of DHKP—C in two attempted military operations during November 2004. In June 2006 four members of the organization were arrested following the shooting of a police officer in İstanbul. In January 2007 a further five DHKP—C members (including Karatas) were detained by the Turkish authorities.

In 1984 the outlawed PKK, seeking the creation of a Kurdish national homeland in Turkey, launched a violent guerrilla campaign against the Turkish authorities in the south-eastern provinces. The Government responded by arresting suspected Kurdish leaders, sending in more security forces, establishing local militia groups and imposing martial law (and later states of emergency) in the troubled provinces. Violence continued to escalate, however, and in April and May 1990 clashes between rebel Kurds, security forces and civilians resulted in the deaths of 140 people. The conflict entered a new phase when, in August and October 1991, and March 1992 (in retaliation for continuing cross-border attacks on Turkish troops), government fighter planes conducted numerous sorties into northern Iraq in order to attack suspected PKK bases there. In the course of these raids many civilians and refugees (including Iraqi Kurds) were reportedly killed, prompting international observers and relief workers publicly to call into question the integrity of the exercises. The Iraqi Government lodged formal complaints with the UN, denouncing Turkish violations of Iraq's territorial integrity.

Violence in the south-eastern provinces, resulting from ethnic tension, persisted throughout 1992 and 1993, despite the stated commitment of the Demirel administration to foster new initiatives for improved relations with ethnic minorities. In late 1992 Turkish air and ground forces (in excess of 20,000 troops), conducted further attacks upon PKK bases inside northern Iraq, hoping to take advantage of losses inflicted on the Kurdish rebels by an offensive in October initiated by Iraqi Kurdish *peshmerga* forces, aimed at forcing the PKK from Iraq. Hopes that a negotiated resolution to the conflict might be achieved, following the unilateral declaration of a cease-fire by the PKK in March 1993, were frustrated by renewed fighting in May and an intensification of the conflict in June. The bombing of several coastal resorts and of tourist attractions in central İstanbul confirmed the PKK's intention to disrupt the country's economy and to attract international attention to the conflict. PKK activists and supporters also conducted protests and attacked Turkish property throughout Europe.

In November 1993 a 10,000-strong élite anti-terrorist force was created to counter the PKK forces, in addition to the estimated 150,000–200,000 troops already positioned in the area of conflict. In 1994 the security forces mounted a heavy offensive against the separatists, and again conducted air attacks on suspected PKK strongholds in south-eastern Turkey and in northern Iraq. Reports that an estimated 6,000 Kurds were forcibly displaced into northern Iraq as a result of the destruction of their villages by security forces were denied by the Minister of Foreign Affairs. In September security forces initiated an operation in the eastern Munzur mountains to destroy PKK stores and supply routes. In November a Kurdish proposal for a cease-fire, accompanied by international mediation, to achieve a peaceful settlement to the conflict was rejected by the Government, which emphasized the success of its anti-terrorist campaign.

On 20 March 1995 a massive offensive, involving 35,000 air and ground force troops, was initiated against PKK targets in northern Iraq. Turkish forces advanced some 40 km across the border, prompting protests from Iraq, as well as concern on the part of the USA and the EU that the military intervention should not be consolidated into a permanent occupation force. The Turkish Government insisted that the offensive was designed to destroy PKK base camps and to force the separatists from northern Iraq (where, it claimed, the PKK had taken advantage of a power vacuum in the region to become securely established). The UN assisted in the evacuation of several thousand Kurds from the northern Iraqi town of Zakho, amid reports of intimidation by the occupying Turkish troops. Under increasing international pressure, Turkey undertook a complete withdrawal of its troops by May. Official figures stated that 555 Kurdish separatists and 58 Turkish soldiers were killed as a result of the operation. Earlier, in April, the PKK had obtained permission to convene in the Netherlands, in an attempt to establish a Kurdish parliament-in-exile, prompting Turkey temporarily to recall its ambassador to the Netherlands. Fighting was again resumed in the south-east of the country in June, and in July a further week-long offensive was conducted against Kurdish bases in northern Iraq. In December the PKK leader, Abdullah Öcalan, announced a unilateral cease-fire on the part of his organization. By March 1996, having received no assurances of a cease-fire from the Turkish authorities, Öcalan advised tourists against visiting the country, warning of possible renewed attacks against major tourist sites. During April an estimated 400 PKK members were killed in the renewed military operation. In the following months PKK activists were frequently pursued into northern Iraq by Turkish ground and air forces, provoking protests from the Iraqi Government, and fighting in the south-eastern provinces escalated. In June five soldiers were killed in a suicide bomb attack in Tunceli, eastern Turkey. A further two suicide attacks, reportedly by PKK members, were perpetrated in October, killing 10 people. In response, Turkish security forces conducted air raids against PKK targets in northern Iraq, which continued into early 1997. An estimated 2,800 PKK activists were killed during 1996 as a result of the conflict, in addition to 532 members of the security forces and 145 civilians.

In May 1997 Turkey again launched a massive military offensive against the PKK in northern Iraq, involving the mobilization of 50,000 troops. Turkey claimed that the incursion was in response to an appeal by the Iraqi-based Kurdistan Democratic Party (KDP), which co-operated with the Turkish attack. The operation elicited rigorous condemnation from Iraq, Iran and Syria, but the response from members of NATO was muted. By June Turkish military officials claimed that the attack had achieved its objectives of destroying several PKK bases in northern Iraq and estimated that more than 3,000 PKK troops had been killed. A further offensive, launched in September, was speculated to be part of a Turkish plan to establish a security zone in northern Iraq to prevent cross-border attacks by the PKK. This assumption was apparently confirmed by the lifting of the state of emergency in three of the nine south-eastern provinces in October.

Despite PKK threats to extend the separatist struggle throughout Turkey if the Turkish Government refused to seek a political solution to the conflict, further Turkish troops entered northern Iraq in February 1998. Further operations against the PKK took place in April, including the capture of a former PKK commander, Semdin Sakik. Sakik had surrendered to the DPK in March, following a disagreement with Öcalan, which fuelled speculation concerning internal dissent within the movement. In August the PKK declared a unilateral cease-fire; this was, however, rejected by the Government.

Relations with Syria, which had already deteriorated in July 1998 (owing to Syria's repeated claim to the Hatay region of Turkey), worsened in early October, after Turkey threatened the use of force if Syria did not expel Öcalan and close down terrorist training camps in both Syria and the Beka'a valley in Lebanon. It was reported that 10,000 Turkish troops had been deployed near the border; the Turkish ambassador to Syria was also recalled. Egypt and Iran both attempted to mediate in the dispute, and, following a meeting of Turkish and Syrian officials in late October, an agreement was signed under which Syria would not allow the PKK to operate on its territory; Öcalan was thus forced to leave the country, and he arrived in Italy in November. Turkey had already temporarily recalled its ambassador to Italy in October, after a meeting of the Kurdish parliament-in-exile was hosted there. Relations deteriorated further when Italy refused to extradite Öcalan to Turkey and Öcalan applied for asylum. Demonstrations were held in Turkey against Italy, and Italian goods were boycotted; Turkey also threatened to end diplomatic relations with Italy if Öcalan's asylum request was granted. However, in January 1999 Öcalan was reported to have left Italy after his application was turned down. In the following month he was captured at the Greek embassy in Kenya and returned to Turkey. Widespread Kurdish protests were held throughout Europe.

At the end of February 1999 Öcalan was formally charged, in the absence of defence counsel, and the first hearing was set for late March. PKK violence in protest at the trial continued in that month, and there were also threats of violence against tourists in Turkey. A series of bomb attacks in İstanbul were later attributed to a new Kurdish group, the Nationalist Kurdish Revenge Teams. In April a further operation was launched against the PKK, involving the deployment of some 15,000 Turkish troops in northern Iraq. Semdin Sakik, the former PKK commander who had been captured in March 1998, was sentenced to death in May 1999; his sentence was upheld by the Supreme Court in October. In June Öcalan was convicted on treason charges and sentenced to death; violent demonstrations were held in protest at his sentence. A third PKK leader, Cevat Soysal, was arrested in Moldova in July.

The PKK agreed to a cease-fire in early August 1999, at which time Öcalan announced that the PKK was prepared to surrender its arms in exchange for Kurdish rights; PKK fighters withdrew from Turkey at the end of the month. However, the Government insisted that the PKK cease hostilities entirely in order for Turkey to reassess the situation. Following a statement issued by Öcalan in September in which he urged PKK rebels to show their commitment to the end of hostilities by surrendering to Turkish forces, two eight-member PKK delegations travelled to Ankara where they were arrested and detained by the authorities.

In September 1999 the Kurdish parliament-in-exile convened in Brussels, where it voted to dissolve and to join the Kurdistan National Congress. Following the cease-fire the number of armed confrontations in the south-east had declined substantially and in October the Government reduced the number of checkpoints in the region. In November Öcalan's death sentence was upheld on appeal and the chief prosecutor rejected his application for a final appeal; his lawyers referred the case to the ECHR. A second trial against Öcalan, together with 101 other defendants, began in Ankara in December for a series of offences including extortion and murder allegedly carried out in the 1970s; the trial was adjourned until February 2000. In January 2000 the parties of the governing coalition announced that they had agreed to delay Öcalan's execution until a ruling had been given by the ECHR.

The PKK announced formally the end to its war against Turkey in February 2000, and stated that it would campaign for Kurdish rights within a framework of peace and democracy. In February three HADEP mayors were arrested and charged with aiding the PKK; they were released on bail, following protests both from within Turkey and internationally. Relations with the EU deteriorated further in February, when Turkey denied EU politicians permission to visit Öcalan in prison. At that time 18 people, including the HADEP leader, Ahmet Turan Demir, were sentenced to almost four years' imprisonment for organizing demonstrations in support of Öcalan. Despite the PKK's cease-fire declaration, Turkish troops continued to push into Kurdish strongholds throughout the year. In September at least 38 civilians were reported to have been killed, following sorties by Turkish fighter planes into northern Iraq targeting suspected PKK bases, and in early 2001 Turkish troops advanced into Kurdish northern Iraq in an attempt to suppress PKK activities. Some 2,500 PKK rebels were believed to be based along the Iran–Iraq border at this time.

In June 2000 there were reports of increased tension within the PKK leadership, with some members, including (according to some sources) Öcalan's brother, Osman, no longer acknowledging Abdullah Öcalan as leader of the organization. In September Selahattin Celik, a founder member of the PKK, formed a breakaway group, styling itself 'the Initiative', to continue the PKK's military campaign. However, Celik, who was based in Germany, lacked the resources and forces to wage a guerrilla war. The hearing of the appeal against Öcalan's death sentence began at the ECHR in November. Öcalan's appeal was based on the grounds that he had not received a fair trial in Turkey under the terms of the European Convention on Human Rights.

In April 2002 the PKK formally announced a change of name to the Congress for Freedom and Democracy in Kurdistan (KADEK), under the leadership of Öcalan, and asserted its wish to campaign peacefully for Kurdish rights. Although the movement had abandoned its initiative for an independent Kurdish state, the announcement was received with scepticism on the part of the Turkish Government. However, KADEK was not included in the EU's list of organizations designated as 'terrorist', and it was believed that its agenda had been designed to win support from the EU. In June the ECHR awarded compensation to 13 Kurdish former members of the TGNA who had been imprisoned by the Government in 1994 for supporting the PKK. In November 2002, in a sign that the Government had acknowledged the conversion of the PKK, the state of emergency that prevailed in the two remaining south-eastern provinces of Diyarbakır and Sirnak was finally ended.

In October 2002, meanwhile, the State Security Court officially commuted Öcalan's death sentence to life imprisonment, in accordance with the abolition of the death penalty in peacetime by the TGNA in August. The court's decision was controversial, since Öcalan was widely despised by the Turkish public for his armed insurrections during the 1980s and 1990s. In March 2003 the ECHR issued a non-binding ruling that Öcalan had not received a fair trial, and criticized Turkey for violating some of Öcalan's rights; however, the ECHR rejected accusations by Öcalan's lawyers of inhumane treatment and illegal detention. Turkey immediately appealed against the ECHR, fearing renewed pressure from the EU to hold a retrial if the ruling was upheld. Despite its success in defeating Kurdish separatism, the Government continued to fear the possible emergence of a Kurdish state in northern Iraq after the USA's war against Iraqi President Saddam Hussain's regime in March–April 2003 (see below). A partial amnesty offered to supporters of KADEK by the Government in July failed, apparently owing to the effective exclusion of the movement's leadership, with only eight members accepting the terms by the end of August. In September, following renewed attacks by the organization in eastern Turkey, KADEK formally ended the cease-fire declared in February 2000, accusing the authorities of failing to address demands for improved Kurdish rights and freedom of expression. In November 2003 KADEK was reconstituted as the Kongreya Gelê Kurdistanê (KONGRA-GEL—Kurdistan People's Congress), which, in January 2004, the US Administration added to its list of designated 'terrorist' organizations.

After revoking its cease-fire, KONGRA-GEL organized sporadic attacks during 2004. In July government troops launched an offensive against KONGRA-GEL positions at the border with Iraq. In November further clashes between security forces and KONGRA-GEL militants, in which six rebels were killed, were reported in south-eastern Turkey. In early 2005 security forces repelled an attack staged from northern Iraq by suspected KONGRA-GEL members, and also arrested two KONGRA-GEL militants who had been planning a bomb attack in Mersin. In April the KONGRA-GEL leadership announced that the organization was to revert to its original name, PKK (although it appeared that not all elements of the movement did so). In May the ECHR ruled that the trial of Öcalan had been unfair, on the grounds that he had not been tried by an independent tribunal (owing to the presence of a military judge on the panel); the Turkish Government indicated that a further trial would be conducted.

A series of bomb attacks in July and August 2005 were attributed to Kurdish militants (although the PKK denied responsibility), including one on a tourist bus in the Aegean Sea resort of Kuşadası, in which five people died, and another against an army unit in south-eastern Turkey. In September some 88 PKK supporters were arrested in İstanbul, after protesting at being prevented from attending a rally in support of Öcalan (who was said to have been placed in solitary confinement). Despite the PKK's extension until early October of a unilateral cease-fire, which it had declared in August, clashes between rebels and government forces continued in the east of the country. Later in October Kurdish protests erupted in the north-western town of Eskişehir, where the trial was in process of four security officers accused of killing two civilians, including a minor, while in pursuit of rebels. In November rioting erupted in the south-eastern town of Şemdinli, after three suspected perpetrators of a bomb attack apparently aimed against a PKK supporter, in which one person was killed, were discovered to be police intelligence agents. The Government subsequently pledged that an investigation would be conducted into the incident. Security forces continued to stage operations in eastern Turkey against members of the PKK and its re-emerged military wing, Hezên Parastina Gel (HPG—People's Defence Forces). In March 2006 some 50 suspected militants were detained after a security operation in central Turkey. Between 28 March and 1 April the funeral of four suspected PKK supporters in the south-eastern town of Viranşehir precipitated large-scale Kurdish rioting in the regional capital, Diyarbakır; some 12 people were killed in the disturbances. In April a series of bomb attacks in İstanbul resulted in three deaths, and in August the coastal resorts of Marmaris and Antalya were also targeted: a further three people were killed in the Antalya blast and in both bombings there were dozens of casualties, including many foreign nationals. Responsibility for the attacks was claimed by a group called the Kurdistan Freedom Falcons (TAK), which purported to be linked to the PKK. In September Erdoğan emphatically rejected a call from the imprisoned Öcalan for a cease-fire to be imposed by the organization on 1 October. Öcalan was reported to have demanded a retrial against his sentence in the following month. A suicide bomb attack carried out at a shopping centre in Ankara in May 2007 resulted in the deaths of six people. Turkish security officials claimed that the attack had been perpetrated by Kurdish extremists, although spokesmen for the PKK denied responsibility.

Turkey has been a member of NATO since 1952, and is widely considered to have fulfilled a crucial role in NATO defence strategy in south-eastern Europe. During the 1990s Turkey's importance to its key ally, the USA, increased as its strategic location allowed it to co-operate with the USA in regional security issues. The Turkish Government responded positively to requests from the USA for logistical aid, following the forcible annexation of Kuwait by Iraq in August 1990, and complied with UN proposals for economic sanctions against Iraq by closing its border to all non-essential trade and, later, to traffic. In September Turkey and the USA extended an agreement to allow the USA access to more than 25 military establishments, in return for military and economic aid, that had been initially signed in 1980, and renewed in 1987. In January 1991 a resolution to extend the war powers of the Government and effectively endorse the unrestricted use of Turkish airbases by coalition forces was agreed by the TGNA. US aircraft subsequently embarked upon bombing missions into north-eastern Iraq from NATO bases inside south-eastern Turkey. In February and March the US Government announced substantial increases in military and economic aid to Turkey. In April an estimated 600,000 Kurds attempted to flee northern Iraq into Turkey. Following a massive international relief effort and the subsequent repatriation of the majority of refugees, the Turkish Government agreed to the deployment in south-east Turkey of a 3,000-strong multi-national 'rapid reaction force', which would respond to any further acts of aggression by Iraq against the Kurds in the newly created 'safe havens'. While all ground forces were withdrawn in October, the Turkish Government agreed to the continued use of its airbases by a small allied air-strike force to conduct patrols of northern Iraq under the mandate of 'Operation Provide Comfort'. The mandate was granted six-month extensions, despite increasing unease on the part of the Turkish authorities that the Kurdish enclave was providing a refuge for PKK separatists. Difficulties in Turkey's relations with the USA arose in 1994, following a decision by the US Congress to withhold some military and economic aid in order to encourage greater respect for human rights in the Turkish Government's treatment of Kurdish separatists.

In March 1996 the Turkish Government assured the TGNA that the mandate for the use of Turkish bases for allied aircraft engaged in 'Operation Provide Comfort' would be terminated, following the approval of a final three-month extension. In July, however, the new RP Prime Minister, Necmettin Erbakan, in spite of his earlier election pledge to conclude the arrangement, secured a final extension of the operation's mandate until the end of the year. In September the Turkish Government refused permission for the use of its airbases for a US military operation against Iraqi forces that had violated the Kurdish area in northern Iraq. Turkey amassed an estimated additional 20,000 troops along the border and revealed proposals to establish a temporary security zone in the region in order to stem any influx of refugees from Iraq and to prevent the PKK from exploiting the situation. The Government also undertook to relocate the military co-ordination centre of 'Operation Provide Comfort' from Zakho in northern Iraq to Silopi in south-eastern Turkey. ('Operation Provide Comfort' was superseded by the more limited aerial surveillance operation 'Northern Watch' in January 1997.) In October 1996 the Turkish Government was actively involved in negotiations between the conflicting Kurdish factions in northern Iraq to secure a peace agreement, not least in an attempt to end the power vacuum in that region which threatened Turkey's security. A second round of talks, following the conclusion of a preliminary agreement at the end of October, was initiated in November. During 1996 Turkey pursued diplomatic efforts to secure the reopening of the petroleum pipeline from Kirkuk in northern Iraq to Yumurtalik in Turkey, which had been closed since August 1990 as a result of UN-imposed economic sanctions. The pipeline was finally reactivated in December, in accordance with a UN agreement permitting the export of US $2,000m. of petroleum by Iraq over a six-month period, in order to fund the purchase of essential medical and other humanitarian supplies. As relations between Iraq and the UN deteriorated from the end of 1997, Turkey announced that it opposed the use of its Incirlik airbase for potential US-led strikes against Iraq and urged a peaceful solution to the crisis. Relations deteriorated further in late 1998, and Turkey again urged a diplomatic solution. Although Turkey was informed of the airstrikes against Iraq in December, in January 1999 it announced that Turkish airbases would not be used in any new operation against Iraq.

Following the suicide attacks on the USA in September 2001, perpetrated by Osama bin Laden's al-Qa'ida network, Turkey emerged as a crucial ally in the former's 'war on terror', immediately pledging its co-operation. In October the TGNA agreed in principle to send troops to Afghanistan and allow foreign forces to be stationed in Turkey, and in December US Secretary of State Colin Powell visited Turkey to discuss security and bilateral trade issues. (It was believed that, in return for assisting in the US-led campaign, Turkey would gain financial assistance from the USA and be able to persuade the Administration to pressure the EU into accepting Turkey's membership.) Meanwhile, hundreds of Turkish commandos were deployed in Uzbekistan in preparation for possible combat in Afghanistan, and 90 of these entered northern Afghanistan to train the opposition United National Islamic Front for the Salvation of Afghanistan (the United Front—UF, or 'Northern Alliance'). Turkey had for some years had contacts with the UF's Gen. Abdulrashid Dostam, having given him asylum in the late 1990s. Turkey assumed command of the International Security Assistance Force (ISAF) in Afghanistan in June 2002, raising its troop presence in that country to 1,000. (Turkish command of the ISAF ended in February 2003, whereupon control of the force passed to Germany and the Netherlands.)

In 2002 Turkish leaders became increasingly concerned about the possibility that the USA would open a 'second front' in its military campaign to overthrow the regime of Saddam Hussain. In particular, the Government feared a break-up of the Iraqi state and the creation of a Kurdish state in northern Iraq that could be used to foster Kurdish nationalism in its own territory, and the possible mass exodus of Iraqi Kurds into Turkey. There were also concerns about the disruption to Turkish-Iraqi trade and economic co-operation that any US-led attack would bring. Ecevit's illness and the subsequent preparations for elections to the TGNA in November meant that no agreements between Turkey and the USA were reached over the latter's planned invasion of Iraq. Relations between the two countries were further complicated by the victory of the AKP in the elections, and overwhelming public opposition to war against Iraq. By January 2003 a number of senior US officials had visited Turkey to persuade the Government to accept the deployment of 62,000 US troops in the south-east of the country, and the use of the region as a staging post for a 'northern front' in the planned conflict. Following lengthy negotiations, the US Government offered a financial package of US $6,000m. in direct grants and an additional $20,000m. in loans and trade concessions in compensation for any economic losses incurred during the war; however, the Turkish authorities considered this sum to be insufficient. President Sezer warned in February that US forces could only be deployed in Turkey if the USA obtained a second UN resolution from the UN Security Council authorizing the use of force against Iraq.

On 1 March 2003 the TGNA rejected a motion allowing the USA to deploy troops in Turkey. (Although 264 members of the TGNA had voted in favour of the deployment, with 250 against, the motion was four votes short of a majority of deputies in attendance.) As many as 50 AKP legislators voted against the Government, underscoring the level of opposition to US plans for a military campaign to oust the Iraqi regime. On 20 March the TGNA voted only to allow the use of Turkish airspace for the conflict, but endorsed the deployment of Turkish troops in Iraq if considered necessary. The US-led coalition forces initiated attacks against the Iraqi regime on that day, and shortly thereafter abandoned attempts to negotiate the use of Turkish bases. The aid package was withdrawn following the TGNA vote, but in April the USA offered a new, reduced package totalling a loan of US $8,500m. in order to repair bilateral relations. The US Secretary of State, Colin Powell, visited Ankara at that time and secured Turkish permission for humanitarian aid and US logistical supplies to be delivered to US and coalition troops in Iraq via Turkish territory. In September the Turkish and US Governments signed an agreement approving the loan to compensate for the adverse effects of the March–April conflict in Iraq. In October a motion proposed by the Council of Ministers in favour of contributing peace-keeping troops to the US-led coalition in Iraq was endorsed by the TGNA. Following widespread protests in both Turkey and Iraq, however, Erdoğan announced that he would consider reversing this decision, and in November the planned deployment of Turkish forces in Iraq was cancelled.

Amid an intensification of PKK violence in south-eastern Turkey during 2006, the likelihood grew of a large-scale Turkish military incursion to attempt to defeat PKK rebels in northern Iraq. By July 2007, according to Hoshyar az-Zibari, the Iraqi Minister of Foreign Affairs, Turkish armed forces along the countries' mutual border amounted to some 140,000 personnel. In August, after a reported 12 Turkish soldiers had died during fighting with PKK militants in that month, Erdoğan and the Iraqi Prime Minister, Nuri al-Maliki, reached a memorandum of understanding aimed at ending the 'safe haven' of the PKK in northern Iraq. A further security co-operation pact was signed in late September, although the Iraqi Government refused Turkey's principal demand that its military be permitted to enter Iraqi territory in pursuit of Kurdish fighters. A large number of Turkish soldiers were reported to have been killed during clashes with the PKK in subsequent weeks. In mid-October the TGNA endorsed a decision to allow Turkish military raids into northern Iraq, despite US President Bush and al-Maliki urging the Turkish leadership to show restraint. In November Bush pledged that the USA would increase its military co-operation with Turkey, in an apparent effort to dissuade the Turkish Government from launching a major incursion into Iraqi territory. Nevertheless, in mid-December Turkish troops began an offensive against PKK bases in Iraq's northern region, in response to a series of cross-border raids by armed Kurdish separatists to carry out bomb attacks against Turkish soldiers in south-eastern Turkey. The Iraqi Government protested to its Turkish counterpart that it had not been consulted over the military action, while the President of the Kurdish Autonomous Region, Masoud Barzani, described Turkey's actions as a violation of Iraqi sovereignty. In late February 2008 it was initially reported that up to 10,000 Turkish troops had entered northern Iraq, in what appeared to be a much larger incursion than that of the previous December, and with the additional launching of airstrikes against PKK militant bases; however, it was reported at the end of February that only several hundred forces had participated in the military campaign. Nevertheless, dozens of PKK militants were killed in the week-long offensive, together with several Turkish soldiers. (The Turkish military claimed by this time to have killed at least 230 PKK fighters, and to have lost 27 of its soldiers; however, PKK sources alleged that around 90 Turkish soldiers had died in the recent incursion.)

Meanwhile, in early October 2007 Turkey withdrew its ambassador to Washington, DC, USA, in protest against the adoption by the foreign affairs committee of the US House of Representatives of a non-binding resolution describing as 'genocide' the killing of an estimated 1.5m. Armenians following the First World War (see above).

Although Turkey and Greece are both members of NATO, long-standing disputes over sovereignty in the Aegean Sea and concerning Cyprus have strained relations between the two countries, and tension was exacerbated when Turkey granted recognition to the 'Turkish Republic of Northern Cyprus' ('TRNC'), proclaimed in November 1983 (see the chapter on Cyprus). In April 1988 the Greek Prime Minister, Andreas Papandreou, officially accepted Turkey's status as an associate of the EC by signing the Protocol of Adaptation (consequent on Greece's accession to the EC) to the EC-Turkey Association Agreement, which the Greek Government had hitherto refused to do, and in June Turgut Özal became the first Turkish Prime Minister to visit Greece for 36 years. In February 1990 relations deteriorated again, following violent clashes between Christians and the Muslim minority in western Thrace, in Greece. Throughout the early 1990s Turkey and Greece maintained strong support for their respective communities in Cyprus during the ongoing, but frequently interrupted, negotiations to resolve the issue.

The issue of the demarcation of territorial waters in the Aegean re-emerged as a source of tension with Greece in 1994. Turkey insisted that it would retaliate against any expansion of territorial waters in the region, as provided for under the terms of the UN Convention on the Law of the Sea (UNCLOS), which entered into force in November. Military exercises in the region were undertaken by both Turkish and Greek naval vessels, and resumed in June 1995 following ratification of UNCLOS by the Greek Parliament. Bilateral relations, which remained strained during 1995 over the issue of the treatment of the Muslim minority in western Thrace, deteriorated sharply in early 1996, owing to a series of incidents in the Aegean in which both countries claimed sovereignty of Imia (Kardak), a small, uninhabited island. Turkey's claim was based on a concession granted by Italy prior to the 1947 settlement that awarded the main Dodecanese islands to Greece. The dispute was exploited by nationalist media in both countries; however, the threat of military action was averted in February 1996 when the two sides agreed to a petition of the US Government to withdraw naval vessels from the region and to pursue efforts to conclude a diplomatic solution. Differences remained on the means of achieving a settlement, with Greece proposing to take the dispute to international arbitration, an option endorsed by the EU Council of Ministers, and Turkey advocating bilateral negotiations. Throughout 1996 relations remained strained as a result of several minor confrontations between Greek and Turkish patrol vessels in the Aegean, persistent Greek allegations of violations of its airspace by Turkish aircraft and Turkish concern at the treatment of the ethnic population in western Thrace. From mid-1996 an escalation in intercommunal tension in Cyprus emphasized divisions between the two countries. Turkey remained committed in its support for the 'TRNC' authorities and resolved to respond with military action to the proposed deployment of an anti-aircraft missile system in the Greek Cypriot territory. A joint defence doctrine was agreed by the Turkish and 'TRNC' authorities in January 1997, and in March a co-operation accord, providing for some US $250m. in economic assistance to the 'TRNC', was ratified by the two sides.

In April 1997, following Greece's continued refusal to conduct bilateral discussions with Turkey over sovereignty rights in the Aegean, Turkey rejected proposals to refer the dispute over Imia (Kardak) to the International Court of Justice (ICJ). At the end of April the Greek and Turkish ministers responsible for foreign affairs held bilateral talks in Malta under EU auspices, during which it was agreed that each country would establish a committee of experts to help resolve bilateral disputes. The two committees were to be separate and independent and were to communicate through the EU. In July, at a NATO summit in Madrid, Spain, direct talks took place between Demirel and the Greek Prime Minister, Konstantinos Simitis. The so-called Madrid agreement was signed, in which both sides pledged to respect the other's sovereign rights and to renounce violence, and the threat of violence, in their dealings with each other. Later in July, following earlier statements from Turkey expressing the hope that Greece would revoke its veto on EU aid, Greece stated that the veto would not be removed unless Turkey agreed to international arbitration over the disputed islet of Imia (Kardak).

In July 1997 Turkey announced the formation of a joint committee to implement partial integration between Turkey and the 'TRNC', in response to the EU's agreement to commence accession talks with Cyprus. Turkey also declared in September that should the EU continue to conduct membership talks with the Greek Cypriot Government, then it would seek further integration with the 'TRNC'. Shortly afterwards Turkey banned all Greek Cypriot ships from entering Turkish ports. Following the involvement of Greece in Greek Cypriot military exercises in October, in November Turkish forces engaged in military manoeuvres in the 'TRNC'. However, Yılmaz and Simitis held a cordial meeting later in November and agreed to explore confidence-building measures. Yet relations continued to be strained by accusations of violations of airspace and territorial waters, made by both Greece and Turkey. The most serious incident occurred in October 1997 when Greece accused Turkey of harassing a plane carrying the Greek Minister of Defence. In January 1998 Turkey declared that a Greek plan to extend its territorial waters from six to 12 miles under UNCLOS was unacceptable, as were plans to open several Aegean islets for settlement. Turkey also protested to the UN that the proposed opening of an airbase at Paphos in southern Cyprus would destabilize the military situation on the island. In April Greece again vetoed the release of aid promised to Turkey under the Turkish-EU customs union.

Relations deteriorated in 1998 as a result of a purchase agreement between the Greek Cypriot Government and Russia for anti-aircraft missiles. Turkey maintained that their deployment would be a threat to its territory and in July announced that it planned to deploy missiles in the 'TRNC' if the missiles deal proceeded. In December, however, the Greek Cypriot Government announced that it would not be deploying the missiles in Cyprus and that they would be deployed on Crete, Greece. In January 1999 Turkey refused to pay compensation which had been awarded by the ECHR to a Greek Cypriot woman for land lost as a result of the Turkish occupation of northern Cyprus.

In early 1999 Greece denied Turkish accusations of Greek support for the PKK, although Öcalan was later captured at the Greek embassy in Kenya. In March Turkey alleged that Greece had unilaterally suspended 'confidence-building' talks on the dispute in the Aegean, and denied a claim that Turkish aircraft had violated Greek airspace. In August relations between the two countries improved markedly, following the Greek response to the earthquake that occurred in north-west Turkey at the end of that month. Greek rescue teams were among the first to arrive in Turkey, and Greece agreed to lift its veto on EU development loans and aid to Turkey; Turkey reciprocated the gesture by sending a rescue team to Greece following a smaller-scale earthquake in Athens in September. A joint business council announced that it was to resume its activities in that month, and the Turkish and Greek ministers responsible for foreign affairs met for discussions in Brussels. Train services linking Greece and Turkey were introduced in November. In January 2000 the Greek Minister of Foreign Affairs made the first official visit to Turkey by a Greek foreign minister for 38 years, during which it was agreed that direct talks would be held to reduce military tensions in the Aegean. In February his Turkish counterpart made an equally historic visit, becoming the first Turkish foreign minister to visit Greece in 40 years. In October, however, Greece withdrew from a joint NATO military exercise in the Aegean, after it accused Turkey of preventing Greek aircraft from flying over the disputed islands of Limnos and Ikaria. This followed a joint NATO military exercise with Greek and Turkish troops on a Greek beach in June, which had been considered to be a mark of considerable progress in Greek-Turkish relations. In February 2001 the Greek parliament decreed a 'Genocide Day' to commemorate the Turkish assault on the Greek community in eastern Turkey by Atatürk's forces in 1922. However, in April 2001 both Turkey and Greece announced major reductions in their weapons-procurement programmes, and in May Greece announced measures to improve the rights of its ethnic Turks (mainly in Thrace). In June the two countries discussed the possibility of allowing Turkish nationals to visit Greek islands in the Aegean for day trips without the need for visas, and the Minister of Foreign Affairs, İsmail Cem, received his Greek counterpart, Georgios Papandreou, to discuss friendship-building measures such as the demining of their mutual border and co-hosting the 2008 European Football Championship. In November 2001 Turkey and Greece signed an agreement that allowed Greece to repatriate illegal Turkish immigrants.

None the less, Cyprus continued to overshadow bilateral relations, and in May 2001 Cem warned that there would be 'no limits' to Turkey's response were Cyprus to be admitted to EU membership before a political settlement had been reached; in November Ecevit warned that Turkey could annex the 'TRNC' if this were to occur. In February 2002 the Turkish and Greek foreign ministers recommenced talks, following the resumption of negotiations between the Greek and Turkish Cypriot sides on the island. In mid-March Turkey and Greece discussed ongoing disputes over the Aegean Sea, including the control of the continental shelves and the resources beneath them. Later in the month the two Governments signed an agreement to build a 285-km natural gas pipeline from Ankara to Komotini, Greece, thereby allowing Iranian gas to flow to the EU via the existing Tabriz–Ankara pipeline. In October Greece offered its support for the scheduling of EU accession negotiations with Turkey.

Following the elections to the TGNA in November 2002, Reçep Tayyip Erdoğan stated that a final peace agreement over Cyprus would accelerate Turkey's chances of joining the EU. Erdoğan, whose political priority was Turkey's EU membership, was increasingly in conflict with Turkish Cypriot leader Rauf Denktaş's unyielding stance on reaching a political solution. In January 2003 Erdoğan publicly criticized Denktaş and stated that he was in favour of a new policy for Cyprus, with a view to achieving a solution by 28 February 2003 in order to allow the 'TRNC' to join the EU in 2004 at the same time as the Greek part of the island. During late 2002 and early 2003 the Turkish- and Greek-Cypriot leaders had made significant progress towards reaching a final agreement, which would permit the entire island to accede to the EU on 1 May 2004. However, negotiations on the peace plan failed in March 2003 (see the chapter on Cyprus). Following further UN-sponsored discussions in New York, on 13 February 2004 agreement was reached on a reunification plan based on proposals drafted by the UN Secretary-General, Kofi Annan. The Greek Cypriot President, Tassos Papadopoulos, and Denktaş, resumed UN-sponsored negotiations in the Cypriot capital, Nicosia, on 19 February. Greece and Turkey joined the negotiations later in March; however, both Papadopoulos and Denktaş subsequently opposed a final resolution, which was to be submitted for approval by both the Greek- and Turkish-Cypriot communities at a referendum. On 24 April the reunification plan was endorsed by Turkish Cypriots by 64.9% of votes cast at the referendum, but rejected by Greek Cypriots by an overwhelming majority of 75.8% of the votes; consequently, only the Greek part of Cyprus was admitted to the EU on 1 May. EU officials subsequently announced measures to alleviate the economic sanctions in force against the 'TRNC'.

In April 2005 the Turkish Cypriot Prime Minister, Mehmet Ali Talat, who strongly supported reunification of the island and full participation in the EU, was elected to the 'TRNC' presidency, replacing Denktaş. In late January 2008 the Greek Prime Minister, Dr Konstantinos (Kostas) Karamanlis, undertook an official three-day visit to Turkey—the first such visit by a Greek premier since 1959. In February 2008 Papadopoulos was defeated at the first round of the Greek Cypriot presidential elections, and at the second round Demetris Christofias was elected to succeed him. It was strongly hoped that the election of Christofias, who became the EU's first communist head of state, would facilitate the procurement of a swift and lasting resolution to Cyprus's long-running division, and, therefore, prove advantageous to Turkish hopes of EU accession. In mid-March it was announced that Christofias was to meet with Talat in Nicosia in order to discuss the resumption of reunification talks. The announcement followed a meeting, held earlier in March, between the two leaders' aides, during which convergence was reported to have been reached on a number of disputed issues. At their discussions in Nicosia on 21 March, Christofias and Talat agreed to: open the Ledra Street crossing as a symbol of reconciliation between their two communities (this occurred on 3 April); establish a number of working groups and technical committees; and devise a precise agenda for UN-sponsored reunification negotiations to take place. A subsequent meeting between Christofias and Talat was scheduled for June.

Following the 1980 military coup, the EC-Turkish Association Council (which had been established in 1963) was suspended, together with all community aid to the country. Turkey was readmitted to associate membership of the EC in September 1986, but failed to gain access to the suspended EC aid or to extend the rights of the large number of Turkish workers in Europe. In April 1987 Turkey made a formal application to become a full member of the EC. In December 1989 the application was effectively rejected, at least until 1993, by the Commission of the European Communities. The Commission cited factors including Turkey's unsatisfactory human rights record, high rate of inflation, dependence upon the rural population and inadequate social security provisions as falling short of EC expectations. During informal discussions in 1993 representatives of the EC reiterated their concern at abuses of human rights in Turkey and the lack of progress in the political negotiations regarding Cyprus; however, they recognized the strategic importance of Turkey's role as a stable regional influence.

The Turkish Government began to implement measures to construct a customs union with the EU, which was to become effective on 1 January 1995. Human rights issues remained the main obstacle to securing an agreement, and in December 1994 the customs union was postponed on these grounds. In February 1995 Greece withdrew its veto on the customs union, having received assurance on the accession of Cyprus to the EU, and the agreement was signed in March; however, it was to be subject to ratification by the European Parliament. The Turkish Government subsequently pursued efforts to introduce new democratization legislation and to secure the support of European leaders for the customs union by extending guarantees on human rights and treatment of its Kurdish population. The final terms of the arrangement were agreed at a meeting of the EU-Turkish Association Council in October, and were approved by the European Parliament in December. The EU was expected to provide a total of ECU 1,800m. over a five-year period, in order to assist the implementation of the new trade regime and to alleviate any initial hardships resulting from the agreement. The customs union came into effect on 1 January 1996. Its implementation was, however, delayed, owing to Greek opposition to the release of ECU 375m. in aid, claiming that Turkish action in the Aegean was a violation of the agreement. In July Greece withdrew its opposition to Turkey's participation in an EU-Mediterranean assistance programme, although the block on funds from the customs union remained in effect. Throughout 1996 the Turkish Government criticized the EU for its failure to adhere to the terms of the economic agreement. In January 1997 Turkey warned that it would disrupt any expansion of NATO if the EU refused to consider the Turkish membership application. Previously, Turkey had prevented the use of NATO facilities by members of Western European Union, owing to Greek opposition to Turkey's full participation in the regional defence grouping.

Relations with the EU were tense in 1997 as the next group of EU applicants was selected. In December, following EU announcements that Turkey would not be invited to join the EU, but that it would be invited to a newly created EU Conference, which was to include both EU and non-EU states, Turkey stated that it would not attend such a conference and that it would also cease negotiations on Cyprus, human rights and the Aegean disputes. It further threatened to boycott EU goods and to withdraw its application to the EU if it was not included in a list of candidates by June. On 20 December Turkey announced a six-month freeze in relations with the EU. The EU later announced it was withholding all aid to Turkey for 1998, owing to the situation in the south-east of the country and its human rights problems. Turkey officially declined its invitation to the EU Conference in March 1998 and in May also declined to attend a scheduled meeting of the EU-Turkish Association Council. Relations with France deteriorated in May when the French National Assembly adopted a motion recognizing the Turkish 'genocide' against the Armenians in 1915–23; a number of bilateral military and commercial contracts were suspended as a result. However, in February 2000 the French Senate decided not to place the draft law recognizing the Armenian 'genocide' (approved by the National Assembly in 1998) on its agenda for discussion.

In October 1999 an EU report declared Turkey to be a suitable candidate to join that body, although Turkey stated that it would not accept any extraordinary conditions attached to such a candidacy, particularly with relation to Öcalan and the Kurdish problem. A number of EU members offerred their support to Turkey in late 1999, including Greece and Italy. In December Turkey was invited to attend the EU summit in Helsinki, Finland, and to accept formal status as a candidate for membership. The Government initially objected, owing to attached conditions concerning Cyprus and the Aegean dispute with Greece, but following a visit to Turkey by Javier Solana, the Secretary-General of the Council of the European Union, decided to accept. It announced at that time that it would seek an end to its territorial disputes with Greece by 2004, the deadline set by the EU for a review.

In August 2000 Turkey signed the International Covenant of Civil and Political Rights and the International Covenant on Economic, Social and Cultural Rights. This was described as a positive step by the EU in its progress to accession report on Turkey in November, although it pointed out that Turkey had not yet acceded to a number of other major human rights instruments, such as the abolition of the death penalty and the Convention on the Elimination of All Forms of Racial Discrimination. The report concluded that Turkey did not yet meet the Copenhagen criteria (which state that a country must have achieved 'stability of institutions guaranteeing democracy, the rule of law, human rights and respect for and protection of minorities'), thus making accession negotiations impossible, and described the overall human rights record in Turkey as worrying. It also stated that although Turkey had the basic features of a democratic system, it was slow to implement institutional reforms. Accession was also conditional on a satisfactory settlement of the Cyprus problem. This condition led to the Turkish withdrawal from the UN-sponsored proximity talks in protest. Prime Minister Ecevit accused the EU of 'deception' over Turkey's membership application, stating that it had reneged on a promise not to link Turkey's application to a resolution of the Cyprus problem and disputes with Greece over territorial rights in the Aegean Sea. A reworking of the Cyprus condition was later approved by Turkey; however, further tension was caused by Turkey's obstruction of an EU-NATO agreement enabling the EU's planned Rapid Reaction Force to use NATO assets, despite

Turkey's offer to contribute up to 6,000 troops to the Rapid Reaction Force.

Meanwhile, the Armenian 'genocide' question continued to provoke tension between Turkey and the international community. In April 2000 Turkey complained to Israel after the Israeli education minister stated that he believed school pupils should be taught of the 'genocide' of the Armenians; the minister was speaking at a meeting to mark the 85th anniversary of the massacre. In October the TGNA threatened not to renew the USA's mandate to use a Turkish airbase if the US Congress backed a draft resolution which referred to the killing of the 1.5m. Armenians in Turkey in 1915–23 as 'genocide'. Following intervention by President Bill Clinton, the House of Representatives agreed to withdraw the resolution. The European Parliament adopted a resolution in November that formally accused Turkey of genocide against Armenians in 1915 (at the same time it also called on Turkey to pull its forces out of the 'TRNC'). Turkey reacted angrily, with the FP proposing a legislative investigation 'with the aim of removing wrong and biased opinions'. Relations with France were, however, more seriously damaged in January 2001, after the French National Assembly unanimously voted to recognize the 1915–23 massacre of Armenians under the Ottoman Empire as 'genocide', against the wishes of the Government. In November 2000 the French Senate had already voted to recognize the massacre as genocide; none the less, the French Government attempted to reassure Turkey that bilateral relations remained intact. Following the National Assembly vote, however, Ecevit stated that the French action would damage relations and recalled Turkey's ambassador to France immediately after the vote for consultations. In late January 2001 Turkey cancelled a surveillance satellite contract with a French firm, and another French company was barred from tendering for a major defence contract. Turkey also removed a French telecommunications group from the list of bidders for the privatization of the state-owned telecommunications company. The Government further announced plans to erect a 'genocide' monument to the 1.5m. Algerians killed in the 1954–62 war of independence against the French.

Relations between Turkey and the EU received a setback in early May 2001 when the ECHR ruled that Turkey had grossly violated the human rights of thousands of Greek Cypriots during its invasion, and subsequent occupation of northern Cyprus since 1974. The court highlighted the failure of the Turkish Government to investigate the fate of missing Greek Cypriots, and their forcible eviction from the north and the subsequent confiscation of their property.

In late May 2001 Turkey nominally agreed to grant the EU's Rapid Reaction Force access to NATO assets for future operations. Although Turkey would be consulted on such matters, it would not have the same participation rights or veto powers as the existing 15 EU members. However, Turkish officials remained dissatisfied at the arrangements, having lobbied strongly for a greater influence in EU security planning. Turkey also feared that an upsurge of violence in Cyprus would necessitate the deployment of the Rapid Reaction Force on the island, placing the EU directly against itself, and had unsuccessfully sought guarantees against such an eventuality. In December Turkey finally reached agreement with the EU regarding the Rapid Reaction Force after months of British diplomacy.

In August 2001, meanwhile, the ECHR ruled that the Government's decision to ban the Islamist FP did not violate human rights laws. In October the TGNA passed constitutional amendments designed to facilitate EU membership but stopped short of abolishing the death penalty, a crucial EU demand. The issue of capital punishment placed the EU at odds with the ultra-nationalist MHP in the ruling coalition, which had pledged to exact the death penalty imposed on PKK leader Abdullah Öcalan. In August 2002 the EU welcomed the TGNA's vote to abolish the death penalty in peacetime, as part of a broader package of reforms, and, similarly, reacted positively to the commutation of Öcalan's death sentence to life imprisonment in October of that year (see above). The new AKP Government elected in November pledged to accelerate efforts to join the EU. However, in that month Valéry Giscard d'Estaing, the Chairman of the Convention on the Future of Europe, stated publicly that Turkey should never be allowed to join the EU, and that its accession would mean the 'end of the European Union'. Senior EU officials distanced themselves from the remarks, which were also dismissed by Erdoğan. At the EU summit in Copenhagen, Denmark, in December, EU leaders agreed to delay negotiations on Turkish membership until after December 2004, and to resume discussions then only if Turkey had fulfilled all the entry obligations. Several EU members, notably France and Germany, remained less enthusiastic about Turkish membership, citing its poor human rights record, which Turkey again pledged to improve. Erdoğan warned that continuing delays to negotiations and attempts to exclude Turkey from the EU could cause increased anti-Muslim sentiments against the organization.

A further complication to Turkish ambitions for EU membership emerged with the failure of a UN plan for the reunification of Cyprus in April 2004 (see above). The resultant accession of only Greek Cypriot Cyprus to the EU on 1 May presented complications for Turkey's EU aspirations, although the Greek Cypriot Government declared that it would not veto Turkey's membership application, provided that it met the standards stipulated by the EU. An official visit to Greece by Erdoğan in May—the first by a Turkish premier in 16 years—reflected the improvement in relations between the two countries. An EU summit in Brussels in June reaffirmed that a decision would be taken in December on whether Turkey had made sufficient progress on the EU's criteria for membership and that formal accession negotiations would be initiated if standards were considered to have been met. However, severe doubts about Turkey's qualifications had been presented in a European Parliament resolution, which had been adopted overwhelmingly in April, drawing attention to Turkey's continued use of torture, to the persecution of minorities and other contraventions.

Nevertheless, in October 2004 the European Commission announced its approval of Turkey's qualification for accession negotiations, on condition that reforms continued. In many EU member states, however, there was increasing popular opposition to the admission of Turkey, especially in Germany and France, where the opposition was believed to reflect concern over the accession of a predominantly Muslim country; some favoured an option that Turkey be offered 'privileged member' status, rather than full membership. On 17 December the EU extended a provisional invitation to Turkey to commence accession negotiations on 3 October 2005, subject to the Turkish Government's fulfilment of a number of criteria, including continued progress in political and economic reforms. Erdoğan accepted an EU requirement to sign a customs accord with member states by that date, but insisted that the protocol would not constitute official Turkish recognition of the authorities of Greek Cyprus; instead he agreed to a compromise arrangement, whereby Turkey made a commitment for future recognition. The British Prime Minister welcomed the agreement; however, both the French and Austrian Governments pledged to conduct national referendums on Turkish entry, while a demonstration in protest at Turkish membership was conducted in Italy. In June 2005 the German Bundestag (Federal Assembly) became the latest EU legislature to attract Turkish anger by condemning the Armenian 'genocide' and accusing the Turkish Government of failing to address the issue.

In July 2005, pending an EU decision on the opening of accession negotiations in October, the Turkish Government signed the requisite customs protocol with Cyprus and the other nine new EU member states, but appended a declaration reaffirming that the accord did not constitute official recognition of Greek Cyprus. In September EU member states adopted a draft declaration stating that Turkish recognition of Cyprus was necessary to the accession process, but without stipulating a date for this (thereby posing no obstacle to the beginning of negotiations). At the beginning of October intensive debate took place between EU member states to resolve the impasse over Austria's insistence that Turkey be offered the lesser option of 'privileged partnership' (to which the Turkish Government remained opposed), rather than full membership. Austria withdrew its veto to the admission of Turkey, after Croatia was unexpectedly declared eligible to enter into membership negotiations (see the chapter on Croatia). Turkey's accession negotiations with the EU were officially approved on 3 October, and opened on the following day.

In early November 2005 an EU report, while welcoming Turkey's economic performance (see Economic Affairs), criticized a lack of progress in political reforms, citing continued human rights violations, including torture, and the necessity for further judicial reforms. Furthermore, the subsequent reluctance of the Turkish authorities to open ports and airports to Greek Cypriot-registered traffic by the end of 2006, in adherence to the customs protocol and as a condition to progress in the accession negotiations, prompted criticism from EU officials and repeated threats from the Greek Cypriot Government to veto

Turkey's membership. Nevertheless, EU ministers responsible for foreign affairs formally opened the first chapter of accession negotiations with Turkey in June. Attempts by the Finnish presidency of the EU to broker a deal under which the EU would take charge of the port of Famagusta in the 'TRNC' while the nearby town of Varosha would be returned to Greek Cypriot control were eventually abandoned in late November. Meanwhile, relations with France worsened in October 2006, when the French National Assembly endorsed a bill making it a crime to deny that Armenians suffered genocide at the hands of Turks in 1915–23; the vote was criticized by the EU. In the same month the EU advised Turkey that safeguarding freedom of expression in the country was to be regarded as a matter of urgency. During 2005–06 court proceedings were initiated against several prominent novelists who were accused of 'insulting Turkishness' under Article 301 of the penal code.

In late November 2006 the European Commission recommended the suspension of negotiations on eight of 35 chapters of the accession talks (these included trade, financial services and transport), a decision that was endorsed at the summit meeting of the European Council in early December. At the end of December Turkey pledged to implement a six-year 'roadmap' and reform programme and to continue implementing all the required judicial and military reforms, even in those areas where negotiations had been suspended. In March 2007 the EU resumed negotiations with Turkey on the accession chapter relating to enterprise and industry. However, in June, following the inauguration as French President of Nicolas Sarkozy in the previous month, France blocked the commencement of negotiations on the accession chapter relating to economic and monetary union, apparently in a further move to prevent Turkey's eventual accession to the EU. (French officials later asserted that they were not opposed to the commencement of further negotiating chapters with Turkey, but that they believed that all options, including that of 'preferential partnership', should be considered.) Later in June the EU did extend membership discussions with Turkey on two new, smaller chapters concerning financial controls and statistics. In November the European Commission urged the Turkish Government to accelerate its political and social reform process, citing the treatment of the minority Kurdish population and Article 301 as particular areas where further progress was required. Accession talks concerning health and consumer affairs, as well as inter-European transport links, were initiated in mid-December. The TGNA approved amendments to Article 301 at the end of April 2008, although critics of the Government countered that the changes were not as far-reaching as they had hoped. Under the newly revised legislation, it would become a crime to insult 'the Turkish nation' rather than 'Turkishness', while the maximum sentence for someone convicted of such a crime was to be shortened from three to two years.

Following the formal dissolution of the USSR in December 1991, the Turkish Government sought to further its political, economic and cultural influence in the Caucasus and Central Asia, in particular with Azerbaijan, Kazakhstan, Kyrgyzstan, Turkmenistan and Uzbekistan, all of which share ethno-linguistic ties with Turkey. Following the outbreak of war between Armenia and Azerbaijan in 1991, Turkey blockaded Armenia and provided support to its 'Turkic' ally, Azerbaijan. In April 1992 Prime Minister Demirel undertook an official visit to several former Soviet republics, pledging aid of more than US $1,000m. in the form of credits for the purchase of Turkish goods and contracts. At the same time programmes broadcast by the Turkish national television company began to be relayed, by satellite, to the region. In June leaders of 11 nations, including Turkey, Greece, Albania and six former Soviet republics, established the Organization of the Black Sea Economic Co-operation (see p. 367), and expressed their commitment to promoting greater co-operation with regard to transport, energy, information, communications and ecology. In October 1994 a meeting of the heads of state of Turkey, Azerbaijan, Turkmenistan, Uzbekistan, Kazakhstan and Kyrgyzstan took place in İstanbul, in an effort to develop and improve relations among the 'Turkic' republics. Summit meetings have subsequently been convened each year. In the late 1990s Turkey sought to encourage Western firms to build a new petroleum pipeline from Baku, Azerbaijan, to the Turkish port of Ceyhan, thereby allowing the transportation of petroleum from the Caspian Sea to the Mediterranean, via Azerbaijan and Georgia. Such a scheme would also increase Turkey's importance to the EU by making it the centre of the Transport Corridor Europe–Caucasus–Asia (TRACECA) project. Despite the cost of the pipeline, construction began in June 2002. In October 2000 President Sezer signed military co-operation pacts with Kyrgyzstan and Uzbekistan, allowing Turkey to train and equip their armed forces. In mid-2001 work began on a new natural gas pipeline from Dzhubga, Russia, to Samsun, Turkey, beneath the Black Sea, which would increase Turkey's dependency on Russian natural gas. During a significant visit to Turkey in December 2004 the Russian President, Vladimir Putin, signed co-operation agreements in the fields of trade, defence and finance.

In late 1995 a long-standing dispute with Syria and Iraq concerning the water supply from the Euphrates and Tigris rivers re-emerged as a major source of tension in Turkey's external relations. (Hostilities with Syria had already intensified during the year over that country's apparent support for the PKK, with the Turkish Government accusing Syria of supplying armaments to the separatist organization.) In December Syria issued a formal protest at the construction of a new hydroelectric dam on the Euphrates river (as part of the extensive southern Anatolia project—GAP) arguing that it would adversely affect the supply of water flowing into Syria. Further protests by Syria and Iraq that Turkey was storing their share of water from the two rivers and restricting flow, in contravention of previous agreements, resulted in a ruling, in March 1996, by the Council of the Arab League that the waters of the rivers should be shared equally between the three countries. In September 1997 President Demirel appealed for talks with Syria and Iraq on the use of the waters of the Euphrates. In August 1998, however, the Government refused to revive water talks with Syria and Iraq, citing issues that had first to be improved between the countries, primarily that of terrorism. Relations between Syria and Turkey improved during 1999 and in October officials from the two countries reportedly agreed to open a new border crossing. However, in January 2000 Turkey appealed to the USA not to remove Syria from its list of nations accused of sponsoring terrorism, until such time as all PKK bases had been removed from Syria, and ruled out any concessions on the water issue in order to aid talks between Israel and Syria. In March Turkey and Syria announced a new framework for bilateral relations and discussed the basic principles that would apply to them, although in that month Turkey warned against the use of a map, prepared by Syria for use at a trade fair, which showed the Turkish region of Hatay as Syrian territory. A major rapprochement materialized in early 2002 when Turkey signed an agreement with Syria allowing for joint military exercises. In early 2003 Turkey and Syria agreed to co-operate in bringing about a peaceful solution to the crisis over Iraq's alleged weapons of mass destruction and the US pursuit of regime change in Iraq. President Bashar al-Assad became the first Syrian Head of State to undertake an official visit to Turkey in January 2004.

In early 1996 Turkey signed a new military and intelligence co-operation agreement with Israel, which permitted the use of Turkish airbases and airspace for military training purposes. The pact stemmed from common concerns about Iran, Iraq, and Syria, and received support from the USA, a strong ally of both Turkey and Israel. The Arab League denounced the agreement as 'an act of aggression'. Business deals quickly followed, especially those concerning the supply of Turkish water to Israel. However, the gradual improvement in Turkey's relations with its Arab neighbours from 2000 made the pact with Israel less significant, and, in response to the increasing violence between Israelis and Palestinians in the West Bank and Gaza, Prime Minister Ecevit in April 2002 accused Israel of 'genocide' against the Palestinians. None the less, in August Turkey signed an agreement with Israel according to which it would sell the latter 50m. cu m of water every year for the next 20 years. In May 2004 relations with Israel became further strained, when Prime Minister Erdoğan condemned an Israeli offensive in Gaza. In January 2005, however, the Turkish Deputy Prime Minister and Minister of Foreign Affairs made an official visit to Israel—the first by a Turkish politician since the AKP Government was elected in November 2002.

In April 1996 the Turkish and Iranian authorities ordered the expulsion of diplomatic personnel following accusations of Iranian involvement in Islamist terrorist attacks committed in Turkey in the early 1990s. In August relations with Iran were strengthened by the conclusion of an agreement providing for the construction of a 320-km pipeline between the two countries and the export of substantial supplies of natural gas from Iran by 1999 (later revised to 1998). In December 1996 the Presidents of Turkey and Iran agreed to pursue greater economic and security co-operation. A trade agreement was concluded granting each other the status of most favoured nation. In February 1997 the Iranian ambassador to Turkey provoked a diplomatic crisis by advocating the introduction of Islamic law in Turkey. Criticism of the actions of the Turkish military by an Iranian consul-general later in that month resulted in both men being asked to leave the country. Iran responded by expelling two Turkish diplomats. However, both countries immediately undertook diplomatic initiatives to restore relations, and in March it was agreed that all bilateral agreements were to be pursued. Following negotiations, it was announced in September that full diplomatic relations were to be resumed.

In October 1998 Iran and Turkey established a committee to demarcate their joint border; they later signed a memorandum to increase customs co-operation at their main border crossing. In February 1999 the two countries agreed to implement measures aimed at more effective co-operation on border security. In June a meeting of the Turkish-Iranian border committee was held for the first time since 1994; a number of issues were discussed and it was agreed that the committee should meet every year. In July, however, the Turkish chargé d'affaires was twice summoned to the Iranian Ministry of Foreign Affairs following the alleged bombing of an Iranian border region by Turkey in which five people died, although Turkey claimed that its air force had bombed Kurdish targets in Iraq not Iran. In August a meeting of the Turkish-Iranian security commission ended with the signing of a memorandum of understanding in which the two countries agreed to combat illegal organizations within their respective territories. In October Turkey announced it would contribute to compensation for the Iranian bomb damage; a Turkish report into the incident concluded that Turkey had bombed Iraq not Iran, although some people with Iranian citizenship, living in northern Iraq, might have been affected. In October Iran's President Muhammad Khatami welcomed the improvement in ties with Turkey, although in that month Iran expressed concern about Turkey's co-operation with Israel. In December Turkey protested to Iran following the death of a soldier in a clash on the border. In January 2000 the Iranian and Turkish ministers responsible for foreign affairs held talks in Ankara and signed a memorandum of understanding to promote bilateral co-operation. During 2001 both countries sought to improve co-operation in combating drugs-trafficking and organized crime. However, rising tensions between Azerbaijan and Iran over claims to the Caspian Sea, Turkey's strong support for Azerbaijan, its continuing alliance with Israel, and competition for influence in the Caucasus and Central Asia, threatened to bring occasional tensions to the relationship. In early 2003 both Turkey and Iran were seeking to increase their influence in Iraq during the build-up of US military forces in the region, and after the subsequent collapse of the regime of Saddam Hussain, Turkey sought to develop ties with Iraq's ethnic Turkoman minority, with Iran favouring the majority Shi'a population.

Government

Under the Constitution approved by referendum in November 1982 (with subsequent amendments), legislative power is vested in the unicameral Turkish Grand National Assembly (TGNA), with 550 deputies, who are elected by universal adult suffrage for a five-year term. Executive power is vested in the President, to be elected by the TGNA for a seven-year term and empowered to appoint a Prime Minister and senior members of the judiciary, the Central Bank and broadcasting organizations; to dissolve the TGNA; and to declare a state of emergency entailing rule by decree. For administrative purposes, Turkey comprises 81 provinces and 2,074 municipalities.

Defence

Turkey joined the North Atlantic Treaty Organization (NATO) in 1952. Military service in the army lasts for 15 months. The total strength of the active armed forces, as assessed at November 2007, was 510,600 (including 359,500 conscripts), comprising an army of 402,000, a navy of 48,600 and an air force of 60,000. There was a gendarmerie numbering 150,000 and a coast guard of 3,250 (including 1,400 conscripts). Reserve forces totalled 378,700 in the armed forces and 50,000 in the gendarmerie. In April 2005 the Governments of Greece and Turkey announced military co-operation measures, including the establishment of direct communications between two air force bases, in an effort to ease tension concerning air space violations over the Aegean Sea. Increased military co-operation between Greece and Turkey was agreed in December 2007; the new measures included the formation of a joint military unit for multinational peace-keeping missions. Defence expenditure for 2007 was budgeted at about US $10,880m.

Economic Affairs

In 2006, according to estimates by the World Bank, Turkey's gross national income (GNI), measured at average 2004–06 prices, was US $393,903m., equivalent to $5,400 per head (or $9,060 per head on an international purchasing-power parity basis). During 1996–2006, it was estimated, the population increased at an average annual rate of 1.5%, while gross domestic product (GDP) per head rose, in real terms, by an average of 2.5% per year. Overall GDP increased, in real terms, by an annual average of 4.0% in 1996–2006. According to official figures, GDP increased by 4.5% in 2007.

Agriculture (including forestry and fishing) contributed 8.7% to GDP in 2007, and engaged 27.3% of the employed population in 2006. The country is self-sufficient in most basic foodstuffs. The principal agricultural exports are cotton, tobacco, wheat, fruit and nuts. Other important crops are barley, maize, sugar beet, potatoes and onions. The raising of sheep, goats, cattle and poultry is also an important economic activity. During 1998–2007 agricultural GDP increased by an annual average of 0.4%; however, the agricultural sector contracted by 6.8% in 2007, owing to adverse conditions engendered by drought.

Industry (including mining, manufacturing, construction and power) contributed 27.8% to GDP in 2007, and engaged 25.4% of the employed population in 2006. During 1998–2007 industrial GDP increased by an annual average of 4.3%; growth in the industrial sector was 5.4% in 2007.

Mining contributed 1.4% to GDP in 2007, and engaged 0.6% of the employed population in 2006. Chromium, copper and borax are the major mineral exports. Coal, petroleum, natural gas, bauxite, iron ore, manganese and sulphur are also mined. The development and expansion of Turkey's gold-mining facilities was in progress in the mid-2000s. During 1998–2007 mining GDP increased by an annual average of 0.6%; growth in the mining sector was reported at 8.1% in 2007.

Manufacturing contributed 18.7% to GDP in 2007, and employed 18.7% of the employed population in 2006. The most important branches, measured by gross value of output, are textiles, food-processing, petroleum refineries, iron and steel, and industrial chemicals. During 1998–2007 manufacturing GDP increased by an annual average of 4.2%; growth in the manufacturing sector was 5.4% in 2007.

Energy is derived principally from thermal power plants. In 2004 41.3% of energy was derived from natural gas, 30.6% from hydroelectric power, 22.9% from coal and a further 5.1% from petroleum. The energy sector contributed 2.1% to GDP in 2007, and employed 0.4% of the employed population in 2006. Total domestic output of crude petroleum and natural gas accounts for some 12% of the country's hydrocarbon requirements. Imports of crude petroleum comprised 19.9% of the value of total imports in 2007. A major development project for south-east Anatolia, scheduled for completion in 2010, was to increase Turkey's energy production by 70% and to irrigate 1.6m. ha of uncultivable or inadequately irrigated land, by constructing dams and hydroelectric plants on the Tigris and Euphrates rivers and their tributaries. In July 2006 the second largest petroleum pipeline in the world—transporting oil between Baku, Azerbaijan, and the Turkish terminal at Ceyhan, via Tbilisi, Georgia—was formally inaugurated. In 2005 a new 'blue stream' natural gas pipeline running between Russia and Turkey under the Black Sea was also opened. In early 2006 the Government confirmed that the country's first nuclear installation was to be constructed in the Black Sea province of Sinop, with its completion envisaged for 2012; two further nuclear power plants were scheduled to be built by 2015.

The services sector contributed 63.5% of GDP in 2007, and engaged 47.3% of the employed population in 2006. Tourism is one of Turkey's fastest growing sources of revenue. Total tourist arrivals increased to more than 23.3m. in 2007, according to provisional figures, and tourists generated some US $16,851m. in revenue in 2006. Remittances from Turkish workers abroad also make an important contribution to the economy, amounting to $2,835m. in 2001. During 1998–2007 the GDP of the services sector increased by an annual average of 4.9%; growth in the sector was 6.3% in 2007.

In 2006 Turkey recorded a visible trade deficit of US $41,238m., and there was a deficit of $32,774m. on the current account of the balance of payments. In 2007 the principal source of imports (13.8%) was Russia; other major suppliers were Germany, the People's Republic of China and Italy. Germany was the principal market for exports in that year (11.2%); other important purchasers were the United Kingdom, Italy and France. Exports in 2007 were dominated by machinery and transport equipment, basic manufactures (mainly textiles), and clothing and accessories. In that year the principal imports were machinery and transport equipment, mineral fuels (particularly crude petroleum), basic manufactures and chemical products.

In 2005 there was a budgetary deficit of 3,995m. new Turkish liras. Turkey's external debt at the end of that year was US $171,059m., of which $62,580m. was long-term public debt. In that year the cost of debt-servicing was equivalent to 39.1% of the value of exports of goods and services. The annual rate of inflation averaged 56.2% in 1992–2005. Consumer prices increased by 9.6% in 2006 and by 8.8% in 2007. In 2006 the rate of unemployment was estimated at 9.9%.

Turkey is a member of numerous international and regional organizations, including the Developing Eight (D-8, see p. 412), the Economic Co-operation Organization (ECO, see p. 238), and the Organization of the Black Sea Economic Co-operation (see p. 367). Turkey was accepted as a candidate for membership of the European Union (EU, see p. 244) in December 1999. (For details regarding Turkey's accession negotiations with the EU, see Recent History.)

Turkey's economy has been afflicted by persistently high rates of inflation, an expanding public sector deficit, ongoing political instability and a poor rate of tax collection. The country experienced a severe financial crisis in November 2000 and again in February 2001, resulting in soaring interest rates and an effective devaluation of the lira. In April 2007 the main share price index and the Turkish lira again declined sharply, amid the political instability surrounding the presidential election (see Recent History). The Turkish authorities have in recent years, and particularly since the election in late 2002 of the pro-European AKP, made the focus of economic planning the achievement of the levels of macroeconomic stability required for attaining membership of the EU. In November 2005 an EU report granted Turkey the status of a functioning market economy, a declaration that contributed to stimulating investor confidence. The Government's national development plan for 2007–13, approved by the TGNA in July 2006, had this as its principal aim. The plan set the target for average annual GDP growth at 7%. At the beginning of 2005 the Government established a new monetary unit, the new Turkish lira, as part of ongoing efforts to restrain inflation (the old currency remained in circulation until the end of the year). In May 2005 a three-year stand-by arrangement was approved with the IMF to support the Government's economic and financial programme. According to the IMF's sixth review under the arrangement, carried out in November 2007, the Turkish economy had strengthened significantly since the 2001 crisis. The current account deficit, although higher than desired as a result of strong domestic demand growth, higher international oil prices and lower receipts from tourism, appeared to have peaked in 2006, at 7.9% of gross national income; the previously high net public debt ratio was falling steadily; and growth rates, although predicted to decline slightly, stood close to the level predicted under the IMF programme. However, inflation, despite falling massively from its 2001 level of some 70%, continued to be a problem, standing at 8.8% in 2007 (significantly higher than the target rate of 4%).

Education

Legislation took effect in 1997 to increase the duration of compulsory primary education from five to eight years, for children between six and 14 years of age. All state education up to University or Higher Institute levels is co-educational and provided free of charge. The number of primary schools, according to provisional figures, reached 34,093 in 2007/08, compared with 12,511 in 1950. Secondary education, which lasts for at least three years, may be undertaken in general high schools, open high schools or vocational and technical high schools. According to provisional figures, there were 3,830 general high schools in 2007/08. In 2004/05, according to UNESCO estimates, enrolment at primary schools included 89.4% of pupils in the relevant age group, while 66.8% of pupils in the appropriate age group were enrolled at secondary schools. In 2005/06 almost 2.2m. students attended 1,306 higher education institutes. Government expenditure on education was budgeted at about US $6,700m in 2004.

Public Holidays

2008: 1 January (New Year's Day), 23 April (National Sovereignty and Children's Day), 19 May (Commemoration of Atatürk, and Youth and Sports Day), 30 August (Victory Day), 1–3 October* (Şeker Bayram—End of Ramadan), 29 October (Republic Day), 9–12 December* (Kurban Bayram—Feast of the Sacrifice).
2009: 1 January (New Year's Day), 23 April (National Sovereignty and Children's Day), 19 May (Commemoration of Atatürk, and Youth and Sports Day), 30 August (Victory Day), 20–22 September* (Şeker Bayram—End of Ramadan), 29 October (Republic Day), 27–30 November* (Kurban Bayram—Feast of the Sacrifice).

* These holidays are dependent on the Islamic lunar calendar and may vary by one or two days from the dates given.

Weights and Measures

The metric system is in force.

Statistical Survey

Sources (unless otherwise stated): T.C. Başbakanlık Türkiye İstatistik Kurumu (Turkish Statistical Institute), Necatibey Cad. 114, 06580-Yücetepe/Ankara; tel. (312) 400410; internet www.turkstat.gov.tr.

Area and Population

AREA, POPULATION AND DENSITY

Area (sq km)	
Land	769,604
Inland water	13,958
Total	783,562*
Population (census results)	
21 October 1990	56,473,035
22 October 2000	
Males	34,346,735
Females	33,457,192
Total	67,803,927
Population (official estimates at mid-year)	
2004	71,152,000
2005	72,065,000
2006	72,974,000
Density (per sq km) at mid-2006	94.8†

* 302,535 sq miles.
† Land area only.

PROVINCES
(2000 census)

	Area (sq km)	Population	Density (per sq km)
Adana	14,046	1,849,478	131.7
Adıyaman	7,606	623,811	82.0
Afyon	14,719	812,416	55.2
Ağri	11,499	528,744	46.0
Aksaray	7,966	396,084	49.7
Amasya	5,704	365,231	64.0
Ankara	25,402	4,007,860	157.8
Antalya	20,791	1,719,751	82.7
Ardahan	4,968	133,756	26.9
Artvin	7,367	191,934	26.1
Aydın	7,904	950,757	120.3
Balıkesir	14,473	1,076,347	74.4
Bartın	2,080	184,178	88.5
Batman	4,659	456,734	98.0
Bayburt	3,739	97,358	26.0
Bilecik	4,307	194,326	45.1
Bingöl	8,254	253,739	30.7

TURKEY

—continued	Area (sq km)	Population	Density (per sq km)
Bitlis	7,095	388,678	54.8
Bolu	8,323	270,654	32.5
Burdur	7,135	256,803	36.0
Bursa	10,886	2,125,140	195.2
Çanakkale	9,950	464,975	46.7
Çankırı	7,492	270,355	36.1
Çorum	12,796	597,065	46.7
Denizli	11,804	850,029	72.0
Diyabakır	15,204	1,362,708	89.6
Düzce	2,593	314,266	121.2
Edirne	6,098	402,606	66.0
Elazığ	9,281	569,616	61.4
Erzincan	11,728	316,841	27.0
Erzurum	25,331	937,389	37.0
Eskişehir	13,902	706,009	50.8
Gaziantep	6,845	1,285,249	187.8
Giresun	6,832	523,819	76.7
Gümüşhane	6,437	186,953	29.0
Hakkari	7,179	236,581	33.0
Hatay	5,831	1,253,726	215.0
Iğdir	3,588	168,634	47.0
Isparta	8,871	513,681	57.9
İçel	15,512	1,651,400	106.5
İstanbul	5,315	10,018,735	1,885.0
İzmir	12,016	3,370,866	280.5
Kahramanmaraş	14,457	1,002,384	69.3
Karabük	4,109	225,102	54.8
Karaman	8,869	243,210	27.4
Kars	10,139	325,016	32.1
Kastamonu	13,158	375,476	28.5
Kayseri	17,109	1,060,432	62.0
Kırıkkale	4,570	383,508	83.9
Kırklareli	6,300	328,461	52.1
Kırşehir	6,530	253,239	38.8
Kilis	1,428	114,724	80.3
Kocaeli	3,625	1,206,085	332.7
Konya	40,814	2,192,166	53.7
Kütahya	12,014	656,903	54.7
Malatya	12,103	853,658	70.5
Manisa	13,229	1,260,169	95.3
Mardin	8,806	705,098	80.1
Muğla	12,949	715,328	55.2
Muş	8,067	453,654	56.2
Nevşehir	5,392	309,914	57.5
Niğde	7,365	348,081	47.3
Ordu	5,952	887,765	149.2
Osmaniye	3,196	458,782	143.5
Rize	3,922	365,938	93.3
Sakarya	4,880	756,168	155.0
Samsun	9,364	1,209,137	129.1
Siirt	5,473	263,676	48.2
Sinop	5,817	225,574	38.8
Sivas	28,567	755,091	26.4
Şanlıurfa	19,336	1,443,422	74.6
Şırnak	7,152	353,197	49.4
Tekirdağ	6,342	623,591	98.3
Tokat	10,073	828,027	82.2
Trabzon	4,664	975,137	209.1
Tunceli	7,686	93,584	12.2
Uşak	5,363	322,313	60.1
Van	22,983	877,524	38.2
Yalova	850	168,593	198.3
Yozgat	14,074	682,919	48.5
Zonguldak	3,310	615,599	186.0
Total	783,562	67,803,927	86.5

PRINCIPAL TOWNS
(population at census of 22 October 2000, within municipal boundaries)

İstanbul	8,803,468	Erzurum	361,235
Ankara (capital)	3,203,362	Kahramanmaraş	326,198
İzmir (Smyrna)	2,232,265	Van	284,464
Bursa	1,194,687	Sakarya	283,752
Adana	1,130,710	Denizli	275,480
Gaziantep	853,513	Elazığ	266,495
Konya	742,690	Gebze	253,487
Antalya	603,190	Sivas	251,776
Diyarbakır	545,983	Batman	246,678
Mersin (İçel)	537,842	Tarsus	216,382
Kayseri	536,392	Balıkesir	215,436
Eskişehir	482,793	Trabzon	214,949
Şanlıurfa	385,588	Manisa	214,345
Malatya	381,081	Kinkkale	205,078
Samsun	363,180		

Mid-2007 ('000, incl. suburbs, UN estimates): İstanbul 10,061; Ankara 3,716; İzmir 2,587; Bursa 1,492; Adana 1,293; Gaziantep 1,044; Konya 919; Antalya 783 (Source: UN, *World Urbanization Prospects: The 2007 Revision*).

BIRTHS, MARRIAGES AND DEATHS

	Live births		Marriages		Deaths	
	Number*	Rate (per 1,000)	Number	Rate (per 1,000)	Number*	Rate (per 1,000)
2002	1,362,000	19.6	519,044	7.5	429,000	6.2
2003	1,361,000	19.4	575,257	8.2	436,000	6.2
2004	1,360,000	19.1	625,635	8.8	443,000	6.2
2005	1,361,000	18.9	651,896	9.1	450,000	6.2
2006	1,362,000	18.7	650,233	8.9	456,000	6.3

* Figures are projected estimates.

Expectation of life (years at birth, WHO estimates): 71.2 (males 69.0; females 73.6) in 2005 (Source: WHO, *World Health Statistics*).

ECONOMICALLY ACTIVE POPULATION*
(sample surveys, '000 persons aged 15 years and over)

	2004	2005	2006
Agriculture, hunting, forestry and fishing	7,400	6,493	6,088
Mining and quarrying	105	119	128
Manufacturing	3,800	4,084	4,186
Electricity, gas and water	82	79	93
Construction	1,030	1,171	1,267
Wholesale and retail trade; repair of motor vehicles, motorcycles and personal and household goods; restaurants and hotels	4,179	4,547	4,730
Transport, storage and communications	1,100	1,131	1,163
Financial intermediation, real estate, renting and business activities	786	871	1,011
Community, social and personal service activities	3,309	3,551	3,664
Total employed	21,791	22,046	22,330
Unemployed	2,498	2,519	2,446
Total labour force	24,289	24,565	24,776
Males	17,902	18,213	18,297
Females	6,388	6,352	6,480

* Excluding armed forces.

TURKEY

WORKERS ABROAD

	2000	2001	2002
Turkish citizens working abroad (number)	1,170,226	1,178,412	1,200,725
Workers' remittances from abroad (US $ million)	4,560	2,786	1,936

Turkish citizens working abroad (number): 1,197,968 in 2003; 1,195,612 in 2004.

Sources: Undersecretariat of the Prime Ministry for Foreign Trade; Secretariat of the State Planning Organization.

Health and Welfare

KEY INDICATORS

Total fertility rate (children per woman, 2005)	2.4
Under-5 mortality rate (per 1,000 live births, 2005)	29
HIV/AIDS (% of persons aged 15–49, 2001)	<0.1
Physicians (per 1,000 head, 2003)	1.35
Hospital beds (per 1,000 head, 2005)	2.60
Health expenditure (2004): US $ per head (PPP)	556.8
Health expenditure (2004): % of GDP	7.7
Health expenditure (2004): public (% of total)	72.3
Access to water (% of persons, 2004)	96
Access to sanitation (% of persons, 2004)	88
Human Development Index (2005): ranking	84
Human Development Index (2005): value	0.775

For sources and definitions, see explanatory note on p. vi.

Agriculture

PRINCIPAL CROPS
('000 metric tons)

	2004	2005	2006
Wheat	21,000	21,500	20,010
Rice (paddy)	490	600	696
Barley	9,000	9,500	9,551
Maize	3,000	4,200	3,811
Rye	270	270	246
Oats	270	270	271
Potatoes	4,800	4,090	4,397
Sugar beet	13,517	15,181	14,452
Dry beans	250	210	196
Chick peas	620	600	552
Lentils	540	570	623
Walnuts	126	150	130
Hazelnuts (Filberts)	350	530	661
Olives	1,600	1,200	1,600*
Sunflower seed	900	975	1,118
Cottonseed†	1,350	1,125	1,350
Cabbages and other brassicas	700	675	687
Lettuce and chicory	362	372	391
Spinach	213	238	242
Tomatoes	9,440	10,050	9,855
Cauliflowers and broccoli	117	126	136
Pumpkins, squash and gourds	364	368	365
Cucumbers and gherkins	1,725	1,745	1,800
Aubergines (Eggplants)	900	930	924
Green chillies and peppers	1,700	1,829	1,842
Green onions and shallots	207	200	201
Dry onions	2,040	2,070	1,765
Garlic	109	100	100*
Leeks and other alliacious vegetables	295	320	320
Green beans	582	555	564
Carrots and turnips	439	390	402
Watermelons	3,825	3,970	3,805
Cantaloupes and other melons	1,825	1,766	1,766*
Bananas	130	150	178
Oranges	1,300	1,445	1,536
Tangerines, mandarins, etc.	670	715	791
Lemons and limes	600	600	710
Grapefruit and pomelo	135	150	180
Apples	2,100	2,570	2,002

—continued	2004	2005	2006
Pears	320	360	318
Quinces	80	100	106
Apricots	320	860	460
Sweet cherries	245	280	310
Sour cherries	138	140	121
Peaches and nectarines	372	510	553
Plums	210	220	214
Strawberries	155	200	211
Grapes	3,500	3,850	4,000
Figs	275	285	290
Cotton (lint)	936	864	900
Tea (made)	202	218	205
Anise, badian and fennel	26	24	20
Tobacco (leaves)	134	135	140

* FAO estimate.
† Unofficial figures.

Aggregate production ('000 metric tons, may include official, semi-official or estimated data): Total cereals 34,075 in 2004, 36,386 in 2005, 34,598 in 2006; Total roots and tubers 4,800 in 2004, 4,090 in 2005, 4,398 in 2006; Total pulses 1,584 in 2004, 1,565 in 2005, 1,550 in 2006; Total spices 91 in 2004, 103 in 2005; 99 in 2006; Total vegetables (incl. melons) 25,348 in 2004, 26,290 in 2005, 25,723 in 2006; Total fruits (excl. melons) 11,063 in 2004, 12,998 in 2005, 12,563 in 2006.

Source: FAO.

LIVESTOCK
('000 head, year ending September)

	2004	2005	2006
Horses	227	212	208
Asses, mules or hinnies	490	452	423
Cattle	9,788	10,069	10,526
Buffaloes	113	104	105
Camels	1	1	1
Pigs	7	4	2
Sheep	25,432	25,201	25,304
Goats	6,772	6,610	6,517
Chickens	277,533	296,876	317,497
Ducks	811	770	656
Geese	1,337	1,251	1,067
Turkeys	3,994	3,902	3,697

Source: FAO.

LIVESTOCK PRODUCTS
('000 metric tons)

	2003	2004	2005
Cattle meat	290.5	365.0	321.7
Buffalo meat	1.7	2.0	1.6
Sheep meat*	267	273	272
Goat meat*	45.0	45.0	45.0
Horse meat*	1.7	2.0	2.0
Chicken meat	872.4	876.8	936.7
Cows' milk	9,514.3	9,609.3	10,026.2
Buffalo milk	48.8	39.3	38.1
Sheep milk	770.0	771.7	789.9
Goats' milk	278.1	259.1	253.8
Hen eggs	791.7	691.0	753.3
Honey	69.5	73.9	82.3

* FAO estimates.

2006: Figures assumed to be unchanged from 2005 (FAO estimates).

Source: FAO.

Forestry

ROUNDWOOD REMOVALS
('000 cubic metres, excl. bark)

	2004	2005	2006
Sawlogs, veneer logs and logs for sleepers	5,235	5,107	5,649
Pulpwood	4,278	4,403	4,747
Other industrial wood	1,712	1,692	1,865
Fuel wood	5,278	4,983	4,552
Total	16,503	16,185	16,813

Source: FAO.

SAWNWOOD PRODUCTION
('000 cubic metres, incl. railway sleepers)

	2004	2005	2006
Coniferous (softwood)	3,625	3,787	4,323
Broadleaved (hardwood)	2,590	2,658	2,756
Total	6,215	6,445	7,079

Source: FAO.

Fishing

('000 metric tons, live weight)

	2003	2004	2005
Capture	507.8	550.5	426.5
Blue whiting	7.5	4.4	4.1
Mullets	26.0	27.5	25.5
European anchovy	295.0	340.0	138.6
Bluefish	22.0	19.9	18.4
Mediterranean horse mackerel	16.4	18.1	13.5
Striped venus	19.7	16.9	10.8
Aquaculture	79.9	94.0	119.2
Trout	40.9	45.1	49.3
Seabasses	21.0	26.3	37.5
Gilthead seabream	16.7	20.4	28.3
Total catch	587.7	644.5	545.7

Source: FAO.

Mining

('000 metric tons, unless otherwise indicated)

	2003	2004	2005[1]
Hard coal	3,090	2,843	3,050
Lignite	43,749	43,754	55,626
Crude petroleum ('000 barrels)	16,980	16,270	16,500
Natural gas ('000 cu m)[2]	275,947	344,196	n.a.
Iron ore: gross weight	3,429	4,120	4,598
Iron ore: metal content	1,830	2,200	2,450
Copper[1,3]	58.0	49.0	48.0
Bauxite[4]	364.3	365.8	475.3
Lead: mine output[3]	17.5	18.7	21.0
Lead: concentrates[1,3]	16.0	17.0	19.0
Chromium[5]	229.3	506.4	700.0
Silver (kilograms)[4,6]	95,000	73,000[1]	80,000
Gold (kilograms)[1,3,7]	6,500	4,500	5,000
Marble ('000 cu m)	544.6	669.0	800.0
Limestone[6]	28,609	30,963	35,000
Quartzite	2,908.6	2,961.9	3,200
Dolomite	1,158.5	2,109.4	2,200
Bentonite	831.1	850.0[1]	925.0
Kaolin	370.5	536.0	580.0
Silica sand[8]	1,283	1,188	1,200

—continued	2003	2004	2005[1]
Gypsum[6]	196.7	250.1	250.0
Magnesite: mine output	3,224.3	3,733.0	3,400
Feldspar: mine output	1,862.3	1,983.3	2,200
Borate minerals: mine output	2,207.1	2,878.9	2,900
Borate minerals: concentrates	1,399.0	1,697.0	1,700
Nitrogen[9]	289.3	329.4	330.0
Perlite: mine output	136.7	133.8	140.0
Pumice	895.6	1,036.0	1,000.0
Pyrites[8]	1,103.9	765.4	800.0
Sodium sulphate: concentrates	556.6	523.3	550.0

[1] Estimated production.
[2] Marketed production only.
[3] Figures refer to metal content of ores and concentrates.
[4] Figures refer to public sector production only. Data for private sector production are not available, but production is estimated to have been 30,000 metric tons in each year.
[5] Figures refer to gross weight of ores.
[6] Excluding production used for making cement.
[7] Figures include estimated output from the by-products of refining other base metals.
[8] Figures refer to gross weight of minerals.
[9] Nitrogen content of ammonia.

Source: US Geological Survey.

Industry

SELECTED PRODUCTS
('000 metric tons, unless otherwise indicated)

	2005	2006	2007*
Margarine	625.5	612.7	577.8
Refined sunflower seed oil	240.1	264.0	258.1
Flour	2,297.5	2,205.4	2,374.0
Sugar	1,927.9	1,805.5	1,666.1
Beer (million litres)	893.6	905.9	920.5
Raki (million litres)	44.1	37.8	38.1
Cigarettes (with filter)	104.2	128.3	119.6
Cotton yarn	458.8	532.0	542.9
Wool yarn	41.6	37.6	38.0
Products of the paper industry	553.0	600.2	622.8
Wood block flooring ('000 sq m)	3,371.5	5,182.8	4,930.6
Calf skins ('000 sq m)	580.6	490.1	544.8
Leather for clothing and gloves ('000 sq m)	287.4	506.3	385.7
Leather shoes ('000 pairs)	47,206.8	60,701.0	58,732.2
Crude steel	20,961.2	23,307.5	25,760.9
Pig-iron	178.4	122.0	264.8
Cement	41,100.3	47,906.4	49,552.6
Polyethylene	273.6	384.6	393.9
Propylene	140.8	198.7	240.5
Ammonia	370.6	111.5	—
Sulphuric acid	164.6	304.3	331.4
Ethylene	314.4	488.8	486.3
Motor oil	7,549.2	7,616.5	7,338.4
Motor gasoline	3,733.7	3,760.8	4,147.3
Naphthas	1,467.3	1,527.6	990.6
Jet fuel	1,997.0	2,119.4	2,557.7
Liquefied petroleum gas	767.3	800.7	761.2
Asphalt	1,763.6	2,225.3	2,291.0
Fuel oil (No. 6)	6,388.6	6,192.3	6,023.3
Kerosene	57.2	36.3	71.9
Composed fertilizers	1,599.5	1,272.6	1,379.7
Other fertilizers	1,623.3	1,723.0	1,534.7
Domestic refrigerators ('000)	5,098.9	6,222.7	6,161.5
Domestic washing machines ('000)	4,433.8	5,410.2	5,407.8
Ovens ('000)	4,540.9	5,646.0	5,769.7
Vacuum cleaners ('000)	1,206.7	1,487.8	1,575.9
Television receivers ('000, colour)	20,790.1	17,930.4	12,591.6
Tyres for automobiles ('000 units)	17,535.2	17,489.2	17,557.9
Tractors (number)	38,800	42,496	37,524
Passenger motor cars (number)	635,137	756,381	855,460
Pick-up trucks (number)	128,426	136,594	154,979
Buses and minibuses (number)	59,070	46,510	38,264
Electricity (million kWh)	161,956.2	n.a.	n.a.

* Preliminary.

TURKEY

Statistical Survey

Finance

CURRENCY AND EXCHANGE RATES

Monetary Units
100 kuruş = 1 new Turkish lira.

Sterling, Dollar and Euro Equivalents (31 December 2007)
£1 sterling = 2.328 new liras;
US $1 = 1.162 new liras;
€1 = 1.711 new liras;
100 new Turkish liras = £42.95 = US $86.05 = €58.45.

Average Exchange Rate (new Turkish liras per US $)
2005   1.3436
2006   1.4285
2007   1.3033

Note: A new currency, the new Turkish lira, equivalent to 1,000,000 of the former units, was introduced on 1 January 2005. Figures in this survey have been converted retrospectively to reflect this development.

CONSOLIDATED BUDGET
(million new Turkish liras)

Revenue	2001	2002	2003
General budget	50,890.5	74,603.7	98,558.7
Taxation	39,735.9	59,631.9	84,316.2
Taxes on income	15,647.6	19,343.2	25,716.0
Taxes on wealth	433.3	734.3	2,092.1
Taxes on goods and services	18,103.2	30,064.0	43,927.0
Taxes on foreign trade	5,551.1	9,487.2	12,578.7
Non-tax revenue	7,418.4	10,874.5	10,222.8
Special revenue and funds	3,736.2	4,097.3	4,019.8
Annexed budget revenues	652.5	988.6	1,691.7
Total	51,543.0	75,592.3	100,250.4

Expenditure	2001	2002	2003
Current expenditure	20,448.0	31,108.0	38,513.9
Personnel	15,211.9	23,089.2	30,209.5
Other current expenditure	5,236.1	8,018.8	8,304.4
Investment expenditure	4,149.6	6,891.8	7,179.7
Transfers	55,981.5	77,682.6	94,761.3
Interest payments	41,062.2	51,870.7	58,609.2
Domestic debt interest	37,494.3	46,807.0	52,718.9
Foreign debt interest	3,567.9	5,063.6	5,890.3
Transfers to state-owned economic enterprises	1,107.1	2,170.0	1,881.0
Tax rebates	2,918.2	5,665.8	8,335.9
Social security payments	5,112.0	11,205.0	15,922.0
Other transfers	5,268.8	6,746.1	9,973.2
Total	80,579.1	115,682.4	140,454.8

2004 (million new Turkish liras): Total revenue 121,869.9; Total expenditure 152,169.9.

2005 (million new Turkish liras): Total revenue 150,462.7; Total expenditure 158,579.4.

2006 (million new Turkish liras, central management budget): Total revenue 171,309.3; Total expenditure 175,304.0.

Source: Ministry of Finance, İstanbul.

INTERNATIONAL RESERVES
(US $ million at 31 December)

	2005	2006	2007
Gold (national valuation)	1,912	2,373	3,123
IMF special drawing rights	16	12	50
Reserve position in IMF	161	170	178
Foreign exchange	50,402	60,710	73,156
Total	52,491	63,265	76,507

Source: IMF, *International Financial Statistics*.

MONEY SUPPLY
(million new Turkish liras at 31 December)

	2004	2005	2006
Currency outside banks	12,312	17,852	23,881
Demand deposits at deposit money banks	16,211	24,429	43,235
Total money (incl. others)	28,631	42,370	67,218

Source: IMF, *International Financial Statistics*.

COST OF LIVING
(Consumer Price Index; base: 2003 = 100)

	2005	2006	2007
Food and non-alcoholic beverages	112.08	122.95	138.21
Alcoholic beverages and tobacco	135.18	163.54	179.77
Clothing and footwear	110.44	110.35	115.33
Housing, water, electricity, gas and other fuels	120.00	135.18	150.34
Household goods	113.64	120.01	129.13
Health	112.64	116.95	122.53
Transport	123.73	136.44	144.09
Communications	104.89	107.61	106.71
Recreation and culture	117.06	122.88	127.38
Education	135.16	145.65	156.14
Restaurants and hotels	133.49	152.08	169.10
Miscellaneous goods and services	117.71	137.05	144.66
All items	117.48	128.76	140.03

NATIONAL ACCOUNTS
(million new Turkish liras at current prices)

National Income and Product

	2003	2004	2005
Compensation of employees	93,978.0	113,261.8	129,713.7
Operating surplus	179,960.2	214,252.1	238,887.7
Domestic factor incomes	273,938.2	327,513.9	368,601.4
Consumption of fixed capital	27,294.2	30,169.0	31,715.4
Gross domestic product (GDP) at factor cost	301,232.4	357,682.9	400,316.8
Indirect taxes	59,481.0	73,633.0	87,909.9
Less Subsidies	950.5	804.4	1,024.3
GDP in purchasers' values	359,762.9	430,511.5	487,202.4
Factor income received from abroad	8,415.6	10,040.1	11,907.9
Less Factor income paid abroad	11,497.7	11,619.2	12,709.2
Gross national product (GNP)	356,680.9	428,932.3	486,401.0
Less Consumption of fixed capital	27,294.2	30,169.0	31,715.4
National income in market prices	329,386.7	398,763.4	454,685.7

Expenditure on the Gross Domestic Product

	2005	2006	2007
Government final consumption expenditure	76,498.6	93,525.3	104,465.8
Private final consumption expenditure	465,401.8	534,849.2	605,236.8
Increase in stocks	−6,756.4	−1,782.7	5,729.1
Gross fixed capital formation	136,475.1	169,044.7	184,126.0
Total domestic expenditure	671,619.1	795,636.5	899,557.7
Exports of goods and services	141,826.5	171,926.5	187,952.7
Less Imports of goods and services	164,513.9	209,172.1	231,123.1
GDP in purchasers' values	648,931.7	758,390.8	856,386.7
GDP at constant 1998 prices	90,499.7	96,738.3	101,045.5

TURKEY

Gross Domestic Product by Economic Activity

	2005	2006	2007
Agriculture, forestry and fishing	60,713.7	62,662.8	65,906.3
Mining and quarrying	7,628.5	8,952.4	10,536.6
Manufacturing	112,051.7	130,393.1	141,545.1
Electricity, gas and water	11,956.7	13,452.1	15,621.6
Construction	28,694.1	35,849.3	42,748.2
Wholesale and retail trade	80,211.9	94,856.3	103,322.1
Hotels and restaurants	14,528.3	17,041.9	19,323.3
Transport, storage and communications	89,087.3	104,123.0	117,306.8
Financial institutions	18,293.4	21,860.6	27,234.0
Ownership of dwellings	60,120.2	74,467.2	90,963.5
Real estate, renting and business activities	22,614.0	27,822.9	34,412.6
Public administration and defence; compulsory social security	26,018.8	29,620.6	33,092.5
Education	17,773.4	21,241.9	24,564.6
Health and social work	10,339.6	12,061.1	14,128.7
Other community, social and personal services	10,687.0	12,784.0	14,534.0
Private households with employed persons	995.9	1,229.1	1,487.8
Sub-total	571,714.5	668,418.3	756,727.7
Taxes, less subsidies	86,571.1	100,462.6	112,587.7
Less Financial intermediation services indirectly measured	9,353.8	10,490.1	12,928.7
GDP in purchasers' values	648,931.7	758,390.8	856,386.7

Balance of Payments
(US $ million)

	2004	2005	2006
Exports of goods f.o.b.	67,047	76,949	91,937
Imports of goods f.o.b.	−90,925	−110,479	−133,175
Trade balance	−23,878	−33,530	−41,238
Exports of services	22,960	26,648	24,547
Imports of services	−10,163	−11,376	−11,186
Balance on goods and services	−11,081	−18,258	−27,877
Other income received	2,651	3,684	4,473
Other income paid	−8,288	−9,483	−11,057
Balance on goods, services and income	−16,718	−24,057	−34,461
Current transfers received	1,155	1,475	1,764
Current transfers paid	−38	−21	−77
Current balance	−15,601	−22,603	−32,774
Direct investment abroad	−859	−1,078	−934
Direct investment from abroad	2,883	9,801	20,070
Portfolio investment assets	−1,388	−1,233	−4,029
Portfolio investment liabilities	9,411	14,670	11,402
Other investment assets	−6,955	259	−12,420
Other investment liabilities	14,660	21,268	31,705
Net errors and omissions	2,109	2,092	−2,399
Overall balance	4,260	23,176	10,621

Source: IMF, *International Financial Statistics*.

External Trade

PRINCIPAL COMMODITIES
(distribution by SITC, US $ million, excl. military goods)

Imports c.i.f.	2005	2006	2007
Crude materials (inedible) except fuels	7,660.5	9,190.8	12,240.2
Metalliferous ores and metal scrap	3,600.7	4,602.6	6,390.1
Mineral fuels, lubricants, etc.	21,254.8	28,858.8	33,881.0
Petroleum, petroleum products, etc.	12,412.5	16,608.3	19,339.2
Chemicals and related products	16,438.8	18,407.5	22,104.8
Organic chemicals	3,292.4	3,434.0	3,792.9
Medicinal and pharmaceutical products	3,183.8	3,343.1	3,838.4
Plastics in primary forms	4,468.2	5,367.9	6,835.0
Basic manufactures	19,989.7	24,883.8	32,163.1
Textile yarn, fabrics, etc.	4,440.5	4,686.0	6,152.2
Iron and steel	6,746.6	8,140.7	11,341.0
Machinery and transport equipment	38,028.1	43,036.6	49,856.4
Power-generating machinery and equipment	3,647.0	3,960.3	5,067.4
Machinery specialized for particular industries	5,181.4	5,740.4	6,759.7
General industrial machinery, equipment and parts	4,469.8	5,619.9	6,970.5
Road vehicles	10,378.8	11,145.2	12,035.4
Miscellaneous manufactured articles	6,705.9	7,941.2	9,874.0
Non-monetary gold, unwrought or semi-manufactured	3,894.8	4,012.7	5,325.1
Total (incl. others)	116,774.2	139,576.2	170,057.2

Exports f.o.b.	2005	2006	2007
Food and live animals	6,512.3	6,594.5	7,821.5
Vegetables and fruit	4,373.6	4,260.9	4,901.5
Chemicals and related products	3,060.5	3,923.1	4,736.7
Basic manufactures	20,408.9	23,854.9	29,947.6
Textile yarn, fabrics, etc.	7,075.5	7,584.7	8,945.2
Non-metallic mineral manufactures	2,390.1	2,477.2	3,060.7
Iron and steel	5,827.0	7,239.3	9,562.2
Machinery and transport equipment	21,609.0	26,385.9	34,241.3
Road vehicles	9,428.9	11,730.3	15,701.0
Miscellaneous manufactured articles	16,051.5	16,745.8	20,009.3
Clothing and accessories (excl. footwear)	11,833.1	12,051.9	13,885.5
Total (incl. others)	73,476.4	85,534.7	107,213.7

PRINCIPAL TRADING PARTNERS
(US $ million, excl. military goods*)

Imports c.i.f. (excl. grants)	2005	2006	2007
Algeria	1,695.0	1,864.5	2,108.5
Austria	940.1	1,077.2	1,351.4
Belgium	2,241.1	2,476.9	2,868.7
China, People's Republic	6,885.4	9,669.1	13,234.1
France (incl. Monaco)	5,887.8	7,240.0	7,849.7
Germany	13,633.9	14,768.2	17,540.0
India	1,280.5	1,579.4	2,299.7
Iran	3,469.7	5,626.6	6,613.8
Italy	7,566.3	8,663.5	9,967.8
Japan	3,109.2	3,216.7	3,703.4
Korea, Republic	3,485.4	3,556.3	4,369.9
Libya	1,989.3	2,297.4	399.7
Netherlands	2,151.6	2,160.1	2,655.0

TURKEY

Statistical Survey

Imports c.i.f. (excl. grants)—continued	2005	2006	2007
Romania	2,285.6	2,669.0	3,112.8
Russia	12,905.6	17,806.2	23,508.5
Saudi Arabia	1,888.8	2,252.1	2,440.0
Spain	3,555.1	3,832.6	4,342.8
Sweden	1,427.1	1,488.1	1,716.1
Switzerland	4,054.0	4,014.8	5,268.9
Ukraine	2,651.0	3,059.1	4,519.1
United Kingdom	4,695.6	5,137.6	5,477.1
USA	5,375.5	6,260.9	8,163.6
Total (incl. others)	116,774.2	139,576.2	170,057.2

Exports f.o.b.	2005	2006	2007
Algeria	807.1	1,020.7	1,231.7
Austria	659.1	709.9	844.0
Belgium	1,292.3	1,381.1	1,735.8
Bulgaria	1,179.3	1,568.0	2,060.2
China, People's Republic	549.8	693.0	1,039.5
Denmark	733.2	827.1	1,008.5
Egypt	687.3	709.4	902.7
France	3,805.8	4,604.3	5,974.2
Germany	9,455.1	9,686.2	11,993.1
Greece	1,126.7	1,602.6	2,262.7
Iran	912.9	1,066.9	1,387.4
Iraq	2,750.1	2,589.4	2,844.7
Israel	1,466.9	1,529.2	1,658.2
Italy	5,616.8	6,752.3	7,479.7
Netherlands	2,469.6	2,539.2	3,018.9
Poland	830.5	1,060.1	1,436.4
Romania	1,785.4	2,350.5	3,644.2
Russia	2,377.1	3,237.6	4,726.9
Saudi Arabia	962.2	982.2	1,486.9
Spain	3,010.9	3,720.5	4,579.6
United Arab Emirates	1,675.2	1,985.7	3,240.9
United Kingdom	5,917.2	6,814.3	8,626.5
USA	4,910.7	5,060.9	4,168.2
Total (incl. others)	73,476.4	85,534.7	107,213.7

*Imports by country of origin, exports by country of last consignment.

Transport

RAILWAYS
(traffic)

	2004	2005	2006
Passengers carried ('000)	76,756	76,306	77,414
Passenger-km (million)	5,237	5,036	5,277
Freight carried ('000 metric tons)*	17,708	18,945	19,745
Freight ton-km (million)	9,417	9,152	9,676

*Excluding parcels and departmental traffic.

ROAD TRAFFIC
(motor vehicles by use)

	2004	2005	2006
Passenger cars	5,400,440	5,772,745	6,140,992
Minibuses	318,954	338,539	357,523
Buses and coaches	152,712	163,390	175,949
Small trucks	1,259,867	1,475,057	1,695,624
Trucks	647,420	676,929	709,535
Motorcycles and mopeds	1,218,677	1,441,066	1,822,831
Special purpose vehicles	28,004	30,333	34,260

SHIPPING
Merchant Fleet
(registered at 31 December)

	2004	2005	2006
Number of vessels	1,114	1,156	1,184
Total displacement ('000 grt)	4,678.9	5,044.7	4,848.8

Source: Lloyd's Register-Fairplay, *World Fleet Statistics*.

International Sea-borne Traffic

	1999	2000	2001
Vessels entered (number)	23,097	25,199	20,431
Passengers disembarked (number)	482,715	600,948	590,454
Goods unloaded ('000 metric tons)*	71,453	79,337	68,342
Vessels cleared (number)	18,097	18,385	18,916
Passengers embarked (number)	484,244	593,493	599,474
Goods loaded ('000 metric tons)*	25,075	25,477	34,137

*Including timber.

CIVIL AVIATION
(scheduled services)

	2003	2004	2005
Domestic services:			
Kilometres flown ('000)	28,180	28,489	35,886
Number of passengers	4,991,517	5,805,291	7,151,491
Passenger-km ('000)	2,751,910	3,223,299	3,991,885
Freight handled (metric tons)	29,146	30,710	31,504
Total ton-km ('000)	275,681	321,118	392,055
International services:			
Kilometres flown ('000)	101,738	109,038	122,899
Number of passengers	4,802,897	5,617,506	6,486,320
Passenger-km ('000)	12,223,997	14,227,375	16,359,597
Freight handled (metric tons)	88,993	93,736	87,851
Total ton-km ('000)	1,617,729	1,849,177	2,104,407

Tourism

VISITOR ARRIVALS BY NATIONALITY
(provisional)

Country	2005	2006	2007
Austria	486,051	429,708	472,482
Azerbaijan	411,652	380,132	434,577
Belgium	485,758	451,426	542,712
Bulgaria	1,621,704	1,177,903	1,239,667
France	701,190	657,859	768,167
Georgia	367,339	549,328	630,979
Germany	4,240,122	3,762,469	4,149,805
Greece	548,784	412,819	447,950
Iran	957,245	865,942	1,058,206
Israel	393,805	362,501	511,435
Italy	401,852	402,573	514,803
Netherlands	1,253,885	997,466	1,057,403
Russia	1,864,682	1,853,442	2,465,336
Sweden	405,956	326,255	338,182
Ukraine	380,392	487,917	593,302
United Kingdom	1,757,843	1,678,845	1,916,130
USA	434,991	532,404	642,911
Total (incl. others)	21,124,886	19,819,833	23,340,911

Tourism receipts (million US $, excl. passenger transport, incl. expenditure of Turkish nationals residing abroad): 18,153.5 in 2005; 16,850.9 in 2006; n.a. in 2007.

TURKEY

Communications Media

	2004	2005	2006
Telephones ('000 main lines in use)	19,125.2	18,978.2	18,831.6
Mobile cellular telephones ('000 subscribers)	34,707.5	43,609.0	52,662.7
Personal computers ('000 in use)	3,703	n.a.	n.a.
Internet users ('000)	10,220.0	11,204.3	12,283.5
Broadband subscribers ('000)	577.9	1,589.8	2,773.7

Radio receivers ('000 in use): 11,300 in 1997.

Television receivers ('000 in use): 21,152 in 2001.

Facsimile machines (number in use): 108,014 in 1997.

Book production (titles): 2,920 in 1999.

Daily newspapers (number): 588 in 2004.

Non-daily newspapers (number): 1,771 in 2004.

Sources: International Telecommunication Union; UNESCO Institute for Statistics; UN, *Statistical Yearbook*.

Education

(2007/08 unless otherwise indicated, provisional figures)

	Institutions	Teachers	Students
Pre-primary	22,506	25,901	701,762
Primary	34,093	445,452	10,870,570
Secondary:			
general	3,830	106,270	1,980,452
vocational and teacher training	4,450	84,771	1,264,870
Higher*	1,306	84,785	2,181,217

*Figures for 2005/06.

Adult literacy rate (UNESCO estimates): 87.4% (males 95.3%; females 79.6%) in 2004 (Source: UNESCO Institute for Statistics).

Directory

The Constitution

In October 1981 the National Security Council (NSC), which took power in September 1980, announced the formation of a Consultative Assembly to draft a new constitution, replacing that of 1961. The Assembly consisted of 40 members appointed directly by the NSC and 120 members chosen by the NSC from candidates put forward by the governors of the 67 provinces; all former politicians were excluded. The draft Constitution was approved by the Assembly in September 1982 and by a national referendum in November. Its main provisions are summarized below:

Legislative power is vested in the unicameral Grand National Assembly, which (following an amendment in July 1995) comprises 550 deputies. The election of deputies is by universal adult suffrage for a five-year term. Executive power is vested in the President, who is elected by the Grand National Assembly for a seven-year term and is empowered to: appoint a Prime Minister and senior members of the judiciary, the Central Bank and broadcasting organizations; dissolve the Assembly; and declare a state of emergency entailing rule by decree. Strict controls on the powers of trades unions, the press and political parties were also included. An appended 'temporary article' automatically installed the incumbent President of the NSC as Head of State for a seven-year term, assisted by a Presidential Council comprising members of the NSC.

In July 2003 the Grand National Assembly approved an amendment reducing the number of NSC members from 13 to six. The NSC was henceforth to be a predominantly civilian advisory body, comprising the President, Prime Minister, Chief of General Staff, and Ministers of Foreign Affairs, National Defence and Internal Affairs. Amendments approved by the Assembly in May 2004 included guarantees of equal rights between men and women, the removal of references to capital punishment and the abolition of State Security Courts. (For details regarding further constitutional amendments, see Recent History.)

The Government

HEAD OF STATE

President: ABDULLAH GÜL (took office 28 August 2007).

COUNCIL OF MINISTERS
(April 2008)

Prime Minister: REÇEP TAYYIP ERDOĞAN.

Deputy Prime Ministers: CEMIL ÇIÇEK, HAYATI YAZICI, NAZIM EKREN.

Ministers of State: Prof. Dr MEHMET AYDIN, MURAT BAŞESGIOĞLU, KÜRŞAT TÜZMEN, NIMET ÇUBUKÇU, MEHMET ŞIMŞEK, MUSTAFA SAIT YAZICIOĞLU.

Minister of Foreign Affairs and Chief Negotiator of Turkey for European Union Affairs: ALI BABACAN.

Minister of Justice: MEHMET ALI ŞAHIN.

Minister of National Defence: MEHMET VECDI GÖNÜL.

Minister of Internal Affairs: Dr BEŞIR ATALAY.

Minister of Finance: KEMAL UNAKITAN.

Minister of National Education: Dr HÜSEYIN ÇELIK.

Minister of Public Works and Settlement: FARUK NAFIZ ÖZAK.

Minister of Health: Prof. Dr REÇEP AKDAĞ.

Minister of Transport: BINALI YILDIRIM.

Minister of Agriculture and Rural Affairs: Dr MEHMET MEHDI EKER.

Minister of Labour and Social Security: FARUK ÇELIK.

Minister of Industry and Trade: MEHMET ZAFER ÇAĞLAYAN.

Minister of Energy and Natural Resources: Dr MEHMET HILMI GÜLER.

Minister of Culture and Tourism: ERTUĞRUL GÜNAY.

Minister of the Environment and Forestry: Prof. Dr VEYSEL EROĞLU.

MINISTRIES

President's Office: Cumhurbaşkanlığı Köşkü, 06689 Çankaya, Ankara; tel. (312) 4685030; fax (312) 4413816; e-mail cumhurbaskanligi@tccb.gov.tr; internet www.cankaya.gov.tr.

Prime Minister's Office: Başbakanlık, Bakanlıklar, Ankara; tel. (312) 4189056; fax (312) 4180476; e-mail bilgi@basbakanlik.gov.tr; internet www.basbakanlik.gov.tr.

Deputy Prime Ministers' Office: Başbakan yard. ve Devlet Bakanı, Bakanlıklar, Ankara; tel. (312) 4191621; fax (312) 4191547.

Ministry of Agriculture and Rural Affairs: Tarım ve Köyişleri Bakanlığı, Kampüsü Eskişehir Yolu 9km Lodumlu, Ankara; tel. (312) 2873360; fax (312) 2863964; e-mail admin@tarim.gov.tr; internet www.tarim.gov.tr.

Ministry of Culture and Tourism: Kültür ve Turizm Bakanlığı, Atatürk Bul. 29, 06050 Opera, Ankara; tel. (312) 3090850; fax (312) 3124359; e-mail info@kulturturizm.gov.tr; internet www.kultur.gov.tr.

Ministry of Energy and Natural Resources: Enerji ve Tabii Kaynaklar Bakanlığı, İnönü Bul. 27, Bahçelievler, Ankara; tel. (312) 2126420; fax (312) 2156586; e-mail bilgi@enerji.gov.tr; internet www.enerji.gov.tr.

Ministry of the Environment and Forestry: Çevre ve Orman Bakanlığı, Söğütözü Cad. 14E, Ankara; tel. (312) 2075000; fax (312) 2150094; e-mail webmaster@cevreorman.gov.tr; internet www.cevreorman.gov.tr.

Ministry of Finance: Maliye Bakanlığı, Dikmen Cad., Ankara; tel. (312) 4250018; fax (312) 4250058; e-mail bshalk@maliye.gov.tr; internet www.maliye.gov.tr.

Ministry of Foreign Affairs: Dişişleri Bakanlığı, Dr Sadık Ahmet Cad. 12, 06100 Balgat, Ankara; tel. (312) 2921000; fax (312) 2873869; e-mail webmaster@mfa.gov.tr; internet www.mfa.gov.tr.

Ministry of Health: Sağlık Bakanlığı, Mithatpasa Cad. 3 Sihhiye, 06434 Ankara; tel. (312) 5852250; fax (312) 4339885; e-mail info@saglik.gov.tr; internet www.saglik.gov.tr.

Ministry of Industry and Trade: Sanayi ve Ticaret Bakanlığı, Eskişehir Yolu üzeri 7 km, Ankara; tel. (312) 2860365; fax (312) 2864005; e-mail webmaster@sanayi.gov.tr; internet www.sanayi.gov.tr.

Ministry of Internal Affairs: Içişleri Bakanlığı, Bakanlıklar, Ankara; tel. (312) 4181368; fax (312) 4181795; internet www.icisleri.gov.tr.

Ministry of Justice: Adalet Bakanlığı, 06659 Kizilay, Ankara; tel. (312) 4177770; fax (312) 4193370; e-mail info@adalet.gov.tr; internet www.adalet.gov.tr.

Ministry of Labour and Social Security: Çalışma ve Sosyal Güvenlik Bakanlığı, İnönü Bul. 42, 06100 Emek, Ankara; tel. (312) 2966000; fax (312) 4179765; tel. webmaster@csgb.gov.tr; internet www.calisma.gov.tr.

Ministry of National Defence: Milli Savunma Bakanlığı, 06100 Ankara; tel. (312) 4254596; fax (312) 4184737; internet www.msb.gov.tr.

Ministry of National Education: Milli Eğitim Bakanlığı, Atatürk Bul., Bakanlıklar, Ankara; tel. (312) 4191410; fax (312) 4177027; e-mail meb@meb.gov.tr; internet www.meb.gov.tr.

Ministry of Public Works and Settlement: Bayındırlık ve İskan Bakanlığı, Vekaletler Cad. 1, 06100 Ankara; tel. (312) 4186443; fax (312) 4251288; e-mail webadmin@bayindirlik.gov.tr; internet www.bayindirlik.gov.tr.

Ministry of Transport: Ulaştırma Bakanlığı, Hakkı Turayliç Cad. 5, 06338 Emek, Ankara; tel. (312) 2031010; fax (212) 2124930; internet www.ubak.gov.tr.

Legislature

BÜYÜK MILLET MECLISI
(Grand National Assembly)

Speaker: KÖKSAL TOPTAN.
General Election, 22 July 2007.

Party	Valid votes cast	% of valid votes	Seats
Adalet ve Kalkınma Partisi (AKP)	16,340,534	46.66	341
Cumhuriyet Halk Partisi (CHP)	7,300,234	20.85	112
Milliyetçi Hareket Partisi (MHP)	5,004,003	14.29	70
Independents	1,822,253	5.20	26
Demokrat Parti (DP)	1,895,807	5.41	0
Genç Parti (GP)	1,062,352	3.03	0
Saadet Partisi (SP)	817,843	2.34	0
Others	774,289	2.21	0
Total	35,017,315*	100.00	549†

* Excluding 870,653 invalid votes.
† One of the elected representatives of the MHP died on 26 July 2007, thus one seat remained vacant.

Election Commission

Yüksek Seçim Kurulu (YSK) (High Electoral Board): Kızılırmak Cad. 9, 06640 Küçükesat, Ankara; tel. (312) 4191040; fax (312) 4195308; internet www.ysk.gov.tr/ysk/index.html; independent; Chair. MUHAMMER AYDIN.

Political Organizations

Political parties were banned from 1980–83. Legislation enacted in March 1986 stipulated that a party must have organizations in at least 45 provinces, and in two-thirds of the districts in each of these provinces, in order to take part in an election. A political party is recognized by the Government as a legitimate parliamentary group only if it has at least 20 deputies in the Grand National Assembly.

In mid-1992, following the adoption of less restrictive legislation concerning the formation of political parties, several new parties were established, and the left-wing CHP, dissolved in 1981, was reactivated.

Adalet ve Kalkınma Partisi (AKP) (Justice and Development Party): Söğütözü Cad. 6, Çankaya, Ankara; tel. (312) 2045000; fax (312) 2045020; internet www.akparti.org.tr; f. 2001; Islamist-orientated; Leader RECEP TAYYIP ERDOĞAN.

Anavatan Partisi (ANAVATAN) (Motherland Party): 13 Cad. 3, Balgat, Ankara; tel. (312) 2865000; fax (312) 2865019; e-mail anavatan@anavatan.org.tr; internet www.anavatan.org.tr; f. 1983; supports freedom of thought and expression, of religion and of enterprise; Chair. ERKAN MUMCU.

Bağımsız Türkiye Partisi (BTP) (Independent Turkey Party): Bestekar Sok. 45 Kavaklıdere, Ankara; tel. (312) 4269146; fax (312) 4262908; e-mail btp@btp.org.tr; internet www.btp.org.tr; f. 2001; Chair. Prof. Dr HAYDAR BAŞ.

Büyük Birlik Partisi (BBP) (Great Unity Party): Tuna Cad. 28, Yenişehir, Ankara; tel. (312) 4340923; fax (312) 4355818; e-mail bbp@bbp.org.tr; internet www.bbp.org.tr; f. 1993; Chair. MUHSIN YAZICIOĞLU.

Cumhuriyet Halk Partisi (CHP) (Republican People's Party): Anadolu Bul. 12 Söğütözü, Ankara; tel. and fax (312) 2074000; e-mail chpbim@chp.org.tr; internet www.chp.org.tr; f. 1923 by Kemal Atatürk; dissolved in 1981 and reactivated in 1992; merged with Sosyal Demokrat Halkçı Parti (Social Democratic Populist Party) in Feb. 1995 and with the Yeni Türkiye Partisi in Oct. 2004; left-wing; Leader DENIZ BAYKAL; Sec.-Gen. TARHAN ERDEM.

Değişen Türkiye Partisi (DEPAR) (Changing Turkey Party): Aşağlı Öveçler 6, Cad. 78, Sok. 15/2, Dikmen, Ankara; tel. (312) 4794875; fax (312) 4795964; f. 1998; Chair. GÖKHAN ÇAPOĞLU.

Demokrasi ve Barış Partisi (DBP) (Democracy and Peace Party): Menekşe 1, Sok. 10-A/7, Kızılay, Ankara; tel. (312) 4173587; f. 1996; pro-Kurdish; Leader REFIK KARAKOÇ.

Demokrat Parti (DP) (Democratic Party): Çetýn Emeç Bul. 117, Balgat, Ankara; tel. (312) 4441946; fax (312) 2898783; e-mail dp@dp.org.tr; internet www.dp.org.tr; f. 1983 as Doğru Yol Partisi (True Path Party); renamed as above in May 2007, amid planned merger with Anavatan Partisi (Motherland Party); however, merger subsequently failed; centre-right; Chair. SÜLEYMAN SOYLU.

Demokratik Sol Parti (DSP) (Democratic Left Party): Fevzi Çakmak Cad. 17, Ankara; tel. (312) 2124950; fax (312) 2124188; e-mail dsp@dsp.org.tr; internet www.dsp.org.tr; f. 1985, drawing support from mems of the fmr Republican People's Party; centre-left; Sec.-Gen. ZEKI SEZER.

Demokratik Toplum Partisi (DTP) (Democratic Society Party): Barışmançо Cad. 32, Sok. 37 Balgat, Ankara; tel. (12) 2863200; fax (12) 2851819; f. 2004 as Democratic Society Movement; registered as pol. party 2005; Pres LEYLA ZANA, SELMA IRMAK.

Emek Partisi (EMEP) (Labour Party of Turkey): Kocamustafapaşa Cad., Turan Topal Sok., Findikoba Ishani 2/2, Fatih, İstanbul; tel. (212) 5884332; fax (212) 5884341; e-mail international@emep.org; internet www.emep.org; f. 1996; advocates scientific socialism; Pres. LEVENT TÜZEL.

Emekci Halk Partisi (EHP) (Working People's Party): f. Jan. 2004.

Genç Parti (GP) (Youth Party): İller Sok. 7, Mebusevleri, 06580 Tandoğan, Ankara; tel. (312) 2969700; fax (312) 2969757; internet www.gencpartiliyiz.com; f. 2002; populist, nationalist; Leader CEM UZAN.

Halkın Yükselişi Partisi (HYP) (People's Ascent Party): Filistin Sok. 30, Ankara; tel. (312) 4480621; fax (312) 4476968; e-mail hypgenelmerkez@hyp.org.tr; internet www.hyp.org.tr; f. 2005; advocates social democratic principles; Leader YAŞAR NURI ÖZTÜRK.

İşçi Partisi (IP) (Workers' Party): Toros Sok. 9, Sıhhiye, Ankara; tel. (312) 2318111; fax (312) 2292994; e-mail ip@ip.org.tr; internet www.ip.org.tr; f. 1992; Chair. DOĞU PERINÇEK.

Liberal Demokratik Parti (LDP) (Liberal Democratic Party): Gazi Mustafa Kemal Bul., 108/18 Maltepe, 06570 Ankara; tel. (312) 2323374; fax (312) 4687597; e-mail info@ldp.org.tr; internet www.ldp.org.tr; f. 1994; Chair. CEM TOKER.

Millet Partisi (MP) (Nation Party): İstanbul Cad., Rüzgarlı Gayret Sok. 2, Ankara; tel. (312) 3127626; fax (312) 3127651; internet www.milletpartisi.org; f. 1992; Chair. AYKUT EDIBALI.

Milliyetçi Hareket Partisi (MHP) (Nationalist Action Party): Ceyhun Atıf Kansu Cad. 128, Balgat, Ankara; tel. (312) 4725555; fax (312) 4731544; e-mail bilgi@mhp.org.tr; internet www.mhp.org.tr; f. 1983; fmrly the Democratic and Conservative Party; Leader DEVLET BAHÇELI; Sec.-Gen. FARUK BAL.

Özgürlük ve Dayanisma Partisi (ODP) (Freedom and Solidarity Party): GMK Bul. 87/18, Maltepe, Ankara; tel. (312) 2317232; fax 2320347; e-mail odp@odp.org.tr; internet www.odp.org.tr; f. 1996; Leader UFUK URAZ.

Özgür Toplum Parti (OTP) (Free Society Party): f. June 2003; assoc. with Halkın Demokrasi Partisi; Leader AHMET TURAN DEMIR.

Saadet Partisi (SP) (Felicity Party): Ziyabey Cad. 2, Sok. 15, 06520 Balgat, Ankara; tel. (312) 2848800; fax (312) 2856246; e-mail info@

saadet.org.tr; internet www.saadet.org.tr; f. 2001; replaced conservative wing of Islamist fundamentalist and free-market advocating Fazilet Partisi (Virtue Party), which was banned in that year; Chair. RECAI KUTAN.

Türkiye Komünist Partisi (TKP) (Communist Party of Turkey): Osmanağa Mahallesi Nüzhet Efendi Sok. 4, Kadıköy, İstanbul; tel. (216) 3455480; fax (216) 3461137; e-mail tkp@tkp.org.tr; internet www.tkp.org.tr; f. 1981 as the Party of Socialist Power; name changed as above in 2001; Gen. Sec. AYDEMIR GÜLER.

Yurt Partisi (Homeland Party): Necatibey Cad. 61/15, Kızılay, Ankara; tel. (312) 2325166; fax (312) 2324909; e-mail genelmerkez@yurtpartisi.org.tr; internet www.yurtpartisi.org.tr; f. 2002; nationalist and conservative party; Leader SAADETIN TANTAN.

The following proscribed organizations were engaged in an armed struggle against the Government:

Devrimci Halk Kurtuluş—Cephesi (DHKP—C) (Revolutionary People's Liberation Party—Front): e-mail dhkc@ozgurluk.org; left-wing faction of Dev-Sol; subsumed parent org. in 1996.

Partiya Karkeren Kurdistan (PKK) (Kurdistan Workers' Party): internet www.pkk.org; f. 1978; 57-member directorate; launched struggle for an independent Kurdistan in 1984; declared cease-fire 2000; renamed Congress for Freedom and Democracy in Kurdistan (KADEK) April 2002 and KONGRA-GEL Nov. 2003; return to fmr name, PKK, announced April 2005, following resumption of armed struggle; name KONGRA-GEL continued to be used by some elements; re-emerged military wing, Hezên Parastina Gel (HPG—People's Defence Forces); Leader ABDULLAH ÖCALAN; Chair. ZÜBEYIR AYDAR.

Diplomatic Representation

EMBASSIES IN TURKEY

Afghanistan: Cinnah Cad. 88, 06551 Çankaya, Ankara; tel. (312) 4422523; fax (312) 4422269; Ambassador MASOOD KHALILI.

Albania: Ebuziya Tevfik Sok. 17, Çankaya, Ankara; tel. (312) 4416103; fax (312) 4416109; e-mail embassy.ankara@mfa.gov.al; Ambassador ALTIN KODRA.

Algeria: Şehit Ersan Cad. 42, 06680 Çankaya, Ankara; tel. (312) 4687719; fax (312) 4687593; e-mail cezayirbe@yahoo.fr; Ambassador SMAÏL ALLAOUA.

Argentina: Uğur Mumcu Cad. 60/3, 06700 Gaziosmanpaşa, Ankara; tel. (312) 4462062; fax (312) 4462063; e-mail embargturquia@yahoo.com.ar; Ambassador SEBASTIÁN BRUGO MARCÓ.

Australia: Uğur Mumcu Cad. 88, 7th Floor, 06700 Gaziosmanpaşa, Ankara; tel. (312) 4599500; fax (312) 4464827; e-mail dima-ankara@dfat.gov.au; internet www.turkey.embassy.gov.au; Ambassador PETER LEO DOYLE.

Austria: Atatürk Bul. 189, Kavaklıdere, Ankara; tel. (312) 4190431; fax (312) 4189454; e-mail ankara-ob@bmeia.gv.at; Ambassador Dr HEIDEMARIA GÜRER.

Azerbaijan: Cemal Nadir Sok. 20 Celikler Apt, Çankaya, Ankara; tel. (312) 4412620; fax (312) 4412600; e-mail azer-tr@tr.net; internet www.azembassy.org.tr/english.htm; Ambassador ZAKIR HASHIMOV.

Bangladesh: Cinnah Cad. 78/7–10, 06690 Çankaya, Ankara; tel. (312) 4392750; fax (312) 4422561; e-mail bdootankara@superonline.com; Ambassador Maj.-Gen. MUHAMMAD ISHTIAQ.

Belarus: Abidin Daver Sok. 17, 06550 Çankaya, Ankara; tel. (312) 4416769; fax (312) 4416674; e-mail turkey@belembassy.org; Ambassador NATALYA ZHYLEVICH.

Belgium: Mahatma Gandhi Cad. 55, Gaziosmanpaşa, Ankara; tel. (312) 4056166; fax (312) 4468251; e-mail ankara@diplobel.org; internet www.diplomatie.be/ankara; Ambassador MARC VAN RYSELBERGHE.

Bosnia and Herzegovina: Turan Emeksiz Sok. 3/9, Park Evleri B Blok, Gaziosmanpaşa, Ankara; tel. (312) 4273602; fax (312) 4273604; e-mail bh_emb@kablonet.com.tr; Ambassador NADA JANKOVIĆ.

Brazil: Reşit Galip Cad., İlkadım Sok. 1, 06700 Gaziosmanpaşa, Ankara; tel. (312) 4481840; fax (312) 4481838; e-mail brasemb@brasembancara.org; internet www.brasembancara.org; Ambassador CESÁRIO MELANTONIO NETO.

Bulgaria: Atatürk Bul. 124, 06680 Kavaklıdere, Ankara; tel. (312) 4672071; fax (312) 4672574; e-mail bulankemb@ttnet.com; Ambassador BRANIMIR MLADENOV.

Canada: Cinnah Cad. 58, 06690 Çankaya, Ankara; tel. (312) 4092700; fax (312) 4092811; e-mail ankra@international.gc.ca; internet geo.international.gc.ca/canada-europa/turkey; Chargé d'affaires a.i. GRAEME MCINTYRE.

Chile: Reşit Galip Cad., İrfanli Sok. 14/1–3, 06700 Gaziosmanpaşa, Ankara; tel. (312) 4473418; fax (312) 4474725; e-mail embassy@chile.org.tr; internet www.chile.org.tr; Ambassador FRANCISCO MARAMBIO.

China, People's Republic: Gölgeli Sok. 34, 06700 Gaziosmanpaşa, Ankara; tel. (312) 4360628; fax (312) 4464248; e-mail chinaemb_tr@mfa.gov.cn; internet www.chinaembassy.org.tr; Ambassador SUN GUOXIANG.

Croatia: Kelebek Sok. 15/A, 06700 Gaziosmanpaşa, Ankara; tel. (312) 4469460; fax (312) 4464700; e-mail ankara@mvpei.hr; internet tr.mvp.hr; Ambassador GORDAN BAKOTA.

Cuba: Şölen Sok. 8, 06550 Çankaya, Ankara; tel. (312) 4428970; fax (312) 4414007; e-mail embacubatur@tr.net; Ambassador ERNESTO GÓMEZ ABASCAL.

Czech Republic: Kaptanpaşa Sok. 15, 06700 Gaziosmanpaşa, Ankara; tel. (312) 4056139; fax (312) 4463084; e-mail ankara@embassy.mzv.cz; internet www.mzv.cz/ankara; Ambassador EVA FILIPI.

Denmark: Mahatma Gandhi Cad. 74, 06700 Gaziosmanpaşa, Ankara; tel. (312) 4466141; fax (312) 4472498; e-mail ankamb@um.dk; internet www.ambankara.um.dk; Ambassador JESPER VAHR.

Egypt: Atatürk Bul. 126, 06680 Kavaklıdere, Ankara; tel. (312) 4261026; fax (312) 4270099; e-mail egankara@yahoo.com; Ambassador Dr ALAA ELDIN A. SHAWKY ELHADIDI.

Estonia: Gölgeli Sok. 16, 06700 Gaziosmanpaşa, Ankara; tel. (312) 4056970; fax (312) 4056976; e-mail ankara@mfa.ee; internet www.estemb.org.tr/embassy; Ambassador MÄRT VOLMER.

Ethiopia: Reşit Galip Cad., Gökçek Sok. 11, Ankara; tel. (312) 4360400; fax (312) 4481938; e-mail ethembank@ttnet.net.tr; Ambassador MULATU TESHOME WIRTU.

Finland: Kader Sok. 44, 06700 Gaziosmanpaşa, Ankara; tel. (312) 4261930; fax (312) 4680072; e-mail sanomat.ank@formin.fi; internet www.finland.org.tr; Ambassador MARIA SERENIUS.

France: Paris Cad. 70, 06540 Kavaklıdere, Ankara; tel. (312) 4554545; fax (312) 4554527; e-mail ambaank@yahoo.fr; internet www.ambafrance-tr.org; Ambassador BERNARD EMIÉ.

Georgia: Kılıç Ali Sok. 12, Oran, Ankara; tel. (312) 4918030; fax (312) 4426507; e-mail ankara.emb@mfa.gov.ge; Ambassador GRIGOL MGALOBLISHVILI.

Germany: Atatürk Bul. 114, 06690 Kavaklıdere, Ankara; tel. (312) 4555100; fax (312) 4266959; e-mail infomail@germanembassyank.com; internet www.ankara.diplo.de; Ambassador Dr ECKART CUNTZ.

Greece: Zia ür-Rahman Cad. 9–11, 06670 Gaziosmanpaşa, Ankara; tel. (312) 4480873; fax (312) 4463191; e-mail gremb.ank@mfa.gr; Ambassador FOTIOS-JEAN XYDAS.

Holy See: Apostolic Nunciature, Birlik Mah. 3, Cad. 37, PK 33, 06552 Çankaya, Ankara; tel. (312) 4953514; fax (312) 4953540; e-mail vatican@tr.net; Apostolic Nuncio Most Rev. ANTONIO LUCIBELLO (Titular Archbishop of Thurio).

Hungary: Sancak Mah. Layoş, Koşut Cad. 2, Yıldız, Çankaya, Ankara; tel. (312) 4422273; fax (312) 4415049; e-mail huembtur@isnet.net.tr; internet www.mfa.gov.hu/kulkepviselet/TR/hu; Ambassador ISTVÁN SZABÓ.

India: Cinnah Cad. 77/A, 06680 Çankaya, Ankara; tel. (312) 4382195; fax (312) 4403429; e-mail chancery@indembassy.org.tr; internet www.indembassy.org.tr; Ambassador CHITRA NARAYANAN.

Indonesia: Abdullah Cevdet Sok. 10, 06680 Çankaya, Ankara; tel. (312) 4382190; fax (312) 4382193; e-mail indoank@indoank.org; Ambassador AWANG BAHRIN.

Iran: Tahran Cad. 10, Kavaklıdere, Ankara; tel. (312) 4682821; fax (312) 4682823; e-mail iranembassy_ankara@hotmail.com; Ambassador GHOLAMREZA BAQERI-MOQADDAM (acting).

Iraq: Turan Emeksiz Sok. 11, 06700 Gaziosmanpaşa, Ankara; tel. (312) 4687421; fax (312) 4684832; e-mail ankemb@iraqmofamail.net; Ambassador SABAH J. OMRAN.

Ireland: Uğur Mumcu Cad. 88, MNG Binası B Blok Kat 3, Gaziosmanpaşa 06700 Ankara; tel. (312) 4466172; fax (312) 4468061; e-mail ankaraembassy@dfa.ie; Ambassador ANTONY MANNIX.

Israel: Mahatma Gandhi Cad. 85, 06700 Gaziosmanpaşa, Ankara; tel. (312) 4597500; fax (312) 4597555; e-mail info@ankara.mfa.gov.il; internet ankara.mfa.gov.il; Ambassador GAVRIEL LEVY.

Italy: Atatürk Bul. 118, 06680 Kavaklıdere, Ankara; tel. (312) 4574200; fax (312) 4574280; e-mail ambasciata.ankara@esteri.it; internet www.italian-embassy.org.ae/Ambasciata_Ankara; Ambassador CARLO MARSILI.

Japan: Reşit Galip Cad. 81, 06692 Gaziosmanpaşa, Ankara; tel. (312) 4460500; fax (312) 4371812; e-mail culture@jpn-emb.org.tr; internet www.tr.emb-japan.go.jp; Ambassador NOBUAKI TANAKA.

Jordan: Dede Korkut Sok. 18 Mesnevi, 06690 Çankaya, Ankara; tel. (312) 4402054; fax (312) 4404327; e-mail jordembank@superonline.com; Ambassador FARIS SHAWKAT AL-MUFTI.

Kazakhstan: Kiliç Ali Sok. 6, Oran Sitesi, Çankaya, Ankara; tel. (312) 4919100; fax (312) 4904455; e-mail kazank@kazakhstan.org.tr; internet www.kazakhstan.org.tr; Chargé d'affaires a.i. YERZHAN ISSIN.

Korea, Republic: Cinnah Cad., Alaçam Sok 5, 06690 Çankaya, Ankara; tel. (312) 4684822; fax (312) 4682279; e-mail turkey@mofat.go.kr; internet tur-ankara.mofat.go.kr; Ambassador KIM CHANG-YEOB.

Kuwait: Reşit Galip Cad. Kelebek Sok. 110, Gaziosmanpaşa, Ankara; tel. (312) 4450576; fax (312) 4466839; e-mail kuwait@ada.net.tr; Ambassador ABDULLAH ABD AL-AZIZ AD-DUWAIKH.

Kyrgyzstan: Boyabat Sok. 11, Ankara; tel. (312) 4468408; fax (312) 4468411; e-mail kirgiz-o@tr.net; Ambassador MAMBETJUNUS ABYLOV.

Latvia: Reşit Galip Cad. 95, Çankaya, Ankara; tel. (312) 4056136; fax (312) 4056137; e-mail embassy.turkey@mfa.gov.lv; Ambassador IVARS PUNDURS.

Lebanon: Kızkulesi Sok. 44, Gaziosmanpaşa, 06700 Ankara; tel. (312) 4467487; fax (312) 4461023; e-mail lebembas@ttnet.net.tr; Chargé d'affaires WAJIB ABD AS-SAMAD.

Libya: Cinnah Cad. 60, 06690 Çankaya, Ankara; tel. (312) 4381110; fax (312) 4403862; e-mail ashaabiankara@hotmail.com; Chargé d'affaires a.i. MUHAMMAD ZENATI.

Lithuania: Mahatma Gandhi Cad. 17/8–9, 06700 Gaziosmanpaşa, Ankara; tel. (312) 4470766; fax (312) 4470663; e-mail lrambasd@ada.net.tr; Ambassador DARIUS PRANCKEVIČIUS.

Macedonia, former Yugoslav republic: Karaca Sok. 24/5–6, 06700 Gaziosmanpaşa, Ankara; tel. (312) 4399204; fax (312) 4399206; e-mail macemb@ttnet.net.tr; Ambassador MELPOMENI KORNETI.

Malaysia: Mahatma Gandhi Cad. 58, 06700 Gaziosmanpaşa, Ankara; tel. (312) 4463547; fax (312) 4464130; e-mail malankara@kln.gov.my; internet www.kln.gov.my/perwakilan/ankara; Ambassador Dato' SAIPUL ANWAR ABD AL-MUIN.

Mexico: Kırkpınar Sok. 8/6, 06540 Çankaya, Ankara; tel. (312) 4423033; fax (312) 4420221; e-mail mexico@embamextur.com; internet www.mexico.org.tr; Ambassador SALVADOR CAMPOS ICARDO.

Moldova: Kaptanpaşa Sok. 49, 06700 Gaziosmanpaşa, Ankara; tel. (312) 4465527; fax (312) 4465816; e-mail ankara@mfa.md; Ambassador MIHAIL BARBULAT.

Mongolia: Koza Sok. 109, 06700 Gaziosmanpaşa, Ankara; tel. (312) 4467977; fax (312) 4467791; e-mail mogolelc@ttnet.net.tr; internet web.ttnet.net.tr/mogolelc; Ambassador OCHIRYN OCHIRJAV.

Morocco: Reşit Galip Cad., Rabat Sok. 11, 06700 Gaziosmanpaşa, Ankara; tel. (312) 4376020; fax (312) 4471405; e-mail sifamatr@tr.net; Ambassador ABDELLAH ZAGOUR.

Netherlands: Hollanda Cad. 3, 06550 Yıldız, Ankara; tel. (312) 4091800; fax (312) 4091898; e-mail ank@minbuza.nl; internet www.nl.org.tr; Ambassador P. M. KURPERSHOEK.

New Zealand: PK 162, İran Cad. 13/4, 06700 Kavaklıdere, Ankara; tel. (312) 4679054; fax (312) 4679013; e-mail nzembassyankara@ttnet.net.tr; internet www.nzembassy.com/turkey; Ambassador HAMISH COOPER.

Nigeria: Uğur Mumcu Sok. 56, 06700 Gaziosmanpaşa, Ankara; tel. (312) 4481077; fax (312) 4481082; Chargé d'affaires a.i. IBUKUN A. OLATIDOYE.

Norway: Kirkpinar Sok. 18, 06540 Çankaya, Ankara; tel. (312) 4058010; fax (312) 4430544; e-mail emb.ankara@mfa.no; internet www.norway.org.tr; Ambassador CECILIE LANDSVERK.

Oman: Mahatma Gandhi Cad. 63, 06700 Gaziosmanpaşa, Ankara; tel. (312) 4470630; fax (312) 4470632; e-mail omanembassy@yahoo.com; Ambassador MUHAMMAD NASSER AL-WOHAIBI.

Pakistan: İran Cad. 37, 06700 Gaziosmanpaşa, Ankara; tel. (312) 4271410; fax (312) 4671023; e-mail parepank@yahoo.com; Ambassador Lt-Gen. (retd) SYED IFTIKHAR HUSSAIN SHAH.

Philippines: Mahatma Gandhi Cad. 56, 06700 Gaziosmanpaşa, Ankara; tel. (312) 4465831; fax (312) 4465733; e-mail ankarape@dfa.gov.ph; Ambassador BAHNARIM A. GUINOMLA.

Poland: Atatürk Bul. 241, 06650 Kavaklıdere, Ankara; tel. (312) 4675619; fax (312) 4678963; e-mail polamb@superonline.com; internet www.polonya.org.tr; Chargé d'affaires a.i. KRZYSZTOF LEWANDOWSKI.

Portugal: Kuleli Cad. 26, 06700 Gaziosmanpaşa, Ankara; tel. (312) 4056028; fax (312) 4463670; e-mail embaixada@portugal.org.tr; Ambassador JOSÉ MANUEL DE CARVALHO LAMEIRAS.

Qatar: Bakü Sok. 6, Diplomatic Site, Oran, Ankara; tel. (312) 4907274; fax (312) 4906757; e-mail ankara@mofa.gov.qa; Ambassador ABD AR-RAZAK ABD AL-GHANI.

Romania: Bükreş Sok. 4, 06680 Çankaya, Ankara; tel. (312) 4271243; fax (312) 4271530; e-mail romanyabyk@dsl.ttnet.net.tr; Chargé d'affaires a.i. PETRE STOICESCU.

Russia: Karyağdı Sok. 5, 06692 Çankaya, Ankara; tel. (312) 4392122; fax (312) 4383952; e-mail rus-ankara@yandex.ru; internet www.turkey.mid.ru; Ambassador VLADIMIR E. IVANOVSKII.

Saudi Arabia: Turan Emeksiz Sok. 6, 06700 Gaziosmanpaşa, Ankara; tel. (312) 4685540; fax (312) 4274886; e-mail tremb@mofa.gov.sa; Ambassador MUHAMMAD AL-HUSSAINI ASH-SHARIF.

Senegal: İran Cad. 47/5, Gaziosmanpaşa, Ankara; tel. (312) 4663086; fax (312) 4272213; Chargé d'affaires a.i. MARCELLINE PELEVALA SYLLA.

Serbia: Paris Cad. 47, 06450 Kavaklıdere, Ankara; tel. (312) 4260236; fax (312) 4278345; e-mail embserank@tr.net; Ambassador VLADIMIR CURGUS.

Slovakia: Atatürk Bul. 245, 06692 Kavaklıdere, Ankara; tel. (312) 4675075; fax (312) 4682689; e-mail emb.ankara@mzv.sk; Ambassador VLADIMÍR JAKABČÍN.

Slovenia: Kırlangıç Sok. 36, 06700 Gaziosmanpaşa, Ankara; tel. (312) 4054221; fax (312) 4260216; e-mail van@gov.si; Ambassador MITJA ŠTRUKELJ.

South Africa: Filistin Sok. 27, 06700 Gaziosmanpaşa, Ankara; tel. (312) 4464056; fax (312) 4466434; e-mail political@southafrica.org.tr; internet www.southafrica.org.tr; Ambassador TEBOGO JOSEPH SEOKOLO.

Spain: Abdullah Cevdet Sok. 8, 06680 Çankaya, Ankara; tel. (312) 4380392; fax (312) 4426991; e-mail emb.ankara@mae.es; Ambassador LUIS FELIPE FERNÁNDEZ DE LA PEÑA.

Sudan: Sancak Mah. 12 Cad. 16, 06550 Çankaya, Ankara; tel. (312) 4413885; fax (312) 4413886; e-mail ankara@mfa.gov.sd; Ambassador MUHAMMAD AL-HASSAN AHMED AL-HAJ.

Sweden: Katip Çelebi Sok. 7, 06692 Kavaklıdere, Ankara; tel. (312) 4554100; fax (312) 4554120; e-mail ambassaden.ankara@foreign.ministry.se; internet www.swedenabroad.com/ankara; Ambassador CHRISTER ASP.

Switzerland: Atatürk Bul. 247, 06692 Kavaklıdere, Ankara; tel. (312) 4675555; fax (312) 4671199; e-mail ank.vertretung@eda.admin.ch; internet www.eda.admin.ch/ankara; Ambassador WALTER B. GYGER.

Syria: Sedat Simavi Sok. 40, 06680 Çankaya, Ankara; tel. (312) 4409657; fax (312) 4385609; Ambassador KHALED RAAD.

Tajikistan: Cayhane Cad. 24, Gaziosmanpaşa, Ankara; tel. (312) 4461602; fax (312) 4463621; e-mail tajemb_turkey@inbox.ru; Ambassador SHUKHRAT M. SULTONOV.

Thailand: Çankaya Cad. Kader Sok. 45/3–4, 06700 Gaziosmanpaşa, Ankara; tel. (312) 4673059; fax (312) 4277284; Ambassador KANYA CHAIMAN.

Tunisia: Kuleli Sok. 12, 06700 Gaziosmanpaşa, Ankara; tel. (312) 4377812; fax (312) 4377100; e-mail at.ankara@superonline.com; Ambassador GHAZI JOMAA.

'Turkish Republic of Northern Cyprus': Rabat Sok. 20, 06700 Gaziosmanpaşa, Ankara; tel. (312) 4376031; fax (312) 4465238; e-mail kktcbe@superonline.com; Ambassador TAMER GAZIOĞLU.

Turkmenistan: Koza Sok. 28, 06700 Gaziosmanpaşa, Ankara; tel. (312) 4416122; fax (312) 4417125; e-mail tmankara@ttnet.net.tr; Ambassador NURBERDY AMANMURADOV.

Ukraine: Sancak Mahallesi 206 Sok. 17, 06550 Çankaya, Ankara; tel. (312) 4415499; fax (312) 4406815; e-mail emb_tr@mfa.gov.ua; internet www.mfa.gov.ua/turkey; Ambassador OLEKSANDR MISCHENKO.

United Arab Emirates: Turan Güneş Bul. 15, Cad. 290, Sok. 3, Sancak Mah., Çankaya, Ankara; tel. (312) 4901414; fax (312) 4912333; e-mail uaeemb@uaeemb.net; internet www.uaeemb.net; Chargé d'affaires a.i. ISMAIL AZ-ZAABI.

United Kingdom: Şehit Ersan Cad. 46/A, 06680 Çankaya, Ankara; tel. (312) 4553344; fax (312) 4553356; e-mail britembinf@fco.gov.uk; internet www.britishembassy.gov.uk/turkey; Ambassador NICK BAIRD.

USA: Atatürk Bul. 110, 06100 Kavaklıdere, Ankara; tel. (312) 4555555; fax (312) 4670019; e-mail webmaster_ankara@state.gov; internet turkey.usembassy.gov; Ambassador ROSS WILSON.

Uzbekistan: Sancak Mah. 211 Sok. 3, 06550 Çankaya, Ankara; tel. (312) 4413871; fax (312) 4427058; e-mail embankara@post.mfa.uz; Ambassador ULFAT S. KADYROV.

Venezuela: Koza Sok. 91/3, 06700 Gaziosmanpaşa, Ankara; tel. (312) 4478131; fax (312) 4470711; e-mail embveank@tarassul.sy; Chargé d'affaires a.i. RAÚL JOSÉ BETANCOURT SEELAND.

Viet Nam: Çayhane Sok. 34, Gaziosmanpaşa, Ankara; tel. (312) 4468049; fax (312) 4465623; e-mail dsqvnturkey@yahoo.com; Ambassador NGUYEN SY XUNG.

TURKEY

Yemen: Fethiye Sok. 2, 06700 Gaziosmanpaşa, Ankara; tel. (312) 4462637; fax (312) 4461778; e-mail yemenemb@superonline.com; Ambassador NORIA ABDULLAH AL-HAMAMI.

Judicial System

Until the foundation of the Turkish Republic, a large part of the Turkish civil law—the laws affecting the family, inheritance, property, obligations, etc.—was based on the Koran, and this holy law was administered by special religious (*Shari'a*) courts. The legal reform of 1926 was not only a process of secularization, but also a radical change of the legal system. The Swiss Civil Code and the Code of Obligation, the Italian Penal Code and the Neuchâtel (Cantonal) Code of Civil Procedure were adopted and modified to fit Turkish customs and traditions.

According to current Turkish law, the power of the judiciary is exercised by judicial (criminal), military and administrative courts. These courts render their verdicts in the first instance, while superior courts examine the verdict for subsequent rulings.

SUPERIOR COURTS

Constitutional Court: Consists of 11 regular and four substitute members, appointed by the President. Reviews the constitutionality of laws, at the request of the President of the Republic, parliamentary groups of the governing party or of the main opposition party, or of one-fifth of the members of the National Assembly, and sits as a high council empowered to try senior members of state. The rulings of the Constitutional Court are final. Decisions of the Court are published immediately in the Official Gazette, and shall be binding on the legislative, executive and judicial organs of the state; Chief Justice HAŞIM KILIÇ.

Court of Appeals: The court of the last instance for reviewing the decisions and verdicts rendered by judicial courts. It has original and final jurisdiction in specific cases defined by law. Members are elected by the Supreme Council of Judges and Prosecutors; Chief Justice HASAN GERÇEKER.

Council of State: An administrative court of the first and last instance in matters not referred by law to other administrative courts, and an administrative court of the last instance in general. Hears and settles administrative disputes and expresses opinions on draft laws submitted by the Council of Ministers. Three-quarters of the members are appointed by the Supreme Council of Judges and Public Prosecutors, the remaining quarter is selected by the President of the Republic.

Military Court of Appeals: A court of the last instance to review decisions and verdicts rendered by military courts, and a court of first and last instance with jurisdiction over certain military persons, stipulated by law, with responsibility for the specific trials of these persons. Members are selected by the President of the Republic from nominations made by the Military Court of Appeals.

Supreme Military Administrative Court: A military court for the judicial control of administrative acts concerning military personnel. Members are selected by the President of the Republic from nominations made by the Court.

Court of Jurisdictional Disputes: Settles disputes among judicial, administrative and military courts arising from disagreements on jurisdictional matters and verdicts.

Court of Accounts: A court charged with the auditing of all accounts of revenue, expenditure and government property, which renders rulings related to transactions and accounts of authorized bodies on behalf of the National Assembly.

Supreme Council of Judges and Public Prosecutors: The President of the Council shall be the Minister of Justice, and the Under-Secretary to the Minister of Justice shall serve as an ex officio member of the Council. Three regular and three substitute members from the Court of Appeals, together with two regular and two substitute members of the Council of State, shall be appointed to the Supreme Council by the President of the Republic for a four-year term. Decides all personnel matters relating to judges and public prosecutors.

Public Prosecutor: The law shall make provision for the tenure of public prosecutors and attorneys of the Council of State and their functions. The Chief Prosecutor of the Republic, the Chief Attorney of the Council of State and the Chief Prosecutor of the Military Court of Appeals are subject to the provisions applicable to judges of higher courts.

Military Trial: Military trials are conducted by military and disciplinary courts. These courts are entitled to try the military offences of military personnel and those offences committed against military personnel or in military areas, or offences connected with military service and duties. Military courts may try non-military persons only for military offences prescribed by special laws.

Religion

ISLAM

More than 99% of the Turkish people are Muslims. However, Turkey is a secular state. Although Islam was stated to be the official religion in the Constitution of 1924, an amendment in 1928 removed this privilege. Since 1950 subsequent Governments have tried to re-establish links between religion and state affairs, but secularity was protected by the revolution of 1960, the 1980 military takeover and the 1982 Constitution.

Diyanet İşleri Başkanlığı (Presidency of Religious Affairs): Eskişehir Yolu 9 km Çankaya, Ankara; tel. (312) 2957000; e-mail diyanet@diyanet.gov.tr; internet www.diyanet.gov.tr; Pres. Prof. Dr ALI BARDAKOĞLU.

CHRISTIANITY

The town of Antioch (now Antakya) was one of the earliest strongholds of Christianity, and by the 4th century had become a patriarchal see. Formerly in Syria, the town was incorporated into Turkey in 1939. Constantinople (now İstanbul) was also a patriarchal see, and by the 6th century the Patriarch of Constantinople was recognized as the Ecumenical Patriarch in the East. Gradual estrangement from Rome developed, leading to the final breach between the Catholic West and the Orthodox East, usually assigned to the year 1054.

There are estimated to be about 100,000 Christians in Turkey.

The Orthodox Churches

Armenian Patriarchate: Ermeni Patrikliği, 34130 Kumkapı, İstanbul; tel. (212) 5170970; fax (212) 5164833; e-mail info@lraper.org; internet www.lraper.org; f. 1461; 100,000 adherents (incl. workers from Armenia—2007); Patriarch MESROB II.

Bulgarian Orthodox Church: Bulgar Ortodoks Kilisesi, Halâskâr Gazi Cad. 319, Şişli, İstanbul; Rev. Archimandrite GANCO ÇOBANOF.

Greek Orthodox Church: The Ecumenical Patriarchate (Rum Ortodoks Patrikhanesi), Sadrazam Ali Paşa Cad. 35, 34220 Fener-Haliç, İstanbul; tel. (212) 5255416; fax (212) 5316533; e-mail patriarchate@ec-patr.org; internet www.ec-patr.org; Archbishop of Constantinople (New Rome) and Ecumenical Patriarch BARTHOLOMEW I.

The Roman Catholic Church

At 31 December 2005 there were an estimated 24,949 adherents in the country.

Bishops' Conference: Conferenza Episcopale di Turchia, Satırcı Sok 2, Harbiye, 34373 İstanbul; tel. (212) 2190089; fax (212) 2411543; f. 1987; Pres. Most Rev. RUGGERO FRANCESCHINI (Archbishop of İzmir).

Armenian Rite

Patriarchate of Cilicia: f. 1742; Patriarch NERSES BEDROS TARMOUNI XIX (resident in Beirut, Lebanon).

Archdiocese of İstanbul: Sakızağacı Cad. 31, PK 183, 80072 Beyoğlu, İstanbul; tel. (212) 2441258; fax (212) 2432364; f. 1928; Archbishop HOVHANNES TCHOLAKIAN.

Byzantine Rite

Apostolic Exarchate of İstanbul: Hamalbaşı Cad. 44, PK 259, 80070 Beyoğlu, İstanbul; tel. (212) 2440351; fax (212) 2411543; f. 1911; Apostolic Admin. LOUIS PELÂTRE (Titular Bishop of Sasima).

Bulgarian Catholic Church: Bulgar Katolik Kilisesi, Eski Parmakkapı Sok. 15, Galata, İstanbul.

Latin Rite

Metropolitan Archdiocese of İzmir: Church of St Polycarp, Necatibey Bul. 2, PK 267, 35210 İzmir; tel. (232) 4840531; fax (232) 4845358; e-mail curiaves@yahoo.it; f. 1818; Archbishop of İzmir Most Rev. RUGGERO FRANCESCHINI.

Apostolic Vicariate of Anatolia: Mithat Paša Cad. 5, PK 75, 31200 Iskenderum; tel. (326) 6175916; fax (326) 6139291; e-mail curiaves@yahoo.it; f. 1990; Vicar Apostolic LUIGI PADOVESE (Titular Bishop of Monteverde).

Apostolic Vicariate of İstanbul: Papa Roncalli Sok. 83, 80230 Harbiye, İstanbul; tel. (212) 2480775; fax (212) 2411543; e-mail vapostolique@yahoo.fr; f. 1742; Vicar Apostolic LOUIS PELÂTRE (Titular Bishop of Sasima).

Maronite Rite

The Maronite Patriarch of Antioch, Cardinal Nasrallah Pierre Sfeir, is resident in Lebanon.

TURKEY

Melkite Rite
The Greek Melkite Patriarch of Antioch, Grégoire III Laham, is resident in Damascus, Syria.

Syrian Rite
The Syrian Catholic Patriarch of Antioch, Ignace Pierre VIII Abdel Ahad, is resident in Beirut, Lebanon.

Patriarchal Exarchate of Turkey: Sarayarkası Sok 15, PK 84, 80090 Ayazpaşa, İstanbul; tel. (212) 2432521; fax (212) 2490261; f. 1908; Patriarchal Exarch Fr. MARZENA ESHAK.

The Anglican Communion
Within the Church of England, Turkey forms part of the diocese of Gibraltar in Europe. The Bishop is resident in the United Kingdom.

Anglican Chaplaincy in İstanbul: Christ Church, Serdar Ekram Sok. 82, Karaköy, İstanbul; tel. (212) 2515616; fax (212) 2435702; e-mail parson@tnn.net; internet www.anglicanistanbul.com; Chaplain Rev. Canon IAN SHERWOOD.

JUDAISM
There are estimated to be about 23,000 Jews in Turkey.

Jewish Community of Turkey: Türkiye Hahambaşılığı, Yemenici Sok 23, Beyoğlu, 34430 Tünel, İstanbul; tel. (212) 2938794; fax (212) 2441980; e-mail info@musevicemaati.com; internet www.musevicemaati.com; Chief Rabbis ISAK HALEVA, DAVID ASSEO.

The Press

Almost all İstanbul papers are also printed in Ankara and İzmir on the same day, and some in Adana. Among the most serious and influential papers are the dailies *Milliyet* and *Cumhuriyet*. The weekly *Gırgır* is noted for its political satire. The most popular dailies are the İstanbul papers *Sabah*, *Hürriyet*, *Milliyet* and *Zaman*; *Yeni Asır*, published in İzmir, is the best-selling quality daily of the Aegean region. There are numerous provincial newspapers with a limited circulation.

PRINCIPAL DAILIES

Adana
Yeni Adana: Abidinpaşa Cad. 70, 01010 Adana; tel. (322) 3599984; fax (322) 3593655; e-mail yeniadana@ttnet.net.tr; internet www.yeniadana.net; f. 1918; political; Propr ÇETIN REMZI YÜREĞIR; Chief Editor AHMET YAHŞI; circ. 2,000.

Ankara
Ankara Ticaret: Rüzgârlı Caddesi, Ibrahim Müteferrika Sok. 2/10, Ankara; tel. (312) 3112131; fax (312) 3116690; f. 1954; commercial; Chief Editor ZEKI OCAK; Gen. Man. ISTIKLAL YARADILIŞ; circ. 2,470.

Belde: Rüzgarlı Gayret Sok. 7/1, Ulus, Ankara; tel. (312) 3106820; f. 1968; Propr İLHAN İŞBILEN; circ. 3,399.

The New Anatolian: Şehit Ersan Cad. 4/15–16 Kavaklıdere, Ankara; tel. (312) 4674151; fax (312) 4674156; e-mail tna@thenewanatolian.com; internet www.thenewanatolian.com; English language; Founder ILHAN ÇEVIK; Editor-in-Chief METE BELOVACIKLI.

Tasvir: Rüzgarlı Plevne Sok. 14, Ulus, Ankara; tel. (312) 3101443; fax (312) 3122209; f. 1960; conservative; Editor ENDER YOKDAR; circ. 3,055.

Turkish Daily News: Sogutozu Mahallesi Dumlupinar Bul. 102, 06510 Çankaya, Ankara; tel. (312) 2070090; fax (312) 2070094; e-mail tdn@tdn.com.tr; internet www.turkishdailynews.com; f. 1961; English language; CEO NURI M. ÇOLAKOĞLU; Exec. Editor EYÜP CAN SAĞLIK; circ. 54,500.

Türkiye Ticaret Sicili: Karanfil Sok. 56, Bakanlıklar, Ankara; tel. (312) 4138000; fax (312) 4258173; e-mail ttsgmd@tobb.org.tr; internet www.ticaretsicil.gov.tr; f. 1957; commercial; Publr KEMAL CIRAK; Editor YALÇIN KAYA AYDOS.

Vakit: Ada 55, İstoç Bağcılar, İstanbul; tel. (212) 6592056; fax (212) 4474209; e-mail haber@vakit.com.tr; internet www.vakit.com.tr; f. 1978; Man. Editor AHMET KARAHASANOĞLU; circ. 3,384.

Yeni Tanin: Ankara; f. 1964; political; Propr BURHANETTIN GÖĞEN; Man. Editor AHMET TEKEŞ; circ. 3,123.

Yirmidört Saat: Gazeteciler Cemiyeti Çevre Sok. 35, Çankaya, Ankara; tel. (312) 1682384; f. 1978; Propr BEYHAN CENKÇI.

Eskişehir
Istikbal: İstiklal Mah. Porsuk Bulvarı Adalar Sok. 5, Eskişehir; tel. (222) 2201901; fax (222) 2201902; e-mail info@istikbalgazetesi.com; internet www.istikbalgazetesi.com; f. 1950; morning; Editor MURAT TAŞKIN.

Gaziantep
Olay (Event): Olay Medya Plaza, Topraklik, Gaziantep; tel. (342) 2206666; fax (342) 2206670; e-mail olay@olaymedya.com; internet www.olaymedya.com; f. 1992; Man. EROL MARAS.

İstanbul
Akşam: Davutpaşa Cad. 34, 34020 Zeytinburnu, İstanbul; tel. (212) 4493000; fax (212) 4819561; e-mail editor@aksam.com.tr; internet www.aksam.com.tr; Man. Dir SERDAR TURGUT.

Apoyevmatini: İstiklâl Cad., Suriye Pasajı 348, Beyoğlu, İstanbul; tel. (212) 2437635; f. 1925; Greek language; Publr EUSEVIA ADOSOGLOU; Editor MICHAEL VASSILIADIS; circ. 580.

Bugün: Medya Plaza Basın Ekspres Yolu, 34540 Güneşli, İstanbul; tel. (212) 5504850; fax (212) 5023340; e-mail bugun@bugun.com.tr; internet www.bugun.com.tr; f. 1989; Propr ONAY BILGIN; circ. 184,884.

Cumhuriyet (Republic): Prof. Nurettin Mazhar Öktel Sok. 2, 34381 Şişli, İstanbul; tel. (212) 3437274; fax (212) 3437264; e-mail postakutusu@cumhuriyet.com.tr; internet www.cumhuriyet.com.tr; f. 1924; morning; liberal; Man. Editor HIKMET ÇETINKAYA; circ. 75,000.

Dünya (World): Basınevi Balamir Sok. 7, İstanbul; tel. (216) 6811800; fax (216) 6803975; e-mail dunya@dunyagazetesi.com.tr; internet www.dunyagazetesi.com.tr; f. 1952; morning; economic; Editor-in-Chief OSMAN S. AROLAT; circ. 60,000.

Fotomaç: Medya Plaza, Basın Ekspres Yolu, 34540 Güneşli, İstanbul; tel. (212) 5504900; fax (212) 5028217; internet www.fotomac.com.tr; f. 1991; sport; Chief Officer İBRAHIM SETEN; circ. 250,000.

Günaydın-Tan: Alayköşkü, Cad. Eryilmaz Sok. 13, Cağaloğlu, İstanbul; tel. (212) 5120050; fax (212) 5260823; f. 1968; Editor-in-Chief SECKIN TURESAY.

Hürriyet: Babiali Cad. 15–17, Guneslikoy, 34540 Bakırköy, İstanbul; tel. (212) 5550050; fax (212) 5156705; e-mail editor@hurriyet.com.tr; internet www.hurriyet.com.tr; f. 1948; morning; independent political; Propr AYDIN DOĞAN; Chief Editor ERTUĞRUL ÖZKÖK; circ. 542,797.

Meydan (Nationalism): Yüzyıl Mahallesi, Mahmutbey Viyadüğü Altı, İkitelli, 34410 Cağaloğlu, İstanbul; tel. (212) 5056111; fax (212) 5056436; f. 1990; Propr REFIK ARAS; Editor UFUK GULDEMIR.

Milli Gazete: Cemal Ulusoy Cad. 38/A, 34620 Bahçelievler, İstanbul; tel. (212) 6971000; fax (212) 6931801; e-mail milli@milligazete.com.tr; internet www.milligazete.com.tr; f. 1973; pro-Islamist; right-wing; Editor-in-Chief EKREM KIZILTAŞ; circ. 51,000.

Milliyet: Doğan Medya Center, Bağcılar, 34204 İstanbul; tel. (212) 5056111; fax (212) 5056233; e-mail webadmin@milliyet.com.tr; internet www.milliyet.com.tr; f. 1950; morning; political; Editor-in-Chief DERYA SAZAK; circ. 630,000.

Nor Marmara: İstiklâl Cad., Solakzade Sok. 5, PK 507, İstanbul; tel. (212) 2444736; e-mail info@normarmara.com; internet www.normarmara.com; f. 1940; Armenian language; Propr and Editor-in-Chief ROBER HADDELER; Gen. Man. ARI HADDELER; circ. 2,200.

Sabah (Morning): Medya Plaza, Basın Ekspres Yolu, Günesli, İstanbul; tel. (212) 5504810; fax (212) 5028143; internet www.sabah.com.tr; assets seized by the state Savings Deposit Insurance Fund in April 2007; transfer to ownership of Turkuvaz Radyo Televizyon ve Gazetecilik AŞ (a subsidiary of Çalık Holding) was approved by the Fund in Feb. 2008, for completion by May; Editor-in-Chief ERGUN BABAHAN; circ. 550,000.

Tercüman: Davutpaşa Cad. 34, Zeytinbumu, İstanbul; tel. (212) 4493000; fax (212) 4819550; internet www.tercuman.com.tr; f. 1961; right-wing; Propr SEDAT COLAK; Chief Editor BÜLENT CAN; circ. 32,869.

Türkiye (Turkey): Ekim Cad. 29, 34197 Yenibosna, İstanbul; tel. (212) 4543000; fax (212) 4543100; e-mail info@tg.com.tr; internet www.turkiyegazetesi.com.tr; f. 1970; Dir of Publs NUH ALBAYRAK; circ. 450,000.

Yeni Nesil (New Generation): Sanayi Cad., Selvi Sok. 5, Yenibosna, Bakırköy, İstanbul; tel. (212) 5846261; fax (212) 5567289; f. 1970; as Yeni Asya; political; Editor-in-Chief UMIT SIMSEK.

Yeni Şafak: Yenidoğan Mah., Şenay Sok. 2, Kat 1, Bayrampaşa, İstanbul; tel. (212) 6122390; fax (212) 6121903; internet yenisafak.com.tr; Editor-in-Chief YUSUF ZIYA CÖMERT.

Yeniyüzyıl: Medya Plaza Basın Ekspres Yolu, 34540 Güneşli, İstanbul; tel. (212) 5028877; fax (212) 5028295; Editor KEREM ÇALISKAN.

Zaman (Time): Ahmet Taner Kislali Cad. 6, 34194 Yenibosna, İstanbul; tel. (212) 4541454; fax (212) 4548634; e-mail zaman@zaman.com.tr; internet www.zaman.com.tr; f. 1962; morning; political, independent; CEO EKREM DUMANLI; Editor-in-Chief BÜLENT KENEŞ; circ. 210,000.

İzmir

Rapor: Gazi Osman Paşa Bul. 5, İzmir; tel. (232) 4254400; f. 1949; Owner DINÇ BILGIN; Man. Editor TANJU ATEŞER; circ. 9,000.

Ticaret Gazetesi: 1571 Sok. 16, 35110 Çınarlı, 35110 İzmir; tel. (232) 4619642; fax (232) 4619646; e-mail ticinfo@unimedya.net.tr; internet www.ticaretgazetesi.com; f. 1942; commercial news; Editor-in-Chief AHMET SÜKUTI TÜKEL; Man. Editor CEMAL M. TÜKEL; circ. 5,009.

Yeni Asır (New Century): Gaziosmanpaşa Bul. 5, 35210 Çankaya, İzmir; tel. (232) 4415000; fax (232) 4464222; e-mail yasir@yeniasir.com.tr; internet www.yeniasir.com.tr; f. 1895; political; Man. Editor AYDIN BILGIN; Editorial Dir HAMDI TÜRKMEN; circ. 60,000.

Konya

Yeni Konya: Şeref Şirin Mah. İstanbul Cad., Ay İşhanı 3/167, Karatay/Konya; tel. (332) 3507575; fax (332) 3509920; internet www.yenikonya.com.tr; f. 1945; political; Gen. Man. MUSTAFA TATLISU; Chief Editor ALI SAKAL; monthly circ. 1,657.

Yeni Meram: Konya; tel. (332) 3452424; e-mail yenimeram@yenimeram.com.tr; internet www.yenimeram.com.tr; f. 1949; political; Propr ÇETYN REMZY YÜREĎYR; Chief Editor YALÇIN REMZY YÜREĎYR; monthly circ. 44,000.

WEEKLIES

Ankara

EBA Briefing: Bestekar Sok. 21/8, Kavaklıdere, Ankara; tel. (312) 4180628; fax (312) 4180432; f. 1975; publ. by Ekonomik Basın Ajansı (Economic Press Agency); political and economic survey; Publrs ORHAN TOLUN, YAVUZ TOLUN.

Ekonomi ve Politika: Kavaklıdere, Ankara; f. 1966; economic and political; Publr ZIYA TANSU.

Turkish Economic Gazette: Atatürk Bul. 149, Bakanlıklar, Ankara; tel. (312) 4177700.

Turkish Probe: Hülya Sok. 45, 06700 GOP, Ankara; tel. (312) 4475647; fax (312) 4468374; English language; Publr A. ILHAN ÇEVIK; Editor-in-Chief ILNUR ÇEVIK; circ. 2,500.

Türkiye İktisat Gazetesi: Karanfil Sok 56, 06582 Bakanlıklar, Ankara; tel. (312) 4184321; fax (312) 4183268; f. 1953; commercial; Chief Editor MEHMET SAĞLAM; circ. 11,500.

Antalya

Pulse: PK 7, Kemer, Antalya; tel. and fax (242) 8180105; e-mail uras@ada.net.tr; internet www.turkpulse.com; politics and business; English; publ. online; Publr VEDAT URAS.

İstanbul

Aktüel: Medya Plaza Basın Ekspres Yolu, 34540 Güneşli, İstanbul; tel. (212) 5504870; e-mail aktuel@birnumara.com.tr; internet aktuel.birnumara.com.tr; f. 1991; Gen. Man. GÜLAY GÖKTÜRK; Man. Editor ALEV ER.

Bayrak: Çatalçeşme Sok. 50/5, 34410 Cağaloğlu, İstanbul; tel. (212) 5275575; fax (212) 5268363; f. 1970; political; Editor MEHMET GÜNGÖR; circ. 10,000.

Elegans Magazine: Valikonağı Cad. Y.K.V. Binası K:5 D:3 34365 Nişantaşı, İstanbul; tel. (212) 2336506; fax (212) 2312878; e-mail elegans@elegans.com.tr; internet www.elegans.com.tr; f. 1985; social, economic and global issues; Publr ÖMER TAYFUN YUMAK.

Ekonomik Panaroma: Büyükdere Cad. Ali Kaya Sok. 8, 80720 Levent, İstanbul; tel. (212) 2696680; f. 1988; Gen. Man. AYDIN DEMIRER.

Ekonomist: Hürriyet Medya Towers, 34212 Güneşli, İstanbul; tel. (212) 4103256; fax (212) 4103255; e-mail ekonomist@doganburda.com; internet www.ekonomist.com.tr; f. 1991; CEO MEHMET Y. YILMAZ.

Gırgır: Alayköşkü Cad., Çağaloğlu, İstanbul; tel. (212) 2285000; satirical; Propr and Editor OĞUZ ARAL; circ. 500,000.

İstanbul Ticaret: İstanbul Chamber of Commerce, Ragip Gümüşpala Cad. 84, 34378, Eminönü, İstanbul; tel. (212) 5114150; fax (212) 5131565; f. 1958; commercial news; Publr MEHMET YILDIRIM.

Tempo: Hürriyet Medya Towers 34212 Güneşli, İstanbul; tel. (212) 4103282; fax (212) 4103311; e-mail tempo@doganburda.com; www.tempodergisi.com.tr; f. 1987; Editor NEVAL BATLAS.

Türk Dünyası Araştırmalar Dergisi: Hürgüç Gazetecilik AŞ Hürriyet Tesisleri, Güneşli, İstanbul; tel. (212) 5500081; Dir SEDAT SIMAVI; Gen. Man. MEHMET Y. YILMAZ.

PERIODICALS

Ankara

Azerbaycan Türk Kültür Dergisi: Vakıf İş Hanı 324, Anafartalar, Ankara; f. 1949; literary and cultural periodical of Azerbaijani Turks; Editor Dr AHMET YAŞAT.

Bayrak Dergisi: Bestckar Sok. 44/5, Kavaklıdere, Ankara; f. 1964; Publr and Editor HAMI KARTAY.

Bilim ve Teknik: Bilim ve Teknik Dergisi Tübitak, Atatürk Bul. 221, Kavaklıdere, 06100 Ankara; tel. (312) 4270625; fax (312) 4276677; e-mail bteknik@tubitak.gov.tr; internet www.biltek.tubitak.gov.tr; f. 1967; monthly; science; Propr Prof. NÜKET YETIS; Man. Editor RAŞIT GÜRDILEK.

Devlet Opera ve Balesi Genel Müdürlüğü: Ankara; tel. (312) 3241476; fax (312) 3107248; f. 1949; state opera and ballet; Gen. Dir. RENGIM GOKMEN.

Devlet Tiyatrosu: Devlet Tiyatrosu Um. Md., Ankara; f. 1952; art, theatre.

Eğitim ve Bilim: Kızılırmak Sok. 8, Kocatepe, Ankara; tel. (312) 4180614; fax (312) 4175365; e-mail ipekt@ted.org.tr; f. 1928; quarterly; education and science; publ. by the Turkish Educational Asscn; Editors Prof. AYDAN ERSÖZ, Dr GÜLTEKIN ÖZDEMIR, ANDREW DAVENTRY; circ. 500.

Karınca: Türk Kooperatifçilik Kurumu, Mithatpaşa Cad. 38/A, 06420 Kızılay, Ankara; tel. (312) 4359899; fax (312) 4304292; f. 1934; monthly review publ. by the Turkish Co-operative Asscn; Editor Prof. Dr RASIH DEMIRCI; circ. 5,000.

Maden Tetkik Arama Genel Müdürlüğü: MTA Dergisi Editörlüğü, MTA Geological Research Dept, G Blok, 06520 Ankara; e-mail editorluk@mta.gov.tr; internet www.mta.gov.tr; f. 1935; 2 a year; publ. by General Directorate of Mineral Research and Exploration of Turkey; English edn *Bulletin of Mineral Research and Exploration* (2 a year); Gen. Dir MEHMET ÜZER; Editor-in-Chief Prof. Dr ERGUN GÖKTEN.

Mimarlık (Architecture): Konur Sok. 4/2, Kızılay, Ankara; tel. (312) 4173727; fax (312) 4180361; e-mail mimarlikdergisi@mimarlarodasi.org.tr; internet www.mimarlarodasi.org.tr; f. 1963; every 2 months; publ. by the Chamber of Architects of Turkey; Editor N. MÜGE CENGÍZKAN; circ. 20,000.

Mühendis ve Makina: Sümer 2 Sok. 36/1A, 06640 Demirtepe, Ankara; tel. (312) 2313159; fax (312) 2313165; e-mail mmo@mmo.org.tr; internet www.mmo.org.tr/muhendismakina; f. 1957; engineering; monthly; publ. by the Chamber of Mechanical Engineers; Propr MEHMET SOĞANCI; Editor YÜKSEL KÖKEN; circ. 30,000.

Teknik ve Uygulama: Konur Sok. 4/4, 06442 Kızılay, Ankara; tel. (312) 4182374; f. 1986; engineering; every 2 months; publ. by the Chamber of Mechanical Engineers; Propr İSMET RIZA ÇEBI; Editor UĞUR DOĞAN; circ. 3,000.

Türk Arkeoloji ve Etnoğrafya Dergisi (General Directorate of Monuments and Museums): Kültür ve Turizm Bakanlığı, Kültür Varlıkları ve Müzeler Genel Müdürlüğü-II. Meclis Binası Ulus, 06100 Ankara; tel. (312) 3104960; fax (312) 3115085; e-mail kulturvarlikmuze@kulturturizm.gov.tr; internet www.kulturturizm.gov.tr; archaeological.

Türk Dili: Türk Dil Kurumu, Atatürk Bul. 217, 06680 Kavaklıdere, Ankara; tel. (312) 4286100; fax (312) 4285288; e-mail tdili@tdk.gov.tr; internet www.tdk.gov.tr; f. 1951; monthly; Turkish literature and language; Editor Prof. Dr ŞÜKRÜ HALUK AKALIN.

Turkey—Economic News Digest: Karanfil Sok. 56, Ankara; f. 1960; Editor-in-Chief BEHZAT TANIR; Man. Editor SADIK BALKAN.

Türkiye Bankacılık: PK 121, Ankara; f. 1955; commercial; Publr MUSTAFA ATALAY.

Türkiye Bibliyografyası: Milli Kütüphane Başkanlığı, 06490 Bahçelievler, Ankara; tel. (312) 2126200; fax (312) 2230451; e-mail katalog@mkutup.gov.tr; internet www.mkutup.gov.tr; f. 1928; monthly; Turkish national bibliography; publ. by the Turkish National Library, Cataloguing and Classification Dept; Dir AHMET ÇELENKOĞLU.

Türkiye Makaleler Bibliyografyası (Bibliography of Articles in Turkish Periodicals): Milli Kütüphane Başkanlığı, 06490 Bahçelievler, Ankara; tel. (312) 2126200; fax (312) 2230451; e-mail bibliografya@mkutup.gov.tr; internet www.mkutup.gov.tr; f. 1952; monthly; Turkish articles, bibliography; publ. by the Turkish National Library, Bibliography Preparation Dept; Dir SEMA AKINCI.

İstanbul

Arkeoloji ve Sanat Dergisi (Archaeology and Art Magazine): Hayriye Cad. 3/4 Çorlu Apt., 34425 Beyoğlu, İstanbul; tel. (212) 2456838; fax (212) 2456877; e-mail info@arkeolojisanat.com; internet arkeolojisanat.com; f. 1978; bi-monthly; publ. by Archaeology and Art Publications; Publr and Editor NEZIH BAŞGELEN; English-Language Submissions Editor BRIAN JOHNSON.

Bankacılar: Nıspetıye Cad. Akmerkez, B3 Blok. Kat 13–14, 80630 Etiler, İstanbul; tel. (212) 2820973; fax (212) 2820946; publ. by the Banks' Asscn of Turkey; quarterly.

İstanbul Ticaret Odası Mecmuası: Gümüşpala Cad. 84, 34378 Eminönü, İstanbul; tel. (212) 5114150; fax (212) 5131565; f. 1884; quarterly; journal of the İstanbul Chamber of Commerce (ICOC); English; Editor-in-Chief CENGIZ ERSUN.

Musiki Mecmuası (Music Magazine): POB 336, Sem'i Bey Sok. 19/3, Yıldızbakkal, Kadiköy, İstanbul; tel. (216) 3306299; e-mail etemungor@hotmail.com; f. 1948; monthly; music and musicology; Editor ETEM RUHI ÜNGÖR.

Nûr (The Light): Nuruosmaniye Cad., Sorkun Han 28/2, 34410, Cağaloğlu, İstanbul; tel. (212) 5277607; fax (212) 5208231; e-mail sozler@ihlas.net.tr; internet www.sozler.com.tr; f. 1986; religion; Publr MEHMET NURI GÜLEÇ; Editor CEMAL UŞAK.

Pirelli Mecmuası: Büyükdere Cad. 117, Gayrettepe, İstanbul; tel. (212) 2663200; fax (212) 2520718; e-mail bilyay@ibm.net; f. 1964; monthly; Publr Türk-Pirelli Lastikleri AŞ; Editor UĞUR CANAL; circ. 24,500.

Ruh ve Madde Dergisi (Spirit and Matter): Ruh ve Madde Publications and Health Services Co, Hasnun Galip Sok., Pembe Çıkmazı 4, D 6/8, 80072 Beyoğlu, İstanbul; tel. (212) 2431814; fax (212) 2520718; e-mail info@ruhvemadde.com; internet www.ruhvemadde.com; f. 1959; organ of the Foundation for Spreading the Knowledge to Unify Humanity; Editor HALUK HACALOĞLU.

Sevgi Dünyası (World of Respect): Aydede Cad. 4/5, 80090 Taksimi, İstanbul; tel. (212) 2504242; fax (212) 2702252; e-mail editor@dostlik.org; internet www.dostluk.org; f. 1963; monthly; social, psychological and spiritual; Publr and Editor Dr REFET KAYSERILIOĞLU.

Turkey: Ihlas Holding Merkez Binası 29, Ekim Cad. 23, 34197 Yenibosna, İstanbul; tel. (212) 4542520; fax (212) 4542555; e-mail info@img.com.tr; internet www.img.com.tr/turkey; f. 1982; monthly; English language; economics; Editor MEHMET SÖZTUTAN; circ. 43,000.

Varlık Yayınları AŞ: Ayberk Ap. Piyerloti Cad. 7–9, Çemberlitaş, 34400 İstanbul; tel. (212) 5162004; fax (212) 5162005; e-mail varlik@varlik.com.tr; internet www.varlik.com.tr; f. 1933; monthly; literary; Editors FILIZ NAYIR DENIZTEKIN, ENVER ERCAN; circ. 4,000.

İzmir

İzmir Ticaret Odası Dergisi: Atatürk Cad. 126, 35210 İzmir; tel. (232) 4417777; fax (232) 4837853; f. 1927; every 2 months; publ. by Chamber of Commerce of İzmir; Sec.-Gen. Prof. Dr İLTER AKAT; Man. ÜMIT ALEMDAROĞLU.

NEWS AGENCIES

Anadolu Ajansı: Mustafa Kemal Bul. 128/C, Tandogan, Ankara; tel. (312) 2317000; fax (312) 2312174; e-mail aa1@anadoluajansi.com.tr; internet www.aa.com.tr; f. 1920; Chair. ALI AYDIN DUNDAR; Gen. Dir BEHIÇ EKŞI.

ANKA Ajansı: Cinnah Cad. 11/5 Kavaklıdere, Ankara; tel. (312) 4682500; fax (312) 4268471; e-mail anka@ankaajansi.com.tr; internet www.ankaajansi.com.tr; Dir-Gen. VELI ÖZDEMIR.

Bagımsız Basın Ajansı (BBA): Saglam Fikir Sok. 11, Esentepe, 80300 İstanbul; tel. (212) 2122936; fax (212) 2122940; e-mail bba@bba.tv; internet www.bba.tv; f. 1971; provides camera crewing, editing and satellite services in Turkey, the Balkans, the Middle East and the former Soviet republics to broadcasters world-wide.

Cihan News Agency: Cobancesme Mah. Kalender Sok. 16, 34590 Yenibosna, İstanbul; tel. (212) 5524057; fax (212) 4541456; e-mail cihannews@cihan.com.tr; internet www.cihannews.com; f. 1992; part of Feza Media Corpn.

Hürriyet Haber Ajansı: Hürriyet Medya Towers, Güneşli, 34544 İstanbul; tel. (212) 6770365; fax (212) 6770372; e-mail ucebeci@hurriyet.com.tr; f. 1963; Dir-Gen. UĞUR ÇEBECI.

İKA Haber Ajansı (Economic and Commercial News Agency): Atatürk Bul. 199/A-45, Kavaklıdere, Ankara; tel. (312) 1267327; f. 1954; Dir ZIYA TANSU.

Milha News Agency: Doğan Medya Center, Bağcılar, 34554 İstanbul; tel. (212) 5056111; fax (212) 5056233.

TEBA—Türk Ekonomik Basın Ajansı (Turkish Economic Press Agency): Süleyman Hacı Abdullahoğlu Cad. 5, D3 Balgat, Ankara; tel. (312) 2842006; fax (312) 2840638; e-mail teba@tebahaber.com.tr; internet www.tebahaber.com.tr; f. 1981; private economic news service; Propr ORHAN TOLUN; Editor YAVUZ TOLUN.

Ulusal Basın Ajansı (UBA): Meşrutiyet Cad. 5/10, Ankara; Man. Editor OĞUZ SEREN.

JOURNALISTS' ASSOCIATION

Türkiye Gazeteciler Cemiyeti: Türkocağı Cad. 1, Cağaloğlu, İstanbul; tel. (212) 5138300; fax (212) 5268046; e-mail tgc@tgc.org.tr; internet www.tgc.org.tr; f. 1946; Pres. ORHAN ERINÇ; Sec. RIDVAN YELE.

Publishers

Altın Kitaplar Yayınevi Anonim ŞTİ: Celal Ferdi Gökçay Sok., Nebioğlu Han, Kat. 1, Cağaloğlu, İstanbul; tel. (212) 5268012; fax (212) 5268011; e-mail info@altinkitaplar.com.tr; internet www.altinkitaplar.com.tr; f. 1959; fiction, non-fiction, biography, children's books, encyclopaedias, dictionaries; Publrs FETHI UL, TURHAN BOZKURT; Chief Editor MÜRSIT UL.

Arkadas Co Ltd: Yuva Mah. 3702, Sok. 4, Yenimahalle, Ankara; tel. (312) 3946270; fax (312) 3946285; e-mail info@arkadas.com.tr; internet www.arkadas.com.tr; f. 1980; fiction, educational and reference books; Gen. Man. CUMHUR OZDEMIR.

Arkeoloji ve Sanat Yayınları (Archaeology and Art Publications): Yeniçarşı Hayriye Cad. 3/4 Çorlu Apt., Galatasaray, 80060 İstanbul; tel. (212) 2456838; fax (212) 2456877; e-mail info@arkeolojisanat.com; internet www.arkeolojisanat.com; f. 1978; classical, Byzantine and Turkish studies, art and archaeology, numismatics and ethnography books; Publr NEZIH BASGELEN; Senior Editor BRIAN JOHNSON.

Bilgi Yayınevi: Meşrutiyet Cad. 46/A, Yenişehir, 06420 Ankara; tel. (312) 4318122; fax (312) 4317758; e-mail info@bilgiyayinevi.com.tr; internet www.bilgiyayinevi.com.tr.

Doğan Burda Derg: Hürriyet Medya Towers, 34212 Güneşli, İstanbul; tel. (212) 4780300; fax (212) 4103512; e-mail abone@doganburda.com; internet www.doganburda.com.

IKI NOKTA (Research Press & Publications Industry & Trade Ltd): Eğitim M. Kasap İsmail S. Öğün İş Merkezi 5/2, 34722 Kadıköy, İstanbul; tel. (216) 3490141; fax (216) 3376756; e-mail info@ikinokta.com; internet www.ikinokta.com; humanities; Pres. YÜCEL YAMAN.

Iletisim Yayınları: Binbirdirek Meydanı Sok., Iletisim Han 7/2, 34122 Cağaloğlu, İstanbul; tel. (212) 5162260; fax (212) 5161258; e-mail iletisim@iletisim.com.tr; internet www.iletisim.com.tr; f. 1984; fiction, non-fiction, encyclopaedias, reference; Gen. Man. NIHAT TUNA.

Inkilap Kitabevi: Çobançeşme Mah. Altay Sok. 8 Yenibosna, İstanbul; tel. (212) 4961111; fax (212) 4961112; e-mail posta@inkilap.com; internet www.inkilap.com; f. 1935; general reference and fiction; Man. Dir A. FIKRI; Dir of Foreign Rights S. DIKER.

Kabalcı Yayınevi: Ankara Cad. 47, Cağaloğlu, İstanbul; tel. (212) 5226305; fax (212) 5268495; e-mail info@kabalci.com.tr; internet www.kabalci.com.tr; art, history, literature, social sciences; Pres. SABRI KABALCI.

Metis Yayınları: Ipek Sok. 9, 80060 Beyoğlu, İstanbul; tel. (212) 2454509; fax (212) 2454519; e-mail metis@turk.net; internet www.metisbooks.com; f. 1982; fiction, literature, non-fiction, social sciences; Dir SEMIH SÖKMEN.

Nobel Medical Publishing: Millet Cad. 111 Çapa, İstanbul; tel. (212) 6328333; fax (212) 5870217; e-mail destek@nobeltip.com; internet kurumsal.nobeltip.com; f. 1974; medical books and journals; CEO RIFKI BIROĞLU; Dir ERSAL BINGÖL.

Nurdan Yayınları Sanayi ve Ticaret Ltd Sti: Prof. Kâzim Ismail Gürkan Cad. 13, Kati 1, 34410 Cağaloğlu, İstanbul; tel. (212) 5225504; fax (212) 5125186; e-mail info@nurdan.com.tr; internet www.nurdan.com.tr; f. 1980; children's and educational; Dir NURDAN TÜZÜNER.

Parantez Yayınları AŞ: Istikal Cad. 212 Alt Kat 8, Beyoğlu, İstanbul; tel. and fax (212) 2528567; e-mail parantez@parantez.net; internet www.parantez.net; f. 1991; Publr METIN ZEYNIOĞLU.

Payel Yayınevi: Cağaloğlu Yokusu Evren han Kat 3/51, 34400 Cağaloğlu, İstanbul; tel. (212) 5284409; fax (212) 5124353; f. 1966; science, history, literature; Editor AHMET ÖZTÜRK.

Remzi Kitabevi AŞ: Akmerkez E3 Blok Kat. 14, Etiler, İstanbul; tel. (212) 2822080; fax (212) 2822090; e-mail post@remzi.com.tr; internet www.remzi.com.tr; f. 1927; general and educational; Dirs EROL ERDURAN, ÖMER ERDURAN, AHMET ERDURAN.

Seckin Yayınevi: Saglik Sok. 19B, 06410 Sihhiye, Ankara; tel. (312) 4353030; fax (312) 4355088; e-mail satis@seckin.com.tr; internet www.seckin.com.tr; f. 1959; accounting, computer science, economics, law; Dir KORAY SEÇKIN.

Türk Dil Kurumu (Turkish Language Institute): Atatürk Bul. 217, 06680 Kavaklıdere, Ankara; tel. (312) 4268124; fax (312) 4285288; e-mail bilgi@tdk.gov.tr; internet tdk.gov.tr; f. 1932; non-fiction, research, language; Pres. Prof. Dr ŞÜKRÜ HALUK AKALIN.

Varlık Yayınları AŞ: Ayberk Ap. Piyerloti Cad. 7–9, Çemberlitaş, 34400 İstanbul; tel. (212) 5162004; fax (212) 5162005; e-mail varlik@varlik.com.tr; internet www.varlik.com.tr; f. 1933; fiction and non-fiction books, and cultural monthly review; Dirs FILIZ NAYIR DENIZTEKIN, OSMAN DENIZTEKIN.

GOVERNMENT PUBLISHING HOUSE

Ministry of Culture and Tourism: Directorate of Publications, Necatibey Cad. 55, 06440 Kızılay, Ankara; tel. (312) 2315450; fax

TURKEY

(312) 2315036; e-mail yayimlar@kutuphanelergm.gov.tr; internet www.kultur.gov.tr; f. 1973; Dir ALI OSMAN GÜZEL.

PUBLISHERS' ASSOCIATION

Türkiye Yayıncılar Birliği Derneği (Publishers' Association of Turkey): Kazım Ismail Gürkan Cad. 12, Ortaklar Han Kat 3/17, Cağaloğlu, İstanbul; tel. (212) 5125602; fax (212) 5117794; e-mail info@turkyaybir.org.tr; internet www.turkyaybir.org.tr; f. 1985; Pres. ÇETIN TÜZÜNER; Sec. METIN CELÂL ZEYNIOĞLU; 230 mems.

Broadcasting and Communications

TELECOMMUNICATIONS

Regulatory Authorities

General Directorate of Communications: Hakkı Turayliç Cad. 5 Kat 7–8, Emek, Ankara; tel. (312) 2031000; fax (312) 2121775; e-mail soytas@ubak.opr.tr; internet www.ubak.gov.tr/tr/hgm; Dir-Gen. CABIR BILIRGEN.

Telekomünikasyon Kurumu (Telecommunications Authority): Yeşilırmak Sok., 16 Demirtepe, 06430 Ankara; tel. (312) 2947400; fax (312) 2947145; e-mail info@tk.gov.tr; internet www.tk.gov.tr; f. 2000; Chair. Dr TAYFUN ACARER; Dir FETHI SIMSEK.

Principal Operators

Turkcell: Mesrutiyet Cad. 71, 34430 Tepebaşi, İstanbul; tel. (212) 3131000; fax (212) 2925393; e-mail musteri.hizmetleri@turkcell.com.tr; internet www.turkcell.com.tr; provides mobile cellular services; 40.3% held by the Cukurova Group, 37.1% by Sonera Holding; 35.4m. subscribers at Dec. 2007; CEO SÜREYYA CILIV.

Türksat AŞ: Konya Yolu 40 km, Gölbaşı, Ankara; tel. (312) 6153000; fax (312) 4995115; e-mail info@turksat.com.tr; internet www.turksat.com.tr.

Turk Telekom: İstanbul; tel. (212) 3493939; fax (212) 3529499; e-mail iletisim@turktelekom.com.tr; internet www.turktelekom.com.tr; 55% owned by Oger Telecoms Joint Venture Group; Chair. Dr PAUL DOANY.

BROADCASTING

Regulatory Authority

Radyo ve Televizyon Üst Kurulu (RTÜK) (Radio and Television Supreme Council): Bilkent Plaza B2 Blok, Bilkent, 06530 Ankara; tel. (312) 2975000; fax (312) 2661985; e-mail rtuk@rtuk.org.tr; internet www.rtuk.org.tr; responsible for assignment of channels, frequencies and bands, controls transmitting facilities of radio stations and TV networks, draws up regulations on related matters, monitors broadcasting and issues warnings in case of violation of the Broadcasting law; Pres. ZAHID AKMAN.

Radio

Türkiye Radyo ve Televizyon Kurumu (TRT) (Turkish Radio and Television Corpn): Turan Güneş Bul., 06450 Oran, Ankara; tel. (312) 4904300; fax (312) 4912817; e-mail trthaber@trt.net.tr; internet www.trt.net.tr; f. 1964; controls Turkish radio and television services, incl. four national radio channels; Dir-Gen. İBRAHIM ŞAHIN; Head of Radio ÇETIN TEZCAN.

Voice of Turkey: PK 333, 06443 Yenişehir, Ankara; tel. (312) 4909800; fax (312) 4909845; e-mail tsr@trt.net.tr; internet www.trt.net.tr/wwwtrt/tsr.aspx; f. 1937; external service of the TRT; Head of External Service OSMAN DILEKCI.

There are also more than 50 local radio stations, an educational radio service for schools and a station run by the Turkish State Meteorological Service. The US forces have their own radio and television service.

Television

Türkiye Radyo ve Televizyon Kurumu (TRT): (Turkish Radio and Television Corpn): Oran Sitesi Turan Güneş Bul. A Block Kat 6, 06450 Oran, Ankara; e-mail nilgun.artun@trt.net.tr; internet www.trt.net.tr; five national channels in 2000 and two satellite channels broadcasting to Europe; Dir-Gen. İBRAHIM ŞAHIN; Head of Television NILGÜN ARTUN; Dir Ankara TV GÜRKAN ELÇI.

In addition there are also 11 other television stations, including cable networks. These are: ATV (www.atv.com.tr), Cine 5 (www.cine5.com.tr), Kanal D (www.kanald.com.tr), Kanal 6 (www.kanal6.com.tr), Kral TV (www.kraltv.com.tr), No1 TV (www.levi.com.tr/no1tv), NTV Online (www.ntv.com.tr), Show TV (www.showtv.net), Star (www.startv.com.tr), TGRT (www.tgrt.com.tr) and NTVMSNBC (www.ntvmsnbc.com).

Finance

(cap. = capital; res = reserves; dep. = deposits; m. = million; brs = branches; amounts in new Turkish liras unless otherwise indicated; note: figures have been converted retrospectively to reflect the introduction on 1 January 2005 of the new unit of currency, equivalent to 1,000,000 of the old Turkish lira)

The Central Bank of the Republic of Turkey (Türkiye Cumhuriyet Merkez Bankası AŞ) was founded in 1931, and constituted in its present form in 1970. The Central Bank is the bank of issue and is also responsible for the execution of monetary and credit policies, the regulation of the foreign and domestic value of the Turkish lira jointly with the Government, and the supervision of the credit system. In 1987 a decree was issued to bring the governorship of the Central Bank under direct government control. In 2001 the Central Bank was granted policy independence.

In June 1999 an independent supervisory body, the Regulatory and Supervisory Board for Banking, was established by law to monitor the financial sector. The treasury, the Ministry of Finance, the Central Bank, the state planning organization, the Capital Markets Board and the Banks' Association of Turkey were each to nominate one member to the Board for a six-year term. The Board was operational from mid-2000. Other legislation passed in June 1999 incorporated core principles of the Basle Committee on Banking Supervision relating to risk-based capital requirements, loan administration procedures, auditing practices and credit risk issues.

The largest of the private-sector Turkish banks is the Türkiye İş Bankası AŞ, which operates 918 branches in the country.

There are several credit institutions in Turkey, including the Türkiye Sınai Kalınma Bankası AŞ (Industrial Development Bank of Turkey), which was founded in 1950, with the assistance of the World Bank, to encourage private investment in industry by acting as underwriter in the issue of share capital.

There are numerous co-operative organizations, including agricultural co-operatives in rural areas. There are also a number of savings institutions.

In 1990 the Turkish Government announced plans to establish a structure for offshore banking. A decree issued in October of that year exempted foreign banks, operating in six designated free zones, from local banking obligations.

At the end of 1999 the number of banks operating in Turkey (excluding the Central Bank) totalled 81, of which seven were state owned. Following a number of liquidations, mergers and acquisitions in the banking system after 2000, the number of banks had been reduced to 48 by the end of 2004. By March 2008 this number had been further reduced, to 46. Of this total, 13 were development and investment banks; the number of state-owned banks had been reduced to three, with the control of Birleşik Fon Bankasi AŞ (formerly Bayindirbank) passing to the Savings Deposit Insurance Fund. There were 11 private commercial banks and 18 foreign-owned banks.

BANKING

Regulatory Authority

Bancacılık Düzenleme ve Denetleme Kurumu (BDDK) (Banking Regulation and Supervisory Agency): Atatürk Bul. 191, 06680 Kavaklidere, Ankara; tel. (312) 4556500; fax (312) 4241733; e-mail bilgi@bddk.org.tr; internet www.bddk.org.tr; Chair. TEVFIK BILGIN.

Central Bank

Türkiye Cumhuriyet Merkez Bankası AŞ (Central Bank of the Republic of Turkey): Head Office, İstiklal Cad. 10 Ulus, 06100 Ankara; tel. (312) 3103646; fax (312) 3107434; e-mail iletisimbilgi@tcmb.gov.tr; internet www.tcmb.gov.tr; f. 1931; bank of issue; cap. 46.2m., res 779.5m., dep. 84,232.2m. (Dec. 2006); Gov. DURMUŞ YILMAZ; 21 brs.

State Banks

Türkiye Cumhuriyeti Ziraat Bankası (Agricultural Bank of the Turkish Republic): Doğanbey Mah., Atatürk Bul. 8, 06107 Ulus, Ankara; tel. (312) 5842000; fax (312) 3101134; e-mail zbmail@ziraatbank.com.tr; internet www.ziraat.com.tr; f. 1863; absorbed Türkiye Emlâk Bankası AŞ (Real Estate Bank of Turkey) in July 2001; cap. 6,729.1m., res 3,702.1m., dep. 52,634.8m. (Dec. 2005); Chair. Prof. Dr İLHAN ULUDAĞ; Gen. Man. CAN AKIN ÇAĞLAR; 1,177 brs in Turkey, 9 brs abroad.

Türkiye Halk Bankası AŞ: Esikişehir Yolu, 2 Cad. 63, Söğütözü, 06520 Ankara; tel. (312) 2892000; fax (312) 2893575; e-mail info@halkbank.com.tr; internet www.halkbank.com.tr; f. 1938; absorbed Türkiye Öğretmenler Bankası TAŞ in 1992; acquired 96 brs of Türkiye Emlak Bankası in 2001; merged with Pamukbank TAŞ in 2004; cap. 1,150.0m., res 1,514.7m., dep. 21,961.8m. (Dec. 2005); Chair. HASAN CEBECI; Gen. Man. HÜSEYIN AYDIN; 586 brs in Turkey, 2 brs abroad.

TURKEY

Türkiye Vakıflar Bankası TAO (Vakifbank) (Foundation Bank of Turkey): Camlik Cad. Cayir Cimen Sok. 2, 34330 1 Levent, İstanbul; tel. (212) 3167116; fax (212) 3167126; e-mail international@vakifbank.com.tr; internet www.vakifbank.com.tr; f. 1954; cap. 1,279.0m., res 2,265.1m., dep. 23,411.2m. (Dec. 2005); Chair. YUSUF BEYAZIT; Gen. Man. BILAL KARAMAN; 302 brs in Turkey, 1 br. abroad.

Principal Commercial Banks

Akbank TAŞ: Sabancı Center, 34330 4 Levent, 80745 İstanbul; tel. (212) 2700044; fax (212) 2697383; e-mail investor.relations@akbank.com; internet www.akbank.com; f. 1948; absorbed Ak Uluslararası Bankası AŞ in Sept. 2005; 20% owned by Citigroup; cap. 1,800.0m., res 3,114.9m., dep. 36,839.0m. (Dec. 2005); Chair. and Man. Dir EROL SABANCI; Pres. and CEO ZAFER KURTUL; 671 brs in Turkey, 2 brs abroad.

Alternatifbank AŞ: Cumhuriyet Cad. 22–24, Elmadağ, 34367 İstanbul; tel. (212) 3156500; fax (212) 2331500; e-mail sakir.somek@abank.com.tr; internet www.abank.com.tr; f. 1991; 95.6% owned by Anadolu Group; cap. 224.3m., res –45.7m., dep. 1,162.5m. (Dec. 2006); Chair. TUNCAY OZILHAN; CEO MURAT ARIĞ; 40 brs.

Oyak Bank AŞ: Eski Büyükdere Cad., Ayazaga Köyyolu 6, Maslak, 34398 İstanbul; tel. and fax (212) 4440600; e-mail contactcenter@oyakbank.com.tr; internet www.oyakbank.com.tr; f. 1990; merged with Sümerbank in 2001; owned by ING Groep NV (Netherlands); cap. 803.4m., res 338.4m., dep. 8,931.5m. (Dec. 2006); Chair. ŞERIF COŞKUN ULUSOY; Gen. Man. HAKAN EMINSOY; 365 brs in Turkey, 1 br. in Bahrain.

Şekerbank TAŞ: Büyükdere Cad. 171, Metrocity İş Merkezi, A-Blok 34330 1 Levent, İstanbul; tel. (212) 3197000; fax (212) 3197162; e-mail intdiv@sekerbank.com.tr; internet www.sekerbank.com.tr; f. 1953; cap. 125.0m., res 280.9m., dep. 2,615.5m. (Dec. 2005); 33.98% owned by TuranAlem Securities, Kazakhstan; Chair. HASAN BASRI GÖKTAN; Gen. Man. MERIÇ ULUŞAHIN; 203 brs.

Tekstilbank AŞ: Büyükdere Cad. 63, 34398 Maslak, İstanbul; tel. (212) 3355335; fax (212) 3281328; e-mail ir@tekstilbank.com.tr; internet www.tekstilbank.com.tr; f. 1986; cap. 175.0m., res 22.3m. dep. 1,381.5m. (Dec. 2005); 75.4% owned by GSD Holdings; Chair. and Gen. Man. ÇIM GÜZELAYDINLI; 51 brs.

Türk Ekonomi Bankası AŞ (TEB): Meclısı Mebusan Cad. 35, 34427 Fındıklı, İstanbul; tel. (212) 2512121; fax (212) 2525058; internet www.teb.com.tr; f. 1927; fmrly Kocaeli Bankası TAŞ; 84.25% owned by TEB Mali Yatırımlar AŞ (in 2005 BNP Paribas acquired 50% of TEB Mali Yatırımlar, making it an indirect 42.125% shareholder in TEB); cap. 57.8m., res 450.8m., dep. 5,158.5m. (Dec. 2005); Chair. YAVUZ CANEVI; Gen. Man. VAROL CIVIL; 129 brs.

Türkiye Garanti Bankası AŞ (Garantibank): Nispetiye Mah, Aytar Cad. 2, 34340 Levent Beşiktaş, İstanbul; tel. and fax (212) 3181818; fax (212) 3181888; e-mail mutlus@garanti.com.tr; internet www.garantibank.com; f. 1946; owned by Doğuş Group; cap. 3,046.4m., res 244.7m., dep. 28,808.4m. (Dec. 2005); Chair. FERIT FAIK ŞAHENK; Pres., CEO and Gen. Man. ERGUN ÖZEN; 487 brs in Turkey, 5 brs abroad.

Türkiye İş Bankası AŞ (İşbank): İş Kuleleri, 34330 Levent, İstanbul; tel. (212) 3160000; fax (212) 3160900; e-mail halkla.iliskiler@isbank.com.tr; internet www.isbank.com.tr; f. 1924; cap. 2,326.2m., res 6,960.3m., dep. 36,708.1m. (Sept. 2007); Chair. CANER ÇIMENBIÇER; CEO and Gen. Man. H. ERSIN ÖZINCE; 933 brs in Turkey, 11 abroad.

Yapı ve Kredi Bankası AŞ: Yapı Kredi Plaza, Blok D, 80620 İstanbul; tel. (212) 3397000; fax (212) 3396000; internet www.ykb.com.tr; f. 1944; cap. 3,516.3m., res 54.4m., dep. 18,372.4m. (Dec. 2005); merged with Koçbank AŞ in 2006; CEO and Gen. Man. TAYFUN BAYAZIT; COO ALESSANDRO DECIO; 598 brs.

Development and Investment Banks

İller Bankasi Genel Müdürülüğü: Atatürk Bul. 21, 06053 Opera, Ankara; tel. (312) 3103141; fax (312) 3107459; e-mail ilbank@ilbank.gov.tr; internet www.ilbank.gov.tr; CEO HIDAYET ATASOY; 19 brs.

Türkiye Kalkınma Bankası (Development Bank of Turkey): İzmir Cad. 35, 06440 Kızılay Ankara; tel. (312) 4179200; fax (312) 4183967; e-mail tkbhaberlesme@tkb.com.tr; internet www.tkb.com.tr; Chair. and Gen. Dir ABDULLAH ÇELIK.

Türkiye Sınai Kalkınma Bankası AŞ (Industrial Development Bank of Turkey): Meclisi Mebusan Cad. 81, Findikli, 34427 İstanbul; tel. (212) 3345050; fax (212) 3345234; e-mail info@tskb.com.tr; internet www.tskb.com; f. 1950; cap. 200.0m., res 254.1m., dep. 475.9m. (Dec. 2005); Chair. CAHIT KOCAÖMER; CEO and Pres. HALIL EROĞLU; 2 brs.

Savings Deposit Insurance Fund Bank

Birleşik Fon Bankasi AŞ: Büyükdere Cad. 143, 34394 Esentepe, İstanbul; tel. (212) 3401000; fax (212) 3473217; e-mail callcenter@fonbank.com.tr; internet www.fonbank.com.tr; fmrly Bayindirbank; name changed as above 2005; control passed to Savings Deposit Insurance Fund in 2001.

Banking Organization

Banks' Association of Turkey: Nıspetıye Cad. Akmerkez B3 Blok. Kat 13–14, 34340 Etiler, İstanbul; tel. (212) 2820973; fax (212) 2820946; e-mail gensek@tbb.org.tr; internet www.tbb.org.tr; f. 1958; Chair. ERSIN ÖZINCE; Sec.-Gen. Dr EKREM KESKIN.

STOCK EXCHANGE

İstanbul Menkul Kıymetler Borsası (İMKB): Resitpaşa Mah., Tuncay Artun Cad., 34467 Emirgan, İstanbul; tel. (212) 2982100; fax (212) 2982500; e-mail info@ise.org; internet www.ise.org; f. 1866; revived in 1986 after being dormant for about 60 years; 104 mems of stock market, 132 mems of bond and bills market (April 2008); Chair. and CEO HÜSEYIN ERKAN; Senior Vice-Chair. ARIL SEREN.

INSURANCE

AKSigorta: Meclis-i Mebusan Cad. 147 Fındıklı, 34427 İstanbul; tel. (212) 3934300; fax (212) 3343900; e-mail info@aksigorta.com.tr; internet www.aksigorta.com.tr; f. 1960; Chair. M. AKIN KOZANOĞLU; Gen. Man. I. RAGIP YERGIN.

Anadolu Sigorta TAŞ (Anadolu Insurance Co): Büyükdere Cad. İş Kuleleri Kule 2 Kat. 23–26 34330 4 Levent, İstanbul; tel. (212) 3500350; fax (212) 3500355; e-mail bilgi@anadolusigorta.com.tr; internet www.anadolusigorta.com.tr; f. 1925; Chair. BURHAN KARAGÖZ; CEO MUSTAFA ALI SU.

Ankara Sigorta TAŞ (Ankara Insurance Co): Bankalar Cad. 80, 80020 Karaköy, İstanbul; tel. (212) 2521010; fax (212) 2525044; internet www.ankarasigorta.com.tr; f. 1936; Chair. ÖZKAN ELGIN; Gen. Man. ŞABAN ÇAĞIRANY (acting).

AXA Oyak AŞ: Meclis-i Mebusan Cad. Oyak İş Hanı 15, 34433 Salıpazarı, İstanbul; tel. (212) 3342424; fax (212) 2521515; internet www.axaoyak.com.tr; Chair. Dr MEHMET AYDIN MÜDERRISOĞLU; Gen. Man. HAKKI CEMAL ERERDI; 10 brs.

Başak Groupama Sigorta AŞ: Halaskargazi Cad. 15, 34373 Harbiye, İstanbul; tel. (212) 2316000; fax (212) 2307604; e-mail sigorta@basakgroupama.com.tr; internet www.basakgroupama.com.tr; Gen. Man. ENIS BASIM.

Ergoisviçre Sigorta AŞ: Kısıklı Cad. 30, Altunizade 34662, İstanbul; tel. (216) 5548100; fax (216) 4741387; e-mail ergoisvicre@ergoisvicre.com.tr; internet www.ergoisvicre.com.tr; f. 1926 as La Suisse Umum Sigorta, acquired by İsviçre in 1981; jt venture between Ergo and Isviçre in 2006; fire, accident, marine, engineering, agricultural; Chair. OKAN BALCI; Gen. Man. MURAT BALCI; 11 regional brs.

Eureko Sigorta: Mete Cad. Parkhan 34, Taksim İstanbul; tel. (212) 3931000; fax (212) 2490104; e-mail esmusterihizmetleri@eurekosigorta.com.tr; internet www.eurekosigorta.com.tr; f. 1989 as Garanti Sigorta; renamed as above in Oct. 2007; 80% owned by Eureko BV (Netherlands) and 20% by Türkiye Garanti Bankası AŞ; Chair. ERGUN ÖZEN; CEO OKAN UTKUERI.

Fiba Sigorta AŞ: Rüzgalıbahçe Mah. Cumhuriyet Cad. Acarlar İş Merkezi 12 C Blok, 34805 Kavacık, Beykoz İstanbul; tel. (216) 5386000; fax (216) 5386290; e-mail info@fibasigorta.com.tr; internet www.fibasigorta.com.tr; Pres. YENER DINÇMEN.

Güneş Sigorota: Güneş Plaza, Büyükdere Cad. 110, 34384 Esentepe, İstanbul; tel. (212)3556565; fax (212)3556464; e-mail gunes@gunessigorta.com.tr; internet www.gunessigorta.com.tr; f. 1957; Chair. YUSUF BEYAZIT; Gen. Man. MEHMET AYDOĞDU.

Güven Sigorta TAŞ: Bankalar Cad. 81, 34420 Karaköy, İstanbul; tel. (212) 3135555; fax (212) 2378085; e-mail info@guvensigorta.com.tr; internet www.guvensigorta.com.tr; f. 1924; owned by Turkish Agricultural Credit Co-operatives Central Union; all brs of insurance; Gen. Man. BÜLENT SOMUNCU.

Hür Sigorta AŞ: Büyükdere Cad., Hür Han 15/A, 80260 Şişli, İstanbul; tel. (212) 2322010; fax (212) 2463673; e-mail hursigorta@hursigorta.com.tr; internet www.hursigorta.com.tr; Chair. BÜLENT SEMILER; Gen. Man. GÜNER YALÇINER.

Işık Sigorta AŞ: Küçüksu Cad. Akçakoca Sok. 6 Kat 2, 34768 Ümraniye, İstanbul; tel. (216) 6337100; fax (216) 6318448; e-mail bilgi@isiksigorta.com.tr; internet www.isiksigorta.com.

Koç Allianz Sigorta AŞ: Bağlarbaşı, Kısıklı Cad. 11, 34662 Altunizade, İstanbul; tel. (216) 5566666; fax (216) 5566777; e-mail info@kocallianz.com.tr; internet www.kocallianz.com.tr; f. 1923; Chair. RAHMI M. KOÇ; CEO GEORGE D. SARTOREL.

Liberty Sigorta AŞ: Meclisi Mebusan Cad. 21, Karaköy, İstanbul; tel. (212) 2514035; fax (212) 2491046; e-mail info@sekersigorta.com.tr; internet www.libertysigorta.com.tr; f. 1954 as Şeker Sigorta AŞ; renamed as above in 2006; 90.43% owned by Liberty Mutual Group (USA); Gen. Man. Dr MUSTAFA AKAN.

TURKEY

Milli Reasürans TAŞ: Teşvikiye Cad. 43–57, 34368 Teşvikiye, İstanbul; tel. (212) 2314730; fax (212) 2308608; e-mail info@millire.com.tr; internet www.millire.com.tr; f. 1929; premium income 576.0m., total assets 616.4m. (Dec. 2004); Chair. Prof. Dr AHMET KIRMAN; Dir and Gen. Man. CAHIT NOMER.

Ray Sigorta: Haydar Aliyev Cad. 35, Tarabya 34457 Sarıyer, İstanbul; tel. (212) 3632500; fax (212) 2994849; e-mail info@raysigorta.com.tr; internet www.raysigorta.com.tr; f. 1958; Doğan Group is major shareholder.

TEB Sigorta: Meclis-i Mebusan Cad. 47/6, 34427 Findikli, İstanbul; tel. (212) 3931600; fax (212) 2928761; e-mail info@tebsigorta.com.tr; internet www.tebsigorta.com.tr; owned by Zurich Financial Services Group (Switzerland); Chair. ANNETTE ELIZABETH COURT; Gen. Man. ALI ERTUĞRUL BUL.

Türkiye Genel Sigorta AŞ: Meclisi Mebusan Cad. 25, 34433 Salıpazarı, İstanbul; tel. (212) 3349000; fax (212) 3349019; e-mail genel@genelsigorta.com; internet www.genelsigorta.com; f. 1948; 80% owned by Mapfre Internacional (Spain); Chair. ANGEL ALONSO BATRES; Gen. Man. HULUSI TAŞKIRAN.

Yapi Kredi Sigorta AŞ: Yapi Kredi Plaza, Blok A, Büyükdere Cad., 34330 Levent, İstanbul; tel. (212) 3360606; fax (212) 3360808; e-mail yksigorta@yksigorta.com.tr; internet www.yksigorta.com.tr; f. 1944; Chair. TAYFUN BAYAZIT; Gen. Man. MURAT GÜVENEL.

Trade and Industry

GOVERNMENT AGENCIES

Özelleştirme İdaresi Başkanlığı (OIB) (Privatization Administration): Ziya Gökalp Cad. 80, Kurtuluş Ankara; tel. (312) 4304560; fax (312) 4403271; e-mail info@oib.gov.tr; internet www.oib.gov.tr; co-ordinates privatization programme; Pres. METIN KILCI.

Rekabet Kurumu (Turkish Competition Authority): Bilkent Plaza B3 Blok PK, 06800 Bilkent, Ankara; tel. (312) 2914444; fax (312) 2667920; e-mail rek@rekabet.gov.tr; internet www.rekabet.gov.tr; f. 1997; prevents restriction of competition, oversees mergers and monitors state aid; Pres. and Chair. Prof. Dr NURETTIN KALDIRIMCI.

DEVELOPMENT ORGANIZATION

Turkish Atomic Energy Authority: Prime Minister's Office, Eskişehir Yolu 9km, 06530 Lodumlu, Ankara; tel. (312) 2958700; fax (312) 2878761; e-mail bilgi_taek@taek.gov.tr; internet www.taek.gov.tr; f. 1956; controls the development of peaceful uses of atomic energy; 11 mems; Pres. OKAY ÇAKIROĞLU; Vice-Pres. ALI ALAT.

CHAMBERS OF COMMERCE AND INDUSTRY

Union of Chambers and Commodity Exchanges of Turkey (UCCET) (Türkiye Odalar Borsalar Birliği—TOBB): Atatürk Bul. 149, 06640 Bakanlıklar, Ankara; tel. (312) 4138000; fax (312) 4183268; e-mail info@tobb.org.tr; internet www.tobb.org.tr; f. 1950; represents 364 chambers and commodity exchanges; Pres. RIFAT HISARCIKLIOĞLU.

Ankara Chamber of Commerce (Ankasa Tabip Odasi—ATO): Mithatpaşa Cad. 62/18 Kızılay, 06420 Ankara; tel. (312) 4188700; fax (312) 4187794; e-mail ato@ato.org.tr; internet www.ato.org.tr.

Ankara Chamber of Industry: Çetin Emeç Bul. 4, Cad. 71, Sok. 11, Öveçler, Ankara; tel. (312) 4171200; fax (312) 4175205; e-mail aso@aso.org.tr; internet www.e-aso.org.tr; f. 1963; Chair. TARIK ARTUMAÇ; Dir M. NURETTIN ÖZDEBIR.

İstanbul Chamber of Commerce (ICOC): Reşadiye Cad. 34112 Eminönü, İstanbul; tel. (212) 4556000; fax (212) 5131565; e-mail ito@ito.org.tr; internet www.ito.org.tr; f. 1882; more than 300,000 mems; Pres. MURAT YALÇINTAŞ.

İstanbul Chamber of Industry: Meşrutiyet Cad. 62, 34430 Tepebaşı, İstanbul; tel. (212) 2522900; fax (212) 2495084; e-mail info@iso.org.tr; internet www.iso.org.tr; f. 1952; more than 12,500 mems (2006); Chair. C. TANIL KÜÇÜK; Gen. Sec. METE MELEKSOY.

İzmir Chamber of Commerce: Atatürk Cad. 126, 35210 İzmir; tel. (232) 4984200; fax (232) 4837853; e-mail info@izto.org.tr; internet www.izto.org.tr; f. 1885; Pres. EKREM DEMIRTAŞ; Sec.-Gen. ADNAN YILDIRIM.

EMPLOYERS' ASSOCIATIONS

Türk Sanayicileri ve İşadamları Derneği (TÜSİAD) (Turkish Industrialists' and Businessmen's Association): Meşrutiyet Cad. 74, 34420 Tepebaşı, İstanbul; tel. (212) 2495448; fax (212) 2933783; e-mail tusiad@tusiad.org; internet www.tusiad.org; f. 1971; 451 mems; Chair. ARZUHAN YALÇINDAĞ; Sec.-Gen. Dr HALUK R. TÜKEL.

Türkiye İşveren Sendikaları Konfederasyonu (TİSK) (Turkish Confederation of Employer Associations): Hoşdere Cad. Reşat Nuri Sok. 108, 06540 Çankaya, Ankara; tel. (312) 4397717; fax (312) 4397592; e-mail tisk@tisk.org.tr; internet www.tisk.org.tr; f. 1962; represents (on national level) 22 employers' asscns, with 8,300 affiliated enterprises; official representative in labour relations; Pres. TUĞRUL KUDATGOBILIK; Sec.-Gen. BÜLENT PIRLER.

UTILITIES

In November 2007 the Ministry of Finance stated that it intended to implement the delayed privatization of Turkey's electricity distribution grid in 2008.

Electricity

Elektrik Üretim Anonim Şirketi (EÜAŞ) (Electricity Generation Co Inc): İnönü Bul. 27, Bahçelievler, 06490 Ankara; tel. (312) 2126900; fax (312) 2130103; e-mail basinhalk@euas.gov.tr; internet www.euas.gov.tr; f. 2001, following devolution of responsibilities of fmr Elektrik Üretim-İletim AŞ into separate entities for generation, transmission and wholesale activities; responsible for electricity generation; Gen. Man. SEFER BÜTÜN.

Türkiye Elektrik Iletim Anonim Şirketi (TEIAŞ) (Turkish Electricity Transmission Company): İnönü Bul. 27, Bahçelievler, 06490 Ankara; tel. (312) 2126915; fax (312) 2138870; internet www.teias.gov.tr; f. 2001 (see EÜAŞ, above); responsible for electricity transmission; Chair. and Gen. Man. İLHAMI ÖZŞAHIN.

Water

General Directorate of State Hydraulic Works (DSI): İnönü Bul., Yücetepe, 06100 Ankara; tel. (312) 4178300; fax (312) 4182498; e-mail idarim@dsi.gov.tr; internet www.dsi.gov.tr; f. 1953; controlled by the Ministry of Energy and Natural Resources; responsible for the planning and devt of water resources; Dir-Gen. HAYDAR KOÇAKER.

TRADE UNIONS

Confederations

DİSK (Türkiye Devrimci İşçi Sendikaları Konfederasyonu) (Confederation of Progressive Trade Unions of Turkey): Cad. Abide-I Hürriyet 117, Kat. 5-6-7, Şişli, İstanbul; tel. (212) 2910005; fax (212) 2342075; e-mail disk@disk.org.tr; internet www.disk.org.tr; f. 1967; member of ITUC, European Trade Union Confed. and Trade Union Advisory Cttee; 26 affiliated unions; Pres. SÜLEYMAN ÇELEBI; Sec.-Gen. TAYFUN GÖRGÜN.

Türk-İş (Türkiye İşçi Sendikaları Konfederasyonu Genel Başkanlığı) (Confederation of Turkish Trade Unions): Bayındır Sok 10, 06410 Kizilay, Ankara; tel. (312) 4333125; fax (312) 4336809; e-mail turkis@turkis.org.tr; internet www.turkis.org.tr; f. 1952; mem. of ITUC, European Trade Union Confed. and OECD/Trade Union Advisory Cttee; 32 national unions and federations with 1.7m. mems; Pres. SALIH KILIÇ; Gen. Sec. MUSTAFA KUMLU.

Principal DİSK Trade Unions

BASS (Türkiye Devrimci Banka ve Sigorta İşçileri Sendikası) (Bank and Insurance Employees Unionı): Sumer 2 Sok. 29 Kat. 4, 06640 Kizilay, Ankara; tel. (312) 2325009; fax (312) 2316730; e-mail bass-w@tr.net; internet www.bass-sen.org.tr; Pres. TURGUT YILMAZ; 15,000 mems.

Basın-İş (Türkiye Basın,Yayın, Grafiker ve Ambalaj İşçileri Sendikası) (Press, Publishing, Graphical and Packing Workers): Necatibey Cad., Hanimeli Sok. 26/7, 06430 Sihhiye, Ankara; tel. (312) 2302908; fax (312) 2294315; e-mail basinis@basin-is.org; internet www.basin-is.org; f. 1963; Pres. YAKUP AKKAYA; Gen. Sec. ISMAIL HAKKI KÜTÜKÇÜ; 5,000 mems.

Birlesik Metal-İs (Birlesik Metal İşçileri Sendikası): Tünel Yolu Cad. 2, 34744 Bostancı, Kadıköy, İstanbul; tel. (216) 3808590; fax (216) 3736502; e-mail info@birlesikmetal.org; internet www.birlesikmetal.org; Pres. ADNAN SERDAROĞLU; Gen. Sec. SELÇUK GÖKTAŞ; 58,800 mems.

Demiryol-İş (Türkiye Demiryolu İşçileri Sendikası) (Railway Workers): Necatibey Cad., Sezenler Sok 5, 06430 Yenişehir, Ankara; tel. (312) 2318029; fax (312) 2318032; e-mail demiryolis@demiryolis.org.tr; internet www.demiryolis.org.tr; f. 1952; Pres. ERGÜN ATALAY; Gen. Sec. HÜSEYIN KAYA; 25,000 mems.

Deri-İş (Türkiye Deri İşçileri Sendikası) (Leather Industry): Ahmet Kutsi Tecer Cad. 12/6, Merter, İstanbul; tel. (212) 5048083; fax (212) 5061079; f. 1948; Pres. NUSRETTIN YILMAZ; Gen. Sec. ALI SEL; 11,000 mems.

Dev. Sağlık-İş (Türkiye Devrimci Sağlık İşçileri Sendikası) (Health Employees): Millet Cad., Sadi Çeşme Sok. Başak İş Merkezi 25 Kat 1, Aksaray, İstanbul; tel. (212) 5337719; fax (212) 6315904; e-mail bilgi@devsaglikis.org.tr; internet www.devsaglikis.org.tr; f. 1961; Pres. ARZU ÇERKEZOĞLU; Gen. Sec. TUFAN SERTLEK; 15,000 mems.

Genel-Iş (Türkiye Genel Hizmet İşçileri Sendikası) (Municipal Workers): Çankırı Cad. 28, Kat 5–9, Ulus, Ankara; tel. (312)

3091547; fax (312) 3091046; e-mail bilgi@genel-is.org.tr; internet www.genel-is.org.tr; f. 1983; Pres. EROL EKICI; Gen. Sec. KANI BEKO; 50,000 mems.

Gıda-İş (Türkiye Gıda Sanayii İşçileri Sendikası): Molla Şeref Mah. Ali Yeşim Sok. 13 D/5 Fındıkzade-Fatih, İstanbul; tel. (212) 5233620; fax (212) 5233621; e-mail disk_gidais@mynet.com; Pres. CELAL OVAT; Gen. Sec. SEYIT ASLAN; 31,000 mems.

Koop-İş (Türkiye Kooperatif ve Büro İşçileri Sendikası) (Co-operative and Office Workers): Özveren Sok. 6, Maltepe, Ankara; tel. (312) 2320910; fax (312) 2295836; e-mail bilgi@koopis.org.tr; internet www.koopis.org.tr; f. 1964; Pres. EYÜP ALEMDAR; Gen. Sec. AHMET GÜVEN; 29,000 mems.

Lastik-İş (Türkiye Petrol, Kimya ve Lastik Sanayii İşçileri Sendikası): Bulgurlu Mah. Üçpınarlar Cad. Enver Sok. 1 Rıza Kuas Merkez Binası, 34696 Üsküdar, İstanbul; tel. (216) 3390400; fax (216) 3392313; e-mail lastik-is@lastik-is.org.tr; internet www.lastik-is.org.tr; Pres. ABDULLAH KARACAN; Gen. Sec. NURI SERIM; 18,000 mems.

Limter-İş (Liman, Tersane Gemi Yapım Onarım İşçileri Sendikası) (Harbour, Shipyard, Ship Building and Repairs): Evliya Çelebi Mah. Deniz Sok. 1 K2 D3, Tuzla, İstanbul; tel. (216) 4467545; fax (216) 4467546; e-mail limteris@gmail.com; f. 1947; Pres. CEM DINÇ; Gen. Sec. ZAFER TEKTAŞ; 7,000 mems.

Nakliyat-İş (Nakliye İşçileri Sendikası) (Transportation Workers): Kemalpaşa Mah., Atatürk Bul. Emlak Kredi Bankası Blokları 146 B Blok Kat 4 Daire 16, Eminönü, İstanbul; tel. (212) 5142671; fax (212) 5142669; e-mail nakliyatis@ttnet.net.tr; Pres. ALI RIZA KÜÇÜKOSMANOĞLU; Gen. Sec. YURDAL ŞENOL.

OLEYİS (Otel, Lokanta, Eğlence Yerleri İşçileri Sendikası) (Hotel, Restaurant and Places of Entertainment Workers): Cumhuriyet Cad. 37/4 Beyoğlu, İstanbul; tel. (212) 2356393; fax (212) 3615139; e-mail bilgi@oleyis.org.tr; internet www.oleyis.org.tr; f. 1947; Pres. KAMER AKTAŞ; Gen. Sec. MEHMET EMIN ÜNAL; 4,000 mems.

Sosyal-İş (Türkiye Sosyal Sigortalar, Eğitim, Büro, Ticaret Kooperatif Banka ve Güzel Sanatlar İşçileri Sendikası) (Banking, Insurance and Trading): Mithatpaşa Cad. 56/10 Kızılay, Ankara; tel. (312) 4301773; fax (312) 4323963; e-mail sosyal-is@sosyal-is.org.tr; internet www.sosyal-is.org.tr; Pres. ÖZCAN KESGEÇ; Gen. Sec. TAMER ATIŞ; 31,000 mems.

Tekstil İşçileri Sendikası: M. Nezihi Özmen Mah., Akçay Sok. 22 D2 Güngören, İstanbul; tel. (212) 6372900; fax (212) 6372909; e-mail esgudum@disktekstil.org; internet www.disktekstil.org; Pres. SÜLEYMAN ÇELEBI; Gen. Sec. MUHARREM KILIÇ; 45,000 mems.

Tümka-İş (Türkiye Tüm Kağıt Selüloz Sanayii İşçileri Sendikası): Kınalıtepe Sok. Simitaş 4, Blok 16 D15, Merter, İstanbul; tel. (212) 6776334; fax (212) 5390551; Pres. KEMAL YILMAZ; Gen. Sec. İLHAN ÖZEL; 3,000 mems.

Other Principal Trade Unions

Denizciler (Türkiye Denizciler Sendikası) (Seamen): Rıhtım Cad. Denizciler Sok. 5 Tophane, Karaköy, İstanbul; tel. (212) 2929081; fax (212) 2933938; e-mail kul@cakakul.av.tr; internet www.turkiyedenizcilersendikasi.org.tr; f. 1959; Pres. TURHAN UZUN; Gen. Sec. ŞÜKRÜ AKARDAŞ; 4,272 mems.

Fındık-İş (Fiskobirlik İşçileri Sendikası) (Hazelnut producers): Giresun; Pres. AKÇIN KOÇ; Gen. Sec. ERSAIT ŞEN.

Hava-İş (Türkiye Sivil Havacılık Sendikası) (Civil Aviation): İncirli Cad., Volkan Apt, 68/1 Bakırköy, İstanbul; tel. (212) 6602095; fax (212) 5719051; e-mail havais@havais.org.tr; internet www.havais.org.tr; Pres. ATILAY AYÇIN; Gen. Sec. MUSTAFA YAĞCI; 11,200 mems.

Liman-İş (Türkiye Liman ve Kara Tahmil İşçileri Sendikası) (Longshoremen): Necatibey Cad., Sezenler Sok. 4, Kat. 5, Sıhhıye, Ankara; tel. (312) 2317418; fax (312) 2302484; e-mail liman-is@tr-net.net.tr; f. 1963; Pres. RAIF KILIÇ; Gen. Sec. ERDING ÇAKIR; 5,000 mems.

Şeker-İş (Türkiye Şeker Sanayii İşçileri Sendikası) (Sugar Industry): Karanfil Sok. 59, Bakanlıklar, Ankara; tel. (312) 4184273; fax (312) 4259258; e-mail info@sekeris.org.tr; internet www.sekeris.org.tr; f. 1952; Pres. İSA GÖK; Gen. Sec. FETHI TEKIN; 35,000 mems.

Tarım-İş (Türkiye Orman, Topraksu, Tarım ve Tarım Sanayii İşçileri Sendikası) (Forestry, Agriculture and Agricultural Industry Workers): Bankacı Sok. 10, 06700 Kocatepe, Ankara; tel. (312) 4190456; fax (312) 4193113; e-mail tarim-is@tr.net; internet www.tarimis.org.tr; f. 1961; Pres. BEDRETTIN KAYKAÇ; Gen. Sec. MUSTAFA ÇARDAKÇI; 15,000 mems.

Tekgıda-İş (Türkiye Tütün, Müskirat Gıda ve Yardımcı İşçileri Sendikası) (Tobacco, Drink, Food and Allied Workers): 4 Levent Konaklar Sok., İstanbul; tel. (212) 2644996; fax (212) 2789534; e-mail bilgi@tekgida.org.tr; internet www.tekgida.org.tr; f. 1952; Pres. MUSTAFA TÜRKEL; Gen. Sec. MECIT AMAÇ; 176,000 mems.

Teksif (Türkiye Tekstil, Örme ve Giyim Sanayii İşçileri Sendikası) (Textile, Knitting and Clothing): Ziya Gökalp Cad. Aydoğmuş Sok. 1, Kurtuluş, Ankara; tel. (312) 4312170; fax (312) 4357826; internet www.teksif.org.tr; f. 1951; Pres. NAZMI IRGAT; Gen. Sec. MEHMET ÇAKAN; 60,000 mems.

Tez-Koop-İş (Türkiye, Ticaret, Kooperatif, Eğitim, Büro ve Güzel Sanatlar İşçileri Sendikası) (Commercial and Clerical Employees): Üç Yıldız Cad. 29, Subayevleri, Ayınlıkevler, 06130 Ankara; tel. (312) 3183979; fax (312) 3183988; e-mail sendika@tezkoopis.org; internet www.tezkoopis.org.tr; f. 1962; Pres. GÜRSEL DOĞRU; Gen. Sec. SEDAT ÖLMEZ; 30,000 mems.

Türk Harb-İş (Türkiye Harb Sanayii ve Yardımcı İşkolları İşçileri Sendikası) (Defence Industry and Allied Workers): İnkılap Sok. 20, Kızılay, Ankara; tel. (312) 4175097; fax (312) 4171364; internet www.harb-is.org.tr; f. 1956; Pres. AHMET KALFA; Gen. Sec. SALIM TILDICI; 25,000 mems.

Türk-Metal (Türkiye Metal, Çelik, Mühimmat, Makina ve Metalden Mamul, Eşya ve Oto, Montaj ve Yardımcı İşçileri Sendikası) (Auto, Metal and Allied Workers): Kızılırmak Mah., Adalararası Sok. 3, Eskişehir Yolu 1 km, 06560 Söğütözü, Ankara; tel. (312) 2926400; fax (312) 2844018; e-mail bilgiislem@turkmetal.org.tr; internet www.turkmetal.org.tr; f. 1963; Pres. MUSTAFA ÖZBEK; Gen. Sec. MUHARREM ASLIYÜCE; 247,000 mems.

Yol-İş (Türkiye Yol, Yapı ve İnşaat İşçileri Sendikası) (Road, Construction and Building Workers): Sümer 1 Sok. 18, Kızıloy, Ankara; tel. (312) 2324687; fax (312) 2324810; e-mail yildirimkoc@yol-is.org.tr; internet www.yol-is.org.tr; f. 1963; Pres. FIKRET BARIN; Gen. Sec. TEVFIK OZCELIK; 70,000 mems.

Transport

RAILWAYS

The total length of the railways in operation within the national frontiers was 10,984 km in 2005, of which 8,697 km were main lines, 2,336 km were electrified and 3,111 km were signalled. There are direct rail links with Bulgaria to Iran and Syria. Construction of a new line connecting Turkey with Georgia and Azerbaijan commenced in late 2007, with an anticipated completion date of 2009/10. İstanbul operates an 18-km light railway system, and opened its first metro line in September 2000. Both systems are being expanded. Ankara and İzmir both operate metro railways.

Türkiye Cumhuriyeti Devlet Demiryolları İşletmesi Genel Müdürlüğü (TCDD) (Turkish State Railways): Talatpaşa Bul., 06330 Gar, Ankara; tel. (312) 3090515; fax (312) 3123215; e-mail tcddapk@tcdd.gov.tr; internet www.tcdd.gov.tr; f. 1924; operates all railways and connecting ports (see below) of the State Railway Administration, which acquired the status of a state economic enterprise in 1953, and a state economic establishment in 1984; 470 main-line diesel locomotives, 74 main-line electric locomotives, 965 passenger coaches and 16,070 freight wagons; Chair. of Bd and Gen. Dir SÜLEYMAN KARAMAN.

ROADS

In January 2008 the total road network was estimated at 63,899 km of classified roads, of which 1,987 km were motorways, 31,333 km were highways and 30,579 km were secondary roads.

Bayındırlık ve İskan Bakanlığı, Karayolları Genel Müdürlüğü (KGM) (General Directorate of Highways): İnönü Bul., Yücetepe, 06100 Ankara; tel. (312) 4157000; fax (312) 4186996; e-mail info@kgm.gov.tr; internet www.kgm.gov.tr; f. 1950; Dir-Gen. MEHMET CAHIT TURHAN.

SHIPPING

At the end of 2006 Turkey's merchant fleet comprised 1,184 vessels and had an aggregate displacement of 4,848,839 grt.

General-purpose public ports are operated by two state economic enterprises. The ports of Bandırma, Derince, Haydarpaşa (İstanbul), İskenderun, İzmir and Samsun, all of which are connected to the railway network, are operated by Turkish State Railways (see above), while the smaller ports of Antalya, Giresun, Hopa, Tekirdağ and Trabzon are operated by the Turkish Maritime Organization. Control of the port of Mersin was transferred to the private sector in 2007 under a 36-year concession agreement. However, a similar arrangement involving the port of İzmir was suspended in March 2008.

Turkish Maritime Organization (TDI): Genel Müdürlüğü, Rıhtım Cad. Merkez Han 4, 34443 Karaköy, İstanbul; tel. (212) 2515000; fax (212) 2495391; e-mail tdi@tdi.gov.tr; internet www.tdi.com.tr; Gen. Man. BURHAN KÜLÜNK.

Port of Bandırma: TCDD Liman İşletme Müdürlüğü, Bandırma; tel. (266) 7187530; fax (266) 7136011; e-mail bandirmaliman@tcdd.gov.tr; Port Man. OKKES DEMIREL; Harbour Master RUSEN OKAN.

TURKEY

Port of Derince: TCDD Liman İşletme Müdürlüğü, Derince; tel. (262) 2399021; e-mail derinceliman@tcdd.gov.tr; Port Man. ALI ARIF AYTAÇ; Harbour Master HAYDAR DOĞAN.

Port of Haydarpaşa (İstanbul): TCDD Liman İşletme Müdürlüğü Haydarpaşa, İstanbul; tel. (216) 3488020; fax (216) 3451705; e-mail haydarpasaliman@tcdd.gov.tr; Port Man. NEDIM OZCAN; Harbour Master İSMAIL SAFAER.

Port of İskenderun: TCDD Liman İşletme Müdürlüğü, İskenderun; tel. (326) 6140044; fax (326) 6132424; e-mail iskenderunliman@tcdd.gov.tr; Port Man. HILMI SÖNMEZ; Harbour Master İSHAK ÖZDEMIR.

Port of İzmir: TCDD Liman İşletme Müdürlüğü, İzmir; tel. (232) 4631600; fax (232) 4632248; e-mail izmirliman@tcdd.gov.tr; Port Man. GÜNGÖR ERKAYA; Harbour Master MEHMET ONGEL.

Port of Mersin: Liman İşletmesi Yolcu, Mersin; tel. (324) 2390939; fax (324) 2390849; e-mail marketing@mersinport.com.tr; internet www.mersinport.com.tr; managed since 2007 by a consortium of PSA International (Singapore) and Akfen (Turkey) under a 36-year concession; Port Man. PETER ONG KIM PONG; Harbour Master RACI TARHUSOĞLU.

Port of Samsun: TCDD Liman İşletme Müdürlüğü, Samsun; tel. (362) 2332293; fax (362) 4451626; e-mail samsunliman@tcdd.gov.tr; Port Man. SAFFET YAMAK; Harbour Master Capt. ARIF H. UZUNOĞLU.

Private Companies

Akmar Shipping Group: Küçükbakkalköy Mah. Cicek Sok. 4, Aksoy Plaza, 34750 Kadıköy, İstanbul; tel. (216) 5762666; fax (216) 5727195; e-mail info@akmar.com.tr; internet www.akmar.com.tr; f. 2004; Chair. NECDET AKSOY.

Deniz Nakliyatı TAŞ (Turkish Cargo Lines): Fahrettin Kerim Gökay Cad. Denizciler İş Merkezi No. 14, A Blok Kat. 1, Altunizade/Üsküdar, İstanbul; tel. (216) 4747400; fax (216) 4747430; e-mail tcl@tcl.com.tr; internet www.tcl.com.tr; f. 1955; bulk carriers; Gen. Man. CEMIL GÜCÜYENER; 2 large and 2 small handy bulk/ore carriers.

İstanbul Deniz Otobusleri Sanayi ve Ticaret AŞ: Kennedy Cad., Yenikapı Hızlı Feribot Iskelesi, Eminönü, İstanbul; tel. (212) 4556900; fax (212) 5173958; e-mail info@ido.com.tr; internet www.ido.com.tr; f. 1987; ferry company; Chair. MUSTAFA ACIKALIN; Man. Dir AHMET PAKSOY; 82 vessels.

Kiran Group of Shipping Companies: Fahrettin Kerim Gorkay Cad. 18, Denizciler İş Merkezi B Blok Kat 2, 34662 Altunizade, İstanbul; tel. (216) 5541400; fax (216) 5541414; e-mail kiran@kiran.com.tr; internet www.kiran.com.tr; f. 1959; Chair. TURGUT KIRAN; Man. Dir TAMER KIRAN; 19 vessels.

Ozsay Seatransportation Co Inc: Güzelyalı, E-5 Üzeri 18, 34903 Pendik, İstanbul; tel. (216) 4933610; fax (216) 4930306; e-mail ozsay@tnn.net; internet www.ozsay.com; Pres. RECEP KALKAVAN; Man. Dir OMER KALKAVAN; 10 vessels.

Pinat Gida Sanayi ve Ticaret AŞ: Pak Ismerkezi Prof. Dr Bulent Tarcan Sok 5/3, 80290 Gayrettepe, İstanbul; tel. (212) 2747533; fax (212) 2750317; e-mail pinat@pinat.com.tr; Pres. ENGIN PAK; Man. Dir ALPAY CITAK; 7 vessels.

Türkiye Denizcilik İşletmeleri Denizyolları İşletmesi Müdürlüğü (TDI): Meclisi Mebusan Cad. 18, 80040 Salıpazarı, İstanbul; tel. (212) 2521700; fax (212) 2515767; e-mail bilgiedinme@tdi.gov.tr; internet www.tdi.com.tr; ferry company; Chair. ERKAN ARIKAN; Man. Dir KADIR KURTOĞLU; 5 vessels.

Vakif Deniz Finansal Kiralama AŞ: Rihtim Cad. 201 Tahir Han kat 6, PK 853, 80040 Karaköy, İstanbul; 15 vessels.

Yardimci Shipping Group of Companies: Aydintepe Mah. Tersaneler Cad. 50 Sok 7, 81700 Tuzla, İstanbul; tel. (216) 4938000; fax (216) 4928080; e-mail info@yardimci.gen.tr; internet www.yardimci.gen.tr; f. 1976; Chair. KEMAL YARDIMCI; Man. Dir HUSEYIN YARDIMCI; 6 vessels.

Shipping Associations

SS Gemi Armatörleri Motorlu Taşıyıcılar Kooperatifi (Turkish Shipowners' Asscn): Meclisi Mebusan Cad., Dursun Han, Kat. 7, No 89, Salıpazarı İstanbul; tel. (212) 2510945; fax (212) 2492786; f. 1960; Pres. GÜNDÜZ KAPTANOĞLU; Man. Dir A. GÖKSU; 699 vessels.

Türk Armatörler Birliği (Turkish Shipowners' Union): Meclisi Mebusan Cad. Dursun Han, Kat. 7 No. 89, Salıpazarı, İstanbul; tel. (212) 2453022; fax (212) 2492786; f. 1972; 460 mems; Pres. ŞADAN KALKAVAN; Co-ordinator HAKAN ÜNSALER.

Vapur Donatanları ve Acenteleri Derneği (Turkish Shipowners' and Shipping Agents' Asscn): Kiliç Ali Pasa Mah. Ilyas Celebi Sok. No.23, 34433 Cihangir-Beyoğlu, İstanbul; tel. (212) 2443294; fax (212) 2432865; e-mail vapurd@vda.org.tr; internet www.vda.org.tr; f. 1902; world-wide agency service; Pres. RUHI DUMAN; Man. Dir NESLIHAN BAŞARSLAN.

CIVIL AVIATION

The management of Turkey's airports and provision of the air traffic service and its control in Turkish airspace is performed by the Devlet Hava Meydanları İşletmesi Genel Müdürlüğü (General Directorate of State Airports Authority). Atatürk (İstanbul), Esenboğa (Ankara), Adnan Menderes (İzmir and Trabzon), Antalya, Adana, Trabzon, Milas–Bodrum, Süleyman Demirel and Nevşehir–Kapadokya airports are open for international and domestic flights, both regular and charter. Adıyaman, Ağrı, Ferit Melen, Gaziantep, Kahraman Maraş, Kars, Körfez, Mardin, Samsun–Çarşamba, Siirt, Tokat, Uşak and Şanlıurfa Aerodromes are open only for domestic flights.

Devlet Hava Meydanları İşletmesi Genel Müdürlüğü (General Directorate of State Airports Authority): Konya Yolu Üzeri, 06330 Etiler, Ankara; tel. (312) 2126120; fax (312) 2123917; e-mail dhmi@dhmi.gov.tr; internet www.dhmi.gov.tr; f. 1984; Chair. of Bd and Dir-Gen. ORHAN BIRDAL.

Sivil Havacılık Genel Müdürlüğü (Directorate General of Civil Aviation): Bosna Hersek Cad. 5 Emek, Ankara; tel. (312) 2154400; fax (312) 2124684; internet www.shgm.gov.tr; Gen. Man. ALI ARIDURU.

Atlasjet Havacilik AŞ (Alfa Airlines Inc): Yesilyurt Mah. Eski Halkali Yolu Alacati Evleri Yani 5/B, 34153 Florya, İstanbul; tel. (212) 6632000; fax (212) 6632751; internet www.atlasjet.com; f. 2001; passenger and cargo; 12 aircraft; Chair. TUNCAY DOĞANER; CEO ORHAN COŞKUN.

Fly Air (ESN): Cevizli Sok. 7 Senlikkoy Mah., 34153 Florya, İstanbul; tel. (212) 4243837; fax (212) 5149902; e-mail info@flyair.com.tr; internet www.flyair.com.tr; f. 2002; charter and scheduled flights, international and cargo; 13 aircraft.

Inter Airlines (Istanbul Airlines): Çağlayan Mah. 2004, Sok. 26, Barınaklar, Antalya; tel. (242) 3104400; fax (242) 3240928; e-mail info@interekspres.com; internet www.interekspres.com; f. 1999; charter flights to European destinations; Chair. ÖMER TOROSLUOĞLU; Gen. Man. ERCÜMENT FILIZ.

Onur Air Taşımacılık AŞ: Senlikköy Mah., Çatal Sok. 3, 34153 Florya, İstanbul; tel. (212) 6632300; fax (212) 6632319; e-mail info@onurair.com.tr; internet www.onurair.com.tr; f. 1992; regional and domestic passenger and cargo charter services; Chair. CANKUT BAGANA.

Pegasus Airlines: Basın Ekspres Yolu 2, Halkalı, İstanbul; tel. (212) 6977777; fax (212) 6939777; internet www.flypgs.com; f. 1990; charter services; 17 aircraft; Chair. ALI SABANCI; Gen. Man. SERTAÇ HAYBAT; 17 planes.

Sky Airlines: Güzeloba Mah. Ay 1 Sok. 1, 07230 Anatalya; tel. (242) 3108800; fax (242) 3108805; e-mail info@skyairlines.net; internet www.skyairlines.net; f. 2000; regional passenger charter flights; seven aircraft; Chair. TALHA GÖRGÜLÜ; Gen. Man. TAHIR GÖRGÜLÜ.

Sonmez Hava Yolları: 9 km Yeni Yalova Yolu, PK 189, Bursa; tel. (224) 2610440; fax (224) 2610428; e-mail helikopter@sonmezholding.com.tr; internet www.sonmezholding.com.tr; f. 1984; scheduled flights and dedicated freight; Chair. ALI OSMAN SÖNMEZ.

SunExpress (Güneş Ekspres Havacilik AŞ): Mehmetçik Mah. Aspendos Bul. Aspendos İş Merkezi 63/1–2, 07300 Antalya; tel. (242) 3102626; fax (242) 3102650; e-mail travelcenter@sunexpress.com.tr; internet www.sunexpress.com.tr; f. 1990; charter and scheduled passenger and freight; serves European destinations; Man. Dir PAUL SCHWAIGER.

Türk Hava Yolları AO (THY) (Turkish Airlines Inc): Genel Müdürlük Binas, Atatürk Hava Limanı, 34830 Yeşilköy, İstanbul; tel. (212) 4636363; fax (212) 4652121; e-mail customer@thy.com; internet www.thy.com.tr; f. 1933; 49.12% state-owned; extensive internal network and scheduled and charter flights to destinations in the Middle East, Africa, the Far East, Central Asia, the USA and Europe; 102 aircraft; Chair. CANDAN KARLITEKIN; Gen. Man. TEMEL KOTIL.

Tourism

Visitors to Turkey are attracted by the climate, fine beaches and ancient monuments. With government investment, the country has rapidly become a leading holiday destination for European tourists (particularly from the United Kingdom and Germany). In 2007 the number of tourists increased to a provisional 23.3m. (compared with 7.5m in 1999), while receipts from tourism reached US $16,851m. in 2006.

Ministry of Culture and Tourism: See The Government—Ministries; Dir-Gen. of Information MUSTAFA SYAHHAN; Dir-Gen. of Investments and Establishments KUDRET ASLAN.

TURKMENISTAN

Introductory Survey

Location, Climate, Language, Religion, Flag, Capital

Turkmenistan is situated in the south-west of Central Asia. It is bordered to the north by Uzbekistan, to the north-west by Kazakhstan, to the west by the Caspian Sea, to the south by Iran and to the south-east by Afghanistan. The climate is severely continental, with extremely hot summers and cold winters. The average temperature in January is −4°C (25°F), but winter temperatures can fall as low as −33°C (−27°F). In summer temperatures often reach 50°C (122°F) in the south-eastern Kara-Kum desert; the average temperature in July is 28°C (82°F). Precipitation is slight throughout much of the country: average annual rainfall ranges from only 80 mm (3.1 ins) in the north-west to about 300 mm (11.8 ins) in mountainous regions. Turkmen, a member of the Southern Turkic group, is the official language. Most of the population are Sunni Muslims. Islam in Turkmenistan has traditionally featured elements of Sufi mysticism and shamanism, and pilgrimages to local religious sites are reported to be common. The national flag (proportions 2 by 3) consists of a maroon stripe bearing a vertical design of five different carpet patterns above a wreath of olive branches on a green background, with five white, five-pointed stars framed by a narrow white crescent moon, in its upper dexter corner. The capital is Aşgabat.

Recent History

In 1877 Russia began a campaign against the Turkmen, which culminated in the battle of Gök Tepe in 1881, at which some 20,000 Turkmen are estimated to have been killed. In 1895 the Russian conquest was confirmed by agreement with the British; the international boundary thus established divided some Turkmen under Russian rule from others in the British sphere of influence. In 1917 the Bolsheviks attempted to take power in the region, but there was little support from among the local population. An anti-Bolshevik Russian Provisional Government of Transcaspia was formed, and a Turkmen Congress was also established. Soviet forces were sent to Aşgabat, and a Turkestan Autonomous Soviet Socialist Republic, which included Transcaspia, was declared on 30 April 1918. In July, however, nationalists, aided by British forces, ousted the Bolshevik Government and established an independent Government in Aşgabat, protected by a British garrison. After the British withdrew, however, the Government was soon removed, and by 1920 Red Army troops, led by Gen. Mikheil Frunze, were in control of Aşgabat. As part of the National Delimitation of Central Asia, the Turkmen Soviet Socialist Republic (SSR) was established on 27 October 1924. In May 1925 it became a constituent republic of the USSR. Political power in the republic became the preserve of the Communist Party of Turkmenistan (CPT).

The Soviet agricultural collectivization programme, which was begun in 1929 and entailed the forcible settlement of traditionally nomadic people in collective farms, provoked military resistance, and guerrilla warfare against Soviet power continued until 1936. In 1928 a campaign against the practice of religion in Turkmenistan was launched: almost all Islamic institutions were closed, including schools, courts and mosques. In the early 1930s there was a campaign among the Turkmen intelligentsia for greater political autonomy for Turkmenistan. In response, many intellectuals were imprisoned or executed. The scope of the purges widened in the late 1930s to include government and CPT officials, including a Chairman of the republican Supreme Soviet (Supreme Council—legislature).

After the early 1930s there was little development in the industrial sector. Agriculture was encouraged and irrigation extended. Irrigation projects such as the Kara-Kum Canal, the largest such scheme in the USSR, enabled rapid development of cotton-growing, especially after 1945. The immigration of Russians into the urban areas of Turkmenistan, from the 1920s, gradually diminished the proportion of Turkmen in leading posts in the republic.

In the late 1980s Turkmenistan's role as a provider of raw materials (mainly natural gas and cotton) to more developed regions of the USSR provoked strong criticism of the relationship between republican and the all-Union authorities. The environmental and health hazards connected with intensive agriculture were also widely discussed in the republican media. However, the geographical remoteness of the republic inhibited its involvement in the political changes occurring in other Soviet republics. In the absence of any significant pro-democracy movement, the CPT dominated the republic's elections to the all-Union Congress of People's Deputies in the Soviet and Russian capital, Moscow, in early 1989. In September, however, Turkmen intellectuals formed Unity (Agzybirlik), a 'popular front' organization concerned with the status of Turkmen language and culture and environmental matters, which initially gained official registration but was banned in January 1990. Only the CPT and its approved organizations were permitted to participate in elections to the republican Supreme Soviet on 7 January. When the new Supreme Soviet convened, Saparmyrat Niyazov, the First Secretary of the CPT since 1985, was elected Chairman of the Supreme Soviet, the highest government office in the republic.

In May 1990 Turkmen officially became the state language, replacing Russian; Turkmenistan was the last of the Soviet republics to introduce such legislation. On 22 August the Turkmenistani Supreme Soviet adopted a declaration of sovereignty. On 27 October Niyazov was elected, by direct ballot, to the new post of executive President of Turkmenistan. He was unopposed in the election and reportedly received 98.3% of the votes cast. In late 1990 and early 1991 Turkmenistan participated in negotiations towards a new Union Treaty, which was to redefine the status of the republics within the structure of the USSR. The underdeveloped state of the economy, and the republic's dependence on the central Government for subsidies, ensured that the republic's leadership was one of the most enthusiastic proponents of the preservation of the USSR. At the all-Union referendum on the status of the USSR in March 1991, 95.7% of eligible voters in Turkmenistan approved the preservation of the USSR as a 'renewed federation', the highest proportion of any Soviet republic.

President Niyazov made no public announcements either opposing or supporting the attempted coup by conservative communist elements in Moscow of August 1991. However, opposition groups, including Unity, publicly opposed the coup, which led to the arrest of several of their leaders. Following the failure of the coup attempt, Niyazov remained in power and announced that the CPT would be retained as the ruling party; however, in December the CPT changed its name to the Democratic Party of Turkmenistan (DPT), with Niyazov as its Chairman. On 18 October Turkmenistan was among the signatories of the treaty establishing an economic community of eight republics. This was followed on 26 October by a national referendum at which, according to the official results, 94.1% of the electorate voted for independence. On the following day the Turkmenistani Supreme Council adopted a law on independence. The name of the republic was changed from the Turkmen SSR to Turkmenistan. On 21 December Turkmenistan became a signatory, with 10 other republics, of the Alma-Ata (Almaty) Declaration, which formally established the Commonwealth of Independent States (CIS, see p. 215); this decision was subsequently ratified by the Turkmenistani Supreme Council.

The DPT and Niyazov came to dominate independent Turkmenistan, particularly in the Council of Ministers and the Supreme Council. Although Niyazov reportedly continued to enjoy widespread popular support, there was some criticism of his increasingly authoritarian style of leadership, which involved rigid control of the media and the restriction of opposition activity. The promotion of a presidential 'cult of personality' was reported to have prompted the resignation, in mid-1992, of the Minister of Foreign Affairs, Abdy Kuliyev. The new Constitution, adopted on 18 May, further enhanced presidential authority, making Niyazov Chairman of the Government (Prime Minister), as well as Head of State, and giving him certain legislative prerogatives. He was also to act concurrently as the Supreme Commander of the Armed Forces. In June Niyazov was re-elected, unopposed, to the presidency, receiving a purported 99.5% of the votes cast in a direct ballot.

Other significant structural changes were introduced under the new Constitution. The Supreme Council was to be replaced as Turkmenistan's legislature by a 50-member Majlis (Assembly); however, until the expiry of its five-year term, the Supreme Soviet elected in 1990 (renamed as the Majlis), was to be retained as the republican legislature. The Khalk Maslakhaty (People's Council) was established as the 'supreme representative body of popular power'. The Khalk Maslakhaty was to act in a supervisory capacity, and would not diminish the authority of the President or the Majlis; however, it was to debate and decide important political and economic issues, and would also be empowered to demand changes to the Constitution and to vote to express 'no confidence' in the President, if it found his actions to be at variance with the law. The Khalk Maslakhaty was to comprise the 50 deputies of the Majlis in addition to 50 elected and 10 appointed representatives from the electoral districts of Turkmenistan (the former were directly elected in November–December 1992); it was also to include other members of local government and prominent figures, including the members of the Government and the Chairman of the Supreme Court, and was to be headed by the President.

After the new Constitution was adopted, there were fears that the rights of Turkmenistan's ethnic minorities (the most numerous of which, Russians and Uzbeks, represented some 10% and 9%, respectively, of the total population in the early 1990s) were in jeopardy, as the document stipulated that only ethnic Turkmen would be eligible for employment in state enterprises. Moreover, the Russian language was to lose the status of 'language of inter-ethnic communication' that it had held since 1990. Although the population is predominantly Muslim, Turkmenistan's Constitution guaranteed state secularism, a principle that was strongly emphasized by President Niyazov.

The presidential personality cult was strengthened during 1993, with numerous institutions, streets and public buildings being named after Niyazov. Notably, the Caspian Sea port of Krasnovodsk was renamed Türkmenbaşi ('Head of the Turkmen', a recently introduced mode of address for Niyazov). In December the Majlis voted to extend Niyazov's term of office until 2002, on the grounds that the republic's political and economic stability depended on the realization of Niyazov's '10 Years of Prosperity' programme of gradual reforms. The extension of Niyazov's presidency was endorsed by a reported 99.99% of the electorate in a referendum held on 15 January 1994.

Elections to the new, 50-member Majlis were held in December 1994, officially with the participation of 99.8% of the registered electorate. It was reported that 49 of the 50 deputies had been elected unopposed. The Majlis convened later in the month; the overwhelming majority of the deputies were believed to be members of the DPT.

Despite the result of the referendum of January 1994, elements of opposition to Niyazov were believed to be active in Turkmenistan, as well as in exile in other republics of the CIS, in particular Russia, where Abdy Kuliyev led an opposition group known as the Turkmenistan Foundation. In June 1995 the Turkmenistani Supreme Court sentenced two opposition leaders to respective terms of 12 and 15 years' imprisonment in a labour colony, having found them guilty of involvement in an alleged plot to assassinate Niyazov. In July 1995 a protest rally took place in Aşgabat (reportedly the first to be held in Turkmenistan since independence), at which up to 1,000 demonstrators criticized Niyazov's leadership and the continuing economic hardships. In August, in what was interpreted as a response to the previous month's unrest, Niyazov dismissed 10 of Turkmenistan's 50 local etrap (district or raion) administrative leaders. In October the President also dismissed several senior members of the Council of Ministers.

In 1996 and 1997 Niyazov effected widespread dismissals of government officials, as well as local administrative leaders and members of the judiciary. In February 1998 the President revealed that he planned to amend the Constitution after the legislative elections of December 1999, devolving certain presidential powers to the Majlis and relinquishing the post of prime minister (although in the event he retained the latter position). In April 1998 elections to the Khalk Maslakhaty were held, with the reported participation of 99.5% of the electorate.

Turkmenistan continued to attract the censure of international human rights organizations during the late 1990s. In April 1998 a delegation of the Organization for Security and Co-operation in Europe (OSCE, see p. 354) appealed to Niyazov to release eight political prisoners who had been detained since the demonstration of July 1995. Niyazov agreed to their release, following which he made his first official visit to the USA where he met President Bill Clinton. Niyazov's systematic purging of government and other officials continued in May 1998. An attempted military rebellion that occurred in western Turkmenistan in September was followed by the dismissal of the Minister of Defence, and the comprehensive reorganization of senior personnel of the armed forces and border troops.

The promotion of the presidential cult of personality appeared to intensify during 1998: in October Niyazov was honoured with his third 'hero of Turkmenistan' award (the country's highest honour) and in December a giant ceremonial arch, the 'Arch of Independence', surmounted by a revolving gold-plated statue of the President, was inaugurated in central Aşgabat, and Niyazov was unanimously re-elected Chairman of the DPT. In what was interpreted as an effort to counter growing international accusations of dictatorial methods, the President declared, in December, that the elections to the Majlis scheduled for late 1999 would be contested on a multi-party basis, and that the establishment of new political parties would be permitted in advance of the poll. In December the Khalk Maslakhaty voted to abolish the death penalty; Turkmenistan thus became the first Central Asian state to proscribe capital punishment.

Elections to the Majlis were conducted on 12 December 1999. According to official reports, some 99% of the registered electorate participated in the poll. In the event, the DPT was the only party represented and the OSCE declined an invitation to monitor the poll, claiming that there was little evidence of a genuinely democratic process. In late December the new Majlis approved an amendment to the Constitution whereby Niyazov's presidential term was extended indefinitely. Niyazov had made repeated claims that the success of democratic and economic reform would be dependent on the continuity of successive 10-year plans. Following the Majlis' endorsement of the amendment, Niyazov announced that the creation of opposition political parties would not be contemplated before 2010. These developments further aroused the concerns of the international community, and there was considerable outrage when, in March 2000, the leader of the unofficial popular opposition front, Unity, Nurberdy Nurmamedov, was sentenced to five years' imprisonment on charges of hooliganism and intent to murder, after he protested that the December 1999 amendment to the Constitution was undemocratic.

On 1 January 2000 Turkmenistan formally adopted a revised form of the Latin script, replacing the Cyrillic script that had been introduced for the Turkmen language in the 1920s. In July Niyazov issued an order declaring that, henceforth, knowledge of the Turkmen language would be a mandatory requirement for all government officials; heads of state organizations, ministries and higher-education institutions were given 30 days to learn the language or lose their positions. Furthermore, all candidates for leadership posts were to have their genealogies over the previous three generations verified.

In January and June 2000 President Niyazov dismissed a number of prominent government officials, including three Deputy Chairmen. Niyazov also instructed Turkmenistani citizens and government organizations to close any bank accounts held abroad, in order to curtail the flow of capital from Turkmenistan. At the end of July the President dismissed Boris Shikhmuradov, the Minister of Foreign Affairs; he was replaced by Batyr Berdiyev. It was also announced that all officials, including government ministers, would henceforth to be appointed for a six-month probation period.

In the early 2000s Niyazov oversaw the introduction of a number of policies intended to develop a strong Turkmen national identity, including the closure of the opera and ballet theatre in Aşgabat, which Niyazov denounced as 'alien' to Turkmen culture. A principal element of Niyazov's proposals to promote a Turkmen national culture was the publication of the *Ruhnama*, or national code of spiritual conduct, a volume purportedly written by the President. This text became a key element of the school curriculum, and was in effect elevated to the status of a holy text, with display of the volume required in mosques and citations from the work included in inscriptions in religious and public buildings, with knowledge of the text, moreover, becoming a prerequisite for entry into various professions. (A second volume of the *Ruhnama* was published in September 2004.)

In July 2001 Berdiyev was dismissed as Minister of Foreign Affairs, and replaced by Rashid Merepov. In late October Shikhmuradov was dismissed as ambassador to the People's Republic of China. He fled to exile in Moscow from where, in early

November, he issued a statement condemning Niyazov's rule. Meanwhile, it was reported that a warrant for Shikhmuradov's arrest on charges of the misappropriation of state property had been issued by the Prosecutor-General, Gurbanbibi Atajanova, along with a request for his extradition from Russia. Although Shikhmuradov denied the charges, Turkmenistani officials claimed that his actions were an attempt to avoid prosecution; it was also widely speculated that Shikhmuradov intended to replace Niyazov by means of a coup. In January 2002 he established the People's Democratic Movement of Turkmenistan, with the aim of deposing Niyazov. In early February Nurmuhamed Khanamov resigned as ambassador to Turkey in order to join the opposition movement. In mid-February a former Deputy Chairman, Khudayberdy Orazov, announced his support for the opposition-in-exile. The Turkmenistani authorities subsequently issued a request for the extradition of Khanamov and accused Orazov of embezzling state funds. Meanwhile, in March Niyazov dismissed a number of senior officials from the defence, intelligence and security services (including the Minister of Defence), whom he accused of plotting to remove him from power. In addition, the State Border Service was placed under the direct control of the President. A new Minister of Internal Affairs was appointed in May, and in the same month Seitbay Gandimov was dismissed as Deputy Chairman and Chairman of the central bank, following allegations of links to Orazov. A further cabinet reorganization followed in August. Government changes in September included the appointment of three new ministers and the creation of a Ministry of National Security, under Batyr Busakov, to replace the Committee for National Security. In late September the newly appointed Chairman of the central bank was dismissed, following the theft from the bank of US $41.5m. In the same month Niyazov announced the creation of so-called 'labour armies', comprising 20,000 men under the age of 35, which were to be drafted to work without remuneration on public projects; the term of service was to be two years, irrespective of previous army service. Further government changes took place in mid-November, and Ovezgeldy Atayev was elected Chairman of the Majlis.

On 25 November 2002 it was widely reported that an assassination attempt had been made against the presidential motorcade, as it travelled through Aşgabat. An emergency cabinet meeting was held, and Niyazov publicly accused former officials Shikhmuradov and Khanamov, among others, of an attempted coup. An official announcement the following day reported the arrest of 16 suspects, although international human rights organizations reported hundreds of detentions in subsequent days. Also on 25 November Shikhmuradov, who had clandestinely returned to Turkmenistan, was arrested in Aşgabat. Following a televised confession, a one-day trial at the Supreme Court on 30 December found Shikhmuradov guilty of the attempt on Niyazov's life, and he was sentenced to 25 years' imprisonment (subsequently increased to a life sentence by the Majlis). Orazov and Khanamov were also convicted *in absentia*, and former Minister of Foreign Affairs Batyr Berdiyev was detained and sentenced in early 2003 to 25 years' imprisonment for his alleged involvement in the assassination attempt; the opposition-in-exile subsequently indicated that Berdiyev may have died. Meanwhile, opposition leader Murad Esenov, in exile in Sweden, claimed that the assassination attempt had been staged as a pretext for the arrest of Shikhmuradov and other members of the opposition, and the OSCE, concerned at the circumstances surrounding Shikhmuradov's trial and confession, sent a fact-finding mission to Aşgabat. In late December the Uzbekistani ambassador to Turkmenistan (the embassy of which country had been searched, in violation of the Vienna Convention on Diplomatic Relations) was expelled from the country, having been accused of harbouring Shikhmuradov immediately after the attack (see below). In June 2003 Orazov reportedly stated that Shikhmuradov and his opposition allies had intended to stage a coup, but that they had no intention of killing Niyazov.

In February 2003 Niyazov issued decrees that temporarily reinstated the requirement for exit visas (which had been abolished in December 2001), and imposed severe restrictions on the exchange of Turkmenistani currency. (The requirement for exit visas was abolished again in March 2004.) The import of foreign periodicals was prohibited, and more severe restrictions were imposed on journalists. Meanwhile, on 6 April 2003 elections to the Khalk Maslakhaty and to district and village councils took place, with the participation of some 89.3% of the electorate. The OSCE, which had accused the authorities of widespread human rights abuses in a report issued in March, questioned the legitimacy of the electoral process.

On 15 August 2003 amendments to the Constitution elevated the Khalk Maslakhaty, which was henceforth to comprise 2,507 members, to the status of a 'permanently functioning supreme representative body of popular authority', and required it to remain in continuous session. The Khalk Maslakhaty was also accorded a number of legislative powers, which enabled it to pass constitutional laws, thus effectively displacing the Majlis as the country's leading legislative body. Other changes to the Constitution forbade Turkmenistani citizens from holding dual nationality, superseding an agreement on dual nationality reached with Russia in December 1993 (see below).

Government changes in September 2003 included the appointment of Maj.-Gen. Agageldy Mamatgeldiyev as Minister of Defence. As part of further restructuring in November, two new Deputy Chairmen and a new Minister of National Security were appointed. Also in November a new law was passed restricting the activities of religious groups by criminalizing any confession not registered with the Ministry of Justice (at that time the only state-registered faiths were Sunni Islam and Russian Orthodox Christianity). The formation of political parties on religious grounds was also prohibited. (These laws were revised in March 2004.) In the same month a new law came into force, which severely restricted the activities of non-governmental organizations, imposing fines, prison sentences and periods of 'corrective labour' for those convicted under the new guide-lines. In late November the UN General Assembly adopted a resolution (which was, notably, supported by Russia), expressing grave concerns over human rights violations in Turkmenistan. At the end of the month Niyazov pardoned more than 7,000 prisoners.

In December 2003 President Niyazov reorganized the state broadcasting organizations. Further government changes were made in January 2004, including the appointment of a new Minister of Petroleum, Natural Gas and Mineral Resources. In February Niyazov replaced 15,000 medical workers with army conscripts, in an attempt to reduce government expenditure on health care. In April the Minister of the Economy and Finance, the Minister of Education and the heads of two state-controlled banks were dismissed. In May Niyazov signed a decree prohibiting the use of child labour in the cotton industry. A further presidential decree, issued in June, invalidated all higher-education degrees received abroad; all teachers with such degrees were to be dismissed. Niyazov implemented further government changes in July, appointing a new Minister of Trade and Foreign Economic Relations. In August Geldimuhammet Ashirkulov was appointed Minister of Internal Affairs. (In early December Ashirkulov was, in turn, replaced by Akmamed Rahmanov.) Meanwhile, in October Niyazov removed Enebai Atayeva as Deputy Chairman and Governor of the cotton-producing Ahal Velayat (Region). This dismissal reportedly reflected dissatisfaction with the nation-wide cotton harvest; the regional deputy governor and four heads of cotton-producing associations were also replaced. In early November President Niyazov adopted what was apparently Turkmenistan's first law preventing the illegal use and trafficking of drugs. In the same month the UN General Assembly adopted a second resolution criticizing human rights violations in Turkmenistan; on this occasion Russia abstained from voting, while Uzbekistan voted against the resolution, despite its explicit condemnation of discrimination by the Government of Turkmenistan against Russians, Uzbeks and other minority ethnic groups in the country.

Elections to the Majlis were conducted on 19 December 2004. According to official reports, 76.9% of the registered electorate participated in the poll, at which the DPT was the only party represented. (A second round of voting took place on 9 January 2005 in seven districts, where candidates had failed to obtain the required 50% plus one of the votes cast.) In April 2005 Niyazov declared that a multi-candidate presidential election would be conducted in 2009, following elections for district governors in 2006, regional governors in 2007 and parliamentary deputies in 2008. However, in October 2005 President Niyazov was the only member of the Khalk Maslakhaty to vote in favour of retaining on the Council's agenda a discussion of his proposal to hold a presidential election in 2009.

Meanwhile, in February 2005 Niyazov announced plans to close all hospitals outside Aşgabat, stating that the provision of hospitals outside the capital was unnecessary, particularly given the shortage of doctors. Niyazov also ordered the closure of rural libraries, asserting that the rural Turkmenistani population was largely illiterate and therefore made limited use of the existing facilities. The President imposed further restrictions in April, prohibiting the import and circulation of all foreign print media, and refusing to renew the licences of international shipping firms and express couriers. In June a report published by the London School of Hygiene and Tropical Medicine (United Kingdom) expressed concern at the 'systematic dismantling' of Turkmenistan's health-care system, asserting that people were dying because they could not afford health-care fees; the report urged the international community to apply pressure on Turkmenistan to improve services.

Throughout 2005 and in the first months of 2006 President Niyazov frequently replaced state officials; many of those dismissed were accused of corruption or other abuses of office, and sentenced to long custodial terms. Notably, in late May 2005 the deputy prime minister for the Fuel and Energy Sector, Yolly Gurbanmuradov, was dismissed, having been accused of 'serious shortcomings' and of having abused his position for personal gain when he had served as head of the State Bank for Foreign Economic Activities in 1993–2001. Despite conflicting reports that Gurbanmuradov had either hanged himself in prison or been killed during interrogation, in July 2005 it was reported that he had been sentenced to 25 years' imprisonment. Meanwhile, at the end of May 2005 Niyazov also removed Shekersoltan Muhammedova from the chairmanship of the Central Bank, accusing her of corruption. She was replaced by Jumaniyaz Annaorazov, hitherto the Minister of the Economy and Finance. Niyazov further reorganized the energy sector in August and September of that year. In mid-April 2006 Niyazov appointed Muhammetguly Ogshukov, previously First Deputy Prosecutor-General, to replace Atajanova as Prosecutor-General. Although Niyazov initially stated that Atajanova was to retire (having occupied the post since 1997), later in the month Atajanova admitted to charges made by Niyazov that she had taken bribes and stolen state property. In early May Niyazov declared invalid the presidential decree relieving her of her post in connection with her retirement, instead decreeing that she was relieved of her duties for having committed 'shameful' deeds and having damaging the title of the office of Prosecutor-General. In the same month work was completed on a palace made of ice, the construction of which had cost some US $21.5m. in Aşgabat, while work commenced on the construction of a huge artificial lake in the Kara-Kum desert. Elections to the 625 municipal councils (gengeşes) took place on 23 July; 5,320 deputies were elected to local gengeşes from a field of 12,200 contenders.

On 21 December 2006 President Niyazov died, having suffered a heart attack. Under the terms of the Constitution, the role of acting President should have been assumed by Ovezgeldy Atayev, Chairman of the Majlis; however, Atayev was dismissed from his post shortly after Niyazov's death, when state prosecutors announced they would be investigating Atayev on criminal charges. Subsequently, the State Security Council appointed the Deputy Chairman of the Government and Minister of Health and the Medical Industry, Gurbanguly Berdymuhamedov, to act as President until presidential elections had been held. Meanwhile, Akja Nurburdiyeva succeeded Atayev as Chairman of the Majlis. Six candidates contested the presidential elections, which were held on 11 February 2007. As had widely been predicted, Berdymuhamedov was the clear winner, receiving 89.2% of the votes cast; turn-out was a reported 98%. Berdymuhamedov was inaugurated as President on 14 February and from mid-February the appointment of government ministers and other senior state officials was announced, including several ministers who had served under Niyazov. Among the principal appointments were those of Rashid Meredov as deputy premier and Minister of Foreign Affairs, Mamatgeldiyev as Minister of Defence and Murad Karryev as Minister of Justice; Muhammetgeldy Annaamanov was appointed Minister of Education, replacing Hydyr Saparliev, who was promoted to the position of deputy premier. New appointments were also made to regional governorships and to the chairmanship of the Supreme Court and to the Office of the Prosecutor-General.

The most significant of President Berdymuhamedov's early decrees was the Code of Social Guarantees, signed into law on 19 March 2007, which restored pension rights that had been removed from an estimated 100,000 senior citizens in the previous year. On 31 March Berdymuhamedov was elected Chairman of the Khalk Maslakhaty. In a speech to the body the President announced a programme of agricultural reforms and plans to extend public access to the internet, which hitherto had been severely restricted, in Turkmenistan. (The first public access point to the internet in the country had been opened in February in Aşgabat.) In April the Minister of Internal Affairs appointed in February was dismissed, reportedly for failure to address corruption within the ministry and an increase in drug abuse within the country, and was replaced by Khodjamyrat Annagurbanov. In July Berdymuhamedov effected a limited government reorganization and replaced a number of other senior officials. In early October Berdymuhamedov dismissed Minister of Internal Affairs Annagurbanov and the Minister of National Security, both of whom, according to an official announcement, were to be subject to criminal proceedings on undisclosed charges. Charymyrat Amanov was appointed to the Ministry of National Security, while Orazgeldy Amanmyradov received the internal affairs portfolio. In November Berdymuhamedov appointed a new Deputy Chairman of the Government, responsible for Trade and Textiles. On 9 December elections were conducted to councils in each of Turkmenistan's Velayats. In April 2008 Hojamyrat Geldimyradov, hitherto Minister of Finance, was appointed as Deputy Chairman of the Government, responsible for Economic Affairs, while the deputy premier responsible for Transport and Communications, Gurbannazar Ashyrov, was dismissed, having been subject to criticism for the conduct of his actions by the President; the Chairman of the Central Bank was also replaced. Later in April Berdymuhamedov established a special commission to revise the Constitution, and officially abolished the names of the months introduced by Niyazov (which had included various titles of Niyazov and his parents). In early May it was announced that the gold revolving statue of Niyazov and the Arch of Independence constructed in 1998 were to be relocated to a less prominent location on the outskirts of the capital.

One of the fundamental principles of Turkmenistan's foreign policy is that of 'permanent neutrality', a concept that is enshrined in the Constitution. The republic's neutral status was recognized by the UN General Assembly in December 1995, two months after Turkmenistan became the first of the former Soviet republics to join the Non-aligned Movement (see p. 424). The policy of neutrality has led Turkmenistan to adopt a somewhat equivocal attitude towards its membership of the CIS. President Niyazov consistently expressed opposition to centralized structures within the Commonwealth, preferring to regard it as a 'consultative body'. Moreover, the republic refused to sign a number of CIS agreements on closer political, military and economic integration, and at the beginning of September 2005 Niyazov confirmed that Turkmenistan intended to withdraw from full membership of the CIS, but would remain an associate member of the organization.

None the less, Turkmenistan's most important political ally and economic partner remains Russia, the leading CIS state. In December 1993 Turkmenistan became the first of the former Soviet republics to sign an agreement on dual citizenship with Russia; it was hoped that this would further strengthen bilateral relations, while helping to stem the exodus of ethnic Russians from the republic. However, at a meeting in Moscow in April 2003, Niyazov and President Vladimir Putin of Russia agreed to rescind the agreement (which was believed to have facilitated the ability of Niyazov's opponents to operate from exile). Later in April Niyazov decreed that the estimated 95,000 dual passport holders in Turkmenistan should renounce either their Russian or Turkmenistani citizenship within two months, prompting protests from the Russian Ministry of Foreign Affairs, which insisted that the new agreement was not meant to apply retroactively and, moreover, had not yet been ratified by Russia. In June the Russian Gosudarstvennaya Duma (State Duma) adopted a resolution condemning Niyazov's unilateral revocation of dual citizenship, and the Russian Government subsequently deemed Turkmenistan unsafe for its citizens. Nevertheless, in August the Khalk Maslakhaty passed constitutional amendments forbidding Turkmenistani citizens from holding dual citizenship, and placing any dual citizens remaining in the country in breach of the law.

Meanwhile, Turkmenistan's natural gas exports were a persistent cause of friction between the two countries. Transport of natural gas from Turkmenistan was dependent on the use of the former Soviet pipeline system, which remained largely under Russian control. In 1993 Turkmenistan's access to European markets via this system was effectively curbed by Russia's decision to direct Turkmenistani gas exports to Ukraine and the South Caucasus. However, as a result of the recipient countries' delay in paying for their gas imports, Turkmenistan suspended all deliveries in 1993–95, which in turn was severely detrimental to the Turkmenistani economy. Although gas exports to Ukraine and the South Caucasus were resumed in 1996, in March 1997 Niyazov announced the dissolution of the Turkmenistani-Russian company, Türkmenrosgaz (which held a monopoly on the sale and export of Turkmenistani gas), because the company was in severe debt. In response, the Russian Government denied Turkmenistan access to the regional pipeline system. Although Ukraine began to repay its outstanding debt to Turkmenistan, delivery was hampered by Russia's refusal to lower its transport tariffs to the level demanded by Turkmenistan. However, in December 1998 Turkmenistan reached an agreement with Russia regarding the transport of natural gas, and deliveries to Ukraine were resumed in January 1999, only to be suspended again in May, owing to further payment problems. In May 2000 the Turkmenistani authorities agreed to increase its deliveries of natural gas to Russia annually for the following three to four years. At the beginning of 2001 Turkmenistan halted its deliveries to Russia, owing to the failure of the two sides to agree on a mutually acceptable price; agreement was finally reached in February with Itera, an affiliate of the Russian gas monopoly, Gazprom. Turkmenistan also signed an agreement with Itera and a Russian energy company, Zarubezhneft, for the development of Turkmenistan's onshore and offshore hydrocarbons deposits.

Turkmenistan resumed natural gas deliveries to Ukraine in November 2000, and in May 2001 Turkmenistan agreed to supply Ukraine with 250,000m. cu m of natural gas in 2002–06. In April 2003 Turkmenistan agreed to supply Russia with more than 2,000,000m. cu m of natural gas over 25 years; a similar agreement was reached with Ukraine in late 2003. However, in early January 2005 Turkmenistan stopped supplying Russia with natural gas, in an attempt to force Gazprom to agree to an increase in the price of gas sold by Turkmenistan. Russia refused to negotiate gas prices until 2007, under the terms of the bilateral agreement signed in 2003, and Turkmenistan resumed gas supplies to Russia after 10 days. However, Turkmenistan did manage to persuade Ukraine to accept an increase in the price of gas from US $44 per 1,000 cu m to $58 per 1,000 cu m, after Niyazov briefly suspended gas supplies to that country. The impasse between Russia and Turkmenistan was resolved in April 2005, when Gazprom agreed to make all payments for gas from Turkmenistan in cash, abandoning the previous partial barter system. In late 2005 Turkmenistan attempted to secure a new agreement on gas prices, and at the end of the year Gazprom agreed to purchase 30,000m. cu m of natural gas in 2006 at $65 per 1,000 cu m. The two states subsequently signed a new, 18-month contract, which required Ukraine to pay for its gas in cash only, instead of using bartering arrangements. Ukraine was to purchase 59,500m. cu m of gas at $44 per 1,000 cu m (lower than the rate agreed to in January 2005), and to repay its arrears for past exports in commodities, without increasing their prices. In March 2006 Ukraine confirmed that it owed Turkmenistan $169.6m. ($46.8m. in cash, and $122.8m. in commodities) for gas supplied in 2003–05, and the two countries agreed a schedule of repayment.

In September 2006 President Niyazov declared that Russia and the People's Republic of China were priority customers for gas, while casting grave doubts on the prospects for the proposed trans-Caspian and trans-Afghanistan pipelines. Turkmenistan's success in convincing Russia to agree to a substantial price increase for gas in the same month underscored the latter's need to continue to exert control over Turkmenistani gas supplies, on which it was dependent in order to meet its own export commitments to Western Europe and elsewhere. Following Niyazov's death in late December, in May 2007 President Berdymuhamedov met Presidents Putin of Russia and Nursultan Nazarbayev of Kazakhstan in the port-city of Türkmenbaşi, where an agreement was reached to export Turkmenistani gas to Russia by way of Kazakhstan; Russia accepted a 40% price increase for imports of Turkmenistani gas over the following year.

Of the remaining CIS member states, Turkmenistan has concentrated on developing closer relations with the neighbouring Central Asian republics of Kazakhstan, Kyrgyzstan, Tajikistan and Uzbekistan. Turkmenistan remained neutral regarding the civil war in Tajikistan (q.v.), and it did not contribute troops to the joint CIS peace-keeping forces in the region, although Aşgabat did become one of the venues for the Tajikistani peace negotiations. In July 2001 Turkmenistan and Kazakhstan signed a treaty demarcating their shared border. In September 2000 Turkmenistan and Uzbekistan had signed a treaty defining their 1,867 km-border and, under President Niyazov's orders, a 1,700-km fence was installed along the border in 2001 (although increased control of the border was reported to have led to local tensions). Relations with Uzbekistan deteriorated sharply in December 2002, following the alleged coup attempt of 25 November (see above). In mid-December the Uzbekistani embassy in Aşgabat was searched for evidence, and Uzbekistan's ambassador to Turkmenistan was subsequently declared *persona non grata*, on the grounds that he supported the alleged instigator of the coup, Boris Shikhmuradov. The Uzbekistani authorities reacted with hostility, and troops from both countries were deployed along their common border. Stricter border controls were subsequently implemented. In mid-November 2004 President Niyazov and President Islam Karimov of Uzbekistan met for their first presidential summit in more than four years in Buxoro, Uzbekistan, where they signed three bilateral agreements, pledging friendship between the two countries, mutual trust, and co-operation; simplifying regulations concerning cross-border travel for residents of border zones; and agreeing on a framework for sharing regional water resources. The Presidents declared that all bilateral issues had been resolved, and in early December they celebrated the demarcation of the border between the two countries. A new Uzbekistani ambassador to Turkmenistan was appointed in January 2005.

The legal status of the Caspian Sea, and the ownership of the extensive deposits of petroleum and natural gas beneath it, provoked controversy from the mid-1990s between all five of the littoral states (Turkmenistan, Azerbaijan, Iran, Kazakhstan and Russia). At a special conference on the Sea's status, held in Aşgabat in November 1996, the Ministers of Foreign Affairs of all five countries established a working group to formulate the demarcation of national boundaries. Nevertheless, in early 1997 Turkmenistan and Azerbaijan were engaged in a dispute over the status of two Caspian oilfields (the Azeri and Çirağ fields—known as the Khazar and Kaverochkin fields in Turkmenistan), which were being developed by Azerbaijan and a consortium of international companies. The situation deteriorated in July 1997, when Azerbaijan announced its intention to develop, in conjunction with a consortium of Russian companies, a third oilfield, which both countries laid claim to, known as Kyapaz to the Azeris and as Serdar to the Turkmen. Although Russia subsequently withdrew from the project, Azerbaijan refused to abandon its claim to the field. Apparently in response, in September Turkmenistan launched its first international tender for petroleum and gas exploration in the Caspian Sea, and announced that it expected Azerbaijan to compensate it for developing the Azeri and Çirağ fields. The commercial exploitation of the latter field began in November. Although Kazakhstan and Russia signed an agreement in October 2000 defining the legal status of the Caspian Sea, the remaining littoral states made limited progress. In November 2003 representatives of the five littoral states, meeting in Tehran, Iran, signed a UN-sponsored framework Convention for the Protection of the Marine Environment of the Caspian Sea, which sought to alleviate environmental damage in the Caspian Sea region. In mid-January 2005 President Niyazov approved a proposal from a Canadian company, Buried Hill Energy and Petroleum, to develop the Serdar oilfield, prompting protests from Azerbaijan. In November Niyazov agreed that a production-sharing agreement would be signed with Buried Hill Energy and Petroleum for the development of the Turkmenistani sector of the Caspian Sea.

Iran plays the most important role in Turkmenistan's foreign relations outside the CIS. In 1992 a number of agreements on closer political, economic and cultural integration were signed, including an accord to construct a railway line between Iran and Turkmenistan. The line, which linked the Turkmenistani city of Tejen with the northern Iranian city of Mashad, was opened in May 1996, thus affording Turkmenistan access both to the Persian (Arabian) Gulf and to İstanbul, Turkey. Turkmenistan and Iran also signed an agreement on the construction of a 140-km gas pipeline between the Korpeje natural gas deposit in south-western Turkmenistan and the city of Kord Kuy in northern Iran. The pipeline was to be the first segment on a route, which, it was envisaged, would eventually transport Turkmenistani gas via Iran to Turkey and thence to western Europe. The inauguration of the pipeline in December 1997 opened the first alternative export route for Turkmenistan's natural gas, and thus promised greater economic independence for the republic from Russia. In April 2006 Iran reached agreement with Turkmenistan on gas imports, which were expected to total some 6,000m. cu m in 2006 and some 8,000m. cu m in 2007.

In March 2003 work on a project, conceived in 1999, to construct an underwater trans-Caspian gas export pipeline to Turkey, via Azerbaijan and Georgia, was suspended indefinitely, owing to disagreement between Turkmenistan and Azerbaijan over the division of the pipeline's anticipated throughput. Meanwhile, in late April 2002 President Niyazov requested UN support for the construction of a proposed 1,680-km gas pipeline from Dauletabad in Turkmenistan to Fazilka, a village on the Pakistan–India border, via Afghanistan, led by the US company Unocal. In May 2002 the leaders of Turkmenistan, Afghanistan and Pakistan signed a memorandum of understanding on a feasibility study for the project. In December 2002 an agreement was signed on the construction of the pipeline, which was expected to be able to carry some 708,000m. cu m of gas per year. The project was subject to prolonged delays, and in 2008 it was announced that construction of the pipeline, which was additionally to supply gas to India, would commence in 2010. Meanwhile, in February 2006 Pakistan and Turkmenistan signed a memorandum of understanding, according to which Turkmenistan agreed to supply Pakistan with some 90.6m. cu m of gas per day for 30 years.

President Niyazov confirmed his country's neutrality by developing equal relations with the Taliban and their opponents, the United National Islamic Front for the Salvation of Afghanistan, commonly known as the United Front or the 'Northern Alliance', in the late 1990s. Turkmenistan was central in organizing peace negotiations between the Taliban and United Front in both July 1999 and December 2000. Niyazov maintained the country's neutrality following the large-scale suicide attacks in the USA in September 2001, which were attributed to the Saudi Arabian-born leader of the Islamist militant al-Qa'ida (Base) organization, Osama bin Laden, who had developed a close association with the Taliban. None the less, Niyazov gave his consent to the use of Turkmenistan's ground and air transport 'corridors' for the delivery of humanitarian aid to Afghanistan during airstrikes against al-Qa'ida and its Taliban hosts; Niyazov refused US troops access to Turkmenistan's military bases, however, reaffirming the country's policy of non-interference.

In April 2006 Turkmenistan and the People's Republic of China signed an agreement to construct a natural gas pipeline from Turkmenistan to China; details of the pipeline's construction were to have been finalized by the end of the year. According to the agreement, China was to purchase 30,000m. cu m of Turkmenistani gas per year for 30 years from 2009 (when the pipeline was scheduled to be completed). In August 2007 the Turkmenistani Government awarded China rights to develop gas reserves in the east of the country for the project.

Turkmenistan enjoys close relations with Turkey (which has been regarded as competing with Iran for political and economic influence in the region), not least owing to the Turkmens' ethnic and linguistic ties with the Turks. Turkmenistan is a member, with both Turkey and Iran (among others), of the Economic Co-operation Organization (ECO, see p. 238).

In September 2007 President Berdymuhamedov, addressing the UN General Assembly, announced that he planned to develop co-operation with the international community in all areas of activity; he and other members of the Turkmenistani Government also met with US officials to discuss reforms and private investment. At the end of February 2008 further discussions on energy co-operation were conducted during a visit to Aşgabat by a senior US official. In April, following a visit to Turkmenistan by the EU external relations commissioner, the Government pledged to supply 10,000m. cu m of gas for the EU's planned Nabucco pipeline project from 2009, together with opportunity for investments in new fields.

Government

Under the terms of the 1992 Constitution, the President of the Republic is directly elected, by universal adult suffrage, for five years, although in December 1993 the legislature voted to extend President Niyazov's mandate—due to expire in 1997—until 2002 (this was endorsed in a national referendum in January 1994). In December 1998 the Khalk Maslakhaty endorsed an amendment to the Constitution whereby Niyazov's mandate was extended indefinitely. The President is both Head of State and Head of Government (Prime Minister in the Council of Ministers), holding executive power in conjunction with the Council of Ministers (which is appointed by the President), and is concurrently Supreme Commander of the Armed Forces. The supreme legislative body is the Majlis (Assembly), the 50 members of which are directly elected for a term of five years. The deputies of the Majlis also sit on the Khalk Maslakhaty (People's Council), a supervisory organ, which includes a further 50 directly elected and 10 appointed representatives from all districts of Turkmenistan, the members of the Council of Ministers and other prominent figures, and is headed by the President of the Republic. In August 2003 a constitutional law and a constitutional amendment were passed elevating the Khalk Maslakhaty to the status of 'permanently functioning supreme representative body of popular authority', and requiring it to remain in continuous session. The constitutional changes ascribed to the Khalk Maslakhaty, which was, henceforth, to comprise 2,507 members, a number of legislative powers, including the passing of constitutional laws, thereby effectively displacing the Majlis as the country's leading legislative body. Turkmenistan is divided into five velayats (regions), which are subdivided into 50 etraps (districts) and 625 gengeşes (municipalities).

Defence

In mid-1992 Turkmenistan began the establishment of national armed forces, based upon the former Soviet military units still stationed in the republic; under an agreement with Russia, these forces were initially under joint Turkmenistani and Russian command. Since 1993 Turkmenistan has co-operated with Russia and Kazakhstan in the operation of the Caspian Sea Flotilla, another former Soviet force, based, under Russian command, at Astrakhan, Russia. In May 1994 Turkmenistan became the first Central Asian republic of the former USSR to join the North Atlantic Treaty Organization's 'Partnership for Peace' (see p. 342) programme. However, one of the fundamental principles of Turkmenistan's foreign policy is that of 'permanent neutrality', which is enshrined in the Constitution. The republic's neutrality was recognized by the UN General Assembly in December 1995, two months after Turkmenistan became the first former Soviet republic to join the Non-aligned Movement (see p. 424). As assessed at November 2007, the armed forces numbered 22,000, comprising an army of 18,500, an air force of 3,000 and a navy (largely coastguard units) of 500. Military service lasts for 24 months. The budget for 2006 allocated US $181m. to defence.

Economic Affairs

In 2004, according to estimates by the World Bank, Turkmenistan's gross national income (GNI), measured at average 2002–04 prices, was US $6,615m., equivalent to $1,340 per head (or $6,910 per head on an international purchasing-power parity basis). During 1996–2006, it was estimated, the population increased at an average annual rate of 1.4%. Gross domestic product (GDP) per head increased, in real terms, by an average of 8.3% per year in 1995–2005. Overall GDP increased, in real terms, at an average annual rate of 10.3% per year in 1995–2004. According to the Asian Development Bank (ADB, see p. 182), GDP increased by 10.0% in 2007.

Agriculture contributed an estimated 19.6% of GDP in 2004, according to the World Bank. The sector employed 31.5% of the total economically active population at mid-2005, according to FAO. Although the Kara-Kum desert covers some 80% of the country's territory, widespread irrigation has enabled rapid agricultural development; however, over-intensive cultivation of the principal crop, cotton, together with massive irrigation projects, have led to serious ecological damage. In 1996 cotton contributed an estimated 11.5% of GDP, although the Government planned to reduce cotton production in favour of food production by 2010. Other important crops include grain, vegetables and fruit (in particular grapes and melons), although the country remains heavily dependent on imports of foodstuffs. Livestock husbandry (including the production of astrakhan and karakul wools) plays a central role in the sector, and silkworms are bred. According to the World Bank, agricultural production increased, in real terms, by an annual average of 5.8% in 1995–2003. Real agricultural GDP increased by 9.5% in 2002 and by 9.9% in 2003.

Industry (including mining, manufacturing, construction and power) contributed an estimated 40.1% of GDP in 2004, when, according to the ADB, 13.8% of the employed labour force were engaged in the sector. During 1995–2003, according to the World Bank, industrial GDP increased, in real terms, at an average annual rate of 10.1%. However, real industrial GDP increased by 13.2% in 2002 and by 16.2% in 2003.

Turkmenistan is richly endowed with mineral resources, in particular natural gas and petroleum (recoverable reserves of which were estimated at some 2,860,000m. cu m and 100m.

metric tons, respectively, at the end of 2006). In 2006 Turkmenistan produced approximately 62,200m. cu m of gas, and production of petroleum averaged 163,000 barrels per day. A new power installation, constructed at a cost of US $120m. in the town of Daşoguz, commenced production in December 2007; it was expected to generate more than 1,500m. kWh of electricity a year. In addition, Turkmenistan has large deposits of iodine, bromine, sodium sulphate, clay, gypsum and different types of salt.

The manufacturing sector contributed 21.7% of GDP in 2004. The principal branches of manufacturing are the processing of mineral resources (predominantly petroleum and natural gas) and textiles (mainly cotton products). Petroleum is refined at three refineries, at Türkmenbaşi, Seidi and Türkmenabat. According to the World Bank, manufacturing GDP increased by 24.0% in 1998–2003. Sectoral growth was estimated at 25.6% in 2002 and 34.7% in 2003.

In 2003 an estimated 10,800m. kWh of electricity was produced domestically; of electricity produced in 1994, some 20% was reported to have been exported, while a proportion of the remainder was distributed free of charge to domestic users. (Some charges for domestic electricity use were introduced in 1996; however, the 2006 budget provided for free distribution.) In 2003 mineral fuels accounted for just 0.7% of the value of merchandise imports, according to ADB estimates.

The services sector provided an estimated 40.3% of GDP in 2004, and employed some 38.0% of the working population in 2003. Trade and catering services form the major part of the sector, providing some 6% of employment in 1998. According to the World Bank, services GDP increased, in real terms, at an average annual rate of 11.7% in 1995–2003. Real services GDP increased by 34.1% in 2002 and by 22.2% in 2003.

According to the ADB, in 2006 Turkmenistan recorded a surplus of US $1,295m. on the current account of the balance of payments. In 2006 the principal source of imports (accounting for 14.0% of the total) was the United Arab Emirates; other major suppliers were Turkey (9.9%), Russia (8.0%) and Ukraine (7.8%). The principal markets for exports were Ukraine (46.3%) and Iran (16.8%). In 2003 the principal exports were basic manufactures. The principal imports in that year were machinery and transport equipment, basic manufactures, chemicals, miscellaneous manufactured articles, and food and live animals.

In 2004 there was a budgetary surplus estimated at 11,800m. manats (equivalent to some 0.02% of GDP). At the end of 2005 Turkmenistan's total external debt was US $1,092m., of which $912m. was long-term public debt. Consumer prices increased by an annual average of 1,150% in 1993 and by 1,748% in 1994, but the inflation rate declined to 1,005% in 1995, to 992% in 1996 and to an estimated 84% in 1997. Average prices rose by 16.8% in 1998 and by 24.2% in 1999. The inflation rate declined again in 2000, to an annual average of 7.4%, and in 2001, to 4.0%. According to estimates by the European Bank for Reconstruction and Development (EBRD, see p. 239), deflation of 3.5% in 2002 and 1.9% in 2003 was recorded. Inflation declined from 8.2% in 2006 to 6.5% in 2007, according to the ADB. In 2004 some 62,000 people were registered as unemployed (about 2.6% of the labour force); however, unofficial sources estimated the rate to be considerably higher.

Turkmenistan became a member of the IMF and the World Bank in 1992. It also joined the EBRD as a 'Country of Operations' and, with five other former Soviet republics, the Economic Co-operation Organization (ECO, see p. 238). In 1994 Turkmenistan became a member of the Islamic Development Bank (IDB, see p. 329), and it joined the ADB in 2000.

The disruptions in inter-republican trade that followed the dissolution of the USSR in December 1991 damaged Turkmenistan's industrial sector, which relied heavily on imported finished and intermediate goods. Moreover, the failure, or delay, of many of Turkmenistan's CIS trading partners to pay for imports of natural gas (the mainstay of the republic's economy) resulted in huge arrears, and Turkmenistan was forced to suspend deliveries several times throughout the 1990s and early 2000s, with adverse consequences for the economy. The opening of a new gas pipeline to Iran in late 1997 did, however, contribute to some revival in the economically crucial gas sector. In 2003 Turkmenistan concluded major agreements with both Russia and Ukraine to supply them with natural gas for 25 years. In December 2007 Turkmenistan signed an agreement for the construction of a new gas pipeline link to Russia via Kazakhstan, and negotiated a significant increase in the price paid by Russia for Turkmenistani gas. A pipeline link with China was expected to be completed in 2009. The rate of inflation decreased significantly and GDP grew strongly from 2000, largely owing to the export of natural gas, petroleum and cotton, and, in particular, to an increase in international prices of natural gas, and a sustained increase in output (although a small decline in production, of 0.9%, was recorded in 2004). From the mid-1990s the Government sought to increase the value of the country's traditional exports, based on natural resources and crops; however, in 2007 it appeared that cotton and wheat production had fallen short of official targets. Moreover, an inefficient tax system and a poorly regulated banking sector, largely under state control, continued to hinder economic stability, and estimates of the private sector's contribution to GDP in 2003 varied between 20% and 30%, reflecting the lack of structural reform or market liberalization. Following the death of President Niyazov in 2006, there were signs that the country's new leadership intended to pursue significant reforms and greater international integration. Although the economic situation remained healthy during 2007, the official figure of 20% GDP growth, cited by the Government, is likely to have been overestimated, with the IMF estimating that growth in that year more probably amounted to around 10%. The Asian Development Bank (ADB) projected GDP growth of 10%–11% for 2008.

Education

A state-funded education system was introduced under Soviet rule. Although some schools provided instruction in Russian, Uzbek and Kazakh, President Niyazov pledged to eradicate teaching in languages other than Turkmen. Following the death of Niyazov, in February 2007 the new President increased the period of primary and secondary education from nine to 10 years (effective from the beginning of the 2007/08 school year). In 1990 the total enrolment at higher schools was equivalent to 21.8% of the relevant age-group. The 1999 budget allocated 26.9% of total expenditure (1,048,700m. manats) to education. Free education at Turkmenistan's 16 universities was apparently abolished in 2003, while it was reported that the number of places for students in educational establishments had been sharply reduced since the mid-1990s. In 2004 a presidential decree invalidating all higher-education degrees received abroad came into effect; all teachers with such degrees were to be dismissed.

Public Holidays

2008: 1 January (New Year's Day), 12 January (Memorial Day), 19 February (National Flag Day; President Niyazov's Birthday), 8 March (International Women's Day), 21 March (Novrus Bairam, Spring Holiday), 8–9 May (Victory Day), 18 May (Revival and Unity Day), 1 October* (Oraza Bairam—Id al-Fitr, end of Ramadan), 6 October (Remembrance Day), 27–28 October (Independence Day), 8 December* (Kurban Bairam—Id al-Adha, Feast of the Sacrifice), 12 December (Turkmenistan Neutrality Day).

2009: 1 January (New Year's Day), 12 January (Memorial Day), 19 February (National Flag Day; President Niyazov's Birthday), 8 March (International Women's Day), 21 March (Novrus Bairam, Spring Holiday), 8–9 May (Victory Day), 18 May (Revival and Unity Day), 6 October (Remembrance Day), 20 September* (Oraza Bairam—Id al-Fitr, end of Ramadan), 27–28 October (Independence Day), 27 November* (Kurban Bairam—Id al-Adha, Feast of the Sacrifice), 12 December (Turkmenistan Neutrality Day).

* These holidays are dependent on the Islamic calendar and may vary by one or two days from the dates given.

Weights and Measures

The metric system is in force.

Statistical Survey

Principal sources (unless otherwise stated): IMF, *Turkmenistan, Economic Review, Turkmenistan—Recent Economic Developments* (December 1999); World Bank, *Statistical Handbook: States of the Former USSR*.

Area and Population

AREA, POPULATION AND DENSITY

Area (sq km)	488,100*
Population (census results)	
12 January 1989	3,533,925
10 January 1995	
Males	2,225,331
Females	2,257,920
Total	4,483,251
Population (UN estimates at mid-year)†	
2005	4,833,000
2006	4,899,000
2007	4,965,000
Density (per sq km) at mid-2007	10.2

* 188,456 sq miles.
† Source: UN, *World Population Prospects: The 2006 Revision*; these estimates are substantially lower than those produced by the state statistics institute (see below).

Population (official estimate): 6,800,200 at 1 April 2006 (Source: National Institute of State Statistics and Information).

POPULATION BY ETHNIC GROUP
(official estimates at 1 January 1993)

	Number	%
Turkmen	3,118,000	73.3
Russian	419,000	9.8
Uzbek	382,000	9.0
Kazakh	87,000	2.0
Others	248,000	5.8
Total	**4,254,000**	**100.0**

Ethnic groups (percentage of total, at census of 1995): Turkmen 77.0; Uzbek 9.2; Russian 6.7; Kazakh 2.0; Others 5.1 (Source: US Embassy in Turkmenistan).

PRINCIPAL TOWNS
(estimated population at 1 January 1999)

Aşgabat (capital)	605,000	Türkmenbaşi‡	70,000	
Türkmenabat*	203,000	Bayramaly	60,000	
Daşoguz	165,000	Tejen	54,000	
Mari	123,000	Serdar§	51,000	
Balkanabat†	119,000			

* Formerly Charjew (Chardzhou).
† Formerly Nebit-Dag.
‡ Formerly Krasnovodsk.
§ Formerly Gyzylarbat (Kizyl-Arvat).

1 July 2002 (official estimate): Aşgabat 743,000.

Mid-2007 (incl. suburbs, UN estimate): Aşgabat 744,000 (Source: UN, *World Urbanization Prospects: The 2007 Revision*).

BIRTHS, MARRIAGES AND DEATHS

	Registered live births		Registered marriages		Registered deaths	
	Number	Rate (per 1,000)	Number	Rate (per 1,000)	Number	Rate (per 1,000)
1987	126,787	37.2	31,484	9.2	26,802	7.9
1988	125,887	36.0	33,008	9.4	27,317	7.8
1989	124,992	34.9	34,890	9.8	27,609	7.7

Registered deaths: 25,755 (death rate 7.0 per 1,000) in 1990; 27,403 (7.3 per 1,000) in 1991; 27,509 (6.8 per 1,000) in 1992; 31,171 (7.2 per 1,000) in 1993; 32,067 (7.3 per 1,000) in 1994.

1998 (provisional): Live births 98,461 (birth rate 20.3 per 1,000); Marriages 26,361 (marriage rate 5.4 per 1,000); Deaths 29,628 (death rate 6.1 per 1,000).

Source: UN, *Demographic Yearbook*.

Births (annual averages, UN estimates): Birth rate (per 1,000): 32.5 in 1990–95; 24.5 in 1995–2000; 22.9 in 2000–05 (Source: UN, *World Population Prospects: The 2006 Revision*).

Deaths (annual averages, UN estimates): Death rate (per 1,000): 8.4 in 1990–95; 8.0 in 1995–2000; 8.3 in 2000–05 (Source: UN, *World Population Prospects: The 2006 Revision*).

2002: Birth rate 22.2 per 1,000; death rate 6.4 per 1,000 (Source: UN, *Statistical Yearbook for Asia and the Pacific*).

Expectation of life (years at birth, WHO estimates): 60.8 (males 56.9; females 65.0) in 2005 (Source: WHO, *World Health Statistics*).

EMPLOYMENT
('000 persons at 31 December)

	1996	1997	1998*
Agriculture	769.8	778.8	890.5
Forestry	2.5	2.9	1.9
Industry†	172.0	188.1	226.8
Construction	136.2	122.8	108.2
Trade and catering	91.8	101.2	115.8
Transport and communications	77.7	77.9	90.7
Information-computing services	1.3	1.0	1.2
Housing and municipal services	50.2	46.8	48.3
Health care and social security	97.4	100.4	89.2
Education, culture and arts	183.8	185.9	190.5
Science, research and development	9.2	6.9	5.2
General administration	24.7	25.3	28.8
Finance and insurance	8.7	9.6	12.6
Other activities	41.5	28.3	29.0
Total	**1,666.8**	**1,675.9**	**1,838.7**

* Provisional.
† Comprising manufacturing (except printing and publishing), mining and quarrying, electricity, gas, water, logging and fishing.

2004 ('000 persons at 31 December, estimates): Employed 2,110 (Agriculture 1,017, Industry 291, Other 802); Unemployed 62; Total labour force (incl. those not registered) 2,389 (Source: Asian Development Bank, *Key Indicators of Developing Asian and Pacific Countries*).

Mid-2005 (estimates): Agriculture, etc. 716,000; Total (incl. others) 2,276,000 (Source: FAO).

TURKMENISTAN

Health and Welfare

KEY INDICATORS

Total fertility rate (children per woman, 2005)	2.6
Under-5 mortality rate (per 1,000 live births, 2005)	104
HIV/AIDS (% of persons aged 15–49, 2005)	<0.1
Physicians (per 1,000 head, 2004)	4.18
Hospital beds (per 1,000 head, 2004)	4.90
Health expenditure (2004): US $ per head (PPP)	245.2
Health expenditure (2004): % of GDP	4.8
Health expenditure (2004): public (% of total)	68.9
Access to water (% of persons, 2004)	71
Access to sanitation (% of persons, 2004)	62
Human Development Index (2005): ranking	109
Human Development Index (2005): value	0.713

For sources and definitions, see explanatory note on p. vi.

Agriculture

PRINCIPAL CROPS
('000 metric tons)

	2004	2005	2006*
Wheat	2,600	2,834†	3,260
Rice (paddy)	110	120†	135
Barley	60	65†	78
Potatoes	149*	151*	175
Sugar beet*	274	295	235
Cottonseed*	660	660	460
Cabbages	50*	56†	58
Tomatoes	250*	278†	282
Dry onions	85*	94†	96
Carrots	53*	58†	60
Watermelons*	250	253	250
Grapes*	180	170	180
Apples	35*	35*	43
Cotton (lint)*	330	330	230

* FAO estimate(s).
† Unofficial figure.
Source: FAO.

LIVESTOCK
('000 head at 1 January)

	2004	2005	2006
Horses*	16	16	17
Asses, mules or hinnies*	25	25	26
Camels*	40	40	41
Cattle	2,000	2,025	2,065†
Pigs	30	30*	29*
Sheep†	13,150	14,267	15,694
Goats†	750	822	904
Chickens†	7,000	7,000	7,500
Turkeys*	200	200	200

* FAO estimate(s).
† Unofficial figure(s).
Source: FAO.

LIVESTOCK PRODUCTS
('000 metric tons)

	2004*	2005	2006*
Cattle meat	106	100*	102
Sheep meat	95	90*	93
Goat meat	7	7*	7
Chicken meat	14	12*	14
Cows' milk	1,400	1,140†	1,197
Hen eggs	35	35*	37
Honey*	10	10	9
Wool: greasy*	20	20	20

* FAO estimate(s).
† Unofficial figure.
Source: FAO.

Fishing

(metric tons, live weight)

	2003	2004	2005*
Capture	14,543	14,992	15,000
Azov sea sprat	14,276	14,674	14,680
Aquaculture	24	16	16
Total catch	14,567	15,008	15,016

* FAO estimates.
Source: FAO.

Mining

('000 metric tons, unless otherwise indicated)

	2003	2004	2005
Crude petroleum*	10,000	10,100	9,500
Natural gas (million cu metres)*	55,100	54,600	58,800
Bentonite†	50	50	50
Salt (unrefined)†	215	215	215
Gypsum (crude)†	100	100	100

* Source: BP, *Statistical Review of World Energy*.
† Estimates from US Geological Survey.

2006 ('000 metric tons, unless otherwise indicated): Crude petroleum 8,100; Natural gas (million cu metres) 62,200 (Source: BP, *Statistical Review of World Energy*).

TURKMENISTAN

Industry

SELECTED PRODUCTS
('000 metric tons, unless otherwise indicated)

	2000	2001	2002
Cottonseed oil	48	45	26
Wheat flour	544	579	400
Woven cotton fabrics (million sq metres)	34	61	78
Woven silk fabrics ('000 sq metres)	216	115	283
Blankets	14	7	10
Knotted wool carpets and rugs ('000 sq metres)	1,040	1,434	1,475
Footwear, excl. rubber ('000 pairs)	478	444	253
Nitric acid (100%)	192	151	212
Ammonia (nitrogen content)	117	99	130
Nitrogenous fertilizers (a)*	89	72	103
Phosphate fertilizers (b)*†	11	11	17
Soap	3.0	2.5	1.6
Motor spirit (petrol)	1,132	1,283	1,292
Gas-diesel (distillate fuel) oil	2,247	2,547	2,360
Residual fuel oils	1,536	1,586	1,640
Clay building bricks (million)	309	269	279
Quicklime	17	17	15
Cement	420	448	486
Electric energy (million kWh)	9,845	10,825	11,200

* Production in terms of (a) nitrogen or (b) phosphoric acid.
† Official figures.

Source: mainly UN, *Industrial Commodity Statistics Yearbook*.

Woven woollen fabrics (million sq metres): 2.8 in 1996; 3.2 in 1997; 2.5 in 1998 (Source: UN, *Industrial Commodity Statistics Yearbook*).

Ethyl alcohol ('000 hectolitres): 2 in 1997; 1 in 1998; 1 in 1999 (Source: UN, *Industrial Commodity Statistics Yearbook*).

2003 ('000 metric tons, unless otherwise indicated, estimates): Wheat flour 503; Nitrogenous fertilizers 96; Gas-diesel (distillate fuel) oil 1,750; Cement 239; Electric energy (million kWh) 10,800 (Source: Asian Development Bank, *Key Indicators of Developing Asian and Pacific Countries*).

Finance

CURRENCY AND EXCHANGE RATES

Monetary Units
100 tenge = 1 Turkmen manat.

Sterling, Dollar and Euro Equivalents (30 November 2007)
£1 sterling = 10,745.3 manats;
US $1 = 5,200.0 manats;
€1 = 7,675.7 manats;
10,000 Turkmenistani manats = £0.93 = $1.92 = €1.30.

Note: The Turkmenistani manat was introduced on 1 November 1993, replacing the Russian (formerly Soviet) rouble at a rate of 1 manat = 500 roubles. Following the introduction of the Turkmenistani manat, a multiple exchange rate system was established. The foregoing information refers to the official rate of exchange. This rate was maintained at US $1 = 4,165 manats between May 1997 and April 1998. It was adjusted to $1 = 5,200 manats in April 1998. In addition to the official rate, there was a commercial bank rate of exchange until this market was closed in December 1998. There is also a 'parallel' market rate, which averaged $1 = 6,493 manats in 1998 and reached $1 = 14,200 manats at mid-1999.

BUDGET
('000 million manats)

Revenue*	1997	1998	1999†
State budget	2,067.3	1,867.5	2,382.3
Personal income tax	108.3	157.4	224.9
Profit tax	579.6	412.0	422.0
Value-added tax	797.9	714.9	946.3
Natural resources tax	231.2	43.1	201.1
Excise tax	92.4	221.3	377.8
Other receipts*	257.9	318.8	210.1
Pension and Social Security Fund	471.0	711.0	832.5
Medical Insurance Fund	32.7	8.2	0.0
Repayments on rescheduled gas debt	246.6	474.1	478.3
Total	**2,817.6**	**3,060.8**	**3,693.1**

Expenditure	1997	1998	1999‡
National economy	843.9	461.1	623.3
Agriculture	632.5	331.4	223.2
Transport and communications	121.1	63.4	190.0
Other	90.3	66.3	210.1
Socio-cultural services†	975.7	1,850.0	1,907.9
Education	435.3	919.2	1,048.7
Health	443.1	493.8	550.6
Communal services	9.1	337.9	188.6
Culture, recreation and other purposes	88.2	99.1	120.0
Defence§	440.2	435.8	582.0
Pension and Social Security Fund	387.8	511.5	605.9
Interest payments	72.1	11.1	18.0
Public administration and other purposes	94.3	153.4	157.2
Total	**2,814.0**	**3,422.8**	**3,894.3**

* Including grants received and road fund revenues.
† Approved budget.
‡ Excluding expenditure of the Pension and Social Security Fund.
§ Variable coverage, owing to changes in classification.

1997 ('000 million manats, revised figures): Revenue 2,761.5; Expenditure 2,781.8 (Source: Asian Development Bank, *Key Indicators of Developing Asian and Pacific Countries*).

1998 ('000 million manats, revised figures): Revenue 3,077.5; Expenditure 3,440.3 (Source: Asian Development Bank, *Key Indicators of Developing Asian and Pacific Countries*).

1999 ('000 million manats, revised figures): Revenue 3,895.4; Expenditure 3,890.3 (Source: Asian Development Bank, *Key Indicators of Developing Asian and Pacific Countries*).

2000 ('000 million manats): Revenue 6,034.1 (Tax revenue 5,909.0); Expenditure 6,121.0 (Current expenditure 5,831.0, Capital expenditure 290.0) (Source: Asian Development Bank, *Key Indicators of Developing Asian and Pacific Countries*).

2001 ('000 million manats): Revenue 7,824.0 (Tax revenue 7,783.0); Expenditure 7,605.0 (Current expenditure 7,223.0, Capital expenditure 382.0) (Source: Asian Development Bank, *Key Indicators of Developing Asian and Pacific Countries*).

2002 ('000 million manats): Revenue 8,243.1 (Current revenue 8,243.1, incl. Tax revenue 7,827.0); Expenditure 8,166.0 (Current expenditure 7,684.0, Capital expenditure 482.0) (Source: Asian Development Bank, *Key Indicators of Developing Asian and Pacific Countries*).

2003 ('000 million manats): Revenue 10,716.0 (Current revenue 10,716.0, incl. Tax revenue 10,222.0); Expenditure 11,497.0 (Current expenditure 10,811.0, Capital expenditure 686.0) (Source: Asian Development Bank, *Key Indicators of Developing Asian and Pacific Countries*).

2004 ('000 million manats): Revenue 14,262.4 (Current revenue 14,262.4, incl. Tax revenue 13,454.0); Expenditure 14,250.6 (Current expenditure 13,496.6, Capital expenditure 754.0) (Source: Asian Development Bank, *Key Indicators of Developing Asian and Pacific Countries*).

TURKMENISTAN

INTERNATIONAL RESERVES
(US $ million at 31 December)

	2003	2004	2005
Total	2,673.0	2,714.0	3,600.0

Source: Asian Development Bank, *Key Indicators of Developing Asian and Pacific Countries*.

MONEY SUPPLY
('000 million manats at 31 December)

	1996	1997	1998
Currency in circulation	270.2	407.7	1,040.2
Demand deposits at banks	130.0	423.4	259.8

Total money ('000 million manats at 31 December): 1,672 in 1999; 2,651 in 2000; 3,062 in 2001; 3,394 in 2002; 5,354 in 2003; 6,142 in 2004 (Source: Asian Development Bank, *Key Indicators of Developing Asian and Pacific Countries*).

COST OF LIVING
(Consumer Price Index; base: previous year at 31 December = 100)

	2003	2004*	2005*
All items	106.5	110.0	110.5

* Preliminary.

Source: European Bank for Reconstruction and Development.

NATIONAL ACCOUNTS
('000 million manats at current prices)

Expenditure on the Gross Domestic Product

	2003	2004	2005
Final consumption expenditure	36,040.7	42,017.1	48,679.4
Households / Non-profit institutions serving households	28,480.7	33,150.8	38,194.2
General government	7,560.0	8,866.3	10,485.2
Gross capital formation	15,059.1	16,380.1	24,060.6
Total domestic expenditure	51,099.8	58,397.2	72,740.0
Exports of goods and services	35,554.1	42,715.1	61,795.8
Less Imports of goods and services	30,944.6	36,767.9	53,237.5
GDP in market prices	55,709.2	64,344.4	81,298.2

Gross Domestic Product by Economic Activity

	2003	2004	2005
Agriculture	11,221.0	14,495.6	17,939.0
Mining and quarrying / Manufacturing / Electricity, gas and water	19,391.8	21,991.4	28,231.5
Construction	4,455.2	4,949.3	5,518.6
Trade	2,101.3	2,490.2	3,114.9
Transport and communications	3,297.8	3,962.4	4,920.6
Finance / Public administration / Other activities	15,242.2	16,455.4	21,573.6
Total	55,709.2	64,344.4	81,298.2

Source: Asian Development Bank, *Key Indicators of Developing Asian and Pacific Countries*.

BALANCE OF PAYMENTS
(US $ million)

	1996	1997	1998
Exports of goods f.o.b.	1,692.0	774.0	614.1
Imports of goods f.o.b.	−1,388.3	−1,005.0	−1,137.1
Trade balance	303.7	−230.9	−523.0
Services (net)	−323.4	−402.5	−471.0
Balance on goods and services	−19.7	−633.5	−994.0
Other income (net)	16.7	84.8	32.6
Balance on goods, services and income	−3.0	−548.7	−961.4
Current transfers (net)	4.8	−31.2	26.9
Current account	1.8	−579.9	−934.5
Direct investment	108.1	102.4	64.1
Trade credit (net)	60.8	−266.5	56.5
Other (net)	−211.6	1,035.9	749.7
Net errors and omissions	46.4	−71.4	33.9
Overall balance	5.4	220.6	−30.3

Current balance (US $ million): 84 in 2004; 616 in 2005; 1,295 in 2006 (Source: Asian Development Bank, *Key Indicators of Developing Asian and Pacific Countries*).

External Trade

PRINCIPAL COMMODITIES
(US $ million)

Imports c.i.f.	2001	2002	2003
Food and live animals	129.4	114.3	130.3
Beverages and tobacco	56.8	70.1	67.4
Mineral fuels, lubricants, etc.	39.1	25.7	17.7
Chemicals	178.6	210.8	271.2
Basic manufactures	448.7	394.2	487.7
Machinery and transport equipment	1,204.7	857.6	1,125.6
Miscellaneous manufactured articles	128.1	112.7	165.2
Total (incl. others)	2,348.8	2,119.4	2,450.0*

Exports f.o.b.	2001	2002	2003
Food and live animals	4.7	3.4	2.9
Beverages and tobacco	—	0.6	0.3
Mineral fuels, lubricants, etc.	123.7	83.8	152.4
Chemicals	7.0	28.4	55.0
Basic manufactures	141.6	150.6	169.6
Machinery and transport equipment	14.5	17.1	16.9
Miscellaneous manufactured articles	52.8	74.1	80.8
Total (incl. others)	2,620.2	2,855.6	3,320.0*

* Estimate.

Source: Asian Development Bank, *Key Indicators of Developing Asian and Pacific Countries*.

TURKMENISTAN

PRINCIPAL TRADING PARTNERS
(US $ million)

Imports	2004	2005	2006
Azerbaijan	157.8	300.9	353.1
China, People's Repub.	93.9	99.5	178.7
France	136.4	97.0	95.5
Germany	219.5	146.3	216.3
Iran	123.4	167.8	211.0
Japan	56.2	n.a.	n.a.
Kazakhstan	100.8	120.3	n.a.
Russia	266.6	246.5	248.0
Turkey	236.3	198.7	309.3
Ukraine	247.6	205.9	241.5
United Arab Emirates	252.3	343.3	431.5
USA	323.8	260.9	124.1
Total (incl. others)	2,737.2	2,709.0	3,111.6

Exports	2004	2005	2006
Afghanistan	96.9	110.7	129.9
Hungary	56.7	300.3	159.3
Iran	660.6	841.1	1,038.3
Italy	158.2	201.1	194.1
Romania	137.3	129.0	151.4
Russia	39.3	57.7	n.a.
Turkey	159.7	145.9	170.8
Ukraine	1,776.1	2,434.6	2,856.4
United Arab Emirates	123.8	157.7	194.6
USA	78.7	132.5	73.6
Total (incl. others)	4,062.3	5,694.2	6,174.0

Source: Asian Development Bank, *Key Indicators of Developing Asian and Pacific Countries*.

Transport

RAILWAYS
(traffic)

	1996	1997	1999*
Passenger journeys (million)	7.8	6.4	3.1
Passenger-km (million)	2,104	958	701
Freight transported (million metric tons)	15.9	18.5	17.2
Freight ton-km (million)	6,779	7,445	7,337

* Data for 1998 were not available.

Source: *Railway Directory*.

SHIPPING

Merchant Fleet
(registered at 31 December)

	2004	2005	2006
Number of vessels	41	45	53
Total displacement ('000 grt)	42.9	48.5	53.4

Source: Lloyd's Register-Fairplay, *World Fleet Statistics*.

CIVIL AVIATION
(estimated traffic on scheduled services)

	2001	2002	2003
Kilometres flown (million)	22	22	22
Passengers carried ('000)	1,407	1,407	1,412
Passenger-kilometres (million)	1,608	1,608	1,538
Total ton-kilometres (million)	156	156	150

Source: UN, *Statistical Yearbook*.

Tourism

FOREIGN VISITOR ARRIVALS*

Country of nationality	2003	2004	2005
France	298	636	683
Germany	466	1,191	1,028
Iran	5,623	9,341	7,173
Japan	269	770	428
Netherlands	84	324	453
Russia	115	318	13
USA	181	343	332
Total (incl. others)	8,214	14,799	11,611

* Arrivals of non-resident tourists at national borders.

Tourism receipts (US $ million): 66 in 1996; 74 in 1997; 192 in 1998.

Source: World Tourism Organization.

Communications Media

	2004	2005	2006
Telephones ('000 main lines in use)	376.1	398.1	398.1
Mobile cellular telephones ('000 subscribers)	50.1	105.0	105.0
Internet users ('000)	36	48	65

Television receivers ('000 in use): 880 in 2001.

Book production (including pamphlets): 450 titles (5,493,000 copies) in 1994.

Radio receivers ('000 in use): 1,225 in 1997.

Personal computers ('000 in use): 2 in 1999.

Sources: International Telecommunication Union; UNESCO, *Statistical Yearbook*.

Education

1990/91: 76,000 students at higher schools (Source: UNESCO, *Statistical Yearbook*).

Institutions (2005): Secondary schools 1,704; Secondary specialized schools 15; Higher schools (incl. universities) 16 (Source: Permanent Mission of Turkmenistan to the United Nations).

Students enrolled at universities (2003): 14,859 (Source: UNICEF).

Adult literacy rate (UNESCO estimates): 98.8% (males 99.3%; females 98.3%) in 1995 (Source: UNESCO Institute for Statistics).

Directory

The Constitution

A new Constitution was adopted on 18 May 1992. The Constitution was organized into eight sections (detailing: fundamentals of the constitutional system; fundamental human and civil rights, freedoms and duties; the system of state governmental bodies; local self-government; the electoral system and provisions for referendum; judicial authority; the Office of the Prosecutor-General; and final provisions), and included the following among its main provisions:

The President of the Republic is directly elected by universal adult suffrage for a five-year term. A President may hold office for a maximum of two terms. The President is not only Head of State, but also Chairman of the Government (Prime Minister in the Council of Ministers) and Supreme Commander-in-Chief of the National Armed Forces. The President must ratify all parliamentary legislation and in certain circumstances may legislate by decree. The President appoints the Council of Ministers and chairs sessions of the Khalk Maslakhaty (People's Council).

Supreme legislative power resides with the 50-member Majlis, a unicameral parliament which is directly elected for a five-year term. Sovereignty, however, is vested in the people of Turkmenistan, and the supreme representative body of popular power is the Khalk Maslakhaty. This is described as a supervisory organ with no legislative or executive functions, but it is authorized to perform certain duties normally reserved for a legislature or constituent assembly. Not only does it debate and approve measures pertaining to the political and economic situation in the country, but it examines possible changes to the Constitution and may vote to express 'no confidence' in the President of the Republic, on grounds of unconstitutionality. The Khalk Maslakhaty comprises all the deputies of the Majlis, a further 50 directly elected and 10 appointed representatives from all districts of the country, the members of the Council of Ministers, the respective Chairmen of the Supreme Court and the Supreme Economic Court, the Prosecutor-General and the heads of local councils.

The Constitution, which defines Turkmenistan as a democratic state, also guarantees the independence of the judiciary and the basic human rights of the individual. The age of majority is 18 years (parliamentary deputies must be aged at least 21). Minority ethnic groups are granted equality under the law, although Turkmen is the only official language. A central tenet of Turkmenistan's foreign policy is that of 'permanent neutrality'.

Note: On 15 January 1994 a referendum confirmed President Saparmyrat Niyazov's exemption from the need to be re-elected in 1997. An amendment to the Constitution, approved by the Khalk Maslakhaty in December 1999, extended the term of Niyazov's presidency indefinitely. In February 2001, following Niyazov's announcement that he would retire by 2010, the Khalk Maslakhaty endorsed a resolution to hold open presidential elections in 2008–10, following his retirement. In August 2003 a constitutional law and a constitutional amendment were passed elevating the Khalk Maslakhaty to the status of 'permanently functioning supreme representative body of popular authority', and requiring it to remain in continuous session. The constitutional changes ascribed to the Khalk Maslakhaty a number of legislative powers, including the passing of constitutional laws, thereby effectively displacing the Majlis as the country's leading legislative body. The Khalk Maslakhaty was to comprise 2,507 members.

Following the death of President Niyazov on 20 December 2006, the Khalk Maslakhaty approved a number of constitutional amendments. It was determined that, in the event of presidential incapacity, the duties of the Head of State were to be assumed, in an acting capacity, by a Deputy Chairman of the Government. The Constitution was amended to permit an acting Head of State to contest presidential elections, which must be held no more than 60 days after the presidency had become vacant.

The Government

HEAD OF STATE

President of the Republic: GURBANGULY BERDYMUHAMEDOV (elected 11 February 2007; inaugurated 14 February 2007).

COUNCIL OF MINISTERS
(April 2008)

Chairman of the Government: GURBANGULY BERDYMUHAMEDOV.
Deputy Chairman, responsible for Petroleum and Natural Gas: TACHBERDY TAGIYEV.
Deputy Chairman, responsible for Transport and Communications: NAZARGULY SHAGULYYEV.
Deputy Chairman, responsible for Economic Affairs: KHOJAMYRAT GELDYMYRADOV.
Deputy Chairman and Minister of Foreign Affairs: RASHID MEREDOV.
Deputy Chairman, responsible for Education, Science, Health, Culture, Sport, the Mass Media and Social Organizations: HYDYR SAPARLIEV.
Deputy Chairman, responsible for the Textile Industry, Trade and the Chamber of Commerce and Industry: HOJAMUHAMMET MUHAMMEDOV.
Minister of National Security: CHARYMYRAT AMANOV.
Minister of Defence: Maj.-Gen. AGAGELDY MAMATGELDIYEV.
Minister of Justice: MURAD KARRYEV.
Minister of Internal Affairs: ORAZGELDY AMANMYRADOV.
Minister of Finance: ANNAMUHAMMET GOCHIYEV.
Minister of Social Security: GURBANGELDY KAKALIYEV.
Minister of Construction: SHAMUHAMMET DURDYLYYEV.
Minister of Culture, Television and Radio: GULMYRAT MEREDOV.
Minister of Energy and Industry: GURBANNUR ANNAVELIYEV.
Minister of Railways: ORAZBERDY HUDAIBERDIEV.
Minister of Communications: RESULBERDY KHOZHAGURBANOV.
Minister of Road Transport and Highways: GURBANMYRAT HANGULIYEV.
Minister of the Petroleum Industry and Mineral Resources: BAYMYRAT HOJAMUHAMMEDOV.
Minister of Trade and Foreign Economic Relations: NOKERGULY ATAGULYEV.
Minister of the Textile Industry: JEMAL GEOKLENOVA.
Minister of Health and the Medical Industry: ATA SERDAROV.
Minister of Education: MUHAMMETGELDY ANNAAMANOV.
Minister of Water Resources: MYRATGELDY AKMAMMEDOV.
Minister of Agriculture: ESENMYRAT ORAZGELDIYEV.
Minister of the Economy and Development: GURBANMYRAT GURBANMYRADOV.
Minister of Environmental Protection: MAGTYMGULY AKMURADOV.

Note: The Chairmen of the three state concerns Türkmennebit (Turkmenneft—Turkmen Oil), Türkmengaz (Turkmengaz—Turkmen Gas) and Türkmenhaky (Turkmenkover—Turkmen Carpets) have the status of State Ministers.

MINISTRIES

Office of the President and the Council of Ministers: 744000 Aşgabat; tel. (12) 35-45-34; fax (12) 35-51-12; internet www.turkmenistan.gov.tm.
Ministry of Agriculture: 744000 Aşgabat, ul. Azad 63; tel. (12) 35-66-91; fax (12) 35-01-18; e-mail minselhoz@online.tm.
Ministry of Communications: 744000 Aşgabat, ul. Gurungan 40; tel. (12) 35-21-52; fax (12) 35-05-95; e-mail mincom@telecom.tm.
Ministry of Construction: 744000 Aşgabat, ul. 2049; tel. (12) 51-23-59.
Ministry of Culture, Television and Radio: 744000 Aşgabat, ul. Pushkin 14; tel. (12) 35-30-61; fax (12) 35-35-60.
Ministry of Defence: 744000 Aşgabat, ul. Galkynyş 4; tel. (12) 35-22-59.
Ministry of the Economy and Development: Aşgabat.
Ministry of Education: 744000 Aşgabat, ul. Gurungan 2; tel. (12) 35-58-03; fax (12) 39-88-11.
Ministry of Energy and Industry: 744000 Aşgabat, ul. 2008 6; tel. (12) 35-38-70; fax (12) 39-06-82.
Ministry of Environmental Protection: 744000 Aşgabat, ul. 2035 102; tel. (12) 35-43-17; fax (12) 51-16-13; e-mail ministr@nature-tm.org.
Ministry of Finance: 744000 Aşgabat, ul. 2008 4; tel. (12) 51-05-63; fax (12) 51-18-23.
Ministry of Foreign Affairs: 744000 Aşgabat, pr. Magtymguly 83; tel. (12) 26-62-11; fax (12) 35-42-41; e-mail mfatm@online.tm.
Ministry of Health and the Medical Industry: 744000 Aşgabat, pr. Magtymguly 90; tel. (12) 35-60-47; fax (12) 35-50-32.
Ministry of Internal Affairs: 744000 Aşgabat, pr. Magtymguly 85; tel. (12) 35-59-23.
Ministry of Justice: 744000 Aşgabat, ul. 2022 86; tel. (12) 38-04-11.

TURKMENISTAN

Ministry of National Security: 744000 Aşgabat, pr. Magtymguly 91; fax (12) 51-07-55.

Ministry of the Petroleum Industry and Mineral Resources: 744000 Aşgabat, ul. Gurungan 28; tel. (12) 39-38-27; fax (12) 39-38-21; e-mail ministryoilgas@online.tm.

Ministry of Railways: 744000 Aşgabat, ul. S. Türkmenbaşi 9.

Ministry of Road Transport and Highways: 744000 Aşgabat, ul. 1916 141; tel. (12) 35-02-36; fax (12) 35-18-43; e-mail tcentr@online.tm.

Ministry of Social Security: 744007 Aşgabat, ul. 2003 3; tel. (12) 25-30-03.

Ministry of the Textile Industry: 744000 Aşgabat, ul. Annadurdiyeva 52; tel. (12) 51-03-03.

Ministry of Trade and Foreign Economic Relations: 744000 Aşgabat, ul. Gurungan 1; tel. (12) 35-10-47; fax (12) 35-73-24; e-mail mtfer@online.tm.

Ministry of Water Resources: 744000 Aşgabat, ul. 2005 1; tel. (12) 39-06-15; fax (12) 39-85-39.

President

Following the death of President Gen. SAPARMYRAT NIYAZOV on 20 December 2006, the hitherto Deputy Chairman and Minister of Health and the Medical Industry, GURBANGULY BERDYMUHAMEDOV, assumed the presidency in an acting capacity, before being elected President in an election held on 11 February 2007. BERDYMUHAMEDOV was elected by 89.2% of votes cast, with a participation rate of some 98% of registered voters, according to official results; he was inaugurated on 14 February.

Legislature

Khalk Maslakhaty
(People's Council)

744000 Aşgabat.

Chairman: President of Turkmenistan GURBANGULY BERDYMUHAMEDOV.

Under the Constitution of May 1992, the Khalk Maslakhaty was established as the supreme representative body in the country. Formally, it is neither a legislative nor an executive body, although its decisions supersede those of both parliament and presidency. The 2,507-member body consists of the President, the Majlis deputies, the Chairman of the Supreme Court, the Prosecutor-General, the members of the Council of Ministers, the hakims (governors) of the five velayats (regions) and the hakim of the city of Aşgabat; the elected people's representatives of each district; the chairpersons of parties, the Youth Association, trade unions, and the Women's Union, who are members of the All-national Galkynyş National Revival Movement of Turkmenistan; the chairpersons of public organizations; representatives of the Council of Elders; the hakims of cities that are the administrative centres of the velayats and etraps (districts); and the heads of the municipal councils (archins) of the towns and villages that are the administrative centres of the districts. It is headed by the President of the Republic. Elections for the 50 district representatives were held in November and December 1992; the Council convened for the first time later in December. Fresh elections were held in April 1998 and on 6 April 2003. On the latter occasion, according to official reports, 99.8% of eligible voters participated. It was also reported that all candidates were members of the Democratic Party of Turkmenistan. A constitutional law and constitutional amendment passed in August 2003 elevated the Khalk Maslakhaty to the status of 'permanently functioning supreme representative body of popular authority'. The Khalk Maslakhaty was henceforth required to remain in continuous session, and effectively displaced the Majlis as the country's leading legislative body.

Majlis
(Assembly)

744000 Aşgabat, ul. Bitarap Türkmenistan 17; tel. (12) 35-31-25; fax (12) 35-31-47.

Chairman: AKJA NURBERDIYEVA.

The 50-member Majlis is directly elected for a term of five years. Elections to the Majlis were held on 19 December 2004, officially with the participation of 76.88% of the registered electorate. A second round of voting took place in seven districts on 9 January 2005, where candidates had failed to obtain an absolute majority of votes. All contestants were believed to be members of the ruling party, the Democratic Party of Turkmenistan. The deputies of the Majlis also form part of the Khalk Maslakhaty.

Election Commission

Central Commission for Elections and Referendums: Aşgabat; comprises a chairman, two vice-chairmen, a secretary and 12 mems, all appointed by the President of the Republic; Chair. MURAT KARIYEV; Sec. JEREN TAIMOVA.

Political Organizations

Democratic Party of Turkmenistan: 744014 Aşgabat, ul. Gurungan 28; tel. (12) 25-12-12; name changed from Communist Party of Turkmenistan in 1991; Chair. GURBANGULY BERDYMUHAMEDOV; Sec. ONJIK MUSAYEV.

Unity (Agzybirlik): 744000 Aşgabat; e-mail agzybirlik@hotmail.com; internet hem.lidnet.se/~agzybirlik/; f. 1989; popular front organization; denied official registration except from Oct. 1991 to Jan. 1992; Leader NURBERDY NURMAMEDOV.

Turkmenistan is effectively a one-party state, with the Democratic Party of Turkmenistan (led by the President of the Republic) dominant in all areas of government. The President of the Republic is also the leader of the **National Revival Movement of Turkmenistan (Galknyş)**. There are, however, several unregistered opposition groups, such as **Unity (Agzybirlik)**. A **Social Democratic Party** was reportedly established in Aşgabat in August 1996, upon the merger of several small unofficial groups.

Other opposition elements are based in other republics of the Commonwealth of Independent States, in particular Russia. A leading opposition figure in exile is a former Minister of Foreign Affairs, ABDY KULIYEV, whose **United Democratic Opposition of Turkmenistan (ODOT)** is based in Moscow, Russia, while the **Movement for Democratic Reform**, founded in 1996, is based in Sweden. The **Fatherland (Watan)**, movement is also based in Sweden; e-mail info@watan.ru; internet watan.ru) and comprises Turkmen and other Central Asian oppositionists. In January 2002 a former Minister of Foreign Affairs, BORIS SHIKHMURADOV, established the opposition **People's Democratic Movement of Turkmenistan** (PDMT; internet gundogar.org); however, he was imprisoned in December, having been convicted of orchestrating the attempted assassination of President Saparmyrat Nizayov in November. Another opposition leader accused of conspiring with Shikhmuradov was NURMUKHAMMED KHANAMOV, founder of the **Republican Party of Turkmenistan** (RPT; internet tmrepublican.org; Co-Chair. NURMUKHAMMET HANAMOV; SAPAR YKLYMOV).

Opposition leaders met in Prague, Czech Republic, in September 2003 and announced the formation of the Union of **Democratic Forces of Turkmenistan (UDFT)**, comprising four main groups: the RPT; Fatherland; the ODOT; and the **Revival Social Political Movement**.

Diplomatic Representation

EMBASSIES IN TURKMENISTAN

Afghanistan: 744000 Aşgabat, Gerogly 14; tel. (12) 39-58-21; fax (12) 39-58-20; Ambassador ABDUL KARIM KHADAM.

Armenia: 744000 Aşgabat, Gerogly 14; tel. (12) 35-44-18; fax (12) 39-55-38; e-mail eat@online.tm; Ambassador (vacant).

Azerbaijan: 744000 Aşgabat, M. Kosayev 62A; tel. (12) 39-11-02; fax (12) 39-14-47; e-mail azsefir_ashg@online.tm; internet www.azembassyashg.com; Ambassador ELKHAN BAKHADUR OĞLU GUSEYINOV.

Belarus: 744000 Aşgabat, ul. Esgerler 35; tel. (12) 36-46-88; fax (12) 36-46-91; e-mail turkmenistan@belembassy.org; Ambassador YURIY H. MALUMOV.

China, People's Republic: 744036 Aşgabat, Berzengi raion, ul. Archabil, Hotel 'Kuwwat'; tel. (12) 48-81-31; fax (12) 48-18-13; e-mail chemb@online.tm; Ambassador LU GUICHENG.

France: 744000 Aşgabat, ul. Esgerler 35; tel. (12) 36-35-50; fax (12) 36-36-40; e-mail cad.achgabat-amba@diplomatie.gouv.fr; Ambassador CHRISTIAN LECHERVY.

Georgia: 744000 Aşgabat, ul. Azadi 139A; tel. (12) 34-48-38; fax (12) 34-32-48; e-mail georgia@online.tm; internet www.turkmenistan.mfa.gov.ge; Ambassador ALEKSI PETRIASHVILI.

Germany: 744000 Aşgabat, ul. Hydyr Derzhazhev, Hotel 'Ak Altin'; tel. (12) 36-35-15; fax (12) 36-35-22; e-mail grembtkm@online.tm; Ambassador HANS MONDORF.

Holy See: 744000 Aşgabat, Merkezi Poçta, POB 98; tel. (12) 39-11-40; fax (12) 35-36-83; e-mail aszomi@online.tm; internet www.catholic-turkmenistan.org; Apostolic Nuncio ANTONIO LUCIBELLO (Titular Archbishop of Thurio) (resident in Ankara, Turkey).

TURKMENISTAN

India: 744000 Aşgabat, ul. Yu. Emre 2/1, Imperial International Business Centre; tel. (12) 45-81-52; fax (12) 45-61-56; e-mail indembhoc@online.tm; Ambassador Prof. RAM PAL KAUSHIK.

Iran: 744000 Aşgabat, ul. 2072 3; tel. (12) 35-02-37; fax (12) 35-05-65; e-mail isroiref@online.tm; Ambassador MOHAMMAD REZA FORQANI.

Japan: 744000 Aşgabat, ul. Hydyr Derzhazhev, Hotel 'Ak Altin'; tel. (12) 47-70-81; fax (12) 47-70-83; Ambassador YASUO SAITO (resident in Moscow, Russia).

Kazakhstan: 744036 Aşgabat, ul. Garaşizlik 11/13; tel. (12) 48-04-68; fax (12) 48-04-76; e-mail embkaz@online.tm; Ambassador MURAT M. ATANOV.

Korea, Republic: Aşgabat; Ambassador KIM CHONG YUL.

Kyrgyzstan: 744000 Aşgabat, ul. Gerogly 85; tel. and fax (12) 35-55-06; e-mail kg@online.tm; internet kyrgtm.by.ru; Ambassador BORUBEK ASHIROV.

Libya: 744000 Aşgabat, ul. Azad 17A; tel. (12) 35-49-17; fax (12) 39-35-26; Chargé d'affaires a.i. RAGAB BEN KHAMADI.

Pakistan: 744000 Aşgabat, ul. Garaşizlik 4/1; tel. (12) 48-21-28; fax (12) 48-21-30; e-mail parepashgabat@online.tm; Ambassador SAID AKBAR AFRIDI.

Poland: 744005 Aşgabat, ul. Azadi 17A; tel. (12) 27-40-35; fax (12) 27-31-22; Ambassador MACIEJ LANG.

Romania: 744000 Aşgabat, ul. Kusayeva 107; tel. (12) 34-76-55; fax (12) 34-76-20; e-mail ambromas@online.tm; Chargé d'affaires a.i. CIOCAN LAURENŢIU.

Russia: 744004 Aşgabat, pr. S. Türkmenbaşi 11; tel. (12) 35-39-57; fax (12) 39-84-66; e-mail emb-rus@online.tm; Ambassador IGOR A. BLATOV.

Saudi Arabia: 744000 Aşgabat, ul. Yu. Emre 2/1, Imperial International Business Centre; tel. (12) 45-49-63; fax (12) 45-49-70; e-mail tmemb@mofa.gov.sa; Ambassador ABD AL-AZIZ IBRAHIM AL-GHADEER.

Switzerland: 744000 Aşgabat; Ambassador ALAN GIDETTI.

Tajikistan: 744000 Aşgabat, ul. Gurungan 19; tel. (12) 35-56-96; fax (12) 39-31-74; e-mail tadjemb_tm@mail.ru; Ambassador KOZIDAVLAT KOIMDODOV.

Thailand: 744000 Aşgabat; Ambassador KANYA CHAIMAN.

Turkey: 744007 Aşgabat, ul. Gerogly 9; tel. (12) 35-41-18; fax (12) 39-19-14; e-mail askabat.be@mfa.gov.tr; Ambassador HAKKI AKIL.

Ukraine: 744001 Aşgabat, ul. Azadi 49; tel. (12) 39-13-73; fax (12) 39-10-28; e-mail emb_tm@mfa.gov.ua; internet www.mfa.gov.ua/turkmenistan; Ambassador VIKTOR A. MAYKO.

United Arab Emirates: 744000 Aşgabat, Khalifa Centre, pr. S. Türkmenbaşi 124; tel. (12) 45-69-15; fax (12) 45-69-16; Ambassador HASSAN ABDULLAH AL-ADHAB.

United Kingdom: 744001 Aşgabat, Four Points Ak Altin Hotel, 3rd Floor, Office Bldg; tel. (12) 36-34-62; fax (12) 36-34-65; e-mail beasb@online.tm; internet www.britishembassy.gov.uk/turkmenistan; Ambassador PETER BUTCHER.

USA: 744000 Aşgabat, ul. Pushkin 9; tel. (12) 35-00-45; fax (12) 39-26-14; e-mail irc-ashgabat@iatp.edu.tm; internet turkmenistan.usembassy.gov; Chargé d'affaires a.i. RICHARD E. HOAGLAND.

Uzbekistan: 744006 Aşgabat, ul. Gerogly 50A; tel. (12) 33-10-55; fax (12) 34-23-37; Ambassador ALISHER K. KODIROV.

Judicial System

Chairman of the Supreme Court: YARANMURAT YAZMYRADOV.

Prosecutor-General: CHARY HOJAMYRADOV, 744000 Aşgabat, ul. Seidi; fax (12) 35-44-82.

Religion

The majority of the population are adherents of Islam. In June 1991 the Supreme Soviet of the Turkmen SSR adopted a Law on Freedom of Conscience and Religious Organizations. In April 1994 a council (gengeş) for religious affairs was established, within the office of the President; it was chaired by the *qazi* (supreme Islamic judge) of Turkmenistan, with the head of the Orthodox Church in Turkmenistan serving as Deputy Chairman. In November 2003 new legislation, replacing that of 1991, was approved, restricting the activities of religious groups, although registration requirements for religious communities were made more flexible by a presidential decree, issued in early 2004. Further legislation, approved in March of that year, reduced the membership threshold required for a group to register from 500 to five. Prior to these amendments, only Sunni Muslim and Russian Orthodox Christian groups had been permitted to register. By mid-2004 groups of Seventh-day Adventist and Baptist Christians, Hare Krishnas and Baha'is had also registered.

ISLAM

Turkmen are traditionally Sunni Muslims, but with elements of Sufism. Islam was severely persecuted by the Soviet regime from the late 1920s. Until July 1989 Aşgabat was the only Central Asian capital without a functioning mosque. The Muslims of Turkmenistan are officially under the jurisdiction of the Muslim Board of Central Asia, based in Tashkent, Uzbekistan, but, in practice, the Government permits little external influence in religious affairs. The Board is represented in Turkmenistan by a qazi, who is responsible for appointing Muslim clerics in all rural areas.

Qazi of Turkmenistan: ROVSHEN ALLABERDIYEV.

CHRISTIANITY

The Russian Orthodox Church (Moscow Patriarchate)

The Church in Turkmenistan comes under the jurisdiction of the Eparchy of Tashkent and Central Asia, headed by the Metropolitan of Tashkent and Central Asia, VLADIMIR (IKIM), based in Uzbekistan.

Roman Catholic Church

The Church is represented in Turkmenistan by a Mission, established in September 1997. There were an estimated 70 adherents at 31 December 2005.

Superior: Fr ANDRZEJ MADEJ, 744000 Aşgabat, ul. Gerogly 20A, POB 98; tel. (12) 39-11-40; fax (12) 35-36-83; e-mail amadej@oblaci.pl.

The Press

All publications listed below are in Turkmen, except where otherwise stated.

PRINCIPAL NEWSPAPERS

Adalat (Justice): 744005 Aşgabat, ul. 2033 1/4; tel. (12) 39-79-04; weekly; Editor-in-Chief DOVLET H. GURBANGELDIYEV; circ. 42,575.

Aşgabat/Ashkhabad: 744004 Aşgabat, ul. Galkynyş 20; tel. (12) 22-33-04; f. 1960; 3 a week; journal of the Union of Writers of Turkmenistan; popular; in Turkmen and Russian; Editor-in-Chief SAPARMYRAT GARAKHANOV; Deputy Editor-in-Chief ORAZ AKGAYEV; circ. 6,832.

Beyik Türkmenbaşiyn Nesli (Generation of Turkmenbashi the Great): 744064 Aşgabat, ul. Galkynyş 20; tel. (12) 39-17-64; f. 1922; 3 a week; for young people; Editor ANNAGUL NARLIEVA; circ. 21,591.

Dogry yöl (True Path): 744000 Aşgabat; internet www.dogryyol.com; in Russian, news of Turkmenistan and Central Asia; online only; pro-opposition.

Edebiyat we sungat (Literature and Art): 744004 Aşgabat, ul. Galkynyş 20; tel. (12) 35-30-34; f. 1958; weekly; Editor ANNAMYRAT POLADOV; circ. 19,111.

Esger (Soldier): 744004 Aşgabat, ul. 2038 29; tel. (12) 35-68-09; f. 1993; weekly; organ of the Council of Ministers; military newspaper; Editor-in-Chief AGAMYRAT GELDYEV; circ. 40,200.

Galkynyş (Revival): 744604 Aşgabat, ul. Galkynyş 20; tel. (12) 22-34-23; weekly; Editor-in-Chief KHUDAIBERDI DIVANGULIYEV; circ. 44,586.

Habarlar: 744004 Aşgabat, ul. Galkynyş 20; tel. (12) 46-84-70; weekly; in Russian and Turkmen; television and radio; business; advertisements; Editor-in-Chief R. BALABAN; circ. 3,596.

Mugallymlar gazeti (Teachers' Newspaper): 744004 Aşgabat, ul. G. Kuliyev20; tel. (12) 35-09-66; f. 1952; 3 a week; organ of the Ministry of Education; Editor REJEPNUR GURBANNAZAROV; circ. 75,226.

Neitralnyi Turkmenistan (Neutral Turkmenistan): 744004 Aşgabat, ul. Galkynyş 20; tel. and fax (12) 39-42-76; fax (12) 22-34-37; e-mail nt@online.tm; internet www.tmpress.gov.tm; f. 1924; 6 a week; organ of the Majlis and the Council of Ministers; in Russian; Editor-in-Chief JEREN TAIMOVA; circ. 30,091.

Novosti Turkmenistana (Turkmenistan News): 744000 Aşgabat, ul. Gurungan 24A; tel. (12) 39-12-21; fax (12) 51-02-34; f. 1994; weekly; in Russian, English and Turkmen; publ. by Dowlet Khabarlar Gullugy news agency; circ. 500.

Syyasy sokhbetdeş (Political Symposium): 744604 Aşgabat, ul. Galkynyş 20; tel. (12) 25-10-84; f. 1992; weekly; organ of the Democratic Party of Turkmenistan; Editor AKBIBI YUSUPOVA; circ. 14,500.

Turkmenistan: Zolotoi Vek (Turkmenistan: The Golden Age): 744000 Aşgabat; internet www.turkmenistan.gov.tm; online only; in Russian; publ. by Democratic Union of Journalists of Turkmenistan.

Türkmening yupekyoli (Turkmen Railwayman): 744007 Aşgabat, ul. Chary Nurymov 3; tel. (12) 35-06-52; f. 1936; weekly; organ of the Turkmenistan State Railways; covers transport and communications; Editor BAYRAM SAHEDOV; circ. 7,000.

TURKMENISTAN

Türkmenistan: 744004 Aşgabat, ul. Galkynyş 20; tel. (12) 39-14-55; f. 1920; 6 a week; organ of the Council of Ministers and the Majlis; Editor-in-Chief JEREN TAIMOVA; circ. 25,591.

Watan (Fatherland): 744604 Aşgabat, ul. Galkynyş 20; tel. (12) 22-34-56; f. 1925; 3 a week; Editor-in-Chief AMANMUHAMMET REPOW; circ. 25,419.

PRINCIPAL PERIODICALS

Monthly, unless otherwise indicated.

Diller duniesi (World of Languages): 744014 Aşgabat, ul. O. Kuliyeva 22; tel. (12) 29-15-41; f. 1972; 6 a year; publ. by the Ministry of Education; in Russian and Turkmen.

Diyar: 744604 Aşgabat, ul. Galkynyş 20; tel. (12) 35-53-97; f. 1992; foreign policy and international relations; publ. by the President of the Republic and the Council of Ministers; Editor-in-Chief ASHIRBERDY GURBANOV; circ. 12,881.

Finansovye vesti (Financial News): 744004 Aşgabat, ul. Galkynyş 20; tel. (12) 29-42-76; f. 1994; in Russian, English and Turkmen; publ. by the Ministry of the Economy and Finance.

Garagum (Kara-Kum): 744005 Aşgabat, ul. Galkynyş 20; tel. (12) 35-11-15; f. 1928; literary; Editor SAPAR ORAYEV; circ. 2,546.

Guneş (The Sun): 744000 Aşgabat, ul. Galkynyş 20; tel. (12) 22-33-05; for children; Editor-in-Chief SHADURDY CHARYGYLLYEV; circ. 44,696.

Gurbansoltan Eje: 744604 Aşgabat, ul. Galkynyş 20; tel. (12) 22-33-09; f. 1931; fmrly *Ovadan* (Beautiful); for women; Editor AKBIBI YUSUBOVA; circ. 56,626.

Izvestiya Akademii Nauk Turkmenistana (Academy of Sciences of Turkmenistan News): 744000 Aşgabat, ul. Azad 59; f. 1946; 6 a year; in Russian and Turkmen.

Politicheskii sobesednik (Political Colloquium): 744604 Aşgabat, ul. Galkynyş 20; tel. (12) 25-10-84; f. 1937; in Russian; publ. by the Democratic Party of Turkmenistan; circ. 2,300.

Saglyk (Health): 744000 Aşgabat, ul. Kerbabayeva 39/57; tel. (12) 39-16-21; f. 1990; 6 a year; publ. by the Ministry of Health and the Medical Industry; Editor-in-Chief BAYRAMAMMED TACHMAMEDOV; circ. 35,071.

Türkmen dili khem edebiyati (Turkmen Language and Literature): 744000 Aşgabat; tel. (12) 41-88-03; f. 1991; 6 a year; publ. by the Ministry of Education.

Türkmen dunyasi: 744004 Aşgabat, ul. Azad 20; tel. (12) 47-81-18; organ of the Humanitarian Association of World Turkmen; Editor-in-Chief ANNABERDY AGABAYEV; circ. 11,956.

Türkmen medeniyeti (Turkmen Culture): 744007 Aşgabat, ul. O. Kuliyeva 21; tel. (12) 25-37-22; f. 1993; 2 a year; publ. by the Ministry of Culture, Television and Radio Broadcasting; Editor GELDYMYRAT NURMUKHAMMEDOV.

Türkmen sporty/Sport Turkmenistana (Turkmen Sport): 744004 Aşgabat, ul. Galkynyş 20; tel. (12) 22-33-72; weekly; in Turkmen and Russian; Editor-in-Chief VIKTOR MIHAYLOV; circ. 2,500.

Türkmenistanyn Lukmancykygy: 744004 Aşgabat, ul. A. Gulmammedov 4A; tel. (12) 35-25-40; every two months; health-care policy; Editor-in-Chief O. SERDAROV.

Türkmenistanyn oba khozhalygy (Agriculture of Turkmenistan): 744000 Aşgabat, ul. Azad 63; tel. (12) 35-19-38; f. 1929; Editor BYASHIM TALLYKOV; circ. 3,500.

Türkmenistanyng Mejlisining Maglumatlary (Bulletin of the Majlis of Turkmenistan): 744000 Aşgabat, ul. Garaşizlik 110; tel. (12) 35-50-39; fax (12) 35-31-47; e-mail mejlis@online.tm; f. 1960; 4 a year; in Russian and Turkmen.

Vozrozhdeniye (Rebirth): 744604 Aşgabat, ul. Galkynyş 20; tel. (12) 35-10-84; in Russian; political; Editor-in-Chief H. DIVANGULYEV; circ. 1,500.

NEWS AGENCIES

Türkmen Dowlet Khabarlar Gullugy (Turkmen State News Service): 744000 Aşgabat, ul. Gurungan 24A; tel. (12) 39-12-21; fax (12) 51-02-34; e-mail tpress@online.tm; f. 1967; Dir JEREN TAIMOVA.

Publishers

Magaryf Publishing House: 744000 Aşgabat; Dir N. ATAYEV.

Turkmenistan State Publishing Service: 744000 Aşgabat, ul. Galkynyş 20; tel. (12) 46-90-13; f. 1965; politics, science and fiction; Chair. ANNANUR CHARYYAROV.

Ylym Publishing House: 744000 Aşgabat, ul. Azad 59; tel. (12) 29-04-84; f. 1952; desert development, science; Dir N. I. FAIZULAYEVA.

Broadcasting and Communications

TELECOMMUNICATIONS

Türkmentelekom: 744000 Aşgabat, ul. Asudalyk 36; tel. (12) 51-12-77; fax (12) 51-02-40; e-mail admin@telecom.tm; internet www.telecom.tm; f. 1993; Dir-Gen. ANNALY CH. BERDINOBATOV.

BROADCASTING

Turkmen State Information Agency (Türkmen Dovlet Habarlary): 744004 Aşgabat, ul. Gurungan; tel. (12) 39-12-21; fax (12) 51-02-34; e-mail tpress@online.tm; Head JEREN TAIMOVA.

Radio

Turkmen National Radio Co: 744000 Aşgabat, ul. Navoi 5; tel. (12) 39-25-20; Chair. MURAD ORAZOV.

Char Tarapdan (From All Sides): tel. (12) 39-86-72; Dir BERDIMYRAT ABDYYEV.

Miras (Heritage): tel. (12) 35-68-50; Dir GURBANDURDY REJEPOV.

Watan (Fatherland): tel. (12) 51-12-96; Dir YAILIM I. ORAZOV.

Television

Turkmen National Television Co: 744000 Aşgabat, ul. Navoi 5; tel. (12) 39-25-20; Chair. MURAD ORAZOV.

Altyn Asyr (Golden Age): tel. (12) 39-85-06; Dir SHADURDY ALOVOV (acting).

Miras (Heritage): tel. (12) 35-20-43; Dir BYAGUL CH. NURMURADOVA.

Türkmenistan: tel. (12) 35-00-86; Dir MURAD A. ORAZOV.

Yaşlyk (Youth): tel. (12) 35-00-86; Dir (vacant).

Finance

(cap. = capital; res = reserves; dep. = deposits; m. = million; brs = branches; amounts in Turkmen manats)

BANKING

In late 2002 there were 12 commercial banks operating in Turkmenistan. The state retains substantial interests and involvement in banking.

Central Bank

Central Bank of Turkmenistan: 744000 Aşgabat, ul. Bitarap Türkmenistan; tel. (12) 38-10-27; fax (12) 51-08-12; e-mail merkez3@online.tm; f. 1991; central monetary authority, issuing bank and supervisory authority; Chair. GUVANCH B. GEOKLENOV; 5 brs.

Other Banks

Daihanbank: 744000 Aşgabat, ul. 2067 60; tel. and fax (12) 41-98-68; e-mail daybank@online.tm; f. 1989 as independent bank, Agroprombank, reorganized 1999; specializes in agricultural sector; Chair. of Bd TUMAR MAMMEDOV; 70 brs.

Garagum International Joint-Stock Bank: 744000 Aşgabat, ul. O. Kuliyeva 3; tel. (12) 35-22-01; fax (12) 35-38-54; f. 1993 as International Bank for Reconstruction, Development and Support of Entrepreneurship, name changed 2000; Chair. BEKMAMED SOLTANMEMEDOV.

Garaşyslyk Bank: 744000 Aşgabat, ul. Gerogly 30A; tel. (12) 35-48-75; fax (12) 39-01-24; e-mail garash@cbtm.net; f. 1999 following merger of Gas Bank and Aşgabat Bank; cap. US $5m. (Oct. 2003); Chair. (vacant); 5 brs.

Kreditbank: 744000 Aşgabat, pr. Magtymguly; tel. (12) 35-02-22; fax (12) 35-03-09; e-mail kreditbank@online.tm; f. 1995; fmrly Rossiiskii Kredit; Chair. BATYR BAYRIYEV.

President Bank: 744000 Aşgabat, ul. Gurungan 22; tel. (12) 35-79-43; fax (12) 51-08-12; e-mail presidentbank@cbtm.net; f. 2000; cap. US $60m.; Exec. Dir (vacant).

Savings Bank of Turkmenistan (Sberbank): 744000 Aşgabat, pr. Magtymguly 86; tel. (12) 35-46-71; fax (12) 35-40-04; f. 1923, reorganized 1989; wholly state-owned; Chair. BEGENCH BAYMUKHAMEDOV; 120 brs.

Senagatbank: 744013 Aşgabat, pr. S. Türkmenbaşi 42; tel. (12) 45-31-33; fax (12) 45-44-09; e-mail senagat@online.tm; f. 1989; cap. 31,200m., res 1,394m., dep. 32,547m. (Feb. 2005); Chair. EYEBERDI ATAYEV; 5 brs.

Turkmen Turkish Commercial Bank: 744000 Aşgabat, pr. Magtumguly 111/2, POB 15; tel. (12) 51-14-07; fax (12) 51-11-23; e-mail ttcb@online.tm; f. 1993, with 50% Turkish ownership; cap. 26,000.0m., res 2,220.8m., dep. 34,463.5m. (Dec. 2005); Chair. BATIR SAHATOV.

Türkmenvnesheconombank—State Bank for Foreign Economic Affairs of Turkmenistan: 744000 Aşgabat, ul. Garaşizlik 32; tel. (12) 40-60-40; fax (12) 40-65-63; e-mail tveb@online.tm; f. 1992 as independent bank, from Soviet Vneshekonombank; wholly state-owned; cap. 344,064m., dep. 4,599,973m., total assets 5,059,082m. (Dec. 2006); Chair. Rahimberdi Jepbarov; 5 brs.

Türkmenbank—State Commercial Bank 'Türkmenistan': 744000 Aşgabat, ul. Gurungan 10A; tel. (12) 51-07-21; fax (12) 39-67-35; e-mail turkmenbank@ctbm.net; f. 1992; Chair. Atamyrat Atalykov.

Türkmenbaşi Bank: 744000 Aşgabat, ul. Annadurdiyeva 54; tel. (12) 51-24-50; fax (12) 51-11-11; e-mail mail@investbank.org; f. 1992 as Investbank, renamed in 2000; Chair. Amanmurat Pajayev; 23 brs.

COMMODITY EXCHANGE

State Commodity and Raw Materials Exchange of Turkmenistan: 744000 Aşgabat, pr. Magtymguly 111; tel. (12) 35-43-21; fax (12) 51-03-04; e-mail info@exchange.gov.tm; internet www.turkmenbusiness.org; f. 1994; Chair. Yagmyrgeldy Myratlyev.

Trade and Industry

GOVERNMENT AGENCIES

National Institute of State Statistics and Information on Turkmenistan (Türkmenmillihasabat): 744000 Aşgabat, ul. 2033 72; tel. (12) 39-42-65; fax (12) 35-43-79; e-mail staff@natstat.gov.tm; f. 1997; Dir Kakamyrat Mommadov.

State Agency for Foreign Investment (SAFI): 744000 Aşgabat, ul. Azad 53; tel. and fax (12) 35-04-16; e-mail saffi@online.tm; f. 1996; monitors and regulates all foreign investment in Turkmenistan; registers foreign cos in Turkmenistan; Dir (vacant).

DEVELOPMENT ORGANIZATION

Small and Medium Enterprise Development Agency (SMEDA): 744000 Aşgabat, ul. 2015 8; tel. (12) 34-42-59; fax (12) 34-51-49; e-mail smeda@cat.glasnet.ru; jt venture between Turkmen Govt and the European Union (EU); Dir Serdar Babayev.

CHAMBER OF COMMERCE

Chamber of Commerce and Industry of Turkmenistan: 744000 Aşgabat, ul. 2037 17; tel. (12) 35-64-03; fax (12) 35-13-52; e-mail mission@online.tm; f. 1959; Chair. Arslan F. Nepesov.

UTILITIES

Electricity

Kuvvat Turkmen State Energy Technology Corpn: 744000 Aşgabat, ul. 2008 6; tel. (12) 35-68-04; fax (12) 39-06-82; e-mail kuvvat@online.tm; state electrical power generation co and agency; Chair. Yusup Davydov.

STATE HYDROCARBONS COMPANIES

Türkmenbaşi Oil Refinery: 745000 Balkan Velayat, Türkmenbaşi, POB 5; tel. (00222) 7-45-45; fax (00222) 7-45-44; production and refining of petroleum; sales of petroleum and liquefied natural gas; Dir (vacant).

Türkmengaz: 744036 Aşgabat, ul. 1939 56; tel. (12) 40-32-00; fax (12) 40-32-54; e-mail annam@online.tm; f. 1996; govt agency responsible for natural gas operations, inc. development of system of extraction, processing of gas and gas concentrate and gas transportation and sale; Chair. Yagshygeldy Kakayev.

Türkmengeologiya: 744000 Aşgabat, ul. 2023 7/32; tel. (12) 35-13-46; fax (12) 35-50-15; govt agency responsible for natural gas and petroleum exploration; Chair. Sapargeldi Jumayev.

Türkmenneft: 745100 Balkan Velayat, Balkanabat, pr. Magtymguly 49; tel. (00243) 2-19-45; govt agency responsible for petroleum operations and production; Chair. Karyagdy Tashliyev; Gen. Dir Khakim Imamov.

Türkmenneftegazstroi: 744036 Aşgabat, ul. Arçabil 56; tel. (12) 40-35-01; fax (12) 40-35-01; e-mail tngg@online.tm; govt agency for construction projects in the hydrocarbons sector; Chair. Gurbanberdy Orazmuradov.

TRADE UNIONS

Federation of Trade Unions of Turkmenistan: 744000 Aşgabat, pr. S. Türkmenbaşi 13; tel. (12) 35-62-08; fax (12) 35-21-30; Chair. Enebay G. Atayeva.

Committee of Trade Unions of Ahal Velayat: 744000 Ahal Velayat, pos. Anau, Gyaver etrap; tel. 41-39-19; Dir A. Taganov.

Committee of Trade Unions of Daşoguz Velayat: 746311 Daşoguz Velayat, Niyazovsk, S. Türkmenbaşi shayoly 8; Dir Sh. Igamov.

Transport

RAILWAYS

The main rail line in the country runs from Türkmenbaşi (formerly Krasnovodsk), on the Caspian Sea, in the west, via Aşgabat and Mari, to Türkmenabat (formerly Charjew) in the east. From Türkmenabat one line runs further east, to the other Central Asian countries of the former USSR, while another runs north-west, via Uzbekistan and Kazakhstan, to join the Russian rail network. In 2007 the total length of rail track in use in Turkmenistan was 2,523 km. A 203-km rail link from Türkmenabat to Atamarut was opened in 1999. In 1996 a rail link was established with Iran (on the route Tejen–Serakhs–Mashhad), thus providing the possibility of rail travel and transportation between Turkmenistan and İstanbul, Turkey, as well as giving access to the Persian (Arabian) Gulf. A 540-km railway line, running south–north across the country from Aşgabat to Daşoguz, via Garagum, was completed in early 2006.

Turkmenistan State Railways (Türkmendemorjollari): 744007 Aşgabat, pr. S. Türkmenbaşi 7; tel. (12) 35-55-45; fax (12) 51-06-32; f. 1992; Pres. B. P. Redjepov.

ROADS

In 1999 there was an estimated total of 24,000 km of roads, of which some 19,500 km were hard-surfaced. In early 2008 construction was underway on a principal road of 1,200 km, which was to link Türkmenbaşi with the eastern town of Farap.

SHIPPING

Shipping services link Türkmenbaşi (formerly Krasnovodsk) with Baku (Bakı, Azerbaijan), Makhachkala (Dagestan, Russia) and the major Iranian ports on the Caspian Sea. The Amu Dar'ya river is an important inland waterway. From 2000 Türkmenbaşi port was undergoing an extensive process of modernization.

Shipowning Companies

Neftec: 745100 Balkan Velayat, Türkmenbaşi; tel. (2) 765-81; fax (2) 766-89.

Turkmen Maritime Steamship Co: 745100 Balkan Velayat, Türkmenbaşi, ul. Shagadama 8; tel. (2) 767-34.

Turkmen Shipping Co: 745100 Balkan Velayat, Türkmenbaşi, ul. Shagadama 8; tel. (2) 972-67; fax (2) 767-85.

Türkmenderyayollary: 746000 Lebap Velayat, Türkmenabat, ul. Gyamichiler 8; tel. (2) 223-12; fax (2) 23-46-88; f. 1992 as Turkmen River Shipping Co; renamed as above in 1998.

Türkmennefteflot: 745100 Balkan Velayat, Türkmenbaşi, POB 6; tel. (2) 762-62.

CIVIL AVIATION

Turkmenistan's international airport is at Aşgabat. In December 2007 it was announced that the National Civil Aviation Authority of Turkmenistan (Türkmenhovayollary) was to sign an agreement with the Turkish company Polimeks on the construction of an airport in Türkmenbaşi, at a cost of €125m.

National Civil Aviation Authority of Turkmenistan (Türkmenhovayollary): 744000 Aşgabat, ul. 2007 3A; tel. (12) 35-10-52; fax (12) 35-44-02; e-mail aviahead@online.tm; f. 1992; Dir-Gen. Merdan Ayazov.

Turkmenistan Airlines: 744000 Aşgabat, ul. Magtymguly 80; tel. (12) 35-10-52; fax (12) 35-44-02; f. 1992; domestic and international scheduled and charter passenger flights, incl. services to Europe, Central and South-East Asia, and the Middle East; three divisions: Ahal Air Co, Khazar Air Co and Lebap Air Co; Gen. Dir Aleksei P. Bondarev.

Tourism

Although the tourism sector in Turkmenistan remains relatively undeveloped, owing, in part, to the vast expanse of the Kara-Kum desert (some 80% of the country's total area), the Government has made efforts to improve the standard of visitor accommodation (there are a number of new luxury hotels in Aşgabat) and to improve the capacity and efficiency of the capital's international airport). The scenic Kopet Dagh mountains, the Caspian Sea coast, the archaeological sites and mountain caves of Kugitang, and the hot subterranean mineral lake at Kov-Ata are among the country's natural

TURKMENISTAN

attractions, while the ancient cities of Mari and Nisa—former capitals of the Seljuk and Parthian empires, respectively—are of considerable historical interest. In addition, Kunya-Urgench is an important site of Muslim pilgrimage. In 2005, according to the World Tourism Organization, there were 11,611 visitors from abroad; receipts from tourism totalled US $192m. in 1998.

State Committee for Tourism and Sport: 744000 Aşgabat, ul. Pushkin 17; tel. (12) 35-47-77; fax (12) 39-67-40; e-mail turkmentan@online.tm; internet www.tourism-sport.gov.tm; founded on the basis of the State Tourist Corpn Turkmensyyakhat; f. 2000; Chair. (vacant).

National Institute of Sport and Tourism: 744001 Aşgabat, ul. 2038 15A; tel. (12) 36-25-40; fax (12) 36-24-56; f. 1981; activities include the provision of training in 15 types of sport, catering and tourism; Rector AŞIR MOMMADOV.

TUVALU

Introductory Survey

Location, Climate, Language, Religion, Flag, Capital

Tuvalu is a scattered group of nine small atolls (five of which enclose sizeable lagoons), extending about 560 km (350 miles) from north to south, in the western Pacific Ocean. Its nearest neighbours are Fiji to the south, Kiribati to the north and Solomon Islands to the west. The climate is warm and pleasant, with a mean annual temperature of 30°C (86°F), and there is very little seasonal variation. The average annual rainfall is about 3,500 mm (140 ins), the wettest months being November to February. The inhabitants speak Tuvaluan and English. Almost all of them profess Christianity, and about 98% are Protestants. The national flag (proportions 1 by 2) is light blue with the United Kingdom flag as a rectangular canton in the upper hoist, occupying one-quarter of the area, and nine five-pointed yellow stars (arranged to symbolize a map of the archipelago) in the fly. The flag was reintroduced in February 1997 to replace a design, adopted in October 1995, omitting the British union flag. The capital is on Funafuti Atoll.

Recent History

Tuvalu was formerly known as the Ellice (or Lagoon) Islands. Between about 1850 and 1875 many of the islanders were captured by slave-traders and this, together with European diseases, reduced the population from about 20,000 to 3,000. In 1877 the United Kingdom established the Western Pacific High Commission (WPHC), with its headquarters in Fiji, and the Ellice Islands and other groups were placed under its jurisdiction. In 1892 a British protectorate was declared over the Ellice Islands, and the group was linked administratively with the Gilbert Islands to the north. In 1916 the United Kingdom annexed the protectorate, which was renamed the Gilbert and Ellice Islands Colony (GEIC). During the Japanese occupation of the Gilbert Islands in 1942–43, the administration of the GEIC was temporarily moved to Funafuti in the Ellice Islands. (For more details of the history of the GEIC, see the chapter on Kiribati.)

A series of advisory and legislative bodies prepared the GEIC for self-government. In May 1974 the last of these, the Legislative Council, was replaced by the House of Assembly, with 28 elected members (including eight Ellice Islanders) and three official members. A Chief Minister was elected by the House and chose between four and six other ministers, one of whom had to be from the Ellice Islands.

In January 1972 the appointment of a separate GEIC Governor, who assumed most of the functions previously exercised by the High Commissioner for the Western Pacific, increased the long-standing anxiety of the Ellice Islanders over their minority position as Polynesians in the colony, dominated by the Micronesians of the Gilbert Islands. In a referendum held in the Ellice Islands in August and September 1974, more than 90% of the voters favoured separate status for the group, and in October 1975 the Ellice Islands, under the old native name of Tuvalu ('eight standing together', which referred to the eight populated atolls), became a separate British dependency. The Deputy Governor of the GEIC took office as Her Majesty's Commissioner for Tuvalu. The eight Ellice representatives in the GEIC House of Assembly became the first elected members of the new Tuvalu House of Assembly. They elected one of their number, Toaripi Lauti, to be Chief Minister. Tuvalu was completely separated from the GEIC administration in January 1976. The remainder of the GEIC was renamed the Gilbert Islands and achieved independence, as Kiribati, in July 1979.

Tuvalu's first separate elections took place in August 1977, when the number of elective seats in the House of Assembly was increased to 12. An independence Constitution was finalized at a conference in London in February 1978. After five months of internal self-government, Tuvalu became independent on 1 October 1978, with Lauti as the first Prime Minister. The pre-independence House of Assembly was redesignated Parliament. In September 2000 Tuvalu was formally admitted to the UN.

In 1983 the USA formally renounced its claim, dating from 1856, to the four southernmost atolls. Following elections to Parliament in September 1981, Lauti was replaced as Prime Minister by Dr Tomasi (later Sir Tomasi) Puapua. Puapua was re-elected Prime Minister following subsequent elections in September 1985.

In February 1986 a nation-wide poll was conducted to establish public opinion as to whether Tuvalu should remain an independent constitutional monarchy, with the British monarch at its head, or become a republic. Only on one atoll did the community appear to be in favour of the adoption of republican status. In March Tupua (later Sir Tupua) Leupena, a former Speaker of Parliament, was appointed Governor-General, replacing Sir Penitala Teo, who had occupied the post since independence in 1978.

At a general election in September 1989 supporters of Puapua were reported to have been defeated in the election, and an opponent, Bikenibeu Paeniu (who had been appointed Minister of Community Services within the previous year), was elected Prime Minister. In October 1990 Toaripi Lauti succeeded Sir Tupua Leupena as Governor-General.

Legislation approved by Parliament in mid-1991, which sought to prohibit all new religions from the islands and to establish the Church of Tuvalu as the State Church, caused considerable controversy and extensive debate. A survey showed the population to be almost equally divided over the matter, although Paeniu firmly opposed the motion, describing it as incompatible with basic human rights.

In August 1991 the Government announced that it was to prepare a compensation claim against the United Kingdom for the allegedly poor condition of Tuvalu's economy and infrastructure at the time of the country's achievement of independence in 1979. Moreover, Tuvalu was to seek additional compensation for damage caused during the Second World War when the United Kingdom gave permission for the USA to build airstrips on the islands (some 40% of Funafuti was uninhabitable because of large pits created by US troops during the construction of an airstrip on the atoll). Relations with the United Kingdom deteriorated further in late 1992, when the British Government harshly criticized the financial policy of Paeniu's Government. Paeniu defended his Government's policies, and stated that continued delays in the approval of aid projects from the United Kingdom meant that Tuvalu would not be seeking further development funds from the British Government.

At a general election held in September 1993, three of the 12 incumbent members of Parliament lost their seats. At elections to the premiership held in the same month, however, Paeniu and Puapua received six votes each. When a second vote produced a similar result, the Governor-General dissolved Parliament, in accordance with the Constitution. Paeniu and his Cabinet remained in office until the holding of a further general election in November. At elections to the premiership in the following month Kamuta Latasi defeated Paeniu by seven votes to five. Puapua, who had agreed not to challenge Paeniu in the contest in favour of supporting Latasi, was elected Speaker of Parliament. In June 1994 Latasi removed the Governor-General, Toomu Malaefono Sione, from office, some seven months after he had been appointed to the position, and replaced him with Tulaga (later Sir Tulaga) Manuella. Latasi alleged that Paeniu's appointment of Sione had been politically motivated.

In December 1994, in what was widely regarded as a significant rejection of its political links with the United Kingdom, the Tuvaluan Parliament voted to remove the British union flag from the Tuvalu national flag. A new design was selected and the new flag was inaugurated in October 1995. Speculation that the British monarch would be removed as Head of State intensified during 1995, following the appointment of a committee to review the Constitution. The three-member committee was to examine the procedure surrounding the appointment and removal of the Governor-General, and, particularly, to consider the adoption of a republican system of government.

In late 1996 the Deputy Prime Minister, Otinielu Tausi, and the parliamentary Speaker, Dr Tomasi Puapua, both announced their decision to withdraw their support for Latasi's Government, thereby increasing the number of opposition members in Parliament from five to seven. This reversal appeared to be in response to increasing dissatisfaction among the population with Latasi. This had been perceived firstly with his unpopular initiative to replace the country's national flag, and was exacerbated by revelations that the leasing of Tuvalu's telephone code to a foreign company had resulted in the use of the islands' telephone system for personal services considered indecent by the majority of islanders. (It was announced by the Government in October 2000 that the lease was to be terminated by the end of the year.) Opponents of the Prime Minister submitted a parliamentary motion of no confidence in his Government in December, which was approved by seven votes to five. Paeniu subsequently defeated Latasi, by a similar margin, to become Prime Minister, and a new Cabinet was appointed. The new premier acted promptly to restore the country's original flag, by proposing a parliamentary motion in February 1997, which was approved by seven votes to five.

A total of 35 candidates contested a general election on 26 March 1998. The period prior to the election had been characterized by a series of bitter disputes between Paeniu and Latasi, in which both had made serious accusations of sexual and financial misconduct against the other. Five members of the previous Parliament were returned to office, although Latasi unexpectedly failed to secure re-election. Paeniu was subsequently re-elected Prime Minister by 10 votes to two. In June the new Government announced a series of development plans and proposals for constitutional reform, including the introduction of a code of conduct for political leaders and the creation of an ombudsman's office. Paeniu stated that his administration intended to consult widely with the population before any changes were implemented. Also in 1998 Puapua was appointed Governor-General, replacing Manuella.

On 13 April 1999 Paeniu lost a parliamentary vote of confidence and was forced to resign. Later in the month Ionatana Ionatana, hitherto the Minister of Health, Education, Culture, Women and Community Affairs, was elected by Parliament as the new Prime Minister. On his appointment Ionatana immediately effected a reorganization of the Cabinet.

Potentially the most significant new source of revenue for many years was established in September 1998 when the Government signed an agreement to lease the country's national internet suffix '.tv' to a Canadian information company. The company, which defeated several other business interests to secure the deal, was expected to market the internet address to international television companies. Although that arrangement subsequently failed, it was announced in February 2000 that a US $50m. deal on the sale of the '.tv' suffix had been concluded with a US company. The sale was expected to generate some $10m. annually in revenue. The funds generated from the sale enabled Tuvalu officially to join the UN, and participate in the 55th annual UN General Assembly Meeting, held in September 2000.

In early December 2000 Prime Minister Ionatana Ionatana died unexpectedly. The Deputy Prime Minister, Lagitupu Tuilimu was immediately appointed as interim Prime Minister, pending the election of a replacement. In late February 2001 Parliament elected as Prime Minister the Minister of Internal Affairs and Rural and Urban Development, Faimalaga Luka; he assumed responsibility for the additional portfolios of foreign affairs, finance and economic planning, and trade and commerce, and immediately named a new cabinet. A vote of no confidence was upheld against Luka in December 2001 while he was away in New Zealand, undergoing a medical examination. Koloa Talake, a former Minister of Finance, was elected Prime Minister in the same month, winning eight of the 15 votes cast (the number of parliamentary seats having been increased from 12 to 15). He appointed an entirely new Cabinet.

Talake announced in March 2002 that lawyers were preparing evidence for further legal action against the United Kingdom, seeking compensation for the alleged inequality of the division of assets between Tuvalu and Kiribati when the two nations had achieved independence in the late 1970s. Following the general election held on 25 July 2002, Saufatu Sopoanga, a former Minister of Finance, defeated Amasone Kilei, the opposition candidate, by eight votes to seven to become the new Prime Minister. Sopoanga subsequently announced his intention to hold a referendum on the adoption of a republican system of Government in Tuvalu.

In May 2003 two by-elections resulted in the loss of the Government's one-seat majority. The Government's subsequent refusal to convene Parliament (allegedly in order to evade a vote of no confidence) was strongly criticized by the opposition. The Government maintained that it would regain its majority with an imminent defection from the opposition and would then convene Parliament. In July, however, the situation remained unchanged and the opposition consequently sought a court order obliging Sopoanga to convene Parliament. The appointment, in early September, of Faimalaga Luka, hitherto Speaker and a member of Parliament, as the country's new Governor-General necessitated an additional by-election, which resulted in a further delay to Parliament's being convened. However, following the success of its candidate at the by-election, and (as anticipated) the defection of an opposition member, the Government regained its majority in mid-October. Parliament was finally convened in early November.

In April 2004 the Government announced that a team of officials was touring the outer islands to canvas opinion on the adoption of republican status for Tuvalu. If islanders indicated sufficient support for the proposal, a referendum would be held. In March 2005 the Prime Minister indicated that he expected the referendum to go ahead, stating that he had encountered widespread concern among Tuvaluans that the British Government was failing to meet its financial obligations to the islands.

In August 2004 the Prime Minister, Saufatu Sopoanga, was ousted by nine parliamentary votes to five in a vote of no confidence after a member of the Government crossed the floor to vote with the opposition and was joined by the Speaker. The election of a new Prime Minister, however, was delayed by Sopoanga's decision to relinquish his seat, thus necessitating the organization of a by-election before Parliament could select a premier. Deputy Prime Minister Maatia Toafa assumed the role of acting Prime Minister in the interim. Sopoanga regained his seat in a by-election in early October, and on 11 October acting Prime Minister Maatia Toafa was elected to the premiership, defeating Sopoanga by eight votes to seven.

In April 2005 it was announced that Sio Patiale, a member of Parliament, was to resign on grounds of ill health. The consequent by-election was expected to be very significant, owing to the possibility that it might result in a majority for the opposition in Parliament. In the same month the Governor-General, Faimalaga Luka, resigned, having reached the maximum permitted age for the post of 65, and was replaced by Filiomea Telito. Luka died in August of that year. A further by-election in September, caused by the resignation of another member of Parliament, was won by a candidate who decided to support the Government, thus consolidating its majority.

In May 2005 the President of Taiwan visited three countries in the Pacific, including Tuvalu, in an attempt to improve diplomatic relations. During his brief visit, the Prime Minister signed a joint communiqué with his Tuvaluan counterpart.

Tuvalu's annual visitor arrival numbers were greatly increased by a meeting of ministers which the country hosted in Funanfuti in June 2005. Some 80 delegates from 14 Pacific island countries attended the meeting to discuss issues concerned with economic development in the region.

The legislative election held on 3 August 2006 resulted in major changes to the composition of Parliament, with the entry of eight new members. Maatia Toafa was the only cabinet member to retain a seat, and was subsequently replaced as Prime Minister by Apisai Ielemia in mid-August. Ielemia assumed additional responsibility for the foreign affairs portfolio, while Taavau Teii was appointed Deputy Prime Minister and Minister for Natural Resources. Other appointments to the new Government included Lotoala Metia as Minister of Finance, Economic Planning and Industries and Willie Telavi as Minister of Home Affairs and Rural Development.

On 30 April 2008 a referendum on Tuvalu's system of government was conducted. The level of participation was reportedly low, at approximately 21% of the electorate. The majority of voters rejected proposals for a republican system, with a president as head of state: according to reports, 1,260 voters (or 65%) out of a total of 1,939 preferred the retention of the existing system of constitutional monarchy.

In 1989 a UN report on the 'greenhouse effect' (the heating of the earth's atmosphere) listed Tuvalu as one of the island groups which would completely disappear beneath the sea in the 21st century, unless drastic action were taken. At the UN World Climate Conference, held in Geneva in late 1990, Paeniu appealed for urgent action by developed nations to combat the environmental changes caused by the 'greenhouse effect', which were believed to include a 10-fold increase in cyclone frequency (from two in 1940 to 21 in 1990), an increase in salinity in ground water and a considerable decrease in the average annual rainfall. However, the Government remained critical of the inertia with which it considered certain countries had reacted to its appeal for assistance and reiterated the Tuvaluan people's fears of physical and cultural extinction. The subsequent Prime Minister, Kamuta Latasi, was similarly critical of the industrial world's apparent disregard for the plight of small island nations vulnerable to the effects of climate change, particularly when Tuvalu was struck by tidal waves in 1994 (believed to be the first experienced by the islands). The Government of Tuvalu was strongly critical of Australia's refusal to reduce its emission of pollutant gases (known to contribute to the 'greenhouse effect') at the Conference of the Parties to the UN Framework Convention on Climate Change (UNFCCC, see UN Environment Programme, see p. 62) in Kyoto, Japan, in late 1997. However, in July 2001 Australia adopted the Kyoto Protocol, which urged industrial nations to reduce carbon-dioxide emissions by 5.2% from 1990 levels by 2012. In March 2001 Tuvalu, Kiribati and the Maldives announced their decision to take legal action against the USA for its refusal to sign the Kyoto Protocol. In August Tuvalu was one of six states at the Pacific Islands Forum to demand a meeting with US President George W. Bush to try to enlist his support for the Kyoto Protocol. (The USA produced nearly one-third of the industrialized countries' carbon-dioxide emissions and had repeatedly refused to adopt the Protocol.)

The installation of a new sea-level monitoring station began in December 2001 as part of the South Pacific Sea Level and Climate Monitoring Project administered by the Australian aid agency, AusAID. In January 2002 it was reported that the Government had engaged a US law firm to prosecute the USA and other nations for failing to meet their commitments to the UNFCCC. In September 2003 Tuvalu's Prime Minister addressed the 58th session of the UN General Assembly in New York and appealed for collective action to mitigate the impact of climate change and rising sea-levels on the islands. He once again urged all industrialized nations, particularly the USA, to sign the Kyoto Protocol. The option of resettlement on neighbouring islands, including Fiji, was under consideration, but only as a last resort, and the Government was also considering the purchase of land in other countries for economic reasons, while declaring that this might be a useful long-term solution should the problems caused by climate change worsen. In December 2007 it was reported that water from wells was becoming increasingly unsuitable for consumption, while high tides were causing frequent flooding.

Tuvalu was subject to considerable international criticism in mid-2004 regarding its decision to join the International Whaling Commission (IWC, see p. 404). Environmental and animal welfare groups accused the Tuvaluan Government of accepting financial incentives from Japan in return for agreeing to use its vote to support a removal of the ban on commercial whaling at the commission's annual meeting in Italy in July 2004. In early 2006 the US ambassador to Tuvalu, Larry Dinger, received a petition from Greenpeace, the international environmentalist group, urging Tuvalu to cease voting with Japan at the IWC. In May of the same year, however, prior to the IWC's annual meeting in Japan, Tuvalu reiterated its stance. Tuvalu later denied that Japan had secured its vote at the meeting through its financing of infrastructure projects in Tuvalu after IWC delegates voted narrowly in favour of the resolution calling for a resumption of commercial whaling.

Government

Tuvalu is a constitutional monarchy. Executive authority is vested in the British sovereign, as Head of State, and is exercisable by her representative, the Governor-General, who is appointed on the recommendation of the Prime Minister and acts, in almost all cases, on the advice of the Cabinet. Legislative power is vested in the unicameral Parliament, with 15 members elected by universal adult suffrage for four years (subject to dissolution). The Cabinet is led by the Prime Minister, who is elected by and from the members of Parliament. On the Prime Minister's recommendation, other ministers are appointed by the Governor-General. The Cabinet is responsible to Parliament. Each of the inhabited atolls has its own elected Island Council, which is responsible for local government.

Economic Affairs

In 2006 the UN's Economic and Social Commission for Asia and the Pacific (ESCAP) estimated Tuvalu's gross domestic product (GDP) at current prices to be US $16.2m., equivalent to $1,545 per head. During 1995–2005, it was estimated, the population increased at an average annual rate of 0.9%. According to figures from ESCAP, overall GDP increased, in real terms, at an average annual rate of 1.9% in 1995–2000, and by an average rate of 5.7% in 2000–05. Compared with the previous year, GDP rose by 1.0% in 2006.

Agriculture (including fishing) is, with the exception of copra production, of a basic subsistence nature. According to ESCAP estimates the sector contributed some 16.7% of GDP in 2006; the GDP of the agricultural sector increased at an average annual rate of 0.2% in 1995–2000, and 1.3% in 2000–05. Compared with the previous year, agricultural GDP increased by 3.9% in 2006. In 2005, according to FAO, the sector engaged some 25% of the labour force. Coconuts (the source of copra) are the only cash crop. Pulaka, taro, papayas, the screw-pine (*Pandanus*) and bananas are cultivated as food crops and honey is produced. In the late 1990s and early 2000s agriculture became increasingly affected by climate change and rising sea-levels. More frequent high tides caused flooding which damaged crops, particularly the important taro crop, and killed tree roots, which reduced the harvest of coconuts and other fruits. Livestock comprises pigs, poultry and goats. Fish and other sea products are staple constituents of the islanders' diet. The sale of fishing licences to foreign fleets is an important source of income and earned $A11.8m. in 2001 (compared with $A3.6m. in 1997), equivalent to 50.3% of current revenue. Revenue from this source, however, declined in subsequent years, owing to decreases in catches.

Industry (including mining, manufacturing, construction and utilities) accounted for 13.6% of GDP in 2006, according to ESCAP estimates. In 1995–2000, according to the same figures, industrial GDP expanded at an average annual rate of 6.4%, and the average annual rate of growth was 5.1% in 2000–05. Compared with the previous year, the sector's GDP increased by 1.1% in 2006. Manufacturing is confined to the small-scale production of coconut-based products, soap and handicrafts. The manufacturing sector contributed some 3.7% of GDP in 2002.

Energy is derived principally from a power plant (fuelled by oil) and, on the outer islands, solar power. In 1989 mineral fuels accounted for almost 13% of total import costs. With financial assistance from the Japanese Government, construction work on the electricity station on Funafuti was proceeding in 2006/07.

The Government is an important employer (engaging 1,185 people in 2001, equivalent to about one-half of the labour force) and consequently the services sector makes a relatively large contribution to Tuvalu's economy (providing some 69.7% of GDP in 2006, according to ESCAP estimates). In 1995–2000, according to ESCAP, the GDP of the services sector increased at an average annual rate of 8.4%, and the annual average growth rate was estimated at 4.3% in 2000–05. Compared with the previous year, the sector's GDP expanded by 1.6% in 2006. The islands' remote situation and lack of amenities have hindered the development of a tourist industry. Visitor arrivals were reported to total 1,130 in 2007, in comparison with 1,131 in 2006. An important source of revenue has been provided by remittances from Tuvaluans working abroad. Remittances from Tuvaluan seafarers employed on foreign vessels were estimated at $A4m. in 2006. In 2001 receipts from the leasing of the islands' internet domain address reached US $1.6m., while revenue from telecommunication licence fees totalled $0.31m.

Tuvalu recorded a visible trade deficit of US $28.6m. in 2003; in that year the cost of imports exceeded $24.0m., while export revenue totalled only $147,100. The principal source of imports in 2005 was Fiji (47.0%). The principal market for exports were Italy and Fiji. The principal imports in 2005 were mineral products, prepared foodstuffs, machinery, mechanical appliances and electrical equipment, and transport equipment.

According to ADB figures, the 2006 budget allowed for expenditure of $A30.6m., while revenue (including grants) totalled $A28.6m. in the same year (some 12.0% higher than in 2005). With the support of the Consolidated Investment Fund (a depository of the Tuvalu Trust Fund—TTF), in 2006 the budget deficit was reduced to $A2.0m. The TTF was established in 1987, with assistance from New Zealand, Australia and the United Kingdom, to generate funding, through overseas investment, for development projects. By September 2006 the assets of the TTF were estimated to total $A77m. In 2006 the TTF contributed more than $A11m. to the Consolidated Investment Fund. In 2007/08 New Zealand budgeted for bilateral assistance worth $NZ2.3m. Aid from Australia was budgeted at $A5.6m. for the same year. Tuvalu has also received significant financial assistance from Taiwan since the establishment of diplomatic relations. The annual rate of inflation averaged 2.7% in 1996–2006.

According to the ADB, the average inflation rate decreased from 3.8% in 2006 to 3.0% in 2007.

Tuvalu is a member of the Pacific Community (see p. 377), the Pacific Islands Forum (see p. 380) and the UN Economic and Social Commission for Asia and the Pacific (ESCAP, see p. 35). In 1993 the country was admitted to the Asian Development Bank (ADB, see p. 182).

The islands have continued to suffer from the increasing impact of climate change (see Recent History). In February 2005 high tides flooded homes, government buildings and the airport, also causing damage to agricultural produce. Conversely, the country is also vulnerable to drought. Tuvalu's high dependence on imports has resulted in a persistent trade deficit. In February 2000 the sale of the '.tv' internet suffix (see Recent History) substantially increased the islands' income. Proceeds from the sale were used to develop the country's infrastructure. The Government of Apisai Ielemia, which took office in August 2006, hoped to reduce the disparities in living standards between Funafuti and the outer islands. In an effort to raise remittances from overseas workers, with external assistance the Tuvalu Maritime Training Institute was to be substantially upgraded. The expansion of the institute was aimed at significantly increasing the number of graduates. The Government's short-term development strategy has been formulated within a programme known as Te Kakeega II, eight strategic areas of focus being identified. However, the achievement of these aims was largely dependent upon the performance of the TTF. Revenue from the sale of fishing licences was becoming more vulnerable to the fluctuations in fish stocks caused by the increasing frequency of the climatic phenomena known as El Niño and La Niña. Income from fishing licence fees rose by 34.4% in 2007, while revenues from the '.tv' internet domain facility reportedly declined by 19.8% in the same year. Tuvalu has remained reliant on income from overseas and has continued to depend on foreign assistance for its development budget. In addition to the substantial aid received from Japan for the purposes of infrastructural improvements, Taiwan and the European Union were to contribute $A2.6m. and $A2.2m. respectively in 2007. In 2006 it was reported that the UN was considering raising Tuvalu's status to developing country from its least developed country (LDC) status by 2013. According to the ADB, the economy expanded by 2.0% in 2007, and the same rate of GDP growth was projected for 2008.

Education

Education is provided by the Government, and is compulsory between the ages of six and 15 years. In 2001 there were 10 primary schools, with a total of 2,067 pupils and 103 teachers in 2006. There were two secondary schools in 2006, with 52 teachers and 629 pupils in 2004. Enrolment in pre-primary level education in 2003/04 was equivalent to 99% of children from the relevant age-group while enrolment in primary schools was equivalent to 98.5% of children from the relevant age-group. In 2000/01 enrolment in secondary schools was equivalent to 84.4% of children from the relevant age-group. The only tertiary institution is the Tuvalu Maritime Training Institute at Amatuku on Funafuti. Further training or vocational courses are available in Fiji and Kiribati. The University of the South Pacific (based in Fiji) has an extension centre on Funafuti. A programme of major reforms in the education system in Tuvalu, begun in the early 1990s, resulted in the lengthening of primary schooling (from six to eight years) and a compulsory two years of secondary education, as well as the introduction of vocational, technical and commerce-related courses at the Maritime Training School. Adult literacy was estimated at 98% at the 1991 census. Total government expenditure on education in 2001 was equivalent to some 35% of total budgetary expenditure. The education sector received funding US $10.5m. in 2005, as part of a joint grant provided by the New Zealand Government and the World Bank.

Public Holidays

2008: 1 January (New Year's Day), 10 March (Commonwealth Day), 21–24 March (Easter), 9 June (Queen's Official Birthday), 4 August (National Children's Day), 1–2 October (Tuvalu Day, anniversary of independence), 14 November (Prince of Wales's Birthday), 25 December (Christmas Day), 26 December (Boxing Day).

2009: 1 January (New Year's Day), 13 March (Commonwealth Day), 10–13 April (Easter), 8 June (Queen's Official Birthday), 4 August (National Children's Day), 1–2 October (Tuvalu Day, anniversary of independence), 14 November (Prince of Wales's Birthday), 25 December (Christmas Day), 26 December (Boxing Day).

Weights and Measures

The metric system has been introduced, but the imperial system is still employed.

Statistical Survey

Source (unless otherwise indicated): Central Statistics Division, Ministry of Finance and Economic Planning, Private Bag, Vaiaku, Funafuti; tel. 20107; fax 21210; e-mail statistics@tuvalu.tv; internet http://www.spc.int/prism/country/tv/stats/.

AREA AND POPULATION

Land Area: 25.6 sq km (9.9 sq miles).

Population: 9,043 at census of 17 November 1991; 9,561 (males 4,729, females 4,832) at census of 1 November 2002; 10,219 (official estimate) at 31 December 2005. *By Atoll* (at census of 1 November 2002): Funafuti 4,492; Vaitupu 1,591; Niutao 663; Nanumea 664; Nukufetau 586; Nanumaga 589; Nui 548; Nukulaelae 393; Niulakita 35. *Mid-2004* (official estimate): Funafuti 5,394.

Density (at 31 December 2005): 399.2 per sq km.

Principal Towns (population at 2002 census): Alapi 1.024; Fakaifou 1,007; Senala 589; Teone 540; Vaiaku (capital) 516; Motufoua 506. Source: Thomas Brinkhoff, *City Population* (internet www.city-population.de).

Births and Deaths: Registered live births 185 in 2003, 190 in 2004, 191 in 2005; Registered deaths 83 in 2003, 89 in 2004, 59 in 2005.

Expectation of Life (years at birth, WHO estimates): 62.0 (males 61.3; females 63.4) in 2005. Source: WHO, *World Health Report*.

Economically Active Population: In 1979 there were 936 people in paid employment, 50% of them in government service. In 1979 114 Tuvaluans were employed by the Nauru Phosphate Co, with a smaller number employed in Kiribati and about 255 on foreign ships. At the 1991 census the total economically active population (aged 15 years and over) stood at 2,383 (males 1,605, females 778). *Mid-2005* (estimates): Agriculture, etc. 1,000; Total labour force 4,000 (Source: FAO).

HEALTH AND WELFARE

Key Indicators

Total Fertility Rate (children per woman, 2005): 3.6.
Under-5 Mortality Rate (per 1,000 live births, 2005): 38.
Physicians (per 1,000 head, 2002): 0.55.
Hospital Beds (per 1,000 head, 2001): 4.0.
Health Expenditure (2004): US $ per head (PPP): 257.1.
Health Expenditure (2004): % of GDP: 16.6.
Health Expenditure (2004): public (% of total): 94.8.
Access to Sanitation (% of persons, 2004): 90.

For sources and definitions, see explanatory note on p. vi.

AGRICULTURE, ETC.

Principal Crops (metric tons, 2005, FAO estimates): Coconuts 1,139; Copra 150; Roots and tubers 140; Vegetables 530; Bananas 284; Other fruits (excl. melons) 465. Note: Data were not available for 2006.

Livestock ('000 head, year ending September 2004, FAO estimates): Pigs 13.5; Chickens 45; Ducks 15. Note: Data were not available for 2005–06.

Livestock Products (metric tons, 2005, FAO estimates): Chicken meat 47; Pig meat 97; Hen eggs 22; Honey 3. Note: Data were not available for 2006.

Fishing (metric tons, live weight, 2005): Total catch 2,561 (Skipjack tuna 1,200; Yellowfin tuna 1,000).

Source: FAO.

FINANCE

Currency and Exchange Rates: Australian and Tuvaluan currencies are both in use. Australian currency: 100 cents = 1 Australian dollar ($A). *Sterling, US Dollar and Euro Equivalents* (31 December 2007): £1 sterling = $A2.2725; US $1 = $A1.1343; €1 = $A1.6698; $A100 = £44.01 = US $88.16 = €59.89. *Average Exchange Rate* ($A per US dollar): 1.3095 in 2005; 1.3280 in 2006; 1.1951 in 2007.

Budget ($A '000, 2006): Current revenue 14,677 (Revenue from taxation 5,717, Non-tax revenue 8,960); Expenditure 30,612. Source: Asian Development Bank, *Key Indicators of Developing Asian and Pacific Countries*.

Official Development Assistance (US $ million, 2002): Bilateral 11.2; Multilateral 0.5; Total 11.7 (all grants). *2005:* Total assistance 9.0. Source: UN, *Statistical Yearbook for Asia and the Pacific*.

Cost of Living (Consumer Price Index for Funafuti; base: July–Sept. 2003 = 100): 101.8 in 2004; 105.1 in 2005; 109.1 in 2006. Source: Asian Development Bank, *Key Indicators of Developing Asian and Pacific Countries*.

Gross Domestic Product ($A '000 at constant 1988 factor cost): 16,947 in 2002; 17,286 in 2003 (estimate); 17,805 in 2004 (estimate).

Gross Domestic Product by Economic Activity ($A '000 at current prices, 2002): Agriculture 4,565; Mining 237; Manufacturing 1,016; Electricity, gas and water 1,433; Construction 1,370; Trade, restaurants and hotels 3,700; Transport, storage and communications 3,429; Finance and real estate 4,055; Public administration 7,188; Others (incl. community and personal services) 1,794; *Less* Imputed bank charges 1,295; *Total* 27,490. Source: Asian Development Bank, *Key Indicators of Developing Asian and Pacific Countries*.

Balance of Payments ($A '000, 2003): Exports of goods f.o.b. 444; Imports of goods f.o.b. −28,995; *Trade balance* −28,552; Exports of services and other income 7,403; Imports of services and other income −17,687; *Balance on goods, services and income* −38,836; Current transfers (net) 20,833; *Current balance* −18,003. Source: Asian Development Bank, *Key Indicators of Developing Asian and Pacific Countries*.

EXTERNAL TRADE

Principal Commodities ($A '000, 2005): *Imports:* Animals and animal products 1,473.8; Vegetable products 1,224.2; Prepared foodstuffs 2,385.1; Mineral products 3,661.2; Chemical products 734.5; Textiles and textile articles 759.2; Base metals and articles thereof 695.1; Machinery, mechanical appliances and electrical equipment 2,318.9; Transportation equipment 884.8; Total (incl. others) 16,908.0. *Exports:* Mineral products 5.9; Wood and wood products 10.0; Base metals and articles thereof 12.3; Machinery, mechanical appliances and electrical equipment 13.9; Transportation equipment 9.3; Instruments—measuring, musical 14.9; Total (incl. others) 80.0.

Principal Trading Partners (US $ million, 2005): *Imports:* Australia 3.49; China, People's Republic 6.99; Fiji 18.48; Japan 7.26; New Zealand 1.90; Total (incl. others) 39.36. *Exports:* Denmark 0.03; Fiji 0.19; Germany 0.04; Italy 0.53; Poland 0.02; Total (incl. others) 0.98.

Source: Asian Development Bank, *Key Indicators of Developing Asian and Pacific Countries*.

TRANSPORT

Shipping: *Merchant Fleet* (registered at 31 December 2006): Vessels 131; Total displacement ('000 grt) 359.3. Source: Lloyd's Register-Fairplay, *World Fleet Statistics*.

TOURISM

Tourist Arrivals: 1,377 in 2003; 1,290 in 2004; 1,085 in 2005.

Tourist Arrivals by Country of Residence (2005): Australia 186; Fiji 223; Japan 118; New Zealand 117; United Kingdom 37; USA 83; Total (incl. others) 1,085.

Source: World Tourism Organization.

COMMUNICATIONS MEDIA

Non-daily Newspapers (1996): 1; estimated circulation 300*.

Telephones (main lines, 2005): 900 in use†.

Mobile Cellular Telephones (subscribers, 2005): 1,300.

Internet Users (2005): 1,700.

Radio Receivers (1997): 4,000 in use*.

Facsimile Machines (1993): 10 in use‡.

* Source: UNESCO, *Statistical Yearbook*.
† Source: International Telecommunication Union.
‡ Source: UN, *Statistical Yearbook*.

EDUCATION

Pre-school (2005): 57 teachers; 647 pupils.

Primary (2001, unless otherwise indicated): 9 government schools, 1 private school; 103 teachers (2005); 2,010 pupils (2005).

General Secondary (2005): 2 government schools; 56 teachers; 593 pupils. A maritime school offers training for 60 merchant seamen per year, with vocational, technical and commerce-related courses. The University of the South Pacific has an extension centre in Funafuti offering diploma and vocational courses and the first two years of degree courses (the latter requiring completion in Suva, Fiji).

Directory

The Constitution

A new Constitution came into effect at independence on 1 October 1978. Its main provisions are as follows:

The Constitution states that Tuvalu is a democratic sovereign state and that the Constitution is the Supreme Law. It guarantees protection of all fundamental rights and freedoms and provides for the determination of citizenship.

The British sovereign is represented by the Governor-General, who must be a citizen of Tuvalu and is appointed on the recommendation of the Prime Minister. The Prime Minister is elected by Parliament, and up to four other ministers are appointed by the Governor-General from among the members of Parliament, after consultation with the Prime Minister. The Cabinet, which is directly responsible to Parliament, consists of the Prime Minister and the other ministers, whose functions are to advise the Governor-General upon the government of Tuvalu. The Attorney-General is the principal legal adviser to the Government. Parliament is composed of 15 members directly elected by universal adult suffrage for four years, subject to dissolution, and is presided over by the Speaker (who is elected by the members). The Constitution also provides for the operation of a Judiciary (see Judicial System) and for an independent Public Service. Under a revised Constitution that took effect on 1 October 1986, the Governor-General no longer has the authority to reject the advice of the Government.

The Government

HEAD OF STATE

Sovereign: HM Queen ELIZABETH II.

Governor-General: FILOIMEA TELITO (took office 15 April 2005).

CABINET
(April 2008)

Prime Minister and Minister of Foreign Affairs: APISAI IELEMIA.

Deputy Prime Minister and Minister of Natural Resources: TAAVAU TEII.

Minister of Finance and Economic Planning: LOTOALA METIA.

Minister of Health: IAKOBA ITALELI.

Minister of Communications, Transport and Tourism: TAUKELINA FINIKASO.

Minister of Home Affairs: WILLIE TELAVI.

Minister of Public Utilities and Industries: KAUSEA NATANO.

Minister of Education, Youth and Sports: Dr FALESA PITOI.

MINISTRIES

Office of the Prime Minister: Private Mail Bag, Vaiaku, Funafuti; tel. 20101; fax 20820.

TUVALU

Ministry of Education, Sports and Culture: Vaiaku, Funafuti; tel. 20405; fax 20832.

Ministry of Finance and Economic Planning: PMB, Vaiaku, Funafuti; tel. 20202; fax 20210; e-mail secfin@tuvalu.tv.

Ministry of Foreign Affairs: Vaiaku, Funafuti; tel. 20102; fax 20820.

Ministry of Health: Vaiaku, Funafuti; tel. 20403; fax 20832.

Ministry of Home Affairs and Rural Development: Vaiaku, Funafuti; tel. 20172; fax 20821.

Ministry of Local Government, Women and Youth: Vaiaku, Funafuti.

Ministry of Natural Resources, Energy and Environment: Vaiaku, Funafuti; tel. 20827; fax 20826.

Ministry of Trade, Tourism and Commerce: PMB, Vaiaku, Funafuti; tel. 20182; fax 20829.

Ministry of Works, Communications and Transport: PMB, Vaiaku, Funafuti; tel. 20052; fax 20772; e-mail tuvmet@tuvalu.tv.

Legislature

PARLIAMENT

Parliament has 15 members, who hold office for a term of up to four years. A general election was held on 3 August 2006. There are no political parties.

Speaker: KAMUTA LATASI.

Diplomatic Representation

There are no embassies or high commissions in Tuvalu. The British High Commissioner in Fiji is also accredited as High Commissioner to Tuvalu. Other Ambassadors or High Commissioners accredited to Tuvalu include the Australian, New Zealand, US, French and Japanese Ambassadors in Fiji.

Judicial System

The Supreme Law is embodied in the Constitution. The High Court is the superior court of record, presided over by the Chief Justice, and has jurisdiction to consider appeals from judgments of the Magistrates' Courts and the Island Courts. Appeals from the High Court lie with the Court of Appeal in Fiji or, in the ultimate case, with the Judicial Committee of the Privy Council in the United Kingdom.

There are eight Island Courts with limited jurisdiction in criminal and civil cases.

High Court: Vaiaku, Funafuti; tel. 20837.

Chief Justice: VINCENT LUNABEK.

Attorney-General: ESE APINELU (acting).

Religion

CHRISTIANITY

Te Ekalesia Kelisiano Tuvalu (The Christian Church of Tuvalu): POB 2, Funafuti; tel. 20755; fax 20651; f. 1861; autonomous since 1968; derived from the Congregationalist foundation of the London Missionary Society; some 91% of the population are adherents; Pres. Rev. TOFIGA FALANI; Gen. Sec. Rev. KITIONA TAUSI.

Roman Catholic Church: Catholic Centre, POB 58, Funafuti; tel. and fax 20527; e-mail cathcent@tuvalu.tv; 121 adherents (31 Dec. 2005); Superior Fr CAMILLE DESROSIERS.

Other churches with adherents in Tuvalu include the Church of Jesus Christ of Latter-day Saints (Mormons), the Jehovah's Witnesses, the New Apostolic Church and the Seventh-day Adventists.

BAHÁ'Í FAITH

National Spiritual Assembly: POB 48, Funafuti; tel. 20860; mems resident in 8 localities.

The Press

Tuvalu Echoes: Broadcasting and Information Office, Vaiaku, Funafuti; tel. 20138; fax 20732; f. 1984; fortnightly; English; Editor MELAKI TAEPE; circ. 250.

Te Lama: Ekalesia Kelisiano Tuvalu, POB 2, Valuku, Funafuti; tel. and fax 20755; e-mail gs_ekt@yahoo.com; quarterly; religious; Pres. Rev. TOFIGA FALANI; Editor Rev. KITIONA TAUSI; circ. 1,000.

Broadcasting and Communications

TELECOMMUNICATIONS

Tuvalu Telecommunications Corporation: Vaiaku, Funafuti; tel. 20001; fax 20800; e-mail media@tuvalu.tv; f. 1994.

BROADCASTING

Tuvalu Media Corporation: PMB, Vaiaku, Funafuti; tel. 20731; fax 20732; e-mail media@tuvalu.tv; internet www.tuvalu-news.tv/tmc; f. 1999; govt-owned; Chief Broadcasting and Information Officer PUSINELLI LAAFAI.

Radio

Radio Tuvalu: Broadcasting and Information Office, PMB, Vaiaku, Funafuti; tel. 20138; fax 20732; f. 1975; daily broadcasts in Tuvaluan and English, 43 hours per week; Programme Producer RUBY S. ALEFAIO.

Finance

BANKS

Development Bank of Tuvalu: PMB 9, Vaiaku, Funafuti; tel. 20199; fax 20850; f. 1993; replaced the Business Development Advisory Bureau.

National Bank of Tuvalu: POB 13, Vaiaku, Funafuti; tel. 20803; fax 20802; e-mail nbt@tuvalu.tv; f. 1980; commercial bank; govt-owned; ($A '000) cap. 471.0, res 2,964.3, dep. 16,585.1 (Dec. 2003); Chair. AUNESE SIMATI; Gen. Man. SIOSE P. TEO; brs on all atolls.

Trade and Industry

GOVERNMENT AGENCIES

National Fishing Corporation of Tuvalu (NAFICOT): POB 93, Funafuti; tel. 20724; fax 20152; fishing vessel operators; seafood processing and marketing; agents for diesel engine spare parts, fishing supplies and marine electronics; Gen. Man. SEMU SOPOANGA TAAFAKI.

Tuvalu Philatelic Bureau: POB 24, Funafuti; tel. 20224; fax 20712; e-mail philatelic@tuvalu.tv.

CHAMBER OF COMMERCE

Tuvalu Chamber of Commerce: POB 27, Vaiaku, Funafuti; tel. 20917; fax 20646; e-mail tpasefika@hotmail.com; Chair. MATANILE IOSEFA; Sec. TEO PASEFIKA.

UTILITIES

Electricity

Tuvalu Electricity Corporation (TEC): POB 32, Vaiaku, Funafuti; tel. 20352; fax 20351; e-mail thomas@tuvalu.tv; Gen. Man. MAFALU LOTOLUA.

CO-OPERATIVES

Tuvalu Co-operative Society Ltd: POB 11, Funafuti; tel. 20747; fax 20748; e-mail mlaafai@tuvalu.tv; f. 1979; by amalgamation of the eight island socs; controls retail trade in the islands; Gen. Man. MONISE LAAFAI; Registrar SIMETI LOPATI.

Tuvalu Coconut Traders Co-operative: Contact TAAI KATALAKE.

TRADE UNION

Tuvalu Overseas Seamen's Union (TOSU): POB 99, Funafuti; tel. 20609; fax 20610; e-mail tosu@tuvalu.tv; f. 1988; Gen. Sec. TOMMY ALEFAIO.

Transport

ROADS

Funafuti has some impacted-coral roads totalling some 8km in length; elsewhere, tracks exist.

SHIPPING

There is a deep-water lagoon at the point of entry, Funafuti, and ships are able to enter the lagoon at Nukufetau. Irregular shipping services connect Tuvalu with Fiji and elsewhere. The Government operates an inter-island vessel.

TUVALU

CIVIL AVIATION

In 1992 a new runway was constructed with aid from the European Union to replace the grass landing strip on Funafuti. Air Marshall Islands operates a three-weekly service between Funafuti, Nadi (Fiji) and Majuro (Marshall Islands). In June 1995 Tuvalu, Kiribati, the Marshall Islands and Nauru agreed to begin discussions on the establishment of a joint regional airline. The Government of Tuvalu purchased a substantial shareholding (estimated at some US $2m.) in Air Fiji in 2001.

Tourism

In 2004 there was one hotel, with 16 rooms, on Funafuti and three guest houses. Visitor arrivals were estimated to total 1,130 in 2007. The majority of visitors are from Fiji, Australia, Japan and New Zealand.

Tuvalu Tourism Office: Ministry of Finance, Economic Planning and Industries, PMB, Funafuti; tel. 20408; fax 20210; e-mail lleneuoti@yahoo.com; internet www.timelesstuvalu.com; Tourism Officer LONO LENEUOTI.

UGANDA

Introductory Survey

Location, Climate, Language, Religion, Flag, Capital

The Republic of Uganda is a land-locked equatorial country in East Africa, bordered by Sudan to the north, the Democratic Republic of the Congo to the west, Kenya to the east and Rwanda, Tanzania and Lake Victoria to the south. The climate is tropical, with temperatures, moderated by the altitude of the country, varying between 15°C and 30°C. The official language is English and there are many local languages, the most important of which is Luganda. About 75% of the population follow Christian beliefs, while some 15% are Muslims. The national flag (proportions 2 by 3) has six horizontal stripes: black, gold, red, black, gold and red. In the centre is a white disc containing a crested crane. The capital is Kampala.

Recent History

Formerly a British protectorate, Uganda became an independent member of the Commonwealth on 9 October 1962. The Government was led by Dr Milton Obote, leader of the Uganda People's Congress (UPC) from 1960 and Prime Minister from April 1962. At independence the country comprised four regions, including the kingdom of Buganda, which had federal status. Exactly one year after independence Uganda became a republic, with Mutesa II, Kabaka (King) of Buganda, as first President. In February 1966 Obote led a successful coup against the Kabaka, and in April he became executive President. In September 1967 a new Constitution was introduced, establishing a unitary republic, and Buganda was brought under the control of the central Government. In 1969 all opposition parties were banned.

Obote was overthrown in January 1971 by the army, led by Maj.-Gen. (later Field Marshal) Idi Amin Dada, who assumed full executive powers and suspended political activity. The National Assembly was dissolved in February, when Amin declared himself Head of State, took over legislative powers and suspended parts of the 1967 Constitution. In August 1972 Amin, proclaiming an 'economic war' to free Uganda from foreign domination, undertook a mass expulsion of non-citizen Asians (who comprised the majority of the resident Asian population), thereby incurring widespread international condemnation.

Amin's regime was characterized by the ruthless elimination of suspected opponents, mass flights of refugees to neighbouring countries and periodic purges of the army (which, in turn, perpetrated numerous atrocities). Relations within the East African Community (EAC), comprising Uganda, Kenya and Tanzania, deteriorated during the 1970s. In February 1976 Amin claimed that large areas of western Kenya were historically part of Uganda, and in November 1978 Uganda annexed the Kagera salient from Tanzania. In early 1979 an invasion force comprising Tanzanian troops and the Uganda National Liberation Army (UNLA) gained control of the southern region of Uganda. Amin's forces capitulated, and in April a Tanzanian assault force entered Kampala. The remaining pro-Amin troops were defeated in June. Amin fled initially to Libya and in 1980 took up permanent residence in Saudi Arabia. He remained in exile there until his death in August 2003.

A provisional Government, the National Executive Council (NEC), was established in April 1979 from the ranks of the Uganda National Liberation Front (UNLF, a coalition of 18 previously exiled groups), with Dr Yusuf Lule, a former vice-chancellor of Makerere University, as President. Lule was succeeded in June by Godfrey Binaisa (a former Attorney-General), who was, in turn, overthrown by the Military Commission of the UNLF in May 1980, after he had decided to allow only UNLF members to stand in parliamentary elections and attempted to reorganize the leadership of the UNLA. The elections, in December, were contested by four parties and won by the UPC, with Obote, who remained its leader, becoming President for the second time. The defeated parties complained of gross electoral malpractice by UPC supporters.

The Obote Government was subject to constant attack from guerrilla groups operating inside the country. Hundreds of Obote's opponents were detained, including Democratic Party (DP) members of the National Assembly. Following the withdrawal of Tanzanian troops in June 1981, there were reports from the West Nile Region of further atrocities by Ugandan soldiers. In January 1982 the Uganda Popular Front was formed to co-ordinate, from abroad, the activities of the main opposition groups in exile: the Uganda Freedom Movement (UFM), the Uganda National Rescue Front and the National Resistance Movement (NRM), led by Lule and his former Minister of Defence, Lt-Gen. Yoweri Museveni. The NRM had a military wing, the National Resistance Army (NRA), led by Museveni. Lule died in 1985, whereupon Museveni became sole leader of the NRM and NRA. From 1982 thousands of Ugandans were reported to have fled the country, to escape fighting between guerrilla forces and UNLA troops. In March 1983, during a campaign by the UNLA to repel an NRA offensive, attacks on refugee camps resulted in the deaths of hundreds of civilians and more than 100,000 people were displaced. The NRA denied involvement in the massacres.

In July 1985 Obote was overthrown in a military coup, led by Brig. (later Lt-Gen.) Basilio Okello. (Obote was subsequently granted political asylum by Zambia.) A Military Council, headed by Lt-Gen. (later Gen.) Tito Okello, the Commander-in-Chief of the army, was established to govern the country, pending elections to be held one year later. In subsequent months groups that had been in opposition to Obote, with the exception of the NRA and the NRM (see below), reached agreement with the new administration and accepted positions on the Military Council. An amnesty was declared for exiles who had supported Amin.

In August 1985 the NRA, led by Museveni, entered into negotiations with the Government (under the auspices of President Daniel arap Moi of Kenya), while conducting a simultaneous military campaign to overthrow Okello. During the following two months the NRA gained control of large areas of the country and in January 1986 the NRA took control of Kampala by force and dissolved the Military Council. Okello fled to Sudan, and then to Tanzania. On 29 January Museveni was sworn in as President, and in February he announced the formation of a new Cabinet, comprising mainly members of the NRA and NRM, but also representatives of other political groups including the DP, the UPC, the UFM, the Federal Democratic Movement (FEDEMO), and three members of the previous administration. A National Resistance Council (NRC) was formed to act in place of a legislature for an indefinite period. All party political activity was banned in March, although political organizations were not proscribed. At a summit meeting in March the Heads of State of all the countries adjoining Uganda pledged their support for Museveni.

Initial attempts to integrate defeated rebel forces into the NRA were only partially successful, and guerrilla groups remained active in northern Uganda. An association of opposition groups, the Uganda People's Democratic Movement (UPDM), was formed in May 1986.

In June 1987 the NRC offered an amnesty to rebels (except those accused of murder or rape). In August, however, the UPDM joined with a faction of the FEDEMO and another opposition group, the United National Front, to form an alliance seeking Museveni's overthrow. The most widespread source of disruption during 1987 was a rebellion that had arisen in northern and eastern Uganda in late 1986 by the cultish 'Holy Spirit' movement; between December 1986 and November 1987 some 5,000 ill-equipped 'Holy Spirit' fighters were reportedly killed in clashes with the NRA. By December 1987 the rebellion had been suppressed and its leader had escaped to Kenya. Surviving members of the movement, however, regrouped as the Lord's Resistance Army (LRA—see below). In early 1988 the NRC extended the period of its amnesty to guerrilla groups: by mid-April it was reported that almost 30,000 rebels had surrendered. Many of these were integrated into the NRA.

In February 1989 the first national election since 1980 was held. The NRC, hitherto composed solely of presidential nominees, was expanded from 98 to 278 members, to include 210 elected representatives. While 20 ministerial posts were reserved for nominated members of the NRC, 50 were allocated to elected members. Also in February Museveni appointed a constitutional commission to assess public opinion on Uganda's political future and to draft a new constitution.

In October 1989 (despite opposition from the DP) the NRC approved draft legislation to prolong the Government's term of office by five years from January 1990 (when its mandate had been due to expire): the NRM justified seeking to extend its rule by claiming that it required further time in which to prepare a new constitution, organize elections, eliminate guerrilla activity, improve the judiciary, police force and civil service and rehabilitate the country's infrastructure. In March 1990 the NRM extended the national ban on party political activity (imposed in March 1986) for a further five years. In July the leader of the UPDM, Eric Otema Allimadi, signed a peace accord with the Government. During April 1991 the NRA initiated a campaign to combat continuing rebel activity in the north and east: by July it was reported that at least 1,500 guerrillas had been killed and more than 1,000 arrested. In May Museveni formally invited all former resident Asians expelled at the time of the Amin regime to return, pledging the restitution of expropriated property.

In December 1992 the Constitutional Commission presented its draft Constitution to the Government. The draft was published in March 1993, and in the following month the NRC passed legislation authorizing the establishment of a Constituent Assembly (see below). In July the NRC adopted a constitutional amendment revoking the abolition of traditional rulers, as provided for under the 1967 Constitution. Restored traditional rulers would, however, have only ceremonial significance.

In January 1994 the Ugandan National Democratic Alliance and the Ugandan Federal Army agreed to suspend their armed struggle, under the provisions of a government amnesty, and in March the surrender of senior members of the Ruwenzururu Kingdom Freedom Movement in the south-west signified the end of a conflict dating from independence. During January the Government took part in negotiations with the LRA. However, following the collapse of the discussions, the LRA intensified guerrilla activities in northern Uganda. From 1994 large numbers of security forces were deployed in the region, representing a considerable burden on national resources; they failed, however, to suppress the rebellion (see below).

At elections to the 288-member Constituent Assembly, which took place on 28 March 1994, more than 1,500 candidates contested the 214 elective seats. Although the elections were officially conducted on a non-party basis, NRM members were believed to have secured the majority of votes in the centre, west and south-west of the country, whereas UPC and DP members, who advocated an immediate return to multi-party politics, secured the most seats in the north and east. The Constituent Assembly, which also comprised nominated representatives of the armed forces, political parties, trade unions, and youth and disabled organizations, debated and amended the draft Constitution, finally enacting it in September 1995. The Constitution, under whose terms a national referendum on the future introduction of a multi-party political system took place in 2000 (see below), was promulgated in October 1995.

A presidential election took place in May 1996, at which Museveni was returned to office, winning 74.2% of the votes cast. The election was pronounced free and fair by international observers. Museveni's main rival, Paul Ssemogerere (the Chairman of the DP), took 23.7% of the votes. As the unofficial representative of an electoral alliance between the DP and the UPC, Ssemogerere was widely perceived to be associated with the UPC's exiled leader, Obote. Legislative elections took place in June 1996. The total membership of the NRC, redesignated the Parliament under the new Constitution, was reduced from 278 to 276, comprising 214 elected and 62 nominated representatives. Also in June elections were held for new local councils (to replace the resistance committees). In July Museveni appointed an enlarged Government.

During 1993–98 the LRA was alleged to have killed as many as 10,000 people, while some 220,000 sought refuge in protected camps; economic activity in the region was devastated. The LRA's use of abducted children as soldiers (reportedly some 10,000 by early 1999) attracted widespread international condemnation. The Government strongly resisted pressure to resume negotiations with the LRA, prompting some speculation that Museveni (a southerner) might be prepared to profit from the disablement of opposition strongholds in the northern region. In May 1999, however, the Government appeared to modify its policy towards the LRA by offering it an amnesty and promising its leader, Joseph Kony, a cabinet post in the event of his being democratically elected. In the west, meanwhile, the Uganda People's Defence Forces (UPDF, as the NRA had been restyled) fought intermittently with two rebel groups: the Allied Democratic Front (ADF), mainly comprising Ugandan Islamic fundamentalist rebels, exiled Rwandan Hutu militiamen and former soldiers from Zaire (which became the Democratic Republic of the Congo—DRC—in May 1997), and the West Nile Bank Front (WNBF). Although WNBF activities subsided in mid-1997, following the killing of several hundred of its members by Sudanese rebels, the ADF mounted a persistent terror campaign from mid-1997 against western Ugandan targets, threatening tourism to the region and disrupting economic activity. In August 1999, confronted by escalating security problems on various fronts, the Government was reported to have recalled for military service some 10,000 demobilized troops, and in September the command structure of the UPDF was reorganized. In November the UPDF launched a new offensive against the ADF in the Ruwenzori region. In December the Parliament adopted legislation that extended (not without conditions, in some cases) an amnesty to all rebels in opposition to President Museveni. The ADF's response was apparently to intensify its struggle. In February 2000 President Museveni was reported to be personally co-ordinating military operations against the ADF in western Uganda, and to have renewed his appeal to the rebels to avail themselves of the new amnesty legislation.

In July 1999 legislation was enacted providing for the proposed referendum on a multi-party political system to take place in 2000 as planned. However, most political parties announced that they would boycott the referendum on the grounds that it would be manipulated by the NRM for its own objectives. In October a US-based human rights organization, Human Rights Watch, criticized Uganda's political system and claimed that the country was moving away from democracy. Ugandan political leaders had criticized the readiness of some Western donors (in particular those that formed the Referendum 2000 Group in December 1999) to support the referendum process, claiming that by so doing they were legitimizing the prevailing suspension of active political opposition. In February 2000 Uganda's Multi-Party National Referendum Committee appealed for a postponement of the referendum on the grounds that the Electoral Commission had not made funds available to some advocates of a return to political pluralism. In the same month the Referendum 2000 Group expressed concern at the Government's failure to implement measures on which it had made conditional its support of the referendum process. At the referendum, which proceeded on 29 June, 90.7% of participants voted in favour of retaining the existing 'no-party' political system. However, the result was effectively nullified by the Constitutional Court in 2004 (see below).

A presidential election was held on 12 March 2001. The election had been scheduled for 7 March, but was delayed to allow the Electoral Commission time to check and amend the electoral register after it was found to contain about 2.5m. more voters than there were citizens eligible to vote. At the election, which had a participation rate of 70%, Museveni was re-elected President, winning 69.3% of the votes cast. His main challenger, Kizza Besigye, won 27.8%.

Legislative elections were held on 26 June 2001, at which 50 parliamentarians, including 10 ministers, failed to secure re-election. The rate of voter participation was reported as being low. The total number of seats in Parliament was increased to 292 (comprising 214 elected and 78 nominated representatives), of which the NRM reportedly secured more than 70%. In July Museveni appointed a new Cabinet, which included the 10 ministers who had failed to retain their parliamentary seats in June. Notably, Amama Mbabazi was appointed as Minister of Defence, a portfolio hitherto held by Museveni.

In May 2002 Parliament approved the Political Parties and Organizations Act 2002, which severely curtailed the activities of political parties, while classifying the NRM as a 'political system' rather than a party. The Act also provided for the dissolution of all parties not registered by 17 January 2003. However, in March 2003 opposition leaders successfully challenged two clauses of the Act in the Constitutional Court, which ruled that the NRM was not a system, but a political party, and suspended the section of the Act that required parties to register, pending the outcome of a further petition against the Act. (The Attorney-General later clarified that parties would still be obliged to register, but not by a particular time.) The ruling allowed political parties to operate nationally for the first time in 17 years. The NRM became the first party to apply for registration, in June 2003, under the modified name of the National Resistance Movement Organisation (NRM-O). Meanwhile, in late May Museveni effected a cabinet reorganization, notably appointing Prof. Gilbert Bukenya as Vice-President, following the resignation of the incumbent, Dr Speciosa Kazibwe, and dismissing a number of ministers who had recently expressed opposition to a proposal to revoke the current two-term limit on the presidential mandate. This proposal was endorsed by the Cabinet in August. By April 2004 some 60 new political parties had emerged, although only 13 had applied for registration. Also in April Museveni was promoted to the rank of General, before formally retiring from the military in order to comply with legislation barring serving members of the armed forces from active membership of a political party. Museveni retained his position as Commander-in-Chief of the armed forces.

In June 2004 the Constitutional Court issued a ruling that annulled the Referendum (Political System) Act of 2000 and effectively nullified the June 2000 referendum at which a return to a multi-party system had been rejected. Thus, legislative elections, scheduled to be held concurrently with the presidential election in 2006, would be held under the new system—subject to approval at a referendum, which was to be held in July 2005 (see below). The referendum appeared to be unnecessary, however, as in November 2004 the Constitutional Court repealed legislation preventing political parties from contesting elections. The Court also rejected an appeal from opposition parties against mandatory registration and ruled that parties would have six months to register prior to the 2006 elections.

Meanwhile, it was reported in August 2004 that a new opposition party, the Forum for Democratic Change (FDC), had been formed by a merger of Reform Agenda, the Parliamentary Advocacy Forum and the National Democratic Forum. Several parliamentarians affiliated to the UPC had apparently joined the new party.

In February 2005 the Constitution (Amendment) Bill, which provided for a return to multi-party democracy, was presented to the Parliament. The Bill also contained a provision for the removal of the two-term limit on the presidency. Throughout 2004 Museveni had engaged in what amounted to a tacit campaign for re-election: he abolished an unpopular local tax on 'boda bodas' (motorcycle taxis) in Kampala and offered deputies who openly supported his re-election funds to be used ostensibly to enable them to consult with their constituents on the Constitution (Amendment) Bill. Furthermore, in mid-January 2005 Museveni effected a cabinet reshuffle, in which several ministers who had advocated a third presidential term were promoted. Parliament approved the removal of the two-term limit on the presidency in June, and voted in favour of the holding of a national referendum on the restoration of multi-party democracy. At the referendum, which took place on 28 July, 92.5% of participants approved the motion. The rate of voter participation was low, however, at just 47%. The opposition had called for a boycott of the referendum.

In October 2005 Besigye returned from four years of self-imposed exile in South Africa in order to contest the presidential election as the FDC's candidate. (He had left Uganda following the presidential elections of 2001 claiming to fear for his safety.) Besigye was arrested in November 2005 and charged with rape and treason. The FDC claimed the charges against Besigye were politically motivated and designed to prevent him from contesting the election. Large numbers of his supporters gathered to demonstrate outside the police station where he was being detained and two days of violence ensued, with the security forces resorting to the use of tear gas in order to disperse the crowds. Later that month 14 people who, with Besigye, were also being tried for treason were granted bail by the High Court. However, a group of armed men, not in regular army uniform, arrived and waited for them outside court and the 14 opted to remain in custody. The following week Besigye and a number of others appeared before a military tribunal and were charged with terrorism and illegally possessing weapons. Besigye's lawyers contested the tribunal's jurisdiction and refused to enter a plea. His trial by court martial was to begin following the conclusion of his civil trial. In December Besigye pleaded not guilty to the treason charge at the High Court; his trial was postponed until early January, raising fears that it might not conclude in time for the election. The High Court ruled that the military should suspend its trial until the Constitutional Court had examined its legality; however, the military stated its intention to proceed, noting that it was not subordinate to the High Court. (Although the High Court had granted Besigye bail, he remained in military custody.) In January 2006 the High Court ruled that the military tribunal's authority to detain Besigye had expired and ordered his release. The Constitutional Court judged that the military did not have the jurisdiction to try Besigye, and that the charges related to terrorism and the illegal possession of weapons could only be heard by the High Court. It also ruled that the deployment of troops to the High Court in November was unconstitutional. In February a High Court jury found Besigye not guilty of rape. Under Ugandan law a jury can advise a judge but its decision is not binding. The High Court adjourned Besigye's trial until after the election.

Meanwhile, in April 2005 it was reported that former President Obote was considering a return from exile in Zambia. However, the Ugandan Government stated that it had yet to receive a formal request from Obote for permission to re-enter Uganda, and that until it did so it would not declare its position on the issue. Obote died in October, still in exile. His body was returned to Uganda where he was accorded a state funeral. In mid-November President Museveni confirmed his intention to stand for a third term in office. He was subsequently elected unopposed as the NRM-O candidate.

At the presidential election, held on 23 February 2006, Museveni won 59.3% of the valid votes cast and was elected for a third term. Besigye was the only other candidate to mount a credible challenge, receiving 37.4% of the votes. While international observers did not condemn the process outright, they reported a number of serious flaws and concluded that a law passed in 1997 that effectively granted the NRM-O access to public funds for campaigning did not provide a fair basis for multi-party elections. (Parliamentary elections were held concurrently with the presidential election; according to preliminary results, the NRM-O secured 191 seats in the 319-member Parliament, while the FDC took 37 seats.)

In March 2006 Besigye was acquitted of rape. The military conceded that Besigye would not have to face a court martial while on trial for treason, but did not drop the charges against him and appealed against the ruling that the terrorism and weapons charges must be heard in the High Court. In April Besigye challenged the results of the presidential election in the Supreme Court. The Court unanimously decided that the Electoral Commission had not conducted the election in compliance with the Constitution and other relevant legislation. However, it further ruled (by four votes to three) that this had not substantially affected the final outcome of the election. Besigye's trial for treason commenced in April; he and his 22 co-defendants denied the charges. In late May Museveni unveiled his new Cabinet. Most notably, Gen. Ali Moses was replaced as First Deputy Prime Minister by Eriya Kategaya.

In March 2007 security agents raided the High Court and arrested six supporters of Besigye who had been granted bail. One lawyer was beaten unconscious during the heavily armed raid. In response, the judiciary commenced industrial action and only agreed to return to work after Museveni expressed regret for the incident one week later. Violence erupted on the streets of Kampala in April after protests against plans to allocate one-third of the Mabira forest to an Asian-owned sugar company turned hostile, forcing police to protect Asian businesses and a Hindu temple. An Asian man and two other people were killed. In October Besigye announced that he was to relinquish the presidency of the FDC in 2010, allowing sufficient time for a new leader to be selected ahead of the presidential elections scheduled for 2011.

During 1987 Uganda's relations with neighbouring Kenya deteriorated, with the Museveni Government accusing the regime of President Moi of sheltering and supporting Ugandan rebels. When, in October, Uganda stationed troops at the two countries' common border, Kenya threatened to retaliate with force against any attempts by Ugandan military personnel to cross the frontier in pursuit of rebels. In December there were clashes between Kenyan and Ugandan security forces and the border was temporarily closed. In late December, following the intervention of the Organization of African Unity (now the African Union—AU, see p. 164), discussions between the Heads of State of the two countries led to a resumption of normal traffic across the border. However, several incursions into Kenya by Ugandan troops were subsequently reported. In November 1994 the Presidents of Uganda, Kenya and Tanzania met in Arusha, Tanzania, and established a permanent commission for co-operation between the three countries. In March 1996 Museveni, Moi and President Benjamin Mkapa of Tanzania, meeting in Nairobi, Kenya, formally inaugurated the Secretariat of the Permanent Tripartite Commission for East African Co-operation, which aimed to revive the EAC (see p. 412). A treaty for the re-establishment of the EAC, providing for the creation of a free trade area (with the eventual introduction of a single currency), for the development of infrastructure, tourism and agriculture within the Community and for the establishment of a regional legislature and court was ratified by the three Heads of State in November 1999. Museveni, Mkapa and President Mwai Kibaki of Kenya signed a protocol in March 2004 on the creation of a customs union, whereby most duties on goods within the EAC would be eliminated. The customs union was established on 1 January 2005.

During 1988 tension arose along Uganda's border with Zaire (now the DRC—see above), owing to a number of attacks by Zairean troops on NRA units; further border clashes occurred in 1992. In November 1996 Ugandan rebels were reportedly operating from within Zaire with the support of Zairean troops. In late 1996 and early 1997 the Ugandan authorities repeatedly denied allegations that Ugandan forces were occupying territory in eastern Zaire; however, it was widely reported that the Museveni Government supplied armaments and tactical support to Laurent-Désiré Kabila's Alliance des forces démocratiques pour la libération du Congo-Zaïre, which took power in Zaire in May 1997. The Museveni administration, however, subsequently withdrew its support from the new regime in the DRC, as President Kabila made no attempt to sever the ongoing supply of armaments to Ugandan guerrilla groups operating in the DRC–Uganda border region. In August 1998 the Museveni administration, in co-operation with the Rwandan Government, formed a joint military command in November 1998. The Kabila regime accused Uganda and Rwanda of creating, with DRC rebels, a Tutsi-dominated alliance with expansionist ambitions; it was also alleged that the DRC's two eastern neighbours were illegally exploiting mineral interests in the area occupied by their forces. In July 1999 a comprehensive cease-fire agreement was concluded in Lusaka, Zambia, by the Heads of State of all the countries engaged militarily in the civil war in the DRC, including those of Angola, Namibia and Zimbabwe, who had supported the DRC Government. The cease-fire was to be monitored by a joint military commission, while a UN peace-keeping force was to be deployed on the withdrawal from the DRC of all foreign troops. However, the implementation of the Lusaka accord did not proceed smoothly. In mid-August tensions escalated into hostilities between Ugandan and Rwandan armed forces around the city of Kisangani, in the DRC. In May 2000 the DRC Government signed an agreement in which it consented to the deployment of 500 UN military observers and 5,000 support troops, the UN Mission in the Democratic Republic of the Congo (MONUC, see p. 85), to monitor the frequently violated cease-fire that had been inaugurated by the Lusaka accord. Almost immediately afterwards, however, hostilities erupted again between Ugandan and Rwandan troops in Kisangani. In mid-May Uganda and Rwanda withdrew their troops in Kisangani to prepare the way for its eventual cession to the control of MONUC. In December all parties in the conflict signed an agreement under which all forces would withdraw 15 km from positions of military engagement by January 2001, to allow UN peace-keepers to ensure the observance of the cease-fire. In January 2001 President Kabila was assassinated by one of his bodyguards; he was succeeded by his son, Joseph Kabila, who immediately engaged in international efforts to end the conflict. In mid-March the groups involved in the conflict, under the aegis of the UN Security Council, commenced the military disengagement of their forces. However, factions subsequently refused to proceed with the withdrawal from military positions until MONUC guaranteed security in the region. Following the publication of a UN report, in April, alleging that Burundi, Rwanda and Uganda were illegally exploiting the DRC's mineral reserves, Museveni announced that Uganda would withdraw its remaining troops from the DRC and pull out of the UN-sponsored Lusaka accord. In late 2001 Rwandan troops occupied positions in the eastern DRC that had been vacated by the UPDF in June of that year, prompting fears that clashes would again erupt between Rwandan and Ugandan forces. Despite the redeployment of Ugandan troops in the north-east of the DRC in January 2002, to prevent escalating fighting between the rebel factions from reaching the border with Uganda, negotiations between Uganda and Rwanda continued, with British mediation, and in April the two countries signed a peace agreement in Kigali. In September a peace accord was signed by Uganda and the DRC in Luanda, Angola, providing for the normalization of relations between the two countries and the complete withdrawal of Ugandan troops from the DRC. Uganda subsequently began the withdrawal of its troops, although the UN permitted some of them to remain near the north-eastern town of Bunia to assist with maintaining security. In March 2003 the Governments of Uganda and the DRC and local rebel groups signed a cease-fire agreement, although later that month the Rwandan Government threatened to resume military engagement in eastern DRC if the UN failed to secure the withdrawal of all Ugandan troops. In response to the continuing violence around Bunia, which was in contravention of the peace agreement, the UN Security Council issued a resolution calling for increased numbers of military and humanitarian observers to be stationed in the DRC under the MONUC mandate, and the immediate withdrawal of Ugandan troops. The Ugandan Government subsequently pledged to withdraw forces from the DRC, and all remaining Ugandan troops left the north-east of the country in May. In April 2005 the International Criminal Court (ICC, see p. 314), based in The Hague, Netherlands, began proceedings against Uganda following accusations by the DRC Government that Ugandan troops had violated human rights and massacred Congolese civilians while deployed in the country. The DRC also demanded reparations for destruction and looting allegedly carried out by the UPDF. The Ugandan Government denied the claims. In early September 2007 Uganda and the DRC agreed to the establishment of a joint force, supported by MONUC and tasked with removing LRA fighters from the DRC by December. However, later in September an incident was reported in which Ugandan troops were alleged to have opened fire on a passenger boat from the DRC, killing several people. A number of LRA soldiers were captured in October and a senior LRA official surrendered to UN peace-keepers. Four other high-ranking LRA members had previously been indicted by the ICC for crimes against humanity.

From the late 1980s Sudanese troops reportedly made repeated incursions into Ugandan territory in pursuit of Sudanese rebels. Relations between the two countries deteriorated seriously in 1994, when each Government accused the other of harbouring and supporting their respective outlawed guerrilla groups; in April 1995 Uganda severed diplomatic relations with Sudan. Relations between the two countries remained strained: in September 1996 and in February 1997 it was alleged that Sudanese aircraft had attacked northern Uganda, and in April, despite a continuing dialogue mediated by Iran and Libya, the Sudanese authorities claimed that their forces had killed several hundred Ugandan soldiers who had been assisting Sudanese rebels from within Sudanese territory. In February 1998 Uganda deployed troops along the Uganda–Sudan border, with the aim of preventing LRA rebels from taking captives over the frontier into Sudan. In December, in Kenya, the Presidents of Uganda and Sudan unexpectedly signed an accord that set out a comprehensive resolution of the two countries' differences. The Nairobi Agreement committed Uganda and Sudan to the renunciation of force as a means of settling disputes; to the disarmament and disbandment of terrorist groups and the cessation of support for rebel groups; to the repatriation of prisoners of war; and to the restoration of full diplomatic relations by the end of February 2000. Joint committees were to be established to oversee the implementation of the Agreement from January 2000. In September Uganda and Sudan agreed to disarm the LRA, which had been active throughout 2000, and to relocate it at least 1,000 km deeper within Sudanese territory. It was also agreed that the Governments of Uganda, Sudan, Libya and Egypt, in collaboration with the Carter Center, Canada, the UN Children's Fund and the office of the UN High Commissioner for Refugees (UNHCR), would set up a body to find and repatriate all children abducted from Sudan by rebel groups. Rebel attacks continued in northern Uganda, however, and in January 2001 President Museveni threatened to send troops to pursue rebel groups into Sudanese territory. Following a Libyan diplomatic initiative in that month, Sudan and Uganda agreed to restore diplomatic relations. In August the Ugandan embassy reopened in the Sudanese capital, Khartoum, and a chargé d'affaires was appointed; relations were upgraded to an ambassadorial level in April 2002. In August 2001 the Sudanese President, Lt-Gen. Omar Hassan Ahmad al-Bashir, announced that his Government would no longer provide support for the LRA, and in December bank accounts used by the LRA in London, United Kingdom, were frozen. Negotiations between Sudan and Uganda continued successfully throughout early 2002, with both countries remaining committed to implementing the Nairobi Agreement. In March it was announced that Sudan was to allow the

UPDF to deploy forces within its borders in order to pursue operations against the LRA, and later that month the Ugandan Government announced that its troops had captured all four main bases in Sudan belonging to the LRA. In November the Sudanese authorities agreed to extend permission for Ugandan troops to remain on its territory for as long as Uganda deemed necessary.

In early 2003 Museveni agreed to a cease-fire and appointed a delegation to commence peace negotiations with the LRA, but these soon collapsed. The Government ordered 800,000 people in northern Uganda to enter refugee camps for their protection; however, the LRA continued to attack the camps. In October LRA attacks, which had begun to spread further south and east, intensified, and a counter-offensive by the UPDF in December had little success. Nevertheless, Museveni claimed in January 2004 that the LRA had been 'defeated decisively' and that his forces were on the verge of killing its leader, Kony. Also in January the ICC announced that it was to initiate plans for an investigation into the activities of the LRA, referred for consideration by the Court in the previous month by Museveni. In late February, in one of the worst attacks in recent years, the LRA massacred more than 200 civilians sheltering in a refugee camp near Lira, in northern Uganda. In the following weeks the UPDF launched assaults on two LRA groups in two villages near the camp, killing 16 rebels in one attack and five in the other. Thousands demonstrated in Lira against the Government's failure to protect civilians, and the protests rapidly became violent. The UPDF commenced a new offensive in southern Sudan, and in March killed more than 50 rebels entering Uganda from Sudan. Despite the UPDF's continued claims of imminent victory, the LRA attacks continued unabated. The Government introduced legislation in mid-2004 that allowed the prosecution by the ICC of Ugandans suspected of war crimes. In June it was reported that at least 12 high-ranking LRA commanders had taken advantage of an amnesty offered by the Government and surrendered; among them was Kony's personal secretary. In July the ICC investigation into the activities of the LRA began; in April 2005 it was reported that the ICC was to establish a field office in Kampala in order to expedite its investigation.

Meanwhile, in November 2004 an LRA spokesman stated that the group no longer believed a military end to the conflict was possible, and that the LRA was thus willing to negotiate towards a peace accord. A cease-fire was agreed, although fighting continued outside the cease-fire zone. Delegations representing the Government and the LRA met in December in Kitgum, in northern Uganda, and Museveni subsequently extended the cease-fire until the end of December. Although there were indications at the end of December that the Government and LRA were close to agreeing a permanent truce, the LRA postponed the signing of a memorandum of understanding in order to continue internal consultations. Shortly afterwards a UPDF force was ambushed, for which Museveni blamed the LRA. The Government refused to extend the cease-fire, and UPDF troops re-occupied the cease-fire zone in order to prevent attacks on civilians. A cease-fire was agreed in February 2005, during which an amnesty was offered to LRA fighters who wished to surrender. Later that month Brig. Sam Kolo, the LRA's chief negotiator in the recent peace talks, escaped an attack by LRA combatants with the help of the UPDF, to whom he surrendered. The UPDF stated that Kolo's life was in danger following a dispute with the LRA's deputy leader, Vincent Otti. The Government's chief negotiator confirmed that Otti would take Kolo's place in any future negotiations. However, many observers regarded Kolo as one of the LRA's most rational commanders, and attributed to him the success of recent negotiations. In March, following a government request, the ICC agreed to delay issuing arrest warrants for LRA commanders after concerns were raised that they would be reluctant to negotiate if they feared arrest once peace had been established. The cease-fire agreed in February lapsed in March and fighting resumed. The UPDF began an offensive against LRA bases, while the LRA, in turn, attacked villages and resumed its abduction of children.

In September 2005 two groups of LRA fighters, one led by Otti, entered the DRC from southern Sudan. Representatives of the UN met for first time with the LRA and urged the group to disarm. The meeting was also attended by senior members of DRC military. In October the ICC issued arrest warrants for Kony, Otti and three other LRA commanders. Kony was indicted on 12 counts of crimes against humanity, including sexual enslavement, and 21 counts of war crimes. The UPDF claimed to have recently killed one of the five indicted LRA commanders. Shortly after the warrants were issued the LRA altered its tactics and began to attack humanitarian workers. In November it killed two UN mine clearance experts in southern Sudan. Later that month Otti offered to enter into peace negotiations, stating he was willing to be tried by the ICC, but added that the UPDF had also committed crimes during the conflict for which the Government should be tried. In April 2006 it was announced that refugee camps in the Lango and Teso sub-regions were to close (but not those in the Acholi sub-region). Also in that month the Ugandan Parliament approved legislation that enabled the Government to exclude Kony and others from the amnesty offered to the LRA.

In July 2006 peace talks between the LRA and the Government commenced in Juba, southern Sudan. On 26 August both sides agreed on a truce and a cease-fire came into force on 29 August. By September UNHCR estimated that more than 300,000 people had left displacement camps in recent months. However, it emerged in October that both the Ugandan army and the LRA had violated the terms of their truce, according to a report by a peace process monitoring team. The LRA rebels had pledged to assemble at two neutral points in southern Sudan by mid-September in return for an amnesty. In December President Museveni held direct talks with a member of the LRA for the first time when he spoke by satellite telephone with Otti. A cessation of hostilities agreement, signed by both sides, was also extended in the same month for a second time, until 28 February 2007. However, the LRA withdrew from the talks in January, citing security fears after al-Bashir apparently indicated that he sought to eradicate the LRA from Sudan. The issues of reconciliation and accountability also remained contentious. It was believed that the LRA would not sign a peace deal while warrants for the arrest of Kony and his commanders remained in place. Following a meeting between the UN Special Envoy for areas affected by the LRA, the former President of Mozambique, Joaquim Chissano, and Kony in mid-March, the LRA agreed to resume negotiations on condition that other African mediators join the talks along with Sudan. In mid-April the LRA signed a new cease-fire with the Government. Under the new agreement the LRA was granted six weeks in which to assemble its fighters at Ri-Kwangba near the border with the DRC. Peace talks resumed in Juba at the end of May. In November Kony appointed Okot Odhiambo as deputy leader of the LRA amid unconfirmed reports that Otti had been executed alongside his family and several commanders who remained loyal to him. Sources within the LRA insisted that Otti was still alive and that rumours of Otti's death were unfounded. Observers raised concerns that the LRA was taking a more radical stance, which could threaten the success of the peace talks. In January 2008 Otti's death was confirmed, although it remained unclear whether he had been killed or had died from natural causes. A new cease-fire was agreed between the Government and the LRA in late January 2008, ahead of peace talks which were to resume at the end of the month. Violence had largely subsided during the latest round of peace negotiations and refugees had begun to return home. Negotiations were ongoing in March to determine a timescale for demobilization, however, mediators were confident that they were close to agreeing a final peace deal to end the conflict.

During the late 1980s an estimated 250,000 Rwandan refugees were sheltering in Uganda. Relations with Rwanda deteriorated in October 1990, following the infiltration of northern Rwanda by an invasion force of some 4,000 Rwandan rebels who had been based in Uganda. In February 1991 a conference was held on the Rwandan security situation; an amnesty was agreed for all Rwandans who were exiled abroad, and the rebels were urged to observe a cease-fire. Nevertheless, the allegedly Uganda-based Rwandan rebels continued to operate in northern Rwanda during 1991–93. The victory in Rwanda of the Front patriotique rwandais (FPR) in mid-1994 brought about a significant change in bilateral relations; Maj.-Gen. Paul Kagame, Rwandan Vice-President and Minister of National Defence, had previously served in the Ugandan NRA, as had other members of the FPR administration. In August 1995 Museveni made an official visit to Rwanda, and both countries made commitments to enhance economic and social co-operation. In August 1998 Uganda and Rwanda jointly deployed troops in the DRC (see above). Relations between the two countries worsened again during their involvement in the hostilities in the DRC; there were frequent reports of fighting, especially around the town of Kisangani. However, this tension eased when both armies withdrew from Kisangani during May 2000 (see above), and in July Museveni and Kagame met to discuss relations between their respective countries. In January 2001 at least 15,000 Rwandan refugees, most of them Hutu, entered Uganda following an order in Tanzania to expel all non-citizens. A further 7,000 Rwandan refugees had entered Uganda through Tanzania by July. In July 2003 the Rwandan Government signed a tripartite agreement with the Ugandan authorities and UNHCR, providing for the voluntary repatriation of some 26,000 Rwandans resident in refugee camps in western Uganda. In February 2004 an improvement in diplomatic relations between Rwanda and Uganda (following progress in the situation in the DRC) was demonstrated by a bilateral agreement to strengthen co-operation in several fields.

At the end of 2006, according to UNHCR, the number of refugees in Uganda totalled 222,330, including 171,565 from Sudan, 28,766 from the DRC and 17,000 from Rwanda.

Following a two-day summit in Nairobi in December 2006, the Presidents of Burundi, the DRC, Kenya, Zambia, Tanzania and Uganda signed a regional security, stability and development treaty. Provisions included a development plan, estimated to cost in excess of US $2,000m. to be funded from contributions by member states and donors in conjunction with the African Development Bank. Measures to disarm remaining rebel groups, prevent arms trafficking and assist refugees were also included.

In March 2007 1,700 Ugandan peace-keepers were deployed in Somalia as part of the AU Mission in Somalia to assist with the stabilization of that country.

Government

Following the January 1986 coup, power was vested in a broad-based interim Government, headed by an executive President. A National Resistance Council (NRC) was formed to legislate by decree. In addition, resistance committees were formed at local and district level. Political activity was suspended, although political parties were not banned. National elections were held in February 1989. Representatives were elected directly to local-level resistance committees; these elected representatives to district-level resistance committees, and these, in turn, elected representatives to the NRC. The NRC was expanded from 98 members, all nominated by the President, to 278 members, of whom 68 were nominated by the President and 210 were elected. In October 1989 the NRC approved legislation prolonging the Government's term of office by five years from January 1990, when its mandate had been due to expire. A new Constitution was enacted by an elected Constituent Assembly in September 1995 and came into force in the following month. The first direct presidential election was held in May 1996, and national legislative elections took place in the following month to a 276-member Parliament, as the NRC became—comprising 214 directly elected and 62 nominated members. Voting also took place in June for local councils (which replaced the resistance committees). Further local elections were held in November 1997 and January 2002. Under the terms of the new Constitution, a national referendum on the future introduction of a multi-party political system took place in June 2000, at which voters overwhelmingly endorsed the retention of the existing 'no-party' system (this was nullified by the Constitutional Court in 2004—see Recent History). Legislation to amend the Constitution in order to allow multi-party politics, and to remove the two-term limit on the presidency, was approved by the Parliament in early 2005 and by 92.5% of voters at a referendum held on 28 July 2005. Following legislative elections in June 2006, the number of seats in Parliament stood at 319, comprising 215 directly elected representatives and 104 nominated members, including 69 women.

Defence

As assessed at November 2007, the Uganda People's Defence Forces was estimated to number 45,000 men, including paramilitary forces (a border defence unit of about 600 men, a police air wing of about 800 men, about 400 marines and local defence units of about 3,000 men, with a further 7,000 reportedly under training). Defence was allocated an estimated 396,000m. shillings by the central Government in 2007. The Lord's Resistance Army (LRA) was thought to have about 1,500 members, with about 600 in Uganda and the remainder in Sudan. The Allied Democratic Front was believed to comprise some 200 men. The West Nile Bank Front was thought to number 1,000, but had not launched any attacks in the previous 12 months and was therefore considered dormant.

Economic Affairs

In 2006, according to estimates by the World Bank, Uganda's gross national income (GNI), measured at average 2004–06 prices, was US $8,917m., equivalent to $300 per head (or $1,490 per head on an international purchasing-power parity basis). During 1996–2006, it was estimated, the population increased at an average annual rate of 3.3%, while gross domestic product (GDP) per head increased, in real terms, by an average of 2.3% per year. Overall GDP increased, in real terms, at an average annual rate of 5.7% in 1996–2006; growth was 5.3% in 2006.

Agriculture (including hunting, forestry and fishing) contributed 20.8% of GDP in 2006 and engaged 68.7% of the employed labour force in 2003. The principal cash crops are coffee, tobacco, tea and cotton. Maize, sugar cane and cocoa are also cultivated, and the production of cut flowers is an important activity. Together, coffee, tea, cocoa and spices provided 27.5% of export earnings in 2005. The main subsistence crops are plantains, cassava, sweet potatoes, maize, millet, sorghum, beans, groundnuts and rice. In addition, livestock (chiefly cattle, goats, sheep and poultry) are reared, and freshwater fishing is an important rural activity. Agricultural GDP increased by an average of 4.0% per year in 1996–2006, according to the World Bank; it increased by 5.0% in 2006.

Industry (including mining, manufacturing, construction and power) contributed 25.3% of GDP in 2005, and employed 7.8% of the working population in 2003. Industrial GDP increased at an average annual rate of 7.8% in 1996–2006, according to the World Bank; it increased by 3.4% in 2006.

Mining has made a negligible contribution to GDP since the 1970s (1.1% in 2006) and in 2003 it employed just 0.3% of the working population. The Government aims to encourage renewed investment in the sector. Output of copper, formerly an important export, virtually ceased during the late 1970s. However, the state-owned Kilembe copper mine in western Uganda was transferred to private ownership and the first phase of preparations to reopen the mine was expected to be completed during 2005; the second phase was expected to take a further 10 months to complete. In 2006 Uganda Gold Mining Ltd (UGM) signed an agreement with Kilembe Mines Ltd transferring ownership of 70% of the Kilember copper mine to UGM. That company was to complete a feasibility study for renewed copper exploitation by 2009. The production of cobalt from stockpiled copper pyrites commenced in 1999. Uganda is believed to possess the world's second largest deposit of gold, which began to be exploited again in the mid-1990s. Apatite and limestone are also mined. There are, in addition, reserves of iron ore, magnetite, tin, tungsten, beryllium, bismuth, asbestos, graphite, phosphate and tantalite. Mining GDP increased by 8.9% in 1998/99.

Manufacturing contributed 10.4% of GDP in 2006 and in 2003 it employed 6.1% of the working population. The most important manufacturing activities are the processing of agricultural commodities, brewing, vehicle assembly and the production of textiles, cement, soap, fertilizers, paper products, metal products, shoes, paints, matches and batteries. Manufacturing GDP increased by an average of 7.4% per year in 1996–2006, according to the World Bank. The sector's GDP increased by 11.1% in 2005; however, it contracted by 1.6% in 2006.

Energy is derived principally from hydroelectric power. In 1998 Uganda generated only about two-thirds of national energy requirements. However, plans are under way to expand hydroelectric production. Imports of petroleum and petroleum products accounted for 16.7% of the value of Uganda's merchandise imports in 2005.

The services sector contributed 53.8% of GDP in 2006, and engaged 23.5% of the employed labour force in 2003. Trade is the most important aspect of the sector. Services GDP increased by an average of 7.5% per year in 1996–2006, according to the World Bank. GDP in the sector increased by 9.7% in 2006.

In 2006 Uganda recorded a visible trade deficit of US $1,235.3m., and there was a deficit of $240.1m. on the current account of the balance of payments. In 2005 the principal sources of imports were Kenya (25.3%), Japan, South Africa, the United Arab Emirates (UAE), India and the People's Republic of China; The Netherlands (10.5%) the UAE, Switzerland, Kenya, the DRC and Sudan were the main markets for exports in that year. The Common Market for Eastern and Southern Africa (COMESA, see p. 205) and the European Union (EU, see p. 244) are important trading partners: in 2003 they took 28.3% and 17.7%, respectively, of total imports and provided 27.7% and 26.3%, respectively, of total exports. The principal exports in

2005 were coffee, fish, gold, tobacco and tea; the main imports in that year were petroleum products, road vehicles, cereals and cereal preparations, iron and steel and medical and pharmaceutical products.

In the financial year ending 30 June 2006 Uganda's central government budgetary deficit was an estimated 119,000m. shillings, equivalent to 0.6% of GDP. Uganda's external debt totalled US $4,463m. at the end of 2005, of which $4,250m. was long-term public debt. In that year the cost of debt-servicing was equivalent to 9.2% of the value of exports of goods and services. The annual average rate of inflation was 6.8% in 1996–2006; consumer prices increased by 2.4% in 2006.

Uganda is a member of the COMESA, the African Development Bank (see p. 162) and the East African Community (EAC, see p. 412).

Uganda is regarded as having an open, deregulated economy, with conditions favourable to investment. As such, Uganda has enjoyed good relations with international donors, and during 1998–2000 Uganda secured international aid and debt-relief, including assistance under the IMF's initiative for heavily indebted poor countries (HIPC), to the value of US $1,500m. It was estimated that these funds would reduce Uganda's annual debt-servicing obligations by about 65%–75%. In March 2000 donor countries commended Uganda for having focused its economic policies on the reduction of poverty and for its commitment to reduce defence spending to 2% of GDP. However, a large part of Uganda's GDP growth is offset by the rapid annual increase in population. Moreover, the conflict with the LRA in the north of the country has led to continued high expenditure on defence and has hampered growth in the region. The conflict is estimated to have cost Uganda over $100m. worth of production capacity annually. Following the conclusion of an IMF arrangement in 2005, the IMF announced that Uganda's economy had improved to the point where it no longer qualified for aid. Nevertheless, Uganda remains one of poorest nations in the world, and the country's economy faces two main challenges. Firstly, to sustain growth (which is still largely dependent on agricultural exports) at a sufficient level to enable the reduction of poverty, with income distributed more evenly throughout the country; and secondly to reduce its reliance on foreign aid, which finances around one-half of the country's expenditure. GDP growth in 2005–07 was hampered by prolonged drought and power shortages, and as a result of the power deficits in the previous two years, in August 2007 construction of a hydroelectric power station at Bujagali with financial assistance from the World Bank began. The facility, which was expected to be operational by 2011 was to have a generating capacity of 250 MW. Construction of a further hydroelectric power station at Karuma was expected to commence in September 2008. The IMF forecast GDP growth of 6.5% in 2007 and of 7.1% in 2008.

Education

Education is not compulsory. Most schools are supported by the Government, although a small proportion are sponsored by missions. Traditionally all schools have charged fees. In 1997, however, the Government introduced an initiative known as Universal Primary Education (UPE), whereby free primary education was to be phased in for up to four children per family. Primary education begins at six years of age and lasts for seven years. Secondary education, beginning at the age of 13, lasts for a further six years, comprising a first cycle of four years and a second of two years. In 2002/03, according to UNESCO, enrolment at pre-primary level was 3% (for both boys and girls). In that year, 141% of children in the appropriate age-group (males 142%; females 139%) were enrolled at primary schools. According to UNESCO estimates, enrolment at secondary schools was 16% (males 17%; females 16%), while just 3% of those in the relevant age group (males 4%; females 2%) were enrolled in tertiary education. In addition to Makerere University in Kampala there is a university of science and technology at Mbarara, and a small Islamic university is located at Mbale. In 2004 58,823 students were enrolled in university. Education expenditure in the financial year ending 30 June 1997 accounted for 24.9% of government current expenditure.

Public Holidays

2008: 1 January (New Year's Day), 26 January (Liberation Day), 8 March (International Women's Day), 21–24 March (Easter), 1 May (Labour Day), 3 June (Martyrs' Day), 9 June (National Heroes' Day), 1 October* (Id al-Fitr, end of Ramadan), 9 October (Independence Day), 9 December* (Id al-Adha, Feast of the Sacrifice), 25 December (Christmas), 26 December (Boxing Day).

2009: 1 January (New Year's Day), 26 January (Liberation Day), 8 March (International Women's Day), 10–13 April (Easter), 1 May (Labour Day), 3 June (Martyrs' Day), 9 June (National Heroes' Day), 20 September* (Id al-Fitr, end of Ramadan), 9 October (Independence Day), 27 November* (Id al-Adha, Feast of the Sacrifice), 25 December (Christmas), 26 December (Boxing Day).

* These holidays are dependent on the Islamic lunar calendar and the exact dates may vary by one or two days from those given.

Weights and Measures

The metric system is in force.

Statistical Survey

Sources (unless otherwise stated): Uganda Bureau of Statistics, POB 13, Entebbe; tel. (41) 320165; fax (41) 320147; e-mail ubos@infocom.co.ug; internet www.ubos.org; Statistics Department, Ministry of Finance, Planning and Economic Development, POB 8147, Kampala.

Area and Population

AREA, POPULATION AND DENSITY

Area (sq km)	
Land	197,323
Inland water and swamp	44,228
Total	241,551*
Population (census results)	
12 January 1991	16,671,705
12 September 2002	
Males	11,929,803
Females	12,512,281
Total	24,442,084
Population (official estimates at mid-year)	
2005	26,494,600
2006	27,356,900
2007	28,247,300
Density (per sq km) at mid-2007	116.9

* 93,263 sq miles.

PRINCIPAL ETHNIC GROUPS
(at census of 12 September 2002)*

Acholi	1,145,357	Basoga	2,062,920
Baganda	4,126,370	Iteso	1,568,763
Bagisu	1,117,661	Langi	1,485,437
Bakiga	1,679,519	Lugbara	1,022,240
Banyakole	2,330,212		

* Ethnic groups numbering more than 1m. persons, excluding population enumerated in hotels.

UGANDA

DISTRICTS
(population, official estimates at mid-2004)

Central	7,015,300	Northern		5,812,700
Kalangala	41,400	Adjumani		225,100
Kampala	1,290,500	Apac		716,800
Kayunga	306,800	Arua		915,500
Kiboga	249,200	Gulu		491,000
Luwero	496,100	Kitgum		307,500
Masaka	777,300	Kotido		705,400
Mpigi	424,300	Lira		805,200
Mubende	742,400	Moroto		185,500
Mukono	845,800	Moyo		229,800
Nakasongola	129,200	Nakapiripirit		170,500
Rakai	485,700	Nebbi		453,500
Sembabule	190,700	Pader		315,300
Wakiso	1,035,800	Yumbe		291,500
Eastern	6,712,400	Western		6,761,500
Bugiri	464,800	Bundibugyoi		232,900
Busia	239,500	Bushenyi		746,400
Iganga	757,300	Hoima		380,000
Jinja	436,100	Kabale		479,400
Kaberamaido	130,600	Kabarole		368,300
Kamuli	753,200	Kamwenge		312,300
Kapchorwa	208,600	Kanungu		212,300
Katakwi	343,800	Kasese		568,600
Kumi	417,500	Kibaale		454,100
Mayuge	346,900	Kisoro		224,300
Mbale	760,800	Kyenjojo		405,700
Pallisa	552,000	Masindi		512,900
Sironko	305,700	Mbarara		1,142,500
Soroti	406,800	Ntungamo		400,000
Tororo	589,300	Rukungiri		322,000

PRINCIPAL TOWNS
(population according to provisional results of census of 12 September 2002)*

Kampala (capital)	1,208,544	Entebbe	57,518
Gulu	113,144	Kasese	53,446
Lira	89,971	Njeru	52,514
Jinja	86,520	Mukono	47,305
Mbale	70,437	Arua	45,883
Mbarara	69,208	Kabale	45,757
Masaka	61,300	Kitgum	42,929

* According to administrative divisions of 2002.

Mid-2007 ('000, incl. suburbs, UN estimate): Kampala 1,420 (Source: UN, *World Urbanization Prospects: The 2007 Revision*).

BIRTHS AND DEATHS
(annual averages, UN estimates)

	1990–95	1995–2000	2000–05
Birth rate (per 1,000)	49.6	48.2	47.3
Death rate (per 1,000)	16.0	17.7	15.5

Source: UN, *World Population Prospects: The 2006 Revision*.

Expectation of life (years at birth, WHO estimates): 49.7 (males 48.5; females 51.0) in 2005 (Source: WHO, *World Health Statistics*).

EMPLOYMENT
(persons aged 10 years and over, census of 12 September 2002)*

	Males	Females	Total
Agriculture, hunting and forestry	2,545,962	2,649,779	5,195,741
Fishing	102,043	16,743	118,786
Mining and quarrying	13,613	6,127	19,740
Manufacturing	108,653	45,594	154,247
Electricity, gas and water supply	12,860	1,509	14,369
Construction	105,769	2,939	108,708
Wholesale and retail trade, repair of motor vehicles, motorcycles and personal and household goods	191,191	143,145	334,336
Hotels and restaurants	23,741	64,099	87,840
Transport, storage and communications	119,437	5,798	125,235
Financial intermediation / Real estate, renting and business activities	14,539	7,562	22,101
Public administration and defence, compulsory social security	146,319	27,278	173,597
Education	124,167	85,015	209,182
Health and social work	54,327	53,108	107,435
Other community, social and personal service activities	22,736	26,734	49,470
Private households with employed persons	14,019	19,115	33,134
Not classifiable by economic activity	120,219	76,167	196,386
Total employed	3,719,595	3,230,712	6,950,307

* Excluding population enumerated at hotels.

2003 ('000 persons aged 10 years and over): Agriculture, hunting and forestry 6,278.3; Fishing 83.3; Mining and quarrying 27.8; Manufacturing 564.9; Electricity, gas and water supply 9.3; Construction 120.4; Wholesale and retail trade, repair of motor vehicles, motorcycles and personal and household goods 1,074.2; Hotels and restaurants 240.8; Transport, storage and communications 175.9; Real estate, renting and business activities 37.0; Public administration and defence, compulsory social security 74.1; Education 240.8; Health and social work 74.1; Other community, social and personal service activities 148.2; Private households with employed persons 111.1; *Total employed* 9,260.0; Unemployed 346.0; *Total labour force* 9,606.0 (Source: ILO).

Health and Welfare

KEY INDICATORS

Total fertility rate (children per woman, 2005)	7.1
Under-5 mortality rate (per 1,000 live births, 2005)	136
HIV/AIDS (% of persons aged 15–49, 2005)	6.7
Physicians (per 1,000 head, 2004)	0.08
Hospital beds (per 1,000 head, 2004)	0.70
Health expenditure (2004): US $ per head (PPP)	135.3
Health expenditure (2004): % of GDP	7.6
Health expenditure (2004): public (% of total)	32.7
Access to water (% of persons, 2004)	60
Access to sanitation (% of persons, 2004)	43
Human Development Index (2005): ranking	154
Human Development Index (2005): value	0.505

For sources and definitions, see explanatory note on p. vi.

UGANDA

Agriculture

PRINCIPAL CROPS
('000 metric tons)

	2004	2005	2006
Rice (paddy)	121	153	154
Maize	1,080	1,170	1,258
Millet	659	672	687
Sorghum	399	449	440
Potatoes	573	585	628
Sweet potatoes	2,650	2,478	2,628
Cassava (Manioc)	5,500	5,576	4,926
Sugar cane	2,203*	2,150*	1,950†
Dry beans	455	478	424
Cow peas, dry	69	71	71
Pigeon peas	84	85	88
Soybeans	158	158	175
Groundnuts (in shell)	155	159	154
Sesame seed	125	161	166
Seed cotton†	78	108	88
Onions, dry†	147	147	147
Bananas†	615	624	624
Plantains	9,686	9,045	9,054
Coffee (green)	170	158	133
Tea (made)	36	38	34
Tobacco (leaves)	33	31	32†
Cotton (lint)*	30	44	37

* Unofficial figure(s).
† FAO estimate(s).

Aggregate production ('000 metric tons, may include official, semi-official or estimated data): Total cereals 2,274 in 2004, 2,459 in 2005, 2,557 in 2006; Total roots and tubers 8,723 in 2004, 8,765 in 2005, 8,182 in 2006; Total vegetables (incl. melons) 557 in 2004, 557 in 2005, 557 in 2006; Total fruits (excl. melons) 10,354 in 2004, 9,722 in 2005, 9,731 in 2006.

Source: FAO.

LIVESTOCK
('000 head, year ending September)

	2004	2005	2006
Asses, mules or hinnies*	18	18	18
Cattle	6,567	6,770	6,973
Sheep	1,552	1,600	1,648
Goats	7,566	7,800	8,034
Pigs	1,940	2,000	2,000*
Chickens	31,622	25,174	22,849

* FAO estimate(s).

Source: FAO.

LIVESTOCK PRODUCTS
('000 metric tons, FAO estimates)

	2004	2005	2006
Cattle meat	106	106	106
Sheep meat	8	6	6
Goat meat	29	29	29
Pig meat	76	79	79
Chicken meat	38	44	44
Cows' milk	700	700	760
Poultry eggs	20	20	20

Source: FAO.

Forestry

ROUNDWOOD REMOVALS
('000 cubic metres, excl. bark, FAO estimates)

	2004	2005	2006
Sawlogs, veneer logs and logs for sleepers	1,055	1,055	1,055
Other industrial wood	2,120	2,120	2,120
Fuel wood	36,235	36,797	37,343
Total	39,410	39,972	40,518

Source: FAO.

SAWNWOOD PRODUCTION
('000 cubic metres, incl. railway sleepers)

	2004*	2005	2006
Coniferous (softwood)	67	24	24
Broadleaved (hardwood)	197	101	93
Total	264	125	117

* FAO estimates.

Source: FAO.

Fishing

('000 metric tons, live weight)

	2003	2004	2005
Capture	241.8	372.4	417.1
Cyprinids	8.3	22.9	25.7
Tilapias	97.3	138.8	155.6
African lungfishes	4.6	12.9	14.5
Characins	9.5	20.0	22.4
Nile perch	112.8	156.3	175.2
Aquaculture	5.5	5.5	10.8
Total catch	247.3	377.9	427.9

Source: FAO.

Mining

('000 metric tons, unless otherwise indicated)

	2003	2004	2005
Cement (hydraulic)	507.1	559.0	630.0*
Tantalum and niobium (columbium) concentrates (kilograms)	16,240	376	273
Cobalt (metric tons)	0	436	638
Gold (kilograms)	40	1,447	46
Limestone	226.4	228.8	540.8
Salt (unrefined)*	5	5	5

* Estimate(s).

Source: US Geological Survey.

UGANDA

Statistical Survey

Industry

SELECTED PRODUCTS
('000 metric tons, unless otherwise indicated)

	2003	2004	2005
Soft drinks (million litres)	78.5	111.5	163.5
Sugar	139.5	189.5	182.9
Soap	101.3	93.4	127.6
Cement	507.1	559.0	692.7
Paint (million litres)	1.9	2.2	8.2
Edible oil and fat	56.0	58.1	43.3
Animal feed	20.9	19.6	17.3
Footwear (million pairs)	3.4	3.6	46.3
Wheat flour	42.2	25.7	20.3
Processed milk (million litres)	14.9	19.6	18.5
Cotton and rayon fabrics (million sq metres)	11.1	10.1	13.6
Clay bricks, tiles, etc.	33.3	15.4	36.2
Corrugated iron sheets	39.2	48.8	61.6

Source: Bank of Uganda.

Finance

CURRENCY AND EXCHANGE RATES

Monetary Units
100 cents = 1 new Uganda shilling.

Sterling, Dollar and Euro Equivalents (31 October 2007)
£1 sterling = 3,598.6 new Uganda shillings;
US $1 = 1,735.5 new Uganda shillings;
€1 = 2,507.2 new Uganda shillings;
10,000 new Uganda shillings = £2.78 = $5.76 = €3.99.

Average Exchange Rate (new Uganda shillings per US $)
2004 1,810.3
2005 1,780.7
2006 1,831.5

Note: Between December 1985 and May 1987 the official exchange rate was fixed at US $1 = 1,400 shillings. In May 1987 a new shilling, equivalent to 100 of the former units, was introduced. At the same time, the currency was devalued by 76.7%, with the exchange rate set at $1 = 60 new shillings. Further adjustments were implemented in subsequent years. Foreign exchange controls were mostly abolished in 1993.

BUDGET
(million new shillings, year ending 30 June)

Revenue	2003/04	2004/05	2005/06
Revenue*	1,669,200	1,948,000	2,267,000
Grants	1,188,000	1,198,000	1,136,000
Total	2,857,200	3,146,000	3,403,000

Expenditure	2003/04	2004/05	2005/06
Recurrent expenditure	1,868,000	1,977,900	2,234,000
Wages and salaries	683,000	774,000	867,000
Interest payments	264,000	229,000	250,000
Development expenditure	1,094,000	1,187,100	1,262,000
External expenditure	439,000	487,100	519,000
Domestic expenditure	635,000	700,000	743,000
Net lending and investment	80,700	47,400	26,000
Total	3,042,700	3,212,400	3,522,000

*Tax revenue excludes tax refunds and government payments.

INTERNATIONAL RESERVES
(US $ million at 31 December)

	2004	2005	2006
IMF special drawing rights	0.7	1.1	0.1
Foreign exchange	1,307.4	1,343.1	1,801.8
Total	1,308.1	1,344.2	1,801.9

Source: IMF, *International Financial Statistics*.

MONEY SUPPLY
('000 million new shillings at 31 December)

	2004	2005	2006
Currency outside banks	588.61	710.22	885.87
Demand deposits at commercial banks	752.63	894.22	1,020.61
Total money	1,341.24	1,604.45	1,906.49

Source: IMF, *International Financial Statistics*.

COST OF LIVING
(Consumer Price Index for all urban households; base: 2000 = 100)

	2004	2005	2006
Food	111.4	126.1	139.1
Clothing	100.5	102.3	106.8
Rent, fuel and light	121.0	130.1	n.a.
All items (incl. others)	114.5	124.1	133.3

Source: ILO.

NATIONAL ACCOUNTS
(million new shillings at current prices)

Expenditure on the Gross Domestic Product

	2004	2005	2006
Government final consumption expenditure	2,055,645	2,356,983	2,676,574
Private final consumption expenditure	10,790,811	12,344,208	14,860,021
Increase in stocks	15,338	51,390	58,277
Gross fixed capital formation	3,227,081	3,696,936	4,510,215
Total domestic expenditure	16,088,875	18,449,517	22,105,087
Exports of goods and services	1,884,120	2,350,966	2,327,573
Less Imports of goods and services	3,862,172	4,601,102	5,952,580
Statistical discrepancy	−29,267	68,939	128,350
GDP in purchasers' values	14,081,557	16,268,320	18,608,430
GDP at constant 1997/98 prices	11,004,238	11,606,298	12,393,135

Gross Domestic Product by Economic Activity

	2004	2005	2006
Agriculture, hunting, forestry and fishing	2,305,118	2,665,779	2,946,685
Mining and quarrying	106,317	112,402	149,460
Manufacturing	1,201,543	1,350,166	1,468,481
Electricity, gas and water	165,425	180,045	171,027
Construction	1,283,379	1,496,825	1,795,422
Wholesale and retail trade	1,418,825	1,648,988	1,925,792
Hotels and restaurants	400,588	464,567	528,547
Transport, storage and communications	1,010,031	1,287,910	1,656,035
General government services	570,512	638,701	695,900
Education	870,960	1,003,333	1,162,376
Health	333,096	406,644	497,513
Other services	957,803	1,065,422	1,154,623
Total monetary GDP	10,623,596	12,320,782	14,151,862
Non-monetary GDP			
Agriculture	1,700,122	1,993,882	2,202,455
Construction	66,731	74,771	82,853
Owner-occupied dwellings	482,526	508,359	538,738
Total GDP at factor cost	12,872,975	14,897,795	16,975,908
Taxes on production and imports (net)	1,208,581	1,370,525	1,632,522
GDP at market prices	14,081,557	16,268,320	18,608,430

UGANDA

BALANCE OF PAYMENTS
(US $ million)

	2004	2005	2006
Exports of goods f.o.b.	708.9	864.2	1,003.9
Imports of goods f.o.b.	−1,461.1	−1,780.4	−2,239.1
Trade balance	−752.2	−916.2	−1,235.3
Exports of services	358.3	507.7	489.8
Imports of services	−651.2	−786.7	−990.0
Balance on goods and services	−1,045.1	−1,195.1	−1,735.5
Other income received	35.7	49.8	71.9
Other income paid	−328.8	−298.9	−296.6
Balance on goods, services and income	−1,338.2	−1,444.2	−1,960.2
Current transfers received	1,233.1	1,365.2	2,022.0
Current transfers paid	−183.3	−306.5	−301.9
Current balance	−288.4	−385.5	−240.1
Direct investment from abroad	295.4	379.8	391.6
Portfolio investment assets	—	—	—
Portfolio investment liabilities	6.2	−13.4	21.7
Other investment assets	0.1	−7.1	−10.1
Other investment liabilities	113.1	106.0	128.5
Net errors and omissions	−3.9	1.9	41.5
Overall balance	122.5	81.7	332.9

Source: IMF, *International Financial Statistics*.

External Trade

PRINCIPAL COMMODITIES
(distribution by SITC, US $ '000)

Imports c.i.f.	2003	2004	2005
Food and live animals	144,836	189,910	212,121
Cereals and cereal preparations	106,698	134,431	141,194
Crude materials (inedible) except fuels	47,703	49,504	54,197
Mineral fuels, lubricants, etc.	188,770	219,745	348,474
Petroleum, petroleum products and related materials	187,255	217,762	343,159
Animal and vegetable oils, fats and waxes	64,523	72,070	73,707
Chemicals and related products	180,354	224,882	268,415
Medicinal and pharmaceutical products	74,920	80,137	85,721
Plastics in primary forms	28,332	43,886	62,606
Basic manufactures	270,623	322,438	362,764
Non-metallic mineral manufactures	51,862	57,269	68,576
Iron and steel	77,755	96,020	118,823
Machinery and transport equipment	344,098	473,729	537,299
Telecommunications and sound recording/reproducing apparatus	48,936	82,764	100,410
Electrical machinery, apparatus, etc.	52,178	61,971	56,843
Road vehicles (incl. air-cushion vehicles) and parts (excl. tyres, engines and electrical parts)	115,096	144,695	192,198
Miscellaneous manufactured articles	130,046	155,222	186,404
Total (incl. others)	1,375,106	1,726,238	2,054,137

Exports f.o.b.	2003	2004	2005
Food and live animals	272,838	318,434	419,261
Fish, crustaceans, molluscs and preparations thereof	84,649	100,028	139,864
Cereals and cereal preparations	17,592	26,360	31,040
Coffee, tea, cocoa, spices and manufactures	157,646	174,832	223,691
Beverages and tobacco	45,764	43,698	39,509
Tobacco and tobacco manufactures	43,212	40,805	32,281
Crude materials (inedible) except fuels	61,726	94,649	106,478
Textile fibres (not wool tops) and their wastes (not in yarn)	22,180	49,329	39,267
Crude animal and vegetable materials n.e.s.	29,845	35,234	39,823
Mineral fuels, lubricants and related materials	41,664	40,219	37,839
Petroleum, petroleum products and related materials	27,884	28,145	32,979
Basic manufactures	19,394	31,068	52,193
Iron and steel	11,035	18,123	29,699
Machinery and transport equipment	19,208	25,713	42,582
Miscellaneous manufactured articles	18,515	27,143	13,343
Gold, non-monetary (excl. gold ores and concentrates)	33,726	61,200	73,074
Total (incl. others)	534,106	665,090	812,857

PRINCIPAL TRADING PARTNERS
(US $ '000)

Imports c.i.f.	2003	2004	2005
Argentina	2,191	17,806	24,507
Belgium	23,087	35,321	31,073
Canada	8,283	19,115	27,150
China, People's Repub.	70,248	103,090	109,217
France	15,596	35,525	35,317
Germany	39,151	36,346	49,256
Hong Kong	16,805	13,377	16,511
India	102,160	121,773	131,813
Italy	23,320	20,433	49,222
Japan	90,361	121,984	146,552
Kenya	357,327	399,198	520,686
Malaysia	42,062	67,430	47,214
Netherlands	25,015	37,165	43,875
Saudi Arabia	12,270	14,893	22,776
Sweden	8,811	30,343	22,643
South Africa	98,984	140,899	143,676
United Arab Emirates	80,416	84,881	136,702
United Kingdom	86,411	84,422	99,405
USA	78,129	103,390	78,143
Total (incl. others)	1,375,106	1,726,238	2,054,137

UGANDA

Exports f.o.b.

	2003	2004	2005
Australia	9,214	3,417	3,967
Belgium	12,899	26,685	33,147
Burundi	10,076	18,113	20,801
Congo, Democratic Repub.	12,891	28,913	60,404
France	5,116	22,702	39,581
Germany	12,024	17,677	33,768
Hong Kong	12,300	15,845	12,936
Japan	10,006	5,975	5,220
Kenya	78,432	76,903	72,437
Netherlands	48,955	57,860	85,413
Rwanda	20,803	24,683	36,088
Saudi Arabia	12,527	1,625	14
Singapore	13,859	22,799	28,945
South Africa	29,632	9,250	9,796
Spain	14,526	13,914	17,988
Sudan	13,765	22,676	50,487
Switzerland	72,993	108,779	74,857
Tanzania	5,832	12,155	15,445
United Arab Emirates	345	33,458	84,389
United Kingdom	33,883	29,438	26,831
USA	12,693	15,714	15,892
Total (incl. others)	534,106	665,090	812,857

Transport

RAILWAYS
(traffic)

	1994	1995	1996
Passenger-km (million)	35	30	28
Freight ton-km (million)	208	236	187

Freight traffic ('000 ton-km): 212,616 in 2003; 229,439 in 2004; 185,559 in 2005.

ROAD TRAFFIC
(vehicles in use)

	2003	2004	2005
Passenger cars	56,837	59,786	65,472
Buses and coaches	20,572	23,443	28,436
Lorries and vans	64,650	70,215	71,887
Motorcycles	80,088	89,212	108,207

CIVIL AVIATION
(traffic on scheduled services)

	2001	2002	2003
Kilometres flown (million)	2	2	2
Passengers carried ('000)	41	41	40
Passenger-km (million)	235	237	237
Total ton-km (million)	42	42	44

Source: UN, *Statistical Yearbook*.

Tourism

FOREIGN TOURIST ARRIVALS

Country of residence	2003	2004	2005
India	6,639	9,366	10,691
Kenya	114,499	220,062	138,346
Rwanda	50,143	65,298	80,522
Tanzania	30,534	67,885	50,723
United Kingdom	17,181	22,402	28,227
USA	13,179	18,898	21,968
Total (incl. others)	305,719	512,379	467,728

Tourism receipts (US $ million, incl. passenger transport): 185 in 2003; 257 in 2004; 357 in 2005 (Source: World Tourism Organization).

Communications Media

	2004	2005	2006
Telephones ('000 main lines in use)	71.6	87.5	108.1
Mobile cellular telephones ('000 subscribers)	1,165.0	1,315.3	2,008.8
Personal computers ('000 in use)	120	250	n.a.
Internet users ('000)	200	500	750
Broadband subscribers	—	800	1,200

Source: partly International Telecommunication Union.

Television receivers ('000 in use, 2000): 610.

Radio receivers ('000 in use, 1997): 2,600.

Facsimile machines (number in use, year ending 30 June 1996): 3,000 (estimate).

Book production (titles, excl. pamphlets and govt publications, 1996): 288.

Daily newspapers: 2 titles (average circulation 40,000 copies) in 1996; 7 titles in 2004.

Sources: mainly UNESCO, *Statistical Yearbook*; UN, *Statistical Yearbook*; UNESCO Institute for Statistics.

Education

(2004)

	Institutions	Teachers	Students
Primary	n.a.	147,291	7,377,292
Secondary	n.a.	29,061	697,507
Teacher training colleges	10	n.a.	16,170
Technical schools and institutes	25	n.a.	7,999
Universities	18	n.a.	58,823

Adult literacy rate (UNESCO estimates): 66.8% (males 76.8%; females 57.7%) in 2002 (Source: UNESCO Institute for Statistics).

Directory

The Constitution

Following the military coup in July 1985, the 1967 Constitution was suspended, and all legislative and executive powers were vested in a Military Council, whose Chairman was Head of State. In January 1986 a further military coup established an executive Presidency, assisted by a Cabinet of Ministers and a legislative National Resistance Council (NRC). In September 1995 a Constituent Assembly (comprising 214 elected and 74 nominated members) enacted a draft Constitution. The new Constitution was promulgated on 8 October 1995. Under its terms, a national referendum on the introduction of a multi-party political system was to take place in 2000. The referendum produced an overwhelming vote in favour of retaining the existing 'no-party' system; however, the referendum was annulled by the Constitutional Court in 2004. A direct presidential election took place in May 1996, followed in June of that year by legislative elections to the Parliament. This body, comprising 214 elected members and 62 nominated members, replaced the NRC. At the general election of June 2001 the number of nominated members was increased to 78. Legislation outlining the transition to multi-party politics was passed by the Parliament on 28 June 2005 and approved by 92.5% of voters in a national referendum held on 28 July 2005. The legislation also removed the two-term limit on the presidency.

The Government

HEAD OF STATE

President: Gen. (retd) YOWERI KAGUTA MUSEVENI (took office 29 January 1986; elected 9 May 1996, re-elected 12 March 2001 and 23 February 2006).

Vice-President: Prof. GILBERT BALIBASEKA BUKENYA.

THE CABINET
(March 2008)

Prime Minister: Prof. APOLLO NSIBAMBI.

First Deputy Prime Minister and Minister in Charge of East African Affairs: ERIYA KATEGAYA.

Second Deputy Prime Minister and Minister of Public Service: HENRY MUGANWA KAJURA.

Third Deputy Prime Minister and Minister of Information and National Guidance: KIRUNDA KIVEJINJA.

Minister for Security: AMAMA MBABAZI.

Minister in Charge of the Presidency: BEATRICE WABUDEYA.

Minister in the Office of the Prime Minister: ADOLF MWESIGE.

Minister of Agriculture, Animal Industry and Fisheries: HILLARY ONEK.

Minister of Defence: Dr CRISPUS KIYONGA.

Minister of Relief and Disaster Preparedness: TARSIS KABWEGYERE.

Minister of Education and Sports: NAMIREMBE BITAMAZIRE.

Minister of Energy and Minerals: DAUDI MIGEREKO.

Minister of Internal Affairs: Dr RUHAKANA RUGUNDA.

Minister of Finance: Dr EZRA SURUMA.

Minister of Works: JOHN NASASIRA.

Minister of Justice and Constitutional Affairs and Attorney-General: GERALD KIDDU MAKUBUYA.

Minister of Gender, Labour and Social Services: SYDA BUMBA.

Minister of Trade and Industry: JANAT MUKWAYA.

Minister of Water and Environment: MARIA MUTAGAMBA.

Minister of Lands, Housing and Urban Development: OMARA ATUBO.

Minister of Health: Dr STEVEN MALLINGA.

Minister of Foreign Affairs: SAM KUTESA.

Minister of Information Communication Technology: HAMU MULIIRA.

Minister of Local Government: Maj.-Gen. KAHINDA OTAFIIRE.

Minister without Portfolio: DOROTHY HYUHA.

In addition to the Cabinet Ministers, there are 44 Ministers of State. The Chief Whip is also a member of the Cabinet.

MINISTRIES

Office of the President: Parliament Bldg, POB 7168, Kampala; tel. (41) 4258441; fax (41) 4256143; e-mail aak@statehouse.go.ug; internet www.statehouse.go.ug.

Office of the Prime Minister: POB 341, Kampala; tel. (41) 4259518; fax (41) 4242341.

Ministry of Agriculture, Animal Industry and Fisheries: POB 102, Entebbe; tel. (41) 4320987; fax (41) 4321255; e-mail mosagr@hotmail.com; internet www.agriculture.go.ug.

Ministry of Defence: Bombo, POB 7069, Kampala; tel. (41) 4270331; fax (41) 4245911.

Ministry of Education and Sports: Embassy House and Development Bldg, Plot 9/11, Parliament Ave, POB 7063, Kampala; tel. (41) 4234451; fax (41) 42230437; e-mail pro@education.go.ug; internet www.education.go.ug.

Ministry of Energy and Minerals: Amber House, Kampala Rd, Kampala; tel. (41) 4311111; e-mail psmemd@energy.go.ug; internet www.energyandminerals.go.ug.

Ministry of Finance: Appollo Kaggwa Rd, Plot 2/4, POB 8147, Kampala; tel. (41) 4234700; fax (41) 4230163; e-mail webmaster@finance.go.ug; internet www.finance.go.ug.

Ministry of Foreign Affairs: Embassy House, POB 7048, Kampala; tel. (41) 4345661; fax (41) 4258722; e-mail info@mofa.go.ug; internet www.mofa.go.ug.

Ministry of Gender, Labour and Social Affairs: Udyam House, Jinja Rd, POB 7168, Kampala; tel. (41) 4258334.

Ministry of Health: Plot 6, Lourdel Rd, Wandegeya, POB 7272, Kampala; tel. (41) 4340884; fax (41) 4340887; e-mail info@health.go.ug; internet www.health.go.ug.

Ministry of Information Communication Technology: Kampala.

Ministry of Information and National Guidance: Kampala.

Ministry of Internal Affairs: Plot 75 Jinja Rd, POB 7191, Kampala; tel. (41) 4231059; fax (41) 4231063; e-mail info@mia.go.ug; internet www.mia.go.ug.

Ministry of Justice and Constitutional Affairs: Parliament Bldg, POB 7183, Kampala; tel. (41) 4230538; fax (41) 4254829; e-mail mojca@africaonline.co.ug; internet www.justice.go.ug.

Ministry of Lands, Housing and Urban Development: Kampala.

Ministry of Local Government: Uganda House, 8/10 Kampala Rd, POB 7037, Kampala; tel. (41) 4341224; fax (41) 4258127; e-mail info@molg.go.ug; internet www.molg.go.ug.

Ministry of Security: Kampala.

Ministry of Disaster Preparedness, Relief and Refugees: POB 341, Kampala; tel. (41) 4236967.

Ministry of Trade and Industry: 6/8 Parliament Ave, POB 7103, Kampala; tel. (41) 4232971; fax (41) 4242188; e-mail ps@mintrade.org.

Ministry of Water and Environment: POB 7096, Kampala; tel. (41) 4342931; e-mail mwle@mwle.go.ug; internet www.mwle.go.ug.

Ministry of Works: POB 10, Entebbe; tel. (42) 4320101; fax (42) 4320135; e-mail mowhc@utlonline.co.ug; internet www.miniworks.go.ug.

President and Legislature

PRESIDENT

Election, 23 February 2006

Candidate	Votes	% of votes
Gen. (Retd) Yoweri Kaguta Museveni (NRM-O)	4,078,677	59.28
Kizza Besigye (FDC)	2,570,572	37.36
John Ssebaana Kizito (DP)	109,055	1.59
Abed Bwanika (Ind.)	65,344	0.95
Miria Obote Kalule (UPC)	56,584	0.82
Total	**6,880,232**	**100.00**

PARLIAMENT

Speaker: EDWARD SSEKANDI.

Deputy Speaker: REBECCA KADAGA.

The National Resistance Movement, which took office in January 1986, established a National Resistance Council (NRC), initially comprising 80 nominated members, to act as a legislative body. National elections were held on 11–28 February 1989, at which 210 members of an expanded NRC were elected by members of district-level Resistance Committees (themselves elected by local-level Resistance Committees, who were directly elected by universal adult suffrage). The remaining 68 seats in the NRC were reserved for candidates nominated by the President (to include 34 women and representatives of youth organizations and trades unions). Political parties were not allowed to participate in the election campaign. In October 1989 the NRC approved legislation extending the Government's term of office by five years from January 1990, when its mandate was to expire. The Constituent Assembly (see Constitution) extended further the NRM's term of office in November 1994. Under the terms of the Constitution that was promulgated in October 1995, the NRC was restyled as the Ugandan Parliament. Legislative elections to the Parliament took place in June 1996 (again officially on a 'no-party' basis). The total membership of the Parliament was reduced from 278 to 276, comprising 214 elected and 62 nominated representatives. A national referendum on the future introduction of a multi-party political system was staged in June 2000, at which 90.7% of participants voted in favour of retaining the 'no-party' political system—the referendum was nullified in mid-2004 (see Recent History). Legislation was adopted by the Parliament in June 2005, and ratified by a national referendum on 28 July of that year, restoring multi-party politics and lifting the two-term limit on the presidency. Multi-party legislative elections were held on 23 February 2006, following which the number of seats in Parliament stood at 319, comprising 215 directly elected representatives, 69 nominated female representatives, 10 nominated representatives from the UPDF, five nominated representatives for young people, five nominated representatives for people with disabilities, five nominated representatives for workers and 10 ex officio members.

UGANDA

Election Commission

Electoral Commission: 53–56 Jinja Rd, POB 22678, Kampala; tel. (41) 4337500; fax (41) 4341907; e-mail info@ec.or.ug; internet www.ec.or.ug; f. 1997; independent; Chair. Dr BADRU M. KIGGUNDU.

Political Organizations

Political parties were ordered to suspend active operations, although not formally banned, in March 1986. At a referendum on the future restoration of a plural political system, which took place on 29 June 2000, the retention of the existing 'no-party' system was overwhelmingly endorsed by voters. However, the result was nullified by the Constitutional Court in mid-2004. Following a successful challenge to the Political Parties and Organisations Act 2002, political parties were permitted to resume their activities nationally from March 2003. Discussions on a proposed transition to multi-party politics commenced in 2004. By April of that year some 60 new political parties had emerged, but only 13 had sought registration. In mid-2005 legislation was passed allowing for a return to full multi-party democracy; the legislation was approved by 92.5% of voters in a national referendum held on 28 July 2005. By mid-2006 33 parties had been officially registered.

Bazzukulu ba Buganda (Grandchildren of Buganda): Bagandan separatist movement.

Buganda Youth Movement: f. 1994; seeks autonomy for Buganda; Leader STANLEY KATO.

Conservative Party (CP): f. 1979; Leader JEHOASH MAYANJA-NKANGI.

Democratic Party (DP): City House, Plot 2/3 William St, POB 7098, Kampala; tel. and fax (41) 4252536; e-mail info@dpuganda.org; internet www.dpuganda.org; f. 1954; main support in southern Uganda; seeks a multi-party political system; Pres. JOHN SSEBAANA KIZITO; Vice-Pres. ZACHARY OLUM.

Federal Democratic Movement (FEDEMO): Kampala.

Forum for Democratic Change (FDC): f. 2004 by a merger of the Reform Agenda, the Parliamentary Advocacy Forum and the National Democratic Forum; Leader KIZZA BESIGYE.

Forum for Multi-Party Democracy: Kampala; Gen. Sec. JESSE MASHATTE.

Justice Forum: Leader MUHAMMAD KIBIRIGE MAYANJA.

Movement for New Democracy in Uganda: based in Zambia; f. 1994 to campaign for multi-party political system; Leader DAN OKELLO-OGWANG.

National Resistance Movement Organisation (NRM-O): f. as National Resistance Movement to oppose the UPC Govt 1980–85; also opposed the mil. Govt in power from July 1985 to Jan. 1986; its fmr mil. wing, the National Resistance Army (NRA), led by Lt-Gen. (later Gen. retd) Yoweri Kaguta Museveni, took power in Jan. 1986; name changed as above on registration in 2003; Chair. Dr SAMSON KISEKKA.

Nationalist Liberal Party: Kampala; f. 1984 by a breakaway faction of the DP; Leader TIBERIO OKENY.

Uganda Democratic Alliance (UDA): Leader APOLO KIRONDE.

Uganda Democratic Freedom Front: Leader Maj. HERBERT ITONGA.

Uganda Freedom Movement (UFM): Kampala; mainly Baganda support; withdrew from NRM coalition Govt in April 1987; Sec.-Gen. (vacant).

Uganda Independence Revolutionary Movement: f. 1989; Chair. Maj. OKELLO KOLO.

Uganda Islamic Revolutionary Party (UIRP): Kampala; f. 1993; Chair. IDRIS MUWONGE.

Uganda National Unity Movement: Chair. Alhaji SULEIMAN SSALONGO.

Uganda Patriotic Movement (UPM): Kampala; f. 1980; Sec.-Gen. JABERI SSALI.

Uganda People's Congress (UPC): POB 1951, Kampala; internet www.members.home.net/upc; f. 1960; socialist-based philosophy; mainly northern support; ruling party 1962–71 and 1980–85, sole legal political party 1969–71; Nat. Leader Dr JAMES RWANYARARE.

Ugandan People's Democratic Movement (UPDM): seeks democratic reforms; support mainly from north and east of the country; includes mems of fmr govt armed forces; signed a peace accord with the Govt in 1990; Chair. ERIC OTEMA ALLIMADI; Sec.-Gen. EMMANUEL OTENG.

Uganda Progressive Union (UPU): Kampala; Chair. ALFRED BANYA.

In August 2006 12 parties merged to form an opposition group styled The People's Platform (TPP). Those parties included the **Forum for Integrity in Leadership (FIL)**, the **Movement for Democratic Change (MDC)** and the **National Peasant Party (NPP)**. The Chairman of the FIL, EMMANUEL TUMUSIIME, assumed the chairmanship of TPP

The following organizations are in armed conflict with the Government:

Alliance of Democratic Forces (ADF): active since 1996 in southeastern Uganda; combines Ugandan Islamic fundamentalist rebels, exiled Rwandan Hutus and guerrillas from the Democratic Republic of the Congo; Pres. Sheikh JAMIL MUKULU.

Lord's Resistance Army (LRA): f. 1987; claims to be conducting a Christian fundamentalist 'holy war' against the Govt; forces est. to number up to 1,500, operating mainly from bases in Sudan; Leader JOSEPH KONY; a breakaway faction (LRA—Democratic) is led by RONALD OTIM KOMAKECH.

Uganda National Rescue Front Part Two (UNRF II): based in Juba, Sudan; Leader ALI BAMUZE.

Uganda People's Freedom Movement (UPFM): based in Tororo and Kenya; f. 1994 by mems of the fmr Uganda People's Army; Leader PETER OTAI.

West Nile Bank Front (WNBF): operates in northern Uganda.

Diplomatic Representation

EMBASSIES AND HIGH COMMISSIONS IN UGANDA

Algeria: 14 Acacia Ave, Kololo, POB 4025, Kampala; tel. (41) 4232918; fax (41) 4341015; e-mail ambalgka@imul.com; Ambassador ABDELKADER AZIRIA.

Belgium: Rwenzori House, 3rd Floor, Plot 1, Lumumba Ave, POB 7043, Kampala; tel. (41) 4345559; fax (41) 4347212; e-mail kampala@diplobel.org; internet www.diplomatie.be/kampala; Ambassador JAN DE BRUYNE.

China, People's Republic: 37 Malcolm X Ave, Kololo, POB 4106, Kampala; tel. (41) 4259881; fax (41) 4235087; e-mail chinaemb_ug@mfa.gov.cn; internet ug.china-embassy.org; Ambassador SUN HEPING.

Congo, Democratic Republic: 20 Philip Rd, Kololo, POB 4972, Kampala; tel. (41) 4250099; fax (41) 4340140; Chargé d'affaires a.i. BISELELE WA MUTSHIPAYI.

Cuba: KAR Dr., 16 Lower Kololo Terrace, POB 9226, Kampala; tel. (41) 4233742; fax (41) 4233320; e-mail ecuba@africaonline.co.ug; Ambassador RICARDO ANTONIO DANZA SIGAS.

Denmark: Plot 3, Lumumba Ave, POB 11243, Kampala; tel. (31) 2263211; fax (31) 2264624; e-mail kmtamb@um.dk; internet www.ambkampala.um.dk; Ambassador STIG BARLYNG.

Egypt: 33 Kololo Hill Dr., POB 4280, Kampala; tel. (41) 4254525; fax (41) 4232103; e-mail egyembug@utlonline.co.ug; Ambassador REDA ABDEL RAHMAN BEBARS.

Ethiopia: 3L Kitante Close, off Kira Rd, POB 7745, Kampala; tel. (41) 4348340; fax (41) 4341885; Ambassador Ato TERFA MENEGESHA.

France: 16 Lumumba Ave, Nakasero, POB 7212, Kampala; tel. (41) 4342120; fax (41) 4341252; e-mail ambafrance.kampala@diplomatie.gouv.fr; internet www.ambafrance-ug.org; Ambassador BERNARD GARANCHER.

Germany: 15 Philip Rd, Kololo, POB 7016, Kampala; tel. (41) 4501111; fax (41) 4501115; e-mail info@kampala.diplo.de; internet www.kampala.diplo.de; Ambassador REINHARD BUCHHOLZ.

Holy See: Chwa II Rd, Mbuya Hill, POB 7177, Kampala (Apostolic Nunciature); tel. (41) 4505619; fax (41) 4441774; Apostolic Nuncio (vacant).

India: 11 Kyaddondo Rd, Nakasero, POB 7040, Kampala; tel. (41) 4457368; fax (41) 4454943; e-mail hoc@hicomindkampala.org; High Commissioner SIBARATA TRIPATHI.

Iran: 9 Bandali Rise, Bugolobi, POB 24529, Kampala; tel. (41) 4441689; fax (41) 4443590; Ambassador ABOUTALEBI MORTEZA.

Ireland: 25 Yusuf Lule Rd, Nakasero, POB 7791, Kampala; tel. (41) 4340400; fax (41) 4344353; e-mail kampalaembassy@dfa.ie; Chargé d'affaires a.i. AINE HEARNS.

Italy: 11 Lourdel Rd, Nakasero, POB 4646, Kampala; tel. (41) 4250442; fax (41) 4250448; e-mail segreteria.kampala@esteri.it; internet www.ambkampala.esteri.it; Ambassador UMBERTO PLAJA.

Japan: Plot 8, Kyaddondo Rd, Nakasero, POB 23553, Kampala; tel. (41) 4349542; fax (41) 4349547; e-mail jembassy@jembassy.co.ug; Ambassador RYUUZI KIKUCHI.

Kenya: 41 Nakasero Rd, POB 5220, Kampala; tel. (41) 4458235; fax (41) 4458239; e-mail kenyahicom@africaonline.co.ug; High Commissioner JAPHETH R. GETUGI.

UGANDA

Directory

Korea, Democratic People's Republic: 10 Prince Charles Dr., Kololo, POB 5885, Kampala; tel. (41) 4546033; fax (41) 4450224; Ambassador Pak Hyon Jae.

Libya: 26 Kololo Hill Dr., POB 6079, Kampala; tel. (41) 4344924; fax (41) 4344969; Sec. of People's Bureau Abdalla Abdulmaula Bujeldain.

Netherlands: Rwenzori Courts, 4th Floor, Plot 2, Nakasero Rd, POB 7728, Kampala; tel. (41) 2346000; fax (41) 2231861; e-mail kam@minbuza.nl; internet www.netherlandsembassyuganda.org; Ambassador Jeroen Verheul.

Nigeria: 33 Nakasero Rd, POB 4338, Kampala; tel. (41) 4433691; fax (41) 4432543; e-mail nighicom-sgu@africaonline.co.ug; High Commissioner Chukudi Dixon Orike.

Norway: 8A John Babiiha Ave, Kololo, POB 22770, Kampala; tel. (41) 4343621; fax (41) 4343936; e-mail emb.kampala@mfa.no; internet www.norway.go.ug; Ambassador Bjørg Schonhowd Leite.

Russia: 28 Malcolm X Ave, Kololo, POB 7022, Kampala; tel. (41) 4433676; fax (41) 4345798; Ambassador Valery I. Utkin.

Rwanda: 2 Nakaima Rd, POB 2468, Kampala; tel. (41) 4344045; fax (41) 4458547; Ambassador Ignace Kamali Karegesa.

Saudi Arabia: 3 Okurut Close, Kololo, POB 22558, Kampala; tel. (41) 4340614; fax (41) 4454017; Chargé d'affaires Majed Abdulrahman M. Martha al-Otaibi.

South Africa: Plot 15A, Nakasero Rd, POB 22667, Kampala; tel. (41) 4343543; fax (41) 4348216; e-mail kampala.sahc@foreign.gov.za; High Commissioner Thanduyise Henry Chiliza.

Sweden: 24 Lumumba Ave, Nakasero, POB 22669, Kampala; tel. (41) 4340970; fax (41) 4340979; e-mail ambassaden.kampala@foreign.ministry.se; internet www.swedenabroad.com/kampala; Ambassador Anders Johnson.

Tanzania: 6 Kagera Rd, Nakasero, POB 5750, Kampala; tel. (41) 4456272; fax (41) 4343973; High Commissioner Rajab H. Gamaha.

United Kingdom: Plot 4, Windsor Loop Rd, POB 7070, Kampala; tel. (31) 4312000; fax (41) 4257304; e-mail bhcinfo@starcom.co.ug; internet www.britishhighcommission.gov.uk/uganda; High Commissioner Francois Gordon.

USA: Plot 1577, Ggaba Rd, POB 7007, Kampala; tel. (41) 4259791; fax (41) 4259794; e-mail KampalaWebContact@state.gov; internet kampala.usembassy.gov; Ambassador Steven A. Browning.

Judicial System

Courts of Judicature: High Court Bldg, POB 7085, Kampala; tel. (41) 4233420; e-mail info@judicature.go.ug; internet www.judicature.go.ug.

The Supreme Court

Kabaka Anjagala Rd, Mengo.

Hears appeals from the Court of Appeal. Also acts as a Constitutional Court.

Chief Justice: Benjamin Odoki.

Deputy Chief Justice: L. E. M. Mukasa-Kikonyogo.

The Court of Appeal: 5 Parliament Ave, Kampala; hears appeals from the High Court; the Court of Appeal consists of the Deputy Chief Justice and no fewer than seven Justices of Appeal, the number thereof being prescribed by Parliament.

The High Court

POB 7085, Kampala; tel. (41) 4233422.

Has full criminal and civil jurisdiction and also serves as a Constitutional Court. The High Court consists of the Principal Judge and 27 Puisne Judges.

Principal Judge: James Ogoola.

Magistrates' Courts: These are established under the Magistrates' Courts Act of 1970 and exercise limited jurisdiction in criminal and civil matters. The country is divided into magisterial areas, presided over by a Chief Magistrate. Under the Chief Magistrate there are two categories of Magistrates. The Magistrates preside alone over their courts. Appeals from the first category of Magistrates' Court lie directly to the High Court, while appeals from the second categories of Magistrates' Court lie to the Chief Magistrate's Court, and from there to the High Court. There are 27 Chief Magistrates' Courts, 52 Magistrates' Grade I Courts and 428 Magistrates' Grade II Courts.

Religion

Christianity is the majority religion—its adherents constitute approximately 75% of the population. Muslims account for approximately 15% of the population. A variety of other religions, including traditional indigenous religions, several branches of Hinduism, the Bahá'í Faith and Judaism, are practised freely and, combined, make up approximately 10% of the population. There are few atheists in the country. In many areas, particularly in rural settings, some religions tend to be syncretistic: deeply held traditional indigenous beliefs are blended into or observed alongside the rites of recognized religions, particularly in areas that are predominantly Christian. Missionary groups of several denominations are present and active in the country, including the Pentecostal Church, the Baptist Church, the Episcopal Church/Church of Uganda, the Church of Christ and the Mormons.

CHRISTIANITY

The Roman Catholic and Anglican Churches claim approximately the same number of followers, accounting for approximately 90% of the country's professed Christians. The Seventh-day Adventist Church, the Church of Jesus Christ of Latter-day Saints (Mormons), the Orthodox Church, Jehovah's Witnesses, the Baptist Church, the Unification Church and the Pentecostal Church, among others, are also active.

The Anglican Communion

Anglicans are adherents of the Church of the Province of Uganda, comprising 29 dioceses. In 2002 there were about 8m. adherents.

Archbishop of Uganda and Bishop of Kampala: Most Rev. Livingstone Mpalanyi-Nkoyoyo, POB 14123, Kampala; tel. (41) 4270218; fax (41) 4251925; e-mail couab@uol.co.ug.

Greek Orthodox Church

Archbishop of East Africa: Nicademus of Irinoupoulis (resident in Nairobi, Kenya); jurisdiction covers Kenya, Tanzania and Uganda.

The Roman Catholic Church

Uganda comprises four archdioceses and 15 dioceses. At 31 December 2005 there were an estimated 11,910,108 adherents (equivalent to some 42.7% of the total population).

Uganda Episcopal Conference

Uganda Catholic Secretariat, POB 2886, Kampala; tel. (41) 4510398; fax (41) 4510545.

f. 1974; Pres. Most Rev. Matthias Ssekamanya (Archbishop of Lugazi).

Archbishop of Gulu: Most Rev. John Baptist Odama, Archbishop's House, POB 200, Gulu; tel. (77) 2700996; e-mail metrog@africaonline.co.ug.

Archbishop of Kampala: Cyprian Kizito Lwanga, Archbishop's House, POB 14125, Mengo, Kampala; tel. (41) 4270183; fax (41) 4345441; e-mail klarchdioc@utlonline.co.ug.

Archbishop of Mbarara: Most Rev. Paul Bakyenga, POB 150, Mbarara; tel. (485) 420052; fax (485) 421249; e-mail mbarchd@utlonline.co.ug.

Archbishop of Tororo: Most Rev. James Odongo, Archbishop's House, Plot 17 Boma Ave, POB 933, Mbale; tel. (45) 44433269; fax (45) 44433754; e-mail tororoad@africaonline.co.ug.

ISLAM

Muslims are mainly Sunni, although there are Shi'a followers of the Aga Khan among the Asian community.

The Uganda Muslim Supreme Council: POB 1146, Kampala; tel. (41) 4344499; fax (41) 4256500; Mufti of Uganda Sheikh Shaban Mubajje; Chief Kadi and Pres. of Council Husayn Rajab Kakooza.

BAHÁ'Í FAITH

National Spiritual Assembly: POB 2662, Kampala; tel. (31) 2262681; e-mail ugangabahai@gmail.com; mems resident in 2,721 localities.

JUDAISM

There is a small Jewish community, the Abayudaya, in central Uganda, with 600 members and six synagogues.

The Press

DAILY AND OTHER NEWSPAPERS

The Citizen: Kampala; official publ. of the Democratic Party; English; Editor John Kyeyune.

The Economy: POB 6787, Kampala; weekly; English; Editor Roland Kakooza.

UGANDA

Financial Times: Plot 17/19, Station Rd, POB 31399, Kampala; tel. (41) 4245798; bi-weekly; English; Editor G. A. ONEGI OBEL.
Focus: POB 268, Kampala; tel. (41) 4235086; fax (41) 4242796; f. 1983; publ. by Islamic Information Service and Material Centre; 4 a week; English; Editor HAJJI KATENDE; circ. 12,000.
Guide: POB 5350, Kampala; tel. (41) 4233486; fax (41) 4268045; f. 1989; weekly; English; Editor-in-Chief A. A. KALIISA; circ. 30,000.
The Monitor: Plot 29–35, 8th St, POB 12141, Kampala; tel. (41) 4232367; fax (41) 4232369; e-mail editorial@monitor.co.ug; internet www.monitor.co.ug; f. 1992; daily; English; Man. Dir CONRAD NKUTU; Exec. Editor Dr PETER MWESIGE; circ. 22,000 (Mon.–Sat.), 24,000 (Sun.).
Mulengera: POB 6787, Kampala; weekly; Luganda; Editor ROLAND KAKOOZA.
Munnansi News Bulletin: POB 7098, Kampala; f. 1980; weekly; English; owned by the Democratic Party; Editor ANTHONY SGEKWEYAMA.
Munno: POB 4027, Kampala; f. 1911; daily; Luganda; publ. by the Roman Catholic Church; Editor ANTHONY SSEKWEYAMA; circ. 7,000.
New Vision: POB 9815, Kampala; tel. (41) 4337000; fax (41) 4232050; e-mail editorial@newvision.co.ug; internet www.newvision.co.ug; f. 1986; official govt newspaper; daily; English; Editor-in-chief ELS DE TERMMERMAN; circ. 34,000 (Mon.–Sat.), 42,000 (Sun.).

Bukedde: e-mail bukeddekussande@newvision.co.ug; daily; Luganda; Editor MAURICE SSEKWAUNGU; circ. 16,000.
Etop: e-mail etop@newvision.co.ug; weekly; vernacular; Editor KENNETH OLUKA; circ. 5,000.
Orumuri: tel. (485) 421265; internet www.orumuri.co.ug; weekly; vernacular; Editor JOSSY MUHANGI; circ. 11,000.
Rupiny: e-mail rupiny@newvision.co.ug; weekly; vernacular; Editor CHRIS BANYA; circ. 5,000.

Ngabo: POB 9362, Kampala; tel. (41) 4242637; f. 1979; daily; Luganda; Editor MAURICE SEKAWUNGU; circ. 7,000.
The Star: POB 9362, Kampala; tel. (41) 4242637; f. 1980; revived 1984; daily; English; Editor SAMUEL KATWERE; circ. 5,000.
Taifa Uganda Empya: POB 1986, Kampala; tel. (41) 4254652; f. 1953; daily; Luganda; Editor A. SEMBOGA; circ. 24,000.
Weekly Topic: POB 1725, Kampala; tel. (41) 4233834; weekly; English; Editor JOHN WASSWA; circ. 13,000.

PERIODICALS

Eastern Africa Journal of Rural Development: Dept of Agricultural Economics and Agribusiness, Makerere University, POB 7062, Kampala; tel. (77) 2616540; fax (41) 4530858; e-mail bkiiza@infocom.co.ug; annual; Editor BARNABAS KIIZA; circ. 800.
The Exposure: POB 3179, Kampala; tel. (41) 4267203; fax (41) 4259549; monthly; politics.
Leadership: POB 2522, Kampala; tel. (41) 4422407; fax (41) 4421576; f. 1956; 11 a year; English; Roman Catholic; circ. 7,400; Editor Fr CARLOS RODRÍGUEZ.
Mkombozi: c/o Ministry of Defence, Republic House, POB 3798, Kampala; tel. (41) 4270331; f. 1982; military affairs; Editor A. OPOLOTT.
Musizi: POB 4027, Mengo, Kampala; f. 1955; monthly; Luganda; Roman Catholic; Editor F. GITTA; circ. 30,000.
Pearl of Africa: POB 7142, Kampala; monthly; govt publ.
Uganda Confidential: POB 5576, Kampala; tel. (41) 4250273; fax (41) 4255288; e-mail ucl@swiftuganda.com; internet www.swiftuganda.com/~confidential; f. 1990; monthly; Editor TEDDY SSEZI-CHEEYE.

NEWS AGENCY

Uganda News Agency (UNA): POB 7142, Kampala; tel. (41) 4232734; fax (41) 4342259; Dir CRISPUS MUNDUA (acting).

Publishers

Centenary Publishing House Ltd: POB 6246, Kampala; tel. (41) 4241599; fax (41) 4250427; f. 1977; religious (Anglican); Man. Dir Rev. SAM KAKIZA.
Fountain Publishers Ltd: POB 488, Kampala; tel. (41) 4259163; fax (41) 4251160; e-mail fountain@starcom.co.ug; internet www.fountainpublishers.co.ug; f. 1989; general, school textbooks, children's books, academic, scholarly; Man. Dir JAMES TUMUSIIME.
Longman Uganda Ltd: POB 3409, Kampala; tel. (41) 4242940; f. 1965; Man. Dir M. K. L. MUTYABA.

Uganda Printing and Publishing Corporation: POB 33, Entebbe; tel. (41) 4220639; fax (41) 4220530; f. 1993; Man. Dir P. A. BAKER.

Broadcasting and Communications

TELECOMMUNICATIONS

Celtel Uganda: Celtel House, 40 Wampewo Ave, Kololo, POB 6771, Kampala; tel. (75) 2230110; fax (41) 4230106; e-mail customercare@ug.celtel.com; internet www.ug.celtel.com; f. 1995; Man. Dir YESSE OENGA.
MTN Uganda Ltd: POB 24624, Kampala; tel. and fax (31) 2212333; e-mail mtn@mtn.co.ug; internet www.mtn.co.ug; f. 1998.
Uganda Communications Commission: Communications House, 12th Floor, 1 Colville St, POB 7376, Kampala; tel. (41) 4339000; fax (41) 4348832; e-mail ucc@ucc.co.ug; internet www.ucc.co.ug; f. 1998; regulatory body; Chair. Dr A. M. S. KATAHOIRE; Exec. Dir PATRICK MASAMBU.
Uganda Telecom Ltd (UTL): Rwenzori Courts, Plot 2/4A, Nakasero Rd, POB 7171, Kampala; tel. (41) 4333200; fax (41) 4345907; e-mail info@utlonline.co.ug; internet www.utl.co.ug; f. 1998; state-owned; privatization pending; Man. Dir ABDULBASET ELAZZABI.

BROADCASTING

Regulatory Body

Uganda Broadcasting Council (UBC): Broadcasting Council Secretariat, Worker's House, Northern wing, 6th Floor, Plot 1 Pilkington Rd, POB 27553, Kampala; tel. (41) 4251452; fax (41) 4250612; e-mail info@broadcastug.com; internet www.broadcastug.com; f. 1998; statutory body enacted by the Electronic Media Act of 2000; main functions include licensing and regulating radio and television stations, video and cinema operators and libraries for hiring out video recordings or cinema films; consists of 12 mems appointed by the Minister of Information Communication Technology; Chair. GODFREY MUTABAAZI; Dir-Gen. EDGAR TABAARO.

Radio

91.3 Capital FM: POB 7638, Kampala; tel. (41) 4235092; fax (41) 4344556; f. 1993; independent music station broadcasting from Kampala, Mbarara and Mbale; Chief Officers WILLIAM PIKE, PATRICK QUARCOO.
Central Broadcasting Service (CBS): POB 12760, Kampala; tel. (41) 4272993; fax (41) 4340031; f. 1996; independent station broadcasting in local languages and English to most of Uganda.
Radio One: POB 4589, Kampala; tel. (41) 4348211; fax (41) 4348311.
Radio Uganda: POB 7142, Kampala; tel. (41) 4257256; fax (41) 4256888; f. 1954; state-controlled; broadcasts in 24 languages, including English, Swahili and Ugandan vernacular languages; Commr for Broadcasting JACK TURYAMWIJUKA.
Sanyu Radio: Katto Plaza, Nkrumah Rd, Kampala; f. 1993; independent station broadcasting to Kampala and its environs.
Voice of Toro: POB 2203, Kampala.

Television

Sanyu Television: Naguru; f. 1994; independent station broadcasting to Kampala and its environs.
Uganda Television (UTV): POB 7142, Kampala; tel. (41) 4254461; f. 1962; state-controlled commercial service; programmes mainly in English, also in Swahili and Luganda; transmits over a radius of 320 km from Kampala; five relay stations are in operation, others are under construction; Controller of Programmes FAUSTIN MISANVU.

Finance

(cap. = capital; res = reserves; dep. = deposits; m. = million; brs = branches; amounts in new Uganda shillings, unless otherwise indicated)

BANKING

Central Bank

Bank of Uganda: 37–43 Kampala Rd, POB 7120, Kampala; tel. (41) 4258441; fax (41) 4255983; e-mail info@bou.or.ug; internet www.bou.or.ug; f. 1966; bank of issue; cap. 20,000m., res 291,993m., dep. 2,659,751m. (June 2005); Gov. EMMANUEL TUMUSIIME-MUTEBILE; Dep. Gov. DAVID G. OPIOKELLO (acting).

UGANDA

State Bank

Uganda Development Bank Ltd (UDBL): 15A Clement Hill Rd, Ruth Towers, POB 7210, Kampala; tel. (414) 355555; fax (414) 355556; e-mail info@udbl.co.ug; f. 1972; state-owned; reorg. 2001; privatization pending; cap. 11m. (Dec. 1993); CEO ANTHONY K. APPIAH.

Commercial Banks

Bank of Africa—Uganda Ltd: Plot 45 Jinja Rd, POB 2750, Kampala; tel. (41) 4236535; fax (41) 4230439; e-mail boa@boa-uganda.com; internet www.boa-uganda.com; f. 1986 as Allied Bank International (Uganda); name changed as above in 2005; 46% owned by Bank of Africa—Kenya, 22% by FMO, 22% by Aureos Capital, 10% by Central Holdings Ltd; cap. 4,001m., res 5,361m., dep. 60,553m. (Dec. 2006); Chair. JOHN CARRUTHERS; Man. Dir KWAME AHADZI; 5 brs.

Cairo International Bank: 30 Kampala Rd, POB 7052, Kampala; tel. (41) 4235666; fax (41) 4230130; e-mail cib@spacenetuganda.com; 44.4% owned by Banque du Caire, 36.1% owned by Kato Aromatics SAE, 6.5% each owned Bank of Egypt, Bank Misr and Bank of Alexandria; cap. 7,135m. (Dec. 2003); Chair. Dr IBRAHIM KAMEL; Man. Dir NABIL GHANEM.

Crane Bank Ltd: Crane Chambers, 38 Kampala Rd, POB 22572, Kampala; tel. (41) 4231337; fax (41) 4231578; e-mail cranebank@cranebanklimited.com; internet www.cranebanklimited.com; 17% by M/S Meera Investments Ltd, remainder owned by private investors; cap. 5,000m., dep. 107,435m. (Dec. 2003); Chair. SAMSON MUWANGUZI; Man. Dir A. R. KALAN (acting).

DFCU Bank Ltd: Impala House, 13 Kimathi Ave, POB 70, Kampala; tel. (41) 4231784; fax (41) 4231687; e-mail dfcubank@dfcugroup.com; internet www.dfcugroup.com; f. 1984 as Gold Trust Bank Ltd; current name adopted 2000; cap. 5,200m., res 5,097m., dep. 172,645m. (Dec. 2004); Chair. Dr WILLIAM KALEMA; Man. Dir COLIN MCCORMACK.

Diamond Trust Bank (Uganda) Ltd: Diamond Trust Bldg, Plot 17–19, Kampala Rd, POB 7155, Kampala; tel. (41) 4259331; fax (41) 4342286; e-mail info@dtbuganda.co.ug; 40% owned by The Diamond Jubilee Investment Trust, 33.3% owned by Aga Khan Fund for Economic Development, 26.7% owned by Diamond Trust Bank Kenya Ltd; cap. 4,000m., dep. 31,757m. (Dec. 2005); Chair. MAHMOOD MANJI; CEO MANMATH K. DALAI.

Mercantile Credit Bank Ltd: Plot 10, Old Port Bell Rd, POB 620, Kampala; tel. and fax (41) 4235967; e-mail mcb@afsat.com; cap. 1,000m. (Dec. 2003); Chair. PALLE MOELLER; Man. NELSON LUGOLOBI.

National Bank of Commerce (Uganda) Ltd: Cargen House, Plot 13A, Parliament Ave, POB 23232, Kampala; tel. (41) 2347699; fax (41) 2347701; e-mail nbc@swiftuganda.com; cap. 4,631m. (Dec. 2003); Chair. AMOS NZEYI; Man. Dir G. BANGERA.

Nile Bank Ltd: Spear House, Plot 22, Jinja Rd, POB 2834, Kampala; tel. (41) 4346904; fax (41) 4257779; e-mail info@nilebank.co.ug; internet www.nilebank.co.ug; f. 1988; 15.88% owned by East African Development Bank, remainder owned by private investors; cap. 4,000m., res 889m., dep. 111,053m. (Dec. 2005); Chair. J. B. BYAMUGISHA; Man. Dir RICHARD P. BYARUGABA; 8 brs.

Orient Bank Ltd: Orient Plaza, Plot 6/6A, Kampala Rd, POB 3072, Kampala; tel. (41) 4236012; fax (41) 4236066; e-mail mail@orient-bank.com; internet www.orient-bank.com; f. 1993; cap. 5,000m., res 3,377m., dep. 91,020m. (Dec. 2005); Chair. KETAN MORJARIA; Man. Dir SAMWIRI H. K. NJUKI; 6 brs.

Post Bank Uganda Ltd: Plot 11/13, Nkrumah Rd, POB 7189, Kampala; tel. (41) 4258551; fax (41) 4347107; e-mail postbank@imul.com; wholly state-owned; cap. 2,000m. (Dec. 2003); Chair. STEPHEN MWANJE.

Development Banks

Capital Finance Corpn Ltd: 4 Pilkington Rd, POB 21091, Kampala; tel. (41) 4345200; fax (41) 4258310; 70% owned by City Credit Bank Ltd; Chair. KEMAL LALANI; Man. Dir and CEO GHULAM HAIDER DAUDANI.

Centenary Rural Development Bank: 7 Entebbe Rd, POB 1892, Kampala; tel. (41) 4251276; fax (41) 4251273; e-mail info@centenarybank.co.ug; internet www.centenarybank.co.ug; cap. 4,110m. (Dec. 2003); Chair. Dr JOHN DDUMBA SSENTAMU; CEO HUNG LIHN.

Development Finance Co of Uganda Ltd: Rwenzori House, 1 Lumumba Ave, POB 2767, Kampala; tel. (41) 4231215; fax (41) 4259435; e-mail dfcu@dfcugroup.com; internet www.dfcugroup.com; owned by Commonwealth Devt Corpn (60%), Uganda Devt Corpn (18.5%) and International Finance Corpn (21.5%); cap. 3,978m. (Dec. 2003); Chair. WILLIAM S. KALEMA; Man. Dir C. MCCORMACK.

East African Development Bank (EADB): East African Development Bank Bldg, 4 Nile Ave, POB 7128, Kampala; tel. (41) 4230021; fax (41) 4259763; e-mail dg@eadb.org; internet www.eadb.org; f. 1967; Govts of Kenya, Uganda and Tanzania 25.46% each; remaining 23.62% shared between FMO (Netherlands); Deutsche Investitions- und Entwicklungs-GmbH (Germany); SBIC—Africa Holdings; Commercial Bank of Africa (Kenya); Nordea AB (Sweden); Standard Chartered Bank (United Kingdom); Barclays Bank PLC (United Kingdom); provides financial and tech. assistance to promote industrial development within Uganda, Kenya and Tanzania; regional offices in Nairobi and Dar es Salaam; cap. US $69m., res US $8m. (Dec. 2005); Chair. GRAY S. MGONJA.

Housing Finance Co Uganda Ltd: Investment House, 25 Kampala Rd, POB 1539, Kampala; tel. (41) 4341227; fax (41) 4341429; internet www.housingfinance.co.ug; 45% owned by Govt, 50% owned by National Social Security Fund, 5% owned by National Housing and Construction Corpn; cap. 1,000m. (Dec. 2003); Chair. KEITH MUHAKANIZI; Man. Dir NICHOLAS OKWIR.

Foreign Banks

Bank of Baroda (Uganda) Ltd (India): 18 Kampala Rd, POB 7197, Kampala; tel. (41) 4233680; fax (41) 4230781; e-mail bobho@spacenetuganda.com; internet www.bankofbaroda.com; f. 1969; wholly owned by Bank of Baroda (India); cap. 4,000m., res 5,647m., dep. 126,995m. (Dec. 2004); Chair. M. B. SAMANT; Man. Dir K. K. SHUKLA; 6 brs.

Barclays Bank of Uganda Ltd (United Kingdom): POB 7101, Barclay House, Plot 4, Harrington Rd, Kampala; tel. (31) 2218300; fax (31) 2218393; e-mail uganda.barclays@barclays.com; internet www.barclays.com/uganda.htm; f. 1969; wholly owned by Barclays Bank PLC (United Kingdom); cap. 4,000m., res 15,236m., dep. 328,553m. (Dec. 2005); Chair. GEORGE EGADU; Man. Dir NICK MBUVI; 4 brs.

Citibank (Uganda) Ltd (USA): Plot 4, Centre Court, Ternan Ave, Nakasero, POB 7505, Kampala; tel. (41) 4305500; fax (41) 4340624; internet www.citibank.com/eastafrica/uganda.htm; 99.9% owned by Citicorp Overseas Investment Corpn, 0.1% owned by Foremost Investment; cap. 21,285m. (Dec. 2003); Chair. Prof. J. M. L. SSEBUWUUFU; Man. Dir SHIRISH BHIDE.

Stanbic Bank Uganda Ltd (United Kingdom): Crested Towers, Short Tower, 17 Hannington Rd, POB 7131, Kampala; tel. (41) 2231152; fax (41) 2231116; e-mail ugandainfo@stanbic.com; internet www.stanbic.co.ug; f. 1906 as National Bank of India Uganda; adopted present name 1993; wholly owned by Stanbic Africa Holdings Ltd (United Kingdom); merged with Uganda Commercial Bank Ltd 2002; cap. 5,119m., res 50,703m., dep. 828,150m. (Dec. 2005); Chair. Dr MARTIN ALIKER; Man. Dir KITILI MBATHI; 2 brs.

Standard Chartered Bank Uganda Ltd (United Kingdom): 5 Speke Rd, POB 7111, Kampala; tel. (41) 4341623; fax (41) 4231473; internet www.standardchartered.com/ug; f. 1912; wholly owned by Standard Chartered Bank PLC; cap. 4,000m., res 15,553m., dep. 544,863m. (Dec. 2005); Chair. JAMES MULWANA; CEO LAMIN MANJANG; 5 brs.

Tropical Africa Bank Ltd (Libya): Plot 27, Kampala Rd, POB 9485-7292, Kampala; tel. (41) 2341408; fax (41) 2232296; e-mail tabu10@calva.com; f. 1972; 50% govt-owned, 50% owned by Libyan Arab Foreign Bank; cap. 7,000m. (Dec. 2003); Chair. C. M. KASSAMI; Gen. Man. and CEO MOHAMED A. WAHRA.

STOCK EXCHANGE

Uganda Securities Exchange: Workers' House, 2nd Floor, Northern Wing, 1 Pilkington Rd, POB 23552, Kampala; tel. (41) 4343297; fax (41) 4343841; internet www.use.or.ug; f. 1997; Chair. GEOFFREY A. ONEGI-OBEL; Chief Exec. SIMON RUTEGA.

INSURANCE

East Africa General Insurance Co Ltd: Plot 14, Kampala Rd, POB 1392, Kampala; tel. (31) 22262221; fax (41) 4343234; e-mail vkrishna@eagen.co.ug; internet www.eagen.co.ug; f. 1949; public shareholding co; fire, life, motor, marine and accident; CEO VYASA KRISHNA.

National Insurance Corporation: Plot 3, Pilkington Rd, POB 7134, Kampala; tel. (41) 4258001; fax (41) 4259925; f. 1964; general and life; Man. Dir S. SEBUUFU.

NICO Insurance (Uganda) Ltd: 3rd Floor Greenland Towers, Kampala Rd, Opposite Bank of Uganda, POB 24256, Kampala; tel. (31) 2264720; fax (31) 2264723; internet www.nicomw.com; subsidiary of NICO Holdings Ltd (based in Malawi); Man. Dir RONALD ZAKE.

Pan World Insurance Co Ltd: POB 7658, Kampala; tel. (41) 4341618; fax (41) 4341593; Gen. Man. GORDON SENTIBA.

Uganda American Insurance Co Ltd: POB 7077, Kampala; tel. and fax (41) 4533781; f. 1970; Man. Dir STAN MENSAH.

UGANDA

Uganda Co-operative Insurance Ltd: Plot 10, Bombo Rd, POB 6176, Kampala; tel. (41) 4241836; fax (41) 4258231; f. 1982; general; Chair. EPHRAIM KAKURU; Gen. Man. (vacant).

Trade and Industry

GOVERNMENT AGENCIES

Capital Markets Authority: 8th Floor, Jubilee Insurance Centre, 14 Parliament Ave, POB 24565, Kampala; tel. (41) 4342788; fax (41) 4342803; e-mail info@cmauganda.co.ug; internet www.cmauganda.co.ug; f. 1996 to develop, promote and regulate capital markets sector; Chair. TWAHA KIGONGO KAAWAASE.

Enterprise Development Unit (EPD): Kampala; oversees privatization programme; Exec. Dir LEONARD MUGANWA.

Export and Import Licensing Division: POB 7000, Kampala; tel. (41) 4258795; f. 1987; advises importers and exporters and issues import and export licences; Prin. Commercial Officer JOHN MUHWEZI.

Uganda Advisory Board of Trade: POB 6877, Kampala; tel. (41) 4233311; f. 1974; issues trade licences and service for exporters.

Uganda Export Promotion Board: POB 5045, Kampala; tel. (41) 4230233; fax (41) 4259779; e-mail uepc@starcom.co.ug; internet www.ugandaexportsonline.com; f. 1983; provides market intelligence, organizes training, trade exhbns, etc.; Exec. Dir FLORENCE KATE.

Uganda Investment Authority: Investment Centre, Plot 28, Kampala Rd, POB 7418, Kampala; tel. (41) 4251561; fax (41) 4342903; e-mail info@ugandainvest.com; internet www.ugandainvest.com; f. 1991; promotes foreign and local investment, assists investors, provides business information, issues investment licences; Exec. Dir Dr MAGGIE KIGOZI.

DEVELOPMENT ORGANIZATIONS

Agriculture and Livestock Development Fund: f. 1976; provides loans to farmers.

National Housing and Construction Corpn: Crested Towers, POB 659, Kampala; tel. (41) 4330002; fax (41) 4258708; e-mail sales@nhcc.co.ug; internet www.nhcc.co.ug; f. 1964; govt agent for building works; also develops residential housing; Chair. Dr COLIN SENTONGO; Gen. Man. M. S. KASEKENDE.

Uganda Industrial Development Corpn Ltd (ULDC): 9–11 Parliament Ave, POB 7042, Kampala; tel. (41) 4234381; fax (41) 4241588; f. 1952; Chair. SAM RUTEGA.

CHAMBER OF COMMERCE

Uganda National Chamber of Commerce and Industry: Plot 2, 1st Floor, Parliament Ave, Jumbo Plaza, POB 3809, Kampala; tel. (41) 4503024; fax (41) 4230231; e-mail info@ugandachamber.com; internet www.chamberuganda.com; Chair. BONEY KATATUMBA.

INDUSTRIAL AND TRADE ASSOCIATIONS

CMB Ltd (Coffee Marketing Board): POB 7154, Kampala; tel. (41) 4254051; fax (41) 4230790; state-owned; privatization pending; purchases and exports coffee; Chair. Dr DDUMBA SSENTAMU; Man. Dir SAM KIGGUNDU.

Cotton Development Organization: POB 7018, Kampala; tel. (41) 4232968; fax (41) 4232975; Man. Dir JOLLY SABUNE.

Produce Marketing Board: POB 3705, Kampala; tel. (41) 4236238; Gen. Man. ESTHER KAMPAMPARA.

Uganda Coffee Development Authority (UCDA): Coffee House, Plot 35, Jinja Rd, POB 7267, Kampala; tel. (41) 4256940; fax (41) 4256994; e-mail ucdajc@ugandacoffee.org; internet www.ugandacoffee.org; f. 1991; enforces quality control and promotes coffee exports, maintains statistical data, advises Govt on local and world prices and trains processors and quality controllers; Man. Dir HENRY NGABIRANO.

Uganda Importers', Exporters' and Traders' Association: Kampala.

Uganda Manufacturers' Association (UMA): Lugogo Show Grounds, POB 6966, Kampala; tel. (41) 4221034; fax (41) 4220285; e-mail information@uma.or.ug; internet www.uma.or.ug; promotes mfrs' interests; Chair. JAMES KALIBALA.

Uganda Tea Authority: POB 4161, Kampala; tel. (41) 4231003; state-owned; controls and co-ordinates activities of the tea industry; Gen. Man. MIRIA MARGARITA MUGABI.

EMPLOYERS' ORGANIZATION

Federation of Uganda Employers: POB 3820, Kampala; tel. (41) 4220201; fax (41) 4221257; e-mail fue@infocom.co.ug; internet www.employers.co.ug; Chair. ALOYSIUS K. SSEMMANDA; Exec. Dir ROSEMARY N. SSENABULYA.

UTILITIES

Electricity

Uganda Electricity Board (UEB): POB 7059, Kampala; tel. (41) 4254071; fax (41) 4235119; f. 1948; privatization pending; Chair. J. E. N. KAGULE-MAGAMBO; 36 brs.

Water

National Water & Sewerage Corpn: Plot 39, Jinja Rd, POB 7053, Kampala; tel. (41) 4315100; fax (41) 4258299; e-mail info@nwsc.co.ug; internet www.nwsc.co.ug; f. 1972; privatization pending; Man. Dir WILLIAM TSIMWA MUHAIRWE; 12 brs.

CO-OPERATIVES

In 2000 there were 6,313 co-operative societies, grouped in 34 unions. There is at least one co-operative union in each administrative district.

Uganda Co-operative Alliance: Kampala; co-ordinating body for co-operative unions, of which the following are among the most important:

Bugisu Co-operative Union Ltd: Palisa Rd, Private Bag, Mbale; tel. (45) 4233027; f. 1954; processors and exporters of Bugisu arabica coffee; 226 mem. socs; Gen. Man. WOMUTU.

East Mengo Growers' Co-operative Union Ltd: POB 7092, Kampala; tel. (41) 4270383; fax (41) 4243502; f. 1968; processors and exporters of coffee and cotton; 280 mem. socs; Chair. FRANCIS MUKAMA; Man. JOSEPH SSEMOGERERE.

Kakumiro Growers' Co-operative Union: POB 511, Kakumiro; processing of coffee and cotton; Sec. and Man. TIBIHWA-RUKEERA.

Kimeeme Livestock Co-operative Society: Mwanga II Rd, POB 6670, Kampala; f. 1984; farming and marketing of livestock; Chair. SAMUSI LUKIMA.

Lango Co-operative Union: POB 59, Lira; f. 1956; ginning and exporting of conventional and organic cotton produce; Gen. Man. PATRICK ORYANG.

Masaka Co-operative Union Ltd: POB 284, Masaka; tel. (481) 420260; f. 1951; coffee, dairy farming, food processing, carpentry; 245 primary co-operative socs; Chair. J. M. KASOZI; Gen. Man. EDWARD C. SSERUUMA.

Nyakatonzi Growers Co-operative Union: Fort Portal Rd, POB 32, Kasese; tel. (483) 444370; fax (483) 444135; f. 1957; processors and exporters of coffee and cotton; Gen. Man. ADAM BWAMBALE.

South Bukedi Co-operative Union: 6 Busia Rd, POB 101, Tororo; tel. (45) 4244327; f. 1952; ginning and export of cotton lint; Gen. Man. MICHAEL O. OGUNDY.

South-west Nile Co-operative Union: POB 33, Pakwach, Nebbi; f. 1958; ginning and export of cotton; Gen. Man. PHILIP UPAKRWOTH.

Uganda Co-operative Savings and Credit Society: 62 Parliament Ave, POB 9452, Kampala; tel. (41) 4257410; f. 1973; Chair. PATRICK KAYONGO.

Uganda Co-operative Transport Union: 41 Bombo Rd, POB 5486, Kampala; tel. and fax (41) 456506; e-mail uctultd@infocom.co.ug; f. 1971; general transport, imports of motor vehicles, vehicle repair and maintenance; Gen. Man. NUWAGIRA NABOTH MWEJUNE.

Wamala Growers' Co-operative Union Ltd: POB 99, Mityana; tel. (46) 4222036; f. 1968; coffee and cotton growers, real estate agents, cattle ranchers, printers, mfrs of edible oils, bricks, tiles and clay products; 250 mem. socs; Gen. Man. HERBERT KIZITO.

West Mengo Growers' Co-operative Union Ltd: POB 7039, Kampala; tel. (41) 4567511; f. 1948; cotton growing and buying, coffee buying and processing, maize milling; 250 mem. socs; Chair. H. E. KATABALWA MIIRO.

West Nile Tobacco Co-operative Union: Wandi, POB 71, Arua; f. 1965; growing, curing and marketing of tobacco; Gen. Man. ANDAMAH BABWA.

TRADE UNION

National Organization of Trade Unions (NOTU): POB 2150, Kampala; tel. (41) 4256295; f. 1973; Chair. E. KATURAMU; Sec.-Gen. MATHIAS MUKASA.

Transport

RAILWAYS

In 1997 there were 1,250 km of 1,000-mm-gauge track in operation. A programme to rehabilitate the railway network is under way.

Uganda Railways Corporation (URC): Nasser Rd, POB 7150, Kampala; tel. (41) 4254961; fax (41) 4344405; f. 1977 following the dissolution of East African Railways; management of operations assumed by Rift Valley Railways consortium in Nov. 2006; Man. Dir D. C. Murungi.

ROADS

Uganda's road network consists of approximately 10,000 km of national or trunk roads (of which some 2,200 km are bituminized, the rest being gravel), 25,000 km of district or feeder roads, 2,800 km of urban roads (comprising roads in Kampala City, the 13 municipal councils and the 50 town councils in the country) and 30,000 km of community roads. There are also private roads, some of which are open to the general travelling public. Road transport remains the dominant mode of transport in terms of scale of infrastructure and the volume of freight and passenger movement. The National (Trunk) Road Network carries 80% of Uganda's passenger and freight traffic and includes international routes linking Uganda to neighbouring countries and to the sea (via Kenya and Tanzania), and internal roads linking areas of high population and large administrative and commercial centres. It provides the only form of access to most rural communities. The Government is implementing a programme of continuous upgrading of key gravel roads to bitumen standard.

INLAND WATERWAYS

A rail wagon ferry service connecting Jinja with the Tanzanian port of Tanga, via Mwanza, was inaugurated in 1983, thus reducing Uganda's dependence on the Kenyan port of Mombasa. In 1986 the Uganda and Kenya Railways Corporations began the joint operation of Lake Victoria Marine Services, to ferry goods between the two countries via Lake Victoria.

CIVIL AVIATION

The international airport is at Entebbe, on Lake Victoria, some 40 km from Kampala. There are also several small airfields.

Civil Aviation Authority (CAA): POB 5536, Kampala; Passenger Terminal Bldg, 2nd floor, Entebbe International Airport; tel. (41) 4320516; fax (41) 4320571; e-mail info@caa.co.ug; internet www.caa.co.ug; Man. Dir Ambrose Akandonda.

Principal Airlines

Air Uganda (AU): Kampala; f. 2007; services to Africa; CEO Peter de Waal.

Dairo Air Cargo Services: 24 Jinja Rd, POB 5480, Kampala; tel. (41) 4257731.

Eagle Air Ltd: Entebbe International Airport, POB 7392, Kampala; tel. (41) 4344292; fax (41) 4344501; e-mail eagle@swiftuganda.com; internet www.eagleuganda.com; f. 1994; domestic services, charter flights to neighbouring countries; Man. Dir Capt. Anthony Rubombora.

Inter Air: Nile Ave, POB 22658, Kampala; tel. (41) 4255508.

Tourism

Uganda's principal attractions for tourists are the forests, lakes, mountains and wildlife and an equable climate. A programme to revive the tourist industry by building or improving hotels and creating new national parks began in the late 1980s. There were 467,728 tourist arrivals in 2005 (compared with 12,786 in 1983). Revenue from the sector in that year was estimated at US $357m., including revenue from the transport of passengers.

Uganda Tourist Board: Impala House, 13/15 Kimatti Ave, POB 7211, Kampala; tel. (41) 4342196; fax (41) 4342188; e-mail utb@visituganda.com; internet www.visituganda.com; Chair. Peter Kamya; Gen. Man. Ignatius Nakishero.

UKRAINE

Introductory Survey

Location, Climate, Language, Religion, Flag, Capital

Ukraine is situated in east-central Europe. It is bordered by Poland, Slovakia, Hungary, Romania and Moldova to the west, by Belarus to the north, and by Russia to the north-east and east. To the south lie the Black Sea and the Sea of Azov. The climate is temperate, especially in the south. The north and north-west share many of the continental climatic features of Poland or Belarus. Average temperatures in Kyiv (Kiev) range from −6.1°C (21°F) in January to 20.4°C (69°F) in July, and average annual rainfall is 615 mm (24 ins). The official state language is Ukrainian, although Russian is widely spoken, except in the west. Most of the population are adherents of Orthodox Christianity, and there are many adherents to the Roman Catholic Church (mostly followers of Eastern rites) in western regions. There are also a number of Protestant churches and small communities of Jews and Muslims, the latter principally comprising Crimean Tatars. The national flag (proportions 2 by 3) has two equal horizontal stripes, of pale blue over yellow. The capital is Kyiv.

Recent History

The original East Slavic state, Kyivan (Kievan) Rus, founded in the late 10th century, was based in what is now Ukraine ('the Borderlands'), and is claimed as the precursor of Russia, Belarus and Ukraine. Following the fall of the Rus principalities, in the 13th and 14th centuries, during the Mongol invasions, the Ukrainians (sometimes known as Little Russians or Ruthenians), mainly under Polish and Lithuanian rulers, developed distinctively from the other Eastern Slavs. Ukrainians first entered the Russian Empire in 1654, when a Cossack state east of the Dnipro (Dniepr) River, led by Hetman Bohdan Khmelnytsky, sought Russian protection from Polish invasion. In 1667 Ukraine was divided: the regions east of the Dnipro became part of Russia, while Western Ukraine was annexed by Poland. Russia gained more Ukrainian lands as a result of subsequent partitions of Poland (1793 and 1795) and, in the south, from the Ottoman Empire; the western regions were acquired by Austria.

When the Russian Empire collapsed, in 1917, Ukrainian nationalists set up a central Rada (council or soviet) in Kyiv and demanded autonomy from the Provisional Government in Petrograd (St Petersburg). After the Bolshevik coup, in November, the Rada proclaimed a Ukrainian People's Republic. In December the Bolsheviks established a rival Government in Kharkiv, and by February 1918 much of Ukraine was occupied by Soviet forces. In March, however, the Bolsheviks were forced to cede Ukraine to Germany, under the terms of the Treaty of Brest-Litovsk. Ukraine was the battleground for much of the fighting in the Civil War over the next two years, but in December 1920 a Ukrainian Soviet Socialist Republic (SSR) was established.

The Treaty of Rīga, which formally ended the Soviet–Polish War in 1921, assigned territories in western Ukraine to Poland, Czechoslovakia and Romania. Eastern and central lands formed the Ukrainian SSR, one of the founding members of the Union of Soviet Socialist Republics (USSR), in December 1922. The collectivization of agriculture from 1929 had severe consequences for the republic; at least 5m. Ukrainians were estimated to have died in a famine in 1933, which resulted from collectivization. In the 1930s advocates of the wider Ukrainian cultural or political autonomy were arrested, and by the late 1930s almost the entire Ukrainian cultural and political élite had been imprisoned, killed or exiled. Ukraine also suffered greatly during the Second World War, which resulted in an estimated 6m. deaths in the republic.

Soviet victory in the war, and the annexing of territories from Czechoslovakia, Poland and Romania resulted in the uniting of the western and eastern areas of Ukraine, and the republic gained representation, nominally separate from that of the USSR, at the UN. In 1954 Crimea (formerly part of Russia), the Tatar inhabitants of which had been deported *en masse* to Soviet Central Asia in 1944, was transferred to Ukrainian control.

During the 1960s there was an increase in covert opposition to the regime, manifested in the production of independent publications, known as *samvydav* (*samizdat*—self-publishing). In 1973 Petro Shelest, the First Secretary (leader) of the Communist Party of Ukraine (CPU) was dismissed and replaced by Vladimir Shcherbitsky, a loyal ally of the Soviet leader, Leonid Brezhnev.

The accession of the reformist Mikhail Gorbachev to the Soviet leadership, in 1985, had little initial effect in Ukraine. On 26 April 1986 a serious explosion occurred at the Chornobyl (Chernobyl) nuclear power station, in northern Ukraine. Only after unusually high levels of radiation were reported in other European countries did Soviet officials admit that large amounts of radioactivity had leaked into the atmosphere. Some 135,000 people were evacuated from a 50-km (30-mile) exclusion zone around Chornobyl (including large areas within neighbouring Belarus). Thirty-one people were killed in the initial explosion, but in 1996 it was reported that an estimated 2,500 deaths in Ukraine may have been caused by the accident, while a further 3.2m. people had been affected by the disaster, as a result of increased numbers of cancers and other related illnesses. Official secrecy surrounding the Chornobyl accident led to greater public support for opposition movements in Ukraine, such as the liberal nationalist Ukrainian People's Movement for Restructuring (Rukh), which was founded in 1988 by a group of prominent writers and intellectuals. Similarly, economic problems contributed to a growing militancy among mining communities in the Donbass region (around Donetsk, in eastern Ukraine), producing 11 strikes in the first three months of 1989, and the revival of hitherto 'underground' religious groups from 1988 resulted in the legalization of the Ukrainian (Byzantine rite) Catholic Church in December 1989.

Shcherbitsky was dismissed in September 1989; he was replaced by Volodymyr Ivashko. In local and republican elections, held on 4 March 1990, candidates supported by the Democratic Bloc, a coalition led by Rukh, won 108 of the 450 seats in the Verkhovna Rada (Supreme Council—republican legislature). Independents supported by the Bloc won about 60 seats, although an estimated 280 supported the CPU leadership. In June Ivashko was elected Chairman of the Verkhovna Rada (the highest state post in the Republic); he resigned later in the month as First Secretary of the CPU. On 16 July the Verkhovna Rada adopted a declaration of sovereignty. Later in the month Ivashko resigned as Chairman of the Verkhovna Rada, following his appointment as Deputy General Secretary of the Communist Party of the Soviet Union; he was replaced by Leonid Kravchuk, hitherto Second Secretary of the CPU. In October Vitold Fokin, a moderate reformist, succeeded Vitaliy Masol as Chairman of the Council of Ministers (Prime Minister).

The Government participated in negotiations on a new union treaty and signed the protocol to a draft treaty in March 1991. The Government also agreed to conduct the all-Union referendum on the future of the USSR (see the chapter on the Russian Federation), but appended a further question, asking if Ukraine's declaration of sovereignty should form the basis for participation in a renewed federation. Of the electorate, 84% participated in the referendum, 70% of whom approved Gorbachev's proposal to preserve the USSR as a 'renewed federation'. However, Ukraine's own question received greater support (80%), and an additional question in certain western regions, which asked voters if they supported a fully independent Ukraine, secured the support of 90% of those voting.

Following the attempted coup by conservative communists in Moscow, the Russian and Soviet capital, on 19 August 1991, the Verkhovna Rada, on 24 August, adopted a declaration of independence, pending confirmation by a referendum on 1 December, when direct presidential elections were also scheduled. The CPU was banned at the end of August. Despite his background in the CPU, Kravchuk's support for Ukrainian independence ensured his election as President of the Republic on 1 December 1991, with 62% of the votes cast. In the referendum, some 90% of votes were cast in favour of independence (84% of the electorate participated), which thereby took effect. In early December an independent Ukrainian armed forces was established. In January 1992 a new interim currency coupon, which retained the Ukrainian name of the Soviet currency, the karbovanets, was introduced.

The Government was subject to intense criticism as inflation increased sharply following the withdrawal of subsidies from foodstuffs in July 1992, and resigned in September, having been conclusively defeated in a vote of no confidence. In October Leonid Kuchma, hitherto director-general of a missile factory in Dnipropetrovsk, was appointed Prime Minister, and a new Government was formed. Kuchma proposed a programme of economic reform, which was strongly opposed by left-wing groups, including the Socialist Party of Ukraine (SPU), which had been formed from elements of the CPU. In January 1993 Viktor Yushchenko, a leading exponent of market reform, was appointed Governor of the National Bank of Ukraine (NBU). As Ukraine began to experience 'hyperinflation', more than 2m. miners and factory workers, mainly in the Donbass region, joined a strike, in June 1993, demanding a referendum of confidence in the President and in the Verkhovna Rada. In September Kuchma again tendered his resignation, which was accepted by the legislature; Yufym Zvyahylsky, the First Deputy Prime Minister, was appointed as Prime Minister, in an acting capacity, although after several days President Kravchuk assumed direct control of the Government.

Elections to the new, 450-member Verkhovna Rada were held on 27 March 1994, with two subsequent rounds of voting in April, in constituencies where candidates had failed to secure 50% of the votes cast. The CPU was permitted to contest the elections and won 86 seats, more than any other group, and, in alliance with the SPU and the Peasants' Party of Ukraine (PPU), formed the largest bloc in the Verkhovna Rada; 170 nominally independent candidates were elected. A notable political division between eastern (where left-wing parties obtained greater support) and western (where moderate nationalist parties won the greatest share of the votes) regions was evident in the election results. Further rounds of voting, held in late 1994 to fill the 112 vacant seats, failed to elect candidates in more than 50 seats. In May Oleksandr Moroz, the leader of the SPU, was elected Chairman of the Verkhovna Rada, which in June elected Masol as Prime Minister.

A presidential election held on 26 June 1994 was inconclusive, as no candidate secured the minimum 50% of the votes necessary for election. Kravchuk received the greatest share of votes cast, with 37.7%, followed by Kuchma, with 31.3%. In a second round of voting, held on 10 July, Kuchma was elected President, securing 52.1% of the votes. A continuing polarity in voting patterns was recorded between the east, where voters largely supported Kuchma, and the west, where Kravchuk secured a majority of votes cast. In March 1995 Masol resigned as Prime Minister and was replaced, in an acting capacity, by Yevhen Marchuk. In June the President and the Verkhovna Rada signed a Constitutional Agreement, announcing the cancellation of a referendum of confidence in the President and the legislature, previously announced by Kuchma, but granting the President additional powers, including the right to appoint leading officials without the approval of the Verkhovna Rada, and to issue decrees with the force of legislation. These provisions were to remain in effect until the adoption of a new Constitution. The President was to retain the prerogative to legislate economic reform by decree until the expiry of his term in 1999.

In May 1996 Kuchma dismissed Marchuk as premier, appointing Pavlo Lazarenko in his place, and the new Constitution was adopted on 28 June. It confirmed the extensive new powers of appointment granted to the President in the interim Constitutional Agreement. In July the Cabinet of Ministers resigned; Lazarenko retained the premiership in the new Government. As unrest in the coal-mining industry continued, the Government commenced a structural reorganization of the sector, and in mid-July an agreement was reached with the trade unions to end an ongoing strike. The attempted assassination of Lazarenko, shortly after the signing of the agreement, was linked by some observers to his role in resolving the dispute. The introduction of a new currency, the hryvnya, in the same month, was regarded as an indication that the serious economic difficulties that had affected Ukraine for several years were beginning to relent. Lazarenko resigned in early July 1997. In mid-July the legislature approved Valeriy Pustovoytenko as the new Prime Minister. In September the legislature approved a new electoral law, which provided for 225 seats in the 450-member Verkhovna Rada to be allocated by proportional representation on the basis of party lists, subject to a minimum threshold of 4% of the total votes cast, and for the remaining 225 to be elected from single-seat constituencies. Meanwhile, it was announced that Lazarenko was to be prosecuted on charges of embezzlement.

A total of 30 parties and electoral blocs contested the legislative elections to the Verkhovna Rada, held on 29 March 1998, in which 70.8% of the electorate participated. The CPU obtained 123 seats, becoming the largest party in the legislature. Eight parties secured representation on the basis of party lists, and some 136 independent deputies were elected. Oleksandr Tkachenko, the leader of the PPU, was elected as Chairman of the legislature in July. Lazarenko was arrested in early December as he attempted to enter Switzerland, and charged with money-laundering. In February 1999 the Verkhovna Rada endorsed a resolution allowing for Lazarenko to be charged, and shortly afterwards he was detained in the USA.

In the first round of voting in the presidential election, held on 31 October 1999, Kuchma won the largest proportion of the votes cast for any candidate, with 36.5%; his opponent in the second round was Petro Symonenko of the CPU, who had obtained 22.2% of the first round votes. The rate of participation was 70%. In early November Kuchma undertook a number of measures that were regarded as being intended to ensure his re-election in the second round, including the dismissal of governors of three oblasts (regions) in which Symonenko or the third-placed candidate, Moroz, had won the vote. In the second ballot, on 14 November, Kuchma retained the presidency, receiving some 57.7% of the votes cast; he was inaugurated on 30 November. The regional division in voting patterns evident in earlier presidential and parliamentary elections was not repeated.

In mid-December 1999 the Verkhovna Rada endorsed the nomination of Yushchenko as premier; his appointment was widely welcomed by centre-right factions, as he had obtained a reputation as a competent and trustworthy economic reformer during his tenure as Governor of the NBU. Yushchenko's appointment, however, precipitated discontent within left-wing factions in the legislature who, in January 2000, compelled the new centrist parliamentary majority led by Kravchuk to hold a separate session in an exhibition centre near the parliamentary building, where it voted unanimously to remove Tkachenko and his deputy from the chairmanship of the legislature. The opposition continued to meet in the Verkhovna Rada building, although the faction was insufficient to constitute a quorum. In February the majority faction elected Ivan Plyushch, an ally of Pustovoytenko, as legislative Chairman. After several days, deputies of the majority grouping gained entry to the parliamentary building, and normal activity resumed.

Meanwhile, a presidential decree issued in January 2000, scheduling a referendum on proposed constitutional amendments for 16 April, was widely condemned; more than 3m. signatures had reportedly been collected in favour of this proposal, which appeared to be intended to strengthen the constitutional position of the President. Of the six questions initially intended to feature in the referendum, two were excluded from the plebiscite by the Constitutional Court. The four remaining questions—on the dissolution of the Verkhovna Rada should deputies fail to approve the state budget within three months of its submission; the reduction of the number of deputies from 450 to 300; the establishment of a bicameral legislature; and the placing of limitations on the immunity enjoyed by deputies—were approved by a majority of the 81% of the electorate that participated in the referendum. However, no proposal to implement these decisions ensued, and it thus appeared that the referendum had served primarily to increase the President's authority over the legislature.

In June 2000 Lazarenko was convicted, *in absentia*, of money-laundering by a court in Switzerland, and given an 18-month suspended prison sentence. In July the Deputy Prime Minister, responsible for Energy Issues, Yuliya Tymoshenko, a prominent instigator of reforms in the energy sector and the leader of the Fatherland party, was charged with corruption, as a result of investigations into her former ally, Lazarenko, in the USA.

In early November 2000 a decapitated corpse, believed to be that of an investigative journalist, Heorhiy Gongadze, missing since mid-September, was discovered near Kyiv, by police. Gongadze, who had edited an online news site, *Ukrainska Pravda* (Ukrainian Truth), which had investigated incidents of high-level political corruption, had been a vocal critic of Kuchma; he had also made allegations of harassment by state officials. In late November Moroz released tape recordings in which Kuchma, the head of the presidential administration,

Volodymyr Lytvyn, and the Minister of Internal Affairs, Yuriy Kravchenko, were alleged to discuss possible means of killing Gongadze. Controversy surrounded the authenticity of these, and other, recordings, which a former presidential security adviser, Maj. Mykola Melnychenko, claimed to have made over a period of several months, prior to fleeing Ukraine.

In January 2001 Kuchma dismissed Tymoshenko, as an investigation into her alleged involvement in tax evasion and the smuggling of Russian gas proceeded. In February further audio recordings were made public. After initially denying the authenticity of the recordings, Kuchma admitted that the recordings were of his voice, but stated that they had been edited in an attempt to incriminate him. Demonstrations in Kyiv to demand Kuchma's resignation continued for several weeks, of which Tymoshenko, leading a loose coalition of opposition movements, the National Salvation Forum (NSF), was the most prominent leader. In February, in an apparent concession to the demands of the protesters, Kuchma dismissed the head of the national security service, Gen. Leonid Derkach, and the head of the presidential bodyguard. In mid-February Tymoshenko was arrested on charges of tax evasion. In late February Gongadze's body was formally identified by the Prosecutor-General's office, and a murder inquiry was opened. In May Gongadze's death was officially attributed to a criminal attack, with no political motives, and it was announced that the investigation into his death was to be closed. Meanwhile, in March a demonstration by up to 18,000 anti-Kuchma protesters in Kyiv degenerated into violent clashes and was dispersed by police with tear gas; several prominent members of the extreme nationalist Ukrainian National Assembly-Ukrainian National Self-Defence Organization (UNA-UNSO), including its leader, Andriy Shkil, were arrested and subsequently charged with provoking unrest. In late March, in an apparent conciliatory gesture towards the opposition, Kuchma dismissed Kravchenko as Minister of Internal Affairs, replacing him with Yuriy Smirnov. At the end of the month Tymoshenko was released from prison, and all charges against her were dismissed; in April the Supreme Court suspended Tymoshenko's re-arrest, although the charges against her remained a subject of investigation (several of the charges against her were abandoned in September).

In April 2001 the Verkhovna Rada approved a motion of no confidence in the Prime Minister and his Cabinet of Ministers. Yushchenko's position had been regarded as particularly vulnerable, despite the economic growth achieved during his premiership: in 2000 economic growth had been recorded for the first time since independence. In May Anatoliy Kinakh, hitherto First Deputy Prime Minister, responsible for Economic Policy, was appointed to succeed Yushchenko as Prime Minister. In the second half of 2001 a number of electoral blocs were formed in preparation for the forthcoming legislative elections. In late September Tymoshenko issued an appeal for other opposition groupings to join the NSF, but rejected the suggestion that the group unite with the Our Ukraine bloc of centrist and nationalist parties headed by Yushchenko; her supporters subsequently become known as the Yuliya Tymoshenko Bloc (YuTB). Meanwhile, supporters of Kuchma formed the For a United Ukraine (FUU) bloc, headed by Lytvyn, which incorporated five parties, including several generally regarded as sympathetic to business interests; among the members of FUU were: Kinakh's Party of Industrialists and Entrepreneurs of Ukraine and the Party of the Regions (PR).

In February 2002 Ukrainian prosecutors charged Lazarenko, *in absentia*, with having ordered the murders of two parliamentary deputies in 1996 and 1998; in March 2002 the Prosecutor-General was reported to have rejected a motion approved by the Verkhovna Rada for the initiation of a legal investigation into Kuchma's alleged role in the case. Also in March the Government's director of arms exports, Valeriy Malev, was killed in an automobile collision. It subsequently emerged that several days before Malev's death Kuchma had been informed of the discovery of audio recordings made by Melnychenko, in which Kuchma and Malev were allegedly heard to discuss the sale of air-defence equipment to Iraq, in violation of UN sanctions.

In the legislative elections, held on 31 March 2002, Our Ukraine, which by this time comprised 10 moderate and nationalist parties, including two factions of Rukh, obtained both the largest share of the votes (23.6%) and the largest number of seats to be won by any party, receiving 112; FUU received the second largest number of seats (101), but only 11.8% of the votes cast. The CPU obtained 20.0% of the votes cast, but received only 66 seats. The Social-Democratic Party of Ukraine—United (SDPU—U) received 24 seats and 6.3% of the votes cast, the SPU 23 seats and 6.9% of the votes, and the YuTB 22 seats and 7.3% of the votes. A total of 93 independent candidates were elected. Opposition spokesmen alleged that incidents of electoral fraud had been perpetrated, and a report by observers from the Organization for Security and Co-operation in Europe (OSCE, see p. 354) indicated 'important flaws' in the organization of the elections. After the elections, Viktor Medvedchuk, the Chairman of the SDPU—U, was appointed to head the presidential administration, following the election of the incumbent, Lytvyn, as Chairman of the Verkhovna Rada.

In August 2002 Kuchma announced that a Constitutional Commission was to be formed to investigate the possibility of introducing constitutional reforms, with the intention of surmounting the executive–parliamentary tensions that had characterized much of Ukrainian politics since independence. In October a senior judge in Kyiv opened a criminal investigation into Kuchma, who was charged with violating 11 articles of the criminal code, including charges of corruption, abuse of power and the sale of military radar equipment to Iraq; the Supreme Court rejected an appeal by the Office of the Prosecutor-General declaring the case to be illegal. However, in early November an ally of Kuchma, Vasyl Malyarenko, was elected as Chairman of the Supreme Court, replacing Vitaliy Boyko, and in late December the Court ruled that the investigation into Kuchma had indeed been opened illegally.

In mid-November 2002 Kuchma dismissed Kinakh as Prime Minister; he was replaced, on 16 November, by Viktor Yanukovych, latterly Governor of Donetsk Oblast. A new Government, in which several principal positions remained unchanged, was appointed later in the month. In early December a stable pro-presidential majority was finally established in the Verkhovna Rada.

In February 2003 Yushchenko issued a public statement, addressed to Kuchma, Yanukovych and Lytvyn, urging an end to what was described as 'political terror', including physical assaults against a number of political activists and the unsolved murders of several journalists. Later in the month anti-Kuchma demonstrations were held in several major cities. In mid-February the Verkhovna Rada rejected draft legislation on constitutional reform presented by deputies of the SDPU—U and the SPU, providing for the election of all 450 deputies by proportional representation on the basis of party lists, within the existing 225 constituencies; the draft, which was supported by deputies of Our Ukraine, the CPU and the YuTB, in addition to allies of the Government, was again rejected by the Verkhovna Rada in April. However, in March Kuchma submitted a draft on constitutional reform to the legislature: the draft envisaged that the Verkhovna Rada be replaced with a 300-seat State Assembly elected under a party list system, and an 81-member House of the Regions; moreover, the parliament was to be granted the power to dismiss the Prime Minister, and the President the power to dissolve parliament. In April the two highest-ranking members of the Government were elected to senior positions in the PR: Yanukovych was elected as party Chairman and the First Deputy Prime Minister and Minister of Finance, Mykola Azarov, became the Chairman of the party's Political Council.

In June 2003 Lazarenko was released on bail in the USA (Lazarenko's trial, on charges of money-laundering, commenced in mid-March 2004). In mid-June Kuchma submitted revised draft legislation on constitutional reform to the Verkhovna Rada; however, following the failure of the Verkhovna Rada to support either the constitutional amendments proposed by Kuchma or those presented by a group of opposition deputies, the President stated that he was prepared to co-operate with members of the legislative opposition. In early September a new draft, prepared by members of the pro-presidential and CPU legislative factions (widely known as the Medvedchuk-Symonenko draft), was presented to the Verkhovna Rada; the draft envisaged the extension of the mandate of the existing legislature by one year, until 2007, when its replacement would be elected by a system of proportional representation. The draft also provided for the direct election, in 2004, of an interim President with reduced powers, until 2006, when a President would be elected by the Verkhovna Rada.

Meanwhile, in August 2003 Kuchma dismissed Smirnov as Minister of Internal Affairs; he was replaced by Mykola Bilokon. In September Anatoliy Zlenko retired from the post of Minister of Foreign Affairs. He was replaced by Kostyantyn Hryshchenko, hitherto Ukraine's ambassador to the USA. In October Kuchma dismissed the Prosecutor-General, Svyatoslav Pyskun, nominating Hennadiy Vasilyev, hitherto the First Deputy Chairman of the Verkhovna Rada and a former Chief Prosecutor in Donetsk Oblast, as his replacement; the legislature approved the appointment in mid-November. There were renewed concerns about the use of force to inhibit political debate, after Our Ukraine was prevented from holding a conference in Donetsk at the end of October. Reports stated that as many as 2,000 people had prevented members and supporters of the grouping from entering the building where the meeting was to have been held, and that material linking Yushchenko with Nazi symbols and ideology had been widely disseminated around the city. Our Ukraine, the YuTB and the SPU subsequently issued a statement accusing the Kuchma administration of dictatorial methods. In mid-November members of Our Ukraine were refused permission to hold a meeting in Sumy, and the electricity supply to the offices of a newspaper in the town was reportedly disconnected for the duration of a visit by Yushchenko. (In late October Kuchma had ordered the Ministry of Internal Affairs and the State Security Service to investigate allegations made by Yushchenko that he was the target of an assassination plot.)

In an apparent attempt to encourage the legislature to approve constitutional reforms, in November 2003 Kuchma requested that the Constitutional Court rule on the circumstances under which the President could dissolve the Verkhovna Rada. On 24 December the Verkhovna Rada gave provisional approval to the Medvedchuk-Symonenko draft on constitutional reform (however, the 274 votes cast in favour of the proposals, although sufficient to enable the bill to receive a second reading in the legislature, fell short of the 300 votes required for the approval of a constitutional amendment). The leadership of the Our Ukraine, YuTB and SPU factions did not support the proposals. On 30 December the Constitutional Court declared that Kuchma would be eligible to seek re-election upon the expiry of his term of office in October 2004, ruling that the constitutional provision that prevented the President from holding more than two consecutive mandates introduced during Kuchma's first term did not apply retroactively. On 3 February 2004 the Verkhovna Rada voted to amend the Medvedchuk-Symonenko draft on constitutional reform, removing those proposals pertaining to the election of the president by the legislature, which had attracted international criticism. This amendment, which was approved by 304 votes, was supported by the SPU, although Our Ukraine and the YuTB refused to participate in the voting.

In March 2004 the Verkhovna Rada approved legislation, supported by the SPU and the CPU, which introduced a proportional representation system for the election of all 450 parliamentary deputies, within the existing 225 constituencies; the percentage of the votes required for a party to obtain election was to be reduced from 4% to 3%. The vote was boycotted by the Our Ukraine and YuTB factions; the legislation was signed into law by Kuchma in early April. Also in March legislation was approved to modify the presidential election procedure, requiring candidates to submit the signatures of 500,000 eligible voters, rather than the 1m. required under legislation adopted in 1999. On 7 April the Verkhovna Rada failed to approve the competing proposals for reform embodied in the amended Medvedchuk-Symonenko draft. In accordance with the Constitution, the draft could not be reintroduced to the legislature for the period of one year. In June Lazarenko was convicted of money-laundering, fraud and extortion by a federal court in Los Angeles, CA, USA.

Politics in 2004 were dominated by preparations for the presidential election. In April Yanukovych was named as the candidate for the pro-presidential bloc, while Yushchenko's candidacy was officially registered in August; a total of 24 candidates were eventually registered to contest the poll. On 20 August two bombs exploded in a Kyiv market, and a further explosion occurred on 3 September; the authorities suggested that the explosions were connected to members of Our Ukraine, while the opposition claimed that the secret services had orchestrated the attacks in an attempt to discredit the opposition. In September Yushchenko was admitted to a clinic in Vienna, Austria, and subsequently emerged with his face severely scarred by lesions; it emerged that this resulted from his poisoning during a meal with senior members of the secret services, and Yushchenko himself accused the incumbent administration of seeking to murder him. Shortly before the first round of the election Yanukovych, in his capacity as Prime Minister, announced that the rate of state pensions was to be increased. In his capacity as presidential candidate, meanwhile, Yanukovych pledged to grant Russian the status of a joint official language and work towards permitting dual Ukrainian-Russian citizenship. Yushchenko, conversely, made it clear that he would, if elected, seek the closer integration of Ukraine into the European Union (EU, see p. 244) and the North Atlantic Treaty Organization (NATO, see p. 340).

After the first round of voting, held on 31 October 2004, no candidate secured a majority of votes cast. The Central Electoral Commission (CEC) published the final results of the poll, awarding Yushchenko 39.9% of the votes cast, and Yanukovych 39.3%, on 10 November. Yushchenko and Yanukovych were, therefore, to proceed to a second round on 21 November. The CEC initially indicated that Yanukovych led by nearly 3% in the second round, with more than 99% of the votes counted, contradicting several exit polls endorsed by the opposition. Large-scale protests at the allegedly fraudulent conduct of the count, and in support of both Yushchenko and Tymoshenko, commenced in central Kyiv on 22 November, focused around the central Maidan Nezalezhnosti (Independence Square). The youth group Pora! (Enough!) played a principal role in the organization of the protests. The demonstrators established a tent settlement along Kyiv's main thoroughfare, and adopted the colour orange as a unifying symbol, leading what became known as the 'orange revolution'. Protests were almost entirely peaceful, with several hundred thousand people reportedly present at the height of the demonstrations. Meanwhile, a number of local administrations, including the city councils of Kyiv and Lviv, declared that they did not accept the results announced by the CEC and that they regarded Yushchenko as the legitimate Head of State, while demonstrations against the conduct of the election were reported across the country. The OSCE condemned the conduct of both rounds of voting. On 23 November Yushchenko took a symbolic oath of office in front of the Verkhovna Rada. On 24 November the CEC officially announced the preliminary results of the second round: Yanukovych was declared the winner, with 49.5% of the votes cast, while Yushchenko was deemed to have received 46.6%. Opposition protests persisted, however, with demands for a general strike the following day, and speeches and demonstrations continued in freezing conditions in central Kyiv, led by Yushchenko and Tymoshenko; protesters blockaded numerous government buildings. Smaller protests in favour of Yanukovych were also held, principally in eastern Ukraine, where the administrations of several oblasts (notably Donetsk and Luhansk) expressed their intention to hold referendums on autonomy or secession should Yushchenko be declared president.

Following an appeal to the Supreme Court regarding the conduct of the second round of voting, on 25 November 2004 the Court announced that it would suspend the publication of the election results until the opposition's complaints could be considered. A significant shift in the allegiances of the mass media was also observed, with staff at state-owned broadcasting outlets, which had hitherto been reported to demonstrate a clear pro-Yanukovych bias, announcing that they would begin 'full and impartial' coverage of the events surrounding the disputed vote. On 27 November the Verkhovna Rada voted to declare the 21 November ballot invalid and to express a lack of confidence in the CEC, while a subsequent motion of no confidence in Yanukovych's Government was passed on 1 December (these resolutions, however, carried no legal force, as they required the signature of President Kuchma to be binding). On 29 November it was reported that Serhiy Tihipko, hitherto the manager of Yanukovych's presidential campaign, had resigned from the position of Governor of the NBU, and considered his role within Yanukovych's campaign to have concluded. Meanwhile, Polish President Aleksander Kwaśniewski, Lithuanian President Valdas Adamkus and the EU High Representative for Common Foreign and Security Policy, Javier Solana Madariaga, arrived in Kyiv to attempt mediation between the two parties in the crisis. Yushchenko repeatedly stated that the only resolution that he considered acceptable was a repeat run of the second round of voting, a course of action described by Kuchma as lacking domestic or international precedent. On 3 December the Supreme Court ruled that the results of the second round of voting, as announced by the CEC on 24 November, were invalid, and ordered that a repeat election be conducted within three weeks.

Following extensive negotiations, on 8 December 2004 the Verkhovna Rada voted to support a series of amendments to the Constitution and electoral law, with some 420 deputies voting in favour of the proposals. The constitutional amendments incorporated several of the changes included in the Medvedchuk-

Symonenko draft of amendments, among them the transfer of several powers of appointment from the President to the Prime Minister and the legislature. The amendments also provided for the expulsion from the legislature of any deputy who left the party or bloc on whose list he or she had been elected. Immediately after the vote, Kuchma signed the amendments into law, although they were not fully to take effect until after the legislative elections due to be held in March 2006. Kuchma also announced the dismissal of the Prosecutor-General, Hennadiy Vasilyev (who was replaced by his predecessor, Pyskun, after he won a court case declaring his dismissal in 2003 to be illegal), and approved a substantial reconstitution of the CEC. Yanukovych was granted leave from his position as Prime Minister in order to campaign for the repeated second round of voting; he was replaced in an acting capacity by Azarov. The repeat ballot was held on 26 December. Preliminary results suggested a victory for Yushchenko; however, Yanukovych lodged complaints against the conduct of the election with the CEC and, subsequently, the Supreme Court, thus causing the official publication of the results to be delayed until all legal means of protest had been exhausted. Meanwhile, on 27 December Minister of Transport and Communications Heorhiy Kirpa was found dead, apparently as a result of multiple bullet wounds. Earlier in the month Yuriy Lyakh, Chairman of the Ukrainian Credit Bank, had been found dead in his office, from neck wounds apparently inflicted with a paper knife. Both cases were officially described as suicide, despite widespread speculation that both deaths had been political assassinations. On 31 December Yanukovych resigned as Prime Minister, and on 6 January 2005 Kuchma signed a decree dismissing the Cabinet of Ministers. On that date Yanukovych's complaints were rejected by the Supreme Court, and four days later Yushchenko was officially declared to have won the ballot of 26 December 2004, receiving 52.0% of the votes cast, compared with the 44.2% awarded to Yanukovych. A clear regional divide was evident in the results: in 16 of the 27 primary administrative divisions of Ukraine, the most popular candidate in that region had obtained more than 75% of the votes cast; Yushchenko obtained such support in 12 administrative divisions, mainly in western and central Ukraine, including Kyiv City, while Yanukovych received similarly overwhelming majorities in four divisions: the eastern oblasts of Donetsk and Luhansk, the Autonomous Republic of Crimea, and in Sevastopol City. A final appeal, lodged by Yanukovych with the Supreme Court, was rejected on 20 January 2005, and Yushchenko was inaugurated as President on 23 January.

On 4 February 2005 the Verkhovna Rada voted to approve Yushchenko's nomination of Tymoshenko as Prime Minister and a new Cabinet of Ministers was announced, notably including Kinakh (who had announced his support for Yushchenko after the first round of voting) as First Deputy Prime Minister. Other ministerial appointments included Yuriy Lutsenko as Minister of Internal Affairs and Anatoliy Hrytsenko as Minister of Defence. Yushchenko also appointed many new regional governors, and named Petro Poroshenko, a prominent business executive, as Chairman of the National Security and Defence Council. Yanukovych, meanwhile, expressed his intention of leading a 'harsh opposition' to Yushchenko's administration. The new Government declared combating corruption to be a priority, and several privatizations conducted during Kuchma's presidency were targeted for investigation; the extent to which they should be investigated became a significant source of tension between the various parties and elements represented within the new administration. Similar tensions existed over other policy matters between the three main political groupings represented within the Government: nationalists and populists, associated chiefly with Tymoshenko; statist socialists linked with the SPU; and those elements regarded as more sympathetic to business interests, associated more closely with Yushchenko. The latter formed a new political party, People's Union Our Ukraine; Yushchenko was named as the Honorary Chairman of the party, Roman Bezsmertnyi (Yushchenko's electoral campaign manager and a Deputy Prime Minister) became the Chairman of the party's Council, and Yuriy Yekhanurov (a former First Deputy Prime Minister and Minister of the Economy, and the recently appointed Governor of Dnipropetrovsk Oblast) the Chairman of the party's Executive Committee.

Yushchenko also endorsed a reopening of the investigation into the death of Gongadze. On 4 March 2005 former Minister of Internal Affairs Kravchenko, who was alleged to be one of the officials who had discussed the killing of Gongadze on the audio recordings released in 2000, was found dead, reportedly as the result of suicide, shortly before he had been due to be questioned at the office of the Prosecutor-General. It was subsequently announced that four people were to be charged in connection with Gongadze's death. The trial of three men, all former police officers, commenced in January 2006; the fourth man, suspected of being Gongadze's killer, was believed to have fled Ukraine. (In March 2008 the three men were found guilty of murdering Gongadze, each receiving custodial sentences of 12–13 years, although the investigations failed to discover who had ordered the killing.)

Meanwhile, it soon became apparent that some of the new administration's policy decisions had been instrumental in reducing the hitherto strong rate of economic growth. Increases in social spending (introduced by both the new Government, and by the Yanukovych administration prior to the first round of voting in late 2004) led to heightened inflation. Moreover, Tymoshenko's decision, in April 2005, to maintain at existing levels the retail prices of petroleum (for which Ukraine was heavily dependent on Russia) resulted in several Russian companies limiting their supplies to Ukraine, purportedly in order to carry out repairs to pipelines, causing a severe shortfall relative to demand. Later in May Yushchenko issued a decree criticizing the Government's action in restraining prices as incompatible with the principles of market economics, and ordered that the limits imposed be rescinded as a matter of urgency. Meanwhile, inter-factional disagreements in the Verkhovna Rada meant that several items of legislation, which had been intended to expedite Ukraine's application for membership of the World Trade Organization (WTO, see p. 396), were not approved by the legislature before the beginning of its summer recess.

The growing tensions between the constituent groupings that had supported the 'orange revolution' resulted in a series of resignations in early September 2005, amid accusations of corruption. On 1 September an adviser to Tymoshenko, Mykola Brodsky, alleged that elements close to Yushchenko were engaged in corrupt practices; one day later the Chief of the Presidential Staff, Oleksandr Zinchenko, announced his resignation, criticizing the corrupt actions of Poroshenko, in particular. On 8 September Mykola Tomenko announced his resignation as Deputy Prime Minister. Later the same day Yushchenko dismissed Tymoshenko and her Government, and also announced that Poroshenko had resigned from the National Security and Defence Council. In a statement generally understood to pertain specifically to Tymoshenko, Yushchenko stated that the Government had been dismissed because it had failed to operate cohesively, having been undermined by factionalism and machinations. Tymoshenko subsequently gave a lengthy televised interview in which she expressed regret at her dismissal, criticized several close associates of Yushchenko, and stated that, as a result of her dismissal, the YuTB would effectively go into opposition and present its own list of candidates, separate from those of Our Ukraine, at the 2006 elections to the Verkhovna Rada.

The split between the YuTB and Our Ukraine was demonstrated on 20 September 2005, when the Verkhovna Rada narrowly failed to approve Yushchenko's nomination of Yekhanurov as Prime Minister. Consequently, in order to obtain support for Yekhanurov's nomination from the sizable PR faction within the legislature, Yushchenko and Yanukovych agreed a 10-point memorandum; among the controversial measures provided for by the document were an amnesty for all those involved in electoral fraud at the annulled second round of presidential voting in 2004, and an extension of the immunity from prosecution enjoyed by legislative deputies to members of regional and local councils. On 22 September Yekhanurov was confirmed as Prime Minister, having received 289 votes in favour of his nomination in the Verkhovna Rada, compared with the 223 votes obtained prior to the signature of the memorandum. Several ministers holding principal positions in the former administration retained their portfolios. New appointments included that of Arseniy Yatsenyuk as Minister of the Economy, and Stanislav Stashevskyi as First Deputy Prime Minister, replacing Kinakh, who became the Chairman of the National Security and Defence Council. The dismissal of Pyskun as Prosecutor-General, on 14 October, was a further significant personnel change; his replacement, in an acting capacity, was Serhiy Vynokurov, who subsequently announced that all criminal charges against Poroshenko had been abandoned. On 31 October the Verkhovna Rada approved the appointment of Oleksandr Medvedko as Prosecutor-General.

The issue of Ukraine's dependence on other countries, and particularly Russia, for energy supplies assumed renewed significance in late 2005, as a result of demands issued by the Russian state-controlled gas monopoly, Gazprom, that Ukraine pay market prices (US $230 per 1,000 cu m) for the supply of natural gas, rather than the heavily subsidized rate (of $50 per 1,000 cu m) that it had paid hitherto. Following the failure of the Ukrainian authorities and Gazprom to reach agreement, on 1 January 2006 Gazprom suspended supplies to Ukraine, a measure that caused considerable hardship in Ukraine, as well as resulting in the loss of supplies to other European countries that received gas from pipelines traversing Ukraine. On 4 January supplies of natural gas to Ukraine were restored, after Ukraine agreed to pay $95 per 1,000 cu m for a mixture of Russian and Turkmenistani natural gas, which was to be supplied to Ukraine by a Swiss-registered company, RosUkrEnergo. This agreement was to be subject to renegotiation after six months.

The new arrangements for the purchase of natural gas were a source of considerable controversy within Ukraine and were instrumental in bringing about a vote of no confidence in the Government on 10 January 2006, which was approved by 250 votes to 50 against. (Tymoshenko stated that she would withdraw from the agreement in the event of her again becoming Prime Minister.) Although such a vote should, theoretically, have resulted in the Government's removal from office, the constitutional position at this time was obscure (the transfer of many of the powers of appointment from the President to the Prime Minister and the Chairman of the Verkhovna Rada, agreed in late 2004, had taken effect on 1 January 2006), and in the absence of a functioning Constitutional Court, President Yushchenko requested that the Yekhanurov administration remain in office until after the forthcoming legislative elections.

The legislative elections proceeded, as scheduled, on 26 March 2006, contested by 45 parties and blocs. The changes that had taken place in Ukrainian politics since the previous elections in 2002, and the introduction of a system of full proportional representation and the exclusion of nominally independent deputies, meant that the new Verkhovna Rada had a very different composition to the one that it replaced. The results of voting did, however, confirm the persistence of the division in support for parties between, on one hand, eastern and southern regions, and on the other hand, central and western regions. Yanukovych's PR became the largest party in the new legislature, with 32.1% of the total votes cast, receiving 186 seats. The YuTB was placed second, with 22.3% and 129 seats, while the Our Ukraine bloc (comprising several smaller, generally liberal or nationalist parties, in addition to Our Ukraine) obtained 14.0% and 81 seats, considerably less, in both percentage and seat terms, than the Our Ukraine electoral alliance of 2002 had received. Only two other groupings—the SPU, with 5.7% (33 seats), and the CPU, with 3.7% (21 seats)—surpassed the 3% quota required to obtain representation. Although there were some suspicions of malpractice in the concurrent elections to the Crimean Supreme Council (see below), and some other minor flaws, the elections to the Verkhovna Rada were described by international monitors as free and fair. The failure of any party or bloc to obtain a majority of legislative seats necessitated the formation of a coalition government. However, the formation of a coalition proved to be a protracted process, meaning that Ukraine was effectively without a functioning parliament or government for several months.

In late June 2006 it was announced that Our Ukraine, the YuTB and the SPU were to form a governing coalition supportive of Yushchenko, with Tymoshenko as premier. However, when the coalition declined to nominate Moroz of the SPU to the chairmanship of the Verkhovna Rada, that party announced its withdrawal from the coalition, which thereby ceased to hold a majority of legislative seats. The SPU subsequently announced that it would support a so-called 'anti-crisis coalition' headed by Yanukovych and the PR and also comprising the CPU and the SPU; these three parties controlled 240 of the 450 parliamentary seats. Subsequently, the anti-crisis coalition was also dissolved, and at the end of July, following protracted negotiations, a 'national unity coalition' was formed after Yushchenko and leaders of four of the five parliamentary parties signed a document titled the 'Universal of National Unity' that outlined various domestic and foreign policy aims. The remaining political faction, the YuTB, refused to sign the Universal and announced its intention to remain in opposition. The Universal was signed shortly before Yushchenko was constitutionally required either to submit a nomination for the premiership to a parliamentary vote of confidence or to dissolve parliament and call fresh elections (in the event that a government had not been formed).

Yushchenko decided against dissolving the Verkhovna Rada and accepted Yanukovych's nomination as Prime Minister, subject to the proviso that Yanukovych accepted the principles of the Universal, among which were the retention of Ukrainian as the sole official state language (outwith Crimea), the rejection of any restructuring of Ukraine on a federal basis, and the aspiration towards the eventual incorporation of Ukraine into European and Atlantic organizations (subject to approval on these matters in national referendums). On 4 August 2006 the Verkhovna Rada approved the nomination of Yanukovych as Prime Minister and the formation of a new Government, comprising representatives of the PR, Our Ukraine, the SPU and the CPU. (This was the first Government in post-Soviet Ukraine to include members of the CPU.) Officially, Our Ukraine did not enter into the coalition agreement, although four members of the new Government belonged to the bloc, in addition to non-party allies of Yushchenko. Meanwhile, on 25 August a US court sentenced former Prime Minister Lazarenko to nine years imprisonment, following his conviction in June 2004 for money-laundering, fraud and extortion (see above).

Despite the apparent political settlement suggested by the signing of the Universal and subsequent formation of a ruling coalition, tensions between President Yushchenko and Prime Minister Yanukovych were still evident, while the balance of powers between the President, Prime Minister and Verkhovna Rada, provided for by the amended Constitution, remained uncertain; in particular, several of Yanukovych's actions as Prime Minister appeared to overstep the responsibilities of that office. In September 2006 Yanukovych refused to sign several presidential decrees (which, in order to become valid, require the approval of the Prime Minister and Chairman of the Verkhovna Rada). In mid-September, moreover, Yanukovych expressed Ukraine's unpreparedness to enter into a closer relationship with NATO at a meeting of the Alliance in Brussels, Belgium (see below), despite such remarks being contrary both to the stated policy of Yushchenko (who, as President, was constitutionally responsible for foreign affairs) and to the terms of the Universal. Furthermore, later in September the Verkhovna Rada voted to abolish a prohibition on parliamentary deputies switching party allegiance or becoming independent that had been introduced prior to the March legislative elections with the expectation that it would ease the development of a more coherent party system and permit the formation of more stable governments. At the end of the month Yanukovych demanded the dismissal of the governors of five eastern regions who were members of Our Ukraine, a demand which required presidential endorsement. In early October Our Ukraine announced its decision to withdraw its members from the Government and enter into the opposition; however, both Yushchenko and Yanukovych refused to accept the ministers' resignations, which were subject to a certain amount of constitutional confusion regarding the dismissal and appointment of ministers.

On 15 November 2006 Minister of Foreign Affairs Borys Tarasyuk and Minister of Defence Anatoliy Hrytsenko (both of whom were strongly opposed to Yanukovych's intervention at NATO) had been due to present reports to the Verkhovna Rada, which had then been expected to vote to dismiss the two ministers, but these presentations (and the vote) were postponed for at least two weeks. However, on 1 December the Verkhovna Rada voted in favour of the dismissal of Tarasyuk and the Minister of Internal Affairs, Lutsenko; Tarasyuk, who was, in the mean time, prevented from attending government meetings, went on to have his dismissal overturned by a district court (on the grounds that his post, in common with a small number of principal ministerial appointments, was answerable to the President, rather than to the Verkhovna Rada and the Government), although his dismissal was upheld by the appeals court in Kyiv on 10 January 2007. Consequently, on 30 January Tarasyuk resigned from the Government.

There was continued instability within the governing coalition: on 20 March 2007 the Verkhovna Rada rejected Yushchenko's nomination of Volodymyr Ohryzko as Minister of Foreign Affairs. The legislature approved the appointment of Yatsenyuk to that position on the following day, alongside several other ministerial appointments. Later in the month a group of deputies hitherto loyal to Yushchenko, and most notably including Kinakh, announced that they would henceforth form part of the PR faction in the Verkhovna Rada. Frustrated at the inability to govern effectively, on 2 April Yushchenko issued a decree dissolving the Verkhovna Rada and scheduling pre-term parliamentary elections for 27 May. Yanukovych initially refused to accept the presidential decree and asked the Constitutional Court to rule on the constitutionality of the dissolution of parliament. Meanwhile, the Verkhovna Rada continued to meet, refusing to recognize the legitimacy of its dissolution. Supporters of Yanukovych staged demonstrations in Kyiv and set up encampments in front of the Verkhovna Rada and at other locations in central Kyiv. (Subsequent reports appeared to confirm allegations that supporters of Yanukovych were being paid to travel to Kyiv and take part in demonstrations.) On 25 April Yushchenko announced that the parliamentary elections were to be delayed until 24 June, as a result of the Government having failed to agree on funding for the elections, and as a result of the inaction of the CEC. On 30 April the Verkhovna Rada approved a resolution calling for the concurrent holding of fresh presidential and legislative elections, to be held no later than December 2007 and subject to the introduction of a number of constitutional amendments. Yushchenko continued to insist, however, that the Constitution required any pre-term elections to be held no later than 60 days following the dissolution of the Verkhovna Rada. Meanwhile, the Constitutional Court had failed to issue any ruling on the legitimacy of the dissolution of the legislature within one month, as required; the acting Chairman of the Court, Ivan Dombrovsky, resigned in May, while several other judges of the Court were absent, resigned, or were dismissed, effectively rendering the Court unable to conduct its work. (In early July the Constitutional Court elected Andriy Stryzhak as the new Chairman.) Meanwhile, it was reported on 4 May that Yushchenko and Yanukovych had agreed to fresh parliamentary elections being held later in the year, subject to the agreement of several constitutional amendments by the outgoing legislature; Yanukovych had abandoned demands for a presidential election to be held concurrently with the parliamentary polling.

On 1 June 2007 Yushchenko again dismissed Pyskun, who had been reappointed to the Office of Prosecutor-General in April, and replaced him, again, with Medvedko. On 5 June Yushchenko issued a further decree rescheduling legislative elections for 30 September, following a compromise arrangement, reached on 27 May, between Yushchenko, Yanukovych and Moroz. Our Ukraine and YuTB deputies subsequently withdrew from the Verkhovna Rada. (A further decree, issued on 1 August, stipulated electoral conditions.) In early July Our Ukraine formed an electoral alliance with the People's Self-Defence group of Lutsenko and several smaller parties, which became known as Our Ukraine-People's Self-defence bloc. Tymoshenko demanded that a national referendum to resolve the constitutional impasse be conducted to coincide with the elections, and began to organize a petition in support of the poll. However, the CEC ruled against the organization of an early constitutional referendum, on the grounds that it allowed insufficient time for preparation. In August the YuTB succeeded, after a legal appeal, in reversing a decision by the CEC to refuse to register it for the elections, on the grounds that it had submitted incomplete documentation. By the end of that month 21 political associations had registered with the CEC to contest the elections.

According to official results of the legislative elections on 30 September 2007, released by the CEC in mid-October, Yanukovych's PR won 34.4% of the votes and 175 seats, the YuTB 30.7% and 156 seats, the Our Ukraine-People's Self-defence bloc 14.2% and 72 seats, the CPU 5.4% and 27 seats, and the Lytvyn bloc 4.0% and 20 seats. The SPU, with 2.9% of the votes, narrowly failed to secure the minimum for parliamentary representation. Tymoshenko and the leader of the Our Ukraine-People's Self-defence bloc, Vyacheslav Kyrylenko, subsequently announced their intention to sign a coalition agreement, which would allow the two groupings a narrow parliamentary majority; Tymoshenko would be returned to the office of Prime Minister, while ministerial portfolios were to be divided equally between the two blocs. After Yushchenko urged co-operation with the PR, however, it was reported that Yanukovych's party had been offered deputy ministerial and other official posts in the new administration, prompting fears of further protracted coalition discussions. Although the elections were regarded by international observers to have met democratic standards, the official publication of the final results was delayed, pending the outcome of a legal challenge submitted by five small parties, including the SPU, based on alleged violations concerning the inclusion of Ukrainians resident abroad on voting lists. The Verkhovna Rada was convened on 23 November, when Yanukovych formally relinquished the presidency. On 29 November, following further protracted negotiations, it was announced that the coalition agreement announced in October had been finalized. In early December a parliamentary vote on Tymoshenko's nomination to the premiership narrowly failed, owing, according to her supporters, to a fault in the electronic voting system; a further attempt was prevented by a blockade by PR deputies. On 18 December Tymoshenko's nomination as Prime Minister was finally approved by 226 votes in the Verkhovna Rada. Her Government comprised 12 representatives of the YuTB and 11 of the Our Ukraine-People's Self-defence bloc; the Minister of Foreign Affairs, Volodymyr Ohryzko, who, together with the Minister of Defence, had been nominated by the President in accordance with the Constitution, was independent.

In January 2008 it was reported that Lutsenko, who had been reappointed Minister of Internal Affairs, had physically assaulted the Mayor of Kyiv, Leonid Chernovetsky, following an altercation over allegedly corrupt agreements relating to the transfer of land ownership in the city. In March the Verkhovna Rada approved a resolution, supported by the YuTB, scheduling early mayoral elections in Kyiv, following a report by a government investigative commission on the activities of the Kyiv City authorities. Legislation under debate that strengthened presidential powers while reducing those of the Cabinet of Ministers was a subject of great controversy in the legislature, and served to exacerbate tensions between Tymoshenko and Yushchenko, who continued to criticize the Prime Minister's economic policies and accused her of encouraging corrupt practices in land auctions. Also in March a new pro-presidential association, United Centre, chaired by a strenuous opponent of Tymoshenko, Ihor Kril, was established; Lutsenko also announced that his parliamentary People's Self-defence bloc would form the basis for a new party, and that it would not merge into Our Ukraine, as had previously been considered. In April the Constitutional Court ruled that the constitutional system could be amended by a national referendum (although the Verkhovna Rada would first be required to amend certain aspects of the existing Constitution). A protracted dispute between the President and the Cabinet of Ministers over the State Property Fund escalated in late April, when Yushchenko issued decrees in an effort to reverse a government decision to dismiss the head of the Fund, who had objected to privatization plans. Following continued denunciations of Tymoshenko by Yushchenko and his close associate, head of the presidential secretariat Viktor Baloha, in mid-May YuTB deputies blockaded the Verkhovna Rada, preventing Yushchenko from making his annual parliamentary address.

Despite the political differences between the Ukrainian-speaking western regions and the Russian-speaking eastern regions that were evident during the 1990s and 2000s, only in the Crimean peninsula did any significant movement for reunification with Russia emerge. (Speculation that several eastern and southern regions would hold referendums for autonomy in late 2004 appeared to be largely transient, and associated with the disputed presidential election, rather than representing any long-term political aspirations.) The situation was further complicated by the status of the Crimean Tatars, who had been forcibly deported to Soviet Central Asia in 1944, and who began to return to Crimea from late 1989. In a referendum held in January 1991, residents of Crimea (which then had the status of an ordinary oblast) voted to restore it to the status of a nominally autonomous republic. The decision, although it had no legal basis, was ratified by the Verkhovna Rada. In June Crimean Tatars established 'parallel' institutions to those of the state, without any constitutional or legal status. The Kurultay (Assembly) was a popular assembly that was intended to convene once a year, the Qırımtatar Milly Meclisi (Crimean Tatar National Assembly) was to meet throughout the year, and a number of local assemblies were also established. In February 1992 the Crimean Supreme Council, the regional legislature, voted to transform the region into the Republic of Crimea, and in May declared Crimea an independent state, adopting a new Constitution. However, following threats from the Verkhovna Rada to impose an economic blockade and direct rule on Crimea, the independence declaration was rescinded. In June the Ukrainian Government confirmed Crimea's status as an autonomous republic within Ukraine, which was otherwise to remain a unitary state. (The city of Sevastopol was not, however, to form part of the autonomous republic.) Meanwhile, relations between the local leadership and Crimean Tatars, some 250,000 of whom had returned to Crimea by late 1992, deteriorated steadily, primarily as a result of disputes over the ownership of land and property, and the right to gain Ukrainian citizenship. In October a Tatar encampment was dispersed on the orders of the Crimean Government, and in response some 6,000 Tatars stormed the Crimean parliament building.

With the election of Yurii Meshkov as President of Crimea in January 1994, it appeared likely that the region would renew efforts towards sovereignty, as well as establish closer links with Russia. In response, the Verkhovna Rada approved constitutional amendments, according to which the Ukrainian President could nullify any measures taken by the Crimean authorities that he deemed to be illegal. In March a referendum was held in Crimea, simultaneously with the Ukrainian legislative elections; 70% of those voting in the referendum supported broader autonomous powers for Crimea. In May, following a vote by the Crimean parliament to restore the suspended Constitution of May 1992, the Ukrainian Government ordered the Crimean legislature to rescind its decision; the crisis appeared to have been defused by June 1994, when delegations from the Ukrainian and Crimean parliaments met in Simferopol, the Crimean capital, where it was agreed that Crimea would continue to be subject to Ukrainian law. In September the Crimean legislature voted to restrict the Crimean President's executive authority, in response to which Meshkov temporarily suspended parliament. Meanwhile, the Verkhovna Rada approved a constitutional amendment, permitting it to nullify any legislation adopted by the Crimean parliament that contravened the Ukrainian Constitution. In March 1995 the Ukrainian legislature voted to abolish both the Crimean Constitution of May 1992 and the Crimean presidency, and in April 1995 Kuchma imposed direct rule on Crimea.

In October 1995 the Crimean legislature approved a new Constitution. Before its final adoption by the Verkhovna Rada in December 1996, the Constitution underwent several amendments; notably, Ukrainian was recognized as the state language, although Russian was to be the language of all official correspondence of the autonomous republic. In February 1997, contrary to national law, which stipulates that the appointment of the Crimean Prime Minister is the prerogative of the Ukrainian President, the Crimean parliament arrogated to itself the power to appoint the regional Government. In April it appointed Anatolii Franchuk as the new Crimean premier, in place of Arkadii Demydenko. Kuchma suspended this resolution, declaring it to be a violation of the Ukrainian Constitution, but, following the approval of a second motion of no confidence in Demydenko, in June Kuchma consented to his dismissal. A new Council of Ministers headed by Franchuk was subsequently approved by the Crimean legislature. In October 1997 Kuchma exercised his veto over items of legislation approved by the Crimean Supreme Council—the adoption of Russian as the peninsula's official language of business communication, and the realignment of Crimea's time zone with that of Moscow—that were regarded as an assertion of the primacy of Crimea's links with Russia. Further conflict arose between the national Government and the Crimean legislature in February 1998, following the approval of legislation by the Verkhovna Rada, whereby all Ukrainian citizens were to be eligible to contest the seats in the Crimean legislature—hitherto, only citizens resident in Crimea had been eligible. In addition, the new legislation stated that elections to the Crimean parliament were to be held simultaneously with the elections to the Verkhovna Rada in March and not in September, as had previously been decided by the Crimean Supreme Council.

Elections to the Crimean legislature in March 1998 brought the issue of the status of the Crimean Tatars to the fore, when demonstrations were staged by Tatars appealing for the right to vote. The OSCE estimated that about one-half of the 165,000 Tatars resident in Crimea did not have Ukrainian citizenship and were, therefore, ineligible to vote. Leonid Grach, the leader of the CPU in Crimea, was elected Chairman of the new Crimean Supreme Council. In May a new Council of Ministers was appointed, with Sergei Kunitsyn as Chairman. In January 1999 a new Crimean Constitution came into effect, which granted the Crimean authorities the right to manage its own property and to pass a budget. Although citizenship had recently been granted to a number of Crimean Tatars, representatives of the group held a demonstration in May in Simferopol, demanding constitutional changes to ensure better representation and rights for Crimean Tatars and for the Crimean Tatar language to be recognized as a state language; subsequent protests culminated in a 20,000-strong demonstration in Simferopol in May 2000. In mid-July 2001 the Supreme Council dismissed Kunitsyn from the premiership for the third time. Although Kuchma had refused to recognize the previous dismissals, in late July Kuchma accepted Kunitsyn's removal from office, and expressed support for the new premier elected by the Crimean Supreme Council, Valerii Gorbatov of the Working Ukraine party.

As campaigning for the concurrent elections to the Verkhovna Rada and the Crimean Supreme Council, to be held on 31 March 2002, commenced, controversy was provoked at the end of February by the invalidation of Grach's candidacy for a seat in the Supreme Council, on technical grounds. Despite his disqualification, Grach's name appeared on ballot papers, and he was re-elected to the Supreme Council in defiance of the decision of the Crimean Court of Appeal. The elections to the Crimean Supreme Council demonstrated a sizeable shift in support away from the communists, towards centrists, whose grouping, known as the Kunitsyn Team, after its leader, won 39 of the 100 seats in the Council; a pro-communist electoral alliance, the Grach bloc, received 28 seats. Three other parties obtained representation, and 29 independent candidates were elected. In late April the Ukrainian Supreme Court approved Grach's appeal, thereby serving to legitimize his status as a deputy of the Crimean legislature. However, Grach was unsuccessful in his campaign for re-election as Chairman of the Crimean legislature, being defeated by a former Deputy Chairman, Boris Deich. The new parliament also voted for the dismissal of Gorbatov and the reappointment of Kunitsyn as Prime Minister, and reformists loyal to Kunitsyn were successful in establishing a majority in the legislature. None the less, in the concurrent elections to the Verkhovna Rada, the CPU remained the most popular party on the peninsula. Notably, for the first time, Crimean Tatar deputies were elected to the Verkhovna Rada, within the Our Ukraine bloc. Russian nationalists only successfully attracted votes in the Crimean city of Sevastopol.

In early 2004 concern was expressed by ethnic Russians resident in Crimea that a measure, approved by the Crimean Government in 2000, which ordered foreign citizens resident in Crimea to pay higher rates for utilities and accommodation than those paid by Ukrainian citizens, was being applied to Russian citizens resident in the Republic. Meanwhile, an increase in ethnic tensions between Crimean Tatars and the Slavic inhabitants of the peninsula was reported in early 2004. Although it appeared that disputes over land were the principal source of tensions, some reports suggested that violence had been provoked by groups of Russian right-wing extremists and militant Cossack groups resident in neighbouring regions of Russia. In the first few months of the year, in advance of the 60th anniversary of the deportation of the Tatars from the peninsula, several clashes and violent incidents occurred, and in early April a petition, signed by over 35,000 Crimean Tatars, which alleged that the police force in Crimea were ignoring incidents of interethnic violence against Tatars, was presented to President Kuchma. The continuing tension in Crimean society was reflected in the allegiances displayed in the presidential election of late 2004, when the peninsula's Russophone majority overwhelmingly supported Yanukovych, while the Crimean Tatar minority was reported to have voted principally for the victorious candidate, Yushchenko, in the hope that he would act to address their grievances regarding land distribution and greater ethnic autonomy. In late April 2005 Kunitsyn resigned as Prime Minister of Crimea, following his appointment as an adviser to President Yushchenko; the Crimean Supreme Council voted to approve Anatolii Matviyenko as his replacement. Matviyenko's appointment caused some controversy on the peninsula, both because he had never held any position of responsibility in Crimea and because of his affiliations with both Ukrainian nationalists and the YuTB, which did not enjoy significant support in the Republic. Matviyenko was subject to frequent criticism as Prime Minister, particularly for failing to resolve concerns about widespread corruption or the issue of land allocation to returning Crimean Tatars, and his premiership proved short-lived. Following the dismissal of Tymoshenko as Prime Minister of Ukraine, in early September, the Crimean Supreme Council voted to dismiss the republican Government; Matviyenko duly resigned on 20 September. On 23 September the Crimean Supreme Council approved the appointment of Anatolii Burdyugov, the leader of the Crimean branch of Yushchenko's People's Union Our Ukraine party, as Prime Minister, and a new Government was formed at the end of the month. In late February 2006 the Crimean legislature voted to hold a referendum on the proposed introduction of Russian as a state language within the peninsula; however, President Yushchenko stated that the referendum would be unconstitutional, and this ruling was subsequently confirmed by the CEC.

Elections to the Crimean Supreme Council, held concurrently with local elections and with those to the Verkhovna Rada on 26 March 2006, were marred by allegations of electoral fraud; moreover, one candidate was killed on polling day and, in early April, the body of a local councillor was found in unexplained circumstances, after his apparent abduction (however, police stated that the latter killing did not appear to have a political motive). At the end of March the President's Representative in Crimea, Volodomyr Kulich, announced that a commission comprising senior officials of several ministries and law-enforcement bodies was to be established to investigate the apparent electoral violations. Meanwhile, protesters outside the Crimean Parliament demanded that elections in districts where violations were found, be declared null and void. (No official results of the Crimean elections had been released by this time.) The national Prosecutor-General and Matviyenko (in his role as deputy head of the presidential secretariat, to which he had been appointed in November 2005) also became involved in the investigation of the alleged irregularities. The results of the elections were finally announced on 19 April. The For Yanukovych bloc (principally comprising the Party of the Regions) obtained the largest proportion of the votes cast, with 32.6%; it was awarded 44 of the 100 seats in the Supreme Council. The second-placed party was the pro-Russian Union party, with 7.6% of the votes and 10 seats. The Kunitsyn bloc obtained 10 seats, the CPU nine, the People's Movement of Ukraine-Rukh and the YuTB each obtained eight seats, the Nataliya Vitrenko People's Opposition bloc obtained seven seats, and the 'Ne Tak' Opposition bloc (which comprised several centrist parties associated with allies of former President Kuchma, most notably the SDPU—U) obtained four.

In late May 2006 the proposed staging of military exercises off the coast of Crimea, under the aegis of NATO and with the participation of the defence forces of 12 countries, were a focus for protests in the port of Feodosiya, in the east of Crimea, principally by Russian nationalists opposed to Ukrainian involvement with NATO. It was also reported that the local branches of the CPU and the PR supported the protests. Although similar exercises had taken place in the region on an annual basis since 1997, on each occasion, in accordance with the national Constitution, they had required the specific approval of the Verkhovna Rada. As the outgoing Verkhovna Rada had failed to vote to approve the exercises on three occasions, and the prolonged coalition negotiations following the elections to that body on 26 March had prevented the new legislature from convening, it became apparent that the forthcoming exercises had no legal standing. In early June the Crimean Supreme Council was reported to have voted to approve a statement declaring the peninsula a 'NATO-free territory'. (Some reports suggested, however, that this vote had not been taken within a formal parliamentary session, and, in any case, the statement had no constitutional meaning.) On 11 June some 200 US reserve troops began to leave Crimea, having been prevented from undertaking the construction work for which they had been contracted, and the proposed exercises were abandoned. Meanwhile, there were heightened ethnic tensions on the peninsula during 2006, mostly relating to questions of land ownership. In the first half of the year clashes broke out on several occasions in protest at the operations of a market located on a traditional Crimean Tatar burial site. (The market was moved to a new location later in the year.) In late December the Crimean branch of the CPU organized a 'people's referendum' on the peninsula (which was not, however, recognized as having any official status) on Ukraine's aspirations towards NATO membership. According to the results of the poll issued by the CPU, some 58% of eligible voters participated in the 'referendum', of whom almost 99% rejected the notion of Ukrainian accession to NATO.

Following the dissolution of the Verkhovna Rada and scheduling of pre-term elections for 30 September 2007, it was announced in July that Kunitsyn was again to head the pro-presidential coalition, reconstituted as Our Ukraine-People's Self-defence bloc, in Crimea. A number of electoral irregularities were reported in the Republic on 30 September; at the elections to the Verkhovna Rada, Yanukovych's PR secured some 61.0% of votes cast in the Republic, followed by the Our Ukraine-People's Self-defence bloc, with only 8.2%, the CPU, with 7.6%, and the YuTB, with about 6.9%. Following the elections, a temporary ban on demonstrations was ended by the Crimean authorities; in mid-October some 2,000 Crimean Tatars demonstrated in Simferopol to demand land for resettlement, and a further series of protests was planned. In May 2008 the Ukrainian authorities prevented the Mayor of Moscow, Yurii Luzhkov, from entering the country, after he declared that Sevastopol had not formed part of the territory of Crimea formally transferred from Russian to Ukrainian control in 1954.

Following the collapse of the USSR in 1991, the Ukrainian leadership was notably reluctant to sign any union agreement with the other former Soviet republics that might compromise its declaration of independence. It was this reluctance to enter into a renewed political union that led to the establishment of the Commonwealth of Independent States (CIS, see p. 215) by President Kravchuk, and the leaders of Russia and Belarus, on 8 December. Although relations with Russia, as Ukraine's major trading partner and a country with close ethnic, historic, cultural and familial links with Ukraine, remained generally good following independence, tensions existed between those who sought to renew closer relations with Russia and countries of 'Eurasia', and those who sought to emphasize Ukraine's independence and 'European' status. Ukraine agreed to a unified command for the strategic (principally nuclear-armed) forces of the former USSR, but began to establish its own conventional armed forces. In January 1994 a trilateral agreement on the removal of nuclear weapons from Ukraine was signed by Ukraine, Russia and the USA, and in November the Verkhovna Rada voted to ratify the Treaty on the Non-Proliferation of Nuclear Weapons (see p. 107). In December Kuchma formally signed the Treaty, and the Strategic Arms' Reduction Treaty (START) I entered into force. The transfer to Russia of Ukraine's nuclear weapons was completed by June 1996.

Throughout the 1990s Ukraine consistently refused to participate in organizations that it perceived as being dominated by Russia, although it became an associate member of the CIS Air Defence Agreement in 1995. In 1997 Ukraine initiated the establishment of the GUAM (Georgia-Ukraine-Azerbaijan-Moldova) grouping. In 2001 a permanent office of the grouping (known as GUUAM in 1999–2005, when Uzbekistan was also a member) was opened in Yalta, Crimea. In 2006, at a summit held in Kyiv, the grouping was formally inaugurated as a full international organization concerned with the promotion of democracy, energy security and strengthening relations; it was also redesignated as the Organization for Democracy and Economic Development—GUAM (see p. 425). As the Kuchma administration became increasingly isolated internationally in the early 2000s, particularly in response to allegations that it had illegally sold military equipment to the Iraqi regime of Saddam Hussain, Ukraine's relationship with Russia appeared to strengthen. In January 2003 Kuchma was elected as Chairman of the CIS, becoming the first non-Russian to hold that post. (He was, however, replaced by Russian President Vladimir Putin in 2004.) Later in 2003 proposals to form a 'single economic zone' with Belarus, Kazakhstan and Russia became increasingly popular, and were approved by the Verkhovna Rada in September, on the condition that participation did not contravene the Ukrainian Constitution, although interest in Ukraine's participation in such a zone waned following the election of Yushchenko as President in late 2004. In August 2005 Yushchenko and President Mikheil Saakashvili of Georgia, meeting in Borjomi, Georgia, signed the Borjomi Declaration, on the creation of a new Community of Democratic Choice, an alliance that intended to remove divisions and resolve conflicts in the Baltic, Black Sea and Caspian regions. The new, nine-country grouping was officially launched in December, at a meeting in Kyiv.

The principal controversy between Ukraine and Russia concerned ownership of the former Soviet Black Sea Fleet, based in Sevastopol, on the Crimean peninsula. Although both countries agreed in July 1992 to exercise joint control over the fleet for a transitional period of three years, in April 1995 the Russian parliament imposed a moratorium on plans to divide the fleet. Nevertheless, in June Russian President Boris Yeltsin and Kuchma agreed to the equal division of the fleet, with separate Ukrainian and Russian bases. The main Russian base was to be at Sevastopol, although the exact legal status of the city was left unresolved. Yeltsin and Kuchma signed an agreement on 31 May 1997, in accordance with which the Russian fleet was to lease three bays in Sevastopol for 20 years, while the Ukrainian fleet was to use the remainder. Upon expiry, the treaty could be renewed for five years, but would then be subject to renegotiation. A bilateral Treaty of Friendship, Co-operation and Partnership was also signed, in which, significantly, Russia for the first time recognized the sovereignty of Ukraine. Russia finally ratified the treaty in February 1999, and in June of that year and in March 2000 further agreements were signed between Russia and Ukraine pertaining to the fleet and the operations and services of jointly used facilities. In January 2003 a treaty delineating the land boundary between Russia and Ukraine (which remained largely unmarked and unregulated) was signed by Kuchma and President Vladimir Putin of Russia, although discussions on the status of the Sea of Azov, which lies between the two countries, remained unresolved. Work on the construction of a Russian dam in the Sea precipitated considerable controversy, and raised concerns that the territorial integrity of Ukraine was being violated. In December Presidents Kuchma and Putin signed an agreement on the use of the Sea of Azov, the entirety of which was defined as comprising the internal waters of both countries. Agreement was also reached on the maritime state boundary of Russia and Ukraine in the region.

The Ukrainian presidential election of 2004 caused considerable upheaval in diplomatic relations with Russia. During the course of the campaign, the Russian Government was accused by the Ukrainian opposition and external commentators of interference in favour of Yanukovych; notably, President Putin visited Ukraine before each round of voting to appear publicly with Yanukovych and Kuchma, and telephoned Yanukovych to congratulate him on his apparent victory after the second round before the official (and subsequently annulled) results had been announced. Some US $300m. were reported to have been donated to the Yanukovych campaign by the Russian authorities, and Putin described the demonstrations that resulted in the election being re-run as constitutionally illegitimate. Symbolically, and in accordance with promises made during his election campaign, President Yushchenko visited Moscow one day after his inauguration in January 2005, and emphasized the importance of maintaining co-operative relations with Russia. However, further diplomatic tension was caused by the appointment of Tymoshenko as Prime Minister in February, in part as a result of a warrant existing in Russia for her arrest on charges of the attempted bribery of Russian officials during her time as head of a Ukrainian natural gas trading company in the 1990s.

The appointment of Yanukovych as Prime Minister in August 2006 facilitated an improvement in relations between Ukraine and Russia: on 15 August Yanukovych met Prime Minister Mikhail Fradkov of Russia at the Black Sea port of Sochi, and on 22 December President Putin visited Ukraine for the first time since Yushchenko's election. However, as a counterpoint to Ukraine's close economic ties with Russia, particularly with regard to gas supplies, in March 2007 Yushchenko and President Lech Kaczyński of Poland announced their intention to stage a summit in May, also involving Azerbaijan, Georgia and Kazakhstan, to discuss the extension of the Odesa–Brody pipeline as part of a wider initiative to reduce both Ukrainian and Polish reliance on Russian fuel imports. On 3 October Gazprom threatened again to suspend natural gas supplies to Ukraine, on the grounds that it was owed US $1,300m.; on 9 October, however, it was announced that a compromise agreement had been reached, whereby Ukraine was to repay $1,200m. by transferring gas from underground storage facilities in Ukraine to Gazprom for further export. Tymoshenko, who had recently returned to the office of Prime Minister, strenuously criticized an agreement reached between Russia and Ukraine, which retained the intermediary trading company in gas supplies to Ukraine, the Swiss-registered RosUkrEnergo. Meanwhile, Russia strongly criticized Ukraine's formal request for NATO membership (see below). Putin subsequently warned that, in the event that Ukraine joined NATO and agreed to the deployment on its territory of elements of the planned US national missile defence system, Russia would be prepared to target its missiles at Ukraine. In February 2008 Gazprom warned that it would reduce supplies to Ukraine, in response to debts incurred during the previous month; it was subsequently announced that Ukraine and Russia had reached a debt settlement, and also agreed to discontinue use of RosUkrEnergo as an intermediary. Later in February, however, Gazprom claimed that Ukraine had failed to sign the negotiated agreements. After further discussions, in April the Ukrainian Government announced that agreement had been reached on a new payment scheme; at the insistence of the Russian authorities, RosUkrEnergo was to remain the intermediary company, operating within Russia.

Ukraine sought to counterbalance its close relations with Russia by a policy of engagement with Western nations and organizations, as part of what was termed a 'multi-vector' foreign policy. In 1994 Ukraine joined NATO's 'Partnership for Peace' (see p. 342) programme; a 'Charter on a Distinctive Relationship' was signed with the Organization in 1997, envisaging enhanced co-operation with the Alliance. In April 1999, in protest at NATO air-strikes against Yugoslavia (Serbia and Montenegro), the Verkhovna Rada voted to withdraw from the 'Partnership for Peace' programme. When the conflict ended, Ukraine rejoined the programme, and in July sent troops to form part of the peacekeeping force in the Serbian province of Kosovo.

Following pressure from the USA, in 1998 Ukraine cancelled an agreement to supply turbines to Bushehr nuclear power station in Iran. The USA, in return, pledged to allocate additional investment to the development of Ukraine's energy sector. In March 2000 the USA, one of the major aid donors to Ukraine in the mid-1990s, became concerned about allegations that Ukraine had misused IMF funds, and demanded a full audit of the central bank before any more assistance would be forthcoming. During a visit to Ukraine in June, US President Bill Clinton pledged aid towards the decommissioning of the Chornobyl reactor, which was closed in December. Relations with the USA deteriorated somewhat during 2002, following allegations that Ukraine, with the complicity of President Kuchma, had transferred military equipment to Iraq. In October a joint British-US inquiry failed to determine the veracity of the allegations, which the Ukrainian Government continued to deny. However, in March 2003, following the commencement of US-led military action in Iraq, Ukraine agreed to a request by the USA to dispatch an anti-nuclear, anti-biological and anti-chemical warfare unit, comprising 448 troops, to Kuwait. The Verkhovna Rada approved this measure in mid-March, although it also approved a motion condemning the US-led intervention. In June the Verkhovna Rada approved proposals to dispatch up to 1,800 troops to serve in the Polish-administered stabilization zone in southern Iraq; some 1,650 Ukrainian troops entered service in the zone from September. The participation of Ukrainian forces in Iraq appeared to lead to an improvement in relations with the USA, and in October Prime Minister Viktor Yanukovych visited Washington, DC, and met Vice-President Richard B. Cheney and Secretary of State Colin Powell. Yushchenko's inauguration as President was widely expected to lead to an improvement in US-Ukrainian relations, and the 'orange revolution' that had brought Yushchenko to power was generally regarded favourably in the USA. In early April 2005 Yushchenko visited the USA, meeting President George W. Bush and addressing the US Senate. Relations with the USA did not appear to be affected negatively by Yushchenko's approval, later that month, of a decree authorizing the withdrawal of Ukrainian peacekeeping troops from Iraq by the end of the year, as had been approved by the Verkhovna Rada in the previous year. In September 2007 the Ukraine authorities signed a US $505m. contract with a French company for the construction of a steel covering to protect the damaged concrete encasing the decommissioned Chornobyl nuclear reactor.

Ukraine signed a trade agreement with the EU in June 1995, and was formally admitted to the Council of Europe (see p. 225) in November. The Ukrainian leadership had long expressed an intention to pursue full membership of the EU; however, the failure to abolish capital punishment (which is prohibited by the conditions of membership of the organization) before March 2000 was a source of tension, as was the slow pace of political and economic reform and, in particular, concerns that President Kuchma may have been implicated in the murder of investigative journalist Heorhiy Gongadze in 2000. President Yushchenko, who was elected in late 2004, emphasized in his earliest diplomatic pronouncements that he regarded the integration of Ukraine into both the EU and NATO as fundamental goals of his presidency. However, the return of Yanukovych as Prime Minister in August 2006 delayed Ukraine's attempts to enter into a Membership Action Plan with NATO, which the USA was apparently eager to support. This trend was affirmed by remarks made by Yanukovych in September, at a meeting of NATO representatives in Brussels, Belgium, to the effect that Ukraine was not ready to join NATO. Yanukovych's remarks were disowned by Yushchenko and the Minister of Defence, Anatoliy Hrytsenko, and furthermore were regarded as a breach of both the Universal covenant and national Constitution (which states that the President is responsible for foreign policy). In 2007–08 Ukraine was due to complete a 10-year Partnership and

Co-operation Agreement (PCA) with the EU. The PCA was then expected to be replaced by an Enhanced Agreement that would, however, not include a provision for future membership. Ukraine's membership application to the WTO (submitted in 1993) was formally approved on 5 February 2008, and was ratified by the legislature in April. Ukraine's accession to the WTO was expected to allow discussions on a free-trade agreement with the EU to proceed. In January 2008 the Ukraine Government formally requested a NATO Membership Action Plan (MAP), which was regarded as preparatory to membership. (Opposition parties, notably the PR and the CPU, strongly criticized Ukraine's request for NATO membership.) At a NATO summit meeting, which was convened in Bucharest, Romania, on 2 April, Ukraine and Georgia were not offered a MAP, although the Alliance made clear that it welcomed a closer relationship with both countries and would consider offering a MAP to each of them in due course; Russia's permanent representative to NATO had criticized US support for the aspirations towards NATO accession of those countries.

Government

Executive power is vested in the President and the Prime Minister, and legislative power is the prerogative of the 450-member Verkhovna Rada. The President is elected by direct, popular vote for a five-year term. Prior to constitutional amendments agreed in late 2004, the President appointed the Prime Minister and the members of the Cabinet of Ministers. However, with effect from 2006 several presidential powers of appointment were to be transferred to the Prime Minister, who was to be elected by the Verkhovna Rada. The President was to retain the right to appoint certain principal ministers, and, in certain circumstances, to dissolve the legislature. Ukraine is a unitary state, divided for administrative purposes into 24 oblasts (regions), one autonomous republic (Crimea), and two metropolitan areas (Kyiv and Sevastopol). The Constitution guarantees local self-government to regions, cities, settlements and villages. Regional governors are appointed by the President.

Defence

In December 1991 the Verkhovna Rada adopted legislation establishing independent Ukrainian armed forces. As assessed at November 2007, there were 129,925 active personnel in the Ukrainian armed forces, including 70,753 ground forces, 45,240 in the air force, and an estimated 13,932 (including conscripts) in the navy. There were also paramilitary forces, comprising 45,000 in the Border Guard and an estimated 39,900 serving under the Ministry of Internal Affairs. In addition, some 9,500 were serving in civil defence troops answerable to the Ministry for Emergency Situations and Protection of the Population from the Consequences of the Chornobyl Catastrophe. There were, additionally, some 1m. reserves. Military service is compulsory for males over 18 years of age, for a period of 18 months in the ground forces and air forces, and two years in the navy. Legislation approved in March 2005 provided for the reduction by six months of the terms of conscription to the ground forces and the navy. The 2007 budget allocated an estimated 9,100m. hryvnyas to defence.

Economic Affairs

In 2006, according to the World Bank, Ukraine's gross national income (GNI), measured at average 2004–06 prices, was US $90,616m., equivalent to $1,950 per head (or $7,520 per head, on an international purchasing-power parity basis). During 1996–2006 gross domestic product (GDP) per head increased, in real terms, at an average rate of 5.5% per year. Over the same period, the population decreased by an annual average of 0.9%. Ukraine's GDP increased, in real terms, by an average of 4.5% annually during 1996–2006. Real GDP increased by 7.1% in 2006.

Agriculture (including forestry and fishing) contributed 8.4% of GDP and provided 17.6% of employment in 2006. Ukraine has large areas of extremely fertile land, forming part of the 'black earth' belt, and the country is self-sufficient in almost all aspects of agricultural production. The principal crops are grain, potatoes, sugar beet and other vegetables. A programme to transfer state collective farms to private ownership was initiated in 1991. In January 1997 only 14% of land was managed by private farms, although in that year private farms contributed some 46% of total agricultural output. During 1996–2006, according to the World Bank, agricultural GDP increased by an annual average of 1.4%, in real terms. In 2006 the GDP of the sector increased by 0.2%.

Industry (including mining, manufacturing, construction and power) contributed an estimated 35.2% of GDP and provided 24.2% of employment in 2006. Heavy industry dominates the sector, particularly metal-working, mechanical engineering, chemicals and machinery products. By 1997 some 80% of the defence industry factories operating at the end of the Soviet period had been converted to non-military production. According to the World Bank, industrial GDP increased by an average of 5.3% annually, in real terms, in 1996–2006. Real industrial GDP increased by 6.7% in 2006.

In 2003 some 3.7% of the work-force were engaged in mining and quarrying; the sector contributed 4.5% of GDP in 2006. Ukraine has large deposits of coal (mainly in the huge Donbass coal basin) and high-grade iron ore, and there are also significant reserves of manganese, titanium, graphite, natural gas and petroleum. Production of coal declined by some 53% in 1989–95, and in 1996 the Government implemented a major reorganization of the coal-mining industry, including the closure of several loss-making mines.

The manufacturing sector contributed 22.5% of GDP in 2006 and provided 17.6% of employment in 2003. During 1995–2004 manufacturing GDP increased by an annual average of 7.2%, in real terms. The GDP of the sector increased by 14.6% in 2004.

Ukraine is highly dependent on imports of energy products, of which Russia and Turkmenistan are the principal suppliers. Imports of mineral fuels comprised 30.0% of the value of total imports in 2006. Ukraine is also vitally important as an energy transit country, situated as it is between the mineral resource-rich countries of the former USSR and the developed economies of Europe. A pipeline from a new oil terminal at Odesa, on the Black Sea coast, to Brody, near the border with Poland, which was originally intended to carry petroleum from the Caspian Sea to central and western Europe, was completed in 2001; however, following Ukraine's failure to secure petroleum suppliers from the Caspian region, the pipeline entered operation in reverse direction, permitting Russian companies to pump their petroleum to the Black Sea for export. Ukraine has five nuclear power stations. However, following the accident at the Chornobyl station in 1986, the viability of the country's nuclear power programme was called into question. Nevertheless, two new nuclear reactors, the first to be completed since the Chornobyl accident, began energy production in 2004. In 2004 nuclear power accounted for 47.8% of Ukraine's electricity production; coal accounted for 24.7% and natural gas for 20.7%.

The services sector contributed 56.4% of GDP and engaged 58.2% of the employed labour force in 2006. During 1996–2006 the GDP of the sector increased by an average of 3.6% annually, in real terms. The real GDP of the sector declined by under 0.2% in 2005, before increasing by 9.6% in 2006. A significant event for the development of the tourist sector in Ukraine was the announcement, in April 2007, that the country was to co-host, with Poland, the 2012 football European Championship finals.

In 2006 Ukraine recorded a trade deficit of US $5,194m., while there was a deficit of $1,617m. on the current account of the balance of payments. In 2006 the principal markets for exports were Russia (accounting for 22.5%), Italy (6.5%) and Turkey (6.2%). The principal source of imports in that year was Russia (providing 30.6% of all imports), followed by Germany (9.5%), Turkmenistan (7.8%) and the People's Republic of China (5.1%). The principal imports in 2006 were mineral products (which accounted for 30.0% of the total), machinery, mechanical and electrical equipment, vehicles and transportation equipment, chemical products, base metals, and plastics and rubbers. The principal exports in that year were base metals (some 42.8% of the total, comprising principally iron and steel), mineral products, chemical products, and machinery, mechanical and electrical equipment.

In 2006 a budgetary surplus of 3,602m. hryvnyas was recorded, equivalent to 0.7% of GDP. Ukraine's total external debt was US $33,297m. at the end of 2005, of which $10,458m. was long-term public debt. In that year the cost of debt-servicing was equivalent to 13.0% of the value of exports of goods and services. In 1996–2006 the average annual inflation rate was 12.4%. According to official figures, consumer prices increased by 16.6% in 2007. Some 6.8% of the labour force were unemployed in 2006.

Ukraine became a member of the IMF and the World Bank in 1992. It also joined the European Bank for Reconstruction and Development (EBRD, see p. 239) as a 'Country of Operations'. In June 1994 Ukraine signed an agreement of partnership and co-operation with the European Union (EU, see p. 244), which was ratified in 1998. An interim trade accord was signed with the EU in June 1995. Ukraine is a member of the Organization of the Black Sea Economic Co-operation (see p. 367), and acceded to the World Trade Organization (see p. 396) in 2008.

In 2001 recorded GDP was equivalent to just 44% of the level recorded in 1991, although the existence of a large informal sector meant that the extent of the decline may have been overstated. The economy showed significant signs of improvement from 2000, when GDP registered positive growth for the first time since the USSR's collapse. The disruption to the national economy caused by the disputed presidential election of late 2004 and tensions over economic policy in the Government formed in February 2005 resulted in the rate of growth recorded in that year being markedly lower than that recorded in the previous three years. One of the most controversial privatizations to be carried out under the former regime of President Leonid Kuchma, that of Kryvorizhstal, Ukraine's largest steel plant, was annulled under the new administration, one of a small number of disputed privatizations of the post-Soviet period that were to be investigated. A 90% stake in the company, which had been sold for US $800m. in June 2004, to a consortium headed by close allies and relations of Kuchma, was returned to state control, prior to its re-sale, in October 2005, to Mittal Steel (of the Netherlands) for $4,800m. Substantial increases in the payments for the supply of Russian and Turkmenistani natural gas had a detrimental effect on the Ukrainian economy from 2006. These payments increased in 2007 by some 40%, and a similar increase was anticipated in 2008. None the less, real GDP growth in 2007 was estimated at 7.3%, and the IMF predicted growth of 7.0% in 2008. Ukraine's accession to the WTO, ratified in April 2008, was expected to have a significant advantageous effect on the economy, particularly benefiting foreign investment and steel exports to the EU, although other sectors, such as agriculture and automobile manufacturing, were expected to suffer. Inflation rose sharply in the second half of 2007 and early 2008, driven by rising food and energy costs, and by the impact of certain policies of the incoming Tymoshenko administration, including the payment of token sums by way of compensation to Ukrainians who had lost their savings following the collapse of the national savings bank (and 'hyper-inflation') in the early 1990s. Overdependence on steel exports and vulnerability to further increases in the price of natural gas from Russia and Turkmenistan remained significant weaknesses in the Ukrainian economic situation, as did lingering doubts over political stability and the durability of Tymoshenko's second premiership.

Education

After Ukrainian was decreed the state language in 1990, policies were adopted to ensure that all pupils were granted the opportunity of tuition in Ukrainian. In 2001 there was also tuition in Russian, as well as in Romanian, Hungarian, Moldovan, Crimean Tatar and Polish. In the early 1990s there were significant changes to the curriculum, with a greater emphasis on Ukrainian history and literature. Some religious and private educational institutions were established in the early 1990s. Education is officially compulsory between seven and 15 years of age. Primary education begins at seven years of age and lasts for four years. Secondary education, beginning at 11, lasts for a maximum of seven years, comprising a first cycle of five years and a second of two years. In 2005 enrolment at primary schools included 83.3% of children in the relevant age-group. In that year enrolment in secondary education included 79.5% of the relevant age group. In 2006/07 there were 2,786,600 students enrolled in higher education. In 2006 government expenditure on education totalled 33,274m. hryvnyas (13.7% of the total budgetary expenditure).

Public Holidays

2008: 1 January (New Year), 7 January (Orthodox Christmas), 8 March (International Women's Day), 28 April (Orthodox Easter Monday), 1–2 May (Labour Day), 9 May (Victory Day), 28 June (Constitution Day), 24 August (Independence Day).
2009: 1 January (New Year), 7 January (Orthodox Christmas), 8 March (International Women's Day), 20 April (Orthodox Easter Monday), 1–2 May (Labour Day), 9 May (Victory Day), 28 June (Constitution Day), 24 August (Independence Day).

Weights and Measures

The metric system is in force.

Statistical Survey

Principal source (unless otherwise stated): State Committee for Statistics, 01023 Kyiv, vul. Sh. Rustaveli 3; tel. (44) 226-20-21; fax (44) 235-37-39; e-mail info@ukrstat.gov.ua; internet www.ukrstat.gov.ua.

Area and Population

AREA, POPULATION AND DENSITY

Area (sq km)	603,700*
Population (census results)	
12 January 1989	51,706,742
5 December 2001	
Males	22,441,344
Females	26,015,758
Total	48,457,102
Population (official estimates at 1 July)	
2005	47,075,295
2006	46,756,618
2007	46,490,819
Density (per sq km) at 1 July 2007	77.0

* 233,090 sq miles.

POPULATION BY ETHNIC GROUP
(permanent inhabitants, census of 5 December 2001)

	'000	%
Ukrainian	37,541.7	78.13
Russian	8,334.1	17.34
Belarusian	275.8	0.57
Moldovan	258.6	0.54
Crimean Tatar	248.2	0.52
Others	1,393.9	2.90
Total	**48,052.3**	**100.00**

UKRAINE

ADMINISTRATIVE DIVISIONS

	Area ('000 sq km)	Population (at 1 July 2007)*	Density (per sq km)
Regions			
Cherkasy	20.9	1,322,088	63.3
Chernihiv	31.9	1,143,816	35.9
Chernivtsi	8.1	905,061	80.7
Dnipropetrovsk	31.9	3,408,488	106.8
Donetsk	26.5	4,557,770	172.0
Ivano-Frankivsk	13.9	1,383,544	99.5
Kharkiv	31.4	2,800,406	89.2
Kherson	28.5	1,112,685	39.0
Khmelnytsky	20.6	1,356,426	65.8
Kirovohrad	24.6	1,046,958	42.6
Kyiv	28.1	1,744,694	62.1
Luhansk	26.7	2,367,983	88.7
Lviv	21.8	2,562,603	117.6
Mykolayiv	24.6	1,207,776	49.1
Odesa	33.3	2,392,540	71.8
Poltava	28.8	1,532,783	53.2
Rivne	20.1	1,153,266	57.4
Sumy	23.8	1,204,213	50.6
Ternopil	13.8	1,101,960	79.9
Transcarpathia	12.8	1,242,717	97.1
Vinnytsia	26.5	1,679,556	63.4
Volyn	20.2	1,037,225	51.3
Zaporizhzhia	27.2	1,839,508	67.6
Zhytomyr	29.9	1,311,863	43.9
Cities			
Kyiv	0.8	2,721,739	3,402.2
Sevastopol	0.9	378,970	421.0
Autonomous Republic			
Crimea	26.1	1,974,181	75.6
Total	603.7	46,490,819	77.0

* Official estimates.

PRINCIPAL TOWNS
(population at census of 5 December 2001, rounded figures)

Kyiv (Kiev, capital)	2,611,000	Poltava	318,000
Kharkiv	1,470,000	Chernihiv	305,000
Dnipropetrovsk	1,065,000	Cherkasy	295,000
Odesa	1,029,000	Sumy	293,000
Donetsk	1,016,000	Horlivka	292,000
Zaporizhzhia	815,000	Zhytomyr	284,000
Lviv	733,000	Dniprodzerzhynsk	256,000
Kryvyi Rih	669,000	Khmelnytsky	254,000
Mykolayiv	514,000	Kirovohrad	254,000
Mariupol*	492,000	Rivne	249,000
Luhansk†	463,000	Chernivtsi	241,000
Makiyivka	390,000	Kremenchuk	234,000
Vinnytsia	357,000	Ternopil	228,000
Simferopol	344,000	Ivano-Frankivsk	218,000
Sevastopol	342,000	Lutsk	209,000
Kherson	328,000	Bila Tserkva	200,000

* Known as Zhdanov from 1948 to 1989.
† Known as Voroshylovhrad from 1935 to 1958 and from 1970 to 1989.

BIRTHS, MARRIAGES AND DEATHS*

	Registered live births Number	Rate (per 1,000)	Registered marriages Number	Rate (per 1,000)	Registered deaths Number	Rate (per 1,000)
2000	385,126	7.8	274,523	5.5	758,082	15.3
2001	376,479	7.8	309,602	6.4	745,953	15.4
2002	390,687	8.1	317,228	6.6	754,911	15.7
2003	408,591	8.5	370,966	7.8	765,408	16.0
2004	427,259	9.0	278,230	5.9	761,263	16.0
2005	426,085	9.0	332,138	7.1	781,964	16.6
2006	460,368	9.8	354,959	7.6	758,093	16.2
2007	472,657	10.2	416,427	9.0	762,877	16.4

* Rates for 1997–2000 are based on unrevised population estimates.

Expectation of life (years at birth, WHO estimates): 67.0 (males 61.2; females 73.1) in 2005 (Source: WHO, *World Health Statistics*).

Statistical Survey

IMMIGRATION AND EMIGRATION

	2005	2006	2007
Immigrants	39,580	44,227	46,507
Emigrants	34,997	29,982	29,669

ECONOMICALLY ACTIVE POPULATION
(annual averages, '000 persons aged 15–70 years)

	2004	2005	2006
Agriculture, hunting, forestry and fishing	3,998.3	4,005.5	3,649.1
Mining and quarrying; manufacturing; electricity, gas and water supply	4,077.1	4,072.4	4,036.9
Construction	907.5	941.5	987.1
Wholesale and retail trade; repair of motor vehicles, motorcycles and personal and household goods; hotels and restaurants	3,971.2	4,175.2	4,406.9
Transport, storage and communications	1,374.9	1,400.5	1,428.8
Financial intermediation	216.1	247.9	286.0
Real estate, renting and business activities	919.9	966.6	1,041.9
Public administration and defence; compulsory social security	1,050.2	1,028.9	1,033.7
Education	1,648.7	1,668.2	1,690.5
Health and social work	1,348.9	1,356.6	1,356.7
Other community, social and personal service activities; private households with employed persons; extra-territorial organizations and bodies	782.9	816.7	812.8
Total employed	20,295.7	20,680.0	20,730.4
Total unemployed	1,906.7	1,600.8	1,515.0
Total labour force	22,202.4	22,280.8	22,245.4

Source: ILO.

Health and Welfare

KEY INDICATORS

Total fertility rate (children per woman, 2005)	1.1
Under-5 mortality rate (per 1,000 live births, 2005)	17
HIV/AIDS (% of persons aged 15–49, 2005)	1.4
Physicians (per 1,000 head, 2004)	2.95
Hospital beds (per 1,000 head, 2005)	8.7
Health expenditure (2004): US $ per head (PPP)	426.6
Health expenditure (2004): % of GDP	6.5
Health expenditure (2004): public (% of total)	56.7
Access to water (% of persons, 2004)	96
Access to sanitation (% of persons, 2004)	96
Human Development Index (2005): ranking	76
Human Development Index (2005): value	0.788

For sources and definitions, see explanatory note on p. vi.

Agriculture

PRINCIPAL CROPS
('000 metric tons)

	2004	2005	2006
Wheat	17,520.2	18,699.2	14,000.0
Barley	11,084.4	8,975.1	11,316.0
Maize	8,866.8	7,166.6	6,320.0
Rye	1,592.5	1,054.2	920.0*
Oats	1,007.0	790.7	700.0*
Millet	458.8	140.6	108.0*
Buckwheat	293.6	274.7	212.0*
Potatoes	20,754.8	19,462.4	19,467.0
Sugar beet	16,600.4	15,467.8	22,421.0
Dry peas	636.3	616.0	485.0*

UKRAINE

—continued	2004	2005	2006
Sunflower seed	3,050.1	4,706.1	5,324.0
Cabbages	1,544.5	1,475.4	1,465.0*
Tomatoes	1,145.7	1,471.8	1,461.0*
Pumpkins, squash and gourds	1,023.2	1,072.0*	1,064.0*
Cucumbers and gherkins	712.5	687.9	685.0*
Chillies and green peppers	128.2	131.5	130.0*
Dry onions	721.7	751.1	746.0*
Garlic	130.7	145.6	14.0
Carrots	674.9	645.3	640.0*
Watermelons	307.1	256.4	255.0*
Apples	716.9	719.8	475.0*
Pears	151.7	177.3	116.0*
Apricots	99.3	94.2	62.0*
Sweet cherries	85.3	100.2	66.0*
Sour (Morello) cherries	178.5	181.8	120.0*
Plums	173.3	165.9	110.0*
Grapes	374.0	442.6	370.0*

* Unofficial figure.

Aggregate production ('000 metric tons, may include official, semi-official or estimated data): Total cereals 40,997 in 2004, 37,258 in 2005, 33,698 in 2006; Total roots and tubers 20,755 in 2004, 19,462 in 2005, 19,467 in 2006; Total vegetables (incl. melons) 7,832 in 2004, 8,110 in 2005, 8,055 in 2006; Total fruits (excl. melons) 1,918 in 2004, 2,041 in 2005, 1,424 in 2006.

Source: FAO.

LIVESTOCK
('000 head at 1 January)

	2004	2005	2006
Horses	637	591	585
Cattle	7,712	6,903	6,514
Pigs	7,322	6,466	7,053
Sheep	893	875	872
Goats	965	894	758
Chickens	122,026	131,976	140,500

* FAO estimate.

Source: FAO.

LIVESTOCK PRODUCTS
('000 metric tons)

	2004	2005	2006
Cattle meat	618.0	561.8	591.5
Pig meat	558.8	493.7	520.0
Chicken meat	375.5	496.6	522.5
Cows' milk	13,390.1	13,423.8	12,988.0
Sheep's milk	30.4	24.1	23.7
Goats' milk	289.0	266.5	258.0
Poultry eggs	683.7	756.3	828.4
Hen eggs	677.4	748.1	819.5
Honey	57.9	71.5	n.a.

Source: FAO.

Forestry

ROUNDWOOD REMOVALS
('000 cubic metres, excl. bark)

	2004	2005	2006
Sawlogs, veneer logs and logs for sleepers	4,571	4,632	4,888
Pulpwood	954	953	1,000
Other industrial wood*	941	876	865
Fuel wood*	8,396	8,146	8,494
Total	14,862	14,606	15,247

* Unofficial figures.

Source: FAO.

SAWNWOOD PRODUCTION
('000 cubic metres, incl. railway sleepers)

	2004	2005	2006
Coniferous (softwood)	1,670	1,743	1,581
Broadleaved (hardwood)	722	673	611
Total	2,392	2,416	2,192

* Unofficial figures.

Source: FAO.

Fishing

('000 metric tons, live weight)

	2003	2004	2005
Capture	222.3	202.7	244.9
Azov sea sprat	11.1	8.5	14.6
Southern hake	7.5	1.0	n.a.
Blue grenadier	10.6	6.3	n.a.
Gobies	6.6	12.4	11.7
Snoek	7.5	7.4	n.a.
Sardinellas	5.5	2.4	5.0
European pilchard (sardine)	20.1	28.1	38.0
European sprat	31.4	30.9	35.7
European anchovy	13.1	9.4	6.9
Greenback horse mackerel	25.0	22.6	n.a.
Other jack and horse mackerels	9.4	1.6	0.7
Other mackerels	7.6	3.8	0.5
Antarctic krill	17.7	12.3	22.4
Wellington flying squid	10.4	20.1	n.a.
Aquaculture	25.6	26.2*	28.7
Common carp	15.0	14.8	16.2
Silver carp	7.0	7.0*	7.5
Total catch	248.0	229.0*	273.7

* FAO estimate.

Source: FAO.

Mining

('000 metric tons, unless otherwise indicated)

	2003	2004	2005
Hard (incl. coking) coal	63,866	62,100	58,000
Brown coal (incl. lignite)	950*	3,000	3,000
Crude petroleum	3,975	4,179	4,269
Natural gas (million cu m)	19,460	19,000	19,300
Iron ore: gross weight	62,497.6	65,540.0	68,569.6
Manganese ore*†	880	810	770
Ilmenite concentrate	421	370	370
Rutile concentrate	60	60	60
Zirconium concentrates*	35.0	35.0	35.0
Uranium concentrate (metric tons)†	800	800	800
Bentonite*	300	300	300
Kaolin	225	225	225
Potash salts (crude)*‡	60	50	65
Native sulphur*	142	136	135
Salt (unrefined)*	2,757	3,339	3,400
Graphite (metric tons)*	7,500	7,500	7,500
Peat*	1,000	1,000	1,000

* Estimated production.
† Figures refer to the metal content of ores and concentrates.
‡ Figures refer to potassium oxide content.

Source: US Geological Survey.

UKRAINE

Industry

SELECTED PRODUCTS
('000 metric tons, unless otherwise indicated)

	2001	2002	2003
Margarine	167	170	123
Flour	2,686	2,724	2,540
Raw sugar*	1,947	1,621	2,486
Ethyl alcohol ('000 hectolitres)	2,643	2,840	2,546
Wine ('000 hectolitres)	1,425	2,081	2,045
Beer ('000 hectolitres)	13,059	15,000	17,012
Cigarettes (million)	69,731	81,088	96,776
Wool yarn: pure and mixed	3.7	3.5	3.0
Cotton yarn: pure and mixed	11.0	10.7	8.7
Flax yarn	1.3	0.8	0.2
Woven cotton fabrics (million sq metres)	46	57	27
Woven woollen fabrics (million sq metres)	7.4	7.0	6.5
Linen fabrics (million sq metres)	5.7	4.1	0.3
Footwear, excl. rubber ('000 pairs)	15,155	15,016	15,939
Hydrochloric acid	66.8	60.5	76.9
Sulphuric acid	1,040	935	1,131
Nitric acid	6	4	436
Phosphoric acid	30.9	18.5	31.3
Caustic soda (Sodium hydroxide)	134	133	160
Soda ash (Sodium carbonate)	651	679	656
Nitrogenous fertilizers (a)†	2,153	2,311	2,473
Phosphatic fertilizers (b)†	61	28	38
Potassic fertilizers (c)†	20	8	14
Rubber tyres ('000)‡	6,862	6,244	6,107
Rubber footwear ('000 pairs)	2,527	2,665	3,588
Clay building bricks (million)	1,382	1,462	1,563
Quicklime	4,367	4,456	4,962
Cement	5,786	4,456	4,962
Pig-iron	26,379	27,633	29,529
Crude steel: for castings	500	872	1,514
Crude steel: ingots	33,523	34,543	37,524
Tractors (number)§	3,640	2,980	4,531
Household refrigerators ('000)	509	583	340
Household washing machines ('000)	166	232	251
Radio receivers ('000)	26	33	21
Television receivers ('000)	148	159	415
Passenger motor cars ('000)	26	44	102
Buses and motor coaches (number)	2,474	2,102	2,655
Lorries (number)	6,747	2,343	1,265
Bicycles ('000)‖	109	245	281
Electric energy ('000 million kWh)	173	174	180

* Production from home-grown sugar beet.
† Production of fertilizers is in terms of (a) nitrogen; (b) phosphoric acid; or (c) potassium oxide.
‡ Tyres for road motor vehicles.
§ Tractors of 10 horse-power and over, excluding industrial tractors and road tractors for tractor-trailer combinations.
‖ Excluding children's bicycles.

Source: UN, *Industrial Commodity Statistics Yearbook*.

Raw sugar ('000 metric tons): 2,147 in 2004; 2,139 in 2005; 2,592 in 2006.

Sulphuric acid ('000 metric tons): 1,425 in 2004; 1,606 in 2005; 1,493 in 2006.

Caustic soda (Sodium hydroxide) ('000 metric tons): 210 in 2004; 209 in 2005; 183 in 2006.

Nitrogenous fertilizers (nitrogen content, '000 metric tons): 2,407 in 2004; 2,633 in 2005; 2,566 in 2006.

Rubber tyres ('000): 7,940 in 2004; 7,531 in 2005; 7,093 in 2006.

Cement ('000 metric tons): 10,600 in 2004; 12,200 in 2005; 13,700 in 2006.

Pig-iron ('000 metric tons): 31,000 in 2004; 30,700 in 2005; 32,900 in 2006.

Tractors (number): 5,806 in 2004; 5,543 in 2005; 3,703 in 2006.

Household refrigerators ('000): 581 in 2004; 711 in 2005; 731 in 2006.

Household washing machines ('000): 345 in 2004; 322 in 2005.

Television receivers ('000): 443 in 2004; 651 in 2005; 431 in 2006.

Passenger motor cars ('000): 174 in 2004; 192 in 2005; 267 in 2006.

Buses and motor coaches (number): 2,598 in 2004; 4,655 in 2005; 7,660 in 2006.

Electric energy ('000 million kWh): 182 in 2004; 186 in 2005; 193 in 2006.

Finance

CURRENCY AND EXCHANGE RATES

Monetary Units
100 kopiykas = 1 hryvnya.

Sterling, Dollar and Euro Equivalents (31 December 2007)
£1 sterling = 10.1171 hryvnyas;
US $1 = 5.0500 hryvnyas;
€1 = 7.4341 hryvnyas;
100 hryvnyas = £9.88 = $19.80 = €13.45.

Average Exchange Rate (hryvnyas per US $)
2005 5.1247
2006 5.0500
2007 5.0500

Note: Following the dissolution of the USSR in December 1991, Russia and several other former Soviet republics retained the rouble (known as the karbovanets—KRB in Ukraine) as their monetary unit. In November 1992 this currency ceased to be legal tender in Ukraine, and was replaced (initially at par) by a currency coupon, also known as the karbovanets, or kupon, for a transitional period. Following the introduction of the transitional currency, Ukraine operated a system of multiple exchange rates, but in October 1994 the official and auction rates were merged. The unified exchange rate at 31 December 1995 was US $1 = 179,400 KRB. On 2 September 1996 Ukraine introduced a new currency, the hryvnya, at a rate of 100,000 KRB per hryvnya (1.750 hryvnyas per $).

GOVERNMENT FINANCE
(general government transactions, million hryvnyas)

Summary of Balances

	2004	2005	2006
Revenue	127,509	183,407	234,374
Less Expense	130,946	183,071	230,772
Net operating balance	–3,437	336	3,602
Less Net acquisition of non-financial assets	8,331	6,225	9,113
Net lending/borrowing	–11,768	–5,889	–5,511

Revenue

	2004	2005	2006
Taxes	63,614	98,351	126,414
Taxes on income, profits and capital gains	30,539	42,328	50,448
Taxes on goods and services	25,444	46,592	65,713
Social contributions	40,912	55,460	70,413
Grants	428	199	163
Other revenue	22,555	29,397	37,385
Total	127,509	183,407	234,374

Expense/Outlays

Expense by economic type	2004	2005	2006
Compensation of employees	33,511	43,729	56,470
Use of goods and services	20,627	29,667	36,874
Interest	3,147	3,462	3,702
Subsidies	8,215	10,268	17,622
Grants	218	194	140
Social benefits	53,590	85,437	102,817
Other expense	11,640	10,315	13,148
Total	130,946	183,071	230,772

UKRAINE

Statistical Survey

Outlays by functions of government*	2004	2005	2006
General public services	12,116	14,798	19,899
Defence	5,111	5,066	5,547
Public order and safety	7,855	10,210	12,701
Economic affairs	21,520	20,864	27,344
Environmental protection	889	890	1,541
Housing and community amenities	3,008	4,630	8,696
Health	13,313	16,805	20,954
Recreation, culture and religion	2,802	3,586	4,501
Education	17,999	26,374	33,274
Social protection	57,205	88,891	108,645
Total	**141,818**	**192,112**	**243,102**

* Including net acquisition of non-financial assets.

Source: IMF, *Government Finance Statistics Yearbook*.

INTERNATIONAL RESERVES
(US $ million at 31 December)

	2004	2005	2006
Gold (national valuation)	224.1	402.5	513.5
IMF special drawing rights	1.2	1.0	1.5
Foreign exchange	9,489.5	18,987.0	21,843.2
Total	**9,714.8**	**19,390.5**	**22,358.2**

Source: IMF, *International Financial Statistics*.

MONEY SUPPLY
(million hryvnyas at 31 December)

	2004	2005	2006
Currency outside banks	42,344.9	60,231.4	74,983.6
Demand deposits at banks	24,669.1	38,243.0	48,110.0
Total money (incl. others)	**67,090.3**	**98,572.6**	**123,275.6**

Source: IMF, *International Financial Statistics*.

COST OF LIVING
(Consumer Price Index; base: previous year = 100)

	2005	2006	2007
Food and beverages	110.7	103.5	122.9
Other consumer goods	104.0	102.5	106.0
Services	115.8	149.4	112.0
All goods and services	**110.3**	**111.6**	**116.6**

NATIONAL ACCOUNTS
(million hryvnyas at current prices)

National Income and Product

	2004	2005	2006
Compensation of employees	157,450	216,600	268,631
Net operating surplus and mixed income	105,924	118,230	143,771
Domestic primary incomes	**263,374**	**334,830**	**412,402**
Consumption of fixed capital	46,576	50,545	58,265
Gross domestic product (GDP) at factor cost	**309,950**	**385,375**	**470,667**
Taxes on production and imports	40,018	62,777	82,377
Less Subsidies	4,855	6,700	8,891
GDP in market prices	**345,113**	**441,452**	**544,153**
Primary incomes received from abroad	2,040	3,822	6,684
Less Primary incomes paid abroad	5,467	8,863	15,378
Gross national income (GNI)	**341,686**	**436,411**	**535,459**
Less Consumption of fixed capital	46,576	50,545	58,265
Net national income	**295,110**	**385,866**	**477,194**
Current taxes and transfers from abroad	14,481	16,185	18,245
Less Current transfers paid abroad	803	1,358	1,818
Net national disposable income	**308,788**	**400,696**	**493,621**

Expenditure on the Gross Domestic Product

	2004	2005	2006
Final consumption expenditure	**245,556**	**337,879**	**424,906**
Households	180,399	252,624	319,383
Non-profit institutions serving households	4,547	4,727	5,173
General government	60,610	80,528	100,350
Gross capital formation	**73,070**	**99,876**	**134,740**
Gross fixed capital formation	77,820	96,965	133,874
Changes in inventories	−4,883	2,736	655
Acquisitions, less disposals, of valuables	133	175	211
Total domestic expenditure	**318,626**	**437,755**	**559,646**
Exports of goods and services	219,607	227,252	253,707
Less Imports of goods and services	193,120	223,555	269,200
GDP in market prices	**345,113**	**441,452**	**544,153**

Gross Domestic Product by Economic Activity

	2004	2005	2006
Agriculture, hunting, forestry and fishing	37,258	40,542	41,006
Mining and quarrying	12,518	17,939	22,064
Manufacturing	64,124	86,863	109,416
Electricity, gas and water supply	12,423	15,169	18,610
Construction	14,463	16,370	21,168
Wholesale and retail trade; repair of motor vehicles, motorcycles and personal goods	41,057	56,041	68,573
Transport, storage and communication	42,694	47,435	56,053
Education	16,252	20,882	26,243
Health and social work	10,952	13,965	17,722
Other economic activities	66,580	80,797	106,277
Sub-total	**318,321**	**396,003**	**487,132**
Less Financial intermediation services indirectly measured	5,275	7,402	13,009
Gross value added in basic prices	**313,046**	**388,601**	**474,123**
Taxes on products	33,122	54,183	71,618
Less Subsidies on products	1,055	1,332	1,588
GDP in market prices	**345,113**	**441,452**	**544,153**

BALANCE OF PAYMENTS
(US $ million)

	2004	2005	2006
Exports of goods f.o.b.	33,432	35,024	38,949
Imports of goods f.o.b.	−29,691	−36,159	−44,143
Trade balance	**3,741**	**−1,135**	**−5,194**
Exports of services	7,859	9,354	11,290
Imports of services	−6,622	−7,548	−9,164
Balance on goods and services	**4,978**	**671**	**−3,068**
Other income received	389	758	1,332
Other income paid	−1,034	−1,743	−3,054
Balance on goods, services and income	**4,333**	**−314**	**−4,790**
Current transfers received	2,671	3,111	3,533
Current transfers paid	−95	−266	−360
Current balance	**6,909**	**2,531**	**−1,617**
Capital account (net)	7	−65	3
Direct investment abroad	−4	−275	133
Direct investment from abroad	1,715	7,808	5,203
Portfolio investment assets	−6	—	−3
Portfolio investment liabilities	2,073	2,757	3,586
Other investment assets	−12,313	−7,936	−15,424
Other investment liabilities	4,196	5,749	10,189
Net errors and omissions	−54	156	339
Overall balance	**2,523**	**10,725**	**2,409**

Sources: IMF, *International Financial Statistics*.

UKRAINE

External Trade

PRINCIPAL COMMODITIES
(distribution by Harmonized System, US $ million)

Imports f.o.b.	2004	2005	2006
Vegetable products	439.5	525.5	671.7
Prepared food, beverages, spirits, tobacco	1,004.6	1,454.9	1,654.5
Mineral products	10,845.4	11,567.8	13,506.2
Mineral fuels, oils, waxes and bituminous substances	10,160.9	10,661.9	12,711.6
Coal	900.3	714.3	760.6
Crude petroleum	4,837.4	4,600.5	4,403.6
Natural gas	3,591.4	3,946.0	4,769.4
Chemicals and related products	2,248.4	3,097.0	3,888.6
Plastics, rubbers, and articles thereof	1,406.6	1,937.8	2,527.5
Plastic and articles thereof	1,070.9	1,497.3	1,988.7
Wood pulp, paper, paperboard, scrap and waste paper and articles thereof	785.2	1,003.9	1,173.3
Paper and paperboard, articles of paper pulp	664.8	866.5	1,014.2
Textiles and textile articles	992.2	1,406.2	1,365.5
Base metals and articles thereof	1,752.9	2,468.7	3,327.4
Iron and steel	814.7	1,151.1	1,468.9
Machinery and mechanical appliances, electrical equipment and appliances, parts and accessories	4,740.7	6,340.0	7,877.7
Machinery and mechanical appliances, computers, etc.	3,214.3	4,050.2	5,195.7
Electrical machinery, equipment and parts, etc.	1,526.4	2,289.9	2,682.0
Vehicles, aircraft, vessels and associated transportation equipment	2,493.6	3,219.5	5,147.3
Vehicles other than railway or tramway rolling stock	2,246.1	3,022.9	4,898.5
Total (incl. others)	28,996.0	36,136.3	45,038.6

Exports f.o.b.	2004	2005	2006
Vegetable products	1,137.4	1,694.8	1,950.5
Cereals	844.3	1,383.1	1,353.7
Prepared food, beverages, spirits, tobacco	1,140.7	1,290.8	1,394.2
Mineral products	4,323.7	4,705.4	3,871.6
Ores, slag and ash	679.4	1,045.2	912.3
Mineral fuels, oils, waxes and bituminous substances	3,386.7	3,343.0	2,553.4
Chemicals and related products	2,782.0	2,988.3	3,387.2
Textiles, textile articles, etc.	882.6	914.0	915.3
Base metals and articles thereof	13,050.8	14,085.5	16,426.2
Iron and steel	10,768.3	11,451.2	13,057.4
Articles of iron and steel	1,448.0	1,848.3	2,361.6

Exports f.o.b.—continued	2004	2005	2006
Machinery and mechanical appliances, electrical equipment and appliances, parts and accessories	3,031.0	2,838.7	3,330.5
Machinery and mechanical appliances, computers, etc.	1,801.9	1,922.0	2,051.5
Electrical machinery, equipment and parts, etc.	1,229.1	916.7	1,279.0
Vehicles, aircraft, vessels and associated transportation equipment	2,037.3	1,648.0	2,078.5
Railway or tramway locomotives, rolling stock, track fixtures and fittings, signals, etc.	1,492.8	964.2	1,067.0
Total (incl. others)	32,672.3	34,284.4	38,368.0

PRINCIPAL TRADING PARTNERS
(US $ million)

Imports f.o.b.	2004	2005	2006
Austria	344.4	458.4	547.2
Belarus	538.2	939.8	1,255.2
Brazil	264.0	312.5	279.8
China, People's Republic	733.3	1,810.4	2,310.4
Czech Republic	419.7	594.0	825.1
Finland	255.7	351.1	391.8
France (incl. Monaco)	653.0	798.9	989.8
Germany	2,731.8	3,384.0	4,268.3
Hungary	362.3	647.7	802.2
Italy	806.0	1,030.2	1,467.4
Japan	422.0	548.2	848.7
Kazakhstan	388.5	186.4	965.7
Korea, Republic	322.0	648.5	935.4
Netherlands	352.2	464.1	641.3
Poland	968.7	1,406.0	2,109.2
Russia	11,811.8	12,842.5	13,787.0
Sweden	418.4	547.4	565.0
Switzerland	300.0	252.5	283.2
Turkey	368.4	607.7	769.2
Turkmenistan	1,953.7	2,678.1	3,492.0
United Kingdom	733.6	502.7	620.6
USA	763.6	710.0	879.1
Total (incl. others)	28,996.0	36,136.3	45,038.6

Exports f.o.b.	2004	2005	2006
Algeria	593.8	617.2	466.7
Belarus	550.8	891.1	1,222.7
Bulgaria	498.5	543.0	595.7
China, People's Republic	831.4	711.1	544.7
Cyprus	168.4	217.0	251.8
Czech Republic	299.1	376.9	341.6
Egypt	367.6	798.8	748.2
Estonia	278.4	125.1	123.4
Germany	1,891.0	1,285.2	1,283.8
Hungary	807.6	688.8	946.1
India	481.8	736.9	850.1
Iran	434.8	576.9	318.3
Italy	1,620.4	1,892.6	2,500.3
Kazakhstan	622.9	667.1	826.3
Korea, Republic	358.4	202.2	88.6
Latvia	377.3	311.4	286.1
Lithuania	468.6	209.3	278.3
Moldova	659.8	678.6	671.1
Netherlands	525.0	515.3	708.1
Poland	997.9	1,010.4	1,344.5
Romania	731.7	488.8	625.8
Russia	5,888.7	7,490.1	8,650.7
Saudi Arabia	241.6	386.5	537.0

UKRAINE

Statistical Survey

Exports f.o.b.—*continued*	2004	2005	2006
Singapore	286.4	489.6	211.5
Slovakia	398.1	507.7	549.6
Spain	521.8	573.5	445.1
Switzerland	472.9	395.8	112.1
Syria	603.8	672.1	602.2
Turkey	1,869.2	2,026.7	2,390.0
United Arab Emirates	426.1	345.2	392.6
United Kingdom	346.6	358.2	387.6
USA	1,506.9	956.5	1,208.8
Total (incl. others)	32,672.3	34,228.4	38,368.0

Transport

RAILWAYS
(traffic)

	2004	2005	2006
Passengers carried ('000 journeys)	452,200	444,700	448,800
Freight carried ('000 metric tons)	460,900	448,700	476,800
Passenger-km (million)	51,800	52,400	53,400
Freight ton-km (million)	233,600	223,400	240,600

ROAD TRAFFIC
(motor vehicles in use)

	1998	1999	2000
Passenger cars	4,877,787	5,210,774	5,250,129
Motorcycles and mopeds	2,609,201	2,432,787	2,251,505

2004: Passenger cars 5,445,830; Buses 175,945; Lorries and vans 917,427; Motorcycles 1,145,407.

Source: IRF, *World Road Statistics*.

INLAND WATERWAYS

	2004	2005	2006
Passengers carried ('000 journeys)	11,800	13,600	12,900
Freight carried ('000 metric tons)	20,600	21,400	23,000
Passenger-km (million)	100	100	100
Freight ton-km (million)	14,900	15,900	18,600

SHIPPING
Merchant Fleet
(registered at 31 December)

	2004	2005	2006
Number of vessels	647	658	655
Total displacement ('000 grt)	1,144.8	1,154.0	1,136.5

Source: Lloyd's Register-Fairplay, *World Fleet Statistics*.

International Sea-borne Freight Traffic
('000 metric tons, incl. transit departures)

	2002	2003	2004
Goods loaded	62,196	55,704	65,424
Goods unloaded	6,648	7,860	11,400

Source: UN, *Monthly Bulletin of Statistics*.

CIVIL AVIATION
(traffic on scheduled services)

	2001	2002	2003
Kilometres flown (million)	30	32	38
Passengers carried ('000)	986	1,120	1,476
Passenger-kilometres (million)	1,418	1,578	2,351
Total ton-kilometres (million)	149	156	231

Source: UN, *Statistical Yearbook*.

Tourism

TOURIST ARRIVALS
('000 non-resident persons)

Country of residence	2007
Belarus	2,919
Hungary	1,252
Moldova	3,999
Poland	4,430
Romania	1,010
Russia	7,258
Total (incl. others)	23,122

Receipts from tourism (US $ million, incl. passenger transport): 1,204 in 2003; 2,931 in 2004; 3,542 in 2005.

Source: World Tourism Organization.

Communications Media

	2004	2005	2006
Book production (titles)	14,790	15,720	15,867
Newspapers (titles)	3,014	2,974	2,918
Magazines and other periodicals (titles)	2,385	2,182	2,301
Telephones ('000 main lines in use)	12,142.0	11,666.6	12,341.0
Mobile cellular telephones ('000 subscribers)	13,735.0	29,999.9	49,076.2
Personal computers ('000 in use)	1,327	1,810	n.a.
Internet users ('000)	3,750	4,560	5,545

Radio receivers ('000 in use): 45,050 in 1997.

Television receivers ('000 in use): 23,000 in 2000.

Facsimile machines (number in use): 42,161 in 2000.

Sources: mainly UNESCO, *Statistical Yearbook*; International Telecommunication Union.

Education

(2006/07, unless otherwise indicated)

	Institutions	Teachers	Students
Pre-primary	15,100*	191,500†	1,081,000
Primary *and* General secondary	21,400	537,000	5,120,000
Specialized secondary: vocational	1,021	289,300	473,800
Higher	920	121,300†	2,786,600

* Including some 2,600 with activities suspended.
† 1993/94 figure.

Adult literacy rate (UNESCO estimates): 99.4% (males 99.7%; females 99.2%) in 2001 (Source: UNESCO Institute for Statistics).

Directory

Constitution

The Constitution of Ukraine, summarized below, was adopted at the Fifth Session of the Verkhovna Rada on 28 June 1996. It replaced the Soviet-era Constitution (Fundamental Law), originally approved on 12 April 1978, but amended several times after Ukraine gained independence in 1991, and entered into force the day of its adoption. On 8 December 2004, following the disputed (and subsequently annulled) second round of voting in the presidential election, the Verkhovna Rada approved a number of constitutional amendments, principally concerned with transferring a number of presidential powers, including the appointment of the majority of ministerial posts, to the Prime Minister and to the Verkhovna Rada. These amendments, which were signed into law on the same day by the outgoing President, Leonid Kuchma, were scheduled to take effect either conditionally on 1 September 2005 (subject to various reforms to local government having been approved by that date) or unconditionally on 1 January 2006. As the reforms to local government had not been agreed, the constitutional amendments took effect from the latter date, excepting those pertaining to the Verkhovna Rada or Prime Minister, which entered into force in May 2006, following the assembly of a legislature after the general election held in March.

FUNDAMENTAL PRINCIPLES

Ukraine is a sovereign and independent, unitary and law-based state, in which power is exercised directly by the people through the bodies of state power and local self-government. The life, honour, dignity and health of the individual are recognized as the highest social value. The Constitution is the highest legal authority; the power of the State is divided between the legislative, the executive and the judicial branches. The state language is Ukrainian. The use and protection of Russian and other languages of national minorities, and the development of minorities' ethnic and cultural traditions is guaranteed. The State ensures protection of all forms of ownership rights and management, as well as the social orientation of the economy. The state symbols of Ukraine, its flag, coat of arms and anthem, are established.

THE RIGHTS, FREEDOMS AND DUTIES OF CITIZENS

The rights and freedoms of individuals are declared to be unalienable and inviolable regardless of race, sex, political or religious affiliation, wealth, social origin or other characteristics. Fundamental rights, such as the freedoms of speech and association and the right to private property, are guaranteed. Citizens have the right to engage in political activity and to own private property. All individuals are entitled to work and to join professional unions to protect their employment rights. The Constitution commits the State to the provision of health care, housing, social security and education. All citizens have the right to legal assistance. Obligations of the citizenry include military service and taxes. The age of enfranchisement for Ukrainian citizens is 18 years. Elections to organs of state authority are declared to be free and conducted on the basis of universal, equal and direct suffrage by secret ballot.

THE VERKHOVNA RADA

The Verkhovna Rada (Supreme Council) is the sole organ of legislative authority in Ukraine. It consists of 450 members, elected for a four-year term on the basis of proportional representation. The constitutional reforms approved in late 2004 prohibit deputies from leaving the party or bloc for whom they have been elected during the term of their elective mandate. Only Ukrainian citizens aged over 21 years, who have resided in Ukraine for the five previous years are eligible for election to parliament. The Verkhovna Rada is a permanently acting body, which elects its own Chairman and Deputy Chairmen.

The most important functions of the legislature include: the enactment of laws; the approval of the state budget and other state programmes; the scheduling of presidential elections; the removal (impeachment) of the President; the appointment of the Prime Minister; the declaration of war or conclusion of peace; the foreign deployment of troops; and consenting to international treaty obligations within the time limit prescribed by law. Within 15 days of a law passed by the Verkhovna Rada being received by the President, the President shall officially promulgate it or return it for repeat consideration by parliament. If, during such consideration, the legislature re-adopts the law by a two-thirds' majority, the President is obliged to sign it and officially promulgate it within 10 days. The President of Ukraine may terminate the authority of the Verkhovna Rada if, within 30 days of a single, regular session a plenary session cannot be convened, except within the last six months of the President's term of office.

THE PRESIDENT

The President of Ukraine is the Head of State, and is guarantor of state sovereignty and the territorial integrity of Ukraine. The President is directly elected for a period of five years. A presidential candidate must be aged over 35 years and a resident of the country for the 10 years prior to the election. The President may hold office for no more than two consecutive terms.

The President's main responsibilities include: the scheduling of elections and of referendums on constitutional amendments; the conclusion of international treaties; and the promulgation of laws. The President appoints certain senior members of the Cabinet of Ministers; the constitutional reforms agreed in late 2004 transferred responsibility for the appointment of the majority of Ministers to the Prime Minister.

The President is the Supreme Commander of the Armed Forces of Ukraine and chairs the National Security and Defence Council. The President may be removed from office by the Verkhovna Rada by impeachment, for reasons of state treason or another crime. The decision to remove the President must be approved by at least a three-quarters' majority in the Verkhovna Rada. In the event of the termination of the authority of the President, the Prime Minister executes the duties of the President until the election and entry into office of a new President.

THE CABINET OF MINISTERS

The principal organ of executive government is the Cabinet of Ministers, which is responsible before the President and accountable to the Verkhovna Rada. The Cabinet supervises the implementation of state policy and the state budget and the maintenance of law and order. The Cabinet of Ministers is headed by the Prime Minister. The duties of the Prime Minister include the submission of proposals to the President on the creation, reorganization and liquidation of ministries and other central bodies of executive authority. The Cabinet of Ministers must resign when a new President is elected, or in the event of the adoption of a vote of 'no confidence' by the Verkhovna Rada.

JUDICIAL POWER

Justice in Ukraine is administered by the Constitutional Court and by courts of general jurisdiction. The Supreme Court of Ukraine is the highest judicial organ of general jurisdiction. Judges hold their position permanently, except for justices of the Constitutional Court and first judicial appointments, which are made by the President for a five-year term. Other judges, with the exception of justices of the Constitutional Court, are elected by the Verkhovna Rada. Judges must be at least 25 years of age, have a higher legal education and at least three years' work experience in the field of law, and have resided in Ukraine for no fewer than 10 years. The Procuracy of Ukraine is headed by the General Procurator, who is appointed with the consent of parliament and dismissed by the President. The term of office of the General Procurator is five years.

A Superior Justice Council, responsible for the submission of proposals regarding the appointment or dismissal of judges, functions in Ukraine. The Council consists of 20 members. The Chairman of the Supreme Court of Ukraine, the Minister of Justice, and the General Procurator are ex officio members of the Superior Justice Council.

LOCAL SELF-GOVERNMENT

The administrative and territorial division of Ukraine consists of the Autonomous Republic of Crimea, 24 provinces (oblasts), the cities of Kyiv and Sevastopol (which possess special status), districts (raions), cities, settlements and villages. Local self-government is the right of territorial communities. The principal organs of territorial communities are the district and provincial councils, which, with their chairmen, are directly elected for a term of four years. The chairmen of district and provincial councils are elected by the relevant council and head their executive structure. Provincial and district councils monitor the implementation of programmes of socio-economic and cultural development of the relevant provinces and districts, and adopt and monitor the implementation of district and provincial budgets, which are derived from the state budget.

THE AUTONOMOUS REPUBLIC OF CRIMEA

The Autonomous Republic of Crimea is an inseparable, integral part of Ukraine. It has its own Constitution, which is adopted by the Supreme Council of the Autonomous Republic of Crimea (the representative organ of Crimea) and approved by the Verkhovna Rada.

UKRAINE

Legislation adopted by the Autonomous Republic's Supreme Council and the decisions of its Council of Ministers must not contravene the Constitution and laws of Ukraine. The Chairman of the Council of Ministers is appointed and dismissed by the Supreme Council of the Autonomous Republic of Crimea with the consent of the President of Ukraine. Justice in Crimea is administered by courts belonging to the single court system of Ukraine. An Office of the Representative of the President of Ukraine functions in Crimea.

The jurisdiction of the Autonomous Republic of Crimea includes: organizing and conducting local referendums; implementing the republican budget on the basis of the state policy of Ukraine; ensuring the function and development of the state and national languages and cultures; participating in the development and fulfilment of programmes for the return of deported peoples.

THE CONSTITUTIONAL COURT

The Constitutional Court consists of 18 justices, six of whom are appointed by the President, six by the Verkhovna Rada and six by the Assembly of Judges of Ukraine. Candidates must be citizens of Ukraine, who are at least 40 years of age and have resided in Ukraine for the previous 20 years. Justices of the Constitutional Court serve a term of nine years, with no right to reappointment. A Chairman is elected by a secret ballot of the members for a single three-year term.

The Constitutional Court provides binding interpretations of the Constitution. It rules on the constitutionality of: parliamentary legislation; acts of the President and the Cabinet of Ministers; the official interpretation of the Constitution of Ukraine; international agreements; and the impeachment of the President of Ukraine.

CONSTITUTIONAL AMENDMENTS AND THE ADOPTION OF A NEW CONSTITUTION

A draft law on amending the Constitution may be presented to the Verkhovna Rada by the President or at least one-third of the constitutional composition of the parliament. A draft law on amending the Constitution, which has been given preliminary approval by a majority of the constitutional composition of the Verkhovna Rada, is considered adopted if it receives the support of at least a two-thirds' parliamentary majority. In the case of its approval it is confirmed by a nation-wide referendum designated by the President.

The Government

HEAD OF STATE

President: VIKTOR A. YUSHCHENKO (elected 26 December 2004; inaugurated 23 January 2005).

CABINET OF MINISTERS
(April 2008)

Prime Minister: YULIYA V. TYMOSHENKO.
First Deputy Prime Minister: OLEKSANDR V. TURCHYNOV.
Deputy Prime Minister: IVAN V. VASYUNYK.
Deputy Prime Minister: HRYHORIY M. NEMYRYA.
Minister of Education and Science: IVAN O. VAKARCHUK.
Minister of Transport and Communications: YOSYP V. VINSKY.
Minister of Culture and Tourism: VASYL V. VOVKUN.
Minister of the Economy: BOHDAN M. DANYLYSHYN.
Minister of Labour and Social Policy: LYUDMYLA L. DENISOVA.
Minister of Defence: YURIY I. YEKHANUROV.
Minister of the Protection of Health: VASYL M. KNYAZEVYCH.
Minister of Regional Development and Construction: VASYL S. KUYBIDA.
Minister of Housing and Communal Services: OLEKSIY YU. KUCHERENKO.
Minister of Internal Affairs: YURIY V. LUTSENKO.
Minister of Agrarian Policy: YURIY F. MELNYK.
Minister of Industrial Policy: VOLODYMYR S. NOVYTSKY.
Minister of Justice: MYKOLA V. ONISHCHUK.
Minister of Foreign Affairs: VOLODYMYR S. OHRYZKO.
Minister of the Family, Youth and Sports: YURIY O. PAVLENKO.
Minister of Finance: VIKTOR M. PYNZENYK.
Minister of the Coal Industry: VIKTOR I. POLTAVETS.
Minister of Fuel and Energy: YURIY V. PRODAN.
Minister of the Protection of the Environment: HEORHIY H. FILIPCHUK.
Minister for Emergency Situations and the Protection of the Population from the Consequences of the Chornobyl Catastrophe: VOLODYMYR M. SHANDRA.
Minister of the Cabinet of Ministers: PETRO M. KRUPKO.

MINISTRIES

Office of the President: 01021 Kyiv, vul. Shovkovichna 12; tel. (44) 226-20-77; fax (44) 293-61-61; e-mail president@adm.gov.ua; internet www.president.gov.ua.

Office of the Cabinet of Ministers: 01008 Kyiv, vul. M. Hrushevskoho 12/2; tel. and fax (44) 254-05-84; e-mail pr@kmu.gov.ua; internet www.kmu.gov.ua.

Ministry of Agrarian Policy: 01008 Kyiv, vul. Hrushevskoho 12/2; tel. (44) 278-71-18; fax (44) 229-87-56; e-mail minister@minapk.kiev.ua; internet www.minagro.gov.ua.

Ministry of the Coal Industry: 01601 Kyiv, vul. Khmelnytskoho 4; tel. (44) 594-62-27; fax (44) 206-37-19; e-mail DSher@mvp.gov.ua; internet www.mvp.gov.ua.

Ministry of Culture and Tourism: 01601 Kyiv, vul. Ivana Franka 19; tel. (44) 226-26-45; fax (44) 235-32-57; e-mail minister@mincult.gov.ua; internet www.mincult.gov.ua.

Ministry of Defence: 03168 Kyiv, Povitroflotskyi pr. 6; tel. (44) 226-26-56; fax (44) 226-20-15; e-mail pressmou@pressmou.kiev.ua; internet www.mil.gov.ua.

Ministry of the Economy: 01008 Kyiv, vul. M. Hrushevskoho 12/2; tel. (44) 253-93-94; fax (44) 226-31-81; e-mail meconomy@me.gov.ua; internet www.me.gov.ua.

Ministry of Education and Science: 01601 Kyiv, bulv. T. Shevchenka 16; tel. (44) 226-26-61; fax (44) 274-10-49; e-mail press@mon.gov.ua; internet www.mon.gov.ua.

Ministry of Emergency Situations and the Protection of the Population from the Consequences of the Chornobyl Catastrophe: 01030 Kyiv, vul. O. Honchara 55A; tel. (44) 247-31-44; e-mail main@mns.gov.ua; internet www.mns.gov.ua.

Ministry of the Family, Youth and Sport: 01019 Kyiv, vul. Esplanadna 42; tel. (44) 289-12-64; fax (44) 289-12-94; e-mail correspond@mms.gov.ua; internet www.kmu.gov.ua/sport/control.

Ministry of Finance: 01008 Kyiv, vul. M. Hrushevskoho 12/2; tel. (44) 253-62-56; fax (44) 253-82-43; e-mail infomf@minfin.gov.ua; internet www.minfin.gov.ua.

Ministry of Foreign Affairs: 01018 Kyiv, pl. Mykhailivska 1; tel. (44) 238-15-06; fax (44) 226-31-69; internet www.mfa.gov.ua.

Ministry of Fuel and Energy: 01601 Kyiv, vul. Khreshchatik 30; tel. (44) 206-38-00; fax (44) 462-05-61; e-mail kanc@mintop.energy.gov.ua; internet mpe.kmu.gov.ua.

Ministry of Housing and Communal Services: 03150 Kyiv, vul. Dymytrova 24; tel. (44) 287-23-84; fax (44) 289-01-66; e-mail minjkg@ukr.net; internet www.minjkg.gov.ua.

Ministry of Industrial Policy: 03035 Kyiv, vul. Surikova 3; tel. (44) 246-32-20; fax (44) 245-47-78; e-mail minister@industry.gov.ua; internet industry.kmu.gov.ua.

Ministry of Internal Affairs: 01024 Kyiv, vul. Ak. Bohomoltsya 10; tel. (44) 256-03-33; fax (44) 256-16-33; e-mail mail@centrmia.gov.ua; internet mvs.gov.ua.

Ministry of Justice: 01001 Kyiv, vul. Horodetskoho 13; tel. and fax (44) 228-37-23; e-mail themis@minjust.gov.ua; internet www.minjust.gov.ua.

Ministry of Labour and Social Policy: 01023 Kyiv, vul. Esplanadna 8/10; tel. (44) 220-90-97; fax (44) 220-90-64; e-mail public@subs-mspp.kiev.ua; internet www.minpraci.gov.ua.

Ministry of the Protection of the Environment: 03035 Kyiv, vul. Uritskoho 35; tel. (44) 228-06-44; fax (44) 229-83-83; internet www.menr.gov.ua.

Ministry of the Protection of Health: 01021 Kyiv, vul. M. Hrushevskoho 7; tel. and fax (44) 253-00-56; internet www.moz.gov.ua.

Ministry of Regional Development and Construction: 01205 Kyiv, vul. V. Zhytomyrska 9; tel. (44) 226-22-08; fax (44) 226-20-97; e-mail zinaidak@ukr.net; internet www.minregionbud.gov.ua.

Ministry of Transport and Communications: 01135 Kyiv, pr. Peremohy 14; tel. (44) 226-22-04; fax (44) 216-72-06; e-mail portal@mtu.gov.ua; internet www.mintrans.gov.ua.

UKRAINE

President

Presidential Election, First Ballot, 31 October 2004

Candidates	Votes	%
Viktor A. Yushchenko (Independent)	11,188,675	39.91
Viktor F. Yanukovych (Party of the Regions)	11,008,731	39.27
Oleksandr O. Moroz (Socialist Party of Ukraine)	1,632,098	5.82
Petro M. Symonenko (Communist Party of Ukraine)	1,396,135	4.98
Nataliya M. Vitrenko (Progressive Socialist Party of Ukraine)	429,794	1.53
Others	988,363	3.53
Against all candidates	556,962	1.99
Total*	28,035,184	100.00

* Including 834,426 invalid votes (2.98% of the total).

Second Ballot, 26 December 2004*

Candidates	Votes	%
Viktor A. Yushchenko (Independent)	15,115,712	52.00
Viktor F. Yanukovych (Party of the Regions)	12,848,528	44.20
Against all candidates	682,239	2.35
Total†	29,068,971	100.00

* The results of an initial second round of voting, conducted on 21 November 2004, in which the Central Electoral Commission had declared Yanukovych the winner, were annulled by the Supreme Court.

† Including 422,492 invalid votes (1.45% of the total).

Legislature

Verkhovna Rada (Supreme Council)
01008 Kyiv, vul. M. Hrushevskoho 5; tel. (44) 255-21-15; fax (44) 253-32-17; e-mail umz@rada.gov.ua; internet www.rada.gov.ua.

Chairman: ARSENIY P. YATSENYUK.

General Election, 30 September 2007

Parties and blocs	Votes	% of votes	Seats
Party of the Regions	8,013,895	34.37	175
Yuliya Tymoshenko bloc*	7,162,193	30.71	156
Our Ukraine-People's Self-defence bloc†	3,301,282	14.15	72
Communist Party of Ukraine	1,257,291	5.39	27
Lytvyn bloc‡	924,538	3.96	20
Socialist Party of Ukraine	668,234	2.86	—
Progressive Socialist Party of Ukraine	309,008	1.32	—
Others	661,928	2.78	—
Total§	23,315,257	100.00	450

* Electoral bloc comprising Fatherland, the Reforms and Order Party and the Ukrainian Social Democratic Party.

† Electoral bloc comprising nine parties, including Our Ukraine People's Union, the 'Enough!' Civic Party, the People's Movement of Ukraine-Rukh, the Synod Ukrainian Republican Party and the Ukrainian People's Party.

‡ Electoral bloc comprising the People's Party and the Labour Party of Ukraine.

§ The total number of votes cast was 23,315,257, including 379,703 invalid votes (representing 1.73% of the total), and 637,185 votes 'against all lists' (2.73% of the total).

Election Commission

Central Electoral Commission of Ukraine (CEC) (Tsentralna vyborcha Komisiya Ukrainy): 01196 Kyiv, pl. L. Ukrainky 1; tel. (44) 286-84-62; e-mail post@cvk.gov.ua; internet www.cvk.gov.ua; Head VOLODYMYR SHAPOVAL.

Political Organizations

Since the 1990s Ukrainian politics has been characterized by frequent changes of formation and allegiance within and between various factions or blocs. At 1 February 2008 there were 144 political parties registered in Ukraine, of which the following were the most important:

Communist Party of Ukraine (CPU) (Komunistychna Partiya Ukrainy): 04070 Kyiv, vul. Borysohlibska 7; tel. (44) 425-54-87; e-mail press@kpu.net.ua; internet www.kpu.net.ua; banned 1991–93; advocates state control of economy and confederation with Russia; Sec. of Cen. Cttee PETRO M. SYMONENKO.

'Enough!' Civic Party (Hromadyanska Partiya 'Pora!'): 01025 Kyiv, vul. Desyatynna 1/3; tel. (44) 594-20-20; e-mail info@pora.org.ua; internet www.pora.org.ua; f. 2005 on the basis of the 'Yellow Pora' civil organization; supports expansion of democratic freedoms and greater integration with the West; contested 2006 legislative elections as mem. of the Enough!-Party of Reforms and Order civic bloc and 2007 legislative elections as mem. of the Our Ukraine-National Self-defence bloc; Chair. of Political Council VLADYSLAV V. KASKIV.

Fatherland (Batkivshchyna): 01133 Kyiv, bulv. Lesi Ukrainky 26, POB 81; tel. (44) 286-65-42; fax (44) 285-69-07; e-mail sector@byti.org.ua; internet www.tymoshenko.com.ua; f. 1999; merged with Conservative Republican Party (led by STEPAN KHMARA) in 2002, and with Yabluko party in 2004; nationalist, populist, supportive of socially-orientated economics; contested 2006 and 2007 legislative elections as mem. of Yuliya Tymoshenko bloc; Chair. YULIYA V. TYMOSHENKO; 275,000 mems (2005).

Green Party of Ukraine (Partiya Zelenykh Ukrainy): 01030 Kyiv, vul. Chapayeva 2/16; tel. and fax (44) 278-26-63; e-mail sekretariat@greenparty.ua; internet www.greenparty.ua; f. 1990; Pres. VOLODYMYR O. KOSTERIN.

Our Ukraine People's Union (Our Ukraine) (Narodnyi Soyuz 'Nasha Ukraina') (Nasha Ukraina): 04070 Kyiv, vul. Spaska 37A; tel. (44) 206-60-97; e-mail tak@ua.org.ua; internet www.razom.org.ua; f. 2005 as People's Union Our Ukraine to support administration of Pres. Yushchenko; present name adopted 2007; contested 2006 legislative elections as mem. of the Our Ukraine bloc and 2007 legislative elections as mem. of Our Ukraine-National Self-defence bloc; Hon. Pres. VIKTOR A. YUSHCHENKO; Chair. of Council VYACHESLAV A. KYRYLENKO; 7,789 mems (Apr. 2005).

Party of the Regions (PR) (Partiya Regioniv): 01021 Kyiv, vul. Lypska 10; tel. (44) 254-29-20; fax (44) 254-33-70; e-mail partreg@ln.ua; internet www.partyofregions.org.ua; f. 1997 as the Workers' Solidarity Party of Regional Rebirth of Ukraine; present name adopted 2001; Chair. VIKTOR F. YANUKOVYCH.

People's Movement of Ukraine-Rukh (PMU-R) (Narodnyi Rukh Ukrainy): 01034 Kyiv, vul. O. Honchara 33; tel. (44) 246-47-67; fax (44) 531-30-42; e-mail org@nru.org.ua; internet www.nru.org.ua; f. 1989 as popular movement (Ukrainian People's Movement for Restructuring); registered as political party in 1993; contested 2006 legislative elections as mem. of Our Ukraine bloc and 2007 legislative elections as mem. of Our Ukraine-National Self-defence bloc; national democratic party; Chair. BORYS I. TARASYUK.

People's Party (Narodna Partiya): 01034 Kyiv, vul. Reitarska 6 A; tel. (44) 270-61-86; fax (44) 270-65-91; e-mail info@narodna.org.ua; internet www.narodna.info; f. 1996 as Agrarian Party of Ukraine; renamed People's Agrarian Party of Ukraine in 2004; present name adopted 2005; contested 2006 legislative elections as mem. of Lytvyn's People's bloc and 2007 legislative elections as mem. of Lytvyn bloc; centrist; Leader VOLODYMYR M. LYTVYN.

Progressive Socialist Party of Ukraine (Prohresyvna Sotsialistychna Partiya Ukrainy): 01011 Kyiv, vul. Panas Mirnoho 27/51; tel. (44) 254-18-40; fax (44) 278-54-91; e-mail pspu@svitonline.com; internet www.vitrenko.org; f. 1996 by members of the Socialist Party of Ukraine; contested 2006 legislative elections as mem. of the Nataliya Vitrenko People's Opposition bloc; favours extension of Belarus-Russia Union to incorporate Ukraine; opposed to Ukraine seeking membership of NATO; Chair. NATALIYA M. VITRENKO.

Reforms and Order Party (Partiya 'Reformy i poryadok'): 01021 Kyiv, vul. Institutska 28; tel. (44) 536-91-26; fax (44) 536-91-27; e-mail ref_ord@i.com.ua; internet www.prp.org.ua; f. 1997 as Reforms and Order Party; changed name to Our Ukraine in mid-2004; in July 2005 the Ministry of Justice ruled that the party had acted unlawfully in adopting the name 'Our Ukraine', and the party reverted to its original name; contested 2006 legislative elections as part of the Enough!-Party of Reforms and Order civic bloc and 2007 legislative elections as part of the Yuliya Tymoshenko bloc; Chair. VIKTOR M. PYNZENYK.

Socialist Party of Ukraine (SPU) (Sotsialistychna Partiya Ukrainy): 02100 Kyiv, vul. Bazhova 12; tel. and fax (44) 573-58-97; e-mail pr@spu.in.ua; internet www.spu.in.ua; f. 1991; formed as partial successor to the CPU; advocates democratic socialism; Leader and First Sec. OLEKSANDR O. MOROZ.

Ukrainian People's Party (UPP) (Ukrainska Narodna Partiya): 01601 Kyiv, vul. Pushkinska 28A; tel. (44) 234-59-17; fax (44) 234-05-68; e-mail office@unp-ua.org; internet www.unp-ua.org; f. 1999 as

UKRAINE

breakaway faction of People's Movement of Ukraine-Rukh by fmr leader Vyacheslav Chornovil; fmrly Ukrainian People's Movement-Rukh; present name adopted 2003; contested 2006 legislative elections as mem. of Kostenko and Plyushch's Ukrainian People's bloc and 2007 legislative elections as mem. of Our Ukraine-National Self-defence bloc; Chair. YURIY I. KOSTENKO.

Ukrainian Social Democratic Party (Ukrainska Sotsial-demokratychna Partiya): 03150 Kyiv, vul. Antonovycha 154; tel. (44) 286-49-90; fax (44) 254-47-13; internet www.usdp.kiev.ua; f. 1998; contested 2007 legislative elections as mem. of the Yuliya Tymoshenko bloc; Leader YEVHEN V. KORNIYCHUK.

Diplomatic Representation

EMBASSIES IN UKRAINE

Afghanistan: 01037 Kyiv, pr. Chervonozoryanyi 42; tel. and fax (44) 245-81-04; e-mail sm_kh2003@yahoo.com; Ambassador MOHAMMED ASIF DILAWAR.

Algeria: 01001 Kyiv, vul. B. Khmelnytskoho 64; tel. (44) 216-70-79; fax (44) 216-70-08; e-mail ambkv@ksv.net.ua; Ambassador MOKADDEM BAFDAL.

Argentina: 01901 Kyiv, vul. Ivana Franka 36, POB 217; tel. (44) 490-25-16; fax (44) 238-69-22; e-mail eucra@mrecic.gov.ar; Ambassador OLGA LILA ROLDÁN VÁZQUEZ.

Armenia: 01901 Kyiv, vul. Volodymyrska 45; tel. (44) 224-90-05; fax (44) 235-05-00; e-mail despanut@visti.com; Ambassador ARMEN KHACHATRIAN.

Austria: 01030 Kyiv, vul. Ivana Franka 33; tel. (44) 288-09-43; fax (44) 230-23-52; e-mail kiew-ob@bmeia.gv.at; internet www.aussenministerium.at/kiew; Ambassador JOSEF MARKUS WUKETICH.

Azerbaijan: 04050 Kyiv, vul. Hlubochytska 24; tel. (44) 484-69-39; fax (44) 484-69-46; e-mail embass@faust.kiev.ua; internet www.azembassy.org.ua; Ambassador TALYAT MUSEIB OĞLU ALIYEV.

Belarus: 01030 Kyiv, vul. M. Kotsyubynskogo 3; tel. (44) 537-52-00; fax (44) 537-52-13; e-mail inbox@belembassy.org.ua; internet www.belembassy.org.ua; Ambassador VALENTYN V. VELICHKO.

Belgium: 01030 Kyiv, vul. Leontovicha 4; tel. (44) 238-26-00; fax (44) 238-26-01; e-mail kiev@diplobel.org; internet www.diplomatie.be/kiev; Ambassador MARC VINCK.

Brazil: 01010 Kyiv, vul. Suvorova 14/12, POB 471; tel. (44) 280-63-01; fax (44) 280-95-68; e-mail kievbrem@brasil.kiev.ua; internet brasil.kiev.ua; Ambassador RENATO LUIZ RODRIGUES MARQUES.

Bulgaria: 01023 Kyiv, vul. Hospitalna 1; tel. (44) 246-72-37; fax (44) 235-51-19; e-mail embuln@i.kiev.ua; internet www.mfa.bg/kyiv; Ambassador DIMITAR VLADIMIROV.

Canada: 01901 Kyiv, vul. Yaroslaviv Val 31; tel. (44) 590-31-00; fax (44) 590-31-57; e-mail kyiv@international.gc.ca; internet www.kyiv.gc.ca; Ambassador ABINA M. DANN.

China, People's Republic: 01901 Kyiv, vul. M. Hrushevskoho 32; tel. (44) 253-31-54; fax (44) 253-73-71; internet ua.china-embassy.org; Ambassador ZHOU LI.

Croatia: 01091 Kyiv, vul. Artema 51/50; tel. (44) 486-58-62; fax (44) 484-69-43; e-mail croemb.ukraine@mvpei.hr; internet ua.mvp.hr; Ambassador ŽELJKO KIRINČIĆ.

Cuba: 01901 Kyiv, prov. Bekhterevskyi 5; tel. (44) 486-57-43; fax (44) 486-19-07; e-mail embacuba@naverex.kiev.ua; Ambassador JULIO GARMENDÍA PEÑA.

Czech Republic: 01901 Kyiv, vul. Yaroslaviv Val 34A; tel. (44) 272-04-31; fax (44) 272-62-04; e-mail kiev@embassy.mzv.cz; internet www.mzv.cz/kiev; Ambassador JAROSLAV BAŠTA.

Denmark: 01901 Kyiv, vul. B. Khmelnytskoho 56; tel. (44) 200-12-60; fax (44) 200-12-81; e-mail ievamb@um.dk; Ambassador UFFE ANDERSSON BALSLEV.

Egypt: 01901 Kyiv, vul. Observatorna 19; tel. (44) 212-13-27; fax (44) 216-94-28; e-mail eg.emb_kiev@mfa.gov.eg; internet www.mfa.gov.eg/Missions/ukraine/kiev/embassy/en-GB/default/; Ambassador YOUSSEF MOUSTAFA ZADA.

Estonia: 01901 Kyiv, vul. Volodymyrska 61/11–37; tel. (44) 590-07-80; fax (44) 590-07-81; e-mail embassy.kiev@mfa.ee; internet www.estemb.kiev.ua; Ambassador JAAN HEIN.

Finland: 01901 Kyiv, vul. Striletska 14; tel. (44) 278-70-49; fax (44) 278-20-32; e-mail sanomat.kio@formin.fi; internet www.finland.org.ua; Ambassador CHRISTER MICHELSSON.

France: 01034 Kyiv, vul. Reitarska 39; tel. (44) 590-36-00; fax (44) 590-36-24; e-mail pressefr@carrier.kiev.ua; internet www.ambafrance-org.ua; Ambassador JEAN-PAUL VEZIANT.

Georgia: 04119 Kyiv, vul. Melnikov 83D; tel. (44) 451-43-53; fax (44) 451-43-56; e-mail posta@georgia.com.ua; Ambassador MERAB ANTADZE.

Germany: 01901 Kyiv, vul. B. Khmelnytskoho 25; tel. (44) 247-68-00; fax (44) 247-68-18; e-mail kanzlei@german-embassy.kiev.ua; internet kiew.diplo.de; Ambassador REINHARD SCHAEFERS.

Greece: 01901 Kyiv, vul. Panfilovtsev 10; tel. (44) 254-54-71; fax (44) 254-39-98; e-mail greece@kiev.relc.com; internet www.greece.kiev.ua; Ambassador CHARALAMBOS DIMITRIOU.

Holy See: 01901 Kyiv, vul. Turhenyevska 40; tel. (44) 482-35-57; fax (44) 482-35-53; e-mail nuntius@visti.com; internet www.nuntiatura.kiev.ua; Apostolic Nuncio Most Rev. IVAN JURKOVIČ (Titular Archbishop of Corbavia).

Hungary: 01034 Kyiv, vul. Reitarska 33; tel. (44) 230-80-00; fax (44) 272-20-90; e-mail kev.missions@kum.hu; internet www.mfa.gov.hu/emb/kiev; Ambassador ANDRÁS BÁRSONY.

India: 01901 Kyiv, vul. Teryokhina 4; tel. (44) 468-66-61; fax (44) 468-66-19; e-mail india@public.ua.net; internet www.indianembassy.org.ua; Ambassador DEBABRATA SAHA.

Indonesia: 04107 Kyiv, vul. Nahirna 27B; tel. (44) 206-54-46; fax (44) 206-54-40; e-mail kbri@indo.ru.kiev.ua; internet www.kbri.kiev.ua; Ambassador ALBERTUS EMANUEL ALEXANDER LATURIUW.

Iran: 01901 Kyiv, vul. Kruhlouniversytetska 12; tel. (44) 229-44-63; fax (44) 229-32-55; Ambassador SEYYED MUSSA KAZEMI.

Israel: 01901 Kyiv, bulv. L. Ukrainky 34; tel. (44) 586-15-00; fax (44) 586-15-55; e-mail info@kiev.mfa.gov.il; internet ukraine.mfa.gov.il; Ambassador ZINA KALAY-KLEITMAN.

Italy: 01901 Kyiv, vul. Yaroslaviv Val 32B; tel. (44) 230-31-00; fax (44) 230-31-03; e-mail ambasciata.kiev@esteri.it; internet www.ambkiev.esteri.it; Ambassador PETRO GIOVANNI DONNICI.

Japan: 01901 Kyiv, Muzeiniy prov. 4; tel. (44) 490-55-00; fax (44) 490-55-02; e-mail jpembua7f@sovamua.com; internet www.ua.emb-japan.go.jp; Ambassador MUTSUO MABUCHI.

Kazakhstan: 01901 Kyiv, vul. Melnykova 26; tel. (44) 489-18-58; fax (44) 483-11-98; e-mail post@kazakh.kiev.ua; internet www.kazembassy.com.ua; Ambassador AMANGELDY ZH. ZHUMABAYEV.

Korea, Republic: 01034 Kyiv, vul. Volodymyrska 43; tel. (44) 246-37-59; fax (44) 246-37-57; e-mail korea@koremb.kiev.ua; internet ukr.mofat.go.kr; Ambassador HUR SEUNG-CHUL.

Kuwait: 04210 Kyiv, vul. Obolonska nab. 19; tel. (44) 391-51-60; fax (44) 391-51-64; e-mail kuwait_embassy@ukr.net; Ambassador HAMOOD YOUSSEF AL-ROUDHAN.

Kyrgyzstan: 01901 Kyiv, vul. Artema 51/50; tel. (44) 482-08-89; fax (44) 482-13-97; e-mail embassy.kg.kiev@silvercom.net; Ambassador ERKIN B. MAMKULOV.

Latvia: 01901 Kyiv, vul. I. Mazepy 6B; tel. (44) 490-70-30; fax (44) 490-70-35; e-mail embassy.ukraine@mfa.gov.lv; internet www.am.gov.lv/ukraine; Ambassador ATIS SJANITS.

Libya: 04050 Kyiv, vul. Ovrutska 6; tel. (44) 238-60-70; fax (44) 238-60-68; Chargé d'affaires FURJANI ABD AS-SALAM.

Lithuania: 01901 Kyiv, vul. Buslivska 21; tel. (44) 254-09-20; fax (44) 254-09-28; e-mail amb.ua@urm.lt; internet ua.mfa.lt; Ambassador ALGIRDAS KUMŽA.

Macedonia, former Yugoslav republic: 03150 Kyiv, vul. I. Fedorova 12; tel. (44) 238-66-16; fax (44) 238-66-17; e-mail embmac@carrier.kiev.ua; Ambassador (vacant).

Malaysia: 1042 Kyiv, vul. Rayevskoho 4; tel. (44) 390-95-43; fax (44) 390-95-45; e-mail malkiev@kln.gov.my; internet www.kln.gov.my/perwakilan/kiev; Ambassador Dato ABDULLAH SANI OMAR.

Moldova: 01010 Kyiv, vul. I. Mazepy 6; tel. (44) 290-77-21; fax (44) 290-77-22; e-mail moldoukr@sovamua.com; Ambassador SERGIU STATI.

Morocco: 03680 Kyiv, pr. Fedorov 12; tel. (44) 284-33-26; fax (44) 568-58-84; e-mail morocco@voilacable.com; Ambassador ABDELJALIL SAUBRY.

Netherlands: 01901 Kyiv, Kontraktova pl. 7; tel. (44) 490-82-00; fax (44) 490-82-09; e-mail kie@minbuza.nl; internet www.netherlands-embassy.com.ua; Ambassador RON KELLER.

Nigeria: 01015 Kyiv, bulv. Panfiliovtsiv 36; tel. (44) 254-58-50; fax (44) 254-53-71; Ambassador IGNATIUS HEKAYRE AJURU.

Norway: 01901 Kyiv, vul. Striletska 15; tel. (44) 590-04-70; fax (44) 234-06-55; e-mail emb.kiev@mfa.no; internet www.norway.com.ua; Ambassador OLAV BERSTAD.

Pakistan: 01015 Kyiv, pr. Panfilovtsiv 7; tel. (44) 280-25-77; fax (44) 254-45-30; e-mail parepkyiv@mail.kar.net; Ambassador GHAZANFAR ALI KHAN.

Poland: 01034 Kyiv, vul. Yaroslaviv Val 12; tel. (44) 230-07-00; fax (44) 270-63-36; e-mail ambasada@polska.com.ua; internet www.kijow.polemb.net; Ambassador JACEK KLUCZKOWSKI.

Portugal: 01901 Kyiv, vul. I. Fedorova 12/2; tel. (44) 287-58-61; fax (44) 230-26-25; e-mail geral@embport.kiev.ua; Ambassador JOSÉ MANUEL DA ENCARNAÇÃO PESSANHA VIEGAS.

UKRAINE

Romania: 01030 Kyiv, vul. M. Kotsyubynskoho 8; tel. (44) 234-00-40; fax (44) 235-20-25; e-mail romania@adamant.net; internet kiev.mae.ro; Ambassador TRAIAN LAURENȚIU HRISTEA.

Russia: 03049 Kyiv, Povitroflotskyi pr. 27; tel. (44) 244-09-63; fax (44) 246-34-69; e-mail embrus@public.icyb.kiev.ua; internet www.embrus.org.ua; Ambassador VIKTOR S. CHERNOMYRDIN.

Serbia: 04070 Kyiv, vul. Voloska 4; tel. (44) 425-60-60; fax (44) 425-60-47; e-mail ambars@optima.com.ua; Ambassador GORAN ALEKSIĆ.

Slovakia: 01901 Kyiv, vul. Yaroslaviv Val 34; tel. (44) 212-03-10; fax (44) 272-32-71; e-mail embassy@kiev.mfa.sk; internet www.slovakia.kiev.ua; Ambassador URBAN RUSNÁK.

Slovenia: 01030 Kyiv, vul. B. Khmelnytskoho 48; tel. (44) 585-23-31; fax 585-23-43; e-mail vki@gov.si; internet kijev.veleposlanistvo.si; Ambassador PRIMOŽ ŠELIGO.

South Africa: 01004 Kyiv, vul. V. Vasylkivska 9/2, POB 7; tel. (44) 287-71-72; fax (44) 287-72-06; e-mail kiev.admin@foreign.gov.za; Ambassador ANDRIES VENTER.

Spain: 01901 Kyiv, vul. Zhoriva 46; tel. (44) 391-30-24; fax (44) 492-73-27; e-mail emb.kiev@maec.es; Ambassador LUIS JAVIER GIL CATALINA.

Sweden: 01901 Kyiv, vul. Ivana Franka 34/33; tel. (44) 494-42-70; fax (44) 494-42-71; e-mail ambassaden.kiev@foreign.ministry.se; internet www.swedenabroad.com/kiev; Ambassador JOHN-CHRISTER ÅHLANDER.

Switzerland: 01015 Kyiv, vul. Kozyatynska 12, POB 114; tel. (44) 281-61-28; fax (44) 280-14-48; e-mail kie.vertretung@eda.admin.ch; internet www.eda.admin.ch/kiev; Ambassador GEORG ZUBLER.

Syria: 03050 Kyiv, vul. Biloruska 5; tel. (44) 489-55-51; fax (44) 483-97-88; e-mail syrian-emb@ukr.net; Chargé d'affaires a.i. SULEIMAN ABUDIAB.

Turkey: 01901 Kyiv, vul. Arsenalna 18; tel. (44) 281-07-51; fax (44) 285-64-23; e-mail kievbe@binet.com.ua; Ambassador ALI BILGE CANKOREL.

Turkmenistan: 01901 Kyiv, vul. Pushkinska 6; tel. (44) 229-34-49; fax (44) 229-30-34; e-mail ambturkm@ukrpack.net; Ambassador ARSLAN S. NEPESOV.

United Kingdom: 01025 Kyiv, vul. Desyatynna 9; tel. (44) 490-36-60; fax (44) 490-36-62; e-mail ukembinf@sovamua.com; internet www.britishembassy.gov/ukraine; Ambassador TIM BARROW.

USA: 01901 Kyiv, vul. Yu. Kotsyubynskoho 10; tel. (44) 490-40-00; fax (44) 490-40-85; e-mail press@usembassy.kiev.ua; internet kiev.usembassy.gov; Ambassador WILLIAM B. TAYLOR, Jr.

Uzbekistan: 01901 Kyiv, vul. Volodymyrska 16; tel. (44) 501-50-00; fax 501-50-01; Ambassador ILHOM O. HAYDAROV.

Viet Nam: 01011 Kyiv, vul. Leskova 5; tel. (44) 254-45-89; fax (44) 294-80-87; e-mail dsq@dsqvn.kiev.ua; Ambassador NGUYEN VAN THANEM.

Judicial System

Constitutional Court of Ukraine (Konstytutsiyniy sud Ukrainy): 01033 Kyiv, vul. Zhylianska 14; tel. (44) 289-05-53; fax (44) 287-20-01; e-mail idep@ccu.gov.ua; internet www.ccu.gov.ua; f. 1996; Chair. ANDRIY A. STRYZHAK.

Supreme Court (Verkhovnyi sud Ukrainy): 01024 Kyiv, vul. P. Orlyka 4; tel. (44) 253-63-08; internet www.scourt.gov.ua; Chair. VASYL V. OPONENKO; Chair. of Civil Chamber ANDRIY V. HNATENKO; Chair. of Criminal Chamber MYKOLA YE. KOROTKEVYCH; Chair. of Economic Chamber VALENTYN P. BARBARA; Chair. of Administrative Chamber VIKTOR V. KRYVENKO; Chair. of Military Judicial Commission OLEKSANDR F. VOLKOV.

Supreme Economic Court (Vyshyi hospodarskyi sud Ukrainy): 01011 Kyiv, vul. Kopylenka 6; tel. (44) 536-05-00; fax (44) 536-18-18; e-mail kantselariya@vasu.arbitr.gov.ua; internet www.arbitr.gov.ua; f. 1991; Chair. SERHIY F. DEMCHENKO.

Office of the Prosecutor-General: 01011 Kyiv, vul. Riznytska 13/15; tel. (44) 226-20-27; fax (44) 280-28-51; e-mail ilrd@gp.gov.ua; internet www.gp.gov.ua; Prosecutor-General OLEKSANDR L. MEDVEDKO.

Religion

State Department for Ethnic and Religious Affairs (Derzhavnyi departament u spravakh natsionalnostei ta religii): 01025 Kyiv, vul. Volodymyrska 9; tel. (44) 278-17-18; e-mail mail@scnm.gov.ua; internet www.scnm.gov.ua; Chair. OLEKSANDR N. SAHAN.

CHRISTIANITY

The Eastern Orthodox Church

Eastern Orthodoxy is the principal religious affiliation in Ukraine. Until 1990 all legally constituted Orthodox church communities in Ukraine were part of the Ukrainian Exarchate of the Russian Orthodox Church (Moscow Patriarchate). In that year the Russian Orthodox Church in Ukraine was renamed the Ukrainian Orthodox Church (UOC), partly to counter the growing influence of the previously prohibited Ukrainian Autocephalous Orthodox Church (UAOC). A new ecclesiastical organization was formed in June 1992, when Filaret (Denisenko), the disgraced former Metropolitan of Kyiv, united with a faction of the UAOC to form the Kyiv Patriarchate. In July 1995 Filaret was elected as Patriarch, prompting some senior clergy to leave the church and join the UAOC. In the mid-2000s the UOC (Moscow Patriarchate) remained the largest church organization in Ukraine.

Ukrainian Autocephalous Orthodox Church: 01001 Kyiv, vul. Tryokhsvyatytelska 8A; e-mail uapc-ptr@uapc-ptr.kiev.ua; internet www.uaoc.kiev.ua; f. 1921; forcibly incorporated into the Russian Orthodox Church (Moscow Patriarchate) in 1930; continued to operate clandestinely; formally revived in 1990; 1,178 parishes in 2008; Administrator Archbishop IHOR (ISICHENKO).

Ukrainian Orthodox Church (Moscow Patriarchate): 01015 Kyiv, vul. I. Mazepy 25/49; tel. (44) 255-12-04; fax (44) 254-53-01; e-mail mitropolia@svitonline.com; internet www.pravoslavye.org.ua; exarchate of the Russian Orthodox Church (Moscow Patriarchate); 11,233 parishes in 2008; Metropolitan of Kyiv and All-Ukraine VLADIMIR (SABODAN).

Ukrainian Orthodox Church (Kyiv Patriarchate): 01004 Kyiv, vul. Pushkinska 36; tel. (44) 234-10-96; fax (44) 234-30-55; e-mail patz@ukrpack.net; internet www.cerkva.info; f. 1992 by factions of the Ukrainian Orthodox Church (Moscow Patriarchate) and Ukrainian Autocephalous Orthodox Church; 3,963 parishes in 2008; 'Patriarch of Kyiv and all Rus-Ukraine' FILARET (DENISENKO).

Russian Orthodox Old Belief (Old Ritual) Church (Russkaya Pravoslavnaya Staroobryadcheskaya Tserkov): 49017 Dnipropetrovsk, pr. K. Marksa 60/8; tel. (562) 52-17-75; internet www.staroobryad.narod.ru; f. 1652 by separation from the Moscow Patriarchate; divided into two main branches: the *popovtsi* (which have priests) and the *bespopovtsi* (which reject the notion of ordained priests and the use of all sacraments, other than that of baptism). Both branches are further divided into various groupings. The largest group of *popovtsi* are those of the Belokrinitskii Concord; 56 parishes of the Belokrinitskii Concord in Ukraine in 2008, and 10 parishes of *bezpopovtsi* at that time; Bishop of Kyiv and all Ukraine SAVVAYIYE.

The Roman Catholic Church

Most Roman Catholics in Ukraine are adherents of the Byzantine Rites, the so-called 'Greek' Catholic Church, which is based principally in Western Ukraine and Transcarpathia. Some controversy arose, in August 2005, when the seat of the head of the Byzantine-rite Church, was relocated from Lviv to the Ukrainian capital, Kyiv. In 2008 there were 3,681 parishes of the Byzantine rites in Ukraine, 895 Roman Catholic parishes of the Latin rite and 24 parishes of the Armenian rite. Ukraine comprises one archbishopric-major (of the Byzantine rite), three archdioceses (including one each for Catholics of the Latin, Byzantine and Armenian rites) and 15 dioceses (of which one is directly responsible to the Holy See). At 31 December 2005 there were an estimated 4,623,981 adherents (excluding adherents of the Armenian rite, for whom figures were not available), equivalent to some 8.4% of the population. Of that number, around 82% followed the Byzantine rites.

Bishops' Conference: Bishops' Conference of Ukraine, 79008 Lviv, pl. Katedralna 1; tel. (32) 276-94-15; fax (32) 296-61-14; f. 1992; Pres. Cardinal MARIAN JAWORSKI (Metropolitan Archbishop of Lviv).

Byzantine Ukrainian Rite

Archbishop-Major of Kyiv and Halych: Cardinal LUBOMYR HUSAR, 01000 Kyiv, vul. Riznytska 11 B/28–29; tel. and fax (44) 2540-56-10; e-mail arkyrparh-kv@voliacable.com; internet www.ugcc.org.ua; head of Ukrainian Greek Catholic Church; established in 1596 by the Union of Brest; forcibly integrated into the Russian Orthodox Church (Moscow Patriarchate) in 1946, but continued to function in an 'underground' capacity; regalized in 1989; in 2005 the seat of the head of the Church was relocated from Lviv, in western Ukraine, to Kyiv.

Archbishop of Lviv: Most Rev. IHOR VOZNIAK, 79000 Lviv, pl. Sv. Yura 5; tel. and fax (32) 272-25-24; e-mail cerkvalviv@ugcc.org.ua.

UKRAINE

Latin Rite

Metropolitan Archbishop of Lviv: Cardinal MARIAN JAWORSKI, 79008 Lviv, ul. Vynnitsenka 32; tel. (32) 240-37-47; fax (32) 240-37-48; e-mail rku@lviv.farlep.net; internet www.rkc.lviv.ua.

Armenian Rite

Archbishop of Lviv: (vacant).

Protestant Churches

There were 8,417 Protestant communities registered in Ukraine in 2008.

All-Ukrainian Union of Christians of the Evangelical Faith—Pentecostalists: 01033 Kyiv, vul. Karyerna 44; 1,433 parishes in 2008.

All-Ukrainian Union of Associations of Evangelical Christians-Baptists: 01004 Kyiv, vul. L. Tolstoho 3B; tel. (44) 234-82-41; fax (44) 234-16-76; e-mail union@baptist.kiev.ua; 2,487 parishes in 2008, 134,757 adherents in 2006; affiliated to the Euro-Asiatic Federation of the Union of Evangelical Christians-Baptists; Pres. VYACHESLAV V. NESTERUK.

Embassy of the Blessed Kingdom of God for All Nations (Posolstvo Blagoslovennoho Tsarstva Bozhyeho dlya Vsekh Narodov Mira): 02152 Kyiv, vul. Tychchyny 18, Legkoatletletichesky manezh; tel. (44) 553-15-38; e-mail mail@godembassy.org; internet www.godembassy.org; f. 1994 as Word of Faith (Slovo Very); Pastor SUNDAY ADELAJA; 25,000 mems (2005).

Ukrainian Lutheran Church: 01004 Kyiv, vul. V. Vasylkivska 14/15; tel. (44) 235-77-21; fax (44) 234-08-00; e-mail vhorpynchuk@yahoo.com; internet www.ukrlc.org; 40 parishes in 2008; Leader of Church Bishop Dr VYACHESLAV HORPYNCHUK.

ISLAM

In 2008 there were 512 Islamic communities officially registered in Ukraine, of which 341 were members of the Religious Administration of Muslims of Crimea. An Islamic University was established in Donetsk in 1998.

All-Ukrainian Association of Muslim Social Organizations (Arraid): 04119 Kyiv, vul. Dekhtyarivska 25A; tel. (44) 490-99-00; fax (44) 490-99-22; e-mail office@arraid.org; internet www.arraid.org; f. 1997; brs in Dnipropetrovsk, Donetsk, Kharkiv, Luhansk, Lviv, Odesa, Simferopol, Vinnytsya and Zaporizhzhya; publishes periodical *Arraid (Pioneer)* in Arabic and Russian and educational material in Russian, Tatar and Ukrainian; undertakes charitable and educational work; Chair. ISMAIL KADI.

Religious Administration of Muslims of Crimea: 95000 Crimea, Simferopol, Kebir Çami Mosque; 341 communities in 2008; Mufti AJE NURALI ABLAIYEV.

Religious Administration of Muslims of Ukraine: 04071 Kyiv, vul. Lukyanovska; tel. (44) 465-18-77; fax (44) 456-17-70; e-mail islam@i.kiev.ua; internet www.islamyat.org; f. 1992; 68 communities in 2008; Mufti Sheikh AHMED TAMIM.

JUDAISM

In 2001 there were 103,600 Jews in Ukraine (according to census results), despite high levels of emigration from the 1970s. From 1989 there was a considerable revival in the activities of Jewish communities. In 2005 there were 263 Jewish religious communities registered in Ukraine (of which 106 were members of the Chabad-Lubavitch sect), compared with 12 synagogues in 1989.

All-Ukrainian Jewish Congress: 01023 Kyiv, vul. Mechnykova 14/1; tel. (44) 235-71-20; fax (44) 235-10-67; e-mail vek@i.kiev.ua; internet www.jewish.kiev.ua; f. 1997; affiliated to the Federation of Jewish Communities of the CIS and the Baltic states; unites 183 communities; Chief Rabbi of Ukraine AZRIEL CHAIKIN.

Jewish Confederation of Ukraine: 04071 Kyiv, vul. Shekavystka 29; tel. (44) 536-12-21; e-mail eku@jewukr.org; internet www.jewukr.org; Chief Rabbi of Kyiv and All Ukraine YAAKOV DOV BLEICH.

The Press

In 2006 there were a total of 2,918 newspapers and 2,301 periodicals published in Ukraine. In addition to newspapers published in Ukraine, several newspapers and magazines published in Russia have a large circulation in Ukraine.

The publications listed below are in Ukrainian, except where otherwise stated.

PRINCIPAL NEWSPAPERS

Demokratychna Ukraina (Democratic Ukraine): 03047 Kyiv, pr. Peremohy 50; tel. (44) 454-88-30; fax (44) 456-91-21; e-mail du@uct.ua; internet www.dua.com.ua; f. 1918; fmrly *Radyanska Ukraina* (Soviet Ukraine); 4 a week; Editor VITALIY ADAMENKO; circ. 62,400 (2005).

Den (The Day): 04212 Kyiv, vul. Marshala Tymoshenka 2L; tel. (44) 414-40-66; fax (44) 414-49-20; e-mail master@day.kiev.ua; internet www.day.kiev.ua; f. 1998; in Ukrainian and Russian; 5 a week; publ. by the Presa Ukrainy (Press of Ukraine) Publishing House; Editor-in-Chief LARYSA IVSHYNA.

Fakty i Kommentarii (Facts and Commentaries): 04116 Kyiv, vul. V. Vasylevskoy 27–29; tel. (44) 244-57-81; fax (44) 246-85-50; e-mail info@facts.kiev.ua; internet www.facts.kiev.ua; daily; politics, economics, sport, law, culture; in Russian.

Gazeta po-Kiyevski (Kyiv Newspaper): 04080 Kyiv, vul. Frunze 104A; tel. (44) 205-43-85; e-mail tsn@pk.kiev.ua; internet pk.kiev.ua; in Russian; six a week; Chief Editor SERGEI TIKHII.

Holos Ukrainy/Golos Ukrainy (Voice of Ukraine): 03047 Kyiv, vul. Nesterova 4; tel. (44) 441-88-11; fax (44) 224-72-54; e-mail mail@golos.com.ua; f. 1991; organ of the Verkhovna Rada; in Ukrainian and Russian; 5 a week; Editor SERHIY M. PRAVDENKO; circ. 150,000 (2002).

Kiyevskiye Vedomosti (Kyiv Gazette): 04086 Kyiv, vul. Olzhycha 29; tel. (44) 238-28-07; internet www.kv.com.ua; f. 1992; national daily; in Russian; also weekly edition (Fridays), in Ukrainian, *Kyivski Vidomosti*; Dir-Gen. VLADIMIR P. DERIKIT; Editor-in-Chief NIKOLAI V. ZAKREVSKII.

Kommersant-Ukraina (Businessman-Ukraine): Kyiv; internet www.kommersant.ua; f. 2005; owned by Kommersant Publishing House (Russia); in Russian; Dir-Gen. KAZBEK BEKTURSUNOV; Editor-in-Chief ANDREI VALILYEV.

Kyiv Post: 02140 Kyiv, pr. Bazhava 14A; tel. and fax (44) 496-45-63; e-mail editor@kyivpost.com; internet www.kyivpost.com; f. 1995; weekly; in English; Publr JED SUNDEN; Chief Editor STEFAN LADANAY; circ. 22,000 (2007).

Literaturna Ukraina (Literary Ukraine): 01061 Kyiv, bulv. L. Ukrainky 20; tel. (44) 286-36-39; e-mail lit_ukraine@ukr.net; f. 1927; weekly; organ of Union of Writers of Ukraine; Editor PETRO PEREBYJNIS; circ. 7,150 (2007).

Molod Ukrainy (The Youth of Ukraine): 03047 Kyiv, pr. Peremohy 50; tel. (44) 454-83-83; fax (44) 235-31-52; e-mail mu@pressa.com.ua; f. 1925; 3 a week; Editor-in-Chief V. I. NIKIPYELOV; circ. 24,000 (2007).

Pravda Ukrainy (The Truth of Ukraine): 03047 Kyiv, pr. Peremohy 50; tel. (44) 441-85-34; f. 1938; 5 a week; in Russian; Editor-in-Chief OLHA PRONINA; circ. 40,000.

Robitnycha Hazeta/Rabochaya Gazeta (Workers' Gazette): 03047 Kyiv, pr. Peremohy 50; tel. (44) 441-83-33; fax (44) 446-68-85; f. 1957; 5 a week; publ. by the Cabinet of Ministers and Inter-regional Association of Manufacturers; Ukrainian and Russian edns; Editor-in-Chief IVAN G. LITVIN.

Silski Visti (Rural News): 03047 Kyiv, pr. Peremohy 50; tel. (44) 441-86-32; fax (44) 446-93-71; e-mail ssk@silvist.kiev.ua; internet www.silskivisti.kiev.ua; f. 1920; 3 a week; Chief Editor V. D. HRUZIN.

Ukraina Moloda (Ukraine The Young): 03047 Kyiv, pr. Peremohy 50; tel. and fax (44) 454-83-92; e-mail post@umoloda.kiev.ua; internet www.umoloda.kiev.ua; 5 a week; independent; Editor MYKHAYLO DOROSHENKO; circ. 163,650 (2007).

Ukrainska Pravda (Ukrainian Truth): Kyiv; e-mail ukrpravda@gmail.com; internet www.pravda.com.ua; online only; in English, Russian and Ukrainian; Editor-in-Chief OLENA PRYTULA.

Ukrainske Slovo (The Ukrainian Word): 01010 Kyiv, vul. I. Mazepy 6; tel. (44) 280-70-59; fax (44) 280-62-65; e-mail info@ukrslovo.gu.ua; internet www.ukrslovo.com.ua; f. 1933; weekly; nationalist; Editor-in-Chief VOLODYMYR HAPTAR.

Uryadoviy Kuryer (Official Courier): 01008 Kyiv, vul. Sadova 1; tel. (44) 253-12-95; fax (44) 253-39-50; e-mail letter@ukcc.com.ua; internet www.ukcc.com.ua; f. 1990; 5 a week; organ of the Cabinet of Ministers; Editor-in-Chief MYKHAYLO M. SOROKA; circ. 125,000 (2002).

Vechirniy Kyiv (Evening Kyiv): 04136 Kyiv, vul. Marshala Hrechka 13; tel. (44) 434-61-09; fax (44) 443-96-09; e-mail office@vechirka.kiev.ua; internet www.vechirka.kiev.ua; f. 1906; 5 a week; Editor-in-Chief OLEKSANDR BALABKO; circ. 45,000 (2005).

Vlada i Polityka/Vlast i Politika (Power and Politics): 01042 Kyiv, vul. P. Lumumby 4v/200; tel. (44) 201-01-28; fax (44) 201-01-29; e-mail vip@vipnews.com.ua; internet www.vipnews.com.ua; f. 2001; weekly; in Ukrainian and Russian; Dir-Gen. ANDRIY V. NAKONECHNYI; Editor-in-Chief YURIY L. UZDEMYR; circ. 22,000 (2002).

Za Vilnu Ukrainu (For a Free Ukraine): 79000 Lviv, vul. Voronoho 3; tel. (32) 297-92-49; fax (32) 272-95-27; e-mail zwuky@mail.lviv.ua; f. 1990; 5 a week; independent; Editor-in-Chief MYKHAYLO SIRKIV; circ. 30,058 (2001).

UKRAINE

PRINCIPAL PERIODICALS

Avto-Tsentr (Autocentre): 03047 Kyiv, pr. Peremohy 50, POB 2; tel. (44) 206-56-01; fax (44) 458-44-04; e-mail info@autocentre.ua; internet www.autocentre.ua; f. 1997; weekly; motoring; in Russian; Editor-in-Chief Sergei Tarnavskii; circ. 200,000.

Barvinok (Periwinkle): 04119 Kyiv, vul. Dekhtyarivska 38–44; tel. (44) 213-99-13; fax (44) 211-04-36; e-mail barvinok@kievweb.com.ua; f. 1928; fortnightly; illustrated popular fiction for school-age children; in Ukrainian; Editor Vasyl Voronovych; circ. 40,000.

Berezil: 61002 Kharkiv, vul. Chernyshevskoho 59; tel. (57) 700-32-23; fax (57) 700-54-37; f. 1956; fmrly Prapor; monthly; journal of Union of Writers of Ukraine; fiction and socio-political articles; Editor-in-Chief Volodymyr Naumenko; circ. 5,000.

Delovaya Stolitsya (Capital City Business): 01135 Kyiv, vul. Pavlovska 29; tel. (44) 461-91-32; fax (44) 461-91-40; e-mail dsnews@dsnews.com.ua; internet www.dsnews.com.ua; f. 2001; weekly; in Russian; Editor-in-Chief Inna Kovtun; circ. 46,700 (2003).

Delovaya Ukraina (Business Ukraine): 01133 Kyiv, vul. Kutuzova 18/7/2; tel. and fax (44) 201-03-90; e-mail delukr@email.kiev.ua; internet www.delukr.kiev.ua; f. 1992; 2 a week; business issues; in Ukrainian and Russian; Editor Allal Kovtum.

Dnipro (The Dnieper): 04119 Kyiv, vul. Dekhtyarivska 38–44; tel. (44) 446-11-42; f. 1927; 2 a month; novels, short stories, essays, poetry, social and political topics; Editor Mykola Lukiv.

Donbas/Donbass: 83055 Donetsk, vul. Artema 80A; tel. (622) 93-82-26; f. 1923; monthly; journal of Union of Writers of Ukraine; fiction; in Ukrainian and Russian; circ. 20,000 (1991).

Dzerkalo Tyzhnya/Zerkalo Nedyeli (Mirror of the Week): 03680 Kyiv, vul. Tverska 6; tel. (44) 536-02-44; fax (44) 269-74-52; e-mail info@mirror.kiev.ua; internet www.zerkalo-nedeli.com; weekly; politics, economics, the arts; Ukrainian and Russian edns; also English edition (online only); Editor-in-Chief Vladimir Mostovoi; circ. 30,000 (Russian edn), 12,000 (Ukrainian edn).

Dzvin (Bell): 79005 Lviv, vul. Kn. Romana 6; tel. (32) 272-36-20; f. 1940; monthly; journal of Union of Writers of Ukraine; fiction; Editor Roman Fedoriv; circ. 152,500.

Interesna Hazeta (Interesting Newspaper): 03047 Kyiv, pr. Peremohy 50; tel. (44) 441-82-59; e-mail postmail@avkpress.kiev.ua; 2 a month; general; circ. 700,000.

Kompanyon (Companion): 01103 Kyiv, vul. Kykbydze 39; tel. (44) 494-25-01; fax (44) 494-25-05; e-mail komp@companion.ua; internet www.companion.ua; f. 1996; weekly; in Russian; economics, politics, business; Editor-in-Chief A. Pohorelov; circ. 25,000 (2004).

Kyiv: 01025 Kyiv, vul. Desyatinna 11; tel. (44) 229-02-80; f. 1983; monthly; journal of the Union of Writers of Ukraine and the Kyiv Writers' Organization; fiction; Editor-in-Chief Petro M. Perebyjnis.

Malyatko (Child): 04119 Kyiv, vul. Dekhtyarivska 38–44; tel. and fax (44) 483-98-91; e-mail malyatko_1@online.com.ua; f. 1960; monthly; illustrated; for pre-school children; Editor-in-Chief Zinaida Leshenko; circ. 35,780 (2005).

Nataly: 02156 Kyiv, vul. Kyoto 25; tel. (44) 519-34-33; fax (44) 518-77-90; internet www.nataly.com.ua; monthly; women's interest; Editor-in-Chief Zhanna Lavrova; circ. 679,115 (2002).

Natsionalna Bezpeka i Oborona (National Security and Defence): 01034 Kyiv, vul. Volodymyrska 46, Olekander Razumkov Ukrainian Centre for Economic and Political Studies; tel. (44) 201-11-98; fax (44) 201-11-99; e-mail info@uceps.com.ua; internet www.uceps.com.ua; f. 2000; monthly; politics, economics, international relations; in Ukrainian and English; Pres. Anatoliy Grytsenko.

Obrazotvorche Mistetstvo (Fine Arts): 04055 Kyiv, vul. Artema 1–5; tel. (44) 272-02-86; fax (44) 272-14-54; e-mail spilka@nbi.com.ua; f. 1933; 4 a year; publ. by the National Union of Artists of Ukraine; Editor-in-Chief Oleksandr Fedoruk; circ. 1,500 (2007).

Perets (Pepper): 03047 Kyiv, pr. Peremohy 50; tel. (44) 454-82-14; fax (44) 234-35-82; e-mail prudnyk@bigmir.net; f. 1922; monthly; publ. by the Presa Ukrainy Publishing House; satirical; Editor Mykhaylo Prudnyk; circ. 15,000 (2007).

Politychna Dumka/Politicheskaya Mysl/Political Thought: 01030 Kyiv, vul. Leontovycha 5; tel. and fax (44) 235-02-29; e-mail politdumka@bigmir.net; internet www.politdumka.kiev.ua; f. 1993; current affairs and political analysis; Ukrainian, Russian and English edns; Editor-in-Chief Volodymyr Polokhalo.

Polityka i Chas/Politics and the Times: 02160 Kyiv, pr. Vozyednanaya 15–17; tel. and fax (44) 550-31-44; e-mail times@uct.kiev.ua; f. 1994 to replace *Pid praporam Lenina* (Under the Banner of Lenin); monthly; organ of the Ministry of Foreign Affairs; international relations and foreign affairs; in Ukrainian (monthly) and English (quarterly); Editor-in-Chief Leonid Baidak; circ. 6,000 (2003).

Ukraina (Ukraine): 03047 Kyiv, pr. Peremohy 50; tel. and fax (44) 454-88-31; internet ukraina-magazine.com.ua; f. 1907; monthly; social, political and cultural life in Ukraine; illustrated; Editor-in-Chief Ihor Parymsky; circ. 40,000 (2007).

Ukraina Business (Ukraine Business): 01004 Kyiv, vul. Pushkinska 20/24; tel. and fax (44) 224-25-55; f. 1990; weekly; Editor-in-Chief Yuriy Vasylchuk.

Ukrainskiy Teatr (Ukrainian Theatre): Kyiv; tel. (44) 228-24-74; f. 1936; 6 a year; journal of the Ministry of Art and Culture, and the Union of Theatrical Workers of Ukraine; Editor-in-Chief Yuriy Bohdashevskiy; circ. 4,100.

Vitchyzna (Fatherland): 01021 Kyiv, vul. M. Hrushevskoho 34; tel. (44) 253-28-51; f. 1933; 6 a year; Ukrainian prose and poetry; Editor Oleksandr Hlushko; circ. 50,100.

Vsesvit (The Whole World): 01021 Kyiv, vul. M. Hrushevskoho 34/1; tel. (44) 253-13-18; fax (44) 253-06-13; e-mail myk@vsesvit-review.kiev.ua; internet www.vsesvit-journal.com; f. 1925; monthly; foreign fiction, literary criticism and reviews of foreign literature and art; Exec. Editor Oleh Mykytenko; circ. 2,000–3,000 (2007).

Yeva (Eve): 04050 Kyiv, vul. Melnykova 12A/8; tel. (44) 568-59-53; fax (44) 568-58-96; e-mail info@evamag.com; f. 1998; 6 a year; fashion, design; Editor-in-Chief Iryna B. Danylevska; circ. 10,000 (2002).

Zhinka (Woman): 03047 Kyiv, pr. Peremohy 50; tel. and fax (44) 446-90-34; e-mail zhinka@cki.ipri.kiev.ua; f. 1920; monthly; publ. by Presa Ukrainy Publishing House; social and political subjects, fiction; for women; Editor Lidiya Mazur; circ. 250,000.

NEWS AGENCIES

Interfax-Ukraina (Interfax-Ukraine): 01034 Kyiv, vul. Reitarska 8/5A; tel. (44) 464-04-65; fax (44) 464-05-69; e-mail news@interfax.kiev.ua; internet www.interfax.kiev.ua; f. 1992; Dir Oleksandr Martynenko.

Respublika Ukrainian Independent Information Agency (UNIAR): 02005 Kyiv, vul. Mechnykova 14/1; tel. (44) 246-46-34; e-mail naboka@uniar.kiev.ua; internet www.uniar.com.ua; independent press agency; Dir S. Naboka.

Ukrainian Independent Information and News Agency (UNIAN): 01001 Kyiv, vul. Khreshchatyk 4; tel. (44) 279-33-53; fax (44) 461-91-11; e-mail info@unian.net; internet www.unian.net; f. 1993; press agency and monitoring service; selected services are provided in Ukrainian, Russian and English; Gen. Dir Oleh I. Nalivaiko; Editor-in-Chief Oleksandr A. Kharchenko.

Ukrainski Novyni Informatsyonnoye Ahentstvo (Ukrainian News Information Agency): 01033 Kyiv, vul. Volodymyrska 61/11/41; tel. (44) 494-31-60; fax (44) 494-31-67; e-mail office@ukranews.com; internet www.ukranews.com; f. 1993; economic and political news; in Ukrainian, Russian and English.

UkrInform–Ukrainian National Information Agency: 01001 Kyiv, vul. B. Khmelnytskoho 8/16B; tel. (44) 279-81-52; fax (44) 279-86-65; e-mail office@ukrinform.com; internet news.ukrinform.com.ua; f. 1918; Dir-Gen. Viktor Chamara.

Publishers

In 1996 there were 6,460 book titles (including pamphlets and brochures) published in Ukraine (total circulation 50.9m.). By 2006 the number of book titles published in Ukraine had increased to 15,867.

Budivelnik (Builder): 04053 Kyiv, vul. Observatorna 25; tel. (44) 212-10-90; f. 1947; books on building and architecture; in Ukrainian and Russian; Dir S. N. Balatskii.

Dnipro (The Dnieper): 01034 Kyiv, vul. Volodymyrska 42; tel. (44) 224-31-82; e-mail dnipro-pbl@svitonline.com; internet www.dnipro-publ.kiev.ua; f. 1919; classics, fiction, art and popular editions; in Ukrainian and Russian; Dir Taras I. Sergiychuk.

Donbas/Donbass: 83002 Donetsk, vul. B. Khmelnytskoho 102; tel. (622) 93-25-84; fiction and criticism; in Ukrainian and Russian; Dir B. F. Kravchenko.

Folio: Kharkiv; tel. and fax (572) 47-61-25; e-mail foliosp@kharkov.ukrpack.net; internet folio.com.ua; f. 1992; classic and contemporary fiction in Russian, Ukrainian and French; Gen. Man. Aleksandr V. Krasovitskii.

Kamenyar (Stonecrusher): 79000 Lviv, vul. Pidvalna 3; tel. and fax (32) 272-19-49; e-mail vyd_kamenyar@mail.lviv.ua; fiction and criticism; in Ukrainian; Dir Dmytro I. Sapiga.

Karpaty (The Carpathians): 88000 Transcarpathian obl., Uzhhorod, Radyanska pl. 3; tel. (312) 23-25-13; fiction and criticism; in Ukrainian and Russian; Dir V. I. Dankanich.

Konsum: 61057 Kharkiv, POB 9123; tel. (572) 17-01-19; fax (572) 23-76-75; e-mail book@konsum.kharkov.ua; internet konsum.kharkov.ua; politics, economics, human rights, legal and medical books.

UKRAINE

Lybid (Swan): 01001 Kyiv, vul. Pushkinska 32; tel. (44) 228-10-93; fax (44) 229-11-71; e-mail info@lybid.org.ua; internet www.lybid.org.ua; f. 1835; University of Kyiv press; Dir OLENA A. BOIKO.

Medytsyna Svitu (Medicines of the World): 79071 Lviv, vul. Kulparkivska 131; tel. (32) 263-34-65; fax (32) 261-34-65; e-mail msvitu@mail.lviv.ua; internet www.msvitu.lviv.ua; f. 1996; medical journals and books, history, art and religion; Dirs VOLODYMYR PAVLIUK, ZINOVIY MATCHAK.

Mystetstvo: 01034 Kyiv, vul. Zolotovoritska 11; tel. (44) 235-53-92; fax (44) 279-05-64; e-mail mystetstvo@ukr.net; f. 1932; fine art criticism, theatre and screen art, tourism, Ukrainian culture; in Ukrainian, Russian, English, French and German; Dir NINA PRYBEHA.

Molod (Youth): 04119 Kyiv, vul. Dekhtyarivska 38–44; tel. (44) 213-11-60; fax (44) 213-11-92; in Ukrainian; Dir O. I. POLONSKA.

Muzichna Ukraina (Musical Ukraine): 01034 Kyiv, vul. Pushkinska 32; tel. (44) 225-63-56; fax (44) 224-63-00; f. 1966; books on music; in Ukrainian; Dir N. P. LINNIK; Editor-in-Chief B. R. VERESHCHAGIN.

Naukova Dumka (Scientific Thought): 01601 Kyiv, vul. Tereshchenkivska 3; tel. (44) 234-40-68; fax (44) 234-70-60; e-mail ndumka@i.kiev.ua; internet www.ndumka.kiev.ua; f. 1922; scientific books and periodicals in all branches of science; research monographs; Ukrainian literature; dictionaries and reference books; in Ukrainian, Russian and English; Dir I. R. ALEKSEYENKO.

Osvita (Education): 04053 Kyiv, vul. Yu. Kotsyubynski 5; tel. and fax (44) 216-54-44; e-mail osvita@kv.ukrtel.net; internet www.osvitapublish.com.ua; f. 1920; state-owned; educational books for schools of all levels; Dir-Gen. IRAYIDA PODOLYUK.

Prapor (Flag): 61002 Kharkiv, vul. Chubarya 11; tel. (572) 47-72-52; fax (572) 43-07-21; fmrly Berezil; general; in Ukrainian and Russian; Dir V. S. LEBETS.

Prosvita (Enlightenment): 01032 Kyiv, bulv. Shevchenka 46; tel. (44) 234-15-86; fax (44) 234-95-23; internet www.prosvita.kiev.ua; f. 1990; textbooks for all levels of education from pre-school to higher education.

Rino (Beacon): 65026 Odesa, vul. Zhukovskoho 14; tel. and fax (482) 722-35-95; e-mail rino@farlep.net; fiction and criticism; in Ukrainian and Russian; Dir D. A. BUKHANENKO.

Rodovid: 01001 Kyiv, POB 548; tel. and fax (44) 220-48-29; e-mail rodovid@ln.ua; internet www.rodovid.net; history, ethnography, poetry, cultural history.

Sich (Camp): 49070 Dnipropetrovsk, pr. K. Marksa 60; tel. (562) 45-22-01; fax (562) 45-44-04; f. 1964; fiction, juvenile, socio-political, criticism; in Ukrainian, English, German, French and Russian; Dir V. A. SIROTA; Editor-in-Chief V. V. LEVCHENKO.

Tavria: 95000 Crimea, Simferopol, vul. Gorkogo 5; tel. (652) 27-45-66; fax (652) 27-65-74; e-mail ingvi@ukr.net; fiction, criticism, folklore and geography; in Ukrainian, Russian and Crimean Tatar; Dir Y. IVANICHENKO.

Tekhnika (Technology): Kyiv; tel. (44) 228-22-43; f. 1930; industry and transport books, popular science, posters and booklets; in Ukrainian and Russian; Dir M. G. PISARENKO.

Tsentr Yevropy (The Centre of Europe): 79000 Lviv, vul. Kostyushko 18/317; tel. (32) 272-35-66; fax (32) 272-76-71; e-mail centrevr@is.lviv.ua; internet www.centrevtr@is.lviv.ua; f. 1994; books relating to the history and culture of Halychyna (Galicia); Dir SERHIY E. FRUKHT.

Ukraina: 01054 Kyiv, vul. Hoholivska 7H; tel. (44) 216-36-02; fax (44) 216-97-35; e-mail ua@alfacom.net; internet www.ua.alfacom.net; f. 1922; humanities, science, reference and literary works; Dir MYKOLA V. STETYUHA; Editor-in-Chief OLEKSANDR P. KOSYUK.

Ukrainska Ensyklopedia (Ukrainian Encyclopedia): 01030 Kyiv, vul. B. Khmelnytskoho 51; tel. (44) 224-80-85; encyclopedias, dictionaries and reference books; Dir A. V. KUDRITSKIY.

Ukrainskiy Pysmennyk (Ukrainian Writer): 01054 Kyiv, vul. O. Honshara 52; tel. (44) 486-25-92; e-mail ukps@ln.ua; f. 1933; publishing house of the National Union of Writers of Ukraine; fiction; in Ukrainian; Dir A. O. SAVCHUK.

Urozhai (Harvest): 03035 Kyiv, vul. Uritskoho 45; tel. (44) 220-16-26; f. 1925; books and journals about agriculture; Dir V. G. PRIKHODKO.

Veselka (Rainbow): 04050 Kyiv, vul. Melnikova 63; tel. (44) 483-95-01; fax (44) 483-33-59; e-mail veskiev@iptelecom.net.ua; internet www.veselka-ua.com; f. 1934; books for pre-school and school-age children; in Ukrainian and foreign languages; Dir YAREMA HOYAN.

Vyscha Shkola (High School): 01054 Kyiv, vul. Hoholivska 7; tel. and fax (44) 216-33-05; f. 1968; educational, scientific, reference, etc.; Dir V. P. KHOVKHUN; Editor-in-Chief V. V. PIVEN.

Zdorovya (Health): Kyiv; tel. (44) 216-89-08; books on medicine, physical fitness and sport; in Ukrainian; Dir A. P. RODZIYEVSKIY.

Znannya (Knowledge): 01034 Kyiv, vul. Striletska 28; tel. (44) 234-80-43; fax (44) 238-82-65; e-mail znannia@society.kiev.ua; internet www.znannia.com.ua; f. 1948; general non-fiction; Dir VOLODOMYR KARASOV.

Broadcasting and Communications

TELECOMMUNICATIONS

Regulatory Authorities

State Committee for Communication and Information: 01001 Kyiv, vul. Khreshchatyk 22; tel. (44) 228-15-00; fax (44) 228-61-41; e-mail mailbox@stc.gov.ua; internet www.stc.gov.ua; Chair. IHOR V. KRAVETS.

Major Service Providers

Astelit: 03110 Kyiv, vul. Solomyanska 11A; tel. (44) 233-31-31; internet www.life.com.ua; f. 2005; 51% owned by TurkCell (Turkey); provides mobile cellular telecommunications services under the brand name 'Life'.

Golden Telecom GSM: 01021 Kyiv, vul. Khreshchatyk 19A; tel. (44) 490-00-90; fax (44) 490-00-70; e-mail info@goldentele.com; internet www.goldentele.com; mobile cellular telephone services; Gen. Man. YURIY BEZBORODIV.

KyivStar GSM: Kyiv, vul. I. Mazepy 24; tel. (44) 466-04-66; internet www.kyivstar.net; f. 1997; 54.2% owned by Telenor (Norway); provides mobile cellular telecommunications services under the brand names 'Ace & Base' and 'Djuice' in major cities and other regions across Ukraine; Pres. IHOR LITOVCHENKO; 15.1m. subscribers (May 2006).

MTS Ukraina: 01015 Kyiv, vul. Leiptsizka 15; fax (44) 230-02-56; e-mail slavik@umc.com.ua; internet www.umc.com.ua; f. 1991; fmrly Ukrainian Mobile Communications; present name adopted 2007; 100% owned by MTS (Russia); Gen. Man. ANDRIY DUBOVSKOV.

UkrTelecom: 01030 Kyiv, bulv. Shevchenka 18; tel. (44) 226-25-41; fax (44) 234-39-57; e-mail ukrtelecom@ukrtelecom.net; internet www.ukrtelecom.ua; f. 1993; national fixed telecommunications network operator; provides national and international telecommunications services; Chair. of Bd HEORHIY B. DZEKON.

BROADCASTING

Regulatory Authorities

State Committee for Television and Radio Broadcasting (Derzhavnyi komitet telebachennya i radiomovlennya Ukrainy): 01001 Kyiv, vul. Khreshchatyk 26/206; tel. (44) 239-63-89; internet comin.kmu.gov.ua; responsibilities include the supervision of 27 state-controlled television and radio companies; Chair. EDUARD PRUTNIK.

National Council of Ukraine for Television and Radio Broadcasting: 01025 Kyiv, vul. Desyatynna 14; tel. (44) 278-68-32; fax (44) 228-75-75; e-mail shevch@ukr.net; internet www.nrada.gov.ua; f. 1994; monitoring and supervisory functions; issues broadcasting licences; Chair. VITALIY F. SHEVCHENKO.

Radio

Hromadske (Community) Radio: 01025 Kyiv, vul. Volodymyrska 61/11/50; tel. (44) 494-40-14; information, news and discussion programmes.

National Radio Co of Ukraine-Ukrainian Radio (Natsionalna Radiokompaniya Ukrainy-Ukrainske Radio): 01001 Kyiv, vul. Khreshchatyk 26; tel. (44) 279-33-79; fax (44) 279-34-77; e-mail krutouz@nrcu.gov.ua; internet www.nrcu.gov.ua; state-owned; domestic broadcasts; also international broadcasts in English, German, Romanian and Ukrainian; Pres. VIKTOR I. NABRUSKO.

Several independent radio stations broadcast to the major cities of Ukraine.

Television

Ukrainian State Television and Radio Co (Derzhavna Teleradiomovna Kompaniya Ukrainy): 01001 Kyiv, vul. Khreshchatyk 26; tel. (44) 481-43-86; Chair. VITALIY DOKALENKO.

1+1: 01001 Kyiv, vul. Khreshchatyk 7/11; tel. and fax (44) 490-01-01; e-mail contact@1plus1.tv; internet www.1plus1.tv; f. 1995; independent; broadcasts for 24 hours daily to 95% of Ukrainian population; Chair. of Bd of Dirs OLEKSANDR YU. RODNYANSKY.

5 Kanal: 04176 Kyiv, vul. Elektrykiv 26; tel. (44) 239-16-86; internet 5.ua; terrestrial broadcasts to 14 cities, and cable and satellite broadcasts; 24-hour news broadcasts; Dir-Gen. IVAN ADAMCHUK.

Inter: 01601 Kyiv, vul. Dmitriyevska 30; tel. and fax (44) 490-67-65; e-mail pr@inter.ua; internet www.inter.kiev.ua; f. 1996.

UKRAINE

Novy Kanal (New Channel): 04107 Kyiv, vul. Nahorna 24/1; tel. (44) 238-80-28; fax (44) 238-80-20; e-mail post@novy.tv; internet www.novy.tv; f. 1998; broadcasts in Ukrainian and Russian; Chair. OLEKSANDR M. TKACHENKO.

STB: 03113 Kyiv, vul. Shevtsova 1; tel. (44) 501-98-99; e-mail y@stb.ua; internet stb.ua; Chair. of Bd VOLODYMYR BORODYANSKY.

Finance

(cap. = capital; res = reserves; dep. = deposits; brs = branches; m. = million; amounts in hryvnyas, unless otherwise indicated)

In June 2004 there were 158 banks registered in Ukraine, of which two were state-owned, and 18 were majority or wholly foreign-owned. Some 127 of the banks had assets worth less than US $150m., and the largest 25 banks accounted for 72.3% of the total banking assets.

BANKING

Central Bank

National Bank of Ukraine (Natsionalny Bank Ukrainy): 01601 Kyiv, vul. Institutska 9; tel. (44) 253-38-22; fax (44) 230-20-33; e-mail postmaster@bank.gov.ua; internet www.bank.gov.ua; f. 1991; cap. 10m., res 1,710m., dep. 40,169m. (Dec. 2005); Gov. VOLODYMYR S. STELMAKH.

Other State Banks

Republican Bank of Crimea: 95000 Crimea, Simferopol, ul. Gorkogo; tel. (652) 51-09-46; e-mail webmaster@rbc.crimea.ua.

UkrExImBank—State Export-Import Bank of Ukraine: 03150 Kyiv, vul. Horkoho 127; tel. (44) 247-80-70; fax (44) 247-80-82; e-mail bank@eximb.com; internet www.eximb.com; f. 1992; fmrly br. of USSR Vneshekonombank (External Trade Bank); cap. 1,457.2m., dep. 8,994.5m., total assets 10,187.9m. (Dec. 2005); Chair. of Bd VIKTOR V. KAPUSTIN; 29 brs.

Commercial Banks

Alfa-Bank (Ukraine): 01025 Kyiv, vul. Desyatinna 4/6; tel. (44) 490-46-00; fax (44) 490-46-01; e-mail mail@alfabank.kiev.ua; internet www.alfabank.com.ua; f. 1993; cap. US $72.6m., res $24.0m., dep. $964.5m. (Dec. 2006); Chair. ANDRIY VOLKOV.

Brokbiznesbank: 03057 Kyiv, pr. Peremohy 41; tel. (44) 206-29-83; fax (44) 459-67-80; e-mail bank@bankbb.com; internet www.bankbb.com; f. 1991; dep. US $766m., total assets $1,540m. (Jun. 2007); Chair. of Council NIKOLAY STRILA; Chair. of Bd SERHIY P. MISHTA; 235 brs.

Calyon Bank Ukraine: 01034 Kyiv, vul. Volodymyrska 23A; tel. (44) 490-14-01; fax (44) 490-14-02; e-mail ukr-general@ua.calyon.com; internet www.calyon.kiev.ua; f. 1993; 100% owned by Crédit Lyonnais (France); cap. 172m., res 96m., dep. 1,800m. (Dec. 2007); Pres. and Dir-Gen. JACQUES MOUNIER.

Dongorbank: 83086 Donetsk, vul. Artema 38; tel. (62) 332-73-03; fax (62) 332-73-24; e-mail pr_financing@dongorbank.com; internet www.dongorbank.com; f. 1992; cap. 228.7m., res 15.2m., dep. 1,884.3m. (Dec. 2005); Head of Management Bd VLADIMIR POPOVICH.

Finance and Credit Bank (Bank 'Financy ta Kredyt'): 04050 Kyiv, vul. Artema 60; tel. (44) 490-68-70; fax (44) 238-24-65; e-mail common@fc.kiev.ua; internet www.fc.kiev.ua; f. 1990; cap. 675.1m., res dep. 6,111.7m., total assets 7,297.8m. (Dec. 2006); Chair. VLADIMIR G. KHLYVNYUK; 11 brs.

First Ukrainian International Bank/Pershyi Ukrainskyi Mizhnarodnyi Bank (FUIB): 83000 Donetsk, vul. Universitetska 2A; tel. (623) 32-45-03; fax (623) 32-47-00; e-mail info@fuib.com; internet www.fuib.com; f. 1991; cap. US $90.8m., res $42.5m., dep. $555.2m. (Dec. 2006); Chair. of Bd ALEKSANDR I. DOVGOPOLYUK.

Forum Bank (Bank Forum): 02100 Kyiv, bulv. Verkhovnoi Rady 7; tel. (44) 552-05-55; fax (44) 554-70-90; e-mail market@forum.com.ua; internet www.forum.com.ua; f. 1994; cap. 639.7m., res 40.3m., dep. 5,879.2m. (Dec. 2006); Chair. YAROSLAV V. KOLESNYK; 28 brs.

HVB Bank Ukraine: 01034 Kyiv, vul. Yaroslaviv Val 14A; tel. (44) 230-33-00; fax (44) 230-33-91; e-mail hvb-kiev@hvb-cee.com; internet www.hvb.com.ua; f. 1997; present name adopted 2002; 91.2% owned by Bayerische Hypo- und Vereinsbank AG (HypoVereinsbank, Germany); cap. 126.5m., res 1.3m., dep. 1,238.2m. (Dec. 2005); Chair. GERD WRIEDT.

Khreshchatyk Bank: 01001 Kyiv, vul. Khreshchatyk 8A; tel. and fax (44) 464-12-28; e-mail bank@xbank.com.ua; internet www.xcitybank.com.ua; f. 1993; present name adopted 1998; 51% owned by Kyiv City Administration; cap. US $109.0m., res $9.1m., dep. 584.1m. (Dec. 2006); Chair. of Bd DMYTRO M. GRYDZHYK; 87 brs.

Kredobank: 79026 Lviv, vul. Sakharova 78; tel. (32) 297-23-20; fax (32) 297-08-37; e-mail office@kredobank.com.ua; internet www.kredobank.com.ua; f. 1990; present name adopted 2006; 98.2% owned by PKO Bank Polski SA (Poland); cap. 273.4m., dep. 2,379.6m. (Jul. 2007), res 0.0m. (Dec. 2005); Pres. STEPAN I. KUBIV.

Kredytprombank: 01014 Kyiv, bulv. Druzhby Narodiv 38; tel. (44) 490-27-79; fax (44) 490-72-28; e-mail kpb@kreditprombank.com; internet www.kreditprombank.com; f. 1997, as Inkombank-Ukraina; present name adopted 1999; cap. 149.8m., res 86.2m. (Dec. 2004), dep. 2,510.0m. (Dec. 2005); Chair. of Bd NIKOLAI P. ROZHKO; Chief Exec. LYUDMILA V. RASPUTNA.

Nadra Bank: 04053 Kyiv, vul. Artema 15; tel. (44) 238-84-00; fax (44) 246-48-40; e-mail pr@nadrabank.kiev.ua; internet www.nadra.com.ua; f. 1993; cap. US $56.5m., res $38.1m., dep. $1,038.4m. (Dec. 2005); Pres. and Chair. of Bd IGOR V. GILENKO; 552 brs and sub-brs.

OTP Bank: 01033 Kyiv, vul. Zhylyanska 43; tel. (44) 490-05-00; fax (44) 490-05-01; e-mail infobox.rbu@rbu-kiev.raiffeisen.at; internet www.rbua.com; f. 1998; present name adopted 2006; 100% owned by OTP Bank plc (Romania); cap. 540.0m., res 2.7m., dep. 10,009.3m. (Dec. 2006); Chair. of Bd DMITRI ZINKOV.

Pivdennyi Bank (Southern Bank): 65059 Odesa, vul. Krasnova 6/1; tel. (482) 30-70-37; fax (482) 30-70-82; e-mail naa@pivdenny.odessa.ua; internet en.bank.com.ua; f. 1993; cap. 527m., total assets 4,410m. (Jul. 2007); Chair. of Bd VADYM V. MOROKHOVSKIY; 16 brs.

PrivatBank: 49094 Dnipropetrovsk, nab. Peremohy 50; tel. (562) 39-05-11; fax (56) 778-54-74; e-mail privatbank@pbank.dp.ua; internet www.privatbank.com.ua; cap. 2,335.3m., res 448.8m., dep. 28,902.3m. (Dec. 2006); Chair. of Bd ALEXANDER DUBILET; 51 brs.

ProCredit Bank Ukraine (ProKredyt Bank Ukraine): 03115 Kyiv, pr. Peremohy 107A; tel. (44) 590-10-00; fax (44) 590-10-01; e-mail procreditbank@procreditbank.com.ua; internet www.procreditbank.com.ua; f. 2000; present name adopted 2003; 60% owned by ProCredit Holding AG (Germany), 20% by Western NIS Enterprise Fund (Germany), 20% by European Bank for Reconstruction and Development (United Kingdom); cap. US $29.7m., res $0.2m., dep. $213.8m. (Dec. 2006); Gen. Man. DIRK HABOECK.

Prominvestbank (Industrial-Investment Bank): 01001 Kyiv, prov. Shevchenka 12; tel. (44) 201-51-20; fax (44) 201-50-44; e-mail bank@pib.com.ua; internet www.pib.com.ua; f. 1922 as Stroibank, name changed 1992; cap. 1,573.0m., total assets 17,595.8m. (Dec. 2006); Chair. VOLODYMYR P. MATVYENKO; 600 brs.

Raiffeisenbank Aval: 01011 Kyiv, vul. Leskova 9; tel. (44) 490-88-01; fax (44) 490-87-55; e-mail info@aval.ua; internet www.aval.ua; f. 1992 under the name Aval Bank; present name adopted 2006 following 2005 acquisition by Raiffeisen International Bank AG (Austria); cap. US $307.7m., res $24.1m., dep. $3,336.7m. (Dec. 2005); Pres. VOLODYMYR I. LAVRENCHUK; 1,400 brs.

Rodovid Bank: 04070 Kyiv, vul. P. Sahaidachniy 17; tel. (44) 255-86-47; fax (44) 255-86-54; e-mail info@rodovidbank.com; internet www.rodovidbank.com; f. 1990; present name adopted 2004; cap. 350.0m., res 77.6m., dep. 3,138.3m.(Dec. 2006); Chair. of Bd DENIS V. GORBUNENKO; 2 brs.

TAS-Kommertsbank: 01032 Kyiv, vul. Kominterna 30; tel. (44) 238-38-83; fax (44) 238-38-85; e-mail office@tas-combank.com.ua; internet www.tas-combank.com.ua; f. 1991; cap. US $97.2m., res $12.0m., dep. $708.9m. (Dec. 2006); Chair. of Bd SERHIY TIHIPKO.

Ukrgazbank: 01004 Kyiv, vul. Chervonoarmiyska 39; tel. (44) 594-11-63; fax (44) 239-28-44; e-mail office@ukrgasbank.com; internet www.ukrgasbank.com; f. 1993; cap. 312.8m., res 147.8m., dep. 3,743.6m. (Dec. 2006); Chair. VADYM P. LYASHKO.

Ukrprombank (Ukrainsky Promyslovy Bank): 01133 Kyiv, bulv. L. Ukrainky 26; tel. (44) 537-47-00; fax (44) 295-17-00; e-mail secretary@ukrprombank.kiev.ua; internet www.ukrprombank.com.ua; f. 1989; cap. 842.0m., res 12.9m., dep. 5,562.6m. (Dec. 2006); Chair. OLEKSANDR SOLTUS.

UkrSibbank: 04070 Kyiv, vul. Andriyevksa 2/12; tel. (44) 230-48-88; fax (44) 230-48-98; e-mail office@ukrsibbank.com; internet www.ukrsibbank.com; f. 1990; commercial and investment banking, non-banking financial services; 51% owned by BNP Paribas SA (France); cap. 2,693.7m., res 13.9m., dep. 18,499.0m. (Dec. 2006); Chair. of Bd OLEKSANDR E. ADARYCH; 1,000 brs and sub-brs.

UkrSotsBank—Bank for Social Development: 03150 Kyiv, vul. Kovpaka 29; tel. (44) 230-32-24; fax (44) 230-32-23; e-mail info@ukrsotsbank.com; internet www.usb.com.ua; f. 1990; cap. 496.7m., res 387.6m., dep. 10,960m. (Dec. 2006); Chair. of Supervisory Council IHOR YUSHKO; Chair. of Bd BORIS TIMONKIN; over 500 brs.

VA Bank-Vseukrainsky Aktsionerny Bank (All-Ukrainian Share Bank): 04119 Kyiv, vul. Zoolohichna 5; tel. (44) 481-33-47; fax (44) 481-33-49; e-mail fi@vab.ua; internet www.vab.ua; f. 1992; cap. 128.6m., dep. 757.2m., total assets 1,345.0m. (Dec. 2007); Pres. SERHIY MAKSIMOV; Chair. PETR RASOCHA; 25 brs.

VTB Bank: 01601 Kyiv, vul. Hoholevskaya 24; tel. (44) 486-04-90; e-mail post@mriya.com; internet www.vtb.com; f. 1992; cap. 163.6m., res −0.6m., dep. 2,232.4m. (Dec. 2006); Chair. of Bd VADIM PUSHKAROV; 20 brs.

Savings Bank

State Savings Bank of Ukraine—Oschadbank (Derzhavnyi Oshchadnyi Bank Ukrainy): 01023 Kyiv, vul. Hospitalna 12 G; tel. (44) 247-85-69; fax (44) 247-85-68; internet www.oschadnybank.com; f. 1991; cap. 878.5m., res 484.7m., dep. 7,400m. (2006); Chair. ANATOLIY GULEY; 6,300 brs.

Banking Association

Association of Ukrainian Banks (Asotsiatsiya Ukrainskykh Bankiv): 02002 Kyiv, vul. M. Raskova 15/703; tel. (44) 516-87-75; fax (44) 516-87-76; e-mail aub@carrier.kiev.ua; internet www.aub.com.ua; fmrly Commercial Bank Asscn; Pres. OLEKSANDR SUGONIAKO.

COMMODITY EXCHANGES

Carpathian Commodity Exchange: 78200 Ivano-Frankivsk obl., Kolomiya, vul. Vahylevycha 1, POB 210; tel. and fax (343) 32-19-61; f. 1996; Gen. Man. IVAN P. VATUTIN.

Crimea Universal Exchange: 95050 Crimea, Simferopol, vul. L. Chaikinoy 1/421; tel. (652) 22-04-32; fax (652) 22-12-73; f. 1923 as Simferopol Commodity Exchange; present name adopted 1991; Pres. NATALIYA S. SYUMAK.

Dnipro (Pridniprovska) Commodity Exchange: 49094 Dnipropetrovsk, vul. Nab. Peremohy 15A; tel. (562) 35-77-45; fax (56) 744-27-16; e-mail ptb@pce.dp.ua; originally founded 1908 as Katerinoslav Commodity Exchange; re-established with present name in 1991; brs in Dniprodzerzhynsk, Kryvyi Rih, Marhanets, Pavlohrad and Synelnykove; Gen. Man. VADYM F. KAMEKO.

Donetsk Commodity Exchange: 83086 Donetsk, vul. Pershotravnevska 12; tel. (62) 338-10-93; fax (62) 335-92-91; e-mail oltradex@pub.dn.ua; f. 1991; Gen. Man. PETRO O. VYSHNEVSKYI.

Kharkiv Commodity Exchange: 61003 Kharkiv, vul. Universytetska 5; tel. (572) 12-33-21; fax (572) 12-74-95; e-mail ss@htb.kharkov.ua; f. 1993; Pres. IHOR V. ZOTOV.

Kyiv Universal Exchange: 01103 Kyiv, Zaliznychne shose 57; tel. (44) 295-11-29; fax (44) 295-44-36; e-mail nva@iptelecom.net.ua; internet www.kue.kiev.ua; f. 1990; Pres. KONSTANTIN LAPUSHEN.

Odesa Commodity Exchange: 65114 Odesa, vul. Lyustdorfska doroha 140A; tel. (482) 61-89-92; fax (482) 47-72-84; e-mail yuri@oce.odessa.ua; f. 1796; re-established 1990; Gen. Man. MYKOLA O. NIKOLISHEN.

Ukrainian Universal Commodity Exchange: 03680 Kyiv, pr. Akadmika Hlushkova 1/6; tel. (44) 251-94–90; fax (44) 251-95-40; e-mail birga@uutb.kiev.ua; internet www.uutb.com.ua; f. 1991; Pres. OLEKSANDR M. BORKOVSKYI.

Zaporizhzhya Commodity Exchange 'Hileya': 69037 Zaporizhzhya, vul. 40 rokiv Radyanskoyi Ukrainy 41; tel. (612) 33-32-73; fax (612) 34-76-62; f. 1991; re-established 1996; Gen. Man. ANTON A. KHULAKHSIZ.

INSURANCE

In March 2004 there were 360 insurance companies operating in Ukraine, of which the following were among the most important:

State Insurance Companies

Crimean Insurance Co: 99011 Sevastopol, vul. Butakov 4; tel. (692) 55-30-28; fax (692) 54-23-00; e-mail ksk@ksk.in.ua; internet www.ksk.in.ua; f. 1993; Dir ISABELLA BILDER.

DASK UkrinMedStrakh: 01601 Kyiv, vul. O. Honshara 65; tel. (44) 216-30-21; fax (44) 216-96-92; e-mail ukrmed@ukrpack.com; f. 1999; provides compulsory medical insurance to foreigners and stateless persons temporarily resident in Ukraine.

Oranta Insurance Co: 01015 Kyiv, vul. Sichnevogo Povstannya 34B; tel. (44) 537-58-00; fax (44) 537-58-83; e-mail oranta@oranta.ua; internet www.oranta.ua; f. 1921; Chair. of Bd OLEG SPILKA.

Commercial Insurance Companies

AIG Ukraine: 01004 Kyiv, vul. Shovkovychna 42–44; tel. (44) 490-65-50; fax (44) 490-65-48; e-mail reception@aig.com.ua; internet www.aig.com.ua; f. 2000; affiliated to American International Group (USA); Gen. Man. IHOR KOVALENKO.

AKB Garant Insurance Co: 03062 Kyiv, pr. Peremohy 67; tel. (44) 459-52-00; fax (44) 459-52-07; e-mail akb@garant.kiev.ua; internet www.garant.kiev.ua; f. 1994; general insurance services; Gen. Man. OLEKSANDR I. DYACHENKO.

Alcona Insurance Co: 03150 Kyiv, vul. Chervonoarmiyska 102; tel. and fax (44) 247-44-77; e-mail alcona@alcona.kiev.ua; internet www.alcona.com.ua; f. 1992; insurance and reinsurance.

Aska Insurance Co: 03186 Kyiv, vul. Antonova 5; tel. (44) 241-11-67; e-mail office@aska.com.ua; internet www.aska.com.ua; life and non-life insurance; Chair. HALINA N. TRETYAKOVA; Gen. Man. A. SOSYS.

Dask Insurance Co: 49000 Dnipropetrovsk, vul. K. Libknekhta 4D; tel. (562) 32-09-75; fax (562) 32-09-81; e-mail dask@dask.dp.ua; internet www.dask.com.ua; f. 1993; affiliated to Dask Insurance Group; Dir IRINA MURASCHKO.

Disco Insurance Co: 49000 Dnipropetrovsk, vul. K. Libknekhta 4D; tel. (562) 32-09-78; fax (562) 32-09-81; e-mail disco@disco.dp.ua; internet www.disco.dp.ua; f. 1992; affiliated to Dask Insurance Group.

ECCO Insurance Co: 01034 Kyiv, vul. Prorizna 4/23; tel. (44) 228-10-82; e-mail insurance@ecco-alpha.kiev.ua; internet www.ecco-insurance.at; f. 1991; affiliated to ECCO (Austria); life and non-life insurance.

EnergoPolis Insurance Co: 03049 Kyiv, vul. Bohdanivska 10; tel. (44) 244-02-36; fax (44) 244-05-94; e-mail office@enpolis.com.ua; internet www.enpolis.com.ua; Chair. of Bd and Dir-Gen. VIKTOR MYKOLAYCHUK.

Galinstrakh Insurance Co: 79012 Lviv, vul. Ak. Sakharova 34; tel. (32) 275-70-30; fax (32) 297-10-40; e-mail gis@is.lviv.ua; internet www.gis.com.ua; f. 1991; general insurance services; Chair. of Bd STEPHAN SOVINSKIY.

Ingo—Ukraina Insurance Co: 01054 Kyiv, vul. Vorovskogo 33; tel. (44) 490-27-44; fax (44) 490-27-48; e-mail office@ingo.com.ua; internet www.ingo.com.ua; f. 1994; fmrly Ostra-Kyiv Insurance Co; re-insurance, medical, travel, property and cargo insurance; Chair. of Bd IHOR N. HORDYENKO.

Inter-Policy Insurance Co: 01033 Kyiv, vul. Volodymyrska 69; tel. (44) 287-70-96; fax (44) 289-74-45; e-mail office@inter-policy.com; f. 1993.

Kyiv Insurance Co: 04053 Kyiv, vul. Yu. Kotsubynskoho 20; tel. (44) 461-92-41; fax (44) 461-92-43; e-mail info@kic.kiev.ua; internet www.kic.kiev.ua; f. 1998.

Ostra Insurance Co: 65026 Odesa, vul. Pushkinska 13; tel. (482) 22-38-87; fax (482) 24-18-37; e-mail main@ostra.com.ua; internet www.ostra.com.ua; f. 1990; non-life; Chair. KHYRACH MAHDYEV.

QBE Ukraina Insurance: 01033 Kyiv, vul. Saksahanskoho 36D; tel. (44) 537-53-90; fax (44) 537-53-99; e-mail insurance@qbe-ukraine.com; internet www.qbe-ukraine.com; f. 1998; affiliate of QBE Insurance (New Zealand).

Skide Insurance Co: 04050 Kyiv, vul. Hlybochytska 72; tel. (44) 417-40-04; fax (44) 228-40-33; e-mail skide@iptelecom.net.ua; f. 1991; Pres. VOLODYMYR BESARAB.

Skide-West Insurance Co: 04053 Kyiv, vul. Artema 40; tel. (44) 238-62-38; fax (44) 246-96-25; e-mail mail@skide-west.com; internet www.skide-west.com; f. 1993; cap. US $389.1m. (2004); Pres. ANDRIY PERETYAZHKO; 37 brs and rep. offices.

Sun Life Ukraine: 01032 Kyiv, vul. Starovokzalna 17; tel. (44) 235-20-02; fax (44) 235-89-17; e-mail office@sunlife.com.ua; internet www.sunlife.com.ua; f. 1993; life; Pres. ROSTYSLAV B. TALSKYI.

UkrGazPromPolis Insurance Co: 01034 Kyiv, vul. O. Honshara 41; tel. (44) 235-25-00; e-mail office@ugpp.com.ua; internet www.ugpp.com.ua; f. 1996; jointly owned by UkrGazProm, UkrGazPromBank and KyivTransGaz; Pres. KONSTANTYN O. YEFYMENKO.

Insurance Association

League of Insurance Organizations of Ukraine: 02660 Kyiv, vul. M. Roskovoyi 11; tel. and fax (44) 516-82-30; internet www.uainsur.com; f. 1992; non-profit asscn of insurance cos; Pres. ALEKSANDR FILONYUK.

Trade and Industry

GOVERNMENT AGENCY

State Property Fund of Ukraine (Fond Derzhavnoho Maina Ukrainy): 01133 Kyiv, vul. Kutuzova 18/9; tel. (44) 200-33-33; fax (44) 286-79-85; e-mail marketing@spfu.kiev.ua; internet www.spfu.gov.ua; Head ANDRIY PORTNOV (acting).

NATIONAL CHAMBER OF COMMERCE

Ukrainian Chamber of Commerce and Industry (Torgovo-Promyslova Palata Ukrainy/Torgovo-Promyshlennaya Palata Ukrainy): 01601 Kyiv, vul. V. Zhytomyrska 33; tel. (44) 272-29-11; fax (44) 212-33-53; e-mail ucci@ucci.org.ua; internet www.ucci.org.ua; f. 1972; Chair. SERHIY P. SKRYPCHENKO; 27 regional brs with a total of c. 7,500 mems.

REGIONAL CHAMBERS OF COMMERCE

Chambers of Commerce are located in every administrative region of Ukraine, including the following:

UKRAINE

Chamber of Commerce and Industry of Crimea: 95013 Crimea, Simferopol, ul. Sevastopolskaya 45; tel. (652) 24-86-38; fax (652) 49-33-45; e-mail cci@cci.crimea.ua; internet www.cci.crimea.ua; f. 1974; sub-brs in Armyansk, Dzhankoi, Feodosiya, Kerch, Yalta and Yevpatoriya; Pres. NEONILA M. GRACHEVA.

Dnipropetrovsk Chamber of Commerce: 49044 Dnipropetrovsk, vul. Shevchenka 4; tel. (562) 36-22-58; fax (562) 36-22-59; e-mail miv@dcci.dp.ua; internet www.dcci.dp.ua; brs at Kryvyi Rih and Dniprodzerzhynsk; Pres. VYTALIY H. ZHMURENKO.

Donetsk Chamber of Commerce: 83007 Donetsk, pr. Kyivsky 87; tel. (62) 387-80-00; fax (62) 387-80-01; e-mail dcci@dttp.donetsk.ua; internet www.cci.donbass.com; f. 1964; brs at Artemovsk, Horlivka, Kramatorsk, Makiyivka and Mariupol; Pres. GENNADII D. CHIZHIKOV.

Kharkiv Chamber of Commerce: 61037 Kharkiv, pr. Moskovksky 122; tel. (57) 714-96-90; fax (57) 738-64-79; e-mail info@kcci.kharkov.ua; internet www.kcci.kharkov.ua; Pres. VIKTOR I. LOBODA.

Kyiv Chamber of Commerce and Industry: 01504 Kyiv-54, vul. B. Khmelnytskoho 55; tel. (44) 246-83-01; fax (44) 246-99-66; e-mail info@kiev-chamber.org.ua; internet www.kiev-chamber.org.ua; Pres. MYKOLA V. ZASULSKIY.

Lviv Chamber of Commerce and Industry: 79011 Lviv, Stryiskiy park 14; tel. and fax (32) 276-46-11; e-mail lcci@cci.com.ua; internet www.lcci.com.ua; f. 1850; Pres. DMYTRO D. AFTANAS.

Odesa Chamber of Commerce: 65011 Odesa, vul. Bazarna 47; tel. (48) 777-20-96; fax (482) 49-63-07; e-mail oav@orcci.odessa.ua; internet www.orcci.odessa.ua; f. 1924; brs at Illichivsk, Izmayil and Reni; Pres. SERHIY SHUVALOV.

Sevastopol Chamber of Commerce and Industry: 99011 Sevastopol, ul. B. Morskaya 34; tel. (692) 54-35-36; fax (692) 54-06-44; e-mail stpp@optima.com.ua; internet www.stpp.org.ua; f. 1963; Pres. LYUDMILA I. VISHNYA.

Transcarpathian (Zakarpatska) Chamber of Commerce and Industry: 88015 Transcarpathian obl., Uzhhorod, vul. Hrushevskoho 62; tel. (312) 66-22-14; fax (312) 66-44-77; e-mail tpp@tpp.uzhgorod.ua; internet www.tpp.uzhgorod.ua; br. at Mukachevo; Pres. OTTO O. KOVCHAR.

Zaporizhzhya Chamber of Commerce: 69000 Zaporizhzhya, bulv. Tsentralnyi 4; tel. (612) 13-50-24; fax (612) 33-11-72; e-mail cci@cci.zp.ua; internet www.cci.zp.ua; brs at Berdyansk and Melitopol; Pres. VOLODOMYR I. SHAMYLOV.

EMPLOYERS' ORGANIZATION

Congress of Business Circles of Ukraine: 01061 Kyiv, vul. Prorizna 15; tel. (44) 228-64-81; fax (44) 229-52-84; Pres. VALERIY G. BABICH.

UTILITIES

Regulatory Bodies

National Electricity Regulatory Commission of Ukraine: 03057 Kyiv, vul. Smolenska 19; tel. (44) 241-90-01; fax (44) 241-90-47; e-mail box@nerc.gov.ua; f. 1994; promotion of competition and protection of consumer interests; Chair. YURIY PRODAN.

State Committee for Nuclear Regulation (Derzhanvnyi komitet yadernoho rehulyuvannya Ukrainy): 01011 Kyiv, vul. Arsenalna 9/11; tel. (44) 254-33-47; fax (44) 254-33-11; e-mail pr@hq.snrc.gov.ua; internet www.snrc.gov.ua; Chair. OLENA A. MYKOLAICHUK.

Electricity

EnergoAtom: 01032 Kyiv, vul. Vetrova 3; tel. (44) 281-48-83; e-mail pr@nae.atom.gov.ua; internet www.energoatom.kiev.ua; f. 1996; responsible for scientific and technical policy within the nuclear power industry; manages all five nuclear power producing installations in Ukraine; Pres. ANDRIY L. DERKACH.

Kyivenergo: 01001 Kyiv, pl. Ivana Franka 5; tel. (44) 201-58-67; fax (44) 239-47-06; e-mail pubrel@kievenergo.com.ua; internet www.kievenergo.com.ua; power generation and distribution; Chair. SERHIY M. TITENKO.

Zakhidenergo (West Energy): 79011 Lviv, vul. Sventitskoho 2; tel. (32) 279-89-41; fax (32) 278-90-59; e-mail z_vtv@rdc.west.energy.gov.ua; f. 1995; power generation; Pres. and Gen. Dir VOLODYMYR PAVLYUK.

Gas

Naftogaz Ukrainy (Oil and Gas of Ukraine): 01001 Kyiv, vul. B. Khmelnytskoho 6B; tel. (44) 461-25-37; fax (44) 220-15-26; e-mail ngu@naftogaz.net; internet www.naftogaz.com; f. 1998; state-owned; production and distribution of gas and petroleum; storage of gas; gas- and condensate-processing; Chair. of Bd OLEH DUBYNA.

UkrGazEnergo: Kyiv; f. 2006; 50% owned by RosUkrEnergo (itself 50% owned by Gazprom, Russia), 50% owned by Naftogaz Ukrainy; exclusive provider of natural gas to industrial concerns; Co-Chair. ALEKSANDR RYAZANOV, IHOR VORONIN.

TRADE UNION FEDERATIONS

Confederation of Free Trade Unions of Ukraine (CFTUU) (Konfederatsiya Vilnykh Profspilok Ukrainy—KVPU): 03150 Kyiv, vul. V. Vasylkivska 54; tel. (44) 287-33-38; fax (44) 287-72-83; e-mail info@kvpu.org.ua; internet www.kvpu.org.ua; f. 1997; independent; Chair. MYKHAYLO YA. VOLYNETS.

Federation of Trade Unions of Ukraine (FTUU): 01012 Kyiv, Maidan Nezalezhnosti 2; tel. (44) 278-87-88; fax (44) 278-87-98; e-mail fpsu@fpsu.ozg.ua; f. 1990; fmr Ukrainian branch of General Confederation of Trade Unions of the USSR; affiliation of 40 trade union brs; Chair. OLEKSANDR YURKIN.

Transport

RAILWAYS

In 2002 there were 22,078 km of railway track in use, of which more than 9,000 km were electrified. Lines link most towns and cities in the country, and with various major cities in other European countries.

State Railway Transport Administration—Ukrzaliznytsia: 03680 Kyiv, vul. Tverska 5; tel. (44) 223-00-10; fax (44) 258-80-11; e-mail ci@uz.gov.ua; internet www.uz.gov.ua; Dir-Gen. VOLODYMYR KOZAK.

Ukrreftrans: 03049 Kyiv, vul. Furmanova 1/7; tel. (44) 245-47-22; e-mail sekretar@interntrans.com.ua; internet www.intertrans.com.ua; state-owned freight transportation service.

Dnipropetrovsk Metro: 49038 Dnipropetrovsk, vul. Kurchatova 8; tel. (562) 42-37-68; fax (56) 778-65-33; e-mail metrodp@ukr.net; internet gorod.dp.ua/metro; f. 1995; one line with six stations; total length 8 km; total planned network of 74 km.

Kharkiv Metro: 61012 Kharkiv, vul. Engelsa 29; tel. (572) 12-59-83; fax (572) 23-21-41; e-mail metro@tender.kharkov.com; internet www.metro.kharkov.ua; f. 1975; three lines with 26 stations; total length 34 km; Gen. Man. LEONID A. ISAYEV.

Kyiv Metro: 03055 Kyiv, pr. Peremohy 35; tel. (44) 238-44-21; fax (44) 238-44-46; e-mail nto@metro.kiev.ua; internet www.metro.kiev.ua; f. 1960; three lines with 42 stations; Dir MYKOLA M. SHAVLOVSKIY.

ROADS

At 31 December 2002 there were 169,678 km of roads, of which 96.8% were paved.

INLAND WATERWAYS

The Dnipro (Dniepr—Dnieper) River, which links Kyiv, Cherkasy, Dnipropetrovsk and Zaporizhzhya with the Black Sea, is the most important route for river freight.

SHIPPING

The main ports are Yalta and Yevpatoriya in Crimea, and Odesa. In addition to long-distance international shipping lines, there are services to the Russian ports of Novorossiisk and Sochi, and Batumi and Sukhumi in Georgia. Although many passenger routes on the Black Sea ceased to operate in the 1990s, there are regular passenger services from Odesa to Haifa (Israel) and Istanbul (Turkey), and, in the summer months, between Odesa and Crimea. At December 2006 Ukraine's merchant fleet (655 vessels) had a total displacement of 1.1m. grt.

Port Authority

Odesa Commercial Sea Port: 65026 Odesa, pl. Mytna 1; tel. (48) 729-35-55; fax (48) 729-36-27; e-mail welcome@port.odessa.ua; internet www.port.odessa.ua; f. 1794; state-owned; cargo handling and storage, marine passenger terminal services; Gen. Man. MYKOLA P. PAVLYUK.

Shipping Companies

Azov Shipping Co: 87510 Donetsk obl., Mariupol, pr. Admirala Lunina 89; tel. (629) 31-15-00; fax (629) 31-12-25; e-mail admin@c2smtp.azsco.anet.donetsk.ua; f. 1871; Pres. SERHIY V. PRUSIKOV.

State Black Sea Shipping Co: 65026 Odesa, vul. Lanzheronovska 1; tel. (482) 25-21-60; fax (482) 60-57-33; Pres. BORIS SCHERBAK.

Ukrainian Danube Shipping Co: 68600 Odesa obl., Izmayil, vul. Chervonaflotska 28; tel. (4841) 2-55-50; fax (4841) 2-53-55; e-mail udp_t@udp.izmail.uptel.net; f. 1944; cargo and passenger services; Pres. PETR S. SUVOROV.

Ukrainian Shipping Co (UkrShip): 65014 Odesa, vul. Marazlyevska 8; tel. (48) 734-73-50; fax (48) 777-07-00; e-mail admin@ukrship.odessa.ua; f. 1996; Pres. A. SAVITSKIY.

Ukrrechflot Co: 04071 Kyiv, Nizhny val. 51; tel. (44) 416-88-79; fax (44) 417-86-82; jt-stock co; Pres. NIKOLAY A. SLAVOV.

Yugreftransflot: 99014 Crimea, Sevastopol, ul. Rybakov 5; tel. (692) 41-25-41; fax (692) 42-39-19; e-mail jsc@urtf.com; jt-stock co; Chair. VOLODYMYR ANDREYEV.

CIVIL AVIATION

The principal international airport is at Boryspil (Kyiv), but several other airports, including those at Dnipropetrovsk and Odesa, also service international flights.

AeroSvit Airlines: 01032 Kyiv, bulv. Shevchenko 58A; tel. (44) 246-50-70; fax (44) 246-50-46; e-mail av@aswt.kiev.ua; internet www.aerosvit.com; f. 1994; operates scheduled and charter passenger services to domestic and international destinations; Chief Exec. and Dir-Gen. GRYGORIY GURTOVOY.

ARP 410—Kyiv Aircraft Repair Plant (ARP 410—Kyivsky Aviyaremontny Zavod): 03151 Kyiv, Vozdukhoflotsky pr. 94; tel. (44) 246-26-64; fax (44) 243-40-33; e-mail arp410-cs@svitonline.com; internet www.arp410.com.ua; f. 1999; domestic passenger and international cargo flights; Dir-Gen. ANATOLIY P. KUDRIN.

Donbassaero Airlines (Donbass-Vostochnye Aviyalinii Ukrainy—Donbassaero): 83021 Donetsk, Donetsk International Airport; tel. (62) 385-61-68; fax (62) 332-00-55; e-mail info@donbass.aero; internet www.donbass.aero; f. 1991; present name adopted 2003; passenger and cargo flights between Donetsk and domestic and international destinations; Dir-Gen. ALEKSANDR HRECHKO.

Khors Air Company: 01133 Kyiv, vul. L. Ukrainki 34; tel. (44) 294-94-11; fax (44) 573-86-72; e-mail aircargo@khors.com.ua; internet www.khors.com.ua; f. 1990; operates international, regional and domestic cargo and passenger services; Gen. Dir ANATOLIY VYSOCHANSKIY.

Ukraine International Airlines (Mizhnarodni Avialinyi Ukraini): 01054 Kyiv, ul. B. Khmelnytskogo 63A; tel. (44) 461-56-56; fax (44) 230-88-66; e-mail uia@ps.kiev.ua; internet www.ukraine-international.com; f. 1992; 61.6% state-owned, 22.5% owned jointly by SAir (Switzerland) and Austrian Airlines (Austria); operates domestic services, and international services to European and Middle Eastern destinations from Kyiv, Dnipropetrovsk, Kharkiv, Lviv, Odesa and Simferopol; Pres. VITALIY M. POTEMSKIY.

Tourism

The Black Sea coast of Ukraine has several popular resorts, including Odesa and Yalta. The Crimean peninsula is a popular tourist centre in both summer and winter, owing to its temperate climate. Kyiv, Lviv and Odesa have important historical attractions, and there are many archaeological monuments on the Black Sea coast, including the remains of ancient Greek and Ottoman settlements. However, the tourist industry remains relatively undeveloped. There were 23.1m. foreign tourist arrivals in Ukraine in 2007; receipts from tourism (including passenger transport) totalled US $3,542m. in 2005.

Ministry of Culture and Tourism: see The Government (Ministries).

Ministry of Health Resorts and Tourism of the Autonomous Republic of Crimea: 95005 Crimea, Simferopol, pr. Kirova 13; tel. (652) 54-46-68; fax (652) 25-94-38; e-mail tourism_crimea@ukr.net; internet www.tourism.crimea.ua; Minister VLADIMIR A. SOVOLYEV.

State Tourism Administration of Ukraine (Derzhavna turystychna administratsiya Ukrainy): 01034 Kyiv, vul. Yaroslaviv val 36; tel. (44) 272-42-15; fax (44) 272-42-77; e-mail info@tourism.gov.ua; internet www.tourism.gov.ua; f. 1999; Chair. VALERIY I. TSYBUKH.

THE UNITED ARAB EMIRATES

Introductory Survey

Location, Climate, Language, Religion, Flag, Capital

The United Arab Emirates (UAE) lies in the east of the Arabian peninsula. It is bordered by Saudi Arabia to the west and south, and by Oman to the east. In the north the UAE has a short frontier with Qatar and a coastline of about 650 km on the southern shore of the Persian (Arabian) Gulf, separated by a detached portion of Omani territory from a small section of coast on the western shore of the Gulf of Oman. The climate is exceptionally hot in summer, with average maximum temperatures exceeding 40°C, and humidity is very high. Winter is mild, with temperatures ranging from 17°C to 20°C. Average annual rainfall is very low: between 100 mm and 200 mm. The official language is Arabic, spoken by almost all of the native population. Arabs are, however, outnumbered by non-Arab immigrants, mainly from India, Pakistan, Bangladesh and Iran. According to official census results, UAE nationals represented about 20% of the total population in 2005. Most of the inhabitants are Muslims, mainly of the Sunni sect. The national flag (proportions 1 by 2) has three equal horizontal stripes, of green, white and black, with a vertical red stripe at the hoist. The capital is Abu Dhabi.

Recent History

Prior to independence the UAE was Trucial Oman, also known as the Trucial States, and the component sheikhdoms of the territory were under British protection. Although from 1892 the United Kingdom assumed responsibility for the sheikhdoms' defence and external relations, they were otherwise autonomous and followed the traditional form of Arab monarchy, with each ruler having virtually absolute power over his subjects.

In 1952 the Trucial Council, comprising the rulers of the seven sheikhdoms, was established in order to encourage the adoption of common policies in administrative matters, possibly leading to a federation of the states. Petroleum, the basis of the area's modern prosperity, was first discovered in 1958, when deposits were located beneath the coastal waters of Abu Dhabi, the largest of the sheikhdoms. Onshore petroleum was found in Abu Dhabi in 1960, and commercial exploitation of petroleum began in 1962, providing the state with greatly increased revenue. However, Sheikh Shakhbut bin Sultan an-Nahyan, the Ruler of Abu Dhabi since 1928, failed to use the income from petroleum royalties to develop his domain. As a result, the ruling family deposed him in August 1966 and installed his younger brother, Sheikh Zayed bin Sultan. Under the rule of Sheikh Zayed, Abu Dhabi was transformed, with considerable income from the petroleum industry allocated for public works and the provision of welfare services. In 1966 petroleum was discovered in neighbouring Dubai (the second largest of the Trucial States), which also underwent a rapid development.

In January 1968 the United Kingdom announced its intention to withdraw British military forces from the area by 1971. In March 1968 the Trucial States joined nearby Bahrain and Qatar (which were also under British protection) in what was named the Federation of Arab Emirates. It was intended that the Federation should become fully independent, but the interests of Bahrain and Qatar proved to be incompatible with those of the smaller sheikhdoms, and both seceded from the Federation in August 1971 to become separate independent states. In July six of the Trucial States (Abu Dhabi, Dubai, Sharjah, Umm al-Qaiwain, Ajman and Fujairah) had agreed on a federal Constitution for achieving independence as the United Arab Emirates (UAE). The United Kingdom accordingly terminated its special treaty relationship with the States, and the UAE became independent on 2 December 1971. The remaining sheikhdom, Ras al-Khaimah, joined the UAE in February 1972. At independence Sheikh Zayed of Abu Dhabi took office as the first President of the UAE. Sheikh Rashid bin Said al-Maktoum, the Ruler of Dubai since 1958, became Vice-President, while his eldest son, Sheikh Maktoum bin Rashid al-Maktoum (Crown Prince of Dubai), became Prime Minister in the federal Council of Ministers. A 40-member consultative assembly, the Federal National Council (FNC), was also inaugurated.

In January 1972 the Ruler of Sharjah, Sheikh Khalid bin Muhammad al-Qasimi, was killed by rebels under the leadership of his cousin, Sheikh Saqr bin Sultan, who had been deposed as the sheikhdom's Ruler in June 1965. However, the rebels were defeated, and Sheikh Khalid was succeeded by his brother, Sheikh Sultan bin Muhammad al-Qasimi.

Sheikh Zayed, disappointed with progress towards centralization, reportedly announced in August 1976 that he was not prepared to accept another five-year term as President. In November, however, the highest federal authority, the Supreme Council of Rulers (comprising the Rulers of the seven emirates), re-elected him unanimously, following agreements granting the federal Government greater control over defence, intelligence services, immigration, public security and border control.

Owing to a dispute over a senior appointment in February 1978, the forces of Dubai and Ras al-Khaimah refused to accept orders from the Federal Defence Force. Although Ras al-Khaimah later reintegrated with the Federal Defence Force, Dubai's armed forces effectively remained a separate entity. In March 1979 a 10-point memorandum from the National Council, containing proposals for increased unity, was rejected by Dubai, which, together with Ras al-Khaimah, boycotted a meeting of the Supreme Council. In April Sheikh Maktoum resigned as Prime Minister; he was replaced by his father, Sheikh Rashid, who formed a new Council of Ministers in July, while retaining the post of Vice-President. Sheikh Ahmad bin Rashid al-Mu'alla, the Ruler of Umm al-Qaiwain (the smallest of the emirates) since 1929, died in February 1981, and was succeeded by his son, Rashid. Sheikh Rashid bin Humaid an-Nuaimi, the Ruler of Ajman since 1928, died in September 1981, and was succeeded by his son, Humaid.

The UAE was a founder member of the Co-operation Council for the Arab States of the Gulf (the Gulf Co-operation Council—GCC, see p. 219) in May 1981. The GCC aims to achieve greater political and economic integration between Gulf countries (for further details, see below).

There was an attempted coup in Sharjah in June 1987, when Sheikh Abd al-Aziz, a brother of Sheikh Sultan, announced (in his brother's absence) the abdication of the Ruler, on the grounds that he had mismanaged the economy. The Supreme Council of Rulers intervened to endorse Sheikh Sultan's claim to be the legitimate Ruler of Sharjah, effectively restoring him to power. Sheikh Abd al-Aziz was given the title of Crown Prince and was granted a seat on the Supreme Council. In February 1990, however, Sheikh Sultan removed his brother from the post of Crown Prince and revoked his right to succeed him as Ruler. In July Sheikh Sultan appointed Sheikh Ahmad bin Muhammad al-Qasimi, the head of Sharjah's petroleum and mineral affairs office, as Deputy Ruler of Sharjah, although he was not given the title of Crown Prince.

The UAE became involved in a major international financial scandal in July 1991, when regulatory authorities in seven countries abruptly closed down the operations of the Bank of Credit and Commerce International (BCCI), in which the Abu Dhabi ruling family and agencies had held a controlling interest (77%) since April 1990. The termination of the bank's activities followed the disclosure of systematic, large-scale fraud by BCCI authorities prior to April 1990. By July 1991 BCCI's activities had been suspended in all 69 countries in which it had operated. At the conclusion of fraud trials in May 1994 all but one of the defendants were sentenced to terms of imprisonment ranging from three to 14 years. (In June 1995 a court of appeal overturned the guilty verdicts of two of those imprisoned.) New legislation was subsequently prepared to strengthen the role of the Central Bank and to enforce stricter regulation of the Emirates' financial sector.

Meanwhile, in October 1990, upon the death of his father, Sheikh Maktoum acceded to the positions of Ruler of Dubai and Vice-President and Prime Minister of the UAE. In January 1995 Sheikh Maktoum issued a decree naming Sheikh Muhammad bin Rashid al-Maktoum as Crown Prince, and Sheikh Hamdan bin Rashid al-Maktoum as Deputy Ruler of Dubai. In June 1996 legislation designed to make the provisional Constitution permanent was endorsed by the FNC, following its approval by the Supreme Council of Rulers. At the same time Abu Dhabi was formally designated capital of the UAE.

In October 2003 Sheikh Zayed appointed Sheikh Hamdan bin Zayed an-Nayhan as a Deputy Prime Minister, in addition to his existing responsibilities as Minister of State for Foreign Affairs. In the following month Sheikh Zayed issued a decree installing Sheikh Muhammad bin Zayed an-Nahyan, the Chief of Staff of Federal Armed Forces, as Deputy Crown Prince of Abu Dhabi. Meanwhile, in June Sheikh Saqr bin Muhammad al-Qasimi, the ruler of Ras al-Khaimah, deposed his eldest son, Khalid, as Crown Prince and appointed a younger son, Sa'ud, in his place. Sheikh Khalid, a noted reformist, reportedly claimed that the decision had been influenced by his father's ill health. Tanks from the federal UAE armed forces arrived in Ras al-Khaimah city, apparently in an attempt to prevent supporters of Sheikh Khalid from demonstrating against the decision. Tension in the emirate quickly eased, however, after the departure of Sheikh Khalid to Oman. In January 2004 Sheikh Sa'ud ordered the release of 124 prisoners, including several of the protesters who had demonstrated against his appointment.

Sheikh Zayed died on 2 November 2004, following several years of ill health. His son, Sheikh Khalifa bin Zayed an-Nahyan, automatically succeeded him as Ruler of Abu Dhabi and was elected by the Supreme Council to the presidency the following day. The day before Sheikh Zayed's death a restructuring had been implemented of the Council of Ministers (the first such reorganization since 1997). The most significant changes were the appointment as Minister of Economy and Planning of Sheikha Lubna bint Khalid al-Qasimi, who became the first woman to hold a cabinet position in the UAE, and the combining of the petroleum and mineral resources ministry with the electricity and water portfolio to form a new Ministry of Energy, headed by Muhammad bin Dhaen al-Hamili. In December Sheikh Khalifa announced a similarly rare restructuring of the Abu Dhabi Executive Council, to be chaired by the new Crown Prince, Sheikh Muhammad, who also remained the Chief of Staff of Federal Armed Forces.

Sheikh Maktoum, who had reportedly suffered from heart problems, died suddenly in January 2006. He was immediately succeeded as Ruler of Dubai by his brother, Sheikh Muhammad bin Rashid al-Maktoum, who had been Dubai's Crown Prince since 1995. Sheikh Muhammad also replaced Sheikh Maktoum as Vice-President and Prime Minister of the UAE. His first Council of Ministers, approved by the President on 9 February, contained nine new ministers (including a second female minister) and several new portfolios; however, most of the key ministries remained unchanged. Sheikh Muhammad retained control of the Ministry of Defence, a position he has held since 1971.

In December 2005 Sheikh Khalifa announced tentative proposals to open one-half of the 40 seats in the FNC to indirect election via new national councils in each of the emirates. The President envisaged that this represented the first step towards wider participatory democracy and the federation's first general election. Officials indicated that the gradual democratization of the GCC states had created both external and internal pressure on the Government to adopt constitutional change. The partial elections to the FNC were held on 16, 18 and 20 December 2006: four members of the Council were elected from from each of Abu Dhabi and Dubai, three each from Sharjah and Ras al-Khaimah, and two each from Fujairah, Umm al-Qaiwain and Ajman. The 20 seats were contested by 450 candidates, including 65 women. Just 6,689 selected UAE nationals (among them 1,189 women) were eligible to participate in the polls as members of the new electoral colleges (these had been chosen by the National Electoral Committee, established in August). The elected members included one woman, selected in Abu Dhabi. Overall voter turnout in the seven emirates was reported to be 74.4%. The new FNC was inaugurated in February 2007. (Of its 20 appointed members, nine were women.) At the opening session, Abd al-Aziz Abdullah al-Ghurair was elected Speaker.

In late September 2007 Sheikh Muhammad issued a directive that was interpreted as instructing that journalists in the UAE would no longer be liable for imprisonment for libel. None the less, existing legislation governing press and publications remained in place. In response to the directive, the UAE's journalists' association drafted a code of conduct, which was to be binding for all journalists working in the UAE, including foreign journalists.

In early February 2008 Sheikh Muhammad issued a decree appointing his son, Sheikh Hamdan bin Muhammad bin Rashid al-Maktoum, as Crown Prince of Dubai. The new Crown Prince and his younger brother, Sheikh Maktoum, were also named as Deputy Rulers of Dubai. Sheikh Hamdan had been appointed Chairman of the Dubai Executive Council in September 2006. The appointments were followed, in mid-February 2008, by a reorganization of the federal Council of Ministers. While the strategic portfolios of energy, foreign affairs and defence remained unchanged, other appointments were regarded as reflecting Sheikh Muhammad's policy priorities in further developing the business sector. Sheikha Lubna al-Qasimi was transferred from the post of Minister of Economy to the new position of Minister of Foreign Trade; she was replaced in her former role by Sultan bin Said al-Mansour, previously Minister of Governmental Sector Development; his ministry was also to take responsibility for industrial affairs. The appointment of Ghobash Said Ghobash, hitherto ambassador to the USA, as Minister of Labour was interpreted as a significant indicator that Sheikh Muhammad was seeking to address perceived international concerns regarding workers' rights in the UAE. Hadif Jowan adh-Dhahiri was appointed Minister of Justice, while Muhammad bin Abdullah al-Gargawi, the chief executive of Dubai Holding, who was regarded as a close associate of Sheikh Muhammad, was promoted to the position of Minister of Cabinet Affairs (having previously held the position of Minister of State). The new administration included four women. In March, following the amendment of pertinent legislation earlier in the year, the UAE's first female judge was appointed by the Ruler of Abu Dhabi.

Conflict arose between the UAE and Iran in 1992 concerning the sovereignty of Abu Musa, an island situated between the states in the Persian (Arabian) Gulf. The island had been administered since 1991 under a joint agreement between Iran and Sharjah, in accordance with which an Iranian garrison was stationed on the island. In that year Iran had also seized the smaller neighbouring islands of Greater and Lesser Tunb. In April 1992 the Iranian garrison on Abu Musa was said to have seized civilian installations on the island. There were further allegations that Iranian officials were attempting to force expatriate workers employed by the UAE to leave the island, preventing the entry of other expatriates, and increasing the number of Iranian nationals there. However, in April 1993 all those who had been expelled from or refused entry to Abu Musa in 1992 were reportedly permitted to return. In October 1993 Sheikh Zayed announced the introduction of a federal law standardizing the limits of the UAE's territorial waters to 12 nautical miles (22.2 km) off shore, in response to a similar announcement by the Iranian authorities. In December 1994 the UAE announced its intention to refer the dispute to the International Court of Justice in The Hague, Netherlands, and in February 1995 it was alleged that Iran had deployed air defence systems on the islands. In November officials from the UAE and Iran, meeting in Qatar, failed to reach agreement on establishing an agenda for ministerial-level negotiations.

In March–April 1996 bilateral relations deteriorated further when Iran opened an airport on Abu Musa and a power station on Greater Tunb. In February 1999 the UAE protested at the construction by Iran of municipal facilities on Abu Musa and at recent Iranian military exercises near the disputed islands. Iran subsequently complained to the UN that, in disputing the location of its military exercises, the UAE was interfering in Iranian internal affairs. During 1999 the UAE was increasingly critical of the rapprochement between Saudi Arabia and Iran, considering that it was at the expense of Saudi relations with the UAE. In November a tripartite committee, established by the GCC and comprising representatives of Oman, Qatar and Saudi Arabia, announced that it would continue efforts to facilitate a settlement. Sheikh Zayed boycotted a meeting of GCC leaders in Saudi Arabia, in protest at the lack of attention given to the dispute with Iran by the other GCC members at a time when they were increasingly moving towards improved relations with Iran. In December the UAE renewed its request for Iran to enter into direct negotiations or agree to international arbitration over the islands. In March 2000, following a statement by Iran that it would be prepared to negotiate over the islands, the UAE asserted that it would refer it to the GCC tripartite committee. No significant progress had been reached concerning a resolution of the territorial dispute by early 2008. Meanwhile, however, commercial links between the two countries remained strong, with the UAE having particular importance as a supplier of imports to Iran. President Mahmoud Ahmadinejad of Iran made the first visit to the UAE by an Iranian head of state in May 2007. Prior to the visit, the UAE authorities released from custody 12 Iranian divers who had been detained earlier in the month in waters off Abu Musa. Sheikh Muhammad visited Iran in February 2008 (he was the most senior UAE official to visit the country since the Iranian Revolution in 1979). In an interview with the Dubai-based *Khaleej Times* in April 2008, Iran's ambassador to the UAE emphasized positive developments in bilateral co-operation, and indicated his country's preparedness to discuss and resolve issues through dialogue with the UAE.

Meanwhile, relations between the UAE and Saudi Arabia had also become strained by the UAE's trade negotiations with the USA (see below); Saudi Arabia considered that the GCC should negotiate any trade agreement as a single body. In December 2005 the relationship was weakened further in relation to a long-standing border dispute between the UAE and Saudi Arabia concerning the Shaybah oilfield in the Rub al-Khali desert region. The dispute was the principal focus of discussions between the UAE's President and the Saudi Minister of the Interior in June 2006.

In response to Iraq's occupation of Kuwait in August 1990, the UAE (which supported the US-led multinational effort against Iraq) announced that foreign armed forces opposing the Iraqi invasion would be provided with military facilities in the Emirates. By the mid-1990s, however, the UAE was among those states questioning the justification for the continued maintenance of international sanctions (imposed in 1990) against Iraq, in view of the resultant humanitarian consequences for the Iraqi population. Following the restoration of diplomatic ties with Iraq in 1998, the UAE's embassy in the Iraqi capital was reopened in April 2000. However, the Ruler of Fujairah was criticized in Iraq after a speech, at the UN Millennium Summit in New York in September, in which he called on Iraq to apply all pertinent UN Security Council resolutions, particularly those related to the issue of prisoners of war. Although Iraq's Minister of Trade visited Abu Dhabi in December, where he was received by Sheikh Zayed, the UAE lent its support to a declaration of the GCC annual summit meeting that urged Iraq to conform with UN resolutions: it was generally considered that the UAE had been compelled to endorse the declaration in return for GCC support in its territorial dispute with Iran. Addressing the Arab Inter-Parliamentary Union in February 2001, Sheikh Zayed none the less urged Arab states to work jointly towards an end to the sanctions regime in force against Iraq. In November the UAE and Iraq signed a free trade agreement, which was ratified by Sheikh Zayed in May 2002.

The UAE severed diplomatic relations with the Taliban regime in Afghanistan in late September 2001, in response to the suicide attacks against New York and Washington, DC, on 11 September. Hitherto, the UAE had been one of only three states to maintain ties with the Taliban (the UAE's relations with the Taliban being at chargé d'affaires level). The Saudi Arabian-born Osama bin Laden, whose al-Qa'ida (Base) organization was at that time based in Afghanistan, was the USA's principal suspect in having orchestrated the September 2001 attacks. After diplomatic relations were severed, the UAE's Minister of Foreign Affairs stated that the his Government had sought to persuade the Taliban to hand over bin Laden so that he might stand trial in an international court. In common with other GCC members, the UAE pledged support for the USA in its efforts to bring to justice the perpetrators of terrorism. None the less, the UAE emphasized that the success of the US-led 'coalition against terror' must be linked to a resumption of the Arab-Israeli peace process, and expressed concerns that military action should not target any Arab state. The UAE's banking sector came under international scrutiny after US investigators claimed to have evidence of transactions between banks in the UAE and the USA linking bin Laden with the suicide attacks. At the end of September the Emirates' Central Bank ordered that the assets in the UAE of 27 individuals and organizations accused by the USA of involvement in terrorism be frozen; in November the Central Bank reportedly ordered a freeze on the assets of a further 62 entities. Following the swift defeat of the Taliban regime in the US-led military offensive, which began in October, and the inauguration of a new Afghan interim administration in December 2001, the Afghan embassy in the UAE was reopened in February 2002; the opening of the UAE's embassy in Kabul was announced in March. In November the Central Bank tightened regulations on the informal money-transfer system known as *hawala*, after the practice was criticized by Western law enforcement agencies as an important element in the financing of terrorism.

At the summit meeting of the Council of the League of Arab States (the Arab League, see p. 332) convened in Beirut, Lebanon, in March 2002, the Minister of State for Foreign Affairs, Sheikh Hamdan bin Zaid an-Nahyan, declared the UAE to be opposed to any future US-led campaign to oust the regime of Saddam Hussain in Iraq as a potential second phase in the USA's declared 'war on terror'. The UAE continued to urge a diplomatic solution to the crisis, and promoted a plan for the Iraqi leader to go into exile in order to prevent a war to oust his regime; however, in March 2003 the UAE disregarded appeals by some members of the Arab League to refuse to provide facilities for military action in Iraq. At the commencement of the conflict later in that month some 3,000 US air force personnel and 72 combat aircraft were stationed in the UAE. Following the overthrow of Iraq's Baathist regime by the US-led coalition in early April and the subsequent announcement that US forces were to be withdrawn from Saudi Arabia, the USA stated that it would develop the adh-Dhafra airport in Abu Dhabi for use by its military aircraft. In the immediate aftermath of the ousting of the regime of Saddam Hussain, the UAE provided significant humanitarian aid to Iraq, and made clear its intention to participate in the reconstruction of the country. In early 2004 the UAE agreed to write off most of Iraq's US $3,800m. bilateral debt.

In July 2004 the UAE signed a Trade and Investment Framework Agreement with the USA—regarded as a preliminary step towards a bilateral free trade agreement. Free trade negotiations with the USA duly commenced in March 2005. However, the talks were postponed in March 2006, as a result of a disagreement between the two countries regarding the acquisition by the state-owned Dubai Ports World (DP World) of a British-based ports and ferries operator, P&O, whose holdings included six major US ports. DP World agreed to sell the six US ports after the House Appropriations Committee of the US House of Representatives, in opposition to the US executive, adopted an amendment that would prevent the operation of the US ports by DP World; it was considered a risk to US security that the ports should be held by UAE interests. Meanwhile, the Court of Appeal in the United Kingdom had rejected an attempt by a US partner of P&O to block the acquisition on the grounds that this would be harmful to its business. DP World reached an agreement to sell the US ports to a US company in December of that year. Trade negotiations meanwhile resumed. In late 2007, however, the Office of the US Trade Representative announced that the two countries had agreed that they would be unable to conclude a free trade accord during the tenure of the incumbent US Administration; a new round of negotiations was expected to commence following the inauguration of a new US president in 2009. The USA indicated its expectation that further progress on issues of labour rights would be a prerequisite to an eventual agreement. In January 2008 US President George W. Bush delivered the key address of his first tour of the Middle East from Abu Dhabi. In April the UAE's Minister of Foreign Affairs, Sheikh Abdullah bin Zayed an-Nahyan, and the US Secretary of State, Condoleezza Rice, meeting in Bahrain in advance of a GCC-US summit, signed a memorandum of understanding governing co-operation in the peaceful use of nuclear energy. Prior to this agreement, the UAE (which had in January 2008 ratified the International Convention for the Suppression of Acts of Nuclear Terrorism) issued a policy document regarding plans for the potential development of nuclear energy for civilian use, including a commitment to forgo any domestic enrichment or reprocessing capability in exchange for the long-term supply of fuel from external sources.

Bilateral co-operation accords signed during the course of a visit to the UAE by President Nicolas Sarkozy of France in January 2008 included an arrangement whereby France would assist in the development of a civilian nuclear energy programme in the UAE. Agreement was also reached on the establishment by France of a permanent military base in Abu Dhabi, capable of accommodating some 500 armed forces personnel. A memorandum of understanding on co-operation in nuclear energy for civilian purposes was signed by the UAE and the United Kingdom in May.

The UAE established diplomatic relations, at ambassadorial level, with the Democratic People's Republic of Korea in September 2007.

Government

The highest federal authority is the Supreme Council of Rulers, comprising the hereditary rulers of the seven emirates, each of whom is virtually an absolute monarch in his own domain. Decisions of the Supreme Council require the approval of at least five members, including the rulers of both Abu Dhabi and Dubai. From its seven members, the Supreme Council elects a President and a Vice-President. The President appoints the Prime Minister and the federal Council of Ministers, responsible to the Supreme Council, to hold executive authority. The legislature is the Federal National Council (FNC), a consultative assembly that considers laws proposed by the Council of Ministers. The FNC comprises 40 members—of whom one-half are appointed by the emirates and the remainder are chosen by electoral colleges—who serve two-year terms. There are no political parties.

Defence

As assessed at November 2007, the armed forces totalled an estimated 51,000 men (of whom some 30% were thought to be expatriates): an army of 44,000, an air force of 4,500 and a navy of around 2,500. The Union Defence Force and the armed forces of Abu Dhabi, Dubai, Ras al-Khaimah and Sharjah were formally merged in 1976, although Dubai still maintains a degree of independence (as to a lesser extent do other emirates). Military service is voluntary. The defence budget for 2007 was estimated at AED 37,000m. Forces of the US Central Command, including 58 air force personnel (as assessed at November 2007), were also stationed in the UAE.

Economic Affairs

In 2004, according to estimates by the World Bank, the UAE's gross national income (GNI), measured at average 2002–04 prices, was US $103,461m., equivalent to $23,950 per head (or $23,990 on an international purchasing-power parity basis). During 1996–2006, it was estimated, the population increased by an average annual rate of 6.4%. Gross domestic product (GDP) per head decreased, in real terms, by an average of 0.2% per year during 1996–2005. Overall GDP increased, in real terms, by an average annual rate of 6.7% in 1996–2005. According to preliminary Central Bank figures, real GDP increased by 8.2% in 2005, and by 9.4% in 2006.

According to preliminary Central Bank figures, agriculture (including livestock and fishing) contributed 2.0% of GDP in 2006, and engaged 6.8% of the employed population in the same year. The principal crops are dates, tomatoes, aubergines, and pumpkins, squash and gourds. The UAE imports some 70% of food requirements. Some agricultural products are exported on a small scale. Livestock-rearing and fishing are also important. During 1996–2005 agricultural GDP, according to World Bank data, increased, in real terms, at an average annual rate of 8.0%. The GDP of the sector increased by 5.0% in 2006, according to data published by the IMF.

Industry (including mining, manufacturing, construction and power) contributed 57.9% of GDP in 2006, according to preliminary Central Bank figures, and engaged 38.0% of the working population in the same year. During 1996–2005, according to World Bank data, industrial GDP increased by an average of 5.4% per year. The GDP of the sector expanded by 14.5% in 2006, according to IMF data.

Mining and quarrying contributed 36.9% of GDP in 2006, according to preliminary Central Bank data, and employed 1.4% of the working population in the same year. Petroleum production is the most important industry in the UAE, with balance of payments data as published by the IMF indicating that exports of crude petroleum and related products contributed 44.2% of total export revenues in 2006. At the end of 2006 the UAE's proven recoverable reserves of petroleum were 97,800m. barrels, representing 8.1% of world reserves. Production levels in 2006 averaged 2.97m. barrels per day (b/d). As a member of the Organization of the Petroleum Exporting Countries (OPEC, see p. 373), the UAE is subject to production quotas agreed by the Organization's Conference. The UAE has large natural gas reserves, estimated at 6,060,000m. cu m at the end of 2006 (3.3% of world reserves). Most petroleum and natural gas reserves are concentrated in Abu Dhabi. Dubai is the UAE's second largest producer of petroleum. Marble and sand are also quarried. According to IMF data, the GDP of the mining sector increased by 17.0% in 2006.

Manufacturing contributed 12.1% of GDP in 2006, according to preliminary Central Bank figures, and employed 12.7% of the working population in the same year. The major heavy industries in the UAE are related to hydrocarbons, and activities are concentrated in the Jebel Ali Free Zone (in Dubai) and the Jebel Dhanna-Ruwais industrial zone in Abu Dhabi. The most important products are liquefied petroleum gas, distillate fuel oils and jet fuels. There are two petroleum refineries in Abu Dhabi, and the emirate has 'downstream' interests abroad. The most important activities in the non-hydrocarbons manufacturing sector are aluminium, steel and chemicals. During 1996–2005, according to World Bank data, manufacturing GDP increased at an average annual rate of 12.0%. Figures published by the IMF indicated that the GDP of the sector increased by 13.5% in 2006.

Each of the emirates is responsible for its own energy production. Electric energy is generated largely by thermal power stations, utilizing the UAE's own hydrocarbons resources. In early 2008 the UAE signed an agreement with France regarding co-operation in the development of a civilian nuclear power programme; memoranda of understanding were subsequently also signed with the USA and the United Kingdom regarding civilian nuclear co-operation.

The services sector contributed 40.0% of GDP in 2006, according to preliminary Central Bank figures, and engaged 55.2% of the working population in the same year. The establishment of the Jebel Ali Free Zone in 1985 enhanced Dubai's reputation as a well-equipped entrepôt for regional trade, and significant growth in both re-exports and tourism has been recorded in recent years. The financial services and real estate sectors have also expanded rapidly as the UAE has pursued economic diversification. During 1996–2005, according to World Bank data, the GDP of the services sector increased by an average of 7.9% per year. According to figures published by the IMF, the sector's GDP increased by 8.7% in 2006.

In 2006, according to preliminary Central Bank figures, the UAE recorded a visible trade surplus of AED 207,070m., and there was a surplus of AED 129,110m. on the current account of the balance of payments. In 2006 the principal source of imports was India, which supplied 10.7% of total imports. Other important suppliers in that year were the People's Republic of China, the USA, Germany and Japan. India was also the principal market for non-petroleum exports in 2006, taking 15.2% of the total. The other member states of the Co-operation Council for the Arab States of the Gulf (the Gulf Co-operation Council—GCC, see p. 219) together took 11.4% of non-petroleum exports in that year. Largely through its re-export trade, the UAE is of particular importance as a supplier of goods to Iran. Excluding hydrocarbons and free trade exports, the principal exports in 2006 were base metals and articles of base metal, plastics, rubber and related articles, and prepared foodstuffs and beverages. The principal imports in that year were machinery and electrical equipment, pearls, precious or semi-precious stones and precious metals, and vehicles and other transport equipment.

Preliminary Central Bank figures for 2006 indicated a surplus of AED 72,466m. on the consolidated government budget, equivalent to 12.1% of GDP. The federal budget, to which Abu Dhabi is the major contributor, represents about one-quarter of the country's total public expenditure, as the individual emirates have their own budgets for municipal expenditure and local projects. Annual inflation averaged 4.9% in 2000–06. Consumer prices increased by an annual average of 9.3% in 2006. Some 2.3% of the labour force were recorded as unemployed in 2000. About 90% of the work-force are estimated to be non-UAE nationals.

In addition to its membership of OPEC (see p. 373) and the GCC (see p. 219), the UAE also belongs to the Organization of Arab Petroleum Exporting Countries (OAPEC, see p. 366) and the Arab Fund for Economic and Social Development (AFESD, see p. 174). The UAE, and Abu Dhabi in particular, is a major aid donor. Abu Dhabi disburses loans through the Abu Dhabi Fund for Development (ADFD). GCC member states established a unified regional customs tariff in January 2003, and agreed to create a single market and currency no later than January 2010. The economic convergence criteria for the monetary union were agreed at a GCC summit in Abu Dhabi in December 2005, and in January 2008 the GCC common market was launched.

The sustained high level of international petroleum prices contributed substantially to very rates of economic growth and strong fiscal and balance of payments surpluses in the UAE in 2003–06. None the less, successful efforts at diversification of economic activity, hitherto particularly in Abu Dhabi and Dubai (each emirate retains considerable autonomy in its economic affairs), has resulted in less reliance on the hydrocarbons sector than in many other petroleum-producing countries. Highly developed infrastructure and low import tariffs have enhanced the UAE's position as a centre for regional trade, with Central Bank figures indicating in 2007 that the rate of growth of re-exports was exceeding that of domestic exports. Meanwhile, the tourism, real estate and financial services sectors also expanded

THE UNITED ARAB EMIRATES

rapidly, and the strong performance of the construction sector reflected the rapid expansion of infrastructure. Growth of the non-oil sector during 2003–06 averaged some 10% annually. It was anticipated that the UAE's banking sector, measured by value of assets, would become the largest in the region (surpassing that of Saudi Arabia) during 2008. The Government's strategic plan for the remainder of the decade envisaged the continuing diversification of the economy, and placed emphasis on social issues and labour reform. It was aimed to strengthen co-operation between the federal and emirate governments, and improve efficiency in the public sector. Legislation was issued in late 2007 establishing a new federal body, the Emirates Investment Authority, with responsibility for making investments on behalf of the federal Government. Following the initial public offering on the Dubai International Financial Exchange of a 23% stake in Dubai Ports World (the proceeds of the sale were to be transferred to the state-owned parent company, Dubai World, which had funded its subsidiary's acquisition of the British-based P&O in 2006), further issues from government holdings were anticipated. The Government was confident of meeting convergence criteria for GCC monetary union, and plans for the introduction of a value-added tax were well advanced. The federal budget for 2008 envisaged a 24% increase in overall expenditure, with strong petroleum revenues allowing for enhanced investment in education, health and infrastructure. There were concerns at this time regarding the ability of infrastructure to keep pace with demand, especially, and despite rapid expansion, in the housing and transport sectors and in the supply of electricity and water. The level of demand for rental properties among the large expatriate community was a particular factor contributing to a high rate of inflation, while provision for a 70% increase in salaries for federal government employees in the 2008 budget was expected to place upward pressure on salaries in other sectors. Meanwhile, industrial action by workers in the construction sector in late 2007, in support of demands for improved pay and conditions, was reported to have impeded progress on some infrastructure projects.

Education

Primary education is compulsory, beginning at six years of age and lasting for six years. Secondary education, starting at the age of 12, also lasts for six years, comprising two equal cycles of three years. According to UNESCO estimates, enrolment at primary schools in 2004/05 included 70.5% of children in the relevant age group, while 57.4% of pupils in the appropriate age group were enrolled at secondary schools. Most of the teachers are from other Arab countries, notably Kuwait, Jordan and Egypt. The UAE has three universities: two in Abu Dhabi (one of which, Zayed University, enrols female nationals only) and the third in Sharjah. In 2002/03 16,128 students were enrolled at the University of Al-Ain in Abu Dhabi. Four higher colleges of technology (two for male and two for female students) opened in 1988 and admitted a total of 1,150 students by 1992/93, all of whom were citizens of the UAE. In 2002/03 71,194 students were enrolled in university and other higher education. A branch of the Sorbonne University, based in Paris, France, opened in Abu Dhabi in October 2006, following an agreement signed earlier that year with the Ministry of Higher Education and Scientific Research. Many other students receive higher education abroad. Budgeted federal government expenditure by the Ministries of Education and of Higher Education and Scientific Research in the 2006/07 fiscal year totalled AED 7,220m. (36.6% of total expenditure by the central Government).

Public Holidays

2008: 1 January (New Year's Day), 10 January*† (Muharram, Islamic New Year), 20 March* (Mouloud, Birth of Muhammad), 30 July* (Leilat al-Meiraj, Ascension of Muhammad), 2 September* (first day of Ramadan), 1 October* (Id al-Fitr, end of Ramadan), 2 December (National Day), 9 December* (Id al-Adha, Feast of the Sacrifice), 25 December (Christmas Day), 29 December*† (Muharram, Islamic New Year).

2009: 1 January (New Year's Day), 9 March* (Mouloud, Birth of Muhammad), 19 July* (Leilat al-Meiraj, Ascension of Muhammad), 22 August* (first day of Ramadan), 20 September* (Id al-Fitr, end of Ramadan), 27 November* (Id al-Adha, Feast of the Sacrifice), 2 December (National Day), 18 December* (Muharram, Islamic New Year), 25 December (Christmas Day).

* These holidays are dependent on the Islamic lunar calendar and may vary slightly from the dates given.

† This festival occurs twice (marking the start of the Islamic years AH 1429 and 1430) within the same Gregorian year.

Weights and Measures

The imperial, metric and local systems are all in use.

Statistical Survey

Source (unless otherwise stated): Central Bank of the UAE, POB 854, Abu Dhabi; tel. (2) 6652220; fax (2) 6667494; e-mail uaecbadm@cbuae.gov.ae; internet www.centralbank.ae.

Area and Population

AREA, POPULATION AND DENSITY

Area (sq km)	77,700*
Population (census results)	
17 December 1995	2,411,041
6 December 2005	
UAE nationals	824,921
Males	418,057
Females	406,864
Non-UAE nationals	3,279,774†
Total	4,104,695
Population (official estimate at mid-year)	
2006 (preliminary)	4,229,000
Density (per sq km) at 2006	54.4

* 30,000 sq miles.

† Including 335,615 non-national groups not enumerated on 6 December; the enumerated total of non-nationals was 2,944,159 (total enumerated population of UAE was 3,769,080).

POPULATION BY EMIRATE
(mid-2003, preliminary figures)

	Area (sq km)	Population	Density (per sq km)
Abu Dhabi	67,350	1,591,000	23.6
Dubai	3,900	1,204,000	308.7
Sharjah	2,600	636,000	244.6
Ajman	250	235,000	940.0
Ras al-Khaimah	1,700	195,000	114.7
Fujairah	1,150	118,000	102.6
Umm al-Qaiwain	750	62,000	82.7
Total	**77,700**	**4,041,000**	**52.0**

PRINCIPAL TOWNS
(estimated population at mid-2003)

Dubai	1,171,000	Ras al-Khaimah	102,000
Abu Dhabi (capital)	552,000	Fujairah	54,000
Sharjah	519,000	Umm Al-Quwain	38,000
Al-Ain	348,000	Khor-Fakkan	32,000
Ajman	225,000		

Mid-2006 (official estimate): Dubai 1,241,000 (Source: Statistics Centre, Municipality of Dubai, *Dubai in Figures*).

THE UNITED ARAB EMIRATES

BIRTHS, MARRIAGES AND DEATHS

	Live births		Marriages*		Deaths	
	Number	Rate (per 1,000)	Number	Rate (per 1,000)	Number	Rate (per 1,000)
1996	47,050	18.9	6,275	2.5	4,785	1.9
1997	46,360	17.5	6,573	2.5	4,878	1.8
1998	48,136	17.0	6,920	2.4	5,033	1.8
1999	49,659	16.4	10,182	3.4	5,194	1.7
2000	53,686	16.5	8,965	2.8	5,396	1.7
2001	56,136	16.1	9,697	2.8	5,758	1.8
2002	58,070	15.5	11,285	3.0	5,994	1.6
2003	61,165	15.1	12,277	3.0	6,002	1.5

* Muslim marriages only.

Expectation of life (years at birth, WHO estimates): 77.5 (males 76.4; females 79.3) in 2005 (Source: WHO, *World Health Statistics*).

EMPLOYMENT
(persons aged 15 years and over)

	2004	2005	2006*
Agriculture, hunting, forestry and fishing	168,574	191,091	193,059
Mining and quarrying	35,575	38,303	38,930
Oil and gas	30,015	32,864	33,127
Manufacturing	319,384	333,180	361,766
Electricity, gas and water supply	28,848	33,861	34,142
Construction	497,974	528,991	647,132
Wholesale and retail trade; repair of motor vehicles, motorcycles and personal and household goods	478,716	497,345	518,546
Hotels and restaurants	109,931	115,435	123,995
Transport, storage and communications	147,807	161,122	174,489
Financial intermediation	27,011	30,701	36,525
Real estate, renting and business activities	73,817	77,070	83,923
Public administration and defence; compulsory social security	264,568	283,210	284,441
Community, social and personal service activities	106,700	113,576	121,102
Private households with employed persons	200,240	220,255	225,593
Total employed	2,459,145	2,624,139	2,843,643

* Preliminary figures.

Health and Welfare

KEY INDICATORS

Total fertility rate (children per woman, 2005)	2.4
Under-5 mortality rate (per 1,000 live births, 2005)	9
HIV/AIDS (% of persons aged 15–49, 1994)	0.18
Physicians (per 1,000 head, 2004)	2.02
Hospital beds (per 1,000 head, 2002)	2.20
Health expenditure (2004): US $ per head (PPP)	502.7
Health expenditure (2004): % of GDP	2.9
Health expenditure (2004): public (% of total)	69.9
Human Development Index (2005): ranking	39
Human Development Index (2005): value	0.868

For sources and definitions, see explanatory note on p. vi.

Agriculture

PRINCIPAL CROPS
('000 metric tons)

	2003	2004	2005
Potatoes	7.1	7.1	7.1
Cabbages	14.3	45.6	56.3
Lettuce	0.8	0.3*	0.0
Spinach	0.9	86.3*	127.9*
Tomatoes	134.0	502.6*	663.9*
Cauliflowers and broccoli	5.5	11.8*	13.6*
Pumpkins, squash and gourds	19.8	29.8*	34.4*
Cucumbers and gherkins	11.3	21.5*	24.0*
Aubergines (Eggplants)	14.1	9.6*	5.3*
Chillies and green peppers	5.4	5.5*	5.5*
Green onions and shallots	15.9	—	—
Green beans	1.1	1.2*	1.2*
Carrots and turnips	1.1	1.4*	1.4*
Watermelons	2.3	6.6*	8.0*
Cantaloupes and other melons	4.7	43.6*	61.6*
Lemons and limes	11.3	11.3*	11.5*
Mangoes, mangosteens and guavas	4.3	4.3*	4.5*
Dates	757.6	814.8*	859.2*

* FAO estimate.

Aggregate production ('000 metric tons, may include official, semi-official or estimated data): Total vegetables (incl. melons) 381 in 2003, 931 in 2004, 1,169 in 2005; Total fruits (excl. melons) 783 in 2003, 841 in 2004, 886 in 2005.

Note: Data for 2006 were not available.

Source: FAO.

LIVESTOCK
('000 head, year ending September)

	2003	2004*	2005*
Cattle	113	115	115
Camels	259	250	250
Sheep	583	590	580
Goats	1,495	1,500	1,520
Chickens*	18,000	15,000	15,000

* FAO estimates.

Note: Data for 2006 were not available.

Source: FAO.

LIVESTOCK PRODUCTS
('000 metric tons)

	2003	2004*	2005*
Cattle meat*	9.5	9.8	9.8
Camel meat*	15.4	15.4	15.4
Sheep meat*	7.2	13.5	13.5
Goat meat*	10.4	14.4	15.2
Chicken meat*	41.0	34.8	36.0
Cows' milk	11.5	11.5	11.5
Camels' milk	39.2	39.4	39.4
Sheep's milk	11.6	12.0	12.0
Goats' milk	34.8	35.0	35.5
Hen eggs	16.7†	17.0	17.0

* FAO estimates.
† Unofficial figure.

Note: Data for 2006 were not available.

Source: FAO.

THE UNITED ARAB EMIRATES

Statistical Survey

Fishing

('000 metric tons, live weight of capture)

	2002	2003	2004
Capture	97.6	95.2	90.0*
Groupers and seabasses	22.8	18.8	18.2*
Grunts and sweetlips	4.5	3.8	3.7*
Emperors (Scavengers)	21.1	20.3	19.6*
King soldier bream	4.8	5.9	5.7*
Sardinellas	3.5	4.1	4.0*
Stolephorus anchovies	6.4	3.5	3.4*
Narrow-barred Spanish mackerel	3.8	5.7	5.1
Jacks and crevalles	4.8	1.6	1.6*
Carangids	1.2	3.3	3.2*
Indian mackerel	2.1	2.9	2.9*
Aquaculture*	—	2.3	0.6
Total catch (incl. others)*	97.6	97.5	90.6

* FAO estimate(s).
2005: Figures assumed to be unchanged from 2004 (FAO estimates).
Source: FAO.

Mining

(estimated production)

	2004	2005	2006
Crude petroleum (million barrels)	820	830	900
Natural gas (million cu metres)*	45,400	46,400	47,000

* On a dry basis.
Source: US Geological Survey.

Industry

SELECTED PRODUCTS
('000 barrels, unless otherwise indicated, estimates)

	2004	2005	2006
Cement ('000 metric tons)	9,000	9,800	9,800
Aluminium ('000 metric tons)	683	722	861
Motor spirit (petrol)	20,000	20,000	30,000
Kerosene	50,000	50,000	50,000
Gas-diesel (distillate fuel) oil	45,000	45,000	48,000
Residual fuel oils	20,000	20,000	19,000
Liquefied petroleum gas	88,000	n.a.	n.a.

Source: US Geological Survey.

Electric energy (million kWh): 48,163 in 2003 (preliminary).

Finance

CURRENCY AND EXCHANGE RATES

Monetary Units
100 fils = 1 UAE dirham (AED).

Sterling, Dollar and Euro Equivalents (31 December 2007)
£1 sterling = 7.357 dirhams;
US $1 = 3.673 dirhams;
€1 = 5.406 dirhams;
100 UAE dirhams = £13.59 = $27.23 = €18.50.

Exchange Rate: The Central Bank's official rate was set at US $1 = 3.671 dirhams in November 1980. This remained in force until December 1997, when the rate was adjusted to $1 = 3.6725 dirhams.

BUDGET OF THE CONSOLIDATED GOVERNMENTS
(million UAE dirhams)

Revenue	2004	2005	2006*
Tax revenue	9,566	6,810	8,490
Custom revenue	3,040	3,852	4,693
Non-tax revenue	85,185	137,095	192,214
Revenue from petroleum and natural gas	73,322	111,377	161,516
Profit of joint stock corporations	3,322	4,624	5,702
Total	94,751	143,905	200,704

Expenditure	2004	2005	2006*
Current expenditure	80,984	84,255	100,691
Salaries and wages	15,628	16,654	17,764
Goods and services	25,032	24,383	26,076
Subsidies and transfers	11,666	18,916	30,295
Development expenditure	15,207	14,042	16,748
Loans and equity	83	6,133	10,799
Total	96,274	104,430	128,238

* Preliminary figures.

INTERNATIONAL RESERVES
(US $ million at 31 December, excluding gold)

	2004	2005	2006
IMF special drawing rights	5.4	9.6	12.2
Reserve position in IMF	315.5	133.0	93.3
Foreign exchange*	18,209.0	20,867.7	27,511.9
Total	18,529.9	21,010.3	27,617.4

* Figures exclude the Central Bank's foreign assets and accrued interest attributable to the governments of individual emirates.
Source: IMF, *International Financial Statistics*.

MONEY SUPPLY
(million UAE dirhams at 31 December)

	2004	2005	2006
Currency outside banks	15,778	17,522	21,837
Demand deposits at commercial banks	65,040	86,927	98,183
Total money	80,818	104,449	120,020

Source: IMF, *International Financial Statistics*.

COST OF LIVING
(Consumer Price Index; base: 2000 = 100)

	2004	2005	2006*
Food, beverages and tobacco	112.0	117.0	123.5
Clothing and footwear	112.0	114.8	119.2
Housing (incl. rent)	119.0	130.1	150.1
Furniture, etc.	106.9	110.5	113.2
Medical care and health services	117.0	123.4	127.5
Transport and communications	111.5	116.6	127.7
Recreation and education	117.1	121.7	124.6
All items (incl. others)	114.6	121.7	133.0

* Preliminary figures.

THE UNITED ARAB EMIRATES

Statistical Survey

NATIONAL ACCOUNTS
(million UAE dirhams at current prices)

National Income and Product

	2002	2003	2004*
Compensation of employees	79,102	88,926	94,395
Operating surplus	157,785	193,950	242,972
Domestic factor incomes	236,887	282,876	337,367
Consumption of fixed capital	35,969	38,876	41,394
Gross domestic product (GDP) at factor cost	272,856	321,752	378,761
Indirect taxes, *less* subsidies	2,430	3,396	3,928
GDP in purchasers' values	275,286	325,148	382,689
Net factor income from abroad	−11,805	−16,261	−16,135
Gross national income	263,481	308,887	366,554
Less Consumption of fixed capital	35,969	38,876	41,394
National income in market prices	227,512	270,011	325,160
Less Net current transfers from abroad	1,050	1,000	1,500
National disposable income	226,462	269,011	323,660

* Preliminary figures.

Expenditure on the Gross Domestic Product

	2004	2005	2006*
Government final consumption expenditure	48,850	53,979	60,646
Private final consumption expenditure	198,800	233,486	275,344
Increase in stocks	4,505	5,724	6,663
Gross fixed capital formation	81,255	93,798	121,000
Total domestic expenditure	333,410	386,987	463,653
Net exports of goods and services	57,072	103,596	141,812
Less Net indirect taxes	3,947	5,071	6,234
GDP in purchasers' values	386,535	485,513	599,231

* Preliminary figures.

Gross Domestic Product by Economic Activity

	2004	2005	2006*
Agriculture, hunting, forestry and fishing	10,100	11,028	12,241
Mining and quarrying	124,089	174,114	224,552
Oil and gas	123,261	173,195	223,422
Manufacturing	50,159	61,194	73,433
Electricity and water	6,720	7,935	9,522
Construction	28,971	34,980	45,124
Wholesale and retail trade, and repairs	43,458	52,998	62,538
Restaurants and hotels	7,343	8,946	10,431
Transport, storage and communications	27,263	32,642	38,517
Financial institutions and insurance	23,374	28,426	35,674
Real estate and business services	30,018	35,920	46,121
Government services	32,463	34,735	39,025
Community, social and personal services	7,113	7,607	8,706
Private households with employed persons	2,126	2,382	2,627
Sub-total	393,197	492,908	608,511
Less Imputed bank service charge	6,662	7,395	9,280
GDP in purchasers' values	386,535	485,513	599,231

* Preliminary figures.

BALANCE OF PAYMENTS
('000 million UAE dirhams)

	2004	2005*	2006*
Exports of goods f.o.b.	334.19	430.74	523.35
Imports of goods f.o.b.	−232.96	−273.58	−316.28
Trade balance	101.23	157.15	207.07
Services (net)	−44.35	−53.56	−65.26
Income (net)	0.57	10.60	17.40
Balance on goods, services and income	57.45	114.19	159.21
Current transfers (net)	−18.57	−24.70	−30.10
Current balance	38.89	89.49	129.11
Capital and financial accounts (net)	−23.87	−53.88	−58.99
Net errors and omissions	−2.19	−26.11	−46.24
Overall balance	12.83	9.50	23.89

* Preliminary figures.

External Trade

PRINCIPAL COMMODITIES
(distribution by HS, million UAE dirhams)

Imports c.i.f.	2004	2005	2006
Vegetable products	6,653.2	8,304.5	9,041.2
Prepared foodstuffs, beverages, spirits and tobacco	6,062.9	7,057.2	7,895.6
Chemical products, etc.	11,152.1	12,729.6	15,754.7
Plastics, rubber and articles thereof	7,484.4	8,932.1	10,693.4
Textiles and textile articles	13,272.0	13,476.0	14,805.0
Pearls, precious or semi-precious stones, precious metals, etc.	38,058.7	50,693.6	52,475.3
Base metals and articles of base metal	17,947.5	22,924.6	32,689.5
Machinery and electrical equipment	45,627.9	57,443.7	66,439.9
Vehicles and other transport equipment	23,635.5	30,388.7	36,786.7
Total (incl. others)	195,703.9	242,421.9	284,453.2

Exports f.o.b.*	2004	2005	2006
Vegetable products	493.0	503.0	298.2
Prepared foodstuffs, beverages, spirits and tobacco	1,173.3	2,035.1	2,576.7
Mineral products	552.3	817.8	1,060.1
Chemical products, etc.	546.2	879.2	997.7
Plastics, rubber and articles thereof	2,078.7	2,574.3	2,860.1
Textiles and textile articles	673.7	727.2	980.4
Stone, plaster, cement, ceramic and glassware	651.5	804.0	1,199.7
Base metals and articles of base metal	3,224.2	3,561.5	4,489.0
Machinery and electrical equipment	292.1	480.7	969.1
Vehicles and other transport equipment	164.4	146.4	709.3
Total (incl. others)†	12,536.3	14,650.9	23,180.8

* Excluding petroleum exports and excluding re-exports; re-exports amounted to 66,236.6m. dirhams in 2004; 94,004.1m. dirhams in 2005 and 91,163.0m. dirhams in 2006.
† Excluding free zone exports.

THE UNITED ARAB EMIRATES

SELECTED MAJOR TRADING PARTNERS
(million UAE dirhams)

Imports	2005	2006
Australia	3,663.0	5,245.5
Belgium/Netherlands/Luxembourg	7,532.0	9,603.8
Brazil	2,972.9	3,858.4
Canada	1,297.7	1,958.3
China, People's Republic	23,760.5	30,390.1
France (incl. Monaco)	8,540.9	8,681.5
GCC countries	10,536.5	16,887.9
Germany	16,344.2	20,970.9
India	31,685.4	30,426.3
Italy (incl. San Marino)	8,417.2	12,249.8
Japan	17,027.1	20,660.6
Korea, Republic	6,489.8	7,600.8
New Zealand	401.8	554.6
South Africa	2,355.2	1,779.9
United Kingdom	15,962.7	14,692.6
USA	18,514.7	23,222.6
Total (incl. others)	242,421.9	284,453.2

Exports*	2005	2006
Australia	329.4	381.5
Belgium/Netherlands/Luxembourg	5,400.4	3,252.6
Brazil	20.7	36.9
Canada	90.2	117.1
GCC countries	16,225.8	13,051.6
Germany	1,612.7	888.7
India	19,588.6	17,354.6
New Zealand	108.1	135.4
United Kingdom	876.2	1,519.2
USA	2,224.3	2,140.2
Total (incl. others)	108,655.0	114,343.8

* Data for non-petroleum exports and all re-exports.

Transport

ROAD TRAFFIC
('000 registered motor vehicles in use)

	2000	2001	2002
Passenger cars (incl. taxis)	561.9	654.2	606.1
Trucks (incl. public)	83.3	66.2	66.2
Buses (incl. public)	14.7	13.3	16.0
Other	13.2	11.2	13.1

Total vehicles in use: 767 in 2002; 792 in 2003.

SHIPPING
Merchant Fleet
(registered at 31 December)

	2004	2005	2006
Number of vessels	384	406	417
Total displacement ('000 grt)	799.2	839.2	870.3

Source: Lloyd's Register-Fairplay, *World Fleet Statistics*.

International Sea-borne Shipping
(estimated freight traffic, '000 metric tons)

	1988	1989	1990
Goods loaded	63,380	72,896	88,153
Crude petroleum	54,159	63,387	78,927
Other cargo	9,221	9,509	9,226
Goods unloaded	8,973	8,960	9,595

Source: UN, *Monthly Bulletin of Statistics*.

Statistical Survey

CIVIL AVIATION
(traffic on scheduled services)*

	2001	2002	2003
Kilometres flown (million)	136	159	207
Passengers carried ('000)	7,676	9,667	11,610
Passenger-km (million)	26,202	33,125	41,504
Total ton-km (million)	4,148	5,261	6,760

* Figures include an apportionment (one-quarter) of the traffic of Gulf Air, a multinational airline with its headquarters in Bahrain.

Source: UN, *Statistical Yearbook*.

Tourism

FOREIGN TOURIST ARRIVALS*

Country	2001	2002	2003
Canada	36,742	95,878	55,297
Egypt	96,002	111,822	121,221
France	69,620	90,735	98,624
Germany	194,079	236,660	235,147
India	246,335	336,046	357,941
Iran	194,140	270,350	334,453
Jordan	58,844	73,140	76,553
Lebanon	61,133	74,225	83,137
Pakistan	117,116	154,711	183,724
Russia	205,126	267,655	324,484
United Kingdom	384,443	491,604	496,147
USA	98,893	123,112	175,116
Total (incl. others)†	4,133,531	5,445,367	5,871,023

* Figures refer to international arrivals at hotels and similar establishments.
† Total includes domestic tourists.

Receipts from tourism (US $ million, incl. passenger transport): 1,200 in 2001; 1,332 in 2002; 1,439 in 2003; 1,594 in 2004; 2,200 in 2005.

Source: World Tourism Organization.

Communications Media

	2004	2005	2006
Telephones ('000 main lines in use)	1,187.7	1,236.9	1,309.7
Mobile cellular telephones ('000 subscribers)	3,683.1	4,534.1	5,519.3
Personal computers ('000 in use)	450	850	n.a.
Internet users ('000)	1,185.0	1,321.7	1,708.5
Broadband subscribers ('000)	56.1	129.3	240.6

Daily newspapers (titles): 9 in 2004.
Radio receivers ('000 in use): 820 in 1997.
Television receivers ('000 in use): 780 in 2001.
Facsimile machines ('000 in use): 50 in 1997.

Sources: partly UNESCO, *Statistical Yearbook*; UN, *Statistical Yearbook*; International Telecommunication Union.

Education

(Government schools only)

	2001/02	2002/03	2003/04
Institutions	740	744	755
Teachers*	27,616	27,954	27,855
Students			
Pre-primary	22,219	22,596	20,561
Primary	204,760	214,235	218,739
Secondary	65,195	65,202	64,618
Other schools	3,487	4,607	5,154

* Includes administrative and technical staff.

Adult literacy rate (UNESCO estimates): 88.7% (males 89.0%; females 87.8%) in 2004 (Source: UNESCO Institute for Statistics).

Directory

The Constitution

A provisional Constitution for the UAE took effect in December 1971. This laid the foundation for the federal structure of the Union of the seven emirates, previously known as the Trucial States.

The highest federal authority is the Supreme Council of Rulers, which comprises the Rulers of the seven emirates. It elects the President and Vice-President from among its members. The President appoints a Prime Minister and a Council of Ministers. Proposals submitted to the Council require the approval of at least five of the Rulers, including those of Abu Dhabi and Dubai. The legislature is the Federal National Council (FNC), a consultative assembly comprising 40 members, of whom one-half are appointed by the emirates and the remainder are chosen by electoral colleges for a two-year term.

In July 1975 a committee was appointed to draft a permanent federal constitution, but the FNC decided in 1976 to extend the provisional document for five years. The provisional Constitution was extended for another five years in December 1981, and for further periods of five years in 1986 and 1991. In November 1976, however, the Supreme Council amended Article 142 of the provisional Constitution so that the authority to levy armed forces was placed exclusively under the control of the federal Government. Legislation designed to make the provisional Constitution permanent was endorsed by the FNC in June 1996, after it had been approved by the Supreme Council of Rulers.

The Government

HEAD OF STATE

President: Sheikh KHALIFA BIN ZAYED AN-NAHYAN (Ruler of Abu Dhabi, elected by the Supreme Council of Rulers as President of the UAE on 3 November 2004).
Vice-President: Sheikh MUHAMMAD BIN RASHID AL-MAKTOUM (Ruler of Dubai).

SUPREME COUNCIL OF RULERS
(with each Ruler's date of accession)

Ruler of Abu Dhabi: Sheikh KHALIFA BIN ZAYED AN-NAHYAN (2004).
Ruler of Dubai: Sheikh MUHAMMAD BIN RASHID AL-MAKTOUM (2006).
Ruler of Sharjah: Sheikh SULTAN BIN MUHAMMAD AL-QASIMI (1972).
Ruler of Ras al-Khaimah: Sheikh SAQR BIN MUHAMMAD AL-QASIMI (1948).
Ruler of Umm al-Qaiwain: Sheikh RASHID BIN AHMAD AL-MU'ALLA (1981).
Ruler of Ajman: Sheikh HUMAID BIN RASHID AN-NUAIMI (1981).
Ruler of Fujairah: Sheikh HAMAD BIN MUHAMMAD ASH-SHARQI (1974).

COUNCIL OF MINISTERS
(April 2008)

Prime Minister and Minister of Defence: Sheikh MUHAMMAD BIN RASHID AL-MAKTOUM.
Deputy Prime Ministers: Sheikh SULTAN BIN ZAYED AN-NAHYAN, Sheikh HAMDAN BIN ZAYED AN-NAHYAN.
Minister of Finance and Industry: Sheikh HAMDAN BIN RASHID AL-MAKTOUM.
Minister of the Interior: Lt-Gen. Sheikh SAIF BIN ZAYED AN-NAHYAN.
Minister of Presidential Affairs: Sheikh MANSOUR BIN ZAYED AN-NAHYAN.
Minister of Foreign Affairs: Sheikh ABDULLAH BIN ZAYED AN-NAHYAN.
Minister of Higher Education and Scientific Research: Sheikh NAHYAN BIN MUBARAK AN-NAHYAN.
Minister of Public Works: Sheikh HAMDAN BIN MUBARAK AN-NAHYAN.
Minister of Economy: SULTAN BIN SAID AL-MANSOURI.
Minister of Foreign Trade: Sheikha LUBNA BINT KHALID AL-QASIMI.
Minister of Justice: Dr HADIF JOWAN ADH-DHAHIRI.
Minister of Energy: MUHAMMAD BIN DHAEN AL-HAMILI.
Minister of Labour: SAQR GHOBASH SAID GHOBASH.
Minister of Social Affairs: Dr MARIAM MUHAMMAD KHALFAN AR-ROUMI.
Minister of Education: Dr HANIF HASSAN ALI.
Minister of Health: HUMAID MUHAMMAD OBAID AL-QATTAMI.
Minister of the Environment and Water: Dr RASHID AHMAD AL-FAHD.
Minister of Culture, Youth and Community Development: ABD AR-RAHMAN MUHAMMAD AL-OWAIS.
Minister of Cabinet Affairs: MUHAMMAD BIN ABDULLAH AL-GARGAWI.
Minister of State for Financial Affairs: OBAID HUMAID AT-TAYER.
Minister of State for Foreign Affairs and for Federal National Council Affairs: Dr ANWAR MUHAMMAD GARGASH.
Ministers of State: Dr KHALIFA BAKHIT AL-FALASI, REEM IBRAHIM AL-HASHEMI, Dr MAITHA SALIM ASH-SHAMSI.

FEDERAL MINISTRIES

Office of the Prime Minister: POB 12848, Dubai; tel. (4) 3534550; fax (4) 3530111.
Office of the Deputy Prime Minister: POB 831, Abu Dhabi; tel. (2) 4451000; fax (2) 4450066.
Ministry of Cabinet Affairs: POB 899, Abu Dhabi; tel. (2) 6268100; fax (2) 6268033; e-mail csb@csb.ae; internet www.csb.gov.ae.
Ministry of Culture, Youth and Community Development: POB 17, Abu Dhabi; tel. (2) 4453000; fax (2) 4452504.
Ministry of Defence: POB 46616, Abu Dhabi; tel. (4) 4461300; fax (4) 4463286.
Ministry of Economy: POB 901, Abu Dhabi; tel. (2) 6265000; fax (2) 6260000; e-mail moep@moep.gov.ae; internet www.moep.gov.ae.
Ministry of Education: POB 295, Abu Dhabi; tel. (2) 6213800; fax (2) 6351164; e-mail moe@uae.gov.ae; internet www.moe.gov.ae.
Ministry of Energy: POB 59, Abu Dhabi; tel. (2) 6262288; fax (2) 6272291; e-mail moew@uae.gov.ae; internet www.uae.gov.ae/moew.
Ministry of the Environment and Water: POB 213, Abu Dhabi; tel. (2) 4495100; fax (2) 4495150; e-mail adarchieve@moew.gov.ae; internet www.moew.gov.ae.
Ministry of Finance and Industry: POB 433, Abu Dhabi; tel. (2) 6726000; fax (2) 66663088; e-mail mofi@uae.gov.ae; internet www.uae.gov.ae/mofi.
Ministry of Foreign Affairs: POB 1, Abu Dhabi; tel. (2) 4444488; fax (2) 4449100; e-mail mofa@mofa.gov.ae; internet www.mofa.gov.ae.
Ministry of Foreign Trade: Abu Dhabi.
Ministry of Health: POB 848, Abu Dhabi; tel. (2) 6330000; fax (2) 6726000; e-mail postmaster@moh.gov.ae; internet www.moh.gov.ae/intro.
Ministry of Higher Education and Scientific Research: POB 45253, Abu Dhabi; tel. (2) 6428000; fax (2) 6427262; e-mail mohe@uae.gov.ae; internet www.uae.gov.ae/mohe.
Ministry of the Interior: POB 398, Abu Dhabi; tel. (2) 4414666; fax (2) 4414938; e-mail moi@uae.gov.ae.
Ministry of Justice: POB 260, Abu Dhabi; tel. (2) 6814000; fax (2) 6810680; e-mail moj@uae.gov.ae.
Ministry of Labour: POB 809, Abu Dhabi; tel. (2) 6671700; fax (2) 6665889; e-mail minister@mol.gov.ae; internet www.mol.gov.ae.
Ministry of Presidential Affairs: Abu Dhabi.
Ministry of Public Works: POB 878, Abu Dhabi; tel. (2) 6260606; fax (2) 6260026; e-mail falshamsi@mpw.ae; internet www.mopw.gov.ae.
Ministry of Social Affairs: POB 809, Abu Dhabi; tel. (2) 6332355; fax (2) 6333659.
Ministry of State for Federal National Council Affairs: POB 130000, Abu Dhabi; tel. (2) 4041000; fax (2) 4041155; e-mail mfnca@mfnca.ae; internet www.mfnca.ae.
Ministry of State for Financial Affairs: POB 433, Abu Dhabi; tel. (2) 771133; fax (2) 793255.
Ministry of State for Foreign Affairs: POB 1, Abu Dhabi; tel. (2) 6660888; fax (2) 6652883.

Legislature

FEDERAL NATIONAL COUNCIL

Formed under the provisional Constitution, the Council is composed of 40 members from the various emirates (eight each from Abu Dhabi and Dubai, six each from Sharjah and Ras al-Khaimah, and four each from Ajman, Fujairah and Umm al-Qaiwain). Each emirate appoints its own representatives separately. The Council studies laws proposed by the Council of Ministers and can reject them or suggest amendments. In December 2005 Sheikh Khalifa announced that elections would be introduced to choose one-half of the members of the FNC, which would also be expanded and granted enhanced powers. In August 2006 a National Electoral Committee was established to preside over the elections, which were held during 16–20 December.

Speaker: ABD AL-AZIZ ABDULLAH AL-GHURAIR.

Diplomatic Representation

EMBASSIES IN THE UNITED ARAB EMIRATES

Afghanistan: POB 5687, Abu Dhabi; tel. (2) 6655560; fax (2) 6655576; Ambassador FARID ZEKRIA.

Algeria: POB 3070, Abu Dhabi; tel. (2) 448949; fax (2) 4470686; Ambassador HAMID CHEBIRA.

Argentina: POB 3325, Abu Dhabi; tel. (2) 4436838; fax (2) 4431392; e-mail embar@emirates.net.ae; Ambassador RUBÉN EDUARDO CARO.

Australia: POB 32711, Al-Muhairy Centre, Level 14, Sheikh Zayed I St, Abu Dhabi; tel. (2) 6346100; fax (2) 6393525; e-mail abudhabi.embassy@dfat.gov.au; internet www.uae.embassy.gov.au; Ambassador JEREMY BRUER (also accredited to Qatar).

Austria: POB 35539, Al-Khazna Tower, 7th Floor, Najda St, Abu Dhabi; tel. (2) 6766611; fax (2) 6715551; internet www.austrianembassy.ae; Ambassador Dr GERALD KRIECHBAUM.

Azerbaijan: POB 45766, Plot N-297, Villa Sector W/16, Al-Bateen Area, Abu Dhabi; tel. (2) 6662848; fax (2) 6663150; e-mail azembassy@emirates.net.ae; Ambassador (vacant).

Bahrain: POB 3367, Abu Dhabi; tel. (2) 6657500; fax (2) 6674141; e-mail bahrain1@emirates.net.ae; Ambassador MUHAMMAD SAQR AL-MAAWDA.

Bangladesh: POB 2504, Villa 32, Khlaidya, Abu Dhabi; tel. (2) 668375; fax (2) 667324; e-mail banglaad@emirates.net.ae; Ambassador A. T. M. NAZIMULLAH CHOWDHURY.

Belarus: POB 30337, Villa 434, 26th St, Ar-Rouda Area, Abu Dhabi; tel. (2) 4453399; fax (2) 4451131; e-mail uae@belembassy.org; Ambassador VLADIMIR SULIMSKY.

Belgium: POB 3686, Al-Masood Tower, 6th Floor, Hamdan St, Abu Dhabi; tel. (2) 6319449; fax (2) 6319353; e-mail abudhabi@diplobel.org; internet www.diplomatie.be/abudhabi; Ambassador PHILIPPE DARTOIS.

Bosnia and Herzegovina: POB 43362, Abu Dhabi; tel. (2) 6444164; fax (2) 6443619; e-mail abhad@bhmc.ae; internet www.bhmc.ae; Ambassador MILUTIN VASILJEVIĆ.

Brazil: POB 3027, St 5, Villa 3, Madinat Zayed, Abu Dhabi; tel. (2) 6320606; fax (2) 6327727; e-mail abubrem@emirates.net.ae; internet www.brazilembuae.ae; Ambassador FLAVIO MOREIRA SAPHA.

Brunei: POB 5836, Plot 8, Villa 1, St 27, E-33, Abu Dhabi; tel. (2) 4486999; fax (2) 4486333; e-mail kbdauh98@emirates.net.ae; Ambassador Dato Paduka Haji ADNAN BIN Haji ZAINAL.

Canada: POB 6970, Abu Dhabi Trade Towers, West Tower, 9th and 10th Floors, Abu Dhabi; tel. (2) 4071300; fax (2) 4071399; e-mail abdbi@international.gc.ca; internet www.dfait-maeci.gc.ca/abudhabi; Ambassador SARA HRADECKY.

China, People's Republic: POB 2741, Plot 26, W-22, Abu Dhabi; tel. (2) 4434276; fax (2) 4436835; e-mail chinaemb_ae@mfa.gov.cn; internet ae.chineseembassy.org; Ambassador GAO YUNSHENG.

Czech Republic: POB 27009, City Bank Bldg, Corniche Plaza, Abu Dhabi; tel. (2) 6782800; fax (2) 6795716; e-mail abudhabi@embassy.mzv.cz; internet www.mzv.cz; Ambassador VĚRA JEŘÁBKOVÁ.

Egypt: POB 4026, Abu Dhabi; tel. (2) 4445566; fax (2) 4449878; e-mail egemb_abudhabi@mfa.gov.eg; Ambassador MUHAMMAD SAID OBAID.

Eritrea: POB 2597, Abu Dhabi; tel. (2) 6331838; fax (2) 6346451; Ambassador OSMAN MUHAMMAD OMAR.

Finland: POB 3634, Al-Masood Tower, Hamdan St, Abu Dhabi; tel. (2) 6328927; fax (2) 6325063; e-mail sanomat.abo@formin.fi; internet www.finland.ae; Chargé d'affaires a.i. ESA HURTIG.

France: POB 4014, Abu Dhabi; tel. (2) 4435100; fax (2) 4434158; e-mail ambafr@emirates.net.ae; internet www.ambafrance-eau.org; Ambassador PATRICE PAOLI.

The Gambia: Abu Dhabi; tel. (2) 6678030; Ambassador KEBBA NJIE.

Germany: POB 2591, Abu Dhabi Mall, West Tower, 14th Floor, Abu Dhabi; tel. (2) 6446693; fax (2) 6446942; e-mail info@abu-dhabi.diplo.de; internet www.abu-dhabi.diplo.de; Ambassador KLAUS-PETER BRANDES.

Greece: POB 5483, Plot 141, Villa 1, E-48, Moroor, Abu Dhabi; tel. (2) 6654847; fax (2) 6656008; e-mail grembauh@emirates.net.ae; Ambassador GEORGE KOSTOLAS.

Hungary: POB 44450, Abu Dhabi; tel. (2) 6766190; fax (2) 6766215; e-mail mission.abu@kum.hu; Ambassador JÁNOS GÖNCI.

India: POB 4090, Abu Dhabi; tel. (2) 4492700; fax (2) 4444685; e-mail indiauae@indembassyuae.org; internet www.indembassyuae.org; Ambassador TALMIZ AHMAD.

Indonesia: POB 7256, Abu Dhabi; tel. (2) 4454448; fax (2) 4455453; e-mail indoemb@emirates.net.ae; internet www.indoemb.org/kbri; Chargé d'affaires a.i. JOKO SANTOSO.

Iran: POB 4080, Abu Dhabi; tel. (2) 4447618; fax (2) 4448714; e-mail iranemb@eim.ae; internet www.iranembassy.org.ae; Ambassador HAMID REZA ASEFI.

Iraq: Manhal St, Haoudh 55, St 32, Abu Dhabi; tel. (2) 6655215; fax (2) 6655214; e-mail iraqiemb@emirates.net.ae; Ambassador FARES UJAIL AL-YAWER.

Italy: POB 46752, Villa 438–439, St 26, Al-Manaseer Area, Abu Dhabi; tel. (2) 4435622; fax (2) 4434337; e-mail italianembassy.abudhabi@esteri.it; internet www.ambabudhabi.esteri.it; Ambassador PAOLO DIONISI.

Japan: POB 2430, Abu Dhabi; tel. (2) 4435696; fax (2) 4434219; e-mail embjpn@japanembassyauh.com; internet www.uae.emb-japan.go.jp; Ambassador TAKUMA HATANO.

Jordan: POB 4024, Abu Dhabi; tel. (2) 4447100; fax (2) 4449157; e-mail jordan2@emirates.net.ae; Ambassador EID KAMAL AR-RODAN.

Kazakhstan: POB 39556, Al-Mushrif, W-52, Villa 61B, Abu Dhabi; tel. (2) 4476623; fax (2) 4476624; e-mail kazemb@emirates.net.ae; Ambassador ASLAR A. MUSINOV.

Kenya: POB 3854, Abu Dhabi; tel. (2) 6666300; fax (2) 6652827; e-mail kenyarep@emirates.net.ae; Ambassador BISHAR ABDI RAHMAN HUSSEIN.

Korea, Republic: POB 3270, Abu Dhabi; tel. (2) 4435337; fax (2) 4435348; e-mail keauhlee@emirates.net.ae; Ambassador JOON-JAE LEE.

Kuwait: POB 926, Abu Dhabi; tel. (2) 4446888; fax (2) 4444990; Ambassador FAISAL ABDULLAH IBRAHIM AL-MISHAAN.

Lebanon: POB 4023, Abu Dhabi; tel. (2) 4492100; fax (2) 4493500; e-mail libanamb@emirates.net.ae; Ambassador FAUZI FAWAZ.

Libya: POB 5739, Abu Dhabi; tel. (2) 4450030; fax (2) 4450033; e-mail libyandh@emirates.net.ae; Chargé d'affaires ABD AL-HAMID ALI SHAIKHY.

Malaysia: POB 3887, Abu Dhabi; tel. (2) 4482775; fax (2) 4482779; e-mail mwabudhabi@eim.ae; internet www.kln.gov.my/perwakilan/abudhabi; Ambassador Dato' ABD AL-MUBIN RAZALI.

Mauritania: POB 2714, Abu Dhabi; tel. (2) 4462724; fax (2) 4465772; Ambassador MUHAMMAD AL-MUKHTAR OULD M. YAHAYA.

Morocco: POB 4066, Abu Dhabi; tel. (2) 4433963; fax (2) 4433917; e-mail sifmabo@emirates.net.ae; Ambassador ABDELKADER AZ-ZAOUI.

Netherlands: POB 46560, Al-Masood Tower, 6th Floor, Abu Dhabi; tel. (2) 6321920; fax (2) 6313158; e-mail abu@minbuza.nl; internet www.netherlands.ae; Ambassador GILLES ARNOUT BESCHOOR PLUG.

Norway: POB 47270, Abu Dhabi; tel. (2) 6211221; fax (2) 6213313; e-mail emb.abudhabi@mfa.no; internet www.norway.ae; Ambassador ARNE RIKTER-SVENDSEN.

Oman: POB 2517, Said bin Tahnon Sq., Al-Mushraf Area, Abu Dhabi; tel. (2) 4463333; fax (2) 4464633; Ambassador Sheikh MUHAMMAD BIN ABDULLAH AL-QATABI.

Pakistan: POB 846, Abu Dhabi; tel. (2) 4447800; fax (2) 4492076; e-mail pakem@emirates.net.ae; AHSAN ULLAH KHAN.

Philippines: POB 3215, Plot 97, Villa 2, St 5, E-18/02, Abu Dhabi; tel. (2) 6415922; fax (2) 6412559; e-mail auhpe@emirates.net.ae; Ambassador LIBRAN N. CABACTULAN.

Poland: POB 2334, Abu Dhabi; tel. (2) 4465200; fax (2) 4462967; e-mail polcon99@emirates.net.ae; internet www.plembassy.gov.ae; Ambassador ROMAN CHAKACZKIEWICZ.

Qatar: POB 3503, 26th St, Al-Minaseer, Abu Dhabi; tel. (2) 4493300; fax (2) 4493311; e-mail abudhabi@mofa.gov.qa; Ambassador ABDULLAH M. AL-UTHMAN.

Romania: 9 POB 70416, Abu Dhabi; tel. (2) 4459919; fax (2) 4461143; e-mail romaniae@emirates.net.ae; Ambassador NIKOLAI JOYA.

Russia: POB 8211, Abu Dhabi; tel. (2) 6721797; fax (2) 6728713; e-mail ruconsl@emirates.net.ae; Ambassador SERGEI YAKOVLEV.

Saudi Arabia: POB 4057, Abu Dhabi; tel. (2) 4445700; fax (2) 4448491; Ambassador Dr ABDULLAH BIN MUAMMAR.

Somalia: POB 4155, Abu Dhabi; tel. (2) 6669700; fax (2) 6651580; e-mail somen@emirates.net.ae; Ambassador HUSSEIN MUHAMMAD BULLALEH.

South Africa: POB 29446, Abu Dhabi; tel. (2) 4473446; fax (2) 4473031; e-mail saemb@emirates.net.ae; internet www.southafrica.ae; Chargé d'affaires MMUTLANE SAMSON MAKENA.

THE UNITED ARAB EMIRATES

Spain: POB 46474, Abu Dhabi; tel. (2) 6269544; fax (2) 6274978; e-mail emb.abudhabi@mae.es; Ambassador Manuel Piñeiro.

Sri Lanka: POB 46534, Abu Dhabi; tel. (2) 6426666; fax (2) 6428289; e-mail lankemba@emirates.net.ae; Ambassador Muhammad Nabavi Junaid.

Sudan: POB 4027, Abu Dhabi; tel. (2) 6666788; fax (2) 6654231; e-mail sudembll@emirates.net.ae; Ambassador Ahmad Mahjoub.

Sweden: POB 31867, Abu Dhabi; tel. (2) 6210162; fax (2) 6394941; e-mail ambassaden.abudhabi@foreign.ministry.se; internet www.swedenabroad.com/abudhabi; Ambassador Bruno S. Beijer.

Switzerland: POB 46116, Abu Dhabi; tel. (2) 6274636; fax (2) 6269627; e-mail vertretung@adh.rep.admin.ch; internet www.eda.admin.ch/uae; Ambassador Peter Vogler.

Syria: POB 4011, Abu Dhabi; tel. (2) 4448768; fax (2) 4449387; Ambassador Dr Rustum az-Zobi, (vacant).

Thailand: POB 47466, Abu Dhabi; tel. (2) 6421772; fax (2) 6421773; e-mail thaiauh@emirates.net.ae; Ambassador Karn Chiranond.

Tunisia: POB 4166, Abu Dhabi; tel. (2) 6811331; fax (2) 6812707; e-mail ambtunad@emirates.net.ae; Ambassador Muhammad as-Sediri.

Turkey: POB 3204, Abu Dhabi; tel. (2) 4454864; fax (2) 4452522; e-mail tcadbe@eim.ae; Ambassador Umur Apaydin.

Ukraine: POB 45714, Abu Dhabi; tel. (2) 6327586; fax (2) 6327506; e-mail emb_ae@mfa.gov.ua; internet www.oae.mfa.gov.ua/oae; Ambassador Sergiy O. Pas'ko.

United Kingdom: POB 248, Abu Dhabi; tel. (2) 6101100; fax (2) 6101586; e-mail chancery.abudhabi@fco.gov.uk; internet www.britishembassy.gov.uk/uae; Ambassador Edward Oakden.

USA: POB 4009, Abu Dhabi; tel. (2) 4142200; fax (2) 4142469; e-mail webmasterabudhabi@state.gov; internet uae.usembassy.gov; Chargé d'affaires a.i. Martin R. Quinn.

Yemen: POB 2095, Abu Dhabi; tel. (2) 4448457; fax (2) 4447978; e-mail yemenemb@emirates.net.ae; Ambassador Dr Abd al-Wahid Muhammad Farea.

Judicial System

The 95th article of the Constitution of 1971 provided for the establishment of the Union Supreme Court and Union Primary Tribunals as the judicial organs of State.

The Union has exclusive legislative and executive jurisdiction over all matters that are concerned with the strengthening of the federation, such as foreign affairs, defence and Union armed forces, security, finance, communications, traffic control, education, currency, measures, standards and weights, matters relating to nationality and emigration, Union information, etc.

The late President Sheikh Zayed signed the law establishing the new federal courts on 9 June 1978. The new law effectively transferred local judicial authorities into the jurisdiction of the federal system.

Primary tribunals in Abu Dhabi, Sharjah, Ajman and Fujairah are now primary federal tribunals, and primary tribunals in other towns in those emirates have become circuits of the primary federal tribunals.

The primary federal tribunals may sit in any of the capitals of the four emirates and have jurisdiction on all administrative disputes between the Union and individuals, whether the Union is plaintiff or defendant. Civil disputes between Union and individuals will be heard by primary federal tribunals in the defendant's place of normal residence.

The law requires that all judges take a constitutional oath before the Minister of Justice and that the courts apply the rules of *Shari'a* (Islamic religious law) and that no judgment contradicts the *Shari'a*. All employees of the old judiciaries will be transferred to the federal authority without loss of salary or seniority.

In February 1994 President Sheikh Zayed ordered that an extensive range of crimes, including murder, theft and adultery, be tried in *Shari'a* courts rather than in civil courts.

Chief Shari'a Justice: Ahmad Abd al-Aziz al-Mubarak.

Religion

ISLAM

Most of the inhabitants are Muslims of the Sunni sect, while about 16% of Muslims are Shi'ites.

CHRISTIANITY

Roman Catholic Church

Apostolic Vicariate of Arabia: POB 54, Abu Dhabi; tel. (2) 4461895; fax (2) 4465177; e-mail vicapar@emirates.net.ae; responsible for a territory covering most of the Arabian peninsula (including Saudi Arabia, the UAE, Oman, Qatar, Bahrain and Yemen), containing an estimated 1,900,000 Catholics (31 December 2007); Vicar Apostolic Bishop Paul Hinder (Vicar Apostolic of Arabia).

The Anglican Communion

Within the Episcopal Church in Jerusalem and the Middle East, the UAE forms part of the diocese of Cyprus and the Gulf. The Anglican congregations in the UAE are entirely expatriate. The Bishop in Cyprus and the Gulf resides in Cyprus, while the Archdeacon in the Gulf is resident in Bahrain.

Chaplain, St Andrew's Church: Rev. Clive Windebank, St Andrew's Church, POB 262, Abu Dhabi; tel. (2) 4461631; fax (2) 4465869; e-mail standrew@emirates.net.ae; internet www.standrewauh.org.

The Press

The state regulator for the sector is the National Media Council, under the Chairmanship of Sheikh Abdullah bin Zayed an-Nahyan (Minister of Foreign Affairs).

ABU DHABI

Abu Dhabi Magazine: POB 662, Abu Dhabi; tel. (2) 6214000; fax (2) 6348954; f. 1969; Arabic, some articles in English; monthly; Editor Zuhair al-Qadi; circ. 18,000.

Adh-Dhafra: POB 4288, Abu Dhabi; tel. (2) 6328103; Arabic; weekly; independent; publ. by Dar al-Wahdah.

The Emirates Eveningpost: Alquos Indest Area, Dubai; tel. (4) 2405588; e-mail it@eveningpost.ae; internet www.wadi.ae; f. 2004; daily (evenings); English; Editor Saira Menezes; circ. 30,000.

Emirates News: POB 791, Abu Dhabi; tel. (2) 4451446; fax (2) 4453662; e-mail emrtnews@emirates.net.ae; f. 1975; English; daily; publ. by Al-Ittihad Press, Publishing and Distribution Corpn; Chair. Sheikh Abdullah bin Zayed an-Nahyan; Man. Editor Peter Hellyer; circ. 21,150.

Hiya (She): POB 2488, Abu Dhabi; tel. (2) 4474121; Arabic; weekly for women; publ. by Dar al-Wahdah.

Al-Ittihad (Unity): POB 791, Abu Dhabi; tel. (2) 4455555; fax (2) 4455126; internet www.alittihad.ae; f. 1972; Arabic; daily and weekly; publ. by Al-Ittihad Press, Publishing and Distribution Corpn; Man. Editor Ali Abu ar-Rish; circ. 58,000 daily, 60,000 weekly.

Majed: POB 791, Abu Dhabi; tel. (2) 4451804; fax (2) 4451455; e-mail majid-magazine@emi.co.ae; internet www.emi.co.ae; Arabic; f. 1979; weekly; children's magazine; Man. Editor Ahmad Omar; circ. 145,300.

Ar-Riyada wa-Shabab (Sport and Youth): POB 2710, Dubai; tel. (4) 4444400; fax (4) 4445973; Arabic; weekly; general interest.

UAE and Abu Dhabi Official Gazette: POB 899, Abu Dhabi; tel. (2) 6660604; Arabic; daily; official reports and papers.

UAE Press Service Daily News: POB 2035, Abu Dhabi; tel. (2) 4444292; f. 1973; English; daily; Editor Rashid al-Mazroui.

Al-Wahdah (Unity): POB 2488, Abu Dhabi; tel. (2) 4478400; fax (2) 4478937; f. 1973; daily; independent; Man. Editor Rashid Aweidha; Gen. Man. Khalifa al-Mashwi; circ. 20,000.

Zahrat al-Khaleej (Splendour of the Gulf): POB 791, Abu Dhabi; tel. (2) 4461600; fax (2) 4451653; f. 1979; Arabic; weekly; publ. by Al-Ittihad Press, Publishing and Distribution Corpn; women's magazine; Editor-in-Chief Talal Tohme; circ. 10,000.

DUBAI

Akhbar Dubai (Dubai News): Department of Information, Dubai Municipality, POB 1420, Dubai; f. 1965; Arabic; weekly.

Al-Bayan (The Official Report): POB 2710, Dubai; tel. (4) 6688222; fax (4) 6688222; internet www.albayan.ae; f. 1980; owned by Dubai authorities; Arabic; daily; CEO Sami al-Qamzi; Editor-in-Chief Da'en Shahin; circ. 82,575.

Emirates Woman: POB 2331, Dubai; tel. (4) 2824060; fax (4) 2827593; e-mail annabel@motivate.co.ae; f. 1979; publ. by Motivate Publishing; English; monthly; fashion, health and beauty; Editor Annabel Kantaria; circ. 18,690.

Gulf News: Sheikh Zayed Rd, POB 6519, Dubai; tel. (4) 3447100; fax (4) 3446515; e-mail editorial@gulfnews.com; internet www.gulfnews.com; f. 1978; publ. by An-Nisr Publishing; English; daily; two weekly

THE UNITED ARAB EMIRATES

Directory

supplements, Junior News (Wed.), Gulf Weekly (Thur.); Editor-in-Chief ABD-AL HAMID AHMAD; Editor FRANCIS MATTHEW; circ. 86,900.

Al-Jundi (The Soldier): POB 2838, Dubai; tel. (4) 3433033; fax (4) 3433343; e-mail mod5@emirates.net.ae; f. 1973; Arabic; monthly; military and cultural; Editor-in-Chief Col MUHAMMAD ALI ABDULLAH AL-EASSA; circ. 5,000–7,000.

Khaleej Times: POB 11243, Dubai; tel. (4) 3383535; fax (4) 3383345; e-mail ktimes@emirates.net.ae; internet www.khaleejtimes.com; f. 1978; a Galadari enterprise; English; daily; distributed throughout the region and in India, Pakistan and the United Kingdom; free weekly supplement, Weekend (Fri.); Publr and Editor-in-Chief MUHAMMAD A. R. GALADARI; Man. Dir QASSIM MUHAMMAD YOUSUF; circ. 70,000.

Trade and Industry: POB 1457, Dubai; tel. (4) 2280000; fax (4) 2211646; e-mail dcciinfo@dcci.org; internet www.dcci.org; f. 1975; Arabic and English; monthly; publ. by Dubai Chamber of Commerce and Industry; circ. 26,000.

UAE Digest: POB 500595, Dubai; tel. (4) 3672245; fax (4) 3678613; e-mail info@sterlingp.ae; internet www.sterlingp.ae; English; monthly; publ. by Sterling Publications; current affairs; Man. Editor K. RAVEENDRAN.

Viva: POB 500024, Dubai; tel. (4) 2108000; fax (4) 2108080; e-mail viva-enquiries@itp.com; internet www.vivamagazine.ae; f. 2004; publ. by ITP; Editor MANDIE GOWER; circ. 23,000.

What's On: POB 2331, Dubai; tel. (4) 2824060; fax (4) 2824436; e-mail editor-wo@motivate.co.ae; f. 1979; publ. by Motivate Publishing; English; monthly; Exec. Editor IAN FAIRSERVICE; circ. 17,905.

RAS AL-KHAIMAH

Akhbar Ras al-Khaimah (Ras al-Khaimah News): POB 87, Ras al-Khaimah; Arabic; monthly; local news.

Al-Ghorfa: POB 87, Ras al-Khaimah; tel. (7) 2333511; fax (7) 2330233; f. 1970; Arabic and English; free monthly; publ. by Ras al-Khaimah Chamber of Commerce; Editor ZAKI H. SAQR.

Ras al-Khaimah Magazine: POB 200, Ras al-Khaimah; Arabic; monthly; commerce and trade; Chief Editor AHMAD AT-TADMORI.

SHARJAH

Al-Azman al-Arabia (Times of Arabia): POB 5823, Sharjah; tel. (6) 5356034.

The Gulf Today: POB 30, Sharjah; tel. (6) 5591919; fax (6) 5532737; e-mail tgtmkt@alkhaleej.co.ae; internet www.godubai.com/gulftoday; f. 1995; English; daily; circ. 38,000.

Al-Khaleej (The Gulf): POB 30, Sharjah; tel. (6) 5625304; fax (6) 5598547; internet www.alkhaleej.co.ae; f. 1970; Arabic; daily; political, independent; Editor GHASSAN TAHBOUB; circ. 82,750.

Sawt al-Khaleej (Voice of the Gulf): Sharjah; tel. (6) 5358003.

Ash-Sharooq (Sunrise): POB 30, Sharjah; tel. (6) 5598777; fax (6) 5599336; f. 1970; Arabic; weekly; general interest; Editor YOUSUF AL-HASSAN.

At-Tijarah (Commerce): Sharjah Chamber of Commerce and Industry, POB 580, Sharjah; tel. (6) 5116600; fax (6) 5681119; e-mail scci@sharjah.gov.ae; internet www.sharjah.gov.ae; f. 1970; Arabic/English; monthly magazine; circ. 50,000; annual trade directory; circ. 100,000.

NEWS AGENCIES

Emirates News Agency (WAM): POB 3790, Abu Dhabi; tel. (2) 4454545; fax (2) 4044200; e-mail wamnews@eim.ae; internet www.wam.org.ae; f. 1977; operated by the Govt; Dir-Gen. IBRAHIM AL-ABED.

UAE Press Service: POB 2035, Abu Dhabi; tel. (2) 6820424.

Publishers

All Prints: POB 857, Abu Dhabi; tel. (2) 6336999; fax (2) 6320844; e-mail allprints@allprints.co.ae; internet web.allprints.ae; f. 1968; publishing and distribution; Partners BUSHRA KHAYAT, TAHSEEN S. KHAYAT.

ITP: POB 500024, Dubai; tel. (4) 2108000; fax (4) 2108080; e-mail info@itp.com; internet www.itp.com.

Al-Ittihad Press, Publishing and Distribution Corpn: POB 791, New Airport Rd, Abu Dhabi; tel. (2) 4455555; fax (2) 4451653; Chair. KHALFAN BIN MUHAMMAD AR-ROUMI.

Motivate Publishing: POB 2331, Dubai; tel. (4) 2824060; fax (4) 2820428; e-mail motivate@motivate.ae; internet www.motivatepublishing.com; f. 1979; books and magazines; Man. Partner and Group Editor IAN FAIRSERVICE.

Sterling Publications: POB 500595, Dubai; tel. (4) 3672245; fax (4) 3678613; e-mail info@sterlingp.ae; internet www.sterlingp.ae; magazines; Publr and Man. Dir SANKARANARAYANAN; Man. Editor K. RAVEENDRAN.

Broadcasting and Communications

TELECOMMUNICATIONS

Telecommunications Regulatory Authority (TRA): POB 26662, Abu Dhabi; tel. (2) 6212222; fax (2) 6212227; e-mail info@tra.ae; internet www.tra.ae; f. 2004; Chair. MUHAMMAD BIN AHMAD AL-QAMZI; Dir-Gen. MUHAMMAD AL-GHANEM.

Emirates Integrated Telecommunications Co (du): POB 502666, Dubai; tel. (4) 3600000; fax (4) 3604440; e-mail talk-to-us@du.ae; internet www.du.ae; f. 2006; commenced operations under the brand name 'du' in Feb. 2007; 40% owned by the federal Govt, 20% by Mubadala Development Co, 40% by TECOM Investment and 20% by public shareholders; provides telecommunications services throughout the UAE; Chair. AHMAD BIN BYAT; CEO OSMAN SULTAN.

Emirates Telecommunications Corpn (Etisalat): POB 300, Abu Dhabi; tel. (2) 6333111; fax (2) 6344432; e-mail prd@etisalat.co.ae; internet www.etisalat.co.ae; provides telecommunications services throughout the UAE; Pres. and CEO MUHAMMAD OMRAN.

BROADCASTING

Radio

Abu Dhabi Radio: Abu Dhabi; tel. (2) 4451111; fax (2) 4451155; f. 1968; broadcasts in Arabic over a wide area; also broadcasts in French, Bengali, Filipino and Urdu; Dir-Gen. ABD AL-WAHAB AR-RADWAN.

Capital Radio: POB 63, Abu Dhabi; tel. (2) 4451000; fax (2) 4451155; English-language FM music and news station, govt-operated; Station Man. AIDA HAMZA.

Dubai Radio and Colour Television: POB 1695, Dubai; tel. (4) 3370255; fax (4) 3374111; broadcasts domestic Arabic and European programmes; Chair. Sheikh HASHER MAKTOUM; Dir-Gen. ABD AL-GHAFOOR SAID IBRAHIM.

Ras al-Khaimah Broadcasting Station: POB 141, Ras al-Khaimah; tel. (7) 2851151; fax (7) 2353441; two transmitters broadcast in Arabic and Urdu; Dir Sheikh ABD AL-AZIZ BIN HUMAID.

Sharjah Broadcasting Station: POB 155, Sharjah; broadcasts in Arabic and French.

UAE Radio and Television—Dubai: POB 1695, Dubai; tel. (4) 3369999; fax (4) 3374111; e-mail dubairtv@emirates.net.ae; broadcasts in Arabic and English to the USA, India and Pakistan, the Far East, Australia and New Zealand, Europe and North and East Africa; Chair. Sheikh HASHEM MAKTOUM; Dir-Gen. AHMAD SAID AL-GAOUD; Controller of Radio HASSAN AHMAD.

Umm al-Qaiwain Broadcasting Station: POB 444, Umm al-Qaiwain; tel. (6) 7666044; fax (6) 7666055; e-mail uaqfm@emirates.net.ae; f. 1978; broadcasts music and news in Arabic, Malayalam, Sinhala and Urdu; Gen. Man. ALI JASSEM.

Television

Dubai Radio and Colour Television: see Radio.

UAE Radio and Television—Dubai: see Radio; Controller of Programmes NASIB BITAR.

UAE TV—Abu Dhabi: POB 637, Abu Dhabi; tel. (2) 4452000; fax (2) 4451470; f. 1968; broadcasts programmes incorporating information, entertainment, religion, culture, news and politics; Dir-Gen. ALI OBAID.

UAE Television—Sharjah: POB 111, Sharjah; tel. (6) 5361111; fax (6) 5541755; f. 1989; broadcasts in Arabic and Urdu in the northern emirates; Executive Dir MUHAMMAD DIAB AL-MUSA.

Finance

(cap. = capital; res = reserves; dep. = deposits; m. = million; brs = branches; amounts in dirhams, unless otherwise indicated)

BANKING

Central Bank

Central Bank of the United Arab Emirates: POB 854, Abu Dhabi; tel. (2) 6652220; fax (2) 6667494; e-mail admin@cbuae.gov.ae; internet www.centralbank.ae; f. 1973; acts as issuing authority for local currency; superseded UAE Currency Board in Dec. 1980; cap. 300.0m., res 1,260.0m., dep. 57,579.8m. (Dec. 2005); Chair.

Muhammad Eid al-Muraikhi; Gov. Sultan bin Nasser as-Suwaidi; 6 brs.

Principal Banks

Abu Dhabi Commercial Bank (ADCB): POB 939, Abu Dhabi; tel. (2) 6962222; fax (2) 6450384; e-mail info@adcb.com; internet www.adcb.com; f. 1985 by merger; 65% govt-owned, 35% owned by private investors; cap. 4,000m., res 5,315.5m., dep. 51,367.0m. (Dec. 2006); Chair. Said Mubarak Rashid al-Hajeri; CEO Eirvin Knox; 40 brs in the UAE, 2 in India.

Abu Dhabi Islamic Bank: POB 313, As-Sultan Tower, Baniyas St (Najda), Abu Dhabi; tel. (2) 6100600; fax (2) 6654340; e-mail adib@adib.co.ae; internet www.e-adib.com; f. 1997; cap. 1,000.0m., res 747.6m., dep. 19,733.1m. (Dec. 2005); Chair. Majid Salem Khalifa ar-Romaithi; Man. Dir Khamis Buharoon.

Arab Emirates Investment Bank PJSC: POB 5503, Office 904, Twin Towers, Baniyas St, Deira, Dubai; tel. (4) 2222191; fax (4) 2274351; e-mail aeibank@emirates.net.ae; internet www.aeibank.com; f. 1976 as Arab Emirate Investment Bank Ltd; name changed as above in 2000; cap. 40.9m., res 323.9m., dep. 244.5m. (Dec. 2005); Chair. Omar Abdullah al-Futtaim; Gen. Man. and CEO Kalim ar-Rahman.

Bank of Sharjah Ltd: POB 1394, Sharjah; tel. (6) 5694411; fax (6) 5694422; e-mail bankshj@emirates.net.ae; internet www.bankofsharjah.com; f. 1973; cap. 1,000m., res 905.0m., dep. 3,721.9m. (Dec. 2005); Chair. Ahmad an-Noman; Gen. Man. Varouj Nerguizian; brs in Abu Dhabi, Dubai and Al-Ain.

Commercial Bank of Dubai PSC: POB 2668, Mankhool St, Dubai; tel. (4) 2121000; fax (4) 2121911; e-mail cbd-ho@cbd.ae; internet www.cbd.ae; f. 1969; 20% owned by Govt of Dubai; cap. 627.5m., res 2,145.4m., dep. 11,790.2m. (Dec. 2005); Chair. Ahmad Humaid at-Tayer; CEO Peter Baltussen; 16 brs.

Commercial Bank International PSC: POB 4449, Ar-Riqah St, Dubai; tel. (4) 2275265; fax (4) 2279038; e-mail cbiho@emirates.net.ae; internet www.cbiuae.com; f. 1991; cap. 299.1m., res 171.7m., dep. 4,066.4m. (Dec. 2005); Chair. Hamad Abdullah al-Mutawaa; CEO Khamis Buharoom; 9 brs.

Dubai Bank PJSC: POB 65555, Sheikh Zayed Rd, Dubai; e-mail info@dubaibank.ae; internet www.dubaibank.ae; tel. (4) 3328989; fax (4) 3290071; f. 2002 by Emaar Properties, a real estate developer; cap. 500.0m., res 35.5m., dep. 3,919.0m. (Dec. 2005); Chair. Muhammad ash-Shaibani; CEO Abd al-Aziz al-Muhairi.

Dubai Islamic Bank PJSC: POB 1080, Airport Rd, Deira, Dubai; tel. (4) 2953000; fax (4) 2954111; e-mail contactus@alislami.ae; internet www.alislami.ae; f. 1975; cap. 2,800.0m., res 5,694.0m., dep. 52,382.4m. (Dec. 2006); Chair. Dr Muhammad Khalfan bin Kharbash; Man. Dir Khaled al-Kamda; 44 brs.

Emirates Islamic Bank PJSC: POB 5547, Beniyas Rd, Deira, Dubai; tel. (4) 2287474; fax (4) 2272172; e-mail info@emiratesislamicbank.ae; internet www.emiratesislamicbank.ae; f. 1976 as Middle East Bank; became a Public Joint Stock Co (PJSC) in 1995; changed name as above in 2004; subsidiary (99.8% owned) of Emirates Bank Int.; cap. 650.0m., res 188.7m., dep. 9,102.1m. (Dec. 2006); Chair. Sayed Muhammad Rashid ash-Sharid; CEO Ibrahim Fayez ash-Shamsi; 16 brs.

Emirates NBD PJSC: POB 2923, Beniyas Rd, Deira, Dubai; tel. (4) 2256256; fax (4) 2227662; e-mail saeedy@emiratesbank.com; internet www.emiratesbank.com; f. 2007 by merger of Emirates Bank International PJSC with National Bank of Dubai PJSC; 56% owned by Govt of Dubai; total assets 254,000m. (Dec. 2007); Chair. Ahmad Humaid at-Tayer; CEO Rick Pudner.

First Gulf Bank: POB 6316, Sheikh Zayed St, Abu Dhabi; tel. (2) 6816666; fax (2) 6814282; e-mail info@fgb.ae; internet www.fgb.ae; f. 1979; cap. 1,250.0m., res 6,739.0m., dep. 34,731.8m. (Dec. 2006); Chair. Sheikh Mansour bin Zayed an-Nahyan; CEO Abd al-Hamid Said; 5 brs.

Investbank PSC: POB 1885, Sharjah; tel. (6) 5693030; fax (6) 5694442; e-mail custserv@invest-bank.com; internet www.invest-bank.com; f. 1975; cap. 1,000.0m., res 313.1m., dep. 4,761.3m. (Dec. 2006); Chair. Dr Abdullah Omran Taryam; Gen. Man. Sami R. Farhat; 7 brs.

Mashreqbank PSC: POB 1250, Omer bin al-Khattab St, Deira, Dubai; tel. (4) 2223333; fax (4) 2226061; internet www.mashreqbank.com; f. 1967 as Bank of Oman; name changed as above in 1993; cap. 866.2m., res 954.2m., dep. 41,644.3m. (Dec. 2006); Chair. Abdullah bin Ahmad al-Ghurair; CEO Abd al-Aziz Abdullah al-Ghurair; 36 brs in the UAE, 6 abroad.

Al-Masraf: POB 46733, ARBIFT Bldg, Hamdan St, Tourist Club Area, Abu Dhabi; tel. (2) 6721900; fax (2) 6777550; e-mail arbiftho@emirates.net.ae; internet www.arbift.com; f. 1976 as Arab Bank for Investment and Foreign Trade; renamed as above in 2007; jointly owned by the UAE Govt, the Libyan Arab Foreign Bank and the Banque Extérieure d'Algérie; cap. 660.0m., res 760.7m., dep. 5,155.5m. (Dec. 2006); Pres. and Chair. Dr Abd al-Hafid M. Zlitni; Gen. Man. Ibrahim Nasser Rashid Lootah; 7 brs in the UAE.

National Bank of Abu Dhabi (NBAD): POB 4, Tariq ibn Ziad St, Abu Dhabi; tel. (2) 6111111; fax (2) 6655329; e-mail CustomerSupport@nbad.com; internet www.nbad.com; f. 1968; 73% owned by Abu Dhabi Investment Council, 3% by foreign institutions and the remainder by UAE citizens; cap. 1,224.1m., res 7,131.2m., dep. 82,816.6m. (Dec. 2006); Chair. Khalifa Muhammad al-Kindi; CEO Michael H. Tomalin; 60 brs in the UAE, 19 abroad.

National Bank of Fujairah PSC: POB 887, Hamad bin Abdullah St, Fujairah; tel. (9) 2224518; fax (9) 2224516; e-mail nbfho@nbf.ae; internet www.nbf.ae; f. 1982; owned jointly by Govt of Fujairah (36.78%), Govt of Dubai (9.78%), and UAE citizens and cos (51.25%); cap. 1,000.0m., res 486.6m., dep. 6,424.0m. (Dec. 2006); Chair. Sheikh Saleh bin Muhammad ash-Sharqi; Gen. Man. Asad Ahmed; 6 brs.

National Bank of Ras al-Khaimah PSC (RAKBANK): POB 5300, Rakbank Bldg, Oman St, al-Nakheel, Ras al-Khaimah; tel. (7) 2281127; fax (7) 2283238; e-mail nbrakho@emirates.net.ae; internet www.rakbank.ae; f. 1976; 52.75% owned by Govt of Ras al-Khaimah; cap. 536.3m., res 476.2m., dep. 7.366.3m. (Dec. 2006); Chair. Sheikh Omar bin Saqr al-Qasimi; Gen. Man. Graham Honeybill; 16 brs.

National Bank of Umm al-Qaiwain PSC: POB 800, Umm al-Qaiwain Private Properties Dept Bldg, King Faisal St, Umm al-Qaiwain; tel. (6) 7655225; fax (6) 7655440; e-mail nbuq@nbq.ae; internet www.nbq.ae; f. 1982; cap. 600.0m., res 520.1m., dep. 3,429.7m. (Dec. 2006); Chair. Sheikh Sa'ud bin Rashid al-Mu'alla; Man. Dir and CEO Sheikh Nasser bin Rashid al-Mu'alla; 12 brs.

Sharjah Islamic Bank: POB 4, Al-Borj Ave, Sharjah; tel. (6) 5681000; fax (6) 5680101; e-mail sibmail@sib.ae; internet www.sib.ae; f. 1976 as National Bank of Sharjah; name changed as above in 2005, reflecting the bank's conversion to *Shari'a*-compliant operations; commercial bank; cap. 1,100m., res 789.3m., dep. 4,506.1m. (Dec. 2006); Chair. Sheikh Sultan bin Muhammad bin Sultan al-Qassimi; CEO Muhammad Ahmad Abdullah; 13 brs.

Union National Bank: POB 3865, Salam St, Abu Dhabi; tel. (2) 6741600; fax (2) 6786080; e-mail feedback@unb.ae; internet www.unb.co.ae; f. 1983; fmrly Bank of Credit and Commerce (Emirates); cap. 1,562.5m., res 2,283.4m., dep. 30,568.7m. (Dec. 2006); Chair. Sheikh Nahyan bin Mubarak an-Nahyan; CEO Muhammad Nasr Abdeen; 26 brs in the UAE.

United Arab Bank: POB 25022, 6th Floor, HE Sheikh Abdullah bin Salem al-Qassimi Bldg, al-Qassimi St, Sharjah; tel. (6) 5733900; fax (6) 5733907; e-mail uarbae@emirates.net.ae; internet www.uab.ae; f. 1975; affiliated to Société Générale, France; 35% owned by Commercial Bank of Qatar; cap. 635.5m., res 457.3m., dep. 3,601.4m. (Dec. 2006); Chair. Sheikh Faisal bin Sultan bin Salem al-Qassimi; CEO Bertrand Giraud; 9 brs.

Development Bank

Emirates Industrial Bank: POB 2722, 6th Floor, Arab Monetary Fund Bldg, Corniche Rd, Abu Dhabi; tel. (2) 6339700; fax (2) 6319191; e-mail projects_auh@emiratesindustrialbank.net; internet www.emiratesindustrialbank.net; f. 1982; offers low-cost loans to enterprises with at least 51% local ownership; 51% state-owned; cap. 200m.; Chair. Muhammad Khalfan Khirbash; Gen. Man. Muhammad Abd al-Baki Muhammad.

Bankers' Association

United Arab Emirates Bankers' Association: POB 44307, Abu Dhabi; tel. (2) 6272541; fax (2) 6274155; e-mail ebauae@emirates.net.ae; internet www.eba-ae.com; f. 1983; Chair. Abdullah Ahmad al-Ghurair (Chair., Mashreqbank PSC); Gen. Man. Fathi M. Skaik.

STOCK EXCHANGES

Abu Dhabi Securities Market (ADSM): POB 54500, Abu Dhabi; tel. (2) 6277777; fax (2) 6128782; e-mail info@adsm.co.ae; internet www.adsm.co.ae; f. 2000; Chair. Nasser Ahmad as-Suwaidi; Dir-Gen. Tom Healy.

Dubai Financial Market (DFM): POB 9700, Dubai; tel. (4) 3055555; fax (4) 3314924; e-mail helpdesk@dfm.co.ae; internet www.dfm.co.ae; f. 2000; restructured to comply with *Shari'a* principles in 2006; 14 listed cos, two bonds, six mutual funds; market capitalization AED 61,370m. (Feb. 2004); Dir-Gen. Essa Abd al-Fattah Kazim.

Dubai International Financial Exchange (DIFX): POB 53536, Level 7, The Exchange Bldg, Gate District, Dubai International Financial Centre, Dubai; tel. (4) 3612222; fax (4) 3612130; e-mail contact@difx.ae; internet www.difx.ae; f. 2005; Chair. Soud Ba'alawy.

THE UNITED ARAB EMIRATES   Directory

INSURANCE

Abu Dhabi National Insurance Co (ADNIC): POB 839, Abu Dhabi; tel. (2) 6264000; fax (2) 6268600; e-mail adnic@adnic.ae; internet www.adnic.ae; f. 1972; subscribed 25% by the Govt of Abu Dhabi and 75% by UAE nationals; all classes of insurance; Chair. KHALIFA MUHAMMAD AL-KINDI.

Al-Ahlia Insurance Co: POB 128, Ras al-Khaimah; tel. (7) 2221479; f. 1977; Chair. Sheikh OMAR BIN ABDULLAH AL-QASSIMI; 3 brs.

Al-Ain Ahlia Insurance Co: POB 3077, Abu Dhabi; tel. (2) 4459900; fax (2) 4456685; e-mail alainins@emirates.net.ae; internet www.alaininsurance.com; f. 1975; Chair. MUHAMMAD BIN J. R. AL-BADIE ADH-DHAHIRI; Gen. Man. MUHAMMAD MAZHAR HAMADEH; brs in Dubai, Sharjah, Tarif, Ghouifat and al-Ain.

Dubai Insurance Co PSC: POB 3027, Dubai; tel. (4) 2693030; fax (4) 2693727; e-mail dubins@emirates.net.ae; f. 1970; Chair. MAJID AL-FUTTAIM.

Sharjah Insurance Co: POB 792, Sharjah; tel. (6) 5686690; fax (6) 5686545; e-mail sirco@emirates.net.ae; f. 1970; Gen. Man. MUHAMMAD FAWZI NAJI.

Union Insurance Co: POB 3196, Abu Dhabi; POB 460, Umm al-Qaiwain; POB 4623, Dubai; tel. (6) 666223; Gen. Man. L. F. DOKOV.

Trade and Industry

DEVELOPMENT ORGANIZATIONS

Abu Dhabi Development Finance Corpn: POB 814, Abu Dhabi; tel. (2) 6441000; fax (2) 6440800; e-mail opadfdmn@emirates.net.ae; provides finance to the private sector; Chair. Sheikh KHALIFA BIN ZAYED AN-NAHYAN; Dir-Gen. SAID KHALFAN MATAR AR-ROMAITHI.

Abu Dhabi Fund for Development (ADFD): POB 814, as-Salam St, Abu Dhabi; tel. (2) 6441000; fax (2) 6440800; e-mail opadfdmn@emirates.net.ae; f. 1971; offers economic aid to other Arab states and other developing countries in support of their development; cap. AED 4,000m.; Dir-Gen. SAID KHALFAN MATAR AR-ROMAITHI.

Abu Dhabi Investment Company (ADIC): POB 46309, Abu Dhabi; tel. (2) 6658100; fax (2) 6650575; e-mail adic@emirates.net.ae; internet www.adic.ae; f. 1977; investment and merchant banking activities in the UAE and abroad; 98% owned by ADIC and 2% by National Bank of Abu Dhabi; total assets AED 5,947m. (1997); Chair. KHALIFA M. AL-KINDI; CEO JASEM S. AZ-ZAABI.

Abu Dhabi Investment Council (ADIC): POB 3600, Abu Dhabi; tel. (2) 4150000; fax (2) 4151100; f. 2006 as successor to Abu Dhabi Investment Authority (f. 1976); responsible for co-ordinating Abu Dhabi's investment policy; Chair. Sheikh KHALIFA BIN ZAYED AN-NAHYAN; 1 br. overseas.

Abu Dhabi Planning Department: POB 12, Abu Dhabi; tel. (2) 6727200; fax (2) 6727749; f. 1974; supervises Abu Dhabi's Development Programme; Chair. MUSALLAM SAID ABDULLAH AL-QUBAISI; Under-Sec. AHMAD M. HILAL AL-MAZRUI.

Dubai Development and Investment Authority (DDIA): Dubai; CEO MUHAMMAD AL-GARGAWI.

Dubai Holding: Dubai; internet www.dubaiholding.com; f. 2004; supervises major construction projects in Dubai; cap. AED 25,000m. (Oct. 2004); CEO MUHAMMAD BIN ABDULLAH AL-GARGAWI.

General Industry Corpn (GIC): POB 4499, Abu Dhabi; tel. (2) 6214900; fax (2) 6325034; e-mail info@gic.co; f. 1979; responsible for the promotion of non-petroleum-related industry; Chair. Sheikh HAMAD BIN TAHNOON AN-NAHYAN; Dep. Dir-Gen. SUHAIL MUHAMMAD AL-AMERI.

International Petroleum Investment Co (IPIC): POB 7528, Abu Dhabi; tel. (2) 6336200; fax (2) 6216045; f. 1984; cap. US $200m.; state-owned venture to develop overseas investments in energy and energy-related projects; Chair. Sheikh MANSUR BIN ZAYED AN-NAHYAN; Man. Dir KHADEM AL-QUBAISI.

CHAMBERS OF COMMERCE

Federation of UAE Chambers of Commerce and Industry: POB 3014, Abu Dhabi; tel. (2) 6214144; fax (2) 6339210; e-mail fcciauh@emirates.net.ae; internet www.fcci.gov.ae; POB 8886, Dubai; tel. (4) 2212977; fax (4) 2235498; e-mail fccidxb@emirates.net.ae; internet www.fcci-uae.com; f. 1976; seven mem. chambers; Chair. ABDULLAH RAHED AL-KHARJI; Sec.-Gen. ABDULLAH SULTAN ABDULLAH.

Abu Dhabi Chamber of Commerce and Industry: POB 662, Abu Dhabi; tel. (2) 6214000; fax (2) 6215867; e-mail services@adcci.gov.ae; internet www.adcci-uae.com; f. 1969; 45,000 mems; Pres. SALAH SALEM BIN OMAIR ASH-SHAMSI; Dir-Gen. AHMAD HASSAN AL-MANSOURI (acting).

Ajman Chamber of Commerce and Industry: POB 662, Ajman; tel. (6) 7422177; fax (6) 7427591; e-mail info@ajcci.gov.ae; internet www.ajcci.gov.ae; f. 1977; Chair. KHALIFA MUHAMMAD AL-MOAJEY; Dir-Gen. MUHAMMAD AL-HAMRANI.

Dubai Chamber of Commerce and Industry: POB 1457, Dubai; tel. (4) 2280000; fax (4) 2211646; e-mail dcci@dcci.gov.ae; internet www.dcci.org; f. 1965; 87,829 mems; Chair. OBAID HUMAID AT-TAYER; Dir-Gen. HAMAD BUAIMIM.

Fujairah Chamber of Commerce, Industry and Agriculture: POB 738, Fujairah; tel. (9) 2222400; fax (9) 2221464; e-mail fujccia@emirates.net.ae; Pres. SAID ALI KHAMAS; Dir-Gen. SHAHEEN ALI SHAHEEN.

Ras al-Khaimah Chamber of Commerce, Industry and Agriculture: POB 87, Ras al-Khaimah; tel. (7) 2333511; fax (7) 2330233; e-mail a.alshayeb@rakchamber.ae; internet www.rakchamber.com/English/index.htm; f. 1967; 17,840 mems (Dec. 2007); Chair. YOUSUF AL-NEAIMI; Dir-Gen. Dr ABD AL-RAHMAN ASH-SHAYEB AN-NAQPI.

Sharjah Chamber of Commerce and Industry: POB 580, Sharjah; tel. (6) 5116600; fax (6) 5681119; e-mail scci@sharjah.gov.ae; internet www.sharjah.gov.ae; f. 1970; 33,500 mems; Chair. AHMAD MUHAMMAD AL-MIDFA'A; Dir-Gen. SAID OBAID AL-JARWAN.

Umm al-Qaiwain Chamber of Commerce and Industry: POB 436, Umm al-Qaiwain; tel. (6) 7656915; fax (6) 7657056; Pres. ABDULLAH RASHID AL-KHARJI; Man. Dir SHAKIR AZ-ZAYANI.

STATE HYDROCARBONS COMPANIES

Abu Dhabi

Supreme Petroleum Council: POB 898, Abu Dhabi; tel. (2) 602000; fax (2) 6023389; f. 1988; assumed authority and responsibility for the administration and supervision of all petroleum affairs in Abu Dhabi; Chair. Sheikh KHALIFA BIN ZAYED AN-NAHYAN; Sec.-Gen. YOUSUF BIN OMEIR BIN YOUSUF.

Abu Dhabi National Oil Co (ADNOC): POB 898, Abu Dhabi; tel. (2) 6020000; fax (2) 6023389; e-mail adnoc@adnoc.com; internet www.adnoc.com; f. 1971; cap. AED 7,500m.; state company; deals in all phases of oil industry; owns two refineries: one on Umm an-Nar island and one at Ruwais; Habshan Gas Treatment Plant (scheduled for partial privatization); gas pipeline distribution network; a salt and chlorine plant; holds 60% participation in operations of ADMA-OPCO and ADCO, and 88% of ZADCO; has 100% control of Abu Dhabi National Oil Co for Oil Distribution (ADNOC-FOD), Abu Dhabi National Tanker Co (ADNATCO), National Drilling Co (NDC) and interests in numerous other companies, both in the UAE and overseas; ADNOC is operated by Supreme Petroleum Council, Chair. Sheikh KHALIFA BIN ZAYED AN-NAHYAN; CEO YOUSUF BIN OMEIR BIN YOUSUF.

Subsidiaries include:

Abu Dhabi Co for Onshore Oil Operations (ADCO): POB 270, Abu Dhabi; tel. (2) 6040000; fax (2) 6669785; shareholders are ADNOC (60%), British Petroleum, Shell and Total (9.5% each), Exxon and Mobil (4.75% each) and Partex (2%); oil exploration, production and export operations from onshore oilfields; average production (1990): 1.2m. b/d; Chair. YOUSUF BIN OMEIR BIN YOUSUF; Gen. Man. ANDRE VAN STRIJP.

Abu Dhabi Drilling Chemicals and Products Ltd (ADDCAP): POB 46121, Abu Dhabi; tel. (2) 6029000; fax (2) 6029010; e-mail addcap@emirates.net.ae; f. 1975; production of drilling chemicals and provision of marine services; wholly-owned subsidiary of ADNOC; Chair. YOUSUF BIN OMEIR BIN YOUSUF; Gen. Man. MAHFOUD A. DARBOUL ASH-SHEHHI.

Abu Dhabi Gas Industries Co (GASCO): POB 665, Abu Dhabi; tel. (2) 6030000; fax (2) 6037414; e-mail info@gasco.ae; internet www.gasco.ae; f. 1978; started production in 1981; recovers condensate and LPG from Asab, Bab and Bu Hasa fields for delivery to Ruwais natural gas liquids fractionation plant; capacity of 22,000 metric tons per day; ADNOC has a 68% share; Total, Shell Gas and Partex have a minority interest; Chair. YOUSUF OMEIR BIN YOUSUF; Gen. Man. MUHAMMAD A. SAHOO.

Abu Dhabi Gas Liquefaction Co (ADGAS): POB 3500, Abu Dhabi; tel. (2) 6061111; fax (2) 6065500; e-mail info@adgas.com; internet www.adgas.com; f. 1973; owned by ADNOC, 70%; Mitsui and Co, 15%; British Petroleum (BP), 10%; Total, 5%; operates LGSC and the LNG plant on Das Island which uses natural gas produced in association with oil from offshore fields and has a design capacity of approx. 2.3m. metric tons of LNG per year and 1.29m. tons of LPG per year; the liquefied gas is sold to the Tokyo Electric Power Co, Japan; Chair. A. N. AS-SUWEIDI; Gen. Man. SAIF AHMAD AL-GHAFLI.

Abu Dhabi Marine Operating Co (ADMA-OPCO): POB 303, Abu Dhabi; tel. (2) 6060000; fax (2) 6065062; operates a concession 60% owned by ADNOC, 40% by Abu Dhabi Marine Areas Ltd; f. 1977 as an operator for the concession; production (1984): 67,884,769 barrels (8,955,721 metric tons); Chair. YOUSUF BIN OMEIR BIN YOUSUF; Gen. Man. HENRY BACCONNIER.

Abu Dhabi Oil Refining Co (TAKREER): POB 3593, Abu Dhabi; tel. (2) 6027000; fax (2) 6027001; e-mail publicrelation@takreer.com; internet www.takreer.com; refining of crude oil; production of chlorine and related chemicals; Chair. YOUSUF BIN OMEIR BIN YOUSUF; Gen. Man. ALI SAEED AL-BADI.

ADNOC Distribution: POB 4188, Abu Dhabi; tel. (2) 6771300; fax (2) 6722322; e-mail Information@adnoc-dist.ae; internet www.adnoc-dist.ae; 100% owned by ADNOC; distributes petroleum products in UAE and world-wide; Chair. YOUSUF BIN OMEIR BIN YOUSUF; Gen. Man. JAMAL JABER ADH-DHAREEF.

National Drilling Co (NDC): POB 4017, Abu Dhabi; tel. (2) 6316600; fax (2) 6317045; e-mail ndcisc@emirates.net.ae; drilling operations; Chair. ABDULLAH NASSER AS-SUWAIDI; Gen. Man. NAJEEB HASSAN AZ-ZAABI.

National Petroleum Construction Co (NPCC): POB 2058, Abu Dhabi; tel. (2) 5549000; fax (2) 5549111; e-mail npccnet@eim.ae; internet www.npcc.ae; f. 1973; 'turnkey' construction and maintenance of offshore facilities for the petroleum and gas industries; cap. AED 100m.; Chair. HUSSAIN JASEM AN-NOWAIS; CEO AQEEL A. MADHI.

Ajman

Ajman National Oil Co (AJNOC): POB 410, Ajman; tel. (6) 7421218; f. 1983; 50% govt-owned, 50% held by Canadian and private Arab interests.

Dubai

DUGAS (Dubai Natural Gas Co Ltd): POB 4311, Dubai (Location: Jebel Ali); tel. (4) 3846000; fax (4) 3846118; wholly owned by Dubai authorities; Dep. Chair. and Dir SULTAN AHMAD BIN SULAYEM.

Dubai Petroleum Establishment: POB 2222, Dubai; tel. (4) 3846000; fax (4) 3846118; internet dubaipetroleum.ae; responsible for managing Dubai's offshore petroleum assets; wholly owned by Dubai authorities.

Emirates General Petroleum Corpn (Emarat): POB 9400, Dubai; tel. (4) 3434444; fax (4) 3433393; e-mail info@emarat.ae; internet www.emarat.ae; f. 1981; wholly owned by Ministry of Finance and Industry; distribution of petroleum; Chair. MUHAMMAD BIN DHAEN AL-HAMILI; Gen. Man. RASHID ASH-SHAMSI.

Emirates National Oil Co (ENOC): POB 6442, ENOC Complex, Sheikh Rashid Rd, Dubai; tel. (4) 3374400; fax (4) 3134702; e-mail webmaster@enoc.com; internet www.enoc.com; f. 1993; responsible for management of Dubai-owned cos in petroleum-marketing sector; Chief Exec. HUSSAIN M. SULTAN.

Emirates Petroleum Products Co Pvt. Ltd: POB 5589, Dubai; tel. (4) 372131; fax (4) 3031605; f. 1980; jt venture between Govt of Dubai and Caltex Alkhaleej Marketing; sales of petroleum products, bunkering fuel and bitumen; Chair. Sheikh HAMDAN BIN RASHID AL-MAKTOUM.

Sedco-Houston Oil Group: POB 702, Dubai; tel. (4) 3224141; holds onshore concession of over 400,000 ha as well as the offshore concession fmrly held by Texas Pacific Oil; Pres. CARL F. THORNE.

Sharjah

A Supreme Petroleum Council was established in Sharjah in 1999; it was to assume the responsibilities of the Petroleum and Mineral Affairs Department.

Petroleum and Mineral Affairs Department: POB 188, Sharjah; tel. (6) 5541888; Dir ISMAIL A. WAHID.

Sharjah Liquefied Petroleum Gas Co (SHALCO): POB 787, Sharjah; tel. (6) 5286333; fax (6) 5286111; e-mail shalco@shalco.ae; f. 1984; gas processing; producer of liquified commercial propane and commercial butane; 60% owned by Sharjah authorities, 25% BP Sharjah LPG Co, 7.5% each Itochu Corpn and Tokyo Boeki of Japan; Gen. Man. SALEH AL-ALI.

Umm al-Qaiwain

Petroleum and Mineral Affairs Department: POB 9, Umm al-Qaiwain; tel. (6) 7666034; Chair. Sheikh SULTAN BIN AHMAD AL-MU'ALLA.

UTILITIES

Abu Dhabi

Abu Dhabi Water and Electricity Authority (ADWEA): POB 6120, Abu Dhabi; tel. (2) 6943333; fax (2) 6943491; e-mail webmaster@adwea.gov.ae; internet www.adwea.gov.ae; f. 1999 to oversee the privatization of the water and electricity sectors; Chair. Sheikh DIAB BIN ZAYED AN-NAHYAN.

    Abu Dhabi Distribution Co: POB 219, Abu Dhabi; tel. (2) 6423000; fax (2) 6426033; e-mail contactcenter@addc.ae; internet www.addc.ae; f. 1999; distribution of water and electricity; Chair. Sheikh DIAB BIN ZAYED AN-NAHYAN.

Abu Dhabi National Energy Co (TAQA): POB 55224, Abu Dhabi; tel. (2) 6943662; fax (2) 6422555; e-mail info@taqa.ae; internet www.taqa.ae; f. 2005; 51% owned by Abu Dhabi Water and Electricity Authority; owns assets in power, water, petroleum and mineral sectors in the UAE and abroad; provides more than 85% of the water and electricity produced in Abu Dhabi; CEO PETER BARKER-HOMEK.

Abu Dhabi Transmission and Dispatch Co: POB 173, Abu Dhabi; tel. (2) 6414000; fax (2) 6426333; internet www.transco.ae; f. 1999.

Abu Dhabi Water and Electricity Co (ADWEC): POB 51111, Abu Dhabi; tel. (2) 6943333; fax (2) 6425773; e-mail webmaster@adwec.ae; internet www.adwec.ae; f. 1999; Chair. Sheikh DHIYAB BIN ZAYED AN-NAHYAN.

Al-Ain Distribution Co: POB 1065, al-Ain; tel. (3) 7636000; fax (3) 7632025; e-mail customercare@aadc.ae; internet www.aadc.ae; f. 1999; distribution of water and electricity; Chair. Sheikh DIAB BIN ZAYED AN-NAHYAN.

Bayounah Power Co: POB 33477, Abu Dhabi; tel. (2) 6731100; fax (2) 6730403; internet www.bpc.ae; f. 1999; Chair. AHMAD HILAL AL-KUWAITI; Man. Dir ABD AL-JALEEL AL-KHOURY.

Al-Mirfa Power Co: POB 32277, Abu Dhabi; tel. (2) 8833044; fax (2) 8833011; e-mail info@ampc.ae; internet www.ampc.ae; f. 1999 to control Mirfa and Madinat Zayed plants; capacity 300 MW electricity per day, 37m. gallons water per day; Chair. ABDULLAH AL-AHBABI; Gen. Man. PHILIP GRAHAM TILSON.

Emirates CMS Power Co: POB 47688, Abu Dhabi; tel. (2) 5067100; fax (2) 5067157; e-mail zgdesouza@cmsenergy.com; internet www.adwea.gov.ae/ecpc; f. 1999; owns and operates the Al-Taweelah 'A2' plant; Man. Dir BRIAN S. JACKSON.

Taweelah Asia Power Co (TAPCO): POB 32255, Abu Dhabi; tel. (2) 5627000; fax (2) 5627055; internet tapco.ae; subsidiary of Abu Dhabi National Energy Co; manages the Taweelah B water and power project; Exec. Man. Dir TOM SAMSON.

Umm an-Nar Power Co: POB 33488, Abu Dhabi; tel. (2) 5582700; fax (2) 5582405; f. 1999.

Dubai

Dubai Electricity and Water Authority (DEWA): POB 564, Dubai; tel. (4) 3244444; fax (4) 3248111; e-mail dewa@dewa.gov.ae; internet www.dewa.gov.ae; Gen. Man. SAID MUHAMMAD AHMAD AT-TAYER.

Northern Emirates (Ajman, Fujairah, Ras al-Khaimah and Umm al-Qaiwain)

Ministry of Energy: see Ministries.

Sharjah

Sharjah Electricity and Water Authority (SEWA): Sharjah; tel. (2) 5288888; fax (2) 5288000; e-mail contactus@sewa.gov.ae; internet www.sewa.gov.ae.

Transport

RAILWAYS

In mid-2005 Dubai Municipality awarded the construction contract for an urban light-railway system, provisionally known as Dubai Metro, to Mitsubishi Corpn of Japan. The first phase of the project was due to open in 2009, and full operation of the system was scheduled for 2012. Construction of a monorail linking the Palm Jumeirah development and the Atlantis station on the crescent began in 2006, under the title Palm Monorail, with completion expected in late 2009. In September 2006 it was reported that the Abu Dhabi authorities had approved plans for the construction of a 30-km monorail, projected for completion by 2020. Plans were announced in late 2007 for the construction of an 800-km railway network for passengers and freight, linking the seven emirates. Completion was anticipated in 2012, with the possibility of eventual linking to a planned railway network for the member countries of the Co-operation Council for the Arab States of the Gulf (Gulf Co-operation Council).

ROADS

Roads are rapidly being developed in the UAE, and Abu Dhabi and Dubai are linked by a good road which is dual carriageway for most of its length. This road forms part of a west coast route from Shaam, at the UAE border with the northern enclave of Oman, through Dubai and Abu Dhabi to Tarif. An east coast route links Dibba with Muscat.

Other roads include the Abu Dhabi–al-Ain highway and roads linking Sharjah and Ras al-Khaimah, and Sharjah and Dhaid. An underwater tunnel links Dubai Town and Deira by dual carriageway and pedestrian subway. Plans for the construction of a causeway between the UAE and Qatar were announced in December 2004; however, the project was subsequently delayed owing to objections from Saudi Arabia. An extensive development plan announced in July 2006, the Dubai Strategic Plan, was to allocate AED 44,000m. to road infrastructure up to 2020 and was to include the construction of 500 km of new roads, more than 95 new interchanges and upgrades of the emirate's existing road network. In 2003 there was a total paved-road network of 4,030 km.

SHIPPING

Dubai has been the main commercial centre in the Gulf for many years. Abu Dhabi has also become an important port since the opening of the first section of its artificial harbour, Port Zayed. There are smaller ports in Sharjah, Fujairah, Ras al-Khaimah and Umm al-Qaiwain. Dubai possesses two docks capable of handling 500,000-ton tankers, seven repair berths and a third dock able to accommodate 1,000,000-ton tankers. The Dubai port of Mina Jebel Ali, which was to be expanded at a cost of some US $1,362m., has the largest man-made harbour in the world. Plans are under way to expand facilities at Sharjah's Khor Fakkan Port and Ras al-Khaimah's Mina Saqr Port. The first phase of the Mina Saqr project was completed in 2007, increasing the port's annual capacity to 350,000 TEUs; upon completion of the second phase, capacity would increase to 1.7m. TEUs per year.

Abu Dhabi

Abu Dhabi Seaport Authority: POB 422, Port Zayed, Abu Dhabi; tel. (2) 6730600; fax (2) 6731023; e-mail mrktdept@emirates.net.ae; f. 1972; administers Port Zayed under the ownership of Dubai Ports World; facilities at the port include 21 deep-water berths and five container gantry cranes of 40 metric tons capacity; cold storage 20,500 tons; in 2000 Port Zayed handled 315,810 20-ft equivalent units (TEUs); Chair. Sheikh SAID BIN ZAYED AN-NAHYAN; Asst Under-Sec. for Operations MUBARAK MUHAMMAD AL-BU AINAIN.

Abu Dhabi National Tanker Co (ADNATCO): POB 2977, 11th and 12th Floors Takreer Tower, Khalifa St, Abu Dhabi; tel. (2) 6028400; fax (2) 6028323; e-mail adnatco@adnatco.ae; internet www.adnatco.com; subsidiary co of ADNOC, operating owned and chartered tankships, and transporting crude petroleum, refined products and sulphur; Chair. NASSER AHMAD AS-SUWAIDI; Gen. Man. MUHAMMAD SALEM OBAID ADH-DHAHERI.

Abu Dhabi Petroleum Ports Operating Co (IRSHAD): POB 61, Abu Dhabi; tel. (2) 6028000; fax (2) 6742094; e-mail info@irshad.ae; internet www.irshad.ae; f. 1979; manages Jebel Dhanna, Ruwais, Das Island, Umm an-Nar and Zirku Island SPM terminal, Mubarraz; operates fleet of 36 vessels; cap. AED 50m.; 60% owned by ADNOC, 40% by LAMNALCO Kuwait; Chair. YOUSUF BIN OMEIR BIN YOUSUF; Gen. Man. KHALIFA M. AL-GOBAISI.

National Marine Services Co (NMS): POB 7202, Abu Dhabi; tel. (2) 6339800; fax (2) 6211239; operate, charter and lease specialized offshore support vessels; cap. AED 25m.; owned 60% by ADNOC and 40% by Jackson Marine Corpn USA; Chair. SOHAIL FARES AL-MAZRUI; Gen. Man. Capt. HASSAN A. SHARIF.

Dubai

Dubai Ports World (DP World): POB 17000, 5th Floor, JAFZA 17, Dubai; tel. (4) 8811110; fax (4) 48811331; e-mail info@dpworld.com; internet www.dpworld.ae; f. 2005 by the merger of Dubai Ports Authority (f. 1991 by the merger of Mina Jebel Ali and Mina Rashid) and Dubai Ports International (f. 1999); subsidiary of state-controlled Dubai World; 23% sold via initial public offering Nov. 2007; storage areas and facilities for loading and discharge of vessels; operates ports of Mina Jebel Ali and Mina Rashid in Dubai, Port Zayed in Abu Dhabi, Fujairah Port and numerous other int. facilities; handled 42m. TEUs world-wide in 2006; CEO MUHAMMAD SHARAF; Exec. Vice-Pres. and COO ANIL WATS.

Dubai Drydocks: POB 8988, Dubai; tel. (4) 3450626; fax (4) 3450116; e-mail drydocks@drydocks.gov.ae; internet www.drydocks.gov.ae; f. 1983; state-owned; dry-docking and repairs, tank cleaning, construction of vessels and floating docks, conversions, galvanizing, dredging, etc.; Chief Exec. GEOFF TAYLOR.

Sea Bridge Shipping: POB 8458, Dubai; tel. (4) 3379858; fax (4) 3372600; cargo ships; Chair. S. RAMAKRISHNAN; Man. Dir L. B. CULAS.

Vela International Marine: POB 26373, City Towers 2, Sheikh Zayed Rd, Dubai; tel. (4) 3123100; fax (4) 3310585; internet www.vela.ae; subsidiary of Saudi Arabian Oil Co; operates tankers; Pres. and CEO SALEH B. K'AKI.

Fujairah

Fujairah Port: POB 787, Fujairah; tel. (9) 2228800; fax (9) 2228811; f. 1982; operated by Dubai Ports World; offers facilities for handling container, general cargo and 'roll on, roll off' traffic; handled 565,723 TEUs in 1999; Chair. Sheikh SALEH BIN MUHAMMAD ASH-SHARQI; Gen. Man. Capt. MOUSA MURAD; Harbour Master Capt. TAMER MASOUD.

Ras al-Khaimah

Saqr Port Authority: POB 5130, Ras al-Khaimah; tel. (7) 2668444; fax (7) 2668533; e-mail info@saqrport.com; internet www.saqrport.com; port operators handling bulk cargoes, containers, general cargo and 'roll on, roll off' traffic; govt-owned; Chair. Sheikh SAQR BIN MUHAMMAD AL-QASIMI; CEO VEN GOVINDA.

Sharjah

Department of Seaports and Customs: POB 510, Sharjah; tel. (6) 5281327; fax (6) 5281425; e-mail shjports@eim.ae; internet www.sharjahports.ae; the authority administers Port Khalid, Hamriyah Port and Port Khor Fakkan and offers specialized facilities for container and 'roll on, roll off' traffic, reefer cargo and project and general cargo; in 2003 Port Khalid handled 145,482 TEUs of containerized shipping, and Port Khor Fakkan 1,444,451 TEUs; Port Khalid and Hamriyah Port together handled over 4m. metric tons of non-containerized cargo; Chair. (Ports and Customs) Sheikh KHALID BIN ABDULLAH AL-QASIMI; Dir-Gen. ISSA JUMA AL-MUTAWA.

Fal Shipping Co Ltd: POB 6600, Sharjah; tel. (6) 5286666; fax (6) 5280861; internet www.falgroup.com/htm/shipping.htm; operates tankships; Chair. ABDULLAH JUMA AS-SARI; Gen. Man. MUHAMMAD OSMAN FADUL.

Umm al-Qaiwain

Ahmed bin Rashid Port and Free Zone Authority: POB 279, Umm al-Qaiwain; tel. (6) 7655882; fax (6) 7651552; e-mail abrpaftz@emirates.net.ae; Pres. KHALID BIN RASHID AL-MOALLA; Gen. Man. MURTAZA K. MOOSAJEE.

CIVIL AVIATION

There are six international airports at Abu Dhabi, al-Ain (Abu Dhabi), Dubai (DIA), Fujairah and Ras al-Khaimah, and a smaller one at Sharjah, which forms part of Sharjah port, linking air, sea and overland transportation services. Owing to space constraints at DIA, construction work began in 2005 on a new airport, with an eventual capacity of 120m. passengers and 12m. metric tons of freight per year, at Jebel Ali (Dubai). The new airport, Dubai World Central, was expected to accommodate its first flights in mid-2008. Meanwhile, an expansion project at DIA, to increase annual capacity from 30m. to 70m. passengers, was scheduled for completion in 2010. As part of this project, a new terminal was due to open in mid-2008. An expansion project at Abu Dhabi was expected to increase annual passenger capacity there to 20m. by 2010. A project to redevelop Sharjah International Airport, at a cost of US $61m., was also under way. In 1995 a total of 11.6m. passengers used the six UAE airports, 3.3m. of them passing through Abu Dhabi airports; in 2005 a record 23m. passengers used Dubai airport alone. Abu Dhabi withdrew from Gulf Air, which it had owned jointly with Bahrain and Oman (and previously with Qatar), in September 2005.

Civil Aviation Department: POB 20, Abu Dhabi; tel. (2) 6757500; responsible for all aspects of civil aviation; Chair. Sheikh HAMDAN BIN MUBARAK AN-NAHYAN.

Abu Dhabi Aviation: POB 2723, Abu Dhabi; tel. (2) 5758000; fax (2) 5757775; e-mail adava@emirates.net.ae; internet www.adaviation.com; f. 1976; domestic charter flights; Chair. Sheikh HAMDAN BIN MUBARAK AN-NAHYAN; Gen. Man. MUHAMMAD IBRAHIM AL-MAZROUI.

> **Emirates Air Service:** POB 2723, Abu Dhabi; tel. (2) 6757021; fax (2) 4449100; f. 1976 as Abu Dhabi Air Services; overhaul, engine and avionics servicing, component repairs and complete refurbishment.

Air Arabia: POB 132, Sharjah; tel. (6) 5088888; fax (6) 5580244; e-mail hraydan@airarabia.com; internet www.airarabia.com; f. 2003; owned by the Sharjah Govt; low-fare airline; operates three aircraft and serves 16 destinations; Chair. Sheikh ABDULLAH BIN MUHAMMAD ATH-THANI; CEO ADEL ALI.

Emirates Airline: POB 686, Dubai; tel. (4) 2951111; fax (4) 2955817; e-mail corpcom@emiratesairline.com; internet www.emirates.com; f. 1985; owned by the Dubai Govt; operates services to 92 destinations in 59 countries; carried 17.5m. passengers in 2006/07 and 1.2m. metric tons of freight in 2006/07; Chair. and CEO Sheikh AHMAD BIN SAID AL-MAKTOUM; Exec. Vice-Chair. MAURICE FLANAGAN.

Etihad Airways: POB 35566, Abu Dhabi; tel. (2) 5058000; fax (2) 5058111; internet www.etihadairways.com; f. 2003; owned by the Abu Dhabi Govt; operates 37 aircraft serving 45 short- and long-haul destinations; carried 4.6m. passengers in 2007; Chair. Sheikh AHMAD BIN SAIF AN-NAHYAN; CEO JAMES HOGAN.

Falcon Express Cargo Airlines (FECA): Dubai International Airport, POB 93722, Dubai; tel. (4) 2826886; fax (4) 2823125; e-mail admin@feca.bz; internet www.feca.bz/home.htm; f. 1995; dedicated courier freight.

RAK Airways: POB 31457, Ras al-Khaimah; tel. (7) 2075000; fax (7) 2447387; e-mail info@rakairways.com; internet www.rakairways.com; f. 2005; flights commenced 2007; owned by Govt. of Ras al-Khaimah; operates from Ras al-Khaimah Int. Airport; Man. Dir Dr KHATER MASSAAD.

Tourism

Tourism is an established industry in Dubai and Sharjah, and plans are being implemented to foster tourism in other emirates, notably in Abu Dhabi. In 2003 foreign visitors to the UAE totalled almost 5.9m., compared with 616,000 in 1990. Receipts from tourism totalled US $2,200m. in 2005.

Abu Dhabi Tourism Authority: POB 94000, Abu Dhabi; tel. (2) 4440444; fax (2) 4440400; e-mail info@abudhabitourism.ae; internet www.exploreabudhabi.ae; f. 2004; Chair. Sheikh SULTAN BIN TAHNUN AN-NAHYAN.

Department of Tourism and Commerce Marketing: POB 594, Dubai; tel. (4) 2230000; fax (4) 2230022; e-mail info@dubaitourism.co.ae; internet www.dubaitourism.co.ae; f. 1997; Chair. Sheikh MUHAMMAD BIN RASHID AL-MAKTOUM (Ruler of Dubai); Dir-Gen. KHALID A. BIN SULAYEM.

Dubai Information Department: POB 1420, Dubai; Dir OMAR DEESI.

Fujairah Tourism Bureau: POB 829, Fujairah; tel. (9) 2231554; fax (9) 2231006; e-mail fujtourb@emirates.net.ae; internet www.fujairah-tourism.ae; f. 1995; Chair. Sheikh SAID BIN SAID ASH-SHARQI; Dir WAHID BIN YOUSUF.

National Corporation for Tourism and Hotels (NCTH): POB 6942, Abu Dhabi; tel. (2) 4099999; fax (2) 4099990; e-mail ncth@emirates.net.ae; internet www.ncth.com; 20% owned by Govt of Abu Dhabi.

Ras al-Khaimah Information and Tourism Department: POB 141, Ras al-Khaimah; tel. (7) 2751151; Chair. Sheikh ABD AL-AZIZ BIN HUMAID AL-QASIMI.

Ras al-Khaimah Tourism Promotion Board: POB 11940, Ras Al Khaimah; tel. (7) 2445125; fax (7) 2288022; internet www.raktourism.com; f. 2006; CEO Dr KHATER MASSAAD.

Sharjah Commerce and Tourism Development Authority: POB 26661, 9th Floor, Crescent Tower, Buheirah Corniche, Sharjah; tel. (6) 5566777; fax (6) 5563000; e-mail sctda@sharjah.org; internet www.sharjah-welcome.com; f. 1980; Dir. MUHAMMAD SAIF AL-HAJRI.

THE UNITED KINGDOM

Introductory Survey

Location, Climate, Language, Religion, Flag, Capital

The United Kingdom of Great Britain and Northern Ireland lies in north-western Europe, occupying the major portion of the British Isles. The country's only land boundary is with Ireland. Great Britain, consisting of one large island and a number of smaller ones, comprises England, Scotland to the north and Wales to the west. It is separated from the coast of western Europe by the English Channel to the south and by the North Sea to the east. The northern and western shores are washed by the Atlantic Ocean. Ireland lies to the west across the Irish Sea. Northern Ireland, which is a constitutionally distinct part of the United Kingdom, is situated in the north-east of Ireland and is composed of six of the nine counties in the Irish province of Ulster, with the rest of the island comprising the state of Ireland. The climate of the United Kingdom is generally temperate but variable. The average temperature is about 15°C (59°F) in summer and about 5°C (41°F) in winter. The annual average rainfall is 1,125 mm (44.3 ins). The official language is English, but Welsh is spoken by about one-fifth of the Welsh population. The Church of England is the established church in England. Other large Christian denominations are Roman Catholicism, Methodism, the United Reformed Church and the Baptists. The national flag (proportions 1 by 2), known as the Union Jack, is a superimposition of the red cross of Saint George of England, the white saltire of Saint Andrew of Scotland and the red saltire of Saint Patrick of Ireland, all on a blue background. The capital is London.

Recent History

At the end of the Second World War the United Kingdom still ruled a vast overseas empire, and successive British Governments, in response both to nationalist aspirations and world pressure, gradually granted independence to the colonies; almost all of these became members of the Commonwealth (see p. 206). Britain's dominance diminished over the Commonwealth, which became a free association of states, and by the end of the 1970s the country looked exclusively to the North Atlantic Treaty Organization (NATO, see p. 340) and to the European Community (EC, now European Union—EU, see p. 244) for its future security.

Following the general election of 1945, the Labour Party formed a Government under its Leader, Clement Attlee. The general election of 1951 was won by the Conservative Party, which subsequently formed a Government under Winston Churchill, the wartime Prime Minister. The Conservatives remained in power for 13 years, led successively by Churchill, Sir Anthony Eden (1955–57), Harold Macmillan (1957–63) and Sir Alec Douglas-Home (1963–64). The election of 1964 gave a small parliamentary majority to the Labour Party, led by Harold Wilson. The Labour Party was re-elected in 1966, but in 1970 a Conservative Government, under Edward Heath, was returned.

After the general election of February 1974 Wilson formed a minority Government; at a further election in October the Labour Party achieved a small majority in the House of Commons. Wilson resigned as Prime Minister in April 1976, and was succeeded by James Callaghan. His Labour Government immediately encountered a serious monetary crisis and, following a series of by-election defeats, became a minority Government again.

In the general election of May 1979 the Conservative Party won a parliamentary majority. A Government was formed under Margaret Thatcher, who became the United Kingdom's first female Prime Minister. Thatcherite policy proved controversial, owing to the austerity of certain economic measures and an accompanying increase in unemployment. New legislation restricted the power of the trade unions.

Michael Foot was elected Leader of the Labour Party in November 1980. The increasing prominence of extreme left-wing members caused serious rifts in the Labour Party, and in March 1981 four former ministers from the right wing of the party formed the Social Democratic Party (SDP). The SDP formed a political alliance with the Liberals later that year.

In April 1982 Argentine forces invaded the British dependency of the Falkland Islands (q.v.). The successful military campaign to recover the islands in June increased the Government's popularity, despite rising unemployment and strict monetary control of the economy. In the general election of June 1983 the Conservative Party increased its majority in the House of Commons to 146 seats. The Labour Party's parliamentary representation fell and Neil Kinnock subsequently replaced Foot as the Labour Leader.

At a general election in June 1987 the Conservative Party won an overall majority of 102 seats in the House of Commons. In March 1988 the SDP-Liberal Alliance formally merged as the Social and Liberal Democrats (later known as the Liberal Democrats), and in July Paddy Ashdown (of the former Liberal Party) was elected as party Leader.

In mid-1990 the introduction of a local tax, the community charge (or 'poll tax'), in conjunction with an economic recession, and the unpopularity of changes to the education system and of proposed reforms to the National Health Service (NHS), contributed to considerable national dissatisfaction with the Thatcher administration. The Government was also divided, chiefly over policy on integration with the EC. In November Sir Geoffrey Howe resigned as the Lord President of the Council, Leader of the House of Commons and Deputy Prime Minister, in protest against Thatcher's hostility towards economic and political union within the EC. Michael Heseltine (who had resigned as Secretary of State for Defence in 1986) announced that he would challenge Thatcher for the leadership of the Conservative Party. In the first ballot of the leadership election (conducted among Conservative Members of Parliament—MPs) Thatcher failed to achieve an outright victory and subsequently withdrew her candidacy. John Major, Chancellor of the Exchequer since October 1989, finally won the contest and was officially appointed Prime Minister in November 1990. (The community charge was replaced with a local 'council tax', based on property values, in April 1993.)

In a general election held in April 1992 the Conservative Party was re-elected with an overall, but substantially reduced, majority in the House of Commons. Economic recession continued and the Government's economic policies were criticized by political opponents and by industrial and business leaders. Divisions within the Conservative Party over the provisions of the Treaty on European Union (the Maastricht Treaty) were exacerbated by the United Kingdom's departure from the exchange rate mechanism (ERM) of the European Monetary System (see p. 288) in September. The Treaty was endorsed by the House of Lords, the non-elected upper chamber, in July 1993, despite fierce opposition from some Conservatives. However, in a vote to ratify the Treaty, by adopting a motion on its so-called 'social chapter', conducted in the House of Commons later in July, 'rebel' Conservatives joined the Opposition to defeat the motion. The Prime Minister introduced a confidence motion the following day, and speculation that Major would call a general election in the event of a defeat for the Government ensured the support of dissident MPs.

Following the Labour Party's fourth successive general election defeat, in April 1992, Kinnock announced his resignation as party Leader. In July John Smith was elected to replace him. Prior to his death, in May 1994, Smith reformed the relationship between the Labour Party and the trade unions, reducing the unions' influence over policy formulation and the election of party chiefs and parliamentary candidates. In July Tony Blair, Labour's parliamentary spokesman on home affairs, was elected Leader by the party's electoral college. Blair's initiative to abandon Labour's socialist commitment to common ownership of the means of production provoked a much-publicized reassessment of party ideology, and became a test of support for the new leadership. In April 1995 a special party conference endorsed a draft text to replace the relevant clause of the party's constitution.

By May 1995 the Government's majority in the House of Commons had been reduced to 10 members. In June Major announced his resignation as Leader of the Conservative Party, asserting that speculation regarding a challenge to his leadership was undermining both his authority as Prime Minister and that of the Government. The Secretary of State for Wales, John Redwood, resigned from the Cabinet in order to challenge Major as party Leader. In the ballot for the leadership, held in July, Major obtained 218 of the 329 votes of the parliamentary party (compared with Redwood's 89). By April 1996 the Government's majority in the House of Commons had declined to a single seat.

In March 1996 the imposition by the EU of a comprehensive trade ban on British beef products, in response to a major public health alert (see below), emboldened those Conservative MPs demanding a limitation in the country's convergence with the EU. In April Major committed a future Conservative administration to conducting a popular referendum on the country's participation in a European single currency. In June more than 70 Conservative MPs declared their support for a wider referendum on EU membership, demonstrating the increasing prominence of the so-called Eurosceptic faction of the party.

In December 1996 the Government officially lost its majority in the House of Commons when the Labour Party won a by-election for a previously Conservative-held seat. In February 1997 the Labour Party attempted to force a government defeat, in order to prompt a general election, by introducing a parliamentary censure motion against the Minister of Agriculture, Fisheries and Food, Douglas Hogg, for his administration of the bovine spongiform encephalopathy (BSE) crisis (see below). However, the Ulster Unionists upheld the Government's position by abstaining. By March the Conservatives' parliamentary minority had deepened, following a further Labour by-election victory and the defection of a Eurosceptic MP.

At a general election held on 1 May 1997 the Labour Party (now frequently referred to as New Labour, emphasizing the reforms undertaken under Blair's leadership) secured an overwhelming victory, winning 418 of the 659 parliamentary seats, with 44.3% of the votes cast in Britain. The Conservative Party won only 165 seats, with 31.5% of the vote. Moreover, for the first time in its history, the Conservative Party failed to win any parliamentary representation in Scotland or Wales. The Liberal Democrats increased their number of seats to 46, although with a slightly reduced share of the votes (17.2%, compared with 17.9% in 1992). Major immediately announced his resignation as Leader of the Conservative Party: William Hague, hitherto Secretary of State for Wales, was elected to the post (and thus as Leader of the Opposition) by Conservative MPs in June.

In the new Labour Government Gordon Brown, who had been prominent in the creation of New Labour, was named as Chancellor of the Exchequer and Robin Cook became the new Secretary of State for Foreign and Commonwealth Affairs, while the Labour Party's Deputy Leader, John Prescott, was appointed Deputy Prime Minister, assuming additional responsibility for the environment, transport and the regions. Peter Mandelson, one of Blair's closest advisers, and regarded as highly influential in the organization of Labour's election campaign, was appointed Minister without Portfolio, with responsibility for co-ordinating government policy (a non-Cabinet post). The new administration announced a series of radical policy proposals and government reforms, including an employment initiative, aimed initially at long-term unemployed 18–24 year olds, which was to be financed by a single taxation levy on the profits of privatized industries. Brown announced changes to the management and regulation of the economy and the financial sector (including a transfer of operational responsibility for monetary policy to the Bank of England), while Cook defined the Government's broad approach to foreign affairs, with greater emphasis on the country's role in international organizations and the incorporation of human rights concerns into foreign policy and trade decisions. A new Department for International Development was established, to assume the functions of the former Overseas Development Administration (previously under the authority of the Foreign and Commonwealth Office) at cabinet level. The Government's parliamentary programme included additional legislation intended to improve standards in education, the adoption of a national minimum wage, and constitutional reform.

In July 1997 the Government formally published its proposals for the establishment of devolved legislative authorities in Scotland and Wales. For Scotland a proposed new elected Parliament was envisaged as having powers to legislate on all domestic matters, including education, health, local government, law and order, and the possible mandate to vary taxes set by the United Kingdom Government. An executive level of government was to be headed by a First Minister. The 129 Members of the Scottish Parliament (MSPs) were to be elected every four years by a combined system of direct voting and a form of proportional representation. The Welsh Assembly, like the Scottish body, was envisaged as assuming control of the annual block grant for the region from central government, and as undertaking responsibility for issues covered by the Welsh Office. The 60-member Assembly was to be elected under the same system as in Scotland. In a referendum held in Scotland in September, 74.3% of those voting supported a new Parliament, while 63.5% approved its having tax-raising powers. The results, although representing only an estimated 44.7% and 38.1% of eligible voters, respectively, were considered by the Government as being an endorsement of its proposals. The referendum in Wales, held one week later, was less conclusive, with only 50.3% of participants (or some 25% of eligible voters) endorsing the Assembly. None the less, the Government declared its intention to implement the majority decision. A political settlement on the future governance of Northern Ireland (see below), concluded in April 1998, provided for new constitutional arrangements regarding the status of Northern Ireland within the United Kingdom and for the establishment of a British-Irish Council.

In October 1998 the Leader of the Government in the House of Lords, Baroness Jay of Paddington, announced that legislation was to be introduced to remove the voting rights of hereditary peers, and that a Royal Commission was to be appointed to consider options for a definitive reform of the second chamber. Opposition from within the House of Lords was appeased in December when a compromise agreement was reached under which 92 hereditary peers were to retain their seats in an interim second chamber pending the definitive reform. Draft legislation for the abolition of hereditary peerages and the establishment of an interim chamber was published in January 1999. In October the upper chamber approved the House of Lords Bill, and in November it received royal assent. In January 2000 the Royal Commission published its proposals for the definitive reform of the upper house, recommending that the new chamber should comprise some 550 members, the majority of whom would be chosen by an independent commission, while a 'significant minority' (between 65 and 195) would be elected by regional proportional representation.

At elections to the new legislative authorities in Scotland and Wales, held in May 1999, the Labour Party, while securing the greatest number of seats, failed to gain an overall majority in either assembly. In Scotland the Labour Party obtained 56 of the total of 129 seats, while the SNP won 35 seats, the Conservative Party 18 seats, and the Liberal Democrats 17 seats; the remaining three seats were won by independent candidates. The Labour Party and the Liberal Democrats subsequently formed a coalition administration, headed by Labour's Donald Dewar as First Minister. In Wales the Labour Party secured 28 of the total of 60 seats, while Plaid Cymru obtained 17 seats, the Conservative Party nine seats and the Liberal Democrats six seats. Despite Labour's lack of an overall majority, in mid-May the Welsh First Minister, Alun Michael, opted to form a minority administration rather than a formal coalition. Powers were transferred to both the Scottish and the Welsh legislatures on 1 July 1999.

During 2000 there was considerable political upheaval in both Wales and Scotland. In February Rhodri Morgan succeeded Alun Michael as Welsh First Minister. Michael had resigned shortly before the Welsh Assembly adopted a vote of no confidence in his leadership. In May the Leader of Plaid Cymru, Dafydd Wigley, resigned owing to ill health; he was replaced by Ieuan Wyn Jones in August. In October the ruling Labour Party entered into a coalition agreement with the Liberal Democrats, who obtained two portfolios, including that of Deputy First Minister, in the reorganized nine-member Welsh Cabinet. Meanwhile, in Scotland the unexpected resignation of Alex Salmond as Leader of the SNP in July precipitated a leadership contest in which John Swinney was elected as Salmond's successor. Following the death in October of Dewar, the Labour Party in Scotland elected Henry McLeish, the Minister for Enterprise and Lifelong Learning, to succeed him as their Leader. Later in that month McLeish was elected to succeed Dewar as First Minister.

In August 1999 the Liberal Democrats elected Charles Kennedy to succeed Paddy Ashdown as their Leader. In October Blair conducted a government reorganization in which Peter Mandelson replaced Mo Mowlam as Secretary of State for Northern Ireland. Mandelson had been appointed President of the Board of Trade and Secretary of State for Trade and Industry in July 1998, but had resigned in December following allegations of financial impropriety. In January 2001 Mandelson resigned as

Secretary of State for Northern Ireland after his initial denial of any direct involvement in an enquiry to the Home Office in June 1998, regarding the application for British citizenship of an Indian business executive, appeared to be false. Dr John Reid, hitherto Secretary of State for Scotland, was appointed to succeed Mandelson, thus becoming the first Roman Catholic to hold the Northern Ireland portfolio.

In February 2001 incidences of foot-and-mouth disease (FMD—a non-fatal yet highly contagious virus carried by cloven-hoofed animals) in south-east England prompted the European Commission to impose a temporary ban on the export of live animals, meat and dairy products from the United Kingdom. A continuing rise in the number of cases of FMD throughout the country, mounting pressure from agricultural interest groups and popular opposition to the timing of the polls led the Government to announce in April that emergency legislation would be introduced to provide for a five-week postponement of the local elections due to be held in May (the first time such legislation had been required during peacetime).

In early May 2001 Blair announced that a general election (as well as the postponed local elections) would be conducted on 7 June, although new incidences of FMD continued to be discovered. The last case of FMD was identified in September and in January 2002 the Government announced that the United Kingdom was free of the disease. In February the European Commission agreed to lift remaining restrictions on the import and export of British meat, animal products and livestock. A report published by the National Audit Office in June 2002 confirmed that the losses to the British economy resulting from the FMD outbreak totalled some £5,000m. In July the report of an inquiry into the Government's handling of the crisis was published, which was highly critical of the Government's response to the outbreak, stating that FMD spread far wider than it should have as a result of inadequate contingency plans and the Government's slow response.

At the general election held on 7 June 2001 the Labour Party won a further comprehensive victory, securing 413 of the 659 parliamentary seats with 40.7% of the votes cast. The Conservative Party won 166 seats with 31.7% of the votes cast, while the Liberal Democrats increased their parliamentary representation to 53 seats, with 18.3% of the votes cast. The election, however, attracted the lowest rate of voter participation, 59.4%, since 1918. Following his party's poor performance, Hague announced his intention to resign the leadership of the Conservative Party; in September Iain Duncan Smith, hitherto the Conservative Party's parliamentary spokesman on defence, was elected to replace Hague as Leader of the Conservative Party. Meanwhile, in a major reorganization of the Cabinet, Jack Straw, hitherto Secretary of State for the Home Department, replaced Cook as Secretary of State for Foreign and Commonwealth Affairs and David Blunkett, formerly Secretary of State for Education, assumed Straw's portfolio. The Ministry of Agriculture, Fisheries and Food, which had been heavily criticized for its handling of the FMD outbreak, was replaced by the Department for the Environment, Food and Rural Affairs and a new Department for Work and Pensions was created. Furthermore, Blair removed the responsibility for transport, environment and the regions from the Deputy Prime Minister, Prescott, appointing Stephen Byers, previously Secretary of State for Trade and Industry, as head of the newly formed Department for Transport, Local Government and the Regions (DTLR).

Upon their release in November 2001, the Government's proposals for the reform of the House of Lords encountered fierce opposition from both Labour and opposition MPs concerning the number of directly elected members envisaged in the plans. The public consultation process on the proposals ended in January 2002. In May the Government effectively abandoned the recommendations, and in December a new joint committee of MPs and peers presented seven options for the future proportion of elected members in the House of Lords, ranging from a wholly elected chamber to a wholly appointed house. However, in February 2003 all seven options were rejected by MPs voting in the House of Commons.

In December 2001 a Labour MP defected to the Liberal Democrats, citing the Government's continued failure to improve public services and the decision to approve military action in Afghanistan (see below). Blair also encountered criticism for allegedly neglecting domestic issues and increasingly concentrating on foreign policy. Also in December anti-terrorism legislation was introduced in response to the events of 11 September in the USA (see below), which, most notably, provided for the detention of suspected international terrorists without trial if their deportation was not deemed possible. However, in July 2002 the legislation was declared unlawful and in breach of the European Convention on Human Rights by the Special Immigration Appeals Committee (SIAC). In October the British Court of Appeal ruled against the July decision and in May 2003 Blunkett announced proposals that would allow police to hold terrorist suspects without charge for up to 14 days. In October the SIAC rejected appeals by 10 foreign nationals who had been detained indefinitely without trial.

In May 2002 Byers resigned as Secretary of State for Transport, Local Government and the Regions, having incurred criticism of his actions for his decision to place the heavily indebted rail infrastructure operating company, Railtrack, into administration in October 2001. (Byers had initially declared that he would not use public funds to compensate Railtrack shareholders, but the funding arrangements that he announced in March 2002 for the proposed successor company, Network Rail, were perceived as a reversal of this policy.) There followed a major reorganization of several government departments. The DTLR was abolished and a new Department for Transport was created, which was headed by Alistair Darling, hitherto Secretary of State for Work and Pensions.

In mid-March 2003 Clare Short announced her intention to resign as Secretary of State for International Development if Blair approved British participation in the US-led campaign to oust the regime of Saddam Hussain in Iraq (see below) without a pertinent UN resolution. Following the failure to secure a second UN resolution authorizing military action in Iraq and the announcement that British troops would be deployed as part of the US-led coalition to remove Hussain, Cook resigned as Leader of the House of Commons, citing his unwillingness to accept collective responsibility for the decision to commit the United Kingdom to military action without international agreement or domestic support. Two ministers of state and a number of ministerial aides also resigned in protest at Blair's decision. Blair suffered another major reverse when 139 Labour MPs voted in favour of a motion stating that there was no moral justification for an attack on Iraq, although another motion endorsing his strategy was approved by 412 votes to 149. In April Blair appointed Reid to replace Cook. Short finally resigned from the Cabinet in May, accusing Blair of reneging on assurances he had made to her concerning the need for a UN mandate to establish a legitimate Iraqi government. She was succeeded by Baroness Amos of Brondesbury.

At elections to the Scottish and Welsh legislative authorities, held on 1 May 2003, the Labour Party again won the largest number of seats in both assemblies. In Wales Labour secured 30 of the 60 available seats, Plaid Cymru won 12 seats, the Conservatives 11, and the Liberal Democrats six; the remaining seat was taken by an independent candidate. Morgan subsequently appointed a new, all-Labour Cabinet. In Scotland the Labour Party obtained 50 of the total of 129 seats, while the SNP took 27, the Conservatives 18, the Liberal Democrats 17, the Scottish Green Party seven, and the Scottish Socialist Party six; the remaining four seats were won by independent candidates. In mid-May Jack McConnell, who had succeeded McLeish as Leader of the Labour Party in Scotland and First Minister in November 2001, announced a reorganized coalition administration, again comprising Labour and the Liberal Democrats.

In May 2003 Straw indicated that evidence that Iraq had possessed weapons of mass destruction might never be found, prompting allegations from a number of anti-war MPs that the perceived threat posed by that country had been exaggerated, and that the House of Commons had been misled. The British Broadcasting Corporation (BBC) came into conflict with the Government in the same month, when a BBC journalist alleged that a dossier published by the Government in September 2002 to explain the case for the removal of the Iraqi regime, had made exaggerated claims concerning Iraq's possession of chemical and biological weapons: he claimed that the Prime Minister's Director of Communications and Strategy, Alastair Campbell, was responsible for including misleading information in the dossier, against the wishes of the intelligence agencies. Blair denied the accusations and stated that the evidence had been compiled and approved by the Joint Intelligence Committee (JIC). In June 2003 it was announced that the parliamentary Foreign Affairs Select Committee (FASC) was to conduct an inquiry into whether the Government had provided accurate and complete information to Parliament in the period leading up to military action in Iraq, while the parliamentary Intelligence and Security Committee (ISC) was to investigate the role played by the intelligence agencies. In mid-June the ISC censured the Prime Minister's Office for having published (in February) a second dossier which contained outdated material, but in September its report exonerated the Government of political interference in the assessment of secret intelligence. In July the FASC concluded that Campbell had not exerted improper influence on the drafting of the first dossier, but criticized his role in the production of the second, which had led Blair unwittingly to misinform Parliament that further intelligence existed on Iraq's alleged concealment of weapons of mass destruction. The BBC, however, while refusing to reveal its source, rejected Campbell's demand that it retract the story. Also in July the Ministry of Defence confirmed that Dr David Kelly, a senior adviser to the ministry, was the source of the BBC's information pertaining to Iraq's weapons. Later in that month Dr Kelly committed suicide. The Secretary of State for Defence, Geoff Hoon, denied responsibility for revealing Kelly's identity. Blair ordered an independent judicial inquiry, under Lord Hutton, into his death: its report, published in January 2004, concluded that there had been no duplicitous strategy on the part of the Government to reveal Dr Kelly's name to the media, but that the Ministry of Defence had erred by failing to inform Kelly that his name would be confirmed if journalists suggested it, and that its treatment of Kelly after his public exposure had been unsatisfactory. The report criticized the management and editorial systems of the BBC, whose Director-General, together with the Chairman of the Board of Governors, then resigned. In early February 2004 Blair announced the establishment of a further inquiry, under Lord Butler of Brockwell, into the accuracy of the intelligence gathered on Iraqi weapons of mass destruction, which would examine any discrepancies between the information collected, evaluated and used by the Government before the conflict in Iraq and intelligence discovered by the Iraq Survey Group (see below) since the end of major combat operations in May 2003. In July 2004 Lord Butler published the findings from his inquiry, which revealed that intelligence surrounding the compilation of the first dossier was 'seriously flawed' and criticized the intelligence services for using unreliable sources of information within Iraq. It also disclosed that before the start of the war there was no proof that Iraq had any significant stocks of weapons of mass destruction. While it suggested that the next Chairman of the JIC should be a person 'with experience of dealing with ministers in a senior role', it stressed that there was no evidence of 'deliberate distortion or culpable negligence' on the part of the JIC.

In June 2003, meanwhile, an extensive reorganization of the Cabinet included plans to effect major changes to the British legal and judicial system. Under the proposals the post of Lord Chancellor, which had been in existence for some 1,400 years, was to be abolished and a US-style supreme court was to replace the judicial function of the House of Lords as the United Kingdom's highest court of appeal. The Lord Chancellor's Office was replaced by a newly created Department for Constitutional Affairs, which also assumed responsibility for the abolished Scottish and Welsh Offices. Officials from those offices were located within the new department, although Darling assumed the position of Secretary of State for Scotland in addition to the transport portfolio, and Peter Hain, who replaced Reid as Leader of the House of Commons, retained the post of Secretary of State for Wales. Reid subsequently replaced Alan Milburn as Secretary of State for Health. Lord Falconer of Thoroton was appointed to head the Department for Constitutional Affairs, while also assuming temporarily the functions of the Lord Chancellor—although he would not sit as a judge—pending the full implementation of the reforms. Furthermore, an independent commission would assume responsibility for appointing judges. The decision to abolish such a historic position without prior consultation was heavily criticized by a number of MPs and Lords, and Blair was requested by the Speaker of the House of Commons to appear before the chamber to clarify the decisions and their repercussions. Consultation papers regarding the further reform of the House of Lords, which proposed the removal of the remaining 92 hereditary peers and the creation of a wholly appointed upper chamber with unchanged revising powers, and the abolition of the position of Lord Chancellor and the creation of a supreme court, were published by the Government in September 2003. In March 2004 the House of Lords determined by 216 votes to 183 to refer the Constitutional Reform Bill to a Lords select committee for further scrutiny. The Government announced later in that month that it was postponing plans to abolish the remaining 92 hereditary peerages; it intended, however, to continue with plans to establish a supreme court and remove the post of Lord Chancellor. In July the Lords select committee revealed that it had made several amendments to the bill; however, the clause providing for the removal of the Lord Chancellor was rejected by the House of Lords later in that month. The Government subsequently agreed only to modify the Lord Chancellor's role. In March 2005 an attempt by the Government to separate the Lord Chancellor's roles as supreme judge, Speaker of the House of Lords and government minister failed when a new amendment to the bill, proposing that the Lord Chancellor need not be a member of the House of Lords or a lawyer, was rejected by the upper house. However, the House of Lords subsequently voted by a majority of 12 to allow an MP who was not necessarily a lawyer to take on the role of Lord Chancellor, and the Constitutional Reform Bill received royal assent in late March. As part of the reform of the role of Lord Chancellor, in January 2006 the House of Lords formally agreed to elect a Speaker, the Lord Chancellor having hitherto traditionally presided over debates. In April the Constitutional Reform Act came into force, and the Lord Chief Justice of England and Wales, Lord Phillips of Worth Matravers, assumed control of the judiciary in England and Wales from the Lord Chancellor. The new Supreme Court was not scheduled to commence operations until October 2009.

In September 2003 the Labour Party candidate at a by-election in a previously safe Labour constituency was defeated by the Liberal Democrats' candidate. In early October Blair effected a minor reshuffle of the Cabinet, following the death of the Leader of the House of Lords, Lord Williams of Mostyn. Baroness Amos was appointed to replace Lord Williams and Hilary Benn succeeded Amos as Secretary of State for International Development. In late October Duncan Smith announced his resignation as Leader of the Conservative Party after Conservative MPs approved a vote of no confidence in his leadership. He was replaced by Michael Howard, a former Secretary of State for the Home Department, who was elected Leader unopposed.

Dissent from within the Labour Party continued to threaten to undermine Blair's authority and in January 2004, in the most notable Labour revolt since Blair became Prime Minister, 72 Labour MPs voted against the Government's Higher Education Bill, which proposed to introduce repayable and variable university tuition fees from 2006. Only intense lobbying by a number of cabinet ministers secured the passage of the Bill—by five votes. On 10 June 2004, at elections to the European Parliament and at local elections, the Labour Party suffered significant losses. In the local elections Labour lost 464 seats and eight councils, leaving them with control of 39 councils, while the Conservatives gained 263 seats and 13 councils, increasing their total to 51 councils, and the Liberal Democrats suffered a net loss of two councils, leaving them with control of nine. The Labour Party's poor performance was widely attributed to popular dissatisfaction with the Government's decisions concerning the Iraq war. In the European elections the Conservatives won 27 of the 78 seats allocated to the United Kingdom (compared with 36 in 1999) and Labour won 19 (a decline of 10 seats). The Liberal Democrats won 12 seats (compared with 10 in 1999), while the Eurosceptic UK Independence Party increased its representation in the European Parliament from three seats to 12. Electoral participation was registered at 38.2%, compared with 24% in 1999.

In late November 2004 an inquiry was established to investigate accusations that the Secretary of State for the Home Department, David Blunkett, had expedited a visa application for the employee of his former lover. In early December the report of the inquiry revealed a 'chain of events' linking Blunkett to the dispatch of the application, although no evidence was uncovered of his direct intervention. Despite asserting his innocence of any deliberate wrongdoing, Blunkett resigned from the Cabinet. Charles Clarke, hitherto Secretary of State for Education and Skills, was appointed to replace him, while Ruth Kelly, the former Minister for the Cabinet Office, was allocated Clarke's role. Also in December the Law Lords ruled that the detention without trial under the 2001 Anti-Terrorism, Crime and Security Act of the remaining nine foreign suspects who could not be deported was discriminatory and in breach of their human rights, overturning an earlier ruling by SIAC. Clarke presented a new anti-terrorism bill to Parliament in February 2005 since the powers of detention under the 2001 Act were due to expire in March, as a result of the legal ruling. The new bill encountered strong criticism from human rights groups, which claimed it infringed civil liberties. The House of Lords adopted the bill in mid-March after the Government had made significant amendments to it in response to its repeated rejection by the upper house.

In early April 2005 Blair announced that a general election would take place on 5 May. Prior to this announcement a Labour candidate had defected to the Liberal Democrats, having become disillusioned with Blair's 'increasingly authoritarian' style of Government. The following day, however, a Liberal Democrat MP defected to Labour, having left the party four years earlier. Blair's credibility was adversely affected by continuing controversy about Iraq, which was exacerbated by the publication of the initial (previously undisclosed) advice of the Attorney-General on the legality of the war.

At the general election on 5 May 2005 the Labour Party was re-elected for a third term, albeit with a substantially reduced majority, securing 356 of the 645 parliamentary seats contested, with 35.2% of the votes cast. The Conservative Party and the Liberal Democrats both increased their representation in the House of Commons, securing 197 seats (with 32.3% of the votes cast) and 62 seats (with 22.0%), respectively. Voting in one further constituency was postponed, owing to the death of a candidate. The rate of participation by eligible voters was 61.3%. Following the election, Michael Howard announced his intention to step down as Leader of the Conservative Party. Blair commenced a major reorganization of ministerial portfolios on 6 May. David Blunkett returned to the Cabinet as Secretary of State for Work and Pensions, Reid was named as the new Secretary of State for Defence, replacing Hoon (who became Lord Privy Seal and Leader of the House of Commons), while Patricia Hewitt (hitherto Secretary of State for Trade and Industry and Minister for Women) took on Reid's former post as Secretary of State for Health. Alan Johnson, hitherto Secretary of State for Work and Pensions, was allocated the trade and industry portfolio, while David Miliband assumed the newly created post of Minister of Communities and Local Government.

On 7 July 2005 52 people were killed and more than 700 injured in four attacks—three on London Underground trains and one on a bus—perpetrated by suicide bombers in London. Of the four bombers, all of whom also died in the attacks, three were subsequently discovered to have been native British Muslims of Pakistani descent, while the fourth was a convert to Islam of Jamaican origin. In September Al-Jazeera, a Qatar-based television station, broadcast a videotaped communiqué, supplied to it by the militant Islamist al-Qa'ida (Base) organization, in which Mohammad Sidique Khan, who had been identified as one of the four 7 July bombers, cited the United Kingdom's participation in the invasion of Iraq in 2003 as one of the motivations for the attacks. In a separate part of the communiqué al-Qa'ida claimed responsibility for the attacks. On 21 July 2005 at least four further attempts to attack London Underground trains and a bus with bombs were unsuccessful owing to the failure of the bombs to explode. By the end of the month four men suspected of involvement in the 21 July attacks had been arrested in the United Kingdom. A fifth man was arrested a week later in the Italian capital, Rome, having fled to Italy following the attacks. Of the five initial detainees, all of whom were of African origin, two had obtained British citizenship in recent years, while a third had been granted indefinite leave to remain in the United Kingdom in 2000. In September 2005 Italy agreed to extradite the fifth suspect to the United Kingdom. In December a sixth man suspected of assisting in the failed attacks was extradited to the United Kingdom from Ethiopia, having been arrested in that country in the previous month. The trial of the six men on charges of conspiracy to murder commenced in January 2007. In early July four of the defendants were found guilty and were each sentenced to life imprisonment. A retrial was expected to take place in the case of the two remaining defendants after the jury failed to reach a verdict. However, in November the two men each admitted lesser charges: one was convicted of conspiracy to cause explosions and the other of collecting information useful to a person committing or preparing an act of terrorism. The men were sentenced later that month, receiving prison terms of 33 years, and six years and nine months, respectively.

In April 2007 five British Muslims (who had been arrested in 2004) were convicted of conspiracy to cause explosions, having planned to detonate explosives made from fertilizer at a shopping centre, a night-club and gas installations. It was revealed during the trial that two men, who later perpetrated the suicide bombings in London on 7 July 2005, had been under surveillance by the security services in the course of the investigation, but had not been regarded as posing a serious threat. The trial of eight men charged in connection with an alleged plot to detonate improvised explosive devices aboard several transatlantic airliners commenced at a court in London in early April 2008.

The internal security service—known as MI5—was criticized for its failure to prevent the attacks of July 2005 and, in particular, for its decision, in June, to reduce its estimation of the threat to the United Kingdom from international terrorism to its lowest level since 11 September 2001. For its part, in response to the attacks, the Government sought the support of both the Conservatives and the Liberal Democrats for proposed new legislation to counter terrorism, and requested the assistance of moderate Muslim leaders in the United Kingdom to combat Islamic radicalism. In mid-September 2005 the Government published a new Terrorism Bill. The draft legislation sought to establish new offences of preparing terrorist acts or assisting others to commit them; attendance at terrorist training facilities in any part of the world or providing such training; and 'direct or indirect encouragement' of terrorist acts and the release of communications that 'glorify, exalt or celebrate' acts of terrorism committed over the past 20 years. It was further proposed that the maximum period for which suspected terrorists could be detained without charge should be extended from 14 to 90 days. While a number of the bill's provisions were supported by both the Conservatives and the Liberal Democrats, representatives of those parties claimed that the Government had failed to justify the proposed extension of the maximum period of detention without charge to 90 days. Civil liberties organizations, meanwhile, claimed that such an extension would infringe suspects' human rights. In November the 90-day extension was emphatically rejected by the House of Commons. The rejection of the proposed legislation, which 49 Labour MPs had also refused to support, marked the first defeat that the Labour Government had suffered in the Commons since it assumed power in 1997. The defeat was followed by a vote in favour of extending the maximum permissible period of detention of terrorist suspects without charge to 28 days.

Despite opposition from 25 Labour MPs, the Government's contentious Identity Cards Bill secured passage through the House of Commons in mid-October 2005. Later that month, however, the House of Lords adopted wide-ranging amendments to the Government's Racial and Religious Hatred Bill, with a view to guaranteeing freedom of speech in respect of religion. The proposed legislation was intended to afford to religious groups legal safeguards similar to those already enjoyed by ethnic groups. Also in late October the Government published a white paper in which it detailed proposals for the reform of the state school system. Strong opposition to the proposed reforms was expressed by elements within the Labour Party, who feared they would have a damaging effect on comprehensive secondary school education. In the same month the Secretary of State for Trade and Industry, Johnson, announced that he had concluded an agreement with public sector trade unions whereby a retirement age of 65 would apply for civil servants, nurses and teachers who joined those professions from April 2007, while the retirement age of those already so employed at April 2007 would remain fixed at 60. The reform was intended to reduce the Government's unfunded public sector pension deficit, which had been estimated at £400,000m.–£700,000m. At the end of November 2005 a government-appointed commission published recommendations on the longer-term reform of state pension arrangements, which included, notably, a proposal to increase the state pensionable age from 65 to 68 by 2050.

In early November 2005 David Blunkett resigned as Secretary of State for Work and Pensions after it transpired that aspects of his tenure of appointments by private companies, following his resignation from the Cabinet in December 2004 had contravened guide-lines for former ministers accepting such positions within two years of relinquishing office. Blunkett was succeeded by John Hutton, previously Chancellor of the Duchy of Lancaster and Minister for the Cabinet Office. In December members of the Conservative Party elected David Cameron to be the new Leader of the party and, thus, of the Opposition. In early January 2006, two days after he had issued a statement in which he admitted that he had received treatment for alcoholism, Charles Kennedy resigned as Leader of the Liberal Democrats. Sir Menzies Campbell, the Deputy Leader of the party under Kennedy, was elected as the Liberal Democrats' new Leader in March.

In December 2005 Blair dismissed calls that had been made by human rights organizations for a public inquiry into allegations that the United Kingdom's airspace and air transport facilities had been used in the transfer ('extraordinary rendition') of detainees, in particular terrorist suspects, by the US Central Intelligence Agency (CIA) to third countries where it was possible that they might be subjected to torture during interrogation. At a press conference in December Blair insisted that he had no evidence to suggest that anything illegal had occurred in connection with the so-called rendition flights. In January 2006, however, the *New Statesman* magazine published a Foreign and Commonwealth Office memorandum it had obtained in which it was stated that rendition flights were probably illegal under international law. The memorandum further stated that the Office's own investigations had discovered at least two instances of such flights across British airspace, but that there 'could be more'. In February the foreign affairs committee of the House of Commons stated in its annual report on human rights that the Government had been too slow to investigate allegations that as many as 200 rendition flights had crossed British airspace. According to the committee, the Government was obliged, under the UN Convention against Torture and Other Cruel, Inhuman or Degrading Treatment or Punishment, to investigate such allegations, together with other claims that the USA had established secret prisons in third countries for the purpose of interrogating detainees. Also in February Blair referred to the US camp for detained 'enemy combatants' at Guantánamo Bay, Cuba, as an anomaly that would eventually have to be addressed. On the previous day the High Court had granted three former residents of the United Kingdom who were detained at Guantánamo Bay permission to seek through the courts a petition by the British Government for their release, as it had already done in nine previous cases. In a statement to the House of Commons in February 2008, the Secretary of State for the Foreign and Commonwealth Office, Miliband, admitted that a number of so-called rendition flights had in fact used facilities at Diego Garcia, in the Indian Ocean (the coral atoll was a British dependency, but had been leased by the USA for use as a military base since the 1960s).

In January 2006 two clauses of the Government's Racial and Religious Hatred Bill were rejected by the House of Commons when MPs voted in favour of amendments to the bill that had been introduced by the House of Lords with the aim of guaranteeing freedom of speech in respect of religion. The bill received royal assent in the following month. Also in that month the House of Lords introduced five amendments to the Government's Identity Cards Bill, including, notably, one that stipulated that the new cards should not become compulsory without new primary legislation. In February the House of Commons rejected one of the amendments introduced by the House of Lords that would have made identity cards wholly voluntary, while accepting the requirement for new primary legislation before the proposed identity cards could be made compulsory. Following a series of votes in which the House of Lords repeatedly rejected the Government's proposals, returning the bill to the Commons, in March both chambers accepted a compromise whereby all passport applicants would have their details placed on a national identity register from 2008, but could choose not to be issued an identity card until 2010. In late March the House of Lords finally approved the Terrorism Bill, including the clause outlawing the glorification of terrorism (which it had twice rejected earlier in that year), and the Terrorism Act came into force in April.

In March 2006, after the House of Lords Appointments Commission had expressed concern over a number of Labour nominations for peerages, it was revealed that four of the nominees had made unpublicized loans totalling at least £4.5m. to the Labour Party. A police investigation was subsequently launched into whether, effectively, the Labour Party had illegally sold 'titles of honour'. Although the police investigation was widened to examine the funding of both the Conservatives and the Liberal Democrats, the nominations called into question the Labour Party's commitment to transparency in political party funding, the reform of which it had begun after its election in 1997. Labour had in fact been under no legal obligation—as it would have been had they been donations—to declare the loans, but the fact that the party's treasurer, Jack Dromey, had been unaware of them strengthened the impression of duplicity. In July 2006 the Labour Party's principal fund-raiser, Lord Levy, was arrested in the course of the investigation, while during the year the Prime Minister was among about 90 others (including members of all three main political parties) who were interviewed by the police. However, in July 2007, the Crown Prosecution Service announced that no charges would be brought in relation to the allegations.

At local elections held on 4 May 2006 the Labour Party performed poorly, most notably in London, losing 319 seats and 17 councils, leaving them in overall control of 30 councils. The Conservative Party gained 316 seats and 11 councils, increasing their total to 68 councils. The Liberal Democrats failed to make any significant impact with net gains of two seats and one council, giving them control of 13 councils. On 5 May Blair effected a major reorganization of the Cabinet. Clarke was dismissed as Secretary of State for the Home Department, following criticism over the revelation in late April that a number of foreign nationals convicted and imprisoned for crimes committed while living in Britain had not been considered for deportation following their release. Reid was appointed to the vacant position, and was replaced as Secretary of State for Defence by Des Browne (previously Chief Secretary to the Treasury). Margaret Beckett (hitherto Secretary of State for the Environment, Food and Rural Affairs) was appointed Secretary of State for Foreign and Commonwealth Affairs, succeeding Straw, who took the title of Lord Privy Seal and Leader of the House of Commons. Prescott remained as Deputy Prime Minister, although most of his policy responsibilities were allocated to a new Department for Communities and Local Government.

In December 2006 the Government attracted widespread criticism when the Attorney-General announced that a two-year investigation by the Serious Fraud Office into sales of military aircraft and equipment to Saudi Arabia by a British company, BAE Systems, had been abandoned in the interests of national security and foreign policy objectives in the Middle East. It had been alleged that BAE had provided millions of pounds in bribes to the Saudi royal family in order to secure sales contracts, in contravention of a law adopted in 2002. In March 2007 the Organisation for Economic Co-operation and Development (OECD, see p. 347) announced its intention to investigate whether the United Kingdom had contravened OECD's convention on combating bribery in international business transactions. In June the US Department of Justice instituted an inquiry into the allegations of corrupt payments by BAE Systems to secure Saudi arms contracts. Also in March the Government faced a rebellion among Labour MPs who were opposed to the renewal of the country's nuclear deterrent, and was obliged to rely on the support of opposition MPs in a vote on the construction of new Trident submarines carrying nuclear warheads.

New legislative proposals on the reform of the House of Lords, published in February 2007, suggested the abolition (over a transitional period) of all hereditary and life peerages and the reduction of the total membership of the upper house to 540, while MPs were to choose between a range of options on the proportion of members that would be elected and appointed. In a non-binding vote on these options, conducted in March, a majority of MPs favoured an upper house that would be entirely elected, while a smaller majority voted for one with 80% elected and 20% appointed members; in the House of Lords itself all the options were rejected and the house voted to retain a non-elected upper chamber.

At local and regional elections on 4 May 2007 the Labour Party incurred considerable losses. In Scotland the SNP gained 20 new seats, thus obtaining 47 of the 129 seats in the legislature, while Labour won 46, the Conservatives 17, the Liberal Democrats 16 and the Scottish Green Party two: the complexity of the voting procedure was blamed for the fact that about 7% of the ballot papers were declared invalid. On 16 May 2007 members of the Scottish Parliament elected the SNP Leader, Alex Salmond (who had regained that role in 2004), as First Minister, at the head of a minority SNP administration (with partial support from the Green members). In the election to the Welsh Assembly Labour lost four seats, but remained the largest party in the legislature with 26 of the 60 seats, while Plaid Cymru won 15, the Conservative Party 12 and the Liberal Democrats six. Initial discussions between the outgoing First Minister, Labour's Rhodri Morgan, and the Leader of Plaid Cymru, Ieuan Wyn Jones, regarding the possible formation of a coalition ended in May without an agreement having been reached. However, despite subsequent talks between Plaid Cymru, the Conservative Party and the Liberal Democrats over the formation of a so-called 'rainbow' coalition, in June Labour and Plaid Cymru finally agreed to form a coalition administration, with Morgan as First Minister and Wyn Jones as his Deputy

In May 2007 a new Ministry of Justice, headed by the Lord Chancellor, Lord Falconer, was established to take over responsibility for prisons, probation services and sentencing from the Home Office, which was to remain responsible for policing, internal security, counter-terrorism and immigration. On 10 May Blair made the long-anticipated announcement that he would resign as Leader of the Labour Party, with effect from 27 June. As the sole candidate, Brown was confirmed as the new Leader of the Labour Party on 24 June. The election to the deputy leadership of the party, which took place on the same day, was closely contested by six candidates and was won in the fifth round of voting by the former Secretary of State for Social Security, Harriet Harman, who was also appointed party Chairman. Brown assumed the role of Prime Minister three days later, following Blair's resignation. At the end of June Brown announced an extensive reorganization of the Cabinet. Alistair Darling, previously the Secretary of State for Trade and Industry, replaced Brown as Chancellor of the Exchequer, while Miliband was appointed Secretary of State for Foreign and Commonwealth Affairs. Straw was appointed Minister of Justice and Lord Chancellor for the transitional period and Jacqui Smith was named as Secretary of State for the Home Department. The Department for Education and Skills was divided to create two new departments: Children, Schools and Families and Innovation, Universities and Skills. The new portfolios were assumed by Ed Balls and John Denham, respectively. Harman was appointed Leader of the House of Commons, Lord Privy Seal and Minister for Women and Equality. Brown's appointments included five ministers who were not members of the Labour Party, among them the former Director-General of the Confederation of British Industry, Sir Digby Jones, and a former UN Deputy Secretary-General, Sir Mark Malloch Brown, as part of a strategy to create a government that extended beyond political affiliations to include talented experts from other fields.

The first week of Brown's premiership was marked by two failed bomb attacks, thought to have been perpetrated by Islamist terrorists. At the end of June 2007 two car bombs placed in central London failed to detonate, while a day later two men were arrested after driving a vehicle containing explosive materials into a terminal building at Glasgow Airport. (One of the men arrested in Glasgow died in August, having sustained severe injuries during the attack.) In early July the Prime Minister announced a number of proposals for constitutional reform, including the transfer to Parliament of powers to approve military action overseas. Brown also indicated his preference for the creation of a so-called 'British bill of rights' to complement the existing Human Rights Act. In late October the Government published three consultation papers, in which the proposals were further outlined.

High public approval ratings for Brown in the first months of his premiership led to speculation that he might call an early general election in late 2007. His popularity was in part due to his effective response to domestic crises, including the attempted terrorist attacks in London and Glasgow, extensive flooding in June and an outbreak of foot and mouth disease in August. This was compounded by his influence in securing a UN resolution at the end of July to send international troops to Darfur, Sudan, to help end the humanitarian crisis. However, following the announcement of new policy initiatives by the Conservative Party, including an increase in the threshold for inheritance tax and a levy on business executives with non-domicile status, who benefited from favourable income tax rules in the United Kingdom, Brown's standing in opinion polls declined. Brown's political reputation was adversely affected by his belated confirmation in October that there would not be an early general election. The Government suffered a further reverse with the admission in November that two compact discs containing the personal and banking details of 25m. individuals in the child benefit system had been lost by HM Revenue and Customs. Also in November the Labour Party was embroiled in a second funding scandal, when it was revealed that donations totalling £670,000 by a property developer, David Abrahams, were illegally channelled through third parties. The General-Secretary of the Labour Party, Peter Watt, submitted his resignation and Brown pledged to return the money. The Electoral Commission requested that the Metropolitan Police conduct an investigation into possible illegal party funding.

In November 2007 the legislative reforms planned by the Government during the following 12 months were presented in the Queen's Speech. They included a further extension of counter-terrorism powers, restrictions on the entry requirements for migrant workers from countries outside of the European Economic Area (EEA—comprising the 27 member states of the EU, as well as Iceland, Liechtenstein and Norway) and reforms to the education system. However, a 'British bill of rights' was not among the measures announced. The new Counter-Terrorism Bill, which was published in January 2008, contained provisions for the extension of the maximum period of pre-charge detention of terrorist suspects from 28 to 42 days in exceptional circumstances, subject to judicial and parliamentary approval. Although this was significantly shorter than the 56 days that had previously been under consideration, it provoked intense criticism from both opposition MPs and a number of Labour backbenchers. Meanwhile, in October 2007 Campbell unexpectedly announced his resignation as Leader of the Liberal Democrats, following criticism of his performance by some senior party members. He was replaced in mid-December by Nick Clegg.

In January 2008 the Secretary of State for Work and Pensions, Peter Hain (who concurrently held the post of Secretary of State for Wales), resigned following allegations of financial impropriety concerning donations to his campaign for election as Deputy Leader of the Labour Party. In a subsequent cabinet reorganization, James Purnell (hitherto Secretary of State for Culture, Media and Sport) was appointed to replace Hain. The Chief Secretary for the Treasury, Andy Burnham, assumed Purnell's portfolio, while Paul Murphy rejoined the Cabinet as Secretary of State for Wales.

In mid-February 2008 the Government announced the nationalization of a major commercial bank, Northern Rock, which had received emergency funds from the Bank of England in late 2007, owing to credit problems precipitated by the US mortgage crisis. Despite opposition from the Conservative Party, the Banking (Special Provisions) Bill was approved by the House of Commons on 20 February, by 293 votes to 167. The bill received royal assent on the following day.

Local elections on 1 May 2008 demonstrated the decline in popularity of the Government, which was exacerbated by public opposition to the abolition of the 10 pence starting rate of income tax in April 2008, which adversely affected those on low wages. At elections to 159 councils in England and Wales the Labour Party suffered significant losses, losing a total of 331 seats and nine councils. The Conservative Party performed well, gaining 294 seats and 12 councils, while the Liberal Democrats made a net gain of one council. In separate elections for the Mayor of London, the Conservative Party candidate, Boris Johnson, defeated the incumbent, Ken Livingstone of the Labour Party, winning 53.2% of the votes cast under a supplementary vote system.

In 1920, faced with mounting popular support for independence in Ireland, where a guerrilla campaign was being waged by the clandestine Irish Republican Army (IRA), in an attempt to force British withdrawal, the British Government conceded to demands for Home Rule, but only to a limited extent, since this was strongly opposed by Protestants in the province of Ulster, who did not wish to become part of a Catholic-dominated all-Ireland state. The Government of Ireland Act (1920) thus provided for two parliaments in Ireland: one in Dublin, for 26 of the 32 counties of Ireland, which obtained dominion status as the Irish Free State, now Ireland (q.v.), in 1922, and one in Belfast, for the remaining six counties, which collectively became known as Northern Ireland and remained an integral part of the United Kingdom.

With the support of the Protestant majority in Northern Ireland, the Ulster Unionist Council (UUC), which had campaigned for the continuation of union with Great Britain, retained permanent control of the Belfast Parliament. Northern Ireland was governed by a one-party administration, with an all-unionist Cabinet headed by a provincial Prime Minister. The British monarch was represented by a Governor. Since Catholics were not only effectively excluded from political power, but also suffered discrimination in civil matters, a state of sectarian tension continued.

During the late 1960s an active civil rights movement emerged, which sought to end the Catholics' grievances by non-violent means. However, Protestant extremists viewed the movement as a republican threat, and resorted to violence against Catholic activists. The IRA was originally a small element in the civil rights movement, but, after increasingly serious disturbances, a breakaway group, calling itself the Provisional IRA, embarked on a campaign of violence with the aim of reuniting Ireland on its own terms. In April 1969 the Northern Ireland Government requested that British army units be assigned to protect important installations and in August the British and Northern Ireland Governments agreed that all security forces in the territory would be placed under

British command. In March 1972, as a result of increased violence, the British Government assumed direct responsibility for law and order. Finding this unacceptable, the Northern Ireland Government resigned. The British Government prorogued the Northern Ireland Parliament and introduced direct rule from London, thus alienating many Protestants.

In 1973 new legislation abolished the office of Governor and the Northern Ireland Parliament, and provided for new constitutional arrangements. In June elections were conducted for a 78-member Northern Ireland Assembly, and an Executive was subsequently constituted from its members. An important part of this new 'power-sharing' arrangement was the establishment of a limited role for the Irish Government in Northern Ireland's affairs. Accordingly, in December, at Sunningdale (in southern England), the British and Irish Governments and the Northern Ireland Executive finalized an agreement to form a Council of Ireland (with members drawn from the Governments of Northern Ireland and Ireland), which would have a range of economic and cultural responsibilities in both parts of Ireland. However, the 'Sunningdale Agreement' and the new devolved authority in Northern Ireland were rejected by many Protestants, and led, in 1974, to a general strike. A state of emergency was declared and the Executive was forced to resign. The Assembly was prorogued, and Northern Ireland returned to direct rule by the British Government. The collapse of the Sunningdale Agreement led to a rise in popularity of the more extreme Democratic Unionist Party (DUP—founded in 1971, and led by Rev. Dr Ian Paisley), which established itself as the main rival to the previously dominant Ulster Unionist Party (UUP—the 'official' Unionists).

Throughout the 1970s the Provisional IRA and the Irish National Liberation Army (INLA, which emerged in 1975) continued their terrorist attacks on both British military and civilian targets, while Protestant 'loyalist' paramilitary groups engaged in attacks on Roman Catholics.

Discussions between the Governments of the United Kingdom and Ireland in 1984–85 culminated in the signing of the Anglo-Irish Agreement in November 1985. The Agreement established the Intergovernmental Conference, through which British and Irish ministers were to meet regularly to discuss political, security, legal and cross-border matters relating to Northern Ireland. While giving the Irish Government a formal consultative role in Northern Ireland affairs, the Agreement recognized that the constitutional status of Northern Ireland remained unchanged and would not be altered without the consent of a majority of Northern Ireland's population. The Agreement had the support of the predominantly Catholic Social Democratic and Labour Party (SDLP), and was approved by the Irish and British Parliaments. However, it was strongly opposed by most unionist politicians, who organized mass demonstrations and violent protests against the Agreement. In June 1986 the Northern Ireland Assembly was dissolved.

The Provisional IRA's campaign of violence in Northern Ireland escalated during 1987, and in 1988 IRA members conducted a successful campaign against British military targets, particularly in Western Europe. Between late 1988 and early 1991 a series of terrorist attacks took place against British Army personnel and politicians in both Great Britain and in continental Europe.

In September 1989 the Irish Government demanded a review of the Ulster Defence Regiment (UDR), the main security force in Northern Ireland, following allegations that it had passed information to loyalist paramilitary groups, which had subsequently been used to target and murder members of the IRA. In May 1990 the allegations were confirmed. During the resulting prosecution of a member of the Ulster Defence Association (UDA) in January 1992, fresh evidence emerged of collusion between the security forces and loyalist paramilitary organizations, and details of events leading to the murder by the UDA in 1989 of a republican lawyer, Patrick Finucane, were revealed. In June 1999 a former British soldier, William Stobie, was charged with Finucane's murder. He subsequently claimed to have been working as a police informer at the time and to have warned them of the impending killing. Furthermore, it was revealed that Stobie had confessed to his involvement in the murder to the Royal Ulster Constabulary (RUC—the Northern Ireland police force) nine years earlier. In November 2001, however, Stobie was acquitted of any involvement in Finucane's murder, after it was ruled that, owing to medical reasons, the main prosecution witness was incapable of testifying. In August 2002, at the behest of the British Government, a former Canadian supreme court judge, Peter Cory, began investigating whether six cases where collusion between the security forces and paramilitary organizations had been alleged (including the Finucane murder) would be subject to public inquiries. Meanwhile, in December 2001 Stobie was assassinated by loyalist paramilitaries.

In April 2003 the interim results of an inquiry established in 1999, under the Commissioner of the Metropolitan Police Force, Sir John Stevens, were published. Stevens stated that he had found evidence of 'widespread collusion' between the security forces and loyalist paramilitaries in the murder of innocent civilians, and that the murders of Finucane and Adam Lambert, who had been killed by the UDA in 1987, could have been prevented. The report concluded that the RUC's investigation of Finucane's murder should have resulted in the early detection and arrest of his killers, and it was highly critical of the withholding of intelligence and evidence by the RUC and the British Army's Force Research Unit (FRU—a secret agency that recruited and controlled agents within loyalist and republican paramilitary organizations). In addition, it was revealed that the RUC had failed to warn or protect nationalists known to be at risk from attack by loyalist paramilitaries. Stevens also announced that a number of investigations remained ongoing and that 57 files had been sent to the Northern Ireland Director of Public Prosecutions. In May 2003 Kenneth Barrett, a senior member of the UDA, was arrested and charged with Finucane's murder. In June 2007 the Director of Public Prosecutions announced that no further prosecutions would be brought in the Finucane case.

In early July 2003 the European Court of Human Rights in Strasbourg, France, ruled that the United Kingdom was guilty of a serious breach of the Human Rights Convention for failing to carry out an adequate investigation into Finucane's death. In March 2004 the Finucane family launched a court action against the British Government to force it to publish the Cory report and to set up a public inquiry into the murders of Patrick Finucane and three other people in the late 1990s. The report was published on 1 April and inquiries were immediately set up into the deaths of these people. However, a public investigation into Finucane's killing was delayed until Barrett's trial had been completed. In September Barrett was convicted of Finucane's murder, having pleaded guilty; he was sentenced to 22 years' imprisonment. Following the conclusion of the trial, pressure was again placed on the Government to open a public inquiry. In late September the Secretary of State for Northern Ireland, Paul Murphy, announced that an inquiry would be held under restrictions after the introduction of new legislation intended to address national security requirements. The Finucane family, however, insisted that a public investigation should take place. When the proposed bill on inquiries was announced in November, the Finucane family expressed concern that a large proportion of evidence in the case would have to be considered in private under its terms. The bill was also criticized by Cory and human rights organizations. Nevertheless, the Inquiries Act received royal assent in April 2005. The Finucane family continued to campaign for a public inquiry and to oppose any inquiry held under the terms of the Inquiries Act.

In January 1990, meanwhile, the British Government launched an initiative to convene meetings between representatives from the major political parties in Northern Ireland and the British and Irish Governments to discuss devolution in Northern Ireland and the future of its relations with Ireland. Sinn Féin (the political wing of the Provisional IRA) was to be excluded from the talks because of its refusal to denounce the IRA's campaign of violence. Bilateral discussions between the British Government and the DUP, the UUP, the SDLP and the Alliance Party eventually began in April 1991, and talks subsequently commenced between all the Northern Ireland parties and the Irish Government. The principal point of contention was the unionists' demand that Ireland hold a referendum on Articles 2 and 3 of its Constitution, which laid claim to the territory of Northern Ireland. The Irish Government, however, remained unwilling to make such a concession except as part of an overall settlement. In the absence of an agreement, the negotiations formally ended in November 1992, and the Anglo-Irish Conference resumed.

In August 1992 the British Government announced the proscription of the UDA under the Emergency Provisions Act, a measure that was widely regarded as long overdue in the light of the UDA's paramilitary activities from the early 1970s onwards (some committed under the name of Ulster Freedom Fighters—UFF). In late 1993 and early 1994 police in Great Britain made several large seizures of explosives, which the Government claimed to be evidence of improving anti-terrorist surveillance. During this period frequent discoveries of IRA devices and bomb alerts caused much disruption, especially to public transport services.

In October 1993 the British and Irish Prime Ministers, John Major and Albert Reynolds, issued a joint statement setting out the principles on which future negotiations were to be based. The statement emphasized the precondition that Sinn Féin permanently renounce violence before being admitted to the negotiations. In December Major and Reynolds made a joint declaration, known as the 'Downing Street Declaration', which provided a specific framework for a peace settlement. The initiative, which was widely supported by opposition parties in Britain and Ireland, referred to the possibility of a united Ireland and accepted the legitimacy of self-determination, while insisting on majority consent within Northern Ireland. The DUP, the UUP and Sinn Féin rejected the document, which effectively removed any confidence of achieving an imminent peace settlement. However, the British and Irish Governments reiterated their intention to pursue the peace process.

On 31 August 1994 the IRA announced 'a complete cessation of violence'. On 13 October the loyalist paramilitary groups declared a suspension of military activity, which was effectively to be linked to that of the IRA. Later that month Major announced new measures to restart the peace process, adopting the 'working assumption' that the IRA cease-fire was permanent. The first public meeting between Sinn Féin and government officials was held in December, marking the start of exploratory talks between the two sides. In February 1995 Major and the new Irish Prime Minister, John Bruton, presented a Framework Document, together with a separate British government paper on a new Northern Ireland Assembly. The Framework Document reaffirmed the principles of the Downing Street Declaration, and included provisions for the co-operation and involvement of both Governments in the peace settlement. In addition, the Document proposed the establishment of a cross-border body in which elected representatives of the Irish Parliament and a Northern Ireland Assembly might create and implement policy on issues agreed by the two Governments, in consultation with the Northern Ireland parties. The proposals for the Northern Ireland Assembly envisaged an elected authority with wide legislative and executive responsibility (except, initially, over taxation, and law and order), although it was to be monitored by a three-member elected panel. Both Governments emphasized that the proposals were to form the basis of negotiations and public consideration, and any final agreement was to be subject to parliamentary approval and popular consent by means of a referendum.

Despite a positive Sinn Féin response to the Framework Document, the issue of decommissioning paramilitary weapons remained the major obstacle to peace negotiations. The Government repeatedly objected to Sinn Féin's linking of IRA decommissioning with the demilitarization of Northern Ireland. In May 1995, having agreed that these would be discussed as separate issues, the Secretary of State for Northern Ireland, Sir Patrick Mayhew, and the Sinn Féin President, Gerry Adams, met (the most senior-level encounter of the two sides in 20 years) at an investment conference for Northern Ireland, held in Washington, DC, USA. Further political dialogue was hindered by Sinn Féin's opposition to the British Government's insistence that decommissioning by paramilitary organizations be a precondition to conducting all-party negotiations.

In November 1995 the British and Irish Governments agreed to initiate preliminary talks (provisionally scheduled to commence in February 1996) with all the parties in Northern Ireland and to establish an international commission to assess the practicalities of the decommissioning of armaments and other aspects of the peace process. US President Bill Clinton endorsed this initiative during a visit later that month, and the commission, chaired by one of Clinton's advisers, George Mitchell, began meetings with all sides involved in the peace process in December. The final report of the international commission was issued in January 1996, and recommended proceeding with all-party talks on the condition that all sides endorse the eventual complete disarmament of paramilitary organizations, the renunciation of violence and the cessation of paramilitary 'punishment' attacks. According to the report, arms decommissioning was to be considered in parallel with the negotiations, while the eventual surrender of weaponry was to be conducted under international supervision, with those involved being free from prosecution. The report was generally supported by all sides.

In February 1996 the IRA abruptly terminated its cease-fire by exploding a large bomb in London. The organization blamed the British Government for the resumption of hostilities, citing its inflexible response to the Mitchell report. The security forces subsequently uncovered details of a revived bombing campaign in Great Britain. Bruton and Major declared that they would suspend all ministerial dialogue with Sinn Féin, but would intensify efforts to achieve a peaceful settlement. At the end of the month the leaders announced an initiative to pursue the peace process, incorporating nationalist and unionist demands. Consultations were to commence immediately on an electoral format to establish a forum for intersectoral dialogue prior to the initiation of comprehensive political negotiations, to be based on the 1995 Framework Document. In March the British Cabinet approved a 'hybrid' electoral system for the Northern Ireland forum, in an attempt to accommodate demands from all sides and to ensure a wide representation of the region's political groupings. Participants in the all-party negotiations were to be selected from among the 110 forum members. In the election, held on 30 May, the UUP secured 24% of the votes cast and the largest number of seats (30), while the DUP and the SDLP took 21 and 17 seats respectively. Sinn Féin's 15% share of the votes secured the party 17 seats. In addition, seven seats were won by the Alliance Party, three by the United Kingdom Unionist Party (UKUP) and two each by the Progressive Unionist Party (PUP), the Ulster Democratic Party (UDP), the Women's Coalition of Northern Ireland and representatives of Labour (a coalition of left-wing individuals and associations). The multi-party discussions, which commenced on 10 June, were undermined by Sinn Féin's exclusion, in the absence of a new IRA cease-fire declaration, and by unionist opposition to the appointment of Mitchell as Chairman, which they claimed was part of a nationalist agenda. Further political uncertainty followed an IRA bomb attack in Manchester in June.

In July 1996 political events in Northern Ireland were dominated by sectarian disputes regarding the organization of traditional Protestant marches. The peace process suffered a further reverse when the SDLP announced that it was to withdraw from the recently elected forum, owing to the British Government's management of the crisis to which the disputes gave rise. In July and September raids by the security forces on suspected IRA bases in southern England resulted in the seizure of explosives, and were reported by the police to have averted planned attacks on infrastructural and political targets.

In October 1996 the UUP and the SDLP agreed on a draft agenda, based on the provisions of the Mitchell report, to enable substantive multi-party talks to proceed without being dominated by the issue of weapons decommissioning. In November Sinn Féin revealed a set of proposals, formulated with the SDLP in order to bolster the peace process, which included the implementation by the British Government of confidence-building measures, such as the release of IRA prisoners, and a guarantee that Sinn Féin would be admitted to the talks in the event of a renewed IRA cease-fire. In response, Major defined the terms by which the party could join the talks, namely, a credible and lasting restoration of the IRA cease-fire and an end to all paramilitary training activities and punishment attacks. In January 1997 all-party talks resumed, but were suspended in March until after the general election in the United Kingdom, scheduled to be held in May. Prior to the poll the IRA undertook a co-ordinated programme of disruption in Great Britain, while sectarian tensions increased in Northern Ireland.

In the general election, held on 1 May 1997, the UUP secured 10 of the 18 seats available, with 32.7% of the votes cast in Northern Ireland. Sinn Féin regained a parliamentary mandate, winning two seats (with 16.1% of the votes). The SDLP won three seats, with 24.1% of the votes. The DUP lost two of its previously held seats, securing two seats (13.6%), and the UKUP won its first seat in a general election (1.6%).

The newly elected Labour Government generated renewed optimism that a peace settlement could be achieved. The Prime Minister, Tony Blair, proposed a timetable for the talks, and reiterated that he envisaged their conclusion no later than May 1998, when the results were to be put to a popular referendum. In June 1997 the British and Irish Governments announced a new initiative to accelerate the peace process, whereby the decommissioning of paramilitary weapons, together with other confidence-building measures, would be undertaken concurrently with political negotiations, in an attempt to facilitate Sinn Féin's participation in the process, and clarified that Sinn Féin would be eligible to join substantive negotiations six weeks after a new IRA cease-fire announcement.

In July 1997 the IRA announced a restoration of its cease-fire. A few days later the Irish and British Governments issued a joint statement that the all-party negotiations would commence on 15 September, with the participation of Sinn Féin. At the same time, however, the unionist parties rejected the measures for weapons decommissioning that had been formulated by the two Governments. At the end of August the new Secretary of State for Northern Ireland, Mo Mowlam, concluded that the restoration of the IRA cease-fire was 'unequivocal' and invited Sinn Féin to join the talks. Accordingly, in September Sinn Féin endorsed the so-called Mitchell principles, which committed participants to accepting the outcome of the peace process and renouncing violence as a means of punishment or resolving problems. The UUP, together with the DUP and UKUP, which had already declared their boycott of any discussions with Sinn Féin, and other loyalist representatives, failed to attend the opening session of the talks when they resumed in September, owing partly to a statement by the IRA that undermined Sinn Féin's endorsement of the Mitchell principles. The talks were further jeopardized by the explosion of a republican bomb in Co Armagh for which a proscribed dissident paramilitary faction, the Continuity Army Council, claimed responsibility. Nevertheless, the UUP rejoined the peace negotiations a few days later. In late September all eight parties to the talks signed a procedural agreement to pursue substantive negotiations. At the same time the Independent International Commission on Decommissioning (IICD) was inaugurated, under the chairmanship of the former head of the Canadian armed forces, Gen. John de Chastelain. The first meeting between a British Prime Minister and Sinn Féin leaders in more than 70 years took place at the talks in October, when Blair held private discussions with Adams and Martin McGuinness. In December the murder of the leader of the proscribed Loyalist Volunteer Force (LVF), Billy Wright, in the Maze Prison by INLA prisoners prompted an escalation of sectarian violence throughout Northern Ireland. In January 1998 Mowlam took the unprecedented action of meeting loyalist paramilitary prisoners within the Maze prison, which secured their continued endorsement of PUP and UDP participation in the peace discussions.

In January 1998 Blair and the Irish Prime Minister, Bertie Ahern, published a document outlining a framework for negotiations: this envisaged 'balanced constitutional change' by both Governments and proposed a devolved form of government within Northern Ireland. After intensive negotiations, on 10 April a settlement was announced. The Good Friday Agreement (or Belfast Agreement) envisaged radical reform of the political structures of Northern Ireland, its relations with Ireland, and its constitutional standing within the United Kingdom. The main provisions of the Agreement were as follows: the establishment of a 108-member elected Northern Ireland Assembly, with authority to legislate on all domestic matters currently administered by the Northern Ireland Office; an Executive Committee, to be elected by the Assembly and headed by a First Minister and Deputy First Minister; an obligation that the Assembly establish, within one year, a North/South Ministerial Council at which representatives of the Irish Government and the executive authority in Northern Ireland might consider issues of cross-border concern; regular meetings of representatives of the Irish Government with members of the British Parliament, the Northern Ireland Assembly and other regional assemblies of the United Kingdom, under a new British-Irish Council, with the objective of promoting co-operation, information exchange and agreement on issues of mutual interest; amendment of Articles 2 and 3 of the Irish Constitution; replacement of the 1985 Anglo-Irish Agreement with a new bilateral accord, incorporating a British-Irish Intergovernmental Council to oversee the Assembly and North/South Council; and a commitment by all parties to achieve the decommissioning of paramilitary weapons within two years. David Trimble, the Leader of the UUP, secured the critical support of his party for the settlement, although several dissident UUP politicians later joined the DUP and UKUP in their campaign to prevent an endorsement of the accord, and the Protestant Orange Order urged its members to oppose the Agreement. Sinn Féin approved the accord. Some 71.1% of voters in Northern Ireland and 94.4% of voters in Ireland approved the proposed peace settlement in referendums conducted on 22 May, securing its immediate future. Parties in Northern Ireland began almost immediately to prepare for the elections to the Northern Ireland Assembly, which were scheduled to be held on 25 June. Voting was to be conducted using the single transferable vote system of proportional representation, providing for six members to be elected from each of the 18 Westminster parliamentary constituencies, with a broad representation of political preferences.

In the elections to the Northern Ireland Assembly, conducted on 25 June 1998, the UUP won 28 of the 108 seats, while the SDLP took 24, despite having won the largest share of first-preference votes under the new voting system. Sinn Féin won 18 Assembly seats. Those opposed to the Good Friday Agreement secured a total of 28 seats, including 20 representatives of the DUP, five of the UKUP and three dissident UUP politicians. The remaining seats were won by the Alliance Party (six), the PUP (two) and the Women's Coalition (two). At the inaugural meeting of the Assembly, on 1 July, Trimble was elected as First Minister of the executive body, while Seamus Mallon of the SDLP was elected as Deputy First Minister. Sectarian violence soon threatened to disrupt the peace process following confrontations between the security forces and members of the Orange Order who, in defiance of the newly established Parades Commission, sought to march its traditional route along the predominantly Roman Catholic-inhabited Garvaghy Road in Portadown, Co Armagh, to the church at nearby Drumcree. However, following the deaths of three young Roman Catholics in a petrol bomb attack in Ballymoney, Co Antrim, in July the majority of the loyalists in Portadown abandoned their protest. In August the peace process again came under threat when 29 people in Omagh, Co Tyrone, were killed by an explosive device, planted by a dissident republican group, the Real IRA, representing the single largest toll of deaths in any incident since the onset of unrest associated with Northern Ireland. Later that month Ahern announced a series of anti-terrorism measures in an effort to facilitate convictions against terrorists based in Ireland. Similarly, Blair announced legislation, which was approved in September, including heightened powers to convict anyone conspiring within the United Kingdom to commit terrorist offences.

Progress in the peace process continued to be obstructed throughout late 1998 by a dispute between unionists and Sinn Féin concerning the decommissioning of paramilitary weapons, with Trimble insisting that the admittance of Sinn Féin representatives to the Executive Committee be conditional on progress in the demilitarization of the IRA. For its part, Sinn Féin insisted that the Good Friday Agreement did not specify when decommissioning should begin, only that it should be completed by May 2000. As a result of the dispute the deadline of 21 October 1998 for the formation of the Executive Committee and the North/South bodies was not met. In December agreement was finally reached on the responsibilities of the 10 government departments of the Executive Committee and of six North/South 'implementation' bodies. This was endorsed by the Northern Ireland Assembly in February 1999.

During 1999 the date for the devolution of powers to the new Northern Ireland institutions, envisaged as 10 March in the Good Friday Agreement, was postponed several times, and negotiations were halted in July when Trimble announced that the UUP would not participate in a devolved administration with Sinn Féin until some decommissioning had taken place. A review of the peace process, headed by George Mitchell, began in September. In that month the former Chairman of the Conservative Party, Chris Patten, who had been appointed in April 1998 to head an independent commission charged with conducting a review of policing in Northern Ireland, published his report. Recommended changes to the RUC included the establishment of an elected body of representatives, drawn from all sections of the community, to which the new force would be accountable, the active recruitment of Roman Catholic officers in order that the force should achieve a balanced representation, and a reduction in the number of serving officers from 13,500 to 7,500, subject to the successful conclusion of the peace process. The report provoked anger from unionists, who particularly objected to plans to change the force's name, oath and symbols. Sinn Féin, meanwhile, renewed its demand that the force be disbanded.

In November 1999 Mitchell concluded the review of the peace process, producing an agreement providing for the devolution of powers to the Executive Committee. The agreement followed a statement by the IRA that it would appoint a representative to enter discussions with the IICD. Trimble persuaded his party to approve the agreement. On 29 November the Northern Ireland Assembly convened to appoint the 10-member Executive Committee. On 2 December power was officially transferred from Westminster to the new Northern Ireland executive at Stormont Castle and, in accordance with the Good Friday Agreement, the Irish Government removed from the Irish Constitution its territorial claim over Northern Ireland. In mid-December the inaugural meeting was held of the North/South Ministerial Council. The British-Irish Council met for the first time later that month. In late December Peter Mandelson, the new Secretary of State for Northern Ireland, announced a review of security procedures in Northern Ireland and the withdrawal of some 2,000 troops from Northern Ireland, and in January 2000 he adopted the majority of the recommendations contained in the Patten report, provoking an angry response from unionists. In that month Adams dismissed the possibility of immediate IRA decommissioning, and a report by the IICD confirmed that there had been no disarmament. With the prospect of the collapse of the peace process, the British and Irish Governments engaged in intensive negotiations. On 1 February the IRA released a statement giving assurances that its cease-fire would not be broken and expressing support for the peace process. However, it failed to comply with an 11 February deadline to begin decommissioning, and legislation came into effect on that day suspending the new executive, legislative and co-operative institutions and returning Northern Ireland to direct rule. The IRA subsequently announced its withdrawal from discussions with the IICD. Adams refused to participate in any further review of the peace process until the suspended institutions had been restored.

Direct talks between the British and Irish Governments and the principal parties resumed in early May 2000, with the Government promising to restore the Northern Ireland institutions on 22 May and postpone the deadline for decommissioning until June 2001, subject to a commitment by the IRA on the arms issue. On 6 May the IRA responded by offering to 'initiate a process that will completely and verifiably put arms beyond use'. Under the offer a number of IRA arms depositories were to be regularly inspected by two independent international figures, Martti Ahtisaari, the former President of Finland, and Cyril Ramaphosa, a principal figure in the South African peace process. Trimble narrowly succeeded in securing the approval of the UUP of a return to power sharing, and on 30 May power was once again transferred from Westminster to the new Northern Ireland institutions. In accordance with their continued policy of attempting to impede the functioning of the Assembly, DUP ministers agreed to retake their places in the Assembly but announced their intention periodically to resign their posts in order to disrupt parliamentary business. In June the IRA allowed three arms depositories to be inspected by Ramaphosa and Ahtisaari and announced that it had also resumed contact with the IICD. The two inspectors affirmed that the arms they had seen were 'safely and adequately stored' and that they had installed devices at the depositories, which would enable them to detect if the weapons were subsequently tampered with.

In July 2000 the decision again to prohibit the Orange Order from marching along the Garvaghy Road in Portadown provoked renewed sectarian violence and numerous attacks on the security forces. Later in that month, under the terms of the Good Friday Agreement, the final group of 86 convicted terrorists was freed from prison in Northern Ireland. Their release was widely criticized as it had been conditionally linked to the commencement of IRA arms' decommissioning, which had yet to begin. In August Mandelson warned feuding loyalist paramilitary groups that they risked further delaying IRA decommissioning if they continued their retaliatory attacks. In an attempt to quell unrest, troops were once again deployed on the streets of Belfast, and John Adair, the Leader of the UFF, who was widely believed to be responsible for many of the incidents, was arrested and imprisoned; he had been released under the provisions of the Good Friday Agreement in September 1999. Nevertheless, revenge attacks continued throughout late 2000. In December, however, the feud was declared to be at an end by three of the four groups involved.

Meanwhile, in November 2000 the Northern Ireland Policing Bill received royal assent, and later in that month the House of Lords approved controversial legislation that would enable members of the Irish Parliament to stand for election to the Northern Ireland Assembly as well as to the British Parliament.

In March 2001 the IRA unexpectedly announced that it had re-established contact with the IICD. In an attempt further to disrupt the peace process, the Real IRA exploded two bombs outside the BBC's Television Centre building in London in March and April. The incident was widely condemned by all parties democratically involved in the peace process. The Real IRA had also been responsible for four previous attacks on Great Britain during 2000 and early 2001. In May 2001 the US Government designated the Real IRA as a foreign terrorist organization and froze its assets in the USA. In April 2003 five members of the Real IRA were sentenced to terms of imprisonment ranging from 16 to 22 years for their roles in the London bombings.

At the general election to the British Parliament held on 7 June 2001 the UUP won six seats (compared with 10 in 1997), with 26.8% of the votes cast in Northern Ireland. The DUP secured five seats, gaining three at the expense of the UUP, with 22.5% of the votes cast. Sinn Féin increased its parliamentary representation, winning four seats, with 21.7% of the votes, while the SDLP took only three seats, with 21.0% of the votes. The UUP suffered a further significant reverse at local elections held in Northern Ireland later in June, with Sinn Féin and the DUP making substantial gains at the UUP's expense.

Following Trimble's announcement of his intention to resign as First Minister on 1 July 2001 if the IRA had not commenced a process of decommissioning, Blair and Ahern held emergency talks with representatives from the UUP, Sinn Féin and the SDLP in June. On 1 July Trimble duly resigned. The administrative functions of the office of the First Minister were assumed on a caretaker basis by the Minister of Enterprise, Trade and Investment, Sir Reg Empey of the UUP. (Mallon's position of Deputy First Minister became vacant, although he continued to exercise the functions of his office.) Trimble's resignation triggered a six-week period at the end of which, barring the resolution of the impasse between the parties and the election of a First Minister and Deputy First Minister, new elections to the Assembly would have to be held. Later in July the IICD stated that the IRA had yet to decommission a single weapon, and had failed to outline how it intended to put its arms beyond use.

In early August 2001 the British and Irish Governments unveiled their joint 'Proposals for the Implementation of the Good Friday Agreement'. The proposals stipulated that while decommissioning was not a precondition of the Agreement, it remained indispensable to a political resolution and must be resolved in a manner 'acceptable to and verified by the IICD'. However, while Trimble stated that he would 'carefully consider' the proposals, he remained adamant that in the continued absence of IRA decommissioning of weapons there would be no progress. A few days later both the IICD and the IRA issued statements confirming that they had agreed upon a confidential decommissioning scheme, and de Chastelain announced that he was satisfied that the IRA had begun a process that would put arms 'completely and verifiably' beyond use. Trimble described the announcement as a 'step forward', but insisted that it was not sufficient for him to retract his resignation and demanded evidence of the destruction of weapons. Faced with the impending collapse of the Northern Ireland institutions, on 10 August the British Government suspended the Northern Ireland institutions for a 24-hour period. Under a legal loophole contained within the Good Friday Agreement, this decision allowed for a six-week extension to the previously imposed deadline for the election of a First Minister and Deputy. In response to the suspension, the IRA withdrew the offer to commence the process of decommissioning.

Also in August 2001 speculation that the RUC had ignored warnings of an imminent bomb attack in Omagh, prior to the atrocity in August 1998 (see above), prompted an inquiry by the Police Ombudsman for Northern Ireland, Nuala O'Loan, into the police force's investigation of the bombing. O'Loan's report, which was published in December 2001, stated that the RUC's Special Branch had failed to pass on two separate warnings from informants, and that a number of grave errors were made during the subsequent police investigation into the attack. In mid-August the British Government had announced revised policing proposals, which envisaged the equal division of recruitment to the police force between Protestants and Roman Catholics and allowed for the possibility of ex-paramilitary prisoners sitting on the 29 District Police Partnership Boards, providing they relinquished their support for terrorist organizations. Sinn Féin had rejected the proposals before their publication and insisted that they would refuse to nominate members to the new 19-member Northern Ireland Policing Board (NIPB), which would be responsible for overseeing the police. On 4 November the RUC was officially renamed the Police Service of Northern Ireland (PSNI), and three days later the NIPB held its inaugural meeting. The two vacant Sinn Féin seats on the board were allocated to the DUP and the UUP. In early February 2002 the Chairman of the

NIPB issued a joint statement on behalf of the NIPB, O'Loan and the Chief Constable of the PSNI, Sir Ronnie Flanagan (who had been criticized in O'Loan's report), which recognized that 'on the basis of the information available the Omagh bombing could not have been prevented'. Later that month Flanagan announced his resignation. Meanwhile, in January Colm Murphy, the only person to have been charged in relation to the bomb attack, was sentenced to 14 years' imprisonment by the Special Criminal Court in Dublin for conspiracy to cause an explosion. In September Hugh Orde was appointed Chief Constable of the PSNI. In August 2003 the leader of the Real IRA, Kevin McKevitt, was sentenced to 20 years' imprisonment by the Special Criminal Court in Dublin for directing a terrorist organization. Investigations into the Omagh bombing continued in 2003 and 2004 and in March 2004 one of the five men being sued by the relatives of the Omagh victims in a civil court case was sentenced to three and a half years' imprisonment for membership of the Real IRA.

Meanwhile, on 22 September 2001 Dr John Reid, who had succeeded Mandelson as Secretary of State for Northern Ireland earlier in that year (see above), announced a further 24-hour suspension of the Assembly, thus granting the parties a further six weeks in which to overcome the continuing impasse. Trimble subsequently announced that the UUP would table a motion in the Assembly to exclude the two Sinn Féin ministers from the Executive, and that if, as was almost certain, the motion was defeated and there was still no progress on the decommissioning issue by the IRA, UUP ministers would begin to withdraw from the Executive, thus precipitating its collapse. Following continued sectarian clashes in late September (for which Reid held the UDA responsible) and the murder of a journalist in Co Armagh, for which the LVF claimed responsibility, the Secretary of State announced that the British Government no longer recognized the UDA/UFF and LVF cease-fires.

In October 2001 the UUP exclusion motion was duly defeated and the three UUP ministers and the two DUP ministers resigned. Later that month the IRA and the IICD issued separate statements, which affirmed that the IRA had taken the unprecedented step of putting a significant quantity of arms, ammunition and explosives beyond use. The announcement prevented the imminent collapse of the Northern Ireland institutions and was widely welcomed by all pro-Agreement parties. Trimble immediately announced that he would reappoint the three UUP ministers to the Executive and seek re-election to the post of First Minister. On 24 October the UUP ministers resumed their posts and on the following day the DUP resumed its two portfolios. Later in October Trimble received approval from the UUP Executive to resume his post as First Minister, with the SDLP Leader-elect, Mark Durkan, announcing his intention to stand for the position of Deputy First Minister. On 2 November, however, Trimble failed in his attempt to be re-elected as First Minister. Although he secured 70.6% of the total votes cast (including all 38 nationalist votes), two anti-Agreement members of the UUP voted against Trimble, thus preventing him from obtaining the constitutionally required majority of unionists in favour of his re-election. Following intensive negotiations, three members of the independent Alliance Party and one member of the Women's Coalition agreed to redesignate themselves temporarily as unionists, and on 6 November Trimble finally regained the post of First Minister. Durkan was returned as Deputy First Minister.

In December 2001 the British Government provoked considerable controversy when it announced that it had agreed to grant Sinn Féin MPs access to the facilities of the House of Commons and that they would receive their full parliamentary allowances and travel expenses, despite the fact that they still refused to take their seats in Parliament or participate in debates, and would not swear allegiance to the Queen. In January 2002 Sinn Féin MPs occupied offices in the House of Commons for the first time.

In mid-2002, despite the announcement in April that the IRA had put a further quantity of arms, ammunition and explosives beyond use, the fragility of the peace process was underscored by unprecedented levels of street violence in north and east Belfast. Adams' refusal to testify before a US investigation into alleged IRA links with left-wing rebels in Colombia, allied with allegations of IRA involvement in the theft of documents from PSNI Special Branch offices in Belfast in March 2002 and the discovery, in June, of an IRA intelligence database listing details of more than 200 judges, politicians and members of the security forces, provoked unionist demands that Sinn Féin ministers be removed from the power-sharing Executive and further 'crisis' meetings between the British and Irish Governments.

In July 2002 the IRA apologized for the deaths and injuries of 'non-combatants' caused as a result of its actions over the previous 30 years. The sincerity of the apology was questioned by Trimble, and senior unionists were sceptical that the IRA remained committed to the peace process in the light of continued sectarian violence in Belfast, for which the UUP maintained that the IRA was primarily responsible. Earlier in July, during talks between the British and Irish Governments and the pro-Agreement parties in Belfast, Trimble had implied that UUP ministers would resign from the Executive by the end of that month if the IRA did not clearly demonstrate its commitment to a 'full transition from violence to democracy'.

Violent sectarian disturbances continued in Belfast during August 2002. Early in that month the Real IRA was suspected to have been responsible for a bomb attack in which a Protestant man was killed—the first fatality caused by the organization since the Omagh bombing in August 1998—and in mid-August a Roman Catholic was murdered in an apparent revenge act for the earlier wounding of a young Protestant. The situation was exacerbated by the escalation of a feud between rival loyalist paramilitary groups, which resulted in a number of shootings, and unionists called for the establishment of an independent body to monitor the paramilitary cease-fires. Later in that month the ruling council of the UUP, the UUC, announced that it would withdraw the UUP's ministers from the Executive in January 2003 if the IRA and Sinn Féin had not demonstrated a complete transition to democracy and non-violence.

In early October 2002 Sinn Féin's offices at the Northern Ireland Assembly were raided by police, who, as part of a major investigation into intelligence-gathering by republicans, suspected that the IRA had infiltrated the Northern Ireland Office and gained access to large numbers of confidential documents. Among a number of people detained was Sinn Féin's Head of Administration, Denis Donaldson, who was charged with possession of documents likely to be of assistance to terrorist organizations. (In 2007 the case collapsed, when it emerged that Donaldson had acted as an informant for the British security services—see below.) Trimble accused Sinn Féin of a 'massive political conspiracy' and threatened to withdraw from the Executive unless the British Government proposed the expulsion of Sinn Féin from the Assembly. Emergency talks between the British and Irish Governments and the Northern Ireland political leaders followed; however, Blair's demands for IRA concessions on the arms issue were not met. On 11 October the two DUP ministers resigned from the Executive, and on 14 October the Assembly was suspended and direct rule imposed. In a joint statement, Blair and Ahern announced that the devolved institutions would only be restored if Sinn Féin ended its link with paramilitary organizations and Blair subsequently called on the IRA to disband. Later that month the IRA announced the suspension of all contact with the IICD and claimed that the British Government was to blame for the current crisis, having failed to honour its commitments under the Good Friday Agreement.

In May 2003 Adams stated that the IRA leadership was determined 'that there will be no activities which will undermine in any way the peace process or the Good Friday Agreement'; however, Blair cited the refusal of the IRA to give him 'absolute clarity' that it had ceased all paramilitary activity as the reason for his decision again to postpone elections. Nevertheless, the British and Irish Governments published their Joint Declaration, which included plans to reduce the security forces from 14,500 to 5,000 by April 2005; to repeal anti-terrorist legislation specific to Northern Ireland; to establish an independent international monitoring body to assess any breaches of the Good Friday Agreement; to transfer policing and judicial powers to a devolved government; and provision that terrorists who had committed crimes for which they had not yet been convicted would have their cases heard at 'special judicial tribunals'. The Declaration also urged a full and permanent cessation of all paramilitary activity, including military attacks, intelligence gathering, weapons procurement and punishment attacks.

In June 2003 Trimble secured a narrow victory at an emergency meeting of the UUC over UUP MP Jeffrey Donaldson, who had attempted to persuade the party to support a motion to reject the Joint Declaration. Donaldson, Rev. Martin Smyth (the party's President) and David Burnside subsequently resigned the UUP Westminster whip, provoking further speculation about a split within the party. Days later the three dissident

MPs were suspended from the party. In July the High Court in Belfast ruled that their suspension was 'unlawful, invalid and of no force or effect', and Trimble suffered a further reverse when more than 37% of the members of his constituency association expressed their lack of confidence in his leadership of the party. In September Trimble succeeded narrowly in passing a motion at the UUC which urged Donaldson, Smyth and Burnside to retake the party whip at Westminster; however, the three MPs insisted they would remain outside the parliamentary party and continue their opposition to the Joint Declaration.

Talks between the British and Irish Governments and the major Northern Ireland political parties continued during late 2003, and in September the four members of the International Monitoring Commission (IMC) were appointed. Trimble and Adams met with Ahern and Blair in London in mid-October, and it was revealed that elections to the Northern Ireland Assembly would take place on 26 November. However, later on the same day Trimble issued a statement in which he maintained that the acts of decommissioning of IRA weapons, witnessed by de Chastelain earlier that day, had lacked the transparency the UUP required to be convinced of the IRA's genuine desire to commit to a lasting peace. Trimble announced that the peace process would be put on hold pending the convening of the UUC, thus preventing the devolution of powers to the Northern Ireland institutions; however, both Blair and Ahern insisted that the elections would proceed on 26 November. The British Government acknowledged in late October that the devolved institutions would not be restored following the elections and that a review of the Good Friday Agreement would take place in early 2004, although Blair stressed that the fundamental principles of the Agreement were not a matter for negotiation. A statement issued by the IRA on 29 October maintained that it had honoured its commitments and that there would be no more acts of decommissioning until the UUP agreed to support the restoration of power sharing.

At the elections to the Northern Ireland Assembly, held on 26 November 2003, the DUP, which was opposed to the Good Friday Agreement, secured 30 of the 108 seats, thus becoming the largest party in the Assembly. The UUP won 27 seats, while Sinn Féin increased its parliamentary representation to 24 seats. The SDLP suffered a significant loss of support, winning just 18 seats. Of the remaining seats, six were won by the Alliance Party, while the PUP, the UKUP and an independent candidate each won one seat. The rate of voter participation was officially recorded at 63.1%. The election results increased the pressure on Trimble from anti-Agreement factions of the UUP, which again called for his resignation. Furthermore, the DUP demanded a full renegotiation of the Good Friday Agreement. However, both Ahern and Blair reiterated that the 'principles and values' of the Agreement would not be changed. In December an independent report into a series of car bombs detonated in Dublin and Monaghan, Ireland, in May 1974 in which 33 people were killed and some 300 were injured, concluded that there were 'grounds for suspecting' that British security forces had helped loyalist paramilitaries to carry out the atrocities. Families of the victims repeated their demands for a public inquiry into the incidents. Later in that month Jeffrey Donaldson resigned from the UUP; two other UUP deputies also left the party and in early January 2004 they confirmed that they would join the DUP. A few days later, however, Burnside and Smyth announced that they had retaken the UUP whip at Westminster.

In January 2004 the DUP Leader, Paisley, met Ahern at the Irish embassy in London, insisting that the DUP would not conduct face-to-face talks with Sinn Féin until the IRA had disbanded. The review of the Good Friday Agreement commenced in early February with Paisley setting out his party's own proposals for power sharing. While acknowledging that the proposals signalled progress on the part of the DUP, they were generally negatively received by Sinn Féin, which feared that they would lead to a return to unionist majority rule. In early March Trimble withdrew his party in protest at the alleged IRA involvement in the recent kidnapping of a dissident republican in Belfast. Later in that month Ahern and Blair met to hold talks with political groups and reiterated their commitment to the conclusion of a power-sharing agreement. In late March Trimble was re-elected as the Leader of the UUP. In April the IMC issued its first report, in which it detailed the levels of ongoing paramilitary activity by both loyalist and republican groups in Northern Ireland. The British Government subsequently announced that it would impose financial sanctions on Sinn Féin and the PUP.

The review of the Good Friday Agreement resumed at Leeds Castle in England in September 2004, having been put on hold for the European elections. As the talks began de Chastelain announced that the IRA would be prepared to decommission its weapons if a political deal were agreed upon; however, the talks ended with no agreement. In November the UDA indicated its intention to end violence and demilitarize following an announcement by the Secretary of State for Northern Ireland, Paul Murphy, that the UDA's February cease-fire would be officially recognized by the Government. On 17 November the British and Irish Governments passed their proposals for restoring the power-sharing executive to the DUP and Sinn Féin for consultation. One week later Paisley conferred with Blair and stated that the disarming of the IRA would only be an acceptable starting point for the power-sharing agreement if it was verified by photographic evidence. At the end of the month Adams met the PSNI Chief Constable, Orde, to discuss decommissioning, while Paisley met de Chastelain in Belfast to review the destruction of the IRA's weapons. On the following day Paisley issued an ultimatum to the IRA that if the peace accord were not restored in the current situation it would become an almost impossible task in the future, and also called for the IRA to repent of its past actions. Adams declared Paisley's comments to be offensive and stated that Sinn Féin would go no further in negotiations. On 8 December, despite being resigned to the collapse of the peace process, Blair and Ahern met in Belfast to reveal their final proposals to restore devolution. On the following day the IRA declared that photographic proof of decommissioning had never been an option and that although the IRA was committed to the peace process, it would not be subjected to a process of humiliation.

In December 2004 an estimated £26.5m. was stolen from the Belfast headquarters of Northern Bank. The PSNI immediately set up an investigation into the robbery and in January 2005 Orde stated that the IRA had been responsible for the robbery. In a report published in mid-February the IMC implicated not only the IRA but also Sinn Féin leaders (these accusations were vehemently denied by Adams). In early February Ahern and Blair warned the IRA that its failure to demilitarize was the only obstacle to an agreement on power sharing; on the following day the IRA withdrew its commitment to decommissioning. In March, responding to Sinn Féin's alleged involvement in the robbery of the Northern Bank, the British Parliament voted to withdraw from the party its entitlement to an allowance payable to Northern Irish political parties, and from Sinn Féin's four MPs their entitlement to personal parliamentary allowances. Early in April, in an initiative that aimed to break the deadlock over the restoration of devolution, Adams urged the IRA to embrace the political alternative to armed struggle that now existed. In May Sean Gerard Hoey, who had already been detained on charges of terrorism and membership of the Real IRA, was charged with the murder of the 29 people who had been killed in the Omagh bombing in 1998; his trial commenced in September 2006. In December 2007 Hoey was acquitted of all charges. At the trial's conclusion, the presiding judge expressed concerns over DNA evidence used by the prosecution and errors committed by the police force during its investigation into the bombings. Immediately following Hoey's acquittal, Orde defended the conduct of his officers, while acknowledging that it was highly unlikely that anyone would be convicted of perpetrating the bombing.

At the general election to the British Parliament held on 5 May 2005 the UUP recorded its worst electoral performance since the formation of Northern Ireland's first government in 1921, retaining only one of the five seats it had previously held, with 17.8% of the votes cast in Northern Ireland. The DUP secured nine seats, gaining four at the expense of the UUP, with 33.7% of the votes cast. Sinn Féin increased its parliamentary representation, winning five seats (compared with four in 2001), with 24.3% of the votes, while the representation of the SDLP, which took three seats with 17.5% of the votes, remained unchanged. Following the election, in which he had himself lost his seat, Trimble resigned as Leader of the UUP. (In June the UUP elected Empey as its new Leader.) In a major reorganization of ministerial portfolios on 6 May, Peter Hain replaced Paul Murphy as the Secretary of State for Northern Ireland. Hain's retention of the office—Secretary of State for Wales—that he had held in the outgoing Cabinet was criticized by the DUP, which claimed that the status of the Northern Ireland portfolio had thereby been diminished.

In May 2005, after he had held seemingly fruitless discussions with, separately, Sinn Féin and unionist leaders in London, Hain emphasized that progress in the peace process could only be achieved on the basis of the Good Friday Agreement. Paisley, however, described the Good Friday Agreement as 'dead', stating that progress would only be achieved through comprehensive, verifiable weapons decommissioning and the abandonment by the IRA of all criminal activities. Meanwhile, on 10 May the European Parliament adopted a resolution that accused members of the IRA of the murder of a Catholic man, Robert McCartney, in Belfast in January. Towards the end of the month a report by the IMC highlighted the IRA's continued military readiness and its recruitment and training campaign. In mid-June the House of Commons voted to extend for one year the withdrawal of parliamentary allowances from Sinn Féin and its MPs.

In July 2005 the IRA issued a communiqué in which it formally renounced its armed struggle and committed itself to the pursuit of its objectives, including the goal of a united Ireland, through peaceful means only. At the same time the IRA undertook to conclude the process of comprehensive, verifiable weapons decommissioning. Welcoming the IRA's communiqué in a joint statement, Blair and Ahern emphasized that the commitments it contained must be authenticated in action. Leading unionists, including Paisley and Empey, together with US President George W. Bush, responded to the IRA's announcement in a similar fashion. Unionist uncertainty over the good faith of the IRA's statement was reflected in the DUP's condemnation of the Government's decision to begin removing security facilities in South Armagh on the day after it had been issued. Hain's announcement, on 1 August, of a plan to reduce within two years the number of British army personnel in Northern Ireland by 50%, and to repeal anti-terrorism measures exclusive to Northern Ireland, likewise provoked condemnation by unionists. Loyalist violence that broke out that day in Belfast and continued sporadically throughout the month was attributed to a feud between the paramilitary Ulster Volunteer Force (UVF) and the LVF. On 10 September the most serious sectarian violence for 10 years erupted in Belfast and continued for three days, after the route of a march by the Orange Order was diverted away from a nationalist area in the west of the city. On 14 September, in view of incontrovertible evidence of the UVF's involvement in the unrest, Hain withdrew the United Kingdom's recognition of the UVF's 11-year cease-fire.

In late September 2005 the IRA formally declared in a communiqué that it had completed the process of weapons decommissioning. De Chastelain, who, together with two clergymen, one Catholic and one Protestant, had witnessed the decommissioning, announced at the same time that he was satisfied that the arms decommissioned represented the totality of the IRA's arsenal. Both Blair and Ahern welcomed the IRA's statement as a significant step towards peace and Hain stated that negotiations on the restoration of devolution should commence in early 2006. In early October 2005 the DUP presented Blair with a list of conditions that it insisted must be met to ensure that the unionist community received equal treatment with the IRA, and without whose fulfilment it would refuse to negotiate with Sinn Féin on power sharing. Unionists criticized a decision to restore to Sinn Féin from 1 November its entitlement to the allowance payable to Northern Ireland political parties, and condemned the Government's intention, announced by Hain in late October, to grant an amnesty to certain categories of suspects who remained at large, claiming that the Government had secretly offered the amnesty to the IRA as an inducement for it to abjure violence. At the end of October the LVF responded to weapons decommissioning by the IRA by disbanding all of its paramilitary units.

The DUP absented itself from talks held in mid-November 2005 between Hain, the Irish Minister for Foreign Affairs, Dermot Ahern, and representatives of Sinn Féin, including the party's chief negotiator, Martin McGuinness, who challenged Paisley to keep his word that he would share power with Sinn Féin after the IRA had decommissioned its arms. In early December, in a further response to the IRA's abandonment of its armed struggle, the Government announced that British military strength in Northern Ireland would be reduced to below 9,000 in the following month. In the same month the Public Prosecution Service retracted allegations that the IRA had infiltrated the Northern Ireland Office in 2002 (see above). After the former Sinn Féin official, Denis Donaldson, had confessed to having been an informer working for the British security services for some 20 years and been expelled from the party, Adams asserted that the allegations of infiltration had been part of an attempt by those within the security services who opposed Sinn Féin's participation in government to wreck the Northern Ireland Assembly. Later in December, however, Hain dismissed calls for an inquiry into the affair.

In January 2006 Blair and the Irish Prime Minister, Bertie Ahern, announced that multi-party discussions would recommence on 6 February. In a report published days before the talks were due to begin the IMC alleged that the process of decommissioning IRA weapons had not been completed in September 2005, as the IRA had claimed and the IICD had verified. The IMC's report also accused some IRA members of organized criminal activity and asserted that the IRA continued to gather intelligence. At the same time, however, the IMC's report stated that the IRA no longer committed acts of terrorism. For its part, the IICD reaffirmed its claim that the IRA had completed the process of weapons decommissioning in September. At a conference of the DUP in early February 2006 Paisley described as a 'blatant lie' the claim that the IRA had completely disarmed and dismissed any question of sharing power with Sinn Féin before it did so. Despite these setbacks, multi-party talks seeking to restart the peace process were initiated on schedule on 6 February near Belfast.

In mid-February 2006 Hain presented to the House of Commons the Northern Ireland (Miscellaneous Provisions) Bill which, if adopted, would allow the Government to transfer responsibility for policing and justice to Northern Ireland politicians. The bill also provided for the organization of immediate elections to the Northern Ireland Assembly, in the event of political agreement being reached, rather than waiting until 2007 for such elections to be held. The body of Denis Donaldson was found in Co Donegal, Ireland, in April. Despite Sinn Féin's condemnation of the apparent murder and the IRA's claim that it had had 'no involvement whatsoever' in Donaldson's death, prominent unionists, including Paisley, blamed republicans for his death.

Two days after Donaldson's body had been discovered Blair and Ahern issued a major joint statement that sought to clarify the course that the renewed peace process should take in 2006. The two Prime Ministers stated their conviction that the IRA no longer represented a terrorist threat and that all parties should engage in political dialogue, and stated that their aim was to set out a practical framework and reasonable timescale for the restoration of devolution. The Northern Ireland Assembly was recalled on 15 May. The Assembly's primary responsibility was to elect a First Minister and a Deputy First Minister as soon as possible, to allocate ministerial portfolios, and to make other preparations for government. Once the Assembly had elected a First Minister and a Deputy First Minister on a cross-community basis and formed an Executive, power would automatically be devolved to the Assembly and at that point the British Government's power to suspend the Assembly would lapse definitively. In the event of the Assembly's being unable to elect First and Deputy First Ministers within the normal six-week period, Blair and Ahern stated that they would be prepared to allow a further period of 12 weeks after the summer recess for the formation of an Executive. However, if by 24 November the Assembly had failed to achieve this, the Prime Ministers' joint view was that no further purpose would be served by another election at that point or in May 2007. They would be obliged, therefore, to cancel salaries and allowances payable to members of the Assembly and to defer restoration of the Assembly and the Executive until a clear political willingness to exercise devolved power existed. Such a deferral would have immediate implications for the British and Irish Governments' joint stewardship of the peace process and detailed work was stated to have already begun on British-Irish partnership arrangements that would become necessary under such circumstances. In June 2006 a Preparation for Government Committee, comprising representatives of the principal parties, was established within the Assembly, to discuss the devolution of policing and justice and other key matters. Dissident republicans continued to use violent tactics, claiming responsibility for a number of arson attacks in August. In October the IMC confirmed that the IRA had dismantled its paramilitary structures and was no longer involved in organized crime; the report acknowledged, however, that dissident republican and loyalist factions and individuals were still engaged in violence and crime. In the same month discussions took place at St Andrews, in Scotland, between Blair, Ahern and the leaders of the principal Northern Ireland parties: the ensuing St Andrews Agreement established a schedule for the restoration of devolved government by March 2007 and the devolution of criminal justice and policing by 2008.

Following qualified approval of the St Andrews Agreement by Sinn Féin and the DUP, legislation giving effect to the accord was adopted by Parliament in late November 2006. The new law provided for the Northern Ireland Assembly to be redesignated as a transitional assembly and to be dissolved in January 2007, pending an election in March, after which parties would nominate assembly members to positions in a devolved executive, to take office on 26 March. In January 2007 Sinn Féin held a special party conference, at which delegates voted to support the PSNI and to take up the party's allocated places on the NIPB, thereby reversing the party's long-standing policy and removing the last obstacle to the process of devolution. In February the UDA (the principal loyalist paramilitary organization) announced that it would accept the participation of Sinn Féin in a future government, while in May the UVF announced that it had renounced paramilitary activity.

At the election to the Assembly, held on 7 March 2007, the DUP won 36 of the 108 seats, Sinn Féin 28, the UUP 18, the SDLP 16 and the Alliance Party two. On 26 March Paisley and Adams committed themselves to forming a new power-sharing executive by 8 May, on which date Paisley was duly sworn in as First Minister and McGuinness as Deputy First Minister. The remaining 10 ministries were allocated in proportion to the number of seats obtained by each party in the Assembly: the DUP four ministries, Sinn Féin three, the UUP two and the SDLP one. During 2007 relations between the two main parties within the Executive were cordial. In mid-July 2007 Paisley and McGuinness led a delegation of the Executive at a meeting of the North/South Ministerial Council in Armagh, the first such meeting since 2002 and the first to be attended by DUP ministers. In early December Paisley and McGuinness, along with members of the Executive, visited the USA. Meanwhile, in November 2007 the UDA announced the cessation of its paramilitary activity.

However, a series of disagreements between the DUP and Sinn Féin in early 2008 threatened to disrupt co-operation within the Executive. In January the Secretary of State for Northern Ireland, Shaun Woodward, was criticized by some senior members of the DUP after he indicated that the British Government envisaged the devolution of powers over the justice system and policing to the Executive by the end of 2008, in accordance with the provisions of the St Andrews Agreement. Paisley insisted that the IRA disband its army council, that arson attacks on Orange Order buildings cease and that financing measures be agreed by the Executive and the British Government before powers could be transferred. Adams, however, welcomed the proposals and accused the DUP of reneging on its commitment to the St Andrews Agreement. In March Adams and the Minister of Finance and Personnel, Peter Robinson of the DUP, held informal talks in an attempt to resolve disagreements between the parties following comments made by McGuinness and the DUP Minister for Enterprise, Trade and Investment, Nigel Dodds, which were deemed to be offensive. Earlier that month a cross-party Assembly committee had failed to reach an agreement over the devolution of powers, and by early May no further progress had been made.

In early March 2008 Paisley announced that he was to resign as Leader of the DUP and as First Minister in May. At a special party conference held in mid-April, Robinson was elected to succeed Paisley as Leader. He was expected to assume the role of First Minister by the end of June.

In November 1988 the European Court of Human Rights ruled in favour of four men who were protesting against being detained without charge in Northern Ireland for more than four days, under the Prevention of Terrorism Act (which allowed detention for up to seven days). In December the Government responded to the ruling by announcing a derogation from the European Convention for the Protection of Human Rights. In November 1991 the UN Committee Against Torture expressed concern over cases of alleged ill-treatment of terrorist suspects in detention and other abuses of human rights in Northern Ireland, which had been detailed in a report compiled by a prominent human rights organization, Amnesty International. In September 1995 the European Court of Human Rights unexpectedly overturned an earlier decision of the European Commission of Human Rights and ruled that the killing of three IRA activists in Gibraltar, in 1988, was in breach of Article 2 of the Convention, defining the 'right of life'. While clearing the Government of operating a 'shoot-to-kill' policy, the Court insisted that excessive and unlawful force had been used. In May 1997 the newly elected Labour Government announced that the European Convention was to be incorporated into United Kingdom law and applied in full in Northern Ireland and that the jurisdiction of British courts would be extended to cover the rights guaranteed in the Convention. The Human Rights Act received royal assent in November 1998 and came into force in October 2000. Meanwhile, in April 1998 a report of a special inquiry of the UN Human Rights Commission, initiated in October 1997, upheld complaints by human rights groups regarding the RUC's intimidation of lawyers defending terrorist suspects and the failure to extend adequate legal rights to those detained under emergency legislation. In particular, the report recommended a new inquiry into the allegations that the RUC failed to prevent the murder, by UDA activists, of the republican lawyer Patrick Finucane in Belfast in 1989 (see above). In May 2001 the European Court of Human Rights awarded compensation to the families of 10 IRA members killed by security forces in Northern Ireland during the 1980s and 1990s, after it agreed that the Government had breached Article 2 of the Convention. It also criticized the investigation into the shootings of eight of those 10 IRA members for its lack of independence.

A new official inquiry into the fatal shooting of 14 republican demonstrators by the security forces in Londonderry in January 1972, conducted by Lord Saville of Newdigate, began hearing evidence in March 2000. The destruction by the British army, prior to the inquiry, of rifles required as evidence prompted lawyers representing the families of the victims to accuse the Ministry of Defence of deliberately attempting to frustrate the process. In a significant development in November the lawyer acting for the 440 soldiers involved in the case accepted, in contrast to the findings of an original inquiry, that none of the civilians officially listed as killed or wounded in the incident had been armed. He did, however, maintain that a second list of at least 34 'untraced or unidentified casualties' who were never publicly acknowledged as injured in the incident could have included in their number gunmen who had fired on the soldiers. In May 2001 Martin McGuinness survived a motion of no confidence in the Northern Ireland Assembly, after he admitted in a written statement presented to the Saville inquiry that he was the IRA's adjutant (effectively second-in-command) in Londonderry in January 1972. McGuinness, however, denied that IRA gunmen had been involved in the exchanges of fire with security forces and rejected the claim of an eyewitness that he had fired the first shot. In January 2003 Sir Edward Heath, British Prime Minister in 1972, appeared before the inquiry and dismissed allegations that the shootings had been premeditated as 'absurd'. In November 2003 McGuinness appeared before the inquiry but refused to disclose the names of IRA members who had been with him in Londonderry on 'Bloody Sunday', despite being warned by Lord Saville that he could face further legal action. McGuinness insisted that the IRA had not conducted any military operations in Londonderry that day and that no IRA members had been killed or injured during the shootings. The inquiry concluded in November 2004 with the tribunal retiring to compile its report; by May 2008 the report had yet to be completed.

In June 2005 the Government published reports compiled, respectively, by the Council of Europe's Commissioner for Human Rights and the European Committee for the Prevention of Torture and Inhuman or Degrading Treatment or Punishment (CPT) that contained strong criticism of the United Kingdom's policies on terrorist suspects and those seeking political asylum in the country. Fault was found in particular with the Anti-Terrorism, Crime and Security Act (2001) because it enabled the Secretary of State for Home Affairs to subject suspects to control orders without trial. The report of the Commissioner also claimed that there were deficiencies in the procedures governing legal appeals by unsuccessful political asylum seekers against deportation. The Government strongly denied a claim by the CPT that detainees had been mistreated. Later in June 2005 human rights groups, with the support of opposition parties and some Labour MPs, sought to persuade the Government not to repatriate Zimbabwean asylum seekers whose applications had failed on the grounds that they risked mistreatment on their return to Zimbabwe. Also in June a report published by Amnesty International alleged that, by detaining them prior to deportation, the Government had infringed the human rights of as many as 25,000 failed applicants for political asylum in the United Kingdom in 2004. In July the Government announced that it had suspended its policy of deporting failed Zimbabwean applicants for political asylum pending a High Court's consideration of its legality. In October, in a 'test case', the Asylum and Immigration Tribunal ruled that an unsuccessful Zimbabwean applicant for political asylum could not be repatriated to Zimbabwe as he would be at risk of mistreatment there. On the following day, in response to the likelihood that British courts would uphold appeals by foreign nationals against deportation to countries where they risked persecution, the Government announced that it would seek to overrule a majority decision by the European Court of Human Rights in 1996 that national security interests could not take precedence over an individual's inalienable human rights.

The United Kingdom became a full member of the EC in January 1973. A referendum in 1975 endorsed British membership by a large majority. The first direct election of British representatives to the European Parliament took place in June 1979. During the 1980s the Thatcher Government demanded controls on spending by the EC, and particularly reform of the Common Agricultural Policy (CAP), and expressed scepticism regarding proposals for greater European economic unity, on the grounds that this was likely to entail a loss of national sovereignty. In October 1990, however, the United Kingdom joined the ERM. Following Major's assumption of the British premiership, relations with individual members of the EC (particularly Germany) improved, and the Government adopted a more pragmatic approach towards European developments. Nevertheless, the British Government agreed to the terms of the Maastricht Treaty only after substantial concessions had been granted for the United Kingdom. In particular, the United Kingdom's participation in the final stage of European Economic and Monetary Union (EMU), including the adoption of a single EC currency by 2000, was made optional.

British relations with the EU were adversely affected by concerns over the safety of beef from British cattle. In March 1996 a report by a government health advisory committee recognized a possible link between BSE, evident in cattle herds in all parts of the country, and a new strain of Creutzfeldt-Jakob disease (CJD), a degenerative disease affecting humans. The findings of the report provoked a serious crisis of consumer confidence within the United Kingdom and abroad, and several countries announced a ban on all imports of beef and related products from the United Kingdom. At the end of March comprehensive restrictions on the export from the United Kingdom of all live cattle, beef and derivatives were imposed by the European Commission. EU ministers of agriculture undertook to support the British Government in compensating farmers for any necessary slaughter of cattle herds, on condition that adequate measures were adopted to eradicate BSE.

The election, in May 1997, of the Labour Government generated expectations of a significant improvement of relations between the United Kingdom and the EU. The Blair administration immediately announced its intention to withdraw the country's option not to participate in the 'social chapter' of the Maastricht Treaty, and to promote completion of the internal economic market and enlargement of the EU. However, the new Government remained opposed to greater EU authority over national borders and immigration controls, and its demands for reform of the CAP. In June 1997 EU heads of state and of government signed the Treaty of Amsterdam, amending the Maastricht Treaty. The new agreement incorporated the social chapter, given the Labour Government's willingness to subscribe to the protocol, although it was not expected to be enforced in the United Kingdom until the new Treaty had been ratified by all members. The United Kingdom, together with Ireland, secured an exemption from obligations with regard to immigration, asylum and visa policies; however, Blair negotiated an option to participate in certain co-operative aspects of the border arrangements.

In July 1999 the European Commission formally ended the ban on British beef exports, with effect from 1 August, subject to the provision that all beef was de-boned and came from animals whose pedigree could be traced. However, despite the Commission's ruling, France announced that it would maintain its embargo on British beef pending a report by its own food safety agency on the advisability of ending restrictions. In October 2002, following a ruling by the European Court of Justice that the French embargo was illegal, the French Government removed the ban on British beef. (In November 2005 the British Department for Environment, Food and Rural Affairs lifted the ban on sales for human consumption of meat from cattle aged over 30 months, and in May 2006 the EU removed the remaining restrictions on the United Kingdom's foreign sales of live cattle and beef products.) Later in October 2002 relations between France and the United Kingdom were again strained following disagreements between Blair and the French President, Jacques Chirac, over EU agricultural policy reform. Bilateral relations deteriorated further after France invited the President of Zimbabwe, Robert Mugabe, to attend a summit of African leaders in Paris, despite the imposition earlier that year of sanctions prohibiting Mugabe and other Zimbabwean political leaders from travelling to EU countries. Relations between the United Kingdom and France were also strained by their differing views on the necessity of military action in Iraq (see below). In October 2003 Chirac visited London for talks with Blair, at which Chirac expressed his reservations over US-British policies in Iraq; however, they agreed to enhance co-operation to combat illegal immigration. In November 2004 Chirac again visited London to celebrate the 100th anniversary of the *entente cordiale* agreement, which had settled outstanding colonial disputes between the two countries. Following the election of Nicolas Sarkozy as President of France in May 2007, relations between the two countries improved. During an official state visit to the United Kingdom in March 2008, Sarkozy reiterated his intention to increase co-operation with the British Government over the construction of new nuclear energy plants, immigration and security.

In October 1997 the Chancellor of the Exchequer, Gordon Brown, attempted to clarify the Government's stance on the European single currency, following a period of intense speculation. He identified five key principles for participation in EMU, relating to its impact on the British economy and employment, and insisted that membership would have to be preceded by a sustained period of economic stability. In December Blair objected to a decision by other EU leaders to establish a new economic policy group, comprising representatives of countries adopting the single currency from 1 January 1999. None the less, the Government emphasized its commitment to the successful introduction of the euro (as the currency was designated). In May 1999 Blair expressed his intention to end what he termed Britain's 'ambivalence' towards the EU and to make the country a 'leading partner' in the bloc. Earlier in the year he had predicted that the relevant conditions for participation in EMU would be in place shortly after the next general election. In June 2003 Brown announced that four of the five key principles for deciding British participation in EMU had not yet been fulfilled. Nevertheless, he stated that the Government remained in favour of joining the single currency once the conditions were in place.

Despite his previously vehement stance opposing such a move, in April 2004 Blair announced plans to hold a referendum on the proposed new draft EU constitutional treaty. The draft had been prepared by a convention, headed by the former French President, Valéry Giscard d'Estaing, during 2002–03, and was finally approved by the leaders of the 25 member states of the EU in mid-June 2004. A bill was published in January 2005 to allow for a referendum on the treaty. In June, however, following the failure of the French and Dutch electorates to endorse the treaty in referendums, Straw announced that the Government would not proceed with a second reading of the bill in the House of Commons. At the same time Straw emphasized the Government's view that the treaty represented 'a sensible new set of rules for the enlarged EU'. In June 2007, at a summit meeting in Brussels, Belgium, EU leaders reached a preliminary agreement providing for a comprehensive reform treaty to replace the constitutional treaty rejected by French and Dutch voters. On 13 December the Reform Treaty (later known as the Treaty of Lisbon) was signed by EU heads of state and of government, including Brown, at a summit meeting in Lisbon, Portugal. A motion by the Conservative Party to ratify the treaty by national referendum was rejected by the House of Commons in early March 2008. (Prior to the 2005 general election, all three main political parties had promised to ratify the constitutional treaty by means of a referendum.) The treaty was due to be ratified by parliamentary vote by the end of 2008.

Following Iraq's forcible annexation of Kuwait in August 1990, the British Government promptly supported the efforts of the USA in defending Saudi Arabia from potential Iraqi aggression and deployed some 42,000 personnel in the subsequent engagement in hostilities against Iraq, under the auspices of the UN. British troops also participated in subsequent humanitarian efforts to protect the Kurdish population within Iraq from persecution by the Iraqi armed forces. In January 1993 British fighter aircraft participated in US-led attacks on military targets in Iraq, launched in response to renewed Iraqi incursions into Kuwait and obstruction of a UN investigation into a suspected

Iraqi nuclear weapons programme. In September 1996 the British Government gave political and logistical support to a series of air-strikes by the USA against targets in Iraq. In December 1998, following Iraq's refusal to co-operate with weapons inspections by the UN Special Commission (UNSCOM), the USA and the United Kingdom conducted a further series of air-strikes in an effort to 'degrade' Iraq's military capabilities. Further airborne attacks were conducted in early 1999 and mid-2000 in response to alleged violations by Iraq of the UN air exclusion zone. In February 2001 the United Kingdom and the USA were again involved in the bombardment of a number of targets in Iraq, in response to a reportedly increased threat to aircraft from those countries in the preceding weeks. The action was, however, condemned by several Western and Arab countries.

In March 2002 Blair faced opposition from within the Labour Party as speculation mounted about the possibility of further military action against Iraq. Blair indicated in July that he had 'tremendous concerns' about any possible military strikes on Iraq and subsequently announced his support for the UN Security Council's proposal that UN weapons inspectors be readmitted to Iraq. He did, however, stress in late August that the British Government was determined to deal with the threat posed by Iraq's possession of weapons of mass destruction. In early September, in response to mounting public opposition to possible military action in Iraq, Blair insisted that no decision on such action had yet been taken, but stated that he would publish a dossier outlining the 'real and unique threat' posed by the regime of the Iraqi President, Saddam Hussain, by the end of the month. Following a meeting with the US President, George W. Bush, Blair announced that the United Kingdom and the USA would attempt to secure a new UN Security Council resolution that would approve military action in Iraq, should that country fail to comply with UN weapons inspectors. Both British and US officials greeted with scepticism Iraq's declaration, made on 16 September, of its willingness to readmit weapons inspectors 'without conditions'; however, the People's Republic of China, France and Russia cautiously welcomed the move. In late September the British Government published the dossier outlining its case against the Iraqi regime and the perceived threat posed by that country's 'illicit weapons programmes' to the security of both the West and the Middle East (see above). However, it appeared that the United Kingdom and the USA were becoming increasingly isolated in their attempts to secure approval for the use of military force against Iraq. On 8 November, after a compromise had been reached between the five permanent members, the UN Security Council unanimously adopted Resolution 1441, which demanded, *inter alia*, that Iraq permit weapons inspectors from UNSCOM's replacement, the UN Monitoring, Verification and Inspection Commission (UNMOVIC), and the International Atomic Energy Agency (IAEA, see p. 107) unrestricted access to sites suspected of holding illegal weapons and required the Iraqi leadership to make a full declaration of its chemical, biological, nuclear and ballistic weapons, as well as related materials used in civilian industries, within 30 days. The resolution warned that this represented a 'final opportunity' for the Iraqi authorities to comply with their disarmament obligations under previous UN resolutions, affirming that Iraq would face 'serious consequences' in the event of non-compliance with the UN inspectors or of any 'false statements and omissions' in its weapons declaration. Later in November the Liberal Democrats' parliamentary motion proposing that no military action should be taken against Iraq without a fresh mandate from the UN and a vote in the House of Commons was defeated by 452 votes to 85; 32 Labour MPs voted in favour of the motion.

In mid-December 2002 the British Secretary of State for Foreign and Commonwealth Affairs, Jack Straw, denounced Hussain's claims that he had destroyed all weapons of mass destruction as an 'obvious falsehood'. The USA also stated that Iraq was in 'material breach' of UN Resolution 1441 since it had failed to give a complete account of its weapons capabilities, citing in particular Iraq's failure to account for stocks of biological weapons such as anthrax. During January 2003 Blair, while asserting that conflict was not inevitable if Iraq complied with the UN's disarmament terms and insisting that UNMOVIC and the IAEA be granted sufficient time in order to complete their inspections, ordered large numbers of troops to the Persian (Arabian) Gulf region to join the increasing number of US forces already in position there. However, it also became apparent that month that disagreements over policy on Iraq within the Government, the Labour Party and Parliament as a whole were increasing, particularly following Blair's refusal in mid-January to guarantee that British troops would not be involved in a military campaign in Iraq should there be no UN resolution approving such action. On 27 January, 60 days after the resumption of UN weapons inspections in Iraq (as stipulated under Resolution 1441), the head of UNMOVIC, Hans Blix, and the Director-General of the IAEA, Muhammad el-Baradei, briefed the UN Security Council on the progress of inspections. El-Baradei stated that IAEA inspectors had found no evidence that Iraq had restarted its nuclear weapons programme, but requested more time for the organization to complete its research. Blix, for his part, claimed that there was no evidence that Iraq had destroyed known stocks of illegal chemical and long-range ballistic weapons, and announced that he was sceptical about Baghdad's willingness to disarm. Following the briefing, Straw declared Iraq to be in 'material breach' of Resolution 1441.

In January 2003, as the likelihood of a US-led military response to the crisis increased, the United Kingdom was one of eight European countries to sign a joint statement expressing support for the USA's stance on Iraq. The following month increasing British popular opposition to military action against Iraq precipitated nation-wide 'anti-war' demonstrations, including a march in London reportedly attended by some 1m. people. Blair continued with his efforts to secure a second UN Security Council resolution authorizing a US-led campaign in Iraq should inspectors from UNMOVIC continue to report Baghdad's non-compliance; however, on 26 February he suffered a damaging reverse when 122 Labour MPs supported an all-party motion in the House of Commons stating that the case for military action against Iraq was 'as yet unproven'. Earlier in February the USA had presented to the Security Council what it claimed to be overwhelming evidence of Iraq's possession of weapons of mass destruction, its attempts to conceal such weapons from the UN inspectorate and its links with international terrorism, including the al-Qa'ida network. Despite signs of progress being reported by Blix in mid-February in his report to the UN Security Council, on 24 February the United Kingdom, the USA and Spain presented a draft resolution to the Security Council effectively authorizing a US-led military campaign against Hussain's regime, in response to Iraq's failure to disarm peacefully. The resolution stated that a deadline of 17 March would be set, by which time Iraq should prove that it was disarming; however, no specific mention was made of consequent military action in the event of the deadline not being met by Iraq, apparently in an effort by the US-led coalition to persuade France, Russia and China not to exercise their right of veto. Officials from France, Russia and Germany responded to the draft resolution by presenting an alternative proposal involving an extended timetable of weapons inspections in order to avert a war. On 7 March Straw submitted an amended draft resolution to the Security Council which concluded that Iraq would have 'failed to take the final opportunity to disarm unless on or before 17 March the Council concludes that Iraq has demonstrated full, unconditional, immediate and active co-operation with its disarmament obligations under resolution 1441'. On 12 March Blair proposed six new conditions that Iraq must meet in order to prove that it was serious about disarmament: this was seen as an attempt at a compromise that might encourage wavering countries in the Security Council to support an amended resolution. The British proposals came a day after President Bush had rejected a suggested 45-day postponement of any decision to go to war by six countries that had the power to influence the Security Council vote, although Blair also indicated that British forces would participate in the anticipated US-led campaign in Iraq without the passing of a second UN resolution.

On 16 March 2003 Blair attended a summit meeting in the Azores, Portugal, along with President Bush and the Spanish Prime Minister, José María Aznar. The following day the United Kingdom, the USA and Spain withdrew their resolution from the UN, stating that they reserved the right to take their own action to ensure Iraqi disarmament. Later that day Bush issued an ultimatum giving Saddam Hussain and his two sons 48 hours to leave Baghdad or face military action. Shortly after the expiry of Bush's 48-hour deadline, on 19 March US and British armed forces launched a 'broad and concerted campaign' (code-named 'Operation Iraqi Freedom') to oust the regime of Saddam Hussain. US-led coalition forces crossed into Iraq from Kuwait and began a steady advance towards the capital. At the same time a campaign of massive air-strikes was launched against the key symbols of the Iraqi regime in and around Baghdad, including selected military bases, communications sites, government buildings and broadcasting headquarters. The US and British forces adopted a simultaneous campaign of issuing leaflets and broadcasting radio messages, in an effort to persuade Iraqi citizens to abandon their support for the incumbent regime: their declared intention was that Operation Iraqi Freedom would precipitate the disintegration of the regime 'from within'. British troops were principally engaged in securing towns in southern Iraq, including Iraq's second largest city, Basra, after the US-led coalition had seized control of the key southern port of Umm Qasr and the Al-Faw Peninsula. During the campaign Blair frequently stressed his desire that the UN should play a central role in the future of Iraq. Baghdad was captured by US forces on 9 April and, following the seizure by US troops of Saddam Hussain's birthplace and power base, Tikrit (to the north of Baghdad), on 14 April, the Iraqi regime appeared to have collapsed. Although the whereabouts of Saddam Hussain and his sons remained unknown, by late April a number of senior Iraqi officials had been captured and on 1 May President Bush officially declared an end to 'major combat operations' in Iraq. Hussain's sons Uday and Qusay were killed in July following an exchange of gunfire with US special forces in Mosul and Saddam Hussain was captured by US special forces on 14 December near Tikrit.

On 22 May 2003 the UN Security Council approved Resolution 1483, which recognized the US- and British-led Coalition Provisional Authority (CPA), headed by US diplomat L. Paul Bremer, III, as the legal occupying power in Iraq, and mandated the CPA to establish a temporary Iraqi governing authority. UN sanctions imposed on Iraq in 1990 were also lifted. However, it soon became clear that the arrest or elimination of the main figures of the old regime was not diminishing the level of armed resistance to coalition forces. In July 2003 the British Government formally assumed command of the multinational task force for southeastern Iraq, with its headquarters in Basra, comprising some 16,000 troops, of whom 11,000 were British. In early September the British Government agreed to dispatch a further 1,200 troops to Iraq while placing another 1,800 soldiers on stand-by. In January 2004 Blair pledged that British troops would remain in Iraq for a minimum of a further two years and that there would be no reduction in the strength of British forces in the country until the transfer of power to a provisional Iraqi administration, scheduled for July that year.

Meanwhile, there appeared to be little sign of the chemical, biological and nuclear weapons which had been the *raison d'être* of the US-led campaign. In early October 2003 the Iraq Survey Group, a group of more than 1,000 experts established by the US-led coalition in May to investigate the presence of illegal weapons in Iraq, which had been given the task of locating supplies of these weapons, published its interim report. This indicated that while no such weapons themselves had been found, there was evidence of weapons-related programmes and of Iraqi attempts to gain nuclear technology on the international black market. In January 2004 the 400-member Joint Captured Material Exploitation Group, led by an Australian brigadier, was withdrawn from Iraq, leading to suggestions that the coalition had failed to locate conventional weapons or sites, such as missiles and launchers, that might be used in conjunction with banned weapons. In mid-September a draft report compiled by the Iraq Survey Group in Washington, DC, USA revealed that no weapons of mass destruction had been found in Iraq. Later that month at a Labour Party conference Blair apologized for the intelligence claim that Iraq possessed weapons of mass destruction; however, he refused to apologize for sending British troops to Iraq, stating that the removal of Saddam Hussain was sufficient justification.

On 28 June 2004, two days ahead of schedule, the USA formally transferred sovereignty to Iraq and the interim Prime Minister, Dr Ayad Allawi, and his cabinet ministers were sworn in. A further 400 British troops were sent to Iraq in preparation for the country's first multi-party elections for over 50 years, which took place on 30 January 2005. By the end of 2006 responsibility for two of the four provinces supervised by British forces had been transferred to the Iraqi security forces; responsibility for Maysan province was transferred in April 2007. In October 2007 the Prime Minister announced that some 1,000 troops were to be withdrawn from Iraq by December that year, upon the transfer of responsibility for Al-Basrah (Basra) province to the Iraqi security services and that further withdrawals would take place in early 2008, reducing the total number of troops to 2,500. In December control of Basra province was duly transferred and around 1,000 troops were withdrawn from the province accordingly. However, in April 2008 the Secretary of State for Defence, Des Browne, confirmed the postponement of further troop withdrawals, citing an increase in attacks on coalition and Iraqi forces by insurgents. By early May 2008 a total of 176 British soldiers had been killed in Iraq since the beginning of the conflict (including those who died from non-combat injuries), and there were some 4,000 British service personnel still stationed in the country.

The International Committee of the Red Cross voiced its concern over the treatment of Iraqi prisoners by coalition forces in a report published in February 2004. In May the Secretary of State for Defence, Geoff Hoon, admitted that British forces had taken part in incidents of assault in Iraq in the form of the forced hooding of detainees and stated that investigations were taking place into 33 incidents of alleged abuse. The Government encountered further criticism in early June when it was revealed that the Ministry of Defence was in fact investigating 75 claims of abuse. In June the House of Commons defence committee announced plans to form a cross-party parliamentary committee to investigate the role of British troops in Iraq, particularly following the transfer of power to Iraq at the end of the month. In mid-June it was announced that four British soldiers from the Royal Regiment of Fusiliers would be tried before a court martial on charges of assault and indecent assault following the emergence of personal photographs depicting incidents of abuse. They were tried in Osnabrück, Germany, in January 2005, convicted and sentenced to terms of imprisonment ranging from four months to two years. In July the Attorney-General announced that 11 British soldiers would appear before a court martial on charges, including unlawful killing, manslaughter and inhuman treatment of persons, that had been brought by the Army Prosecution Authority in connection with military operations in Iraq in 2003. In September 2005 the trial before a court martial began of four serving and three former members of the Parachute Regiment who were charged with murder and violent disorder in connection with a military operation in Iraq in 2003. All seven were acquitted in November 2005 on the grounds of insufficient evidence.

In early 1999 the United Kingdom was one of the principal participants in a NATO air offensive against the Federal Republic of Yugoslavia (now Serbia). The campaign, which began in March, was intended to end the atrocities committed by Serb forces against ethnic Albanians in the Serbian province of Kosovo (see the chapter on Serbia). Although NATO did not have a direct mandate from the UN Security Council for the offensive, it insisted that earlier UN resolutions provided ample justification for the use of force on humanitarian grounds. However, although NATO's stated targets were to be exclusively military, the campaign was widely criticized for the number of civilian casualties caused by NATO errors. It was also widely held that NATO was failing in its stated aim of averting a humanitarian disaster in Kosovo, because the air offensive had prompted Serbia to intensify its attacks on Kosovans, provoking a severe refugee crisis as hundreds of thousands of Kosovans attempted to flee the province. In March Blair announced the establishment of a cross-departmental group to respond to the refugee crisis, and pledged £10m. in aid. Following a visit to Kosovan refugee encampments in the former Yugoslav republic of Macedonia (FYRM) in May, Blair promised to increase aid to £40m. and announced that the United Kingdom would receive 1,000 refugees a week. The Government had earlier been criticized by its NATO partners for its reluctance to accept the refugees. As the military campaign developed Blair was perceived as the most determined of NATO's leaders in his effort to force the Yugoslav President, Slobodan Milošević, to accept the alliance's terms for a cessation of hostilities. In early June Milošević conceded to these demands, and by the end of that month Serb forces had withdrawn from Kosovo. British troops formed part of the force that entered the province to enforce the peace process. In November diplomatic relations between the two countries were restored.

In late August 2001 some 2,000 British troops were deployed in the FYRM as part of a multinational 3,500-strong NATO mission (Operation Essential Harvest) mandated to disarm members of the ethnic Albanian National Liberation Army and destroy their weapons during a 30-day period. The large proportion of British troops involved in the operation provoked criticism from opposition parties and the death under fire of a British member of the mission later that month led to increased popular opposition in the United Kingdom to the British forces' presence in the FYRM. Nevertheless, following the successful completion of Operation Essential Harvest some 3,900 British troops remained in the Balkans as part of NATO's Kosovo Force. In July 2002 it was announced that the majority of the remaining 2,000 British troops in Kosovo would be withdrawn by the end of August.

The terrorist attacks on New York and Washington, DC, on 11 September 2001, for which the USA held the al-Qa'ida organization of Osama bin Laden responsible and in which 78 British citizens were killed, were denounced by Blair as an attack on the democratic world. The Prime Minister pledged that the United Kingdom would stand 'shoulder to shoulder' with the USA in its quest to bring the perpetrators of the attacks to justice and offered to provide military and diplomatic assistance to the US Administration. Blair, who by late October had held talks with more than 50 foreign heads of government, played a significant role in strengthening the international coalition against terrorism and obtaining support for military action against the Islamist Taliban regime in Afghanistan, which was suspected of harbouring senior al-Qa'ida figures, including bin Laden.

On 4 October 2001 the British Government released documents detailing evidence of al-Qa'ida's responsibility for the attacks on the USA, and three days later US and British armed forces commenced the aerial bombardment of suspected al-Qa'ida camps and strategic Taliban positions in Afghanistan. Blair stressed, however, that military strikes were part of a wider, lengthy campaign against terrorism involving diplomatic, economic and political action. In mid-October British military leaders agreed to deploy up to 1,000 ground troops in Afghanistan and the following month the Secretary of State for Defence, Geoff Hoon, confirmed that British troops were involved in ground operations in Afghanistan. In December it was announced that the United Kingdom had agreed to lead the International Security Assistance Force (ISAF), which was granted a six-month mandate by the UN to provide security in Kabul and its environs. ISAF was expected to comprise as many as 5,000 troops from 17 countries, some 2,000 of whom would be from the United Kingdom. The first British peace-keeping troops arrived in Afghanistan later in December. In March 2002 a separate force of 1,700 British combat troops was deployed in Afghanistan to assist US special forces with their pursuit of the remaining Taliban and al-Qa'ida fighters, and later that month Hoon stated that British troops would not be withdrawn from Afghanistan until the threat of al-Qa'ida and the Taliban had been eradicated. By the end of 2006 around 5,300 British troops remained stationed in Afghanistan, either participating in ISAF or assisting US special forces. In mid-2007 an additional 1,400 troops were deployed to Afghanistan. By April 2008 some 7,800 British troops were deployed in Afghanistan, mainly in the south of the country. By early May 2008 95 British soldiers had been killed in Afghanistan since 2001 (including 26 soldiers who died from non-combat injuries).

In November 1991 the United Kingdom and the USA demanded that Libya extradite for trial, either in the United Kingdom or the USA, two suspected intelligence agents who were alleged to be responsible for an explosion that destroyed a US passenger aircraft over Lockerbie, Scotland, in 1988. The United Kingdom subsequently supported the imposition, by the UN, of economic and political sanctions against Libya. In view of Libya's continued refusal to allow the suspects to be tried in Scotland, in August 1998 the United Kingdom and the USA conceded to a Libyan proposal, subsequently endorsed by the UN Security Council, that they be tried on neutral territory in the Netherlands. In March 1999 Libya finally agreed to the extradition of the suspects. The UN sanctions against Libya were subsequently suspended. The trial of Abd al-Baset Ali Muhammad al-Megrahi and Al-Amin Khalifa Fhimah, which was heard under Scottish law by a panel of Scottish judges in the presence of international observers, commenced in May 2000. At the end of January 2001 the judges announced that they had unanimously found al-Megrahi guilty of the murder of 270 people and sentenced him to life imprisonment. Fhimah was, however, acquitted, owing to lack of evidence of his involvement in the bombing, and freed to return to Libya. Despite mounting pressure from Arab League states, the British Secretary of State for Foreign and Commonwealth Affairs, Robin Cook, maintained that sanctions against Libya would not be permanently revoked until Libya accepted responsibility for the bombing and paid 'substantial' compensation. In March 2002, following an appeal that was unanimously rejected by the five judges, al-Megrahi was transferred to a prison in Scotland to begin his sentence; it was ruled in November 2003 that he would serve 27 years in prison before becoming eligible for parole. Also in March 2002 Libya appointed an ambassador to the United Kingdom for the first time in 17 years. In August 2002 a minister of the British Foreign and Commonwealth Office visited Libya for talks with Libyan leader Col al-Qaddafi, representing the first visit by a British government minister to Libya for some 20 years.

In March 2003 it was reported that, following negotiations in London, Libya had agreed to accept civil responsibility for the actions of its officials in the Lockerbie case and would pay compensation to the families of the victims, in stages, conditional upon the removal of UN and US sanctions. In August Libya informed the President of the UN Security Council that it accepted 'responsibility for the actions of its officials' in the Lockerbie bombing; agreed to pay compensation to the families of the victims; pledged co-operation in any further Lockerbie inquiry; and agreed to continue its co-operation in the 'war against terror' and to take practical measures to ensure that such co-operation was effective. Following the transfer of US $2,700m. in compensation to the International Bank of Settlements, the United Kingdom submitted a draft resolution to the Security Council requesting the formal lifting of UN sanctions against Libya. On 12 September 13 of the 15 members of the UN Security Council approved the lifting of the sanctions imposed against Libya; France and the USA abstained from the vote.

In December 2003 Blair announced that Libya had agreed to disclose and dismantle its programme to develop weapons of mass destruction and long-range ballistic missiles. The statement was the culmination of nine months of clandestine negotiations between Qaddafi and British and US diplomats during which the Libyan authorities had reportedly shown evidence of a 'well advanced' nuclear weapons programme, as well as the existence of large quantities of chemical weapons and bombs designed to carry poisonous gas. Libya also agreed to adhere to the Chemical Weapons Convention and to sign an additional protocol allowing the IAEA to carry out random inspections of its facilities. In February 2004 the first meeting between cabinet-level ministers of the United Kingdom and Libya for more than 20 years took place in London. In March Blair visited Tripoli and held talks with Qaddafi, after which the British Prime Minister stated that there was genuine hope for a 'new relationship', while Qaddafi insisted that he was willing to join the international 'war against terror'. It was also announced that British police officers would travel to Libya in April to continue investigations into the murder of a British police officer outside the Libyan People's Bureau in London in 1984. In September Qaddafi announced that Libya had dismantled its weapons of mass destruction programme and in December, with the unilateral sanctions imposed upon Libya by the USA having consequently been lifted, Libya paid the second instalment of its compensation to the families of those killed in the Lockerbie bombing. In May 2006 Libya was removed from the US list of states deemed to support international terrorism, the condition for the payment of the final instalment of compensation. In October 2005 a memorandum of understanding signed by Libya and the United Kingdom guaranteed that Libya would not subject to torture or execute any person who was repatriated to it from the United Kingdom. A further memorandum of understanding was signed by Qaddafi and Blair at the end of May 2007, which provided for negotiations on the transfer of prisoners, extradition and mutual assistance in criminal law. A final agreement was to be signed within 12 months.

In February 1990 diplomatic relations (severed in 1982) were restored between the United Kingdom and Argentina. While both countries continued to indicate that their respective claims to sovereignty over the Falkland Islands were not negotiable, political dialogue was able to proceed under a mutual arrangement to circumvent the issue of sovereignty. In September 1995 the two sides concluded an accord to allow exploration for offshore petroleum and gas deposits in the disputed waters around the Islands. A joint commission was to be established to supervise licensing and revenue-sharing. (The first licences were awarded in October 1996.) In October 1995 Major met with the Argentine President, Carlos Menem, at the UN headquarters in New York, USA (the first meeting at this level since the 1982 war). In October 1998 Menem made an official visit to the United Kingdom, the first by an Argentinian President in almost 40 years. In June 2000 relatives of the 323 Argentinians who were killed when a British submarine sank an Argentinian battleship during the Falklands conflict in 1982 announced their intention to take their claim for compensation from the British Government to the European Court of Human Rights. However, the claim was judged inadmissible in the following month, owing to the amount of time that had elapsed between the incident and the claim being lodged. In July 2001 Blair became the first serving British Prime Minister to visit Argentina.

The long-standing dispute with Spain over the sovereignty of Gibraltar has frequently strained relations between the two countries (see the chapters on Spain and Gibraltar). Dialogue between the United Kingdom and Spain over the future of Gibraltar resumed in July 2001 for the first time since 1998, and further discussions were held in Luxembourg in October 2001, although Gibraltar's Chief Minister, Peter Caruana, refused to attend either meeting. In November the British Government announced that it would be willing to consider joint sovereignty of the territory with Spain. This statement angered Caruana, who again boycotted talks between the British and Spanish Foreign Ministers, held in Barcelona, Spain, later that month at which the British and Spanish Governments concluded that they would reach an agreement on the future of the territory by mid-2002. In January 2002 Caruana agreed to attend discussions scheduled for the following month, on the condition that Gibraltar was granted equal status at the meeting and that Britain and Spain guaranteed that any proposal regarding British-Spanish joint sovereignty of the territory would be withdrawn if rejected at a referendum. Caruana's conditions were not met and he was again absent from talks held in early February. In March some 25,000 people protested in Gibraltar against the proposed power-sharing arrangement; nevertheless, both the Spanish and British Governments reiterated their determination to proceed with plans for a joint sovereignty agreement. However, in April, shortly before talks on the future of Gibraltar were scheduled to recommence, the Spanish Prime Minister stated that Spain would never cede its claim to sovereignty over the territory. In response to this announcement, Caruana insisted that if the British Government entered an agreement with Spain granting concessions over sovereignty, the Gibraltar Government would organize its own referendum, thus making it even more difficult for the British and Spanish Governments to secure popular approval for their proposals. In May Jack Straw, the British Secretary of State for Foreign and Commonwealth Affairs, visited Gibraltar and stated that he would not enter into an agreement with Spain that was not in the best interests of the citizens of Gibraltar. In July Straw confirmed that the United Kingdom was willing to share sovereignty of the territory with Spain, subject to approval by the residents of Gibraltar at a referendum, provoking angry protests in Gibraltar, and later in July Caruana announced that Gibraltar would conduct its own referendum on the sovereignty issue by the end of October. Both the Spanish and the British Governments condemned Caruana's decision to hold a referendum and stated that it would lack any validity. The Gibraltar referendum, held on 7 November, which explicitly asked if Gibraltarians approved 'of the principle that Britain and Spain should share sovereignty over Gibraltar' resulted in an overwhelming rejection of the Spanish and British proposals. Of those voting, 99.0% rejected shared sovereignty; the rate of voter participation was recorded at 87.9%. In June 2003 the British Government announced that talks with Spain regarding the possibility of sharing the sovereignty of Gibraltar had failed and suspended any further negotiations over the issue indefinitely. In December 2004 a tripartite meeting between the United Kingdom, Spain and Gibraltar was held in the United Kingdom, and it was subsequently announced that, henceforth, decisions on the territory's future must be agreed by all three parties. In March 2006 Straw sought to reassure Spain that, in the view of the British Government, Spanish rights over Gibraltar would not be affected by a proposed new constitution for the territory, despite the inclusion of references to the right to self-determination of Gibraltarians. In September agreements were signed by representatives of the three Governments allowing easier border crossings in and out of Gibraltar, direct commercial flights to Gibraltar from Spain, and improved telecommunications links. At a referendum held on 30 November 60.2% of those that voted approved the new Constitution; the rate of voter participation was 60.4%. The Constitution entered into force on 2 January 2007.

Relations with Iran, which had improved during the early 2000s, were strained following the arrest in August 2003 in northern England of Hadi Soleimanpour, a former Iranian ambassador to Argentina, on suspicion of involvement in a terrorist attack in Buenos Aires in 1994 in which 85 people were killed. Shots were fired at the British embassy in Tehran on several occasions later in 2003, prompting the Foreign and Commonwealth Office to protest strongly to the Iranian authorities. In November the United Kingdom rejected Argentina's request for extradition and Soleimanpour, who had earlier been released on bail, subsequently returned to Iran. In May 2004 demonstrators demanded the closure of the embassy and the removal of the ambassador, in protest against British policy in Iraq, and threw petrol bombs at the building. Diplomatic relations were further strained in June when three British patrol crafts and eight Royal Navy personnel were captured on the Shatt al-Arab waterway by Iranian authorities who claimed the servicemen had entered Iranian territorial waters. After intense negotiations between British and Iranian diplomats, the men were released four days later and claimed that they had been forcibly escorted into Iranian waters. In October 2005 Blair warned Iran against supporting rebel factions in Iraq. The Iranian Government denied that it was doing so, and accused British forces stationed in Iraq of assisting Arab separatists responsible for recent bomb explosions in the Iranian city of Ahvaz. The United Kingdom, together with the USA and other Western governments, expressed suspicion during the early 2000s that Iran's programme of uranium enrichment was not, as Iran claimed, purely for peaceful purposes. In November 2004, after discussions with representatives of France, Germany and the United Kingdom, acting on behalf of the EU, Iran agreed to suspend its uranium enrichment programme, but in January 2006 it announced that it was resuming nuclear research and development. In December and again in March 2007 the UN Security Council imposed sanctions on Iran for refusing to comply with requests to desist from uranium enrichment. In April the Iranian navy arrested 15 British naval personnel whom it accused of intruding into Iranian territorial waters; they were released after almost two weeks in captivity.

Government

The United Kingdom is a constitutional monarchy. The Sovereign is the Head of State and the monarchy is hereditary. Parliament consists of the House of Commons and the House of Lords. The 646 members of the Commons are elected for a maximum of five years by direct suffrage by all citizens of 18 years and over, using single-member constituencies. The House of Lords is composed of hereditary Peers of the Realm and Life Peers and Peeresses created by the Sovereign for outstanding public service. Legislation may be initiated in either House but it usually originates in the Commons. Each bill has three readings in the Commons and it is then passed to the House of Lords who may return it to the Commons with amendments or suggestions. The House of Lords may delay, but cannot prevent, any bill from becoming law once it has been passed by the Commons. Executive power is held by the Cabinet, headed by the Prime Minister. The Cabinet is responsible to the House of Commons.

The Northern Ireland Act 1974 made the Secretary of State for Northern Ireland and his ministers answerable to Parliament at Westminster for the government of Northern Ireland, under a parliamentary order, renewable annually. In October 1982 a 78-member Northern Ireland Assembly was elected, in accordance with the Northern Ireland Act 1982: its role was primarily consultative, pending the devolution of executive power. The 1985 Anglo-Irish Agreement, signed by the Prime Ministers of the United Kingdom and of Ireland in November, left the constitutional status of Northern Ireland unaltered, but gave Ireland a consultative role in Northern Ireland affairs, through an Intergovernmental Conference. In June 1986 the British Government announced the dissolution of the Northern Ireland Assembly, four months before the end of its four-year term, following a boycott of meetings by some members, in protest at the Anglo-Irish Agreement. Elections to a new 108-member Assembly were held on 25 June 1998, as part of the multi-party agreement on the future governance of Northern Ireland, approved by a popular referendum in May. An Executive Committee, headed by a First Minister, was constituted from among the legislative members. Responsibility for all matters formerly implemented by the Northern Ireland Office was transferred to the devolved authority under new parliamentary legislation implemented in December 1999. The 1998 Agreement also provided for the establishment of a North/South Ministerial Council, to facilitate co-operation between the Irish Government and representatives of the Northern Ireland Executive on specific cross-border and all-island concerns, and of a British-Irish Council, comprising representatives of British and Irish Governments, members of the devolved authorities in Northern Ireland, Scotland and Wales, and representatives of the Isle of Man and the Channel Islands. The arrangements of the Anglo-Irish Agreement were replaced by a British-Irish Intergovernmental Conference, with responsibility to oversee the new political institutions. The new Northern Ireland institutions were suspended in February 2000, owing to a political impasse concerning the decommissioning of paramilitary weapons and Northern Ireland was returned to direct rule. On 30 May, following an agreement on the issue of decommissioning, power was once again transferred from Westminster to the new Northern Ireland institutions. The Northern Ireland Executive was suspended again on 14 October 2002 and Northern Ireland was returned to direct rule from Westminster, until the restoration of devolved government on 8 May 2007.

In 1999 devolved legislative authorities were established in Scotland and Wales. In Scotland a new elected parliament, based in Edinburgh, was established with powers to legislate on all domestic matters (incl. education, health, local government and law and order) and with a mandate to vary taxes set by the Government of the United Kingdom by 3%. The Assembly has 129 members, elected every four years by a combined system of direct voting, on the basis of Westminster parliamentary constituencies, and a form of proportional representation, whereby additional members are elected from a party list on the basis of the larger constituencies used for elections to the European Parliament. The Welsh Assembly, located in Cardiff, undertook responsibility for issues covered by the Welsh Office of the Government of the United Kingdom. The 60-member Assembly was elected under the same system as in Scotland. Elections to the two Assemblies took place simultaneously in May 1999 and the transfer of powers took place on 1 July.

Legislation providing for the abolition of all but 92 hereditary peers and the establishment of an interim second chamber pending a definitive reform of the House of Lords was passed in November 1999.

Defence

The United Kingdom is a member of the North Atlantic Treaty Organization (NATO, see p. 340) and maintains a regular army. The total strength of the armed forces in November 2007, including those enlisted outside Britain (3,330), was 191,030 (army 104,980, navy 40,840, air force 45,210). In November 2004 the European Union (EU, see p. 244) ministers responsible for defence agreed to create 13 'battlegroups' (each numbering about 1,500 men), which could be deployed at short notice to crisis areas around the world. The EU battlegroups, two of which were to be ready for deployment at any one time, following a rotational schedule, reached full operational capacity from 1 January 2007. The United Kingdom committed troops to two battlegroups (one comprising solely British troops and one in conjunction with the Netherlands). Military service is voluntary. The United Kingdom possesses its own nuclear weapons. Government-budgeted defence expenditure for 2007 totalled £29,900m.

Economic Affairs

In 2006, according to estimates by the World Bank, the United Kingdom's gross national income (GNI), measured at average 2004–06 prices, was US $2,425,210m., equivalent to $40,180 per head (or $35,580 per head on an international purchasing-power parity basis). During 1996–2006, it was estimated, the population increased at an average annual rate of 0.3%, while gross domestic product (GDP) per head increased, in real terms, by an average of 2.4% per year over the same period. Overall GDP increased, in real terms, at an average annual rate of 2.8% in 1996–2006. Real GDP increased by 2.9% in 2006 and by 3.0% in 2007, according to official figures.

Agriculture (including hunting, forestry and fishing) contributed 0.9% of GDP in 2006 and accounted for 1.4% of work-force jobs in December 2007. The principal crops include wheat, sugar beet, potatoes and barley. Livestock-rearing (particularly poultry and cattle) and animal products are important, as is fishing. The GDP of the agricultural sector increased, in real terms, by an average of 0.9% per year during 1996–2005; it declined by 2.1% in 2003, but recovered to record growth of 2.8% in 2006 and 0.9% in 2007.

Industry (including mining, manufacturing, construction and power) contributed 22.9% of GDP in 2006 and accounted for 17.6% of work-force jobs in December 2007. Industrial GDP increased, in real terms, at an average annual rate of 0.4% during 1996–2005; in 2005 (excluding construction) it declined by 2.0%, but in 2006 and 2007 growth of 0.3% was recorded.

Mining (including petroleum and gas extraction) contributed 2.3% of GDP in 2006 and engaged 0.8% of the employed labour force in 1990; together with the energy and water industries, the sector accounted for 0.6% of work-force jobs in December 2007. Natural gas, sand and gravel, limestone, crude petroleum, igneous rock and coal are the principal minerals produced. The GDP of the mining sector decreased, in real terms, at an average annual rate of 4.4% during 1998–2006; the GDP of extractive industries decreased by 8.0% in 2006 and by 1.7% in 2007.

Manufacturing provided 12.6% of GDP in 2006 and accounted for 10.0% of work-force jobs in December 2007. The principal branches of manufacturing include transport equipment, food products, machinery, chemical products and metals and metal products. In real terms, the GDP of the manufacturing sector increased at an average annual rate of 0.2% during 1998–2006; manufacturing GDP declined by 2.6% in 2002, but the sector recovered to record growth of 1.5% in 2006 and 0.6% in 2007.

Energy is derived principally from natural gas, petroleum and, to a lesser degree in recent years, coal. Of the United Kingdom's total consumption of energy in 2006, 45.0% was derived from petroleum, 33.4% was from natural gas, 18.7% from electricity (including nuclear power, hydroelectric power), 1.6% from solid fuels and 0.4% was from renewable and waste sources. At the end of 2007 19 nuclear power reactors were operating in the United Kingdom (a further 26 had been permanently shut down). In 2006 mineral fuels accounted for about 9.7% of the value of total merchandise imports. In mid-2003 plans were announced for the construction of three new offshore wind farms, which would provide sufficient energy to power 15% of British homes upon their completion. It was anticipated that they would supply some 5% of the United Kingdom's electric power by 2010.

Services accounted for 76.2% of GDP in 2006 and accounted for 81.0% of work-force jobs in December 2007. The United Kingdom is an important international centre for business and financial services. Financial intermediation and other business services (including renting and real estate) contributed 32.6% of GDP in 2006. Receipts from tourism totalled £16,002m. in 2006. Wholesale and retail trade (including the motor trade) and repairs (11.5% of GDP in 2006) and transport and communications (6.8% of GDP in 2006) are also major contributors to the economy. In real terms, the GDP of the services sector increased at an average annual rate of 3.7% during 1996–2005; the sector's GDP increased by 3.7% in 2006 and 2007.

According to preliminary seasonally adjusted figures, in 2007 the United Kingdom recorded a visible trade deficit of £87,649m., and there was a deficit of £57,795m. on the current account of the balance of payments. In 2006 the principal source of imports (13.0%) was France, while the principal market for exports in that year was the USA (13.1%). Other major trading partners include Germany, the Netherlands, Ireland and Belgium-Luxembourg. The principal imports in 2006 were road vehicles, petroleum and petroleum products and mechanical and electrical machinery. These items also constituted the United Kingdom's principal exports in the same year.

According to preliminary official estimates for the 2007 calendar year, there was a budgetary deficit of £39,400m. (equivalent to 2.8% of GDP). At the end of December 2007 general government debt was £618,800m. (equivalent to 43.8% of GDP). The annual rate of inflation, according to the retail price index, averaged 2.8% in 1995–2007; retail prices increased by 4.3% in 2007, while consumer prices (excluding owner-occupier housing costs and council tax) increased by 2.3%. The rate of unemployment averaged 5.2% in November 2007–January 2008.

The United Kingdom is a member of the European Union (EU, see p. 244). It is also a member of the Organisation for Economic Co-operation and Development (OECD, see p. 347).

Following a period of recession in the early 1990s, the United Kingdom economy experienced a prolonged period of expansion, with sustained growth in GDP accompanied by a declining rate of unemployment and low rates of inflation. However, the worldwide economic slowdown in 2007/08 had an adverse effect on the economy of the United Kingdom. The shortage of credit in the global financial system, which originated in a crisis in the US low-income mortgage sector, caused substantial losses in the British financial sector, and led, notably, to the nationalization of a major commercial bank, Northern Rock, in February 2008. The 2008 budget forecast a slowing in GDP growth, to 1.75-2.25% in 2008, after growth of 3.0% was recorded in 2007. Additionally, a decline in consumer spending was expected, with growth due to fall to 1.75% in 2008 and 1.5% in 2009, compared with 3% in 2007.

This lowering of personal disposable incomes came as house prices began to fall in 2008, following 12 consecutive years of price increases. Annual inflation in 2006 exceeded the target of 2%, principally owing to high international energy prices and rising food costs, and the rate continued to increase, reaching 3.0% in the year to March 2008. In an effort to address inflationary pressures, from August 2006 the Bank of England implemented a series of increases in policy interest rates, bringing the rate to 5.75% in July 2007 (the highest level since early 2001); however, the rate was reduced to 5.0% in April 2008. Net public sector debt, which at March 2008 was equivalent to 36.7% of GDP, from 36.6% a year earlier, remained beneath the Treasury's targeted ceiling of 40%. The deficit on the current account of the balance of payments widened in 2007, to the equivalent of 4.2% of GDP, as a result of the appreciation of the currency and slower growth in the USA and other major export markets. Economic policy remained broadly unchanged following the assumption, in June 2007, of the office of Prime Minister by Gordon Brown, the Chancellor of the Exchequer under the Labour Government since 1997. However, Brown faced growing criticism of his policy decisions in light of the uncertain economic environment, and, in particular, following the entering into force of the abolition of the 10 pence starting rate of income tax in April 2008.

Education

Education in the United Kingdom is compulsory for all children between the ages of five (four in Northern Ireland) and 16 and takes place in several stages: nursery (now part of the foundation stage in England), primary, secondary, further and higher education. Further education, the non-compulsory fourth stage, covers non-advanced education, which can be taken at both further (including tertiary) education colleges, higher education institutions and increasingly in secondary schools. Higher education, the fifth stage, is study beyond the General Certificate of Education (GCE) Advanced Level (A Level) and its equivalent, which, for most full-time students, takes place in higher education institutions. In November 2007 the Government announced plans to introduce an Education and Skills Bill, under which, most notably, the school leaving age would be increased from 16 to 18 for pupils in England and Wales, by 2015.

Responsibility for education is substantially devolved: the Secretary of State for Children, Schools and Families is responsible, in principle, for all sectors of education in England, excluding further education, the responsibility for which rests with the Secretary of State for Innovation, Universities and Skills. From 2006 responsibility for all sectors of education in Wales was devolved to the Welsh Assembly Government. Since 1999 the Scottish Executive has had full responsibility for education in Scotland. Responsibility for education in Northern Ireland was devolved to the Northern Ireland Department of Education in May 2007, except for higher and further education, which are administered by the Northern Ireland Department for Employment and Learning. Assessment of the quality of schools is undertaken in England by the Office for Standards in Education (OFSTED), in Wales by Her Majesty's Chief Inspectorate For Education and Training in Wales, in Scotland by Her Majesty's Inspectorate of Education and in Northern Ireland by the Education and Training Inspectorate.

In recent years there has been a major expansion of pre-school education. Many children under the age of five attend state nursery schools or nursery schools attached to primary schools. Others may attend playgroups in the voluntary sector or privately run nurseries. In England and Wales many primary schools also operate an early admission policy where they admit children under the age of five into 'reception classes'. The primary stage covers three age ranges: nursery (under five), infant (five to seven or eight) and junior (up to 11 or 12), but in Scotland and Northern Ireland there is generally no distinction between infant and junior schools. Most public sector primary schools take both boys and girls in mixed classes.

Secondary education generally begins at the age of 11, although in England many areas have middle schools for children aged eight to 12 years or nine to 13 years. In most areas, the state-maintained system of comprehensive schools prevails. Pupils are admitted to such schools without reference to ability. Some localities, however, retain a system of grammar and secondary modern schools, to which admission is determined through a test of ability. Specialist schools covering 10 areas (arts, business and enterprise, engineering, humanities, language, mathematics and computing, music, science, sports and technology) also operate in England. The Specialist Schools Programme helps schools, in partnership with private-sector sponsors and supported by additional government funding, to establish distinctive identities through their chosen specialisms and achieve their target to raise standards. Specialist schools have a special focus on their chosen subject area, but must meet the requirements of the National Curriculum and deliver a broad and balanced education to all pupils. Schools can also combine any two specialisms. In 2000 the Department for Education and Skills announced the introduction of Academies, which were to be mixed-ability schools, located mainly in disadvantaged urban areas. Academies were to be partially financed by private individual or institutional investors, faith groups or other organizations in the voluntary sector. By May 2008 there were 83 Academies in England. Special schools (day or boarding) are provided by local education authorities (LEAs) for certain children with special educational needs, although the vast majority are educated in ordinary schools. All children attending special schools are offered a curriculum designed to overcome their learning difficulties and to enable them to become self-reliant.

Examinations for the single-system General Certificate of Secondary Education (GCSE) may be taken (usually at the age of 16) in as many subjects as a candidate wishes. In 1989 the Government implemented legislation introduced under the Education Reform Act (1988), which provided for a National Curriculum and national testing of pupils aged seven, 11 and 14 years in state schools in England and Wales (Key Stages 1, 2 and 3, respectively). All state schools in England, Wales and Northern Ireland must conform to the national curriculums, which set out which subjects pupils should study, what they should be taught and what standards they should achieve. In Scotland the curriculum in state schools is not prescribed by statute, but the Secretary of State for Scotland issues national advice and guidance to schools and Scottish Local Authorities. The Qualifications and Curriculum Authority is the statutory body which advises the Government on all matters concerned with the curriculum and all aspects of school examinations and assessment in state schools in England. It is also responsible for vocational qualifications. Similar arrangements operate for Wales, Scotland and Northern Ireland. The A Level, generally taken at the age of 18, was introduced in the early 1950s, and serves as a qualification for entrance to higher education. Over the years there have been attempts to broaden the curriculum and experience of those taking A Levels (e.g. the Advanced Supplementary examination in 1989). In September 2000, however, a completely revised approach to A Level was introduced, based entirely on a modular approach. Candidates are now able to take modules as they proceed through the course, rather than being examined in a single session at the end of the course. The new A Level qualification consists of two parts, the AS (Advanced Subsidiary), which can also be taken as a free-standing qualification, and A2. All students now take the AS and then, where appropriate, proceed to the more challenging A2 to complete their A level. In 1999/2000 National Qualifications (NQ) were introduced in Scotland. NQs include Standard Grades, Intermediate 1 and 2 and Higher Grades. Pupils study for the Scottish Certificate of Education (SCE)/NQ Standard Grade, approximately equivalent to GCSE, in their third (S3) and fourth (S4) years of secondary schooling (roughly ages 14 and 15), with courses taking two years to complete. Each subject has several elements, some of which are internally assessed in school, and Standard Grade courses are offered at three levels: Credit (grades 1–2), General (grades 3–4) and Foundation (grades 5–6). The Higher Grade requires one further year of study and, for the more able candidates, the range of subjects taken may be as wide as at Standard Grade, with as many as five or six subjects spanning both arts and science. Three or more Highers are regarded as being approximately the equivalent of two or more A Levels.

Since 1986 the National Council for Vocational Qualifications (NCVQ) has established a framework of National Vocational Qualifications (NVQ) in England, Wales and Northern Ireland. The framework is based on five defined levels of achievement, ranging from Level 1, broadly equating to foundation skills in semi-skilled occupations, to Level 5, equating to professional/senior management occupations. The competence-based system has also been extended in Scotland through a system of Scottish Vocational Qualifications (SVQ) along similar lines to the NVQs. General National Vocational Qualifications (GNVQ), along with General Scottish Vocational Qualifications (GSVQ) have also been introduced. GNVQs, which are normally studied in school or college, aim to incorporate skills required by employers and are designed to develop the skills and understanding needed in vocational areas such as business, engineering or health and social care, in order to provide an introduction into both further education and employment. They are awarded at Foundation and Intermediate levels and through Vocational Certificates of Education (VCEs—more commonly known as vocational A levels), which replaced the Advanced level GNVQ. GSVQs are awarded on the basis of a modular framework of National Certificate Units, which give candidates practical and knowledge-based vocational skills and are taken in secondary schools and colleges.

Further and higher education may be pursued through vocational or academic courses, on a full-time, part-time or 'sandwich' basis. The decision to admit students is made by each institution according to its own entrance requirements. The term 'further education' may be used in a general sense to cover all non-advanced courses taken after the period of compulsory education, but more commonly it excludes those staying on at secondary school and those in higher education, i.e. courses in universities and colleges leading to qualifications above A Level, SCE Higher Grade, GNVQ/NVQ level three, and their equivalents. Since 1 April 1993 sixth-form colleges have been included in the further education sector.

Higher education is defined as courses that are of a standard that is higher than A Level, the SCE Higher Grade of the SCE, GNVQ/NVQ Level 3 or the Edexcel (formerly BTEC) or SQA National Certificate/Diploma. Higher education students are most likely to be working towards one of the following qualifications. An Honours degree: the most common of these are Bachelor of Arts (BA Hons) and Bachelor of Science (BSc Hons). These are usually full-time three-year courses but can also be taken as longer part-time courses and may be available through distance learning. In Scotland, where students usually start a year earlier, a full-time first-degree generally takes four years for Honours and three years for the broad-based Ordinary degree. A Foundation degree: this is a new vocationally focused higher education qualification. It aims to increase the number of people qualified at higher technician and associate professional level (e.g. legal executives, engineering technicians, personnel officers, laboratory technicians, teaching assistants). Both full- and part-time courses are offered in a variety of work-related subjects and offer progression to a full Honours degree. A Higher National Diploma (HND) or Diploma of Higher Education (Dip HE): these take two years full-time, and there is the option of turning them into an Honours degree by studying for a further year. Some students go on to do postgraduate studies, usually leading to a Masters degree, such as a Master of Arts (MA), or Master of Science (MSc), or to a Doctorate (PhD). A Masters degree usually lasts one year full-time or two years part-time. A PhD usually lasts three years full-time or six years part-time.

In 2003/04 there were 89 universities (47 traditional universities and 42 former polytechnics and colleges awarded university status in 1992—including the London and Manchester Business Schools, as well as the Open University and the privately funded University of Buckingham) and 60 other higher education institutions offering courses of higher education in the United Kingdom. The Open University, founded in 1969, and funded mainly by the Higher Education Funding Council for England, provides degree courses by means of printed texts, television broadcasts, audio/visual materials, correspondence tuition and, for some courses, short residential schools. No formal qualifications are required for entry to its courses. Some British universities and colleges also now offer study through distance learning, usually learning at home or work.

Educational establishments in the United Kingdom are administered and financed in several ways. Most schools are controlled by LEAs, which are part of the structure of local government, but some are 'assisted', receiving grants direct from central government sources and being controlled by governing bodies, which have a substantial degree of autonomy. Alongside the state system, there are independent schools, which do not receive grants from public funds but are financed by fees and endowments; many of these schools are administered by charitable trusts and church organizations.

The Learning and Skills Council (LSC) is responsible for funding the further education sector in England. The LSC is also responsible for funding provision for non-prescribed higher education in further education sector colleges and further education provided by LEA maintained and other institutions, referred to as 'external institutions'. Until 2006 the National Council for Education and Training for Wales (part of Education and Learning Wales—ELWa) largely funded further education provision made by further education institutions via a third party or sponsored arrangements. In 2006 the functions of ELWa were assumed by the Welsh Assembly Government, including the funding of higher education institutions in Wales. The Scottish Funding Council funds further education colleges in Scotland, while the Department for Employment and Learning funds further education colleges in Northern Ireland.

Government finance for publicly funded higher education institutions (to help meet the costs of teaching, research and related activities) is distributed by the Higher Education Funding Councils (HEFC) in England and Wales, the Scottish Funding Council, and the Department of Education in Northern Ireland. In addition, some designated higher education (mainly Higher National Diplomas/Higher National Certificates and Certificates of Higher Education) is also funded by these sources. The further education sources mentioned above fund the remainder.

Student loans are the main form of support for assistance with living costs for higher education students. The maximum loan in 2005/06 for full-time students was £5,175. The amount of loan paid also depends on the student's and their family's income. Loans are repaid on the basis of income after the student has left their course, and only when the student's annual income exceeds £15,000. From September 2004 a full-time undergraduate would have to pay up to £1,150 towards the tuition fees for each year of the course. The level of the contribution is means-tested, although those on lower family incomes are entitled to free tuition. Since September 2006 universities in England have been entitled to set variable fees for individual courses, up to a maximum of £3,000, which will rise in line with inflation. However, any rise above the 2005/06 level of £1,175 was to be subject to an access agreement in partnership with the Office for Fair Access. Since the academic year 2000/01, eligible full-time Scottish-domiciled or EU students who are studying in Scotland no longer pay tuition fees. Other additional forms of student support include: dependant's allowances; young and mature student bursaries; hardship funds; disabled students' allowance and care leavers' grant; and the Maintenance Grant, which was introduced in September 2006.

Budgetary expenditure on education and training in 2004/05 totalled an estimated £65,300m, representing 13.5% of total expenditure.

Public Holidays

2008: 1 January (New Year's Day), 2 January* (Scotland only), 17 March (St Patrick's Day, Northern Ireland only), 21 March* (Good Friday), 24 March† (Easter Monday), 5 May* (Early May Holiday), 26 May (Spring Holiday), 14 July (Battle of the Boyne, Northern Ireland only), 4 August* (Summer Bank Holiday, Scotland only), 25 August† (Late Summer Bank Holiday), 25 December (Christmas Day), 26 December* (Boxing Day).

2009: 1 January (New Year's Day), 2 January* (Scotland only), 17 March (St Patrick's Day, Northern Ireland only), 10 April* (Good Friday), 13 April† (Easter Monday), 4 May* (Early May Holiday), 25 May (Spring Holiday), 13 July (Battle of the Boyne, Northern Ireland only), 3 August* (Summer Bank Holiday, Scotland only), 31 August† (Late Summer Bank Holiday), 25 December (Christmas Day), 28 December* (Boxing Day).

*Bank Holidays but not national holidays in Scotland.
† Excluding Scotland.

Weights and Measures

The metric system of weights and measures is now the primary system in force, although the imperial system is still used in limited areas.

Weight

1 pound (lb) = 16 ounces (oz) = 453.59 grams.
14 pounds = 1 stone = 6.35 kilograms.
112 pounds = 1 hundredweight (cwt) = 50.8 kilograms.
20 hundredweights = 1 ton = 1,016 kilograms.

Length

1 yard (yd) = 3 feet (ft) = 36 inches (ins) = 0.9144 metre.
1,760 yards = 1 mile = 1.609 kilometres.

Capacity

1 gallon = 4 quarts = 8 pints = 4.546 litres.

THE UNITED KINGDOM

Statistical Survey

Source (unless otherwise stated): Office for National Statistics, 1 Drummond Gate, London SW1V 2QQ; internet www.statistics.gov.uk.

Statistics refer to the United Kingdom unless otherwise indicated.

Area and Population

AREA, POPULATION AND DENSITY

Land area (sq km)	242,495*
Population usually resident (census results)	
21 April 1991	56,466,700
29 April 2001	
Males	28,581,233
Females	30,207,961
Total	58,789,194
Population (official estimates at mid-year)	
2004	59,834,900
2005	59,834,300
2006	60,587,300
Density (per sq km) at mid-2006	249.8

*93,628 sq miles.

DISTRIBUTION OF POPULATION
(at mid-2006, '000)

	Land area (sq km)	Population	Density (per sq km)
Great Britain	228,919	58,845.7	257.1
England	130,279	50,762.9	389.6
Wales	20,733	2,965.9	143.1
Scotland	77,907	5,116.9	65.7
Northern Ireland	13,576	1,741.6	128.3
Total	242,495	60,587.3	249.8

ADMINISTRATIVE AREAS
('000, population estimates at mid-2006)

England

Greater London	7,512
Metropolitan Counties:	
Greater Manchester	2,554
Merseyside	1,354
South Yorkshire	1,293
Tyne and Wear	1,088
West Midlands	2,600
West Yorkshire	2,161
Unitary Authorities:	
Bath and North-east Somerset	176
Blackburn with Darwen	141
Blackpool	143
Bournemouth	161
Bracknell Forest	112
Brighton and Hove	251
Bristol	411
Darlington	99
Derby	236
East Riding of Yorkshire	331
Halton	120
Hartlepool	91
Herefordshire	178
Isle of Wight	139
Kingston upon Hull	256
Leicester	290
Luton	187
Medway	252
Middlesbrough	138
Milton Keynes	225
North Lincolnshire	159
North Somerset	201
North-east Lincolnshire	159
Nottingham	286
Peterborough	163
Plymouth	248
Poole	137
Portsmouth	196
Reading	143
Redcar and Cleveland	140
Rutland	38
Slough	120
South Gloucestershire	254
Southampton	229
Southend-on-Sea	160
Stockton-on-Tees	189
Stoke-on-Trent	240
Swindon	187
Telford and Wrekin	162
Thurrock	149
Torbay	133
Warrington	194
West Berkshire	149
Windsor and Maidenhead	139
Wokingham	154
York	192
Non-Metropolitan Counties:	
Bedfordshire	404
Buckinghamshire	487
Cambridgeshire	590
Cheshire	686
Cornwall/Isles of Scilly	526
Cumbria	496
Derbyshire	754
Devon	741
Dorset	403
Durham	501
East Sussex	506
Essex	1,361
Gloucestershire	579
Hampshire	1,266
Hertfordshire	1,059
Kent	1,383
Lancashire	1,166
Leicestershire	635
Lincolnshire	686
Norfolk	832
North Yorkshire	592
Northamptonshire	669
Northumberland	310
Nottinghamshire	769
Oxfordshire	632
Shropshire	289
Somerset	519
Staffordshire	823
Suffolk	702
Surrey	1,085
Warwickshire	522
West Sussex	771
Wiltshire	449
Worcestershire	553

Wales

Unitary Authorities:	
Blaenau Gwent	69
Bridgend	133
Caerphilly	171
Cardiff	318
Carmarthenshire	178
Ceredigion	77
Conwy	111
Denbighshire	96
Flintshire	150
Gwynedd	118
Isle of Anglesey	69
Merthyr Tydfil	56
Monmouthshire	88
Neath Port Talbot	137
Newport	140
Pembrokeshire	117
Powys	131
Rhondda, Cynon, Taff	234
Swansea	227
Torfaen	91
Vale of Glamorgan	123
Wrexham	131

Scotland

Unitary Authorities:	
Aberdeen City	207
Aberdeenshire	236
Angus	109
Argyll and Bute	91
Clackmannanshire	49
Comhairle nan Eilean Siar (Western Isles)	26
Dumfries and Galloway	148
Dundee City	142
East Ayrshire	119
East Dunbartonshire	106
East Lothian	93
East Renfrewshire	89
Edinburgh, City of	464
Falkirk	150
Fife	359
Glasgow City	581
Highland	215
Inverclyde	82
Midlothian	79
Moray	87
North Ayrshire	136
North Lanarkshire	324
Orkney Islands	20
Perth and Kinross	140
Renfrewshire	170
Scottish Borders	110
Shetland Islands	22
South Ayrshire	112
South Lanarkshire	308
Stirling	88
West Dunbartonshire	91
West Lothian	166

Northern Ireland

Unitary Authorities:	
Antrim	52
Ards	76
Armagh	57
Ballymena	61
Ballymoney	29
Banbridge	46
Belfast	268
Carrickfergus	40
Castlereagh	66
Coleraine	57
Cookstown	35
Craigavon	87
Derry	108
Down	68
Dungannon	52
Fermanagh	61
Larne	31
Limavady	34
Lisburn	113
Magherafelt	42
Moyle	17
Newry and Mourne	93
Newtownabbey	81
North Down	79
Omagh	51
Strabane	39

Sources: Office for National Statistics.

THE UNITED KINGDOM

Statistical Survey

PRINCIPAL LOCALITIES*
('000, population estimates at mid-2006)

Locality	Pop.	Locality	Pop.
Greater London (capital)	7,512	Newcastle upon Tyne	271
Birmingham	1,007	Belfast	267
Leeds	750	Bolton	262
Glasgow City	581	Kingston upon Hull	256
Sheffield	526	Walsall	255
Bradford	493	South Gloucestershire	254
Edinburgh	464	Rotherham	253
Manchester	452	Medway	252
Liverpool	436	Brighton and Hove	251
Bristol	411	Plymouth	248
Kirklees	398	Stoke-on-Trent	240
Fife	359	Wolverhampton	237
East Riding of Yorkshire	331	Aberdeenshire	236
North Lanarkshire	324	Derby	236
Wakefield	321	Rhondda, Cynon, Taff	234
Cardiff	318	Southampton	229
Wirral	311	Swansea	227
South Lanarkshire	308	Milton Keynes	225
Coventry	307	Barnsley	224
Wigan	306	Oldham	220
Dudley	305	Salford	218
Sunderland	291	Highland	215
Leicester	290	Tameside	214
Doncaster	290	Trafford	212
Sandwell	288	Rochdale	207
Nottingham	286	Aberdeen City	207
Stockport	281	Solihull	203
Sefton	277		

* Local authority areas with populations greater than 200,000.

Sources: Office for National Statistics.

BIRTHS, MARRIAGES AND DEATHS*

	Registered live births Number	Rate (per 1,000)	Registered marriages Number	Rate (per 1,000)	Registered deaths Number	Rate (per 1,000)
1999	699,976	12.0	310,083	5.3	629,476	10.7
2000	697,029	11.6	305,912	5.2	610,579	10.4
2001	669,123	11.4	286,133	4.9	604,393	10.2
2002	668,777	11.3	293,021	4.9	608,045	10.2
2003	695,549	11.7	308,620	5.1	612,085	10.3
2004	715,996	12.0	313,550	5.2	583,082	9.7
2005	722,549	12.0	286,826	n.a.	582,964	9.7
2006	748,563	12.4	275,137†	n.a.	572,224	9.4

* In England and Wales, figures for births are tabulated by year of occurrence, while figures for Scotland and Northern Ireland are tabulated by year of registration. Births to non-resident mothers in Northern Ireland are excluded from the figures for the United Kingdom.
† Preliminary.

Sources: Office for National Statistics; General Register Office for Scotland; Northern Ireland Statistics and Research Agency.

Expectation of life (years at birth, WHO estimates): 78.9 (males 76.6; females 81.1) in 2005 (Source: WHO, *World Health Statistics*).

IMMIGRATION AND EMIGRATION*

Immigrants
('000)

Origin†	2003	2004	2005
EU‡	101	139	180
Ireland	5	5	4
Commonwealth countries	207	255	223
Australia, New Zealand, Canada	68	63	64
South Africa	28	37	29
India, Bangladesh, Sri Lanka	45	60	64
Pakistan	13	29	22
Caribbean	4	6	2
Other§	49	60	42
Other territories|	205	189	161
USA	28	28	25
Middle East	27	26	19
Total	**513**	**582**	**565**

Emigrants
('000)

Destination†	2003	2004	2005
EU‡	122	121	134
Ireland	13	13	13
Commonwealth countries	131	138	141
Australia, New Zealand, Canada	90	95	95
South Africa	14	10	14
India, Bangladesh, Sri Lanka	7	6	10
Pakistan	4	4	7
Caribbean	1	3	3
Other§	15	20	12
Other territories|	109	100	104
USA	27	27	27
Middle East	7	12	12
Total	**362**	**359**	**380**

* Figures are compiled in accordance with the Total International Migration (TIM) methodology, which supplements International Passenger Survey (IPS) data (whereby small samples of detailed passenger numbers are extrapolated according to a weighting system) with estimates of migration between the UK and Ireland (agreed between the Irish Central Statistics Office and the UK Office for National Statistics), and with Home Office data on asylum seekers and their dependents. In addition, two adjustments are estimated to account for 'visitor switchers' (who stay longer than their stated intention) and 'migrant switchers' (who stay for less time than intended).
† Figures refer to the country of immigrants' last permanent residence or emigrants' intended future residence.
‡ Figures for all years show the EU as it was constituted at 31 December of year shown.
§ From 2004 excludes Cyprus and Malta.
| From 2004 excludes Czech Republic, Estonia, Hungary, Latvia, Lithuania, Poland, Slovakia and Slovenia.

WORK-FORCE JOBS BY INDUSTRY
('000 at December)

	2005	2006	2007
Agriculture, hunting, forestry and fishing	453	454	451
Mining, energy and water	169	177	183
Manufacturing	3,319	3,224	3,172
Construction	2,149	2,215	2,208
Distribution, hotels and restaurants	7,078	7,014	7,117
Transport and communications	1,866	1,853	1,854
Banking, finance, insurance, etc.	6,364	6,503	6,651
Public administration, education and health*	7,892	7,967	7,991
Other services	1,962	2,004	1,992
Total	**31,253**	**31,412**	**31,620**
Males	16,671	16,748	16,789
Females	14,582	14,664	14,831

* Including public and private sectors.

Note: Since data correspond to jobs rather than employees, a single worker may be counted more than once; figures include armed forces personnel.

Economically active population (labour force survey, '000 persons aged 16 years and over, excl. armed forces, Nov. 2007–Jan. 2008): Total employed 29,457; Unemployed 1,608; Total labour force 31,065 (males 16,827, females 14,238).

THE UNITED KINGDOM

Health and Welfare

KEY INDICATORS

Total fertility rate (children per woman, 2005)	1.7
Under-5 mortality rate (per 1,000 live births, 2005)	6
HIV/AIDS (% of persons aged 15–49, 2005)	0.2
Physicians (per 1,000 head, 2004)	2.3
Hospital beds (per 1,000 head, 2004)	3.9
Health expenditure (2004): US $ per head (PPP)	2,559.9
Health expenditure (2004): % of GDP	8.1
Health expenditure (2004): public (% of total)	86.3
Human Development Index (2005): ranking	16
Human Development Index (2005): value	0.946

For sources and definitions, see explanatory note on p. vi.

Agriculture

PRINCIPAL CROPS
('000 metric tons)

	2004	2005	2006
Wheat	15,473	14,863	14,735
Barley	5,816	5,495	5,239
Oats	627	532	728
Rye	33	40	43
Triticale (wheat-rye hybrid)	62	53	61
Potatoes	6,317	5,961	5,684
Sugar beet	9,042	8,687	7,150
Rapeseed	1,609	1,902	1,870
Dry peas	215	161	200
Dry broad beans*	131	130	130
Dry onions	340.9	383.4	383.4*
Mushrooms	74	74	74*
Carrots and turnips	768.3	832.6	832.6*
Cabbages and other brassicas	266.1	308.2	308.2*
Cauliflower and broccoli	233.8	218.7	218.7*
Green peas	135.9	133.1	133.1*
Linseed	52	89	49
Lettuce and chicory	150.2	139.9	139.9*
Tomatoes	78.3	79.5	79.5*
Cucumbers and gherkins	61.4	59.0	59.0*
Apples	170.0	218.5	218.5*
Pears	22.7	23.8	23.8*
Strawberries	52.4	62.6	62.6*

*FAO estimate(s).

Aggregate production (may include official, semi-official or estimated data): Total cereals 22,028 in 2004, 20,998 in 2005, 20,820 in 2006; Total pulses 866 in 2004, 791 in 2005, 830 in 2006; Total roots and tubers 6,317 in 2004, 5,961 in 2005, 5,684 in 2006; Total vegetables (incl. melons) 2,635 in 2004, 2,772 in 2005, 2,772 in 2006; Total fruits (excl. melons) 295 in 2004, 355 in 2005, 355 in 2006.

Source: FAO.

LIVESTOCK
('000 head, year ending September)

	2004	2005	2006
Cattle	10,551	10,378	10,160
Sheep and lambs	35,848	35,253	34,722
Pigs	5,159	4,862	4,933
Chickens	167,824	160,509	158,202
Ducks and geese*	2,790	2,680	2,980
Turkeys*	11,145	10,720	11,900

*Unofficial figures.

Source: FAO.

LIVESTOCK PRODUCTS
('000 metric tons, unless otherwise indicated)

	2004	2005	2006
Cattle meat	719	762	762*
Sheep meat	312	331	331*
Pig meat	708	706	706*
Chicken meat	1,294.6	1,331.3	1,331.3*
Cows' milk	14,555†	14,577	14,577*
Hen eggs	620.8	615.3	595.0
Wool: greasy	60	60	60*

*FAO estimate.
†Unofficial figure.

Source: FAO.

Forestry

ROUNDWOOD REMOVALS
('000 cubic metres, excl. bark)

	2004	2005	2006
Sawlogs, veneer logs and logs for sleepers	5,051	5,003	5,271
Pulpwood	2,617	2,705	2,369
Other industrial wood	394	457	448
Fuel wood	229	317	317
Total	8,291	8,482	8,405

Source: FAO.

SAWNWOOD PRODUCTION
('000 cubic metres, incl. railway sleepers)

	2004	2005	2006
Coniferous (softwood)	2,711	2,716	2,850
Broadleaved (hardwood)	61	53	45
Total	2,783	2,770	2,895

Source: FAO.

Fishing

('000 metric tons, live weight)

	2003	2004	2005
Capture	635.6	653.3	669.5
Atlantic cod	21.5	21.2	20.0
Haddock	41.4	46.0	31.7
Blue whiting	29.4	59.8	126.1
Atlantic herring	90.3	96.3	130.8
Atlantic mackerel	183.0	174.7	126.6
Norway lobster	27.8	30.2	27.1
Common edible cockle	26.8	12.9	13.2
Aquaculture	181.8*	207.2	172.8
Atlantic salmon	145.6	158.1	129.8
Total	817.5*	860.5	842.3

*FAO estimate.

Note: Figures exclude aquatic mammals, recorded by number rather than weight. The number of whales caught was: 142 in 2003; 467 in 2004; nil in 2005.

Source: FAO.

THE UNITED KINGDOM

Mining and Quarrying

('000 metric tons, unless otherwise indicated)

	2004	2005	2006*
Hard coal (incl. slurries)	25,096	20,498	18,588
Natural gas and petroleum:			
Methane—colliery	70	65	} 79,947
Methane—North Sea[1]	95,937	87,517	
Crude petroleum	87,516	72,121	69,665
Condensates and others[2]	7,858	7,543	6,913
Iron ore[3]	1*	0	0
China clay (sales)[4]	1,945	1,911	1,762
Ball clay (sales)	965	1,011	1,015
Fireclay[5]	402	395	400
Fuller's earth (sales)*[6]	28	6	—
Common clay and shale[5]	11,164	10,898	10,000
Slate[7]	901	928	900
Limestone[8]	81,641	77,596	} 90,000
Dolomite[8]	12,226	11,514	
Chalk[5]	7,997	7,105	7,000
Sandstone[9]	18,844	18,685	19,000
Common sand and gravel[10]	97,333	94,666	93,000
Igneous rock[11]	53,037	53,104	54,000
Gypsum	1,686	1,700*	1,700
Rock salt*	2,000	2,000	2,000
Salt from brine*	1,000	1,000	1,000
Salt in brine*[12]	2,800	2,800	2,800
Fluorspar*	50	61	60
Barytes	61	62	47
Talc	4	6	4
Potash[13]	912	732	716

* Estimate(s).
[1] 2005 figure refers to all methane.
[2] Includes ethane, propane and butane, in addition to condensates (pentane and hydrocarbons).
[3] Figures refer to gross weight. The estimated iron content is 55%.
[4] Dry weight.
[5] Excluding production in Northern Ireland.
[6] Estimates based on data from producing companies.
[7] Including waste used for constructional fill and powder and granules used in industry.
[8] Dolomite included with limestone for 2006.
[9] Including grit and conglomerate.
[10] Including marine-dredged sand and gravel for both home consumption and export.
[11] Excluding production in Northern Ireland and the Channel Islands.
[12] Used for purposes other than salt-making.
[13] Chloride (K$_2$O content).

Source: British Geological Survey.

Industry

SELECTED PRODUCTS
('000 metric tons, unless otherwise indicated)

	2003	2004	2005
Wheat flour	5,572	5,576	5,611
Refined sugar[1]	1,368	1,390	1,300
Margarine and other table spreads	442	431	n.a.
Crude seed and nut oil[2]	769	747	n.a.
Beer ('000 hectolitres)	58,014	57,459	56,255
Cigarettes ('000 million)	49.1	48.2	45.9
Butane and propane[3]	2,281	2,152	2,424
Petroleum naphtha[3]	3,503	3,168	3,019
Motor spirit (petrol)[3]	22,627	24,589	22,620
Aviation turbine fuel[3]	5,277	5,615	5,167
Burning oil[3]	3,521	3,613	3,325
Diesel fuel and gas oil[3]	27,380	28,647	28,486
Fuel oil[3]	9,495	11,308	10,155
Lubricating oils[3]	576	1,136	936

Statistical Survey

—continued	2003	2004	2005
Petroleum bitumen (asphalt)[3]	1,925	2,196	1,912
Cement	11,215	11,405	11,216
Pig-iron[4]	10,228	10,180	10,189
Crude steel (usable)	13,268	13,766	13,234
Aluminium—(wrought remelt)	548.1	565.0	573.8
Refined lead—unwrought[5]	364.6	245.9	304.3
Zinc—unwrought: primary	16.6	—	—
Passenger motor cars ('000)	1,657.6	1,646.8	1,595.7
Road goods vehicles ('000)	188.9	209.3	206.8
Electric energy (million kWh)	398,209	395,306	400,525

[1] Production from home-grown sugar beet only.
[2] Including maize oil.
[3] Refinery production only (excluding supplies from other sources).
[4] Including blast-furnace ferro-alloys.
[5] Excluding hard lead.

2006: Cement ('000 metric tons) 11,460; Beer ('000 hectolitres) 53,763; Cigarettes ('000 million) 44.4; Passenger motor cars ('000) 1,442.1; Road goods vehicles ('000) 207.7.

Finance

CURRENCY AND EXCHANGE RATES

Monetary Units
100 pence (pennies) = 1 pound sterling (£).

Dollar and Euro Equivalents (31 December 2007)
US $1 = 49.92 pence;
€1 = 73.48 pence;
£10 = $20.03 = €13.61.

Average Exchange Rate (pound sterling per US $)
2005   0.5500
2006   0.5435
2007   0.4998

BUDGET
(general government transactions, non-cash basis, year ending 31 March, £ '000 million)

Revenue

	2003/04	2004/05	2005/06
Inland revenue	227.8	249.8	277.2
Income tax (net)	113.6	122.5	130.5
Corporation tax	28.3	33.7	42.0
National insurance contributions	72.5	78.1	85.5
Customs and excise	115.6	121.0	120.7
Value added tax	69.1	73.0	72.9
Fuel duties	22.8	23.3	23.4
Business rates	18.4	18.7	19.8
Council tax	18.7	20.0	20.9
Other taxes and royalties	16.1	17.2	17.6
Interest and dividends	4.6	6.0	6.7
Gross operating surplus and rent	20.2	20.6	23.4
Other receipts and adjustments	1.2	—	0.3
Total current revenue	**422.5**	**453.1**	**486.8**

Source: HM Treasury, *Public Sector Finances Databank* (August 2007).

THE UNITED KINGDOM

Statistical Survey

Outlays

Outlays by function of government*	2003/04	2004/05	2005/06†
General public services	11.1	12.4	13.1
EU transactions	−2.1	−0.9	−0.6
International services	5.1	5.5	6.1
Public-sector debt interest	22.9	24.7	26.6
Defence	28.8	30.0	30.7
Public order and safety	26.5	28.4	29.4
Enterprise and economic development	6.4	6.8	6.4
Science and technology	2.3	2.5	2.9
Employment policies	3.2	3.2	3.4
Agriculture, fisheries and forestry	5.2	5.4	5.6
Transport	16.2	16.0	16.8
Environment protection	6.3	7.0	8.5
Housing and community amenities	6.8	8.2	10.7
Health	74.9	82.8	88.9
Recreation, culture and religion	9.6	10.0	10.6
Education and training	60.4	64.5	69.3
Social protection	155.6	164.1	171.0
Accounting adjustments	16.3	21.0	25.5
Less Public sector net investment	15.4	20.1	22.7
Total current expenditure‡	**440.2**	**471.5**	**502.3**

* Including net acquisition of non-financial assets.
† Estimates.
‡ Including depreciation.

Source: HM Treasury, *Public Expenditure Statistical Analyses* (July 2007).

OFFICIAL RESERVES
(US $ million at 31 December)*

	2005	2006	2007
Gold	5,126	6,341	8,344
IMF special drawing rights	287	396	360
Foreign currencies	37,349	40,990	44,315
Reserve position in IMF	1,765	1,414	1,099
Other reserve assets	3,569	4,074	3,060
Total	**48,096**	**53,214**	**57,178**

* Reserves are revalued at 31 March each year.

Source: Bank of England.

MONEY SUPPLY
(£ million at 31 December)

	2005	2006	2007
Retail deposits and cash	922,687	996,671	1,073,021
Notes and coin in private sector	38,508	40,565	44,606
Bank deposits	709,941	768,053	817,865
Building society deposits	174,238	188,053	210,550
Wholesale deposits	405,633	500,888	600,716
Bank deposits	390,022	482,013	579,640
Building society deposits	15,612	18,875	21,075
Total broad money	**1,328,320**	**1,497,559**	**1,673,736**

Source: Bank of England.

COST OF LIVING
(General Index of Retail Prices, annual averages; base: January 1987 = 100)

	2005	2006	2007
Food	153.8	157.1	164.3
Catering	239.2	245.6	253.6
Alcoholic drink	207.7	212.7	219.0
Tobacco	328.7	343.4	361.6
Housing	287.5	302.1	330.7
Fuel and light	159.8	199.1	213.2
Household goods	145.2	147.1	150.5
Household services	184.3	190.8	197.3
Clothing and footwear	95.7	94.5	93.7
Personal goods and services	203.6	209.1	215.2
Motoring expenditure	184.2	186.9	189.2
Fares and other travel costs	225.9	229.9	244.2
Leisure goods	94.5	92.2	89.8
Leisure services	261.2	266.8	275.6
All items	**192.0**	**198.1**	**206.6**

NATIONAL ACCOUNTS
(£ million at current prices)

National Income and Product

	2004	2005	2006
Compensation of employees	648,717	686,805	721,287
Gross operating surplus	314,405	320,794	340,331
Mixed income	71,958	75,675	78,864
Gross domestic product (GDP) at factor cost	**1,035,080**	**1,083,274**	**1,140,482**
Taxes on production and imports	158,587	162,059	171,518
Less Subsidies	9,371	10,441	−11,827
Statistical discrepancy	—	−916	−551
GDP at market prices	**1,184,296**	**1,233,976**	**1,299,622**
Primary incomes received from abroad *Less* Primary incomes paid abroad	25,548	24,746	17,334
Gross national income	**1,209,844**	**1,258,722**	**1,316,956**
Less Consumption of fixed capital	128,427	131,093	133,936
Net national income	**1,081,417**	**1,127,629**	**1,183,020**
Current transfers from abroad *Less* Current transfers paid abroad	−9,920	−11,087	−10,697
Net national disposable income	**1,071,497**	**1,116,542**	**1,172,323**

Expenditure on the Gross Domestic Product

	2004	2005	2006
Final consumption expenditure	1,012,192	1,061,355	1,114,893
Households	732,531	760,869	794,768
Non-profit institutions serving households	28,953	31,585	33,313
General government	250,708	268,901	286,812
Gross capital formation	207,079	215,556	238,531
Gross fixed capital formation	202,260	211,862	234,751
Changes in inventories	4,856	4,071	3,735
Acquisitions, less disposals, of valuables	−37	−377	45
Total domestic expenditure	**1,219,271**	**1,276,911**	**1,353,424**
Exports of goods and services	298,694	326,790	369,691
Less Imports of goods and services	333,669	370,968	424,128
Statistical discrepancy	—	1,243	635
GDP in purchasers' values	**1,184,296**	**1,233,976**	**1,299,622**
GDP at constant 2003 prices	**1,154,685**	**1,175,916**	**1,209,344**

THE UNITED KINGDOM

Gross Domestic Product by Economic Activity*

	2005	2006
Agriculture, hunting, forestry and fishing	10,253	10,577
Mining and quarrying	25,110	28,093
Manufacturing	149,818	152,255
Electricity, gas and water supply	25,066	31,532
Construction	65,232	65,921
Wholesale and retail trade; repair of motor vehicles, motorcycles and personal and household goods	132,793	139,807
Hotels and restaurants	32,710	35,576
Transport, storage and communication	82,205	82,950
Financial intermediation	96,693	108,877
Real estate, renting and business activities	270,791	286,270
Public administration and defence	54,772	58,776
Education	63,290	64,698
Health and social work	80,985	84,806
Other community, social and personal services†	58,830	62,390
Sub-total	1,148,548	1,212,528
Less Financial intermediation services indirectly measured	51,922	57,566
Gross value added at basic prices	1,096,629	1,154,959
Value added taxes on products	83,382	87,679
Other taxes on products	59,076	62,752
Less Subsidies on products	−5,111	−5,768
GDP in purchasers' values	1,233,976	1,299,622

*These data are described by the ONS as 'experimental', and include estimates for private investment in own account computer software which were not included in these accounts prior to 2005.
† Including private households with employees, and extra-territorial organizations.

Note: Totals may not be equal to the sum of component parts, owing to rounding.

BALANCE OF PAYMENTS
(£ million)

	2004	2005	2006
Exports of goods f.o.b.	190,877	211,608	245,105
Imports of goods f.o.b.	−251,770	−280,397	−328,736
Trade balance	−60,893	−68,789	−83,631
Exports of services	107,817	115,182	124,586
Imports of services	−81,899	−90,571	−95,392
Balance on goods and services	−34,975	−44,178	−54,437
Other income received	142,201	187,487	241,350
Other income paid	−115,605	−161,753	−222,795
Balance on goods, services and income	−8,379	−18,444	−35,882
Current transfers received	12,917	17,255	16,165
Current transfers paid	−23,866	−29,263	−28,064
Current balance	−19,328	−30,452	−47,781
Capital account (net)	2,063	1,491	830
Direct investment abroad	−53,831	−49,999	−69,496
Direct investment from abroad	42,416	107,794	76,891
Portfolio investment abroad	−140,853	−160,332	−199,118
Portfolio investment from abroad	87,247	130,869	155,631
Financial derivatives (net)	−7,875	9,556	7,449
Other investment abroad	−325,588	−505,032	−393,843
Other investment from abroad	404,321	508,711	454,865
Net errors and omissions	11,624	−11,950	14,146
Overall balance	196	656	−426

GROSS PUBLIC EXPENDITURE ON OVERSEAS AID
(£ million, year ending 31 March)

	2003/04	2004/05	2005/06
Total bilateral aid*	2,598.0	3,111.7	4,401.8
DFID† bilateral programmes	1,960.9	2,111.6	2,504.5
Poverty reduction budget support	313.5	421.9	524.7
Other financial aid	367.9	283.4	361.1
Technical co-operation	484.0	465.4	483.6
Grants and other aid in kind	469.8	589.7	684.9
Humanitarian assistance	310.1	336.2	410.6
DFID debt relief	15.5	14.9	39.5
Other bilateral programmes	637.1	1,000.1	1,897.3
CDC investments	350.4	238.3	156.1
Debt relief	175.5	618.4	1,588.2
Other‡	111.2	143.5	153.0
Total multilateral aid	1,866.3	1,839.1	1,956.6
DFID multilateral programmes	1,788.7	1,558.5	1,674.4
European Community	1,031.4	951.5	916.9
World Bank Group	382.6	206.5	272.2
International Monetary Fund	9.4	1.8	23.7
Global Environmental Assistance	61.1	47.5	50.0
HIPC Trust Fund	19.9	42.1	11.1
Regional development banks	80.4	82.2	77.7
UN agencies	189.1	201.0	298.9
Commonwealth	6.7	8.6	5.3
International research organizations	8.1	17.4	18.5
Other multilateral programmes	77.6	280.6	282.2
EC/EU	54.2	258.9	255.7
Global Environmental Assistance	0.1	0.1	0.1
UN agencies	22.3	20.6	25.3
Commonwealth	0.8	0.8	0.8
International research organizations	0.2	0.2	0.2
Administrative costs	249.4	226.8	253.9
Total gross expenditure on aid	4,713.7	5,177.7	6,612.3

* Excluding official advances to Commonwealth Development Corporation.
† Department for International Development (DFID).
‡ Mainly non-DFID debt relief.

Source: Department for International Development, *Statistics on International Development*.

External Trade

(Note: Figures include the Isle of Man and the Channel Islands)

PRINCIPAL COMMODITIES
(£ million)

Imports c.i.f.	2004	2005	2006
Food and live animals	17,208	18,594	19,930
Mineral fuels, lubricants, etc.	17,547	25,920	31,727
Petroleum, petroleum products, etc.	15,307	21,988	26,814
Chemicals and related products	27,927	29,208	31,927
Basic manufactures*	32,299	33,469	37,654
Machinery and transport equipment	103,883	117,321	146,751
Mechanical machinery and equipment	19,725	21,851	22,771
Electrical machinery, apparatus, etc.	45,497	55,736	81,701
Road vehicles and parts†	30,732	31,434	32,955
Other transport equipment	7,929	8,300	9,324
Miscellaneous manufactured articles	39,820	42,176	45,079
Clothing and footwear	10,639	11,297	11,856
Scientific and photographic apparatus	7,256	7,415	7,704
Total (incl. others)	251,770	280,399	328,233

THE UNITED KINGDOM

Statistical Survey

Exports f.o.b.	2004	2005	2006
Food and live animals	6,462	6,550	6,826
Mineral fuels, lubricants, etc.	17,885	21,497	25,242
Petroleum, petroleum products, etc.	16,200	19,795	23,124
Chemicals and related products	32,008	33,389	37,385
Organic chemicals	6,040	6,703	8,055
Medicinal products	12,326	12,321	13,787
Basic manufactures*	24,458	26,494	27,789
Machinery and transport equipment	78,377	89,382	110,643
Mechanical machinery and equipment	23,810	25,797	28,373
Electrical machinery, apparatus, etc.	28,623	37,120	55,458
Road vehicles and parts†	18,489	19,440	19,430
Other transport equipment	7,455	7,025	7,382
Miscellaneous manufactured articles	22,919	25,108	26,204
Scientific and photographic apparatus	7,041	7,245	7,417
Total (incl. others)	190,877	211,616	244,542

* Sorted industrial diamonds, usually classified with natural abrasives (under 'crude materials'), are included with 'basic manufactures'.
† Excluding tyres, engines and electrical parts.

PRINCIPAL TRADING PARTNERS
(£ million)

Imports c.i.f.	2004	2005	2006
Austria	2,354	2,463	2,912
Belgium-Luxembourg	13,845	15,153	18,858
Canada	4,187	4,155	5,012
China, People's Republic	10,405	12,963	15,330
Denmark	3,357	4,395	6,247
Finland	2,336	2,432	2,862
France	20,132	22,185	50,535
Germany	35,380	39,171	42,764
Hong Kong	5,771	6,601	7,384
India	2,290	2,783	3,140
Ireland	10,133	10,410	10,737
Italy	12,186	12,675	13,287
Japan	8,106	8,670	7,932
Korea, Republic	3,083	3,064	3,094
Netherlands	18,195	20,437	23,660
Norway	8,479	12,078	14,440
Russia	3,511	5,009	5,770
Singapore	3,382	3,829	3,781
South Africa	2,344	2,225	3,927
Spain (excl. Canary Is)	9,120	11,452	13,638
Sweden	5,118	5,461	6,340
Switzerland	3,439	3,882	4,380
Turkey	3,246	3,511	3,952
USA	22,067	22,184	25,852
Total (incl. others)	251,770	280,399	328,233

Exports f.o.b.	2004	2005	2006
Australia	2,455	2,580	2,479
Belgium-Luxembourg	10,511	11,396	14,885
Canada	3,339	3,277	3,879
China	2,372	2,811	3,268
Denmark	2,042	2,314	3,886
France	18,564	19,933	29,251
Germany	21,671	23,026	27,456
Hong Kong	2,632	3,087	2,863
India	1,389	1,352	1,307
Ireland	14,133	16,297	17,516
Italy	8,401	8,791	9,624
Japan	3,862	3,900	4,111
Netherlands	12,030	12,718	16,749
Norway	1,937	2,211	2,094
Spain (excl. Canary Is)	9,100	10,678	12,597
Sweden	4,355	4,586	5,224
Switzerland	2,840	4,985	4,105
USA	28,576	30,912	31,960
Total (incl. others)	190,877	211,616	244,542

Transport

RAILWAYS

	2003/04	2004/05	2005/06
Passenger journeys (million):			
Great Britain national railways	1,012	1,045	1,082
Northern Ireland railways	6.9	6.9	7.7
Underground railways (London and Glasgow)	961	989	984
Light rail	160	172	175
Passenger-kilometres (million):			
Great Britain national railways	40,937	41,762	43,211
Northern Ireland railways	233.0	225.2	240.5
Underground railways (London and Glasgow)	7,383	7,649	7,628
Light rail	945	1,033	1,052
Freight carried (million metric tons)*	89	102	104
Freight ton-kilometres ('000 million)*	19	21	22

* Great Britain only. Figures exclude parcels and materials for rail infrastructure. From 2004/05, figures for freight carried are not strictly comparable with those for previous years.

Sources: Department for Transport (Great Britain); Department for Regional Development (Northern Ireland).

ROAD TRAFFIC
('000 licensed vehicles in Great Britain at 31 December)

	2003	2004	2005
Private motor cars	24,985	25,754	26,208
Motorcycles, scooters and mopeds	1,005	1,060	1,075
Light goods vehicles*	2,730	2,900	3,019
Heavy goods vehicles	426	434	433
Public passenger vehicles	96	100	103

* Goods vehicles less than 3,500 kg in weight.

Source: Department for Transport.

SHIPPING

Merchant Fleet
(registered at 31 December)

	2004	2005	2006
Number of vessels	1,569	1,563	1,598
Total displacement ('000 grt)	11,122.9	11,194.0	12,150.0

Source: Lloyd's Register-Fairplay, *World Fleet Statistics*.

THE UNITED KINGDOM

International Sea-borne Freight Traffic
('000 metric tons)

	2003	2004	2005
Goods imported	323,800	342,400	354,400
Goods exported	231,900	230,600	231,300

Source: Department for Transport.

CIVIL AVIATION
(United Kingdom airlines)

	2002	2003	2004
All scheduled services:			
Aircraft stage flights (number)	911,518	895,095	927,040
Aircraft-kilometres flown (million)	1,047.1	1,088.0	1,138.0
Passengers carried (million)	72.2	76.3	82.8
Passenger-kilometres flown (million)	156,493.9	164,806.3	173,816.0
Total cargo carried (metric tons)	768,736	800,645	842,993
Total metric ton-kilometres (million)	4,997.0	5,242.0	5,371.8
Freight metric ton-kilometres (million)	4,940.5	5,187.0	5,297.0
Mail metric ton-kilometres (million)	56.6	54.5	74.8
Domestic scheduled services:			
Aircraft stage flights (number)	359,400	345,954	373,858
Aircraft-kilometres flown (million)	126.0	123.0	134.5
Passengers carried (million)	19.8	20.8	21.9
Passenger-kilometres flown (million)	8,321.9	8,903.7	9,262.6
Total cargo carried (metric tons)	16,755	17,248	14,862
Total metric ton-kilometres (million)	6.4	6.5	5.2
Freight metric ton-kilometres (million)	3.6	3.4	2.6
Mail metric ton-kilometres (million)	2.8	3.1	2.6
International scheduled services:			
Aircraft stage flights (number)	552,118	549,141	553,182
Aircraft-kilometres flown (million)	921.1	965.0	1,003.4
Passengers carried (million)	52.4	55.5	60.8
Passenger-kilometres flown (million)	148,172.1	155,902.6	164,553.4
Total cargo carried (metric tons)	751,975	783,397	828,132
Total metric ton-kilometres (million)	4,990.7	5,235.1	5,366.6
Freight metric ton-kilometres (million)	4,936.9	5,183.6	5,294.4
Mail metric ton-kilometres (million)	53.8	51.5	72.2

Source: Civil Aviation Authority.

Tourism

FOREIGN VISITORS BY REGION OF ORIGIN
('000 unless otherwise indicated)

	2004	2005	2006
Europe	19,424	21,565	23,377
North America	4,356	4,234	4,764
Other countries	3,975	4,171	4,572
Total	27,755	29,970	32,713
Total expenditure (£ million)	13,047	14,248	16,002

Source: International Passenger Survey, Office for National Statistics, *Travel Trends*.

VISITS BY COUNTRY OF PERMANENT RESIDENCE
('000)

	2004	2005	2006
Australia	787	919	956
Belgium	1,104	1,112	997
Canada	740	796	868
France	3,254	3,324	3,693
Germany	2,968	3,294	3,411
Ireland	2,578	2,806	2,909
Italy	1,348	1,186	1,477
Netherlands	1,620	1,720	1,791
Poland	528	1,041	1,326
Spain	1,465	1,786	1,981
Sweden	585	728	714
Switzerland	597	699	745
USA	3,616	3,438	3,896
Total (incl. others)	27,755	29,970	32,713

Source: International Passenger Survey, Office for National Statistics, *Travel Trends*.

Communications Media

	2004	2005	2006
Telephones ('000 main lines in use)	34,576.5	34,068.4	33,602.5
Mobile cellular telephones ('000 subscribers)	59,687.9	65,471.7	69,656.6
Personal computers ('000 in use)	35,890	n.a.	n.a.
Internet users ('000)	28,094.0	32,076.0	33,534.0
Broadband subscribers ('000)	6,123.9	9,894.2	12,995.1

1996: Facsimile machines (number in use) 1,992,000.

1997: Radio receivers ('000 in use) 84,500.

1999: Book production (titles) 110,965.

2000: Daily newspapers 108 (average circulation 19,159,000); Non-daily newspapers 467 (average circulation 6,246,000).

Sources: UNESCO, *Statistical Yearbook*; UN, *Statistical Yearbook* and International Telecommunication Union.

THE UNITED KINGDOM

Education

PRE-PRIMARY, PRIMARY AND SECONDARY EDUCATION

	2004/05	2005/06	2006/07
Schools	34,388	34,101	33,892
Public sector mainstream	29,998	29,711	29,470
Nursery	3,425	3,349[1]	3,326[1]
Primary	22,343	22,156	21,968
Secondary (incl. specialist)	4,230	4,206	4,176
Middle deemed secondary	260	250	248
Modern	124	115	113
Grammar	234	233	233
Technical	2	2	2
Comprehensive	3,427	3,424	3,398
Other	183	182	182
Non-maintained mainstream	2,476	2,493	2,542
Academies	17	27	46
Special schools	1,436	1,416	1,391
Maintained	1,329	1,311	1,285
Non-maintained	107	105	106
Pupil referral units	478	481	489
Teachers ('000):[2]	578.6	585.3	n.a.
Maintained nursery and primary schools	236.0	238.8[3]	n.a.
Maintained secondary schools	253.1	255.3[3]	n.a.
Non-maintained mainstream	67.8	68.8[3]	n.a.
All special schools	21.8	22.4[3]	n.a.
Full-time and part-time pupils ('000):	9,963.3	9,893.5	9,812.6
Maintained schools	9,305.3	9,229.1	9,136.1[3]
Nursery	141.9	150.8	157.1[3]
Primary	5,044.9	4,974.9	4,921.9[3]
Nursery classes	307.8	308.7	316.8[3]
Other classes	4,737.1	4,666.1	4,605.0[3]
Secondary	4,002.2	3,987.5	3,941.6[3]
Special schools	101.4	100.3	99.8[3]
Pupil referral units[4]	14.9	15.6	15.7[3]
Non-maintained schools	658.0	664.4	676.5[3]
Special schools	6.0	5.9	5.8[3]
Other	652.0	658.5	670.7[3]

[1] Excluding pre-school education centres not in partnership with a local authority.
[2] Qualified teachers only. Full-time teachers and the full time equivalent of part-time teachers. Excluding Pupil Referral Unit teachers.
[3] Preliminary.
[4] England and Wales only; excluding pupils registered elsewhere.

Source: Department for Children, Schools and Families, London.

POST-COMPULSORY EDUCATION

	2004/05	2005/06	2006/07
Universities	119	123	124
Other higher education institutes	47	43	45
Further education institutes/colleges	480	476	459
Sixth form colleges	102	102	96
Full-time teaching and research staff ('000)	170	171	n.a.
Students (incl. from overseas) taking higher education courses:			
full-time students ('000)	1,083.5	1,055.0	n.a.
part-time students ('000)	3,963.7	3,395.4	n.a.

Note: Figures for institutions include, but for teaching staff exclude, the Open University.

Source: Department for Children, Schools and Families, London.

Directory

The Constitution

The United Kingdom is a constitutional monarchy. In the ninth century, when England was first united under a Saxon King, the monarchy was the only central power and the Constitution did not exist. Today, the Sovereign acts on the advice of her Ministers which she cannot, constitutionally, ignore; power, which has been at various times and in varying degrees in the hands of kings, feudal barons, ministers, councils and parliaments, or of particular groups or sections of society, is vested in the people as a whole, and the Sovereign is an essential part of the machinery of government which has gradually been devised to give expression to the popular will.

Both the powers of the Government and the functions of the Sovereign are determined by the Constitution, by the body of fundamental principles on which the State is governed and the methods, institutions and procedures which give them effect. But the United Kingdom has no written Constitution: there is no document, no one law or statute, to which reference can be made. The Constitution is an accumulation of convention, precedent and tradition which, although continually changing as the times change, is at any one moment binding and exact.

Some of the principles and many of the practices are secured by Statute, some are avowed by Declaration or Manifesto and many are incorporated in the Common Law. Magna Carta, in 1215, began the process by which the law of the land acquired a status of its own, independent of King and Parliament; the Bill of Rights of 1689 ended the long era of rivalry between Crown and Parliament and began the story of their co-operation; and the Reform Act of 1832 dramatically broadened the basis of representative government and prepared the way for further changes. The Constitution is, above all, based on usage. It has been modified to match changing customs and to meet successive situations. Any one Parliament could, if it chose, revise or repeal every law and disown every convention that has constitutional significance. It could destroy the whole fabric of political and social existence, including its own; because, according to the Constitution, Parliament, which represents the people, is supreme. The work of one Parliament is not binding on its successors, except in so far as changes must be made by constitutional means. Parliament cannot disobey the law, but it can change it.

It would be impossible to enumerate the principles which are extant in the British Constitution. In constitutional as in legal practice, the way has been to admit the general principle in quite practical terms related to specific practical problems: the Habeas Corpus Act, for example, which establishes the principle of no imprisonment without trial, makes no mention of the principle itself but lays down in most concrete terms the punishments that shall be inflicted on a judge, or other law officer, if he fails to issue the Writ (commanding the prisoner to be brought before the court) when applied for. The principles of the Constitution and constitutional practice are in fact inherent in the Common Law on the one hand and in the structure, functions and procedures of the various instruments of government on the other: of the Crown, of Parliament, of the Privy

Council, of the Government and the Cabinet and of the government departments.

THE SOVEREIGN

The monarchy is hereditary, descending to the sons of the Sovereign in order of seniority or, if there are no sons, to the daughters.

The constitutional position of the Queen as head of the State, quite apart from her position as head of the Commonwealth, demands that she keep herself informed on all aspects of the life of her subjects, that she maintain absolute impartiality and that she should personally visit the different parts of her realm as often as it is possible for her to do so, but she has also quite specific functions, all exercised on ministerial advice: she summons, prorogues and dissolves Parliament; she must give Royal Assent to a Bill which has passed through both Houses of Parliament, before it becomes law; she is head of the judiciary (although the judiciary is now quite independent of the executive); she appoints all important state officials, including judges, officers of the forces and representatives abroad, and she confers honours and awards. Her formal consent is necessary before a Minister can take up office or a Cabinet be formed; and before a treaty may be concluded, war declared or peace made. These are some of the more essential functions. However, the Queen also has many residuary responsibilities, such as the guardianship of infants and persons of unsound mind, the creation of corporations, granting of printing rights for the Bible and Prayer Book and for state documents; and her signature and consent are necessary to many important state papers. Constitutional government cannot in fact be carried on without the Sovereign, so much so that provision has been made by Act of Parliament for the appointment of a Regent should the Sovereign be incapacitated or under age and for Counsellors of State to act in the temporary absence of the Queen.

PARLIAMENT

The Queen in Parliament—the House of Commons and the House of Lords—is the supreme legislative authority in the United Kingdom. Under the Parliament Act of 1911 the maximum life of one Parliament was fixed at five years: if, that is, Parliament has not meanwhile been dissolved for any other reason, such as the fall of the Government, then a general election is at the end of five years necessary by law. During its lifetime, the power of Parliament is theoretically absolute; it can make or unmake any law. In practice, of course, it must take account of the electorate. Parliament is prorogued at intervals during its life, which therefore consists of a number of sessions; by present custom, a session has normally 160 sitting days and is divided into five periods: from November (when the session is opened) until Christmas (about 30 days), from January till Easter (50), from Easter till Whitsun (30), from Whitsun until the end of July (40) and 10 days in October.

The House of Commons has 646 members, each elected for one geographical constituency. The Speaker, who is elected by the members immediately a new parliament meets, presides. Members of Parliament may be elected either at a general election or at a by-election (held in the event of the death, resignation or expulsion of the sitting member) and in either case hold their seats during the life of the existing parliament. All British subjects who are more than 18 years of age (and subjects of any Commonwealth country and of Ireland who are resident in the United Kingdom) have the vote unless legally barred (e.g. for insanity). Anyone who has the vote may stand as a candidate for election except clergymen of the Church of England, the established Churches of Scotland and Northern Ireland and the Roman Catholic Church, and certain officers of the Crown; civil servants must resign from the service if they wish to stand as a Member of Parliament.

There are over 700 members of the House of Lords, including 12 Lords of Appeal in Ordinary (appointed for life to carry out the judicial duties of the House); the two archbishops and the 24 senior diocesan bishops of the Church of England are also members. The House of Lords Act 1999 ended the right of hereditary peers to sit and vote in the House of Lords. An amendment to the Act provided for 92 of the existing hereditary peers to remain as members until the next stage of reform.

Members of Parliament whose views coincide form parties which agree in each case to support the policies put forward by their chosen leaders, and to present a common front on all important issues both in Parliament and to the electorate. This system evolved during the 17th and 18th centuries and is now essential to the working of the British Constitution. Under the party system, the Queen sends for the leader of the party which wins the majority of seats (although not necessarily of votes) at a general election and asks him or her to form a government. The party with the second largest number of seats forms the Opposition, which has quite specific functions. Members of other minority parties and independents may support the Government or Opposition as they choose. Each party has its own Whips, officials whose duty it is to arrange, (in consultation with the Whips of other parties), matters of procedure and organization; to ensure that members attend debates; and to muster for their party its maximum voting strength. In addition, each party has its own national and local organizations outside Parliament.

Parliamentary procedure, like the Constitution itself, is determined by rules, customs, forms and practices which have accumulated over many centuries. The Speaker is responsible for their application, and generally for controlling the course of business and debates in the house.

It is the duty of Parliament to make the laws which govern the life of the community, to appropriate the necessary funds for the various services of state and to criticize and control the Government. Parliament is also consulted before the ratification of certain international treaties and agreements.

Legislation may (with some exceptions) be initiated in either House and on either side of the House. In practice, most Public Bills are introduced into the House of Commons by the Government in power (the chief exceptions are Private Members' Bills) as the result of Cabinet decisions. Each Bill which is passed by the Commons at its third reading is sent to the House of Lords, who either accept it or return it to the Commons with suggested amendments. The Lords cannot in any instance prevent Bills passed by the Commons from becoming law: over Money Bills or Bills affecting the duration of Parliament they have no power at all, and by the Parliament Act of 1949 any other Bill passed by the Commons in two successive sessions may be presented for Royal Assent without the consent of the Lords, provided one year has elapsed between the date of the second reading in the Commons and the date of its final passing. In practice, the House of Lords is extremely unlikely to delay matters thus far, and its main function is to scrutinize the work of the Commons, to caution and suggest. Bills of a non-controversial kind are sometimes introduced initially in the House of Lords.

Northern Ireland

Following the prorogation of the Northern Ireland Parliament in 1972, responsibility for the Government of Northern Ireland rested with the Secretary of State for Northern Ireland. Direct rule continued until 1973, when the Northern Ireland Executive was established under the provisions of the Northern Ireland Constitution Act (1973). The Northern Ireland Executive assumed responsibility for the administration of Northern Ireland and was answerable to the Northern Ireland Assembly, elected in June 1973. The Executive collapsed in May 1974, and the Secretary of State resumed control of the Northern Ireland departments.

In October 1982 a new Northern Ireland Assembly was elected under the provisions of the Northern Ireland Act 1982. Under the Act, the Assembly was eventually to resume legislative and executive functions, provided that it produced proposals for the resumption of its powers, deemed to be acceptable to the people of Northern Ireland by Parliament. In June 1986 the Assembly was dissolved.

In November 1985 the Anglo-Irish Agreement was signed by the Prime Ministers of the United Kingdom and Ireland, leaving the status of Northern Ireland unaltered and confirming that the status of Northern Ireland would not be altered without the consent of a majority of its inhabitants. The Agreement provided for the establishment of an intergovernmental conference, through which the Government of Ireland was permitted to make proposals on matters relating to Northern Ireland affairs.

New constitutional arrangements for Northern Ireland were agreed by the leaders of Northern Ireland's political parties (with the exception of the Democratic Unionist Party and the United Kingdom Unionist Party) and by the British and Irish Governments in April 1998, and were approved in a popular referendum conducted in May. Accordingly, legislation was introduced into the United Kingdom Parliament to provide for the transfer of responsibility for the administration of Northern Ireland to an elected Assembly and Executive. A North/South Ministerial Council was established by the Assembly to undertake consideration of all-Ireland issues. Representatives of the Irish and British Governments, of the devolved authorities in Northern Ireland, Scotland and Wales and of the Channel Islands and Isle of Man were to convene under a British-Irish Council, to consider the development of the islands and formulate common policies, although with no legislative or administrative powers. A new bilateral agreement between the United Kingdom and Ireland subsumed the 1985 accord and established a new British-Irish Intergovernmental Conference. The new Northern Ireland institutions were suspended in February 2000, owing to a political impasse concerning the decommissioning of paramilitary weapons, and Northern Ireland was returned to direct rule. In May, following an agreement on the issue of decommissioning, power was once again transferred from Westminster to the new Northern Ireland institutions. The Northern Ireland Assembly and Executive were suspended again in October 2002 and Northern Ireland was returned to direct rule from Westminster. The Assembly was recalled on 15 May 2006. Elections to the Assembly took place on 7 March 2007 and the Assembly was recalled on 8 May.

Scotland and Wales

In 1999 devolved legislative authorities were established in Scotland and Wales. In Scotland a new elected Parliament, based in Edinburgh, was established with powers to legislate on all domestic matters (including education, health, local government and law and order) and with a mandate to vary taxes set by the Government of the United Kingdom by 3%. The Parliament has 129 members, elected every four years by a combined system of direct voting, on the basis of Westminster parliamentary constituencies, and a form of proportional representation, whereby additional members are elected from a party list on the basis of the larger constituencies used for elections to the European Parliament. The Welsh Assembly, located in Cardiff, undertook responsibility for issues covered by the Welsh Office of the Government of the United Kingdom. The 60-member Assembly was elected under the same system as in Scotland. Elections to the two assemblies took place simultaneously in May 1999 and the transfer of powers took place on 1 July.

THE PRIVY COUNCIL

The power of the Privy Council has declined with the development of the Cabinet and its main function today is to give effect to decisions made elsewhere. There are at present over 500 Privy Counsellors, including Cabinet Ministers (who are automatically created Privy Counsellors), and people who have reached eminence in some branch of public affairs. Meetings are presided over by the Queen, and the responsible minister is the Lord President of the Council, an office which, since 1600, has always been held by a member of the party in power, who is usually also a leading member of the Cabinet. The Privy Council is responsible for making Orders in Council, of which there are two kinds: those made in virtue of the Royal prerogative, e.g. the ratification of treaties, and those which are authorized by Act of Parliament and are, in fact, a form of delegated legislation. It has also various advisory functions which cover such subjects as scientific, industrial, medical and agricultural research. An important organ of the Privy Council is the Judicial Committee.

HER MAJESTY'S GOVERNMENT

The Government is headed by the Prime Minister, who is also the leader of the party which holds the majority in the House of Commons. It includes ministers who are in charge of government departments and those who hold traditional offices which involve no special departmental duties; the Chancellor of the Exchequer and the Lord Chancellor, who are specially responsible for financial and economic and legal affairs, respectively; the law officers of the Crown (the Attorney-General and Solicitor-General, the Lord Advocate for Scotland and the Solicitor-General for Scotland); the Ministers of State, who are usually appointed to assist Ministers in charge of departments; and Parliamentary Secretaries and Under-Secretaries.

The cabinet system developed during the 18th century from the informal meetings of Privy Counsellors who were also ministers, and who formed a committee of manageable size which could take decisions far more quickly and simply than larger bodies. The Cabinet today has between 15–25 members at the discretion of the Prime Minister—its main duty is to formulate policy for submission to Parliament.

The doctrine of ministerial responsibility has also evolved gradually, but was generally accepted by the middle of the last century. Each Minister must take full responsibility, particularly in Parliament, for the work of his own department; if his department fails over any important matter, he will be expected to resign. Ministers also assume collective responsibility for the work of the Government and for any advice which it may offer to the Crown.

The Government

HEAD OF STATE

Sovereign: Her Majesty Queen ELIZABETH II (succeeded to the throne 6 February 1952).

THE MINISTRY
(April 2008)

The Cabinet

Prime Minister, First Lord of the Treasury and Minister for the Civil Service: GORDON BROWN.
Chancellor of the Exchequer: ALISTAIR DARLING.
Secretary of State for Foreign and Commonwealth Affairs: DAVID MILIBAND.
Secretary of State for Justice and Lord Chancellor for the transitional period: JOHN (JACK) STRAW.
Secretary of State for the Home Department: JACQUELINE (JACQUI) SMITH.
Secretary of State for Defence and Secretary of State for Scotland: DES BROWNE.
Secretary of State for Health: ALAN JOHNSON.
Secretary of State for the Environment, Food and Rural Affairs: HILARY BENN.
Secretary of State for International Development: DOUGLAS ALEXANDER.
Secretary of State for Business, Enterprise and Regulatory Reform: JOHN HUTTON.
Leader of the House of Commons and Lord Privy Seal and Minister for Women and Equality: HARRIET HARMAN.
Secretary of State for Work and Pensions: JAMES PURNELL.
Secretary of State for Transport: RUTH KELLY.
Secretary of State for Communities and Local Government: HAZEL BLEARS.
Parliamentary Secretary to the Treasury and Chief Whip: GEOFFREY (GEOFF) HOON.
Secretary of State for Children, Schools and Families: EDWARD (ED) BALLS.
Chancellor of the Duchy of Lancaster and Minister for the Cabinet Office: EDWARD (ED) MILIBAND.
Secretary of State for Northern Ireland: SHAUN WOODWARD.
Leader of the House of Lords and Lord President of the Council: Baroness ASHTON OF UPHOLLAND.
Secretary of State for Innovation, Universities and Skills: JOHN DENHAM.
Secretary of State for Wales: PAUL MURPHY.
Secretary of State for Culture, Media and Sport: ANDY BURNHAM.
Chief Secretary to the Treasury: YVETTE COOPER.

Also attending Cabinet

Lords Chief Whip and Captain of the Honourable Corps of Gentlemen at Arms: Baroness ROYALL OF BLAISDON.
Attorney-General: Baroness SCOTLAND OF ASTHAL.
Minister of State for the Olympics and for London and Paymaster-General: TESSA JOWELL.
Minister of State for Africa, Asia and the United Nations, Foreign and Commonwealth Office: Lord MALLOCH-BROWN.
Minister of State for Housing, Department for Communities and Local Government: CAROLINE FLINT.
Minister of State for Children and Youth Justice, Department for Children, Schools and Families, and Minister for the North-West of England: BEVERLEY HUGHES.

Law Officers

Attorney-General: Baroness SCOTLAND OF ASTHAL.
Solicitor-General: VERA BAIRD.
Advocate-General for Scotland: Lord DAVIDSON OF GLEN CLOVA.

Ministers not in the Cabinet

Financial Secretary to the Treasury: JANE KENNEDY.
Economic Secretary to the Treasury: KITTY USSHER.
Exchequer Secretary to the Treasury: ANGELA EAGLE.
Minister of State for Europe, Foreign and Commonwealth Office: JIM MURPHY.
Minister of State for the Middle East, Foreign and Commonwealth Office: Dr KIM HOWELLS.
Minister of State for Trade, Foreign and Commonwealth Office and Department for Business, Enterprise and Regulatory Reform: Lord JONES OF BIRMINGHAM.
Ministers of State, Ministry of Justice: MICHAEL WILLS, DAVID HANSON.
Minister of State for Security, Counter-terrorism and Policing, Home Office: TONY MCNULTY.
Minister of State for Immigration and Asylum, Home Office, Minister of State, HM Treasury and Minister for the West Midlands: LIAM BYRNE.
Minister of State, Ministry of Defence: BOB AINSWORTH.
Minister of State, Scotland Office: DAVID CAIRNS.
Minister of State, Department for Health: DAWN PRIMAROLO.
Minister of State, Department of Health and Minister for the South-West of England: BEN BRADSHAW.
Ministers of State, Department for Environment, Food and Rural Affairs: PHIL WOOLAS, Lord ROOKER.

THE UNITED KINGDOM

Ministers of State, Department for Business, Enterprise and Regulatory Reform: Pat McFadden, Malcolm Wicks.
Minister of State for Pensions Reform, Department for Work and Pensions: Mike O'Brien.
Minister of State for Employment and Welfare Reform, Department for Work and Pensions: Stephen Timms.
Minister of State for Transport, Department for Transport and Minister for Yorkshire and the Humber: Rosie Winterton.
Minister of State, Department for Communities and Local Government: John Healey.
Minister of State for Schools, Department for Children, Schools and Families: Jim Knight.
Minister of State, Northern Ireland Office: Paul Goggins.
Ministers of State, Department for Innovation, Universities and Skills: Bill Rammell, Ian Pearson.
Minister of State and Minister for Sport, Department for Culture, Media and Sport: Margaret Hodge.
Deputy Chief Whip and Minister for the North-East of England: Nick Brown.
Minister for the East of England: Barbara Follett.
Minister for the East Midlands: Phil Hope.
Minister for the South-East of England: Jonathan Shaw.

MINISTRIES

Prime Minister's Office: 10 Downing St, London, SW1A 2AA; tel. (20) 7270-3000; fax (20) 7295-0918; internet www.number10.gov.uk.
Department of Business, Enterprise and Regulatory Reform: 1 Victoria St, London, SW1H 0ET; tel. (20) 7215-5000; fax (20) 7215-0105; e-mail enquiries@berr.gsi.gov.uk; internet www.berr.gov.uk.
Cabinet Office: 70 Whitehall, London, SW1A 2AS; tel. (20) 7276-1234; e-mail pscdl@cabinet-office.x.gsi.gov.uk; internet www.cabinet-office.gov.uk.
Department for Children, Schools and Families: Sanctuary Bldgs, Great Smith St, London, SW1P 3BT; tel. 0870-000-2288; fax (1928) 794248; e-mail info@dcsf.gsi.gov.uk; internet www.dcsf.gov.uk.
Department for Communities and Local Government: Eland House, Bressenden Place, London, SW1E 5DU; tel. (20) 7944-4400; fax (20) 7944-4101; e-mail contactus@communities.gsi.gov.uk; internet www.communities.gov.uk.
Department for Culture, Media and Sport: 2–4 Cockspur St, London SW1Y 5DH; tel. (20) 7211-6200; fax (20) 7211-6032; e-mail enquiries@culture.gov.uk; internet www.culture.gov.uk.
Ministry of Defence: Main Bldg, Whitehall, London, SW1A 2HB; tel. (20) 7218-9000; e-mail public@ministers.mod.uk; internet www.mod.uk.
Department for Environment, Food and Rural Affairs: Nobel House, 17 Smith Sq., London, SW1P 3JR; tel. (20) 7238-6000; fax (20) 7238-6609; e-mail helpline@defra.gsi.gov.uk; internet www.defra.gov.uk.
Foreign and Commonwealth Office: King Charles St, London, SW1A 2AH; tel. (20) 7008-1500; internet www.fco.gov.uk.
Department of Health: Richmond House, 79 Whitehall, London, SW1A 2NS; tel. (20) 7210-4850; fax (20) 7210-5523; e-mail dhmail@dh.gsi.gov.uk; internet www.dh.gov.uk.
Home Office: 2 Marsham St, London, SW1P 4DF; tel. (20) 7035-4848; fax (20) 7035-4745; e-mail public.enquiries@homeoffice.gsi.gov.uk; internet www.homeoffice.gov.uk.
Department for Innovation, Universities and Skills: Kingsgate House, 66–74 Victoria St, London, SW1E 6SW; tel. (020) 7215-5555; e-mail info@dius.gsi.gov.uk; internet www.dius.gov.uk.
Department for International Development: 1 Palace St, London, SW1E 5HE; tel. (20) 7023-0000; fax (1355) 843632; e-mail enquiry@dfid.gov.uk; internet www.dfid.gov.uk.
Ministry of Justice: Selborne House, 54 Victoria St, London, SW1E 6QW; tel. (20) 7210-8500; fax (20) 7210-0647; e-mail general.queries@justice.gsi.gov.uk; internet www.justice.gov.uk.
Northern Ireland Office: 11 Millbank, London, SW1P 4PN; tel. (20) 7210-0260; fax (20) 7210-0213; e-mail info@nio.gov.uk; internet www.nio.gov.uk.
Scotland Office: Dover House, Whitehall, London, SW1A 2AU; tel. (20) 7270-6754; fax (20) 7270-6812; e-mail scotlandoffice.ministers@scotland.gsi.gov.uk; internet www.scotlandoffice.gov.uk.
Department for Transport: Great Minster House, 76 Marsham St, London, SW1P 4DR; tel. (20) 7944-8300; fax (20) 7944-9643; e-mail fax9643@dft.gsi.gov.uk; internet www.dft.gov.uk.
HM Treasury: 1 Horse Guards Rd, London, SW1A 2HQ; tel. (20) 7270-4558; fax (20) 7270-4861; e-mail public.enquiries@hm-treasury.gov.uk; internet www.hm-treasury.gov.uk.

Wales Office: Gwydyr House, Whitehall, London, SW1A 2ER; tel. (20) 7270-0534; e-mail wales.office@walesoffice.gsi.gov.uk; internet www.walesoffice.gov.uk.
Department for Work and Pensions: Caxton House, Tothill St, London, SW1H 9DA; tel. (20) 7712-2171; fax (20) 7712-2386; internet www.dwp.gov.uk.

Legislature

PARLIAMENT

House of Commons

Speaker: Michael Martin.
Chairman of Ways and Means: Sir Alan Haselhurst.
Leader of the House: Harriet Harman.

General Election, 5 May 2005

	Votes	% of votes	Seats
Labour Party	9,556,183	35.2	356*
Conservative Party	8,772,598	32.3	198†
Liberal Democrats	5,982,045	22.0	62
Democratic Unionist Party	241,856	0.9	9
Scottish National Party	412,267	1.5	6
Sinn Féin	174,530	0.6	5
Plaid Cymru (Party of Wales)	174,838	0.6	3
Social Democratic and Labour Party	125,626	0.5	3
Ulster Unionist Party	127,314	0.5	1
Others	1,565,070	5.9	3
Total	**27,132,327**	**100.0**	**646†**

* Including the Speaker.
† Including the representative for the South Staffordshire constituency, for which the election was postponed until 24 June 2005, owing to the death of the Liberal Democrat candidate.

House of Lords
(April 2008)

Lord Speaker: Baroness Hayman.
Lord Chairman of Committees: Lord Brabazon of Tara.
Leader of the House: Baroness Ashton of Upholland.

	Seats
Archbishops and Bishops	26
Life Peers under the Appelate Jurisdiction Act 1876	23
Life Peers under the Life Peerages Act 1958	605
Peers under the House of Lords Act 1999	91
Total	**745**

The Legislative Authorities and Executive Bodies of Northern Ireland, Scotland and Wales

New constitutional arrangements for Northern Ireland were agreed by the leaders of Northern Ireland's political parties (with the exception of the Democratic Unionist Party and the United Kingdom Unionist Party) and by the British and Irish Governments in April 1998, and were approved in a popular referendum conducted in May. Accordingly, legislation was introduced into the United Kingdom Parliament to provide for the transfer of responsibility for the administration of Northern Ireland to an elected Assembly and Executive. Elections to a new 108-member Assembly were held on 25 June 1998. An Executive Committee, headed by a First Minister, was constituted from among the legislative members. Responsibility for all matters formerly implemented by the Northern Ireland Office was transferred to the devolved authority under new parliamentary legislation implemented in December 1999. The new Northern Ireland institutions were suspended in February 2000, owing to a political impasse concerning the decommissioning of paramilitary weapons, and Northern Ireland was returned to direct rule. On 30 May, following an agreement on the issue of decommissioning, power was once again transferred from Westminster to the new Northern Ireland institutions. However, the Northern Ireland Executive was suspended again on 14 October 2002 and Northern Ireland was returned to direct rule. Following an agreement between the main Northern Ireland political parties and the British and Irish Governments in November 2006, elections to the Assembly were held on 7 March 2007. A power-sharing Executive Committee, headed by a First Minister, was again constituted and on 8 May power was transferred from Westminster to the Northern Ireland institutions.

In 1999 devolved legislative authorities were established for Scotland and Wales. An executive level of government, headed by a First Minister, was also established for each country. The Scottish Parliament assumed powers to legislate on all domestic matters, including education, health, local government and law and order. It also had a mandate to vary taxes set by the United Kingdom Government by 3%. The Welsh Assembly (Cynulliad Cenedlaethol Cymru) assumed responsibility for issues covered by the Welsh Office of the United Kingdom Government. Both assemblies were elected, for a term of four years, by a combined system of direct voting, on the basis of Westminster parliamentary constituencies, and a form of proportional representation, whereby additional members were elected from a party list on the basis of the larger constituencies used for election to the European Parliament. The transfer of powers to both the Scottish and the Welsh authorities took place on 1 July.

NORTHERN IRELAND

Legislature

Northern Ireland Assembly

On 14 October 2002 the Assembly was suspended and Northern Ireland was returned to direct rule from Westminster. Elections, scheduled to have taken place in May 2003, were subsequently postponed until November. Following the elections, the Assembly remained suspended. The Assembly was recalled on 15 May 2006, under temporary rules that precluded the enacting of legislation, in order to elect a multi-party devolved executive by the deadline imposed by the British Government of 24 November. The Assembly reconvened on 24 November, following the signing by all the major political parties and the British and Irish Governments of the St Andrews Agreement, which was intended to precipitate the full restoration of devolution to Northern Ireland. Elections to the Assembly took place on 7 March 2007 and the Assembly was recalled on 8 May.

Presiding Officer: WILLIAM HAY.

Election, 7 March 2007

	First preference votes	% of first preference votes	Seats
Democratic Unionist Party	207,721	30.1	36
Sinn Féin	180,573	26.2	28
Ulster Unionist Party	103,145	14.9	18
Social Democratic and Labour Party	105,164	15.2	16
Alliance Party	36,139	5.2	7
Independents	21,993	2.8	1
Green Party	11,985	1.7	1
Progressive Unionist Party	3,822	0.6	1
Total (incl. others)	690,313	100.0	108

Executive Committee
(April 2008)

A power-sharing executive, comprising the Democratic Unionist Party (DUP), Sinn Féin (SF), the Ulster Unionist Party (UUP) and the Social Democratic and Labour Party (SDLP).

First Minister: Rev. Dr IAN R. K. PAISLEY (DUP).
Deputy First Minister: MARTIN MCGUINNESS (SF).
Minister of Finance and Personnel: PETER ROBINSON (DUP).
Minister of Education: CAITRÍONA RUANE (SF).
Minister of Enterprise, Trade and Investment: NIGEL DODDS (DUP).
Minister of Health, Social Services and Public Safety: MICHAEL MCGIMPSEY (UUP).
Minister for Social Development: MARGARET RITCHIE (SDLP).
Minister for Regional Development: CONOR MURPHY (SF).
Minister of the Environment: ARLENE FOSTER (DUP).
Minister of Agriculture and Rural Development: MICHELLE GILDERNEW (SF).
Minister of Culture, Arts and Leisure: EDWIN POOTS (DUP).
Minister for Employment and Learning: Sir REG EMPEY (UUP).

SCOTLAND

Legislature

Scottish Parliament

Presiding Officer: ALEX FERGUSSON.

Election, 3 May 2007

	Total votes	%	Seats
Scottish National Party	1,297,628	33.1	47
Labour Party	1,259,642	32.1	46
Conservative Party	618,748	15.8	17
Liberal Democrats	556,903	14.2	16
Green Party	85,555	2.2	2
Others	104,023	2.7	1
Total	3,922,499	100.0	129

Cabinet
(April 2008)

First Minister: ALEX SALMOND.
Cabinet Secretary for Finance and Sustainable Growth: JOHN SWINNEY.
Cabinet Secretary for Education and Lifelong Learning: FIONA HYSLOP.
Cabinet Secretary for Health and Wellbeing: NICOLA STURGEON.
Cabinet Secretary for Justice: KENNY MACASKILL.
Cabinet Secretary for Rural Affairs and the Environment: RICHARD LOCHHEAD.
Minister for Parliamentary Business: BRUCE CRAWFORD.
Minister for Europe, External Affairs and Culture: LINDA FABIANI.
Minister for Enterprise, Energy and Tourism: JIM MATHER.
Minister for Transport, Infrastructure and Climate Change: STEWART STEVENSON.
Minister for Schools and Skills: MAUREEN WATT.
Minister for Children and Early Years: ADAM INGRAM.
Minister for Public Health: SHONA ROBISON.
Minister for Communities and Sport: STEWART MAXWELL.
Minister for Community Safety: FERGUS EWING.
Minister for Environment: MICHAEL RUSSELL.
Lord Advocate: ELISH ANGIOLINI.
Solicitor-General: FRANK MULHOLLAND.

WALES

Legislature

Welsh Assembly

Presiding Officer: Lord DAFYDD ELIS-THOMAS.

Election, 3 May 2007

	Total votes	%	Seats
Labour Party	519,682	30.7	26
Plaid Cymru	423,878	25.0	15
Conservative Party	427,883	25.3	12
Liberal Democrats	258,950	15.3	6
Others	63,593	3.8	1
Total	1,693,986	100.0	60

Cabinet
(April 2008)

A coalition of the Labour Party and Plaid Cymru (PC).

First Minister: RHODRI MORGAN (Labour).
Deputy First Minister and Minister for the Economy and Transport: IEUAN WYN JONES (PC).
Minister for Finance and Public Service Delivery: ANDREW DAVIES (Labour).
Minister for Social Justice and Local Government: Dr BRIAN GIBBONS (Labour).
Minister for Children, Education, Lifelong Learning and Skills: JANE HUTT (Labour).
Minister for Rural Affairs: ELIN JONES (PC).
Minister for Health and Social Services: EDWINA HART (Labour).
Minister for Environment, Sustainability and Housing: JANE DAVIDSON (Labour).
Minister for Heritage: RHODRI GLYN THOMAS (PC).

THE UNITED KINGDOM

Counsel-General, Leader of the House, responsible for Assembly Business and Communications: CARWYN JONES (Labour).

Election Commission

The Electoral Commission: Trevelyan House, Great Peter St, London SW1P 2HW; tel. (20) 7271-0500; fax (20) 7271-0505; e-mail info@electoralcommission.org.uk; internet www.electoralcommission.gov.uk; f. 2000; independent; Chair. SAM YOUNGER; Chief Exec. PETER WARDLE.

Political Organizations

Alliance Party: 88 University St, Belfast, BT7 1HE; tel. (28) 9032-4274; fax (28) 9033-3147; e-mail alliance@allianceparty.org; internet www.allianceparty.org; f. 1970; non-sectarian and non-doctrinaire party of the centre, attracting support from within both Catholic and Protestant sections of the community in Northern Ireland; 1,500 mems; Leader DAVID FORD.

British National Party: POB 14, Welshpool, Powys, SY21 0WE; tel. (870) 757-6267; e-mail enquiries@bnp.org.uk; internet www.bnp.org.uk; f. 1982 as a breakaway faction from the National Front; National Chair. NICK GRIFFIN.

Communist Party of Britain: Ruskin House, 23 Coombe Rd, Croydon, CR0 1BD; tel. (20) 8686-1659; e-mail office@communist-party.org.uk; internet www.communist-party.org.uk; f. 1920; re-established 1988; Marxist-Leninist; Gen.-Sec. ROBERT GRIFFITHS.

Conservative and Unionist Party: 30 Millbank, London, SW1P 4DP; tel. (20) 7222-9000; fax (20) 7222-1135; internet www.conservatives.com; f. 1870 as Conservative Central Office; aims to uphold the Crown and the Constitution; to build a sound economy based on freedom and enterprise; to encourage personal responsibility and a wider spread of ownership of property; to look after those most in need; to ensure respect for law and order; to improve educational standards and widen parents' choice; to strengthen Britain's defences, maintain its interests and increase its influence abroad, not least through commitment to the European Union; member of the International Democrat Union and the European Democrat Union; in the European Parliament part of the European People's Party-European Democrat Group; 320,000 mems (adherent on a local, rather than national, basis); Leader DAVID CAMERON; Chair. CAROLINE SPELMAN.

Co-operative Party: 77 Weston St, London, SE1 3SD; tel. (20) 7367-4150; fax (20) 7407-4476; e-mail mail@party.coop; internet www.party.coop; f. 1917; under an Agreement with the Labour Party it is recognized as the political party representing the co-operative movement, and fields candidates, jointly with the Labour Party, who are Labour and Co-operative candidates at local and British parliamentary elections; promotes the principles of the co-operative movement; seeks to extend co-operative enterprise and cares for the interests of the consumer; individual mems in 200 brs; 47 societies are affiliated; Chair. GARETH THOMAS; Sec. PETER HUNT.

Democratic Unionist Party (DUP): 91 Dundela Ave, Belfast, BT4 3BU; tel. (28) 9052-1323; fax (28) 9052-1289; e-mail info@dup.org.uk; internet www.dup.org.uk; f. 1971; pro-British party of Northern Ireland; Leader Rev. IAN R. K. PAISLEY; Chief Exec. ALLAN EWART; Party Sec. NIGEL DODDS.

Green Party: 1A Waterlow Rd, London, N19 5NJ; tel. (20) 7272-4474; fax (20) 7272-6653; e-mail office@greenparty.org.uk; internet www.greenparty.org.uk; f. 1973 as People, adopted the name Ecology Party in 1975; present name adopted 1985; campaigns for the protection of the environment and the promotion of social justice; approx. 7,000 mems; Chair. RICHARD MALLENDER; Principal Speakers CAROLINE LUCAS, DEREK WALL.

Labour Party: 39 Victoria St, London, SW1H 0HA; tel. (8705) 900200; fax (20) 7802-1234; e-mail info@new.labour.org.uk; internet www.labour.org.uk; f. 1900; a democratic socialist party affiliated to the Socialist International and the Party of European Socialists; aims to achieve a dynamic economy, serving the public interest, with a strong private sector and high quality public services; a just society, with full equality of opportunity; an open democracy, guaranteeing fundamental human rights and governmental accountability and a healthy environment; committed to co-operating with European institutions, the UN, the Commonwealth and other international bodies to secure peace, freedom, democracy, economic security and environmental protection for all; also committed to pursuing these aims with trade unions, co-operative societies, voluntary organizations, consumer groups and other representative bodies; supports European economic and political union; Leader GORDON BROWN; Deputy Leader and Chair. HARRIET HARMAN; Gen. Sec. (vacant).

Liberal Democrats: 4 Cowley St, London, SW1P 3NB; tel. (20) 7222-7999; fax (20) 7799-2170; e-mail info@libdems.org.uk; internet www.libdems.org.uk; f. 1988 following the merger of the Liberal Party (f. 1877) and the Social Democratic Party (f. 1981, disbanded 1990); c. 70,000 mems; Leader NICHOLAS (NICK) CLEGG; Pres. SIMON HUGHES.

Plaid Cymru—Party of Wales: Tŷ Gwynfor, 18 Park Grove, Cardiff, CF10 3BN; tel. (29) 2064-6000; fax (29) 2064-6001; e-mail post@plaidcymru.org; internet www.plaidcymru.org; f. 1925; promotes Welsh interests and seeks independence for Wales; formed a parliamentary alliance with the SNP in April 1986; 10,000 mems; Leader IEUAN WYN JONES; Pres. DAFYDD IWAN.

Progressive Unionist Party: 299 Newtownards Rd, Belfast, BT4 1AG; tel. (28) 9022-5040; fax (28) 9022-5041; e-mail movingforward@pup-ni.org.uk; internet www.pup-ni.org.uk; loyalist party in Northern Ireland; Leader DAWN PURVIS.

Respect—The Unity Coalition: 209 Coborn House, 3 Coborn Rd, London, E3 2DA; tel. (020) 8983-9671; e-mail office@respectcoalition.org; internet www.respectcoalition.org; f. 2004; Chair. LINDA SMITH; National Sec. JOHN REES.

Scottish Liberal Democrats: 4 Clifton Terrace, Edinburgh, EH12 5DR; tel. (131) 337-2314; fax (131) 337-3566; e-mail administration@scotlibdems.org.uk; internet www.scotlibdems.org.uk; Leader NICOL STEPHEN.

Scottish National Party (SNP): 107 McDonald Rd, Edinburgh, EH7 4NW; tel. (131) 525-8900; fax (131) 525-8901; e-mail snp.hq@snp.org; internet www.snp.org; f. 1934; advocates independence for Scotland as a member of the EU and Scottish control of national resources; Leader ALEX SALMOND; Pres. IAN HUDGHTON.

Scottish Socialist Party: Suite 308, 93 Hope St, Glasgow, G2 6LD; tel. (141) 221-7470; e-mail ssp.glasgow@btconnect.com; internet www.scottishsocialistparty.org; f. 1998; Convener COLIN FOX.

Sinn Féin (We Ourselves): 53 Falls Rd, Belfast, BT12 4PD; tel. (28) 9022-3000; fax (28) 9022-3001; e-mail sfadmin@eircom.net; internet www.sinnfein.ie; f. 1905; seeks the reunification of Ireland and the establishment of a 32-county democratic socialist state; engages in community politics; Chair. MARY LOU MCDONALD; Pres. GERRY ADAMS; Gen. Sec. RITA O'HARE.

Social Democratic and Labour Party (SDLP): 121 Ormeau Rd, Belfast, BT7 1SH; tel. (28) 9024-7700; fax (28) 9023-6699; e-mail info@sdlp.ie; internet www.sdlp.ie; f. 1970; radical, left-of-centre principles with a view to the eventual reunification of Ireland by popular consent; Leader MARK DURKAN.

Socialist Labour Party: POB 112, Leigh, WN7 4WS; tel. and fax (870) 8503576; e-mail info@socialist-labour-party.org.uk; internet www.socialist-labour-party.org.uk; f. 1996; supports renationalization of industry, constitutional reform, withdrawal from the European Union; Leader ARTHUR SCARGILL; Pres. PAUL HARDMAN; Gen. Sec. IAN JOHNSON.

Socialist Party: POB 24697, London, E11 1YD; tel. (20) 8988-8777; e-mail info@socialistparty.org.uk; internet www.socialistparty.org.uk; f. 1991 as Militant Labour by fmr members of the Militant tendency (an extreme-left faction within the Labour Party); present name adopted 1997; registered with the Electoral Commission under the name Socialist Alternative; mem. of the Committee for a Workers' International (CWI); Gen. Sec PETER TAAFFE.

Socialist Workers' Party (SWP): POB 42184, London, SW8 2WD; tel. (20) 7819-1170; fax (20) 7819-1179; e-mail enquiries@swp.org.uk; internet www.swp.org.uk; f. 1950; advocates workers' control through revolution, not reform; c. 9,000 mems; Nat. Sec. MARTIN SMITH.

Solidarity—Scotland's Socialist Movement: POB 7565, Glasgow, G42 2DN; e-mail info@solidarityscotland.org; internet www.solidarityscotland.org; f. 2006 by disaffected members of the Scottish Socialist Party; Leaders TOMMY SHERIDAN, ROSEMARY BYRNE.

Ulster Unionist Party: Cunningham House, 429 Holywood Rd, Belfast, BT4 2LN; tel. (28) 9076-5500; fax (28) 9076-9416; e-mail uup@uup.org; internet www.uup.org; f. 1905; governed Northern Ireland 1921–72; supports parity and equality for Northern Ireland within the United Kingdom; Pres. JOHN WHITE; Leader Sir REG EMPEY.

UK Independence Party: POB 408, Newton Abbot, Devon, TQ12 9BG; tel. (1626) 831290; fax (1626) 831348; e-mail mail@ukip.org; internet www.ukip.org; f. 1993; advocates withdrawal from the European Union; 27,000 mems; Leader NIGEL FARAGE; Chair. JOHN WHITTAKER.

United Kingdom Unionist Party (UKUP): 10 Central Ave, Bangor, BT20 3AF; tel. (28) 9052-1482; fax (28) 9052-1483; e-mail info@ukup.org; seeks to preserve the union between Great Britain and Northern Ireland; Leader ROBERT MCCARTNEY.

Veritas: POB 4775, Atherstone, CV9 9AY; tel. (1827) 881287; e-mail veritasparty@btconnect.com; internet www.veritasparty.com; f. 2005; advocates withdrawal from the European Union; Leader PATRICK ESTON.

The following paramilitary organizations in Northern Ireland are proscribed: (nationalist) the Provisional Irish Republican Army (IRA), the Irish National Liberation Army, Cumann na mBan (women's section of the IRA), Fianna na hEireann (youth section of the IRA), Saor Eire and the Irish People's Liberation Organization; (loyalist) the Ulster Freedom Fighters, the Ulster Volunteer Force, the Red Hand Commando, the Ulster Defence Association (UDA), the Loyalist Volunteer Force (LVF), the Continuity Army Council, the Red Hand Defenders and the Orange Volunteers.

Diplomatic Representation

EMBASSIES AND HIGH COMMISSIONS IN THE UNITED KINGDOM

Afghanistan: 31 Prince's Gate, London, SW7 1QQ; tel. (20) 7589-8891; fax (20) 7584-4801; e-mail london@mfa.gov.af; internet www.afghanembassyuk.org; Ambassador Dr MUHAMMAD RAHIM SHERZOY.

Albania: 2nd Floor, 24 Buckingham Gate, London, SW1E 6LB; tel. (20) 7828-8897; fax (20) 7828-8869; e-mail embassy.london@mfa.gov.al; internet www.albanianembassy.co.uk; Ambassador ZEF MAZI.

Algeria: 54 Holland Park, London, W11 3RS; tel. (20) 7221-7800; fax (20) 7221-0448; e-mail info@algerianembassy.org.uk; internet www.algerianembassy.org.uk; Ambassador MUHAMMAD SALAH DEMBRI.

Andorra: 63 Westover Rd, London, SW18 2RF; tel. (20) 8874-4806; fax (20) 8874-4902; Ambassador MARIA ROSA PICART DE FRANCIS.

Angola: 22 Dorset St, London, W1U 6QY; tel. (20) 7299-9850; fax (20) 7486-9397; e-mail embassy@angola.org.uk; internet www.angola.org.uk; Ambassador ANA MARIA TELES CARREIRA.

Antigua and Barbuda: 2nd Floor, 45 Crawford Pl., London, W1H 4LP; tel. (20) 7258-0070; fax (20) 7258-7486; e-mail enquiries@antigua-barbuda.com; internet www.antigua-barbuda.com; High Commr Dr CARL ROBERTS.

Argentina: 65 Brook St, London, W1K 4AH; tel. (20) 7318-1300; fax (20) 7318-1301; e-mail info@argentine-embassy-uk.org; internet www.argentine-embassy-uk.org; Ambassador FEDERICO MIRRÉ.

Armenia: 25A Cheniston Gdns, London, W8 6TG; tel. (20) 7938-5435; fax (20) 7938-2595; e-mail armemb@armenianembassyuk.com; Ambassador Dr VAHE GABRIELYAN.

Australia: Australia House, Strand, London, WC2B 4LA; tel. (20) 7379-4334; fax (20) 7240-5333; internet www.uk.embassy.gov.au; High Commr FRANCES ADAMSON (acting).

Austria: 18 Belgrave Mews West, London, SW1X 8HU; tel. (20) 7344-3250; fax (20) 7344-0292; e-mail london-ob@bmeia.gv.at; internet www.bmeia.gv.at/london; Ambassador Dr GABRIELE MATZNER-HOLZER.

Azerbaijan: 4 Kensington Court, London, W8 5DL; tel. (20) 7938-3412; fax (20) 7937-1783; e-mail london@mission.mfa.gov.az; internet www.azembassy.org.uk; Ambassador FAKHRADDIN GURBANOV.

Bahamas: 10 Chesterfield St, London, W1J 5JL; tel. (20) 7408-4488; fax (20) 7499-9937; e-mail information@bahamashclondon.net; internet www.bahamashclondon.net; High Commr BASIL G. O'BRIEN.

Bahrain: 30 Belgrave Sq., London, SW1X 8QB; tel. (20) 7201-9170; fax (20) 7201-9183; e-mail information@bahrainembassy.co.uk; internet www.bahrainembassy.co.uk; Ambassador (vacant).

Bangladesh: 28 Queen's Gate, London, SW7 5JA; tel. (20) 7584-0081; fax (20) 7581-7477; e-mail bhclondon@btconnect.com; internet www.bhclondon.org.uk; High Commr SHAFI U. AHMED.

Barbados: 1 Great Russell St, London, WC1B 3ND; tel. (20) 7631-4975; fax (20) 7323-6872; e-mail london@foreign.gov.bb; High Commr L. EDWIN POLLARD.

Belarus: 6 Kensington Court, London, W8 5DL; tel. (20) 7937-3288; fax (20) 7361-0005; e-mail uk@belembassy.org; internet www.uk.belembassy.org; Ambassador ALEKSANDR MIKHNEVICH.

Belgium: 17 Grosvenor Cres., London, SW1X 7EE; tel. (20) 7470-3700; fax (20) 7470-3795; e-mail london@diplobel.be; internet www.diplomatie.be/london; Ambassador JEAN-MICHEL VERANNEMAN DE WATERVLIET.

Belize: 3rd Floor, 45 Crawford Pl., London, W1H 4LP; tel. (20) 7723-3603; fax (20) 7723-9637; e-mail bzhc-lon@btconnect.com; internet www.belizehighcommission.com; High Commr LAWRENCE SYLVESTER.

Bolivia: 106 Eaton Sq., London, SW1W 9AD; tel. (20) 7235-4248; fax (20) 7235-1286; e-mail info@embassyofbolivia.co.uk; internet www.embassyofbolivia.co.uk; Ambassador MARÍA BEATRIZ SOUVIRON CRESPO.

Bosnia and Herzegovina: 5–7 Lexham Gdns, London, W8 5JJ; tel. (20) 7373-0867; fax (20) 7373-0871; e-mail embassy@bhembassy.co.uk; internet www.bhembassy.co.uk; Ambassador TANJA MILASINOVIĆ.

Botswana: 6 Stratford Pl., London, W1C 1AY; tel. (20) 7499-0031; fax (20) 7495-8595; e-mail bohico@govbw.com; High Commr ROY BLACKBEARD.

Brazil: 32 Green St, London, W1K 7AT; tel. (20) 7399-9000; fax (20) 7399-9100; e-mail info@brazil.org.uk; internet www.brazil.org.uk; Ambassador CARLOS AUGUSTO REGO SANTOS-NEVES.

Brunei: 19–20 Belgrave Sq., London, SW1X 8PG; tel. (20) 7581-0521; fax (20) 7235-9717; e-mail bhcl@brunei-high-commission.co.uk; High Commr Pengiran Dato' MAIDIN HASHIM.

Bulgaria: 186–188 Queen's Gate, London, SW7 5HL; tel. (20) 7584-9400; fax (20) 7584-4948; e-mail ambass.office@bulgarianembassy.org.uk; internet www.bulgarianembassy.org.uk; Ambassador Dr LACHEZAR NIKOLOV MATEV.

Cambodia: 64 Brondesbury Park, Willesden Green, London, NW6 7AT; tel. (20) 8451-7850; fax (20) 8451-7594; e-mail cambodianembassy@btconnect.com; internet www.cambodianembassy.org.uk; Ambassador HOR NAMBORA.

Cameroon: 84 Holland Park, London, W11 3SB; tel. (20) 7727-0771; fax (20) 7792-9353; High Commr SAMUEL LIBOCK MBEI.

Canada: MacDonald House, 1 Grosvenor Sq., London, W1K 4AB; tel. (20) 7258-6600; fax (20) 7258-6533; e-mail ldn@international.gc.ca; internet www.dfait-maeci.gc.ca/london; High Commr JAMES R. WRIGHT.

Chile: 12 Devonshire St, London, W1G 7DS; tel. (20) 7580-6392; fax (20) 7436-5204; e-mail embachile@embachile.co.uk; internet www.echileuk.demon.co.uk; Ambassador RAFAEL MORENO.

China, People's Republic: 49–51 Portland Pl., London, W1B 4JL; tel. (20) 7299-4049; fax (20) 7636-5578; e-mail press@chinese-embassy.org.uk; internet www.chinese-embassy.org.uk; Ambassador FU YING.

Colombia: 3 Hans Cres., London, SW1X 0LN; tel. (20) 7589-9177; fax (20) 7589-4718; e-mail mail@colombianembassy.co.uk; internet www.colombianembassy.co.uk; Ambassador NOEMÍ SANÍN POSADA.

Congo, Democratic Republic: 281 Gray's Inn Rd, London, WC1X 8QF; tel. (20) 7278-9825; fax (20) 7833-9967; Ambassador EUGÉNIE TSHIELA COMPTON.

Costa Rica: Flat 1, 14 Lancaster Gate, London, W2 3LH; tel. (20) 7706-8844; fax (20) 7706-8655; e-mail costarica@btconnect.com; Ambassador PILAR SABORÍO DE ROCAFORT.

Côte d'Ivoire: 2 Upper Belgrave St, London, SW1X 8BJ; tel. (20) 7235-6991; fax (20) 7259-5320; e-mail info@ambaci-uk.org; internet www.ambaci-uk.org; Ambassador PHILIPPE D. DJANGONÉ-BI.

Croatia: 21 Conway St, London, W1T 6BN; tel. (20) 7387-2022; fax (20) 7387-0310; e-mail croemb.london@mvpei.hr; internet uk.mfa.hr; Ambassador JOŠKO PARO.

Cuba: 167 High Holborn, London, WC1V 6PA; tel. (20) 7240-2488; fax (20) 7836-2602; e-mail embacuba@cubaldn.com; internet www.cubaldn.com; Ambassador RENÉ JUAN MUJICA CANTELAR.

Cyprus: 13 St James' Sq., London, SW1Y 4LB; tel. (20) 7321-4100; fax (20) 7321-4164; e-mail cyphclondon@dial.pipex.com; internet www.mfa.gov.cy/highcomlondon; High Commr DIMITRIS HATZIARGIROU (acting).

Czech Republic: 26 Kensington Palace Gdns, London, W8 4QY; tel. (20) 7243-1115; fax (20) 7727-9654; e-mail london@embassy.mzv.cz; internet www.mzv.cz/london; Ambassador JAN WINKLER.

Denmark: 55 Sloane St, London, SW1X 9SR; tel. (20) 7333-0200; fax (20) 7333-0270; e-mail lonamb@um.dk; internet www.amblondon.um.dk; Ambassador BIRGER RIIS-JØRGENSEN.

Dominica: 1 Collingham Gdns, London, SW5 0HW; tel. (20) 7370-5194; fax (20) 7373-8743; e-mail dominicahighcom@btconnect.com; High Commr AGNES ADONIS (acting).

Dominican Republic: 139 Inverness Terrace, London, W2 6JF; tel. (9065) 508945; fax (20) 7727-3693; e-mail info@dominicanembassy.org.uk; internet www.dominicanembassy.org.uk; Ambassador ANIBAL DE CASTRO.

Ecuador: Flat 3B, 3 Hans Cres., Knightsbridge, London, SW1X 0LS; tel. (20) 7584-1367; fax (20) 7823-9701; e-mail eecugranbretania@mmrree.gov.ec; Chargé d'affaires a.i. DÉBORAH SALGADO CAMPAÑA.

Egypt: 26 South St, London, W1K 1DW; tel. (20) 7499-3304; fax (20) 7491-1542; e-mail embassy@embassyofegypt.co.uk; internet www.egyptianconsulate.co.uk; Ambassador GEHAD MADI.

El Salvador: 1st and 2nd Floors, 8 Dorset Sq., London, NW1 6PU; tel. (20) 7224-9800; fax (20) 7224-9878; e-mail elsalvador.embassy@gmail.com; Ambassador Dr VLADIMIRO P. VILLALTA.

THE UNITED KINGDOM

Equatorial Guinea: 13 Park Pl., St. James's, London, SW1A 1LP; tel. (20) 7499-6867; fax (20) 7499-6782; internet www.embarege-londres.org; Ambassador AGUSTIN NZE NFUMU.

Eritrea: 96 White Lion St, London, N1 9PF; tel. (20) 7713-0096; fax (20) 7713-0161; e-mail eriemba@erimbauk.com; Ambassador TESFAMICAEL GERAHTU OGBAGHIORGHIS.

Estonia: 16 Hyde Park Gate, London, SW7 5DG; tel. (20) 7589-3428; fax (20) 7589-3430; e-mail embassy.london@estonia.gov.uk; internet www.estonia.gov.uk; Ambassador Dr MARGUS LAIDRE.

Ethiopia: 17 Prince's Gate, London, SW7 1PZ; tel. (20) 7589-7212; fax (20) 7584-7054; e-mail info@ethioembassy.org.uk; internet www.ethioembassy.org.uk; Ambassador BERHANU KEBEDE.

Fiji: 34 Hyde Park Gate, London, SW7 5DN; tel. (20) 7584-3661; fax (20) 7584-2838; e-mail mail@fijihighcommission.org.uk; internet www.fijihighcommission.org.uk; High Commr MACA TULAKEPA (acting).

Finland: 38 Chesham Pl., London, SW1X 8HW; tel. (20) 7838-6200; fax (20) 7235-3680; e-mail sanomat.lon@formin.fi; internet www.finemb.org.uk; Ambassador JAAKKO LAAJAVA.

France: 58 Knightsbridge, London, SW1X 7JT; tel. (20) 7073-1000; fax (20) 7073-1004; e-mail presse.londres-amba@diplomatie.fr; internet www.ambafrance-uk.org; Ambassador MAURICE GORDAULT-MONTAGNE.

Gabon: 27 Elvaston Pl., London, SW7 5NL; tel. (20) 7823-9986; fax (20) 7584-0047; Ambassador (vacant).

The Gambia: 57 Kensington Court, London, W8 5DG; tel. (20) 7937-6316; fax (20) 7937-9095; e-mail gambia@gamhighcom.wanadoo.co.uk; High Commr ELIZABETH YA ELI HARDING.

Georgia: 4 Russell Gdns, London, W14 8EZ; tel. (20) 7603-7799; fax (20) 7603-6682; e-mail embassy@geoemb.plus.com; internet www.geoemb.org.uk; Ambassador GELA CHARKVIANI.

Germany: 23 Belgrave Sq., London, SW1X 8PZ; tel. (20) 7824-1300; fax (20) 7824-1449; e-mail mail@german-embassy.org.uk; internet www.london.diplo.de; Ambassador (vacant).

Ghana: 13 Belgrave Sq., London, SW1X 8PN; tel. (20) 7235-4142; fax (20) 7245-9552; e-mail information@ghanahighcommissionuk.com; internet www.ghanahighcommissionuk.com; High Commr ANNAN ARKYIN CATO.

Greece: 1A Holland Park, London, W11 3TP; tel. (20) 7229-3850; fax (20) 7229-7221; e-mail political@greekembassy.org.uk; internet www.greekembassy.org.uk; Ambassador VASSILIS-ACHILLEAS PISPINIS.

Grenada: The Chapel, Archel Rd, West Kensington, London, W14 9QH; tel. (20) 7385-4415; fax (20) 7381-4807; e-mail grenada@high-commission.demon.co.uk; High Commr JOSEPH STEPHEN CHARTER.

Guatemala: 13 Fawcett St, London, SW10 9HN; tel. (20) 7351-3042; fax (20) 7376-5708; e-mail ambassador.gtm@btconnect.com; Ambassador EDMUNDO RENÉ URRUTIA GARCIA.

Guinea: 48 Onslow Gdns, London, SW7 3PY; tel. and fax (20) 7594-4819; e-mail ambaguineeuk@yahoo.co.uk; Ambassador LANSANA KEÏTA.

Guyana: 3 Palace Court, Bayswater Rd, London, W2 4LP; tel. (20) 7229-7684; fax (20) 7727-9809; e-mail ghc.l@ic24.net; High Commr LALESHWAR K. N. SINGH.

Holy See: 54 Parkside, London, SW19 5NE (Apostolic Nunciature); tel. (20) 8944-7189; fax (20) 8947-2494; e-mail nuntius@globalnet.co.uk; Apostolic Nuncio Most Rev. FAUSTINO SAINZ MUÑOZ (Titular Archbishop of Novaliciana).

Honduras: 115 Gloucester Pl., London, W1U 6JT; tel. (20) 7486-4880; fax (20) 7486-4550; e-mail hondurasuk@lineone.net; Ambassador IVÁN ROMERO-MARTÍNEZ.

Hungary: 35 Eaton Pl., London, SW1X 8BY; tel. (20) 7235-5218; fax (20) 7823-1348; e-mail office@huemblon.org.uk; internet www.mfa.gov.hu/emb/london/; Ambassador BORBÁLA CZAKÓ.

Iceland: 2A Hans St, London, SW1X 0JE; tel. (20) 7259-3999; fax (20) 7245-9649; e-mail icemb.london@utn.stjr.is; internet www.iceland.org/uk; Ambassador SVERRIR HAUKUR GUNNLAUGSSON.

India: India House, Aldwych, London, WC2B 4NA; tel. (20) 7836-8484; fax (20) 7836-4331; e-mail info@hcilondon.net; internet www.hcilondon.net; High Commr SHIV SHANKAR MUKHERJEE.

Indonesia: 38 Grosvenor Sq., London, W1X 2HW; tel. (20) 7499-7661; fax (20) 7491-4993; e-mail kbri@btconnect.com; internet www.indonesianembassy.org.uk; Ambassador YURI OCTAVIAN THAMRIN.

Iran: 16 Prince's Gate, London, SW7 1PT; tel. (20) 7225-3000; fax (20) 7589-4440; e-mail info@iran-embassy.org.uk; internet www.iran-embassy.org.uk; Ambassador RASOUL MOVAHEDIAN ATTAR.

Iraq: 9 Holland Villas Rd, London, W14 8BP; tel. (20) 7602-8456; fax (20) 7371-1652; e-mail lonemb@iraqmofamail.net; Chargé d'affaires a.i. ABD AL-MUHAIMEN AL-ORAIBI.

Ireland: 17 Grosvenor Pl., London, SW1X 7HR; tel. (20) 7235-2171; fax (20) 7245-6961; internet www.embassyofireland.co.uk; Ambassador DAVID COONEY.

Israel: 2 Palace Green, Kensington, London, W8 4QB; tel. (20) 7957-9500; fax (20) 7957-9555; e-mail public3@london.mfa.gov.il; internet london.mfa.gov.il; Ambassador RON PROSOR.

Italy: 14 Three Kings Yard, London, W1K 4EH; tel. (20) 7312-2200; fax (20) 7312-2230; e-mail ambasciata.londra@esteri.it; internet www.amblondra.esteri.it; Ambassador GIANCARLO ARAGONA.

Jamaica: 1–2 Prince Consort Rd, London, SW7 2BZ; tel. (20) 7823-9911; fax (20) 7589-5154; e-mail jamhigh@jhcuk.com; internet www.jhcuk.com; High Commr BURCHELL ANTHONY WHITEMAN.

Japan: 101–104 Piccadilly, London, W1J 7JT; tel. (20) 7465-6500; fax (20) 7491-9348; e-mail info@jpembassy.org.uk; internet www.uk.emb-japan.go.jp; Ambassador YOSHIJI NOGAMI.

Jordan: 6 Upper Phillimore Gdns, London, W8 7HA; tel. (20) 7937-3685; fax (20) 7937-8795; e-mail info@jordanembassyuk.org; internet www.jordanembassyuk.org; Ambassador Dr ALIA BOURAN.

Kazakhstan: 33 Thurloe Sq., London, SW7 2SD; tel. (20) 7581-4646; fax (20) 7584-8481; e-mail london@kazakhstan-embassy.org.uk; internet www.kazakhstanembassy.co.uk; Chargé d'affaires a.i. Dr DASTAN YELEUNEKOV.

Kenya: 45 Portland Pl., London, W1N 4AS; tel. (20) 7636-2371; fax (20) 7323-6717; e-mail knganga@kenyahighcommission.net; internet www.kenyahighcommission.net; High Commr JOSEPH KIRUGUMI MUCHEMI.

Korea, Democratic People's Republic: 73 Gunnersbury Ave, London, W5 4LP; tel. (20) 8992-4965; fax (20) 8992-2053; Ambassador JA SONG-NAM.

Korea, Republic: 60 Buckingham Gate, London, SW1E 6AJ; tel. (20) 7227-5500; fax (20) 7227-5503; internet www.koreanembassy.org.uk; Chargé d'affaires a.i. SUK-IN CHOI.

Kuwait: 2 Albert Gate, London, SW1X 7JU; tel. (20) 7590-3400; fax (20) 7823-1712; e-mail kuwait@dircon.co.uk; internet www.kuwaitinfo.org.uk; Ambassador KHALID AD-DUWAISAN.

Kyrgyzstan: Ascot House, 119 Crawford St, London, W1U 6BJ; tel. (20) 7935-1462; fax (20) 7935-7449; e-mail mail@kyrgyz-embassy.org.uk; internet www.kyrgyz-embassy.org.uk; Ambassador Dr KUBAN ILYASOVICH MAMBETALIEV.

Latvia: 45 Nottingham Pl., London, W1U 5LY; tel. (20) 7312-0040; fax (20) 7312-0042; e-mail embassy.uk@mfa.gov.lv; internet www.london.mfa.gov.lv; Ambassador INDULIS BĒRZIŅŠ.

Lebanon: 21 Palace Gardens Mews, London, W8 4RB; tel. (20) 7227-6696; fax (20) 7243-1699; e-mail emb.leb@btinternet.com; Chargé d'affaires a. i. INAAM OSSEIRAN.

Lesotho: 7 Chesham Pl., London, SW1 8HN; tel. (20) 7235-5686; fax (20) 7235-5023; e-mail lhc@lesotholondon.org.uk; internet www.lesotholondon.org.uk; High Commissioner Prince SEEISO BERENG SEEISO.

Liberia: 23 Fitzroy Sq., London, W1 6EW; tel. (20) 7388-5489; fax (20) 7380-1593; e-mail liberianembassy@yahoo.co.uk; internet www.embassyofliberia.org.uk; Ambassador WESLEY MOMO JOHNSON.

Libya: 15 Knightsbridge, London, SW1X 7LY; tel. (20) 7201-8280; fax (20) 7245-0588; Chargé d'affaires a.i. OMAR R. JELBAN.

Lithuania: 84 Gloucester Pl., London, W1U 6AU; tel. (20) 7486-6401; fax (20) 7486-6403; e-mail amb.uk@urm.lt; internet uk.mfa.lt; Ambassador VYGAUDAS UŠACKAS.

Luxembourg: 27 Wilton Cres., London, SW1X 8SD; tel. (20) 7235-6961; fax (20) 7235-9734; e-mail londres.amb@mae.etat.lu; Ambassador HUBERT WURTH.

Macedonia, former Yugoslav republic: Suites 2.1 and 2.2, 2nd Floor, Buckingham Court, Buckingham Gate, London, SW1E 6PE; tel. (20) 7976-0535; fax (20) 7976-0539; e-mail info@macedonianembassy.org.uk; internet www.macedonianembassy.org.uk; Ambassador MARIJA EFREMOVA.

Madagascar: 8–10 Hallam St, London W1W 6JE; tel. (20) 3008-4550; fax (20) 3008-4551; e-mail embamadlon@yahoo.co.uk; internet www.embassy-madagascar-uk.com; Chargé d'affaires IARY BERTHINE RAVAOARIMANANA.

Malawi: 70 Winnington Rd, London, N2 0TX; tel. (20) 8455-5624; fax (20) 3235-1066; e-mail malawihighcom@btconnect.com; internet www.malawihighcom.org.uk; High Commr Dr FRANCIS MOTO.

Malaysia: 45 Belgrave Sq., London, SW1X 8QT; tel. (20) 7235-8033; fax (20) 7235-5161; e-mail mwlon@btconnect.com; internet www.kln.gov.my/mission/london; High Commr Datuk ABD AZIZ MOHAMMED.

Maldives: 22 Nottingham Pl., London, W1U 5NJ; tel. (20) 7224-2135; fax (20) 7224-2157; e-mail info@maldiveshighcommission.org; internet www.maldiveshighcommission.org; High Commr Dr MOHAMED ASIM.

Malta: Malta House, 36–38 Piccadilly, London, W1J 0LE; tel. (20) 7292-4800; fax (20) 7734-1831; e-mail maltahighcommission.london@gov.mt; High Commr Dr Michael Refalo.

Mauritania: 8 Carlos Pl., London, W1K 3AS; tel. (20) 7478-9323; fax (20) 7478-9339; e-mail ambarim@aol.com; Ambassador Ould Moctar Neche Mélaïnine.

Mauritius: 32–33 Elvaston Pl., London, SW7 5NW; tel. (20) 7581-0294; fax (20) 7823-8437; e-mail londonmhc@btinternet.com; High Commr Abhimanu Mahendra Kundasamy.

Mexico: 16 St George St, Hanover Sq., London, W1S 1FD; tel. (20) 7499-8586; fax (20) 7495-4035; e-mail mexuk@sre.gob.mx; internet www.sre.gob.mx/reinounido; Ambassador Juan José Bremer de Martino.

Moldova: 5 Dolphin Sq., Edensor Rd, London, W4 2ST; tel. (20) 8995-6818; fax (20) 8995-6927; e-mail londra@mfa.md; internet www.moldovanembassy.org.uk; Ambassador Mariana Durleşteanu.

Mongolia: 7 Kensington Court, London, W8 5DL; tel. (20) 7937-0150; fax (20) 7937-1117; e-mail office@embassyofmongolia.co.uk; internet www.embassyofmongolia.co.uk; Ambassador Bulgaagiin Altangerel.

Montenegro: 11 Waterloo Pl., London, SW1Y 4AU; tel. (20) 7863-8806; fax (20) 7863-8807; Ambassador Dragiša Burzan.

Morocco: 49 Queen's Gate Gdns, London, SW7 5NE; tel. (20) 7581-5001; fax (20) 7225-3862; e-mail mail@sifamaldn.org; Ambassador Muhammad Belmahi.

Mozambique: 21 Fitzroy Sq., London, W1T 6EL; tel. (20) 7383-3800; fax (20) 7383-3801; e-mail sandra@mozambiquehc.co.uk; internet www.mozambiquehc.org.uk; High Commr António Gumende.

Myanmar: 19A Charles St, London, W1J 5DX; tel. (20) 7499-4340; fax (20) 7409-7043; e-mail melondon@btconnect.com; Ambassador U Nay Win.

Namibia: 6 Chandos St, London, W1G 9LU; tel. (20) 7636-6244; fax (20) 7637-5694; e-mail namibia.hicom@btconnect.com; High Commr George Mbanga Liswaniso.

Nepal: 12A Kensington Palace Gdns, London, W8 4QU; tel. (20) 7229-1594; fax (20) 7792-9861; e-mail eon@nepembassy.org.uk; internet www.nepembassy.org.uk; Ambassador Murari Raj Sharma.

Netherlands: 38 Hyde Park Gate, London, SW7 5DP; tel. (20) 7590-3200; fax (20) 7225-0947; e-mail london@netherlands-embassy.org.uk; internet www.netherlands-embassy.org.uk; Ambassador Pieter Willem Waldeck.

New Zealand: New Zealand House, 80 Haymarket, London, SW1Y 4TQ; tel. (20) 7930-8422; fax (20) 7839-4580; e-mail aboutnz@newzealandhc.org.uk; internet www.nzembassy.com/uk; High Commr Jonathan Hunt.

Nicaragua: Suite 31, Vicarage House, 58–60 Kensington Church St, London, W8 4DB; tel. (20) 7938-2373; fax (20) 7937-0952; e-mail embanic1@yahoo.co.uk; Ambassador Piero Paolo Coen Ubilla.

Nigeria: Nigeria House, 9 Northumberland Ave, London, WC2N 5BX; tel. (20) 7839-1244; fax (20) 7839-8746; e-mail chancery@nigeriahc.org.uk; internet www.nigeriahc.org.uk; High Commr Dr Dalhatu Sarki Tafida.

Norway: 25 Belgrave Sq., London, SW1X 8QD; tel. (20) 7591-5500; fax (20) 7245-6993; e-mail emb.london@mfa.no; internet www.norway.org.uk; Ambassador Bjarne Lindstrøm.

Oman: 167 Queen's Gate, London, SW7 5HE; tel. (20) 7225-0001; fax (20) 7589-2505; Ambassador Hussain Ali Abdullatif.

Pakistan: 34–36 Lowndes Sq., London, SW1X 9JN; tel. (20) 7664-9200; fax (20) 7664-9224; e-mail pareplondon@supanet.com; internet www.pakmission-uk.gov.pk; High Commr Maleeha Lodhi.

Panama: 40 Hertford St, London, W1J 7SH; tel. (20) 7493-4646; fax (20) 7493-4333; e-mail panama1@btconnect.com; Ambassador Liliana Fernándes.

Papua New Guinea: 3rd Floor, 14 Waterloo Pl., London, SW1R 4AR; tel. (20) 7930-0922; fax (20) 7930-0828; internet www.pnghighcomm.org.uk; High Commr Jean L. Kekedo.

Paraguay: 3rd Floor, 344 Kensington High St, London, W14 8NS; tel. (20) 7610-4180; fax (20) 7371-4279; e-mail embapar@btconnect.com; internet www.paraguayembassy.co.uk; Chargé d'affaires a.i. Maria Christina Acosta Alvarez.

Peru: 52 Sloane St, London, SW1X 9SP; tel. (20) 7235-1917; fax (20) 7235-4463; e-mail postmaster@peruembassy-uk.com; internet www.peruembassy-uk.com; Ambassador Ricardo Luna Mendoza.

Philippines: 9A Palace Green, London, W8 4QE; tel. (20) 7937-1600; fax (20) 7937-2925; e-mail londonpe@dfa.gov.ph; internet www.philemb.org.uk; Ambassador Edgardo B. Espiritu.

Poland: 47 Portland Pl., London, W1B 1JH; tel. (870) 774-2700; fax (20) 7291-3575; e-mail polishembassy@polishembassy.org.uk; internet www.london.polemb.net; Ambassador Barbara Tuge-Erecińska.

Portugal: 11 Belgrave Sq., London, SW1X 8PP; tel. (20) 7235-5331; fax (20) 7235-0739; e-mail london@portembassy.co.uk; Ambassador António Nunes de Carvalho Santana Carlos.

Qatar: 1 South Audley St, London, W1K 1NB; tel. (20) 7493-2200; fax (20) 7493-2661; Ambassador Khalid bin Rashid bin Salim al-Hamoudi al-Mansouri.

Romania: Arundel House, 4 Palace Green, London, W8 4QD; tel. (20) 7937-9666; fax (20) 7937-8069; e-mail roemb@roemb.co.uk; internet londra.mae.ro; Ambassador Ion Jinga.

Russia: 13 Kensington Palace Gdns, London, W8 4QX; tel. (20) 7229-6412; fax (20) 7727-8625; e-mail office@rusemblon.org; internet www.great-britain.mid.ru; Ambassador Yurii V. Fedotov.

Rwanda: 120–122 Seymour Pl., London, W1H 1NR; tel. (20) 7724-9832; fax (20) 7724-8642; e-mail uk@ambarwanda.org.uk; internet www.ambarwanda.org.uk; Ambassador Claver Gatete.

Saint Christopher and Nevis: 2nd Floor, 10 Kensington Court, London, W8 5DL; tel. (20) 7937-9718; fax (20) 7937-7484; e-mail sknhighcomm@btconnect.com; High Commr James E. Williams.

Saint Lucia: 1 Collingham Gdns, London, SW5 0HW; tel. (20) 7370-7123; fax (20) 7370-1905; e-mail hcslu@btconnect.com; High Commr Maura Felix (acting).

Saint Vincent and the Grenadines: 10 Kensington Court, London, W8 5DL; tel. (20) 7565-2874; fax (20) 7937-6040; e-mail info@svghighcom.co.uk; High Commr Cenio E. Lewis.

Saudi Arabia: 30 Charles St, London, W1J 5DZ; tel. (20) 7917-3000; fax (20) 7917-3330; e-mail ukemb@mofa.gov.sa; internet www.saudiembassy.org.uk; Ambassador Prince Muhammad bin Nawaf bin Abdulaziz.

Senegal: 39 Marloes Rd, London, W8 6LA; tel. (20) 7937-7237; fax (20) 7938-2546; e-mail senegalembassy@hotmail.co.uk; internet www.senegalembassy.co.uk; Ambassador Abdou Sourang.

Serbia: 28 Belgrave Sq., London, SW1X 8QB; tel. (20) 7235-9049; fax (20) 7235-7092; internet www.serbianembassy.org.uk; Chargé d'affaires Dragan Županjevac.

Sierra Leone: 41 Eagle St, London, WC1R 4TL; tel. (20) 7404-0140; fax (20) 7430-9862; e-mail info@slhc-uk.org.uk; internet www.slhc-uk.org.uk; High Commr Melvin H. Chalobah.

Singapore: 9 Wilton Cres., London, SW1X 8SP; tel. (20) 7235-8315; fax (20) 7245-6583; e-mail singhc_lon@sgmfa.gov.sg; internet www.mfa.gov.sg/london; High Commr Michael Eng Cheng Teo.

Slovakia: 25 Kensington Palace Gdns, London, W8 4QY; tel. (20) 7313-6470; fax (20) 7313-6481; e-mail emb.london@mzv.sk; internet www.slovakembassy.co.uk; Ambassador Juraj Zervan.

Slovenia: 10 Little College St, London, SW1P 3SH; tel. (20) 7222-5400; fax (20) 7222-5277; e-mail vlo@gov.si; internet london.embassy.si; Ambassador Iztok Mirošić.

South Africa: South Africa House, Trafalgar Sq., London, WC2N 5DP; tel. (20) 7451-7299; fax (20) 7451-7284; e-mail webdesk@southafricahouse.com; internet www.southafricahouse.com; High Commr Dr Lindiwe Mabuza.

Spain: 39 Chesham Pl., London, SW1X 8SB; tel. (20) 7235-5555; fax (20) 7259-5392; e-mail embespuk@mail.mae.es; internet www.mae.es/embajadas/londres; Ambassador Carlos Miranda y Elío.

Sri Lanka: 13 Hyde Park Gdns, London, W2 2LU; tel. (20) 7262-1841; fax (20) 7262-7970; e-mail mail@slhc-london.co.uk; internet www.slhclondon.org; High Commr Kshenuka Senewiratne.

Sudan: 3 Cleveland Row, St James's, London, SW1A 1DD; tel. (20) 7839-8080; fax (20) 7839-7560; e-mail admin@sudanembassy.co.uk; internet www.sudanembassy.co.uk; Ambassador Omar Muhammad Ahmad Siddig.

Swaziland: 20 Buckingham Gate, London, SW1E 6LB; tel. (20) 7630-6611; fax (20) 7630-6564; e-mail enquiries@swaziland.org.uk; High Commr Mary Madzandza Kanya.

Sweden: 11 Montagu Pl., London, W1H 2AL; tel. (20) 7917-6400; fax (20) 7724-4174; e-mail ambassaden.london@foreign.ministry.se; internet www.swedenabroad.com/london; Ambassador Staffan Carlsson.

Switzerland: 16–18 Montagu Pl., London, W1H 2BQ; tel. (20) 7616-6000; fax (20) 7724-7001; e-mail swissembassy@lon.rep.admin.ch; internet www.swissembassy.org.uk; Ambassador Alexis P. Lautenberg.

Syria: 8 Belgrave Sq., London, SW1X 8PH; tel. (20) 7245-9012; fax (20) 7235-4621; e-mail info@syrianembassy.co.uk; internet www.syrianembassy.org.uk; Ambassador Dr Sami Khiyami.

Tanzania: 3 Stratford Pl., London, W1C 1AS; tel. (20) 7569-1470; fax (20) 7491-3710; e-mail hom@tanzania-online.gov.uk; internet www.tanzania-online.gov.uk; High Commr Mwanaidi S. Maajar.

Thailand: 29–30 Queen's Gate, London, SW7 5JB; tel. (20) 7589-2944; fax (20) 7823-7492; e-mail thaiduto@btinternet.com; internet www.thaiembassyuk.org.uk; Ambassador Kitti Wasinondh.

Tonga: 36 Molyneux St, London, W1H 5BQ; tel. (20) 7724-5828; fax (20) 7723-9074; e-mail enquiries@tongahighcom.co.uk; High Commr Dr SIONE NGONGO KIOA.

Trinidad and Tobago: 42 Belgrave Sq., London, SW1X 8NT; tel. (20) 7245-9351; fax (20) 7823-1065; e-mail tthc.info@btconnect.net; High Commr GLENDA P. MOREAN-PHILLIP.

Tunisia: 29 Prince's Gate, London, SW7 1QG; tel. (20) 7584-8117; fax (20) 7584-3205; Ambassador HAMIDA MRABET LAÂBIDI.

Turkey: 43 Belgrave Sq., London, SW1X 8PA; tel. (20) 7393-0202; fax (20) 7393-0066; e-mail turkish.emb@btclick.com; internet www.turkishembassylondon.org; Ambassador MEHMET YIĞIT ALPOGAN.

Turkmenistan: 2nd Floor South, St George's House, 14–17 Wells St, London, W1P 3FP; tel. (20) 7255-1071; fax (20) 7323-9184; Ambassador YAZMURAD SERYAEV.

Uganda: Uganda House, 58/59 Trafalgar Sq., London, WC2N 5DX; tel. (20) 7839-5783; fax (20) 7839-8925; internet www.ugandahighcommission.co.uk; High Commr JOAN KAKIMA NYAKATUURA RWABYOMERE.

Ukraine: 60 Holland Park, London, W11 3SJ; tel. (20) 7727-6312; fax (20) 7792-1708; e-mail emb_gb@mfa.gov.ua; internet www.ukremb.org.uk; Ambassador IHOR KHARCHENKO.

United Arab Emirates: 30 Princes Gate, London, SW7 1PT; tel. (20) 7581-1281; fax (20) 7581-9616; e-mail information@uaeembassyuk.net; internet www.uaeembassyuk.net; Ambassador ISSA SALEH AL-GURG.

USA: 24–32 Grosvenor Sq., London, W1A 1AE; tel. (20) 7499-9000; internet london.usembassy.gov; Ambassador ROBERT HOLMES TUTTLE.

Uruguay: 2nd Floor, 140 Brompton Rd, London, SW3 1HY; tel. (20) 7589-8835; fax (20) 7581-9585; e-mail emburuguay@emburuguay.org.uk; Ambassador RICARDO VARELA.

Uzbekistan: 41 Holland Park, London, W11 2RP; tel. (20) 7229-7679; fax (20) 7229-7029; e-mail info@uzbekembassy.org; internet www.uzbekembassy.org; Ambassador OTABEK H. AKBAROV.

Venezuela: 1 Cromwell Rd, London, SW7 2HW; tel. (20) 7584-4206; fax (20) 7589-8887; e-mail info@venezlon.co.uk; internet www.venezlon.co.uk; Ambassador SAMUEL MONCADA.

Viet Nam: 12–14 Victoria Rd, London, W8 5RD; tel. (20) 7937-1912; fax (20) 7937-6108; e-mail embassy@vietnamembassy.org.uk; internet www.vietnamembassy.org.uk; Ambassador TRAN QUANG HOAN.

Yemen: 57 Cromwell Rd, London, SW7 2ED; tel. (20) 7584-6607; fax (20) 7589-3350; e-mail yemenembassy@btconnect.com; internet www.yemenembassy.org.uk; Ambassador MUHAMMAD TAHA MUSTAFA.

Zambia: Zambia House, 2 Palace Gate, London, W8 5NG; tel. (20) 7589-6655; fax (20) 7581-1353; e-mail immzhcl@btconnect.com; internet www.zhcl.org.uk; High Commr ANDERSON KASEBA CHIBWA.

Zimbabwe: Zimbabwe House, 429 Strand, London, WC2R 0QE; tel. (20) 7836-7755; fax (20) 7379-1167; e-mail zimlondon@yahoo.co.uk; Ambassador GABRIEL MHARADZE MACHINGA.

Judicial System

There are, historically, three sources of the law as administered in the law courts today: Statute Law, which is written law and consists mainly of Acts of Parliament; Common Law, which originated in ancient usage and has not been formally enacted; and Equity, which was the system evolved by the Lord Chancellor's court (Court of Chancery) to mitigate the strictness of some of the common law rules. The law of the European Community has now been added to these.

Scottish common and statute law differ in some respects from that current in the rest of the United Kingdom, owing to Scotland's retention of its own legal system under the Act of Union with England of 1707.

Three factors help to ensure a fair trial: the independence of judges, who, in the case of High Court Judges, are outside the control of the executive and can be removed from office only after an address from Parliament to the Sovereign (Circuit Judges can be removed by the Lord Chancellor); the participation of private citizens in all important criminal and some civil cases, in the form of a summoned jury of 12 persons, who judge, if necessary by a majority, the facts of a case, questions of law being decided by the judge; and the system of appeals to a higher court, including the Criminal and Civil Divisions of the Court of Appeal, and, thereafter, the House of Lords.

The Courts and Legal Services Act 1990 provided for radical change in the legal profession, including legislation permitting solicitors to appear in higher courts, and extensive reform of the civil courts, whereby the civil cases formerly heard in the High Court could be transferred to the county courts.

In June 2003 the Government announced its intention to create a new free-standing Supreme Court to take over the judicial functions of the House of Lords and the Judicial Committee of the Privy Council. The proposed legislation was adopted in March 2005, although the Supreme Court was not expected to commence operations until October 2009.

MAGISTRATES' COURTS OR PETTY SESSIONS

The criminal courts of lowest jurisdiction are presided over by Justices of the Peace, who are unpaid lay people appointed by the Lord Chancellor. They have power to try all non-indictable offences, and some of the less serious indictable offences, if the defendant agrees. The trial of nearly all criminal offences begins in the magistrates' court. Approximately 95% of all criminal offences are dealt with solely by magistrates' courts. In the vast majority of committals for trial in the Crown Court magistrates are not required to consider evidence.

In London and in certain other large towns there are a small number of professional salaried magistrates, known as metropolitan stipendiary magistrates in London and as stipendiary magistrates in the provinces, who sit alone, whereas lay justices normally sit in threes when acting judicially.

Youth Courts, composed of specially trained justices selected by the justices of each petty sessional division (in London, by the Lord Chancellor), have power to try most charges against children under 18 years. The general public is excluded and there are restrictions on newspaper reports of the proceedings.

Magistrates also have power to grant, renew, transfer or remove or order the forfeiture of licences for the sale of alcoholic drinks, and to control the structural design of premises where alcohol is sold for consumption on the premises. They also control the licensing of betting shops, and grant bookmakers' permits.

COUNTY COURTS

A high proportion of civil actions are tried in these courts, which are presided over by a circuit judge, or, in some cases, a district judge, sitting alone. From 1 July 1991 county courts were granted unlimited jurisdiction.

THE CROWN COURT

The Crown Court came into being on 1 January 1972, under the Courts Act 1971, replacing Quarter Sessions and Assizes, to deal with serious criminal cases where trial by jury is required. The Crown Court sits at various centres throughout England and Wales. Court centres have been administratively divided into three tiers. The most serious offences are tried at first and second tier centres presided over by High Court Judges, Circuit Judges or Recorders. Circuit Judges or Recorders preside over third tier centres, where the less serious offences are tried. The Crown Court for the City of London is the Central Criminal Court (the Old Bailey).

HIGH COURT OF JUSTICE

Certain civil cases are heard in the three divisions of this court—Chancery, Queen's Bench and Family. The Chancery Division deals with litigation about property, patents, family trusts, companies, dissolution of partnerships and disputed estates. The Queen's Bench Division hears cases involving damage to property, personal injuries, etc. and also includes the Commercial and Admiralty Courts. The Family Division hears contested or complex divorce and separation cases and matters relating to children such as adoption, wardship or guardianship of minors.

Chancery Division

President: Sir ROBERT ANDREW MORRITT (Chancellor).

Judges: Sir JOHN EDMUND FREDERIC LINDSAY, Sir EDWARD CHRISTOPHER EVANS-LOMBE, Sir WILLIAM ANTHONY BLACKBURNE, Sir NICHOLAS JOHN PATTEN, Sir TERRENCE MICHAEL ELKAN BARNET ETHERTON (also Chairman of the Law Commission), Sir PETER WINSTON SMITH, Sir KIM MARTIN JORDAN LEWISON, Sir DAVID ANTHONY STEWART RICHARDS, Sir GEORGE ANTHONY MANN, Sir NICHOLAS ROGER WARREN, Sir DAVID JAMES TYSON KITCHIN, Sir MICHAEL TOWNLEY FEATHERSTONE BRIGGS, Sir LAUNCELOT DINADIN JAMES HENDERSON, Sir PAUL HYACINTH MORGAN, Sir ALASTAIR HUBERT NORRIS, Sir GERALD EDWARD BARLING, Sir CHRISTOPHER DAVID LLOYD.

Queen's Bench Division

President: Sir IGOR JUDGE.

Judges: Sir STUART NEIL MCKINNON, Sir JOHN THAYNE FORBES, Sir ANDREW DAVID COLLINS, Sir ALEXANDER NEIL LOGIE BUTTERFIELD, Sir ROBERT FRANKLYN NELSON, Sir DAVID EADY, Sir JEREMY MIRTH SULLIVAN, Sir DAVID HERBERT PENRY-DAVEY, Sir DAVID WILLIAM STEEL, Sir NICOLAS DUŠAN BRATZA (Judge of the European Court of Human Rights), Sir MICHAEL JOHN BURTON, Sir RUPERT MATTHEW JACKSON, Sir PATRICK ELIAS, Sir RICHARD JOHN PEARSON AIKENS, Sir

THE UNITED KINGDOM *Directory*

Stephen Robert Silber, Sir John Bernard Goldring, Dame Anne Judith Rafferty, Sir Geoffrey Douglas Grigson, Sir Richard Henry Quixano Henriques, Sir Stephen Miles Tomlinson, Sir Andrew Charles Smith, Sir Christopher John Pitchford, Sir Duncan Brian Walter Ouseley, Sir Richard George Bramwell McCombe, Sir Raymond Evan Jack, Sir Robert Michael Owen, Sir Colin Crichton Mackay, Sir John Edward Mitting, Sir David Roderick Evans, Sir Nigel Anthony Lamert Davis, Sir Peter Henry Gross, Sir Brian Richard Keith, Sir Jeremy Lionel Cooke, Sir Richard Alan Field, Sir Colman Maurice Treacy, Sir Peregrine Charles Hugo Simon, Sir Roger John Royce, Dame Laura Mary Cox, Sir Adrian Bruce Fulford, Sir Jack Beatson, Sir Michael George Tugendhat, Sir David Clive Clarke, Dame Elizabeth Gloster, Sir David Michael Bean, Sir Alan Fraser Wilkie, Dame Linda Penelope Dobbs, Sir Henry Egar Garfield Hodge, Sir Paul James Walker, Sir David Calvert-Smith, Sir Christopher Simon Courtenay Stephenson Clarke, Sir Charles Peter Lawford Openshaw, Dame Caroline Jane Swift, Sir Brian Frederick James Langstaff, Sir David Lloyd Jones, Sir Vivian Arthur Ramsay, Sir Nicholas Edward Underhill, Sir Stephen John Irwin, Sir Nigel John Martin Teare, Sir John Griffith Williams, Sir Wyn Lewis Williams, Sir Timothy Roger Alan King, Sir John Henry Boulton Saunders, Sir Julian Martin Flaux, Sir Nicholas Felix Stadlen, Sir Robert Akenhead, Sir David Robert Foskett, Sir Nicholas John Gorrod Blake, Sir Ross Frederick Cranston, Sir Peter David William Coulson, Sir David Maddison, Sir Richard Owen Plender, Sir William James Lynton Blair, Sir Alistair Geoffrey MacDuff.

Family Division

President: Sir Mark Howard Potter.

Judges: Sir Jan Peter Singer, Sir Andrew Tristam Hammett Kirkwood, Sir Hugh Peter Derwyn Bennett, Sir Edward James Holman, Dame Mary Claire Hogg, Sir Arthur William Hessin Charles, Sir David Roderick Lessiter Bodey, Dame Jill Margaret Black, Sir James Lawrence Munby, Sir Paul James Duke Coleridge, Sir Mark Hedley, Dame Anna Evelyn Hamilton Pauffley, Sir Roderic Lionel James Wood, Dame Florence Jacquelene Baron, Sir Ernest Nigel Ryder, Sir Andrew Ewart McFarlane, Dame Julia Wendy Macur, Sir Andrew John Gregory Moylan, Dame Eleanor Warwick King.

COURT OF APPEAL

An appeal lies in civil cases to this court from County Courts and the High Court of Justice and in criminal cases from the Crown Courts. The Master of the Rolls is the effective head of the court.

Ex Officio Judges

Lord Chief Justice of England and Wales: Lord Phillips of Worth Matravers.

Master of the Rolls: Sir Anthony Peter Clarke.

President of the Queen's Bench Division: Sir Igor Judge.

President of the Family Division: Sir Mark Howard Potter.

Chancellor of the High Court: Sir Robert Andrew Morritt.

Lords Justices of Appeal: Sir Malcolm Thomas Pill, Sir Alan Hylton Ward, Sir Mathew Alexander Thorpe, Sir George Mark Waller (Vice-President Civil Division of the Court of Appeal), Sir John Frank Mummery, Sir Richard Joseph Buxton, Sir Anthony Tristram Kenneth May (Vice-President Queen's Bench Division of the High Court), Sir Simon Lane Tuckey, Sir John Grant McKenzie Laws, Sir Stephen John Sedley, Sir David Nicholas Ramsey Latham (Vice-President Criminal Division of the Court of Appeal), Sir Bernard Anthony Rix, Dame Mary Howarth Arden, Sir David Wolfe Keene, Sir John Anthony Dyson, Sir Andrew Centlivres Longmore, Sir Robert John Anderson Carnwath, Sir Thomas Scott Gillespie Baker, Dame Janet Hilary Smith, Sir Roger John Laugharne Thomas, Sir Robert Raphael Hayim (Robin) Jacob, Sir Nicholas Peter Rathbone Wall, Sir Maurice Ralph Kay, Sir Anthony Hooper, Sir William Marcus Gage, Sir Timothy Andrew Wigram Lloyd, Sir Martin James Moore-Bick (Deputy Head of Civil Justice), Sir Nicholas Allan Roy Wilson, Sir Alan George Moses, Sir Stephen Price Richards, Dame Heather Carol Hallett, Sir Anthony Phillip Gilson Hughes, Sir Brian Henry Leveson, Sir Lawrence Anthony Collins, Sir Roger Grenfell Toulson, Sir Colin Percy Farquharson Rimer, Sir Stanley Jeffrey Burnton.

HOUSE OF LORDS

In civil and criminal cases this is the final court of appeal.

Senior Lord of Appeal in Ordinary: Lord Bingham of Cornhill.

Second Senior Lord of Appeal in Ordinary: Lord Hoffmann.

Lords of Appeal in Ordinary: Lord Hope of Craighead, Lord Saville of Newdigate, Lord Scott of Foscote, Lord Rodger of Earlsferry, Lord Walker of Gestingthorpe, Lady Hale of Richmond, Lord Carswell, Lord Brown of Eaton-under-Heywood, Lord Mance, Lord Neuberger of Abbotsbury.

JUDICIAL COMMITTEE OF THE PRIVY COUNCIL

Final court of appeal for appeals from certain Commonwealth territories; also exercises domestic jurisdiction in ecclesiastical matters and appeals from disciplinary tribunals of certain professions.

Northern Irish Judicial System

The judicial system of Northern Ireland, so far as the Supreme Court is concerned, is a miniature of the English system, and is based on the Judicature (Northern Ireland) Act 1978. It consists, as in England, of the High Court, the Court of Appeal, and the Crown Court (which has jurisdiction in criminal matters). The jurisdiction of the Magistrates' Courts (Courts of Summary Jurisdiction) is exercised by a permanent judiciary of legally qualified resident magistrates.

COUNTY COURTS

The county court system corresponds to its English counterpart, but there is no system of pleadings, as is found in the English county court. There are also variations in jurisdiction levels. County court judges share with the judges of the High Court the exercise of the jurisdiction of the Crown Court.

HIGH COURT

The Lord Chief Justice of Northern Ireland: Sir Brian Kerr (President), Royal Courts of Justice, Chichester St, Belfast, BT1 3JF; tel. (28) 9023-5111; fax (28) 9031-3508; e-mail adminoffice@courtsni.gov.uk; internet www.courtsni.gov.uk.

Judges: Sir Patrick Coghlin, Sir John Gillen, Sir Richard McLaughlin, Sir Ronald Weatherup, Sir Reginald Weir, Sir Charles Morgan, Sir Donnell Deeny, Sir Anthony Ronald Hart, Sir William Benjamin Synge Stephens, Sir Seamus Treacy.

COURT OF APPEAL

President: The Lord Chief Justice of Northern Ireland

Judges: Sir Malachy Higgins, Sir Paul Frederick Girvan, Sir Anthony Campbell.

Scottish Judicial System

CRIMINAL COURTS

Minor offences are dealt with in District courts.

Sheriff Court

Most criminal actions, including all but the most serious offences, are tried in this court. Each of the six sheriffdoms of Scotland has a Sheriff Principal and a number of Sheriffs, who hear the cases.

High Court of Justiciary

This is the supreme criminal court in Scotland: all the most serious cases are taken there. Appeal may be made to it from the Sheriff Court and from the District courts; there is, however, no further appeal to the House of Lords.

The 32 judges of this court are known as Lords Commissioners of Justiciary and are headed by the Lord Justice General and the Lord Justice Clerk. Apart from their criminal jurisdiction in this court, these judges are also judges of the Court of Session (see below) in civil cases. The Lord Justice General is also the President of the Court of Session.

High Court in Edinburgh: Lawnmarket, Edinburgh, EH1 2PE; tel. (131) 240-6900; fax (131) 240-6915; e-mail supreme.courts@scotcourts.gov.uk; internet www.scotcourts.gov.uk.

High Court in Glasgow: Saltmarket, Glasgow, G1 5JU; tel. (141) 552-3795; fax (140) 559-4519; e-mail supreme.courts@scotcourts.gov.uk; internet www.scotcourts.gov.uk.

CIVIL COURTS

Sheriff Court

This court hears civil as well as criminal cases, and in civil cases its jurisdiction is practically unlimited. It has concurrent jurisdiction with the Court of Session in divorce actions. Appeal may be made to the Court of Session or the Sheriff Principal.

THE UNITED KINGDOM

Court of Session

This is the supreme civil court in Scotland. It has an Inner House and an Outer House.

The Inner House has two divisions of equal standing, each consisting of five judges (the quorum is three although due to pressure of business an extra division of three judges frequently sits) under the presidency of the Lord President and the Lord Justice Clerk respectively; it is mainly an appeal court, whence further appeal may be made to the House of Lords.

Court of Session: Parliament House, Parliament Sq., Edinburgh, EH1 1RQ; tel. (131) 225-2595; fax (131) 240-6755; e-mail supreme.courts@scotcourts.gov.uk; internet www.scotcourts.gov.uk.

First Division

Lord Justice General and President of the Court of Session: Lord HAMILTON.

Judges: Lord NIMMO SMITH, Lord REED, Lord KINGARTH, Lord EASSIE.

Second Division

Lord Justice Clerk: Lord GILL.

Judges: Lord OSBORNE, Lord JOHNSTON, Lord WHEATLEY, Lady PATON.

The Outer House deals with the major civil cases and divorce actions. The judges are those of the High Court of Justiciary, sitting in a civil capacity as judges of the Court of Session.

Judges: Lord CARLOWAY, Lord CLARKE, Lord HARDIE, Lord MACKAY OF DRUMADOON, Lord MCEWAN, Lord MENZIES, Lord DRUMMOND YOUNG, Lord EMSLIE, Lady SMITH, Lord BRODIE, Lord BRACADALE, Lady DORRIAN, Lord HODGE, Lord MACPHAIL, Lord GLENNIE, Lord KINCLAVEN, Lord TURNBULL, Lady CLARK OF CALTON, Lord BRAILSFORD, Lord UIST, Lord MALCOLM, Lord MATTHEWS, Lord WOOLMAN.

Religion

CHRISTIANITY

Churches Together in Britain and Ireland: Bastille Court, 2 Paris Garden, London, SE1 8ND; tel. (20) 7654-7254; fax (20) 7654-7222; e-mail info@ctbi.org.uk; internet www.ctbi.org.uk; f. 1990 as successor to the British Council of Churches; co-ordinates the activities of its 38 member churches and liaises with ecumenical bodies in Britain and Ireland. Its work divisions include Church Life, Church and Society and International Affairs, Spirituality, Racial Justice, Mission and Inter-faith Relations. It provides a forum for joint decision-making and enables the churches to take action together; Gen. Sec. Rev. Canon BOB FYFFE.

Action of Churches Together in Scotland (ACTS): Inglewood House, Alloa, FK15 2HU; tel. (1259) 216980; fax (1259) 215964; e-mail ecumenical@acts-scotland.org; internet www.acts-scotland.org; aims to encourage and express unity of Christian Churches in Scotland; Convener Rev. MARY BUCHANAN; Gen. Sec. STEPHEN SMYTH.

Churches Together in England (CTE): 27 Tavistock Sq., London, WC1H 9HH; tel. (20) 7529-8131; fax (20) 7529-8134; e-mail office@cte.org.uk; internet www.churches-together.org.uk; f. 1990; 29 mem. bodies; Pres Most Rev. and Rt Hon. Dr ROWAN WILLIAMS, ELIZABETH MATEAR, Rt Rev. NATHAN HOVHANNISIAN, H.E. Cardinal CORMAC MURPHY-O'CONNOR; Gen. Sec. Rev. DAVID CORNICK.

Churches Together in Wales (Cytûn): 58 Richmond Rd, Cardiff, CF24 3UR; tel. (29) 2046-4204; e-mail post@cytun.org.uk; internet www.cytun.org.uk; fmrly the Council of Churches for Wales; Chief Exec. Rev. ALED EDWARDS.

Irish Council of Churches: Inter-Church Centre, 48 Elmwood Ave, Belfast, BT9 6AZ; tel. (28) 9066-3145; fax (28) 9066-4160; e-mail michael@irishchurches.org; internet www.irishchurches.org; f. 1922 (present name adopted 1966); 15 mem. churches; the organization of the churches in Ireland takes no account of the partition of the island into two separate political entities, with Ireland and Northern Ireland thus subject to a unified jurisdiction for ecclesiastical purposes; Pres. Rev. TONY DAVIDSON; Gen. Sec. MICHAEL EARLE.

The Anglican Communion

The Church of England

The Church of England is the Established Church, and as such acknowledges the authority of Parliament in matters in which secular authority is competent to exercise control. Queen Elizabeth I was declared 'supreme Governor on Earth' of the Church of England, and the Sovereign is consecrated to this office at coronation.

In England, there are two Provinces, Canterbury and York. The former contains 30, the latter 14, dioceses. Each Province has its ancient Convocations, the Upper and Lower House. By the Enabling Act the Constitution of the National Assembly of the Church of England ('Church Assembly') received statutory recognition in 1920, with power, subject to the control and authority of Parliament, of initiating legislation on all matters concerning the Church of England. Measures passed by the Assembly and approved by Parliament were submitted for the Royal Assent, having the force of Acts of Parliament.

In 1970, by the Synodical Government Measure (1969), the Church Assembly was reconstituted as the General Synod and was also given authority to exercise most of the functions of the Convocations. The House of Bishops consists of members of the Upper House of the Convocations (53 persons). The House of Clergy consists of the Lower Houses (a maximum of 259 persons). The House of Laity consists almost entirely of representatives of the dioceses elected by the deanery synods (a maximum of 258 persons).

In 2001 there were 1,372,000 people on the Church's electoral rolls. The Archbishops and the 24 senior Bishops sit in the House of Lords.

Archbishop of Canterbury, Primate of All England and Metropolitan: Most Rev. and Rt Hon. Dr ROWAN WILLIAMS, Lambeth Palace, London, SE1 7JU; tel. (20) 7898-1200; fax (20) 7261-9836; internet www.archbishopofcanterbury.org.

Archbishop of York, Primate of England and Metropolitan: Rt Rev. and Rt Hon. JOHN SENTAMU, Bishopthorpe Palace, Bishopthorpe, York, YO23 2GE; tel. (1904) 707021; fax (1904) 709204; e-mail office@archbishopofyork.org; internet www.archbishopofyork.org.

General Synod of the Church of England: Church House, Great Smith St, London, SW1P 3AZ; tel. (20) 7898-1000; fax (20) 7898-1369; e-mail synod@c-of-e.org.uk; internet www.cofe.anglican.org; 467 mems; Sec.-Gen. WILLIAM FITTALL.

The Church of Ireland

The See House, Cathedral Close, Armagh, BT61 7EE; tel. (28) 3752-7144; fax (28) 3752-7823; e-mail enquiries@ireland.anglican.org; internet www.ireland.anglican.org.

Ireland (including Northern Ireland) comprises two archdioceses and 10 dioceses; in 2006 there were 275,000 members of the Church of Ireland in Northern Ireland.

Archbishop of Armagh and Primate of All Ireland: Most Rev. ALAN HARPER, The See House, Cathedral Close, Armagh, BT61 7EE; tel. (28) 3752-7144; fax (28) 3752-7823; e-mail archbishop@armagh.anglican.org.

The Church in Wales

39 Cathedral Rd, Cardiff, CF11 9XF; tel. (29) 2034-8200; fax (29) 2038-7835; e-mail information@churchinwales.org.uk; internet www.churchinwales.org.uk.

The Province of Wales was created as a result of the Welsh Church Act of 1914, which took effect on 31 March 1920 and separated the four Welsh Dioceses from the Province of Canterbury. It is divided into six Dioceses served by 620 stipendiary clerics. The number of Easter communicants is approximately 75,000. The Church in Wales has an administrative governing body which is a legislative assembly composed of bishops, clergy and laity, and a representative body incorporated by Royal Charter, which holds and manages the property and central funds of the Church; Provincial Sec. JOHN SHIRLEY.

Archbishop of Wales: Most Rev Dr BARRY C. MORGAN, Llys Esgob, Cathedral Green, Llandaff, Cardiff, CF5 2YE; tel. (29) 2056-2400; fax (29) 2056-8410; e-mail archbishop@churchinwales.org.uk.

The Scottish Episcopal Church

21 Grosvenor Cres., Edinburgh, EH12 5EE; tel. (131) 225-6357; fax (131) 346-7247; e-mail office@scotland.anglican.org; internet www.scotland.anglican.org.

Formerly the Established Church of Scotland, was disestablished and disendowed in 1689; is in full communion with all branches of the Anglican Communion; seven dioceses: Aberdeen and Orkney, Argyll and The Isles, Brechin, Edinburgh, Glasgow and Galloway, Moray, Ross and Caithness, and St Andrews, Dunkeld and Dunblane. There is a Bishop in each diocese; one of them is elected by the other Bishops as the Primus; Churches, mission stations, etc. 310, clergy 402, communicants 29,810; Sec.-Gen. to the General Synod JOHN STUART.

Primus: Most Rev. IDRIS JONES (Bishop of Glasgow and Galloway), The Diocesan Centre, 5 St Vincent Pl., Glasgow, G1 2DH; tel. (141) 2215720; fax (141) 2217014; e-mail office@glasgow.anglican.org; internet www.glasgow.anglican.org.

The Roman Catholic Church

For ecclesiastical purposes Great Britain comprises seven archdioceses and 23 dioceses. There is also an apostolic exarchate for the

THE UNITED KINGDOM

Ukrainian Rite. Ireland (including Northern Ireland) comprises four archdioceses and 22 dioceses. The dioceses of Down and Connor and Dromore are completely in Northern Ireland, while the archdiocese of Armagh and the dioceses of Derry and Clogher are partly in Northern Ireland and partly in Ireland. At 31 December 2005 there were an estimated 4,060,003 adherents in England and Wales, of whom about 50,000 were of the Ukrainian Rite, and an estimated 709,743 adherents in Scotland. At the 2001 census 40.3% of the population of Northern Ireland gave their religion as Catholic or Roman Catholic.

Latin Rite

Bishops' Conference of England and Wales

39 Eccleston Sq., London, SW1V 1BX; tel. (20) 7630-8220; fax (20) 7901-4821; e-mail secretariat@cbcew.org.uk; internet catholicchurch.org.uk; President H.E. Cardinal CORMAC MURPHY-O'CONNOR (Archbishop of Westminster); Gen. Sec. Mgr ANDREW SUMMERSGILL.

Archbishop of Westminster: H.E. Cardinal CORMAC MURPHY-O'CONNOR, Archbishop's House, Westminster, London, SW1P 1QJ; tel. (20) 7798-9033; fax (20) 7798-9077; e-mail archbishop@rcdow.org.uk; internet www.rcdow.org.uk/archbishop.

Archbishop of Birmingham: Most Rev. VINCENT NICHOLS, Archbishop's House, 8 Shadwell St, Queensway, Birmingham, B4 6EY; tel. (121) 236-9090; fax (121) 212-0171; e-mail archbishop@rc-birmingham.org; internet www.birminghamdiocese.org.uk.

Archbishop of Liverpool: Most Rev. PATRICK ALTHAM KELLY, Archbishop's House, Lowood, Carnatic Road, Mossley Hill, Liverpool, L18 8BY; tel. (151) 724-6398; fax (151) 724-6405; e-mail archbishop.liverpool@rcaolp.co.uk; internet www.archdiocese-of-liverpool.co.uk.

Archbishop of Southwark: Most Rev. KEVIN JOHN MCDONALD, Archbishop's House, 150 St George's Rd, Southwark, London, SE1 6HX; tel. (20) 7928-2495; fax (20) 7928-7833; e-mail secswk@rcsouthwark.co.uk; internet www.rcsouthwark.co.uk.

Archbishop of Cardiff: Most Rev. PETER SMITH, Archbishop's House, 41–43 Cathedral Rd, Cardiff, South Glamorgan, CF11 9HD; tel. (29) 2022-0411; fax (29) 2037-9036; e-mail arch@rcacd.org; internet www.rcacd.org.

Archbishop of Armagh and Primate of All Ireland: Cardinal SEÁN B. BRADY, Ara Coeli, Armagh, BT61 7QY; tel. (28) 3752-2045; fax (28) 3752-6182; e-mail admin@aracoeli.com; internet www.armagharchdiocese.org.

Bishops' Conference of Scotland

64 Aitken St, Airdrie, ML6 6LT; tel. (1236) 764061; fax (1236) 762489; e-mail gensec@bpsconfscot.com; internet www.bpsconfscot.com; President HE Cardinal KEITH MICHAEL PATRICK O'BRIEN (Archbishop of St Andrews and Edinburgh); Gen. Sec. Rev. PAUL M. CONROY.

Archbishop of St Andrews and Edinburgh: HE Cardinal KEITH MICHAEL PATRICK O'BRIEN, Archbishop's House, 42 Greenhill Gdns, Edinburgh, EH10 4BJ; tel. (131) 447-3337; fax (131) 447-0816; e-mail cardinal@staned.org.uk; internet www.archdiocese-edinburgh.com.

Archbishop of Glasgow: Most Rev. MARIO JOSEPH CONTI, Curial Offices, 196 Clyde St, Glasgow, G1 4JY; tel. (141) 226-5898; fax (141) 225-2600; e-mail info@rcag.org.uk; internet www.rcag.org.uk.

Ukrainian Rite

Apostolic Exarch: (vacant), Bishop's House, 22 Binney St, London, W1Y 1YN; tel. (20) 7629-1073; fax (20) 7355-3314; e-mail frben@catholic.org; internet www.cerkva.org.uk.

Protestant Churches

Association of Baptist Churches in Ireland: 19 Hillsborough Rd, Moira, Craigavon, County Armagh, BT67 0HG; tel. (28) 9261-9267; e-mail abc@thebaptistcentre.org; internet www.baptistireland.org; 111 churches; 93 ministers; 8,446 mems; Pres. Pastor DEREK BAXTER; Dir Pastor WILLIAM COLVILLE.

Baptist Union of Great Britain: Baptist House, POB 44, 129 Broadway, Didcot, Oxfordshire, OX11 8RT; tel. (1235) 517700; fax (1235) 517715; e-mail info@baptist.org.uk; internet www.baptist.org.uk; f. 1813; the Baptist form of church government is congregational; baptism by immersion of believers is practised; the Churches are grouped in associations; mems (2005) 138,364; Gen. Sec. Rev. JONATHAN P. EDWARDS.

Church of Scotland: 121 George St, Edinburgh, EH2 4YN; tel. (131) 225-5722; fax (131) 220-3113; e-mail lturnbull@cofscotland.org.uk; internet www.churchofscotland.org.uk; the national Church of Scotland was reformed in 1560, and became Presbyterian in doctrine and constitution. In 1921 the Church of Scotland Act was passed, by which the articles declaring the full spiritual freedom of the Church are recognized as lawful. In 1925 the Church of Scotland (Property and Endowments) Act became law, and made over to the Church of Scotland places of worship, manses and endowments in absolute property, vesting the future control of them in Trustees. The union of the Church of Scotland and the United Free Church was effected in 1929; Moderator Rev. SHELAGH KESTING; Lord High Commr to the 2007 General Assembly HRH THE DUKE OF YORK; 600,000 mems.

Elim Pentecostal Church: PO Box 38, Cheltenham, Glos, GL50 3HN; tel. (1242) 519904; fax (1242) 222279; e-mail info@elimhq.org.net; internet www.elim.org.uk; f. 1915; c. 580 churches and 60,000 adherents in Great Britain; Gen. Superintendent Rev. JOHN GLASS.

Free Church of Scotland: 15 North Bank St, The Mound, Edinburgh, EH1 2LS; tel. (131) 226-5286; fax (131) 220-0597; e-mail catherine@freechurchofscotland.org.uk; internet www.freechurch.org; f. 1843; 103 congregations; Principal Clerk of Assembly Rev. JAMES MACIVER.

Free Churches Group, Churches Together in England: 27 Tavistock Sq., London, WC1H 9HH; tel. (20) 7529-8131; fax (20) 7529-8134; e-mail office@cte.org.uk; internet www.churches-together.net; central body for the co-ordination of the work of the Free Churches throughout England and Wales; Moderator Cmmr ELIZABETH MATEAR; Exec. Sec. Rev. MARK FISHER.

Lutheran Council of Great Britain: 30 Thanet St, London, WC1H 9QH; tel. (20) 7554-2900; fax (20) 7383-3081; e-mail enquiries@lutheran.org.uk; internet www.lutheran.org.uk; Chair. Rev. JUHA RINTAMÄKI; Gen. Sec. Rev. THOMAS BRUCH.

Methodist Church: Methodist Church House, 25 Marylebone Rd, London, NW1 5JR; tel. (20) 7486-5502; fax (20) 7224-5228; e-mail enquiries@methodistchurch.org.uk; internet www.methodist.org.uk; f. 1739 by Rev. John Wesley, a priest of the Church of England; the governing body of the Church is the Annual Conference, which consists of ministers and lay representatives. The Church throughout Great Britain is divided into 33 Districts, and these hold their Synod Meetings in the autumn and the spring. The Districts are divided into Circuits, which hold regular Circuit Meetings, made up of representatives from the churches within the Circuit. There are also local Church Councils; 293,661 mems (2004); Pres. of the Methodist Conference (2007/08) Rev. Dr MARTIN ATKINS (designate); Gen. Sec. of the Methodist Conference Rev. DAVID DEEKS.

Methodist Church in Ireland: 1 Fountainville Ave, Belfast, BT9 6AN; tel. (28) 9032-4554; fax (28) 9023-9467; e-mail secretary@irishmethodist.org; internet www.irishmethodist.org; 220 churches; 303 ministers; 53,990 mems; Pres. Rev. ROBERT COOPER; Sec. Rev. DONALD P. KER.

Moravian Church: 5 Muswell Hill, London, N10 3TJ; tel. (20) 8883-3409; fax (20) 8365-3371; e-mail office@moravian.org.uk; internet www.moravian.org.uk; f. 1457; Sec. Provincial Board JACKIE MORTEN.

Moravian Church in Ireland: 37 Deramore Park South, Malone Rd, Belfast, BT9 5JY; tel. (28) 9068-1554; e-mail derick.woods@btinternet.com; f. 1746; Chair. of Conf. DERICK WOODS.

Non-Subscribing Presbyterian Church of Ireland: 41A Rosemary St, Belfast, BT1 1QB; tel. and fax (28) 9032-5365; e-mail info@nspresbyterian.org; internet www.nspresbyterian.org; Moderator Rt. Rev. TOM BANHAM; Clerk Rev. NIGEL PLAYFAIR.

Presbyterian Church in Ireland: Church House, Fisherwick Pl., Belfast, BT1 6DW; tel. (28) 9032-2284; fax (28) 9041-7301; e-mail info@presbyterianireland.org; internet www.presbyterianireland.org; 549 churches; 382 ministers; 262,000 mems, 28,000 in 550 Sunday Schools; Moderator of the Gen. Assembly Rev. Dr JOHN FINLAY; Clerk of Assembly and Gen. Sec. Rev. Dr DONALD WATTS.

Presbyterian Church of Wales: 81 Merthyr Rd, Whitchurch, Cardiff, CF14 1DD; tel. (29) 2062-7465; fax (29) 2061-6188; e-mail swyddfa.office@ebcpcw.org.uk; internet www.ebcpcw.org.uk; f. 1811; 832 churches, 77 full-time ministers, 34,819 mems (2005); Moderator of General Assembly Rev. JOHN OWEN; Gen. Sec. Rev. IFAN RH ROBERTS.

The Religious Society of Friends (Quakers) in Britain: Friends House, 173 Euston Rd, London, NW1 2BJ; tel. (20) 7663-1000; fax (20) 7663-1001; e-mail enquiries@quaker.org.uk; internet www.quaker.org.uk; f. mid-17th century by George Fox; the Quakers have 15,800 mems and 8,400 'attenders' in Great Britain; Recording Clerk (Sec.) HELEN GRIFFITH.

Salvation Army: 101 Newington Causeway, London, SE1 6BN; tel. (20) 7367-4500; fax (20) 7367-4728; e-mail info@salvationarmy.org.uk; internet www.salvationarmy.org.uk; f. 1865; Territorial Commdr JOHN MATEAR.

Union of Welsh Independents: Tŷ John Penri, 5 Axis Court, Riverside Business Park, Swansea Vale, Swansea, SA7 0AJ; tel. (1792) 795888; fax (1792) 795376; e-mail undeb@annibynwyr.org; internet www.annibynwyr.org; Pres. Rev. DEWI MYRDDIN HUGHES; Gen. Sec. Rev. Dr GERAINT TUDUR.

United Free Church of Scotland: 11 Newton Place, Glasgow, G3 7PR; tel. (141) 332-3435; fax (141) 333-1973; e-mail office@ufcos.org

THE UNITED KINGDOM

.uk; internet www.ufcos.org.uk; f. 1900; 64 congregations, 32 ministers and pastors, 4,000 mems; Moderator Rev. DAVID CARTLEDGE; Gen. Sec. Rev. JOHN O. FULTON.

United Reformed Church: United Reformed Church House, 86 Tavistock Pl., London, WC1H 9RT; tel. (20) 7916-2020; fax (20) 7916-2021; e-mail urc@urc.org.uk; internet www.urc.org.uk; f. 1972 by union of the Congregational Church in England and Wales and the Presbyterian Church of England; joined by the Churches of Christ 1981 and by the Scottish Congregational Church 2000; approx. 1,800 churches and 250,000 mems; Moderator Rev. Dr STEPHEN ORCHARD; Gen. Sec. Rev. Dr DAVID CORNICK.

Orthodox Churches

Council of Oriental Orthodox Churches: 34 Chertsey Rd, Church Sq., Shepperton, Middx, TW17 9LF; tel. and fax (1932) 232913; Sec. Deacon AZIZ M. A. NOUR.

Armenian Apostolic Church: POB 46207, London, W5 2YE; tel. (20) 7937-0152; fax (20) 7937-9049; e-mail info@accc.org.uk; internet www.accc.org.uk; Primate Bishop NATHAN HOVHANNISIAN.

Greek Orthodox Church (Archdiocese of Thyateira and Great Britain of the Oecumenical Patriarchate): Thyateira House, 5 Craven Hill, London, W2 3EN; tel. (20) 7723-4787; fax (20) 7224-9301; e-mail mail@thyateira.org.uk; internet www.thyateira.org.uk; f. 1922; Archbishop of Thyateira and Great Britain GREGORIOS; Chancellor Bishop ATHANASIOS OF TROPAEOU.

Russian Orthodox Patriarchal Church in Great Britain: Cathedral of the Assumption and All Saints, Ennismore Gdns, London, SW7 1NH; tel. (20) 7584-0096; fax (20) 7584-9864; e-mail sourozh@mail.ru; internet www.sourozh.org; Bishop ELISEY OF SOUROZH.

Serbian Orthodox Church: 131 Cob Lane, Bournville, Birmingham, B30 1QE; tel. (121) 458-5273; fax (121) 458-4986; Very Rev. MILENKO ZEBIĆ.

Other Christian Churches

First Church of Christ, Scientist: 8 Wright's Lane, Kensington, London, W8 6TA; tel. (20) 7937-3389; fax (20) 7937-3341; e-mail fccslon@tiscali.co.uk; internet www.ccs.org.uk; f. 1879; the Mother Church is the First Church of Christ, Scientist, in Boston, MA (USA); approx. 150 churches in Great Britain; District Man. for Great Britain and Ireland TONY LOBL.

Church of Jesus Christ of Latter-day Saints (Mormon): Press Office, 751 Warwick Rd, Solihull, West Midlands, B91 3DQ; tel. (121) 712-1202; fax (121) 712-1126; e-mail mclavertymw@ldschurch.org; internet www.lds.org.uk; f. 1830; c. 181,000 mems (2004); Area Pres. ELDER KENNETH JOHNSON.

General Assembly of Unitarian and Free Christian Churches: Essex Hall, 1–6 Essex St, London, WC2R 3HY; tel. (20) 7240-2384; fax (20) 7240-3089; e-mail ga@unitarian.org.uk; internet www.unitarian.org.uk; f. 1928; Chief Exec. STEVE DICK.

Jehovah's Witnesses: Watch Tower House, The Ridgeway, London, NW7 1RN; tel. (20) 8906-2211; fax (20) 8371-0051; internet www.watchtower.org; f. 1900; there were an estimated 130,000 Jehovah's Witnesses in the UK in 2007.

Seventh-day Adventist Church Headquarters: Stanborough Park, Watford, Herts, WD25 9JZ; tel. (1923) 672251; fax (1923) 893212; e-mail info@adventist.org.uk; internet www.adventist.org.uk; f. 1863; there were an estimated 28,000 mems. in approx. 300 congregations across the UK and Ireland in late 2007; Communication Dir VICTOR HULBERT.

Spiritualists' National Union: Redwoods, Stansted Hall, Stansted Mountfitchet, Essex, CM24 8UD; tel. (845) 458-0768; fax (1279) 812034; e-mail snu@snu.org.uk; internet www.snu.org.uk; f. 1891 (and inc. 1901); for the advancement of Spiritualism as a religion and a religious philosophy, it is a trust corporation officially recognized as the central and national body representing the Spiritualists of Great Britain; conducts the Arthur Findlay College of Psychic Science; c. 400 Spiritualist churches, societies and 20,000 individual mems; Pres. DUNCAN P. GASCOYNE; Gen. Sec. CHARLES S. COULSTON.

ISLAM

The Muslim community in the United Kingdom, which according to the 2001 census numbered 1.59m., consists mainly of people from the Indian sub-continent and their British-born descendants. The chief concentrations of Muslims are in London, the Midlands, South Wales, Lancashire and Yorkshire. There are more than 900 mosques in the United Kingdom; the oldest is the Shah Jehan Mosque in Woking, Surrey.

London Central Mosque Trust and Islamic Cultural Centre: 146 Park Rd, London, NW8 7RG; tel. (20) 7725-2213; fax (20) 7724-0493; e-mail info@iccuk.org; internet www.iccuk.org; Dir-Gen. Dr AHMAD AD-DUBAYAN.

Muslim Council of Britain: POB 57330, London, E1 2WJ; tel. (845) 2626786; fax (20) 7247-7079; e-mail admin@mcb.org.uk; internet www.mcb.org.uk; f. 1997; Sec.-Gen. Dr MUHAMMAD ABDUL BARI.

SIKHISM

According to the 2001 census, there were 336,000 Sikhs in the United Kingdom, who originally came from the Punjab region of the Indian sub-continent as well as from East Africa, although many are now British-born. Each gurdwara (temple) is independent, and there is no central national body.

Sikh Missionary Society, UK: 10 Featherstone Rd, Southall, Middx, UB2 5AA; tel. (20) 8574-1902; fax (20) 8574-1912; e-mail info@sikhmissionarysociety.org; internet www.sikhmissionarysociety.org; promotes Sikhism and acts as a resource centre for information and literature; Hon. Gen. Sec. SURINDER SINGH PUREWAL.

HINDUISM

According to the 2001 census, there were 559,000 Hindus in the United Kingdom, with their origins in India, East Africa and Sri Lanka, although many are now British by birth. Hindus in the United Kingdom are concentrated in London, the Midlands and Yorkshire.

JUDAISM

The Jewish community in the United Kingdom numbered 267,000, according to the 2001 census. There are about 350 synagogues in the United Kingdom.

Chief Rabbi of the United Hebrew Congregations of the Commonwealth: Rabbi Prof. Sir JONATHAN SACKS, Office of the Chief Rabbi, Alder House, 735 High Rd, London, N12 0US; tel. (20) 8343-6301; fax (20) 8343-6310; e-mail info@chiefrabbi.org; internet www.chiefrabbi.org.

Court of the Chief Rabbi (Beth Din): 735 High Rd, London, N12 0US; tel. (20) 8343-6270; fax (20) 8343-6257; e-mail info@bethdin.org.uk; Registrar D. FREI.

There is no comprehensive organization of synagogues covering the country as a whole. In London and the South-East there are the following major synagogue organizations:

Liberal Judaism: The Montagu Centre, 21 Maple St, London, W1T 4BE; tel. (20) 7580-1663; fax (20) 7631-9838; e-mail montagu@liberaljudaism.org; internet www.liberaljudaism.org; f. 1902; 9,300 mems, 31 affiliated synagogues, 3 assoc. communities; Chief Exec. Rabbi DANNY RICH.

Movement for Reform Judaism: The Sternberg Centre for Judaism, 80 East End Rd, Finchley, London, N3 2SY; tel. (020) 8349-5640; fax (20) 8349-5699; e-mail admin@reformjudaism.org.uk; internet www.reformjudaism.org.uk; Head Rabbi Dr TONY BAYFIELD.

Spanish and Portuguese Jews' Congregation: 2 Ashworth Rd, London, W9 1JY; tel. (20) 7289-2573; fax (20) 7289-2709; e-mail howardmiller@spsyn.org.uk; internet www.sandp.org; f. 1657; Pres. of the Bd of Elders BERNARD MOCATTA; Chief Exec. HOWARD MILLER.

Union of Orthodox Hebrew Congregations (UOHC): 140 Stamford Hill, London, N16 6QT; tel. (20) 8802-6226; fax (20) 8809-6590; e-mail ck@uohc.org.uk; f. 1926; over 100 affiliated synagogues in the United Kingdom and other Commonwealth countries; Gen. Sec. CHAI SCHNECK.

United Synagogue: Adler House, 735 High Rd, London, N12 0US; tel. (20) 8343-8989; fax (20) 8343-6262; internet www.theus.org.uk; f. 1870 by Act of Parliament; Pres. Dr SIMON HOCHHAUSER; Chief Exec. STUART TAYLOR (acting).

West London Synagogue of British Jews: 33 Seymour Pl., London, W1H 5AU; tel. (20) 7723-4404; fax (20) 7224-8258; e-mail admin@wls.org.uk; internet www.wls.org.uk; f. 1840; c. 4,000 mems; Senior Rabbi MARK L. WINER; Exec. Dir ALAN SHAPIRO.

BUDDHISM

According to the 2001 census, the Buddhist community in the United Kingdom numbered 152,000.

Buddhist Society: 58 Eccleston Sq., London, SW1V 1PH; tel. (20) 7834-5858; fax (20) 7976-5238; e-mail info@thebuddhistsociety.org; internet www.thebuddhistsociety.org; f. 1924; Registrar LOUISE MARCHANT.

BAHÁ'Í FAITH

National Spiritual Assembly of the Bahá'ís of the United Kingdom: 27 Rutland Gate, London, SW7 1PD; tel. (20) 7584-2566; fax (20) 7584-9402; e-mail nsa@bahai.org.uk; internet www.bahai.org.uk; f. 1923; Sec. Dr KISHAN MANOCHA; Chair. SHIRIN TAHZIB.

The Press

The United Kingdom has some of the highest circulation figures in the world for individual newspapers (*Daily Mail* 2.2m., *The Sun* 3.0m., *News of the World* 3.0m.). At 1 January 2004 there were more than 2,600 regional and local daily and weekly newspapers (including free titles) in the United Kingdom and the total weekly circulation of all newspapers was 136.4m.

There is no law which specifies the operations of the press but several items of legislation bear directly on press activities. Although exact reporting of legal proceedings appearing at the time of trial is protected from later charges of defamation, the freedom to report cases is subject to certain restrictions as defined in the Judicial Proceedings Act of 1926, in the Children's and Young Persons' Act of 1933 and in the Criminal Justice Act 1967. The strict laws of contempt of court and of libel somewhat limit the scope of the press. Journalists are subject to the former if they publish material liable to interfere with a matter which is *sub judice* but this law is qualified by the Administration of Justice Act of 1960 which declares an editor not guilty of contempt if, after taking reasonable care, he remained ignorant of the fact that proceedings were pending. The Scottish law of contempt is more severe than the English. Libel cases can involve the awarding of punitive damages against the press. The Defamation Act of 1952 lessened the possible repercussions of unintentional libel and made provision for the claim of fair comment by the defence.

The Official Secrets Act of 1911 prohibits the publication of secret information where this is judged not to be in the national interest. The Secretary of State for the Home Department is empowered to require a person with information about a violation of the Act to disclose his source. Journalists have no exemption here. The publication of morally objectionable and harmful material is treated in the Children's and Young Persons' (Harmful Publications) Act of 1955 and in the Obscene Publications Act.

Legislative measures have been taken to limit the excessive development of concentrations of newspaper ownership and the extent of the control by newspaper owners over other mass media such as the television. The Television Act of 1964 provided for intervention by the Postmaster-General or the Independent Broadcasting Authority where investments by newspaper owners in television companies are judged liable to lead to abuses. The Monopolies and Mergers Act of 1965 requires the written consent of the Department of Trade and Industry (now Department for Business, Enterprise and Regulatory Reform) for the transfer of daily or weekly papers with an aggregate average of over 500,000 copies per day of publication. The Department's decision is based on the conclusions of the Monopolies Commission to which, with the exception of cases of papers judged to be uneconomical and of papers with an average daily circulation of no more than 25,000 copies, all cases are referred for investigation.

The Press Complaints Commission, which replaced the Press Council in 1991, has an independent chairman and 16 members, drawn from the lay public and the press. It deals with complaints from the public and upholds an 18-point Code of Practice.

Among the most influential newspapers may be included: *The Times*, *The Guardian*, *The Independent*, *Daily Telegraph* and *Financial Times* (daily), *The Observer*, *The Independent on Sunday*, *The Sunday Times* and *Sunday Telegraph* (Sunday newspapers). Prominent among the popular press are: *Daily Mail*, *Daily Mirror*, *The Express* and *The Sun* (daily), *Sunday Mirror*, *News of the World* and *The People* (Sunday newspapers).

No important newspaper is directly owned by a political party. The great rate of news consumption has fostered the growth of large national groups or chains of papers controlled by a single organization or individual. The largest of these chains are as follows:

Daily Mail and General Trust PLC: Northcliffe House, 2 Derry St, London, W8 5TT; tel. (20) 7938-6000; fax (20) 7938-4626; e-mail webmaster@dmgt.co.uk; internet www.dmgt.co.uk; controls through Associated Newspapers one national daily, *Daily Mail*, one national Sunday, *The Mail on Sunday*, three London dailies, *Evening Standard*, *London Lite* and *Metro*; through Northcliffe Media controls 18 daily titles, 28 weekly titles and 50 free newspapers; Group Chair. Viscount ROTHERMERE; Group CEO CHARLES SINCLAIR (until 30 September 2008), MARTIN MORGAN (from 1 October 2008).

Guardian Media Group PLC: 60 Farringdon Rd, London, EC1R 3GA; tel. (20) 7239-9711; fax (20) 7713-4709; internet www.gmgplc.co.uk; f. 1821; owned by the Scott Trust; subsidiary publishing cos include Guardian Newspapers Ltd (controls *The Guardian*, *The Observer*) and GMG Regional Media (controls *Manchester Evening News*); Chair. PAUL MYNERS; CEO CAROLYN MCCALL.

Independent Newspapers UK: Independent House, 191 Marsh Wall, London, E14 9RS; tel. (20) 7005-2000; internet www.inmplc.com; British subsidiary of Ireland's Independent News & Media PLC; publishes one national daily, *The Independent*, and one national Sunday paper, *The Independent on Sunday*; Chief Exec. Sir ANTHONY O'REILLY; Chair. Dr B. HILLERY.

News International PLC: 1 Virginia St, London, E98 1XY; tel. (20) 7782-6000; fax (20) 7782-6097; internet www.newsint.co.uk; British subsidiary of USA's News Corporation; subsidiary cos: News Group Newspapers Ltd (controls *The Sun* and *News of the World*), Times Newspapers Ltd (controls *The Times* and *The Sunday Times*); Exec. Chair. LESLIE HINTON.

Trinity Mirror PLC: 1 Canada Sq., Canary Wharf, London, E14 5AP; tel. (20) 7293-3000; fax (20) 7293-3280; internet www.trinitymirror.com; f. 1999; by merger of Mirror Group Newspapers Ltd and Trinity International Holdings; controls a total of over 200 newspapers, including one national daily paper, *Daily Mirror*, two national Sunday papers, *The People*, *Sunday Mirror*, two Scottish national papers, *Daily Record* and *Sunday Mail*, and numerous regional and local papers; Chair. Sir IAN GIBSON; Chief Exec. SYLVIA (SLY) BAILEY.

United Business Media PLC: Ludgate House, 245 Blackfriars Rd, London, SE1 9UY; tel. (20) 7921-5000; e-mail communications@unitedbusinessmedia.com; internet www.unitedbusinessmedia.com; f. 1996 by merger of United Newspapers and MAI group; international media and information group; three core business divisions—professional media, market research, news distribution; Chair. GEOFF UNWIN; CEO DAVID LEVIN.

PRINCIPAL NATIONAL DAILIES
(average net circulation figures, in the United Kingdom only, as at April 2008, unless otherwise stated)

Daily Express: The Northern & Shell Bldg, 10 Lower Thames St, London, EC3R 6EN; tel. (871) 4341010; e-mail expressletters@express.co.uk; internet www.express.co.uk; f. 1900; Propr Northern and Shell Group; Editor PETER HILL; circ. 688,856.

Daily Mail: Northcliffe House, 2 Derry St, London, W8 5TT; tel. (20) 7938-6000; fax (20) 7937-4463; e-mail news@dailymail.co.uk; internet www.dailymail.co.uk; f. 1896; inc. *News Chronicle* (1960) and *Daily Sketch* (1971); Propr Associated Newspaper Holdings; Editor-in-Chief PAUL DACRE; Man. Dir GUY ZITTER; circ. 2,160,775.

Daily Mirror: 1 Canada Sq., Canary Wharf, London, E14 5AP; tel. (20) 7293-3000; fax (20) 7293-3280; e-mail mailbox@mirror.co.uk; internet www.mirror.co.uk; f. 1903; Propr Trinity Mirror PLC; Editor RICHARD WALLACE; circ. 1,368,808.

Daily Sport: 19 Gt Ancoats St, Manchester, M60 4BT; tel. (161) 236-4466; fax (161) 236-4535; internet www.dailysport.net; f. 1988; Propr Sport Media Group; Editor-in-Chief BARRY MCILHENEY; circ. 95,060.

Daily Star: The Northern & Shell Bldg, 10 Lower Thames St, London, EC3R 6EN; tel. (8714) 341010; fax (20) 7922-7960; e-mail news@dailystar.co.uk; internet www.dailystar.co.uk; f. 1978; Propr Express Newspapers PLC; Editor DAWN NEESOM; circ. 608,768.

Daily Telegraph: 111 Buckingham Palace Rd, London, SW1W 0DT; tel. (20) 7931-2000; e-mail dtletters@telegraph.co.uk; internet www.telegraph.co.uk; *Daily Telegraph*, f. 1855, *Morning Post*, f. 1772; amalgamated 1937; Propr Press Acquisitions Ltd; Chief Exec. MURDOCH MACLENNAN; Editor WILLIAM LEWIS; circ. 821,466.

Financial Times: Number One Southwark Bridge, London, SE1 9HL; tel. (20) 7873-3000; fax (20) 7873-3076; internet www.ft.com; f. 1880; Propr Pearson PLC; CEO JOHN RIDDING; Editor LIONEL BARBER; circ. 133,126.

The Guardian: 119 Farringdon Rd, London, EC1R 3ER; and 164 Deansgate, Manchester, M3 3GG; tel. (20) 7278-2332; fax (20) 7837-2114; e-mail userhelp@guardian.co.uk; internet www.guardian.co.uk; tel. (161) 832-7200; fax (161) 832-5351; f. 1821; Propr Guardian Newspapers Ltd; Editor ALAN RUSBRIDGER; circ. 306,199.

The Independent: Independent House, 191 Marsh Wall, London, E14 9RS; tel. (20) 7005-2000; fax (20) 7005-2999; e-mail customerservices@independent.co.uk; internet www.independent.co.uk; f. 1986; Editor ROGER ALTON; circ. 186,278.

Racing Post: 1 Canada Sq., Canary Wharf, London, E14 5AP; tel. (20) 7293-3000; fax (20) 7293-3758; e-mail editor@racingpost.co.uk; internet www.racingpost.co.uk; f. 1986; covers national and international horse racing, greyhound racing, general sport and betting; Editor BRUCE MILLINGTON; circ. 61,962.

The Sun: 1 Virginia St, London, E98 1SN; tel. (20) 7782-4000; fax (20) 7782-4108; e-mail corporate.info@the-sun.co.uk; internet www.thesun.co.uk; f. 1921 as *Daily Herald*; present name since 1964; Propr News International PLC; Editor REBEKAH WADE; Man. Dir MIKE ANDERSON; circ. 2,979,580.

The Times: 1 Pennington St, London, E98 1TT; tel. (20) 7782-5000; fax (20) 7782-5046; internet www.timesonline.co.uk; f. 1785; Propr News International PLC; Editor JAMES HARDING; circ. 588,006.

THE UNITED KINGDOM

LONDON DAILIES
(average net circulation figures as at April 2008, unless otherwise stated)

Evening Standard: Northcliffe House, 2 Derry St, London, W8 5TT; tel. (20) 7938-6000; fax (20) 7937-2648; internet www.standard.co.uk; f. 1827; merged with *Evening News* 1980; Mon.–Fri.; evening; Propr Associated Newspaper Holdings PLC; Editor VERONICA WADLEY; Man. Dir ANDREW MULLINS; circ. 281,187.

London Lite: Northcliffe House, 2 Derry St, London, W8 5TT; tel. (20) 7651-5450; internet www.thisislondon.co.uk; f. 2006; evening; distributed free of charge; Propr Associated Newspapers Holdings PLC; Editor MARTIN CLARKE; circ. 402,281.

Metro: Northcliffe House, 2 Derry St, London, W8 5TT; tel. (20) 7651-5200; fax (20) 7651-5342; e-mail mail@ukmetro.co.uk; internet www.metro.co.uk; f. 1999; Mon.–Fri.; morning; distributed free of charge; also distributed in Bath, Birmingham, Brighton, Bristol, Cardiff, Derby, Edinburgh, Glasgow, Leeds, Leicester, Liverpool, Manchester, Newcastle, Nottingham and Sheffield; Propr Associated Newspaper Holdings PLC; Editor KENNY CAMPBELL; Man. Dir STEVE AUCKLAND; circ. 747,006 (London); 1,360,685 (total UK).

thelondonpaper: 1 Pennington St, London, E98 1XY; tel. (20) 7782-4835; e-mail laura.tait@newsint.co.uk; internet www.thelondonpaper.com; evening; distributed free of charge; Propr News International; f. 2006; Editor STEFANO HATFIELD; circ. 500,911.

PRINCIPAL PROVINCIAL DAILIES
(average net circulation figures as at December 2007, unless otherwise stated)

Aberdeen

Evening Express: Aberdeen Journals Ltd, Lang Stracht, Mastrick, Aberdeen, AB15 6DF; tel. (1224) 690222; fax (1224) 699575; e-mail ee.news@ajl.co.uk; internet www.eveningexpress.co.uk; f. 1879; Editor DAMIAN BATES; circ. 53,384.

Press and Journal: Aberdeen Journals Ltd, Lang Stracht, Mastrick, Aberdeen, AB15 6DF; tel. (1224) 690222; fax (1224) 663575; e-mail pj.newsdesk@ajl.co.uk; internet www.pressandjournal.co.uk; f. 1747; morning; Editor DEREK TUCKER; circ. 80,177.

Belfast

Belfast Telegraph: 124–144 Royal Ave, Belfast, BT1 1EB; tel. (28) 9026-4000; fax (28) 9055-4506; e-mail newseditor@belfasttelegraph.co.uk; internet www.belfasttelegraph.co.uk; f. 1870; independent; evening; Proprs Independent News and Media PLC; Editor MARTIN LINDSAY; circ. 75,602.

Irish News: 113–117 Donegall St, Belfast, BT1 2GE; tel. (28) 9032-2226; fax (28) 9033-7505; e-mail newsdesk@irishnews.com; internet www.irishnews.com; f. 1855; Irish nationalist; morning; Editor NOEL DORAN; circ. 47,790.

News Letter: 2 Esky Drive, Carn Industrial Estate, Craigavon, BT63 5YY; tel. (28) 9089-7700; fax (28) 9066-9910; e-mail darwin.templeton@jpress.co.uk; internet www.newsletter.co.uk; f. 1737; unionist; morning; Editor DARWIN TEMPLETON; circ. 26,477.

Birmingham

Birmingham Mail: POB 78, Weaman St, Birmingham, B4 6AY; tel. (121) 236-3366; fax (121) 233-0271; e-mail steve_dyson@mrn.co.uk; internet www.birminghammail.net; f. 1870; evening; independent; Propr Trinity Mirror PLC; Editor STEVE DYSON; circ. 67,231.

Bradford

Telegraph & Argus: Hall Ings, Bradford, BD1 1JR; tel. (1274) 729511; fax (1274) 723634; e-mail newsdesk@bradford.newsquest.co.uk; internet www.thetelegraphandargus.co.uk; f. 1868; evening; Editor PERRY AUSTIN-CLARKE; circ. 36,839.

Brighton

The Argus: Argus House, Crowhurst Rd, Hollingbury, Brighton, BN1 8AR; tel. (1273) 544544; fax (1273) 566114; e-mail editor@theargus.co.uk; internet www.theargus.co.uk; f. 1880; Propr Newsquest Media Group; Man. Dir MARTYN WILLIS; Editor MICHAEL BEARD; circ. 32,874.

Bristol

Evening Post: Temple Way, Bristol, BS99 7HD; tel. (117) 934-3000; fax (117) 934-3575; e-mail epnews@bepp.co.uk; internet www.thisisbristol.com; f. 1932; inc. the *Evening World*; Propr Northcliffe Newspapers; independent; Editor-in-Chief MIKE NORTON; circ. 51,287.

Western Daily Press: Temple Way, Bristol, BS99 7HD; tel. (117) 934-3000; fax (117) 934-3574; e-mail wdnews@bepp.co.uk; internet www.westpress.co.uk; f. 1858; Propr Northcliffe Newspapers; morning; independent; Editor ANDY WRIGHT; circ. 41,639.

Cardiff

South Wales Echo: Havelock St, Cardiff, CF10 1XR; tel. (29) 2022-3333; fax (29) 2058-3624; e-mail echo.newsdesk@mediawales.co.uk; internet www.icwales.co.uk; f. 1884; Propr Trinity Mirror PLC; evening; independent; Editor MIKE HILL (acting); circ. 46,127.

The Western Mail: Havelock St, Cardiff, CF10 1XR; tel. (29) 2022-3333; fax (29) 2058-3652; e-mail newsdesk@mediawales.co.uk; internet www.icwales.co.uk; f. 1869; independent; Editor ALAN EDMUNDS; circ. 37,576.

Coventry

Coventry Telegraph: Corporation St, Coventry, CV1 1FP; tel. (24) 7663-3633; fax (24) 7655-0869; e-mail alan.kirby@coventrytelegraph.net; internet www.coventrytelegraph.net; f. 1891 as *Midland Daily Telegraph*; Propr. Trinity Mirror PLC; independent; morning; Editor ALAN KIRBY; circ. 46,933.

Darlington

Northern Echo: POB 14, Priestgate, Darlington, Co Durham, DL1 1NF; tel. (1325) 505065; e-mail newsdesk@nne.co.uk; internet www.thisisthenortheast.co.uk; f. 1869; morning; independent; Editor PETER BARRON; circ. 50,256.

Derby

Derby Evening Telegraph: Northcliffe House, Meadow Rd, Derby, DE1 2DW; tel. (1332) 291111; fax (1332) 253027; e-mail newsdesk@derbytelegraph.co.uk; internet www.thisisderbyshire.co.uk; f. 1932; inc. *Derby Daily Telegraph*, f. 1879, *Derby Daily Express*, f. 1884; Editor STEVE HALL; circ. 42,726.

Dundee

Courier and Advertiser: Albert Sq., Dundee, DD1 9QJ; tel. (1382) 223131; fax (1382) 225511; e-mail editor@thecourier.co.uk; internet www.thecourier.co.uk; f. 1810; morning; Editor WILLIAM HUTCHEON; circ. 73,485.

Edinburgh

Edinburgh Evening News: Barclay House, 108 Holyrood Rd, Edinburgh, EH8 8AS; tel. (131) 620-8703; fax (131) 620-8696; e-mail jmclellan@edinburghnews.com; internet www.edinburghnews.com; f. 1873; Propr Johnston Press PLC; Editor JOHN McLELLAN; circ. 50,847.

The Scotsman: Barclay House, 108 Holyrood Rd, Edinburgh, EH8 8AS; tel. (131) 620-8620; fax (131) 620-8616; e-mail enquiries@scotsman.com; internet www.scotsman.com; f. 1817; morning; Propr Johnston Press PLC; Editor MIKE GILSON; circ. 52,009.

Glasgow

Daily Record: 1 Central Quay, Glasgow, G3 8DA; tel. (141) 309-3000; fax (141) 309-3340; internet www.dailyrecord.co.uk; morning; independent; f. 1895; Propr Trinity Mirror PLC; Editor-in-Chief BRUCE WADDELL; circ. 383,589.

Glasgow Evening Times: 200 Renfield St, Glasgow, G2 3Q3; tel. (141) 302-7000; fax (141) 302-6600; e-mail times@eveningtimes.co.uk; internet www.eveningtimes.co.uk; f. 1876; Propr Newsquest; Editor DONALD MARTIN; circ. 74,466.

The Herald: 200 Renfield St, Glasgow, G2 3QB; tel. (141) 302-7000; fax (141) 302-7171; e-mail news@theherald.co.uk; internet www.theherald.co.uk; f. 1783; morning; independent; Propr Newsquest; Editor CHARLES McGHEE; circ. 65,745.

Scottish Daily Express: Citypoint Z, 25 Tyndrum St, Glasgow, G4 0JY; tel. (141) 332-4600; fax (141) 332-2555; e-mail scot.news@express.co.uk; internet www.express.co.uk/scottish; morning; regional edition of *Daily Express*; Propr Northern and Shell Group; Editor DAVID HAMILTON.

Grimsby

Grimsby Telegraph: 80 Cleethorpe Rd, Grimsby, DN31 3EH; tel. (1472) 360360; fax (1472) 372257; e-mail newsdesk@grimsbytelegraph.co.uk; internet www.thisisgrimsby.co.uk; f. 1898; evening; Editor MICHELLE LALOR; circ. 34,288.

Ipswich

East Anglian Daily Times: 30 Lower Brook St, Ipswich, IP4 1AN; tel. (1473) 230023; e-mail news@eadt.co.uk; internet www.eadt.co.uk; morning; Editor TERRY HUNT; circ. 34,392.

THE UNITED KINGDOM   *Directory*

Kingston upon Hull

Hull Daily Mail: Blundell's Corner, Beverley Rd, Kingston upon Hull, HU3 1XS; tel. (1482) 327111; fax (1482) 584353; e-mail news@mailnewsmedia.co.uk; internet www.thisishullandeastriding.co.uk; f. 1885; evening; Editor JOHN MEEHAN; circ. 56,208.

Leeds

Yorkshire Evening Post: POB 168, Wellington St, Leeds, LS1 1RF; tel. (113) 243-2701; fax (113) 238-8536; e-mail eped@ypn.co.uk; internet www.yorkshireeveningpost.co.uk; f. 1890; Propr Johnston Press PLC; Editor PAUL NAPIER; circ. 55,732.

Yorkshire Post: POB 168, Wellington St, Leeds, LS1 1RF; tel. (113) 243-2701; fax (113) 244-3430; e-mail yp.newsdesk@ypn.co.uk; internet www.yorkshirepost.co.uk; f. 1754; morning; Propr Johnston Press PLC; Editor PETER CHARLTON; circ. 49,031.

Leicester

Leicester Mercury: St George St, Leicester, LE1 9FQ; tel. (116) 251-2512; fax (116) 253-0645; e-mail newsdesk@leicestermercury.co.uk; internet www.thisisleicestershire.co.uk; f. 1874; evening; Editor NICK CARTER; circ. 70,028.

Liverpool

Liverpool Echo: POB 48, Old Hall St, Liverpool, L69 3EB; tel. (151) 227-2000; fax (151) 472-2474; e-mail letters@liverpoolecho.co.uk; internet www.liverpoolecho.co.uk; f. 1879; evening; independent; Propr Trinity Mirror PLC; Editor ALASTAIR MACHRAY; circ. 106,401.

Manchester

Manchester Evening News: 1 Scott Pl., Hardman St, Manchester, M3 3RN; tel. (161) 832-7200; fax (161) 831-7418; e-mail newsdesk@men-news.co.uk; internet www.manchestereveningnews.co.uk; f. 1868; independent; Editor PAUL HORROCKS; circ. 81,326.

Middlesbrough

Evening Gazette: Borough Rd, Middlesbrough, TS1 3AZ; tel. (1642) 245401; fax (1642) 210565; e-mail darren.thwaites@eveninggazette.co.uk; internet www.gazettelive.co.uk; f. 1869; Propr Trinity Mirror PLC; Editor DARREN THWAITES; circ. 50,920.

Newcastle upon Tyne

Evening Chronicle: Groat Market, Newcastle upon Tyne, NE1 1ED; tel. (191) 232-7500; fax (191) 232-2256; e-mail ec.news@ncjmedia.co.uk; internet www.chroniclelive.co.uk; f. 1885; Propr Trinity Mirror PLC; Editor PAUL ROBERTSON; circ. 74,107.

The Journal: Groat Market, Newcastle upon Tyne, NE1 1ED; tel. (191) 232-7500; fax (191) 230-4144; e-mail jnl.newsdesk@ncjmedia.co.uk; internet www.journallive.co.uk; f. 1832; morning; Propr Trinity Mirror PLC; Editor BRIAN AITKEN; circ. 34,013.

Norwich

Eastern Daily Press: Prospect House, Rouen Rd, Norwich, NR1 1RE; tel. (1603) 628311; fax (1603) 623872; e-mail edp@archant.co.uk; internet www.edp24.co.uk; f. 1870; independent; Propr Archant Regional Ltd; Editor PETER FRANZEN; circ. 64,700.

Nottingham

Nottingham Evening Post: Castle Wharf House, Nottingham, NG1 7EU; tel. (115) 948-2000; fax (115) 964-4032; e-mail newsdesk@nottinghameveningpost.co.uk; internet www.thisisnottingham.co.uk; f. 1878; Editor MALCOLM PHEBY; circ. 57,699.

Plymouth

Western Morning News: 17 Brest Rd, Derriford, Plymouth, PL6 5AA; tel. (1752) 765500; fax (1752) 765535; e-mail wmnnewsdesk@westernmorningnews.co.uk; internet www.westernmorningnews.co.uk; f. 1860; Editor ALAN QUALTROUGH; circ. 41,154.

Portsmouth

The News: The News Centre, London Rd, Hilsea, Portsmouth, PO2 9SX; tel. (23) 9266-4488; e-mail newsdesk@thenews.co.uk; internet www.portsmouth.co.uk; f. 1877; evening; Editor MARK WALDRON; circ. 52,531.

Preston

Lancashire Evening Post: Oliver's Place, Preston, PR2 9ZA; tel. (1772) 254841; fax (1772) 880173; e-mail lep.newsdesk@lep.co.uk; internet www.lep.co.uk; f. 1886; Editor SIMON REYNOLDS; circ. 30,467.

Sheffield

The Star: York St, Sheffield, S1 1PU; tel. (114) 276-7676; fax (114) 272-5978; e-mail starnews@sheffieldnewspapers.co.uk; internet www.thestar.co.uk; f. 1887; evening; independent; Propr Johnston Press PLC; Editor ALAN POWELL; circ. 52,180.

Southampton

Southern Daily Echo: Newspaper House, Test Lane, Redbridge, Southampton, SO16 9JX; tel. (23) 8042-4777; fax (23) 8042-4545; e-mail newsdesk@dailyecho.co.uk; internet www.dailyecho.co.uk; f. 1888; Propr Newsquest; Editor IAN MURRAY; circ. 39,174.

Stoke-on-Trent

The Sentinel: Staffordshire Sentinel News & Media Ltd, Sentinel House, Etruria, Stoke-on-Trent, ST1 5SS; tel. (1782) 602525; fax (1782) 602616; e-mail newsdesk@thesentinel.co.uk; internet www.thisisthesentinel.co.uk; f. 1854; Editor-in-Chief MIKE SASSI; circ. 61,910.

Sunderland

Sunderland Echo: Echo House, Pennywell, Sunderland, Tyne and Wear, SR4 9ER; tel. (191) 501-5800; fax (191) 534-3807; e-mail echo.news@northeast-press.co.uk; internet www.sunderlandecho.com; f. 1873; evening; Editor ROB LAWSON; circ. 42,910.

Swansea

South Wales Evening Post: Adelaide St, Swansea, SA1 1QT; tel. (1792) 510000; fax (1792) 514197; e-mail postnews@swwmedia.co.uk; internet www.thisissouthwales.co.uk; f. 1930; Editor SPENCER FEENEY; circ. 51,329.

Telford

Shropshire Star: Waterloo Rd, Ketley, Telford, Shropshire, TF1 5HU; tel. (1952) 242424; fax (1952) 254605; e-mail newsroom@shropshirestar.co.uk; internet www.shropshirestar.com; f. 1964; evening; Propr Shropshire Newspapers Ltd; Editor SARAH-JANE SMITH; circ. 71,513.

Wolverhampton

Express and Star: 51–53 Queen St, Wolverhampton, West Midlands, WV1 1ES; tel. (1902) 313131; fax (1902) 710106; e-mail newsdesk@expressandstar.co.uk; internet www.expressandstar.co.uk; f. 1874; evening; Propr The Midland News Association Ltd; Editor ADRIAN FABER; circ. 138,780.

York

The Press: POB 29, 76–86 Walmgate, York, YO1 9YN; tel. (1904) 653051; fax (1904) 612853; e-mail newsdesk@ycp.co.uk; internet www.thepress.co.uk; morning; Editor KEVIN BOOTH; circ. 33,045.

PRINCIPAL WEEKLY NEWSPAPERS

(average net circulation figures as at April 2008, unless otherwise stated)

Asian Times: Ethnic Media Group, Whitechapel Technology Centre, Unit 2, 65 Whitechapel Rd, London, E1 1DU; tel. (20) 7650-2000; fax (20) 7650-2001; internet www.asiantimesonline.co.uk; Editor HAMANT VERMA; Man. Dir WAYNE BOWER.

Daily Star Sunday: Ludgate House, 245 Blackfriars Rd, London, SE1 9UX; tel. (20) 7928-8000; fax (20) 7633-0244; e-mail dailystarnewsdesk@dailystar.co.uk; internet www.dailystar.co.uk/sunday; f. 1978; Propr Express Newspapers PLC; Editor GARETH MORGAN; circ. 296,892.

The Independent on Sunday: Independent House, 191 Marsh Wall, London, E14 9RS; tel. (20) 7005-2000; fax (20) 7005-2627; internet www.independent.co.uk; f. 1990; Propr Independent Newspapers UK; Editor JOHN MULLIN; circ. 178,228.

The Mail on Sunday: Northcliffe House, 2 Derry St, London, W8 5TS; tel. (20) 7938-6000; fax (20) 7937-3829; internet www.mailonsunday.co.uk; f. 1982; Propr Associated Newspapers Ltd; Editor PETER WRIGHT; Man. Dir STEPHEN MIRON; circ. 2,073,286.

News of the World: 1 Virginia St, London, E1 9XR; tel. (20) 7782-1000; fax (20) 7583-9504; e-mail newsdesk@notw.co.uk; internet www.notw.co.uk; f. 1843; Propr News International; Sunday; Editor COLIN MYLER; Man. Dir MIKE ANDERSON; circ. 2,985,443.

The Observer: 3-7 Herbal Hill, London, EC1R 5EJ; tel. (20) 7278-2332; fax (20) 7713-4250; e-mail userhelp@guardian.co.uk; internet observer.guardian.co.uk; f. 1791; owned by Guardian Newspapers Ltd; Sunday; Editor JOHN MULHOLLAND; circ. 400,627.

The People: 1 Canada Sq., Canary Wharf, London, E14 5AP; tel. (20) 7293-3000; fax (20) 7293-3887; internet www.people.co.uk;

THE UNITED KINGDOM

f. 1881; Propr Trinity Mirror PLC; Editor Lloyd Embley (acting); circ. 608,568.

Scotland on Sunday: Barclay House, 108 Holyrood Rd, Edinburgh, EH8 8AS; tel. (131) 620-8620; fax (131) 620-8491; e-mail letters_sos@scotlandonsunday.com; internet scotlandonsunday.scotsman.com; f. 1988; Propr Johnston Press PLC; Editor Les Snowdon; circ. 67,067.

Sunday Express: Ludgate House, 245 Blackfriars Rd., London, SE1 9UX; tel. (8714) 341010; fax (20) 7620-1656; internet www.express.co.uk; f. 1918; inc. *Sunday Despatch* 1961; independent; Propr Northern and Shell Group; Editor-in-Chief Martin Townsend; circ. 630,626.

Sunday Herald: 200 Renfield St, Glasgow, G2 3QB; tel. (141) 302-7800; e-mail editor@sundayherald.com; internet www.sundayherald.com; f. 1999; Propr Newsquest Media Group; Editor Richard Walker; circ. 47,921.

Sunday Life: 124–144 Royal Ave, Belfast, BT1 1EB; tel. (28) 9026-4300; fax (28) 9054-4507; e-mail writeback@belfasttelegraph.co.uk; internet www.sundaylife.co.uk; f. 1988; Editor Martin Lindsay; circ. 67,608 (July–Dec. 2007).

Sunday Mail: 1 Central Quay, Glasgow, G3 8DA; tel. (141) 309-3000; fax (141) 242-3587; e-mail mailbox@sundaymail.co.uk; internet www.sundaymail.co.uk; Propr Trinity Mirror PLC; Editor Allan Rennie; circ. 467,331.

Sunday Mercury: Weaman St, Birmingham, B4 6AZ; tel. (121) 234-5567; e-mail sundaymercury@mrn.co.uk; internet www.icbirmingham.co.uk; Propr Trinity Mirror PLC; f. 1918; Editor David Brookes; circ. 59,339 (July–Dec. 2007).

Sunday Mirror: 1 Canada Sq., Canary Wharf, London, E14 5AP; tel. (20) 7293-3000; fax (20) 7822-3587; e-mail mailbox@mirror.co.uk; internet www.sundaymirror.co.uk; f. 1915; Propr Trinity Mirror PLC; independent; Editor Tina Weaver; circ. 1,260,687.

The Sunday Post: 144 Port Dundas Rd, Glasgow, G4 0HZ; tel. (141) 332-9933; fax (141) 331-1595; e-mail mail@sundaypost.com; internet www.sundaypost.com; f. 1919; Propr D.C. Thomson & Co. Ltd; Editor David Pollington; circ. 396,604.

Sunday Sport: 19 Gt Ancoats St, Manchester, M60 4BT; tel. (161) 236-4466; fax (161) 236-4535; f. 1986; Propr Sport Media Group; Editor-in-Chief Barry McIlheney; circ. 86,205.

Sunday Sun: Groat Market, Newcastle upon Tyne, NE1 1ED; tel. (191) 201-6251; fax (191) 230-0238; e-mail colin.patterson@ncjmedia.co.uk; internet www.sundaysun.co.uk; f. 1919; Propr Trinity Mirror PLC; independent; north-east England; Editor Colin Patterson; circ. 68,033 (July–Dec. 2007).

Sunday Telegraph: 111 Buckingham Palace Rd, London, SW1W 0DT; tel. (20) 7931-2000; e-mail stletters@telegraph.co.uk; internet www.telegraph.co.uk; f. 1961; Propr Press Acquisitions Ltd; Editor Ian McGregor; circ. 606,229.

The Sunday Times: 1 Pennington St, London, E98 1ST; tel. (20) 7782-5000; fax (20) 7782-5658; internet www.sunday-times.co.uk; f. 1822; Propr News International; Editor John Witherow; circ. 1,038,279.

Wales on Sunday: Thomson House, Havelock St, Cardiff, CF1 1XR; tel. (29) 2058-3583; e-mail wosmail@mediawales.co.uk; internet www.icwales.co.uk; f. 1991; Editor Tim Gordon; circ. 41,199 (July–Dec. 2007).

SELECTED PERIODICALS
(circulation figures as at June 2007, unless otherwise stated)

Arts and Literature

Apollo: 22 Old Queen St, London, SW1H 9HP; tel. (20) 7961-0150; fax (20) 7961-0110; e-mail editorial@apollomag.com; internet www.apollo-magazine.com; f. 1925; owned by Press Holdings; monthly; fine and decorative art; Publr Celia Bailey; Editor Michael Hall.

Architects' Journal: Greater London House, Hampstead Rd, London, NW1 7EJ; tel. (20) 7728-4574; fax (20) 7391-3435; e-mail kieran.long@emap.com; internet www.architectsjournal.co.uk; f. 1895; Thursday; Editor Kieran Long; circ. 13,491 (July 2005).

Architectural Review: Greater London House, Hampstead Rd, London, NW1 7EJ; tel. (20) 7728-5000; e-mail paul.finch@emap.com; internet www.arplus.com; f. 1896; monthly; Editor Paul Finch; circ. 18,544 (July 2005).

The Artist: Caxton House, 63–65 High St, Tenterden, Kent, TN30 6BD; tel. (1580) 763673; fax (1580) 765411; e-mail sally@tapc.co.uk; internet www.theartistmagazine.co.uk; f. 1931; monthly; Editor Sally Bulgin.

ArtReview: 1 Sekforde St, London, EC1R 0BE; tel. (20) 7107-2760; fax (20) 7107-2761; e-mail editorial@artreview.com; internet www.art-review.com; f. 1949; monthly; Editor Rebecca Wilson.

BBC Music Magazine: Origin Publishing Ltd, 14th Floor, Tower House, Fairfax St, Bristol, BS1 3BN; tel. (117) 927-9009; fax (117) 934-9008; e-mail music@bbcmagazinesbristol.com; internet www.bbcmusicmagazine.com; f. 1992; monthly; classical music; Editor Oliver Condy; circ. 47,091 (Dec. 2006).

The Bookseller: Endeavour House, 189 Shaftesbury Ave, London, WC2H 8TJ; tel. (20) 7420-6006; fax (20) 7420-6103; e-mail letters.to.editor@bookseller.co.uk; internet www.thebookseller.com; f. 1858; incorporates *Bent's Literary Advertiser* (f. 1802); Friday; Propr VNU Entertainment Media UK Ltd; Editor Neill Denny.

The Burlington Magazine: 14–16 Dukes Rd, London, WC1H 9SZ; tel. (20) 7388-1228; fax (20) 7388-1229; e-mail burlington@burlington.org.uk; internet www.burlington.org.uk; f. 1903; monthly; all forms of art, ancient and modern; Editor Richard Shone.

Classical Music: Rhinegold Publishing Ltd, 241 Shaftesbury Ave, London, WC2H 8TF; tel. (20) 7333-1742; fax (20) 7333-1769; e-mail classical.music@rhinegold.co.uk; internet www.rhinegold.co.uk; f. 1976; fortnightly; Editor Keith Clarke; circ. 18,000 (July 2005).

Dancing Times: 45–47 Clerkenwell Green, London, EC1R 0EB; tel. (20) 7250-3006; fax (20) 7253-6679; e-mail dt@dancing-times.co.uk; internet www.dancing-times.co.uk; f. 1910; monthly; ballet and modern dance; Editor Mary Clarke.

Empire: Endeavour House, 189 Shaftesbury Ave, WC2H 8JG; tel. (20) 7182-8781; internet www.empireonline.com; monthly; film; Editor Mark Dinning; circ. 179,373.

Film Review: Visual Imagination Ltd, 9 Blades Court, Deodar Rd, London, SW15 2NU; tel. (20) 8875-1520; fax (20) 8875-1588; e-mail filmreview@visimag.com; internet www.visimag.com/filmreview; f. 1955; monthly; Editor Nikki Baughan.

Folklore: The Folklore Society, c/o The Warburg Institute, Woburn Sq., London, WC1H 0AB; tel. (20) 7862-8564; e-mail enquiries@folklore-society.com; internet www.folklore-society.com; f. 1878; 3 a year; Editor Prof. Patricia Lysaght.

Gramophone: Teddington Studios, Broom Rd, Teddington, Middlesex, TW11 9BE; tel. (20) 8267-5136; fax (20) 8267-5844; e-mail gramophone@haymarket.com; internet www.gramophone.co.uk; f. 1923; monthly; Publr Simon Temlett; Editor James Inverne; circ. 40,089 (Dec. 2006).

Granta: 12 Addison Ave, London, W11 4QR; tel. (20) 7605-1360; fax (20) 7704-0474; e-mail editorial@granta.com; internet www.granta.com; quarterly; Editor Jason Cowley; circ. 80,000 (July 2005).

Index on Censorship: 6–8 Amwell St, London, EC1R 1UQ; tel. (20) 7278-2313; fax (20) 7278-1878; e-mail contact@indexoncensorship.org; internet www.indexoncensorship.org; f. 1972; four a year; concerned with freedom of expression throughout the world; Editor Jo Glanville.

Jazz Journal International: Jazz Journal Ltd, 3 & 3A Forest Rd, Loughton, Essex IG10 1DR; tel. (20) 8532-0456; fax (20) 8532-0440; f. 1948; monthly; Editor Janet Cook.

Language Learning Journal: Association for Language Learning, 150 Railway Terrace, Rugby, CV21 3HN; tel. (1788) 546443; fax (1788) 544149; e-mail info@all-languages.org.uk; internet www.all-languages.org.uk; f. 1990; 2 a year; Editors Dr Norbert Pachler, Dr Douglas Allford; circ. 4,000 (July 2005).

mixmag: 90–92 Pentonville Rd, London, N1 9HS; tel. (20) 7078-8400; fax (20) 7833-9900; e-mail mixmag@mixmag.net; internet www.mixmag.net; f. 1983; publ. by Development Hell Ltd; monthly; dance music and club culture; Editor Andrew Harrison; circ. 37,139.

Mojo: Endeavour House, 189 Shaftesbury Ave, London, WC2H 8JG; tel. (20) 7436-1515; fax (20) 7182-8596; internet www.mojo4music.com; f. 1993; monthly; popular music; Editor Phil Alexander; circ. 112,037.

NME: IPC Media Ltd, The Blue Fin Bldg, 110 Southwark St, London, SE1 0SU; tel. (20) 7261-5000; fax (20) 7261-6022; e-mail conor_mcnicholas@ipcmedia.com; internet www.nme.com; f. 1952; Wednesday; popular music; Editor Conor McNicholas; circ. 68,151.

Opera: 36 Black Lion Lane, London, W6 9BE; tel. (20) 8563-8893; fax (20) 8563-8635; e-mail editor@opera.co.uk; internet www.opera.co.uk; f. 1950; monthly; Editor John Allison.

Poetry Review: 22 Betterton St, London, WC2H 9BX; tel. (20) 7420-9883; fax (20) 7240-4818; e-mail poetryreview@poetrysociety.co.uk; internet www.poetryreview.co.uk; f. 1909; quarterly; Editor Fiona Sampson.

Q Magazine: Endeavour House, 189 Shaftesbury Ave, London, WC2H 8JG; tel. (20) 7182-8000; fax (20) 7182-8547; internet www.q4music.com; f. 1986; monthly; music, general features; Editor Paul Rees; circ. 130,179.

Sight and Sound: British Film Institute, 21 Stephen St, London, W1T 1LN; tel. (20) 7255-1444; fax (20) 7436-2327; e-mail s&s@bfi.org.uk; internet www.bfi.org.uk/sightandsound; f. 1932; monthly; international film review; Editor Nick James; circ. 20,303 (Dec. 2006).

The Stage: Stage House, 47 Bermondsey St, London, SE1 3XT; tel. (20) 7403-1818; fax (20) 7357-9287; e-mail editor@thestage.co.uk; internet www.thestage.co.uk; f. 1880; Thursday; theatre, light entertainment, television, opera, dance; Man. Dir CAROLINE COMERFORD; circ. 34,000.

The Times Literary Supplement: Times House, 1 Pennington St, London, E98 1BS; tel. (20) 7782-5000; fax (20) 7782-4966; e-mail letters@the-tls.co.uk; internet www.the-tls.co.uk; f. 1902; Friday; weekly journal of literary criticism; Editor Sir PETER STOTHARD; circ. 34,673.

Top of the Pops: 80 Wood Lane, London, W12 0TT; tel. (020) 8433-1296; e-mail totp.magazine@bbc.co.uk; internet www.totpmag.com; monthly; popular music; Editor PETER HART; circ. 102,997.

Current Affairs and History

Antiquity: King's Manor, York, YO1 7EP; tel. and fax (1904) 433994; e-mail editor@antiquity.ac.uk; internet antiquity.ac.uk; f. 1927; quarterly; archaeology; Editor Prof. MARTIN CARVER.

The Big Issue: 1–5 Wandsworth Rd, London, SW8 2LN; tel. (20) 7526-3200; fax (20) 7526-3201; e-mail press@bigissue.com; internet www.bigissue.com; also offices based in Bristol, Cardiff, Glasgow, Manchester and the Midlands producing regional weekly editions; f. 1991; weekly; current affairs, social issues; Editor-in-Chief A. JOHN BIRD; total circ. 158,581.

Classical Quarterly: Journals Group, Cambridge University Press, The Edinburgh Bldg, Shaftesbury Rd, Cambridge, CB2 2RU; tel. (1223) 326070; fax (1223) 325150; e-mail journals@cambridge.org; internet journals.cambridge.org/jid_caq; f. 1906; 2 a year; language, literature, history and philosophy; Editors Dr RHIANNON ASH, Prof. JUDITH MOSSMAN.

Contemporary Review: POB 1242, Oxford, OX1 4FJ; tel. and fax (1865) 201529; e-mail editorial@contemporaryreview.co.uk; internet www.contemporaryreview.co.uk; f. 1866; monthly; publ by Contemporary Review Co Ltd; politics, international affairs, social subjects, the arts; Editor Dr RICHARD MULLEN.

English Historical Review: Oxford University Press, Gt Clarendon St, Oxford, OX2 6DP; e-mail ehr@oup.com; internet www3.oup.co.uk/enghis; f. 1886; 6 a year; learned articles and book reviews; Editors G. W. BERNARD, MARTIN CONWAY.

The Historian: The Historical Association, 59A Kennington Park Rd, London, SE11 4JH; tel. (20) 7735-3901; fax (20) 7582-4989; e-mail enquiry@history.org.uk; internet www.history.org.uk; f. 1906; 4 a year; Editors Prof. BILL SPECK, IAN MASON; circ. 3,500 (July 2005).

History Today: 20 Old Compton St, London, W1D 4TW; tel. (20) 7534-8000; fax (20) 7534-8008; e-mail p.furtado@historytoday.com; internet www.historytoday.com; f. 1951; monthly; illustrated general historical magazine; Editor PETER FURTADO; circ. 26,191 (Dec. 2006).

International Affairs: Royal Institute of International Affairs, Chatham House, 10 St James's Sq., London, SW1Y 4LE; tel. (20) 7957-5724; fax (20) 7957-5710; e-mail csoper@chathamhouse.org.uk; internet www.chathamhouse.org.uk; f. 1922; six per year; publ. by Wiley-Blackwell; original articles, and reviews of publications on international affairs; Editor CAROLINE SOPER.

Journal of Contemporary History: Unit 24A, The Bardfield Centre, Great Bardfield, Essex, CM7 4SL; tel. (1371) 811608; fax (80) 280-0620; e-mail office@jch.org.uk; internet www.jch.org.uk; f. 1966; quarterly; publ. by SAGE Publications Ltd; Editors RICHARD J. EVANS, NIALL FERGUSON, STANLEY PAYNE.

London Gazette: POB 7923, London, SE1 5ZH; tel. (20) 7394-4517; fax (20) 7394-4572; e-mail london.gazette@tso.co.uk; internet www.londongazette.co.uk; f. 1665; 5 a week; the oldest continuously published newspaper in the UK; government journal of official, legal and public notices.

New Left Review: 6 Meard St, London, W1F 0EG; tel. (20) 7734-8830; fax (20) 7439-3869; e-mail mail@newleftreview.org; internet www.newleftreview.org; f. 1960; 6 a year; international politics, economics and culture; Editor SUSAN WATKINS.

New Statesman: 3rd Floor, 52 Grosvenor Gardens, London, SW1W 0AU; tel. (20) 7730-3444; fax (20) 7259-0181; e-mail info@newstatesman.co.uk; internet www.newstatesman.com; f. 1913; weekly; current affairs, politics and the arts; Editor SUE MATTHIAS (acting); circ. 29,041.

People in Power: Cambridge International Reference on Current Affairs Ltd (CIRCA), 13–17 Sturton St, Cambridge, CB1 2SN; tel. (1223) 568017; fax (1223) 354643; e-mail pip@circaworld.com; internet www.peopleinpower.com; f. 1987; bi-monthly; current worldwide government listings; Man. Dir. ROGER EAST; Producer ROSEMARY PAYNE.

The Political Quarterly: Blackwell Publishing Ltd, 9600 Garsington Rd, Oxford, OX4 2DQ; tel. (1865) 476303; fax (1865) 476770; internet www.blackwellpublishing.com; f. 1930; Editors ANDREW GAMBLE, ANTHONY WRIGHT.

Private Eye: 6 Carlisle St, London, W1D 3BN; tel. (20) 7437-4017; fax (20) 7437-0705; e-mail strobes@private-eye.co.uk; internet www.private-eye.co.uk; f. 1961; fortnightly; satirical; Editor IAN HISLOP; circ. 208,945.

Prospect: 2 Bloomsbury Pl., London, WC1A 2QA; tel. (20) 7255-1281; fax (20) 7255-1279; e-mail editorial@prospect-magazine.co.uk; internet www.prospect-magazine.co.uk; f. 1995; monthly; political and cultural; Editor DAVID GOODHART; circ. 24,900.

Race & Class: The Institute of Race Relations, 2–6 Leeke St, London, WC1X 9HS; tel. (20) 7837-0041; fax (20) 7278-0623; e-mail info@irr.org.uk; internet www.irr.org.uk; f. 1959; quarterly; journal on racism, empire and globalization; Editors A. SIVANANDAN, HAZEL WATERS.

The Spectator: 22 Old Queen St, London, SW1H 9HP; tel. (20) 7961-0200; fax (20) 7961-0058; e-mail editor@spectator.co.uk; internet www.spectator.co.uk; f. 1828; Propr Press Holdings; Thursday; independent political and literary review; Editor MATTHEW D'ANCONA; circ. 73,204.

Tribune: 9 Arkwright Rd, London, NW3 6AN; tel. (20) 7433-6410; fax (20) 7433-6419; e-mail mail@tribunemagazine.co.uk; internet www.tribuneweb.co.uk; f. 1937; Friday; Labour's independent weekly; politics, current affairs, arts; Editor CHRIS MCLAUGHLIN.

Economics and Business

Accountancy Age: Incisive Media, 32–34 Broadwick St, London, W1A 2HG; tel. (20) 7316-9000; fax (20) 7316-9250; e-mail news@accountancyage.com; internet www.accountancyage.co.uk; f. 1969; weekly; Editor GAVIN HINKS; circ. 70,092 (July 2005).

The Banker: Number One Southwark Bridge, London, SE1 9HL; tel. (20) 7775-6359; e-mail stephen.timewell@ft.com; internet www.thebanker.com; f. 1926; monthly; monetary and economic policy, international and domestic banking and finance, banking technology, country surveys; Propr Pearson PLC; Editor-in-Chief STEPHEN TIMEWELL; circ. 26,089 (July 2005).

Campaign: Haymarket Marketing Publications Ltd, 174 Hammersmith Rd, London, W6 7JP; tel. (20) 8267-4656; fax (20) 8267-4915; e-mail campaign@haymarket.com; internet www.brandrepublic.com/campaign; f. 1968; advertising, marketing and media; Thursday; Editor CLAIRE BEALE; circ. 10,585 (July 2005).

Crops: Farmers Weekly Group, 2nd Floor, Quadrant House, The Quadrant, Sutton, Surrey, SM2 5AS; tel. (20) 8652-4934; fax (20) 8652-8928; e-mail crops@rbi.co.uk; internet www.fwi.co.uk; f. 1984; fortnightly; publ. by Reed Business Information; Editor ROBERT HARRIS; circ. 16,003.

Economic Journal: Wiley-Blackwell, 9600 Garsington Rd, Oxford, OX4 2QD; tel. (1865) 791100; fax (1865) 791347; e-mail rchandler@wiley.com; internet www.blackwellpublishing.com; f. 1891; nine a year; Editors ANTONIO CICCONE, LEONARDO FELLI, JÖRN-STEFFEN PISCHKE, STEVE MACHIN, ANDREW SCOTT, DAVID MYATT.

The Economist: 25 St James's St, London, SW1A 1HG; tel. (20) 7830-7000; fax (20) 7839-2968; e-mail letters@economist.com; internet www.economist.com; f. 1843; 50% owned by Pearson PLC, 50% by individual shareholders; Friday; Editor JOHN MICKLETHWAIT; Publr and Man. Dir ANDREW RASHBASS; circ. 172,842.

Euromoney: Nestor House, Playhouse Yard, London, EC4V 5EX; tel. (20) 7779-8888; fax (20) 7779-8653; e-mail hotline@euromoneyplc.com; internet www.euromoney.com; f. 1969; monthly; Editor CLIVE HORWOOD; circ. 27,712 (July 2005).

Farmers Weekly: Farmers Weekly Group, Quadrant House, 2nd Floor, The Quadrant, Sutton, Surrey, SM2 5AS; tel. (20) 8652-4911; fax (20) 8652-4005; e-mail farmers.weekly@rbi.co.uk; internet www.fwi.co.uk; f. 1934; Friday; publ. by Reed Business Information; Editor JANE KING; circ. 70,315.

Investors Chronicle: FT Business, 1 Southwark Bridge, London, SE1 9HL; tel. (20) 7382-3000; fax (20) 7775-6501; e-mail ic.customer.services@ft.com; internet www.investorschronicle.co.uk; f. as *Money Market Review* 1860; amalgamated with *Investors Chronicle* 1914; amalgamated with the *Stock Exchange Gazette* 1967; Friday; independent financial and economic review; Editor MATTHEW VINCENT; circ. 35,046.

Management Today: 174 Hammersmith Rd, London, W6 7JP; tel. (20) 8267-4629; fax (20) 8267-4680; e-mail editorial@mtmagazine.co.uk; internet www.managementtoday.co.uk; f. 1966; monthly; Editor MATTHEW GWYTHER; circ. 100,464 (July 2005).

Education

Higher Education Quarterly: Blackwell Publishing, 9600 Garsington Rd, Oxford, OX4 2DQ; tel. (1865) 776868; fax (1865) 714591; e-mail sarah.phibbs@oxon.blackwellpublishing.com; internet www.blackwellpublishing.com; f. 1946; Editor LEE HARVEY.

The Teacher: Hamilton House, Mabledon Pl., London, WC1H 9BD; tel. (20) 7380-4708; fax (20) 7383-7230; e-mail teacher@nut.org.uk; internet www.teachers.org.uk/theteacher; f. 1872; magazine of the

NUT; news, comments and articles on all aspects of education; eight a year; Editor ELLIE CAMPBELL-BARR.

The Times Educational Supplement: 26 Red Lion Sq., London, WC1R 4HQ; tel. (20) 3194-3000; fax (20) 3194-3333; e-mail wendy.berliner@tes.co.uk; internet www.tes.co.uk; f. 1910; Friday; Editor WENDY BERLINER (acting); circ. 69,153.

The Times Higher Education Supplement: 26 Red Lion Sq., London, WC1R 4HQ; tel. (20) 3194-3000; fax (20) 3194-3300; e-mail editor@thes.co.uk; internet www.thes.co.uk; f. 1971; Thursday; Editor GERARD KELLY; circ. 22,194 (Dec. 2006).

Home, Fashion and General

Arena: Endeavour House, 189 Shaftesbury Ave, London, WC2H 8JG; tel. (20) 7437-9011; fax (20) 7520-6500; internet www.arenamagazine.co.uk; monthly; men's interest; Editor GILES HATTERSLEY; circ. 30,886.

Bella: H. Bauer Publishing Ltd, 1st Floor, 24–28 Oval Rd, London, NW1 7DT; tel. (20) 7241-8000; fax (20) 7241-8056; internet www.bauer.co.uk; f. 1987; weekly, Tuesday; fashion, beauty, health, cookery, handicrafts; Editor JULIA DAVIS; circ. 247,390.

Best: National Magazine Company, 72 Broadwick St, London, W1F 9EP; tel. (20) 7439-5000; fax (20) 7439-4580; e-mail best@acp-natmag.co.uk; internet www.natmags.co.uk; f. 1987; weekly; women's interest; Editor MICHELLE HATHER; circ. 340,793.

Chat: IPC Connect Ltd, The Blue Fin Bldg, 110 Southwark St, London, SE1 0SU; tel. and fax (20) 3148-6153; e-mail ingrid_millar@ipcmedia.com; internet www.ipcmedia.com; weekly; women's interest; Editor GILLY SINCLAIR; circ. 511,510.

Company: National Magazine House, 72 Broadwick St, London, W1F 9EP; tel. (20) 7439-5000; fax (20) 7439-6886; e-mail company.mail@natmags.co.uk; internet www.natmags.co.uk; monthly; Editor CLAIRE IRVINE (acting); circ. 264,494.

Cosmopolitan: National Magazine House, 72 Broadwick St, London, W1F 9EP; tel. (20) 7439-5000; fax (20) 7439-5232; e-mail contact@natmags.co.uk; internet www.cosmopolitan.co.uk; f. 1972; monthly; women's interest; Editor LOUISE COURT; circ. 450,952.

Elle: 64 North Row, London, W1K 7LL; tel. (20) 7150-7000; fax (20) 7150-7001; e-mail lorraine.candy@hf-uk.com; internet www.hachettefilipacchiuk.co.uk; f. 1985; monthly; women's interest; Editor-in-Chief LORRAINE CANDY; circ. 203,302.

Esquire: National Magazine House, 72 Broadwick St, London, W1F 9EP; tel. (20) 7439-5000; fax (20) 7439-5675; e-mail info@esquire.co.uk; internet www.esquire.co.uk; f. 1991; monthly; men's interest; Editor JEREMY LANGMEAD; circ. 53,537.

Eve: Griffin House, 161 Hammersmith Rd, London, W6 8BS; tel. (20) 8267-5000; fax (20) 8267-8222; e-mail evemagazine@haymarket.com; internet www.evemagazine.co.uk; f. 2000; monthly; Editor NIC MCCARTHY; circ. 163,415.

FHM: Endeavour House, 189 Shaftesbury Ave, London, WC2H 8JG; tel. (20) 7436-1515; fax (20) 7182-8021; e-mail help@fhm.com; internet www.fhm.com; f. 1987; monthly; men's interest; Editor-in-Chief ANTHONY NOGUERA; circ. 311,590.

Glamour: Vogue House, Hanover Sq., London, W1S 1JU; tel. (20) 7499-9080; e-mail glamour-editorial@condenast.co.uk; internet www.glamour.com; f. 2001; monthly; women's interest; Editor JO ELVIN; circ. 544,653.

Good Housekeeping: National Magazine House, 72 Broadwick St, London, W1F 9EP; tel. (20) 7439-5000; fax (20) 7437-6886; e-mail contact@goodhousekeeping.co.uk; internet www.goodhousekeeping.co.uk; f. 1922; monthly; Editor-in-Chief LOUISE CHUNN; circ. 435,238.

GQ: The Condé Nast Publications Ltd, Vogue House, Hanover Sq., London, W1S 1JU; tel. (20) 7499-9080; fax (20) 7495-1679; internet www.gq-magazine.co.uk; f. 1988; monthly; Editor DYLAN JONES; circ. 127,886.

Grazia: Endeavour House, 189 Shaftesbury Ave, London, WC2H 8JG; tel. (20) 7437-9011; e-mail feedback@graziamagazine.co.uk; internet www.graziamagazine.co.uk; f. 2005; weekly; Editor JANE BRUTON; circ. 220,125.

Harper's Bazaar: National Magazine House, 72 Broadwick St, London, W1F 9EP; tel. (20) 7439-5000; fax (20) 7439-6886; internet www.harpersbazaar.co.uk; f. 1929; Propr National Magazine Co Ltd; monthly; international fashion, beauty, general features; Editor LUCY YEOMANS; circ. 105,834.

Heat: Endeavour House, 189 Shaftesbury Ave, London, WC2H 8JG; tel. (20) 7437-9011; internet www.heatworld.com; f. 1999; Tuesdays; celebrity news, TV, radio, films; Editor JULIAN LINLEY (acting); circ. 558,365.

Hello!: Hello! Ltd, Wellington House, 69–71 Upper Ground, London, SE1 9PQ; tel. (20) 7667-8700; fax (20) 7667-8716; e-mail hello@hellomagazine.com; internet www.hellomagazine.com; Propr. Hola, SA (Spain); weekly; Publishing Dir CHARLOTTE STOCKTING; Editor KAY GODDARD; circ. 419,814.

Homes and Gardens: The Blue Fin Bldg, 110 Southwark St, London, SE1 0SU; tel. (20) 7261-6202; fax (20) 7261-6247; internet www.homesandgardens.com; f. 1919; monthly; Editor DEBORAH BARKER; circ. 139,100.

House & Garden: The Condé Nast Publications Ltd, Vogue House, Hanover Sq., London, W1S 1JU; tel. (20) 7499-9080; fax (20) 7629-2907; e-mail harriet.bindloss@condenast.com; internet www.houseandgarden.co.uk; f. 1920; monthly; Editor SUSAN CREWE; circ. 141,782.

Ideal Home: IPC Media Ltd, The Blue Fin Bldg, 110 Southwark St, London, SE1 0SU; tel. (20) 3148-5000; e-mail ideal_home@ipcmedia.com; internet www.idealhomemagazine.co.uk; f. 1920; 11 a year; Editor ISOBEL MCKENZIE-PRICE; circ. 233,360.

InStyle: The Blue Fin Bldg, 110 Southwark St, London, SE1 0SU; tel. (20) 7261-4747; fax (20) 7261-6664; internet www.instylemagazine.co.uk; f. 2001; monthly; fashion, beauty; Editor TRISH HALPIN; circ. 178,699.

The Lady: 39–40 Bedford St, London, WC2E 9ER; tel. (20) 7379-4717; fax (20) 7497-2137; e-mail admin@lady.co.uk; internet www.lady.co.uk; f. 1885; Tuesday; Editor ARLINE USDEN; circ. 31,572 (2006).

Loaded: IPC Media Ltd, The Blue Fin Bldg, 110 Southwark St, London, SE1 0SU; tel. (20) 3148-6751; e-mail jo_smalley@ipcmedia.com; internet www.loaded.co.uk; f. 1994; monthly; men's interest; Editor MARTIN DAUBNEY; circ. 120,492.

Marie Claire: IPC Media Ltd, The Blue Fin Bldg, 110 Southwark St, London, SE1 0SU; tel. (20) 3148-7664; e-mail marieclaire@ipcmedia.com; internet www.marieclaire.co.uk; f. 1988; monthly; women's interest; Man. Editor MARIE O'RIORDAN; circ. 332,705.

Maxim: 30 Cleveland St, London, W1T 4JD; tel. (20) 7907-6000; fax (20) 7907-6020; e-mail editorial@maxim-magazine.co.uk; internet www.maxim-magazine.co.uk; f. 1995; monthly; health, fitness, fashion, finance; Editor MICHAEL DONLEVY; circ. 107,687.

My Weekly: D. C. Thomson & Co Ltd, 80 Kingsway East, Dundee, DD4 8SL; tel. (1382) 223131; fax (1382) 452491; e-mail myweekly@dcthomson.co.uk; f. 1910; Thursday; women's interest; Editor SALLY HAMPTON; circ. 171,392.

Now: The Blue Fin Bldg, 110 Southwark St, London, SE1 0SU; tel. (20) 3148-6373; fax (20) 3148-8110; internet www.nowmagazine.co.uk; weekly; celebrity news, TV, radio, films; Editor ABIGAIL BLACKBURN; circ. 494,229.

Nuts: The Blue Fin Bldg, 110 Southwark St, London, SE1 0SU; tel. (20) 7261-6174; e-mail nutsmagazine@ipcmedia.com; internet www.nutsmag.co.uk; f. 2004; weekly; Editor DOMINIC SMITH; circ. 279,269.

OK!: The Northern & Shell Bldg, 10 Lower Thames St, London, EC3R 6EN; tel. (871) 434-1010; e-mail editor@ok-magazine.com; internet www.ok-magazine.co.uk; weekly; Editor LISA BYRNE; circ. 557,014.

The People's Friend: D. C. Thomson & Co Ltd, 80 Kingsway East, Dundee, DD4 8SL; tel. (1382) 223131; fax (1382) 452491; e-mail peoplesfriend@dcthomson.co.uk; f. 1869; Wednesday; women's fiction, home, crafts, general; Editor MARGARET MCCOY; circ. 337,898.

Prima: 72 Broadwick St, London, W1F 9EP; tel. (20) 7439-5000; fax (20) 7312-4100; e-mail prima@natmags.co.uk; internet www.prima.co.uk; f. 1986; monthly; Editor MAIRE FAHEY; circ. 300,025.

Reader's Digest: Reader's Digest Association Ltd, (British Edition) 11 Westferry Circus, Canary Wharf, London, E14 4HE; tel. (20) 7715-8000; fax (20) 7715-8716; e-mail theeditor@readersdigest.co.uk; internet www.readersdigest.co.uk; f. 1938; monthly; Editor KATHERINE WALKER; circ. 712,815.

The Scots Magazine: D. C. Thomson & Co. Ltd, 2 Albert Sq., Dundee, DD1 9QJ; tel. (1382) 223131; fax (1382) 322214; e-mail mail@scotsmagazine.com; internet www.scotsmagazine.com; f. 1739; monthly; Scottish interest; circ. 39,588.

She: 72 Broadwick St, London, W1F 9EP; tel. (20) 7439-5000; fax (20) 7437-6886; e-mail sian.rees@natmags.co.uk; internet www.natmags.co.uk; f. 1955; monthly; Editor SIÂN REES; circ. 169,112.

Take a Break: H. Bauer Publishing Ltd, 24–28 Oval Rd, London, NW1 7DT; tel. (20) 7241-8000; fax (20) 7241-8052; e-mail tab.features@bauer.co.uk; internet www.bauer.co.uk; f. 1990; Thursday; Editor JOHN DALE; circ. 1,028,423.

Tatler: The Condé Nast Publications Ltd, Vogue House, Hanover Sq., London, W1S 1JU; tel. (20) 7499-9080; fax (20) 7409-0451; internet www.tatler.co.uk; f. 1709; monthly; Editor GEORDIE GREIG; circ. 90,125.

That's Life!: H. Bauer Publishing Ltd, 24–28 Oval Rd, London, NW1 7DT; tel. (20) 7241-8000; fax (20) 7241-8008; e-mail sales@tpc-london.com; internet www.bauer.co.uk; f. 1995; Thursday; Editor JO CHECKLEY; circ. 443,604.

Vanity Fair: The Condé Nast Publications Ltd, Vogue House, Hanover Sq., London, W1R 0AD; tel. (20) 7499-9080; fax (20)

7499-4415; internet www.vanityfair.co.uk; monthly; Editor HENRY PORTER; circ. 98,190.

Viz: Dennis Publishing Ltd, 30 Cleveland St, London, W1T 4JD; tel. (20) 7907-6000; fax (20) 7907-6020; e-mail viz@viz.co.uk; internet www.viz.co.uk; f. 1979; monthly; Publr WILL WATT; Editor SIMON DONALD; circ. 94,364 (Dec. 2006).

Vogue: The Condé Nast Publications Ltd, Vogue House, Hanover Sq., London, W1S 1JU; tel. (20) 7499-9080; fax (20) 7408-0559; internet www.vogue.co.uk; f. 1916; monthly; Editor ALEXANDRA SHULMAN; circ. 220,084.

The Voice: GV Media Group Ltd, Northern & Shell Tower, 6th Floor, 4 Selsdon Way, London, E14 9GL; tel. (20) 7510-0340; fax (20) 7510-0341; e-mail letters@gvmedia.co.uk; internet www.voice-online.co.uk; f. 1982; Monday; black interest; Group Editor DEIRDRE FORBES.

Wallpaper*: 7th Floor, The Blue Fin Bldg, 110 Southwark St, London, SE1 0SU; tel. (20) 3148-5000; fax (20) 3148-8119; e-mail marketing@wallpaper.com; internet www.wallpaper.com; f. 1996; 11 times a year; Editor TONY CHAMBERS; circ. 112,871 (Dec. 2006).

Woman: The Blue Fin Bldg, 110 Southwark St, London, SE1 0SU; tel. (20) 3148-6491; e-mail woman@ipcmedia.com; internet www.ipcmedia.com/brands/woman; f. 1937; Tuesday; Editor JACKIE HATTON; circ. 369,982.

Woman and Home: The Blue Fin Bldg, 110 Southwark St, London, SE1 0SU; tel. (20) 3148-7836; e-mail woman&home@ipcmedia.com; internet www.ipcmedia.com/brands/womanhome; f. 1926; monthly; Editor SUE JAMES; circ. 320,934.

Woman's Own: The Blue Fin Bldg, 110 Southwark St, London, SE1 0SU; tel. (20) 3148-6552; fax (20) 3148-8112; internet www.ipcmedia.com/brands/womansown; f. 1932; Tuesday; Editor-in-Chief KAREN LIVERMORE; circ. 344,765.

Woman's Weekly: The Blue Fin Bldg, 110 Southwark St, London, SE1 0SU; tel. (20) 3148-6628; internet www.ipcmedia.com/brands/womansweekly; f. 1911; Wednesday; Editor DIANE KENWOOD; circ. 369,926.

Zoo: Endeavour House, 189 Shaftesbury Ave, London, WC2H 8JG; tel. (20) 7208-3797; internet www.zooweekly.co.uk; f. 2004; weekly; Editor BEN TODD; circ. 186,732.

Law

Law Quarterly Review: 100 Avenue Rd, London, NW3 3PF; tel. (20) 7393-7000; fax (20) 7393-7010; internet www.sweetandmaxwell.co.uk; f. 1885; quarterly; Editor Prof. FRANCIS M. B. REYNOLDS.

Law Society's Gazette: 113 Chancery Lane, London, WC2A 1PL; tel. (20) 7242-1222; e-mail gazette-editorial@lawsociety.org.uk; internet www.lawgazette.co.uk; f. 1903; weekly; Editor-in-Chief PAUL ROGERSON; circ. 115,576.

The Lawyer: St Giles House, 50 Poland St, London, W1V 7AX; tel. (20) 7970-4614; fax (20) 7970-4640; e-mail catrin.griffiths@thelawyer.com; internet www.thelawyer.com; weekly; Editor CATRIN GRIFFITHS; circ. 31,507.

Leisure Interests and Sport

Autocar Magazine: Haymarket Consumer Media, Broom Rd, Teddington, Middx, TW11 9BE; tel. (20) 8267-5630; fax (20) 8267-5759; e-mail autocar@haynet.com; internet www.autocar.co.uk; f. 1895; Wednesday; Editor CHAS HALLETT; circ. 59,427.

Autosport: Haymarket Consumer Media, Broom Rd, Teddington, Middx, TW11 9BE; tel. (20) 8267-5118; e-mail rob.aherne@haymarket.com; internet www.autosport.com; f. 1950; Thursday; covers all aspects of motor sport; Editor-in-Chief ANDY VAN DE BURGT; circ. 38,495 (Dec. 2006).

Car: Media House, Lynchwood Business Park, Lynchwood, Peterborough, PE2 6EA; tel. (1733) 468485; fax (1733) 468660; internet www.carmagazine.co.uk; f. 1962; monthly; Editor PHIL MCNAMARA; circ. 80,312.

Country Life: 9th Floor, The Blue Fin Bldg, 110 Southwark St, London, SE1 0SU; tel. (20) 3148-4445; fax (20) 3148-8129; e-mail milly_cumming@ipcmedia.com; internet www.countrylife.co.uk; f. 1897; Thursday; Editor MARK HEDGES; circ. 40,408 (Dec. 2006).

The Countryman: The Water Mill, Broughton Hall, Skipton, BD23 3AG; tel. (1756) 701381; fax (1756) 701326; e-mail editorial@thecountryman.co.uk; internet www.thecountryman.co.uk; f. 1927; monthly; independent; Editor PAUL JACKSON; circ. 20,600.

FourFourTwo: Haymarket Consumer Media, Broom Rd, Teddington, TW11 9BE; tel. (20) 8267-5848; fax (20) 8267-5354; e-mail martyn.jones@haymarket.com; internet www.fourfourtwo.com; f. 1994; monthly; football; Editor HUGH SLEIGHT; circ. 103,669.

BBC Gardeners' World Magazine: BBC Worldwide Ltd, Room AG193, 80 Wood Lane, London, W12 0TT; tel. (20) 8433-3959; fax (20) 8433-3986; e-mail gweditorial@bbc.co.uk; internet www.gardenersworld.com; f. 1991; monthly; Editor ADAM PASCO; circ. 303,448.

Golf Monthly: The Blue Fin Bldg, 110 Southwark St, London, SE1 0SU; tel. (20) 7148-4530; e-mail golfmonthly@ipcmedia.com; internet www.golf-monthly.co.uk; f. 1911; monthly; Editor MICHAEL HARRIS; circ. 74,801.

BBC Good Food: BBC Worldwide Ltd, 80 Wood Lane, London, W12 0TT; tel. (20) 8433-1316; fax (20) 8433-1277; e-mail goodfoodrs@galleon.co.uk; internet www.bbcmagazines.com/goodfood; f. 1989; monthly; Editor GILLIAN CARTER; circ. 338,395.

Hi-Fi News: Leon House, 10th Floor, 233 High St, Croydon, Surrey, CR9 1HZ; tel. (20) 8726-8310; fax (20) 8726-8397; e-mail hi-finews@ipcmedia.com; internet www.hifinews.com; f. 1956; monthly; all aspects of high quality sound reproduction, record reviews; Editor PAUL MILLER; circ. 13,176.

Men's Health: 72 Broadwick St, London, W1F 9EP; tel. (20) 7339-4400; fax (20) 7339-4444; e-mail nicky.williams@natmag-rodale.co.uk; internet www.menshealth.co.uk; f. 1995; monthly; lifestyle, health, general features; Editor MORGAN REES; circ. 238,980.

Practical Photography: Media House, Lynchwood Business Park, Lynchwood, Peterborough, PE2 6EA; tel. (1733) 264666; fax (1733) 465246; internet www.practicalphotography.co.uk; monthly; Editor-in-Chief ANDREW JAMES; circ. 61,078 (Dec. 2006).

Radio Times: BBC Worldwide Ltd, Woodlands, 80 Wood Lane, London, W12 0TT; tel. 0870 608 4455; fax (20) 8433-3160; e-mail radio.times@bbc.co.uk; internet www.radiotimes.com; f. 1923; weekly; programme guide to television and radio broadcasts; Editor GILL HUDSON; circ. 1,046,601.

Rugby World: The Blue Fin Bldg, 110 Southwark St, London, SE1 0SU; tel. (20) 3148-4702; e-mail paul_morgan@ipcmedia.com; internet www.rugbyworld.com; monthly; Editor PAUL MORGAN; circ.41,896 (Dec. 2006).

Time Out: Time Out Magazine Ltd, Universal House, 251 Tottenham Court Rd, London, W1T 7AB; tel. (20) 7813-3000; fax (20) 7813-6001; e-mail net@timeout.co.uk; internet www.timeout.com; f. 1968; weekly; listings and reviews of events in London; Time Out Group also publishes city guides and specialized London guides; Editor GORDON THOMSON; circ. 87,308.

TVTimes: The Blue Fin Bldg, 110 Southwark St, London, SE1 0SU; tel. (20) 3148-5570; e-mail tvtimes_letters@ipcmedia.com; internet www.ipcmedia.com/brands/tvtimes; f. 1955; features and listings of all television broadcasts; Editor IAN ABBOTT; circ. 353,014.

What Car?: Teddington Studios, Broom Rd, Teddington, Middx, TW11 9BE; tel. (20) 8267-5688; fax (20) 8267-5750; e-mail whatcar@haymarket.com; internet www.whatcar.com; f. 1973; 13 a year; Group Editor STEVE FOWLER; circ. 109,372.

What's On TV: The Blue Fin Bldg, 110 Southwark St, London, SE1 0SU; tel. (20) 3148-5928; e-mail wotv-postbag@ipcmedia.com; internet www.ipcmedia.com/brands/whatsontv; f. 1991; weekly; television programme guide and features; Editor COLIN TOUGH; circ. 1,422,486.

The Wisden Cricketer: 1.4 Shepherds Bldg, Charecroft Way, London, W14 0EE; internet www.cricinfo.com/wisdencricketer; f. 1921; monthly; acquired by BSkyB Publications Ltd in 2007; Editor JOHN STERN; circ. 35,442 (Dec. 2006).

Zest: 72 Broadwick St, London, W1F 9EP; tel. (20) 7439-5000; fax (20) 7437-6886; e-mail contact@zest.co.uk; internet www.zest.co.uk; health, beauty, fitness and nutrition; Editor ALISON PYLKKANEN; circ. 102,261.

Medicine, Science and Technology

Biochemical Journal: Portland Press Ltd, 3rd Floor, Eagle House, 16 Procter St, London, WC1V 6NX; tel. (20) 7280-4110; fax (20) 7280-4169; e-mail editorial@portlandpress.com; internet www.biochemj.org; f. 1906; 2 a month; publ. by Portland Press on behalf of the Biochemical Society; Chair. Editorial Board PETER SHEPHERD; Publr P. J. STARLEY.

British Journal of Psychiatry: 17 Belgrave Sq., London, SW1X 8PG; tel. (20) 7235-2351; fax (20) 7259-6507; e-mail bjp@rcpsych.ac.uk; internet bjp.rcpsych.org; monthly; original articles, reviews and correspondence; publ. by the Royal College of Psychiatrists; Editor PETER TYRER; circ. 14,100 (July 2005).

British Journal of Psychology: St Andrew's House, 48 Princess Rd East, Leicester, LE1 7DR; tel. (116) 254-9568; fax (116) 247-0787; e-mail journals@bps.org.uk; internet www.bps.org.uk; f. 1904; quarterly; publ. by the British Psychological Society; Editor Prof. PETER MITCHELL.

British Journal of Sociology: 9600 Garsington Rd, Oxford, OX4 2DQ; tel. (1865) 776868; fax (1865) 714591; internet www.blackwellpublishing.com/bjos; f. 1950; quarterly; Editor BRIDGET HUTTER.

BMJ: BMA House, Tavistock Sq., London, WC1H 9JP; tel. (20) 7387-4499; fax (20) 7383-6418; e-mail editor@bmj.com; internet www.bmj.com; f. 1840; Saturday; 10 overseas editions; Editor Dr FIONA GODLEE; circ. 122,982 (July 2005).

Computer Weekly: Reed Business Information, Quadrant House, The Quadrant, Sutton, Surrey, SM2 5AS; tel. (20) 8652-8642; fax (20) 8652-8979; e-mail cwnews@rbi.co.uk; internet www.computerweekly.com; f. 1966; Tuesday; Editor BRIAN MCKENNA.

Computing: VNU Business Publications, VNU House, 32–34 Broadwick St, London, W1A 2HG; tel. (20) 7316-9000; fax (20) 7316-9160; e-mail computing@vnu.co.uk; internet www.computing.co.uk; f. 1973; Thursday; Editor BRYAN GLICK; circ. 115,000 (July 2005).

The Ecologist: Unit 102D, Lana House Studios, 116–118 Commercial St, London, E1 6NF; tel. (20) 7422-8100; fax (20) 7422-8101; e-mail editorial@theecologist.org; internet www.theecologist.org; f. 1970; 10 per year; all aspects of ecology, the environment, etc.; Editor PAT THOMAS.

Flight International: Reed Business Information, Quadrant House, The Quadrant, Sutton, Surrey, SM2 5AS; tel. (20) 8652-3842; fax (20) 8652-3840; e-mail flight.international@rbi.co.uk; internet www.flightinternational.com; f. 1909; Tuesday; Editor MURDO MORRISON.

The Geographical Magazine: Circle Publishing, 1 Victoria Villas, Richmond, Surrey, TW9 2GW; tel. (20) 8332-2713; fax (20) 8332-9307; e-mail magazine@geographical.co.uk; internet www.geographical.co.uk; f. 1935; monthly; Editor GEORDIE TORR; circ. 21,684.

Lancet: 32 Jamestown Rd, London, NW1 7BY; tel. (20) 7424-4910; fax (20) 7424-4911; e-mail editorial@lancet.com; internet www.lancet.com; f. 1823; Saturday; medical; Editor Dr RICHARD HORTON.

Nature: Macmillan Magazines Ltd, 4 Crinan St, London, N1 9XW; tel. (20) 7833-4000; fax (20) 7843-4640; e-mail nature@nature.com; internet www.nature.com/nature; f. 1869; Thursday; scientific; Editor-in-Chief Dr PHILIP CAMPBELL.

New Scientist: Lacon House, 84 Theobald's Rd, London, WC1X 8NS; tel. (20) 7611-1200; fax (20) 7611-1250; e-mail news@newscientist.com; internet www.newscientist.com; f. 1956; Thursday; science and technology; Editor JEREMY WEBB; circ. 178,854 (world-wide).

Nursing Times: Greater London House, Hampstead Rd, London, NW1 7EJ; tel. (20) 7874-0500; fax (20) 7874-0505; e-mail rachel.downey@emap.com; internet www.nursingtimes.net; f. 1905; Tuesday; professional nursing journal; Editor RACHEL DOWNEY; circ. 48,388.

The Practitioner: Ludgate House, 245 Blackfriars Rd, London, SE1 9UY; tel. (20) 7921-8113; e-mail cchapman@cmpmedica.com; internet www.thepractitioner.co.uk; f. 1868; monthly; medical journal for General Practitioners; Editor CORINNE SHORT; circ. 35,656.

Religion and Philosophy

Catholic Herald: Herald House, 15 Lamb's Passage, Bunhill Row, London, EC1Y 8TQ; tel. (20) 7448-3602; fax (20) 7256-9728; e-mail editorial@catholicherald.co.uk; internet www.catholicherald.co.uk; f. 1888; Catholic weekly newspaper; Friday; Editor LUKE COPPEN.

Church Times: 13–17 Long Lane, London, EC1A 9PN; tel. (20) 7776-1060; fax (20) 7776-1086; e-mail editor@churchtimes.co.uk; internet www.churchtimes.co.uk; f. 1863; Church of England and world-wide Anglican news; Friday; Editor PAUL HANDLEY.

Jewish Chronicle: Jewish Chronicle Newspaper Ltd, 25 Furnival St, London, EC4A 1JT; tel. (20) 7415-1500; fax (20) 7405-9040; e-mail jconline@thejc.com; internet www.thejc.com; f. 1841; Friday; Editor DAVID ROWAN; circ. 33,441.

Methodist Recorder: 122 Golden Lane, London, EC1Y 0TL; tel. (20) 7251-8414; fax (20) 7608-3490; e-mail editorial@methodistrecorder.co.uk; internet www.methodistrecorder.co.uk; f. 1861; Thursday; Man. Editor MOIRA SLEIGHT.

New Blackfriars: Blackfriars, Oxford, OX1 3LY; tel. (1865) 776868; fax (1865) 714591; e-mail fergus.kerr@english.op.org; internet www.blackwellpublishing.com; f. 1920; monthly; religious and cultural; Editor Rev. FERGUS KERR.

Philosophy: Royal Institute of Philosophy, 14 Gordon Sq., London, WC1H 0AR; tel. (20) 7387-4130; e-mail j.garvey@royalinstitutephilosophy.org; internet www.royalinstitutephilosophy.org; f. 1925; quarterly; Editor ANTHONY O'HEAR.

The Universe: 1st Floor, St James's Bldgs, Oxford St, Manchester, M1 6FP; tel. (161) 236-8856; fax (161) 236-8530; e-mail newsdesk@totalcatholic.com; internet www.totalcatholic.com; f. 1860; Sunday; illustrated Catholic newspaper and review; publ. by Gabriel Communications Ltd; Editor JOSEPH KELLY.

Woman Alive: Christian Publishing and Outreach, Garcia Estate, Canterbury Rd, Worthing, West Sussex, BN13 1BW; tel. (1903) 264556; fax (1903) 821081; e-mail womanalive@cpo.org.uk; internet www.womanalive.co.uk; f. 1982; monthly; Editor JACKIE STEAD.

PRESS ORGANIZATION

Press Complaints Commission: Halton House, 20–23 Holborn, London, EC1 2JD; tel. (20) 7831-0022; fax (20) 7831-0025; e-mail complaints@pcc.org.uk; internet www.pcc.org.uk; f. 1991 to replace the Press Council, following the report of the Committee on Privacy and Related Matters; an independent organization established by the newspaper and magazine industry through the Press Standards Board of Finance to deal with complaints from the public about the contents and conduct of newspapers and magazines; the Commission has an independent chairman and 17 members, drawn from the lay public (who are in the majority) and the press. It upholds a 16-point Code of Practice, agreed by a committee of editors representing the newspaper and magazine industry. It aims to ensure that the British press maintains the highest professional standards, having regard to generally established press freedoms; Chair. Sir CHRISTOPHER MEYER; Dir TIM TOULMIN.

NEWS AGENCIES

Associated Press Ltd: Associated Press House, 12 Norwich St, London, EC4A 1BP; tel. (20) 7353-1515; fax (20) 7353-8118; f. 1931; British subsidiary of Associated Press of USA; delivers a world-wide foreign news and photographic service to Commonwealth and foreign papers; Chair. LOUIS D. BOCCARDI; Bureau Chief BARRY RENFREW.

Press Association Ltd: 292 Vauxhall Bridge Rd, London, SW1V 1AE; tel. (870) 120-3200; fax (870) 120-3201; e-mail info@pa.press.net; internet www.pa.press.net; f. 1868; national news agency of the United Kingdom and Ireland; Chair. Sir HARRY ROCHE; CEO and Editor-in-Chief PAUL POTTS; Editor JONATHAN GRUN.

Reuters Group PLC: Reuters Bldg, 30 The South Colonnade, Canary Wharf, London, E14 5EP; tel. (20) 7250-1122; fax (20) 7324-5400; e-mail editor@reuters.com; internet www.reuters.co.uk; f. 1851; world-wide news and information service to media and business clients in 57,900 organizations and media clients in 157 countries; Chair. NIALL FITZGERALD; CEO TOM GLOCER; Editor-in-Chief DAVID SCHLESINGER.

United Press International (UPI): Empire House, Empire Way, Middlesex, HA9 0EW; tel. (20) 8970-2604; fax (20) 8970-2613; internet www.upi.com; supplies world-wide news and news-picture coverage in English and Arabic to newspapers, radio and television stations throughout the world; Editor-in-Chief MICHAEL MARSHALL.

INSTITUTIONS

Chartered Institute of Journalists: 2 Dock Offices, Surrey Quays Rd, London, SE16 2XU; tel. (20) 7252-1187; fax (20) 7232-2302; e-mail memberservices@cioj.co.uk; internet www.cioj.co.uk; f. 1884; Pres. JOHN THORPE; Gen. Sec. DOMINIC COOPER.

The Journalists' Charity (Newspaper Press Fund): Dickens House, 35 Wathen Rd, Dorking, Surrey, RH4 1JY; tel. (1306) 887511; fax (1306) 888212; e-mail enquiries@journalistscharity.org.uk; internet www.journalistscharity.org.uk; f. 1864; charity for journalists and their dependants; Chair. ROBERT WARREN; Dir DAVID ILOTT; 5,500 mems.

Newspaper Publishers' Association (NPA): 8th Floor, St Andrew's House, 18-20 St Andrew St, London, EC4A 3AY; tel. (20) 7636-7014; fax (20) 7631-5119; f. 1906; comprises 8 national newspaper groups; Chair. TIM BROOKS; Dir DAVID NEWELL.

Newspaper Society (NS): St Andrew's House, 18-20 St Andrew St, London, EC4A 3AY; tel. (20) 7632-7400; fax (20) 7632-7401; e-mail ns@newspapersoc.org.uk; internet www.newspapersoc.org.uk; f. 1836; represents the regional and local press; Pres. RUSSELL WHITEHAIR; Dir DAVID NEWELL.

Periodical Publishers' Association Ltd: Queen's House, 28 Kingsway, London, WC2B 6JR; tel. (20) 7404-4166; fax (20) 7404-4167; e-mail info1@ppa.co.uk; internet www.ppa.co.uk; f. 1913; trade association for the British magazine industry; Chair. HELEN ALEXANDER; Chief Exec. IAN LOCKS; more than 350 mems.

Association of Publishing Agencies (APA): Queen's House, 3rd Floor, 55–56 Lincoln's Inn Fields, London, WC2A 3LJ; tel. (20) 7404-4166; fax (20) 7404-4167; e-mail info@apa.co.uk; internet www.apa.co.uk; f. 1993; trade association for the customer publishing industry; Chair. SEAN KING; CEO PATRICK FULLER.

UK Association of Online Publishers (AOP): Queen's House, 55–56 Lincoln's Inn Fields, London, WC2A 3LJ; tel. (20) 7404-4166; fax (20) 7404-4167; e-mail ruth.brownlee@ukaop.org.uk; internet www.ukaop.org.uk; f. 2002; represents the interests of online content providers; Chair. SIMON WALDMAN.

THE UNITED KINGDOM

Scottish Daily Newspaper Society: 21 Lansdowne Cres., Edinburgh, EH12 5EH; tel. (131) 535-1064; fax (131) 535-1063; e-mail info@sdns.org.uk; f. 1915; Dir JAMES B. RAEBURN.

Scottish Newspaper Publishers' Association: 48 Palmerston Pl., Edinburgh, EH12 5DE; tel. (131) 220-4353; fax (131) 220-4344; e-mail info@snpa.org.uk; internet www.snpa.org.uk; Dir SIMON M. L. FAIRCLOUGH.

See also under Employers' Organizations and Trade Unions.

Principal Publishers

Publishing firms in the United Kingdom are mainly located in London and many are members of large publishing groups, notably Random House, Reed Elsevier, the Pearson Group and Thomson Reuters. Fiction remains the largest category. The United Kingdom publishes more new titles every year than any other European country. In 2002 125,390 new titles were issued.

Anova Books Group Ltd: 10 Southcombe St, London, W14 0RA; tel. (20) 7605-1400; fax (20) 7605-1401; e-mail info@anovabooks.com; internet www.anovabooks.com; f. 2005; fmrly Chrysalis Books; imprints: Batsford, Collins & Brown, Conway, National Trust Books, Paper Tiger, Pavilion, Portico, Robson; Chief Exec. ROBIN WOOD.

Asean Academic Press Ltd: POB 13945, London, E5 0XY; fax (20) 8533-5856; e-mail aapub@attglobal.net; internet www.aseanacademicpress.com; educational, technical, professional and scientific books on Asia.

Ashgate Publishing Ltd: Gower House, Croft Rd, Aldershot, Hants, GU11 3HR; tel. (1252) 331551; fax (1252) 368595; e-mail info@ashgatepublishing.com; internet www.ashgate.com; f. 1967; social sciences and humanities, art, business and public sector management books; imprints: Ashgate, Gower, Lund Humphries, Variorum; Chair. N. FARROW.

Batsford: 10 Southcombe St, London, W14 0RA; tel. (20) 7314-1400; fax (20) 7314-1594; e-mail krichardson@anovabooks.com; internet www.anovabooks.com/imprint/batsford; f. 1843; imprint of Anova Books Group; crafts, design, architecture, art techniques, fashion, film, chess, bridge, gardening, English heritage, historic Scotland.

BBC Worldwide Ltd: Woodlands, 80 Wood Lane, London, W12 0TT; tel. (20) 8433-2000; fax (20) 8749-0538; e-mail bbcworldwide@bbc.co.uk; internet www.bbcworldwide.com; Chief Exec. JOHN SMITH.

Berlitz Publishing Co Ltd: 58 Borough High St, London, SE1 1XF; tel. (20) 7403-0284; fax (20) 7403-0290; e-mail publishing@berlitz.co.uk; internet www.berlitzpublishing.com; f. 1970; travel, languages, reference, leisure, children's books; owned by Apa Publications (Germany); Group Man. Dir JEREMY WESTWOOD.

A. & C. Black Publishers Ltd: 37 Soho Sq., London, W1D 3QZ; tel. (20) 7758-0200; fax (20) 7758-0222; e-mail enquiries@acblack.com; internet www.acblack.com; f. 1807; inc. Adlard Coles Nautical, Christopher Helm, Herbert Press, Pica Press, T & AD Poyser, Thomas Reed, Methuen Drama; children's and educational books, music, arts and crafts, drama, reference, sport, theatre, travel, sailing, ornithology; owned by Bloomsbury Publishing PLC; Chair. NIGEL NEWTON; Editorial Dir JANET MURPHY.

Bloomsbury Publishing PLC: 36 Soho Sq., London, W1D 3DY; tel. (20) 7494-2111; fax (20) 7434-0151; e-mail csm@bloomsbury.com; internet www.bloomsbury.com; f. 1986; fiction, non-fiction and children's; Chair. JEREMY WILSON; CEO NIGEL NEWTON.

Bowker (UK) Ltd: 1st Floor, Medway House, Cantelupe Rd, East Grinstead, West Sussex, RH19 3BJ; tel. (1342) 310450; fax (1342) 310486; e-mail sales@bowker.co.uk; internet www.bowker.co.uk; owned by the Cambridge Information Group; business, general reference and bibliographic information; Man. Dir DOUG MCMILLAN.

Marion Boyars Publishers Ltd: 24 Lacy Rd, London, SW15 1NL; tel. (20) 8788-9522; fax (20) 8789-8122; e-mail catheryn@marionboyars.com; internet www.marionboyars.co.uk; f. 1975; fiction, plays, cinema, music, translations, literary criticism, sociology; Man. Dir CATHERYN KILGARRIFF.

Calder Publications Ltd: London House, 243-253 Lower Mortlake Rd, Richmond, Surrey, TW9 2LL; tel. (20) 8948-9550; fax (20) 8948-5599; e-mail info@oneworldclassics.com; internet www.calderpublications.com; f. 1950; acquired by Oneworld Publications in 2007; fiction, plays, music, opera, European classics, translations, general books, social science, politics; Calderbooks, Journal of Beckett Studies, English National Opera studies.

Cambridge University Press: The Edinburgh Bldg, Shaftesbury Rd, Cambridge, CB2 2RU; tel. (1223) 312393; fax (1223) 315052; e-mail information@cambridge.org; internet www.cambridge.org; f. 1534; academic and scientific monographs and textbooks, educational, English language teaching materials, microsoftware, bibles, prayer books and academic journals; Chief Exec. STEPHEN R. R. BOURNE.

Canongate Books: 14 High St, Edinburgh, EH1 1TE; tel. (131) 557-5111; fax (131) 557-5211; e-mail info@canongate.co.uk; internet www.canongate.net; f. 1973; general, fiction, non-fiction; Chair. JAMIE BYNG.

Jonathan Cape Ltd: Random House, 20 Vauxhall Bridge Rd, London, SW1V 2SA; tel. (20) 7840-8563; fax (20) 7233-6117; e-mail enquiries@randomhouse.co.uk; internet www.randomhouse.co.uk; f. 1921; imprint of The Random House Group Ltd; general, biography, travel, belles-lettres, fiction, history, poetry; subsidiary imprint: The Bodley Head (biography, current affairs, humour); Publishing Dir DAN FRANKLIN.

Carlton Books: 20 Mortimer St, London W1T 3JW; tel. (20) 7612-0400; fax (20) 7612-0401; e-mail sales@carltonbooks.co.uk; internet www.carltonbooks.co.uk; f. 1992; Man. Dir JONATHAN GOODMAN.

Century: Random House, 20 Vauxhall Bridge Rd, London, SW1V 2SA; tel. (20) 7840-8554; fax (20) 7233-6127; e-mail enquiries@randomhouse.co.uk; internet www.randomhouse.co.uk; f. 1987; imprint of The Random House Group Ltd; general, biography, travel, current affairs, fiction, memoirs, music, philosophy; Man. Dir RICHARD CABLE.

Chatto and Windus: 20 Vauxhall Bridge Rd, London, SW1V 2SA; tel. (20) 7840-8540; fax (20) 7233-6117; internet www.randomhouse.co.uk; imprint of The Random House Group Ltd; general, academic, biography, memoirs, politics, history, literary criticism, current affairs, cultural studies and fiction; imprint: Hogarth Press; Dir ALISON SAMUEL.

Church House Publishing: Church House, Great Smith St, London, SW1P 3AZ; tel. (20) 7898-1451; fax (20) 7898-1449; e-mail publishing@c-of-e.org.uk; internet www.chpublishing.co.uk; Publ. Man. Dr THOMAS ALLAIN-CHAPMAN.

James Clarke and Co Ltd: POB 60, Cambridge, CB1 2NT; tel. (1223) 350865; fax (1223) 366951; e-mail publishing@jamesclarke.co.uk; internet www.jamesclarke.co.uk; f. 1859; religious, reference and academic; imprints: Acorn Editions, Lutterworth Press, Patrick Hardy Books; acquired James Nisbet & Co in 2008; Man. Dir ADRIAN BRINK.

CMP Information (CMPi): Riverbank House, Angel Lane, Tonbridge, Kent, TN9 1SE; tel. (1732) 364422; internet www.cmpi.biz; magazines and information services; CEO GARY HUGHES.

Collins Bartholomew: Westerhill Rd, Bishopbriggs, Glasgow, G64 2QT; tel. (141) 306-3752; fax (141) 306-3130; e-mail collinsbartholomew@harpercollins.co.uk; internet www.bartholomewmaps.com; f. 1826; cartographic division of Harper-Collins Publishers; maps, atlases, bespoke mapping services and data; Exec. Dir SHEENA BARCLAY.

Conran Octopus: 2–4 Heron Quays, London, E14 4JP; tel. (20) 7531-8400; fax (20) 7531-8627; e-mail info@conran-octopus.co.uk; internet www.conran-octopus.co.uk; illustrated reference books; imprint of Octopus Publishing Group Ltd; Publr LORRAINE DICKEY.

Constable and Robinson Ltd: 3 The Lanchesters, 162 Fulham Palace Rd, London, W6 9ER; tel. (20) 8741-3663; fax (20) 8748-7562; e-mail enquiries@constablerobinson.com; internet www.constablerobinson.com; biography and autobiography, general and military history, current affairs, psychology and self-help, health, popular science, and crime fiction; Man. Dir NICHOLAS ROBINSON.

Continuum International Publishing Group: The Tower Bldg, 11 York Rd, London, SE1 7NX; tel. (20) 7922-0880; fax (20) 7922-0881; e-mail rbairdsmith@continuumbooks.com; internet www.continuumbooks.com; f. 1994; popular culture, religion, humanities, social sciences, philosophy and education; imprints: Burns & Oates, Continuum, T&T Clark, Thoemmes Continuum, Hambledon Continuum and Network Continuum; Chair. PATRICK AUSTEN; CEO OLIVER GADSBY.

James Currey Publishers: 73 Botley Rd, Oxford, OX2 0BS; tel. (1865) 244111; fax (1865) 246454; e-mail editorial@jamescurrey.co.uk; internet www.jamescurrey.co.uk; African and world anthropology; Chair. JAMES CURREY; Man. Dir DOUGLAS H. JOHNSON.

Darton, Longman and Todd Ltd: 1 Spencer Court, 140–142 Wandsworth High St, London, SW18 4JJ; tel. (20) 8875-0155; fax (20) 8875-0133; e-mail tradesales@darton-longman-todd.co.uk; internet www.darton-longman-todd.co.uk; f. 1959; theology, spirituality, religious biography and history, Bibles; Editorial Dir BRENDAN WALSH.

David & Charles Ltd: Brunel House, Forde Close, Newton Abbot, Devon, TQ12 4PU; tel. (870) 990-8222; fax (870) 442-2034; e-mail postmaster@davidandcharles.co.uk; internet www.davidandcharles.co.uk; f. 1960; owned by F+W Publications, Inc. (USA); general, trade and reference; Group Chair. and CEO DAVID NUSSBAUM.

André Deutsch Ltd: 20 Mortimer St, London, W1T 3JW; tel. (20) 7612-0400; fax (20) 7612-0401; e-mail enquiries@carltonbooks.co.uk; internet www.carltonbooks.co.uk; f. 1950; biography, memoirs, humour, art, politics, history, travel, sport; imprint of Carlton Books.

Dorling Kindersley PLC: 80 Strand, London, WC2R ORL; tel. (20) 7010-3000; fax (20) 7010-6060; internet www.dorlingkindersley-uk.co.uk; f. 1974; holding co Pearson PLC; illustrated reference books; CEO GARY JUNE.

Gerald Duckworth and Co Ltd: 1st Floor, East Wing, Greenhill House, 90–93 Cowcross St, London, EC1M 6BF; tel. (20) 7490-7300; fax (20) 7490-0080; e-mail info@duckworth-publishers.co.uk; internet www.ducknet.co.uk; f. 1898; fiction, academic; Propr PETER MAYER; COO GILLIAN HALKINS.

Edinburgh University Press: 22 George Sq., Edinburgh, EH8 9LF; tel. (131) 650-4218; fax (131) 662-0053; e-mail timothy.wright@eup.ed.ac.uk; internet www.eup.ed.ac.uk; learned books and journals; Chair. TIM RIX; Chief Exec. TIMOTHY WRIGHT.

Edward Elgar Publishing Ltd: Glensanda House, Montpellier Parade, Cheltenham, GL50 1UA; tel. (1242) 226934; fax (1242) 262111; e-mail info@e-elgar.co.uk; internet www.e-elgar.com; f. 1986; economics, law, business and management; Man. Dir E. ELGAR.

Elsevier Ltd: The Boulevard, Langford Lane, Kidlington, Oxford, OX5 1GB; tel. (1865) 843000; fax (1865) 843010; e-mail directenquiries@elsevier.com; internet www.elsevier.com; f. 1958; academic and professional reference books; imprints: Academic Press, Architectural Press, Bailliere Tindall, Butterworth-Heinemann, Churchill Livingstone, Digital Press, Elsevier, Elsevier Advanced Technology, Focal Press, Gulf Professional, JAI, Made Simple Books, Morgan Kaufmann, Mosby, Newnes, North-Holland, Pergamon, Saunders; part of Reed Elsevier Group PLC; Man. Dir ANNA MOON.

Encyclopaedia Britannica UK Ltd: 2nd Floor, Unity Wharf, 13 Mill St, London, SE1 2BH; tel. (20) 7500-7800; fax (20) 7500-7878; e-mail enquiries@britannica.co.uk; internet www.britannica.co.uk; f. 1768; publs Encyclopaedia Britannica , Britannica Book of the Year, Great Books of the Western World, Britannica Learning Library, Britannica Almanac; Man. Dir IAN GRANT.

Euromonitor International: 60–61 Britton St, London, EC1M 5UX; tel. (20) 7251-8024; fax (20) 7608-3149; e-mail info@euromonitor.com; internet www.euromonitor.com; f. 1972; business and commercial reference; Chair. R. N. SENIOR; Man. Dir T. J. FENWICK.

Evans Publishing Group: 2A Portman Mansions, Chiltern St, London, W1U 6NR; tel. (20) 7487-0920; fax (20) 7487-0921; e-mail sales@evansbrothers.co.uk; internet www.evansbooks.co.uk; f. 1906; educational, children's, general and overseas books; Man. Dir S. T. PAWLEY; Publr SU SWALLOW.

Everyman's Library: Northburgh House, 10 Northburgh St, London, EC1V 0AT; tel. (20) 7566-6350; fax (20) 7490-3708; e-mail books@everyman.uk.com; internet www.randomhouse.co.uk/knopf/classics; f. 1906; publ. in United Kingdom by The Random House Group Ltd.

Faber and Faber Ltd: 3 Queen Sq., London, WC1N 3AU; tel. (20) 7465-0045; fax (20) 7465-0034; internet www.faber.co.uk; f. 1929; biography, autobiography, children's, film, drama, popular science, economics, fiction, history, music, poetry; Man. Dir STEPHEN PAGE.

The Folio Society Ltd: 44 Eagle St, London, WC1R 4FS; tel. (20) 7400-4200; fax (20) 7400-4242; internet www.foliosociety.com; f. 1947; fine illustrated editions of children's, fiction, food, gardening, history, biographies, poetry and travel books; Publishing Dir DAVID HAYDEN.

Footprint Handbooks Ltd: 6 Riverside Court, Lower Bristol Rd, Bath, BA2 3DZ; tel. (1225) 469141; fax (1225) 469461; e-mail discover@footprintbooks.com; internet www.footprintbooks.com; Dirs ANDY RIDDLE, PATRICK DAWSON.

W. Foulsham & Co Ltd: The Publishing House, Bennetts Close, Slough, Berks, SL1 5AP; tel. (1753) 526769; fax (1753) 535003; e-mail reception@foulsham.com; internet www.foulsham.com; f. 1819; finance, reference; Man. Dir BARRY BELASCO.

Fourth Estate: 77–85 Fulham Palace Rd, London, W6 8JB; tel. (20) 8741-4414; fax (20) 8307-4466; e-mail general@4thestate.co.uk; internet www.4thestate.co.uk; f. 1984; literature, humour, general reference, current affairs, literary and commercial fiction, cookery; imprint of HarperCollins Publishers; Pub. Dir NICHOLAS PEARSON.

Samuel French Ltd: 52 Fitzroy St, London, W1T 5JR; tel. (20) 7387-9373; fax (20) 7387-2161; e-mail theatre@samuelfrench-london.co.uk; internet www.samuelfrench-london.co.uk; f. 1830; drama; Chair. LEON F. EMBRY; Man. Dir VIVIEN GOODWIN.

Victor Gollancz Ltd: Orion House, 5 Upper St Martin's Lane, London, WC2H 9EA; tel. (20) 7240-3444; fax (20) 7379-6158; internet www.orionbooks.co.uk; f. 1928; imprint of Orion Publishing Group Ltd; science fiction and fantasy; Dirs JO FLETCHER, SIMON SPANTON.

Granta Books: 12 Addison Ave, London, W11 4QR; tel. (20) 7605-1360; fax (20) 7605-1361; e-mail publicity@granta.com; internet www.granta.com; fiction, political non-fiction; Editorial Dir GEORGE MILLER.

Gresham Books Ltd: 46 Victoria Rd, Summertown, Oxford OX2 7QD; tel. (1865) 513582; fax (1865) 512718; e-mail info@gresham-books.co.uk; internet www.gresham-books.co.uk; f. 1978; hymn books, school histories, music folders; Chief Exec. P. A. LEWIS.

Guinness World Records Ltd: 184-192 Drummond St, 3rd Floor, London, NW1 3HP; tel. (20) 7891-4567; fax (20) 7891-4501; internet www.guinnessworldrecords.com; f. 1954; acquired by Gullane Entertainment in 2001; music and general interest; CEO STEPHEN NELSON; Man. Dir CHRISTOPHER IRWIN.

Hachette Livre UK: 338 Euston Rd, London, NW1 3BH; tel. (20) 7873-6000; fax (20) 7873-6124; internet www.hachettelivre.co.uk; f. 1993 as Hodder Headline; present name adopted 2007; divisions: Hodder Education, John Murray Ltd, Headline Publishing Group, Hodder and Stoughton Ltd, Hachette Children's Books, Orion, Octopus Publishing Group, Little, Brown Book Group, Chambers Harrap; Group Chief Exec. TIM HELY HUTCHINSON.

Robert Hale Ltd: Clerkenwell House, 45–47 Clerkenwell Green, London, EC1R 0HT; tel. (20) 7251-2661; fax (20) 7490-4958; e-mail enquire@halebooks.com; internet www.halebooks.com; f. 1936; memoirs, biography, travel, sport, fiction, belles-lettres, general non-fiction; Man. Dir JOHN HALE.

Hamlyn: 2–4 Heron Quays, London, E14 4JP; tel. (20) 7531-8400; fax (20) 7531-8650; e-mail info-ho@hamlyn.co.uk; internet www.hamlyn.co.uk; imprint of Octopus Publishing Group Ltd; cookery, DIY, gardening, sports, health, animals; Publishing Dir JANE BIRCH.

Harlequin Mills and Boon Ltd: Eton House, 18–24 Paradise Rd, Richmond, Surrey, TW9 1SR; tel. (20) 8288-2800; fax (20) 8288-2899; internet www.millsandboon.co.uk; f. 1908; romantic fiction; Man. Dir GUY HALLOWES.

HarperCollins Publishers Ltd: 77–85 Fulham Palace Rd, London, W6 8JB; tel. (20) 8307-4000; fax (20) 8307-4440; e-mail contact@harpercollins.co.uk; internet www.harpercollins.co.uk; f. 1819; owned by News International; fiction and non-fiction of all classes, including biographies, history, travel, nature, sport, art, children's, classics, atlases, reference, religion; imprints: Armada, Bartholomew, Collins, Collins Bibles, Collins Cartographic, Collins Classics, Collins Crime, Collins English Dictionaries, Collins Liturgical, Flamingo, Fontana, HarperCollins, HarperCollins Audio, HarperCollins Paperbacks, HarperCollins Science Fiction and Fantasy, Jets, Lions, Marshall Pickering, Nicholson, Times Books, Tolkien, Tracks, Young Lions; CEO and Publr VICTORIA BARNSLEY.

Harvill Secker: The Random House Group Ltd, 20 Vauxhall Bridge Rd, London, SW1V 2SA; tel. (20) 7840-8540; fax (20) 7233-6117; e-mail enquiries@randomhouse.co.uk; internet www.randomhouse.co.uk/harvillsecker; fiction, non-fiction, illustrated books; imprint of The Random House Group Ltd.

Haynes Publishing: Sparkford, Yeovil, Somerset, BA22 7JJ; tel. (1963) 440635; fax (1963) 440001; e-mail sales@haynes.co.uk; internet www.haynes.co.uk; f. 1960; transport, manuals etc.; Chair. J. H. HAYNES; CEO E. OAKLEY.

Headline Publishing Group: 338 Euston Rd, London, NW1 3BH; tel. (20) 7873-6000; fax (20) 7873-6124; e-mail headline.books@headline.co.uk; internet www.headline.co.uk; f. 1986; division of Hachette Livre UK; fiction, autobiography, biography, food and wine, gardening, popular science, sport and TV tie-ins; Man. Dir MARTIN NEILD.

Heinemann: Halley Court, Jordan Hill, Oxford, OX2 8EJ; tel. (1865) 311366; fax (1865) 310043; e-mail enquiries@pearson.com; internet www.heinemann.co.uk; imprint of Pearson Education; educational textbooks for UK and abroad; Man. Dir JOHN FALLON.

William Heinemann: Random House, 20 Vauxhall Bridge Rd, London, SW1V 2SA; tel. (20) 7840-8548; fax (20) 7233-6127; e-mail enquiries@randomhouse.co.uk; internet www.randomhouse.co.uk; arts, biography, fiction, history, science, travel; imprint of The Random House Group Ltd.

Hodder Arnold: 338 Euston Rd, London, NW1 3BH; tel. (20) 7873-6000; fax (20) 7873-6325; e-mail feedback.arnold@hodder.co.uk; internet www.hoddereducation.co.uk; f. 1890; imprint of Hodder Education; medical, nursing, health sciences; Man. Dir PHILIP WALTERS.

Hodder Education: 338 Euston Rd, London, NW1 3BH; tel. (20) 7873-6000; fax (20) 7873-6299; e-mail educationenquiries@hodder.co.uk; internet www.hoddereducation.co.uk; f. 1906; division of Hachette Livre UK; imprints: Hodder Arnold, Hodder Gibson, Hodder Murray and Teach Yourself; Chief Exec. PHILIP WALTERS.

Hodder and Stoughton: 338 Euston Rd, London, NW1 3BH; tel. (20) 7873-6000; fax (20) 7873-6024; internet www.hodder.co.uk; f. 1868; division of Hachette Livre UK; imprints: Mobius, Sceptre; general, biography, travel, fiction, current affairs; Man. Dir JAMIE HODDER-WILLIAMS.

Informa PLC: Mortimer House, 37–41 Mortimer St, London, W1T 3JH; tel. (20) 7017-5000; internet www.informa.com; journals and

THE UNITED KINGDOM

books; commercial, professional, academic and scientific, reference; Chair. DEREK MAPP; Chief Exec. PETER RIGBY.

IOP Publishing: Dirac House, Temple Back, Bristol, BS1 6BE; tel. (117) 929-7481; fax (117) 929-4318; e-mail info@iop.org; internet publishing.iop.org; f. 1874; scientific and technical publishers; Man. Dir J. R. COWHIG.

Jane's Information Group Ltd: Sentinel House, 163 Brighton Rd, Coulsdon, Surrey, CR5 2YH; tel. (20) 8700-3700; fax (20) 8763-1006; e-mail info.uk@janes.com; internet www.janes.com; owned by IHS, Inc (USA); intelligence and analysis on national and international defence, security and risk developments; Pres. and COO SCOTT KEY.

Jordan Publishing Ltd: 21 St Thomas St, Bristol, BS1 6JS; tel. (117) 923-0600; fax (117) 923-0486; e-mail achim.bosse@jordanpublishing.co.uk; internet www.jordanpublishing.co.uk; f. 1863; practical law books covering family law, litigation, company, property and private client law; Man. Dir CAROLINE VANDRIDGE-AMES.

Michael Joseph Ltd: 80 Strand, London, WC2R 0RL; tel. (20) 7010-3000; fax (20) 7010-6060; internet www.penguin.co.uk; f. 1936; general, fiction, non-fiction; division of Penguin; Publishing Dir LOUISE MOORE.

Richard Joseph Publishers Ltd: POB 15, Torrington, EX38 8ZJ; tel. (1805) 625750; fax (1805) 625376; e-mail info@sheppardsworld.co.uk; internet www.sheppardsworld.co.uk; reference and directories; publishes the weekly journal *Sheppard's Confidential*; Man. Dir RICHARD JOSEPH.

Kenyon-Deane: 10 Station Rd, Industrial Estate, Malvern, Worcs., WR13 6RN; tel. and fax (1684) 540154; e-mail simon@cressrelles.co.uk; internet www.cressrelles.co.uk; f. 1971; owned by Cressrelles Publishing Company Ltd; incorporates Kenyon House Press, H. F. W. Deane Ltd; plays and drama textbooks, specialists in all-women plays and plays for young people; Man. Dir LESLIE SMITH.

Kingfisher Publications PLC: New Penderel House, 283–288 High Holborn, London, WC1V 7HZ; tel. (20) 7903-9999; fax (20) 7242-4979; e-mail sales@kingfisherpub.com; internet www.kingfisherpub.com; children's books; imprints: Kingfisher; owned by Pan Macmillan Ltd; Man. Dir JOHN PICKETT.

Kogan Page Ltd: 120 Pentonville Rd, London, N1 9JN; tel. (20) 7278-0433; fax (20) 7837-6348; e-mail kpinfo@kogan-page.co.uk; internet www.kogan-page.co.uk; f. 1967; business, management, accountancy, textbooks, transport, careers, personal development, training, marketing, consumer, reference; Man. Dir HELEN KOGAN.

Lawrence and Wishart Ltd: 99A Wallis Rd, London, E9 5LN; tel. (20) 8533-2506; fax (20) 8533-7369; e-mail info@lwbooks.co.uk; internet www.lwbooks.co.uk; f. 1936; politics, history, feminism, race, economics, Marxist theory, cultural studies; Managing Editor SALLY DAVISON.

Letts Educational: 4 Grosvenor Pl., London, SW1X 7DL; tel. (20) 8996-3333; fax (20) 8742-8390; e-mail mail@lettsed.co.uk; internet www.lettsed.co.uk; children's, educational, textbooks; Man. Dir NIGEL WARD.

LexisNexis Butterworths: Halsbury House, 35 Chancery Lane, London, WC2A 1EL; tel. (20) 7400-2500; fax (20) 7400-2842; internet www.lexisnexis.co.uk; f. 1818; part of Reed Elsevier PLC; law, tax, accountancy, banking books and journals; Group Man. Dir JOSH BOTTOMLEY.

Frances Lincoln: 4 Torriano Mews, Torriano Ave, London, NW5 2RZ; tel. (20) 7284-4009; fax (20) 7485-0490; e-mail reception@franceslincoln.com; internet www.franceslincoln.com; f. 1977; illustrated non-fiction, children's fiction and non-fiction; Man. Dir JOHN NICOLL.

Little, Brown Book Group UK: Brettenham House, Lancaster Pl., London, WC2E 7EN; tel. (20) 7911-8000; fax (20) 7911-8100; e-mail email.uk@littlebrown.co.uk; internet www.littlebrown.co.uk; division of Hachette Livre UK; imprints: Abacus, Virago, Sphere, Orbit, little, brown; CEO and Publr URSULA MACKENZIE.

Liverpool University Press: 4 Cambridge St, Liverpool, L69 7ZU; tel. (151) 794-2233; fax (151) 794-2235; e-mail lup@liv.ac.uk; internet www.liverpool-unipress.co.uk; f. 1899; European and American literature, social, political, economic and ancient history, planning, hispanic studies, population studies, architecture, art, art history, cultural studies, science fiction criticism series; Dir ROBIN BLOXSIDGE.

Lonely Planet Publications: 2nd Floor, 186 City Rd, London, EC1V 2NT; tel. (20) 7106-2100; fax (20) 7106-2101; internet www.lonelyplanet.com; f. 1973; travel, languages; 75% share acquired by BBC Worldwide in 2007; Publr STEPHEN PALMER.

Lund Humphries: Gower House, Croft Rd, Aldershot, Hants, GU11 3HR; tel. (1252) 331551; fax (1252) 344405; e-mail info@lundhumphries.com; internet www.lundhumphries.com; f. 1969; arts, graphic arts, design, architecture, photography, scholarly, Arabic language; Dir NIGEL FARROW.

Lutterworth Press: POB 60, Cambridge, CB1 2NT; tel. (1223) 350865; fax (1223) 366951; e-mail sales@lutterworth.com; internet www.lutterworth.com; f. 1799; imprint of James Clarke & Co Ltd; the arts, crafts, biography, educational, environmental, history, theology, travel, sport, juvenile fiction and non-fiction; Man. Dir ADRIAN BRINK.

McGraw-Hill Education: McGraw-Hill House, Shoppenhangers Rd, Maidenhead, Berks., SL6 2QL; tel. (1628) 502500; fax (1628) 770224; internet www.mcgraw-hill.co.uk; technical, scientific, computer studies, professional reference, general and medical books; Pres. HENRY HIRCHBERG.

Macmillan Education Ltd: Between Towns Rd, Oxford, OX4 3PP; tel. (1865) 405700; fax (1865) 405701; e-mail elt@macmillan.com; internet www.macmillaneducation.com; a division of Macmillan Publishers Ltd; English Language Teaching and educational books; Chair. CHRISTOPHER PATERSON; Man. Dir CHRIS HARRISON.

Manchester University Press: Oxford Rd, Manchester, M13 9NR; tel. (161) 275-2310; fax (161) 274-3346; e-mail d.rodgers@manchester.ac.uk; internet www.manchesteruniversitypress.co.uk; f. 1904; all branches of higher education, arts, science and social sciences; Chief Exec. DAVID RODGERS.

Methuen Publishing Ltd: 8 Artillery Row, London, SW1P 1RZ; tel. (20) 7802-0018; fax (20) 7828-1244; e-mail info@methuen.co.uk; internet www.methuen.co.uk; f. 1889; literature, fiction, non-fiction, biography, sport, theatre, drama, humour, music; imprint: Politico's Publishing; Man. Dir PETER TUMMONS.

Mitchell Beazley: 2–4 Heron Quays, London, E14 4JP; tel. (20) 7531-8400; fax (20) 7531-8650; e-mail info@mitchell-beazley.co.uk; internet www.mitchell-beazley.co.uk; f. 1969; imprint of Octopus Publishing Group Ltd; Miller's antiques, arts and design, interiors and style, gardening, reference, wine and food; Publr DAVID LAMB.

John Murray Publishers: 338 Euston Rd, London, NW1 3BH; tel. (20) 7873-6000; fax (20) 7873-6446; internet www.hachettelivre.co.uk; f. 1768; division of Hachette Livre UK (see above); biography, autobiography, memoir, history, travel, fiction, current affairs; Man. Dir MARTIN NEILD.

Nelson Thornes Ltd: Delta Pl., 27 Bath Rd, Cheltenham, GL53 7TH; tel. (1242) 267100; fax (1242) 221914; e-mail cservices@nelsonthornes.com; internet www.nelsonthornes.com; educational; Man. Dir FRED GRAINGER.

Novello and Co Ltd: 14–15 Berners St, London, W1T 3LJ; tel. (20) 7612-7400; fax (20) 7612-7545; e-mail promotion@musicsales.co.uk; internet www.chesternovello.com; music; Man. Dir JAMES RUSHTON.

Octopus Publishing Group Ltd: 2–4 Heron Quays, London, E14 4JP; tel. (20) 7531-8400; fax (20) 7531-8650; e-mail info@octopus-publishing.co.uk; internet www.octopus-publishing.co.uk; division of Hachette Livre UK; imprints: Bounty, Cassel Illustrated, Conran Octopus, Gaia Books, Godsfield Press, Hamlyn, Miller's, Mitchell Beazley, MQP, Philip's; Chief Exec. ALISON GOFF.

Open University Press, McGraw-Hill Education: Shoppenhangers Rd, Maidenhead, SL6 2QL; tel. (1628) 502500; fax (1628) 770224; e-mail enquiries@openup.co.uk; internet www.openup.co.uk; academic, study skills, politics, sociology, psychology, education, higher education, media, film and cultural studies, health and social welfare, counselling and psychotherapy, management and public policy; Man. Dir SHONA MULLEN.

Orion Publishing Group: Orion House, 5 Upper St Martin's Lane, London, WC2H 9EA; tel. (20) 7240-3444; fax (20) 7240-4822; e-mail info@orionbooks.co.uk; internet www.orionbooks.co.uk; f. 1991; division of Hachette Livre UK; imprints: Gollancz, Orion, Orion Children's, Phoenix, Weidenfeld & Nicolson; CEO PETER ROCHE.

Peter Owen Publishers: 73 Kenway Rd, London, SW5 0RE; tel. (20) 7373-5628; fax (20) 7373-6760; e-mail admin@peterowen.com; internet www.peterowen.com; f. 1951; general publishers of fiction, autobiography, biography, translations, history, the arts, etc.; Man. Dir PETER OWEN; Editorial Dir ANTONIA OWEN.

Oxford University Press: Gt Clarendon St, Oxford, OX2 6DP; tel. (1865) 556767; fax (1865) 556646; e-mail webenquiry@oup.com; internet www.oup.com; f. c. 1478; Bibles, prayer books, Oxford English Dictionary, the Dictionary of National Biography and many other dictionaries and books of reference, learned and general works from the humanities to the sciences, educational, electronic, music and children's books and audio-visual and English language teaching material; Sec. to the Delegates of the Press and Chief Exec. Dr HENRY REECE.

Palgrave Macmillan Ltd: Houndmills, Basingstoke, Hants., RG21 6XS; tel. (1256) 329242; fax (1256) 479476; e-mail bookenquiries@palgrave.com; internet www.palgrave.com; academic, professional, textbooks and journals; Man. Dir D. J. G. KNIGHT.

Pan Macmillan Ltd: 20 New Wharf Rd, London, N1 9RR; tel. (20) 7014-6000; fax (20) 7014-6001; e-mail books@macmillan.co.uk; internet www.panmacmillan.com; fiction and non-fiction, children's, general reference; imprints: Macmillan, Pan, Picador, Sidgwick &

THE UNITED KINGDOM

Jackson, Boxtree, Tor, Macmillan Children's Books, Campbell Books, Young Picador, Rodale; Chief Exec. RICHARD CHARKIN.

Pavilion Books: Anova Books Group Ltd, 10 Southcombe St, London, W14 0RA; tel. (20) 7605-1400; fax (20) 7605-1401; e-mail epreece-morrison@anovabooks.com; internet www.anovabooks.com/imprint/pavilion; general, arts, non-fiction.

Pearson Education Ltd: Edinburgh Gate, Harlow, Essex, CM20 2JE; tel. (1279) 623623; fax (1279) 431059; e-mail enquiries@pearson.com; internet www.pearsoned.co.uk; Propr Pearson PLC; acquired Harcourt Education International in 2007; imprints include: Ginn, Heinemann, Longman, Payne-Gallway, Prentice Hall, Raintree, Rigby and Scott Prentice; CEO JOHN FALLON.

Pearson Publishing Group: Pearson Publishing Group, Chesterton Mill, French's Rd, Cambridge, CB4 3NP; tel. (1223) 350555; fax (1223) 356484; e-mail info@pearson.co.uk; internet www.pearson.co.uk; Chair. GEORGE PEARSON.

Penguin Books Ltd: 80 The Strand, London, WC2R 0RL; tel. (20) 7010-3000; fax (20) 7416-3099; e-mail editor@penguin.co.uk; internet www.penguin.co.uk; f. 1936; holding co Pearson PLC; paperback imprints: Penguin and Puffin; reprints and original works of fiction and non-fiction including travel, biography, science and social studies, reference books, handbooks, plays, poetry, classics and children's books; Penguin Group UK is made up of Penguin Press (Allen Lane, Reference, Penguin Classics and Penguin Modern Classics), Penguin General (imprints: Penguin, Hamish Hamilton, Michael Joseph, Viking, Fig Tree) and the children's division (imprints: Puffin, Ladybird, Warne); Chair. and Chief Exec. JOHN MAKINSON; CEO (UK) PETER FIELD.

Phaidon Press Ltd: Regent's Wharf, All Saints St, London, N1 9PA; tel. (20) 7843-1000; fax (20) 7843-1010; e-mail enquiries@phaidon.com; internet www.phaidon.com; art, architecture, children's, contemporary culture, cookery, design, decorative arts, fashion, photography and music, film, fine art; Chair. RICHARD SCHLAGMAN.

Philip's: 2–4 Heron Quays, London, E14 4JP; tel. (20) 7644-6940; fax (20) 7644-8464; e-mail philips@philips-maps.co.uk; internet www.philips-maps.co.uk; imprint of Octopus Publishing Group Ltd; maps, atlases, astronomy, encyclopaedias; Man. Dir JOHN GAISFORD.

Pluto Press: 345 Archway Rd, London, N6 5AA; tel. (20) 8348-2724; fax (20) 8348-9133; e-mail beech@plutobooks.com; internet www.plutobooks.com; academic, scholarly, current affairs and reference; Man. Dir ROGER VAN ZWANENBERG; Editorial Dir ANNE BEECH.

Proquest Information and Learning: The Quorum, Barnwell Rd, Cambridge, CB5 8SW; tel. (1223) 215512; fax (1223) 215514; e-mail marketing@proquest.co.uk; internet www.proquest.co.uk; f. 1973 as Chadwyck-Healey Ltd; changed name as above in 2001; academic; Chair. ALAN ALDWORTH; Gen. Man. STEVEN HALL.

The Random House Group Ltd: Random House, 20 Vauxhall Bridge Rd, London, SW1V 2SA; tel. (20) 7840-8400; fax (20) 7233-6115; e-mail enquiries@randomhouse.co.uk; internet www.randomhouse.co.uk; imprints: Arrow, Jonathan Cape, Cedar, Century, Chatto & Windus, Ebury Press, Everyman, Harvill Secker, William Heinemann, Hutchinson, Mainstream, Pimlico, Random House Children's Books, Rider, Vermilion, Vintage, Yellow Jersey; Chair. and CEO GAIL REBUCK.

Reader's Digest Association Ltd: 11 Westferry Circus, Canary Wharf, London, E14 4HE; tel. (20) 7715-8000; fax (20) 7715-8181; internet www.readersdigest.co.uk; various non-fiction, condensed and series fiction; Chair THOMAS RYDER; Man. Dir ANDREW LYNAM-SMITH.

Reed Business Information: Quadrant House, The Quadrant, Sutton, Surrey, SM2 5AS; tel. (20) 8652-3500; fax (20) 8652-8932; e-mail information@reedinfo.co.uk; internet www.reedbusiness.co.uk; f. 1866; business directories and online services; CEO KEITH JONES.

Reed Elsevier Group PLC: 1–3 Strand, London, WC2N 5JR; tel. (20) 7930-7077; fax (20) 7166-5799; internet www.reedelsevier.com; f. 1992; books, journals, magazines and electronic resources; divisions: science and medical, education, legal and business; Chair. JAN HOMMEN; Chief Exec. Sir CRISPIN DAVIS.

Routledge: 2 Park Sq., Milton Park, Abingdon, Oxfordshire OX14 4RN; tel. (20) 7017-6000; fax (20) 7017-6699; e-mail webmaster.books@tandf.co.uk; internet www.routledge.com; f. 1988; imprint of Taylor and Francis Group; professional, academic, reference; Man. Dir JEREMY NORTH.

SAGE Publications Ltd: 1 Oliver's Yard, 55 City Rd, London, EC1Y 1SP; tel. (20) 7324-8500; fax (20) 7324-8600; e-mail info@sagepub.co.uk; internet www.sagepub.co.uk; f. 1971; academic and professional social sciences, sciences and humanities; imprint: Sage Education; Man Dir STEPHEN BARR.

Schofield and Sims Ltd: Dogley Mill, Penistone Rd, Fenay Bridge, Huddersfield, West Yorks., HD8 0NQ; tel. (1484) 607080; fax (1484) 606815; e-mail post@schofieldandsims.co.uk; internet www.schofieldandsims.co.uk; f. 1901; educational; Chair. NICK PLATTS.

Directory

Scholastic Ltd: Villiers House, Clarendon Ave, Leamington Spa, Warwickshire, CV32 5PR; tel. (1926) 887799; fax (1926) 883331; internet www.scholastic.co.uk; f. 1964; direct marketing, educational and children's books; Group Man. Dir KATE WILSON.

SCM-Canterbury Press Ltd: St Mary's Works, St Mary's Plain, Norwich, NR3 3BH; tel. (1603) 612914; fax (1603) 624483; e-mail admin@scm-canterburypress.co.uk; internet www.scm-canterburypress.co.uk; f. 1929; religious, theological; Group CEO ANDREW MOORE.

Scripture Union: 207–209 Queensway, Bletchley, Milton Keynes, Bucks, MK2 2EB; tel. (1908) 856000; fax (1908) 856111; e-mail info@scriptureunion.org.uk; internet www.scriptureunion.org.uk; f. 1867; Christian education and Bible reading guides; Chief Exec. KEITH CIVVAL.

Simon and Schuster: Africa House, 64–78 Kingsway, London, WC2B 6AH; tel. (20) 7316-1900; fax (20) 7316-0331; e-mail enquiries@simonandschuster.co.uk; internet www.simonsays.co.uk; f. 1986; owned by CBS Corpn (USA); fiction, non-fiction, music, travel; imprints: Pocket Books, Touchstone, Scribner, Free Press; Man. Dir IAN S. CHAPMAN.

Society for Promoting Christian Knowledge: 36 Causton St, London, SW1P 4ST; tel. (20) 7592-3900; fax (20) 7592-3939; e-mail spck@spck.org.uk; internet www.spck.org.uk; f. 1698; religious; imprints: SPCK, Triangle, Azure, Sheldon Press; Publishing Dir JOANNA MORIARTY.

Souvenir Press Ltd: 43 Great Russell St, London, WC1B 3PD; tel. (20) 7580-9307; fax (20) 7580-5064; e-mail souvenirpress@ukonline.co.uk; general; Man. Dir ERNEST HECHT.

The Stationery Office: St Crispins, Duke St, Norwich, NR3 1PD; tel. (1603) 622211; e-mail book.enquiries@tso.co.uk; internet www.tso.co.uk; f. 1786 as His Majesty's Stationery Office (govt publishing house); privatized in 1996; acquired by Williams Lea in 2007; business and publishing services; publishes *Hansard*, *Highway Code*, *British Pharmacopoeia*; Chief Exec. RICHARD DELL.

Sweet and Maxwell Ltd: 100 Avenue Rd, London, NW3 3PF; tel. (20) 7393-7000; fax (20) 7393-7010; e-mail customer.services@sweetandmaxwell.co.uk; internet www.sweetandmaxwell.co.uk; f. 1799; imprints: Stevens and Sons Ltd, W. Green, Round Hall, ESC Publishing, the European Law Centre; holding co Thomson Reuters; law books; Man. Dir PETER LAKE.

Taylor and Francis Group Ltd: 4 Park Sq., Milton Park, Abingdon, Oxfordshire, OX14 4RN; tel. (20) 7017-6000; fax (20) 7017-6699; e-mail info@tandf.co.uk; internet www.taylorandfrancisgroup.com; division of Informa PLC; imprints: Taylor and Francis, Routledge, Garland Science, CRC Press and Psychology Press; professional, academic, scientific, technical, reference; books and journals; Chief Exec. ROGER HORTON.

Thames and Hudson Ltd: 181A High Holborn, London, WC1V 7QX; tel. (20) 7845-5000; fax (20) 7845-5050; e-mail sales@thameshudson.co.uk; internet www.thamesandhudson.com; art, archaeology, history, etc.; Chair. THOMAS NEURATH; Man. Dir JAMIE CAMPLIN.

Thomson Reuters: The Quadrangle, 180 Wardour St, London, W1A 4YG; tel. (20) 7437-9787; e-mail general.info@thomsonreuters.com; internet www.thomsonreuters.com; f. 2008 by merger of Thomson Corpn and Reuters Group PLC (f. 1865); legal, financial; also owns Reuters news agency; Chair. DAVID THOMSON; CEO THOMAS H. GLOCER.

Transworld Publishers Ltd: 61–63 Uxbridge Rd, London, W5 5SA; tel. (20) 8579-2652; fax (20) 8579-5479; e-mail info@transworld-publishers.co.uk; internet www.booksattransworld.co.uk; imprints: Corgi, Bantam Books, Black Swan, Bantam Press, Doubleday, Expert Books, Eden Project Books, Channel 4 Books; all types of fiction and non-fiction; division of The Random House Group Ltd; Man. Dir LARRY FINLAY.

University of Wales Press: 10 Columbus Walk, Brigantine Pl., Cardiff, CF10 4UP; tel. (29) 2049-6899; fax (29) 2049-6108; e-mail post@uwp.co.uk; internet www.uwp.co.uk; f. 1922; academic and educational (Welsh and English); Dir ASHLEY DRAKE.

Usborne Publishing: Usborne House, 83–85 Saffron Hill, London, EC1N 8RT; tel. (20) 7430-2800; fax (20) 7430-1562; e-mail mail@usborne.co.uk; internet www.usborne.com; f. 1973; educational and children's publishing; Man. Dir T. P. USBORNE.

Virgin Books: Thames Wharf Studios, Rainville Rd, London, W6 9HA; tel. (20) 7386-3300; fax (20) 7386-3360; e-mail info@virgin-books.co.uk; internet www.virginbooks.com; 90% owned by The Random House Group Ltd; general, popular culture, film, music, humour, biography, fiction, non-fiction, erotica; imprints: Virgin, Black Lace and Nexus; Man. Dir RICHARD CABLE.

Frederick Warne (Publishers) Ltd: 80 Strand, London, WC2R 0RL; tel. (20) 7010-3000; fax (20) 7010-6707; e-mail peterrabbit@penguin.co.uk; internet www.peterrabbit.com; f. 1865; a division of

THE UNITED KINGDOM

Penguin Books since 1983; classic illustrated children's books (including Beatrix Potter); Man. Dir SALLY FLOYER.

Wiley-Blackwell: 9600 Garsington Rd, Oxford, OX4 2DQ; tel. (1865) 776868; fax (1865) 714591; e-mail customerservices@oxon.blackwellpublishing.com; internet www.blackwellpublishing.com; f. 2001 as Blackwell Publishing Ltd, by merger of Blackwell Publishing and Blackwell Science; acquired by John Wiley & Sons, Inc. (USA) in 2007; academic, professional, business, medical and science books and journals; CEO ERIC A. SWANSON.

The Women's Press: 27 Goodge St, London, W1T 2LD; tel. (20) 7636-3992; fax (20) 7637-1866; e-mail david@the-womens-press.com; internet www.the-womens-press.com; f. 1978; feminist; Man. Dir CHARLOTTE GASCOIGNE.

Yale University Press: 47 Bedford Sq., London, WC1B 3DP; tel. (20) 7079-4900; fax (20) 7079-4901; e-mail sales@yaleup.co.uk; internet www.yalebooks.co.uk; f. 1973; the only US university press to operate a separate publishing co in Europe; Man. Dir ROBERT BALDOCK.

Zed Books Ltd: 7 Cynthia St, London, N1 9JF; tel. (20) 7837-0384; fax (20) 7833-3960; e-mail editorial@zedbooks.net; internet www.zedbooks.co.uk; f. 1977; academic, current affairs; Editors ELLEN MCKINLAY, TAMSINE O'RIORDAN.

PUBLISHERS' ORGANIZATIONS

Booktrust: Book House, 45 East Hill, London, SW18 2QZ; tel. (20) 8516-2977; fax (20) 8516-2978; e-mail query@booktrust.org.uk; internet www.booktrust.org.uk; non-profit-making organization funded by voluntary donations and membership fees; f. 1945; originally f. 1925 as The National Book Council to extend the use and enjoyment of books; renamed Book Trust 1986; publishes annotated book lists; postal book information service; administers book prizes, including the Orange Broadband Prize for Fiction and the John Llewellyn Rhys Prize; runs www.booktrusted.com, a website dedicated to children's books; Chair. ALISON MORRISON; Exec. Dir VIV BIRD.

The Publishers' Association: 29B Montague St, London, WC1B 5BW; tel. (20) 7691-9191; fax (20) 7691-9199; e-mail mail@publishers.org.uk; internet www.publishers.org.uk; f. 1896; represents book, journal and electronic publishers in the UK and seeks to promote the sales of British books; Pres. MIKE BOSWOOD; Chief Exec. SIMON JUDEN; 127 mems.

Publishing Scotland: Scottish Book Centre, 137 Dundee St, Edinburgh, EH11 1BG; tel. (131) 228-6866; fax (131) 228-3220; e-mail enquiries@publishingscotland.org; internet www.publishingscotland.org; f. 1973 as Scottish Publishers' Association; present name adopted 2007; assists member publishers in the promotion and marketing of their books; offers export services, consultancy and training; Chief Exec. LORRAINE FANNIN.

Broadcasting and Communications

REGULATORY AUTHORITY

Office of Communications (Ofcom): Riverside House, 2A Southwark Bridge Rd, London, SE1 9HA; tel. (20) 7981-3000; fax (20) 7981-3333; e-mail contact@ofcom.org.uk; internet www.ofcom.org.uk; f. 2003 to replace the Office of Telecommunications, the Broadcasting Standards Commission, the Radio Authority, the Radiocommunications Agency and the Independent Television Commission; the independent regulator for the British communications industries, with responsibilities across television, radio, telecommunications and wireless communications services; promotes choice, quality and value in electronic communications services, where appropriate, by encouraging competition between the providers of those services; ensures the most efficient use of the radiocommunications spectrum (the airwaves used for the transmission of all non-military wireless communications services); ensures that a wide range of electronic communications services, including broadband, is available across the United Kingdom; ensures that a wide range of television and radio programmes of high quality and wide appeal are broadcast; maintains plurality in the media by ensuring a sufficiently broad range of ownership; protects audiences against offensive or harmful material, unfairness or the infringement of privacy on television and radio; Chair. Lord CURRIE OF MARYLEBONE; Chief Exec. ED RICHARDS.

TELECOMMUNICATIONS

British Telecommunications PLC: BT Centre, 81 Newgate St, London, EC1A 7AJ; tel. (20) 7356-5000; fax (20) 7356-6630; e-mail btgroup@bt.com; internet www.bt.com; wholly owned subsidiary of BT Group PLC; Chair. Sir MICHAEL RAKE; Chief Exec. BEN VERWAAYEN (until 31 May 2008); IAN LIVINGSTON (from 1 June 2008).

Cable and Wireless PLC: 7th Floor, The Point, 37 North Wharf Rd, Paddington Basin, London, W2 1LA; tel. (20) 7315-4000; internet www.cwcom.co.uk; acquired rival co Energis in mid-2005; Chair. RICHARD LAPTHORNE; UK and International Chair. and Joint Group Man. Dir JOHN PLUTHERO; Joint Group Man. Dir TONY RICE.

Hutchison 3G UK Ltd (3): Star House, 20 Grenfell Rd, Maidenhead, SL6 1EH; tel. (8707) 330333; internet www.three.co.uk; f. 2003; mobile cellular telecommunications; owned by Hutchison Whampoa Ltd (Hong Kong); CEO KEVIN RUSSELL.

Kingston Communications: 37 Carr Lane, Hull, HU1 3RE; tel. (1482) 602100; fax (1482) 219289; e-mail publicrelations@kcom.com; internet www.kcom.com; f. 1904; Chair. MICHAEL ABRAHAMS; Chief Exec. MALCOLM FALLEN.

National Grid Wireless: Wireless House, Warwick Technology Park, Heathcote Lane, Warwick, CV34 6DD; tel. (1926) 416000; fax (20) 416600; e-mail marketinguk@ngridwireless.com; internet www.nationalgridwireless.com; fmrly known as Crown Castle UK Ltd; present name adopted 2004; acquired by Macquarie UK Broadcast Ventures April 2007; CEO JOHN WARD.

O$_2$: 260 Bath Rd, Slough, Berks, SL1 4DX; tel. (113) 2722000; e-mail feedback@o2.com; internet www.o2.co.uk; formerly BT Cellnet; demerged from BT Group in October 2002 and became part of the mmO$_2$ group; acquired by Telefónica, SA (Spain) in March 2006; Chair. PETER ERSKINE.

Orange: St James Court, Gt Park Rd, Almondsbury Park, Bradley Stoke, Bristol, BS32 4QJ; tel. (870) 376-8888; internet www.orange.co.uk; f. 1994; acquired by France Telecom in 2000; part of the Orange SA (France) group; Chief Exec. TOM ALEXANDER; Group Chair. DIDIER LOMBARD.

T-Mobile (UK) Ltd: Hatfield Business Park, Hatfield, Herts, AL10 9BW; tel. (1707) 315000; internet www.t-mobile.co.uk; owned by Deutsche Telekom AG (Germany); fmrly One2One; CEO JIM HYDE.

THUS Group PLC: 1–2 Berkeley Sq., 99 Berkeley St, Glasgow, G3 7HR; tel. (141) 567-1234; fax (141) 566-3035; e-mail thus.enquiries@thus.net; internet www.thus.co.uk; f. 1994 as Scottish Power Telecommunications Holdings, restyled THUS PLC in 1999; demerged from ScottishPower and renamed as above in 2002; Chair. PHILIP ROGERSON; Chief Exec. BILL ALLAN.

Tiscali UK Ltd: 20 Broadwick St, London, W1F 8HT; tel. (20) 7087-2000; fax (20) 7087-2282; e-mail info@tiscali.com; internet www.tiscali.co.uk; f. 2001; provides fixed-line telecommunications, digital television services and broadband internet access; subsidiary of Tiscali SpA (Italy); CEO MARY TURNER; 1.7m. subscribers (2006).

Virgin Media: Media House, Bartley Wood Business Park, Bartley Way, Hook, Reading, RG27 9UP; tel. (1256) 752000; fax (1256) 752100; internet www.virginmedia.com; f. 2007 by merger of NTL Inc and Virgin Mobile; Chair. JAMES F. MOONEY; CEO NEIL BURKETT (acting).

Vodafone Group PLC: The Connection, Newbury, Berks, RG14 2FN; tel. (1635) 33251; fax (1635) 676147; internet www.vodafone.com; Chair. Sir JOHN BOND; Chief Exec. ARUN SARIN.

BROADCASTING

British Broadcasting Corporation (BBC): Broadcasting House, London, W1A 1AA; tel. (20) 7580-4468; fax (20) 7637-1630; internet www.bbc.co.uk; f. 1922; operates under Royal Charter; financed by the television licence fees; governed by BBC Trust, which replaced fmr Board of Governors in January 2007; Chair. of BBC Trust Sir MICHAEL LYONS; Dir-Gen. MARK THOMPSON; COO CAROLINE THOMSON; CEO of BBC Worldwide JOHN SMITH; Dir of Vision JANA BENNETT; Dir of Marketing, Communications and Audiences TIM DAVIE; Dir of BBC People STEPHEN KELLY; Dir of Audio and Music JENNY ABRAMSKY; Dir of Future Media and Technology ASHLEY HIGHFIELD.

Radio

British Broadcasting Corporation

BBC Radio provides a service of five national networks throughout the United Kingdom, 40 local radio stations in England and the Channel Islands, Radio Scotland, Radio Wales, Radio Cymru, broadcasting in Welsh, and Radio Ulster and Radio Foyle (in Northern Ireland); it also offers a number of specialist digital services; Dir of Audio and Music JENNY ABRAMSKY.

Radio 1: broadcasts 24 hours a day of contemporary music programmes; Controller ANDY PARFITT.

Radio 2: broadcasts popular music and culture; Controller LESLEY DOUGLAS.

Radio 3: provides 24-hour broadcasts of classical music, drama, talks and documentaries; Controller ROGER WRIGHT.

Radio 4: broadcasts news and current affairs and also provides a wide range of features, drama and discussions; Controller MARK DAMAZER.

Radio Five Live: began broadcasting in March 1994, replacing Radio 5; provides a 24-hour service of news and sports programmes;

THE UNITED KINGDOM

Directory

also operates **Five Live Sports Extra**, a part-time digital network for sports events not broadcast elsewhere on BBC Radio; Controller ADRIAN VAN KLAVEREN.

6 Music: began broadcasting in 2002, digital station playing pop and rock music; Controller LESLEY DOUGLAS.

1Xtra: began broadcasting in 2002; digital station playing contemporary urban music for a young audience; Controller ANDY PARFITT.

Asian Network: began broadcasting in 2002, digital station aimed at the Asian communities in the United Kingdom; Controller ANDY PARFITT.

BBC7: digital radio station featuring archive material and original spoken-word programming, began broadcasting in 2002; Controller MARK DAMAZER.

BBC World Service: Bush House, Strand, London, WC2B 4PH; tel. (20) 7240-3456; fax (20) 7557-1258; e-mail worldservice@bbc.co.uk; internet www.bbc.co.uk/worldservice; the World Service in English is broadcast for 24 hours daily and is directed to all areas of the world. In addition, there are special services, in 33 languages, to: the Far East (in Mandarin, Cantonese, Burmese, Indonesian, Thai and Vietnamese); the Indian sub-continent (in Bengali, Hindi, Nepali, Sinhala, Tamil and Urdu); the Caucasus and Central Asia (in Azeri, Kyrgyz and Uzbek); the Middle East and North Africa (in Arabic, Pashto, Farsi and Turkish); Africa (in Arabic, English, French, Hausa, Kinyarwanda/Kirundi, Portuguese, Somali and Swahili); and the Western Hemisphere (in Portuguese for Brazil and Spanish for Latin America). Services in the following languages are transmitted for listeners in Europe: Albanian, Macedonian, Romanian, Russian, Serbian, and Turkish; Dir NIGEL CHAPMAN.

Independent Radio

Classic FM: 30 Leicester Sq., London, WC2H 7LA; tel. (20) 7343-9000; fax (20) 7344-2703; e-mail enquiries@classicfm.com; internet www.classicfm.com; began broadcasting September 1992; popular classical music; owned by GCap Media PLC; Station Man. DARREN HENLEY.

Independent Radio News (IRN): 200 Gray's Inn Rd, 6th Floor, London, WC1X 8XZ; tel. (20) 7430-4090; fax (20) 7430-4092; e-mail news@irn.co.uk; internet www.irn.co.uk; f. 1973; produced by ITN Radio; news agency for the independent local radio network; Chair. TERRY SMITH; Man. Dir JOHN PERKINS.

The Local Radio Company: 11 Duke St, High Wycombe, Buckinghamshire, HP13 6EE; tel. (1494) 688200; fax (1494) 688201; internet www.thelocalradiocompany.com; owns and operates 28 local radio licences across the United Kingdom; f. 2004 to purchase the entire share capital of Radio Investments Ltd; Chief Exec. RICHARD WHEATLY.

TalkSport UK: 18 Hatfields, London, SE1 8DJ; tel. (20) 7959-7800; fax (20) 7959-7808; internet www.talksport.net; began broadcasting February 1995 as Talk Radio UK; name changed as above January 2000; Propr UTV PLC; Man. Dir SCOTT TAUNTON.

Virgin Radio (Virgin 1215): 1 Golden Sq., London, W1F 9DJ; tel. (20) 7434-1215; fax (20) 7434-1197; internet www.virginradio.co.uk; began broadcasting April 1993; popular music; Propr SMG PLC; Exec. Chair. RICHARD HUNTINGFORD.

Television

British Broadcasting Corporation

BBC Television: Television Centre, Wood Lane, London, W12 7RJ; tel. (20) 8743-8000; internet www.bbc.co.uk; operates two terrestrial services, BBC-1 and BBC-2, and six digital channels, BBC-3, BBC-4, CBeebies, CBBC, BBC News 24 and BBC Parliament; Dir of Vision JANA BENNETT.

BBC-1: internet www.bbc.co.uk/bbcone; provides a coverage of over 99% of the population of the United Kingdom. Colour service began in 1969; a breakfast-time television service began in 1983; Controller JAY HUNT.

BBC-2: internet www.bbc.co.uk/bbctwo; began broadcasting in 1964, and is available to 99% of the population. Colour service began in 1967; Controller ROLY KEATING.

BBC-3: internet www.bbc.co.uk/bbcthree; digital entertainment channel; Controller DANNY COHEN.

BBC-4: internet www.bbc.co.uk/bbcfour; digital channel showing in-depth cultural programmes; Controller GEORGE ENTWISTLE (acting).

CBBC: internet www.bbc.co.uk/cbbc; digital service for children aged six to 13; Controller RICHARD DEVERELL.

CBeebies: internet www.bbc.co.uk/cbeebies; digital service aimed at under-fives.

BBC News 24: internet www.bbc.co.uk/news24; 24–hour digital news service; Dir of News HELEN BOADEN; Controller KEVIN BAKHURST.

BBC Parliament: internet www.bbc.co.uk/parliament; provides coverage from the Houses of Parliament and the devolved Parliament and Assemblies in Scotland, Wales and Northern Ireland; Controller PETER KNOWLES.

Independent Television

In October 1991 the Independent Television Commission (ITC), in accordance with the provisions of the Broadcasting Act of 1990, awarded the 16 licences that constituted the renamed Channel 3 (ITV 1). The franchises were allocated by a system of competitive tendering, although the ITC was empowered to select a company presenting a lower bid in 'exceptional circumstances'. The new licences came into force on 1 January 1993, when Channel 4 (q.v.) also became an ITC licensee. By the end of 1995 the ITC had also issued 183 non-domestic satellite and licensable programme service licences. In October 1995 the ITC awarded the licence for the fifth terrestrial channel to Channel 5 Broadcasting; broadcasting commenced in March 1997. In June the ITC awarded the British Digital Broadcasting consortium (ONdigital, later renamed ITV Digital) three licences to operate digital terrestrial television (DTT) services in the United Kingdom. The first digital television services became available in the following year. However, following the collapse of ITV Digital in April 2002, the ITC withdrew the consortium's licences and in May it announced that they were to be re-tendered; in August one licence was awarded to the BBC and two to Crown Castle International (now National Grid Wireless). DTV Services Ltd, a consortium of the BBC, Crown Castle International and BSkyB, subsequently announced its plans to launch Freeview, which would provide a wide range of free-to-view digital television channels. Freeview commenced broadcasting in late 2002. The ITC became part of Ofcom in late 2003. In early 2005 Ofcom published a provisional timetable outlining plans for the country to switch entirely from analogue to digital television region by region between 2008 and 2012. In June 2007 there were 9,139,000 households in the United Kingdom receiving digital terrestrial television (Freeview).

Channel Four Television: 124 Horseferry Rd, London, SW1P 2TX; tel. (20) 7306-8333; internet www.channel4.com; f. 1980; began broadcasting 1982; national television service; available to 97% of the population; financed by advertising; in accordance with the Broadcasting Act (1990), Channel Four became a public corporation and ITC licensee, responsible for selling its own advertising, from January 1993; Chair. LUKE JOHNSON; Chief Exec. ANDY DUNCAN.

five: 22 Long Acre, London, WC2E 9LY; tel. (8457) 050505; e-mail customerservices@five.tv; internet www.five.tv; awarded licence for fifth national terrestrial channel in October 1995; commenced broadcasting on 30 March 1997 as Channel 5; renamed as above in 2002; owned by RTL Group (Luxembourg); Chair. DAVID ELSTEIN; Chief Exec. (vacant); Dir of Programmes BEN GALE.

Freeview: Broadcast Centre, 201 Wood Lane, London, W12 7TP; tel. (8708) 809980; internet www.freeview.co.uk; f. 2002; a consortium of the BBC, National Grid Wireless, ITV, Channel 4 and BSkyB providing Freeview, a digital service offering more than 40 television stations and additional interactive services; commenced transmission in late 2002.

Independent Television News Ltd (ITN): 200 Gray's Inn Rd, London, WC1X 8XZ; tel. (20) 7833-3000; fax (20) 7430-4305; internet www.itn.co.uk; f. 1955; ITV PLC holds a 40% stake, with Daily Mail and General Trust PLC, Reuters Holdings and United Business Media each holding a 20% stake; provides all national and international news programming for ITV 1 and the London region, plus news programming for Channel 4 and Independent Radio News (IRN); also operates the ITN Archive, ITN Factual, ITN On and ITN Source; became a profit-making company in 1993; Chief Exec. MARK WOOD.

ITV PLC: 200 Gray's Inn Rd, London, WC1V 8HF; tel. (20) 7620-1620; internet www.itvplc.com; f. 2004 following the merger of Carlton and Granada; owns all of the regional Channel 3 licences in England and Wales; Exec. Chair. MICHAEL GRADE.

SMG PLC: Pacific Quay, Glasgow, G51 1PQ; tel. (141) 300-3300; e-mail communications@smg.plc.uk; internet www.smg.plc.uk; owns stv and Virgin Radio; Chair. RICHARD FINDLAY; Chief Exec. ROB WOODWARD.

S4C Welsh Fourth Channel Authority (Awdurdod Sianel Pedwar Cymru): Parc Tŷ Glas, Llanishen, Cardiff, CF14 5DU; tel. (29) 2074-7444; fax (29) 2075-4444; e-mail hotline@s4c.co.uk; internet www.s4c.co.uk; f. 1980; commenced broadcasting in 1982; television service for Wales; Chair. JOHN WALTER JONES; Chief Exec. IONA JONES.

Independent Television (ITV—Channel 3) Regional Licencees

Independent Television Association Ltd (ITV): ITV Network Centre, 200 Grays Inn Rd, London, WC1V 8HF; tel. (20) 7843-8000; fax (20) 7843-8158; e-mail info@itv.co.uk; internet www.itv.com;

THE UNITED KINGDOM

f. 1956; from 1992 the central co-ordinating body for Channel 3 (ITV 1); Dir of Television PETER FINCHAM.

GMTV: c/o London Television Centre, Upper Ground, London, SE1 9TT; tel. (20) 7827-7000; fax (20) 7827-7001; internet www.gm.tv; nationwide breakfast-time service; began broadcasting in January 1993 (replacing TV-am PLC); 75% owned by ITV PLC; Man. Dir PAUL CORLEY.

ITV Anglia: Anglia House, Norwich, NR1 3JG; tel. (1603) 615151; fax (1603) 631032; e-mail anglia@itvlocal.com; internet www.itvlocal.com/anglia; East of England; Propr ITV PLC; began broadcasting in 1959; Man. Dir NEIL THOMPSON.

ITV Border: Television Centre, Carlisle, CA1 3NT; tel. (1228) 525101; fax (1228) 541384; e-mail border@itvlocal.com; internet www.itvlocal.com/border; Borders and the Isle of Man; Propr ITV PLC; Chief Exec. PADDY MERRALL.

ITV Central: Gas St, Birmingham, B1 2JT; tel. (870) 600-6766; fax (844) 556-3820; e-mail central@itvlocal.com; internet www.itvlocal.com/central; East and West Midlands; Propr ITV PLC.

ITV Granada: Granada TV Centre, Quay St, Manchester, M60 9EA; tel. and fax (161) 832-7211; fax (161) 827-2180; e-mail granada@itvlocal.com; internet www.itvlocal.com/granada; north-west England; Propr ITV PLC; Man. Dir SUSAN WOODWARD.

ITV London: London Television Centre, Upper Ground, London, SE1 9LT; fax (20) 7261-8163; e-mail london@itvlocal.com; internet www.itvlocal.com/london; London area, Monday to Thursday, Friday to 5.15 p.m; formed by a merger of Carlton and LWT in February 2004; Propr ITV PLC; Man. Dir CHRISTY SWORDS.

ITV Meridian: Solent Business Park, Whiteley, Hants, PO15 7PA; tel. and fax (1489) 442000; e-mail meridian@itvlocal.com; internet www.itvregions.com/meridian; south and south-east England and Thames Valley; began broadcasting in January 1993; Propr ITV PLC; Man. Dir MARK SOUTHGATE.

ITV Tyne Tees: Television House, The Watermark, Gateshead, NE11 9SZ; tel. (844) 881-5000; e-mail tynetees@itvlocal.com; internet www.itvlocal.com/tynetees; f. 1959; north-east England; Propr ITV PLC; Man. Dir and Controller of Programmes GRAEME THOMPSON.

ITV Wales: Television Centre, Culverhouse Cross, Cardiff, CF5 6XJ; tel. (844) 881-0100; fax (29) 2059-7183; e-mail wales@itvlocal.com; internet www.itvlocal.com/wales; fmrly HTV Wales; Propr ITV PLC; Man. Dir ELIS OWEN.

ITV West: The Television Centre, 470 Bath Rd, Bristol, BS4 3HG; tel. (844) 881-2345; fax (844) 881-2346; e-mail west@itvlocal.com; internet www.itvlocal.com/west; fmrly HTV West; Bristol, Gloucestershire, north Dorset, Somerset and Wiltshire; Propr ITV PLC; Man Dir MARK HASKELL.

ITV Westcountry: Language Science Park, Western Wood Way, Plymouth, PL7 5BQ; tel. and fax (844) 881-4900; e-mail westcountry@itvlocal.com; internet www.itvlocal.com/westcountry; Cornwall, Devon, Somerset and west Dorset; began broadcasting in January 1993; Propr ITV PLC; Man. Dir MARK HASKELL.

ITV Yorkshire: Television Centre, Kirkstall Rd, Leeds, LS3 1JS; tel. (113) 243-8283; fax (113) 243-3655; internet www.itvlocal.com/yorkshire; Propr ITV PLC; Man. Dir DAVID M. B. CROFT.

stv: Pacific Quay, Glasgow, G51 1PQ; tel. (141) 300-3000; fax (141) 300-3030; internet www.stv.tv; f. 1957; operates two services in central and northern Scotland; Propr SMG PLC; Man. Dir, SMG Television BOBBY HAIN.

UTV PLC: Havelock House, Ormeau Rd, Belfast, BT7 1EB; tel. (28) 9032-8122; fax (28) 9024-6695; e-mail info@utvplc.com; internet www.u.tv; started transmission 1959; Chair. JOHN B. MCGUCKIAN; Chief Exec. JOHN MCCANN.

Satellite and Cable Broadcasting

By June 2007 11,279,571 households in the United Kingdom paid to subscribe to multi-channel satellite or cable television services. Of these, 8,085,000 subscribed to digital satellite television with a further 3,405,025 households subscribing to cable television (digital 3,132,571; analogue 272,454). Some 945,000 households received free-to-view digital satellite television services. The major satellite and cable television companies are listed below.

BBC Worldwide Television: Woodlands, 80 Wood Lane, London, W12 0TT; tel. (20) 8433-2000; fax (20) 8749-0538; internet www.bbcworldwide.com; began broadcasting in 1991; part of BBC Worldwide Ltd; broadcasts 24-hour news and information ('BBC World') and light entertainment programmes to Europe ('BBC Prime'); other news programmes broadcast to Africa, Asia (including a Japanese-language service to Japan), the Middle East, Australia and New Zealand; Chief Exec. JOHN SMITH.

British Sky Broadcasting Group PLC (BSkyB): Grant Way, Isleworth, Middlesex, TW7 5QD; tel. (20) 7705-3000; fax (20) 7705-

Directory

3030; internet www.sky.com; f. 1990 by merger of British Satellite Broadcasting (BSB) and Sky TV PLC (a subsidiary of News International); satellite broadcaster and programme provider; multi-channel digital television service SkyDigital (see below); Chair. JAMES MURDOCH; CEO JEREMY DARROCH.

SkyDigital: 6 Centaurs Business Park, Grant Way, Isleworth, Middlesex, TW7 5QD; tel. (20) 7705-3000; fax (20) 7705-3030; internet www.sky.com; owned by British Sky Broadcasting Group PLC; Chief Exec. JEREMY DARROCH.

Eurosport UK: 55 Drury Lane, London, WC2B 5SQ; tel. (20) 7468-7777; fax (20) 7468-0023; e-mail dorman@eurosport.com; internet www.eurosport.co.uk; began broadcasting in 1989; Man. Dir SIMON CRANE.

Freesat: 4th Floor, 58-60 Berners St, London, W1T 3NQ; tel. (845) 313-0052; internet www.freesat.co.uk; f. 2007; commenced broadcasting in May 2008; free-to-air digital satellite service, offering more than 80 digital television and radio channels; jointly owned by the BBC and ITV PLC; Man. Dir EMMA SCOTT.

MTV Networks Europe: 180 Oxford St, London, W1D 1DS; tel. (20) 7478-6000; fax (20) 7284-7788; internet www.mtv.co.uk; began broadcasting in 1987; popular music; Pres. BRENT HANSEN.

UKTV: 160 Great Portland St, London, W1W 5QA; tel. (20) 7299-6200; fax (20) 7299-6000; internet www.uktv.co.uk; began broadcasting 1992; nine channels: Dave, UKTV Documentary, UKTV Drama, UKTV Food, UKTV Gardens, UKTV Gold, UKTV History, UKTV People and UKTV Style; satellite, cable and DTT; Chief Exec. DAVID ABRAHAM.

Finance

The United Kingdom's central bank is the Bank of England, which was established by Act of Parliament and Royal Charter in 1694 and nationalized under the Bank of England Act 1946. The Scottish and Northern Ireland banks issue their own notes but these are largely covered by holdings of Bank of England notes.

The Bank of England holds the main government accounts, acts as registrar of government stocks and as agent of the Government for a number of financial operations. It is also banker to a number of commercial banks. The London clearing banks maintain a substantial proportion of their total cash holdings in the form of balances at the Bank and these are used in the settlement of daily cheque and credit clearings. The Bank has traditionally been responsible for advising the Government on the formulation of monetary policy and for its subsequent execution. A new Bank of England Act, which accorded the Bank statutory operational independence for monetary policy, within agreed government economic targets, received Royal Assent in April 1998, and entered into force on 1 June. The Act provided for the establishment of a Monetary Policy Committee (MPC), with responsibility for analysing and formulating monetary policy within the framework of maintaining price stability and supporting the Government's economic policies. The Treasury was to reserve the right to direct the Bank with respect to monetary decisions in extreme circumstances. The MPC was to comprise the Governor of the Bank, the two newly-created Deputy-Governors, two other Bank officials and four members appointed by the Chancellor of the Exchequer. The Bank's Court of Directors was to review the MPC's procedures and produce an annual report, to be presented to Parliament, under new measures to promote greater accountability and transparency of the Bank's operations. The 1998 Act also transferred, to the Financial Services Authority, the Bank's functions with regard to the supervision of banks.

The commercial banks may be divided into two broad categories: clearing banks and other banks. Clearing banks play the main part in operating the money transmission system throughout the United Kingdom. The other banks comprise accepting houses (taking their name from their business of accepting bills of exchange for payment) and other British-owned banks, overseas-owned banks and consortium banks. As the use of bills of exchange has declined, all accepting houses have assumed the specialist financial services of merchant banks, which include the management of investment trusts, foreign currency trading and company mergers and acquisitions. Since the late 1980s several merchant banks have been incorporated into larger banking organizations to provide a full range of financial, including retail, banking services.

Consortium banks have been formed in the United Kingdom by groups of banks, mostly from overseas, but including some British clearing banks. Initially they were set up to afford shareholders access to the Eurocurrency markets. More recently consortia have been formed as a means of combining institutions from similar geographical areas, when a London operation would be uneconomic for individual banks. Consortium banks are important participants in the major inter-bank markets in sterling and currency deposits and certificates of deposit.

THE UNITED KINGDOM

The discount houses are a specialized group of institutions peculiar to London. They raise the greater part of their funds from within the banking sector. These funds are borrowed by the houses at call or short notice (thereby providing the lending banks with a highly liquid interest-bearing investment) and are used to purchase correspondingly liquid assets—mainly Treasury and commercial bills, short-dated government stocks, certificates of deposit, local authority debt, etc. The discount houses are now more generally incorporated as part of the group of banks authorized by the Bank as listed money market institutions under the 1986 Financial Services Act. The United Kingdom's official reserves, comprising gold, convertible currencies and special drawing rights on the International Monetary Fund, are held in the Exchange Equalization Account operated since 1932 by the Bank of England as agent for the Treasury.

The London Gold Market engages in the trading, transporting, refining, melting, assaying and vaulting of gold. The unique feature of the London market is the 'fixing', which determines the price of gold on a twice-daily basis by matching orders from customers and markets throughout the world. In September 1996 the London Commodity Exchange merged with the London International Financial Futures and Options Exchange (LIFFE), which has since become unique as an exchange trading options on individual equities and on financial, agricultural, soft commodity and equity index products. In October 2001 the French-based Euronext security market acquired LIFFE for a sum of £555m.

The building society movement is important both as a medium of savings (the largest in the United Kingdom) and for the finance of house purchase in a country where more than two-thirds of dwellings are owner-occupied. The expansion of building societies into banking was a characteristic of the late 1980s. This trend was furthered in the 1990s with several large building societies converting to banks through public share offers or opting to merge with similar institutions or with retail banks in order to provide a comprehensive range of financial services. In 2001 there were 48 societies registered in the United Kingdom, compared with 190 in 1984. By June 2007 that number had increased to 59.

National Savings are administered by the Department for National Savings and the Trustee Savings Banks. Through the Department for National Savings the Government administers the National Savings Bank 'investment' and 'ordinary' accounts, National Savings certificates, Premium bonds and other securities, all aimed primarily at the small saver. The outlets for these services are some 14,500 post offices in the United Kingdom.

There are certain institutions set up to provide finance for specific purposes; the more important of these are the 3i Group PLC (which provides investment capital to companies which do not have ready access to capital markets) and the Agricultural Mortgage Corporation (loans against mortgages on agricultural property).

The main capital market is the London Stock Exchange, and since October 1986 the volume of business transacted has greatly expanded with the introduction of the Stock Exchange Automated Quotations system (SEAQ), an electronic trading system which allows off-floor trading. The process of automating trading was completed in October 1997 when the Stock Exchange Electronic Trading Service (Sets) became operational.

The United Kingdom has a highly developed insurance market, located primarily in London. Lloyd's, with its unique system of underwriting syndicates (of which there were 66 in September 2007) has an international reputation for marine and aviation insurance, and reinsurance, as well as a significant share of the British motor insurance market. Much of Lloyd's premium income comes from outside the United Kingdom through Lloyd's 169 accredited brokers. There are over 800 authorized insurance companies in the United Kingdom, dealing with life and general insurance, as well as international reinsurance.

BANKING

(cap. = capital; p.u. = paid up; auth. = authorized; m. = million; res = reserves; dep. = deposits; subs. = subscribed; brs = branches; amounts in pounds sterling)

The 1987 Banking Act replaced the Banking Act of 1979 under which a statutory framework for the supervision of the banking sector was established. The 1987 Act defines new criteria by which an institution can be authorized to accept deposits. The administrative authority for the Act is the Bank of England.

Central Bank

Bank of England: Threadneedle St, London, EC2R 8AH; tel. (20) 7601-4444; fax (20) 7601-5460; e-mail enquiries@bankofengland.co.uk; internet www.bankofengland.co.uk; inc by Royal Charter in 1694, and nationalized by Act of Parliament on 1 March 1946; amended by 1998 Bank of England Act (see above); the Government's banker and on its behalf manages the note issue and sets the official Bank rate; also the bankers' bank; mem. of the Cheque and Credit Clearing Company; cash centre at Leeds and Debden; agencies in Belfast, Birmingham, Bristol, Cambridge, Cardiff, Exeter, Glasgow, Greater London, Leeds, Liverpool, Manchester, Newcastle upon Tyne, Nottingham and Southampton; capital stock amounting to 14.6m. is held by the Treasury; cap. 15m., res 1,845m., dep. 33,380m. (Feb. 2007); Gov. MERVYN KING; Dep. Govs Sir JOHN GIEVE, RACHEL LOMAX.

Principal Banks Incorporated in the United Kingdom

Abbey National Plc: Abbey National House, 2 Triton Sq., Regent's Pl., London, NW1 3AN; tel. (870) 607-6000; e-mail feedback@abbey.com; internet www.abbey.com; f. 1944 as Abbey National Building Society; current status assumed in 1989; owned by Banco Santander Central Hispano, SA (Spain); cap. 148m., res 1,857m., dep. 178,146m. (Dec. 2006); Chair. Lord BURNS; Chief Exec. ANTÓNIO HORTA-OSÓRIO; 793 brs.

Alliance & Leicester PLC: Carlton Park, Narborough, Leicester, LE19 0AL; tel. (116) 201-1000; fax (116) 200-4040; internet www.alliance-leicester.co.uk; fmrly a building society; assumed banking status in 1997; broad-based financial services provider incl. business banking services through wholly-owned subsidiary, Girobank; cap. 823.6m., res 200.2m., dep. 64,280.1m. (Dec. 2006); Chair. Sir DEREK HIGGS; Chief Exec. RICHARD A. PYM; 256 brs.

Bank of Scotland PLC: POB 5, The Mound, Edinburgh, EH1 1YZ; tel. (131) 470-2000; fax (131) 243-7082; internet www.bankofscotland.co.uk; f. 1695 by Act of Scots Parliament; merged with Halifax plc to create HBOS in 2001; adopted current name in 2007; 100% owned by HBOS; cap. 436m., res. 5,032m., dep. 427,372m (Dec. 2006); Chair. Lord STEVENSON; Chief Exec. ANDY HORNBY.

Barclays Bank PLC: 1 Churchill Place, London, E14 5HP; tel. (20) 7699-5000; fax (20) 7699-3463; internet www.barclays.co.uk; inc. 1896; clearing bank; principal operating co of Barclays PLC (group holding co); cap. 1,634m., res 6,208m., dep. 937,825m. (Dec. 2006); Group Chair. MARCUS AGIUS; Chief Exec. JOHN VARLEY; 3,500 brs in 76 countries.

Cheltenham and Gloucester PLC (C&G): Barnett Way, Gloucester, GL4 3RL; tel. (1452) 372372; fax (1452) 373955; internet www.cheltglos.co.uk; f. 1850 as Cheltenham and Gloucester Benefit Building Society; current name and status assumed in 1995; mem. of the Lloyds TSB Group; cap. 508.3m., res 1,084.6m., dep. 79,380m. (Dec. 2006); Chair. DAVID PRITCHARD; Man. Dir JON PAIN.

Clydesdale Bank PLC: 30 St Vincent Pl., Glasgow, G1 2HL; tel. (141) 248-7070; fax (141) 204-0828; internet www.cbonline.co.uk; f. 1838; wholly-owned by National Australia Bank Ltd; clearing bank; cap. 232.0m., res 618.0m., dep. 25,278.0m. (Dec. 2006); Chair. MALCOLM WILLIAMSON; Chief Exec. (Europe) LYNNE PEACOCK; 230 brs.

The Co-operative Bank PLC: POB 101, 1 Balloon St, Manchester, M60 4EP; tel. (161) 832-3456; fax (161) 829-4475; e-mail customerservice@co-operativebank.co.uk.; internet www.co-operativebank.co.uk; f. 1872; clearing bank; cap. 55m., res 13.9m., dep. 11,476.4m. (Jan. 2007); Chair. GRAHAM R. BENNETT; Chief Exec. PIERS WILLIAMSON; 158 brs.

Coutts and Co: 440 Strand, London, WC2R 0QS; tel. (20) 7753-1000; fax (20) 7753-1050; internet www.coutts.com; f. 1692; private clearing bank and asset management; parent co Royal Bank Of Scotland Group PLC; cap. 41.3m., dep. 7,390.8m. (Dec. 1996); Chair. DAVID DOUGLAS-HOME, Earl of Home; Chief Exec. SARAH DEAVES; 24 brs.

First Trust Bank: First Trust Centre, POB 123, 92 Ann St, Belfast, BT1 3AY; tel. (28) 9032-5599; fax (28) 9032-1754; internet www.firsttrustbank.co.uk; f. 1991 following merger of Northern Ireland operations of AIB Group, Ireland and TSB Northern Ireland; trading name of AIB Group (UK) PLC in Northern Ireland; Group Chair. (UK) JOHN B. MCGUCKIAN; Man. Dir TERRY MCDAID; 57 brs.

HSBC Bank PLC: 8 Canada Sq., London, E14 5HQ; tel. (20) 7991-8888; internet www.hsbc.co.uk; f. 1836; from 1992 subsidiary of HSBC Holdings PLC; clearing bank; cap. 797m., res 14,636m., dep. 400,664m. (Dec. 2005); Chair. STEPHEN GREEN; Group Chief Exec. D. D. J. JOHN; 1,700 brs.

Lloyds TSB Bank PLC: 25 Gresham St, London, EC2V 7HN; tel. (20) 7626-1500; fax (20) 7661-4790; internet www.lloydstsb.co.uk; f. 1995 by merger of Lloyds Bank PLC (f. 1765) and TSB Group (f. 1973), name changed as above June 1999; clearing bank; cap. 1,429m., res 1,621m., dep. 237,582m. (Dec. 2006); Chair. Sir VICTOR BLANK; Chief Exec. ERIC DANIELS; 2,500 brs.

Lloyds TSB Scotland PLC: POB 177, Henry Duncan House, 120 George St, Edinburgh, EH2 4LH; tel. (131) 225-4555; fax (131) 220-4217; internet www.lloydstsb.com/scotland; f. 1983 as TSB Bank Scotland PLC following merger of four Scottish TSBs; wholly-owned subsidiary of Lloyds TSB Group PLC; cap. 75m., dep. 9,859.2m. (Dec. 2006); Chair. Prof. EWAN BROWN; Chief Exec. SUSAN RICE; 184 brs.

National Westminster Bank PLC: 135 Bishopsgate, London, EC2M 3UR; tel. (20) 7726-1000; fax (20) 7375-5050; internet www.natwest.com; f. 1968; clearing bank; acquired by The Royal Bank of Scotland Group PLC in 2000; cap. 1,678m., res 8,495m., dep.

266,086m. (Dec. 2006); Chair. Sir GEORGE ROSS MATHEWSON; Group Chief Exec. FRED GOODWIN; 1,631 brs.

Northern Bank Limited: Donegall Sq. West, Belfast, BT1 6JS; tel. (28) 9004-5000; fax (28) 9089-3214; internet www.northernbank.co.uk; f. 1960; owned by Danske Bank Group; cap. 88m., res 20.7m., dep. 3,831.2m. (Dec. 2005); Chair. PETER STRAARUP; Chief Exec. DONALD PRICE; 94 brs.

Northern Rock PLC: Northern Rock House, Gosforth, Tyne and Wear, NE3 4PL; tel. (845) 600-8401; fax (191) 284-8470; internet www.northernrock.co.uk; taken under state ownership in Feb. 2008; cap. 123.9m., res 25.2m., dep. 78,190.1m. (Dec. 2005); Exec. Chair. RON SANDLER; Chief Exec. ANDY KUIPERS; 90 brs.

The Royal Bank of Scotland PLC: POB 1000, Gogaburn, Edinburgh, EH12 1HQ; tel. (131) 556-8555; fax (131) 557-6565; internet www.rbs.co.uk; f. 1985 as result of merger of Royal Bank of Scotland and Williams & Glyn's Bank. The Royal Bank of Scotland (est. by Royal Charter in 1727) merged with National Commercial Bank of Scotland in 1969. Williams & Glyn's Bank was result of merger of Glyn Mills & Co (est. 1753) and Williams Deacon's Bank (est. 1771); subsidiary of The Royal Bank of Scotland Group PLC; clearing bank; cap. 815m., res 39,412., dep. 720,440m. (Dec. 2006); Chair. Sir TOM MCKILLOP; Group Chief Exec. Sir FRED GOODWIN; 639 brs.

Standard Chartered Bank: 1 Aldermanbury Sq., London, EC2V 7SB; tel. (20) 7280-7500; fax (20) 7280-7791; internet www.standardchartered.com; f. 1853; holding co Standard Chartered PLC; cap. US $692m., res $7,845m., dep. $220,801m. (Dec. 2006); Chair. MERVYN DAVIES; 570 brs.

Ulster Bank Ltd: 11–16 Donegall Sq. East, Belfast, BT1 5UB; tel. (28) 9027-6000; fax (28) 9027-5661; e-mail morrow@ulsterbank.com; internet www.ulsterbank.co.uk; f. 1836; mem. of Royal Bank of Scotland Group; cap. 717m., res 2,245m., dep. 40,841m. (Dec. 2006); Chair. Dr ALAN GILLESPIE; Group Chief Exec. CORMAC MCCARTHY; 214 brs.

Yorkshire Bank PLC: 20 Merrion Way, Leeds, LS2 8NZ; tel. (113) 247-2000; fax (113) 242-0733; internet www.ybonline.co.uk; f. 1859; wholly owned by National Australia Bank Ltd; cap. 251.1m., res 91.4m., dep. 7,691.1m. (Sept. 2002); Chief Exec. (Europe) LYNNE PEACOCK; Operations Gen. Man. GLENN KING; 260 brs.

Principal Merchant Banks

Ansbacher & Co Ltd: 2 London Bridge, London, SE1 9RA; tel. (20) 7089-4700; fax (20) 7089-4850; e-mail info@ansbacher.com; internet www.ansbacher.com; f. 1894; cap. 59.0m., res 1.0m., total assets 561.6m. (Dec. 2006); Chair. HUGH TITCOMB.

Barclays Capital: 5 The North Colonnade, Canary Wharf, London, E14 4BB; tel. (20) 7623-2323; e-mail publisher@barclayscapital.com; internet www.barcap.com; investment banking division of Barclays PLC; Chief Exec. ROBERT E. DIAMOND, Jnr.

Brown, Shipley & Co Ltd: Founders Court, London, EC2R 7HE; tel. (20) 7606-9833; fax (20) 7282-3274; e-mail marketing@brownshipley.com; internet www.brownshipley.com; f. 1810; owned by KBC Group NV (Belgium); cap. issued 86.4m., dep. 573.7m. (Dec. 2001); Chair. DAVID ROUGH; Man. Dir S. BLANEY.

Butterfield Bank (UK) Ltd: 99 Gresham St, London, EC2V 7NG; tel. (20) 7776-6700; fax (20) 7776-6701; e-mail info@butterfieldprivatebank.co.uk; internet www.butterfieldprivatebank.co.uk; f. 1919; acquired by Bermuda's Bank of Butterfield in February 2004; cap. 13.0m., res 13.7m., dep. 928.7m. (Dec. 2006); Man. Dir GEORGE BOGUCKI.

Cater Allen Ltd: 9 Nelson St, Bradford, BD1 5AN; tel. (114) 228-2407; e-mail info@caterallen.co.uk; internet www.caterallen.co.uk; f. 1981 by merger of Cater Ryder and Co Ltd (f. 1816) and Allen Harvey and Ross Ltd (f. 1888); acquired by Abbey National Treasury Services in 1997; cap. 100m., dep. 1,411.6m. (Dec. 2001); Chair. MALCOLM MILLINGTON; Man. Dir RICHARD J. DUNN.

Citibank International PLC: POB 242, Citigroup Centre, 33 Canada Sq., Canary Wharf, London, E14 5LB; tel. (20) 7500-5000; fax (20) 7500-1695; internet www.citibank.co.uk; f. 1972; cap. 1,505m., res 538m., dep. 25,430m. (Dec. 2005); Chair. and Chief Exec. WILLIAM J. MILLS.

Citigroup: 33 Canada Sq., Canary Wharf, London, E14 5LB; tel. (20) 7986-2925; internet www.citigroup.com; f. 2000 by merger of J. Henry Schroder & Co Ltd and Salomon Smith Barney; present name adopted 2001; Chairs CHARLES MCVEIGH, DAVID CHALLEN.

Close Brothers Ltd: 10 Crown Pl., London, EC2A 4FT; tel. (20) 7426-4000; fax (20) 7426-4044; e-mail enquiries@closebrothers.co.uk; internet www.closebrothers.co.uk; cap. 82.5m., res 207.0m., dep. 2,940.2m. (July 2006); Chair. S. R. HODGES.

DB UK Bank Limited: 23 Great Winchester St, London, EC2P 2AX; tel. (20) 7545-8000; fax (20) 7545-6155; internet www.deutsche-bank.com; f. 1838; as George Peabody & Co; renamed Morgan Grenfell & Co Ltd in 1910; present name adopted 2004; acquired by Deutsche Bank Group in 1989; cap. 385m., res 4.2m., dep. 7,279.2m. (Dec. 2004); Chair. S. J. DOBBIE; Chief Exec. D. G. PENFOLD; 1 br.

Dresdner Kleinwort Ltd: 30 Gresham St, London, EC2V 7PG; tel. (20) 7623-8000; fax (20) 7623-4069; internet www.dresdnerkleinwort.com; wholly owned subsidiary of Kleinwort Benson Group; ultimate holding co Dresdner Bank AG; share cap. 548.6m., res 67.5m., dep. 602.2m. (Dec. 2004); Chair. ALLAN C. D. YARROW.

Investec Bank (UK) Ltd: 2 Gresham St, London, EC2V 7QP; tel. (20) 7597-4000; fax (20) 7597-4070; internet www.investec.com; f. 1977 as Allied Arab Bank Ltd, name changed as above 1997; acquired Guinness Mahon & Co Ltd 1998; cap. 354.0m., res 44.3m., dep. 5,867.9m. (March 2006); Chair. H. HERMAN; CEO B. FRIED.

Kaupthing Singer & Friedlander Ltd: 1 Hanover St, London, W1S 1AX; tel. (20) 7623-3000; fax (20) 7623-2122; internet www.kaupthingsingers.co.uk; f. 1907; acquired by Kaupping Banki hf (Iceland) in 2005; cap. 155m., res 40m., dep. 2,589m. (Dec. 2006); CEO ARMAN THORVALDSSON; 4 brs.

N M Rothschild & Sons Limited: New Court, St Swithin's Lane, London, EC4P 4DU; tel. (20) 7280-5000; fax (20) 7929-1643; internet www.nmrothschild.com; f. 1804; cap. 50.0m., res 4.1m., dep. 4,649.6m. (March 2006); Chair. Baron DAVID DE ROTHSCHILD; 4 brs.

UBS Limited: 1 Finsbury Ave, London, EC2M 2PP; tel. (20) 7567-8000; fax (20) 7568-4800; internet www.ubs.com/investmentbank; Chair. MARCEL OSPEL; CEO MARCEL ROHNER.

West Merchant Bank Ltd: 33–36 Gracechurch St, London, EC3V 0AX; tel. (20) 7623-8711; fax (20) 7626-1610; f. 1964 as Standard Chartered Merchant Bank Ltd; renamed Chartered West LB Ltd in 1990; present name adopted 1993; subsidiary of Westdeutsche Landesbank Girozentrale; cap. 90.0m., res 7.3m., dep. 5,148.4m. (Dec. 1997); Chief Exec. RICHARD BRIANCE.

Savings Organization

National Savings & Investments: 375 Kensington High St, London, W14 8SD; tel. (845) 9645-0000; e-mail pressoffice@nationalsavings.co.uk; internet www.nsandi.com; govt department and Executive Agency of the Chancellor of the Exchequer; money placed in National Savings and Investments is used by the Treasury to help cost-effectively manage the national debt and contribute towards the Government's financing needs; Chief Exec. JAN PLATT; Man. Dir PAUL SPENCER.

National Savings regional offices: Glasgow, G58 1SB; Durham, DH99 1NS; Blackpool, FY3 9ZW; Lytham St Annes, FY0 1YN; f. 1861; Chief Exec. PETER BAREAU.

Credit Institutions

ECI Ventures: 1st Floor, Brettenham House, Lancaster Pl., London, WC2E 7EN; tel. (20) 7606-1000; fax (20) 7240-5050; e-mail ecivmail@eciv.co.uk; internet www.eciv.co.uk; f. 1976; advises and manages ECI5 (£78m. UK Ltd Partnership), ECI6 (£100m. UK Ltd Partnership) and EC17 (£175m. UK Ltd Partnership) to provide equity capital, mainly for management buy-outs; Chair. Sir JOHN BANHAM.

Permira: 20 Southampton St, London, WC2E 7QH; tel. (20) 7632-1000; fax (20) 7497-2174; e-mail carl.parker@permira.com; internet www.permira.com; fmrly Schroder Ventures Europe; present name adopted 2001; advises 19 Permira Funds world-wide to provide equity capital for financial acquisitions, leveraged buy-outs and buy-ins, growth buy-outs, public-to-private transactions, 'turnarounds'; Chair. DAMON BUFFINI.

3i Group PLC: 16 Palace St, London, SW1E 5JD; tel. (20) 7928-3131; fax (20) 7928-0058; e-mail general_enquiries@3i.com; internet www.3i.com; f. 1945 as the Industrial and Commercial Finance Corpn Ltd by the English and Scottish clearing banks, renamed Finance for Industry PLC, renamed Investors in Industry Group PLC in 1983, and renamed as above in 1988; provides long-term and permanent financial advice; cap. 292.1m., res 1,757.1m., dep. 1,385.0m. (March 1995); Chair. Baroness HOGG; Chief Exec. PHILIP YEA.

Banking and Finance Organizations

Association of Foreign Banks (AFB): 1 Bengal Ct, London, EC3V 9DD; tel. (20) 7283-8300; fax (20) 7283-8302; e-mail secretariat@foreignbanks.org.uk; internet www.foreignbanks.org.uk; f. 1947; incorporated mems of the British Overseas and Commonwealth Banks' Association (f. 1917) in 1996; name changed as above in 2002; approx. 185 mem. banks; Chair. ROGER GIFFORD; Man. Dir JOHN TREADWELL.

Banking Code Standards Board: Level 12, City Tower, 40 Basinghall St, London, EC2V 5DE; tel. (845) 230-9694; fax (20) 7374-4414; e-mail helpline@bcsb.org.uk; internet www.bankingcode.org.uk; fmrly Independent Review Body; self-regulatory body which monitors and enforces Banking Code (for personal customers) and

… Business Banking Code; Chair. GERARD LEMOS; Chief Exec. ROBERT SKINNER.

British Bankers' Association: Pinners Hall, 105–108 Old Broad St, London, EC2N 1EX; tel. (20) 7216-8800; fax (20) 7216-8811; internet www.bba.org.uk; f. 1919; Pres. STEPHEN GREEN; Chief Exec. ANGELA KNIGHT.

Building Societies Association (BSA): 6th Floor, York House, 23 Kingsway, London, WC2B 6UJ; tel. (20) 7520-5900; fax (20) 7240-5290; e-mail web.master@bsa.org.uk; internet www.bsa.org.uk; represents building societies; Chair. IAIN CORNISH; Dir-Gen. ADRIAN COLES.

The Chartered Institute of Bankers in Scotland: Drumsheugh House, 38B Drumsheugh Gardens, Edinburgh, EH3 7SW; tel. (131) 473-7777; fax (131) 473-7788; e-mail info@ciobs.org.uk; internet www.ciobs.org.uk; f. 1875; professional examinations, courses and publications; approx. 13,000 mems; Pres. MILLER MCLEAN; Chief Exec. SIMON THOMPSON.

Institute of Financial Services: 4–9 Burgate Lane, Canterbury, CT1 2XJ; tel. (1227) 818609; fax (1227) 784331; e-mail customerservices@ifslearning.com; internet www.ifslearning.com; f. 1879 as the Chartered Institute of Bankers, current name adopted 2001; a registered charity and one of the leading bodies for the provision of financial education and life-long career support to both the financial services industry and the wider community; Pres. MICHAEL KIRKWOOD; Chief Exec. GAVIN SHREEVE.

London Investment Banking Association: 6 Frederick's Pl., London, EC2R 8BT; tel. (20) 7796-3606; fax (20) 7796-4345; e-mail liba@liba.org.uk; internet www.liba.org.uk; mems c. 60 British and foreign banks and securities houses; Chair. A. C. D. YARROW; Dir-Gen. JONATHAN TAYLOR.

London Money Market Association: 2 Gresham St, London, EC2V 7QP; tel. (20) 7597-4485; fax (20) 7597-4491; e-mail rvardy@investec.co.uk; internet www.lmma.co.uk; f. 1998; mems include international banks, securities houses, building societies; 22 mems; Chair. IAN MAIR; Dep. Chair. R. J. VARDY, I. FOX.

STOCK EXCHANGE

The London Stock Exchange: 10 Paternoster Sq., London, EC4M 7LS; tel. (20) 7797-1000; fax (20) 7334-8916; e-mail infosales@londonstockexchange.com; internet www.londonstockexchange.com; had its origins in the coffee houses of 17th-century London, when those wishing to invest or raise money bought and sold shares in joint-stock companies; formally constituted in 1802. By 1890 an association of stock exchanges had been formed. In 1965 a process of federation began which led to the amalgamation of all stock exchanges in the UK and Ireland in 1973. The Irish Stock Exchange officially ended its 200-year-old association with the London Stock Exchange in December 1995. In November 1986 the Exchange became a private limited company and member firms became shareholders of the Exchange with one vote each. In 1991, the 1875 Deed of Settlement was superseded as the Exchange's constitutional document by a Memorandum and Articles of Association. The governing council of the Exchange was replaced with a Board of Directors drawn from the Exchange's executive and from its customer and user base. In October 1996 an electronic quotation and trading system was introduced, which allowed for off-floor trading and direct global access to share price information. The old mandatory separation of the functions of brokers and jobbers and the system of fixed minimum commissions were then abolished. The Exchange regulates the operation of the market-place as a Recognised Investment Exchange and also regulates listed companies as the United Kingdom's Competent Authority for Listing. The Official List is the Exchange's main market. In June 1995 an Alternative Investment Market (AIM) was established to accommodate smaller and expanding companies. In March 2000 the member institutions voted to end 199 years of mutual status and convert the London Stock Exchange into a public limited company. Its own shares were fully listed from July 2001. In September 2000 plans for the proposed merger with its German counterpart, Deutsche Börse, were abandoned following a hostile takeover bid for the Exchange by the Swedish technology company Om Gruppen. The bid was rejected by shareholders in November. In October 2002 the London Stock Exchange opened a new derivatives trading platform, which would enable private investors to purchase covered warrants. The London Stock Exchange merged with its Italian counterpart, Borsa Italiana, in October 2007. In April 2008 there were 3,224 companies listed on the London Stock Exchange, including 1,218 UK-listed companies, 332 overseas-listed companies and 1,674 companies on AIM; Chair. CHRIS GIBSON-SMITH; Chief Exec. CLARA FURSE.

SUPERVISORY BODIES

In May 1997 the Government announced its intention to establish a single statutory supervisory authority for the financial services sector. Accordingly, in November the then Securities and Investment Board was transformed into a new Financial Services Authority (FSA). From 1 June 1998, when the new Bank of England Act entered into force, the FSA incorporated the Board of Banking Supervision, which advises on supervision policy. The FSA also assumed responsibility for the supervision of insurance companies from the Department of Trade and Industry. On 1 December 2001 the FSA formally incorporated the activities of the existing regulatory bodies as well as the Building Societies Commission, the Registry of Friendly Societies and the Friendly Societies Commission following the enactment of the 2000 Financial Services and Markets Act.

The Financial Ombudsman Service: South Quay Plaza, 183 Marsh Wall, London, E14 9SR; tel. (20) 7964-1000; fax (20) 7964-1001; e-mail complaint.info@financial-ombudsman.org.uk; internet www.financial-ombudsman.org.uk; f. 2001 to replace The Personal Investment Authority Ombudsman Bureau, The Insurance Ombudsman Bureau, The Office of the Banking Ombudsman, The Office of the Building Societies Ombudsman, The Office of the Investment Ombudsman, The Securities and Futures Authority Complaints Bureau, The Financial Services Authority Complaints Unit and The Personal Insurance Arbitration Service; Chair. Sir CHRISTOPHER KELLY; Chief Ombudsman WALTER MERRICKS.

Financial Services Authority (FSA): 25 The North Colonnade, Canary Wharf, London, E14 5HS; tel. (20) 7066-1000; fax (20) 7066-1099; e-mail consumerhelp@fsa.gov.uk; internet www.fsa.gov.uk; f. 1998 to undertake supervision, regulation and market surveillance of all areas of financial activity as defined under the 2000 Financial Services and Markets Act; single statutory regulator responsible for promoting orderly, efficient and fair markets, promoting public understanding of the financial system and reducing financial crime; Chair. CALLUM MCCARTHY; Chief Exec. HECTOR SANTS.

Securities & Investment Institute: 8 Eastcheap, London, EC3M 1AE; tel. (20) 7645-0600; fax (20) 7645-0601; e-mail info@sii.org.uk; internet www.sii.org.uk; f. 1992; aims to promote professional standards and ethics in the securities industry; Chair. SCOTT DOBBIE; Chief Exec. SIMON CULHANE.

INSURANCE

Lloyd's: 1 Lime St, London, EC3M 7HA; tel. (20) 7327-1000; fax (20) 7327-5229; e-mail helpdesk@lloyds.com; internet www.lloyds.com; had its origins in the coffee house opened c. 1688 by Edward Lloyd and was incorporated by Act of Parliament (Lloyd's Acts 1871–1982); an international insurance market and Society of Underwriters, consisting of about 1,124 individual and (since January 1994) 1,017 corporate members grouped into syndicates who accept risks on the basis of unlimited and limited liability, respectively; business is effected through firms of accredited Lloyd's brokers who alone are permitted to place insurances either directly or by way of reinsurance, and some three-quarters of the annual premium income is from overseas business. Lloyd's accounts for approximately half of all international insurance premiums underwritten in the London market. The Lloyd's market is administered by the Corporation of Lloyd's through an 18-member Council, mostly elected by and from the underwriting membership. Lloyd's is regulated by the Financial Services Authority (FSA), under the Financial Services and Markets Act of 2000; capacity to accept insurance premiums of more than £16,100m. in 2007; 66 syndicates underwriting insurance in 2007, covering all classes of business from more than 200 countries and territories world-wide; Chair. Lord LEVENE; CEO RICHARD WARD.

Principal Insurance Companies

Allianz Insurance PLC: 57 Ladymead, Guildford, Surrey, GU1 1DB; tel. (1483) 568161; fax (1483) 300952; internet www.allianz.co.uk; part of the Allianz Group (Germany); f. 1905, fmrly Cornhill Insurance Co PLC; Chair. Lord WALKER OF WORCESTER; Chief Exec. ANDREW TORRANCE.

Aviva PLC: POB 420, St Helen's, 1 Undershaft, London, EC3P 3DQ; tel. (20) 7283-2000; e-mail aviva_info@aviva.com; internet www.aviva.com; formed by merger of Commercial Union and General Accident in 1998; merged with Norwich Union PLC in 2000; renamed as above in 2002; Chair. Lord SHARMAN OF REDLYNCH; Group Chief Exec. ANDREW MOSS.

AXA Insurance PLC: 1 Aldgate, London, EC3N 1RE; tel. (20) 7702-3109; fax (20) 7369-3909; e-mail customerservice@axa-insurance.co.uk; internet www.axa-insurance.co.uk; f. 1903; Chair. ANTHONY HAMILTON; CEO NICOLAS MOREAU.

Co-operative Insurance Society Ltd (CIS): Miller St, Manchester, M60 0AL; tel. (161) 832-8686; fax (161) 837-4048; e-mail ibis@co-operativeinsurance.co.uk; internet www.co-operativeinsurance.co.uk; f. 1867; Chair. SIMON BUTLER; Chief Exec. DAVID ANDERSON.

Direct Line Group: 3 Edridge Rd, Croydon, Surrey, CR9 1AG; tel. (20) 8686-3313; fax (20) 8681-0512; internet www.directline.com; wholly owned by The Royal Bank of Scotland; Man. Dir CHRIS MOAT.

Ecclesiastical Insurance Office PLC: Beaufort House, Brunswick Rd, Gloucester, GL1 1JZ; tel. (1452) 528533; fax (1452) 423557; e-mail information@eigmail.com; internet www.ecclesiastical.co.uk; f. 1887; Chair. NICHOLAS SEALY; Chief Exec. MICHAEL TRIPP.

Equitable Life Assurance Society: Walton St, Aylesbury, Buckinghamshire, HP21 7QW; tel. (845) 603-6771; fax (1296) 386383; e-mail enquiries@equitable.co.uk; internet www.equitable.co.uk; f. 1762; Chair. VANNI TREVES; Chief Exec. CHARLES THOMSON.

Friends Provident PLC: 100 Wood St, London, EC2V 7AN; tel. (870) 608-3678; fax (1306) 740150; e-mail customer.services@friendsprovident.co.uk; internet www.friendsprovident.co.uk; f. 1832; Exec. Chair. Sir ADRIAN A. MONTAGUE.

Legal and General Group PLC: Temple Court, 11 Queen Victoria St, London, EC4N 4TP; tel. (20) 7528-6200; fax (20) 7528-6222; internet www.legalandgeneral.com; f. 1836; Group CEO TIM BREEDON; Group Chair. ROB MARGETTS; Sec. DAVID BINDING.

    Legal and General Insurance Ltd: Temple Court, 11 Queen Victoria St, London, EC4N 4TP; tel. (20) 7528-6200; fax (20) 7528-6222; f. 1946 as British Commonwealth Insurance Co; Chair. TIM BREEDON; Sec. JEAN WEBB.

Liverpool Victoria Friendly Society Ltd: County Gates, Bournemouth, BH1 2NF; tel. (1202) 292333; fax (1202) 292253; internet www.lv.co.uk; f. 1843; Chair. and Acting Chief Exec. DENNIS HOLT.

MGM Assurance (Marine and General Mutual Life Assurance Society): MGM House, Heene Rd, Worthing, Sussex, BN11 3AT; tel. (1903) 836067; fax (1903) 836004; e-mail customercentre@mgm-assurance.co.uk; internet www.mgm-assurance.co.uk; f. 1852; Chair. CHRISTOPHER REEVES; CEO GERARD P. N. HEALY.

The National Farmers Union Mutual Insurance Society Ltd: Tiddington Rd, Stratford upon Avon, Warwicks., CV37 7BJ; tel. (1789) 204211; fax (1789) 298992; internet www.nfumutual.co.uk; f. 1910; Chair. Sir DONALD CURRY; Group Chief Exec. IAN GEDEN.

Pearl: The Pearl Centre, Lynch Wood, Peterborough, Cambridgeshire, PE2 6FY; tel. (1733) 470470; fax (1733) 472300; internet www.pearl.co.uk; f. 1864; part of Pearl Group Limited; present name adopted Dec. 2003; Chair. JONATHAN EVANS.

Phoenix Life Ltd: 1 Wythall Green Way, Wythall Green, Birmingham, B47 6WG; tel. (845) 002-0036; internet www.phoenixlifegroup.co.uk; f. 2005 by a merger of Swiss Life UK and Royal & Sun Alliance UK life business; merged with Britannic Assurance PLC in 2007; subsidiary of Resolution PLC; Chair. DUNCAN FERGUSON; Group CEO PAUL THOMPSON.

The Prudential Assurance Co Ltd: 250 Euston Rd, London, NW1 2PQ; tel. (20) 7405-9222; fax (20) 7548-3465; internet www.prudential.co.uk; f. 1848; holding co: Prudential Corpn PLC; Group Chair. Sir DAVID CLEMENTI; CEO MARK TUCKER.

Royal and Sun Alliance Insurance Group PLC: 9/F, 1 Plantation Place, 30 Venture St, London, EC3M 3BD; tel. (20) 7111-7000; internet www.royalsunalliance.com; f. 1996 by merger of Royal Insurance Holdings PLC (f. 1845) and Sun Alliance Group PLC; Chair. JOHN NAPIER; CEO ANDY HASTE.

Royal Liver Assurance Ltd: Royal Liver Bldg, Pier Head, Liverpool, L3 1HT; tel. (151) 236-1451; fax (151) 236-2122; internet www.royalliverassurance.com; f. 1850; Chair. DAVID E. WOODS; Chief Exec. STEVE BURNETT.

The Royal London Mutual Insurance Society Ltd: 55 Gracechurch St, London, EC3A ORL; tel. (870) 850-6070; fax (1625) 605400; e-mail info@royal-london.co.uk; internet www.royal-london.co.uk; f. 1861; Chair. HUBERT REID; CEO MIKE YARDLEY.

    Scottish Life: POB 54, 19 St Andrew Sq., Edinburgh, EH2 1YE; tel. (131) 456-7777; fax (131) 456-7880; e-mail e-face@scottishlife.co.uk; internet www.scottishlife.co.uk; f. 1881; re-inc as a Mutual Company 1968; became part of Royal London Mutual Insurance Society in July 2001; Chief Exec. BRIAN DUFFIN.

Scottish Widows' PLC: POB 17036, 69 Morrison St, Edinburgh, EH3 8YF; tel. (131) 655-6000; fax (131) 662-4053; internet www.scottishwidows.co.uk; f. 1815 as Scottish Widows' Fund and Life Assurance Society; name changed as above March 2000 following acquisition by Lloyds TSB; Chair. Lord LEITCH; CEO ARCHIE KANE.

The Standard Life Assurance Co: Standard Life House, 30 Lothian Rd, Edinburgh, EH1 2DH; tel. (845) 606-0100; e-mail customer_service@standardlife.com; internet www.standardlife.co.uk; f. 1825; assets under management £96,000m. (Feb. 2004); Chair. GERRY GRIMSTONE; Group CEO SANDY CROMBIE.

Swiss Re UK Ltd: 30 St Mary Axe, London, EC3A 8EP; tel. (20) 7933-3000; fax (20) 7933-5000; internet www.swissre.com; CEO (life and health) CRAIG THORNTON; CEO (property and casualty) PHILIPPE REGAZZONI.

Wesleyan Assurance Society: Colmore Circus, Birmingham, B4 6AR; tel. (121) 335-3487; fax (121) 200-2971; internet www.wesleyan.co.uk; f. 1841; Chair. LOWRY D. MACLEAN; CEO CRAIG ERRINGTON.

Zurich Assurance Ltd: UK Life Centre, Station Rd, Swindon, SN1 1EL; tel. (1793) 511227; fax (1793) 506625; internet www.zurich.co.uk; f. 1872; Group Chair. MANFRED GENTZ; CEO JAMES SCHIRO.

Insurance Associations

Associated Scottish Life Offices: POB 25, Craigforth, Stirling, FK9 4UE; tel. (1786) 448844; fax (1786) 450427; constituted 1841 as an Association of General Managers of Scottish Offices transacting life assurance business; 7 full mems; Chair. GRAHAM POTTINGER; Dep. Chair. DAVID HENDERSON.

Association of British Insurers: 51 Gresham St, London, EC2V 7HQ; tel. (20) 7600-3333; fax (20) 7696-8999; e-mail info@abi.org.uk; internet www.abi.org.uk; f. 1985; principal trade association for insurance companies; protection, promotion, and advancement of the common interests of all classes of insurance business; c. 390 mems; Chair. ARCHIE KANE; Dir-Gen. STEPHEN HADDRILL.

British Insurance Brokers' Association (BIBA): BIBA House, 14 Bevis Marks, London, EC3A 7NT; tel. (870) 950-1790; fax (20) 7626-9676; e-mail enquiries@biba.org.uk; internet www.biba.org.uk; f. 1977; Chair. DEREK THORNTON; Chief Exec. ERIC GALBRAITH.

Chartered Insurance Institute: 20 Aldermanbury, London, EC2V 7HY; tel. (20) 8989-8464; fax (20) 8530-3052; e-mail knowledge@cii.co.uk; internet www.cii.co.uk; f. 1897; inc 1912; approx. 90,000 mems; Pres. MICHAEL BRIGHT; Dir-Gen. Dr A. SCOTT.

Fire Protection Association: London Rd, Moreton-in-Marsh, Gloucestershire, GL56 0RH; tel. (1608) 812500; fax (1608) 812501; e-mail fpa@thefpa.co.uk; internet www.thefpa.co.uk; f. 1946; Man. Dir JON O'NEILL.

Fire and Risk Services: BRE Garston, Watford, Hertfordshire, WD25 9XX; tel. (1923) 664000; fax (1923) 664910; e-mail enquiries@brecertification.co.uk; internet www.bre.co.uk/frs; f. 1986; incorporates the Loss Prevention Council, fire division of the Building Research Establishment; Dir CHRIS BROADBENT.

Insurance Institute of London: 20 Aldermanbury, London, EC2V 7HY; tel. (20) 7600-1343; fax (20) 7600-6857; e-mail iil.london@cii.co.uk; internet www.iilondon.co.uk; f. 1907; Pres. TOM DOHERTY.

International Underwriting Association (IUA): London Underwriting Centre, 3 Minster Ct, Mincing Lane, London, EC3R 7DD; tel. (20) 7617-4444; fax (20) 7617-4440; e-mail info@iua.co.uk; internet www.iua.co.uk; f. 1998; Chair. STEPHEN RILEY; Chief Exec. DAVE J. MATCHAM.

Associations of Actuaries

Faculty of Actuaries: 18 Dublin St, Edinburgh, EH1 3PP; tel. (131) 240-1300; fax (131) 240-1313; e-mail faculty@actuaries.org.uk; internet www.actuaries.org.uk; f. 1856; 1,275 Fellows, 13 Honorary Fellows; Pres. STEWART RITCHIE; Chief Exec. CAROLINE INSTANCE.

Institute of Actuaries: Staple Inn Hall, High Holborn, London, WC1V 7QJ; tel. (20) 7632-2100; fax (20) 7632-2111; e-mail institute@actuaries.org.uk; internet www.actuaries.org.uk; f. 1848; Royal Charter 1884; 15,369 mems (May 2007); Pres. NICHOLAS DUMBRECK (until 30 June 2008), NIGEL MASTERS (from 1 July 2008); Chief Exec. CAROLINE INSTANCE.

Trade and Industry

GOVERNMENT AGENCIES

Advisory, Conciliation and Arbitration Service (Acas): Brandon House, 180 Borough High St, London, SE1 1LW; tel. (20) 7210-3613; fax (20) 7210-3615; internet www.acas.org.uk; f. 1975; an independent organization, under the direction of a council comprising employers, trade union representatives and independent members, appointed by the Sec. of State for Business, Enterprise and Regulatory Reform. The service aims to improve organizations and working life through good employment relations. Acas provides collective conciliation, arbitration, mediation, advisory, training and information services, and conciliates in individual employment rights issues; Chair. ED SWEENEY; Chief Exec. JOHN TAYLOR.

Central Arbitration Committee: POB 51547, London, SE1 1ZG; tel. (20) 7904-2300; fax (20) 7904-2301; e-mail enquiries@cac.gov.uk; internet www.cac.gov.uk; f. 1976 as an independent body under the 1975 Employment Protection Act, in succession to Industrial Court/Industrial Arbitration Board; adjudicates on claims for statutory trade union recognition and de-recognition under the 1999 Employment Relations Act; determines disclosure of information complaints and considers applications and complaints received under the Information and Consultation of Employees Regulations 2004; considers applications in relation to the establishment and operation of European Works Councils, European Companies and European Co-operative Societies; Chair. Sir MICHAEL BURTON; Chief Exec. GRAEME CHARLES.

THE UNITED KINGDOM
Directory

Charity Commission for England and Wales: Harmsworth House, 13–15 Bouverie St, London, EC4Y 8DP; tel. (845) 300-0218; fax (20) 7674-2300; e-mail enquiries@charitycommission.gsi.gov.uk; internet www.charitycommission.gov.uk; statutory organization responsible for the regulation of registered charities; Chief Exec. ANDREW HIND; Chair. SUZI LEATHER.

Competition Appeal Tribunal: Victoria House, Bloomsbury Pl., London, WC1A 2EB; tel. (20) 7979-7979; fax (20) 7979-7978; e-mail info@catribunal.org.uk; internet www.catribunal.org.uk; f. 2002; a specialist tribunal established to hear certain cases in the sphere of British competition and economic regulatory law; hears appeals against decisions of the Office of Fair Trading and the regulators in the telecommunications, electricity, gas, water, railways and air traffic services sectors under the Competition Act of 1998; reviews decisions of the Office of Fair Trading, the Competition Commission and the Secretary of State made pursuant to the merger control and market investigation provisions of the Enterprise Act of 2002; also has jurisdiction, under the Competition Act of 1998, to award damages in respect of infringements of EC or British competition law and, under the Communications Act of 2003, to hear appeals against decisions of OFCOM; headed by the President and a panel of Chairmen and 19 mems with backgrounds in law, economics, business, accountancy and regulation who sit with the President or a mem. of the panel of Chairmen to hear cases; Pres. Sir GERALD BARLING; Registrar CHARLES DHANOWA.

Competition Commission: Victoria House, Southampton Row, London, WC1B 4AD; tel. (20) 7271-0100; fax (20) 7271-0367; e-mail info@cc.gsi.gov.uk; internet www.competition-commission.org.uk; conducts in-depth inquiries into mergers, markets and the regulation of the major regulated industries; Chair. PETER FREEMAN; Chief Exec. MARTIN STANLEY.

Competition Service: Victoria House, Bloomsbury Pl., London, WC1A 2EB; tel. (20) 7979-7979; fax (20) 7979-7978; e-mail info@catribunal.org.uk; internet www.catribunal.org.uk; f. 2003 under the Enterprise Act 2002; a corporate and executive non-departmental public body, whose purpose is to fund and provide support services to the Competition Appeal Tribunal; Dir of Operations JEREMY STRAKER.

Environment Agency: Rio House, Waterside Drive, Aztec West, Almondsbury, Bristol, BS32 4UD; tel. (8708) 506506; e-mail enquiries@environment-agency.gov.uk; internet www.environment-agency.gov.uk; f. 1996; incorporated former National Rivers Authority; Chair. of Board Sir JOHN HARMAN (until July 2008), Lord SMITH (from July 2008); Chief Exec. BARONESS YOUNG OF OLD SCONE.

Food Standards Agency: Aviation House, 125 Kingsway, London, WC2B 6NH; tel. (20) 7276-8000; fax (20) 7276-8004; e-mail helpline@foodstandards.gsi.gov.uk; internet www.food.gov.uk; f. 2000; Chair. Dame DEIRDRE HUTTON; Chief Exec. TIM SMITH.

Forestry Commission: Silvan House, 231 Corstorphine Rd, Edinburgh, EH12 7AT; tel. (131) 334-0303; fax (131) 334-3047; e-mail enquiries@forestry.gsi.gov.uk; internet www.forestry.gov.uk; government department responsible for protecting and expanding the forests and woodlands of England, Scotland and Wales and increasing their value to society and the environment; implements the Government's forestry policy within the framework of the Forestry Acts, administers the Woodland Grant Scheme, controls tree-felling through the issue of licences, administers plant health regulations to protect woodlands against tree-pests and diseases, and conducts research; responsible for the management of the national forests; Chair. Lord CLARK OF WINDERMERE; Dir-Gen. TIM ROLLINSON.

GLE oneLondon: New City Court, 20 St Thomas St, London, SE1 9RS; tel. (20) 7403-0300; fax (20) 7940-1742; e-mail info@gle.co.uk; internet www.gle.co.uk/onelondon; f. 2001 following merger between London Enterprise Agency and Greater London Enterprise; jointly owned by all 33 London borough councils; Man. Dir PETER THACKWRAY.

Health and Safety Executive: Caerphilly Business Park, Caerphilly, CF83 3GG; tel. (845) 345-0055; fax (845) 408-9566; e-mail hse.infoline@natbrit.com; internet www.hse.gov.uk; Chief Exec. GEOFFREY PODGER.

Learning and Skills Council: Cheylesmore House, Quinton Rd, Coventry, CV1 2WT; tel. (845) 019-4170; fax (24) 7682-3675; e-mail info@lsc.gov.uk; internet www.lsc.gov.uk; Chair. CHRIS BANKS; Chief Exec. MARK HAYSOM.

National Audit Office: 151 Buckingham Palace Rd, London, SW1W 9SS; tel. (20) 7798-7000; fax (20) 7798-7894; e-mail enquiries@nao.gsi.gov.uk; internet www.nao.org.uk; audits the financial statements of all government departments and agencies, certain public bodies and international organizations; the Comptroller and Auditor-General is responsible for controlling receipts into, and issues from, the Consolidated and National Loans Funds and reports to Parliament on value for money issues or on important issues arising from the financial statements; Comptroller and Auditor-General TIM BURR.

National Consumer Council: 20 Grosvenor Gdns, London, SW1W 0DH; tel. (20) 7730-3469; fax (20) 7730-0191; e-mail info@ncc.org.uk; internet www.ncc.org.uk; f. 1975; 12 mems; Chair. LARRY WHITTY.

Natural England: 1 East Parade, Sheffield, S1 2ET; tel. (114) 241-8920; fax (114) 241-8921; e-mail enquiries@naturalengland.org.uk; internet www.naturalengland.org.uk; f. 2006 by merger of English Nature, landscape, access and recreation sections of the Countryside Agency and the environmental land management functions of the Rural Development Service; advises Government and acts on issues relating to the environmental, economic and social well-being of the English countryside; Chair. Sir MARTIN DOUGHTY; Chief Exec. Dr HELEN PHILLIPS.

Office of Fair Trading: Fleetbank House, 2–6 Salisbury Sq., London, EC4Y 8JX; tel. (20) 7211-8000; fax (20) 7211-8800; e-mail enquiries@oft.gsi.gov.uk; internet www.oft.gov.uk; f. 1973; monitors consumer affairs, competition policy, consumer credit, estate agencies, etc.; Chair. PHILIP COLLINS; Chief Exec. JOHN FINGLETON.

Postal Services Commission (Postcomm): Hercules House, 6 Hercules Rd, London, SE1 7DB; tel. (20) 7593-2100; fax (20) 7593-2142; e-mail info@psc.gov.uk; internet www.psc.gov.uk; f. 2000 under the Postal Services Act of 2000 as an independent regulator for postal services in the UK; duties include ensuring the provision of a universal postal service, licensing postal operators, introducing competition into mail services, regulating Royal Mail and advising the Govt on the Post Office network; Chair. NIGEL STAPLETON; Chief Exec. SARAH CHAMBERS.

UK Statistics Authority: Statistics House, Tredegar Park, Newport, Gwent, NP10 8XG; tel. (0845) 601-3034; e-mail info@statistics.gov.uk; internet www.statisticsauthority.gov.uk; f. 2008; advises on the quality, quality assurance and priority-setting for National Statistics and on the procedures designed to deliver statistical integrity, to ensure National Statistics are trustworthy and responsive to public needs; Chair. Sir MICHAEL SCHOLAR; Chief Exec. KAREN DUNNELL.

United Kingdom Atomic Energy Authority (UKAEA): Harwell Science and Innovation Campus, Didcot, Oxfordshire, OX11 0RA; tel. (1235) 820220; fax (1235) 434452; internet www.ukaea.org.uk; f. 1954 to take responsibility for British research and development into all aspects of atomic energy; separated into AEA Technology, which operated as the Authority's commercial division, and UKAEA; AEA Technology transferred to the private sector in 1996. UKAEA's core task is to manage the decommissioning of reactors and other facilities used for the nuclear research and development programme. It also carries out fusion research. These activities are conducted at sites at Windscale (Cumbria), Dounreay (Caithness), Harwell and Culham (Oxfordshire) and Winfrith (Dorset); Chair. Lady BARBARA THOMAS; Chief Exec. NORMAN HARRISON.

DEVELOPMENT ORGANIZATIONS

Economic Research Institute of Northern Ireland (ERINI): Floral Buildings, 2–14 East Bridge St, Belfast, BT1 3NQ; tel. (28) 9072-7350; fax (28) 9031-9003; e-mail contact@erini.ac.uk; internet www.erini.ac.uk; f. 2004 to replace the Northern Ireland Economic Council (f. 1977); provides independent economic research, analysis and advice aimed at challenging and developing public policy-making and strategic thinking on issues facing Northern Ireland society; 15 mems representing trade union, employer and independent interests; Chair. JOHN BEATH; Dir VICTOR HEWITT.

Invest Northern Ireland (Invest NI): Bedford Sq., Bedford St, Belfast, BT1 7ES; tel. (28) 9023-9090; fax (28) 9043-6536; e-mail eo@investni.com; internet www.investni.com; f. 2002 to assume responsibility for the activities of the Industrial Development Board for Northern Ireland, the Local Enterprise Development Unit, the Industrial Research and Technology Unit, the Company Development Programme and the business support activities of the Northern Ireland Tourist Board; Invest NI is the main economic development agency in Northern Ireland and, sponsored by the Dept of Enterprise, Trade and Investment, aims to accelerate economic growth in Northern Ireland; Chair. STEPHEN KINGON; Chief Exec. LESLIE MORRISON.

London First: 1 Hobhouse Court, Suffolk St, London, SW1Y 4HH; tel. (20) 7665-1500; fax (20) 7665-1501; e-mail staff@london-first.co.uk; internet www.london-first.co.uk; promotes London as a business centre; Chair. HARVEY MCGRATH; Pres. Lord SHEPPARD OF DIDGEMERE.

Overseas Development Institute: 111 Westminster Bridge Rd, London, SE1 7JD; tel. (20) 7922-0300; fax (20) 7922-0399; e-mail odi@odi.org.uk; internet www.odi.org.uk; f. 1960; independent policy unit on international development and humanitarian issues; Chair. Lord TURNER; Dir SIMON MAXWELL.

Scottish Enterprise: 5 Atlantic Quay, 150 Broomielaw, Glasgow, G2 8LU; tel. (141) 248-2700; fax (141) 221-3217; e-mail network

.helpline@scotent.co.uk; internet www.scottish-enterprise.com; economic development agency for lowland Scotland; Chair. Sir JOHN WARD; Chief Exec. JACK PERRY.

CHAMBERS OF COMMERCE

British Chambers of Commerce (BCC): 65 Petty France, London, SW1H 9EU; tel. (20) 7654-5800; fax (20) 7654-5819; e-mail info@britishchambers.org.uk; internet www.britishchambers.org.uk; f. 1860; in January 1993 subsumed National Chamber of Trade (f. 1897); represents the new Approved Chamber Network in the United Kingdom (comprising 58 Chambers at June 2007); Pres. PETER MILEHAM; Dir-Gen. DAVID FROST.

International Chamber of Commerce (ICC) United Kingdom: 12 Grosvenor Pl., London, SW1X 7HH; tel. (20) 7838-9363; fax (20) 7235-5447; e-mail info@iccorg.co.uk; internet www.iccuk.net; f. 1920; British affiliate of the world business org.; Dir ANDREW HOPE.

London Chamber of Commerce and Industry: 33 Queen St, London, EC4R 1AP; tel. (20) 7248-4444; fax (20) 7489-0391; e-mail lc@londonchamber.co.uk; internet www.londonchamber.co.uk; Pres. STEPHEN GREENE; Chief Exec. JEFFREY ADAMS.

Northern Ireland Chamber of Commerce and Industry: Chamber of Commerce House, 22 Great Victoria St, Belfast, BT2 7BJ; tel. (28) 9024-4113; fax (28) 9024-7024; e-mail mail@northernirelandchamber.com; internet www.nicci.co.uk; f. 1783; Pres. Dr MARK SWEENEY; Chief Exec. FRANK HEWITT; 4,000 mems.

INDUSTRIAL AND TRADE ASSOCIATIONS

Aluminium Federation: National Metalforming Centre, 47 Birmingham Rd, West Bromwich, B70 6PY; tel. (121) 601-6363; fax (870) 138-9714; e-mail alfed@alfed.org.uk; internet www.alfed.org.uk; f. 1962; Pres. HENRY DICKINSON; Sec.-Gen. WILL SAVAGE.

Association of the British Pharmaceutical Industry: 12 Whitehall, London, SW1A 2DY; tel. (20) 7930-3477; fax (20) 7747-1414; e-mail abpi@abpi.org.uk; internet www.abpi.org.uk; f. 1930; Pres. NIGEL BROOKSBY; Dir-Gen. Dr RICHARD BARKER.

Association of Manufacturers of Domestic Appliances: Rapier House, 40–46 Lamb's Conduit St, London, WC1N 3NW; tel. (20) 7405-0666; fax (20) 7405-6609; e-mail info@amdea.org.uk; internet www.amdea.org.uk; f. 1969; 27 mem. cos; Chief Exec. DOUGLAS HERBISON.

BFM (British Furniture Manufacturers Association): Wycombe House, 9 Amersham Hill, High Wycombe, Bucks HP13 6NR; tel. (149) 4523-021; fax (149) 4474-270; e-mail info@bfm.org.uk; internet www.bfm.org.uk; merged in January 1993 with BFM Exhibitions and BFM Exports; Man. Dir ROGER MASON.

British Beer and Pub Association: Market Towers, 1 Nine Elms Lane, London, SW8 5NQ; tel. (20) 7627-9191; fax (20) 7627-9123; e-mail enquiries@beerandpub.com; internet www.beerandpub.com; f. 1904; 73 mems; trade association for British brewing industry and multiple pub chains; Chief Exec. PATRICK BROWNE.

British Cable Association: 3–30 Lingfield Rd, Wimbledon, SW19 4PU; tel. and fax (20) 8946-6978; e-mail peter.smeeth@btconnect.com; internet www.bcauk.org; f. 1903; fmrly British Cable Makers' Confederation; Sec.-Gen. PETER SMEETH.

British Cement Association: Riverside House, 4 Meadows Business Park, Station Approach, Blackwater, Camberley, Surrey, GU17 9AB; tel. (1276) 608700; fax (1276) 608701; e-mail info@bca.org.uk; internet www.bca.org.uk; Chair. CLIVE JAMES; Chief Exec. PAL CHANA.

British Ceramic Confederation: Federation House, Station Rd, Stoke-on-Trent, Staffs., ST4 2SA; tel. (1782) 744631; fax (1782) 744102; e-mail bcc@ceramfed.co.uk; internet www.ceramfed.co.uk; f. 1984; 125 mems; Chief Exec. KEVIN FARRELL.

British Clothing Industry Association: 5 Portland Pl., London, W1B 1PW; tel. (20) 7636-7788; fax (20) 7636-7515; e-mail bcia@dial.pipex.com; f. 1980; Chair. JAMES MCADAM; Dir JOHN R. WILSON.

British Electrotechnical and Allied Manufacturers' Association (BEAMA Ltd): Westminster Tower, 3 Albert Embankment, London, SE1 7SL; tel. (20) 7793-3000; fax (20) 7793-3003; e-mail info@beama.org.uk; internet www.beama.org.uk; f. 1905 as British Electrical and Allied Manufacturers' Association Ltd, present name from 2002; 460 mems; Pres. and Chair. RICHARD DICK; CEO DAVID DOSSETT.

British Exporters' Association: Broadway House, Tothill St, London, SW1H 9NQ; tel. (20) 7222-5419; fax (20) 7799-2468; e-mail bexamail@aol.com; internet www.bexa.co.uk; Pres. Sir RICHARD NEEDHAM; Chair. RICHARD HILL; Dir HUGH BAILEY.

British Footwear Association: 3 Burystead Place, Wellingborough, Northants, NN8 1AH; tel. (1933) 229005; fax (1933) 225009; e-mail info@britfoot.com; internet www.britfoot.com; f. 1898; Exec. Officer ELAINE DAVIES.

British Glass: 9 Churchill Way, Chapeltown, Sheffield, S35 2PY; tel. (114) 290-1850; fax (114) 290-1851; e-mail info@britglass.co.uk; internet www.britglass.co.uk; over 100 mems; Dir-Gen. DAVID WORKMAN.

British Hospitality Association: Queen's House, 55/56 Lincoln's Inn Fields, London, WC2A 3BH; tel. (845) 880-7744; fax (20) 7404-7799; e-mail bha@bha.org.uk; internet www.bha-online.org.uk; f. 1907; Pres. Sir DAVID MICHELS; Chief Exec. ROBERT COTTON.

British Non-Ferrous Metals Federation: 5 Grovelands Business Centre, Boundary Way, Hemel Hempstead, HP2 7TE; tel. (1442) 275705; fax (1442) 275716; e-mail bnfmf@copperuk.org.uk; f. 1945; Dir DAVID PARKER.

The British Precast Concrete Federation Ltd: 60 Charles St, Leicester, LE1 1FB; tel. (116) 253-6161; fax (116) 251-4568; e-mail info@britishprecast.org; internet www.britishprecast.org; f. 1918; approx. 125 mems; Chief Exec. MARTIN A. CLARKE.

British Printing Industries Federation: Farringdon Point, 29–35 Farringdon Rd, London, EC1M 3JF; tel. (870) 240-4085; fax (20) 7405-7784; e-mail andrew.brown@bpif.org.uk; internet www.britishprint.com; f. 1900; 2,500 mems; Pres. MIKE TAYLOR; Chief Exec. MICHAEL JOHNSON.

British Rubber Manufacturers' Association: 6 Bath Pl., Rivington St, London, EC2A 3JE; tel. (20) 7457-5040; fax (20) 7972-9008; e-mail mail@brma.co.uk; f. 1968; Pres. JAMES RICKARD; Dir A. J. DORKEN.

The Carpet Foundation: MFC Complex, 60 New Rd, Kidderminster, Worcs., DY10 1AQ; tel. (1562) 755568; fax (1562) 865405; internet www.comebacktocarpet.com; 11 manufacturer and 1,100 retailer mems; Chair. JOHN DUNCAN; Chief Exec. MIKE HARDIMAN.

CBI: Centre Point, 103 New Oxford St, London, WC1A 1DU; tel. (20) 7379-7400; fax (20) 7240-1578; internet www.cbi.org.uk; f. 1965 as the Confederation of British Industry, name changed as above in 2001; acts as a national point of reference for all seeking views of industry and is recognized internationally as the representative organization of British industry and management; advises the Government on all aspects of policy affecting the interests of industry; has a direct corporate membership employing more than 4m., and a trade association membership representing more than 6m. of the workforce; Pres. MARTIN BROUGHTON; Dir-Gen. RICHARD LAMBERT.

Chemical Industries Association: King's Buildings, Smith Sq., London, SW1P 3JJ; tel. (20) 7834-3399; fax (20) 7834-4469; e-mail enquiries@cia.org.uk; internet www.cia.org.uk; Pres. ALISTAIR STEEL; Dir-Gen. JUDITH HACKITT.

Construction Confederation: 55 Tufton St, London, SW1P 3QL; tel. (870) 898-9090; fax (870) 898-9095; e-mail enquiries@thecc.org.uk; internet www.thecc.org.uk; f. 1878; 5,000 mems; Chair. JAMES WATES; Chief Exec. STEPHEN RATCLIFFE.

Dairy UK: 93 Baker St, London, W1U 6QQ; tel. (20) 7486-7244; fax (20) 7487-4734; e-mail info@dairyuk.org; internet www.dairyuk.org; f. 1933; Pres. DAVID CURRY; Dir-Gen. JIM BEGG.

Electrical Contractors' Association: ESCA House, 34 Palace Court, London, W2 4HY; tel. (20) 7313-4800; fax (20) 7221-7344; e-mail info@eca.co.uk; internet www.eca.co.uk; f. 1901; Pres. ROBERT HALL; Dir DAVID R. J. POLLOCK.

Energy Networks Association: 18 Stanhope Pl., London, W2 2HH; tel. (20) 7706-5100; e-mail info@energynetworks.org; internet 2008.energynetworks.org; f. 2003; represents British gas and electricity transmission and distribution licence holders; Chair. PAUL CUTTILL; CEO DAVID SMITH.

Engineering Employers' Federation (EEF): Broadway House, Tothill St, London, SW1H 9NQ; tel. (20) 7222-7777; fax (20) 7222-2782; e-mail enquiries@eef-fed.org.uk; internet www.eef.org.uk; f. 1896; 5,700 mems through 14 associations; Pres. ALAN WOOD; Dir-Gen. MARTIN TEMPLE.

Farmers' Union of Wales: Llys Amaeth, Plas Gogerddan, Aberystwyth, Ceredigion, SY23 3BT; tel. (1970) 820820; fax (1970) 820821; e-mail head.office@fuw.org.uk; internet www.fuw.org.uk; f. 1955; 14,000 mems; Pres. GARETH VAUGHAN.

Food and Drink Federation: 6 Catherine St, London, WC2B 5JJ; tel. (20) 7836-2460; fax (20) 7836-0580; e-mail generalenquiries@fdf.org.uk; internet www.fdf.org.uk; Dir-Gen. MELANIE LEECH.

Glass and Glazing Federation: 44–48 Borough High St, London, SE1 1XB; tel. (870) 042-4255; fax (870) 042-4266; e-mail info@ggf.org.uk; internet www.ggf.org.uk; f. 1977; trade organization for employers and cos in the flat glass, glazing, home improvement, plastic and window film industries; Chief Exec. NIGEL REES.

Institute of Export: Export House, Minerva Business Park, Lynch Wood, Peterborough, PE2 6FT; tel. (1733) 404400; fax (1733) 404444; e-mail institute@export.org.uk; internet www.export.org.uk; f. 1935; professional educational organization devoted to the development of British export trade and the interests of those associated with it;

more than 6,000 mems; Pres. Sir MARTIN LAING; Chair. LESLEY BALCHELOR; Dir ANDY GIBSON.

Labour Relations Agency: 2-8 Gordon St, Belfast, BT1 2LG; tel. (28) 9032-1442; fax (28) 9033-0827; e-mail info@lra.org.uk; internet www.lra.org.uk; f. 1976; provides an impartial and confidential employment relations service to those engaged in industry, commerce and the public services in Northern Ireland; provides advice on good employment practices and assistance with the development and implementation of employment policies and procedures; also active in resolving disputes through its conciliation, mediation and arbitration services.

National Association of British and Irish Millers Ltd: 21 Arlington St, London, SW1A 1RN; tel. (20) 7493-2521; fax (20) 7493-6785; e-mail info@nabim.org.uk; internet www.nabim.org.uk; trade assoc. of the British flour milling industry; f. 1878; Dir-Gen. ALEXANDER WAUGH; Sec. NIGEL BENNETT.

National Farmers' Union: Agriculture House, Stoneleigh Park, Warwickshire CV8 2TZ; tel. (24) 7685-8500; fax (24) 7685-8501; e-mail nfu@nfu.org.uk; internet www.nfuonline.com; f. 1904 as Lincolnshire Farmers' Union, adopted present name in 1908; Pres. PETER KENDALL; Dir-Gen. RICHARD MACDONALD.

National Metal Trades Federation: Savoy Tower, 77 Renfrew St, Glasgow, G2 3BZ; tel. (141) 332-0826; fax (141) 332-5788; e-mail alex.shaw@nmtf.org.uk; internet www.nmtf.org.uk; Sec. ALEX SHAW.

Northern Ireland Hotels Federation: Midland Bldg, Whitla St, Belfast, BT15 1JP; tel. (28) 9035-1110; fax (28) 9035-1509; e-mail office@nihf.co.uk; internet www.nihf.co.uk; Pres. RODNEY WATSON; Chief Exec. JANICE GAULT.

Northern Ireland Textiles and Apparel Asscn: 5C The Square, Hillsborough, BT26 6AG; tel. (28) 9268-9999; fax (28) 9268-9968; e-mail info@nita.co.uk; internet www.nita.co.uk; f. 1993; Dir LINDA MACHUGH; 30 mems.

Producers Alliance for Cinema and Television (PACT) Ltd: 2nd Floor, 1 Procter St, London, WC1V 6DW; tel. (20) 7067-4367; fax (20) 7067-4377; e-mail enquiries@pact.co.uk; internet www.pact.co.uk; film and TV producers; represents 1,000 companies; Chief Exec. JOHN MCVAY; Chair. ANDREW ZEIN.

Quarry Products Association: Gillingham House, 38–44 Gillingham St, London, SW1V 1HU; tel. (20) 7963-8000; fax (20) 7963-8001; e-mail info@qpa.org; internet www.qpa.org; fmrly British Ready Mixed Concrete Asscn., and the British Aggregate Construction Materials Industry Ltd; Chair LYNDA THOMPSON; Dir SIMON VAN DER BYL.

Scottish Building Federation: Crichton House, Crichton's Close, Edinburgh, EH8 8DT; tel. (131) 556-8866; fax (131) 558-5247; e-mail info@scottish-building.co.uk; internet www.scottish-building.co.uk; Pres. BILL IMLACH; Gen. Man. DOUGLAS FERGUS.

Scottish Enterprise—Textiles: Apex House, 99 Haymarket Terrace, Edinburgh, EH12 5DH; tel. (131) 313-6243; fax (131) 313-4231; internet www.scottish-textiles.co.uk; present name since 1991.

Sea Fish Industry Authority (Seafish): 18 Logie Mill, Logie Green Rd, Edinburgh, EH7 4HS; tel. (131) 558-3331; fax (131) 558-1442; e-mail seafish@seafish.co.uk; internet www.seafish.org; non-departmental public body sponsored by the four United Kingdom Government fisheries departments and funded by a levy on seafood; works with all sectors of the British seafood industry to satisfy consumers, raise standards, improve efficiency and secure a sustainable future; Chair. ANDREW DEWAR-DURIE; Chief Exec. JOHN RUTHERFORD.

Society of British Aerospace Companies Ltd: Unit 7, Salamanca Sq, 9 Albert Embankment, London, SE1 7SP; tel. (20) 7091-4500; fax (20) 7091-4545; e-mail post@sbac.co.uk; internet www.sbac.co.uk; f. 1916; national trade association for the British aerospace industry; Pres. CHRIS GEOGHEGAN; Dir-Gen. Dr SALLY HOWES.

Society of Motor Manufacturers and Traders: Forbes House, Halkin St, London, SW1X 7DS; tel. (20) 7235-7000; fax (20) 7235-7112; e-mail smmt@smmt.co.uk; internet www.smmt.co.uk; Pres. ROGER PUTNAM; Chief Exec. CHRISTOPHER MACGOWAN.

The Sugar Bureau: Duncan House, 6 Catherine St, London, WC2B 5JJ; tel. (20) 7379-6830; fax (20) 7836-4113; e-mail info@sugar-bureau.co.uk; internet www.sugar-bureau.co.uk; represents sugar companies in the UK, provides technical, educational and consumer information about sugar and health; Dir Dr ALISON BOYD.

Timber Trade Federation: Building Centre, 26 Store St, London, WC1E 7BT; tel. (20) 3205-0067; fax (20) 7291-5379; e-mail ttf@ttf.co.uk; internet www.ttf.co.uk; Chief Exec. JOHN WHITE.

Ulster Chemists' Asscn: 5 Annadale Ave, Belfast, BT7 3JH; tel. (28) 9069-0456; fax (28) 9069-0457; e-mail adrienne@uca.org.uk; internet www.uca.org.uk; f. 1901; promotion and protection of interests of community pharmacies in Northern Ireland; Pres. PAUL MCDONAGH.

Ulster Farmers' Union: Dunedin, 475 Antrim Rd, Belfast, BT15 3DA; tel. (28) 9037-0222; fax (28) 9037-1231; e-mail info@ufuhq.com; internet www.ufuni.org; f. 1918; Pres. KENNETH SHARKEY; Chief Exec. CLARKE BLACK; 12,500 mems.

United Kingdom Petroleum Industry Association: 9 Kingsway, London, WC2B 6XF; tel. (20) 7240-0289; fax (20) 7379-3102; e-mail info@ukpia.com; internet www.ukpia.com; f. 1978; Pres. NICK THOMAS; Dir-Gen. CHRIS HUNT.

EMPLOYERS' ASSOCIATIONS

British Retail Consortium: 2nd Floor, 21 Dartmouth St, London, SW1H 9BP; tel. (20) 7854-8900; fax (20) 7854-8901; e-mail info@brc.org.uk; internet www.brc.org.uk; f. 1975; represents retailers; Dir-Gen. KEVIN HAWKINS; Man. Dir JEREMY BEADLES.

Chartered Management Institute: Management House, Cottingham Rd, Corby, NN17 1TT; tel. (1536) 204222; fax (1536) 201651; e-mail enquiries@managers.org.uk; internet www.managers.org.uk; f. 1992 as the Institute of Management by amalgamation of British Institute of Management (f. 1947) and Institution of Industrial Managers (f. 1931); changed name as above in 2002; represents 71,000 individual mems and 450 corporate mems; Pres. Sir JOHN SUNDERLAND; Chief Exec. MARY CHAPMAN.

Federation of Small Businesses: Sir Frank Whittle Way, Blackpool Business Park, Blackpool, Lancashire FY4 2FE; tel. (1253) 336000; fax (1253) 348046; e-mail membership@fsb.org.uk; internet www.fsb.org.uk; f. 1974; represents the interests of British small businesses and the self-employed; 185,000 mems; Policy Chair. JOHN WRIGHT.

Institute of Directors: 116 Pall Mall, London, SW1Y 5ED; tel. (20) 7766-8888; fax (20) 7766-8833; e-mail enquiries@iod.com; internet www.iod.com; f. 1903; 53,000 mems; Chair. Dr NEVILLE BAIN; Dir-Gen. MILES TEMPLEMAN.

UTILITIES

Regulatory Authorities

Northern Ireland Authority for Energy Regulation: Queens House, 10–18 Queens St, Belfast, BT1 6ED; tel. (28) 9031-1575; e-mail ofreg@nics.gov.uk; internet ofreg.nics.gov.uk; independent public body to regulate the electricity and natural gas industries in Northern Ireland; Chair. PETER MATTHEWS; Chief Exec. IAIN OSBOURNE.

Office of Gas and Electricity Markets (Ofgem): 9 Millbank, London, SW1P 3GE; tel. (20) 7901-7000; fax (20) 7901-7066; e-mail consumeraffairs@ofgem.gov.uk; internet www.ofgem.gov.uk; f. 1999 following merger of Offer and Ofgas; regulates the gas and electricity industries in England, Scotland and Wales and aims to promote the interests of all gas and electricity customers by promoting competition and regulating monopolies; Chair. Sir JOHN MOGG; Chief Exec. ALISTAIR BUCHANAN.

Electricity

Principal Electricity Companies

British Energy PLC: GSO Business Park, East Kilbride, G74 5PG; tel. (1355) 846000; fax (1355) 846001; e-mail john.mcnamara@british-energy.com; internet www.british-energy.com; Chair. Sir ADRIAN MONTAGUE; Chief Exec. BILL COLEY.

CE Electric UK: 98 Aketon Rd, Castleford, WF10 5DS; tel. (1977) 605934; fax (1977) 605944; internet www.ceelectricuk.com; subsidiary of MidAmerican Energy Holdings Co; delivers electricity to 3.6m. homes in the north-east of England, Yorkshire and Humberside; Dir J. M. FRANCE.

Central Networks: Herald Way, Pegasus Business Park, East Midlands Airport, Castle Donnington, DE74 2TU; tel. (1332) 393415; internet www.central-networks.co.uk; subsidiary of E.ON UK PLC; fmrly East Midlands Electricity PLC; merged with Midlands Electricity PLC in 2004 and name changed to above; Man. Dir BOB TAYLOR.

EDF Energy: 40 Grosvenor Pl., London, SW1X 7GN; tel. (20) 7242-9050; e-mail info@edfenergy.com; internet www.edfenergy.com; supplies electricity and gas through London Energy, SWEB Energy and Seeboard Energy; Chair. DANIEL CAMUS; Chief Exec. VINCENT DE RIVAZ.

E.ON UK PLC: Westwood Way, Westwood Business Park, Coventry, CV4 8LG; tel. (24) 7642-4000; fax (24) 7642-5432; e-mail jonathan.smith@eon-uk.com; internet www.eon-uk.com; f. 2004; fmrly Powergen UK PLC; supplies, distributes and sells electricity; also retailer of gas; subsidiary of E.ON AG (Germany); Chair. Dr WULF H. BERNOTAT; Chief Exec. Dr PAUL GOLBY.

Green Energy (UK) PLC: 190 Strand, London, WC2 8JN; e-mail newconnections@greenenergy.uk.com; internet www.greenenergy.uk.com; Chair. Sir PETER THOMPSON; CEO DOUGLAS STEWART.

THE UNITED KINGDOM

National Grid PLC: 1–3 Strand, London, WC2N 5EH; tel. (20) 7004-3000; fax (20) 7004-3004; internet www.nationalgrid.com; Chair. Sir JOHN PARKER; CEO STEVE HOLLIDAY.

Northern Ireland Electricity PLC: 120 Malone Rd, Belfast, BT9 5HT; tel. (28) 9066-1100; e-mail customercontact@nie.co.uk; internet www.nie.co.uk; holding co Viridian Group; Chair. DIPESH SHAH; Man. Dir HARRY MCCRACKEN.

npower: Oak House, Bridgwater Rd, Warndon, Worcester, WR4 9FP; tel. (1793) 877777; fax (1793) 892525; internet www.npower.com; f. 1999 to combine the electricity and gas supply business of six companies; launched in 2000; retail arm of RWE npower PLC; CEO DAVID THRELFALL.

Powergen UK: Westwood Way, Westwood Business Park, Coventry, CV4 8LG; tel. (24) 7642-4000; fax (24) 7642-5432; subsidiary of E.ON UK PLC; CEO Dr PAUL GOLBY.

RWE npower plc: Windmill Hill Business Park, Whitehill Way, Swindon, Wiltshire, SN5 6PB; tel. (1793) 877777; fax (1793) 893955; internet www.rwenpower.com; Group CEO ANDREW DUFF.

Scottish and Southern Energy PLC: Inveralmond House, 200 Dunkeld Rd, Perth, PH1 3AQ; tel. (1738) 456660; fax (1738) 455281; e-mail info@scottish-southern.co.uk; internet www.scottish-southern.co.uk; Chair. Sir ROBERT SMITH; CEO IAN MARCHANT.

ScottishPower PLC: Corporate Office, 1 Atlantic Quay, Glasgow, G2 8SP; tel. (141) 248-8200; fax (141) 248-8300; internet www.scottishpower.com; acquired by Iberdrola, SA (Spain) in 2007; Chair. JOSÉ IGNACIO SÁNCHEZ GALÁN; CEO JOSÉ LUIS DEL VALLE.

South Wales Electricity PLC: POB 7506, Perth, PH1 3QR; internet (800) 052-5252; internet www.swalec.co.uk; part of Scottish and Southern Energy Group; CEO JOHN ROBINS.

Southern Electric: 55 Vastern Rd, Reading, Berks, RG1 8BU; internet www.southern-electric.co.uk; part of Scottish and Southern Energy Group; Group CEO IAN MARCHANT.

Gas

Principal Gas Suppliers

British Gas: Centrica PLC, Millstream, Maidenhead Rd, Windsor, Berkshire, SL4 5GD; tel. (845) 070-9010; e-mail house@britishgas.co.uk; internet www.britishgas.co.uk; part of Centrica Group; Chair. ROGER CARR; Man. Dir PHIL BENTLEY.

EDF Energy: see Electricity.

npower: see Electricity.

Phoenix Natural Gas Ltd: 197 Airport Rd West, Belfast, BT3 9ED; tel. (28) 9055-5555; fax (28) 9055-5500; e-mail info@phoenix-natural-gas.com; internet www.phoenix-natural-gas.com; f. 1997; CEO PETER DIXON.

ScottishPower: see Electricity.

Southern Electric: see Electricity.

SWEB Energy: Freepost 3805, Plymouth, PL1 1WN; tel. (800) 365000; fax (1392) 448-9111; internet www.sweb.co.uk; part of EDF Energy group; Chief Exec. VINCENT DE RIVAZ.

Water

Regulatory Authority

Water Services Regulation Authority (Ofwat): Centre City Tower, 7 Hill St, Birmingham, B5 4UA; tel. (121) 625-1300; fax (121) 625-1400; e-mail enquiries@ofwat.gsi.gov.uk; internet www.ofwat.gov.uk; independent economic regulator of the water and sewerage cos in England and Wales; ensures compliance with the functions specified in the Water Industry Act of 2003; Chair. PHILIP FLETCHER; Chief Exec. REGINA FINN.

Principal Companies

Anglian Water Services Ltd: POB 770, Lincoln, LN5 7WX; tel. (8457) 919155; fax (1480) 326981; internet www.anglianwater.co.uk; Chair. JONSON COX; CEO PETER SIMPSON.

Mid-Kent Water PLC: Rocfort Rd, Snodland, Kent, ME6 5AH; tel. (1634) 873033; fax (1634) 242764; e-mail water@midkent.co.uk; internet www.midkentwater.co.uk; Propr Hastings Fund Management; Chair. GORDON MAXWELL; Gen. Man. PAUL BUTLER.

Northern Ireland Water: Northland House, 3 Frederick St, Belfast, BT1 2NR; tel. (8457) 440088; e-mail waterline@niwater.com; internet www.niwater.com; Chief Exec. KATHARINE BRYAN.

Scottish Water: Castle House, 6 Castle Drive, Carnegie Campus, Dunfermline, KY11 8GG; tel. 0845 601 8855; e-mail customer.service@scottishwater.co.uk; internet www.scottishwater.co.uk; f. 2002; Chair. RONNIE MERCER; Chief Exec. RICHARD K. ACKROYD.

Severn Trent Water Ltd: 2297 Coventry Rd, Birmingham, B26 3PU; tel. (121) 722-4000; fax (121) 722-4800; internet www.stwater.co.uk; Chair. Sir JOHN EGAN; Chief Exec. TONY WRAY.

South East Water: 3 Church Rd, Haywards Heath, West Sussex, RH16 3NY; tel. (845) 301-8045; e-mail contactcentre@southeastwater.co.uk; internet www.southeastwater.co.uk; merged with Mid Kent Water in 2007; owned by Hastings Diversified Utilities Fund and the Utilities Trust of Australia; Chair. GORDON MAXWELL; Man. Dir PAUL BUTLER.

South Staffordshire Water PLC: POB 63, Walsall, WS2 7PJ; tel. (1922) 616239; internet www.south-staffs-water.co.uk; Exec. Chair. DAVID SANKEY; Man. Dir Dr JACK CARNELL.

South West Water Ltd: Peninsula House, Rydon Lane, Exeter, EX2 7HR; tel. (1392) 446688; fax (1392) 434966; internet www.southwestwater.co.uk; part of Pennon Group; Chair. KENNETH HARVEY; CEO CHRISTOPHER LOUGHLIN.

Southern Water PLC: POB 41, Worthing, West Sussex, BN13 3NZ; tel. (1903) 264444; fax (1903) 691435; e-mail customerservices@southernwater.co.uk; internet www.southernwater.co.uk; Chair. MIKE WELTON; CEO LES DAWSON.

Thames Water Utilities Ltd: POB 286, Swindon, SN38 2RA; tel. (845) 920-0888; internet www.thameswateruk.co.uk; acquired by Kemble Water Ltd in 2006; Chair. Sir PETER MASON; CEO DAVID OWENS.

Three Valleys Water PLC: POB 48, Bishops Rise, Hatfield, Herts, AL10 9HL; tel. (1707) 268111; fax (1707) 277188; internet www.3valleys.co.uk; Chair. Sir ALAN THOMAS; Man. Dir ANDREW SMITH.

United Utilities PLC: Dawson House, Great Sankey, Warrington, WA5 3LW; tel. (1925) 237000; fax (1925) 237073; internet www.uuplc.co.uk; Chair. Sir RICHARD EVANS; Chief Exec. PHILIP GREEN.

Welsh Water (Dwr Cymru Cyfyngedig): Pentwyn Rd, Nelson, Treharris, Mid Glamorgan, CF46 6LY; tel. (1443) 452300; fax (1443) 452809; e-mail enquiries@dwrcymru.com; internet www.dwrcymru.com; f. 1989; Chair. Lord BURNS; Man. Dir NIGEL ANNETT.

Wessex Water Services Ltd: Claverton Down Rd, Bath, BA2 7WW; tel. (1225) 526000; e-mail info@wessexwater.co.uk; internet www.wessexwater.co.uk; Propr YTL (Malaysia); Chair. and CEO COLIN SKELLETT.

Yorkshire Water Services Ltd: POB 500, Bradford, BD6 2SZ; tel. (845) 124-2424; fax (1274) 372800; internet www.yorkshirewater.com; Chair. JOHN NAPIER; Man. Dir KEVIN WHITEMAN.

CO-OPERATIVE ORGANIZATIONS

Co-operatives UK: Holyoake House, Hanover St, Manchester, M60 0AS; tel. (161) 246-2900; fax (161) 831-7684; e-mail info@cooperatives-uk.coop; internet www.cooperatives-uk.coop; f. 1869; co-ordinates, informs and advises the 45 retail consumer co-operative societies and 700 worker co-operatives and employee-owned businesses; Chair. BEN REID; Society Sec. JOHN BUTLER; Chief Exec. Dame PAULINE GREEN.

Co-operative Group Ltd: New Century House, POB 53, Manchester, M60 4ES; tel. (161) 834-1212; fax (161) 834-4507; internet www.co-operative.co.uk; f. 1863; merged with United Co-operatives in 2007; Chair. LEN WARDLE.

National Association of Co-operative Officials (NACO): 6A Clarendon Pl., Hyde, Cheshire, SK14 2QZ; tel. (161) 351-7900; fax (161) 366-6800; internet www.nacoco-op.org; Nat. Pres. ROGER DAVIES.

TRADE UNIONS

Central Organizations

Trades Union Congress (TUC): Congress House, Great Russell St, London, WC1B 3LS; tel. (20) 7636-4030; fax (20) 7636-0632; e-mail info@tuc.org.uk; internet www.tuc.org.uk; f. 1868; a voluntary association of trade unions, the representatives of which meet annually to consider matters of common concern to their members. A General Council of 57 members is elected at the annual Congress to keep watch on all industrial movements, legislation affecting labour and all matters touching the interest of the trade union movement, with authority to promote common action on general questions and to assist trade unions in the work of organization. Through the General Council and its Executive Committee, the TUC campaigns on issues of concern to employees and provides services for affiliated unions. It also makes nominations to various bodies such as the Health and Safety Commission, the Equal Opportunities Commission and the Advisory, Conciliation and Arbitration Service Council. In mid-2007 66 unions, with a total membership of almost 7.0m., were affiliated to the TUC. The TUC is affiliated to the ITUC and the ETUC, and nominates the British Workers' Delegate to the International Labour Organization; Pres. DAVE PRENTIS; Gen. Sec. BRENDAN BARBER.

Irish Congress of Trade Unions (Northern Ireland Committee): 4–6 Donegall Street Pl., Belfast, BT1 2FN; tel. (28) 9024-7940; fax (28) 9024-6898; e-mail info@ictuni.org; internet www.ictuni.org; 36 affiliated unions in Northern Ireland, with a membership of 215,478 (2006); Gen. Sec. DAVID BEGG.

THE UNITED KINGDOM

Scottish Trades Union Congress: 333 Woodlands Rd, Glasgow, G3 6NG; tel. (141) 337-8100; fax (141) 337-8101; e-mail info@stuc.org.uk; internet www.stuc.org.uk; f. 1897; 633,462 individual mems affiliated through 39 trade unions and 20 trades union councils (2007); Gen. Sec. GRAHAME SMITH.

Wales Trades Union Council: 1 Cathedral Rd, Cardiff; tel. (29) 2034-7010; fax (29) 2022-1940; e-mail wtuc@tuc.org.uk; internet www.wtuc.org.uk; f. 1973; Gen. Sec. FELICITY WILLIAMS.

General Federation of Trade Unions: Central House, Upper Woburn Pl., London, WC1H 0HY; tel. (20) 7388-0852; fax (20) 7383-0820; e-mail gftuhq@gftu.org.uk; internet www.gftu.org.uk; f. 1899 by the TUC; 35 affiliated orgs; Pres. DOUG NICHOLLS.

Principal Trade Unions Affiliated to the TUC

Includes all affiliated unions whose membership is in excess of 10,000.

ACCORD: Simmons House, 46 Old Bath Rd, Charvil, Reading, Berks, RG10 9QR; tel. (118) 934-1808; fax (118) 932-0208; e-mail info@accordhq.org; internet www.accord-myunion.org; Gen. Sec. GED NICHOLS; 27,477 mems (2006).

Associated Society of Locomotive Engineers and Firemen (ASLEF): 9 Arkwright Rd, London, NW3 6AB; tel. (20) 7317-8600; fax (20) 7794-6406; e-mail info@aslef.org.uk; internet www.aslef.org.uk; f. 1880; Gen. Sec. KEITH NORMAN; 16,482 mems (2006).

Association of Teachers and Lecturers (ATL): 7 Northumberland St, London WC2N 5RD; tel. (20) 7930-6441; fax (20) 7930-1359; e-mail info@atl.org.uk; internet www.atl.org.uk; f. 1978; Pres. JULIE NEAL; Gen. Sec. Dr MARY BOUSTED; 113,161 mems.

Bakers, Food and Allied Workers' Union (BFAWU): Stanborough House, Great North Rd, Stanborough, Welwyn Garden City, Herts., AL8 7TA; tel. (1707) 260150; fax (1707) 261570; e-mail info@bfawu.org; internet www.bfawu.org; f. 1861; Pres. RONNIE DRAPER; Gen. Sec. JOSEPH MARINO; 28,426 mems.

Broadcasting, Entertainment, Cinematograph and Theatre Union (BECTU): 373–377 Clapham Rd, London, SW9 9BT; tel. (20) 7346-0900; fax (20) 7346-0901; e-mail info@bectu.org.uk; internet www.bectu.org.uk; f. 1991 as a result of merger between Asscn of Cinematograph, Television and Allied Technicians (f. 1933) and the Broadcasting and Entertainment Trades Alliance (f. 1984); Pres. TONY LENNON; Gen. Sec. GERRY MORRISSEY; 26,543 mems (2006).

Chartered Society of Physiotherapy (CSP): 14 Bedford Row, London, WC1R 4ED; tel. (20) 7306-6666; fax (20) 7306-6611; e-mail enquiries@csp.org.uk; internet www.csp.org.uk; f. 1894; Pres. Baroness FINLAY OF LLANDAFF; Chief Exec. PHIL GRAY; 47,000 mems.

Communications Workers' Union (CWU): 150 The Broadway, Wimbledon, London, SW19 1RX; tel. (20) 8971-7200; fax (20) 8971-7300; e-mail info@cwu.org; internet www.cwu.org; f. 1995 by merger of the National Communications Union and the Union of Communication Workers; Pres. JANE LOFTUS; Gen. Sec. BILLY HAYES; 200,000 mems.

Community: Swinton House, 324 Gray's Inn Rd, London, WC1X 8DD; tel. (20) 7239-1200; fax (20) 7278-8378; e-mail info@community-tu.org; internet www.community-tu.org; f. 2004 by the merger of the Iron and Steel Trades Confed. and the National Union of Knitwear, Footwear and Apparel Trades; Gen. Sec. MICHAEL J. LEAHY; 67,488 mems (2006).

Connect: 30 St George's Rd, Wimbledon, London, SW19 4BD; tel. (20) 8971-6000; fax (20) 8971-6002; e-mail union@connectuk.org; internet www.connectuk.org; trade union for professionals in the communications industry; fmrly Society of Telecom Executives, name changed as above in 2000; Pres. DENISE MCGUIRE; Gen. Sec. ADRIAN ASKEW; 19,472 mems (2006).

Educational Institute of Scotland (EIS): 46 Moray Pl., Edinburgh, EH3 6BH; tel. (131) 225-6244; fax (131) 220-3151; e-mail enquiries@eis.org.uk; internet www.eis.org.uk; f. 1847; professional and trade union org. for teachers and lecturers in schools, colleges and universities; Pres. KIRSTY DEVANEY; Gen. Sec. RONALD A. SMITH; 59,978 mems.

Equity: Guild House, Upper St Martin's Lane, London, WC2H 9EG; tel. (20) 7379-6000; fax (20) 7379-7001; e-mail info@equity.org.uk; internet www.equity.org.uk; represents artists and performers; Pres. HARRY LANDIS; Gen. Sec. CHRISTINE PAYNE; 35,942 mems (2006).

FDA: 8 Leake St, London, SE1 7NN; tel. (20) 7401-5555; fax (20) 7401-5550; e-mail oliver@fda.org.uk; internet www.fda.org.uk; f. 1919; Pres. DAVID WATTS; Gen. Sec. JONATHAN BAUME; 17,218 mems.

Fire Brigades Union (FBU): Bradley House, 68 Coombe Rd, Kingston upon Thames, Surrey, KT2 7AE; tel. (20) 8541-1765; fax (20) 8546-5187; e-mail office@fbu.org.uk; internet www.fbu.org.uk; f. 1918; Pres. MICK SHAW; Gen. Sec. MATT WRACK; 47,071 mems.

GMB—Britain's General Union: 22–24 Worple Rd, Wimbledon, London, SW19 4DD; tel. (20) 8947-3131; fax (20) 8944-6552; e-mail info@gmb.org.uk; internet www.gmb.org.uk; f. 1982; Pres. MARY TURNER; Gen. Sec. PAUL KENNY; 600,106 mems.

Musicians' Union (MU): 60–62 Clapham Rd, London, SW9 0JJ; tel. (20) 7582-5566; fax (20) 7582-9805; e-mail info@musiciansunion.org.uk; internet www.musiciansunion.org.uk; f. 1893; Gen. Sec. JOHN F. SMITH; 32,461 mems (2006).

National Association of Schoolmasters Union of Women Teachers (NASUWT): Hillscourt Education Centre, Rose Hill, Rednal, Birmingham, B45 8RS; tel. (121) 453-6150; fax (121) 457-6208; e-mail nasuwt@mail.nasuwt.org.uk; internet www.nasuwt.org.uk; f. 1919; merged with UWT 1976; Pres. JOHN MAYES; Gen. Sec. CHRIS KEATES; 251,763 mems.

National Union of Journalists (NUJ): Headland House, 308-312 Gray's Inn Rd, London, WC1X 8DP; tel. (20) 7278-7916; fax (20) 7837-8143; e-mail info@nuj.org.uk; internet www.nuj.org.uk; f. 1907; Pres. CHRIS MORLEY; Gen. Sec. JEREMY DEAR; 38,000 mems.

National Union of Rail, Maritime and Transport Workers (RMT): 39 Chalton Rd, London, NW1 1JD; tel. (20) 7387-4771; fax (20) 7387-4123; e-mail info@rmt.org.uk; internet www.rmt.org.uk; f. 1990 through merger of National Union of Railwaymen (f. 1872) and National Union of Seamen (f. 1887); Pres. JOHN LEACH; Gen. Sec. BOB CROW; 74,539 mems (2006).

National Union of Teachers (NUT): Hamilton House, Mabledon Pl., London, WC1H 9BD; tel. (20) 7388-6191; fax (20) 7387-8458; internet www.teachers.org.uk; Pres. JUDY MOORHOUSE; Gen. Sec. STEVE SINNOTT; 270,436 mems (2006).

Nationwide Group Staff Union (NGSU): Middleton Farmhouse, 37 Main Rd, Middleton Cheney, Banbury, OX17 2QT; tel. (1295) 710767; fax (1295) 712580; e-mail ngsu@ngsu.org.uk; internet www.ngsu.org.uk; Gen. Sec. TIM POIL; 12,627 mems (2007).

Nautilus UK: Oceanair House, 750–760 High Rd, Leytonstone, London, E11 3BB; tel. (20) 8989-6677; fax (20) 8530-1015; e-mail enquiries@nautilus.org; internet www.nautilusuk.org; f. 1936; fmrly the National Union of Marine, Aviation and Shipping Transport Officers; present name adopted 2006; Sec. BRIAN ORRELL; 18,000 mems.

Prison Officers' Association (POA): Cronin House, 245 Church St, London, N9 9HW; tel. (20) 8803-0255; fax (20) 8803-1761; internet www.poauk.org.uk; f. 1939; Chair. COLIN MOSES; Gen. Sec. BRIAN CATON; 35,772 mems (2006).

Prospect: New Prospect House, 8 Leake St, London, SE1 7NN; tel. (20) 7902-6600; fax (20) 7902-6667; e-mail enquiries@prospect.org.uk; internet www.prospect.org.uk; f. 1919 as the Institution of Professionals, Managers and Specialists; name changed as above in 2001; Pres. GRAEME HENDERSON; Gen. Sec. PAUL NOON; 101,532 mems (2006).

Public and Commercial Services Union (PCS): 160 Falcon Rd, London, SW11 2LN; tel. (20) 7924-2727; fax (20) 7924-1847; internet www.pcs.org.uk; f. 1998 by merger of Civil and Public Services Asscn (f. 1903) and Public Services, Tax and Commerce Union (f. 1996); Pres. JANICE GODRICH; Gen. Sec. MARK SERWOTKA; 311,274 mems (2006).

Society of Radiographers (SoR): 207 Providence Sq., Mill St, London, SE1 2EW; tel. (20) 7740-7200; fax (20) 7740-7204; e-mail info@sor.org; internet www.sor.org; f. 1920; Pres. ZENA MITTON; Chief Exec. RICHARD EVANS; 18,840 mems.

Transport Salaried Staffs' Association (TSSA): Walkden House, 10 Melton St, London, NW1 2EJ; tel. (20) 7387-2101; fax (20) 7383-0656; internet www.tssa.org.uk; f. 1897; Pres. ANDY BAIN; Gen. Sec. GERRY DOHERTY; 29,231 mems (2006).

Union of Construction, Allied Trades and Technicians (UCATT): UCATT House, 177 Abbeville Rd, Clapham, London, SW4 9RL; tel. (20) 7622-2442; fax (20) 7720-4081; e-mail info@ucatt.org.uk; internet www.ucatt.info; f. 1971; Pres. JOHN THOMPSON; Gen. Sec. ALAN RITCHIE; 128,914 mems (2006).

Union of Shop, Distributive and Allied Workers (USDAW): 188 Wilmslow Rd, Manchester, M14 6LJ; tel. (161) 224-2804; fax (161) 257-2566; e-mail enquiries@usdaw.org.uk; internet www.usdaw.org.uk; Pres. JEFF BROOME; Gen. Sec. JOHN HANNETT; 341,291 mems (2006).

UNISON: 1 Mabledon Pl., London, WC1H 9AJ; tel. (845) 355-0845; fax (20) 7551-1101; e-mail direct@unison.co.uk; internet www.unison.org.uk; f. 1993 through merger of Confederation of Health Service Employees (COHSE—f. 1910), National and Local Government Officers Asscn (NALGO—f. 1905) and National Union of Public Employees (NUPE—f. 1888); Pres. NORMA STEPHENSON; Gen. Sec. DAVE PRENTIS; 1,031,000 mems.

Unite—Amicus Section: 35 King St, London, WC2E 8JG; tel. (20) 7420-8900; fax (20) 7420-8998; e-mail simon.dubbins@amicustheunion.org; internet www.amicustheunion.org.uk; f. 2002 by merger of Amalgamated Engineering and Electrical Union and Manufacturing, Science, Finance; merged with UNIFI in 2004;

merger with T&G approved in May 2007 and due to be completed in November 2008; Joint Gen. Sec. DEREK SIMPSON; 1,080,046 mems.

Unite—Transport and General Workers' Section (T&G): Transport House, 128 Theobalds Rd, London, WC1X 8TN; tel. (20) 7611-2500; fax (20) 7611-2555; e-mail tgwu@tgwu.org.uk; internet www.tgwu.org.uk; merger with Amicus approved in May 2007 and due to be completed in November 2008; Joint Gen. Sec. TONY WOODLEY; 820,118 mems.

United Road Transport Union (URTU): Almond House, Oak Green, Stanley Green Business Park, Cheadle Hulme, SK8 6QL; tel. (800) 526639; fax (161) 485-3109; e-mail info@urtu.com; internet www.urtu.com; f. 1890 as United Carters' Asscn; present name adopted 1964; Gen. Sec. ROBERT MONKS; 16,800 mems.

University and College Union (UCU): 27 Britannia St, London, WC1X 9JP; Egmont House, 25–31 Tavistock Place, London, WC1H 9UT; tel. (20) 7837-3636; fax (20) 7837-4403; e-mail hq@ucu.org.uk; internet www.ucu.org.uk; f. 2006 by merger of the Association of University Teachers and NATFHE—The University & College Lecturers' Union; Pres. LINDA NEWMAN; Gen. Sec. SALLY HUNT; 117,804 mems (2006).

Unions not affiliated to the TUC

Irish National Teachers' Organization (INTO): 23 College Gardens, Belfast, BT9 6BS (headquarters in Dublin); tel. (28) 9038-1455; fax (28) 9066-2803; e-mail infoni@into.ie; internet www.into.ie; f. 1868; affiliated to the Irish Congress of Trade Unions (Northern Ireland Committee); Northern Sec. FRANK BUNTING; 6,149 mems (Dec. 2006).

National Farmers' Union (NFU): see Industrial and Trade Associations.

Northern Ireland Public Service Alliance: Harkin House, 54 Wellington Park, Belfast, BT9 6DP; tel. (28) 9066-1831; fax (28) 9066-5847; e-mail info@nipsa.org.uk; internet www.nipsa.org.uk; affiliated to the Irish Congress of Trade Unions; Pres. (2007/08) BILLY LYNN; Gen. Sec. JOHN COREY; 43,300 mems.

Services Industrial Professional Technical Union (SIPTU): 3 Antrim Rd, Belfast, BT15 2BE; tel. (28) 9031-4000; fax (28) 9031-4044; e-mail belfast@siptu.ie; internet www.siptu.ie; affiliated to the Irish Congress of Trade Unions (Northern Ireland Committee); Regional Sec. JOE CUNNINGHAM; 7,000 members.

Ulster Teachers' Union: 94 Malone Rd, Belfast, BT9 5HP; tel. (28) 9066-2216; fax (28) 9068-3296; e-mail office@utu.edu; internet www.utu.edu; f. 1919; affiliated to the Irish Congress of Trade Unions (Northern Ireland Committee); Pres. STANLEY POOTS; Gen. Sec. AVRIL HALL-CALLAGHAN; 6,700 mems (Dec. 2006).

Union of Democratic Mineworkers (UDM): The Sycamores, Moor Rd, Bestwood, Nottingham, NG6 8UE; tel. (115) 976-3468; fax (115) 976-3474; f. 1986; Pres. and Gen. Sec. NEIL GREATREX; c. 1,500 mems.

National Federations

Confederation of Shipbuilding and Engineering Unions: 5th Floor, 35 King St, London, WC2E 8JG; tel. (20) 7420-8988; fax (20) 7420-1488; 750,000 mems in 7 affiliated trade unions; Gen. Sec. JOHN WALL.

Federation of Entertainment Unions: 1 Highfield, Twyford, Hampshire, SO21 1QR; tel. and fax (1962) 713134; e-mail harris.s@btconnect.com; f. 1990; seven affiliated unions; Sec. STEVE HARRIS.

General Federation of Trade Unions (GFTU): Central House, Upper Woburn Pl., London, WC1H OHY; tel. (20) 7387-2578; fax (20) 7383-0820; e-mail gftuhq@gftu.org.uk; internet www.gftu.org.uk; f. 1899; represents specialist unions; Pres. DOUG NICHOLLS; Gen. Sec. MIKE BRADLEY; 34 affiliated unions with total membership of 225,687 (Dec. 2006).

Transport

RAILWAYS

The Railways Act 1993, providing for a process of rail privatization, received royal assent in November 1993. A separate, government-owned company, Railtrack, was set up on 1 April 1994 to take responsibility for infrastructure (track, signals and stations) and levy charges on train operators for track access. As a result of the 1993 Railways Act, 25 Train Operating Units (TOUs) came into being on 1 April 1994. The Director of Passenger Rail Franchises was responsible for awarding franchises for the 25 TOUs as early as practicable and was to monitor the franchises to ensure compliance with the agreed contracts. The first passenger train franchises were awarded in December 1995, and two TOUs were transferred to private operators in February 1996; the final TOU transferred to the private sector in March 1997. Railtrack was transferred to the private sector in May 1996. In October 2001 the Government placed the heavily-indebted Railtrack in administration. In March 2002 Network Rail, a 'not-for-profit' Government-supported company, offered £500m. for Railtrack, and in July Railtrack shareholders voted to accept Network Rail's offer. Railtrack remained in administration until October 2002, when the final takeover by Network Rail proceeded.

In July 1987 the Channel Tunnel Treaty was signed between the Governments of France and the United Kingdom, providing the constitutional basis for the construction of a cross-channel tunnel between the two countries, comprising a fixed link of two rail tunnels and one service tunnel, at an estimated cost of £4,700m. Of the total length of 31 miles (50 km), 23 miles are under the seabed. The tunnel was opened in May 1994. The rail services provider, Eurostar UK, moved all London operations from Waterloo International to St Pancras station in November 2007.

DfT Rail and National Networks: Department for Transport, Great Minster House, 76 Marsham St, London SW1P 4DR; tel. (20) 7944-8300; fax (20) 7944-9643; e-mail rail@dft.gsi.gov.uk; internet www.dft.gov.uk/pgr/rail; f. 2005; strategic and financial responsibility for the railways, assumed many functions of the Strategic Rail Authority (SRA), which was dissolved in August 2005 following a national rail review in July 2004; Dir-Gen. MIKE MITCHELL.

Office of Rail Regulation: 1 Kemble St, London, WC2B 4AN; tel. (20) 7282-2000; fax (20) 7282-2040; e-mail rail.library@orr.gsi.gov.uk; internet www.rail-reg.gov.uk; Chair. CHRIS BOLT.

Network Rail Ltd: 40 Melton St, London, NW1 2EE; tel. (20) 7557-8000; fax (20) 7557-9000; e-mail enquiries@networkrail.com; internet www.networkrail.co.uk; f. 2002 as a 'not-for-profit' company by train operators, rail unions and passenger groups to take over responsibility for running the UK rail network from Railtrack PLC; Chair. IAN MCALLISTER; Chief Exec. IAIN COUCHER.

Northern Ireland Railways Co Ltd: Central Station, East Bridge St, Belfast, BT1 3PB; tel. (28) 9089-9400; fax (28) 9089-9401; internet www.nirailways.co.uk; f. 1967; subsidiary of Northern Ireland Transport Holding Co (see under Roads) and part of the Translink rail and bus network; operates rail services for passenger traffic over 342 km and for freight traffic over 268 km of railway track; a high-speed passenger service between Belfast and Dublin, launched in co-operation with Irish Rail, began operations in 1997; Chief Exec. CATHERINE MASON; Gen. Man., Rail Services MALACHY MCGREEVY.

Channel Tunnel Rail Link

Eurotunnel Group: UK Terminal, Ashford Rd, Folkestone, Kent, CT18 8XX; tel. (1303) 282222; fax (1303) 850360; e-mail press@eurotunnel.com; internet www.eurotunnel.com; Anglo-French consortium contracted to design, finance and construct the Channel Tunnel under a concession granted for a period up to 2052 (later extended to 2086); receives finance exclusively from the private sector; operates a service of road vehicle 'shuttle' trains and passenger and freight trains through the Channel Tunnel; Chair. and Chief Exec. JACQUES GOUNON.

Eurostar UK/Eurostar Group Ltd: Times House, Bravingtons Walk, Regent Quarter, London, N1 9AW; tel. (20) 7902-3658; e-mail press.office@eurostar.co.uk; internet www.eurostar.com; commenced international high-speed passenger rail services in 1994; provides services from London, and Ebbsfleet and Ashford (both in Kent), direct to Paris, Brussels, Lille, Calais-Frethun, Disneyland Paris, Avignon and Bourg St Maurice; Chair. GUILLAUME PEPY; CEO RICHARD BROWN.

Associations

Railway Industry Association: 22 Headfort Pl., London, SW1X 7RY; tel. (20) 7201-0777; fax (20) 7235-5777; e-mail ria@riagb.org.uk; internet www.riagb.org.uk; f. 1875; represents UK-based railway suppliers, with a free sourcing service for products and services; Chair. TONY KING; Dir-Gen. JEREMY CANDFIELD; 141 mems.

Association of Train Operating Companies: 3rd Floor, 40 Bernard St, London, WC1N 1BY; tel. (20) 7841-8000; e-mail atocnews@atoc.org; internet www.atoc.org; f. 1994; Chair. MIKE ALEXANDER; Dir-Gen. MICHAEL ROBERTS.

ROADS

Total road length in Great Britain in 2005 was 388,008 km (241,097 miles), of which 3,519 km (2,187 miles) was motorway. In 2005 there were 24,930 km (15,491 miles) of roads of all classes in Northern Ireland, including some 110 km (68 miles) of motorway.

Highways Agency: 123 Buckingham Palace Rd, London, SW1W 9HA; tel. and fax (8459) 556575; e-mail ha_info@highways.gsi.gov.uk; internet www.highways.gov.uk; executive agency of the Department for Transport; responsible for maintaining, operating and improving the motorway and trunk road network in England; Chief Exec. ARCHIE ROBERTSON.

THE UNITED KINGDOM

Northern Ireland Transport Holding Co: Chamber of Commerce House, 22 Great Victoria St, Belfast, BT2 7LX; tel. (28) 9024-3456; fax (28) 9033-3845; internet www.translink.co.uk/nithco.asp; publicly owned; owns Metro, Northern Ireland Railways Co Ltd and Ulsterbus, all part of the Translink rail and bus network; Chair. VERONICA PALMER; Chief Exec. CATHERINE MASON.

Ulsterbus Ltd: Milewater Rd, Belfast, BT3 9BG; Central Station, Belfast, BT1 3PB; tel. (28) 9089-9400; fax (28) 9035-1474; internet www.translink.co.uk/atulsterbus.asp; responsible for almost all bus transport in Northern Ireland, except Belfast city; services into Ireland; assoc. co Flexibus Ltd (minibus contract hire); Chief Exec. CATHERINE MASON.

METROPOLITAN TRANSPORT

Docklands Light Railway: POB 154, Castor Lane, London, E14 0DS; tel. (20) 7363-9700; fax (20) 7363-9532; e-mail cservice@dlr.co.uk; internet www.dlr.co.uk; opened 1987; in 1992 responsibility was transferred from London Transport to the London Docklands Development Corpn; in 1998 the Railway was again transferred to the Dept for Environment, Transport and the Regions and in July 2000 the Railway became part of Transport for London; franchised to a private co, Docklands Railway Management (now Serco Docklands), in 1997; comprises a 38-station system bounded by Bank, Tower Gateway, King George V (North Woolwich), Beckton, Stratford and Lewisham; construction of an extension from King George V to Woolwich Arsenal due to be completed in February 2009; further extension from Canning Town to Stratford International due to open in July 2010; Man. Dir, London Rail IAN BROWN.

Metro: Milewater Rd, Belfast, BT3 9BG; tel. (28) 9035-1201; fax (28) 9035-1474; internet www.translink.co.uk/metro.asp; responsible for operating municipal transport in the City of Belfast; subsidiary of Northern Ireland Transport Holding Co (see under Roads); Chief Exec. CATHERINE MASON.

Metrolink: Metrolink House, Queens Rd, Manchester, M8 0RY; tel. (161) 205-2000; e-mail customerservices@metrolink.co.uk; internet www.metrolink.co.uk; opened 1992; owned by the Greater Manchester Passenger Transport Executive (GMPTE); operated by Serco Metrolink; 37-station hybrid tram and rail network in Greater Manchester, bounded by Altrincham, Bury, Eccles and Manchester Piccadilly; Chief Exec. DAVID LEATHER (acting).

Transport for London (TfL): Windsor House, 42–50 Victoria St, London, SW1H 0TL; tel. (20) 7941-4500; fax (20) 7649-9121; e-mail enquire@tfl.gov.uk; internet www.tfl.gov.uk; f. 2000; executive arm of Greater London Authority (GLA), responsible for activities of former London Transport; Chair. BORIS JOHNSON (Mayor of London); Commr PETER HENDY.

London Underground: 55 Broadway, London, SW1H 0BD; tel. (20) 7222-5600; internet www.tfl.gov.uk/tube; f. 1985; however, underground railway network dates back to 1863; responsible for providing and securing the services of underground rail in Greater London; Man. Dir TIM O'TOOLE.

SPT Subway: Consort House, 12 West George St, Glasgow, G2 1HN; tel. (141) 332-6811; e-mail enquiry@spt.co.uk; internet www.spt.co.uk/subway; f. opened 1896; electrified in 1923; owned and operated by Strathclyde Partnership for Transport (SPT); 10-km, 15-station underground rail network in central Glasgow; Dir, Subway Operations DAVID WALLACE.

Tyne and Wear Metro: Nexus House, St James' Blvd, Newcastle upon Tyne, NE1 4AX; tel. (191) 203-3333; fax (191) 203-3180; e-mail metro.communications@nexus.org.uk; internet www.tyneandwearmetro.co.uk; opened 1980; 77.5-km, 60-station light rail network serving Newcastle, Gateshead, North Tyneside, South Tyneside and Sunderland; owned and operated by Tyne and Wear Passenger Transport Executive (Nexus); Dir-Gen. BERNARD GARNER.

INLAND WATERWAYS

There are some 3,540 km (2,200 miles) of inland waterways in Great Britain under the control of British Waterways, varying from the river navigations and wide waterways accommodating commercial craft to canals taking small holiday craft.

British Waterways: 6 Clarendon Rd, Watford, Hertfordshire, WD17 1DA; tel. (1923) 201120; fax (1923) 201400; e-mail enquiries.hq@britishwaterways.co.uk; internet www.britishwaterways.co.uk; f. 1963; Chair. TONY HALES; Chief Exec. ROBIN EVANS.

SHIPPING

There are more than 400 ports in the United Kingdom, of which Grimsby and Immingham, the Tees and Hartlepool ports, London (Tilbury), Southampton, Milford Haven, Liverpool, the Forth ports, Felixstowe, Dover and Sullom Voe are the largest (in terms of the tonnage of goods traffic handled). Twenty-one ports, including Grimsby and Immingham, Hull, Southampton and five ports in South Wales, are owned and administered by Associated British Ports. The majority of the other large ports are owned and operated by public trusts, including London, which is administered by the Port of London Authority, and Belfast, administered by the Belfast Harbour Commissioners. Under the Ports Act (1991), trust ports were permitted to become private, commercial enterprises. By mid-1995 five major trust ports, including the Port of London Authority and the Medway Ports Authority, had been transferred to the private sector. In May 1998 the Government announced that the port of Belfast was to be transferred to the private sector. Sullom Voe, Bristol and a number of smaller ports are under the control of local authorities, and there are more than 100 ports owned and administered by statutory or private companies; of these, Liverpool (owned by Mersey Docks and Harbour Co), Felixstowe and Manchester are the largest.

Britain is linked to the rest of Europe by an extensive passenger and vehicle ship ferry service. There are regular freight services from Belfast, Larne and Warrenpoint, in Northern Ireland, to ports in Great Britain and Europe; passenger services operate daily between Northern Ireland and Great Britain.

Associated British Ports (ABP): 150 Holborn, London, EC1N 2LR; tel. (20) 7430-1177; fax (20) 7430-1384; e-mail pr@abports.co.uk; internet www.abports.co.uk; f. 1983; controls 21 UK ports; Chair. CHRIS CLARK; Chief Exec. PETER JONES.

The Baltic Exchange Ltd: 38 St Mary Axe, London, EC3A 8BH; tel. (20) 7623-5501; fax (20) 7369-1622; e-mail enquiries@balticexchange.co.uk; internet www.balticexchange.com; world market for chartering ships, charters aircraft, buys and sells ships and aircraft; Chair. MICHAEL DRAYTON; Chief Exec. JEREMY PENN.

British Ports Association (BPA): Africa House, 64–78 Kingsway, London, WC2B 6AH; tel. (20) 7242-1200; fax (20) 7430-7474; e-mail info@britishports.org.uk; internet www.britishports.org.uk; promotes and protects the general interests of port authorities, comments on proposed legislation and policy matters; Dir DAVID WHITEHEAD.

Port of London Authority: London River House, Royal Pier Rd, Gravesend, Kent, DA12 2BG; tel. (1474) 562200; fax (1474) 562281; internet www.portoflondon.co.uk; Chair. SIMON SHERRARD; Chief Exec. RICHARD EVERITT.

Principal Shipping Companies

Belfast Freight Ferries Ltd: Victoria Terminal 1, Dargan Rd, Belfast, BT3 9LJ; tel. (28) 9077-0112; fax (28) 9078-1217; ro-ro service to Heysham; Chair. ANGUS FRASER; Man. Dir ALAN PEACOCK.

Bibby Line Ltd: 105 Duke St, Liverpool, L1 5JQ; tel. (151) 708-8000; fax (151) 794-1000; e-mail enquiries@bibbyline.co.uk; internet www.bibbyline.co.uk; f. 1807; operates chemical carriers and shallow water accommodation units; Chair. S. P. SHERRARD; Man. Dir CY GREEN.

Boyd Line: 7 The Orangery, Hesslewood Country Office Park, Ferriby Rd, Hessle, HU13 0LH; tel. (1482) 324024; fax (1482) 323737; e-mail jon.carden@boydline.co.uk; internet www.boydline.co.uk; vessel owners and managers; Man. Dir JONATHAN CARDEN; 2 vessels.

BP Shipping Ltd: Chertsey Rd, Sunbury on Thames, Middlesex, TW16 7LN; tel. (1932) 771652; internet www.bpshipping.co.uk; f. 1915; division of BP PLC; Group Vice-Pres. and Chief Exec. DAVID BALDRY; 56 vessels.

Caledonian MacBrayne Ltd: The Ferry Terminal, Gourock, Renfrewshire, PA19 1QP; tel. (1475) 650100; fax (1475) 637607; e-mail info@calmac.co.uk; internet www.calmac.co.uk; holding co owned by Scottish Govt.; extensive car and passenger services on Firth of Clyde, to Western Isles of Scotland and a service between Ballycastle, in Northern Ireland, and Rathlin Island; 31 ro-ro vessels; Chair. PETER TIMMS; Man. Dir LAWRIE SINCLAIR.

Clipper Marine Services Ltd: Brunswick House, 8–13 Brunswick Pl., Southampton, SO15 2AP; tel. (23) 8063-9777; fax (23) 8063-9888; e-mail cmsukmgt@clipper-group.com; internet www.clipper-group.com; f. 1899 as Crescent Marine Services; Gen. Man. MIKE JENNINGS.

Coastal Container Line Ltd: Coastal House, Victoria Terminal 3, West Bank Rd, Belfast, BT3 9JL; tel. (28) 9037-3200; fax (28) 9037-1333; internet www.coastalcontainer.co.uk; container services from Belfast and Dublin to Cardiff and Liverpool; Operations Dir JOHN FORRESTER.

James Fisher & Sons PLC: Fisher House, POB 4, Barrow-in-Furness, Cumbria, LA14 1HR; tel. (1229) 615400; fax (1229) 836761; e-mail b.reception@james-fisher.co.uk; internet www.james-fisher.co.uk; f. 1847; provider of marine services operating in all sectors; also supplier of engineering services to the nuclear energy industry; Exec. Chair. TIMOTHY C. HARRIS; CEO NICHOLAS P. HENRY.

Fyffes Group Ltd: Houndmills Rd, Houndmills Industrial Estate, Basingstoke, Hampshire, RG21 6XL; tel. (1256) 383200; fax (1256) 383259; e-mail info@fyffes.com; internet www.fyffes.co.uk; f. 1901.

Geest Line: 3700 Parkway, Whiteley, Fareham, PO15 7AL; tel. (1489) 873575; fax (1489) 873562; e-mail quotes@geestline.com;

internet www.geestline.com; container cargo transportation between the UK and the Caribbean; Man. Dir BILL SALMOND.

Goulandris Brothers (Chartering) Ltd: 34A Queen Anne's Gate, London, SW1H 9AB; tel. (20) 7222-5244; fax (20) 7222-6817; e-mail chartering@goulanbros.co.uk; internet www.goulanbros.co.uk; f. 1968; ship chartering and brokerage; Man. Dir BASIL GOULANDRIS.

Heyn Handling Solutions: 1 Corry Pl., Belfast Harbour, Belfast, BT3 9AH; tel. (28) 9035-0035; fax (28) 9035-0011; e-mail info@heyn.co.uk; internet www.heyn.co.uk; liner and port agency; Man. Dir DAVID CLARKE.

Holbud Ship Management Ltd: Hydery House, 66 Leman St, London, E1 8EU; tel. (20) 7488-4901; fax (20) 7265-0654; ship agents; Dir B. D. SABARWAL.

Norfolkline Irish Sea Ferries: 12 Quays Terminal, Tower Rd, Birkenhead, Wirral, CH41 1FE; tel. (151) 906-2700; fax (151) 906-2718; internet www.norfolkline.com; fmrly Norse Merchant Ferries; owned by Norfolk Line BV (Netherlands); ro-ro freight, car and passenger services from Birkenhead–Belfast and Dublin, and Dover–Dunkirk (France).

OSG Ship Management (UK) Ltd: Moreau House, 116 Brompton Rd, London, SW3 1JJ; tel. (20) 7591-6660; fax (870) 607-9546; internet www.osg.com; bulk carriers, parcels tankers, conventional tankers; transportation of crude petroleum, petroleum products and liquified natural gas; Man. Dir Capt. IAN T. BLACKLEY.

P & O Ferries: Channel House, Channel View Rd, Dover, Kent, CT17 9TJ; tel. (1304) 863000; fax (1304) 863223; e-mail customer.services@poferries.com; internet www.poferries.com; car and passenger services across the English Channel and North Sea; subsidiary of DP World (Dubai, UAE); parent co of P&O Irish Sea Ferries; frmly P&O Stena Line; CEO HELEN DEEBLE.

Shell International Trading and Shipping Co Ltd: Shell Centre, York Rd, London, SE1 7NA; tel. (20) 7934-1234; e-mail shelltradingcommunications@shell.com; internet www.shell.com/shipping; world-wide operations trading and transporting crude petroleum and supplying petroleum products; incorporates Shell Tankers (UK) Ltd.

Stena Line Ltd: Stena House, Station Approach, Holyhead, Anglesey, LL65 1DQ; tel. (8705) 707070; e-mail info.uk@stenaline.com; internet www.stenaline.com; parent co Stena AB (Sweden); services from Great Britain to Northern Ireland, Ireland and the Netherlands; Group CEO GUNNAR BLOMDAHL; Area Dir, Irish Sea MICHAEL McGRATH.

Stephenson Clarke Shipping Ltd: Eldon Court, Percy St, Newcastle upon Tyne, NE99 1TD; tel. (191) 232-2184; fax (191) 261-1156; e-mail all@scsbulk.co.uk; internet www.scsbulk.com; f. 1730; ship operators, agency and management services; Man. Dir TREVOR KINGSLEY-SMITH.

Andrew Weir & Co Ltd: Dexter House, 2 Royal Mint Court, London, EC3N 4XX; tel. (20) 7575-6000; fax (20) 7481-4784; e-mail aws@aws.co.uk; internet www.aws.co.uk; f. 1885; shipowners, ship managers; Man Dir STEVE CORKHILL.

Shipping Associations

Chamber of Shipping Ltd: Carthusian Court, 12 Carthusian St, London, EC1M 6EZ; tel. (20) 7600-1534; fax (20) 7726-2080; e-mail postmaster@british-shipping.org; internet www.british-shipping.org; Pres. MARTIN WATSON (2008); Dir-Gen. MARK BROWNRIGG.

Passenger Shipping Association Ltd (PSA): 1st Floor, 41–42 Eastcastle St, London W1W 8DU; tel. (20) 7436-2449; fax (20) 7636-9206; e-mail h.tapping@psa-psara.org; internet www.the-psa.org; formerly Ocean Travel Development (f. 1958); 50 mems; Chair. JOHN CRUMMIE; Dir WILLIAM GIBBONS.

CIVIL AVIATION

In addition to many international air services into and out of the country, an internal air network operates from more than 20 main commercial airports.

The principal airports are Heathrow and Gatwick serving London, and Manchester, Birmingham and Glasgow, which in 2006 handled 67.3m., 34.1m., 22.1m., 9.1m. and 8.8m. passengers, respectively. In March 1991 a new development was opened at Stansted, including a new terminal, cargo centre and rail link to central London. In 2006 Stansted handled 23.7m. passengers. A new £30m. London City Airport opened in 1987, providing domestic and international flights to and from city centres, mainly for business travellers. In 2007 London City handled 2.9m. passengers. In March 2008 a fifth terminal building opened at Heathrow, increasing capacity at the airport to some 90m. passengers a year.

BAA PLC: 130 Wilton Rd, London, SW1V 1LQ; tel. (20) 7834-9449; fax (20) 7932-6699; e-mail baamediacentre@baa.com; internet www.baa.com; f. 1966 as British Airports Authority; privatized in 1987; propr of Heathrow, Stansted, Gatwick, Southampton, Glasgow, Aberdeen and Edinburgh airports; Chair. Sir NIGEL RUDD; CEO COLIN MATTHEWS.

Civil Aviation Authority (CAA): CAA House, 45–59 Kingsway, London, WC2B 6TE; tel. (20) 7379-7311; internet www.caa.co.uk; f. 1972; public service enterprise and a regulatory body responsible for economic and safety regulation of civil aviation; advises Govt on aviation issues; conducts economic and scientific research; produces statistical data; regulates British airspace; represents consumer interests and manages airspace users' needs; Chair. Sir ROY McNULTY.

NATS Ltd: Corporate and Technical Centre, 4000 Parkway, Whiteley, Fareham, Hants, PO15 7FL; tel. (1489) 616001; fax (1489) 615734; internet www.nats.co.uk; f. 1960 as National Air Traffic Control Services; name changed as above in 1972 when the org. became part of the CAA (q.v.); public-private partnership between the Airline Group (a consortium of British Airways, BMI, Virgin Atlantic, Britannia, Monarch, easyJet and Airtours), British airport operator BAA plc, NATS employees and the British Government; provides air traffic control services over the UK and North Atlantic, at 15 British airports and at Gibraltar Airport. It operates and maintains a nation-wide communications, surveillance and navigation network; Chair. JOHN DEVANEY; CEO PAUL BARRON.

Principal Private Airlines

Air Southwest: Plymouth City Airport, Crownhill, Plymouth, PL6 8BW; tel. (870) 043-4553; e-mail other-queries@airsouthwest.com; internet www.airsouthwest.com; f. 2003; scheduled flights from Plymouth, Newquay and Bristol to destinations in the UK, France and Ireland; owned by Sutton Harbour Group; Group Man. Dir NIGEL GODEFROY.

British Airways PLC: Waterside, POB 365, Harmondsworth, Middlesex, UB7 0GB; tel. (845) 779-9977; internet www.britishairways.com; f. 1972; operates extensive domestic, European and worldwide services, scheduled services to more than 250 destinations in 99 countries; Chair. MARTIN BROUGHTON; Chief Exec. WILLIE WALSH.

bmi: Donington Hall, Castle Donington, Derby, DE74 2SB; tel. (1332) 854000; fax (1332) 854662; internet www.flybmi.com; f. 1938 as Air Schools Ltd; name changed to British Midland Airways Ltd in 1964 and as above in 2002; scheduled services to 47 destinations world-wide; cargo and charter flights; Chair. Sir MICHAEL BISHOP; CEO NIGEL TURNER.

bmibaby: Donington Hall, Castle Donington, Derby, DE74 2SB; tel. (1332) 854000; internet www.bmibaby.com; f. 2002; low-cost passenger services to 30 European destinations; Man. Dir DAVID BRYON.

easyJet PLC: Hangar 89, London Luton Airport, Luton, LU2 9LS; tel. (1582) 445566; fax (1582) 443355; internet www.easyjet.co.uk; f. 1995; low-cost scheduled domestic and European passenger services from 15 UK airports; Chair. Sir COLIN CHANDLER; Chief Exec. ANDREW HARRISON.

First Choice Airways: Commonwealth House, Chicago Ave, Manchester Airport, M90 3DP; tel. (161) 489-0321; fax (161) 908-2275; e-mail eteam@firstchoice.co.uk; internet www.firstchoice.co.uk/flights; f. 1987 as air2000; present name adopted 2004; scheduled services from 15 airports in the United Kingdom to 60 destinations world-wide; subsidiary of TUI Travel PLC; Man. Dir, UK and Ireland DERMOT BLASTLAND.

Flybe: Jack Walker House, Exeter International Airport, Exeter, EX5 2HL; tel. (1392) 366669; fax (1392) 366151; e-mail customerrelationsadmin@flybe.com; internet www.flybe.com; f. 1979 as Jersey European Airways; name changed as above 2002; acquired BA Connect in 2007; independent regional airline providing low-cost domestic and European services; Chair. and CEO JIM FRENCH.

flyglobespan: Atlantic House, 38 Gardners Cres., Edinburgh, EH3 8DQ; tel. (870) 556-1522; internet www.flyglobespan.com; f. 2003; low-cost scheduled lights to 23 destinations world-wide, operating from eight UK airports; Chair. TOM DALRYMPLE.

Loganair Ltd: St Andrews Drive, Glasgow Airport, Abbotsinch, Paisley, Renfrewshire, PA3 2TG; tel. (141) 848-7594; fax (141) 887-6020; internet www.loganair.co.uk; f. 1962; operating as British Airways franchisee until October 2008; signed franchise agreement with Flybe in 2008; Scottish domestic services; Chair. SCOTT GRIER; Chief Exec. PETER TIERNEY.

Monarch Airlines: Prospect House, Prospect Way, London Luton Airport, Luton, LU2 9NU; tel. (1582) 400000; fax (1582) 411000; internet www.flymonarch.com; f. 1967; scheduled and charter services to the Mediterranean; CEO PETER BROWN.

Thomsonfly: London Luton Airport, Luton, LU2 9ND; tel. (870) 190-0737; e-mail lynn.houghton@thomson.co.uk; internet www.thomsonfly.com; f. 2004; propr TUI AG (Germany); operates

THE UNITED KINGDOM

scheduled services from 20 UK airports to 80 destinations worldwide; Chief Commercial Officer ALEX HUNTER.

Virgin Atlantic Airways: Manor Royal, Crawley, West Sussex, RH10 2NU; tel. (1293) 562345; fax (1293) 561721; internet www.virgin-atlantic.com; f. 1984; operates services to destinations in the USA, the Caribbean and the Far East; Chair. Sir RICHARD BRANSON; Chief Exec. STEVE RIDGWAY.

Tourism

In 2006 there were 32.7m. arrivals by foreign visitors to the United Kingdom; receipts from tourism totalled £16,002m. in that year.

Northern Ireland Tourist Board: St Anne's Court, 59 North St, Belfast, BT1 1NB; tel. (28) 9023-1221; fax (28) 9024-0960; e-mail info@nitb.com; internet www.discovernorthernireland.com; Chair. TOM MCGRATH; Chief Exec. ALAN CLARKE.

VisitBritain: Thames Tower, Black's Rd, London, W6 9EL; tel. (20) 8846-9000; fax (20) 8563-0302; e-mail corporatepr@visitbritain.org; internet www.visitbritain.com; markets Great Britain overseas and England to the British; Chair. CHRISTOPHER RODRIGUES; Chief Exec. TOM WRIGHT.

Visit London: 6th Floor, 2 More London Riverside, London, SE1 2RR; tel. (20) 7234-5800; fax (20) 7234-5751; e-mail enquiries@visitlondon.com; internet www.visitlondon.com; f. 1963; promotes and markets London to leisure and business visitors; Chair. TAMARA INGRAM; CEO JAMES BIDWELL.

VisitScotland: Ocean Point One, 94 Ocean Drive, Leith, Edinburgh, EH6 6JH; tel. (131) 472-2207; e-mail info@visitscotland.com; internet www.visitscotland.com; Chair. PETER LEDERER; Chief Exec. PHILIP RIDDLE.

Visit Wales: Brunel House, 2 Fitzalan Rd, Cardiff, CF24 0UY; tel. (845) 010-3300; fax (29) 2048-5031; e-mail info@visitwales.co.uk; internet www.visitwales.co.uk; Dir, Tourism and Marketing JONATHAN JONES.

UNITED KINGDOM CROWN DEPENDENCIES

The Channel Islands and the Isle of Man lie off shore from the United Kingdom but are not integral parts of the country. They are dependencies of the British Crown and have considerable self-government in internal affairs.

THE CHANNEL ISLANDS

The Channel Islands lie off the north-west coast of France to the west of Normandy, in the English Channel (la Manche). The bailiwicks of the Channel Islands (Guernsey and its dependencies, and Jersey) are the remnants of the Duchy of Normandy, which was in permanent union with the English (now British) Crown from 1106. They do not, however, form part of the United Kingdom. The islands have their own legislative assemblies and legal and administrative systems, their laws depending for their validity on Orders made by the Queen in Council. Her Majesty's Government in the United Kingdom is responsible for the defence and international relations of the islands, and the Crown is ultimately responsible for their good government. The bailiwicks do not form part of the European Union.

Guernsey

Introduction

The civil flag of Guernsey is white, bearing a red cross of St George, with a yellow couped cross superimposed on the cross. The capital is St Peter Port. English is the language in common use, but the Norman *patois* is spoken in some rural parishes. Dependencies of Guernsey are Alderney, Brecqhou, Herm, Jethou, Lihou and Sark. In addition to the British public holidays, Guernsey celebrates 9 May (Liberation Day).

Statistical Survey

including Herm and Jethou

Source (unless otherwise stated): Policy and Research Unit, Sir Charles Frossard House, La Charroterie, St Peter Port, Guernsey, GY1 1FH; tel. (1481) 717012; fax (1481) 717157; internet www.gov.gg.

AREA AND POPULATION

Area: 63.4 sq km (24.4 sq miles).

Population: 59,807 (males 29,138, females 30,669) at census of 29 April 2001. *2006* (estimate): 61,029.

Density (2006): 962.6 per sq km.

Parishes (2001 census): St Peter Port 16,488; Vale 9,573; Castel 8,975; St Sampson 8,592; St Martin 6,267; St Saviour 2,696; St Andrew 2,409; St Pierre du Bois 2,188; Forest 1,549; Torteval 973; Herm 95; Jethou 2; Total 59,807.

Births and Deaths (2000): Live births 644; Deaths 565.

Economically Active Population (at 31 December 2007): Horticulture and other primary 924; Manufacturing 1,225; Construction 3,160; Utilities 365; Transport 1,164; Hostelry 2,085; Supplier and wholesale selling 633; Retail 3,716; Personal services 889; Recreation and culture 509; Finance 7,731; Miscellaneous business 1,698; Information services 773; Health 1,307; Education 305; Public administration 5,350; Non-profit 279; Unallocated 60; *Total employed* 32,173 (males 17,592, females 14,581); Unemployed 223; *Total labour force* 32,396.

AGRICULTURE

The principal crops are flowers, much of which are grown under glass. About 16.3 sq km (6.2 sq miles) are cultivated.

FINANCE

Currency and Exchange Rates: 100 pence = 1 pound sterling (£). *Dollar and Euro Equivalents* (31 December 2007): US $1 = 49.92 pence; €1 = 73.48 pence; £10 = $20.03 = €13.61.

Note: Guernsey is in monetary union with the United Kingdom. It has its own coins and notes but United Kingdom coins and notes are also legal tender.

Budget (£ million, 2005): General revenue income 310; General revenue expenditure 292.

Cost of Living: (Retail Price Index at mid-year; base: 31 December 1999 = 100) All items 123.9 in 2005; 128.1 in 2006; 134.1 in 2007.

Gross Domestic Product by Economic Activity (£ '000, 2006, estimates): Horticulture 11,267; Other primary 12,931; Manufacturing 39,566; Construction 153,579; Utilities 14,583; Transport 30,057; Hostelry 48,363; Wholesale 49,489; Retail 118,712; Recreation 13,150; Information 50,819; Financial services 491,514; Legal, business and personal services 225,891; Health, education and public administration 219,001; Non-profit 6,068; *Total factor incomes* 1,484,990; *Less* Pensions 35,976; Other income 203,476; *Less* Adjustment to profit account 500; *Total* 1,651,990.

EXTERNAL TRADE

Principal Commodities: *Imports* (1999): Petroleum and oil 168,026,000 litres. *Exports* (1998, £ million): Light industry 47.0; Total flowers 34.0; Total vegetables 5.0.

TRANSPORT

Road Traffic (vehicles registered, 2006): Private vehicles 40,504; Commercial vehicles 7,733; Motorcycles 5,793.

Shipping (2006): Passenger movements 342,075.

Civil Aviation (2006): Passenger movements 869,076.

TOURISM

Number of Visitors (2006): 220,000.

COMMUNICATIONS MEDIA

Telephones (2004): 55,100 main lines in use.

Mobile Cellular Telephones (2004): 43,800.

Internet Users (2004): 36,000.

Source: International Telecommunication Union.

EDUCATION

Primary (2007): 4,456 pupils.

Secondary (2007): 4,449 pupils.

Directory

The Constitution

The Lieutenant-Governor and Commander-in-Chief of Guernsey is the personal representative of the Sovereign and the channel of communication between the Crown and the Insular Government. He is appointed by the Crown. He is entitled to sit and speak in the Assembly of the States, but not to vote.

The Bailiff is appointed by the Crown and is President both of the Assembly of the States (the insular legislature), where he has a casting vote, and of the Royal Court of Guernsey.

UNITED KINGDOM CROWN DEPENDENCIES 　　*The Channel Islands (Guernsey)*

The government of the island is conducted by a Policy Council, 10 departments and five 'specialist' committees. The Chief Minister may nominate a Deputy Chief Minister and Ministers for each of the 10 departments. Ministers and committee chairmen are elected by the members of the States of Deliberation.

The States of Deliberation is composed of the following members:

(*a*) The Bailiff, who is President ex officio.

(*b*) HM Procureur (Attorney-General) and HM Comptroller (Solicitor-General) Law Officers of the Crown, who are appointed by the Crown. They are entitled to sit in the States and to speak, but not to vote.

(*c*) The 45 People's Deputies elected by popular franchise.

(*d*) The two Alderney Representatives elected by the States of Alderney.

Projets de Loi (Permanent Laws) require the sanction of Her Majesty in Council.

The function of the States of Election is to elect persons to the office of Jurat. It is composed of the following members:

(*a*) The Bailiff (President ex officio).

(*b*) The 12 Jurats or 'Jures-Justiciers'.

(*c*) The 10 Rectors of the Parishes.

(*d*) HM Procureur and HM Comptroller.

(*e*) The 45 People's Deputies.

(*f*) The 34 Douzaine Representatives.

Meetings of the States and of the Royal Court, formerly conducted in French, are now conducted in English, but the proceedings in both are begun and ended in French.

The Government

Lieutenant-Governor and Commander-in-Chief of the Bailiwick of Guernsey: Sir FABIAN MALBON.

Secretary and ADC to the Lieutenant-Governor: Col R. H. GRAHAM.

Bailiff of Guernsey: GEOFFREY ROBERT ROWLAND.

Deputy Bailiff: RICHARD JOHN COLLAS.

HM Procureur (Attorney-General): JOHN NIKOLAS VAN LEUVEN.

HM Comptroller (Solicitor-General): HOWARD EDWARD ROBERTS.

Chief Executive of the States: MIKE BROWN.

POLICY COUNCIL
(May 2008)

Chief Minister: LYNDON TROTT.

Deputy Chief Minister and Minister of Public Services: BERNARD FLOUQUET.

Minister of the Treasury and Resources: CHARLES PARKINSON.

Minister of the Home Department: GEOFF MAHY.

Minister of Education: CAROL STEERE.

Minister of Health and Social Services: HUNTER ADAM.

Minister of Housing: DAVID JONES.

Minister of Commerce and Employment: CARLA MCNULTY BAUER.

Minister of Social Security: MARK DOREY.

Minister of the Environment: PETER SIRETT.

Minister of Culture and Leisure: MIKE O'HARA.

Judicial System

Justice is administered in Guernsey by the Royal Court, which consists of the Bailiff and the 12 Jurats. The Royal Court also deals with a wide variety of non-contentious matters. A Stipendiary Magistrate deals with minor civil and criminal cases. The Guernsey Court of Appeal deals with appeals from the Royal Court.

Religion

CHRISTIANITY

The Church of England

The Church of England in Guernsey is the established church. The Deanery includes the islands of Alderney, Sark, Herm and Jethou; it forms part of the diocese of Winchester.

Dean of Guernsey: Very Rev. Canon K. PAUL MELLOR, The Deanery, Cornet St, St Peter Port, GY1 1BZ; tel. (1481) 720036; e-mail paul@townchurch.org.gg.

The Roman Catholic Church

The diocese of Portsmouth includes the Channel Islands and part of southern England. In Guernsey there are three Roman Catholic churches, of which the senior is St Joseph and St Mary, Cordier Hill, St Peter Port.

Catholic Dean of Guernsey: Fr MICHAEL HORE, Ampthill House, Cordier Hill, St Peter Port, GY1 1JH; tel. (1481) 720196; fax (1481) 711247; e-mail sjoss.guernsey@virgin.net; internet catholic.org.gg.

Other Christian Churches

The Presbyterian Church and the Church of Scotland are represented by St Andrew's Church, The Grange, St Peter Port. The Baptist, Congregational, Elim and Methodist Churches are also represented in the island.

The Press

Guernsey Press and Star: The Guernsey Press Co, POB 57, Braye Rd, Vale, GY1 3BW; tel. (1481) 240240; fax (1481) 240235; e-mail newsroom@guernsey-press.com; internet www.guernsey-press.com; f. 1897; daily; independent; Editor RICHARD DIGARD; circ. 16,249 (Dec. 2006).

Guernsey Weekly Press: The Guernsey Press Co, POB 57, Braye Rd, Vale, GY1 3BW; tel. (1481) 240240; fax (1481) 240235; e-mail editorial@thisisguernsey.com; internet www.thisisguernsey.com; f. 1902; Thursday; independent; Editor RICHARD DIGARD.

Publishers

Toucan Press: The White Cottage, route de Carteret, Castel, GY5 7YG; tel. (1481) 257017; f. 1850; history, Thomas Hardy, Channel Islands; Man. Dir G. STEVENS COX.

Broadcasting and Communications

TELECOMMUNICATIONS

Cable and Wireless Guernsey Ltd: POB 3, Telecoms House, Upland Rd, St Peter Port, GY1 3AB; tel. (1481) 700700; fax (1481) 724640; e-mail contact@surecw.com; internet www.surecw.com/guernsey; operates under brand name *Sure*; fixed-line and mobile telecommunications services, as well as broadband internet services; Chief Exec. GEOFFREY HOUSTON.

Wave Telecom: POB 537, 24 High St, St Peter Port, GY1 2JU; tel. (1481) 818181; internet www.wavetelecom.com; f. 2002; subsidiary of Jersey Telecom; offers fixed-line and mobile telecommunications services; Man. Dir TIM RINGSDORE.

BROADCASTING

Radio

BBC: Radio and Television (see United Kingdom).

BBC Radio Guernsey: Television House, Bulwer Ave, St Sampson, GY2 4LA; tel. (1481) 200600; fax (1481) 200361; e-mail radio.guernsey@bbc.co.uk; internet www.bbc.co.uk/guernsey; f. 1982; Man. Editor DAVID MARTIN.

Island FM: 12 Westerbrook, St Sampson, GY2 4QQ; tel. (1481) 242000; fax (1481) 241120; e-mail studio@islandfm.guernsey.net; internet www.islandfm.com; Programme Controller GARY BURGESS.

Television

Channel Television: Television House, Bulwer Ave, St Sampson, GY2 4LA; tel. (1481) 241888; fax (1481) 241889; e-mail broadcast@channeltv.co.uk; internet www.channelonline.tv; Chair. DAVID FORDHAM; Man. Dir MIKE ELSEY.

(See also under Jersey.)

Finance

(cap. = capital; res = reserves; dep. = deposits; brs = branches; amounts in pounds sterling, unless otherwise indicated.)

Guernsey Financial Services Commission: POB 128, La Plaiderie Chambers, La Plaiderie, St Peter Port, GY1 3HQ; tel. (1481) 712706; fax (1481) 712010; e-mail info@gfsc.gg; internet www.gfsc.gg; f. 1988; regulates banking, investment, insurance and fiduciary activities; Dir-Gen. PETER NEVILLE.

BANKING

At December 2007 total bank deposits in Guernsey were £119,200m. in 47 financial institutions.

British Clearing Banks

The banks listed below are branches of British banks, and details concerning directors, capital, etc. of the parent bank will be found under the appropriate section in the pages dealing with the United Kingdom.

Barclays Bank PLC: POB 41, Le Marchant House, Le Truchot, St Peter Port, GY1 3BE; tel. (1481) 705600; fax (1481) 713712; e-mail guernsey@internationalbanking.barclays.com; internet www.internationalbanking.barclays.com; Dir STEPHEN JONES; 2 brs.

HSBC Bank PLC: POB 31, HSBC House, Lefebvre St, St Peter Port, GY1 3AT; tel. (1481) 717717; fax (1481) 717700; internet www.hsbc.co.uk; Area Man. G. JOHN DAVIES; 5 brs.

Lloyds TSB Offshore Ltd: POB 53, 1 Smith St, St Peter Port, GY1 4BD; tel. (1481) 724061; fax (1481) 712247; e-mail gsypersbkg@lloydstsb-offshore.com; internet www.lloydstsb-offshore.com; part of Lloyds TSB banking group; Chair. DAVID J. S. OLDFIELD; 5 brs.

Other Banks

Adam and Company International Ltd: POB 402, Royal Bank Pl., 1 Glategny Esplanade, St Peter Port, GY1 3GB; tel. (1481) 715055; fax (1481) 726919; e-mail john.judge@adambank.com; internet www.adambank.com; f. 1990; cap. 0.5m., res 0.6m., dep. 102.6m. (Dec. 2005); Chair. D. J. CATHIE; Man. Dir J. JUDGE.

Bank of Ireland (I.O.M.) Ltd: POB 611, High St, St Peter Port, GY1 4NY; tel. (1481) 741742; fax (1481) 741740; e-mail info@boioffshore.com; internet www.boiiom.com; f. 1964; cap. 5.0m., res 0.1m., dep. 2,655.8m. (March 2007); COO MICHAEL MCKAY.

Butterfield Bank (Guernsey) Ltd: POB 25, Regency Court, Glategny Esplanade, St Peter Port, GY1 3AP; tel. (1481) 711521; fax (1481) 714533; e-mail info@butterfield.gg; internet www.butterfieldbank.gg; f. 1989; subsidiary of Bank of N. T. Butterfield & Son Ltd (Bermuda); cap. 38.8m., res 16.5m., dep. 839.3m. (Dec. 2006); Man. Dir ROBERT MOORE.

Close Bank Guernsey Ltd: POB 116, Trafalgar Court, Admiral Park, St Peter Port, GY1 3EZ; tel. (1481) 711594; fax (1481) 726645; e-mail infogsy@closepb.com; internet www.closepb.com; f. 1965 as Rea Brothers (Guernsey) Ltd; present name adopted 1999; cap. 1.0m., dep. 336.9m. (July 2006); Chair. C. N. FISH; Man. Dir PHIL O'SHEA.

Crédit Suisse (Guernsey) Ltd: POB 368, Helvetia Court, South Esplanade, St Peter Port, GY1 3JY; tel. (1481) 719000; fax (1481) 724676; e-mail csguernsey.info@credit-suisse.com; internet www.credit-suisse.com/guernsey; f. 1986; cap. US $6.1m., res $211.7m., dep. $4,432.2m. (Dec. 2006); CEO R. MCGREGOR.

EFG Private Bank (Channel Islands) Ltd: POB 603, EFG House, St Julian's Ave, St Peter Port, GY1 4NN; tel. (1481) 723432; fax (1481) 723488; internet www.efggroup.com; f. 1992 as The Private Bank & Trust Co (Guernsey) Ltd; present name adopted 1997; cap. 5.0m., res 33.1m., dep. 818.5m. (Dec. 2004); Man. Dir D. G. GARDNER.

Fortis Bank (CI) Ltd: POB 119, Martello Court, Admiral Park, St Peter Port, GY1 3HB; tel. (1481) 751000; fax (1481) 751001; e-mail enquiries@gg.fortis.com; internet www.gg.fortis.com; fmrly Mees-Pierson Reads; present name adopted 2006; cap. 3.2m., res 93.2m., dep. 843.0m. (Dec. 2006); Man. Dir GRAHAM THOURNE.

SG Hambros Bank (Channel Islands) Ltd: POB 6, Hambro House, St Julian's Ave, St Peter Port, GY1 3AE; tel. (1481) 726521; fax (1481) 727139; e-mail channelislands@sghambros.com; internet www.sghambros.com; f. 1967; formerly SG Hambros Bank and Trust (Guernsey) Ltd; name changed in 2005 following merger with SG Hambros Bank and Trust (Jersey) Ltd; merchant bankers; cap. 4.5m., res 129.3m., dep. 1,696.5m. (Dec. 2005); Chair. WARWICK J. NEWBURY; Chief Exec. RICHARD A. OLLIVER.

HSBC Private Bank (Guernsey) Ltd: HSBC Private Bank Bldg, rue du Pré, St Peter Port, GY1 1LU; tel. (1481) 710901; fax (1481) 711824; internet www.hsbcprivatebank.com; f. 1985; cap. US $22.0m., res $465.0m., dep. $3,841.9m. (Dec. 2006); CEO GARY MILLER.

Investec Bank (Channel Islands) Ltd: POB 188, La Vieille Cour, St Peter Port, GY1 3LP; tel. (1481) 723506; fax (1481) 741147; e-mail enquiries@investec-ci.com; internet www.investec.com; f. 1977 as Guinness Mahon Guernsey Ltd; present name adopted 1999; cap. 14.7m., res 60.7m., dep. 1,721.2m. (March 2006); Chair. A. TAPNACK; Gen. Man. MORT MIRGHAVAMEDDIN.

Lloyds TSB Offshore Ltd Private Banking Office: POB 136, Sarnia House, Le Truchot, St Peter Port, GY1 4EN; tel. (1481) 708000; fax (1481) 727416; e-mail pvtbankingg@lloydstsb-offshore.com; internet www.privatebanking.lloydstsb-offshore.com; Head of Sales and Relationships MARK JACKSON.

N. M. Rothschild & Sons (CI) Ltd: POB 58, St Julian's Court, St Julian's Ave, St Peter Port; tel. (1481) 713713; fax (1481) 727705; e-mail private.banking@rothschild.co.uk; internet www.rothschild.gg; f. 1967; subsidiary of N. M. Rothschild & Sons Ltd, London; cap. 5m., res 0.1m., dep. 1,167.6m. (March 2007); Chair. CHRISTOPHER COLEMAN; Man. Dir PETER ROSE.

Rothschild Bank Switzerland (CI) Ltd: POB 330, St Julian's Court, St Julian's Ave, St Peter Port, GY1 3UA; tel. (1481) 710521; fax (1481) 711272; internet www.rothschildbank.com; Man. Dir R. VAN BEEK.

Royal Bank of Canada (Channel Islands) Ltd: POB 48, Canada Court, St Peter Port, GY1 3BQ; tel. (1481) 744000; fax (1481) 744001; e-mail infogpb@rbc.com; internet www.rbcprivatebanking.com; f. 1973; subsidiary of Royal Bank of Canada; cap. 5m., res 264.6m., dep. 5,310.2m. (Oct. 2006); Chair. M. J. LAGOPOULOS; Man. Dir C. C. BLAMPIED.

Schroders (CI) Ltd: POB 334, Regency Court, Glategny Esplanade, St Peter Port, GY1 3UF; tel. (1481) 703700; fax (1481) 703600; internet www.schroders.com/ci; f. 1992; cap. 0.5m., res 4.5m., dep. 828.8m. (Dec. 2006); Chair. P. D. WHITE.

Banking Organization

Association of Guernsey Banks: c/o Kleinwort Benson, POB 44, Fairbairn House, Rohais, St Peter Port, GY1 6DS; tel. (1481) 746434; fax (1481) 716900; e-mail alan.bougourd@skiptonguernsey.com; internet www.agb.org.gg; f. 1988; Chair. JIM GILLIGAN.

STOCK EXCHANGE

Channel Islands Stock Exchange (CISX): 1 Lefebvre St, St Peter Port, GY1 4PJ; tel. (1481) 713831; e-mail info@cisx.com; internet www.cisx.com; 50 cos listed; Chief Exec. TAMARA MENTESHVILI.

INSURANCE

At 30 April 2008 there were 368 international insurers and 25 domestic insurers operating in Guernsey.

Generali Worldwide Insurance Co Ltd: POB 613, Generali House, Hirzel St, St Peter Port, GY1 4PA; tel. (1481) 715400; fax (1481) 715390; e-mail enquiries@generali-guernsey.com; internet www.generali-gw.com; Chair. CHRISTOPHER SPENCER; CEO GAVIN TRADELIUS.

Heritage Group: POB 225, Polygon Hall, Le Marchant St, St Peter Port, GY1 4HY; tel. (1481) 716000; fax (1481) 728452; e-mail info@heritage.co.gg; internet www.heritage.co.gg.

Insurance Corpn of the Channel Islands Ltd: POB 160, Dixcart House, Sir William Pl., St Peter Port, GY1 4EY; tel. (1481) 707551; e-mail icci@insurancecorporation.com; internet www.insurancecorporation.com; mem. of the Royal Sun Alliance Group; Man. Dir PETER GALLAGHER.

Islands' Insurance Co Ltd: Lancaster Court, Forest Lane, St Peter Port, GY1 1WJ; tel. (1481) 710731.

Norwich Union Insurance Group: Hirzel Court, St Peter Port, GY1 2NQ; tel. (1481) 724864.

Trade and Industry

CHAMBER OF COMMERCE

Guernsey Chamber of Commerce: Suite 3, 16 Glategny Esplanade, St Peter Port, GY1 1WN; tel. (1481) 727483; fax (1481) 710755; e-mail office@guernseychamber.com; internet www.guernseychamber.com; f. 1808; Pres. MARK TRENCHARD.

UTILITIES

Electricity

Guernsey Electricity: POB 4, Electricity House, Northside, Vale, GY1 3AD; tel. (1481) 200700; fax (1481) 246942; e-mail admin@electricity.gg; internet www.electricity.gg; Chair. KEN GREGSON; Man. Dir IAN WATSON.

Gas

Guernsey Gas: POB 70, Rue du Commerce, St Peter Port, GY1 3BZ; tel. (1481) 724811; internet www.gsygas.com; Dir PAUL GARLICK.

Water

Guernsey Water: POB 30, South Esplanade, St Peter Port, GY1 3AS; tel. (1481) 724552; fax (1481) 715094; fmrly States of Guernsey Waterboard; name changed as above 2004; Dir of Water Services ANDREW REDHEAD.

Transport

SHIPPING

Alderney Shipping Co Ltd: POB 77, White Rock, St Peter Port, GY1 4BN; tel. (1481) 724810; fax (1481) 712081; e-mail annika@aldshp.co.uk; internet www.aldshp.co.uk.

Condor Ltd: 3rd Floor, La Plaiderie House, La Plaiderie, St Peter Port, GY1 1WD; tel. (1481) 729666; fax (1481) 712555; internet www.condorferries.co.uk; f. 1964; regular passenger service operating between the Channel Islands and St Malo (France), and between the Channel Islands and Poole, Weymouth and Portsmouth; Man. Dir ROBERT PROVAN; Gen. Man. NICK DOBBS.

Condorferries Freight: 3rd Floor, La Plaiderie House, La Plaiderie, St Peter Port, GY1 1WD; tel. (1481) 728620; fax (1481) 728521; e-mail jeff.vidamour@condorferries.co.uk; internet www.condorferries.co.uk; regular ro-ro freight services between Portsmouth, Guernsey, Jersey and St Malo (France); Freight Dir JEFF VIDAMOUR.

Herm Seaway Express: Albert Pier, St Peter Port; tel. (1481) 724161; fax (1481) 700226; Contact PETER WILCOX.

Isle of Sark Shipping Co Ltd: White Rock, St Peter Port, GY1 2LN; tel. (1481) 724059; fax (1481) 713999; e-mail shipping@sark.info; internet www.sarkshipping.info; operates daily services between Guernsey and Sark.

Trident Charter Co Ltd: Woodville, Les Dicqs, Vale, GY6 8JW; tel. (1481) 245253; fax (1481) 700226; e-mail peterwilcox@cw.gsy.net; Man. PETER WILCOX.

CIVIL AVIATION

Aurigny Air Services Ltd: States Airport, La Planque Lane, Forest, GY8 0DT; tel. (1481) 266444; fax (1481) 266446; e-mail customerrelations@aurigny.com; internet www.aurigny.com; f. 1968; scheduled passenger services from Guernsey to Alderney, Jersey, Bristol, London, Manchester and Dinard (France); freight services, tour operation, ambulance charters and third party handling; Man. Dir MALCOLM HART.

Blue Islands: Century House, 12 Victoria St, St Anne, Alderney, GY9 3UF; tel. (1481) 711321; fax (1481) 735235; e-mail enquiries@blueislands.com; internet www.blueislands.com; f. 1999 as Le Cocqs Air Link; name changed as above in 2006; scheduled passenger flights between Alderney, Guernsey and Jersey, and to Bournemouth, Brighton, Cardiff, Southampton, the Isle of Man and Paris (France); Chair. DEREK COATES; Man. Dir PAUL SABIN.

Tourism

A total of 220,000 tourists visited Guernsey during 2006.

VisitGuernsey: POB 459, St Martin, GY1 6AF; tel. (1481) 234567; fax (1481) 238755; e-mail enquiries@visitguernsey.com; internet www.visitguernsey.com; Dir of Marketing and Tourism CHRIS ELLIOTT.

Islands of the Bailiwick of Guernsey

Alderney

The area of Alderney is 7.9 sq km (3.1 sq miles) and at the 2001 census the population was 2,294. The principal town is St Anne's.

The President, who is elected for a four-year term, is the civic head of Alderney and has precedence on the island over all persons except the Lieutenant-Governor of Guernsey, and the Bailiff of Guernsey or his representative. He presides over meetings of the States of Alderney, which are responsible for the administration of the island with the exception of policing, public health and education, which are administered by the States of Guernsey. The States consist of 10 members who hold office for four years and are elected by universal suffrage of residents.

President of the States: Sir NORMAN BROWSE.

Chief Executive of the States: DAVID JEREMIAH.

Greffier: SARAH KELLY.

States of Alderney: POB 1, Alderney, GY9 3AA; tel. (1481) 822811; fax (1481) 822436; e-mail states@alderney.net; internet www.alderney.gov.gg.

Brecqhou and Lihou

Brecqhou (measuring 1.2 km by 0.5 km) is a dependency of Sark. Lihou (area 0.2 sq km) is, for administrative purposes, part of Guernsey.

Herm

Herm is held on a 100-year lease from the States of Guernsey by Wood of Herm Island Ltd, with a duty to preserve the island's outstanding natural beauty and peacefulness. Farming and tourism are the chief sources of income. The island has an area of 2.0 sq km (0.8 sq miles). At the 2001 census the population of Herm was 95.

Herm Island Administration Office: Herm Island, Guernsey, GY1 3HR; tel. (1481) 722377; fax (1481) 700334; e-mail admin@herm-island.com; internet www.herm-island.com; Island Man. ADRIAN HEYWORTH.

Jethou

Jethou has an area of 0.2 sq km (0.07 sq miles) and is leased by the Crown to a tenant who has no official functions. At the 2001 census the population of Jethou was 2.

Sark

The area of the island is 5.5 sq km (2.1 sq miles) and at the 2001 census the population was 589. No motor vehicles are permitted apart from a small number of tractors. In summer a daily boat service runs between Guernsey and Sark, and in winter a limited service is provided. There are two harbours on the island.

The Seigneur of Sark is the hereditary civic head of the island and thereby entitled to certain privileges. The Seigneur is a member of the Chief Pleas of Sark, the island's parliament, and has a suspensory veto on its ordinances. The Seigneur has the right, subject to the approval of the Lieutenant-Governor of Guernsey, to appoint the Seneschal of Sark, who is President of the Chief Pleas and Chairman of the Seneschal's Court, which is the local Court of Justice.

In March 2006 the Chief Pleas voted in favour of reducing the number of its members from 52 (comprising the owners of the island's 40 tenements—known as tenants—and 12 elected 'deputies of the people') to 28, of whom 14 were to be tenants and the remaining 14 residents. Under the reformed system the members of the Chief Pleas would be elected by universal suffrage of residents. An official opinion poll on the composition of the Chief Pleas was conducted between mid-August and early September. Some 56.0% of the valid votes cast (234 of a total of 418) supported open elections for all 28 seats in the Chief Pleas, while 44.0% of voters favoured the option of reserving 12 of the 28 seats specifically for residents and eight for tenants. A participation rate of 89.5% was recorded for the opinion poll, which was subsequently approved by the Chief Pleas. In February 2008 the Chief Pleas ratified the reform law, which would allow for the introduction of an elected chamber. The Privy Council of the United Kingdom approved the proposed changes in April, and elections for a fully elected, 28-member Chief Pleas were due to take place by December.

Seigneur of Sark: JOHN MICHAEL BEAUMONT.

Seneschal: Lt-Col REGINALD J. GUILLE.

Greffier: T. J. HAMON.

Sark Committee Office: La Chasse Marette, GY9 0SF; tel. (1481) 832118; fax (1481) 833086; e-mail seigneur@sark.gov.gg; internet www.sark.info.

Sark Tourism: Harbour Hill, Sark, GY9 0SB; tel. (1481) 832345; fax (1481) 832483; e-mail contact@sark.info; internet www.sark.info.

UNITED KINGDOM CROWN DEPENDENCIES   *The Channel Islands (Jersey)*

JERSEY

Introduction

Jersey, the largest of the Channel Islands, is situated to the south-east of Guernsey, from which it is separated by 27 km (17 miles) of sea. The official language of Jersey is English (since 1960), although French is still used in the courts. The state and civil flag is white with a red saltire and coat of arms bearing three yellow lions and surmounted by a yellow crown. The capital is St Helier. In addition to the British public holidays, Jersey celebrates 9 May (Liberation Day).

Statistical Survey

Source (unless otherwise stated): States of Jersey Statistics Department, Cyril Le Marquand House, POB 140, JE4 8QT; tel. (1534) 440426; fax (1534) 440409; e-mail statistics@gov.je; internet www.gov.je/statistics.

AREA AND POPULATION

Area: 118.2 sq km (45.6 sq miles).

Population (census of 11 March 2001): 87,186 (males 42,484, females 44,702). *2006* (official estimate at 31 December): 89,300.

Density (per sq km, 2006): 755.5.

Principal Towns (2001): St Helier 28,310; St Saviour 12,491; St Brelade 10,134; St Clement 8,196.

Births and Deaths (2006): Live births 950 (10.6 per 1,000); Deaths 760 (8.5 per 1,000). *2007:* Live births 1,030; Deaths 707.

Economically Active Population (at June 2007, rounded estimates): Agriculture and fishing 2,240; Manufacturing, electricity, gas and water 2,100; Construction and quarrying 5,180; Wholesale and retail 8,440; Hotels, restaurants etc. 6,260; Transport, storage and communication 2,750; Financial services 12,660; Miscellaneous business activities (incl. computers) 3,720; Public administration 6,730; Education, health and other services 5,060; *Total employed* 55,140; Unemployed 330; *Total labour force* 55,470.

AGRICULTURE, ETC.

Principal Crops: Some 56.5% of total land area was classified as agricultural in 2006. The principal crops are potatoes, cauliflowers and tomatoes. Dairy and cattle farming are important activities.

Fishing ('000 metric tons, 2006): Capture 1,721 (Wet fish 179, Brown crab 349, Lobster 131, Spider crab 129, Scallops 304, Whelk 621, Others 5); Aquaculture 772 (Oysters 651, Scallops 3, Mussels 118); *Total catch* 2,493.

FINANCE

Currency and Exchange Rates: 100 pence = 1 pound sterling (£). *Dollar and Euro Equivalents* (31 December 2007): US $1 = 49.92 pence; €1 = 73.48 pence; £10 = $20.03 = €13.61.

Note: Jersey is in monetary union with the United Kingdom. It has its own coins and notes but United Kingdom coins and notes are also legal tender.

Budget (£ million, 2006): States General Funds income 526 (Income tax 398); Expenditure 504 (States net revenue expenditure 465; Capital expenditure 39).

Money Supply (currency in circulation, £ million at 31 December 20056): Notes 69.6; Coins 6.4; *Total* 75.9.

Cost of Living (Retail Price Index at June; base June 2000 = 100, all items): 122.6 in 2005; 126.2 in 2006; 131.6 in 2007.

Gross National Income (£ million, 2006): 3,400.

Gross Value Added by Economic Activity (£ million at constant 2003 prices, 2006): Agriculture 45; Manufacturing 50; Electricity, gas and water 34; Construction 180; Wholesale and retail trade 221; Hotels, restaurants and bars 109; Transport, storage and communications 142; Finance 1,780; Other business activities 619; Public administration 237; *Total* 3,418.

TRANSPORT

Road Traffic (vehicles registered at 31 December 2001): Motor cars 71,059; Motorcycles 5,676; Mopeds 2,200; Buses and minibuses 691; Tractors 2,369; Vans 7,562; Trucks 3,617; Total (incl. others) 94,538. *2007* (vehicles registered at 31 December): Total 107,996.

Shipping (2007): Passenger movements 782,000; Containerized freight ('000 metric tons handled) 337.

Civil Aviation (2005): Aircraft movements 70,012; Total passengers carried 1,483,477 (Arrivals 741,969, Departures 741,508). *2007:* Total passenger arrivals 781,563 (from UK 680,505).

TOURISM

Tourist Arrivals (2004): *Holiday and Leisure Visitors* (staying in paid accommodation): 377,820 (UK mainland 301,460; Other Channel Islands 14,900; France 29,380; Germany 10,060); *Total Arrivals*: 731,310. *2006:* Total visitor arrivals 729,900 (number staying in paid accommodation 365,500); Total revenues £222m.

COMMUNICATIONS MEDIA

Telephones (2006, estimate): 71,500 main lines in use.
Mobile Cellular Telephones (2006, estimate): 102,000.
Internet Users (2004): 27,000.

Source: partly International Telecommunication Union.

EDUCATION

Pupils (2006): Primary 6,972 (state schools 5,679, private 1,293); Secondary 6,284 (state schools 5,220, private 1,064).

Directory

The Constitution

The Lieutenant-Governor and Commander-in-Chief of Jersey is the personal representative of the Sovereign, the Commander of the Armed Forces of the Crown, and the channel of communication between the Crown and the Insular Government. He is appointed by the Crown, and is entitled to sit and speak in the Assembly of the States of Jersey, but not to vote. He has a veto on certain forms of legislation.

The Bailiff is appointed by the Crown, and is President both of the Assembly of the States (the insular legislature) and the Royal Court of Jersey. In the States, he has a right of dissent and a casting vote.

The Deputy Bailiff is appointed by the Crown, and, when authorized by the Bailiff to do so, he may discharge any function appertaining to the office of Bailiff.

The government of the island is conducted by a Council of Ministers, which consists of a Chief Minister and nine other ministers. The Chief Minister is elected by the States and nominates the other ministers, subject to the approval of the States. The States consist of 12 Senators (elected for six years, six retiring every third year), 12 Connétables (triennial), and 29 Deputies (triennial). They are elected by universal suffrage. The Dean of Jersey, the Attorney-General and Solicitor-General are appointed by the Crown and are entitled to sit and speak in the States, but not to vote. Permanent laws passed by the States require the sanction of Her Majesty in Council, but Triennial Regulations do not.

The Government

Lieutenant-Governor and Commander-in-Chief of Jersey: Lt-Gen. ANDREW RIDGEWAY.
Secretary to the Lieutenant-Governor and Aide-de-Camp: Lt-Col A. J. C. WOODROW.
Bailiff: Sir PHILIP MARTIN BAILHACHE.
Deputy Bailiff: MICHAEL CAMERON ST JOHN BIRT.
Dean of Jersey: Very Rev. ROBERT FREDERICK KEY.
Attorney-General: WILLIAM JAMES BAILHACHE.
Solicitor-General: TIMOTHY JOHN LE COCQ.
Greffier of the States: MICHAEL NELSON DE LA HAYE.

COUNCIL OF MINISTERS
(April 2008)

Chief Minister: FRANK HARRISON WALKER.
Minister for the Treasury and Resources: TERENCE LE SUEUR.
Minister for Home Affairs: WENDY KINNARD.
Minister for Education, Sport and Culture: MICHAEL VIBERT.
Minister for Health and Social Services: BEN SHENTON.

UNITED KINGDOM CROWN DEPENDENCIES   The Channel Islands (Jersey)

Minister for Social Security: PAUL ROUTIER.
Minister for Economic Development: PHILLIP OZOUF.
Minister for Transport and Technical Services: GUY DE FAYE.
Minister for Housing: TERENCE LE MAIN.
Minister for Planning and the Environment: FREDERICK ELLYER COHEN.

Judicial System

Justice is administered in Jersey by the Royal Court, which consists of the Bailiff or Deputy Bailiff and 12 Jurats elected by an Electoral College. There is a Court of Appeal, which consists of the Bailiff (or Deputy Bailiff) and two Judges, selected from a panel appointed by the Crown. A final appeal lies to the Privy Council in certain cases.

A Stipendiary Magistrate deals with minor civil and criminal cases. He also acts as an Examining Magistrate in some criminal matters.

Religion

CHRISTIANITY

The Church of England

The Church of England is the established church. The Deanery of Jersey is an Ecclesiastical Peculiar, governed by its own canons, the Dean being the Ordinary of the Island; it is attached to the diocese of Winchester for episcopal purposes.

Dean of Jersey: Very Rev. ROBERT FREDERICK KEY, The Deanery, David Place, St Helier, JE2 4TE; tel. (1534) 720001; fax (1534) 617488; e-mail deanofjersey@jerseymail.co.uk.

The Roman Catholic Church

The diocese of Portsmouth includes the Channel Islands and part of southern England. The Episcopal Vicar for the Channel Islands resides at St Peter Port, Guernsey. In Jersey there are 12 Roman Catholic churches, including St Mary and St Peter's, Wellington Rd, St Helier (English), and St Thomas, Val Plaisant, St Helier (French).

Other Christian Churches

The Baptist, Congregational New Church, Methodist and Presbyterian churches are also represented.

The Press

Jersey Evening Post: POB 582, JE4 8XQ; tel. (1534) 611611; fax (1534) 611622; e-mail editorial@jerseyeveningpost.com; internet www.jerseyeveningpost.com; f. 1890; independent; Propr The Claverley Company; Editor CHRIS BRIGHT; circ. 21,237 (Dec. 2006).

Jersey Weekly Post: POB 582, JE4 8XQ; tel. (1534) 611611; fax (1534) 611622; e-mail editorial@jerseyeveningpost.com; internet www.thisisjersey.com; Thursday; Propr The Claverley Company; Editor CHRIS BRIGHT; circ. 1,200.

Publishers

Ashton & Denton Publishing Co (CI) Ltd: 3 Burlington House, St Saviour's Rd, St Helier, JE2 4LA; tel. (1534) 735461; fax (1534) 875805; e-mail asden@supanet.com; f. 1957; local history, holiday guides, financial; Man. Dir A. MACKENZIE.

Barnes Publishing Ltd: 18 Great Union Rd, St Helier, JE2 3YA; tel. (1534) 618166; fax (1534) 607029; e-mail ian.barnes@barnespublishing.com; internet barnespublishing.com; f. 1993 as Apache Publishing; present name adopted 1998; Man. Dir IAN BARNES.

Broadcasting and Communications

TELECOMMUNICATIONS

Cable and Wireless Jersey: Richmond House, 8 David Pl., St Helier, JE2 4TD; tel. (1534) 888291; fax (1534) 888292; e-mail solutions@cwjersey.com; internet www.cw.com/jersey; Chief Exec. DAVID SMITH.

Jersey Telecom: POB 53, No. 1 The Forum, Grenville St, St Helier, JE4 8PB; tel. (1534) 882882; fax (1534) 882883; e-mail enquiries@jerseytelecom.com; internet www.jerseytelecom.com; Chair. JOHN HENWOOD; Man. Dir BOB LAWRENCE.

BROADCASTING

Radio

BBC: Radio and Television (see United Kingdom).

BBC Radio Jersey: 18 Parade Rd, St Helier, JE2 3PL; tel. (1534) 870000; e-mail jersey@bbc.co.uk; internet www.bbc.co.uk/jersey; f. 1982; broadcasts 77 hours a week.

Channel 103 FM: 6 Tunnell St, St Helier, JE2 4LU; tel. (1534) 888103; fax (1534) 877177; e-mail admin@channel103.com; internet www.channel103.com; f. 1992; Man Dir RICHARD JOHNSON.

Television

Channel Television: Television Centre, St Helier, JE1 3ZD; tel. (1534) 816816; fax (1534) 816777; e-mail broadcast@channeltv.co.uk; internet www.channelonline.tv; f. 1962; daily transmissions; Chair. DAVID FORDHAM; Man. Dir MIKE ELSEY.

Programmes are also received from the BBC, Channel 4 and five in the United Kingdom and also from France.

Finance

Jersey Financial Services Commission: POB 267, 14–18 Castle St, St Helier, JE4 8TP; tel. (1534) 822000; fax (1534) 822001; e-mail info@jerseyfsc.org; internet www.jerseyfsc.org; f. 1998; financial services regulator; Dir-Gen. JOHN HARRIS.

BANKING

(cap. = capital; auth. = authorized; res = reserves; dep. = deposits; m. = million; br./brs = branch(es); amounts in pounds sterling, unless otherwise indicated)

In June 2007 total bank deposits in Jersey were £211,746m. in 47 institutions.

British Clearing Banks

The banks listed below are branches of British banks, and details concerning directors, capital, etc. of the parent bank will be found under the appropriate section in the pages dealing with the United Kingdom.

Barclays Bank PLC: POB 8, 13 Library Pl., St Helier, JE4 8NE; tel. (1534) 812000; fax (1534) 813500; Jersey Man. MARTYN SCRIVEN; 4 brs.

National Westminster Bank PLC: POB 11, 16 Library Pl., St Helier, JE4 8NH; tel. (1534) 282828; fax (1534) 282730; Man. P. TAYLOR; 6 brs.

Other Banks

ABN AMRO Private Banking: POB 255, 7 Castle St, St Helier, JE4 8TB; tel. (1534) 604000; fax (1534) 759041; e-mail pbclients@uk.abnamro.com; internet www.abnamroprivatebanking.com/jersey; f. 1997; Gen. Man. MARK HENNY.

AIB Bank (CI) Ltd: POB 468, AIB House, 25 Esplanade, St Helier, JE1 2AB; tel. (1534) 883000; fax (1534) 883112; e-mail one@aib.je; internet www.aib.je; f. 1981; cap. 10.0m., res 0.5m., dep. 1,587.0m. (Dec. 2005); Man. Dir D. J. MOYNIHAN.

Ansbacher (Channel Islands) Ltd: POB 393, 7–11 Britannia Pl., Bath St, St Helier, JE4 8US; tel. (1534) 504504; fax (1534) 504575; e-mail info@ansbacher.co.je; internet www.ansbacher.com/channelislands.html; f. 1984 as Westpac Banking Corpn (Jersey) Ltd; acquired by Henry Ansbacher Group in 1995; cap. 2.5m., res 9.1m., dep. 278.0m. (Dec. 2005); Man. Dir MARK BRIGHT.

Bank Leumi (Jersey) Ltd: POB 510, 27 Hill St, St Helier, JE4 5TR; tel. (1534) 702525; fax (1534) 617446; e-mail dlieberman@leumijersey.com; internet www.bankleumi.co.uk; f. 1993; cap. 10.5m., res 2.7m., dep. 193.4m. (Dec. 2005).

Bank of Scotland International Ltd: Halifax House, 31–33 New St, St Helier, JE4 8YW; tel. (1534) 613500; fax (1534) 759280; e-mail enquiry@bankofscotlandint.co.uk; internet www.bankofscotland-international.com; cap. 15.0m., dep. 822.8m. (Feb. 2001); f. 1986; Man. Dir GRAEME HALL.

Banque Transatlantique (Jersey) Ltd: POB 206, 47–49 La Motte St, St Helier, JE4 0XR; tel. (1534) 881471; fax (1534) 881473; e-mail btjersey@psilink.co.je; internet www.transat.tm.fr.

BHF-Bank (Jersey) Ltd: 6 Wests Centre, St Helier, JE2 4ST; tel. (1534) 879044; fax (1534) 879246; f. 1981; cap. €4.0m., res €16.5m., dep. €1,200.0m. (Dec. 2006); Man. JOHN M. ALCOCK.

Citibank (Channel Islands) Ltd: POB 104, 38 The Esplanade, St Helier, JE4 8ZT; tel. (1534) 608000; fax (1534) 608190; internet www.citibank.com/privatebank/index.htm; f. 1969; cap. US $0.9m., res $7.6m., dep. $216.4m. (Dec. 2005); Chair. PHILIP HOOPER.

Coutts Channel Islands: POB 6, 23–25 Broad St, St Helier, JE4 8ND; tel. (1534) 282380; fax (1534) 282400; internet www.coutts.com; f. 1969; Dir NICHOLAS LANE.

Deutsche Bank International Ltd: POB 727, St Paul's Gate, New St, St Helier, JE4 8ZB; tel. (1534) 889900; fax (1534) 889911; internet www.dboffshore.com; f. 1972; cap. 15.0m., res 172.7m., dep. 4,008.1m. (Dec. 2006); CEO MARK HIRST.

Dexia Private Bank Jersey Ltd: POB 12, 2–6 Church St, St Helier, JE4 9NE; tel. (1534) 834400; fax (1534) 834411; e-mail dexiapbjsy@localdial.com; internet www.dexia-privatebank.je; f. 1996; Man. Dir DAVID G. SMITH.

Fairbairn Private Bank Ltd: Fairbairn House, 31 The Esplanade, St Helier, JE1 1FB; tel. (1534) 887889; fax (1534) 509725; e-mail jer@fairbairnpb.com; internet www.fairbairnpb.com; f. 1994 as Flemings (Jersey) Ltd, name changed as above in 2004; cap. 0.4m., res 10.9m., dep. 821.0m. (Dec. 2006); Man. Dir G. J. HORTON.

SG Hambros Bank (Channel Islands) Ltd: POB 78, SG Hambros House, 18 The Esplanade, St Helier, JE4 8PR; tel. (1534) 815555; fax (1534) 815640; e-mail channelislands@sghambros.com; internet www.sghambros.com; f. 1967 as Hambros (Jersey) Ltd; previously SG Hambros Bank and Trust (Jersey) Ltd; name changed in 2005 following merger with SG Hambros Bank and Trust (Guernsey) Ltd; subsidiary of SG Hambros Bank and Trust Ltd, London; cap. 4.5m., res 129.3m., dep. 1,696.5m. (Dec. 2005); Chair. WARWICK J. NEWBURY; Man. Dir RICHARD A. OLLIVER.

HSBC Bank International Ltd: HSBC House, St Helier, JE1 1HS; tel. (1534) 616000; fax (1534) 616001; e-mail offshore@hsbc.com; internet www.offshore.hsbc.com; f. 1967 as Midland Bank Finance Corpn (Jersey) Ltd; cap. 1.4m., res. 34.2m, dep. 5,939.0m. (Dec. 2006); Chief Exec. MARTIN DAVID SPURLING.

HSBC Bank Middle East Ltd: POB 315, HSBC House, The Esplanade, St Helier, JE4 8UB; tel. (1534) 606512; fax (1534) 606149; e-mail chris.keirle@hsbc.com; internet www.middleeast.hsbc.com; cap. US $431.1m., res $15.2m., dep. $22,126.7m. (Dec. 2006); Chair. DAVID HOWARD HODGKINSON.

HSBC Private Bank (Jersey) Ltd: POB 88, 1 Grenville St, St Helier, JE4 9PF; tel. (1534) 672000; fax (1534) 672020; internet www.hsbcprivatebank.com; fmrly HSBC Republic Bank (Jersey) Ltd; name changed as above in Jan. 2004; cap. 1.1m., res 63.9m., dep. 1,639.2m. (Dec. 2006); Man. Dirs STUART TAYLOR, GEORGE KEAN.

ING Bank (Jersey) Ltd: 3rd Floor, Forum House, Grenville St, St Helier, JE2 4UF; tel. (1534) 880888; fax (1534) 880777; internet www.ing.je; f. 1988; name changed as above in 2003; Man. Dir PAUL VAN NESTE.

Kleinwort Benson (Channel Islands) Ltd: POB 76, Kleinwort Benson House, Wests Centre, St Helier, JE4 8PQ; tel. (1534) 613000; fax (1534) 613141; internet www.kleinwortbenson.com; f. 1962; mem. of the Dresdner Bank Group; cap. 5.0m., res 20.0m., dep. 2,190.6m. (Dec. 2005); Man. Dir MARTIN ANGUS TAYLOR.

Lloyds TSB Offshore Ltd: POB 311, 25 New St, St Helier, JE4 8ZU; tel. (800) 638000; fax (1534) 284331; e-mail jerseyoffc@lloydstsb-offshore.com; internet www.lloydstsb-offshore.com; part of Lloyds TSB banking group; cap. 207.8m., res 111.6m., dep. 6,626.7m. (Dec. 2006); Chair. DAVID J. S. OLDFIELD; 5 brs.

JPMorgan Chase Bank: POB 127, JPMorgan House, Grenville St, St Helier, JE4 8QH; tel. (1534) 626262; fax (1534) 626301; Gen. Man. L. C. WORTHAM.

JP Morgan Trust Co (Jersey): POB 127, JPMorgan House, Grenville St, St Helier; tel. (1534) 626262; fax (1534) 626300; Chair. T. TODMAN; Man. Dir L. C. WORTHAM.

The Royal Bank of Scotland International Ltd: POB 64, 71 Bath St, St Helier, JE4 8PJ; tel. (1534) 285200; fax (1534) 285222; internet www.rbsint.com; f. 1966; cap. 86.5m., res 686.3m., dep. 14,216.7m. (Dec. 2002); Chief Exec. IAN HENDERSON.

Standard Bank Jersey Ltd: POB 583, Standard Bank House, 47–49 La Motte St, St Helier, JE4 8XR; tel. (1534) 881188; fax (1534) 881199; e-mail sbj@sboff.com; internet www.sboff.com; f. 1977 as Brown Shipley (Jersey); present name adopted 2000; cap. 10.0m., res 10.5m., dep. 683.4m. (Dec. 2005); Chair. R. A. G. LEITH; CEO IAN GIBSON.

Standard Chartered (Jersey) Ltd: 15 Castle St, St Helier, JE4 8PT; tel. (1534) 704000; fax (1534) 704600; internet www.standardchartered.com/je; f. 1966 as Julian S. Hodge Bank (Jersey) Ltd; present name adopted 2004; cap. 7.3m., res 83.2m., dep. 4,922.9m. (Dec. 2004); CEO ALISON MACFADYEN.

INSURANCE

Jersey Mutual Insurance Soc.: 74 Halkett Pl., St Helier, JE1 1BT; tel. (1534) 734246; fax (1534) 733381; e-mail info@jerseymutual.com; internet www.jerseymutual.com; f. 1869; general, household and travel; Pres. G. DE GRUCHY; Sec. R. A. JEANNE.

Trade and Industry

CHAMBER OF COMMERCE

Jersey Chamber of Commerce: Chamber House, 25 Pier Rd, St Helier, JE1 4HF; tel. (1534) 724536; fax (1534) 734942; e-mail admin@jerseychamber.com; internet www.jerseychamber.com; f. 1768; Pres. CLIVE SPEARS; Head, Marketing and Operations CATHERINE HARGREAVES; 600 mems.

Utilities

Electricity

Jersey Electricity Co Ltd: POB 45, Queen's Rd, St Helier, JE4 8NY; tel. (1534) 505460; fax (1534) 505565; e-mail jec@jec.co.uk; internet www.jec.co.uk; f. 1924; Chair. GEOFFREY GRIME; CEO MIKE LISTON.

Gas

Jersey Gas Co Ltd: POB 169, Thomas Edge House, Tunnell St, St Helier, JE4 8RE; tel. (1534) 755500; fax (1534) 769822; e-mail jerseygas@jsy-gas.com; internet www.jsygas.com; Man. Dir PAUL GARLICK.

Water

Jersey New Waterworks Co Ltd (Jersey Water): Mulcaster House, Westmount Rd, St Helier, JE1 1DG; tel. (1534) 707300; fax (1534) 707400; e-mail info@jerseywater.je; internet www.jerseywater.je; Chair. DAVID NORMAN; Man. Dir HOWARD SNOWDEN.

Transport

SHIPPING

The harbour of St Helier has 1,400 m of cargo working quays, with 10 berths in dredged portion (2.29 m) and eight drying berths.

Condor Jersey Ltd: Elizabeth Terminal and Albert Quay, St Helier; tel. (1534) 607080; fax (1534) 280767; e-mail reservations@condorferries.co.uk; internet www.condorferries.co.uk; head office in Guernsey; daily services to mainland Britain; also regular services to Guernsey and St Malo (France); Gen. Man. NICK DOBBS.

CIVIL AVIATION

The States of Jersey Airport is at St Peter, Jersey.

Airline

Flybe: States Airport, St Peter; tel. (871) 7000535; internet www.flybe.com; f. 1983 as Jersey European Airways; present name adopted 2002; services between Jersey and Guernsey, London, Belfast, Birmingham, Bristol, Edinburgh, Exeter, Glasgow, Inverness, Leeds/Bradford, Liverpool, Manchester, Norwich, Southampton, Dublin (Ireland) and Geneva (Switzerland); Chair. and CEO JIM FRENCH.

Tourism

In 2006 Jersey recorded some 729,900 tourist arrivals; 365,000 visitors stayed in paid accommodation. Tourist expenditure in that year was £222m.

Jersey Tourism: Liberation Sq., St Helier, JE1 1BB; tel. (1534) 448800; fax (1534) 448898; e-mail info@jersey.com; internet www.jersey.com; Dir DAVID DE CARTERET.

THE ISLE OF MAN

Introduction

The Isle of Man lies in the Irish Sea between the Cumbrian coast of England and Northern Ireland. It is a dependency of the Crown and does not form part of the United Kingdom. It has its own legislative assembly and legal and administrative systems, its laws depending for their validity on Orders made by the Queen in Council. Her Majesty's Government in the United Kingdom is responsible for the defence and international relations of the island, and the Crown is ultimately responsible for its good government. However, control of direct taxation is exercised by the Manx Government and, although most rates of indirect taxation are the same on the island as in the United Kingdom, there is some divergence of rates. The capital is Douglas. In addition to the British public holidays, the Isle of Man also celebrates Senior Race Day of the annual Isle of Man Tourist Trophy (TT) Races (which, in 2008, falls on 6 June) and Tynwald Day (7 July).

Statistical Survey

Source: Isle of Man Government Offices, Bucks Rd, Douglas; tel. (1624) 685711; internet www.gov.im.

AREA AND POPULATION

Area: 572 sq km (221 sq miles).

Population (census, 23–24 April 2006): 80,058 (males 39,523, females 40,535).

Density (per sq km, 2006 census): 140.0.

Principal Localities (2006 census): Douglas (capital) 26,218; Onchan 9,172; Ramsey 7,309; Peel 4,280; Port Erin 3,575; Braddan 3,151; Castletown 3,109.

Births and Deaths (2005): Live births 901 (birth rate 11.3 per 1,000); Deaths 775 (death rate 10.5 per 1,000). *2006:* Live births 905; Deaths 768.

Economically Active Population (2006 census): Agriculture, etc. 642; Manufacturing 2,248; Construction 3,374; Electricity, gas and water 603; Transport and communication 3,171; Wholesale and retail trade 4,550; Entertainment, catering and tourist accommodation 2,259; Banking and finance 7,010; Real estate and renting 1,072; Other professional, business and scientific services 3,741; Education 2,805; Medical and health services 3,316; Public administration 2,898; Other services 3,075; Activities not adequately defined 19; *Total employed* 40,783 (males 22,020, females 18,763); Unemployed 1,010 (males 634, females 376); *Total labour force* 41,793 (males 22,654, females 19,139).

AGRICULTURE, ETC.

Crops (area in acres, 2006): Cereals and potatoes 11,807; Grass 64,616; Rough grazing 27,101.

Livestock (2006): Cattle 29,654; Sheep 136,751; Pigs 601; Poultry 20,169.

Fishing (2006 unless otherwise indicated): *Amount Landed* (metric tons): Scallops 1,522; Queen scallops 1,133 (2005); *Value of Landings:* Scallops £1.5m.; Queen scallops £0.8m.; Total first-hand sale value of all landings: £3.1m.

FINANCE

Currency and Exchange Rates: 100 pence = 1 pound sterling (£). *Dollar and Euro Equivalents* (31 December 2007): US $1 = 49.92 pence; €1 = 73.48 pence; £10 = $20.03 = €13.61.

Note: The Isle of Man is in monetary union with the United Kingdom. It has its own coins and notes, but United Kingdom coins and notes are also legal tender.

Budget: (£ million, 2008/09, estimates): *Total Revenue* 599.0 (Customs and excise 434.1; Income and other taxes 161.0); *Total Expenditure* 566.5 (Health and social security 233.5).

Cost of Living: (Retail Price Index at September; base: January 2000 = 100) All items 116.5 in 2004; 120.2 in 2005; 124.1 in 2006.

Gross Domestic Product (GDP) (£ million at constant 2005/06 factor cost): 1,467.6 in 2003/04; 1,543.3 in 2004/05; 1,634.1.

GDP by Economic Activity (£ million at current factor cost, 2005/06): Agriculture, hunting, forestry and fishing 19.2; Mining and quarrying 8.7; Manufacturing 126.9; Electricity, gas and water supply 32.2; Construction 134.1; Wholesale and retail trade, repair of motor vehicles, motorcycles and personal and household goods 135.6; Transport and communications 110.4; Catering and entertainment and tourist accommodation 52.6; Financial services, real estate, renting and business activities 670.7; Other professional, educational, scientific and medical service activities 402.4; Public administration 85.0; Other services 71.7; *Sub-total* 1,849.4; Ownership of dwellings, less adjustments –215.2; *Total* 1,634.1.

TRANSPORT

Road Traffic (registered vehicles, 2001): Private 45,195; Engineering 385; Goods 4,489; Agricultural 931; Hackney 790; Public service 146; Motorcycles, scooters and tricycles 4,519.

Shipping (2005/06, unless otherwise indicated): Passengers handled 598,108; Registered merchant vessels 316; Other registered vessels 613; Total displacement ('000 grt, 2006) 9,192.

Civil Aviation: Passengers handled 789,155 (2006); Freight carried 4,594 metric tons (2003).

TOURISM

Tourist Arrivals (2006): Staying visitors 219,100; Day visitors 5,214; Business travellers 82,276.

COMMUNICATIONS MEDIA

Telephone Connections (2001): Fixed 56,000; Mobile 32,000.

Television Licences (2000): 28,601.

EDUCATION

State Primary (2004/05): 35 schools, 6,653 students.

State Secondary (2004/05): 5 schools, 4,788 students.

College (2004/05): 1 college, 8,300 students.

There are, in addition, two private schools.

Directory

The Constitution

The Head of State of the Isle of Man is the British monarch as the Lord of Mann. The Lieutenant-Governor, who is the Crown's personal representative on the island, is appointed by the Head of State for a five-year term. The legislature is Tynwald, comprising two branches, the Legislative Council and the House of Keys, sitting together as one body, but voting separately on all questions except in certain eventualities. The House of Keys, the lower chamber, has 24 members, who represent single member and multi-member constituencies and are elected by adult suffrage for five years. Eight of the 11 members of the Legislative Council are elected by the House of Keys. The remainder are ex officio members: the Lord Bishop of Sodor and Man, the Attorney-General and the President of Tynwald, who is elected by all the members of Tynwald.

The Government

HEAD OF STATE

Lord of Mann: HM Queen ELIZABETH II.
Lieutenant-Governor: Sir PAUL HADDACKS.

COUNCIL OF MINISTERS
(April 2008)

Chief Minister: ANTHONY (TONY) BROWN.
Minister of Agriculture, Fisheries and Forestry: PHIL GAWNE.
Minister of Education: ANNE CRAINE.
Minister of Health and Social Security: EDDIE TEARE.
Minister of Home Affairs: MARTYN QUAYLE.
Minister of Local Government and the Environment: JOHN SHIMMIN.
Minister of Tourism and Leisure: ADRIAN EARNSHAW.
Minister of Trade and Industry: DAVID CRETNEY.
Minister of Transport: DAVID ANDERSON.
Minister of the Treasury: ALLAN BELL.

UNITED KINGDOM CROWN DEPENDENCIES   The Isle of Man

GOVERNMENT OFFICES

Isle of Man Government: Government Office, Bucks Rd, Douglas; tel. (1624) 6856711; fax (1624) 685710; e-mail chiefsecs@gov.im; internet www.gov.im.

Department of Agriculture, Fisheries and Forestry: Rose House, 51–59 Circular Rd, Douglas, IM1 1AZ; tel. (1624) 685835; e-mail daff@gov.im; internet www.gov.im/daff.

Department of Education: St George's Court, Upper Church St, Douglas, IM1 2SG; tel. (1624) 685820; fax (1624) 685834; e-mail admin@doe.gov.im; internet www.gov.im/education.

Department of Health and Social Security: Markwell House, Market St, Douglas, IM1 2RZ; tel. (1624) 685028; fax (1624) 685130; e-mail minister@dhss.gov.im; internet www.gov.im/dhss.

Department of Home Affairs: Homefield, 88 Woodbourne Rd, Douglas, IM2 3AP; tel. (1624) 694300; fax (1624) 621298; e-mail generalenquiries.dha@gov.im; internet www.gov.im/dha.

Department of Local Government and Environment: Murray House, Mount Havelock, Douglas, IM1 2SF; tel. (1624) 685954; e-mail ceo.dlge@gov.im; internet www.gov.im/dlge.

Department of Tourism and Leisure: St Andrew's House, Douglas, IM1 2PX; tel. (1624) 686801; e-mail dotl@gov.im; internet www.gov.im/tourism.

Department of Trade and Industry: Hamilton House, Peel Rd, Douglas, IM1 5EP; tel. (1624) 682354; fax (1624) 682355; e-mail dti@gov.im; internet www.gov.im/dti.

Department of Transport: Sea Terminal, Douglas, IM1 2RF; tel. (1624) 686600; e-mail enquiries@dot.gov.im.

Department of the Treasury: Government Office, Bucks Rd, Douglas; tel. (1624) 685586; e-mail treasuryadmin@gov.im; internet www.gov.im/treasury.

External Relations Division: Government Office, Bucks Rd, Douglas, IM1 3PN; tel. (1624) 685397; fax (1624) 685710; e-mail anne.shimmin@cso.gov.im; internet www.gov.im/cso/externalrelations.

Legislature

TYNWALD

President: NOEL QUAYLE CRINGLE.
Deputy President: STEPHEN CHARLES RODAN.

Legislative Council (Upper House)

President of the Council: NOEL QUAYLE CRINGLE.
Lord Bishop of Sodor and Man: (vacant).
Attorney-General: WILLIAM JOHN HOWARTH CORLETT.
Members appointed by the House of Keys: GEORGE HENRY WAFT, EDWARD ALAN CROWE, EDWARD GEORGE LOWEY, CLARE MARGARET CHRISTIAN, DAVID ALEXANDER, DUDLEY MICHAEL WILLIAM BUTT, ALEXANDER FRANK DOWNIE, JUAN RICHARD TURNER.
Clerk: JONATHAN KING.

House of Keys (Lower House)

Speaker: STEPHEN CHARLES RODAN.
Clerk of Tynwald, Secretary of the House and Counsel to the Speaker: MALACHY CORNWELL-KELLY.

The House of Keys consists of 24 members, elected by adult suffrage for five years—eight for Douglas, two for Ramsey, one each for Peel and Castletown, and 12 for rural districts. The last general election took place on 23 November 2006. The next general election was scheduled to be held in November 2011. Most members of the House of Keys are elected as independents. However, a small number are affiliated to political parties.

Political Organizations

Liberal Vannin: White Cot, King Edward's Rd, Onchan; tel. (1624) 626379; e-mail peter.karran@liberalvannin.org; internet www.liberalvannin.org; f. 2006; Leader PETER KARRAN.

Manx Labour Party: f. 1918.

Mec Vannin: internet www.mecvannin.im; f. 1962; advocates the establishment of the Isle of Man as a sovereign republic; Pres. BERNARD MOFFATT; Chair. MARK KERMODE.

Judicial System

The Isle of Man is, for legal purposes, an autonomous sovereign country under the British Crown, with its own legislature and its own independent judiciary administering its own common or customary and statute law. The law of the Isle of Man is, in most essential matters, the same as the law of England and general principles of equity administered by the English Courts are followed by the Courts of the Isle of Man unless they conflict with established local precedents. Her Majesty's High Court of Justice of the Isle of Man is based upon the English system but modified and simplified to meet local conditions. Justices of the Peace are appointed by the Lord Chancellor of Great Britain usually on the nomination of the Lieutenant-Governor. The Deemsters (see below), the High Bailiff, the Mayor of Douglas, and the Chairmen of the Town and Village Commissioners are ex-officio Justices of the Peace. The Manx Court of Appeal consists of the Deemsters and the Judge of Appeal.

First Deemster and Clerk of the Rolls: J.M. KERRUISH.
Second Deemster: D.C. DOYLE.
Judge of Appeal: G. F. TATTERSALL.

Religion

CHRISTIANITY

The Church of England

The Isle of Man forms the diocese of Sodor and Man, comprising 27 parishes. The parish church at Peel was designated a cathedral in 1980.

Lord Bishop of Sodor and Man: (vacant), Bishop's House, The Falls, Tromode Road, Cronkbourne, IM4 4PZ; tel. (1624) 622108; fax (1624) 672890; e-mail bishop-sodor@mcb.net.

Roman Catholic Church

The deanery of the Isle of Man is part of the archdiocese of Liverpool. There are eight Catholic churches on the island.

Dean of the Isle of Man: Very Rev. Canon BRENDAN ALGER, St Mary of the Isle, Douglas, IM1 3EG; tel. (1624) 675509.

Other Churches

There are also congregations of the following denominations: Baptist, Bethel Non-Denominational, Christadelphian, Congregational, Greek Orthodox, Independent Methodist, Methodist, Presbyterian, Elim Pentecostal, United Reformed, and Religious Society of Friends (Quakers); also Christian Science, Jehovah's Witnesses and the Church of Jesus Christ of Latter-day Saints.

There are small Bahá'í, Jewish and Muslim communities on the island.

The Press

Isle of Man Courier: Publishing House, Peel Rd, Douglas, IM1 5PZ; tel. (1624) 695695; fax (1624) 661041; e-mail john.sherrocks@newsiom.co.im; internet www.iomonline.co.im; f. 1884; weekly; Editor JOHN SHERROCKS; circ. 36,018.

Isle of Man Examiner: Publishing House, Peel Rd, Douglas, IM1 5PZ; tel. (1624) 695695; fax (1624) 661041; e-mail john.sherrocks@newsiom.co.im; internet www.iomonline.co.im; f. 1880; weekly; Editor JOHN SHERROCKS; circ. 14,436.

The Manx Independent: Publishing House, Peel Rd, Douglas, IM1 5PZ; tel. (1624) 695695; fax (1624) 661041; e-mail john.sherrocks@newsiom.co.im; internet www.iomonline.co.im; f. 1987; Friday; Editor JOHN SHERROCKS; circ. 12,711.

Manx Tails Magazine: Media House, Cronkbourne, Douglas, IM4 4SB; tel. (1624) 696560; fax (1624) 625623; e-mail mail@manninmedia.co.im; internet www.manninmedia.co.im/tails.html; monthly; Editor SIMON RICHARDSON.

Sea Breezes Magazine: Media House, Cronkbourne, Douglas, IM4 4SB; tel. (1624) 696573; fax (1624) 661655; e-mail seabreezes@manninmedia.co.im; internet www.seabreezes.co.im; f. 1919; Editor ANDREW DOUGLAS.

Publishers

Amulree Publications: Lossan y Twoaie, Glen Rd, Laxey, IM4 7AN; tel. (1624) 862238; e-mail amulree@mcb.net; internet www.mcb.net/amulree; Propr BILL SNELLING.

Electrochemical Publications Ltd: Asahi House, 10 Church Rd, Port Erin, IM9 6AQ; tel. (1624) 834941; fax (1624) 835400; e-mail sales@elchempub.com; internet www.elchempub.com; Man. Dir WILLIAM GOLDIE.

Grove Publishing Co: The Ballacrosha, Ballaugh, Sulby, IM7 5BP; tel. (1624) 897355.

Lily Publications Ltd: POB 33, Ramsey, IM99 4LP; tel. (1624) 898446; fax (1624) 898449; e-mail sales@lilypublications.co.uk; internet www.lilypublications.co.uk; f. 1991; Man. Dir MILES COWSILL.

Mannin Media Group Ltd: Media House, Cronkbourne, Douglas, IM4 4SB; tel. (1624) 696560; fax (1624) 625623; e-mail mail@manninmedia.co.im; internet www.manninmedia.co.im; Chief Exec. STEVEN BROWN.

The Manx Experience: Sunnybank Ave, Birch Hill, Onchan, IM3 3BW; tel. (1624) 627727; fax (1624) 663627; e-mail mail@manxexperience.co.uk; Man. Dirs GWYNNETH BROWN, COLIN BROWN.

Pines Press: The Pines, Ballelin, Maughold, Ramsey, IM7 1HJ; tel. (1624) 862030.

Keith Uren Publishing: 12 Manor Lane, Farmhill, Braddan, IM2 2NX; tel. and fax (1624) 611100; e-mail portfolio@manxe.net.

Vathek Publishing Ltd: Bridge House, Dalby, IM5 3BP; tel. (1624) 844056; fax (1624) 845043; e-mail mlw@vathek.com; internet www.vathek.com; legal journals; Man. Dir MAIRWEN LLOYD-WILLIAMS.

Broadcasting and Communications

Isle of Man Communications Commission: Salisbury House, Victoria St, Douglas, IM1 2LW; tel. (1624) 677022; fax (1624) 626499; e-mail margaret.king@cc.gov.im; internet www.gov.im/government/boards/cc.xml; appointed by the Isle of Man Government to represent the island's interests in all matters of telecommunications, radio and television; Chair. MARTYN QUAYLE; Dir ANTHONY HEWITT.

TELECOMMUNICATIONS

Manx Telecom Ltd: Isle of Man Business Park, Cooil Rd, Braddan, IM99 1HX; POB 100, Douglas, IM99 1HX; tel. (1624) 624624; fax (1624) 636011; e-mail mail@manx-telecom.com; internet www.manx-telecom.com; subsidiary of O$_2$ PLC; Man. Dir CHRIS HALL.

BROADCASTING
Radio and Television

BBC: Radio and Television (see United Kingdom).

ITV Border: Television (see United Kingdom).

Manx Radio: POB 1368, Douglas, IM99 1SW; tel. (1624) 682600; fax (1624) 682604; e-mail postbox@manxradio.com; internet www.manxradio.com; commercial station operated (by agreement with the Isle of Man Government) by Radio Manx Ltd; Chair. DAVID NORTH; Man. Dir ANTHONY PUGH.

The Isle of Man also receives television programmes from Channel 4 and five.

Finance

Isle of Man Government Financial Supervision Commission: POB 58, Finch Hill House, Bucks Rd, Douglas, IM99 1DT; tel. (1624) 689300; fax (1624) 689399; e-mail fsc@gov.im; internet www.fsc.gov.im; responsible for the licensing, authorization and supervision of banks, building societies, investment businesses, collective investment schemes and fiduciary service providers; also responsible for the Companies Registry; Chair. ROSEMARY PENN; Chief Exec. JOHN ASPDEN.

Treasury: Government Office, Bucks Rd, Douglas, IM1 3PU; tel. (1624) 685586; fax (1624) 685662; e-mail treasuryadmin@gov.im; internet www.gov.im/treasury; Minister ALLAN BELL; Chief Financial Officer P. M. SHIMMIN.

BANKING
(cap. = capital; res = reserves; dep. = deposits; m. = million; brs = branches; amounts in pounds sterling)

At 31 December 2007 total bank deposits in the Isle of Man amounted to some £50,540m., and there were 41 licensed banks and three building societies. The Financial Supervision Commission may allow a major bank to establish a presence on the island on a managed bank basis, by awarding an 'offshore' banking licence.

AIB Bank (CI) Ltd: POB 186, 10 Finch Rd, Douglas, IM99 1QE; tel. (1624) 639639; fax (1624) 639636; e-mail one@aiboffshore.com; internet www.alliedirishoffshore.com; f. 1977; cap. 10.0m., res 0.5m., dep. 1,587.0m. (Dec. 2005); Man. Dir D. J. MOYNIHAN.

Alliance & Leicester International Ltd: POB 226, 19–21 Prospect Hill, Douglas, IM99 1RY; tel. (1624) 663566; fax (1624) 663577; internet www.alil.co.im; Man. Dir SIMON HULL.

Anglo Irish Bank Corpn (IOM) PLC: Jubilee Bldgs, Victoria St, Douglas, IM1 2SH; tel. (1624) 698000; fax (1624) 698001; e-mail enquiries@angloirishbank.co.im; internet www.angloirishbank.co.im; Man. Dir STEWART DAVIES.

Bank of Ireland (IOM) Ltd: POB 246, Christian Rd, Douglas, IM99 1XF; tel. (1624) 644222; fax (1624) 644298; e-mail info@boiiom.com; internet www.boiiom.com; f. 1981; cap. 5m., res 0.06m., dep. 2,655.8m. (March 2007); Chair. J. L. M. QUINN; Chief Operating Officer MICHAEL MCKAY.

Barclays Private Bank and Trust (Isle of Man) Ltd: POB 48, Queen Victoria House, Victoria St, Douglas, IM99 1DF; tel. (1624) 682828; fax (1624) 620905; internet www.barclays.co.uk/privatebank; Man. Dir ALAN R. PATRICK.

Barclays Private Clients International Ltd: POB 213, Eagle Court, 25 Circular Rd, Douglas, IM99 1RH; tel. (1624) 684000; fax (1624) 684321; international banking services; Man. Dir T. PARKES; 6 brs.

Britannia International Ltd: POB 231, Britannia House, Athol St, Douglas, IM99 1SD; tel. (1624) 681100; fax (1624) 681105; e-mail enquiries@britanniainternational.com; internet www.britanniainternational.com; offshore subsidiary of Britannia Building Society; Man. Dir MARK BERESFORD.

Cayman National Bank and Trust Co (Isle of Man) Ltd: 4–8 Hope St, Douglas, IM1 1AQ; tel. (1624) 646900; fax (1624) 662192; e-mail banking@cnciom.com; internet www.cnciom.com; f. 1985; subsidiary of Cayman National Corpn, Cayman Islands; cap. 2.0m., dep. 12.5m (Sep. 2006); Man. Dir IAN BANCROFT.

Celtic Bank Ltd: POB 114, Celtic House, Victoria St, Douglas, IM99 1JW; tel. (1624) 622856; fax (1624) 620926; f. 1977; issued cap. 6.8m., res 7.9m., dep. 465.2m. (March 2007); Chair. RICHARD G. DANIELSON; Chief Exec. SIMON YOUNG.

Close Bank (Isle of Man) Ltd: POB 203, St George's Court, Upper Church St, Douglas, IM99 1RB; tel. (1624) 643200; fax (1624) 622039; e-mail infoiom@closepb.com; internet www.closepb.com; f. 1976 as Rea Brothers (Isle of Man) Ltd; present name adopted 1999; merchant bank; cap. 5.0m., dep. 269.0m. (July 2006); Man. Dir ANDREW HENTON.

Conister Trust PLC: Conister House, 16–18 Finch Rd, Douglas, IM1 2PT; tel. (1624) 694694; fax (1624) 624278; e-mail info@conistertrust.com; internet www.conistertrust.com; f. 1935; specializes in asset finance; cap. 7.1m., dep. 52.9m. (Dec. 2005); Chair. PETER HAMMONDS; CEO JERRY LINEHAN; 1 br.

Duncan Lawrie (IOM) Ltd: 14–15 Mount Havelock, Douglas, IM1 2QG; tel. (1624) 620770; fax (1624) 676315; e-mail iom@duncanlawrie.com; internet www.duncanlawrie.com; cap. 6.0m., dep. 100.2m. (Dec. 2005); Chair. P. J. FIELD; Man. Dir ALAN M. MOLLOY.

Fairbairn Private Bank (IOM) Ltd: St Mary's Court, 20 Hill St, Douglas, IM1 1EU; tel. (1624) 645000; fax (1624) 627218; e-mail iom@fairbairnpb.com; internet www.fairbairnpb.com; f. 1987 as Robert Fleming (IOM) Ltd; present name adopted 2004; cap. 5.0m., res 2.90m., dep. 485.6m. (Dec. 2006); Chair. H. ASKARI; Man. Dir G. J. HORTON.

Habib European Bank Ltd: 14 Athol St, Douglas, IM1 1JA; tel. (1624) 622554; fax (1624) 627135; e-mail habibbank@manx.net; internet www.habibbank.com; f. 1982; subsidiary of Habib Bank AG (Switzerland); cap. 5.0m., dep. 85.0m. (Dec. 2006); Gen. Man. A. SHAIKH.

Kaupthing Singer & Friedlander (Isle of Man) Ltd: POB 197, Samuel Harris House, 5–11 St George's St, Douglas, IM99 1SN; tel. (1624) 699222; fax (1624) 699200; e-mail international@kaupthing.com; internet www.kaupthing.co.im; f. 1971; private bank; owned by Kaupþing banki hf (Iceland); cap. 5.0m., res 32.1m., dep. 348.9m. (Dec. 2005); Chair. L. DOHERTY; Man. Dir A. A. DOHERTY.

Lloyds TSB Offshore Ltd: Victory House, Prospect Hill, Douglas, IM99 1AH; tel. (1624) 638000; fax (1624) 673435; e-mail iiompersbkg@lloydstsb-offshore.com; internet www.lloydstsb-offshore.com; cap. 207.8m., res 11.6m., dep. 626.7m (Dec. 2006); 5 brs.

Nationwide International Ltd: POB 217, 5–11 St George's St, Douglas, IM99 1RN; tel. (1624) 696000; fax (1624) 696001; internet www.nationwideinternational.com; f. 1990; Chair. MATTHEW CARTER; Man. Dir CARL GANDY.

Standard Bank Isle of Man Ltd: Standard Bank House, 1 Circular Rd, Douglas, IM1 1SB; tel. (1624) 643643; fax (1624) 643800; e-mail sbiom@standardbank.com; internet www.sboff.com; f. 1972 as Standard Chartered Bank (Isle of Man) Ltd; present name adopted 1995; cap. 5.0m., res 11.9m., dep. 974.7m. (Dec. 2005); Man. Dir J. COYLE.

Zurich Bank International Ltd: POB 422, Lord St, Douglas, IM99 3AF; tel. (1624) 671666; fax (1624) 627526; e-mail relationship.banking@zurich.com; internet www.zurichbankinternational.com; f. 1983 as Dunbar International Ltd; present name adopted 2003; Chair. CHRIS GIBSON; Man. Dir GRAHAM SHEWARD.

'Offshore' Banks

AbbeyInternational: POB 150, Abbey House, Circular Rd, Douglas, IM99 1NH; tel. (1624) 644800; fax (1624) 644691; e-mail customerservices@abbeyinternational.com; internet www.abbeyinternational.com; Man. Dir P. BRACKPOOL.

Bank of Scotland International Ltd: POB 19, Prospect Hill, Douglas, IM99 1AT; tel. (1624) 613500; fax (1624) 759280; e-mail enquiry@bankofscotlandint.com; internet www.bankofscotlandinternational.com; f. 1976; Chair. PETER JACKSON.

Bradford & Bingley International Ltd: 30 Ridgeway St, Douglas, IM1 1TA; tel. (1624) 695000; fax (1624) 695001; e-mail enquiries@bbi.co.im; internet www.bbi.co.im; f. 1989; subsidiary of Bradford & Bingley PLC; cap. and res 266m. (Dec. 2006); Man. Dir JOHN SHEATH.

Coutts (IOM) International Ltd: 1 Prospect Hill, Douglas, IM1 1ES; tel. (1624) 632276; fax (1624) 620988; internet www.coutts.com; Gen. Man. P. WEYNANDT.

Isle of Man Bank Ltd: POB 13, 2 Athol St, Douglas IM99 1AN; tel. (1624) 637000; fax (1624) 624686; internet www.iombank.com; f. 1865; cap. 7.5m., res 137.7m., dep. 1,519.2m. (Dec. 2006); bankers to Isle of Man Govt; mem. of the Royal Bank of Scotland Group; Chair. JAMES MORRIS; 11 brs.

The Royal Bank of Scotland International Ltd: POB 151, Royal Bank House, 2 Victoria St, Douglas, IM99 1NJ; tel. (1624) 646464; fax (1624) 646497; e-mail marketingiom@rbsint.com; internet www.rbsint.com; Chief Exec. IAN HENDERSON.

Restricted Banks

Irish Permanent International: 12–14 Ridgeway St, Douglas, IM1 1EN; tel. (1624) 641641; fax (1624) 676795; e-mail info@irishpermanentintl.com; internet www.irishpermanentintl.com; Man. Dir PHILIP MURRAY.

Merrill Lynch Bank and Trust Co (Cayman) Ltd: Belgravia House, 34–44 Circular Rd, Douglas, IM1 1QW; tel. (1624) 688600; fax (1624) 688601; Man. N. ORDERS.

INSURANCE

There were 184 authorized insurance companies in the Isle of Man at 31 December 2006, including:

Canada Life International Ltd: St Mary's, The Parade, Castletown, IM9 1RJ; tel. (1624) 820200; fax (1624) 820201; e-mail customer.support@canadalifeint.com; internet www.canadalifeint.com; f. 1987; Man. Dir TONY PARRY.

Castletown Insurance Services Ltd: Compton House, Parliament Sq., Castletown, IM9 1LA; tel. (1624) 827710; fax (1624) 827709; e-mail rdrinkwater@castletowninsurance.com; internet www.castletowninsurance.com; f. 1998; Jt Man. Dirs CHRISTINE CROWTHER, RICHARD DRINKWATER.

CMI Insurance Co Ltd: Clerical Medical House, Victoria Rd, Douglas, IM99 1LT; tel. (1624) 638888; fax (1624) 625900; e-mail iom.policyadministration1@clericalmedical.com; part of the HBOS Group.

Friends Provident International Ltd: Royal Court, Castletown, IM9 1RA; tel. (1624) 821212; fax (1624) 824405; e-mail servicedesk@fpiom.com; internet www.fpinternational.com; Man. Dir PAUL QUIRK.

Hansard International Ltd: POB 192, Harbour Court, Lord St, Douglas, IM99 1QL; tel. (1624) 688000; fax (1624) 688008; e-mail enquiries@hansard.com; internet www.hansard.com; Exec. Chair. Dr LEONARD S. POLONSKY.

Isle of Man Assurance Ltd: IOMA House, Hope St, Douglas, IM1 1AP; tel. (1624) 681200; fax (1624) 681391; e-mail info@ioma.co.im; internet www.ioma.co.im; Chair. ROBIN BIGLAND; Man. Dir NIGEL WOOD.

Royal Insurance Service Co (IOM) Ltd: Jubilee Bldgs, 1 Victoria St, Douglas, IM99 1BF; tel. (1624) 645947; fax (1624) 620934; Man. DAVID STACEY.

Royal Skandia Life Assurance Ltd: POB 159, Skandia House, King Edward Rd, Onchan, IM99 1NU; tel. (1624) 655555; fax (1624) 611715; e-mail support@royalskandia.com; internet www.royalskandia.com.

Scottish Provident International Life Assurance Ltd: Provident House, Ballacottier Business Park, Cooil Rd, Douglas, IM2 2SP; tel. (1624) 681681; fax (1624) 677336; e-mail csc@spila.com; internet www.spila.com; f. 1991; subsidiary of Resolution PLC; Man. Dir LILLIAN BOYLE.

Tower Insurance Co Ltd: POB 27, Jubilee Bldgs, 1 Victoria St, Douglas, IM99 1BF; tel. (1624) 673446; fax (1624) 663664; e-mail tower.insurance@uk.royalsun.com; internet www.towerinsurance.co.im; subsidiary of Royal and Sun Alliance PLC; Dir DAVID STACEY.

Zurich International Life Ltd: 43–51 Athol St, Douglas, IM99 1EF; tel. (1624) 662266; fax (1624) 662038; internet www.zurichintlife.com.

Insurance Association

Insurance and Pensions Authority: 4th Floor, HSBC House, Ridgeway St, Douglas, IM1 1ER; tel. (1624) 646000; fax (1624) 646001; e-mail ipa@gov.im; internet www.gov.im/ipa; Chief Exec. DAVID VICK.

Trade and Industry

CHAMBER OF COMMERCE

Isle of Man Chamber of Commerce: 17 Drinkwater St, Douglas, IM1 1PP; tel. (1624) 674941; fax (1624) 663367; e-mail enquiries@iomchamber.org.im; internet www.iomchamber.org.im; 400 mems; Pres. STUART MCCUDDEN; Chair. JOHN HOLLIS; Chief Exec. BARBARA O'HANLON.

UTILITIES

Electricity

Manx Electricity Authority: POB 177, Douglas, IM99 1PS; tel. (1624) 687687; fax (1624) 687612; e-mail mea@gov.im; internet www.gov.im/mea; Chair. EDDIE TEARE; Chief Exec. ASHTON LEWIS.

Gas

Manx Gas Ltd: Murdoch House, South Quay, Douglas, IM1 5PA; tel. (1624) 644444; fax (1624) 626528; e-mail info@manxgas.co.im; internet www.manxgas.com; f. 1999 by merger of Douglas Gas and Calor Manx Gas; Man. Dir C. J. SIDLEY.

Water

Isle of Man Water Authority: Drill Hall, Tromode Rd, Douglas, IM2 5PA; tel. (1624) 695949; fax (1624) 695956; e-mail water@gov.im; internet www.gov.im/water; Chair. DAVID CANNAN; Chief Exec. JOHN SMITH.

TRADE UNIONS

In 1991 the Trade Union Act was approved by Tynwald, providing for the registration of trade unions. Although trade unions had been active previously on the Isle of Man, they had not received legal recognition.

Manx Fish Producers' Organization Ltd: Heritage Centre, The Quay, Peel, IM5 1TA; tel. (1624) 842144; fax (1624) 844395; e-mail manx.fa@lineone.net; Chair. GEOFF COMBER.

Manx National Farmers' Union: Agriculture House, Ballafletcher Farm Rd, Tromode, IM4 4QE; tel. (1624) 662204; e-mail gensec@manx-nfu.org; internet www.manx-nfu.org; Pres. HOWARD QUAYLE.

Unite—T&G Section: 25 Fort St, Douglas, IM2 2LJ; tel. (1624) 621156; fax (1624) 673115; Regional Industrial Organizer MICK HEWER.

Transport

RAILWAYS

Isle of Man Transport: Transport Headquarters, Banks Circus, Douglas, IM1 5PT; tel. (1624) 662525; fax (1624) 663637; e-mail info@busandrail.dtl.gov.im; internet www.iombusandrail.info; 29 km (18 miles) of electric track; also 25 km (16 miles) of steam railway track, and Snaefell Mountain Railway (7 km of electric track); 85 buses; Head of Rail Services (vacant); Head of Bus Services STEVE HOWSON.

ROADS

There are over 805 km (500 miles) of roads on the Isle of Man.

Dept of Transport: Sea Terminal, Douglas, IM1 2RF; tel. (1624) 686600; fax (1624) 686617; e-mail enquiries@dot.gov.im; internet www.gov.im/transport; Chief Exec. IAN THOMPSON.

Isle of Man Transport: see above.

SHIPPING

Isle of Man Steam Packet Co Ltd: Imperial Bldgs, Douglas, IM1 2BY; tel. (1624) 645645; fax (1624) 645609; internet www.steam-packet.com; f. 1830; daily services operate all the year round between Douglas and Heysham and Liverpool; during the summer there are frequent services between the island and Dublin and Belfast; Chair. JUAN KELLY; Man. Dir MARK WOODWARD; fleet of 1 passenger/car ferry, 1 ro-ro passenger/freight ferry and 2 Seacat Fastcraft.

Mezeron Ltd: East Quay, Ramsey, IM8 1BG; tel. (1624) 812302; fax (1624) 815613; e-mail mezeron@mezeronuk.co.uk; f. 1983; cargo services; Man. Dir N. A. LEECE.

Ramsey Steamship Co Ltd: 8 Auckland Terrace, Parliament St, Ramsey, IM8 1AF; tel. (1624) 816202; fax (1624) 816206; e-mail tony@ramsey-steamship.com; internet www.ramsey-steamship.com; f. 1913; cargo services; Man. Dir A. G. KENNISH.

Tufton Oceanic Investments Ltd: 2nd Floor, St George's Court, Upper Church St, Douglas, IM1 1EE; tel. (1624) 663616; fax (1624)

663918; e-mail tufton@tuftonoceanic.com; internet www.tuftonoceanic.com; Chair. TAKIS KLERIDES; Man. Dir CATO BRAHDE.

CIVIL AVIATION

Eastern Airways: Ronaldsway Airport, Ballasalla, IM9 2AS; tel. (1652) 680600; e-mail information@easternairways.com; internet www.easternairways.com; daily scheduled passenger services to Birmingham, Bristol, Newcastle and Southampton.

Island Aviation and Travel Ltd: Ronaldsway Airport, Ballasalla, IM9 2AS; tel. (1624) 824300; fax (1624) 824946; e-mail enquiries@iaat.co.uk; internet www.iaat.co.uk; provides executive charters to world-wide destinations, runs air-ambulance services, aircraft management, handling.

Manx2: Ronaldsway Airport, Ballasalla, IM9 2AS; tel. (1624) 822111; e-mail customer.services@manx2.com; internet www.manx2.com; scheduled passenger flights to Belfast, Blackpool, Gloucester, Jersey and Leeds/Bradford; Chair. NOEL HAYES; Gen. Man. DYLAN EVANS.

Tourism

In 2006 a total of 219,100 tourists stayed at least one night on the Isle of Man.

Dept of Tourism and Leisure, Tourism Division: St Andrew's House, Douglas, IM1 2PX; tel. (1624) 686801; fax (1624) 686800; e-mail tourism@gov.im; internet www.visitisleofman.com; responsibilities of tourist board, also operates modern and vintage transport systems, a Victorian theatre and an indoor and outdoor sport and leisure complex; f. 1896; CEO CAROL GLOVER.

UNITED KINGDOM OVERSEAS TERRITORIES

From February 1998 the British Dependent Territories were referred to as the United Kingdom Overseas Territories, following the announcement of the interim findings of a British government review of the United Kingdom's relations with the Overseas Territories. In March 1999 draft legislation confirming this change was published by the British Government: under the proposed legislation, the citizens of Overseas Territories would be granted the rights, already enjoyed by the citizens of Gibraltar and the Falkland Islands, to British citizenship and of residence in the United Kingdom. These entitlements were not reciprocal, and British citizens would not enjoy the same rights with regard to the Overseas Territories. The British Overseas Territories Act entered effect in May 2002. The British Government meanwhile announced its determination to ensure that legislation in the Overseas Territories adhered to British and European Union standards, particularly in the areas of financial regulation and human rights.

ANGUILLA

Introductory Survey

Location, Climate, Language, Religion, Flag, Capital

Anguilla, a coralline island, is the most northerly of the Leeward Islands, lying 113 km (70 miles) to the north-west of Saint Christopher (St Kitts) and 8 km (5 miles) to the north of St Maarten/St Martin. Also included in the territory are the island of Sombrero, 48 km (30 miles) north of Anguilla, and several other uninhabited small islands. The climate is sub-tropical, the heat and humidity being tempered by the trade winds. Temperatures average 27°C (80°F) and mean annual rainfall is 914 mm (36 ins), the wettest months being September to December. English is the official language. Many Christian churches are represented, the principal denominations being the Anglican and Methodist Churches. The flag (proportions 3 by 5 on land, 1 by 2 at sea) has a dark blue field with the Union flag in the upper hoist corner and, in the centre of the fly, a white shield bearing three orange circling dolphins above a light blue base. The capital is The Valley.

Recent History

Anguilla, previously inhabited by Arawaks and Caribs, was a British colony from 1650 until 1967. From 1825 the island became increasingly associated with Saint Christopher (St Kitts) for administrative purposes (also see chapter on Saint Christopher and Nevis). The inhabitants of Anguilla petitioned for separate status in 1875 and 1958. In February 1967, however, St Christopher-Nevis-Anguilla assumed the status of a State in Association with the United Kingdom, as did four other former British colonies in the Eastern Caribbean. These Associated States became independent internally, while the British Government retained responsibility for external affairs and defence.

In May 1967 the Anguillans, under the leadership of Ronald Webster, a local businessman and head of the only political party, the People's Progressive Party (PPP), repudiated government from Saint Christopher. After attempts to repair the breach between Saint Christopher and Anguilla had failed, British security forces were deployed in Anguilla in March 1969 to install a British Commissioner. Members of London's Metropolitan Police Force remained on the island until the Anguilla Police Force was established in 1972. In July 1971 the British Parliament approved the Anguilla Act, one clause of which stipulated that, should Saint Christopher-Nevis-Anguilla decide to end its associated status, Anguilla could be separated from the other islands. In August the British Government's Anguilla Administration Order 1971 determined that the British Commissioner would continue to be responsible for the direct administration of the island, with the co-operation of a local elected council. The terms of this Order were superseded by the introduction of a new Constitution in February 1976. Anguilla formally separated from Saint Christopher-Nevis-Anguilla on 19 December 1980, assuming the status of British Dependent Territory. In accordance with the terms of the British Government's Anguilla Constitution Order of 1982, a new Constitution came into operation in Anguilla on 1 April 1982.

Legislative elections were held in March 1976, and Webster was appointed Chief Minister. In February 1977, following his defeat on a motion of confidence, he was replaced by Emile Gumbs as Chief Minister and as leader of the PPP (renamed the Anguilla National Alliance—ANA—in 1980). Webster was returned to power, to lead the recently formed Anguilla United Party (AUP), at a general election in May 1980. The dismissal of the Minister of Agriculture in May 1981 led to serious divisions within the Government, and the resignation in sympathy of another minister precipitated the collapse of Webster's administration. Webster subsequently formed a new political party, the Anguilla People's Party (APP), which won five of the seven seats in a general election in June. An early general election in March 1984 resulted in a conclusive defeat for the APP, including the loss of Webster's own seat. Gumbs became Chief Minister, and pursued a policy of revitalizing the island's economy, mainly through tourism and attracting foreign investment. Webster resigned from the leadership of the APP, which was renamed the Anguilla Democratic Party (ADP).

The majority of the population expressed no desire for independence, but the new Government appealed for wider powers for the Executive Council, and for more aid and investment from the United Kingdom in the island's economy and infrastructure. In October 1985 the Governor appointed a committee to review the Constitution, in response to an earlier unanimous request from the House of Assembly for modifications, particularly concerning the status of women and of persons born overseas of Anguillan parents. The amendments, which provided for the appointment of a Deputy Governor and designated international financial affairs (the 'offshore' banking sector) as the Governor's responsibility, came into effect in May 1990.

Gumbs remained Chief Minister following a general election in February 1989. The ANA won only three seats in the House of Assembly but was supported by the independent member, Osbourne Fleming, who retained his cabinet portfolio. The ADP secured one seat and the revived AUP won two.

In May 1991 the British Government abolished capital punishment for the crime of murder in Anguilla (as well as in several other British Dependent Territories).

A general election in March 1994 failed to produce a clear majority for any one party, and a coalition was subsequently formed by the ADP and the AUP, which had each won two seats and, respectively, secured 31% and 11% of total votes cast. The ANA, under the leadership of Eric Reid, won two seats with 36% of the vote, while the remaining seat was secured by Fleming. The AUP leader, Hubert Hughes, was subsequently appointed Chief Minister, replacing Sir Emile Gumbs (as he had become). On becoming Chief Minister, Hughes immediately stated that he might seek Anguilla's independence from the United Kingdom.

In October 1995 the island suffered severe damage from 'Hurricane Luis'. Destruction of buildings and infrastructure, as well as damage to the agricultural sector, was estimated to be worth some EC $72m. Hughes was highly critical of the British Government's response to the hurricane, which he alleged was inadequate. In May 1997 Robert Harris, hitherto Deputy Governor, assumed office as Governor.

The announcement by the British Government in January 1997 that it was considering the extension of its powers in the Dependent Territories of the Caribbean attracted further criticism from Hughes. The proposed reintroduction of reserve powers, whereby the Governor (with the consent of the British Government) can amend, veto or introduce legislation without the agreement of the local legislature, provoked accusations from Hughes that the United Kingdom hoped to create a situation in which territories would be forced to seek independence. The British Government, however, maintained that the initiative had been prompted largely by a desire to secure Anguilla's financial services sector from exploitation by criminal organizations, particularly drugs-traffickers (which had remained a problem, owing to the territory's bank secrecy laws).

In September 1997 Hughes publicly denounced Robert Harris for being oblivious to his country's needs, and, furthermore, made allegations of corruption within the Civil Service Association (CSA). The CSA denied the claim and immediately requested a public apology. Meanwhile Osbourne Fleming pressed for Hughes' resignation, claiming that the remarks were unjustified and jeopardized public and investor confidence in the Government.

In May 1998 Hughes announced that public consultations would be undertaken on a proposal to reform Anguilla's constitutional status in the hope that a reformed Constitution could be in place before the general election, scheduled for March 1999. Hughes criticized the current Constitution for vesting executive authority in the Governor rather than in locally elected ministers. Hughes ruled out any prospect of creating a Senate on the grounds of the cost involved. In September 1998, however, the British Government announced that its Overseas Dependencies were to be renamed United Kingdom Overseas Territories. In March 1999 the British Government issued a policy document confirming the change of name, and guaranteeing citizens of Overseas Dependencies the right to British citizenship. The proposals also included the requirement that the Constitutions of Overseas Territories should be revised in order to conform to British and international standards. The process of revision of the Anguillan Constitution began in September 1999.

Following the general election of 4 March 1999 the composition of the legislature remained unaltered. The AUP-ADP coalition therefore kept control of the House of Assembly, and the four members of the Executive Council retained their portfolios.

In May 1999 the two ADP ministers threatened to withdraw from the coalition Government, accusing Hughes of excluding them from the decision-making process, and in June the ADP leader, Victor Banks, resigned his post as Minister of Finance and Economic Development, and withdrew from the ruling coalition. The other ADP minister, Edison Baird, refused, however, to resign his post, and was subsequently expelled from the party. Although Banks' resignation deprived the AUP-ADP coalition of its majority in the House of Assembly, Hughes announced that he did not intend to resign his position. Banks and the three members of the opposition ANA therefore withdrew from the House, demanding that fresh elections be held. Lacking the necessary quorum in the legislature, the Government was unable to implement policy or to introduce a budget for 1999/2000.

In January 2000 legal proceedings begun by Hughes, in an attempt to compel the Speaker to convene the House of Assembly, were rejected by the High Court. Hughes therefore announced that he would hold legislative elections in March 2000. At the elections, held on 3 March, the ANA won three seats, the AUP two, and the ADP one, while Edison Baird was elected as an independent. The ANA and the ADP, which had formed an electoral alliance, known as the Anguilla United Front, prior to the elections, therefore gained control of the House of Assembly. The leader of the ANA, Osbourne Fleming, was subsequently appointed the Chief Minister of an Executive Council that included two other ANA ministers, while Victor Banks was again appointed Minister of Finance, Economic Development, Investment and Commerce.

In February 2000 the Governor, Robert Harris, departed the island. Harris, who had reportedly been extremely frustrated by the island's political crisis, suggested that he had found it very difficult to work closely with the Government of Anguilla. Peter Johnstone replaced Harris as Governor, who, in turn, was replaced by Alan Huckle in May 2004.

Following Anguilla's inclusion on an Organisation for Economic Co-operation and Development (OECD, see p. 347) blacklist of tax havens in 2000, the Government introduced a number of articles of legislation to combat money-laundering on the island, including the establishment of a 'Money Laundering Reporting Authority'. OECD removed Anguilla from the list in March 2002, declaring that the Government had made sufficient commitments to improve transparency and effective exchange of information on tax matters by the end of 2005. In late 2002, however, the burgeoning financial sector faced further disruption when the United Kingdom, under pressure from the European Union (EU, see p. 244), as part of its effort to investigate tax evasion, demanded that Anguilla disclose the identities and account details of Europeans holding private savings accounts on the island. Anguilla, along with some other British Overseas Territories facing similar demands, claimed it was being treated unfairly compared with more powerful European countries, such as Switzerland and Luxembourg. In February 2004 a new financial regulatory body, the Anguilla Financial Services Commission, commenced operations. The Commission replaced the Financial Services Department of the Ministry of Finance and represented a further commitment to transparency within the sector.

In June 2001 the Government officially approved the draft of its National Telecommunications Policy, which would liberalize the sector. Although the legislation still needed to pass through parliament, in April 2003 Cable & Wireless, the country's sole telecommunications provider, signed an agreement with the Government to open the market for competition. The opposition argued that a single operator was more suitable in a country as small as Anguilla, where economies of scale were not achievable. It was argued that the proposed legislation could lead to a reduction in investment and consequent job losses.

In August 2003 the Government sold 6m. shares at US $1 each in the Anguilla Electricity Company, a profit-making public utility, in order to raise funds for the US $20m. expansion and reconstruction of Wallblake Airport. The proceeds of the sale were to go towards lengthening the airport's runway in order to accommodate larger aircraft. The AUP leader Hubert Hughes criticized the sale as unnecessary and questioned the transparency of the process.

In May 2004 Edison Baird replaced Hubert Hughes as Leader of the Opposition after Albert Hughes resigned from the AUP and transferred his support to Baird. Baird later formed a new political party, the Anguilla National Strategic Alliance (ANSA), in advance of the general election, which was constitutionally due by June 2005.

At the general election, which was held on 21 February 2005, the Anguilla United Front (the AUF, comprising the ANA and the ADP) secured four seats and 38.9% of the votes cast; the remaining three seats were shared by the Anguilla United Movement (as the AUP had been renamed, with one seat and 19.4% of the votes) and the ANSA (two seats and 19.2% of the ballot). The remaining 23% of the votes were shared between independent candidates and the Anguilla Progressive Party. Turn-out was 74.6%—considerably higher than expected. Analysts were also surprised by the scale of the AUF's victory; a closer contest had been expected, but the alliance campaigned strongly on the success of its infrastructural improvements, particularly the expansion of Wallblake Airport, during its previous administration. Fleming announced a new Executive Council on 22 February. The only change was the replacement as Minister of Education, Health, Social Development and Lands of Eric Reid, who retired and did not contest the election. Evans Rogers succeeded him.

In December 2005 the Government announced its intention to establish a new Constitutional and Electoral Reform Commission, to build on the work done by the previous electoral commission in 2001–04 in ascertaining the views of the people of Anguilla. The Commission began work in February 2006; key issues to be addressed were the fundamental rights and freedoms outlined in the Constitution, the powers of the Governor and the size of the House of Assembly. A report detailing the Commission's recommendations was submitted to the Governor in August, but elicited no publicly acknowledged response until March 2007, a delay which provoked anti-Government criticism—albeit limited and peaceful—from Anguillans. A public announcement by the Office of the Chief Minister in that month indicated that the Government was to receive a delegation from the British Foreign and Commonwealth Office (FCO) in July to facilitate discussions towards constitutional reform. This necessitated a preliminary review of the Commission's recommendations, together with public consultations, prior to the FCO representatives' arrival. The first in an extensive series of such reviews was convened in early March and attended by parliamentary representatives and the Chairman of the Constitutional and Electoral Reform Commission. While several sections of the extant Constitution were regarded by the Commission as still relevant and adequate, areas identified as problematic and in most urgent need of amendment included the administration of justice—particularly to reflect the abolition of the death penalty—transparency in judicial proceedings, enforcement of constitutional rights, and the appointment of the island Governor and deputies.

In addition, concern had been expressed that the existing number of ministers in the Executive Council (or 'Cabinet', in accordance with the Commission's proposals) was insufficient for the dispatch of governmental responsibilities and should be increased, but that the ratio of ministers to non-ministerial representatives in the House of Assembly should not exceed 50%; it was proposed that members of the Council be increased from three to five ministers, in addition to the Chief Minister (or 'Premier' under the recommendations). The Cabinet would comprise these six members, each awarded a vote, together with the Deputy Governor and the Attorney-General, who would remain without voting authority. The Premier would replace the Governor as chairman of the Cabinet, although the latter would retain the right to be informed by, consult and advise the Cabinet. Further, it was suggested that the size of the Assembly be increased from seven elected members to 13. (Should it be concluded that seven ministers be appointed in addition to the Chief Minister, the Assembly should grow to 15 members in order to accommodate the recommended majority of non-ministerial members.) An expanded Assembly, it was suggested, would also obviate the need for a Parliamentary Secretary. It was also proposed that, in the event of a motion of 'no confidence' being brought in the Assembly, there would be recourse to the pre-1982 Constitution, whereby the Governor would exercise discretion as to whether to call a general election. Such a motion might be upheld by a simple majority vote, as opposed to the existing two-thirds' majority requirement. An existing provision, reportedly not yet exercised, affording the Governor alternative powers to force legislation through the House of Assembly was considered a threat to democracy and the Commission urged for its repeal; similarly, the rescision of powers previously vested in the Secretary of State to disallow legislation passed by the Governor was advised, on the basis that such a provision was no longer required.

The Commission also proposed extensive electoral reform: *inter alia*, the institution of an independent Boundaries Commission was put forward, as was thorough revision of the Election Act. The abolition of the Judicial Services Commission and establishment of a Judicial and Legal Services Commission as its successor, endowed with powers to influence the Governor's judicial appointments, was also suggested and constituted a measure more consistent with other Caribbean states under the jurisdiction of the Eastern Caribbean Supreme Court. The embedding of the Financial Services Commission and its regulatory authority within the constitution was also promulgated in order to enhance supervision of the financial services industry in Anguilla.

Interpreted broadly, the Commission's recommendations sought to advance Anguilla's ambitions towards greater self-determination and the democratic, inclusive administration of its own affairs, gradually reducing the influence of the Government of the United Kingdom—upon whose unilateral authority so many of its existing constitutional statutes were premised. The institution of independent public service and advisory bodies, was intended to equip a future government with the appropriate consultative resources to generate more comprehensive and effective legislative proposals for the advancement of Anguilla and the protection of its people.

Alan Huckle was succeeded by Andrew George as Governor in July 2006. The country's first indigenous Deputy Governor, lawyer Stanley Everton Reid, was sworn in later that month.

The proposed visit by a five-member delegation from the FCO to discuss constitutional reform, scheduled to take place between 23 and 27 July 2007, was postponed—only days in advance—by the Anguillan Government in order that further public consultations might be conducted. The Government confirmed, however, that it would be seeking 'full internal self-government' for Anguilla, and at the end of April 2008 it announced the commencement of work on a draft constitution.

In May 2002 the British Overseas Territories Act, having received royal assent in the United Kingdom in February, came into force and granted British citizenship to the people of its Overseas Territories, including Anguilla. Under the new law Anguillans would be able to hold British passports and work in the United Kingdom and anywhere else in the EU.

In July 2005 the Governments of Anguilla and the British Virgin Islands announced the formal establishment of the maritime boundary between the two territories. The boundary had been agreed in 2002 following discussions facilitated by the British Government. Co-operation between British Virgin Islands customs officials and their Anguillan counterparts enabled the recovery of a substantial quantity of drugs from a container vessel impounded in Anguilla in July 2006; the haul, comprising over 140 packages of compressed cannabis with an estimated street value of over US $1,500 per pound, was thought to be the largest ever seized on the island and an indication of the success of joint law enforcement initiatives in the region.

Government

The Constitution vests executive power in a Governor, appointed by the British monarch. The Governor is responsible for external affairs, international financial affairs, defence and internal security. In most other matters the Governor acts on the advice of the Executive Council, led by the Chief Minister. Legislative power is held by the House of Assembly, comprising 11 members: two *ex officio*, two nominated by the Governor, and seven elected for five years by universal adult suffrage. The Executive Council is responsible to the House. A review of the Constitution was ongoing in 2008.

Economic Affairs

In 2006 the gross national income (GNI) of Anguilla, measured at current prices, was EC $594.75m., equivalent to EC $42,837 per head. During 1998–2006, it was estimated, the population increased at an average annual rate of 3.1%, while gross domestic product (GDP) per head increased, in real terms, by an average of 4.0% per year. Overall GDP increased, in real terms, at an average annual rate of 7.2% in 1998–2006; growth was 21.6% in 2006.

Agriculture (including crops, livestock and fishing) contributed 1.8% to GDP in 2006 and agriculture, fishing and mining engaged 3.3% of the employed labour force in 2002. Smallholders grow vegetables and fruit for domestic consumption; the principal crops are pigeon peas, sweet potatoes and maize. Livestock-rearing traditionally supplies significant export earnings, but the principal productive sector is the fishing industry (which is also a major employer). Real agricultural GDP increased by an annual average of 0.5% during 1998–2006, although growth was an estimated 5.1% in 2006.

Industry (including mining, manufacturing, construction, and power), which accounted 24.9% of GDP in 2006 and (not including the small mining sector) engaged 18.8% of the employed labour force in 2001, is traditionally based on salt production and shipbuilding. Real industrial GDP increased by an annual average of 9.9% in 1998–2006; the sector expanded dramatically in 2006, by 30.2%.

The mining and quarrying sector, contributed 1.8% of GDP in 2006 and engaged only 0.2% of the working population in 1992. Anguilla's principal mineral product is salt. Mining GDP increased by an annual average of 16.6% during 1998–2006; growth was 36.0% in 2006.

The manufacturing sector, accounting for 2.4% of employment in 2003 and for only 1.9% of GDP in 2006, consists almost entirely of boat-building and fisheries processing. Real manufacturing GDP increased by an annual average of 17.9% in 1998–2006. Sectoral GDP increased by 9.0% in 2006.

The construction industry, which engaged 14.9% of the employed labour force in 2001, accounted for 16.7% of GDP in 2006. Until a slowdown in the late 1990s, growth in the construction industry was very high, owing to reconstruction work necessitated by the effects of 'Hurricane Luis'. GDP in the construction sector increased at an annual average of 8.4% during 1998–2006, in real terms; the sector expanded dramatically in 2006, by an estimated 36.6%. Imported hydrocarbon fuels meet most energy needs.

The services sector accounted for 73.3% of GDP in 2006 and engaged 77.9% of the employed labour force in 2001. Tourism is increasingly the dominant industry of the economy, and is a catalyst for growth in other areas. The hotel and restaurant sector is the largest contributor to GDP, accounting for 25.7% of GDP in 2006. The hotel and restaurant sector increased by 17.5% in 2006. In 2006 tourism expenditure totalled EC $271.6m. The USA provided 53.6% of visitors (including excursionists) in 2005. The opening of Anguilla's first championship-standard golf course in late 2006 was expected further to contribute to tourism revenues. The 'offshore' financial institutions are also important contributors to the GDP of the service industry, with the banking and insurance sector contributing 10.7% of GDP in 2006. The real GDP of the services sector increased at an annual average of 6.4% in 1998–2006; growth was 10.5% in 2006.

In 2005 Anguilla recorded a merchandise trade deficit of EC $99.3m., and a deficit on the current account of the balance of payments of EC $53.3m. The trade deficit was partly offset by receipts from the 'invisibles' sector: tourism, financial services, remittances from Anguillans abroad and official assistance. The principal sources of imports are the USA, Puerto Rico and the Netherlands Antilles. The principal markets for exports are the USA and St Maarten. The main commodity exports are lobsters, fish, livestock and salt. Imports, upon which Anguilla is highly dependent, consist of foodstuffs, construction materials, manufactures, machinery and transport equipment. In late 2004 Anguilla began refining sugar for export, resulting in an increase in manufactured exports in the first six months of 2005.

In 2006, according to preliminary figures from the Eastern Caribbean Central Bank (ECCB, see p. 415), a budgetary deficit of EC $34.8m. was recorded (equivalent to 8.2% of GDP). Anguilla's external public debt totalled an estimated US $32.64m. in 2006. Development assistance was estimated to total US $3.1m. in 1998. Consumer prices increased by an annual average of 3.3% in 1996–2006; the average annual rate of inflation increased by 8.1% in 2006. Some 7.8% of the labour force were unemployed in July 2002 (compared with 26% in 1985).

In April 1987 Anguilla became the eighth member of the ECCB and in 2001 joined the regional stock exchange, the Eastern Caribbean Securities Exchange (based in Saint Christopher and Nevis), established in the same year. The territory is also a member of the Organisation of Eastern Caribbean States (OECS, see p. 425) and an associate member of the Association of Caribbean States (ACS, see p. 411) and the Economic Community for Latin America and the Caribbean (ECLAC, see p. 38). As a dependency of the United Kingdom, Anguilla has the status of Overseas Territory in association with the EU (see p. 244). In 1999 Anguilla was granted associate membership of the Caribbean Community and Common Market (CARICOM, see p. 196).

The island has developed its limited resources in recent years. Both tourism—which has become the dominant industry, resulting in a high level of activity in the construction industry during the 1990s—and the international financial sector have apparently benefited from the perceived stability of dependent status. However, Anguilla remains particularly vulnerable to adverse climatic conditions. This was demonstrated in October 1995, when 'Hurricane Luis' devastated the island, and again in November 1999, when damage caused by 'Hurricane Lenny' forced the temporary closure of the island's two largest tourist resorts. The Government of Osbourne Fleming, which took office in 2000, committed itself to increased expenditure and increased state investment in tourism, financial services and fisheries. The Government also hoped to establish the island as a centre for information technology and electronic commerce, and to raise revenue from the sale and leasing of internet domain names. A total of 3,041 new International Business Companies had been registered by the end of 2003. In February 2005 the Financial Services Commission introduced procedures, under the Anguilla Mutual Funds Act 2004, to allow the formation of mutual and hedge funds within 24 hours; it was hoped the new provisions would provide a further boost to the financial sector. In 2004 the banking and insurance sector expanded by an estimated 25.8%. Nevertheless, tourism remains the most important sector of the economy. Visitor arrivals in 2006 increased by some 12.5%, stimulating strong economic growth that year. Similar GDP growth was recorded in the first nine months of 2007, particularly in the construction and tourism industries. Consumer prices rose by just 1.1% over the same period, compared with 11.4% a year earlier, while tourism arrivals from the USA increased by 11.6%. There were concerns, however, that the island would not be able to maintain such a rapid growth rate. Demands on the labour supply, together with significantly increased imports and the rising cost of oil, have increased pressure on the economy.

Education

Education is free and compulsory between the ages of five and 16 years. Primary education begins at five years of age and lasts for six years. Secondary education, beginning at eleven years of age, lasts for a further six years. There are six government primary schools and one government secondary school. In 2004/05 enrolment at primary schools included 88.6% of children in the relevant age-group, while enrolment at secondary schools for that year included 80.8% of pupils in the relevant age-group. A 'comprehensive' secondary school education system was introduced in September 1986. Post-secondary education is undertaken abroad. According to the 2005 budget address, recurrent government expenditure on education in 2000–04 averaged 13.8% of total recurrent expenditure, the second largest government expenditure in a single sector after health.

Public Holidays

2008: 1 January (New Year's Day), 21 March (Good Friday), 24 March (Easter Monday), 1 May (Labour Day), 12 May (Whit Monday), 30 May (Anguilla Day), 16 June (Queen's Official Birthday), 4 August (August Monday), 7 August (August Thursday), 8 August (Constitution Day), 19 December (Separation Day), 25–26 December (Christmas).

2009: 1 January (New Year's Day), 10 April (Good Friday), 13 April (Easter Monday), 1 May (Labour Day), 30 May (Anguilla Day), 1 June (Whit Monday), 15 June (Queen's Official Birthday), 3 August (August Monday), 6 August (August Thursday), 7 August (Constitution Day), 19 December (Separation Day), 25–26 December (Christmas).

Weights and Measures

The metric system has been adopted, although imperial weights and measures are also used.

Statistical Survey

Source (unless otherwise stated): Government of Anguilla, The Secretariat, The Valley; tel. 497-2451; fax 497-3389; e-mail stats@gov.ai; internet gov.ai/statistics.

AREA AND POPULATION

Area (sq km): 96 (Anguilla 91, Sombrero 5).

Population: 11,561 (males 5,705, females 5,856) at census of 9 May 2001. *Mid-2006* : 13,884 (Source: Eastern Caribbean Central Bank).

Density (at mid-2006): 144.6 per sq km.

Principal Towns (population at 2001 census): South Hill 1,495; North Side 1,195; The Valley (capital) 1,169; Stoney Ground 1,133. *Mid-2003* (UN estimate, incl. suburbs): The Valley 1,380 (Source: UN, *World Urbanization Prospects: The 2003 Revision*).

Births, Marriages and Deaths (2006 unless otherwise indicated): Registered live births 183 (birth rate 12.8 per 1,000); Registered marriages 75 (marriage rate 6.1 per 1,000) in 2003; Registered deaths 59 (death rate 4.1 per 1,000). Source: partly UN, *Population and Vital Statistics Report*.

Expectation of Life (years at birth): 77.1 (males 74.2; females 80.1) in 2005 (Source: Pan American Health Organization).

Economically Active Population (persons aged 15 years and over, census of 9 May 2001): Agriculture, fishing and mining 183; Manufacturing 135; Electricity, gas and water 81; Construction 830; Trade 556; Restaurants and hotels 1,587; Transport, storage and communications 379; Finance, insurance, real estate and business services 433; Public administration, social security 662; Education, health and social work 383; Other community, social and personal services 164; Private households with employed persons 164; Activities not stated 871; *Total employed* 5,644 (males 3,014, females 2,630); Unemployed 406 (males 208, females 198); *Total labour force* 6,050 (males 3,222, females 2,828). *July 2002:* Total employed 5,496 (males 3,009, females 2,487); Unemployed 465 (males 204, females 261); Total labour force 5,961 (Source: ILO).

HEALTH AND WELFARE

Under-5 Mortality Rate (per 1,000 live births, 1997): 34.0.

Physicians (per 1,000 head, 2003): 1.2.

Health Expenditure (% of GDP, 1998): 4.92.

Sources: Caribbean Development Bank, *Social and Economic Indicators 2004* and Pan American Health Organization.

For definitions, see explanatory note on p. vi.

AGRICULTURE, ETC.

Fishing (metric tons, live weight, 2005, FAO estimates): Marine fishes 180, Caribbean spiny lobster 60, Stromboid conchs 10; Total catch 250. Source: FAO.

INDUSTRY

Electric Energy (million kWh): 55.33 in 2002; 58.39 in 2003; 62.07 in 2004.

FINANCE

Currency and Exchange Rates: 100 cents = 1 Eastern Caribbean dollar (EC $). *Sterling, US Dollar and Euro Equivalents* (30 November 2007): £1 sterling = EC $5.579; US $1 = EC $2.700; €1 = EC $3.985; EC $100 = £17.92 = US $37.04 = €27.09. *Exchange Rate:* Fixed at US $1 = EC $2.70 since July 1976.

Budget (EC $ million, 2006, preliminary): *Revenue:* Tax revenue 153.6 (Taxes on domestic goods and services 78.7, Taxes on international trade and transactions 74.3, Taxes on property 0.6); Non-tax revenue 27.6; Total 181.2. *Expenditure:* Current expenditure 145.2 (Personal emoluments 49.1, Other goods and services 52.2, Transfers and subsidies 37.6, Interest payments 6.3); Capital expenditure 43.2; Total 188.4. Source: Eastern Caribbean Central Bank, *Annual Economic and Financial Review 2006*.

Cost of Living (Consumer Price Index; base: 2000 = 100): All items 108.3 in 2004; 113.5 in 2005; 122.7 in 2006. Source: ILO.

Gross Domestic Product (EC $ million at constant 1990 prices): 221.39 in 2004; 245.17 in 2005; 281.88 in 2006. Source: Eastern Caribbean Central Bank.

Expenditure on the Gross Domestic Product (EC $ million at current prices, 2006): Government final consumption expenditure 117.23; Private final consumption expenditure 490.96; Gross fixed capital formation 222.31; *Total domestic expenditure* 830.50; Export of goods and services 340.56; *Less* Import of goods and services 592.58; *GDP in purchasers' values* 578.49. Source: Eastern Caribbean Central Bank.

Gross Domestic Product by Economic Activity (EC $ million at current prices, 2006): Agriculture (including crops, livestock and fishing) 8.45; Mining and quarrying 8.36; Manufacturing 8.89; Electricity and water 20.91; Construction 77.43; Wholesale and retail 27.91; Hotels and restaurants 119.56; Transport and Communications 60.04; Banks and insurance 49.64; Real estate and housing 9.22; Government services 67.12; Other services 7.46; *Sub-total* 464.99; *Less* Imputed bank service charge 39.73; *GDP at factor cost* 425.26. Source: Eastern Caribbean Central Bank.

Balance of Payments (EC $ million, 2005): Export of goods f.o.b. 15.02; Imports of goods f.o.b. −114.30; *Trade balance* −99.29; Exports of services 98.99; Imports of services −56.29; *Balance on goods and services* −56.59; Other income received 11.68; Other income paid −9.26; *Balance on goods, services and income* −54.17; Current transfers received 10.74; Current transfers paid −9.68; *Current balance* −53.10; Capital account (net) 12.81; Direct investment from abroad 98.86; Portfolio investment liabilities 0.59; Other investment assets −9.24; Other investment liabilities −48.57; Net errors and omissions 4.10; *Overall balance* 5.45. Source: IMF, *International Financial Statistics*.

EXTERNAL TRADE

Principal Commodities (EC $ million, 2005): *Imports:* Food and live animals 57.4; Beverages and tobacco 25.1; Mineral fuels, lubricants, etc. 34.6; Chemicals and related products 22.7; Basic manufactures 61.9; Machinery and transport equipment 101.6; Miscellaneous manufactured articles 36.4; Total (incl. others) 350.6. *Exports* (incl. re-exports): Food and live animals 13.9; Beverages and tobacco 7.5; Basic manufactures 1.5; Machinery and transport equipment 14.8; Miscellaneous manufactured articles 1.9; Total (incl. others) 39.8.

Principal Trading Partners (EC $ million, 2005): *Imports:* Barbados 3.7; Guadeloupe 7.3; Guyana 6.6; Netherlands Antilles 22.3; Puerto Rico 27.4; Trinidad and Tobago 29.8; United Kingdom 16.1; USA 177.6; US Virgin Islands 5.6; Total (incl. others) 350.6. *Exports* (incl. re-exports): British Virgin Islands 1.7; Guadeloupe 0.8; Guyana 4.8; Netherlands Antilles 9.9; Saint Lucia 2.1; United Kingdom 10.7; USA 3.7; Total (incl. others) 39.8.

TRANSPORT

Road Traffic (motor vehicles licensed, 2003): Private cars 3,198; Hired cars 830; Buses/trucks/jeeps/pickups 2,002; Motor cycles 53; Tractors 5; Heavy equipment 168; Other 7.

Shipping: *Merchant Fleet* (registered at 31 December 2006): 4; Total displacement 805 grt. Source: Lloyd's Register-Fairplay, *World Fleet Statistics*.

TOURISM

Visitor Arrivals: 120,788 (stop-overs 53,987, excursionists 66,801) in 2004; 143,186 (stop-overs 62,084, excursionists 81,102) in 2005; 161,091 (stop-overs 72,084, excursionists 89,007) in 2006 (preliminary). Source: Eastern Caribbean Central Bank, *Annual Economic and Financial Review 2006*.

Visitor Arrivals by Country of Residence (2005): Canada 6,856; Caribbean 10,956; Germany 1,249; Italy 2,585; United Kingdom 7,084; USA 76,787; Total (incl. others) 143,186.

Tourism Receipts (EC $ million): 186.2 in 2004; 232.3 in 2005; 271.6 in 2006 (preliminary). Source: Eastern Caribbean Central Bank, *Annual Economic and Financial Review 2006*.

COMMUNICATIONS MEDIA

Radio Receivers (1997): 3,000 in use.

Television Receivers (1999): 1,000 in use.

Telephones (2002): 5,796 main lines in use.

Facsimile Machines (1993): 190 in use.

Mobile Cellular Telephones (2000): 15,000 subscribers.

Internet Connections (2002): 1,391.

Sources: partly UN, *Statistical Yearbook*; International Telecommunication Union.

EDUCATION

Pre-primary (2003): 11 schools; 38 teachers; 499 pupils.

Primary (2003): 8 schools; 92 teachers; 1,438 pupils.

General Secondary (2002/03): 1 school; 91 teachers; 1,102 pupils.

Adult Literacy Rate (UNESCO estimates): 95.4% (males 95.1%; females 95.7%) in 1995. Source: UNESCO, *Statistical Yearbook*.

Directory

The Constitution

The Constitution, established in 1976, accorded Anguilla the status of a British Dependent Territory. It formally became a separate dependency on 19 December 1980, and is administered under the Anguilla Constitution Orders of 1982 and 1990. British Dependent Territories were referred to as United Kingdom Overseas Territories from February 1998 and draft legislation confirming this change and granting citizens rights to full British citizenship and residence in the United Kingdom was published in March 1999. The British Overseas Territories Act entered into effect in May 2002. The British Government proposals also included the requirement that the Constitutions of Overseas Territories should be revised in order to conform to British and international standards. The process of revision of the Anguillan Constitution began in September 1999.

The British monarch is represented locally by a Governor, who presides over the Executive Council and the House of Assembly. The Governor is responsible for defence, external affairs (including international financial affairs), internal security (including the police), the public service, the judiciary and the audit. The Governor appoints a Deputy Governor. On matters relating to internal security, the public service and the appointment of an acting governor or deputy governor, the Governor is required to consult the Chief Minister. The Executive Council consists of the Chief Minister and not more than three other ministers (appointed by the Governor from the elected members of the legislative House of Assembly) and two *ex officio* members (the Deputy Governor and the Attorney-General). The House of Assembly is elected for a maximum term of five years by universal adult suffrage and consists of seven elected members, two *ex officio* members (the Deputy Governor and the Attorney-General) and two nominated members who are appointed by the Governor, one upon the advice of the Chief Minister, and one after consultations with the Chief Minister and the Leader of the Opposition. The House elects a Speaker and a Deputy Speaker.

The Governor may order the dissolution of the House of Assembly if a resolution of 'no confidence' is passed in the Government, and elections must be held within two months of the dissolution.

The Constitution provides for an Anguilla Belonger Commission, which determines cases of whether a person can be 'regarded as belonging to Anguilla' (i.e. having 'belonger' status). A belonger is someone of Anguillan birth or parentage, someone who has married a belonger, or someone who is a citizen of the United Kingdom Overseas Territories from Anguilla (by birth, parentage, adoption or naturalization). The Commission may grant belonger status to those who have been domiciled and ordinarily resident in Anguilla for not less than 15 years.

The Government

Governor: ANDREW GEORGE (took office 10 July 2006).

EXECUTIVE COUNCIL
(April 2008)

Chief Minister and Minister of Home Affairs, Gender Affairs, Immigration, Labour, Lands and Physical Planning and Environment: OSBOURNE FLEMING (AUF).

Minister of Finance, Economic Development, Investment, Tourism and Commerce: VICTOR F. BANKS (AUF).

Minister of Social Development and Education: EVANS MCNEIL ROGERS (AUF).

Minister of Infrastructure, Communications, Utilities, Housing, Agriculture and Fisheries: KENNETH HARRIGAN (AUF).

Attorney-General: WILHELM C. BOURNE.

Deputy Governor: STANLEY EVERTON REID.

Parliamentary Secretary with responsibility for Water, Agriculture and Fisheries: ALBERT HUGHES.

MINISTRIES

Office of the Governor: Government House, POB 60, The Valley; tel. 497-2622; fax 497-3314; e-mail govthouse@anguillanet.com.

Office of the Chief Minister: The Secretariat, The Valley; tel. 497-2518; fax 497-3389; e-mail chief-minister@gov.ai.

All ministries are based in The Valley, mostly at the Secretariat (tel. 497-2451; internet www.gov.ai).

Legislature

HOUSE OF ASSEMBLY

Speaker: DAVID CARTY.

Clerk to House of Assembly: ADELLA RICHARDSON.

Election, 21 February 2005

Party	% of votes	Seats
Anguilla United Front (AUF)	38.9	4
Anguilla United Movement (AUM)	19.4	1
Anguilla National Strategic Alliance (ANSA)	19.2	2
Anguilla Progressive Party (APP)	9.5	—
Total (incl. others)	100.0	7

There are also two *ex officio* members and two nominated members.

Political Organizations

Anguilla National Strategic Alliance (ANSA): The Valley; Leader EDISON BAIRD.

Anguilla Progressive Party (APP): The Valley; Leader ROY ROGERS.

Anguilla United Front (AUF): The Valley; internet www.unitedfront.ai; f. 2000; Leader OSBOURNE FLEMING; alliance comprising:

  Anguilla Democratic Party (ADP): The Valley; f. 1981 as Anguilla People's Party; name changed 1984; Leader VICTOR F. BANKS.

  Anguilla National Alliance: The Valley; f. 1980 by reconstitution of People's Progressive Party; Leader OSBOURNE FLEMING.

Anguilla United Movement (AUM): The Valley; f. 1979; revived 1984; previously known as the Anguilla United Party—AUP; conservative; Leader HUBERT B. HUGHES.

UNITED KINGDOM OVERSEAS TERRITORIES   Anguilla

Judicial System

Justice is administered by the High Court, Court of Appeal and Magistrates' Courts. One of the 16 puisne judges of the Eastern Caribbean Supreme Court's High Court division, concurrently accredited to Montserrat, arbitrates in sittings of the High Court.

Puisne Judge: JANICE MESADIS GEORGE-CREQUE.

Religion

CHRISTIANITY

The Anglican Communion

Anglicans in Anguilla are adherents of the Church in the Province of the West Indies, comprising nine dioceses. Anguilla forms part of the diocese of the North Eastern Caribbean and Aruba.

Bishop of the North Eastern Caribbean and Aruba: Rt Rev. LEROY ERROL BROOKS, St Mary's Rectory, POB 180, The Valley; tel. 497-2235; fax 497-8555; e-mail brookx@anguilla.net.com.

The Roman Catholic Church

The diocese of St John's-Basseterre, suffragan to the archdiocese of Castries (Saint Lucia), includes Anguilla, Antigua and Barbuda, the British Virgin Islands, Montserrat and Saint Christopher and Nevis. The Bishop resides in St John's, Antigua.

Roman Catholic Church: St Gerard's, POB 47, The Valley; tel. 497-2405.

Protestant Churches

Methodist Church: POB 5, The Valley; tel. 497-2612; fax 497-8460; e-mail methodism@anguillanet.com; Supt Minister Rev. Dr H. CLIFTON NILES.

The Seventh-day Adventist, Baptist, Church of God, Pentecostal, Apostolic Faith and Jehovah's Witnesses Churches and sects are also represented.

The Press

Anguilla Life Magazine: Caribbean Commercial Centre, POB 109, The Valley; tel. 497-3080; fax 497-2501; 3 a year; Publr and Editor CLAIRE DEVENER; circ. 10,000.

The Anguillian Newspaper: POB 98, The Valley; tel. 497-3823; fax 497-8706; internet www.anguillian.com; Editor A. NAT HODGE.

The Light: Herbert's Commercial Centre, POB 1373, The Valley; tel. 497-5641; fax 497-5795; e-mail thelight@anguillanet.com; f. 1993; weekly; newspaper; Editor GEORGE C. HODGE.

Official Gazette: The Valley; tel. 497-5081; monthly; govt news-sheet.

What We Do in Anguilla: Herbert's Commercial Centre, POB 1373, The Valley; tel. 497-5641; fax 497-5795; e-mail thelight@anguillanet.com; f. 1987; monthly; tourism; Editor GEORGE C. HODGE; circ. 50,000.

Broadcasting and Communications

TELECOMMUNICATIONS

Cable & Wireless Anguilla: POB 77, The Valley; tel. 497-3100; fax 497-2501; internet www.anguillanet.com; Gen. Man. SUTCLIFFE HODGE.

Wireless Ventures (Anguilla) Ltd: Babrow Bldg, The Valley; tel. 498-7500; fax 498-7510; e-mail customercareanguilla@digicelgroup.com; owned by Digicel Ltd (Bermuda); fmrly AT&T Wireless.

BROADCASTING

Radio

Caribbean Beacon Radio: Long Rd, POB 690, The Valley; Head Office: POB 7008, Columbus, GA 31908, USA; tel. 497-4340; fax 497-4311; f. 1981; privately owned and operated; religious and commercial; broadcasts 24 hours daily; Pres. Dr GENE SCOTT; CEO B. MONSELL HAZELL.

Heart Beat Radio: The Valley; tel. 497-3354; fax 497-5995; e-mail hbr1075@anguillanet.com; internet hbr1075.com; f. 2001; commercial; music and news programmes.

Klass 92.9 FM: POB 339, The Valley; tel. 497-3791; e-mail request@klass929.com; internet www.klass929.com; f. 2006; commercial; Owner ABNER BROOKS, Jr.

Kool FM: North Side, The Valley; tel. 497-0103; fax 497-0104; e-mail kool@koolfm103.com; internet www.koolfm103.com; commercial.

Radio Anguilla: Dept of Information and Broadcasting, Treasury Dept, The Valley; tel. 497-2218; fax 497-5432; e-mail radioaxa@anguillanet.com; internet www.radioaxa.com; f. 1969; owned and operated by the Govt of Anguilla since 1976; 250,000 listeners throughout the north-eastern Caribbean; broadcasts 17 hours daily; Dir of Information and Broadcasting KENNETH HODGE; News Editor WYCLIFFE RICHARDSON.

Voice of Creation Station: The Valley; internet www.voiceofcreation.com; f. 2000; religious station with devotional and gospel music; Owner 'GRANTI' GRANT.

ZJF FM: The Valley; tel. 497-3157; f. 1989; commercial.

Television

Anguilla Television: terrestrial channels 3 and 9; 24-hour local and international English language programming.

Caribbean Cable Communications (Anguilla): Edwin Wallace Rey Dr., POB 336, The Valley; tel. 497-3600; fax 497-3602; e-mail alisland@anguillanet.com; internet www.caribcable.com; also broadcasts to Nevis; Pres. LEE BERTMAN.

Finance

(cap. = capital; res = reserves; dep. = deposits; m. = million; amounts in EC dollars)

CENTRAL BANK

Eastern Caribbean Central Bank: Fairplay Commercial Complex, POB 1385, The Valley; tel. 497-5050; fax 497-5150; e-mail eccbaxa@anguillanet.com; internet www.eccb-centralbank.org; HQ in Basseterre, Saint Christopher and Nevis; bank of issue and central monetary authority for Anguilla, Antigua and Barbuda, Dominica, Grenada, Montserrat, Saint Christopher and Nevis, Saint Lucia and Saint Vincent and the Grenadines; Gov. Sir K. DWIGHT VENNER; Country Man. MARILYN BARTLETT-RICHARDSON.

COMMERCIAL BANKS

Caribbean Commercial Bank (Anguilla) Ltd: POB 23, The Valley; tel. 497-3917; fax 497-3570; e-mail service@ccb.ai; internet www.ccb.ai; f. 1976; Chair. OSBOURNE B. FLEMING; Man. Dir STARRY WEBSTER-BENJAMIN.

FirstCaribbean International Bank Ltd: POB 140, The Valley; tel. 497-2301; fax 497-2980; e-mail care@firstcaribbeanbank.com; internet www.firstcaribbeanbank.com; f. 2002 following merger of Caribbean operations of Barclays Bank PLC and CIBC; Exec. Chair. MICHAEL MANSOOR; CEO CHARLES PINK.

National Bank of Anguilla Ltd (NBA): POB 44, The Valley; tel. 497-2101; fax 497-3310; e-mail nbabankl@anguillanet.com; internet www.nba.ai; f. 1985; 5% owned by Govt of Anguilla; cap. 30.7m., res 14.5m., dep. 570.3m. (March 2005); CEO E. VALENTINE BANKS.

Scotiabank Anguilla Ltd: Fairplay Commercial Centre, POB 250, The Valley; tel. 497-3333; fax 497-3344; e-mail bns.anguilla@scotiabank.com; internet www.scotiabank.com; Man. Dir KERWIN BAPTISTE.

There are 'offshore' foreign banks based on the island, but most are not authorized to operate in Anguilla. There is a financial complex known as the Caribbean Commercial Centre in The Valley.

TRUST COMPANIES

Barwys Trust Anguilla Ltd: Caribbean Suite, The Valley; tel. 497-2189; fax 497-5007; e-mail info@barwys.com; internet www.barwys.com; Man. JOSEPH BRICE.

Codan Trust Co (Anguilla) Ltd: NBA Corporate Bldg, Caribbean Suite, POB 147, The Valley; tel. 498-4126; fax 498-8423; e-mail anguilla@conyersdillandpearman.com; internet conyersdillandpearman.com; subsidiary of Conyers, Dill and Pearman, Bermuda; Man. GARETH THOMAS.

First Anguilla Trust Co Ltd: Mitchell House, POB 174, The Valley; tel. and fax 498-8800; e-mail information@firstanguilla.com; internet www.firstanguilla.com; Man. Dir JOHN DYRUD.

Fortis Intertrust (Anguilla) Ltd: National Bank Corporate Bldg, Airport Rd, POB 1388, The Valley; tel. 497-2189; fax 497-5007; e-mail anneke.soedhoe@fortisintertrust.com; internet www.fortisintertrust.com; Gen. Man. ANNEKE SOEDHOE.

GenevaTrust: National Bank Corporate Bldg, Caribbean Suite, Airport Rd, The Valley; tel. 870-3178; fax 870-3949; e-mail geneva@genevatrust.com; internet www.genevatrust.com; f. 2005 as the GenevaTrust Corporation; subsidiary of Geneva Assurance Ltd; CEO NADINE DE KOKER.

Global Trustees (Anguilla) Ltd: 201 The Rogers Office Bldg, Edwin Wallace Rey Dr., George Hill; tel. 498-5858; fax 497-5504; e-mail anguilla@gcsl.info; internet www.gcsl.info; fmrly Hansa Bank and Trust Co; Man. Dir CARLYLE K. ROGERS.

Harney Westwood & Riegels (Anguilla) (HWR Services (Anguilla) Ltd): Harlaw Chambers, POB 1026, The Valley; tel. 498-5000;

fax 498-5001; e-mail anguilla@harneys.com; internet www.harneys.com; Man. KIMBERLY FLEMING.

Lutea (Anguilla) Ltd: Caribbean Suite, POB 1533, The Valley; tel. 498-0340; fax 498-0341; e-mail acharles@lutea.com; internet www.lutea.com; owned by the Lutea Group of Cos, administered in Jersey; Man. AINE CHARLES.

Mossack Fonseca & Co (British Anguilla) Ltd: Quantum Bldg, Suite 29, Caribbean Commercial Centre, The Valley; tel. 498-7777; fax 497-3727; e-mail anguilla@mossfon.com; internet www.mossfon.com; Man. SHERMA BAPTISTE.

Sinel Trust (Anguilla) Ltd: Sinel Chambers, POB 1269, The Valley; tel. 497-3311; fax 497-5659; e-mail arichardson@sineltrust.com; internet www.sineltrust-anguilla.com; CEO ALEX RICHARDSON.

REGULATORY AUTHORITY

Anguilla Financial Services Commission: The Secretariat, POB 1575, The Valley; tel. 497-5881; fax 497-5872; e-mail info@fsc.org.ai; internet www.fsc.org.ai; f. 2004 to replace the Financial Services Dept of the Ministry of Finance, Economic Development, Investment, Tourism and Commerce; Chair. DENNIS CROSS.

STOCK EXCHANGE

Eastern Caribbean Securities Exchange: based in Basseterre, Saint Christopher and Nevis; tel. (869) 466-7192; fax (869) 465-3798; e-mail info@ecseonline.com; internet www.ecseonline.com; f. 2001; regional securities market designed to facilitate the buying and selling of financial products for the eight member territories—Anguilla, Antigua and Barbuda, Dominica, Grenada, Montserrat, Saint Christopher and Nevis, Saint Lucia and Saint Vincent and the Grenadines; Gen. Man. TREVOR E. BLAKE.

INSURANCE

A-Affordable Insurance Services Inc: Old Factory Plaza, POB 6, The Valley; tel. 497-5757; fax 497-2122.

British American Insurance Co Ltd: Herbert's Commercial Centre, POB 148, The Valley; tel. 497-2653; fax 497-5933; e-mail britam@anguillenet.com.

Caribbean Alliance Insurance Co Ltd: POB 1377, The Valley; tel. 497-3525; fax 497-3526.

D-3 Enterprises Ltd: Caribbean Commercial Complex, POB 1377, The Valley; tel. 497-3525; fax 497-3526; e-mail d-3ent@anguillanet.com; internet www.d-3enterprises.com; Man. Dir CLEMENT RUAN.

Gulf Insurance Ltd: c/o Ferry Boat Inn, POB 189, Blowing Point; tel. 497-6613; fax 497-6713; internet wwwgulfinsuranceltd.com; Contact MARJORIE MCCLEAN.

Malliouhana-Anico Insurance Co Ltd (MAICO): Herbert's Commercial Centre, POB 492, The Valley; tel. 497-3712; fax 497-3710; e-mail maico@anguillanet.com; Man. MONICA HODGE.

National Caribbean Insurance Co Ltd: Herbert's Commercial Centre, POB 323, The Valley; tel. 497-2865; fax 497-3783.

National General Insurance Co N.V. (NAGICO): c/o Fairplay Management Services, POB 79, The Valley; tel. 497-2976; fax 497-3303; e-mail fairplay@anguillanet.com; internet www.nagico.com.

Nem West Indies Insurance Ltd (Nemwil): Old Factory Plaza, POB 6, The Valley; tel. 497-5757; fax 497-2122.

Trade and Industry

DEVELOPMENT ORGANIZATION

Anguilla Development Board: POB 285, Wallblake Rd, The Valley; tel. 497-3690; fax 497-2959.

CHAMBER OF COMMERCE

Anguilla Chamber of Commerce and Industry: POB 321, The Valley; tel. 497-2839; fax 497-2839; e-mail acoci@caribcable.com; internet www.anguillachamber.com; Pres. JOHN BENJAMIN; Exec. Dir CALVIN BARTLETT.

INDUSTRIAL AND TRADE ASSOCIATION

Anguilla Financial Services Association (AFSA): POB 1071, The Valley; tel. 497-8367; fax 497-3096; e-mail info@anguillafinance.com; internet www.anguillafinance.com; Pres. GRAHAM CRABTREE.

UTILITIES

Electricity

Anguilla Electricity Co Ltd: POB 400, The Valley; tel. 497-5200; fax 497-5440; e-mail info@anglec.com; internet www.anglec.com; f. 1991; operates a power-station and 12 generators; Chair. RODNEY REY; Gen. Man. NEIL MCCONNIE.

Transport

ROADS

Anguilla has 140 km (87 miles) of roads, of which 100 km are tarred.

SHIPPING

The principal port of entry is Sandy Ground on Road Bay. There is a daily ferry service between Blowing Point and Marigot (St Martin). The first phase of the Anguilla ports Development Project commenced in July 2006 with the development of Road Bay; upon completion in October, extensive work began at Blowing Point to create three new piers, two of which were to be devoted to ferry and passenger services. Construction of the new facilities was completed in 2007.

Link Ferries: Little Harbour; tel. 497-2231; fax 497-3290; e-mail fbconnor@anguillanet.com; internet www.link.ai; f. 1992; daily services to Julianna International Airport (St Martin) and charter services to neighbouring islands and offshore quays; Owner FRANKLYN CONNOR.

CIVIL AVIATION

Wallblake Airport, 3.2 km (2 miles) from The Valley, has a bitumen-surfaced runway with a length of 1,100 m (3,600 ft). In 1996 Anguilla signed an agreement with the Government of Aruba providing for the construction of a new jet airport on the north coast of the island, with finance of some US $30m. from the Aruba Investment Bank. Reconstruction and expansion of Wallblake Airport was completed in late 2004. Most of the cost of the EC $49.2m. project was allocated to the extension of the runway to accommodate mid-range aircraft. LIAT and Winair regional airlines also operate from Wallblake airport.

American Eagle: POB 659, Wallblake Airport; tel. 497-3131; fax 497-3502; regional partner co of American Airlines; operates scheduled flights from Puerto Rico 3 times a day (December to April) and once daily (May to November).

Anguilla Air Services: POB 559, Wallblake Airport; tel. 498-5922; fax 498-5921; e-mail info@anguillaairservices.com; internet www.anguillaairservices.com; f. Dec. 2006; operates passenger and cargo charter flights from Anguilla to neighbouring islands; Man. Dir CARL THOMAS.

Trans Anguilla Airways (2000) Ltd (TAA): POB 1329, Wallblake Airport; tel. 497-8690; fax 497-8689; e-mail transang@anguillanet.com; internet www.transanguilla.com; f. 1996; air charter service in the Eastern Caribbean; Chair. JOSHUA GUMBS.

Tyden Air: POB 107, Wallblake Airport; tel. 497-3419; fax 497-3079; charter company servicing whole Caribbean.

Tourism

Anguilla's sandy beaches and unspoilt natural beauty attract tourists and also day visitors from neighbouring St Martin/St Maarten. In November 1999 'Hurricane Lenny' badly affected Anguilla, forcing the temporary closure of the island's two largest hotels. Tourism receipts totalled an estimated EC $271.6m. in 2006 and there were 746 hotel rooms on the island in 2005; in the latter year 54% of visitors were from the USA, 8% were from other Caribbean countries, while most of the remainder were from the United Kingdom, Canada, Italy and Germany. Visitor numbers totalled an estimated 161,091 in 2006.

Anguilla Hotel and Tourism Association: Coronation Ave, POB 1020, The Valley; tel. 497-2944; fax 497-3091; e-mail ahta@anguillanet.com; internet www.ahta.ai; f. 1981; Exec. Dir TRUDY NIXON.

Anguilla Tourist Board: Coronation Ave, POB 1388, The Valley; tel. 497-2759; fax 497-2710; e-mail atbtour@anguillanet.com; internet www.anguilla-vacation.com; Dir AMELIA VANTERPOOL-KUBISCH.

BERMUDA

Introductory Survey

Location, Climate, Language, Religion, Flag, Capital

The Bermudas or Somers Islands are an isolated archipelago, comprising about 138 islands, in the Atlantic Ocean, about 917 km (570 miles) off the coast of South Carolina, USA. Bridges and causeways link seven of the islands to form the principal mainland. The climate is mild and humid. Temperatures are generally between 8°C (46°F) and 32°C (90°F), with an average annual rainfall of 1,470 mm (58 ins). The official language is English, but there is a small community of Portuguese speakers. Most of the inhabitants profess Christianity, and numerous denominations are represented, the principal one being the Anglican Church. The flag (proportions 1 by 2) is the British 'Red Ensign' (this usage being unique among the British colonies), with, in the fly, the colony's badge: a seated red lion holding a shield (with a gold baroque border), which depicts the wreck off Bermuda of the ship of the first settlers. The capital is Hamilton.

Recent History

Bermuda was first settled by the British in 1609. It has had a representative assembly since 1620 (and thus claims one of the oldest parliaments in the world), and became a British crown colony in 1684. Bermuda was granted internal self-government by the Constitution introduced in 1968, although the British Government retains responsibility in certain matters. Various amendments to the 1968 Constitution were made in 1973, the most important being the establishment of the Governor's Council, through which the Governor exercises responsibility for external affairs, defence, internal security and the police. In 1974 the Government Leader was restyled Premier and the Executive Council became the Cabinet.

The first general election under the new Constitution, which took place in May 1968 against a background of rioting and racial tension (some 60% of the population are of African origin, the rest mostly of European extraction), was won by the United Bermuda Party (UBP), a moderate, multi-racial party whose policies were based on racial co-operation and continued support for dependent status. The underlying racial tensions were emphasized in 1972 and 1973 by shooting incidents which resulted in the deaths of the Governor, the Commissioner of Police and three others. In December 1977 the Governor's assassin and another convicted murderer were executed, and further rioting and arson ensued. A state of emergency was declared, and British troops were flown to Bermuda to restore order.

At the general election of May 1976, the UBP was returned to power with a decreased majority, winning 26 of the 40 seats in the House of Assembly. The remaining seats were won by the mainly black, left-wing Progressive Labour Party (PLP), which campaigned for independence. In August 1977 Sir John Sharpe, Premier and leader of the UBP since December 1975, resigned both posts and was succeeded by David Gibbons, the Minister of Finance.

In February 1978 a Royal Commission was established to investigate the causes of racial violence, and in August the Commission published a report which suggested the redrawing of constituency boundaries to improve the PLP's prospects for winning seats. Despite this, the UBP won the December 1980 election. Gibbons resigned as Premier and UBP leader in January 1982 and was succeeded by John Swan, the Minister of Home Affairs. At a general election in February 1983, the UBP increased its majority in the House of Assembly. Internal divisions within the PLP led to the expulsion from the party of four PLP members of the House of Assembly. These members, after sitting as independents, formed a new centre party, the National Liberal Party (NLP), in August 1985. In October Swan called an early general election, hoping to take advantage of the divided opposition. The UBP was decisively returned to power, securing 31 of the 40 seats in the House of Assembly, while the PLP retained only seven seats and the NLP won two. Following a general election in February 1989, the UBP remained in power, but with a reduced representation in the House of Assembly. By contrast, the PLP increased its representation.

Constitutional amendments introduced in 1979 included provision for closer consultation between the Premier and the Leader of the Opposition on the appointment of members of the Public Service Commission and the Boundaries Commission, and on the appointment of the Chief Justice. The 1978 Royal Commission recommended early independence for Bermuda, but the majority of the population at that time seemed to oppose such a policy. Swan had declared himself in favour of eventual independence for the colony, but only with the support of the Bermudian people.

In August 1992 Lord Waddington (former leader of the British House of Lords) replaced Sir Desmond Langley as Governor. Waddington remained in office until June 1997, when he was succeeded by Thorold Masefield.

At a general election on 5 October 1993 (the first to be held since the voting age was lowered from 21 to 18 years in 1990), the UBP was returned to power, winning 22 seats in the House of Assembly, while the PLP secured 18. In February 1994 legislation providing for the organization of a referendum on independence for Bermuda was narrowly approved in the House of Assembly. The debate on independence was believed to have intensified as a result of the announcement in late 1993 that British and US forces would close their facilities and withdraw permanently from the island by April 1995 and September 1995, respectively. The PLP, which advocates independence for Bermuda, consistently opposed the organization of a referendum on the subject, believing that the independence issue should be determined by a general election. In May 1994 a PLP legislative motion to reject a proposed government inquiry into the possibilities for independence was narrowly approved, effectively halting further progress towards a referendum. However, the debate continued, and in October a government delegation travelled to London for official discussions on the subject. Further legislation regarding the proposed referendum was narrowly approved in March 1995, and it was subsequently announced that a vote would be held in August. The PLP encouraged its supporters to boycott the poll, which required not only a majority of votes, but also the approval of 40% of eligible voters in order to achieve a pro-independence result.

The referendum, which was delayed briefly owing to the passage of 'Hurricane Felix', took place on 16 August 1995. Some 59% of eligible voters participated in the poll (a relatively low level for Bermuda), of which 74% registered their opposition to independence from the United Kingdom, and 26% expressed their support for independence. The following day Swan resigned as Premier and as leader of the UBP. Factions within the governing party were perceived to have become considerably polarized during the independence debate, which had resulted in the division of opinion along racial lines. The Minister of Finance, Dr David Saul (who had remained neutral on the independence issue), was subsequently elected leader of the UBP, and Saul was therefore sworn in as Premier on 25 August. Saul stated that his principal objectives were to re-establish a climate of political stability (thus reassuring the international business community), to encourage the continued development of the financial services and tourism sectors and to reunite the UBP. However, under Saul's leadership divisions within the party appeared to deepen, culminating in June 1996 in the approval of a motion of censure against him in the House of Assembly. The motion, which was supported by five UBP members, had been prompted by disagreement with Saul's decision to authorize the establishment of a foreign-owned restaurant in the Territory, in contravention of a ruling by the Bermuda Monetary Authority regarding the granting of franchises to such businesses.

In an attempt to restore a measure of unity within the UBP, Saul announced a reallocation of cabinet portfolios in January 1997. In the reorganization three of the five party members who had supported a motion of censure against Saul in June of the previous year were appointed to positions in the Cabinet. In March, however, Saul announced his resignation as Premier, as a member of the House of Assembly and as the leader of the party. He was replaced by Pamela Gordon, who was elected to the party leadership (and thus as Premier) unopposed.

In May 1998 Gordon effected a major reorganization of the Cabinet with the expressed aim of making the Government 'more efficient and effective'. In the following month the Court of Appeal upheld the constitutionality of the Prohibited Restaurants Act, passed by the House of Assembly in response to a further attempt by a group of Bermudian entrepreneurs, including Sir John Swan, to introduce fast-food franchises to Bermuda. The debate on the bill in the House of Assembly had been highly contentious, and was reported to have caused deep divisions within the ruling UBP. The Supreme Court had previously ruled that the Act was contrary to the provisions of the Constitution, as it made no provision for compensation. In July 1999 the Judicial Committee of the Privy Council upheld the constitutionality of the Prohibited Restaurants Act, rejecting a final appeal by the consortium.

Elections to the House of Assembly took place in November 1998. The PLP won its first ever majority in the House of Assembly, taking 26 seats, while the UBP obtained 14 seats. On 10 November a new Cabinet was appointed and party leader Jennifer Smith was sworn in as Bermuda's first PLP Premier. In her subsequent public address she sought to reassure the international business community that her Government would seek to enhance Bermuda's attraction as an international business centre, and that she would resist any attempts to alter the island's tax status. Smith further promised that, although independence for Bermuda remained a stated aim of her party, no immediate moves towards independence were planned.

In February 1999 Smith met members of the Organisation for Economic Co-operation and Development (OECD, see p. 347) to reassure them that Bermuda was determined to improve regulation of the 'offshore' financial services sector. In March the British Government published draft legislation redesignating its Dependencies as United Kingdom Overseas Territories, and guaranteeing their citizens' rights to a British passport and to residence in the United Kingdom. The document also stated, however, that the Overseas Territories would be obliged to reform their legislation to ensure compliance with European standards on human rights and on financial regulation. In October it was announced that in accordance with the proposed reforms, corporal and capital punishment were to be removed from the statute book.

A report by the Financial Action Task Force on Money Laundering (see p. 416) concluded in June 2000 that Bermuda appeared 'to have effective regulations and supervision' in place in its financial services sector. In the same month the Government agreed to co-operate with OECD in an international effort to reduce tax evasion, promising to end within five years the 'harmful' practices that had given the island a reputation as a tax haven. Measures included a pledge to exchange information about tax in Bermuda with other nations, the introduction of legislation for companies to audit accounts and for these to be made available to the Bermudian authorities, and in the opening up of previously sheltered sectors of the economy to international companies. The Government had, however, pledged to maintain its existing tax system, which included no income tax. In December the members of the House of Assembly agreed, for the first time, to declare their assets and financial interests.

In October 2000 the opposition UBP boycotted the opening of parliament in protest at government plans to reduce the number of seats in the House of Assembly. Pamela Gordon claimed that there had not been adequate public consultation on the matter. Premier Smith had rejected calls for a constitutional conference or a referendum on the proposals, which included replacing the two-member constituencies with single-member ones, although she did announce that the Government would hold a public meeting to discuss the issue. The PLP believed that the existing system was weighted in favour of the UBP, which was considered the party of the white population. The UBP claimed that changes made without proper consultation and a referendum would mean a move towards a 'black dictatorship'. In December the House of Assembly approved a motion requesting the British Government to approve the establishment of a boundaries commission, which would recommend the size of the island's constituencies. Any changes would be subject to ratification by the United Kingdom's Foreign and Commonwealth Office (FCO). In January 2001 the UBP submitted an 8,500-signature petition to the British Government, demanding a constitutional conference or referendum before any changes were made. Gordon also claimed that some Bermudians had refused to sign the petition fearing recriminations. The FCO, however, stated that a constitutional conference was unnecessary, and in April it began consultations over the proposed changes. The commission recommended reducing the number of seats in the House of Assembly by four, to 36. In addition, whereas deputies had previously been elected from 20 two-member constituencies, under the proposed scheme each member of parliament would be elected by a separate constituency. The FCO approved the changes before the July 2003 general election.

In October 2001 Gordon resigned as leader of the UBP. The party elected Grant Gibbons as her successor. In November Sir John Vereker succeeded Sir Thorold Masefield as Governor of Bermuda.

In May 2002 the British Overseas Territories Act, having received royal assent in the United Kingdom in February, came into force and granted British citizenship to the people of its Overseas Territories, including Bermuda. Under the new law Bermudians would be able to hold British passports and work in the United Kingdom and anywhere else in the European Union (see p. 244).

In mid-2002 the issue of financial transparency and corporate governance in Bermuda re-emerged following the disastrous collapse of the US energy concern Enron and several other multinationals in late 2001 and early 2002. The indictment on tax-evasion charges of Dennis Kozlowski, the former CEO of Tyco International Ltd, a manufacturer of electronic security systems with a nominal headquarters on the island, fuelled a growing campaign in the US media and the US Congress against the perceived lack of financial regulation and scrutiny in Bermuda. The Corporate Patriot Enforcement Act of 2005, approved by the US Congress in that year, sought to discourage US corporations to relocate their headquarters from the USA to offshore sites such as Bermuda, by making them still liable to pay tax in the USA.

At an election to the smaller 36-seat House of Assembly in July 2003, the PLP retained its parliamentary majority, securing 22 seats, but its share of the popular vote was reduced to 52% (compared with 48% for the UBP). Smith resigned as Premier following pressure from 11 'rebel' PLP MPs after it emerged that she had retained her seat, in what was regarded as a 'safe' PLP constituency, by just eight votes. She was replaced by the erstwhile Minister of Works and Engineering, William Alexander Scott. Scott's first Cabinet, announced a few days after the elections, consisted of 12 members, despite the PLP's pre-election pledge to reduce the size of the executive to eight in order to reduce costs.

In December 2004 Scott announced that a Bermuda Independence Commission would be established in order to foment debate regarding the island's future. This Commission was duly established in January 2005 and in November it submitted its report; however, its findings were criticized for being biased, as they failed to include contributions from the UBP, including only the ruling PLP's submission. In an attempt to quell the criticism, Scott declared that discussions would take place in 2006 regarding the future status of Bermuda. However, public opinion remained strongly in favour of maintaining links with the United Kingdom: according to opinion polls in June 2006, only 20% of the public supported independence, while a significant 65% opposed complete secession from the United Kingdom. In March both the UN and the British Government indicated their support for a referendum on the issue; however, Scott maintained that the question of independence should be decided at the next general election, which was constitutionally due by 2008. The issue of independence created political tension between the population's black majority, from which the PLP drew much of its support, and the white minority.

Scott's premiership was abruptly curtailed on 27 October 2006 after he was defeated in a PLP leadership contest; party delegates voted for former Minister of Transport and Tourism and Deputy Premier Ewart Brown to succeed the incumbent Premier. Demonstrating his intention to compete for the party leadership, Brown had resigned from his ministerial responsibilities earlier in the month; he was formally inaugurated as party leader on 30 October, resuming the portfolio for Transport and Tourism and announcing limited changes to the Government's composition. The most notable of these was the creation of a ministerial post for matters of social rehabilitation, to be occupied by erstwhile Minister of Community Affairs and Sports Dale Butler, whose newly vacated portfolio was assumed by Wayne Perinchief. Paula Ann Cox, the Minister of Finance, assumed the additional role of Deputy Premier. Brown emphasized the fundamental importance of a responsive social welfare framework to the future prosperity of Bermuda, pledging to invest substantially in the country's care system and confirming his commitment to addressing disruptive racial tensions among the island's communities. The latter concern proved of particular pertinence to the opposition UBP, embroiled as it was in an internal racial discrimination controversy which, in January 2007, precipitated the resignations of House of Assembly member Jamahl Simmons and party Chairwoman Gwyneth Rawlins. Both alleged serious charges of racial discrimination against factions within the party. Simmons claimed that a white élite within the UBP was attempting to remove him from his seat; the departure of two black party members only exacerbated public scepticism about the party's professed allegiance to an integrated Bermudian society. Calls for the resignation of leader Wayne Furbert ensued, with senior members asserting that intra-party schisms and dissension arising from the racism dispute threatened to undermine the UBP's political power. Such public wrangling further provoked speculation of an early general election—ahead of the 2008 deadline dictated constitutionally—whereby Premier Brown might take advantage of an opposition in disarray. The Premier suggested, in March 2007, that future independence for Bermuda was 'inevitable', but that the issue might not feature prominently during the impending election campaign; he indicated that constitutional revisions must be effected and the entrenchment of economic dependence upon the United Kingdom in the national ideology be reversed before advances towards such a momentous development could be achieved.

The unauthorized disclosure, from a source within the Bermuda police, of documents implicating the Premier and a number of other high-ranking government officials in a corruption scandal, served to compromise relations with the United Kingdom in May 2007. Brown maintained that a previous inquiry, in 2004, into the alleged dubious arrangement between government personnel (including himself) and the state-owned Bermuda Housing Corporation—whereby considerable public funds were appropriated for private enrichment—had discharged him of any misconduct. Moreover, he blamed Governor Vereker for failing to ensure the documents' safe custody, and thereby allowing the information to enter into the public realm.

On 12 December 2007 Richard Gozney was inaugurated as Governor of Bermuda. At a general election held on 18 December, the PLP secured a third consecutive term in office with 52.5% of the votes cast, while the UBP won 47.3% of the ballot. The parties' representation in the legislature remained as at the 2003 election: 22 seats for the PLP and 14 seats for the UBP. Brown was duly sworn in as Prime Minister two days later, and his new Cabinet included the reappointment of Nelson Bascome as Minister of Health. Bascome had resigned from the post in February amid a criminal investigation into his business practices during his tenure as Minister of Health and Family Services (in the late 1990s); he had been charged with two counts of theft and one of corruption in June, and the case was proceeding through the courts in mid-2008. Allegations of corruption and issues of race featured prominently in the election campaign, with PLP candidates employing inflammatory rhetoric to suggest that the UBP, if elected, would install a regime oppressive to the black population. After failing to win the constituency seat he contested, Michael Dunkley was replaced as leader of the UBP by Kim Swan, who had been the party's leader in the Senate for six years.

Following increased drugs-smuggling and immigration violations by Jamaican nationals, in January 2003 it was announced that Jamaican visitors to Bermuda would henceforth require visas. In February 2005 a Supreme Court judge ruled as unlawful the Government's policy of deferring the right to apply for parole for prisoners convicted of drugs-smuggling until they had served one-half of their sentence. Prisoners convicted of non-drugs, non-sexual or non-violent offences were allowed to apply for parole after serving one-third of their sentence. In July the Misuse of Drugs Amendment Act introduced legislation allowing courts to fine those convicted of drugs offences up to US $1m. and to impose prison sentences of between 10 years and life. Despite the designation of a dedicated cabinet minister and employment of an eminent British police officer as Assistant Commissioner specializing in drugs crime prevention, drugs-related violent crime escalated during 2006. Police authorities had valued Bermuda's drugs trade at an estimated US $200m. by August of that year.

Concerns about the regulation of Bermuda's burgeoning financial services industry also intensified in 2006, with increased incidences of money-laundering and embezzlement. The arrest in Bermuda of Dutch businessman and oil magnate, John Deuss, in October of that year attracted considerable local and international media interest; Deuss was compelled to resign as Chairman and Chief Executive Officer of Bermuda Commercial Bank (BCB) following allegations of money-laundering, among other illegal practices, and extradited to the Netherlands. It had transpired in September the principal shareholder in BCB, First Curaçao International Bank, was being investigated by Dutch and Caribbean regulators in relation to similar charges of financial malpractice. Despite these troubling developments, the House of Assembly ratified the Investment Funds Act 2006 in December, designed to facilitate the registration and license of investment funds in the territory by eliminating 'unnecessary' administrative protocols and to encourage further expansion in a sector already attractive to international fund operators. Bermuda's financial sector was criticized in February 2007 for its resistance to regulatory mechanisms and reluctance to engage in transparency exercises accepted, albeit hesitantly, by its Cayman Islands counterparts.

Government

Bermuda is a crown colony of the United Kingdom, with a wide measure of internal self-government. An appointed Governor, responsible for external affairs, defence and internal security, represents the British monarch. The bicameral legislature comprises the Senate (11 nominated members) and the House of Assembly, with 36 members representing separate constituencies elected for five years by universal adult suffrage. The Governor appoints the majority leader in the House as Premier, and the latter nominates other ministers. The Cabinet is responsible to the legislature. For the purposes of local government, the island has long been divided into nine parishes (originally known as 'tribes', except for the 'public land' of St George's, the capital until 1815). The town of St George's and the city of Hamilton constitute the two municipalities of the territory.

Defence

The local defence force is the Bermuda Regiment, with a strength of some 630 men and women in 1999. The Regiment employs selective conscription.

Economic Affairs

In 1997, according to estimates by the World Bank, Bermuda's gross national income (GNI), measured at average 1995–97 prices, was US $2,128m. During 1996–2006, it was estimated, the population increased at an average annual rate of 0.3%, while overall gross domestic product (GDP) increased, in real terms, at an average annual rate of 3.5% in 1996–2005; growth was estimated at 5.4% in 2006. In 2000 GDP per head was estimated to be equivalent to some US $34,600, one of the highest levels in the world.

Agriculture (including fishing, mining and quarrying) engaged only 1.7% of the employed labour force in 2007 and contributed 0.8% of GDP in 2006. The principal crops were potatoes, carrots, bananas, vegetables and melons. Flowers (notably lilies) are grown for export. Other vegetables and fruit are also grown, but Bermuda remains very dependent upon food imports, which, with beverages and tobacco, accounted for 18.1% of total imports in 2004. Livestock-rearing includes cattle and goats (both mainly for dairy purposes), pigs and poultry. There is a small fishing industry, mainly for domestic consumption. In 1996–2005 agricultural GDP increased by an annual average of 5.2%; the sector grew by 1.3% in 2005.

Industry (including manufacturing, construction, quarrying and public utilities) contributed 8.8% of GDP in 2006 and engaged an estimated 12.2% of the employed labour force in 2007. The main activities include ship repairs, boat-building and the manufacture of paints and pharmaceuticals. The principal industrial sector is construction (in which an estimated 8.9% of the total labour force were engaged in 2007). Most of Bermuda's water is provided by privately collected rainfall. Energy requirements are met mainly by the import of mineral fuels (fuels accounted for 10.9% of total imports in 2004). An explosion at Bermuda's only power plant in July 2005 reduced electricity production to just 85 MW from its full capacity of 165 MW. The cost of repairing the damage was estimated at B $10m. Industrial GDP increased by an average of 3.4% per year in 1996–2005; the sector expanded by 10.2% in 2005.

Bermuda is overwhelmingly a service economy, with service industries contributing an estimated 90.3% of GDP in 2006 and engaging 86.0% of the employed labour force in 2007. In the latter year, 12.1% of the employed labour force worked in restaurants and hotels, but tourism is estimated to account for some 60% of all employment, directly and indirectly. The total number of tourists, particularly of cruise-ship passengers, is strictly controlled, in order to maintain Bermuda's environment and its market for wealthier visitors. Most tourists come from the USA (some 75.7% of total arrivals by air in 2005). In 2007 659,572 tourists visited Bermuda, an increase of 3.8% on the previous year's figure. In September 2003 the impact of 'Hurricane Fabian' led to the cancellation of several cruise-ship visits and the temporary closure of the international airport to commercial aircraft. In addition, two leading hotels suffered extensive damage. Largely as a consequence of the hurricane, tourism revenue declined to B $342.5m. in 2003, from B $378.8m. the previous year, before recovering slightly to B $353.7m. in 2004. In 1996–2005 the GDP of the services sector increased by an annual average of 4.1%; services GDP increased by 6.4% in 2005.

There is a significant commercial and 'offshore' financial sector, and in 2000 Bermuda was the world's third largest insurance market, having doubled in size during the 1990s. In late 2001 the industry came under huge pressure from claims made in connection to the September terrorist attacks in the USA, although increased demand for insurance and reinsurance services led to a number of new companies being formed at the same time. It was estimated that, in 1995, the entire financial sector contributed more than one-third of foreign exchange earnings. An estimated 31.2% of the employed labour force were engaged directly in the finance, insurance, real estate and business sectors in 2007. International business was estimated to account for 23.3% of GDP in 2006. In 2007 the number of companies registered in Bermuda totalled 15,358. The GDP of the international business sector increased by an annual average of 10.0% in 1996–2005; the sector increased by 8.7% in 2004 and by a further 9.0% in 2005. Another important source of income is the 'free-flag' registration of shipping, giving Bermuda one of the largest fleets in the world. In 1999 Bermuda passed the Electronic Transactions Act, designed to create an infrastructure to support the country's burgeoning 'e-commerce' sector, which was intended to become Bermuda's third major service industry, alongside financial services and tourism.

Bermuda is almost entirely dependent upon imports, has very few commodity exports and, therefore, consistently records a large visible trade deficit (B $1,068m. in 2006). Receipts from the service industries normally ensure a surplus on the current account of the balance of payments (recorded at $901m. in 2006). The USA is the principal source of imports (79.0% of total imports in 2004) and the principal market for exports. Other important trading partners include the United Kingdom, Canada and France. The main exports are rum, flowers, medicinal and pharmaceutical products and the re-export of petroleum products. The principal imports are machinery and food, beverages and tobacco.

In 2007/08 Bermuda recorded an estimated budgetary surplus of some B $48.0m. (excluding debt and sinking fund contributions). A surplus of $53.6m. was projected for the 2008/09 financial year. The average annual rate of inflation was 2.7% in 1996–2006. The rate averaged 3.0% in 2006. In February 2001 government figures indicated that unemployment had fallen for the first time since 1993.

Bermuda, the oldest colony of the United Kingdom, has the status of Overseas Territory in association with the European Union (see p. 244) and has also been granted Designated Territory status by the British Government (this allows Bermudian-based funds and unit trusts access to the British market). Bermuda's financial services also benefit from a special tax treaty with the USA. A similar agreement was signed in November 2005 with Australia, in which both parties would share tax information on a specific subject under investigation or audit. In 2000 Bermuda joined the Caribbean Tourism Organization. In July 2003 Bermuda became an associate member of the Caribbean Community and Common Market (CARICOM, see p. 196).

Bermudians enjoy a high standard of living, although addressing the inequality of the distribution of wealth was a key objective of the PLP Government that took office in 2003, as is local disquiet at the cost of property. The Government borrowed B $85m. to underpin the 2004/05 budget, which was mostly intended for expenditure on social projects, such as housing for the homeless and health services. Proximity to the USA and the parity of the US and Bermuda dollars

UNITED KINGDOM OVERSEAS TERRITORIES — Bermuda

help both tourism and financial industries, and Bermuda's status as a United Kingdom Overseas Territory remains a perceived contributor to political stability and financial integrity. The territory's insurance industry has experienced a period of rapid expansion and remains the most important component of the financial sector. Following a decline in the tourism sector in 2001, partly owing to the repercussions of the terrorist attacks on the USA in September, the Bermuda Alliance for Tourism launched a rebranding of Bermuda as a luxury destination, in order to attract higher-spending visitors. Against expectations, however, tourism expenditures continued to decline, in part owing to 'Hurricane Fabian', which caused several million Bermudian dollars-worth of damage in late 2003. In January 2005 the Minister of Tourism and Transport, Dr Ewart Brown, announced plans to extend the tourist season into the winter months in order to increase tourism revenue by 7% over the following three years. One proposed measure to achieve this target was the revival of the African Diaspora Heritage Trail. In the long term, the Government will need to address the differences between the requirements of the international businesses domiciled on Bermuda and the needs of Bermudians employed in other sectors. Concerns were also raised over how much further the international business sector could expand without putting excessive strain on the local infrastructure. Furthermore, commentators regarded the islands' continuing heavy dependence on the tourism and 'offshore' finance sectors as potentially risky; in particular, discussion of changes to Bermuda's tax exemption laws resulted in several International Business Companies indicating their intentions to move to other regimes if financial conditions were to deteriorate. Bermuda was estimated to have the highest rate of GDP per head of anywhere in the world in 2007, at US $64,255. This was forecast to rise further, to $67,927 during 2008. However, with tourist arrivals from the important US market expected to decline owing to a contraction in that country's economy, and a decline in global 'hedge fund' finance (which had supported Bermudian economic growth in recent years), the expansion of the economy was estimated to have reached only 2.2% in 2007. GDP growth was forecast to increase to 2.5% in 2008, with inflation anticipated to fall to 3.6%, compared with 3.8% in the previous year.

Education

There is free compulsory education in government schools between the ages of five and 16 years, and a number of scholarships are awarded for higher education and teacher training. There are also seven private secondary schools which charge fees. In 2004/05 enrolment at primary and secondary level institutions was equivalent to 95.4% of children in the relevant age-groups. The Bermuda College, founded in 1972, accepts students over the age of 16, and is the only post-secondary educational institution. Extramural degree courses are available through Queen's University, Canada, and Indiana and Maryland Universities, USA. A major programme to upgrade the education system, involving the establishment of five new primary and two secondary schools, was implemented between 1996 and 2002.

Public Holidays

2008: 1 January (New Year's Day), 21 March (Good Friday), 24 May (Bermuda Day), 16 June (Queen's Official Birthday), 31 July (Cup Match), 1 August (Somers' Day), 1 September (Labour Day), 13 October (Heroes' Day), 11 November (Remembrance Day), 25–26 December (Christmas).

2009: 1 January (New Year's Day), 10 April (Good Friday), 24 May (Bermuda Day), 30 July (Cup Match), 31 July (Somers' Day), 7 September (Labour Day), 13 October (Heroes' Day), 11 November (Remembrance Day), 25–26 December (Christmas).

Weights and Measures

The metric system has been widely adopted but imperial and US weights and measures are both used in certain fields.

Statistical Survey

Source: Dept of Statistics, POB HM 3015, Hamilton HM MX; tel. 297-7761; fax 295-8390; e-mail statistics@gov.bm; internet www.gov.bm.

AREA AND POPULATION

Area: 53.3 sq km (20.59 sq miles).

Population (civilian, non-institutional): 58,460 at census of 20 May 1991; 62,059 (males 29,802, females 32,257) at census of 20 May 2000. *Mid-2005* (UN estimate): 63,797 (Source: UN, *Population and Vital Statistics Report*).

Density (mid-2005): 1,196.9 per sq km.

Principal Towns (population at 1991 census): St George's 1,648; Hamilton (capital) 1,100.

Births, Marriages and Deaths (2002): Live births 830 (birth rate 13.4 per 1,000); Marriage rate 15.1 per 1,000; Deaths 404 (death rate 6.5 per 1,000). *2007:* Birth rate 11.3; Death rate 7.8 (Source: Pan American Health Organization).

Expectation of Life (years at birth, 2007): 78.1 (males 76.0; females 80.3). Source: Pan American Health Organization.

Employment (excluding unpaid family workers, 2007, preliminary data): Agriculture, forestry, fishing, mining and quarrying 693; Manufacturing 935; Electricity, gas and water 394; Construction 3,538; Wholesale and retail trade 4,750; Hotels and restaurants 4,829; Transport and communications 2,754; Financial intermediation 2,952; Real estate 614; Business activities 4,176; Public administration 4,113; Education, health and social services 3,245; Other community, social and personal services 2,152; International business activity 4,687; *Total employed* 39,832.

HEALTH AND WELFARE

Physicians (per 1,000 head, 2005): 2.1.

Hospital Beds (per 1,000 head, 2004): 21.1.

Health Expenditure (% of GDP, 2004): 4.3.

Health Expenditure (public, % of total, 1995): 53.2.

Source: partly Pan American Health Organization.

For other sources and definitions, see explanatory note on p. vi.

AGRICULTURE, ETC.

Principal Crops (metric tons, 2006, FAO estimates): Potatoes 820; Carrots 340; Vegetables and melons 2,100; Bananas 330.

Livestock (2005, FAO estimates): Cattle 600; Horses 900; Pigs 600.

Livestock Products (metric tons, 2006, FAO estimates): Cows' milk 1,350; Hen eggs 280.

Fishing (metric tons, live weight, 2005): Groupers 48; Snappers and jobfishes 35; Wahoo 83; Yellowfin tuna 61; Carangids 46; Caribbean spiny lobster 30; Total catch (incl. others) 406.

Source: FAO.

INDUSTRY

Electric Energy (consumption, million kWh): 595 in 2004.

FINANCE

Currency and Exchange Rates: 100 cents = 1 Bermuda dollar (B $). *Sterling, US Dollar and Euro Equivalents* (31 December 2007): £1 sterling = B $2.003; US $1 = B $1.000; €1 = B $1.472; B $100 = £49.92 = US $100.00 = €67.93. *Exchange Rate:* The Bermuda dollar is at par with the US dollar. Note: US and Canadian currencies are also accepted.

Budget (B $ million, 2008/09): Total current account revenue 985.3; Total current account expenditure 931.7. Note: Figures exclude interest on debt (21.5), sinking fund contribution (8.6), surplus available for capital expenditure (23.4) and capital expenditure (154.9).

Cost of Living (Consumer Price Index; base: 2000 = 100): 112.5 in 2004; 116.0 in 2005; 119.5 in 2006. Source: ILO.

Gross Domestic Product (US $ million at constant 1996 prices): 3,578.4 in 2004; 3,769.3 in 2005; 3,971.0 in 2006.

Expenditure on the Gross Domestic Product (B $ million at current prices, year ending 31 March 2001): Government final consumption expenditure 367; Private final consumption expenditure 2,079; Gross fixed capital formation 679; *Total domestic expenditure* 3,125; Exports of goods and services 1,597; *Less* Imports of goods and services 1,325; *GDP in purchasers' values* 3,397. Source: UN, *National Accounts Statistics*.

Gross Domestic Product by Economic Activity (B $ million at current prices, 2006): Agriculture, forestry and fishing 46.4; Manufacturing 91.2; Electricity, gas and water 89.9; Construction and quarrying 312.3; Wholesale and retail trade and repair services 403.3; Restaurants and hotels 299.0; Transport and communications 295.9; Financial intermediation 770.5; Real estate and renting activities 762.6; Business activities 517.4; Public administration 261.1; Education, health and social work 328.5; Other community, social and personal services 111.1; International business activity 1,301.5; *Sub-total* 5,590.7; *Less* Imputed bank service charges 475.0; Indirect taxes, less subsidies 239.2; *GDP in purchasers' values* 5,354.8.

Balance of Payments (B $ million, 2006, estimates): Exports of goods f.o.b. 26; Imports of goods f.o.b. −1,094; *Trade Balance* −1,068; Exports of services 1,477; Imports of services −914; *Balance on goods and services* −505; Other income received 1,742; Other income paid

–331; *Balance on goods, services and income* 906; Current transfers (net) –5; *Current balance* 901; Direct investment (net) –313; Portfolio investment (net) 407; Other investments (net) 1,339; Reserve assets (net) –10; *Overall balance* 2,324.

EXTERNAL TRADE

Principal Commodities (B $ million, 2004): *Imports:* Food, beverages and tobacco 175.0; Clothing 42.5; Fuels 105.4; Chemicals 108.4; Basic material and semi-manufacturing 144.4; Machinery 183.8; Transport equipment 64.6; Finished equipment 144.8; Miscellaneous 0.3; Total (incl. others) 969.1. *Exports* (2003, preliminary estimate): Total 52.0.

Principal Trading Partners (US $ million): *Imports* (2004): Canada 38.6; Caribbean countries 48.2; United Kingdom 28.9; USA 762.3; Total (incl. others) 965.0. *Exports* (1995): France 7.5; United Kingdom 3.9; USA 31.3; Total (incl. others) 62.9. *2003:* Total exports 57.

Source: partly UN, *International Trade Statistics Yearbook.*

TRANSPORT

Road Traffic (vehicles in use, 2005): Private cars 21,978; Motorcycles 19,087; Buses, taxis and limousines 815; Trucks and tank wagons 4,058; Other 1,177; *Total* 47,115.

Shipping: *Ship Arrivals* (2004): Cruise ships 161; Cargo ships 186; Oil and gas tankers 21. *Merchant Fleet* (registered at 31 December 2006): 149; Total displacement 8,413,173 grt (Source: Lloyd's Register-Fairplay, *World Fleet Statistics*). *International Freight Traffic* ('000 metric tons, 1990): Goods loaded 130; Goods unloaded 470 (Source: UN, *Monthly Bulletin of Statistics*).

Civil Aviation (1999): Aircraft arrivals 6,024; Passengers 354,026; Air cargo 4,761,444 kg; Air mail 422,897 kg.

TOURISM

Visitor Arrivals: 516,827 (arrivals by air 269,568, cruise-ship passengers 247,259) in 2005; 635,272 (arrivals by air 298,973, cruise-ship passengers 336,299) in 2006; 659,572 (arrivals by air 305,548, cruise-ship passengers 354,024) in 2007.

Tourism Receipts (B $ million, estimated): 342.5 in 2003; 353.7 in 2004; 392.3 in 2004.

COMMUNICATIONS MEDIA

Radio Receivers (1997): 82,000 in use.
Television Receivers (1999): 70,000 in use.
Telephones (2006): 57,700 main lines in use.
Mobile Cellular Telephones (2006): 60,100 subscribers.
Personal Computers (2002): 34,000 in use.
Internet Users (2006): 42,000.
Broadband Subscribers (2006): 23,600.
Daily Newspapers (2000): 1 (estimated circulation 17,700).
Non-daily Newspapers (2000): 2 (estimated circulation 11,600).

Sources: mainly UNESCO, *Statistical Yearbook*; UN, *Statistical Yearbook*; International Telecommunication Union.

EDUCATION

Pre-primary (1999, unless otherwise indicated): 12 schools (2006); 191 teachers; 429 pupils.

Primary (1999, unless otherwise indicated): 17 (and 5 middle) schools (2006); 368 teachers; 4,980 pupils.

Senior (1999): 18 schools; 399 teachers; 2,335 pupils*.

Higher (2002): 1 institution; 544 students.

* Including six private schools.

2004: Local student enrolment 10,594 (government schools including pre-school 6,370, private schools excluding pre-school 3,512, Bermuda college 712); Teachers 1,310.

Adult Literacy Rate (UNESCO estimates): 99% (males 98%; females 99%) in 1998 (Source: UNESCO, *Statistical Yearbook*).

Directory

The Constitution

The Constitution, introduced on 8 June 1968 and amended in 1973 and 1979, contains provisions relating to the protection of fundamental rights and freedoms of the individual; the powers and duties of the Governor; the composition, powers and procedure of the Legislature; the Cabinet; the judiciary; the public service and finance.

The British monarch is represented by an appointed Governor, who retains responsibility for external affairs, defence, internal security and the police.

The Legislature consists of the monarch, the Senate and the House of Assembly. Three members of the Senate are appointed at the Governor's discretion, five on the advice of the Government leader and three on the advice of the Opposition leader. The Senate elects a President and Vice-President. The House of Assembly, consisting of 36 members elected under universal adult franchise, elects a Speaker and a Deputy Speaker, and sits for a five-year term.

The Cabinet consists of the Premier and at least six other members of the Legislature. The Governor appoints the majority leader in the House of Assembly as Premier, who in turn nominates the other members of the Cabinet. They are assigned responsibilities for government departments and other business and, in some cases, are assisted by Permanent Cabinet Secretaries.

The Cabinet is presided over by the Premier. The Governor's Council enables the Governor to consult with the Premier and two other members of the Cabinet nominated by the Premier on matters for which the Governor has responsibility. The Secretary to the Cabinet, who heads the public service, acts as secretary to the Governor's Council.

Voters must be British subjects aged 18 years or over (lowered from 21 years in 1990), and, if not possessing Bermudian status, must have been registered as electors on 1 May 1976. Candidates for election must qualify as electors, and must possess Bermudian status.

Under the British Overseas Territories Act, which entered into effect in May 2002, Bermudian citizens have the right to United Kingdom citizenship and the right of abode in the United Kingdom. British citizens do not enjoy reciprocal rights.

The Government

Governor and Commander-in-Chief: Sir RICHARD GOZNEY (took office 12 December 2007).
Deputy Governor: MARK ANDREW CAPES.

CABINET
(April 2008)

Premier and Minister of Tourism and Transport: Dr EWART FREDERICK BROWN.
Deputy Premier, Minister of Finance and Economic Development: PAULA A. COX.
Minister of Health: NELSON BASCOME.
Minister of the Environment and Sports: ELVIN JAMES.
Minister of Education: RANDOLPH HORTON.
Minister of Labour, Home Affairs and Housing: DAVID BURCH.
Minister of Energy, Telecommunications and E-Commerce: TERRY LISTER.
Minister of Works and Engineering: DERRICK BURGESS.
Minister of Culture and Social Rehabilitation: DALE D. BUTLER.
Attorney-General: Sen. KIM WILSON.

MINISTRIES

Office of the Governor: Government House, 11 Langton Hill, Pembroke HM 13; tel. 292-3600; fax 292-6831; e-mail depgov@ibl.bm; internet www.gov.bm.

Office of the Premier: Cabinet Office, Cabinet Bldg, 105 Front St, Hamilton HM 12; tel. 292-5501; fax 292-0304; e-mail premier@gov.bm; internet www.gov.bm.

Ministry of Culture and Social Rehabilitation: Melbourne House, Suite 304, 11 Parliament St, POB HM 788, Hamilton HM CX; tel. 296-1574; fax 295-2066; internet www.gov.bm.

Ministry of Education: Dundonald Pl., 14 Dundonald St, POB HM 1185, Hamilton HM EX; tel. 278-3300; fax 278-3348; internet www.moe.bm.

Ministry of Energy, Telecommunications and E-Commerce: F. B. Perry Bldg, 2nd Floor, 40 Church St, Hamilton HM 12; tel. 292-4595; fax 295-1462; e-mail gtelecom@gov.bm; internet www.mtec.bm.

Ministry of the Environment and Sports: Government Administration Bldg, 30 Parliament St, Hamilton HM 12; tel. 297-7590; internet www.gov.bm.

Ministry of Finance: Government Administration Bldg, 30 Parliament St, Hamilton HM 12; tel. 295-5151; fax 295-5727.

UNITED KINGDOM OVERSEAS TERRITORIES   Bermuda

Ministry of Health: Continental Bldg, 25 Church St, Hamilton HM 12; tel. 278-4900; fax 292-2622; e-mail wjones@gov.bm; internet www.health.gov.bm.

Ministry of Justice and Attorney-General's Chambers: 1st Floor, Global House, 43 Church St, Hamilton HM 12; tel. 292-2463; fax 292-3608; e-mail agc@gov.bm.

Ministry of Labour, Home Affairs and Housing: Government Administration Bldg, 1st Floor, 30 Parliament St, Hamilton HM 12; tel. 297-7819; internet www.gov.bm.

Ministry of Tourism and Transport: Global House, 43 Church St, Hamilton HM 12; tel. 295-3130; fax 295-1013; e-mail mtelemaque@gov.bm; internet www.gov.bm.

Ministry of Works and Engineering: General Post Office Bldg, 3rd Floor, 56 Church St, POB HM 525, Hamilton HM 12; tel. 297-7699; fax 295-0170; e-mail nfox@bdagov.bm; internet www.wae.gov.bm.

Legislature

SENATE

President: ALFRED OUGHTON.
Vice-President: Dr IDWAL WYN (WALWYN) HUGHES.
There are 11 nominated members.

HOUSE OF ASSEMBLY

Speaker: STANLEY W. LOWE.
Deputy Speaker: Dr JENNIFER M. SMITH.
Clerk to the Legislature: SHERNETTE WOLFE; tel. 292-7408; fax 292-2006; e-mail smwolffe@gov.bm.
General Election, 18 December 2007

Party	% of votes	Seats
Progressive Labour Party	52.5	22
United Bermuda Party	47.3	14
Total (incl. others)	100.0	36

Political Organizations

National Liberal Party (NLP): POB HM 2190, Hamilton HM FX; tel. 236-9438; fax 236-5472; f. 1985; Leader DESSALINE WALDRON; Chair. GRAEME OUTERBRIDGE.

Progressive Labour Party (PLP): Alaska Hall, 16 Court St, POB 1367, Hamilton HM 17; tel. 292-2264; fax 295-7890; e-mail info@plp.bm; internet www.plp.bm; f. 1963; advocates the 'Bermudianization' of the economy, more equitable taxation, a more developed system of welfare and preparation for independence; Leader Dr EWART FREDERICK BROWN; Chair. DAVID BURT.

United Bermuda Party (UBP): Central Office, 3rd Floor, Bermudiana Arcade, 27 Queen St, Hamilton HM 11; tel. 295-0729; fax 292-7195; e-mail info@ubp.bm; internet www.ubp.bm; f. 1964; policy of participatory democracy, supporting system of free enterprise; Leader KIM SWAN; Chair. MICHAEL FAHY.

Judicial System

Chief Justice: RICHARD GROUND.
President of the Court of Appeal: EDWARD ZACCA.
Registrar of Supreme Court and Court of Appeal: MICHAEL J. MELLO.
Director of Public Prosecutions: RORY FIELD.

The Court of Appeal was established in 1964, with powers and jurisdiction of equivalent courts in other parts of the Commonwealth. The Supreme Court has jurisdiction over all serious criminal matters and has unlimited civil jurisdiction. The Court also hears civil and criminal appeals from the Magistrates' Courts. The three Magistrates' Courts have jurisdiction over all petty offences, and have a limited civil jurisdiction.

Religion

CHRISTIANITY

In 2000 it was estimated that 23% of the population were members of the Anglican Communion, 15% were Roman Catholics, 11% were African Methodist Episcopalians, 7% were Seventh-day Adventists and 4% were Wesleyan Methodists. The Presbyterian Church, the Baptist Church and the Pentecostal Church are also active in Bermuda.

The Anglican Communion

The Anglican Church of Bermuda consists of a single, extra-provincial diocese, directly under the metropolitan jurisdiction of the Archbishop of Canterbury, the Primate of All England. There are about 23,000 Anglicans and Episcopalians in Bermuda.

Bishop of Bermuda: Rt Rev. EWEN RATTERAY, Bishop's Lodge, 18 Ferrar's Lane, Pembroke HM 08, POB HM 769, Hamilton HM CX; tel. 292-6987; fax 292-5421; e-mail bishopratteray@ibl.bm; internet www.anglican.bm.

The Roman Catholic Church

Bermuda forms a single diocese, suffragan to the archdiocese of Kingston in Jamaica. At 31 December 2005 there were an estimated 9,275 adherents in the Territory. The Bishop participates in the Antilles Episcopal Conference (currently based in Port of Spain, Trinidad and Tobago).

Bishop of Hamilton in Bermuda: ROBERT JOSEPH KURTZ, 2 Astwood Rd, POB HM 1191, Hamilton HM EX; tel. 232-4414; fax 232-4447; e-mail rjkurtz@northrock.bm.

Protestant Churches

Baptist Church: Emmanuel Baptist Church, 35 Dundonald St, Hamilton HM 10; tel. 295-6555; fax 296-4491; Pastor RONALD K. SMITH.

Wesley Methodist Church: 41 Church St, Hamilton HM 12; tel. 292-0418; fax 295-9460; e-mail info@wesley.bm; internet www.wesley.bm; Rev. (vacant).

The Press

Bermuda Magazine: POB HM 283, Hamilton HM HX; tel. 295-0695; fax 295-8616; e-mail cbarclay@ibl.bm; f. 1990; quarterly; Editor-in-Chief CHARLES BARCLAY.

The Bermuda Sun: 19 Elliott St, POB HM 1241, Hamilton HM FX; tel. 295-3902; fax 292-5597; e-mail feedback@bermudasun.bm; internet www.bermudasun.bm; f. 1964; 2 a week; official govt gazette; Publr RANDY FRENCH; Editor TONY MCWILLIAM; circ. 12,500.

The Bermudian: 13 Addendum Lane, Pitt's Bay Rd, Pembroke HM 07; POB HM 283, Hamilton HM AX; tel. 232-7041; fax 232-7042; e-mail info@thebermudian.com; f. 1930; monthly; pictorial and lifestyle magazine; Editor TINA STEVENSON; circ. 7,500.

Bermudian Business Online: POB HM 283, Hamilton HM AX; tel. 232-7041; fax 232-7042; e-mail info@thebermudian.com; internet www.bermudianbusiness.com; f. 1996; publ. by The Bermudian Publishing Co Ltd; Publr TINA STEVENSON; circ. 2,500.

Cable TV Guide: 41 Victoria St, Hamilton HM 12; tel. 295-3902; fax 295-5597.

The Mid-Ocean News: 2 Par-la-Ville Rd, POB HM 1025, Hamilton HM DX; tel. 295-5881; fax 295-1513; f. 1911; weekly with TV Guide; sister publication of The Royal Gazette; Editor TIM HODGSON; Gen. Man. KEITH JENSEN; circ. 14,500.

Preview Bermuda: POB HM 3273, Hamilton HM PX; tel. 292-4155; fax 292-4156; e-mail info@previewbermuda.com; internet www.previewbermuda.com; monthly magazine; caters to tourists and visitors to Bermuda; Publr JACKIE STEVENSON; circ. 15,000 per month.

The Royal Gazette: 2 Par-la-Ville Rd, POB HM 1025, Hamilton HM DX; tel. 295-5881; fax 292-2498; e-mail letters@royalgazette.bm; internet www.theroyalgazette.com; f. 1828; morning daily; incorporates The Colonist and Daily News (f. 1866); Editor WILLIAM J. ZUILL; Gen. Man. KEITH JENSEN; circ. 17,500.

TV Week: 2 Par-la-Ville Rd, Hamilton HM 08; tel. 295-5881.

The Worker's Voice: 49 Union Sq., Hamilton HM 12; tel. 292-0044; fax 295-7992; e-mail biu@ibl.bm; fortnightly; organ of the Bermuda Industrial Union; Editor Dr B. B. BALL.

Publisher

Bermudian Publishing Co Ltd: POB HM 283, Hamilton HM AX; tel. 232-7041; fax 232-7042; e-mail info@thebermudian.com; internet www.thebermudian.com; social sciences, sociology, sports; Editor (vacant).

Broadcasting and Communications

TELECOMMUNICATIONS

Bermuda Digital Communications: 22 Reid St, Hamilton HM 11; tel. 296-4010; fax 296-4020; e-mail info@bdc.bm; internet www.bdc.bm; f. 1998; mobile cellular telephone operator; Chair. and CEO KURT EVE.

UNITED KINGDOM OVERSEAS TERRITORIES

Bermuda

Bermuda Telephone Co (BTC): 30 Victoria St, POB 1021, Hamilton HM DX; tel. 295-1001; fax 295-1192; e-mail customersupport@btc.bm; internet www.btc.bm; f. 1987; Pres. and CEO FRANCIS R. MUSSENDEN.

Cable & Wireless (Bermuda) Ltd: 1 Middle Rd, Smith's FL 03, POB HM 151, Hamilton HM AX; tel. 297-7000; fax 297-7159; e-mail helpdesk@bda.cwplc.com; internet www.cw.com/bermuda; new fibre-optic submarine cable, 'Gemini Bermuda', to replace satellite dish in October 2007 as facilitator of Cable & Wireless' global communications services; CEO EDDIE SAINTS.

Digicel Bermuda: Washington Mall, 22 Church St, Phase II, POB 896, Hamilton HM 11; tel. 500-5000; fax 295-3235; e-mail info.bermuda@digicelgroup.com; internet www.digicelbermuda.com; f. 2005; Country Man. DAVID HUNTER.

TeleBermuda International Ltd (TBI): Bermuda Monetary House, 2nd Floor, 43 Victoria St, Hamilton HM 12; POB HM 3043, Hamilton HM NX; tel. 296-9000; fax 296-9010; e-mail save@telebermuda.com; internet www.telebermuda.com; f. 1997; a division of GlobeNet Communications, provides an international service; owns a fibre-optic network connecting Bermuda and the USA; Pres. and CEO GREGORY SWAN.

BROADCASTING

Radio

Bermuda Broadcasting Co: POB HM 452, Hamilton HM BX; tel. 295-2828; fax 295-4282; e-mail zbmzfb@bermudabroadcasting.com; f. 1982 as merger of ZBM (f. 1943) and ZFB (f. 1962); operates 4 radio stations; Man. Dir ULRIC P. (RICK) RICHARDSON; Comptroller MALCOLM R. FLETCHER.

DeFontes Broadcasting Co Ltd (VSB): POB HM 1450, Hamilton HM FX; tel. 292-0050; fax 295-1658; e-mail mbishop@vsbbermuda.com; internet www.vsbbermuda.com; f. 1981 as St George's Broadcasting Co; commercial; 4 radio stations; Pres. KENNETH DEFONTES; Station Man. MIKE BISHOP.

Television

Bermuda Broadcasting Co: see Radio; operates 2 TV stations (Channels 7 and 9).

Bermuda Cablevision Ltd: 19 Laffan St, POB 1642, Hamilton HM GX; tel. 292-5544; fax 295-3023; e-mail info@cablevision.bm; internet www.cablevision.bm; f. 1988; 180 channels; Pres. DAVID LINES; Gen. Man. TERRY ROBERSON.

DeFontes Broadcasting Co Ltd (VSB): see Radio; operates 1 TV station.

Finance

(cap. = capital; res = reserves; dep. = deposits; m. = million; brs = branches; amounts in Bermuda dollars)

BANKING

Central Bank

Bermuda Monetary Authority: BMA House, 43 Victoria St, Hamilton, HM 12; tel. 295-5278; fax 292-7471; e-mail info@bma.bm; internet www.bma.bm; f. 1969; central issuing and monetary authority; cap. 20.0m., res 18.7m., total assets 165.3m. (Dec. 2006); Chair. ALAN F. RICHARDSON; CEO MATTHEW ELDERFIELD.

Commercial Banks

Bank of Bermuda Ltd: 6 Front St, POB HM 1020, Hamilton HM DX; tel. 299-5613; fax 299-6559; e-mail kim.l.wheddon@bob.hsbc.com; internet www.bankofbermuda.bm; f. 1889; 100% acquired by HSBC Asia Holdings BV (Netherlands) in Feb. 2004; cap. 29.0m., res 390.4m., dep. 10,165.2m. (Dec. 2002); CEO PHILIP BUTTERFIELD; COO MICHAEL COLLINS; 6 brs.

Bank of N. T. Butterfield & Son Ltd: 65 Front St, POB HM 195, Hamilton HM 12; tel. 295-1111; fax 292-4365; e-mail contact@bntb.bm; internet www.bankofbutterfield.com; f. 1858; inc. 1904; cap. 29.9m., res 442.8m., dep. 10,042.8m. (Dec. 2006); Chair. ROBERT MULDERIG; Pres. and CEO ALAN R. THOMPSON; 5 brs.

Bermuda Commercial Bank Ltd: Bermuda Commercial Bank Bldg, 19 Par-la-Ville Rd, POB 1748, Hamilton HM GX; tel. 295-5678; fax 295-8091; e-mail enquiries@bcb.bm; internet www.bcb.bm; f. 1969; cap. 10.4m., res 11.0m., dep. 803.1m. (Dec. 2005); COO DOMINIQUE SMITH; Chief Financial Officer GREG REID.

STOCK EXCHANGE

Bermuda Stock Exchange: 3rd Floor, Washington Mall, Church St, Hamilton HM FX; tel. 292-7212; fax 292-7619; e-mail info@bsx.com; internet www.bsx.com; f. 1971; 427 listed equities, funds, debt issues and depositary programmes; Chair. DAVID BROWN; Pres. and CEO GREG WOJCIECHOWSKI.

INSURANCE

Bermuda had a total of some 1,600 registered insurance companies in 2002, the majority of which are subsidiaries of foreign insurance companies, or owned by foreign industrial or financial concerns. Many of them have offices on the island.

Insurance Information Office: Cedarpark Centre, 48 Cedar Ave, POB HM 2911, Hamilton HM LX; tel. 292-9829; fax 295-3532; e-mail biminfo@bii.bm; internet www.bermuda-insurance.org; division of the Bermuda Insurance Development Council; Dir DAVID FOX.

Major Companies

ACE Bermuda: ACE Global HQ, 17 Woodbourne Ave, POB HM 1015, Hamilton HM DX; tel. 295-5200; fax 298-9620; e-mail info@acebermuda.com; internet www.acebermuda.com; total revenue $13,328m. (Dec. 2006); Pres. and CEO G. REES FLETCHER; Chair. EVAN G. GREENBERG; Regional Exec. ALLISON TOWLSON.

Argus Insurance Co Ltd: Argus Insurance Bldg, 12 Wesley St, POB HM 1064, Hamilton HM EX; tel. 295-2021; fax 292-6763; e-mail insurance@argus.bm; internet www.argus.bm; Pres. and CEO GERALD D. E. SIMONS; Chair. JAMES A. C. KING.

Bermuda Insurance Development Council: c/o Bermuda Insurance Institute, The Cedar Parkade Bldg, 48 Cedar Ave, POB HM 2911, Hamilton HM LX; tel. 526-6353; fax 295-3532; e-mail biminfo@bii.bm; internet www.bermuda-insurance.org.

Bermuda Insurance Management Association (BIMA): POB HM 1752, Hamilton HM GX; tel. 295-4864; fax 292-7375; manages over 1,200 insurance and reinsurance cos; liaises with govt and other financial orgs with regard to insurance industry issues; Pres. PHILIP BARNES.

Paumanock Insurance Co Ltd: POB HM 2267, Hamilton HM JX; tel. 292-2404; fax 292-2648.

X. L. Insurance Co Ltd: 1 Bermudiana Rd, Hamilton HM 11; tel. 292-8515; fax 292-5226; e-mail info@xl.bm; internet www.xlinsurance.com; Pres. and Chief Exec. BRIAN O'HARA.

Trade and Industry

GOVERNMENT AGENCY

Bermuda Registrar of Companies: Government Administration Bldg, 30 Parliament St, Hamilton HM HX; tel. 297-7530; fax 292-6640; e-mail jfsmith@gov.bm; internet www.roc.gov.bm; Registrar of Companies STEPHEN LOWE.

DEVELOPMENT ORGANIZATION

Bermuda Small Business Development Corpn: POB HM 637, Hamilton HM CX; tel. 292-5570; fax 295-1600; e-mail bdasmallbusiness@gov.bm; internet www.bsbdc.bm; f. 1980; funded jtly by the Govt and private banks; guarantees loans to small businesses; Gen. Man. MICHELLE KHALDUN.

CHAMBER OF COMMERCE

Bermuda Chamber of Commerce: 1 Point Pleasant Rd, POB HM 655, Hamilton HM CX; tel. 295-4201; fax 295-5779; e-mail info@bermudacommerce.com; internet www.bermudacommerce.com; f. 1907; Pres. PETER EVERSON; Exec. Vice-Pres. DIANE GORDON; 750 mems.

INDUSTRIAL AND TRADE ASSOCIATION

Bermuda International Business Association (BIBA): Cedar House, Ground Floor, 20 Victoria St, Hamilton HM 12; tel. 292-0632; fax 292-1797; e-mail info@biba.org; internet www.biba.org; Chair. LLOYD WIGGAN; CEO CHERYL PACKWOOD.

EMPLOYERS' ASSOCIATIONS

Bermuda Employers' Council: Reid House, Ground Floor, 31 Church St, Hamilton HM 12; tel. 295-5070; fax 295-1966; e-mail twarner@bec.bm; internet www.bec.bm; f. 1960; advisory body on employment and labour relations; Pres. WILLIAM DESILVA; Exec. Dir MARTIN LAW; 420 mems.

Construction Association of Bermuda: POB HM 238, Hamilton HM AX; tel. 292-0633; fax 292-0564; e-mail administrator@constructionbermuda.com; internet www.constructionbermuda.com; f. 1968; Pres. ALEX M. DECOUTO; 90 mems.

Hotel Employers of Bermuda: c/o Bermuda Hotel Asscn, 'Carmel', 61 King St, Hamilton HM 19; tel. 295-2127; fax 292-6671; e-mail johnh@ibl.bm; f. 1968; Pres. FRANK STOCEK; CEO JOHN HARVEY; 8 mems.

UTILITY

BELCO Holdings Ltd: 27 Serpentine Rd, POB HM 1026, Hamilton HM DX; tel. 295-5111; fax 292-8975; e-mail info@belco.bhl.bm; internet www.belcoholdings.bm; f. 1906; holding co for Bermuda Electric Light Co Ltd, and Bermuda Gas and Utility Co Ltd; Chair. J. MICHAEL COLLIER; Pres. and CEO A. L. VINCENT INGHAM.

TRADE UNIONS

In 2007 trade union membership was estimated at approximately 9,140. There are nine registered trade unions, eight of which profess membership of the Bermuda Trades Union Congress:

Bermuda Industrial Union: 49 Union Sq., Hamilton HM 12; tel. 292-0044; fax 295-7992; e-mail biu@biu.bm; f. 1946; Pres. CHRIS FURBERT; Gen. Sec. HELENA BURGESS; 5,202 mems.

Bermuda Trades Union Congress (BTUC): POB 2080, Hamilton HM HX; tel. 292-6515; fax 292-0697; e-mail mcharles@but.bm; Pres. ANTHONY WOLFFE; Gen. Sec. MICHAEL CHARLES; principal mems of the BTUC include:

Bermuda Federation of Musicians and Variety Artists: Reid St, POB HM 6, Hamilton HM AX; tel. 291-0138; Sec.-Gen. LLOYD H. L. SIMMONS; 318 mems.

Bermuda Public Services Union: POB HM 763, Hamilton HM CX; tel. 292-6985; fax 292-1149; e-mail osimmons@bpsu.bm; internet www.bpsu.bm; re-formed 1961; Pres. ARMELL L. THOMAS; Gen. Sec. EDWARD G. BALL, Jr; 3,454 mems.

Bermuda Union of Teachers: POB HM 726, Hamilton HM CX; tel. 292-6515; fax 292-0697; e-mail butunion@ibl.bm; internet www.but.bm; f. 1919; Pres. LISA TROTT; Gen. Sec. MICHAEL A. CHARLES; 700 mems.

Transport

ROADS

There are some 225 km (140 miles) of public highways and 222 km of private roads, with almost 6 km reserved for cyclists and pedestrians. Each household is permitted only one passenger vehicle, and visitors may only hire mopeds, to limit traffic congestion.

SHIPPING

The chief port of Bermuda is Hamilton, with a secondary port at St George's. Both are used by freight and cruise ships. There is also a 'free' port, Freeport, on Ireland Island. In 2000 it was proposed to enlarge Hamilton docks in order to accommodate larger cruise ships. There remained, however, fears that such an enlargement would place excessive strain on the island's environment and infrastructure. Bermuda is a free-flag nation, and at December 2006 the shipping register comprised 149 vessels, totalling 8,413,173 grt.

Department of Marine and Ports Services: POB HM 180, Hamilton HM AX; tel. 295-6575; fax 295-5523; e-mail marineports@bolagov.bm; Dir of Marine and Ports Services FRANCIS RICHARDSON; Deputy Dir and Habour Master MICHAEL DOLDING.

Department of Maritime Administration: Magnolia Pl., 2nd Floor, 45 Victoria St, POB HM 1628, Hamilton HM GX; tel. 295-7251; fax 295-3718; e-mail maradros@gov.bm; internet www.bermudashipping.bm; Chief Surveyor DUNCAN CURRIE; Registrar of Shipping ANGELIQUE BURGESS.

Principal Shipping Companies

B & H Ocean Carriers Ltd: Par-la-Ville Pl., 3rd Floor, 14 Par-la-Ville Rd, POB HM 2257 HM JX, Hamilton; tel. 295-6875; fax 295-6796; e-mail info@bhcousa.com; internet www.bhocean.com; f. 1987; Chair. MICHAEL S. HUDNER.

Benor Tankers Ltd: Cedar House, 41 Cedar Ave, HM 12 Hamilton; Pres. CARL-ERIK HAAVALDSEN; Chair. HARRY RUTTEN.

Bermuda Forwarders Ltd: 2 Mills Creek Park, POB HM 511, Hamilton HM CX; tel. 292-4600; fax 292-1859; e-mail info@bermudaforwarders.com; internet www.bermudaforwarders.com; international import and export handlers; Pres. TOBY KEMPE.

Bermuda International Shipping Ltd: Waverley Bldg, 35 Church St, Hamilton HM 12; tel. 296-9798; fax 295-4556; e-mail meyershipping@ibl.bm; internet www.meyer.bm; Dir J. HENRY HAYWARD.

BEST Shipping: 6 Addendum Lane South, POB HM 335, Hamilton HM BX; tel. 292-8080; fax 295-1713; e-mail dsousa@best.bm; internet www.best.bm; f. 1987 as Bermuda Export Sea Transfer Ltd; sea and air freight services; Pres. and Man. Dir DAVID SOUSA.

Container Ship Management Ltd: 14 Par-la-Ville Rd, POB HM 2266, Hamilton HM JX; tel. 295-1624; fax 295-3781; e-mail csm@csm.bm; internet www.bcl.bm/csm; Pres. GEOFFREY FRITH.

Dorchester Atlantic Marine Limited Partnership: Richmond House, 12 Par-la-Ville Rd, POB HM 2089, Hamilton HM HX; tel. 295-0614; fax 292-1549; e-mail contact@dorchesteratlantic.com; internet www.dorchesteratlantic.com; f. 1970; fmrly Atlantic marine Limited Partnership; Man. Dir JENS ALERS.

Gearbulk Holding Ltd: Par-la-Ville Pl., 14 Par-la-Ville Rd, Hamilton HM JX; tel. 295-2184; fax 295-2234; internet www.gearbulk.com; Pres. ARTHUR E. M. JONES.

Golden Ocean Management: Par-la-Ville Pl., 14 Par-la-Ville Rd, POB HM 1593, Hamilton HM 08; tel. 295-6935; fax 295-3494; internet www.goldenocean.no; Chair. and Pres. JOHN FREDRIKSON; CEO HERMAN BILLUNG.

Norwegian Cruise Line: 3rd Floor, Reid House, Church St, POB 1564, Hamilton; internet www.ncl.com; Chair. EINAR KLOSTER.

Shell Bermuda (Overseas) Ltd: Shell House, Ferry Reach, POB 2, St George's 1.

Unicool Ltd: POB HM 1179, Hamilton HM EX; tel. 295-2244; fax 292-8666; Pres. MATS JANSSON.

Worldwide Shipping Managers Ltd: 7 Reid St, Suite 402, POB HM 1862, Hamilton HM 11; tel. 295-3770; fax 295-3801.

CIVIL AVIATION

The former US Naval Air Station (the only airfield) was returned to the Government of Bermuda in September 1995, following the closure of the base and the withdrawal of US forces from the islands. Bermuda does not have its own airline. From May 2006 the island was served by the low-cost US airline JetBlue, in addition to other British, Canadian and US airlines.

Department of Civil Aviation: POB GE 218, St George's GE BX; tel. 293-1640; fax 293-2417; e-mail info@dca.gov.bm; internet www.dca.gov.bm; responsible for all civil aviation matters; Dir of Civil Aviation THOMAS DUNSTAN.

Bermuda International Airport: 3 Cahow Way, St George's GE CX; tel. 293-2470; e-mail dao@gov.bm; internet www.bermudaairport.com; Gen. Man. AARON ADDERLEY.

Tourism

Tourism is the principal industry of Bermuda and is government-sponsored. The great attractions of the islands are the climate, scenery, and facilities for outdoor entertainment of all types. In 2007 a total of 659,572 tourists (including 354,024 cruise-ship passengers) visited Bermuda. In 2005 the industry earned an estimated B $392.3m. In 2006 there were 56 licensed hotels, 2,824 rooms and 5,698 beds; government projections were for 65 licensed hotels, 4,229 rooms and 8,870 beds to be available by the end of 2009.

Bermuda Department of Tourism: Tulip House, Suite 9, 70 Borough High St; tel. 864-9924; fax 864-9966; e-mail ukEurope@bermudatourism.com; internet www.bermudatourism.com; Dir of Tourism IAN MACINTYRE (acting).

Bermuda Hotel Association: 'Carmel', 61 King St, Hamilton HM 19; tel. 295-2127; fax 292-6671; e-mail johnh@ibl.bm; internet www.experiencebermuda.com; Chair. MICHAEL WINFIELD; Exec. Dir JOHN HARVEY; 37 mem. hotels.

THE BRITISH ANTARCTIC TERRITORY

The British Antarctic Territory lies within the Antarctic Treaty area (i.e. south of latitude 60° S). The Territory, created by an Order in Council which came into force on 3 March 1962, consists of all islands and territories south of latitude 60° S, between longitudes 20° W and 80° W, and includes the South Orkney Islands, the South Shetland Islands, the Antarctic Peninsula and areas south and east of the Weddell Sea. With the island of South Georgia and the South Sandwich Islands (now forming a separate territory, q.v.), this area had been constituted by the United Kingdom as the Falkland Islands Dependencies in 1908. The flag of the British Antarctic Territory (proportions 1 by 2) has a white field bearing the union flag of the United Kingdom in the canton and, in the centre of the fly half of the flag, the arms of the territory, which consists of a white shield with three wavy blue horizontal lines at the top overlapped by a red triangle, apex downwards, bearing a brown and yellow torch with red-bordered yellow flames framed by golden rays, the shield supported by a golden lion and a black and white penguin with a yellow throat, both supporters surmounted by a scroll of yellow and light blue with a red reverse and the red inscription 'Research and Discovery'; above the shield, a helmet of grey, light blue and white supporting a torse, alternately of white and light blue, is depicted below a sailing ship of black flying the British Blue Ensign at the gaff. The Territory has its own legal system and postal administration, and is financially self-sufficient owing to revenue derived from income tax and the sale of postage stamps.

Area: Land covers about 1,709,400 sq km (660,003 sq miles).

Population: There is no permanent population, but scientists and support personnel staff the British Antarctic Survey stations. *2005/06:* Summer 200 (Rothera 148, Halley 37, Signy 15); Winter 37.

Acting Commissioner, Head of Overseas Territories Directorate and Head of Polar Regions Unit: JANE RUMBLE, Polar Regions Unit, Overseas Territories Directorate, Foreign and Commonwealth Office, King Charles St, London, SW1A 2AH, United Kingdom; tel. (20) 7008-1921; fax (20) 7008-2086; e-mail katherine.henry@fco.gov.uk; internet www.fco.gov.uk/antarctica.

British Antarctic Survey: High Cross, Madingley Rd, Cambridge, CB3 0ET, United Kingdom; tel. (1223) 221400; fax (1223) 362616; e-mail basweb@bas.ac.uk; internet www.antarctica.ac.uk; f. 1962 to replace Falkland Islands Dependencies Survey; responsible for almost all British scientific activities in Antarctica; operates two ice-strengthened ocean-going vessels (RRS *Ernest Shackleton* and RRS *James Clark Ross*), four de Havilland Twin Otter and one Dash-7 aircraft; Total Budget £61.4m. in 2007/08; Dir Prof. NICHOLAS OWENS.

RESEARCH STATIONS

	Latitude	Longitude
Halley	75° 35′ S	26° 34′ W
Rothera	67° 34′ S	68° 08′ W
Signy (summer only)	60° 43′ S	45° 36′ W

THE BRITISH INDIAN OCEAN TERRITORY (BIOT)

The British Indian Ocean Territory (BIOT) was formed in November 1965, through the amalgamation of the former Seychelles islands of Aldabra, Desroches and Farquhar with the Chagos Archipelago, a group of islands 1,930 km north-east of Mauritius, previously administered by the Governor of Mauritius. Aldabra, Desroches and Farquhar were ceded to Seychelles when that country was granted independence in June 1976. Since then BIOT has comprised only the Chagos Archipelago, including the coral atoll Diego Garcia, with a total land area of 60 sq km (23 sq miles), together with a surrounding area of some 54,400 sq km (21,000 sq miles) of ocean.

BIOT was established to meet British and US defence requirements in the Indian Ocean. Previously, the principal economic function of the islands was the production of copra: the islands, together with the coconut plantations, were owned by a private company. The copra industry declined after the Second World War, and, following the purchase of the islands by the British Crown in 1967, the plantations ceased to operate and the inhabitants were offered the choice of resettlement in Mauritius or in Seychelles. The majority (which numbered about 1,200) went to Mauritius, the resettlement taking place during 1969–73, prior to the construction of the military facility. Mauritius subsequently campaigned for the immediate return of the Territory, and received support from the Organization of African Unity (now the African Union) and from India. A protracted dispute with the United Kingdom over compensation for those displaced ended in 1982 when the British Government agreed to an *ex-gratia* payment of £4m. In July 2000 a judicial review of the validity of the Immigration Ordinance of 1971, under which the islanders were removed from BIOT, and which continued to prevent them from resettling in the Territory, was instigated. Meanwhile, in March 1999 it was disclosed that the displaced islanders and their families, now estimated to number up to 4,000, were not to be included in the offer of full British citizenship, with the right of abode in the United Kingdom, that was to be extended to residents of other United Kingdom Overseas Territories by legislation pending in the British Parliament.

In November 2000 the British High Court ruled that the Chagos islanders (Ilois) had been illegally evicted from the Chagos Archipelago, and quashed Section 4 of the 1971 Ordinance, which prevented the return of the Ilois to BIOT. During the case it transpired that the British Government had received a subsidy of US $11m. on the purchase of Polaris submarines in the 1960s from the USA, in return for the lease of Diego Garcia for the US military. Furthermore, the Government had apparently termed the Ilois 'contract workers' in order to persuade the UN that the islanders were not an indigenous population with democratic rights. However, memorandums of the Foreign and Commonwealth Office revealed government knowledge of some of the Ilois living in the Chagos Archipelago for two generations. The British Secretary of State for Foreign and Commonwealth Affairs declined an appeal, thereby granting the islanders an immediate right to return to BIOT. Despite this, a new ordinance, issued in January 2001, allowed the residents to return to any of the islands in the Archipelago, except Diego Garcia, easing US fears of a population near its military base. The British Overseas Territories Act came into effect in May 2002, allowing the displaced islanders to apply for British citizenship. At that time the British Government was also examining the feasibility of a return to the Chagos Archipelago for the islanders, who continued to seek compensation. (However, a report had concluded that resettlement on the atolls of Salomon and Peros Banhos was logistically possible, if not necessarily economically viable.) In October 2003 the High Court ruled that although the islanders could claim to have been ill-treated, the British Government had not known at the time that its actions were unlawful and their claims for compensation were dismissed. Many of the islanders subsequently moved to the United Kingdom.

In December 2000 the Ilois announced their intention to sue the US Government for US $6,000m. in compensation. The hearing of the case, in which the Ilois alleged genocide, torture and forced relocation, opened in December 2001. In mid-2002 the Chagos islanders initiated legal action against the recruitment consultancy that supplies civilian employees for the US naval base on Diego Garcia, alleging that the company had discriminated against them when appointing staff to the base; the consultancy was the first of 12 entities that the islanders intended to sue in the USA. (In April 2006 the US Federal Court of Appeals of the District of Columbia ruled that it had no authority to order compensation to those evicted in order to make way for the establishment of a US military base on Diego Garcia.)

In June 2004 the British Government issued two decrees explicitly stating the country's control of immigration services within the archipelago and banning the Ilois from returning. Nevertheless, in November the Chagossian group reached agreement for some 100 people to travel to Diego Garcia for the purpose of visiting the graves of relatives. In early April 2006 102 Chagossians commenced a visit to the archipelago. On 11 May the British High Court ruled that the exclusion of the islanders from their territory was irrational and unlawful. The British Government commenced proceedings to overturn the May ruling at the Court of Appeal in February 2007; however, in May that court confirmed that the residents of the Chagos Archipelago had been unlawfully removed and upheld the displaced islanders' immediate right to return. In November the House of Lords granted the British Government the right to appeal against the Court of Appeal's decision, on the condition that the Chagossian's costs were met by the British Government. The appeal was scheduled to take place in June 2008. It was estimated that only approximately 500 of the 2,000 deported during the 1960s and 1970s were still alive.

A 1966 agreement between the United Kingdom and the USA provided for BIOT to be used by both countries over an initial period of 50 years, with the option of extending this for a further 20 years. The United Kingdom undertook to cede the Chagos Archipelago to Mauritius when it was no longer required for defence purposes. Originally the US military presence was limited to a communications centre on Diego Garcia. In 1972, however, construction of a naval support facility was begun, apparently in response to the expansion of the Soviet maritime presence in the Indian Ocean. In August 1987 the US navy began to use Diego Garcia as a facility for minesweeping helicopters taking part in operations in the Persian (Arabian) Gulf. Following Iraq's invasion of Kuwait in August 1990, Diego Garcia was used as a base for US B-52 aircraft, which were deployed in the Gulf region. Runway facilities on Diego Garcia were again used in September 1996 and December 1998 as a base for US support aircraft during US missile attacks on Iraq. In October 2001 US forces used the Diego Garcia base to launch strikes on Afghanistan with B-52 aircraft. In March–April 2003 the base was used to launch bombing raids on Iraq in the US-led military campaign to oust the regime of Saddam Hussain.

In January 1988 Mauritius renewed its campaign to regain sovereignty over the Chagos Archipelago. In November 1989, following an incident in which a military aircraft belonging to the US Air Force accidentally bombed a US naval vessel near Diego Garcia, a demonstration was held outside the US embassy in Mauritius, demanding the withdrawal of foreign military forces from the area. However, the US Assistant Secretary of State for African Affairs reiterated during an official visit to Mauritius, in the same month, that the USA would maintain its military presence in the Indian Ocean. In December 2000, following the British High Court's ruling, Mauritius once again staked its claim for sovereignty over the Chagos Archipelago. In April 2004 Paul Bérenger, the recently installed Prime Minister of Mauritius, renewed the campaign to reclaim sovereignty after specialists in international law advised him that the decree by which the United Kingdom separated the Chagos Archipelago from Mauritius was illegal. An attempt was made to block the Mauritian Government from pursuing the case at the International Court of Justice on the basis of a long-standing ruling, whereby members of the Commonwealth could not take the United Kingdom to court; in July the ruling was extended to former members of the Commonwealth, in order to prevent Mauritius from circumventing the obstacle by withdrawing from that organization. Mauritius announced that it would pursue the matter at the General Assembly of the UN.

The civil administration of BIOT is the responsibility of a non-resident commissioner in the Foreign and Commonwealth Office in London, United Kingdom, represented on Diego Garcia by a Royal Navy commander and a small British naval presence. A chief justice, a senior magistrate and a principal legal adviser (who performs the functions of an attorney-general) are resident in the United Kingdom.

Land Area: about 60 sq km.

Population: There are no permanent inhabitants. In November 2004 there were about 4,000 US and British military personnel and civilian support staff stationed in the Territory.

Currency: The official currency is the pound sterling, but the US dollar is also accepted.

Acting Commissioner: JANE RUMBLE, Head of Overseas Territories Dept, Foreign and Commonwealth Office, King Charles St, London SW1A 2AH, United Kingdom; tel. (20) 7008-2890.

Administrator: TONY HUMPHRIES, Overseas Territories Dept, Foreign and Commonwealth Office, King Charles St, London SW1A 2AH, United Kingdom; tel. (20) 7008-2890.

Commissioner's Representative: Commdr NEIL HINCH, RN, Diego Garcia, c/o BFPO Ships.

THE BRITISH VIRGIN ISLANDS

Introductory Survey

Location, Climate, Language, Religion, Flag, Capital

The British Virgin Islands consist of more than 60 islands and cays, of which only 16 are inhabited. The islands, most of which are mountainous and of volcanic origin (the only exception of any size is the coralline island of Anegada), lie at the northern end of the Leeward Islands, about 100 km (62 miles) to the east of Puerto Rico and adjoining the United States Virgin Islands. The climate is subtropical but extremes of heat are relieved by the trade winds. The average annual rainfall is 1,000 mm (39 ins). The official language is English. Most of the inhabitants profess Christianity. The flag is the British 'Blue Ensign', with the territory's badge (a green shield, with a white-clad virgin and 12 oil lamps, above a scroll bearing the motto 'vigilate') in the fly. The capital, Road Town, is situated on the island of Tortola.

Recent History

Previously peopled by Caribs, and named by the navigator Christopher Colombus after St Ursula and her 11,000 fellow-martyrs, the islands were settled by buccaneers and the Dutch, but were finally annexed by the British in 1672. In 1872 they became part of the British colony of the Leeward Islands, which was administered under a federal system. The federation was dissolved in July 1956, but the Governor of the Leeward Islands continued to administer the British Virgin Islands until 1960, when an appointed Administrator (restyled Governor in 1971) assumed direct responsibility. Unlike the other Leeward Islands, the British Virgin Islands did not join the Federation of the West Indies (1958–62), preferring to develop its links with the US Virgin Islands.

A new Constitution was introduced in April 1967, when H. Lavity Stoutt became the islands' first Chief Minister. He was later replaced by Willard Wheatley. At an election in September 1975 Stoutt's Virgin Islands Party (VIP) and the United Party (UP) each won three of the seven elective seats on the Legislative Council. Wheatley, sitting as an independent member, held the balance of power and he continued in office, with Stoutt as Deputy Chief Minister.

An amended Constitution took effect in June 1977, giving more extensive internal self-government; some electoral changes were also made (see Constitution). In the first election to the enlarged Legislative Council to take place under the new Constitution, in November 1979, independent candidates won five of the nine elective seats, with the VIP winning the remainder. Stoutt secured enough support to be reinstated as Chief Minister. In the November 1983 election the VIP and the UP each secured four seats. The one successful independent candidate, Cyril Romney, became Chief Minister and formed a coalition Government with members of the UP.

In August 1986 the Governor dissolved the Legislative Council six days before a scheduled council debate on a motion of no confidence against Romney (who had allegedly been involved with a company under investigation by the British police and the US Department of Justice's Drug Enforcement Administration). At a general election in the following month the VIP won five of the nine elective seats, with the UP and independent candidates (including Romney) taking two seats each. Stoutt was appointed Chief Minister.

The Deputy Chief Minister, Omar Hodge, was dismissed from the Executive Council in March 1988, following an official inquiry into allegations of financial malpractice (he continued to protest his innocence, and won a libel suit in January 1990). Hodge was replaced by Ralph O'Neal, formerly leader of the UP, who joined the VIP.

At a general election in November 1990 the VIP increased its majority, while the UP lost both its seats. Stoutt retained the post of Chief Minister.

The principal concern of the Stoutt administration in the early 1990s was the trade in, and increasing local use of, illicit drugs. In late 1990 the Stoutt administration introduced legislation to impose more stringent regulations governing the 'offshore' financial sector, while plans to review immigration policy were under discussion, in an attempt to reduce the number of illegal immigrants entering the territory. Both areas had previously been considered to be insufficiently protected from exploitation by traffickers seeking to introduce illicit drugs into the islands or to divert funds from their sale through the financial sector.

In August 1993 the British Government appointed three commissioners to review the territory's Constitution at the request of the Legislative Council. Proposed changes included the introduction of direct elections for the position of Chief Minister, the enlargement of the Legislative Council and the adoption of a bill of rights. The British Government's decision in early 1994 to accept the commission's proposal to enlarge the Legislative Council to 13 seats (by the creation of four seats representing the territory 'at large') was strongly criticized by Stoutt. His opposition to the changes intensified in July, when he failed to obtain a deferral of the decision in order that the Legislative Council could debate the issue. Discussions on various recommendations in the review continued in 1995 and 1996.

At elections to the newly enlarged legislature on 20 February 1995 the VIP won six seats, the UP and the Concerned Citizens' Movement (CCM—formerly IPM) each secured two seats and independent candidates won the remaining three seats. One of the successful independents, Alvin Christopher, subsequently gave his support to the VIP, thus providing the party with the majority required to form a Government, again headed by Stoutt. However, in May, the Deputy Chief Minister, Ralph O'Neal, was appointed Chief Minister, following the sudden death of Stoutt.

In July 1996 the Governor, David Mackilligin, recommended that there should be a public debate on the continued use of judicial corporal punishment in the territory (the British Virgin Islands being the only British Dependent Territory in which the practice remained in force). The issue was raised owing to concern that, as a signatory to the European Convention on Human Rights, the United Kingdom was potentially in violation of the accord every time that a sentence of corporal punishment was passed in the islands.

In March 1999 the Government of the United Kingdom published draft legislation pertaining to its relationship with its Overseas Dependencies, which were to be renamed United Kingdom Overseas Territories (and had been referred to as such since February 1998). The legislation proposed the extension of British citizenship to the citizens of Overseas Territories, although it also required its Overseas Territories to amend their legislation on human rights and on the regulation of the financial services sector to meet international standards. In July the British Government appointed a consultant, Alan Hoole, a former Governor of Anguilla, to review the Constitution of the British Virgin Islands. In September Hoole proposed several changes to the Constitution, including the introduction of more frequent meetings of the Legislative Council and the removal of the Governor's powers to veto legislation. Under the terms of the proposed changes, the Governor was also to be obliged to consult with the Executive Council before implementing policy in his areas of special responsibility (foreign affairs, the civil service and defence). It was also suggested that members of the Legislative Council and senior civil servants should be obliged to declare their interests. In August the Governor outlined the Government's legislative programme. The main aim of the proposed legislation was to ensure that the regulation of the financial services sector conformed to international standards. Savage, who also announced the introduction of a comprehensive review of the education system, announced that the drafting of the proposed amendments to the Constitution would continue throughout the year.

Elections to the Legislative Council took place on 17 May 1999. The VIP retained control of the legislature, increasing its representation to seven seats. The recently founded National Democratic Party (NDP) took five seats, while the CCM retained one seat. The UP and several independent candidates also contested the elections. O'Neal subsequently re-appointed the members of the previous Executive Council.

In September 2000 the Legislative Council passed legislation abolishing judicial corporal punishment on the British Virgin Islands, in keeping with the United Kingdom's acceptance of the European Convention of Human Rights. In November the Legislative Council voted in favour of making 7 March, the birth date of H. Lavity Stoutt, a public holiday; this was to replace, from 2002, the public holiday of 14 November, the birthday of the Prince of Wales.

The Organisation for Economic Co-operation and Development (see p. 347) announced in April 2002 that the British Virgin Islands had made sufficient commitments to improve the transparency of its tax and regulatory systems to be removed from an updated list of 'un-co-operative' tax havens, first published in 2000. Also in April, a tax information exchange agreement, designed to reduce the potential for abuse of the tax system, was signed with the USA. In the same month, the financial secretary, L. Allen Wheatley, was arrested in connection with the mishandling of government contracts relating to the Beef Island Airport development project, and in May the Government survived a motion of no confidence brought against it in connection with the airport development project. In November 2002 some of the charges against Wheatley were dropped after the prosecution was unable to provide sufficient evidence of fraud or breach of trust; however, the presiding magistrate determined there was enough evidence for Wheatley to answer related charges of theft and corruption. The trial of Wheatley and four other men began in November 2003; four of the five defendants pleaded guilty to approving an airport telecommunications contract based on inflated prices that cost the Government some US $450,000. In January 2004 Wheatley was sentenced to nine months in gaol; in return for the guilty pleas, prosecutors withdrew theft charges, which carried much harsher jail terms. (Wheatley had already been sentenced to five years' imprisonment on separate corruption charges in February 2003.)

In late 2002 the recovering financial sector faced further disruption when the United Kingdom, under pressure from a European Union (EU, see p. 244) investigation into tax evasion, demanded that the British Virgin Islands disclose the identities and account details of Europeans holding private savings accounts on the islands. The British Virgin Islands, along with some other British Overseas Territories facing similar demands, claimed it was being treated unfairly compared with more powerful European countries, such as Switzerland and Luxembourg. In January 2005 the Business Companies Act came into force, which eliminated the distinction between laws governing local and 'offshore' businesses. Further reform to the tax system also took place.

In May 2002 the British Overseas Territories Act, having received royal assent in the United Kingdom in February, came into force and granted British citizenship to the people of its Overseas Territories, including the British Virgin Islands. Under the new law British Virgin Islanders would be able to hold British passports and work in the United Kingdom and anywhere else in the EU.

In October 2002 Tom Macan succeeded Frank Savage as Governor.

A general election was held on 16 June 2003. The NDP secured eight seats compared with the VIP's five after a campaign that was dominated by the issues of alleged corruption, management of public sector capital projects, and relations with the United Kingdom. Orlando Smith became the new Chief Minister.

Following the scandal over the Beef Island Airport development scheme, and in an attempt to hold public offices more accountable for their expenditure and renew public trust in the executive, in late September 2003 the new Government passed an Audit Act. A commission for constitutional review was appointed in April 2004, which was to consider, *inter alia*, the criteria for qualification for residency status, the reserve powers of the Governor, the duties of the Attorney-General and the introduction of an article relating to human rights into the Constitution. A Constitutional Review Report was released in 2005, based on the commission's findings. Among the suggestions included in the report were the reform of the legal system (including the introduction of legal aid), and a move towards a cabinet system of government, with the title of Chief Minister changing to Premier. The possibility of renaming the Legislative Council a Parliament was also examined. A first round of negotiations to discuss the proposed constitutional reform, between representatives of the British Government and the Chief Minister, was held in Barbados in March 2006. Negotiations continued throughout 2006, with subsequent rounds of discussions in June and October. These were augmented by two public consultations in September to obtain contributions towards a proposed Fundamental Rights Chapter within the new constitution. A fourth and final forum, conducted in London, United Kingdom, on 26–28 February 2007, sought to examine the provisions of a draft constitution document prepared by the Constitutional Review Commission and conclude debate upon the proposed new statutes. The British Foreign and Commonwealth Office Minister with responsibility for Overseas Territories, Lord David Triesman, endorsed the successful completion of negotiations, announcing the formulation of a new constitution for the territory that would simultaneously afford greater autonomy to the country while maintaining harmonious relations with the United Kingdom; Chief Minister Smith expressed his satisfaction that '95 per cent' of the Review Commission's stated objectives for constitutional reform had been achieved.

The principal features of the proposed constitution included the institution of a cabinet system of government (whereby the Executive Council would be renamed 'the Cabinet'), within which the Premier (formerly Chief Minister) would command influence in the determination of the cabinet agenda, previously the subject of the Governor's sole arbitration, and a Cabinet Secretary would be appointed to set the Cabinet's agenda; the establishment of a National Security Council—to be comprised of the Governor, the Premier, a named government minister, the Attorney-General and the Commissioner of Police—conferring matters of internal security and policing of the islands from the sole remit of the British Government to that of the British Virgin Islands also, and upon whose recommendations the Governor would be obliged to act; the institution of an Office for Public Prosecutions; a reduction in the Governor's powers of veto; the inclusion of a Fundamental Rights Chapter to ensure the promotion and protection of citizens' human rights and freedoms; and provision for the creation of a sixth government ministry to accommodate the requirements of the territory's expanding population. The United Kingdom would retain some residual authority in order to regulate the development of the British Virgin Islands, embracing issues such as the observation of international standards in relation to the burgeoning financial services sector and the islands' natural disaster preparedness. Chief Minister Smith announced his Government's intention, at the end of March, to launch a constitutional education programme following finalization of the new constitution. After being approved by the United Kingdom Privy Council on 14 June, the Virgin Islands Constitutional Order 2007 became effective on 15 June, subsequent to the dissolution of the Legislative Council.

In February 2005 the Legislative Council approved the Firearms Amendment Act designed to reduce levels of gun crime committed with illegal weapons. New proposed legislation regarding the liberalization of the telecommunications sector was under discussion in Parliament in early 2006; however, the bill was subsequently withdrawn after disagreement over which members should vote. At the following parliamentary sitting, at the beginning of May, the bill was again presented for debate, but members voted for it to be removed from the order paper for a second time. The Minister for Communications and Works, J. Alvin Christopher, failed to vote in favour of withdrawing the proposed legislation, instead abstaining along with members of the opposition. The following week Christopher was dismissed from his government post; he was replaced by Elmore Stoutt.

Proposals for the liberalization of the telecommunications sector continued to feature in parliamentary discussion during 2006 and, in October, some tangible progress was made towards ending the 'three-way monopoly' within the territory's communications and broadcasting market, with the establishment of a Telecommunications Regulatory Commission (TRC). The authority, a statutory body affiliated to the Ministry of Communications and Works, was instituted under the Telecommunications Act 2006, which was ratified in June and effected on 24 October of that year. It was proposed that three or four operators would be awarded licences for the provision of a comprehensive range of telecommunications services and, in early March 2007, the sole mobile provider in the British Virgin Islands, Cable & Wireless, signed an Interconnection Agreement memorandum of understanding with CCT Global Communications (operating locally as CCT Boatphone). In late April the Government announced that it was inviting unitary licence applications—permitting operation in all sectors of the telecommunications market for 15 years—from only the three current providers. A fourth company, Digicel, initiated court proceedings against the TRC in respect of the restriction after its licence application was rejected.

The High Court ruled in favour of Digicel, which was granted a licence to operate mobile services in December 2007.

On 18 April 2006 David Pearey was sworn in as Governor in succession to Tom Macan.

In an effort to enhance immigration monitoring in the British Virgin Islands, the Government implemented a new visa regime in April 2007 requiring that Jamaican nationals without residency or 'belonger' status obtain a visa to enter the territory; the passport office had commenced issuing of visas on 1 March, since which time over 850 such documents had been granted to Jamaicans. The measure followed the apprehension, during a border security initiative in February, of 49 illegal immigrants originating from Haiti and the Dominican Republic.

The VIP achieved a convincing victory at a general election held on 20 August 2007, securing ten seats while the NDP won two. An independent candidate won the remaining seat in the renamed legislature, the House of Assembly. The leader of the VIP, Ralph O'Neal, became the British Virgin Islands' first Premier, the title accorded to him under the terms of the new Constitution. O'Neal assumed responsibilities for the portfolios of finance and tourism, and Dancia Penn Sallah became the Deputy Premier and Minister of Health and Social Development. The new Premier also appointed Andrew Fahie as Minister of Education and Culture, Julian Fraser as Minister of Communications and Works, and Omar Hodge as Minister of Natural Resources and Labour. On assuming office, O'Neal pledged to address the increase in serious crime by reviewing levels of funding for the police force and the customs and immigration departments, and to enact a period of fiscal transparency and responsibility, particularly with regard to construction projects, owing to a predicted budget deficit of US $13m. for 2007.

Government

Under the provisions of the 2007 Constitution, the Governor is appointed by the British monarch and is responsible for external affairs, defence and internal security, terms and conditions of service of public officers, and the administration of the Courts. The Governor also fulfils the role of Presiding Officer at meetings of the Cabinet, which comprises the Premier and five other members. The House of Assembly comprises 15 members: a Speaker, one ex officio member, and 13 members elected by universal adult suffrage.

Defence

The United Kingdom is responsible for the defence of the islands. In September 1999 it was announced that Royal Air Force patrols were to be undertaken from the islands in order to intercept drugs-traffickers. Central government expenditure on defence totalled US $0.4m. in 1997.

Economic Affairs

In 2006, according to UN estimates, the British Virgin Islands' gross domestic product (GDP) was US $1,034m., equivalent to some $46,404 per head. The population doubled during 1984–94, to 17,903, primarily owing to a large influx of immigrants from other Caribbean Islands, the United Kingdom and the USA. During 1995–2005, according to the Caribbean Development Bank (CDB), it was estimated, the population increased at an average annual rate of 3.1%, while GDP increased, in real terms, by some 5.9% per year during 1996–2006. Estimated growth was some 4.1% in 2006.

Agriculture (including forestry and fishing) contributed 1.0% of GDP in 2006, and engaged 0.5% of the employed labour force in 2005. The islands produces fruit and vegetables for domestic consumption or export to the US Virgin Islands, and some sugar cane (for the production of rum). Food imports accounted for 18.9% of total import costs in 1997. The fishing industry caters for local consumption and export, and provides a sporting activity for tourists, although the Government has been looking to develop deep-sea fishing commercially for domestic and export markets.

Industry (including mining, manufacturing, construction and public utilities) accounted for 10.7% of GDP in 2006 and engaged 11.4% of the employed labour force in 2005. The mining sector is negligible, consisting of the extraction of materials for the construction industry and of some salt. Manufacturing, which provided 3.0% of GDP in 2006, consists mainly of light industry; there is one rum distillery, two factories for the production of ice, some plants producing concrete blocks and other construction materials, small boat manufacture and various cottage industries. Construction activity accounted for 5.6% of GDP in 2006. Most energy requirements must be imported (mineral fuels accounted for an estimated 8.5% of total imports in 1997).

Services, primarily tourism and financial services, constitute the principal economic sector of the British Virgin Islands, contributing 88.2% of GDP in 2006, and accounting for 88.1% of employment in 2005. The tourism industry earned some US $437m. in 2005, and employed about one-third of the working population, directly or indirectly. The British Virgin Islands is the largest 'bareboat' chartering centre in the Caribbean, and approximately 60% of stop-over visitors stay aboard yachts. Nevertheless, in 2002 the restaurants and hotels sector contributed 13.5% of GDP. The number of stop-over visitors reached 337,134 in 2005 (most of whom were from the USA), an 11.0% increase on the previous year's total; the ratio of tourists to local population is therefore higher than at any other Caribbean destination. The 2001 budget included $53m. to be spent on renovations to the Beef Island airport, in addition to further investment to the country's infrastructure, which was expected to provide a boost to tourism revenue in the second half of the decade.

Financial services expanded rapidly as a result of legislative measures adopted in 1984, and in 2004 the 'offshore' sector contributed over one-half of direct government revenue (some US $110m.). There were a cumulative total of 544,000 International Business Company (IBC) registrations in the islands in 1984–2004. The islands have also recorded significant growth in the establishment of mutual funds and of insurance companies. In January 2002 the Government created the Financial Services Commission, an independent regulatory authority for the sector, in order to meet international demands for a clear separation between the Government and financial services regulation.

In 2003, according to the CDB, the British Virgin Islands recorded a trade deficit of US $158.1m. The trade deficit is normally offset by receipts from tourism, development aid, remittances from islanders working abroad (many in the US Virgin Islands) and, increasingly, from the 'offshore' financial sector. The principal sources of imports (most of the islands' requirements must be imported) are the USA (which provided 56.9% of imports in 1997), Trinidad and Tobago, Antigua and Barbuda, and also the United Kingdom. The principal markets for the limited amount of exports are the US Virgin Islands and the USA and Puerto Rico; rum is exported to the USA. Machinery and transport equipment are the main imports (accounting for 28.3% of total imports in 1997), and fruit and vegetables, rum, sand and gravel are the main exports.

The budget for the 2004 financial year recorded revenue at US $204.7m. against recurrent and capital expenditure of $214.2m. In 1996/97 there was a surplus of $56m. on the current account of the balance of payments. British budgetary support ceased in 1977, but the United Kingdom grants assistance for capital development. In 2004 total external debt was calculated to be $44.1m. In 1998 the territory received $1.2m. in development assistance. Central Government debt to GDP ratio was estimated at 10.0% in the same year. The average annual rate of inflation was 3.1% in 1995–2005; consumer prices increased by an average 0.7% in 2004 and by 2.3% in 2005. The rate of unemployment was estimated to be 3.5% in 2005.

The British Virgin Islands became an associate member of the Caribbean Community and Common Market (CARICOM, see p. 196) in 1991; it is a member of CARICOM's Caribbean Development Bank (CDB, see p. 201) and an associate member of the Organisation of Eastern Caribbean States (OECS, see p. 425). In economic affairs the territory has close affiliations with the neighbouring US Virgin Islands, and uses US currency. As a dependency of the United Kingdom, the islands have the status of Overseas Territory in association with the European Union (EU, see p. 244).

The economy of the British Virgin Islands is largely dominated by tourism and by the provision of international financial services. The 'offshore' financial sector, which developed rapidly in the last two decades of the 20th century, is an important source of employment and provided 54% of direct government revenue in 2004. Despite ongoing efforts to attract insurance and trust companies to the islands, it was estimated that in early 2000 IBCs still accounted for around 90% of government revenues from financial services. International attempts, notably by the Organisation for Economic Co-operation and Development (OECD, see p. 347), to encourage the reform of 'offshore' financial centres are therefore of great concern to the British Virgin Islands, particularly as IBCs, which are not taxed and which are not obliged to disclose their directors or shareholders, have been singled out for particular criticism. Nevertheless, revenue from annual licence fees paid by 'offshore' companies remained strong in the early 21st century. Despite the rise of the financial sector, tourism remains the most important sector of the economy, as the construction and retail sectors, among others, are to a certain extent dependent on its performance. In the long term, however, the Government hoped to encourage greater diversification of the economy, in order to reduce reliance on tourism and financial services, both of which remained vulnerable to external pressures. Nevertheless, according to reports, cruise-ship passenger numbers increased by 23.9% year on year in January–November 2007, to 472,743. Moreover, the implementation of a new passenger departure tax, which was approved in 2007, was likely further to increase tourism revenue. Although the aftermath of the September 2001 terrorist attacks in the USA adversely affected tourism revenues in 2002, which was only partially offset by increased activity in the 'offshore' banking sector, the economy performed strongly in 2003. In 2004 legislation was approved eliminating the distinction between 'onshore' and 'offshore' taxation regimes, in order to bring the economic structure of the Virgin Islands into confirmity with EU and OECD requirements; a transitional period ended in January

UNITED KINGDOM OVERSEAS TERRITORIES — The British Virgin Islands

2007. In late 2006 the British Virgin Islands Ports Authority announced plans to improve the territory's port facilities. The budget for 2007 recorded the highest revenues ever for the British Virgin Islands, and included some measures to provide tax relief to those on lower incomes. Economic growth in the early and mid-2000s was attributed to tourism (particularly eco-tourism) and the burgeoning financial sector.

Education

Primary education is free, universal and compulsory between the ages of five and 11. Secondary education is also free and lasts from 12 to 16 years of age. In 2004/05 enrolment at primary schools included 95.1% of children in the relevant age-group; enrolment at secondary schools included 88.2% of students in the relevant age category during the same academic period. Higher education is available at the University of the Virgin Islands (St Thomas, US Virgin Islands) and elsewhere in the Caribbean, in North America and in the United Kingdom. Central government expenditure on education in 1997 was US $17.1m.

Public Holidays

2008: 1 January (New Year's Day), 3 March (H. Lavity Stoutt's Birthday), 10 March (Commonwealth Day), 21 March (Good Friday), 24 March (Easter Monday), 12 May (Whit Monday), 14 June (Queen's Official Birthday), 1 July (Territory Day), 4–6 August (Festival Monday, Tuesday and Wednesday), 21 October (Saint Ursula's Day), 25–26 December (Christmas).

2009: 1 January (New Year's Day), 2 March (H. Lavity Stoutt's Birthday), 9 March (Commonwealth Day), 10 April (Good Friday), 13 April (Easter Monday), 1 June (Whit Monday), 13 June (Queen's Official Birthday), 29 June (Territory Day), 3–5 August (Festival Monday, Tuesday and Wednesday), 21 October (Saint Ursula's Day), 25–26 December (Christmas).

Weights and Measures

The imperial system is used.

Statistical Survey

Source: Development Planning Unit, Central Administrative Complex, Road Town, Tortola VG1110; tel. 494-3701; fax 494-3947; e-mail dpu@dpu.org; internet dpu.gov.vg.

AREA AND POPULATION

Area: 153 sq km (59 sq miles). *Principal Islands* (sq km): Tortola 54.4; Anegada 38.8; Virgin Gorda 21.4; Jost Van Dyke 9.1.

Population: 16,644 at census of 12 May 1991; 20,647 (males 10,627, females 10,020) at census of 21 May 2001 (Source: UN, *Demographic Yearbook*); 25,800 (estimate) at mid-2005; *By Island* (1980): Tortola 9,119; Virgin Gorda 1,412; Anegada 164; Jost Van Dyke 134; Other islands 156; (1991) Tortola 13,568 (Source: partly Caribbean Development Bank, *Social and Economic Indicators*).

Density (mid-2005): 168.6 per sq km.

Principal Town: Road Town (capital), population 13,000 (UN estimate, incl. suburbs, mid-2005). Source: UN, *World Urbanization Prospects: The 2005 Revision*.

Births, Marriages and Deaths (registrations, 2004): 316 live births (birth rate 14.7 per 1,000); 426 marriages (marriage rate 19.6 per 1,000); 120 deaths (death rate 5.5 per 1,000). *2007:* Crude birth rate 14.8 per 1,000; Crude death rate 4.4 per 1,000. Sources: Caribbean Development Bank, *Social and Economic Indicators*; Pan American Health Organization.

Expectation of Life (years at birth, estimates): 76.9 (males 75.7; females 78.1) in 2007. Source: Pan American Health Organization.

Employment (2005): Agriculture, hunting and forestry 78; Fishing 14; Mining and quarrying 37; Manufacturing 404; Electricity, gas and water supply 145; Construction 1,260; Wholesale and retail trade 1,624; Hotels and restaurants 2,573; Transport, storage and communications 454; Financial intermediation 797; Real estate, renting and business activities 1,307; Public administration and social security 5,142; Education 1,119; Health and social work 141; Other community, social and personal service activities 724; Private households with employed persons 404; Not classifiable by economic activity 9; Total 16,232.

HEALTH AND WELFARE

Physicians (per 1,000 head, 1999): 1.15.

Hospital Beds (per 1,000 head, 2005): 1.9.

Health Expenditure (% of GDP, 1995): 3.9. *2003* (public expenditure only): 3.1.

Health Expenditure (public, % of total, 1995): 36.5.

Source: Pan American Health Organization.

For definitions, see explanatory note on p. vi.

AGRICULTURE, ETC.

Livestock ('000 head, 2006, FAO estimates): Cattle 2.4; Sheep 6.1; Goats 10.0; Pigs 1.5.

Fishing (metric tons, live weight, 2005, FAO estimates): Snappers 370; Boxfishes 35; Jacks and crevalles 25; Caribbean spiny lobster 50; Marine fishes 800; Total catch (incl. others) 1,300.

Source: FAO.

INDUSTRY

Electric Energy (production, million kWh, estimates): 40 in 2002; 45 in 2003; 45 in 2004. Source: UN, *Industrial Commodity Statistics Yearbook*.

FINANCE

Currency and Exchange Rate: United States currency is used: 100 cents = 1 US dollar ($). *Sterling and Euro Equivalents* (31 December 2007): £1 sterling = US $2.0034; €1 = US $1.4721; US $100 = £49.92 = €67.93.

Budget (US $ million, 2004): *Revenue:* Tax revenue 72.6 (Import duties 24.2, Income and property tax 41.7, Passenger and hotel tax 6.7); Non-tax revenue 132.1 (Financial services sector 109.8); Total recurrent revenue 204.7. *Expenditure:* Recurrent expenditure 180.4 (Goods and services 62.9; Wages and salaries 83.6; Subsidies and transfers 32.9); Capital expenditure 33.8; Total expenditure 214.2.

Cost of Living (Consumer Price Index; base: 1995 = 100): 131.8 in 2003; 132.7 in 2004; 135.7 in 2005.

Gross Domestic Product (US $ million at constant 1990 prices): 842 in 2004; 919 in 2005; 957 in 2006. Source: UN Statistics Division, National Accounts Main Aggregates Database.

Expenditure on the Gross Domestic Product (US $ million at current prices, 2006): Government final consumption expenditure 97; Private final consumption expenditure 389; Gross capital formation 248; Changes in inventories −15; *Total domestic expenditure* 719; Exports of goods and services 1,119; *Less* Imports of goods and services 805; *GDP in purchasers' values* 1,034. Source: UN Statistics Division, National Accounts Main Aggregates Database.

Gross Domestic Product by Economic Activity (rounded figures in current prices, US $ million, 1999): Agriculture, hunting and forestry 4.1; Fishing 5.4; Mining and quarrying 0.4; Manufacturing 27.0; Electricity, gas and water 11.1; Construction 49.0; Wholesale and retail trade 90.0; Hotels and restaurants 98.0; Transport, storage and communications 79.0; Financial intermediation 43.0; Real estate, renting and business services 188.0; Public administration 35.0; Education 13.6; Health and social work 9.5; Other community, social and personal services 15.8; Private households with employed persons 6.0; *Sub-total* 674.0; *Less* Imputed bank service charges 35.0; Indirect taxes, less subsidies 23.0; *GDP in purchasers' values* 662.0. Source: UN, *National Accounts Statistics*. *2006* (US $ million): Agriculture, hunting, forestry and fishing 11; Mining, manufacturing and utilities 54 (Manufacturing 32); Construction 60; Wholesale, retail trade, restaurants and hotels 289; Transport, storage and communication 119; Other activities 530; *Total gross value added* 1,063 (Source: UN Statistics Division, National Accounts Main Aggregates Database).

EXTERNAL TRADE

Principal Commodities ($ '000): *Imports c.i.f.* (1997): Food and live animals 31,515; Beverages and tobacco 8,797; Crude materials (inedible) except fuels 1,168; Mineral fuels, lubricants, etc. 9,847; Chemicals 8,816; Basic manufactures 31,715; Machinery and transport equipment 47,019; Total (incl. others) 116,379. *Exports f.o.b.* (1996): Food and live animals 368; Beverages and tobacco 3,967; Crude materials (inedible) except fuels 1,334; Total (incl. others) 5,862. *2001* (exports, $ million) Animals 0.1; Fresh fish 0.7; Gravel and sand 1.4; Rum 3.6; Total 28.13.

Principal Trading Partners ($ '000): *Imports c.i.f.* (1997): Antigua and Barbuda 1,807; Trinidad and Tobago 2,555; United Kingdom 406; USA 94,651; Total (incl. others) 166,379. *Exports f.o.b.* (1996): USA and Puerto Rico 1,077; US Virgin Islands 2,001; Total (incl. others) 5,862. *1999:* Imports 208,419; Exports 2,081.

Source: mainly UN, *International Trade Statistics Yearbook*.

TRANSPORT

Road Traffic (motor vehicles registered and licensed, 2005): 13,392 (Private vehicles 9,201, Commercial vehicles 2,102, Rental vehicles 1,196, Taxis 483, Government 275, Motorcycles 135).

Shipping: *International Freight Traffic* ('000 metric tons, 2002): Goods unloaded 145.6. *Cargo Ship Arrivals* (2002): 2,027. *Merchant Fleet* (vessels registered, at 31 December 2006): 13; Total displacement 16,535 grt (Sources: British Virgin Islands Port Authority; Lloyd's Register-Fairplay, *World Fleet Statistics*).

Civil Aviation (passenger arrivals): 153,391 in 2003; 220,239 in 2004 (estimate); 220,116 in 2005 (estimate).

TOURISM

Visitor Arrivals ('000): 317.8 stop-over visitors, 300.4 cruise-ship passengers in 2003; 303.8 stop-over visitors, 466.6 cruise-ship passengers in 2004; 337.1 stop-over visitors, 449.2 cruise-ship passengers in 2005.

Visitor Expenditure (US $ million): 342 in 2003; 393 in 2004; 437 in 2005. Source: World Tourism Organization.

COMMUNICATIONS MEDIA

Radio Receivers (1997): 9,000 in use.
Television Receivers (1999): 4,000 in use.
Telephones (2002): 12,000 main lines in use.
Facsimile Machines (1996): 1,200 in use.
Non-daily Newspapers (1996): 2 (estimated circulation 4,000).
Sources: UNESCO, *Statistical Yearbook*; UN, *Statistical Yearbook*.

EDUCATION

Pre-primary: 5 schools (1994/95); 45 teachers (2004/05); 577 pupils (2004/05).
Primary: 20 schools (1993/94); 194 teachers (2004/05); 2,898 pupils (2004/05).
Secondary: 4 schools (1988); 147 teachers (2004/05); 1,882 pupils (2004/05).
Tertiary (2004/05): 110 teachers; 1,200 pupils.
Sources: UNESCO Institute for Statistics; Caribbean Development Bank, *Social and Economic Indicators*.

Directory

The Constitution

The British Virgin Islands have had a representative assembly since 1774. Following a United Kingdom Government invitation in 2001 for its Overseas Territories to institute programs of constitutional reform, a new Constitution for the British Virgin Islands was finalized in May 2007 and formally ratified by the Privy Council of the United Kingdom in June. The Virgin Islands Constitutional Order 2007 became effective (largely—see below) from 15 June and represented the first comprehensive revision of the Territory's constitution since that which had precipitated the 1977 Constitution, which it replaced. Under the terms of the 2007 Constitution, the Governor is responsible for defence and internal security (including the police force), external affairs, terms and conditions of service of public officers, and the administration of the Courts. The Governor also possesses reserved legislative powers in respect of legislation necessary in the interests of his special responsibilities and fulfils the role of Presiding Officer at meetings of the Cabinet (formerly the 'Executive Council'). The Cabinet comprises the Premier (formerly 'Chief Minister'), one ex officio member (the Attorney-General), and four other ministers (appointed by the Governor on the advice of the Premier); a Cabinet Secretary sets the Cabinet's agenda under consultation with the Premier. The House of Assembly (formerly 'Legislative Council') consists of a Speaker, chosen from among the elected members of—or those eligible for election to—the Assembly, one ex officio member (the Attorney-General) and 13 elected members (nine members from one-member electoral districts and four members representing the territory 'at large').

The new Constitution also makes provision for the formation of a sixth government ministry, while a National Security Council, comprised of the Governor, Premier, Attorney-General, Commissioner of Police and a named government minister, advises the Governor upon matters of internal security and policing of the territory. A Fundamental Rights Chapter, ensuring the protection of citizens' human rights and freedoms, is also in effect. By mid-2008 a Public Service Commission and Judicial and Legal Services Commission had been instituted, while preparations for a Human Rights Commission were ongoing.

The division of the islands into nine electoral districts, instead of seven, came into effect at the November 1979 general election. The four 'at large' seats were introduced at the February 1995 general election. The minimum voting age was lowered from 21 years to 18 years.

Under the British Overseas Territories Act, which entered into effect in May 2002, British Virgin Islanders have the right to United Kingdom citizenship and the right of abode in the United Kingdom. British citizens do not enjoy reciprocal rights.

The Government

Governor: DAVID PEAREY (assumed office 18 April 2006).
Deputy Governor: ELTON GEORGES.

CABINET
(April 2008)

Premier and Minister of Finance and Tourism: RALPH TELFORD O'NEAL.
Deputy Premier and Minister of Health and Social Development: DANCIA PENN SALLAH.
Minister of Natural Resources and Labour: OMAR HODGE.
Minister of Education and Culture: ANDREW FAHIE.
Minister of Communications and Works: JULIAN FRASER.
Attorney-General: KATHLEEN QUARTEY AYENSU.

MINISTRIES

Office of the Governor: 1 Government House Dr, POB 702, Road Town, Tortola VG1110; tel. 494-2345; fax 494-5790; e-mail bvigovernor@gov.vg; internet www.bvi.gov.vg.

Office of the Deputy Governor: Central Administration Bldg, West Wing, 33 Admin Dr., Road Town, Tortola VG1110; tel. 494-3701; fax 494-6481; e-mail webmaster@dgo.gov.vg; internet www.dgo.gov.vg.

Office of the Premier: 33 Admin Dr., Wickham's Cay 1, Road Town, Tortola VG1110; tel. 468-3701; fax 468-4435; e-mail premieroffice@gov.vg; internet www.bvigazette.org.

Ministry of Communications and Works: 33 Admin Dr., Wickham's Cay 1, Road Town, Tortola VG1110; tel. 468-0629; fax 494-3873; e-mail mcw@mail.bvi.org.

Ministry of Education and Culture: 33 Admin Dr., Wickham's Cay 1, Road Town, Tortola VG1110; tel. 468-0632; fax 494-5421; e-mail bvimecgov@hotmail.com.

Ministry of Finance and Economic Development: Central Administration Bldg, West Atrium, 2nd Floor, Road Town, Tortola VG1110; tel. 494-3701; fax 494-6180; e-mail finance@gov.vg; internet www.finance.gov.vg.

Ministry of Health and Welfare: West Atrium, Central Administration Bldg, Road Town, Tortola VG1110; tel. 494-3701; fax 494-5018; e-mail min.health@bvigovvernment.org.

Ministry of Natural Resources and Labour: 33 Administration Dr., Wickham's Cay 1, Road Town, Tortola VG1110; tel. 468-3701; e-mail nrl@gov.vg.

HOUSE OF ASSEMBLY

Speaker: V. INEZ ARCHIBALD.
Clerk: ALVA MCCALL; tel. 468-6908; e-mail almccall@gov.vg.
General Election, 20 August 2007

Party	% of vote	Seats
Virgin Islands Party	45.2	10
National Democratic Party	39.6	2
Independent	15.2	1
Total	100.0	13

Political Organizations

Concerned Citizens' Movement (CCM): Road Town, Tortola VG1110; f. 1994 as successor to Independent People's Movt; Leader ETHLYN SMITH.

National Democratic Party (NDP): Road Town, Tortola VG1110; f. 1998; Chair. RUSSELL HARRIGAN; Leader ORLANDO SMITH.

United Party (UP): POB 3068, Road Town, Tortola VG1110; tel. 495-2656; fax 494-1808; e-mail liberatebvi@msn.com; f. 1967; Chair. CONRAD MADURO; Pres. HENRY KETTLE.

Virgin Islands Party (VIP): Road Town, Tortola VG1110; Leader RALPH T. O'NEAL.

Judicial System

Justice is administered by the Eastern Caribbean Supreme Court, based in Saint Lucia, which consists of two divisions: the High Court of Justice and the Court of Appeal. There are two resident High Court Judges. A visiting Court of Appeal, comprised of the Chief Justice and two Judges of Appeal, sits twice a year in the British Virgin Islands. There is also a Magistrates' Court, which hears prescribed civil and criminal cases. The final Court of Appeal is the Privy Council in the United Kingdom. Under the terms of the 2007 Constitution, a Judicial and Legal Services Commission, chaired by the Chief Justice, was established to counsel the Governor in matters relating to judicial appointments and regulation of the territory's legal system.

Resident Judges: INDRA HARIPRASHAD-CHARLES, RITA JOSEPH-OLIVETTI.

Magistrate: VALERIE STEPHENS.

Registrar: PAULA AJARIE (acting).

Magistrate's Office: Magistrates Court, POB 140, Road Town, Tortola VG1110; tel. 494-3460; fax 494-2499; e-mail magistrate@vigilate.org.

Religion

CHRISTIANITY

The Roman Catholic Church

The diocese of St John's-Basseterre, suffragan to the archdiocese of Castries (Saint Lucia), includes Anguilla, Antigua and Barbuda, the British Virgin Islands, Montserrat and Saint Christopher and Nevis. The Bishop is resident in St John's, Antigua. In 2005 it was estimated that 10.4% of the population were Roman Catholic.

The Anglican Communion

The British and US Virgin Islands form a single, missionary diocese of the Episcopal Church of the United States of America. The Bishop of the Virgin Islands is resident on St Thomas in the US Virgin Islands. In 2005 it was estimated that 16.7% of the population were Anglican.

Protestant Churches

Various Protestant denominations are represented, principally the Methodist Church (an estimated 32.9% of the population in 2005). Others include the Seventh-day Adventist (6.3%), Church of God (9.2%) and Baptist Churches (4.7%).

The Press

The BVI Beacon: 10 Russell Hill Rd, POB 3030, Road Town, Tortola VG1110; tel. 494-3434; fax 494-6267; e-mail bvibeacn@surfbvi.com; internet www.bvibeacon.com; f. 1984; Thursdays; covers local and international news; also operates from the US Virgin Islands; Editor LINNELL M. ABBOTT; circ. 3,400.

The BVI StandPoint: Wickhams Cay, POB 4311, Road Town, Tortola VG1110; tel. 494-8106; fax 494-8647; e-mail editorial@bvistandpoint.net; internet www.bvistandpoint.net; fmrly BVI PennySaver, adopted current name in 2001; Tuesdays and Fridays; covers local and international news; Editor CARMILITA JAMIESON; circ. 18,000.

The Island Sun: 112 Main St, POB 21, Road Town, Tortola VG1110; tel. 494-2476; fax 494-5854; e-mail issun@candwbvi.net; internet islandsun.com; f. 1962; Fridays; publ. by Sun Enterprises (BVI) Ltd; Editor VERNON W. PICKERING; circ. 3,000.

The Welcome (The British Virgin Islands Welcome Tourist Guide): POB 133, Road Town, Tortola; tel. 494-2413; fax 494-4413; e-mail jim@bviwelcome.com; internet www.bviwelcome.com; f. 1971; every 2 months; general, tourist information; Publr PAUL BACKSHALL; Editor CLAUDIA COLLI; annual circ. 185,000.

Publishers

Caribbean Publishing Co (BVI) Ltd: POB 3403, Road Town, Tortola VG1110; tel. 494-2060; fax 494-3060; e-mail bvi-sales@caripub.com; Gen. Man. MICHAEL ARNOLD.

Island Publishing Services Ltd: POB 133, Road Town, Tortola VG1110; tel. 494-2413; fax 494-4413; e-mail cpcips@surfbvi.com; internet www.caribbeanprinting.com/islandp.html.com; publishes *The Welcome (The British Virgin Islands Welcome Tourist Guide)* (q.v.), *BVI Restaurant and Food Guide* (annual), and *The Limin' Times* (weekly entertainment guide).

Broadcasting and Communications

TELECOMMUNICATIONS

A Telecommunications Regulatory Commission was established under the Telecommunications Act 2006 in October to facilitate the liberalization of the telecommunications sector, which had commenced earlier that year. In April 2007 a Telecommunications Liberalization Act was ratified by the Government; the legislation prepared the market for the addition of further operators after a period of three years until which time the market would be restricted to the existing three service providers. However, the market was subsequently opened to applications from alternative operators after Digicel pursued a successful lawsuit against the restriction: the first unitary licences were issued in June 2007, and Digicel was granted a mobile licence in December.

Regulatory Bodies

Telecommunications Regulatory Commission: Road Town, Tortola; f. Oct. 2006; regulatory body; Chair. COLLIN SCATLIFFE; CEO DAVID IVERSON.

Telephone Services Management Unit: Central Administration Bldg, Road Town, Tortola VG1110; tel. 494-4728; fax 494-6551; e-mail tsmu@bvigovernment.org; govt agency.

Principal Companies

Cable & Wireless (WI) Ltd: Cutlass Bldg, Wickhams Cay 1, POB 440, Road Town, Tortola VG1110; tel. 494-4444; fax 494-2506; e-mail support@candwbvi.net; internet www.cwcaribbean.com/bvi; f. 1967; CEO VANCE LEWIS.

Caribbean Cellular Telephone (CCT Boatphone): Geneva Pl., Road Town, Tortola VG1110; tel. 494-5639; internet www.cctwireless.com; mobile cellular telephone operator.

Digicel: Road Town, Tortola; internet www.digicelgroup.com; granted licence to operate mobile cellular telephone network in British Virgin Islands in Dec. 2007; CEO COLM DELVES.

BROADCASTING

Radio

Virgin Islands Broadcasting Ltd—Radio ZBVI: Baughers Bay, POB 78, Road Town, Tortola VG1110; tel. 494-2250; fax 494-1139; e-mail zbvi@caribsurf.com; internet www.zbvi.vi; f. 1965; commercial; Gen. Man. HARVEY HERBERT; Operations Man. SANDRA POTTER WARRICAN.

Television

BVI Cable TV: Fishlock Rd, POB 694, Road Town, Tortola VG1110; tel. 494-3205; fax 494-2952; operated by Innovative Communication Corporation, based in the US Virgin Islands; programmes from US Virgin Islands and Puerto Rico; secured a licence to compete in the newly liberalized telecommunications market in June 2007; 53 channels; Gen. Man. LUANNE HODGE.

Television West Indies Ltd (ZBTV): Broadcast Peak, Chawell, POB 34, Tortola VG1110; tel. 494-3332; commercial.

Finance

BANKING

Regulatory Authority

Financial Services Commission: Pasea Estate, POB 418, Road Town, Tortola VG1110; tel. 494-1324; fax 494-5016; e-mail commissioner@bvifsc.vg; internet www.bvifsc.vg; f. 2002; independent financial services regulator; Chair. ROBIN GAUL; Man. Dir and CEO ROBERT MATHAVIOUS.

Commercial Banks

Ansbacher (BVI) Ltd: International Trust Bldg, POB 659, Road Town, Tortola VG1110; tel. 494-3215; fax 494-3216.

Banco Popular de Puerto Rico: POB 67, Road Town, Tortola VG1110; tel. 494-2117; fax 494-5294; e-mail internet@bppr.com; internet www.bancopopular.com; Pres. and CEO RICHARD L. CARRIÓN; Man. SANDRA SCATLIFFE.

Bank of East Asia (BVI) Ltd: East Asia Chambers, POB 901, Road Town, Tortola VG1110; tel. 494-6775; fax 495-5088; internet www.hkbea.com; Gen. Man. PATRICK ANDREW NICHOLAS.

UNITED KINGDOM OVERSEAS TERRITORIES — The British Virgin Islands

Bank of Nova Scotia (Canada): Wickhams Cay 1, POB 434, Road Town, Tortola VG1110; tel. 494-2526; fax 494-4657; e-mail joycelyn.murraine@scotiabank.com; internet www.bvi.scotiabank.com; f. 1967; Man. Dir JOYCELYN MURRAINE.

Citco Fund Services (BVI) Ltd: Citco Bldg, Wickhams Cay, POB 662, Road Town, Tortola VG1110; tel. 494-2218; fax 494-3917; e-mail bvi-fund@citco.com; internet www.citco.com; f. 1978; Man. NICOLA GILLESPIE.

DISA Bank (BVI) Ltd: POB 985, Road Town, Tortola VG1110; tel. 494-4977; fax 494-4980; Man. ROSA RESTREPO.

First Bank Virgin Islands: Road Town Business Centre, Wickham's Cay 1, Road Town, Tortola VG1110; tel. 494-2662; fax 494-2379; internet www.firstbankvi.com; f. 1994 as a commercial bank in Puerto Rico.

FirstCaribbean International Bank Ltd: Wickhams Cay 1, POB 70, Road Town, Tortola VG1110; tel. 494-2171; fax 494-4315; e-mail marion.blyden@firstcaribbeanbank.com; internet www.firstcaribbeanbank.com; f. 2003 following merger of Caribbean operations of Barclays Bank PLC and CIBC; Barclays relinquished its stake in June 2006; CEO CHARLES PINK.

HSBC Guyerzeller Bank (BVI) Ltd: POB 3162, Road Town, Tortola VG1110; tel. 494-5414; fax 494-5417; e-mail rhbvi@surfbvi.com; Dir KENNETH W. MORGAN.

Rathbone Bank (BVI) Ltd: POB 986, Road Town, Tortola VG1110; tel. 494-6544; fax 494-6532; e-mail cornel.baptiste; Man. Dir CORNEL BAPTISTE.

VP Bank (BVI) Ltd: Sir Francis Drake's Hwy, POB 3463, Road Town, Tortola VG1110; tel. 494-1100; fax 494-1199; e-mail vpbank@surfbvi.com; internet www.vpbank.vg; Man. Dir Dr PETER REICHENSTEIN.

Development Bank

Development Bank of the British Virgin Islands: New Social Security Bldg, Wickhams Cay 1, POB 275, Road Town, Tortola VG1110; tel. 494-3737; fax 494-3119; e-mail vanterpooldbvi@candwbvi.net; state-owned; Chair. MEADE MALONE.

TRUST COMPANIES

Abacus Trust and Management Services Ltd: 333 Waterfront Dr., Road Town, Tortola VG1110; tel. 494-4388; fax 494-3088; e-mail info@mwmabacus.com; internet www.mwmabacus.com; f. 1994; Man. MEADE MALONE.

Aleman, Cordero, Galindo and Lee Trust (BVI) Ltd: POB 3175, Road Town, Tortola VG1110; tel. 494-4666; fax 494-4679; e-mail alcogalbvi@alcogal.com; Man. GABRIELLA CONTE.

AMS Trustees Ltd: Sea Meadow House, POB 116, Road Town, Tortola VG1110; tel. 494-3399; fax 494-3041; internet www.amsbvi.com; subsidiary of the AMS Group (British Virgin Islands); Man. (vacant).

Belmont Trust Ltd: Belmont Chambers, Tropic Isle Bldg, Nibbs St, POB 3443, Road Town, Tortola VG1110; tel. 494-5800; fax 494-2545; e-mail info@belmontbvi.net; internet www.belmontbvi.com; Man. ANDREA DOUGLAS.

CCP Financial Consultants Ltd: Ellen Skelton Bldg, Fishers Lane, POB 681, Road Town, Tortola VG1110; tel. 494-6777; fax 494-6787; e-mail ccp@surfbvi.com; internet www.ccpbvi.com; Man. JOSEPH ROBERTS.

Citco BVI Ltd: Wickhams Cay, POB 662, Road Town, Tortola VG1110; tel. 494-2217; fax 494-3917; e-mail bvi-trust@citco.com; internet www.citcotrust.com; Man. NICOLA GILLESPIE.

HSBC International Trustee (BVI) Ltd: Woodbourne Hall, POB 916, Road Town, Tortola VG1110; tel. 494-5414; fax 494-5417; e-mail kenneth.morgan@htvg.vg; Dir KENNETH MORGAN.

Hunte & Co Services Ltd: Omar Hodge Bldg, 3rd Floor, Wickhams Cay I, POB 3504, Road Town, Tortola; tel. 495-0232; fax 495-0229; internet www.hunteandco.com; Office Man. DEBORAH BLANFORD.

Maples Finance BVI Ltd: Sea Meadow House, POB 173, Road Town, Tortola VG1110; tel. 494-3384; fax 494-4643; e-mail bviinfo@maplesandcalder.com; internet www.maplesandcalder.com; Man. ROBERT MCINTYRE.

Midocean Management and Trust Services (BVI) Ltd: POB 805, Road Town, Tortola VG1110; tel. 494-4567; fax 494-4568; e-mail midocean@maitlandbvi.com; Man. ELIZABETH WILKINSON.

Moore Stephens International Services (BVI) Ltd: Palm Grove House, Wickhams Cay I, POB 3186, Road Town, Tortola VG1110; tel. 494-3503; fax 494-3592; e-mail moorestephens@moorestephensbvi.com; internet www.moorestephens.com; Man. SELINA O'NEAL.

TMF (BVI) Ltd: POB 964, Road Town, Tortola VG1110; tel. 494-4997; fax 494-4999; e-mail bvi@tmf-group.com; internet www.tmf-group.com; Man. GRAHAM COOK.

Totalserve Trust Company Ltd: 197 Main St, POB 3540, Road Town, Tortola VG1110; tel. 494-6900; fax 494-6990; e-mail bvi@totalservecy.com; internet www.totalservecy.com; Man. RONELLE BOBB.

Tricor Services (BVI) Ltd: POB 3340, Road Town, Tortola VG1110; tel. 494-6004; fax 494-6404; e-mail info@bvi.tricorservices.com; Man. PATRICK A. NICHOLAS.

Trident Trust Company (BVI) Ltd: Trident Chambers, Wickhams Cay, POB 146, Road Town, Tortola VG1110; tel. 494-2434; fax 494-3754; e-mail bvi@tridenttrust.com; internet www.tridenttrust.com; Man. BARRY R. GOODMAN.

At the beginning of 2007 there were some 2,600 active mutual and hedge funds registered with the British Virgin Islands International Finance Centre.

INSURANCE

Albion Insurance Management Ltd: POB 4623, Road Town, Tortola VG1110; tel. 494-9670; fax 495-9690; e-mail gtaylor@albionbvi.com; internet www.albionbvi.com; Man. GREGORY TAYLOR.

ALTA Insurance Management (BVI) Ltd: POB 4623, Road Town, Tortola VG1110; tel. 494-9670; fax 494-9690; e-mail gtaylor@altaholdings.com; internet www.altaholdings.com; Man. GREGORY TAYLOR.

AMS Insurance Management Services Ltd: Sea Meadow House, POB 116, Road Town, Tortola VG1110; tel. 494-4078; fax 494-2519; e-mail amsins@amsbvi.com; internet www.amsbvi.com; Man. DEREK LLOYD.

Belmont Insurance Management Ltd: POB 3443, Road Town, Tortola VG1110; tel. 494-5800; fax 494-2545; e-mail info@belmontbvi.com; internet www.belmontbvi.com; Man. SIMON OWEN.

Caledonian Insurance Services (BVI) Ltd: POB 4428, Road Town, Tortola VG1110; tel. 494-4111; fax 494-4222; e-mail insurance@caledonian.com; internet www.caledonian.com; Dir HARRY THOMPSON.

Captiva Global Ltd: POB 4428, Road Town, Tortola VG1110; tel. 494-4111; fax 494-4222; e-mail info@captiva.vg; internet www.captiva.vg; Man. Dir HARRY J. THOMPSON.

Caribbean Insurers Ltd (CIL): Mirage Bldg, POB 129, Road Town, Tortola VG1110; tel. 494-2728; fax 494-4393; e-mail info@caribbins.com; internet www.caribbeaninsurers.com; f. 1973; part of the Caribbean Insurers Group; Chair. and CEO JOHN WILLIAMS.

Euro-American Insurance Management Ltd: Euro American Bldg, R. G. Hodge Plaza, Wickham's Cay I, POB 3161, Road Town, Tortola VG1110; tel. 494-4692; fax 494-4695; e-mail eamsbvi@surfbvi.com; internet www.eamsonline.com; Man. Dir KAY REDDY.

Hunte & Co Insurance Management Services Ltd: POB 3504, Road Town, Tortola VG1110; tel. 495-0232; fax 495-0229; internet www.hunteandco.com; Man. ROSINA ANN-MARIE KNIGHT.

HWR Insurance Management Services Ltd (Harneys Insurance): POB 71, Road Town, Tortola VG1110; tel. 494-2233; fax 494-3547; e-mail insurance@harneys.com; internet www.harneys.com; Man. Dir DAVID SPYER.

Marine Insurance Office (BVI) Ltd (MIO): POB 874, Road Town, Tortola VG1110; tel. 494-3795; fax 494-4540; e-mail marinein@surfbvi.com; f. 1985; Man. WESLEY WOOLHOUSE.

Osiris Insurance Management Ltd: POB 2221, Road Town, Tortola VG1110; tel. 494-9820; fax 494-6934; e-mail osiristrust@surfbvi.com; internet osiristrust.com; Man. HARRY THOMPSON.

Trident Insurance Management (BVI) Ltd: POB 146, Road Town, Tortola VG1110; tel. 494-4078; fax 494-2519; e-mail trident@surfbvi.com; Man. DEREK LLOYD.

TSA Insurance Management Ltd: POB 3443, Road Town, Tortola VG1110; tel. 494-5800; fax 494-6563; e-mail jwilliams@surfbvi.com; Man. JOHN WILLIAMS.

USA Risk Group (BVI) Inc: POB 3140, Road Town, Tortola VG1110; tel. 494-4111; fax 494-4222; e-mail sgrayston@vim.usarisk.com; internet www.usarisk.com; Man. STUART H. GRAYSTON.

Several US and other foreign companies have agents in the British Virgin Islands. In 2006 57 new 'captive' insurers were registered by the British Virgin Islands International Financial Centre, increasing the total such registered to more than 400.

Trade and Industry

GOVERNMENT AGENCY

Trade and Investment Promotion Department: Central Administration Bldg, 33 Administration Dr., Road Town, Tortola VG1110; tel. 494-3701; fax 494-5676; e-mail trade@bvigovernment.org.

UNITED KINGDOM OVERSEAS TERRITORIES

CHAMBER OF COMMERCE

British Virgin Islands Chamber of Commerce and Hotel Association: James Frett Bldg, Wickhams Cay 1, POB 376, Road Town, Tortola VG1110; tel. 494-3514; fax 494-6179; e-mail averil@bviccha.org; internet www.bviccha.org; f. 1986; Exec. Dir AVERIL HENRY; Pres. (Business and Commerce) JOHN SHIRLEY; Pres. (Hotels and Tourism) ROMNEY PENN.

UTILITIES

Electricity

British Virgin Islands Electricity Corpn (BVIEC): Long Bush, POB 268, Road Town, Tortola VG1110; tel. 494-3911; fax 494-4291; e-mail bviecgm@bvielectricity.com; internet www.bvielectricity.com; f. 1979; state-owned, privatization pending; Chair. MARGARET PENN.

Water

Water and Sewerage Dept: POB 130, Baughers Bay, Road Town, Tortola VG1110; tel. 468-3416; fax 494-6746; e-mail water@surfbvi.com.

Transport

ROADS

In 2002 there were 132 km (82 miles) of access roads, 77 km of primary roads, 37 km of secondary roads and 90 km of tertiary roads. In 2005 13,392 vehicles were licensed, 9,201 of which were private vehicles.

Public Works Department: Baughers Bay, Tortola; tel. 494-2722; fax 494-4740; e-mail pwd@bvigovernment.org; responsible for road maintenance.

SHIPPING

There are two direct steamship services, one from the United Kingdom and one from the USA. Motor launches maintain daily mail and passenger services with St Thomas and St John, US Virgin Islands. A new cruise-ship pier, built at a cost of US $6.9m. with assistance from the Caribbean Development Bank, was opened in Road Town in 1994 and was later expanded. Further expansion work was due to be completed in December 2008.

British Virgin Islands Ports Authority: Port Purcell, POB 4, Road Town, Tortola VG1110; tel. 494-3435; fax 494-2642; e-mail bviports@bviports.org; internet www.bviports.org; f. 1991; Chair. CARL DAWSON; Man. Dir VICTOR O'NEAL.

Tropical Shipping: Port Purcell Seaport, Island Shipping and Trading, POB 250, Road Town, Tortola VG1110; tel. 494-2674; fax 494-3505; e-mail lmoses@tropical.com; internet www.tropical.com; Man. LEROY MOSES.

CIVIL AVIATION

Beef Island Airport, about 16 km (10 miles) from Road Town, has a runway with a length of 1,100 m (3,700 ft). A new US $65m. airport terminal was opened at the airport in March 2002. In October 2003 work began to lengthen the runway to 1,500 m. Upon completion of the renovation in May 2004 the airport was renamed Terrence B. Lettsome Airport. Captain Auguste George Airport on Anegada has been designated an international point of entry and was resurfaced in the late 1990s. The airport runway on Virgin Gorda was to be extended to 1,200 m to allow larger aircraft to land. The Government announced that a budgetary allocation of $500,000 would be assigned to secure state-ownership of Virgin Gorda airport in 2007.

Director of Civil Aviation: DENNISTON FRAZER, Terrance B. Lettsome International Airport, Suite 217–19, Beef Island; tel. 468-6492; fax 468-6493; e-mail aviation@bvigovernment.org.

Tourism

The main attraction of the islands is their tranquillity and clear waters, which provide excellent facilities for sailing, fishing, diving and other water sports. In 2004 there were an estimated 1,370 hotel rooms. There are also many charter yachts offering overnight accommodation. There were some 337,134 stop-over visitors and 449,152 cruise-ship passengers in 2005. The majority of tourists are from the USA. Receipts from tourism totalled an estimated US $391.3m. in 2004.

British Virgin Islands Chamber of Commerce and Hotel Association: see Chamber of Commerce.

British Virgin Islands Tourist Board: 2nd Floor, AKARA Bldg, DeCastro St, Road Town, Tortola VG1110; tel. 494-3134; fax 494-3866; e-mail info@bvitourism.com; internet www.bvitourism.com; Dir JANIS BRAITHWAITE-EDWARDS.

THE CAYMAN ISLANDS

Introductory Survey

Location, Climate, Language, Religion, Flag, Capital

The Cayman Islands lie about 290 km (180 miles) west-north-west of Jamaica and consist of three main islands: Grand Cayman and, to the north-east, Little Cayman and Cayman Brac. The climate is tropical but is tempered by the trade winds, with a cool season between November and March, when temperatures average 24°C (75°F). The rainy season lasts from May until October. Mean annual rainfall is 1,524 mm (60 ins). The official language is English. Many Christian churches are represented. The flag is the British 'Blue Ensign', with the islands' coat of arms (a golden lion on a red background above three stars in green, representing the three main islands, superimposed on wavy lines of blue and white, the shield surmounted by a torse of white and blue bearing a yellow pineapple behind a green turtle, and with the motto 'He hath founded it upon the seas' on a scroll beneath) on a white roundel in the fly. The capital is George Town, on the island of Grand Cayman.

Recent History

The Cayman Islands came under acknowledged British rule in 1670 and were settled mainly from Jamaica and by privateers and buccaneers. The islands of Little Cayman and Cayman Brac were permanently settled only in 1833, and until 1877 there was no administrative connection between them and Grand Cayman. A representative assembly first sat in 1832. The islands formed a dependency of Jamaica until 1959, and the Governor of Jamaica held responsibility for the Cayman Islands until Jamaican independence in 1962, when a separate administrator was appointed (the title was changed to that of Governor in 1971). The 1959 Constitution was revised in 1972, 1992 and 1994.

For many years there have been no formal political parties on the islands, despite the emergence of a nascent party political system during the 1960s with the formation, in 1961, of the National Democratic Party (NDP), as part of a campaign for self-government. The Christian Democratic Party was formed as a conservative opposition. Both parties disappeared within a few years despite the electoral success of the NDP, largely owing to the system of gubernatorial nomination to the Executive Council. In the 1970s elections for the 12 elective seats in the Legislative Assembly came to be contested by 'teams' of candidates, as well as by independents. Two such teams were formed, Progress and Dignity (the more conservative) and Unity, but all candidates were committed to augmenting the economic success of the Caymans, and favoured continued dependent status. There are no plans for independence, and the majority of the population wish to maintain the islands' links with the United Kingdom.

At elections in November 1980 the Unity team, led by Jim Bodden, took eight of the 12 seats. In the November 1984 elections opposition independents won nine seats, aided by public disquiet at the rapid growth of the immigrant work-force, and the implications of the recent US challenges to the Cayman Islands' bank secrecy laws. In 1987 the Legislative Assembly successfully sought stricter regulations of status and residency for those able to participate in elections, in an attempt to protect the political rights of native Caymanians (in view of the very large immigrant population). At a general election in November 1988 seven of the existing members were returned, and five new members were elected. Prior to the election the teams had regrouped into more informal coalitions, indicating the primacy of personal over 'party' affiliations.

In July 1990 the Legislative Assembly approved proposals to review the Constitution, and in January 1991 the British Government sent two commissioners to the territory to discuss possible amendments. The implementation of most recommendations, including the appointment of a Chief Minister, was postponed pending a general election to be held in 1992. One of the amendments, however, which involved increasing the number of elective seats in the Legislative Assembly to 15, was adopted in March 1992. The proposed reforms had prompted the formation, in mid-1991, of the territory's first political organization since the 1960s, the Progressive Democratic Party (PDP). During 1992 the organization developed into a coalition and was renamed the National Team. At the general election in November 1992 National Team members secured 12 of the elective seats in the newly enlarged Legislative Assembly, while independent candidates won the remaining three. In November of that year James Ryan was appointed Chief Secretary, following the retirement of Lemuel Hurlston. The new Government opted to revoke the provisions in the Constitution for a Chief Minister; however, in 1994 it introduced a ministerial system and created a fifth ministerial portfolio.

At a general election in November 1996 the governing National Team remained in power, although with a reduced majority, winning nine seats in the Legislative Assembly. Two new groupings, the Democratic Alliance and Team Cayman (which had formed in opposition to the Government's alleged mismanagement of the public debt and of Cayman Airways) secured two seats and one seat, respectively. Independent candidates won three seats.

In November 1997 the Minister of Community Development, Sport, Youth Affairs and Culture, McKeeva Bush, was dismissed from his post after it was alleged that a bank of which he was a director had authorized fraudulent loans totalling some US $1.1m. Bush (who denied any knowledge of the alleged corruption) was replaced by Julianna O'Connor Connolly, the first female minister on the island.

In March 1999 the Government of the United Kingdom published draft legislation pertaining to its relationship with its Overseas Dependencies, which were to be renamed United Kingdom Overseas Territories (and had been referred to as such since February 1998). The legislation proposed the extension of British citizenship to the citizens of Overseas Territories, although it also required the Tterritories to amend their legislation on human rights and on the regulation of the financial services sector to meet international standards. The Cayman Islands were praised for the introduction in 1998 of laws on tax evasion, and for strengthening the regulatory powers of the Monetary Authority, although concern was expressed that homosexuality remained a criminal offence in the islands. The issue of the legal status of homosexuality in the Cayman Islands had been highlighted in January 1998 by the authorities' refusal to permit a stop-over by a US cruise liner whose 900 passengers were homosexual men.

In late April 1999 representatives of the European Union (EU, see p. 244) held meetings with the overseas territories of member states to discuss proposed reforms of legislation relating to the financial services sector. The Cayman Islands delegation defended the islands' standards of regulation, arguing that the islands had implemented some of the strictest laws in the world against money-laundering, and that proposals to abolish the Cayman Islands' laws on banking secrecy would place the islands at a disadvantage, compared with the financial centres of Switzerland and Luxembourg. In early June the Cayman Islands announced that it was to seek certification under the UN's Offshore Initiative, and that consequently a UN agency, the Global Programme against Money Laundering, was to undertake a review of the islands' financial systems and regulations.

In August 1999 a US citizen, John Matthewson, was sentenced to five years' probation by a US court on charges of money-laundering in the Cayman Islands. Matthewson had reportedly escaped a prison sentence by revealing to US investigators the extent of his activities in the Cayman Islands and the extent to which the islands' financial system benefited those seeking to evade US taxation. The US Government subsequently charged several of Matthewson's clients with tax evasion, and it was widely believed that the case had seriously damaged the islands' reputation both for secrecy and as a reputable financial centre. However, the island authorities claimed that the Royal Cayman Islands Police had co-operated fully with the US investigators, and also observed that in 1998 the islands' policy of co-operation with US investigators in their efforts to prevent money-laundering had been singled out for praise in the US *International Narcotics Control Strategy Report*.

Drugs-related crime continued to be a serious problem in the 1990s, when an estimated 75% of all thefts and burglaries in the islands were attributed, directly or indirectly, to the drugs trade. The Mutual Legal Assistance Treaty (signed in 1986, and ratified by the US Senate in 1990) between the Cayman Islands and the USA provides for the mutual exchange of information for use in combating crime (particularly drugs-trafficking and the diversion of funds gained illegally from the drugs trade). Further legislation relating to the abuse of the financial sector by criminal organizations was approved in November 1996. In October 2005 the Government introduced longer sentences for possession of illegal firearms or bullet-proof vests. Offenders would be sentenced to a minimum of 10 years in prison and fined CI $100,000.

In a general election held on 8 November 2000 the governing National Team suffered a heavy defeat, losing six of its nine seats, including that held by Truman Bodden, the Leader of Government Business. The newly elected Legislative Assembly appointed Kurt Tibbetts of the Democratic Alliance as Leader of Government Business.

In an unprecedented development in November 2001, several members of the Legislative Assembly, dissatisfied with the Government's leadership during the economic slowdown, formed the United Democratic Party (UDP). McKeeva Bush, the leader of the new party and Deputy Leader of Government Business and Minister of Tourism, Environment and Transport, claimed that at least 10 members of the 15-member Assembly were UDP supporters. Subsequently, the passing of a motion of 'no confidence' against the Leader of Government Business resulted in Tibbetts and Edna Moyle, the Minister of Community Development, Women's Affairs, Youth and Sport, leaving the Executive Council. Bush became the new Leader of Government Business, while two other legislators, Gilbert McLean and Frank McField, both members of the UDP, joined the Cabinet. In May 2002, at the UDP's inaugural convention, Bush was formally elected leader of the party. In the same month it was announced that the five opposition members of the legislative assembly had formed a new political party, the People's Progressive Movement (PPM), led by Tibbetts.

In March 2002 the three-member Constitutional Review Commission, appointed by the Governor in May 2001, submitted a new draft constitution. The proposed document had to be debated by the Legislative Assembly and then approved by the British Parliament before being formally adopted. The draft constitution included the creation of the office of Chief Minister, proposed a full ministerial government, and incorporated a bill of rights. The opposition demanded a referendum on the recommendations, on the grounds that the UDP had rejected several of the proposals, despite strong public support for the changes, but Bush forwarded the proposals to the British Foreign and Commonwealth Office (FCO), via the Governor's office. In December Bush and the leader of the opposition, Tibbetts, travelled to the United Kingdom in order to review the proposed constitution with FCO officials. Consensus, however, proved impossible to achieve. While the PPM called for a public referendum on issue, the UDP announced in February 2004 that it would not participate in the constitutional review process before the next election. These were originally scheduled to be held in November 2004, but were postponed, owing to the damage caused by 'Hurricane Ivan' in September 2004 (see below). In March 2006 an FCO delegation visited the Cayman Islands for informal discussions aimed at restarting the process of constitutional reform.

In May 2002 the British Overseas Territories Act, having received royal assent in the United Kingdom in February, came into force and granted British citizenship to the people of its Overseas Territories, including the Cayman Islands. Under the new law Caymanians would be able to hold British passports and work in the United Kingdom and elsewhere in the EU. Also in May, the Cayman Islands became an associate member of the Caribbean Community and Common Market (CARICOM, see p. 196). In the same month Bruce Dinwiddy succeeded Peter Smith as Governor.

In January 2003 Bush accused the United Kingdom of undermining the course of Cayman Islands' justice, after a routine money-laundering case was dismissed amid allegations of espionage and obstruction of justice by British intelligence agents. The trial collapsed after it was alleged that the Director of the Cayman Islands Financial Reporting Unit (and a key witness in the trial) had passed information about the case to an unnamed agency of the British Government, understood to be the Secret Intelligence Service (MI6). It was claimed that MI6 wished to protect the names of its sources within the Caribbean 'offshore' banking community. Bush demanded the British Government pay for the failed trial, estimated to cost some US $5m., and for any negative repercussions the affair might have for the reputation of the islands' banking sector. The United Kingdom, however, refused to compensate the Cayman Islands and maintained that although its intelligence agencies might have helped in the investigation, they had never interfered in the case. In March the Attorney-General, David Ballantyne, resigned amid accusations that he was aware that British intelligence agents were working covertly in the Cayman Islands; Samuel W. Bulgin, the erstwhile Solicitor-General, was appointed as Ballantyne's permanent successor in July.

The opposition PPM won a resounding victory at the general election of 11 May 2005, securing nine of the 15 legislative seats. The ruling UDP won only five seats, with the remaining seat going to an independent. The outgoing UDP Government had been criticized for its handling of the aftermath of 'Hurricane Ivan', which had caused an estimated CI $2,800m. of damage in September 2004, and also for its decision, in the same month, to grant 'belonger' status to some 3,000 people, a move interpreted by many as an attempt to increase the party's electoral support. The Leader of Government Business, Kurt Tibbetts, pledged to hold a referendum on increased autonomy for the islands. In November he announced a Freedom of Information Bill, to be debated in the Legislative Assembly, prior to a public consultation exercise. The proposed legislation was intended to promote government transparency and accountability, thus increasing constitutional democracy, and in January 2007 revisions to a draft version of the document were under discussion pending submission to the Cabinet for approval in March. However, anticipated consideration of the amendments to the bill was postponed beyond the fourth governmental convention of the 2006/07 fiscal year, conducted on 23 March; the 'logistics' of implementing the necessary personnel training for the introduction of a dedicated Freedom of Information office and creation of an Information Commissioner role, with the equivalent governmental rank of the Auditor General, was cited as the principal delaying factor. The legislation was finally approved at the end of August and in the following month the Freedom of Information Unit was officially opened. The law was scheduled to become effective on 1 January 2009 in order to grant adequate preparation time for the administration of requests for information to the relevant government departments.

In November 2005 Stuart Jack succeeded Bruce Dinwiddy as Governor. Governor Jack indicated in January 2007 that a general election would not be called before May 2009, and may be postponed until November of that year to allow the elected government sufficient opportunity to prepare for the June deadline by which the next budget should be announced. The opposition UDP, however, contended that an election was constitutionally due by November 2008, the previous ballot having been postponed from the corresponding month in 2004 owing to disruption caused by 'Hurricane Ivan'.

In mid-February 2007 the Government announced the establishment of a Constitutional Review Secretariat to initiate renewed efforts towards constitutional reform in the territory from March. The mandate of the government-administered body, to be presided over by Cabinet Secretary Orrett Connor, was stated as promoting public awareness, disseminating information and expediting the public consultation process through education and the institution of an effective communication framework. Formal embarkation upon constitutional modernization—facilitated by the counsel of a British constitutional lawyer, Professor Jeffrey Jowell—was expected to commence once the Secretariat became fully operational, entailing a national referendum and negotiations with the United Kingdom in the advanced stages. In January 2008 the Government launched a series of public consultations ahead of a referendum scheduled to be held in May. The FCO affirmed in early April that the new Constitution must include a bill of rights and, in response, the Government postponed the referendum to allow a longer period of public deliberation. The ballot was expected to be held before September.

The US Senate Finance Committee reported in June 2007 that it had identified more than 14,000 registered companies purportedly maintaining headquarters at a single address in the Caribbean island nation, and subsequently commissioned an inquiry into the anomaly by the Government Accountability Office. It was estimated that evasion of US tax obligations by such entities—achieved by establishing 'offshore' subsidiaries on the islands—had resulted in a US $100,000m. shortfall in tax-based revenue and precipitated a growing sentiment of hostilities between the two nations' respective regulatory authorities.

Amendments to the Cayman Islands immigration regime in November 2005 required that persons originating from Costa Rica, El Salvador, Guatemala and Jamaica hold a visa in order to enter the territory. The maximum fine for living illegally in the Cayman Islands was CI $20,000. Amendments to the 2004 Term Limit Policy, or 'rollover law', which limited the term for which work permits may be granted to seven years, were promulgated in October 2006.

Government

Under the revised Constitution of 1994, the Governor, who is appointed by the British monarch, is responsible for external affairs, defence, internal security and the public service. The Governor is Chairman of the Cabinet, comprising three members appointed by the Governor and five members elected by the Legislative Assembly. The Legislative Assembly comprises three official members and 15 members elected by universal adult suffrage for a period of four years. A constitutional review was under way in 2008.

Defence

The United Kingdom is responsible for the defence of the Cayman Islands.

Economic Affairs

In 2006, according to official estimates, the Cayman Islands' gross domestic product (GDP) was CI $2,035m., equivalent to some $39,100 per head. During 1996–2006, according to official estimates, the population increased at an average annual rate of 4.2%, while GDP increased, in real terms, by 5.4% per year during 1998–2006; growth was 4.6% in 2006.

Agriculture (which engaged only 2.3% of the employed labour force in 2006 and accounted for 0.4% of value added in the same year) is limited by infertile soil, low rainfall and high labour costs. The principal crops are citrus fruits and bananas, and some other produce for local consumption. Flowers (particularly orchids) are produced for export. Livestock-rearing consists of beef cattle, poultry (mainly for eggs) and pigs. The traditional activity of turtle-hunting has virtually disappeared; the turtle farm (the only commercial one in the world) now produces mainly for domestic consumption (and serves as a research centre), following the imposition of US restrictions on the trade in turtle products in 1979. Fishing is mainly for lobster and shrimp.

Industry, engaging 21.3% of the employed labour force and, according to the UN, accounting for 15.0% of value added in 2006, consists mainly of construction and related manufacturing, some food-processing and tourist-related light industries. The construction sector contributed 9.7% of value added in 2006, while manufacturing activities accounted for only about 1.7% of the total in that year. Energy requirements are satisfied by the import of petroleum products and gas (7.7% of total imports in 2006).

Service industries dominate the Caymanian economy, accounting for 76.4% of employment (excluding unclassified activities) in 2006 and contributing 84.6% of value added in the same year. The tourism industry is the principal economic activity, and in 1991 accounted for 22.9% of GDP and employed, directly and indirectly, some 50% of the working population. The industry earned an estimated US $353.0m. in 2006, compared to $518.0m. the year previous. Most visitors are from the USA (81.3% of tourist arrivals in 2006). The Cayman Islands is one of the largest 'offshore' financial centres in the world; during the 2005/06 fiscal year there were 709 banks and trust companies and 6,527 mutual funds on the islands, according to the Cayman Islands Monetary Authority. In 2006 the financial services sector engaged 9.2% of the working population, and in 1999 contributed about 36.0% of GDP.

In 2006 the Cayman Islands recorded a trade deficit of CI $895.4m. Receipts from tourism and the financial sector, remittances and capital inflows normally offset the trade deficit. The principal source of imports is the USA (which provided some 71.2% of total imports in 2006), which is also one of the principal markets for exports (34.6% in 1994). Other major trading partners in 2006 included the Netherlands Antilles (8.0% of total imports). Principal exports in the 1990s were fish and cut flowers. The principal imports in 2006 were miscellaneous manufactured articles (53.3%), machinery and transport equipment (10.5%), petroleum products and gas (7.7%) and basic manufactures (6.2%).

An estimated government budget surplus of CI $67.3m. was recorded in 2006. In 1998 official development assistance totalled US $0.2m. At the end of 1999 the public debt stood at US $114.8m. The average annual rate of inflation was 3.1% in 1996–2006; consumer prices increased by an annual average of 3.1% in 2007. According to official census figures, only 61% of the resident population of the islands were Caymanian in 2005 (compared with 79% in 1980). Some 3.3% of the labour force were unemployed in 2005.

The United Kingdom is responsible for the external affairs of the Cayman Islands, and the dependency has the status of Overseas Territory in association with the European Union (EU, see p. 244). The Cayman Islands gained associate member status in Caribbean Community and Common Market (CARICOM, see p. 196) in 2002; the territory is also a member of CARICOM's Caribbean Development Bank (CDB, see p. 201).

Both the principal economic sectors, 'offshore' finance and tourism, benefit from the Cayman Islands' political stability, good infrastructure and extensive development. Tourism continued to expand in the early 2000s, although the Government attempted to limit tourist numbers in order to minimize damage to the environment, particularly the coral reef, and to preserve the islands' reputation as a destination for visitors of above-average wealth. The sector, nevertheless, was adversely affected by the damage caused by 'Hurricane Ivan' in September 2004. The financial sector, which benefits from an absence of taxation and of foreign exchange regulations, recorded consistently high levels of growth during the 1990s, and provided an estimated 30% of GDP in 1998. The banking sector was reckoned to be the world's fifth largest in 2000, owing to the absence of direct taxation, lenient regulation and strict confidentiality laws. The Cayman Islands have a policy of openly confronting the issues of financial transparency and of money-laundering, and an information exchange treaty with the USA was ratified in 1990. However, despite the efforts of the authorities, the vulnerability of the islands' financial services sector to exploitation by criminal organizations continued to cause concern. In June 2000 the Cayman Islands were included on a list of harmful tax regimes compiled by an agency of the Organisation for Economic Co-operation and Development (OECD, see p. 347) and were urged to make legislative changes, introducing greater legal and administrative transparency. The Government pledged to adopt international standards of legal and administrative transparency by 2005, and in 2001, following stricter regulation of the private banking sector, the Cayman Islands were removed from the blacklist. The Government's decision to increase the annual licensing fee charged to 'offshore' financial institutions in the 2002 budget was widely criticized as being potentially damaging to the industry. In late 2002 the financial sector faced disruption when the United Kingdom, under pressure from an EU investigation into tax evasion, demanded that the Cayman Islands disclose the identities

UNITED KINGDOM OVERSEAS TERRITORIES — The Cayman Islands

and account details of Europeans holding private savings accounts on the islands. The Cayman Islands, along with some other British Overseas Territories facing similar demands, claimed it was being treated unfairly, and refused to make any concessions. Nevertheless, the Legislative Assembly, after the British Government pledged to safeguard the territory's interests, voted to accept British/EU demands by 1 January 2005. Damage resulting from 'Hurricane Ivan'—which swept across the islands in September 2004—contributed to slow economic growth in 2005 (0.9%) and required imports of capital equipment and construction materials to facilitate the reconstruction process. An associated shortage of housing coupled with a rise in insurance costs produced a marked increase in inflation during 2005, which stood at some 7.0%. In June 2006 the Government assigned US $2m. in hurricane relief funding, primarily aimed at providing housing. The European Commission (EC) later agreed to assist the authorities to this end; pledging €3.7m. in 2007, and a further €3.3m. in 2008. Inflation subsided in 2006–07, but was expected increase once more in 2008, owing to the high international prices for food and mineral fuels. The Government sought to protect per caput incomes by reducing import duties on a number of staple items. Real GDP was forecast to expand by 1.7% in 2008 and by 1.9% in 2009.

Education

Schooling is compulsory for children between the ages of five and 15 years. It is provided free in 10 government-run primary schools, and there are also three state secondary schools, as well as six church-sponsored schools (five of which offer secondary as well as primary education). Primary education, from five years of age, lasts for six years; in 2004/05 enrolment at primary schools included an estimated 81.1% of pupils in the relevant age-group. Secondary education lasts for seven years and enrolment at secondary-level institutions in 2004/05 included an estimated 95.6% of students in the relevant age-group. Some CI $100m. was allocated for education in the 2006/07 budget.

Public Holidays

2008: 1 January (New Year's Day), 28 January (National Heroes' Day), 6 February (Ash Wednesday), 21 March (Good Friday), 24 March (Easter Monday), 19 May (Discovery Day), 16 June (Queen's Official Birthday), 7 July (Constitution Day), 17 November (Remembrance Day), 25–26 December (Christmas).

2009: 1 January (New Year's Day), 26 January (National Heroes' Day), 25 February (Ash Wednesday), 10 April (Good Friday), 13 April (Easter Monday), 18 May (Discovery Day), 15 June (Queen's Official Birthday), 6 July (Constitution Day), 16 November (Remembrance Day), 25–26 December (Christmas).

Weights and Measures

The imperial system is in use.

Statistical Survey

Sources: Government Information Services, Cricket Sq., Elgin Ave, George Town, Grand Cayman; tel. 949-8092; fax 949-5936; The Information Centre, Economic and Statistics Office, Government Administration Bldg, Grand Cayman; tel. 949-0940; fax 949-8782; e-mail infostats@gov.ky; internet www.eso.ky.

AREA AND POPULATION

Area: 262 sq km (102 sq miles). The main island of Grand Cayman is about 197 sq km (76 sq miles), about one-half of which is swamp. Cayman Brac is 39 sq km (15 sq miles); Little Cayman is 26 sq km (11 sq miles).

Population: 39,410 (males 19,311, females 20,099) at census of 10 October 1999 (Grand Cayman 37,473, Cayman Brac 1,822, Little Cayman 115). *2006* (estimated population at 31 December): 53,172.

Density (31 December 2006): 202.9 per sq km.

Principal Towns (population at 1999 census): George Town (capital) 20,626; West Bay 8,243; Bodden Town 5,764. *Mid-2005* (UN estimate, incl. suburbs): George Town 26,000 (Source: partly UN, *World Urbanization Prospects: The 2005 Revision*).

Births, Marriages and Deaths (2006): Live births 710 (birth rate 13.7 per 1,000); Marriages 1,938 (marriage rate 37.3 per 1,000); Deaths 182 (death rate 3.5 per 1,000).

Expectation of Life (years at birth, 2007): 80.2 (males 77.6; females 82.9). Source: Pan-American Health Organization.

Economically Active Population (sample survey, persons aged 15 years and over, April 2006): Agriculture and fishing 805; Manufacturing 383; Construction 6,344; Electricity, water and quarrying 726; Wholesale and retail trade 4,232; Restaurants and hotels 3,779; Transport, post and telecommunication 1,477; Financial services 3,205; Public administration 2,380; Education, health and social work 2,421; Other community, social and personal service activities 1,817; Private households with employed persons 3,004; Business services 4,443; *Total employed* 35,016; Unemployed 943; *Total labour force* 35,959 (Caymanian 18,303, non-Caymanian 17,656).

HEALTH AND WELFARE

Physicians (per 1,000 head, 2005): 1.4.

Health Expenditure: % of GDP (1997): 4.2.

Health Expenditure: public (% of total, 1997): 53.2.

Source: mainly Pan American Health Organization.

For definitions, see explanatory note on p. vi.

AGRICULTURE, ETC.

Livestock ('000 head, 2006, FAO estimates): Cattle 1.3; Goats 0.3; Pigs 0.4; Chickens 6.

Fishing (metric tons, live weight, 2005): Total catch 125 (all marine fishes).

Source: FAO.

INDUSTRY

Electric Energy (production, million kWh): 433.4 in 2004; 463.2 in 2005; 535.7 in 2006.

FINANCE

Currency and Exchange Rates: 100 cents = 1 Cayman Islands dollar (CI $). *Sterling, US Dollar and Euro Equivalents* (31 December 2007): £1 sterling = CI $1.670; US $1 = 83.3 CI cents; €1 = CI $1.23; CI $100 = £59.90 = US $120.00 = €81.52. *Exchange rate:* Fixed at CI $1 = US $1.20.

Budget (CI $ million, 2006): *Revenue:* Taxes on international trade and transactions 187.0; Taxes on other domestic goods and services 193.7; Taxes on property 47.2; Other tax revenue 17.1; Non-coercive revenue 55.4 (Sales of goods and services 53.8); Total 500.4. *Expenditure:* Current expenditure 384.3 (Personnel costs 182.6, Supplies and consumable goods 109.0, Subsidies 66.9, Transfer payments 16.9, Interest payments 8.9); Extraordinary expenses 7.2; Other executive expenses 2.0; Capital expenditure and net lending 39.6; Total 433.1.

Cost of Living (Consumer Price Index; base: September 1994 = 100): 142.5 in 2005; 143.5 in 2006; 148.0 in 2007.

Gross Domestic Product (CI $ million at constant 1986 prices): 854.5 in 2004; 910.0 in 2005; 951.9 in 2006.

Gross Domestic Product by Economic Activity (CI $ million in current prices, 1991): Primary industries 5; Manufacturing 9; Electricity, gas and water 19; Construction 54; Trade, restaurants and hotels 138; Transport, storage and communications 65; Finance, insurance, real estate and business services 210; Community, social and personal services 42; Government services 63; Statistical discrepancy 1; *Sub-total* 606; Import duties less imputed bank service charge 11; *GDP in purchasers' values* 617. *2006* (CI $ million): Agriculture, hunting, forestry and fishing 8; Mining, manufacturing and utilities 105 (Manufacturing 34); Construction 195; Wholesale, retail trade, restaurants and hotels 472; Transport, storage and communication 221; Other activities 1,005; *Total gross value added* 2,006 (Source: UN Statistics Division, National Accounts Main Aggregates Database).

EXTERNAL TRADE

Principal Commodities (CI $ million, 2006): *Imports c.i.f.:* Food and live animals 44.9; Beverages and tobacco 44.3; Petroleum products and gas 70.0; Chemicals and related products 22.1; Basic manufactures 56.2; Machinery and transport equipment 94.9; Miscellaneous manufactured articles 482.6; Total (incl. others) 906.1. *Exports f.o.b.:* Total 10.7.

Principal Trading Partners (CI $ million): *Imports c.i.f.* (2006): Japan 6.3; Netherlands Antilles 73.0; United Kingdom 4.5; USA 656.6; Total (incl. others) 914.2. *Exports f.o.b.* (1994): USA 0.9; Total 2.6.

TRANSPORT

Road Traffic ('000 motor vehicles in use, 2002): Passenger cars 23.8; Commercial vehicles 6.4.

Shipping: *International Freight Traffic* ('000 metric tons): Goods loaded 735 (1990); Goods unloaded 239,138 (2000). *Cargo Vessels* (1995): Vessels 15, Calls at port 266. *Merchant Fleet* (vessels registered at 31 December 2006): 157; Total displacement 2,889,842 grt. (Source: Lloyd's Register-Fairplay, *World Fleet Statistics*).

TOURISM

Visitor Arrivals ('000): 1,953.2 (arrivals by air 259.9, cruise-ship passengers 1,693.3) in 2004; 1,966.8 (arrivals by air 167.8, cruise-ship passengers 1,799.0) in 2005; 2,197.4 (arrivals by air 267.3, cruise-ship passengers 1,930.1) in 2006.

Stay-over Arrivals by Place of Origin ('000, 2006): Canada 14.9; Europe 17.4; USA 217.4; Total (incl. others) 267.3.

Tourism Receipts (US $ million, incl. passenger transport): 518.0 in 2003; 519.0 in 2004; 353.0 in 2005. Source: World Tourism Organization.

COMMUNICATIONS MEDIA

Radio Receivers: 36,000 in use in 1997.
Television Receivers: 23,239 in use in 1999.
Telephones: 32,967 main lines in use in 2003.
Facsimile Machines: 116 in use in 1993.
Mobile Cellular Telephones (subscribers): 33,800 in 2004.
Fixed and Mobile Telecommunication Lines (number in service): 110,656 in 2005.
Internet Connections: 9,909 in 2003.
Daily Newspapers: 2 (circulation 15,400) in 2004.

EDUCATION
(30 September 2006)

Institutions: Government 18; Private 11; Total 29.

Enrolment: *Government:* Pre-primary 41; Primary 2,339; Middle 1,171; Secondary 948; Total 4,499. *Private:* Pre-primary 292; Primary 1,253; Middle 558; Secondary 415; Total 2,518.

Directory

The Constitution

The Constitution of 1959 was revised in 1972, 1992 and 1994. Under its terms, the Governor, who is appointed for four years, is responsible for defence and internal security, external affairs, and the public service. The Cabinet (known as the Executive Council until 2003) comprises the Chairman (the Governor), the Chief Secretary, the Financial Secretary, the Attorney-General, the Cabinet Secretary (all four of whom are appointed by the Governor) and five other Ministers elected by the Legislative Assembly from their own number. The Governor assigns ministerial portfolios to the elected members of the Cabinet. There are 15 elected members of the Legislative Assembly (elected by direct, universal adult suffrage for a term of four years) and three official members appointed by the Governor. The Speaker presides over the Assembly. The United Kingdom retains full control over foreign affairs. In May 2001 the Governor appointed a Constitutional Review Commission to make recommendations on changes to the Cayman Islands' political structure and processes. A government-administered Constitutional Review Secretariat was established in March 2007 to resume evaluation of the Cayman Islands' Constitution following the disruption to previous efforts caused by 'Hurricane Ivan'.

The Government

Governor: STUART JACK (assumed office November 2005).

CABINET
(May 2008)

Chairman: STUART JACK (The Governor).
Chief Secretary and Minister of Internal and External Affairs*: GEORGE A. MCCARTHY.
Attorney-General and Minister of Legal Affairs*: SAMUEL W. BULGIN.
Financial Secretary*: KENNETH JEFFERSON.
Cabinet Secretary*: ORRETT CONNOR.
Leader of Government Business and Minister for District Administration, Planning, Agriculture and Housing: D. KURT TIBBETTS.
Minister of Health and Human Services: ANTHONY S. EDEN.
Minister of Education, Training, Employment, Youth, Sports and Culture: ALDEN MCNEE MCLAUGHLIN.
Minister of Communications, Works and Infrastructure: V. ARDEN MCLEAN.
Minister of Tourism, Environment, Investment and Commerce: CHARLES CLIFFORD.

A District Commissioner, Ernie Scott, represents the Governor on Cayman Brac and Little Cayman.
* Appointed by the Governor.

LEGISLATIVE ASSEMBLY

Legislative Assembly: 33 Fort St, POB 890, George Town, Grand Cayman; tel. 949-4236; fax 949-9514; e-mail wendy.lauer@gov.ky; internet www.legislativeassembly.ky; Clerk WENDY LAUER.

Members: The Chief Secretary, the Financial Secretary, the Attorney-General, and 15 elected members. The most recent election to the Assembly was on 11 May 2005. In February 1991 a Speaker was elected to preside over the Assembly (despite provision for such a post in the Constitution, the functions of the Speaker had hitherto been assumed by the Governor).

Speaker: EDNA MOYLE.
Leader of Government Business: D. KURT TIBBETTS.

GOVERNMENT OFFICES

Office of the Governor: Aall Bldg, 4th Floor, North Church St, George Town, Grand Cayman; tel. 244-2401; fax 945-4131; e-mail staffoff@candw.ky; internet www.gov.ky.

All official government offices and ministries are located in the Government Administration Bldg, Elgin Ave, George Town, Grand Cayman.

Election Commission

Elections Office: Kirk House Bldg, 4th Floor, George Town, Grand Cayman; tel. 949-8047; fax 949-0631; e-mail electionsoffice@electionsoffice.ky; internet www.electionsoffice.ky; Supervisor of Elections KEARNEY SIDNEY GOMEZ.

Political Organizations

People's Progressive Movement (PPM): POB 10526 APO, Grand Cayman; tel. 945-1776; f. 2002; Leader D. KURT TIBBETTS; Chair. ANTONY DUCKWORTH.

United Democratic Party (UDP): Edge Plaza, Unit 3, 6 Ashgo St, POB 10009, Grand Cayman; e-mail info@udp.ky; internet www.udp.ky; tel. 943-3338; fax 943-3339; f. 2001; Leader W. MCKEEVA BUSH; Chair. BILLY REID.

Judicial System

There is a Grand Court of the Islands (with Supreme Court status), a Summary Court, a Youth Court and a Coroner's Court. The Grand Court has jurisdiction in all civil matters, admiralty matters, and in trials on indictment. Appeals lie to the Court of Appeal of the Cayman Islands and beyond that to the Privy Council in the United Kingdom. The Summary Courts deal with criminal and civil matters (up to a certain limit defined by law) and appeals lie to the Grand Court.

Chief Justice: ANTHONY SMELLIE.
President of the Court of Appeal: EDWARD ZACCA.
Solicitor-General: CHERYLL RICHARDS.
Clerk of the Courts of the Islands: VALDIS FOLDATS, Court's Office, Edward St, George Town, Grand Cayman KY1-1106; tel. 949-4296; fax 949-9856; e-mail valdis.foldats@gov.ky.

Religion

CHRISTIANITY

The oldest-established denominations are (on Grand Cayman) the United Church of Jamaica and Grand Cayman (Presbyterian), and (on Cayman Brac) the Baptist Church. Anglicans are adherents of the Church in the Province of the West Indies (Grand Cayman forms part of the diocese of Jamaica). Within the Roman Catholic Church, the Cayman Islands forms part of the archdiocese of Kingston in Jamaica. Other denominations include the Church of God, Church of God (Full Gospel), Church of Christ, Seventh-day Adventist, Wesleyan Holiness, Jehovah's Witnesses, Church of the Latter Day Saints, Bahá'í and Church of God (Universal). In 1999 there were an estimated 90 churches in the Cayman Islands, including seven churches on Cayman Brac, and a Baptist Church on Little Cayman.

The Press

Cayman Islands Journal: The Compass Centre, Shedden Rd, POB 1365, George Town, Grand Cayman; tel. 949-5111; fax 949-7675; internet www.cayjournal.com; publ. by the Cayman Free Press; monthly; broadsheet business newspaper; Publr BRIAN UZZELL.

Cayman Net News: 85 North Sound Rd, Alissta Towers, POB 10707, Grand Cayman; tel. 946-6060; fax 949-0679; e-mail news@caymannetnews.com; internet www.caymannetnews.com; internet news service; publishes weekly newspaper (f. 2006); Publr and Editor-in-Chief DESMOND SEALES.

Caymanian Compass: The Compass Centre, Shedden Rd, POB 1365, George Town, Grand Cayman; tel. 949-5111; fax 949-7675; internet www.caycompass.com; f. 1965; publ. by the Cayman Free Press; 5 a week; Publr BRIAN UZZELL; circ. 10,000.

Chamber in Action: POB 1000, George Town, Grand Cayman; tel. 949-8090; fax 949-0220; e-mail info@caymanchamber.ky; internet www.caymanchamber.ky; f. 1965; monthly; newsletter of the Cayman Islands Chamber of Commerce; Editor WIL PINEAU; circ. 5,000.

The Executive: Crewe Rd, George Town, POB 173 GT; tel. 949-5111; fax 949-7033; e-mail cfp@candw.ky; quarterly; circ. 7,500.

Gazette: Gazette Office, Government Information Service, Cayman Islands Government, Craicket Square, Elgin Ave, Grand Cayman; tel. 949-8092; fax 949-5936; e-mail caymangazette@gov.ky; internet www.gazettes.gov.ky; official newspaper of the govt; publ. fortnightly on Monday; Editor-in-Chief PATRICIA EBANKS.

Key to Cayman: The Compass Centre, Shedden Rd, POB 1365 George Town, Grand Cayman KY1 1108; tel. 949-5111; fax 949-7675; e-mail info@cfp.ky; internet www.caymanfreepress.com; 2 a year; free tourist magazine; publ. by the Cayman Free Press; Cayman Free Press also publs bi-weekly *Caymanian Compass* newspaper and accompanying supplements, *Cayman Islands Journal*, *Cayman Islands Yearbook & Business Directory*, *Cayman Islands Map*, and *Inside Out*, a home and living magazine.

The New Caymanian: Grand Cayman; tel. 949-7414; fax 949-0036; weekly; Publr and Editor-in-Chief PETER JACKSON.

Publishers

Caribbean Publishing Co (Cayman) Ltd: 1 Paddington Pl., Suite 306, North Sound Way, POB 688, George Town, Grand Cayman; tel. 949-7027; fax 949-8366; internet www.caribbeanwhitepages.com; f. 1978.

Cayman Free Press Ltd: The Compass Centre, Shedden Rd, POB 1365, George Town, Grand Cayman; tel. 949-5111; fax 949-7675; e-mail info@cfp.ky; internet www.caymanfreepress.com; f. 1965.

Government Information Service: Gazette Office, Cayman Islands Govt, Cricket Sq., Elgin Avenue, Grand Cayman; tel. 949-8092; fax 949-5936; e-mail caymangazette@gov.ky; internet www.gazettes.gov.ky; publr of official govt releases, *Gazette*.

Progressive Publications Ltd: Economy Printers Bldg, POB 764, George Town, Grand Cayman; tel. 949-5780; fax 949-7674.

Tower Marketing and Publishing: tel. 946-6000; fax 946-6001; e-mail info@tower.com.ky; internet www.tower.com.ky.

Broadcasting and Communications

REGULATORY AUTHORITY

Information and Communications Technology Authority (ICTA): Alissta Towers, 3rd Floor, 85 North Sound Rd, POB 2502, Grand Cayman KY1 1104; tel. 946-4282; fax 945-8284; e-mail info@icta.ky; internet www.icta.ky; f. 2002; responsible for the regulation and licensing of telecommunications, broadcasting, and all forms of radio which includes ship, aircraft, mobile and amateur radio and the management of the Cayman Islands internet domain; Chair. SAMUEL JACKSON; Man. Dir DAVID ARCHBOLD.

TELECOMMUNICATIONS

Cable & Wireless (Cayman Islands) Ltd: Anderson Sq. Bldg, Anderson Sq., Sheddon Rd, POB 293, George Town, Grand Cayman; tel. 949-7800; fax 949-7962; e-mail cs@candw.ky; internet www.candw.ky; f. 1966; Cable & Wireless' monopoly over the telecommunications market ended in 2004; Man. Dir TONEY HEART; CEO TIMOTHY ADAM.

Digicel Cayman: Cayman Financial Centre, 36A Roys Dr., POB 700, George Town, Grand Cayman; tel. 345-9433; fax 945-1351; e-mail caycustomercare@digicelgroup.com; internet www.digicelcayman.com; f. 2003; owned by an Irish consortium; acquired the operations of Cingular Wireless (fmrly those of AT & T Wireless) in the country in 2005 (www.cingular.ky); CEO DENIS O'BRIEN.

TeleCayman: Cayman Corporate Centre, 4th Floor, POB 704 GT, Grand Cayman; tel. 769-1000; fax 769-0999; e-mail sales@telecaymen.com; internet www.telecayman.com; provides telephone and internet services; Senior Vice-Pres. GILBERT CHALIFOUX.

WestTel Ltd: Trinity Sq., Eastern Ave, George Town, Grand Cayman; tel. 745-5555; fax 743-3334; e-mail support@westtel.ky; internet www.westtel.ky; f. 2003; provides telephone and internet services; independent affiliate of WestStar TV Ltd cable television co; Chief Technical Officer MICHAEL EDENHOLM.

BROADCASTING

Radio

Radio Cayman: Elgin Ave, POB 1110 GT, George Town, Grand Cayman; tel. 949-7799; fax 949-6536; e-mail rcnews@gov.ky; internet www.radiocayman.gov.ky; started full-time broadcasting 1976; govt-owned commercial radio station; service in English; operates Radio Cayman One and Radio Cayman Two; Dir LOXLEY E. M. BANKS.

Radio Heaven 97 FM: GKF Industrial Park, Godfrey Nixon Way, POB 31481 SMB, George Town, Grand Cayman; tel. 949-9797; fax 949-2707; e-mail steve.koranda@heaven97.com; internet www.heaven97.com; f. 1997; owned by Christian Communications Association; Christian broadcasting, music and news; commercial station; Station Man. STEVE KORANDA.

Radio ICCI-FM: International College of the Cayman Islands, POB 136, Grand Cayman KY1-1501; tel. 947-1100; fax 947-1210; e-mail icci@icci.edu.ky; internet www.icci.edu.ky; f. 1973; radio station of the International College of the Cayman Islands; educational and cultural; Pres. Dr ELSA M. CUMMINGS.

Radio Ocean 95: 38 Earth Close, POB 425, Grand Cayman KY1-1502; e-mail gregg_a@candw.ky; internet www.ocean95.com; operated by Cerentis Broadcasting Systems; Station Man. GREGG ANDERSON.

Radio Vibe: POB 236, Grand Cayman KY1-1104; tel. 946-9898; e-mail kenny@vibefm.ky; internet www.vibefm.ky; operated by Paramount Media Services, in addition to Spin FM; Man. KENNY RANKINE.

Radio Z99.9 FM: 256 Crewe Rd, Suite 201, Crighton Bldg, POB 30110, Grand Cayman KY1-1201; tel. 945-1166; fax 945-1006; e-mail info@z99.ky; internet www.z99.ky; owned by Hurley's Entertainment Corpn Ltd; Man. Dir RANDY MERREN.

Television

Cayman Adventist Television Network (CATN/TV): POB 515, Grand Cayman KY1-1106; tel. 949-2739; e-mail mission@candw.ky; internet www.tagnet.org/cayman/tv.html; f. 1996; local and international programmes, mainly religious; Pres. JEFFREY THOMPSON.

Cayman Christian TV Ltd: POB 964, Grand Cayman KY1-1102; relays Christian broadcasting from the Trinity Broadcasting Network (USA); Vice-Pres. FRED RUTTY.

CITN Cayman 27: Sound Way, George Town, Grand Cayman; tel. 945-2739; fax 945-1373; e-mail citn@Cayman27.com.ky; internet www.cayman27.com.ky; f. 1992 as Cayman International Television Network; 24 hrs daily; local and international news and US entertainment; 10-channel cable service of international programmes by subscription; Mans COLIN WILSON, JOANNE WILSON.

Weststar TV Ltd: 45 Eclipse Way, POB 31117, Grand Cayman KY1-1205; tel. 745-5555; e-mail info@weststartv.com; internet www.weststartv.com; f. 1993; operates wireless cable television service; affiliated to WestTel Ltd; Operations Man. RICHARD CORBIN.

Finance

(cap. = capital; res = reserves; dep. = deposits; m. = million; brs = branches)

Banking facilities are provided by commercial banks. The islands have become an important centre for 'offshore' companies and trusts. At July 2007 there were some 73,000 companies registered in the Cayman Islands. In 2005 there were also 438 licensed banks and trusts and 6,268 registered mutual funds. At the end of March 2008 there were 347 licensed banks and trusts and a total of 9,018 registered mutual funds. The islands were well-known as a tax haven because of the absence of any form of direct taxation. In mid-June 2006 assets held by banks registered in the Cayman Islands totalled US $1,413,000m.

Cayman Islands Monetary Authority (CIMA): 80E Shedden Rd, Elizabethan Sq., POB 10052 APO, George Town, Grand Cayman KY1 1001; tel. 949-7089; fax 945-2532; e-mail cima@cimoney.com.ky; internet www.cimoney.com.ky; f. 1997; responsible for managing the territory's currency and reserves and for regulating the financial services sector; cap. CI $8.1m., res CI $8.8m., dep. CI $54.8m. (Dec. 2004); Chair. TIMOTHY RIDLEY; Man. Dir CINDY SCOTLAND.

UNITED KINGDOM OVERSEAS TERRITORIES — The Cayman Islands

PRINCIPAL BANKS AND TRUST COMPANIES

AALL Trust and Banking Corpn Ltd: AALL Bldg, POB 1166, George Town, Grand Cayman; tel. 949-5588; fax 949-8265; Chair. ERIC MONSEN; Man. Dir KEVIN DOYLE.

Appleby Trust (Cayman) Ltd: Artemis House, 67 Fort St, POB 1350, George Town, Grand Cayman KY1-1108; tel. 814-2015; e-mail jfletcher@applebyglobal.com; internet www.applebyglobal.com; f. 2006 following acquisition of business interests of Ansbacher (Cayman) Ltd; offices in Bermuda; Man. Dir JOHN FLETCHER.

Atlantic Security Bank: POB 10340, George Town 1097, Grand Cayman; internet www.asbnet.com; f. 1981 as Banco de Crédito del Peru International, name changed as above 1986; Chair. DIONISIO ROMERO; Pres. CARLOS MUÑOZ.

Julius Baer Bank and Trust Co Ltd: Windward Bldg 3, Regatta Office Park, Seven Mile Beach, POB 1100, George Town, Grand Cayman; tel. 949-7212; fax 949-0993; internet www.juliusbaer.ch; f. 1974; 100% owned by Julius Baer Holding Ltd (Switzerland); Man. Dir CHARLES FARRINGTON.

Banco Português do Atlântico: POB 30124, Grand Cayman; tel. 949-8322; fax 949-7743; e-mail bcpjvic@candw.ky; Gen. Man. HELENA SOARES CARNEIRO.

Banco Safra (Cayman Islands) Ltd: c/o Bank of Nova Scotia, POB 501, George Town, Grand Cayman; tel. 949-2001; fax 949-7097; f. 1993; cap. US $60.0m., res US $124.5m., dep. US $726.1m. (Dec. 2003).

BANIF-Banco Internaçional do Funchal (Cayman) Ltd: Genesis Bldg, 3rd Floor, POB 32338 SMB, George Town, Grand Cayman; tel. 945-8060; fax 945-8069; e-mail banifcay@candw.ky; internet www.banif.pt; Chair. and CEO Dr JOAQUIM FILIPE MARQUES DOS SANTOS; Gen. Man. VALDEMAR B. LOPES.

Bank of America Trust and Banking Corpn (Cayman) Ltd: BankAmerica Bldg, Fort St, POB 1092, George Town, Grand Cayman; tel. 949-7888; fax 949-7883; f. 1999; Man. Dir CHARLES FARRINGTON.

Bank of Bermuda (Cayman) Ltd: British American Tower, 3rd Floor, POB 513, George Town, Grand Cayman; tel. 949-9898; fax 949-7959; internet www.bankofbermuda.bm; f. 1968 as a trust; converted to a bank in 1988; total assets US $1,041m. (July 2001); Chair. HENRY B. SMITH; Man. Dir ALLEN BERNARDO.

Bank of Nova Scotia: 6 Cardinal Ave, POB 689, George Town, Grand Cayman; tel. 949-7666; fax 949-0020; e-mail scotiaci@candw.ky; internet www.scotiabank.com; also runs trust company; Man. Dir FARRIED SULLIMAN.

BankBoston Trust Co (Cayman Islands) Ltd: The Bank of Nova Scotia Trust Co (Cayman) Ltd, Scotiabank Bldg, 6 Cardinal Ave, POB 501, George Town, Grand Cayman; tel. 949-8066; fax 949-8080; e-mail info@maples.candw.ky; internet www.bankboston international.com; f. 1997.

Bermuda Trust (Cayman) Ltd: 5th Floor, Bermuda House, POB 513, George Town, Grand Cayman; tel. 949-9898; fax 949-7959; internet www.bankofbermuda.bm; f. 1968 as Arawak Trust Co; became subsidiary of Bank of Bermuda in 1988; bank and trust services; Chair. JOSEPH JOHNSON; Man. Dir KENNETH GIBBS.

BFC Bank (Cayman) Ltd: Trafalgar Pl., POB 1765, George Town, Grand Cayman; tel. 949-8748; fax 949-8749; e-mail bfc@candw.ky; f. 1985; FC Financière de la Cité, Geneva, 99.9%; cap. US $0.8m., res US $3.7m., dep. US $33.5m. (March 2001); Chair. SIMON C. TAY; Resident Man. CHERRYLEE BUSH.

Butterfield Bank (Cayman) Ltd: Butterfield House, 68 Fort St, POB 705, George Town, Grand Cayman; tel. 949-7055; fax 949-7761; e-mail info@butterfieldbank.ky; internet www.butterfieldbank.ky; f. 1967; name changed as above in 2004, fmrly Bank of Butterfield International (Cayman) Ltd; subsidiary of Bank of N. T. Butterfield & Son Ltd, Bermuda; cap. US $16.5m., res US $0.05m., dep. US $2,182.3m. (June 2004); Chair. ALAN THOMPSON; Man. Dir CONOR J. O'DEA; 3 brs.

Caledonian Bank and Trust Ltd: POB 1043, George Town, Grand Cayman; tel. 949-0050; fax 949-8062; e-mail info@caledonian.com; internet www.caledonian.com; f. 1970; Chair. WILLIAM S. WALKER; Man. Dir DAVID S. SARGISON.

Cayman National Bank Ltd: Cayman National Bank Bldg, 4th Floor, 200 Elgin Ave, POB 1097, George Town, Grand Cayman; tel. 949-4655; fax 949-7506; e-mail cnb@caymannational.com; internet www.caymannational.com; f. 1974; subsidiary of Cayman National Corpn; cap. CI $2.4m., res CI $41.4m., dep. CI $466.0m. (Sept. 2002); Chair. BENSON O. EBANKS; Pres. STUART DACK; 6 brs.

CITCO Bank and Trust Co Ltd: Regatta Office Park, West Bay Rd, POB 31105 SMB, Grand Cayman; tel. 945-3838; fax 945-3888; e-mail cayman-bank@citco.com; internet www.citco.com.

Coutts (Cayman) Ltd: Coutts House, 1446 West Bay Rd, POB 707, George Town, Grand Cayman; tel. 945-4777; fax 945-4799; internet www.rbscoutts.com; f. 1967; fmrly NatWest International Trust Corpn (Cayman) Ltd; 100% owned by Royal Bank of Scotland International (Holdings) Ltd (Jersey); Chair. CHRIS BURTON; Man. Dir DAVID NEUSCHAFFER.

Deutsche Bank (Cayman) Ltd: Elizabethan Sq., POB 1984, George Town, Grand Cayman; tel. 949-8244; fax 949-8178; e-mail dmg-cay@candw.ky; internet www.dboffshore.com; f. 1983 as Morgan Grenfell (Cayman) Ltd; name changed to Deutsche Morgan Grenfell (Cayman) Ltd in 1996; name changed as above in 1998; cap. US $5.0m., res US $20.3m., dep. US $129.3m. (Dec. 1998); Chair. MARK HIRST; Branch Man. JANET HISLOP.

Deutsche Bank International Trust Co (Cayman) Ltd: POB 1984, George Town, Grand Cayman; tel. 949-8244; fax 949-7866; f. 1999; Regional Man. TIM GODBER.

Deutsche Girozentrale Overseas Ltd: POB 694, George Town, Grand Cayman; tel. 914-9483; fax 949-0626; Man. Dir RAINER MACH.

Fidelity Bank (Cayman) Ltd: POB 914, George Town, Grand Cayman KY1 1103; tel. 949-7822; fax 949-6064; e-mail bank@fidelitycayman.com; internet www.fidelitycayman.com; f. 1979; Pres. and CEO BRETT HILL.

FirstCaribbean International Bank Ltd: POB 68, George Town, Grand Cayman; tel. 949-7300; fax 815-2292; internet www.firstcaribbeanbank.com; f. 2002 following merger of Caribbean operations of Barclays Bank PLC and CIBC; Barclays relinquished its stake to CIBC in June 2006; Exec. Chair. MICHAEL MANSOOR; CEO CHARLES PINK; Cayman Islands Contact MARK MCINTYRE.

Fortis Bank (Cayman) Ltd: Grand Pavilion Commercial Centre, West Bay Rd, POB 2003, George Town, Grand Cayman; tel. 949-7942; fax 949-8340; e-mail phil.brown@ky.fortisbank.com; internet www.fortis.com; f. 1984 as Pierson, Heldring & Pierson (Cayman) Ltd; name changed to Mees Pierson (Cayman) Ltd in 1993; present name adopted in June 2000; Man. Dir ROGER HANSON.

HSBC Financial Services (Cayman) Ltd: Strathvale House, 2nd Floor, 90 North Church St, POB 1109, George Town, Grand Cayman; tel. 949-7755; fax 949-7634; e-mail hfsc.info@ky.hsbc.com; internet www.hsbc.ky; f. 1982; Dirs TOM CLARK, DAVID A. WHITEFIELD.

IBJ Whitehall Bank and Trust Co: West Wind Bldg, POB 1040, George Town, Grand Cayman; tel. 949-2849; fax 949-5409; Man. ROGER HEALY.

Intesa Bank Overseas Ltd: c/o Coutts (Cayman) Ltd, Coutts House, West Bay Rd, POB 705, George Town, Grand Cayman; tel. 945-4777; fax 945-4799; f. 1994 as Ambroveneto International Bank; name changed as above in March 1999; cap. US $10.0m., total assets US $1,339.8m. (Dec. 1999); Chair. FRANCESCO DE VECCHI; Man. Dirs RICHARD AUSTIN, ANDREW GALLOWAY.

LGT Bank in Liechtenstein (Cayman) Ltd: UBS House, 227 Elgin Ave, POB 852, George Town, Grand Cayman; tel. 949-7676; fax 949-8512; e-mail lgt.cayman@lgt.com; internet www.lgt-bank-in-liechtenstein.com.

Lloyds TSB Bank and Trust (Cayman) Ltd: Grand Cayman; tel. 949-7854; fax 949-0090; Man. ROGER C. BARKER.

Mercury Bank and Trust Ltd: POB 2424, George Town, Grand Cayman; tel. 949-0800; fax 949-0295; Man. VOLKER MERGENTHALER.

Merrill Lynch Bank and Trust Co (Cayman) Ltd: POB 1164, George Town, Grand Cayman; tel. 949-8206; fax 949-8895; internet www.ml.com.

Royal Bank of Canada: 24 Shedden Rd, POB 245, Grand Cayman; tel. 949-4600; fax 949-7396; internet www.royalbank.com; Man. HARRY C. CHISHOLM.

Royal Bank of Canada Trust Co (Cayman) Ltd: 24 Shedden Rd, POB 1586 GT, Grand Cayman; tel. 949-9107; fax 949-5777; internet www.rbcprivatebanking.com/cayman-islands.html; Man. Dir RALPH AWREY.

Scotiabank and Trust (Cayman) Ltd: Scotia Centre, 6 Cardinal Ave, POB 501 GT, George Town, Grand Cayman; tel. 949-2001; fax 949-7097; e-mail cayman@scotiatrust.com; internet www.cayman.scotiabank.com; fmrly Bank of Novia Scotia Trust Company (Cayman) Ltd; present name adopted Dec. 2003; Man. Dir FARRIED SULLIMAN.

UBS (Cayman Islands) Ltd: UBS House, 227 Elgin Ave, POB 852, George Town, Grand Cayman; tel. 914-1060; fax 914-4060; internet www.ubs.com/cayman-funds; CEO WALTER EGGENSCHWILER.

Development Bank

Cayman Islands Development Bank: Cayman Financial Centre, 36B Dr Roy's Dr., POB 1271 GT, George Town; tel. 949-7511; fax 949-6168; e-mail angela.miller@gov.ky; f. 2002; replaced the Housing Devt Corpn and the Agricultural and Industrial Devt Bd; under the jurisdiction of the Ministry of Tourism, Environment, Investment and Commerce; Devt Finance Institution Gen. Man. ANGELA J. MILLER.

UNITED KINGDOM OVERSEAS TERRITORIES

Banking Association

Cayman Islands Bankers' Association: Macdonald Sq., Fort St, POB 676, George Town, Grand Cayman; tel. 949-0330; fax 945-1448; e-mail ciba@candw.ky; Pres. Timothy Godber; 86 full mems, 250 assoc. mems.

STOCK EXCHANGE

Cayman Islands Stock Exchange (CSX): 4th Floor, Elizabethan Sq., POB 2408, George Town, Grand Cayman; tel. 945-6060; fax 945-6061; e-mail csx@csx.com.ky; internet www.csx.com.ky; f. 1996; 1,477 cos listed (July 2007); CEO Valia Theodoraki.

INSURANCE

Several foreign companies have agents in the islands. A total of 934 insurance companies were registered at the end of March 2008. In particular, the islands are a leading international market for health insurance. Local companies include the following:

British Caymanian Insurance Agency Ltd: Elizabethan Sq., POB 74 GT, Grand Cayman KY1-1002; tel. 949-8699; fax 949-8411; e-mail gderry@candw.ky; Man. Derry Graham.

Cayman National Insurance Brokers Ltd: POB 10042, George Town, Grand Cayman KY1-1001; tel. 949-0111; fax 949-8163; e-mail cnib@caymannational.com; internet www.caymannational.com; part of the Cayman National Corpn; Gen. Man. Mary Mellin.

Cayman Insurance Centre: POB 10056, Cayman Business Park; tel. 814-7230; e-mail trisha.anthony@cic.com.ky; internet www.cic.com.ky; Pres. Linda Chapman-Key.

Cayman Islands National Insurance Co (CINICO): Phase 3, 1st Floor, Elizabethan Sq., POB 512 GT, Grand Cayman KY1-1106; tel. 949-8101; fax 949-8226; e-mail debanks@cinico.ky; internet www.cinico.ky; CEO and Pres. Gordon Rowell.

Insurance Company of the West Indies (Cayman) Ltd (ICWI): 93 Hospital Rd, POB 461, Grand Cayman KY1-1106; tel. 949-6970; fax 949-6929; e-mail icwi@candw.ky; internet www.icwi.net; subsidiary of Insurance Company of the West Indies, Jamaica; Man. Heather Lanigan.

Island Heritage Insurance Co Ltd: 802 West Bay Rd, Grand Pavilion Centre, POB 2501, Grand Cayman KY1-1104; tel. 949-7280; fax 945-6765; e-mail info@islandheritage.com.ky; internet www.island-heritage.com; property insurance; Chair. Conor O'Dea.

Sagicor Life of the Cayman Islands Ltd: 198 North Church St, POB 1087, George Town, Grand Cayman KY1-1102; tel. 949-8211; fax 949-8262; e-mail customerservice@sagicor.com; internet www.sagicor.com; f. 2004 by merger between Global Life and Capital Life; Country Man. Claudette Saint-Reid.

Trade and Industry

GOVERNMENT AGENCY

Cayman Islands Investment Bureau: Cayman Corporate Centre, 1st Floor, Hospital Rd., POB 10087 APO, Grand Cayman KY1-1001; tel. 945-0943; fax 945-0941; e-mail info@investcayman.gov.ky; internet www.investcayman.gov.ky; f. 2003; Exec. Dir Dr Dax Basdeo.

CHAMBER OF COMMERCE

Cayman Islands Chamber of Commerce: Macdonald Sq., 2nd Floor, Fort St, POB 1000, George Town, Grand Cayman KY1 1102; tel. 949-8090; fax 949-0220; e-mail info@caymanchamber.ky; internet www.caymanchamber.ky; f. 1965; Pres. James Tibbetts; Chief Exec. Wil Pineau; 594 corporate mems and 78 associates.

TRADE ASSOCIATION

Cayman Islands Financial Services Association (CIFSA): POB 11048, Grand Cayman; tel. 623-6700; fax 623-6731; e-mail info@caymanfinances.com; internet www.caymanfinances.com; f. 2003; Dir Eduardo D'Angelo P. Silva.

EMPLOYERS' ORGANIZATION

Labour Office: 4th Floor, Tower Bldg, Grand Cayman; tel. 949-0941; fax 949-6057; Dir Dale M. Banks.

UTILITIES

Electricity

Caribbean Utilities Co Ltd (CUC): Corporate HQ & Plant, North Sound Rd, POB 38, George Town, Grand Cayman; tel. 949-5200; fax 949-4621; e-mail info@cuc.ky; internet www.cuc-cayman.com; Pres. and CEO J. F. Richard Hew; Chair. David Ritch.

Cayman Brac Power and Light Co Ltd (CBP&L): Stake Bay Point, POB 95, Stake Bay, Cayman Brac; tel. 948-2224; fax 948-2204; Gen. Man. Jonathan Tibbetts.

Water

Cayman Islands Water Authority: 13G Red Gate Rd, POB 1104 GT, George Town, Grand Cayman; tel. 949-6352; fax 949-0094; e-mail wac@candw.ky; Dir Dr Gelia Frederick-van Genderen.

Consolidated Water Co Ltd (CWCO): Windward 3, 4th Floor, Regatta Business Park, POB 1114, George Town, KY1-1102 Grand Cayman; tel. 945-4277; fax 949-2957; e-mail info@cwco.com; internet www.cwco.com; f. 1973; Pres. and CEO Frederick W. McTaggart; Dir and Chair. Jeffrey M. Parker.

Transport

ROADS

There are some 406 km (252 miles) of motorable roads, of which 304 km are surfaced with tarmac. The road network connects all districts on Grand Cayman and Cayman Brac (which has 76 km of motorable road), and there are 43 km of motorable road on Little Cayman (of which about 18 km are paved). According to the 2008 budget address, US $8.8m. was to be allocated for ongoing improvements to the islands' road network.

SHIPPING

George Town is the principal port and a new port facility was opened in July 1977. Cruise liners, container ships and smaller cargo vessels ply between the Cayman Islands, Florida, Jamaica and Costa Rica. There is no cruise-ship dock in the Cayman Islands. Ships anchor off George Town and ferry passengers ashore to the North or South Dock Terminals in George Town. The number of cruise-ship passengers is limited to 6,000 per day. The port of Cayman Brac is Creek; there are limited facilities on Little Cayman. In December 2006 the shipping register comprised 157 vessels, with combined displacement totalling 2,889,842 grt.

Maritime Authority of Cayman Islands (MACI): Kirk House, 3rd Floor, 22 Albert Panton St, George Town, Grand Cayman; tel. 949-8831; fax 949-8849; e-mail maci.consulting@cishipping.com; internet www.cishipping.com; f. 2005; wholly govt-owned; legal entity responsible for: enforcement of international maritime laws and conventions; implementation of maritime safety and security, Cayman Islands marine environment laws; formation of national maritime policy; representation and protection of national maritime interests at international forums; also undertakes vessel and mortgage registration, advisory and marine survey and audit services fmrly administered by CISR; Chair. Sharon E. Roulstone; CEO A. Joel Walton.

Port Authority of the Cayman Islands: Harbour Dr., POB 1358 GT, George Town, Grand Cayman; tel. 949-2055; fax 949-5820; e-mail info@caymanport.com; internet www.caymanport.com; Port Dir Paul Hurlston.

Principal Shipping Companies

Cayman Freight Shipping Ltd: Mirco Commercial Centre, 2nd Floor, Industrial Park, POB 1372, George Town, Grand Cayman; tel. 949-4977; fax 949-8402; e-mail cfssl@candw.ky; internet www.seaboardmarinecayman.ky; Man. Dir Robert Foster.

Cayman Islands Shipping Registry: Kirk House, 3rd Floor, 22 Albert Panton St, POB 2256, George Town, Grand Cayman KY1-1107; tel. 949-8831; fax 949-8849; e-mail cisrky@cishipping.com; internet www.cishipping.com; f. 1993; dept of Maritime Authority of Cayman Islands (MACI); Dir A. Joel Walton.

Thompson Shipping Co Ltd: Cayman Shipping Centre, 2nd Floor, 432 Eastern Ave, POB 188, George Town, Grand Cayman KY1-1004; tel. 949-8044; fax 949-8349; e-mail info@thompsonshipping.com; internet www.thompsonshipping.com; f. 1977.

CIVIL AVIATION

There are two international airports in the Territory: Owen Roberts International Airport, 3.5 km (2 miles) from George Town, and Gerrard Smith International Airport on Cayman Brac. Both are capable of handling jet-engined aircraft. Edward Bodden Airport on Little Cayman can cater for light aircraft. Several scheduled carriers serve the islands.

Civil Aviation Authority of the Cayman Islands: Unit 4, Cayman Grand Harbour, POB 10277 APO, George Town, Grand Cayman; tel. 949-7811; fax 949-0761; e-mail civil.aviation@caacayman.com; internet www.caacayman.com; f. 1987; Dir-Gen. Richard Smith; Chair. Sheridan Brooks-Hurst.

Cayman Airways Ltd: 91 Owen Roberts Dr., POB 10092 APO, Grand Cayman KY1 1001; tel. 949-8200; fax 949-7607; e-mail customerrelations@caymanairways.net; internet www

.caymanairways.com; f. 1968; wholly govt-owned since 1977; operates local services and scheduled flights to Jamaica, Honduras and the USA; Chair. ANGELYN HERNANDEZ; CEO PATRICK STRASBURGER.

Island Air: Airport Rd, POB 2433, George Town, Grand Cayman; tel. 949-5252; fax 949-7044; e-mail iair@candw.ky; internet www.islandaircayman.info; operates daily scheduled services between Grand Cayman, Cayman Brac and Little Cayman.

Tourism

The Cayman Islands are a major tourist destination, the majority of visitors coming from North America. The tourism industry was badly affected by the damage caused by 'Hurricane Ivan' in September 2004, severely reducing available accommodation and a major reconstruction effort was undertaken in 2005. The beaches and opportunities for diving in the offshore reefs form the main attraction for most tourists. In 2006 there were an estimated 3,907 hotel rooms. In the same year there were 267,257 arrivals by air (compared with 167,801 in the preceding year) and some 1,930,136 cruise visitors (following the redirection of some cruise ships from ports elsewhere, damaged by 'Hurricane Wilma'). The USA remained the core market for stay-over visitors to the islands (81.3%). In 2005 the tourism industry earned an estimated US $353.0m.

Cayman Islands Department of Tourism: Cricket Sq., POB 67, George Town, Grand Cayman KY1-1102; tel. 949-0623; fax 949-4053; internet www.caymanislands.ky; f. 1965; Dir PILAR BUSH.

Cayman Islands Tourism Association (CITA): Largatos Bldg, 73 Lawrence Blvd, POB 31086 SMB, Grand Cayman; tel. and fax 949-8522; fax 946-8522; e-mail info@cita.ky; internet www.cita.ky; f. 2001 as a result of the amalgamation of the Cayman Tourism Alliance and the Cayman Islands Hotel and Condominium Asscn; Pres. KARIE BERGSTROM; Exec. Dir KEN THOMPSON.

Sister Islands Tourism Association (SITA): POB 187, Cayman Brac KY2-2101; tel. and fax 948-1345; e-mail sita@candw.ky; internet www.sisterislands.com; Pres. PETER HILLENBRAND (acting).

THE FALKLAND ISLANDS

Introductory Survey

Location, Climate, Language, Religion, Flag, Capital

The Falkland Islands, comprising two large islands and about 200 smaller ones, are in the south-western Atlantic Ocean, about 770 km (480 miles) north-east of Cape Horn, South America. The climate is generally cool, with strong winds (mainly westerly) throughout the year. The mean annual temperature is 6°C (42°F), while average annual rainfall is 635 mm (25 ins). The language is English. Most of the inhabitants profess Christianity, with several denominations represented. The flag is the British 'Blue Ensign', with the colony's coat of arms (a shield showing a white and violet ram standing in green grass, on a blue background, above a sailing ship bearing red crosses on its pennants and five six-pointed stars on its central sail, on three white horizontal wavy lines, with the motto 'Desire the Right' on a scroll beneath) on a white disc in the centre of the flag. The capital is Stanley, on East Falkland Island.

Recent History

The first recorded landing on the islands was made from a British ship in 1690, when the group was named after Viscount Falkland, then Treasurer of the Royal Navy. French sailors named the islands 'Les Malouines' (after their home port of Saint-Malo), from which the Spanish name 'Islas Malvinas' is derived. A French settlement was established in 1764 on the island of East Falkland, but in 1767 France relinquished its rights to the territory to Spain, which then ruled the adjacent regions of South America. Meanwhile, a British expedition annexed West Falkland in 1765, and a garrison was established. The British settlement, formed in 1765–66, was recognized by Spain in 1771 but withdrawn in 1774. The Spanish garrison was withdrawn in 1811.

When the United Provinces of the River Plate (now Argentina) gained independence from Spain in 1816, the Falkland Islands had no permanent inhabitants, although they provided temporary bases for sealing and whaling activities by British and US vessels. In 1820 an Argentine ship was sent to the islands to proclaim Argentine sovereignty as successor to Spain. An Argentine settlement was founded in 1826 but most of its occupants were expelled by a US warship in 1831. The remaining Argentines were ejected by a British expedition in 1832, and British sovereignty was established in 1833.

The islands became a Crown Colony of the United Kingdom, administered by a British-appointed Governor. However, Argentina did not relinquish its claim, and negotiations to resolve the dispute began in 1966 at the instigation of the UN. The inhabitants of the islands, nearly all British by descent, consistently expressed their desire to remain under British sovereignty.

After routine talks between delegations of the British and Argentine Governments in New York in February 1982, the Argentine foreign ministry announced that it would seek other means to resolve the dispute. Rumours of a possible invasion had begun in the Argentine press in January, and Argentina's military regime took advantage of a British protest at the presence of a group of Argentine scrap merchants, who had made an unauthorized landing on South Georgia in March and had raised an Argentine flag, to invade the Falkland Islands on 2 April. A small contingent of British marines was overwhelmed, the British Governor, Rex (later Sir Rex) Hunt, was expelled and an Argentine military governorship was established. The USA and the UN attempted (unsuccessfully) to mediate, in an effort to prevent military escalation. British forces, which had been dispatched to the islands immediately after the Argentine invasion, recaptured South Georgia on 25 April. The Argentine forces on the Falklands formally surrendered on 14 June, after a conflict in the course of which about 750 Argentine, 255 British and three Falklanders' lives were lost.

The Governor returned to the islands as Civil Commissioner on 25 June 1982, and Britain established a 'protection zone' around the islands, extending 150 nautical miles (278 km) off shore, as well as a garrison of about 4,000 troops. The British Government began an investigation into the possibilities of developing the islands' economy, and in November agreed to grant the Falkland Islanders full British citizenship. In November 1983 the post of Chief Executive of the Falkland Islands Government was created, in combination with the executive vice-chairmanship of the newly formed Falkland Islands Development Corporation. The Civil Commissioner, Sir Rex Hunt, retired in September 1985, whereupon a new Governor was appointed.

The issue of the sovereignty of the Falkland Islands remained a major impediment to the normalization of relations between Argentina and the United Kingdom. The Argentine Government refused to agree to a formal declaration that hostilities were ended until the United Kingdom agreed to participate in negotiations over sovereignty, while the United Kingdom refused to negotiate until Argentina had formally ended hostilities.

Following the return to civilian rule in Argentina in December 1983, the newly elected President, Dr Raúl Alfonsín, stated his Government's desire to seek a negotiated settlement to the dispute over the Falkland Islands. In October 1984 the Argentine Government removed restrictions on British companies and interests in Argentina as a possible prelude to resuming negotiations.

The British Government's refusal to discuss the issue of sovereignty, and its insistence on the paramountcy of the Falkland Islanders' wishes, were reflected in the new Constitution for the Falklands (approved by the islands' Legislative Council in January 1985), which guaranteed the islanders' right to self-determination.

The number of British troops stationed on the islands was reduced, following the opening, in mid-1985, of a new military airport at Mount Pleasant, about 30 km south-west of Stanley, enabling rapid reinforcement of the garrison, if necessary. In July the British Government ended its ban on Argentine imports, which had been in force since 1982. In October elections took place on the Falklands for a new Legislative Council. In the same month, South Georgia and the South Sandwich Islands ceased to be dependencies of the Falkland Islands, although the Governor of the Falkland Islands was to be (*ex officio*) Commissioner for the territory.

In 1986 parliamentary delegations from the United Kingdom and Argentina conducted exploratory talks. However, the British Government remained intransigent on the issue of the sovereignty of the islands. In early 1986 Argentina's continued claim to the naval 'protection zone' was manifested in attacks on foreign fishing vessels by Argentine gunboats. In October Britain unilaterally declared a fisheries conservation and management zone extending 150 nautical miles (278 km) around the islands, with effect from February 1987, to prevent the over-fishing of the waters. The imposition of this zone, whose radius coincided with that of the naval protection zone, was condemned by the majority of UN members, as was Britain's rejection, in November 1986, of an offer by Argentina to declare a formal end to hostilities in exchange for the abolition of the protection zone.

The resignation, in June 1989, of three members of the Legislative Council, in protest against a proposed agricultural grants scheme, prompted the dissolution of the legislative body. In the ensuing parliamentary elections in October, eight independent candidates, all of whom vigorously opposed renewing links, at any level, with Argentina, defeated 10 other candidates to take all the elective seats.

The successful independent candidates in elections to the eight elective seats of the Legislative Council in October 1993 and October 1997 expressed their reluctance to develop closer contacts with Argentina and their determination not to enter into negotiations with that country regarding the islands' sovereignty.

On 22 November 2001 a general election took place to elect members to a new Legislative Council. Of the eight elected, only three members had not served on the Legislative Council before. In a concurrent referendum the electorate voted against changing the two-constituency system (the Stanley constituency and the Camp constituency) to a single constituency for legislative elections.

A general election was held on 17 November 2005 in which eight independent candidates, of whom five were new members, were elected to the Legislative Council.

Beginning in 1982 the UN General Assembly voted annually, by an overwhelming majority, in favour of the resumption of negotiations between Argentina and the United Kingdom. The British Government consistently declined to engage in such dialogue. However, relations between Argentina and the United Kingdom improved, following the election, in May 1989, of a new Argentine President, Carlos Saúl Menem, who initially indicated that his country would be willing to suspend temporarily its demand that the issue of the sovereignty of the Falkland Islands be discussed, in the interests of the restoration of full diplomatic and commercial relations with the United Kingdom. In October a meeting of British and Argentine representatives, which took place in Madrid, Spain, culminated in the formal cessation of all hostilities, and the re-establishment of diplomatic relations at consular level. Restrictions on Argentine merchant vessels with regard to the naval protection zone around the Falkland Islands were also eased. In the following month, however, the United Kingdom announced that it was to increase the extent of its territorial waters around the islands from three to 12 nautical miles, in spite of protests from the Argentine authorities. In February 1990 Argentina and the United Kingdom conducted further negotiations in Madrid, as a result of which the two countries re-established full diplomatic relations. It was also announced that the naval protection zone around the Falkland Islands was to be modified in March, and that mutually agreed military procedures, that would ensure the security of the region, would take effect. In mid-1993 the further reduction of military restrictions around the islands was announced by both Governments.

Following successful negotiations between Argentina and the United Kingdom in Madrid in November 1990, an agreement regarding the protection and conservation of the South Atlantic fishing area was announced, whereby a temporary ban on fishing was to be extended, from late December, to an area incorporating an additional 50-mile (93-km) semicircular region to the east of the islands, beyond the existing 150-mile fishing zone. (The agreement was renewed in December 1991 and 1992.) The two sides also agreed to establish a South Atlantic Fisheries Commission, which was to meet at least twice in every year that the ban remained in place, in order to discuss fishing activity and conservation in the region. Throughout 1990 the Falkland Islands Government had appealed to the British Government to exercise its legal right under international law to extend the fisheries conservation and management zone, claiming that over-fishing of the previously well-stocked waters just beyond the 150-mile limit by vessels from Taiwan and the Republic of Korea (ignoring previously agreed voluntary restraints on fishing in the area) had seriously depleted stocks and posed a threat to the islands' lucrative squid-fishing industry.

In May 1993 the British Government announced that it would extend from 12 to 200 nautical miles its territorial jurisdiction in the waters surrounding South Georgia and the South Sandwich Islands. In December the Argentine Government indicated its acceptance of the United Kingdom's proposed extension of fishing rights around the Falkland Islands from 150 to 200 miles, in order to allow the islanders to fulfil an annual squid-fishing quota of 150,000 metric tons (effective from January 1994). The Argentine quota was agreed at 220,000 tons (compared with an estimated catch of 130,000 tons in 1992). In August 1994 the British Government unilaterally decided to extend its fisheries conservation zone north of the islands, thereby annexing a small but lucrative fishing ground (not previously protected by British or Argentine legislation) that was being plundered by foreign fishing vessels. In January 1997 the United Kingdom and Argentina agreed to resume negotiations on a long-term fisheries agreement that would include the disputed waters around the islands. Following the release of a Joint Declaration between the two Governments on 14 July 1999, both Governments agreed to co-operate to combat illegal fishing in the South West Atlantic and to ensure the sustainability of fish stocks in the region.

In November 1991 the Governments of both Argentina and the United Kingdom claimed rights of exploration and exploitation of the sea-bed and the subsoil of the continental shelf around the Falkland Islands (which are believed to be rich in petroleum reserves). In April 1992 the Falkland Islands Government invited tenders for seismic reports of the region. In December 1993 the British Geological Survey reported that preliminary seismic investigations indicated deposits in excess of those located in British North Sea oilfields. A bilateral agreement on petroleum and gas exploration in an area of 18,000 sq km, to the south-west of the islands, was concluded in New York in September 1994. A joint hydrocarbons commission would regulate licensing in the area, examining bids from Anglo-Argentine joint ventures (in which case taxes would be levied on operators by the respective Governments) or by third countries (from which royalties on revenues would be exacted by the Falkland Islands Government at a rate expected to approach 9%). The successful conclusion of the agreement appeared to dissipate Argentine objections, voiced earlier in the year, to the Falkland Islands' unilateral offer of rights to drill in 19 areas (comprising 44,000 sq km not covered by the Anglo-Argentine agreement) to the north and south of the islands. Licences to explore for hydrocarbons were awarded to five international consortia in October 1996. The possibility that commercial quantities of petroleum might be discovered prompted renewed discussion as to the amount of any future royalties exacted by the Falkland Islands Government that should be returned to the Government of the United Kingdom. In early 1997 the British Government indicated that it expected to benefit considerably from any such royalties, while the Falkland Islands administration proposed that some of the revenue could be used to finance the islands' defence expenditure (currently funded by the United Kingdom). Meanwhile, the Argentine Government claimed that it should be entitled to benefit from the discovery of petroleum in the region: draft legislation presented to Congress provided for the imposition of sanctions on petroleum companies and fishing vessels operating in Falkland Islands waters without Argentine authorization, in addition to the levying of 3% royalties from the sale of petroleum discovered in the area.

In late 1996 the Argentine Government suggested, for the first time, that it might consider shared sovereignty of the Falkland Islands with the United Kingdom. The proposal was firmly rejected by the British Government and by the Falkland Islanders, who reiterated their commitment to persuading the UN Special Political and Decolonization Committee to adopt a clause granting the islanders the right to self-determination.

In May 1999 formal negotiations between the Falkland Islands and Argentina took place in the United Kingdom. Issues under discussion included co-operation in fishing and petroleum exploration, Argentine access to the islands and the resumption of air links with mainland South America. (In March Chile had ended its country's regular air services to the islands in protest at the British Government's continued detention of Gen. Pinochet; Uruguay subsequently agreed not to establish an air link with the islands unless flights were routed via the Argentine capital.) The sovereignty of the Falkland Islands was not scheduled for discussion. Four of the islands' councillors also attended the three days of talks, thereby occasioning the first direct talks between Falkland Islanders and the Argentine Government. The dialogue continued in July in New York and London. On 14 July a joint Argentine-British declaration was issued that eliminated the restrictions on travel by Argentine citizens to the Falkland Islands and re-established airline services by the Chilean carrier LanChile between South America and the Falkland Islands (with a stop-over in Argentina). It was also agreed to increase bilateral co-operation between Argentina and the Falkland Islands on combating illegal fishing and conservation of fish stocks. Symbolic gestures included allowing the construction of a monument to the Argentine war dead at their cemetery on the islands (permission was finally granted in March 2002), while in return the Argentine Government would cease to use the Spanish names given to Falklands locations during the 1982 occupation. The agreement did not affect claims to sovereignty. Even so, the round of talks provoked demonstrations by an estimated 500 people on the Falkland Islands. The protests resumed on 16 October when the first flights carrying Argentine visitors arrived in the Falklands. In July 2000 the Anglo-Argentine dialogue on joint petroleum and gas exploration was suspended by mutual agreement for an indefinite period of time.

On 3 December 2002 Howard Pearce succeeded Donald Lamont as Governor of the Falkland Islands and Commissioner of South Georgia and the Sandwich Islands. In March 2003 Chris Simpkins became the new Chief Executive; he replaced Michael Blanch, who had reached the end of his three-year contract.

In May 2003 the new Argentine President, Néstor Carlos Kirchner, promised in his inaugural speech to maintain his country's claim to the Falkland Islands; he reiterated that commitment in January 2005, and once more appealed for the resumption of bilateral negotiations. In November 2003 Argentina began to demand that the increasingly frequent air-charter services flying from the Falkland Islands to Chile obtain permission to use Argentine airspace.

The decision was intended to pressure the British Government into reversing its policy of not allowing Argentine airlines to fly to the Falkland Islands. The services were suspended in January 2004 after the British Government lodged objections to the Argentine demands; the situation seemed likely to damage the territory's burgeoning tourism trade. In March a British proposal for the resumption of direct charter flights from Argentina to the Falkland Islands was rejected by the Kirchner Government, which continued to demand that an Argentine carrier be authorized to benefit from the increased passenger traffic between the Falkland Islands and mainland South America. A reference to the islands was included in a draft of the constitutional treaty of the European Union, to which Argentina strongly objected. At a meeting of the UN's Special Committee on Decolonization, held in mid-2005, the Falkland Islands appealed for the right to self-determination; the Committee requested that the Governments of Argentina and the United Kingdom resume negotiations.

Alan Huckle succeeded Howard Pearce as Governor of the Falkland Islands in August 2006. Melanie Chilton, Principal Crown Counsel, succeeded David Lang as Attorney-General on 1 November following the latter's retirement. However, Chilton resigned in the following month, citing family health reasons, and on 1 September 2007 David Pickup, Director-General of Her Majesty's Revenue and Customs, assumed the role. In January 2008 Dr Tim Thorogood replaced Chris Simpkins as Chief Executive.

A constitutional review process, initiated by the British Government Department of Overseas Territories in 1997, which promulgated greater self-governance for the islands, was well advanced in mid-2008. A number of changes to the administration of the territory were proposed; a Constitutional Select Committee was convened on 2 February 2007 to complete the review discussions and final proposals were submitted to the British Foreign and Commonwealth Office (FCO) for deliberation in June. Most notable among the amendments proposed were the insertion of citizens' right to self-determination within the main body of the Constitution, the updating of provisions in accordance with the United Kingdom's obligations under the European Convention on Human Rights, and clarification of the Governor's and Chief Executive's roles as head of the Public Service and head of the Civil Service, respectively. Proposals for the establishment of an ombudsman, Public Accounts Committee, the consolidation of electoral districts into a single constituency and the determination of the extent of self-government to be exercised by the territory were designated as matters requiring further consultation with the FCO before being written into statute. Officials from the FCO held two rounds of talks with the Constitutional Select Committee in December 2007 and February 2008 to discuss the draft new constitution and a further public consultation was expected to follow.

In enforcing the statutes of the Ottawa Convention, adopted under the Landmines Act 1998, the United Kingdom was required to identify and eliminate all mine devices within its territory and overseas jurisdictions within 10 years of the Convention's enactment. The resultant deadline for the destruction of all anti-personnel landmines in the Falkland Islands was established as March 2009, although progress towards achieving this objective had been impeded by the shifting nature of the islands' terrain and consequent inappropriateness of the conventional mine-detection techniques employed. Of the 127 minefields laid by Argentine forces in 1982, 101 remained by February 2007; the minefields were enclosed by cordons and there had been no reported civilian fatalities from mine explosions since the end of the conflict. An assessment of the feasibility of eliminating the remaining landmines was conducted in October 2007 and revealed that the process would be technically possible but was expected to require a considerable amount of funding. The project was under review in early 2008.

The Argentine Government formed a Congressional Observatory in June 2006 with the express function of actively reclaiming the Falkland Islands, which it continued to refer to as Argentine territory. In January 2007 the Argentine Minister of Foreign Affairs, International Trade and Worship had sought to enlist the support of the UN Secretary-General, Ban Ki-Moon, asserting that the United Kingdom had seized the archipelago by illegal means. President Kirchner maintained that the islanders possessed no right to self-determination, contending that the present population displaced indigenous Argentine residents upon settlement in 1833 with the intention of establishing a British colonial state, a claim strenuously refuted by the United Kingdom. In February Argentina rejected an invitation by the British Government to participate in joint commemorative celebrations to mark the 25th anniversary of the conflict's end. A joint hydrocarbon exploratory contract between Argentina and the United Kingdom was abandoned in the following month; the Argentine Government accused the British of pursuing a 'unilateral' approach to oil exploration initiatives and averred that there would be no further developments on the matter until the United Kingdom had agreed to resume negotiations over the islands' sovereignty. The original agreement, signed by former Argentine President Carlos Saúl Menem in 1995, followed the restoration of diplomatic relations between the two countries in 1990 and had been regarded as Argentine acknowledgment of Britain's claim to the sea floor surrounding the Falkland Islands. In April 2007 the Kirchner administration reiterated its claim to the territory and enjoined the British Government to cede to international demands to engage in dialogue over the future of the islands. The United Kingdom stated that it would not consider amendments to the governance or affiliations of the Falkland Islands unless and until a request to this effect was registered by the populace; it was asserted that no such request had been expressed by the islanders and, further, that they opposed Argentina's territorial offensive.

New legislation approved by the Argentine legislature on 11 April 2007 effectively required fishing companies wishing to operate in the maritime exclusion zone surrounding the islands to choose between Argentine or British authorities when making permit applications, and included restrictions against fishing in Argentine jurisdictional waters where a permit issued by the corresponding issuing authority was not held. A recent decision by the Falkland Islands authorities to begin issuing 25-year licences—as opposed to the one-year permits issued previously—had provoked protest from Argentina, which claimed its territorial rights had been disregarded.

The Argentine Government continued to seek a favourable resolution with regard to its claims of sovereignty over the Falkland Islands throughout 2007 and early 2008. During her inauguration speech in December 2007, the new President of Argentina, Cristina Fernández de Kirchner, stated that she was not prepared to make concessions in those claims and her Government once again urged the United Kingdom to relaunch the negotiations process. However, in mid-October 2007 the British Government announced its intention to submit a claim to the UN Commission on the Limits of the Continental Shelf for Atlantic seabed territory around the Falkland Islands. The Argentine Minister of Foreign Affairs, International Trade and Worship, Jorge Taiana, insisted that his Government would challenge any such claim made by the United Kingdom, which would conflict with the 1959 Antarctic Treaty, to which both countries were a signatory. The Treaty prevents the exploration of oil, gas and minerals in the region, other than for scientific purposes. Furthermore, tensions between the two countries were exacerbated in early May 2008 when Taiana, accused the British Government of 'illegitimately' issuing licences for hydrocarbon exploration and extraction activities in an area north of the Falkland Islands, part of the Argentine continental shelf. The British Government refused to concede to any of the claims made by its Argentine counterpart and maintained that it held sovereignty over the disputed area.

Government

Administration is conducted by the appointed Governor (who is the personal representative of the British monarch), aided by the Executive Council, comprising two *ex-officio* members and three members elected by the Legislative Council. The Legislative Council is composed of two *ex-officio* members and eight elected members. Voting is by universal adult suffrage. A constitutional review was under way in 2008.

Defence

According to official sources, in May 2008 there were approximately 1,200 British troops stationed on the islands (450 army, 650 air force and 100 navy). The total cost of the conflict in 1982 and of building and maintaining a garrison for four years was estimated at £2,560m. The current annual cost of maintaining the garrison is approximately £65m. Total expenditure in 1999/2000 was £71.1m. The cost of maintaining British military personnel in the territory was £143.3m. in 2005/06. There is a Falkland Islands Defence Force, composed of islanders.

Economic Affairs

According to government estimates, gross domestic product (GDP) was some £70m. in 2001, with GDP per head of £24,030 and annual growth of an estimated 2%. Gross national income was estimated to have increased from £5m. in 1980 to more than £50m. in 2000.

Most of the agricultural land on the Falkland Islands is devoted to the rearing of sheep. However, the land is poor and more than four acres are required to support one animal. In the late 1990s annual exports of wool were valued at some £3.5m. Declining international wool prices encouraged agricultural diversification, such as the pursuit of organic farming, the breeding of cashmere goats and also the development of meat production (an abattoir was constructed to meet European Union standards, incurring expenditure of £372,332 in 2002 and a further £678,371 in 2003). Some vegetables are produced (notably in a hydroponic market garden), and there are small dairy herds (672 dairy cows in 2006/07). From 1987, when a licensing system was introduced for foreign vessels fishing within a 150-nautical-mile conservation and management zone (see Recent History), the economy was diversified and the islands' annual income increased considerably. Although revenue from the sale of licences declined in the 1990s following the Argentine Government's commencement of the sale of fishing licences in 1993, licences (and transshipments) totalled £22.9m. in 2001/02, equivalent to 51.5% of total budget revenue in that year. The revenue funds social provisions and economic development programmes. In the late 1980s about one-third of the world's total catch of *illex* and *loligo* squid was derived from this fishing zone. However, over-fishing in the area surrounding the conservation zone had a detrimental effect on stocks of fish in the islands' waters, and frequently the Government has been obliged to call an early halt to the exploitation of both squid types, as it did in both 2004 and 2005. The 2006 season for *illex* squid fishing began in mid-February and by the end of March approximately 40 licences had been sold. Revenues from fishing licences and transshipment increased to approximately £16.1m. in 2005/06, approximately 37% of total revenues in that fiscal year.

Manufacturing activity on the islands reflects the predominance of the agricultural sector: a wool mill on West Falkland produces yarns for machine knitting, hand knitting and weaving. Several small companies in the Falklands produce garments for local and export sales. Some fish-processing also takes place on East Falkland.

The Falkland Islands are heavily dependent on imports of all fuels, except peat; households primarily depend on kerosene and diesel for heating purposes. Wind power is used in many remote locations to offset this dependence and reduce pollution of the atmosphere. The Falkland Islands Government licensed five consortia to explore for hydrocarbons in waters north of the islands in 1996. These companies, including Shell, Amerada Hess and LASMO, drilled six exploration wells in 1998. Five of the six wells had minor traces of hydrocarbons present, but no commercial quantities of petroleum were found in the initial phase of drilling. A British prospecting company has been granted an exploration licence to search for minerals on the islands. Mineral sands including garnet and rutile were being appraised, while more valuable minerals such as gold were being sought. In July 2002 the Falkland Islands Government granted 10 petroleum exploration licences to the Falklands Hydrocarbon Consortium (comprising Global Petroleum Ltd, Hardman Resources Ltd and Falkland Islands Holdings) for an area covering 57,700 sq km to the south of the islands. Activity was renewed in both the minerals and hydrocarbons sectors in 2005.

The Falkland Islands Development Corporation oversees the islands' economic development on behalf of the Government. Since the 1980s the Government has sought to promote the development of the tourism sector. Tourism, and in particular 'eco-tourism', was developing rapidly in this century, and the number of visitors staying on the Falklands Islands had grown to some 3,000 a year, while around 40,000 tourists per year sail through Stanley harbour on their way to Antarctica and sub-antarctic islands such as South Georgia. The sale of postage stamps and coins represents a significant source of income; the value of sales of the former was £296,229 in 1996/97, while the value of sales of the latter totalled £49,351 in 1995/96.

In 2000 the islands recorded an estimated trade surplus of £28,041,897. Fish, most of which is purchased by the United Kingdom, Spain and Chile, is the islands' most significant export. The principal imports are fuel, provisions, alcoholic beverages, building materials and clothing. In early 2001 the Government brought 100 reindeer from the South Georgia Islands (with the aim of increasing the number to 10,000 over the following 20 years) in order to export venison to Scandinavia and Chile.

The budget for the financial year 2005/06 provided for revenue of £43.5m. and expenditure of £43.9m. The islands are generally self-sufficient in all areas of the economy (although expenditures associated with defence are the responsibility of the British Government). The annual rate of inflation averaged 2.5% in 1995–2003; consumer prices increased by 0.7% in 2002 and by 1.2% in 2003. There is a significant shortage of local labour on the islands.

Since 1982 the economy of the Falkland Islands has enjoyed a period of strong and sustained growth, partly owing to substantial investment by the British Government during the 1980s, but primarily as a result of the introduction of the fisheries licensing scheme in 1987. It was anticipated that royalties derived from the sale of licences for the exploration and exploitation of hydrocarbons would strengthen the economy further. The services sector expanded rapidly during the late 1990s, while the importance of the agricultural sector decreased, not least because of its reliance on direct and indirect subsidies. A government development plan emphasized agricultural diversification and the promotion of tourism as its main economic aims; it also sought to develop services and to encourage the growth of industries related to the fishing industry (such as freezer plants and mussel farms). A progress report on economic developments during 2004–07 was released in March 2008 and focused on successes in increasing the profitability of small businesses (an increase of 155% between 2001 and 2006), growth in the number of tourist arrivals (39% growth in the number of long-stay tourists between 2003/04 and 2006/07) and achievements in maintaining lower than average rates of unemployment (3.7% in 2006). However, the review accepted that target GDP growth of 3% had not been achieved (largely as a result of disappointing revenues from the fishery sector) and that the proportion of GDP represented by government spending had only been reduced by 2% (to 42%) and not by the 5% originally predicted. (A medium-term financial plan, also launched in early 2008, sought to reduce annual expenditure by £0.5m. and increase revenue by the same amount each year during the next four years.) At the same time a new social and economic development programme for 2008–12 was published which identified the need to reduce over-reliance on the public sector and to increase, through the encouragement of entrepreneurs, the economic contribution of the private sector, in order to help achieve target GDP growth of 5% over the four-year period in question.

Education

Education is compulsory, and is provided free of charge, for children between the ages of five and 16 years. Facilities are available for further study beyond the statutory school-leaving age. In 2003 203 pupils were instructed by 18 teachers at the primary school in Stanley, while 160 pupils received instruction from 18 teachers at the secondary school in the capital; further facilities existed in rural districts, with six peripatetic teachers visiting younger children for two out of every six weeks (older children boarded in a hostel in Stanley). Total expenditure on education and training was estimated at £3.5m. for 2001/02.

Public Holidays

2008: 1 January (New Year's Day), 21 March (Good Friday), 21 April (HM the Queen's Birthday), 14 June (Liberation Day), 6 October (Spring Holiday), 8 December (Anniversary of the Battle of the Falkland Islands in 1914), 25–29 December (Christmas).
2009: 1 January (New Year's Day), 10 April (Good Friday), 21 April (HM the Queen's Birthday), 14 June (Liberation Day), 5 October (Spring Holiday), 8 December (Anniversary of the Battle of the Falkland Islands in 1914), 25–29 December (Christmas).

Weights and Measures

Both the imperial and metric systems are in general use.

Statistical Survey

Source (unless otherwise stated): The Treasury of the Falkland Islands Government, Stanley, FIQQ 1ZZ; tel. 27143; fax 27144; internet www.falklands.gov.fk/7.htm.

AREA AND POPULATION

Area: approx. 12,173 sq km (4,700 sq miles): East Falkland and adjacent islands 6,760 sq km (2,610 sq miles); West Falkland and adjacent islands 5,413 sq km (2,090 sq miles).

Population: 2,478 at census of 8 October 2006. Note: Figure excludes military personnel and civilians based at Mount Pleasant military base and the 84 residents absent on the night of the census.

Density (2006 census): 0.20 per sq km.

Principal Town (2006 census): Stanley (capital), population 2,115.

Births and Deaths (2000): Live births 27; Deaths 6.

Economically Active Population (persons aged 15 years and over, 2001 census): 2,475 (males 1,370, females 1,105).

AGRICULTURE, ETC.

Livestock (2007, official figures at 31 May): Sheep 530,009; Cattle 6,251; Goats 502; reindeer 124; Horses 644; Poultry 3,419.

Livestock Products (metric tons, 2006, FAO estimates): Cattle meat 130; Sheep meat 774; Cows' milk 1,500; Wool (greasy) 2,340. Source: FAO.

Fishing ('000 metric tons, live weight of capture, 2005): Southern blue whiting 1.7; Argentine hake 4.9; Patagonian grenadier 6.0; Patagonian squid 54.3; Argentine shortfin squid 6.8; Total catch (incl. others) 84.5. Source: FAO.

FINANCE

Currency and Exchange Rates: 100 pence (pennies) = 1 Falkland Islands pound (FI £). *Sterling, Dollar and Euro Equivalents* (31 May 2007): £1 sterling = FI £1.00; US $1 = 49.92 pence; €1 = 73.48 pence; FI £100 = £100.00 sterling = $200.32 = €136.09. *Average Exchange Rate* (FI £ per US dollar): 0.5500 in 2005; 0.5345 in 2006; 0.4998 in 2007. Note: The Falkland Islands pound is at par with the pound sterling.

Budget (FI £ million, 2005/06): *Revenue:* Sales and services 14.6; Fishing licences and transshipment 16.1; Investment income 4.9; Taxes and duties 7.9; Total 43.5. *Expenditure:* Operating expenditure 36.2 (Public works 8.1, Fisheries 6.6, Health care 5.3, Education

5.0, Aviation 2.0, Police and justice 1.3, Agriculture 1.1, Central administration 3.8, Other 3.0); Capital expenditure 7.7; Total 43.9.

Cost of Living (Consumer Price Index for Stanley; base: 2000 = 100): 101.3 in 2001; 102.0 in 2002; 103.2 in 2003. Source: ILO.

EXTERNAL TRADE

2000 (estimates): Total imports £18,958,103; Total exports £47,000,000. Fish is the principal export. Trade is mainly with the United Kingdom, Spain and Chile.

TRANSPORT

Shipping: *Merchant Fleet* (at 31 December 2006): Vessels 29; Displacement 51,596 grt. Source: Lloyd's Register-Fairplay, *World Fleet Statistics*.

Road Traffic: 3,065 vehicles in use in 1995.

TOURISM

Day Visitors (country of origin of cruise-ship excursionists, 2006/07 season): Canada 4,862; United Kingdom 6,736; USA 21,298; Total (incl. others) 51,282. *2007/08:* Total 62,200 (Source: Falkland Islands Tourist Board).

EDUCATION

2003 (Stanley): *Primary:* Teachers 18; Pupils 203, *Secondary:* Teachers 18; Pupils 160.

Directory

The Constitution

The present Constitution of the Falkland Islands came into force on 3 October 1985 (replacing that of 1977) and was amended in 1997. The Governor, who is the personal representative of the British monarch, is advised by the Executive Council, comprising six members: the Governor (presiding), three members elected by the Legislative Council, and two *ex-officio* members, the Chief Executive and the Financial Secretary of the Falkland Islands Government, who are non-voting. The Legislative Council is composed of eight elected members and the same two (non-voting) *ex-officio* members. One of the principal features of the Constitution is the reference in the preamble to the islanders' right to self-determination. The separate post of Chief Executive (responsible to the Governor) was created in 1983. The electoral principle was introduced, on the basis of universal adult suffrage, in 1949. The minimum voting age was lowered from 21 years to 18 years in 1977. A constitutional review process was ongoing at mid-2008.

The Government
(May 2008)

Governor: ALAN HUCKLE (took office 25 August 2006).
Chief Executive of the Falkland Islands Government: Dr TIM THOROGOOD.
Government Secretary: PETER T. KING.
Financial Secretary: DEREK F. HOWATT.
Attorney-General: DAVID PICKUP.
Commander, British Forces South Atlantic Islands: Brig. NICK DAVIS.

EXECUTIVE COUNCIL

The Council consists of six members (see Constitution, above).

LEGISLATIVE COUNCIL

Comprises the Governor, two *ex-officio* (non-voting) members and eight elected members.

GOVERNMENT OFFICES

Office of the Governor: Government House, Stanley, FIQQ 1ZZ; tel. 27433; fax 27434; e-mail gov.house@horizon.co.fk.
General Office: Legislature Dept, Gilbert House, Stanley, FIQQ 1ZZ; tel. 27455; e-mail clerkofcouncils@sec.gov.fk; internet www.falklands.gov.fk.
London Office: Falkland Islands Government Office, Falkland House, 14 Broadway, London SW1H 0BH, United Kingdom; tel. (020) 7222-2542; fax (020) 7222-2375; e-mail representative@falklands.gov.fk; internet www.falklandislands.com; f. 1983.

Judicial System

The judicial system of the Falkland Islands is administered by the Supreme Court (presided over by the non-resident Chief Justice), the Magistrate's Court (presided over by the Senior Magistrate) and the Court of Summary Jurisdiction. The Court of Appeal for the Territory sits in England and appeals therefrom may be heard by the Judicial Committee of the Privy Council.

Chief Justice of the Supreme Court: CHRISTOPHER GARDNER, QC.
Judge of the Supreme Court and Senior Magistrate: ALISON THOMPSON.
Courts Administrator: CHERILYN KING, Ross Rd, Stanley, FIQQ 1ZZ; tel. 27271; fax 2720.
Registrar-General: JOHN ROWLAND, Town Hall, Stanley, FIQQ 1ZZ; tel. 27272; fax 27270.

FALKLAND ISLANDS COURT OF APPEAL

President: Judge APPLEBY.
Registrar: MICHAEL J. ELKS.

Religion

CHRISTIANITY

The Anglican Communion, the Roman Catholic Church and the United Free Church predominate. Also represented are the Evangelist Church, Jehovah's Witnesses, the Lutheran Church, Seventh-day Adventists and the Bahá'í faith.

The Anglican Communion

The Archbishop of Canterbury, the Primate of All England, exercises episcopal jurisdiction over the Falkland Islands and South Georgia.

Rector: Rev. Dr RICHARD HINES, The Deanery, Christ Church Cathedral, Stanley, FIQQ 1ZZ; tel. 21100; fax 21842; e-mail deanery@horizon.co.fk.

The Roman Catholic Church

Prefect Apostolic of the Falkland Islands: MICHAEL BERNARD MCPARTLAND, St Mary's Presbytery, 12 Ross Rd, Stanley, FIQQ 1ZZ; tel. 21204; fax 22242; e-mail stmarys@horizon.co.fk; internet www.southatlanticrcchurch.com; f. 1764; 250 adherents (2004).

The Press

The Falkland Islands Gazette: Stanley, FIQQ 1ZZ; tel. 27242; fax 27109; e-mail atomlinson@sec.gov.fk; internet www.falklands.gov.fk; govt publ.
Falkland Islands News Network: POB 141, Stanley, FIQQ 1ZZ; tel. and fax 21182; e-mail finn@horizon.co.fk; internet www.falklandnews.com; relays news daily online and via fax as FINN(COM) Service; Man. JUAN BROCK; publishes:

Teaberry Express: Stanley, FIQQ 1ZZ; tel. 21182; weekly.

Penguin News: Ross Rd, Stanley, FIQQ 1ZZ; tel. 22684; fax 22238; e-mail pnews@horizon.co.fk; internet www.penguin-news.com; f. 1979; weekly; independent newspaper; Man. Editor JENNY COCKWELL; circ. 1,550.

Broadcasting and Communications

TELECOMMUNICATIONS

In 1989 Cable & Wireless PLC installed a £5.4m. digital telecommunications network covering the entire Falkland Islands. The Government contributed to the cost of the new system, which provides international services as well as a new domestic network. Further work to improve the domestic telephone system was completed in the late 1990s at a cost of £3.3m.

Cable & Wireless PLC: Ross Rd, POB 584, Stanley, FIQQ 1ZZ; tel. 20820; fax 208011; e-mail info@cwfi.co.fk; internet www.cwfi.co.fk; f. 1989; exclusive provider of national and international telecommunications services in the Falkland Islands under a licence issued by the Falkland Islands Govt; CEO RICHARD HALL.

BROADCASTING
Radio

Falkland Islands Radio Service: Broadcasting Studios, John St, Stanley, FIQQ 1ZZ; tel. 27277; fax 27279; e-mail cbichop@firs.co.fk; internet www.firs.co.fk; fmrly Falklands Islands Broadcasting Station; 24-hour service, financed by local Govt in association with

SSVC of London, United Kingdom; broadcasts in English; Station Man. CORINA BISHOP; Programme Controller LIZ ELLIOT.

British Forces Broadcasting Service (BFBS): BFBS Falkland Islands, Mount Pleasant, BFPO 655; tel. 32179; fax 32193; e-mail chris.pearson@bfbs.com; internet www.bfbs.com; 24-hour satellite service from the United Kingdom; Station Man. CHRIS PEARSON; Sr Engineer ADRIAN ALMOND.

Television

British Forces Broadcasting Service: BFBS Falkland Islands, Mount Pleasant, BFPO 655; tel. 32179; fax 32193; daily four-hour transmissions of taped broadcasts from BBC and ITV of London, United Kingdom; Sr Engineer COLIN MCDONALD.

KTV: 16 Ross Rd West, Stanley, FIQQ 1ZZ; tel. 22349; fax 21049; e-mail kmzb@horizon.co.fk; satellite television broadcasting services; Man. MARIO ZUVIC BULIC.

Finance

BANK

Standard Chartered Bank: Ross Rd, POB 597, Stanley, FIQQ 1ZZ; tel. 22220; fax 22219; e-mail bank.info@fk.standardchartered.com; internet www.standardchartered.com/fk; branch opened in 1983; Man. RINO DONOSEPOETRO.

INSURANCE

The British Commercial Union, Royal Insurance and Norman Tremellen companies maintain agencies in Stanley.

Consultancy Services Falklands Ltd: 44 John St, Stanley, FIQQ 1ZZ; tel. 22666; fax 22639; e-mail consultancy@horizon.co.uk; Man. ALISON BAKER.

Trade and Industry

DEVELOPMENT ORGANIZATION

Falkland Islands Development Corporation (FIDC): Shackleton House, West Hillside, Stanley, FIQQ 1ZZ; tel. 27211; fax 27210; e-mail mbrunet@fidc.co.fk; internet www.fidc.co.fk; f. 1983; provides loans and grants; encourages private sector investment, inward investment and technology transfer; Gen. Man. (vacant).

CHAMBER OF COMMERCE

Chamber of Commerce: POB 378, Stanley, FIQQ 1ZZ; tel. 22264; fax 22265; e-mail commerce@horizon.co.fk; internet www.falklandislandschamberofcommerce.com; f. 1993; promotes private industry; operates DHL courier service; runs an employment agency; Pres. ROGER SPINK; 87 mems.

TRADING COMPANIES

Falkland Islands Co Ltd (FIC): Crozier Pl., Stanley, FIQQ 1ZZ; tel. 27600; fax 27603; e-mail fic@horizon.co.fk; internet www.the-falkland-islands-co.com; f. 1851; part of Falkland Islands Holding PLC; the largest trading co; retailing, wholesaling, shipping, insurance and Land Rover sales and servicing; operates as agent for Lloyd's of London and general shipping concerns; travel services and hoteliers; wharf owners and operators; Dir and Gen. Man. ROGER KENNETH SPINK.

Falkland Islands Meat Co: Sand Bay, East Falklands, FIQQ 1ZZ; tel. 27013; fax 27113; e-mail manager@falklands-meat.com; internet www.falklands-meat.com; exporters of lamb and mutton meat; Gen. Man. JOHN FERGUSON.

Falkland Oil and Gas Ltd (FOGL): 56 John St, Stanley, F1QQ 1ZZ; e-mail info@fogl.co.uk; internet www.fogl.co.uk; f. 2004; Falkland Islands Holdings PLC (16%), Global Petroleum (14%) and RAB Capital PLC (33%); operates an offshore petroleum exploration programme with 8 licences covering 65,354 sq km; Chair. RICHARD LIDDELL; CEO TIM BUSHELL.

EMPLOYERS' ASSOCIATION

Sheep Owners' Association: Coast Ridge Farm, Fox Bay, FIQQ 1ZZ; tel. 42094; fax 42084; e-mail n.knight.coastridge@horizon.co.fk; f. 1967; asscn for sheep station owners; limited liability private co; Company Sec. N. KNIGHT.

TRADE UNION

Falkland Islands General Employees Union: Ross Rd, Stanley, FIQQ 1ZZ; tel. 21151; e-mail geu@horizon.co.fk; f. 1943; Chair. GAVIN SHORT; 100 mems.

CO-OPERATIVE SOCIETY

Stanley Co-operative Society: Stanley, FIQQ 1ZZ; tel. 21215; f. 1952; open to all members of the public; Man. NORMA THOM.

Transport

RAILWAYS

There are no railways on the islands.

ROADS

There are 29 km (18 miles) of paved road in and around Stanley. There are 54 km of all-weather road linking Stanley and the Mount Pleasant airport (some of which has been surfaced with a bitumen substance), and a further 37 km of road as far as Goose Green. There are 300 km of arterial roads in the North Camp on East Falkland linking settlements, and a further 197 km of road on West Falkland. An ongoing roads network project to link remote farms was almost complete by early 2007. Where roads have still not been built, settlements are linked by tracks, which are passable by all-terrain motor vehicle or motorcycle except in the most severe weather conditions.

SHIPPING

There is a ship on charter to the Falkland Islands Co Ltd which makes the round trip to the United Kingdom four or five times a year, carrying cargo. A floating deep-water jetty was completed in 1984. The British Ministry of Defence charters ships, which sail for the Falkland Islands once every three weeks. There are irregular cargo services between the islands and southern Chile and Uruguay. The Falkland Islands Development Corpn commissioned a port development plan in February 2007 for the upgrade of existing facilities to reflect growth in containerized traffic, cruise ship arrivals and to accommodate proposed further oil exploration in territorial waters.

The Falkland Islands merchant fleet numbered 29 vessels, with a total displacement of 51,596 grt, at December 2006; the majority of vessels registered are deep-sea fishing vessels.

Stanley Port Authority: c/o Dept of Fisheries, POB 598, Stanley, FIQQ 1ZZ; tel. 27260; fax 27265; e-mail jclark@fisheries.gov.fk; Marine Officer and Harbour Master JON CLARK.

Private Companies

Byron Marine Ltd: 3 H Jones Rd, Stanley, FIQQ 1ZZ; tel. 22245; fax 22246; e-mail info@byronmarine.co.fk; internet www.byronmarine.co.fk; f. 1992; additional activites include oil exploration support services, deep-sea fishing and property; contracted managers of the Falkland Islands Government Port Facility (email: portservices@byronmarine.co.fk); island-wide pilotage services; vessel agent; Man. Dir LEWIS CLIFTON.

Darwin Shipping Ltd: Stanley, FIQQ 1ZZ; tel. 27629; fax 27603; e-mail darwin@horizon.co.fk; internet www.the-falkland-islands-co.com; subsidiary of the Falkland Islands Co Ltd (q.v.); Man. ANDY WATSON.

Falkland Islands Co Ltd (FIC): see Trade and Industry—Trading Companies.

Seaview Ltd: 37 Fitzroy Rd, POB 215, Stanley, FIQQ 1ZZ; tel. 22669; fax 22670; e-mail seaview.agent@horizon.co.fk; internet www.fis.com/polar; operates subsidiary co, Polar Ltd (f. 1989); Man. Dir DICK SAWLE; Operations Man. ALEX REID.

Sulivan Shipping Services Ltd: Davis St, POB 159, Stanley, FIQQ 1ZZ; tel. 22626; fax 22625; e-mail sulivan@horizon.co.fk; internet www.sulivanshipping.com; f. 1987; provides port-agency and ground-handling services; Man. Dir JOHN POLLARD.

CIVIL AVIATION

There are airports at Stanley and Mount Pleasant; the latter has a runway of 2,590 m (8,497 ft), and is capable of receiving wide-bodied jet aircraft. The British Royal Air Force operates two weekly flights from the United Kingdom. The Chilean carrier LAN Airlines (formerly LanChile) operates weekly return flights from Punta Arenas. An 'air bridge', operated by charter carriers subcontracted to the British Ministry of Defence, provides a link via Ascension Island between the Falkland Islands and the United Kingdom.

Falkland Islands Government Air Service (FIGAS): Stanley Airport, Stanley, FIQQ 1ZZ; tel. 27219; fax 27309; e-mail fwallace@figas.gov.fk; f. 1948 to provide social, medical and postal services between the settlements and Stanley; aerial surveillance for Dept of Fisheries since 1990; operates four nine-seater aircraft to over 35

GIBRALTAR

Introductory Survey

Location, Climate, Language, Religion, Flag

The City of Gibraltar lies in southern Europe. The territory consists of a narrow peninsula of approximately 4.8 km (3 miles) in length, running southwards from the south-west coast of Spain, to which it is connected by an isthmus. About 8 km (5 miles) across the bay, to the west, lies the Spanish port of Algeciras, while 32 km (20 miles) to the south, across the Strait of Gibraltar, is Morocco. The Mediterranean Sea lies to the east. The climate is temperate, and snow or frost are extremely rare. The mean minimum and maximum temperatures during the winter are 13°C (55°F) and 18°C (65°F), respectively, and during the summer they are 13°C (55°F) and 29°C (85°F) respectively; the average annual rainfall is 890 mm (35 ins). The official language is English, although most of the population is bilingual in English and Spanish. More than three-quarters of the population are Roman Catholic. The flag (proportions 1 by 2) bears the arms of Gibraltar (a red castle with a pendant golden key) on a background, the upper two-thirds of which are white and the lower one-third red.

Recent History

Since the Second World War, this Overseas Territory has achieved considerable social and economic progress, through intensive development of its social and economic infrastructure, and by the expansion of commerce and the encouragement of tourism. Gibraltar has exercised control over most internal matters since 1969.

The Spanish Government lays claim to Gibraltar as a part of its territory, while the United Kingdom maintains that the Treaty of Utrecht (1713) granted sovereignty over Gibraltar to the United Kingdom in perpetuity (with the stipulation that, if the United Kingdom relinquished the colony, it would be returned to Spain). In 1963 the Spanish Government began a campaign, through the UN, for the cession of Gibraltar to Spain. It also imposed restrictions against Gibraltar, culminating in the closure of the frontier in 1969, the withdrawal of the Spanish labour force, and the severing of transport and communication links with Spain.

Following a referendum held in the territory in 1967, in which the overwhelming majority voted in favour of retaining British sovereignty, a new Constitution, promulgated in 1969, contained a provision that the British Government undertook never to enter into arrangements whereby the people of Gibraltar would pass under the sovereignty of another state against their freely and democratically expressed wishes. Gibraltar joined the European Community (EC, now European Union—EU, see p. 244) with the United Kingdom in 1973.

By 1977, a more flexible attitude by Spain towards Gibraltar became apparent. At talks held between Spanish and British ministers in November representatives of the Gibraltar Government were included for the first time as part of the British delegation. In December 1979 Spain requested new negotiations, and at meetings in April 1980 it was agreed, in principle, to reopen the frontier by June. However, the reopening was delayed by the Spanish Government's insistence that Spanish workers in Gibraltar should be allowed equal status with nationals of EC countries. In October the British Parliament granted Gibraltarians the right to retain full British citizenship. Negotiations for the full opening of the frontier continued in 1982, but a change of attitudes in both countries, following the war between the United Kingdom and Argentina over the sovereignty of the Falkland Islands (q.v.), resulted in an indefinite postponement. In December Spain reopened the border to pedestrians of Spanish nationality and to British subjects resident in Gibraltar.

In a general election held in January 1984, the Gibraltar Labour Party—Association for the Advancement of Civil Rights (GLP—AACR), led by Sir Joshua Hassan, retained a majority of one seat in the House of Assembly. The Gibraltar Socialist Labour Party (GSLP), led by Joseph (Joe) Bossano, secured the remaining seven seats, replacing the Democratic Party of British Gibraltar as the opposition party in the House of Assembly. (Under the terms of the Constitution, the party with the largest share of the vote obtained a maximum of eight seats in the House of Assembly.)

In November 1984 the British and Spanish Governments agreed to provide equal rights for Spaniards in Gibraltar and for Gibraltarians in Spain; to allow free movement for all traffic between Gibraltar and Spain; and to conduct negotiations on the future of the territory, including (for the first time) discussions on sovereignty. Border restrictions were finally ended in February 1985, and negotiations took place between the British and Spanish Governments to improve cross-border co-operation, especially in tourism and civil aviation. In December, however, Spanish proposals for an interim settlement of the territory's future were rejected by the British Government as unacceptable since they implied the eventual automatic cession of Gibraltar to Spain. Subsequent discussions concerning principally Spain's demands for access to the Gibraltar airport (which the Spanish Government claimed was situated on land not covered by the terms of the Treaty of Utrecht) were inconclusive, owing to the Gibraltar Government's insistence that the airport remain exclusively under the control of the British and Gibraltar authorities. In December 1987 negotiators concluded an agreement that recommended increased co-operation between Spain and Gibraltar in the area of transport, in particular the joint administration of Gibraltar's airport. It was announced that Gibraltar's inclusion in an EC directive concerning air transport regulation was subject to the Gibraltar Government's approval of the British-Spanish agreement. However, Gibraltar's House of Assembly rejected the agreement, on the grounds that it would represent an infringement of British sovereignty, and voted unanimously to contest Gibraltar's exclusion from the EC directive.

In December 1987 Hassan resigned as Chief Minister and leader of the GLP—AACR and was succeeded by Adolfo Canepa, the Deputy Chief Minister. At a general election held in March 1988, the GSLP received 58.2% of the votes cast, obtaining eight seats in the House of Assembly, and the GLP—AACR received 29.3% of the vote, securing seven seats. Bossano replaced Canepa as Chief Minister, at the head of Gibraltar's first socialist Government. Bossano announced that he would not participate in British-Spanish negotiations concerning Gibraltar, on the grounds that the territory's sovereignty was not a matter for negotiation between Spain and the United Kingdom, and that the December 1987 agreement would, in his view, result in the absorption of Gibraltar into Spain.

In January 1989, in an unprecedented gesture of co-operation between Gibraltar and Spain, Bossano met the mayor of La Línea, the Spanish town bordering Gibraltar, and offered to assist in financing an economic revival in the region. In February 1990 the British and Spanish Governments agreed to contest a legal action that was to be brought by Gibraltar in the European Court of Justice against Gibraltar's exclusion from measures adopted to liberalize European air transport, which prevented the territory from expanding its air links with Europe. The decision to contest the action was considered to be a further attempt by the United Kingdom to persuade Gibraltar to co-operate with Spain. In March 1991 the United Kingdom withdrew the majority of British army personnel from Gibraltar, although the Royal Navy and Royal Air Force detachments remained.

In May 1991 the Spanish Prime Minister made an official visit to the United Kingdom, and was reported to have proposed a plan for joint sovereignty over Gibraltar, whereby the dependency would become effectively autonomous, with the British and Spanish monarchs as joint heads of state. Although it represented a significant concession by the Spanish Government (which had hitherto demanded full sovereignty over Gibraltar), the plan was rejected by the Gibraltar Government in July. At the EC summit meeting held at Maastricht, Netherlands, in December, Spain continued to refuse to recognize Gibraltar's status as part of the EC, and remained determined to exclude it from the External Frontiers Convention (EFC), which was designed to strengthen common controls on entry into countries belonging to the EC. The continued failure to reach an agreement, particularly concerning the administration of Gibraltar airport, prevented the ratification of the EFC.

At a general election held in January 1992 the GSLP retained eight seats in the House of Assembly, and Bossano was returned for a second term as Chief Minister. The Gibraltar Social Democrats (GSD), which supported Gibraltar's participation in British-Spanish negotiations, secured the remaining seven seats. In February 1992, prior to discussions with British ministers in London, Bossano announced that Gibraltar was to attempt to obtain a revision of the 1969 Constitution, with the aim of achieving self-determination within four years. The British Government, however, stated that it would not consider granting independence to Gibraltar, unless the Spanish Government was prepared to accept the agreement, and excluded the possibility of formal negotiations on the issue.

In January 1993 Gibraltarians lodged a formal protest after increasingly stringent monitoring of vehicles by Spanish customs officials resulted in severe delays at the frontier. In March an official meeting between the foreign ministers of the United Kingdom and Spain achieved little progress; it was agreed, however, that contacts between British and Spanish officials were to be maintained. In early 1994 Bossano accused the British Government of subordinating the interests of Gibraltar to the promotion of harmonious relations with Spain, and demanded a renegotiation of the 1987 airport agreement on the grounds that its provisions had subsequently become redundant and contrary to EU law.

In late 1994 Spain alleged that insufficient action was being taken by Gibraltar to curtail the smuggling of tobacco from Gibraltar to Spain and of illegal narcotics between Morocco and Spain by Gibraltar-based speedboats. The imposition in October of stringent border inspections by Spain, leading to lengthy delays in commercial and visitor traffic, prompted a protest by the British Government. These border checks were eased following assurances that measures were being taken to curtail the activities of the speedboats operating from Gibraltar. Spain reimposed frontier controls in March 1995, precipitating further criticism by the British Government. In May, however, it emerged that the Gibraltar Government had brought into effect only about one-quarter of EU directives governing health and safety regulations, public procurement procedures, environmental matters and the regulation of the banking and financial services sectors, and Gibraltar was warned by the British Government that substantial progress should be made by June. Bossano, however, declared that the House of Assembly had the right to interpret EU legislation as it saw fit, and that any interference by the United Kingdom would be challenged in the British courts. In July 1996 the Gibraltar authorities extended offences of money-laundering, hitherto applicable solely to proceeds from drugs-trafficking, to those from all crimes.

In July 1995, following the confiscation of more than 60 speedboats, alleged to be used in the transport of contraband, the Spanish Government eased frontier controls. The seizures provoked two days of riots and looting in Gibraltar, followed by a peaceful mass demonstration organized by Gibraltar business interests and trade unions in support of the continuing implementation of anti-smuggling measures. Although the British and Spanish Governments jointly agreed in September that the anti-smuggling measures were proving effective, the death of a Spanish civil guard in pursuit of smugglers in April 1996 led to the renewal of border controls by Spain.

Campaign debates in advance of legislative elections in May 1996 focused on Gibraltar's external relations. Bossano and the GSLP proposed that the territory's status be replaced before the year 2000 by a form of 'free association' with the United Kingdom, while the GSD declared as its aims the achievement of improved relations with both Spain and the United Kingdom and the modernization of Gibraltar's Constitution. The election attracted an unusually high turn-out (87.7% of eligible voters), and resulted in the GSD receiving 48% of the vote and the maximum of eight seats in the House of Assembly; the GSD leader, Peter Caruana, became Chief Minister. The GSLP received 39% of the vote and the Gibraltar National Party obtained 13%.

In November 1996 the Spanish Government lodged a complaint with the EU Commission over a private visit to Gibraltar by the EU Commissioner responsible for Immigration and Home and Judicial Affairs to view the operation of Spanish border controls. In the same month Chief Minister Caruana renewed his demand that Gibraltar be accorded equal status with the United Kingdom in future negotiations concerning the territory's interests. In January 1997 Caruana refused to attend discussions on Gibraltar, held in Madrid, Spain, between the United Kingdom and Spain, on the grounds that Gibraltar would not be granted power of veto. A suggestion by Spain that sovereignty over Gibraltar be shared between Spain and the United Kingdom for a 100-year period, with full control then passing to Spain, was rejected by the British Government.

In October 1997 Caruana informed the Decolonization Committee of the UN General Assembly that he was to seek from the British Government an extensive review of the territory's 1969 Constitution. It was to be proposed that Gibraltar would obtain additional autonomy in the conduct of its affairs while remaining in a close political and constitutional relationship with the United Kingdom, similar to that held by the Crown Dependencies of the Channel Islands and the Isle of Man (q.v.). During 1997 new tensions arose between the United Kingdom and Spanish Governments over the long-standing refusal by Spain to permit military aircraft from the United Kingdom and the North Atlantic Treaty Organization (NATO, see p. 340) to cross Spanish airspace on their approach to Gibraltar airport. In July the British Secretary of State for Foreign and Commonwealth Affairs indicated that the United Kingdom would oppose the full incorporation of Spain into NATO unless the ban was lifted. An indication by Spain of its willingness to open its airspace to these flights in return for joint military control of the airport was strongly opposed by Caruana and rejected by the British Government. In July 1998 Spain reversed its long-standing refusal to participate in NATO manoeuvres that were based in, or passed through, Gibraltar. In that month the Spanish Government unsuccessfully requested the British Government to consider a revived proposal for the shared sovereignty of Gibraltar for a period of 50 years, to be followed by the territory's full integration into Spain.

In November 1998 complaints by the Gibraltar Government arose over the conduct of Spanish fishing vessels in the Bay of Gibraltar, which were stated to be operating in violation of the territory's nature protection ordinance. In January 1999 a Spanish trawler was impounded by the Gibraltar authorities, and Spain began to intensify delays in road motor traffic crossing the frontier. An agreement reached in February between the Gibraltar authorities and the Spanish fishermen was not recognized by the Spanish Government.

At the general election held in February 2000 the GSD secured 58.7% of the vote, against 40.8% obtained by an electoral coalition of the GSLP and the Gibraltar Liberal Party (GLP). Caruana was reconfirmed as Chief Minister, and the GSD retained its eight seats in the House of Assembly. The rate of participation was again high, at 83.6%

Extended negotiations between the Spanish and British Governments were concluded in April 2000 with a compromise agreement whereby Spain was to recognize the validity of Gibraltar identity cards and of the territory's financial institutions, provided that the 'competent authority' responsible for their supervision was the United Kingdom rather than the Gibraltar Government. It was also agreed that the British authorities would provide a facility, based in London, through which the Spanish and Gibraltar authorities could have indirect communication. An incidental effect of the agreement was to terminate the long-standing refusal by Spain to adopt any legislation by the EU that might have required it to deal directly with Gibraltar's police or financial regulatory authorities.

In March 2001 the Gibraltar political parties reached an agreement to request the previously proposed reforms to the 1969 Constitution, allowing self-determination, and to hold a referendum on decolonization. However, the move was condemned by Spain as a breach of the Treaty of Utrecht. In July 2001 the British and Spanish Governments renewed discussions on Gibraltar's future status for the first time since 1998. In response, the Gibraltarian legislature requested that a UN decolonization mission visit the territory. At a subsequent meeting in October, the British Secretary of State for Foreign and Commonwealth Affairs, Jack Straw, and his Spanish counterpart, Josep Piqué i Camps, agreed to work towards achieving a settlement on the issue by December 2002 (this was later modified to September 2002). Amid public criticism of proposals of joint British-Spanish sovereignty, Caruana rebuffed an invitation to attend the next round of negotiations in November, claiming that he would not be accorded equal status in the discussions. The Chief Minister also stated that the territory would not accept any change in sovereignty, the sharing of responsibility for its external affairs between Spain and the United Kingdom, nor Spanish military presence.

At the negotiations in November 2001, Piqué announced that Spain was prepared to increase the number of telephone lines available to Gibraltar from 35,000 to 100,000 and provide greater access to the Spanish health care system. However, the issue of the right of the citizens of Gibraltar to vote on the terms of an agreement regarding the future status of the territory remained one of the main points of contention between Spain and the United Kingdom. At the end of the month the British Government announced that Gibraltarians would be given the right to vote in elections to the European Parliament, but ruled out the possibility of the territory's further integration into the United Kingdom. In an open letter published in the local press, Piqué attempted to allay Gibraltarians' fears of the implications of Spanish rule and urged Caruana to attend the negotiations. The following month, however, most of the territory's 300,000 citizens took part in a public demonstration against the proposals. Following further public protests in March 2002, EU leaders agreed to a joint British-Spanish request for a grant of £37m. to fund the development of Gibraltar's port, infrastructure and airport. Caruana rejected the proposals and threatened to organize a referendum.

Shortly before negotiations on the sovereignty issue were due to resume in May 2002, the Spanish Prime Minister, José María Aznar, asserted that Spain would never withdraw its territorial claim to Gibraltar. During a subsequent visit, Straw's efforts to persuade Gibraltar of the benefits of joint sovereignty, and to reassure its residents that any such agreement would be subject to approval by referendum, were met with scepticism. Also in May, the Overseas Territories Act, having received royal assent in the United Kingdom in February, came into force, granting British citizenship rights to the people of its Overseas Territories, including Gibraltar. Under the new law Gibraltarians would be able to hold British passports and work in the United Kingdom and other EU countries.

Negotiations between the Spanish and British Governments progressed in mid-2002, although discussions stalled over Spain's claims to eventual sovereignty rather than permanent co-sovereignty and its refusal to allow British control over the military base. In response, Caruana called a referendum for November 2002. Talks recommenced in September, but with no certain deadline. The referendum, held on 7 November, in which 87.9% of the electorate voted, demonstrated overwhelming (98.97%) opinion against joint sovereignty with Spain; it was, however, not recognized, by either Spain or the United Kingdom. Relations deteriorated later that month when the Spanish Minister of Foreign Affairs claimed that Gibraltar was partly responsible for the sinking of the oil tanker *Prestige* off the coast of Galicia in Spain, as Gibraltarian maritime officials had allegedly failed properly to examine the vessel when it had docked near the territory in June. The British Government, however, refuted these accusations. In January 2003 Caruana proposed constitutional reforms that would establish a decolonized status for the enclave but maintain its links with the United Kingdom. In June Denis MacShane, the British Minister of State for Europe, admitted the plan for joint sovereignty was practically unenforceable given the almost unanimous opposition of Gibraltar's population.

At a general election held on 28 November 2003 the GSD secured 51.5% of the vote, a significant decrease from the 2000 election, against 39.7% secured by the GSLP-GLP coalition. (79.2% of the electorate pariticpated.) The balance of seats in the House of Assembly, however, remained unchanged, with the GSD holding eight seats and the opposition seven seats. Caruana remained as Chief Minister.

For the purposes of the 2004 elections to the European Parliament, in late 2003 the British Parliament adopted legislation incorporating Gibraltar into the South-West region of the United Kingdom; for the first time, Gibraltarians were thus eligible to vote in European elections. Approximately 58% of the Gibaltarian electorate participated in the elections. Following the elections the Spanish Government announced that it would legally challenge the results; the complaint was heard at the European Court of Justice in July 2005.

In February 2004 three Gibraltarian soldiers from the Royal Gibraltar Regiment were charged with attempting to smuggle a large amount of hashish into Spain. The allegations were a considerable embarrassment to the Gibraltarian authorities, which had repeatedly denied claims that the territory was extensively used as a conduit for illegal drugs-trafficking. Celebrations by the Government and the people of Gibraltar to commemorate 300 years of British rule, held in mid-2004, and attended by the British Secretary of State for Defence, Geoff Hoon, were criticised by the Spanish authorities.

In October 2004 Straw and his recently appointed Spanish counterpart, Miguel Angel Moratinos, held discussions in Madrid, at which they addressed the issue of the future format for talks on Gibraltar, which were to include Gibraltarian representation for the first time. Talks involving the three parties took place in the United Kingdom in December further to define this new forum, and in February 2005 the first official trilateral session took place in Málaga, Spain. As a result, a number of Technical Working Groups were established to focus on the most significant issues: the airport, border control, nuclear submarines, telecommunications and pensions. Following several further rounds of discussions, in September 2006 Caruana, Moratinos and the British Minister of State for Europe, Geoff Hoon, signed a series of agreements in Córdoba, Spain: allowing for the operation of flights from Spain and the rest of Europe to Gibraltar; increasing the number of telephone lines to the territory; addressing the issue of outstanding pension payments to Spaniards formerly employed in Gibraltar; and easing border restrictions between Spain and Gibraltar. Moratinos also stated that the Spanish Government had received written assurances from the United Kingdom that nuclear submarines would no longer be docked in Gibraltar. The question of sovereignty was not addressed.

Meanwhile, following lengthy negotiations between the United Kingdom and Gibraltar, it was announced in March 2006 that agreement had been reached on the main provisions of a new draft constitution for the territory. The British authorities stressed that the proposals did not diminish British sovereignty over Gibraltar, which would remain a United Kingdom Overseas Territory. The preamble to the new constitution also made clear that the British Government would never enter into arrangements under which the people of Gibraltar would pass under the sovereignty of another state against their freely and democratically expressed wishes. The draft constitution confirmed that the people of Gibraltar had the right of self-determination (according to the provisions of the UN Charter); this right was not constrained by the Treaty of Utrecht, except in so far as Spain would have the right of refusal should Britain ever renounce sovereignty. Thus, Gibraltarian independence would be an option only with Spanish consent. The remainder of the text introduced substantial reforms. The main elements included limiting the responsibilities of the Governor to the areas of external affairs, defence, internal security and public services, thereby reversing the existing practice and giving Gibraltar much greater control over its internal affairs. The House of Assembly was to be restyled the Gibraltar Parliament and would be allowed to determine its own size. The Governor's powers to withhold assent to legislation passed by the Gibraltarian authorities would be streamlined and his power to disallow proposed new laws would be removed (although his mandate to make Orders in Council would be retained). New commissions were to be created to deal with appointments to the judiciary and to public services, and a new Police Authority for Gibraltar was to be established. In a referendum held on 30 November 2006 the Constitution was approved by 60.2% of valid votes, with 37.8% votes against and 1.7% blank ballots, with a participation rate of 60.4%. The new Constitution entered into force on 2 January 2007 (except for those provisions relating to the Parliament, which would take effect following legislative elections). Meanwhile, in September 2006 Lt-Gen. Sir Robert Fulton took office as Governor and Commander-in-Chief, succeeding Sir Francis Richards.

In February 2007 Caruana created two new ministries, the Ministry of Finance and the Ministry of Justice. The Chief Minister, who already had responsibility for financial affairs, formally became Minister of Finance and also assumed ministerial responsibility for justice, which had been the preserve of the unelected Attorney-General under the previous constitution. The approval of legislation, in July, that provided for transfer of the post of head of the judiciary from the Chief Justice (Head of the Supreme Court) to the President of the Court of Appeal, as provided for by the new Constitution, provoked some controversy. The Chief Justice, Derek Schofield, made known his opposition to the reform, stating that it threatened the independence of the judiciary; he was consequently suspended from office in mid-September; a public hearing into the matter was due to commence in July 2008. Meanwhile, on 7 September 2007 Caruana dissolved the House of Assembly and called elections to the new Gibraltar Parliament for 11 October. Following the elections, the GSD remained the largest party in the legislature, holding 10 of the 17 seats, having obtained 49.3% of the votes cast. The only other grouping to obtain representation was the GSLP-GLP alliance, with seven seats and 45.5% of the votes cast. Some 81.4% of the electorate voted. Caruana re-assumed office as Chief Minister and Minister of Finance, but appointed a Minister of Justice, Daniel Feetham, to undertake the duties formerly the domain of the Attorney-General. Upon his inauguration, Caruana made a speech to Parliament in which he described the new constitutional arrangements as having 'placed Gibraltar and the United Kingdom in a constitutional relationship with each other that is modern and non-colonial in nature', and pledged to explore the possibility of implementing further democratic reforms.

Government

Gibraltar is a United Kingdom Overseas Territory. Executive authority is vested in the British Sovereign and is exercised by the Council of Ministers, presided over by the Chief Minister, except in areas reserved to the Governor. These are defined by the 2006 Constitution as external affairs, defence, internal security and public offices. The Gibraltar Parliament comprises the Speaker (who is elected by, but not from, the Parliament) and 17 members who are elected for a four-year term.

Defence

There is a local defence force, the Royal Gibraltar Regiment, which, following the abolition of conscription, was reorganized as a predominantly volunteer reserve unit; as assessed at November 2007, it comprised 175 members. British army personnel stationed in Gibraltar numbered 40 and there were about 70 Royal Air Force personnel and 20 Royal Navy personnel. There is one Royal Navy base located in Gibraltar.

Economic Affairs

In 2004/05 Gibraltar's gross domestic product (GDP), measured at current prices, was £599.2m., equivalent to £20,820 per head. Gibraltar's population totalled some 28,231 at the census of May 2001, and was estimated to be 28,875 in 2006.

Gibraltar lacks agricultural land and natural resources, and the territory is dependent on imports of foodstuffs and fuels. Foodstuffs were estimated to account for 6% of total imports (excluding petroleum products) in 2004.

The industrial sector (including manufacturing, construction and power) employed 14.8% of the working population at October 2006.

Manufacturing employed 2.4% of the working population at October 2006. The most important sectors are shipbuilding and ship-repairs, and small-scale domestic manufacturing (mainly bottling, coffee-processing, pottery and handicrafts).

Gibraltar is dependent on imported petroleum for its energy supplies. Mineral fuels (excluding petroleum products) accounted for about 55% of the value of total imports in 2004.

Tourism and banking make a significant contribution to the economy. In 2006 revenue from tourism was estimated at G£210.5m. Visitor arrivals by air in 2006 totalled some 165,200, according to official figures. The number of visitor arrivals via the land frontier also reached a record high in 2005; 7,790,800 people crossed into Gibraltar during that year. In 2006 this figure increased further, to 8,185,100. Many cross-border day visitors come to the country with the purpose of shopping. At October 2006 the financial sector employed about 9.2% of the working population. Several Spanish banks have established offices in Gibraltar, encouraging the growth of the territory as an 'offshore' banking centre, while the absence of taxes for non-residents has also encouraged the use of Gibraltar as a financial centre. The value of bank deposits increased by more than 480% in the period 1987–95. By March 2007 there were 18 banks and 56 licensed insurance companies operating in Gibraltar. In November 2002, however, the European Commission ruled that Gibraltar's tax-free status was illegal and ordered Gibraltar to close its tax 'haven', which was unique in the European Union (EU, see p. 244). In March 2005 the Commission ruled that Gibraltar could extend the tax-exempt status of 8,464 companies registered in the territory until December 2010. In the intervening period the Gibraltar Government was to introduce a new taxation structure.

In 2006 Gibraltar recorded a visible trade deficit of £235.5m. The principal sources of imports in that year (excluding petroleum products) were the United Kingdom (accounting for 32.0% of the total) and Spain (24.7%). The principal imports in 2004 were mineral fuels and manufactured goods. The principal re-exports in that year were petroleum products, manufactured goods and wines, spirits, malt and tobacco.

In the year 2005/06 there was an estimated budgetary surplus of £17.99m. The annual rate of inflation averaged 1.8% during 1996–2006. The rate averaged 2.8% in 2006. Less than 5.0% of the labour force was unemployed in 2004.

Gibraltar joined the European Community (now EU, see p. 244) with the United Kingdom in 1973.

The Gibraltar economy is based on revenue from the British defence forces, tourism, shipping, and banking and finance. In 1988 the Gibraltar Government declared its aim to develop the territory as an 'offshore' financial centre, to stimulate private investment, and to promote the tourism sector. A project to build a new financial and administrative centre on land reclaimed from the sea commenced in 1990, and in the same year a Financial Services Commission was appointed to regulate financial activities in Gibraltar. Following the reduction in British military personnel in Gibraltar in the early 1990s, revenue from the British defence forces (which had accounted for some 60% of the economy in 1985) declined sharply. In 1994 British defence forces contributed only 10% to total government revenue. In 1999 there was a sudden increase in gambling outlets in Gibraltar, as leading operations transferred from the United Kingdom. By mid-2004 the Government had issued 11 new licences. In early 2008 it was announced that a new casino and bingo development would be built in Gibraltar, at a cost of around £6m. The project was due to begin construction in February and last for five months. The three main sectors of the economy in the early 2000s were financial services, tourism and shipping, and manufacturing. Gibraltar was to be the recipient of some €8m. in EU Structural Funds during 2000–06, the purpose of which was the encouragement of sustainable economic diversification. Gibraltar was allocated a further €8m. in EU Structural Funds to enhance competitiveness and employment covering the period 2007–13. The Gibraltar Stock Exchange, known as GibEX, was launched in 2006, and was expected to become fully operational in 2008.

Education

Education is compulsory between the ages of five and 15 years, and is provided free in government schools. The language of instruction is English. There are four nursery schools, 11 primary schools (of which one is private), one Service school (administered by the Ministry of Defence for the children of military personnel) and two secondary comprehensive schools—one for boys and one for girls. Scholarships for students in higher education are provided by both government and private sources. There is also one college providing technical and vocational training, and a special school for handicapped children. Government expenditure on education, employment and training in 2005/06 was forecast at G£21.5m. (equivalent to 11.7% of total spending).

Public Holidays

2008: 1 January (New Year's Day), 10 March (Commonwealth Day), 21 March (Good Friday), 24 March (Easter Monday), 5 May (May Day), 26 May (Spring Bank Holiday), 16 June (Queen's Official Birthday), 25 August (Late Summer Bank Holiday), 10 September (Gibraltar National Holiday), 25–26 December (Christmas).
2009: 1 January (New Year's Day), 9 March (Commonwealth Day), 10 April (Good Friday), 13 April (Easter Monday), 4 May (May Day), 25 May (Spring Bank Holiday), 15 June (Queen's Official Birthday), 31 August (Late Summer Bank Holiday), 10 September (Gibraltar National Holiday), 25–26 December (Christmas).

Weights and Measures

Imperial weights and measures are in use, but the metric system is gradually being introduced.

Statistical Survey

Source (unless otherwise indicated): Statistics Office, 99 Harbours Walk, The New Harbours, Gibraltar; tel. 20075515; fax 20051160; e-mail gibstats@gibtelecom.net; internet www.gibraltar.gov.gi .

AREA AND POPULATION

Area: 6.5 sq km (2.5 sq miles).

Population (excl. armed forces): 27,495 (males 13,644, females 13,851) at census of 12 November 2001 (Gibraltarians 22,882, Other British 2,627, Non-British 1,986). *2006* (official figure): 28,875 (Gibraltarians 23,447, Other British 3,284, Non-British 2,144).

Density (2006): 4,442.3 per sq km.

Births, Marriages and Deaths (2006, excl. armed forces): Live births 373 (birth rate 12.9 per 1,000); Marriages 834 (residents 182) (marriage rate 5.6 per 1,000); Deaths 230 (death rate 8.0 per 1,000).

Expectation of Life (years at birth at census of 2001): Males 78.5; Females 83.3.

Employment (October 2006): Manufacturing 460 (Shipbuilding 268); Construction 2,124; Electricity, gas and water 295; Wholesale and retail trade, and repair of goods 2,747; Restaurants and hotels 1,067; Transport, storage and communications 1,042; Financial intermediation 1,738; Real estate, renting and business activities 2,059; Public administration and defence 2,214; Education 804; Health and social work 1,438; Other community, social and personal services 2,497; Total 18,485 (males 10,811, females 7,674). Figures cover only non-agricultural activities, excluding mining and quarrying.

INDUSTRY

Electric Energy (2006): 151.2m. kWh.

FINANCE

Currency and Exchange Rates: 100 pence (pennies) = 1 Gibraltar pound (G£). *Sterling, Dollar and Euro Equivalents* (31 December 2007): £1 sterling = G£1.0000; US $1 = 49.92 pence; €1 = 73.48 pence; G£10 = £10.00 sterling = $20.03 = €13.61. *Average Exchange Rate* (G£ per US dollar): 0.5462 in 2004; 0.5500 in 2005; 0.5435 in 2006; 0.4998 in 2007. Note: The Gibraltar pound is at par with sterling.

Budget (G£ '000, year ending 31 March 2006, forecasts): *Recurrent Revenue:* Taxes 112.000; Duties 38,160; Gambling fees 6,945; Rates 15,300; Departmental fees and receipts 16,769; Government earnings 8,388; Total 197,562. *Recurrent Expenditure:* Education, employment and training 21,051; Heritage, culture, youth and sport 4,020; Housing 9,222; Environment, roads and utilities 24,470; Social and civic affairs 19,392; Trade, industry and communications 12,499; Health and civil protection 34,271; Administration 9,489; Finance 11,602; Law officers 532; Judiciary 965; House of Assembly 925; Office of Principal Auditor 522; Consolidated fund charges 30,612; Total 179,572.

Cost of Living (Retail Price Index at January; base: April 1998 = 100): 108.6 in 2004; 111.7 in 2005; 114.8 in 2006.

Gross National Product (G£ million, at factor cost): 458.94 in 2002/03; 497.59 in 2003/04; 551.50 in 2004/05.

Gross Domestic Product (G£ million, at factor cost): 507.17 in 2002/03; 560.06 in 2003/04; 599.18 in 2004/05.

EXTERNAL TRADE

Imports c.i.f. (G£ million, excluding petroleum products): 292.0 in 2004; 303.0 in 2005; 366.4 in 2006.

Exports f.o.b. (G£ million, excluding petroleum products): 108.4 in 2004; 110.0 in 2005; 130.9 in 2006.

Principal Trading Partners (G£ '000, 2006, excluding petroleum products): *Imports:* United Kingdom 117,117; Spain 90,604; Denmark 4,386; Netherlands 4,335; USA 3,250; Japan 3,227; Total (incl. others) 366,364. Note: Figures for exports are not available.

TRANSPORT

Road Traffic (licences current at 31 December 2006): Private vehicles 14,746; Commercial vehicles 2,255; Motorcycles 7,129.

Shipping (merchant vessels, 2006): Tonnage entered ('000 grt) 223,481; Vessels entered 8,988.

Civil Aviation (2006): Passenger arrivals ('000) 165.2; Passenger departures ('000) 166.0; Freight loaded 52 metric tons; Freight unloaded 296 metric tons. Figures exclude military passengers and freight.

TOURISM

Visitor Arrivals ('000): 7,628.7 in 2004; 7,790.8 in 2005; 8,185.1 in 2006.

Tourism Receipts (G£ million): 229.15 in 2004; 209.77 in 2005; 210.50 in 2006.

COMMUNICATIONS MEDIA

Radio Receivers (1997): 37,000 in use (Source: UNESCO, *Statistical Yearbook*).

Television Licences (2005): 5,965.

Daily Newspapers (1999): 1.

Telephone Stations (2004): 34,476.

Facsimile Machines (1997): 322 in use (Source: UN, *Statistical Yearbook*).

Mobile Cellular Telephones (2000): 5,558 subscribers (Source: International Telecommunication Union).

Internet Connections (31 March 2007): 7,853.

EDUCATION

Primary (state schools, 2004, unless otherwise indicated): 11 schools (1999), 2,975 pupils.

Secondary (state schools, 2004, unless otherwise indicated): 2 schools (1999), 1,995 pupils.

Total Teaching Staff at Primary and Secondary Schools (state schools, 2006): 334.

Technical and Vocational (1999): 1 college, 201 full-time students.

Directory

The Constitution

Gibraltar is a United Kingdom Overseas Territory. Executive authority is vested in the British monarch and is exercisable by the elected Gibraltar Government, except in the specified areas of the Governor's responsibilities; the Governor is the representative of the British monarch. Relations with the British Government are maintained through the Foreign and Commonwealth Office.

Following the referendum of 10 September 1967 (in which the people of Gibraltar voted in favour of retaining British sovereignty), a new Constitution was introduced on 11 August 1969, containing a code of human rights and providing for its enforcement by the Supreme Court of Gibraltar. Following a referendum held on 30 November 2006, this Constitution was revoked in favour of a new one, effective from 2 January 2007. The text regarding human rights was further updated, among other developments enumerated below. Gibraltar controls the majority of its domestic affairs, while the United Kingdom is responsible for matters of external affairs, defence and internal security. The other main provisions are as follows:

BRITISH SOVEREIGNTY

The Preamble to the Gibraltar Constitution Order contains assurances that Gibraltar will remain part of the dominions of the British Crown (unless these provisions are amended by further legislation adopted by the British Parliament), and that the United Kingdom will never enter into arrangements under which the people of Gibraltar would pass under the sovereignty of another State against their freely and democratically expressed wishes.

THE GOVERNOR AND COMMANDER-IN-CHIEF

As a representative of the British monarch, the Governor and Commander-in-Chief is responsible for matters which directly relate to external affairs, defence and internal security (including certain police matters), and such functions in relation to appointments to public offices and related matters as are conferred on him by the Constitution. Any matter which falls outside these special responsibilities is the responsibility of the Council of Ministers. The Governor is also head of the executive and administers Gibraltar, acting generally on the advice of the Council of Ministers. In exceptional circumstances, the Governor has special powers to refuse any advice from the Council of Ministers which, in the Governor's opinion, may not be in the interests of maintaining financial and economic stability. The Governor's formal assent, on behalf of the Crown, is required for all legislation. In some cases, the prior concurrence of the Crown, conveyed through the Secretary of State for Foreign and Commonwealth Affairs, is also required.

GOVERNMENT

The Government is defined as the Council of Ministers together with the British monarch, who is represented in Gibraltar by the Governor. The Council of Ministers comprises the Chief Minister and between four and 10 other ministers appointed from the elected members of the Assembly by the Governor, in consultation with the Chief Minister. (If the number of elected members of parliament exceeds 17, then the number of ministers should equate to one-half of the total, not exceeding 15.) Ministers are collectively responsible to the Parliament. The Government is presided over by the Chief Minister; individual ministers may be given responsibility for specific business. A Minister of Finance holds responsibility for public finances (as opposed to the previous, unelected Financial and Development Secretary). Parliament is to scrutinize and approve all public expenditure, not just expenditure incurred through the Consolidated Fund. Heads of Departments and other government officials appear before it when required.

THE GIBRALTAR PARLIAMENT

Under the 2006 Constitution the former House of Assembly received the status of Parliament and the legislation it produces became 'Acts' rather than 'Ordinances', and the right of British Ministers to disallow such legislation was revoked. With effect from the Parliament elected in October 2007, Parliament comprises the Speaker and at least 17 elected members. The Principal Auditor, the Ombudsman and the Clerk to the Parliament must be officers of Parliament. The Speaker, who cannot be an elected member of Parliament, is elected by Parliament.

The normal term of Parliament is four years. Elections are open to all adult British subjects and citizens of Ireland who have been ordinarily resident in Gibraltar for a continuous period of six months prior to the date for registration as an elector. The minimum voting age is 18 years. Each elector may vote for a maximum of 10 candidates and up to 10 candidates from each party may stand for election.

The elected members of Parliament elect and appoint the Mayor, who carries out ceremonial and representational functions on behalf of the City of Gibraltar.

APPOINTMENTS TO THE PUBLIC SERVICE

From 2007 a Judicial Appointments Commission (under the Chairmanship of the President of the Court of Appeal) and a Specified Appointments Commission (dealing with the most senior office holders) were instituted, in addition to the already existing Public Service Commission. The Governor makes all appointments and dismissals but must accept and implement the advice he receives from these Commissions, except under exceptional circumstances, and may not act at his own discretion.

The Government

Governor and Commander-in-Chief: Lt-Gen. Sir ROBERT FULTON (took office 27 September 2006).

COUNCIL OF MINISTERS
(April 2008)

Chief Minister and Minister of Finance: PETER CARUANA.

UNITED KINGDOM OVERSEAS TERRITORIES

Minister of Justice: DANIEL FEETHAM.
Minister for Trade, Industry, Employment and Communications: JOE J. HOLLIDAY.
Minister for Education, Training, Civic and Consumer Affairs: Dr BERNARD LINARES.
Minister for Health: ERNEST BRITTO.
Minister for Housing: CLIVE BELTRAN.
Minister for Social and Civic Affairs: YVETTE DEL AGUA.
Minister for Heritage, Culture, Youth and Sport: FABIAN VINET.
Minister for the Environment: JAIME NETTO.

MINISTRIES

Office of the Governor: The Convent, Main St; tel. 20045440; fax 20047823; e-mail enquiry.gibraltar@fco.gov.uk.
Office of the Chief Minister: 6 Convent Pl.; tel. 20070071; fax 20076396; e-mail govsec@gibnet.gi; internet www.gibraltar.gov.gi/chief_minister/chief_minister_index.htm.
Ministry of Education, Training, Civic and Consumer Affairs: 40 Town Range; tel. 20077486; fax 20071564; e-mail teachers@gibnynex.gi.
Ministry of the Environment: Joshua Hassan House, Secretary's Lane; tel. 20059800; fax 20076223; e-mail ministry@env.gov.gi.
Ministry of Finance: 6 Convent Pl.; tel. 20070071; fax 20076396.
Ministry of Health: Gibraltar.
Ministry of Heritage, Culture, Youth and Sport: 310 Main St; tel. 20041687; fax 20052589; e-mail minculture@gibtelecom.net.
Ministry of Housing: City Hall, John Mackintosh Sq.; tel. 20075603; fax 20052947.
Ministry of Justice: 6 Convent Pl.; tel. 20070071; fax 20076396.
Ministry of Social and Civic Affairs: 14 Governor's Parade; tel. 20078566; fax 20042509; e-mail dss@gibraltar.gov.gi.
Ministry of Trade, Industry, Employment and Communications: Suite 771, Europort; tel. 20052052; fax 20071406; e-mail gibdti@gibtelecom.net.

Legislature

Gibraltar Parliament
156 Main St; tel. 20078420; fax 20042849; e-mail parliament@gibtelecom.net; internet www.gibraltar.gov.gi.
Speaker: HARESH K. BUDHRANI.

General Election, 11 October 2007

Party	Votes*	% of votes	Seats
Gibraltar Social Democrats	76,334	49.3	10
Gibraltar Socialist Labour Party }	70,397	45.5	7
Gibraltar Liberal Party }			
Progressive Democratic Party	5,799	3.7	—
New Gibraltar Democracy	1,210	0.8	—
Independent	1,003	0.6	—
Total	**154,743**	**100.0**	**17**

* Each voter was permitted to vote for a maximum of 10 candidates. The total number of ballots cast was 16,004.

Political Organizations

All political organizations in Gibraltar advocate self-determination for the territory.

Gibraltar Liberal Party (GLP): 93 Irish Town, POB 225; tel. 20076959; fax 20074664; e-mail libparty@gibnet.gi; internet www.gib.gi/liberalparty; f. 1991 as the Gibraltar National Party; Leader Dr JOSEPH GARCÍA; Chair. JONATHAN STAGNETTO; Sec.-Gen. DAMON BOSSINO.
Gibraltar Social Democrats (GSD): 3/5 Horse Barrack Court; tel. and fax 20070786; e-mail info@gsd.gi; internet www.gsd.gi; f. 1989; holds a majority of seats in the House of Assembly; absorbed the Gibraltar Labour Party in 2005; Leader PETER CARUANA; Gen. Sec. LAURA V. CORREA.
Gibraltar Socialist Labour Party (GSLP): Suite 16, Block 3, Watergardens; tel. 20050700; fax 20078983; e-mail hqgslp@gibtelecom.net; internet www.gslp.gi; f. 1976; Leader JOSEPH (JOE) BOSSANO.
New Gibraltar Democracy (NGD): f. 2005; Christian democratic; Leader CHARLES GOMEZ.

Progressive Democratic Party (PDP): POB 1373; tel. 20049000; e-mail info@pdp.gi; internet www.pdp.gi; f. 2006; Leader KEITH AZOPARDI.

Judicial System

The 2006 Constitution provides for the protection of the fundamental rights and freedoms of the individual and the maintenance of a Supreme Court with unlimited jurisdiction to hear and determine any civil or criminal proceedings under any law. The Courts of Law of Gibraltar comprise a Court of Appeal, the Supreme Court and the Magistrates' Court.

The substantive law of Gibraltar is contained in Orders in Council which apply to Gibraltar, enactments of the Parliament of the United Kingdom which apply to or have been extended or applied to Gibraltar, locally enacted acts and subsidiary legislation, and common law and the rules of equity from time to time in force in the England so far as they may be applicable and subject to all necessary modification.

Court of Appeal
277 Main St.
holds three sessions each year; The Justices of Appeal are drawn from the English Court of Appeal.
President: Sir MURRAY STUART-SMITH.
Justices of Appeal: Sir PAUL KENNEDY, Sir PHILIP OTTON, Sir WILLIAM ALDOUS.

Supreme Court
277 Main St.
includes the office of Admiralty Marshal.
Chief Justice: ANTHONY E. DUDLEY (acting).
Justice: (vacant).

Magistrates' Court
Stipendiary Magistrate: CHARLES PITTO.

Religion

At the 2001 census 78.1% of the population were Roman Catholic, 7.0% Church of England, 4.0% Muslim, 2.1% Jewish and 1.8% Hindu.

CHRISTIANITY

The Roman Catholic Church
Gibraltar forms a single diocese, directly responsible to the Holy See. At 31 December 2005 there were an estimated 21,470 adherents in the territory.
Bishop of Gibraltar: Rt Rev. CHARLES CARUANA, 215 Main St; e-mail epis.carroca@gibnynex.gi; internet www.catholicdiocese.gi; tel. 20076688; fax 20043112.

The Church of England
The diocese of Gibraltar in Europe, founded in 1980, has jurisdiction over the whole of continental Europe, Turkey and Morocco.
Bishop of Gibraltar in Europe: Rt Rev. Dr GEOFFREY ROWELL, Bishop's Lodge, Church Rd, Worth, RH10 7RT, United Kingdom; tel. (1293) 883051; fax (1293) 884479; e-mail bishop@dioceseineurope.org.uk; internet europe.anglican.org.
Dean of the Cathedral of the Holy Trinity: Very Rev. ALAN WOODS, The Deanery, Bomb House Lane; tel. 20078377; fax 20078463; e-mail deangib@gibnet.gi.

Other Christian Churches
Church of Scotland (St Andrew's Presbyterian): Governor's Parade; tel. and fax 20077040; e-mail scotskirk@gibraltar.gi; internet www.scotskirkgibraltar.com; f. 1800; Minister Rev. STEWART LAMONT (St Andrew's Manse, 29 Scud Hill); 50 mems.
Methodist Church: Wesley House, 297 Main St; tel. and fax 20040870; e-mail minister@methodist.org.gi; internet www.methodist.org.gi; Minister Rev. FIDEL PATRON; f. 1769; 80 mems.

ISLAM
A mosque to serve the Islamic community in Gibraltar and financed by the Government of Saudi Arabia was constructed in the late 1990s.

JUDAISM
Jewish Community: Managing Board, 10 Bomb House Lane, POB 318; tel. 20072606; fax 20040487; e-mail mbjc@gibtelecom.net; Pres. H. J. M. LEVY; Hon. Sec. G. E. BELILO; Admin. Sec. E. BENADY; 600 mems.

UNITED KINGDOM OVERSEAS TERRITORIES — Gibraltar

The Press

Gibraltar Chronicle: Watergate House, POB 27; tel. 20047063; fax 20079927; e-mail letters@chronicle.gi; internet www.chronicle.gi; f. 1801; daily (except Sunday); English; Man. Editor Dominique Searle; circ. 6,000.

Gibraltar Gazette: 6 Convent Pl.; tel. 20047932; fax 20074524; e-mail legisunit@gibnynex.gi; f. 1949; weekly; publ. by Gibraltar Chronicle; official notices; circ. 375.

Gibraltar Magazine: PMB 6377, POB 561, Irish Town; tel. and fax 20077748; e-mail gibmag@gibnet.gi; internet www.thegibraltarmagazine.com; f. 1995; monthly; English; business and leisure; Editor Andrea Morton.

Insight: tel. 40913; e-mail advert@insight-gibraltar.com; internet www.insight-gibraltar.com; f. 1992; print and internet magazine; circ. 6,000.

Panorama: 75–77 Irish Town; tel. 79797; fax 74664; e-mail contacts@panorama.gi; internet www.panorama.gi; f. 1975; weekly, on Monday; English; news and features; Editor Joe García; circ. 4,000.

The New People: Suite 1, 3rd Floor Seclane House, 5 Secretary's Lane; tel. 54374000; e-mail thenewpeople@gibtelecom.net; internet www.thenewpeople.net; f. 1996; weekly; English with Spanish section; Editor Clive Golt; circ. 1,000.

Vox: Unit 91, Harbours Walk, New Harbours, POB 306; tel. 20077414; fax 20072531; e-mail editor@vox.gi; internet www.vox.gi; f. 1955; weekly; independent; in English and Spanish; Editor Derek McGrail; circ. 1,800.

Broadcasting and Communications

TELECOMMUNICATIONS

Gibraltar Regulatory Authority (GRA): Suite 811, Europort; tel. 20074636; fax 20072166; e-mail info@gra.gi; internet www.gra.gi; f. 2000; statutory body responsible for the regulation of the radio spectrum, data protection and gambling; Chief Exec. Paul Canessa.

GibNet Ltd: Suite 121, Eurotowers, POB 797; tel. 20047200; fax 20047272; e-mail enquiries@gibnet.net; internet www.gibnet.gi; f. 1994; internet service provider.

Gibtelecom Ltd: Suite 942, Europort; tel. 20052200; fax 20071673; e-mail info@gibtele.com; internet www.gibtele.com; f. 1990; jointly owned by Govt and Telekom Slovenije (Slovenia); operates local and international telephone and telecommunications services; provides range of digital, satellite, mobile and internet services; Chair Fabian Vinet; CEO Tim Bristow.

BROADCASTING

Gibraltar Broadcasting Corporation (GBC): Broadcasting House, 18 South Barrack Rd; tel. 20079760; fax 20078673; e-mail gbc@gibraltar.gi; internet www.gbc.gi; f. 1963; responsible for television and radio broadcasting; Gen. Man. S. Neish.

Radio

GBC—Radio (Radio Gibraltar): 24 hours daily in English and Spanish, including commercial broadcasting. In addition to local programmes, the BBC World Service programme is relayed.

Television

GBC—TV: operates in English for 24 hours daily; GBC and relayed BBC programmes are transmitted.

Finance

(cap. = capital; res = reserves; dep. = deposits; m. = million; brs = branches; amounts in G£)

BANKING

There were 18 banks operating in Gibraltar in March 2007.

Regulatory Authority

Financial Services Commission: Suite 943, Europort, POB 940; tel. 20040283; fax 20040282; e-mail info@fsc.gi; internet www.fsc.gi; f. 1989; regulates the activities of the financial sector; CEO Marcus Killick.

Banks

ABN AMRO Private Banking NV: Suite 731–734, Europort; tel. 20074474; fax 20078512; e-mail private.banking@gi.abnamro.com; internet www.abnamroprivatebanking.com/gi-welcome.htm; f. 1964; Chair. J. J. W. Zweegers; Man. Dir Hans Diederen.

BBVA Privanza International (Gibraltar) Ltd: 260–262 Main St, POB 488; tel. 20079420; fax 20073870; e-mail bbvpring@gibnet.gi; Man. Tonino Leto.

Barclays Private Clients International (Gibraltar) Ltd: Regal House, 3 Queensway, POB 187; tel. 20052378; fax 20079987; e-mail gibraltar@barclays.co.uk; Chief Man. Douglas Reyes.

Credit Suisse (Gibraltar) Ltd: 1st Floor, Neptune House, Marina Bay, POB 556; tel. 20078399; fax 20076027; e-mail csg.mail@credit-suisse.com; f. 1987; Chair. M. Salzmann; Man. Dir Thomas Westh Olsen.

EFG Bank (Gibraltar) Ltd: Eurolife Bldg, 1 Corral Rd, POB 561; tel. 20040117; fax 20040110; e-mail atlaco@gibnet.gi; formerly Banco Atlántico (Gibraltar) Ltd; Man. Emilio Martínez Priego.

S. G. Hambros Bank & Trust (Gibraltar) Ltd: Hambro House, 32 Line Wall Rd, POB 375; tel. 20074850; fax 20079037; e-mail gibraltar@sghambros.com; internet www.sghambros.com; est. 1981; cap. 1.5m., res 10.2m., dep. 245.0m. (June 2005); Chair. Warwick J. Newbury; Man. Dir Emma Perez.

Jyske Bank (Gibraltar) Ltd: 76 Main St, POB 143; tel. 20072782; fax 20072732; e-mail jyskebank@jyskebank.ltd.gi; internet www.jbpb.com; f. 1855 as Galliano (A. L.) Bankers; in 1988 name changed as above; cap. 26.5m., res 0.9m., dep. 1,788.4m. (Dec. 2004); Chair. Jens Lauritzen; Man. Dir Tim Marshall.

Lloyds TSB Bank PLC: 323 Main St, POB 482; tel. 20077373; fax 20070023; internet www.lloydstsb.gi; Man. Albert Douglas Langston.

Lombard Odier Darier Hentsch Private Bank Ltd: Suite 921, Europort, POB 407; tel. 20073350; fax 20073475; e-mail william.jardim@lombardodier.com.

NatWest Offshore Ltd: NatWest House, 57/63 Line Wall Rd, POB 707; tel. 20077737; fax 20074557; e-mail natwestgib@gibnynex.gi; internet www.natwestoffshore.com; f. 1988; Chief Man. Pete Yeoman.

Royal Bank of Scotland (Gibraltar) Ltd: 1 Corral Rd, POB 766; tel. 20073200; fax 20070152; e-mail marvincartwright@rbsint.com; internet www.rbsint.com.

Turicum Private Bank Ltd: Turicum House, 315 Main St, POB 619; tel. 20044144; fax 20044145; e-mail info@turicumprivatebank.com; internet www.turicumprivatebank.com; f. 1993; cap. and res €5.0m., dep. €15.7m. (Dec. 2003); Chair. Dr Raymond Bisang; Chief Exec. Urs Hüni.

Savings Bank

Gibraltar Savings Bank: Treasury Dept, Treasury Bldg, 23 John Mackintosh Sq.; tel. 20048396; fax 20077147; e-mail treasury@gibtelecom.net; dep. 232.2m. (March 2006); Dir C. Victory.

Association

Gibraltar Bankers' Association (GBA): POB 380; tel. 20073200; fax 20070152; e-mail langham@mercuryin.es; internet www.gba.gi; f. 1982; Pres. Kerry Blight; 17 mem. banks.

INSURANCE

There were 56 licensed insurance companies operating in Gibraltar in March 2007.

BMI Insurance Services Limited: Unit 7, Portland House, Glacis Rd, POB 469; tel. 20051010; internet www.bmigroup.gi.

Capurro Insurance and Investments Ltd: 20 Line Wall Rd, POB 130; tel. 20040850; fax 20040851; e-mail info@capurroinsurance.com; internet www.capurroinsurance.com.

Castiel Winser Insurance and Financial Consultants: Natwest House, 57/63 Line Wall Rd, POB 464; tel. 20077723; fax 20079257; e-mail financialservices@castielwinser.com; f. 1985; Man. Dir Sydney Attias.

Eurolife Assurance (International) Ltd: Eurolife Bldg, 1 Corral Rd, POB 233; tel. 20073495; fax 20073120; e-mail eurolife@gibnet.gi; Man. A. Smith.

Eurolinx (Gibraltar) Ltd: Suites 21–22, Victoria House, 26 Main St, POB 671; tel. 20040240; fax 20040241; e-mail eurolinx@sapphirenet.gi; internet www.eurolinx.gi; f. 1990; Dir Alan Joseph Montegriffo.

Gibro Insurance Services Ltd: Gibro House, 4 Giros Passage, POB 693; tel. 20043777; fax 20043538; e-mail gibroins@gibtelecom.net.

Middle Sea Insurance PLC: Suite 1A, 143 Main St, POB 502; tel. 20076434.

Norwich Union International Insurance Ltd: Regal House, 3 Queensway, POB 45; tel. 20079520; fax 20070942; e-mail nugib@gibnet.gi; f. 1984; cap. 1,600,000; CEO. Eric D. Chaloner; Chair. Paul L. Savignon.

Ophir Insurance Services Ltd: 123 Main St, POB 914; tel. 20073871; fax 20050411; e-mail ophir@gibtelecom.net.

Association

Gibraltar Insurance Association: c/o NatWest House, 57/63 Line Wall Rd, POB 464; tel. 77723; fax 79257; f. 1995.

Trade and Industry

GOVERNMENT AGENCY

Finance Centre: Suite 761, Europort; tel. 20050011; fax 20051818; e-mail info@financecentre.gov.gi; f. 1997; marketing and promotion of financial services; liaison between regulator and private sector.

CHAMBER OF COMMERCE

Gibraltar Chamber of Commerce: Watergate House, Casemates Sq. 2/6, POB 29; tel. 20078376; fax 20078403; e-mail info@gibraltarchamberofcommerce.com; internet www.gibraltarchamberofcommerce.com; f. 1882; Pres. NICHOLAS RUSSO; 300 mems.

EMPLOYERS' ORGANIZATIONS

Gibraltar Federation of Small Businesses: GFSB House, POB 211, 112 Irish Town; tel. 20047722; fax 20047733; e-mail gfsb@gfsb.gi; internet www.gfsb.gi; f. 1996; Chair. KEN ROBINSON.

Gibraltar Hotel Association: c/o Caleta Hotel; tel. 20076501; fax 20071050; e-mail caleta@gibnynex.gi; internet www.caletahotel.com; f. 1960; Chair. FRANCO OSTUNI; seven mems.

Gibraltar Licensed Victuallers' Association: c/o Watergate Restaurant, Queensway Quay; tel. 20074195; f. 1976; Chair. M. OTON; 120 mems.

Gibraltar Motor Traders' Association: POB 167; tel. 20079004; f. 1961; Gen. Sec. G. BASSADONE; six mems.

Hindu Merchants' Association: POB 357; tel. 20079000; fax 20071966; e-mail vikram.nagrani@hassans.gi; f. 1964; Pres. VIKRAM NAGRANI; 125 mems.

PRINCIPAL TRADE UNIONS

Gibraltar Taxi Association: 19 Waterport Wharf; tel. 20070052; fax 20076986; f. 1957; Pres. CLIVE ZAMMIT; 100 mems.

Gibraltar Trades Council: 7 Hargraves Ramp, POB 279; tel. 20076930; fax 20079646; e-mail prospect.ggca@gibtelecom.net; comprises unions representing 70% of the working population; affiliated to the United Kingdom Trades Union Congress; Sec. MICHAEL J. A. TAMPIN; Pres. JOSEPH J. CORTES.

Affiliated unions:

Gibraltar General and Clerical Association (GGCA): 7 Hargrave's Ramp, POB 279; tel. 20076930; fax 20079646; e-mail prospect.ggca@gibtelecom.net; internet www.prospectbranches.org.uk/gibraltar; f. 1947; Pres. JOSÉ LUIS GARCÍA; Nat. Sec. MICHAEL J. A. TAMPIN; 1,030 mems (2007).

NASUWT (Gibraltar): 98 Harbours Walk, New Harbours; tel. 20076308; fax 77608; e-mail gtateachers@gibtelecom.net; f. 1962; fmrly known as the Gibraltar Teachers' Association; Pres. JOSEPH J. CORTES; 350 mems.

Unite—T&G Section (United Kingdom) (Gibraltar District): tel. 20074185; fax 20071596; f. 1924; Dist. Officer CHARLES SISARELLO; 4,239 mems.

UTILITIES

Electricity

Gibraltar Electricity Authority: Waterport Power Station, North Mole; tel. 20048908; fax 20077408; govt-owned; generation, distribution and supply of electricity.

Water

AquaGib Ltd: Leanse Pl., Suite 10B, 50 Town Range; tel. 20040880; fax 20040881; e-mail main.office@aquagib.gi; internet www.aquagib.gi; fmrly known as Lyonnais des Eaux (Gibraltar) Ltd; present name adopted 2003; Man. Dir P. LATIN.

Transport

There are no railways in Gibraltar. There is a total road length of 53.1 km, including 12.9 km of highways and 6.8 km of footpaths.

ROADS

Ministry of the Environment: see Ministries.

SHIPPING

The Strait of Gibraltar is a principal ocean route between the Mediterranean and Black Sea areas and the rest of the world.

Gibraltar is used by many long-distance liners, and has dry dock facilities and a commercial ship-repair yard. Tax concessions are available to ship-owners who register their ships at Gibraltar.

Gibraltar Maritime Administration: Watergate House, 2/8 Casemate Sq.; tel. 20047771; fax 20047770; e-mail maritadmin@gibtelecom.net; internet www.gibmaritime.com.

Gibraltar Port Authority: Port Office, North Mole; tel. 20077254; fax 20051513; e-mail ceo.gpa@gibtelecom.net; internet www.gibraltarport.com; CEO Capt. CLIFF BRAND.

Cammell Laird (Gibraltar) Ltd: Main Wharf Rd, The Dockyard, POB 858; tel. 20059400; fax 20044404; e-mail mail@lairds.gi; internet www.lairds.gi; drydock facilities and general ship repairing; CEO MARTIN LOVERIDGE.

M. H. Bland & Co Ltd: Cloister Bldg, Market Lane, POB 554; tel. 20075009; fax 20071608; f. 1810; ship agents, salvage and towage contractors; Chair. JOHN G. GAGGERO.

Association

Gibraltar Shipping Association: c/o Inchcape Shipping Services, POB 194; tel. 20046315; fax 20046316; e-mail mark.porral@iss-shipping.com; f. 1957; Sec. P. L. IMOSSI; 11 mems.

CIVIL AVIATION

The airport is at North Front, on the isthmus, 2.5 km from the city centre. An agreement reached in September 2006 by Gibraltar, the United Kingdom and Spain allowed for the operation of flights from Spain and the rest of Europe to Gibraltar. Hitherto Spain had blocked direct air links between Gibraltar and European countries other than the United Kingdom. Commercial flights between Gibraltar and Spain began in December 2006. In accordance with the 2006 agreement, plans were announced in 2007 for a new airport terminal straddling the border between Gibraltar and Spain, which was expected to be completed in late 2008.

Gibraltar Civil Aviation Advisory Board: Air Terminal, Winston Churchill Ave; tel. 20073026; fax 20073925; e-mail info@gibraltar-airport.com; Sec. JOHN GONÇALVES.

Tourism

Gibraltar's tourist attractions include its climate, beaches and a variety of amenities. Following the reopening of the border with Spain in February 1985, the resumption of traffic by day-visitors contributed to the expansion of the tourist industry. In 2006 visitor arrivals numbered some 8.19m. (by sea: 225,567; air: 143,914; and land: 7,815,661), while revenue from tourism totalled G£210.50m.

Gibraltar Tourist Board: Duke of Kent House, Cathedral Sq.; tel. 20074950; fax 20074943; e-mail tourism@gibraltar.gi; internet www.gibraltar.gov.gi; CEO NICHOLAS GUERRERO.

MONTSERRAT

Introductory Survey

Location, Climate, Language, Religion, Flag, Capital

Montserrat is one of the Leeward Islands in the West Indies. A mountainous, volcanic island, it lies about 55 km (35 miles) north of Basse-Terre, Guadeloupe, and about 43 km south west of Antigua. The climate is generally warm, with a mean maximum temperature of 30°C (86°F) and a mean minimum of 23°C (73°F), but the island is fanned by sea breezes for most of the year. The average annual rainfall is about 1,475 mm (58 ins), although there is more rain in the central and western areas. English is the official language. Many Christian churches are represented, but the principal denominations are the Anglican, Roman Catholic and Methodist Churches. The flag is the British 'Blue Ensign', with the island's badge (a shield depicting a woman dressed in green holding a harp and a cross) on a white roundel in the fly. The capital is Plymouth.

Recent History

Montserrat was first settled by the British (initially Roman Catholic exiles) in 1632, by which time the few original Carib inhabitants had disappeared. It formed part of the federal colony of the Leeward Islands from 1871 until 1956, when the federation was dissolved and the presidency of Montserrat became a separate colony. Montserrat participated in the short-lived Federation of the West Indies (1958–62) and, from 1960, the island had its own Administrator (the title was changed to that of Governor in 1971). The Constitution (see below) came into force in 1960.

The first priority of successive legislatures has been to improve infrastructure and maintain a healthy economy. Between 1952 and 1970 William Bramble dominated island politics. His son, Austin Bramble, leader of the Progressive Democratic Party (PDP), opposed and succeeded him as Chief Minister. In November 1978 the People's Liberation Movement (PLM) won all seven elective seats in the Legislative Council, and the PLM's leader, John Osborne, became Chief Minister. In the general election of February 1983 the PLM was returned to government with five seats. The remainder were won by the PDP, whose commitment to development projects, agriculture and education complemented those of the PLM.

Attempts to form an opposition alliance between the PDP and the National Development Party (NDP—formed by business interests and former members of the PDP) were unsuccessful. Against a divided opposition, the PLM won four of the seven elective seats in the Legislative Council at an early general election in August 1987. The NDP won two seats, and the PDP one (Bramble lost his seat and announced his retirement from politics). Osborne was returned to office as Chief Minister.

Osborne was an advocate of independence from the United Kingdom, despite the apparent lack of popular support for this policy. A referendum on the issue was planned for 1990, but the devastation caused by 'Hurricane Hugo' in September 1989, meant that any plans for independence were postponed. Furthermore, the Osborne Government and the British authorities were embarrassed by controversy surrounding the hitherto lucrative 'offshore' financial sector. In early 1989 the Governor's office announced that the British police were investigating serious allegations against certain banks (involving the processing of illegal funds from a variety of criminal activities). Registration was suspended, several people were charged with criminal offences and, at the end of 1989, most banking licences were revoked. The Montserrat Government agreed to introduce recommended provisions for the regulation of the financial services industry, but Osborne objected strongly to a proposed amendment to the Constitution which transferred responsibility for the sector from the Chief Minister to the Governor. Agreement was subsequently reached, however, when Osborne acknowledged that 'offshore' finance was part of the British Government's responsibility for external affairs.

In late 1990 a dispute arose between the Chief Minister and his deputy, Benjamin Chalmers, who was reported to have accused Osborne of dishonesty in his relations with the Executive Council. Allegations of corruption continued in 1991, and in June an inquiry was undertaken by the British police to investigate the possible involvement of members of the Executive Council in the 1989 banking scandal, as well as in fraudulent land transfers.

The resignation of Chalmers in September 1991, following a further dispute with Osborne, resulted in the loss of the Government's majority in the Legislative Council. This prompted an early election in the following month, when the National Progressive Party (NPP), which had been formed only two months prior to the election, secured a majority of seats. The leader of the NPP, Reuben Meade, became Chief Minister.

In December 1991 the Legislative Council approved legislation allowing the re-establishment of a comprehensive 'offshore' financial centre. Despite considerably improved regulation, more than 90% of the island's 'offshore' and commercial banks were again closed down, following further investigations by British inspectors in mid-1992.

The eruption of Chance's Peak volcano in July 1995, which had been dormant for more than 100 years, caused severe disruption to the island and threatened to devastate Plymouth and surrounding areas in southern Montserrat. In late August the threat of a more serious eruption prompted the evacuation of some 5,000 people to the north of the island, and the declaration by the Government of a state of emergency and a night curfew. As volcanic activity subsided in September, evacuated islanders returned to Plymouth and villages near the volcano. However, by December the area was again deemed to be unsafe, and 4,000 people were evacuated for a further period of several weeks. The Governor and Chief Minister secured an agreement from the British Government for the provision of assistance with evacuation and rehabilitation programmes. A third evacuation took place in April 1996, following a further series of eruptions, and it was announced that some 5,000 evacuees living in 'safe areas' would remain there at least until the end of the year. In that month the British Government announced that Montserratians would be granted residency and the right to work in the United Kingdom for up to two years. In August the British Government announced that it was to provide assistance worth £25m. to finance housing construction projects, infrastructure development, the provision of temporary health and education facilities and other public services in the northern 'safe areas' of the island. By the end of 1996 it was estimated that some 5,000 islanders had left the territory since the onset of volcanic activity in mid-1995.

In September 1996 the Government announced that the general election would take place, despite the continued disruption in the territory. The Deputy Chief Minister, Noel Tuitt, resigned from his post and from the NPP later that month, stating that he was disillusioned with Meade's leadership. Disagreement over the Government's management of the volcano crisis and its handling of aid funds led to the proposal, by an opposition member in early October, of a motion of 'no confidence' in the Chief Minister. Meade, however, avoided a vote on the motion by dissolving the Legislative Council.

No party won an overall majority at the election on 11 November 1996. The NPP secured only one seat (won by Meade). The recently formed People's Progressive Alliance (PPA), led by John Osborne, secured two seats, as did both the Movement for National Reconstruction (MNR), led by Austin Bramble, and independent candidates. A four-member coalition cabinet (which included Meade, but did not include either PPA member) was subsequently formed under the leadership of Bertrand Osborne, who was sworn in as Chief Minister on 13 November.

In June 1997 the scale of volcanic activity on the island increased dramatically with the eruption of the Soufrière Hills volcano, which left some two-thirds of the island uninhabitable, destroyed the capital and resulted in the deaths of 19 people. Islanders were evacuated to 'safe areas' in the north of the country. The British Government responded to the crisis by releasing emergency aid in order to finance the construction of emergency shelters for evacuees, and for repairs to temporary hospital facilities. In July it was announced that a package of options for Montserratians was being formulated, which would offer islanders resettlement grants and assisted passage either to other islands within the Caribbean or to the United Kingdom. The 'safe area' in the north was to be developed for those wishing to remain on the island. By the end of July the population of Montserrat was estimated to have declined to 5,800; in the month since the eruption of the Soufrière Hills volcano some 800 islanders had moved to Antigua, bringing the total number who had moved there since the onset of volcanic activity in 1995 to some 3,000. Many more had resettled on other Caribbean islands or in the United Kingdom.

On 21 August 1997 Bertrand Osborne resigned as Chief Minister following four days of public demonstrations in protest at his handling of the volcano crisis, in particular at uncertainty surrounding the future of the islanders and at poor conditions in emergency shelters. On the same day the British Government announced the financial details of its voluntary evacuation scheme for those wishing to leave Montserrat. The offer, which comprised a relocation grant of £2,400 for adults and £600 for minors, in addition to travel costs, provoked an angry response from islanders, who protested that the grants were severely inadequate. Osborne's successor as Chief Minister, David Brandt, an independent member of the Legislative Council, criticized the British Government's offer while also accusing it of attempting to depopulate Montserrat by showing insufficient commitment to the redevelopment of the island. The British Secretary of State for International Development, Clare Short, denied that the United Kingdom was encouraging people to leave Montserrat. However, accusations made by Short, to the effect that the island's leaders were making unreasonable demands, caused considerable offence to the island Government and the controversy was assuaged only when the British Secretary of State for Foreign and Commonwealth Affairs, Robin Cook, announced the formation of a special inter-departmental committee charged with co-ordinating assistance to Montserrat. At the end of August George Foulkes, the Under-Secretary of State for International Development, visited the island for discussions with the Montserrat Government, during which he announced a five-year sustainable development plan for the north of the island, to include finance for new housing, social services and improved infrastructure. In September Tony Abbott was inaugurated as Governor of Montserrat, replacing Frank Savage.

In January 1998 Brandt renewed his accusations that the British Government was attempting to depopulate Montserrat by delaying the release of development funds. Prompted by these accusations, in February Cook made a formal visit to Montserrat and it was subsequently announced that the United Kingdom would provide further finance of £4.8m. for housing on the island. The new funding brought the total amount committed by the British Government in 1995–98, since the beginning of the volcano crisis, to £59m.

In May 1998 the British Government announced that all citizens of Montserrat, except those already resident in other countries, would be entitled to settle in the United Kingdom. The estimated 3,500 refugees already in the United Kingdom on temporary visas were to be allowed to apply for permanent residency. In early July the

Soufrière Hills volcano erupted again, covering much of the island in ash, and postponing plans to re-open parts of Plymouth to residents. In August part of the central zone of Montserrat was re-opened, following operations to remove ash and debris.

In January 1999 an inquest into the 19 deaths during the eruptions found that in nine cases, the British Government was in part to blame for the deaths. The jury criticized the public shelters provided, where conditions were described as 'deplorable', and the Government's failure to provide farming land in the 'safe area', which had led to some farmers' choosing to risk their lives rather than abandon their farms. The Department for International Development, denied culpability for the deaths, and announced that it was to spend a further £75m. on a three-year redevelopment programme in the north of the island.

In February 1999 studies were published confirming that the volcanic ash covering much of Montserrat contained significant amounts of silica, the cause of the lung disease silicosis. It was suggested that the threat to health from long-term exposure to the ash might further limit the number of areas of the island suitable for redevelopment. In July a bulletin from the Montserrat Volcano Observatory noted that there were no signs of decline in residual volcanic activity, warning that it would take decades for the lava still present to cool to ambient temperatures. Further explosions of ash and minor eruptions of lava continued throughout the rest of the year.

In September 1999 public consultations took place to discuss government proposals to establish a new capital at Little Bay, in the north-west of the island. The new town would take an estimated 10 years to construct. Progress on the project was finally achieved with the establishment of the Montserrat Development Corporation in 2007, whose mandate included the advancement of plans for the construction of the new capital, and the issuing of a contract to a local company to develop the infrastructure. Also in September 1999 the British Government announced further assistance for the construction of housing and expressed support for Government plans to establish Montserrat as a centre for international financial services. In March 2000 the dome of lava, which had been covering the Soufrière Hills volcano, collapsed, producing lava flows and mudslides in the west of the island, and covering much of the 'safe zone' with ash.

In May 2000 an advisory commission on electoral reform recommended the replacement of the constituency system, which was deemed to be redundant following the abandonment of much of the island, by a nine-member single constituency. It was intended that the new system would be in place prior to the general election, scheduled for late 2001.

In July 2001 there was a further partial collapse of the dome of lava covering the Soufrière Hills volanco. Hot ash and volcanic pebbles affected the communities of Salem and Olveston, and ash clouds severely disrupted air travel in the north-eastern Caribbean. In the following month Montserrat signed up to a British mortgage assistance programme, which would provide housing subsidies and loans to residents who had been made homeless as a result of volcanic activity. Many residents were still paying mortgages on homes in an off-limits zone of the island as well as paying rent for new accommodation.

In February 2001 Chief Minister Brandt's coalition Government collapsed following the resignations of two members, who accused Brandt of making decisions, in particular about a proposed new airport, without consulting other ministers. Their resignations forced Brandt to dissolve the Executive Council and announce that an early general election would be held on 2 April, under the new system of the nine-member single constituency (see above). At the election former Chief Minister John Osborne's newly formed New People's Liberation Movement (NPLM) won seven of the nine seats while the NPP won the remaining two seats. Osborne was sworn in as Chief Minister on 5 April.

In May 2001 Anthony Longrigg was inaugurated as Governor of Montserrat, replacing Tony Abbott.

In February 2002 the Organisation of Eastern Caribbean States (OECS, see p. 425) countries, including Montserrat, agreed to allow nationals of member states to travel freely within the OECS area and to remain in a foreign territory within the area for up to six months. In May 2002 the British Overseas Territories Act, having received royal assent in the United Kingdom in February, came into force and granted British citizenship to the people of its 14 Overseas Territories, including Montserrat. Under the new law Montserratians would be able to hold British passports and work in the United Kingdom and anywhere else in the European Union. In October 2003 the British Government formally backed plans for Montserrat to particpate fully in the Caribbean Single Market and Economy (CSME) proposed by the Caribbean Community and Common Market (CARICOM, see p. 196), of which Montserrat was a founder member. (As a United Kingdom Overseas Territory, Montserrat required prior approval from the British Government before undertaking international commitments.) The CSME came into force at the beginning of 2006, although Montserrat was not a founding member.

A massive volcanic eruption, reported to be the largest since 1995, occurred on 12 July 2003, causing infrastructural damage, and the destruction of numerous buildings in Salem, which is on the edge of the 'safe zone'. Further, minor eruptions occurred in April 2005 and May 2006.

In May 2004 Deborah Barnes-Jones took over as Governor from Anthony Longrigg.

In the general election of 31 May 2006 no political parties secured a decisive majority. The Movement for Change and Prosperity (MCAP) gained the largest representation, with four seats, followed by the NPLM with three seats. The Montserrat Democratic Party (MDP) secured one seat, as did former Chief Minister David Brandt, again standing as an independent. Lowell Lewis of the MDP assembled a coalition Government comprising the three NPLM representatives (including former Chief Minister John Osborne) and Brandt. The new Government was sworn into office on 2 June, although allegations of corruption and mismanagement levelled against candidates from both the former government and opposition had overshadowed the election process and doubts were expressed about the new administration's compositional stability.

Concerns emerged in November 2006 relating to the ongoing constitutional revision process, which had been under negotiation with the Government of the United Kingdom since 1997. A series of Legislative Council debates examining a report of the Constitutional Review Commission, first submitted in 2002, and negotiations with Ian Hendry of the British Constitutional Review Team, provoked an angry response from some members of the Chief Minister's Constitutional Advisory Committee. They alleged that Montserrat's increased reliance upon budgetary assistance from the United Kingdom—necessitated by volcanic disruption—was being exploited as a 'coercive tool' in the reform process. While the United Kingdom had encouraged Montserrat to express its preferences and recommendations towards the drafting of a new constitution, it was emphasized that ultimate authority would reside with the British Government, eliciting accusations that the British were offering only a token democracy and had disregarded the Montserratian public consultations. Requests for a system of 'free association', permitting self-determination from the United Kingdom—drafting its own constitution without recourse to the administering nation, but retaining links with that country—and the appointment of an indigenous Deputy Governor who would assume some of the responsibilities of the British Governor in Montserrat, were similarly declined. That other former British colonial territories, including Bermuda, had been granted associated statehood instigated a consultation of the former Saint Christopher and Nevis-United Kingdom Associated Statehood Constitution as a template for Montserrat's submission to the British Constitutional Review Team. However, it was advised that any recommendations found not to concur with the United Kingdom's objective of securing the removal of Montserrat from the UN's Special Committee on Decolonization's list of prospective colonies would be rejected. Chief Minister Lowell Lewis stated in early 2008 that further meetings to discuss the constitutional reform process would not be conducted until the end of that year.

Also in November 2006, Montserrat became a signatory to the UN Convention Against Corruption during the eighth meeting of the Overseas Territories Consultative Council hosted in London, United Kingdom, by the British Overseas Territories Minister, Lord Triesman.

Peter Waterworth succeeded Deborah Barnes-Jones as Governor of Montserrat in July 2007.

Lewis disbanded the coalition Government on 21 February 2008 and formed a new political alliance with the MCAP. Minister of Communications and Works Idabelle Meade and Minister of Agriculture, Lands, Housing and the Environment Margaret Dyer-Howe, both members of the NPLM, were replaced by MCAP members Charles Kirnon and Reuben Meade respectively. Lewis also announced that John Osborne, Minister of Education, Health and Community Services, would be replaced by a member of the MCAP by 31 March, giving the new coalition Government a majority in the Legislative Council, with six seats. Osborne's ministerial responsibilities were, accordingly, assigned to Roselyn Cassell-Sealy.

Meade and two former members of the Legislative Council expressed dissatisfaction in late March 2008 with the reformed electoral system during a public meeting to discuss proposed constitutional changes. They acknowledged that the voting tendencies of most residents of Montserrat were to respond to party personalities rather than to vote for the party itself, and that this was precluded by the present system. Meade proposed the adoption of a system in which four constituencies would be represented by two members, while the Chief Minister would be elected at large. He claimed that the implementation of such measures would aid community development and the rebuilding of the country.

Following a Cuban Government-sponsored diplomatic excursion to Havana by Chief Minister Lowell in January 2007, Montserrat and Cuba pledged to strengthen bilateral relations, particularly in consideration of the burgeoning threat posed by the Soufrière Hills volcanic dome, which had been expanding consistently in the preceding months. However, by mid-April volcanic activity had reportedly abated and in July the exclusion zone, which had been expanded to include settlements bordering Belham Valley to the north, was reduced to its extent at the start of the year.

Government

Under the provisions of the 1960 Constitution and subsequent legislation, the Governor is appointed by the British monarch and is responsible for defence, external affairs and internal security. The Governor is President of the seven-member Executive Council. The Legislative Council comprises 12 members: a Speaker, two official members, two nominated and seven elected by universal adult suffrage. A constitutional review was begun in 2002 and was continuing in 2008.

Economic Affairs

In 2006 Montserrat's gross domestic product (GDP) at market prices was an estimated EC $122.52m., equivalent to approximately EC $24,372 per head. In 1997–2005 real GDP decreased by an annual average of 2.5%; GDP increased by 0.4% in 2005 before declining by 4.9% in 2006.

Agriculture (including forestry and fishing) contributed an estimated 1.1% of GDP in 2006, and engaged 6.6% of the employed labour force in 1992. The sector was almost destroyed by the volcanic eruptions of 1997, which caused an 81.3% decline in agricultural production, and a return to subsistence farming. The sector's GDP contracted by a further 33.3% in 1998, in real terms, but increased by 7.6% in 1999 and by a massive 46.5% in 2000. A contraction of 17.3% in agricultural GDP in 2001 was followed, in 2002, by a 38.4% recovery. However, no growth was recorded in the sector in 2003, and the sector contracted by 17.8% in 2004, largely owing to a further eruption of the Soufrière Hills volcano in July 2003 that destroyed some 95% of that year's food crop. Prior to the volcanic eruption the principal crops grown were white potatoes, onions, rice and sea-island cotton. Cattle, goats, sheep and poultry were also farmed. Montserrat's fisheries are under-exploited, owing to the absence of a sheltered harbour. The sector declined by 12.5% in 2005.

Industry (including mining, manufacturing, construction and public utilities) contributed some 15.9% to GDP in 2006, and engaged some 30.9% of the employed labour force in 1987. Mining and quarrying contributed less than 0.6% of GDP in 2006. Manufacturing contributed 0.7% of GDP in 2006, engaged 5.6% of the employed labour force (together with mining) in 1992, and accounted for about 70% of exports in the early 1990s. Many industrial sites were destroyed in 1997, causing a decline in real manufacturing GDP of 45.2% in that year and of 85.0% in 1998. In 1999 the sector's GDP improved by 10.6%, but growth was static in 2000–05. Light industries comprise the processing of agricultural produce (also cotton and tropical fruits), as well as spring-water bottling and the manufacture of garments and plastic bags. The assembly of electrical components, which accounted for 69% of export earnings in 1993, ceased in 1998, following further volcanic activity. In May 2006 the Government signed a 25-year contract with a British plastics recycling company to supply volcanic ash, to be used in the blending of recycled plastics. Exports of digital data-processing machines comprised 16.7% of total exports in 2003.

Construction contributed an estimated 8.0% of GDP in 2006 and employed 17.5% of the working population in 1988. The sector enjoyed growth in the early 1990s, owing to reconstruction programmes in response to the devastation caused by 'Hurricane Hugo' in 1989. Activity in the sector declined in the mid-1990s, before increasing in the middle of the decade, as a result of further reconstruction work following the volcanic eruptions. In 2000, however, real construction GDP fell by 35.8%. It continued to decrease, by 7.7%, in 2001, before increasing by 40.9% in 2002, although there was another contraction, of 2.9%, in 2003. The trend was reversed yet again in 2004, with the sector increasing by an estimated 2.4%, although it then contracted by 4.3% in 2005. Energy requirements are dependent upon the import of hydrocarbon fuels (15.5% of total imports in 2003).

It is hoped to re-establish Montserrat as a data-processing centre, and as a centre for financial services, which previously provided an important source of government revenue. The tourism sector, which in 2004 contributed an estimated EC $23.2m. in gross visitor expenditure, remains important to the island, and it is hoped to establish Montserrat as a centre for environmental tourism, with the volcano itself as the premier attraction. The GDP of the hotel and restaurant sector increased by an annual average of 10.3% between 1997–2005. The sector recorded a 31.6% contraction in 2003, followed by an expansion of 33.8% in 2004, and 30.9% in 2005. The real GDP of the services sector increased by an annual average of 0.6% during 1997–2005, increasing by 6.4% in 2004, but falling by 0.5% in 2005. Services contributed 83.0% of GDP in 2006.

In 2006 Montserrat recorded an estimated trade deficit of EC $99.3m. Earnings from the services sector, mainly tourism receipts and net transfers (in particular, the remittances from Montserratians abroad and the income of foreign retired people), generally offset persistent trade deficits. There was an estimated deficit on the current account of the balance of payments of EC $43.3m. in 2006. The principal trading partner is the USA (providing 56.4% of imports and receiving 21.4% of exports in 2005). Other trading partners of importance include the United Kingdom, Japan, Trinidad and Tobago and Antigua and Barbuda. The export of rice and of electrical components, previously the most important of the island's few exports, ceased in 1998 following further volcanic activity. Export receipts were, however, estimated to have increased to some US $1.8m. by 2003. Food, beverage and tobacco imports constituted 18.1% of total imports in 2005; the principal imports are machinery and transport equipment and basic manufactures.

In 2005, according to preliminary figures, there was a budgetary deficit of EC $4.5m (including grants of $63.6m.). The capital budget is funded almost entirely by overseas aid, notably from the United Kingdom and Canada. The United Kingdom initially provided aid worth £14.5m. for 1995–98 (additional assistance for emergency housing and other services necessitated by continued volcanic activity had brought this total to £59m. by the end of 1998). In 1999 official development assistance totalled US $65.6m, with British budgetary assistance of £75m. being made available for the three-year reconstruction programme agreed in January 1999. A £55m. programme for 2001–04 was followed by a further three-year £40m. programme extending to 2007. The aid programme for 2006 was valued at £14m., of which £10.2m. was a grant to cover the recurrent budget deficit. Montserrat's total external public debt was estimated to be around EC $10.2m. in 2006, according to government figures. Consumer prices increased by 3.1% in 2004, and by 2.7% in 2005. The Caribbean Development Bank (see p. 201) estimated the unemployment rate to stand at some 13% of the labour force in 2001.

Montserrat is a member of the Eastern Caribbean Central Bank (ECCB), the Caribbean Community and Common Market (CARICOM, see p. 196), the Organisation of Eastern Caribbean States (OECS, see p. 425) and, as a dependency of the United Kingdom, has the status of Overseas Territory in association with the European Union (EU, see p. 244). The territory is also a member of the regional stock exchange, the Eastern Caribbean Securities Exchange (based in Saint Christopher and Nevis), established in 2001.

The eruption of the Soufrière Hills volcano in June 1997, and subsequent volcanic activity, rendered the southern two-thirds of Montserrat, including the capital, Plymouth, uninhabitable. Much of the country's infrastructure, including the main port and airport, was destroyed, and the island's agricultural heartland devastated. The implications for the island's principal industry, tourism, were extremely severe. In August the British Government announced a five-year reconstruction programme for the development of the 'safe areas' in the north of the island. However, by mid-February 1998 the population of Montserrat had declined to just 2,850 (the population was an estimated 11,581 in 1994), owing to the lack of employment prospects and to poor living conditions. Of the remaining work-force, some 25% were employed by the Government or statutory bodies. The population was enumerated at 4,482 in the census of May 2001, and it was hoped that a reduction in volcanic activity would encourage Montserratians resident abroad to return home, thereby stimulating the economy. By 2004, however, the population was estimated to have reached just 4,690. It was anticipated that the ongoing reconstruction efforts and the development of the island as a centre for environmental tourism would stimulate short-term economic growth, while in the long term it was hoped to re-establish Montserrat as a centre for international financial services. At the end of 2003 some 22 International Business Companies and two banks were registered in the Territory. However, Montserrat's economic prospects depended entirely on the activity of the volcano, and although reconstruction work was in progress, other areas of the economy were likely to remain at extremely low levels of output for some years. The Government set aside EC $7m. of the 2004 budget for a three-year 'tourism repositioning strategy', aimed at capitalizing on Montserrat's considerable environmental assets; this amount was in addition to $9m. provided in October 2003 by the British Government for development of the local tourism industry. New port infrastructure was brought into operation during 2004 and an air terminal, which included a 600 m airstrip, suitable for small aircraft bound for neighbouring islands, and funded by the EU and the United Kingdom, was opened in early 2005. The tourism sector was adversely affected by a series of problems in 2005, including the suspension of ferry services. In mid-2008 Montserrat was named as one of the Caribbean economies at risk from illegal financial practice owing to a dearth of qualified investigators within the financial system. Although an estimated 150 people were working in the financial sector in Montserrat, only one employee was believed to be capable of investigating fraudulent behaviour. The economy contracted during 2006, but was estimated to have grown by 1.7% in 2007, with forecasts expecting growth to rise towards 2.0% in 2008. The potential for further volcanic activity remains a threat to the economy, with the Government considering a relocation fund as part of future budget expenditure.

Education
Education, beginning at five years of age, is compulsory up to the age of 14. In 1993 there were 11 primary schools, including 10 government schools. Secondary education begins at 12 years of age, and comprises a first cycle of five years and a second, two-year cycle. In 1989 there was one government secondary school and one private secondary school. In addition, in 1993 there were 12 nursery schools, sponsored by a government-financed organization, and a Technical College, which provided vocational and technical training for school-leavers. There was also an extra-mural department of the University of the West Indies in Plymouth. In 2002 the European Union (EU) and the United Kingdom contributed a total of EC $6m. to the construction of a further education college, the Montserrat Community College, which was completed in late 2003. A nursery school was constructed in 2002 with a further nursery school opened in Salem in September 2005 as part of the Government's commitment to providing increased access to early childhood education. Three 'offshore' medical schools were licensed in 2003. The Ministry of Education was allocated a total of EC $8.3m. in the 2008 budget.

Public Holidays
2008: 1 January (New Year's Day), 17 March (St Patrick's Day), 21 March (Good Friday), 24 March (Easter Monday), 5 May (Labour Day), 12 May (Whit Monday), 14 June (Queen's Official Birthday), 4 August (August Monday), 23 November (Liberation Day), 25–26 December (Christmas), 31 December (Festival Day).

2009: 1 January (New Year's Day), 17 March (St Patrick's Day), 10 April (Good Friday), 13 April (Easter Monday), 4 May (Labour Day), 1 June (Whit Monday), 13 June (Queen's Official Birthday), 3 August (August Monday), 23 November (Liberation Day), 25–26 December (Christmas), 31 December (Festival Day).

Weights and Measures
The imperial system is in use but the metric system is being introduced.

Statistical Survey

Sources (unless otherwise stated): Government Information Service, Media Centre, Chief Minister's Office, Old Towne; tel. 491-2702; fax 491-2711; Eastern Caribbean Central Bank, POB 89, Basseterre, Saint Christopher; internet www.eccb-centralbank.org; OECS Economic Affairs Secretariat, *Statistical Digest*.

AREA AND POPULATION
Area: 102 sq km (39.5 sq miles).

Population: 10,639 (males 5,290, females 5,349) at census of 12 May 1991; 4,491 at census of 12 May 2001 (Source: UN, *Population and Vital Statistics Report*). 2006 (projected estimate at mid-year): 5,027.

Density (mid-2006): 49.3 per sq km.

Principal Towns: Plymouth, the former capital, was abandoned in 1997. Brades is the interim capital.

Births and Deaths (1999): 45 live births (birth rate 9.4 per 1,000); 59 deaths (death rate 12.4 per 1,000) (Source: UN, *Population and Vital Statistics Report*). 2003: Crude birth rate 9.6 per 1,000; Crude death rate 12.3 per 1,000 (Source: Caribbean Development Bank, *Social and Economic Indicators*). 2007: Crude birth rate 17.5 per 1,000; Crude death rate 7.0 per 1,000 (Source: Pan American Health Organization).

Expectation of Life (years at birth, estimates): 79.0 (males 76.8; females 81.3) in 2007. Source: Pan American Health Organization.

Employment (1992): Agriculture, forestry and fishing 298; Mining and manufacturing 254; Electricity, gas and water 68; Wholesale and retail trade 1,666; Restaurants and hotels 234; Transport and communication 417; Finance, insurance and business services 242; Public defence 390; Other community, social and personal services 952; *Total* 4,521 (Source: *The Commonwealth Yearbook*). 1998 (estimate): Total labour force 1,500.

HEALTH AND WELFARE
Physicians (per 1,000 head, 1999): 0.18.

Hospital Beds (per 1,000 head, 2004): 3.3.

Health Expenditure (public, % of GDP, 2000): 7.7.

Health Expenditure (public, % of total, 1995): 67.0.

Source: Pan American Health Organization.

For sources and definitions, see explanatory note on p. vi.

AGRICULTURE, ETC.
Principal Crops (metric tons, 2006, FAO estimates): Vegetables 475; Fruit (excl. melons) 710.

Livestock ('000 head, 2006, FAO estimates): Cattle 9.7; Sheep 4.7; Goats 7.0; Pigs 1.1.

Livestock Products ('000 metric tons, 2006, FAO estimates): Cattle meat 0.7; Cows' milk 2.3.

Fishing (metric tons, live weight, 2005, FAO estimate): Total catch 50 (all marine fishes).

Source: FAO.

INDUSTRY
Electric Energy (million kWh): 10.6 in 2004; 11.3 in 2005; 11.4 in 2006.

FINANCE
Currency and Exchange Rates: 100 cents = 1 East Caribbean dollar (EC $). *Sterling, US Dollar and Euro Equivalents* (30 November 2007): £1 sterling = EC $5.579; US $1 = EC $2.700; €1 = EC $3.985; EC $100 = £17.92 = US $37.04 = €25.09. *Exchange Rate:* Fixed at US $1 = EC $2.70 since July 1976.

Budget (EC $ million, 2006, provisional figures): *Revenue:* Revenue from taxation 31.8 (Taxes on income and profits 13.5, Taxes on property 1.4, Taxes on domestic goods and services 3.5, Taxes on international trade and transactions 13.4); Non-tax revenue 2.7; Total 34.5 (excl. grants 63.6). *Expenditure:* Current expenditure 84.0 (Personal emoluments 35.5, Goods and services 25.7, Interest payments 1.2, Transfers and subsidies 21.6); Capital expenditure 18.6; Total 102.6.

International Reserves (US $ million at 31 December 2007): Foreign exchange 14.50. Source: IMF, *International Financial Statistics*.

Money Supply (EC $ million at 31 December 2007): Currency outside banks 15.07; Demand deposits at deposit money banks 33.24; *Total money* 48.32. Source: IMF, *International Financial Statistics*.

Cost of Living (Consumer Price Index; base: previous year = 100): 99.2 in 2003; 104.3 in 2004; 101.76 in 2005. Source: partly Caribbean Development Bank, *Social and Economic Indicators*.

Gross Domestic Product (EC $ million at constant 1990 prices): 60.8 in 2004; 60.6 in 2005; 58.9 in 2006. Source: Caribbean Development Bank, *Social and Economic Indicators*.

Expenditure on the Gross Domestic Product (EC $ million at current prices, 2006): Government final consumption expenditure 74.91; Private final consumption expenditure 114.47; Gross fixed capital formation 32.48; *Total domestic expenditure* 221.86; Export of goods and services 41.69; *Less* Imports of goods and services 141.04; *GDP at market prices* 122.52.

Gross Domestic Product by Economic Activity (EC $ million at current prices, 2006): Agriculture, forestry and fishing 1.22; Mining and quarrying 0.64; Manufacturing 0.81; Electricity and water 7.63; Construction 9.19; Wholesale and retail trade 4.67; Restaurants and hotels 1.13; Transport 8.84; Communications 3.68; Banks and insurance 10.69; Real estate and housing 14.48; Government services 43.72; Other services 8.08; *Sub-total* 114.78; *Less* Financial intermediation services indirectly measured 8.63; *Gross value added at basic prices* 106.15; Taxes, less subsidies, on products 16.37; *GDP at market prices* 122.52.

Balance of Payments (EC $ million, 2006, provisional): Goods (net) –66.9; Services (net) –32.4; *Balance on goods and services* – 99.3; Income (net) –8.7; *Balance on goods, services and income* – 108.0; Current transfers (net) 64.8; *Current balance* –43.3; Capital account (net) 36.2; Direct investment (net) 2.2; Portfolio investment (net) 0.0; Public sector long-term investment (net) –0.4; Commercial banks –1.0; Other investment assets –5.7; Other investment liabilities (incl. net errors and omissions) 13.8; *Overall balance* 1.6.

EXTERNAL TRADE
Principal Commodities (US $ million, 2005): *Imports c.i.f.:* Food and live animals 3.8; Beverages and tobacco 1.6; Crude materials (inedible) except fuels 0.9; Mineral fuels, lubricants, etc. 7.4; Chemicals 1.5; Manufactured goods 4.9; Machinery and transport equipment 7.0; Miscellaneous manufactured articles 2.3; Total (incl. others) 29.8. *Exports f.o.b.:* Mineral fuels, lubricants, etc. 0.3; Machinery and transport equipment 0.5; Miscellaneous manufactured articles 0.2; Total (incl. others) 1.4.

Principal Trading Partners (US $ million, 2005): *Imports c.i.f.:* Barbados 0.6; Canada 0.6; Dominica 0.3; Japan 1.4; Netherlands 0.3; Trinidad and Tobago 4.3; United Kingdom 2.3; USA 16.8; Total (incl. others) 29.8. *Exports f.o.b.:* Antigua and Barbuda 0.4; United Kingdom 0.2; USA 0.3; Total (incl. others) 1.4.

Source: UN Statistics Division.

TOURISM

Tourist Arrivals (2005, revised figures): Stay-over arrivals 9,690 (USA 2,034, Canada 404, United Kingdom 2,968, Caribbean 3,987, Others 297); Excursionists 3,137; Cruise-ship passengers 169; *Total visitor arrivals* 12,996.

Tourism Receipts (EC $ million): 24.8 in 2004; 24.3 in 2005; 20.9 in 2006 (provisional figure).

TRANSPORT

Road Traffic (vehicles in use, 1990): Passenger cars 1,823; Goods vehicles 54; Public service vehicles 4; Motorcycles 21; Miscellaneous 806.

Shipping ('000 metric tons, 1990): *International Freight Traffic:* Goods loaded 6; Goods unloaded 49. Source: UN, *Monthly Bulletin of Statistics*.

Civil Aviation (1985): Aircraft arrivals 4,422; passengers 25,380; air cargo 132.4 metric tons.

COMMUNICATIONS MEDIA

Radio Receivers (1997): 7,000 in use.
Television Receivers (1999): 3,000 in use.
Telephones (2000): 2,811 main lines in use.
Mobile Cellular Telephones (2000): 489 subscribers.
Non-daily Newspapers (1996): 2 (estimated circulation 3,000).

Sources: UNESCO, *Statistical Yearbook*; International Telecommunication Union.

EDUCATION

Pre-primary (1993/94): 12 schools; 31 teachers; 407 pupils.
Primary: 2 schools (1999); 85 teacher (1993/94); 460 pupils (2003).
Secondary: 1 school (1999); 80 teachers (1993/94); 308 pupils (2003).

Sources: UNESCO, *Statistical Yearbook*; Caribbean Development Bank, *Social and Economic Indicators*, *The Commonwealth Yearbook*.

Directory

The eruption in June 1997 of the Soufrière Hills volcano, and subsequent volcanic activity, rendered some two-thirds of Montserrat uninhabitable and destroyed the capital, Plymouth. Islanders were evacuated to a 'safe zone' in the north of the island.

The Constitution

The present Constitution came into force on 19 December 1989 and made few amendments to the constitutional order established in 1960. The Constitution now guarantees the fundamental rights and freedoms of the individual and grants the Territory the right of self-determination. Montserrat is governed by a Governor and has its own Executive and Legislative Councils. The Governor retains responsibility for defence, external affairs (including international financial affairs) and internal security. The Executive Council consists of the Governor as President, the Chief Minister and three other Ministers, the Attorney-General and the Financial Secretary. The Legislative Council consists of the Speaker (chosen from outside the Council), nine elected, two official and two nominated members. Owing to the disruption caused by evacuation from the south of the island, both the 2001 and 2006 general elections were conducted according to a new 'at large' voting system, without constituencies, but still choosing nine members of the legislature. A constitutional review process was ongoing in early 2008.

The Government

Governor: PETER ANDREW WATERWORTH (took office in July 2007).

EXECUTIVE COUNCIL
(April 2008)

President: PETER ANDREW WATERWORTH (The Governor).
Official Members:
Attorney-General: EUGENE OTUONYE.
Financial Secretary: JOHN SKERRIT.
Chief Minister and Minister of Finance and Economic Development: Dr LOWELL LEWIS.
Minister of Agriculture, Lands, Housing and the Environment: REUBEN T. MEADE.
Minister of Communications and Works: CHARLES KIRNON.
Minister of Education, Labour, Health and Community Services: ROSELYN CASSELL-SEALY.
Clerk to the Executive Council: (vacant).

MINISTRIES

Office of the Governor: Farara Plaza, Brades; tel. 491-2688; fax 491-8867; e-mail govoff@candw.ms; internet www.gov.ms/index/governor.htm.
Office of the Chief Minister: Govt HQ, POB 292, Brades; tel. 491-3378; fax 491-6780; e-mail ocm@gov.ms; internet www.gov.ms/index/chief_minister.htm.
Ministry of Agriculture, Lands, Housing and the Environment: Govt HQ, POB 272, Brades; tel. 491-2546; fax 491-9275; e-mail malhe@gov.ms; internet www.malhe.gov.ms.
Ministry of Communications and Works: Woodlands; tel. 491-2521; fax 491-3475; e-mail mcw@gov.ms; internet www.gov.ms/commsworks.
Ministry of Education, Health, Community Services and Labour: Govt HQ, POB 103, Brades; tel. 491-2541; fax 491-6941; e-mail deped@gov.ms; internet www.mehcs.gov.ms.
Ministry of Finance and Economic Development: Govt HQ, POB 292, Brades; tel. 491-2777; fax 491-2367; e-mail minfin@gov.ms; internet www.finance.gov.ms.

LEGISLATIVE COUNCIL

Speaker: Dr JOSEPH MEADE.
Election, 31 May 2006

Party	Seats
Movement for Change and Prosperity	4
New People's Liberation Movement	3
Montserrat Democratic Party	1
Independent	1
Total	9

There are also two ex officio members (the Attorney-General and the Financial Secretary) and two nominated members.

Political Organizations

Montserrat Democratic Party (MDP): c/o Kelsick & Kelsick, Woodlands Main Rd, POB 185, Brades; tel. 491-2102; e-mail kelkel@candw.ms; internet www.mdp.ms; Leader Dr LOWELL LEWIS; Chair. JEAN KELSICK.
Movement for Change and Prosperity (MCAP): POB 419, Brades; e-mail mail@mcap.ms; internet www.mcap.ms; f. 2005 by fmr mems of the National Progressive Party (NPP); Leader ROSELYN CASSELL-SEALY; Chair. RANDOLPH RILEY.
New People's Liberation Movement (NPLM): f. 1997 as successor party to People's Progressive Alliance and the Movement for National Reconstruction (MNR); opposition party; Leader DAVID BRANDY; Chair. IDABELLE MEADE.

Judicial System

Justice is administered by the Eastern Caribbean Supreme Court (based in Saint Lucia—comprised of the Court of Appeal and the High Court), the Court of Summary Jurisdiction and the Magistrate's Court. A revised edition of the Laws of Montserrat came into force on 15 April 2005, following five years of preparation by a Law Revision Committee.

Puisne Judge (Montserrat Circuit): JANICE MESADIS GEORGE-CREQUE (concurrently accredited to Anguilla).
Magistrate: CLIFTON WARNER, Govt HQ, Brades; tel. 491-4056; fax 491-8866; e-mail magoff@gov.ms.
Registrar: AMILA DALEY, Govt HQ, Brades; tel. 491-3827; fax 491-4687; e-mail courtreg@candw.ms.

Religion

CHRISTIANITY

The Montserrat Christian Council: St Peter's, POB 227; tel. 491-4864; fax 491-2139; Chair. Rev. B. RUTH ALLEN.

The Anglican Communion

Anglicans are adherents of the Church in the Province of the West Indies, comprising eight dioceses. Montserrat forms part of the diocese of the North Eastern Caribbean and Aruba. The Bishop is resident in The Valley, Anguilla.

The Roman Catholic Church

Montserrat forms part of the diocese of St John's-Basseterre, suffragan to the archdiocese of Castries (Saint Lucia). The Bishop is resident in St John's, Antigua and Barbuda.

Other Christian Churches

There are Baptist, Methodist, Pentecostal and Seventh-day Adventist churches and other places of worship on the island.

The Press

Montserrat Newsletter: Farara Plaza, Unit 8, Brades; tel. 491-2688; fax 491-8867; e-mail richard.aspin@fco.gov.uk; internet www.montserrat-newsletter.com; f. 1998; govt information publ; Publicity Officer RICHARD ASPIN.

The Montserrat Reporter: POB 306, Davy Hill; tel. 491-4715; fax 491-2430; e-mail editor@montserratreporter.org; internet www.themontserratreporter.com; weekly on Fridays; circ. 2,000; Editor BENNETTE ROACH.

Broadcasting and Communications

TELECOMMUNICATIONS

Cable & Wireless (West Indies) Ltd: POB 219, Sweeney's; tel. 491-1000; fax 491-3599; e-mail venus.george@cwni.cwplc.com; internet www.cwmontserrat.com.

BROADCASTING

Prior to the volcanic eruption of June 1997 there were three radio stations operating in Montserrat. Television services can also be obtained from Saint Christopher and Nevis, Puerto Rico and from Antigua and Barbuda (ABS).

Radio

Gem Radio Network: POB 488, Barzey's; tel. 491-5728; fax 491-5729; f. 1984; commercial; Station Man. KEVIN LEWIS; Man. Dir KENNETH LEE.

Radio Antilles: POB 35/930; tel. 491-2755; fax 491-2724; f. 1963; in 1989 the Govt of Montserrat, on behalf of the OECS, acquired the station; has one of the most powerful transmitters in the region; commercial; regional; broadcasts in English and French; Chair. Dr H. FELLHAUER; Man. Dir KRISTIAN KNAACK; Gen. Man. KEITH GREAVES.

Radio Montserrat (ZJB): POB 51, Sweeney's; tel. 491-2885; fax 491-9250; e-mail zjb@gov.ms; internet www.zjb.gov.ms; f. 1952; first broadcast 1957; govt station; Station Man. ROSE WILLOCK; CEO LOWELL MASON.

Television

Cable Television of Montserrat Ltd: POB 447, Olveston; tel. 491-2507; fax 491-3081; Man. SYLVIA WHITE.

People's Television (PTV): POB 82, Brades; tel. 491-5110; Man. DENZIL EDGECOMBE.

Finance

The Eastern Caribbean Central Bank, based in Saint Christopher and Nevis, is the central issuing and monetary authority for Montserrat.

Eastern Caribbean Central Bank—Montserrat Office: 2 Farara Plaza, POB 484, Brades; tel. 491–6877; fax 491-6878; e-mail eccbmni@candw.ms; internet www.eccb-centralbank.org; Resident Rep. CHARLES T. JOHN.

Financial Services Commission: Phoenix House, POB 188, Brades; tel. 491-6887; fax 491-9888; e-mail enquiries@fsc.ms; internet www.fsc.ms; f. 2002; the Commission consists of the Commissioner and three other mems appointed by the Governor; Chair. JOHN LAWRENCE.

BANKING

Bank of Montserrat Ltd: Hilltop, POB 10, St Peters; tel. 491-3843; fax 491-3163; e-mail bom@candw.ag; Man. ANTON DOLDRON.

Montserrat Building Society: POB 101, Brades Main Rd, Brades; tel. 491-2391; fax 491-6127; e-mail mbsl@candw.ms.

St Patrick's Co-operative Credit Union Ltd: POB 337, Brades; tel. 491-3666; fax 491-6566; e-mail monndf@candw.ms; Exec. Dir ROSELYN CASSELL-SEALY.

STOCK EXCHANGE

Eastern Caribbean Securities Exchange: based in Basseterre, Saint Christopher and Nevis; tel. (869) 466-7192; fax (869) 465-3798; e-mail info@ecseonline.com; internet www.ecseonline.com; f. 2001; regional securities market designed to facilitate the buying and selling of financial products for the eight member territories—Anguilla, Antigua and Barbuda, Dominica, Grenada, Montserrat, Saint Christopher and Nevis, Saint Lucia and Saint Vincent and the Grenadines; Gen. Man. TREVOR E. BLAKE.

INSURANCE

British American Insurance Co Ltd: POB 77, St Peter's; tel. 491-2361; fax 491-9361.

Insurance Services (Montserrat) Ltd: POB 185, Brades; tel. 491-2103; fax 491-6013; e-mail ismcall@candw.ag; Gen. Man. STEPHEN FRANCOIS.

NAGICO: Ryan Investments, Brades; tel. 491-3403; fax 491-7307; e-mail talicj@yahoo.com.

N. E. M. (West Indies) Insurance Ltd (NEMWIL): POB 287, Brades; tel. 491-3813; fax 491-3815.

United Insurance Co Ltd: Jacquie Ryan Enterprises Ltd, POB 425, Brades; tel. 491-2055; fax 491-3257; e-mail united@candw.ms; CEO JACQUIE RYAN.

Trade and Industry

GOVERNMENT AGENCY

Montserrat Economic Development Unit: Govt HQ, POB 292, Brades; tel. 491-2066; fax 491-4632; e-mail devunit@gov.ms; internet www.devunit.gov.ms.

CHAMBER OF COMMERCE

Montserrat Chamber of Commerce and Industry (MCCI): Vue Pointe Hotel, Old Towne, POB 384, Brades, Plymouth; tel. 491-3640; fax 491-6602; e-mail chamber@candw.ms; refounded 1971; 31 company mems, 26 individual mems; Pres. BRUCE FARARA; Sec.-Treas. FLORENCE GRIFFITH-JOSEPH.

UTILITIES

Electricity

Montserrat Electricity Services Ltd (MONLEC): POB 16, St John's; tel. 491-3148; fax 491-3143; e-mail monlec@candw.ms; domestic electricity generation and supply; the permanent power station at Plymouth was abandoned in 1995; an emergency facility was established in Salem and subsequently relocated to Brades; plans for the formation of a state-owned co, Montserrat Utilities Ltd, by the merger Monlec and Montserrat Water Authority (MWA) were well advanced by early 2008 although the terms of the amalgamation had yet to be finalized; Montserrat Utilities Ltd was operating a third office, in addition to those of Monlec and MWA, during the transition period

Montserrat Utilities Ltd (MUL): c/o Montserrat Water Authority, POB 324, Davy Hill; tel. 491-2538; internet www.mul.ms.

Gas

Grant Enterprises and Trading: POB 350, Brades; tel. 491-9654; fax 491-4854; e-mail granten@candw.ms; domestic gas supplies.

Water

Montserrat Water Authority: POB 324, Davy Hill; tel. 491-2527; fax 491-4904; e-mail mwa@candw.ms; f. 1972; domestic water supplies; negotiations towards finalizing a merger with Montserrat Electricity Services Ltd remained ongoing in 2008 (see Electricity); Chair. LYNDELL GREER; Man. EMILE DUBERRY.

TRADE UNIONS

Montserrat Allied Workers' Union (MAWU): POB 245, Dagenham, Plymouth; tel. 491-5049; fax 491-6145; e-mail bramblehl@candw.ag; f. 1973; private-sector employees; Pres. CHARLES RYAN; Gen. Sec. HYLROY BRAMBLE; 1,000 mems.

UNITED KINGDOM OVERSEAS TERRITORIES

Montserrat Civil Service Association: POB 468, Plymouth; tel. 491-6797; fax 491-5655; e-mail lewisp@gov.ms; Pres. PAUL LEWIS.

Montserrat Seamen's and Waterfront Workers' Union: tel. 491-6335; fax 491-6335; f. 1980; Sec.-Gen. CHEDMOND BROWNE; 100 mems.

Montserrat Union of Teachers: POB 460, Plymouth; tel. 491-4382; fax 491-5779; f. 1978; Pres. JOSEPH H. MEADE; Gen. Sec. HYACINTH BRAMBLE-BROWNE; 46 mems.

Transport

The eruption in June 1997 of the Soufrière Hills volcano, and subsequent volcanic activity, destroyed much of the infrastructure in the southern two-thirds of the island, including the country's principal port and airport facilities, as well as the road network.

ROADS

Prior to the volcanic eruption of June 1997 Montserrat had an extensive and well-constructed road network. There were 203 km (126 miles) of good surfaced main roads, 24 km of secondary unsurfaced roads and 42 km of rough tracks. Government expenditure on road rehabilitation works in 2006 amounted to more than US $3m., while a further US $0.5m. was allocated to the maintenance budget of the Public Works Department for surfacing of the secondary road network. The 2007 budget allocated funds of over US $5m. for continued road and infrastructure improvements, particularly in areas to become more densely populated through housing developments carried out under the Emergency Resettlement Strategy. A five-year roads development project proposal, to cost $20m., was also submitted to the British Department for International Development in that year.

SHIPPING

The principal port at Plymouth was destroyed by the volcanic activity of June 1997. An emergency jetty was constructed at Little Bay in the north of the island. Regular transshipment steamship services are provided by Harrison Line and Nedlloyd Line. The Bermuth Line and the West Indies Shipping Service link Montserrat with Miami, USA, and with neighbouring territories. Local protest followed the discontinuation of a ferry service with Antigua, which occurred at the end of July 2005, as a result of the inauguration of the new airport facilities. Negotiations were ongoing in mid-2008 towards reinstating the ferry service, however, owing to the dramatic impact its suspension had effected upon tourist arrivals.

Port Authority of Montserrat: Little Bay, POB 383, Plymouth; tel. 491-2791; fax 491-8063; e-mail monpa@candw.ms; Man. SHAWN O'GARRO.

Montserrat Shipping Services: POB 46, Carr's Bay; tel. 491-3614; fax 491-3617.

CIVIL AVIATION

The main airport, Blackburne at Trants, 13 km (8 miles) from Plymouth, was destroyed by the volcanic activity of June 1997. A helicopter port at Gerald's in the north of the island was completed in 2000. A new, temporary international airport at Gerald's, financed at a cost of EC $51.95m. by the European Union and the British Department for International Development, was completed in 2005; a new terminal building was opened in February and the airport officially opened in July, to be serviced by Windward Islands Airways International (WINAIR). Despite complaints over the high ticket prices—given WINAIR's monopoly on transport to and from the island and the apparent failure of tourists to take up the new facility—in mid-2007 WINAIR was awarded a one-year licence extension to operate scheduled flights into and out of Gerald's Airport until July 2008. In the longer term, the Government intended to construct a permanent international airport at Thatch Valley. Montserrat is linked to Antigua by a helicopter service, which operates three times a day. The island is also a shareholder in the regional airline, LIAT (based in Antigua and Barbuda), which acquired its troubled rival, Caribbean Star Airlines, in October 2007.

Air Montserrat: tel. 491-6728; fax 491-6729; internet www.airmontserrat.com; f. 2006; operated by Trans Anguilla Airways (2000) Ltd; operates charter services to neighbouring islands, incl. four daily flights to Antigua.

Montserrat Airways Ltd: Plymouth; tel. 491-5342; charter services; subsidiary of Love Air, United Kingdom; Man. Dir NIGEL HARRIS.

Tourism

Since the 1997 volcanic activity, Montserrat has been marketed as an eco-tourism destination. Known as the 'Emerald Isle of the Caribbean', Montserrat is noted for its Irish connections, and for its range of flora and fauna. In 2005 there were 9,690 stay-over tourist arrivals. In that year some 46% of tourist arrivals were from Caribbean countries, 28% from the United Kingdom, 20% from the USA and 3% from Canada. In addition there were 3,137 excursionists and 169 cruise-ship passengers. A large proportion of visitors are estimated to be Montserrat nationals residing overseas. The sector experienced a downturn in 2005 and 2006, partly attributed to increased volcanic activity on the island, when total visitor arrivals were reported as 12,996 and 9,500, respectively. A decline in the number of excursionists making day-trips to the island in these years (falling to 1,509 in 2006) was blamed on the discontinuation of the ferry service between Montserrat and Antigua, and transport links continued to pose a challenge to the sector. Plans to reinstate the ferry service were under discussion in early 2007 in an attempt to reverse this trend, although no progress had been made by mid-2008. It was similarly hoped that the introduction of a new air charter service, Air Montserrat, from December 2006 would precipitate an upturn in future tourist arrivals. Tourism earnings of EC $20.9m. were recorded in 2006.

Montserrat Tourist Board: 7 Farara Plaza, Bldgs B and C, POB 7, Brades; tel. 491-2230; fax 491-7430; e-mail info@montserrattourism.ms; internet www.visitmontserrat.com; f. 1993; Chair. JOHN PONTEEN; Dir of Tourism ERNESTINE CASSELL.

THE PITCAIRN ISLANDS

Introduction

The Pitcairn Islands consist of Pitcairn Island and three uninhabited islands, Henderson, Ducie and Oeno. Pitcairn, situated at 25°04′ S, and 130°06′ W, and about midway between Panama and New Zealand, has an area of 4.5 sq km (1.75 sq miles) and had a population of 46 in mid-2005.

Discovered in 1767 and first settled by the British in 1790, Pitcairn officially became a British settlement in 1887. In 1893 a parliamentary form of government was adopted, and in 1898 responsibility for administration was assumed by the High Commissioner for the Western Pacific. Pitcairn came under the jurisdiction of the Governor of Fiji in 1952, and, from 1970 onwards, of the British High Commissioner in New Zealand acting as Governor, in consultation with an Island Council, presided over by the Island Magistrate (who is elected triennially) and comprising one ex-officio member (the Island Secretary), five elected and three nominated members.

In 1987 the British High Commissioner in Fiji, acting on behalf of Pitcairn, the United Kingdom's last remaining dependency in the South Pacific, joined representatives of the USA, France, New Zealand and six South Pacific island states in signing the South Pacific Regional Environment Protection Convention, the main aim of which is to prevent the dumping of nuclear waste in the region.

In 1989 uninhabited Henderson Island was included on the UNESCO 'World Heritage List'. The island, 168 km (104 miles) east-north-east of Pitcairn, was to be preserved as a bird sanctuary. There are five species of bird unique to the island: the flightless rail or Henderson chicken, the green Henderson fruit dove, the Henderson crake, the Henderson warbler and the Henderson lorikeet. However, concern was expressed in 1994 following claims by scientists studying the island that its unique flora and fauna were threatened by the accidental introduction of foreign plant species by visitors and by an increase in the rat population.

Following some structural changes in the local government of Pitcairn, Steve Christian was elected to the position of Mayor in December 1999, presiding over the Island Council (a role previously fulfilled by the Island Magistrate).

In early 2000 British detectives began an investigation into an alleged rape case on the island. The British team was joined by the New Zealand police force in early 2001, when the case was widened to include 15 alleged sexual assaults, amid reports claiming that sexual abuse, particularly of children, was commonplace on the island. The trial, which was expected to take place in Auckland, New Zealand, would represent the first significant criminal case on Pitcairn since a murder trial in 1897. In November 2000 Auckland's Crown Solicitor, Simon Moore, was appointed Pitcairn's first Public Prosecutor, with the task of deciding whether to bring charges against 20 Pitcairn

Islanders. His decision was delayed by the fact that many of the complainants now lived in New Zealand and by the logistical problems of a trial that could potentially involve the entire populace. However, in April 2003 a judicial delegation of eight people visited Pitcairn and nine men on the island were charged with a total of 64 offences, some of which dated back about 40 years. Many islanders expressed serious concern that their community would not be able to manage if the men (who constituted virtually the entire male workforce) were extradited to New Zealand to stand trial. In early June a further four men, all now resident in New Zealand, were charged with a total of 32 offences, including 10 charges of rape, which were alleged to have taken place on Pitcairn between five and 40 years previously. In April 2004 the Supreme Court of Pitcairn (sitting for only the second time in its history, at a special session in Auckland) rejected the accused men's application to be tried on Pitcairn, reiterating that they should stand trial in New Zealand. However, in late June Pitcairn's Court of Appeal (sitting for the first time in its history) overruled this decision and stated that, despite the logistical problems involved, the trial would be conducted on Pitcairn. Meanwhile, lawyers for the accused men argued that the trial should be abandoned as the islanders were all descendants of the *Bounty* mutineers, who had renounced all allegiance to the British Crown. Their claims that Pitcairn Islanders were not subject to British jurisdiction appeared to be supported by historical documents discovered in London. Moreover, a group of women from Pitcairn issued a public statement claiming that sexual relations between men and girls below the British legal age of consent were commonplace on the island, and not considered to be a criminal offence by either party or by the community as a whole. However, in late September 2004 the trial of seven of the defendants began in converted school premises on Pitcairn. Some 25 lawyers, police officers and journalists travelled to the island, and witnesses in New Zealand gave evidence via live satellite video link. The trial concluded in late October. Six of the seven defendants were found guilty of many of the 51 charges against them. One islander was acquitted of the charges against him. Among those convicted was the Mayor of Pitcairn, Steve Christian, who was found guilty of five counts of rape. The convicted men, four of whom were given prison sentences of between two and six years while two received non-custodial sentences, began a legal challenge against their convictions in February 2005. Their defence was based on a previous claim that Pitcairn Islanders were not subject to British jurisdiction. In May their appeal was rejected by the Pitcairn Supreme Court, sitting in Auckland, New Zealand. In 2006 the men took their appeal to the United Kingdom's highest court, the Privy Council, arguing that they were not British subjects and that English law did not apply on Pitcairn. In October the judges rejected their appeal, declaring that Pitcairn had been ruled by the Crown as a British possession for more than 100 years, and was thus unable to reject a law affirming it as such. Furthermore, the judges decided that there was absolutely no doubt that the laws on sexual offences applied to the six men. The convicted men helped to build a new prison. Seven New Zealand prison officers were dispatched to staff the new facility. In 2008 there were fears that the serious rift created in the island community by the repercussions of the trial might contribute to an eventual decline in the viability of Pitcairn.

At elections to the Island Council in December 2004 five new Council members were elected and Jay Warren, the only defendant to be acquitted in the recent trials, was elected as the island's Mayor. In April 2006 George Fergusson, the newly appointed British High Commissioner to New Zealand, replaced Richard Fell as Governor of Pitcairn, Henderson, Ducie and Oeno Islands. Michael Warren was elected Mayor in December 2007, defeating the incumbent, Jay Warren, and one other candidate.

The island's population increased in March 2006 after the birth of only the second baby in more than 18 years. The child's father was Randy Christian, one of the six men convicted in 2004 on charges of rape.

In early 2007 a retired British police sergeant, Malcolm Gilbert from the Orkney Islands, was recruited by the Foreign and Commonwealth Office on a 12-month contract to police the island.

The British Overseas Territories Act, which took effect in May 2002, granted citizenship rights in the United Kingdom to residents of the Overseas Territories, including Pitcairn. The legislation also entitled Pitcairn Islanders to hold British passports and to work in the United Kingdom and elsewhere in the European Union.

The economy has been based on subsistence gardening, fishing, handicrafts and the sale of postage stamps. Attempts to increase revenue from the island's agricultural output by producing dried fruits (notably bananas, mangoes and pineapples) began in 1999. Diversification of this sector to include production of jam, dried fish and coffee was subsequently under consideration. In early 1999 the Pitcairn Island police and customs office requested that no honey or beeswax be sent to the Territory in order to protect from disease the island's growing honey industry, which was being developed as a source of foreign exchange. Pitcairn honey, which was pronounced to be 'exceptionally pure' by the New Zealand Ministry of Agriculture, began to be exported, largely through internet sales, in late 1999. A new stamp was issued to commemorate the launch of the industry.

A reafforestation scheme, begun in 1963, concentrated on the planting of miro trees, which provide a rosewood suitable for handicrafts. An exclusive economic zone (EEZ) extending 370 km (200 nautical miles) off shore was designated in 1980 and officially declared in 1992. In 1987 the Governor of the islands signed a one-year fishing agreement with Japan, whereby the Japan Tuna Fisheries Co-operative Association was granted a licence to operate vessels within Pitcairn's EEZ. The agreement was subsequently renewed, but lapsed in 1990.

In early 1992 it was reported that significant mineral deposits, formed by underwater volcanoes, had been discovered within the islands' EEZ. The minerals, which were believed to include manganese, iron, copper, zinc, silver and gold, could (if exploited) dramatically affect the Territory's economy.

New Zealand currency is used. There is no taxation (except for small licensing fees on guns and vehicles), and government revenue has been derived mainly from philatelic sales (one-half of current revenue in 1992/93), and from interest earned on investments. In 1998/99 revenue totalled $NZ492,000 and expenditure $NZ667,000. In the early 2000s revenue was estimated to total about $NZ415,000 annually. Capital assistance worth an average of £100,000 annually is received from the United Kingdom. In 2003/04 exports from Pitcairn to New Zealand were worth $NZ6,000, while imports from that country cost $NZ739,000. Exports to Australia totalled $A21,000 in 2000/01, while imports from Australia, consisting mainly of food, totalled $A7,000 in that year. Pitcairn's imports from the USA totalled US $5.5m. in 2001, while exports to the USA were worth US $0.2m. It was hoped that Pitcairn might find an additional source of revenue through the sale of website addresses in early 2000 when the island won a legal victory to gain control of its internet domain name suffix '.pn'. Hopes have also been expressed that the development of the tourism sector might provide some impetus to economic growth in the near future, and initiatives to facilitate this through the improvement of cruise-ship berthing facilities were under discussion in 2008.

Development projects have been focused on harbour improvements, power supplies, telecommunications and road-building. Pitcairn's first radio-telephone link was established in 1985, and a modern telecommunications unit was installed in 1992. A new health clinic was established, with British finance, in 1996. Major improvements to the jetty and slipway at Bounty Bay and to the Hill of Difficulty road, which leads to the landing area, were carried out in 2005. In the same year a museum was constructed on the island to house some of Pitcairn's historical artefacts, including the Bounty cannon, which had been raised from Bounty Bay several years previously.

A steady decline in the population, due mainly to emigration to New Zealand, has been a major problem. In March 2001 a New Zealand company expressed an interest in acquiring development rights on Pitcairn with the aim of establishing fishing and tourism projects. In May 2002 the company's director reportedly announced that the development would begin within the next 12 months, describing plans for a lodge on Pitcairn and for a floating hotel off Oeno Island. The British High Commission in Wellington, however, emphasized that any such developments remained subject to the approval of Pitcairn Island Council, but that the company was welcome to submit proposals.

In August 2004 the British Government announced the provision of US $6.5m. in emergency assistance for the Territory in order to avert a financial crisis. The aid programme included a grant (partly financed by the European Union) to fund improvements to the road between Bounty Bay and Adamstown, which were carried out in mid-2005, and to investigate the potential for ecotourism as a possible source of future revenue. In 2008 the island's telephone system was upgraded and islanders were given constant internet access, while television became available for the first time. In addition to these improvements in the field of communications, other plans for infrastructural development included the building of a breakwater at Bounty Bay. It was hoped that the project, jointly funded by the British Government and the European Development Fund, would make the island more accessible to passenger and cargo ships. Proposals for the use of wind power as an alternative energy source were also discussed.

Statistical Survey

Source: Office of the Governor of Pitcairn, Henderson, Ducie and Oeno Islands, c/o British Consulate-General, Pitcairn Islands Administration, Private Box 105-696, Auckland, New Zealand; tel. (9) 366-0186; fax (9) 366-0187; e-mail pitcairn@iconz.co.nz.

The Pitcairn Islands

AREA AND POPULATION

Area: 35.5 sq km. *By Island*: Pitcairn 4.35 sq km; Henderson 30.0 sq km; Oeno is less than 1 sq km and Ducie is smaller.

Population: 66 at census of 31 December 1991. *Mid-2005*: (estimate): 46.

Density (Pitcairn only, mid-2005): 10.6 per sq km.

Employment (able-bodied men, 2002): 9.

FINANCE

Currency and Exchange Rates: 100 cents = 1 Pitcairn dollar. The Pitcairn dollar is at par with the New Zealand dollar ($NZ). New Zealand currency is usually used.

Budget ($NZ, 1998/99): Revenue 492,000; Expenditure 667,000.

EXTERNAL TRADE

Trade with New Zealand ($NZ '000, year ending 30 June): *Imports*: 32 in 2000/01; 342 in 2001/02; 100 in 2002/03. *Exports*: 134 in 2000/01; 85 in 2001/02; 38 in 2002/03.

TRANSPORT

Road Traffic (motor vehicles, 2002): Passenger vehicles 29 (two-wheeled 1, three-wheeled 6, four-wheeled 23); Tractors 3; Bulldozer 1; Digger 1.

Shipping: *Local Vessels* (communally-owned open surf boats, 2000): 3. *International Shipping Arrivals* (visits by passing vessels, 1996): Ships 51; Yachts 30.

COMMUNICATIONS

Telephones (2002): a party-line service with 15 telephones in use; 2 public telephones; 2 digital telephones. Most homes also have VHF radio.

Directory

THE CONSTITUTION AND GOVERNMENT

Pitcairn is a British settlement under the British Settlements Act 1887, although the islanders reckon their recognition as a colony from 1838, when a British naval captain instituted a Constitution with universal adult suffrage and a code of law. That system served as the basis of the 1904 reformed Constitution and the wider reforms of 1940, effected by Order in Council. The Constitution of 1940 provides for a Governor of Pitcairn, Henderson, Ducie and Oeno Islands (who, since 1970, is concurrently the British High Commissioner in New Zealand), representing the British monarch. A Mayor is elected every three years to preside over the Island Council. The Local Government Ordinance 1964 constituted an Island Council of 10 members: in addition to the Mayor, five members are elected annually; three are nominated for terms of one year (the Governor appoints two of these members at his own discretion); and the Island Secretary is an *ex-officio* member. In addition to the Island Council there is an Island Magistrate who presides over the Magistrate's Court of Pitcairn, and is appointed by the Governor. Liaison between the Governor and the Island Council is conducted by a Commissioner, usually based in the Office of the British Consulate-General in Auckland, New Zealand.

Customary land tenure provides for a system of family ownership (based upon the original division of land in the 18th century). Alienation to foreigners is not forbidden by law, but in practice this is difficult. There is no taxation, and public works are performed by the community.

Governor of Pitcairn, Henderson, Ducie and Oeno Islands: GEORGE FERGUSSON (British High Commissioner in New Zealand—took office April 2006).

Office of the Governor of Pitcairn, Henderson, Ducie and Oeno Islands: c/o British High Commission, 44 Hill St, POB 1812, Wellington, New Zealand; tel. (4) 924-2888; fax (4) 473-4982; e-mail ppa.mailbox@fco.gov.uk; Gov. GEORGE FERGUSSON; Deputy Gov. (vacant); Commissioner LESLIE JAQUES.

Pitcairn Islands Office: Private Box 105-696, Auckland, New Zealand; tel. (9) 366-0186; fax (9) 366-0187; e-mail admin@pitcairn.gov.pn; internet www.government.pn.

Island Council
(April 2008)

Mayor: MICHAEL WARREN.

Island Secretary (ex officio): HEATHER MENZIES.

Government Treasurer: NADINE CHRISTIAN.

Island Auditor: MICHELE CHRISTIAN (acting).

Chairman of Internal Committee: DAVE BROWN.

Other Members: LEA BROWN, BRENDA CHRISTIAN, TURI GRIFFITHS, KARI YOUNG, CAROL WARREN (Governor's Appointee).

Elections to the Island Council take place each December. Meetings are held at the Court House in Adamstown.

Office of the Island Secretary: The Square, Adamstown.

JUDICIAL SYSTEM

Chief Justice: CHARLES BLACKIE.

Island Magistrate: LEA BROWN.

Public Prosecutor: SIMON MOORE.

Public Defender: PAUL DACRE.

RELIGION

Christianity

Since 1887 many of the islanders have been adherents of the Seventh-day Adventist Church.

Pastor: JOHN O'MALLEY, SDA Church, The Square, POB 24, Adamstown; fax 872-7620/9763.

THE PRESS

Pitcairn Miscellany: e-mail admin@miscellany.pn; internet www.miscellany.pn; monthly four-page mimeographed news sheet; f. 1959; edited by the Education Officer; circulation 1,400 in 2002; Editor P. FOLEY.

FINANCE, TRADE AND INDUSTRY

There are no formal banking facilities. A co-operative trading store was established in 1967. Industry consists of handicrafts, and the production of honey and dried fruit.

TRANSPORT

Roads

There are approximately 14 km (9 miles) of dirt road suitable for two-, three- and four-wheeled vehicles. In 2002 Pitcairn had one conventional motor cycle, six three-wheelers and 22 four-wheeled motor cycles, one four-wheel-drive motor car, three tractors, a five-ton digger and a bulldozer; traditional wheelbarrows are used occasionally. In 1995 a total of £79,000 was received from individual donors for work to improve the road leading to the jetty at Bounty Bay. Work to concrete the road, known as the Hill of Difficulty, was completed in mid-2006.

Shipping

No passenger ships have called regularly since 1968, and sea communications are restricted to cargo vessels operating between New Zealand and Panama, which make scheduled calls at Pitcairn three times a year, as well as a number of unscheduled calls. A shipping route between French Polynesia and Pitcairn was opened in 2006. There are also occasional visits by private yachts. The number of cruise ships calling at Pitcairn increased in the late 1990s, and 10 such vessels visited the island in 2000 (compared with just two or three annually in previous years). Two cruise ships called at Pitcairn in April 2005 before stopping at Oeno Island for the tourists to witness a solar eclipse near the island. Bounty Bay, near Adamstown, is the only possible landing site, and there are no docking facilities; in mid-2007 plans to build a breakwater at Bounty Bay were announced. In 1993 the jetty derrick was refitted with an hydraulic system. The islanders have three aluminium open surf boats. Major work to repair the slipway and jetty was carried out by the islanders in mid-2005.

SAINT HELENA AND DEPENDENCIES

Saint Helena

Introduction

Saint Helena lies in the South Atlantic Ocean, about 1,930 km (1,200 miles) from the south-west coast of Africa. Governed by the British East India Co from 1673, the island was brought under the direct control of the British Crown in 1834. At general elections held in September 1976, the Saint Helena Progressive Party, advocating the retention of close economic links with the United Kingdom, won 11 of the 12 elective seats in the Legislative Council. This policy has been advocated by almost all members of the Legislative Council brought to office at subsequent general elections (normally held every four years) up to and including that held in August 2005.

In October 1981 a commission was established by the Governor to review the island's constitutional arrangements. The commission reported in 1983 that it was unable to identify any proposal for constitutional change that would command the support of the majority of the islanders. In 1988, however, a formal Constitution was introduced to replace the Order in Council and Royal Instructions under which Saint Helena had been governed since 1967. The Constitution entered into force on 1 January 1989.

Owing to the limited range of economic activity on the island (see below), Saint Helena is dependent on development and budgetary aid from the United Kingdom. Since 1981, when the United Kingdom adopted the British Nationality Act, which effectively removed the islanders' traditional right of residence in Britain, opportunities for overseas employment have been limited to contract work, principally in Ascension and the Falkland Islands. In 1992 an informal 'commission on citizenship' was established by a number of islanders to examine Saint Helena's constitutional relationship with the United Kingdom, with special reference to the legal validity of the 1981 legislation as applied to Saint Helena. In April 1997 the commission obtained a legal opinion from a former Attorney-General of Saint Helena to the effect that the application of the Act to the population of Saint Helena was in contravention of the Royal Charter establishing British sovereignty in 1673. The commission indicated that it intended to pursue the matter further. In July 1997 private legislation was introduced in the British Parliament to extend full British nationality to 'persons having connections with' Saint Helena. In the following month the British Government indicated that it was considering arrangements under which islanders would be granted employment and residence rights in the United Kingdom. In February 1998, following a conference held in London of representatives of the British Dependent Territories, it was announced that a review was to take place of the future constitutional status of these territories, and of means whereby their economies might be strengthened. It was subsequently agreed that the operation of the 1981 legislation in relation to Saint Helena would also be reviewed. As an immediate measure to ameliorate the isolation of Saint Helena, the British Government conceded permission for civilian air landing rights on Ascension Island, which, with the contemplated construction of a small airstrip on Saint Helena, could facilitate the future development of the island as a tourist destination. In March 1999 the British Government published draft legislation proposing that full British nationality, including the right of abode in the United Kingdom, was to be restored to the population of Saint Helena and its dependencies, under the reorganization of the British Dependent Territories as the United Kingdom Overseas Territories. However, this had still not been implemented by July 2000, when the citizens took their case to the UN Committee on Decolonization, seeking British passports, a new Constitution and administration as a Crown dependency rather than as a colony. In May 2002 the British Overseas Territories Act, which granted British citizenship to the people of the Overseas Territories, including Saint Helena and dependencies, came into effect, having received royal assent in February. Under the new legislation these citizens acquired the right to hold a British passport and to work in the United Kingdom, but not the other benefits of citizenship (such as reduced fees for education). The Act restored those rights removed by the British Nationality Act of 1981. In September 2002 an independent constitutional adviser visited Saint Helena and consulted extensively with the island's residents on the options for future constitutional development. A consultative poll on the draft for a new constitution, which, *inter alia*, proposed the creation of a ministerial form of government, took place on 25 May 2005. The draft document was rejected by 52.6% of voters. Concern was expressed at the low rate of voter participation, recorded at 43% of registered voters. Nevertheless, it was indicated that elements of the rejected constitution were expected to be adopted, including a change to the number of constituencies on Saint Helena. The British Government subsequently stated that it wished to identify any possible improvements to the existing Constitution in conjunction with the new Executive Council, which took office following the elections held on 31 August 2005.

On 4 February 2002 a referendum was held by the Government in Saint Helena, Ascension Island, the Falkland Islands and on RMS *Saint Helena* on future access to the island; 71.6% of votes cast were in favour of the construction of an airport (28.4% opting for a shipping alternative). Plans for the airport and associated commercial developments were cancelled in February 2003, on the grounds of unprofitability and environmental concerns; however, following protests by islanders, in April the Executive Council invited tenders for the construction of the airport. In late January 2006 the Airport Development Bill was presented to the Legislative Council for approval and the following month it was announced that three consortia had pre-qualified to contest for the contract to construct the airport. The project was expected to cost some £40m., of which the British Government was reported to have agreed to contribute some £26.3m., approximately equal to the cost of replacing the mail ship in 2010. The airport, to be located on the eastern coast of the island, was scheduled to be fully functional by 2012. Construction was to begin in 2008. It was hoped that the airport would bring strong benefits to the local economy, particularly through the development of tourism.

The economy of Saint Helena is heavily reliant on British aid. In 2006/07 the assistance totalled £14.76m. and consisted of direct budgetary aid (£6.9m.), an annual subsidy for the operation of the RMS *St Helena* (£3.1m.) and support for bilateral development assistance. Budget revenue totalled £21.30m. in 2006/07, and expenditure in that year was £16.96m. According to official estimates, Saint Helena's gross national product (GNP) totalled £15.6m. in 2005/06. Gross domestic product (GDP) was estimated to have decreased, in real terms, by an annual average of 1.6% during 1999/00–2005/06; a decline of 10.1%, in real terms, was recorded for 2005/06. The population declined by an annual average of 3.2% during 1999/00–2005/06, and, largely as a result of this, per-capita GDP increased, in real terms, by an annual average of 1.9% over the same period. The annual rate of inflation averaged 3.7% in 1990–2001, and the rate, influenced to a large extent by the prevailing rates in its two most important trading partners, South Africa and the United Kingdom, has remained between 3% and 5% in recent years. In 2004 the rate of unemployment (including community work scheme placements) was estimated at 7.6%.

Saint Helena's persistently high rate of unemployment has resulted in widespread reliance on welfare benefit payments and a concurrent decline in living standards for the majority of the population (although an increase in economic migration in recent years has done much to alleviate this situation). Evidence of underlying social discontent emerged in April 1997, when minor public disorders broke out in Jamestown following the refusal of the Governor (who exercises full executive and legislative authority in Saint Helena) to accept the nomination of a prominent critic of government policy to the post of Director of the Department of Social Welfare. Two members of the Executive Council (which acts in an advisory capacity) resigned in protest at the action of the Governor, who subsequently announced that elections to the Legislative Council were to take place in July. Following the elections, held on 9 July, the Governor agreed to the nomination as Chairman of the Education Committee of the candidate he had previously refused to nominate to the Social Welfare Directorate. The newly elected Legislative Council became the first in which members were to receive a fixed salary to serve on a full-time basis, relinquishing any other employment during their term of office.

At the 1998 census 10.2% of the employed labour force were engaged in agriculture and fishing, 19.7% in industry (predominantly construction), 65.6% in services and 4.5% in unspecified activities. Employment in the public sector was estimated to be at 55% of the working population in 2004. In 2000 exports of fish (which, apart from a small quantity of coffee, is the only commodity exported) totalled 43.1 metric tons (compared with 27.2 tons in 1985) and export earnings from this source amounted to £113,000. Improvements in vessel capacity have helped increase fish exports in recent years. An increase in overseas philatelic sales has also generated significant revenues (£80,000 in 2006/07), as has a fledgling tourist industry (£426,000 in 2005/06). Timber production is being developed, with sales amounting to 390 cu m in 1999. However, a large

UNITED KINGDOM OVERSEAS TERRITORIES   Saint Helena and Dependencies

proportion of the labour force (approximately 1,000) must seek employment overseas, principally on Ascension and the Falkland Islands. In March 2001 551 Saint Helenians were working on Ascension, and in December 1999 371 were working on the Falkland Islands; according to the British Foreign and Commonwealth Office, approximately 1,700 members of the work-force were employed offshore at the beginning of 2005.

Saint Helena is of interest to naturalists for its rare flora and fauna. The island has about 40 species of flora that are unique to Saint Helena.

Statistical Survey

Source (unless otherwise indicated): Development and Economic Planning Dept, Government of Saint Helena, Saint Helena Island, STHL 1ZZ; tel. 2777; fax 2830; e-mail depd@helanta.sh.

AREA AND POPULATION

Area: 122 sq km (47 sq miles).

Population: 5,644 at census of 22 February 1987; 5,157 (males 2,612, females 2,545) at census of 8 March 1998; 4,030 at 31 December 2006.

Density (at 31 December 2006): 33.0 per sq km.

Principal Town (UN estimate, incl. suburbs): Jamestown (capital), population 1,787 in mid-2003 (Source: UN, *World Urbanization Prospects: The 2003 Revision*).

Births and Deaths (2006): Registered live births 35; Registered deaths 52. *2005:* Crude birth rate 8.4 per 1,000; Crude death rate 9.7 per 1,000.

Economically Active Population (1998 census): Agriculture, hunting and related activities 187; Fishing 20; Manufacturing 87; Electricity, gas and water 48; Construction 267; Wholesale and retail trade 344; Hotels and restaurants 24; Transport, storage and communications 181; Financial intermediation 17; Real estate, renting and business activities 7; Public administration and defence 293; Education 187; Health and social work 196; Other community services 87; Private household 74; Extra-territorial organizations 11; *Total employed* 2,037 (males 1,146; females 891); Unemployed 449 (males 290; females 159); *Total labour force* 2,486 (males 1,436, females 1,050). *2004:* Employed 1,813; Unemployed (incl. community work scheme) 150; Total labour force 1,963.

AGRICULTURE, ETC.

Livestock (2006 livestock census): Cattle 865; Sheep 1,007; Pigs 654; Goats 630; Donkeys 110; Poultry 7,505.

Fishing (metric tons, live weight, including Ascension and Tristan da Cunha, 2005): Skipjack tuna 321; Yellowfin tuna 255; Tristan da Cunha rock lobster 373; Total catch (incl. others) 1,130. Figures include catches of rock lobster from Tristan da Cunha during the 12 months ending 30 April of the year stated. Source: FAO.

FINANCE

Currency and Exchange Rate: 100 pence (pennies) = 1 Saint Helena pound (£). *Sterling, Dollar and Euro Equivalents* (31 December 2007): £1 sterling = Saint Helena £1; US $1 = 49.91 pence; €1 = 73.48 pence; £10 = $20.03 = €13.61. *Average Exchange Rate* (£ per US dollar): 0.5500 in 2005; 0.5435 in 2006; 0.4998 in 2007. Note: The Saint Helena pound is at par with the pound sterling.

Budget (2006/07): *Revenue:* £21.30m. (United Kingdom assistance £14.76m., Local revenue £6.5m.); *Expenditure:* £16.96m.

Gross Domestic Product (£ '000 at constant 2002 prices): 11,869 in 2003/04; 12,466 in 2004/05; 11,210 in 2005/06.

Money Supply (£ '000, 2006/07): Currency in circulation 3,618 (excl. commemorative coins valued at 514).

Cost of Living (Consumer Price Index; base: 1990 = 100): 142.0 in 1999; 144.0 in 2000; 149.0 in 2001. Source: ILO.

EXTERNAL TRADE

Principal Commodities: *Imports* (1994/95, £ '000): Total 5,076 (Food and live animals 27.9%; Beverages and tobacco 8.5%; Mineral fuels, lubricants, etc. 8.5%; Chemicals and related materials 11.4%; Basic manufactures 12.7%; Machinery and transport equipment 11.7%; Miscellaneous manufactured articles 13.0%; Other commodities and transactions 3.3%); *Exports* (2000): Fish £113,000; Coffee n.a. Trade is mainly with the United Kingdom and South Africa. *2005/06:* Imports f.o.b. £7.8m.; Exports £0.3m.

TRANSPORT

Road Traffic (2005): 1,916 licensed vehicles.

Shipping: *Vessels Entered* (1999): 214. *Merchant Fleet* (31 December 2006): 2 vessels; Total displacement 2,322 grt (Source: Lloyd's Register-Fairplay, *World Fleet Statistics*).

COMMUNICATIONS MEDIA

Radio Receivers ('000 in use, 1997): 3. Source: UNESCO, *Statistical Yearbook*.

Television Subscribers (April 2007): 1,161.

Telephones (main lines in use, April 2007): 2,283.

EDUCATION

Primary (2006/07): 2 schools; 14 teachers; 115 pupils.
Amalgamated School (2006/07): 1 school; 15 teachers; 116 pupils.
Intermediate (2006/07): 2 schools; 17 teachers; 119 pupils.
Secondary (2006/07): 1 school; 42 teachers; 324 pupils.

Directory

The Constitution

The Saint Helena Constitution Order 1988, which entered into force on 1 January 1989, replaced the Order in Council and Royal Instructions of 1 January 1967. Executive and legislative authority is reserved to the British Crown, but is ordinarily exercised by others in accordance with provisions of the Constitution. The Constitution provides for the office of Governor and Commander-in-Chief of Saint Helena and its dependencies (Ascension Island and Tristan da Cunha). The Legislative Council for Saint Helena consists of the Speaker, three ex officio members (the Chief Secretary, the Financial Secretary and the Attorney-General) and 12 elected members; the Executive Council is presided over by the Governor and consists of the above ex officio members and five of the elected members of the Legislative Council. The elected members of the legislature choose from among themselves those who will also be members of the Executive Council. Although a member of both the Legislative Council and the Executive Council, the Attorney-General does not vote on either. Members of the legislature provide the Chairmen and a majority of the members of the various Council Committees. Executive and legislative functions for the dependencies are exercised by the Governor (although an advisory Island Council was inaugurated on Ascension in November 2002).

The Government

(March 2008)

Governor and Commander-in-Chief: ANDREW GURR.
Chief Secretary: ETHEL YON (acting).
Financial Secretary: LINDA CLEMETT.
Chairmen of Council Committees:
Agriculture and Natural Resources: STEDSON GRAHAM FRANCIS.
Education: ERIC WILLIAM BENJAMIN.
Employment and Social Security: BRIAN WILLIAM ISAAC.
Public Health and Social Services: WILLIAM ERIC DRABBLE.
Public Works and Services: BERNICE ALICIA OLSSON.
Speaker of the Legislative Council: ERIC GEORGE.

GOVERNMENT OFFICES

Office of the Governor: The Castle, Jamestown, STHL 1ZZ; tel. 2555; fax 2598; e-mail ocs@helanta.sh; internet www.sainthelena.gov.sh.

Office of the Chief Secretary: The Castle, Jamestown, STHL 1ZZ; tel. 2555; fax 2598; e-mail ocs@helanta.sh.

Political Organizations

There are no political parties in Saint Helena. Elections to the Legislative Council, the latest of which took place in August 2005, are conducted on a non-partisan basis.

Judicial System

The legal system is derived from English common law and statutes. There are four Courts on Saint Helena: the Supreme Court, the Magistrate's Court, the Small Debts Court and the Juvenile Court. Provision exists for the Saint Helena Court of Appeal, which can sit in Jamestown or London.

Chief Justice: B. W. MARTIN (non-resident).
Attorney-General: KEN BADDON.
Sheriff: G. P. MUSK.

Religion

The majority of the population belongs to the Anglican Communion.

CHRISTIANITY

The Anglican Communion

Anglicans are adherents of the Anglican Church of Southern Africa (formerly the Church of the Province of Southern Africa). The Metropolitan of the Province is the Archbishop of Cape Town, South Africa. St Helena forms a single diocese.

Bishop of Saint Helena: Rt Rev. JOHN SALT, Bishopsholme, POB 62, Saint Helena, STHL 1ZZ; tel. and fax 4471; e-mail bishop@helanta.sh; diocese f. 1859; has jurisdiction over the islands of Saint Helena and Ascension.

The Roman Catholic Church

The Church is represented in Saint Helena, Ascension and Tristan da Cunha by a Mission, established in August 1986. There were an estimated 87 adherents in the islands at 31 December 2000.

Superior: Rev. Fr MICHAEL MCPARTLAND (also Prefect Apostolic of the Falkland Islands); normally visits Tristan da Cunha once a year and Ascension Island two or three times a year; Vicar Delegate Rev. Fr JOSEPH WHELAN, Sacred Heart Church, Jamestown, STHL 1ZZ; tel. and fax 2535.

Other Christian Churches

The Salvation Army, Seventh-day Adventists, Baptists, New Apostolics and Jehovah's Witnesses are active on the island.

BAHÁ'Í FAITH

There is a small Bahá'í community on the island.

The Press

St Helena Herald: Saint Helena News Media Board, Broadway House, Jamestown, STHL 1ZZ; tel. 2612; fax 2802; e-mail sthelena.herald@helanta.sh; internet www.news.co.sh; f. 1986; govt-sponsored, independent; weekly; Chief Exec. VERNON QUICKFALL; circ. 1,600.

The St Helena Independent: St Helena Media Productions Ltd, 2nd Floor, Association Hall, Main St, Jamestown, STHL 1ZZ; tel. 2488; e-mail independent@helanta.sh; internet www.saint.fm; f. 2005; independent; weekly.

Broadcasting and Communications

TELECOMMUNICATIONS

Cable & Wireless (St Helena) PLC: POB 2, Bishops Rooms, Jamestown, STHL 1ZZ; tel. 2155; fax 2206; e-mail webmaster@helanta.sh; internet www.cw.com/sthelena; f. 1899; provides national and international telecommunications.

BROADCASTING

Cable & Wireless PLC: The Moon, Jamestown, STHL 1ZZ; tel. 2200; f. 1995; provides a three channel television service 24 hours daily from five satellite channels.

Saint FM: Association Hall, Main St, Jamestown, STHL 1ZZ; tel. 2660; e-mail fm@helanta.sh; internet www.saint.fm; f. 2004; independent FM radio station; also broadcasts on Ascension Island, Falkland Islands and Tristan da Cunha; Dir MIKE OLSSON.

Radio St Helena: Saint Helena Information Office, Broadway House, Jamestown, STHL 1ZZ; tel. 4669; fax 4542; e-mail radio.sthelena@helanta.sh; internet www.sthelena.se/radiosth.htm; independent service; providing broadcasts for 24 hours per day; local programming and relays of British Broadcasting Corporation World Service programmes; Station Man. TONY LEO.

Finance

BANK

Bank of Saint Helena: Post Office Bldg, Main St, Jamestown STHL 1ZZ; tel. 2390; fax 2553; e-mail jamestown@sthelenabank.com; internet www.sainthelenabank.com; f. 2004; replaced the Government Savings Bank; total assets £30,182,375 (31 March 2006); 1 br. on Ascension; Chair. LYN THOMAS; Man. Dir JOHN TURNER.

INSURANCE

Solomon & Co PLC: Jamestown, STHL 1ZZ; tel. 2682; fax 2755; e-mail insurance@solomons.co.sh; internet www.solomons-sthelena.com; Solomon & Co operated an insurance agency on behalf of Royal SunAlliance Insurance Group during 1933–2002, until the latter co withdrew its interest from Saint Helena; negotiations for the foundation of a mutual insurance company on the island commenced in 2004; CEO TONY GREEN.

Trade and Industry

GOVERNMENT AGENCY

St Helena Development Agency: 2 Main St, POB 117, Jamestown, STHL 1ZZ; tel. 2920; fax 2166; e-mail enquiries@shda.co.sh; internet www.shda.helanta.sh; f. 1995; Man. Dir DAVE TYLER.

CHAMBER OF COMMERCE

St Helena Chamber of Commerce: Jamestown, STHL 1ZZ; tel. 2258; fax 2598; internet www.chamber.co.sh.

CO-OPERATIVE

St Helena Growers' Co-operative Society: Jamestown, STHL 1ZZ; tel. and fax 2511; vegetable marketing; also suppliers of agricultural tools, seeds and animal feeding products; 108 mems (1999); Chair. STEDSON FRANCIS; Sec. PETER W. THORPE.

Transport

There are no railways in Saint Helena. In 2004 the Government conducted initial surveys for the construction of an airport, which was scheduled to be completed by 2012 and was to be situated on Prosperous Bay Plain.

ROADS

In 2002 there were 118 km of bitumen-sealed roads, and a further 20 km of earth roads, which can be used by motor vehicles only in dry weather. All roads have steep gradients and sharp bends.

SHIPPING

St Helena Line Ltd: Andrew Weir Shipping, Dexter House, 2 Royal Mint Court, London, EC3N 4XX, United Kingdom; tel. (20) 7265-0808; fax (20) 7481-4784; internet www.aws.co.uk; internet www.rms-st-helena.com; five-year govt contract renewed in August 2006; service subsidized by the British Govt by £1.5m. annually; operates two-monthly passenger/cargo services by the RMS *St Helena* to and from the United Kingdom and Cape Town, South Africa, calling at the Canary Islands, Ascension Island and Vigo, Spain, and once a year at Tristan da Cunha; also operates programme of shuttle services between Saint Helena and Ascension Island and the St Helena Liner Shipping Service; Chair. GARRY HOPCROFT.

Tourism

Although Saint Helena possesses flora and fauna of considerable interest to naturalists, as well as the house (now an important museum) in which the French Emperor Napoleon I spent his final years in exile, the remoteness of the island, which is a two-day sea voyage from Ascension Island, has inhibited the development of tourism. The construction of an airport on Saint Helena, which was scheduled to be fully operational by 2012, should greatly increase the island's accessibility to the limited number of visitors that can currently be accommodated. A total of 8,968 tourists visited Saint Helena in 1997. There are three hotels and a range of self-catering facilities.

St Helena Tourist Office: The Canister, Main St, Jamestown, STHL 1ZZ; tel. 2158; fax 2159; e-mail sthelena.tourism@helanta.sh; internet www.sthelenatourism.com; f. 1998; provides general information about the island; Dir PAMELA YOUNG.

Ascension

The island of Ascension lies in the South Atlantic Ocean, 1,131 km (703 miles) north-west of Saint Helena, of which it is a dependency. Discovered by Portuguese navigators in 1501, the island is a semi-barren, rocky peak of purely volcanic origin. Britain took possession of Ascension in 1815, in connection with Napoleon's detention on Saint Helena. The island is famous for green turtles, and is also a breeding ground for the sooty tern. Under an agreement with the British Government, US forces occupy Wideawake Airfield, which is used as a tracking station for guided missiles. Ascension has no indigenous population, being inhabited by British and US military personnel, *émigré* workers and government administrative staff from Saint Helena. There are also a number of expatriate civilian personnel of Merlin Communications International (MCI), which operates the British Broadcasting Corporation (BBC) Overseas World Service Atlantic relay station, Cable and Wireless PLC, which provides international communications services and operates the 'Ariane' satellite tracking station of the European Space Agency, and staff providing the island's common services. The island is an important communications centre. Ascension does not raise its own finance; the costs of administering the island are borne collectively by the user organizations, supplemented by income from philatelic sales. The island is developing a modest eco-tourism sector. Some revenue, which is remitted to the Saint Helena administration, is derived from fishing licences (estimated to be around £1m. in 1999). Facilities on Ascension underwent rapid development in 1982 to serve as a major staging post for British vessels and aircraft on their way to the Falkland Islands (q.v.), and the island has continued to provide a key link in British supply lines to the South Atlantic. On 31 March 2001 the joint venture between the BBC and Cable and Wireless to provide public services to the island was dissolved. The Ascension Island Government took over responsibility for health and education, the Ascension Island Works and Services Agency, a statutory body, was established to maintain transport and infrastructure, and any remaining services were taken over by the new Ascension Island Commercial Services Ltd (AICS) company. AICS was jointly owned by the Ascension Islands Government, the BBC and Cable and Wireless and had the declared aim of privatizing the new enterprises by April 2002. This development was regarded as reorientating public-service provision towards the demands of the resident population rather than the needs of those organizations using the island. The privatization process was ongoing in 2008.

Dissent developed among the resident population in June 2002, following the decision of the Foreign and Commonwealth Office to impose taxes for the first time on the island (including income tax, property tax and tax on alcohol and tobacco). The primary objection of the population was that this was 'taxation without representation', as the islanders do not possess the right to vote, to own property or even to live on the island. The Governor responded with plans to introduce a democratically elected council that would have a purely advisory function and no decision-making powers, claiming that the islanders initially needed to acquire experience of governance. On 22–23 August a vote on the democratic options took place on the island, with 95% of the votes cast being in favour of an Island Council, rather than an Inter-Island Council plus Island Council structure; 50% of those eligible to vote did so. The Council was to be chaired by the Administrator, on behalf of the Governor, and was to comprise seven elected members, the Attorney-General, the Director of Finance and one or two appointed members. Elections for councillors took place in October, and the Island Council was inaugurated in the following month. A joint consultative council was also to be established, with representatives from both Ascension and Saint Helena, in order to develop policy relating to economic development and tourism common to both islands.

The British Government subsequently stated its intention to enact legislation granting the islanders right of abode and the right to own property. However, following a visit to the island by a delegation of British officials in November 2005, it was announced that the proposed reforms would not be carried out. The British Government cited its reluctance fundamentally to change the nature of the territory and also maintained that granting such rights would impose greater financial liabilities on British taxpayers and would bring an unacceptable level of risk to the United Kingdom. In January 2006 The Island Council announced that it intended to seek clarification regarding the legality of the British Government's decision and reiterated its commitment to securing the islanders' right to abode and the right to purchase property.

In May 2007 the Island Council was suspended and the Ascension Island Advisory Group was established to provide advice to the administrator on certain policy issues. The suspension was expected to remain in place until May 2008, after which elections would be held. It was anticipated that the Advisory Group would meet on a monthly basis, to be supplemented by informal meetings as necessary. Consultation papers were to be issued to encourage the people of Ascension to participate in the decision-making process.

As of early 2004 Ascension Island had a balanced fiscal budget, although with minimal reserves. Government expenditure funds one school, one hospital (offering limited services), police and judicial services; these services are provided without charge to local taxpayers. The Saint Helena-based firm Solomons has a primary role in the incipient private sector and a sports-fishing industry was in the process of being established.

In October 2003 the British Government concluded negotiations with the US authorities over the signing of an agreement to allow US air-charter access to the airfield.

Area: 88 sq km (34 sq miles).

Population: There are no indigenous inhabitants, but some 1,100 personnel and employees and their families are permanently resident (mostly nationals of Saint Helena, with some 200 UK nationals and 150 US nationals).

Budget: (2003/04, £ million, year ending 31 March, estimates): Revenue 4.3; Expenditure 4.0 (Recurrent expenditure 3.3, Capital expenditure 0.7). *2007/08* (Consolidated Fund, £ million, year ending 31 March): Revenue 5.54.

Government: The Governor of Saint Helena, in his capacity as Governor of Ascension Island, is represented by an Administrator. Two advisory groups, one comprising senior managers of resident organizations, and one comprising their employees' representatives, assist the Administrator, who also has professional financial and technical advisers. In November 2002 an advisory Island Council, chaired by the Administrator and comprising seven elected members, the Attorney-General, the Director of Finance and two appointed members, was inaugurated.

Administrator: MICHAEL HILL, The Residency, Georgetown Ascension, ASCN 1ZZ; tel. 7000; fax 6152; e-mail aigenquiries@ascension.gov.ac; internet www.ascension-island.gov.ac.

Magistrate: (vacant).

Justices of the Peace: G. F. THOMAS, A. FOWLER, J. PETERS, C. PARKER-YON.

Religion: Ascension forms part of the Anglican diocese of Saint Helena, which normally provides a resident chaplain who is also available to minister to members of other denominations. There is a Roman Catholic chapel served by visiting priests, as well as a small mosque.

Transport: *Road vehicles* (1998): 830. *Shipping* (1998): ships entered and cleared 105. The St Helena Line Ltd (q.v.) serves the island with a two-monthly passenger/cargo service between Cardiff, in the United Kingdom, and Cape Town, in South Africa. A vessel under charter to the British Ministry of Defence visits the island monthly on its United Kingdom–Falkland Islands service. A US freighter from Cape Canaveral calls at three-month intervals. *Air services*: A twice-weekly Royal Air Force Tristar service between the United Kingdom and the Falkland Islands transits Ascension Island both southbound and northbound. There is a weekly US Air Force military service linking the Patrick Air Force Base in Florida with Ascension Island, via Antigua and Barbuda.

Tourism: Small-scale eco-tourism is encouraged, although accommodation on the island is limited and all visits require written permission from the Administrator. Access is available by twice-weekly flights operated from the United Kingdom by the Royal Air Force (see above), and by the RMS *St Helena* (see Saint Helena—Shipping).

Tristan da Cunha

The island of Tristan da Cunha lies in the South Atlantic Ocean, 2,800 km (1,740 miles) west of Cape Town, South Africa. It comes under the jurisdiction of Saint Helena, 2,300 km (1,430 miles) to the north-east. Also in the group are Inaccessible Island, 37 km (23 miles) west of Tristan; the three Nightingale Islands, 37 km (23 miles) south; and Gough Island (Diego Alvarez), 425 km (264 miles) south. Tristan da Cunha was discovered in 1506, but remained uninhabited until occupied by US whalers during 1790–1811. The British Navy took possession of the island in 1817. Tristan's population was evacuated in 1961, after volcanic eruptions, but was resettled in 1963. The island's major source of revenue derives from a royalty for a crayfishing concession, supplemented by income from the sale of postage stamps and other philatelic items, and handicrafts. The fishing industry and the administration employ all of the working population. Some 20 power boats operating from the island land their catches to a fish-freezing factory built by the Atlantic Islands Development Corpn, whose fishing concession was transferred in January 1997 to a new holder, Premier Fishing (Pty) Ltd, of Cape Town. Premier also operates two large fishing vessels exporting the catch to the USA, France and Japan. Budget estimates for 2005/06 projected a deficit of £147,507. Development aid from the United Kingdom ceased in 1980; since then the island has financed its own projects. In April 2008, prompted by concerns surrounding the island's dwindling capital reserves, Administrator David Morley warned that the island could be bankrupt within four years unless economic austerity measures were implemented immediately. Chief among these proposals was the introduction, with effect from 1 June 2008, of an incremental system of income tax (with a maximum rate of 13%). In June 2001 a hurricane in the main settlement of Edinburgh of the Seven Seas destroyed the hospital, community centre and numerous homes, and also killed many cattle; the satellite phone link was lost and the island was without electricity for one week, although no serious injuries were sustained. The British Department for International Development granted a £75,000 emergency aid package in response to the disaster. However, the cost of repairs surpassed that figure considerably. Furthermore, the problem of poaching in the island's waters resulted in much of Tristan da Cunha's limited resources being used to fund fishing patrols rather than swiftly restoring the damaged infrastructure.

Area: Tristan da Cunha 98 sq km (38 sq miles); Inaccessible Island 10 sq km (4 sq miles); Nightingale Islands 2 sq km (3/4 sq mile); Gough Island 91 sq km (35 sq miles).

Population: (April 2005): 276 (including 10 expatriates) on Tristan; there is a small weather station on Gough Island, staffed, under agreement, by personnel employed by the South African Government.

Fishing: Catch (metric tons, year ending 30 April): Tristan da Cunha rock lobster 534 in 2003; 377 in 2004; 373 in 2005. Source: FAO.

Budget: (2005/06, estimates): Revenue £711,320; Expenditure £858,827 (with excess expenditure financed from capital reserves of £1.2m.).

Government: The Administrator, representing the Governor of Saint Helena, is assisted by an Island Council of eight elected members (of whom at least one must be a woman) and three appointed members, which has advisory powers in legislative and executive functions. The member receiving the largest number of votes at elections to the Council is appointed Chief Islander. The Council's advisory functions in executive matters are performed through 11 committees of the Council dealing with the separate branches of administration. Elections are held every three years. The last elections were held in March 2007.

Administrator: DAVID MORLEY, The Administrator's Office, Edinburgh of the Seven Seas, Tristan da Cunha, TDCU 1ZZ; tel. (satellite) 874-1445434; fax (satellite) 874-1445435; e-mail admin@tristandc.com; internet www.tristandc.com/administator.php.

Legal System: The Administrator is also the Magistrate and Coroner.

Religion: Adherents of the Anglican church predominate on Tristan da Cunha, which is within the Church of the Province of Southern Africa, and is under the jurisdiction of the Archbishop of Cape Town, South Africa. There is also a small number of Roman Catholics.

Transport: The St Helena Line Ltd (q.v.), the MV *Hanseatic*, and MS *Explorer* and the SA *Agulhas* each visit the island once each year, and two lobster concession vessels each make three visits annually, remaining for between two and three months. Occasional cruise ships also visit the island. There is no airfield.

Tourism: Permission from the Administrator and the Island Council is required for visits to Tristan da Cunha. Facilities for tourism are limited, although some accommodation is available in island homes.

SOUTH GEORGIA AND THE SOUTH SANDWICH ISLANDS

South Georgia, an island of 3,592 sq km (1,387 sq miles), lies in the South Atlantic Ocean, about 1,300 km (800 miles) east-south-east of the Falkland Islands. The South Sandwich Islands, which have an area of 311 sq km, lie about 750 km south-east of South Georgia.

The United Kingdom annexed South Georgia and the South Sandwich Islands in 1775. With a segment of the Antarctic mainland and other nearby islands (now the British Antarctic Territory), they were constituted as the Falkland Islands Dependencies in 1908. Argentina made formal claim to South Georgia in 1927, and to the South Sandwich Islands in 1948. In 1955 the United Kingdom unilaterally submitted the dispute over sovereignty to the International Court of Justice (based in the Netherlands), which decided not to hear the application in view of Argentina's refusal to submit to the Court's jurisdiction. South Georgia was the site of a British Antarctic Survey base (staffed by 22 scientists and support personnel) until it was invaded in April 1982 by Argentine forces, who occupied the island until its recapture by British forces three weeks later. The South Sandwich Islands were uninhabited until the occupation of Southern Thule in December 1976 by about 50 Argentines, reported to be scientists. Argentine personnel remained until removed by British forces in June 1982.

In mid-1989 it was reported that the British Government was considering the imposition of a conservation zone extending to 200 nautical miles (370 km) around South Georgia, similar to that which surrounds the Falkland Islands, in an attempt to prevent the threatened extinction of certain types of marine life.

Under the provisions of the South Georgia and South Sandwich Islands Order of 1985, the islands ceased to be governed as dependencies of the Falkland Islands on 3 October 1985. The Governor of the Falkland Islands is, ex officio, Commissioner for the territory.

In May 1993, in response to the Argentine Government's decision to commence the sale of fishing licences for the region's waters, the British Government announced an extension, from 12 to 200 nautical miles, of its territorial jurisdiction in the waters surrounding the islands, in order to conserve crucial fishing stocks.

In September 1998 the British Government announced that it would withdraw its military detachment from South Georgia in 2000, while it would increase its scientific presence on the island with the installation of a permanent team from the British Antarctic Survey to investigate the fisheries around the island for possible exploitation. The small military detachment finally withdrew in March 2001. The British garrison stationed in the Falkland Islands would remain responsible for the security of South Georgia and the South Sandwich Islands. In August 2006 Alan Huckle succeeded Howard Pearce as Governor of the Falkland Islands and Commissioner of South Georgia and the South Sandwich Islands. During a restructuring of the South Georgia Government in May 2007, Assistant Commissioner and Director of Fisheries Harriet Hall was appointed to the newly created role of Chief Executive Officer; Hall assumed office in July, while retaining her responsibilities as Director of Fisheries.

Previously thought to be dormant, increased volcanic activity on Montagu Island, in the South Sandwich Islands, had been monitored closely by the British Antarctic Survey since 2001. In late 2005 Mount Belinda erupted, adding some 50 acres to the island's land area in just one month. The island is largely ice-covered and the eruption allowed scientists the rare opportunity to make direct observations of volcanic activity under ice sheets.

Budget revenue for 2005/06 amounted to £4.4m., while expenditure totalled £4.5m. The main sources of revenue are the sale of fishing licences, incomes from visitor landing charges and philatelic and commemorative coin sales.

At the close of the 2006/07 cruise-ship season on 31 March 2007, South Georgia had recorded a total of 50 ship calls and 5,226 passengers to the island. Greater numbers of visitors to this inhospitable territory—coupled with a growing recognition of the climate change phenomenon—prompted the Government to review its existing biosecurity policy in an effort to prevent the introduction, or translocation, of potentially destructive species of flora and fauna to the island. Furthermore, a major legislative review was underway in early 2008, as a result of which the Government expected to implement changes to legislation governing tourism and visitor management.

The British Antarctic Survey maintains two research stations on South Georgia, at King Edward Point (winter personnel 9, summer personnel 12 in 2007/08) and Bird Island (winter personnel 4, summer personnel 10 in 2007/08).

Commissioner: ALAN HUCKLE (took office on 25 August 2006).

Assistant Commissioner and Director of Fisheries: HARRIET HALL (Stanley, Falkland Islands).

THE TURKS AND CAICOS ISLANDS

Introductory Survey

Location, Climate, Language, Religion, Flag, Capital

The Turks and Caicos Islands consist of more than 30 low-lying islands forming the south-eastern end of the Bahamas chain of islands, and lying about 145 km (90 miles) north of Haiti. Eight islands are inhabited: Grand Turk and Salt Cay (both in the smaller Turks group to the east of the Caicos), South Caicos, Middle (Grand) Caicos, North Caicos, Providenciales (Provo), Pine Cay and Parrot Cay. The climate is warm throughout the year but tempered by constant trade winds. The average annual temperature is 27°C (82°F) and rainfall ranges from 530 mm (21 ins) in the eastern islands to 1,000 mm (40 ins) in the west. The official language is English, though some Creole is spoken by Haitian immigrants. Many Christian churches are represented, the largest denomination being the Baptist Union (25.5% of the population at the census of May 1990). The flag is the British 'Blue Ensign', with the shield from the islands' coat of arms, bearing a shell, a lobster and a cactus, in the fly. The capital is Cockburn Town, on Grand Turk island.

Recent History

The Turks and Caicos Islands were first settled by Amerindian peoples. The islands were then inhabited by privateers, and were settled from Bermuda and by exiled 'Loyalists' from the former British colonies in North America. A Jamaican dependency from 1874 to 1959, the Turks and Caicos Islands became a separate colony in 1962, following Jamaican independence. After an administrative association with the Bahamas, the islands received their own Governor in 1972. The first elections under the present Constitution took place in 1976, and were won by the pro-independence People's Democratic Movement (PDM). In 1980 an agreement was made with the United Kingdom whereby, if the governing PDM won the 1980 elections, the islands would receive independence and a payment of £12m. However, lacking the leadership of J. A. G. S. McCartney, the Chief Minister (who had been killed in an aircraft accident in May 1980), the PDM lost the election in November to the Progressive National Party (PNP), which is committed to continued dependent status. At a subsequent general election, in May 1984, the PNP, led by the Chief Minister, Norman Saunders, won eight of the 11 elective seats.

In March 1985 the Chief Minister, the Minister for Development and Commerce and a PNP member of the Legislative Council were arrested in Miami, Florida, USA, on charges involving illicit drugs and violations of the US Travel Act. All three men were subsequently convicted and imprisoned (with Saunders receiving an eight-year sentence). Saunders resigned and was replaced as Chief Minister by Nathaniel Francis, hitherto the Minister of Public Works and Utilities.

In July 1986 a commission of inquiry into allegations of arson and administrative malpractice following the destruction by fire of a government building in December 1985 concluded that Francis and two of his ministers were unfit for ministerial office; all three ministers subsequently resigned. Two members of the PDM were also deemed to be unfit for public office. In the same month the Governor dissolved the Government, and the Executive Council was replaced by an interim advisory council, comprising the Governor and four members of the former Executive Council. A constitutional commission was appointed in September to review the future administration of the islands.

A general election, preceding the return to ministerial rule, took place in March 1988, following the British Government's acceptance of the principal recommendations of the constitutional commission in the previous year. Under a new multi-member system of representation (see Constitution, below), the PDM won 11 of the 13 seats on the Legislative Council, and the PNP won the remaining two. Oswald O. Skippings, the leader of the PDM, was appointed Chief Minister. The new Constitution strengthened the reserve powers of the Governor, but otherwise the form of government was similar to the provisions of the 1976 Constitution.

In April 1991 a general election took place, at which the PNP secured eight seats, defeating the PDM (which won the remaining five). Skippings was replaced as Chief Minister by C. Washington Misick, the leader of the PNP.

At a general election in January 1995 the PDM secured eight seats, while the PNP won four. Derek Taylor, leader of the PDM, was appointed Chief Minister.

A serious dispute arose between the Legislative Council and the Governor in August 1995, following the latter's decision to reappoint Kipling Douglas to the position of Chief Justice. Taylor, who claimed that Douglas did not enjoy the confidence of his Government, described the decision as provocative and disrespectful. Relations deteriorated in subsequent months, and in February 1996 a petition requesting the immediate removal of the Governor, signed by all members of the Government and opposition, was presented to the British Foreign and Commonwealth Office (FCO). A delegation of politicians from the territory travelled to the United Kingdom to reinforce the views of the Legislative Council, which were believed to be shared by a majority of islanders. In the following month, however, their demands were rejected by the British Government, which deployed a frigate in the islands' waters and ordered 100 police officers to prepare for immediate transfer to the territory in the event of civil disturbance. A climate of animosity between the Governor and the islanders persisted during 1996, and in September Bourke departed from the territory, without formal ceremony, following the expiry of his term of office. He was replaced by John Kelly.

At a general election held on 4 March 1999 the PDM increased its representation in the Legislative Council to nine seats. The PNP won the other four seats.

In June 2000 the Turks and Caicos Islands were included on a list of territories regarded as operating harmful tax regimes. The Organisation for Economic Co-operation and Development (OECD, see p. 347), which compiled the list, urged the Government to make legislative changes, in order to introduce greater legal and administrative transparency to prevent companies using the country's tax system for money-laundering or tax-evasion purposes. OECD removed the Turks and Caicos Islands from the list in March 2002, declaring that the Government had made sufficient commitments to improve transparency and effective exchange of information on tax matters by the end of 2005. In late 2002, however, the recovering financial sector faced further disruption when the United Kingdom, under pressure from a European Union (EU, see p. 244) investigation into tax evasion, demanded that the Turks and Caicos Islands disclose the identities and account details of Europeans holding private savings accounts on the islands. The Turks and Caicos Islands, along with some other British Overseas Territories facing similar demands, claimed it was being treated unfairly, but pledged to introduce the necessary legislation to implement the EU's Savings Tax Directive in 2004, provided it was granted the same allowances as powerful European countries, such as Switzerland and Luxembourg.

In April 2002 the Governor established a Constitutional Modernisation Review Body to discuss changes to the islands' Constitution. This all-party panel presented a report in September. Discussions on a new constitution took place in 2004 between representatives of the Turks and Caicos Islands and British Governments. Following further negotiations between government ministers in October 2005, it was agreed that a draft text of a modernized constitution would be drawn up by the FCO. This proposed document would be subject to approval by both the PDM and the PNP, after which a public consultation period would be held. Adoption of the amendments would be subject to approval by the Legislative Council.

In May 2002 the British Overseas Territories Act, having received royal assent in the United Kingdom in February, came into force and granted British citizenship rights to the people of its Overseas Territories, including the Turks and Caicos Islands. Under the new law, Turks and Caicos Islanders would be able to hold British passports and work in the United Kingdom and anywhere else in the EU. In March 2005 a delegation from the Turks and Caicos Islands made an official visit to the Bahamas in a bid to forge closer ties between the two Governments.

In October 2002 capital punishment for treason and piracy, the only remaining capital crime in the United Kingdom Overseas Territories, was abolished in the Turks and Caicos Islands. In December Jim Poston replaced Mervyn Jones as Governor.

At a general election in 24 April 2003 the PDM won seven of the 13 seats in the Legislative Council. The PNP took the remaining six seats, but challenged the results in two of the more closely fought constituencies. By-elections were held in the two constituencies on 7 August after evidence emerged of bribery and irregularities in voter registration lists; the PNP secured victory in both ballots and therefore wrested overall control of the Legislative Council from the PDM. Misick replaced Taylor as Chief Minister on 15 August.

In July 2005 James Poston was succeeded by Richard Tauwhare as Governor.

In spite of ongoing discussions regarding a new constitution, in April 2006 the Chief Minister met with members of the UN's Special Committee on Decolonization to discuss options for self-determination. Three directions were outlined: independence; independence by free association; or independence by way of integration. However, it was not clear how many islanders wanted independence, and the opposition questioned Misick's motives behind the talks. Misick subsequently issued a statement indicating that the PNP would not pursue independence during the constitutional discussions, nor would the matter feature as an objective of their electoral campaign ahead of the general election, scheduled for February 2007. A public consultation was conducted over a draft constitution, formulated pursuant to an agreement upon greater self-government for the territory, between United Kingdom and island representatives in October 2005, and approved by the Legislative Council on 28 June 2006. Following final submission to the FCO and endorsement by Queen Elizabeth II, the Council decreed the Turks and Caicos Constitutional Order 2006, adopting the new Constitution on 19 July. The Constitution was finally enacted on 9 August, when Chief Minister Misick and Deputy Chief Minister Floyd Hall were inaugurated as Premier and Deputy Premier, respectively. The new administrative regime instituted a new office of Deputy Governor, to which former Chief Secretary Mahala Wynns was appointed; the assignment complied with a new constitutional requirement that the position be occupied by a 'belonger' of the Turks and Caicos Islands. Notable amendments under the new Constitution included the investiture of a unicameral parliament, which would replace and enlarge upon the former Legislative Council. The new House of Assembly would comprise of 21 members, 15 of whom were to be elected for a four-year term and four of whom were to be nominated from the Cabinet (formerly the Executive Council). The new legislature would also include the Attorney-General (an ex officio member) and the Speaker. The Cabinet was to be formed of the Premier, one ex officio member (the Attorney-General), and six ministers—to be appointed by the Governor from the elected House of Assembly—and would be presided over by the Governor. An Electoral District Boundaries 2006 Bill, in accordance with a provision within the new Constitution for the revision of electoral boundaries upon the recommendations of a dedicated commission, was also approved by the legislature, affording the creation of two new constituencies to reflect the two additional elected members of the House of Assembly. The legislation was ratified by the House of Assembly on 8 January 2007, creating two new electoral districts on the island of Providenciales.

A general election was held on 9 February 2007. The PNP were returned to office for a second term, winning 13 of the 15 seats in the House of Assembly. The PDM secured the remaining two seats. Misick was reappointed Premier. The ballot followed a bitterly fought election campaign, in which the PDM made allegations of corruption against the ruling party.

In July 2007 it was alleged that the Premier had assaulted an opposition member of Parliament, Arthur Robinson, in response to criticism of Misick's despatch of his governmental responsibilities. It was claimed that Misick spent a significant proportion of time away from the islands, provoking PDM accusations that he had become an 'absentee premier'. The leader of the PDM, Floyd Seymour, subsequently demanded Misick's resignation. The Premier refused to yield to further calls to stand down when, in early April 2008, allegations of sexual assault surfaced against him by a US citizen who had been visiting the islands. He denied all the claims.

The United Kingdom's House of Commons Foreign Affairs Committee expressed concern in late March 2008 at allegations of corruption and poor governance on the Turks and Caicos Islands. A series of arson attacks had taken place in the preceding months, targeting court buildings and the Attorney-General's office. According to the Committee, when he requested additional security from the FCO, the Attorney-General was told that this was not the responsibility of that office; the FCO had also failed to appoint a new Chief Auditor to the recently vacant position. The Committee recommended the establishment of a committee of inquiry. Misick responded by denying the allegations and particularly blamed opposition opponents for their inception.

Relations with Haiti were severely damaged on 4 May 2007 when a vessel carrying an estimated 160 Haitian migrants capsized in Turks and Caicos jurisdictional waters during an interception operation by the islands' coastguard. 61 of those originally on board were reported dead, while over 20 migrants remained unaccounted for when the search and rescue effort was abandoned on 7 May. Survivors alleged that a police vessel, ostensibly part of the rescue mission, had rammed the overburdened vessel twice prior to its capsize, claims that were vehemently denied by the Turks and Caicos authorities. However, suspicion remained that a 'deliberate criminal action' had been committed. In late February 2008 newspaper reports claimed that over 1,000 Haitian nationals had landed on the islands since the beginning of the year, most of whom had been repatriated.

Government

Under the provisions of the 2006 Constitution (amending the 1988 revision of the 1976 Constitution), executive power is vested in the Governor, appointed by the British monarch. The Governor is responsible for external affairs, internal security, defence, international financial services and the appointment of public officers; other matters are resolved by the Governor upon the advice of the Cabinet. The Governor is President of the Cabinet, which comprises nine members: one ex officio (the Attorney-General), the Premier, and six appointed by the Governor from among the elected members of the House of Assembly. The House of Assembly comprises the Speaker, four nominated members, the ex officio member of the Cabinet and 15 members elected by universal adult suffrage.

Economic Affairs

In 2006, according to official estimates, the Turks and Caicos Islands' gross domestic product (GDP) was a preliminary US $721m., equivalent to some $21,743 per head. During 2001–02, it was estimated, the population increased at an average annual rate of 10.8%, when GDP increased, in real terms, by 10.0% per year; growth in 2006 was 16.7%.

Agriculture is not practised on any significant scale in the Turks Islands or on South Caicos (the most populous island of the territory). None the less, the sector contributed a preliminary 1.0% to GDP in 2006. The other islands of the Caicos group grow some beans, maize and a few fruits and vegetables. There is some livestock-rearing, but the islands' principal natural resource is fisheries, which accounts for almost all commodity exports, the principal species caught being the spiny lobster (an estimated 388 metric tons in 2005) and the conch (an estimated 5,103 metric tons in that year). Conchs were being developed commercially (on the largest conch farm in the world) in 2007, and there was potential for larger-scale fishing. Exports of lobster and conch earned US $3.4m. in 1995, which constituted an increase of more than 14% compared with the previous year's earnings.

Industrial activity consists mainly of construction (especially for the tourism industry) and fish-processing. The sector contributed a preliminary 21.8% to GDP in 2006. The islands possess plentiful supplies of aragonite. The islands are dependent upon the import of mineral fuels to satisfy energy requirements.

The principal economic sector is the service industry, which, in 2006 contributed an estimated 77.1% to GDP. This is dominated by tourism, which is concentrated on the island of Providenciales. The market is for wealthier visitors, most of whom come from the USA. Tourist arrivals increased from approximately 117,600 in 1999 to 165,400 in 2001 and this level was maintained with figures of 155,600 in 2002 and 163,600 in 2003, even in the face of weakened global demand in the aftermath of the September 2001 terrorist attacks on the USA and the subsequent US-led 'war on terror'. Tourism arrivals continued to rise, reaching 264,900 in 2006, while tourism receipts were US $355.1m. in 2005. The depreciation in value of the US dollar, the official currency of the Turks and Caicos, in 2003–04, prompted an increase in non-US visitors to the islands. In January 2004 it was announced that a new US $35m. cruise-ship terminal would be constructed in Grand Turk, enabling, for the first time, large passenger liners to stop in the Territory. The terminal was inaugurated in February 2006. An 'offshore' financial sector was encouraged in the 1980s, and new regulatory legislation was ratified at the end of 1989. In 2000 there were some 8,000 overseas companies registered in the islands.

In 2003 the Turks and Caicos Islands recorded a trade deficit of US $160.9m. (exports were 5.7% of the value of imports). This deficit is normally offset by receipts from tourism, aid from the United Kingdom and revenue from the 'offshore' financial sector. The USA is the principal trading partner, but some trade is conducted with the United Kingdom and with neighbouring nations.

According to figures from the Caribbean Development Bank (CDB), there was an overall budget deficit of US $7.9m. in 2003. In the Government's 2006/07 budget plan, there was an overall budgetary surplus of $13.6m. The islands received a total of $8.2m. in British development assistance in 1999/2000. The total external public debt was $20.0m. in 2003. The rate of inflation, which stood at about 4% in 1995, is dependent upon the movement of prices in the USA, the islands' principal trading partner. Unemployment increased to an estimated 10% in the late 1990s. A large number of Turks and Caicos 'belongers' have emigrated, many to the Bahamas, especially in search of skilled labour (there is no tertiary education in the territory). In July 2000 the CDB announced a loan to the Government of some $4m. to assist the Turks and Caicos Investment Agency.

The Turks and Caicos Islands, as a dependency of the United Kingdom, have the status of Overseas Territory in association with the European Union (EU, see p. 244). The islands are also a member of the CDB (see p. 201) and an associate member of the Caribbean Community and Common Market (CARICOM, see p. 196). The Territory became an associate member of the Association of Caribbean States (ACS, see p. 411) in April 2006.

The economy and the population of the Turks and Caicos Islands were estimated to have doubled in size during the 1990s, making the islands one of the region's most dynamic economies. The remarkable economic growth experienced by the islands was chiefly owing to the increasing significance of the tourism and international financial services sectors, both of which benefited from the perceived stability of United Kingdom Overseas Territory status. In the past decade the 'offshore' financial sector successfully rehabilitated its international reputation through the introduction, in 2002, of a supervisory body, the Financial Services Commission, and the implementation of more stringent regulatory legislation based on the maxim of 'privacy not secrecy'. In early 2004 the financial sector faced further regulatory disruption when the islands came under pressure to implement the EU's Savings Tax Directive (see Recent History). Tourism also grew steadily in the late 1990s, and as a result many new hotels and resorts were developed. Concern has, however, been expressed that the islands are in danger of becoming overdeveloped and thereby of damaging their reputation as an unspoilt tourist location. A further source of disquiet has been the exclusion of many inhabitants from the benefits of economic growth; it was estimated that the economic situation of the majority of 'belongers' improved only marginally during the 1990s, as newly created jobs were often taken by low-wage migrant workers or by highly skilled expatriate workers. It has also been noted that the territory's growth, which is driven more by inward investment than by domestic production, is highly dependent on exterior factors, and international proposals to force comprehensive reforms of 'offshore' financial services centres were, therefore, of particular concern. A 10-year National Development Plan was launched in October 2005, an initiative between the Department of Planning and the Department of Economic Planning and Statistics. The tourism industry was expected to suffer following the introduction of new US legislation in January 2007, which required all passengers travelling between the Caribbean and the USA to hold valid passports. However, tourist arrivals were expected to continue to rise as the US dollar lost value in the second half of 2007, making the islands a cheaper destination for many foreign visitors. Meanwhile, the Government expressed its intention to develop other areas of the economy, including joint business ventures with foreign investors and the expansion of the 'offshore' banking sector. GDP growth rates for 2007 and 2008 were forecast to reach 7.6% and 6.5%, respectively, the latter a consequence of the possible recession in the US economy. GDP per head is expected to decline from 2010 as a result of a growing population, fuelled by increased immigration.

Education

Primary education, beginning at seven years of age and lasting seven years, is compulsory, and is provided free of charge in government schools. Secondary education, from the age of 14, lasts for five years, and is also free. In 1997 there were 21 primary schools, and in 1990 one private secondary school and four government secondary schools. In 1997 the Caribbean Development Bank approved a loan of just under US $4m. to fund the establishment of a permanent campus for the Turks and Caicos Community College.

Public Holidays

2008: 1 January (New Year's Day), 12 March (Commonwealth Day), 21 March (Good Friday), 24 March (Easter Monday), 26 May (National Heroes' Day), 9 June (Queen's Official Birthday), 4 August (Emancipation Day), 26 September (National Youth Day), 13 October (Columbus Day), 24 October (International Human Rights Day), 25–26 December (Christmas).

2009: 1 January (New Year's Day), 12 March (Commonwealth Day), 10 April (Good Friday), 13 April (Easter Monday), 25 May (National Heroes' Day), 8 June (Queen's Official Birthday), 3 August (Emancipation Day), 28 September (National Youth Day), 12 October (Columbus Day), 24 October (International Human Rights Day), 25–26 December (Christmas).

Weights and Measures

The imperial system is in use.

Statistical Survey

Source: Department of Economic Planning and Statistics, Ministry of Finance, South Base, Grand Turk; tel. 946-2801; fax 946-2557; e-mail info@depstc.org; internet www.depstc.org.

AREA AND POPULATION

Area: 948 sq km (366 sq miles). Note: Area includes low water level for all islands, but excludes area to high water mark.

Population: 7,413 at census of 12 May 1980; 11,465 at census of 31 May 1990; 19,886 (males 9,897, females 9,989) at census of 20 August 2001; *2008* (estimate): 36,605. *By Island* (2006, estimates): Grand Turk 5,718; South Caicos 1,118; Middle Caicos 307; North Caicos 1,537; Salt Cay 114; Parrot Cay 60; Providenciales 24,348.

Density (2008 estimate): 38.6 per sq km.

Principal Towns: Cockburn Town (capital, on Grand Turk), population 2,500 (1987 estimate); Cockburn Harbour (South Caicos), population 1,000. *Mid-2003* (UN estimate, incl. suburbs): Grand Turk 5,680 (Source: UN, *World Urbanization Prospects: The 2003 Revision*).

Births, Marriages and Deaths (2006): Live births 409 (birth rate 12.3 per 1,000); Marriages 636 (marriage rate 19.20 per 1,000); Deaths 73 (death rate 2.3 per 1,000).

Expectation of Life (years at birth, 2007): 75.0 (males 72.7; females 77.3). Source: Pan American Health Organization.

Economically Active Population (2005): Agriculture and fishing 247; Mining and quarrying 56; Manufacturing 202; Utilities 269; Construction 2,402; Wholesale and retail trade 1,298; Hotels and restaurants 2,935; Transport, storage and communications 650; Financial intermediation 496; Real estate, renting and business services 1,607; Public administration 2,310; Education, health and social work 496; Other community, social and personal services 971; Private household employment 1,608; Activities not adequately defined 1,895; *Total employed* 17,442; Unemployed 1,524; *Total labour force* 18,966. *2006* (preliminary): Total employed 18,195; Unemployed 1,464; Total labour force 19,659.

HEALTH AND WELFARE

Total Fertility Rate (children per woman, 2007): 3.0.

Under-5 Mortality Rate (per 1,000 live births, 1997): 22.0.

Hospital Beds (per 1,000 head, 2006): 1.4.

Physicians (per 1,000 head, 2001): 7.3.

Health Expenditure (public, % of total, 2004): 12.6.

Health Expenditure (US $ per head, 2004): 741.2.

Access to Sanitation (% of persons, 2004): 96.

Source: partly Pan American Health Organization.

For other sources and definitions see explanatory note on p. vi.

AGRICULTURE, ETC.

Fishing (metric tons, live weight, 2005): Capture 5,491 (Caribbean spiny lobster 388, Stromboid conchs 5,103); Aquaculture 4; *Total catch* 5,495. Figures exclude aquatic plants and mammals.

Source: FAO.

INDUSTRY

Electric Energy (production, million kWh): 10 in 1999–2004. Source: UN, *Industrial Commodity Statistics Yearbook*.

FINANCE

Currency and Exchange Rate: United States currency is used: 100 cents = 1 US dollar ($). Sterling and Euro Equivalents (31 December 2007): £1 sterling = US $2.0034; €1 = US $1.4721; $100 = £49.92 = €67.93.

Budget (US $ million, 2006/07): Total revenue and grants 288.63 (Current revenue 202.52, Capital revenue and grants 86.11); Total expenditure 274.99 (Current expenditure 199.49, Capital expenditure 75.50).

Gross Domestic Product (US $ million at constant 2000 prices): 421.3 in 2004; 481.9 in 2005; 568.1 in 2006 (preliminary).

Expenditure on the Gross Domestic Product (US $ million, 2006, preliminary): Government final consumption expenditure 138.9; Private final consumption expenditure 383.2; Gross capital formation 337.4; *Total domestic expenditure* 859.5; Exports of goods and services 453.5; *Less* Imports of goods and services 591.0; *GDP in market prices* 721.9.

Gross Domestic Product by Economic Activity (US $ million, 2006, preliminary): Agriculture and fishing 7.0; Mining and quarrying 8.0; Manufacturing 12.4; Utilities 25.2; Construction 100.4; Wholesale and retail trade 28.0; Hotels and restaurants 193.8; Transport, storage and communications 57.7; Financial intermediation 77.8; Real estate, renting and business activities 56.1; Public administration, defence and social security 48.4; Education 19.6; Health and social work 16.3; Other community, social and personal services 18.5; *Sub-total* 669.2; *Less* Financial intermediation services indirectly measured 52.5; *Gross value added in basic prices* 616.7; Taxes, less subsidies, on products 105.2; *GDP in market prices* 721.9.

Balance of Payments (US $ million, 2002): Exports of goods f.o.b. 8.7; Imports of goods f.o.b. −177.5; *Trade balance* −168.8; Exports of services 163.1; Imports of services −81.8; *Balance on goods and services* −87.5. Source: Caribbean Development Bank, *Social and Economic Indicators*.

EXTERNAL TRADE

Principal Commodities (US $ million, 2007, provisional): *Imports:* Food and beverages 74.0; Consumer goods 118.0 (Durables 35.4, Non-durables 53.5, Semi-durables 29.0); Fuels and lubricants 48.3; Industrial supplies 185.0; Transport equipment and parts thereof 68.1; Capital goods 86.0 ; Total (incl. others) 580.6. *Exports:* Domestic exports 15.8 (Lobster 2.9; Conch 2.7); Re-exports 0.5; Total exports 16.3.

Principal Trading Partners (US $ million, 2004, provisional): *Imports c.i.f.:* Bahamas 3.8; USA 216.2; Total 220.6. *Exports f.o.b.:* USA 10.8; Total 10.8.

TRANSPORT

Road Traffic (1984): 1,563 registered motor vehicles.

Shipping: *International Freight Traffic* (estimates in '000 metric tons, 1990): Goods loaded 135; Goods unloaded 149. *Merchant Fleet* (vessels registered at 31 December 2006): 5; Total displacement 975 grt. Sources: UN, *Monthly Bulletin of Statistics*; Lloyd's Register-Fairplay, *World Fleet Statistics*.

TOURISM

Tourist Arrivals ('000): 176.1 (of which USA 123.3) in 2005; 248.3 (of which USA 169.7) in 2006; 264.9 in 2007.

Tourism Receipts (estimates, US $ million): 275.6 in 2003; 317.9 in 2004; 355.1 in 2005.

Source: Caribbean Development Bank, *Social and Economic Indicators*.

COMMUNICATIONS MEDIA

Radio Receivers (1997): 8,000 in use.

Telephones (2000, estimate): 6,000 main lines in use.

Facsimile Machines (1992): 200 in use.

Non-daily Newspapers (1996): 1 (estimated circulation 5,000).

Sources: UNESCO, *Statistical Yearbook*; UN, *Statistical Yearbook*.

EDUCATION

Pre-primary (2004/05, unless otherwise indicated): 21 schools (1996/97); 87 teachers (estimate); 672 pupils.

Primary (2004/05, unless otherwise indicated): 10 government schools (2005); 148 teachers; 2,220 pupils.

General Secondary (2004/05, unless otherwise indicated): 4 government schools (2005); 174 teachers (estimate); 1,558 pupils.

Vocational Education (2004/05, estimates): 12 teachers; 128 pupils.

Adult Literacy Rate (UNESCO estimates): 99% (males 99%; females 98%) in 1998.

Sources: partly UNESCO Institute for Statistics; Caribbean Development Bank, *Social and Economic Indicators*.

Directory

The Constitution

The Order in Council of July 1986 enabled the Governor to suspend the ministerial form of government, for which the Constitution of 1976 made provision. Ministerial government was restored in March 1988, following amendments to the Constitution, recommended by a constitutional commission. A further revision to the Constitution, whereby the islands acquired greater self-government, was passed by a resolution of the Legislative Council on 28 June 2006 and formally adopted on 19 July. The Turks and Caicos Islands Constitution Order 2006 became effective from 9 August.

The revised Constitution of 2006 provides for a Cabinet (formerly the Executive Council) and a House of Assembly (formerly the Legislative Council). Executive authority is vested in the British monarch and is exercised by the Governor (the monarch's appointed representative), who also holds responsibility for external affairs, internal security, defence, the appointment of any person to any public office and the suspension and termination of appointment of any public officer.

The Cabinet comprises: one ex officio member (the Attorney-General); the Premier (formerly the Chief Minister—appointed by the Governor) who is, in the judgement of the Governor, the leader of the political party represented in the House of Assembly that commands the support of a majority of the elected members of the House; and six other ministers from among the elected or nominated members of the House of Assembly, appointed by the Governor on the advice of the Premier. The Cabinet is presided over by the Governor.

The House of Assembly consists of the Speaker, the ex officio member of the Cabinet, 15 members elected by residents aged 18 and over, and four nominated members (appointed by the Governor, two on the advice of the Premier, one on the advice of the Leader of the Opposition and one at the Governor's discretion).

Provision was also included under the revised Constitution for the establishment of an Advisory National Security Council, mandated to advise the Governor on matters relating to defence and internal security, external affairs, and international financial services regulation. The Council would also make recommendations for the dispatch of the Governor's responsibilities in the event of a public emergency.

For the purposes of elections to the enlarged House of Assembly, an Electoral District Boundaries (Amendment) Bill was ratified on 8 January 2007, dividing the islands into 15 electoral districts. In 1988 and 1991 a multiple voting system was used, whereby three districts elected three members each, while the remaining five districts each elected two members. However, from the 1995 election a single-member constituency system was used.

The Government

Governor: RICHARD TAUWHARE (sworn in 11 July 2005).
Deputy Governor: MAHALA WYNNS.

CABINET
(April 2008)

President: RICHARD TAUWHARE (The Governor).

Premier and Minister of Planning, Tourism, Development and District Administration: Dr MICHAEL EUGENE MISICK.

Deputy Premier and Minister of Finance, National Insurance and Economic Planning: FLOYD BASIL HALL.

Minister of Housing, Agriculture, Works and Telecommunications: JEFFREY CHRISTOVAL HALL.

Minister of Health and Human Services: LILLIAN ELAINE BOYCE.

Minister of Education, Youth, Sports and Culture: Dr CARLTON MILLS.

Minister of Natural Resources, Fisheries and the Environment: McALLISTER EUGENE HANCHELL.

Minister of Home Affairs and Public Safety: GALMO WILLIAMS.

Ex Officio Member: Attorney-General: KURT DE FREITES.

GOVERNMENT OFFICES

Office of the Governor: Govt House, Grand Turk; tel. 946-2308; fax 946-2903; e-mail govhouse@tciway.tc.

Office of the Premier: Govt Sq., Grand Turk; tel. 946-2801; fax 946-2777.

Office of the Deputy Governor: South Base, Grand Turk; tel. 946-2702; fax 946-2886; e-mail cso@gov.tc.

Office of the Permanent Secretary: Finance Dept, Premier's Office, Govt Bldgs, Front St, Grand Turk; tel. 946-1115; fax 946-2777.

UNITED KINGDOM OVERSEAS TERRITORIES   The Turks and Caicos Islands

Attorney-General's Chambers: South Base, Grand Turk; tel. 946-2096; fax 946-2588; e-mail attorneygeneral@tciway.tc; internet www.lawsconsolidated.tc.

HOUSE OF ASSEMBLY
Speaker: GLENNEVANS CLARKE.
Clerk to the Councils: RUTH BLACKMAN.

Election, 9 February 2007

Party	Seats
Progressive National Party (PNP)	13
People's Democratic Movement (PDM)	2
Total	15

There is one ex officio member (the Attorney-General), four appointed members, and a Speaker (assisted by a Deputy Speaker).

Political Organizations

People's Democratic Movement (PDM): POB 38, Grand Turk; favours internal self-govt and eventual independence; Chair. SHAWN MALCOLM; Leader FLOYD SEYMOUR.

Progressive National Party (PNP): Providenciales; tel. 941-4663; fax 946-3673; e-mail pnp@tciway.tc; supports full internal self-govt; Chair. SANDRA GARLAND; Leader MICHAEL EUGENE MISICK.

United Democratic Party (UDP): Grand Turk; f. 1993; Leader WENDAL SWANN.

Judicial System

Justice is administered by the Supreme Court of the islands, presided over by the Chief Justice. There is a Chief Magistrate resident on Grand Turk, who also acts as Judge of the Supreme Court. There are also three Deputy Magistrates.

The Court of Appeal held its first sitting in February 1995. Previously the islands had shared a court of appeal in Nassau, Bahamas. In certain cases, appeals are made to the Judicial Committee of the Privy Council (based in the United Kingdom).

Judicial Department
Grand Turk; tel. 946-2114; fax 946-2720.
Chief Justice: CHRISTOPHER GARDNER.
Chief Magistrate: (Providenciales) RICHARD WILLIAMS.
Resident Magistrate: (Grand Turk) JOAN F. JOYNER.

Religion

CHRISTIANITY

The Anglican Communion
Within the Church in the Province of the West Indies, the territory forms part of the diocese of Nassau and the Bahamas. The Bishop is resident in Nassau. According to census results, there were 1,465 adherents in 1990.

Anglican Church: St Mary's Church, Front St, Grand Turk; tel. 946-2289; internet bahamas.anglican.org; Archbishop Rev. DREXEL GOMEZ.

The Roman Catholic Church
The Bishop of Nassau, Bahamas (suffragan to the archdiocese of Kingston in Jamaica), has jurisdiction in the Turks and Caicos Islands as Superior of the Mission to the Territory (founded in June 1984).

Roman Catholic Mission: Leeward Highway, POB 340, Providenciales; tel. and fax 941-5136; e-mail info_rcm@catholic.tc; internet www.catholic.tc; churches on Grand Turk, South and North Caicos, and on Providenciales; 132 adherents in 1990 (according to census results); Chancellor Fr PETER BALDACCHINO.

Other Christian Churches
Baptist Union of the Turks and Caicos Islands: South Caicos; tel. 946-3220; 3,153 adherents in 1990 (according to census results).

Jehovah's Witnesses: Kingdom Hall, Intersection of Turtle Cove and Bridge Rd, POB 400, Providenciales; tel. 941-5583.

Methodist Church: The Ridge, Grand Turk; tel. 946-2115; 1,238 adherents in 1990 (according to census results).

New Testament Church of God: Orea Alley, Grand Turk; tel. 946-2175.

Seventh-day Adventists: Grand Turk; tel. 946-2065; Pastor PETER KERR.

The Press

Times of the Islands Magazine: Southwind Plaza, POB 234, Providenciales; tel. and fax 946-4788; e-mail timespub@tciway.tc; internet www.timespub.tc; f. 1988; quarterly; circ. 10,000; Editor KATHY BORSUK.

Turks and Caicos Free Press: Market Pl., POB 179, Providenciales; tel. 941-5615; fax 941-3402; e-mail freepress@tciway.tc; internet www.tcifreepress.com; f. 1991; Vox-Global Télématique; weekly; circ. 3,000; Editor Dr GILBERT MORRIS; Man. BARBARA SMITH.

Turks & Caicos Islands Real Estate Association Real Estate Magazine: Southwind Plaza, POB 234, Providenciales; tel. and fax 946-4788; e-mail timespub@tciway.tc; internet www.timespub.tc; 3 a year; circ. 15,000; Editor KATHY BORSUK.

Turks and Caicos Sun: Airport Plaza, Suite 5, POB 439, Providenciales; tel. 946-8542; fax 946-3281; e-mail turksandcaicossun@express.tc; internet www.suntci.com; f. 2005; publ. by Island Publishing Co Ltd; weekly; Publr and Editor-in-Chief HAYDEN BOYCE.

Turks and Caicos Weekly News: Leeward Highway, Cheshire House, POB 52, Providenciales; tel. 946-4664; fax 946-4661; e-mail tcnews@tciway.tc; Editor BLYTHE DUNCANSON.

Where, When, How: The Saltmills, Unit 6, POB 192, Providenciales; tel. 946-4815; fax 941-3497; e-mail info@wwhtci.com; internet www.wherewhenhow.com; f. 1994; bi-monthly; travel magazine; Co-Editor CHARLES ZDENEK; Co-Editor BRENDA ZDENEK; circ. 70,000 a year.

Broadcasting and Communications

TELECOMMUNICATIONS

Telecommunication Commission: Business Solutions Bldg, Leeward Hwy, Providenciales; tel. 946-1900; fax 946-1119; e-mail info@tcitelecommission.tc; internet www.tcitelecom.gov.tc; f. 2004; regulates telecommunications; Telecommunications Officer JOHN WILLIAMS.

Cable & Wireless (Turks and Caicos) Ltd: Leeward Hwy, POB 78, Providenciales; tel. 946-2200; fax 946-2497; e-mail cwtci@tciway.tc; internet www.cw.tc; f. 1973; monopoly ended in Jan. 2006; Country Chief Exec. DREXWELL SEYMOUR.

Digicel: Graceway House, Unit 207, Leeward Hwy, Providenciales; tel. 941-7600; fax 941-7601; e-mail tcicustomercare@digicelgroup.com; internet www.digiceltci.com; owned by an Irish consortium; granted licence in 2006 to provide mobile telecommunications services in Turks and Caicos; Chair. DENIS O'BRIEN.

Radio

Power 92.5 FM: Providenciales; e-mail kenny@power925fm.com; internet www.power925fm.com.

Radio Providenciales: Leeward Hwy, POB 32, Providenciales; tel. 946-4496; fax 946-4108; commercial.

Radio Turks and Caicos (RTC): POB 69, Grand Turk; tel. 946-2007; fax 946-1600; e-mail rtc@tciway.tc; internet www.turksandcaicos.tc/rtc; govt-owned; commercial; broadcasts 105 hrs weekly; Man. LYNETTE SMITH.

Radio Visión Cristiana Internacional: North End, South Caicos; tel. 946-6601; fax 946-6600; e-mail radiovision@tciway.tc; internet www.radiovision.net; commercial; Man. WENDELL SEYMOUR.

Television

Television programmes are available from a cable network, and broadcasts from the Bahamas can be received in the islands.

TCI New Media Network: Providenciales; f. 2008; govt-owned; Gen. Man. AVA-DAYNE KERR.

Turks and Caicos Television: Pond St, POB 80, Grand Turk; tel. 946-1530; fax 946-2896.

WIV Cable TV: Tower Raza, Leeward Hwy, POB 679, Providenciales; tel. 946-4273; fax 946-4790.

Finance

(cap. = capital; res = reserves; dep = deposit; br(s). = branch(es); amounts in US $ unless otherwise indicated)

REGULATORY AUTHORITY

Financial Services Commission (FSC): Harry E. Francis Bldg, Pond St, POB 173, Grand Turk; tel. 946-2791; fax 946-2821; e-mail

UNITED KINGDOM OVERSEAS TERRITORIES   The Turks and Caicos Islands

fsc@tciway.tc; f. 2002; regulates local and 'offshore' financial services sector; Man. Dir NEVILLE CADOGAN.

BANKING

Belize Bank: The Centre Mews, POB 270, Providenciales; tel. 941-5028; fax 941-5029; e-mail belizebank@tciway.tc; internet www.belizebank.com.

Bordier International Bank and Trust Ltd: Caribbean Pl., Leeward Hwy, POB 5, Providenciales; tel. 946-4535; fax 946-4540; e-mail enquiries@bibt.com; internet www.bibt.com; Chair. FRANÇOIS BOHN; Man. ELISE HARTSHORN.

FirstCaribbean International Bank (Bahamas) Ltd: Leeward Hwy, POB 698, Providenciales; tel. 946-2831; fax 946-2695; e-mail care@firstcaribbeanbank.com; internet www.firstcaribbeanbank.com; f. 2002 following merger of Caribbean operations of Barclays Bank PLC and CIBC; Barclays relinquished its stake to CIBC in June 2006; Exec. Chair. MICHAEL MANSOOR; CEO CHARLES PINK.

Scotiabank (Canada): Cherokee Rd, POB 15, Providenciales; tel. 946-4750; fax 946-4755; e-mail bns.turkscaicos@scotiabank.com; Man. Dir DAVID TAIT; br. on Grand Turk.

Turks and Caicos Banking Co Ltd: Duke St North, Cockburn Town, POB 123, Grand Turk; tel. 946-2368; fax 946-2365; e-mail services@tcbc.tc; internet www.turksandcaicosbanking.tc; f. 1980; cap. $2.7m., dep. $9.7m.; Man. Dir ANTON FAESSLER; COO STEFAN O. STOTZ.

TRUST COMPANIES

Berkshire Trust Co Ltd: Caribbean Pl., POB 657, Providenciales; tel. 946-4324; fax 946-4354; e-mail berkshire.trust@tciway.tc; internet www.berkshire.tc; Pres. GORDON WILLIAMSON.

Chartered Trust Co: Town Centre Bldg, Mezzanine Floor, Butterfield Sq., POB 125, Providenciales; tel. 946-4881; fax 946-4041; e-mail reception@chartered-tci.com; internet www.chartered-tci.com; Man. Dir PETER A. SAVORY.

Meridian Trust Co Ltd: Caribbean Pl., Leeward Hwy, POB 599, Providenciales; tel. 941-3082; fax 941-3223; e-mail mtcl@tciway.tc; internet www.meridiantrust.tc; Man. Dir KEITH BURANT.

M & S Trust Co Ltd: Butterfield Sq., POB 260, Providenciales; tel. 946-4650; fax 946-4663; e-mail mslaw@tciway.tc; internet www.mslaw.tc/trusts.htm; Man. Dir TIMOTHY P. O'SULLIVAN; Man. STEVE ROSS.

Temple Trust Co Ltd: 228 Leeward Hwy, Providenciales; tel. 946-5740; fax 946-5739; e-mail info@templefinancialgroup.com; internet www.templefinancialgroup.com; f. 1985; CEO DAVID C. KNIPE.

INSURANCE

Turks and Caicos Islands National Insurance Board: Misick's Bldg, POB 250, Grand Turk; tel. 946-1048; fax 946-1362; e-mail nib@tciway.tc; internet www.nib.tc; 4 brs.

Turks and Caicos Association of Insurance Managers (TC-AIM): Southwinds Pl., Unit 6, Leeward Hwy, Providenciales; tel. 946-4987; fax 946-4621; internet turksandcaicos.tc/aim; f. 2000 as Association of Insurance Managers; name changed as above in 2003 when registered as a non-profit asscn; protects interests of domestic and 'offshore' insurance cos in the islands; Pres. GARY BROUGH; Treas. ROSS BLUMENTRITT.

Several foreign (mainly US and British) companies have offices in the Turks and Caicos Islands. More than 2,000 insurance companies were registered at the end of 2002.

Trade and Industry

GOVERNMENT AGENCIES

Financial Services Commission (FSC): see Finance.

General Trading Company (Turks and Caicos) Ltd: PMBI, Cockburn Town, Grand Turk; tel. 946-2464; fax 946-2799; shipping agents, importers, air freight handlers; wholesale distributor of petroleum products, wines and spirits.

Turks Islands Importers Ltd (TIMCO): Front St, POB 72, Grand Turk; tel. 946-2480; fax 946-2481; f. 1952; agents for Lloyds of London, importers and distributors of food, beer, liquor, building materials, hardware and appliances; Dir H. E. MAGNUS.

DEVELOPMENT ORGANIZATION

Turks and Caicos Islands Investment Agency (TC Invest): Hon. Headley Durham Bldg, Church Folly, POB 105, Grand Turk; tel. 946-2058; fax 946-1464; e-mail tcinvest@tciway.tc; internet www.tcinvest.tc; f. 1974 as Devt Bd of the Turks and Caicos Islands; statutory body; devt finance for private sector; promotion and management of internal investment; Chair. LILLIAN MISICK; Pres. and CEO COLIN R. HEARTWELL.

CHAMBERS OF COMMERCE

Grand Turk Chamber of Commerce: POB 148, Grand Turk; tel. 946-2324; fax 946-2504; e-mail gtchamberofcommerce@tciway.tc; internet www.turksandcaicos.tc/GrandTurkChamber; f. 1974; 57 mem. cos; Pres. and Exec. Dir GLENNEVANS CLARKE; Hon. Sec. SHERLIN WILLIAMS.

North Caicos Chamber of Commerce: tel. 231-1232; Pres. FRANKLYN ROBINSON; Sec. LLEWYN HANDFIELD.

Providenciales Chamber of Commerce: POB 361, Providenciales; tel. 232-3210; fax 946-4582; internet www.provochamber.com; 131 mems (2006); Pres. TINA FENIMORE; Treas. WILLIAM ELLIOT.

UTILITIES

Electricity and Gas

Atlantic Equipment and Power (Turks and Caicos) Ltd: New Airport Rd, Airport Area, South Caicos; tel. and fax 946-3201; Fortis Inc (Bermuda) completed its acquisition of 100% shares in the co in August 2006; cos referred to collectively as Fortis Turks and Caicos; sole provider of electricity in South Caicos; Pres. and CEO EDDINTON POWELL (designate).

PPC Ltd: Town Centre Mall, POB 132, Providenciales; tel. 946-4313; fax 946-4532; Fortis Energy (Bermuda) completed its acquisition of 100% shares in the co, together with those of its sister co Atlantic Equipment and Power (Turks and Caicos) Ltd, in August 2006; cos referred to collectively as Fortis Turks and Caicos; sole supplier of electricity to Providenciales, North Caicos and Middle Caicos; Pres. and CEO EDDINTON POWELL (designate).

Turks and Caicos Utilities Ltd: Pond St, POB 80, Grand Turk; tel. 946-2402; fax 946-2896; e-mail ewiggins@wrbenterprises.com.

Water

Provo Water Co: Grace Bay Rd, POB 39, Providenciales; tel. and fax 946-5205; e-mail provowater@tciway.tc.

Turks and Caicos Water Co: Provo Golf Clubhouse, Grace Bay Rd, POB 124, Providenciales; tel. 946-5126; fax 946-5127.

TRADE UNION

Turks and Caicos Service Workers Union: POB 369, Blue Mountain, Providenciales; tel. 3360; fax 8516; Pres. E. CONRAD HOWELL.

Transport

ROADS

There are 121 km (75 miles) of roads in the islands, of which 24 km, on Grand Turk, South Caicos and Providenciales, are surfaced with tarmac. A causeway linking the North and Middle Caicos islands was completed in late 2007.

SHIPPING

There are regular freight services from Miami, Florida, USA. The main sea ports are Grand Turk, Providenciales, Salt Cay and Cockburn Harbour on South Caicos. A new US $40m. cruise-ship terminal in Grand Turk, which would enable large passenger liners to stop in the territory, opened in February 2006.

Cargo Express Shipping Service Ltd: South Dock Rd, Providenciales; tel. 941-5006; fax 941-5062.

Seacair Ltd: Churchill Bldg, Front St, POB 170, Grand Turk; tel. 946-2591; fax 946-2226.

Tropical Shipping: c/o Cargo Express Services Ltd, South Dock Rd, Providenciales; tel. 941-5006; fax 941-5062; e-mail nbeen@tropical.com; internet www.tropical.com; Pres. RICK MURRELL.

CIVIL AVIATION

There are international airfields on Grand Turk, South Caicos, North Caicos and Providenciales, the last being the most important; there are also landing strips on Middle Caicos, Pine Cay, Parrot Cay and Salt Cay. An expansion project at Providenciales airport was underway in 2008 and included a new terminal building and the lengthening of the runway in order for the airport to accommodate trans-Atlantic flights.

Civil Aviation Authority: Hibiscus Sq., POB 168, Grand Turk; tel. 946-1607; fax 946-1659; e-mail cad@tciway.tc; Man. Dir THOMAS SWANN.

Air Turks and Caicos (2003) Ltd: 1 InterIsland Plaza, Old Airport Rd, POB 191, Providenciales; tel. 941-5481; fax 946-4040; e-mail fly@airturksandcaicos.com; internet www.airturksandcaicos.com.

Caicos Caribbean Airlines: South Caicos; tel. 946-3283; fax 946-3377; freight to Miami (FL, USA).

Cairsea Services Ltd: Old Airport Rd, POB 138, Providenciales; tel. 946-4205; fax 946-4504; e-mail cairsea@tciway.tc; internet www.cairsea.com; Man. Dir RODNEY THOMPSON.

Global Airways Ltd: POB 359, Providenciales; tel. 941-3222; fax 946-7290; e-mail global@tciway.tc; internet www.globalairways.tc; operates inter-island connections and Caribbean charter flights; Man. Dir LINDSEY GARDINER.

SkyKing Ltd: POB 398, Providenciales; tel. 941-5464; fax 941-5127; e-mail info@skyking.tc; internet skyking.tc; f. 1985; daily inter-island passenger services, and services to Haiti and the Dominican Republic; Pres. HAROLD CHARLES; Gen. Man. MALLORY MCCOMISH.

Turks Air Ltd: Providenciales; tel. 946-4504; fax 946-4504; e-mail turksair@earthlink.net; twice-weekly cargo service to and from Miami (USA); Grand Turk Local Agent CRIS NEWTON.

Turks and Caicos Airways Ltd: Providenciales International Airport, POB 114, Providenciales; tel. 946-4255; fax 946-4438; f. 1976 as Air Turks and Caicos; privatized 1983; scheduled daily inter-island service to each of the Caicos Islands, charter flights; Chair. ALBRAY BUTTERFIELD; Dir-Gen. C. MOSER.

Tourism

The islands' main tourist attractions are the numerous unspoilt beaches, and the opportunities for diving. Salt Cay has been designated a World Heritage site by UNESCO. Hotel accommodation is available on Grand Turk, Salt Cay, South Caicos, Parrot Cay, Pine Cay and Providenciales. In 2007 there were some 264,900 tourist arrivals. In 2006 68.3% of tourists were from the USA. In 2003 there were 2,473 hotel rooms (some 80% of which were on Providenciales). Revenue from the sector in 2005 totalled an estimated US $355.1m.

Turks and Caicos Hotel and Tourism Association: Ports of Call, Providenciales; tel. 941-5787; fax 946-4001; e-mail tchta@tciway.tc; internet www.tchta.com; fmrly Turks and Caicos Hotel Asscn; over 90 mem. orgs; Pres. BUTCH CLARE; CEO CAESAR CAMPBELL.

Turks and Caicos Islands Tourist Board: Front St, POB 128, Grand Turk; tel. 946-2321; fax 946-2733; e-mail grandturk@turksandcaicostourism.com; internet www.turksandcaicostourism.com; f. 1970; br. in Providenciales; Dir LINDSEY MUSGROVE.

THE UNITED STATES OF AMERICA

Introductory Survey

Location, Climate, Language, Religion, Flag, Capital

The United States of America comprises mainly the North American continent between Canada and Mexico. Alaska, to the north-west of Canada, and Hawaii, in the central Pacific Ocean, are two of the 50 States of the USA. There is considerable climatic variation, with mean annual average temperatures ranging from 29°C (77°F) in Florida to −13.3°C (10°F) in Alaska. Average annual rainfall ranges from 1,831 mm (72.1 in) in Arkansas to 191 mm (7.5 in) in Nevada. Much of Texas, New Mexico, Arizona, Nevada and Utah is desert. The official language is English, although there are significant Spanish-speaking minorities. Christianity is the predominant religion. The national flag (proportions 10 by 19) has 13 alternating stripes (seven red and six white) with a dark blue rectangular canton, containing 50 white five-pointed stars, in the upper hoist. The capital is Washington, DC.

Recent History

Concern at the spread of communist influence in Asia dominated US foreign policy during the 1960s and early 1970s. From 1961, until their termination in 1973 by President Richard Nixon, US military operations against communist forces in South Viet Nam led to considerable political division within the USA and were widely criticized internationally. Following a series of scandals involving Nixon and senior administration officials in allegations of corruption and obstruction of justice, known as the 'Watergate' affair, Nixon resigned in August 1974 and was replaced by the Vice-President, Gerald Ford. In November 1976 Jimmy Carter, a Democrat, was elected President. Efforts by the new Administration to resolve tensions in the Middle East culminated in the signing in 1979 of a peace treaty between Egypt and Israel. In 1978 the USA severed formal links with Taiwan and established diplomatic relations with the People's Republic of China. Domestically, economic recession and inflation preoccupied the Carter Administration, and the President's management of the economy was a decisive factor in his defeat by the Republican candidate, Ronald Reagan, in the 1980 presidential election. Although economic recession and high unemployment persisted in the early period of the new Administration, the Republicans retained their previous level of congressional representation in the November 1982 elections. With the resumption of economic growth in 1983, and its strong resurgence through 1984, unemployment and inflation fell, and in November Reagan was re-elected for a further four-year term, securing the largest majority of electoral votes in US history.

In foreign affairs, the Reagan Administration generally pursued a firmly anti-communist line, notably in its active support of right-wing regimes in Latin America, where the US military occupation of Grenada in November 1983 attracted considerable international criticism, and in Africa and the Middle East. Generally friendly relations were, however, maintained with the People's Republic of China. The change of leadership in the USSR in November 1982 was followed by a period of deterioration in contacts between the two countries. Formal disarmament negotiations were renewed following the assumption of leadership in the USSR by Mikhail Gorbachev in 1985. However, US–Soviet relations were overshadowed by Reagan's pursuit of his Strategic Defense Initiative (SDI). Initiated in 1983, this advanced-technology research programme aimed to create a space-based system of defences against nuclear attack. The Reagan Government consistently refused to negotiate the termination of SDI, which was viewed by the USSR as a potential source of arms escalation and a first step in the militarization of space. US–Soviet relations experienced further strain following Soviet military intervention in Afghanistan in 1979.

During the Reagan period the USA adopted a forceful stance (generally welcomed by other Western governments) on international air and sea terrorism. However, in 1985 a ban on trade with Libya, which Reagan alleged to be promoting terrorist activity, received little support from other Western countries. In April 1986, following a terrorist attack on US military personnel in West Berlin, Reagan ordered the selective bombing of government offices and military installations in Tripoli and Benghazi. Direct US military involvement in the Middle East, which had been minimized since its withdrawal in 1984 from peace-keeping operations in Lebanon, was reactivated in July 1987, when Reagan agreed to a request by Kuwait to provide military protection for its petroleum tankers in the Persian (Arabian) Gulf, following attacks on them by Iran. Subsequent incidents in the Gulf brought the USA and Iran into armed confrontations. In April 1988 the USA was a signatory, with the USSR, Afghanistan and Pakistan, to an agreement for the phased withdrawal of Soviet troops from Afghanistan, which was completed in February 1989.

In November 1986 the USA abandoned the weapon deployment limits set by the 1979 Strategic Arms Limitation Treaty (SALT II), which, although never ratified by Congress, had been informally observed by both the USA and the USSR. In March 1987, however, the US Government responded favourably to an indication by the USSR of its willingness to expedite an agreement to eliminate medium-range nuclear missiles from Europe by 1992. Bilateral discussions in 1986 and 1987 resulted in ratification, in 1988, of an Intermediate Nuclear Forces treaty, the first to terminate an entire class of offensive nuclear weapon. The two leaders also agreed to pursue negotiations towards a new Strategic Arms Reduction Treaty (START) to reduce long-range nuclear weaponry by up to 50%. The further advancement of SDI, meanwhile, had become increasingly conjectural: the US Congress proved reluctant to allocate its high funding requirements, and during 1988 and 1989 expressed doubts about the feasibility of the project's goals. The USSR, while maintaining its objections to SDI, agreed in 1990 to exclude it from the ambit of negotiations on START. In July 1991 the USA and USSR signed START, providing for a 30% reduction in long-range nuclear weapons over a seven-year period.

In November 1986 details began to emerge of covert foreign policy operations by senior members of the Reagan Administration in relation to US contacts with the Government of Iran. The ensuing scandal, known as the 'Irangate' or 'Iran-Contra' affair, developed into a major political embarrassment for the President. Subsequent investigations by an independent commission, and by the US Congress, concluded that secret arms sales had been made to the Iranian Government, in return for an undertaking by Iran to help to secure the release of US hostages held by pro-Iranian Islamic groups in Lebanon, and that Reagan had been misled by officials of the security services into authorizing the arms transactions, and bypassing the required congressional consultative procedures. The report also upheld allegations that funds derived from the arms sales had been secretly diverted into bank accounts held by the Nicaraguan Contra rebels. Reagan, who accepted full personal responsibility for the 'Iran-Contra' affair, was exonerated of any deliberate attempt to misrepresent his role in the events. The closing months of Reagan's presidency were clouded by further political scandals involving senior presidential appointees.

At the November 1988 presidential election, Reagan was succeeded by his Vice-President, George Bush, although the Senate and House of Representatives both retained Democratic majorities. The initial months of the Bush Administration were dominated by concern over the formulation of effective measures to contain the federal budget deficit, and over the future course of arms reduction negotiations with the USSR. In June 1989, following an agreement to resume START discussions, President Bush proposed the initiation of new negotiations aimed at achieving substantial reductions in North Atlantic Treaty Organization (NATO) and Warsaw Pact countries' conventional ground forces in Europe. In September the USA and USSR finalized agreements on the monitoring of chemical weapons and procedures for the verification of limits on strategic forces and nuclear tests. A summit meeting between Bush and Gorbachev followed at Valletta, Malta, in December, which marked the opening of a new era in US–Soviet relations. Under discussion were the prospects for new agreements by the mid-1990s for reductions of 50% in nuclear strategic arms, together with substantial reductions in the size of conventional forces based in Europe.

THE UNITED STATES OF AMERICA

The withdrawal by the USSR in late 1989 and early 1990 from the exercise of direct political influence on the internal affairs of the countries of Eastern Europe was accompanied by a further improvement in US–Soviet relations, and by the implementation of programmes of US economic aid for several of the former Soviet 'client' states. In September 1990 the USA and USSR, with France and the United Kingdom (the other powers that occupied Germany at the end of the Second World War) formally agreed terms for the unification of the two post-war German states, which took effect in the following month. In July the USA, together with the world's six largest industrial democracies, agreed to provide the USSR with economic and technical assistance in undertaking a change-over to a market economy. In the same month, a summit meeting of NATO members proposed that the USSR and the other members of the Warsaw Pact alliance join in a formal declaration that the two military groupings were no longer adversaries and would refrain from the threat or use of force. This initiative was followed in November by the signing in Paris, by members of NATO and the Warsaw Pact, of a Treaty on Conventional Armed Forces in Europe (CFE), which provided for bilateral limits to be placed on the number of non-nuclear weapons sited between the Atlantic Ocean and the Ural Mountains. Immediately following the signing of the CFE Treaty, Presidents Bush and Gorbachev were present at a meeting of the Conference on Security and Co-operation in Europe (CSCE, now the Organization for Security and Co-operation in Europe—OSCE, see p.), at which the USA, the USSR and 32 other countries signed a charter declaring the end of the post-war era of confrontation and division in Europe.

In December 1989, following the failure of an internal coup attempt that received non-military US support, the USA carried out an armed invasion of Panama and subsequently installed an elected government. US troops were withdrawn in February 1990. In Nicaragua the defeat of the Sandinista Government in a general election in February 1990 was followed by the resumption of cordial relations with the US Government.

Following the invasion of Kuwait by Iraqi forces on 2 August 1990, and the subsequent annexation of that country by Iraq, the US Government assumed a leading international role in the implementation of political, economic and military measures to bring about an Iraqi withdrawal. The imposition of mandatory economic sanctions against Iraq by the UN Security Council on 6 August was quickly followed by 'Operation Desert Shield', in which US combat troops and aircraft were dispatched to Saudi Arabia, at that country's request, to secure its borders against a possible attack by Iraq. An offer, subsequently repeated, by President Saddam Hussain of Iraq to link withdrawal from Kuwait with a resolution of other outstanding Middle East problems, was rejected, and in late August the UN Security Council endorsed the use of military action to enforce its economic sanctions. Despite intense diplomatic activity, in which the USSR was prominent, the crisis deepened. In early September Presidents Bush and Gorbachev jointly demanded an Iraqi withdrawal, although the USSR expressed reluctance to support military operations by the UN. In late September the UN Security Council intensified its economic measures against Iraq. However, the ineffectiveness both of economic sanctions and of diplomatic negotiation had become evident by late November, and the USSR gave its assent to the use of force against Iraq, although it did not participate in the multinational force that was now arrayed in the Gulf region and included, under US command, air, sea and ground forces from the United Kingdom, France, Italy, Egypt, Morocco, Kuwait and the other Arab Gulf states. Jordan, which was active throughout the crisis in seeking to promote a negotiated settlement, was perceived by the US Government as sympathetic to Iraq, and US financial aid programmes to that country were suspended.

On 29 November 1990 the UN Security Council authorized the use of 'all necessary means' to force Iraq to withdraw from Kuwait, unless it did so by 15 January 1991. By early January 1991 the USA had established a considerable military presence in the Gulf region, and on 17 January 'Operation Desert Storm' was launched, with massive air and missile attacks against Iraqi positions, both in Iraq and Kuwait. In the course of the conflict, more than 110,000 attacking air missions were flown over Kuwait and Iraq by multinational air forces, while naval support operations were conducted from the Gulf. In the following weeks severe damage was inflicted on Iraqi military and economic targets, while counter-attacks by its air force, and attempts to draw Israel into the conflict by launching missile attacks on population centres, proved ineffective. A ground offensive by the multinational force was launched on 23–24 February, and Iraqi positions were quickly overrun. Hostilities were suspended on 28 February. The Government of Iraq accepted cease-fire terms on 3 March, leaving the multinational forces in control of Kuwait, together with an area of southern Iraq, comprising about 15% of that country's total national territory. Troop withdrawals from the occupied area of Iraq commenced in March, with the remaining US troops evacuated in early May, to be replaced by a UN peace-keeping force.

Following the termination of hostilities, in which 148 US troops died in combat, internal rebellions broke out within Iraq by groups opposed to President Saddam Hussain. The severity with which these were suppressed, particularly in the northern region among the Kurdish ethnic group, and the subsequent flight of refugees into neighbouring areas of Turkey and Iran, prompted large-scale international relief operations. The US Government was widely criticized for its refusal to support the anti-Government insurgents and to take action to depose Saddam Hussain. In May 1991 the USA began airlifting troops to northern Iraq to establish 'safe' enclaves, to which Kurdish refugees were encouraged to return. The US military continued to monitor events in these Kurdish areas from operational bases in Turkey and other strategic points in the region. In September 1996 the USA launched missile strikes from naval vessels in the Gulf at military targets in Iraq, in retaliation for attacks by Iraqi forces against Kurds in northern Iraq.

In the period following the Gulf War the US Government actively pursued initiatives to convene a regional conference, with joint and Soviet sponsorship, to seek a permanent solution to the wider problems of the Middle East. In August 1991 the US Secretary of State, James Baker, obtained the agreement of Egypt, Israel, Jordan, Lebanon and Syria to take part in such a conference, the opening session of which was convened in October. Successive negotiations failed to make any substantive progress, and traditionally close relations between Israel and the USA subsequently came under strain, following pressure by the US Government on Israel to suspend the construction of Jewish settlements in occupied territories, pending the eventual outcome of the peace negotiations.

In December 1991, following the replacement of the USSR by the Commonwealth of Independent States (CIS) comprising 11 of the republics of the former Soviet Union, the independence of each republic was recognized by the USA. In January 1992 a meeting was held between President Bush and President Yeltsin of Russia, the dominant republic within the CIS. President Bush expressed concern that effective measures should be taken by the Russian Government to ensure that the nuclear weapons and related technical expertise of the former USSR did not become available to countries not in possession of nuclear weapons capability, or to nations in the Middle East or to the Democratic People's Republic of Korea (DPRK—North Korea). At a subsequent meeting held in February, the Russian leader assured President Bush that immediate safeguards were in force, and that all short-range nuclear warheads would be moved into Russia from sites in other CIS republics by July 1992. President Yeltsin also proposed that the USA and Russia should share in the joint future development of the SDI project (see above), and further reductions in nuclear arsenals were agreed by the two leaders. At a summit meeting held between Presidents Bush and Yeltsin in June 1992 in Washington, DC, agreement was reached on further substantial reductions in nuclear arms, under which, by 2003, total holdings of nuclear warheads would be reduced to less than one-half of the quotas contained in START.

In its relations with the former communist countries in Europe, the USA augmented its commitment to the CSCE with economic support, and promoted the membership of former members of the Warsaw Pact in the North Atlantic Co-operation Council, an offshoot of NATO. Contacts were also revived between the USA and Viet Nam, and in May 1992 there was a partial relaxation of a trade embargo in force since 1975. Relations with Iraq remained tense following the discovery, made in November 1991 by UN representatives, that President Saddam Hussain's regime was seeking to conceal its continuing development of nuclear weapons capability.

Following the conclusion of the Gulf War in early 1991, Bush's political popularity fell sharply, amid growing public perception that the Government was assigning greater priority to foreign affairs than to addressing the problems of the US economy, which had been in recession since early 1989. In April 1992 serious rioting broke out in Los Angeles and spread briefly to several other cities. The underlying causes of the disorders were widely ascribed to the worsening economic and social plight of the impoverished urban black minority.

The 1992 presidential election campaign, in which Bush was opposed by Bill Clinton, a Democratic state governor, and Ross Perot, a populist independent, was dominated by social and economic issues. Bush's record of economic management, particularly in relation to the persistence of federal budget deficits, provided the major line of attack by the opposing candidates. The turn-out of voters, at 55%, was the highest at any presidential election since 1968, and gave a decisive majority, of 43% to 37%, to Clinton. Perot, whose campaign had concentrated on the question of federal deficit spending, obtained almost 19% of the popular vote.

Foreign affairs dominated the final months of the Bush Administration. In July 1992 contention arose between the Government of Iraq and the UN over the rights of UN observers to inspect Iraqi nuclear facilities, and in the following month the US Government sought to limit internal military operations by the Iraqi Government by imposing an air exclusion zone south of latitude 32°N. This was followed, in January 1993, by US participation in selective bombings of Iraqi missile sites. In December 1992 relations with the People's Republic of China, which had been strained since 1989 by the Chinese Government's persistent suppression of political dissent, were revived by the removal of a US embargo on sales of military equipment. In the same month President Bush launched 'Operation Restore Hope', under which 24,000 US troops were sent to Somalia, as part of an international force under US command, to protect shipments of food aid and to assist in the restoration of civil order.

Shortly before the transfer of the presidency to Bill Clinton in January 1993, Presidents Bush and Yeltsin met in Moscow to sign a second Nuclear Arms Reduction Treaty (START II), which provided for the elimination by 2003 of almost 75% of all US and CIS-held nuclear warheads. Clinton announced the termination of SDI, although there was subsequent discussion within the USA of its possible reactivation (see below). Although ratified by the US Senate in 1993, START II remained unratified by the Russian legislature until April 2000. However, arrangements agreed in late 1997 by the US and Russian Governments had extended by five years the period allowed for the elimination of Russia's long-range nuclear missiles.

The initial preoccupation of the Clinton Administration was the formulation of an economic recovery plan, to be phased over a five-year period, to reduce the federal budget deficit by means of increased taxation and economies in the cost of government, rather than by reduced levels of federal spending. Military expenditure was a particular area in which economies were proposed, while additional spending was planned for infrastructural projects and measures to stimulate economic activity. A major restructuring of the US health care system was also planned, and a commission to formulate proposals was placed under the chairmanship of President Clinton's wife, Hillary. Certain aspects of the economic recovery plan, particularly those relating to higher income tax and a new energy tax, encountered initial opposition in the Democrat-controlled Congress, but were eventually approved, in a modified form, by the House of Representatives in May 1993. Approval by the Senate, following further amendments, took place in June. By mid-1993, however, the President's initial popularity had fallen sharply, owing in part to perceptions of indecisiveness by Clinton in formulating effective policies. There was also widespread criticism of the competence of some of his advisers and appointees.

By mid-1993 the crisis in former Yugoslavia had assumed increased importance as a foreign policy issue, leading to disagreements between the USA and the Western European powers, which opposed US proposals to launch direct air strikes against military positions held by Bosnian Serbs. The US Administration, while avoiding any direct military commitment, gave its support, through NATO, to peace-keeping operations in Bosnia and Herzegovina. Clinton was unsuccessful, however, in efforts to secure the removal of the international embargo on arms sales to the Bosnian Muslims. In June 1994 the US Government endorsed proposals by the European Union (EU) countries for the tripartite partition of Bosnia and Herzegovina.

The Clinton Administration made renewed efforts to restore to power Fr Jean-Bertrand Aristide, the first democratically elected President of Haiti, who had taken refuge in the USA following his overthrow by a military junta in 1991. An economic embargo imposed by the Organization of American States (OAS, see p. 360), together with implied threats of military intervention by the US Government, had failed to displace the military regime, and conditions within Haiti had led large numbers of refugees to seek asylum in the USA, many of whom were forcibly repatriated by the US authorities. In June 1994, following the imposition in the previous month of international sanctions against Haiti by the UN Security Council, Clinton announced the suspension of all commercial and financial transactions with Haiti. In September, following a diplomatic mission led by former President Carter, a UN-sponsored multinational force, composed almost entirely of US troops, arrived in Haiti with the agreement of the military junta, which relinquished power in October. US troops were withdrawn from the UN force in March 1995. In January 2004 the Administration of George W. Bush (2001–) condemned attacks on thousands of demonstrators protesting against the Aristide Government. In March, in the face of growing violence and under international pressure, Aristide resigned and went into exile, although he claimed that he had been unconstitutionally removed from office by the USA. Several hundred US marines were deployed in Haiti in March–June 2004 as the vanguard of a multinational UN Stabilization Mission in Haiti to disarm rebel forces and stabilize the country.

During 1993 the Clinton Administration continued to foster efforts to promote a general resolution of tensions in the Middle East. With US assistance, but as a direct result of secret diplomatic mediation by Norway, the Palestine Liberation Organization (PLO) and the Government of Israel signed an agreement providing for Palestinian self-government in the Occupied Territories and for mutual recognition by Israel and the PLO. In January 1994, following a meeting held in Geneva, Switzerland, between Clinton and President Assad of Syria, negotiations were initiated for a settlement between Israel and Syria.

Political and economic contacts with Russia continued on a cordial level, with the two countries adopting a co-operative stance in many areas of foreign policy. In February 1994 the US Government lifted the remaining sanctions on trade with Viet Nam (see above) and in the following July the USA established full diplomatic relations with that country. Little progress, however, was made in the resolution of the persistently adverse US balance of trade with Japan, despite an agreement between the two countries in July 1993 to implement measures to reduce the trade deficit.

The prevention of nuclear proliferation, which remained a prime objective of US foreign policy, led in 1993 and early 1994 to a serious confrontation between the USA and North Korea. In March 1993 the DPRK, which is a signatory of the Nuclear Non-Proliferation Treaty (NPT) and is subject, by virtue of its membership of the International Atomic Energy Agency (IAEA, see p. 107), to the monitoring of its nuclear installations, refused to grant the IAEA inspectorate full access to its nuclear power facility. It cited as its reasons the existence of joint military exercises between the Republic of Korea (South Korea) and the USA and 'unjust acts' by the IAEA. The US Government stated that it had reason to suspect that the DPRK had been diverting nuclear plant material for the development of atomic weapons. In July Clinton visited South Korea, and warned the DPRK that any use of nuclear weapons by them would be met with military force. Despite increasing international pressure, and attempts at mediation by the UN, the DPRK repeatedly asserted its refusal to comply with the treaty's inspection requirements. The crisis steadily worsened during early 1994, and in June the US Government, after seeking unsuccessfully to offer the DPRK economic aid, investment and diplomatic recognition, began to seek support for the imposition of UN economic sanctions. Later in the same month, following a visit to the DPRK by former President Carter (acting as an unofficial representative of the Government), the DPRK agreed to a temporary suspension of its nuclear programme, pending formal discussions with the US Government. These meetings were convened in July. Negotiations aimed at improving relations between the USA and the DPRK, and at fostering a political settlement between the DPRK and the Republic of Korea, were pursued throughout both Clinton Administrations. In March 1999 the US and DPRK Governments agreed on terms whereby US officials would receive unrestricted access to inspect DPRK nuclear facilities.

The collapse of Clinton's plans for health care reform following congressional opposition in 1994, together with increasing public concern about the domestic economy and the effectiveness of Clinton's policies on social issues (notably in the areas of welfare expenditure, law enforcement and the protection of traditional social values), led to a sharp rise in support for the conservative doctrines of politicians representing the right wing of the Republican Party. At congressional elections in November 1994, the Republicans gained control both of the Senate (for the first time since 1986) and the House of Representatives (which had been controlled by the Democrats since 1954). As a result, in 1995 serious divisions began to emerge between President Clinton and Congress. In June tensions arose over proposals to achieve a balanced federal budget. Negotiations proved inconclusive, and in November Clinton, in an effort to resolve the deadlock, refused to renew the temporary funding arrangements, causing an eight-day shutdown of all non-essential operations of the federal government. Agreement on the 1995/96 budget was eventually reached in April 1996, although disagreements on the timetable for, and the method of achieving, a balanced budget remained unresolved.

In the presidential election that was held in November 1996, Clinton decisively secured a second term in office, obtaining 49% of the popular vote, compared with 43% in the 1992 election. Robert Dole, the Republican nominee, obtained 41% of the votes, while Ross Perot, who was nominated by the Reform Party, an organization founded by him to seek radical reductions in federal government spending, attracted 8%. The Republicans retained control of the Senate and House of Representatives.

Following his inauguration in January 1997, Clinton declared the enhancement of educational standards to be a primary aim of his second term. Proposals were also announced to achieve further reductions in welfare dependency, by providing tax credits and other incentives to employers. Financial savings were to be achieved by further reductions in defence expenditure, and by the implementation of additional cuts in spending on health care for the elderly. Clinton reiterated his intention, however, of seeking improved provisions for insured health care, and of achieving a balanced federal budget by 2002. Agreement between Clinton and the Republican congressional leadership on the general terms of these budgetary measures was reached in May 1997.

In foreign affairs, the Clinton Administration continued to support economic reform in Russia and the successor states of the former USSR, with particular emphasis on fostering the changeover from defence to consumer production. Prior to the cease-fire declared in August 1996, the US Government expressed disapproval of the scale of Russian military operations in Chechnya, and in May 1995 the Clinton Administration was refused Russian co-operation in its ban on US trade and investment in Iran, in retaliation for that country's alleged involvement in international terrorism. Concerns expressed by Russia at the proposed enlargement of NATO were addressed at a summit meeting of Presidents Yeltsin and Clinton in Helsinki, Finland, in March 1997. (See the chapter on Russia for details of the subsequent agreement between NATO and Russia.)

The reluctance of the Clinton Administration to participate directly in UN military operations in Bosnia and Herzegovina was modified in June 1995 with a statement by Clinton that US ground troops would be sent to Bosnia and Herzegovina in 'emergency' circumstances on a 'limited basis' if required to assist in the redeployment of existing UN forces, or to participate in monitoring an eventual peace settlement. In November, following US-sponsored negotiations held in Dayton, Ohio, a peace agreement was reached by the opposing sides. As part of its implementation, the US Government agreed to contribute 20,000 troops to a multinational supervisory force of 60,000 troops under the command of NATO. The USA committed about 8,500 troops in an extended NATO peace-keeping operation in Bosnia and Herzegovina until mid-1998 and about 1,000 soldiers served as part of NATO's Stabilization Force until December 2004. A small contingent of US troops remained in Bosnia and Herzegovina in 2008.

Relations with the People's Republic of China pursued an uneven course under the Clinton Administration, owing to disagreements over trade matters and criticism by the USA of alleged abuses by the Chinese Government of human rights. Relations between the two countries declined sharply in February 1996, following US protests over Chinese military operations near Taiwan. Relations between the two countries were enhanced in October 1997 by a state visit to the USA by President Jiang Zemin, following which the US Government revoked a ban, in force since 1989, on the export of US nuclear technology to China. China, together with Russia and the USA, refused in December 1997 to sign an international treaty—the Ottawa Convention—banning the manufacture and use of anti-personnel landmines; the US Government based its objection to the arrangements on its requirement for landmines to protect its troops stationed in the Republic of Korea. It was stated that the USA proposed to develop an alternative weapons technology to replace landmines by 2003. (Following a two and a half year review of landmine policy, in late February 2004 the Bush Administration announced that it would not sign the treaty and would continue to use, indefinitely, 'non-persistent' landmines that would self-destruct or self-deactivate after a certain period of time.) Following the settlement in June 1999 of a dispute over infringements of US copyright and other intellectual property rights, Chinese enhanced trading privileges were granted permanent status in May 2000, opening the way for the People's Republic of China to join the World Trade Organization (WTO, see p. 396).

Successive US Governments remained unwilling to restore relations with Cuba. Relations between the two countries deteriorated in March 1996, after two civilian aircraft carrying Cuban exiles protesting against the Castro Government were shot down by the Cuban air force over international waters. In response, Clinton acceded to congressional demands to strengthen the US commercial and economic embargo that has been in force since 1962. Under the new measure, the Cuban Liberty and Solidarity (Helms-Burton) Act, the USA was to penalize foreign investors whose business in any way involved property in Cuba that was confiscated from US citizens following the 1959 revolution. In June legislation was approved by Congress to impose penalties on foreign companies investing in Iran and Libya, both of which were accused by the US Government of sponsoring international terrorism. In July a number of Canadian, Mexican and Italian companies were informed that sanctions were to be imposed on them under the Helms-Burton legislation, barring their senior executives and certain shareholders from visiting the USA. In response to intense international pressure, Clinton declared a temporary moratorium on certain provisions of the Helms-Burton Act, and in April 1997 the US Government and the EU, which had protested the measure, announced that a compromise had been agreed, subject to the abandonment by the US Government of certain sections of the Act. The moratorium on Title III of the Act was subsequently extended at six-monthly intervals and remained in operation in 2008. In late 2001 the USA lifted temporarily the trade embargo against Cuba to allow the purchase of food and medicines necessary for the reconstruction and aid effort following the devastation caused by 'Hurricane Michelle'. In April 2004 a motion, supported by the USA, condemning Cuba for human rights violations, was approved by the UN General Assembly; similar US-backed motions had been passed by the UN in 2002 and 2003. In April 2005 a milder, US-proposed motion requesting that the mandate of the UN's Special Rapporteur on Human Rights in Cuba be extended was approved by the General Assembly. In July Secretary of State Condoleezza Rice appointed Caleb McCarry Cuba Transition Co-ordinator, a position created at the behest of a special panel charged with directing the US Government's actions 'in support of a free Cuba' and hastening the end to President Castro's premiership.

In December 1994 President Clinton proposed the formation, by 2006, of a Free Trade Area of the Americas (FTAA), comprising 34 countries of the Western hemisphere, although excluding Cuba. Negotiations were scheduled to conclude by January 2005, but stalled in November 2004; in early November 2005, at a Fourth Summit of the Americas, in Mar del Plata, Argentina, an agreement was reached to resume talks in 2006, although negotiations had not progressed by mid-2008. By that time, however, the Venezuelan President, Lt-Col (retd) Hugo Chavéz Frías, had commenced implementation of an alternative free trade initiative for the Americas, the Bolivarian Alternative for the Americas (Alternativa Bolivariana para las Américas—ALBA), in direct challenge to the moribund FTAA.

At the end of 1998 President Clinton and the President of Colombia, Andrés Pastrana Arango, signed a Counter-Narcotics Alliance, in an attempt to promote the ongoing war against drugs-trafficking. In January 2000 the Clinton Administration announced an aid package for the Andean region worth $1,300m., the largest ever aid programme for Latin America. The main portion of the programme, which became known as the 'Plan Colombia', was to provide some $860m. to Colombia, three-quarters of which was allocated to the security forces in that country. The size of the military component of the Plan caused controversy internationally, as did the proposed aerial destruction of crops in the region. As a result, in 2001 the incoming

Administration of George W. Bush implemented an Andean Counterdrug Initiative to complement Plan Colombia, the focus of which would be on improving social and economic conditions in the region. Nevertheless, the objective remained the same: to reduce significantly the flow of drugs from the Andean region into the USA.

International concern at the effects on world climate of emissions of carbon dioxide and other gases that have a warming effect on the atmosphere ('greenhouse gases') has, in recent years, brought the USA and other industrialized countries under pressure to implement measures to reduce the use of these substances. In December 1997, at the third Conference of the Parties to the Framework Convention on Climate Change (see UN Environment Programme, see p. 62), held in Kyoto, Japan, the USA undertook to implement reductions of its emissions of 'greenhouse gases' to 7% below 1990 levels by the year 2012. However, in view of the problems inherent in the cost-effective phasing-out of these substances, ratification of the Kyoto arrangements encountered strong opposition in Congress and among business leaders. Soon after taking office in 2001 President George W. Bush announced that his Government did not support the ratification of the agreement (see below).

In November 1997 the Government of Iraq demanded the immediate removal of US inspectors of the UN Special Commission (UNSCOM, see the chapter on Iraq), carrying out the identification and elimination of biological, chemical and other weapons of mass destruction allegedly held by Iraq. This action was strongly resisted by the UN, amid increasing concern in the USA and internationally at subsequent actions by Iraq to disrupt the weapons inspection programme. Following repeated threats of military action by the USA against Iraq to enforce the inspections arrangements, substantial US military forces were dispatched to the Gulf region. The Government of Iraq agreed, pursuant to extended negotiations, to restore unrestricted access to UN inspectors, and to withdraw its objection to the presence of US personnel. The US Government accepted the agreement, but warned of 'serious consequences' in the event of future violations by Iraq.

US policy continued to encourage political reform and economic development in the former communist countries of Eastern Europe, and in 1998 the Senate gave formal approval for the accession to NATO membership in 1999 of the Czech Republic, Hungary and Poland. Foreign policy concerns involving South Asia were revived in June, when successive tests of nuclear weapons were carried out by the Governments of India and Pakistan. The tests, which were condemned by the five states with nuclear armaments (the USA, France, Russia, the United Kingdom and the People's Republic of China), prompted Clinton to impose economic sanctions on both countries, while pursuing efforts to obtain their accession to the NPT.

During his second term as President, Clinton was confronted by a number of other allegations, which he consistently denied, of perjury and obstruction of justice arising from accusations of sexual harassment, dating from prior to 1992 and extending throughout his presidency. These matters, which related to Clinton's period as a state official in Arkansas, were brought within the ambit of a congressionally mandated independent counsel, Kenneth Starr, who began in 1994 to examine the legal ramifications of the 'Whitewater' affair (President Clinton and his wife were accused of financial irregularities in their alleged involvement in a savings bank and property development company that collapsed in 1989, during Clinton's tenure as Governor of Arkansas). In January 1998 a former White House intern, Monica Lewinsky, was required to give evidence in a civil action by Paula Jones, who had alleged that she had been sexually harassed by Clinton in 1991. In that month Starr was authorized by the Attorney-General to investigate whether a sexual relationship alleged by Lewinsky had taken place with the President in 1995. Clinton vehemently denied any improper conduct with Lewinsky, and, following his private testimony to a grand jury, declared in late January 1998 that he had made no attempt to induce Lewinsky or others to give perjured testimony. In August, however, following an offer of immunity from prosecution by Starr to Lewinsky, the President submitted new testimony to the grand jury; he subsequently made a public statement to the effect that an inappropriate relationship had taken place with Lewinsky, although he had at no time sought to obstruct legal processes. Nevertheless, Starr's report to Congress alleged that Clinton had committed 11 offences of perjury and obstruction of justice, constituting grounds for his removal from office. No evidence, however, was offered of wrongdoing by Clinton in relation to the 'Whitewater' affair. In October the House of Representatives voted to commence an impeachment inquiry against the President. Nevertheless, in February 1999 the Senate acquitted Clinton on the first and second articles of impeachment. A subsequent attempt in the Senate to obtain a vote of censure on Clinton was unsuccessful. (In January 2001, shortly before he left office, Clinton agreed to admit giving misleading testimony to an Arkansas court regarding his relationship with Lewinsky and to make a contribution towards the cost of the investigation into his alleged obstruction of justice in the matter. In return, the investigation was discontinued.)

In August 1998 bomb attacks on US embassy buildings in Nairobi, Kenya, and Dar es Salaam, Tanzania, claimed 258 lives, and were followed by US air missile attacks on a factory site in Khartoum, Sudan (which was alleged to be a manufactory of chemicals for use in toxic gases), and on targets in Afghanistan, which were stated by the US Government to be operational centres for Osama bin Laden, a fugitive Saudi Arabian-born Islamist activist whom the USA believed to be responsible for past assaults on US forces and facilities in Somalia, Yemen and Saudi Arabia. Bin Laden was also held responsible for terrorist operations within the USA, including the 1993 bombing of the World Trade Center in New York. In October 2001 four associates of bin Laden were sentenced to life imprisonment by a US court for their involvement in the bomb attacks in Nairobi and Dar es Salaam.

In December 1998, following the termination by Iraq of international weapons inspections in its territory, the USA and the United Kingdom conducted a series of missile raids on Iraqi military sites. In March 1999 the US Government initiated and led, under NATO auspices, a sustained campaign of missile raids on military and related installations in Serbia and Montenegro, in support of international demands that the President of the Federal Republic of Yugoslavia, Slobodan Milošević, desist from the mass expulsion of members of the ethnic Albanian population of the Serbian province of Kosovo. NATO air attacks on Belgrade during May resulted in the accidental bombing by US aircraft of the diplomatic mission in the Yugoslav capital of the People's Republic of China, which, despite a subsequent apology and the payment of compensation by the US Government, led to a period of strained relations between the two countries. Following the military withdrawal of Serbian forces from Kosovo in June, US forces took a leading role in subsequent UN peace-keeping operations in the region.

Throughout Clinton's presidency the USA continued to pursue an active role in efforts to secure the settlement of conflicts in the Middle East (with particular reference to matters at issue between Israel, Syria and Lebanon) and in December 1999, under Clinton's auspices, the first substantive negotiations since 1996 between the Governments of Israel and Syria took place in Washington, DC. In March 2000 the US Government sought to move towards a rapprochement with Iran with the announcement that it was to ease some of the trade sanctions against Iran that had been in force since 1979.

In January 1999 the Clinton Administration indicated that it was considering an allocation of $7,000m. over a three-year period from 2000 for new research into the SDI programme (see above), which had been initiated by President Reagan in 1983 and on which an estimated $55,000m. had been spent prior to its termination by Clinton in 1995. Under the new proposals, which attracted considerable congressional support from Republicans, the original concept of a space-based missile defence system was to be replaced by a network of ground- or sea-based interceptor rockets with the capability of destroying intercontinental ballistic missiles either accidentally launched or fired by a hostile power. This modification of the SDI, which was redesignated as the National Missile Defence (NMD) system, would require the agreement of Russia to amend prior anti-nuclear treaties. In May 2000 the USA, together with the United Kingdom, France, Russia and the People's Republic of China, announced a commitment to global nuclear disarmament, although no timetable was set out for the eventual elimination of stockpiles of these weapons. In early September 2001, in return for China's acceptance of NMD, the USA pledged to keep China informed of its development and agreed to recognize that the Chinese might, in the future, want to resume nuclear weapons testing. The USA also urged China not to transfer ballistic missile technology to countries which the USA considered to be 'rogue states' (deemed by the Department of State to be those countries with the capabilities to use weapons of mass destruction without adherence to traditional international conventions).

THE UNITED STATES OF AMERICA

Introductory Survey

A presidential election was held on 7 November 2000. Vice-President Al Gore was the Democratic Party candidate, while George W. Bush, the Governor of Texas and a son of former President Bush, was the Republican Party's nominee. Following voting, it emerged that the possession of an overall majority in the presidential Electoral College would depend on the 25 college mandates from the state of Florida, where the result of the ballot was in dispute. The state was initially declared in favour of Governor Bush, pending the result of a mandatory automated recount of the votes; however, the Democrats challenged the declaration (and the state government's refusal to permit the ballots to be recounted by electoral staff following the automated recount) in the Florida Supreme Court, claiming that a significant number of votes in certain counties had been incorrectly registered by the automated counting system. The Court ruled that the ballots in the counties concerned should be recounted by electoral staff and allowed an additional 12 days for this process to be completed. The US Supreme Court disallowed this ruling, however, and returned the matter to the Florida Supreme Court for further consideration. Only one county completed its 'manual' recount and the result remained in Governor Bush's favour (by 537 votes). The Democrats began further legal action, claiming that the importance of recounting of all disputed ballots transcended time limits. The Florida Supreme Court upheld the appeal and ordered the recounting of some 45,000 disputed ballots. The Republicans challenged the verdict, claiming that no provision for such 'manual' recounts was made in the electoral legislation. The US Supreme Court upheld the Republican appeal, by a margin of five judges to four. With all legal options exhausted, and with the Florida legislature having voted to endorse a list of Republican electors irrespective of the outcome of further legal action, Vice-President Gore conceded defeat in Florida (and thereby nationally) on 13 December.

Final results subsequently indicated that Vice-President Gore obtained 48.4% of the valid votes cast, compared with 47.9% obtained by Governor Bush. Thus, the latter became the first contender since 1876 to win a majority in the Electoral College while losing the national popular ballot. In the concurrently held elections to the Senate, the Democrats made a net gain of five seats, resulting in both parties holding 50 of the 100 seats (Hillary Rodham Clinton, the wife of President Clinton, was elected as a Democratic Senator representing New York). The Republicans retained their effective majority in the chamber, however, owing to the casting vote of the President of the Senate, the incoming Vice-President, Dick Cheney. In May 2001 Senator James Jeffords of Vermont left the Republican Party to sit in the Senate as an Independent, thus establishing a Democratic majority of one in that chamber.

President Bush's first Cabinet contained several individuals who had served in his father's Administration, as well as one member of Clinton's Cabinet. His Administration immediately suspended the implementation of a number of environmental regulations issued by Clinton shortly before his departure from office. The Administration's first budget, presented in February 2001, included provisions for reductions in levels of personal taxation. Environmental campaigners (who had expressed reservations over President Bush's attitude to environmental issues) and numerous foreign governments and international organizations strongly criticized the new President in March when his Administration withdrew support for the ratification process of the Kyoto Protocol on climate change, claiming it would be detrimental to US economic interests. In February 2002 Bush proposed voluntary, less far-reaching, measures to reduce emissions of 'greenhouse gases'. A government report on energy policy in May 2001, which included a proposal to introduce legislation authorizing exploratory drilling for oil in the Arctic National Wildlife Refuge in Alaska (ANWR), also prompted criticism from the environmental lobby. In August the House of Representatives voted in favour of the proposal by a narrow majority; however, the proposed legislation was rejected by the Senate in April 2002. The Administration subsequently introduced a provision to allow drilling to start in 2004, whereby federal revenue would be raised from the sale of leases to petroleum companies; however, in March 2003 Congress passed an amendment to remove the provision. In August the Government proposed further controversial amendments to regulations governing carbon emissions; under the new legislation, energy companies would no longer be required to install anti-pollution measures when upgrading equipment. The announcement prompted criticism from environmental groups, and legal contests against the proposals were immediately begun in 13 states.

In March–April 2005 Congress narrowly approved a proposal to begin drilling in the ANWR. However, in its final version, the relevant legislation was part of a wider budget reconciliation bill that was only approved by both houses in late December once the ANWR provision had been removed. In what appeared to be a repetition of the previous year's events, in March 2006 the Senate narrowly approved legislation that would permit the opening of parts of the ANWR to drilling; however, the outcome was again contingent on congressional approval of another budget reconciliation bill. Government proposals for the inclusion of the ANWR in the USA's Strategic Petroleum Reserve were presented in March 2007 as a means of expediting the long-debated exploitation of the Refuge for its oil wealth. Conversely, proposed legislation to designate the coastal region of the ANWR as a wilderness area to be permanently exempted from oil exploration was introduced, by independent Senator Joseph Lieberman, to the Senate Natural Resources Committee for discussion in November, but was rejected before reaching the wider Senate. Despite ratification of minor amendments to existing ANWR legislation during that year, and the President's reiteration in April 2008 of the Refuge's potential as a resource for bolstering the Strategic Petroleum Reserve—with regard to the effects of escalating international oil prices upon the domestic economy—the issue remained unresolved at mid-2008. According to the US Geological Survey, recoverable oil reserves in the ANWR were estimated at 10,400m. barrels of oil in 2005; during that period the USA was consuming 20m. barrels per day.

President Bush's strong personal support for the NMD programme, expressed throughout the electoral campaign and in the period after his inauguration, caused further concern both within the USA and abroad. In November 2001, following a summit meeting in Washington, DC, President Bush and Russian President Vladimir Putin both pledged to reduce their nation's nuclear arsenals by approximately two-thirds over the following decade; a formal agreement was signed in May 2002. In June 2002 the USA formally withdrew from the Anti-Ballistic Missile Treaty (ABM), signed with the USSR in 1972, claiming that its adherence prevented the development of NMD. President Bush emphasized that the USA's withdrawal from the ABM would not undermine US–Russian relations. Putin described the withdrawal as a mistake, but insisted it would not damage Russian security. In December 2001, the USA received fierce criticism from EU member states after forcing the collapse of an international conference convened to reinforce the terms of the Biological and Toxic Weapons Convention, signed in 1972; the USA opposed plans which would have allowed international inspectors to monitor its military and industrial facilities. The USA attracted further international criticism by its refusal to sign up to the terms of the International Criminal Court (ICC), established to try war criminals, which was inaugurated at The Hague, Netherlands, in March 2003. The USA defended its position by claiming that members of its military could be put on trial on political grounds, and, in response, in the same month, Congress passed the American Service Member and Citizen Protection Act, which would enable the USA to free, by force if necessary, any member of its military arrested by the ICC. In mid-June the UN Security Council granted US forces exemption from prosecution by the ICC for one year. Early in the following month the USA reduced military aid to some 35 countries that refused to sign agreements that would give US citizens immunity from prosecution. In March 2006 Secretary of State Condoleezza Rice acknowledged that the retraction of such aid to Latin American countries had disadvantaged the USA's regional security strategy, while in July legislation was introduced into the House of Representatives by Democrats proposing a repeal of military assistance prohibitions against signatories to the ICC. By the following month some 101 Bilateral Immunity Agreements had been signed, exempting certain such US citizens from referral to the ICC. The deterioration of the crisis in Darfur, Sudan (see chapter on Sudan), later that year prompted appeals that the US Administration endorse the jurisdiction of the ICC in prosecuting Sudanese leaders, indicating the USA's recognition of the Court's importance in administering international justice. Following allegations of abuse and torture of Iraqi prisoners by US soldiers (see below), in June 2004 the USA withdrew a proposed resolution at the UN Security Council to give US personnel immunity from prosecution at the ICC.

On 11 September 2001 four commercial passenger aircraft were hijacked shortly after take-off from Boston, New York and Washington, DC. The two aircraft originating in Boston, both bound for Los Angeles, were diverted to New York and each was flown into one of the two towers of the World Trade Center, both of which subsequently collapsed. The third aircraft was flown into the Pentagon building (the headquarters of the Department of Defense) in Washington, DC, and the fourth aircraft, also apparently heading for Washington, DC, crashed in farmland near Pittsburgh, Pennsylvania. The death toll was eventually put at 2,752, including 266 passengers and crew (including the hijackers) on the four aircraft, 190 at the Pentagon, and the remainder in New York, principally those unable to escape from the towers before they collapsed, and members of the emergency services. On 13 September the Secretary of State, Gen. Colin Powell, identified Osama bin Laden (see above) and his al-Qa'ida (Base) organization, a network of fundamentalist Islamist militants, as responsible for the attacks. However, bin Laden, who was believed to be in Afghanistan, where he was harboured by the extremist Islamist Taliban regime, had already denied accusations that he had ordered the hijackings, although he expressed his approval of the attacks. In late 2002 an independent bipartisan inquiry, the National Commission on Terrorist Attacks Upon the United States, was established to investigate the circumstances surrounding the attacks (see below). In early March 2003 security forces in Rawalpindi, Pakistan, arrested the Kuwaiti-born Khalid Sheikh Mohammed, accused of being the operational planner behind the attacks, and released him into US custody for interrogation. In late March 2006, in a court in Virginia, Moroccan-born Zacarias Moussaoui pleaded guilty to charges of conspiracy to commit acts of terrorism, in relation to the attacks. Moussaoui had pleaded guilty to conspiracy charges in July 2002, but subsequently retracted his plea. In early May 2006 he was sentenced to life imprisonment without parole. In March 2007 Khalid Sheikh Mohammed, regarded as one of the principal agents of al-Qa'ida's operations, was tried by military commission, along with two other alleged key al-Qa'ida operatives. The US Department of Defense released a partial transcript of Sheikh Mohammed's trial at the detention centre in Guantánamo Bay, Cuba (see below), in which the suspect claimed involvement in 31 separate international terrorism plots and attacks, including orchestration of the 1993 and 2001 attacks on the World Trade Center, the beheading of US journalist Daniel Pearl in 2002 and numerous assassination attempts against international political leaders. However, speculation that such admissions had been obtained under duress, or torture, tarnished any belief in the international community that justice had been achieved and provoked further criticism of the interrogation methods employed at Guantánamo Bay. Charges brought by the US Government in February 2008 against six prisoners being held in Guantánamo Bay, including Khalid Sheikh Mohammed, elicited similar censure. The charges, for which military prosecutors were to seek the death penalty, related to the detainees' alleged involvement in the 2001 attacks and included conspiracy, murder, attacking civilians, destruction of property and terrorism.

In the immediate wake of the attacks on New York and Washington, DC, President Bush declared that those responsible should be captured 'dead or alive'. Both houses of Congress unanimously approved emergency anti-terrorism legislation, which made provision for increased military spending and US $20,000m. for reconstruction in New York, and passed a resolution authorizing the President to use 'all necessary and appropriate force' against those who organized the attacks. Congress also approved the so-called 'Patriot Act' (Uniting and Strengthening America by Providing the Appropriate Tools Required to Intercept and Obstruct Terrorism—PATRIOT—Act of 2001), which was signed into law in late October 2001, giving wide-ranging powers to the Government to investigate citizens and non-citizens alike. The Act was viewed by critics as a threat to civil liberties. (The Patriot Act was scheduled to expire at the end of 2005, but was temporarily extended by Congress until February 2006. A continuance of the law, the USA Patriot Act Improvement and Reauthorization Act of 2005, was signed into law by the President in March 2006.) The Government began to form an international coalition against terrorism, for which most Western Governments pledged their support. NATO invoked Article Five of the NATO Charter (which states that an attack on a member state is an attack on all 19 members), which required members to assist the USA, according to judgement and resources; the Governments of the United Kingdom, France and Germany, among others, offered military and financial assistance. The Taliban regime in Afghanistan denied involvement in the terrorist attacks, and warned that it would retaliate if attacked. On 17 September the USA issued an ultimatum to the Taliban, via Pakistan (the only state with diplomatic links to the regime), to surrender bin Laden or face an imminent military assault. Several weeks of intense diplomatic activity ensued, during which time international support for the USA's so-called global 'war on terror' increased, and the US Government was apparently able to gather further evidence of the al-Qa'ida network's involvement in the attacks. The Taliban reportedly asked to see evidence of bin Laden's involvement in the attacks, a request rejected by the USA. In the meantime, US military forces increased their presence in the region around Afghanistan. Pakistan and Uzbekistan agreed to grant the US-led forces access to their airbases for emergency operations and Russia allowed access to its airspace for humanitarian missions. Saudi Arabia, although it refused to allow the USA to use its military bases, granted access to its airspace.

On 2 October 2001 NATO declared that it had received evidence from the USA that confirmed bin Laden's responsibility for the terrorist attacks. On 7 October US and British armed forces commenced military operations ('Operation Enduring Freedom') against Taliban military targets and suspected al-Qa'ida training camps in Afghanistan. In addition to military strikes, aircraft released food and medicine parcels to Afghan civilians; leaflets were also dropped offering protection and a reward in return for information on the whereabouts of al-Qa'ida leaders. On 14 October a senior Taliban official offered to surrender bin Laden to a third country in return for a cessation of US bombing, if the USA provided evidence of his involvement in the terrorist attacks, an offer the USA rejected. The US-led forces co-ordinated operations with the military wing of the exiled Afghan Government, the United National Islamic Front for the Salvation of Afghanistan (UIFSA—also known as the Northern Alliance). During November the latter made substantial territorial gains in northern and western Afghanistan, including the Afghan capital, Kabul, and Mazar-i-Sharif, a strategically important town in the north. In late November US ground forces were deployed for the first time, near the southern city of Kandahar, in an attempt to locate bin Laden. Kandahar fell to the US-led forces in early December, leaving only localized areas of Taliban resistance; US forces subsequently intensified their search for bin Laden, who was believed to be in the Tora Bora caves near Jalalabad, in the east of the country. US-led ground forces were still deployed in Afghanistan in May 2002, attempting to overcome a small number of Taliban and al-Qa'ida members who had not surrendered; bin Laden remained at large. The USA refused, however, to deploy peacekeeping troops in Afghanistan to support the interim administration of Hamid Karzai, which had replaced the Taliban regime in early December 2001, although it released previously withheld assets to his Government, and pledged financial aid to rebuild the country's infrastructure. In January 2002 the Bush Government pledged some $296.8m. in funds for the reconstruction of Afghanistan.

In January 2002 the US military began transferring members of the Taliban and al-Qa'ida, who had been captured in battle, to the US naval base in Guantánamo Bay in Cuba. Initially, the USA refused to grant the detainees (numbering almost 300) prisoner-of-war status under the Geneva Convention of 1949 (which guaranteed trial by court martial or a civilian court, as opposed to a military tribunal), prompting criticism from its coalition partners, which intensified following the publication of photographs showing prisoners shackled and blindfolded. In February, following pressure from the British and French Governments, President Bush accorded partial protection of the Convention to captured Taliban fighters (he stopped short of full protection, however, claiming that the soldiers were members of an irregular militia); al-Qa'ida captives were offered no protection, as they were considered to be terrorists with no allegiance to any specific state or government. President Bush also abandoned an earlier demand to make the final judgment on a detainee's guilt or innocence. In late June the Supreme Court ruled that, while the President as Commander-in-Chief had the power to detain enemy combatants, they were entitled to legal representation in a US federal court. The following day the first three prisoners from Guantánamo Bay appeared before a military tribunal.

In November 2005 it was reported that US intelligence services maintained a network of secret prisons—referred to as 'black sites'—in locations which included eastern EU countries. It was further alleged that terrorist suspects were taken from these prisons to countries where torture was tolerated, in a practice known as 'extraordinary rendition'. The following month Secretary of State Condoleezza Rice acknowledged the existence of rendition but denied any toleration of the torture of suspects. However, in January 2005 it had been revealed that, three years previously, the chief legal counsel to the President, Alberto Gonzales (who was appointed Attorney-General in January 2005), had issued a memorandum stating that the USA was not bound by the Geneva Conventions in its treatment of prisoners captured in Afghanistan. In another memorandum ordered by Gonzales in August 2002, it was proposed that Central Intelligence Agency (CIA) officers and other non-military personnel be exempted from a presidential directive for the humane treatment of prisoners. In February 2006 the UN Commission on Human Rights published a report that concluded that the methods used by the US military to interrogate prisoners at Guantánamo Bay amounted to torture, and called on the US Government to close the base and try the remaining detainees before courts on the US mainland. A military report to the Senate's armed forces committee in July found that treatment of the prisoners did not constitute torture, but that it was, however, abusive and degrading. In mid-December President Bush announced that he would approve an amendment proposed by Republican Senator John McCain to ban the 'cruel, inhuman and degrading' treatment of prisoners. Previously Bush had said that he would veto any such amendment and at the signing of the bill, in late December, he appended a presidential signing statement to the effect that the President's authority superseded the new legislation. Department of State officials were summoned to appear before the UN Committee Against Torture in Geneva, Switzerland, in early May to answer inquiries relating to the alleged use of torture employed in extraordinary rendition. The Department of State delegation contended that it had sought assurances that detainees conveyed under this system would not be subjected to torture in their destination country and that US definitions of torture did not infringe those set out in the 1987 Convention. The UN concluded that interrogation methods involving 'waterboarding' (simulated drowning), sexual humiliation and the use of menacing dogs were unacceptable and should be eliminated. It also ruled that the detention of prisoners without charge for extended periods, the use of extraordinary rendition and reports of concealed prisons were issues of grave concern, and it urged that the detention centre at Guantánamo Bay be closed. President Bush stated that a Supreme Court ruling was pending to determine whether Guantánamo detainees should be tried in military or civil courts following their release, before which the closure of the facility could not be pursued. However, in late June the US Supreme Court ruled that military tribunals established for the trial of prisoners at Guantánamo Bay contravened the US uniform code of military justice and Geneva Conventions. The Court rejected the Bush Administration's contention that the President's authority as Commander-in-Chief, and the resolution of Congress approved following the 11 September terrorist attacks, sanctioned the institution of such military tribunals. However, the Department of Defense issued a memorandum in July 2006 declaring that all prisoners at Guantánamo Bay and other US military detention centres world-wide would be protected under Article III of the Geneva Conventions, assuring humane treatment of and basic judicial defence for those facing trial. The announcement corrected previous assertions that the Military Commission Act precluded invocation of Geneva Conventions articles.

The Military Commissions Act of 2006, intended to 'bring to justice' terrorists and other unlawful enemy combatants by means of thorough, fair trials administered by military commissions, was approved by Congress in late September and signed into law by President Bush in mid-October. In March 2007 an Australian, David Hicks—a convert to Islam—became the first detainee to be granted trial by such a commission at Guantánamo Bay and the first convicted of a terrorism offence since the camp's inauguration in 2002. Hicks was sentenced to seven years' imprisonment. However, under a plea bargain, all but nine months of the seven-year term were suspended, with the remaining gaol time to be served in Australia. This was granted on condition that Hicks abandon his allegations of abuse suffered during his period of detention, agree not to seek further legal action against the USA and refrain from speaking to the media about his experience for one year.

At January 2007 14 high-profile terrorist suspects were believed to be detained at Guantánamo Bay. Insufficient evidence for legitimate prosecution meant that up to 100 prisoners were eligible for release at that time. However, before detainees could be freed, the US authorities sought assurances from their respective countries of origin that on repatriation they would not be subject to persecution; many countries to which detainees had fled for protection refused to readmit released captives, resulting in their continued imprisonment, without charge. An appeal by the legal representatives of approximately 60 Guantánamo detainees (facing similar military tribunals), contending that the prisoners had a constitutional right to contest their imprisonment in a US federal court, was rejected, by two votes to one, in the US Court of Appeal in February. The Court's ruling stated that non-citizens without property or residency in the USA were not entitled to US constitutional rights; the dissenting judge maintained that such a ruling contravened the principle of habeas corpus. A subsequent appeal to the Supreme Court challenging the ruling returned an inconclusive result, with the majority decision that the Court would decline to rule on the constitutionality, or otherwise, of Bush's anti-terrorism legislation (ratified in 2006) permitting the indefinite detention of suspected enemy combatants.

Alleged use of 'harsh interrogation' techniques, including 'waterboarding', caused controversy in late 2007 when a report by the *New York Times*, published in October, claimed that the US Department of Justice had privately authorized their use by the CIA against terrorist suspects in 2005 while asserting that such methods did not contravene anti-torture legislation then before Congress. Later in the same month the Director of the CIA, Gen. Michael Hayden, defended the agency's interrogation practices and use of extraordinary rendition as lawful and indispensable means of obtaining information from suspects. However, on 6 December 2007—when an agreement was also reached by Congress negotiators on the terms of legislation to prohibit the use of 'harsh interrogation' techniques by the CIA—Hayden revealed that film tapes documenting the use of such procedures on two al-Qa'ida members in 2002 had been destroyed in November 2005, ostensibly to protect the identity of the CIA interrogators. Critics accused the agency of destroying evidence that might provoke further allegations of torture in relation to their practices. A former CIA officer subsequently attested that 'waterboarding' was used in the interrogation of Abu Zubaydah, the first high-ranking al-Qa'ida member to be captured after the terrorist attacks of 11 September 2001, and that he now considered the practice to constitute torture. In early January 2008 a criminal investigation was launched by Attorney-General Michael B. Mukasey (appointed in November 2007—see below) and in February Hayden, for the first time, admitted the use of 'waterboarding' on three al-Qa'ida detainees, including Khalid Sheikh Mohammed. He declared, however, that the method had not been used in the previous five years and that he had banned its use in 2006. Further, he did not rule out its future employment and admitted he was unsure of its legality under current laws. In early March President Bush vetoed the legislation restricting 'harsh interrogation' techniques already passed by the House of Representatives in December 2007 and by the Senate in February 2008, claiming that such 'specialized interrogation procedures' were of proven effectiveness and, while not practised by the military, should remain available to the CIA.

In late September 2001 the Bush Administration established the Office of Homeland Security to develop and implement a strategy to prevent future terrorist attacks against the USA. The Office was upgraded to a federal Department in November 2002. In October 2001 traces of anthrax (a toxic biological agent) were discovered in items of post sent to senior members of Congress, as well as to government buildings and media organizations in Washington, DC, New York and Florida. The House of Representatives was closed for several days in late October as a precautionary measure. Responsibility for the contamination was initially attributed to al-Qa'ida, although it was subsequently reported that the anthrax had originated in the USA; however, the perpetrators remained unknown. In total, five people died from exposure to anthrax spores (all in mainland USA), and some 300,000 postal workers and civil servants were given precautionary medical treatment in October and November.

In his State of the Union address in January 2002, President Bush described Iran, Iraq and the DPRK as forming an 'axis of evil' that supported international terrorism and sought to develop weapons of mass destruction, and hinted that the USA was considering pre-emptive strikes against them. US allies warned against attacking states unless firm evidence of a link to terrorism could be found. In February Bush faced protests on a visit to South Korea, and members of South Korean

THE UNITED STATES OF AMERICA

President Kim Dae-Jung's ruling party accused Bush of damaging the so-called 'sunshine policy' of reconciliation with North Korea. In the same month Secretary of State Colin Powell made specific mention of removing Saddam Hussain from power in Iraq. In January it was announced that US troops were to be sent to the Philippines to fight against the Abu Sayyaf guerrilla group, which was believed to have links with al-Qa'ida network. In May the 'axis of evil' was extended to include Cuba, Libya and Syria. The Bush Administration accused Cuba of maintaining a biological warfare programme and offering weapons technology to 'rogue states', and claimed that Libya and Syria had violated international weapons treaties. In December the Iranian Government denied US allegations of evidence of the secret manufacture of nuclear weapons. In mid-September 2003 the USA supported an IAEA resolution establishing a deadline of the end of October for Iran to disclose full details of its nuclear programme and provide evidence that it was not developing nuclear weapons. In mid-December Libya agreed to disclose and dismantle its programme to develop weapons of mass destruction and long-range ballistic missiles, following nine months of secret negotiations between the Libyan leader, Col Muammar al-Qaddafi, and US and British diplomats. In January 2004 a US delegation visited Libya to discuss the weapons-dismantling process. As a result, in February the USA ended the restrictions on its citizens travelling to Libya, in place since 1981, and in late June diplomatic relations were officially re-established between the two countries for the first time in 23 years; however, Libya was not removed from the US list of state sponsors of terrorism until mid-May 2006. In February 2005, in protest at what it believed to be Syria's role in the assassination of the Prime Minister of Lebanon, Rafiq Hariri, the USA removed its ambassador to Syria for consultations, and later demanded that all Syrian troops withdraw from Lebanon. (US–Syrian tensions were partly alleviated in September 2006 when an attempted attack on the US embassy in Damascus was foiled by Syrian authorities.) In March 2005, for the first time, the USA agreed with France, Germany and the United Kingdom to offer Iran economic benefits if that country pledged to end its nuclear programme. However, in April 2006 the Iranian President, Mahmoud Ahmadinejad, announced that Iran had successfully achieved the enrichment of uranium for civilian purposes. The Iranian Government claimed that the enriched uranium was not weapons-grade, but rather, to be used as nuclear fuel. Early in May a draft UN resolution was promulgated under which France, Germany, the United Kingdom and the USA again urged Iran to arrest its nuclear enrichment programme and to abandon construction of a heavy-water reactor by the end of August, or face economic sanctions. In return for compliance, a portfolio of incentives was offered, including the provision of light-water nuclear reactors for electricity generation. President Ahmadinejad issued an ambiguous letter in response, denouncing US foreign policy, but failing to confirm or reject the resolution's demands. In August, however, Iran's Supreme Leader, Ayatollah Ali Khamenei, declared that the country's nuclear programme would continue and at the end of that month the heavy-water plant became operational.

A resolution was approved by the UN Security Council on 23 December 2006 imposing sanctions against Iran, which prevented the import or export of materials and technology associated with uranium enrichment enterprises and 'froze' the financial assets of 12 Iranians and 10 institutions associated with the country's nuclear development programme. Nevertheless, in January 2007 Iran announced that production of nuclear fuel for industrial purposes was to commence imminently and declared its intention to enhance economic and military cooperation with Iraq. US suspicions that the Iranian Government was supplying Iraqi Shi'ite militants with ammunition and weapons appeared substantiated in February when US military officials in the Iraqi capital reported the seizure of explosives components manufactured in Iran; however, the Chairman of the Joint Chiefs of Staff, Gen. Peter Pace, later acknowledged that links between the bomb materials and the Iranian administration could not be unequivocally proven. Furthermore, the National Intelligence Estimate, published in December 2007 and compiled using information supplied by the USA's 16 intelligence agencies, reported with 'high confidence' that Iran had ceased its nuclear weapons programme in 2003 and had not recommenced such activities by mid-2007, although it continued to enrich uranium.

In January 2002, following an escalation in the ongoing conflict in the Middle East, the USA brokered talks towards securing a cease-fire agreement between Israel and Palestine. In March the Israeli Prime Minister, Ariel Sharon, agreed to redeploy some Israeli troops from Palestinian areas. The following month Secretary of State Colin Powell visited Israel and held separate talks with Sharon and with Arafat in his besieged headquarters, in an attempt to bring an end to the crisis. However, the mission failed to bring about a cease-fire or the withdrawal of Israeli forces from Palestinian areas. At the end of April 2003 President Bush presented both the Israeli and Palestinian Prime Ministers with a internationally sponsored 'roadmap' for peace, envisaging the phased creation of a sovereign Palestinian state. However, despite acceptance of the plan, Israel continued work on the construction of a 'security fence' in the disputed West Bank region, begun in mid-2002. In July the US Administration threatened to withhold almost US $10,000m. in essential loan guarantees unless construction of the fence ceased. Following approval by the Israeli Government of a further phase of construction, in late November the US Congress cut $290m. from a total $1,400m. in loan guarantees to Israel as a penalty for the continuing expansion of Jewish settlements in the West Bank and Gaza. At a meeting between Bush and Sharon in Crawford, Texas, in April 2005, the President gave his support to Israel's planned withdrawal from the Gaza Strip, but criticized the continued expansion of Jewish settlements in the West Bank. In April 2006 the EU and USA suspended financial aid provisions to the Palestinian Authority, under the leadership of the militant Hamas movement, in response to its continued refusal to recognize the state of Israel. The inauguration of a Fatah and Hamas coalition Government in Palestine in March 2007, while representing a significant advance towards reconciliation, did not herald any immediate improvement in US–Palestinian relations. However, at a Middle East peace conference held in Annapolis, Maryland in November, Israeli Prime Minister Ehud Olmert and Palestinian President Mahmoud Abbas agreed mutually to a deadline of December 2008 for the formulation of a peace settlement. Bush demonstrated his continued commitment to the process in his final year in office by travelling to Israel and the West Bank in January 2008, his first visit to the area since becoming President. Further meetings between the three leaders were expected to take place in April and May. The US Administration's failure to demand an immediate end to the Israeli military offensive against the radical Hezbollah movement in southern Lebanon that began in July 2006 also strained US–Lebanese relations. Instead, the Bush Administration called for joint Lebanese–Israeli negotiations to bring about a long-lasting ceasefire.

In December 2001 Enron Corporation, the largest energy company in the USA, filed for bankruptcy. This was the largest ever bankruptcy in US history, with the immediate loss of 4,000 jobs. It subsequently emerged that Enron's accounts had been falsified over several years. Furthermore, it was revealed that Enron had donated more than US $500,000 to Bush's presidential campaign, and that Vice-President Cheney had met senior Enron executives on several occasions in 2001 while drafting the proposed national energy plan. It was also reported that senior members of the Bush Administration had refused requests from Enron for financial assistance in 2001. An investigation into the bankruptcy was begun by the Department of Justice in early 2002. The firm was found guilty of obstructing justice in June, although the ruling was overturned by the Supreme Court in May 2005. Then, in June 2002 WorldCom, Inc, the second largest long-distance telecommunications company in the USA, revealed that it too had manipulated its accounts to show figures for cash flow and profits that were higher than in reality; the disclosure prompted the Securities and Exchange Commission to announce that the regulation of listed companies and subsequent penalties would become more stringent. WorldCom's Chief Executive, Bernie Ebbers, was arrested in early March 2004 and charged with fraud. Both Enron and WorldCom filed for Chapter 11 bankruptcy protection and continued to trade. In April WorldCom, now part of a restructured MCI, Inc, left Chapter 11 protection following a restatement of its accounts. Ebbers was found guilty of nine criminal charges in March 2005 and, in July, sentenced to 25 years in prison. In May 2006 Enron's founder, Kenneth Lay, and its former CEO, Jeffrey Skilling, were convicted of fraud, conspiracy and insider trading; Lay was found guilty on 10 separate counts, but died from a heart attack in July before sentence could be passed. Skilling was sentenced to 24 years' imprisonment; additionally, the liquidation of Skilling's assets, totalling $60m., was ordered, with $45m. of that sum to be transferred to a restitution fund for victims of the company's bankruptcy.

At mid-term elections held in November 2002, the Republicans assumed control of the Senate and increased their majority in the House of Representatives. Following his party's electoral success, in January 2003 President Bush announced a series of tax reductions worth US $726,000m. over 10 years. The 2004 budget, presented in the following month, included further requests for extensions to tax allowances. However, in March the proposals were vetoed by Congress, which was concerned over increased homeland security expenditure and the cost of the military operation in Iraq (see below). Eventually, in May Congress approved, by one vote, amended legislation that introduced tax cuts of some $350,000m. over the next decade. In early November Congress approved a presidential request for an additional $87,000m. in funding for reconstruction efforts in Iraq and Afghanistan. Also in November Congress enacted legislation extending Medicare (federal health care for the elderly) benefits to cover the cost of most prescription drugs.

In January 2004 the US-Visit programme was implemented, requiring that all visa-holders entering the USA were electronically fingerprinted and photographed on arrival. By January 2005 the programme had been extended to 50 land border crossings and was scheduled to reach a further 115 by the end of that year. In April 2006 some 500,000 people in Los Angeles participated in a march in protest at restrictive new immigration legislation; other protest marches took place in Phoenix, Denver and Milwaukee. The legislation, approved by the House of Representatives in the previous December, made illegal immigration a criminal offence, and approved the construction of a 1,130 km (700 miles) fence on the US–Mexican border. In early April the Senate failed to reach a compromise agreement on the proposed law that would provide 'non-immigrant visas' to some 11m. undocumented workers. The concession had the support of President Bush, but not of the Republican Party, which enjoyed a majority in the Senate. A 'day without immigrants' was declared on 1 May, on which thousands of immigrant workers held a one-day strike as a demonstration of their collective value to the US economy. The Senate ratified immigration legislation at the end of that month authorizing the establishment of a guest worker programme. Provisions were also made for immigrants to attain citizenship, subject to the satisfaction of certain criteria. The 2005 immigration control law had to be reconciled with this new legislation in order for it to become law, although several senior members of the House, in response, had indicated their opposition to any measures in the proposed legislation that might constitute an amnesty for illegal immigrants. By January 2007 it was estimated that there were 11m. illegal immigrants in the USA. In that month a study paper was submitted by the Congressional Research Service to the Department of Homeland Security cautioning that the cost of constructing and maintaining the proposed US–Mexican border security fence could reach US $49,000m.—the Department had been allocated $1,500m. for border security during the 2006/07 fiscal year. The report renewed debate as to the potential effectiveness of such a barrier; a similar measure implemented in the San Diego region had merely transferred immigrant incursions further along the border to southern Arizona, where security was less strictly enforced. During a visit to Mexico in March, President Bush was addressed by the Mexican President, Felipe Calderón Hinojosa, who reiterated his opposition to the proposed security fence. Nevertheless, by March 2008 some 480 km (300 miles) of the fence had been erected with completion of the project scheduled for the end of the year.

Meanwhile, in August 2006 the federal Government implemented 'Operation Jump Start', an immigration control initiative effected in the southern border regions, including Arizona, Texas, California and New Mexico. The initiative entailed the deployment of 6,000 National Guard personnel in support of the Border Patrol, and succeeded in curtailing the illegal border crossings by an estimated 30% by early 2007. The Border Patrol had been expanded from approximately 9,000 operatives in 2001 to almost 13,000 by April 2007. Congressional debate towards devising a comprehensive reform of US immigration policy intensified in early March 2007, with Senate Majority Leader Harry Reid indicating that legislation to, *inter alia*, reinforce border security and offer a programme of 'earned citizenship' to illegal immigrants resident in the USA, would be approved by the Senate before the August recess. However, such approval was not secured and in August 2007 Secretary of Homeland Security Michael Chertoff and Secretary of Commerce Carlos Gutierrez instead outlined a series of measures that could be effected under existing laws. These included addressing border security by deploying additional personnel and an enhanced infrastructure, policing the employment of illegal workers by rendering employers accountable for their recruitment practices, streamlining current guest worker programmes, and facilitating the assimilation of 'newcomers'.

In July 2004 the National Commission on Terrorist Attacks Upon the United States delivered its final report into intelligence failures in the months preceding the attacks of 11 September 2001. It did not lay the blame on either the Clinton or Bush Governments, but asserted that both Administrations had failed to realize the immediacy of the threat posed by the al-Qa'ida network. The report highlighted opportunities to uncover the plot that had been overlooked by both the CIA and the Federal Bureau of Investigation (FBI). However, it did not conclude that the attacks could have been prevented. It also found that, while Osama bin Laden had approved Khalid Sheikh Mohammed's plan in 1999, there was no evidence to link al-Qa'ida with Saddam Hussain (see below). The report recommended, *inter alia*: the creation of a national director of intelligence with overall responsibility for all of the intelligence services; the formation of a national counter-terrorism centre to co-ordinate intelligence-gathering; a reduction in the number of congressional intelligence oversight committees; the establishment of an international network of intelligence-sharing; and the implementation of a national policy to address the threat of militant Islamism. On 17 December 2004, following its approval earlier in the month by both houses of Congress, President Bush enacted the Intelligence Reform and Terrorism Act, which drew on some of the recommendations of the Commission's report. The legislation was designed to restructure the security services and provided for a cabinet-level Director of National Intelligence, to be responsible for co-ordinating the activities of 15 different agencies, including the CIA and the FBI. In April 2005 Bush's nominee to the new post, the erstwhile US ambassador to Iraq, John D. Negroponte, was confirmed by the Senate. An internal investigation by the CIA into intelligence failings, concluded in January of that year, was particularly critical of its former director, George Tenet, who had resigned in June 2004.

Presidential and legislative elections were held on 2 November 2004. The elections were notable for being the first in which unregulated, or so-called 'soft money', donations to the electoral campaigns of political parties from individuals, businesses and unions were banned. These funds were ostensibly intended only for general activities, but had often been used to support the campaigns of particular candidates. In the presidential ballot, President Bush was returned for a second term of office, ultimately securing 286 Electoral College votes (270 votes were necessary to win the presidency). The Democratic challenger, John Kerry, conceded defeat before the final result was confirmed, making a public call for national unity. President Bush took some 51.0% of the popular votes and Kerry 48.1%. In the concurrent legislative elections the Republicans also increased their majority in both houses of Congress. The President was sworn in on 20 January 2005. His new Cabinet included Condoleezza Rice, hitherto Assistant to the President for National Security Affairs, as Secretary of State, and Alberto Gonzales, the President's former chief legal counsel, as Attorney-General. In early February Bush presented a 2006 budget plan to Congress which proposed reductions in funding to 12 out of 23 government agencies. Spending cuts targeted subsidies to farmers, health care payments to the poor and military veterans, as well as education and environment programmes. The budget did not include the cost of a proposed restructuring of the social security system nor the additional cost of military operations overseas: to this last end, in early May a presidential request for a further US $82,000m., principally towards continued military involvement in Afghanistan and Iraq, was approved by Congress.

In late August 2005 'Hurricane Katrina' caused extensive damage to the Gulf coast states of Louisiana, Mississippi and Alabama. Louisiana was the worst affected state: an estimated 80% of the city of New Orleans was flooded. On 2 September President Bush declared a state of emergency in 13 states to release some US $10,500m. in emergency funding; on the same day Congress approved legislation for emergency aid amounting to $51,800m. Damage to infrastructure was blamed for delays in delivering relief to those affected by the hurricane: the first relief convoys took four days to arrive in New Orleans. The US Government appealed to the EU, NATO and the UN for crisis assistance. On 6 September the mayor of New Orleans ordered the evacuation of the entire city, some 480,000 people; however, an estimated 10,000 people, who were either unable or unwilling to move, remained in the city. More than 38,000 members of the National Guard were deployed in affected areas; 7,000 were deployed in New Orleans itself with orders to shoot to kill looters. They were joined by 8,500 soldiers on active duty. Meanwhile, the Government released oil supplies from the Strategic Petroleum Reserve to counter the disruption caused to the region's energy supply network, which accounted for almost one-third of domestic oil production. The impact of another hurricane, 'Hurricane Rita', along the Gulf coast at the end of September, further affected relief efforts. By May 2006 the official death toll as a result of the hurricane was 1,836; a further 705 people remained missing.

The federal Government came under much criticism for its perceived slow reaction to 'Hurricane Katrina': on 9 September 2005 Michael Brown, the Director of the Federal Emergency Management Agency (FEMA), responsible for co-ordinating the relief effort, was relieved of his duties at the head of the recovery operation in Louisiana. Less than a week later, Brown resigned as FEMA Director. A report by the Government Accountability Office (GAO), published in February 2006, criticized government at all levels for its failure adequately to respond to the emergency. It found that relief efforts had been hampered by the absence of a clear chain of command, and compounded by insufficient planning and preparation; it also identified examples of waste and fraud in the appropriation of relief and reconstruction funds. Meanwhile, President Bush appealed to Congress for a further US $19,600m. towards reconstruction along the Gulf coast, particularly the strengthening of the protective levees around New Orleans. President Bush acknowledged that the management of reconstruction and relief efforts in the wake of 'Hurricane Katrina' had been inadequate, and reiterated this sentiment in August when it had emerged that of the $110,000m. designated by Congress to the cause, only $44,000m. had been disseminated.

The Republican Party faced a series of corruption scandals throughout 2005 and 2006. In late September 2005 the Republican Majority Leader in the House of Representatives, Tom DeLay, was indicted on charges of having illegally financed Republican candidates in the 2002 election campaign. DeLay stepped down as Majority Leader, and was replaced in February 2006 by John Boehner. DeLay also resigned his congressional seat in April. (His Deputy Chief of Staff, Tom Rudy, admitted to involvement in the Abramoff case—see below—in the following month, further jeopardizing DeLay's political integrity.) In late October 2005 I. 'Scooter' Lewis Libby, chief of staff to Vice-President Dick Cheney, was indicted on charges that included obstruction of justice and perjury during an investigation into the leaking of the identity of CIA agent Valerie Plame in mid-2003. It was held that Plame's identity had deliberately been made public as a reprisal against her husband and former US Ambassador to Iraq, Senator Joseph Wilson, who had publicly accused the Administration of making selective use of intelligence to justify the invasion of Iraq in 2003. In September 2006 Richard Armitage admitted to being the principal source of the revelation during his tenure as Deputy Secretary of State. The Libby trial commenced in January 2007, although neither Libby nor Vice-President Cheney, also implicated in the scandal, testified. A number of other high-profile political figures became embroiled in proceedings, however, including Karl Rove, the President's political strategist—who was later acquitted of any charges—and President Bush himself. In early March Libby was convicted of four out of five charges of perjury, and in June was sentenced to 30 months in prison. However, the following month President Bush commuted Libby's sentence to a two-year probation period and a US $250,000 fine after describing the original sentence as 'excessive'.

In early January 2006 lobbyist Jack Abramoff pleaded guilty to charges which included conspiracy to bribe public officials, fraud and tax evasion. It was reported that Abramoff had entered a plea bargain to receive a more lenient sentence in return for information with the potential to implicate up to 60 members of Congress in abuse of their positions. Following Abramoff's plea some two dozen members of Congress returned campaign contributions they had received from him. Abramoff was sentenced to 70 months' imprisonment in March. The enactment of legislation banning members of Congress from accepting donations from lobbyists and extending regulation of designated revenue projects was approved by the Senate at the end of March, while a similar, although less far-reaching, law was narrowly approved by the House of Representatives in early May. However, further casualties of the affair were to occur during the course of the year. David Safavian, head of federal procurement policy at the Office of Management and Budget, had been indicted in September 2005 in connection with the scandal and in June 2006 was convicted of perjury and obstruction in the Abramoff investigation; he was sentenced to 18 months' imprisonment. Another Republican to contribute to the catalogue of corruption within the party ranks was Congressman Mark Foley, who resigned his seat in September following allegations of inappropriate and sexual correspondence with former junior congressional employees. A sub-committee of the House Ethics Committee was immediately convened to investigate the affair; it was concluded that several Republican leaders found to have prior knowledge of Foley's transgressions had acted negligently, but had not infringed any House rules. Nevertheless, the party's reputation was damaged ahead of the November mid-term elections.

Although Republican corruption embarrassments persisted throughout 2006 and into 2007, they were partially offset by a Democrat-perpetrated scandal in 2006. The Democratic representative for Louisiana, William Jefferson, was the subject of a corruption investigation by the FBI in March of that year. The FBI's search of Jefferson's Capitol Hill office in May prompted protests from representatives of both political affiliations, who contended that such a raid transgressed boundaries of authority between the executive and the legislature and amounted to a breach of the Constitution. A federal District Court judge ruled in July, however, that the FBI's search adhered to the Constitution.

In 2007 the federal budget proposed reductions in spending on social, health and welfare programmes, while calling for existing tax cuts to be made permanent. There were increases in expenditure on defence and homeland security. However, the budget was criticized for omitting projected expenditure on reconstruction efforts in Iraq and Afghanistan after 2007 and reconstruction in New Orleans following 'Hurricane Katrina'. The budget also included projected revenue from leasing drilling rights in the ANWR (see above), despite the fact that the required legislation had yet to be approved by Congress. The Senate ratified a US $108,900m. emergency spending bill in May. In the same month legislation representing almost $70,000m. in tax reduction, encompassing cuts on stock dividends and capital gains until 2010, was enacted by the Senate. The law had been criticized as favouring affluent families at the expense of the poor.

At mid-term elections in November 2006, the Democrats secured control of both chambers of Congress. According to final results, Democrats controlled 233 seats, while Republicans held 202 seats. The Democrats also secured a further six governorships. The Republican electoral defeat was regarded as indicative of citizens' loss of confidence in Bush's presidency, principally owing to the lack of progress in Iraq and escalating violence in Afghanistan, but also in regard to domestic policy, namely the perceived inadequacy of the federal Government's response to 'Hurricane Katrina', immigration policy, the erratic nature of economic recovery and the numerous cases of corruption within Republican ranks. Nancy Pelosi was appointed as Speaker of the House of Representatives, the first woman to hold the office, while Harry M. Reid was appointed Senate Majority Leader. In its first month in office, in January 2007, the new lower house approved proposals to increase federal funding for embryonic stem cell research; both chambers had previously approved the legislation, but it had been vetoed by President Bush in July 2006.

Immediately following the 2006 mid-term elections, the Secretary of Defense, Donald Rumsfeld, ceded to calls for his resignation, citing the need for a 'fresh perspective' on the ongoing conflict in Iraq. Robert M. Gates, a former CIA Director, succeeded him. Rumsfeld had provoked criticism over strategic policy in Iraq, and had attracted international opprobrium for his apparent approval of 'harsh interrogation' techniques—widely regarded as a euphemism for torture (see above)—in the examination of terrorism suspects. In the following month John Bolton resigned as US Ambassador to the UN; former US Deputy Representative to the UN, Alejandro Daniel Wolff, was appointed to succeed him in an acting capacity.

Further controversy involving the Republican Administration emerged in early 2007 after it was revealed that eight US state attorneys had been summarily dismissed under the direction of Attorney-General Alberto Gonzales. It was alleged that the dismissals, seven of which were effected in December 2006, resulted from the attorneys' failure sufficiently to pursue accusations of voting irregularities against Democratic candidates in the November elections. White House e-mails and documents released in the course of the ensuing investigation corroborated claims that the dismissals were politically motivated; Gonzales' Chief of Staff, D. Kyle Sampson, Karl Rove (now the President's Deputy Chief of Staff), and the then presidential counsel, Harriet Miers, were implicated by the revelations. It was also suggested that Sampson had advocated exploitation of a provision of the recently renewed Patriot Act (see above) that would enable the Attorney-General to effect new appointments to the vacancies created, thereby obviating the need for Senate approval. Miers had resigned from office on 4 January, while Sampson tendered his resignation on 12 March. Gonzales testified before the Senate Judiciary Committee on 20 April when inconsistencies between his various statements regarding his knowledge of, and motivation for, the dismissals were scrutinized and found seriously to undermine his integrity as an impartial arbiter of justice. Both Republican and Democratic senators condemned his conduct and issued calls for his immediate resignation. By May an earlier state attorney dismissal had emerged, dating from January 2006, suggesting that the dismissals had commenced five months earlier than previously thought. On 16 May Deputy Attorney-General Paul J. McNulty became the fourth senior Department of Justice official to resign in connection with the controversy, and on 17 September Gonzales finally stood down from office while maintaining that he had committed no wrongdoing. Karl Rove had relinquished his position as Deputy Chief of Staff in August 2007, citing personal reasons. Michael B. Mukasey was confirmed by the Senate as the new Attorney-General in early November, despite concerns from some Democrat senators arising from his failure to explicitly classify 'waterboarding' as torture, his previous description of the technique as 'repugnant' notwithstanding.

There were a number of further resignations by key personnel in the Bush Administration in 2007 and 2008. Al Hubbard announced his departure from the National Economic Council, of which he was the Director, in November 2007, at a time when the economy of the USA was becoming increasingly unstable. Undersecretary of State for Public Diplomacy, Karen Hughes, who was charged with improving the international perception of the USA, left her position in December. Hughes was the third adviser to President Bush to vacate office in six months, following Counselor to the President Dan Bartlett, in July, and Rove, for whose political consulting firm Bartlett had once worked. Housing and Urban Development Secretary Alphonso Jackson announced his resignation in March 2008, to become effective on 18 April, amid an ongoing FBI investigation into allegations of favouritism in awarding housing contracts and as the US housing market continued to deteriorate, with house prices falling and foreclosure rates rising.

In response to the heightened international concern over global warming and the depletion of energy resources, President Bush signed the Energy Independence and Security Act in December 2007, increasing fuel-efficiency standards for passenger vehicles and stipulating that biofuels should account for 36,000m. gallons of motor fuel by 2022 in order reduce the USA's dependence on imported oil. In his State of the Union address, delivered in January 2008, Bush delineated policy consolidation measures to be enacted during his final term in office, and reaffirmed his commitment to combating climate change with initiatives including the establishment of a US $3,000m. international clean technology fund. He also urged Congress to pass a $150,000m. economic stimulus plan and to ensure that tax relief measures were made permanent, conceding that economic growth in the USA was slowing. Modest domestic policy plans focused on improving educational standards and broadening access to education, specifically through a $300m. scholarship scheme for pupils from low-income households.

Details emerged in March 2008 of a federal investigation into a prostitution ring that implicated the Democrat Governor of New York, Eliot Spitzer. Spitzer had campaigned for office on an anti-corruption mandate and tendered his resignation on 12 March after the Republican Minority Leader of the State Assembly, James Tedisco, threatened to initiate impeachment proceedings.

In September 2002 the Bush Administration attempted to address the new threats faced by the USA internationally and outlined the policies necessary to meet these challenges by issuing a National Security Strategy for the United States. In the same month the Republicans submitted a draft resolution to Congress which would authorize President Bush to use 'any means necessary' to enforce existing UN resolutions against the regime of Saddam Hussain in Iraq and to defend US national interests by depriving Iraq of weapons of mass destruction. It was the first tangible evidence that the Administration was willing to deploy unilateral military action if the UN Security Council did not pass a new resolution authorizing military action against the Iraqi regime. The resolution was approved in October by both houses of Congress, with the provision that the Administration should first exhaust all available channels at the UN and other diplomatic means. As a result of US-led pressure, in November the UN Security Council passed unanimously Resolution 1441, which obliged Iraq, *inter alia*, to declare all weapons of mass destruction within 30 days, to comply with the UN Monitoring, Verification and Inspection Commission (UNMOVIC—the UN weapons inspectors, and successor to UNSCOM), to allow UNMOVIC to resume its work within 45 days (UNSCOM had been expelled from Iraq in 1998—see above), and to allow inspectors unrestricted access within Iraq, including Saddam Hussain's palaces. Later that month UNMOVIC resumed its operations and reported that the Iraqi Government was prepared to comply with Resolution 1441. In December Iraq presented its report on weapons of mass destruction to UNMOVIC; however, US officials declared Iraq to be in 'material breach' of Resolution 1441, for failing to comply with the demand for an accurate and complete account of its weapons programmes, and for resubmitting information that it had previously given to the UN. Following this development, the US and British Governments drew up a timetable to allow UNMOVIC to carry out intensified searches in early 2003, with the threat of military action against Saddam's regime for non-compliance.

In January 2003 some 70,000 US servicemen and -women joined the 60,000 troops already stationed in the Persian (Arabian) Gulf, and military exercises intensified. The French and German Governments expressed their opposition to any eventual conflict and called for a resolution to the problem by diplomatic means. In response, President Bush stated that the USA would lead a 'coalition of the willing' if support was withheld by other UN Security Council members and its traditional allies. The Administration took an increasingly uncompromising stance; the Secretary of Defense, Donald Rumsfeld, described France and Germany as 'old Europe' (as opposed to other more pro-US states in Southern and Eastern Europe), and the Secretary of State, Colin Powell, excluded the possibility of extending the time allocated to inspectors to find prohibited weapons in Iraq. However, Rumsfeld had also suggested the possibility of granting senior Iraqi leaders amnesty and avoiding conflict if they chose exile in a third country. In late January UNMOVIC reported that it had discovered substances and missiles which could be in contravention of UN resolutions. In February the USA, together with the United Kingdom, intensified its efforts to secure a second UN resolution which would authorize military intervention in Iraq; on 5 February Powell presented evidence of, *inter alia*, the alleged existence of weapons of mass destruction in Iraq, and possible links between Saddam Hussain's regime and al-Qa'ida. However, in mid-February UNMOVIC reported greater co-operation on the part of the Iraqi Government and that it had thus far failed to find any weapons of mass destruction. (On 13 February Saddam Hussain issued a presidential decree prohibiting weapons of mass destruction, although some al-Samoud missiles were found with a greater range than permitted under UN resolutions.) On 24 February the USA, with the United Kingdom and Spain, presented a draft resolution, reiterating that Iraq had been warned it would face serious consequences if it failed to disarm, and that it had failed to comply with Resolution 1441. In an effort to win the support of the 10 non-permanent members of the UN Security Council, the draft resolution contained no ultimatum to Iraq or explicit threat of attack. A few days later, however, President Bush insisted that only full disarmament could prevent war. In early March diplomatic efforts to resolve the crisis showed signs of breaking down when Russia and then France declared that they would employ their veto on any resolution leading to conflict, while the UN Secretary-General, Kofi Annan, questioned the legitimacy of a conflict in Iraq without UN approval. Nevertheless, Powell stated that the USA could go to war without a second UN resolution. UNMOVIC, meanwhile, reported that Iraq had destroyed part of its stock of al-Samoud missiles. An amended version of the draft for a second resolution was issued in mid-March and a deadline of 17 March given for Iraq to demonstrate full compliance with Resolution 1441. On 16 March President Bush, the British Prime Minister, Tony Blair, and the Spanish premier, José María Aznar, held an emergency summit in the

Azores, Portugal, at the end of which the three leaders issued an ultimatum giving Saddam Hussain and his two sons 48 hours to leave Iraq or face invasion. The following day the USA, the United Kingdom and Spain decided not to seek a second UN resolution and condemned France for obstructing diplomatic efforts to reach a peaceful outcome. The President of France, Jacques Chirac, responded by criticizing the USA and the United Kingdom for making an 'unjustified' decision to resort to war, and for gravely undermining the UN. The USA announced that some 30 countries had expressed support for its 'coalition of the willing', although only the United Kingdom, Australia, the Czech Republic and Slovakia provided troops.

Shortly after the expiry of President Bush's 48-hour deadline, on 19 March 2003 US and British armed forces launched 'Operation Iraqi Freedom' to oust the regime of Saddam Hussain. A first wave of air-strikes against targets in the southern suburbs of the Iraqi capital, Baghdad, apparently aimed at leading members of the Iraqi regime (including the President himself), failed to achieve their target. Soon afterwards British and US forces crossed into Iraq from Kuwait and generally made a swift advance towards the capital. At the same time, a concerted campaign of massive air-strikes was launched by US-led forces against the key symbols of the Iraqi regime in and around Baghdad, including selected military bases, communications sites, government buildings and broadcasting headquarters. Government and military sites in other prominent Iraqi cities were targeted by the US-led coalition in subsequent days. The US and British forces adopted a simultaneous campaign of issuing leaflets and broadcasting radio messages, in an attempt to persuade Iraqi citizens to abandon their support for Saddam Hussain: their declared intention was that 'Operation Iraqi Freedom' would precipitate the disintegration of the regime 'from within'. Some criticism was made within the US Administration of senior military officials for underestimating the determination of the Iraqi forces. However, by 9 April US forces reached the centre of Baghdad and on 1 May the conflict was officially declared over: Iraq did not formally offer its surrender. In mid-April US Gen. (retd) Jay Garner, Director of the USA's Office of Reconstruction and Humanitarian Assistance in Iraq (ORHA), was appointed Civil Administrator in Iraq, with the intention of overseeing the peaceful transition to civilian rule by Iraqi nationals. An Iraq Survey Group was established to investigate the presence of illegal weapons in the country. In early May a US diplomat, L. Paul Bremer, succeeded Garner as Civil Administrator in Iraq. In late July US special forces killed Saddam Hussain's sons, Uday and Qusay, in Mosul and on 13 December US special forces captured Saddam Hussain himself, in the village of Ad-Dawr near his birthplace, Tikrit: he was accorded prisoner-of-war status and held in US custody, pending his trial by a court to be convened by the Iraqi Governing Council. Legal custody of Saddam Hussain was transferred to the new Iraqi Interim Government in late June 2004 but he remained under US guard. The former Iraqi President's trial began in Baghdad in mid-October 2005, and on 30 December 2006 Saddam Hussain was executed by hanging, following the rejection of his appeal against the death sentence imposed by the Supreme Iraqi Criminal Tribunal on 5 November.

In July 2003 the US Administration admitted that claims, made in January, that the regime of Saddam Hussain had attempted to procure uranium from several African countries as part of its nuclear programme were 'possibly inaccurate'. The claims had formed part of the argument for declaring war on Iraq. In October the Iraq Survey Group published its first report; the report stated that although no weapons of mass destruction had been found thus far, there was evidence of weapons-related programmes. However, in January 2004 David Kay, the head of the Iraq Survey Group, resigned, stating that he did not believe that any stockpiles of weapons of mass destruction ever existed. Kay proposed the establishment of an independent inquiry into US intelligence on Iraqi weapons capability. The Survey Group left Iraq in January 2005. In an interim report to Congress in October 2004, Kay's successor, Charles Duelfer, concluded that Saddam Hussain had destroyed his stocks of weapons of mass destruction 10 years previously. In a report at the end of March 2005 the Survey Group was critical of the restructuring proposed at the CIA and FBI. It also criticized the agencies' failure to provide accurate information on the state of unconventional weapons in Iraq and highlighted weaknesses in their capacity accurately to report on nuclear programmes in Iran and the DPRK in particular. In July 2004 a Senate intelligence committee concluded that the CIA had provided the Bush Administration with flawed intelligence before the invasion of Iraq. At that time the Secretary of Energy, Spencer Abraham, announced that US officials had removed 1.77 metric tons of enriched uranium from Iraq in the previous month.

In late April 2004 photographs, taken in late 2003, were published of US soldiers allegedly abusing prisoners at the Abu Ghraib prison near Baghdad. As further evidence of maltreatment continued to emerge, in early May the Department of Defense revealed that in September 2003 investigations had begun into some 20 cases of the death or alleged torture of prisoners in US custody in Iraq; however, the military denied that there was any evidence of systematic maltreatment of detainees. President Bush publicly condemned the abuse of prisoners. The first prosecution of one of the soldiers involved began in the USA in mid-June. In August an internal military investigation directly implicated 27 soldiers in abuse at Abu Ghraib. In the same month an independent civilian panel confirmed 66 out of some 300 reported cases of prisoner abuse in US-run prisons in Iraq, Afghanistan and at Guantánamo Bay (see above). However, it did not find any systematic policy of abuse or instructions from senior military or government officials. By February 2006 eight US soldiers had been found guilty of the abuse of detainees at Abu Ghraib prison or of dereliction of duty: these included army corporal Charles Graner, found guilty in January 2005 of nine charges of maltreatment of prisoners and sentenced to 10 years' imprisonment; and Private Lynndie England, who was sentenced to three years' imprisonment in September, also on charges including maltreatment of prisoners at Abu Ghraib. In May President Bush ordered the demotion of Brig.-Gen. Janis Karpinski, of the army reserve, who had been in command of the police brigade at Abu Ghraib and was found guilty of dereliction of duty by the US army inspector general. Colonel Thomas Pappas, the officer in charge of intelligence and interrogations at the prison, was also found guilty of dereliction of duty and relieved of his command. In early March it was announced that the USA was to hand over control of the prison to the Iraqi authorities. At that time in Iraq there were an estimated 10,000 prisoners at one British-run and three US-run prisons, including Abu Ghraib.

Incidents of brutality by coalition forces against Iraqi civilians continued to cast a shadow over US operations in that country during 2006. In July a former US soldier was charged with the rape and murder of a young Iraqi girl, as well as the murder of her parents and sister, in Mahmoudiya in March. The case generated intense international concern over both the plight of Iraqi civilians and the psychological impact the conflict was wreaking on troops in the embattled region. On 21 December four US marines were charged by military prosecutors with the murder of 24 civilians in Haditha village in November 2005; four officers were accused of dereliction of duty and failure accurately to report the incident to superior officers. The allegations had arisen during a press conference held by congressman John Murtha who stated that the attack was believed to represent a reprisal for the death of a US marine killed during an earlier bombing.

In late June 2004 L. Paul Bremer officially handed over sovereignty to the Interim Government of Iraq. The event took place in secret two days ahead of schedule, amid fears of terrorist attacks. Full diplomatic relations were restored. In the previous month the US Army had extended the period of duty of thousands of serving troops. In June the Army announced plans to call up 5,600 retired and discharged soldiers to compensate for a lack of trained specialists. As part of the Disabled Soldier Support System, it also hoped to retain soldiers who had been wounded; in December it was estimated that 900 out of 9,300 soldiers injured in Iraq would be eligible for the programme. In January 2005 the Department of Defense revealed that it planned to make cuts of US $60,000m. over the following six years and fundamentally to restructure the armed forces, diverting funds from costly weapons systems to manpower. At that time the cost of the military operation in Iraq had already exceeded $200,000m. In mid-July 2006 Muthanna became the first of Iraq's 18 provinces to be transferred from military control to the full responsibility of the Iraqi Government and signalled a measure of progress in the efforts to achieve stability. Despite fears of an escalation in sectarian violence, in early September authority over the Iraqi armed forces was formally conferred upon the government of Iraq by the US-led coalition.

The Administration came under increasing pressure from 2005 to announce a timetable for the withdrawal of US troops from Iraq; however, President Bush remained adamant that a

THE UNITED STATES OF AMERICA

Introductory Survey

timetable for the withdrawal of troops would not be sought; the assertion was reflected in June 2006 by the Republican-controlled House of Representatives' rejection of a Democrat-sponsored resolution for such a schedule. The House also upheld a non-binding covenant supporting the conflict as integral to the global 'war on terror'. The Senate echoed this sentiment, dismissing by 93 votes to six plans to withdraw most combat troops by the end of the year. Nevertheless, concerns about the misuse of allocated reconstruction funding in Iraq, which precipitated the cancellation of contracts with US companies Parsons, Halliburton and Bechtel during 2006, provoked calls for an inquiry into the incidence of fraud and money-squandering during the execution of infrastructure projects. In June the Senate rejected such a resolution, although the Special Inspector General for Iraq Reconstruction (SIGIR) was, as of 30 April that year, pursuing 72 separate investigations into alleged fraudulence and profiteering by firms involved in the rebuilding efforts. In late July the results of an audit into the practices of the United States Agency for International Development concluded that an accounting scheme had been employed to conceal overspending on reconstruction ventures in Iraq. The disclosure in November by *The New York Times* that President Bush had endorsed a military authorization bill in October, which included a provision for the disbanding of the Office of the SIGIR, precipitated outrage among Democrats who regarded the measure as an executive attempt to conceal the Administration's mismanagement of reconstruction funds.

The bipartisan Iraq Study Group (ISG) was established in March 2006 to conduct an assessment of the situation in Iraq and generate proposals for a revised US strategy towards resolution of the conflict. The ISG submitted its report to Congress in early December, declaring the climate in Iraq to be 'grave and deteriorating', and cautioning that stability and democracy, as opposed to 'victory', should constitute the emphasis of future US military, diplomatic and political initiatives. The report delineated 79 recommendations for consideration by the President in formulating a new strategy for Iraq.

Despite the deployment of 15,600 US troops to Baghdad, the US military conceded in mid-October 2006 that its efforts to secure the Iraqi capital had been unsuccessful, and the UN reported that the number of US and Iraqi fatalities was unremittingly high. In November, the head of US Central Command and leader of US forces in the Middle East, Gen. John Abizaid, advised that additional US troops were required to train the Iraqi military forces. He also opposed the suggestion of imposing a timetable for the withdrawal of US combat personnel. President Bush and his Iraqi counterpart, Nouri al-Maliki, pledged their intention for the expeditious transfer of responsibility from military to Iraqi government authority, with President al-Maliki expressing his ambition for Iraqi forces to have secured full control of the country by June 2007, although no definite timetable was advanced. By the end of 2006 total losses of US military personnel had reached 3,000 since the start of the conflict, while total Iraqi fatalities in 2006 alone, according to a UN report released in January 2007, numbered 34,000.

Bush announced his new strategy for Iraq in January 2007 entitled 'A New Way Forward'; its proposals included the deployment of a further 21,500 troops in Iraq. The new strategy was summarized as one that required greater commitment from the Iraqi Government to quelling sectarian violence and establishing democracy in the country through the attainment of a series of 'benchmarks', in return for US military reinforcements to assist in achieving the security and stability that would enable the Iraqi leaders to resume full responsibility for the territory. Bush cautioned that a withdrawal of US forces before this was accomplished would leave Iraq vulnerable to a 'contagion of violence' engulfing the whole region. A bipartisan 'special advisory council on the war on terror' was to be established to promote the image of a US Government united against terrorism. Expansion of the country's military capabilities was also requested, with the President asking Congress to authorize an increase of 92,000 personnel in the Army and Marine Corps over the next five years. Furthermore, establishment of a voluntary Civilian Reserve Corps was also suggested; this would augment the existing military reserve and ensure sufficient protection for the country in times of conflict. The decision to expand US participation in what was increasingly regarded as a civil war met with strenuous opposition from Democrats and ignited intense debate in Congress in the succeeding weeks. The Senate Foreign Relations Committee adopted a resolution against the deployment of further troops, but Congress failed to achieve unified opposition to the President's proposals—despite the House voting for a non-binding House Concurrent resolution to such effect—when a filibuster in the Senate on 17 February prevented voting on the resolution. Dispatch of US reinforcements began in February. The US Administration indicated its willingness to participate in negotiations with neighbouring Iran and Syria towards resolving the crisis in Iraq, as had been recommended by the ISG report. Members of the UN Security Council, diplomats from all six of Iraq's neighbouring countries, representatives from three international organizations, and US delegates attended a conference convened by Iraqi leaders in early March to discuss strategies for ending the violence in Iraq.

The President's proposed budget for 2008, presented in February 2007, incorporated a request for supplemental funding of US $93,400m. in 2008, and $141,000m. in 2009, to augment the Department of Defense's operations in the ongoing 'war on terror'. In March the House of Representatives voted in favour of emergency spending legislation that would provide $124,000m. for the funding of military operations in Iraq and Afghanistan over the next six months; however, attached to the provision was a timetable for the withdrawal, by 1 September 2008, of combat troops not devoted to security or training functions in Iraq. The Senate subsequently proposed a similar bill allowing $122,000m. in emergency funding and stipulating withdrawal of US troops by an earlier deadline of 31 March 2008; the legislation was narrowly approved. Both versions of the legislation, in harmony with the President's stated new strategy, recommended that 'benchmarks' be reached by the Iraqi Government in order to guarantee continued US support. A final version received congressional approval in late April. However, in early May the President vetoed the law, stating that setting a timetable for troop withdrawal would undermine military efforts and foster further insurgency in Iraq. In mid-May President Bush appointed Lt-Gen. Douglas Lute as deputy national security adviser to oversee developments in Iraq and Afghanistan and to mediate between the various state departments involved in war policy negotiations.

At a joint hearing of the House of Congress armed services and foreign affairs committees in September 2007, Gen. David Petraeus, the leader of US forces in Iraq, testified that the objectives of the 'surge' in troop numbers—30,000 extra US troops were despatched to Iraq between February and June—were largely being met. He claimed that the tactic had reduced sectarian violence, and that in Anbar province in particular Sunni militias were now supporting US forces rather than presenting a hostile resistance. However, he acknowledged the ongoing difficulties of the situation and warned that a premature reduction in troop levels would have 'devastating consequences'. Petraeus advised that US military presence could be scaled down in December 2007 and still further in July 2008, to the 2006 level of 130,000 troops. President Bush subsequently announced that 5,700 troops would be withdrawn from Iraq by the end of 2007 and a total of 21,500 by July 2008, in accordance with Petraeus's recommendations. Bush declined to give a timetable for a full withdrawal of troops, leading Democrats to criticize the scope of the plans. In February 2008 the President's 2009 federal budget presentation to Congress included a proposed 7.5% increase in spending on defence from 2008, to US $515,000m. An additional $70,000m. was allocated to fund the conflicts in Iraq and Afghanistan between the start of the fiscal year in October and January 2009, when the incoming president was due to take office. In a speech on 19 March in recognition of the fifth anniversary of the invasion of Iraq, Bush hailed the success of the 'surge' tactic amid criticism over the rising cost of the war. Estimates in this respect differed widely, with the non-partisan Congressional Budget Office placing the figure at $600,000m. while economist Joseph Stiglitz calculated that the total cost of the war for the USA alone would be $3,000,000m. Democrat consternation was further incited in April when Gen. Petraeus advocated a suspension in troop withdrawals after July in order to undertake a 45-day period of reassessment, as a result of which the President ordered an indefinite suspension to the exit, leaving a US force of around 140,000 combat personnel in the country from August.

Relations with the DPRK were severely strained in late 2002 when it emerged that the DPRK Government had resumed its nuclear energy programme, effectively breaking the accord signed with the USA in 1994. In October the DPRK demanded a treaty of non-aggression with the USA and asserted its right to possess nuclear weapons. In the following month the USA, the

Republic of Korea, Japan and the EU suspended their supply of petroleum to the DPRK until its Government promised to terminate its nuclear weapons programme, although the DPRK denied it operated such a programme. However, in December it announced operations would resume at the Yongbyon nuclear plant, which was capable of producing weapons-grade plutonium. The USA considered that economic sanctions would be an effective means of containing North Korea, although this led to a more uncompromising stance from the DPRK, which said it would consider UN sanctions an 'act of war', and subsequently withdrew from the NPT in January 2003. In mid-July the DPRK claimed that it had made enough plutonium to produce six nuclear bombs. In late August six-party negotiations opened in the Chinese capital, Beijing, between the USA, the DPRK, the People's Republic of China, South Korea, Japan and Russia; however, little progress was achieved. In October President Bush announced that the USA would be prepared to offer security assurances to the DPRK in exchange for verifiable dismantling of any weapons programmes. In January 2004 a group of US nuclear scientists visited the Yongbyon plant, in an unofficial capacity, and announced that they had been shown plutonium but had seen no proof of a nuclear bomb. In February a further round of six-party talks took place in Beijing, but no significant resolutions were reached. Talks in June ended unsuccessfully and in February 2005 the DPRK admitted for the first time that it possessed nuclear weapons. The USA rejected a request in March to hold bilateral talks. Talks eventually resumed in August and the following month it appeared that a breakthrough had been made when the DPRK agreed in principle to end its weapons development programme in exchange for a civilian light-water reactor. However, the DPRK refused to begin dismantling its nuclear programme until it had received the reactor: the USA took the opposite position. Meanwhile, the US Administration alleged that the Banco Asia Delta in Macao, People's Republic of China, was laundering money on behalf of the DPRK Government and imposed a ban on transactions with the bank. The following month US authorities froze the assets of eight North Korean companies, which were accused of supporting the DPRK weapons programme. In October the US Department of Justice charged the DPRK with having forged millions of dollars worth of counterfeit US $100 bills—so-called 'Supernotes'—since 1989. The DPRK Government insisted that six-party negotiations would not resume until the economic sanctions against it were lifted. In April 2006 the USA again rejected a request to hold bilateral talks but, after the DPRK conducted its first nuclear test in October, the USA entered into further talks and in mid-February 2007 significant progress appeared to have been made when the Government of the DPRK agreed to effect the disarmament programme agreed upon in 2005. The process was to begin with the closure of the nuclear reactor in Yongbyon within 60 days but progress once again stalled when the DPRK missed a deadline at the end of 2007 at which it was due to give a full account of its nuclear activities.

Meanwhile, an agreement was reached between President Bush and India's premier, Manmohan Singh, in March 2006 during discussions in New Delhi, under the terms of which India would be permitted to purchase nuclear fuel and technology from the USA in return for the separation of its military and civilian nuclear programmes and consent for UN inspection of its civilian nuclear facilities. US assistance for the advancement of India's nuclear programme, together with those of Pakistan and Israel, had previously been denied under US law as the three were not signatories of the NPT; the new agreement, if approved by Congress, would necessitate the amendment of the US Atomic Energy Act of 1954, although in effectively bypassing the NPT it was argued that the legislation would undermine these international safeguards. Ongoing objections from the Communist Party of India, contending that the agreement would facilitate the exertion of undue US influence over the country's foreign and nuclear policy, presented further obstruction to approval of the agreement which, indeed, remained outstanding in mid-2008.

An escalation in the conflict between Arab *Janjaweed* militia and ethnic groups in the Darfur region of Sudan, which had been ongoing since 2003, prompted protests in Washington, DC and 18 other US cities in April 2006 to demand that the US Administration intervene to alleviate the humanitarian crisis there. In early May the Darfur Peace Agreement—negotiated by the US Deputy Secretary of State, Robert B. Zoellick, African Union representatives and other foreign officials working in Nigeria—was signed between the Sudanese Government and a faction of the Sudan Liberation Army. On 13 October President Bush signed the Darfur Peace and Accountability Act of 2006 into law, imposing sanctions against those responsible for genocide, crimes against humanity and war crimes, supporting strategies to defend civilians and humanitarian exercises, and promoting peace initiatives in Darfur. The legislation was augmented by an executive order—forbidding transactions with, and receipt of property of, the Sudanese Government—which came into effect simultaneously. The order, while specifically prohibiting transactions relating to the oil and petrochemical industries of Sudan, made provision for limited trade to continue with non-governmental concerns in other regions of Sudan. In mid-April 2007 President Bush announced further sanctions to be imposed against Sudan, including restrictions against 29 companies owned or operated by the Sudanese Government and three individuals accused of instigating violence in Darfur. Implementation of the measures was postponed, however, following an appeal from UN Secretary-General Ban Ki-Moon requesting that more time be allowed to negotiate a diplomatic solution. According to the US Department of State, by September 2006 the USA had contributed over US $1,000m. in humanitarian aid—including $400m. over the preceding 12 months for emergency food assistance—to the Sudanese people; the President's State of the Union address to Congress in January 2007 indicated that the US Government would continue to provide assistance to the people of Sudan while enjoining the international community to redouble its efforts in alleviating the crisis.

Government

The USA is a federal republic. Each of the 50 constituent states and the District of Columbia exercises a measure of internal self-government. Defence, foreign affairs, coinage, posts, the higher levels of justice, and internal security are the responsibility of the federal Government. The President is head of the executive and is elected for a four-year term by a college of representatives elected directly from each state. The President appoints the other members of the executive, subject to the consent of the Senate. The Congress is the seat of legislative power and consists of the Senate (100 members) and the House of Representatives (435 members). Two senators are chosen by direct election in each state, to serve a six-year term, and one-third of the membership is renewable every two years. Representatives are elected by direct and universal suffrage for a two-year term. The number of representatives of each state in Congress is determined by the size of the state's population. Ultimate judicial power is vested in the Supreme Court, which has the power to disallow legislation and to overturn executive actions which it deems unconstitutional.

Defence

As assessed at November 2007, US armed forces totalled 1,498,157: army 593,327, air force 336,081, navy 341,588 and 186,661 marine corps; there was also a Coast Guard numbering 40,500 (not including civilians). At the same time active reservists totalled 1,082,718. Proposals for the establishment of Voluntary Civilian Reserve Corps (see Recent History) were presented in early 2007. Military conscription ended in 1973. The Strategic Air Command and Polaris nuclear submarines are equipped with nuclear weapons. The USA is a member of the NATO alliance. Estimated federal defence expenditure for 2007 totalled US $535,943m. (some 19.8% of total federal budgetary expenditure, equivalent to 4.1% of GDP).

Economic Affairs

In 2006, according to estimates by the World Bank, the USA's gross national income (GNI), measured at average 2004–06 prices, was US $13,446,031m., equivalent to $44,970 per head (or $44,260 on an international purchasing-power parity). During 1996–2006, it was estimated, the population increased at an annual average rate of 1.0%, while gross domestic product (GDP) per head increased, in real terms, by an average of 2.3% per year. During the same period, according to official estimates, overall GDP increased, in real terms, at an average annual rate of 3.1%; GDP grew by 3.1% in 2005, but declined to 2.9% in 2006 and further, to 2.2% in 2007.

Agriculture (including forestry, fishing and hunting) contributed 1.0% of GDP in 2006 and engaged 1.5% of the employed civilian population in 2006. The principal crops are hay, potatoes, sugar beet and citrus fruit, which, together with cereals, cotton and tobacco, are important export crops. In recent years the production and export of soybeans has also become significant (a record soybean crop was recorded in 2006). The principal livestock are cattle, pigs and poultry. Food and live animals provided 5.9% of total exports in 2007. The GDP of the sector increased, in real terms, by an average of 4.1% per year in 1996–2006. Real agricultural GDP increased by 5.0% in 2005, while sectoral GDP growth, in real terms, of just 0.9% was recorded in 2006.

Industry (including mining, manufacturing, construction and utilities) provided 20.6% of GDP in 2006 and engaged 20.8% of the employed civilian population in that year. Industrial GDP increased, in real terms, at an average annual rate of 2.1% in 1996–2006. The sector's GDP increased, in real terms, by 0.8% in 2005 and by 0.9% in 2006.

Mining and quarrying contributed 2.0% of GDP in 2006 and engaged 0.5% of the employed civilian population in that year. The USA has significant mineral deposits, specifically of petroleum, natural gas, coal (with 246,643m. metric tons at the end of 2006, the USA had the largest proven recoverable reserves of coal in the world), copper, iron, silver and uranium. At the end of 2006 the USA's proven recoverable reserves of petroleum were 29,900m. barrels, equivalent to 2.5% of the world's proven oil reserves, and sufficient to sustain production at 2006 levels for almost 12 years. Crude petroleum production averaged 6.9m. barrels per day (b/d) in 2006. The USA's proven recoverable reserves of natural gas were estimated at 5,930,000m. cu m at the end of 2006, and production in that year totalled 524,100m. cu m (second only to Russia). Crude materials (excluding fuels) accounted for 5.4% of total exports in 2007; mineral fuels accounted for a further 3.6% of exports in that year. In real terms, the GDP of the sector decreased at an average annual rate of 0.7% during 1996–2006. Real mining GDP decreased by 2.4% in 2005, but increased by 6.2% in 2006.

Manufacturing contributed 11.7% of GDP in 2006 and the sector engaged 11.3% of the employed civilian population in the same year. In 2006 the principal branches of manufacturing (measured by value of output) were chemical products (13.8% of total manufacturing value added) motor vehicles and transport equipment (12.1%), food, beverages and tobacco products (10.4%), computer and electronic equipment (9.0%), fabricated metal products (8.5%) and machinery (7.9%). Manufacturing GDP increased, in real terms, by an average of 3.1% per year in 1996–2006. Sectoral GDP for manufacturing increased by 2.9%, in real terms, in 2006.

According to the US Energy Information Administration (EIA), the USA is the world's largest producer, consumer and net importer of energy. Energy is derived principally from domestic and imported hydrocarbons. The EIA estimated that in 2006 69.6% of total electricity production was provided by fossil fuels (coal 51.8%, natural gas 16.3% and petroleum 1.5%), 21.1% was provided by nuclear power, and some 9.3% was derived from renewable sources. In 2007 fuel imports amounted to 18.5% (petroleum and petroleum products 16.5%) of total merchandise import costs.

Services (including government services) provided 72.8% of GDP in 2006 and engaged 77.7% of the employed civilian population in that year. The combined GDP of all service sectors rose, in real terms, at an average rate of 3.4% per year during 1996–2006. Of non-government services subsectors, the contribution of real estate, rental and leasing was most significant in 2006 (contributing 19.1% the total value of non-government services). Services GDP increased, in real terms, by 3.9% in 2006.

In 2006 the USA recorded a visible trade deficit of $834,600m. (excluding military transactions) and there was a deficit of $811,500m. on the current account of the balance of payments. In 2007 the People's Republic of China (16.5% of total imports) displaced Canada (16.0%) as the USA's main source of imports. Other important supplier nations included Mexico, Japan and Germany. Canada remained the principal export market in 2007, accounting for 21.4% of the total value of exports. Mexico was the USA's second largest export market in that year, taking 11.7% of the value of US exports, followed by the People's Republic of China, Japan and the United Kingdom. In 2007 machinery and transport equipment constituted the most significant category of both imports (accounting for 37.8% of the total value of imports) and exports (46.1% of the total).

A federal budget deficit of $284,181m. was recorded for the financial year ending 30 September 2006, an amount equivalent to 1.9% of GDP in 2006. The deficit was reported to have decreased to $162,002m. in 2007 (1.2% of GDP), but budget forecasts for 2008 and 2009 anticipated deficits equivalent to 2.9% and 2.7% of GDP, respectively. The annual rate of inflation averaged 2.6% in 1995–2007. The average annual rate was 2.8% in 2007. The rate of unemployment averaged 4.6% in 2006.

The USA is a member of the Organisation for Economic Cooperation and Development (OECD, see p. 347), the North American Free Trade Agreement (NAFTA, see p. 338) and the World Trade Organization (WTO, see p. 396). Negotiations towards a free trade agreement, to be known as the Central American Free Trade Agreement (CAFTA), between the USA and Guatemala, Costa Rica, El Salvador, Honduras and Nicaragua were concluded in December 2003 and signed in May 2004 in Washington, DC. The Agreement, which was restyled DR-CAFTA following the inclusion of the Dominican Republic in 2004, was ratified by Congress in late July 2005 and signed by President Bush early in the following month. DR-CAFTA came into effect in El Salvador, Honduras, Nicaragua and Guatemala in 2006, and in the Dominican Republic in 2007. Discussions to establish a Free Trade Area of the Americas, first proposed in 1995, stalled in late 2004, and (although it was agreed in mid-2006 to resume talks) no progress had been made by mid-2008.

The US economy grew strongly throughout the 1990s and early 2000s, despite the persistence of many of the factors that had inhibited growth previously. However, by mid-2008 the country was poised on the edge of recession following the subprime mortgage crisis in late 2006: after house prices began to collapse in that year, many individuals were left unable to refinance mortgages as interest rates rose, leading to unprecedented levels of repossessions. The crisis had the effect of creating a nation-wide, and eventually global, 'credit crunch' as banks and mortgage lenders cut back on giving credit to customers. Real GDP growth slowed to 2.2% in 2007, down from 2.9% in 2006 and, while low, remained positive in the first quarter of 2008, at 0.6%; however, many analysts still asserted that recession remained a very real threat. Inflation, having fallen in 2007, began to increase again in 2008, reaching 3.9% in the year to April as a result of high energy prices, which stood 15.9% higher than the same month in 2007. The federal budget deficit fluctuated in the 2000s. The attacks of 11 September 2001 undermined confidence in the US economy and placed demands on federal budget expenditure for emergency aid and counter-terrorism measures. As a result, a deficit of $157,797m. was recorded in 2002. By 2006 the budget deficit had increased to $248,181m.; however, it fell again in 2007 to $163,000m., the equivalent of 1.2% of GDP. The Bush Administration intended to achieve a balanced budget by 2012 and announced plans as part of the 2008 budget programme to reduce expenditure on the Medicare scheme through health care reforms, a move expected to yield $36,000m. over the following five years. In late April 2008 the Government distributed tax rebates totalling more than $1,000m. to some 117m. homes in an attempt to encourage spending and boost growth. This greatly affected the projected budget deficit for 2008, which was expected to reach $410,000m., or 2.9% of GDP; however, the Administration maintained that a budget surplus would be achieved by 2012. The authorities faced a difficult task in avoiding recession in 2008 and it remained to be seen whether their tactics in drastically reducing interests rates (from 5.25% in June 2006 to 2.0% in April 2008) would be successful.

Education

Education is primarily the responsibility of state and local governments, but some federal funds are available to help meet special needs at primary, secondary and higher education levels. Public education is free in every state from elementary school through high school. The period of compulsory education varies among states, but most states require attendance between the ages of seven and 16 years. In 2006 there were an estimated 33.9m. pupils enrolled in public primary schools and 15.0m. in public secondary schools. Private school enrolment was approximately 4.8m. at primary level and about 1.4m. at secondary level. In 2004 there were 4,216 two-year and four-year universities and colleges, with a total enrolment of an estimated 17.6m. students in 2006. Federal government expenditure on education (including training and employment programmes) totalled US $89.9m. in 2007. Spending on education by state and local government in 2004/05 was $689,376m. (29.1% of total public expenditure).

Public Holidays*

2008: 1 January (New Year's Day), 21 January (Martin Luther King Day), 18 February (Presidents' Day), 26 May (Memorial Day), 4 July (Independence Day), 1 September (Labor Day),

THE UNITED STATES OF AMERICA

13 October (Columbus Day), 11 November (Veterans' Day), 27 November (Thanksgiving Day), 25 December (Christmas Day).

2009: 1 January (New Year's Day), 19 January (Martin Luther King Day), 16 February (Presidents' Day), 25 May (Memorial Day), 3 July (for Independence Day), 7 September (Labor Day), 12 October (Columbus Day), 11 November (Veterans' Day), 26 November (Thanksgiving Day), 25 December (Christmas Day).

* Federal legal public holidays are designated by presidential proclamation or congressional enactment, but need not be observed in individual states, which have legal jurisdiction over their public holidays.

Weights and Measures

With certain exceptions, the imperial system is in force. One US billion equals 1,000 million; one US cwt equals 100 lb; long ton equals 2,240 lb; short ton equals 2,000 lb. A policy of gradual voluntary conversion to the metric system is being encouraged.

Statistical Survey

Source (unless otherwise stated): Statistical Information Office, Population Division, Bureau of the Census, US Dept of Commerce, Washington, DC 20233-0001; internet www.census.gov.

Area and Population

AREA, POPULATION AND DENSITY

Area (sq km)	
Land	9,161,923
Water*	664,706
Total	9,826,630†
Population (census results)‡	
1 April 1990	248,709,873
1 April 2000	
Males	138,053,563
Females	143,368,343
Total	281,421,906
Population (official estimates at mid-year)§	
2005	295,895,897
2006	298,754,819
2007	301,621,157
Density (per sq km) at mid-2007‖	32.9

* Comprises Great Lakes, inland, territorial, and coastal waters.
† 3,794,083 sq miles.
‡ Excluding adjustment for underenumeration; the adjusted total was 281,424,602.
§ Estimates of the resident population, based on adjusted 2000 census results.
‖ Land area only.

RACES
(2000 census)

	Number	%
White	211,460,626	75.14
Black	34,658,190	12.32
Asian	10,242,998	3.64
American Indian and Alaska Native	2,475,956	0.88
Native Hawaiian and Pacific Islander	398,835	0.14
Others*	22,185,301	7.88
Total	**281,421,906**	**100.00**

* Includes those of two or more races.

Hispanic or Latino population (all races): 35,305,818 (12.6%).

STATES
(population at census of 1 April 2000*)

State	Land area (sq km)	Residents ('000)	Density (per sq km)	Capital
Alabama	131,426	4,447	33.8	Montgomery
Alaska	1,481,347	627	0.4	Juneau
Arizona	294,312	5,131	17.4	Phoenix
Arkansas	134,856	2,673	19.8	Little Rock
California	403,933	33,872	83.9	Sacramento
Colorado	268,627	4,301	16.0	Denver
Connecticut	12,548	3,406	271.4	Hartford
Delaware	5,060	784	154.9	Dover
District of Columbia	159	572	3,596.7	Washington
Florida	139,670	15,982	114.4	Tallahassee
Georgia	149,976	8,186	54.6	Atlanta
Hawaii	16,635	1,212	72.9	Honolulu
Idaho	214,314	1,294	6.0	Boise
Illinois	143,961	12,419	86.3	Springfield
Indiana	92,895	6,080	65.5	Indianapolis
Iowa	144,701	2,926	20.2	Des Moines
Kansas	211,900	2,688	12.7	Topeka
Kentucky	102,896	4,042	39.3	Frankfort
Louisiana	112,825	4,469	39.6	Baton Rouge
Maine	79,931	1,275	16.0	Augusta
Maryland	25,314	5,296	209.2	Annapolis
Massachusetts	20,306	6,349	312.7	Boston
Michigan	147,121	9,938	67.5	Lansing
Minnesota	206,189	4,919	23.9	St Paul
Mississippi	121,488	2,845	23.4	Jackson
Missouri	178,414	5,595	31.4	Jefferson City
Montana	376,979	902	2.4	Helena
Nebraska	199,099	1,711	8.6	Lincoln
Nevada	284,448	1,998	7.0	Carson City
New Hampshire	23,227	1,236	53.2	Concord
New Jersey	19,211	8,414	438.0	Trenton
New Mexico	314,309	1,819	5.8	Santa Fe
New York	122,283	18,976	155.2	Albany
North Carolina	126,161	8,049	63.8	Raleigh
North Dakota	178,647	642	3.6	Bismarck
Ohio	106,056	11,353	107.0	Columbus
Oklahoma	177,847	3,451	19.4	Oklahoma City
Oregon	248,631	3,421	13.8	Salem
Pennsylvania	116,074	12,281	105.8	Harrisburg
Rhode Island	2,706	1,048	387.2	Providence
South Carolina	77,983	4,012	51.4	Columbia
South Dakota	196,540	755	3.8	Pierre
Tennessee	106,752	5,689	53.3	Nashville
Texas	678,051	20,852	30.8	Austin
Utah	212,751	2,233	10.5	Salt Lake City
Vermont	23,956	609	25.4	Montpelier
Virginia	102,548	7,079	69.0	Richmond
Washington	172,348	5,894	34.2	Olympia
West Virginia	62,361	1,808	29.0	Charleston
Wisconsin	140,663	5,364	38.1	Madison
Wyoming	251,489	494	2.0	Cheyenne
Total	**9,161,923**	**281,422**	**30.7**	

* Includes armed forces residing in each State.

Note: Totals may not be equal to sum of components, owing to rounding.

PRINCIPAL TOWNS
(population at census of 1 April 2000)

New York	8,008,278	Oklahoma City	506,132
Los Angeles	3,694,820	Tucson	486,699
Chicago	2,896,016	New Orleans	484,674
Houston	1,953,631	Las Vegas	478,434
Philadelphia	1,517,550	Cleveland	478,403
Phoenix	1,321,045	Long Beach, CA	461,522
San Diego	1,223,400	Albuquerque	448,607
Dallas	1,188,580	Kansas City, MO	441,545
San Antonio	1,114,646	Fresno	427,652
Detroit	951,270	Virginia Beach, VA	425,257
San Jose	894,943	Atlanta	416,474
Indianapolis	791,926	Sacramento	407,018
San Francisco	776,733	Oakland	399,484

THE UNITED STATES OF AMERICA

—continued

Jacksonville	735,617	Mesa City, AZ	396,375
Columbus, OH	711,470	Tulsa	393,049
Austin	656,562	Omaha	390,007
Baltimore	651,154	Minneapolis	382,618
Memphis	650,100	Honolulu	371,657
Milwaukee	596,974	Colorado Springs	360,980
Boston	589,141	St Louis	348,189
Washington, DC (capital)	572,059	Wichita	344,284
Nashville-Davidson	569,891	Santa Ana, CA	337,977
El Paso	563,662	Pittsburgh	334,563
Seattle	563,374	Arlington, TX	332,969
Denver	554,636	Cincinnati	331,285
Charlotte	540,828	Anaheim	328,014
Fort Worth	534,694	Toledo, OH	313,619
Portland, OR	529,121	Tampa	303,447

BIRTHS, MARRIAGES, DEATHS

	Registered live births Number ('000)	Rate (per 1,000)	Registered marriages Number ('000)	Rate (per 1,000)	Registered deaths Number ('000)	Rate (per 1,000)
1999	3,959	14.2	2,358	8.6	2,391	8.6
2000	4,059	14.4	2,329	8.3	2,403	8.5
2001	4,026	14.1	2,345	8.2	2,416	8.5
2002	4,022	13.9	2,254	7.8	2,443	8.5
2003	4,090	14.1	2,245	7.7	2,448	8.4
2004	4,112	14.0	2,279	7.8	2,398	8.2
2005*	4,143	14.0	2,249	7.6	2,432	8.2
2006*	4,269	14.3	2,160†	7.3†	2,416	8.1

* Provisional figures.
† Data for Louisiana were not available.

Source: National Center for Health Statistics, US Department of Health and Human Services.

Expectation of life (years at birth, WHO estimates): 77.9 (males 75.3; females 80.4) in 2005 (Source: WHO, *World Health Statistics*).

IMMIGRATION
(year ending 30 September)

Country of birth	2004/05	2005/06	2006/07
Europe	176,516	164,244	120,821
Bosnia and Herzegovina	14,074	3,789	1,569
Poland	15,351	17,051	10,355
Russia	18,055	13,159	9,426
Ukraine	22,745	17,140	11,001
United Kingdom	19,800	17,207	14,545
Asia	400,098	422,284	383,508
Bangladesh	11,487	14,644	12,074
China, People's Republic	69,933	87,307	76,655
India	84,680	61,369	65,353
Iran	13,887	13,947	10,460
Korea, Republic	26,562	24,386	22,405
Pakistan	14,926	17,418	13,492
Philippines	60,746	74,606	72,596
Taiwan	9,196	8,086	8,990
Thailand	5,505	11,749	8,751
Viet Nam	32,784	30,691	28,691
Africa	85,098	117,422	94,711
Egypt	7,905	10,500	9,267
Ethiopia	10,571	16,152	12,786
Nigeria	10,597	13,459	12,448
Somalia	5,829	9,462	6,251
North America, Central America and the Caribbean	345,561	414,075	339,355
Canada	21,878	18,207	15,495
Mexico	161,445	173,749	148,640
Caribbean			
Cuba	36,261	45,614	29,104
Dominican Republic	27,503	38,068	28,024
Haiti	14,524	22,226	30,405
Jamaica	18,345	24,976	19,375

Country of birth—continued	2004/05	2005/06	2006/07
Central America			
El Salvador	21,359	31,782	21,127
Guatemala	16,818	24,133	17,908
South America	103,135	137,986	106,525
Brazil	16,662	17,903	14,295
Colombia	25,566	43,144	33,187
Ecuador	11,608	17,489	12,248
Peru	15,676	21,718	17,699
Venezuela	10,645	11,341	10,692
Total (incl. others and unknown)	1,122,373	1,266,129	1,052,415

Source: US Department of Homeland Security, *Yearbook of Immigration Statistics*.

ECONOMICALLY ACTIVE POPULATION
(annual averages, civilian labour force, '000 persons aged 16 years and over)

	2004	2005	2006
Agriculture, hunting, forestry and fishing	2,232	2,197	2,206
Mining and quarrying	539	624	687
Manufacturing	16,484	16,253	16,377
Electricity, gas and water	1,168	1,176	1,186
Construction	10,768	11,197	11,749
Wholesale and retail trade; repair of motor vehicles, motorcycles and personal and household goods	20,869	21,404	21,328
Hotels and restaurants	9,131	9,306	9,474
Transport, storage and communications	5,844	6,184	6,269
Financial intermediation	6,940	7,035	7,254
Real estate, renting and business activities	17,137	17,461	18,105
Public administration and defence; compulsory social security	6,365	6,530	6,524
Education	12,058	12,264	12,522
Health and social work	16,661	16,910	17,416
Other services	13,056	13,187	13,332
Total employed	139,252	141,730	144,427
Unemployed	8,149	7,591	7,001
Total labour force	147,401	149,320	151,428
Males	78,979	80,033	81,255
Females	68,422	69,288	70,172

Source: ILO.

Health and Welfare

KEY INDICATORS

Total fertility rate (children per woman, 2005)	2.0
Under-5 mortality rate (per 1,000 live births, 2005)	8
HIV/AIDS (% of persons aged 15–49, 2005)	0.6
Physicians (per 1,000 head, 2000)	2.56
Hospital beds (per 1,000 head, 2003)	3.3
Health expenditure (2004): US $ per head (PPP)	6,096.2
Health expenditure (2004): % of GDP	15.4
Health expenditure (2004): public (% of total)	44.7
Human Development Index (2005): ranking	12
Human Development Index (2005): value	0.951

For sources and definitions, see explanatory note on p. vi.

THE UNITED STATES OF AMERICA

Agriculture

PRINCIPAL CROPS
('000 metric tons)

	2004	2005	2006
Wheat	58,738	58,740	57,298
Rice (paddy)	10,540	10,125	8,787
Barley	6,091	6,091	3,920
Maize	299,914	282,311	267,598
Oats	1,679	1,667	1,361
Sorghum	11,523	9,981	7,050
Potatoes	20,686	19,091	19,713
Sweet potatoes	731	714	737
Sugar cane	26,320	25,308	26,835
Sugar beet	27,235	25,087	28,802
Dry beans	807	1,235	1,057
Soybeans (Soya beans)	85,013	85,035	87,670
Groundnuts (in shell)	1,945	2,187	1,479
Sunflower seed	930	1,823	965
Rapeseed	608	717	718
Cottonseed	7,477	7,712	6,666
Cabbages and other brassicas	1,133	1,100	1,100*
Lettuce	4,725	4,659	4,659*
Tomatoes	12,867	11,043	11,250
Cucumbers and gherkins	995	982	982*
Onions (dry)	3,765	3,346	3,346*
Green peas	902	859	859*
String beans	1,020	993	993*
Carrots and turnips	1,600	1,588	1,588*
Green corn (Maize)	3,958	4,116	4,116*
Watermelons	1,673	1,719	1,719*
Cantaloupes and other melons	1,229	1,208	1,208*
Oranges	11,677	9,252	9,000
Tangerines, mandarins, etc.	378	335	417
Lemons and limes	724	870	942
Grapefruit and pomelos	1,964	1,018	1,118
Apples	4,700	4,409	4,569
Pears	792	747	758
Peaches and nectarines	1,344	1,075	916
Plums	295	412	412*
Strawberries	1,004	1,053	1,259
Grapes	5,652	7,088	6,094
Tobacco (leaves)	400	290	338
Cotton (lint)	5,062	5,201	4,498

* FAO estimate.

Aggregate production (may include official, semi-official or estimated data): Total cereals 389,101 in 2004, 369,479 in 2005, 346,562 in 2006; Total fruits (excl. melons) 30,277 in 2004, 28,144 in 2005, 27,327 in 2006; Total oilcrops 108,985 in 2004, 111,082 in 2005, 110,423 in 2006; Total roots and tubers 21,419 in 2004, 19,807 in 2005, 20,451 in 2006; Total vegetables (incl. melons) 39,187 in 2004, 36,845 in 2005, 37,052 in 2006.

Source: FAO.

LIVESTOCK
('000 head at 1 January)

	2004	2005	2006
Cattle	94,888	95,438	96,702
Pigs	60,444	60,975	61,449
Sheep	6,105	6,135	6,230
Horses*	8,000	9,200	9,500
Chickens (million)*	1,985	2,035	2,050
Turkeys (million)	263	252	262

* FAO estimates.
Source: FAO.

LIVESTOCK PRODUCTS
('000 metric tons)

	2004	2005	2006
Cattle meat	11,181	11,243	11,910
Sheep meat	90	85	84
Pig meat	9,313	9,383	9,550
Chicken meat*	15,347	15,945	15,945
Cows' milk	77,535	80,254	82,463
Eggs	5,278	5,330	5,360

* FAO estimates.
Source: FAO.

Forestry

ROUNDWOOD REMOVALS
('000 cubic metres)

	2004	2005	2006
Sawlogs and veneer logs	247,958	253,636	256,036
Pulp wood	161,168	160,815	162,808
Other industrial wood	9,005	9,005	9,005
Fuel wood	43,608	43,891	44,769
Total	461,739	467,347	472,618

Source: FAO.

SAWNWOOD PRODUCTION
('000 cubic metres)

	2004	2005	2006
Coniferous	66,428	69,187	65,549
Broadleaved	26,640	27,833	27,467
Total	93,067	97,020	93,016

Source: FAO.

Fishing

('000 metric tons, live weight)

	2003	2004	2005
Capture	4,939.0	4,959.8	4,888.6
Humpback salmon	151.6	135.2	224.4
Pacific cod	257.4	266.1	248.9
Walleye pollock	1,524.9	1,519.9	1,547.1
North Pacific hake	140.3	215.2	257.2
Atlantic menhaden	203.3	215.2	194.2
Gulf menhaden	522.2	464.1	369.9
American sea scallop	200.5	243.5	214.4
Atlantic surf clam	167.8	149.5	143.3
Aquaculture	544.3	606.5	472.0
Channel catfish	300.1	286.0	275.8
Total catch	5,483.3	5,566.4	5,360.6

Note: Figures exclude aquatic plants (metric tons): 49,496 in 2003; 35,339 in 2004; 35,922 in 2005, corals (metric tons): 1.9 in 2003, and sponges (metric tons): 237.1 in 2003; 253.5 in 2004; 234.3 in 2005. Also excluded are aquatic mammals (recorded by number rather than weight); the number of whales and dolphins caught was: 434 in 2003; 298 in 2004; 67 in 2005. The number of seals and sea lions caught was: 2,242 in 2003; n.a. in 2004; n.a. in 2005. The number of American alligators caught was: 355,789 in 2003; 368,409 in 2004; 356,398 in 2005.

Source: FAO.

THE UNITED STATES OF AMERICA

Mining

('000 metric tons, unless otherwise indicated)

	2004	2005	2006
Crude petroleum (million barrels)[1]	1,983	1,890	n.a.
Natural gas (million cubic feet)[1,2]	19,517	18,951	19,359
Coal (million short tons)[1,3]	1,112	1,131	1,161
Iron ore[4]	54,700	54,300[5]	54,000[5]
Copper[6]	1,160	1,140	1,220[5]
Lead[6]	445	426	430[5]
Zinc[6]	739	748	725[5]
Molybdenum (metric tons)[6]	41,500	58,000[5]	60,500
Silver (metric tons)[6]	1,250	1,230	1,100[5]
Uranium ('000 pounds)[1,7]	2,282	2,689	4,122[8]
Gold (metric tons)[6]	258	256	260[5]
Platinum group metals (kilograms):[6]			
Platinum	4,040	3,920	4,000[5]
Palladium	13,700	13,300	13,600[5]
Lime	20,000	20,000	21,200[5]
Sand and gravel (million metric tons):			
Construction	1,240	1,270	1,280[5]
Industrial	29,700	31,300[5]	n.a.
Stone, crushed (million metric tons)	1,590	1,690	1,670[5]
Bentonite	4,550	4,710	4,620[5]
Fuller's Earth	3,260	2,990	2,980[5]
Kaolin	7,760	7,800	7,740[5]
Phosphate rock[2]	35,800	36,300	30,700[5]
Potash (a)[2,9]	1,300	1,200	1,200[5]
Soda ash	11,000	11,000	10,900[5]
Diatomite	620	653	655[5]
Boron (b)[9]	637	612	612[5]
Salt	46,500	45,100[5]	46,000
Bromine (c)[9]	222	226	226[5]

[1] Source: Energy Information Administration, US Department of Energy.
[2] Figures refer to marketable production.
[3] 1 short ton = 0.907185 metric tons.
[4] Figures refer to the gross weight of usable ore.
[5] Estimate.
[6] Figures refer to metal content of ores and concentrates.
[7] Figures refer to gross weight of uranium oxide ore.
[8] Provisional.
[9] Figures refer to the content of (a) K_2O, (b) B_2O_3 or (c) bromine contained in minerals and compounds.

Source (unless otherwise indicated): US Geological Survey.

Industry

PRINCIPAL MANUFACTURES
(value of shipments in $ '000 million)

	2005	2006
Food	509.8	514.9
Beverages and tobacco products	120.1	120.5
Wood products	106.8	107.2
Paper	156.7	165.2
Printing and related activities	92.6	95.1
Petroleum and coal products	452.0	526.0
Chemicals	568.9	608.2
Plastics and rubber products	193.2	203.5
Non-metallic mineral products	109.7	120.6
Primary metal industries	198.5	227.6
Fabricated metal products	272.2	298.4
Machinery	280.5	303.3
Computers and electronic products	348.7	365.5
Electrical equipment, appliances and components	105.2	113.1
Transportation equipment	672.1	680.5
Total (incl. others)	4,501.6	4,767.7

Source: Bureau of the Census, US Department of Commerce, *Annual Survey of Manufactures*.

Statistical Survey

Finance

CURRENCY AND EXCHANGE RATES

Monetary Units
100 cents = 1 United States dollar ($).

Sterling and Euro Equivalents (31 December 2007)
£1 sterling = US $2.003;
€1 = $1.472;
US $100 = £49.92 = €67.93.

FEDERAL BUDGET
($ million, year ending 30 September, mid-session estimates published in July 2007)

Revenue	2005	2006*	2007*
Individual income taxes	927.2	997.6	1,096.4
Corporation income taxes	278.3	277.1	260.6
Social insurance taxes and contributions	794.1	841.1	884.1
Excise taxes	73.1	73.5	74.6
Estate and gift taxes	24.8	27.5	23.7
Customs duties and fees	23.4	25.9	28.1
Miscellaneous receipts	33.0	42.8	48.4
Total	2,153.9	2,285.5	2,415.9

Expenditure	2005	2006*	2007*
National defence	495.3	505.9	466.0
International affairs	34.6	34.8	32.5
General science, space research and technology	23.7	24.0	25.0
Energy	0.4	2.6	1.1
Natural resources and environment	28.0	32.7	33.1
Agriculture	26.6	26.8	27.0
Commerce and housing credit	7.6	7.9	9.6
Transportation	67.9	71.6	76.9
Community and regional development	26.3	47.0	26.8
Education, training, employment and social services	97.5	109.7	89.9
Health	250.6	267.1	276.4
Medicare	298.6	343.0	394.5
Income security	345.8	360.6	367.0
Social security	523.3	554.7	586.1
Veterans' benefits and services	70.2	70.4	72.6
Administration of justice	40.0	41.3	43.5
General government	17.0	19.0	20.1
Allowances	—	—	—
Net interest	184.0	218.8	243.7
Undistributed offsetting receipts	−65.2	−69.4	−91.2
Total	2,472.2	2,668.5	2,700.7

*Including social security and postal service receipts and expenditures, which are extrabudgetary.

Sources: Office of Management and Budget, Executive Office of the President; Financial Management Service, US Department of the Treasury.

THE UNITED STATES OF AMERICA

Statistical Survey

STATE AND LOCAL GOVERNMENT FINANCES
($ million, fiscal years*)

Revenue	2002/03	2003/04	2004/05
From federal government	389,264	425,683	438,156
From state and local governments	1,658,073	2,009,454	2,084,850
General revenue from own sources	1,373,948	1,464,058	1,582,770
Taxes	938,972	1,010,277	1,096,385
Property	296,683	318,242	335,678
Sales and gross receipts	337,787	360,629	383,264
Individual income	199,407	215,214	240,930
Corporation income	31,369	33,716	43,138
Other	73,726	82,475	93,374
Charges and miscellaneous	434,976	453,781	486,386
Utility and liquor stores	108,388	114,324	119,874
Insurance trust revenue	175,737	431,342	382,205
Employee retirement	120,157	365,318	316,204
Unemployment compensation	35,335	38,362	35,374
Other	20,245	27,662	30,627
Total	**2,047,337**	**2,435,137**	**2,523,006**

Expenditure	2002/03	2003/04	2004/05
General expenditure	1,817,513	1,903,194	2,009,644
Education	621,335	655,361	689,376
Elementary and secondary	428,503	452,055	473,520
Institutions of higher education	164,187	173,086	182,268
Other	28,645	30,220	33,587
Libraries	8,911	9,201	9,871
Public welfare	306,463	335,257	362,007
Hospitals	93,175	96,551	103,314
Health	61,703	63,125	66,930
Social insurance administration	5,267	4,679	4,383
Veterans' services	1,017	1,504	1,349
Highways	117,696	118,179	123,900
Other transportations	24,559	23,780	23,729
Police	67,361	69,707	74,659
Fire protection	27,854	28,330	30,739
Correction	55,471	56,521	59,253
Protective inspection	11,593	11,498	12,873
Natural resources	22,808	23,299	23,914
Parks and recreation	31,765	30,467	31,890
Housing and community development	35,275	37,221	39,995
Sewerage	32,540	35,535	36,372
Solid waste management	19,183	20,373	21,279
Financial administration	34,911	36,163	36,549
Judicial and legal services	32,460	32,993	34,963
General public buildings	11,951	11,763	11,972
Other government administration	19,336	19,823	23,116
Interest on general debt	77,277	81,723	80,980
Other and unallocable	97,602	100,143	106,231
Utility and liquor stores	148,996	159,732	162,181
Insurance trust expenditure	193,263	197,405	195,542
Unemployment compensation	51,547	43,278	29,880
Employee retirement	127,197	137,537	145,796
Other	14,520	16,590	19,866
Total†	**2,164,176**	**2,265,051**	**2,372,080**

* Figures refer to the fiscal year of individual state governments, normally ending 30 June, or, in the case of the following exceptions, ending on some date within the previous 12 months: the state government of Texas and Texas school districts (31 August); the state governments of Alabama and Michigan, all local governments in the District of Columbia and Alabama school districts (30 September); all state and local governments of New York (31 March).
† Including intergovernmental expenditure ($ million): 4,404 in 2002/03; 4,721 in 2003/04; 4,714 in 2004/05.

Sources: Governments Division, Bureau of the Census, US Department of Commerce, *Survey of Government Finances*.

INTERNATIONAL RESERVES
($ '000 million at 31 December)

	2005	2006	2007
Gold (national valuation)	11.04	11.04	11.04
IMF special drawing rights	8.21	8.87	9.48
Reserve position in IMF	8.04	5.04	4.24
Foreign exchange	37.84	40.94	45.80
Total	**65.13**	**65.89**	**70.56**

Source: IMF, *International Financial Statistics*.

CURRENCY AND COIN IN CIRCULATION*
($ million at end of June)

	2005	2006	2007
Total	764,628.2	797,131.3	812,760.5

* Currency outside Treasury and Federal Reserve banks, including currency held by commercial banks.

Source: Financial Management Service, US Department of the Treasury.

COST OF LIVING
(Consumer Price Index for all urban consumers, average of monthly figures. Base: 1982–84 = 100, unless otherwise indicated)

	2005	2006	2007
Food and beverages	191.2	195.7	203.3
Housing	195.7	203.2	209.6
Clothing	119.5	119.5	119.0
Transport	173.9	180.9	184.7
Medical care	323.2	336.2	351.1
Recreation*	109.4	110.9	111.4
Education and communication*	113.7	116.8	119.6
Other goods and services	313.4	321.7	333.3
All items	**195.3**	**201.6**	**207.3**

* Base: December 1997 = 100.

Source: Bureau of Labor Statistics, US Department of Labor.

NATIONAL ACCOUNTS
($ '000 million at current prices)

National Income and Product

	2005	2006	2007
Compensation of employees	7,036.0	7,454.8	7,881.2
Operating surplus	2,920.0	3,225.3	3,282.7
Domestic factor incomes	**9,956.0**	**10,680.1**	**11,163.9**
Consumption of fixed capital	1,609.5	1,615.2	1,686.6
Statistical discrepancy	5.4	−18.1	29.4
Gross domestic product (GDP) at factor cost	**11,570.8**	**12,277.1**	**12,880.4**
Taxes on production and imports	921.6	967.3	1,008.5
Less Subsidies on production and imports	58.5	49.7	47.1
GDP in purchasers' values	**12,433.9**	**13,194.7**	**13,841.8**
Factor income received from abroad	544.1	691.4	817.5
Less Factor income paid abroad	475.6	633.4	721.8
Gross national product (GNP)	**12,502.4**	**13,252.7**	**13,937.1**
Less Consumption of fixed capital	1,609.5	1,615.2	1,686.6
Net national product	**10,893.0**	**11,637.5**	**12,250.5**
Statistical discrepancy	−5.4	18.1	−29.4
National income in market prices	**10,887.6**	**11,655.6**	**12,221.1**

THE UNITED STATES OF AMERICA

Expenditure on Gross Domestic Product

	2005	2006	2007
Government final consumption expenditure	1,965.7	2,089.3	2,221.9
Private final consumption expenditure	8,707.8	9,224.5	9,734.2
Increase in stocks	36.9	46.7	2.9
Gross fixed investment	2,438.1	2,596.3	2,590.3
Total domestic expenditure	13,148.5	13,956.7	14,549.3
Exports of goods and services	1,309.4	1,467.6	1,643.0
Less Imports of goods and services	2,023.9	2,229.6	2,351.0
GDP in purchasers' values	12,433.9	13,194.7	13,841.3
GDP at chained 2000 prices	11,003.4	11,319.4	11,566.8

Gross Domestic Product by Economic Activity*

	2004	2005	2006
Private industries	10,194.3	10,861.5	11,556.0
Agriculture, forestry, fishing and hunting	142.2	128.8	125.4
Agriculture	114.7	100.9	95.7
Forestry, fishing and related activities	27.5	27.9	29.7
Mining	171.3	225.7	262.4
Electricity, gas and water	240.3	249.5	273.4
Construction	539.2	607.9	630.0
Manufacturing	1,427.9	1,483.9	1,549.7
Wholesale trade	686.7	723.7	762.2
Retail trade	776.9	812.7	848.0
Transport and storage	344.6	358.5	385.4
Information	530.6	570.5	598.8
Finance and insurance	907.9	982.5	1,093.7
Real estate and rental and leasing	1,470.9	1,566.5	1,662.8
Professional and business services	1,338.2	1,453.2	1,560.9
Professional, scientific and technical services	792.7	851.9	925.3
Management of companies and enterprises	210.1	234.9	242.1
Administrative and waste management services	335.3	366.4	393.5
Education	108.3	113.9	120.9
Health care and social assistance	808.0	847.6	901.4
Arts, entertainment and recreation	113.7	117.4	126.2
Hotels and restaurants	313.7	331.0	353.6
Other private services	273.9	288.1	301.1
Government	1,491.6	1,568.7	1,649.4
Federal	479.4	502.6	526.4
General government	412.6	438.9	458.6
Government enterprises	66.8	63.7	67.8
State and local	1,012.3	1,066.1	1,122.9
General government	935.8	987.0	1,042.9
Government enterprises	76.4	79.1	80.0
Official adjustment	—	3.7	−10.7
GDP in purchasers' values	11,685.9	12,433.9	13,194.7

* Distribution is based on the 1997 North American Industry Classification System (NAICS), which differs from ISIC.

Source: Bureau of Economic Analysis, US Department of Commerce.

BALANCE OF PAYMENTS
($ '000 million)

	2004	2005	2006
Exports of goods f.o.b.	811.0	898.5	1,026.9
Imports of goods f.o.b.	−1,477.1	−1,681.8	−1,861.4
Trade balance	−666.1	−783.4	−834.6
Exports of services	346.2	384.6	418.9
Imports of services	−292.2	−315.6	−342.8
Balance on goods and services	−612.1	−714.4	−758.5
Other income received	401.9	505.5	650.5
Other income paid	−345.6	−457.4	−613.8
Balance on goods, services and income	−555.7	−666.3	−721.9
Current transfers received	20.3	18.6	24.4
Current transfers paid	−104.7	−107.1	−114.0
Current balance	−640.2	−754.9	−811.5

—*continued*	2004	2005	2006
Capital account (net)	−2.4	−4.1	−3.9
Direct investment abroad	−279.1	7.7	−235.4
Direct investment from abroad	145.8	109.0	180.6
Portfolio investment assets	−153.4	−203.4	−426.1
Portfolio investment liabilities	867.3	832.0	1,017.4
Financial derivatives liabilities	—	—	28.8
Other investment assets	−475.4	−245.2	−396.1
Other investment liabilities	448.6	263.2	661.6
Net errors and omissions	85.8	−18.5	−17.8
Overall balance	−2.8	−14.1	−2.4

Source: IMF, *International Financial Statistics*.

FOREIGN AID
($ million, year ending 30 September)

	2003/04*	2004/05*	2005/06†
Multilateral assistance	1,464.7	1,702.8	1,797.2
Bilateral assistance	15,554.7	31,546.9	14,364.0
Military assistance	6,285.4	4,848.3	5,151.2

* Appropriated.
† Requested.

Source: US Agency for International Development.

External Trade

The customs territory of the USA includes Puerto Rico and the US Virgin Islands. Figures exclude trade with other US possessions.

PRINCIPAL COMMODITIES
(distribution by SITC, $ million)

Imports	2005	2006	2007
Food and live animals	51,440.9	56,102.0	60,879.2
Mineral fuels, lubricants, etc.	286,375.5	333,486.3	360,910.2
Petroleum, petroleum products, etc.	244,407.2	294,361.7	322,876.2
Chemicals and related products	128,386.6	142,899.5	155,358.6
Basic manufactures	190,744.2	222,989.1	227,224.7
Machinery and transport equipment	649,912.6	709,833.7	738,714.8
General industrial machinery, equipment and parts	52,351.8	59,677.0	63,938.8
Office machines and automatic data-processing machines	98,595.8	106,487.9	101,785.9
Telecommunications and sound equipment	104,125.7	115,294.5	129,802.5
Other electrical machinery, apparatus, etc.	99,132.6	109,742.7	113,622.6
Motor vehicles	196,070.3	211,708.3	210,650.4
Miscellaneous manufactured articles	259,753.7	276,409.7	293,818.7
Clothing and accessories (excl. footwear)	76,380.4	79,149.8	81,187.7
Total (incl. others)	1,670,940.4	1,855,119.3	1,953,698.8

THE UNITED STATES OF AMERICA

Exports	2005	2006	2007
Food and live animals	48,292.5	54,259.8	68,250.4
Crude materials (inedible) except fuels	41,192.0	50,149.3	62,432.3
Mineral fuels, lubricants, etc.	26,382.7	34,881.1	41,957.0
Chemicals and related products	123,188.2	138,667.4	158,189.8
Basic manufactures	89,179.1	103,480.7	112,545.6
Machinery and transport equipment	433,665.7	494,452.5	536,409.3
Power-generating machinery and equipment	43,700.5	46,638.8	53,082.2
Machinery specialized for particular industries	35,360.8	40,029.5	51,399.9
General industrial machinery, equipment and parts	41,503.1	47,086.5	51,877.8
Office machines and automatic data-processing machines	46,882.4	49,143.8	46,192.1
Telecommunication equipment, parts and accessories	30,536.1	34,562.0	38,584.9
Other electrical machinery, apparatus, etc.	94,711.5	106,756.3	104,793.7
Motor vehicles	80,026.2	89,347.2	102,812.1
Transport equipment	53,872.5	71,998.7	81,670.0
Miscellaneous manufactured articles	103,808.5	115,968.2	127,064.2
Professional, scientific and controlling instruments, etc.	38,649.6	43,805.7	47,606.3
Total (incl. others)	904,379.8	1,037,143.0	1,162,708.3

Source: Office of Trade and Industry Information (OTII), Manufacturing and Services, International Trade Administration, US Department of Commerce.

PRINCIPAL TRADING PARTNERS
($ million)

Imports	2005	2006	2007
Brazil	24,436.6	26,388.5	25,636.0
Canada	287,870.2	303,416.3	313,110.9
China, People's Republic	243,462.3	287,772.8	321,507.8
France (incl. Monaco)	33,847.4	37,148.6	41,589.0
Germany	84,812.5	89,072.8	94,364.5
India	18,807.5	21,826.3	24,024.4
Ireland	28,621.0	28,640.0	30,346.5
Israel	16,875.2	19,149.9	20,812.0
Italy	31,008.2	32,652.2	35,041.8
Japan	138,091.2	148,091.2	145,463.6
Korea, Republic	43,779.5	45,829.6	47,566.3
Malaysia	33,703.2	36,532.5	32,790.0
Mexico	170,197.9	198,258.6	210,799.0
Nigeria	24,188.3	27,916.4	32,770.2
Russia	15,278.6	19,783.5	19,360.2
Saudi Arabia	27,227.7	31,688.9	35,626.4
Taiwan	34,838.0	38,214.8	38,301.9
Thailand	19,892.4	22,471.5	22,752.9
United Kingdom	51,063.4	53,437.1	56,892.9
Venezuela	33,964.7	37,165.0	39,896.7
Total (incl. others)	1,670,940.4	1,855,119.3	1,953,698.8

Exports	2005	2006	2007
Australia	15,770.9	17,781.8	19,205.1
Belgium	18,604.6	21,347.2	25,291.9
Brazil	15,345.5	19,227.5	24,628.4
Canada	211,420.5	230,256.8	248,437.2
China, People's Republic	41,836.5	55,224.2	65,238.3
France (incl. Monaco)	22,402.2	24,217.2	27,407.1
Germany	31,149.2	41,319.5	49,652.0
Hong Kong	16,322.6	17,778.6	20,120.5
India	7,958.0	10,091.1	17,592.5
Israel	9,731.9	10,964.4	13,018.9
Italy	11,512.2	12,566.7	14,141.3
Japan	55,409.6	59,649.2	62,665.0

Exports—continued	2005	2006	2007
Korea, Republic	27,670.4	32,455.5	34,703.0
Malaysia	10,450.9	12,550.1	11,679.8
Mexico	120,048.9	134,167.1	136,541.3
Netherlands	26,495.6	31,101.8	32,986.0
Singapore	20,646.4	24,683.2	26,284.5
Switzerland	10,740.1	14,376.0	17,039.6
Taiwan	22,049.6	23,023.3	26,358.5
United Arab Emirates	8,476.6	11,921.4	11,609.4
United Kingdom	38,628.7	45,393.0	50,296.2
Total (incl. others)	904,379.8	1,037,143.0	1,162,708.3

Source: Office of Trade and Industry Information (OTII), Manufacturing and Services, International Trade Administration, US Department of Commerce.

Transport

RAILWAYS
(revenue traffic on class I railroads only)

	2002	2003	2004
Passengers carried ('000)*	23,269	24,595	25,215
Passenger-miles (million)*	5,314	5,680	5,511
Freight carried (million short tons)	2,207	2,240	2,398
Freight ton-miles ('000 million)	1,507	1,551	1,663

*AMTRAK passenger traffic only.

Source: Association of American Railroads, Washington, DC.

ROAD TRAFFIC
('000 motor vehicles registered at 31 December)

	2004	2005	2006
Passenger cars	136,431	136,568	135,400
Buses and coaches	795	807	822
Lorries (trucks) and vans	100,017	103,819	107,944
Motorcycles	5,781	6,227	6,679

Source: Federal Highway Administration.

INLAND WATERWAYS
(freight carried, million short tons)

	2003	2004	2005
Lake waterways	89.8	103.5	96.2
Coastal waterways	223.5	220.6	213.7
Internal waterways*	609.6	626.2	624.0
Total†	1,016.1	1,047.1	1,028.9

*Internal refers to freight moved solely within US boundaries, excluding traffic on the Great Lakes system. Figures also exclude waterway improvement materials and fish.
†Totals include intra-port and intra-territorial traffic.

Source: Waterborne Commerce Statistics Center, US Army Corps of Engineers.

THE UNITED STATES OF AMERICA

OCEAN SHIPPING

Sea-going Merchant Vessels

	2001	2002	2003
Number:			
passenger	11	13	11
container	90	91	87
roll-on/roll-off	60	60	64
bulk	15	17	20
tanker	142	130	110
other*	136	132	124
Total	454	443	416
Capacity ('000 dwt):			
passenger	99	104	90
container	3,058	3,201	3,309
roll-on/roll-off	1,260	1,273	1,411
bulk	604	706	837
tanker	8,447	7,532	5,828
other*	2,362	2,162	1,818
Total	15,830	14,978	13,294

* Includes breakbulk, partial container, refrigerated cargo, barge carrier and specialized cargo vessels.

Source: Maritime Administration, US Department of Transportation.

Vessels Entered and Cleared in Foreign Trade in all Ports

	1998	1999	2000
Entered:			
number	61,417	58,374	60,064
displacement ('000 net tons)	619,071	621,204	672,834
Cleared:			
number	60,711	56,599	57,864
displacement ('000 net tons)	630,816	618,990	670,855

Source: Maritime Administration, US Department of Transportation.

CIVIL AVIATION
(US airlines, revenue traffic on scheduled services)

	2003	2004	2005*
Number of departures ('000)	10,839	11,398	11,475
Domestic traffic:			
Passengers enplaned ('000)	592,412	640,683	670,152
Passenger-miles (million)	500,271	551,935	579,661
Freight ton-miles (million)†	12,342	12,756	12,634
Mail ton-miles (million)†	880	819	719
International traffic:			
Passengers enplaned ('000)	53,863	62,222	68,273
Passenger-miles (million)	156,638	181,743	199,326
Freight ton-miles (million)†	13,021	13,926	14,178
Mail ton-miles (million)†	492	477	476

* Provisional figures.

† Short tons (1 short ton = 0.907185 metric tons).

Source: Air Transport Association of America.

Tourism

FOREIGN VISITOR ARRIVALS
(by country of residence, '000)

	2004	2005	2006
Australia	520	582	603
Canada	13,856	14,862	15,992
France	775	879	790
Germany	1,320	1,416	1,386
Italy	471	546	533
Japan	3,748	3,884	3,673
Korea, Republic	627	705	758
Mexico	11,906	12,665	13,317
United Kingdom	4,303	4,345	4,176
Total (incl. others)	46,084	49,206	50,978

Tourism receipts (incl. passenger transport, $ million): 93,398 in 2004; 102,611 in 2005; 107,881 in 2006.

Source: Office of Travel and Tourism Industries, International Trade Administration, US Department of Commerce.

Communications Media

	2004	2005	2006
Telephones ('000 main lines in use)	177,690.7	175,160.9	172,031.9
Mobile cellular telephones ('000 subscribers)	184,819	213,212	233,000
Internet users ('000)	185,000	197,800	208,000
Broadband subscribers ('000)	37,352.5	48,026.6	58,136.6

Personal computers ('000 in use): 223,810 in 2004.

Television receivers ('000 in use): 267,000 in 2001.

Radio receivers ('000 in use): 570,000 in 1996 (estimate).

Facsimile machines ('000 in use): 21,000 in 1997 (estimate).

Books published (number of titles): 96,080 in 2000.

Daily newspapers (2001): 1,468 titles with average circulation of 55,600.

Sources: International Telecommunication Union; UN, *Statistical Yearbook*.

Education

ENROLMENT
('000 students at September of each year, projections)

	2004	2005	2006
Public:			
elementary	34,178	33,823	33,906
secondary	14,617	14,887	15,042
higher	12,980	13,022	13,360
Private:			
elementary	4,812	4,702	4,752
secondary	1,338	1,360	1,375
higher	4,292	4,466	4,288

Total elementary and secondary school teaching staff (projected estimates, '000): 3,537 (public 3,091, private 447) in 2004; 3,593 (public 3,139, private 454) in 2005; 3,635 (public 3,176, private 459) in 2006; 3,671 (public 3,207, private 464) in 2007.

Total higher education teaching staff (projected estimates): 1,237 (public 819, private 418) in 2004; 1,290 (public 841, private 449).

Source: National Center for Education Statistics, US Department of Education.

Directory

The Constitution

Adopted 4 March 1789.

PREAMBLE

We, the people of the United States, in order to form a more perfect Union, establish justice, insure domestic tranquility, provide for the common defence, promote the general welfare, and secure the blessings of liberty to ourselves and our posterity, do ordain and establish this Constitution for the United States of America.

ARTICLE I

Section 1

All legislative powers herein granted shall be vested in a Congress of the United States, which shall consist of a Senate and House of Representatives.

Section 2

1. The House of Representatives shall be composed of members chosen every second year by the people of the several States and the electors in each State shall have the qualifications requisite for electors of the most numerous branch of the State Legislature.

2. No person shall be a Representative who shall not have attained to the age of 25 years and been seven years a citizen of the United States and who shall not, when elected, be an inhabitant of that State in which he shall be chosen.

3. Representatives and direct taxes shall be apportioned among the several States which may be included within this Union according to their respective numbers, which shall be determined by adding to the whole number of free persons, including those bound to service for a term of years, and excluding Indians not taxed, three-fifths of all other persons. The actual enumeration shall be made within three years after the first meeting of the Congress of the United States, and within every subsequent term of 10 years, in such manner as they shall by law direct. The number of Representatives shall not exceed one for every 30,000, but each State shall have at least one Representative; and until such enumeration shall be made, the State of New Hampshire shall be entitled to choose 3; Massachusetts 8; Rhode Island and Providence Plantations 1; Connecticut 5; New York 6; New Jersey 4; Pennsylvania 8; Delaware 1; Maryland 6; Virginia 10; North Carolina 5; South Carolina 5; and Georgia 3.*

4. When vacancies happen in the representation from any State, the Executive Authority thereof shall issue writs of election to fill such vacancies.

5. The House of Representatives shall choose their Speaker and other officers and shall have the sole power of impeachment.

* See Amendment XIV.

Section 3

1. The Senate of the United States shall be composed of two Senators from each State, chosen by the Legislature thereof, for six years; and each Senator shall have one vote.

2. Immediately after they shall be assembled in consequence of the first election, they shall be divided as equally as may be into three classes. The seats of the Senators of the first class shall be vacated at the expiration of the second year, of the second class at the expiration of the fourth year, and of the third class at the expiration of the sixth year, so that one-third may be chosen every second year, and if vacancies happen by resignation or otherwise, during the recess of the Legislature or of any State, the Executive therefore may make temporary appointment until the next meeting of the Legislature, which shall then fill such vacancies.

3. No person shall be a Senator who shall not have attained to the age of 30 years, and been nine years a citizen of the United States, and who shall not, when elected, be an inhabitant of that State for which he shall be chosen.

4. The Vice-President of the United States shall be President of the Senate, but shall have no vote unless they be equally divided.

5. The Senate shall choose their other officers, and also a President *pro tempore*, in the absence of the Vice-President, or when he shall exercise the office of the President of the United States.

6. The Senate shall have the sole power to try all impeachments. When sitting for that purpose, they shall be on oath or affirmation. When the President of the United States is tried, the Chief Justice shall preside; and no person shall be convicted without the concurrence of two-thirds of the members present.

7. Judgment of case of impeachment shall not extend further than to removal from office, and disqualification to hold and enjoy any office of honour, trust, or profit under the United States; but the party convicted shall nevertheless be liable and subject to indictment, trial, judgment, and punishment, according to law.

Section 4

1. The times, places and manner of holding elections for Senators and Representatives shall be prescribed in each State by the Legislature thereof; but the Congress may at any time by law make or alter such regulations, except as to places of choosing Senators.

2. The Congress shall assemble at least once in every year, and such meeting shall be on the first Monday in December, unless they shall by law appoint a different day.

Section 5

1. Each House shall be the judge of the elections, returns, and qualifications of its own members, and a majority of each shall constitute a quorum to do business; but a smaller number may adjourn from day to day, and may be authorized to compel the attendance of absent members in such manner and under such penalties as each House may provide.

2. Each House may determine the rules of its proceedings, punish its members for disorderly behaviour, and with the concurrence of two-thirds, expel a member.

3. Each House shall keep a journal of its proceedings, and from time to time publish the same, excepting such parts as may in their judgment require secrecy; and the yeas and nays of the members of either House on any question shall, at the desire of one-fifth of those present, be entered on the journal.

4. Neither House, during the session of Congress shall, without the consent of the other, adjourn for more than three days, nor to any other place than that in which the two Houses shall be sitting.

Section 6

1. The Senators and Representatives shall receive a compensation for their services to be ascertained by law, and paid out of the Treasury of the United States. They shall in all cases, except treason, felony, and breach of the peace, be privileged from arrest during their attendance at the session of their respective Houses, and in going to and returning from the same; and for any speech or debate in either House they shall not be questioned in any other place.

2. No Senator or Representative shall, during the time for which he was elected, be appointed to any civil office under the authority of the United States which shall have been created, or the emoluments whereof shall have been increased during such time; and no person holding any office under the United States shall be a member of either House during his continuance in office.

Section 7

1. All bills for raising revenue shall originate in the House of Representatives, but the Senate may propose or concur with amendments, as on other bills.

2. Every bill which shall have passed the House of Representatives and the Senate shall, before it becomes a law, be presented to the President of the United States; if he approve, he shall sign it, but if not he shall return it, with his objections to that House in which it shall have originated, who shall enter the objections at large on their journal and proceed to reconsider it. If after such reconsideration two-thirds of that House shall agree to pass the bill, it shall be sent, together with the objections, to the other House, by which it shall likewise be reconsidered; and if approved by two-thirds of that House it shall become a law. But in such cases the votes of both Houses shall be determined by yeas and nays, and the names of the persons voting for and against the bill be entered on the journal of each House respectively. If any bill shall not be returned by the President within 10 days (Sundays excepted) after it shall have been presented to him the same shall be a law in like manner as if he had signed it, unless the Congress by their adjournment prevent its return; in which case it shall not be a law.

3. Every order, resolution, or vote to which the concurrence of the Senate and House of Representatives may be necessary (except on a question of adjournment) shall be presented to the President of the United States, and before the same shall take effect shall be approved by him, or being disapproved by him shall be repassed by two-thirds of the Senate and the House of Representatives, according to the rules and limitations prescribed in the case of a bill.

Section 8

1. The Congress shall have power
To lay and collect taxes, duties, imposts, and excises, to pay the debts and provide for the common defense and general welfare of the United States; but all duties, imposts, and excises shall be uniform throughout the United States.

2. To borrow money on the credit of the United States.

3. To regulate commerce with foreign nations; and among the several States and with the Indian tribes.

4. To establish a uniform rule of naturalization and uniform laws on the subject of bankruptcies throughout the United States.

5. To coin money, regulate the value thereof, and of foreign coin, and fix the standard of weights and measures.

6. To provide for the punishment of counterfeiting the securities and current coin of the United States.

7. To establish post-offices and post-roads.

8. To promote the progress of science and useful arts by securing for limited times to authors and inventors the exclusive rights to their respective writings and discoveries.

9. To constitute tribunals inferior to the Supreme Court.

10. To define and punish piracies and felonies committed on the high seas, and offences against the law of nations.

11. To declare war, grant letters of marque and reprisal, and make rules concerning captures on land and water.

12. To raise and support armies, but no appropriation of money to that use shall be for a longer term than two years.

13. To provide and maintain a navy.

14. To make rules for the government and regulation of the land and naval forces.

15. To provide for calling forth the militia to execute the laws of the Union, suppress insurrections, and repel invasions.

16. To provide for organizing, arming and disciplining the militia, and for governing such part of them as may be employed in the service of the United States, reserving to the States respectively the appointment of the officers, and the authority of training the militia according to the discipline prescribed by Congress.

17. To exercise exclusive legislation in all cases whatsoever over such district (not exceeding 10 miles square) as may, by cession of particular States and the acceptance of Congress, become the seat of Government of the United States and to exercise like authority over all places purchased by the consent of the Legislature of the State in which the same shall be, for the erection of forts, magazines, arsenals, dry-docks, and other needful buildings.

18. To make all laws which shall be necessary and proper for carrying into execution the foregoing powers and all other powers vested by this Constitution in the Government of the United States, or in any department or officer thereof.

Section 9

1. The migration or importation of such persons as any of the States now existing shall think proper to admit shall not be prohibited by the Congress prior to the year 1808, but a tax or duty may be imposed on such importations, not exceeding 10 dollars for each person.

2. The privilege of the writ of habeas corpus shall not be suspended, unless when in cases of rebellion or invasion the public safety may require it.

3. No bill or attainder or *ex post facto* law shall be passed.

4. No capitation or other direct tax shall be laid, unless in proportion to the census or enumeration hereinbefore directed to be taken.

5. No tax or duty shall be laid on articles exported from any State.

6. No preference shall be given by any regulation of commerce or revenue to the ports of one State over those of another, nor shall vessels bound to or from one State be obliged to enter, clear, or pay duties to another.

7. No money shall be drawn from the Treasury but in consequence of appropriations made by law; and a regular statement and account of the receipts and expenditures of all public money shall be published from time to time.

8. No title of nobility shall be granted by the United States. And no person holding any office of profit or trust under them shall, without the consent of the Congress, accept of any present, emolument, office, or title of any kind whatever from any king, prince, or foreign state.

Section 10

1. No State shall enter into any treaty, alliance or confederation, grant letters of marque and reprisal, coin money, emit bills of credit, make anything but gold and silver coin a tender in payment of debts, pass any bill of attainder, *ex post facto* law, or law impairing the obligation of contracts, or grant any title of nobility.

2. No State shall, without the consent of the Congress, lay any impost or duties on imports or exports, except what may be absolutely necessary for executing its inspection laws, and the net produce of all duties and imposts, laid by any State on imports or exports, shall be for the use of the Treasury of the United States; and all such laws shall be subject to the revision and control of the Congress.

3. No State shall, without the consent of Congress, lay any duty of tonnage, keep troops or ships of war in time of peace, enter into agreement or compact with another State, or with a foreign power, or engage in war, unless actually invaded, or in such imminent danger as will not admit of delay.

ARTICLE II

Section 1

1. The Executive power shall be vested in a President of the United States of America. He shall hold his office during the term of four years, and, together with the Vice-President chosen for the same term, be elected as follows

2. Each State shall appoint, in such manner as the Legislature thereof may direct, a number of electors equal to the whole number of Senators and Representatives to which the State may be entitled in the Congress; but no Senator or Representative or person holding an office of trust or profit under the United States shall be appointed an elector.

3. The electors shall meet in their respective States and vote by ballot for two persons, of whom one at least shall not be an inhabitant of the same State with themselves. And they shall make a list of all the persons voted for, and of the number of votes for each, which list they shall sign and certify and transmit, sealed, to the seat of the Government of the United States, directed to the President of the Senate. The President of the Senate shall, in the presence of the Senate and House of Representatives, open all the certificates, and the votes shall then be counted. The person having the greatest number of votes shall be the President, if such number be a majority of the whole number of electors appointed, and if there be more than one who have such a majority, and have an equal number of votes, then the House of Representatives shall immediately choose by ballot one of them for President; and if no person have a majority, then from the five highest on the list the said House shall in like manner choose the President. But in choosing the President, the vote shall be taken by States, the representation from each State having one vote. A quorum, for this purpose, shall consist of a member or members from two-thirds of the States, and a majority of all the States shall be necessary to a choice. In every case, after the choice of the President, the person having the greatest number of votes of the electors shall be the Vice-President. But if there should remain two or more who have equal votes, the Senate shall choose from them by ballot the Vice-President.*

4. The Congress may determine the time of choosing the electors and the day on which they shall give their votes, which day shall be the same throughout the United States.

5. No person except a natural born citizen, or a citizen of the United States, at the time of the adoption of the Constitution, shall be eligible to the office of President; neither shall any person be eligible to that office who shall not have attained to the age of 35 years and been 14 years a resident within the United States.

6. In case of the removal of the President from office, or of his death, resignation, or inability to discharge the powers and duties of the said office, the same shall devolve on the Vice-President, and the Congress may by law provide for the case of removal, death, resignation, or inability, both of the President and Vice-President, declaring what officer shall then act as President, and such officer shall act accordingly until the disability be removed or a President shall be elected.†

7. The President shall, at stated times, receive for his services a compensation which shall neither be increased nor diminished during the period for which he shall have been elected, and he shall not receive within that period any other emolument from the United States, or any of them.

8. Before he enter on the execution of his office he shall take the following oath or affirmation:

'I do solemnly swear (or affirm) that I will faithfully execute the office of President of the United States, and will, to the best of my ability, preserve, protect, and defend the Constitution of the United States.'

* This clause is superseded by Amendment XII.
† This clause is amended by Amendments XX and XXV.

Section 2

1. The President shall be Commander-in-Chief of the Army and Navy of the United States, and of the militia of the several States when called into the actual service of the United States; he may require the opinion, in writing, of the principal officer in each of the executive departments upon any subject relating to the duties of their respective offices, and he shall have the power to grant reprieves and pardons for offences against the United States except in cases of impeachment.

2. He shall have power by and with the advice and consent of the Senate to make treaties, provided two-thirds of the Senators present concur; and he shall nominate and by and with the advice and consent of the Senate shall appoint ambassadors, other public ministers and consuls, judges of the Supreme Court, and all other officers of the United States whose appointments are not herein otherwise provided for, and which shall be established by law; but the Congress may by law vest the appointment of such inferior officers as they think proper in the President alone, in the courts of law, or in the heads of departments.

3. The President shall have power to fill up all vacancies that may happen during the recess of the Senate by granting commissions, which shall expire at the end of their next session.

Section 3

He shall from time to time give to the Congress information of the state of the Union, and recommend to their consideration such measures as he shall judge necessary and expedient; he may, on extraordinary occasions, convene both Houses, or either of them, and in case of disagreement between them with respect to the time of adjournment, he may adjourn them to such time as he shall think proper; he shall receive ambassadors and other public ministers; he shall take care that the laws be faithfully executed, and shall commission all the officers of the United States.

Section 4

The President, Vice-President, and all civil officers of the United States shall be removed from office on impeachment for conviction of treason, bribery or other high crimes and misdemeanours.

ARTICLE III

Section 1

The judicial power of the United States shall be vested in one Supreme Court, and in such inferior courts as the Congress may from time to time ordain and establish. The judges, both of the Supreme and inferior courts, shall hold their offices during good behaviour, and shall at stated times receive for their services a compensation which shall not be diminished during their continuance in office.

Section 2

1. The judicial power shall extend to all cases in law and equity arising under this Constitution, the laws of the United States, and treaties made, or which shall be made, under their authority; to all cases affecting ambassadors, other public ministers and consuls; to all cases of admiralty and maritime jurisdiction; to controversies to which the United States shall be a party; to controversies between two or more States, between a State and citizens of another State, between citizens of different States, between citizens of the same State claiming lands under grants of different States, and between a State, or the citizens thereof, and foreign States, citizens, or subjects.

2. In all cases affecting ambassadors, other public ministers, and consuls, and those in which a State shall be party, the Supreme Court shall have original jurisdiction. In all the other cases before mentioned the Supreme Court shall have appellate jurisdiction both as to law and fact, with such exceptions and under such regulations as the Congress shall make.

3. The trial of all crimes, except in cases of impeachment, shall be by jury, and such trials shall be held in the State where the said crimes shall have been committed; but when not committed within any State the trial shall be at such place or places as the Congress may by law have directed.

Section 3

1. Treason against the United States shall consist only in levying war against them, or in adhering to their enemies, giving them aid and comfort. No person shall be convicted of treason unless on the testimony of two witnesses to the same overt act, or on confession in open court.

2. The Congress shall have power to declare the punishment of treason, but no attainder of treason shall work corruption of blood, or forfeiture except during the life of the person attained.

ARTICLE IV

Section 1

Full faith and credit shall be given in each State to the public acts, records, and judicial proceedings of every other State. And the Congress may by general laws prescribe the manner in which such acts, records, and proceedings shall be proved, and the effect thereof.

Section 2

1. The citizens of each State shall be entitled to all privileges and immunities of citizens in the several States.

2. A person charged in any State with treason, felony, or other crime, who shall flee from justice, and be found in another State, shall, on demand of the Executive authority of the State from which he fled, be delivered up, to be removed to the State having jurisdiction of the crime.

3. No person held to service or labour in one State, under the laws thereof, escaping into another shall in consequence of any law or regulation therein, be discharged from such service or labour, but shall be delivered up on claim of the party to whom such service or labour may be due.

Section 3

1. New States may be admitted by the Congress into this Union; but no new State shall be formed or erected within the jurisdiction of any other State, nor any State be formed by the junction of two or more States, or parts of States, without the consent of the Legislatures of the States concerned, as well as of the Congress.

2. The Congress shall have the power to dispose of and make all needful rules and regulations respecting the territory or other property belonging to the United States; and nothing in this Constitution shall be so construed as to prejudice any claims of the United States, or of any particular State.

Section 4

The United States shall guarantee to every State in this Union a Republican form of government, and shall protect each of them against invasion, and on application of the Legislature, or of the Executive (when the Legislature cannot be convened) against domestic violence.

ARTICLE V

The Congress, whenever two-thirds of both Houses shall deem it necessary, shall propose amendments to this Constitution, or, on the application of the Legislature of two-thirds of the several States, shall call a convention for proposing amendments, which in either case, shall be valid to all intents and purposes, as part of this Constitution, when ratified by the Legislature of three-fourths of the several States, or by conventions in three-fourths thereof, as the one or the other mode of ratification may be proposed by the Congress, provided that no amendment which may be made prior to the year 1808 shall in any manner affect the first and fourth clauses in the Ninth Section of the First Article; and that no State, without its consent, shall be deprived of its equal suffrage in the Senate.

ARTICLE VI

1. All debts contracted and engagements entered into before the adoption of this Constitution shall be as valid against the United States under this Constitution as under the Confederation.

2. This Constitution and the laws of the United States which shall be made in pursuance thereof and all treaties made, or which shall be made, under the authority of the United States, shall be the supreme law of the land, and the judges in every State shall be bound thereby, anything in the Constitution or laws of any State to the contrary notwithstanding.

3. The Senators and Representatives before mentioned, and the members of the several State Legislatures, and all executives and judicial officers, both of the United States and of the several States, shall be bound by oath or affirmation to support this Constitution; but no religious test shall ever be required as a qualification to any office or public trust under the United States.

ARTICLE VII

The ratification of the Conventions of nine States shall be sufficient for the establishment of this Constitution between the States so ratifying the same.

Amendments to the Constitution

Ten Original Amendments, in force 15 December 1791:

AMENDMENT I

Congress shall make no law respecting an establishment of religion, or prohibiting the free exercise thereof; or abridging the freedom of speech or of the Press; or the right of the people peaceably to assemble and to petition the Government for a redress of grievances.

AMENDMENT II

A well-regulated militia being necessary to the security of a free State, the right of the people to keep and bear arms shall not be infringed.

AMENDMENT III

No soldier shall, in time of peace, be quartered in any house without the consent of the owner, nor in time of war but in a manner to be prescribed by law.

AMENDMENT IV

The right of the people to be secure in their persons, houses, papers, and effects, against unreasonable searches and seizures, shall not be violated, and no warrants shall issue but upon probable cause, supported by oath or affirmation, and particularly describing the place to be searched, and the persons or things to be seized.

AMENDMENT V

No person shall be held to answer for a capital or other infamous crime unless on a presentment or indictment of a Grand Jury, except in cases arising in the land or naval forces, or in the militia, when in actual service, in time of war or public danger; nor shall any person be subject for the same offense to be twice put in jeopardy of life or limb; nor shall be compelled in any criminal case to be a witness against himself, nor be deprived of life, liberty, or property, without due process of law; nor shall private property be taken for public use without just compensation.

AMENDMENT VI

In all criminal prosecutions, the accused shall enjoy the right to a speedy and public trial, by an impartial jury of the State and district wherein the crime shall have been committed, which districts shall have been previously ascertained by law, and to be informed of the nature and cause of the accusation; to be confronted with the witnesses against him; to have compulsory process for obtaining witnesses in his favour, and to have the assistance of counsel for his defense.

AMENDMENT VII

In suits at common law, where the value in controversy shall exceed 20 dollars, the right of trial by jury shall be preserved, and no fact tried by a jury shall be otherwise re-examined in any court of the United States than according to the rules of the common law.

AMENDMENT VIII

Excessive bail shall not be required, nor excessive fines imposed, nor cruel and unusual punishments inflicted.

AMENDMENT IX

The enumeration in the Constitution of certain rights shall not be construed to deny or disparage others retained by the people.

AMENDMENT X

The powers not delegated to the United States by the Constitution, nor prohibited by it to the States, are reserved to the States respectively, or to the people.

Subsequent Amendments:

AMENDMENT XI
(became part of the Constitution February 1795)

The judicial power of the United States shall not be construed to extend to any suit in law or equity, commenced or prosecuted against one of the United States, by citizens of another State, or by citizens or subjects of any foreign State.

AMENDMENT XII
(ratified June 1804)

The Electors shall meet in their respective States, and vote by ballot for President and Vice-President, one of whom at least shall not be an inhabitant of the same State with themselves; they shall name in their ballots the person voted for as President, and in distinct ballots the person voted for as Vice-President; and they shall make distinct list of all persons voted for as President, and of all persons voted for as Vice-President, and of the number of votes for each, which list they shall sign and certify, and transmit, sealed, to the seat of the Government of the United States, directed to the President of the Senate; the President of the Senate shall, in the presence of the Senate and House of Representatives, open all the certificates and the votes shall then be counted; the person having the greatest number of votes for President shall be the President, if such number be a majority of the whole number of Electors appointed; and if no person have such majority, then from the persons having the highest number, not exceeding three, on the list of those voted for as President, the House of Representatives shall choose immediately, by ballot, the President. But in choosing the President, the votes shall be taken by States, the representation from each State having one vote; a quorum for this purpose shall consist of a member or members from two-thirds of the States, and a majority of all the States shall be necessary to a choice. And if the House of Representatives shall not choose a President, whenever the right of choice shall devolve upon them, before the fourth day of March next following, then the Vice-President shall act as President, as in the case of the death or other constitutional disability of the President. The person having the greatest number of votes as Vice-President shall be the Vice-President if such number be a majority of the whole number of Electors appointed, and if no person have a majority, then, from the two highest numbers on the list the Senate shall choose the Vice-President; a quorum for the purpose shall consist of two-thirds of the whole number of Senators, and a majority of the whole number shall be necessary to a choice. But no person constitutionally ineligible to the office of President shall be eligible to that of Vice-President of the United States.

AMENDMENT XIII
(ratified December 1865)

1. Neither slavery nor involuntary servitude, except as a punishment for crime whereof the party shall have been duly convicted, shall exist within the United States, or any place subject to their jurisdiction.

2. Congress shall have the power to enforce this article by appropriate legislation.

AMENDMENT XIV
(ratified July 1868)

1. All persons born or naturalized in the United States, and subject to the jurisdiction thereof, are citizens of the United States and of the State wherein they reside. No State shall make or enforce any law which shall abridge the privileges or immunities of citizens of the United States, nor shall any State deprive any person of life, liberty, or property without due process of law, nor deny to any person within its jurisdiction the equal protection of the laws.

2. Representatives shall be apportioned among the several States according to their respective numbers, counting the whole number of persons in each State excluding Indians not taxed. But when the right to vote at any election for the choice of Electors for President and Vice-President of the United States, Representatives in Congress, the executive and judicial officers of a State, or the members of the Legislature thereof, is denied to any of the male inhabitants of such State, being 21 years of age, and citizens of the United States, or in any way abridged, except for participation in rebellion, or other crime, the basis of representation therein shall be reduced in the proportion which the number of such male citizens shall bear to the whole number of male citizens 21 years of age in such State.

3. No person shall be a Senator or Representative in Congress, or Elector of President and Vice-President or hold any office, civil or military, under the United States, or under any State, who, having previously taken an oath as member of Congress or as an officer of the United States, or as a member of any State Legislature, or as an executive or judicial officer of any State, to support the Constitution of the United States, shall have engaged in insurrection or rebellion against the same, or given aid and comfort to the enemies thereof. But Congress may, by vote of two-thirds of each House, remove such disability.

4. The validity of the public debt of the United States, authorized by law, including debts incurred for payment of pensions and bounties for services in suppressing insurrection and rebellion, shall not be questioned. But neither the United States nor any State shall assume or pay any debt or obligation incurred in aid of insurrection or rebellion against the United States, or any claim for the loss or emancipation of any slave; but all such debts, obligations, and claims shall be held illegal and void.

5. The Congress shall have power to enforce by appropriate legislation the provisions of this article.

AMENDMENT XV
(ratified March 1870)

1. The right of the citizens of the United States to vote shall not be denied or abridged by the United States or by any State on account of race, colour, or previous condition of servitude.

2. The Congress shall have power to enforce the provisions of this article by appropriate legislation.

AMENDMENT XVI
(ratified February 1913)

The Congress shall have power to lay and collect taxes on incomes, from whatever sources derived, without apportionment among the several States, and without regard to any census or enumeration.

AMENDMENT XVII
(ratified May 1913)

1. The Senate of the United States shall be composed of two Senators from each State, elected by the people thereof, for six years; and each Senator shall have one vote. The electors in each State shall have the qualifications requisite for electors of the most numerous branch of the State Legislature.

2. When vacancies happen in the representation of any State in the Senate, the executive authority of such State shall issue writs of election to fill such vacancies: provided that the Legislature of any State may empower the Executive thereof to make temporary appointment until the people fill the vacancies by election as the Legislature may direct.

3. This amendment shall not be so construed as to affect the election or term of any Senator chosen before it becomes valid as part of the Constitution.

AMENDMENT XVIII
(ratified January 1919*)

1. After one year from the ratification of this article the manufacture, sale, or transportation of intoxicating liquors within, the importation

thereof into, or the exportation thereof from the United States, and all territory subject to the jurisdiction thereof for beverage purposes is hereby prohibited.

2. The Congress and the several States shall have concurrent power to enforce this article by appropriate legislation.

3. This article shall be inoperative unless it shall have been ratified as an amendment to the Constitution by the Legislatures of the several States, as provided in the Constitution, within seven years from the date of the submission hereof to the States by the Congress.
* Repealed by Amendment XXI.

AMENDMENT XIX
(ratified August 1920)

1. The right of citizens of the United States to vote shall not be denied or abridged by the United States or by any State on account of sex.

2. Congress shall have power, by appropriate legislation to enforce the provisions of this article.

AMENDMENT XX
(ratified January 1933)

Section 1
The terms of the President and Vice-President shall end at noon on the 20th day of January, and the terms of Senators and Representatives at noon on the third day of January, of the years in which such terms would have ended if this article had not been ratified; and the terms of their successors shall then begin.

Section 2
The Congress shall assemble at least once in every year, and such meetings shall begin at noon on the third day of January, unless they shall by law appoint a different day.

Section 3
If, at the time fixed for the beginning of the term of the President, the President elect shall have died, the Vice-President elect shall become President. If a President shall not have been chosen before the time fixed for the beginning of his term, or if the President elect shall have failed to qualify, then the Vice-President elect shall act as President until a President shall have qualified; and the Congress may by law provide for the case wherein neither a President elect nor a Vice-President elect shall have qualified, declaring who shall then act as President, or the manner in which one who is to act shall be selected, and such person shall act accordingly until a President or Vice-President shall have qualified.

Section 4
The Congress may by law provide for the case of the death of any of the persons from whom the House of Representatives may choose a President whenever the right of choice shall have devolved upon them, and for the case of the death of any of the persons from whom the Senate may choose a Vice-President whenever the right of choice shall have devolved upon them.

Section 5
Sections 1 and 2 shall take effect on the 15th day of October following the ratification of this article.

Section 6
This article shall be inoperative unless it shall have been ratified as an amendment to the Constitution by the legislature of three-fourths of the several States within seven years from the date of its submission.

AMENDMENT XXI
(ratified December 1933)

Section 1
The 18th article of amendment to the Constitution of the United States is hereby repealed.

Section 2
The transportation or importation into any State, Territory or Possession of the United States for delivery or use therein of intoxicating liquors, in violation of the laws thereof, is hereby prohibited.

Section 3
This article shall be inoperative unless it shall have been ratified as an amendment to the Constitution by conventions in the several States, as provided in the Constitution, within seven years from the date of the submission hereof to the States by the Congress.

AMENDMENT XXII
(ratified February 1951)

No person shall be elected to the office of President more than twice, and no person who has held the office of President, or acted as President, for more than two years of a term to which some other person was elected President shall be elected to the office of President more than once. But this article shall not apply to any person holding the office of President when this Article was proposed by Congress, and shall not prevent any person who may be holding the office of President, or acting as President, during the term within which this Article becomes operative from holding the office of President or acting as President during the remainder of such term.

AMENDMENT XXIII
(ratified March 1961)

Section 1
The District constituting the seat of Government of the United States shall appoint in such manner as the Congress may direct:

A number of electors of President and Vice-President equal to the whole number of Senators and Representatives in Congress to which the District would be entitled if it were a State, but in no event more than the least populous State; they shall be in addition to those appointed by the States, but they shall be considered, for the purposes of the election of President and Vice-President, to be electors appointed by a State; and they shall meet in the District and perform such duties as provided by the 12th article of amendment.

Section 2
The Congress shall have power to enforce this article by appropriate legislation.

AMENDMENT XXIV
(ratified January 1964)

Section 1
The right of citizens of the United States to vote in any primary or other election for President or Vice-President, for electors for President or Vice-President, or for Senator or Representative in Congress, shall not be denied or abridged by the United States or any State by reason of failure to pay any poll tax or other tax.

Section 2
The Congress shall have power to enforce this article by appropriate legislation.

AMENDMENT XXV
(ratified February 1967)

Section 1
In the case of the removal of the President from office or of his death or resignation, the Vice-President shall become President.

Section 2
Whenever there is a vacancy in the office of the Vice-President, the President shall nominate a Vice-President who shall take office upon confirmation by a majority vote of both Houses of Congress.

Section 3
Whenever the President transmits to the President *pro tempore* of the Senate and the Speaker of the House of Representatives his written declaration that he is unable to discharge the powers and duties of his office, and until he transmits to them a written declaration to the contrary, such powers and duties shall be discharged by the Vice-President as Acting President.

Section 4
Whenever the Vice-President and a majority of either the principal officers of the executive departments or of such other body as Congress may by law provide, transmit to the President *pro tempore* of the Senate and the Speaker of the House of Representatives their written declaration that the President is unable to discharge the powers and duties of his office, the Vice-President shall immediately assume the powers and duties of the office as Acting President.

Thereafter, when the President transmits to the President *pro tempore* of the Senate and the Speaker of the House of Representatives his written declaration that no inability exists, he shall resume the powers and duties of his office unless the Vice-President and a majority of either the principal officers of the executive department or of such other body as Congress may by law provide, transmit within four days to the President *pro tempore* of the Senate and the Speaker of the House of Representatives their written declaration that the President is unable to discharge the powers and duties of his office. Thereupon Congress shall decide the issue, assembling within 48 hours for that purpose if not in session. If the

Congress, within 21 days after receipt of the latter written declaration, or, if Congress is not in session, within 21 days after Congress is required to assemble, determines by two-thirds vote of both Houses that the President is unable to discharge the powers and duties of his office, the Vice-President shall continue to discharge the same as Acting President; otherwise, the President shall resume the powers and duties of his office.

AMENDMENT XXVI
(ratified July 1971)

Section 1

The right of citizens of the United States, who are 18 years of age or older, to vote shall not be denied or abridged by the United States or by any State on account of age.

Section 2

The Congress shall have power to enforce this article by appropriate legislation.

AMENDMENT XXVII
(ratified May 1992)

No law, varying the compensation for the services of the Senators and Representatives, shall take effect, until an election of Representatives shall have intervened.

By Article IV, Section 3 of the Constitution, implemented by vote of Congress and referendum in the territory concerned, Alaska was admitted into the United States on 3 January 1959, and Hawaii on 21 August 1959.

The Executive

HEAD OF STATE

President: GEORGE W. BUSH (took office 20 January 2001; re-elected 2 November 2004).
Vice-President: RICHARD B. CHENEY.

THE CABINET
(April 2008)

Secretary of State: Dr CONDOLEEZZA RICE.
Secretary of the Treasury: HENRY M. PAULSON, Jr.
Secretary of Defense: ROBERT M. GATES.
Attorney-General: MICHAEL B. MUKASEY.
Secretary of the Interior: DIRK KEMPTHORNE.
Secretary of Agriculture: EDWARD SCHAFER.
Secretary of Commerce: CARLOS GUTIERREZ.
Secretary of Labor: ELAINE L. CHAO.
Secretary of Health and Human Services: MICHAEL O. LEAVITT.
Secretary of Homeland Security: MICHAEL CHERTOFF.
Secretary of Housing and Urban Development: ROY A. BERNARDI (acting).
Secretary of Transportation: MARY E. PETERS.
Secretary of Energy: SAMUEL W. BODMAN.
Secretary of Education: MARGARET SPELLINGS.
Secretary of Veterans Affairs: Dr JAMES PEAKE.

Officials with Cabinet Rank

Vice-President: RICHARD B. CHENEY.
Chief of Staff to the President: JOSHUA B. BOLTEN.
Director of the Office of Management and Budget: JIM NUSSLE.
US Trade Representative: SUSAN C. SCHWAB.
Administrator of the Environmental Protection Agency: STEPHEN L. JOHNSON.
Director of the Office of National Drug Control Policy: JOHN P. WALTERS.
Director of National Intelligence: Adm. MIKE MCCONNELL.

GOVERNMENT DEPARTMENTS

Department of Agriculture: 1400 Independence Ave, SW, Washington, DC 20250; tel. (202) 690-0228; fax (202) 720-6314; e-mail agsec@usda.gov; internet www.usda.gov; f. 1889.
Department of Commerce: 1401 Constitution Ave, NW, Washington, DC 20230; tel. (202) 482-2000; e-mail cgutierrez@doc.gov; internet www.commerce.gov; f. 1913.
Department of Defense: 1000 Defense Pentagon, Washington, DC 20301; tel. (703) 428-0711; fax (703) 428-1982; internet www.defenselink.mil; f. 1947.
Department of Education: 400 Maryland Ave, SW, Washington, DC 20202; tel. (202) 401-2000; fax (202) 401-0596; internet www.ed.gov; f. 1979.
Department of Energy: Forrestal Bldg, 1000 Independence Ave, SW, Washington, DC 20585; tel. (202) 586-5000; fax (202) 586-4403; e-mail the.secretary@hq.doe.gov; internet www.energy.gov; f. 1977.
Department of Health and Human Services: 200 Independence Ave, SW, Washington, DC 20201; tel. (202) 619-0257; internet www.os.dhhs.gov; f. 1980.
Department of Homeland Security: 1600 Pennsylvania Ave, NW, Washington, DC 20528; tel. (202) 282-8000; e-mail john.minnick@dhs.gov; internet www.dhs.gov; f. 2002.
Department of Housing and Urban Development: 451 Seventh St, SW, Washington, DC 20410; tel. (202) 708-1112; fax (202) 708-0299; internet www.hud.gov; f. 1965.
Department of the Interior: 1849 C St, NW, Washington, DC 20240; tel. (202) 208-3100; fax (202) 208-5048; internet www.doi.gov; f. 1849.
Department of Justice: 950 Pennsylvania Ave, NW, Washington, DC 20530-0001; tel. (202) 514-2000; fax (202) 307-6777; e-mail askdoj@usdoj.gov; internet www.usdoj.gov; f. 1870; incl. the Office of the Attorney-Gen.
Department of Labor: Frances Perkins Bldg, 200 Constitution Ave, NW, Washington, DC 20210; tel. (202) 693-6000; fax (202) 693-6111; internet www.dol.gov; f. 1913.
Department of State: 2201 C St, NW, Washington, DC 20520; tel. (202) 647-4000; fax (202) 647-6738; internet www.state.gov; f. 1789.
Department of Transportation: 1200 New Jersey Ave, SE, Washington, DC 20590; tel. (202) 366-4000; fax (202) 366-7202; e-mail dot.comments@dot.gov; internet www.dot.gov; f. 1967.
Department of the Treasury: 1500 Pennsylvania Ave, NW, Washington, DC 20220; tel. (202) 622-2000; fax (202) 622-6415; internet www.ustreas.gov; f. 1789.
Department of Veterans Affairs: 810 Vermont Ave, NW, Washington, DC 20420; tel. (202) 273-6000; internet www.va.gov; f. 1989.

EXECUTIVE OFFICE OF THE PRESIDENT

The White House Office: 1600 Pennsylvania Ave, NW, Washington, DC 20500; tel. (202) 456-1414; fax (202) 456-2461; e-mail vice_president@whitehouse.gov; internet www.whitehouse.gov; co-ordinates activities relating to the President's immediate office; Chief of Staff to the Pres. JOSHUA B. BOLTEN.
Central Intelligence Agency: Office of Public Affairs, Washington, DC 20505; tel. (703) 482-0623; fax (703) 482-1739; internet www.cia.gov; f. 1947; Dir Gen. MICHAEL HAYDEN.
Council of Economic Advisers: Eisenhower Executive Office Bldg, 17th St and Pennsylvania Ave, NW, Washington, DC 20502; tel. (202) 395-5042; fax (202) 395-6958; internet www.whitehouse.gov/cea; f. 1946; Chair. Dr EDWARD P. LAZEAR.
Council on Environmental Quality: 722 Jackson Pl., Washington, DC 20503; tel. (202) 395-5750; fax (202) 456-6546; internet www.whitehouse.gov/ceq; f. 1969; Chair. JAMES L. CONNAUGHTON.
National Security Council: Eisenhower Executive Office Bldg, 17th St and Pennsylvania Ave, NW, Washington, DC 20504; tel. (202) 456-9371; internet www.whitehouse.gov/nsc; f. 1947; Asst to the Pres. for Nat. Security Affairs STEPHEN J. HADLEY.
Office of Administration: Eisenhower Executive Office Bldg, 17th St and Pennsylvania Ave, NW, Washington, DC 20503; tel. (202) 395-7235; fax (202) 456-6512; internet www.whitehouse.gov/oa; f. 1977; Dir (vacant).
Office of Faith-Based and Community Initiatives: The White House, Washington, DC 20502; tel. (202) 456-6708; fax (202) 456-7019; internet www.fbci.gov; f. 2001; Dir JAY F. HEIN.
Office of Management and Budget: 725 17th St and Pennsylvania Ave, NW Washington, DC 20503; tel. (202) 395-3080; fax (202) 395-3888; internet www.whitehouse.gov/omb; Dir JIM NUSSLE.
Office of National AIDS Policy: The White House, Rm 464 EEOB, Washington, DC 20502; tel. (202) 456-7320; fax (202) 456-7315; internet www.whitehouse.gov/onap/aids.html; Dir (vacant).
Office of National Drug Control Policy: POB 6000, Rockville, MD 20849-6000; tel. (202) 395-6700; fax (301) 519-5212; internet www.whitehousedrugpolicy.gov; f. 1988; Dir JOHN P. WALTERS.
Office of Policy Development: Executive Office of the President, 1600 Pennsylvania Ave, NW, Washington, DC 20500; tel. (202) 456-6515; fax (202) 456-2878; internet www.whitehouse.gov/dpc; f. 1970; composed of the Domestic Policy Council (f. 1993) and the Nat. Economic Council; Asst to the Pres. for Economic Policy and Dir of the Nat. Economic Council KARL ZINSMEISTER.
Office of Science and Technology Policy: 725 17th St, Rm 5228, NW, Washington, DC, 20502; tel. (202) 456-7116; fax (202) 456-6021;

THE UNITED STATES OF AMERICA

e-mail info@ostp.gov; internet www.ostp.gov; f. 1976; Dir JOHN H. MARBURGER, III.

Office of the United States Trade Representative: Winder Bldg, 600 17th St, NW, Washington, DC 20508; tel. (202) 395-3230; fax (202) 395-4549; e-mail contactustr@ustr.eop.gov; internet www.ustr.gov; f. 1963; US Trade Rep. SUSAN C. SCHWAB.

United States Mission to the United Nations: 799 United Nations Plaza, New York, NY 10017; tel. (212) 415-4404; fax (212) 415-4303; e-mail usa@un.int; internet www.un.int/usa; US Ambassador to the United Nations Dr ZALMAY KHALILZAD.

USA Freedom Corps: 1600 Pennsylvania Ave, NW, Washington, DC 20500; e-mail info@usafreedomcorps.gov; internet www.usafreedomcorps.gov; f. 2002; Dir HENRY C. LOZANO.

White House Military Office: Executive Office of the President, 1600 Pennsylvania Ave, NW, Washington, DC 20500; internet www.whitehouse.gov/whmo; areas of responsibility incl. Camp David (f. 1942) and Air Force One (f. 1962); Dir Rear-Adm. RAYMOND A. SPICER.

President and Legislature

PRESIDENT

Election, 2 November 2004

	Popular votes	% of Popular votes	Electoral College votes
George W. Bush (Republican)	61,872,711	50.57	286
John F. Kerry (Democrat)	58,894,584	48.14	252
Others*	1,582,185	1.29	—
Total	122,349,480	100.00	538

*Including write-in candidates, etc.

CONGRESS

Senate
(April 2008)

The Senate comprises 100 members. Senators' terms are for six years, one-third of the Senate being elected every two years.

President of the Senate: Vice-President RICHARD B. CHENEY.
President Pro Tempore: ROBERT C. BYRD.
Republicans: 49 seats.
Democrats: 49 seats.
Independent: 2 seats.
Majority Leader: HARRY M. REID.
Minority Leader: MITCH McCONNELL.

Members
(With political party and year in which term expires—on 3 January in all cases)

Alabama
Jeff Sessions	Rep.	2009
Richard C. Shelby	Rep.	2011

Alaska
Ted Stevens	Rep.	2009
Lisa Murkowski	Rep.	2011

Arizona
Jon Kyl	Rep.	2013
John McCain	Rep.	2011

Arkansas
Mark L. Pryor	Dem.	2009
Blanche L. Lincoln	Dem.	2011

California
Dianne Feinstein	Dem.	2013
Barbara Boxer	Dem.	2011

Colorado
Wayne Allard	Rep.	2009
Ken Salazar	Dem.	2011

Connecticut
Joe I. Lieberman	Ind.	2013
Chris J. Dodd	Dem.	2011

Delaware
Thomas Carper	Dem.	2013
Joseph R. Biden, Jr	Dem.	2009

Florida
Bill Nelson	Dem.	2013
Mel Martinez	Rep.	2011

Georgia
Saxby Chambliss	Rep.	2009
Johnny Isakson	Rep.	2011

Hawaii
Daniel K. Akaka	Dem.	2013
Daniel K. Inouye	Dem.	2011

Idaho
Larry E. Craig	Rep.	2009
Michael Crapo	Rep.	2011

Illinois
Richard J. Durbin	Dem.	2009
Barack Obama	Dem.	2011

Indiana
Richard G. Lugar	Rep.	2013
Evan Bayh	Dem.	2011

Iowa
Tom Harkin	Dem.	2009
Chuck Grassley	Rep.	2011

Kansas
Pat Roberts	Rep.	2009
Sam Brownback	Rep.	2011

Kentucky
Mitch McConnell	Rep.	2009
Jim Bunning	Rep.	2011

Louisiana
Mary L. Landrieu	Dem.	2009
David Vitter	Rep.	2011

Maine
Olympia J. Snowe	Rep.	2013
Susan M. Collins	Rep.	2009

Maryland
Ben L. Cardin	Dem.	2013
Barbara A. Mikulski	Dem.	2011

Massachusetts
Edward M. Kennedy	Dem.	2013
John F. Kerry	Dem.	2009

Michigan
Debbie Stabenow	Dem.	2013
Carl Levin	Dem.	2009

Minnesota
Amy Klobuchar	Dem.	2013
Norm Coleman	Rep.	2009

Mississippi
Roger Wicker	Rep.	2013
Thad Cochran	Rep.	2009

Missouri
Claire McCaskill	Rep.	2013
Christopher S. (Kit) Bond	Rep.	2011

Montana
Jon Tester	Rep.	2013
Max Baucus	Dem.	2009

Nebraska
E. Benjamin Nelson	Dem.	2013
Chuck Hagel	Rep.	2009

Nevada
John E. Ensign	Rep.	2013
Harry M. Reid	Dem.	2011

New Hampshire
John E. Sununu	Rep.	2009
Judd Gregg	Rep.	2011

New Jersey
Robert Menéndez	Dem.	2013
Frank R. Lautenberg	Dem.	2009

New Mexico
Jeff Bingaman	Dem.	2013
Pete V. Domenici	Rep.	2009

New York
Hillary Rodham Clinton	Dem.	2013
Charles E. Schumer	Dem.	2011

North Carolina
Elizabeth Dole	Rep.	2009
Richard Burr	Rep.	2011

THE UNITED STATES OF AMERICA

North Dakota
Kent Conrad	Dem.	2013
Byron L. Dorgan	Dem.	2011

Ohio
Sherrod Brown	Dem.	2013
George V. Voinovich	Rep.	2011

Oklahoma
James M. Inhofe	Rep.	2009
Tom Coburn	Rep.	2011

Oregon
Gordon Smith	Rep.	2009
Ronald L. Wyden	Dem.	2011

Pennsylvania
Robert P. Casey, Jr	Dem.	2013
Arlen Specter	Rep.	2011

Rhode Island
Sheldon Whitehouse, II	Dem.	2013
Jack Reed	Dem.	2009

South Carolina
Lindsey Graham	Rep.	2009
Jim DeMint	Rep.	2011

South Dakota
Tim Johnson	Dem.	2009
John Thune	Rep.	2011

Tennessee
Robert P. Corker	Rep.	2013
Lamar Alexander	Rep.	2009

Texas
Kay Bailey Hutchison	Rep.	2013
John Cornyn	Rep.	2009

Utah
Orrin G. Hatch	Rep.	2013
Bob F. Bennett	Rep.	2011

Vermont
Bernard Sanders	Ind.	2013
Patrick J. Leahy	Dem.	2011

Virginia
James H. Webb, Jr	Dem.	2013
John W. Warner	Rep.	2009

Washington
Maria Cantwell	Dem.	2013
Patty Murray	Dem.	2011

West Virginia
Robert C. Byrd	Dem.	2013
John D. (Jay) Rockefeller, IV	Dem.	2009

Wisconsin
Herb Kohl	Dem.	2013
Russell D. Feingold	Dem.	2011

Wyoming
Dr John Barrasso	Rep.	2009
Mike B. Enzi	Rep.	2009

House of Representatives
(May 2008)

A new House of Representatives, comprising 435 members, is elected every two years.

Speaker: NANCY PELOSI.

Democrats: 235 seats.

Republicans: 199 seats.

Vacant: 1 seat.

Majority Leader: STENY H. HOYER.

Minority Leader: JOHN BOEHNER.

Election Commission

Federal Election Commission: 999 E St, NW, Washington, DC 20463; tel. (202) 694-1100; fax (202) 219-3880; e-mail webmaster@fec.gov; internet www.fec.gov; f. 1975; independent; Chair. DAVID M. MASON.

Independent Agencies

Advisory Council on Historic Preservation: 1100 Pennsylvania Ave, NW, Suite 803, Old Post Office Bldg, Washington, DC 20004; tel. (202) 606-8503; e-mail achp@achp.gov; internet www.achp.gov; f. 1966; Exec. Dir JOHN M. FOWLER.

African Development Foundation: 1400 I St, NW, Suite 1000, Washington, DC 20005-2248; tel. (202) 673-3916; fax (202) 673-3810; e-mail info@adf.gov; internet www.adf.gov; Pres. RODNEY J. MACALISTER.

American Battle Monuments Commission: Courthouse Plaza II, Suite 500, 2300 Clarendon Blvd, Arlington, VA 22201-3367; tel. (703) 696-6900; fax (703) 696-6666; e-mail info@abmc.gov; internet www.abmc.gov; f. 1923; Chair. Gen. (retd) FREDERICK M. FRANKS, Jr; Sec. and CEO Brig.-Gen. (retd) JOHN W. NICHOLSON.

Appalachian Regional Commission: 1666 Connecticut Ave, NW, Washington, DC 20009-1068; tel. (202) 884-7700; fax (202) 884-7682; e-mail info@arc.gov; internet www.arc.gov; f. 1965; Fed. Co-Chair. ANNE B. POPE; Alt. Fed. Co-Chair. RICHARD J. PELTZ.

Commission on Civil Rights: 624 Ninth St, NW, Washington, DC 20425; tel. (202) 376-7700; fax (202) 376-8116; e-mail publications@usccr.gov; internet www.usccr.gov; f. 1957; Chair. GERALD A. REYNOLDS; Staff Dir KENNETH L. MARCUS.

Commission of Fine Arts: National Bldg Museum, Suite 312, 401 F St, NW, Washington, DC 20001-2728; tel. (202) 504-2200; fax (202) 504-2195; e-mail staff@cfa.gov; internet www.cfa.gov; f. 1910; Chair. EARL A. POWELL, III.

Commodity Futures Trading Commission (CFTC): 3 Lafayette Centre, 1155 21st St, NW, Washington, DC 20581; tel. (202) 418-5000; fax (202) 418-5521; e-mail oea@cftc.gov; internet www.cftc.gov; f. 1974; Chair. WALTER LUKKEN.

Corporation for National and Community Service (CNS): 1201 New York Ave, NW, Washington, DC 20525; tel. (202) 606-5000; fax (202) 565-2799; e-mail info@cns.gov; internet www.nationalservice.gov; Chair. STEPHEN GOLDSMITH; CEO DAVID EISNER; Inspector-Gen. GERALD WALPIN.

Defense Nuclear Facilities Safety Board: 625 Indiana Ave, Suite 700, NW, Washington, DC 20004-2901; tel. (202) 694-7000; fax (202) 208-6518; e-mail mailbox@dnfsb.gov; internet www.dnfsb.gov; f. 1988; Chair. Dr A. J. EGGENBERGER.

Environmental Protection Agency: Ariel Rios Bldg, 1200 Pennsylvania Ave, NW, Washington, DC 20460; tel. (202) 564-4700; internet www.epa.gov; f. 1970; Administrator STEPHEN L. JOHNSON.

Equal Employment Opportunity Commission: 1801 L St, NW, POB 7033, Washington, DC 20507; tel. (202) 663-4900; fax (202) 663-4494; e-mail info@ask.eeoc.gov; internet www.eeoc.gov; f. 1965; Chair. NAOMI C. EARP.

Export-Import Bank of the United States (Ex-Im Bank): see Finance—Banking.

Farm Credit Administration (FCA): 1501 Farm Credit Dr., McLean, VA 22102-5090; tel. (703) 883-4000; fax (703) 790-3260; e-mail info-line@fca.gov; internet www.fca.gov; f. 1933; Chair. and CEO NANCY C. PELLET.

Federal Communications Commission: see Broadcasting and Communications.

Federal Deposit Insurance Corporation (FDIC): 550 17th St, NW, Washington, DC 20429; tel. (202) 736-0000; e-mail publicinfo@fdic.gov; internet www.fdic.gov; f. 1933; Chair. SHEILA C. BAIR; Dir THOMAS J. CURRY.

Federal Election Commission: see Election Commission.

Federal Emergency Management Agency: Federal Center Plaza, 500 C St, SW, Washington, DC 20472; tel. (202) 646-4600; fax (202) 646-2531; internet www.fema.gov; f. 1979; part of the Dept of Homeland Security; Admin. R. DAVID PAULISON.

Federal Housing Finance Board: 1625 I St, NW, 4th Floor, Washington, DC 20006-4001; tel. (202) 408-2500; fax (202) 408-1435; e-mail fhfb@fhfb.gov; internet www.fhfb.gov; Chair. RONALD A. ROSENFELD.

Federal Labor Relations Authority (FLRA): 1400 K St, 4th Floor, NW, Washington, DC 20005; tel. (202) 218-7945; fax (202) 482-6635; e-mail jcrumpacker@flra.gov; internet www.flra.gov; f. 1978; Chair. DALE CABANISS.

Federal Maritime Commission: see Transport—Ocean Shipping.

Federal Mediation and Conciliation Service: 2100 K St, NW, Washington, DC 20427; tel. (202) 606-8100; fax (202) 606-4251; internet www.fmcs.gov; f. 1947; Dir ARTHUR F. ROSENFELD.

Federal Reserve System: see Finance—Banking.

Federal Retirement Thrift Investment Board (FRTIB): 1250 H St, NW, Washington, DC 20005; tel. (202) 942-1600; fax (202) 942-1676; internet www.frtib.gov; f. 1986; Exec. Dir (vacant).

THE UNITED STATES OF AMERICA

Federal Trade Commission: 600 Pennsylvania, NW, Washington, DC 20580; tel. (202) 326-2222; fax (202) 326-2396; internet www.ftc.gov; f. 1914; Chair. WILLIAM E. KOVACIC.

General Services Administration: 1800 F St, NW, Washington, DC 20405; tel. (202) 501-1231; fax (202) 501-1489; internet www.gsa.gov; f. 1949; Administrator DAVID L. BIBB (acting).

Inter-American Foundation: 901 North Stuart St, 10th Floor, Arlington, VA 22203; tel. (703) 306-4319; fax (703) 306-4365; e-mail info@iaf.gov; internet www.iaf.gov; f. 1969; provides grants to non-governmental and community-based orgs in Latin America and the Caribbean; Chair. ROGER W. WALLACE.

Medicare Payment Advisory Commission (MedPAC): 601 New Jersey Ave, NW, Suite 9000, Washington, DC 2001; tel. (202) 220-3700; e-mail webmaster@medpac.gov; internet www.medpac.gov; Chair. GLENN M. HACKBARTH.

Merit Systems Protection Board: 1615 M St, NW, Washington, DC 20419; tel. (202) 653-7200; fax (202) 653-7130; e-mail mspb@mspb.gov; internet www.mspb.gov; f. 1979; Chair. NEIL A. G. MCPHIE.

National Aeronautics and Space Administration (NASA): 300 E St, SW, Washington, DC 20546; tel. (202) 358-0000; fax (202) 358-3251; e-mail info-center@hq.nasa.gov; internet www.nasa.gov; f. 1958; Administrator MICHAEL D. GRIFFIN.

National Archives and Records Administration: 8601 Adelphi Rd, College Park, MD 20740-6001; tel. (301) 837-1600; fax (301) 837-3218; internet www.archives.gov; f. 1934; Archivist of the United States Prof. ALLEN WEINSTEIN.

National Capital Planning Commission: 401 Ninth St, NW, Suite 500, Washington, DC 20004; tel. (202) 482-7200; fax (202) 482-7272; e-mail info@ncpc.gov; internet www.ncpc.gov; f. 1924; Chair. JOHN V. COGBILL, III.

National Commission on Libraries and Information Science: 1800 M St, NW, Suite 350, North Tower, Washington, DC 20036-5841; tel. (202) 606-9200; fax (202) 606-9203; e-mail info@nclis.gov; internet www.nclis.gov; f. 1970; Chair. C. BETH FITZSIMMONS.

National Council on Disability: 1331 F St, NW, Suite 850, Washington, DC 20004-1107; tel. (202) 272-2004; fax (202) 272-2022; e-mail ncd@ncd.gov; internet www.ncd.gov; f. 1978; Chair. JOHN R. VAUGHN.

National Credit Union Administration: 1775 Duke St, Alexandria, VA 22314-3428; tel. (703) 518-6330; fax (703) 518-6409; e-mail pacamail@ncua.gov; internet www.ncua.gov; f. 1970; Chair. JOANN JOHNSON.

National Endowment for the Arts: 1100 Pennsylvania Ave, NW, Washington, DC 20506-0001; tel. (202) 682-5400; fax (202) 682-5611; e-mail webmgr@arts.gov; internet www.arts.gov; f. 1965; Chair. DANA GIOIA.

National Endowment for the Humanities: 1100 Pennsylvania Ave, NW, Rm 503, Washington, DC 20506; tel. (202) 606-8310; e-mail info@neh.gov; internet www.neh.gov; f. 1965; Chair. BRUCE COLE.

National Labor Relations Board: 1099 14th St, NW, Washington, DC 20570-0001; tel. (202) 273-1991; fax (202) 273-1789; internet www.nlrb.gov; f. 1935; Chair. ROBERT J. BATTISTA.

National Mediation Board (NMB): 1301 K St, NW, Suite 250 East, Washington, DC 20005-7011; tel. (202) 692-5010; fax (202) 523-5080; internet www.nmb.gov; f. 1934; Chair. HARRY HOGLANDER.

National Science Foundation (NSF): 4201 Wilson Blvd, Arlington, VA 22230; tel. (703) 292-5111; e-mail info@nsf.gov; internet www.nsf.gov; f. 1950; supports basic scientific and engineering research and education; Dir Dr ARDEN L. BEMENT, Jr.

National Transportation Safety Board: see Transport.

Nuclear Regulatory Commission (NRC): Office of Public Affairs, Washington, DC 20555; tel. (301) 415-8200; e-mail opa@nrc.gov; internet www.nrc.gov; Chair. DALE E. KLEIN.

Occupational Safety and Health Review Commission (OSHRC): 1120 20th St, 9th Floor, NW, Washington, DC 20036-3457; tel. (202) 606-5398; fax (202) 606-5052; internet www.oshrc.gov; f. 1970; Chair. HORACE A. THOMPSON.

Office of Government Ethics: 1201 New York Ave, NW, Suite 500, Washington, DC 20005-3917; tel. (202) 482-9300; fax (202) 482-9237; e-mail contactoge@oge.gov; internet www.usoge.gov; f. 1978; Dir ROBERT I. CUSICK.

Office of Personnel Management (OPM): Theodore Roosevelt Federal Bldg, 1900 E St, NW, Washington, DC 20415; tel. (202) 606-1800; fax (202) 606-2573; e-mail general@opm.gov; internet www.opm.gov; f. 1979; Dir LINDA M. SPRINGER.

Office of Special Counsel: 1730 M St, NW, Suite 300, Washington, DC 20036-4505; tel. (202) 254-3600; fax (202) 653-5151; internet www.osc.gov; Special Counsel SCOTT J. BLOCH.

Peace Corps: Paul D. Coverdell Peace Corps HQ, 1111 20th St, NW, Washington, DC 20526; tel. (202) 692-2100; fax (202) 692-2101; e-mail webmaster@peacecorps.gov; internet www.peacecorps.gov; f. 1961; Dir RONALD A. TSCHETTER.

Pension Benefit Guaranty Corporation: 1200 K St, NW, Suite 12201, Washington, DC 20005-4026; tel. (202) 326-4010; fax (202) 326-4016; e-mail webmaster@pbgc.gov; internet www.pbgc.gov; f. 1974; Dir CHARLES E. F. MILLARD.

Postal Rate Commission: 901 New York Ave, NW, Suite 200, NW, Washington, DC 20268-0001; tel. (202) 789-6800; fax (202) 789-6886; e-mail prc-webmaster@prc.gov; internet www.prc.gov; f. 1970; Chair. DAN G. BLAIR.

Railroad Retirement Board: 844 North Rush St, Chicago, IL 60611-2092; tel. (312) 751-4777; fax (312) 751-7154; e-mail opa@rrb.gov; internet www.rrb.gov; f. 1935; Chair. MICHAEL S. SCHWARTZ.

Securities and Exchange Commission: Station Pl., 100 F St, NE, Washington, DC 20549; tel. (202) 942-8088; fax (202) 942-9646; e-mail help@sec.gov; internet www.sec.gov; f. 1935; Chair. CHRISTOPHER COX.

Selective Service System: 1515 Wilson Blvd, Arlington, VA 22209-2425; tel. (703) 605-4100; fax (703) 605-4106; e-mail information@sss.gov; internet www.sss.gov; f. 1940; Dir WILLIAM A. CHATFIELD.

Small Business Administration: 409 Third St, SW, Washington, DC 20416; tel. (202) 205-6650; fax (202) 205-6802; internet www.sba.gov; f. 1953; Administrator STEVEN C. PRESTON.

Smithsonian Institution: 1000 Jefferson Dr., SW, Washington, DC 20560-0001; tel. (202) 633-1000; e-mail info@si.edu; internet www.si.edu; f. 1846; Sec. CRISTIÁN SAMPER (acting).

Social Security Administration: Office of Public Inquiries, Windsor Park Bldg, 6401 Security Blvd, Baltimore, MD 21235-0001; tel. (410) 965-3120; fax (410) 966-1463; internet www.ssa.gov; Commr MICHAEL J. ASTRUE.

Tennessee Valley Authority: 400 West Summit Hill Dr., Knoxville, TN 37902-1499; tel. (865) 632-2101; e-mail tvainfo@tva.gov; internet www.tva.gov; f. 1933; CEO and Pres. TOM KILGORE.

United States Agency for International Development (USAID): Ronald Reagan Bldg, 1300 Pennsylvania Ave, NW, Washington, DC 20523-0016; tel. (202) 712-4810; fax (202) 216-3524; e-mail pinquiries@usaid.gov; internet www.usaid.gov; f. 1961; Dir HENRIETTA HOLSMAN FORE (acting).

United States Consumer Product Safety Commission: 4330 East-West Hwy, Bethesda, MD 20814-4408; tel. (301) 504-7923; fax (301) 504-0124; e-mail info@cpsc.gov; internet www.cpsc.gov; f. 1972; Chair. NANCY NORD (acting); Commr THOMAS H. MOORE; Exec. Dir PATSY SEMPLE.

United States International Trade Commission: 500 E St, SW, Washington, DC 20436; tel. (202) 205-2000; fax (202) 205-2798; e-mail webmaster@usitc.gov; internet www.usitc.gov; f. 1916; Chair. DANIEL R. PEARSON.

United States Postal Service: 475 L'Enfant Plaza, SW, Washington, DC 20260-0010; tel. (202) 268-2000; fax (202) 268-4860; internet www.usps.com; f. 1970; Postmaster-Gen. and CEO JOHN (JACK) E. POTTER.

United States Trade and Development Agency (USTDA): 1000 Wilson Blvd, Suite 1600, Arlington, VA 22209-3901; tel. (703) 875-4357; fax (703) 875-4009; e-mail info@ustda.gov; internet www.ustda.gov; f. 1961; Dir LEOCADIA I. ZAK (acting).

State Governments

(with expiration date of Governors' current term of office; legislatures at April 2008)

Alabama: Governor BOB RILEY (Rep.—Jan. 2011); Senate: Dem. 22, Rep. 13; House: Dem. 62, Rep. 43.

Alaska: Governor SARAH PALIN (Rep.—Jan. 2011); Senate: Dem. 9, Rep. 11; House: Dem. 17, Rep. 23.

Arizona: Governor JANET NAPOLITANO (Dem.—Jan. 2011); Senate: Dem. 13, Rep. 17; House: Dem. 27, Rep. 33.

Arkansas: Governor MIKE BEEBE (Dem.—Jan. 2011); Senate: Dem. 27, Rep. 8; House: Dem. 75, Rep. 25.

California: Governor ARNOLD SCHWARZENEGGER (Rep.—Jan. 2011); Senate: Dem. 25, Rep. 15; Assembly: Dem. 48, Rep. 32.

Colorado: Governor WILLIAM RITTER, Jr (Dem.—Jan. 2011); Senate: Dem. 20, Rep. 15; House: Dem. 40, Rep. 25.

Connecticut: Governor M. JODI RELL (Rep.—Jan. 2011); Senate: Dem. 23, Rep. 13; House: Dem. 107, Rep. 44.

Delaware: Governor RUTH ANN MINNER (Dem.—Jan. 2009); Senate: Dem. 13, Rep. 8; House: Dem. 19, Rep. 22.

Florida: Governor CHARLIE CRIST (Rep.—Jan. 2011); Senate: Dem. 14, Rep. 26; House: Dem. 42, Rep. 77, Vacant 1.

THE UNITED STATES OF AMERICA

Georgia: Governor George (Sonny) Perdue (Rep.—Jan. 2011); Senate: Dem. 22, Rep. 34; House: Dem. 73, Rep. 107.
Hawaii: Governor Linda Lingle (Rep.—Jan. 2011); Senate: Dem. 21, Rep. 4; House: Dem. 44, Rep. 7.
Idaho: Governor C. L. (Butch) Otter (Rep.—Jan. 2011); Senate: Dem. 7, Rep. 28; House: Dem. 19, Rep. 51.
Illinois: Governor Rod R. Blagojevich (Dem.—Jan. 2013); Senate: Dem. 37, Rep. 22; House: Dem. 67, Rep. 51.
Indiana: Governor Mitchell Daniels (Rep.—Jan. 2009); Senate: Dem. 17, Rep. 33; House: Dem. 51, Rep. 49.
Iowa: Governor Chester (Chet) Culver (Dem.—Jan. 2011); Senate: Dem. 30, Rep. 20; House: Dem. 53, Rep. 47.
Kansas: Governor Kathleen Sebelius (Dem.—Jan. 2011); Senate: Dem. 10, Rep. 30; House: Dem. 47, Rep. 78.
Kentucky: Governor Steve Beshear (Dem.—Jan. 2013); Senate: Dem. 15, Rep. 22, Ind. 1; House: Dem. 63, Rep. 36, Vacant 1.
Louisiana: Governor Bobby Jindal (Rep.—Jan. 2012); Senate: Dem. 23, Rep. 16; House: Dem. 53, Rep. 50, Ind. 2.
Maine: Governor John E. Baldacci, Jr (Dem.—Jan. 2011); Senate: Dem. 18, Rep. 17; House: Dem. 90, Rep. 59, Ind. 2.
Maryland: Governor Martin O'Malley, Jr (Dem.—Jan. 2011); Senate: Dem. 33, Rep. 14; House: Dem. 104, Rep. 37.
Massachusetts: Governor Deval L. Patrick (Dem.—Jan. 2011); Senate: Dem. 35, Rep. 5; House: Dem. 141, Rep. 19.
Michigan: Governor Jennifer M. Granholm (Dem.—Jan. 2011); Senate: Dem. 17, Rep. 21; House: Dem. 58, Rep. 52.
Minnesota: Governor Tim Pawlenty (Rep.—Jan. 2011); Senate: Dem. 45, Rep. 22; House: Dem. 85, Rep. 48, Ind. 1.
Mississippi: Governor Haley Barbour (Rep.—Jan. 2012); Senate: Dem. 27, Rep. 25; House: Dem. 75, Rep. 47.
Missouri: Governor Matt Blunt (Rep.—Jan. 2009); Senate: Dem. 14, Rep. 20; House: Dem. 71, Rep. 92.
Montana: Governor Brian Schweitzer (Dem.—Jan. 2009); Senate: Dem. 26, Rep. 24; House: Dem. 49, Rep. 50, Ind. 1.
Nebraska: Governor Dave Heineman (Rep.—Jan. 2011); Legislature: unicameral body comprising 49 members elected on a non-partisan ballot and classed as senators.
Nevada: Governor James A. Gibbons (Rep.—Jan. 2011); Senate: Dem. 10, Rep. 11; Assembly: Dem. 27, Rep. 15.
New Hampshire: Governor John Lynch (Dem.—Jan. 2011); Senate: Dem. 14, Rep. 10; House: Dem. 236, Rep. 159, Ind. 1, Vacant 4.
New Jersey: Governor Jon S. Corzine (Dem.—Jan. 2010); Senate: Dem. 23, Rep. 17; Assembly: Dem. 48, Rep. 32.
New Mexico: Governor William B. Richardson (Dem.—Jan. 2011); Senate: Dem. 24, Rep. 18; House: Dem. 42, Rep. 28.
New York: Governor David A. Paterson (Dem.—Jan. 2011); Senate: Dem. 30, Rep. 32; Assembly: Dem. 108, Rep. 42.
North Carolina: Governor Mike Easley, Jr (Dem.—Jan. 2009); Senate: Dem. 31, Rep. 19; House: Dem. 68, Rep. 52.
North Dakota: Governor John Hoeven (Rep.—Jan. 2009); Senate: Dem. 21, Rep. 26; House: Dem. 33, Rep. 61.
Ohio: Governor Ted Strickland (Dem.—Jan. 2011); Senate: Dem. 12, Rep. 21; House: Dem. 46, Rep. 53.
Oklahoma: Governor Brad Henry (Dem.—Jan. 2011); Senate: Dem. 24, Rep. 24; House: Dem. 44, Rep. 57.
Oregon: Governor Theodore R. (Ted) Kulongoski (Dem.—Jan. 2011); Senate: Dem. 18, Rep. 11, Ind. 1; House: Dem. 31, Rep. 29.
Pennsylvania: Governor Edward G. Rendell (Dem.—Jan. 2011); Senate: Dem. 21, Rep. 29; House: Dem. 102, Rep. 101.
Rhode Island: Governor Donald L. Carcieri (Rep.—Jan. 2011); Senate: Dem. 32, Rep. 5, Vacant 1; House: Dem. 61, Rep. 13, Ind. 1.
South Carolina: Governor Marshall C. (Mark) Sanford (Rep.—Jan. 2011); Senate: Dem. 19, Rep. 27; House: Dem. 51, Rep. 72, Vacant 1.
South Dakota: Governor M. Michael Rounds (Rep.—Jan. 2011); Senate: Dem. 15, Rep. 20; House: Dem. 20, Rep. 50.
Tennessee: Governor Phil Bredesen (Dem.—Jan. 2011); Senate: Dem. 16, Rep. 16, Ind. 1; House: Dem. 53, Rep. 46.
Texas: Governor Rick Perry (Rep.—Jan. 2011); Senate: Dem. 11, Rep. 20; House: Dem. 71, Rep. 79.
Utah: Governor Jon Huntsman, Jr (Rep.—Jan. 2009); Senate: Dem. 8, Rep. 21; House: Dem. 20, Rep. 55.
Vermont: Governor James H. Douglas (Rep.—Jan. 2011); Senate: Dem. 23, Rep. 7; House: Dem. 93, Rep. 49, Ind. 8.
Virginia: Governor Timothy M. Kaine (Dem.—Jan. 2010); Senate: Dem. 21, Rep. 19; House: Dem. 45, Rep. 53, Ind. 2.
Washington: Governor Christine O. Gregoire (Dem.—Jan. 2009); Senate: Dem. 32, Rep. 17; House: Dem. 63, Rep. 35.
West Virginia: Governor Joe Manchin, III (Dem.—Jan. 2009); Senate: Dem. 23, Rep. 11; House: Dem. 72, Rep. 28.
Wisconsin: Governor James E. Doyle (Dem.—Jan. 2011); Senate: Dem. 18, Rep. 15; Assembly: Dem. 47, Rep. 52.
Wyoming: Governor Dave Freudenthahl (Dem.—Jan. 2011); Senate: Dem. 7, Rep. 23; House: Dem. 17, Rep. 43.

Political Organizations

Communist Party USA (CPUSA): 235 West 23rd St, 7th Floor, New York, NY 10011; tel. (212) 989-4994; fax (212) 229-1713; e-mail cpusa@cpusa.org; internet www.cpusa.org; f. 1919; mems in all 50 states, organized in over 40 states; Nat. Chair. Sam Webb; Exec. Vice-Chair. Jarvis Tyner.

Democratic National Committee: 430 South Capitol St, SE, Washington, DC 20003; tel. (202) 863-8000; fax (202) 863-8174; internet www.democrats.org; f. 1848; Nat. Chair. Howard Dean; Sec. Alice Travis Germond; Treas. Andrew Tobias.

The Green Party of the United States: POB 57065, Washington, DC 20037; tel. (202) 319-7191; fax (202) 319-7193; e-mail info@gp.org; internet www.gp.org; f. 2001; Sec. Holly Hart; Treas. Jody Grage.

The Greens/Green Party USA: POB 408316, Chicago IL 60640; e-mail info@greenparty.org; internet www.greenparty.org; f. 1984 as Greens Cttee of Correspondence; present name adopted in 1991.

Libertarian Party: 2600 Virginia Ave, NW, Suite 200, Washington, DC 20037; tel. (202) 333-0008; fax (202) 333-0072; e-mail info@lp.org; internet www.lp.org; f. 1971; advocates individual freedom, smaller govt and fewer taxes; Exec. Dir Shane Cory.

Prohibition National Committee: POB 2635, Denver, CO 80201; tel. (303) 237-4947; e-mail umalcohol@aol.com; internet www.prohibition.org; f. 1869; opposes the manufacture and sale of alcoholic drinks; opposes abortion, drug abuse and euthanasia; Nat. Chair. Earl F. Dodge; Nat. Sec. Paul B. Scott.

La Raza Unida Party (Partido Nacional La Raza Unida): 483 Fifth St, POB 13, San Fernando, CA 91340; tel. (818) 365-6534; e-mail pnlrunm@yahoo.com; internet larazaunida.tripod.com; f. 1970; aims to achieve self-determination and greater govt representation for Latinos through electoral processes; four state groups, 100 local groups; Nat. Chair. Xenaro G. Ayala.

Reform Party of the USA: POB 3236, Abilene, TX 79604; tel. (325) 672-2575; e-mail info@reformparty.org; internet www.reformparty.org; f. 1996; advocates reform of political system and ethical govt; Nat. Chair. Charles Foster; Sec. Dione Ormond.

Republican National Committee: 310 First St, SE, Washington, DC 20003; tel. (202) 863-8500; fax (202) 863-8820; e-mail info@gop.com; internet www.rnc.org; f. 1854; Chair. Nat. Cttee Mike Duncan; Co-Chair. Jo Ann Davidson.

Social Democrats, USA: 815 15th St, NW, Suite 921, Washington, DC 20005; tel. (202) 638-1515; fax (202) 457-0029; e-mail info@socialdemocrats.org; internet www.socialdemocrats.org; f. 1972 following split from the Socialist Party of America (f. 1901); Pres. David Jessup; Nat. Vice-Chair. Norman Hill.

Socialist Labor Party: POB 218, Mountain View, CA 94042-0218; tel. (408) 280-7226; fax (408) 280-6964; e-mail socialists@slp.org; internet www.slp.org; f. 1876 as the Workingmen's Party; present name adopted in 1877; advocates collective ownership and democratic control of all industries and services through industrial unions; Nat. Sec. Robert Bills.

Socialist Party USA: A. J. Muste Bldg, 339 Lafayette St, Suite 303, New York, NY 10012; tel. and fax (212) 982-4586; e-mail natsec@sp-usa.org; internet www.sp-usa.org; f. 1972 following split from the Socialist Party of the USA (f. 1901); Co-Chairs Andrea Pason, Jerry Levy; Nat. Sec. Greg Pason; 1,800 mems.

Socialist Workers Party: 306 West 37th St, 10th Floor, New York, NY 10018; tel. (212) 736-2540; fax (212) 244-4274; e-mail swpno@mac.com; f. 1938; communist; Nat. Sec. Jack Barnes.

Diplomatic Representation

EMBASSIES IN THE USA

Afghanistan: 2341 Wyoming Ave, NW, Washington, DC 20008; tel. 483-6410; fax 483-6488; e-mail info@embassyofafghanistan.org; internet www.embassyofafghanistan.org; Ambassador Said Tayeb Jawad.

THE UNITED STATES OF AMERICA

Albania: 2100 S St, NW, Washington, DC 20008; tel. (202) 223-4942; fax (202) 628-7342; e-mail info@albanianembassy.org; internet www.albanianembassy.org; Ambassador ALEKSANDER SALLABANDA.

Algeria: 2118 Kalorama Rd, NW, Washington, DC 20008; tel. (202) 265-2800; fax (202) 667-2174; e-mail ambalg2004@yahoo.com; internet www.algeria-us.org; Ambassador AMINE KHERBI.

Andorra: 2 United Nations Plaza, 25th Floor, New York, NY 10017; tel. (212) 750-8064; fax (212) 750-6630; Ambassador CARLES FONT-ROSSELL.

Angola: 2108 16th St, NW, Washington, DC 20009; tel. (202) 785-1156; fax (202) 822-9049; e-mail angola@angola.org; internet www.angola.org; Ambassador JOSEFINA PERPÉTUA PITRA DIAKITÉ.

Antigua and Barbuda: 3216 New Mexico Ave, NW, Washington, DC 20016; tel. (202) 362-5122; fax (202) 362-5225; e-mail embantbar@aol.com; Ambassador DEBORAH MAE LOVELL.

Argentina: 1600 New Hampshire Ave, NW, Washington, DC 20009; tel. (202) 238-6401; fax (202) 332-3171; internet www.embassyofargentina.us; Ambassador HÉCTOR MARCOS TIMERMAN.

Armenia: 2225 R St, NW, Washington, DC 20008; tel. (202) 319-1976; fax (202) 319-2982; e-mail armecon@speakeasy.net; internet www.armeniaemb.org; Ambassador TATOUL MARKARIAN.

Australia: 1601 Massachusetts Ave, NW, Washington, DC 20036-2273; tel. (202) 797-3000; fax (202) 797-3168; internet www.austemb.org; Ambassador DENNIS RICHARDSON.

Austria: 3524 International Court, NW, Washington, DC 20008-3022; tel. (202) 895-6700; fax (202) 895-6750; e-mail obwas@sysnet.net; internet www.austria.org; Ambassador EVA NOWOTNY.

Azerbaijan: 2741 34th St, NW, Washington, DC 20008; tel. (202) 337-3500; fax (202) 337-5911; e-mail azerbaijan@azembassy.com; internet www.azembassy.com; Ambassador YASHAR ALIYEV.

Bahamas: 2220 Massachusetts Ave, NW, Washington, DC 20008; tel. (202) 319-2660; fax (202) 319-2668; e-mail bahemb@aol.com; Ambassador CORNELIUS A. SMITH.

Bahrain: 3502 International Dr., NW, Washington, DC 20008; tel. (202) 342-1111; fax (202) 362-2192; e-mail info@bahrainembassy.org; internet www.bahrainembassy.org; Ambassador NASSER MOHAMED AL BELOOSHI.

Bangladesh: 3510 International Dr., NW, Washington, DC 20008; tel. (202) 244-0183; fax (202) 244-2771; e-mail info@bangladoot.org; internet www.bangladoot.org; Ambassador M. HUMAYUN KABIR.

Barbados: 2144 Wyoming Ave, NW, Washington, DC 20008; tel. (202) 939-9200; fax (202) 332-7467; e-mail washington@foreign.gov.bb; Ambassador MICHAEL IAN KING.

Belarus: 1619 New Hampshire Ave, NW, Washington, DC 20009; tel. (202) 986-1604; fax (202) 986-1805; e-mail usa@belarusembassy.org; internet www.belarusembassy.org; Ambassador MIKHAIL KHVOSTOV.

Belgium: 3330 Garfield St, NW, Washington, DC 20008; tel. (202) 333-6900; fax (202) 333-3079; e-mail washington@diplobel.org; internet www.diplobel.us; Ambassador DOMINICUS STRUYE DE SWIELANDE.

Belize: 2535 Massachusetts Ave, NW, Washington, DC 20008; tel. (202) 332-9636; fax (202) 332-6888; e-mail chancery@embassyofbelize.org; internet www.embassyofbelize.org; Chargé d'affaires a.i. NESTOR MENDEZ.

Benin: 2124 Kalorama Rd, NW, Washington, DC 20008; tel. (202) 232-6656; fax (202) 265-1996; Ambassador SÈGBÉ CYRILLE OGUIN.

Bolivia: 3014 Massachusetts Ave, NW, Washington, DC 20008; tel. (202) 483-4410; fax (202) 328-3712; e-mail webmaster@bolivia-usa.org; internet www.bolivia-usa.org; Ambassador MARIO GUSTAVO GUZMÁN SALDAÑA.

Bosnia and Herzegovina: 2109 E St, NW, Washington, DC 20037; tel. (202) 337-1500; fax (202) 337-1502; e-mail info@bhembassy.org; internet www.bhembassy.org; Ambassador BISERA TURKOVIĆ.

Botswana: 1531-1533 New Hampshire Ave, NW, Washington, DC 20036; tel. (202) 244-4990; fax (202) 244-4164; e-mail cratsiripe@gov.bw; internet www.botswanaembassy.org; Ambassador LAPOLOGANG CAESAR LEKOA.

Brazil: 3006 Massachusetts Ave, NW, Washington, DC 20008; tel. (202) 238-2700; fax (202) 238-2827; e-mail webmaster@brasilemb.org; internet www.brasilemb.org; Ambassador ANTONIO PATRIOTA.

Brunei: 3520 International Court, NW, Washington, DC 20008; tel. (202) 237-1838; fax (202) 885-0560; e-mail info@bruneiembassy.org; internet www.bruneiembassy.org; Ambassador Pengiran INDERA NEGARA P. A. PUTEH.

Bulgaria: 1621 22nd St, NW, Washington, DC 20008; tel. (202) 387-0174; fax (202) 234-7973; e-mail office@bulgaria-embassy.org; internet www.bulgaria-embassy.org; Ambassador ELENA POPTODOROVA.

Burkina Faso: 2340 Massachusetts Ave, NW, Washington, DC 20008; tel. (202) 332-5577; fax (202) 667-1882; e-mail ambawdc@verizon.net; internet www.burkinaembassy-usa.org; Ambassador PARMANGA ERNEST YONLI.

Burundi: 2233 Wisconsin Ave, NW, Suite 212, Washington, DC 20007; tel. (202) 342-2574; fax (202) 342-2575; e-mail burundiembassy@erols.com; internet www.burundiembassy-usa.org; Ambassador CELESTIN NIYONGABO.

Cambodia: 4530 16th St, NW, Washington, DC 20011; tel. (202) 726-7742; fax (202) 726-8381; e-mail mail@embassyofcambodia.org; internet www.embassyofcambodia.org; Ambassador SEREYWATH EK.

Cameroon: 2349 Massachusetts Ave, NW, Washington, DC 20008; tel. (202) 265-8790; fax (202) 387-3826; e-mail cdm@ambacam-usa.org; internet www.ambacam-usa.org; Ambassador JEROME MENDOUGA.

Canada: 501 Pennsylvania Ave, NW, Washington, DC 20001; tel. (202) 682-1740; fax (202) 682-7701; e-mail canada@canadianembassy.org; internet www.canadianembassy.org; Ambassador MICHAEL WILSON.

Cape Verde: 3415 Massachusetts Ave, NW, Washington, DC 20007; tel. (202) 965-6820; fax (202) 965-1207; e-mail ambacvus@sysnet.net; internet www.virtualcapeverde.net; Ambassador JOSE BRITO.

Central African Republic: 1618 22nd St, NW, Washington, DC 20008; tel. (202) 483-7800; fax (202) 332-9893; e-mail car@ambarca.org; Ambassador EMMANUEL TOUABOY.

Chad: 2002 R St, NW, Washington, DC 20009; tel. (202) 462-4009; fax (202) 265-1937; e-mail info@chadembassy.org; internet www.chadembassy.org; Ambassador HASSABALLAH AHMAT SOUBIANE.

Chile: 1732 Massachusetts Ave, NW, Washington, DC 20036; tel. (202) 785-1746; fax (202) 887-5579; e-mail embassy@embassyofchile.org; internet www.chile-usa.org; Ambassador MARIANO FERNÁNDEZ AMUNATEGUI.

China, People's Republic: 2300 Connecticut Ave, NW, Washington, DC 20008; tel. (202) 558-0032; fax (202) 232-7855; e-mail chinaembassy_us@fmprc.gov.cn; internet www.china-embassy.org; Ambassador ZHOU WENZHONG.

Colombia: 2118 Leroy Pl., NW, Washington, DC 20008; tel. (202) 387-8338; fax (202) 232-8643; e-mail enwas@colombiaemb.org; internet www.colombiaemb.org; Ambassador CAROLINA BARCO ISAKSON.

Comoros: 336 East 45th St, 2nd Floor, New York, NY 10017; tel. (212) 750-1637; e-mail comun@undp.org; Ambassador MOHAMED TOIHIRI.

Congo, Democratic Republic: 1800 New Hampshire Ave, NW, Washington, DC 20009; tel. (202) 234-7690; fax (202) 237-0748; Ambassador FAIDA MITIFU.

Congo, Republic: 4891 Colorado Ave, NW, Washington, DC 20011; tel. (202) 726-5500; fax (202) 726-1860; e-mail info@embassyofcongo.org; internet www.embassyofcongo.org; Ambassador SERGE MOMBOULI.

Costa Rica: 2114 S St, NW, Washington, DC 20008; tel. (202) 234-2945; fax (202) 265-4795; e-mail embassy@costarica-embassy.org; internet www.costarica-embassy.org; Ambassador TOMÁS DUEÑAS.

Côte d'Ivoire: 3421 Massachusetts Ave, NW, Washington, DC 20007; tel. (202) 797-0300; fax (202) 462-9444; Ambassador CHARLES KOFFI.

Croatia: 2343 Massachusetts Ave, NW, Washington, DC 20008-2803; tel. (202) 588-5899; fax (202) 588-8936; e-mail public@croatiaemb.org; Ambassador KOLINDA GRABAR-KITAROVIĆ.

Cuba: 'Interests section' in the Embassy of Switzerland, 2630 16th St, NW, Washington, DC 20009; tel. (202) 797-8518; fax (202) 797-8521; e-mail consulcuba@sicuw.org; internet www.eda.admin.ch/eda/en/home/reps/nameri/vusa/wasemb/wacuba.html; Counsellor JORGE ALBERTO BOLAÑOS SUÁREZ.

Cyprus: 2211 R St, NW, Washington, DC 20008; tel. (202) 462-5772; fax (202) 483-6710; e-mail cypembwash@earthlink.net; internet www.cyprusembassy.net; Ambassador ANDREAS KAKOURIS.

Czech Republic: 3900 Spring of Freedom St, NW, Washington, DC 20008; tel. (202) 274-9100; fax (202) 966-8540; e-mail washington@embassy.mzv.cz; internet www.mzv.cz/washington; Ambassador PETR KOLAR.

Denmark: 3200 Whitehaven St, NW, Washington, DC 20008-3616; tel. (202) 234-4300; fax (202) 328-1470; e-mail wasamb@um.dk; internet www.ambwashington.um.dk; Ambassador FRIIS ARNE PETERSEN.

Djibouti: 1156 15th St, NW, Suite 515, Washington, DC 20005; tel. (202) 331-0270; fax (202) 331-0302; Ambassador ROBLÉ OLHAYE.

Dominica: 3216 New Mexico Ave, NW, Washington, DC 20016; tel. (202) 364-6781; fax (202) 364-6791; e-mail embdomdc@aol.com; Chargé d'affaires a.i. JUDITH ANN ROLLE.

Dominican Republic: 1715 22nd St, NW, Washington, DC 20008; tel. (202) 332-6280; fax (202) 265-8057; e-mail embassy@us.serex.gov.do; internet www.domrep.org; Ambassador FLAVIO DARIO ESPINAL.

THE UNITED STATES OF AMERICA

Directory

Ecuador: 2535 15th St, NW, Washington, DC 20009; tel. (202) 234-7200; fax (202) 667-3482; e-mail embassy@ecuador.org; internet www.ecuador.org; Ambassador Luis Benigno Gallegos Chiriboga.

Egypt: 3521 International Court, NW, Washington, DC 20008; tel. (202) 895-5400; fax (202) 244-4319; e-mail Embassy@egyptembassy.net; internet www.egyptembassy.net; Ambassador Nabil M. Fahmy.

El Salvador: 1400 16th St, NW, Suite 100, Washington, DC 20036; tel. (202) 265-9671; fax (202) 232-3763; e-mail correo@elsalvador.org; internet www.elsalvador.org; Ambassador René Antonio León Rodríguez.

Equatorial Guinea: 2020 16th St, NW, Washington, DC 20009; tel. (202) 518-5700; fax (202) 518-5252; Ambassador Purificación Angue Ondo.

Eritrea: 1708 New Hampshire Ave, NW, Washington, DC 20009; tel. (202) 319-1991; fax (202) 319-1304; Ambassador Ghirmai Ghebremariam.

Estonia: 2131 Massachusetts Ave, NW, Washington, DC 20008; tel. (202) 588-0101; fax (202) 588-0108; e-mail info@estemb.org; internet www.estemb.org; Ambassador Väino Reinart.

Ethiopia: 3506 International Dr., NW, Washington, DC 20008; tel. (202) 364-1200; fax (202) 587-0195; e-mail info@ethiopianembassy.org; internet www.ethiopianembassy.org; Ambassador Samuel Assefa.

Fiji: 2000 M St, NW, Suite 710, Washington, DC 20036; tel. (202) 466-8320; fax (202) 466-8325; e-mail info@fijiembassydc.com; internet www.fijiembassy.org; Ambassasdor Ratu Finau Mara.

Finland: 3301 Massachusetts Ave, NW, Washington, DC 20008; tel. (202) 298-5800; fax (202) 298-6030; e-mail sanomat.was@formin.fi; internet www.finland.org; Ambassador Pekka Lintu.

France: 4101 Reservoir Rd, NW, Washington, DC 20007; tel. (202) 944-6166; fax (202) 944-6072; e-mail info@ambafrance-us.org; internet www.ambafrance-us.org; Ambassador Pierre Vimont.

Gabon: 2034 20th St, NW, Suite 200, Washington, DC 20009; tel. (202) 797-1000; fax (202) 332-0668; Ambassador Carlos Boungou.

The Gambia: 1155 15th St, NW, Suite 1000, Washington, DC 20005-2076; tel. (202) 785-1399; fax (202) 785-1430; e-mail info@gambiaembassy.us; internet www.gambiaembassy.us; Chargé d'affaires a.i. Abdul Rahman Cole.

Georgia: 1101 15th St, NW, Suite 602, Washington, DC 20005; tel. (202) 387-2390; fax (202) 387-0864; e-mail embgeorgiausa@yahoo.com; internet www.use.mfa.gov.ge; Ambassador Vasil Sikharulidze.

Germany: 4645 Reservoir Rd, NW, Washington, DC 20007-1998; tel. (202) 298-4000; fax (202) 298-4249; internet www.germany.info; Ambassador Klaus Scharioth.

Ghana: 3512 International Dr., NW, Washington, DC 20008; tel. (202) 686-4520; fax (202) 686-4527; e-mail info@ghanaembassy.org ; internet www.ghana-embassy.org; Ambassador Dr Kwame Bawuah-Edusei.

Greece: 2217 Massachusetts Ave, NW, Washington, DC 20008; tel. (202) 939-1300; fax (202) 939-1324; e-mail greece@greekembassy.org; internet www.greekembassy.org; Ambassador Alexandros P. Mallias.

Grenada: 1701 New Hampshire Ave, NW, Washington, DC 20009; tel. (202) 265-2561; fax (202) 265-2468; internet www.grenadaembassyusa.org; Ambassador Denis G. Antoine.

Guatemala: 2220 R St, NW, Washington, DC 20008; tel. (202) 745-4952; fax (202) 745-1908; e-mail info@guatemala-embassy.org; internet www.guatemala-embassy.org; Ambassador Francisco Villagrán de León.

Guinea: 2112 Leroy Pl., NW, Washington, DC 20008; tel. (202) 483-9420; fax (202) 483-8688; Ambassador (vacant).

Guinea-Bissau: POB 33813, Washington, DC 20033-3813; tel. and fax (301) 947-3958; Chargé d'affaires a.i. (vacant).

Guyana: 2490 Tracy Pl., NW, Washington, DC 20008; tel. (202) 265-6900; fax (202) 232-1297; e-mail guyanaembassydc@verizon.net; internet www.guyanaembassyusa.com; Ambassador Bayney Ram Karran.

Haiti: 2311 Massachusetts Ave, Washington, DC 20008; tel. (202) 332-4090; fax (202) 745-7215; e-mail embassy@haiti.org; internet www.haiti.org; Ambassador Raymond A. Joseph.

Holy See: 3339 Massachusetts Ave, NW, Washington, DC 20008-3687; tel. (202) 333-7121; fax (202) 337-4036; e-mail nuntius@worldnet.att.net; Apostolic Nuncio Most Rev. Pietro Sambi (Titular Archbishop of Bellicastrum).

Honduras: 3007 Tilden St, NW, Suite 4-M, Washington, DC 20008; tel. (202) 966-7702; fax (202) 966-9751; e-mail embassy@hondurasemb.org; internet www.hondurasemb.org; Ambassador Roberto Flores Bermudez.

Hungary: 3910 Shoemaker St, NW, Washington, DC 20008; tel. (202) 362-6730; fax (202) 966-8135; e-mail informacio.was@kum.hu; internet www.huembwas.org; Ambassador Dr Ferenc Somogyi.

Iceland: 1156 15th St, NW, Suite 1200, Washington, DC 20005-1704; tel. (202) 265-6653; fax (202) 265-6656; e-mail icemb.wash@utn.stjr.is; internet www.iceland.org/us; Ambassador Albert Jónsson.

India: 2107 Massachusetts Ave, NW, Washington, DC 20008; tel. (202) 939-7000; fax (202) 265-4351; e-mail information@indiagov.org; internet www.indianembassy.org; Ambassador Ronen Sen.

Indonesia: 2020 Massachusetts Ave, NW, Washington, DC 20036-1084; tel. (202) 775-5200; fax (202) 775-5256; e-mail information@embassyofindonesia.org; internet www.embassyofindonesia.org; Ambassador Sudjadnan Parnohadiningrat.

Iran: 'Interests section' in the Embassy of Pakistan, 2209 Wisconsin Ave, NW, Washington DC 20007; tel. (202) 965-4990; fax (202) 965-1073; e-mail requests@daftar.org; internet www.daftar.org; Dir Ali Jazini.

Iraq: 1801 P St, Washington, DC 20036; tel. (202) 483-7500; fax (202) 462-5066; e-mail admin@iraqiembassy.us; internet www.iraqiembassy.us; Ambassador Samir Shakir Mahmood as-Sumaidaie.

Ireland: 2234 Massachusetts Ave, NW, Washington, DC 20008; tel. (202) 462-3939; fax (202) 232-5993; e-mail embirlus@aol.com; internet www.irelandemb.org; Ambassador Michael Collins.

Israel: 3514 International Dr., NW, Washington, DC 20008; tel. (202) 364-5590; fax (202) 364-5566; e-mail ask@israelemb.org; internet www.israelemb.org; Ambassador Sallai Meridor.

Italy: 3000 Whitehaven St, NW, Washington, DC 20008; tel. (202) 612-4400; fax (202) 518-2151; e-mail stampa@itwash.org; internet www.ambwashingtondc.esteri.it; Ambassador Giovanni Castellaneta.

Jamaica: 1520 New Hampshire Ave, NW, Washington, DC 20006; tel. (202) 452-0660; fax (202) 452-0081; e-mail info@emjamusa.org; internet www.jamaicaembassy.org; Ambassador Anthony Johnson.

Japan: 2520 Massachusetts Ave, NW, Washington, DC 20008-2869; tel. (202) 238-6700; fax (202) 238-2187; e-mail jicc@embjapan.org; internet www.us.emb-japan.go.jp; Ambassador Ryozo Kato.

Jordan: 3504 International Dr., NW, Washington, DC 20008; tel. (202) 966-2664; fax (202) 966-3110; e-mail hkjembassydc@jordanembassyus.org; internet www.jordanembassyus.org; Ambassador HRH Prince Zeid Ra'ad al-Hussein.

Kazakhstan: 1401 16th St, NW, Washington, DC 20036; tel. (202) 232-5488; fax (202) 232-5845; e-mail zakh.embusa@verizon.net; internet www.kazakhembus.com; Ambassador Erlan A. Idrissov.

Kenya: 2249 R St, NW, Washington, DC 20008; tel. (202) 387-6101; fax (202) 462-3829; e-mail information@kenyaembassy.com; internet www.kenyaembassy.com; Ambassador Peter N. Rateng 'Oginga Ogego.

Korea, Republic: KORUS House, 2370 Massachusetts Ave, NW, Washington, DC 20008; tel. (202) 939-5600; fax (202) 797-0595; e-mail webmaster@dynamic-korea.com; internet www.koreaembassyusa.org; Ambassador Tae-Sik Lee.

Kuwait: 2940 Tilden St, NW, Washington, DC 20008; tel. (202) 966-0702; fax (202) 966-0517; e-mail kio@kuwait-info.org; internet www.kuwait-info.org; Ambassador Sheikh Jaber al-Ahmed al-Sabah.

Kyrgyzstan: 2360 Massachusetts Ave, NW, Washington, DC 20008; tel. (202) 449-9822; fax (202) 386 7550; e-mail consul@kgembassy.org; internet www.kgembassy.org; Ambassador Zamira Beksultanovna Sydykova.

Laos: 2222 S St, NW, Washington, DC 20008; tel. (202) 332-6416; fax (202) 332-4923; e-mail laoemb@verizon.net; internet www.laoembassy.com; Ambassador Phiane Philakone.

Latvia: 2306 Massachusetts Ave, NW, Washington, DC 20008; tel. (202) 328-2840; fax (202) 328-2860; e-mail embassy@latvia-usa.org; internet www.latvia-usa.org; Ambassador Andrejs Pildegovics.

Lebanon: 2560 28th St, NW, Washington, DC 20008; tel. (202) 939-6300; fax (202) 939-6324; e-mail info@lebanonembassyus.org; internet www.lebanonembassyus.org; Chargé d'affaires a.i. Dr Antoine Chedid.

Lesotho: 2511 Massachusetts Ave, NW, Washington, DC 20008; tel. (202) 797-5533; fax (202) 234-6815; e-mail lesothoembassy@verizon.net; internet www.lesothoemb-usa.gov.ls; Chargé d'affaires a.i. Mabasia Mohobane.

Liberia: 5201 16th St, NW, Washington, DC 20011; tel. (202) 723-0437; fax (202) 723-0436; e-mail info@liberiaemb.org; internet www.embassyofliberia.org; Ambassador Charles A. Minor.

Libya: Liaison Office, 2600 Virginia Ave, NW, Suite 705, Washington, DC 20037; tel. (202) 944-9601; fax (202) 944-9606; e-mail libya@libyanbureau-dc.org; Chief of Office Ali Suleiman Aujali.

Liechtenstein: 888 17th St, NW, Suite 1250, Washington, DC 20006; tel. (202) 331-0590; fax (202) 331-3221; e-mail tamara

THE UNITED STATES OF AMERICA

.brunhart@was.rep.llv.li; internet www.liechtenstein.li; Ambassador CLAUDIA FRITSCHE.

Lithuania: 4590 MacArthur Blvd, NW, Washington, DC 20007; tel. (202) 234-5860; fax (202) 328-0466; e-mail info@ltembassyus.org; internet www.ltembassyus.org; Ambassador AUDRIUS BRUZGA.

Luxembourg: 2200 Massachusetts Ave, NW, Washington, DC 20008; tel. (202) 265-4171; fax (202) 328-8270; e-mail washington.info@mae.etat.lu; internet www.luxembourg-usa.org; Ambassador JOSEPH WEYLAND.

Macedonia: 2129 Wyoming Ave, NW, Washington, DC 20008; tel. (202) 667-0501; fax (202) 667-2131; e-mail usoffice@macedonianembassy.org; internet www.macedonianembassy.org; Ambassador Dr ZORAN JOLEVSKI.

Madagascar: 2374 Massachusetts Ave, NW, Washington, DC 20008; tel. (202) 265-3034; fax (202) 483-7603; e-mail malagasy.embassy@org; internet www.kln.gov.my/perwakilan/washington; Ambassador JOCELYN RADIFERA.

Malawi: 1029 Vermont Ave, NW, Suite 1000, Washington, DC 20005; tel. (202) 721-0270; fax (202) 721-0288; e-mail malawidc@aol.com; internet www.malawiembassy-dc.org; Ambassador HAWA NDILOWE.

Malaysia: 3516 International Court, NW, Washington, DC 20008; tel. (202) 572-9700; fax (202) 572-9882; e-mail mwalsh@kln.gov.my; Ambassador Datin Paduka RAJMAH HUSSAIN.

Maldives: 800 Second Ave, Suite 400E, New York, NY 10017; tel. (212) 599-6195; fax (212) 661-6405; e-mail maldives@un.int; internet www.maldivesembassy.us; Ambassador MOHAMED HUSSAIN MANIKU.

Mali: 2130 R St, NW, Washington, DC 20008; tel. (202) 332-2249; fax (202) 332-6603; e-mail info@maliembassy.us; internet www.maliembassy.us; Ambassador ABDOULAYE DIOP.

Malta: 2017 Connecticut Ave, NW, Washington, DC 20008; tel. (202) 462-3611; fax (202) 387-5470; e-mail maltaembassy.washington@gov.mt; internet www.foreign.gov.mt; Ambassador MARK MICELI-FARRUGIA.

Marshall Islands: 2433 Massachusetts Ave, NW, Washington, DC 20008; tel. (202) 234-5414; fax (202) 232-3236; e-mail info@rmiembassyus.org; internet www.rmiembassyus.org; Ambassador BENJAMIN GRAHAM.

Mauritania: 2129 Leroy Pl., NW, Washington, DC 20008; tel. (202) 232-5700; fax (202) 319-2623; e-mail info@mauritaniembassy-usa.org; Ambassador IBRAHIMA DIA.

Mauritius: 4301 Connecticut Ave, NW, Suite 441, Washington, DC 20008; tel. (202) 244-1491; fax (202) 966-0983; e-mail mauritius.embassy@prodigy.net; Ambassador KEERTEECOOMAR RUHEE.

Mexico: 1911 Pennsylvania Ave, NW, Washington, DC 20006; tel. (202) 728-1600; fax (202) 234-1698; e-mail mexembusa@sre.gob.mx; internet www.sre.gob.mx/eua; Ambassador ARTURO SARUKHAN CASA-MITJANA.

Micronesia: 1725 N St, NW, Washington, DC 20036; tel. (202) 223-4383; fax (202) 223-4391; e-mail firstsecretary@fsmembassydc.org; internet www.fsmembassydc.org; Ambassador YOSIWO P. GEORGE.

Moldova: 2101 S St, NW, Washington, DC 20008; tel. (202) 667-1130; fax (202) 667-1204; e-mail washington@mfa.md; internet www.embassyrm.org; Ambassador NICOLAE CHIRTOACA.

Monaco: 2314 Wyoming Ave, NW, Washington, DC 20008; tel. (202) 234-1530; Ambassador GILLES ALEXANDRE NOGHES.

Mongolia: 2833 M St, NW, Washington, DC 20007; tel. (202) 333-7117; fax (202) 298-9227; e-mail esyam@mongolianembassy.us; internet www.mongolianembassy.us; Ambassador KHASBAZAR BEKH-BAT.

Montenegro: 1610 New Hampshire Ave, NW, Washington, DC 20009; tel. (202) 234 6108; fax (202) 234 6109; Ambassador MIODRAG VLAHOVIĆ.

Morocco: 1601 21st St, NW, Washington, DC 20009; tel. (202) 462-7980; fax (202) 265-0161; Ambassador AZIZ MEKOUAR.

Mozambique: 1525 New Hampshire Ave, NW, Washington, DC 20036; tel. (202) 293-7146; fax (202) 835-9245; e-mail embamoc@aol.com; internet www.embamoc-usa.org; Ambassador ARMANDO ALEXANDRE PANGUENE.

Myanmar: 2300 S St, NW, Washington, DC 20008; tel. (202) 332-9044; fax (202) 332-9046; e-mail thuriya@aol.com; Chargé d'affaires a.i. LWIN MYINT.

Namibia: 1605 New Hampshire Ave, NW, Washington, DC 20009; tel. (202) 986-0540; fax (202) 986-0443; e-mail info@namibiaembassyusa.org; internet www.namibianembassyusa.org; Ambassador PATRICK NANDAGO.

Nauru: 800 Second Ave, New York, NY 10017; tel. (212) 937-0074; fax (212) 937-0079; Ambassador MARLENE MOSES.

Nepal: 2131 Leroy Pl., NW, Washington, DC 20008; tel. (202) 667-4550; fax (202) 667-5534; e-mail info@nepalembassyusa.org; internet www.nepalembassyusa.org; Ambassador SURESH CHANDRA CHALISE.

Netherlands: 4200 Linnean Ave, NW, Washington, DC 20008; tel. (202) 244-5300; fax (202) 362-3430; e-mail was@minbuza.nl; internet www.netherlands-embassy.org; Ambassador CHRISTIAAN M. J. KRÖNER.

New Zealand: 37 Observatory Circle, NW, Washington, DC 20008; tel. (202) 328-4800; fax (202) 667-5227; e-mail info@nzemb.org; internet www.nzembassy.com; Ambassador ROY FERGUSON.

Nicaragua: 1627 New Hampshire Ave, NW, Washington, DC 20009; tel. (202) 387-4371; fax (202) 939-6545; e-mail nicaraguan.embassy@embanic.org; Ambassador ARTURO JOSÉ CRUZ SEQUEIRA.

Niger: 2204 R St, NW, Washington, DC 20008; tel. (202) 483-4224; fax (202) 483-3169; e-mail ambassadeniger@hotmail.com; internet www.nigerembassyusa.org; Ambassador AMINATA DJIBRILLA MAIGA TOURÉ.

Nigeria: 3519 International Court, NW, Washington, DC 20008; tel. (202) 986-8400; fax (202) 362-6541; e-mail babalola@nigeriaembassyusa.org; internet www.nigeriaembassyusa.org; Ambassador OLUWOLE ROTIMI.

Norway: 2720 34th St, NW, Washington, DC 20008; tel. (202) 333-6000; fax (202) 337-0870; e-mail emb.washington@mfa.no; internet www.norway.org; Ambassador WEGGER CHRISTIAN STRØMMEN.

Oman: 2535 Belmont Rd, NW, Washington, DC 20008; tel. (202) 387-1980; fax (202) 745-4933; Ambassador HUNAINA SULTAN AHMED AL-MUGHAIRY.

Pakistan: 3517 International Court, NW, Washington, DC 20008; tel. (202) 939-6200; fax (202) 387-0484; e-mail info@embassyofpakistan.org; internet www.embassyofpakistan.org; Ambassador MAHMUD ALI DURRANI.

Palau: 1700 Pennsylvania Ave, NW, Suite 400, Washington, DC 20006; tel. (202) 452-6814; fax (202) 452-6281; e-mail info@palauembassy.com; internet www.palauembassy.com; Ambassador HERSEY KYOTA.

Panama: 2862 McGill Terrace, NW, Washington, DC 20008; tel. (202) 483-1407; fax (202) 483-8413; e-mail info@embassyofpanama.org; internet www.embassyofpanama.org; Ambassador FEDERICO A. HUMBERT ARIAS.

Papua New Guinea: 1779 Massachusetts Ave, NW, Suite 805, Washington, DC 20036; tel. (202) 745-3680; fax (202) 745-3679; e-mail info@pngembassy.org; internet www.pngembassy.org; Ambassador EVAN JEREMY PAKI.

Paraguay: 2400 Massachusetts Ave, NW, Washington, DC 20008; tel. (202) 483-6960; fax (202) 234-4508; Ambassador JAMES SPALDING HELLMERS.

Peru: 1700 Massachusetts Ave, NW, Washington, DC 20036; tel. (202) 833-9860; fax (202) 659-8124; e-mail webadmin@embassyofperu.us; internet www.peruvianembassy.us; Ambassador FELIPE ORTIZ DE ZEVALLOS MADUEÑO.

Philippines: 1600 Massachusetts Ave, NW, Washington, DC 20036-2274; tel. (202) 467-9300; fax (202) 467-9417; e-mail info@philippineembassy-usa.org; internet www.philippineembassy-usa.org; Ambassador WILLY C. GAA.

Poland: 2640 16th St, NW, Washington, DC 20009; tel. (202) 234-3800; fax (202) 328-6271; e-mail polemb.info@earthlink.net; internet www.polandembassy.org; Ambassador ROBERT KUPIECKI.

Portugal: 2125 Kalorama Rd, NW, Washington, DC 20008; tel. (202) 328-8610; fax (202) 462-3726; internet www.portugalemb.org; Ambassador JOÃO DE VALLERA.

Qatar: 2555 M St, NW, Washington, DC 20037-1305; tel. (202) 274-1600; fax (202) 237-0061; e-mail info@qatarembassy.net; internet www.qatarembassy.net; Ambassador ALI BIN FAHAD AL-HAJRI.

Romania: 1607 23rd St, NW, Washington, DC 20008; tel. (202) 232-4846; fax (202) 232-4748; e-mail info@roembus.org; internet www.roembus.org; Ambassador ADRIAN COSMIN VIERITA.

Russia: 2650 Wisconsin Ave, NW, Washington, DC 20007; tel. (202) 298-5700; fax (202) 298-5735; e-mail rusembus@erols.com; internet www.russianembassy.org; Ambassador YURII VIKTOROVICH USHA-KOV.

Rwanda: 1714 New Hampshire Ave, NW, Washington, DC 20009; tel. (202) 232-2882; fax (202) 232-4544; e-mail rwandaembassy@rwandaembassy.org; internet www.rwandaembassy.org; Ambassador JAMES KIMONYO.

Saint Christopher and Nevis: 3216 New Mexico Ave, NW, Washington DC 20016; tel. (202) 686-2636; fax (202) 686-5740; e-mail info@stkittsnevis.org; Ambassador (vacant).

Saint Lucia: OECS Bldg, 3216 New Mexico Ave, NW, Washington, DC 20016; tel. (202) 364-6792; fax (202) 364-6723; e-mail eofsaintlu@aol.com; Chargé d'affaires a.i. CLENIE GREER-LACASCADE.

Saint Vincent and the Grenadines: 3216 New Mexico Ave, NW, Washington, DC 20016; tel. (202) 364-6730; fax (202) 364-6736;

THE UNITED STATES OF AMERICA

e-mail mail@embvsg.com; internet www.embvsg.com; Ambassador Ellsworth I. A. John.

Samoa: 800 Second Ave, Suite 800D, New York, NY 10017; tel. (212) 599-6196; fax (212) 599-0797; e-mail samoa@un.int; Ambassador Aliioaiga Feturi Elisaia.

São Tomé and Príncipe: 400 Park Ave, 7th floor, New York, NY 10022; tel. (212) 317-0580; e-mail stp@un.int; Ambassador Ovidio Manuel Barbosa Pequeno.

Saudi Arabia: 601 New Hampshire Ave, NW, Washington, DC 20037; tel. (202) 342-3800; fax (202) 944-5983; e-mail info@saudiembassy.net; internet www.saudiembassy.net; Ambassador Adel din Ahmed al-Jubeir.

Senegal: 2112 Wyoming Ave, NW, Washington, DC 20008; tel. (202) 234-0540; fax (202) 332-6315; Ambassador Dr Amadou Lamine Ba.

Serbia: 2134 Kalorama Rd, NW, Washington, DC 20008; tel. (202) 332-0333; fax (202) 332-3933; e-mail info@serbiaembusa.org; internet www.serbiaembusa.org; Ambassador Dr Ivan Vujačić.

Seychelles: 800 Second Ave, Suite 900C, New York, NY 10017; tel. (212) 687-9766; fax (212) 972-1786; Ambassador Ronald Jean Jumeau.

Sierra Leone: 1701 19th St, NW, Washington, DC 20009; tel. (202) 939-9261; fax (202) 483-1793; Ambassador Bockari Kortu Stevens.

Singapore: 3501 International Pl., NW, Washington, DC 20008; tel. (202) 537-3100; fax (202) 537-0876; e-mail singemb_was@sgmfa.gov.sg; internet www.mfa.gov.sg/washington; Ambassador Heng Chee Chan.

Slovakia: 3523 International Court, NW, Suite 210, Washington, DC 20008; tel. (202) 237-1054; fax (202) 237-6438; e-mail information@slovakembassy-us.org; internet www.slovakembassy-us.org; Ambassador Rastislav Kacer.

Slovenia: 2410 California St, NW, Washington, DC 20008; tel. (201) 667-5363; fax (202) 667-4563; e-mail vwa@gov.si; internet www.embassy.si/washington; Ambassador Samuel Zbogar.

Solomon Islands: 800 Second Ave, Suite 400L, New York, NY 10017; tel. (212) 599-6192; fax (212) 661-8925; e-mail simny@solomons.com; Ambassador Colin D. Beck.

South Africa: 3051 Massachusetts Ave, NW, Washington, DC 20008; tel. (202) 232-4400; fax (202) 265-1607; e-mail info@saembassy.org; internet www.saembassy.org; Ambassador Barbara Masekela.

Spain: 2375 Pennsylvania Ave, NW, Washington, DC 20037; tel. (202) 452-0100; fax (202) 833-5670; e-mail embespus@mail.mae.us; internet www.spainemb.org; Ambassador Carlos Westendorp y Cabeza.

Sri Lanka: 2148 Wyoming Ave, NW, Washington, DC 20008; tel. (202) 483-4025; fax (202) 232-7181; e-mail slembassy@usa.org; internet www.slembassyusa.org; Ambassador Bernard Anton Bandara Goonetilleke.

Sudan: 2210 Massachusetts Ave, NW, Washington, DC 20008; tel. (202) 338-8565; fax (202) 667-2406; e-mail info@sudanembassy.org; internet www.sudanembassy.org; Chargé d'affaires a.i. Prof. John Ukec Lueth Ukec.

Suriname: 4301 Connecticut Ave, NW, Suite 460, Washington, DC 20008; tel. (202) 244-7488; fax (202) 244-5878; e-mail esuriname@covad.net; internet www.surinameembassy.org; Ambassador Jacques R. C. Kross.

Swaziland: 1712 New Hampshire Ave, NW, Washington, DC 20009; tel. (202) 234-5002; fax (202) 234-8254; e-mail swaziland@compuserve.com; Ambassador Ephraim Mandlenkosi M. Hlophe.

Sweden: 2900 K St, NW, Washington, DC 20007; tel. (202) 467-2600; fax (202) 467-2699; e-mail ambassaden.washington@foreign.ministry.se; internet www.swedenabroad.com/washington; Ambassador Jonas Hafström.

Switzerland: 2900 Cathedral Ave, NW, Washington, DC 20008; tel. (202) 745-7900; fax (202) 387-2564; e-mail was.vertretung@eda.admin.ch; internet www.swissemb.org; Ambassador Urs Johann Ziswiler.

Syria: 2215 Wyoming Ave, NW, Washington, DC 20008; tel. (202) 232-6313; fax (202) 234-9548; e-mail info@syrembassy.net; internet www.syrianembassy.us; Chargé d'affaires a.i. Imad Moustapha.

Tajikistan: 1005 New Hampshire Ave, NW, Washington, DC 20037; tel. (202) 223-6090; fax (202) 223-6091; e-mail tajikistan@verizon.net; internet www.tjus.org; Ambassador Abdujabbor Shirinov.

Tanzania: 2139 R St, NW, Washington, DC 20008; tel. (202) 939-6125; fax (202) 797-7408; e-mail ubalozi@tanzaniaembassy-us.org; internet www.tanzaniaembassy-us.org; Ambassador Ombeni Sefue.

Thailand: 1024 Wisconsin Ave, NW, Washington, DC 20007; tel. (202) 944-3600; fax (202) 944-3611; e-mail info@thaiembdc.org; internet www.thaiembdc.org; Ambassador Krit Garnjana-Goonchoor.

Timor-Leste: 3415 Massachusetts Ave, NW, Washington, DC 20008; tel. (202) 965-1515; fax (202) 965-1517; e-mail embtlus@earthlink.net; Ambassador Jose Luis Guterres.

Togo: 2208 Massachusetts Ave, NW, Washington, DC 20008; tel. (202) 234-4212; fax (202) 232-3190; Chargé d'affaires a.i. T. H. Lorempo Landjergue.

Tonga: 250 East 51st St, New York, NY 10022; tel. (917) 369-1025; fax (917) 369-1024; Ambassador Fekitamoeloa 'Utoikamanu.

Trinidad and Tobago: 1708 Massachusetts Ave, NW, Washington, DC 20036; tel. (202) 467-6490; fax (202) 785-3130; e-mail info@ttembwash.com; internet www.bordeglobal.com/ttembassy; Ambassador Marina Annette Valere.

Tunisia: 1515 Massachusetts Ave, NW, Washington, DC 20005; tel. (202) 862-1850; fax (202) 862-1858; Ambassador Mohamed Nejib Hachana.

Turkey: 2525 Massachusetts Ave, NW, Washington, DC 20008; tel. (202) 612-6700; fax (202) 612-6744; e-mail contact@turkishembassy.org; internet www.turkishembassy.org; Ambassador Nabi Şensoy.

Turkmenistan: 2207 Massachusetts Ave, NW, Washington, DC 20008; tel. (202) 588-1500; fax (202) 588-0697; e-mail turkmen@mindspring.com; internet www.turkmenistanembassy.org; Ambassador Meret Bairamovich Orazov.

Uganda: 5911 16th St, NW, Washington, DC 20011; tel. (202) 726-7100; fax (202) 726-1727; e-mail info@ugandaembassyus.org; internet www.ugandaembassy.com; Ambassador Perezi Karukubiro Kamunanwire.

Ukraine: 3350 M St, NW, Washington, DC 20007; tel. (202) 333-0606; fax (202) 333-0817; e-mail infolook@aol.com; internet www.ukraineinfo.us; Ambassador Oleh Shamshur.

United Arab Emirates: 3422 International Court, NW, Washington, DC 20008; tel. (202) 243-2400; fax (202) 243-2432; e-mail info@uaeembassy-usa.org; internet www.uae-embassy.org; Ambassador (vacant).

United Kingdom: 3100 Massachusetts Ave, NW, Washington, DC 20008; tel. (202) 588-7800; fax (202) 588-7870; e-mail washi@fco.gov.uk; internet www.britainusa.com; Ambassador Sir Nigel Sheinwald.

Uruguay: 1913 Eye St, NW, Washington, DC 20006; tel. (202) 331-1313; fax (202) 331-8142; e-mail uruwashi@uruwashi.org; internet www.uruwashi.org; Ambassador Carlos A. Gianelli Derois.

Uzbekistan: 1746 Massachusetts Ave, NW, Washington, DC 20036; tel. (202) 887-5300; fax (202) 293-6804; e-mail info@uzbekistan.org; internet www.uzbekistan.org; Ambassador Abdulaziz Komilov.

Venezuela: 1099 30th St, NW, Washington, DC 20007; tel. (202) 342-2214; fax (202) 342-6820; e-mail apaiva@embavenez-us.org; internet www.embavenez-us.org; Ambassador Bernardo Álvarez Herrera.

Viet Nam: 1233 20th St, NW, Suite 400, Washington, DC 20036; tel. (202) 861-0737; fax (202) 861-0917; e-mail info@vietnamembassy.us; internet www.vietnamembassy-usa.org; Ambassador Le Cong Phung.

Yemen: 2319 Wyoming Ave, NW, Washington, DC 20008; tel. (202) 965-4760; fax (202) 337-2017; e-mail information@yemenembassy.org; internet www.yemenembassy.org; Ambassador Abdulwahab Abdulla Al-Hajjri.

Zambia: 2419 Massachusetts Ave, NW, Washington, DC 20008; tel. (202) 265-9717; fax (202) 332-0826; e-mail info@zambiainfo.org; internet www.zambiaembassy.org; Ambassador Dr Inonge Mbikusita Lewanika.

Zimbabwe: 1608 New Hampshire Ave, NW, Washington, DC 20009; tel. (202) 332-7100; fax (202) 483-9326; e-mail info@zimbabwe-embassy.us; Ambassador Machivenyika Tobias Mapuranga.

Judicial System

Each state has a judicial system structured similarly to the Federal system, with a Supreme Court and subsidiary courts, to deal with cases arising under State Law. These courts have jurisdiction in most criminal and civil actions. Each state has its own bar association of lawyers and its own legal code.

Supreme Court of the United States

Supreme Court Bldg, 1 First St, NE, Washington, DC 20543; tel. (202) 479-3211; fax (202) 479-2971; internet www.supremecourtus.gov.

The Supreme Court is the only Federal Court established by the Constitution. It is the highest court in the nation, comprising a Chief Justice and eight Associate Justices. Appointments, which are for life or until voluntary retirement, are made by the President, subject to confirmation by the US Senate.

THE UNITED STATES OF AMERICA

Chief Justice: JOHN G. ROBERTS, Jr.

Associate Justices: JOHN PAUL STEVENS (1975), ANTONIN SCALIA (1986), ANTHONY M. KENNEDY (1988), DAVID H. SOUTER (1990), CLARENCE THOMAS (1991), RUTH BADER GINSBURG (1993), STEPHEN G. BREYER (1994), SAMUEL A. ALITO, Jr (2006).

US Courts of Appeal

Administrative Office of the US Courts, Washington, DC 20544; tel. (202) 502-2600; internet www.uscourts.gov.

The USA is divided into 12 judicial circuits, in each of which there is one Court of Appeals. The Court of Appeals for the Federal Circuit has nation-wide specialized jurisdiction.

Federal Courts hear cases involving federal law, cases involving participants from more than one state, crimes committed in more than one state and civil or corporate cases that cross state lines. Federal District Courts, of which there are 94, are the courts of first instance for most federal suits.

Federal Circuit: PAUL R. MICHEL (Chief Judge), PAULINE NEWMAN, HALDANE ROBERT MAYER, ALAN D. LOURIE, RANDALL R. RADER, ALVIN A. SCHALL, WILLIAM CURTIS BRYSON, ARTHUR J. GAJARSA, RICHARD LINN, TIMOTHY B. DYK, SHARON PROST, KIMBERLEY MOORE.

District of Columbia Circuit: DAVID B. SENTELLE (Chief Judge), DOUGLAS H. GINSBURG, KAREN LECRAFT HENDERSON, A. RAYMOND RANDOLPH, JUDITH W. ROGERS, DAVID S. TATEL, MERRICK B. GARLAND, JANICE ROGERS BROWN, THOMAS B. GRIFFITH, BRETT M. KAVANAUGH.

First Circuit (Maine, Massachusetts, New Hampshire, Rhode Island, Puerto Rico): MICHAEL BOUDIN (Chief Judge), JUAN R. TORRUELLA, SANDRA L. LYNCH, KERMIT V. LIPEZ, JEFFREY R. HOWARD.

Second Circuit (Connecticut, New York, Vermont): DENNIS JACOBS (Chief Judge), GUIDO CALABRESI, JOSÉ A. CABRANES, CHESTER J. STRAUB, ROSEMARY S. POOLER, ROBERT D. SACK, SONIA SOTOMAYOR, ROBERT A. KATZMANN, BARRINGTON D. PARKER, REENA RAGGI, RICHARD C. WESLEY, PETER W. HALL, DEBRA ANN LIVINGSTON.

Third Circuit (Delaware, New Jersey, Pennsylvania, Virgin Islands): ANTHONY J. SCIRICA (Chief Judge), DOLORES K. SLOVITER, THEODORE A. MCKEE, MARJORIE O. RENDELL, MARYANNE TRUMP BARRY, THOMAS L. AMBRO, JULIO M. FUENTES, D. BROOKS SMITH, D. MICHAEL FISHER, MICHAEL A. CHAGARES, KENT A. JORDAN, THOMAS M. HARDIMAN.

Fourth Circuit (Maryland, North Carolina, South Carolina, Virginia, West Virginia): KAREN J. WILLIAMS (Chief Judge), J. HARVIE WILKINSON, III, PAUL V. NIEMEYER, M. BLANE MICHAEL, DIANA GRIBBON MOTZ, WILLIAM B. TRAXLER, Jr, ROBERT B. KING, ROGER L. GREGORY, DENNIS W. SHEDD, ALLYSON K. DUNCAN.

Fifth Circuit (Louisiana, Mississippi, Texas): EDITH H. JONES (Chief Judge), CAROLYN DINEEN KING, E. GRADY JOLLY, W. EUGENE DAVIS, JERRY E. SMITH, JACQUES L. WIENER, Jr, RHESA H. BARKSDALE, EMILIO M. GARZA, FORTUNATO P. BENAVIDES, CARL E. STEWART, JAMES L. DENNIS, EDITH BROWN CLEMENT, EDWARD C. PRADO, PRISCILLA R. OWEN, JENNIFER W. ELROD, LESLIE SOUTHWICK, CATHARINA HAYNES.

Sixth Circuit (Kentucky, Michigan, Ohio, Tennessee): DANNY J. BOGGS (Chief Judge), BOYCE F. MARTIN, Jr, ALICE M. BATCHELDER, MARTHA CRAIG DAUGHTREY, KAREN NELSON MOORE, RANSEY GUY COLE, Jr, ERIC L. CLAY, RONALD LEE GILMAN, JULIA SMITH GIBBONS, JOHN M. ROGERS, JEFFREY S. SUTTON, DEBORAH L. COOK, DAVID W. MCKEAGUE, RICHARD ALLEN GRIFFIN.

Seventh Circuit (Illinois, Indiana, Wisconsin): FRANK H. EASTERBROOK (Chief Judge), WILLIAM J. BAUER, RICHARD D. CUDAHY, RICHARD A. POSNER, JOHN L. COFFEY, JOEL M. FLAUM, KENNETH F. RIPPLE, DANIEL A. MANION, MICHAEL S. KANNE, ILANA DIAMOND ROVNER, DIANE P. WOOD, TERENCE T. EVANS, ANN CLAIRE WILLIAMS, DIANE S. SYKES, JOHN D. TINDER.

Eighth Circuit (Arkansas, Iowa, Minnesota, Missouri, Nebraska, North Dakota, South Dakota): JAMES B. LOKEN (Chief Judge), ROGER L. WOLLMAN, DIANA E. MURPHY, KERMIT E. BYE, WILLIAM J. RILEY, MICHAEL J. MELLOY, LAVENSKI R. SMITH, STEVEN M. COLLOTON, RAYMOND W. GRUENDER, DUANE BENTON, BOBBY E. SHEPHERD.

Ninth Circuit (Alaska, Arizona, California, Guam, Hawaii, Idaho, Montana, Nevada, Northern Mariana Islands, Oregon, Washington): ALEX KOZINSKI (Chief Judge), HARRY PREGERSON, STEPHEN REINHARDT, MARY M. SCHROEDER, DIARMUID F. O'SCANNLAIN, PAMELA ANN RYMER, ANDREW J. KLEINFELD, MICHAEL DALY HAWKINS, SIDNEY R. THOMAS, BARRY G. SILVERMAN, SUSAN P. GRABER, M. MARGARET MCKEOWN, KIM MCLANE WARDLAW, WILLIAM A. FLETCHER, RAYMOND C. FISHER, RONALD M. GOULD, RICHARD A. PAEZ, MARSHA S. BERZON, RICHARD C. TALLMAN, JOHNNIE B. RAWLINSON, RICHARD R. CLIFTON, JAY S. BYBEE, CONSUELO M. CALLAHAN, CARLOS T. BEA, MILAN D. SMITH, Jr, SANDRA S. IKUTA, N. RANDY SMITH.

Tenth Circuit (Colorado, Kansas, New Mexico, Oklahoma, Utah, Wyoming): ROBERT H. HENRY (Chief Judge), PAUL J. KELLY, DEANELL REECE TACHA, MARY BECK BRISCOE, CARLOS F. LUCERO, MICHAEL R. MURPHY, HARRIS L. HARTZ, TERRENCE L. O'BRIEN, MICHAEL W. MCCONNELL, TIMOTHY M. TYMKOVICH, NEIL M. GORSUCH, JEROME A. HOLMES.

Eleventh Circuit (Alabama, Florida, Georgia): J. L. EDMONSON (Chief Judge), GERALD B. TJOFLAT, R. LANIER ANDERSON, STANLEY F. BIRCH, Jr, JOEL F. DUBINA, SUSAN H. BLACK, EDWARD E. CARNES, ROSEMARY BARKETT, FRANK M. HULL, STANLEY MARCUS, CHARLES R. WILSON, WILLIAM H. PRYOR, Jr.

United States Court of Federal Claims

717 Madison Pl., NW, Washington, DC 20005; tel. (202) 357-6400; internet www.uscfc.uscourts.gov.

Judges: EDWARD J. DAMICH (Chief Judge), CHRISTINE ODELL COOK MILLER, MARIAN BLANK HORN, FRANCIS M. ALLEGRA, LAWRENCE M. BASKIR, LYNN J. BUSH, NANCY B. FIRESTONE, EMILY C. HEWITT, LAWRENCE J. BLOCK, MARY ELLEN COSTER WILLIAMS, CHARLES F. LETTOW, SUSAN G. BRADEN, VICTOR J. WOLSKI, GEORGE W. MILLER, THOMAS C. WHEELER, MARGARET M. SWEENEY.

US Court of International Trade

1 Federal Plaza, New York, NY 10278-0001; tel. (212) 264-2800; fax (212) 264-1085; internet www.cit.uscourts.gov.

Judges: JANE A. RESTANI (Chief Judge), GREGORY W. CARMAN, DONALD C. POGUE, EVAN J. WALLACH, JUDITH M. BARZILAY, DELISSA A. RIDGWAY, RICHARD K. EATON, TIMOTHY C. STANCEU, LEO M. GORDON.

Senior Judges: RICHARD W. GOLDBERG, NICHOLAS TSOUCALAS, R. KENTON MUSGRAVE, THOMAS J. AQUILINO, Jr.

United States Tax Court

400 Second St, NW, Washington, DC 20217; tel. (202) 521-0700; internet www.ustaxcourt.gov.

Judges: JOHN O. COLVIN (Chief Judge), MARY ANN COHEN, MAURICE B. FOLEY, JOSEPH H. GALE, JOSEPH R. GOEKE, HARRY A. HAINES, JAMES S. HALPERN, MARK V. HOLMES, DIANE L. KROUPA, L. PAIGE MARVEL, STEPHEN J. SWIFT, MICHAEL B. THORNTON, JUAN F. VASQUEZ, THOMAS B. WELLS, ROBERT A. WHERRY, Jr.

Religion

Christianity is the predominant religion. The largest single denomination is the Roman Catholic Church. Other major groups in terms of membership are the Baptist, Methodist, Lutheran and Orthodox churches. Numerous other beliefs are represented, the largest in terms of adherents being Judaism, Islam and Buddhism.

CHRISTIANITY

National Council of the Churches of Christ in the USA: 475 Riverside Dr., Suite 880, New York, NY 10115-0050; tel. (212) 870-2025; fax (212) 870-3112; e-mail webmaster@ncccusa.org; internet www.ncccusa.org; f. 1950; an ecumenical org. of 35 Protestant and Orthodox denominations, representing 100,000 congregations of c. 45m. mems; Pres. MICHAEL E. LIVINGSTON; Gen. Sec. Dr ROBERT EDGAR.

The Anglican Communion

The Episcopal Church in the USA: 815 Second Ave, New York, NY 10017-4564; tel. (212) 716-6000; fax (212) 697-5892; e-mail sjcoombs@episcopalchurch.org; internet www.ecusa.anglican.org; f. 1607; mem. of the Worldwide Anglican Communion and World Council of Churches; 7,200 parishes and missions; 2.2m. mems (2004); Presiding Bishop Most Rev. KATHARINE JEFFERTS SCHORI; Exec. Officer and Sec. Rev. Dr GREGORY S. STRAUB.

The Baptist Church

Members (1998 estimate): 33.1m., in 15 bodies, of which the following have the greatest number of members:

American Baptist Association: 4605 North State Line Ave, Texarkana, TX 75503-2928; tel. (903) 792-2783; e-mail bssc@abaptist.org; internet www.abaptist.org; f. 1905; 1,867 churches; 280,973 mems (2000); Pres. Dr NEAL CLARK.

American Baptist Churches in the USA: POB 851, Valley Forge, PA 19482-0851; 588 North Gulph Rd, King of Prussia, PA 19406; tel. (610) 768-2000; fax (610) 768-2275; e-mail cathy.brubaker@abc-usa.org; internet www.abc-usa.org; f. 1907; mem. of the World Council of Churches; 5,740 churches (2005); 1.4m. mems (2003); Pres. Rev. MARY ARMACOST HULST; Gen. Sec. Rev. Dr A. ROY MEDLEY.

Conservative Baptist Association of America: 3686 Stagecoach Rd, Unit F, Longmont, CO 80504-5660; tel. (720) 283-3030; fax (303) 772-5690; e-mail info@cbamerica.org; internet www.cbamerica.org; f. 1947; 1,191 churches; 224,306 mems (2005); Nat. Exec. Dir Rev. STEPHEN LEBAR.

General Association of Regular Baptist Churches: 1300 North Meacham Rd, Schaumburg, IL 60173-4806; tel. (847) 843-1600; fax

THE UNITED STATES OF AMERICA

(847) 843-3757; internet www.garbc.org; 1,330 churches; 245,636 mems (2000); Nat. Rep. Rev. JOHN GREENING.

National Baptist Convention, USA: 1700 Baptist World Center Dr., Nashville, TN 37207; tel. (615) 228-6292; fax (615) 262-3917; e-mail president@nationalbaptist.com; internet www.nationalbaptist.com; f. 1880; mem. of the World Council of Churches; 2,500 churches; 7.5m. mems; Pres. Dr. WILLIAM J. SHAW; Gen. Sec. Rev. ROSCOE COOPER.

Southern Baptist Convention: 901 Commerce St, Nashville, TN 37203-3629; tel. (615) 244-2355; fax (615) 742-8919; e-mail cpmissions@sbc.net; internet www.sbc.net; f. 1845; 42,972 churches; 16.4m. mems (2003); Pres. Exec. Cttee Dr MORRIS H. CHAPMAN.

The Lutheran Church

Members (1998 estimate): 8.3m., in 10 bodies, of which the following have the greatest number of members:

Evangelical Lutheran Church in America: 8765 West Higgins Rd, Chicago, IL 60631; tel. (773) 380-2700; fax (773) 380-1465; e-mail info@elca.org; internet www.elca.org; f. 1988; mem. of the World Council of Churches; 10,549 churches; 4.9m. mems (2007); Leader Bishop Rev. MARK STEPHEN HANSON; Sec. DAVID D. SWARTLING.

Lutheran Church—Missouri Synod: 1333 South Kirkwood Rd, St Louis, MO 63122-7295; tel. (314) 965-9000; e-mail infocenter@lcms.org; internet www.lcms.org; f. 1847; 6,150 churches; 2.5m. mems (2007); Pres. Dr GERALD B. KIESCHNICK; Sec. Dr RAYMOND HARTWIG.

The Methodist Church

Members (1998 estimate): 13.4m. in eight bodies, of which the following have the greatest number of members:

African Methodist Episcopal Church: 500 Eighth Ave South, Nashville, TN 37203; tel. (615) 254-0911; fax (615) 254-0912; e-mail cio@ame-church.com; internet www.ame-church.com; f. 1816; mem. of the Churches Uniting in Christ and World Council of Churches; 4,174 churches; 2.5m. mems (1999); Sr Bishop PHILIP R. COUSIN, Sr; Gen. Sec. Dr CLEMENT W. FUGH.

African Methodist Episcopal Zion Church: 3225 Sugar Creek Rd, POB 32843, Charlotte, NC 28269; tel. (704) 599-4630; e-mail admin@amez.org; internet www.amez.org; f. 1796; mem. of the Churches Uniting in Christ; 3,236 churches; 1.4m. mems (2003); Gen.-Sec. Rev. Dr W. ROBERT JOHNSON, III.

United Methodist Church: POB 320, Nashville, TN 37202; e-mail umc@umcom.org; internet www.umc.org; f. 1968; mem. of the Churches Uniting in Christ and World Council of Churches; 34,892 churches; 8.2m. mems (2003); President of Council of Bishops Bishop JANICE RIGGLE HUIE; Sec. Gen. Conference FITZGERALD REIST.

The Orthodox Churches

Members (2000 estimate): 5.8m. in 12 bodies, of which the following have the greatest number of members:

Antiochian Orthodox Christian Archdiocese of North America (Greek Orthodox Patriarchate of Antioch and all the East): POB 3258, Englewood, NJ 07631-3798; tel. (201) 871-1355; fax (201) 871-7954; e-mail archdiocese@antiochian.org; internet www.antiochian.org; f. 1895; mem. of the World Council of Churches; 210 churches; 82,374 mems (2000); Primate Metropolitan PHILIP (Saliba); Auxiliaries Bishop ANTOUN (Khouri), Bishop BASIL (Essey), Bishop JOSEPH (Zehlaoui), Bishop ALEXANDER (Mufarrij), Bishop MARK (Maymon), Bishop THOMAS (Joseph).

Armenian Apostolic Church of America: *Eastern Prelacy:* 138 East 39th St, New York, NY 10016; tel. (212) 689-7810; fax (212) 689-7168; e-mail email@armenianprelacy.org; internet www.armenianprelacy.org: *Western Prelacy:* 6252 Honolulu Ave, Suite 100, La Crescenta, CA 91214; tel. (818) 248-7737; fax (818) 248-7745; e-mail prelacy@aol.com; f. 1887; mem. of the World Council of Churches; 38 churches; 23,200 mems (2000); Prelate (Eastern Prelacy) Archbishop OSHAGAN CHOLOYAN; Prelate (Western Prelacy) Archbishop MOUSHEGH MARDIROSIAN.

Armenian Church of America: *Eastern Diocese,* 630 Second Ave, New York, NY 10016; tel. (212) 686-0710; fax (212) 686-0245; internet www.armeniandiocese.org; *Western Diocese,* 3325 North Glenoaks Blvd, Burbank, CA 91504; tel. (818) 558-7474; fax (818) 558-6333; e-mail info@armenianchurchwd.com; internet www.armenianchurchwd.com; f. 1889; mem. of the World Council of Churches; 89 churches; 45,840 mems (2000); Primate (Eastern Diocese) Archbishop KHAJAG BARSAMIAN; Primate (Western Diocese) Archbishop HOVNAN DERDERIAN.

Greek Orthodox Archdiocese of America: 8–10 East 79th St, New York, NY 10021-0191; tel. (212) 570-3500; fax (212) 570-3569; e-mail archdiocese@goarch.org; internet www.goarch.org; f. 1921 as Greek Orthodox Archdiocese of North and South America; mem. of the World Council of Churches; 540 churches; 1.5m. mems (2007); Primate Archbishop DIMITRIOS; Chancellor Bishop SAVAS (of Troas).

Orthodox Church in America: POB 675, Syosset, NY 11791; tel. (516) 922-0550; fax (516) 922-0954; e-mail info@oca.org; internet www.oca.org; f. 1794; fmrly Russian Orthodox Greek Catholic Church of North America; mem. of the World Council of Churches; 456 churches; 115,000 mems (2000); Primate Metropolitan HERMAN; Chancellor Archpriest ALEXANDER GARKLAVS.

The Albanian, Bulgarian, Coptic, Romanian, Russian, Serbian, Syrian and Ukrainian Orthodox Churches are also represented.

The Presbyterian Church

Members (1998 estimate): 4.1m. in nine bodies, of which the following have the greatest number of members:

Presbyterian Church in America: 1700 North Brown Rd, Lawrenceville, GA 30043-8143; tel. (678) 825-1000; fax (678) 825-1001; e-mail ac@pcanet.org; internet www.pcanet.org; f. 1973; 1,600 churches; 300,000 mems (2007); Moderator E. J. NUSBAUM; Stated Clerk Dr L. ROY TAYLOR.

Presbyterian Church (USA): 100 Witherspoon St, Louisville, KY 40202-1396; tel. (502) 569-5000; fax (502) 569-8005; e-mail presbytel@pcusa.org; internet www.pcusa.org; f. 1983; mem. of the Churches Uniting in Christ and World Council of Churches; 11,100 churches; 2.4m. mems (2007); Stated Clerk CLIFTON KIRKPATRICK; Moderator JOAN GRAY; Exec. Dir LINDA VALENTINE.

The Roman Catholic Church

At December 2005 there were 194 dioceses and eparchies, with some 65.5m. mems.

United States Conference of Catholic Bishops: 3211 Fourth St, NE, Washington, DC 20017-1194; tel. (202) 541-3000; fax (202) 541-3322; internet www.usccb.org; f. 2001 by merger of the Nat. Conference of Catholic Bishops (f. 1966) and US Catholic Conference (f. 1966); Pres. Cardinal FRANCIS GEORGE (Archbishop of Chicago); Gen. Sec. Mgr DAVID MALLOY.

Archbishops

Anchorage: ROGER L. SCHWIETZ.
Atlanta: WILTON D. GREGORY.
Baltimore: EDWIN F. O'BRIEN.
Boston: SÉAN PATRICK O'MALLEY.
Chicago: Cardinal FRANCIS E. GEORGE.
Cincinnati: DANIEL E. PILARCZYK.
Denver: CHARLES J. CHAPUT.
Detroit: Cardinal ADAM J. MAIDA.
Dubuque: JEROME G. HANUS.
Galveston-Houston: Cardinal DANIEL N. DINARDO.
Hartford: HENRY J. MANSELL.
Indianapolis: DANIEL M. BUECHLEIN.
Kansas City in Kansas: JOSEPH F. NAUMAN.
Los Angeles: Cardinal ROGER M. MAHONY.
Louisville: E. KURTZ.
Miami: JOHN C. FAVALORA.
Milwaukee: TIMOTHY M. DOLAN.
Mobile: OSCAR H. LIPSCOMB.
Newark: JOHN JOSEPH MYERS.
New Orleans: ALFRED C. HUGHES.
New York: Cardinal EDWARD MICHAEL EGAN.
Oklahoma City: EUSEBIUS J. BELTRAN.
Omaha: ELDEN F. CURTISS.
Philadelphia: Cardinal JUSTIN F. RIGALI, STEFAN SOROKA (Ukrainian, Byzantine Rite).
Pittsburgh: BASIL MYRON SCHOTT.
Portland in Oregon: JOHN G. VLAZNY.
Saint Louis: RAYMOND L. BURKE.
Saint Paul and Minneapolis: HARRY J. FLYNN.
San Antonio: JOSÉ H. GÓMEZ.
San Francisco: GEORGE H. NIEDERAUER.
Santa Fe: MICHAEL J. SHEEHAN.
Seattle: ALEXANDER J. BRUNETT.
Washington: DONALD W. WUERL.

Other Christian Churches

Assemblies of God: 1445 North Boonville Ave, Springfield, MO 65802-1894; tel. (417) 862-5554; fax (417) 863-6614; e-mail info@ag.org; internet www.ag.org; f. 1914; 12,311 churches in USA; 2.8m. mems in USA; Gen. Supt GEORGE O. WOOD; Gen. Sec. JOHN M. PALMER.

THE UNITED STATES OF AMERICA

Directory

Christian Church (Disciples of Christ) in the USA and Canada: 130 East Washington St, POB 1986, Indianapolis, IN 46206-1986; tel. (317) 635-3100; fax (317) 635-3700; internet www.disciples.org; f. 1804; 3,750 congregations; 750,000 mems; mem. of the Churches Uniting in Christ and World Council of Churches; Gen. Minister and Pres. Dr SHARON E. WATKINS.

Christian Reformed Church in North America: 2850 Kalamazoo Ave, SE, Grand Rapids, MI 49560; tel. (616) 224-0832; fax (616) 224-5895; e-mail crcna@crcna.org; internet www.crcna.org; f. 1857; Calvinist; 1,023 churches; 273,300 mems (USA and Canada); Exec. Dir Rev. Dr GERARD L. DYKSTRA.

Church of Christ: POB 472, Independence, MO 64051; tel. (816) 833-3995; fax (816) 833-0210; e-mail cofctl@kcnet.com; f. 1830; Sec. Council of Apostles Gen. Church Rep. WILLIAM A. SHELDO.

Church of Christ, Scientist: 210 Massachusetts Ave, Boston, MA 02115; tel. (617) 450-2000; fax (617) 450-3554; e-mail info@churchofchristscientist.org; internet www.tfccs.com; f. 1879; 2,400 congregations world-wide; Pres. MARK SWINNEY; Clerk NATHAN TALBOT.

Church of God in Christ: Mason Temple, 939 Mason St, Memphis, TN 38126; e-mail laity@cogic.org; internet www.cogic.org; f. 1907; 15,300 churches; 5,500,000 mems (1991); Presiding Bishop CHARLES EDWARD BLAKE.

Church of Jesus Christ of Latter-day Saints (Mormon): 47 East South Temple St, Salt Lake City, UT 84150-0001; tel. (801) 240-1000; fax (801) 240-2033; internet www.lds.org; f. 1830; 12,112 wards and brs (congregations) in USA; 5.5m. mems in USA (2003); Pres. THOMAS S. MONSON.

Church of the Nazarene: 6401 The Paseo, Kansas City, MO 64131; tel. (816) 333-7000; fax (816) 361-4983; e-mail gensec@nazarene.org; internet www.nazarene.org; f. 1908; 18,690 churches; 1.6m. mems (2006); Gen. Sec. DAVID P. WILSON.

Friends United Meeting: 101 Quaker Hill Dr., Richmond, IN 47374-1980; tel. (765) 962-7573; fax (765) 966-1293; e-mail info@fum.org; internet www.fum.org; f. 1902; Quaker; mem. of the World Council of Churches; 44,000 mems (USA and Canada); Gen. Sec. SYLVIA GRAVES.

Mariavite Old Catholic Church—Province of North America: 2803 10th St, Wyandotte, MI 48192-4994; tel. and fax (734) 281-3082; e-mail mariaviteocc@hotmail.com; f. 1930; 158 churches; 357,100 mems; Prime Bishop Most Rev. Archbishop Dr ROBERT R. J. M. ZABOROWSKI.

Reformed Church in America: 475 Riverside Dr., New York, NY 10115-0001; tel. (212) 870-3071; fax (212) 870-2499; e-mail questions@rca.org; internet www.rca.org; f. 1628; Calvinist; mem. of the World Council of Churches; 935 churches; 329,437 mems; Gen. Sec. Rev. WESLEY GRANBERG-MICHAELSON.

Seventh-day Adventists: 12501 Old Columbia Pike, Silver Spring, MD 20904-6600; tel. (301) 680-6400; fax (301) 680-6464; internet www.nadadventist.org; f. 1863; 5,026 churches; 998,450 mems (USA and Canada); Pres. H. DON SCHNEIDER; Sec. ROSCOE J. HOWARD, III.

United Church of Christ: 700 Prospect Ave, Cleveland, OH 44115; tel. (216) 736-2100; fax (216) 736-2103; e-mail guessb@ucc.org; internet www.ucc.org; f. 1957; mem. of the Churches Uniting in Christ and World Council of Churches; 5,633 churches; 1.2m. mems; Gen. Minister and Pres. Rev. JOHN H. THOMAS.

United Pentecostal Church International: 8855 Dunn Rd, Hazelwood, MO 63042-2211; tel. (314) 837-7300; fax (314) 837-4503; e-mail info@upci.org; internet www.upci.org; f. 1945 by merger of the Pentecostal Church, Inc, and Pentecostal Assemblies of Jesus Christ; 4,358 churches (USA and Canada); c. 600,000 mems; Gen. Supt Rev. KENNETH N. HANEY; Gen. Sec. JERRY JONES.

BAHÁ'Í FAITH

National Spiritual Assembly of Bahá'ís of the United States: External Affairs Office, 1320 19th St, NW, Suite 701, Washington, DC 20036-1610; tel. (202) 833-8990; fax (202) 833-8988; e-mail bahai-info@usbnc.org; internet www.bahai.us; f. 1844 in Persia (Iran); Chair. JACQUELINE LEFT HAND BULL DELAHUNT; Sec.-Gen. KENNETH E. BOWERS.

BUDDHISM

At mid-2000 there were an estimated 2.5m. Buddhists in the USA.

Association of American Buddhists: 301 West 45th St, New York, NY 10036; tel. (212) 489-1075; e-mail iwanttoknow@buddhismonline.us; internet www.buddhismonline.us; f. 1980; 15 regional groups; Pres. Dr KEVIN R. O'NEIL.

Buddhist Churches of America: 1710 Octavia St, San Francisco, CA 94109-4341; tel. (415) 776-5600; fax (415) 771-6293; e-mail bcahq@pacbell.net; internet www.buddhistchurchesofamerica.org; f. 1899; Hongwanji-ha Jodo Shinshu denomination; c. 230,000 mems; Presiding Bishop KOSHIN OGUI; Exec. Dir HENRY SHIBATA.

HINDUISM

At mid-2000 there were an estimated 1.0m. Hindus in the USA.

Ramakrishna-Vivekananda Center: 17 East 94th St, New York, NY 10128; tel. (212) 534-9445; fax (212) 828-1618; e-mail rvcnewyork@worldnet.att.net; internet www.ramakrishna.org; f. 1933; teachings based on the system of Vedanta; Minister and Spiritual Leader SWAMI YUKTATMANANDA; Dir BARRY ZELIKOVSKY.

ISLAM

At mid-2000 there were an estimated 4.1m. Muslims in the USA, of whom some 40% were African-American.

Council of Masajid of United States (CMUS): 45 Lilac St, Edison, NJ 08817; tel. (732) 985-3304; fax (732) 572-0486; e-mail dawud10@optonline.net; f. 1978; educational agency representing 650 local groups; Pres. DAWUD ASSAD.

Federation of Islamic Associations in the US and Canada: 25351 Five Mile and Aubery Rd, Redford Township, MI 48239; tel. (313) 534-3295; fax (313) 534-1474; f. 1951; co-ordinating agency for 45 affiliated orgs; Gen. Sec. NIHAD HAMED.

Islamic Center of New York: 1711 Third Ave, New York, NY 10029-7303; tel. (212) 722-5234; fax (212) 722-5936; f. 1966; Dir ZIYAD MONAYAIR.

Islamic Mission of America: 143 State St, Brooklyn, NY 11201; tel. (718) 875-6607; f. 1948; maintains an educational and training institute; 15,000 mems; Chair. MOHAMED KABBAJ; Dir Hajj D. A. HAROON.

JUDAISM

In 2003 there were an estimated 6.2m. Jews in North America.

American Jewish Congress: 825 Third Ave, New York, NY 10022; tel. (212) 879-4500; fax (212) 758-1633; e-mail contact@ajcongress.org; internet www.ajcongress.org; f. 1918; 50,000 mems; Chair. JACK ROSEN; Exec. Dir NEIL B. GOLDSTEIN.

Central Conference of American Rabbis: 355 Lexington Ave, New York, NY 10017; tel. (212) 972-3636; fax (212) 692-0819; e-mail info@ccarnet.org; internet www.ccarnet.org; f. 1889; organized rabbinate of Reform Judaism; 1,840 mems; Pres. PETER S. KNOBEL.

The Rabbinical Assembly: 3080 Broadway, New York, NY 10027-4650; tel. (212) 280-6000; fax (212) 749-9166; e-mail info@rabbinicalassembly.org; internet www.rabassembly.org; f. 1901; 1,550 mems; Pres. Rabbi ALVIN K. BERKUN; Exec. Vice-Pres. Rabbi JOEL H. MEYERS.

Union of Orthodox Jewish Congregations of America: 11 Broadway, New York, NY 10004; tel. (212) 563-4000; fax (212) 564-9058; e-mail info@ou.org; internet www.ou.org; f. 1898; 1,000 affiliated congregations representing c. 1.0m. mems; Chair. HARVEY BLITZ; Pres. STEVEN J. SAVITSKY.

Union for Reform Judaism: 633 Third Ave, New York, NY 10017-6778; tel. (212) 650-4000; fax (212) 650-4169; e-mail urj@urj.org; internet urj.org; f. 1873 as the Union of American Hebrew Congregations; present name adopted 2003; more than 900 affiliated congregations representing c. 1.5m. mems; Pres. Rabbi ERIC H. YOFFIE; Sr Vice-Pres. Rabbi LEONARD R. THAL.

United Synagogue of Conservative Judaism: 155 Fifth Ave, New York, NY 10010-6802; tel. (212) 533-7800; fax (212) 353-9439; e-mail info@uscj.org; internet www.uscj.org; f. 1913; 760 affiliated congregations in North America representing c. 1.5m. mems; Pres. Dr RAYMOND GOLDSTEIN; Exec. Vice-Pres. Rabbi JEROME EPSTEIN.

SIKHISM

At mid-2000 there were an estimated 234,000 Sikhs in the USA.

International Sikh Organization: 1901 Pennsylvania Ave, NW, Washington, DC 20006; Pres. Dr GURMIT SINGH AULAKH.

Sikh Center: 2514 West Warner Ave, Santa Ana, CA 92704; tel. (714) 979-9604; e-mail info@sikhcenter.org; internet www.sikhcenter.org; Chief Admin. Siri Singh Sahib HARBHAJAN SINGH KHALSA YOGIJI; Sec.-Gen. SARDANI GURU AMRIT KAUR KHALSA.

The Press

The USA publishes more newspapers and periodicals than any other country. Most dailies give a greater emphasis to local news because of the strong interest in local and regional affairs and the decentralized structure of many government services. These factors, together with the distribution problem inherent in the size of the country, are responsible for the lack of national newspapers. In 2005 the Newspaper Association of America (NAA) estimated that some 51.6% of the adult population read a daily newspaper.

Most influential and highly respected among the few newspapers with a national readership are *USA Today*, the *New York Times*, the *Washington Post*, *Los Angeles Times* and *The Wall Street Journal*

THE UNITED STATES OF AMERICA

(the financial and news daily with editions in New York City, California, Illinois and Texas, and a European and an Asian edition).

In 2005, according to the NAA, 34 daily newspapers had circulations of over 250,000 copies. Among the largest of these, in order of daily circulation in 2004, were *USA Today, The Wall Street Journal, The New York Times, Los Angeles Times, The Washington Post, Chicago Tribune, New York Daily News, The Morning News, The Philadelphia Inquirer* and *The Houston Chronicle*.

In 2005 there were 1,452 English-language daily newspapers, with a total circulation of 53.3m. copies per day. The Sunday edition is an important and distinctive feature of US newspaper publishing; many Sunday newspapers run to over 300 pages. In 2005 there were 914 Sunday newspapers, with a total circulation of about 55.3m. In the same year there were 6,659 weekly newspapers.

The famous tradition of press freedom in the USA is grounded in the First Amendment to the Constitution which declares that 'Congress shall make no law... abridging the freedom of speech or of the Press...' and confirmed in the legislations of many states which prohibit any kind of legal restriction on the dissemination of news.

Legislation affecting the Press is both state and federal. A source of controversy between the Press and the courts has been the threat of the encroachment by judicial decrees on the area of courtroom and criminal trial coverage. In 1972 the Supreme Court ruled that journalists were not entitled to refuse to give evidence before grand juries on information they have received confidentially. Since then the frequent issuing of subpoenas to journalists and the jailing of several reporters for refusing to disclose sources has led to many 'shield' bills being put before Congress and state legislatures calling for immunity for journalists from both federal and state jurisdiction.

In recent years, increased production costs have subjected the industry to considerable economic strain, resulting in mergers and take-overs, a great decline in competition between dailies in the same city, and the appearance of inter-city dailies catering for two or more adjoining centres. A consequence of these trends has been the steady growth of newspaper groups or chains.

The following are among the principal daily newspaper groups:

Advance Publications, Inc: 950 Fingerboard Rd, Staten Island; tel. (212) 286-2860; fax (718) 981-1456; internet www.advance.net; Chair. SAMUEL I. (SI) NEWHOUSE, Jr; Pres. DONALD E. NEWHOUSE; interests in cable television and internet news websites; owns Condé Nast Publications, Parade Publications, Fairchild Publications and American City Business Journals, among others

    Newhouse Newspapers: 711 Third Ave, 15th Floor, New York, NY 10017; tel. (212) 697-8020; fax (212) 972-3146; e-mail toren.beasely@newhouse.com; internet www.newhouse.com; Pres. DONALD E. NEWHOUSE; Man. Editor TOREN BEASELY; 26 daily newspapers incl. *The Star-Ledger, The Plain Dealer* and *The Oregonian*; more than 40 weekly newspapers.

American Community Newspapers: 14875 Landmark Blvd, Suite 110, Dallas, TX 75254; tel. (972) 628-4080; fax (972) 801-3496; e-mail webinfo@mnsun.com; internet www.americancommunitynewspapers.com; CEO GENE M. CARR; 3 daily and 60 weekly newspapers, incl. the Sun Newspapers group, and four speciality pubs; combined circ. c. 950,000.

Block Communications, Inc (BCI): 6450 Monroe St, Sylvania, OH 43560; tel. (419) 724-6212; e-mail info@blockcommunications.com; internet www.blockcommunications.com; f. 1900; Chair. WILLIAM BLOCK, Jr; Man. Dir ALLAN BLOCK; 2 daily newspapers, *The Pittsburgh Post-Gazette* and *The Toledo Blade*; also owns 2 cable cos, 5 television stations and a telephone co; interests in security, cable construction and advertising.

The Copley Press, Inc: 7776 Ivanhoe Ave, La Jolla, CA 92037; tel. (858) 454-0411; fax (858) 729-7629; internet www.copleynewspapers.com; f. 1928; Chair., Pres. and CEO DAVID C. COPLEY; 9 daily newspapers, incl. *The San Diego Union-Tribune*, 8 weekly newspapers and 1 bi-weekly newspaper; owns the Copley News Service syndicate (f. 1955).

Cox Newspapers, Inc: 6205 Peachtree Dunwoody Rd, Atlanta, GA 30328; tel. (678) 645-0000; e-mail christopher.caneles@coxinc.com; internet www.coxnews.com; f. 1898; Pres. JAY R. SMITH; 17 daily newspapers, incl. *The Atlanta Journal-Constitution*, and 26 weekly newspapers; combined weekday circ. 1.2m., combined Sun. circ. 1.6m.

Dow Jones & Co Inc: 1 World Financial Center, 200 Liberty St, New York, NY 10281; tel. (212) 416-2000; fax (212) 416-3478; internet www.dowjones.com; f. 1882; acquired by News Corporation in December 2007; CEO RICHARD F. ZANNINO; pubs incl. *The Wall Street Journal*, the weekly financial magazine *Barron's* and the monthly *Far Eastern Economic Review*; also incl. the community newspaper subsidiary

    Ottaway Newspapers, Inc (ONI): POB 401, Campbell Hall, NY 10916; tel. (845) 294-8181; e-mail dwaterman@ottaway.com; internet www.ottaway.com; f. 1936; merged with Dow Jones in 1970; Chair. and CEO JOHN WILCOX; 8 daily, and 14 weekly newspapers; over 20 other pubs; daily print circ. 280,711, Sun. circ. 303,468 (March 2007).

Freedom Communications, Inc: 17666 Fitch, Irvine, CA 92614-6022; tel. (949) 253-2300; fax (949) 474-7675; e-mail info@link.freedom.com; internet www.freedom.com; Chair. THOMAS W. BASSETT; CEO SCOTT N. FLANDERS; 33 daily newspapers, incl. *The Orange County Register*, and 77 weekly pubs; combined weekday circ. c. 1.2m.; owns 9 television stations.

Gannett Co Inc: 7950 Jones Branch Dr., McLean, VA 22107; tel. (703) 854-6000; fax (703) 854-2046; e-mail gcishare@gannett.com; internet www.gannett.com; f. 1906; Chair., Pres. and CEO CRAIG A. DUBOW; 85 daily newspapers incl. *USA Today, Detroit Free Press* and *The Arizona Republic*, c. 1,000 non-daily pubs; combined weekday circ. 7.2m. (of which c. 2.3m. *USA Today*); owns 23 television stations broadcasting to 18.1% of the USA, and more than 130 internet websites; owns and operates Newsquest Media Group (United Kingdom).

Hearst Corpn: Hearst Tower, 12th Floor, 300 West 57th St, New York, NY 10019; tel. (212) 649-4190; fax (212) 649-2108; internet www.hearstcorp.com; acquired Prime Time, Inc (publr, San Antonio region) in late 2006; Chair. GEORGE R. HEARST, Jr; Pres. and CEO VICTOR F. GANZI; 12 daily newspapers, incl. the *Houston Chronicle* and *San Francisco Chronicle*, and 7 weekly newspapers; 19 monthly magazines incl. *Good Housekeeping, Cosmopolitan, O, The Oprah Magazine* and *Redbook*; owns or operates 29 television stations broadcasting to 18% of the US market; interests in radio broadcasting, cable networks, interactive media and business information publishing.

Lee Enterprises: 201 North Harrison St, Davenport, IA 52801-1939; tel. (563) 383-2100; e-mail dan.hayes@lee.net; internet www.lee.net; f. 1890; Chair., Pres. and CEO MARY E. JUNCK; 50 daily newspapers (jt interest in further 4 dailies) and more than 300 weekly newspapers and speciality pubs; combined weekday circ. 1.6m., combined Sunday circ. 1.9m.; interests in publishing, and purchasing and distribution of raw materials.

The McClatchy Co: 2100 Q St, Sacramento, CA 95816-6899; tel. (916) 321-1855; fax (916) 321-1869; e-mail contact@mcclatchy.com; internet www.mcclatchy.com; acquired Knight Ridder in 2006; established 10 foreign news bureaux in that year; sold largest daily *Star Tribune* to Avista Capital Partners (New York) in early 2007; Chair., Pres. and CEO GARY B. PRUITT; 31 daily newspapers, incl. the *Miami Herald*, and community newspapers.

Media General, Inc: 333 East Franklin St, Richmond, VA 23219; tel. (804) 649-6000; e-mail etucker@mediageneral.com; internet www.mediageneral.com; Chair. J. STEWART BRYAN, III; Pres. and CEO MARSHALL N. MORTON; 25 daily newspapers, incl. *The Tampa Tribune*, and c. 100 weekly newspapers and other pubs; holds a 20% interest in *The Denver Post*; owns 23 network-affiliated television stations.

MediaNews Group: 101 Colfax Ave, Suite 1100, Denver, CO 80202; tel. (303) 954-6360; fax (303) 954-6320; e-mail contact@medianewsgroup.com; internet www.medianewsgroup.com; Vice-Chair. and CEO WILLIAM DEAN SINGLETON; Pres. JOSEPH J. LODOVIC, IV; 57 daily newspapers incl. *The Denver Post* (under a jt operating agreement with *The Rocky Mountain News*, publ. by E. W. Scripps); combined weekday circ. 2.6m., combined Sun. circ. 2.9m.; owns a television station in Arkansas and radio stations in Texas.

New York Times Co: 620 Eighth Ave, New York, NY 10018; tel. (212) 556-1234; internet www.nytco.com; Chair. ARTHUR SULZBERGER, Jr; Pres. and CEO JANET L. ROBINSON; 18 daily newspapers incl. *The New York Times, The International Herald Tribune* and *The Boston Globe*; owns one radio station and c. 50 internet websites; sold Broadcast Media Group to Oak Hill Capital Partners in May 2007.

E. W. Scripps Co: 312 Walnut St, 2800 Scripps Center, Cincinnati, OH 45202; POB 5380, Cincinnati, OH 45201; tel. (513) 977-3000; fax (513) 977-3721; e-mail corpcomm@scripps.com; internet www.scripps.com; Pres. and CEO KENNETH W. LOWE; Exec. Vice-Pres. and COO RICHARD A. BOEHNE; 21 daily newspapers, incl. *The Rocky Mountain News* (under a jt operating agreement with *The Denver Post*, publ. by MediaNews), and 8 community newspapers; owns the Scripps Howard News Service syndicate, 10 television stations, and 6 cable and satellite programming networks.

Tribune Publishing: 435 North Michigan Ave, Chicago, IL 60611; tel. (312) 222-9100; fax (312) 222-4760; e-mail corp.info@tribune.com; internet www.tribune.com; f. 1847; subsidiary of Tribune Co; merged with the Times Mirror Co in 2000; Tribune Co acquired by private investor in April 2007; Chair., Pres. and CEO DENNIS J. FITZSIMONS; 13 daily newspapers incl. *Newsday*, the *Chicago Tribune*, the *Los Angeles Times*, the *Baltimore Sun* and the Spanish-language newspaper *Hoy*; over 130 other pubs; combined weekday circ. 8.0m., combined Sun. circ. 12.0m; operates 23 television stations.

THE UNITED STATES OF AMERICA

PRINCIPAL DAILY AND SUNDAY NEWSPAPERS

Alabama

Birmingham News: 2201 Fourth Ave North, POB 2553, Birmingham, AL 35202; tel. (205) 325-4444; fax (205) 325-3278; internet www.bhamnews.com; f. 1888; Publr Victor H. Hanson, III; Editor Thomas Scarritt; circ. Mon. to Fri. 150,174, Sat. 145,308, Sun. 180,451.

Huntsville Times: 2317 South Memorial Parkway, Huntsville, AL 35801-5623; tel. (256) 532-4000; fax (256) 532-4213; e-mail htimes@htimes.com; internet www.htimes.com; f. 1910; Publr Bob Ludwig; Editor Melinda Gorham; circ. Mon. to Fri. 52,852, Sat. 51,029, Sun. 71,793.

Press-Register: 304 Government St, POB 2488, Mobile, AL 36652-2488; tel. (251) 219-5454; fax (334) 434-8662; e-mail newsroom@press-register.com; internet www.press-register.com; f. 1813; Publr Mike Marshall; Man. Editor Dewey English; circ. Mon. to Fri. 99,742, Sat. 90,953, Sun 114,247.

Montgomery Advertiser: 425 Molton St, Montgomery, AL 36104; tel. (334) 262-1611; fax (334) 261-1521; e-mail advertiser@compuserve.com; internet www.montgomeryadvertiser.com; f. 1828; Publr Scott M. Brown; Exec. Editor Wanda S. Lloyd; circ. Mon. to Fri. 49,703, Sat. 46,610, Sun. 57,955.

Alaska

Anchorage Daily News: 1001 Northway Dr., POB 149001, Anchorage, AK 99514-9001; tel. (907) 257-4200; fax (907) 257-4246; e-mail newsroom@adn.com; internet www.adn.com; f. 1946; Pres. and Publr Michael Sexton; Senior Vice-Pres. and Editor W. Patrick Dougherty; circ. Mon. to Fri. 64,109, Sat. 62,921, Sun. 72,488.

Arizona

Arizona Daily Star: 4850 South Park Ave, POB 26807, Tucson, AZ 85726-6807; tel. (520) 573-4220; fax (520) 573-4107; e-mail jhumenik@azstarnet.com; internet www.azstarnet.com; f. 1877; Publr and Editor John M. Humenik; Exec. Editor Bobbie Jo Buel; circ. Mon. to Fri. 116,345, Sat. 108,960, Sun. 168,861.

Arizona Republic: 200 East Van Buren St, Phoenix, AZ 85004; tel. (602) 444-8000; fax (602) 444-8933; internet www.azcentral.com/arizonarepublic; f. 1890; Exec. Editor Randy Lovely; circ. 1.5m. a week.

Tucson Citizen: 4850 South Park Ave, Tucson, AZ 85714-1637; tel. (520) 573-4561; fax (520) 573-4569; e-mail citizen@tucsoncitizen.com; internet www.tucsoncitizen.com; f. 1870; Publr and Editor Michael Chihak; circ. Mon. to Fri. 25,987, Sat. 24,829.

Arkansas

Democrat-Gazette: 121 East Capitol Ave, POB 2221, Little Rock, AR 72203; tel. (501) 378-3400; fax (501) 372-3908; e-mail fbrooks@arkansasonline.com; internet www2.arkansasonline.com; f. 1819; morning; Publr Walter E. Hussman, Jr; Exec. Editor Griffin Smith; circ. Mon. to Fri. 182,789, Sat. 180,551, Sun. 276,436.

California

Bakersfield Californian: POB 440, Bakersfield, CA 93302-0440; tel. (805) 395-7500; fax (805) 395-7519; internet www.bakersfield.com; f. 1866; Publr and Chair. Ginger Moorhouse; Exec. Editor Mike Jenner; circ. Mon. to Fri. 62,619, Sat. 64,208, Sun. 72,557.

Daily Breeze: Copley Los Angeles Newspapers, 5215 Torrance Blvd, Torrance, CA 90503; tel. (310) 540-5511; e-mail newsroom@dailybreeze.com; internet www.dailybreeze.com; f. 1894; Mon. to Sat. evening, Sun. morning; Publr Liz Gaier; Exec. Editor Philip Sanfield; circ. Mon. to Fri. 69,264, Sat. 74,047, Sun. 70,594.

Daily News: 21221 Oxnard St, Woodland Hills, POB 4200, CA 91365; tel. (818) 713-3000; fax (818) 713-0057; e-mail feedback@dailynews.com; internet www.dailynews.com; f. 1911; publ. by Los Angeles Newspaper Group; morning; Publr John McKeon; Editor Ron Kaye; circ. Mon. to Fri. 145,528, Sat. 130,614, Sun. 166,640.

Fresno Bee: 1626 E St, Fresno, CA 93786; tel. (559) 441-6111; fax (559) 441-6436; internet www.fresnobee.com; f. 1922; Publr and Pres. Ray Steele, Jr; Exec. Editor Betsy Lumbye; circ. Mon. to Fri. 157,546, Sat. 162,811, Sun. 180,043.

Investor's Business Daily: 12655 Beatrice St, Los Angeles, CA 90066; tel. (310) 448-6700; fax (310) 577-7301; e-mail ibdnews@investors.com; internet www.investors.com; f. 1984; morning; Publr W. Scott O'Neill; Editor-in-Chief Wesley F. Mann; circ. Mon. to Fri. 166,669.

Los Angeles Times: 202 West First St, Los Angeles, CA 90012; tel. (213) 237-5000; fax (213) 237-7679; e-mail nancy.sullivan@latimes.com; internet www.latimes.com; f. 1881; Pres. and Publr David D. Hiller; Editor Russ Stanton; circ. Mon. to Fri. 815,723, Sat. 915,423, Sun. 1,173,096.

Modesto Bee: 1325 H St, POB 3928, Modesto, CA 95352; tel. (209) 578-2000; fax (209) 578-2207; e-mail mrandazzo@modbee.com; internet www.modbee.com; f. 1884; Publr Margaret Randazzo; Exec. Editor Mark Vasché; circ. Mon. to Fri. 80,559, Sat. 90,565, Sun. 86,055.

Oakland Tribune: 401 13th St, Alameda, CA 94612; tel. (510) 208-6300; fax (510) 208-6477; internet www.oaklandtribune.com; f. 1874; Editor Pete Wevurksi; circ. Mon. to Fri. 47,768, Sat. 41,187, Sun. 44,346.

Orange County Register: 625 North Grand Ave, POB 11626, Santa Ana, CA 92701-4347; tel. (714) 767-7000; fax (714) 796-3681; e-mail customerservice@ocregister.com; internet www.ocregister.com; CEO and Publr N. Christian Anderson, III; Editor Ken Brusic; circ. Mon. to Fri. 284,613, Sat. 299,385, Sun. 329,549.

Press Democrat: 427 Mendocino Ave, POB 569, Santa Rosa, CA 95402; tel. (707) 546-2020; fax (707) 521-5330; internet www.pressdemocrat.com; f. 1857; Publr Bruce W. Kyse; Exec. Editor Catherine Barnett; circ. Mon. to Fri. 84,014, Sat. 83,424, Sun. 83,436.

Press Enterprise: 3512 14th St, POB 792, Riverside, CA 92501; tel. (951) 368-9403; fax (951) 368-9022; e-mail mdevarenne@pe.com; internet www.pe.com; f. 1878; publ. by Belo Corpn; morning; Publr Ronald R. Redfern; Editor Maria De Varenne; circ. Mon. to Fri. 172,593, Sat. 175,174, Sun. 178,062.

Press-Telegram: 300 Oceangate, Long Beach, CA 90844-0001; tel. (562) 435-1161; fax (562) 437-7892; e-mail mark.stevens@presstelegram.com; internet www.presstelegram.com; Publr Dave Kuta; Exec. Editor Rich Archbold; circ. Mon. to Fri. 87,600, Sat. 75,453, Sun. 86,313.

Sacramento Bee: 2100 Q St, POB 15779, Sacramento, CA 95826; tel. (916) 321-1000; fax (916) 321-1100; e-mail jheapy@sacbee.com; internet www.sacbee.com; f. 1857; Pres. and Publr Janis Heaphy; Exec. Editor Rick Rodriguez; circ. Mon. to Fri. 279,032, Sat. 293,273, Sun. 324,613.

San Bernardino County Sun: 2239 Gannett Parkway, San Bernardino, CA 92407; tel. (909) 889-9666; fax (909) 381-3976; e-mail nancy.kay@sbsun.com; internet www.sbsun.com; f. 1894; Publr Fred Hamilton; Editor Steve Lambert; circ. Mon. to Fri. 60,993, Sat. 58,047, Sun. 67,960.

San Diego Union-Tribune: 350 Camino de la Reina, San Diego, CA 92108; tel. (619) 299-3131; fax (619) 293-1896; e-mail letters@uniontrib.com; internet www.uniontrib.com; f. 1868; Publr David Copley; Sr Editor Bill Osborne; circ. Mon. to Fri. 296,331, Sat. 338,196, Sun. 378,696.

San Francisco Chronicle: 901 Mission St, San Francisco, CA 94103; tel. (415) 777-1111; fax (415) 896-1107; e-mail letters@sfchronicle.com; internet www.sfgate.com; f. 1865; subsidiary of Hearst Communications; Publr and Pres. Frank J. Vega; Exec. Vice-Pres. and Editor Philip Bronstein; circ. Mon. to Fri. 386,564, Sat. 392,375, Sun. 438,006.

San Francisco Examiner: 450 Mission, San Francisco, CA 94105; tel. (415) 359-2600; fax (415) 359-2766; e-mail sfeditor@examiner.com; internet www.examiner.com; f. 1887; Publr John Wilcox; Exec. Editor James Pimentel; circ. Mon. to Fri. 70,000, Sat. 90,000.

San Jose Mercury News: 750 Ridder Park Dr., San Jose, CA 95190-0001; tel. (408) 920-5000; fax (408) 288-8060; internet www.mercurynews.com; f. 1851; owned by MediaNews Group; Publr Jeff Kiel; Editor Carole Leigh Hutton; circ. Mon. to Fri. 230,870, Sat. 207,737, Sun. 251,666.

Stockton Record: 530 East Market St, POB 900, Stockton, CA 95201; tel. (209) 943-6397; fax (209) 547-8186; e-mail newsroom@recordnet.com; internet www.recordnet.com; f. 1895; Publr Roger Coover; Editor Mike Klocke; circ. Mon. to Fri. 58,670, Sat. 56,740, Sun. 62,910.

Colorado

Denver Post: 101 West Colfax Ave, Denver, CO 80202; tel. (303) 954-1010; fax (303) 820-1369; e-mail newsroom@denverpost.com; internet www.denverpost.com; f. 1892; Publr William Dean Singleton; Editor Gregory Moore; circ. Mon. to Fri. 254,058, Sun. 704,168.

The Gazette: 30 South Prospect, Colorado Springs, CO 80903; tel. (719) 632-5511; fax (719) 636-0202; e-mail liz.cobb@gazette.com; internet www.gazette.com; f. 1872; Pres. and Publr P. Scott McKibben; Editor Jeff Thomas; circ. Mon. to Fri. 95,011, Sat. 89,895, Sun. 108,639.

Rocky Mountain News: 101 West Colfax Ave, Suite 500, Denver, CO 80202; tel. (303) 954-5000; fax (303) 892-5081; e-mail subscribe@rockymountainnews.com; internet www.rockymountainnews.com; f. 1859; Publr, Pres. and Editor John R. Temple; circ. Mon. to Fri. 253,834, Sat. 550,088.

THE UNITED STATES OF AMERICA   *Directory*

Connecticut

Connecticut Post: 410 State St, Bridgeport, CT 06604-4501; tel. (203) 333-0161; fax (203) 366-8158; e-mail edit@ctpost.com; internet www.connpost.com; f. 1883; Pres. and Publr ROBERT H. LASKA; Editor JAMES SMITH; circ. Mon. to Fri. 77,015, Sat. 72,249, Sun. 85,815.

Hartford Courant: 285 Broad St, Hartford, CT 06115; tel. (860) 241-6200; fax (860) 520-3176; e-mail letters@courant.com; internet www.courant.com; f. 1764; Publr and CEO STEPHEN D. CARVER; Editor CLIFFORD TEUTSCH; circ. Mon. to Fri. 175,759, Sat. 165,961, Sun. 255,419.

New Haven Register: 40 Sargent Dr., New Haven, CT 06511; tel. (203) 789-5200; fax (203) 865-7894; e-mail kwalsh@nhregister.com; internet www.nhregister.com; f. 1812; Publr KEVIN F. WALSH; Editor JACK KRAMER; circ. Mon. to Fri. 84,778, Sat. 63,161, Sun. 92,947.

Waterbury Republican-American: American-Republican, Inc, 389 Meadow St, POB 2090, Waterbury, CT 06722-2090; tel. (203) 574-3636; fax (203) 596-9277; e-mail falcetti@rep-am.com; internet www.rep-am.com; f. 1844; morning; Publr WILLIAM J. PAPE, II; Exec. Editor JONATHAN F. KELLOGG; circ. Mon. to Fri. 52,100, Sat. 49,267, Sun. 59,173.

Delaware

News Journal: POB 15505, Wilmington, DE 19850; tel. (302) 324-2500; fax (302) 856-3919; e-mail newsroom@newsjournal.com; internet www.newsjournal.com; f. 1871; Publr CURTIS W. RIDDLE; Exec. Editor DAVID LEDFORD; circ. Mon. to Fri. 114,435, Sat. 109,095, Sun. 131,796.

District of Columbia

Washington Post: 1150 15th St, NW, Washington, DC 20071; tel. (202) 334-6000; fax (202) 334-5693; internet www.washingtonpost.com; f. 1877; Chair. BOISFEUILLET JONES; Publr KATHARINE WEYMOUTH; Exec. Editor LEONARD DOWNIE, Jr; Man. Editor PHILIP BENNETT; circ. Mon. to Fri. 699,130, Sat. 636,945, Sun. 929,921.

Washington Times: 3600 New York Ave, NE, Washington, DC 20002-1947; tel. (202) 636-3000; fax (202) 832-2982; internet www.washingtontimes.com; f. 1982; Editor-in-Chief WESLEY PRUDEN; Man. Editor FRANCIS B. COOMBS, Jr; circ. Mon. to Fri. 100,258, Sat. 69,701, Sun. 36,959.

Florida

Daytona Beach News-Journal: 901 Sixth St, Daytona Beach, FL 32117; tel. (386) 252-1511; internet www.news-journalonline.com; f. 1904; morning; Publr, CEO and Pres. GEORGIA M. KANEY; Exec. Editor DON LINLEY; circ. Mon. to Fri. 104,919, Sat. 107,148, Sun. 121,970.

Diario Las Américas: 2900 NW 39th St, Miami, FL 33142; tel. (305) 633-3341; fax (305) 635-7668; internet www.diariolasamericas.com; f. 1953; Spanish; Publr and Editor HORACIO AGUIRRE; circ. Mon. to Sat. 66,000, Sun. 70,000.

Florida Times-Union: 1 Riverside Ave, Jacksonville, FL 32202; POB 1949, Jacksonville, FL 322311; tel. (904) 359-4111; fax (904) 359-4478; e-mail pam.eichholz@jacksonville.com; internet www.jacksonville.com; f. 1864; Publr CARL N. CANNON; Exec. Editor PAT YACK; circ. Mon. to Fri. 155,590, Sat. 166,799, Sun. 214,572.

Florida Today: Cape Publs, Inc, POB 419000, Melbourne, FL 32941-9000; tel. (321) 242-3500; fax (321) 242-6601; internet www.floridatoday.com; f. 1966; morning; Publr and Pres. MARK MIKOLAJCZYK; Exec. Editor TERRY EBERLE; circ. Mon. to Fri. 86,057, Sat. 84,840, Sun. 100,555.

Ledger: POB 408, Lakeland, FL 33802; tel. (863) 802-7099; fax (863) 802-7850; internet www.theledger.com; f. 1924; morning; Publr JEROME FERSON; Exec. Editor SKIP PEREZ; circ. Mon. to Fri. 73,736, Sat. 71,443, Sun. 89,487.

Miami Herald: 1 Herald Plaza, Miami, FL 33132-1693; tel. (305) 350-2111; fax (305) 376-5287; internet www.miamiherald.com; f. 1910; Publr and Pres. DAVID LANDSBERG; Exec. Editor ANDERS GYLLENHAAL; circ. Mon. to Fri. 272,299, Sat. 289,955, Sun. 342,432.

News-Press: 2442 Dr Martin Luther King Jr Blvd, Fort Myers, FL 33901-3987; tel. (941) 335-0200; fax (941) 332-7581; e-mail response@news-press.com; internet www.news-press.com; f. 1884; morning; Publr CAROL HUDLER; Sr Man. Editor CINDY MCCURRY-ROSS; circ. Mon. to Fri. 96,675, Sat. 97,063, Sun. 115,783.

Orlando Sentinel: 633 North Orange Ave, Orlando, FL 32801; tel. (407) 420-5000; fax (407) 420-5350; e-mail insight@orlandosentinel.com; internet www.orlandosentinel.com; f. 1876; morning; Publr, Pres. and CEO KATHLEEN WALTZ; Editor CHARLOTTE HALL; circ. Mon. to Fri. 226,854, Sat. 223,419, Sun. 335,689.

Palm Beach Post: 2751 South Dixie Hwy, West Palm Beach, FL 33405; tel. (561) 820-4100; fax (561) 820-4407; internet www.pbpost.com; f. 1916; Publr TOM GIUFFRIDA; Man. Editor BILL ROSE; Editor JOHN BARTOSEK; circ. Mon. to Fri. 175,495, Sat. 173,970, Sun. 204,847.

Pensacola News Journal: 101 East Romana St, Pensacola, FL 32502; POB 12710, Pensacola, FL 32591; tel. (850) 435-8500; fax (850) 435-8633; e-mail news@pensacolanewsjournal.com; internet www.pnj.com; f. 1889; Publr KEVIN DOYLE; Exec. Editor RICHARD SCHNEIDER; circ. Mon. to Fri. 63,461, Sat. 56,074, Sun. 73,999.

Sarasota Herald-Tribune: 1741 Main St, Sarasota, FL 34236; tel. (941) 953-7755; fax (941) 957-5276; internet www.newscoast.com; f. 1925; Publr DIANE MCFARLIN; Exec. Editor MIKE CONNELLY; circ. Mon. to Fri. 118,328, Sat. 119,083, Sun. 134,101.

St Petersburg Times: 490 First Ave South, POB 1121, St Petersburg, FL 33701; tel. (727) 893-8111; fax (813) 893-8200; e-mail letters@sptimes.com; internet www.sptimes.com; f. 1894; Chair., Editor and CEO PAUL TASH; circ. Mon. to Fri. 323,031, Sat. 341,156, Sun. 422,410 (2006).

Sun-Sentinel: 200 East Las Olas Blvd, Fort Lauderdale, FL 33301-2293; tel. (954) 356-4000; fax (954) 356-4559; internet www.sun-sentinel.com; f. 1960; Publr HOWARD GREENBERG; Editor JEFF GLICK; circ. Mon. to Fri. 226,591, Sat. 241,902, Sun. 319,103.

Tampa Tribune: 200 Parker St, Tampa, FL 33606; POB 191, Tampa, FL 33601; tel. (813) 259-7111; fax (813) 254-4952; internet www.tampatrib.com; f. 1893; morning; Publr and Pres. DENISE E. PALMER; Editor JANET COATS; circ. Mon. to Fri. 226,990, Sat. 225,576.

Georgia

Atlanta Journal-Constitution: 72 Marietta St, POB 4689, Atlanta, GA 30302-4689; tel. (404) 526-5151; fax (404) 526-5746; e-mail access@ajc.com; internet www.ajc.com; f. 1950; Sun. morning; Publr JOHN MELLOT; Editor JULIA WALLACE; circ. Mon. to Fri. 357,399, Sat. 367,110, Sun. 523,687.

Augusta Chronicle: 725 Broad St, POB 1928, Augusta, GA 30903-1928; tel. (706) 823-3258; fax (706) 722-5746; internet chronicle.augusta.com; f. 1785; Morris Communications Co, LLC; Publr. WILLIAM S. MORRIS, III; Exec. Editor DENNIS SODOMKA; circ. Mon. to Fri. 73,561, Sat. 72,650, Sun. 92,418.

Macon Telegraph: 120 Broadway, Macon, GA 31201; POB 4167, Macon, GA 31208; tel. (478) 744-4200; fax (478) 744-4663; e-mail letters@macontel.com; internet www.macon.com; f. 1826; Publr PAMELA J. BROWNING; Exec. Editor SHERRIE MARSHALL; circ. Mon. to Fri. 58,922, Sat. 56,910, Sun. 73,395.

Savannah Morning News: 1375 Chatham Parkway, Savannah, GA 31401; POB 1088, Savannah, GA 31402-1088; tel. (912) 236-9511; fax (912) 234-6522; internet www.savannahnow.com; f. 1850; Publr JULIAN MILLER; Exec. Editor SUSAN CATRON, Jr; circ. Mon. to Fri. 51,456, Sat. 49,030, Sun. 64,308.

Hawaii

Honolulu Advertiser: The News Bldg, 605 Kapi'olani Blvd, POB 3110, Honolulu, HI 96802; tel. (808) 525-7620; fax (808) 535-2415; e-mail hawaii@honoluluadvertiser.com; internet www.honoluluadvertiser.com; f. 1856; Pres. and Publr LEE P. WEBBER; Editor MARK PLATTE; circ. Mon. to Fri. 141,934, Sat. 153,054, Sun. 155,932.

Honolulu Star-Bulletin: Restaurant Row, 7 Waterfront Plaza, Suite 210, 500 Ala Moana, Honolulu, HI 96813; tel. (808) 529-4747; fax (808) 529-4750; e-mail mrovner@starbulletin.com; internet www.starbulletin.com; f. 1882; Pres. DENNIS FRANCIS; Editor FRANK BRIDGEWATER; circ. 66,000.

Idaho

Idaho Statesman: 1200 North Curtis Rd, POB 40, Boise, ID 83707; tel. (208) 377-6200; fax (208) 377-6449; e-mail vgowler@idahostatesman.com; internet www.idahostatesman.com; f. 1864; Publr MI-AI PARRISH; Editor and Vice-Pres. VICKI S. GOWLER; circ. Mon. to Fri. 63,661, Sat. 66,810, Sun. 83,787.

Illinois

Chicago Sun-Times: 350 N. Orleans St, 10th Floor, Chicago, IL 60654; tel. (312) 321-3000; fax (312) 321-3084; e-mail letters@suntimes.com; internet www.suntimes.com; f. 1948; Publr JOHN CRUICKSHANK; Editor-in-Chief MICHAEL COOKE; circ. Mon. to Sat. 600,988, Sun. 445,000.

Chicago Tribune: 435 North Michigan Ave, Chicago, IL 60611-4041; tel. (312) 222-3232; fax (312) 222-4674; internet www.chicagotribune.com; f. 1847; publ. by Chicago Tribune Co; two sister newspapers: *RedEye* and *Hoy Chicago*; Publr, Pres. and CEO SCOTT C. SMITH; Editor ANN MARIE LIPINSKI; circ. Mon. to Fri. 566,827, Sat 473,849, Sun. 940,620.

Daily Herald: POB 280, Arlington Heights, IL 60006; tel. (847) 427-4300; fax (847) 427-4608; internet www.dailyherald.com; f. 1872; owned by Paddock Publications Inc; Publr and Chair. DANIEL E.

BAUMANN; Editor JOHN LAMPINEN; circ. Mon. to Fri. 151,190, Sat. 144,039, Sun. 149,613.

Journal Star: 1 News Plaza, Peoria, IL 61643; tel. (309) 686-3000; fax (309) 686-3296; e-mail kmauser@pjstar.com; internet www.pjstar.com; f. 1855; Publr KEN MAUSER; Man. Editor JACK BRIMEYER; circ. Mon. to Fri. 66,216, Sat. 72,941, Sun. 82,654.

The Pantagraph: 301 West Washington St, POB 2907, Bloomington, IL 61702-2907; tel. (309) 829-9000; fax (309) 829-9104; e-mail linda.lindus@lee.net; internet www.pantagraph.com; f. 1837; Publr LINDA LINDUS; Man. Editor JULIA GERKE; circ. Mon. to Fri. 47,759, Sat. 45,428, Sun. 50,066.

Rockford Register Star: 99 East State St, Rockford, IL 61104; tel. (815) 987-1200; fax (815) 987-1365; internet www.rrstar.com; f. 1888; acquired by GateHouse Media from Gannett Co in 2007; Publr FRITZ JACOBI; Exec. Editor LINDA GRIST CUNNINGHAM; circ. Mon. to Fri. 58,069, Sat. 58,024, Sun. 70,795.

State Journal-Register: 1 Copley Plaza, POB 219, Springfield, IL 62705-0219; tel. (217) 788-1300; fax (217) 788-1551; e-mail sjr@sj-r.com; internet www.sj-r.com; f. 1831; Publr SUE SCHMITT; Editor BARRY J. LOCHER; circ. Mon. to Fri. 52,562, Sat. 51,781, Sun. 61,178.

Indiana

Evansville Courier and Press: 300 Walnut St, POB 268, Evansville, IN 47713; tel. (812) 424-7711; fax (812) 422-8196; e-mail courierpress@evansville.net; internet www.courierpress.com; f. 1845; Publr and Pres. JACK PATE; Man. Editor LINDA NEGRO; circ. Mon. to Fri. 68,344, Sat. 66,571, Sun. 87,771.

Indianapolis Star: POB 145, Indianapolis, IN 46206-0145; tel. (317) 444-8005; fax (317) 633-1038; internet www.indystar.com; Publr and Pres. BARBARA A. HENRY; Editor DENNIS R. RYERSON; circ. Mon. to Fri. 261,405, Sat. 225,926, Sun. 354,312.

Journal-Gazette: 600 West Main St, Fort Wayne, IN 46802; tel. (260) 461-8831; fax (219) 461-8648; e-mail pbeber@jg.net; internet www.journalgazette.net; f. 1863; publ. by Fort Wayne Newspapers; Publr JULIE INSKEEP; Editor CRAIG KLUGMAN; circ. Mon. to Fri. 66,918, Sat. 90,761, Sun. 117,777.

News-Sentinel: 600 West Main St, POB 100, Fort Wayne, IN 46802; tel. (260) 461-8439; fax (260) 461-8817; e-mail nsnews@news-sentinel.com; internet www.news-sentinel.com; f. 1833; publ. by Fort Wayne Newspapers; Publr MICHAEL J. CHRISTMAN; Editor KERRY HUBARTT; circ. Mon. to Fri. 26,385, Sat. 25,979.

Post-Tribune: 1433 East 83rd Ave, Merrillville, IN 46410; tel. (219) 648-3100; fax (219) 881-3249; internet www.post-trib.com; f. 1907; Publr MURDOCH DAVIS; Exec. Editor PAULETTE HADDIX; circ. Mon. to Fri. 66,901, Sat. 63,249, Sun. 67,974.

South Bend Tribune: 225 West Colfax Ave, South Bend, IN 46626; tel. (574) 235-6161; fax (574) 236-1765; e-mail mclein@sbt.sbtinfo.com; internet www.southbendtribune.com; f. 1872; Publr and Editor DAVID C. RAY; circ. Mon. to Fri. 68,901, Sat. 77,651, Sun. 91,862.

The Times: 601 45th Ave, Munster, IN 46325; tel. (219) 932-3100; fax (219) 933-3332; internet www.thetimesonline.com; f. 1906; morning; Publr BILL MASTERSON, Jr; Exec. Editor WILLIAM NANGLE; circ. Mon. to Fri. 82,709, Sat. 79,278, Sun. 89,942.

Iowa

Cedar Rapids Gazette: 500 Third Ave, SE, Cedar Rapids, IA 52401; tel. (319) 398-8211; fax (319) 398-5846; e-mail zack.kucharski@gazettecommunications.com; internet www.gazetteonline.com; f. 1883; Publr and Chair. JOE F. HLADKY, III; Editor MARK BOWDEN; circ. Mon. to Fri. 59,792, Sat. 67,812, Sun. 74,078.

Des Moines Register: 715 Locust St, POB 957, Des Moines, IA 50306-0957; tel. (515) 284-8000; fax (515) 268-2504; e-mail letters@dmreg.com; internet www.dmregister.com; f. 1849; Pres. and Publr LAURA HOLLINGSWORTH; Editor CAROLYN WASHBURN; circ. Mon. to Fri. 146,050, Sat. 142,298, Sun. 233,229.

Quad-City Times: 500 East Third St, POB 3828, Davenport, IA 52801; tel. (563) 383-2200; fax (563) 383-2223; internet www.qctimes.com; f. 1855; division of Lee Enterprises, Inc.; Publr JULIE BECHTEL; Editor STEVE THOMAS; circ. Mon. to Fri. 53,286, Sat. 56,515, Sun. 67,749.

Sioux City Journal: 515 Pavonia St, Sioux City, IA 51102; tel. (712) 293-4250; fax (712) 279-5059; internet www.siouxcityjournal.com; f. 1864; subsidiary of Lee Enterprises, Inc.; Publr RON PETERSON; Editor LARRY MYHRE; circ. Mon. to Fri. 41,092, Sat. 40,229, Sun. 42,323.

Kansas

Topeka Capital-Journal: 616 SE Jefferson St, Topeka, KS 66607; tel. (785) 295-1111; fax (785) 295-1230; e-mail webmaster@cjonline.com; internet www.cjonline.com; f. 1879; Publr MARK NUSBAUM; Exec. Editor PETE GOERING; circ. Mon. to Fri. 44,955, Sat. 45,590, Sun. 54,143.

Wichita Eagle: 825 East Douglas Ave, POB 820, Wichita, KS 67201; tel. (316) 268-6000; fax (316) 268-6438; e-mail wenews@wichitaeagle.com; internet www.kansas.com; f. 1872; Publr LOU HELDMAN; Editor SHERRY CHISENHALL, Jr; circ. Mon. to Fri. 83,903, Sat. 104,320, Sun. 135,998.

Kentucky

Courier-Journal: 525 West Broadway St, Louisville, KY 40202-2137; POB 740031, Louisville, KY 40201; tel. (502) 582-4011; fax (502) 582-4200; e-mail publisher@courier-journal.com; internet www.courier-journal.com; f. 1868; Publr and Pres. DENISE IVEY; Editor BENNIE L. IVORY; circ. Mon. to Fri. 218,796, Sat. 205,009, Sun. 266,594.

Lexington Herald-Leader: 100 Midland Ave, Lexington, KY 40508-1999; tel. (859) 231-3221; e-mail laustin@herald-leader.com; internet www.kentucky.com; f. 1860; Pres. and Publr TIM KELLY; Editor LINDA AUSTIN; circ. Mon. to Fri. 111,124, Sat. 111,663, Sun. 138,986.

Louisiana

Advocate: POB 588, Baton Rouge, LA 70821-0588; tel. (225) 383-1111; fax (225) 388-0371; internet www.2theadvocate.com; f. 1904; morning; Publr DOUGLAS L. MANSHIP; Man. Editor MILFORD FRYER; circ. Mon. to Fri. 96,558, Sat. 101,687, Sun. 123,032.

The Times: 222 Luke St, POB 30222, Shreveport, LA 71130; tel. (318) 459-3200; fax (318) 459-3301; internet www.shreveporttimes.com; f. 1872; Publr PETE ZANMILLER; Exec. Editor ALAN ENGLISH; circ. Mon. to Fri. 54,798, Sat. 55,600, Sun. 68,331.

Times-Picayune: 3800 Howard Ave, New Orleans, LA 70125-1429; tel. (504) 826-3279; fax (504) 826-3700; e-mail pkovacs@timespicayune.com; internet www.nola.com/t-p; f. 1880; Publr ASHTON PHELPS, Jr; Man. Editor PETER KOVACS; Editor JON DONLEY.

Maine

Bangor Daily News: 491 Main St, POB 1329, Bangor, ME 04401; tel. (207) 990-8000; fax (207) 941-9476; e-mail bdnnews@bangordailynews.net; internet www.bangornews.com; f. 1834; Publr RICHARD J. WARREN; Exec. Editor A. MARK WOODWARD; circ. Mon. to Fri. 57,702, Sat. and Sun. 65,374.

Maine Sunday Telegram: 390 Congress St, POB 1460, Portland, ME 04104; tel. (207) 822-4076; fax (207) 879-1042; e-mail info@mainetoday.com; internet www.mainetoday.com; f. 1887; Publr JEAN GANNETT HAWLEY; Exec. Editor LOUIS A. URENECK; circ. 102,904.

Portland Press Herald: 390 Congress St, POB 1460, Portland, ME 04101-5009; tel. (207) 791-6650; fax (207) 791-6931; e-mail herald@portland.com; internet pressherald.mainetoday.com; f. 1862; Publr JEAN GANNETT HAWLEY; Editor and Vice-Pres. JEANNINE A. GUTTMAN; circ. Mon. to Fri. 67,516, Sat. 65,895.

Maryland

Baltimore Sun: 501 North Calvert St, POB 1377, Baltimore, MD 21278; tel. (410) 332-6000; fax (410) 752-6049; e-mail publiceditor@baltsun.com; internet www.baltimoresun.com; f. 1837; Publr, Pres. and CEO TIMOTHY E. RYAN; Editor and Sr Vice-Pres. TIM FRANKLIN; circ. Mon. to Fri. 232,138, Sat. 228,694, Sun. 377,561.

Massachusetts

Boston Globe: 135 Morrissey Blvd, POB 55819, Boston, MA 02205-5819; tel. (617) 929-2000; fax (617) 929-3192; e-mail letters@globe.com; internet www.boston.com; f. 1872; Publr STEVE AINSLEY; Editor MARTIN D. BARON; Exec. Editor HELEN DONOVAN; circ. Mon. to Fri. 382,503, Sat. 355,417, Sun. 562,273.

Boston Herald: 1 Herald Sq., Boston, MA 02118; tel. (617) 426-3000; fax (617) 426-1896; e-mail letterstotheeditor@bostonherald.com; internet www.bostonherald.com; f. 1825; Publr PATRICK PURCELL; Man. Editor KEVIN CONVEY; circ. Mon. to Fri. 201,513, Sat. 146,419, Sun. 110,834.

Christian Science Monitor: 1 Norway St, Boston, MA 02115-3195; tel. (617) 450-2000; internet www.csmonitor.com; f. 1908; publ. by The First Church of Christ Scientist; Editor RICHARD BERGENHEIM; circ. Mon. to Fri. 58,313.

Lowell Sun: 491 Dutton St, Lowell, MA 01853; tel. (978) 458-7100; fax (978) 970-4600; e-mail slaurencio@lowellsun.com; internet www.lowellsun.com; f. 1878; Mon. to Fri. evening, Sat. and Sun. morning; Publr and Pres. MARK O'NEIL; Editor JAMES CAMPANINI; circ. Mon. to Fri. 46,280, Sat. 40,271, Sun. 50,204.

Patriot Ledger: 400 Crown Colony Dr., POB 699159, Quincy, MA 02269-9159; tel. (617) 786-7000; fax (617) 786-7393; e-mail delivery@ledger.com; internet ledger.southofboston.com; f. 1837; mem. of the South of Boston Media Group; Mon. to Fri. evening, weekend; Publr KIRK A. DAVIS; Editor CHAZY DOWALIBY; circ. Mon. to Fri. 52,638, Sat. and Sun. 63,095.

THE UNITED STATES OF AMERICA

The Republican: 1860 Main St, Springfield, MA 01101; tel. (413) 788-1000; fax (413) 788-1301; e-mail blong@repub.com; internet www.repub.com; f. 1824; fmrly Sunday Republican, merged with Union-News in 2003; Publr and CEO LARRY A. MCDERMOTT; Exec. Editor WAYNE E. PHANEUF; circ. Mon. to Fri. 85,798, Sat. 80,053, Sun. 124,492.

Worcester Telegram & Gazette: 20 Franklin St, POB 15012, Worcester, MA 01615-0012; tel. (508) 793-9100; fax (508) 793-9313; e-mail kparent@telegram.com; internet www.telegram.com; f. 1866; Publr BRUCE GAULTNEY; Editor HARRY T. WHITIN; circ. Mon. to Fri. 84,394, Sat. 86,551.

Michigan

Detroit Free Press: 600 West Fort St, Detroit, MI 48226; tel. (313) 222-6400; fax (313) 222-5981; e-mail readrep@freepress.com; internet www.freep.com; f. 1831; Mon. to Fri. morning, Sat. and Sun.; Publr DAVID HUNKE; Exec. Editor CAESAR ANDREWS; circ. Mon. to Fri. 329,989, Sat. 304,850, Sun. 640,356.

The Detroit News: 615 West Lafayette Blvd, Detroit, MI 48226-3197; tel. (313) 222-2300; fax (313) 222-2335; e-mail dave.butler@detnews.com; internet www.detnews.com; f. 1873; Publr and Editor JON WOLMAN; circ. Mon. to Fri. 202,029, Sat. 181,456.

Flint Journal: 200 East First St, Flint, MI 48502-1925; tel. (810) 766-6100; fax (810) 767-7518; e-mail fj@flintjournal.com; internet www.flintjournal.com; f. 1876; Mon. to Fri. evening, Sat. and Sun. morning; Publr DAVID C. SHARP; Editor TONY DEARING; circ. Mon. to Fri. 84,718, Sat. 82,611, Sun. 199,956.

Grand Rapids Press: 155 Michigan St, NW, Grand Rapids, MI 49503-2302; tel. (616) 222-5818; e-mail dgaydou@grpress.com; internet www.grpress.com; f. 1890; Publr DAN GAYDOU; Editor MICHAEL S. LLOYD; circ. Mon. to Fri. 133,107, Sat. 159,187, Sun. 182,252.

Kalamazoo Gazette: 401 South Burdick St, Kalamazoo, MI 49007; tel. (269) 345-3511; fax (269) 345-0583; e-mail jstephanak@kalamazoogazette.com; internet www.kalamazoogazette.com; f. 1883; Publr JAMES STEPHANAK; Editor REBECCA PIERCE; circ. Mon. to Fri. 51,883, Sat. 62,033, Sun. 69,393.

Lansing State Journal: 120 East Lenawee St, Lansing, MI 48919-0001; tel. (517) 377-1000; fax (517) 377-1298; e-mail publisher@lsj.com; internet www.lsj.com; f. 1855; Publr RICHARD RAMHOFF; Exec. Editor MICHAEL HIRTEN; circ. Mon. to Fri. 64,906, Sat. 67,193, Sun. 82,490.

Oakland Press: 48 West Huron St, POB 436009, Pontiac, MI 48343; tel. (248) 332-8181; fax (248) 332-8294; internet www.theoaklandpress.com; f. 1843; Publr and Pres. KEVIN HAEZEBROECK; Exec. Editor GLENN GILBERT; circ. Mon. to Fri. 67,571, Sat. 59,899, Sun. 76,504.

Saginaw News: 203 South Washington Ave, Saginaw, MI 48607; tel. (989) 776-9764; e-mail pchaffee@thesaginawnews.com; internet www.thesaginawnews.com; f. 1859; Mon. to Fri. evening, Sat. and Sun. morning; Publr and Editor PAUL CHAFFEE; circ. Mon. to Fri. 43,093, Sat. 43,089, Sun. 52,057.

Minnesota

Duluth News Tribune: 424 West First St, Duluth, MN 55802; tel. (218) 723-5281; fax (218) 720-4120; e-mail news@duluthnews.com; internet www.duluthnewstribune.com; f. 1869; morning; Publr STEVEN MCLISTER; Exec. Editor ROB KARWATH; circ. Mon. to Fri. 40,305, Sat. 40,082, Sun. 62,468.

Star Tribune: 425 Portland Ave South, Minneapolis, MN 55488; tel. (612) 673-4516; fax (612) 673-4359; e-mail readerrep@startribune.com; internet www.startribune.com; f. 1920; Publr CHRIS HARTE; Editor and Sr Vice-Pres. NANCY BARNES; circ. Mon. to Fri. 345,252, Sat. 368,524, Sun. 574,406.

St Paul Pioneer Press: 345 Cedar St, St Paul, MN 55101; tel. (651) 222-1111; fax (651) 228-5500; e-mail infodesk@pioneerpress.com; internet www.pioneerpress.com; f. 1849; Publr GUY L. GILMORE; Editor THOM FLADUNG; circ. Mon. to Fri. 191,591, Sat. 205,454, Sun. 251,838.

Mississippi

Clarion-Ledger: 201 South Congress St, Jackson, MS 39201; tel. (601) 961-7000; fax (601) 961-7211; e-mail jnewhouse@clarionledger.com; internet www.clarionledger.com; f. 1954; Publr and Pres. LARRY WHITAKER, II; Exec. Editor RONNIE AGNEW; circ. Mon. to Fri. 91,092, Sat. 89,405, Sun. 101,255.

Missouri

Kansas City Star: 1729 Grand Blvd, Kansas City, MO 64108; tel. (816) 234-4741; fax (816) 234-4467; e-mail starinfo@kcstar.com; internet www.kansascity.com; f. 1880; Publr MAC TULLY; Editor MARK ZIEMAN; circ. Mon. to Fri. 260,724, Sat. 265,991, Sun. 359,477.

News-Leader: 651 Boonville Ave, Springfield, MO 65806; tel. (417) 836-1100; fax (417) 837-1381; e-mail rbates@news-leader.com; internet www.springfieldnewsleader.com; f. 1933; morning; Publr THOMAS A. BOOKSTAVER; Exec. Editor DON WYATT; circ. Mon. to Fri. 58,576, Sat. 58,716, Sun. 83,104.

St Louis Post-Dispatch: 900 North Tucker Blvd, St Louis, MO 63101; tel. (314) 340-8000; fax (314) 340-3050; internet www.stltoday.com; f. 1878; Pres. and Publr KEVIN MOWBRAY; Editor ARNIE ROBBINS; circ. Mon. to Fri. 278,999, Sat. 289,576, Sun. 407,754.

Montana

Billings Gazette: POB 36300, Billings, MT 59107; tel. (406) 657-1200; fax (406) 657-1208; internet www.billingsgazette.com; f. 1885; Publr MIKE GULLEDGE; Editor STEVE PROSINSKI; circ. Mon. to Fri. 46,295, Sat. 47,004, Sun. 52,442.

Nebraska

Lincoln Journal Star: Journal Star Printing Co, 926 P St, POB 81609, Lincoln, NE 68501; tel. (402) 475-4200; fax (402) 473-7291; e-mail jmaherk@journalstar.com; internet www.journalstar.com; f. 1867; morning; Publr JOHN F. MAHER; Editor KATHLEEN RUTLEDGE; circ. Mon. to Fri. 77,646, Sat. 72,256, Sun. 82,553.

Omaha World-Herald: 1334 Douglas St, Omaha, NE 68102-1122; tel. (402) 444-1000; fax (402) 345-0183; internet www.omaha.com; f. 1885; CEO and Publr JOHN GOTTSCHALK; Pres. and COO TERRY KROEGER; circ. Mon. to Fri. 184,150, Sat. 170,758, Sun. 222,469.

Nevada

Las Vegas Review-Journal: 1111 West Bonanza Rd, POB 70, Las Vegas, NV 89125; tel. (702) 383-0211; fax (702) 383-4676; e-mail afleming@reviewjournal.com; internet www.lvrj.com; f. 1908; Publr SHERMAN R. FREDERICK; Editor THOMAS MITCHELL; circ. Mon. to Fri. 172,366, Sat. 171,939, Sun. 204,036.

Reno Gazette-Journal: POB 22000, Reno, NV 89520-2000; tel. (775) 788-6200; fax (775) 788-6458; e-mail rgjfeedback@rgj.com; internet www.rgj.com; f. 1870; Publr TED POWER; Exec. Editor BERYL LOVE; circ. Mon. to Fri. 61,201, Sat. 60,654, Sun. 72,388.

New Hampshire

New Hampshire Union Leader, New Hampshire Sunday News: Union Leader Corpn, 100 William Loeb Dr., POB 9555, Manchester, NH 03108-9555; tel. (603) 668-4321; fax (603) 668-0382; e-mail writeus@unionleader.com; internet www.unionleader.com; f. 1863 (New Hampshire Union Leader); f. 1946 (New Hampshire Sunday News); Pres. and Publr JOSEPH W. MCQUAID; Editorial Vice-Pres. CHARLES PERKINS, III; circ. Mon. to Fri. 55,038, Sat. 54,160, Sun. 69,535.

New Jersey

Asbury Park Press: 3601 Hwy 66, POB 1550, Neptune, NJ 07754-1550; tel. (732) 922-6000; fax (732) 918-4818; e-mail garys@app.com; internet www.app.com; f. 1879; Publr and Pres. THOMAS M. DONOVAN; Exec. Editor SKIP HIDLAY; circ. Mon. to Fri. 145,508, Sat. 149,557, Sun. 192,581.

Courier-News: 1201 Route 22 West, Bridgewater, NJ 08807-0600; tel. (908) 722-8800; fax (908) 707-3252; e-mail couriernews@c-n.com; internet www.c-n.com; f. 1884; Publr and Pres. KETAN N. GANDHI; Man. Editor PAUL GRZELLA; circ. Mon. to Fri. 35,790, Sat. 29,194, Sun. 34,910.

Courier-Post: 301 Cuthbert Blvd, POB 5300, Cherry Hill, NJ 08034; tel. (856) 663-3600; fax (856) 663-2831; e-mail thearon@courierpostonline.com; internet www.courierpostonline.com; f. 1875; Pres. and Publr WALT T. LAFFERTY; Exec. Editor EVERETT J. MITCHELL, II; circ. Mon. to Fri. 69,521, Sat. 73,802, Sun. 82,911.

Home News Tribune: 35 Kennedy Blvd, East Brunswick, NJ 08816; tel. (732) 246-5500; fax (732) 565-7208; e-mail hntmetro@thnt.com; internet www.thnt.com; f. 1879; Publr and Pres. KETAN N. GHANDI; Exec. Editor CHARLES PAOLINO; circ. Mon. to Fri. 51,161, Sat. 48,466, Sun. 56,866.

Jersey Journal: 30 Journal Sq., Jersey City, NJ 07306; tel. (201) 653-1000; fax (201) 217-2455; internet www.thejerseyjournal.com; f. 1867; Publr KENDRICK ROSS; Editor JUDITH A. LOCORRIERE; circ. Mon. to Fri. 25,247, Sat. 25,395.

The Record: 150 River St, Hackensack, NJ 07601-7172; tel. (201) 646-4000; fax (201) 646-4135; e-mail newsroom@northjersey.com; internet www.northjersey.com; f. 1895; Chair. MALCOLM A. BORG; Editor and Vice-Pres. FRANK SCANDALE; circ. Mon. to Fri. 170,408, Sat. 172,457, Sun. 194,823.

Star-Ledger: 1 Star-Ledger Plaza, Newark, NJ 07102; tel. (973) 392-4121; e-mail jdennan@starledger.com; internet www.nj.com/starledger; f. 1917; Publr GEORGE ARWADY; Editor JIM WILLSE; circ. Mon. to Fri. 372,629, Sat. 300,732, Sun. 570,523.

The Times: 500 Perry St, POB 847, Trenton, NJ 08605; tel. (609) 989-5454; fax (609) 394-2819; e-mail letters@njtimes.com; internet www.nj.com/times; f. 1882; Publr RICHARD BILOTTI; Exec. Editor BRIAN S. MALONE; circ. Mon. to Fri. 54,578, Sat. 50,979, Sun. 56,356.

Trentonian: 600 Perry St, Trenton, NJ 08602; tel. (609) 989-7800; fax (609) 393-6072; e-mail editor@trentonian.com; internet www.trentonian.com; f. 1946; Publr WILLIAM T. (BILL) MURRAY; Editor (vacant); circ. Mon. to Fri. 40,628, Sat. 32,600, Sun. 28,174.

New Mexico

Albuquerque Journal: Albuquerque Publishing Co, 7777 Jefferson St NE, Albuquerque, NM 87109; tel. (505) 823-3800; e-mail journal@abqjournal.com; internet www.abqjournal.com; f. 1880; Publr T. H. LANG; Editor KENT WALZ; circ. Mon. to Fri. 105,966, Sat. 111,951, Sun. 146,931.

Albuquerque Tribune: 7777 Jefferson St NE, POB T, Albuquerque, NM 87103; tel. (505) 823-3653; fax (505) 823-3689; e-mail editor@abqtrib.com; internet www.abqtrib.com; f. 1922; evening; Editor-in-Chief PHILL CASAUS; Man. Editor KATE NELSON; circ. Mon. to Fri. 10,789, Sat. 12,700.

New York

Albany Times Union: Times Union, News Plaza, POB 15000, Albany, NY 12212; tel. (518) 454-5420; fax (518) 454-5628; e-mail ghearst@timesunion.com; internet www.timesunion.com; f. 1856; Publr MARK E. ALDMAN; Exec. Editor REX SMITH; circ. Mon. to Fri. 92,321, Sat. 70,597, Sun. 140,946.

Buffalo News: 1 News Plaza, POB 100, Buffalo, NY 14240; tel. (716) 856-5555; fax (716) 849-5150; internet www.buffalonews.com; f. 1880; Publr STANFORD LIPSEY; Editor MARGARET M. SULLIVAN; circ. Mon. to Fri. 181,540, Sat. 181,064, Sun. 266,123.

Daily Gazette: 2345 Maxon Rd, Schenectady, NY 12308; POB 1090, Schenectady, NY 12301-1090; tel. (518) 374-4141; fax (518) 395-3089; e-mail gazette@dailygazette.com; internet www.dailygazette.com; f. 1894; Publr and Editor JOHN E. N. HUME, III; circ. Mon. to Fri. 48,585, Sat. 48,593, Sun. 48,191.

Democrat and Chronicle: 55 Exchange Blvd, Rochester, NY 14614-2001; tel. (585) 232-7100; fax (585) 258-3027; internet www.democratandchronicle.com; f. 1833; Publr MICHAEL G. KANE; Editor KAREN MAGNUSON; circ. Mon. to Fri. 154,599, Sat. 168,001, Sun. 215,936.

Newsday: 235 Pinelawn Rd, Melville, NY 11747; tel. (631) 843-2000; fax (516) 843-2953; e-mail editor@newsday.com; internet www.newsday.com; f. 1940; Publr TIMOTHY P. KNIGHT; Editor JOHN MANCINI; circ. Mon. to Fri. 398,231, Sat. 359,113, Sun. 464,169.

Post-Standard: Clinton Sq., POB 4915, Syracuse, NY 13221; tel. (315) 470-0011; fax (315) 470-3081; e-mail mconnor@syracuse.com; internet post-standard.com; f. 1829; Editor and Publr STEPHEN A. ROGERS; Exec. Editor MICHAEL J. CONNOR; circ. Mon. to Fri. 113,991, Sat. 110,809, Sun. 164,702.

Press & Sun-Bulletin: POB 1270, Binghamton, NY 13902-1270; tel. (607) 798-1274; fax (607) 798-1156; internet www.pressconnects.com; f. 1985; Publr SHERMAN M. BODNER; Exec. Editor CALVIN STOVALL; circ. Mon. to Fri. 51,071 Sat. 50,604, Sun. 63,642.

Times Herald-Record ('The Record'): 40 Mulberry St, POB 2046, Middletown, NY 10940; tel. (914) 341-1100; fax (914) 343-2170; internet www.recordonline.com; f. 1956; Publr JOE VANDERHOOF; Exec. Editor DEREK OSENENKO; circ. Mon. to Fri. 80,148, Sat. 75,867, Sun. 86,350.

New York City

New York Daily News: 450 West 33rd St, New York, NY 10001; tel. (212) 210-2100; fax (212) 682-4953; internet www.nydailynews.com; f. 1919; Publr MORTIMER B. ZUCKERMAN; Editor-in-Chief MICHAEL COOKE; circ. Mon. to Fri. 718,174, Sat. 520,708, Sun. 775,543.

New York Post: 1211 Ave of the Americas, New York, NY 10036-8790; tel. (212) 930-8000; fax (212) 930-8540; internet www.nypost.com; f. 1801; Publr RUPERT MURDOCH; Editor-in-Chief COL ALLAN; circ. Mon. to Fri. 724,748, Sat. 472,746, Sun. 439,202.

New York Sun: 105 Chambers St, 2nd Floor, New York, NY 10007; tel. (212) 406-2000; fax (212) 571-9836; e-mail inquiries@nysun.com; internet www.nysun.com; f. 2002; Publr RONALD WEINTRAUB; Editor and Pres. SETH LIPSKY; circ. Mon. to Fri. 132,199.

New York Times: 620 Eighth Ave, New York, NY 10018; tel. (212) 556-1234; e-mail public@nytimes.com; internet www.nytimes.com; f. 1851; Chair. and Publr ARTHUR OCHS SULZBERGER, Jr; Pres. and Gen. Man. SCOTT H. HEEKIN-CANEDY; Exec. Editor BILL KELLER; circ. Mon. to Fri. 1,142,464, Sat. 1,011,900, Sun. 1,529,700.

Staten Island Advance: 950 Fingerboard Rd, Staten Island, New York, NY 10305; tel. (718) 981-1234; fax (718) 981-5679; internet www.silive.com; f. 1886; Mon. to Sat. evening, Sun. morning; Publr CAROLINE DIAMOND HARRISON; Editor BRIAN J. LALINE; circ. Mon. to Fri. 59,461, Sat. 55,481, Sun. 73,203.

The Wall Street Journal: 200 Liberty St, New York, NY 10281; tel. (212) 416-2000; internet www.wsj.com; f. 1889; publ. by Dow Jones & Co Inc; morning; Chair. M. PETER MCPHERSON; CEO RICHARD F. ZANNINO; Man. Editor MARCUS BRAUCHLI; circ. Mon. to Fri. 2,062,312, Sat. 1,968,413.

North Carolina

Charlotte Observer: 600 South Tryon St, POB 32188-28232, Charlotte, NC 28202-1842; tel. (704) 358-5040; fax (704) 358-5036; e-mail acaulkins@charlotteobserver.com; internet www.charlotte.com; f. 1886; Publr and Pres. ANN CAULKINS; Editor RICK THAMES; circ. Mon. to Fri. 215,379, Sat. 231,627, Sun. 270,347.

Citizen-Times: 14 Ohenry Ave, POB 2090, Asheville, NC 28802; tel. (828) 232-5934; fax (828) 251-0585; internet www.citizen-times.com; f. 1870; morning; Publr and Pres JEFFREY P. GREEN; Exec. Editor SUSAN IHNE; circ. Mon. to Fri. 51,512, Sat. 46,281, Sun. 59,511.

Fayetteville Observer-Times: Fayetteville Publishing Co, 458 Whitfield St, POB 849, Fayetteville, NC 28302; tel. (910) 323-4848; fax (919) 486-3531; e-mail cbwell@fayobserver.com; internet www.fayobserver.com; f. 1816; morning; Publr CHARLES BROADWELL; Exec. Editor BRIAN TOLLEY; circ. Mon. to Fri. 64,881, Sat. 64,161, Sun. 69,880.

Greensboro News and Record: 200 East Market St, POB 20848, Greensboro, NC 27420-0848; tel. (336) 373-7000; fax (336) 373-7067; internet www.news-record.com; f. 1905; Publr and Pres. ROBIN SAUL; Exec. Editor JOHN ROBINSON; circ. Mon. to Fri. 89,672, Sat. 88,310, Sun. 106,416.

News and Observer: 215 South McDowell St, POB 191, Raleigh, NC 27602; tel. (919) 829-4500; fax (919) 829-4872; internet www.news-observer.com; f. 1872; Publr ORAGE QUARLES, III; Exec. Editor MELANIE SILL; circ. Mon. to Fri. 177,361, Sat. 172,824, Sun. 213,124.

Winston-Salem Journal: 418 North Marshall St, POB 3159, Winston-Salem, NC 27102-3159; tel. (336) 727-7211; fax (336) 727-4071; e-mail news@wsjournal.com; internet www.wsjournal.com; Publr and Pres. MICHAEL MILLER; Exec. Editor CARL CROTHERS; circ. Mon. to Fri. 83,625, Sat. 91,503, Sun. 94,543.

North Dakota

The Forum: 101 Fifth St North, Box 2020, Fargo, ND 58107; tel. (701) 235-7311; fax (701) 241-5406; internet www.in-forum.com; f. 1878; Publr WILLIAM C. MARCIL; Editor MATT VON PINNON; circ. Mon. to Fri. 48,909, Sat. 54,530, Sun. 59,209.

Ohio

Akron Beacon Journal: 44 East Exchange St, POB 640, Akron, OH 44308; tel. (330) 996-3000; fax (330) 376-9235; internet www.ohio.com; f. 1839; Publr ANDREA MATHEWSON; Editor BRUCE WINGES; circ. Mon. to Fri. 122,388, Sat. 153,630, Sun. 164,902.

Canton Repository: 500 Market Ave South, Canton, OH 44711-2112; tel. (330) 454-5611; fax (330) 454-5610; internet www.cantonrep.com; f. 1815; Publr KEVIN KAMPMAN; Editor JEFF GAUGER; circ. Mon. to Fri. 66,401, Sat. 69,981, Sun. 81,788.

Cincinnati Enquirer: 312 Elm St, Cincinnati, OH 45202; tel. (513) 721-2700; fax (513) 768-8340; e-mail mperry@enquirer.com; internet www.cincinnati.com; f. 1841; Publr and Pres. MARGARET E. BUCHANAN; Exec. Editor HOLLIS TOWNS; circ. Mon. to Fri. 206,320, Sat. 184,074, Sun. 290,500.

Cincinnati Post: 125 East Court St, Cincinnati, OH 45202; tel. (513) 352-2000; fax (513) 621-3962; internet www.cincypost.com; f. 1881; afternoon; publ. by E.W. Scripps Co; due to cease publ. 31 Dec. 2007 following end of 30-yr jt operating agreement with Gannett Co Inc and *The Cincinnati Enquirer*; Editor MIKE PHILIPPS; circ. Mon. to Fri. 26,870, Sat. 37,154.

Cleveland Plain Dealer: 1801 Superior Ave East, Cleveland, OH 44114-2198; tel. (216) 999-3513; fax (216) 999-6354; e-mail circdirector@plaind.com; internet www.plaindealer.com; f. 1842; Pres. and Publr TERRENCE C. Z. EGGER; Editor SUSAN GOLDBERG; circ. Mon. to Fri. 344,704, Sat. 332,247, Sun. 442,482.

Columbus Dispatch: 34 South Third St, Columbus, OH 43215; tel. (614) 461-5000; fax (614) 461-7580; e-mail letters@dispatch.com; internet www.dispatch.com; f. 1871; Pres. MICHAEL FIORILE; Editor BEN MARRISON; circ. Mon. to Fri. 218,940, Sat. 279,407, Sun. 343,616.

Dayton Daily News: 45 South Ludlow St, Dayton, OH 45402; tel. (937) 222-5700; fax (937) 225-2489; e-mail kriley@coxohio.com; internet www.daytondailynews.com; Publr DOUG FRANKLIN; Editor KEVIN RILEY; circ. Mon. to Fri. 121,797, Sat. 113,600, Sun. 166,235.

News-Herald: 7085 Mentor Ave, Willoughby, OH 44094; tel. (440) 951-0000; fax (440) 951-0917; internet www.news-herald.com; f. 1880; Mon. to Sat. evening, Sun. morning; Publr STEVE ROSZCZYK;

THE UNITED STATES OF AMERICA

Exec. Editor TRICIA AMBROSE; circ. Mon. to Fri. 41,261, Sat. 41,674, Sun. 48,318.

Toledo Blade: 541 North Superior St, Toledo, OH 43660-1000; tel. (419) 724-6000; fax (419) 245-6191; internet www.toledoblade.com; f. 1835; Co-Publrs JOHN ROBINSON BLOCK, DIANA E. BLOCK; Exec. Editor RON ROYHAB; circ. Mon. to Fri. 125,956, Sat. 120,847, Sun. 154,566.

The Vindicator: 107 Vindicator Sq., POB 780, Youngstown, OH 44501-0780; tel. (330) 747-1471; fax (330) 747-6712; e-mail news@vindy.com; internet www.vindy.com; Publr BETTY H. BROWN JAGNOW; Gen. Man. MARK BROWN; circ. Mon. to Fri. 57,714, Sat. 61,562, Sun. 79,434.

Oklahoma

Daily Oklahoman: 9000 North Broadway, POB 25125, Oklahoma City, OK 73125; tel. (405) 475-3311; fax (405) 475-3183; internet www.newsok.com; f. 1894; Publr DAVID THOMPSON; Exec. Editor SUE HALE; circ. Mon. to Fri. 216,441, Sat. 194,490, Sun. 282,119.

Tulsa World: 315 South Boulder Ave, POB 1770, Tulsa, OK 74103; tel. (918) 581-8300; fax (918) 581-8353; e-mail letters@tulsaworld.com; internet www.tulsaworld.com; f. 1906; Publr ROBERT E. LORTON; Exec. Editor JOE WORLEY; circ. Mon. to Fri. 120,583, Sat. 136,569, Sun. 171,602.

Oregon

The Oregonian: 1320 SW Broadway, Portland, OR 97201-3469; tel. (503) 221-8150; fax (503) 294-4193; e-mail sengelberg@news.oregonian.com; internet www.oregonian.com; f. 1850; Publr. FRED A. STICKEL; Editor SANDY ROWE; circ. Mon. to Fri. 319,625, Sat. 299,730, Sun. 375,913.

The Register-Guard: 975 High St, POB 10188, Eugene, OR 97440-2188; tel. and fax (541) 485-1234; fax (541) 683-7631; e-mail tbaker@guardnet.com; internet www.registerguard.com; f. 1867; Publr and Editor TONY BAKER; circ. Mon. to Fri. 68,940, Sat. 74,150, Sun. 72,199.

Statesman Journal: 280 Church St, NE, POB 13009, Salem, OR 97309-3009; tel. (503) 399-6611; fax (503) 399-6706; e-mail newsroom@statesmanjournal.com; internet www.statesmanjournal.com; f. 1851; Publr and Pres. BRIAN PRIESTER; Exec. Editor BILL CHURCH; circ. Mon. to Fri. 49,089, Sat. 50,636, Sun. 56,725.

Pennsylvania

Bucks County Courier Times: 8400 Route 13, Levittown, PA 19057-5198; tel. (215) 949-4000; fax (215) 949-4177; internet www.phillyburbs.com; f. 1910; owned by Calkins Media Inc; Publr DALE LARSON; Exec. Editor PATRICIA S. WALKER; circ. Mon. to Fri. 61,086, Sat. 57,674, Sun. 64,738.

Call Chronicle: POB 1260, Allentown, PA 18105; tel. (610) 820-6500; fax (610) 820-6693; f. 1921; Sun.; Publr GARY K. SHORTS; Exec. Editor LAWRENCE H. HYMANS; circ. 189,000.

The Morning Call: 101 North Sixth St, POB 1260, Allentown, PA 18105; tel. (610) 820-6553; fax (610) 820-6693; e-mail publisher@mcall.com; internet www.mcall.com; Publr TIMOTHY R. KENNEDY; Editor ARDITH HILLIARD; circ. Mon. to Fri. 108,886, Sat. 128,351, Sun. 147,696.

Patriot-News: 812 Market St, Harrisburg, PA 17105; tel. (717) 255-8100; fax (717) 255-8456; internet www.patriot-news.com; f. 1854; Publr JOHN KIRKPATRICK; Exec. Editor DAVID NEWHOUSE; circ. 102,467 (morning), 154,021 (Sunday).

Philadelphia Daily News: 400 North Broad St, POB 7788, Philadelphia, PA 19101; tel. (215) 854-5900; fax (215) 854-5910; e-mail dailynews.opinion@phillynews.com; internet www.philly.com; f. 1925; Publr MARK J. FRISBY; Editor MICHAEL DAYS; circ. Mon. to Fri. 113,951, Sat. 69,464.

Philadelphia Inquirer: 400 North Broad St, POB 8623, Philadelphia, PA 19101; tel. (215) 854-2000; fax (215) 854-4974; e-mail inquirer.opinion@phillynews.com; internet www.philly.com/inquirer; f. 1829; Publr BRIAN TIERNY; Editor WILLIAM K. MARIMOW; circ. Mon. to Fri. 352,593, Sat. 360,730, Sun. 688,670.

Pittsburgh Post-Gazette: 34 Blvd of the Allies, Pittsburgh, PA 15222; tel. (412) 263-1100; fax (412) 391-8452; e-mail ssmith@post-gazette.com; internet www.post-gazette.com; f. 1786; Publrs WILLIAM BLOCK, Jr, JOHN ROBINSON BLOCK; Exec. Editor DAVID M. SHRIBMAN, Jr; circ. Mon. to Fri. 213,352, Sat. 196,193, Sun. 341,474.

Sunday News: Lancaster Newspapers, Inc, 8 West King St, POB 1328, Lancaster, PA 17608; tel. (717) 291-8811; fax (717) 399-6506; e-mail madams@lnpnews.com; internet lancasteronline.com/pages/paper/sundaynews; f. 1923; Editor MARV ADAMS; circ. 100,060.

Tribune-Democrat: 425 Locust St, POB 340, Johnstown, PA 15907-0340; tel. (814) 532-5050; fax (814) 539-1409; e-mail newsroom@tribdem.com; internet www.tribune-democrat.com; f. 1853; morning; Publr CHRIS VOCCIO; Editor CHIP MINEMYER; circ. Mon. to Fri. 38,678, Sat. 39,005, Sun. 42,747.

Rhode Island

Providence Journal: 75 Fountain St, Providence, RI 02902-0050; tel. (401) 277-7000; fax (401) 277-7346; e-mail sareson@projo.com; internet www.projo.com; f. 1829; publ. by Belo Corpn; Publr HOWARD G. SUTTON; Exec. Editor JOEL P. RAWSON; circ. Mon. to Fri. 148,700, Sat. 186,912, Sun. 205,102.

South Carolina

Greenville News: 305 South Main St, POB 1688, Greenville, SC 29601-2605; tel. (864) 298-4100; fax (864) 298-4805; e-mail letters@greenvillenews.com; internet www.greenvilleonline.com; f. 1874; Publr STEVEN BRANDT; Editor JOHN S. PITTMAN; circ. Mon. to Fri. 86,499, Sat. 82,930, Sun. 113,386.

The Post and Courier: 134 Columbus St, Charleston, SC 29403-4800; tel. (843) 577-7111; fax (843) 937-5579; e-mail publiceditor@postandcourier.com; internet www.charleston.net; f. 1803; Publr LARRY W. TARLETON, Jr; Exec. Editor BILL HAWKINS; circ. Mon. to Fri. 100,143, Sat. 95,193, Sun. 109,888.

The State: 1401 Shop Rd, POB 1333, Columbia, SC 29202; tel. (803) 771-8380; fax (803) 771-8430; e-mail stateeditor@thestate.com; internet www.thestate.com; f. 1891; Publr HENRY HAITZ, III; Exec. Editor MARK LETT; circ. Mon. to Fri. 106,053, Sat. 116,281, Sun. 139,022.

South Dakota

Argus Leader: 200 South Minnesota Ave, POB 5034, Sioux Falls, SD 57117-5034; tel. (605) 331-2200; fax (605) 331-2294; e-mail editor@argusleader.com; internet www.argusleader.com; f. 1881; Publr ARNOLD GARSON; Exec. Editor RANDALL BECK; circ. Mon. to Fri. 51,211, Sat. 49,026, Sun. 69,767.

Tennessee

Chattanooga Times-Free Press: 400 East 11th St, Chattanooga, TN 37403; tel. (423) 756-6900; fax (423) 757-6383; e-mail tgriscom@timesfreepress.com; internet www.timesfreepress.com; f. 1888; Publr and Exec. Editor TOM GRISCOM; circ. Mon. to Fri. 73,094, Sat. 84,113, Sun. 95,786.

The Commercial Appeal: 495 Union Ave, Memphis, TN 38103; tel. (901) 529-2211; fax (901) 529-2522; internet www.commercialappeal.com; f. 1841; Pres. and Publr JOSEPH PEPE; Editor CHRIS PECK; circ. Mon. to Fri. 146,252, Sat. 138,243, Sun. 184,418.

Knoxville News-Sentinel: 2332 News Sentinel Dr., Knoxville, TN 37921-5731; tel. (865) 523-3131; fax (865) 342-8650; internet www.knoxnews.com; f. 1886; Publr BRUCE HARTMANN; Editor JACK McELROY; circ. Mon. to Fri. 119,172, Sat. 124,293, Sun. 150,147.

The Tennessean: 1100 Broadway St, Nashville, TN 37203; tel. (615) 259-8800; fax (615) 259-8093; e-mail publisher@tennessean.com; internet www.tennessean.com; f. 1812; Publr ELLEN LEIFELD; Editor MARK SILVERMAN; circ. Mon. to Fri. 174,073, Sat. 175,868, Sun. 232,334.

Texas

Austin American-Statesman: 305 South Congress Ave, Austin TX 78704; POB 670, Austin, TX 78767; tel. (512) 445-3500; fax (512) 445-3679; internet www.statesman.com; f. 1871; Publr MICHAEL LAOSA; Editor RICHARD OPPEL; circ. Mon. to Fri. 173,579, Sat. 172,836, Sun. 215,894.

Beaumont Enterprise: 380 Main St, POB 3071, Beaumont, TX 77701-2331; tel. (409) 833-3311; fax (409) 838-2857; e-mail tkelly@hearstnp.com; internet www.beaumontenterprise.com; f. 1880; Publr JOHN E. NEWHOUSE; Editor TIM KELLY; circ. Mon. to Fri. 50,625, Sat. 46,993, Sun. 54,734.

Corpus Christi Caller-Times: 820 North Lower Broadway, POB 9136, Corpus Christi, TX 78469; tel. (361) 884-2011; fax (361) 886-3732; internet www.caller.com; f. 1883; Publr PATRICK J. BIRMINGHAM; Editor LIBBY AVERYT; circ. Mon. to Fri. 52,838, Sat. 58,999, Sun. 73,611.

Dallas Morning News: 508 Young St, Dallas, TX 75202; tel. (214) 977-8222; fax (214) 977-8319; internet www.dallasnews.com; f. 1885; publ. by Belo Corpn; Publr JAMES M. MORONEY, III; Editor ROBERT W. MONG, Jr; circ. Mon. to Fri. 411,919, Sat. 400,214, Sun. 563,079.

El Paso Times: Times Plaza, El Paso, TX 79901-1470; tel. (915) 546-6104; fax (915) 546-6415; internet www.elpasotimes.com; f. 1881; Publr RAY M. STAFFORD; Editor DIONICIO (DON) FLORES; circ. Mon. to Fri. 71,651, Sat. 70,654, Sun. 82,721.

Fort Worth Star-Telegram: POB 1870, Fort Worth, TX 76115; tel. (817) 390-7400; fax (817) 390-7789; e-mail newsroom@star-telegram.com; internet www.star-telegram.com; f. 1909; Publr WESLEY R.

THE UNITED STATES OF AMERICA

TURNER; Exec. Editor JIM WITT; circ. Mon. to Fri. 210,990, Sat. 218,837, Sun. 304,200.

Houston Chronicle: 801 Texas Ave, Houston, TX 77002; tel. (713) 220-7171; fax (713) 220-6677; e-mail online@chron.com; internet www.chron.com; f. 1901; Publr JACK SWEENEY; Editor JEFF COHEN; circ. Mon. to Fri. 503,114, Sat. 476,583, Sun. 677,425.

Lubbock Avalanche-Journal: 710 Ave J, POB 491, Lubbock, TX 79401-1808; tel. (806) 762-8844; fax (806) 744-9603; e-mail terry.greenberg@lubbockonline.com; internet www.lubbockonline.com; f. 1900; Publr STEPHEN A. BEASLEY; Editor TERRY GREENBERG; circ. Mon. to Fri. 54,494, Sat. 50,247, Sun. 60,355.

San Antonio Express-News: 301 Ave E, San Antonio, TX 78205; tel. (210) 250-3000; fax (210) 250-3105; internet www.mysanantonio.com; f. 1864; Publr THOMAS A. STEPHENSON; Editor ROBERT RIVARD; circ. Mon. to Fri. 236,918, Sat. 235,352, Sun. 333,902.

Utah

Deseret Morning News: 30 East 100 South, POB 1257, Salt Lake City, UT 84110; tel. (801) 236-6000; fax (801) 237-2121; e-mail rhall@desnews.com; internet www.deseretnews.com; f. 1850; Publr JIM M. WALL; Editor JOSEPH A. CANNON; circ. Mon. to Fri. 75,026, Sat. 75,237, Sun. 77,487.

Salt Lake Tribune: 90 South 400 West, Suite 700, Salt Lake City, UT 84101; tel. (801) 237-8782; fax (801) 257-8525; e-mail reader.advocate@sltrib.com; internet www.sltrib.com; f. 1871; Exec. Editor TOM BADEN; circ. Mon. to Fri. 128,186, Sat. 123,400, Sun. 149,320.

Standard-Examiner: 332 Standard Way, POB 12790, Ogden, UT 84412-2790; tel. (801) 625-4200; fax (801) 625-4508; e-mail letters@standard.net; internet www.standard.net; f. 1888; Publr LEE CARTER; Man. Editor ANDY HOWELL; circ. Mon. to Fri. 60,956, Sat. 61,595, Sun. 64,324.

Vermont

Burlington Free Press: 191 College St, POB 10, Burlington, VT 05402-0010; tel. (802) 863-3441; fax (802) 660-1802; e-mail letters@bfp.burlingtonfreepress.com; internet www.burlingtonfreepress.com; f. 1827; Publr JAMES CAREY; Exec. Editor MIKE TOWNSEND; circ. Mon. to Fri. 45,176, Sat. 42,072, Sun. 50,575.

Virginia

Daily Press: 7505 Warwick Blvd, Newport News, VA 23607; tel. (757) 247-4600; fax (757) 245-8618; e-mail dpedit@aol.com; internet www.dailypress.com; f. 1896; Publr DIGBY A. SOLOMON; Editor ERNEST C. GATES; circ. Mon. to Fri. 83,367, Sat. 91,962, Sun. 107,701.

Richmond Times-Dispatch: 300 East Franklin St, POB 85333, Richmond, VA 23293; tel. (804) 649-6990; fax (804) 775-8059; e-mail letters@timesdispatch.com; internet www.timesdispatch.com; f. 1850; Publr THOMAS A. SILVESTRI; Exec. Editor GLENN PROCTOR; circ. Mon. to Fri. 186,441, Sat. 184,175, Sun. 214,971.

Roanoke Times: 201 West Campbell Ave, POB 2491, Roanoke, VA 24010-2491; tel. (540) 981-3340; fax (540) 981-3346; internet www.roanoke.com; Publr DEBBIE MEADE; Editor CAROLE TARRANT; circ. Mon. to Fri. 93,803, Sat. 95,825, Sun. 103,483.

USA Today: 7950 Jones Branch Dr., McLean, VA 22108-0605; tel. (703) 276-3400; internet www.usatoday.com; f. 1982; Pres. and Publr CRAIG A. MOON; Editor KENNETH PAULSON; circ. Mon. to Fri. 2,278,022.

Virginian-Pilot: 150 West Brambleton Ave, POB 449, Norfolk, VA 23501-0449; tel. (757) 446-2000; fax (757) 446-2051; e-mail letters@pilotonline.com; internet hamptonroads.com/pilotonline; f. 1876; Publr BRUCE BRADLEY; Man. Editor DENIS FINLEY; circ. Mon. to Fri. 183,024, Sat. 195,827, Sun. 214,995.

Washington

The Herald: 1213 California St, Everett, WA 98201; POB 930, Everett, WA 98206; tel. (425) 339-3000; fax (425) 339-3049; e-mail strick@herald.net; internet www.heraldnet.com; f. 1891; Publr ALLEN B. FUNK; Exec. Editor NEAL PATTISON; circ. Mon. to Fri. 49,072, Sat. 49,573, Sun. 54,743.

News Tribune: 1950 South State St, POB 11000, Tacoma, WA 98411; tel. (253) 597-8742; fax (253) 597-8451; e-mail karen.peterson@thenewstribune.com; internet www.thenewstribune.com; f. 1883; Publr CHERYL DELL; Exec. Editor DAVID A. ZEECK; circ. Mon. to Fri. 119,077, Sat. 113,246, Sun. 131,212.

Seattle Post-Intelligencer: 101 Elliott Ave West, POB 1909, Seattle, WA 98111-1909; tel. (206) 448-8000; fax (206) 448-8165; e-mail editpage@seattlepi.com; internet seattlepi.nwsource.com; f. 1863; Publr and Editor ROGER OGLESBY; Man. Editor DAVID MCCUMBER; circ. Mon. to Fri. 128,012, Sat. 113,759.

Seattle Times: 1120 John St, POB 70, Seattle, WA 98111-0070; tel. (206) 464-2111; fax (206) 464-2261; e-mail pfoote@seattletimes.com; internet seattletimes.nwsource.com; f. 1896; Publr FRANK A. BLETHEN; Exec. Editor DAVID BOARDMAN; circ. Mon. to Fri. 219,722, Sat. 199,938.

Spokesman-Review: 999 West Riverside, POB 2160, Spokane, WA 99210; tel. (509) 459-5000; fax (509) 459-3815; e-mail editor@spokesman.com; internet www.spokesman.com; f. 1883; Publr WILLIAM STACEY COWLES; Editor STEVEN A. SMITH; circ. Mon. to Fri. 93,335, Sat. 104,921, Sun. 119,155.

West Virginia

Charleston Daily Mail: 1001 Virginia St East, Charleston, WV 25301-2835; tel. (304) 348-5140; fax (304) 348-4847; e-mail dmnews@dailymail.com; internet www.dailymail.com; f. 1973; evening; Publr and Editor NANYA FRIEND; Man. Editor BOB KELLY; circ. Mon. to Fri. 22,779.

Wisconsin

Green Bay Press-Gazette: 435 East Walnut St, POB 23430, Green Bay, WI 54305-3430; tel. (920) 435-4411; fax (920) 431-8499; e-mail jdye@greenbaypressgazette.com; internet www.greenbaypressgazette.com; f. 1915; bought by Gannett Co in 1980; Publr WILLIAM T. NUSBAUM; Exec. Editor JOHN DYE; circ. Mon. to Fri. 55,277, Sat. 63,799, Sun. 78,947.

Milwaukee Journal Sentinel: 333 West State St, POB 661, Milwaukee, WI 53201; tel. (414) 224-2000; fax (414) 224-2047; e-mail gstanley@journalsentinel.com; internet www.jsonline.com; f. 1837; Publr ELIZABETH 'BETSY' BRENNER; Editor MARTIN KAISER; circ. Mon. to Fri. 230,220, Sat. 227,445, Sun. 400,317.

Post-Crescent: 306 West Washington St, POB 59, Appleton, WI 54911; tel. (920) 733-4411; fax (920) 733-1983; e-mail gmagno@postcrescent.com; internet www.postcrescent.com; f. 1920; Mon. to Sat evening, Sun. morning; Publr GENIA LOVETT; Exec. Editor DAN FLANNERY; circ. Mon. to Fri. 51,509, Sat. 57,923, Sun. 67,070.

Wisconsin State Journal: 1901 Fish Hatchery Rd, POB 8058, Madison, WI 53713; tel. (608) 252-6100; fax (608) 252-6119; e-mail wsjcity@madison.com; internet www.madison.com/wsj; f. 1839; Publr WILLIAM K. JOHNSTON; Editor ELLEN FOLEY; circ. Mon. to Fri. 88,805, Sat. 96,279, Sun. 143,543.

Wyoming

Star-Tribune: 170 Star Lane, POB 80, Casper, WY 82602; tel. (307) 266-0500; fax (307) 266-0568; e-mail nathan.bekke@casperstartribune.net; internet www.trib.com; f. 1891; Publr NATHAN BEKKE; Editor CLARK WALWORTH; circ. Mon. to Fri. 30,289, Sat. 30,227, Sun. 32,400.

SELECTED PERIODICALS

AARP The Magazine: 601 E St, NW, Washington, DC 20049; tel. (202) 434-2560; e-mail aarpmagazine@aarp.org; internet www.aarpmagazine.org; f. 1958 following merger of *My Generation* and *Modern Maturity* ; publ. of the American Assen of Retired Persons; 6 a year; general interest for the over-50s; Group Publr, Vice-Pres. and Publr JIM FISHMAN; Editor-in-Chief JAMES TOEDTMAN; Editor STEVE SLON; circ. 23,964,332; AARP also publishes *AARP Bulletin* (11 a year, circ. 23,361,340).

Allure: 4 Times Sq., New York, NY 10036; tel. (212) 286-2860; fax (212) 286-4654; internet www.allure.com; f. 1991; publ. by Condé Nast Publications Inc; monthly; women's fashion and wellbeing; Vice-Pres. and Publr NANCY BERGER CARDONE; Editor-in-Chief LINDA WELLS; circ. 1,062,778.

American Heritage: 90 Fifth Ave, New York, NY 10011-8882; tel. (212) 367-3100; fax (212) 367-3149; e-mail mail@americanheritage.com; internet www.americanheritage.com; f. 1954; 8 a year; US history; Publr FRANK ROSA; Editor RICHARD F. SNOW; circ. 318,571; American Heritage also publishes *American Heritage of Inventions and Technology* and quarterly African-American history and culture magazine *American Legacy*.

The American Legion Magazine: 700 North Pennsylvania St, POB 1055, Indianapolis, IN 46206-1055; tel. (317) 630-1200; fax (317) 630-1223; e-mail magazine@legion.org; internet www.legion.org; f. 1919; publ. of The American Legion; monthly; Editor JOHN B. RAUGHTER; circ. 2,557,935 (2007).

American Rifleman: NRA Publications, 11250 Waples Mill Rd, Fairfax, VA 22030; tel. (703) 267-1329; e-mail publications@nrahq.org; internet www.nrapublications.org; f. 1885; official journal of the Nat. Rifle Assen; monthly; Editor-in-Chief MARK A. KEEFE, IV; circ. 1,334,095.

American Teacher: 555 New Jersey Ave, NW, Washington, DC 20001-2079; tel. (202) 879-4400; fax (202) 783-2014; e-mail mailbox@aft.org; internet www.aft.org; f. 1916; 8 a year; Editor ROGER GLASS; circ. 800,000.

Architectural Digest: Condé Nast Publications Inc, 6300 Wilshire Blvd, Los Angeles, CA 90048; tel. (213) 965-3700; fax (213) 965-4975;

THE UNITED STATES OF AMERICA

internet www.architecturaldigest.com; f. 1920; monthly; Vice-Pres. and Publr GIULIO CAPUA; Editor-in-Chief PAIGE RENSE; circ. 846,997.

Arthritis Today: 1330 West Peachtree St, NW, Suite 100, Atlanta, GA 30309; tel. (404) 965-7635; e-mail atmail@arthritis.org; internet www.arthritis.org/resources/arthritistoday; f. 1987; publ. by the Arthritis Foundation; 6 a year; health and lifestyle magazine for sufferers of arthritis; Publr CINDY MCDANIEL; Editor-in-Chief MARCY O'KOON MOSS; circ. 727,734.

Barron's: 4300 North Route 1, South Brunswick, NJ; tel. (609) 514-0870; fax (609) 520-4731; e-mail editors@barrons.com; internet www.barrons.com; f. 1921; publ. by Dow Jones & Co, Inc; acquisition of Dow Jones & Co, Inc by News Corpn pending; weekly; business and finance; Pres. and Editor EDWIN A. FINN, Jr; circ. 312,562.

Better Homes and Gardens: 1716 Locust St, Des Moines, IA 50309-3023; tel. (515) 284-3000; fax (515) 284-3684; internet www.bhg.com; f. 1922; monthly; Vice-Pres. and Publr JAN STUDIN; Editor-in-Chief GAYLE BUTLER; Exec. Editor KITTY MORGAN; circ. 7,675,910.

Bon Appétit: 6300 Wilshire Blvd, 10th Floor, Los Angeles, CA 90048; tel. (323) 965-3658; fax (323) 930-2369; internet www.epicurious.com/bonappetit; f. 1955; monthly; Vice-Pres. and Publr PAUL JOWDY; Editor-in-Chief BARBARA FAIRCHILD; circ. 1,367,478.

Boys' Life: 1325 West Walnut Hill Lane, POB 152079, Irving, TX 75015-2079; tel. (972) 580-2366; fax (972) 580-2079; e-mail boyslifemagazine@netbsa.org; internet www.boyslife.org; f. 1911; publ. by Boy Scouts of America; monthly; Publr J. WARREN YOUNG; Editor J. D. OWEN; circ. 1,244,502.

BusinessWeek: 1221 Ave of the Americas, 43rd Floor, New York, NY 10120; tel. (212) 512-2511; e-mail geoff_dodge@businessweek.com; internet www.businessweek.com; f. 1929; publ. by Business-Week Group, a subsidiary of The McGraw-Hill Cos, Inc; weekly; business, finance and technology; Sr Vice-Pres. and Publr (North America) GEOFFREY DODGE; Editor-in-Chief STEPHEN J. ADLER; circ. 919,343.

Car and Driver: 2002 Hogback Rd, Ann Arbor, MI 48105; tel. (734) 971-3600; fax (734) 971-9188; e-mail editors@caranddriver.com; internet www.caranddriver.com; f. 1956; Publr ROBERT G. HOUGHTLIN, III; Editor-in-Chief CSABA CSERE; circ. 1,300,383.

Catholic Digest: 1 Montauk Ave, Suite 200, New London, CT 06320-4967; tel. (860) 437-3012; fax (860) 437-3013; e-mail dconnors@bayard-inc.com; internet www.catholicdigest.org; f. 1936; monthly; Publr KATHLEEN STAUFFER; Editor DAN CONNORS; circ. 283,548.

Child: 375 Lexington Ave, 9th Floor, New York, NY 10017-5514; tel. (212) 499-2000; fax (212) 499-2038; e-mail mailcenter@child.com; internet www.child.com; f. 1986; 10 a year; Publr RICHARD BERENSON; Editor-in-Chief MIRIAM AROND; circ. 1,020,000.

Condé Nast Traveler: 4 Times Sq., 14th Floor, New York, NY 10036-6561; tel. (212) 286-2860; fax (212) 286-2094; e-mail jason_wagenheim@cntraveler.com; internet www.concierge.com/cntraveler; f. 1954; monthly; Publr LISA HENRIQUES HUGHES; Editor-in-Chief KLARA GLOWCZEWSKA; circ. 808,419.

Congressional Digest: Congressional Digest Corpn, 4416 East West Hwy, Suite 400, Bethesda, MD 20814-4568; tel. (301) 634-3113; fax (301) 634-3189; e-mail info@congressionaldigest.com; internet www.congressionaldigest.com; f. 1921; monthly; Publr PAGE B. ROBINSON THOMAS.

Consumer Reports: 101 Truman Ave, Yonkers, NY 10703-1057; tel. (914) 378-2000; fax (914) 378-2900; e-mail pressroom@consumer.org; internet www.consumerreports.org; f. 1936; monthly; Man. Editor ROBERT TIERNAN; circ. 4,000,000.

Consumers Digest: Consumers Digest Communications, 520 Lake Cook Rd, Suite 500, Deerfield, IL 60015; tel. (847) 607-3000; e-mail postmaster@consumersdigest.com; internet www.consumersdigest.com; f. 1959; 6 a year; Publr RANDY WEBER; circ. 1,200,000.

Cosmopolitan: 300 West 57th St, New York, NY 10019-3299; tel. (212) 649-3570; e-mail cosmo@hearst.com; internet www.cosmomag.com; f. 1886; monthly; women's interest; Publr DONNA KALAJIAN LAGANI; Editor-in-Chief KATE WHITE; circ. 2,915,867.

Country Home: 1716 Locust St, Des Moines, IA 50309; tel. (515) 284-2015; e-mail countryhome@meredith.com; internet www.countryhome.com; f. 1979; publ. by Meredith Corpn; 10 a year; lifestyle; Publr ANTHONY IMPERATO; Editor-in-Chief CAROL SHEEHAN; circ. 1,264,784.

Country Living: 300 West 57th St, New York, NY 10019-3788; tel. (212) 649-3500; e-mail countryliving@hearst.com; internet www.countryliving.com; f. 1978; monthly; Publr STEVEN GRUNE; Editor-in-Chief NANCY MERNIT SORIANO; circ. 1,626,426.

Discover: 90 Fifth Ave, New York, NY 10011; tel. (212) 624-4800; fax (212) 624-4813; e-mail bhostetter@discover.com; internet www.discovermagazine.com; f. 1980; publ. by Discover Media LLC; science and technology; Publr WILLIAM C. HOSTETTER; Editor-in-Chief COREY S. POWELL; circ 716,922.

Ebony: 820 South Michigan Ave, Chicago, IL 60605-2191; tel. (312) 322-9200; fax (312) 322-0039; internet www.ebonyjet.com; f. 1945; monthly; African-American general interest; Publr KENARD GIBBS; Editorial Dir BRYAN MONROE; circ. 1,400,692.

Elks Magazine: 425 West Diversey Pkwy, Chicago, IL 60614-6196; tel. (773) 755-4740; e-mail elksmag@elks.org; internet www.elks.org/elksmag; f. 1922; 10 a year; Editor CHERYL T. STACHURA; circ. 980,000.

Elle: 1633 Broadway, 44th Floor, New York, NY 10019; tel. (212) 767-5800; fax (212) 767-5980; internet www.elle.com; f. 1985; publ. by Hachette Filipacchi Media US, Inc; monthly; women's fashion; Sr Vice-Pres. and Group Publishing Dir CAROL SMITH; Editor-in-Chief ROBERTA MYERS; circ. 1,072,729.

Endless Vacation: 360 Lexington Ave, 19th Floor, New York, NY 10017; tel. (212) 481-3452; fax (212) 213-1287; e-mail barbara.peck@endlessvacation.com; internet www.endlessvacation.com; f. 1975; publ. by Resort Condominiums Int.; 6 a year; Publr MICHAEL PERRY; Editor BARBARA PECK; circ. 1,720,971 (2006).

Entertainment Weekly: 1675 Broadway, 29th Floor, New York, NY 10019; tel. (212) 522-5600; fax (212) 522-4482; e-mail letters@ew.com; internet www.ew.com; f. 1990; Pres. and Publr DAVID S. MORRIS; Man. Editor RICK TETZELI; circ. 1,798,754.

ESPN The Magazine: 19 East 34th St, New York, NY 10016; tel. (212) 515-1000; fax (212) 515-1275; e-mail ms_support@espn.go.com; internet espn.go.com/magazine; f. 1998; fortnightly; subsidiary of Walt Disney DIS; men's sports and lifestyle; Editor-in-Chief GARY HOENIG; circ. 2,108,094.

Esquire: 300 West 57th St, New York, NY 10019-3797; tel. (212) 649-4020; fax (212) 649-4303; e-mail esquire@hearst.com; internet www.esquire.com; f. 1933; monthly; Publr KEVIN O'MALLEY; Editor-in-Chief DAVID GRANGER; circ. 721,133.

Essence: 135 West 50th St, 4th Floor, New York, NY 10020; tel. (212) 642-0600; fax (212) 921-5173; e-mail info@essence.com; internet www.essence.com; f. 1970; monthly; Editor-in-Chief ANGELA BURT-MURRAY; circ. 1,089,495.

Family Circle: 375 Lexington Ave, 9th Floor, New York, NY 10017-5514; tel. (212) 499-2000; fax (212) 499-6740; e-mail support@familycircle.com; internet www.familycircle.com; f. 1932; every 3 weeks; Editor-in-Chief LINDA FEARS; circ. 3,916,247.

FamilyFun: 244 Main St, Northampton, MA 01060; tel. (212) 633-4485; e-mail ellen.antoville@disney.com; internet familyfun.go.com; f. 1991; publ. by Disney Publishing Worldwide; monthly; general interest for families with young children; Editor ANN HALLOCK; circ. 1,794,147.

Family Handyman (Home Service Publications): 2915 Commers Dr., Suite 700, Eagan, MN 55121; tel. (651) 454-9200; fax (651) 994-2250; e-mail fheditor@readersdigest.com; internet www.rd.com/familyhandyman; f. 1951; publ. by Reader's Digest Asscn, Inc; 10 a year; Editor-in-Chief KEN COLLIER; circ. 1,167,304.

Fast Company: 7 World Trade Center, New York, NY 10007-2195; tel. (212) 389-5300; fax (212) 389-5496; e-mail loop@fastcompany.com; internet www.fastcompany.com; f. 1995; monthly; acquired by Mansueto Ventures LLC in 2005; global business practice; Editor-in-Chief ROBERT SAFIAN; circ. 767,900.

FHM: 110 Fifth Ave, New York, NY 10011; tel. (212) 201-6702; fax (212) 201-6965; e-mail andrew.ormson@emapmetrousa.com; internet www.fhmus.com; f. 2000; publ. by Emap Metro LLC; monthly; men's lifestyle, entertainment and fashion; Exec. Publr and Pres. DANA FIELDS; Editor-in-Chief SCOTT GRAMLING; circ. 1,250,275 (2006).

Field & Stream: 2 Park Ave, New York, NY 10016-5601; tel. (212) 779-5000; fax (212) 779-5114; e-mail fsletters@time4.com; internet www.fieldandstream.com; f. 1895; 11 a year; Publr ERIC ZINCZENKO; Editor-in-Chief SID EVANS; circ. 1,532,714.

Fitness: 125 Park Ave, New York, NY 10017-5514; tel. (212) 499-2000; internet www.fitnessmagazine.com; f. 1992; acquired by Meredith Corpn in 2005; women's health and fitness; Publr LEE SLATTERY; Editor-in-Chief DENISE BRODEY; circ. 1,536,211.

Food & Wine: 1120 Ave of the Americas, New York, NY 10036; tel. (212) 382-5600; fax (212) 382-5879; e-mail lynn.m.yoong@aexp.com; internet www.foodandwine.com; f. 1978; publ. by American Express Publishing Corpn; monthly; Publr JULIE MCGOWAN; Editor-in-Chief DANA COWIN; circ. 931,769.

Forbes: 60 Fifth Ave, New York, NY 10011-8802; tel. (212) 620-2200; fax (212) 620-1875; e-mail readers@forbes.com; internet www.forbes.com; f. 1917; fortnightly; Pres. and Editor-in-Chief STEVE FORBES; Publr RICHARD KARLGAARD; Editor WILLIAM BALDWIN; circ. 925,518.

Fortune: 1271 Ave of the Americas, New York, NY 10020; tel. (212) 522-1212; fax (212) 522-0810; e-mail letters@fortune.com; internet www.fortune.com; f. 1930; Man. Editor ANDREW SERWER; circ. 865,850.

Game Informer: 724 North First St, 4th Floor, Minneapolis, MN 55401; tel. (612) 486-6100; fax (612) 486-6101; e-mail andy@

THE UNITED STATES OF AMERICA

gameinformer.com; internet www.gameinformer.com; f. 1991; owned by Sunrise Publs; monthly; computer gaming; Publr CATHY PRESTON; Editor-in-Chief ANDY MCNAMARA; circ. 1,934,859 (2005).

Glamour: 4 Times Sq., 16th Floor, New York, NY 10036; tel. (212) 286-2860; fax (212) 286-8336; e-mail letters@glamour.com; internet us.glamour.com; f. 1939; monthly; Publr WILLIAM WACKERMANN; Editor-in-Chief CYNTHIA LEIVE; circ. 2,262,242.

Golf Digest: 20 Westport Rd, POB 850, Wilton, CT 06897; tel. (800) 438-0491; fax (203) 761-5135; e-mail editor@golfdigest.com; internet www.golfdigest.com; f. 1950; monthly; Vice-Pres. and Publr THOMAS J. BAIR; Editor-in-Chief JERRY TARDE; circ. 1,660,712.

Golf Magazine: Time4 Media, 2 Park Ave, New York, NY 10016-5601; tel. (212) 779-5000; fax (212) 779-5588; e-mail golfletters@golfonline.com; internet www.golfonline.com; f. 1959; monthly; Publr CHARLIE KAMMERER; Editor DAVID CLARKE; circ. 1,414,651.

Good Housekeeping: 300 West 57th St, New York, NY 10019-5288; tel. (212) 649-2000; fax (212) 265-3307; e-mail ghkletters@hearst.com; internet www.goodhousekeeping.com; f. 1885; monthly; Publr PATRICIA HAEGELE; Editor-in-Chief ROSEMARY ELLIS; circ. 4,739,773.

Gourmet: 4 Times Sq., 9th Floor, New York, NY 10036; tel. (212) 286-8050; fax (212) 286-2932; internet www.epicurious.com/gourmet; f. 1941; sister publ. of *Bon Appétit*, under parent publ. *Epicurious*; owned by CondéNet, online affiliate of Condé Nast Publications; monthly; Publr THOMAS H. HARTMAN; Editor RUTH REICHL; circ. 969,308.

GQ: 4 Times Sq., New York, NY 10036; tel. (212) 286-6410; fax (212) 286-7969; internet us.gq.com; f. 1957; publ. by Condé Nast Publs; monthly; men's lifestyle; Vice-Pres. and Publr PETER HUNSINGER; Editor-in-Chief JIM NELSON; circ. 931,694.

Guideposts: 39 Seminary Hill Rd, Carmel, NY 10512; tel. (212) 929-1300; fax (212) 929-9574; e-mail gpeditors@guideposts.org; internet www.guidepostsmag.com; f. 1945; monthly; other publs incl. *Positive Thinking Magazine* (10 a year, circ. 335,000), *Angels on Earth* (6 a year, circ. 600,000) and *Guideposts Sweet 16* (6 a year); personal and spiritual development; Publr JANINE SCOLPINO; Editor-in-Chief EDWARD GRINNAN; circ. 2,377,107.

HANDY: 12301 Whitewater Dr., Minnetonka, MN 55343; tel. (952) 988-7294; fax (952) 988-7486; e-mail lokrend@naminc.com; internet www.handymanclub.com; f. 1993; publ. by North American Media Group Inc; official publ. of the Handyman Club of America; 6 a year; home improvement; Publr TOM SWEENEY; Editor LARRY OKREND; circ. 887,449.

Harper's Bazaar: 300 West 57th St, New York, NY 10019-3799; tel. (212) 903-5000; fax (212) 262-7101; e-mail bazaar@hearst.com; internet www.harpersbazaar.com; monthly; Publr VALERIE SALEMBIER; Editor-in-Chief GLENDA BAILEY; circ. 722,058.

Health: 2100 Lakeshore Dr., Birmingham, AL 35209; tel. (205) 445-6476; fax (205) 445-5123; e-mail health@timeinc.com; internet www.health.com; f. 1987; publ. by Southern Progress Corpn, a subsidiary of Time Inc; 10 a year; women's health and wellbeing; Publr and Vice-Pres. JENNIFER DEANS; Editor-in-Chief ELLEN KUNES; circ. 1,373,292.

Highlights for Children: 803 Church St, Honesdale, PA 18431; tel. (570) 253-1080; fax (570) 253-0179; internet www.highlights.com; f. 1946; monthly; Editor-in-Chief CHRISTINE FRENCH CLARK; circ. 1,800,000 (2007).

Home: 1633 Broadway, 44th Floor, New York, NY 10019; tel. (212) 767-5518; e-mail homemag@hfnm.com; internet www.homemag.com; f. 1981; publ. by Hachette Filipacchi Media US Inc; 10 a year; home improvement and decoration; Vice-Pres. and Publr JOHN H. GRANT; Vice-Pres. and Editor-in-Chief DONNA SAPOLIN; circ. 830,405.

Hot Rod Magazine: 6420 Wilshire Blvd, Los Angeles, CA 90048-5515; tel. (332) 782-2000; fax (323) 782-2223; e-mail hotrod@primedia.com; internet www.hotrod.com; f. 1948; monthly; Sr Vice-Pres. and Group Publr DOUG EVANS; Editor-in-Chief DAVID FREIBURGER; circ. 684,703.

House and Garden: 750 Third Ave, 3rd Floor, New York, NY 10017; tel. (212) 630-2260; fax (212) 630-3280; internet www.houseandgarden.com; f. 1901; publ. by Condé Nast Publs Inc; monthly; Vice-Pres. and Publr JOSEPH LAGANI; Editor-in-Chief DOMINIQUE BROWNING; circ. 976,443.

House Beautiful: 300 West 57th St, 24th Floor, New York, NY 10019-5970; tel. (212) 903-5206; internet www.housebeautiful.com; f. 1896; monthly; Publr KATE KELLY SMITH; Editor-in-Chief STEPHEN DRUCKER; circ. 873,278.

Inc.: 7 World Trade Center, New York, NY 10007-2195; tel. (212) 389-5300; fax (212) 389-5393; e-mail mail@inc.com; internet www.inc.com; f. 1987; acquired by Mansueto Ventures LLC in 2005; monthly; small business resources and advice; Vice-Pres. and Publr GORDON LEE JONES, III; Editor-in-Chief JANE BERENTSON; circ. 696,421.

Directory

In Style: 1271 Ave of the Americas, New York, NY 10020; tel. (212) 522-1212; internet www.instyle.com; f. 1994; publ. by Time Inc; celebrity, women's lifestyle and fashion; Man. Editor CHARLA LAWHON; circ. 1,780,681.

In Touch Weekly: 270 Sylvan Ave, Englewood Cliffs, NJ 07632; tel. (201) 569-6699; fax (201) 569-3584; e-mail contactintouch@intouchweekly.com; internet www.intouchweekly.com; f. 2002; publ. by Bauer Publishing USA; weekly; celebrity and entertainment; Publr MARK OLTARSH; Editor-in-Chief RICHARD SPENCER; circ. 1,310,931.

Jane: 750 Third Ave, New York, NY 10017; tel. (212) 630-4192; e-mail carlos_lamadrid@condenast.com; internet www.janemag.com; f. 1992; publ. by Condé Nast Publications; monthly; women's lifestyle; Vice-Pres. and Publr CARLOS LAMADRID; Editor-in-Chief BRANDON HOLLEY; circ. 706,561 (2005).

Jet: 820 South Michigan Ave, Chicago, IL 60605-2191; tel. (312) 322-9200; fax (312) 322-0951; internet www.ebonyjet.com; f. 1951; weekly; African-American general interest; Man. Editor MALCOLM R. WEST; circ. 909,406.

Junior Scholastic: 557 Broadway, New York, NY 10012; tel. (212) 343-6100; fax (212) 343-6333; e-mail junior@scholastic.com; f. 1937; 18 a year; Editor LEE BAIER; circ. 615,000.

Kiplinger's Personal Finance: 1729 H St, NW, Washington, DC 20006-3904; tel. (202) 887-6400; fax (202) 331-8637; e-mail magazine@kiplinger.com; internet www.kiplinger.com; f. 1947; monthly; Editor FRED FRAILEY; circ. 834,795.

Ladies' Home Journal: 125 Park Ave, New York, NY 10017-5599; tel. (212) 557-6600; fax (212) 455-1010; e-mail lhj@meredith.com; internet www.lhj.com; f. 1883; monthly; Publr JULIE PINKWATER; Editor-in-Chief DIANE SALVATORE; circ. 3,925,756.

The Lion: 300 22nd St, Oak Brook, IL 60523-8842; tel. (630) 571-5466; fax (630) 571-1685; e-mail magazine@lionsclubs.org; f. 1918; 11 a year; business and professional; Editor ROBERT KLEINFELDER; circ. 427,946.

Lucky: 4 Times Sq., 6th Floor, New York, NY 10036; tel. (212) 286-2860; fax (212) 286-4986; internet www.luckymag.com; f. 2000; publ. by Condé Nast Publs Inc; monthly; fashion and shopping; Vice-Pres. and Publr ALEXANDRA 'SANDY' GOLINKIN; Editor-in-Chief KIM FRANCE; circ. 1,167,020.

Marie Claire: 1790 Broadway, 3rd Floor, New York, NY 10019; tel. (212) 649-5000; fax (212) 501-5050; e-mail marieclairepromo@hearst.com; internet www.marieclaire.com; f. 1994; monthly; Publr SUSAN D. PLAGEMANN; Editor-in-Chief JOANNA COLES; circ. 971,348.

Martha Stewart Living: 11 West 42nd St, 25th Floor, New York, NY 10036; tel. (212) 827-8000; fax (212) 827-8204; e-mail mstewart@marthastewart.com; internet www.marthastewart.com; f. 1991; publ. by Martha Stewart Living Omnimedia, Inc; monthly; lifestyle and general interest; Publr SALLY PRESTON; Editor-in-Chief MARGARET ROACH; circ. 2,005,980; other publs incl. *Everyday Food* (f. 2003, circ. 897,647).

Maxim: 1040 Ave of the Americas, New York, NY 10018; tel. (212) 302-2626; fax (212) 302-2631; e-mail editors@maximmag.com; internet www.maximonline.com; f. 1997; publ. by Alpha Media Group; monthly; men's lifestyle and general interest; Editorial Dir JAMES KAMINSKY; circ. 2,568,339.

MediZine Healthy Living: 500 Fifth Ave, Suite 1900, New York, NY 10110; tel. (212) 695-2223; fax (212) 695-2936; e-mail requestinfo@medizine.com; internet www.medizine.com; f. 1994; quarterly; health and wellbeing; other publs incl. *Remedy* (f. 1995, circ. 2,400,000); *Diabetes Focus* (f. 2003, circ. 1,500,000); Editor-in-Chief DIANE UMANSKY; circ. 3,650,000.

Men's Fitness: 1 Park Ave, 10th Floor, New York, NY 10016; tel. (212) 545-4800; fax (212) 685-9644; e-mail jkimmel@amilink.com; internet www.mensfitness.com; f. 1985; publ. by AMI/Weider Publs; 10 a year; men's health, fitness and lifestyle; Publr MARC RICHARDS; Editor-in-Chief ROY S. JOHNSON; circ. 769,426.

Men's Health: 733 Third Ave, 15th Floor, New York, NY 10017; tel. (212) 573-0555; e-mail jon.hammond@rodale.com; internet www.menshealth.com; f. 1988; men's health and general interest; 10 a year; publ. by Rodale Inc; Vice-Pres. and Publr JACK ESSIG; Editor-in-Chief DAVID ZINCZENKO; circ. 1,816,671.

Men's Journal: 1290 Ave of the Americas, New York, NY 10104-0298; tel. (212) 484-1616; fax (212) 484-3429; e-mail eric.bizzak@mensjournal.com; internet www.mensjournal.com; f. 1992; publ. by Wenner Media, Inc; monthly; men's general interest and active lifestyle; Publr WILL SCHENCK; Editor (vacant); circ. 707,808.

Metropolitan Home: 1633 Broadway, 44th Floor, New York, NY 10019-6741; tel. (212) 767-5522; fax (212) 767-5636; e-mail metletters@hfnm.com; internet www.methome.com; f. 1981; publ. by Hachette Filipacchi Media US, Inc; 10 a year; interior design and architecture; Publr DEBORAH BURNS; Editor-in-Chief DONNA WARNER; circ. 565,157.

THE UNITED STATES OF AMERICA — Directory

Midwest Living: 125 Park Ave, New York, NY 10017; tel. (212) 551-7051; fax (212) 551-7115; e-mail brian.kightlinger@meredith.com; internet www.midwestliving.com; f. 1987; publ. by Meredith Corpn; 6 a year; lifestyle with focus on US Midwest; Publr BRIAN KIGHTLINGER; Editor-in-Chief GREG PHILBY; circ. 945,716.

Money: Time & Life Bldg, Rockefeller Center, New York, NY 10020; tel. (212) 522-1210; fax (212) 522-0970; e-mail managing_editor@moneymail.com; internet money.cnn.com; f. 1972; monthly; Man. Editor ERIC SCHURENBERG; circ. 1,933,584.

More: 125 Park Ave, New York, NY 10017-5529; tel. (212) 557-7600; fax (212) 455-1244; internet www.more.com; f. 1998; publ. by Meredith Corpn; 10 a year; women's lifestyle; Publr BRENDA SAGET DARLING; Editor-in-Chief PEGGY NORTHROP; circ. 1,254,273.

Motor Trend: 260 Madison Ave, 8th Floor, New York, NY 10016; tel. (212) 726-4300; fax (917) 256-0025; internet www.motortrend.com; f. 1949; publ. by Primedia, Inc; monthly; Publr IRA GABRIEL; Editor-in-Chief ANGUS MACKENZIE; circ. 1,122,706.

National Enquirer: 600 South East Coast Ave, Lantana, FL 33462-0001; tel. (561) 586-1111; fax (561) 540-1010; e-mail letters@nationalenquirer.com; internet www.nationalenquirer.com; f. 1926; publ. by American Media Inc; weekly; Publr DAVID JACKSON; Editor DAVID PEREL; circ. 1,063,470.

National Geographic Magazine: 1145 17th St, NW, Washington, DC 20036; tel. (212) 610-5500; fax (202) 775-6141; e-mail ngm@nationalgeographic.com; internet ngm.nationalgeographic.com; f. 1888; monthly; Pres. and CEO JOHN FAHEY; Editor-in-Chief CHRIS JOHNS; circ. 5,061,326.

National News: American Legion Auxiliary, 777 North Meridian St, 3rd Floor, Indianapolis, IN 46204-1420; tel. (317) 955-3845; e-mail cbrooks@legion-aux.org; internet www.legion-aux.org; publ. of the American Legion Auxiliary (ALA); 6 a year; information about the ALA; Editor CHRIS BROOKS; circ. 754,932.

The New Yorker: 4 Times Sq., New York, NY 10036-7448; tel. (212) 286-5400; fax (212) 286-4168; e-mail themail@newyorker.com; internet www.newyorker.com; f. 1925; weekly; Publr LOUIS CONA; Editor DAVID REMNICK; circ. 1,069,937.

Newsweek: Newsweek Bldg, 251 West 57th St, New York, NY 10019-1894; tel. (212) 445-4000; fax (212) 445-5068; e-mail webeditors@newsweek.com; internet www.newsweek.com; f. 1933; weekly; Publr PATRICK HAGERTY; Man. Editor JOHN MEACHAM; circ. 3,138,889.

Nick Jr. Family Magazine: 1515 Broadway, 32nd Floor, New York, NY 10036; tel. (212) 654-6198; fax (212) 846-1907; e-mail steven.esformes@nick.com; internet www.nickjr.com; f. 1999; subsidiary of Viacom Int. Inc; monthly; parenting; Editor-in-Chief FREDDI GREENBERG; circ. 1,150,000.

North American Hunter: 12301 Whitewater Dr., Minnetonka, MN 55343; tel. (952) 988-7101; fax (952) 936-9755; e-mail rsundberg@namginc.com; internet www.huntingclub.com; f. 1979; publ. by North American Media Group Inc; 8 a year; official publ. of the North American Hunting Club; hunting and conservation; Publr RICH SUNDBERG; Editor GORDY KRAHN; circ. 743,005.

O, The Oprah Magazine: 300 West 57th St, New York, NY 10019-5915; tel. (212) 903-5366; fax (212) 903-5388; e-mail omail@hearst.com; internet www.oprah.com/omagazine; f. 2001; monthly; Publr JILL SEELIG; Editor-in-Chief AMY GROSS; circ. 2,436,703.

Organic Gardening: 33 East Minor St, Emmaus, PA 18098-0099; tel. (610) 967-5171; fax (610) 967-8963; e-mail og@rodale.com; internet www.organicgardening.com; f. 1942; 6 a year; Editor SCOTT MEYER; circ. 174,560.

Outdoor Life: 2 Park Ave, 10th Floor, New York, NY 10016-5601; tel. (212) 779-5316; fax (212) 779-5118; e-mail olletters@time4.com; internet www.outdoorlife.com; f. 1898; 10 a year; Editor-in-Chief TODD W. SMITH; Exec. Editor JOHN SNOW; circ. 943,129.

Outside: 400 Market St, Santa Fe, NM 87501; tel. (505) 989-7100; fax (505) 989-4700; e-mail letters@outsidemag.com; internet outside.away.com; f. 1976 as Mariah; publ. by Mariah Media Inc; monthly; adventure travel and outdoor recreation; Chair. and Editor-in-Chief LAWRENCE J. BURKE; Vice-Pres. and Publr SCOTT PARMELEE; circ. 664,951.

Parenting: 530 Fifth Ave, 10th Floor, New York, NY 10036; tel. (212) 522-8989; internet www.parenting.com; f. 1987; owned by Time Inc; monthly; other publs. incl. *Babytalk* (f. 1935, circ. 2,006,906 in 2006); Editor-in-Chief JANET CHAN; Publr GREG SCHUMANN; circ. 1,899,833.

Parents' Magazine: 375 Lexington Ave, 10th Floor, New York, NY 10017-5514; tel. (212) 878-8700; fax (212) 986-2656; e-mail support@parents.com; internet www.parents.com; f. 1926; monthly; Publr DIANE NEWMAN; Editor-in-Chief SALLY LEE; circ. 2,073,486.

PC Magazine: 28 East 28th St, New York, NY 10016; tel. (212) 503-5100; fax (212) 503-5000; e-mail jim_mccabe@ziffdavis.com; internet www.pcmag.com; f. 1981; fortnightly; personal computer industry; Publr JIM MCCABE; Editor-in-Chief JIM LOUDERBACK; circ. 708,301.

PC World: PC World Communications, 501 Second St, San Francisco, CA 94107; tel. (415) 243-0500; fax (415) 442-1891; e-mail pcwletters@pcworld.com; internet www.pcworld.com; f. 1982; publ. by PC World Communications, Inc, a subsidiary of International Data Group; monthly; computer technology; Vice-Pres. and Publr MICHAEL CARROLL; Vice-Pres. and Editor-in-Chief HARRY MCCRACKEN; circ. 745,525.

People: Time and Life Bldg, 28th Floor, Rockefeller Center, New York, NY 10020; tel. (212) 522-3347; fax (212) 522-0883; e-mail editor@people.com; internet www.people.com; f. 1974; publ. by Time Inc; weekly; celebrity and entertainment; Publr PAUL CAINE; Man. Editor LARRY HACKETT; circ. 3,738,902.

Playboy: 680 North Lake Shore Dr., Chicago, IL 60611-4402; tel. (312) 751-8000; fax (312) 751-2818; e-mail edit@playboy.com; internet www.playboy.com/magazine-toc.html; f. 1953; monthly; men's interest; Publr LOUIS MOHN; Editor-in-Chief HUGH M. HEFNER; circ. 2,880,337.

Popular Mechanics: 300 West 57th St, New York, NY 10019-5899; tel. (212) 649-2000; e-mail popularmechanics@hearst.com; internet www.popularmechanics.com; f. 1902; monthly; Publr WILLIAM CONGDON; Editor-in-Chief JAMES B. MEIGS; circ. 1,229,998.

Popular Science: 2 Park Ave, 9th Floor, New York, NY 10016; tel. (212) 779-5000; fax (212) 779-5108; e-mail letters@popsci.com; internet www.popsci.com; f. 1872; monthly; Editor MARK JANNOT; circ. 1,364,865.

Prevention: 33 East Minor St, Emmaus, PA 18098-0001; tel. (610) 967-8045; fax (610) 967-9198; e-mail prevention@rodale.com; internet www.prevention.com; f. 1950; monthly; Editor-in-Chief LIZ VACCARIELLO; circ. 3,396,760.

Progressive Farmer: 2204 Lakeshore Dr., Birmingham, AL 35209; tel. (205) 414-4700; fax (205) 414-4705; e-mail jodle@progressivefarmer.com; internet www.progressivefarmer.com; f. 1886; monthly; Publr ADRIAN BLAKE; Editor JACK ODLE; circ. 650,000.

Reader's Digest: Reader's Digest Rd, Pleasantville, NY 10570-7000; tel. (914) 238-1000; fax (914) 238-4559; internet www.rd.com; f. 1922; monthly; Editor-in-Chief PEGGY NORTHROP; circ. 10,700,000 (2007).

Real Simple: 1271 Ave of the Americas, Suite 41–46B, New York, NY 10020; tel. (212) 522-1212; fax (212) 467-1398; internet www.realsimple.com; f. 2000; owned by Time Inc; monthly, plus two special issues; women's lifestyle and general interest; Publr STEVE SACHS; Man. Editor KRISTIN VAN OGTROP; circ. 1,973,306.

Redbook: 224 West 57th St, 6th Floor, New York, NY 10019-3203; tel. (212) 649-3450; fax (212) 581-8114; e-mail redbook@hearst.com; internet www.redbookmag.com; f. 1903; monthly; Publr MARY E. MORGAN; Editor-in-Chief STACY MORRISON; circ. 2,374,237.

RISE Magazine: SchoolSports, Inc, 971 Commonwealth Ave, Boston, MA 02215-1305; tel. (617) 779-9000; fax (617) 779-9100; e-mail feedback@risemag.com; internet www.risemag.com; f. 1997 as *SchoolSports Magazine*; publ. by Scout Publishing; 9 a year; 25 regional edns distributed to c. 6,500 schools; sports and teenage active lifestyle; Publr DAVID WEISS; Editor-in-Chief JONATHAN SEGAL; circ. 912,411.

Road & Track: 1499 Monrovia Ave, Newport Beach, CA 92663-2752; tel. (949) 720-5300; fax (949) 631-2757; e-mail rtletters@hfmus.com; internet www.roadandtrack.com; f. 1947; monthly; Publr JOHN DRISCOLL; Editor THOMAS L. BRYANT; circ. 711,973.

Rolling Stone: 1290 Ave of the Americas, 2nd Floor, New York, NY 10104-0298; tel. (212) 484-1616; fax (212) 484-3429; e-mail feedback@rollingstone.com; internet www.rollingstone.com; f. 1967; fortnightly; Publr RAY CHELSTOWSKI; Man. Editor WILL DANA; circ. 1,445,048.

Scholastic Parent & Child: 557 Broadway, New York, NY 10012; tel. (212) 343-6100; e-mail news@scholastic.com; internet teacher.scholastic.com/products/classmags/parent_child.htm; f. 1995; publ. by Scholastic Inc; a year; Publr RISA CRANDALL; Editor-in-Chief STEPHANIE IZAREK; circ. 1,226,909.

Scientific American: 415 Madison Ave, New York, NY 10017-1179; tel. (212) 451-8200; fax (212) 754-1138; e-mail editors@sciam.com; internet www.sciam.com; f. 1845; monthly; Publr BRUCE BRANDFON; Exec. Editor MARIETTE DICHRISTINA; circ. 593,126.

Scouting Magazine: 1325 West Walnut Hill Lane, POB 152079, Irving, TX 75015-2079; tel. (972) 580-2000; fax (972) 580-2079; e-mail scole@netbsa.org; internet www.scoutingmagazine.org; f. 1913; publ. by Boy Scouts of America; 6 a year; Publr J. WARREN YOUNG; Editor-in-Chief J. D. OWEN; circ. 1,020,466 (2005).

SELF Magazine: 4 Times Sq., 5th Floor, New York, NY 10036; tel. (212) 286-2860; fax (212) 286-6174; e-mail comments@self.com; internet www.self.com; f. 1979; monthly; Vice-Pres. and Publr

THE UNITED STATES OF AMERICA

KIMBERLY ANDERSON KELLEHER; Editor-in-Chief LUCY DANZIGER; circ. 1,486,992.

Seventeen: 300 West 57th St, New York, NY 10019-1798; tel. (212) 649-2000; e-mail mail@seventeen.com; internet www.seventeen.com; f. 1944; publ. by Hearst Corpn; monthly; Publr JAYNE JAMISON; Editor-in-Chief ANN SHOKET; circ. 2,052,666.

Shape: 1 Park Ave, 10th Floor, New York, NY 10016; tel. (212) 545-4800; fax (212) 252-1131; internet www.shape.com; f. 1981; publ. by American Media, Inc; women's health and fitness; Publr SABINE FELDMANN; Editor-in-Chief VALERIE LATONA; circ. 1,747,569.

Sierra: 85 Second St, 2nd Floor, San Francisco, CA 94105; tel. (415) 977-5500; fax (415) 977-5799; e-mail sierra.magazine@sierraclub.org; internet www.sierraclub.org/sierra; f. 1893; official publ. of the Sierra Club; 6 a year; nature and ecology; Editor-in-Chief BOB SIPCHEN; circ. 644,929.

SmartMoney: 1755 Broadway, 2nd Floor, New York, NY 10019; tel. (212) 765-7323; e-mail editors@smartmoney.com; internet www.smartmoney.com; f. 1992; jt venture of Dow Jones & Co, Inc and Hearst Corpn; Publr BILL SHAW; Editor-in-Chief JONATHAN DAHL; circ. 819,812.

Smithsonian Magazine: 420 Lexington Ave, Suite 2335, New York, NY 10170; tel. (212) 916-1300; fax (212) 986-4259; e-mail bianchik@si.edu; internet www.smithsonianmagazine.com; f. 1970; monthly; Publr KERRY BIANCHI; Editor CAREY WINFREY; circ. 2,028,001 (2006).

Southern Living: 2100 Lakeshore Dr., Birmingham, AL 35209-6721; tel. (205) 877-6000; fax (205) 445-7523; internet www.southernliving.com; f. 1966; monthly; Editor JOHN ALEX FLOYD, Jr; circ. 2,813,116.

Sporting News: 475 Park Ave South, 27th Floor, New York, NY 10016; tel. (646) 424-2227; fax (646) 424-2232; e-mail ebaker@sportingnews.com; internet www.sportingnews.com; f. 1886; acquired by American City Business Journals, Inc in 2006; weekly; Publr ED BAKER; Editor JOHN D. RAWLINGS; circ. 710,920.

Sports Illustrated: 1271 Ave of the Americas, 33rd Floor, New York, NY 10020-1339; tel. (212) 522-1212; fax (212) 522-0475; internet sportsillustrated.cnn.com; f. 1954; weekly; Editor TERRY MCDONNELL; circ. 3,250,912.

Star: 1 Park Ave, 3rd Floor, New York, NY 10016; tel. (212) 545-4800; fax (212) 532-0940; internet www.starmagazine.com; f. 1974; weekly; Editor-in-Chief CANDACE TRUNZO; circ. 1,458,104.

Sunset Magazine: 80 Willow Rd, Menlo Park, CA 94025-3691; tel. (650) 321-3600; fax (650) 327-5737; internet www.sunset.com; f. 1898; monthly; Editor KATIE TAMONY; circ. 1,458,628 (2005).

TENNIS: 79 Madison Ave, 8th Floor, New York, NY 10016; tel. (212) 636-2700; fax (212) 636-2720; e-mail jwilliams@tennismagazine.com; internet www.tennis.com; f. 1965; acquired by Miller Publishing Group LLC in 1997; 10 a year; tennis, travel and lifestyle; Publr JEFF WILLIAMS; Editor-in-Chief JAMES MARTIN; circ. 603,096.

This Old House: 1185 Ave of the Americas, 27th Floor, New York, NY 10036; tel. (212) 522-9465; fax (212) 522-9435; e-mail toh_letters@thisoldhouse.com; internet www.thisoldhouse.com; f. 1995; publ. by Time Inc; 10 a year; home improvement; Editor J. SCOTT OMELIANUK; circ. 962,636.

Time: Time and Life Bldg, Rockefeller Center, 1271 Ave of the Americas, New York, NY 10020-1393; tel. (212) 522-1212; fax (212) 522-0023; e-mail letters@time.com; internet www.time.com; f. 1923; weekly; Editor-in-Chief JOHN HUEY; Man. Editor RICHARD STENGEL; circ. 3,399,967.

Traditional Home: 125 Park Ave, New York, NY 10017; tel. (212) 557-6600; fax (212) 551-6914; e-mail traditionalhome@meredith.com; internet www.traditionalhome.com; f. 1978; publ. by Meredith Corpn; 8 a year; Publr PAMELA DANIELS; Editor-in-Chief ANN OMVIG MAINE; circ. 966,173.

Travel & Leisure: 1120 Ave of the Americas, 10th Floor, New York, NY 10036-6770; tel. (212) 382-5600; fax (212) 768-1568; e-mail tlquery@amexpub.com; internet www.travelandleisure.com; f. 1971; monthly; Editor-in-Chief NANCY NOVOGROD; circ. 969,452.

TV Guide: 1211 Ave of the Americas, New York, NY 10036; tel. (212) 852-7500; fax (212) 815-7363; internet www.tvguide.com; f. 1953; weekly; Exec. Editor STEVE SONSKY; circ. 3,265,189.

US Weekly: 1290 Ave of the Americas, 2nd Floor, New York, NY 10104-0298; tel. (212) 484-1616; fax (212) 484-4242; e-mail letters@usmagazine.com; internet www.usmagazine.com; f. 1977; weekly; Publr VICTORIA LASDON ROSE; Editor-in-Chief JANICE MIN; circ. 1,880,291.

US News & World Report: 1050 Thomas Jefferson St, NW, Washington, DC 20007; tel. (202) 955-2000; fax (202) 955-2685; e-mail letters@usnews.com; internet www.usnews.com; f. 1933; weekly; Publr KERRY F. DYER; Pres. WILLIAM D. HOLIBER; Editor BRIAN KELLY; circ. 2,036,261 (2007).

Vanity Fair: 4 Times Sq., 7th Floor, New York, NY 10036; tel. (212) 286-2860; fax (212) 286-7036; e-mail vfmail@vf.com; internet www.vanityfair.com; f. 1983; monthly; Publr EDWARD MENICHESCHI; Editor-in-Chief GRAYDON CARTER; circ. 1,153,517.

VFW Magazine: 406 West 34th St, Kansas City, MO 64111-2736; tel. (816) 756-3390; fax (816) 968-1169; e-mail info@vfw.org; internet www.vfw.org; f. 1912; 11 a year; Editor RICHARD K. KOLB; circ. 1,546,196.

VIA: 150 Van Ness Ave, San Francisco, CA 94102-5208; tel. (415) 565-2451; fax (415) 863-4726; e-mail viamail@csaa.com; internet www.viamagazine.com; f. 1917; publ. by the California State Automobile Asscn; 6 a year; motoring; Editor BRUCE ANDERSON; circ. 2,836,029.

VIBE: 215 Lexington Ave, New York, NY 10016; tel. (212) 448-7300; fax (212) 448-7400; internet www.vibe.com; f. 1993; acquired by Keith Glen Media from VIBE/Spin Ventures in 2006; monthly; urban music and culture; also publ. *VIBE Vixen* (quarterly, circ. 340,000); Publr LEN BURNETT; Editor-in-Chief DANYEL SMITH; circ. 863,283.

Vogue: 4 Times Sq., 12th Floor, New York, NY 10036; tel. (212) 286-2810; fax (212) 286-8593; e-mail voguemail@aol.com; internet www.style.com/vogue; f. 1892; monthly; also publ. *Teen Vogue* (circ. 973,172); Publr THOMAS A. FLORIO; Editor ANNA WINTOUR; circ. 1,301,575.

Weight Watchers Magazine: 360 Lexington Ave, 11th Floor, New York, NY 10017; tel. (212) 370-0644; fax (212) 687-4398; f. 1968; monthly; Publr ANDREW AMILL; Editor KATE GREER; circ. 1,319,514.

WHERE: c/o Miller Publishing Group, 11100 Santa Monica Blvd, Suite 600, Los Angeles, CA, 90025-3384; tel. (310) 893-5400; fax (310) 893-5457; e-mail rick.mollineaux@wheremagazine.com; internet www.wheremagazine.com; f. 1936; acquired by Miller Publishing Group LLC in 1997; monthly; int. visitor information; 23 regional edns; Group Publr PETER BLACKWELL; Editorial Dir MARQ DE VILLIERS; circ. 1,112,766.

Woman's Day: 1633 Broadway, 42nd Floor, New York, NY 10019; tel. (212) 767-6418; e-mail womansday@hfmus.com; internet www.womansday.com; f. 1931; owned by Hachette Filipacchi; 17 a year; women's general interest; Editor-in-Chief JANE CHESNUTT; circ. 3,918,531.

Woman's World: Bauer Publishing, 270 Sylvan Ave, Englewood Cliffs, NJ 07632; tel. (201) 569-6699; fax (201) 569-5303; e-mail tstadnicki@bauer-usa.com; f. 1981; publ. by Bauer Publishing USA; weekly; women's general interest; other pubs incl. *First for Women* (circ. 1,438,672), *J-14* (circ. 462,682) and *Life & Style Weekly* (circ. 753,092); Publr GREG SLATTERY; Editor-in-Chief STEPHANIE SAIBLE; circ. 1,542,394.

Working Mother: 60 East 42nd St, 27th Floor, New York, NY 10165-0001; tel. (212) 351-6400; fax (212) 351-6483; e-mail editors@workingmother.com; internet www.workingmother.com; f. 1978; publ. by Working Mother Media, Inc; lifestyle magazine with focus on working mothers; Pres. and Publr JOAN SHERIDAN LABARGE; Editor-in-Chief SUZANNE RISS; circ. 832,853.

NEWS AGENCIES

Associated Press (AP): 50 Rockefeller Plaza, New York, NY 10020-1666; tel. (212) 621-1500; fax (212) 621-1679; e-mail info@ap.org; internet www.ap.org; f. 1848; Pres. and CEO TOM CURLEY; c. 1,700 newspaper mems in the USA, 6,000 broadcast mems and over 8,500 subscribers abroad.

Bloomberg News: 499 Park Ave, 15th Floor, New York, NY 10022; tel. (212) 318-2000; fax (212) 893-5999; internet www.bloomberg.com; f. 1981; Editor-in-Chief MATTHEW WINKLER.

Dow-Jones Newswires: Harborside Financial Center, 600 Plaza II, Jersey City, NJ 07311-3992; tel. (201) 938-5400; fax (201) 938-5600; e-mail newswires@dowjones.com; internet www.djnewswires.com; Exec. Vice-Pres. CLARE HART.

Jewish Telegraphic Agency, Inc (JTA): 330 Seventh Ave, 17th Floor, New York, NY 10001; tel. (212) 643-1890; fax (212) 643-8498; e-mail info@jta.org; internet www.jta.org; f. 1917; world-wide coverage of Jewish news; offices in Washington, DC, and Jerusalem, Israel; Pres. DANIEL J. KRIFCHER; Exec. Editor and Publr MARK J. JOFFE.

Religion News Service: 1101 Connecticut Ave, NW, Suite 350, Washington, DC 20036; tel. (202) 463-8777; fax (202) 463-0033; e-mail info@religionnews.com; internet www.religionnews.com; Editor KEVIN ECKSTROM.

United Media (UM): 200 Madison Ave, 4th Floor, New York, NY 10016; tel. (212) 293-8500; fax (212) 293-8717; internet www.unitedmedialicensing.com; f. 1978; licensing and syndication of news features; Pres. and CEO DOUGLAS R. STERN.

United Press International (UPI): 1510 H St, NW, Washington, DC 20005; tel. (202) 898-8000; fax (202) 898-8057; internet www.upi

.com; f. 1907; Chair. and Pres. CHUNG HWAN KWAK; serves c. 1,000 newspaper clients world-wide.

NATIONAL ASSOCIATIONS

American Business Media: 675 Third Ave, Suite 415, New York, NY 10017-5704; tel. (212) 661-6360; fax (212) 370-0736; e-mail info@abmmail.com; internet www.americanbusinessmedia.com; f. 1906; Pres. and CEO GORDON T. HUGHES, II; mems: 160 publrs, 900 periodicals, 35 associates (suppliers).

American Society of Magazine Editors (ASME): 810 Seventh Ave, 24th Floor, New York, NY 100192; tel. (212) 872-3700; fax (212) 906-0128; e-mail asme@magazine.org; internet asme.magazine.org; Exec. Dir MARLENE KAHAN; 850 mems.

Audit Bureau of Circulations: 900 North Meacham Rd, Schaumburg, IL 60173-4968; tel. (847) 605-0909; fax (847) 605-0483; internet www.accessabc.com; f. 1914; Chair. ROBERT TROUTBECK; Pres. and Man. Dir MICHAEL J. LAVERY; over 4,000 mems.

Council of Literary Magazines and Presses (CLMP): 154 Christopher St, Suite 3C, New York, NY 10014-9110; tel. (212) 741-9110; fax (212) 741-9112; e-mail info@clmp.org; internet www.clmp.org; f. 1967; provides services to non-commercial US literary magazines and presses; Exec. Dir JEFFREY LEPENDORF; 347 mems.

Magazine Publishers of America (MPA): 810 Seventh Ave, 24th Floor, New York, NY 100192; tel. (212) 872-3700; fax (212) 888-4217; e-mail mpa@magazine.org; internet www.magazine.org; f. 1919; Pres. NINA B. LINK; 320 mem. cos and 100 assoc. mems.

National Newspaper Association: 127–129 Neff Annex, POB 7540, Columbia, MO 65205-7540; tel. (573) 882-5800; fax (573) 884-5490; e-mail info@nna.org; internet www.nna.org; f. 1885; Exec. Dir BRIAN STEFFENS; over 2,500 mems.

Newspaper Association of America: 4401 Wilson Blvd, Suite 900, Arlington, VA 22203-1867; tel. (571) 366-1000; fax (571) 366-1195; internet www.naa.org; f. 1992; Chair. BO JONES; Pres. and CEO JOHN F. STURM; more than 2,000 mems in USA and Canada accounting for over 87% of US daily newspaper circulation.

The Newspaper Guild: 501 Third St, NW, Washington, DC 20001-2760; tel. (202) 434-7177; fax (202) 434-1472; internet www.newsguild.org; f. 1933; journalists' org., organ of the Communications Workers of America trade union; Pres. LINDA K. FOLEY; over 34,000 mems.

Periodical & Book Association of America Inc: 481 Eighth Ave, Suite 826, New York, NY 10001; tel. (212) 563-6502; fax (212) 563-4098; internet www.pbaa.net; Exec. Dir LISA W. SCOTT; 60 mems.

Publishers

Abaris Books: 64 Wall St, Norwalk, CT 06850; tel. (203) 838-8625; fax (203) 857-0730; e-mail abaris@abarisbooks.com; internet www.abarisbooks.com; f. 1973; division of Opal Publishing Corpn; scholarly, fine art reference, philosophy; Publr ANTHONY S. KAUFMANN; Gen. Man. J. C. WEST.

Abbeville Press, Inc: 137 Varick St, New York, NY 10013; tel. (212) 366-5585; fax (212) 366-6966; internet www.abbeville.com; f. 1977; fine arts and illustrated books; Pres. and Publr ROBERT E. ABRAMS.

Abingdon Press: 201 Eighth Ave South, POB 801, Nashville, TN 37202-0801; tel. (615) 749-6290; fax (615) 749-6512; e-mail publicity@abingdonpress.com; internet www.abingdonpress.com; an imprint of The United Methodist Publishing House (f. 1789); religious; Vice-Pres. TAMMY GAINES.

Harry N. Abrams, Inc: 115 West 18th St, New York, NY 10011; tel. (212) 206-7715; fax (212) 519-1210; internet www.hnabooks.com; f. 1949; acquired by Times Mirror Co in 1966; imprints incl. Abrams Books (art, photography, design, architecture), Stewart, Tabori & Chang (f. 1981, cooking, design, gardening, crafts, pets, health, sports, and popular culture) and Amulet Books (f. 2004, youth fiction and non-fiction); owned by Groupe de la Martinière, France; Pres. and CEO MICHAEL JACOBS.

Addison-Wesley and Benjamin Cummings: 75 Arlington St, Suite 300, Boston, MA 02116; tel. (617) 848-6000; fax (617) 944-9338; internet www.aw-bc.com; f. 1942 as Addison-Wesley Press; division of Pearson Education; imprints incl. Addison-Wesley, Allyn & Bacon, Benjamin Cummings, and Longman; computing, economics, finance, mathematics, science and statistics; Chair. and CEO J. LARRY JONES.

AFB Press: 11 Penn Plaza, Suite 300, New York, NY 10001; tel. (212) 502-7651; fax (212) 502-7774; e-mail press@afb.net; internet www.afb.org/store; publishing arm of the American Foundation for the Blind; books, journals, videos, and electronic materials on visual impairment for professionals, researchers and blind or visually impaired individuals and their families; Pres. and CEO CARL R. AUGUSTO; Dir and Editor-in-Chief NATALIE HILZEN.

Alfred Publishing Co, Inc: POB 10003, Van Nuys, CA 91410-0003; fax (818) 891-4875; e-mail customerservice@alfred.com; internet www.alfred.com; f. 1922; educational music, methods and texts; Pres. MORTY MANUS; CEO STEVEN MANUS.

Andrews McMeel Publishing: 4520 Main St, Suite 700, Kansas City, MO 64111; tel. (816) 932-6700; fax (816) 932-6706; e-mail mmm@amuniversal.com; internet www.andrewsmcmeel.com; f. 1970; humour, general trade; Pres. and CEO HUGH T. ANDREWS.

Jason Aronson, Inc: 230 Livingston St, Northvale, NJ 07647; tel. (201) 767-4093; fax (201) 767-4330; e-mail bromer@rowman.com; internet www.aronson.com; f. 1965; psychiatry, psychoanalysis and behavioural sciences; Judaica; Pres. JASON ARONSON.

Augsburg Fortress, Publishers: 100 South Fifth St, POB 1209, Minneapolis, MN 55440; tel. (612) 330-3300; fax (612) 330-3455; e-mail info@augsburgfortress.org; internet www.augsburgfortress.org; f. 1890; publishing arm of the Evangelical Lutheran Church in America; religious (evangelical Lutheran) non-fiction; Pres. and CEO BETH LEWIS.

August House Inc, Publishers: 3500 Piedmont Rd, NE Suite 310, Atlanta, GA 30305; tel. (404) 442-4420; fax (404) 442-4435; e-mail ahinfo@augusthouse.com; internet www.augusthouse.com; f. 1979; Southern regional, history, humour and folklore; CEO STEVE FLOYD.

B&H Publishing Group: 127 Ninth Ave North, Nashville, TN 37234-0143; tel. (615) 251-5614; fax (615) 251-2701; e-mail miriam.evans@bhpublishinggroup.com; internet www.bhpublishinggroup.com; f. 1891; fmrly Broadman & Holman Publrs; present name adopted in 2006; religious (Protestant), fiction, non-fiction, reference and juvenile; Pres. KENNETH H. STEPHENS; Publr DAVID SHEPHERD.

Baker Publishing Group: POB 6287, Grand Rapids, MI 49516; tel. (616) 676-9185; fax (616) 676-9573; e-mail media@bakerbooks.com; internet www.bakerbooks.com; f. 1939; imprints incl. Brazos Press (Protestant and evangelical, Roman Catholic and Eastern Orthodox), Chosen Books (f. 1971, evangelical and charismatic Christian non-fiction), and Revell (Christian fiction and non-fiction); Pres. DWIGHT BAKER.

Ballantine Publishing Group: 1745 Broadway, New York, NY 10019; tel. (212) 572-2713; fax (212) 572-4912; e-mail bfi@randomhouse.com; internet www.randomhouse.com/bb; f. 1952; division of Random House Inc; fiction, non-fiction, reprints; Pres. GINA CENTRELLO.

Barnes and Noble Books: 122 5th Ave, 2nd Floor, New York, NY 10011; tel. (212) 633-3489; fax (212) 675-0413; internet www.barnesandnoble.com; f. 1873; division of Rowman & Littlefield Publrs, Inc; educational and general; Chair. LEONARD RIGGIO; CEO STEPHEN RIGGIO.

Barron's Educational Series, Inc: 250 Wireless Blvd, Hauppauge, NY 11788; tel. (631) 434-3311; fax (631) 434-3723; e-mail fbrown@barronseduc.com; internet www.barronseduc.com; f. 1945; general non-fiction, educational and juvenile; Chair. and CEO MANUEL H. BARRON; Pres. and Publr ELLEN SIBLEY.

Beacon Press: 25 Beacon St, Boston, MA 02108; tel. (617) 742-2110; fax (617) 723-3097; e-mail lriviere@beacon.org; internet www.beacon.org; f. 1854; dept of the Unitarian Universalist Asscn; world affairs, religion and general non-fiction; Dir HELENE ATWAN.

Blackwell Publishing Inc: 350 Main St, Malden, MA 02148; tel. (781) 388-8599; fax (781) 388-8232; e-mail customerservices@blackwellpublishing.com; internet www.blackwellpublishing.com; f. 1970; acquired by John Wiley and Sons, Inc in 2007; academic, medical and scientific, professional society publications; CEO RENÉ OLIVERI; Pres. GORDON TIBBITS, III.

R. R. Bowker LLC: 630 Central Ave, New Providence, NJ 07974; tel. (908) 464-6800; fax (908) 464-3553; e-mail info@bowker.com; internet www.bowker.com; f. 1872; reference and bibliography; Pres. and CEO ANNIE CALLANAN.

Branden Books, Inc: POB 812094, Wellesley, MA 02482; tel. (781) 734-2046; fax (781) 790-1056; internet www.branden.com; f. 1909; art, music, classics, fiction and non-fiction; Pres. ROBERT CASO; Editor and Treas. ADOLPH CASO.

George Braziller, Inc: 171 Madison Ave, New York, NY 10016; tel. (212) 889-0909; fax (212) 689-5405; e-mail info@georgebraziller.com; internet www.georgebraziller.com; f. 1955; art, fiction and non-fiction; Publr GEORGE BRAZILLER.

Brookings Institution Press: 1775 Massachusetts Ave, NW, Washington, DC 20036-2103; tel. (202) 797-6000; fax (202) 536-3623; e-mail bibooks@brookings.edu; internet www.brookings.edu; f. 1927; economics, govt, foreign policy; Dir ROBERT L. FAHERTY.

Cambridge University Press: 32 Ave of the Americas, New York, NY 10013-2473; tel. (212) 337-5000; e-mail newyork@cambridge.org; internet www.cambridge.org/us; scholarly; CEO STEPHEN BOURNE; Pres. RICHARD ZIEMACKI.

Catholic University of America Press: 620 Michigan Ave, NE, Washington, DC 20064; tel. (202) 319-5052; fax (202) 319-4985;

THE UNITED STATES OF AMERICA

e-mail cua-press@cua.edu; internet cuapress.cua.edu; f. 1939; scholarly; Dir DAVID J. MCGONAGLE.

Caxton Press: 312 Main St, Caldwell, ID 83605; tel. (208) 459-7421; fax (208) 459-7450; e-mail sgipson@caxtonpress.com; internet www.caxtonpress.com; f. 1903; Western Americana; Vice-Pres. and Publr SCOTT GIPSON.

Columbia University Press: 61 West 62nd St, New York, NY 10023; tel. (212) 459-0600; fax (212) 459-3678; e-mail cup_publicity@columbia.edu; internet www.columbia.edu/cu/cup; f. 1893; trade, educational, scientific and reference; Pres. and Dir JAMES D. JORDAN.

Concordia Publishing House (CPH): 3558 South Jefferson Ave, St Louis, MO 63118-3968; tel. (314) 268-1000; fax (314) 268-1329; internet www.cph.org; f. 1869; publishing arm of the Lutheran Church-Missouri Synod; religious (Lutheran) children's books, devotionals and curriculum music; Pres. and CEO BRUCE G. KINTZ.

Cornell University Press: Sage House, 512 East State St, POB 250, Ithaca, NY 14850; tel. (607) 257-2338; fax (607) 277-2374; e-mail cupressinfo@cornell.edu; internet www.cornellpress.cornell.edu; f. 1869; scholarly, non-fiction; Dir JOHN G. ACKERMAN.

CQ Press: 1255 22nd St, NW, Suite 400, Washington, DC 20037; tel. (202) 729-1800; fax (202) 729-1403; e-mail lwallace@cqpress.com; internet www.cqpress.com; f. 1945; fmrly Congressional Quarterly Books; business, education and govt; directories; Publr JOHN A. JENKINS.

Creative Co: 123 South Broad St, POB 227, Mankato, MN 56001; tel. (507) 388-6273; fax (507) 388-2746; f. 1932; juvenile; Pres. TOM PETERSON.

F. A. Davis Co: 1915 Arch St, Philadelphia, PA 19103; tel. (215) 568-2270; fax (215) 568-5065; e-mail info@fadavis.com; internet www.fadavis.com; f. 1879; medical, nursing and allied health textbooks; Pres. ROBERT H. CRAVEN, Jr.

Dover Publications, Inc: 31 East Second St, Mineola, NY 11501; tel. (516) 294-7000; fax (516) 742-5049; internet www.doverpublications.com; f. 1941; trade, reprints, scientific, classics, language, arts and crafts; Pres. PAUL NEGRI.

Dufour Editions, Inc: POB 7, Chester Springs, PA 19425-0007; tel. (610) 458-5005; fax (610) 458-7103; e-mail info@dufoureditions.com; internet www.dufoureditions.com; f. 1949; literature, political science, humanities, music and history; Pres. CHRISTOPHER MAY.

Duke University Press: POB 90660, Duke University, Durham, NC 27708-0660; tel. (919) 687-3600; fax (919) 688-4574; e-mail bpublicity@dukeupress.edu; internet www.dukeupress.edu; f. 1921; scholarly; Editor-in-Chief KEN WISSOKER.

Duquesne University Press: 600 Forbes Ave, Pittsburgh, PA 15282; tel. (412) 396-6610; fax (412) 396-5984; e-mail wadsworth@duq.edu; internet www.dupress.duq.edu; f. 1927; scholarly; Dir SUSAN WADSWORTH-BOOTH; Production Editor KATHY MEYER.

Ediciones Universal: 3090 South West Eighth St, Miami, FL 33135; tel. (305) 642-3234; fax (305) 642-7978; e-mail ediciones@ediciones.com; internet www.ediciones.com; f. 1965; Man. JUAN MANUEL SALVAT; Spanish language fiction and non-fiction.

Elsevier: 360 Park Ave South, New York, NY 10010; tel. (212) 989-5800; fax (212) 633-3990; e-mail newsroom@elsevier.com; internet www.elsevier.com; f. 1962; division of Reed Elsevier Group PLC; health sciences imprints incl. Butterworth-Heinemann (f. 1975, technology, medicine and management), Churchill Livingstone (f. 1972, medicine), Hanley & Belfus (f. 1984, medical textbooks and reference materials), Mosby (f. 1906, textbooks and reference materials on medicine, nursing, allied health and veterinary medicine), and W. B. Saunders Co (f. 1888, medicine); science and technology imprints incl. Academic Press (science, technology and business), Architectural Press (architecture), Focal Press (media technology), and Morgan Kaufmann (f. 1984, computing); CEO ERIK ENGSTROM.

Encyclopaedia Britannica, Inc: 331 North LaSalle Street, Chicago, IL 60610; tel. (312) 347-7000; fax (312) 347-7399; internet www.eb.com; f. 1768; encyclopaedias, atlases, dictionaries; CEO JORGE CAUZ.

Facts On File Inc: 132 West 31st St, 17th Floor, New York, NY 10001; tel. (212) 896-4269; fax (917) 339-0323; e-mail lkatz@factsonfile.com; internet www.factsonfile.com; f. 1941; acquired by Veronis Suhler Stevenson in 2005; imprints incl. Ferguson Publishing (f. 1907, children's reference); non-fiction, reference and electronic databases; Publr MARK MCDONNELL.

Farrar, Straus and Giroux, Inc (FSG): 19 Union Sq. West, New York, NY 10003; tel. (212) 741-6900; fax (212) 633-9385; internet www.fsgbooks.com; e-mail fsg.publicity@fsgbooks.com; f. 1946; acquired by Holtzbrinck Publrs, LLC in 1994; imprints incl. Hill and Wang (f. 1956), Faber and Faber, Inc, and North Point Press; literature, international fiction, history, current affairs and science; Chair. ROGER W. STRAUS; Pres. JONATHAN GALASSI.

Fordham University Press: University Box L, Bronx, NY 10458-5172; tel. (718) 817-4795; fax (718) 817-4785; e-mail bkaobrien@fordham.edu; internet www.fordhampress.com; f. 1907; scholarly; Dir ROBERT OPPEDISANO.

W. H. Freeman & Co, Publishers: 41 Madison Ave, 37th Floor, New York, NY 10010; tel. (212) 576-9400; fax (212) 689-2383; e-mail international@whfreeman.com; internet www.whfreeman.com; f. 1946; part of Holtzbrinck Publrs, LLC; textbooks; Pres. ELIZABETH WIDDICOMBE.

Samuel French, Inc: 45 West 25th St, New York, NY 10010; tel. (212) 206-8990; fax (212) 206-1429; e-mail info@samuelfrench.com; internet www.samuelfrench.com; f. 1830; plays; Man. Dir CHARLES R. VAN NOSTRAND.

Gale Cengage Learning: 27500 Drake Rd, Farmington Hills, MI 48331-3535; tel. (248) 669-4253; fax (248) 669-8064; e-mail galeord@gale.com; internet gale.cengage.com; f. 1954; division of Cengage Learning; reference; Pres. GORDON T. MACOMBER.

Garland Science Publishing, Inc: 270 Madison Ave, New York, NY 10016; tel. (917) 351-7100; fax (212) 947-3027; e-mail info@garland.com; internet www.garlandscience.com; f. 1969; part of the Taylor & Francis Group; biology and chemistry textbooks; Vice-Pres. DENISE SCHANCK.

Bernard Geis Associates: 360 E 72nd St, Suite A600, New York, NY 10021; tel. (212) 861-1540; f. 1958; general fiction and non-fiction.

Genealogical Publishing Co: 3600 Clipper Mill Rd, Suite 260, Baltimore, MD 21211; tel. (410) 837-8271; fax (410) 752-8492; e-mail info@genealogical.com; internet www.genealogical.com; f. 1959; genealogy, immigration studies, heraldry and local history; Editor-in-Chief MICHAEL TEPPER.

The K. S. Giniger Co, Inc: 250 West 57th St, Suite 2602, New York, NY 10107; tel. (212) 570-7499; fax (212) 369-6692; f. 1965; general non-fiction; Pres. KENNETH S. GINIGER.

Warren H. Green, Inc: 8356 Olive Blvd, St Louis, MO 63132; tel. (314) 991-8758; fax (314) 997-1788; e-mail editorial@whgreen.com; internet www.whgreen.com; f. 1966; imprints incl. Epoch Press (f. 1986, subsidy publishing, internet www.epoch-press.net); medical, science, technology and philosophy; Pres. LUCY KNAPP; Vice-Pres. PAULINE MUELLER.

Greenwood Publishing Group, Inc: 88 Post Rd West, POB 5007, Westport, CT 06881; tel. (203) 226-3571; fax (203) 222-1502; e-mail webmaster@greenwood.com; internet www.greenwood.com; f. 1967; division of Reed Elsevier Group PLC; comprises Greenwood Press (reference), Heinemann (f. 1978, educational, teaching, professional development), Praeger Publrs (f. 1949, academic and general-interest non-fiction) and Libraries Unlimited (educational and reference); business reference and non-fiction; Pres. WAYNE SMITH.

Grolier Publishing Co, Inc: 90 Sherman Turnpike, Danbury, CT 06816; tel. (203) 797-3500; fax (203) 797-3720; internet www.grolier.com/gi/service/custserve.html; f. 1946; subsidiary of Scholastic, Inc; juvenile educational.

Grove/Atlantic, Inc: 841 Broadway, New York, NY 10003-4793; tel. (212) 614-7850; fax (212) 614-7886; e-mail info@groveatlantic.com; internet www.groveatlantic.com; f. 1993 by merger of Grove Press and Atlantic Monthly Press (f. 1917); fiction, non-fiction, biography, history, social science, poetry; Pres. MORGAN ENTREKIN.

Hammond World Atlas Corpn: 95 Progress St, Union, NJ 07083; tel. (908) 206-1300; fax (908) 206-1104; e-mail customerservice@americanmap.com; internet www.hammondmap.com; f. 1900; division of American Map-Langenscheidt Publishing Group; maps, atlases, cartography; Chair. and CEO STUART DOLGINS.

Harcourt Inc: 6277 Sea Harbor Dr., Orlando, FL 32887; tel. (407) 345-2000; fax (407) 352-3445; internet www.harcourt.com; f. 1919; division of Reed Elsevier Group PLC; fiction, textbooks, general; Pres. and CEO JAMES LEVY.

HarperCollins Publishers: 10 East 53rd St, New York, NY 10022; tel. (212) 207-7000; fax (212) 207-7759; internet www.harpercollins.com; f. 1817; imprints incl. Avon (f. 1941, romantic fiction), Collins (general reference), Rayo (Latino culture) and William Morrow (f. 1926, fiction and non-fiction); fiction, non-fiction, religious, children's, medical, general; Pres. and CEO JANE FRIEDMAN.

Harvard University Press: 79 Garden St, Cambridge, MA 02138; tel. (401) 531-2800; fax (401) 531-2801; e-mail contact_hup@harvard.edu; internet www.hup.harvard.edu; f. 1913; classics, fine arts, philosophy, science, medicine, law, literature, political science, religion, history and govt; Dir WILLIAM P. SISLER.

Hastings House/Daytrips Publishers: POB 908, Winter Park, FL 32790-0908; tel. (407) 339-3600; fax (407) 339-5900; e-mail hastings_daytrips@earthlink.net; internet www.hastingshousebooks.com; f. 1936; travel; Publr PETER LEERS.

Holiday House, Inc: 425 Madison Ave, New York, NY 10017; tel. (212) 688-0085; fax (212) 421-6134; e-mail info@holidayhouse.com;

internet www.holidayhouse.com; f. 1935; juvenile; Pres. JOHN H. BRIGGS, Jr.

Holloway House Book Publishing Co: 8060 Melrose Ave, Los Angeles, CA 90046-7082; tel. (323) 653-8060; fax (323) 655-9452; e-mail info@psiemail.com; internet www.hollowayhousebooks.com; f. 1960; black experience and American Indian literature, gambling, fiction, non-fiction; CEO BENTLEY MORRISS.

Holmes & Meier Publishers, Inc: POB 943, Teaneck, NJ 07666; tel. (201) 833-2270; fax (201) 833-2272; e-mail info@holmesandmeier.com; internet www.holmesandmeier.com; f. 1969; imprints incl. Africana Publishing Co (f. 1969); history, political science, area studies, Africana, Judaica, foreign literature in translation, college texts and scholarly; Publr MIRIAM H. HOLMES.

Hoover Institution Press: Stanford University, Stanford, CA 94305-6010; tel. (650) 723-3373; fax (650) 723-8626; e-mail hooverpress@hoover.stanford.edu; internet www.hoover.org; f. 1962; scholarly; Assoc. Dir JEFFREY BLISS.

Houghton Mifflin Co: 222 Berkeley St, Boston, MA 02116; tel. (617) 351-5000; fax (617) 351-3604; e-mail corporate_communications@hmco.com; internet www.hmco.com; f. 1832; owned by Houghton Mifflin Riverdeep PLC, Ireland; general and educational; Chair., Pres. and CEO ANTHONY LUCKI.

Indiana University Press: 601 North Morton St, Bloomington, IN 47404-3797; tel. (812) 855-8817; fax (812) 855-7931; e-mail iupress@indiana.edu; internet www.iupress.indiana.edu; f. 1950; trade and scholarly non-fiction; Dir JANET RABINOWITCH.

International Universities Press, Inc: 59 Boston Post Rd, Madison, CT 06443; tel. (203) 245-4000; fax (203) 245-0775; e-mail info@iup.com; internet www.iup.com; f. 1943; psychology, psychiatry, medicine, social sciences and journals; Exec. Vice-Pres. Dr MARGARET EMERY.

Islamic Books/Tahrike Tarsile Qur'ān, Inc: POB 731115, Elmhurst, NY 11373-0115; tel. (718) 446-6472; fax (718) 446-4370; e-mail read@koranusa.org; internet www.koranusa.org; f. 1978; Koran and Islamic religious texts; Pres. AUNALI KHALFAN.

Jewish Publication Society: 2100 Arch St, 2nd Floor, Philadelphia, PA 19103; tel. (215) 832-0608; fax (215) 568-2017; e-mail jewishbook@jewishpub.org; internet www.jewishpub.org; f. 1888; Judaica; CEO and Editor-in-Chief Dr ELLEN FRANKEL.

Johns Hopkins University Press: 2715 North Charles St, Baltimore, MD 21218-4319; tel. (410) 516-6900; fax (410) 516-6998; e-mail rr@press.jhu.edu; internet www.press.jhu.edu; f. 1878; social and physical sciences, humanities, health sciences, economics, literary criticism, history; Dir KATHLEEN KEANE.

Kendall/Hunt Publishing Co: 4050 Westmark Dr., POB 1840, Dubuque, IA 52004-1840; tel. (563) 589-1000; fax (563) 589-1253; e-mail webmaster@kendallhunt.com; internet www.kendallhunt.com; f. 1944; business and educational; COO MARK FALB.

Krieger Publishing Co: POB 9542, Melbourne, FL 32902-9542; tel. (321) 724-9542; fax (321) 951-3671; e-mail info@krieger-pubishing.com; internet www.krieger-publishing.com; f. 1970; space technology, adult education, history and natural sciences; Pres. DONALD E. KRIEGER.

Loyola Press: 3441 North Ashland Ave, Chicago, IL 60657; tel. (773) 281-1818; fax (773) 281-0885; e-mail lane@loyolapress.com; internet www.loyolapress.org; f. 1912; religious (Roman Catholic) education and language, religious trade and arts; Pres. GEORGE A. LANE.

McGraw-Hill Companies, Inc: 1221 Ave of the Americas, New York, NY 10020; tel. (212) 512-2000; fax (212) 512-2821; internet www.mcgraw-hill.com; f. 1888; information texts and services for business, industry, govt and the general public; Chair. and CEO HAROLD MCGRAW, III.

Merriam-Webster Inc: 47 Federal St, POB 281, Springfield, MA 01102; tel. (413) 734-3134; fax (413) 731-5979; e-mail jwithgott@merriam-webster.com; internet www.merriam-webster.com; f. 1831; subsidiary of Encyclopaedia Britannica, Inc; dictionaries, reference; Pres. and Publr JOHN M. MORSE.

Michigan State University Press: 1405 South Harrison Rd, Suite 25, East Lansing, MI 48823-5245; tel. (517) 355-9543; fax (517) 432-2611; e-mail msupress@msu.edu; internet www.msupress.msu.edu; f. 1947; scholarly; Dir GABRIEL DOTTO.

The MIT Press: 55 Hayward St, Cambridge, MA 02142; tel. (617) 253-5646; fax (617) 258-6779; internet www.mitpress.mit.edu; f. 1932; computer sciences, architecture, design, linguistics, economics, philosophy, general science, neuroscience, cognitive science and engineering; Dir ELLEN W. FARAN.

Moody Publishers: 820 North LaSalle Blvd, Chicago, IL 60610; tel. (312) 329-2101; fax (312) 329-4157; e-mail pressinfo@moody.edu; internet www.moodypublishers.org; f. 1894; religious; Vice-Pres., Publications GREG THORNTON.

William Morrow & Co Inc: 10 East 53rd St, New York, NY 10022; tel. (212) 207-7000; fax (212) 207-7633; internet www.harpercollins.com; f. 1926; division of HarperCollins; fiction, non-fiction, juvenile; Pres. and CEO JANE FRIEDMAN.

National Academy Press: 500 Fifth St, NW, POB 285, Washington, DC 20055; tel. (202) 334-3180; fax (202) 334-2793; e-mail mlitts@nas.edu; internet www.nap.edu; f. 1863; division of Nat. Academy of Sciences; scientific and technical reports, abstracts, bibliographies, catalogues; Dir BARBARA KLINE POPE.

National Learning Corpn: 212 Michael Dr., Syosset, NY 11791; tel. (516) 921-8888; fax (516) 921-8743; e-mail info@passbooks.com; internet www.passbooks.com; f. 1967; professional and vocational study guides; Pres. MICHAEL P. RUDMAN.

New Directions Publishing Corpn: 80 Eighth Ave, New York, NY 10011; tel. (212) 255-0230; fax (212) 255-0231; e-mail editorial@ndbooks.com; internet www.ndpublishing.com; f. 1936; modern literature, poetry and criticism; Pres. and Publr PEGGY L. FOX.

New York University Press: 838 Broadway, 3rd Floor, New York, NY 10003; tel. (212) 998-2575; fax (212) 995-3833; e-mail customerservice@nyupress.org; internet www.nyupress.org; f. 1916; scholarly and non-fiction; Dir STEVE MAIKOWSKI.

Northwestern University Press: 629 Noyes St, Evanston, IL 60208; tel. (847) 491-2046; fax (847) 491-8150; e-mail nupress@northwestern.edu; internet www.nupress.northwestern.edu; f. 1958; scholarly and trade; Dir DONNA SHEAR.

W. W. Norton & Co Inc: 500 Fifth Ave, New York, NY 10110; tel. (212) 354-5500; fax (212) 869-0856; e-mail srothbard@wwnorton.com; internet www.wwnorton.com; f. 1924; college textbooks, paperbacks, fiction and non-fiction; CEO STEPHEN KING; Pres. DRAKE MCFEELY.

NOVA Publications: 7342 Lee Hwy, No. 201, Falls Church, VA 22046; tel. and fax (703) 237-1591; e-mail novapublic@aol.com; internet www.members.aol.com/novapublic/index.htm; f. 1993; military history, political science, Russian and Middle Eastern studies; Publr ARNOLD C. DUPUY.

Oceana Publications Inc: 75 Main St, Dobbs Ferry, NY 10522-1632; tel. (914) 693-8100; fax (914) 693-0402; e-mail editorial@oceanalaw.com; internet www.oceanalaw.com; f. 1948; international law and trade; division of Oxford University Press, Inc; Pres. DAVID R. COHEN.

The Ohio State University Press: 180 Pressey Hall, 1070 Carmack Rd, Columbus, OH 43210-1002; tel. (614) 292-6930; fax (614) 292-2065; e-mail info@osupress.org; internet www.ohiostatepress.org; f. 1957; scholarly; Dir MALCOLM LITCHFIELD.

Ohio University Press: 19 Circle Dr., The Ridges, Athens, OH 45701; tel. (740) 593-1154; fax (740) 593-4536; e-mail cunningh@ohio.edu; internet www.ohiou.edu/oupress; f. 1964; scholarly and regional studies; Dir DAVID SANDERS.

Open Court Publishing Co: 70 East Lake St, Suite 300, Chicago, IL 60601; tel. (312) 701-1720; fax (312) 701-1728; e-mail opencourt@caruspub.com; internet www.opencourtbooks.com; f. 1887; general non-fiction; Pres. and Publr ANDRE CARUS.

Orbis Books: Walsh Bldg, POB 308, Maryknoll, NY 10545-0308; tel. (914) 941-7590; fax (914) 945-0670; e-mail orbisbooks@maryknoll.org; internet www.orbisbooks.com; f. 1970; theology, religion and social concerns; Publr ROBERT ELLSBERG.

Oxford University Press Inc: 198 Madison Ave, New York, NY 10016; tel. (212) 726-6000; fax (212) 726-6446; e-mail custserv.us@oup.com; internet www.oup.com/us; f. 1896; non-fiction, trade, religious, reference, college textbooks, medical and music; Pres. TIM BARTON.

Paladin Press: Gunbarrel Tech Center, 7077 Winchester Circle, Boulder, CO 80301; tel. (303) 443-7250; fax (303) 442-8741; e-mail service@paladin-press.com; internet www.paladin-press.com; f. 1970; military science and history; Chair. and Pres. PEDER C. LUND.

Paragon House: 1925 Oakcrest Ave, Suite 7, St Paul, MN 55113-2619; tel. (651) 644-3087; fax (651) 644-0997; e-mail info@paragonhouse.com; internet www.paragonhouse.com; f. 1982; academic non-fiction, university texts, reference; Exec. Dir GORDON L. ANDERSON.

Penguin Group (USA) Inc: 375 Hudson St, New York, NY 10014; tel. (212) 366-2000; fax (212) 366-2666; internet us.penguingroup.com; f. 1996 by merger between Penguin Books USA and the Putnam Berkley Group; imprints incl. Ace Books (f. 1953, science fiction), Avery (f. 1976, health, self-help, diet, and fitness), Alpha (f. 1991, general reference) Berkley (f. 1955, mass-market and trade paperback), Dutton (f. 1852, fiction and non-fiction), Gotham (f. 2001, non-fiction), Putnam (f. 1838, fiction and non-fiction), HP Books (automotive, photography, gardening, health and child care), Hudson Street Press (f. 2003, hardcover non-fiction), Jeremy P. Tarcher (f. 1976, non-fiction), NAL (f. 1948, paperback fiction), Penguin (f. 1936, paperback), Plume (f. 1970, paperback), Portfolio (f. 2001, business), Riverhead (f. 1994, fiction), Sentinel (f. 2003, conservative), and Viking (f. 1925, fiction and non-fiction); CEO DAVID SHANKS; Pres. SUSAN PETERSEN KENNEDY.

THE UNITED STATES OF AMERICA

Pennsylvania State University Press: University Support Bldg I, Suite C, 820 North University Dr., University Park, PA 16802; tel. (814) 865-1327; fax (814) 863-1408; e-mail info@psupress.org; internet www.psupress.org; f. 1956; scholarly non-fiction; Dir SANFORD G. THATCHER.

Presbyterian Publishing Corpn (PPC): 100 Witherspoon St, Louisville, KY 40202-1396; tel. (502) 569-5081; fax (502) 569-5113; e-mail publicity@wjkbooks.com; internet www.ppcbooks.com; f. 1938; publishing arm of the Presbyterian Church (USA); imprints incl. Geneva Press (religious trade) and Westminster John Knox Press (f. 1938, non-denominational Christian, modern religious and scholarly); Pres. and Publr DAVIS PERKINS.

Princeton University Press: 41 William St, Princeton, NJ 08540; tel. (609) 258-4900; fax (609) 258-6305; e-mail webmaster@press.princeton.edu; internet press.princeton.edu; f. 1905; scholarly; Dir PETER J. DOUGHERTY; Editor-in-Chief BRIGITTA VAN RHEINBERG.

Quite Specific Media Group Ltd: 7373 Pyramid Pl., Hollywood, CA 90046; tel. (323) 851-5797; fax (323) 851-5798; e-mail info@quitespecificmedia.com; internet www.quitespecificmedia.com; f. 1967; costume, design, fashion and performing arts; Publr RALPH PINE.

Rand McNally: 8255 North Central Park Ave, Skokie, IL 60076; tel. (847) 329-8100; fax (847) 329-6361; e-mail pelsberg@reynoldsgroup.com; internet www.randmcnally.com; f. 1856; maps, atlases, travel guides and educational; Chair. PETER J. NOLAN; Pres. ROBERT APATOFF.

Random House Publishing Group: 1745 Broadway, New York, NY 10019; tel. (212) 782-9000; fax (212) 572-8026; internet www.randomhouse.com; f. 2003 by merger of the Random House Trade Group and Ballantine Books Group; imprints incl. Random House Inc (f. 1925, originals, reprints, paperbacks, juvenile, series, textbooks), Ballantine Books (f. 1952, hardcover, trade and mass-market paperback), Del Rey (f. 1977, science fiction and fantasy), Modern Library (f. 1925, non-fiction and history), One World (f. 1991, multicultural), Presidio Press (military history), and Villard (f. 1983, general fiction and non-fiction); Chair. and CEO PETER OLSON.

Reader's Digest Association: Reader's Digest Rd, Pleasantville, NY 10570-7000; tel. (914) 238-1000; fax (914) 238-4559; internet www.rd.com; reference and non-fiction; Pres. and CEO MARY BERNER.

Rizzoli International Publications: 300 Park Ave South, New York, NY 10010-5399; tel. (212) 387-3400; fax (212) 387-3535; e-mail tkayiatos@rizzoliusa.com; internet www.rizzoliusa.com; f. 1975; division of RCS Media Group (Italy); fine arts, performing arts, architecture; Pres. and CEO MARCO AUSENDA; Vice-Pres. and Publr CHARLES MIERS.

Routledge: 270 Madison Ave, New York, NY 10016-0602; tel. (212) 216-7800; fax (212) 564-7854; e-mail info@taylorandfrancis.com; internet www.routledge-ny.com; f. 1977; imprint of Taylor & Francis Group (q.v.); scholarly, professional, trade, humanities, social sciences.

Rutgers University Press: 100 Joyce Kilmer Ave, Piscataway, NJ 08854; tel. (732) 445-7762; fax (732) 445-7039; e-mail jwi@rutgers.edu; internet rutgerspress.rutgers.edu; f. 1936; scholarly and regional; Dir MARLIE WASSERMAN.

William H. Sadlier Inc: 9 Pine St, New York, NY 10005; tel. (212) 227-2120; fax (212) 267-8696; e-mail wsd@sadlier.com; internet www.sadlier.com; f. 1832; textbooks; Pres. WILLIAM SADLIER DINGER.

St Martin's Press Inc: 175 Fifth Ave, New York, NY 10010; tel. (212) 674-5151; fax (212) 420-9314; e-mail webmaster@stmartins.com; internet www.stmartins.com; f. 1952; part of Holtzbrinck Publrs, LLC; general, scholarly, college textbooks, trade, mass-market and scholarly; Pres. JOHN SARGENT.

Scarecrow Press, Inc: 4501 Forbes Blvd, Suite 200, Lanham, MD 20706; tel. (301) 459-3366; fax (301) 429-5748; e-mail custserv@rowman.com; internet www.scarecrowpress.com; f. 1950; music, film, theatre, reference, textbooks, library and information science; Publr and Editorial Dir EDWARD KURDYLA.

Scholastic, Inc: 555 Broadway, New York, NY 10012; tel. (212) 343-6100; fax (212) 343-6930; e-mail customerservice@scholastic.com; internet www.scholastic.com; f. 1920; children's periodicals, textbooks, educational materials; Chair., Pres. and CEO M. RICHARD ROBINSON.

Harlequin Enterprises Ltd: 233 Broadway, New York, NY 10279; tel. (212) 553-4200; fax (212) 227-8969; e-mail public_relations@harlequin.ca; internet www.eharlequin.com; f. 1979; Harlequin Enterprises, Canada; imprints incl. Harlequin and Silhouette Books; women's fiction, adventure, mystery reprints; Pres. and Publr DONNA HAYES.

Simon & Schuster, Inc: 1230 Ave of the Americas, New York, NY 10020; tel. (212) 698-7000; fax (212) 698-7007; internet www.simonsays.com; f. 1924; trade, juvenile, reference, educational, business and professional; imprints include Aladdin Paperbacks (juvenile fiction), Free Press (politics, history, religion, business, fiction), Howard Books (f. 1969, religion, gift books), Pocket Books (f. 1939, fiction), and Scribner (f. 1846, fiction); Pres. and CEO JACK ROMANOS.

Peter Smith Publisher, Inc: 5 Lexington Ave, Magnolia, MA 01930; tel. (978) 525-3562; fax (978) 525-3674; reprints; Pres. MARY ANN LASH.

Smithsonian Institution Press: 750 Ninth St NW, Suite 4300, Washington, DC 20560-0950; tel. (202) 275-2243; fax (202) 275-2243; e-mail info@sipress.si.edu; internet www.sipress.si.edu; f. 1848; scholarly and general interest, American studies and culture, anthropology, archaeology, natural science and museum studies; Dir DON FEHR.

Southern Illinois University Press: 1915 University Press Dr., Carbondale, IL 62901-4323; 1915 University Press Dr., SIUC Mail Code 6806, Carbondale, IL 62902-6806; tel. (618) 453-2281; fax (618) 453-1221; e-mail ladkins@siu.edu; internet www.siu.edu/~siupress; f. 1953; scholarly non-fiction; Dir ARTHUR M. (LAIN) ADKINS.

Springer: 233 Spring St, New York, NY 10013; tel. (212) 460-1500; fax (212) 460-1575; e-mail service-ny@springer.com; internet www.springer.com; f. 1964; part of Springer Science+Business Media; scientific, technical and medical; CEO DERK HAAK.

Stanford University Press: 1450 Page Mill Rd, Palo Alto, CA 94304; tel. (650) 723-9434; fax (650) 725-3457; e-mail info@www.sup.org; internet www.sup.org; f. 1925; Dir GEOFFREY BURN.

State University of New York Press: 194 Washington Ave, Suite 305, Albany, NY 12210-2384; tel. (518) 472-5000; fax (518) 472-5038; e-mail info@sunypress.edu; internet www.sunypress.edu; f. 1966; scholarly and general interest; Interim Dir JAMES PELTZ.

Sterling Publishing Co, Inc: 387 Park Ave South, New York, NY 10016; tel. (212) 532-7160; fax (212) 213-2495; e-mail publicity@sterlingpub.com; internet www.sterlingpub.com; f. 1949; subsidiary of Barnes and Noble, Inc; non-fiction and illustrated; Chair. BURTON H. HOBSON.

Syracuse University Press: Suite 110, 621 Skytop Rd, Syracuse, NY 13244-5290; tel. (315) 443-5534; fax (315) 443-5545; e-mail supress@syr.edu; internet www.syracuseuniversitypress.syr.edu; f. 1943; scholarly; Dir PETER B. WEBBER.

Taplinger Publishing Co Inc: POB 175, Marlboro, NJ 07746; tel. (305) 256-7880; fax (305) 256-7816; e-mail taplingerpub@yahoo.com; f. 1955; general fiction and non-fiction; Pres. LOUIS STRICK.

Taylor & Francis Group: 270 Madison Ave, New York, NY 10016; tel. (212) 216-7800; fax (212) 564-7854; e-mail info@taylorandfrancis.com; internet www.taylorandfrancis.com; f. 1972; division of Informa PLC; imprints incl. CRC Press (f. 1913, reference, science, engineering and medicine), Garland Science Publishing (f. 1969, molecular biology, immunology and protein science textbooks), Routledge (q.v.), and Taylor & Francis Books (f. 1972, academic, science and reference); Pres. EMMETT DAGES.

Charles C Thomas, Publisher: 2600 South First St, Springfield, IL 62794-9265; tel. (217) 789-8980; fax (217) 789-9130; e-mail books@ccthomas.com; internet www.ccthomas.com; f. 1927; textbooks and reference on education, medicine, psychology and criminology; Pres. MICHAEL P. THOMAS.

Time Life, Inc: POB 4002011, Des Moines, IA 50340-2011; f. 1961; general non-fiction; Pres. and CEO JIM NELSON.

Tuttle Publishing: Airport Business Park, 364 Innovation Dr., North Clarendon, VT 05759; e-mail info@tuttlepublishing.com; internet www.tuttlepublishing.com; f. 1832; the Far East, particularly Japan, languages, art, crafts, martial arts, culture, juvenile, cookery; Publishing Dir EDWARD WALTERS.

United Nations Publications: United Nations Plaza, Room DC2-0853, New York, NY 10017; tel. (212) 963-8302; fax (212) 963-3489; e-mail publications@un.org; internet unp.un.org; f. 1946; world and national economies, international trade, social questions, human rights and international law; Chief of Section CHRISTOPHER WOODTHORPE.

University of Alabama Press: POB 870380, Tuscaloosa, AL 35487; tel. (205) 348-5180; fax (205) 348-9201; e-mail drickman@uapress.ua.edu; internet www.uapress.ua.edu; f. 1945; scholarly; Dir DANIEL J. J. ROSS.

University of Alaska Press: POB 756240, Fairbanks, AK 99775-6240; tel. (907) 474-5831; fax (907) 474-5502; e-mail fypress@uaf.edu; internet www.uaf.edu/uapress; f. 1967; scholarly regional non-fiction, history, anthropology of the circumpolar north; Chair. of Editorial Bd PATRICIA H. PARTNOW.

University of Arizona Press: 355 South Euclid Ave, Suite 103, Tucson, AZ 85719; tel. (520) 621-1441; fax (520) 621-8899; e-mail uapress@uapress.arizona.edu; internet www.uapress.arizona.edu; f. 1959; scholarly, popular, regional and non-fiction; Dir CHRISTINE SZUTER.

THE UNITED STATES OF AMERICA

University of Arkansas Press: McIlroy House, 201 Ozark Ave, Fayetteville, AR 72701; tel. (479) 575-3246; fax (479) 575-6044; e-mail cmoss@uark.edu; internet www.uapress.com; f. 1980; humanities, literature, regional studies, natural history, Middle Eastern studies, poetry, civil rights studies and American history; Dir LARRY MALLEY.

University of California Press: 2120 Berkeley Way, Berkeley, CA 94704-1012; tel. (510) 642-4247; fax (510) 643-7127; e-mail askucp@ucpress.edu; internet www.ucpress.edu; f. 1893; academic and scholarly; Dir LYNNE WITHEY.

University of Chicago Press: 1427 East 60th St, Chicago, IL 60637; tel. (773) 702-7700; fax (773) 702-9756; e-mail general@press.uchicago.edu; internet www.press.uchicago.edu; f. 1891; scholarly and general; Dir PAULA BARKER DUFFY.

University of Georgia Press: 330 Research Dr., Athens, GA 30602-4901; tel. (706) 369-6130; fax (706) 369-6131; e-mail books@ugapress.uga.edu; internet www.ugapress.org; f. 1938; academic, scholarly, poetry, fiction, non-fiction and literary trade; Dir NICOLE MITCHELL.

University of Hawaii Press: 2840 Kolowalu St, Honolulu, HI 96822; tel. (808) 956-8255; fax (808) 988-6052; e-mail uhpbooks@hawaii.edu; internet www.uhpress.hawaii.edu; f. 1947; Asian, Pacific and Hawaiian studies; Dir WILLIAM H. HAMILTON.

University of Idaho Press: 200 South Almon St, Moscow, ID 83844-4416; tel. (208) 885-3300; fax (208) 885-3301; e-mail uipress@uidaho.edu; f. 1972; scholarly, regional studies; Dir IVAR NELSON.

University of Illinois Press: 1325 South Oak St, Champaign, IL 61820; tel. (217) 333-0950; fax (217) 244-8082; e-mail uipress@uillinois.edu; internet www.press.uillinois.edu; f. 1918; scholarly and trade; Dir WILLIS REGIER.

University of Massachusetts Press: POB 429, Amherst, MA 01004-0429; tel. (413) 545-2217; fax (413) 545-1226; e-mail info@umpress.umass.edu; internet www.umass.edu/umpress; f. 1963; scholarly; Dir BRUCE G. WILCOX.

University of Michigan Press: 839 Greene St, Ann Arbor, MI 48104-3209; tel. (734) 764-4388; fax (734) 615-1540; e-mail dshafer@umich.edu; internet www.press.umich.edu; f. 1930; academic, textbooks and paperbacks; Dir PHILIP POCHODA.

University of Minnesota Press: 111 Third Ave South, Suite 290, Minneapolis, MN 55401-5250; tel. (612) 627-1970; fax (612) 627-1980; e-mail ump@umn.edu; internet www.upress.umn.edu; f. 1927; scholarly and general; Dir DOUGLAS M. ARMATO.

University of Missouri Press: 2910 LeMone Blvd, Columbia, MO 65201; tel. (573) 882-7641; fax (573) 884-4498; e-mail upress@umsystem.edu; internet press.umsystem.edu; scholarly; Dir BEVERLY JARRETT.

University of Nebraska Press: 1111 Lincoln Mall, Lincoln, NE 68588-0630; tel. (402) 472-3581; fax (402) 472-6214; e-mail pressmail@unl.edu; internet www.nebraskapress.unl.edu; f. 1941; scholarly and general; Dir GARY DUNHAM.

University of New Mexico Press: 1312 Basehart SE, Suite 200s, Albuquerque, NM 87106; tel. (505) 277-2346; fax (505) 277-7141; e-mail unmpress@unm.edu; internet www.unmpress.com; f. 1929; scholarly and regional studies; Dir LUTHER WILSON.

University of North Carolina Press: 116 South Boundary St, Chapel Hill, NC 27514-3808; tel. (919) 966-3561; fax (919) 966-3829; e-mail uncpress@unc.edu; internet www.uncpress.unc.edu; f. 1922; biography, regional and scholarly; Dir KATE D. TORREY.

University of Notre Dame Press: 310 Flanner Hall, Notre Dame, IN 46556; tel. (574) 631-6346; fax (574) 631-8148; e-mail undpress.1@nd.edu; internet www.undpress.nd.edu; f. 1949; humanities and social sciences; Dir BARBARA J. HANRAHAN.

University of Oklahoma Press: 2800 Venture Dr., Norman, OK 73069-8216; tel. (405) 325-2000; fax (405) 325-4000; internet www.oupress.com; f. 1928; scholarly; Editor-in-Chief CHARLES E. RANKIN; Dir B. BYRON PRICE.

University of Pennsylvania Press: 3905 Spruce St, Philadelphia, PA 19104-4112; tel. (215) 898-6261; fax (215) 898-0404; e-mail custserv@pobox.upenn.edu; internet www.upenn.edu/pennpress; f. 1890; scholarly; Dir ERIC HALPERN.

University of Pittsburgh Press: Eureka Bldg, 3400 Forbes Ave, 5th Floor, Pittsburgh, PA 15260; tel. (412) 383-2456; fax (412) 383-2466; e-mail press@pitt.edu; internet www.upress.pitt.edu; f. 1936; scholarly; Dir CYNTHIA MILLER.

University of South Carolina Press: 1600 Hampton St, 5th Floor, Columbia, SC 29208; tel. (803) 777-5243; fax (803) 777-0160; e-mail lfogle@gwm.sc.edu; internet www.sc.edu/uscpress; scholarly and regional studies; Dir CURTIS L. CLARK.

University of Tennessee Press: Conference Center Bldg, Suite 110, Knoxville, TN 37996-4108; tel. (865) 974-3321; fax (865) 974-3724; e-mail custserv@utk.edu; internet www.utpress.org; f. 1940; scholarly, regional, and literary fiction; Dir JENNIFER M. SILER.

University of Texas Press: POB 7819, Austin, TX 78713-7819; tel. (512) 471-7233; fax (512) 232-7178; e-mail utpress@uts.cc.utexas.edu; internet www.utexas.edu/utpress; f. 1950; general, scholarly non-fiction; Dir JOANNA HITCHCOCK.

University of Utah Press: 1795 East South Campus Dr., 101, Salt Lake City, UT 84112-9402; tel. (801) 581-6771; fax (801) 581-3365; e-mail info@upress.utah.edu; internet www.uofupress.com; f. 1949; scholarly, regional and Middle East studies; Editor-in-Chief JEFFREY GRATHWOHL.

University of Virginia Press: POB 400318, Charlottesville, VA 22904-4318; tel. (434) 924-3469; fax (434) 982-2655; internet www.upress.virginia.edu; f. 1963; scholarly non-fiction, literature, history, Victorian, African and Afro-American studies; Dir PENELOPE KAISERLIAN.

University of Washington Press: POB 50096, Seattle, WA 98145-5096; tel. (206) 543-4050; fax (206) 543-3932; e-mail uwpord@u.washington.edu; internet www.washington.edu/uwpress; f. 1920; general, scholarly, non-fiction and reprints; Dir PAT SODEN.

University of Wisconsin Press: 1930 Monroe St, 3rd Floor, Madison, WI 53711-2059; tel. (608) 263-1110; fax (608) 263-1120; e-mail uwiscpress@uwpress.wisc.edu; internet www.wisc.edu/wisconsinpress; f. 1936; scholarly and trade; Interim Dir SHEILA LEARY.

University Press of America, Inc: 4501 Forbes Blvd, Suite 200, Lanham, MD 20706; tel. (301) 459-3366; fax (301) 429-5749; internet www.univpress.com; f. 1975; scholarly; Vice-Pres. and Dir JUDITH ROTHMAN.

University Press of Florida: 15 North West 15th St, Gainesville, FL 32611-2079; tel. (352) 392-1351; fax (352) 392-7302; internet www.upf.com; f. 1945; general, scholarly, regional; Dir MEREDITH MORRIS-BABB.

University Press of Kansas: 2502 Westbrooke Circle, Lawrence, KS 66045; tel. (785) 864-4155; fax (785) 864-4586; e-mail upress@ku.edu; internet www.kansaspress.ku.edu; f. 1946; scholarly; Dir FRED M. WOODWARD.

University Press of Kentucky: 663 South Limestone St, Lexington, KY 40508-4008; tel. (606) 257-8400; fax (606) 323-1873; internet www.kentuckypress.com; f. 1943; non-fiction, scholarly and regional; Dir STEPHEN M. WRINN.

University Press of Mississippi: 3825 Ridgewood Rd, Jackson, MS 39211; tel. (601) 432-6205; fax (601) 432-6217; e-mail press@ihl.state.ms.us; internet www.upress.state.ms.us; f. 1970; scholarly, non-fiction and regional; Dir SEETHA SRINIVASAN.

University Press of New England: 1 Court St, Lebanon, NH 03766; tel. (603) 448-1533; fax (603) 448-7006; e-mail upneweb@dartmouth.edu; internet www.upne.com; f. 1970; scholarly; Dir MICHAEL P. BURTON (acting).

Vanderbilt University Press: VU Station B 351813, Nashville, TN 37235; tel. (615) 322-3585; fax (615) 343-8823; e-mail vupress@vanderbilt.edu; internet www.vanderbiltuniversitypress.com; f. 1940; scholarly and trade; Dir MICHAEL AMES.

Wayne State University Press: 4809 Woodward Ave, Detroit, MI 48201; fax (313) 577-6131; e-mail jane.hoehner@wayne.edu; internet wsupress.wayne.edu; f. 1941; scholarly; Dir JANE HOEHNER.

Westview Press: 2465 Central Ave, Boulder, CO 80301; tel. and fax (720) 406-7336; e-mail westview.press@perseusbooks.com; internet www.perseusbooksgroup.com/westview; social sciences, humanities, and science textbooks; f. 1976; part of the Perseus Books Group; Publr MARCUS BOGGS.

John Wiley and Sons, Inc: 111 River St, Hoboken, NJ 07030-5774; tel. (201) 748-6000; fax (201) 748-6088; e-mail info@wiley.com; internet www.wiley.com; f. 1807; higher education, scientific, technical, medical, professional and trade; Chair. PETER B. WILEY; Pres. and CEO WILLIAM J. PESCE.

H. W. Wilson Co: 950 University Ave, Bronx, NY 10452; tel. (718) 588-8400; fax (718) 590-1617; e-mail esutter@hwwilson.com; internet www.hwwilson.com; f. 1898; reference and indices; Pres. and CEO HAROLD REGAN.

Wolters Kluwer Health: 161 West Washington St, Suite 1100, Conshohocken, PA 19428; tel. (610) 234-4511; e-mail robert.dekker@wolterskluwer.com; internet www.wkhealth.com; division of Wolters Kluwer; medical and scientific reference; imprints, incl. Lippincott, Williams & Wilkins (f. 1792, dentistry, science, human and veterinary medicine); CEO JEFFERY MCCAULLEY.

Yale University Press: POB 209040, New Haven, CT 06520-9040; tel. (203) 432-0960; fax (203) 432-0948; e-mail alden.ferro@yale.edu; internet www.yale.edu/yup; f. 1908; scholarly; Dir JOHN DONATICH.

THE UNITED STATES OF AMERICA

GOVERNMENT PUBLISHING HOUSE

Government Printing Office: 732 North Capitol St, NW, Washington, DC 20401; tel. (202) 512-0000; fax (202) 512-1293; e-mail contactcenter@gpo.gov; internet www.gpo.gov; Public Printer and CEO ROBERT C. TAPELLA.

ORGANIZATIONS AND ASSOCIATIONS

American Booksellers' Association (ABA): 200 White Plains Rd, Tarrytown, NY 10591; tel. (914) 591-2665; fax (914) 591-2720; e-mail info@bookweb.org; internet www.bookweb.org; f. 1900; 2,500 mems; Pres. RUSS LAWRENCE; CEO AVIN MARK DOMNITZ.

American Medical Publishers' Association (AMPA): 308 East Lancaster Ave, Suite 110, Wynnewood, PA 19096; tel. (610) 642-2810; fax (610) 642-0628; e-mail info@ampaonline.org; internet www.ampaonline.org; f. 1960; 75 mems; Exec. Dirs ROBIN B. BARTLETT, CHRISTINE BOYLAN.

Association of American University Presses, Inc: 71 West 23rd St, New York, NY 10010; tel. (212) 989-1010; fax (212) 989-0275; e-mail info@aaupnet.org; internet www.aaupnet.org; f. 1937; 125 mems; Exec. Dir PETER J. GIVLER.

The Children's Book Council, Inc: 12 West 37th St, 2nd Floor, New York, NY 10018-7480; tel. (212) 966-1990; fax (212) 966-2073; e-mail info@cbcbooks.org; internet www.cbcbooks.org; f. 1945; 75 mems; Chair. SIMON BOUGHTON.

Florida Publishers Association, Inc: POB 430, Highland City, FL 33846-0430; tel. and fax (836) 647-5951; e-mail fpabooks@aol.com; internet www.flbookpub.org; f. 1980; fmrly Nat. Asscn of Independent Publrs; 150 mems; Exec. Dir BETSY WRIGHT-LAMPE.

Independent Book Publishers' Association (PMA): 627 Aviation Way, Manhattan Beach, CA 90266; tel. (310) 372-2732; fax (310) 374-3342; e-mail info@pma-online.org; internet www.pma-online.org; f. 1983 as Publishers' Marketing Asscn; over 4,000 mem. publrs; Pres. FLORRIE BINFORD KICHLER; Exec. Dir JAN NATHAN.

Independent Publishers Group: 814 North Franklin St, Chicago, IL 60610; tel. (312) 337-0747; fax (312) 337-5985; e-mail frontdesk@ipgbook.com; internet www.ipgbook.com; f. 1971; Pres. MARK SUCHOMEL; CEO CURT MATTHEWS.

Music Publishers' Association of the US: 243 5th Ave, Suite 236, New York, NY 10016; tel. (212) 327-4044; internet www.mpa.org; f. 1895; 600 mems; Pres. LAUREN KEISER, CARL FISCHER.

Publishers Group West (PGW): 1700 Fourth St, Berkeley, CA 94710; tel. (510) 528-1444; fax (510) 528-3444; e-mail info@pgw.com; internet www.pgw.com; f. 1976; subsidiary of Publishers Group Worldwide; Vice-Pres. International Sales CHITRA BOPADIKAR.

Small Press Distribution: 1341 Seventh St, Berkeley, CA 94710-1409; tel. (510) 524-1668; fax (510) 524-0852; e-mail spd@spdbooks.org; internet www.spdbooks.org; f. 1969; distributes exclusively independently published literature; Exec. Dir JEFFREY LEPENDORF.

Small Publishers Association of North America (SPAN): 1618 West Colorado Ave, Colorado Springs, CO 80904; tel. (719) 475-1726; fax (719) 471-2182; e-mail span@spannet.org; internet www.spannet.org; f. 1996 to promote the profile and interests of independent publrs and authors; Exec. Dir SCOTT FLORA; over 1,000 mems.

Broadcasting and Communications

Federal Communications Commission (FCC): 445 12th St, SW, Washington, DC 20554; tel. (202) 418-0200; fax (202) 418-0232; e-mail fccinfo@fcc.gov; internet www.fcc.gov; f. 1934; regulates inter-state and foreign communications by radio, television, wire and cable; Chair. KEVIN J. MARTIN.

TELECOMMUNICATIONS

Principal Telecommunications Networks

Alltel Corp. (ALLTEL): Little Rock, AR; tel. (501) 905-6078; e-mail dale.ingram@alltel.com; internet www.alltel.com; f. 1943 as Allied Telephone; merged with Mid-Continent in 1983 when current name adopted; acquired by jt venture of TPG Capital and Goldman Sachs in May 2007; mobile-only service operated from 2006; country's largest mobile network, serving 35 states; Pres. and CEO SCOTT FORD; c. 12m. subscribers.

AT&T, Inc (American Telegraph and Telephone): 175 East Houston St, San Antonio, TX 78205; tel. (212) 387-5400; fax (212) 226-4935; internet www.att.com; f. 1885; bought by SBC Communications in Jan. 2005, merger completed and present name adopted in Nov. 2005; merged with the BellSouth Corpn in Dec. 2006, and acquired full ownership of Cingular Wireless; Chair. and CEO RANDALL L. STEPHENSON.

Cingular Wireless: Glenridge Highlands Two, 5565 Glenridge Connector, Atlanta, GA 30342; tel. (888) 333-6651; internet www.cingular.com; owned by AT&T, Inc; 54.1m. subscribers (2005); Pres. and CEO STANLEY T. SIGMAN.

Comcast Corpn: 1500 Market St, Philadelphia, PA 19102; internet www.comcast.com; tel. (215) 665-1700; e-mail corporate_communications@comcast.com; f. 1963; acquired AT&T Broadband in 2002; acquired part of Adelphia Communications in 2006; 24.1m. cable subscribers in 39 states and the District of Columbia, 12.4m. internet customers, 3.5m. cable telephone subscribers; Chair. and CEO BRIAN L. ROBERTS.

Citizens Communications Co: 3 High Ridge Park, Stamford, CT 06905-1390; tel. (203) 614-5600; fax (203) 614-4602; e-mail citizens@czn.com; internet www.czn.com; f. 1935; 2.4m. access lines in 24 states; operates under brand name Frontier; acquisition of Commonwealth Telephone Enterprises completed in March 2007; Pres. and CEO MAGGIE WILDEROTTER; Exec. Vice-Pres. and COO DANIEL MCCARTHY.

GE American Communications, Inc (GE Americom): 4 Research Way, Princeton, NJ 08540-6684; tel. (609) 987-4000; Chair. and CEO JOHN F. CONNELLY.

Qwest Communications International, Inc: 1801 California St, Denver, CO 80202; tel. (303) 992-1400; fax (303) 896-8515; e-mail qnews@qwest.com; internet www.qwest.com; telephone and internet provider to 21.8m. customers in the USA; acquired US West in 2000; Chair. and CEO EDWARD A. MUELLER; Exec. Vice-Pres. of Operations ROBERT TREGEMBA.

Verizon Communications: 140 West St, New York, NY 10007; tel. (800) 621-9900; internet www.verizon.com; f. 2000 by merger of Bell Atlantic Corpn and GTE Corpn; divisions include Verizon Business, fmrly MCI, Inc; 62.1m. customers (June 2007); Chair. and CEO IVAN G. SEIDENBERG; Pres. and COO DENNIS G. STRIGL.

Associations

United States Telecom Association (USTelecom): 607 14th St, NW, Suite 400, Washington, DC 20005; tel. (202) 326-7300; fax (202) 326-7333; e-mail president@ustelecom.org; internet www.ustelecom.org; Pres. and CEO WALTER B. MCCORMICK, Jr; Chair. RON B. MCCUE.

UTC—Utilities Telecom Council: 1901 Pennsylvania Ave, NW, Washington, DC 20006; tel. (202) 872-0030; fax (202) 872-1331; e-mail utc@utc.org; internet www.utc.org; f. 1948; name changed from United Telecom Council in 2007; non-profit asscn representing telecommunications and information interests of public utilities, natural gas pipelines and other infrastructure cos and their strategic business partners; Pres. and CEO BILL MORONEY.

BROADCASTING

The USA constitutes the world's biggest market for communications and broadcasting systems. The USA has the highest ratio of radio and television receivers per head of population of any country in the world. In 2003 radio sets were in use in 99% of homes and there were an estimated 260m. television receivers in use. There were 9,038 cable systems in operation in the same year, serving an estimated 85.9m. subscribers. In 2003 91.5% of households with television receivers used video cassette recorders.

Radio

In 2003 there were 11,009 licensed commercial AM and FM radio stations operating in the USA. In 2003 the average US household had 8.0 radio sets in use.

Principal Domestic Networks

ABC Radio Networks (American Broadcasting Company Radio Networks): 13725 Montfort Dr., Dallas, TX 75240; tel. (972) 448-3387; fax (214) 991-1071; e-mail omar.thompson@citcomm.com; internet www.abcradionetworks.com; f. 1944; fmrly wholly owned subsidiary of The Walt Disney Company; ABC Radio Business, as a spin-off concern of The Walt Disney Co, merged a wholly owned subsidiary of Citadel Broadcasting Corpn in June 2007; 4,500 affiliated radio stations broadcasting five full service line networks; Pres. JAMES ROBINSON.

Clear Channel Radio: 200 East Basse Rd, San Antonio, TX 78209; tel. (210) 822-2828; e-mail sandacoyle@clearchannel.com; internet www.clearchannel.com/radio; 1,150 radio stations; announced plans in Nov. 2006 to sell 448 radio stations by the end of June 2007 (76 such sales had been confirmed by Feb. that year); Pres. and Chief Financial Officer RANDALL MAYS; CEO MARK MAYS.

CBS RADIO: CBS RADIO, 1515 Broadway, New York, NY 10036; tel. (212) 846-3939; internet www.cbsradio.com; f. 1928; fmrly Infinity Broadcasting; renamed as CBS Radio; division of CBS Corpn; owns CBS Radio Network serving more than 1,500 radio stations; operates 144 radio stations; Pres. and CEO DAN MASON.

National Public Radio (NPR): 635 Massachusetts Ave, NW, Washington, DC 20001; tel. (202) 513-2300; fax (202) 513-3329; e-mail achristopher@npr.org; internet www.npr.org; f. 1970; private

THE UNITED STATES OF AMERICA — Directory

non-profit corpn providing programmes and support facilities to over 800 mem. stations nation-wide; also operates a global programme distribution service by radio, cable and satellite; Chair. TIM EBY; Pres. KEVIN KLOSE.

USA Radio Network, Inc: 2290 Springlake Rd, Suite 107, Dallas, TX 75234; tel. (972) 484-3900; fax (972) 243-3489; e-mail mark@usaradio.com; internet www.usaradio.com; news and information programmes carried by 1,100 affiliates; also broadcasts on short-wave and to US Armed Forces Radio; Pres. MARK MADDOUX.

Westwood One Inc: 40 West 57th St, 5th Floor, New York, NY 10019; tel. (212) 641-2000; internet www.westwoodone.com; f. 1934; managed by CBS Radio, Inc, fmrly Infinity Broadcasting Corpn; subsidiary of Viacom, Inc; largest domestic outsource provider of traffic reporting services, broadcasting to 7,700 radio stations; produces and distributes national news, sports, talk, music and special event programmes, in addition to local news, sports, weather and other information programming; operates BLAISE, CBS, CNN Max, Navigator, NBC, NeXt, Source Max and WONE radio networks; Pres. and CEO PETER KOSANN.

Principal External Radio Services

American Forces Radio and Television Service/American Forces Network (AFRTS/AFN): Defense Media Center (DMC), AFN Broadcast Center, 23755 Z St, Riverside, CA 92518; tel. (951) 413-2319; fax (951) 413-2227; e-mail larry.sichter@dodmedia.osd.mil; internet www.myafn.net; f. 1942; operated by Dept of Defense; provides encrypted US radio and TV programming in English exclusively to US military and Dept of Defense civilian personnel in 177 countries, US territories and aboard US Navy ships; Exec. Dir JEFFREY WHITE (DMC); Dir MELVIN RUSSELL (AFRTS).

RFE/RL (Radio Free Europe/Radio Liberty): 1201 Connecticut Ave, NW, Suite 1100, Washington, DC 20036; tel. (202) 457-6900; fax (202) 457-6992; e-mail jensend@rferl.org; internet www.rferl.org; f. 1950; private, non-profit corpn financed by the federal Govt; broadcasts from Prague, Czech Republic, to Eastern and South-Eastern Europe, Russia, the Caucasus, the Middle East, Central and South-West Asia; c. 1,000 hours weekly in 28 languages; Chair. JAMES K. GLASSMAN; Pres. JEFFREY GEDMIN.

Voice of America: 330 Independence Ave, SW, Washington, DC 20237; tel. (202) 203-4000; fax (202) 203-4960; e-mail publicaffairs@voa.gov; internet www.voanews.com; f. 1942; govt-funded; broadcasts c. 1,000 hours weekly in 45 languages to all areas of the world via, radio, television and the internet; Dir DANFORTH W. AUSTIN.

Television

In 2006 commercial television stations numbered 1,349. The average US household had 2.5 television sets in use in 2005.

In February 2006 Congress approved legislation to end analogue broadcasting by 17 February 2009.

Principal Networks

ABC, Inc (American Broadcasting Co, Inc): 500 South Buena Vista St, Burbank, CA 91521-4551; tel. (818) 460-7477; e-mail netaudr@abc.com; internet abc.go.com; f. 1953; subsidiary of the Walt Disney Co since 1996; 10 owned and 226 affiliated stations; production through Touchstone Television and Disney television content distribution through Buena Vista Television; Pres. Network Operations and Admin. ALEX WALLAU; Pres., Disney-ABC TV Group ANNE SWEENEY.

C-SPAN (Cable-Satellite Public Affairs Network): 400 North Capitol St, Suite 650, Washington, DC 20001; tel. (202) 737-3220; e-mail viewer@c-span.org; internet www.c-span.org; private, non-profit public service; earns its operating revenues through licence fees paid by cable and satellite systems offering the network to their customers; Chair. and CEO BRIAN LAMB; Co-Pres SUSAN SWAIN, ROBERT KENNEDY.

Capital Cities/American Broadcasting Companies, Inc: 77 West 66th St, New York, NY 10023; tel. (212) 456-7777; fax (212) 887-7168; internet www.abctelevision.com; f. 1986; Pres. and CEO THOMAS S. MURPHY; Pres., Radio Network ROBERT F. CALLAHAN.

CBS Television Network (Columbia Broadcasting System Television Network): 51 West 52nd St, New York, NY 10019-6188; tel. (212) 975-4321; internet www.cbs.com; f. 1928; subsidiary of CBS Corpn; serves more than 200 affiliated stations; parent CBS Corpn subsidiary, CBS Television Stations Group, operates 39 stations, incl. 21 CBS, 11 The CW, 3 MyNetworkTV and 4 independents; CBS Corpn Pres. and CEO LESLIE MOONVES; Pres. CBS News and Sports SEAN MCMANUS.

CNN (Cable News Network): 1 CNN Center, POB 105366, Atlanta, GA 30348; tel. (404) 827-1700; fax (404) 827-1099; e-mail public.information@turner.com; internet www.cnn.com; subsidiary of Time Warner; Pres. JONATHAN KLEIN; Pres., CNN News Group JIM WALTON.

FOX Broadcasting Co: 10201 West Pico Blvd, Los Angeles, CA 90035; tel. (310) 369-3553; e-mail scott.grogin@fox.com; internet www.fox.com; f. 1986; subsidiary of News Corpn; more than 900 cable affiliations; Pres. KEVIN REILLY; Chair. PETER LIGUORI.

NBC Universal Television Stations: 30 Rockefeller Plaza, New York, NY 10112; tel. (212) 664-4444; fax (212) 664-5830; internet www.nbcuni.com; f. 1926; subsidiary of NBC Universal; 27 owned and over 200 affiliated stations; Pres. and CEO, NBC Universal JEFF ZUCKER; Pres., Universal Television Group JEFF GASPIN.

PBS (Public Broadcasting Service): 2100 Crystal Dr, Arlington, VA 22202; tel. (703) 739-5000; fax (703) 739-0775; internet www.pbs.org; f. 1969; non-profit-making; financed by private subscriptions and federal govt funds; owned and operated by the 355 public US television stations; Pres. and CEO PAULA KERGER; COO WAYNE GODWIN.

Time Warner Cable, Inc (TWC): 290 Harbor Dr., Stamford, CT 06902-6732; tel. (203) 364-8203; fax (203) 328-0690; internet www.timewarnercable.com; cable television system serving c. 14.7m. subscribers in 33 states; acquired part of Adelphia Communications in 2005; 84% owned by Time Warner; Pres. and CEO GLENN A. BRITT; Chair. DON LOGAN.

Univision Network: 9405 North West 41st St, Miami, FL 33178-2301; tel. (305) 471-3900; fax (305) 471-4065; internet www.univision.com; subsidiary of Univision Communications, Inc; acquired by Broadcasting Media Partners Inc, group of private equity investors, in March 2007; Spanish-language television network; Pres. JOE UVA.

Associations

National Association of Broadcasters (NAB): 1771 N St, NW, Washington, DC 20036; tel. (202) 429-5300; fax (202) 429-4199; e-mail nab@nab.org; internet www.nab.org; f. 1922; trade asscn of radio and TV stations and networks; 8,300 mems; Chair. JOHN L. (JACK) SANDER; Pres. and CEO DAVID K. REHR.

National Cable and Telecommunications Association (NCTA): 25 Massachusetts Ave, NW, Suite 100, Washington, DC 20001-1413; tel. (202) 222-2300; e-mail webmaster@ncta.com; internet www.ncta.com; f. 1952 as Nat. Cable Television Asscn; represents cable operators for over 90% of customers and over 200 cable program networks; internet and digital telephone service provider; c. 3,100 mems; Pres. and CEO KYLE MCSLARROW.

Finance

BANKING

Commercial Banking System

The US banking system is the largest and, in many respects, the most comprehensive and sophisticated in the world. Banking has, however, been largely subject to state rather than federal jurisdiction, and this has created a structure very different from that in other advanced industrial countries. In general, no bank may open branches or acquire subsidiaries in states other than that in which it is based, although in June 1985 the US Supreme Court ruled that federal legislation prohibiting interstate banks does not preclude state governments from permitting regional interstate banking. A number of such mergers have followed, although some states continue to restrict banks to a single branch, or to operating only in certain counties of the state. Federal anti-trust laws also limit mergers of banks within a state. The effect of these measures has been to preserve the independence of a relatively large number of banks. However, the influence of these banks has been increasingly challenged by the formation of several groupings of regional banks. Federal legislation permitting the operation of interstate branch banking networks and the provision of non-banking financial services was enacted in November 1999. In October 2003 the Bank of America announced the acquisition of FleetBoston Financial Corporation, in an agreement that was to create the second largest banking company in the world. In 2006 the restructured Bank of America operated 5,873 branch offices, and controlled total deposits of more than US $937,052m. (or 14.6% of all banking deposits in the USA). The merger in 2004 of JP Morgan Chase & Co and Bank One Corporation established the second largest bank in the USA, with 2,798 branches and total assets in December 2005 of $866,720m.

Following the failure of a number of banks in the late 1980s, the Federal Deposit Insurance Corporation, a government-sponsored body which insures deposits in banks and acts as receiver for national and state banks that have been placed in receivership, was obliged to provide assistance for a large number of institutions. Many banks, meanwhile, have expanded their 'fee income' activities (such as sales of mutual fund investments) to offset declines in customer borrowing, particularly from the industrial and commercial sectors.

The possession of bank accounts and the use of banking facilities are perhaps more widespread among all regions and social groups in

THE UNITED STATES OF AMERICA

the USA than in any other country. This has influenced the formulation of monetary theory and policy, as bank credit has become a more important factor than currency supply in the regulation of the economy. The use of current accounts and credit cards is so common that many authorities claim that the USA can be regarded as, effectively, a cashless society.

Bank Holding Companies

Since 1956 bank holding companies, corporations that control one or more banks in the USA, have become significant elements in the banking system. The proportion of banks owned by holding companies increased from 62% in 1984 to 76% in 2000. In 2004 there were some 5,151 bank holding companies, of which 12% had financial holding company status.

Banking Activities Overseas

From the mid-1960s, the leading banks rapidly expanded their overseas interests. At the end of 1960 there were only eight US banks operating foreign branches, mostly in Latin America and the Far East. The main factors behind this expansion were the geographical limitations imposed by law at home; the rapid expansion of US business interests abroad; the faster economic growth of certain foreign markets; and finally the profitability of the 'Eurodollar' capital markets. The expansion in the overseas activities of US banks reached a high point in 1984. Subsequently declining levels of profitability in this area have resulted in the closure of some overseas offices, although the aggregate total of assets held has continued to rise.

In 1981 the Federal Reserve Board sanctioned the establishment of domestic International Banking Facilities (IBF), permitting commercial banks within the US (including US branches and agencies of foreign banks) to transact certain types of foreign deposit and loan business free of reserve requirements and, in most cases, state income tax liability.

Federal Reserve System: 20th St and Constitution Ave, NW, Washington, DC 20551; tel. (202) 452-3000; fax (202) 452-3819; internet www.federalreserve.gov.

The Federal Reserve System, founded in 1913, comprises the Board of Governors, the Federal Open Market Committee, the Federal Advisory Council, the Consumer Advisory Council, the Thrift Institutions Advisory Council, the 25 branches of the 12 Federal Reserve Banks, together with all member banks.

The Board of Governors is composed of seven members appointed by the President of the United States with the advice and consent of the Senate.

The Reserve Banks are empowered to issue Federal Reserve notes fully secured by the following assets, alone or in any combination: (i) Gold certificates; (ii) US Government and agency securities; (iii) other eligible assets as described by statute; and (iv) Special Drawing Rights certificates. The Reserve Banks may discount paper for depository institutions and make properly secured advances to depository institutions. Federal Reserve Banks were established by Congress as the operating arms of the nation's central banking system. Many of the services performed by this network for depository institutions and for the Government are similar to services performed by banks and thrifts for business customers and individuals. Reserve Banks hold the cash reserves of depository institutions and make loans to them. They move currency and coin into and out of circulation, and collect and process millions of cheques each day. They provide banking services for the Treasury, issue and redeem government securities on behalf of the Treasury, and act in other ways as fiscal agent for the US Government. The Banks also take part in the primary responsibility of the Federal Reserve System, the setting of monetary policy, through participation on the Federal Open Market Committee.

The Comptroller of the Currency (see below) has primary supervisory authority over all federally chartered banks, and the banking supervisors of the States have similar jurisdiction over banks organized under State laws. State member banks are examined by the Federal Reserve.

In 2004 some 2,200 commercial banks were members of the Federal Reserve System.

Board of Governors

Chairman: BEN S. BERNANKE.

Vice-Chairman: DONALD L. KOHN.

Governors: RANDALL S. KROSZNER, FREDERIC S. MISHKIN, KEVIN M. WARSH.

Secretary of the Board: JENNIFER J. JOHNSON.

Directory

Federal Reserve Banks

	Chairman	President
Boston	Lisa M. Lynch	Eric S. Rosengren
New York	Stephen Friedman	Timothy F. Geithner
Philadelphia	William F. Hecht	Charles I. Plosser
Cleveland	Tanny B. Crane	Sandra Pianalto
Richmond	Thomas J. Mackell, Jr	Jeffrey M. Lacker
Atlanta	V. Larkin Martin	Dennis P. Lockhart
Chicago	John A. Canning, Jr	Charles L. Evans
St Louis	Irl F. Engelhardt	James B. Bullard
Minneapolis	James J. Hynes	Gary H. Stern
Kansas City	Lu M. Cordova	Thomas M. Hoenig
Dallas	James T. Hackett	Richard W. Fisher
San Francisco	David K. Y. Tang	Janet L. Yellen

Comptroller of the Currency

Independence Sq., 250 E St, SW, Washington, DC 20219; tel. (202) 874-5000; e-mail Jesse.Stiller@occ.treas.gov; internet www.occ.treas.gov.

The Comptroller of the Currency has supervisory control over all federally chartered banks (see Federal Reserve System).

Comptroller: JOHN C. DUGAN.

Principal Commercial Banks

(cap. = total capital and reserves; dep. = deposits; m. = million; amounts in US dollars)

In general, only banks with a minimum of $2,000m. deposits are listed. In states where no such bank exists, that with the largest deposits is listed.

Alabama

AmSouth Bank NA: 1900 Fifth Ave North, POB 11007, Birmingham, AL 35288; tel. (205) 801-0359; fax (205) 326-5015; internet www.amsouth.com; f. 1873; cap. 0.01m., dep. 45,924.0m. (Dec. 2005); Chair., Pres. and CEO C. DOWD RITTER.

Regions Bank: 417 North 20th St, POB 10247, Birmingham, AL 35202-0247; tel. (205) 326-7697; fax (205) 326-7779; internet www.regionsbank.com; f. 1928; cap. 0.1m., dep. 113,425.0m. (Dec. 2006); Pres. and CEO C. DOWD RITTER.

California

Bank of the West: 180 Montgomery St, San Francisco, CA 94104; tel. (415) 765-4800; fax (415) 434-3470; internet www.bankofthewest.com; f. 1874; cap. 0.005m., dep. 45,921m. (Dec. 2006); Chair. and CEO DON J. MCGRATH; 663 brs.

California Bank and Trust: 11622 El Camino Real, Suite 200, San Diego, CA 92130; tel. (858) 793-7400; fax (858) 793-7438; e-mail info@calbanktrust.com; internet www.calbanktrust.com; f. 1998; cap. 3.2m., dep. 8,804.7m. (Dec. 2006); Chair. and CEO DAVID BLACKFORD.

City National Bank: 400 Roxbury Dr. North, Beverly Hills, CA 90210; tel. (310) 888-6000; fax (310) 888-6045; e-mail contact@cnb.com; internet www.cnb.com; f. 1954; cap. 90.0m., dep. 12,775.5m. (Dec. 2006); Chair. and CEO RUSSELL GOLDSMITH; Pres. CHRISTOPHER J. WARMUTH; 45 brs.

Union Bank of California NA: 400 California St, 1st Floor, San Francisco, CA 94104; tel. (415) 765-3434; fax (415) 765-3507; e-mail Investor.Relations@uboc.com; internet www.uboc.com; f. 1996; cap. 604.6m., dep. 35,067.0m. (Dec. 2002); Pres. and CEO MASAAKI TANAKA; 323 brs.

Connecticut

Citizens Bank of Connecticut: 63 Eugene O'Neill Dr., New London, CT 06320; tel. (860) 638-4419; fax (860) 638-4444; e-mail intbank@citizensbank.com; internet www.citizensbank.com; f. 1996; dep. 4,205.8m., total assets 4,617.0m. (Dec. 2006); Chair., Pres. and CEO RICHARD M. BARRY; 48 brs.

Delaware

Chase Bank USA NA: 200 White Clay Center Dr., 1st Floor, Newark, DE 19711; tel. (302) 758-2600; fax (302) 758-2603; internet www.chase.com; f. 1982 as Chase Manhattan Bank USA; present name adopted 2005; cap. 49.0m., dep. 57,448.1m. (Dec. 2006); Pres. MICHAEL J. BARRETT.

Florida

Northern Trust NA: 700 Brickell Ave, Miami, FL 33131; tel. (305) 372-1000; fax (305) 789-1106; internet www.northerntrust.com; f. 1982; cap. 34.1m., dep. 8,659.5m. (Dec. 2006); Chair., Pres. and CEO WILLIAM L. MORRISON.

Ocean Bank: 780 Northwest 42nd Ave, Miami, POB 441140, FL 33126; tel. (305) 442-2660; fax (305) 444-8153; e-mail obmail@oceanbank.com; internet www.oceanbank.com; f. 1982; cap. 8.5m., dep. 5,190.0m. (Dec. 2006); Pres. and CEO José A. Concepción; 23 brs.

Georgia

SunTrust Bank: 25 Park Pl., POB 4418, Atlanta, GA 30302; tel. (404) 588-7785; fax (404) 302-4782; internet www.suntrust.com; f. 1891; assumed all SunTrust Banks 2000; cap. 21.6m., dep. 155,972.5m. (Dec. 2006); Chair. and Pres. Phillip Humann.

Hawaii

Bank of Hawaii: 111 South King St, Honolulu, HI 96813; tel. (888) 643-3888; fax (808) 537-8440; e-mail info@boh.com; internet www.boh.com; f. 1897; cap. 14.9m., dep. 9,234.9m. (Dec. 2006); Chair., Pres. and CEO Allan R. Landon.

First Hawaiian Bank: 999 Bishop St, Honolulu, HI 96813; tel. (808) 525-7000; fax (808) 525-8182; e-mail bfarias@fhb.com; internet www.fhb.com; f. 1858; cap. 16.2m., dep. 9,380.4m. (Dec. 2006); Chair. Walter A. Dods, Jr; Pres. and CEO Donald G. Horner.

Illinois

First Midwest Bank: 300 Park Blvd, Suite 400, Itasca, IL 60143; internet www.firstmidwest.com; cap. 40.0m., dep. 7,439.7m. (Dec. 2006); Chair. and CEO John O'Meara; 103 brs.

Harris National Association: 111 West Monroe St, 12th Floor, Chicago, IL 60603; tel. (312) 845-2028; fax (312) 845-2199; internet www.harrisbank.com; f. 1882 as N.W. Harris & Co; present name adopted 2005; cap. 143.0m., dep. 36,501.9m. (Dec. 2006); Dirs Pastora San Juan Cafferty, Haven E. Cockerham, Anthony (Tony) Comper, Susan T. Congalton, William A. Downe, David A. Galloway, Wilbur H. Gantz, James J. Glasser, Dr Leo M. Henikoff, Richard M. Jaffee, Karen Maidment, Alan G. McNally, Frank T. Techar, Richard E. Terry.

LaSalle Bank NA: 135 South LaSalle St, Chicago, IL 60603; tel. (312) 904-2000; fax (312) 904-2819; internet www.lasallebank.com; f. 1927; cap. 541.2m., dep. 61,860.4m. (Dec. 2006); Chair. Joost C. L. Kulper; Pres. and CEO Norman R. Bobins.

Northern Trust Co: 50 South LaSalle St, Chicago, IL 60675; tel. (312) 630-6000; fax (312) 444-5244; internet www.northerntrust.com; f. 1889; cap. 3.6m., dep. 46,820.4m. (Dec. 2006); Chair. and CEO William A. Osborn.

Kentucky

First Capital Bank of Kentucky: 293 N. Hubbards Lane, Louisville, KY 40207; tel. (502) 895-5040; e-mail localroots@fcbok.com; internet www.fcbok.com; f. 1996; total assets $319.6m. (Dec. 2007); Chair., Pres. and CEO H. David Hale.

Louisiana

Whitney National Bank: 228 St Charles Ave, New Orleans, LA 70130; tel. (504) 586-7562; fax (504) 586-7412; e-mail lgarza@whitneybank.com; internet www.whitneybank.com; f. 1883; cap. 3,358.0m., dep. 9,024.2m. (Dec. 2006); Chair. and CEO William L. Marks; Pres. and COO John C. Hope, III; 130 brs.

Maryland

Provident Bank of Maryland: 114 East Lexington St, Baltimore, MD 21202-1725; tel. (410) 281-7000; fax (410) 277-2768; internet www.provbank.com; f. 1951; cap. 30.0m., dep. 5,490.6m. (Dec. 2006); Chair. and CEO Peter Martin.

Massachusetts

Citizens Bank of Massachusetts: 28 State St, Boston, MA 02109; tel. (617) 725-5500; fax (617) 725-5877; e-mail intbank@citizensbank.com; internet www.citizensbank.com; f. 1825; dep. 30,403.2m., total assets 35,276.0m. (Dec. 2006); Chair., Pres. and CEO Robert E. Smyth.

Michigan

Citizens Bank: 328 South Saginaw St, Flint, MI 48502; tel. (313) 766-7500; fax (313) 768-6948; internet www.citizensonline.com; f. 1871; cap. 13.9m., dep. 6,754.4m. (Dec. 2006); Chair., Pres. and CEO William R. Hartman.

Comerica Bank: Comerica Tower, Detroit Center, 500 Woodward Ave, Detroit, MI 48226; tel. (313) 222-3300; fax (313) 961-7349; e-mail info@comerica.com; internet www.comerica.com; f. 1849; cap. 378.5m., dep. 49,380.9m. (Dec. 2006); Chair., Pres. and CEO Ralph W. Babb, Jr.

Fifth Third Bank: 111 Lyon NW, Grand Rapids, MI 49503; tel. (616) 771-5000; fax (616) 774-1119; internet www.53.com; f. 1853; cap. 16.4m., dep. 41,097.0m. (Dec. 2006); Chair. George A. Schaefer, Jr; 361 brs.

Minneapolis

US Bank NA: 800 Nicollet Mall, Minneapolis, MN 55402; tel. (612) 303-0799; fax (612) 973-0838; e-mail international.banking@usbank.com; internet www.usbank.com; f. 1853; fmrly Firstar Bank NA, present name adopted in Aug. 2001; cap. 18.2m., dep. 181.577.4m. (Dec. 2006); Chair., CEO and Pres. Richard K. Davis; 2,498 brs.

Mississippi

Trustmark National Bank: 248 East Capitol St, POB 291, Jackson, MS 39201; tel. (601) 354-5863; fax (601) 949-2387; e-mail Trustmark@custhelp.com; internet www.trustmark.com; f. 1889; cap. 13.4m., dep. 7,603.1m. (Dec. 2006); Chair. and CEO Richard G. Hickson.

Missouri

Commerce Bank NA: 1000 Walnut St, POB 13686, Kansas City, MO 64106; tel. (816) 234-2000; fax (816) 234-2799; e-mail mymoney@commercebank.com; internet www.commercebank.com; f. 1865; cap. 10.2m., dep. 12,591.4m. (Dec. 2006); Chair. and CEO Jonathan M. Kemper.

Montana

First Interstate Bank of Montana NA: 2 Main St, POB 7130, Kalispell, MT 59904; tel. (406) 752-5001; internet www.firstinterstatebank.com; f. 1891; cap. 35m., dep. 257.1m. (Dec. 1996); Chair. James Curran; Pres. Bob Schneider.

Nebraska

First National Bank of Omaha: 1620 Dodge St, Omaha, NE 68102; tel. (402) 341-0500; fax (402) 633-3554; e-mail firstnational@fnni.com; internet www.firstnational.com; f. 1857; cap. 5.3m., dep. 6,595.4m. (Dec. 2006); Chair. Bruce R. Lauritzen; 31 brs.

New Hampshire

Citizens Bank of New Hampshire: 875 Elm St, Manchester, NH 03101; tel. (603) 634-7418; fax (603) 634-7481; e-mail intbank@citizensbank.com; internet www.citizensbank.com; f. 1853; cap. 0.8m., dep. 9,250.3m. (Dec. 2006); Chair., Pres. and CEO Thomas M. Metzger; 76 brs.

New York

American Express Bank Ltd: American Express Tower, 23rd Floor, 200 Vesey St, New York, NY 10285-2300; tel. (212) 640-5000; fax (212) 693-1721; internet www.americanexpress.com; f. 1919; cap. 121.0m., res 612.0m., dep. 12,992.0m. (Dec. 2006); Chair. and CEO W. Richard Holmes.

Bank of New York Mellon: 1 Wall St, New York, NY 10286; tel. (212) 495-1784; fax (212) 495-1398; e-mail comments@bankofny.com; internet www.bankofny.com; f. 1784; cap. 1,135.3m., dep. 68,630.0m. (Dec. 2006); Chair. and CEO Thomas A. Renyi; Pres. Gerald L. Hassell.

Bank of Tokyo–Mitsubishi UFJ Trust Co: 1251 Ave of the Americas, New York, NY 10020-1104; tel. (212) 782-4000; fax (212) 782-6415; internet www.btmna.com; f. 1955; cap. 132.9m., dep. 2,910.2m. (Dec. 2006); Chair. Naotaka Obata; Pres. and CEO Yukiharu Kiho.

Citibank NA: 399 Park Ave, New York, NY 10043; tel. (212) 559-1000; fax (212) 223-2681; internet www.citibank.com; f. 1812; cap. 751.0m., dep. 874,793.0m. (Dec. 2006); Chair., Pres. and CEO William R. Rhodes.

Deutsche Bank Trust Company Americas: 60 Wall St, New York, NY 10005; tel. (212) 250-2500; fax (212) 250-4429; internet www.deutsche-bank.com; f. 1903; fmrly Bankers' Trust Co, present name adopted April 2002; cap. 3,627.0m., dep. 22,740.0m. (Dec. 2006); Chair. and CEO Josef Ackerman; Pres. John A. Ross.

HSBC Bank USA NA: POB 2013, Buffalo, NY 14240; fax (716) 841-5391; internet www.banking.us.hsbc.com; f. 1999 following acquisition of Marine Midland Bank by Hongkong & Shanghai Banking Corpn; acquired Republic National Bank of New York in 2000; cap. 2.0m., dep. 146,274.3m. (Dec. 2006); Pres. and CEO Youssef A. Nasr.

M&T Bank Corpn: 1 M & T Plaza, Buffalo, NY 14203-2399; tel. (716) 842-4200; fax (716) 842-5021; internet www.mtb.com; f. 1856; Manufacturers' and Traders' Trust Co; cap. 6,300m., dep. 39,900m. (Dec. 2006); Chair. Robert G. Wilmers; 736 brs.

Trustco Bank NA: 1 Sarnowski Dr., Glenville, NY 12302; tel. (518) 377-3311; fax (518) 381-3668; internet www.trustcobank.com; cap.

29.4m., dep. 2,312.5m. (Dec. 2002); Pres. and CEO ROBERT A. MCCORMICK.

United States Trust Co: 114 West 47th St, New York, NY 10036; tel. (212) 852-1000; fax (212) 995-5642; e-mail info@trust.com; internet www.ustrust.com; f. 1853; cap. 15.0m., dep. 9,585.5m. (Dec. 2006); Chair. and CEO JEFFREY S. MAURER.

North Carolina

Bank of America NA: Bank of America Corporate Center, 100 North Tryon St, Charlotte, NC 28255; tel. (704) 386-5000; fax (704) 386-0981; internet www.bankamerica.com; f. 1904; cap. 2,878.9m., dep. 1,035,586.0m. (Dec. 2006); Chair. and CEO KENNETH D. LEWIS.

Wachovia Bank NA: 301 South College St, Suite 4000, Charlotte, NC 28288-0013; tel. (704) 374-1246; internet www.wachovia.com; f. 1866; cap. 455.0m., dep. 432,927.0m. (Dec. 2006); Chair., Pres. and CEO G. KENNEDY (KEN) THOMPSON.

Ohio

FirstMerit Bank NA: 3 Cascade Plaza, Akron, OH 44308; tel. (330) 996-6300; fax (330) 384-7008; e-mail customerservice@firstmerit.com; internet www.firstmerit.com; cap. 57.6m., dep. 9,092.2m. (Dec. 2006); Chair. and CEO PAUL G. GREIG.

Huntington National Bank: 41 South High St, Columbus, OH 43287; tel. (614) 480-4685; fax (614) 331-5900; e-mail international@huntington.com; internet www.huntington.com; f. 1866; cap. 40.0m., dep. 30,493.3m. (Dec. 2006); Chair. and CEO THOMAS HOAGLIN.

KeyBank NA: 127 Public Sq., Cleveland, OH 44114; tel. (216) 689-3000; fax (216) 689-3683; e-mail Investor_relations@keybank.com; internet www.key.com; f. 1849; cap. 50.0m., dep. 72,956.6m. (Dec. 2006); Chair. and CEO HENRY L. MEYER, III.

National City Bank: 1900 East Ninth St, POB 94750, Cleveland, OH 44114-3484; tel. (216) 575-2000; fax (216) 575-9263; internet www.nationalcity.com; f. 1845; cap. 7.3m., dep. 113,586.8m. (Dec. 2006); Chair. DAVID A. DABERKO; CEO PETER E. RASKIND; c. 1,300 brs.

Oklahoma

Bank of Oklahoma NA: Bank of Oklahoma Tower, POB 2300, Tulsa, OK 74192; tel. (918) 588-6829; fax (918) 588-6026; internet www.bankofoklahoma.com; f. 1933; cap. 52.9m., dep. 12,727.6m. (Dec. 2006); Chair. GEORGE B. KAISER; Pres. and CEO STANLEY A. LYBARGER; 56 brs.

Pennsylvania

PNC Bank, NA: 1 PNC Plaza, 249 Fifth Ave, Pittsburgh, PA 15222-2707; tel. (412) 762-2000; fax (412) 762-5022; internet www.pnc.com; f. 1959; cap. 740.1m., dep. 75,673.3m. (Dec. 2006); Chair., and CEO JAMES E. ROHR; Pres. JOSEPH C. GUYAUX; 854 brs.

Rhode Island

Citizens Bank of Rhode Island: 1 Citizens Plaza, Providence, RI 02903; tel. (401) 454-2441; fax (401) 455-5859; e-mail intbank@citizensbank.com; internet www.citizensbank.com; f. 1996; cap. 1.0m., dep. 12,272.2m. (Dec. 2006); Chair., Pres. and CEO JOSEPH J. MARCAURELE; 78 brs.

South Carolina

Carolina First Bank: 102 South Main St, POB 1029, Greenville, SC 29602; tel. (864) 255-7900; fax (864) 239-6401; e-mail customerassistance@carolinafirst.com; internet www.carolinafirst.com; cap. 7.9m., dep. 7,607.7m. (Dec. 2006); Chair. MACK I. WHITTLE, Jr; Pres. MAURICE J. SPAGNOLETTI.

South Dakota

Citibank USA NA: 701 East 60th St, North, POB 6000, Sioux Falls, SD 57117; tel. (605) 331-2626; internet www.citibank.com; f. 1981; fmrly Citibank (South Dakota), present name adopted in Jan. 2002; cap. 0.04m., dep. 4,768.1m. (Dec. 2005); Gen. Sec. DAVID L. ZIMBECK; Pres. KENDALL E. STORK.

Wells Fargo Bank NA: 101 North Phillips Ave, Sioux Falls, SD 57117; tel. (605) 575-7300; fax (605) 575-4815; e-mail ipb@wellsfargo.com; internet www.wellsfargo.com; f. 1960 as Wells Fargo Bank American Trust Co; fmrly Norwest Bank South Dakota NA, present name adopted in 2004; cap. 520.0m., dep. 330,712.0m. (Dec. 2006); Pres. and CEO JOHN G. STUMPF; 3,000 brs.

Tennessee

First Tennessee Bank NA: 165 Madison Ave, 9th Floor, POB 84, Memphis, TN 38101-0084; tel. (901) 523-4420; fax (901) 523-4438; internet www.firsttennessee.com; f. 1864; cap. 367.3m., dep. 31,700.5m. (Dec. 2006); Chair. and CEO J. KENNETH GLASS; Pres. CHARLES BURKETT; 183 brs.

Texas

Frost National Bank: 100 West Houston St, POB 1600, San Antonio, TX 78296; tel. (210) 220-4011; e-mail frostbank@frostbank.com; internet www.frostbank.com; f. 1899; cap. 8.5m., dep. 11,517.9m. (Dec. 2006); Chair. and CEO T. C. FROST; Pres. PAT FROST.

Virginia

Chevy Chase Bank, FSB: 7926 Jones Branch Dr., McLean, VA 22101; internet www.chevychasebank.com; f. 1955; total assets 14.3m. (Dec. 2005); Chair. and CEO B. FRANCIS SAUL, II.

Washington

Washington Mutual Bank: 1201 Third Ave, Suite 1000, Seattle, WA 95290; tel. (206) 490-8625; internet www.wamu.com; cap. 7.5m., dep. 2,695.2m. (Dec. 2005); Pres. and Chair. KERRY KILLINGER.

Co-operative Bank

CoBank: 5500 South Quebec St, Greenwood Village, CO 80111; tel. (303) 740-4000; fax (303) 740-4366; e-mail webmaster@cobank.com ; internet www.cobank.com; f. 1933; provides loan finance and domestic and international banking services for agricultural and farmer-owned co-operatives; cap. 1,242.4m.(Dec. 2006); Chair. J. ROY ORTON; Pres. and CEO ROBERT B. ENGEL.

Trade Bank

Export-Import Bank of the United States (Ex-Im Bank): 811 Vermont Ave, NW, Washington, DC 20571; tel. (202) 565-3946; fax (202) 565-3380; e-mail bdd@exim.gov; internet www.exim.gov; f. 1934; independent agency since 1945; cap. subscribed by the US Treasury; finances and facilitates US external trade, guarantees payment to US foreign traders and banks, extends credit to foreign governmental and private concerns; cap. 1,000.0m., res. −466.1m. (Sept. 2006); Chair. and Pres. JAMES H. (JIM) LAMBRIGHT.

BANKING ASSOCIATIONS

There is a State Bankers Association in each state.

American Bankers Association: 1120 Connecticut Ave, NW, Washington, DC 20036; tel. (202) 663-5000; fax (202) 828-4547; e-mail custserv@aba.com; internet www.aba.com; f. 1875; Pres. and CEO EDWARD (ED) YINGLING; Chair. BRADLEY E. ROCK.

America's Community Bankers: 900 19th St, NW, Suite 400, Washington, DC 20006; tel. (202) 857-3100; fax (202) 296-8716; e-mail info@acbankers.org; internet www.americascommunitybankers.com; f. 1992; 2,000 mems; Chair. MARK E. MACOMBER; Pres. and CEO DIANE CASEY-LANDRY.

Bank Administration Institute (BAI): 1 North Franklin St, Chicago, IL 60606-3421; tel. (312) 553-4600; fax (312) 683-2426; e-mail info@bai.org; internet www.bai.org; f. 1924; Pres. and CEO DEBORAH L. BIANUCCI.

Bankers' Association for Finance and Trade: 1120 Connecticut Ave, NW, 3rd Floor, Washington, DC 20036; tel. (202) 663-7575; fax (202) 663-5538; e-mail baft@baft.org; internet www.baft.org; affiliated to the American Bankers Asscn; Pres. CRAIG C. WEEKS.

Independent Community Bankers of America: 1615 L St, NW, Suite 900, Washington, DC 20036; tel. (202) 659-8111; e-mail info@icba.org; internet www.icba.org; f. 1930; Pres. and CEO CAMDEN R. FINE; 5,000 banks.

Mortgage Bankers Association of America: 1919 Pennsylvania Ave, Washington, DC 20006; tel. (202) 557-2700; e-mail info@mbaa.org; internet mortgagebankers.org; f. 1914; Chair. JOHN M. ROBBINS; Pres. and CEO JONATHAN L. KEMPNER; 2,700 mems.

PRINCIPAL STOCK EXCHANGES

American Stock Exchange: 86 Trinity Pl., New York, NY 10006; tel. (212) 306-1000; fax (212) 306-1152; e-mail marketdataproducts@amex.com; internet www.amex.com; f. 1849; Chair. and CEO NEAL L. WOLKOFF; Pres. and COO PATRICIA RADO; mems: 661 regular, 160 associate, 203 option principal, 13 limited trading permit-holders.

Boston Stock Exchange Inc: 100 Franklin St, Boston, MA 02110; tel. (617) 235-2000; internet www.bostonstock.com; f. 1834; Chair. and CEO MICHAEL J. CURRAN; 119 mems.

Chicago Stock Exchange: 1 Financial Pl., 440 South LaSalle St, Chicago, IL 60605; tel. (312) 663-2222; e-mail info@chx.com; internet www.chx.com; f. 1882; Chair. MICHAEL H. KERR; CEO DAVID A. HERRON; 445 mems.

Nasdaq Stock Market Inc: 1 Liberty Plaza, 165 Broadway, New York, NY 10006; tel. (212) 401-8700; internet www.nasdaq.com; f. 1998 by the American Stock Exchange and the Nat. Asscn of Securities Dealers (NASD); world-wide electronic trading market; Pres. and CEO ROBERT GREIFELD.

THE UNITED STATES OF AMERICA   *Directory*

National Stock Exchange SM (NSX): 440 South LaSalle St, Suite 2600, Chicago, IL 60605; tel. (312) 786-8803; fax (312) 939-7239; internet www.nsx.com; f. 1885; fmrly Cincinnati Stock Exchange, name changed in Nov. 2003; Chair. DONALD L. CALVIN; CEO JOSEPH S. RIZZELLO.

New York Stock Exchange Euronext: 11 Wall St, New York, NY 10005; tel. (212) 656-3000; fax (212) 656-5646; internet www.nyse.com; f. 1792; Chair. JAN MICHIEL HESSELS; CEO JOHN A. THAIN; 2,800 mems.

Philadelphia Stock Exchange Inc: Stock Exchange Bldg, 1900 Market St, Philadelphia, PA 19103-3584; tel. (215) 496-5000; fax (215) 496-5460; e-mail info@phlx.com; internet www.phlx.com; f. 1790; Chair. and CEO MEYER S. FRUCHER; 505 mems.

INSURANCE

Principal Companies

Acacia Life Insurance Co: 7315 Wisconsin Ave, Bethesda, MD 20814-3202; tel. (301) 280-1000; fax (310) 280-1161; internet www.unificompanies.com; f. 1869; part of UNIFI Mutual Holding Co; life and health; Chair. and CEO HALUK ARITURK.

Allmerica Financial Life Insurance and Annuity Co: 440 Lincoln St, Worcester, MA 01653; internet www.allmerica.com; subsidiary of Allmerica Financial Corpn; life and health, annuities; operates as First Allmerica Financial Life Insurance Co in NY and HI.

Allstate Corpn: 2775 Sanders Rd, Northbrook, IL 60062-6127; tel. (708) 402-5000; fax (708) 402-2351; e-mail directors@allstate.com; internet www.allstate.com; f. 1931; property and casualty, life, fire, indemnity; Pres. and CEO THOMAS J. WILSON.

American Family Insurance Group: 6000 American Pkwy, Madison, WI 53783-0001; tel. (608) 249-2111; internet www.amfam.com; f. 1927; life and annuities through subsidiary, American Family Life Insurance Co; property and casualty through eight other subsidiaries; Chair. and CEO DAVID R. ANDERSON; Pres. and COO JACK SALZWEDEL.

American Family Life Assurance Co of Columbus (AFLAC): 1932 Wynnton Rd, Columbus, GA 31999; tel. (706) 323-3431; internet news@aflac.com; internet www.aflac.com; f. 1955; life and health; Chair. and CEO DANIEL P. AMOS; Pres. KRISS CLONINGER, III.

American General Life and Accident Insurance Co: American General Center, MC 338N, Nashville, TN 37250; internet www.americangeneral.com; f. 1900; wholly owned subsidiary of American International Group, Inc (AIG).

American National Insurance Co: 1 Moody Plaza, Galveston, TX 77550-7999; tel. (409) 763-4661; internet www.anico.com; f. 1905; operating in 50 states, the District of Columbia, Puerto Rico and American Samoa; life and health, annuities, property and casualty, credit insurance and pension plan services; Chair., Pres. and CEO ROBERT L. MOODY.

American United Life Insurance Co: 1 American Sq., POB 368, Indianapolis, IN 46206-0368; tel. (317) 285-1877; internet www.aul.com; f. 1877; part of OneAmerica Financial Partners, Inc; owned by American United Mutual Insurance Holding Company (AUMIHC); life and health, annuities; Pres. and CEO DAYTON H. MOLENDORP.

Ameritas Life Insurance Corpn: 5900 O St, POB 81889, Lincoln, NE 68501-1889; fax (402) 467-7335; internet www.unificompanies.com; part of UNIFI Mutual Holding Co; life and health; Pres. and CEO JOANN M. MARTIN.

AmerUS Group: 699 Walnut St, Des Moines, IA 50309; tel. (515) 362-3600; fax (515) 557-2625; internet www.amerus.com; f. 1896; life and health, annuities; subsidiaries: AmerUS Annuity Group (Topeka, KS), AmerUS Life Insurance Co (Des Moines, IA), Bankers Life Insurance Co of New York (Woodbury, NY), Indianapolis Life Insurance Co (Indianapolis, IN); acquired by Aviva PLC in 2006; Chair., Pres. and CEO THOMAS C. GODLASKY.

Assurant: 1 Chase Manhattan Plaza, New York, NY 10005; tel. (212) 859-7000; internet www.assurant.com; life and health; Chair. JOHN MICHAEL PALMS; Interim Pres. and CEO J. KERRY CLAYTON.

Auto-Owners Insurance Group: 6101 Anacapri Blvd, Lansing, MI 48917; tel. (517) 323-1200; fax (517) 323-8796; internet www.auto-owners.com; f. 1916; property and casualty through Auto-Owners Insurance Co and four other subsidiaries; life through Auto-Owners Life Insurance Co; CEO R. L. LOOYENGA.

AXA-Equitable, Inc: 1290 Ave of the Americas, New York, NY; tel. (212) 554-1234; fax (212) 262-9019; internet www.axa-equitable.com; f. 1859; subsidiary of AXA Financial, Inc; life and health, annuities; Pres. and CEO CHRISTOPHER M. (KIP) CONDRON.

Baltimore Life Insurance Co: 10075 Red Run Blvd, Owings Mills, MD 21117-4871; tel. (410) 581-6600; fax (410) 581-6601; e-mail info@baltlife.com; internet www.baltlife.com; f. 1882; life and health; Chair., Pres. and CEO L. JOHN PEARSON.

W. R. Berkley Corpn: 475 Steamboat Rd, Greenwich, CT 06830; internet www.wrbc.com; f. 1967; property and casualty through subsidiaries, divided into five business sectors: regional, reinsurance, specialty, alternative markets and international; Chair. and CEO WILLIAM R. BERKLEY.

Berkshire Hathaway, Inc: 1440 Kiewit Plaza, Omaha, NE 68131; internet www.berkshirehathaway.com; general insurance through Berkshire Hathaway Group; life insurance through subsidiary, Medical Protective, in Fort Wayne, IN; CEO WARREN E. BUFFETT.

Business Men's Assurance Co of America: BMA Tower, 700 Karnes Blvd, POB 419458, Kansas City, MO 64141; tel. (816) 753-8000; fax (816) 751-5717; e-mail kvincent@bma.com; internet www.bma.com; f. 1909; Chair. and CEO GIORGIO BALZER; Pres. R. T. RAKICH, Jr.

Central United Life Insurance Co: 10700 Northwest Freeway, Houston, TX 77092; tel. (713) 529-0045; fax (713) 529-9425; Pres. DANIEL JAMES GEORGE.

CIGNA Group Insurance: 2 Liberty Pl., 31st Floor, 1601 Chestnut St, Philadelphia, PA 19192; tel. (215) 761-4555; fax (215) 761-5588; internet www.cigna.com; f. 1982; part of CIGNA Corpn; life and health; Chair. and CEO H. EDWARD HANWAY.

CNA Insurance: 333 South Wabash, Chicago, IL 60604; tel. (312) 822-5000; e-mail cna_help@cna.com; internet www.cna.com; part of Loews Corpn; property and casualty; Chair. STEPHEN W. LILIENTHAL; Pres. and CEO JAMES R. LEWIS.

Combined Insurance Co of America (CICA): 1000 North Milwaukee Ave, Glenview, IL 60025; tel. (847) 953-2025; fax (847) 953-8030; internet www.combined.com; f. 1949; life and health; operates as Combined Life Insurance Co of New York in NY; Chair. RICHARD M. RAVIN; CEO DOUG WENDT.

Conseco, Inc: 11825 North Pennsylvania St, Carmel, IN 46032; tel. (317) 817-6100; internet www.conseco.com; f. 1979; life and health; subsidiaries: Conseco Life Insurance Co (IN), Conseco Insurance Co (IL), Conseco Variable Insurance Co (TX), Conseco Health Insurance Co (AZ), Conseco Senior Health Insurance Com (PA), Bankers Life & Casualty Co (Chicago, IL); Chair. R. GLENN HILLIARD; CEO C. JAMES PRIEUR.

Continental Casualty Co: CNA Plaza, 333 South Wabash Ave, Chicago, IL 60685-0001; tel. (312) 822-5000; fax (312) 822-6419; f. 1897; principal subsidiary of CNA; Chair. and CEO DENNIS H. CHOOKASZIAN.

The Continental Insurance Co: 180 Maiden Lane, New York, NY 10038-4925; tel. (212) 440-3000; fax (212) 440-3857; f. 1853; Chair. and CEO J. P. MASCOTTE.

Erie Insurance Group: 100 Erie Insurance Pl., Erie, PA 16530-0001; tel. (814) 870-2000; fax (814) 870-3126; internet www.erieinsurance.com; f. 1925; vehicle, home, commercial and life through network of independent agents; Interim Pres. and CEO JOHN J. BRINLING, Jr.

Farmers Insurance Group of Cos: 4680 Wilshire Blvd, Los Angeles, CA 90010-3807; tel. (213) 930-3200; fax (213) 932-3101; internet www.farmers.com; f. 1928; part of Farmers Group, Inc; owned by Zurich Financial Services; vehicle, home and life; operates in 41 states; subsidiaries: Farmers Insurance Exchange, Truck Insurance Exchange, Fire Insurance Exchange, Farmers New World Life Insurance Co (Mercer Island, WA); acquired Foremost Insurance Co (MI) in 2000; Pres. and CEO MARTIN D. FERNSTEIN.

Federal Insurance Co: POB 1615, Warren, NJ 07061; tel. (908) 903-2000; internet www.chubb.com; CEO DEAN R. O'HARE.

Fidelity National Financial (FNF): 601 Riverside Ave, Jacksonville, FL 32204; tel. (888) 934-3354; internet www.fnf.com; principal subsidiaries: Fidelity National Title Group and Fidelity National Property and Casualty Insurance Group; Chair WILLIAM P. FOLEY, II; CEO AL STINSON.

First American Corpn: 1 First American Way, Santa Ana, CA 92707; tel. (714) 800-3000; e-mail corporate.communications@firstam.com; internet www.firstam.com; f. 1889; Chair. and CEO PARKER S. KENNEDY.

Franklin Life Insurance Co: 1 Franklin Sq., Springfield, IL 62713; tel. (217) 528-2011; fax (217) 528-9106; internet www.americangeneral.com; f. 1884; Chair., Pres. and CEO WILLIAM A. SIMPSON (acting).

General American Life Insurance Co: 700 Market St, POB 396, St Louis, MO 63166; tel. (314) 444-0605; fax (314) 444-0510; internet www.metlife.com; f. 1933; wholly owned subsidiary of MetLife, Inc; Chair., Pres. and CEO KEVIN EICHNER.

Genworth Financial, Inc: 6620 West Broad St, Richmond, VA 23230; e-mail contactus@genworth.com; internet www.genworth.com; f. 1871 as The Life Insurance Co of Virginia; life, long-term care, annuities; Chair., Pres. and CEO MICHAEL D. FRAIZER.

Great Southern Life Insurance Co: 300 West 11th St, Kansas City, MO 64105; fax (816) 391-2018; e-mail dl.customer.service@

americo.com; internet www.greatsouthern.com; f. 1909; Pres. and CEO GARY L. MULLER.

Guarantee Mutual Life Insurance Co: 8801 Indian Hills Dr., Omaha, NE 68114-4066; tel. (402) 390-7300; fax (402) 390-7577; f. 1901; Sr Vice-Pres. RANDY BIGGERSTAFF.

The Guardian Life Insurance Co of America: 7 Hannover Sq., New York, NY 10004; tel. (212) 598-8000; fax (212) 353-7034; internet www.guardianlife.com; f. 1860; life and health through 12 subsidiaries and affiliates; Pres. and CEO DENNIS J. MANNING.

Hanover Insurance Group, Inc: 1440 Lincoln St, Worcester, MA 01653-0002; tel. (508) 855-1000; fax (508) 853-6332; internet www.hanover.com; f. 1852; subsidiary of Allmerica Financial Corpn; property and casualty; operates as The Hanover Insurance Co, and as Citizens Insurance Co of America in MI; Chair. MICHAEL P. ANGELINI; Pres. and CEO FREDERICK H. EPPINGER.

Hartford Financial Services Group, Inc: Hartford Plaza, 690 Asylum Ave, Hartford, CT 06115; internet www.thehartford.com; f. 1810; vehicle, home, life, flood, property and casualty, group benefits, group reinsurance; Chair. and CEO RAMANI AYER; Pres. and COO THOMAS M. MARRA.

Integon General Insurance Corpn: 500 West Fifth St, Winston-Salem, NC 27102-3199; tel. (910) 770-2000; fax (910) 770-2122; f. 1920; part of GMAC Insurance Holdings, Inc since 1997.

John Hancock Life Insurance Co: POB 111, Boston, MA 02117; tel. (617) 572-6000; fax (617) 572-4539; e-mail webmail@jhancock.com; internet www.johnhancock.com; owned by Manulife (Canada); CEO DAVID F. D'ALESSANDRO.

Kansas City Life Insurance Co: 3520 Broadway, Kansas City, MO 64141-6139; tel. (816) 753-7000; internet www.kclife.com; f. 1895; life and health; operates in 48 states and the District of Columbia; subsidiaries: Old American Insurance Co, Sunset Life Insurance Co of America; Chair., Pres. and CEO R. PHILIP BIXBY.

Liberty Mutual Group, Inc: 175 Berkeley St, Boston, MA 02116; tel. (617) 357-9500; fax (617) 350-7648; internet www.libertymutual.com; subsidiaries: Liberty Life Assurance Co of Boston, Liberty Mutual Insurance Co, Liberty Mutual Fire Insurance Co and Employers Insurance Co of Wasusau; Chair., Pres. and CEO EDMUND F. KELLY.

Lincoln National Life Insurance Co: West Tower, Suite 3900, Centre Sq., 1500 Market St, Philadelphia, PA 19102-2112; tel. (877) 275-5462; internet www.lfg.com; f. 1905; part of Lincoln Corpn; life and health; Chair. and CEO JON A. BOSCIA.

Manhattan Life Insurance Co: 5 Waterside Crossing, 3rd Floor, Windsor, CT 06095; tel. (860) 298-9343; fax (877) 626-4281; e-mail cs@manhattanlife.com; f. 1850; part of Manhattan Insurance Group; Chair. and CEO D. M. FORDYCE.

Massachusetts Mutual Life Insurance Co (MassMutual): 1295 State St, Springfield, MA 01111-0001; tel. (413) 788-8411; fax (413) 744-6005; internet www.massmutual.com; f. 1851; part of MassMutual Financial Group; mutual life and health; Chair., Pres. and CEO STUART H. REESE.

Metropolitan Life Insurance Co (MetLife): 1 Madison Ave, New York, NY 10010-3681; tel. (212) 578-2211; fax (212) 689-1980; internet www.metlife.com; f. 1863; life and health; Chair., Pres. and CEO C. ROBERT HENRIKSON.

Minnesota Life Insurance Co: 400 Robert St North, St Paul, MN 55101; tel. (651) 665-3500; fax (651) 665-4488; internet www.minnesotamutual.com; f. 1880; affiliated to Securian Financial Group, Inc; life and health; Chair., Pres. and CEO ROBERT L. SENKLER.

Monarch Life Insurance Co: 1 Monarch Pl., Springfield, MA 01144-1001; tel. (413) 784-2000; fax (413) 784-6271; f. 1901; CEO ROGER T. SERVISON.

Mutual of Omaha Insurance Co: Mutual of Omaha Plaza, Omaha, NE 68175; tel. (402) 342-7600; internet mutualofomaha.com; f. 1909; life and health; operating in 50 states, the District of Columbia, the US Virgin Is, Puerto Rico and Guam; Chair. and CEO DANIEL P. NEARY; Pres. and COO JOHN A. STURGEON.

Nationwide Mutual Insurance Co: 1 Nationwide Plaza, Columbus, OH 43215-2220; tel. (614) 249-7111; internet www.nationwide.com; f. 1925; property and casualty through 18 subsidiaries; life and retirement savings through 25 subsidiaries; also asset management and strategic investment; CEO WILLIAM G. JURGENSEN; Chair. and COO MARK THRESHER.

New York Life Insurance Co: 51 Madison Ave, New York, NY 10010-1603; tel. (212) 576-7000; fax (212) 576-6794; e-mail infonyl@e-mail.com; internet www.newyorklife.com; f. 1845; life and health; Chair. and CEO SEYMOUR (SY) STERNBERG; Pres. TED MATHAS.

The Northwestern Mutual Life Insurance Co: 720 East Wisconsin Ave, Milwaukee, WI 53202-4797; tel. (414) 271-1444; internet www.nmfn.com; f. 1857; mutual life and health; Pres. and CEO EDWARD J. ZORE.

Old Line Life Insurance Co of America: POB 401, Milwaukee, WI 53201; tel. (414) 271-2820; fax (414) 283-5556; f. 1910; Pres. and CEO JAMES A. GRIFFIN.

Pacific Life Insurance Co: 700 Newport Center Dr., Newport Beach, CA 92660-6397; tel. (949) 219-3011; fax (949) 219-7614; e-mail info@pacificlife.com; internet www.pacificlife.com; f. 1868; life and health; Pres. and CEO JAMES T. MORRIS; Chair. THOMAS C. SUTTON.

Penn Mutual Life Insurance Co: 600 Dresher Rd, Horsham, PA 19044; tel. (215) 956-8000; fax (215) 956-7508; internet www.pennmutual.com; f. 1847; Chair. and CEO ROBERT E. CHAPPELL; Pres. and COO DANIEL J. TORAN.

Phoenix Life Insurance Co: 1 American Row, POB 5056, Hartford, CT 06102-5056; tel. (860) 403-5000; e-mail webmaster@phoenixwm.com; internet www.phoenixwm.com; f. 1851; life and health, annuities; operating in all states, the District of Columbia, Puerto Rico, the US Virgin Is and Canada; Chair., Pres. and CEO DONA DAVIS YOUNG.

Pioneer Mutual Life Insurance Co: 101 North 10th St, Fargo, ND 58108; tel. (701) 297-5700; internet www.pmlife.com; part of OneAmerica Financial Partners, Inc, owned by American United Mutual Insurance Holding Co (AUMIHC); life and health, annuities; Pres. and CEO DAYTON H. MOLENDORP.

Principal Financial Group, Inc: 711 High St, Des Moines, IA 50392; tel. (515) 247-5111; internet www.principal.com; life and health; CEO J. BARRY GRISWELL.

The Progressive Group: 6300 Wilson Mills Rd, Mayfield Village, OH 44143; tel. (440) 461-5000; internet www.progressive.com; f. 1937; part of The Progressive Corpn; Pres. and CEO GLENN M. RENWICK.

Protective Life Insurance Co: 2801 Hwy 280 South, Birmingham, AL 35223-2488; tel. (205) 879-9230; fax (205) 268-1000; internet www.protective.com; f. 1907; part of Protective Life Insurance Corpn; life and health; Chair., Pres. and CEO JOHN D. JOHNS.

Provident Life and Accident Insurance Co of America: 1 Fountain Sq., Chattanooga, TN 37402-1389; tel. (423) 755-1011; fax (423) 755-7013; f. 1887; Pres. and CEO WINSTON W. WALKER.

The Prudential Insurance Co of America: 751 Broad St, Newark, NJ 07102-3714; tel. (973) 802-6000; fax (973) 802-7277; internet www.prudential.com; f. 1875; life and health; Chair. and CEO ARTHUR F. RYAN; Pres. RONALD D. BARBARO.

SAFECO Corpn: Safeco Plaza, 4333 Brooklyn Ave, NE, Seattle, WA 98185-0001; tel. (206) 545-5000; fax (206) 548-7117; internet www.safeco.com; f. 1929; subsidiaries: SAFECO Property and Casualty Insurance Cos, SAFECO Surety; Pres. and CEO PAULA ROSPUT REYNOLDS.

Security Mutual Life Insurance Co of New York: 100 Court St, POB 1625, Binghamton, New York, NY 13902-1625; tel. (607) 723-3551; internet www.smlny.com; f. 1886; life and health, annuities; operating in all states; Chair., Pres. and CEO BRUCE W. BOYEA.

Southwestern Life Insurance Co: POB 2699, Dallas, TX 752221; tel. (214) 954-7111; fax (214) 954-7717; f. 1903; subsidiary of Southwestern Life Corpn.

Standard Insurance Co: POB 711, Portland, OR 97207; tel. (503) 248-2700; fax (503) 321-7757; e-mail info@standard.com; internet www.standard.com; f. 1906; principal subsidiary of StanCorp Financial Group, Inc; disability, group diability, group life, group dental, annuities; Chair., Pres. and CEO ERIC E. PARSONS.

Standard Life Insurance Co of New York: POB 5031, White Plains, NY 10602; tel. (914) 989-4400; internet www.standard-ny.com; subsidiary of StanCorp Financial Group, Inc; group life, disability, dental; Chair., Pres. and CEO ERIC E. PARSONS.

State Farm Insurance: 1 State Farm Plaza, Bloomington, IL 61710-0001; tel. (309) 766-2311; fax (309) 766-6169; internet www.statefarm.com; f. 1926; vehicle, fire, life and health insurance; Chair. and CEO EDWARD B. RUST, Jr.

State Life Insurance Co: 1 American Sq., POB 368, Indianapolis, IN 46206-0368; tel. (317) 681-5300; fax (317) 681-5492; internet www.statelife.com; f. 1894; part of OneAmerica Financial Partners, Inc, owned by American United Mutual Insurance Holding Company (AUMIHC); life and health, annuities; Pres. and CEO DAYTON H. MOLENDORP.

Sun Life Insurance Co of America: 11601 Wilshire Blvd, Los Angeles, CA 90025; tel. (213) 312-5000; f. 1897; operating in 48 states and the District of Columbia; Chair. ELI BROAD; Pres. and CEO ROBERT P. SALTZMAN.

Teachers Insurance and Annuity Association-College Retirement Equities Fund (TIAA-CREF): POB 1259, Charlotte, NC 28201; internet www.tiaa-cref.org; mutual life and health; Chair., Pres. and CEO HERBERT M. ALLISON, Jr.

Thrivent Financial for Lutherans: 4321 North Ballard Rd, Appleton, WI 54919-0001; tel. (920) 734-5721; e-mail mail@

THE UNITED STATES OF AMERICA

thrivent.com; internet www.thrivent.com; life and health; Chair., Pres. and CEO BRUCE J. NICHOLSON.

Torchmark Corpn: 3700 South Stonebridge Dr., POB 8080, McKinney, TX 75070-8080; tel. (972) 569-4000; internet www.torchmarkcorp.com; life and health; principal subsidiaries: American Income Life Insurance Co (Waco, TX), First United American Life Insurance Co (Syracuse, NY), Globe Life And Accident Insurance Co (Oklahoma City, OK), Liberty National Life Insurance Co (Birmingham, AL), United American Insurance Co (McKinney, TX), United Investors Life Insurance Co (Birmingham, AL); Chair. and CEO MARK S. MCANDREW.

Transamerica Corpn: 1150 South Olive St, Los Angeles, CA 90015-2290; tel. (213) 741-7629; fax (213) 742-5280; internet www.transamerica.com; f. 1906; part of AEGON Insurance Group; life and health, annuities, reinsurance; subsidiaries: Transamerica Occidental Life Insurance Co, Transamerica Life Insurance Co, Transamerica Financial Life Insurance Co; Pres. RON WAGLEY; COO KAREN MCDONAL.

The Travelers Companies, Inc: 385 Washington St, Saint Paul, MN 55102; tel. (615) 310-7911; fax (860) 277-1970; internet www.travelers.com; f. 2004 as St Paul Travelers by merger of St Paul Coes and Travelers Property and Casualty Corpn; adopted current name in 2007; Chair. and CEO JAY S. FISHMAN.

Unigard Security Insurance Co: 15805 NE 24th St, Bellevue, WA 98008-2409; tel. (425) 641-4321; fax (425) 562-5256; internet www.unigard.com; f. 1901; parent cos: Winterthur Insurance Group, Credit Suisse Group; Pres. and CEO PETER CHRISTEN.

Union Central Life Insurance Co: 1876 Waycross Rd, POB 40888, Cincinnati, OH 45240; tel. (513) 595-2200; fax (513) 595-2559; internet www.unioncentral.com; f. 1867; part of UNIFI Mutual Holding Co; life and health; Chair. JOHN H. JACOBS.

United Insurance Co of America: 1 East Wacker Dr., Chicago, IL 60601-1883; tel. (312) 661-4500; fax (312) 661-4731; f. 1955; subsidiary of Unitrin, Inc; Pres. RICHARD C. VIE.

United States Fidelity & Guaranty Co: 100 Light St, Baltimore, MD 21202-1036; tel. (410) 547-3000; fax (410) 625-2829; f. 1896; Chair. and CEO JACK MOSELEY; Pres. PAUL SCHEEL.

Unitrin, Inc: 1 East Wacker Dr., Chicago, IL 60601; tel. (312) 661-4600; internet www.unitrin.com; life and health through Unitrin Life & Health Insurance Group (five subsidiaries); property and casualty through Unitrin Property & Casualty Insurance Group (19 subsidiaries); two further subsidiaries and five affiliated cos; Chair. RICHARD C. VIE; Pres. and CEO DONALD G. SOUTHWELL.

UnumProvident Corpn: 1 Fountain Sq., Chattanooga, TN 37402; tel. (432) 294-1011; internet www.unumprovident.com; f. 1848; life and health; subsidiaries: Colonial Life Accident and Insurance Co, Paul Revere Life Insurance Co, Provident Life and Accident Insurance Co, Provident Life and Casualty Insurance Co, First Unum Insurance Co and Unum Life Insurance Co of America; Pres. and CEO THOMAS R. WATJEN.

USAA: 9800 Fredericksburg Rd, San Antonio, TX 78288; internet www.usaa.com; f. 1922; property and casualty through seven subsidiaries: United Service Automobile Asscn, USAA Casualty Insurance Co, USAA General Indemnity Co, Garrison Property and Casualty Insurance Co, USAA County Mutual Insurance Co, USAA Texas Lloyd's Co and USAA Ltd; life and annuities through two subsidiaries: USAA Life Insurance Co and USAA Life Insurance Company of New York (Highland Falls, NY).

Washington National Corporation: 300 Tower Pkwy, Lincolnshire, IL 60069; tel. (847) 793-3000; fax (847) 793-3737; f. 1911; Chair. and CEO ROBERT PATIN.

Western & Southern Financial Group: 400 East Fourth St, Cincinnati, OH 45202; tel. (513) 629-1800; fax (513) 629-1220; internet www.westernsouthern.com; f. 1888; operating in 44 states; life and health; subsidiaries: Western & Southern Life Insurance Co, Western-Southern Life Assurance Co, Columbus Life Insurance Co, Integrity Life Insurance Co, Lafayette Life Insurance Co; Chair., Pres. and CEO JOHN F. BARRETT.

Zenith Insurance Co: 21255 Califa St, Woodland Hills, CA 91367; tel. (818) 713-1000; fax (818) 592-0480; e-mail dfreeman@thezenith.com; internet www.thezenith.com ; specializes in workers' compensation; subsidiary: ZNAT Insurance Co; Pres. JACK D. MILLER; Chair. STANLEY R. ZAX.

INSURANCE ORGANIZATIONS

American Council of Life Insurance (ACLI): 101 Constitution Ave, NW, Washington, DC 20001-2133; tel. (202) 624-2000; fax (202) 624-2319; e-mail Media@acli.com; internet www.acli.com; f. 1976; 400 mem. cos; Pres. and CEO FRANK KEATING, Jr.

American Institute of Marine Underwriters (AIMU): 14 Wall St, 21st Floor, New York, NY 10005-2145; tel. (212) 233-0550; fax (212) 227-5102; e-mail aimu@aimu.org; internet www.aimu.org; f. 1898; 105 mems; Chair. RICHARD J. DECKER; Pres. JAMES M. CRAIG.

Directory

American Insurance Association (AIA): 1130 Connecticut Ave, NW, Suite 1000, Washington, DC 20036; tel. (202) 828-7100; fax (202) 293-1219; e-mail info@aiadc.org; internet www.aiadc.org ; f. 1964; 300 mems; Chair. ROBERT P. RESTREPO, Jr; Pres. ROBERT E. VAGLEY.

Casualty Actuarial Society: 4350 North Fairfax Dr., Suite 250, Arlington, VA 22203; tel. (703) 276-3100; fax (703) 276-3108; e-mail office@casact.org; internet www.casact.org; f. 1914; 4,400 mems; Pres. THOMAS G. MYERS.

LIMRA International: 300 Day Hill Rd, Windsor, CT 06095; tel. (860) 688-3358; fax (860) 298-9555; internet www.limra.com; f. 1916; research and consultancy services for insurance cos; Pres. and CEO ROBERT A. KERZNER; 850 mems.

LOMA (Life Office Management Association): 2300 Windy Ridge Pkwy, Suite 600, Atlanta, GA 30339-8443; tel. (770) 951-1770; fax (770) 984-6417; e-mail askloma@loma.org; internet www.loma.org; f. 1924; 1,200 mem. cos; Chair. HOWARD R. FRICKE; Pres. and CEO THOMAS P. DONALDSON.

National Association of Health Underwriters (NAHU): 2000 North 14th St, Suite 450, Arlington, VA 22201; tel. (703) 276-0220; fax (703) 841-7797; e-mail info@nahu.org; internet www.nahu.org; CEO JANET TRAUTWEIN.

National Association of Life Underwriters: 1922 F St, NW, Washington, DC 20006-4387; tel. (202) 331-6000; fax (202) 331-2179; internet www.agents-online.com/nalu/naluhome.html; 108,000 mems; CEO WILLIAM V. REGAN, III.

National Association of Mutual Insurance Cos (NAMIC): 3601 Vincennes Rd, POB 68700, Indianapolis, IN 46268-0700; tel. (317) 875-5250; fax (317) 879-8408; e-mail service@namic.org; internet www.namic.org ; f. 1895; 1,400 mems; Pres. and CEO CHARLES M. CHAMNESS.

Reinsurance Association of America: 1301 Pennsylvania Ave, NW, Suite 900, Washington, DC 20004; tel. (202) 638-3690; fax (202) 638-0936; e-mail infobox@reinsurance.org; internet www.reinsurance.org; f. 1969; 35 mems; Pres. FRANKLIN W. NUTTER.

Trade and Industry

CHAMBER OF COMMERCE

US Chamber of Commerce: 1615 H St, NW, Washington, DC 20062-2000; tel. (202) 659-6000; fax (202) 463-5836; internet www.uschamber.com; f. 1912; mems: c. 3m. cos; over 100 US chambers of commerce in 91 countries; Pres. and CEO THOMAS J. DONOHUE; Chair. PAUL S. SPERANZA, Jr.

EMPLOYERS' ORGANIZATIONS

Chemicals

American Chemistry Council (ACC): 1300 Wilson Blvd, Arlington, VA 22209; tel. (703) 741-5000; fax (703) 741-6000; e-mail helpline@americanchemistry.com; internet www.americanchemistry.com; f. 1872; incl. the Plastics Division and Chlorine Chemistry Division; 135 mems; Pres. and CEO JACK N. GERARD; Sec. DELL PERELMAN.

American Pharmacists Association (APhA): 1100 15th St, NW, Suite 400, Washington, DC 20005-1707; tel. (202) 628-4410; fax (202) 783-2351; e-mail ejefferson@aphanet.org; internet www.aphanet.org; f. 1852; over 57,000 mems; Pres. WINNIE A. LANDIS.

American Plastics Council (APC): 1300 Wilson Blvd, Arlington, VA 22209; tel. (703) 741-5000; fax (703) 741-6093; internet www.americanplasticscouncil.org; affiliate of the American Chemistry Council; 13 mem. cos and 1 affiliated trade asscn; Pres. RODNEY W. LOWMAN.

Consumer Specialty Products Association (CSPA): 900 17th St, NW, Suite 300, Washington, DC 20006; tel. (202) 872-8110; fax (202) 872-8114; e-mail info@cspa.org; internet www.cspa.org; f. 1914; fmrly Chemical Specialities Manufacturers Asscn; over 250 mems; Pres. CHRISTOPHER CATHCART.

Drug, Chemical and Associated Technologies Association, Inc (DCAT): 1 Washington Blvd, Suite 7, Robbinsville, NJ 08691; tel. (609) 448-1000; fax (609) 448-1944; e-mail info@dcat.org; internet www.dcat.org; f. 1890; fmrly Drug, Chemical and Allied Trades Asscn; name changed as above in 2003; 350 mems; Pres. JOSEPH COLLELUORI.

The Fertilizer Institute: Union Center Plaza, 820 First St, NE, Suite 430, Washington, DC 20002; tel. (202) 962-0490; fax (202) 962-0577; e-mail webmaster@tfi.org; internet www.tfi.org; f. 1883; 300 mem. orgs; Pres. FORD B. WEST.

National Community Pharmacists Association (NCPA): 100 Daingerfield Rd, Alexandria, VA 22314; tel. (703) 683-8200; fax (703) 683-3619; e-mail info@ncpanet.org; internet www.ncpanet.org;

THE UNITED STATES OF AMERICA

f. 1898; fmrly Nat. Asscn of Retail Druggists; 25,000 mems; Pres. JOHN E. TILLEY.

Pharmaceutical Research & Manufacturers of America (PhRMA): 950 F St, NW, Suite 900, Washington, DC 20004; tel. (202) 835-3400; fax (202) 835-3414; internet www.phrma.org; f. 1958; 67 mems; Pres. WILLIAM TAUZIN.

Soap and Detergent Association (SDA): 1500 K St, NW, Suite 300, Washington, DC, 20005; tel. (202) 347-2900; fax (202) 347-4110; e-mail info@cleaning101.com; internet www.cleaning101.com; f. 1926; 110 mems; Pres. and CEO ERNIE ROSENBERG.

Synthetic Organic Chemical Manufacturers' Association (SOCMA): 1850 M St, NW, Suite 700, Washington, DC 20036-5810; tel. (202) 721-4100; fax (202) 296-8120; e-mail info@socma.com; internet www.socma.com; f. 1921; 275 mem. cos; Chair. MARGARET WALKER.

Construction
(see also Electricity, and Engineering and Machinery)

American Institute of Constructors (AIC): POB 26334, Alexandria, VA 22314; tel. (703) 683-4999; fax (703) 683-5480; e-mail admin@aicnet.org; internet www.aicnet.org; f. 1971; 1,600 mems; Pres. STEVE BYRNE.

Associated Builders and Contractors, Inc (ABC): 4250 North Fairfax Dr., 9th Floor, Arlington, VA 22203-1607; tel. (703) 812-2000; e-mail gotquestions@abc.org; internet www.abc.org; f. 1950; 24,000 mems; Pres. and CEO M. KIRK PICKEREL.

Associated General Contractors of America (AGC) (AGC of America): 2300 Wilson Blvd, Suite 400, Arlington, VA 22201; tel. (703) 548-3118; fax (703) 548-3119; e-mail info@agc.org; internet www.agc.org; f. 1918; 33,000 mems; Pres. STEVE MASSIE; CEO STEPHEN SANDHERR.

Associated Specialty Contractors, Inc (ASC): 3 Bethesda Metro Center, Suite 1100, Bethesda, MD 20814-5372; tel. (301) 657-3110; fax (301) 215-4500; e-mail dgw@necanet.org; internet www.assoc-spec-con.org; f. 1955; 9 mem. asscns; Pres. DANIEL G. WALTER.

Building Stone Institute (BSI): 551 Tollgate Rd, Suite C, Elgin, IL 60123; tel. (847) 695-0170; fax (847) 695-0174; e-mail jeff@buildingstoneinstitute.org; internet www.buildingstoneinstitute.org; f. 1919; 400 mems; Pres. SCOTT BUECHEL.

Construction Specifications Institute (CSI): 99 Canal Center Plaza, Suite 300, Alexandria, VA 22314; tel. (703) 684-0300; fax (703) 684-8436; e-mail csi@csinet.org; internet www.csinet.org; f. 1948; over 16,000 mems; Pres. EUGENE VALENTINE; Pres.-elect K. M. GILMAN.

Mechanical Contractors Association of America, Inc (MCAA): 1385 Piccard Dr., Rockville, MD 20850-4340; tel. (301) 869-5800; fax (301) 990-9690; e-mail mcaainfo@mcaa.org; internet www.mcaa.org; f. 1889; 2,300 mems; Exec. Vice-Pres. and CEO JOHN R. GENTILLE.

National Association of Home Builders of the US (NAHB): 1201 15th St, NW, Washington, DC 20005; tel. (202) 266-8200; fax (202) 266-8400; internet www.nahb.org; f. 1942; 800 mem. asscns, 220,000 mems; Pres. BRIAN C. CATALDE.

National Association of Plumbing-Heating-Cooling Contractors (PHCC): 180 South Washington St, POB 6808, Falls Church, VA 22046; tel. (703) 237-8100; fax (703) 237-7442; e-mail naphcc@naphcc.org; internet www.phccweb.org; f. 1883; 4,000 mems; Pres. JO RAE WAGNER; Exec. Vice-Pres. IKE CASEY.

National Ready Mixed Concrete Association (NRMCA): 900 Spring St, Silver Spring, MD 20910; tel. (301) 587-1400; fax (301) 585-4219; e-mail info@nrmca.org; internet www.nrmca.org; f. 1930; 1,000 mems; Pres. ELIZABETH TWOHY.

National Tile Contractors Association (NTCA): POB 13629, Jackson, MS 39236; tel. (601) 939-2071; fax (601) 932-6117; internet www.tile-assn.com; f. 1947; Exec. Dir BART BETTIGA.

Tile Council of North America Inc (TCNA): 100 Clemson Research Blvd, Anderson, SC 29625; tel. (864) 646-8453; fax (864) 646-2821; e-mail literature@tileusa.com; internet www.tileusa.com; f. 1945 as Tile Council of America; name changed as above in 2003; 130 mems; Exec. Dir ERIC ASTRACHAN.

US Green Building Council (USGBC): 1015 18th St, NW, Suite 508, Washington, DC 20036; tel. (202) 828-7422; fax (202) 828-5110; e-mail info@usgbc.org; internet www.usgbc.org; over 6,400 mem. orgs; Pres. and CEO S. RICHARD FEDRIZZI; Chair. SANDY WIGGINS.

Electricity
(see also Construction, Electronics and Technology, Engineering and Machinery, and Trade and Industry—Utilities)

Edison Electric Institute (EEI): 701 Pennsylvania Ave, NW, Washington, DC 20004-2696; tel. (202) 508-5000; e-mail feedback@eei.org; internet www.eei.org; f. 1933; mems: 190 investor-owned electric utility cos, 60 int. affiliates; mems generate 60% of electricity produced by US utilities and supply 71% of US customers; Pres. JEFFRY STERBA.

National Association of Electrical Distributors (NAED): 1100 Corporate Sq. Dr., Suite 100, St Louis, MO 63132; tel. (314) 991-9000; fax (314) 991-3060; e-mail info@naed.org; internet www.naed.org; f. 1908; 2,900 mems; Pres. TOM NABER.

National Electrical Contractors Association (NECA): 3 Bethesda Metro Center, Suite 1100, Bethesda, MD 20814-5372; tel. (301) 657-3110; fax (301) 215-4500; internet www.necanet.org; f. 1901; 4,200 mems; Pres. MILNER IRVIN; CEO JOHN M. GRAU.

National Electrical Manufacturers Association (NEMA): 1300 North 17th St, Suite 1752, Rosslyn, VA 22209; tel. (703) 841-3200; fax (703) 841-5900; e-mail webmaster@nema.org; internet www.nema.org; f. 1926; 430 mem. cos; Pres. and CEO JOHN ESTEY.

Electronics and Technology

AeA: 5201 Great America Pkwy, Suite 400, Santa Clara, CA 95054; tel. (408) 987-4200; fax (408) 987-4298; e-mail csc@aeanet.org; internet www.aeanet.org; f. 1943; fmrly American Electronics Asscn; 3,000 mem. cos; Pres. and CEO TIMOTHY A. GUERTIN.

Electronic Industries Alliance: 2500 Wilson Blvd, Arlington, VA 22201-3834; tel. (703) 907-7500; fax (703) 907-7501; internet www.eia.org; f. 1924; 1,300 mem. cos; Pres. MATHEW FLANIGAN (acting).

Institute of Electrical and Electronics Engineers, Inc (IEEE): 445 Hoes Lane, Piscataway, NJ 08854-4141; tel. (732) 981-0060; fax (732) 981-1721; e-mail webmaster@ieee.org; internet www.ieee.org; f. 1963; 365,000 mems world-wide; Pres.-elect and CEO-elect LEWIS M. TERMAN.

IPC (Association Connecting Electronics Industries): 3000 Lakeside Dr., Suite 309, Bannockburn, IL 60015; tel. (847) 615-7100; fax (847) 615-7105; e-mail orderipc@ipc.org; internet www.ipc.org; f. 1957; Chair. C. JAMES HERRING.

Telecommunications Industry Association (TIA): 2500 Wilson Blvd, Suite 300, Arlington, VA 22201; tel. (703) 907-7700; fax (703) 907-7727; e-mail tia@tiaonline.org; internet www.tiaonline.org; f. 1988; Pres. GRANT E. SEIFFERT.

Engineering and Machinery
(see also Electricity and Construction)

Air-Conditioning and Refrigeration Institute (ARI): 4301 North Fairfax Dr., Suite 200, Arlington, VA 22203; tel. (703) 524-8800; fax (703) 528-3816; e-mail ari@ari.org; internet www.ari.org; f. 1953; 220 mems; Pres. WILLIAM G. SUTTON.

American Council of Engineering Companies (ACEC): 1015 15th St, NW, 8th Floor, Washington, DC 20005-2605; tel. (202) 347-7474; fax (202) 898-0068; e-mail acec@acec.org; internet www.acec.org; f. 1905; 6,000 mem. cos; Chair. ORRIN B. MACMURRAY.

American Institute of Chemical Engineers (AIChE): 3 Park Ave, New York, NY 10016-5991; tel. (212) 591-8100; fax (212) 591-8888; e-mail xpress@aiche.org; internet www.aiche.org; f. 1908; over 46,000 mems world-wide; Pres. LARRY EVANS.

American Institute of Mining, Metallurgical and Petroleum Engineers, Inc: 8307 Shaffer Pkwy, Littleton, CO 80127-4012; tel. (303) 948-4255; fax (303) 948-4260; e-mail aime@aimehq.org; internet www.aimehq.org; f. 1871; five constituent socs representing 100,000 mems; Pres. JAMES R. JORDEN.

American Society of Civil Engineers (ASCE): 1801 Alexander Bell Dr., Reston, VA 20191-4400; tel. (703) 295-6300; fax (703) 295-6222; e-mail webmaster@asce.org; internet www.asce.org; f. 1852; over 137,500 mems; Pres. WILLIAM S. MARCUSON, III.

American Society of Heating, Refrigerating and Air Conditioning Engineers (ASHRAE): 1791 Tullie Circle, NE, Atlanta, GA 30329; tel. (404) 636-8400; fax (404) 321-5478; e-mail ashrae@ashrae.org; internet www.ashrae.org; f. 1894; 55,000 mems; Pres. KENT PETERSON.

American Society of Naval Engineers, Inc: 1452 Duke St, Alexandria, VA 22314-3458; tel. (703) 836-6727; fax (703) 836-7491; e-mail asnehq@navalengineers.org; internet www.navalengineers.org; f. 1888; 6,000 mems; Exec. Dir Capt. (retd) DENNIS K. KRUSE.

Association of Coastal Engineers (ACE): c/o Patricia Ehrman, 2770 North West 43rd St, Suite B, Applied Technology and Management Inc, Gainesville, FL 32606; e-mail hugo@coastharborenq.com; internet www.coastalengineers.org; f. 1999; Exec. Sec. PATRICIA EHRMAN.

Association of Home Appliance Manufacturers (AHAM): 1111 19th St, NW, Suite 402, Washington, DC 20036; tel. (202) 872-5955; fax (202) 872-9354; e-mail info@aham.org; internet www.aham.org; f. 1915; Pres. JOSEPH M. MCGUIRE.

AMT (The Association for Manufacturing Technology): 7901 Westpark Dr., McLean, VA 22102-4206; tel. (703) 893-2900; fax (703) 893-

THE UNITED STATES OF AMERICA

1151; e-mail amt@amtonline.org; internet www.amtonline.org; f. 1902; 370 mems; Pres. JOHN B. BYRD, III.

Manufacturers Alliance/MAPI, Inc: 1600 Wilson Blvd, Suite 1100, Arlington, VA 22209-2411; tel. (703) 841-9000; fax (703) 841-9514; e-mail info@mapi.net; internet www.mapi.net; f. 1933; 500 cos; Pres. and CEO THOMAS J. DUESTERBERG.

Petroleum Equipment Institute (PEI): POB 2380, Tulsa, OK 74101-2380; tel. (918) 494-9696; fax (918) 491-9895; e-mail info@pei.org; internet www.pei.org; f. 1951; over 1,600 mems world-wide; Exec. Vice-Pres. ROBERT N. RENKES.

SAE, International (Society of Automotive Engineers): 400 Commonwealth Dr., Warrendale, PA 15096-0001; tel. (724) 776-4841; fax (724) 776-0790; e-mail customerservice@sae.org; internet www.sae.org; f. 1905; over 90,000 mems world-wide; Pres.-elect THOMAS W. RYAN, III.

Society of Naval Architects and Marine Engineers (SNAME): 601 Pavonia Ave, Suite 400, Jersey City, NJ 07306-2907; tel. (201) 798-4800; fax (201) 798-4975; e-mail ccali-poutre@sname.org; internet www.sname.org; f. 1893; over 10,000 mems; Pres. Adm. (retd) ROBERT E. KRAMEK.

United Engineering Foundation: POB 70, Mount Vernon, VA 22121-0070; tel. (973) 244-2328; fax (973) 882-5155; e-mail engfnd@aol.com; internet www.engfnd.org; f. 1914; umbrella org. of engineering socs, incl. ASME International, the Institute of Electrical and Electronics Engineers and the American Institute of Chemical Engineers; Pres. ROBERT E. FREAS; Exec. Dir Dr DAVID L. BELDEN.

Food

American Bakers Association (ABA): 1350 I St, NW, Suite 700, Washington, DC 20005-3300; tel. (202) 789-0300; fax (202) 898-1164; e-mail info@americanbakers.org; internet www.americanbakers.org; f. 1897; Pres. and CEO ROBB MACKIE.

American Beverage Association (ABA): 1101 16th St, NW, Washington, DC 20036-4803; tel. (202) 463-6732; fax (202) 659-5349; e-mail info@ameribev.org; internet www.ameribev.org; f. 1919; fmrly Nat. Soft Drink Asscn; 1,700 mems; Pres. and CEO SUSAN K. NEELY.

American Farm Bureau Federation (FB): 600 Maryland Ave, SW, Suite 1000W, Washington, DC 20024; tel. (202) 406-3600; fax (202) 406-3602; e-mail webmaster@fb.org; internet www.fb.org; f. 1919; 50 mem. states and Puerto Rico; Pres. BOB STALLMAN; Chief Admin. Officer RICHARD NEWPHER.

American Meat Institute: 1150 Connecticut Ave, NW, 12th Floor, Washington, DC 20036; tel. (202) 587-4200; fax (202) 587-4300; e-mail webmaster@meatami.com; internet www.meatami.com; f. 1906; 1,100 mems; Pres. and CEO J. PATRICK BOYLE.

American Council for Food Safety and Quality: 710 Striker Ave, Sacramento, CA 95834; tel. (916) 561-5900; fax (916) 561-5910; e-mail merlej@dfaofca.com; internet www.dfaofca.com; f. 1908; agricultural asscn (dried fruit and tree nuts); 51 mems; Pres. and CEO MERLE JACOBS; Chair. GEORGE SOUSA, Sr.

Commodity Markets Council (CMC): 1300 L St, NW, Suite 1020, Washington, DC 20005; tel. (202) 842-0400; fax (202) 789-7223; e-mail ccochran@cmcmarkets.org; internet www.cmcmarkets.org; f. 1930 as the National Grain Trade Council; reformed as two separate entities, CMC and the Transportation, Elevator and Grain Merchants Asscn in 2006; 38 mems; Dir of Govt Relations CHRISTINE M. COCHRAN.

> **Transportation, Elevator, & Grain Merchants Association (TEGMA):** 1300 L St, NW, Suite 1020, Washington, DC 20005; tel. (202) 842-0400; fax (202) 789-7223; e-mail ccochran@cmcmarkets.org; internet www.tegma.org; f. 2006 following the dissolution of the National Grain Trade Council; promotes efficiency, competitiveness and safety of handling and transportation of North American grain and grain products; 30 mems; Chair. ERIC WILKEY.

Distilled Spirits Council of the US, Inc (DISCUS): 1250 Eye St, NW, Suite 400, Washington, DC 20005; tel. (202) 628-3544; internet www.discus.org; f. 1973; 13 active mems and 23 affiliates; Pres. and CEO Dr. PETER H. CRESSY.

Food Marketing Institute (FMI): 2345 Crystal Dr., Suite 800, Washington, DC 20005; tel. (202) 452-8444; fax (202) 429-4519; e-mail fmi@fmi.org; internet www.fmi.org; f. 1977; 1,500 mems; Pres. and CEO TIMOTHY M. HAMMONDS.

Foodservice Sales and Marketing Association (FSMA): 9192 Red Branch Rd, Suite 200, Columbia, MD 21045; tel. (410) 715-6672; fax (410) 997-9387; e-mail info@fsmaonline.com; internet www.fsmaonline.com; f. 2003; Pres. and CEO RICK ABRAHAM.

Grocery Manufacturers of America, Inc (GMA): 2401 Pennsylvania Ave, NW, 2nd Floor, Washington, DC 20037; tel. (202) 337-9400; fax (202) 337-4508; e-mail info@gmabrands.com; internet www.gmabrands.com; f. 1908; over 185 mems; Pres. and CEO CAL DOOLEY.

Directory

International Foodservice Distributors Association (IFDA): 201 Park Washington Court, Falls Church, VA 22046; tel. (703) 532-9400; fax (703) 538-4673; internet www.ifdaonline.org; f. 1906; over 140 mems; Pres. and CEO ROBERT C. SLEDD.

National Association of Wheat Growers (NAWG): 412 Second St, NE, Suite 300, Washington, DC 20002-4993; tel. (202) 547-7800; fax (202) 546-2638; e-mail wheatworld@wheatworld.org; internet www.wheatworld.org; f. 1950; 20 affiliated mem. states; CEO DAREN COPPOCK.

National Beer Wholesalers Association (NBWA): 1101 King St, Suite 600, Alexandria, VA 22314-2944; tel. (703) 683-4300; fax (703) 683-8965; e-mail info@nbwa.org; internet www.nbwa.org; f. 1938; 1,900 mem. distributor cos; Pres. CRAIG A. PURSER.

National Cattlemen's Beef Association (NCBA): 9110 East Nichols Ave, Suite 300, Centennial, CO 80112; tel. (303) 694-0305; fax (303) 694-2851; e-mail tstokes@beef.org; internet www.beefusa.org; f. 1898; 33,000 mems, plus 45 cattle asscns and 40 breed and industry asscns; Pres. JOHN QUEEN; CEO TERRY L. STOKES.

National Confectioners Association of the US (NCA): 8320 Old Courthouse Rd, Suite 300, Vienna, VA 22182; tel. (703) 790-5750; fax (703) 790-5752; e-mail info@candyusa.org; internet www.candyusa.org; f. 1884; includes Chocolate Manufacturers Asscn; 340 mems; Pres. LAWRENCE T. GRAHAM.

National Dairy Council (NDC): 10255 West Higgins Rd, Suite 900, Rosemount, IL 60018; tel. (847) 803-2000; fax (847) 803-2077; e-mail ndc@dairyinformation.com; internet www.nationaldairycouncil.org; f. 1915; 600 mems.

National Farmers (NFO): 528 Billy Sunday Rd, Ames, IA 50010; tel. 800-247-2110; e-mail info@nfo.org; internet www.nfo.org; f. 1955; c. 35,000 mems; Chair. PAUL OLSON.

National Farmers Union (NFU): 5619 DTC Pkwy, Suite 300, Greenwood Village, CO 80011-3136; tel. (303) 337-5500; fax (303) 771-1770; e-mail dave.frederickson@nfu.org; internet www.nfu.org; f. 1902; 300,000 mems; Pres. TOM BUIS.

National Frozen and Refrigerated Foods Association (NFRA): 4755 Linglestown Rd, Suite 300, POB 6069, Harrisburg, PA 17112; tel. (717) 657-8601; fax (717) 657-9862; e-mail info@nfraweb.org; internet www.nfraweb.org; f. 1945; over 400 mem. cos; Pres. and CEO NEVIN B. MONTGOMERY.

National Grocers Association (NGA): 1005 North Glebe Rd, Suite 250, Arlington, VA 22201-5758; tel. (703) 516-0700; fax (703) 516-0115; e-mail info@nationalgrocers.org; internet www.nationalgrocers.org; f. 1982; 3,000 mems; Pres. and CEO THOMAS K. ZAUCHA.

National Meat Association (NMA): (NMA East) 1400 16th St, NW, Suite 400, Washington, DC 20036; tel. (202) 667-2108; NMA West: 1970 Broadway, Suite 825, Oakland, CA 94612; tel. (510) 763-1533; fax (510) 763-6186; e-mail staff@nmaonline.org; internet www.nmaonline.org; f. 1946; over 600 mems; Chair. TOM CAMPANILE.

North American Millers' Association (NAMA): 600 Maryland Ave, SW, Suite 825 West, Washington, DC 20024; tel. (202) 484-2200; fax (202) 488-7416; e-mail generalinfo@namamillers.org; internet www.namamillers.org; f. 1998; 48 mems and 28 assoc. mems; Pres. BETSY FAGA.

United Fresh Fruit & Vegetable Association: 1901 Pennsylvania Ave, NW, Suite 1100, Washington, DC 20006; tel. (202) 303-3400; fax (202) 303-3433; e-mail united@uffva.org; internet www.uffva.org; f. 1904; 1,300 mems; Pres. and CEO THOMAS E. STENZEL; Pres. TOM LOVELACE.

US Dairy Export Council (USDEC): 2101 Wilson Blvd, Suite 400, Arlington, VA 22201-3061; tel. (703) 528-3049; fax (703) 528-3705; e-mail info@usdec.org; internet www.usdec.org; f. 1995; 62 mems; Pres. THOMAS M. SUBER.

Wine and Spirits Wholesalers of America, Inc (WSWA): 805 15th St, NW, Suite 430, Washington, DC 20005; tel. (202) 371-9792; fax (202) 789-2405; e-mail katrina@wswa.org; internet www.wswa.org; f. 1943; c. 450 mem. cos; Pres. and CEO CRAIG WOLF.

Iron and Steel

American Hardware Manufacturers Association (AHMA): 801 North Plaza Dr., Schaumburg, IL 60173-4977; tel. (847) 605-1025; fax (847) 605-1030; e-mail info@ahma.org; internet www.ahma.org; f. 1901; 500 mems; Pres. and CEO TIMOTHY S. FARRELL; Vice-Chair. WILLIAM P. FARRELL.

American Iron and Steel Institute (AISI): 1140 Connecticut Ave, NW, Suite 705, Washington, DC 20036; tel. (202) 452-7100; e-mail webmaster@steel.org; internet www.steel.org; f. 1908; 29 mem. cos and 125 assoc. and affiliated mems; Chair. WARD J. TIMKEN, Jr.

American Institute of Steel Construction (AISC): 1 East Wacker Dr., Suite 700, Chicago, IL 60601-1802; tel. (312) 670-

4813

2400; fax (312) 670-5403; internet www.aisc.org; f. 1921; Pres. ROGER E. FERCH.

Steel Founders' Society of America (SFSA): 780 McArdle Dr., Unit G, Crystal Lake, IL 60014; tel. (815) 455-8240; fax (815) 455-8241; e-mail monroe@sfsa.org; internet www.sfsa.org; f. 1902; 80 mems; Exec. Vice-Pres. RAYMOND W. MONROE.

Steel Manufacturers Association (SMA): 1150 Connecticut Ave, NW, Suite 715, Washington, DC 20036; tel. (202) 296-1515; fax (202) 296-2506; e-mail stuart@steelnet.org; internet www.steelnet.org; 39 North American mem. cos and six mem. cos world-wide, as well as 107 assoc. mem. cos; Pres. THOMAS A. DANJCZEK.

Leather
(see also Textiles)

Leather Apparel Association (LAA): 19 West 21st St, Suite 403, New York, NY 10010; tel. (212) 727-1210; fax (212) 727-1218; e-mail info@leatherassociation.com; internet www.leatherassociation.com; f. 1990; over 100 mems; Pres. MORRIS GOLDFARB.

Leather Industries of America (LIA): 3050 K St, NW, Suite 400, Washington, DC 20007; tel. (202) 342-8497; fax (202) 342-8583; e-mail info@leatherusa.com; internet www.leatherusa.com; f. 1917; 64 mems; Pres. JOHN WITTENBORN.

Travel Goods Association (TGA): 5 Vaughn Dr., Suite 105, Princeton, NJ 08540; tel. (609) 720-1200; fax (609) 720-0620; e-mail info@travel-goods.org; internet www.travel-goods.org; f. 1938; 400 mems; Pres. MICHELE MARINI PITTENGER.

Lumber
(see also Paper)

American Forest and Paper Association (AF&PA): 1111 19th St, NW, Suite 800, Washington, DC 20036; tel. (202) 463-2700; fax (202) 463-2771; e-mail info@afandpa.org; internet www.afandpa.org; f. 1993; over 250 mems and trade asscns; Pres. W. HENSON MOORE.

APA–The Engineered Wood Association: 7011 South 19th St, Tacoma, WA 98466; tel. (253) 565-6600; fax (253) 565-7265; e-mail help@apawood.org; internet www.apawood.org; f. 1933 as Douglas Fir Plywood Asscn; later became American Plywood Asscn; name changed as above 1994; 109 mems; Pres. DENNIS HARDMAN.

Forest Resources Association Inc: 600 Jefferson Plaza, Suite 350, Rockville, MD 20852-1150; tel. (301) 838-9385; fax (301) 838-9481; e-mail rlewis@forestresources.org; internet www.forestresources.org; f. 1934; 1,300 mems; Pres. R. LEWIS.

National Lumber and Building Material Dealers Association (NLBMDA): 900 Second St, NE, Suite 305, Washington, DC 20002; tel. (202) 547-2230; fax (202) 547-7640; e-mail industrynews@dealer.org; internet www.dealer.org; f. 1915; 20 mem. orgs, representing 8,000 cos; Pres. SHAWN D. CONRAD.

National Wooden Pallet and Container Association (NWPCA): 1421 Prince St, Suite 340, Alexandria, VA 22314-2805; tel. (703) 519-6104; fax (703) 519-4720; e-mail bscholnick@palletcentral.com; internet www.nwpca.com; f. 1916; Pres. and CEO BRUCE N. SCHOLNICK.

North American Wholesale Lumber Association (NAWLA): 3601 Algonquin Rd, Suite 400, Rolling Meadows, IL 60008; tel. (847) 870-7470; fax (847) 870-0201; e-mail info@lumber.org; internet www.lumber.org; f. 1893; over 650 mems; Pres. and CEO NICHOLAS R. KENT.

Southern Forest Products Association: 2900 Indiana Ave, Kenner, LA 70065-4605; tel. (504) 443-4464; fax (504) 443-6612; e-mail mail@spfa.org; internet www.sfpa.org; f. 1915; c. 160 mem. orgs; Pres. DIGGES MORGAN.

Western Wood Products Association (WWPA): Yeon Bldg, 522 South West Fifth Ave, Suite 500, Portland, OR 97204-2122; tel. (503) 224-3930; fax (503) 224-3934; e-mail info@wwpa.org; internet www.wwpa.org; f. 1964; c. 65 mem. orgs; Pres. and CEO MICHAEL R. O'HALLORAN.

Wood Products Manufacturers Association (WPMA): 175 State Rd East, POB 761, Westminster, MA 01473-0761; tel. (978) 874-5445; fax (978) 874-9946; e-mail woodprod@wpma.org; internet www.wpma.org; f. 1929; 664 mems; Pres. TIMOTHY ROCHE.

Metals and Mining
(see also Iron and Steel)

Aluminum Association, Inc: 1525 Wilson Blvd, Suite 600, Arlington, VA 22209; tel. (703) 358-2960; fax (703) 358-2961; e-mail lwilson@aluminum.org; internet www.aluminum.org; f. 1933; 82 mems; Pres. J. STEPHEN LARKIN.

American Zinc Association (AZA): 2025 M St, NW, Suite 800, Washington, DC 20036; tel. (202) 367-1151; fax (202) 367-2232; e-mail zincinfo@zinc.org; internet www.zinc.org; f. 1990; 17 mems; Exec. Dir GEORGE VARY.

ASM International: 9639 Kinsman Rd, Materials Park, OH 44073-0002; tel. (440) 338-5151; fax (440) 338-4634; e-mail customerservice@asminternational.org; internet asmcommunity.asminternational.org/portal/site/asm; f. 1913; fmrly the American Society for Materials; 40,000 mems world-wide; Man. Dir STANLEY C. THEOBALD.

Copper and Brass Fabricators Council, Inc: 1050 17th St, NW, Suite 440, Washington, DC 20036-5518; tel. (202) 833-8575; fax (202) 331-8267; e-mail copbrass@aol.com; f. 1964; 20 mem. cos; Pres. JOSEPH L. MAYER.

Copper Development Association, Inc (CDA): 260 Madison Ave, New York, NY 10016; tel. (212) 251-7200; fax (212) 251-7234; e-mail questions@cda.copper.org; internet www.copper.org; f. 1962; 65 mems; Pres. and CEO ANDREW G. KIRETA, Sr.

Fabricators and Manufacturers Association, International (FMA): 833 Featherstone Rd, Rockford, IL 61107; tel. (815) 399-8775; fax (815) 484-7701; e-mail info@fmanet.org; internet www.fmanet.org; f. 1970; 2,100 mems; Pres. and CEO GERALD M. SHANKEL.

Manufacturing Jewelers and Suppliers of America, Inc (MJSA): 45 Royal Little Dr., Providence, RI 02904; tel. (401) 274-3840; fax (401) 274-0265; e-mail info@mjsa.org; internet www.mjsa.org; f. 1903; 1,800 mems; Pres. and CEO CURTIS LEY.

Metal Powder Industries Federation (MPIF): 105 College Rd East, 1st Floor, Princeton, NJ 08540-6692; tel. (609) 452-7700; fax (609) 987-8523; e-mail info@mpif.org; internet www.mpif.org; f. 1944; 6 feds of 300 corp. mems; Exec. Dir and CEO C. JAMES TROMBINO.

Mining and Metallurgical Society of America (MMSA): POB 810, Boulder, CO 80306-0810; tel. (303) 444-6032; e-mail info@mmsa.net; internet www.mmsa.net; f. 1908; 340 mems; Exec. Dir BETTY L. GIBBS; Pres. ROBERT V. WASHNOCK.

National Mining Association (NMA): 101 Constitution Ave, NW, Suite 500 East, Washington, DC 20001-2133; tel. (202) 463-2600; fax (202) 463-2666; e-mail craulston@nma.org; internet www.nma.org; f. 1995; over 325 mem. cos; Pres. and CEO KRAIG R. NAASZ.

Northwest Mining Association (NWMA): 10 North Post St, Suite 220, Spokane, WA 99201; tel. (509) 624-1158; fax (509) 623-1241; e-mail nwma@nwma.org; internet www.nwma.org; f. 1895; 1,650 mems; Exec. Dir LAURA E. SKAER.

The Silver Institute: 1200 G St, NW, Suite 800, Washington, DC 20005; tel. (202) 835-0185; fax (202) 835-0155; e-mail info@silverinstitute.org; internet www.silverinstitute.org; f. 1971; 30 mems; Pres. ROBERT QUARTERMAN; Exec. Dir MICHAEL DiRIENZO.

Paper
(see also Lumber)

Association of Independent Corrugated Converters (AICC): 113 South West St, POB 25708, Alexandria, VA 22313; tel. (703) 836-2422; fax (703) 836-2795; e-mail info@aiccbox.org; internet www.aiccbox.org; mems: 603 box-makers, 480 associates; Chair. BRIAN P. BUCKLEY.

National Paper Box Association (NPA): 113 South West St, 3rd Floor, Alexandria, VA 22314; tel. (703) 684-2212; fax (703) 683-6920; e-mail npahq@paperbox.org; internet www.paperbox.org; f. 1918; Exec. Vice-Pres. SCOTT MILLER.

NPTA Alliance: 401 North Michigan Ave, Chicago, Illinois IL 60611-4267; tel. (404) 210-3890; e-mail newell@gonpta.com; internet www.gonpta.com; f. 1903; fmrly Nat. Paper Trade Asscn, Inc; restructured Sept. 2007 to operate under management of SmithBucklin Corpn; 2,000 mems; Chair. BILL HIRSCH; CEO NEWELL HOLT.

Paperboard Packaging Council (PPC): 201 North Union St, Suite 220, Alexandria, VA 22314; tel. (703) 836-3300; fax (703) 836-3290; e-mail paperboardpackaging@ppcnet.org; internet www.ppcnet.org; f. 1967; Pres. JEROME T. VAN DE WATER.

Petroleum and Fuel

American Association of Petroleum Geologists (AAPG): 125 West 15th St, POB 979, Tulsa, OK 74101-0979; tel. (918) 584-2555; fax (918) 560-2694; e-mail postmaster@aapg.org; internet www.aapg.org; f. 1917; 30,000 mems world-wide; Exec. Dir WILLARD R. GREEN.

American Association of Petroleum Landmen (AAPL): 4100 Fossil Creek Blvd, Fort Worth, TX 76137-2791; tel. (817) 847-7700; fax (817) 847-7704; e-mail aashton@landman.org; internet www.landman.org; f. 1955; 7,000 mems and 43 affiliated asscns; Pres. M. CRAIG CLARK.

American Petroleum Institute (API): 1220 L St NW, Washington, DC 20005-4070; tel. (202) 682-8000; e-mail mediacenter@api.org; internet www.api.org; f. 1919; 400 corporate mems; Pres. and CEO RED CAVANEY; Vice-Pres. and Dir JIM CRAIG.

Association of Diesel Specialists (ADS): 10 Laboratory Dr., POB 13966, Research Triangle Park, NC 27709-3966; tel. (919) 406-8804; fax (919) 406-1306; e-mail info@diesel.org; internet www.diesel.org; more than 700 corp. and individual mems; Exec. Dir DAVID FEHLING.

Coal Exporters' Association of the US, Inc: 1130 17th St, NW, Washington, DC 20036; tel. (202) 463-2666; fax (202) 833-9636; e-mail eschlecht@nma.org; f. 1945; 35 mems; Exec. Dir MOYA PHELLEPS.

Independent Petroleum Association of America (IPAA): 1201 15th St, NW, Suite 300, Washington, DC 20005; tel. (202) 857-4722; fax (202) 857-4799; e-mail rcarter@ipaa.org; internet www.ipaa.org; f. 1929; 6,000 mems; Pres. BARRY RUSSELL.

National Ocean Industries Association (NOIA): 1120 G St, NW, Suite 900, Washington, DC 20005; tel. (202) 347-6900; fax (202) 347-8650; e-mail mkearns@noia.org; internet www.noia.org; f. 1972; over 300 mem. cos; Pres. TOM FRY.

National Petrochemical and Refiners' Association (NPRA): 1899 L St, NW, Suite 1000, Washington, DC 20036-3896; tel. (202) 457-0480; fax (202) 457-0486; e-mail info@npra.org; internet www.npradc.org; f. 1902; over 450 mems; Pres. BOB SLAUGHTER.

Petroleum Marketers Association of America (PMAA): 1901 North Fort Myer Dr., Suite 500, Arlington, VA 22209-1604; tel. (703) 351-8000; fax (703) 351-9160; e-mail info@pmaa.org; internet www.pmaa.org; 45 mem. asscns; Pres. DANIEL F. GILLIGAN.

Western States Petroleum Association (WSPA): 1415 L St, Suite 600, Sacramento, CA 95814; tel. (916) 498-7750; fax (916) 444-5745; internet www.wspa.org; f. 1907; 30 mem. cos; Pres. JOSEPH SPARANO.

Printing and Publishing
(see also Publishers)

Association for the Suppliers of Printing, Publishing and Converting Technologies (NPES): 1899 Preston White Dr., Reston, VA 22091-4367; tel. (703) 264-7200; fax (703) 620-0994; e-mail npes@npes.org; internet www.npes.org; f. 1933; over 400 mem. cos; Pres. RALPH J. NAPPI.

Binding Industries Association International (BIA): 200 Deer Run Rd, Sewickley, PA 15143-2600; tel. (412) 259-1806; fax (412) 259-1800; e-mail jgoldstein@piagatf.org; internet www.bindingindustries.com; f. 1955; 90 mems; Exec. Dir LAURIE REYNOLDS.

National Association for Printing Leadership (NAPL): 75 West Century Rd, Paramus, NJ 07652-1408; tel. (201) 634-9600; e-mail information@napl.org; internet www.napl.org; f. 1933; 150 assoc. mems; Pres. and CEO JOSEPH P. TRUNCALE.

National Association of Printing Ink Manufacturers (NAPIM): 581 Main St, Woodbridge, NJ 07095; tel. (732) 855-1525; fax (732) 855-1838; e-mail napim@napim.org; internet www.napim.org; f. 1917; Exec. Dir JAMES E. COLEMAN.

Printing Industries of America, Inc/Graphic Arts Information Network (PIA/GATF): 200 Deer Run Rd, Sewickley, PA 15143; tel. (412) 741-6861; fax (412) 741-2311; e-mail piagatf@piagatf.org; internet www.gain.net; f. 1887 and 1924, respectively; consolidated operations in 1999; 12,000 mems; Exec. Vice-Pres. and Exec. Dir MARY GARNETT; Pres. and CEO MICHAEL MAKIN.

Public Utilities
(see also Trade and Industry—Utilities)

American Public Power Association (APPA): 2301 M St, NW, 3rd Floor, Washington, DC 20037-1484; tel. (202) 467-2900; fax (202) 467-2910; e-mail mrufe@appanet.org; internet www.appanet.org; f. 1940; over 2,000 mem. utilities; Chair. TERRY HUVAL.

American Public Works Association (APWA): 2345 Grand Blvd, Suite 700, Kansas City, MO 64108-2625; tel. (816) 472-6100; fax (816) 472-1610; e-mail apwa@apwa.net; internet www.apwa.net; f. 1937; 26,000 mems; Exec. Dir PETER B. KING.

Rubber

Rubber Manufacturers Association (RMA): 1400 K St, NW, Suite 900, Washington, DC 20005-2043; tel. (202) 682-4800; e-mail info@rma.org; internet www.rma.org; f. 1915; over 100 mem. cos; Pres. and CEO DONALD B. SHEA.

Rubber Trade Association of North America, Inc: 220 Maple Ave, POB 196, Rockville Centre, NY 11571-0196; tel. (516) 536-7228; fax (516) 536-2251; f. 1914; 39 mems; Sec. F. B. FINLEY.

Stone, Clay and Glass Products

Glass Association of North America (GANA): 2945 South West Wanamaker Dr., Suite A, Topeka, KS 66614-5321; tel. (785) 271-0208; fax (785) 271-0166; e-mail gana@glasswebsite.com; internet www.glasswebsite.com; f. 1994; 208 mems; Exec. Vice-Pres. STANLEY L. SMITH.

National Glass Association (NGA): 8200 Greensboro Dr., Suite 302, McLean, VA 22102-3881; tel. (703) 342-5642; fax (703) 442-0630; e-mail administration@glass.org; internet www.glass.org; f. 1948; c. 4,000 mem. cos; Pres. and CEO PHILIP J. JAMES.

National Stone, Sand and Gravel Association (NSSGA): 1605 King St, Alexandria, VA 22314; tel. (703) 525-8788; e-mail info@nssga.org; internet www.nssga.org; f. 2000 by merger of Nat. Aggregates Asscn and Nat. Stone Asscn; 950 mems; Pres. and CEO JENNIFER JOY WILSON.

Textiles

American Apparel and Footwear Association (AAFA): 1601 North Kent St, Suite 1200, Arlington, VA 22209; tel. (703) 524-2262; fax (703) 522-6741; e-mail mrust@apparelandfootwear.org; internet www.apparelandfootwear.org; f. 2000 following merger of American Apparel and Manufacturers Asscn and Footwear Industries of America; Pres. and CEO KEVIN M. BURKE.

American Fiber Manufacturers Association, Inc (AFMA): 1530 Wilson Blvd, NW, Suite 690, Arlington, VA 22314; tel. (703) 875-0432; fax (703) 875-0907; e-mail afma@afma.org; internet www.fibersource.com; f. 1933; 34 mems; Pres. PAUL T. O'DAY.

Apparel Retailers of America: 325 Seventh St, Suite 1000, NW, Washington, DC 20004-2801; tel. (202) 347-1932; fax (202) 457-0386; f. 1916; 1,200 mems; Exec. Dir DOUGLAS W. WIEGAND.

Knitted Textile Association: 386 Park Ave South, Suite 901, New York, NY 10016; tel. (212) 689-3807; fax (212) 889-6160; e-mail kta386@aol.com; f. 1965; 140 mems; Exec. Dir PETER ADELMAN.

National Council of Textile Organizations (NCTO): 910 17th St, NW, Suite 1020, Washington, DC 20006; tel. (202) 822-8028; fax (202) 822-8029; e-mail info@ncto.org; internet www.ncto.org; f. 2004; Pres. CASS JOHNSON.

National Knitwear and Sportswear Association: 386 Park Ave South, New York, NY 10016; tel. (212) 683-7520; fax (212) 532-0766; f. 1918; 600 mems; Exec. Dir SETH M. BODNER.

National Textile Association (NTA): 6 Beacon St, Suite 1125, Boston, MA 02108-3812; tel. (617) 542-8220; fax (617) 542-2199; e-mail info@nationaltextile.org; internet www.nationaltextile.org; f. 1854; fmrly Northern Textile Asscn and Knitted Textile Asscn; name changed as above 2002; over 200 mems; Pres. KARL SPILHAUS.

Northern Textile Association: 230 Congress St, Boston, MA 02110; tel. (617) 542-8220; fax (617) 542-2199; e-mail textilenta@aol.com; f. 1854; 300 mems; Pres. KARL SPILHAUS.

United Infants' and Children's Wear Association Inc: 1430 Broadway, Suite 1603, New York, NY 10018; tel. (212) 244-2953; f. 1933; 50 mems; Pres. ALAN D. LUBELL.

Tobacco

Tobacco Associates: 8452 Holly Leaf Dr., McLean, VA 22102-2225; tel. (703) 821-1255; fax (703) 821-1511; e-mail taw@tobaccoassociatesinc.org; internet www.tobaccoassociatesinc.org; f. 1947; Pres. KIRK WAYNE.

Tobacco Merchants Association of the United States (TMA): POB 8019, Princeton, NJ 08543-8019; tel. (609) 275-4900; fax (609) 275-8379; e-mail tma@tma.org; internet www.tma.org; f. 1915; 170 mems; Pres. FARRELL DELMAN.

Transport

Aerospace Industries Association of America, Inc (AIA): 1000 Wilson Blvd, Suite 1700, Arlington, VA 22209-3928; tel. (703) 358-1000; fax (703) 358-1012; e-mail matt.grimison@aia-aerospace.org; internet www.aia-aerospace.org; f. 1919; 105 mems and 174 assoc. mems; Pres. and CEO MARION C. BLAKEY.

Air Transport Association of America, Inc: see Civil Aviation—Associations.

American Bureau of Shipping: see Ocean Shipping—Associations.

Alliance of Automobile Manufacturers (Auto Alliance): 1401 Eye St, NW, Suite 900, Washington, DC 20005; tel. (202) 326-5500; fax (202) 326-5598; internet www.autoalliance.org; f. 1999; asscn of nine car and light truck manufacturers; Pres. and CEO DAVE MCCURDY.

American Bus Association (ABA): 700 13th St, NW, Suite 575, Washington, DC 20005-5923; tel. (202) 842-1645; fax (202) 842-0850; e-mail abainfo@buses.org; internet www.buses.org; f. 1926; c. 3,250 mems; Pres. and CEO PETER J. PANTUSO.

American Institute of Merchant Shipping: see Ocean Shipping—Associations.

American International Automobile Dealers' Association (AIADA): 211 North Union St, Suite 300, Alexandria, VA 22314; tel. (703) 519-7800; fax (703) 519-7810; e-mail goaiada@aiada.org; internet www.aiada.org; f. 1970; 11,000 mems; Pres. CODY LUSK.

THE UNITED STATES OF AMERICA

American Public Transportation Association (APTA): 1666 K St, NW, Suite 1100, Washington, DC 20006; tel. (202) 496-4800; fax (202) 496-4321; e-mail info@apta.com; internet www.apta.com; f. 1882; 1,600 mems; Pres. WILLIAM W. MILLAR.

American Railway Engineering and Maintenance-of-Way Association (AREMA): 10003 Derekwood Lane, Suite 210, MD 20706; tel. (301) 459-3200; fax (301) 459-8077; e-mail fcramer@arema.org; internet www.arema.org; f. 1997; Exec. Dir and CEO Dr CHARLES EMELY.

American Short Line Railroad Association: see Principal Railways—Associations.

American Trucking Associations (ATA): 2200 Mill Rd, Alexandria, VA 22314-4654; tel. (703) 838-1700; e-mail atamembership@trucking.org; internet www.truckline.com; f. 1933; 3,000 mems; Pres. and CEO WILLIAM GRAVES.

Association of American Railroads: see Principal Railways—Associations.

Independent Truck Owner/Operator Association: POB 621, Stoughton, MA 02072; tel. (617) 828-7200; fax (617) 828-6606; f. 1981; 10,000 mems; Pres. MARSHALL SIEGEL.

National Automobile Dealers Association (NADA): 8400 Westpark Dr., McLean, VA 22102-3522; tel. (703) 821-7000; e-mail nadainfo@nada.org; internet www.nada.org; f. 1917; over 20,000 mems; Pres. PHILLIP D. BRADY.

Owner/Operator Independent Drivers' Association (OOIDA): 1 North West OOIDA Dr., Grain Valley, MO 64029; tel. (816) 229-5791; e-mail webmaster@ooida.com; internet www.ooida.com; f. 1973; over 150,000 mems; Pres. JIM JOHNSTON.

Shipbuilders Council of America (SCA): 1455 F St, NW, Suite 225, Washington, DC 20005; tel. (202) 347-5462; fax (202) 347-5464; e-mail mallen@dc.bjllp.com; internet www.shipbuilders.org; f. 1921; absorbed the American Waterways Shipyard Conference (f. 1976) in 1999; 36 mem. cos and 25 affiliate mems; Chair. STEVE WELCH; Pres. ALLEN J. WALKER.

Miscellaneous

American Advertising Federation (AAF): 1101 Vermont Ave, NW, Suite 500, Washington, DC 20005-6306; tel. (202) 898-0089; fax (202) 898-0159; e-mail aaf@aaf.org; internet www.aaf.org; f. 1967; 50,000 mems, 130 corp. mems; Pres. and CEO WALLACE S. SNYDER.

American Association of Exporters and Importers (AAEI): 1050 17th St, NW, Suite 810, Washington, DC 20036; tel. (202) 857-8009; fax (202) 857-7843; e-mail hq@aaei.org; internet www.aaei.org; f. 1921; 1,200 mems; Pres. and CEO HALLOCK NORTHCOTT.

American Marketing Association (AMA): 311 South Wacker Dr., Suite 5800, Chicago, IL 60606; tel. (312) 542-9000; fax (312) 542-9001; e-mail info@ama.org; internet www.marketingpower.com; f. 1937; 38,000 mems; CEO DENNIS L. DUNLAP.

American Society of Association Executives (ASAE): ASAE and the Center for Association Leadership, 1575 I St, NW, Washington, DC 20005-1103; tel. (202) 626-2798; fax (202) 371-8825; e-mail pr@asaecenter.org; internet www.asaenet.org; f. 1920; over 22,000 mems; Pres. and CEO JOHN H. GRAHAM.

Association of Equipment Manufacturers (AEM): 6737 West Washington St, Suite 2400, Milwaukee, WI 53214-5647; tel. (414) 272-0943; fax (414) 272-1170; internet www.aem.org; f. 2002; Pres. DENNIS SLATER.

Consumer Healthcare Products Association (CHPA): 900 19th St, NW, Suite 700, Washington, DC 20006; tel. (202) 429-9260; fax (202) 223-6835; e-mail eassey@chpa-info.org; internet www.chpa-info.org; f. 1881; 165 mem. and assoc. mem. cos; Pres. LYNDA A. SUYDAM.

Cosmetic, Toiletry and Fragrance Association (CTFA): 1101 17th St, NW, Suite 300, Washington, DC 20036-4702; tel. (202) 331-1770; fax (202) 331-1969; internet www.ctfa.org; f. 1894; 600 mem. cos; Pres. and CEO PAMELA G. BAILEY.

Institute for Supply Management (ISM): 2055 East Centennial Circle, POB 22160, Tempe, AZ 85285-2160; tel. (408) 752-6276; fax (408) 752-7890; e-mail pnovak@ism.ws; internet www.ism.ws; f. 1915; 40,000 mems; CEO PAUL NOVAK.

Motion Picture Association of America, Inc (MPAA): 1600 Eye St, NW, Washington, DC 20006; tel. (202) 293-1966; fax (202) 296-7410; internet www.mpaa.org; f. 1922; Chair. and CEO DAN GLICKMAN.

National Association of Manufacturers (NAM): 1331 Pennsylvania Ave, NW, Suite 600, Washington, DC 20004-1790; tel. (202) 637-3000; fax (202) 637-3182; e-mail manufacturing@nam.org; internet www.nam.org; f. 1895; 14,000 mems; Pres. and CEO JOHN ENGLER.

National Association of Realtors (NAR): 430 North Michigan Ave, Suite 500, Chicago, IL 60611-4087; fax (312) 329-8960; e-mail infocentral@realtors.org; internet www.realtor.org; f. 1908; 1,354,468 mems; Pres. PAT V. COMBS.

National Center for Manufacturing Sciences (NCMS): 3025 Boardwalk, Ann Arbor, MI 48108-3230; tel. (734) 995-0300; fax (734) 995-1150; internet www.ncms.org; f. 1986; Pres. and CEO RICHARD F. PEARSON.

National Cooperative Business Association (NCBA): 1401 New York Ave, NW, Suite 1100, Washington, DC 20005-2160; tel. (202) 638-6222; fax (202) 638-1374; e-mail ncba@ncba.coop; internet www.ncba.org; f. 1916; 450 mems; Pres. and CEO PAUL HAZEN.

National Retail Federation (NRF): 325 Seventh St, NW, Suite 1100, Washington, DC 20004-2802; tel. (202) 783-7941; fax (202) 737-2849; e-mail shearmanc@nrf.com; internet www.nrf.com; f. 1911; merged with American Retail Federation in 1990 and incorporated Apparel Retailers of America in 1995; mems: more than 100 state, nat. and trade orgs; Pres. and CEO TRACY MULLIN.

Society of Manufacturing Engineers (SME): 1 SME Dr., Dearborn, MI 48121; tel. (313) 271-1500; fax (313) 425-3401; e-mail service@sme.org; internet www.sme.org; f. 1932; Exec. Dir MARK TOMLINSON.

UTILITIES

Electricity

American Electric Power (AEP): 1 Riverside Plaza, Columbus, OH 43215-2372; tel. (614) 716-1000; internet www.aep.com; f. 1906 as the American Gas and Electricity Co; present name adopted 1958; electricity supplier to Arkansas, Indiana, Kentucky, Louisiana, Michigan, Ohio, Oklahoma, Tennessee, Texas, Virginia and West Virginia; Pres., Chair. and CEO MICHAEL G. MORRIS.

American Public Power Association: 2301 M St, NW, 3rd Floor, Washington, DC 20037-1484; tel. (202) 467-2900; fax (202) 467-2910; e-mail mrufe@appanet.org; internet www.appanet.org; f. 1940; asscn of local publicly owned electric utilities; c. 2,000 mems; Chair. TERRY J. HUVAL.

Association of Edison Illuminating Cos: 600 North 18th St, POB 2641, Birmingham, AL 35291-0992; tel. (205) 257-2530; fax (205) 257-2540; internet www.aeic.org; f. 1885; mems comprise 78 investor-owned public utilities; Exec. Dir EARL B. PARSONS, Jr.

Edison Electric Institute: 701 Pennsylvania Ave, NW, Washington, DC 2004-2696; tel. (202) 508-5000; fax (202) 508-5759; internet www.eei.org; f. 1933; mems comprise 184 investor-owned electric utility cos in the USA and 63 foreign mems; Chair. JAMES E. ROGERS; Pres. THOMAS R. KUHN.

Energy Telecommunications and Electrical Association (ENTELEC): 5005 West Royal Lane, Suite 190, Irving, TX 75063; tel. (888) 503-8700; fax (972) 915-6040; e-mail blaine@entelec.org; internet www.entelec.org; f. 1928 as the Petroleum Industry Electrical Asscn; changed name as above in 1978; 170 mems; Pres. ROBERT BLISS; Exec. Man. BLAINE SISKE.

National Rural Electric Co-operative Association: 4301 Wilson Blvd, Arlington, VA 22203; tel. (703) 907-5500; e-mail patrick.lavigne@nreca.coop; internet www.nreca.org; f. 1942; operates rural electric co-operative systems and public power distribution in 47 states; 900 mems; CEO GLENN ENGLISH.

Gas

American Gas Association (AGA): 400 North Capitol St, NW, Suite 400, Washington, DC 20001; tel. (202) 824-7000; fax (202) 824-7115; e-mail ccussimanio@aga.org; internet www.aga.org; f. 1918; represents 197 local utility cos; Pres. and CEO DAVID N. PARKER.

American Public Gas Association (APGA): 201 Massachusetts Ave, NE, Suite C-4, Washington, DC 20002; tel. (202) 464-2742; fax (202) 464-0246; e-mail lwillsdudich@apga.org; internet www.apga.org; f. 1961; promotes efficiency among public gas systems; 650 mems; Pres. and CEO BERT KALISCH.

Gas Technology Institute: 1700 South Mount Prospect Rd, Des Plaines, IL 60018; tel. (847) 768-0500; fax (847) 768-0501; e-mail membership@gastechnology.org; internet www.gastechnology.org; f. 1976; fmrly Gas Research Institute; 175 mems; Chair. MARY JANE MCCARTNEY.

Natural Gas Supply Association: 805 15th St, NW, Suite 510, Washington, DC 20005-2207; tel. (202) 326-9300; fax (202) 326-9330; internet www.ngsa.org; f. 1967; monitors legislation and economic issues affecting natural-gas producers; Pres. R. SKIP HORVATH.

Water

American Water Works Association: 6666 West Quincy Ave, Denver, CO 80235-3098; tel. (303) 794-7711; fax (303) 347-0804; internet www.awwa.org; f. 1881; 57,000 mems; Pres. NILAKSH KOTHARI; Exec. Dir JACK W. HOFFBUHR.

THE UNITED STATES OF AMERICA

American Water Works Association Research Foundation (AwwaRF): 6666 West Quincy Ave, Denver, CO 80235-3098; tel. (303) 347-6100; fax (303) 730-0851; e-mail info@awwarf.org; internet www.awwarf.org; f. 1966; Exec. Dir ROBERT RENNER.

Association of Metropolitan Water Agencies: 1620 I St, NW, Suite 500, Washington, DC 20006; tel. (202) 331-2820; fax (202) 785-1845; e-mail vandehei@amwa.net; internet www.amwa.net; f. 1981; 63 mems; Pres. MARK PREMO.

National Association of Water Companies: 1725 K St, NW, Suite 200, Washington, DC 20006; tel. (202) 833-8383; fax (202) 331-7442; internet www.nawc.org; f. 1895; privately and commercially owned water cos; 161 mems; Exec. Dir PETER L. COOK.

National Rural Water Association: 2915 South 13th St, Duncan, OK 73533; tel. (580) 252-0629; fax (580) 255-4476; e-mail nrwakc@nwra.org; internet www.nrwa.org; Pres. RODNEY TART; Exec. Man. ROB JOHNSON.

TRADE UNIONS

In 2005 there were approximately 15.7m. union members in the USA, representing 12.5% of the civilian labour force.

Many trade unions based in the USA have members throughout North America. Approximately 30% of Canada's trade union members belong to unions having headquarters in the USA.

American Federation of Labor and Congress of Industrial Organizations (AFL–CIO): 815 16th St, NW, Washington, DC 20006; tel. (202) 637-5000; fax (202) 637-5058; internet www.aflcio.org; f. 1955; Pres. JOHN J. SWEENEY; Sec.-Treas. RICHARD L. TRUMKA; 54 affiliated unions with total membership of 10m. (2007).

AFL–CIO Affiliates
(with 50,000 members and over)

Amalgamated Transit Union: 5025 Wisconsin Ave, NW, Washington, DC 20016; tel. (202) 537-1645; fax (202) 244-7824; e-mail dispatch@atu.org; internet www.atu.org; f. 1892; Int. Pres. WARREN S. GEORGE; Int. Sec.-Treas. OSCAR OWENS; 160,000 mems (2007).

American Federation of Government Employees: 80 F St, NW, Washington, DC 20001; tel. (202) 639-6419; fax (202) 639-6441; e-mail comments@afge.org; internet www.afge.org; f. 1932; Nat. Pres. JOHN GAGE; 600,000 mems.

American Federation of Musicians of the United States and Canada: Paramount Bldg, Suite 600, 1501 Broadway, New York, NY 10036; tel. (212) 869-1330; fax (212) 764-6134; e-mail naglieri@afm.org; internet www.afm.org; f. 1896; Pres. THOMAS F. LEE; Sec.-Treas. SAM FOLIO; 85,000 mems (2006).

American Federation of State, County and Municipal Employees: 1625 L St, NW, Washington, DC 20036-5687; tel. (202) 429-1000; fax (202) 429-1293; internet www.afscme.org; f. 1936; Pres. GERALD W. MCENTEE; Sec.-Treas. WILLIAM LUCY; 1.4m. mems (2007).

American Federation of Teachers (AFT–AFL–CIO): 555 New Jersey Ave, NW, Washington, DC 20001; tel. (202) 879-4400; fax (202) 879-4556; internet www.aft.org; f. 1916; Pres. EDWARD J. MCELROY; Sec.-Treas. NAT LACOUR; 1.3m. mems (2007).

American Federation of Television and Radio Artists: 260 Madison Ave, 7th Floor, New York, NY 10016-2401; tel. (212) 532-0800; fax (212) 545-1238; e-mail nyfilm@ios.com; internet www.aftra.com; f. 1937; Pres. BOB EDWARDS (acting); more than 70,000 mems (2007).

American Postal Workers Union: 1300 L St, NW, Washington, DC 20005; tel. (202) 842-4200; fax (202) 842-4297; internet www.apwu.org; f. 1971; Pres. WILLIAM BURRUS; Sec.-Treas. TERRY STAPLETON; more than 330,000 mems (2007).

Associated Actors and Artistes of America: 165 46th St West, New York, NY 10036; tel. (212) 869-0358; fax (212) 869-1746; f. 1919; Pres. THEODORE BIKEL; 7 nat. unions representing 125,000 mems.

Bakery, Confectionery, Tobacco Workers' and Grain Millers International Union: 10401 Connecticut Ave, Kensington, MD 20895; tel. (301) 933-8600; fax (301) 946-8452; internet www.bctgm.org; f. 1886; Pres. FRANK HURT; Sec.-Treas. DAVID B. DURKEE; 120,000 mems (2006).

Communications Workers of America: 501 Third St, NW, Washington, DC 20001; tel. (202) 434-1100; fax (202) 434-1279; e-mail cwa@capcon.net; internet www.cwa-union.org; f. 1939; Sec.-Treas. BARBARA J. EASTERLING; 740,000 mems (2006).

Glass Molders, Pottery, Plastics & Allied Workers International Union (AFL–CIO, CLC): 608 East Baltimore Pike, POB 607, Media, PA 19063-0607; tel. (610) 565-5051; fax (610) 565-0983; e-mail gmpiu@gmpiu.org; internet www.gmpiu.org; f. 1842; Pres. JOHN P. RYAN; Sec.-Treas. BRUCE R. SMITH; 51,000 mems (2006).

Government Employees, American Federation of: 80 F St, NW, Washington, DC, 20001; tel. (202) 737-8700; fax (202) 639-6441; e-mail comments@afge.org; internet www.afge.org; f. 1932; Nat. Pres. JOHN GAGE; Nat. Sec.-Treas J. DAVID COX; 600,000 mems (2007).

Graphic Communications Conference (GCC): 1900 L St, NW, Washington, DC 20036; tel. (202) 462-1400; fax (202) 721-0600; e-mail webmessenger@gciu.org; internet www.gciu.org; f. 2005; Pres. GEORGE TEDESCHI; Sec.-Treas. ROBERT LACEY (acting); 125,000 mems (2003).

International Alliance of Theatrical Stage Employees, Moving Picture Technicians, Artists and Allied Crafts of the US, its Territories and Canada (IATSE): 1430 Broadway, 20th Floor, New York, NY 10018; tel. (212) 730-1770; fax (212) 730-7809; e-mail webmaster@iatse-intl.org; internet www.iatse-intl.org; f. 1893; Int. Pres. THOMAS C. SHORT; Gen. Sec.-Treas. JAMES B. WOOD; 100,000 mems (2000).

International Association of Bridge, Structural, Ornamental and Reinforcing Iron Workers: 1750 New York Ave, NW, Suite 400, Washington, DC 20006; tel. (202) 383-4800; fax (202) 638-4856; e-mail iwmagazine@iwintl.org; internet www.ironworkers.org; f. 1896; Gen. Pres. JOSEPH HUNT; Gen. Sec. MICHAEL A. FITZPATRICK; 120,000 mems (1997).

International Association of Fire Fighters: 1750 New York Ave, NW, Washington, DC 20006-5395; tel. (202) 737-8484; fax (202) 737-8418; internet www.iaff.org; f. 1918; Gen. Pres. HAROLD SCHAITBERGER; Sec.-Treas. VINCENT J. BOLLON; 281,000 mems.

International Association of Machinists and Aerospace Workers (IAM): 9000 Machinists Pl., Upper Malrboro, MD 20772-2687; tel. (301) 967-4500; fax (301) 967-4588; e-mail websteward@goiam.org; internet www.iamaw.org; f. 1888; Int. Pres. R. THOMAS BUFFENBARGER; Gen. Sec.-Treas. WARREN L. MART; 730,000 mems (2006).

International Brotherhood of Boilermakers, Iron Ship Builders, Blacksmiths, Forgers and Helpers: 753 State Ave, Suite 570, Kansas City, KS 66101; tel. (913) 371-2640; fax (913) 281-8101; e-mail tracy.buck@boilermakers.org; internet www.boilermakers.org; f. 1880; Int. Pres. NEWTON B. JONES; Int. Sec.-Treas. WILLIAM T. CREEDEN; 100,000 mems (2006).

International Brotherhood of Electrical Workers: 900 Seventh St, NW, Washington, DC 20001; tel. (202) 833-7000; fax (202) 728-7676; e-mail web@ibew.org; internet www.ibew.org; f. 1891; Pres. EDWIN D. HILL; Sec.-Treas. JON F. WALTERS; 750,000 mems (2005).

International Longshoremen's Association: 17 Battery Pl., Suite 930, New York, NY 10004; tel. (212) 425-1200; fax (212) 425-2928; e-mail jmcnamara@ilaunion.org; internet www.ilaunion.org; f. 1892; Pres. RICHARD P. HUGHES, Jr; Sec.-Treas. ROBERT E. GLEASON; 65,000 mems (2007).

International Union of Bricklayers and Allied Craftsmen: 1776 Eye St, NW, Washington, DC 20006; tel. (202) 783-3788; fax (202) 393-0219; e-mail askbac@bacweb.org; internet www.bacweb.org; f. 1865; Pres. JOHN J. FLYNN; Sec.-Treas. JAMES BOLAND; 100,000 mems (1999).

International Union of Operating Engineers: 1125 17th St, NW, Washington, DC 20036; tel. (202) 429-9100; fax (202) 778-2616; f. 1896; Gen. Pres. VINCENT J. GIBLIN; Gen. Sec.-Treas. CHRISTOPHER HANLEY; 400,000 mems (2006).

International Union of Painters and Allied Trades: 1750 New York Ave, NW, Washington, DC 20006; tel. (202) 637-0700; f. 1887; Gen. Pres. MICHAEL E. MONROE; Sec.-Treas. JAMES A. WILLIAMS.

International Union of Police Associations: 1549 Ringling Blvd, Suite 600, Sarasota, FL 34236; tel. (941) 487-2560; fax (941) 487-2570; e-mail iupa@iupa.org; internet www.iupa.org; Pres. SAM A. CABRAL; Sec.-Treas. TIMOTHY SCOTT; 80,400 mems (2002).

Marine Engineers' Beneficial Association (MEBA): 444 North Capitol St, NW, Suite 800, Washington, DC 20001; tel. (202) 638-5355; fax (202) 638-5369; e-mail mebahq@d1meba.org; internet www.d1meba.org; f. 1875; Pres. RON DAVIS; Sec.-Treas. BILL VAN LOO; 50,000 mems.

National Association of Letter Carriers (NALC): 100 Indiana Ave, NW, Washington, DC 20001-2144; tel. (202) 393-4695; fax (202) 737-1540; e-mail nalcinf@nalc.org; internet www.nalc.org; f. 1889; Pres. WILLIAM H. YOUNG; Sec.-Treas. JANE E. BROENDEL; 300,058 active mems (2007).

Office and Professional Employees International Union: 265 West 14th St, Suite 610, New York, NY 10011; tel. (212) 675-3210; fax (212) 727-3466; internet www.opeiu.org; f. 1945; Int. Pres. MICHAEL GOODWIN; Sec.-Treas. NANCY WOHLFORTH; 145,000 mems (2006).

Retail, Wholesale and Department Store Union (UFCW): 30 East 29th St, New York, NY 10016; tel. (212) 684-5300; fax (212) 779-2809; internet www.rwdsu.org; f. 1937; Pres. STUART APPELBAUM; Sec.-Treas. JACK WURM; 100,000 mems (1997).

THE UNITED STATES OF AMERICA

Screen Actors Guild: 5757 Wilshire Blvd, Los Angeles, CA 90036-3600; tel. (323) 954-1600; fax (323) 549-6656; internet www.sag.org; f. 1933; Pres. ALAN ROSENBERG; Sec.-Treas. CONNIE STEVENS; 120,000 mems (Feb. 2006).

Seafarers International Union of North America: 5201 Auth Way, Camp Springs, MD 20746; tel. (301) 899-0675; fax (301) 899-7355; e-mail webmaster@seafarers.org; internet www.seafarers.org; f. 1938; Pres. MICHAEL SACCO; Sec.-Treas. DAVID W. HEINDEL; 85,000 mems (1999).

Sheet Metal Workers' International Association: 1750 New York Ave, NW, Washington, DC 20006; tel. (202) 783-5880; fax (202) 662-0894; e-mail info@smwia.org; internet www.smwia.org; f. 1888; Gen. Pres. MICHAEL J. SULLIVAN; Gen. Sec.-Treas. JOSEPH J. NIGRO; 150,000 mems (1999).

Transport Workers' Union of America (TWU): 1700 Broadway, 2nd Floor, New York, NY 10019; e-mail mailbox@twu.org; internet www.twu.org; f. 1934; Int. Pres. JAMES C. LITTLE; Sec.-Treas. JOSEPH C. GORDON; 110,000 mems (2002).

Transportation-Communications International Union: 3 Research Pl., Rockville, MD 20850; tel. (301) 948-4910; fax (301) 948-1369; internet www.goiam.org/tcunion.cfm; f. 1899; affiliated with IAM in 2005, with full merger scheduled before 2012; Pres. ROBERT A. SCARDELLETTI; Sec.-Treas. DANNY L. BIGGS; 46,576 mems (2005).

United Association of Journeymen and Apprentices of the Plumbing and Pipe Fitting Industry of the United States and Canada: 901 Massachusetts Ave, NW, Washington, DC 20001; tel. (202) 628-5823; fax (202) 628-5024; internet www.ua.org; f. 1889; Pres. WILLIAM P. HITE; Sec.-Treas. PATRICK PERNO; 304,000 mems (1999).

United Automobile, Aerospace and Agricultural Implement Workers of America (UAW): Solidarity House, 8000 East Jefferson Ave, Detroit, MI 48214; tel. (313) 926-5000; fax (313) 823-6016; internet www.uaw.org; f. 1935; Pres. RON GETTELFINGER; Sec.-Treas. ELIZABETH BUNN; 640,000 mems (2006).

United Food and Commercial Workers International Union: 1775 K St, NW, Washington, DC 20006; tel. (202) 223-3111; internet www.ufcw.org; f. 1979; Int. Pres. JOSEPH T. HANSEN; Int. Sec.-Treas. ANTHONY M. PERRONE; 1.3m. mems.

United Mine Workers of America (UMWA): 8315 Lee Highway, Fairfax, VA 22031; tel. (703) 208-7200; internet www.umwa.org; f. 1890; Int. Pres. CECIL E. ROBERTS; Sec.-Treas. DAN KANE; 130,000 mems (1999).

United Steelworkers of America (USW): 5 Gateway Center, Pittsburgh, PA 15222; tel. (412) 562-2400; fax (412) 562-2445; e-mail webmaster@usw.org; internet www.usw.org; f. 1936; incorporated PACE International Union in 2005 and Independent Steelworkers Union in 2007; represents workers in the USA, Canada and the Caribbean; Int. Pres. LEO W. GERARD; Sec.-Treas. JAMES D. ENGLISH; 850,000 mems (2007).

United Transportation Union (UTU): 14600 Detroit Ave, Cleveland, OH 44107-4250; tel. (216) 228-9400; fax (216) 228-5755; e-mail pr@utu.org; internet www.utu.org; f. 1969; formed strategic alliance with USW in July 2006; Pres. MALCOLM B. FUTHEY; Gen. Sec. and Treas. KIM N. THOMPSON; 125,000 mems.

Utility Workers Union of America, AFL-CIO: 815 16th St, NW, Washington, DC 20006; tel. (202) 974-8200; fax (202) 974-8201; e-mail rfarley@aflcio.org; internet www.uwua.net; f. 1945; Pres. D. MICHAEL LANGFORD; Sec.-Treas. GARY M. RUFFNER; 50,000 mems (2007).

Independent Unions
(with 50,000 members and over)

American Nurses Association: 8515 Georgia Ave, Suite 400, Silver Spring, MD 20910; tel. (301) 628-5000; fax (301) 628-5001; e-mail ana@ana.org; internet www.nursingworld.org; f. 1896; Pres. REBECCA M. PATTON; 54 constituent mem. state asscns comprising 2.9m. mems (2006).

Change to Win: 1900 L St, NW, Suite 900, Washington, DC 20036; tel. (202) 721-0660; fax (202) 721-0661; e-mail info@changetowin.org; internet www.changetowin.org; f. 2005 following split in the AFL-CIO; Int. Pres. JOSEPH HANSEN; Sec.-Treas. EDGAR ROMNEY.

Affiliates with 50,000 mems and over include:

Brotherhood of Locomotive Engineers and Trainmen (BLET): 1370 Ontario St, Mezzanine, Cleveland, OH 44113-1702; tel. (216) 241-2630; fax (216) 241-6516; e-mail execstaff@ble.org; internet www.ble.org; f. 1863; division of the Rail Conference of the Int. Brotherhood of Teamsters; Pres. DON M. HAHS; Sec.-Treas. WILLIAM C. WALPERT; over 59,000 mems (2006).

International Brotherhood of Teamsters: 25 Louisiana Ave, NW, Washington, DC 20001; tel. (202) 624-6800; fax (202) 624-6918; internet www.teamster.org; f. 1903; withdrew from AFL-CIO in 2005; Pres. JAMES P. HOFFA; Gen. Sec.-Treas. C. THOMAS KEEGEL; 1.4m. mems (2006).

Laborers' International Union of North America: 905 16th St, NW, Washington, DC 20006; tel. (202) 737-8320; fax (202) 737-2754; e-mail rgreer@liuna.org; internet www.liuna.org; f. 1903; Pres. TERENCE M. O'SULLIVAN; Gen. Sec.-Treas. ARMAND E. SABATONI; 820,000 mems (2003).

Service Employees' International Union (SEIU): 1313 L St, NW, Washington, DC 20005; tel. (202) 898-3200; fax (202) 898-3304; internet www.seiu.org; f. 1921; withdrew from AFL-CIO in 2005; Pres. ANDREW L. STERN; Sec.-Treas. ANNA BURGER; 1.8m. mems (2005).

UNITE HERE: 275 Seventh Ave, New York, NY 10001-6708; tel. (212) 265-7000; e-mail acooper@unitehere.org; internet www.unitehere.org; f. 2004 by merger of the Union of Needletrades, Industrial and Textile Employees (UNITE—f. 1995) and Hotel Employees and Restaurant Employees Int. Union (HERE—f. 1891); Gen. Pres. BRUCE S. RAYNOR; Pres. (Hospitality Industries) JOHN W. WILHELM; c. 440,000 mems.

United Brotherhood of Carpenters and Joiners of America: 101 Constitution Ave, NW, Washington, DC 20001; tel. (202) 546-6206; fax (202) 543-5724; internet www.carpenters.org; f. 1881; withdrew from AFL-CIO in 2001; Pres. DOUGLAS J. MCCARRON; Sec.-Treas. ANDRIS J. SILINS; 520,000 mems (2006).

United Food and Commercial Workers International Union: 1775 K St, NW, Washington, DC 20006; tel. (202) 223-3111; internet www.ufcw.org; f. 1979; Int. Pres. JOSEPH T. HANSEN; Int. Sec.-Treas. ANTHONY M. PERRONE; 1.3m. mems.

Fraternal Order of Police: 701 Marriott Dr., Nashville, TN 37214; tel. (615) 399-0900; fax (615) 399-0400; e-mail pyoes@fop.net; internet www.fop.net; Nat. Pres. CHUCK CANTERBURY; Nat. Sec. PATRICK YOES; 324,000 mems (2006).

International Longshore and Warehouse Union: 1188 Franklin St, 4th Floor, San Francisco, CA 94109; tel. (415) 775-0533; fax (415) 775-1302; e-mail info@ilwu.org; internet www.ilwu.org; f. 1937; Pres. ROBERT MCELLRATH; Sec.-Treas. WILLIAM ADAMS; 59,500 mems (2002).

National Education Association of the United States: 1201 16th St, NW, Washington, DC 20036-3290; tel. (202) 833-4000; fax (202) 822-7974; internet www.nea.org; f. 1857; Pres. REG WEAVER; 3.2m. mems (2007).

National Federation of Federal Employees: 805 15th St, NW, Suite 500, Washington, DC 20005; tel. (202) 216-4420; fax (202) 898-1861; e-mail guest@nffe.org; internet www.nffe.org; f. 1917; Pres. RICHARD N. BROWN; Sec.-Treas. JOHN M. PAOLINO; 120,000 mems (1999).

National Rural Letter Carriers' Association: 1630 Duke St, 4th Floor, Alexandria, VA 22314-3465; tel. (703) 684-5545; fax (703) 548-8735; internet www.nrlca.org; f. 1903; Pres. DONNIE PITTS; Sec.-Treas. CLIFFORD T. DAILING; 98,000 mems (1999).

National Treasury Employees Union: 1750 H St, NW, Washington, DC 20006; tel. (202) 572-5500; fax (202) 572-5644; internet www.nteu.org; f. 1938; Nat. Pres. COLLEEN M. KELLEY; 150,000 mems (2006).

Transport

Federal Transit Administration: US Dept of Transportation, 400 Seventh St, SW, Washington, DC 20590; tel. (202) 366-4043; internet www.fta.dot.gov; Administrator JAMES S. SIMPSON.

National Transportation Safety Board: 490 L'Enfant Plaza, SW, Washington, DC 20594; tel. (202) 314-6000; internet www.ntsb.gov; f. 1967; seeks to ensure that all types of transportation in the USA are conducted safely; carries out studies and accident investigations; Chair. MARK V. ROSENKER.

Surface Transportation Board: Mercury Bldg, 1925 K St, NW, Washington, DC 20423-0001; tel. (202) 565-1500; fax (202) 565-9016; internet www.stb.dot.gov; f. 1995; exercises regulatory authority over domestic surface common carriers; jurisdiction extends over rail, inland waterways and motorized traffic; Chair. CHARLES D. NOTTINGHAM.

Transportation Security Administration (TSA): 601 South 12th St, Arlington, VA 22202-4220; internet www.tsa.gov; f. 2001 to ensure the security of the country's transport system against possible terrorist attacks; Asst Sec. of Homeland Security for TSA KIP HAWLEY.

RAILWAYS

In 2005 there were 153,956 km (95,664 miles) of Class I freight railroads, 24,765 km of regional freight railroads and 46,988 km of

THE UNITED STATES OF AMERICA

local freight railroads. In addition, there were 37,015 km of Amtrak passenger railroads.

Federal Railroad Administration: Dept of Transportation, 1120 Vermont Ave, NW, Washington, DC 20590; tel. (202) 493-6000; fax (202) 493-6013; internet www.fra.dot.gov; f. 1966; part of the Dept of Transportation; formulates federal railway policies and administers and enforces safety regulations; Administrator JOSEPH H. BOARDMAN.

Principal Companies

Alaska Railroad Corpn: 327 West Ship Creek Ave, Anchorage, AK 99510; tel. (907) 265-2300; fax (907) 265-2312; e-mail reservation@akrr.com; internet www.akrr.com; f. 1912; independent corpn owned by the State of Alaska; year-round freight service and summer passenger service; operates 845 km of track; Pres. and CEO PATRICK GAMBLE.

Amtrak (National Railroad Passenger Corpn): 60 Massachusetts Ave, NE, Washington, DC 20002; tel. (202) 906-3860; fax (202) 906-3306; internet www.amtrak.com; f. 1970; govt-funded private corpn operating inter-city passenger services over 33,796 track-km in 46 states; Chair. DAVID M. LANEY; Pres. and CEO ALEXANDER KUMMANT.

BNSF Railway: 2650 Lou Menk Dr., Fort Worth, TX 76131-2830; tel. (817) 333-2000; internet www.bnsf.com; fmrly Burlington Northern Santa Fe Corpn; freight services; 51,498 track-km; Pres., Chair. and CEO MATTHEW K. ROSE.

Consolidated Rail Corpn (Conrail): 2001 Market St, Philadelphia, PA 19103; tel. (215) 209-2000; e-mail info@conrail.com; internet www.conrail.com; f. 1976 by fed. govt merger of six bankrupt freight carriers; switching and terminal railroad operating in three locations: Northern NJ, Southern NJ/Philadelphia, and Detroit, MI; Pres. and COO RONALD L. BATORY.

CSX Transportation, Inc (Rail Transport): 500 Water St, Jacksonville, FL 32202; tel. (904) 359-3100; internet www.csx.com; f. 1980 by merger; operates 34,371 km of track (2005); Pres. and CEO MICHAEL J. WARD.

Pan Am Railways: 1700 Iron Horse Park, North Billerica, MA 01862; tel. (978) 663-1130; e-mail customerservice@panamrailways.com; internet www.guilfordrail.com; fmrly Guilford Rail System; name changed as above in 2006; Pres. DAVID FINK.

Kansas City Southern Railway Co: 427 West 12th St, Kansas City, MO 64105; tel. (816) 983-1303; internet www.kcsi.com; Chair. and CEO MICHAEL R. HAVERTY; Pres. and COO ARTHUR L. SHOENER; operates 4,989 km of track.

Long Island Rail Road Co: Jamaica Station, Jamaica, NY 11435-4380; tel. (718) 558-7400; internet www.mta.info/lirr; f. 1834; operates 956 km of track (2005); operated by the Metropolitan Transportation Authority—State of New York; Pres. RAYMOND P. KENNY (acting).

Norfolk Southern Corpn: NS Tower, 3 Commercial Pl., Norfolk, VA 23510; tel. (757) 629-2600; fax (757) 664-5117; e-mail contactus@nscorp.com; internet www.nscorp.com; f. 1988; operates 21,000 miles of track (2007); Pres., Chair. and CEO CHARLES W. MOORMAN.

Union Pacific Railroad Co: 1400 Douglas St, Omaha, NE 68179; tel. (402) 544-5000; fax (402) 350-7362; internet www.uprr.com; f. 1897; division of Union Pacific Corpn; operates 52,143 km of track in 23 states; Pres. and CEO JAMES R. YOUNG.

Associations

American Short Line and Regional Railroad Association: 50 F St, NW, Suite 7020, Washington, DC 20001; tel. (202) 628-4500; fax (202) 628-6430; e-mail aslrra@aslrra.org; internet www.aslrra.org; f. 1913; 418 mems; Pres. and Treas. RICHARD F. TIMMONS.

Association of American Railroads: 50 F St, NW, Washington, DC 20001-1564; tel. (202) 639-2100; fax (202) 639-2558; e-mail ehamberger@aar.org; internet www.aar.org; f. 1934; membership represents virtually all major railroads in the USA, Canada and Mexico, as well as rail industry products and services; Pres. and CEO EDWARD R. HAMBERGER.

ROADS

In 2005 there were 75,432 km (46,871 miles) of interstate highway, 185,882 km of other national highway system roads and 6,194,782 km of other roads. Road network kilometres in that year totalled 6,429,154 of which some 64.5% was classified as paved.

Federal Highway Administration (FHWA): 1200 New Jersey Ave, SE, Washington, DC 20590; tel. (202) 366-0604; fax (202) 366-7493; internet www.fhwa.dot.gov; part of the Dept of Transportation; implements federal highway policy and promotes road safety; Administrator J. RICHARD CAPKA.

INLAND WATERWAYS

In 2005 there were some 41,840 km (26,000 miles) of navigable channels in the USA.

St Lawrence Seaway Development Corpn: US Dept of Transportation, 400 Seventh St, SW, Suite 5424, Washington, DC 20590; tel. (202) 366-0091; fax (202) 366-7147; e-mail tim.downey@sls.dot.gov; internet www.seaway.dot.gov; responsible for the operations and maintenance of sections of the St Lawrence Seaway within the territorial limits of the USA; Administrator COLLISTER JOHNSON, Jr.

Principal Companies

American Commercial Lines, Inc: 1701 East Market St, Jeffersonville, IN 47130; tel. (812) 288-0100; e-mail aclinfo@aclines.com; internet www.aclines.com; f. 1915; operates barge services along c. 24,000 km of the Mississippi and Ohio rivers and tributaries to the Gulf Intracoastal Waterway; fleet of 3,375 barges and 140 towboats; Pres. and CEO MARK R. HOLDEN.

Great Lakes Dredge & Dock Corpn: 2122 York Rd, Oak Brook, IL 60523; tel. (630) 574-3000; fax (630) 574-2909; internet www.gldd.com; f. 1890; dredging, marine construction and reclamation; operates tugboats, drillboats, carfloats, barges and dredges; 180 vessels; Pres. and CEO DOUGLAS B. MACKIE.

Great Lakes Fleet, Inc: 227 West First St, Suite 400, Duluth, MN 55802-1990; tel. (218) 723-2401; fax (218) 723-2455; internet www.cn.ca/specialized/great_lakes/en_KFGreatLakes.shtml; Gen. Man. CHARLES PATTERSON, III; 8 vessels.

Associations

American Waterways Operators: 801 North Quincy St, Suite 200, Arlington, VA 22203; tel. (703) 841-9300; fax (703) 841-0389; internet www.americanwaterways.com; f. 1944; over 400 mems; Pres. THOMAS A. ALLEGRETTI.

Lake Carriers' Association: 614 West Superior St, Suite 915, Cleveland, OH 44113-1383; tel. (216) 621-1107; fax (216) 241-8262; e-mail info@lcaships.com; internet www.lcaships.com/; f. 1892; 18 mem. cos; Pres. JAMES H. I. WEAKLEY.

National Waterways Conference, Inc: 4650 Washington Blvd, Suite 608, Arlington, VA 22201; tel. (703) 243-4090; fax (866) 371-1390; e-mail info@waterways.org; internet www.waterways.org; f. 1960; 200 mems; Chair. GARY LAGRANGE; Pres. AMY W. LARSON.

OCEAN SHIPPING

At 31 December 2006 a merchant fleet of 6,498 vessels, with a total displacement of 11,217,562 grt, was registered in the USA.

Federal Maritime Commission: 800 North Capitol St, NW, Washington, DC 20573; tel. (202) 523-5725; fax (202) 523-0014; e-mail secretary@fmc.gov; internet www.fmc.gov; f. 1961; to regulate the waterborne foreign commerce of the USA; comprises 5 Commrs; Chair. (vacant).

Maritime Administration: 400 Seventh St, SW, Washington, DC 20590; tel. (202) 366-5812; fax (202) 366-3890; internet www.marad.dot.gov; concerned with promoting the US Merchant Marine; also administers subsidy programme to ship operators; Administrator SEAN T. CONNAUGHTON.

Principal Ports

The three largest ports in the USA, in terms of traffic handled, are the Port of South Louisiana, handling 243m. tons in 2005, Houston (200m. tons in 2005) and New York (84.8m. tons in 2005). Many other large ports serve each coast, 24 of them handling between 25m. and 85m. tons of traffic annually. The deepening of channels and locks on the St Lawrence–Great Lakes Waterway, allowing the passage of large ocean-going vessels, has increased the importance of the Great Lakes ports, of which the largest, Duluth-Superior, handled an average annual 40m. tons.

Principal Companies

Alcoa Steamship Co, Inc: 201 Isabella St, Pittsburgh, PA 15212-5858; tel. (412) 553-4545; fax (412) 553-2624; bulk services worldwide; 5 vessels; Pres. R. S. HOSPODAR.

American President Lines Ltd (APL): 1111 Broadway, Oakland, CA 94607-5500; tel. (510) 272-8000; internet www.apl.com; f. 1938; serves east and west coasts of North America, Mexico, Caribbean Basin, Middle East and Far East; wholly owned subsidiary of Neptune Orient Lines (Singapore); 100 vessels; CEO RON WIDDOWS.

Amoco Corpn: 200 East Randolph Dr., Chicago, IL 60601; tel. (312) 856-4511; fax (312) 856-2460; Pres. C. D. PHILLIPS.

Central Gulf Lines, Inc: 1 Whitehall St, New York, NY 10004; tel. (212) 943-4141; fax (212) 809-9036; internet www.intship.com/cgl.htm.

Chevron Shipping Co: 6001 Bollinger Canyon Rd, San Ramon, CA 94583-5177; tel. (925) 842-1000; e-mail comment@chevron.com; internet www.chevron.com; subsidiary of Chevron Corpn; worldwide tanker sevices; regional offices in Houston, London and Singapore; 39 tankers; Chair. and CEO DAVID J. O'REILLY.

THE UNITED STATES OF AMERICA

Colonial Marine Industries, Inc: Hamilton House, 26 East Bryan St, POB 9981, Savannah, GA 31412; tel. (912) 233-7000; fax (912) 232-8216; e-mail colonial@colonialmarine.com; internet www.colonialmarine.com; 5 vessels; Exec. Vice-Pres. RICHARD C. WIGGER.

Coscol Marine Corpn: 9 Greenway Plaza, Houston, TX 77046; tel. (713) 877-3370; fax (713) 877-3433; e-mail edward.knutsen@coastalcorp.com; subsidiary of the Coastal Corpn; 4 tankers; Pres. EDWARD W. KNUTSEN.

Crowley Maritime Corpn: 555 12th St, Suite 2130, Oakland, CA 94607; tel. (510) 251-7500; fax (510) 251-7510; internet www.crowley.com; f. 1892; 280 vessels; Pres., Chair, and CEO THOMAS B. CROWLEY, Jr.

Energy Transportation Group, Inc: 654 Madison Ave, New York, NY 10022; tel. (212) 813-9360; fax (212) 813-6390; e-mail info@etgglobal.com; internet www.etgglobal.com; Chair. and CEO KIMBALL C. CHEN; Pres. and COO ALEX W. EVANS.

Farrell Lines Inc: 1 Whitehall St, New York, NY 10004; tel. (212) 440-4200; fax (212) 440-4645; internet www.farrell-lines.com; f. 1925; freight services from US Atlantic to West Africa, Mediterranean, Middle East and Black Sea; Chair. and CEO JOHN M. WILSON, Jr; Pres. RICHARD GRONDA.

Lykes Lines Ltd: 401 East Jackson St, Suite 3300, POB 31244, Tampa, FL 33631-3244; tel. (813) 276-4600; fax (813) 276-4873; f. 1997; routes from US Gulf and Atlantic ports to United Kingdom and northern Europe, Mediterranean and Africa.

Maritime Overseas Corpn: 511 Fifth Ave, New York, NY 10017; tel. (212) 953-4100; fax (212) 536-3735; manages c. 60 tankers and dry bulk carriers.

Matson Navigation Co: 555 12th St, Suite 700, Oakland, CA 94607; tel. (510) 628-4000; e-mail general_info@matson.com; internet www.matson.com; f. 1901; container and other freight services between US west coast and Hawaii; container leasing world-wide; subsidiary of Alexander & Baldwin, Inc; 17 vessels; Chair. W. ALLEN DOANE; Pres. and CEO JAMES S. ANDRASICK.

ExxonMobil Corpn: 3225 Gallows Rd, Fairfax, VA 22037; tel. (703) 846-3000; 32 vessels; Chair. and CEO REX W. TILLERSON.

OMI Corpn: 1 Station Pl., Stamford, CT 06902; tel. (203) 602-6700; fax (203) 602-6701; e-mail info@omicorp.com; internet www.omicorp.com; acquired by Teekay Corpn and A/S Dampskibsselskabet TORM in June 2007; 43 vessels; Chair. and CEO CRAIG H. STEVENSON, Jr; Pres. and COO ROBERT BUGBEE.

Sea-Land Service, Inc: 6000 Carnegie Blvd, Charlotte, NC 28209-4613; tel. (704) 571-2000; largest US-flag container shipping co; 100 vessels providing containerized services to 80 ports in 120 countries and territories; Pres. and CEO JOHN P. CLANCEY.

Stolt-Nielsen Transportation Group, Inc: 800 Connecticut Ave, 4th Floor, East Norwalk, CT 06854; tel. (203) 838-7100; fax (203) 299-0067; internet www.sntg.com; over 130 tankers; Chair. JACOB B. STOLT-NIELSEN; CEO OTTO H. FRITZNER.

Waterman Steamship Corpn: 1 Whitehall St, New York, NY 10004; tel. (212) 747-8550; fax (212) 747-8588; e-mail waterman@intship.com; internet www.waterman-steamship.com; f. 1919; owned by International Shipholding Corpn; services between the USA and the Middle East.

Associations

American Bureau of Shipping: 16855 Northchase Dr., Houston, TX 77060; tel. (281) 877-5800; fax (281) 877-5803; e-mail abs-worldhq@eagle.org; internet www.eagle.org; f. 1862; 814 mems; Chair. ROBERT D. SOMMERVILLE; Pres. CHRISTOPHER WIERNICKI.

American Maritime Congress: Hall of the States, Suite G-50, 400 North Capitol St, NW, Washington, DC 20001; tel. (202) 347-8020; fax (202) 347-1550; internet www.americanmaritime.org; f. 1977; mems represent major US-flag ship operating cos; Exec. Dir BRIAN W. SCHOENEMAN.

Chamber of Shipping of America: 1730 M St, NW, Suite 407, Washington, DC 20036-4517; tel. (202) 775-4399; fax (202) 659-3795; e-mail omoore@knowships.org; internet www.knowships.org; frmly American Institute of Merchant Shipping; 27 mem. cos; Pres. and CEO JOSEPH J. COX.

CIVIL AVIATION

Federal Aviation Administration: 800 Independence Ave, SW, Washington, DC 20591; tel. (202) 366-4000; internet www.faa.gov; f. 1958; part of the Dept of Transportation; promotes safety in the air, regulates air commerce and assists in development of an effective national airport system; Administrator ROBERT A. STURGELL (acting).

Principal Scheduled Companies

In 2006 there were 5,233 public-use airports in the USA. In 2003 there were 80 registered air carriers operating in the USA; of these, 14 companies were classified as major carriers.

Alaska Airlines: 19300 International Blvd, POB 68900, Seattle, WA 98188; tel. (206) 433-3200; fax (206) 433-7253; internet www.alaskaair.com; f. 1932; scheduled passenger services to 90 destinations in the USA, Canada and Mexico; Pres., Chair. and CEO WILLIAM S. AYER.

   Horizon Air: 19521 Pacific Hwy South, Seattle, WA 98188; tel. (206) 431-3647; internet www.horizonair.com; f. 1981; scheduled cargo services; Pres. and CEO JEFFERY D. PINNEO.

American Airlines, Inc: POB 619616, Dallas/Fort Worth Airport, TX 75261-9616; tel. (817) 967-1234; internet www.aa.com; f. 1934; coast-to-coast domestic routes and services to Canada, Hawaii, Mexico, the Caribbean, South America, Europe and the Far East; acquired Trans World Airlines in 2001; Pres., Chair. and CEO GERARD J. ARPEY.

Continental Airlines, Inc: POB 4607, Houston, TX 77210-4607; 1600 Smith St, Houston, TX 77002; tel. (713) 324-5152; fax (713) 324-2637; e-mail geninfo@coair.com; internet www.continental.com; f. 1934; serves 154 US destinations and 138 international destinations; Pres. JEFF SMISEK.

Delta Air Lines, Inc: 1030 Delta Blvd, POB 20706, Atlanta, GA 30320-6001; tel. (770) 715-2600; internet www.delta.com; f. 1928; domestic and international services to 295 destinations in 46 countries; CEO RICHARD ANDERSON.

Hawaiian Airlines, Inc: 3375 Koapaka St, G-350, Honolulu, HI 96819; tel. (808) 835-3700; fax (808) 835-3690; internet www.hawaiianair.com; f. 1929 as Inter-Island Airways Ltd; inter-island, US mainland and South Pacific services; Pres. and CEO MARK B. DUNKERLEY.

Northwest Airlines, Inc: 2700 Lone Oak Parkway, Eagan, MN 55121-1534; tel. (612) 726-2111; fax (612) 726-0622; internet www.nwa.com; f. 1926; coast-to-coast domestic routes and services to Canada, Europe and the Far East; Chair. ROY BOSTOCK; Pres. and CEO DOUGLAS M. STEENLAND.

Southwest Airlines: 2702 Love Field Dr., POB 36611, Dallas, TX 75235; tel. (214) 792-4000; internet www.southwest.com; f. 1971; scheduled services to 64 cities in 32 states; Pres. COLLEEN BARRETT; Exec. Chair. HERB KELLEHER.

United Airlines Corpn: POB 66100, Chicago, IL 60666; tel. (847) 700-9838; fax (847) 700-4081; internet www.united.com; f. 1931; domestic and international services to over 210 destinations; Pres., Chair. and CEO GLENN F. TILTON, Jr.

US Airways, Inc: 4000 East Sky Harbor Blvd, Phoenix, AZ 85034; tel. (480) 693-0800; internet www.usairways.com; f. 1939 as All-American Airways; merged with America West Airlines in 2005; scheduled passenger services to 237 destinations world-wide; Chair. and CEO DOUG PARKER; Pres. SCOTT KIRBY.

Associations

Air Transport Association of America, Inc: 1301 Pennsylvania Ave, NW, Suite 1100, Washington, DC 20004-1707; tel. (202) 626-4000; fax (202) 626-4181; e-mail ata@airlines.org; internet www.airlines.org; f. 1936; 18 US airlines mems, 3 non-US assoc. mems; Pres. and CEO JAMES C. MAY.

National Air Carrier Association: 1000 Wilson Blvd, Suite 1700, Arlington, VA 22209; tel. (703) 358-8060; e-mail naca@erols.com; internet www.naca.cc; f. 1962; 16 mems; Pres. TOM ZOELLER.

National Air Transportation Association: 4226 King St, Alexandria, VA 22302; tel. (703) 845-9000; fax (703) 845-8176; internet www.nata.aero; f. 1940; Pres. JAMES K. COYNE.

Regional Airline Association: 2025 M St, NW, Suite 800, Washington, DC 20036-3309; tel. (202) 367-1170; fax (202) 367-2170; e-mail raa@raa.org; internet www.raa.org; f. 1975; Pres. ROGER COHEN.

Tourism

American Society of Travel Agents, Inc: 1101 King St, Alexandria, VA 22314; tel. (703) 739-2782; fax (703) 684-8319; e-mail askasta@astahq.com; internet www.astanet.com; f. 1931; Pres. and CEO CHERYL HUDAK; Exec. Vice-Pres. and COO WILLIAM A. MALONEY; over 20,000 mems.

Office of Travel and Tourism Industries: International Trade Administration, US Department of Commerce, 14th and Constitution Ave, NW, Rm 1003, Washington, DC 20230; tel. (202) 482-0140; fax (202) 482-2887; e-mail tinet_info@ita.doc.gov; internet tinet.ita.doc.gov; f. 1996; fed. govt agency; collects and analyses data and develops US tourism policy; Dir HELEN MARANO; Dep. Asst Sec. for Services ANA GUEVARA.

Travel Industry Association of America: 1100 New York Ave, NW, Suite 450, Washington, DC 20005-3934; tel. (202) 408-8422; fax (202) 408-1225; internet www.tia.org; f. 1941; Pres. and CEO ROGER DOW; Chair. JAMES A. RASULO.

UNITED STATES COMMONWEALTH TERRITORIES

There are two US Commonwealth Territories, the Northern Mariana Islands, in the Pacific Ocean, and Puerto Rico, in the Caribbean Sea. A Commonwealth is a self-governing incorporated territory that is an integral part of, and in full political union with, the USA.

THE NORTHERN MARIANA ISLANDS

Introductory Survey

Location, Climate, Language, Religion, Flag, Capital

The Commonwealth of the Northern Mariana Islands comprises 14 islands (all the Marianas except Guam) in the western Pacific Ocean, about 5,300 km (3,300 miles) west of Honolulu (Hawaii). The temperature normally ranges between 24°C (75°F) and 30°C (86°F) in June–November, but is generally cooler and drier from December to May. The average annual rainfall is about 2,120 mm (84 ins). English, Chamorro and Carolinian are the official languages. The population is predominantly Christian, mainly Roman Catholic. The national flag of the United States of America (q.v.) is used by the Northern Mariana Islands. Six islands, including the three largest (Saipan, Tinian and Rota), are inhabited; the principal settlement and the administrative centre are on Saipan.

Recent History

The islands that comprise the Northern Mariana Islands were first sighted by Europeans during the 1520s, and were claimed for Spain in 1565. They were sold to Germany in 1899, but control was transferred to Japan, which had taken the islands from Germany in 1914, by the League of Nations in 1921. The USA captured Saipan and Tinian from the Japanese after fierce fighting in 1944, and the Northern Mariana Islands became a part of the Trust Territory of the Pacific Islands in 1947 (see the chapter on the Marshall Islands).

In June 1975 the Northern Mariana Islands voted for separate status as a US Commonwealth Territory, and in March 1976 US President Gerald Ford signed the Northern Marianas Commonwealth Covenant. In October 1977 President Jimmy Carter approved the Constitution of the Northern Mariana Islands, which provided for the former Marianas District to be internally self-governing from January 1978. In December 1977 elections took place for a bicameral legislature, a Governor and a Lieutenant-Governor. The Northern Marianas were formally admitted to US Commonwealth status in November 1986, after the ending of the Trusteeship in the Territory. At the same time a proclamation issued by US President Ronald Reagan conferred US citizenship on the islands' residents.

At elections in 1989 Republicans retained control of the governorship of the Northern Marianas and ousted a Democrat from the position of the islands' representative in Washington, DC. Larry Guerrero was elected Governor after Pedro Tenorio had decided to resign. However, candidates of the Democratic Party won a majority of seats in the islands' House of Representatives.

In December 1990 the UN Security Council voted to end the Trusteeship of the Northern Marianas, as well as that of two other Pacific Trust Territories. Although the decision to terminate the relationship had been taken in 1986, voting had been delayed. However, Guerrero opposed the termination on the grounds that the new relationship would leave the islands subject to US law while remaining unrepresented in the US Congress.

At elections to the islands' House of Representatives (which had been enlarged by three seats) in 1991 Republicans regained a majority. Similarly, the party increased the number of its senators to eight. Republicans retained their majority at elections to the House of Representatives in 1993. However, in the gubernatorial election a Democrat, Froilan Tenorio, was successful. Similarly, a Democratic candidate, Jesús Borja, was elected as Lieutenant-Governor, while Juan Babauta remained as the Northern Marianas' representative in Washington, DC.

The Territory's reputation was marred in April 1995 when the Government of the Philippines introduced a ban on its nationals accepting unskilled employment in the islands, owing to persistent reports of abuse and exploitation of immigrant workers. Meanwhile, the US Congress announced that it was to allocate US $7m. towards the enforcement of the islands' labour and immigration laws, following the publication of a report in late 1994 that alleged the repeated violations of these regulations, as well as widespread corruption among immigration officials and business leaders.

In May 1997 US President Bill Clinton informed Tenorio of his intention to apply US immigration and minimum wage laws to the Territory, stating that labour practices in the islands were inconsistent with US values. In the previous month Democratic congressman George Miller had proposed legislation (the Insular Fair Wage and Human Rights Act) in the US House of Representatives that would equalize the minimum wage level in the islands with that of the US mainland by 1999. The Territory's Government, which denied many of the claims of exploitation of immigrant workers, responded to the proposed legislation by successfully lobbying the Republican majority in the US House of Representatives to oppose the bill.

In January 1999 the Office of Insular Affairs (OIA) of the US Department of the Interior published a report in which it concluded that the Government's attempts to eradicate abuses of labour and immigration laws had been unsuccessful. In particular, it had failed to reduce the Territory's reliance on alien workers, to enforce US minimum wage laws and to curb evasions of trade legislation governing the export of garments to the USA. In the same month former employees of 18 US clothing retailers initiated legal action against the companies, which were accused of failing to comply with US labour laws in Saipan. In April 2000 a settlement was reached with the garment manufacturers, providing some US $8m. in compensation for the workers. The companies also agreed to conform to regulations established by an independent monitoring system in Saipan.

At legislative elections in November 1997 Republican candidates won 13 of the 18 seats in the House of Representatives and eight of the nine seats in the Senate. At the gubernatorial election, held concurrently, Pedro Tenorio was successful, securing 46% of total votes. Opponents of Pedro Tenorio subsequently initiated a legal challenge to his election on the grounds that it constituted his third term as Governor, thereby violating the Constitution, which stated that a maximum of two gubernatorial terms could be served by any one individual (although the Constitution had been amended to include this provision only during Pedro Tenorio's second term in office). Following legislative elections in November 1999, Democratic candidates held two of the nine seats in the Senate and six of the 18 seats in the House of Representatives.

In February 2000 the US Senate approved a bill granting permanent residency in the Northern Marianas to some 40,000 immigrant workers. However, the bill also included provisions for limiting the stay of all future guest workers. In December 2000 Governor Tenorio announced that he was to oppose the decision by the US Government to bring the Northern Marianas' labour and immigration laws under federal control; Tenorio argued that this might have a negative impact on the Northern Marianas' economy. In May 2001, following intense lobbying by the Northern Marianas Government, the US Congress abandoned the bill. The issue of permanent residency for qualified immigrant workers re-emerged in 2007 with the introduction of minimum wage legislation (see below).

Legislative elections were held in early November 2001, at which the Republican Party secured 12 seats in the House of Representatives, the Democratic Party won five and the Covenant Party took one. The Republican Party won six seats in the Senate, the Democratic Party two and the Covenant Party one. At the concurrent gubernatorial elections Juan Nekai Babauta, the Republican Party candidate and former representative to Washington, won a convincing victory, securing 42.8% of the votes cast. Benigno Fitial, of the Covenant Party, received 24.4%. Babauta was inaugurated as Governor in January 2002, while Diego Benavente, the former Speaker of the House of Representatives, became Lieutenant-Governor.

In January 2002 the Supreme Court suspended deportation proceedings against an immigrant labourer working illegally in the Northern Marianas, after he appealed to the office of the UN High Commissioner for Refugees. The Court warned the Government that it might not be able to order the deportation of up to 10,000 of the Chinese, Sri Lankan and Bangladeshi workers in the Northern Marianas. In late 2002 the Government successfully resisted an attempt by the US Administration to place the Northern Mariana

UNITED STATES COMMONWEALTH TERRITORIES

The Northern Mariana Islands

Islands' immigration and labour legislation under direct federal control. In September 2003 the Northern Mariana Islands announced a new immigration co-operation agreement with the US Department of the Interior, which removed the right of overseas political refugees in the territory to seek asylum in the USA.

In May 2002 the issue of the Northern Marianas' working conditions was raised again by US Senator Edward Kennedy, who proposed a bill that would incrementally increase the minimum wage. In September seven further major US clothing retailers agreed to pay US $11.25m. in compensation to employees alleged to have suffered intolerable working conditions and poor rates of pay. The funds also included sponsorship of independent monitoring of labour conditions in the islands. The case was finally settled in April 2003, when a total of $20m. in compensation was ordered to be made to the claimants. The Garment Oversight Board was constituted in June, with the authority to withdraw certification of working conditions in garment factories supplying major US clothing companies. In March 2004 the Board decertified one of the 26 participating garment manufacturers. In April more than 400 garment workers were referred to the Division of Immigration for probable deportation as a result of their non-co-operation with a Fair Labor Standards Act civil action against garment manufacturers. Nevertheless, a delegate from the US Commission on Civil Rights concluded in May of that year that the situation of garment workers on Saipan appeared to be improving. However, owing to unfavourable external circumstances (see Economic Affairs), in 2005 about a dozen garment factories had ceased operations or reduced their work-force. In early April the repatriation of migrant workers no longer in employment began. In mid-2005 the minimum hourly wage in the Northern Marianas stood at $3.05, some 40% less than the rate prevailing on the US mainland. Legislation seeking to harmonize the minimum wage in the Northern Marianas with that of the USA was introduced to the US Senate in May. The legislation was criticized by the Speaker of the House, Benigno R. Fitial, who believed that the resultant rise in the minimum wage would place the Northern Marianas at a disadvantage with regional competitors. In late July 2005, after further lobbying from the Government and the Saipan Chamber of Commerce, the Northern Marianas were excluded from minimum wage legislation that would have ensured equivalence with the US wage increase to $7.25 an hour. In late January 2007 the Northern Marianas were finally included in the new legislation, while various tax concessions were provisionally approved to ease any losses incurred by small businesses as a result of the increase. The legislation, which was yet to be ratified, also sought to allow qualified immigrant workers to apply for permanent residency. However, within the Northern Marianas strong opposition to the federal legislation continued, as more garment factories risked closure. In early 2008 the islands' once thriving garment industry faced further decline, with the number of operating factories having dwindled to fewer than 10.

A US court order filed by an environmental group, the Center for Biological Diversity, forced military training on the island of Farallon de Medinilla to be suspended for 30 days in mid-2002. Despite environmentalists' concerns about the impact and legality of US military activity—in particular the testing of ordnances—upon the island's wildlife, the Northern Marianas Chamber of Commerce feared that the substantial revenue generated by the visiting US military might be jeopardized.

In May 2002 the Government 'froze' the assets of the Bank of Saipan, pending auditing of its accounts, after the institution's former Chairman was arrested for allegedly attempting to defraud the bank of more than US $6.6m. The bank, which was reported to hold substantial uninsured US government deposits, was placed in receivership and remained closed for 11 months. Following the bank's reopening in April 2003 with assets of some $12m., customers were permitted to retrieve a limited monthly quota of savings deposits. Four defendants were convicted in relation to the case in June.

In September 2002 Governor Babauta proposed reforms to reduce government expenditure. In November the Government announced plans for a US $40m. bond issue to cover the cost of compensating traditional landowners for the loss of property expropriated for government use, and in April 2003 draft legislation was proposed that would substantially reduce government personnel costs. However, in August credit ratings agencies expressed concerns that the Government's other outstanding debts, in particular those to the Northern Mariana Islands' Retirement Fund, would prevent full repayment of the bonds.

At the islands' legislative election of 1 November 2003 the Covenant Party gained a majority in the House of Representatives, winning nine of the 18 seats. The Republican Party secured seven seats, the Democrat Party took one seat and an independent candidate won one seat. The Covenant Party won three seats in the Senate, the Republican Party took two and the Democratic Party won one; three independent candidates were also elected.

Several instances of corruption in public office were reported in 2003; in April Senator Ricardo S. Atalig was found guilty of illegally employing relatives of another Senator, José M. de la Cruz (De la Cruz was suspended from office following his own conviction in July). In August 2004 the Superior Court convicted the chief financial officer of Tinian municipality, Romeo Atalig Diaz, in the first public corruption case lodged by the new anti-corruption unit of the Attorney-General's Office. However, the sentence imposed (fines totalling only US $2,800) was considered derisory by the local press.

At legislative elections held on 5 November 2005 the Covenant Party won eight seats in the House of Representatives, the Republican Party seven seats, the Democratic Party two seats and an independent candidate one seat. Following the election, the Covenant Party and the Republican Party each held three seats in the Senate, the Democratic Party had two seats and there was one independent senator. At the concurrent gubernatorial election Benigno R. Fitial of the Covenant Party and Timothy P. Villagomez, hitherto Vice-Speaker of the House, were elected Governor and Lieutenant-Governor, respectively, winning 3,809 votes (equivalent to 28.0% of valid votes cast). Independent Republican Heinz S. Hofschneider and his vice-gubernatorial candidate, David M. Apatang, came second with 3,710 votes (27.3%), while incumbent Governor Babauta and Lieutenant-Governor Diego Benavente came third with 3,610 votes (26.7%).

In March 2006 Jack Abramoff, who was involved, along with other lobbyists and government officials, in transforming and hindering congressional action regarding the Northern Marianas (particularly with regard to the federal minimum wage issue—see above), was sentenced to five years and 10 months in prison on fraud and conspiracy charges, and ordered to pay restitution of more than US $21m. Abramoff and his law firm had reportedly received large sums of money from the Northern Marianas Government between 1995 and 2001.

Legislative elections were held on 3 November 2007, with the number of seats in the islands' House of Representative having been increased to 20. The Republican Party regained a majority in the House of Representatives, securing 12 seats, while the Covenant Party won four seats, the Democratic Party one seat and independent candidates three seats. In the mid-term Senate elections, three incumbent Senators (two independent candidates and one Covenant Party candidate) were re-elected to the three contested seats. The electorate also voted on several municipal and judicial posts, along with issues such as gaming. In January 2008 the House of Representatives elected Arnold I. Palacios as its Speaker.

Co-operation between the Northern Marianas and the USA continued to increase. In early 2004 the Northern Marianas' representative in Washington, Pete Tenorio, requested authorization for a non-voting delegate to the US Congress from the Northern Marianas. In May four members of the original team of Covenant negotiators considered publicly the possibility of the Northern Marianas becoming the 51st state of the USA. Upon the US House of Representatives' approval of the Northern Mariana Islands Immigration, Security, and Labor Act in December 2007, the bill was transferred to the US Senate, which returned it to the House of Representatives with amendments in April 2008. In May US President George W. Bush approved the legislation, which brought the Northern Marianas under federal immigration laws and create a delegate seat for the Territory in the US House of Representatives.

Government

Legislative authority is vested in the Northern Marianas Commonwealth Legislature, a bicameral body consisting of the Senate and the House of Representatives. There are nine senators, elected for four-year terms, and 20 members of the House of Representatives, elected for two-year terms. Executive authority is vested in the Governor, who is elected by popular vote.

Defence

The USA is responsible for the defence of the Northern Marianas.

Economic Affairs

The Commonwealth of the Northern Mariana Islands' gross national income (GNI) was estimated by the Bank of Hawaii (BOH) to be US $696.3m. in 1999. GNI per head was estimated at $8,582. The population increased at an estimated annual rate of more than 1.5% during 2003–05. According to the BOH, the territory's gross domestic product (GDP) totalled $557.0m. in 2002.

Agriculture is concentrated in smallholdings, important crops being coconuts, breadfruit, tomatoes and melons. Cattle-ranching is practised on Tinian. Vegetables, beef and pork are produced for export. There is little commercial fishing in the islands (the total catch was 163 metric tons in 2003), although there is a major transshipment facility at Tinian harbour. Agriculture (including forestry, fishing and mining) engaged 1.5% of the employed labour force, according to the census of 2000, and its commercial value as a sector is minimal. In 2002 it accounted for only 0.1% of gross business revenues (total revenues generated by business transactions; the Government does not calculate GDP figures).

Industry (including manufacturing and construction) engaged 47.2% of the employed labour force in 2000. Manufacturing alone engaged 40.7% of workers, while construction employed 6.5%. The principal manufacturing activity has been the garment industry, which grew rapidly after its establishment in the mid-1980s to become the islands' leading export sector. Manufacturers benefited from US regulations that permitted duty-free and quota-free imports from the Commonwealth. Garment manufacturing accounted for 23.6% of gross business revenues in 2002, and overall exports of garments were worth US $925.7m. in 2001, compared with $1,017m. in 2000. However, following the liberalization of trade regulations in January 2005, which allowed developing countries to export garments to the USA, about 13 garment factories closed down. Other small-scale manufacturing activities include handicrafts and the processing of fish and copra. Construction is very closely related to the tourist industry and demand for additional hotel capacity.

Service industries dominate the economy, particularly tourism. In 2000 services (including utilities) engaged 51.3% of the employed labour force, and accounted for 29.2% of gross business revenues. However, tourism receipts declined from an estimated US $430m. in 2001 to $225m. in 2002. Japan provided the majority (61.9%) of the islands' visitors in 2006. Other significant sources of tourists were the Republic of Korea, Guam, the USA and the People's Republic of China. A total of 535,224 visitors travelled to the islands in 2004, an increase of 16.5% in relation to the previous year. However, tourism numbers declined in both 2005 and 2006, to just 435,494 in the latter year. It was reported that hotel occupancy in 2004 had increased by some 10% compared with 2003, to reach 71.8%. In 1995 a US company opened the Territory's first casino on Tinian (gambling being prohibited on other islands). The Northern Marianas were expected to receive some $12m. annually in revenue from this casino. In February 2005 it was announced that a South Korean company was shortly to commence construction of a new resort near Tinian International Airport. To comprise 1,000 rooms, the hotel complex was to incorporate a casino and a golf course. This major project, which was to cost $300m., had attracted investment from overseas Asian countries, including the People's Republic of China, as well as from the USA. In late 2005 the US Virgin Islands-based Bridge Investment Group, LLC announced a $150m. project to build a hotel and casino complex on Tinian.

The Northern Marianas are dependent on imports, the value of which totalled US $267.2m. in 2000. The principal imports in that year were clothing (which accounted for 27.6% of the total), beverages (2.8%), construction materials (2.8%) and automobiles and parts (2.2%). In 1991 there was a trade deficit of $126.9m. In 2001 remittances from overseas workers and investments reached $76.7m.

The annual rate of inflation averaged 0.9% in 1996–2006. Consumer prices increased by 4.9% in 2006.

Under the Covenant between the Commonwealth of the Northern Mariana Islands and the USA, the islands receive substantial annual development grants. Loans from the Commonwealth Development Authority totalled more than US $0.5m. in 2001.

The Territory is a member of the Pacific Community (see p. 377) and an associate member of the UN Economic and Social Commission for Asia and the Pacific (ESCAP, see p. 35).

Continued economic problems in the Territory have been largely attributed to the substantial increase in the Northern Marianas' population. The main constraints on development have included the inadequacy of the islands' infrastructure, labour shortages and the dependence on foreign workers, Filipino nationals in particular. However, owing to the large numbers of immigrant workers, wages remained relatively low, amid widespread complaints of poor working conditions. In September 2002 a judgment on a lawsuit against garment manufacturers in Saipan awarded compensation to the affected workers and provided for independent monitoring of labour practices in the Northern Marianas (see Recent History). Although the islands' Government resisted proposals to bring immigration and labour practices into line with the mainland USA, there was concern in the Territory that new World Trade Organization (see p. 396) measures removing import quotas on clothing, which took effect in January 2005, represented a direct threat to the comparative advantage of the garment industry's location within an unincorporated US Territory. None the less, the Northern Mariana Islands have long benefited from their political association with the USA; US federal funding and development assistance totalled some US $13m. in 2001/02, and in January 2004 an agreement was signed whereby the Northern Mariana Islands were to receive some $5.1m. in federal funding in order to offset the impact of migration, under the Compact of Free Association, to the Territory from the Marshall Islands, the Federated States of Micronesia, and Palau. In 2002 the Government introduced tax incentives for new businesses and developers. However, despite improved expenditure controls, the continued recession in the islands was estimated to have led to a deterioration in the Government's fiscal position and an increase in public debt. In May 2008 US President George W. Bush approved legislation granting the Territory the right to a non-voting delegate in the US House of Representatives (see Recent History). More importantly, however, the law also applied US immigration law to the Northern Mariana Islands, thus effectively prohibiting the exploitation of immigrant workers in the garment industry. The development was positively received by the Territory's authorities.

Education

School attendance is compulsory from six to 16 years of age. In 2002/03 there were 12 state primary schools, with a total of 5,849 pupils enrolled, and there were nine state secondary schools, with a total enrolment of 4,705 pupils. There was a total of 18 private schools, with a total enrolment of 2,326 pupils. There was one college of further education, with 1,641 students in 2000/01. Budgetary expenditure on education totalled US $49.6m. in 2000, equivalent to 22.0% of total government expenditure.

Public Holidays

2008: 9 January (Commonwealth Day), 21 January (Martin Luther King Day), 18 February (Presidents' Day), 21 March (Good Friday), 24 March (Covenant Day), 26 May (Memorial Day), 4 July (Liberation Day), 1 September (Labor Day), 13 October (Commonwealth Cultural Day), 4 November (Citizenship Day), 11 November (Veterans' Day), 27 November (Thanksgiving Day), 9 December (Constitution Day), 25 December (Christmas Day).

2009: 9 January (Commonwealth Day), 19 January (Martin Luther King Day), 16 February (Presidents' Day), 23 March (Covenant Day), 10 April (Good Friday), 25 May (Memorial Day), 3 July (for Liberation Day), 7 September (Labor Day), 12 October (Commonwealth Cultural Day), 4 November (Citizenship Day), 11 November (Veterans' Day), 26 November (Thanksgiving Day), 9 December (Constitution Day), 25 December (Christmas Day).

Weights and Measures

With certain exceptions, the imperial system is in force. One US cwt equals 100 lb; one long ton equals 2,240 lb; one short ton equals 2,000 lb. A policy of gradual voluntary conversion to the metric system is being encouraged by the Federal Government.

Statistical Survey

Source: (unless otherwise stated): Department of Commerce, Central Statistics Division, POB 10007, Saipan, MP 96950; tel. 664-3000; fax 664-3001; internet www.commerce.gov.mp.

AREA AND POPULATION

Area: 457 sq km (176.5 sq miles). *By Island*: Saipan 120 sq km (46.5 sq miles); Tinian 102 sq km (39.2 sq miles); Rota 85 sq km (32.8 sq miles); Pagan 48 sq km (18.6 sq miles); Anatahan 32 sq km (12.5 sq miles); Agrihan 30 sq km (11.4 sq miles); Alamagan 11 sq km (4.4 sq miles); Asuncion 7 sq km (2.8 sq miles); Aguijan (Goat Is) 7 sq km (2.7 sq miles); Sarigan 5 sq km (1.9 sq miles); Guguan 4 sq km (1.5 sq miles); Farallon de Pajaros 3 sq km (1.0 sq mile); Maug 2 sq km (0.8 sq mile); Farallon de Medinilla 1 sq km (0.4 sq mile).

Population: 43,345 at census of 1 April 1990; 69,221 (males 31,984, females 37,237) at census of 1 April 2000. *By Island* (2000 census): Saipan 62,392; Rota 3,283; Tinian (with Aguijan) 3,540; Northern Islands 6. *2002* (estimates): Saipan 67,011; Total 74,151. *2006* (UN estimate): 82,128 (Source: UN Economic and Social Commission for Asia and the Pacific).

Density (2006): 179.7 per sq km.

Ethnic Groups (2000 census): Filipino 18,141; Chinese 15,311; Chamorro 14,749; part-Chamorro 4,383; Total (incl. others) 69,221.

Principal Towns (population at 2000 census): San Antonio 4,741; Garapan (capital) 3,588; Koblerville 3,543; San Vincente 3,494; Tanapag 3,318; Chalan Kanoa 3,108; Kagman 3,026. Source: Thomas Brinkhoff, *City Population* (internet www.citypopulation.de).

Births and Deaths (2002): Registered live births 1,289 (birth rate 17.4 per 1,000); Registered deaths 164 (death rate 2.2 per 1,000).

Employment (2000 census, persons aged 16 years and over): Agriculture, forestry, fisheries and mining 623; Manufacturing 17,398; Construction 2,785; Transport, communication and utilities 1,449; Trade, restaurants and hotels 9,570; Financing, insurance and real estate 1,013; Community, social and personal services 9,915; *Total employed* 42,753 (males 19,485, females 23,268); Unemployed 1,712 (males 888, females 824); *Total labour force* 44,465 (males 20,373, females 24,092). *Mid-2005* (estimates): Agriculture, etc. 9,000; Total labour force 38,000 (Source: FAO).

HEALTH AND WELFARE
Key Indicators

Access to Water (% of persons, 2004): 99.

Access to Sanitation (% of persons, 2004): 95.

For sources and definitions, see explanatory note on p. vi.

AGRICULTURE, ETC.

Livestock (1997): Cattle 1,789; Pigs 831; Goats 249; Poultry birds 29,409.

Fishing (metric tons, live weight, 2005): Total catch 196 (Skipjack tuna 93; Yellowfin tuna 19; Common dolphinfish 10). Source: FAO.

FINANCE

Currency and Exchange Rates: United States currency is used: 100 cents = 1 United States dollar (US $). *Sterling and Euro Equivalents* (31 December 2007): £1 sterling = US $2.003; €1 = US $1.472; US $100 = £49.92 = €67.93.

Federal Direct Expenditures (US $ million, year ending September 2006): Retirement and disability 27.1; Total (incl. others) 176.9 (Source: US Census Bureau, *Consolidated Federal Funds Report*).

Budget (US $ million, year ending 30 September 2002, estimates): Total revenue 199.7 (Taxes 166.8, Service fees 28.7, Operating transfers 4.3); Total expenditure 212.1 (Wages, salaries and benefits 108.9; Other expenditure 103.2). Source: Bank of Hawaii, *Commonwealth of the Northern Mariana Islands Economic Report* (October 2003).

Cost of Living (Consumer Price Index for Saipan; base: 2000 = 100): 99.3 in 2004; n.a. in 2005; 104.7 in 2006. Source: ILO.

Gross Domestic Product (US $ million in current prices, estimate): 557.0 in 2002. Source: Bank of Hawaii, *Commonwealth of the Northern Mariana Islands Economic Report* (October 2003).

EXTERNAL TRADE

Principal Commodities (US $ million): *Imports* (1997): Beverages 12.8; Tobacco 5.4; Automobiles (incl. parts) 42.1; Clothing 309.2; Total (incl. others) 836.2. *Exports* (2000): Total 1,000.

Principal Trading Partners (US $ million, 1997): *Imports*: Guam 298.0; Hong Kong 200.5; Japan 118.3; Korea, Republic 80.6; USA 63.3; Total (incl. others) 836.2.

Sources: UN, *Statistical Yearbook for Asia and the Pacific* and *Statistical Yearbook*.

TRANSPORT

Shipping: *Registered Fleet* (2001): 1,029 vessels (791 fishing vessels); *Traffic* ('000 short tons, 1997): Goods loaded 184.1; Goods unloaded 425.9.

Civil Aviation (Saipan Int. Airport, year ending September 1999): 23,853 aircraft landings; 562,364 boarding passengers. Source: Commonwealth Ports Authority.

Road Traffic (registered motor vehicles, 2001): 17,900.

TOURISM

Visitor Arrivals: 589,224 in 2004; 491,701 in 2005; 435,494 in 2006.

Visitor Arrivals by Country (2006): China, People's Republic (incl. Hong Kong) 38,313; Japan 269,780; Korea, Republic 82,891; USA (incl. Guam) 24,579; Total (incl. others) 435,494.

Tourism Receipts (US $ million): 407 in 1999; 430 in 2000; 225 in 2002 (approximate figure). Source: Bank of Hawaii, *Commonwealth of the Northern Mariana Islands Economic Report* (October 2003).

COMMUNICATIONS MEDIA

Radio Receivers (households with access, census of 2000): 10,684.

Television Receivers (estimate, 1995): 15,460 in use.

Telephones (main lines in use, 2006): 30,684.

Mobile Cellular Telephones (2004): 20,500 subscribers*.

Facsimile Machines (1996): 1,200 in use†.

* Source: International Telecommunication Union.
† Source: UN, *Statistical Yearbook*.

EDUCATION

Pre-primary (2002/03, state schools, Headstart programme): 12 schools; 98 teachers; 606 pupils.

Primary (2002/03, state schools): 12 schools; 283 teachers; 5,849 students.

Secondary (2002/03, state schools): 9 schools; 248 teachers; 4,705 students.

Higher (2000/01): 1 college; 1,641 students (full- and part-time students).

Private Schools (2002/03): 18 schools; 186 teachers; 2,326 students.

Directory

The Government
(April 2008)

Governor: BENIGNO R. FITIAL (took office 9 January 2006).
Lieutenant-Governor: TIMOTHY P. VILLAGOMEZ.

DEPARTMENT SECRETARIES

Secretary of the Department of Finance: ELOY S. INOS.

Secretary of the Department of Community and Cultural Affairs: MELVIN FAISAO (acting).

Secretary of the Department of Labor: GIL M. SAN NICOLAS.

Secretary of the Department of Lands and Natural Resources: IGNACIO DELA CRUZ.

Secretary of the Department of Public lands: JOHN S. DEL ROSARIO, Jr.

Secretary of the Department of Public Works: JOSE S. DEMAPAN.

Secretary of the Department of Commerce: JAMES SANTOS.

Commissioner of the Department of Public Safety: REBECCA WARFIELD.

Secretary of the Department of Public Health: JOSEPH KEVIN P. VILLAGOMEZ.

GOVERNMENT OFFICES

Office of the Governor: Caller Box 10007, Capitol Hill, Saipan, MP 96950; tel. 664-2276; fax 664-2290; e-mail gov.frosario@saipan.com; internet www.gov.mp.

Office of the Resident Representative to the USA, Commonwealth of the Northern Mariana Islands: 2121 R St, NW, Washington, DC 20008, USA; tel. (202) 673-5869; fax (202) 673-5873; e-mail rep@resrep.gov.mp; the Commonwealth Govt also has liaison offices in Hawaii and Guam.

Department of the Interior, Office of Insular Affairs (OIA): Field Office of the OIA, Dept of the Interior, POB 502622, Saipan, MP 96950; tel. 234-8861; fax 234-8814; e-mail jeff.schorr@pticom.com; internet www.doi.gov/oia/Islandpages/cnmipage.htm; OIA representation in the Commonwealth; Field Representative JEFFREY SCHORR.

Department of Commerce: Capitol Hill, Saipan, MP 96950; tel. 664-3003; fax 664-3067; e-mail commercedept@pticom.com; internet www.commerce.gov.mp.

Department of Community and Cultural Affairs: Capitol Hill, Saipan, MP 96950; tel. 664-2576; fax 664-2570; e-mail dccaoos@pticom.com; internet www.dcca.gov.mp.

Department of Finance: Capitol Hill, Saipan, MP 96950; tel. 664-1100; fax 664-1115; e-mail procurement@gtepacifica.net; internet www.dof.gov.mp.

Department of Labor: POB 10007, Saipan, MP 96950; tel. 236-0900; fax 236-0991; e-mail webmaster@marianaslabor.net; internet marianaslabor.net.

Department of Lands and Natural Resources: Capitol Hill, Saipan, MP 96950; tel. 322-9830; fax 322-2633.

Department of Public Health: Capitol Hill, Saipan, MP 96950; tel. 234-8950; fax 236-8390; e-mail fbraig@cnmidph.net; internet www.dphsaipan.com.

Department of Public Lands: Capitol Hill, Saipan, MP 96950; tel. 234-2751; fax 234-3755.

Department of Public Safety: Capitol Hill, Saipan, MP 96950; tel. 664-9022; fax 664-9027; internet www.dps.gov.mp.

Department of Public Works: Capitol Hill, Saipan, MP 96950; tel. 235-5827; fax 235-6346.

UNITED STATES COMMONWEALTH TERRITORIES

Legislature

Legislative authority is vested in the Northern Marianas Commonwealth Legislature, a bicameral body consisting of the Senate and the House of Representatives. There are nine senators, elected for four-year terms, and 20 members of the House of Representatives, elected for two-year terms. The most recent legislative election was held on 3 November 2007. The Republican Party won 12 seats in the House of Representatives, the Covenant Party four seats, the Democratic Party one seat and independent candidates three seats. Meanwhile, two independent candidates and one Covenant Party candidate were re-elected to the three Senate seats being contested.

Senate President: PETE P. REYES.
Speaker of the House: ARNOLD I. PALACIOS.
Commonwealth Legislature: Capitol Hill, Saipan, MP 96950; tel. 664-7757; fax 322-6344.

Election Commission

Commonwealth Election Commission: POB 500470, Saipan, MP 96950-0470; tel. 664-8683; fax 664-8689; e-mail executivedirector@votecnmi.gov.mp; internet www.votecnmi.gov.mp; Exec. Dir GREGORIO C. SABLAN.

Political Organizations

Covenant Party: c/o Commonwealth Legislature, Capitol Hill, Saipan, MP 96950; Leader BENIGNO R. FITIAL; Chair. ELOY INOS.
Democratic Party of the Commonwealth of the Northern Mariana Islands, Inc: Saipan, MP 96950; tel. 234-7497; fax 233-0641; Pres. Dr CARLOS S. CAMACHO; Chair. LORENZO CABRERA.
Republican Party of the Northern Marianas: POB 500777, Saipan, MP 96950; tel. 233-1288; fax 233-1288; State Chair. TOM PANGELINAN; Exec. Dir (vacant).

Judicial System

The judicial system in the Commonwealth of the Northern Mariana Islands (CNMI) consists of the Superior Court, the Commonwealth Supreme Court (which considers appeals from the Superior Court) and the Federal District Court. Under the Covenant, federal law applies in the Commonwealth, apart from the following exceptions: the CNMI is not part of the US Customs Territory; the federal minimum-wage provisions do not apply; federal immigration laws do not apply; and the CNMI may enact its own taxation laws.

Chief Justice of the Commonwealth Supreme Court: MIGUEL S. DEMAPAN.
Presiding Judge of the Superior Court: ROBERT C. NARAJA.
Attorney-General: MATTHEW T. GREGORY.
Public Defender: ADAM HARDWICKE.

Religion

The population is predominantly Christian, mainly Roman Catholic. There are small communities of Episcopalians (Anglicans—under the jurisdiction of the Bishop of Hawaii, in the USA) and Protestants.

CHRISTIANITY
The Roman Catholic Church

The Northern Mariana Islands comprise the single diocese of Chalan Kanoa, suffragan to the archdiocese of Agaña (Guam). The Bishop participates in the Catholic Bishops' Conference of the Pacific, based in Suva, Fiji. At 31 December 2005 there were 43,000 adherents, including temporary residents, in the Northern Mariana Islands.

Bishop of Chalan Kanoa: Most Rev. TOMAS AGUON CAMACHO, Bishop's House, Chalan Kanoa, POB 500745, Saipan, MP 96950; tel. 234-3000; fax 235-3002; e-mail diocese@pticom.com.

The Press

The weekly *Focus on the Commonwealth* is published in Guam, but distributed solely in the Northern Mariana Islands.

Marianas Observer: POB 502119, Saipan, MP 96950; tel. 233-3955; fax 233-7040; weekly; Publr JOHN VABLAN; circ. 2,000.
Marianas Review: POB 501074, Saipan, MP 96950; tel. 234-7160; f. 1979 as *The Commonwealth Examiner*; weekly; English and Chamorro; independent; Publr LUIS BENAVENTE; Editor RUTH L. TIGHE; circ. 1,700.
Marianas Variety: POB 500231, Saipan, MP 96950; tel. 234-6341; fax 234-9271; e-mail editorial@mvariety.com; internet www.mvariety.com; Mon.–Fri.; English and Chamorro; independent;

The Northern Mariana Islands

f. 1972; Publrs ABED E. YOUNIS, PAZ C. YOUNIS; Editor ZALDY DANDAN; circ. 7,500.
North Star: Chalan Kanoa, POB 500745, Saipan, MP 96950; tel. 234-3000; fax 235-2531; e-mail north.star@saipan.com; weekly; English and Chamorro; Roman Catholic; f. 1976; Publr BISHOP TOMAS A. CAMACHO; Man. Editor RUY VALENTE M. POLISTICO.
Pacific Daily News (Saipan bureau): POB 500822, Saipan, MP 96950; tel. 234-6423; fax 234-5986; Publr LEE WEBBER; circ. 5,000.
Pacific Star: POB 505815 CHRB, Saipan, MP 96950; tel. 288-0746; fax 288-0747; weekly; Operational Man. NICK LEGASPI; circ. 3,000.
Pacifica: POB 502143, Saipan, MP 96950; monthly; Editor MIKE MALONE.
Saipan Tribune: POB 10001, PMB 34, Saipan, MP 96950-8901; tel. 235-8747; fax 235-3740; e-mail editor.tribune@saipan.com; internet www.saipantribune.com; 2 a week; Editor JAYVEE L. VALLEJERA; Publr JOHN PANGELINAN; circ. 3,500.

Broadcasting and Communications

TELECOMMUNICATIONS

Pacific Telecom Inc: POB 500306 CK, Saipan, MP 96950; tel. 682-1060; fax 682-4555; internet www.pticom.com.
SAIPANCELL Communications: Gualo Rai Commercial Center, Main Bldg, Gualo Rai, Middle Rd, Saipan; tel. 483-2273; fax 235-7640; e-mail service@guamcell.net; internet www.saipancell.com; f. ; fmrly Saipan Cellular & Paging; cellular services; Pres. MARK CHAMBERLIN.

BROADCASTING
Radio

Far East Broadcasting Co, Inc: POB 500209, Saipan, MP 96950; tel. 322-9088; fax 322-3060; e-mail saipan@febc.org; internet www.febc.org; f. 1946; non-commercial religious broadcasts; Chair. Dr DOUG PENNOYER; Field Dir ROBERT L. SPRINGER.
   KSAI-AM: tel. 234-6520; fax 234-3428; e-mail ksai@febc.org; f. 1978; local service; mainly religious broadcasts; Station Man. CHRIS SLABAUGH.
   KFBS-SW: POB 500209, Saipan, MP 96950; tel. 322-9088; fax 322-3060; e-mail saipan@febc.org; internet www.febc.org; f. 1946; international broadcasts in Chinese, Indonesian, Russian, Vietnamese, Mongolian; owned by Far East Broadcasting Co, Inc; Exec. Dir ROBERT SPRINGER.
Inter-Island Communications, Inc: POB 500914, Saipan, MP 96950; tel. 234-7239; fax 234-0447; f. 1984; commercial; station KCNM-AM, or KZMI-FM in stereo; Gen. Man. HANS W. MICKELSON; Programme Dir KEN WARNICK; CEO ANGEL OCAMPO.
KRNM: POB 501250, Saipan, MP 96950; tel. 234-5498; fax 235-0915; internet www.krnm.org; f. 1994; public station based on Northern Marianas Coll. campus; Gen. Man. CARL POGUE.
Magic 100.3: Magic Studio, 1st Floor, Naru Bldg, Susupe; fax 234-2262; e-mail Kwaw100.3@Magic100Radio.com; internet www.magic100radio.com.
Power 99: POB 10000, Saipan, MP 96950; tel. 235-7996; fax 235-7998; e-mail tpalacios@spbguam.com; internet www.power99.net; Station Man. TINA PALACIOS; Gen. Man. CURTIS DANCOE.
The Rock 97.9: POB 10000 Saipan, MP 96950; tel. 235-7996; fax 235-7998; e-mail cdancoe@spbguam.com; Man. ALBERT JUAN.

Television

KMCV-TV: POB 501298, Saipan, MP 96950; tel. 235-6365; fax 235-0965; f. 1992; 52-channel commercial station, with 8 pay channels, broadcasting 24 hours a day; US programmes and local and international news; 5,650 subscribers; Gen. Man. WAYNE GAMBLIN.
Marianas CableVision: Nauru Bldg, 2°, Susupe, Saipan, MP 96950; tel. 235-4628; fax 235-0965; e-mail mcv.service@saipan.com; internet www.mcvcnmi.com; 55-channel cable service provider, broadcasting US and Pacific Rim programmes; Pres. JOHN CRUIKSHANK; Gen. Man. MARK BIRMINGHAM.

Finance

BANKING

Bank of Guam (USA): POB 500678, Saipan, MP 96950; tel. 233-5000; fax 233-5003; internet www.bankofguam.com; Gen. Man. MARCIE TOMOKANE; brs on Tinian and Rota.
Bank of Hawaii: Bank of Hawaii Bldg, El Monte Ave, Garapan, POB 500566, Saipan, MP 96950; tel. 236-8450; fax 235-3913; internet www.boh.com; Man. JOHN SHEATHER; 2 brs.

UNITED STATES COMMONWEALTH TERRITORIES

The Northern Mariana Islands

Bank of Saipan: POB 500690, Saipan, MP 96950; tel. 234-6260; fax 235-1802; e-mail bankofsaipan@gtepacifica.net; internet www.bankofsaipan.com; three-year period of receivership ended Aug. 2005; dep. US $23m. (Dec. 2004); Pres. JON BARGFREDE; 3 brs.

City Trust Bank: Gualo Rai, POB 501867, Saipan, MP 96950; tel. 234-7701; fax 234-8664; e-mail citytrustbank@ctbsaipan.com; Asst Vice-Pres. and Acting Man. MARIA LOURDES JOHNSON.

First Hawaiian Bank: Gualo Rai Commercial Center, Middle Rd, Gualo Rai, Saipan 96950; tel. 235-3090; fax 236-8936; internet www.fhb.com; Area Man. JUAN LIZAMA.

Guam Savings and Loan Bank: POB 503201, Saipan, MP 96950; tel. 233-2265; fax 233-2227; Gen. Man. GLEN PEREZ.

INSURANCE

Allied Insurance/Takagi and Associates, Inc: PPP 602 Box 10000 Saipan, MP 96950; tel. 233-2554; fax 670-2553; Gen. Man. PETER SIBLY.

Aon Insurance: Aon Insurance Micronesia (Saipan) Inc, POB 502177, Saipan, MP 96950; tel. 234-2811; fax 234-5462; e-mail rod.rankin@aon.com.au; internet www.aon.com; Communications Officer RODNEY RANKIN.

Associated Insurance Underwriters of the Pacific, Inc: POB 501369, Saipan, MP 96950; tel. 234-7222; fax 234-5367; e-mail aiup@pticom.com; Gen. Man. MAGGIE GEORGE.

Calvo's Insurance Underwriters, Inc.: Oleai Shopping Center, Saipan, MP 96950; tel. 234-5690; fax 234-5693; e-mail calvospc@vzpacifica.net; internet www.calvosinsurance.com; Man. ELI C. BUENAVENTURA.

Century Insurance (Tan Holdings Corpn): Century Insurance PMB 193, POB 10000, Saipan, MP 96950; tel. 234-0609; fax 234-1845; e-mail nel_matanguihan@cicspn.com; internet www.cicspn.com; Gen. Man. NEL MATANGUIHAN.

General Accident Insurance Asia Ltd (Microl Insurance): POB 502177, Saipan, MP 96950; tel. 234-2811; fax 234-5462; Man. Dir MICHAEL W. GOURLAY.

Marianas Insurance Co Ltd: POB 502505, Saipan, MP 96950-2505; tel. 234-5091; fax 234-5093; e-mail admin@marianasinsurance.com; internet www.marianasinsurance.com; Gen. Man. ROSALIA S. CABRERA.

Midland Insurance Underwriters, Inc.: PMB 219, POB 10000, Capitol Hill, Saipan, MP 96950; tel. 235-3598; fax 235-3597; e-mail midland@vzpacifica.net.

Moylan's Insurance Underwriters (Int.), Inc: POB 500658, Saipan, MP 96950; tel. 234-6571; fax 632-3788; e-mail saipan@moylansinsurance.com; internet www.moylansinsurance.com; Branch Man. TAMARA TALALEMOTOU.

Nichido Insurance: Oleai Central Bldg, San Jose, Saipan, MP 96950; tel. 234-5690; fax 234-5693.

Pacifica Insurance Underwriters, Inc: POB 500168, Saipan, MP 96950; tel. 234-6267; fax 234-5880; e-mail piui@pacificains.com; internet www.pacificains.com; f. 1972; Pres. NORMAN T. TENORIO.

Primerica Financial Services: POB 500964, Saipan, MP 96950; tel. 235-2912; fax 235-7910; Gen. Man. JOHN SABLAN.

Royal Crown Insurance: Royal Crown Bldg, Beach Road, Chalan LauLau, POB 10001, Saipan, MP 96950; tel. 234-2256; fax 234-2258.

Staywell: POB 502050, Saipan, MP 96950; tel. 323-4260; fax 323-4263; e-mail stwspn@ite.net; Man. FRANNY PANGELINAN.

Trade and Industry

GOVERNMENT AGENCIES

Commonwealth Development Authority: POB 502149, Wakins Bldg, Gualo Rai, Saipan, MP 96950; tel. 234-7145; fax 234-7144; e-mail administration@cda.gov.mp; internet www.cda.gov.mp; govt lending institution; funds capital improvement projects and private enterprises; offers tax incentives to qualified investors; Chair. VINCENT M. CALVO; CEO OSCAR C. CAMACHO (acting).

Marianas Public Lands Authority: POB 500380, Saipan, MP 96950; tel. 234-3751; fax 234-3755; manages public land, which constitutes 82% of total land area in the Commonwealth (14% on Saipan).

CHAMBER OF COMMERCE

Saipan Chamber of Commerce: Chalan Kanoa, POB 500806 CK, Saipan, MP 96950; tel. 233-7150; fax 233-7151; e-mail saipanchamber@saipan.com; internet www.saipanchamber.com; Pres. JIM ARENOVSKI; Exec. Dir CHRISTINE PARKE.

EMPLOYERS' ASSOCIATIONS

Association of Commonwealth Teachers (ACT): POB 5071, Saipan, MP 96950; tel. and fax 256-7567; e-mail cnmiteachers@netscape.net; supports the teaching profession and aims to improve education in state schools.

Saipan Garment Manufacturers' Association (SGMA): POB 10001, Saipan, MP 96950; tel. 235-7699; fax 235-7899; e-mail sgmaemy@vzpacifica.net; internet www.sgma-saipan.org; Exec. Dir (vacant).

UTILITIES

Commonwealth Utilities Corporation: POB 501220, Saipan, MP 96950; tel. 235-7025; fax 235-6145; e-mail cucedp@gtepacifica.net; internet www.cuccnmi.com; scheduled for privatization.

TRADE UNION AND CO-OPERATIVES

International Brotherhood of Electrical Workers: c/o Micronesian Telecommunications Corpn, Saipan, MP 96950; Local 1357 of Hawaii branch of US trade union based in Washington, DC.

The Mariana Islands Co-operative Association, Rota Producers and Tinian Producers Associations operate on the islands.

Transport

RAILWAYS

There have been no railways operating in the islands since the Japanese sugar industry railway, on Saipan, ceased operations in the Second World War.

ROADS

In 1991 there were 494 km (307 miles) of roads on the islands, 320 km (199 miles) of which are on Saipan. First grade roads constitute 135 km (84 miles) of the total, 99 km (62 miles) being on Saipan. There is no public transport, apart from a school bus system.

SHIPPING

The main harbour of the Northern Mariana Islands is the Port of Saipan, which underwent extensive renovation in the mid-1990s. There are also two major harbours on Rota and one on Tinian. Several shipping lines link Saipan, direct or via Guam, with ports in Japan, Asia, the Philippines, the USA and other territories in the Pacific.

Commonwealth Ports Authority: POB 501055, Saipan, MP 96950; tel. 664-3500; fax 234-5962; e-mail cpa.admin@saipan.com; internet net.saipan.com/cftemplates/cpa/index.cfm; Exec. Dir CARLOS H. SALAS; Chair. RAMÓN S. PALACIOS.

Mariana Express Lines: POB 501937, CTS Bldg, Saipan, MP 96950; tel. 322-1690; fax 323-6355; e-mail winnie_ong@mariana-express.com; internet www.mariana-express.com; services between Saipan, Guam, Japan and Hong Kong; Man. WINNIE ONG.

Saipan Shipping Co Inc (Saiship): Saiship Bldg, Charlie Dock, POB 500008, Saipan, MP 96950; tel. 322-9706; fax 322-3183; e-mail darlene_cabrera@saipanshipping.com; f. 1956; weekly barge service between Guam, Saipan and Tinian; monthly services to Japan and Micronesia; Gen. Man. DARLENE CABRERA.

Westpac Freight: POB 2048, Puerto Rico, Saipan, MP 96950; tel. 322-8798; fax 322-5536; e-mail westpac@gtepacifica.net; services between Saipan, Guam and the USA; Man. MICHIE CAMACHO.

CIVIL AVIATION

Air services are centred on the main international airport, Isley Field, on Saipan. There are also airports on Rota and Tinian.

Continental Micronesia: POB 508778, A.B. Won Pat International Airport, Tamuning, GU 96911; tel. 647-6595; fax 649-6588; internet www.continental.com; f. 1968, as Air Micronesia, by Continental Airlines (USA); name changed 1992; subsidiary of Continental Airlines; hub operations in Saipan and Guam; services throughout the region and to destinations in the Far East and the mainland USA; Pres. MARK ERWIN.

Freedom Air: POB 500239 CK, Saipan, MP 96950; tel. 234-8328; e-mail freedom@ite.net; internet www.freedomairguam.com; scheduled internal flights.

Tourism

Tourism is one of the most important industries in the Northern Mariana Islands, earning some US $225m. in 2002. In that year there were 4,313 hotel rooms. Most of the islands' hotels are Japanese-owned, and in 2005 69% of tourists came from Japan. The Republic of Korea and the USA are also important sources of tourists. The

UNITED STATES COMMONWEALTH TERRITORIES

islands received a total of 535,224 visitors in 2004 (an increase of some 16.5% on the figure for the previous year). In 2005 there were 506,846 visitors. The islands of Asuncion, Guguan, Maug, Managaha, Sariguan and Uracas (Farallon de Pajaros) are maintained as uninhabited reserves. Visitors are mainly attracted by the white, sandy beaches and the excellent diving conditions. There is also interest in the *Latte* or *Taga* stones (mainly on Tinian), pillars carved from the rock by the ancient Chamorros, and relics from the Second World War.

Hotel Association of the Northern Mariana Islands: POB 5075 CHRB, Saipan, MP 96950; tel. 234-3455; fax 234-3411; e-mail lynn_knight@tanholdings.com; internet www.saipanhotels.org; f. 1983; Chair. LYNN KNIGHT.

Marianas Visitors Authority (MVA): POB 500861 CK, Saipan, MP 96950; tel. 664-3200; fax 664-3237; e-mail mva@mymarianas.com; internet www.mymarianas.com; f. 1976; responsible for the promotion and development of tourism in the Northern Mariana Islands; Chair. JERRY TAN; Man. Dir PERRY TENORIO.

PUERTO RICO

Introductory Survey

Location, Climate, Language, Religion, Flag, Capital

The Commonwealth of Puerto Rico comprises the main island of Puerto Rico, together with the small offshore islands of Vieques and Culebra and numerous smaller islets, lying about 80 km (50 miles) east of Hispaniola (Haiti and the Dominican Republic) in the Caribbean Sea. The climate is maritime-tropical, with an average annual temperature of 24°C (75°F) and a normal range between 17°C (63°F) and 36°C (97°F). The official languages are Spanish and English. Christianity is the dominant religion, and about 73% of the population are Roman Catholics. The flag (proportions 3 by 5) has five alternating red and white horizontal stripes of equal width, with a blue triangle, in the centre of which is a five-pointed white star, at the hoist. The capital is San Juan.

Recent History

Puerto Rico, also known as Borinquen (after the original Arawak Indian name Boriquen), was ruled by Spain from 1509 until 1898, when it was ceded to the USA at the conclusion of the Spanish–American war, and administered as an 'unincorporated territory' of the USA. In 1917 Puerto Ricans were granted US citizenship, and in 1947 Puerto Rico obtained the right to elect its own Governor. A Constitution, promulgated in 1952, assigned Puerto Rico the status of a self-governing 'Commonwealth', or 'Estado Libre Asociado', in its relation to the USA.

The Partido Popular Democrático (PPD) held a majority in both chambers of the legislature from 1944 until 1968, when, following a split within the party, the Partido Nuevo Progresista (PNP), an advocate of statehood, won the governorship and legislative control. This followed a plebiscite in 1967, when 61% of voters had ratified a continuation of Commonwealth status in preference to independence (1%) or incorporation as a State of the USA (39%). In the general election of 1972 the PPD, under the leadership of Rafael Hernández Colón, regained the governorship and legislative control from the PNP, only to lose them again in 1976. The victorious PNP was led by Carlos Romero Barceló, who became Governor in January 1977.

Romero Barceló, who had promised a referendum on statehood if re-elected for a further term in 1980, abandoned this plan following the election, in which he narrowly defeated former Governor Hernández Colón. The PPD, however, gained control of the legislature. The 1984 gubernatorial election, which was contested mainly on economic issues, was won by Hernández Colón by only 50,000 votes, with the PPD retaining substantial majorities in both legislative chambers. In September 1985 Romero Barceló was succeeded as leader of the PNP by Baltasar Corrada del Río.

A gubernatorial election, held in November 1988, resulted in the re-election of Hernández Colón. Electoral participation was unusually high, at almost 90%.

The question of eventual independence for Puerto Rico has been a politically sensitive issue for over 50 years. With the PPD supporting the continuation and enhancement of Commonwealth status and the PNP advocating Puerto Rico's inclusion as a state of the USA, mainstream party encouragement of independence aims has come mainly from the Partido Independentista Puertorriqueño (PIP) and other left-wing groups. There are two small, and occasionally violent, terrorist factions, the Ejército Popular Boricua (Los Macheteros), which operates in Puerto Rico, and the Fuerzas Armadas de Liberación Nacional (FALN), functioning principally on the US mainland.

In the 1988 election campaign, Corrada del Río, whose campaign was endorsed by the successful US presidential candidate, George Bush, advocated the admission of Puerto Rico as the 51st state of the USA, while Hernández Colón reiterated the traditional PPD policy of 'maximum autonomy' for Puerto Rico 'within a permanent union with the USA'. President Bush's open support of the statehood option was criticized by Hernández Colón and the PPD. In January 1989 Hernández Colón promised that a further plebiscite would be held. Although it was initially planned to hold this referendum in June 1991, in February the proposed legislation to make its result binding on the US Government failed to obtain sufficient support in the US Senate to allow it to proceed to full consideration by the US Congress.

In December 1991 the PPD Government organized a referendum on a proposal to adopt a charter of 'democratic rights', which included guarantees of US citizenship regardless of future change in Puerto Rico's constitutional status, and the maintenance of Spanish as the official language. The proposed charter was rejected by a margin of 53% to 45%. This result was widely interpreted as an indication that the majority of voters wished to retain Puerto Rico's Commonwealth status. Hernández Colón announced in January 1992 that he would not seek re-election in the gubernatorial election in November, and in the following month resigned as leader of the PPD. His successor as party leader, Victoria Muñoz Mendoza, was defeated in the election by the PNP candidate, Pedro Rosselló. The leadership of the PPD subsequently passed to Héctor Luis Acevedo.

Rosselló, who took office in January 1993, announced that a further referendum on Puerto Rico's future constitutional status would be held during the year. The Government proceeded with legislation rescinding the removal, in 1991, of English as an official language of the island. The referendum, which took place in November 1993, resulted in a 48% vote favouring the retention of Commonwealth status, with 46% of voters supporting accession to statehood and 4% advocating full independence.

In July 1996 a committee of the US House of Representatives unanimously recommended that Puerto Rican voters be given an opportunity, before 1998, to choose whether to retain the island's present status, or to proceed to statehood or full self-government. A preference for change would be followed by a 10-year 'Transition Plan' based on the result, during which time ballots would be held periodically to confirm the direction of the Plan. These proposals, however, were opposed by the Resident Commissioner representing the Puerto Rican Government in the House of Representatives, and were withdrawn in late 1996.

At elections held in November 1996 Rosselló was re-elected as Governor. The PNP retained control of both chambers of the legislature. During the campaign, the levels of minimum wages on the island, together with the recent abolition by US President, Bill Clinton, of federal tax exemptions for US companies establishing plants in Puerto Rico, formed the main political issues.

Debate on the Territory's constitutional future intensified during 1997. In November, following a decision by the US Supreme Court expressly recognizing Puerto Rican citizenship as distinct from US citizenship, a new political movement, the Pro Patria National Union, was formed to encourage Puerto Ricans formally to renounce their US nationality. In March 1998, by a majority of only one vote, the US House of Representatives passed legislation providing for a referendum to determine the island's future status. Under the referendum plan, a vote in favour of statehood would oblige the US Congress to legislate for a 51st state during 1999, with Puerto Rico's admission to the union following within a 10-year period. In December 1998, however, the Puerto Rican electorate rejected the statehood proposal by a margin of 50% to 47%; 71% of eligible voters participated in the referendum. Rosselló proceeded to describe the result as a reflection of the PNP Government's decline in popularity over domestic issues, and indicated that he was to petition the US Congress to implement measures to facilitate the island's transition to statehood. In June 1999, however, Rosselló unexpectedly announced that he would not seek re-election in the gubernatorial election scheduled to take place in November 2000. In July 2001 the new Governor, Sila María Calderón, voiced support for a further referendum on the island's status during 2002. In July 2002 Calderón announced the creation of a 'Status Committee' to resolve the issue; the Committee was to consist of representatives of the PPD, PNP and PIP, including Colón and Barceló.

An extended period of public protest followed the accidental death, in April 1999, of a civilian security guard during routine US military exercises on the small offshore island of Vieques, the eastern section of which, covering a coastline of 32 km, was used by the US Navy as an ammunition testing range. With support from the PIP, groups of protesters promptly established camps on the firing range, compelling the US Navy temporarily to suspend these operations. Following extended negotiations between the Puerto Rican and US Governments, in January 2000 Rosselló and President Clinton announced a compromise plan to end the protesters' occupation by undertaking that, in return for the resumption of naval exercises in which only dummy ammunition would be used, the US Administration would provide immediate development aid to Vieques of $40m. This figure would rise to $90m. if residents of the island would agree in a referendum (provisionally scheduled for November 2001 but subsequently cancelled—see below) to allow the US Navy to resume live ammunition testing, in which event the Navy would undertake to leave Vieques permanently by 2003. In May 2000, prior to a proposed unilateral resumption of naval exercises (using dummy ammunition), protests on Vieques intensified, and several hundred federal government agents were sent to remove the protesters forcibly. The US Navy subsequently declared a 5-km land and sea 'security area' around the island.

Gubernatorial and legislative elections were held on 7 November 2000. Sila María Calderón of the PPD won 49% of the votes cast and was elected Governor, narrowly defeating Carlos Pesquera of the PNP who obtained 46% of the ballot. The PPD secured 19 seats in the Senate, while the PNP secured eight seats. The PPD also became the largest party grouping in the House of Representatives, securing 27 of the 51 seats. The PNP won 23 seats.

Upon taking office, Calderón announced her administration's repudiation of the agreement on military activity on Vieques signed in January 2000 by Clinton and Rosselló. Military exercises on the island were resumed in April 2001, despite legal challenges and protests. In June the new US President, George W. Bush, announced that the US Navy would end military activity on the island by May 2003. Meanwhile, Calderón announced plans for a referendum on US military activity on Vieques to be held in July 2001; it was postponed until November, but was subsequently cancelled by the US Congress, which ordered the US military to remain on Vieques until an alternative location was found. The US Congress claimed that on-going tests were necessary as part of the US-led 'war on terror' following the terrorist attacks on Washington, DC, and New York in September. (A non-binding referendum had been held in July, in which 68% of voters were in favour of the immediate departure from the island of the US Navy.) Tests resumed in April 2002, amid protests from members of the PIP. In mid-2002 the PIP threatened to call a general strike and instigate a campaign of civil disobedience if the US Navy failed to leave the island by May 2003. The final scheduled bombing exercises took place in February 2003, and the US Navy withdrew from the island on 1 May. The firing range was to become a wildlife reserve. The last remaining base, at Ceiba, was closed on 31 March 2004. In 2006 environmental concerns were raised over underwater detonations carried out by the US Navy as part of its ongoing clean-up operations.

In 2002 several prominent PNP officials who had served in the Rosselló administration went on trial on charges of corruption and in December former education secretary Victor Fajardo was sentenced to 12 years' imprisonment after being convicted of diverting state funds to the PNP. In January 2003 the former Speaker of the House of Representatives under the Rosselló administration, Edison Misla Aldorano, was found guilty of extortion, money-laundering and perverting the course of justice; in the same month a former member of Rosselló's staff was sentenced to 18 months' imprisonment. In March 2004 a legislative ethics committee found Oscar Ramos, a PNP deputy, guilty of bribery charges. However, the party voted not to expel Ramos, prompting the PPD to claim that the PNP was not taking seriously the fight against corruption in public office.

Legislative and gubernatorial elections were held on 2 November 2004. Initial results showed that Aníbal Acevedo Vilá of the ruling PPD won the gubernatorial election by just 3,880 votes, a margin of only 0.2%. Under electoral law a victory by a margin of 0.5% or less was subject to a recount. In December it was announced that, with 99.9% of the votes recounted, Acevedo Vilá had won 48.4% of the ballot, while the PNP's candidate, former Governor Rosselló, attracted 48.2% of the votes cast. The third placed candidate, Rubén Berríos Martínez, representing the PIP, won 2.7%. Having achieved a sufficient margin of votes, Acevedo Vilá was declared the winner and was duly sworn in as Governor on 2 January 2005. In the concurrently held legislative election, the PNP gained control of both houses from the PPD, winning a majority of seats in both the Senate and the House of Representatives (17 and 32, respectively), while the PPD secured nine senate and 18 lower-house seats. The PIP's representation was unchanged, with one member in each chamber of the legislature. Voter turn-out was 81.6%.

In March 2005 both houses of the legislature unanimously approved legislation providing for a referendum in July on whether to petition the US Congress and President Bush to agree to honour the results of a further referendum on how the island's future status should be decided, to be held before the end of 2006. However, the following month, Governor Acevedo Vilá vetoed the legislation on the grounds that it did not make sufficient provision for the option of a constituent assembly, instead of a popular, binding referendum, to decide on the eventual status of the island.

Also in March 2005, there was widespread opposition to the decision by the US Territorial District Court of Puerto Rico to impose the death sentence on two convicted murderers. Capital punishment had been banned in the Territory in 1930, a decision that had been upheld in 2000 by a ruling of the Supreme Court of Puerto Rico that it violated the island's Constitution. However, the ruling was subsequently overturned by the US Court of Appeals, which found that Puerto Rico was subject to US federal law and that the death penalty was applicable in certain cases; this decision was upheld by the US Supreme Court. In early April Acevedo Vilá wrote to the US Attorney-General requesting that the death penalty should not apply to residents of Puerto Rico. In May the jury serving on the trial moved to sentence the two men to life imprisonment.

In May 2005, at the PNP's general assembly, a majority of party members voted that Pedro Rosselló should replace fellow party member Kenneth McClintock Hernández as President of the Senate. McClintock announced that he would refuse to stand down. He received the support of five PNP senators who were consequently suspended from the party, and finally expelled in March 2006, as was McClintock. McClintock continued to serve as President of the Senate and stated that he still considered himself a PNP politician.

In July 2005 Acevedo Vilá vetoed the proposed budget on the grounds that expenses were greater than income and that it was therefore unconstitutional. The Government continued to operate using the previous year's budget. However, in April 2006 Acevedo Vilá announced that the budget was insufficient to provide for the Government's operating expenses until the end of the financial year (30 June) and that non-essential public sector services would be suspended from 1 May unless the legislature approved an emergency loan, to fund the shortfall of US $740m., and the introduction of a 7% sales tax, to finance the loan repayments. The announcement prompted a protest march through San Juan in which more than 45,000 people participated. None the less, it was reported that 45 government agencies closed on 1 May, together with some 1,600 public schools, affecting an estimated 500,000 pupils and rendering some 95,760 workers temporarily unemployed. At a series of demonstrations in the capital, public-sector employees demanded an early resolution to the impasse between the executive and the legislature. However, discussions between Acevedo Vilá and José Aponte Hernández, Speaker of the PNP-controlled House of Representatives, foundered on the proposed rate of tax. An emergency commission was established in May, composed of the Governor, members of the House of Representatives and banking agents, and mediated by the Archbishop of San Juan, Roberto Octavio González Nieves. The initiative resulted in an agreement to secure a loan and to replace excise tax with a general sales and use tax of 5.5%, with revenue to be divided between federal and local government. However, owing to inaccurate phrasing, the legislation that was enacted on 13 May authorized a combined sales tax of 7.0%. A petition filed by PNP deputies in early November requesting the Supreme Court to uphold the intended rate of tax was rejected and the law took effect later that month. In early February 2008 Acevedo Vilá suggested proposals to reduce the sales tax to 2.5% and introduce a new excise tax of 4.5% in order to stimulate the economy, but faced criticism from members of the legislature for failing to reduce government spending.

In September 2005 Filiberto Ojeda Ríos, the leader of the Ejército Popular Boricua (see above), was shot and killed during a raid on his home, in Hormigueros, by agents of the USA's Federal Bureau of Investigation (FBI). The FBI had considered Ojeda Ríos a fugitive since he fled the USA in 1990 while awaiting trial for an armed robbery in 1983. A series of anti-terrorism raids, conducted by the FBI in February 2006 on residences and businesses in San Juan believed to be connected to the Ejército Popular Boricua, led to public anger and demonstrations: the Government had not received prior warning of the operation and, in one raid, pepper spray was used against journalists. No arrests were made, however.

In December 2005 a US presidential task force on the status of Puerto Rico, commissioned by President Bush in December 2003, delivered its findings. It recommended that Congress approve legislation for a two-stage plebiscite to be held in Puerto Rico within a year. In the first stage, the people of Puerto Rico would be given the option to continue as part of the Commonwealth or to seek a change in status. In the event that they chose the latter, a second vote would be held on whether to be incorporated as a state within the USA or become an independent country. Irrespective of the outcome, any decision would have to be approved mutually by the US Congress and the Government of Puerto Rico. While the PNP and the PIP welcomed the report, it was criticized by Governor Acevedo Vilá and the PPD because it omitted autonomy as an option. In January 2006 both houses of the Puerto Rican legislature approved legislation calling on Congress to act on the recommendations of the task force. A series of proposed laws consistent with the findings of the task force was submitted to Congress throughout 2006, while a bill supported by Acevedo Vilá and the PPD was submitted in March 2007. The latter advocated that a constitutional convention choose one of three options: statehood, independence or a new or modified commonwealth status. The proposal provided for a referendum to be held on the recommended option, prior to its submission for debate in Congress.

Acevedo Vilá was the subject of corruption allegations in early 2008 when an investigation by the FBI revealed details of improper campaign financing and tax fraud between 1999 and 2004. On 28 March the Governor was charged on 19 criminal counts relating to the use of illegally obtained donations to eliminate campaign debts and to pay for family holidays and other personal expenses. Among a further 12 associates also indicted were four businessmen from Philadelphia, Pennsylvania (USA), and a Puerto Rican business owner, who were accused of obtaining government contracts in return for making campaign donations. Acevedo Vilá pleaded not guilty to the charges and stated his intention to remain in office—and, indeed, contend for re-election in the November gubernatorial election—despite calls from opposition parties for his resignation.

Government

Executive power is vested in the Governor, elected for a four-year term by universal adult suffrage. The Governor is assisted by an appointed Cabinet. Legislative power is held by the bicameral Legislative Assembly, comprising the Senate (with 27 members) and the House of Representatives (51 members). Additional members may be assigned in each chamber to ensure adequate representation of minority parties. The members of both chambers are elected by direct vote for four-year terms. The Resident Commissioner, also elected for a four-year term, represents Puerto Rico in the US House of Representatives, but is permitted to vote only in committees of the House. Puerto Ricans are citizens of the USA, but those resident in Puerto Rico, while eligible to participate in national party primary elections, may not vote in presidential elections.

Defence

The USA is responsible for the defence of Puerto Rico. Puerto Rico has a paramilitary National Guard numbering about 11,000, which is funded mainly by the US Department of Defense.

Economic Affairs

In the fiscal year ending 30 June 2007, according to official estimates, Puerto Rico's gross national income (GNI) was US $58,712m., equivalent to approximately $14,900 per head. During 1996–2006, it was estimated the population increased at an average annual rate of 0.6%. Gross domestic product (GDP) per head increased, in real terms, by an average of 1.6% per year during 1998–2007, while GDP increased, in real terms, by an average of 2.1% per year over the same period. According to government estimates, GDP increased by 0.9% in 2006 but declined by 1.6% in 2007.

Agriculture, forestry and fishing contributed an estimated 0.5% of GDP in the fiscal year ending 30 June 2007 and employed an average of 1.3% of the working population in the same period, according to preliminary official figures. Dairy produce and other livestock products are the mainstays of the agricultural sector. The principal crops are fruits (principally plantains, bananas and oranges) and coffee. Cocoa cultivation has been successfully introduced, and measures to improve agricultural land use have included the replanting of some sugar-growing areas with rice and the cultivation of plantain trees over large areas of unproductive hill land. Commercial fishing is practised on a small scale. The GDP of the agricultural sector increased, in real terms, at an average rate of 2.1% per year between 1980/81 and 1990/91. Agricultural GDP rose by approximately 1.5% in 1993/94.

According to preliminary official figures, industry (including manufacturing, construction and mining) provided an estimated 43.1% of GDP and employed 18.1% of the working population in 2006/07. Industrial GDP increased, in real terms, at an average annual rate of 2.9% between 1980/81 and 1990/91. It rose by 3.3% in 1993/94.

Mining and construction was estimated to provide about 2.1% of GDP in 2006/07 and construction alone employed 7.4% of the working population in the same fiscal year. Otherwise, Puerto Rico has no commercially exploitable mineral resources, although deposits of copper and nickel have been identified.

Manufacturing is a significant source of income, accounting for an estimated 41.0% of GDP and employing 10.7% of the working population in 2006/07. The principal branch of manufacturing in 2002/03, based on the value of output, was chemical products (accounting for 72.4% of the total sector), mainly drugs and medicines. Other important products were computers, electronic and electrical products (12.6%) and food products (6.0%). The GDP of the manufacturing sector increased, in real terms, by 2.9% per year between 1980/81 and 1990/91. The rate of advance was 3.5% in 1993/94. In 2006 total electricity production stood at 24,870m. kWh.

Services (including electricity, gas and water) provided an estimated 56.4% of GDP and engaged 80.6% of the employed labour force in 2006/07 (including 23.4% employed by the Government). In real terms, the GDP of all service sectors increased at an average rate of 4.9% per year between 1980/81 and 1990/91, and by 4.4% in 1993/94. Tourism is of increasing importance; in 2006/07 tourist arrivals were estimated at 5.1m. visitors (including 1.4m. excursionists), generating revenue totalling US $3,413.9m. Visitors from the US mainland comprised more than 75% of the total number of visitors (excluding excursionists) in 2006/07. The Government planned to add some 5,000 hotel rooms by 2008.

In 2006/07 there was a visible trade surplus of US $14,742.6m. but there was a deficit of $4,861m. on the current account of the balance of payments. In 2006/07 the principal source of imports was the USA (responsible for 50.1% of the total value of imports), which was also the principal market for exports (77.2% of the total). Other important trading partners included Belgium, Germany, Ireland, Japan and the US Virgin Islands. The principal imports in that year were chemicals and related manufactures (particularly pharmaceuticals and medicines, which accounted for 36.4% of the total value of imports), petroleum and coal products and manufactured food products. The principal exports were manufactured chemical products (pharmaceuticals and medicines accounted for 60.9% of total value of exports), medical equipment and supplies and computer and electronic products.

In 2005/06 there was a budget deficit of US $1,801.3m. (excluding other government fund financing), equivalent to 2.1% of GDP in that fiscal year. Puerto Rico's gross public debt at the end of the fiscal year to 30 June 2007 was an estimated $42,818.3m. The annual inflation rate averaged 8.4% in 1996–2006. Consumer prices increased by an average of 14.6% in 2006. Puerto Rico is very densely populated, and unemployment has been a persistent problem, although assisted by the growth in the tourism industry, the jobless rate declined during the 1990s. The average rate of unemployment was estimated at 10.4% in 2006/07.

Puerto Rico holds associate status in the UN Economic Commission for Latin America and the Caribbean (ECLAC, see p. 38) and has observer status in the Caribbean Community and Common Market (CARICOM, see p. 196). Puerto Rico declined to accept associate status in the Association of Caribbean States (ACS), formed in 1994, on the grounds of opposition by the US Government to the inclusion of Cuba. In July 2001 Puerto Rico applied for associate membership of CARICOM; the USA criticized the move, emphasizing that it had authority over the island's foreign policy as long as Puerto Rico held Commonwealth status.

US federal aid programmes are of central importance to the Puerto Rican economy, and the island has also received disaster relief in respect of hurricanes that widely disrupt the Puerto Rican economy intermittently. Economic growth has been inhibited by the lack of an adequate infrastructure. Government programmes of industrial and taxation incentives, aimed at attracting US and foreign investors and encouraging domestic reinvestment of profits and long-term capital investment, have generated growth in the manufacturing and services sectors. However, from 1996 the US Government progressively withdrew a number of important tax exemptions (collectively known as Section 936) enjoyed by US and foreign investors; the last vestiges of Section 936 were ended on 31 December 2006. The Government of Puerto Rico attempted to counteract the economic impact of their removal by seeking to establish the island as a centre for the finishing of Latin American manufactured goods destined for member states of the North American Free Trade Agreement (NAFTA, see p. 338). Following the closure of the US naval base at Ceiba in March 2004 (see Recent History), the former base became the site of the US $6,700m. Portal del Futuro development. The development was expected to create 20,000 direct jobs and a further 50,000 jobs indirectly over the following 30 years. Problems associated with years of local government financial mismanagement crystallized in 2006 when a calamitous budget shortfall precipitated a major political and economic crisis (see Recent History) resulting in a period of economic recession out of step with the region. The introduction of major revisions to the tax system produced some positive results in reducing the fiscal deficit, but the attendant loss in consumer and business confidence prompted Governor Acevedo Vilá, in February 2008, to seek the means by which to effect a compromise upon the scope and relative success of the tax reform initiative. The fiscal balance remained a cause for concern (undermining government investment in industry), and the negative impact in late 2007 and early 2008 of the worsening economic outlook for the USA further depressed the immediate prospects of the potentially lucrative pharmaceuticals and tourism sectors. A further decline in economic growth, exacerbated by political uncertainty surrounding Acevedo Vilá's future in office (see Recent History), seemed likely to exceed 1.0% again in 2007/08.

Education

The public education system is centrally administered by the Department of Education. Education is compulsory for children between six and 16 years of age. In 2005 there were an estimated 563,490 pupils attending public day schools and in 2007/08 an estimated 114,627 pupils attending private schools. The 12-year curriculum, beginning at five years of age, is subdivided into six grades of elementary school, three years at junior high school and three years at senior high school. Vocational schools at the high-school level and kindergartens also form part of the public education system. Instruction is conducted in Spanish, but English is a required subject at all levels. In 2004 there were five universities. The State University system consists of three principal campuses and six regional colleges. In 2005 there were some 101,453 students enrolled in higher education at public institutes. An estimated 31,227 students were enrolled at private institutes of higher education in 2007/08. In 2005/06 US $4,102.0m. of general government expenditure was allocated to education (equivalent to 25.7% of total expenditure).

Public Holidays

2008: 1 January (New Year), 6 January (Epiphany), 14 January (Birthday of Eugenio María de Hostos), 21 January (Martin Luther King Day), 18 February (Presidents' Day), 21 March (Good Friday), 22 March (Emancipation of the Slaves), 21 April (Birthday of José de Diego), 26 May (Memorial Day), 24 June (Feast of St John the Baptist), 4 July (US Independence Day), 21 July (Birthday of Luis Muñoz Rivera), 25 July (Constitution Day), 27 July (Birthday of José Celso Barbosa), 1 September (Labor Day), 13 October (Columbus Day), 11 November (Veterans' Day), 19 November (Discovery of Puerto Rico Day), 27 November (US Thanksgiving Day), 25 December (Christmas Day).

2009: 1 January (New Year), 6 January (Epiphany), 12 January (Birthday of Eugenio María de Hostos), 19 January (Martin Luther King Day), 16 February (Presidents' Day), 22 March (Emancipation of the Slaves), 10 April (Good Friday), 20 April (Birthday of José de Diego), 25 May (Memorial Day), 24 June (Feast of St John the Baptist), 4 July (US Independence Day), 20 July (Birthday of Luis Muñoz Rivera), 25 July (Constitution Day), 27 July (Birthday of José Celso Barbosa), 7 September (Labor Day), 12 October (Columbus Day), 11 November (Veterans' Day), 19 November (Discovery of Puerto Rico Day), 26 November (US Thanksgiving Day), 25 December (Christmas Day).

Weights and Measures

The US system is officially in force. Some old Spanish weights and measures, as well as the metric system, are used in local commerce.

Statistical Survey

Source (unless otherwise stated): Puerto Rico Planning Board, POB 41119, San Juan, 00940-1119; tel. (787) 723-6200; internet www.jp.gobierno.pr.

Area and Population

AREA, POPULATION AND DENSITY

Area (sq km)	8,959*
Population (census results)	
1 April 1990	3,522,037
1 April 2000	
Males	1,833,577
Females	1,975,033
Total	3,808,610
Population (official estimates at mid-year)	
2005	3,912,000
2006	3,928,000
2007†	3,941,000
Density (per sq km) at mid-2007	439.9

* 3,459 sq miles.
† Preliminary.

PRINCIPAL TOWNS
(population estimates at mid-2006)

San Juan (capital)	426,618		Caguas	142,769
Bayamón	221,546		Guaynabo	102,525
Carolina	187,578		Arecibo	102,216
Ponce	181,267			

Source: Government Development Bank for Puerto Rico, *Puerto Rico in Figures*.

BIRTHS, MARRIAGES AND DEATHS

	Registered live births		Registered marriages		Registered deaths	
	Number	Rate (per 1,000)	Number	Rate (per 1,000)*	Number	Rate (per 1,000)
2000	59,460	15.5	25,980	8.9	28,550	7.6
2001	55,983	14.6	28,598	7.4	28,794	7.5
2002	52,871	13.7	25,645	6.6	28,098	7.3

* Rates calculated using estimates of population aged 15 years and over.
Source: Department of Health, Commonwealth of Puerto Rico.

2003 (rounded figures): Births 51,000 (birth rate 13.1 per 1,000); Deaths 28,000 (death rate 7.3 per 1,000).

2004 (rounded figures): Births 51,000 (birth rate 13.2 per 1,000); Deaths 29,000 (death rate 7.5 per 1,000).

2005 (rounded figures): Births 51,000 (birth rate 13.0 per 1,000); Deaths 30,000 (death rate 7.6 per 1,000).

2006 (rounded figures): Births 49,000 (birth rate 12.4 per 1,000); Deaths 28,000 (death rate 7.2 per 1,000).

2007 (rounded figures, preliminary): Births 50,000 (birth rate 12.7 per 1,000); Deaths 29,000 (death rate 7.4 per 1,000).

Source: mainly US Bureau of the Census, Population Division; Department of Health, Commonwealth of Puerto Rico; Puerto Rico Planning Board, Office of the Census.

Expectation of life (years at birth): 76.7 (males 72.4; females 81.0) in 2006 (Source: Pan American Health Organization).

ECONOMICALLY ACTIVE POPULATION
('000 persons aged 16 years and over)

	2004/05	2005/06	2006/07*
Agriculture, forestry and fishing	26	22	16
Mining	1	0	0
Manufacturing	138	136	135
Construction	87	88	94
Trade	261	271	260
Transportation	27	26	23
Communication	17	16	16
Finance, insurance and real estate	43	46	45
Other public utilities	15	16	14
Services	349	355	364
Government	274	280	296
Total employed	1,238	1,256	1,263
Unemployed	147	166	147
Total labour force	1,385	1,422	1,409

* Preliminary figures.

Health and Welfare

KEY INDICATORS

Total fertility rate (children per woman, 2006)	1.9
Under-5 mortality rate (per 1,000 live births, 2004)	11.4
Physicians (per 1,000 head, c. 2001)	1.75
Hospital beds (per 1,000 head, 2002)	3.2
Health expenditure (1994): % of GDP	6.0

Source: mostly Pan American Health Organization.

For other sources and definitions see explanatory note on p. vi.

UNITED STATES COMMONWEALTH TERRITORIES   Puerto Rico

Agriculture

PRINCIPAL CROPS
('000 metric tons)

	2003	2004	2005
Tomatoes	17.9	17.9	18.7
Pumpkins, squash and gourds	13.0	13.0	14.3
Bananas	51.9	56.5	52.2
Plantains	123.2	123.6	76.4
Oranges	17.5	17.7	18.8
Mangoes	12.1	14.0	12.9
Pineapples	17.3	15.3	15.3
Coffee (green)	9.3	10.2	7.9

Aggregate production (may include official, semi-official or estimated data): Total fruits (excl. melons) 232.2 in 2003, 249.3 in 2004, 193.4 in 2005; Total roots and tubers 10.6 in 2003, 12.1 in 2004, 10.8 in 2005; Total vegetables (incl. melons) 51.3 in 2003, 51.2 in 2004, 50.6 in 2005.

2006 Production (incl. aggregates) assumed to be unchanged from 2005 (FAO estimates).

Source: FAO.

LIVESTOCK
('000 head, year ending September)

	2003	2004	2005
Asses, mules or hinnies*	4.5	4.5	4.5
Cattle	420.9	388.2	376.9
Sheep	5.7	5.4	6.1
Goats	4.9	2.9	3.1
Pigs	50.0*	50.0*	48.7
Horses	3.8	5.1	6.4
Chickens	11,140	9,578	12,376

* FAO estimate(s).

2006 Figures assumed to be unchanged from 2005 (FAO estimates).
Source: FAO.

LIVESTOCK PRODUCTS
('000 metric tons)

	2003	2004	2005
Cattle meat	9.7	12.6	9.8
Pig meat	9.2	11.9	10.7
Chicken meat	47.1	49.8	49.6
Cows' milk	361.0	349.6	338.5
Hen eggs	10.7	11.4	11.2

2006 Production assumed to be unchanged from 2005 (FAO estimates).
Source: FAO.

Fishing

(metric tons, live weight)

	2003	2004	2005
Capture	2,919	2,428	2,551
Groupers	90	65	53
Snappers and jobfishes	603	404	498
Seerfishes	94	54	70
Marine fishes	104	41	25
Caribbean spiny lobster	196	158	157
Stromboid conchs	1,141	1,203	1,329
Aquaculture	269	417	417*
Penaeus shrimps	69	166	166*
Total catch	3,188	2,845	2,968*

* FAO estimate.
Source: FAO.

Industry

SELECTED PRODUCTS
(year ending 30 June)

	1995/96	1996/97	1997/98*
Distilled spirits ('000 proof gallons)	25,343	36,292	33,471

* Preliminary.

Electric energy (million kWh): 24,100.1 in 2004; 24,500.0 in 2005; 24,870.0 in 2006 (Source: Government Development Bank for Puerto Rico, *Puerto Rico in Figures*).

Cement ('000 94–lb sacks): 37,173 in 2004; 36,847 in 2005; 36,910 in 2006 (Source: US Geological Survey).

Beer ('000 hectolitres): 317 in 1997; 263 in 1998; 259 in 1999 (Source: UN, *Industrial Commodity Statistics Yearbook*).

Finance

CURRENCY AND EXCHANGE RATES

Monetary Units
United States currency: 100 cents = 1 US dollar (US $).

Sterling and Euro Equivalents (31 December 2007)
£1 sterling = US $2.003;
€1 = US $1.472;
US $100 = £49.92 = €67.93.

BUDGET
(US $ '000, general government operations, year ending 30 June)

Revenue	2003/04	2004/05	2005/06
Income tax	5,061,761	5,564,673	6,181,995
Excise tax	1,924,610	2,101,216	2,013,998
Other taxes	19,211	7,128	15,145
Charges for services	750,978	702,691	828,993
Intergovernmental transfers	3,654,766	4,319,977	4,663,422
Interest	58,914	116,686	117,080
Other revenue	629,426	869,338	334,591
Total	12,099,666	13,681,709	14,155,224

Expenditure	2003/04	2004/05	2005/06
General government services	1,777,365	1,675,428	2,489,093
Public safety	1,765,199	2,409,668	2,108,152
Health	2,176,741	2,344,522	1,429,888
Public housing and welfare	2,738,016	3,320,849	3,130,373
Education	3,474,013	4,177,664	4,101,980
Economic development	868,926	706,066	516,444
Intergovernmental transfers	528,829	—	409,727
Capital outlays	581,788	665,630	502,348
Principal on debt servicing	526,572	391,554	446,281
Interest	737,502	733,931	822,234
Total	15,174,951	16,425,312	15,956,520

* Excluding net financing (US $ '000): 3,239,392 in 2003/04; 2,107,107 in 2004/05; 1,819,389 in 2005/06.

Source: Department of the Treasury, Commonwealth of Puerto Rico.

COST OF LIVING
(Consumer Price Index; base: 2000 = 100)

	2004	2005	2006
Food (incl. beverages)	176.3	212.1	257.1
Fuel and light	110.9	136.5	157.2
Rent	107.5	109.0	110.9
Clothing (incl. footwear)	95.2	95.1	95.5
All items (incl. others)	137.1	156.1	178.9

Source: ILO.

UNITED STATES COMMONWEALTH TERRITORIES Puerto Rico

NATIONAL ACCOUNTS
(US $ million at current prices, year ending 30 June)
Expenditure on the Gross Domestic Product

	2004/05	2005/06	2006/07*
Government final consumption expenditure	10,065.4	10,329.6	10,486.9
Private final consumption expenditure	46,535.4	49,467.8	51,889.4
Gross domestic investment	12,248.5	12,072.0	11,984.7
Net sales to the rest of the world	−15,097.0	−15,136.5	−15,648.6
Gross national product	53,752.4	56,732.9	58,712.4
Exports of goods and services / *Less* Imports of goods and services	29,056.1	30,209.7	30,988.8
GDP in purchasers' values	82,808.5	86,942.6	89,701.2
GDP in constant 1954 prices	11,089.7	11,193.7	11,014.3

* Preliminary.

Gross Domestic Product by Economic Activity

	2004/05	2005/06	2006/07*
Agriculture	374.9	385.0	441.4
Manufacturing	34,534.0	36,546.5	36,716.8
Construction and mining†	1,848.0	1,807.0	1,874.7
Transportation and public utilities‡	5,308.6	5,700.8	5,970.7
Trade	10,216.7	10,708.6	11,060.7
Finance, insurance and real estate	14,267.4	14,998.2	16,335.6
Services	7,964.5	8,241.3	8,529.0
Government	8,150.5	8,424.2	8,586.3
Sub-total	82,664.6	86,811.6	89,515.2
Statistical discrepancy	143.9	131.1	186.0
Total	82,808.5	86,942.6	89,701.2

* Preliminary.
† Mining includes only quarries.
‡ Includes radio and television broadcasting.

BALANCE OF PAYMENTS
(US $ million, year ending 30 June)

	2004/05	2005/06	2006/07*
Merchandise exports	59,900.5	64,999.2	66,077.1
Merchandise imports	−45,998.9	−50,138.0	−51,334.5
Trade balance	13,901.6	14,861.2	14,742.6
Exports of services	6,346.3	6,199.4	6,788.2
Imports of services	−5,205.3	−4,950.5	−5,164.3
Balance on goods and services	15,042.6	16,110.1	16,366.5
Other income received	2,000.3	2,455.6	1,998.6
Other income paid	−32,140.0	−33,702.1	−34,013.8
Balance on goods, services and income	−15,097.4	−15,136.4	−15,648.7
Net transfers and interest	9,296.6	10,040.6	10,787.6
Current balance	−5,800.4	−5,095.9	−4,861.0
Net capital movements	5,631.4	−64.4	4,078.6
Overall balance	−169.0	−5,160.3	−782.4

* Preliminary.

External Trade

PRINCIPAL COMMODITIES
(US $ million, year ending 30 June)

Imports	2004/05	2005/06	2006/07
Mining products	1,347.4	1,231.0	1,510.0
Manufacturing products	35,921.3	39,808.4	42,259.4
Food	2,162.7	2,380.4	2,440.6
Products of petroleum and coal	2,924.5	3,962.1	4,152.8
Chemical products	17,086.8	19,089.0	21,675.9
Basic chemicals	3,211.2	3,543.1	4,150.3
Pharmaceuticals and medicines	12,967.6	14,467.3	16,494.7
Machinery, except electrical	1,111.2	1,267.8	1,266.0
Computer and electronic products	2,833.8	2,707.5	2,932.8
Transport equipment	2,786.2	2,674.3	1,922.3
Motor vehicles	2,454.8	2,325.0	1,608.7
Miscellaneous manufacturing	1,456.0	1,627.5	1,617.9
Total (incl. others)	38,905.2	42,630.2	45,265.8

Exports	2004/05	2005/06	2006/07
Manufacturing products	56,022.9	59,542.1	59,378.1
Food	3,626.0	3,956.2	3,751.5
Chemicals	37,191.0	38,618.9	39,587.8
Pharmaceuticals and medicines	34,712.2	35,970.3	36,567.9
Computer and electronic products	7,090.9	7,452.1	6,885.0
Computers and peripheral equipment	4,144.8	3,838.6	4,023.0
Electrical equipment, appliances and components	1,123.3	1,362.6	1,281.4
Miscellaneous manufacturing	4,010.7	5,164.4	4,788.6
Medical equipment and supplies	3,913.2	4,993.8	4,675.2
Total (incl. others)	56,543.2	60,118.7	60,010.8

PRINCIPAL TRADING PARTNERS
(US $ million, year ending 30 June)

Imports	2004/05	2005/06	2006/07
Brazil	689.9	676.4	672.9
China, People's Republic	n.a.	566.7	644.9
Dominican Republic	643.9	596.4	485.7
Germany	828.0	903.0	871.9
Ireland	7,716.8	7,950.2	9,492.6
Japan	1,554.8	1,834.9	1,661.3
Nigeria	n.a.	n.a.	903.4
Singapore	956.7	592.7	612.2
United Kingdom	524.5	513.4	n.a.
USA	19,133.7	21,502.9	22,662.4
US Virgin Islands	1,264.7	1,486.1	1,377.5
Total (incl. others)	38,905.2	42,629.5	45,265.8

Exports	2004/05	2005/06	2006/07
Belgium	1,335.5	1,464.1	2,013.9
Dominican Republic	845.2	887.0	987.6
France	693.5	410.2	358.8
Germany	544.5	635.5	2,046.3
Italy	414.9	216.3	n.a.
Japan	n.a.	458.3	526.6
Netherlands	1,800.6	2,356.7	2,763.8
Singapore	608.0	849.7	1,119.2
Spain	n.a.	n.a.	353.6
United Kingdom	749.2	693.8	935.0
USA	46,703.0	49,651.8	46,324.0
Total (incl. others)	56,543.2	60,118.7	60,010.8

Transport

ROAD TRAFFIC
(motor vehicles registered at 31 December)

	2004	2006*
Passenger cars	2,210,998	2,341,820
Buses and coaches	3,308	3,503
Lorries (trucks) and vans	36,063†	100,841
Motorcycles	31,770	91,082

* Data for 2005 were not available.
† Privately-owned vehicles only.

Source: Federal Highway Administration, US Department of Transportation, *Highway Statistics*.

SHIPPING
(Port of San Juan, year ending 30 June)

	2004/05	2005/06	2006/07
Cruise passenger movements	1,386,211	1,299,323	1,374,379
Cruise-ship calls	606	550	563
Cargo movements ('000 short tons)	10,041.3	9,707.3	9,609.5

Source: Puerto Rico Ports Authority.

CIVIL AVIATION
(year ending 30 June)

	2004/05	2005/06	2006/07
Luis Muñoz Marín International Airport			
Passenger movements ('000)	10,677.7	10,680.8	10,321.2
Freight (million lbs)	551.8	541.0	521.4
Regional airports			
Passenger movements ('000)	818.5	1,008.1	1,129.5
Freight (million lbs)	257.0	266.3	255.5

Source: Puerto Rico Ports Authority.

Tourism

(year ending 30 June)

	2004/05	2005/06	2006/07*
Total visitors ('000)	3,685.9	3,722.0	3,687.0
From USA	2,828.6	2,910.7	2,867.3
From US Virgin Islands	18.8	19.2	19.4
From elsewhere	838.5	792.1	800.3
Excursionists (incl cruise passengers)	1,386.9	1,300.9	1,375.4
Expenditure ($ million)	3,238.6	3,369.3	3,413.9

* Preliminary figures.

Communications Media

	2003	2004	2005
Telephones ('000 main lines in use)	1,212.8	1,111.9	1,037.7
Mobile cellular telephones ('000 subscribers)	1,860.0	2,682.0	3,353.8
Internet users ('000)	764.0	862.0	915.6
Broadband subscribers ('000)	54.3	86.3	118.3

Television receivers ('000 in use): 1,270 in 1999.

Radio receivers ('000 in use): 2,840 in 1997.

Facsimile machines ('000 in use): 543 in 1993.

Daily newspapers (1996): 3; average circulation ('000 copies) 475.

Non-daily newspapers (1988 estimates): 4; average circulation ('000 copies) 106.

Sources: UNESCO, *Statistical Yearbook*; UN, *Statistical Yearbook*; International Telecommunication Union.

Education

(public education at fall 2005, unless otherwise indicated)

	Institutes	Teachers	Enrolment
Elementary and secondary	1,523*	42,036	563,490
Post-secondary†	17‡	14,557§	67,990

* 2005/06.
† Excluding adult (enrolment 33,463 in 2005) and vocational education.
‡ 2006/07.
§ Four-year full-time equivalent teaching staff.

Adult and vocational education: 80 institutes (private only); 33,463 students enrolled (public only).

Source: National Center for Education Statistics, US Department of Education.

Private education (accredited private institutions, 2007/08 unless otherwise indicated): Institutes 145 (2003/04); Pre-primary enrolment 26,534; Elementary and secondary enrolment 114,627; Post-secondary enrolment 31,227 (Source: Consejo General de Educacíon, San Juan).

Adult literacy rate (UNESCO estimates): 94.1% (males 93.9%; females 94.4%) in 2002 (Source: UNESCO Institute for Statistics).

Directory

The Constitution

RELATIONSHIP WITH THE USA

On 3 July 1950 the Congress of the United States of America adopted Public Law No. 600, which was to allow 'the people of Puerto Rico to organize a government pursuant to a constitution of their own adoption'. This Law was submitted to the voters of Puerto Rico in a referendum and was accepted in the summer of 1951. A new Constitution was drafted in which Puerto Rico was styled as a Commonwealth, or estado libre asociado, 'a state which is free of superior authority in the management of its own local affairs', though it remained in association with the USA. This Constitution, with its amendments and resolutions, was ratified by the people of Puerto Rico on 3 March 1952, and by the Congress of the USA on 3 July 1952; and the Commonwealth of Puerto Rico was established on 25 July 1952.

Under the terms of the political and economic union between the USA and Puerto Rico, US citizens in Puerto Rico enjoy the same privileges and immunities as if Puerto Rico were a member state of the Union. Puerto Rican citizens are citizens of the USA and may freely enter and leave that country.

The Congress of the USA has no control of, and may not intervene in, the internal affairs of Puerto Rico.

Puerto Rico is exempted from the tax laws of the USA, although most other federal legislation does apply to the island. Puerto Rico is represented in the US House of Representatives by a non-voting delegate, the Resident Commissioner, who is directly elected for a four-year term. The island has no representation in the US Senate.

There are no customs duties between the USA and Puerto Rico. Foreign products entering Puerto Rico—with the single exception of coffee, which is subject to customs duty in Puerto Rico, but not in the USA—incur the same customs duties as would be paid on their entry into the USA.

The US social security system is extended to Puerto Rico, except for unemployment insurance provisions. Laws providing for economic co-operation between the Federal Government and the States of the Union for the construction of roads, schools, public health services and similar purposes are extended to Puerto Rico. Such joint programmes are administered by the Commonwealth Government.

Amendments to the Constitution are not subject to approval by the US Congress, provided that they are consistent with the US federal Constitution, the Federal Relations Act defining federal relations with Puerto Rico and Public Law No. 600. Subject to these limitations, the Constitution may be amended by a two-thirds' vote of the Puerto Rican Legislature and by the subsequent majority approval of the electorate.

BILL OF RIGHTS

No discrimination shall be made on account of race, colour, sex, birth, social origin or condition, or political or religious ideas. Suffrage shall be direct, equal and universal for all over the age of 18. Public property and funds shall not be used to support schools other than State schools. The death penalty shall not exist. The rights of the individual, of the family and of property are guaranteed. The

Constitution establishes trial by jury in all cases of felony, as well as the right of habeas corpus. Every person is to receive free elementary and secondary education. Social protection is to be afforded to the old, the disabled, the sick and the unemployed.

THE LEGISLATURE

The Legislative Assembly consists of two chambers, the members of which are elected by direct vote for a four-year term. The Senate is composed of 27 members, who must be over 30 years of age. The House of Representatives is composed of 51 members, of whom 40 are elected on a constituency basis, and a further 11 are at large members, elected by proportional representation. Representatives must be over 25 years of age. The Constitution guarantees the minority parties additional representation in the Senate and the House of Representatives, which may fluctuate from one quarter to one third of the seats in each House.

The Senate elects a President and the House of Representatives a Speaker from their respective members. The sessions of each house are public. A majority of the total number of members of each house constitutes a quorum. Either house can initiate legislation, although bills for raising revenue must originate in the House of Representatives. Once passed by both Houses, a bill is submitted to the Governor, who can either sign it into law or return it, with his reasons for refusal, within 10 days. If it is returned, the Houses may pass it again by a two-thirds' majority, in which case the Governor must accept it.

The House of Representatives, or the Senate, can impeach one of its members for treason, bribery, other felonies and 'misdemeanours involving moral turpitude'. A two-thirds' majority is necessary before an indictment may be brought. The cases are tried by the Senate. If a Representative or Senator is declared guilty, he is deprived of his office and becomes punishable by law.

THE EXECUTIVE

The Governor, who must be at least 35 years of age, is elected by direct suffrage and serves for four years. Responsible for the execution of laws, the Governor is Commander-in-Chief of the militia and has the power to proclaim martial law. At the beginning of every regular session of the Assembly, in January, the Governor presents a report on the state of the treasury, and on proposed expenditure. The Governor chooses the Secretaries of Departments, subject to the approval of the Legislative Assembly. These are led by the Secretary of State, who replaces the Governor at need.

LOCAL GOVERNMENT

The island is divided into 78 municipal districts for the purposes of local administration. The municipalities comprise both urban areas and the surrounding neighbourhood. They are governed by a mayor and a municipal assembly, both elected for a four-year term.

The Government

HEAD OF STATE

Governor: ANÍBAL ACEVEDO VILÁ (took office 2 January 2005).

EXECUTIVE
(April 2008)

Secretary of State: FERNANDO J. BONILLA ORTIZ.
Secretary of the Interior: ANÍBAL JOSÉ TORRES.
Secretary of Justice: ROBERTO SÁNCHEZ RAMOS.
Secretary of the Treasury: JUAN CARLOS MÉNDEZ TORRES.
Secretary of Education: RAFAEL ARAGUNDE TORRES.
Secretary of the Family: FÉLIX MATOS.
Secretary of Labor and Human Resources: ROMÁN M. VELASCO GONZÁLEZ.
Secretary of Transportation and Public Works: GABRIEL ALCARÁZ EMMANUELLI.
Secretary of Health: ROSA PÉREZ PERDOMO.
Secretary of Agriculture: SALVADOR RAMÍREZ CARDONA.
Secretary of Housing: JORGE RIVERA JIMÉNEZ.
Secretary of Natural and Environmental Resources: JAVIER VÉLEZ AROCHO.
Secretary of Consumer Affairs: ALEJANDRO GARCÍA PADILLA.
Secretary of Sports and Recreation: DAVID E. BERNIER RIVERA.
Secretary of Economic Development and Commerce: JORGE P. SILVA PURAS.
Attorney-General: SALVADOR J. ANTONETTI STUTTS.
Resident Commissioner in Washington: LUIS FORTUÑO.

GOVERNMENT OFFICES

Office of the Governor: La Fortaleza, POB 9020082, PR 00902-0082; tel. (787) 721-7000; fax (787) 724-1472; e-mail secretariomail@fortaleza.gobierno.pr; internet www.fortaleza.gobierno.pr.

Department of Agriculture: POB 10163, Santurce, PR 00908-1163; tel. (787) 721-2120; fax (787) 723-8512; e-mail webmaster@agricultura.pr; internet www.agricultura.gobierno.pr.

Department of Consumer Affairs: POB 41059, Minillas Station, San Juan, PR 00940-1059; tel. (787) 722-7555; fax (787) 726-0077; e-mail webmaster@daco.gobierno.pr; internet www.daco.gobierno.pr.

Department of Economic Development and Commerce: 355 Avda Roosevelt, Suite 401, Hato Rey, PR 00918; internet www.ddecpr.com; tel. (787) 765-2900; fax (787) 753-6874.

Department of Education: Avda Teniente César González, esq. Calle Juan Calaf, Urb. Industrial Tres Monjitas, San Juan, PR 00919-0759; POB 190759, Hato Rey, PR 00917; tel. (787) 759-2000; fax (787) 250-0275.

Department of the Family: POB 11398, Santurce, San Juan, PR 00910-1398; tel. (787) 294-4900; fax (787) 294-0732; internet www.familia.gobierno.pr.

Department of Health: POB 70184, San Juan, PR 00936-8184; tel. (787) 274-7676; e-mail webmaster@salud.gov.pr; internet www.salud.gov.pr.

Department of Housing: 606 Avda Barbosa, Juan C. Cordero, San Juan, PR 00928-1365; Apdo 21365, Rio Piedras, PR 00928; tel. (787) 274-2527; fax (787) 758-9263; e-mail mcardona@vivienda.gobierno.pr; internet www.vivienda.gobierno.pr.

Department of Justice: POB 9020192, San Juan, PR 00902-0192; tel. (787) 721-2900; fax (787) 724-4770; e-mail aalamo@justicia.gobierno.pr; internet www.justicia.gobierno.pr; incl. the Office of the Attorney-General.

Department of Labor and Human Resources: Edif. Prudencio Rivera Martínez, 505 Avda Muñoz Rivera, Hato Rey, PR 00918; tel. (787) 754-5353; fax (787) 753-4201; e-mail lortiz@dtrh.gobierno.pr; internet www.dtrh.gobierno.pr.

Department of Natural and Environmental Resources: Carretera 8838, Km 6.3, Sector El Cinco, Río Piedras, POB 366147, San Juan, PR 00936; tel. (787) 999-2200; fax (787) 723-4255; e-mail webmaster@drna.gobierno.pr; internet www.drna.gobierno.pr.

Department of Recreation and Sports: 1611 Antiguo Edif. del Fondo del Seguro del Estado, Avda Fernández Juncos, esq. Calle Bolívar, San Juan, PR 00902-3207; POB 9023207, Rio Piedras, PR 00909; tel. (787) 721-2800; fax (787) 728-0736; e-mail mraffaele@drd.gobierno.pr; internet www.drd.gobierno.pr.

Department of State: Apdo 9023271, San Juan, PR 00902-3271; tel. (787) 721-1768; fax (787) 723-3304; e-mail estado@gobierno.pr; internet www.estado.gobierno.pr.

Department of Transportation and Public Works: POB 41269, San Juan, PR 00940; tel. (787) 722-2929; fax (787) 728-8963; e-mail servciud@act.dtop.gov.pr; internet www.dtop.gov.pr.

Department of the Treasury: POB 9024140, San Juan, PR 00902-4140; tel. (787) 723-7085; e-mail infoserv@hacienda.gobierno.pr; internet www.hacienda.gobierno.pr.

Gubernatorial Election, 2 November 2004

Candidate	Votes	%
Aníbal Acevedo Vilá (PPD)	963,303	48.40
Pedro Rosselló González (PNP)	959,737	48.22
Rubén Berríos Martínez (PIP)	54,551	2.74
Total (incl. others)*	1,990,372	100.00

* Including 4,960 blank votes and 4,042 spoiled votes.

Legislature

LEGISLATIVE ASSEMBLY

Senate

President of the Senate: KENNETH MCCLINTOCK HERNÁNDEZ.

Election, 2 November 2004

Party	Seats
PNP	17
PPD	9
PIP	1
Total	27

UNITED STATES COMMONWEALTH TERRITORIES

Puerto Rico

House of Representatives

Speaker of the House: José Aponte Hernández.

Election, 2 November 2004

Party	Seats
PNP	32
PPD	18
PIP	1
Total	**51**

Election Commission

Comisión Estatal de Elecciones de Puerto Rico (CEE): Avda Arterial B 500, Hato Rey, San Juan, PR 00919; POB 195552, San Juan, PR 00919-5552; tel. (787) 294-1190; e-mail hava@cee.gobierno.pr; internet www.ceepur.org; f. 1977; independent; Pres. Ramón E. Gómez-Colón; Dir Yvonne Rivera Picorelli.

Political Organizations

Frente Socialista: 103 Américo Miranda, POB 70359, San Juan, PR 00936; e-mail informacion@frentesocialista.org; internet es.geocities.com/frentesocialistapr; f. 2001; mem. orgs incl. the Partido Revolucionario de los Trabajadores Puertorriqueños (PRTP—Los Macheteros) and Movimiento Socialista de Trabajadores

 Movimiento Socialista de Trabajadores (MST): Apdo 22699, Estación UPR, San Juan, PR 00931-2699; e-mail info@bandera.org; internet www.bandera.org; f. 1982 by merger of the Movimiento Socialista Popular and Partido Socialista Revolucionario; pro-independence; mainly composed of workers and university students.

Movimiento Independentista Nacional Hostosiano (MINH): f. 2004 by merger of the Congreso Nacional Hostosiano and Nuevo Movimiento Independentista (fmr mems of the Partido Socialista Puertorriqueño); pro-independence; Co-Pres Julio Muriente Pérez, Noel Colón Martínez.

Partido Independentista Puertorriqueño (PIP) (Puerto Rican Independence Party): 963 F. D. Roosevelt Ave, Hato Rey, San Juan PR 00920-2901; e-mail pipnacional@independencia.net; internet www.independencia.net; f. 1946; advocates full independence for Puerto Rico as a socialist-democratic republic; Leader Rubén Berríos Martínez; Exec. Pres. Fernando Martín; Sec.-Gen. Juan Dalmau Ramírez; c. 6,000 mems.

Partido Nuevo Progresista (PNP) (New Progressive Party): POB 1992, Fernández Zuncos Station, San Juan 00910-1992; tel. (787) 289-2000; e-mail dannyls@caribe.net; internet www.pnp.org; f. 1967; advocates eventual admission of Puerto Rico as a federated state of the USA; Pres. Luis G. Fortuño Burset; c. 225,000 mems.

Partido Popular Democrático (PPD) (Popular Democratic Party): Comité Central PPD, Puerta de Tierra, POB 9065788 San Juan, PR 00906-5788; tel. (787) 721-2001; e-mail lherrero@ppdpr.net; internet www.ppdpr.net; f. 1938; supports continuation and improvement of the present Commonwealth status of Puerto Rico; Pres. and Leader Aníbal Acevedo Vilá; c. 950,000 mems.

Partido Puertorriqueños por Puerto Rico (Puerto Ricans for Puerto Rico—PPR): POB 9858, San Juan, PR 00908; tel. (787) 622-0002; fax (787) 725-0001; e-mail contacto@popuertorico.com; internet www.porpuertorico.com; f. 2003 as an ecological ('green') party; formally registered as political party in 2007; promotes citizen participation, sustainable devt and quality of life; Pres. Rogelio Figueroa.

Pro Patria National Union: seeks independence for Puerto Rico; encourages assertion of distinct Puerto Rican citizenship as recognized by US Supreme Court in 1997; Leader Fufi Santori.

Puerto Rican Republican Party: Suite 203, 1629 Avda Piñero, San Juan, PR 00920; tel. (787) 793-8084; e-mail cchardon@goppr.org; internet www.goppr.org; Chair. Dr Tiody de Jesús de Ferré; Exec. Dir Annie J. Mayol.

Puerto Rico Democratic Party: POB 19328, San Juan, PR 00910-3939; tel. (787) 274-2921; fax 759-9075.

Refundación Comunista Puerto Rico: Organización RC, POB 13362, San Juan, PR 00908-3362; e-mail refundacionpcp@yahoo.es; internet www.refundacioncomunistapr.com; f. 2001; Marxist-Leninist; pro-independence; maintains close relations with the Frente Socialista; Contact Aballarde Rojo.

Judicial System

The Judiciary is vested in the Supreme Court and other courts as may be established by law. The Supreme Court comprises a Chief Justice and up to six Associate Justices, appointed by the Governor with the consent of the Senate. The lower Judiciary consists of Superior and District Courts and Municipal Justices equally appointed.

 There is also a US Federal District Court, whose judges are appointed by the President of the USA. Judges of the US Territorial District Court are appointed by the Governor.

Supreme Court of Puerto Rico

POB 2392, Puerta de Tierra, San Juan, PR 00902-2392; tel. (787) 724-3551; fax (787) 725-4910; e-mail buzon@tribunales.gobierno.pr; internet www.tribunalpr.org.

Chief Justice: Federico Hernández Denton.

Justices: Francisco Rebollo López, Efraín E. Rivera Pérez, Liana Fiol Matta, Anabelle Rodríguez Rodríguez.

US Territorial District Court for Puerto Rico

Clemente Ruiz-Nazario US Courthouse & Federico Degetau Federal Bldg, 150 Carlos Chardón St, Hato Rey, PR 00918; tel. (787) 772-3011; fax (787) 766-5693; internet www.prd.uscourts.gov.

Judges: José A. Fusté (Chief Judge), Carmen C. Cerezo, Daniel R. Domínguez, Jay A. García-Gregory, Aida M. Delgado-Colón, Gustavo A. Gelpí, Francisco A. Besosa, Juan R. Torruella.

Religion

About 73% of the population belonged to the Roman Catholic Church at the end of 2005. The Protestant churches active in Puerto Rico include the Episcopalian, Baptist, Presbyterian, Methodist, Seventh-day Adventist, Lutheran, Mennonite, Salvation Army and Christian Science. There is a small Jewish community numbering around 2,500 adherents.

CHRISTIANITY

The Roman Catholic Church

Puerto Rico comprises one archdiocese and four dioceses. At 31 December 2005 there were 2,853,027 adherents.

Bishops' Conference of Puerto Rico

POB 40682, San Juan, PR 00940-0682; tel. (787) 728-1650; fax (787) 728-1654; e-mail ceppr@coqui.net.

f. 1960; Pres. Rt Rev. Roberto Octavio González Nieves (Archbishop of San Juan de Puerto Rico).

Archbishop of San Juan de Puerto Rico: Rt Rev. Roberto Octavio González Nieves, Arzobispado, Calle San Jorge 201, Santurce, POB 00902-1967; tel. (787) 725-4975; fax (787) 723-4040; e-mail cancilleria@arqsj.org.

Other Christian Churches

Episcopal Church of Puerto Rico: POB 902, St Just, PR 00978; tel. (787) 761-9800; fax (787) 761-0320; e-mail iep@episcopalpr.org; internet www.episcopalpr.org; f. 1872; diocese of the Episcopal Church in the USA, part of the Anglican Communion; Leader Bishop Rt Rev. David Andrés Alvarez; 42,000 baptized mems.

Puerto Rico Council of Churches: Calle El Roble 54, Apdo 21343, Río Piedras, San Juan, PR 00928; tel. (787) 765-6030; fax (787) 765-5977; f. 1954 as the Evangelical Council of Puerto Rico; Pres. Rev. Héctor Soto; Exec. Sec. Rev. Cruz A. Negrón Torres; 8 mem. churches.

BAHÁ'Í FAITH

National Spiritual Assembly: POB 11603, San Juan, PR 00910-2703; tel. (787) 763-0982; fax (787) 753-4449; e-mail bahaipr@prtc.net; internet www.bahaipr.org.

JUDAISM

Sha'are Zedek Synagogue-Community Center: 903 Avda Ponce de León, Santurce, San Juan, PR 00907; tel. (809) 724-4157; fax (809) 722-4157; f. 1942; Conservative congregation with 250 familiesRabbi Gabriel Frydman.

There is also a reform congregation with 60 families.

The Press

Puerto Rico has high readership figures for its few newspapers and magazines, as well as for mainland US periodicals. Several newspapers have a large additional readership among the immigrant communities in New York.

DAILIES
(m = morning; s = Sunday)

El Nuevo Día: Parque Industrial Amelia, Carretera 165, Guaynabo; POB 9067512, San Juan, PR 00906-7512; tel. (787) 641-8000; fax

UNITED STATES COMMONWEALTH TERRITORIES

Puerto Rico

(787) 641-3924; e-mail laferre@elnuevodia.com; internet www.endi.com; f. 1970; Chair. and Editor María Luisa Ferré Rangel; Pres. María Eugenia Ferré Rangel; Dir Luis Alberto Ferré Rangel; circ. 202,212 (m), 254,769 (s).

Primera Hora: Parque Industrial Amelia, Calle Diana Lote 18, Guaynabo, PR 00966; POB 2009, Cataño, PR 00963-2009; tel. (787) 641-5454; fax (787) 641-4472; internet www.primerahora.com; Pres. and Editor Antonio Luis Ferré; Dir Jorge Cabezas; Gen. Man. Juan Mario Alvarez Cartaña; circ. 133,483 (m), 92,584 (Sat.).

The San Juan Star: POB 364187, San Juan, PR 00936-4187; tel. (787) 782-4200; fax (787) 783-5788; internet www.thesanjuanstar.com; f. 1959; English; Pres. and Publr Gerry Angulo; Gen. Man. Salvador Hasbún; circ. 50,000.

El Vocero de Puerto Rico: Apdo 7515, San Juan, PR 00906-7515; tel. (787) 721-2300; fax (787) 722-0131; e-mail opinion@vocero.com; internet www.vocero.com; f. 1974; Publr and Editor Gaspar Roca; circ 143,150 (m), 123,869 (Sat.).

PERIODICALS

BuenaVIDA: 1700 Fernández Juncos Ave, San Juan, PR 00909; tel. (787) 728-7325; f. 1990 as Buena Salud; monthly; health and fitness; Editor Ivonne Longueira; circ. 61,000.

Caribbean Business: 1700 Fernández Juncos Ave, San Juan, PR 00909-2938; POB 12130, San Juan, PR 00914-0130; tel. (787) 728-9300; fax (787) 726-1626; e-mail cbeditor@casiano.com; internet www.casiano.com/html/cb.html; f. 1973; weekly; business and finance; Editor Elisabeth Román; circ. 45,000.

Educación: c/o Dept of Education, POB 190759, Hato Rey Station, San Juan, PR 00919; f. 1960; 2 a year; Spanish; Editor José Galarza Rodríguez; circ. 28,000.

La Estrella de Puerto Rico: 165 Calle París, Urb. Floral Park, Hato Rey, PR 00917; tel. (787) 754-4440; fax (787) 754-4457; internet www.estrelladepr.com; f. 1983; weekly; Spanish and English; Editor-in-Chief Frank Gaud; circ. 123,500.

Imagen: 1700 Fernández Juncos Ave, Stop 25, San Juan, PR 00909-2999; tel. (787) 728-4545; fax (787) 728-7325; e-mail imagen@casiano.com; internet www.casiano.com/html/imagen.html; f. 1986; monthly; women's interest; Editor Annette Oliveras; circ. 80,000.

Qué Pasa: Loiza St Station, POB 6338, San Juan, PR 00914; tel. (787) 728-3000; fax (787) 728-1075; internet www.casiano.com/html/quepasa.html; f. 1948; quarterly; English; publ. by Puerto Rico Tourism Co; official tourist guide; Editor Ronald Flores; circ. 120,000.

Resonancias: Instituto de Cultura Puertorriqueña, Oficina de Publicaciones, Ventas y Mercadeo. POB 9024184, San Juan, PR 00902-4184; tel. (787) 724-4215; fax (787) 723-0168; e-mail revista@icp.gobierno.pr; internet www.icp.gobierno.pr; f. 2000; 2 a year; Spanish; Puerto Rican and general culture and music; Editor Gloria Tapia; circ. 3,000.

Revista Colegio de Abogados de Puerto Rico: POB 9021900, San Juan, PR 00902-1900; tel. (787) 721-3358; fax (787) 725-0330; e-mail abogados@prtc.net; f. 1914; quarterly; Spanish; law; Editor Lic. Alberto Medina; circ. 10,000.

Revista del Instituto de Cultura Puertorriqueña: Oficina de Publicaciones, Ventas y Mercadeo, POB 9024184, San Juan, PR 00902-4184; tel. (787) 721-0901; e-mail revista@icp.gobierno.pr; internet www.icp.gobierno.pr; f. 1958; 2 a year; Spanish; arts, literature, history, theatre, Puerto Rican culture; Editor Gloria Tapia; circ. 3,000.

La Semana: Calle Cristóbal Colón, esq. Ponce de León, Casilla 6527, Caguas 00725; tel. (787) 743-6537; e-mail lasemana@lasemana.com; internet www.lasemana.com; weekly; f. 1963; Spanish; regional interest; Gen. Man. Marjorie M. Rivera Rivera.

TeVe Guía: San Juan, PR; weekly; TV listings; circ. 470,000 (monthly).

La Torre: POB 23322, UPR Station, San Juan, PR 00931-3322; tel. (787) 758-0148; fax (787) 753-9116; e-mail ydef@hotmail.com; f. 1953; publ. by University of Puerto Rico; quarterly; literary criticism, linguistics, humanities; Editor Yudit de Ferdinandy; circ. 1,000.

Vea: POB 190240, San Juan, PR 00919-0240; tel. (787) 721-0095; fax (787) 725-1940; f. 1969; weekly; Spanish; TV, films and celebrities; Editor Enrique Pizzi; circ. 92,000.

Vida Actual: 1700 Fernández Juncos Ave, San Juan, PR 00909; tel. (787) 728-3000; fax (787) 268-0135; internet www.casiano.com/html/vida_actual.html; f. 2000; fortnightly; family and general information; Editor Elsa Fernández Miralles; circ. 120,000.

El Visitante: POB 41305, San Juan, PR 00940-1305; tel. (787) 728-3710; fax (787) 268-1748; e-mail director@elvisitante.biz; internet www.elvisitante.net; f. 1975; weekly; Roman Catholic; Dir José R. Ortiz Valladares; Editor Rev. Efraín Zabala; circ. 59,000.

Publishers

Ediciones Huracán Inc: 874 Baldorioty de Castro, San Juan, PR 00925; tel. (787) 763-7407; fax (787) 753-1486; e-mail edhucan@caribe.net; f. 1975; textbooks, literature, social studies, history; Pres. Carmen Rivera-Izcoa.

Editorial Académica, Inc: 67 Santa Anastacia St, El Vigía, Río Piedras, PR 00926; tel. (787) 760-3879; f. 1988; regional history, politics, government, educational materials, fiction; Dir Fidelio Calderón.

Editorial Cordillera, Inc: POB 192363, San Juan, PR 00919-2363; tel. (787) 767-6188; fax (787) 767-8646; e-mail info@editorialcordillera.com; internet www.editorialcordillera.com; f. 1962; Puerto Rican history, culture and literature, educational, trade; Pres. Patricia Gutiérrez; Sec. and Treas. Adolfo R. López.

Editorial Cultural Inc: POB 21056, Río Piedras, San Juan, PR 00928; tel. (787) 765-9767; f. 1949; general literature and political science; Dir Francisco M. Vázquez.

Editorial Edil, Inc: POB 23088, UPR Station, Río Piedras, PR 00931; tel. (787) 753-9381; fax (787) 250-1407; e-mail editedil@coqui.net; internet www.editorialedil.com; f. 1967; univ. texts, literature, technical and official publs; Man. Dir and Publr Consuelo Andino Ortiz.

Instituto de Cultura Puertorriqueña: Oficina de Publicaciones, Ventas y Mercadeo, POB 9024184, San Juan, PR 00902-4184; tel. (787) 724-0700; fax (787) 723-0168; e-mail revista@icp.gobierno.pr; internet www.icp.gobierno.pr; f. 1955; literature, history, poetry, music, textbooks, arts and crafts; Dir Gloria Tapia.

University of Puerto Rico Press (EDUPR): POB 23322, UPR Station, Río Piedras, San Juan, PR 00931-3322; tel. (787) 250-0435; fax (787) 753-9116; e-mail edupr@upr.edu; f. 1947; general literature, children's literature, Caribbean studies, law, philosophy, science, educational; Exec. Dir Manuel G. Sandoval.

Broadcasting and Communications

TELECOMMUNICATIONS

Junta Reglamentadora de Telecomunicaciones de Puerto Rico: Edif. Capital Center II, 235 Avda Arterial Hostos, Suite 1001, San Juan, PR 00918-1453; tel. (787) 756-0804; fax (787) 756-0814; e-mail correspondencia@jrtpr.gobierno.pr; internet www.jrtpr.gobierno.pr; telecommunications regulator; Pres. Miguel Reyes Dávila.

Puerto Rico Telephone Co (PRTC): POB 360998, San Juan, PR 00936-0998; tel. (787) 782-8282; fax (787) 774-0037; internet www.telefonicapr.com; provides all telecommunications services in Puerto Rico; fmrly state-owned; acquired by America Móvil in 2007; Pres. and CEO Cristina Lambert.

BROADCASTING

There were 120 radio stations and 15 television stations operating in 2002. The only non-commercial stations are the radio station and the two television stations operated by the Puerto Rico Department of Education. The US Armed Forces also operate a radio station and three television channels.

Asociación de Radiodifusores de Puerto Rico (Puerto Rican Radio Broadcasters' Asscn): Caparra Terrace, Delta 1305, San Juan, PR 00920; tel. (787) 783-8810; fax (787) 781-7647; e-mail prbroadcasters@centennialpr.net; f. 1947; Pres. Manuel Santiago Santos; Exec. Dir José A. Ribas Dominicci; 102 mems.

Finance

(cap. = capital; res = reserves; dep. = deposits; brs = branches; amounts in US dollars)

BANKING

Government Bank

Government Development Bank for Puerto Rico (Banco Gubernamental de Fomento para Puerto Rico—BGF): POB 42001, San Juan, PR 00940-2001; tel. (787) 722-2525; fax (787) 721-1443; e-mail gdbpr@bgf.gobierno.pr; internet www.gdb-pur.com; f. 1942; independent govt agency; acts as fiscal (borrowing) agent to the Commonwealth Govt and its public corpns and provides long- and medium-term loans to private businesses; cap. 20.5m., res 46.8m., dep. 5,816.5m. (June 2001); Pres. Jorge Irizarry; Chair. Rafael F. Martínez Margarida.

Autoridad para el Financiamiento de la Vivienda de Puerto Rico: Edif. Capital Center, Arterial Hostos 235, Torre Norte, 11° y 12°, Of. 1201, Hato Rey, PR 00918; tel. (787) 765-7577; fax (787) 754-1440; f. 1961; fmrly Banco y Agencia de Financiamiento de la Vivienda de Puerto Rico; present name adopted in 2001; subsidiary of the Government Development Bank for Puerto Rico; finance agency; helps low-income families to purchase houses; Exec. Dir FERNANDO BERIO MUÑIZ.

Commercial Banks

Banco Bilbao Vizcaya Argentaria Puerto Rico: 15th Floor, Torre BBVA, 258 Muñoz Rivera Ave, San Juan 00918; POB 364745, San Juan, PR 00936-4745; tel. (787) 777-2000; fax (787) 777-2999; internet www.bbvapr.com; f. 1967 as Banco de Mayagüez; taken over by Banco Occidental in 1979; merged with Banco Bilbao Vizcaya, S.A. in 1988; named changed from BBV Puerto Rico in 2000; cap. 138.7m., res, surplus and profits 381.0m., dep. 5,598.9m. (Dec. 2006); Pres. ANTONIO UGUINA; 65 brs.

Banco Popular de Puerto Rico: POB 362708, San Juan, PR 00936-2708; tel. (787) 724-3659; e-mail internet@bppr.com; internet www.bppr.com; f. 1893; cap. 7.0m., res, surplus and profits 1,684.0m., dep. 22,448.0m. (Dec. 2006); Chair., Pres. and CEO RICHARD L. CARRIÓN; 195 brs.

Banco Santander Puerto Rico: 207 Ponce de León Ave, Hato Rey, PR 00919; POB 362589, San Juan, PR 00936-0062; tel. (787) 759-7070; fax (787) 767-7913; internet www.santanderpr.com; f. 1976; cap. 101.2m., res, surplus and profits 486.9m., dep. 7,405.1m. (Dec. 2006); Pres. JOSÉ RAMON GONZALEZ; Chair. and CEO MONICA APARICIO; 67 brs.

Citibank NA: 252 Ponce de León Ave, San Juan, PR 00918; tel. (787) 753-5619; fax (787) 766-3880; Gen. Man. HORACIO IGUST; 14 brs.

Doral Bank: Galería Paseos Mall, Grand Blvd Paseos, Suite 107, San Juan, PR 00926; tel. (787) 725-6060; fax (787) 725-6062; e-mail dbcw@doralbank.com; internet www.doralbank.com; cap. 400m., dep. 2,730m., assets 6,726m. (Dec. 2003); subsidiary of local bank-holding co, Doral Financial Corpn, which completed buyout negotiations with financial group, led by Bear Stearn Cos Inc (USA), in July 2007; 90% investor-owned, through Doral Holdings Delaware, LLC, since July 2007; CEO GLEN R. WAKEMAN; Chair. CALIXTO GARCÍA VELEZ; 37 brs.

Scotiabank de Puerto Rico: Plaza Scotiabank, 273 Ponce de León Ave, esq. Calle Méjico, Hato Rey, PR 00918; POB 362230, San Juan PR 00936-2230; tel. (787) 758-8989; fax (787) 766-7879; internet www.scotiabankpr.com; f. 1910; cap. 23.2m., res, surplus and profits 146.2m., dep. 1,333.8m. (Dec. 2006); Chair. PETER CARDINAL; Pres. and CEO BRUCE BOWEN; 19 brs.

Savings Banks

First BanCorp: First Federal Bldg, 1519 Ponce de León Ave, POB 9146, Santurce, PR 00908-0146; tel. (787) 729-8200; fax (787) 729-8139; internet www.firstbankpr.com; f. 1948, adopted current name in 1998; operates FirstBank Puerto Rico; cap. and res 368.3m., dep. 3,363.0m. (Dec. 2000); Chair. LUIS M. BEAUCHAMP; 45 brs.

Oriental Bank and Trust: Ave Fagot, esq. Obispado M-26, Ponce; tel. (787) 259-0000; fax (787) 259-0700; e-mail jllantin@orientalfg.com; internet www.orientalonline.com; total assets 2,039m. (June 2001); Chair., Pres. and CEO JOSÉ ENRIQUE FERNÁNDEZ.

Ponce Federal Bank, FSB: Villa esq. Concordia, POB 1024, Ponce, PR 00733; tel. (787) 844-8100; fax (787) 848-5380; f. 1958; Pres. and CEO HANS H. HERTELL; 19 brs.

R & G Corporation: POB 2510, Guaynabo, PR 00970; tel. (787) 766-6677; fax (787) 766-8175; internet www.rgonline.com; total assets 4,676m. (Dec. 2001); Chair., Pres. and CEO VÍCTOR J. GALÁN.

SAVINGS AND LOAN ASSOCIATIONS

Caguas Central Federal Savings of Puerto Rico: POB 7199, Caguas, PR 00626; tel. (787) 783-3370; f. 1959; total assets 800m.; Pres. LORENZO MUÑOZ FRANCO.

Westernbank Puerto Rico: 19 West McKinley St, Mayagüez, PR 00680; tel. (787) 834-8000; fax (787) 831-5958; internet www.wbpr.com; cap. and res 250.6m., dep. 2,610.4m. (Dec. 2000); Chair. and CEO FRANK C. STIPES; 31 brs.

Banking Organization

Puerto Rico Bankers' Association: 208 Ponce de León Ave, Suite 1014, San Juan, PR 00918-1002; tel. (787) 753-8630; fax (787) 754-6022; e-mail info@abpr.com; internet www.abpr.com; Pres. RAFAEL ARRILLAGA TORRENS; Vice-Pres. ALVARO JARAMILLO.

INSURANCE

Atlantic Southern Insurance Co: POB 362889, San Juan, PR 00936-2889; tel. (787) 767-9750; fax (787) 764-4707; internet www.atlanticsouthern.com; f. 1945; Chair. DIANE BEAN SCHWARTZ; Pres. RAMÓN L. GALANES.

Caribbean American Life Assurance Co: 273 Ponce de León Ave, Suite 1300, Scotiabank Plaza, San Juan, PR 00917; tel. (787) 250-1199; fax (787) 250-7680; internet www.calac.com; Pres. IVÁN C. LÓPEZ.

Cooperativa de Seguros Multiples de Puerto Rico: POB 363846, San Juan, PR 00936-3846; internet www.segurosmultiples.coop; general insurance; Pres. RENÉ A. CAMPOS CARBONELL.

La Cruz Azul de Puerto Rico: Carretera Estatal 1, Km 17.3, Río Piedras, San Juan, PR 00927; POB 366068, San Juan, PR 00936-6068; tel. (787) 272-9898; fax (787) 272-7867; e-mail scliente@cruzazul.com; internet www.cruzazul.com; Exec. Dir MARKS VIDAL.

FirstBank Insurance Agency, Inc: Las Vistas Shopping Village, Suite 11, 300 Felisa Rincón de Gautier, POB 9146, San Juan, PR 00908-0146; tel. (787) 292-4380; fax (787) 292-4355; internet www.firstbankpr.com; owned by First BanCorp.

Great American Life Assurance Co of Puerto Rico: POB 363786, San Juan, PR 00936-3786; tel. (787) 758-4888; fax (787) 766-1985; e-mail galifepr@galifepr.com; known as General Accident Life Assurance Co until 1998; Pres. ARTURA CARIÓN; Sr Vice-Pres. EDGARDO DIAZ.

National Insurance Co: POB 366107, San Juan, PR 00936-6107; tel. (787) 758-0909; fax (787) 756-7360; internet www.nicpr.com; f. 1961; subsidiary of National Financial Group; Chair., Pres. and CEO CARLOS M. BENÍTEZ, Jr.

Pan American Life Insurance Co: POB 364865, San Juan, PR 00936-4865; tel. (787) 620-1414; fax (787) 999-1250; e-mail jortega@panamericanlife.com; internet www.panamericanlife.com; Regional Pres. JUAN A. ORTEGA; Gen. Man. MAITE MUÑOZGUREN.

Puerto Rican-American Insurance Co: POB 70333, San Juan, PR 00936-8333; tel. (787) 250-5214; fax (787) 250-5371; f. 1920; total assets 119.9m. (1993); Chair. and CEO RAFAEL A. ROCA; Pres. RODOLFO E. CRISCUOLO.

Security National Life Insurance Co: POB 193309, Hato Rey, PR 00919; tel. (787) 753-6161; fax (787) 758-7409; Pres. CARLOS FERNÁNDEZ.

Universal Insurance Group: Calle 1, Lote 10, 3°, Metro Office Park, Guaynabo; POB 2145, San Juan, PR 00922-2145; tel. (787) 793-7202; fax (787) 782-0692; internet www.universalpr.com; f. 1972; comprises Universal Insurance Co, Eastern America Insurance Agency and Caribbean Alliance Insurance Co; Chair. and CEO LUIS MIRANDA CASAÑAS.

There are numerous agents, representing Puerto Rican, US and foreign companies.

Trade and Industry

DEVELOPMENT ORGANIZATION

Puerto Rico Industrial Development Co (PRIDCO): POB 362350, San Juan, PR 00936-2350; 355 Roosevelt Ave, Hato Rey, San Juan, PR 00918; tel. (787) 758-4747; fax (787) 764-1415; internet www.pridco.com; public agency responsible for the govt-sponsored industrial devt programme; Exec. Dir BORIS JASKILLE.

CHAMBERS OF COMMERCE

Chamber of Commerce of Puerto Rico: 100 Calle Tetuán, POB 9024033, San Juan, PR 00902-4033; tel. (787) 721-6060; fax (787) 723-1891; e-mail ebigas@camarapr.net; f. 1913; Pres. BARTOLOMÉ GAMUNDI; Exec. Vice-Pres. EDGARDO BIGAS VALLADARES; 1,800 mems.

Chamber of Commerce of the South of Puerto Rico: 65 Calle Isabel, POB 7455, Ponce, PR 00732-7455; tel. (787) 844-4400; fax (787) 844-4705; e-mail info@camarasur.org; internet www.camarasur.org; f. 1885; Pres. ROLANDO EMMANUELLI JIMÉNEZ; 550 mems.

Chamber of Commerce of the West of Puerto Rico Inc: Edif. Doral Bank, Suite 905, 101 Calle Méndez Vigo Oeste, POB 9, Mayagüez, PR 00681; tel. (787) 832-3749; fax (787) 832-4287; e-mail ccopr@coqui.net; internet www.ccopr.com; f. 1962; Pres. WILLIE PHITTS; 300 mems.

Official Chamber of Commerce of Spain: POB 894, San Juan, PR 00902; tel. and fax (787) 212-5333; e-mail cocep@cocep.org.pe; internet www.cocep.org.pe; f. 1966; promotes Spanish goods; provides information for Spanish exporters and Puerto Rican importers; Pres. JAIME SAENZ DE TEJADA; Gen. Sec. CÉSAR LÓPEZ-DÓRIGA; 300 mems.

Puerto Rico/United Kingdom Chamber of Commerce: 102 San Justo, San Juan, PR 00901; tel. (877) 594-7354; fax (787) 721-7333; e-mail iancourt@bivapr.net; internet users.bivapr.net/iancourt; Chair. Dr IAN COURT; 120 mems.

INDUSTRIAL AND TRADE ASSOCIATIONS

Home Builders' Association of Puerto Rico: 1605 Ponce de León Ave, Condominium San Martín, Santurce, San Juan, PR 00909; tel. (787) 723-0279; Exec. Dir María Elena Cristy; 150 mems.

Pharmaceutical Industry Association of Puerto Rico (PIA-PR): City View Plaza, Suite 407, Guaynabo, PR 00968; tel. (787) 622-0500; fax (787) 622-0503; e-mail info@piapr.com; internet www.piapr.com; Chair. David Carberry; Sec. Daneris Fernández; 19 mem. cos.

Puerto Rico Farm Bureau: 1605 Ponce de León Ave, Suite 403, Condominium San Martín, San Juan, PR 00909-1895; tel. (787) 721-5970; fax (787) 724-6932; f. 1925; Pres. Antonio Alvarez; over 1,500 mems.

Puerto Rico Manufacturers' Association (PRMA): POB 195477, San Juan, PR 00919-5477; tel. (787) 759-9445; fax (787) 756-7670; internet www.prma.com; Pres. Edgardo Fábregas; Exec. Vice-Pres. William Riefkohl.

Puerto Rico United Retailers Center: POB 190127, San Juan, PR 00919-0127; tel. (787) 641-8405; fax (787) 641-8406; e-mail cud@centrounido.com; internet www.centrounido.org; f. 1891; represents small and medium-sized businesses; Pres. Elliott Rivera; 20,000 mems.

UTILITIES

Electricity

Autoridad de Energía Eléctrica (AEE): POB 364267, San Juan, PR 00936-4267; tel. (787) 289-3434; fax (787) 289-4690; e-mail director@prepa.com; internet www.aeepr.com; govt-owned electricity corpn, opened to private co-generators in the mid-1990s; installed capacity of 4,389 MW; Dir Jorge A. Rodríguez Ruiz.

TRADE UNIONS

American Federation of Labor–Congress of Industrial Organizations (AFL–CIO): San Juan; internet www.afl-cio.org; Regional Dir Agustín Benítez; c. 60,000 mems.

Central Puertorriqueña de Trabajadores (CPT): POB 364084, San Juan, PR 00936-4084; tel. (787) 781-6649; fax (787) 277-9290; f. 1982; Pres. Federico Torres Montalvo.

Confederación General de Trabajadores de Puerto Rico: 620 San Antonio St, San Juan, PR 00907; f. 1939; Pres. Francisco Colón Gordiany; 35,000 mems.

Federación del Trabajo de Puerto Rico (AFL-CIO): POB S-1648, San Juan, PR 00903; tel. (787) 722-4012; f. 1952; Pres. Hipólito Marcano; Sec.-Treas. Clifford W. Depin; 200,000 mems.

Puerto Rico Industrial Workers' Union, Inc: POB 22014, UPR Station, San Juan, PR 00931; Pres. David Muñoz Hernández.

Sindicato Empleados de Equipo Pesado, Construcción y Ramas Anexas de Puerto Rico, Inc (Construction and Allied Trades Union): Calle Hicaco 95, Urb. Milaville, Río Piedras, San Juan, PR 00926; f. 1954; Pres. Jesús M. Agosto; 950 mems.

Sindicato de Obreros Unidos del Sur de Puerto Rico (United Workers' Union of South Puerto Rico): POB 106, Salinas, PR 00751; f. 1961; Pres. José Caraballo; 52,000 mems.

Unión General de Trabajadores de Puerto Rico: Apdo 29247, Estación de Infantería, Río Piedras, San Juan, PR 00929; tel. (787) 751-5350; fax (787) 751-7604; f. 1965; Pres. Juan G. Eliza-Colón; Sec.-Treas. Osvaldo Romero-Pizarro.

Unión de Trabajadores de la Industría Eléctrica y Riego de Puerto Rico (UTIER): POB 13068, Santurce, San Juan, PR 00908; tel. (787) 721-1700; e-mail utier@coqui.net; internet www.utier.org; Pres. Ricardo Santos Ramos; 6,000 mems.

Transport

In January 2004 a 17-km urban railway (Tren Urbano), capable of carrying some 300,000 passengers per day, was inaugurated in greater San Juan. The railway took eight years to build and cost some US $2,150m. An extension to Carolina and Minillas was proposed in March 2005, at a projected cost of $900m.

Ponce and Guayama Railway: Aguirre, PR 00608; tel. (787) 853-3810; owned by the Corporación Azucarera de Puerto Rico; transports sugar cane over 96 km of track route; Exec. Dir A. Martínez; Gen. Supt J. Rodríguez.

ROADS

The road network totalled 24,431 km (15,181 miles) in 2003, of which some 94% was paved. A modern highway system links all cities and towns along the coast and cross-country. A highways authority oversees the design and construction of roads, highways and bridges. In April 2002 it was announced that some US $585.6m. was to be invested in projects to improve or expand the road network.

Autoridad de Carreteras: Centro Gubierno Minillas, Edif. Norte, Avda de Diego 23, POB 42007, Santurce, San Juan, PR 00940-2007; tel. (787) 721-8787; fax (787) 727-5456; internet www.dtop.gov.pr/act; Exec. Dir Luis Trinidad Garay.

SHIPPING

There are 11 major ports on the island, the principal ones being San Juan, Ponce and Mayagüez. Other ports include Guayama, Guayanilla, Guánica, Yabucoa, Aguirre, Aguadilla, Fajardo, Arecibo, Humacao and Arroyo. San Juan, one of the finest and longest all-weather natural harbours in the Caribbean, is the main port of entry for foodstuffs and raw materials and for shipping finished industrial products. In 2005 it handled more than 10.0m. metric tons of cargo. Under US cabotage laws all maritime freight traffic between the USA and Puerto Rico must be conducted using US-registered vessels. Passenger traffic is limited to tourist cruise vessels. Work on the US $700m. Las Américas 'megaport' was ongoing in 2008. In April 2005 a high-speed ferry service was launched, connecting San Juan to the islands of Vieques and Culebra.

Autoridad de los Puertos (Puerto Rico Ports Authority): Calle Lindbergh, 64 Antigua Base Naval Miramar, San Juan, PR 00907; POB 362829, San Juan, PR 00936-2829; tel. (787) 723-2260; fax (787) 722-7867; e-mail webmaster@prpa.gobierno.pr; internet www.prpa.gobierno.pr; f. 1942 as the Autoridad de Transporte de Puerto Rico; present name adopted in 1955; manages and administers all ports and airports; Exec. Dir Fernando J. Bonilla.

CIVIL AVIATION

There are two international airports on the island (Luis Muñoz Marín at Carolina, San Juan, and Rafael Hernández at Aguadilla) and nine regional airports. There are also six heliports.

Tourism

An estimated 3.7m. tourists visited Puerto Rico in 2006/07, when revenue from this source was estimated at US $3,414m. Almost 78% of all tourist visitors were from the US mainland. In 2004 there were approximately 12,864 hotel rooms. The Government planned to add a further 5,000 rooms by 2008.

Compañía de Turismo (Puerto Rico Tourism Co): Edif. La Princesa, 2 Paseo La Princesa, POB 9023960, San Juan, PR 00902-3960; tel. (787) 721-2400; fax (787) 722-6238; e-mail drodriguez2@prtourism.com; internet www.gotopuertorico.com; f. 1970; Exec. Dir Terestella González Denton.

UNITED STATES EXTERNAL TERRITORIES

The External or Unincorporated Territories of the USA comprise the Pacific Territories of American Samoa and Guam, the Caribbean Territory of the US Virgin Islands, and a number of smaller islands.

AMERICAN SAMOA

Introductory Survey

Location, Climate, Language, Religion, Flag, Capital

American Samoa comprises the seven islands of Tutuila, Ta'u, Olosega, Ofu, Aunu'u, Rose and Swains. They lie in the southern central Pacific Ocean, along latitude 14°S at about longitude 170°W, about 3,700 km (2,300 miles) south-west of Hawaii. The temperature normally ranges between 21°C (70°F) and 32°C (90°F), and the average annual rainfall is 5,000 mm (197 ins), the greatest precipitation occurring between December and March. English and Samoan, a Polynesian language, are spoken. The population is largely Christian, more than 50% being members of the Christian Congregational Church. The flag has a dark blue field, on which is superimposed a red-edged white triangle (with its apex at the hoist and its base at the outer edge of the flag), containing an eagle, representing the USA, grasping in its talons a yellow *fue* (staff) and *uatogi* (club), Samoan symbols of sovereignty. The capital is Pago Pago, on Tutuila (the officially designated seat of government is the village of Fagatogo).

Recent History

The Samoan islands were first visited by Europeans in the 1700s, but it was not until 1830 that missionaries from the London Missionary Society settled there. In 1878 the Kingdom of Samoa, then an independent state, gave the USA the right to establish a naval base at Pago Pago. The islands were also of interest to the United Kingdom and Germany, but the former withdrew in 1899, leaving the western islands for Germany to govern. The chiefs of the eastern islands ceded their lands to the USA in 1904, and the islands officially became an Unincorporated Territory of the USA in 1922.

Until 1978 American Samoa was administered by a Governor, appointed by the US Government, with a legislature comprising the Senate and the House of Representatives. In November 1977 the first gubernatorial election took place, and in January 1978 Peter Coleman was inaugurated as the islands' Governor. He was re-elected for a second term in November 1980, after three years in office instead of the prescribed four, to allow synchronization with mainland US elections in 1980. At the gubernatorial election of November 1984 A. P. Lutali was elected Governor and Eni Hunkin (who subsequently adopted the use of his chiefly name, Faleomavaega) became Lieutenant-Governor. The High Court of American Samoa had previously ruled that Coleman was ineligible to stand for a third successive term as Governor, as legislation restricted tenure by any individual to two successive terms. In October 1986 a constitutional convention completed a comprehensive redrafting of the American Samoan Constitution. The draft revision, however, had yet to be submitted to the US Congress in the early 21st century. In April 2004 it was announced that the Political Status Study Commission was to examine the territory's situation and submit its recommendations prior to the holding of another constitutional convention.

In July 1988 the Territory's delegate to the US House of Representatives, Fofō Sunia, announced that he would not seek re-election, as he was under official investigation for alleged financial mismanagement. In October he received a prison sentence for fraud. Eni F. H. Faleomavaega replaced Sunia as delegate in November. At the gubernatorial election in November Coleman was re-elected Governor for a third term, and Galea'i Poumele replaced Faleomavaega as Lieutenant-Governor.

In November 1992 Peter Coleman was defeated by A. P. Lutali at the gubernatorial election. At elections to the House of Representatives in November 1994 about one-third of those members who sought re-election were defeated. Faleomavaega was re-elected as non-voting delegate.

Gubernatorial and legislative elections took place in November 1996. An estimated 87% of eligible voters participated in the election, at which only eight of the 18 members seeking re-election to the Fono were successful. At a second round of voting the incumbent Lieutenant-Governor, the Democrat Tauese Sunia, was elected Governor with 51.3% of the votes cast, defeating Leala Peter Reid, Jr, who secured 48.7% of votes. Faleomavaega was re-elected as delegate to the US House of Representatives, winning 56.5% of the votes cast, defeating Gus Hannemann, who won 43.5% of votes.

The decision in July 1997 by the Government of neighbouring Western Samoa to change the country's name to simply Samoa caused some controversy. Legislation approved in March 1998 by the Territory's House of Representatives stated that American Samoa should not recognize the new name, which was viewed by many islanders as serving to undermine their own Samoan identity. Also in response to the change of name, legislation prohibiting citizens of the former Western Samoa from owning land in American Samoa was approved. Nevertheless, some rapprochement followed. In August 2004 plans were announced for greater economic co-operation, and in November a twice-weekly air link commenced operations. However, concerns were expressed at the decision of the Samoan Government in March 2005 to require of American Samoan citizens travelling to Samoa a permit and a passport. In April a bilateral meeting was held in the Samoan capital, and leaders began negotiations on the issue of travel requirements. Meanwhile, in late March the Samoan Government announced plans to open a consulate in American Samoa.

In November 1998 Faleomavaega was re-elected as delegate to the US House of Representatives. In the same month, following a dispute lasting several years, five leading US tobacco companies reached a legal settlement with most of the individual states of the USA and several of its territories, including American Samoa. It was agreed that between 1998 and 2025 American Samoa was to receive a total of some US $29m. in compensation for the harmful effects of cigarette-smoking suffered by its inhabitants.

At elections held on 7 November 2000 Tauese Sunia was narrowly re-elected as Governor, receiving 50.7% of the votes cast, compared with 47.9% for the opposition candidate, Senator Lealaifuaneva. However, following the Chief Electoral Officer's refusal to allow a recount, as requested by Lealaifuaneva (who claimed that absentee ballots had not been properly handled), Lealaifuaneva filed a lawsuit against the Government; this was dismissed by the High Court in early December. At congressional elections, held concurrently, no candidate received the necessary 50% majority, Faleomavaega winning 45.7% of votes cast, compared with 30.3% for Hanneman. A second round of polling took place on 21 November, when Faleomavaega was reported to have won 61.1% of the votes.

The issue of US jurisdiction in the Territory was raised again in September 2001, when the islands' Senate approved a resolution urging discussion with the US Government with regard to the conferral of limited federal jurisdiction to the High Court of American Samoa, the only US territory without a sitting federal judge. A congressional public survey, conducted in the same month, registered wide popular support for a Federal Court and Public Prosecutor. At a meeting of the UN General Assembly in January 2002, the UN accepted American Samoa's proposal of May 2001 to be removed from the list of colonized territories. The Governor had sent a resolution to the UN Committee on Decolonization affirming American Samoa's wish to remain a US territory.

In September 2002 the Territory's immigration procedures were amended to give the Attorney-General, rather than the Immigration Board, the ultimate authority to grant permanent residency status to aliens. The House of Representatives of American Samoa also approved a resolution to repeal legislation automatically conferring US citizenship in the Territory to foreign parents. In the same month the Territory's intelligence agencies claimed that the Speaker of the House of Representatives, Tuanaitau Tuia, had used public funds to purchase a car and to finance private travel for his wife. Meanwhile, in June a former president of the Amerika Samoa Bank (now ANZ Amerika Samoa Bank) was convicted of fraud for his involvement in a scheme that had misappropriated US $75m. of investors' money. Further allegations of corruption in the banking sector followed in 2004. The government-owned Development Bank of American Samoa was being investigated in April of that year by an anti-corruption committee of the Senate, after records suggested favouritism in the approval of loans.

In elections for American Samoa's delegate to the Federal Congress on 6 November 2002, Faleomavaega won 41.3% of the votes cast, Fagafaga Daniel Langkilde secured 32.1% and Aumua Amata Coleman won 26.6%. Since none of the candidates received the requisite 50% of votes, Faleomavaega and Langkilde entered a second round of voting on 19 November, at which Faleomavaega secured an eighth term in office. In March 2003 Governor Tauese Sunia died; Lieutenant-Governor Togiola Tulafono replaced him and appointed Aitofele Sunia as his deputy.

In December 2002 legislation was introduced that prohibited nationals of 23 countries deemed to present a terrorist threat from entering the Territory, unless they were granted special permission. Opposition groups in Fiji expressed their displeasure at the inclusion of their country on the list, owing to its large Muslim population.

In January 2003 the Senate approved a motion to begin expulsion hearings against Senator Faamausili Pola. Members of the chamber had already voted to remove him in September 2002, when it was alleged that he had not been elected according to Samoan tradition. In March 2003 it was reported that the South Korean owner of the Daewoosa Samoa clothing factory, Kil Soo Lee, had been convicted by a US court of trafficking in humans. (In June 2005 Lee was sentenced to 40 years' imprisonment; Lee subsequently announced his intention to appeal against the verdict.) The mainly Vietnamese and Chinese factory employees had received very low wages and worked in appalling conditions. The American Samoan High Court had previously ordered Daewoosa to pay workers US $3.5m. in compensation and fined the company an additional $290,000 in April 2002. In March 2004 Governor Tulafono announced plans for legislation that would allow prosecution of human-trafficking offences in the territory. In July it was announced that a US senate committee would hold a hearing on human-trafficking at the site of the closed garment factory.

During 2003 several allegations of official corruption were made against American Samoan government officials. In September an employee of the Territory's Office of Procurement was allowed to return to work despite a recent conviction in an insurance fraud case. In the same month the Senate ordered an official investigation into contracts awarded by Tafua Faau Seumanutafa, the Chief Procurement Officer, and senior officials from the Department of Health and Social Security and the Department of Education. In May 2004 Seumanutafa pleaded guilty in the Hawaii Federal District Court to one count of conspiracy to defraud the US Government, in a case that also implicated senior officials from the Department of Health and Social Security and the Department of Education. Also in May the Senate Select Investigative Committee issued subpoenas to several senators to testify in relation to alleged corruption in the allocation of government contracts. In early September the Committee recommended that, while under investigation for alleged corruption, Lieutenant-Governor Ipulasi Aitofele Sunia be placed on leave and have his name removed from the list of candidates for the forthcoming gubernatorial election. Governor Tulafono claimed that the charges were politically motivated. Meanwhile, in February 2004 the US Federal Bureau of Investigation (FBI) began an investigation into the alleged misuse of US government funds. In March 2005 the FBI effected an unannounced search of the government offices in Pago Pago, forbidding entry to the Governor, Lieutenant-Governor and Attorney-General for the duration of the operation. In mid-March the Government announced its intention to challenge the legality of the search warrants. In October Dr Sili K. Sataua and Patolo Mageo, the former Directors of the Education and Human Resources Departments, respectively, were sentenced in a federal court in Honolulu, Hawaii, to custodial sentences following their conviction on corruption charges. In September 2007 Lieutenant-Governor Sunia and Senator Tulifua Tini Lam Yuen were detained on charges of fraud, bribery and obstruction in relation to business transactions involving the Department of Education. Their trial was scheduled to commence in January 2009.

At the gubernatorial election held on 2 November 2004 incumbent Governor Tulafono received 48.4% of the votes cast in the first round of polling, while Afoa Moega Lutu obtained 39.4%. At the second round of voting, conducted on 16 November, Tulafono was re-elected, having secured 55.72% of the votes; Moega Lutu received 44.28%.

In October 2006 the minimum hourly wage for five industry categories rose by between seven and nine cents. However, plans to raise the hourly rate for the cannery sector encountered strong opposition from the business community and from the Government itself, which argued that the decision would adversely affect companies' cost effectiveness. The tuna-canning industry, as the greatest source of revenue for the islands, was consequently able to exert significant pressure on wage levels. However, supporters of the decision pressed for a greater increase in order to attract and retain employees. Minimum-wage legislation was brought under federal control in 2007, when it was envisaged that the minimum wage in the Territory would increase to US $7.25 per hour by 2014. This rise was to be implemented in phases, with variations between industries. In early 2008, however, the US Senate was investigating proposed legislation to restrict further increases in view of their consequences for the territorial economy.

Eni Faleomavaega, the incumbent delegate to the US Congress, was re-elected for an unprecedented 10th two-year term in office in November 2006, defeating his closest rival, Amata Aumua Coleman, by just 702 votes of the total of 11,033 cast. In February 2008 the Territory's House of Representatives endorsed an amendment to the Constitution that sought to confer ultimate legislative authority to the Fono in the event of a Governor's use of the veto.

Meanwhile, the islands remained vulnerable to adverse weather phenomena. In May 2003 severe flooding and landslides led to the deaths of five people, and in the following month US President George W. Bush declared the Territory a federal disaster area. In January 2004 a state of emergency was declared when a cyclone damaged the islands. The USA allocated US $12.5m. towards the relief effort. In February 2005 Cyclone Olaf caused extensive damage to the territory's Manu'a islands, destroying numerous buildings and interrupting electricity supplies. An estimated 70 homes were destroyed in Manu'a, while some 200 houses suffered major damage. The islands' Governor subsequently declared a state of emergency.

Government

Executive power is vested in the Governor, who is elected by popular vote and has authority which extends to all operations within the Territory of American Samoa. He has the power of veto with respect to legislation approved by the Fono (Legislature). The Fono consists of the Senate and the House of Representatives, with a President and a Speaker presiding over their respective divisions. The Senate is composed of 18 members, elected, according to Samoan custom, from local chiefs, or Matai, for a term of four years. The House of Representatives consists of 20 members who are elected by popular vote for a term of two years, and a non-voting delegate from Swains Island. The Fono meets twice a year, in January and July, for not more than 45 days, and at such special sessions as the Governor may call. The Governor, who serves a four-year term, has the authority to appoint heads of government departments with the approval of the Fono.

Defence

The USA is responsible for the defence of American Samoa.

Economic Affairs

In 2000, according to estimates by the American Samoa National Income and Product Accounts Task Force, American Samoa's gross national income (GNI), measured at constant 1999 prices, was about US $348.6m., equivalent to some $6,332 per head. Between 1973 and 1985, it was estimated, GNI increased, in real terms, at an average rate of 1.7% per year, with real GNI per head rising by only 0.1% per year. Gross domestic product (GDP) was estimated (at constant 1999 prices and allowing for statistical discrepancy) in 1999 at $444.2m. and in 2000 at $437.9m. In 2001–07 the population increased by an average of 2.3% per year. An estimated 91,000 American Samoans live on the US mainland or Hawaii.

Agriculture, hunting, forestry, fishing engaged 32.0% of the total labour force in 2005, according to FAO estimates. Agricultural production provides little surplus for export. Major crops are coconuts, bananas, taro, pineapples, yams and breadfruit. Local fisheries are at subsistence level, but tuna-canning plants at Pago Pago process fish from US, Taiwanese and South Korean vessels. Canned tuna constituted some 98.4% of export revenue in 2005/06, when earnings reached US $431.5m.

Within the industrial sector, manufacturing activities engaged 35.3% of the employed labour force in 2000. Fish-canning is the dominant industry; in 2001 some 70% of those employed in these factories were guest workers from Samoa (formerly Western Samoa). Other manufacturing activities include garment-manufacturing, meat-canning, handicrafts, dairy-farming, orchid-farming and the production of soap, perfume, paper products and alcoholic beverages. Exports of textiles and garments were valued at US $7.3m. in 2000/01, accounting for 3.2% of total exports. The construction sector engaged 6.4% of the employed labour force in 2000.

Service industries engage a majority of the employed labour force in American Samoa (55.2% in 2000). The Government employs almost one-third of workers, although in the mid-1990s a series of reductions in the number of public-sector employees were introduced. The tourist industry is developing slowly, and earned some US $10m. in 1998. The number of tourist arrivals declined from 44,158 in 2000 to 24,496 in 2005. Of those 46.0% were from Samoa, while 27.6% originated from the USA and 12.8% from New Zealand.

In 2005/06 American Samoa recorded a visible trade deficit of US $140.7m. Most of American Samoa's trade is conducted with the USA. Other trading partners in 2005/06 included New Zealand, which supplied 9.1% of total imports (excluding items imported by the Government and goods by the fish-canning sector), and Singapore (8.0%).

A fiscal deficit of US $10,484m. was recorded in the year to September 2006. The annual rate of inflation averaged 3.0% in

1997–2006. The inflation rate reached 3.0% in 2006. An estimated 10.5% of the total labour force were unemployed in 2003.

American Samoa is a member of the Pacific Community (see p. 377), and is an associate member of the UN Economic and Social Commission for Asia and the Pacific (ESCAP, see p. 35).

Economic development has been hindered by the islands' remote location, the limited infrastructure and lack of skilled workers. American Samoa's financial problems have been compounded by the high demand for government services from an increasing population and by the limited economic and tax base, as well as by natural disasters. A controversial minimum wage structure, in which American Samoa has considerably lower minimum hourly rates of pay than the rest of the USA, has been largely attributed to the presence of the two tuna-canning plants on the islands, which employ almost one-half of the labour force and consequently exert substantial influence over the setting of wage levels. However, the remit of US minimum wage legislation was extended to American Samoa from 2007; with annual increases of US $0.50 per hour scheduled until such time that wages complied with terms delineated under the Fair Labour Standards Act. Attempts to achieve a greater measure of financial security for the islands have included severe reductions in the number of public-sector employees, increased fees for government services, and plans to diversify the economy by encouraging tourism and expanding manufacturing activity. In March 2003 the Senate approved a bill to levy tax on foreign tuna meat sold to the Territory's canneries. In December 2003 the USA declared American Samoa eligible for financing from a US $30m. regional fund to offset the economic impact of Marshallese and Micronesian migrants. Despite the concerns of the congressional Government Accountability Office—expressed in its report of December 2004, relating to the auditing and efficiency of federal spending in American Samoa—the US Congress approved the Interior Appropriations bill for 2005/06, which provided American Samoa with some $33m. ($331,000 more than the 2004/05 outlay). Budgeted US funding for American Samoa totalled $22.9m. in 2006/07. In March 2006 Governor Tulafono proposed the issue of government bonds to the value of $20m., in order to raise funds for infrastructural projects. In April 2008 the US Treasury agreed to allocate to the Government the sum of $20.4m. to be redistributed to those members of the population eligible for a personal tax rebate.

Education

Education is officially compulsory for 12 years between six and 18 years of age. Primary education begins at six years of age and lasts for eight years. Secondary education, beginning at the age of 14, lasts for a further four years. In 2004 there were 51 pre-primary schools, 32 primary schools and 12 secondary schools. There was also a community college of further education, with 1,550 students. In 2006 there were 11,100 pupils enrolled at primary schools and 5,074 at secondary schools. Expenditure on education and culture in 2001/02 was US $51.3m., or 28.4% of total government expenditure.

Public Holidays

2008: 1 January (New Year's Day), 21 January (Martin Luther King Day), 18 February (Presidents' Day), 17 April (Flag Day, commemorating the first raising of the US flag in American Samoa), 26 May (Memorial Day), 4 July (Independence Day), 1 September (Labor Day), 13 October (Columbus Day), 11 November (Veterans' Day), 27 November (Thanksgiving Day), 25 December (Christmas Day).

2009: 1 January (New Year's Day), 19 January (Martin Luther King Day), 16 February (Presidents' Day), 17 April (Flag Day, commemorating the first raising of the US flag in American Samoa), 25 May (Memorial Day), 3 July (for Independence Day), 7 September (Labor Day), 12 October (Columbus Day), 11 November (Veterans' Day), 26 November (Thanksgiving Day), 25 December (Christmas Day).

Weights and Measures

With certain exceptions, the imperial system is in force. One US cwt equals 100 lb; one long ton equals 2,240 lb; one short ton equals 2,000 lb. A policy of gradual voluntary conversion to the metric system is being encouraged by the Federal Government.

Statistical Survey

Source (unless otherwise indicated): Statistics Division, Department of Commerce, Pago Pago, AS 96799; tel. 633-5155; fax 633-4195; internet www.asdoc.info/index.htm.

AREA AND POPULATION

Area: 201 sq km (77.6 sq miles); *By Island* (sq km): Tutuila 137; Ta'u 46; Ofu 7; Olosega 5; Swains Island (Olohenga) 3; Aunu'u 2; Rose 1.

Population: 46,773 at census of 1 April 1990; 57,291 (males 29,264, females 28,027) at census of 1 April 2000. *Mid-2007* (official estimate): 68,200. *By Island* (2000): Tutuila 55,400; Manu'a District (Ta'u, Olosega and Ofu islands) 1,378; Aunu'u 476; Swains Island (Olohenga) 37.

Density (mid-2007): 339.3 per sq km.

Ethnic Groups (2000 census): Samoan 50,545; part-Samoan 1,991; Asian 1,631; Tongan 1,598; Total (incl. others) 57,291.

Principal Towns (population at 2000 census): Tafuna 8,409; Nu'uuli 5,154; Pago Pago (capital) 4,278; Leone 3,568; Ili'ili 2,513.

Births, Marriages and Deaths (2006, unless otherwise stated): Registered live births 1,442 (birth rate 21.6 per 1,000); Registered marriages 171 ; Registered deaths 267 (death rate 4.0 per 1,000).

Expectation of Life (years at birth, 1995): Males 68.0; Females 76.0. Source: UN Economic and Social Commission for Asia and the Pacific.

Economically Active Population (persons aged 16 years and over, 2000 census): Agriculture, hunting, forestry, fishing and mining 517; Manufacturing 5,900; Construction 1,066; Trade, restaurants and hotels 2,414; Transport, storage, communications and utilities 1,036; Financing, insurance, real estate and business services 311; Community, social and personal services 5,474; *Total employed* 16,718 (males 9,804, females 6,914); Unemployed 909 (males 494, females 415); *Total labour force* 17,627 (males 10,298, females 7,329) (Source: US Department of Commerce, *2000 Census of Population and Housing*). *2003* (estimates): Total employed 14,319; Unemployed 1,681; Total labour force 16,000 (Source: US Department of State). *Mid-2005* (estimates): Agriculture, etc. 8,000; Total labour force 25,000 (Source: FAO).

AGRICULTURE, ETC.

Principal Crops ('000 metric tons, 2006, FAO estimates): Coconuts 4.6; Taro 1.5; Bananas 0.7.

Livestock (year ending September 2006, FAO estimates): Pigs 10,500; Cattle 103; Chickens 38,000.

Livestock Products (metric tons, 2006, FAO estimates): Pig meat 315; Chicken meat 25; Cows' milk 16; Hen eggs 30.

Fishing (metric tons, live weight, 2005): Total catch 3,943 (Albacore 2,917; Yellowfin tuna 508; Wahoo 207).

Source: FAO.

INDUSTRY

Production (2004): Electric energy 138 million kWh. Source: UN, *Industrial Commodity Statistics Yearbook*.

FINANCE

Currency and Exchange Rates: United States currency is used: 100 cents = 1 United States dollar (US $). *Sterling and Euro Equivalents* (31 December 2007): £1 sterling = US $2.003; €1 = US $1.472; US $100 = £49.92 = €67.93.

Federal Direct Expenditures (US $ million, year ending September 2006): Retirement and disability payments 48.4; Grants 151.7; Total (incl. others) 246.1 (Source: US Census Bureau, *Consolidated Federal Funds Report*).

Budget (US $ '000, year ending September 2005): *Revenue:* Taxes 50,397; Licences and permits 1,160; Intergovernmental 111,783; Charges for services 8,438; Fines and fees 1,869; Total (incl. others) 182,015. *Expenditure:* General government 45,555; Public safety 11,827; Public works 5,801; Health and recreation 31,952; Education and culture 65,881; Economic development 20,083; Capital projects 7,411; Debt-servicing 3,989; Total 192,499.

Cost of Living (Consumer Price Index; annual averages; base: July–Sept. 1997 = 100): All items 121.0 in 2004; 127.2 in 2005; 131.0 in 2006.

Gross Domestic Product (US $ million at constant 1999 prices, provisional estimates): 444.2 in 1999 (with a statistical discrepancy of 6.7%); 437.9 in 2000 (with a statistical discrepancy of 4.4%). Note: Recorded accounts are not available; figures represent the findings of the American Samoa National Income and Product Accounts Task Force, established to produce reliable economic statistics for the territory.

EXTERNAL TRADE

Principal Commodities (US $ million): *Imports* (excl. government purchases and cannery goods, year ending September 2006): Food 141.3 (Fish 74.4); Fuel and oil 35.8 (Diesel fuel 14.4); Textiles and clothing 6.6; Machinery and transport equipment 21.8 (Road motor vehicles and parts 13.7); Miscellaneous manufactured articles 113.7

(Tin plates 48.0); Construction materials 17.5; Total (incl. others) 341.5. *Exports:* Total exports 438.5 (Canned tuna 431.5; Pet food 7).

Principal Trading Partners (US $ million, year ending September 2006): *Imports* (excl. government purchases and cannery goods): Australia 8.4; Fiji 22.5; Japan 2.0; Korea, Republic 21.2; New Zealand 31.1; Samoa 17.0; Singapore 27.2; USA 133.4; Total (incl. others) 341.5. *Exports:* Total 438.5 (almost entirely to the USA).

TRANSPORT

Road Traffic ('000 registered motor vehicles, year ending September 2006): Passenger cars 7.8; Total 9.2.

International Sea-borne Shipping (freight traffic, '000 metric tons, year ending September 2006): Goods loaded 148; Goods unloaded 400.

Civil Aviation (Pago Pago Int. Airport, year ending September 2006): Flights 4,344; Passengers (excl. transit) 157,023 (Boarding 81,907, Disembarking 75,116); Transit 385; Freight and mail ('000 lb) Loaded 3,893, Unloaded 3,939.

TOURISM

Tourist Arrivals by Country (2005): Australia 755; China, People's Republic 501; Fiji 264; New Zealand 3,138; Philippines 317; Samoa 11,277; Tonga 385; United Kingdom 126; USA 6,757; Total (incl. others) 24,496.

Tourism Receipts (US $ million): 9 in 1996; 10 in 1997; 10 in 1998.

Source: World Tourism Organization.

COMMUNICATIONS MEDIA

Daily Newspapers (1996): 2; estimated circulation 5,000*.

Non-daily Newspapers (1996): 1; estimated circulation 3,000*.

Radio Receivers (1997): 57,000* in use.

Television Receivers (1999): 15,000* in use.

Telephones (2006): 10,737 main lines in use.

Facsimile Machines (2006): 686 subscribers.

Mobile Cellular Telephones (2006): 8,525 subscribers.

*Sources: UNESCO, *Statistical Yearbook* and American Samoa Telecommunications Authority.

EDUCATION

Pre-primary (2006): 40 schools ; 140 teachers; 2,038 pupils.

Primary (2006): 35 schools ; 450 teachers; 11,100 pupils.

Secondary (2006): 12 high schools; 213 teachers; 5,074 pupils.

Higher (2006): American Samoa Community College 1,607 students.

Sources: American Samoa Department of Education.

Directory

The Constitution

American Samoa is an Unincorporated Territory of the USA. Therefore, not all the provisions of the US Constitution apply. As an unorganized territory it has not been provided with an organic act by Congress. Instead the US Secretary of the Interior, on behalf of the President, has plenary authority over the Territory and enabled the people of American Samoa to draft their own Constitution.

According to the 1967 Constitution, executive power is vested in the Governor, whose authority extends to all operations within the Territory of American Samoa. The Governor has veto power with respect to legislation passed by the Fono (Legislature). The Fono consists of the Senate and the House of Representatives, with a President and a Speaker presiding over their respective divisions. The Senate is composed of 18 members, elected, according to Samoan custom, from local chiefs, or Matai, for a term of four years. The House of Representatives consists of 20 members who are elected by popular vote for a term of two years, and a non-voting delegate from Swains Island. The Fono meets twice a year, in January and July, for not more than 45 days and at such special sessions as the Governor may call. The Governor has the authority to appoint heads of government departments with the approval of the Fono. Local government is carried out by indigenous officials. In August 1976 a referendum on the popular election of a Governor and a Lieutenant-Governor resulted in an affirmative vote. The first gubernatorial elections took place on 8 November 1977 and the second was held in November 1980; subsequent elections were to take place every four years.

American Samoa sends one non-voting Delegate to the US House of Representatives, who is popularly elected every two years.

The Government

(April 2008)

Governor: TOGIOLA TULAFONO; (took office March 2003, re-elected 16 November 2004).

Lieutenant-Governor: IPULASI AITOFELE SUNIA.

GOVERNMENT OFFICES

Governor's Office: Executive Office Bldg, Third Floor, Utulei, Pago Pago, AS 96799; tel. 633-4116; fax 633-2269; e-mail governorsoffice@asg-gov.net; internet americansamoa.gov/gov_office/gov_office.htm.

Department of the Interior, Office of Insular Affairs (OIA): Field Office of the OIA, Dept of the Interior, POB 1725, Pago Pago, AS 96799; tel. 633-2800; fax 633-2415; internet www.doi.gov/oia/Islandpages/asgpage; Field Representative LYDIA FALEAFINE NOMURA.

Office of the Representative to the Government of American Samoa: Amerika Samoa Office, 1427 Dillingham Blvd, Suite 210, Honolulu HI 96817, USA; tel. (808) 847-1998; fax (808) 847-3420; e-mail hawaiioff@aol.com; Representative SOLOALI'I FA'ALEPO, Jr.

Department of Administrative Services: American Samoa Government, Executive Office Bldg, Utulei, Pago Pago, AS 96799; tel. 633-4158; fax 633-1841; internet americansamoa.gov/departments/depts/admin.htm; Dir NU'UTAI SONNY THOMPSON.

Department of Agriculture: American Samoa Government, Executive Office Building, Utulei, Pago Pago, AS 96799; tel. 699-1497; fax 699-4031; internet americansamoa.gov/departments/depts/agriculture.htm; Dir APEFA'I TAIFANE.

Department of Commerce: American Samoa Government, Executive Office Bldg, 2nd Floor, POB 1147, Utulei, Pago Pago, AS 96799; tel. 633-5155; fax 633-4195; internet www.asdoc.info/IndexCSSDOC.htm; Dir FALESEU ELIU PAOPAO.

Department of Education: American Samoa Government, Executive Office Bldg, Utulei, Pago Pago, AS 96799; tel. 633-1246; fax 633-1247; e-mail luituitele@doe.as; internet www.doe.as; Dir Dr CLAIR POUMELE.

Department of Health: American Samoa Government, Pago Pago, AS 96799; tel. 633-4606; fax 633-5379; internet americansamoa.gov/departments/depts/health.htm; Dir UTO'OFILI ASOFA'AFETAI MAGA.

Department of Homeland Security: tel. 633-2827; fax 633-2979; e-mail mrsala@americansamoa.gov; internet americansamoa.gov/departments/depts/dhs.htm; Dir MICHAEL SALA.

Department of Human Resources: American Samoa Government, Executive Office Bldg, Utulei, Pago Pago, AS 96799; tel. 633-4485; fax 633-1139; internet americansamoa.gov/departments/depts/human_resources.htm; Dir MALU MAGEO.

Department of Human and Social Services: American Samoa Government, Pago Pago, AS 96799; tel. 633-1187; fax 633-7449; internet americansamoa.gov/departments/depts/hss.htm; Dir TALIA FA'AFETAI I'AULUALO.

Department of Legal Affairs: American Samoa Government, Executive Office Bldg, Utulei, Pago Pago, AS 96799; tel. 633-4163; fax 633-1838; internet americansamoa.gov/departments/depts/legal.htm; Dir Attorney-General FEPULEA'I AFA RIPLEY, Jr.

Department of Local Government (Office of Samoan Affairs): American Samoa Government, Pago Pago, AS 96799; tel. 633-5201; fax 633-5590; internet americansamoa.gov/departments/depts/local.htm; Dir MAUGA TASI ASUEGA.

Department of Marine and Wildlife Resources: American Samoa Government, Executive Office Bldg, Utulei, Pago Pago, AS 96799; tel. 633-4456; fax 633-5590; e-mail ray@americansamoa.gov; internet americansamoa.gov/departments/depts/mwr.htm; Dir UFAGAFA RAY TULAFONO.

Department of Parks and Recreation: American Samoa Government, Pago Pago, AS 96799; tel. 699-9614; fax 699-4427; internet americansamoa.gov/departments/depts/parks.htm; Dir TA'AMUVAIGAFA IAKOPO.

Department of Planning and Budget: tel. 633-4201; fax 633-1148; internet americansamoa.gov/departments/depts/budget.htm; Dir MAGALEI LOGOVI'I.

Department of Port Administration: American Samoa Government, Pago Pago, AS 96799; tel. 633-4251; fax 633-5281; internet americansamoa.gov/departments/depts/port.htm; Dir MATAGI MAILO RAY MCMOORE.

American Samoa

Department of Procurement: tel. 699-1170; fax 699-2387; internet americansamoa.gov/departments/depts/procurement.htm; Dir LA'AU M. SEUI.

Department of Public Information: American Samoa Government, Pago Pago, AS 96799; tel. 633-4191; fax 633-1044; internet americansamoa.gov/departments/depts/information.htm; Dir PAOLO SIVIA SIVIA.

Department of Public Safety: American Samoa Government, Pago Pago, AS 96799; tel. 633-1111; fax 633-7296; internet americansamoa.gov/departments/depts/safety.htm; Dir SOTOA M. SAVALI.

Department of Public Works: American Samoa Government, Executive Office Bldg, Utulei, Pago Pago, AS 96799; tel. 633-4141; fax 633-5958; internet americansamoa.gov/departments/depts/works.htm; Dir PUNAOFO TILEI.

Department of Treasury: American Samoa Government, Executive Office Bldg, Utulei, Pago Pago, AS 96799; tel. 633-4155; fax 633-4100; internet americansamoa.gov/departments/depts/treasury.htm; Dir AITOFELE SUNIA.

Department of Youth and Women's Affairs: American Samoa Government, Executive Office Bldg, Utulei, Pago Pago, AS 96799; tel. 633-2836; fax 633-2875; Dir Leiataua Dr LEUGA TURNER.

Environmental Protection Agency: American Samoa Government, Office of the Governor, Pago Pago, AS 96799; tel. 633-2304; fax 633-5801; e-mail tv5551@yahoo.com; internet americansamoa.gov/departments/agencies/epa.htm; Dir Dr TOA'FA VAIAGA'E.

Legislature

FONO

Senate

The Senate has 18 members, elected, according to Samoan custom, from local chiefs, or Matai, for a term of four years.

President: LOLO LETALU MOLIGA.

House of Representatives

The House has 20 members who are elected by popular vote for a term of two years, and a non-voting delegate from Swains Island.

Speaker: SAVALI TALAVOU ALE.

CONGRESS

Since 1980 American Samoa has been able to elect, for a two-year term, a Delegate to the Federal Congress, who may vote in committee but not on the floor of the House of Representatives. At the election to the post in November 2006 incumbent Congressman Eni F. Hunkin Faleomavaega was re-elected for a record 10th two-year term.

Delegate of American Samoa: ENI F. HUNKIN FALEOMAVAEGA, US House of Representatives, 2422 Rayburn House Office Bldg, Washington, DC 20515, USA; tel. (202) 225-8577; fax (202) 225-8757; e-mail faleomavaega@mail.house.gov.

Judicial System

The judicial system of American Samoa consists of the High Court, presided over by the Chief Justice and assisted by Associate Justices (all appointed by the Secretary of the Interior), and a local judiciary in the District and Village Courts. The judges for these local courts are appointed by the Governor, subject to confirmation by the Senate of the Fono. The High Court consists of three Divisions: Appellate, Trial, and Land and Titles. The Appellate Division has limited original jurisdiction and hears appeals from the Trial Division, the Land and Titles Division and from the District Court when it has operated as a court of record. The Trial Division has general jurisdiction over all cases. The Land and Titles Division hears cases involving land or Matai titles.

The District Court hears preliminary felony proceedings, misdemeanours, infractions (traffic and health), civil claims less than US $3,000, small claims, Uniform Reciprocal Enforcement of Support cases, and *de novo* trials from Village Courts. The Village Courts hear matters arising under village regulations and local customs.

Chief Justice: MICHAEL KRUSE.
Associate Justice: LYLE L. RICHMOND.
Attorney-General: FEPULEAI AFA RIPLEY.

High Court

Office of the Chief Justice, High Court, Pago Pago, AS 96799; tel. 633-1261; fax 633-1318; e-mail hcourt@samoatelco.com.

Judge of the District Court: JOHN L. WARD II, POB 427, Pago Pago, AS 96799; tel. 633-1101.

Judge of the Village Court: FAISIOTA TAUANU'U, Pago Pago, AS 96799; tel. 633-1102.

Religion

The population is largely Christian, more than 50% being members of the Congregational Christian Church and about 20% being Roman Catholics.

CHRISTIANITY

American Samoa Council of Christian Churches: c/o CCCAS Offices, POB 1637, Pago Pago, AS 96799; f. 1985; six mem. churches; Pres. (vacant); Gen. Sec. Rev. ENOKA L. ALESANA (Congregational Christian Church in American Samoa).

The Roman Catholic Church

American Samoa comprises the single diocese of Samoa-Pago Pago, suffragan to the archdiocese of Samoa-Apia and Tokelau. At 31 December 2005 there were 15,500 adherents in the islands. The Bishop participates in the Catholic Bishops' Conference of the Pacific, based in Suva, Fiji.

Bishop of Samoa-Pago Pago: Rev. JOHN QUINN WEITZEL, Diocesan Pastoral Center, POB 596, Fatuoaiga, Pago Pago, AS 96799; tel. 699-1402; fax 699-1459; e-mail quinn@samoatelco.com.

The Anglican Communion

American Samoa is within the diocese of Polynesia, part of the Church of the Province of New Zealand. The Bishop of Polynesia is resident in Fiji.

Protestant Churches

Congregational Christian Church in American Samoa (CCCAS): POB 1537, Pago Pago, AS 96799; tel. 699-9810; fax 699-1898; e-mail cccasgensec@samoatelco.com; internet www.cwmission.org.uk/about/view_church.cfm?ChurchID=6; Gen. Sec. Rev SAMUEL TIALAVEA; 40,000 mems (incl. congregations in New Zealand, Australia and USA) in 2004.

Other active Protestant groups include the Baptist Church, the Christian Church of Jesus Christ, the Methodist Church, Assemblies of God, Church of the Nazarene and Seventh-day Adventists. The Church of Jesus Christ of Latter-day Saints (Mormons) is also represented.

The Press

American Samoa Tribune: 5 a week; circ. 4,500 (2006).

News Bulletin: Office of Public Information, American Samoa Government, Utulei; tel. 633-5490; daily (Mon.–Fri.); English; non-commercial; Editor PHILIP SWETT; circ. 1,800.

Samoa Journal and Advertiser: POB 3986, Pago Pago, AS 96799; tel. 633-2399; weekly; English and Samoan; Editor MICHAEL STARK; circ. 3,000.

Samoa News: POB 909, Pago Pago, AS 96799; tel. 633-5599; fax 633-4864; internet www.samoanews.com; 6 a week; English and Samoan; Publr VERA M. ANNESLEY; circ. 4,500.

Broadcasting and Communications

TELECOMMUNICATIONS

American Samoa Telecommunications Authority: Box M, Pago Pago, AS 96799; tel. 633-1211; internet www.samoatelco.com.

Blue Sky Communications: 478 Laufou Shopping Center, Pago Pago, AS 96799; tel. 699-2759; fax 699-6593; e-mail webmaster@bluesky.as; internet www.bluesky.as; mobile-telecommunications provider.

BROADCASTING

Radio

KSBS-FM: POB 793, Pago Pago, AS 96799; tel. 633-7000; fax 622-7839; e-mail helpdesk@ksbsfm.com; internet www.ksbsfm.com; commercial; Gen. Man. ESTHER PRESCOTT.

WVUV: POB 4894, Pago Pago, AS 96799; tel. 688-7397; fax 688-1545; fmr govt-administered station leased to Radio Samoa Ltd in 1975; commercial; English and Samoan; 24 hours a day; Man. VINCENT IULI.

Television

KVZK-TV: Office of Public Information, POB 3511, Pago Pago, AS 96799; tel. 633-4191; fax 633-1044; f. 1964; govt-owned; non-commercial; English and Samoan; broadcasts 18 hours daily on two channels; Gen. Man. PABLO SIVIA SIVIA; Technical Dir JEFFREY ALWIN.

UNITED STATES EXTERNAL TERRITORIES

Malama TV: Malama Communications, Inc., POB AB, Pago Pago 96799; tel. 699-5999; fax 699-6006; e-mail webmaster@malama.tv; internet www.malama.tv/TalofaSamoa.htm.

Finance

(cap. = capital; dep. = deposits; m. = million; amounts in US dollars)

BANKING

Commercial Banks

ANZ Amerika Samoa Bank: POB 3790, Pago Pago, AS 96799; tel. 633-5053; fax 633-5057; internet www.anz.com.au/americansamoa; f. 1979; fmrly Amerika Samoa Bank; joined ANZ group in April 2001; Pres. GARY AYRE; 3 brs.

Bank of Hawaii (USA): POB 69, Pago Pago, AS 96799; tel. 633-4226; fax 633-2918; f. 1897; Man. BRIAN S. GLASS; 3 brs.

Development Bank

Development Bank of American Samoa: POB 9, Pago Pago, AS 96799; tel. 633-4031; fax 633-1163; e-mail dbasinfo@dbas.org; internet www.dbas.org; f. 1969; govt-owned and non-profit-making; Chair. EUGENE G. C. H. REID; Pres. MANUTAFEA E. MEREDITH.

INSURANCE

American International Underwriters (South Pacific) Ltd: Pago Pago, AS 96799; tel. 633-4845.

Mark Solofa, Inc: POB 3149, Pago Pago, AS 96799; tel. 699-5902; fax 699-5904; e-mail marksalofainc@yahoo.com.

National Pacific Insurance Ltd: Centennial Bldg, POB 1386, Pago Pago, AS 96799; tel. 633-4266; fax 633-2964; e-mail contact@npipago.as; f. 1977; Country Man. JASON THOMAS.

Oxford Pacific Insurance Management: POB 1420, Pago Pago, AS 96799; tel. 633-4990; fax 633-2721; e-mail progressive_oxford@yahoo.com; f. 1977; represents major international property and life insurance cos; Pres. GREGG F. DUFFY.

South Seas Financial Services Corporation: POB 1448, Pago Pago, AS 96799; tel. 633-7896; fax 633-7895; e-mail ssfs@samoatelco.com.

Trade and Industry

DEVELOPMENT ORGANIZATIONS

American Samoa Development Corporation: Pago Pago, AS 96799; tel. 633-4241; f. 1962; financed by private Samoan interests.

American Samoa Economic Advisory Commission: Pago Pago; Chair. JOHN WAIHEE.

Department of Commerce: see Government Offices; Dir FALESEU ELIU PAOPAO.

CHAMBER OF COMMERCE

Chamber of Commerce of American Samoa: POB 2446, Pago Pago, AS 96799; tel. 699-1881; fax 699-1197; e-mail info@amsamoachamber.com; internet www.amsamoachamber.com; Pres. DAVID ROBINSON.

UTILITIES

American Samoa Power Authority: Pago Pago, AS 96799; tel. 644-2772; fax 644-5005; internet www.aspower.com; supplies water and electricity throughout the islands; also manages sewer and solid waste collection; Chair. FEPULEAI AFA RIPLEY, Jr; CEO MICHAEL KEYSER (acting).

Transport

ROADS

There are about 150 km (93 miles) of paved and 200 km (124 miles) of secondary roads. Non-scheduled commercial buses operate a service over 350 km (217 miles) of main and secondary roads. There were an estimated 8,100 registered motor vehicles in the islands in 2004.

SHIPPING

There are various passenger and cargo services from the US Pacific coast, Japan, Australia (mainly Sydney) and New Zealand, that call at Pago Pago, which is one of the deepest and most sheltered harbours in the Pacific. Inter-island boats provide frequent services between Samoa and American Samoa.

Hamburg Süd: Samoan Sports Building, No. 1 Main St, Fagatogo, POB 1417, Pago Pago, AS 96799; tel. 633-4665; fax 699-8110; e-mail spsi@samoatelco.com; internet www.hamburgsud.com.

PM&O Line: Suite 202, Fagatogo Sq., POB 5023, Pago Pago, AS 96799; tel. 633-4527; fax 633-4530; e-mail paige@blueskynet.as; internet www.pmoline.com; f. 1978.

Polynesia Shipping: POB 1478, Pago Pago AS 96799; tel. 633-1211; fax 633-1265.

CIVIL AVIATION

There is an international airport at Tafuna, 11 km (7 miles) from Pago Pago, and smaller airstrips on the islands of Ta'u and Ofu. International services are operated by Hawaiian Airlines and Polynesian Blue.

Samoa Aviation: POB 280, Pago Pago Int. Airport, Pago Pago, AS 96799; tel. 699-9106; fax 699-9751; f. 1986; operates service between Pago Pago and Samoa, Tonga and Niue; Pres. ANDRE LAVIGNE.

Tourism

The tourist industry is encouraged by the Government, but suffers from the cost and paucity of air services linking American Samoa with its main sources of custom, particularly the USA. Pago Pago is an important mid-Pacific stop-over for large passenger aircraft. A total of 24,496 tourists visited the islands in 2005. In that year 28% of tourists came from the USA and 13% from New Zealand. In 1992 there were some 542 hotel beds available in the islands. The industry earned an estimated US $10m. in 1998.

Office of Tourism: Convention Center, POB 1147, Tafuna, Pago Pago, AS 96799; tel. 699-9411; fax 699-9414; e-mail asgtourism@samoatelco.com; Deputy Dir VIRGINIA SAMUELU.

Pago Pago Visitors Association (PPVA): f. 2004; Pres. TOM DRABBLE.

GUAM

Introductory Survey

Location, Climate, Language, Religion, Flag, Capital

Guam is the southernmost and largest of the Mariana Islands, situated about 2,170 km (1,350 miles) south of Tokyo (Japan) and 5,300 km (3,300 miles) west of Honolulu (Hawaii). The temperature normally ranges between 24°C (75°F) and 30°C (86°F) in June–November, but it is generally cooler and drier from December to May. The average annual rainfall is about 2,000 mm (79 ins). English is the official language, but Japanese and Chamorro, the local language, are also spoken. The principal religion is Christianity, the majority of the population being Roman Catholics. The national flag of the United States of America (q.v.) is used by Guam. The capital is Hagåtña (formerly Agaña).

Recent History

Members of a Spanish expedition, under the Portuguese navigator, Fernão Magalhães (Ferdinand Magellan), were the first Europeans to discover Guam, visiting the island in 1521. The island was claimed by Spain in 1565, and the first Jesuit missionaries arrived three years later. The native Micronesian population is estimated to have fallen from 100,000 in 1521 to fewer than 5,000 in 1741, owing largely to a combination of aggression by the Spaniards and exposure to imported diseases. The intermarrying of Micronesians, Spaniards and Filipinos resulted in the people now called Chamorros. Guam was ceded to the USA after the Spanish–American War of 1898. In 1941, during the Second World War, Guam was invaded by Japanese troops, but following fierce fighting the island was recaptured by US forces in 1944.

Guam became an Unincorporated Territory of the USA, under the jurisdiction of the US Department of the Interior, in 1950. In 1970 the island elected its first Governor, and in 1972 a new law gave Guam the right to elect one Delegate to the US House of Representatives in Washington, DC. The Delegate was permitted to vote in committee but not on the floor of the House. In 1976 an island-wide referendum decided that Guam should maintain close links with the USA, but that negotiations should be held to improve the island's status. In a further referendum, in 1982, in which only 38% of eligible voters participated, the status of a Commonwealth, in association with the USA, was the most favoured of six options; this was supported by 48% of voters. In 1987, in a referendum on the provisions of a draft law aimed at conferring the status of Commonwealth on the Territory, voters approved the central proposal, while rejecting articles empowering the Guam Government to restrict immigration and granting the indigenous Chamorro people the right to determine the island's future political status. In a further referendum later in the year both outstanding provisions were approved. Negotiations between the Guam Commission for Self Determination and the USA subsequently continued.

In February 1987 the former Governor of Guam, Ricardo Bordallo, was found guilty of charges of bribery, extortion and conspiracy to obstruct justice, and was sentenced to 30 years' imprisonment (later reduced to nine years) in April. In November Bordallo's wife, Madeleine, was elected to replace him in the Guam Legislature; in October 1988 Bordallo won an appeal and his sentence was cancelled. Bordallo was liable for imprisonment in the USA on charges of obstruction and attempting to influence witnesses, but in January 1990 he committed suicide. Madeleine Bordallo was the Democratic candidate at gubernatorial elections in November, when Joseph Ada was re-elected. Concurrent elections to the Guam Legislature resulted in a Democratic majority of one seat.

At legislative elections in November 1992 the Democrats increased their representation to 14 seats, while the Republicans secured only seven. Robert Underwood was elected as the new Democratic Delegate to the US House of Representatives, replacing the Republican Ben Blaz.

In January 1994 the US Congress approved legislation providing for the transfer of 3,200 acres of land on Guam from federal to local control. This was a significant achievement for the Government of Guam, which had campaigned consistently for the return of 27,000 acres (20% of Guam's total area), appropriated by US military forces after the Second World War. However, Chamorro rights activists opposed the legislation, claiming that land should be transferred to the original landowners rather than to the Government of Guam.

At gubernatorial elections in November 1994 the Democratic candidate, Carl Gutierrez, defeated his Republican opponent, Tommy Tanaka, winning 54.6% of total votes cast, while Madeleine Bordallo was elected to the post of Lieutenant-Governor. Legislative elections held concurrently also resulted in a Democratic majority, with candidates of the party securing 13 seats, while the Republicans won eight. Robert Underwood was re-elected unopposed as Delegate to the US House of Representatives.

Reports that Chamorro rights activists had initiated a campaign for independence from the USA were denied by the Governor in July 1995. However, in September Lieutenant-Governor Madeleine Bordallo expressed her support for the achievement of full autonomy for Guam and for the Chamorro people's desire for decolonization.

It was reported in 1995 that US President Bill Clinton had appointed a team of Commonwealth negotiators to review the draft Guam Commonwealth Act. Guam's self-styled Commission on Decolonization was established in 1997, headed by the Governor. A plebiscite on the political status of Guam was originally scheduled for November 2000 but was subsequently deferred, to coincide with the islands' legislative and presidential elections scheduled for November 2004. However, in May 2004 legislation was drafted that would postpone the referendum until the number of Chamorro voters registered by the Guam Elections Committee had reached the requisite 50%.

At elections in November 1996 Republican members regained a majority in the Legislature, winning 11 seats, while Democratic candidates secured 10 seats. In a concurrent referendum voters approved a proposed reduction in the number of Senators from 21 to 15 (effective from November 1998), and plans to impose an upper limit (2.5% of total budgetary expenditure) on legislative expenses. However, a proposal to restrict the number of terms that Senators could seek to serve in the Legislature was rejected by voters. Guam's Delegate to the US House of Representatives, Robert Underwood, was re-elected unopposed.

In June 1998 Underwood secured approval from the US authorities to change the spelling of Guam's capital from Agaña to Hagåtña. The change was effected in order to reflect more accurately the original Chamorro language name for the town.

Robert Underwood was re-elected, with 70.2% of the total votes cast, as Guam's Delegate to the US House of Representatives in November 1998. Concurrent gubernatorial and legislative elections resulted in the return to office of incumbent Governor Carl Gutierrez and of Lieutenant-Governor Madeleine Bordallo. (In December former Governor Joseph Ada alleged that Gutierrez's victory had been achieved by fraudulent means, and later in the month a Guam court invalidated the election result and ordered a new poll to be held. However, in February 1999 the Superior Court of Guam found that there had been no electoral malpractice, and confirmed the appointments of Gutierrez and Bordallo.) In elections to the Legislature, where the number of seats had been reduced from 21 to 15, 12 candidates of the Republican Party and three candidates of the Democratic Party were returned as Senators.

US President Clinton visited Guam in November 1998. During his visit President Clinton approved the transfer of some 1,300 ha of federal land to the local administration and undertook to accelerate the transfer of a further 2,020 ha of former US air force and navy land. In August 2001 the US Army announced plans to move some combat weaponry and equipment from Europe to storage bases in Guam, as well as in Taiwan and Hawaii. During 2004/05 the US Air Force stationed several of its B-52 and B-2 bombers on Guam, following the construction of a new hangar on the island. In May 2005 the US Government announced plans substantially to increase military spending in 2005/06 in Guam, with some US $162m. allocated for new construction projects. Notwithstanding the concerns of some anti-war and Chamorro rights activists, the increased military presence on Guam was widely welcomed as a source of new investment and employment. Rights activists continued to express their opposition after plans were revealed to relocate 8,000 US marines and their families from their base on the Japanese island of Okinawa to Guam, as part of a broader agreement on the redeployment of US forces. While Japan was likely to bear much of the financial burden, US President George W. Bush submitted a proposed budget for 2008 that included $345m. for military construction projects, including the relocation costs of the marines and their dependants. A final agreement on the relocation of troops to Guam was concluded in May 2006. Legislation authorizing funding of some $6,000m. for the relocation had been approved by both chambers of the Japanese legislature by May 2007. The US Government had committed funding of $4,000m. for the realignment, which would also involve a reorganization of US troops within Japan. During a visit to the Territory in February 2007, US Vice-President Richard Cheney emphasized the strategic importance of Guam, while reports suggested that the inflow of funds related to the increased military presence might reach $15,000m. However, in June 2007 it was reported that the relocation of troops would not begin until 2012 at the earliest, with a target completion date of 2014; as many as 15,000 skilled workers would be required to implement the move. Some remained sceptical about the benefits of the relocation, fearing that the influx might lead to an increase in violent crimes and other social and environmental disturbance.

At elections held in November 2000, Underwood was re-elected as Guam's delegate to the US House of Representatives, winning 78.1% of votes cast. At the concurrent legislative election, eight candidates of the Republican Party and seven candidates of the Democratic Party were returned as senators.

Robert Underwood secured the Democratic nomination for the gubernatorial election scheduled for November 2002, but at the poll was defeated by the Republican candidate, Felix P. Camacho, who received 55.4% of the votes cast. (Madeleine Bordallo was designated Guam's Delegate to the US Congress.) In the Legislature, nine Democratic candidates were elected as senators, while the Republican party's representation decreased to six seats. Governor Camacho pledged to halt the widely perceived rise in corruption and misallocation of public funds on Guam.

Also in November 2002 the US Congress approved the Guam War Claims Review Commission Act, which provided for the creation of a body to investigate events that had followed the island's occupation by Japanese forces during the Second World War. Furthermore, the Commission was to determine whether the USA had offered the Islanders sufficient compensation for their mistreatment prior to Guam's liberation in 1944. The War Claims Review Commission, appointed in September 2003, acknowledged the hardship and suffering of the people of Guam, their 'courageous loyalty to the USA' and the inequality in compensation payments with regard to similar claims. In late March 2006 Madeleine Bordallo reintroduced the Guam World War II Loyalty Recognition Act, thus apparently making significant progress in efforts to compel the federal Government to recompense Guam residents for their suffering during the 1940s. The war claims legislation was approved by the US House of Representatives in May 2007; the Congressional Budget Office projected the cost of implementing the provisions of the bill during the period 2008–12 at almost US $130m. In early 2008 the proposed legislation had yet to be debated in the US Senate.

Meanwhile, in May 2004 the US State Department's Radiation Exposure Compensation Program declared Guam eligible for compensation for the effects of nuclear tests carried out in the Pacific region during the 'Cold War' (the long period of mutual hostility between the USA and the Soviet Union). In April 2005 the US Congressional Committee to Assess the Scientific Information for the Radiation Exposure Screening and Education Program published a report recommending, in accordance with the wishes of the Guam delegation, that scientific criteria (including radiation measurements and analyses of public health data) be used for assessing eligibility for compensation, rather than geographical proximity to nuclear testing, which had determined eligibility hitherto. The report concluded that although Guam had been exposed to radiation through wind-borne particles, this exposure had not significantly increased the incidence of cancers and other radiation-related illnesses. Future claims for compensation were therefore thought unlikely to succeed.

At the legislative election held on 2 November 2004 the Republican party secured a majority, winning nine of the 15 seats in the island's legislature; five Democrat incumbents were deposed. At a concurrently held plebiscite, a proposal to legalize casinos on the island was rejected. Later in the month a group of campaigners for the proposal filed an appeal in the Superior Court against the result of the election, alleging electoral malpractice.

Meanwhile, numerous investigations into allegations of official corruption were conducted. In April 2003 a former Republican Senator and gubernatorial candidate, Tommy Tanaka, pleaded guilty to charges of misprision of felony, which related to his alleged involvement in a fraudulent government contract. In the same month Joseph Mafnas, a former chief of the Guam police department, was indicted on forgery charges. However, the case against him foundered in September 2004 owing to the absence from the island of the key witness for the prosecution. In March 2004 former Governor Carl Gutierrez was tried for his involvement in a private property development scheme, which allegedly involved the misappropriation of public funds. All but two minor charges against him were dismissed by a Superior Court judge in April. Although in August charges ranging from theft by deception to official misconduct were filed against the former Governor, these were dismissed in early September. Gutierrez stood trial in June 2005 for alleged improper dealings relating to the island's retirement fund; he was acquitted of all charges in the following month, and in August announced his intention to contest the next gubernatorial election, scheduled for November 2006. However, in December 2005 new corruption charges connected to the retirement fund were filed against Gutierrez and others responsible for its operation. In January 2006 further charges were brought against the former Governor relating to his administration of the Guam Memorial Hospital. Meanwhile, in October 2005 Gutierrez's former Chief of Staff, Gil Shinohara, was convicted of conspiracy to commit fraud.

Legislative and gubernatorial elections took place on 7 November 2006. Felix P. Camacho secured a second term as Governor, defeating Robert Underwood, who later filed an unsuccessful appeal at the US Supreme Court seeking clarification of the results, in a dispute over the exclusion of 'crossover' ballots from the valid votes. Michael W. Cruz was elected Lieutenant-Governor, replacing Kaleo Moylan. Madeleine Bordallo secured a third term as Delegate to the US House of Representatives. The Republicans retained control of the legislature, albeit with a decreased majority, winning eight seats, compared with the Democrats' seven; the incumbent Speaker, Republican Mark Forbes, was re-elected.

In March 1998, meanwhile, delegates from several Pacific island nations and territories met in Hawaii to discuss methods of controlling the increasing population of brown tree snakes in Guam. The venomous reptile, which was accidentally introduced to the island from New Guinea after the Second World War, had been responsible for frequent power cuts, as they were able to ascend electricity poles and short-circuit the lines, as well as for major environmental problems (including the decimation of native bird, rodent and reptile populations). The US Geological Survey estimated the density of tree snakes on Guam to be roughly 13,000 per sq mile (33,670 per sq km) of forested land. By 2004 a team of 25 full-time snake-trappers and nine dog-handlers was capturing an estimated 6,000 tree snakes annually at Guam's five main ports (air and sea), but in September of that year plans were announced to reduce funding to this programme by nearly one-half. Also in September the US House of Representatives approved a bill allocating US $104m. of federal funds towards the eradication of Guam's tree snake population. In October, furthermore, the US Senate authorized expenditure of $77m., to be divided among Guam, Hawaii and other islands, for the purposes of snake-eradication programmes.

The island remained vulnerable to the impact of extreme weather formations. President George W. Bush declared the island a federal disaster area following Typhoon Chata'an in July 2002 and Supertyphoon Pongsona in December 2002. Some 35,000 islanders were homeless in early 2003, and the US Government granted US $10m. towards the recovery effort. In July, in response to the high costs incurred by the recovery programme, the island's Delegate to the US Congress, Madeleine Bordallo, introduced a bill to amend the Organic Act of Guam. The legislation attempted to empower the US Secretary of the Interior to waive Guam's outstanding federal debt, in order to offset social costs caused by migration to Guam from Compact of Free Association countries. The measure was defeated, although the amended Compact of Free Association signed in December approved some $14m. to offset Guam's migration costs and erased $157m. of debt owed to the US federal Government. In February 2006 Governor Camacho announced his intention to restart negotiations on some $60.5m. of debt relief for Guam. Also in that month, legislation seeking to amend the Organic Act of Guam, in order to grant the territory greater autonomy from the US federal Government, was submitted to the island's legislature.

In a landmark decision in January 2006 the US House of Representatives approved an amendment to grant limited voting rights to delegates from Guam. Although delegates would be unable to vote on the final passage of legislation, the ruling would permit them to cast a vote in the 'Committee of the Whole House on the State of the Union', a means by which the House expedites consideration of certain legislation, particularly amendments. The decision was expected to allow for more effective lobbying on the part of Guam's delegate to Congress, and the promotion of Guam's views on a number of important issues within the federal system.

Government

Guam is governed under the Organic Act of Guam of 1950, which gave the island statutory local power of self-government and made its inhabitants citizens of the United States, although they are not permitted to vote in national elections. Guam's non-voting Delegate to the US House of Representatives is elected every two years. Executive power is vested in the civilian Governor, who is elected by popular vote every four years. The heads of the executive departments are appointed by the Governor, with the consent of the Guam Legislature. The Legislature consists of 15 senators elected by popular vote every two years. It is empowered to enact legislation on local matters, including taxation and fiscal appropriations.

Defence

Guam is an important strategic military base for the USA, with 1,706 members of the Air Force and 1,074 naval personnel stationed there, as assessed at November 2007.

Economic Affairs

In 2000, according to estimates by the Bank of Hawaii (BOH), Guam's gross national income (GNI), at current prices, was US $2,772.8m., equivalent to $16,575 per head. Between 1988 and 1993, it was estimated, GNI increased, in real terms, at an average rate of some 10% per year, and by 3.9% in 1994. Official estimates of gross island product (GIP—the official measure of the Territory's economic performance) were recorded at $3,428m. in 2002, equivalent to $21,117 per head. In 1995–2006, according to World Bank figures, the population increased at an average annual rate of 1.4%.

Agriculture (including forestry, fishing and mining) engaged only an estimated 0.3% of the labour force in paid employment in December 2005, according to official payroll records. The principal crops cultivated on the island include watermelons, coconuts, cucumbers, gherkins, bananas, runner beans, aubergines (eggplants), squash, tomatoes and papaya. Livestock reared includes pigs, goats and poultry. The fishing catch totalled an estimated 162 metric tons in 2005.

The industrial sector accounted for some 15% of gross domestic product (GDP) in 1993. According to official payroll records, construction and manufacturing engaged an estimated 10.6% of the labour force in paid employment in December 2005. Construction, which alone engaged 6.1% of the employed labour force in 2002, is the dominant industrial activity, and is closely related to the tourist industry. According to official figures, in 1995 construction contributed 12.6% of GIP. Manufacturing industries, including textile and garment production and boat-building, engaged an estimated 2.9% of the labour force in paid employment in December 2005.

Service industries dominate the economy, engaging 89.2% of the labour force in paid employment in December 2005, according to payroll records. The federal and territorial Governments together employed 25.5% of workers at that time. According to official estimates, the services sector contributed 69.2% of GIP in 1995. Tourism is Guam's most important industry; the sector provided 18% of GDP and engaged an estimated 21.4% of the employed labour force in 1994. In 2005 some 1,227,587 tourists visited the island (of whom 78% were from Japan).

The Territory consistently records a visible trade deficit. According to official annual estimates based on sample months in each quarter, the cost of imports in 2005 was US $532.7m., while export revenues totalled just $51.9m. in 2005, and were estimated at $53.0m. in 2006. Major imports in 2005 included motor cars (16.9% of the total value of imports), beef, beer, luggage items, jewellery and watches. Exports in 2006 were dominated by motor cars (43.0% of the total value of exports) and fish (22.3%). Singapore supplied 39.1% of total imports in 2002. Japan purchased 51.3% of the island's exports in 2003. Guam is a low-duty port, and is an important distribution point for goods destined for Micronesia. Re-exports constitute a high proportion of Guam's exports, major commodities being petroleum and petroleum products, iron and steel scrap, and eggs.

In the year ending September 2005 total budgetary operational expenditure stood at US $735.1m. and revenue at $694.4m. In May 2005 the Office of the Public Auditor reported that some $26m. of public money had been lost in 2004 either through fraud or inefficiency. US federal Government expenditure in Guam totalled $1,380.4m. in 2005/06. The Government's total debt stood at $326.7m. at the end of the financial year 2003/04. According to official figures, the average annual rate of inflation was 3.5% in 1996–2007. Consumer prices increased by 11.6% in 2006 and by 6.8% in 2007. Guam's unemployment rate stood at 7.0% in December 2005, according to the national Bureau of Labor Statistics.

Guam is a member of the Pacific Community (see p. 377) and an associate member of the UN's Economic and Social Commission for Asia and the Pacific (ESCAP, see p. 35). In early 1996 Guam joined representatives of the other countries and territories of Micronesia at a meeting in Hawaii, at which a new regional organization, the Council of Micronesian Government Executives, was established. The body aimed to facilitate discussion of economic developments in the region and to examine possibilities for reducing the considerable cost of shipping essential goods between the islands.

Guam continues to receive considerable financial support from the USA, particularly in the area of defence (federal expenditure on defence in Guam reached US $738.6m. in 2005/06). In the early 2000s a series of natural disasters, notably Typhoon Pongsona in December 2002, severely damaged the island's infrastructure. Moreover, the tourism sector, which had expanded rapidly during the 1990s, was badly affected by the repercussions of the suicide attacks on the mainland USA in September 2001, compounded by the continued economic difficulties in Japan (the principal source of the island's visitors) and the outbreak of Severe Acute Respiratory Syndrome (SARS) in East Asia. By 2005, however, tourist numbers had recovered to pre-2002 levels of 1.2m. The privatization of the Guam Telephone Authority was finalized in December 2004, and in February 2005 Governor Camacho announced his intention to privatize the Guam Waterworks Authority. An agreement worth $72,000m., to sell a number of Guam-based telecommunications companies to a Japanese cellular telephone services provider, was formally approved in November 2006 by the Federal Communications Commission. It was envisaged that the recovery of the tourism industry in 2006 and 2007 and an increasingly buoyant construction sector (the value of building permits increased by 36%, to $167.6m., between 2004 and 2005) would continue to promote economic recovery. Furthermore, development projects costing a total of $86m. were scheduled by the territorial Government's Department of Public Works for 2006 and 2007. The outcome of ongoing discussions surrounding the schedule for a planned relocation of US marines and their families from the Japanese island of Okinawa to Guam (see Recent History), and a further US military proposal to station a Global Strike Task Force at Andersen air force base on Guam (the projected cost of which was $2,000m.), were likely to be crucial in strategic planning for significant economic growth in the future. However, in May 2008 Governor Camacho reiterated concerns that vital federal investment in Guam's infrastructure was required immediately in order to prepare for the potential 30% increase in the island's population over the next five years that was likely to result from the proposed troop deployments.

Education

School attendance is compulsory from six to 16 years of age. There were 26 public elementary schools, seven junior high and four senior high schools, as well as a number of private schools operating on the island in 2003. Total secondary enrolment in public schools in 2004/05 was 16,046 students. Some 3,034 students were enrolled at the university of Guam in that year. In 2000 the rate of adult illiteracy was estimated at 1.0%. Government expenditure on education was US $2,000m. in 2003/04 (equivalent to 29% of total expenditure).

Public Holidays

2008: 1 January (New Year's Day), 21 January (Martin Luther King Day), 18 February (Presidents' Day), 3 March (Guam Discovery Day), 21 March (Good Friday), 26 May (Memorial Day), 4 July (US Independence Day), 21 July (Liberation Day), 1 September (Labor Day), 13 October (Columbus Day), 2 November (All Souls' Day), 11 November (Veterans' Day), 27 November (Thanksgiving Day), 8 December (Immaculate Conception), 25 December (Christmas Day).

2009: 1 January (New Year's Day), 19 January (Martin Luther King Day), 16 February (Presidents' Day), 2 March (Guam Discovery Day), 10 April (Good Friday), 25 May (Memorial Day), 3 July (for US Independence Day), 21 July (Liberation Day), 7 September (Labor Day), 12 October (Columbus Day), 2 November (All Souls' Day), 11 November (Veterans' Day), 26 November (Thanksgiving Day), 8 December (Immaculate Conception), 25 December (Christmas Day).

Weights and Measures

With certain exceptions, the imperial system is in force. One US cwt equals 100 lb; one long ton equals 2,240 lb; one short ton equals 2,000 lb. A policy of gradual voluntary conversion to the metric system is being encouraged by the Federal Government.

Statistical Survey

Sources (unless otherwise stated): Guam Bureau of Statistics and Plans, PO Box 2950, Hagåtña; tel. 472-4201; fax 477-1812; internet www.bsp.guam.gov.

AREA AND POPULATION

Area: 549 sq km (212 sq miles).

Population: 133,152 at census of 1 April 1990; 154,805 (males 79,181, females 75,624) at census of 1 April 2000. *Mid-2008* (official estimate): 175,877.

Density (mid-2008): 320.4 per sq km.

Ethnic Groups (2000 census): Chamorro 57,297; Filipino 40,729; White 10,509; Other Asian 9,600; part-Chamorro 7,946; Chuukese 6,229; Total (incl. others) 154,805.

Regions (population at 2000 census): North 80,466; Central 45,382; South 28,957.

Principal Towns (population at 2000 census): Tamuning 10,833; Mangilao 7,794; Yigo 6,391; Astumbo 5,207; Barrigada 4,417; Hagåtña (capital) 1,122.

Births, Marriages and Deaths (2005, unless otherwise indicated): Registered live births 3,203 (birth rate 19.0 per 1,000); Registered marriages (2004) 1,561; Registered deaths 697 (death rate 4.1 per 1,000). Sources: mostly UN, *Population and Vital Statistics Report* and Office of Insular Affairs, *2004 Guam Statistical Yearbook*.

Expectation of Life (years at birth, UN estimates): 78 (males 76; females 81) in 2004. Source: Office of Insular Affairs, *2004 Guam Statistical Yearbook*.

Economically Active Population (persons aged 16 years and over, excl. armed forces, 2002 estimates): Agriculture, forestry, fishing and mining 290; Manufacturing 1,570; Construction 3,420; Transport, storage and utilities 4,590; Wholesale and retail trade 12,690; Finance, insurance and real estate 2,450; Public administration 16,500; Education, health and social services 14,510; Total employed 56,020; Unemployed 7,070; Total labour force 63,090. *2005* (payroll data at December): Agriculture, forestry, fishing and mining 170; Manufacturing 1,660; Construction 4,460; Transport, storage and utilities 4,970; Wholesale and retail trade 14,240; Finance, insurance and real estate 2,540; Public administration 14,770; Education, health and social services 15,190; Total employed 58,000. Source: Guam Department of Labor.

AGRICULTURE, ETC.

Principal Crops (metric tons, 2005, FAO estimates): Coconuts 57,353; Roots and tubers 3,116; Cucumbers and gherkins 414; Watermelons 2,473; Other melons 495; Bananas 511. Note: Data were not available for 2006.

Livestock (head, year ending September 2005, FAO estimates): Chickens 200,000; Ducks 5,000; Pigs 5,100; Goats 680. Note: Data were not available for 2006.

Livestock Products (metric tons, 2005, FAO estimates): Chicken meat 200; Hen eggs 700; Pig meat 200. Note: Data were not available for 2006.

Fishing (metric tons, live weight, 2005): Common dolphinfish 37; Wahoo 16; Skipjack tuna 15; Total capture (incl. others) 162.

Source: FAO.

INDUSTRY

Electric Energy (million kWh, estimates): 1,603 in 2002; 1,457 in 2003; 1,589 in 2004. Source: UN, *Industrial Commodity Statistics Yearbook*.

FINANCE

Currency and Exchange Rates: US currency is used. For details, see section on the Northern Mariana Islands.

Federal Direct Expenditures (US $ million, year ending September): 1,249.4 (Defence 659.7) in 2004; 1,412.8 (Defence 711.7) in 2005; 1,380.4 (Defence 738.6) in 2006 (Source: US Census Bureau, *Consolidated Federal Funds Report*).

Budget (US $ million, year ending September 2005): *Revenue:* Taxes 440.3; Licences, fees and permits 37.1; Use of money and property 5.6; Federal contributions 196.8; Total (incl. others) 694.4. *Expenditure:* General government 68.2; Public order 84.2; Public health 64.1; Community services 34.4; Individual and collective rights 44.4; Public education 223.7; Debt service 57.3; Total (incl. others) 735.1.

Cost of Living (Consumer Price Index; base: July–September 1996 = 100): All items 122.1 in 2005; 136.2 in 2006; 145.4 in 2007.

Gross Island Product (US $ million at current prices, estimates): 3,428 in 2002.

Gross Island Product by Economic Activity (US $ million, 1995): Construction 379.02; Trade 622.86; Public administration 965.97; Other services 486.94; Other non-services 544.61; Total 2,999.40.

EXTERNAL TRADE

Principal Commodities: *Imports* (US $ '000, estimated averages based on sample months, 2005): Food and non-alcoholic beverages 163,587.9 (Meat and edible offal of beef 18,179.4; Water, containing sugar 18,054.6); Alcoholic beverages 22,752.3 (Beer 16,223.5); Transportation and parts 111,165.4 (Motor cars 90,235.8); Construction materials 19,734.0; Men's and women's apparel 26,132.3; Plastics, leather and paper 93,249.2 (Travel goods, handbags, etc. 74,643.3); Other imports 86,652.6 (Articles of jewellery 15,985.7; Watches 24,497.0); Total (incl. others) 532,687.1. *Exports* (US $ '000, 2006): Motor cars 22,758.7; Fish (chilled, fresh, frozen, dried and salted) 11,830.0; Iron, non-alloy steel bars and rods 2,395.8; Trunks, suitcases and similar bags 2,221.9; Tobacco, cigars, etc. 1,886.9; Aluminium waste, scraps, tubes or fittings 1,659.0; Wrist watches and parts 1,298.4; Total (incl. others) 52,963.3.

Principal Trading Partners (US $ '000, 2002): *Imports:* Hong Kong 36,240; Japan 96,450; Korea, Republic 9,688; Philippines 1,437; Singapore 180,076; Australia 9,770; New Zealand 5,520; Total (incl. others) 527,000. *Exports:* Philippines 1,440; Singapore 500; Korea, Republic 2,280; Japan 30,780; Total (incl. others) 49,380.
Source: UN, *Statistical Yearbook for Asia and the Pacific*.

TRANSPORT

Road Traffic (registered motor vehicles, 2005): Private cars 63,631; Taxis 348; Buses 644; Goods vehicles 24,971; Motorcycles 1,273; Total (incl. others) 96,112. Source: Department of Revenue and Taxation, Government of Guam.

International Sea-borne Shipping (estimated freight traffic, '000 revenue tons, 2005): Goods loaded 246.7; Goods unloaded 1,170.2; Goods transshipped 624.8. *Merchant Fleet* (total displacement, '000 grt at 31 December 1992): 1 (Source: Lloyd's Register-Fairplay, *World Fleet Statistics*).

Civil Aviation (Guam International Airport, 2005): *Passengers:* aArrivals 1,441,248; Departures 1,451,159; In transit 179,043. *Cargo* (metric tons): Unloaded 17,917; Loaded 14,099. *Mail* (metric tons): Incoming 3,996; Outgoing 1,668. *Aircraft Movements:* 34,101 (Source: Guam International Airport Authority).

TOURISM

Foreign Tourist Arrivals: 909,506 in 2003; 1,159,881 in 2004; 1,227,587 in 2005.

Tourist Arrivals by Country of Residence ('000, 2005): Japan 955.2; Korea, Republic 109.3; Philippines 7.1; Taiwan 23.4; USA 45.9; Total (incl. others) 1,227.6.

Tourism Receipts (US $ million): 2,361 in 1998; 1,908 in 1999.
Source: World Tourism Organization.

COMMUNICATIONS MEDIA

Radio Receivers (1997): 221,000 in use.
Television Receivers (1999): 110,000 in use.
Telephones (2004): 69,755 main lines in use.
Mobile Cellular Telephones (2005, estimate): 98,000 subscribers*.
Internet Users (2004): 79,000*.
Daily Newspapers (1997): 1 (circulation 24,457).
Non-daily Newspapers (1988): 4 (estimated circulation 26,000).
*Sources: International Telecommunication Union and UN, *Statistical Yearbook for Asia and the Pacific*.

EDUCATION

Institutions (2005/06): Primary (incl. kindergarten, grades 1–8) 42 (public 27, private 15; Secondary (grades 9–12) 9 (public 4, private 5); ; Guam Community College; University of Guam.

Teachers (2005/06): Primary 1,917 (public 1,405, private 512); Secondary 1,108 (public 470, private 638).

Enrolment (2005/06): Kindergarten (grades 1–5) 18,842 (public 14,555, private 4,287); Primary (grades 6–8) 8,893 (public 6,852, private 2,041); Secondary (grades 9–12) 12,048 (public 9,371, private 2,677); High school (graduates) 1,735 (public 1,218, private 517); Guam Community College 10,268; University of Guam 3,034.

Sources: Department of Education, Guam Community College, Office of Insular Affairs, *2005 Guam Statistical Yearbook* and University of Guam.

Directory

The Constitution

Guam is governed under the Organic Act of Guam of 1950, which gave the island statutory local power of self-government and made its inhabitants citizens of the United States, although they cannot vote in presidential elections. Their Delegate to the US House of Representatives is elected every two years. Executive power is vested in the civilian Governor and the Lieutenant-Governor, first elected, by popular vote, in 1970. Elections for the governorship occur every four years. The Government has 48 executive departments, whose heads are appointed by the Governor with the consent of the Guam Legislature. The Legislature consists of 15 members elected by popular vote every two years (members are known as Senators). It is empowered to pass laws on local matters, including taxation and fiscal appropriations.

The Government
(April 2008)

Governor: FELIX CAMACHO (Republican—took office January 2003; re-elected 7 November 2006).
Lieutenant-Governor: Dr MICHAEL W. CRUZ.

GOVERNMENT OFFICES

Government offices are located throughout the island.
Office of the Governor: POB 2950, Hagåtña, GU 96932; tel. 472-8931; fax 477-4826; e-mail governor@mail.gov.gu; internet governor.guam.gov.
Department of the Interior, Office of Insular Affairs (OIA): Hagåtña, GU 96910; tel. 472-7279; fax 472-7309; Field Representative KEITH A. PARSKY.
Customs and Quarantine Agency: 13–16A Mariner Ave, Tiyan, Barrigada, GU 96913; tel. 475-6202; fax 475-6227; Dir ROBERT D. CAMACHO.
Department of Administration: POB 884, Hagåtña, GU 96932; tel. 475-1110; fax 475-6788; e-mail doadir@mail.gov.gu; Dir LOURDES M. PEREZ.
Department of Agriculture: 192 Dairy Rd, Mangilao, GU 96913; tel. 734-3942; fax 734-6569; e-mail guamagriculture@yahoo.com; Dir PAUL BASSLER.
Department of Chamorro Affairs: tel. 475-4278; fax 475-4227; e-mail dcapres1@chamorroaffairs.org; internet www.chamorroaffairs.org; Pres. ELIZABETH A. P. DIEGO.
Department of Commerce: 102 M St, Tiyan, GU 96913; tel. 475-0321; fax 477-9031; e-mail commerce@mail.gov.gu.
Department of Corrections: POB 3236, Hagåtña, GU 96932; tel. 734-4668; fax 734-4990; Dir JOSÉ PALACIOS (acting).
Environmental Protection Agency: 17-3304 Mariner Ave, Tiyan, GU 96913; tel. 475-1658; fax 477-9402; e-mail mmann@guamepa.govguam.net; internet www.guamepa.govguam.net; Administrator LORILEE T. CRISOSTOMO.
Housing and Urban Renewal Authority: 117 Bien Venida Ave, Sinajana, GU 96910; tel. 472-3910; fax 472-7565; e-mail rdeguzman@netpci.com; internet www.ghura.org; Exec. Dir RONALD DE GUZMAN.
Department of Integrated Services for Individuals with Disabilities: Suite 703, 238 Archbishop F. C. Flores St, Pacific News Bldg, Hagåtña, GU 96910; tel. 475-4645; fax 477-2892; Dir ROSEANNE ADA.
Department of Labor: 414 West Soledad Ave, GCIC Bldg, Hagåtña, GU 96910; tel. 475-7000; fax 475-7045; e-mail connent@ite.net; internet www.guamdol.net; Dir MARIA CONNELLEY.
Department of Land Management: 590 South Marine Corps Dr., Route 1, Tamuning, GU 96913; tel. 649-5390; fax 649-5383; internet dlm.guam.gov; Dir TEREZO R. MORTERO.
Department of Law: Suite 2-200E, Judicial Center Bldg, 120 West O'Brien Drive, Hagåtña, GU 96910; tel. 475-3324; fax 475-2493; e-mail law@ns.gov.gu; internet www.justice.gov.gu/dol.
Department of Mental Health and Substance Abuse: e-mail info@guamdmhsa.com; internet dmhsa.guam.gov; Dir ANDREA M. LEITHEISER (acting).

UNITED STATES EXTERNAL TERRITORIES Guam

Department of Military Affairs: 430 Army Dr., Bldg 300, Barrigada; tel. 735-0406; fax 649-8775; internet dma.guam.gov.

Department of Parks and Recreation: 490 Chalan Palasyo, Agaña Heights, GU 96910; tel. 475-6296; fax 477-0997; e-mail parks@ns.gov.gu; internet www.dpr.guam.gov; Dir JOSEPH W. DUENAS.

Department of Public Health and Social Services: 123 Chalan Kareta, Route 10, Mangilao, GU 96923; tel. 735-7102; fax 734-5910; internet dphss.guam.gov; Dir PETER JOHN D. CAMACHO (acting).

Public School System: POB DE, Hagåtña, GU 96932; tel. 475-0457; fax 472-5003; internet www.gdoe.net; fmrly known as Department of Education.

Department of Public Works: 542 North Marine Drive, Tamuning, GU 96911; tel. 646-3131; fax 646-3233; internet www.dpw.guam.gov; Dir LAWRENCE P. PEREZ.

Department of Revenue and Taxation: 1240 Route 16, Barrigada, GU 96913; tel. 635-1817; fax 633-2643; e-mail pinadm@revtax.gov.gu; internet www.guamtax.com; Dir ARTEMIO ILAGAN.

Department of the Treasury: PDN Bldg, Suite 404, 238 Archbishop Flores St, Hagåtña, GU 96910.

Department of Youth Affairs: POB 23672, Guam Main Facility, GU 96921; tel. 735-5010; fax 734-7536; e-mail ddell@ns.gov.gu; internet guamyouth.org; Dir CHRISTOPHER M. DUENAS.

Office of Civil Defense (Guam Homeland Security): 221-B Chalan Palasyo, Agana Heights, GU 96910; tel. 475-9600; fax 477-3727; internet www.guamhs.org; f. 1999; Administrator CHARLES H. ADA, II (acting).

Legislature

GUAM LEGISLATURE

The Guam Legislature has 15 members, directly elected by popular vote for a two-year term. Elections took place on 7 November 2006, when the Republican Party won eight of the 15 seats and the Democratic Party secured seven.

Speaker: MARK FORBES.

CONGRESS

Guam elects a non-voting Delegate to the US House of Representatives. An election was held on 7 November 2006, when the Democratic candidate, Madeleine Z. Bordallo, was re-elected unopposed as Delegate.

Delegate of Guam: MADELEINE Z. BORDALLO, Cannon House Office Bldg, 427, Washington, DC 20515-5301, USA; tel. (202) 225-1188; fax (202) 226-0341; e-mail madeleine.bordallo@mail.house.gov; internet www.house.gov/bordallo.

Election Commission

Guam Election Commission: Guam Capital Investment Corpn Bldg, 414 West Soledad Ave, Suite 200, Hagåtña 96910; tel. 477-9791; fax 477-1895; e-mail gec@kuentos.guam.net; internet www.guamelection.org; Chair. FREDERICK J. HORECKY; Exec. Dir GERALD A. TAITANO.

Judicial System

Attorney-General: ALICIA LIMTIACO.
US Attorney: LEONARDO M. RAPADAS.

Supreme Court of Guam: Suite 300, Guam Judicial Center, 120 West O'Brien Drive, Hagåtña, GU 96910; tel. 475-3162; fax 475-3140; e-mail justice@guamsupremecourt.com; internet www.guamsupremecourt.com; Chief Justice ROBERT J. TORRES, Jr.

District Court of Guam

4th Floor, US Courthouse, 520 West Soledad Ave, Hagåtña, GU 96910; tel. 473-9180; fax 473-9118; e-mail judith_hattori@gud.uscourts.gov; internet www.gud.uscourts.gov.

Judge appointed by the President of the USA. The court has the jurisdiction of a Federal district court and of a bankruptcy court of the United States in all cases arising under the laws of the United States. Appeals may be made to the Court of Appeals for the Ninth Circuit and to the Supreme Court of the United States.

Magistrate Judge: JOAQUIN V. E. MANIBUSAN, Jr.

Superior Court of Guam

120 West O'Brien Drive, Hagåtña, GU 96910; tel. 475-3250; internet www.justice.gov.gu/superior.html.

Judges are appointed by the Governor of Guam for an initial eight-year term and are thereafter retained by popular vote. The Superior Court has jurisdiction over cases arising in Guam other than those heard in the District Court.

Presiding Judge: ALBERTO C. LAMORENA, III.

There are also Probate, Traffic, Domestic, Juvenile and Small Claims Courts.

Religion

The majority of the population are Roman Catholic, but there are also members of the Episcopal (Anglican) Church, the Baptist churches and the Seventh-day Adventist Church. There are small communities of Muslims, Buddhists and Jews.

CHRISTIANITY

The Roman Catholic Church

Guam comprises the single archdiocese of Agaña. The Archbishop participates in the Catholic Bishops' Conference of the Pacific, based in Suva, Fiji, and the Federation of Catholic Bishops' Conferences of Oceania, based in Wellington, New Zealand.

At 31 December 2005 there were 132,494 adherents in Guam.

Archbishop of Agaña: Most Rev. ANTHONY SABLAN APURON, Chancery Office, Cuesta San Ramón 96910B, Hagåtña, GU 96910; tel. 472-6116; fax 477-3519; e-mail archbishop@mail.archdioceseofguam.com; internet www.archdioceseofagana.com.

BAHÁ'Í FAITH

National Spiritual Assembly: POB Box BA, Hagåtña, GU 96931; tel. 472-9100; fax 472-9101; e-mail nsamar@ite.net; mems resident in 19 localities in Guam and 10 localities in the Northern Mariana Islands.

The Press

NEWSPAPERS AND PERIODICALS

Bonita: POB 11468, Tumon, GU 96931; tel. 632-4543; fax 637-6720; f. 1998; monthly; Publr IMELDA SANTOS; circ. 3,000.

Directions: POB 27290, Barrigada, GU 96921; tel. 635-7501; fax 635-7520; f. 1996; monthly; Publr JERRY ROBERTS; circ. 3,800.

Hospitality Guahan: POB 8565, Tamuning, GU 96931; tel. 649-1447; fax 649-8565; e-mail info@ghra.org; internet www.ghra.org; f. 1996; quarterly; circ. 3,000.

Marianas Business Journal: POB 3191, Hagåtña, GU 96932; tel. 649-0883; fax 649-8883; e-mail glimpses@glimpsesofguam.com; internet www.mbjguam.net; f. 2003; fortnightly; Publr MAUREEN N. MARATITA; Editor PATRICIA SHOOK; circ. 3,000.

Pacific Daily News and Sunday News: POB DN, Hagåtña, GU 96932; tel. 477-1736; fax 472-1512; e-mail cblas@guampdn.com; internet www.guampdn.com; f. 1944; Publr RINDRATY LIMTIACO; Man. Editor DAVID CRISOSTOMO; circ. 28,520 (weekdays), 26,237 (Sunday).

The Pacific Voice: POB 2553, Hagåtña, GU 96932; tel. 472-6427; fax 477-5224; f. 1950; Sunday; Roman Catholic; Gen. Man. TEREZO MORTERA; Editor Rev. Fr HERMES LOSBANES; circ. 6,500.

TV Guam Magazine: 237 Mamis St, Tamuning, GU 96911; tel. 646-4030; fax 646-7445; f. 1973; weekly; Publr DINA GRANT; Man. Editor EMILY UNTALAN; circ. 15,000.

NEWS AGENCY

United Press International (UPI) (USA): POB 1617, Hagåtña, GU 96910; tel. 632-1138; Correspondent DICK WILLIAMS.

Broadcasting and Communications

TELECOMMUNICATIONS

Guam Educational Telecommunication Corporation (KGTF): POB 21449, Guam Main Facility, Barrigada, GU 96921; tel. 734-2207; fax 734-3476; e-mail kgtfl2@ite.net; internet www.kgtf.org.

Guam Telephone Authority: 624 North Marines Corps Dr., POB 9008, Tamuning, GU 96913; tel. 644-4482; fax 649-4821; e-mail ask@gta.net; internet www.gta.net; acquired by TeleGuam Holdings LLC in Dec. 2004; CEO and Pres. DAN MOFFAT.

BROADCASTING

Radio

K-Stereo: POB 20249, Guam Main Facility, Barrigada, GU 96921; tel. 477-9448; fax 477-6411; operates on FM 24 hours a day; Pres. EDWARD H. POPPE; Gen. Man. FRANCES W. POPPE.

KOKU-FM: 424 West O'Brien Drive, Julale Center, Hagåtña, GU 96910; tel. 477-5658; fax 472-7663; e-mail marketing@hitradio100

.com; operates on FM 24 hours a day; Pres. Kurt S. Moylan; Marketing and Sales Man. Vince Limuaco.

KPRG FM: KPRG, UoG Station Mangilao, GU 96923; tel. 734-8930; fax 734-2958; e-mail kprg@kprg.org; internet www.kprg.org; operated by the University of Guam; news and music; Chair. Marie Mesa-Kerlin; Chairs Tod Thompson, Nick Captain; Gen. Man. Chris Hartig (acting).

Radio Guam (KUAM): 600 Harman Loop, Dededo, GU 96912; tel. 637-5826; fax 637-9865; e-mail generalmanager@kuam.com; internet www.kuam.com; f. 1954; operates on AM and FM 24 hours a day; Pres. Paul M. Calvo; Gen. Man. Joey Calvo.

Sorensen Media Group: Suite 800, 111 Chalan Santo Papa, Hagåtña, GU 96910; tel. 477-5700; fax 477-3982; e-mail rex@spbguam.com; internet www.sorensenmediagroup.com; f. 1981; Chair. and CEO Rex Sorensen; Man. Dir Evan Cohen.

Trans World Radio Pacific (TWR): POB CC, Hagåtña, GU 96932; tel. 477-9701; fax 477-2838; e-mail ktwr@twr.org; internet www.guam.net/home/twr; f. 1975; broadcasts Christian programmes on KTWR and one medium-wave station, KTWG, covering Guam and nearby islands, and operates five short-wave transmitters reaching most of Asia, Africa and the Pacific; Chair. Thomas J. Lowell; Pres. Dr David G. Tucker; Station Dir Michael Davis.

Television

KGTF—TV: POB 21449 Guam Main Facility, Barrigada, GU 96921; tel. 734-3476; fax 734-5483; e-mail kgtf12@kgtf.org; internet www.kgtf.org; f. 1970; cultural, public service and educational programmes; Gen. Man. Geraldine 'Ginger' S. Underwood; Operations Man. Benny T. Flores.

KTGM—TV: 692 Marine Dr., Tamuning 96911; tel. 649-8814; fax 649-0371.

KUAM—TV: 600 Harmon Loop, Dededo, Hagåtña, GU 96912; tel. 637-5826; fax 637-9865; e-mail generalmanager@kuam.com; internet www.kuam.com; f. 1956; operates channels 8 and 11; News Dir Sabrina Salas.

Finance

(cap. = capital; res = reserves; = dep. = deposits; m. = million; brs = branches; amounts in US dollars)

BANKING

Commercial Banks

Allied Banking Corpn (Philippines): Suite 104, Bejess Commercial Bldg, 719 South Marine Drive, Tamuning, GU 96913; tel. 649-5001; fax 649-5002; e-mail abcguam@kuentos.guam.net; Asst Vice-Pres. Mario R. Palisoc; 1 br.

Bank of Guam: POB BW, 111 Chalan Santo Papa, Hagåtña, GU 96932; tel. 472-5300; fax 477-8687; e-mail customerservice@bankofguam.com; internet www.bankofguam.com; f. 1972; total assets $704.6m. (2003); Chair. Anthony A. Leon Guerrero; Exec. Vice-Pres. William D. Leon Guerrero; 19 brs.

Bank of Hawaii (USA): PO Box BH, Hagåtña, GU 96932; tel. 479-3500; fax 479-3777; Vice-Pres. Rodney Kimura; 3 brs.

BankPacific, Ltd: 151 Aspinall Ave, Hagåtña, GU 96910; tel. 472-6704; fax 477-1483; e-mail philipf@bankpacific.com; internet www.bankpacific.com; f. 1954; Pres. and CEO Philip J. Flores; Exec. Vice-Pres. Mark O. Fish; 4 brs in Guam; 1 br. in Palau; 1 br. in Northern Mariana Islands.

Citibank NA (USA): 402 East Marine Drive, POB FF, Hagåtña, GU 96932; tel. 477-2484; fax 477-9441; internet www.citibank.com/guam; Vice-Pres. Rashid Habib; 2 brs.

Citizens Security Bank (Guam) Inc: Suite 112, 424 West O'Brien Dr., Julale Shopping Center, Hagåtña, GU 96910; tel. 479-9000; fax 479-9090; internet csb.com.gu; mem. of ANZ Group; Pres. and CEO Daniel L. Webb; 4 brs.

First Commercial Bank (Taiwan): POB 2461, Hagåtña, GU 96932; tel. 472-6864; fax 477-8921; e-mail fcbgu@ite.net; Gen. Man. Jenn-Hwa Wang; 1 br.

First Hawaiian Bank (USA): Compadres Mall 562, Harmon Loop Rd, Dededo, GU 96912; tel. 475-7900; fax 637-9686; internet www.fhb.com; Regional Man. (Guam and Saipan) John K. Lee; 3 brs.

HSBC Ltd: POB 27c, Hagåtña, GU 96932; tel. 647-8588; fax 646-3767; CEO Guy N. de B. Priestley; 2 brs.

Metropolitan Bank and Trust Co: 665 South Marine Drive, Tamuning, GU 96911; tel. 649-9555; fax 649-9558; e-mail mbguam@metrobank.com.ph; f. 1975; Sen. Man. Josephine M. Papelera.

Union Bank of California (USA): 194 Hernan Cortes Ave, POB 7809, Hagåtña, GU 96910; tel. 477-8811; fax 472-3284; Man. Kinji Suzuki; 2 brs.

INSURANCE

American National Insurance Co: POB 3340, Hagåtña, GU 96910; tel. 477-9600.

Chung Kuo Insurance Co: GCIC Bldg, Suite 707, 414 West Soledad Ave, Hagåtña, GU 96910; tel. 477-7696; fax 477-4788; internet www.cki.com.tw.

Midland National Life Insurance Co: Winner Bldg, Suite 20n, Tamuning, GU 96911; tel. 649-0330; internet www.mnlife.com; f. 1906 as Dakota Mutual Life Insurance Company; name changed as above in 1925.

Moylan's Insurance Underwriters, Inc: Suite 102 Julale Shopping Center, 424 West O'Brien Dr., Hagåtña, GU 96910; tel. 477-8613; fax 477-1837; e-mail agana@moylansinsurance.com; internet www.moylansinsurance.com; Pres. Kurt S. Moylan; Admin. Man Cecilia Anas.

Nanbo Insurance: POB 2980, Hagåtña, GU 96910; tel. 477-9754; internet www.nanbo.com.

Pioneer Pacific Financial Services, Inc of Guam: POB EM, Hagåtña, GU 96910; tel. 477-6400.

Trade and Industry

DEVELOPMENT ORGANIZATION

Guam Economic Development and Commerce Authority (GEDCA): Guam International Trade Center Bldg, Suite 511, 590 South Marine Dr., Tamuning, GU 96911; tel. 647-4332; fax 649-4146; e-mail help@investguam.com; internet www.investguam.com; f. 1965; Pres. and Gen. Man. Angel Mendoza; Admin. Anthony Blaz.

CHAMBER OF COMMERCE

Guam Chamber of Commerce: Ada Plaza Center, Suite 101, 173 Aspinall Ave, POB 283, Hagåtña, GU 96932; tel. 472-6311; fax 472-6202; e-mail gchamber@guamchamber.com; internet www.guamchamber.com.gu; f. 1924; Chair. Laura-Lynn Dacanay; Pres. Joey Crisostomo.

EMPLOYERS' ORGANIZATION

The Employers' Council: 718 North Marine Drive, Suite 201, East-West Business Center, Upper Tumon, GU 96913; tel. 649-6616; fax 649-3030; e-mail tecinc@ite.net; internet www.ecouncil.org; f. 1966; private, non-profit asscn providing management development training and advice on personnel law and labour relations; Exec. Dir E. L. Gibson.

UTILITIES

Electricity

Guam Energy Office: 548 North Marine Corps Dr., Tamuning, GU 96913; tel. 646-4361; fax 649-1215; e-mail lucybk@teleguam.net; internet www.guamenergy.com; Dir J. Lawrence M. Cruz.

Guam Power Authority: POB 2977, Hagåtña, GU 96932; tel. 648-3225; fax 649-6942; internet www.guampowerauthority.com; f. 1968; autonomous government agency; supplies electricity throughout the island; Gen. Man. John Benavente.

Water

Guam Waterworks Authority: 578 North Marine Drive, Tamuning, GU 96913; tel. 647-2603; fax 646-2335; e-mail heidi@guamwaterworks.org; internet www.guamwaterworks.org; CEO John Benavente.

TRADE UNIONS

Many workers belong to trade unions based in the USA such as the American Federation of Government Employees and the American Postal Workers' Union.

Guam Federation of Teachers (GFT): Local 1581, POB 2301, Hagåtña, GU 96932; tel. 735-4390; fax 734-8085; e-mail webmaster@gftunion.com; internet www.gftunion.com; f. 1965; affiliate of American Federation of Teachers; Pres. Matt Rector; 2,000 mems.

Guam Hotel and Restaurant Association: POB 8565, Tamuning, GU 96931; tel. 649-1447; e-mail president@ghra.org; internet www.ghra.org; 37 mem. restaurants and hotels; Pres. Mary P. Torre.

Guam Landowners' Association: Hagåtña; Sec. Ronald Teehan.

Transport

ROADS

There are 885 km (550 miles) of public roads, of which some 675 km (420 miles) are paved. A further 685 km (425 miles) of roads are classified as non-public, and include roads located on federal government installations.

SHIPPING

Apra, on the central western side of the island, is one of the largest protected deep-water harbours in the Pacific.

Port Authority of Guam: 1026 Cabras Highway, Suite 201, Piti, GU 96925; tel. 477-5931; fax 477-2689; e-mail webmaster@portofguam.com; internet www.portofguam.com; f. 1975; government-operated port facilities; Gen. Man. JOSEPH W. DUENAS; Chair. MONTE MESA.

Ambyth, Shipping and Trading, Inc: 1026 Cabras Highway, Piti, GU 96915; tel. 477-7250; fax 472-1264; e-mail ops@ambyth.guam.net; internet www.ambyth.com; agents for all types of vessels and charter brokers; Pres. ALFRED LAM; Gen. Man. ANDREW MILLER.

Atkins, Kroll, Inc: 443 South Marine Dr., Tamuning, GU 96913; tel. 649-6410; e-mail atkins_kroll@akguam.com; internet www.akguam.com; f. 1914; vehicle distribution; Pres. ROBERT J. HERNANDEZ; Vice-Pres. and Gen. Man. DAN CAMACHO.

COAM Trading Co Ltd: PAG Bldg, Suite 110, 1026 Cabas Highway, Piti, GU 96925; tel. 477-1737; fax 472-3386.

Dewitt Moving and Storage: Suite 100, 165-1, Guerrero St, Tamuning, GU 96913; tel. 646-4442; fax 646-0034; e-mail ezdewitt@dewittguam.com; internet www.dewittguam.com; Pres. JOHN BURROWS.

Guam Shipping Agency: PO Box GD, Hagåtña, GU 96932; tel. 477-7381; fax 477-7553; Gen. Man. H. KO.

Interbulk Shipping (Guam) Inc: Bank of Guam Bldg, Suite 502, 111 Chalan Santo Papa, Hagåtña, GU 96910; Man. S. GYSTAD.

Maritime Agencies of the Pacific Ltd: Piti, GU 96925; tel. 477-8500; fax 477-5726; e-mail rehmapship@kuentos.guam.net; f. 1976; agents for fishing vessels, cargo, dry products and construction materials; Pres. ROBERT E. HAHN.

Pacific Navigation System: POB 7, Hagåtña, GU 96910; f. 1946; Pres. KENNETH T. JONES, Jr.

Seabridge Micronesian, Inc: 1026 Cabras Highway, Suite 114, Piti, Guam 96925; tel. 477-7345; fax 477-6206; Gen. Man. PAUL L. BLAS.

Sea-Land Service, Inc: POB 8897, Tamuning, GU 96931; tel. 475-8100; internet www.horizon-lines.com; CEO CHUCK RAYMOND.

Tucor Services: 180 Guerrero St, Harmon Industrial Park, POB 6128, Tamuning, GU 96911; tel. 646-6947; fax 646-6945; e-mail boll@tucor.com; general agents for numerous dry cargo, passenger and steamship cos; Pres. MICHELLE BOLL.

CIVIL AVIATION

Guam is served by A. B. Won Pat International Airport.

Guam International Airport Authority: POB 8770, Tamuning, GU 96931; tel. 646-0300; fax 646-8823; e-mail lizb@guamairport.net; internet www.guamairport.com; Chair. FRANK F. BLAS; Exec. Man. JESUS Q. TORRES.

Asia Pacific Airlines (APA): POB 24858, Guam Main Facility, Barrigada, Guam 96921; fax 647-8440; e-mail info@flyapa.com; internet www.flyapa.com; f. 1999; affiliate of Tan Holdings Corpn. (Commonwealth of the Northern Mariana Islands); cargo; serving Guam, Hawaii, Hong Kong, Marshall Islands, Federated States of Micronesia, Palau and the Philippines.

Continental Micronesia Airlines: POB 8778, Tamuning, GU 96931; tel. 649-6594; fax 649-6588; internet www.continental.com; f. 1968, as Air Micronesia, by Continental Airlines (USA); hub operations in Guam and Saipan (Northern Mariana Islands); services throughout the region and to destinations in the Far East and the mainland USA; Pres. and CEO LARRY KELLNER.

Freedom Air: POB 1578, Hagåtña, GU 96932; tel. 647-8359; fax 646-7488; e-mail freedom@ite.net; internet www.freedomairguam.com; f. 1974; Man. Dir JOAQUIN L. FLORES, Jr.

Tourism

Tourism is the most important industry on Guam. In 2005 there were 1,227,587 visitor arrivals. In that year some 78% of arrivals were visitors from Japan; 9% were from the Republic of Korea, and 4% from the USA. Most of Guam's hotels are situated in, or near to, Tumon, where amenities for entertainment are well-developed. Numerous sunken wrecks of aircraft and ships from Second World War battles provide interesting sites for divers. There were 7,561 hotel rooms on Guam in 2004. A total of US $16.2m. was collected in hotel occupancy taxes in 2002. The industry as a whole earned some $1,908m. in 1999.

Guam Visitors Bureau: 401 Pale San Vitores Rd, Tumon, GU 96913; tel. 646-5278; fax 646-8861; internet www.visitguam.org; Chair. DAVID B. TYDINGCO; Gen. Man. GERALD S. A. PEREZ.

THE UNITED STATES VIRGIN ISLANDS

Introductory Survey

Location, Climate, Language, Religion, Flag, Capital

The United States Virgin Islands consists of three main inhabited islands (St Croix, St Thomas and St John) and about 50 smaller islands, mostly uninhabited. They are situated at the eastern end of the Greater Antilles, about 64 km (40 miles) east of Puerto Rico in the Caribbean Sea. The climate is tropical, although tempered by the prevailing easterly trade winds. The temperature averages 26°C (79°F), with little variation between winter and summer. The humidity is low for the tropics. English is the official language, but Spanish and Creole are also widely used. The people of the US Virgin Islands are predominantly of African descent. There is a strong religious tradition, and most of the inhabitants are Christians, mainly Protestants. The flag (proportions 2 by 3) is white, with a modified version of the US coat of arms (an eagle holding an olive branch in one foot and a sheaf of arrows in the other, with a shield, comprising a small horizontal blue panel above vertical red and white stripes, superimposed), between the letters V and I, in the centre. The capital is Charlotte Amalie, on the island of St Thomas.

Recent History

The Virgin Islands, originally inhabited by Carib and Arawak Indians, were discovered by Europeans in 1493. The group subsequently passed through English, French, and Dutch control, before the western islands of St Thomas and St John, colonized by Denmark after 1670, and St Croix, purchased from France in 1733, became the Danish West Indies. In 1917 these islands, which are strategically placed in relation to the Panama Canal, were sold for US $25m. by Denmark to the USA. They now form an unincorporated territory of the USA. Residents of the US Virgin Islands are US citizens, but cannot vote in presidential elections, if resident in the islands. The US Virgin Islands is represented in the US House of Representatives by one popularly elected Delegate, who is permitted to vote only in committees of the House.

The inhabitants of the islands were granted a measure of self-government by the Organic Act, as revised in 1954, which created the elected 15-member Senate. Since 1970, executive authority has been vested in the elected Governor and Lieutenant-Governor. In the first gubernatorial election, in 1970, the Republican incumbent, Melvin Evans, retained office. In 1974 Cyril E. King, leader of the Independent Citizens Movement (a breakaway faction of the Democratic Party), was elected Governor. On King's death in 1978, the former Lieutenant-Governor, Juan Luis, was elected Governor. He was returned to power in the 1982 election. The governorship passed to the Democratic Party with the election of Alexander Farrelly in 1986. Farrelly was re-elected Governor in 1990, and in the 1994 elections was succeeded by an Independent, Dr Roy Schneider. The governorship was regained by a Democrat, Charles Turnbull, in the 1998 elections. Turnbull was re-elected to the post in 2000 and 2002.

Since 1954 there have been five attempts to redraft the Constitution to give the US Virgin Islands greater autonomy. Each draft has, however, been rejected by a referendum. The US Government has expressed the view that it would welcome reform, if approved by the residents, as long as it was economically feasible and did not affect US national security. A non-binding referendum on the islands' future status, which was to take place in November 1989, was postponed following the disruption caused by 'Hurricane Hugo'. Voting, which eventually took place in October 1993, produced support of 80% for retaining the islands' existing status, with 14% favouring full integration with the USA and 5% advocating the termination of US sovereignty. The result of the referendum was, however, invalidated by the low turn-out: only 27% of registered voters took part, falling short of the 50% participation required for the referendum to be valid. Subsequent legislation to create a constitutional convention was presented to the US Virgin Islands Senate, and in May 2000 a committee of the US House of Representatives began consideration of a range of measures to enlarge the scope of local self-government in the Territory. In November 2004 Governor Turnbull approved legislation allowing the creation of a further constituent assembly to redraft the Constitution.

In February 2005 a 7,000-signature petition was submitted to the US Congress by residents of St Croix, in support of making the island a separate US External Territory from St Thomas and St John. Organizers of the petition claimed that such a move would generate more federal funding for the island, which was affected by a higher unemployment rate than the other two islands, despite being the location for one of the world's largest petroleum refineries. In May the Territorial Government brought a court case against the owners of the Hovensa LLC oil refinery (see Economic Affairs) and the defunct St Croix Alumina plant for contaminating the sole groundwater supply on St Croix. Both companies had reached an agreement with the US Environmental Protection Agency (EPA) in 2001 to clean up petroleum spillages; according to the EPA some 2m. gallons of petroleum leaked into the local aquifer between 1978 and 1991.

At a gubernatorial election to the US Virgin Islands' Senate on 7 November 2006 neither of the two leading candidates for the governorship managed to secure a requisite 50% share of the vote. As a result, a run-off election was held on 21 November: John deJongh, representing the Democratic Party of the Virgin Islands, defeated independent candidate Kenneth Mapp by 16,644 votes to 12,402. DeJongh was sworn into office, together with Lieutenant-Governor Gregory Francis, on 1 January 2007. Outgoing Governor Turnbull had been constitutionally precluded from contesting the office, having already served two consecutive four-year terms. The Territory's Delegate to Congress, Donna M. Christensen, formally commenced a sixth consecutive term of office on 4 January during a ceremony in Washington, DC, USA. Appointments to the new cabinet were announced from mid-January and the 13 members of the new Executive were officially inaugurated in early May in St Thomas and St Croix, respectively. Notable appointments included Beverly Nicholson-Doty—former President of the US Virgin Islands Hotel and Tourism Association—as Commissioner of Tourism, James H. McCall as Commissioner of Police, and Robert S. Mathes as Commissioner of Planning and Natural Resources. Attorney-General Vincent Frazer was also re-elected and his appointment formalized on 4 May.

In November 2006 the US Virgin Islands Government exercised its right to establish a territorial appellate court, conferred by a US Congress amendment to the Revised Organic Act in 1984 and signed into law by Governor Turnbull in October 2004, becoming the last US sovereign jurisdiction to do so. A Supreme Court would, from 1 January 2007, administer all appeals transferred from the Superior Court without the need for recourse to the federal judiciary, in accordance with the Islands' state and territorial counterparts. In December the first judicial officers were officially sworn in, with Rhys Hodge, formerly a presiding judge of the Superior Court, appointed Chief Justice of the new judicial body.

Progress towards formulating a new constitution for the territory was furthered in April 2007 when the availability of petitions for prospective delegate candidates to participate in the fifth Constitutional Convention was announced. A special election was held on 12 June to determine the composition of a constitutional development committee; the resultant constitutional development process would facilitate the territory's transition from a US Constitution- and Organic Act-governed state to one enjoying greater autonomy. It was also hoped that a new constitution would precipitate greater distinction between the legislative, executive and judicial branches of government. The Fifth Constitutional Convention was assembled on 23 July 2007 to commence work upon the drafting of a new constitution; a deadline of 27 July 2008 had been established for the adoption of a constitution by the Convention, which would require the approval of two-thirds of all delegates.

In March 2002 the islands were removed from the Organisation for Economic Co-operation and Development's list of tax havens, after pledging to improve the transparency of its financial services sector by the end of 2005. In May 2007 Christensen presented legislation for the institution of a Chief Financial Officer (CFO) in the territory to function as an independent arbiter upon government fiscal policy. Although a similar law had been earlier approved, Christensen proposed a number of amendments to it, including provision for the chairman of the CFO appointment commission, to be elected by a majority vote of the panel (where the Chief Judge of the Superior Court had previously been designated chairman). It was hoped that the new legislation would encourage greater co-operation between the Governor and Legislative Assembly towards reducing the fiscal deficit, and would facilitate and enhance the transparency of financial policy. A number of financial scandals earlier in the year had foregrounded the necessity of financial services regulatory reform: in June 2006 former director of the US Virgin Islands Department of Planning and Natural Resources Division of Environmental Protection, Hollis L. Griffin, was accused, together with two other islanders, of conspiring to defraud the islands Government of US $1.4m. Hollis and his two co-defendants were given custodial sentences at the federal court in Atlanta, Georgia, in early May. Furthermore, an economic development programme, implemented by the Territorial Government and permitting firms operating in the islands to reduce their tax payments by up to 90%, was discovered to have been exploited in March 2007 when four individuals, including one islander, were charged with tax evasions amounting to £74m. Following initial reports in 2003 that the programme was being used as a means of tax evasion, the US federal Government had imposed restrictions on the tax incentive scheme in 2004. Since that time, 23 of 49 registered 'hedge funds' established within the territory had withdrawn or suspended operations. In February 2007 the US Inland Revenue Service announced that the financial affairs of 8,500 high-salaried residents of the US Virgin Islands would be subjected to increased scrutiny. In April Alric Simmonds, Deputy Chief of Staff to erstwhile Governor Turnbull, was indicted on charges of embezzlement, conversion of government property and grand larceny. In November he pleaded guilty to the charges, which detailed the misappropriation of US $1.2m. between 2002 and 2006.

Combating crime and terrorism was a stated objective of Governor deJongh's new administration from January 2007. An anti-crime initiative was announced in February; measures included an increase in the size of the police force and establishment of a forensic facility. Specialized police professionals from external US police jurisdictions were also to be drafted in to support and instruct existing personnel. A previous scheme, the Blue Lightning Marine unit (based on St Thomas), was to be reinstated to address the problem of guns- and drugs-trafficking and illegal immigrant incursions through coastal patrols. Governor deJongh had expressed dismay at his predecessor's decision to grant 26 pardons and 11 sentence commutations in December 2006, several of which related to violent crimes. Despite the enhanced crime prevention measures, according to local news sources a record number of murders, 46, took place in 2007 while the number of incidents involving a firearm increased by 40 from levels in 2006, to 171 cases. In his State of the Territory Address in January 2008 deJongh reiterated his commitment to reducing the crime level, and focused particularly on increasing the effectiveness of law-enforcement. To that end, in March he submitted legislation to abolish the Drug Enforcement Bureau and to redirect funding to the police department, which had proved to be more successful in targeting drugs-trafficking, having seized 20,000 kg of marijuana plants and 20 kg of cocaine in 2007.

Economic Affairs

According to estimates by the Territorial Government, the islands' gross national income (GNI) in 1989 was US $1,344m., equivalent to about $13,100 per head. Average personal income in 2006 was $19,211 per head, or about 55.6% of the US mainland average. GNI increased, in real terms, at an average rate of 2.5% per year during 1980–89. In 1996–2006 the population increased by an annual average of 0.6%.

Most of the land is unsuitable for large-scale cultivation, but tax incentives have encouraged the growing of vegetables, fruit and cereals, which are produced for local consumption. According to the 2000 census figures, 0.7% of the economically active population were engaged in agriculture, forestry, fishing and mining. According to FAO estimates, however, the sector engaged around 21.6% of the labour force in mid-2005.

The islands are heavily dependent on links with the US mainland. There are no known natural resources, and, because of limited land space and other factors, the islands are unable to produce sufficient food to satisfy local consumption. Most goods are imported, mainly from the mainland USA.

Industry (including construction and mining) engaged some 12.0% of the non-agricultural labour force in 2002, according to official figures. The manufacturing sector employed 4.9% of the employed labour force in 2006, an increase of 9.0% over the previous year. The main branch of manufacturing is petroleum-refining.

Services (including public administration) employed some 88.0% of the non-agricultural labour force in 2002, according to official figures, of which about 33% was employed in public administration. Tourism, which is estimated to account for more than 60% of gross domestic product (GDP), is the mainstay of the islands' income and employment, and provides the major source of direct and indirect revenue for other service sectors (including trade and transport). The emphasis is on the visiting cruise-ship business and the advantages of duty-free products for tourist visitors. In 2006 visitor arrivals (including excursionists and cruise passengers) totalled 2.6m.; in 2004 visitor expenditures amounted to US $1,356.9m. In late 2005 an agreement was signed to build a $500m. casino and resort on St Croix; construction was scheduled for completion by 2022. In 2007 work was ongoing on a number of construction projects related to the tourism industry, including a $63m. recreation centre on St Thomas and the addition of a cruise-ship dock at St Croix harbour. Construction of a $47m. marina facility at Gallows Bay was scheduled to commence in that year. A $150m. hotel and marina complex was completed on St Thomas in late 2006; the Yacht Haven Grande facility, equipped to accommodate the largest cruise ships, accepted its first 'mega-yacht' in November of that year, while the complex was officially inaugurated in March 2007.

St Croix has the world's second largest petroleum refinery, Hovensa LLC (a joint venture between the US oil company Amerada Hess and Petróleos de Venezuela, SA) which produced some 484,000 barrels per day (b/d) in 2004. In that year Hovensa exported refined petroleum products to the USA worth US $6,193m. while, in 2005, shipments of refined petroleum products reached 488,747 barrels, representing almost double the volume (253,560 barrels) exported in the previous year. In response to stricter environmental controls, in September 2005 the company began work on a $400m. desulphurization unit. An Energy Efficiency and Renewable Energy Rebate Progam, launched by the US Virgin Islands Energy Office in October 2006, originally was intended to run for a limited number of months, but was extended until September the following year. It sought to promote awareness of and participation in alternative, renewable energy practices in an attempt to reduce utility costs. In January 2007 four solar power sites on St Thomas, constructed by residents with government funding, were certified by the Energy Office as suitable power generation units from which the Water and Power Authority might purchase energy that was surplus to the residents' requirements. Efforts have been made to introduce labour-intensive and non-polluting manufacturing industries. Rum is an important product; the industry, however, was expected to encounter increased competition from Mexico as a result of the North American Free Trade Agreement (NAFTA, see p. 338), which entered into operation in January 1994. In 2003 the industry was based around a single company, Virgin Islands Rum Industries Ltd, which, in that year alone, exported some 5,973.3m. gallons of rum to the USA. Federal excise taxes collected on rum exports to the USA returned $70.8m. of revenue in 2006.

The population increased dramatically from the 1960s. This inflow included people from neighbouring Caribbean countries, together with wealthy white settlers from the US mainland, attracted by the climate and the low taxes. At the 2000 census 31% of the population originated from other Caribbean islands and 14.5% from the mainland USA.

Throughout the 1990s the budget deficit of the Territorial Government increased. By December 1999 the deficit was estimated to have risen to US $305m., and in that year the Territorial Government introduced a Five-Year Strategic and Financial Operating Plan to reduce government expenditure and enhance the effectiveness of procedures for revenue collection. By 2003/04 the budget deficit had been reduced to $4.6m. In 2005/06 the islands' debt amounted to some $1,150m., equivalent to $10,272 per head. The average rate of unemployment stood at to 6.4% in 2006. The islands were expected, in the foreseeable future, to continue to receive grants and other remittances from the US Government, although greater efforts towards achieving enhanced financial accountability were demanded.

In 2003 the islands recorded a trade deficit of US $359.9m. In 2005 the USA provided 11.3% of imports and took 95.0% of exports. Venezuela was also a major source of imports. Of total exports to the USA in 2005, 94.2% were refined petroleum products. Crude petroleum accounted for 83.4% of the islands' total imports in that year.

Owing to the islands' heavy reliance on imported goods, local prices and inflation are higher than on the mainland, and the islands' economy, in contrast to that of the USA, remained in recession for most of the 1990s. It was hoped that amendments to the Western Hemisphere Travel Initiative, ratified by US Congress in October 2006 and requiring all US citizens and foreign nationals travelling to and from the Caribbean to hold a valid passport from 8 January 2007 (with the exception of cruise-ship passengers, who were to be exempted until June 2009), would confer an advantage on US territories in the Caribbean. In October 2004 the US Congress approved legislation to reform corporate tax in the US Virgin Islands. There were concerns that the measures would deter companies from using the territory as a tax haven, at a cost to the local economy of up to US $63m. in lost revenue and as many as 600 jobs. In November 2006 US Treasury Regulations, effecting a relaxation of the residency requirements for companies and individuals in the islands, were implemented in an attempt to address such concerns and encourage greater confidence in the beleaguered Economic Development Commission programme. (The financial services sector had experienced a period of stagnation since early 2005 following the introduction of the 2004 law.) Preliminary figures estimated that in 2005/06 government revenues had totalled $727m. and were expected to increase to $749m. in 2007, despite the departure of numerous international financial services companies from the islands. However, lower than anticipated revenue collections during the first quarter of 2007 prompted fears of a $46.5m. budget deficit by the end of the fiscal year. In December 2006 legislation confirming the right of the US Virgin Islands Government to formulate its own tax policy was approved by the US House of Representatives. While concern had been expressed by the US General Accounting Office and Department of the Interior in December that the governments of US insular territories—including the Virgin Islands—represented 'high-risk' investments for federal funding, owing to their reliance on a narrow range of volatile key industries and scarce natural resources, some limited progress had been made towards diversification and economic independence by that time. In 2006 and 2007 the territory recorded estimated GDP growth of 3.5% and 2.4%, respectively, with growth in 2008 forecast to reach 2.8%. Meanwhile, in spite of budget projections of a $32m. surplus in 2007, burdensome fiscal debts continued to restrict government operations and $392m. in unpaid public sector wages remained an issue in need of urgent address in that year.

The territory is an associate member of the UN Economic Commission for Latin America and the Caribbean (ECLAC, see p. 38).

Education

Education is compulsory up to the age of 16 years. It generally comprises eight years at primary school and four years at secondary school. In 2002 there were 24,934 students enrolled at elementary and secondary schools. The University of the Virgin Islands, with campuses on St Thomas and St Croix, had 2,610 students in 2004. The territorial education system is comprised of a State Education Agency and two Local Education Agencies covering the St Thomas/St John District and the St Croix District. The Department of Education was allocated US $38.2m. in the federal budget for 2007.

Public Holidays

2008: 1 January (New Year's Day), 6 January (Three Kings' Day), 21 January (Martin Luther King Day), 18 February (Presidents' Day), 21–24 March (Easter), 27 March (Transfer Day), 26 May (Memorial Day), 16 June (Organic Act Day), 3 July (Danish West Indies Emancipation Day), 4 July (US Independence Day), 28 July (Hurricane Supplication Day), 1 September (Labor Day), 13 October (for Columbus Day/Puerto Rico Friendship Day), 20 October (Virgin Islands Thanksgiving Day), 1 November (Liberty Day), 11 November (Veterans' Day), 27 November (US Thanksgiving Day), 25–26 December (Christmas).

2009: 1 January (New Year's Day), 6 January (Three Kings' Day), 19 January (Martin Luther King Day), 16 February (Presidents' Day), 27 March (Transfer Day), 10–13 April (Easter), 25 May (Memorial Day), 15 June (Organic Act Day), 3 July (Danish West Indies Emancipation Day), 4 July (US Independence Day), 27 July (Hurricane Supplication Day), 7 September (Labor Day), 12 October (Columbus Day/Puerto Rico Friendship Day), 19 October (Virgin Islands Thanksgiving Day), 1 November (Liberty Day), 11 November (Veterans' Day), 26 November (US Thanksgiving Day), 25–26 December (Christmas).

Statistical Survey

Sources (unless otherwise stated): Office of Public Relations, Office of the Governor, Charlotte Amalie, VI 00802; tel. (340) 774-0294; fax (340) 774-4988; Bureau of Economic Research, Dept of Economic Development and Agriculture, 1050 Norre Gade No. 5, Suite 301, Charlotte Amalie, VI 00802; POB 6400, Charlotte Amalie, VI 00804; tel. (340) 774-8784; e-mail dhazell@usviber.org; internet www.usviber.org.

AREA AND POPULATION

Area: 347.1 sq km (134 sq miles): St Croix 215 sq km (83 sq miles); St Thomas 80.3 sq km (31 sq miles); St John 51.8 sq km (20 sq miles).

Population: 101,809 at census of 1 April 1990; 108,612 (males 51,684, females 56,748) at census of 1 April 2000. *By Island* (2000 census): St Croix 53,234, St Thomas 51,181, St John 4,197. Source: US Bureau of the Census. *2004* (official figures): St Croix 54,629; St Thomas 52,523; St John 4,307; Total 111,459. *2006* (resident population, estimates): St Croix 55,287; St Thomas 53,155; St John 4,359; Total 112,801.

Density (2006, estimate): 325.0 per sq km.

Principal Towns (population at census of 1 April 2000): Charlotte Amalie (capital) 11,004; Christiansted 2,637; Frederiksted 732. Source: Thomas Brinkhoff, *City Population* (internet www.citypopulation.de).

Births and Deaths (2004): Registered live births 1,574; Registered deaths (preliminary) 624 (death rate 6.9 per 1,000) (Source: US National Center for Health Statistics). *2007:* Birth rate 13.4 per 1,000; Death rate 6.6 per 1,000 (Source: Pan American Health Organization).

Expectation of Life (years at birth, estimates): 79.4 (males 75.5; females 83.3) in 2007. Source: Pan American Health Organization.

Economically Active Population (persons aged 16 years and over, 2000 census): Agriculture, forestry, fishing, hunting and mining 324; Manufacturing 2,754; Construction 4,900; Wholesale trade 912; Retail trade 6,476; Transportation, warehousing and utilities 3,321; Information 931; Finance, insurance, real estate, rental and leasing 2,330; Professional, scientific, management, administrative and waste management services 3,058; Educational, health, and social services 6,742; Arts, entertainment, recreation, accommodation and food services 7,351; Public administration 4,931; Other services 2,535; *Total employed* 46,565 (Source: US Bureau of the Census). *2006* (number of waged and salaried jobs, official figures): Construction and mining 3,095; Manufacturing 2,327; Transportation, warehouse and utilities 1,651; Wholesale and retail trade 6,930; Financial activities 2,573; Leisure and hospitality 7,188; Information 825; Other services 9,268; Federal government 831; Territorial government 11,536.

HEALTH AND WELFARE

Total Fertility Rate (children per woman, 2007): 2.1.
Under-5 Mortality Rate (per 1,000 live births, 2005): 10.1.
Physicians (per 1,000 head, 2003): 1.47.
Hospital Beds (per 1,000 head, 1996): 18.7.
Source: Pan American Health Organization.
For definitions, see explanatory note on p. vi.

AGRICULTURE, ETC.

Livestock (2006, FAO estimates): Cattle 8,000; Sheep 3,200; Pigs 2,600; Goats 4,000; Chickens 35,000.

Fishing (metric tons, live weight, 2005): Total catch (all capture) 1,269 (Groupers 54; Snappers, jobfishes, etc. 130; Grunts, sweetlips, etc. 44; Parrotfishes 181; Surgeonfishes 46; Triggerfishes, durgons, etc. 51; Caribbean spiny lobster 106; Stromboid conchs 480).
Source: FAO.

INDUSTRY

Production ('000 metric tons unless otherwise indicated, 2002, estimates): Jet fuels 1,745; Motor spirit (petrol) 2,654; Kerosene 91; Gas-diesel (distillate fuel) oil 5,725; Residual fuel oils 3,550; Liquefied petroleum gas 164; Electric energy (2004) 1,050 million kWh. Source: UN, *Industrial Commodity Statistics Yearbook*.

FINANCE

Currency and Exchange Rates: 100 cents = 1 United States dollar (US $). *Sterling and Euro Equivalents* (31 December 2007): £1 sterling = US $2.003; €1 = US $1.472; US $100 = £49.92 = €67.93.

Budget (projections US $ million, year ending 30 September 2002): Operating budget 580.2 (Net revenues from taxes, duties and other sources 521.8); Rum excise taxes (Federal remittance) 70.9; Direct Federal expenditures 573. *2006:* Operating budget 611.1 (Net revenues from taxes, duties and other sources 718.7); Rum excise taxes (Federal remittance) 70.8.

Cost of Living (Consumer Price Index; base: 2001 = 100): All items 111.5 in 2004; 114.2 in 2005; 117.6 in 2006.

EXTERNAL TRADE

Total Trade (US $ million): *Imports*: 5,651.4 in 2003; 7,546.9 in 2004; 10,243.3 in 2005. *Exports*: 5,560.8 in 2003; 7,906.7 in 2004; 10,476.3 in 2005. Note: The main import is crude petroleum ($8,739.6m. in 2005), while the principal exports are refined petroleum products ($9,375.7m. in 2005).

Trade with the USA (US $ million): *Imports*: 865.0 in 2004; 1,153.6 in 2005; 1,321.4 in 2006. *Exports*: 7,146.1 in 2004; 9,954.1 in 2005; 11,047.4 in 2006.

TRANSPORT

Road Traffic (registered motor vehicles, 2006): 69,330.

Shipping: *Freight Imports* ('000 metric tons) 1,056 in 2002; 879 in 2003; 979 in 2004. *Cruise-ship Arrivals:* 818 in 2005; 782 in 2006; 752 in 2007. *Passenger Arrivals:* 1,912,539 in 2005; 1,903,533 in 2006; 1,917,878 in 2007.

Civil Aviation (visitor arrivals): 693,058 in 2005; 671,361 in 2006; 693,373 in 2007.

TOURISM

Visitor Arrivals ('000): 2,623.3 (arrivals by air 658.6, cruise-ship passengers 1,964.7) in 2004; 2,605.6 (arrivals by air 693.1, cruise-ship passengers 1,912.5) in 2005; 2,574.9 (arrivals by air 671.4, cruise-ship passengers 1,903.5) in 2006.

Visitor Receipts (US $ million, 2004): Total receipts 1,356.9 (tourists 789.8, excursionists 567.2).

COMMUNICATIONS MEDIA

Radio Receivers (1997): 107,100 in use.
Television Receivers (1999): 71,000 in use.
Telephones (2005): 71,700 main lines in use.
Mobile Cellular Telephones (2005): 80,300 subscribers.
Internet Users (2005): 30,000.
Broadband Subscribers (2005): 3,000.
Daily Newspapers (1996): 3 titles; average circulation 42,000 copies.
Non-daily Newspapers (1988, estimates): 2; average circulation 4,000 copies.
Sources: UNESCO, *Statistical Yearbook*; International Telecommunication Union.

EDUCATION

Pre-primary (1992/93, unless otherwise indicated): 62 schools; 121 teachers; 4,714 students (2000).
Elementary (1992/93, unless otherwise indicated): 62 schools; 790 teachers (public schools only); 13,421 students (2001).
Secondary: 541 teachers (public schools only, 1990); 5,359 students (2001).
Higher Education: 266 teachers (2003/04); 2,610 students (2004).
Sources: UNESCO, *Statistical Yearbook*; US Bureau of the Census.

Directory

The Constitution

The Government of the US Virgin Islands is organized under the provisions of the Organic Act of the Virgin Islands, passed by the Congress of the United States in 1936 and revised in 1954 and 1984. Subsequent amendments provided for the popular election of the Governor and Lieutenant-Governor of the Virgin Islands in 1970 and, since 1973, for representation in the US House of Representatives by a popularly elected Delegate. The Delegate has voting powers only in committees of the House. Executive power is vested in the Governor, who is elected for a term of four years by universal adult suffrage and who appoints, with the advice and consent of the legislature, the heads of the executive departments. The Governor may also appoint administrative assistants as his representatives on St John and St Croix. Legislative power is vested in the legislature of the Virgin Islands, a unicameral body comprising 15 Senators, elected for a two-year term by popular vote. Legislation is subject to the approval of the Governor, whose veto can be overridden by a two-thirds vote of the Legislature. All residents of the islands who are citizens of the USA and at least 18 years of age have the right to vote in local elections, but not in national elections. In 1976 the Virgin Islands were granted the right to draft their own constitution, subject to the approval of the US President and Congress. A constitution permitting a degree of autonomy was drawn up in 1978 and gained the necessary approval, but was then rejected by the people of the Virgin Islands in a referendum in March 1979. A fourth draft, providing for greater autonomy than the 1978 draft, was rejected in a referendum in November 1981. At a further attempt, in October 1993, the referendum was invalidated by the insufficient turn-out of registered voters. In November 2004 legislation was approved to allow the creation of a constituent assembly to redraft the Constitution. A constitutional convention, composed of 30 publicly elected delegates, was due to be convened in July 2007 with a view to adopting a new Constitution by July 2008.

The Government

EXECUTIVE
(May 2008)

Governor: JOHN DEJONGH, Jr.
Lieutenant-Governor: GREGORY FRANCIS.
Commissioner of Agriculture: LOUIS E. PETERSON, Jr.
Commissioner of Education: Dr LAVERNE TERRY.
Commissioner of Finance: CLAUDETTE J. WATSON-ANDERSON.

UNITED STATES EXTERNAL TERRITORIES   The United States Virgin Islands

Commissioner of Health: VIVIAN EBBESEN-FLUDD.
Commissioner of Housing, Parks and Recreation: ST CLAIRE N. WILLIAMS.
Commissioner of Human Services: CHRISTOPHER FINCH.
Commissioner of Labor: ALBERT BRYAN, Jr.
Commissioner of Licensing and Consumer Affairs: KENRICK ROBERTSON.
Commissioner of Planning and Natural Resources: ROBERT S. MATHES.
Commissioner of Police: JAMES H. MCCALL.
Commissioner of Property and Procurement: LYNN A. MILLIN.
Commissioner of Public Works: DARRYL SMALLS.
Commissioner of Tourism: BEVERLY NICHOLSON-DOTY.
Attorney-General: VINCENT FRAZER.
US Virgin Islands Delegate to the US Congress: DONNA M. CHRISTENSEN.

GOVERNMENT OFFICES

Office of the Governor: Government House, 21–22 Kongens Gade, Charlotte Amalie, VI 00802; tel. (340) 774-0001; fax (340) 693-4374; e-mail contact@governordejongh.com; internet www.governordejongh.com.

Office of the Lieutenant-Governor: Government Hill, 18 Kongens Gade, Charlotte Amalie, VI 00802; tel. (340) 774-2991; fax (340) 774-6953; e-mail celeste.lawrence@lgo-vi.gov; internet www.ltg.gov.vi.

Department of Agriculture: Estate Lower Love, Kingshill, St Croix, VI 00850; tel. (340) 774-0991; fax (340) 774-1823.

Department of Education: 1834 Kongens Gade, Charlotte Amalie, VI 00802-6746; tel. (340) 774-0100; fax (340) 779-7153; e-mail llarsen@sttj.k12.vi; internet www.doe.vi.

Department of Finance: GERS Bldg, 2nd Floor, 76 Kronprindsens Gade, Charlotte Amalie, VI 00802; tel. (340) 774-4750; fax (340) 776-4028; e-mail candercpa@msn.com.

Department of Health: 1303 Hospital Ground Suite 10, Charlotte Amalie, St Thomas, VI 00802; tel. (340) 774-0117; fax (340) 777-4001; internet www.healthvi.org.

Department of Housing, Parks and Recreation: Property & Procurement Bldg No. 1, Sub Base, 2nd Floor, Rm 206, Charlotte Amalie, VI 00802; tel. (340) 774-0255; fax (340) 774-4600.

Department of Human Services: Knud Hansen Complex Bldg A 1303, Hospital Ground, Charlotte Amalie, VI 00802; tel. (340) 774-0930; fax (340) 774-3466; internet www.dhs.gov.vi.

Department of Justice: GERS Bldg, 2nd Floor, 48B–50C Kronprindsens Gade, Charlotte Amalie, VI 00802; tel. (340) 774-5666; fax (340) 774-9710; e-mail vfrazer@doj.vi.gov.

Department of Labor: St Thomas: POB 302608, St Thomas, VI 00803-2608; St Croix: 2203 Church St, St Croix, VI 00820-4612; tel. (340) 776-3700; fax (340) 774-5908; e-mail customersupport@vidol.gov; internet www.vidol.gov.

Department of Licensing and Consumer Affairs: Property & Procurement Bldg, 1 Sub Base, Rm 205, Charlotte Amalie, St Thomas VI 00802; tel. (340) 774-3130; fax (340) 776-0675; e-mail dlcacommissioner@dlca.gov.vi; internet www.dlca.gov.vi.

Department of Planning and Natural Resources: Terminal Bldg, 2nd Floor, Suite 6, 8100 Lindberg Bay, St Thomas VI 00802; tel. (340) 774-3320; fax (340) 775-5706; internet www.dpnr.gov.vi.

Department of Police: Alexander Farrelly Criminal Justice Center, Charlotte Amalie, St Thomas, VI 00802; tel. (340) 774-2211; fax (340) 715-5517; e-mail police.commissioner@vipd.gov.vi; internet www.vipd.gov.vi.

Department of Property and Procurement: Property & Procurement Bldg No. 1, 3rd Floor, Sub Base, Charlotte Amalie, VI 00802; tel. (340) 774-0828; fax (340) 777-9587; e-mail lnibbs@pnpvi.org; internet www.pnpvi.org.

Department of Public Works: Bldg No. 8, Sub Base, Charlotte Amalie, VI 00802; tel. (340) 776-4844; fax (340) 774-5869; e-mail darryl.smalls@dpw.vi.gov.

Department of Tourism: POB 6400, St Thomas, VI 00804; tel. (340) 774-8784; fax (340) 774-4390; e-mail info@usvitourism.vi; internet www.usvitourism.vi.

Legislature

LEGISLATIVE ASSEMBLY

Senate
(15 members)

President of the Senate: USIE RICHARDS.

Election, 2 November 2004

Party	Seats
Democrats	10*
Independent Citizens Movement	3
Independent	2
Total	**15**

* In late November 2004 three Democrat deputies defected to form a consensus majority coalition with the Independents and Independent Citizens Movement.

Political Organizations

Democratic Party of the Virgin Islands: POB 2033, St Thomas Democratic District, VI 00803; affiliated to the Democratic Party of the USA; Chair. CECIL R. BENJAMIN, Jr.

Independent Citizens' Movement (The ICM Party, VI): POB 305188, St Thomas, VI 00803-5188; tel. (340) 774-0880; Chair. Sen. TERRENCE NELSON.

Republican Party of the Virgin Islands: 6067 Questa Verde, Christiansted, St Croix, VI 00820-4485; tel. (340) 332-2579; e-mail info@virepublicanwomen.com; internet www.vigop.com; f. 1948; affiliated to the Republican Party of the USA since 1952; Chair. HERB SCHOENBOHM; Pres. TRACY PARDO DE ZELA; Sec. MITSOOKO KING; Exec. Dir JIM OLIVER.

Judicial System

Supreme Court of the Virgin Islands: Alexander A. Farrelly Justice Center, 2nd Floor of Southwing, Suite S211; tel. (340) 777-4935; internet www.visupremecourt.org; f. Jan. 2007, pursuant to legislation passed in Oct. 2004; assumed jurisdiction for all appeals formerly administered by the Superior Court; highest local appellate body, established to administer justice independently of the US federal justice system; judges are appointed by the Governor.

Judges: RHYS S. HODGE (Chief Judge), IVE ARLINGTON SWAN, MARIA M. CABRET.

Superior Court of the Virgin Islands: Alexander A. Farrelly Justice Center, 5400 Veteran's Dr., St Thomas, VI 00802; tel. (340) 774-6680; fax (340) 776-9889; e-mail court.administrator@visuperiorcourt.org; internet www.visuperiorcourt.org; f. 1976 as the Territorial Court of the Virgin Islands; name officially changed in 2004; jurisdiction over all local civil actions and criminal matters; court in St Croix also; judges are appointed by the Governor.

Judges: DARRYL DEAN DONOHUE (Presiding), ISHMAEL A. MEYERS, BRENDA J. HOLLAR, AUDREY L. THOMAS, LEON A. KENDALL, PATRICIA D. STEELE, JULIO A. BRADY, FRANCIS J. D'ERAMO, JAMES S. CARROLL, MICHAEL C. DUNSTON.

US Federal District Court of the Virgin Islands: Division of St Thomas/St John: 5500 Veteran's Dr., Charlotte Amalie, St Thomas, VI 00802-6424; Division of St Croix: 3013 Estate Golden Rock, Christiansted, St Croix, VI 00820-4355; tel. (340) 774-0640; fax (340) 774-1293; internet www.vid.uscourts.gov; jurisdiction in civil, criminal and federal actions; judges are appointed by the President of the USA with the advice and consent of the Senate.

Judges: CURTIS V. GOMEZ (Chief Judge), RAYMOND L. FINCH.

Religion

The population is mainly Christian. The main churches with followings in the islands are Baptist, Roman Catholic, Episcopalian, Lutheran, Methodist, Moravian and Seventh-day Adventist. There is also a small Jewish community, numbering around 900 adherents.

CHRISTIANITY

The Roman Catholic Church

The US Virgin Islands comprises a single diocese, suffragan to the archdiocese of Washington, DC, USA. At 31 December 2005 there were an estimated 30,000 adherents in the territory (27.6% of the population).

Bishop of St Thomas: Most Rev. GEORGE V. MURRY, Bishop's Residence, 29A Princesse Gade, POB 301825, Charlotte Amalie, VI 00803-1825; tel. (340) 774-3166; fax (340) 774-5816; e-mail chancery@islands.vi; internet www.catholicvi.com.

The Anglican Communion

Episcopal Church of the Virgin Islands: Bishop: Rt Rev. AMBROSE GUMBS, 13 Commandant Gade, Charlotte Amalie, POB 10437, St Thomas, VI 00801; tel. (340) 776-1797; fax (340) 777-8485;

e-mail episcopal@vipowernet.net; internet www.episcopaldiocese ofthevirginislands.com.

The Press

Pride Magazine: 22A Norre Gade, POB 7908, Charlotte Amalie, VI 00801; tel. (340) 776-4106; f. 1983; monthly; Editor JUDITH WILLIAMS; circ. 4,000.

St Croix Avis: La Grande Princesse, Christiansted, St Croix, VI 00820; tel. (340) 773-2300; f. 1944; morning; Editor RENA BROADHURST-KNIGHT; circ. 10,000.

St John Tradewinds: The Marketplace, Office Suites II, Office 104, POB 1500, Cruz Bay, St John, VI 00831; tel. (340) 776-6496; fax (340) 693-8885; e-mail editor@tradewinds.vi; internet www.stjohnnews.com; f. 1972; weekly; Publr MALINDA NELSON; circ. 2,500.

Virgin Islands Daily News: 9155 Estate Thomas, VI 00802; tel. (340) 774-8772; fax (340) 776-0740; e-mail dailynews@vipowernet.net; internet www.virginislandsdailynews.com; f. 1930; acquired from Gannet Co Inc, USA, by Innovative Communication Corpn in 1997; morning; CEO and Exec. Editor JASON ROBBINS; circ. 15,000.

Virgin Islands Source: St Thomas; tel. (340) 777-8144; fax (340) 777-8136; e-mail source@viaccess.net; internet www.visource.com; f. 1998; comprises the *St Thomas Source*, *St Croix Source* and *St John Source*; daily; digital; Publr SHAUN A. PENNINGTON.

Broadcasting and Communications

TELECOMMUNICATIONS

Innovative Telephone: Bjerget House, POB 1730, St Croix, VI 00821; tel. (340) 777-7700; fax (340) 777-7701; e-mail info@iccvi.com; internet www.iccvi.com; f. 1959 as Virgin Islands Telephone Corpn (Vitelco); acquired by Innovative Communication Corpn in 1987; present name adopted in 2001; provides telephone services throughout the islands; launched internet service, Innovative PowerNet, in 1999; Pres. and CEO CLARKE GARNETT (acting).

Innovative Wireless: 4006 Estate Diamond, Christiansted, St Croix, VI 00820; fax (340) 778-6011; internet www.vitelcellular.com; f. 1989 as VitelCellular; subsidiary of Innovative Communication Corpn; mobile cellular telecommunications; Man. Dir BEULAH JONIS (acting).

RADIO

WDHP 1620 AM, WRRA 1290 AM, WAXJ 103.5 FM: 79A Castle Coakley, Christiansted, St Croix, VI 00820; tel. (340) 719-1620; fax (340) 778-1686; e-mail info@reefbroadcasting.com; internet www.reefbroadcasting.com; operated by Reef Broadcasting, Inc; commercial; English and Spanish; broadcasts to the US and British Virgin Islands, Puerto Rico and the Eastern Caribbean; Owner and Gen. Man HUGH PEMBERTON.

WEVI (Power 101.7 WeVi-FM): 2C Hogensborg, Frederiksted, St Croix, VI 00840; POB 892, Christiansted, VI 00821; tel. (340) 719-9384; e-mail aw@frontlinemissions.org; internet www.wevifm.net; operated by FrontLine Missions International, Inc; non-commercial; Christian programming; English, Spanish and Créole/Patois.

WGOD: Crown Mountain, POB 5012, Charlotte Amalie, VI 00803; tel. (340) 774-4498; fax (340) 776-0877; operated by Moody Broadcasting Network, USA; commercial; Christian religious programming; Pres. Rev. REYNOLD CHARLES.

WIUJ: c/o WTJX-TV (PBS), Mountain Top, Estate Solberg, St Thomas; POB 2477, St Thomas, VI 00803; e-mail information@wiuj.com; internet www.wiuj.com; operated by V. I. Youth Development Radio, Inc; non-commercial; educational and public service programmes; Gen. Man. LEO MORONE.

WJKC (Isle 95-FM), WMNG (Mongoose), WVIQ (Sunny): 5020 Anchor Way, POB 25680, Christiansted, St Croix, VI 00824; tel. (340) 773-0995; e-mail jkc95@aol.com; internet www.isle95.com; e-mail collinhodge@hotmail.com; commercial; Gen. Man. JONATHAN K. COHEN.

WSTA (Lucky 13): 121 Sub Base, POB 1340, St Thomas, VI 00804; tel. (340) 774-1340; fax (340) 776-1316; e-mail addie@wsta.com; internet www.wsta.com; f. 1950; acquired by Ottley Communications Corpn in 1984; commercial; Owner and Gen. Man. ATHNIEL C. OTTLEY.

WVGN: Nisky Mall Center, PMB 105, St Thomas, VI 00802; e-mail info@wvgn.org; internet www.wvgn.org; f. 2002; operated by Caribbean Community Broadcasting Co; non-commercial; news and public affairs programming; affiliated to NBC, USA; CEO KEITH BASS; Gen. Man. LORRAINE BAA-ELISHA.

WVWI (Radio One), WVJZ (Jamz), WWKS (Kiss), WIVI (Pirate Radio) (Ackley Media Group Stations): 13 Crown Bay Fill, St Thomas, VI 00802; tel. (340) 774-5780; fax (340) 776-1036; e-mail support@ackleycomm.com; internet media.amg.vi/wvwilive; f. 1962; acquired from Knight Quality Stations by Ackley Media Group in 2006; commercial; Pres. and CEO GORDON P. ACKLEY.

WZIN (Buzzrocks): Nisky Mall Center, PMB 357, St Thomas 00802; tel. (340) 776-1043; fax (340) 775-446; e-mail cristy@buzrocks.com; internet www.buzzrocks.com; operated by Pan Caribbean Broadcasting, Inc; commercial; Gen. Man. ALAN FRIEDMAN.

Other radio stations include: WIVH, WMYP (Latino 98.3 FM), WSTX (Magic 97X), and WYAC (Voice of the Virgin Islands).

TELEVISION

Innovative Cable Television (St Croix, St Thomas, St John): 4006 Estate Diamond, Christiansted, St Croix, VI 00820; fax (340) 778-6011; e-mail info@iccvi.com; internet www.innovativecable.com; f. 1997 following acquisition of St Croix Cable TV (f. 1981); subsidiary of Innovative Communication Corpn; acquired Caribbean Communication Corpn in 1998; comprises TV2 (f. 2000); broadcasts to seven Caribbean islands and France; Pres. and Gen. Man. JENNIFER MATARANGAS-KING.

WSVI-TV8 (Channel 8): Sunny Isle Shopping Center, POB 6000, Christiansted, St Croix, VI 00823; tel. (340) 778-5008; fax (340) 778-5011; e-mail channel8@wsvitv.com; internet www.wsvi.tv; f. 1965; operated by Alpha Broadcasting Corpn; affiliated to ABC; one satellite channel and one analogue translator.

WTJX-TV (Public Television Service): Barbel Plaza, POB 7879, Charlotte Amalie, VI 00801; tel. (340) 774-6255; fax (340) 774-7092; e-mail pphipps@wtjxtv.org; internet www.wtjxtv.org; f. 1968; educational and public service programmes; affiliated to PBS; broadcasts on one terrestrial and four digital (cable) channels; broadcasts to the US and British Virgin Islands and Puerto Rico; Chair. ROAN CREQUE; Exec. Dir OSBERT POTTER.

Finance

BANKING

Banco Popular of the Virgin Islands: 193 Altona and Welgunst, Charlotte Amalie, VI 00802; tel. (340) 693-2702; fax (340) 693-2782; Regional Man. VALENTINO I. MCBEAN; 8 brs.

Bank of Nova Scotia (Canada): 214C Altona and Welgunst, POB 420, Charlotte Amalie, VI 00804; tel. (340) 774-6393; fax (340) 693-5994; Country Vice-Pres. PETER VAN SCHIE; Man. BERNICE B. HODGE; 10 brs.

Bank of St Croix: POB 24240, Gallows Bay, St Croix 00824; tel. (340) 773-8500; fax (340) 773-8508; Man. JAMES BRISBOIS; 1 br.

Chase Manhattan Bank, NA (USA): Waterfront, POB 6620, Charlotte Amalie, VI 00801; tel. (340) 776-2222; Gen. Man. WARREN BEER; brs in St Croix and St John.

Citibank, NA (USA): Grand Hotel Bldg, 43–46 Norre Gade, POB 5167, Charlotte Amalie, VI 00801; tel. (340) 776-353; fax (340) 774-6609; Vice-Pres. KEVIN SZOT.

FirstBank of Puerto Rico: POB 3126, St Thomas, VI 00803; tel. (340) 774-2022; fax (340) 776-1313; acquired First Virgin Islands Federal Savings Bank in 2000; Pres. and CEO JAMES E. CRITES; 4 brs.

Virgin Islands Community Bank: 12–13 King St, Christiansted, St Croix, VI 00820; tel. (340) 773-0440; fax (340) 773-4028; internet www.communitybank.vi; Pres. and CEO MICHAEL J. DOW; 3 brs.

INSURANCE

A number of mainland US companies have agencies in the Virgin Islands.

Trade and Industry

GOVERNMENT AGENCY

US Virgin Islands Economic Development Authority: Government Development Bank Bldg, 1050 Norre Gade, POB 305038, St Thomas, VI 00803; tel. (340) 774-8104; e-mail edc@usvieda.org; internet www.usvieda.org; semi-autonomous body comprising Government Devt Bank, Economic Devt Commission, Industrial Park Devt Corpn, Small Business Devt Agency and the Enterprise Zone program; offices in St Thomas and St Croix.

CHAMBERS OF COMMERCE

St Croix Chamber of Commerce: 3009 Orange Grove, Suite 12, Christiansted, St Croix, VI 00820; tel. (340) 773-1435; fax (340) 773-8172; e-mail info@stxchamber.net; internet www.stxchamber.net; f. 1924; Pres. OMER ERSELCUK; Exec. Dir MICHAEL DEMBECK; 250 mems.

St Thomas-St John Chamber of Commerce: 6–7 Dronningens Gade, POB 324, Charlotte Amalie, VI 00804; tel. (340) 776-0100; fax (340) 776-0588; e-mail chamber@islands.vi; internet www

.usvichamber.com; Pres. THADDEUS BAST; Exec. Dir JOSEPH S. AUBAIN; c. 700 mems.

UTILITIES
Regulatory Authority

Virgin Islands Energy Office: 45 Estate Mars Hill, Frederiksted, St Croix, VI 00840; tel. (340) 773-1082; fax 772-0063; e-mail dbuchanan@vienergy.org; internet www.vienergy.org; Dir BEVAN R. SMITH, Jr.

Electricity and Water

Virgin Islands Water and Power Authority (WAPA): POB 1450, Charlotte Amalie, VI 00804-1450; tel. (340) 774-3552; fax (340) 774-3422; internet www.viwapa.vi; f. 1964; public corpn; manufactures and distributes electric power and desalinated sea water; Chair. CHERYL BOYNES-JACKSON; Exec. Dir and CEO HUGO HODGE, Jr; c. 50,000 customers.

Transport

ROADS

The islands' road network totals approximately 855.5 km (531.6 miles). Throughout 2004 the Department of Public Works implemented a programme, valued at US $17.5m., to repair roads damaged in storms in November 2003.

SHIPPING

The US Virgin Islands are a popular port of call for cruise ships. The bulk of cargo traffic is handled at a container port on St Croix. A passenger and freight ferry service provides frequent daily connections between St Thomas and St John and between St Thomas and Tortola (British Virgin Islands). In June 2004 the Port Authority approved a US $9.3m. project to expand freight, vehicle and passenger facilities at Red Hook. A $150m. marina restoration project on St Thomas, completed in October 2006, included provision for 'megayacht' docking facilities in addition to conventional moorings which, it was hoped, would invigorate the cruise-ship industry.

Virgin Islands Port Authority: POB 301707, Charlotte Amalie, VI 00803-1707; tel. (340) 774-1629; fax (340) 774-0025; e-mail info@viport.com; internet www.viport.com; f. 1968; semi-autonomous govt agency; maintains, operates and develops marine and airport facilities; Exec. Dir KENN HOBSON (acting).

CIVIL AVIATION

There are airports on St Thomas and St Croix, and an airfield on St John. Seaplane services link the three islands. The runways at Cyril E. King Airport, St Thomas, and Alexander Hamilton Airport, St Croix, can accommodate intercontinental flights.

Tourism

The islands have a well-developed tourism infrastructure, offering excellent facilities for fishing, yachting and other aquatic sports. A National Park covers about two-thirds of St John. There were 4,813 guest rooms in 2006. In that year there were some 2,574,894 visitors to the islands, of whom 671,361 were tourists and 1,903,533 were cruise-ship passengers. Visitors from the USA comprised 75.5% of hotel guests in 2006. Tourism expenditure stood at US $1,356.9m. in 2004.

St Croix Hotel Association: POB 24238, St Croix, VI 00824; tel. (340) 773-7117; fax (340) 773-5883.

US Virgin Islands Hotel and Tourism Association: POB 2300, Charlotte Amalie, St Thomas, VI 00803; tel. (340) 774-6835; fax (340) 774-4993; e-mail stsjhta@vipowernet.net; internet www.virgin-islands-hotels.com; Pres. LISA HAMILTON.

OTHER UNITED STATES TERRITORIES

Baker and Howland Islands

The Baker and Howland Islands lie in the Central Pacific Ocean, about 2,575 km (1,600 miles) south-west of Honolulu, Hawaii; they comprise two low-lying coral atolls without lagoons, and are uninhabited. Both islands were mined for guano in the late 19th century. Settlements, known as Meyerton (on Baker) and Itascatown (on Howland), were established by the USA in 1935, but were evacuated during the Second World War, owing to Japanese air attacks. The islands are National Wildlife Refuges, and since 1974 have been administered by the US Fish and Wildlife Service. In 1990 legislation before Congress proposed that the islands be included within the boundaries of the State of Hawaii. The islands are administered by the US Department of the Interior, US Fish and Wildlife Service, Refuge Complex Office, POB 50167, Honolulu, Hawaii 96850; internet www.doi.gov.

Jarvis Island

Jarvis Island lies in the Central Pacific Ocean, about 2,090 km (1,300 miles) south of Hawaii. It is a low-lying coral island and is uninhabited. The island was mined for guano in the late 19th century. A settlement, known as Millersville, including a weather station for the benefit of trans-Pacific aviation, was established by the USA in 1935, but was evacuated during the Second World War. Legislation before Congress in 1990 proposed that the island be included within the State of Hawaii. The island is a National Wildlife Refuge and is administered by the US Department of the Interior, US Fish and Wildlife Service (details as above, under Baker and Howland Islands).

Johnston Atoll

Johnston Atoll lies in the Pacific Ocean, about 1,319 km (820 miles) west-south-west of Honolulu, Hawaii. It comprises Johnston Island, Sand Island (uninhabited) and two man-made islands, North (Akua) and East (Hikina); area 2.6 sq km (1 sq mile).

Johnston Atoll was designated a Naval Defense Sea Area and Airspace Reservation in 1941, and is closed to public access. In 1985 construction of a chemical weapons disposal facility began on the atoll, and by 1990 it was fully operational. In 1989 the US Government agreed to remove artillery shells containing more than 400 metric tons of nerve gas from the Federal Republic of Germany, and destroy them on Johnston Island. In late 1991, following expressions of protest to the US Government by the nations of the South Pacific Forum (now Pacific Islands Forum, see p. 380), together with many environmental groups, a team of scientists visited the chemical disposal facility to monitor the safety and environmental impact of its activities. In May 1996 it was reported that all nerve gases stored on the atoll had been destroyed. However, 1,000 tons of chemical agents remained contained in land-mines, bombs and missiles at the site. In December 2000 it was announced that the destruction of the remaining stock of chemical weapons had been completed (the original deadline for the destruction of 40,000 weapons stored on the island had been August 1995). The closure and decontamination of the facility was completed in 2004 and, in June of that year, all military personnel left and control of the Atoll was transferred to the US Fish and Wildlife Service, which has reported its intention eventually to create a nature reserve on the atoll. In March 2005 the Department of Defense announced the termination of the Air Force mission in Johnston Atoll. A facility capable of performing atmospheric tests of nuclear weapons remains operational on the atoll. The atoll had an estimated population of 173 in 1990, although this increased to approximately 1,000, mainly military, personnel during weapons disposal operations in previous years. Johnston Atoll falls under the jurisdiction of the Department of the Interior, US Fish and Wildlife Service (details as above, under Baker and Howland Islands). Operational control is the responsibility of the Defense Threat Reduction Agency (DTRA), Office of the General Counsel, 6801 Telegraph Rd, Room 109, Alexandria, VA 22310-3398; tel. (703) 767-5870. Permission to land on Johnston Island must be obtained from the DTRA. The residing military commander of Johnston Island acts as the agent for the DTRA.

Kingman Reef

Kingman Reef lies in the Pacific Ocean, about 1,500 km (925 miles) south-west of Hawaii, and comprises a reef and shoal measuring about 8 km (5 miles) by 15 km (9.5 miles). In 2000 administrative control was transferred from the US Navy to the Department of the Interior. In 2001 the waters around the reef were designated a National Wildlife Refuge, under the jurisdiction of the US Fish and Wildlife Service (details as above, under Baker and Howland Islands).

Midway Atoll

Midway Atoll lies in the northern Pacific Ocean, about 1,850 km (1,150 miles) north-west of Hawaii. A coral atoll, it comprises Sand Island, Eastern Island and several small islets within the reef, has a total area of about 5 sq km (2 sq miles). The islands had a population of 2,200 in 1983, but by 1990 this had declined to 13. Since the transfer of the islands' administration from the US Department of Defense to the Department of the Interior in October 1996, limited tourism is permitted. There is a National Wildlife Refuge on the Territory, which is home to many species of birds. Legislation before Congress in 1990 proposed the inclusion of the Territory within the State of Hawaii. The islands are administered by the US Department of the Interior, US Fish and Wildlife Service (details as above, under Baker and Howland Islands).

Navassa Island

Navassa Island lies in the Caribbean Sea, about 160 km (100 miles) south of Guantánamo Bay, Cuba, and 65 km (40 miles) west of Haiti. It is a raised coral island with a limestone plateau and has an area of 5.2 sq km (2 sq miles). The island is uninhabited. Navassa became a US Insular Area in 1857, and was mined throughout the late 19th century, under the Navassa Phosphate Co. All mining activities were terminated in 1898. In 1996 the US Coast Guard ceased operations of the island's lighthouse, and in January 1997 the Office of Insular Affairs (under the control of the US Department of the Interior) assumed control of the island. A research expedition undertaken in mid-1998 revealed the presence of numerous undiscovered plant and animal species, many of which were thought to be unique to the island. Visits to the island and its surrounding waters were subsequently prohibited, pending further assessment of the island's environment. In December 1999 administrative responsibility for Navassa passed wholly to the US Department of the Interior, US Fish and Wildlife Service (details as above, under Baker and Howland Islands); however, control over political matters was retained by the Office of Insular Affairs.

Palmyra

Palmyra lies in the Pacific Ocean, about 1,600 km (1,000 miles) south of Honolulu, Hawaii. It comprises some 50 low-lying islets, has a total area of 100 ha, is uninhabited and is privately owned. Since 1961 the Territory has been administered by the US Department of the Interior. In 1990 legislation before Congress proposed the inclusion of Palmyra within the boundaries of the State of Hawaii. In mid-1996 it was announced that the owners (the Fullard-Leo family in Hawaii) were to sell the atoll to a US company, which, it was believed, planned to establish a nuclear waste storage facility in the Territory. The Government of neighbouring Kiribati expressed alarm at the proposal, and reiterated its intention to seek the reinclusion of the atoll within its own national boundaries. However, in June one of the Hawaiian Representatives to the US Congress proposed legislation in the US House of Representatives to prevent the establishment of such a facility, and a US government official subsequently announced that the atoll would almost certainly not be used for that purpose. Palmyra was purchased by The Nature Conservancy (internet www.tnc.org) in December 2000. Designated a National Wildlife Refuge, the lagoons and surrounding waters within the 12 nautical mile zone of US territorial seas were transferred to the US Fish and Wildlife Service (details as above, under Baker and Howland Islands) in January 2001; the US Fish and Wildlife Service subsequently undertook negotiations to purchase part of the 680 acres of emergent lands owned by The Nature Conservancy. In November 2005 an international team of scientists joined with The Nature Conservancy to establish a new station on the Palmyra Atoll in order to undertake environmental research.

Wake Island

Wake Island lies in the Pacific Ocean, about 2,060 km (1,280 miles) east of Guam. It is a coral atoll comprising the three islets of Wake, Wilkes and Peale, with an area less than 8 sq km (3 sq miles) and a population estimated to be almost 2,000 in 1988. Legislation before Congress in 1990 proposed the inclusion of the islands within the Territory of Guam. However, the Republic of the Marshall Islands, some 500 km (310 miles) south of Wake, exerted its own claim to the atoll (called Enenkio by the Micronesians), which is a site of great importance for the islands' traditional chiefly rituals. Plans by a US company, announced in 1998, to establish a large-scale nuclear waste storage facility on the atoll were condemned by environmentalists and politicians in the region. In August 2006 Hurricane Ioke severely damaged much of the island's infrastructure. The US Air Force had previously evacuated all 188 residents. Since 1972 the group has been administered by the US Department of Defense, Department of the Air Force (Pacific/East Asia Division), The Pentagon, Washington, DC 20330; tel. (202) 694-6061; fax (703) 696-7273; internet www.af.mil.

URUGUAY

Introductory Survey

Location, Climate, Language, Religion, Flag, Capital

The Eastern Republic of Uruguay lies on the south-east coast of South America, with Brazil to the north and Argentina to the west. The climate is temperate, with an average temperature of 14°C–16°C (57°F–61°F) in winter and 21°C–28°C (70°F–82°F) in summer. The language is Spanish. There is no state religion but Roman Catholicism is predominant. The national flag (proportions 2 by 3) has nine horizontal stripes (five white and four blue, alternating), with a square white canton, containing a yellow sun with 16 alternating straight and wavy rays, in the upper hoist. The capital is Montevideo.

Recent History

Since gaining independence in 1825, domestic politics in Uruguay traditionally has been dominated by two parties: the Colorados ('reds' or Liberals) and the Blancos ('whites' or Conservatives, subsequently also known as the Partido Nacional). Their rivalry resulted in frequent outbreaks of civil war in the 19th century: the names derive from the flags of the 1836 civil war. From 1880 to 1958 the governing Partido Colorado was led by the Batlle family. Owing to the progressive policies of José Batlle y Ordóñez, Colorado President in 1903–07 and in 1911–15, Uruguay became the first welfare state in Latin America. During 1951–66 the presidency was in abeyance, being replaced by a collective leadership.

In December 1967 Jorge Pacheco Areco assumed the presidency. His period in office was notable for massive increases in the cost of living, labour unrest and the spectacular exploits of the Tupamaro urban guerrilla movement. In March 1972 Pacheco was succeeded by Juan María Bordaberry Arocena, a Colorado, who won the presidential election in November 1971. The army took complete control of the campaign against the Tupamaros, and by late 1973 had suppressed the movement. Military intervention in civilian affairs led, in 1973, to the closure of the Congreso (Congress) and its replacement by an appointed 25-member Council of State (subsequently increased to 35 members). The Partido Comunista and other left-wing groups were banned; repressive measures, including strict press censorship, continued. In September 1974 army officers were placed in control of the major state-owned enterprises.

President Bordaberry was deposed by the army in June 1976 because of his refusal to countenance any return, however gradual, to constitutional rule. In July the recently formed Council of the Nation elected Aparicio Méndez Manfredini to the presidency for five years. Despite the Government's announcement that there would be a return to democracy, persecution of political figures continued, and the number of political prisoners held in 1976 was thought to have reached 6,000.

President Méndez introduced constitutional amendments, known as Institutional Acts, to consolidate the internal situation and to create a 'new order'. By 1980 severe economic problems made the army anxious to return executive responsibility to civilian politicians. A new constitution, under which the armed forces would continue to be involved in all matters of national security, was drafted and submitted to a plebiscite in November 1980, but was rejected by 58% of voters. The military leadership was therefore forced to amend the draft document in consultation with leaders of the recognized political parties, and, in September 1981, a retired army general, Gregorio Alvarez Armellino, was appointed by the Joint Council of the Armed Forces to serve as President during the transition period to full civilian government.

The Government's reluctance to permit greater public freedom and to improve observance of human rights caused serious unrest throughout 1983. Popular discontent was further aroused by the rapid deterioration of the economy and by the effect of events in Argentina. In August the authorities suspended all public political activity and reserved the right to impose a new constitution without consultation, insisting, however, that the original electoral timetable would be maintained. The political opposition responded by threatening to boycott the elections and by uniting with proscribed opposition groups to hold a national day of protest. In September the first organized labour protest for 10 years was supported by 500,000 workers.

Political agitation increased during 1984, and the Government threatened to postpone the elections, planned for 25 November, unless the political parties agreed to its proposals for constitutional reform. Tensions increased in June, following the return from exile and the subsequent arrest of Ferreira Aldunate, the proposed presidential candidate of the Partido Nacional. Talks between the Government, the Partido Colorado and the Unión Cívica (a Christian democratic party) resumed in July; the parties obtained several important concessions, including the right to engage in political activity. In August, encouraged by the Government's commitment to the restoration of the democratic process, the parties (with the exception of the Partido Nacional) agreed to the Government's proposals. The Government confirmed that elections would take place, and all restrictions on political activity were withdrawn.

At elections in November 1984 the Partido Colorado, led by Dr Julio María Sanguinetti Cairolo, secured a narrow victory over the opposition. In February 1985 the military regime relinquished power, one month earlier than originally planned. President Sanguinetti was inaugurated on 1 March, as was a Government of national unity, incorporating representatives of the other parties. Concurrently, various outlawed organizations, including the Partido Comunista, were legalized. All political prisoners were released under an amnesty law later in the month.

The new Government announced its commitment to reversing the economic recession; however, its efforts to address the crisis were hampered by frequent industrial stoppages. Discussions between the administration and trade union and business leaders began in August 1985. Although the Government suspended negotiations following another series of strikes, discussions were resumed in September.

A major political issue in 1986 was the investigation into alleged violations of human rights by the armed forces during the military dictatorship. In August the Government proposed legislation that would offer an amnesty for all military and police personnel accused of this type of crime, in accordance with a pact made with the armed forces that human rights trials would not take place. In October the draft legislation was rejected by opposition parties, but in December a revised law (the Ley de Caducidad, or Statute of Limitations Law) was approved, which brought an end to current military trials and made the President responsible for any further investigations. The law was widely opposed and in February 1987 a campaign was initiated to organize a petition containing the signatures of at least 25% of the registered electorate, as required by the Constitution, in order to force a referendum on the issue. The campaign was supported principally by human rights groups, trade unions and the centre-left coalition, the Frente Amplio (FA). A referendum duly took place in April 1989, at which a total of 53% of the votes were cast in favour of maintaining the amnesty law.

The presidential and legislative elections in November 1989 resulted in victory (for the first time since 1962) for the Partido Nacional. In the presidential election, Luis Alberto Lacalle, the party's main candidate (the electoral code permitted each party to present more than one candidate), received 37% of the votes, while his closest rival, Jorge Batlle Ibáñez of the Partido Colorado, won 30%. However, the Partido Nacional failed to obtain an overall majority in the Congreso, thus compelling the President-elect to seek support from a wider political base. Immediately before taking office, in March 1990, he announced the conclusion of an agreement, the 'coincidencia nacional', between the two principal parties, whereby the Partido Colorado undertook to support proposed legislation on economic reform, in return for the appointment of four of its members to the Council of Ministers.

Labour unrest intensified during the early 1990s. The trade union confederation, the Plenario Intersindical de Trabajadores—Convención Nacional de Trabajadores (PIT—CNT), organized a series of general strikes in support of demands for wage increases and in opposition to government austerity measures and privatization plans. Opposition from within the ruling coalition to the planned sale of state enterprises became apparent in May 1991, when former President Sanguinetti, the leader of the Foro Batllista faction of the Partido Colorado, withdrew his support from the Government, thus forcing the resignation of the Minister of Public Health, the faction's sole representative in the Council of Ministers. Reservations were also expressed by elements of the Partido Nacional. In September, none the less, the privatization legislation was narrowly approved by the Congreso. In response, the opposition FA, with the support of another political organization, Nuevo Espacio, and the trade unions, began a campaign to overrule the legislature by way of a referendum. In October 1992, in a special poll, some 30% of the electorate voted for a full referendum to be held on the partial amendment of the Government's privatization legislation. At the referendum, held in December, 72% of voters supported the proposal for a partial repeal of the legislation. The vote was also widely recognized as a vote of censure against the President's economic policy, and in particular his determination to keep public sector wage increases to a minimum. While the result of the referendum did not affect all planned divestments, it was considered to be a serious reverse and served to undermine confidence in government economic policy. Notwithstanding, President Lacalle indicated that he would continue to pursue the privatization programme.

Industrial unrest in the public sector intensified in 1992, owing primarily to the Government's refusal to grant wage increases in line with inflation. In November, however, following a four-day strike by the police, the Government was forced to concede wage increases of up to 50% to the security forces. Encouraged by this concession, transport and public health workers initiated strikes in support of demands for wage increases.

The presidential and legislative elections in November 1994 were notable for the emergence of a third political force to rival the traditional powers of the Partido Nacional and the Partido Colorado. The Encuentro Progresista (EP)—a predominantly left-wing alliance principally comprising the parties of the FA, as well as dissidents of the Partido Nacional and other minor parties—secured 31% of the votes, as did the Partido Nacional, while the Partido Colorado won a narrow victory with 33% of the vote. Subsequently, the leading presidential candidate of the Partido Colorado, Sanguinetti, was pronounced President-elect. Sanguinetti indicated that he planned to appoint a broadly based Council of Ministers in order to ensure legislative support for his administration.

In early 1995, following talks with opposition parties, the Partido Colorado established a 'governability pact' with the Partido Nacional, providing for a coalition Government. The Council of Ministers contained six members of the Partido Colorado, four from the Partido Nacional, one Unión Cívica member, and one representative from the Partido por el Gobierno del Pueblo (Lista 99), which had contested the elections in alliance with Sanguinetti's Foro Batllista faction of the Partido Colorado, and whose leader, Hugo Batalla, had been elected as Sanguinetti's Vice-President.

In July 1995 the Government and the legislative opposition reached an agreement providing for the reform of the electoral system. Under the existing system, known as the Ley de Lemas, parties were permitted to present more than one presidential candidate, with the leading candidate in each party assuming the total number of votes for candidates in that party. According to the proposed reform, each party would present one candidate, selected by means of an internal election, and, in the event of no candidate securing an absolute majority, a second round of voting would be conducted. In October 1996 President Sanguinetti finally secured the necessary two-thirds' support for the reform in the legislature, notwithstanding a degree of opposition from elements of the FA. Besides abolishing the Ley de Lemas and introducing provision for second-round presidential elections, the reform also accorded greater autonomy to municipal administrations, and established a framework for environmental protection. The amendments were approved by 51% of voters in a plebiscite held in December, and came into effect in January 1997.

In May 1997 some 20,000 civilians staged a rally in the capital to demand that the Government and the armed forces provide information on the whereabouts of as many as 140 people who had 'disappeared' during the military dictatorship. In December President Sanguinetti issued a decree that granted an amnesty to 41 former army officers who had been dismissed from service during the dictatorship, owing to their political beliefs. Lt-Gen. Raúl Mermot, the Commander-in-Chief of the Armed Forces, resigned from his post one month ahead of schedule, in protest at the decision. In May 1999 some 15,000 people participated in a further march in support of demands that the authorities account for the disappearance of friends and relatives during the military dictatorship.

In late April 1999, in the first primary elections to be held in Uruguay, Lacalle, Batlle and Tabaré Ramón Vázquez Rosas were selected as the presidential candidates for the Partido Nacional, the Partido Colorado and the EP (subsequently known as Encuentro Progresista—Frente Amplio, EP—FA), respectively. Vázquez, a former Mayor of Montevideo, won a particularly convincing victory, securing 82% of the votes of his party's supporters, while Batlle defeated Sanguinetti's favoured candidate, Luis Hierro López, who was later nominated as the Partido Colorado's candidate for the vice-presidency.

The presidential and legislative elections of October 1999 confirmed the end of the traditional dominance of the Partido Colorado and the Partido Nacional. The EP—FA became the largest single party in both the Cámara de Representantes and the Cámara de Senadores, winning 40 and 12 seats, respectively. The Partido Colorado largely maintained its representation, securing 33 and 10 seats, while support for the Partido Nacional declined considerably, with the party winning only 22 seats in the lower house and seven in the Cámara de Senadores, having held a combined total of 41 seats in the outgoing legislature. Vázquez gained 39% of the vote, compared with 31% for Batlle and 21% for Lacalle. Despite the convincing success of the EP—FA in the first round, Jorge Batlle defeated Vázquez in a second round of voting on 28 November, with 52% of the vote, aided by the support of the Partido Nacional (under a formal accord). Following his inauguration on 1 March 2000, President Batlle appointed a new Council of Ministers, allocating eight portfolios to the Partido Colorado and five to the Partido Nacional.

In early 2000 Batlle held several meetings with Vázquez, in an apparent attempt to achieve a degree of *rapprochement* with the left, and also committed himself to resolving the issue of the 'disappeared', in marked contrast to his predecessor, Sanguinetti, who had consistently resisted pressure to investigate their fate. In April 2000 Batlle dismissed Gen. Manuel Fernández, one of the country's most senior army officials, after he sought to justify the military repression of the 1970s. In August Batlle announced the formation of a commission, composed of representatives from the Government, the opposition, the Church and the victims' families, to investigate the fate of 164 people who 'disappeared' during the military dictatorship. The unexpected dismissal in January 2001 of Gen. Juan Geymonat, Commander-in-Chief of the Armed Forces, was interpreted as a first step in a military reform programme advocated by Batlle. In October 2002 the Commission reported its preliminary findings that 26 of the 33 'disappeared' Uruguayan citizens under its investigation had been murdered by Argentine and Uruguayan military officers.

Against a background of ongoing economic recession, the Batlle administration encountered opposition to its policies from organized labour groups from 1999. In June 2000 a general strike was organized by the PIT—CNT to demand increased action on unemployment and more finance for education and health care, as well as to protest against emergency legislation, approved that month, which would allow the partial privatization of some public services, including the railways and the ports. A more widespread strike was held in December to protest at the same issues. However, an attempt by the EP—FA to force a referendum on the controversial law in February 2001 failed, owing to a lack of public support.

The financial crisis in neighbouring Argentina of December 2001–January 2002 caused additional economic hardship in Uruguay, with continued rural unrest and political and trade-union opposition to the austerity measures introduced by the Government. There was an unprecedented rise in street violence and organized crime, along with accelerated rates of emigration. In May the Argentine Government's imposition of severe restrictions on bank withdrawals prompted many Argentine citizens holding assets in Uruguay to access their funds, precipitating a crisis in Uruguay's financial system. In late June the Government was forced to abandon exchange rate controls in order to maintain the peso uruguayo's competitiveness against the devalued Argentine and Brazilian currencies. However, by late July, following a 30% decline in the peso's value in relation to the US dollar, and amid rising concerns over the viability and transparency of the banking sector, substantial numbers of Uruguayans also began to withdraw their deposits. In an attempt to avert a financial collapse, the Government instructed all banking institutions in Uruguay to close for a period of four days and introduced emergency economic measures, which included an increase in taxation on salaries and pensions. Moreover, three state-owned banks were placed under direct government administration, and restrictions were imposed on their customers' access to long-term foreign exchange deposits. The Government successfully sought an immediate loan of US $1,500m. from the USA to prevent a severe deterioration in international reserves and in November agreement was reached with the IMF on stand-by loans totalling some $2,800m., to be disbursed in 2002 and 2003. Nevertheless, as a result of the financial crisis, in late July Alberto Bensión, the Minister of Economy and Finance, was forced to resign, having lost the support of the Partido Nacional. He was succeeded by Alejandro Atchugarry, a prominent member of the Partido Colorado.

As well as fomenting popular resentment towards the Government's economic strategy and unprecedentedly high levels of unemployment in mid-2002, the financial crisis led to a greater willingness within the Partido Nacional to reconsider its association with the Partido Colorado. In November the Partido Nacional terminated discussions on a new 'governability pact' between the two parties, removed its five ministers from the Government and withdrew from the ruling coalition, leaving the FA as the largest political bloc in the Congreso. President Batlle subsequently appointed non-partisan ministers to the vacant posts and a limited rationalization of ministries was effected.

In November 2002 it was announced that the three suspended state-run banks were to be merged into one: in March 2003 the Nuevo Banco Comercial began operations. The incorporation of the new bank coincided with the resumption of IMF disbursements, suspended in November owing to the Government's perceived lack of progress on the restructuring of the banking sector. (In January 2005 the International Court of Arbitration of the International Chamber of Commerce (ICC, see p. 312) ruled that Uruguay must pay US $100m., in addition to legal expenses and accrued interest, to foreign investors in the liquidated Banco Comercial.)

In August 2003 a series of strikes was held by public sector workers to protest at the Government's reform programme, in particular, plans to increase private sector participation in the economy. In June the EP—FA succeeded in gaining parliamentary approval for a referendum to be held on the proposed partial privatization of the state-run fuel, cement and alcohol monopoly, ANCAP (Administración Nacional de Combustible, Alcohol y Portland). In the referendum, held on 7 December, some 62% voted to repeal the controversial legislation. The high level of opposition to the law was widely interpreted as a further expression of public dissatisfaction with the Batlle administration. Furthermore, the EP—FA pledged to maintain state control of public utilities if successful in the upcoming presidential and legislative elections of 2004.

At the presidential election that was held on 31 October 2004, Tabaré Vázquez, the candidate of the EP—FA, won the presidency in the first round of voting, with 50.7% of the ballot. His nearest rival, Jorge Larrañaga, the candidate of the Partido Nacional, obtained some 34.1% of the votes, while the Partido Colorado's nominee, Guillermo Stirling, attracted 10.3% of the votes cast. The EP—FA coalition also made gains in the concurrent legislative elections, winning a majority in both chambers of the legislature, with 16 of the 30 seats of the Senado and 52 of the 99 seats of the Cámara de Representantes. By contrast, the Partido Colorado's legislative representation fell sharply: from 33 to 10 seats in the lower house, and from 10 to just three seats in the Senado. The Partido Nacional became the second largest party in both chambers, winning a total of 35 seats in the Cámara de Representantes and 11 seats in the Senado. The EP—FA's electoral campaign had centred on pledges to increase social spending dramatically, to effect a radical reform of the tax and pension systems, and to retain state control over utilities and services.

Concurrently with the presidential election a referendum was held on a proposal that the water industry remain under state control. The proposal was supported by the EP—FA, but opposed by the incumbent Colorado administration. In the poll, 64.5% of those voting were in favour of the water sector remaining under state control. However, following the result of the ballot, the outgoing Colorado Government propounded that all private sector contracts in the water industry be rescinded in order to achieve full nationalization, a proposal that was opposed by President-elect Vázquez.

In November 2004 Larrañaga (who was also the leader of the Alianza Nacional faction of the Partido Nacional) and Sanguinetti, leader of the Foro Batllista tendency within the Partido Colorado, indicated that neither the Partido Nacional nor the Partido Colorado would participate in the incoming Government; however, in February 2005 it was announced that the new administration would receive cross-party support for its economic policies (in addition to the support already pledged for its policies on education and foreign affairs). President Vázquez, who took office on 1 March, notably appointed Danilo Astori of the Asamblea Uruguay as Minister of Economy and Finance. The appointment of Astori, an orthodox economist on the right wing of the EP—FA, was widely interpreted as an attempt to strengthen investor confidence in a broadly left-wing administration. In mid-March both opposition parties withdrew their support for the Government's economic policies in protest at their allocation of positions on the governing bodies of state banks, companies and quasi-autonomous agencies, which, they considered, fell short of the number traditionally allocated to members of the opposition.

An immediate priority of the new Governmnent was to eradicate poverty; to this end, in March 2005 President Vázquez announced the Plan de Atención Nacional de Emergencia Social, a programme of social spending, expected to total some US $200m. over two years. The following day the new Minister of National Defence, Azucena Berruti (a former human rights lawyer), announced that the Government had begun investigations into the 'disappearances' that occurred during the years of military rule. In August the heads of Uruguay's armed forces submitted to the President a report admitting the kidnap, torture and murder of political dissidents, and purportedly detailing the whereabouts of their remains. Information in the report led to the exhumation in November of the bodies of two dissidents murdered by members of the air force. Earlier that month President Vásquez had proposed legislation seeking to amend the Ley de Caducidad (see above) in order to facilitate prosecution of members of the military for human rights abuses committed during military rule. In December 35 unidentified corpses were exhumed from a cemetery in a town near the Brazilian border.

The investigation of human rights abuses allegedly committed during the military dictatorship continued during 2006 and 2007. In May six former Uruguayan military officers were arrested in connection with the 'disappearance' and presumed murder in 1976 of María Claudia García, the daughter of the Argentinian poet Juan Gelman, following an extradition request from Argentina. The arrests represented the first occasion on which any individuals had faced legal action for their alleged role in the torture and murder of dissidents during the period of military repression in the 1970s. In November former President Bordaberry and his then foreign minister, Juan Carlos Blanco, were charged with the abduction and murder of four opponents of the authorities in 1976. Furthermore, in February 2007 a former officer of senior rank in the Uruguayan military was arrested in Brazil, and his extradition to Uruguay sought, on charges relating to the murders of three dissidents in 1976, as well as the 'disappearance' of García. In December former President Alvarez was arrested and charged, along with two army captains, with the forced disappearance of up to 40 dissidents in 1978, during which time he was Commander-in-Chief of the Army. Alvarez's arrest was facilitated by legislation, adopted in September 2006, which established that acts of forced disappearance were considered to be permanent, and were therefore not excluded from prosecution by the Ley de Caducidad.

President Vásquez announced an extensive government reorganization in February 2008, involving six cabinet posts. Notably, the Minister of Foreign Affairs, Reinaldo Gargano, who had reportedly maintained a tense relationship with Vázquez and other members of the Government, was replaced by Dr Gonzalo Fernández, while Jorge Bayardi succeeded Berrutti as Minister of National Defence. The new ministers took office in early March. The President stated that the changes were intended to allow the outgoing ministers to concentrate on party political activities ahead of the presidential and legislative elections due in October 2009, and stressed that they were not in response to a crisis or the under-performance of any minister.

Following a summit conference in Paraguay in March 1991, the Governments of Argentina, Brazil, Paraguay and Uruguay agreed to create a common market of the 'Southern Cone'

URUGUAY

countries, the Mercado Común del Sur (Mercosur, see p. 391). The Treaty of Asunción allowed for the dismantling of trade barriers between the four countries, and entered full operation in 1995. However, in February 2002, following the drastic reduction in exports to other Mercosur member states as a result of the devaluation of the Argentine peso at the beginning of that year, President Batlle declared that Uruguay would begin bilateral free trade negotiations with the USA. In January 2006 it was reported that the Government believed Uruguay's interests were not always best served within Mercosur and that, consequently, it would seek negotiations with the USA on a bilateral free trade agreement (FTA). However, in March the US Department of State declared that the US Government had no plans to negotiate such an agreement with Uruguay. None the less, the signing of a trade and investment framework between the two countries in January 2007 was regarded as a step towards eventual FTA negotiations. A series of trade agreements between Chile and overseas nations in 2002 and 2003 also prompted Uruguay to seek international commercial agreements on a unilateral basis.

In April 2002 Uruguay severed diplomatic relations with Cuba, citing insults by the Cuban Government after Uruguay sponsored a motion, which was passed by the UN Human Rights Commission, calling on Cuba to improve its civil and political rights record. Diplomatic relations were restored, however, following the inauguration of the Vázquez administration in March 2005.

Relations with Argentina were strained from April 2005, when a Finnish company began construction of a cellulose plant in the Uruguayan city of Fray Bentos near the River Uruguay, which separates the two countries. The Argentine Government expressed concerns over the environmental impact of this plant and of a further mill scheduled to be built nearby. The two plants were expected to generate some US $1,800m. of investment in Uruguay. (Construction of the second plant was cancelled in 2006 as a result of the dispute, although the company responsible later announced that it would build the mill at a different location.) In January 2006 Argentine demonstrators blocked passage across the three bridges spanning the river in protests that were tolerated by the Argentine authorities, drawing condemnation from the Uruguayan Government. Furthermore, in March reports appeared in Argentine media suggesting that Uruguayan officials had been bribed to approve the plants' construction; the Government denied the accusations. Demonstrations, attended by some 10,000 people claiming that the project would cause serious environmental damage, continued in the Argentine city of Gualeguaychú. The dispute escalated in May when the Argentine Government initiated proceedings at the International Court of Justice (ICJ) on the grounds that the project would contravene the Statute of the River Uruguay treaty, signed by the two countries in 1975. The ICJ declined to order the suspension of construction of the mills in July, but in January 2007 also rejected a request by the Government of Uruguay to order Argentina to end the ongoing blockade of major roads and bridges between the two countries. Uruguay had claimed that Argentina's protests were resulting in economic hardship for Uruguay and had caused a loss of revenue of some US $800m., much of this in the form of lost earnings from tourism. Bilateral relations improved slightly in April following mediation by Spain, as a result of which both countries declared their willingness to reach a resolution to the impasse. None the less, in November President Vázquez authorized the recently inaugurated mill to begin production, provoking condemnation from Argentina, and temporarily closed the border between the countries in anticipation of violent protests. Argentine demonstrations continued to impede cross-border traffic in early 2008, prompting an official complaint from Uruguay regarding the damage caused to its economy.

Government

Uruguay is a republic comprising 19 departments. Under the 1966 Constitution, executive power is held by the President, who is directly elected by universal adult suffrage for a five-year term. The President is assisted by the Vice-President and the appointed Council of Ministers. Legislative power is vested in the bicameral Congreso, comprising the Cámara de Senadores (Senate) and the Cámara de Representantes (Chamber of Representatives), also directly elected for five years. The President, the Vice-President, the Senators (who number 31, including the Vice-President, who is automatically allocated a seat as President of the Cámara de Senadores) and the 99 Deputies are elected nationally.

Defence

As assessed at November 2007, Uruguay's active armed forces totalled 25,400, comprising an army of 16,800, a navy of 5,600 and an air force of 3,000. Paramilitary forces numbered 920. Defence expenditure in 2006 was budgeted at some 5,800m. pesos uruguayos.

Economic Affairs

In 2006, according to estimates by the World Bank, Uruguay's gross national income (GNI), measured at average 2004–06 prices, was US $17,595m., equivalent to $5,310 per head (or $11,150 per head on an international purchasing-power parity basis). During 1996–2006, it was estimated, the population increased by an annual average of 0.2%, while gross domestic product (GDP) per head increased, in real terms, by an annual average of 0.8% per year. According to official figures, overall GDP increased, in real terms, at an average annual rate of 1.9% in 1997–2007; GDP increased by 7.0% in 2006 and by 7.4% in 2007.

Agriculture (including forestry and fishing) contributed 10.1% of GDP in 2007. Some 4.5% of the active labour force were employed in the sector in 2003. The principal crops are rice, sugar cane, wheat, barley, potatoes, sorghum and maize. Livestock-rearing, particularly sheep and cattle, is traditionally Uruguay's major economic activity. Live animals and animal derivatives provided 37.9% of export revenues in 2006, while exports of skins and hides provided a further 8.6% in the same year. Agricultural GDP increased by an annual average of 2.7% per year in 1997–2007. Agricultural GDP increased by 2.5% in 2007.

Industry (including mining, manufacturing, construction and power) contributed 31.8% of GDP in 2007, and employed 21.5% of the working population in 2003. Industrial GDP increased by an annual average of 1.6% in 1997–2007; industrial GDP increased by 7.9% in 2007.

Uruguay has few mineral resources and no proven hydrocarbon reserves. Accordingly, mining and quarrying only contributed 0.3% of GDP in 2007, and employed 0.1% of the working population in 2003. Apart from the small-scale extraction of building materials, industrial minerals and semi-precious stones, there has been little mining activity, although gold deposits are currently being developed. The GDP of the mining sector declined by an annual average of 0.2% in 1997–2007; mining GDP rose by 15.0% in 2006 and by 1.1% in 2007.

Manufacturing contributed 22.6% of GDP in 2007 and employed 14.6% of the working population in 2003. The principal branches of manufacturing were food products, beverages and tobacco, chemicals, metal products, machinery and equipment, and textiles, clothing and leather products. Manufacturing GDP increased by an annual average of 0.8% in 1997–2007. Manufacturing GDP increased by 8.0% in 2007.

Energy is derived principally from hydroelectric power (81.0% of total electricity production in 2005). The first natural gas pipeline between Uruguay and Argentina, with an operating capacity of 4.9m. cu ft per day, began operating in late 1998. A second natural gas pipeline between Uruguay and Argentina, the Gasoducto Cruz del Sur (GCDS—Southern Cross pipeline), with a transportation capacity of 180m. cu ft per day, was completed in 2002. In early 2007 plans were under consideration for a possible extension of the GCDS to reach Porto Alegre, Brazil. Imports of mineral products (including fuels) comprised 28.0% of the value of total imports in 2006. In August 2005 the Venezuelan President, Lt-Col (retd) Hugo Rafael Chávez Frías, agreed to supply Uruguay with petroleum on preferential terms for the next 25 years.

The services sector contributed 58.1% of GDP in 2007, and engaged 73.9% of the working population in 2003. Tourism is a significant source of foreign exchange, earning US $579m. in 2004. The GDP of the services sector increased by an annual average of 1.6% in 1997–2007, according to preliminary figures. The GDP of the services sector increased by 5.9% in 2007.

In 2006 Uruguay recorded an estimated visible trade deficit of US $484.4m., and there was a deficit of $436.4m. on the current account of the balance of payments. In 2006 the principal source of imports was Argentina (22.6%); other major suppliers were Brazil, Venezuela and the People's Republic of China. Brazil was the principal market for exports (14.7%) in that year; other major recipients were the USA and Argentina. The main exports in 2006 were live animals and animal products, and plants and their products. The principal imports in that year were mineral fuels, machinery and equipment, and industrial chemicals.

In 2006 there was a budgetary deficit of 5,904m. pesos uruguayos, equivalent to some 1.1% of GDP. At the end of 2005 Uruguay's total external debt was US $14,551m., of which $7,866m. was long-term public debt. In that year the cost of debt-servicing was equivalent to 38.9% of the value of exports of goods and services. The average annual rate of inflation was 8.4% in 1998–2007. Consumer prices increased by 6.4% in 2006 and by a further 8.1% in 2007. According to the International Labour Organization (ILO), 10.6% of the labour force were unemployed in 2005.

Uruguay is a member of the Inter-American Development Bank (IDB, see p. 308), the Asociación Latinoamericana de Integración (ALADI, see p. 331), the Sistema Económico Latinoamericano (SELA, see p. 413) and the Mercado Común del Sur (Mercosur, see p. 391). In December 2004 Uruguay was one of 12 countries that were signatories to the agreement, signed in Cusco, Peru, creating the South American Community of Nations (Comunidad Sudamericana de Naciones), intended to promote greater regional economic integration. It had been anticipated that the new entity, to be styled after the EU, would become operational by 2007; however, by April 2008 implementation of the necessary legal frameworks remained incomplete. A treaty for the community—referred to as the Union of South American Nations (Unasur) since its reinvention in April 2007—was expected to be initialled in June 2008, with full functionality of economic union tentatively scheduled for 2019.

The recession experienced in Uruguay in 1999–2002 was largely precipitated by external factors, notably the negative impact of the economic crises in Argentina and Brazil, the devaluation of the Brazilian currency at the beginning of 1999 and low world prices for its principal export products. In 2002 the Government announced a plan to reduce the fiscal deficit by tax increases and privatization. In May 2003 the Government successfully issued new bonds to restructure its short-term external debt. In the same month the World Bank disbursed further loans, totalling US $252m., intended to finance infrastructure and social welfare projects. The funds were to complement assistance from the IDB, which had pledged some $160m., in addition to finance from other international financial institutions. Following a return to economic growth in 2003, the recovery continued in 2004–07, owing primarily to improved export prices, banking sector reforms and increased industrial output. However, the level of public debt remained very high, equivalent to some 90% of GDP. The economic priorities of the Government of Tabaré Vázquez, which took office in March 2005, included a dramatic increase in social welfare expenditure. This was partly to be funded by sustained economic growth and increased foreign investment, as well as by a radical reform of the taxation system. In February 2005 the IMF, on completion of its seventh and final review of Uruguay's stand-by arrangement, approved a final disbursement of $213.8m. A new stand-by arrangement with the IMF worth some $1,110m. was agreed in June, contingent on financial reform, increased private sector participation and fiscal prudence. Positive reviews of the Government's economic policy under orthodox Minister of Economy and Finance Danilo Astori led to further disbursements in 2006. Uruguay realized significantly higher rates of growth in 2006–07 (see above), indicating that the economy had recovered from the recession at the beginning of the decade. The impressive recovery was partly fuelled by high agricultural prices (Uruguay was an important exporter of beef and dairy products) and by increased trade with Brazil and Argentina. However, this left Uruguay vulnerable to further economic downturns in those countries (as in 1999–2002). Furthermore, the continuing dispute with neighbouring Argentina over the construction of two paper mills on the River Uruguay (see Recent History) inhibited bilateral trade and tourism in 2007. None the less, once operational, the two mills were expected to deliver an increase in export revenues, owing to the much larger shipments of wood pulp being exported to the EU. Worsening global conditions were likely to temper the performance of Uruguay's exports in 2008, while rising international prices for food and energy were expected to precipitate higher inflation and widen the current account deficit. The IMF forecast that GDP growth would slow, reaching 6.0% in 2008 and 4.0% in 2009.

Education

All education, including university tuition, is provided free of charge. Education is officially compulsory for six years between six and 14 years of age. Primary education begins at the age of six and lasts for six years. Secondary education, beginning at 12 years of age, lasts for a further six years, comprising two cycles of three years each. In 1996 the total enrolment at primary and secondary schools was equivalent to 97% of the school-age population. In that year primary enrolment included 93% of children in the relevant age-group (males 92%; females 93%), while secondary enrolment was equivalent to 85% of the population in the appropriate age-group (males 77%; females 92%). Total enrolment ratio at primary, secondary and tertiary levels in 2004 was equivalent to 88.9% of the population in the relevant age-group. The programmes of instruction are the same in both public and private schools, and private schools are subject to certain state controls. There were six universities in 2003. Central government expenditure on education in that year was 10,558m. pesos uruguayos (11.8% of central government spending).

Public Holidays

2008: 1 January (New Year's Day), 6 January (Epiphany), 4–5 March (Carnival), 17–21 March (Holy Week), 19 April (Landing of the 33 Patriots), 1 May (Labour Day), 18 May (Battle of Las Piedras), 19 June (Birth of José Artigas), 18 July (Constitution Day), 25 August (National Independence Day), 12 October (Discovery of America and Battle of Sarandí), 2 November (All Souls' Day), 25 December (Christmas Day).

2009: 1 January (New Year's Day), 6 January (Epiphany), 23–24 March (Carnival), 6–10 April (Holy Week), 19 April (Landing of the 33 Patriots), 1 May (Labour Day), 18 May (Battle of Las Piedras), 19 June (Birth of José Artigas), 18 July (Constitution Day), 25 August (National Independence Day), 12 October (Discovery of America and Battle of Sarandí), 2 November (All Souls' Day), 25 December (Christmas Day).

Many businesses close for the entirety of Carnival week (4–8 February 2008 and 23–27 March 2009).

Weights and Measures

The metric system is in force.

URUGUAY

Statistical Survey

Sources (unless otherwise stated): Instituto Nacional de Estadística, Río Negro 1520, 11100 Montevideo; tel. (2) 9027303; internet www.ine.gub.uy; Banco Central del Uruguay, Avda Juan P. Fabini, esq. Florida 777, Casilla 1467, 11100 Montevideo; tel. (2) 9085629; fax (2) 9021634; e-mail info@bcu.gub.uy; internet www.bcu.gub.uy; Cámara Nacional de Comercio y Servicios del Uruguay, Edif. Bolsa de Comercio, Rincón 454, 2°, Casilla 1000, 11000 Montevideo; tel. (2) 9161277; fax (2) 9161243; e-mail info@cncs.com.uy; internet www.cncs.com.uy.

Area and Population

AREA, POPULATION AND DENSITY

Area (sq km)	
Land area	175,016
Inland water	1,199
Total	176,215*
Population (census results)†	
22 May 1996	3,163,763
May–July 2004	
Males	1,565,533
Females	1,675,470
Total	3,241,003
Population (official estimates at mid-year)	
2005	3,305,723
2006	3,314,466
2007	3,323,906
Density (per sq km) at mid-2007	18.9

* 68,037 sq miles.
† Excluding adjustment for underenumeration.

DEPARTMENTS
(population estimates at mid-2007)

	Area (sq km)	Population	Density (per sq km)	Capital
Artigas	11,928	79,317	6.6	Artigas
Canelones	4,536	509,095	112.2	Canelones
Cerro Largo	13,648	89,383	6.5	Melo
Colonia	6,106	120,855	19.8	Colonia del Sacramento
Durazno	11,643	60,926	5.2	Durazno
Flores	5,144	25,609	5.0	Trinidad
Florida	10,417	61,883	5.9	Florida
Lavalleja	10,016	69,968	7.0	Minas
Maldonado	4,793	147,391	30.8	Maldonado
Montevideo	530	1,342,474	2,533.0	Montevideo
Paysandú	13,922	115,623	8.3	Paysandú
Río Negro	9,282	55,657	6.0	Fray Bentos
Rivera	9,370	109,267	11.7	Rivera
Rocha	10,551	70,614	6.7	Rocha
Salto	14,163	126,745	8.9	Salto
San José	4,992	107,644	21.6	San José de Mayo
Soriano	9,008	87,073	9.7	Mercedes
Tacuarembó	15,438	94,613	6.1	Tacuarembó
Treinta y Tres	9,529	49,769	5.2	Treinta y Tres
Total	175,016*	3,323,906	19.0	

* Land area only.

PRINCIPAL TOWNS
(population at 22 May 1996 census)

Montevideo (capital)	1,378,707	Mercedes	50,800
Salto	93,420	Maldonado	50,420
Paysandú	84,160	Melo	47,160
Las Piedras	66,100	Tacuarembó	42,580
Rivera	63,370		

Mid-2007 ('000, incl. suburbs, UN estimate): Montevideo 1,513 (Source: UN, *World Urbanization Prospects: The 2007 Revision*).

BIRTHS, MARRIAGES AND DEATHS*

	Registered live births		Registered marriages		Registered deaths	
	Number	Rate (per 1,000)	Number	Rate (per 1,000)	Number	Rate (per 1,000)
2001	51,959	15.7	13,988	4.2	31,228	9.4
2002	51,953	15.7	14,073	4.3	31,628	9.6
2003	50,631	15.3	14,147	4.3	32,587	9.9
2004	50,052	15.2	13,123	4.0	32,222	9.8
2005	46,944†	14.2†	13,075	4.0	32,319†	9.8†
2006	47,410†	14.2†	12,415	3.7	31,056†	9.4†

* Data are tabulated by year of registration rather than by year of occurrence and have not been adjusted to take account of most recent census.
† Preliminary.

Expectation of life (years at birth, WHO estimates): 75.2 (males 71.5; females 78.9) in 2005 (Source: WHO, *World Health Statistics*).

ECONOMICALLY ACTIVE POPULATION
(ISIC major divisions, '000 persons aged 14 years and over, urban areas)

	2001	2002	2003
Agriculture, hunting, forestry and fishing	45.4	43.7	46.9
Mining and quarrying	1.3	1.2	1.2
Manufacturing (incl. electricity, gas and water)	167.1	154.2	151.1
Construction	87.9	77.4	69.6
Trade, restaurants, hotels and repair of vehicles and household goods	240.8	228.9	225.4
Transport, storage and communications	66.8	62.4	61.1
Financing, insurance, real estate and business services	97.4	96.5	91.0
Public administration and defence, compulsory social security	85.1	86.9	91.2
Education	57.2	62.2	61.6
Health and social work	72.5	76.7	76.7
Community, social and personal services	56.2	52.2	54.8
Private households with employed persons	98.5	96.0	100.9
Activities not adequately defined	—	—	0.3
Total employed	1,076.2	1,038.3	1,032.0
Males	617.7	597.9	589.7
Females	458.5	440.4	442.3
Unemployed	193.2	211.3	208.5
Total labour force	1,269.4	1,250.1	1,240.5

Source: ILO.

2006 ('000 persons aged 14 years and over, estimates): Total employed 1,413; Unemployed 167; Total labour force 1,580 (males 892, females 688).

URUGUAY

Health and Welfare

KEY INDICATORS

Total fertility rate (children per woman, 2005)	2.3
Under-5 mortality rate (per 1,000 live births, 2005)	15
HIV/AIDS (% of persons aged 15–49, 2005)	0.5
Physicians (per 1,000 head, 2002)	3.65
Hospital beds (per 1,000 head, 2005)	2.40
Health expenditure (2004): US $ per head (PPP)	783.7
Health expenditure (2004): % of GDP	8.2
Health expenditure (2004): public (% of total)	43.5
Human Development Index (2005): ranking	46
Human Development Index (2005): value	0.852

For sources and definitions, see explanatory note on p. vi.

Agriculture

PRINCIPAL CROPS
('000 metric tons)

	2004	2005	2006
Wheat	532.6	387.5	400.0*
Rice (paddy)	1,262.6	1,214.5	1,300.0*
Barley	406.5	225.0	250.0*
Maize	223.0	251.0	260.0*
Oats	26.3	21.6*	21.6*
Sorghum	69.7	84.7	84.7*
Potatoes	138.0	157.6	157.6*
Sweet potatoes*	67.7	69.6	69.6
Sugar cane	154.2	177.3	177.3*
Sunflower seed	177.0	150.5	81.0†
Tomatoes†	44.4	47.5	47.5
Dry onions	58.0†	35.0†	35.0*
Carrots	33.8†	32.0†	32.0*
Oranges	124.1	176.5	176.5*
Tangerines, mandarins, clementines and satsumas	77.3	94.4	94.4*
Lemons and limes	33.5	46.0	46.0*
Apples	66.7	77.3	77.3*
Pears	17.6	18.4	18.4*
Peaches and nectarines	14.1	15.9	15.9*
Grapes	147.1	124.3	124.3*

* FAO estimate(s).
† Unofficial figure(s).

Aggregate production ('000 metric tons, may include official, semi-official or estimated data): Total cereals 2,523.2 in 2004, 2,186.9 in 2005, 2,318.9 in 2006; Total fruits (excl. melons) 503.5 in 2004, 578.0 in 2005, 578.0 in 2006; Total vegetables (incl. melons) 215.1 in 2004, 198.4 in 2005, 198.4 in 2006.
Source: FAO.

LIVESTOCK
('000 head, year ending September)

	2003	2004	2005
Cattle	11,708	11,958	11,956
Sheep	9,975	9,508	9,712
Pigs	240	220	257
Horses	437	429	432
Chickens	13,300	13,500	14,000

2006: Figures assumed to be unchanged from 2005 (FAO estimates).
Source: FAO.

LIVESTOCK PRODUCTS
('000 metric tons)

	2003	2004	2005
Cattle meat	424.2	496.5	516.0
Sheep meat	26.9	26.5	37.0*
Pig meat	16.8	15.3	18.6
Chicken meat†	30.5	43.0	45.0
Cows' milk	1,507.0	1,641.0	1,770.0
Eggs	34.5	36.2	36.2†
Wool: greasy	34.9	36.0	37.2

* Unofficial figure.
† FAO estimate(s).
2006: Figures assumed to be unchanged from 2005 (FAO estimates).
Source: FAO.

Forestry

ROUNDWOOD REMOVALS
('000 cubic metres, excl. bark)

	2004	2005	2006
Sawlogs and veneer logs	536	580	734
Pulpwood	2,770	3,128	3,128*
Other industrial wood	18	21	23
Fuel wood	1,760	1,973	2,111
Total	5,084	5,702	5,996

* FAO estimate.
Source: FAO.

SAWNWOOD PRODUCTION
('000 cubic metres, incl. railway sleepers)

	2003	2004	2005
Coniferous (softwood)	82	88	91
Broadleaved (hardwood)	148	164	177
Total	230	252	268

2006: Figures assumed to be unchanged from 2005 (FAO estimates).
Source: FAO.

Fishing

('000 metric tons, live weight)

	2003	2004	2005
Capture	117.3	123.1	126.0
Argentine hake	35.2	41.7	41.5
Striped weakfish	7.1	11.0	8.6
Whitemouth croaker	30.7	29.4	27.8
Patagonian toothfish	4.9	2.1	0.8
Argentine shortfin squid	6.4	4.7	7.7
Red crab	3.0	2.7	2.7
Aquaculture	0.0	0.0	0.0
Total catch	117.4	123.0	126.0

Source: FAO.

Mining

('000 metric tons, unless otherwise indicated)

	2003	2004	2005
Gold (kg)	1,550	2,334	3,151
Gypsum*	1,130	1,130	1,130
Feldspar (metric tons)	2,450	2,450	2,150

* Estimates.
Source: US Geological Survey.

URUGUAY

Industry

SELECTED PRODUCTS
('000 metric tons, unless otherwise indicated)

	2002	2003	2004
Raw sugar*	6.7	6.3	n.a.
Wine	71.4	81.8	112.6
Cigarettes (million)	8,449	5,718	n.a.
Motor spirit (petrol) ('000 barrels)†	2,200	2,200	1,793
Kerosene ('000 barrels)†	500	500	75
Distillate fuel oils ('000 barrels)†	4,100	4,200	8,810
Residual fuel oils ('000 barrels)†	3,600	3,650	3,650
Cement (hydraulic)	1,000†	1,050†	1,050
Electric energy (million kWh)	9,605	8,578	5,936

* Unofficial figures.
† US Geological Survey estimate(s).

Sources: FAO; US Geological Survey; UN, *Industrial Commodity Statistics Yearbook*.

2005 ('000 barrels, unless otherwise indicated): Motor spirit (petrol) 1,830 (estimate); Kerosene 67 (estimate); Distillate fuel oil 8,476 (estimate); Residual fuel oils 3,650 (estimate); Cement (hydraulic) 1,050,000 metric tons (Source: US Geological Survey).

Finance

CURRENCY AND EXCHANGE RATES

Monetary Units
100 centésimos = 1 peso uruguayo.

Sterling, Dollar and Euro Equivalents (31 December 2007)
£1 sterling = 43.073 pesos;
US $1 = 21.500 pesos;
€1 = 31.650 pesos;
1,000 pesos uruguayos = £23.22 = $46.51 = €31.60.

Average Exchange Rate (pesos per US $)
2005   24.479
2006   24.073
2007   23.471

Note: On 1 March 1993 a new currency, the peso uruguayo (equivalent to 1,000 former new pesos), was introduced.

BUDGET*
(million pesos uruguayos)

Revenue	2004	2005	2006
Tax revenue	65,850	72,819	100,293
Taxes on income, profits, etc.	15,428	16,377	20,448
Individual taxes	6,011	4,665	6,235
Corporate taxes	8,967	11,271	13,694
Taxes on property	7,340	8,030	7,951
Domestic taxes on goods and services	38,384	43,174	65,804
General sales, take-over or value-added tax	27,555	31,411	51,749
Taxes on international trade and transactions	2,028	2,194	2,524
Taxes on leisure activities	27	31	50
Other taxes and rates	2,644	3,013	3,516
Non-tax revenue	8,222	7,097	7,462
Transfers	2,994	3,832	3,318
Other income	509	611	248
Total	77,574	84,359	111,321

Expenditure	2004	2005	2006
General public services	23,204	25,519	28,230
Government administration	13,444	15,058	16,290
Defence	4,376	4,660	5,187
Public order and safety	5,385	5,801	6,753
Special and community services	37,148	38,747	58,271
Education	11,873	12,573	14,392
Health	6,521	7,135	8,654
Social security and welfare	16,817	17,109	32,375
Housing and community amenities	1,259	1,371	2,029
Recreational, cultural and religious affairs	679	559	821
Economic affairs and services	3,353	5,931	6,435
Fuel and energy	186	179	194
Agriculture, fishing, forestry and hunting	1,421	2,033	1,584
Mining and mineral resources	253	273	275
Transport and communications	2,530	2,728	3,725
Other economic services	964	718	657
Debt-servicing and governmental transfers	22,805	20,322	24,289
Total	88,510	90,519	117,225

* Figures represent the consolidated accounts of the central Government, which include social security revenue and expenditure.

INTERNATIONAL RESERVES
(US $ million at 31 December)

	2005	2006	2007
Gold	4	5	7
IMF special drawing rights	6	1	—
Foreign exchange	3,068	3,084	4,104
Total	3,078	3,090	4,111

Source: IMF, *International Financial Statistics*.

MONEY SUPPLY
(million pesos uruguayos at 31 December)

	2004	2005	2006
Currency outside banks	10,803.7	13,315.1	16,139.3
Demand deposits at commercial banks	10,928.0	15,440.9	19,301.4
Total money (incl. others)	22,225.4	29,680.3	35,625.5

Source: IMF, *International Financial Statistics*.

COST OF LIVING
(Consumer Price Index for Montevideo; base: March 1997 = 100)

	2004	2005	2006
Food and beverages	201.9	210.1	223.2
Housing	201.1	213.5	230.8
Clothing and footwear	147.4	154.5	158.4
Transport and communications	233.9	237.3	251.5
All items (incl. others)	198.0	207.3	220.6

2007: All items 238.4.

NATIONAL ACCOUNTS
(million pesos uruguayos at current prices)

Expenditure on the Gross Domestic Product

	2005	2006	2007
Government final consumption expenditure	44,902.9	51,232.5	60,384.8
Private final consumption expenditure	300,314.8	347,131.2	403,617.8
Increase in stocks	152.5	2,251.2	6,232.4
Gross fixed capital formation	50,849.5	67,539.7	75,344.7
Total domestic expenditure	396,219.7	468,154.6	545,579.7
Exports of goods and services	126,286.5	139,604.2	158,247.5
Less Imports of goods and services	115,800.9	142,956.9	161,958.7
GDP in purchasers' values	406,705.4	464,801.9	541,868.4
GDP at constant 1983 prices	300.1	321.1	344.9

URUGUAY

Gross Domestic Product by Economic Activity

	2005	2006	2007
Agriculture	36,023.2	40,879.2	53,458.7
Fishing	1,411.1	1,773.6	1,488.8
Mining and quarrying	1,004.1	1,317.5	1,490.6
Manufacturing	91,539.6	107,944.7	123,411.0
Electricity, gas and water	20,128.9	21,698.9	26,084.1
Construction	15,606.5	19,701.0	22,361.9
Trade, restaurants and hotels	52,948.6	60,992.1	73,094.3
Transport, storage and communications	39,392.9	44,953.6	49,616.1
Finance and insurance	32,726.3	35,478.7	37,421.7
Real estate and business services	49,648.2	55,045.9	63,629.6
General government services	34,227.7	38,671.1	45,579.3
Other community, social and personal services	37,863.7	42,085.1	47,814.8
Sub-total	412,520.7	470,541.4	545,451.1
Import duties	21,929.2	24,343.6	28,205.4
Less Imputed bank service charge	27,744.5	30,083.1	31,787.8
GDP in purchasers' values	406,705.4	464,801.9	541,868.4

BALANCE OF PAYMENTS
(US $ million)

	2004	2005	2006
Exports of goods f.o.b.	3,145.0	3,774.1	4,375.0
Imports of goods f.o.b.	−2,992.2	−3,753.3	−4,859.4
Trade balance	152.8	20.8	−484.4
Exports of services	1,111.6	1,311.3	1,285.4
Imports of services	−786.1	−939.5	−902.1
Balance on goods and services	478.3	392.6	−101.2
Other income received	372.4	563.1	733.8
Other income paid	−960.4	−1,057.3	−1,202.9
Balance on goods, services and income	−109.7	−101.5	−570.3
Current transfers received	127.2	143.1	153.3
Current transfers paid	−14.3	−17.3	−19.4
Current balance	3.1	24.3	−436.4
Capital account (net)	5.3	3.8	6.5
Direct investment abroad	−17.7	−36.3	2.4
Direct investment from abroad	332.4	847.4	1,319.1
Portfolio investment assets	−695.7	577.8	−77.5
Portfolio investment liabilities	273.4	228.2	1,807.8
Other investment assets	−259.7	−1,112.7	1,387.1
Other investment liabilities	285.4	419.4	−1,663.8
Net errors and omissions	377.9	−173.4	22.1
Overall balance	304.4	778.4	2,367.4

Source: IMF, *International Financial Statistics*.

External Trade

PRINCIPAL COMMODITIES
(US $ million)

Imports c.i.f.	2004	2005	2006
Food preparations, beverages and tobacco	148.9	176.8	223.6
Mineral products	768.4	972.2	1,335.8
Industrial chemicals and related products	499.0	547.8	606.5
Wood pulp, paper and cardboard	93.3	102.3	112.4
Textiles	163.0	182.9	200.3
Base metals and manufactures thereof	149.6	191.6	250.1
Machinery and equipment	438.4	629.7	763.5
Transport equipment	179.6	267.9	354.6
Total (incl. others)	3,118.6	3,878.9	4,774.9

Exports f.o.b.	2004	2005	2006
Live animals and animal derivatives	1,043.2	1,231.6	1,497.4
Plants and plant derivatives (incl. cereals)	454.3	499.9	548.8
Food, beverages and tobacco	105.8	140.4	139.2
Mineral products	137.2	171.9	148.4
Chemicals and manufactures thereof	131.3	152.0	180.0
Plastics, rubber and manufactures thereof	140.3	174.2	202.4
Hides and leather goods	279.9	282.9	340.7
Wood, plant fibres and manufactures thereof	106.5	141.5	186.7
Wood pulp, paper and cardboard	54.7	64.4	65.8
Textiles	236.9	253.6	268.5
Base metals and manufactures thereof	46.1	52.3	74.3
Machines and electrical equipment	27.8	33.6	42.1
Transport goods and materials	56.3	68.1	110.6
Total (incl. others)	2,932.3	3,416.9	3,952.3

PRINCIPAL TRADING PARTNERS
(US $ million, preliminary figures)

Imports c.i.f.	2004	2005	2006
Argentina	686.5	785.7	1,078.5
Brazil	676.5	824.7	1,077.9
Canada	12.0	21.6	18.3
Chile	58.4	69.6	71.2
China, People's Republic	172.7	242.3	350.9
Germany	82.6	87.8	99.3
Iran	114.9	0.7	130.2
Italy	66.2	75.8	81.9
Japan	42.8	42.9	50.4
Mexico	29.6	50.9	60.6
Spain	55.7	48.1	56.0
United Kingdom	28.8	34.1	45.7
USA	220.3	259.2	326.2
Venezuela	1.8	244.7	599.5
Total (incl. others)	3,118.6	3,878.9	4,774.9

Exports f.o.b.	2004	2005	2006
Argentina	223.3	266.9	301.5
Brazil	483.7	460.3	582.5
Canada	105.1	87.1	44.5
Chile	61.1	83.5	165.3
China, People's Republic	112.9	121.7	159.5
France (incl. Monaco)	32.6	30.9	33.1
Germany	151.6	144.6	164.6
Iran	43.4	80.7	51.2
Italy	89.3	92.9	112.4
Japan	15.1	32.1	42.8
Mexico	117.7	139.3	133.9
Netherlands	53.7	47.2	67.4
Paraguay	58.5	56.0	58.1
Spain	95.2	131.2	119.7
United Kingdom	91.4	85.2	95.4
USA	577.3	762.8	520.4
Venezuela	32.7	33.5	78.2
Total (incl. others)	2,932.3	3,416.9	3,952.3

Transport

RAILWAYS
(traffic)

	2002	2003	2004
Passenger-km (million)	8	11	11
Net ton-km (million)	178	188	297

Source: UN, *Statistical Yearbook*.

URUGUAY

ROAD TRAFFIC
(motor vehicles in use at 31 December)

	1995	1996	1997
Passenger cars	464,547	485,109	516,889
Buses and coaches	4,409	4,752	4,984
Lorries and vans	41,417	43,656	45,280
Road tractors	12,511	14,628	15,514
Motorcycles and mopeds	300,850	328,406	359,824

Source: International Road Federation, *World Road Statistics*.

2003: Passenger cars and vans 526,236; Coaches and minibuses 6,681; Lorries and road tractors 53,615; Motorcycles and mopeds 427,286; Taxis and hire cars 5,447.

SHIPPING

Merchant Fleet
(registered at 31 December)

	2004	2005	2006
Number of vessels	94	120	123
Total displacement ('000 grt)	76.0	95.2	97.4

Source: Lloyd's Register-Fairplay, *World Fleet Statistics*.

CIVIL AVIATION
(traffic on scheduled services)

	2004	2005	2006
Kilometres flown (million)	9.3	7.7	7.6
Passenger-km (million)	1,075.9	979.6	940.4
Total ton-km (million)	4.5	4.3	4.2

Source: UN Economic Commission for Latin America and the Caribbean, *Statistical Yearbook*.

Tourism

ARRIVALS BY NATIONALITY*
('000)

	2003	2004	2005
Argentina	866.6	1,108.6	1,107.5
Brazil	151.4	187.7	197.7
Total (incl. others)	1,508.1	1,870.9	1,917.0

* Figures refer to arrivals at frontiers of visitors from abroad, including Uruguayan nationals permanently resident elsewhere.

Tourism receipts (US $ million): 493.9 in 2004; 593.5 in 2005; 596.6 in 2006.

Communications Media

	2004	2005	2006
Telephones ('000 main lines in use)	997.0	1,006.0	987.0
Mobile cellular telephones ('000 subscribers)	600.0	1,154.9	2,330.0
Personal computers ('000 in use)	430	n.a.	n.a.
Internet users ('000)	567	668	756
Broadband subscribers ('000)	27.0	61.2	107.0

Television receivers (2000): 1,770,000 in use.

Radio receivers (1997): 1,970,000 in use.

Book production (1996): 934 titles.

Daily newspapers (1996): 36 (estimated average circulation 950,000).

Facsimile machines (1995): 11,000 in use.

Sources: UNESCO, *Statistical Yearbook*; UN, *Statistical Yearbook*; International Telecommunication Union.

Education

(2006, unless otherwise indicated)

	Institutions	Teachers	Students
Pre-primary	1,302	3,973	106,636
Primary	2,400	17,111	353,528
Secondary: general	436	25,168*†	218,816
Secondary: vocational	124‡	n.a.	69,896
University and equivalent institutions*‡	6	7,723	72,100

* Public education only.
† 2003.
‡ 2005.

Adult literacy rate (UNESCO estimates): 96.8% (males 96.2%; females 97.3%) in 1996 (Source: UNESCO Institute for Statistics).

Directory

The Constitution

The Constitution of Uruguay was ratified by plebiscite, on 27 November 1966, when the country voted to return to the presidential form of government after 15 years of 'collegiate' government. The main points of the Constitution, as amended in January 1997, are as follows:

GENERAL PROVISIONS

Uruguay shall have a democratic republican form of government, sovereignty being exercised directly by the Electoral Body in cases of election, by initiative or by referendum, and indirectly by representative powers established by the Constitution, according to the rules set out therein.

There shall be freedom of religion; there is no state religion; property shall be inviolable; there shall be freedom of thought. Anyone may enter Uruguay. There are two forms of citizenship: natural, being persons born in Uruguay or of Uruguayan parents, and legal, being people established in Uruguay with at least three years' residence in the case of those with family, and five years' for those without family. Every citizen has the right and obligation to vote.

LEGISLATURE

Legislative power is vested in the Congreso (Congress or General Assembly), comprising two houses, which may act separately or together according to the dispositions of the Constitution. It elects in joint session the members of the Supreme Court of Justice, of the Electoral Court, Tribunals, Administrative Litigation and the Accounts Tribunal.

Elections for both houses, the President and the Vice-President shall take place every five years on the last Sunday in October; sessions of the Assembly begin on 1 March each year and last until 15 December (15 September in election years, in which case the new Congress takes office on 15 February). Extraordinary sessions can be convened only in case of extreme urgency.

URUGUAY

CHAMBER OF REPRESENTATIVES

The Chamber of Representatives has 99 members elected by direct suffrage according to the system of proportional representation, with at least two representatives for each Department. The number of representatives can be altered by law by a two-thirds' majority in both houses. Their term of office is five years and they must be over 25 years of age and be natural citizens or legal citizens with five years' exercise of their citizenship. Representatives have the right to bring accusations against any member of the Government or judiciary for violation of the Constitution or any other serious offence.

SENATE

The Senate comprises 31 members, including the Vice-President, who sits as President of the Senate, and 30 members elected directly by proportional representation on the same lists as the representatives, for a term of five years. They must be natural citizens or legal citizens with seven years' exercise of their rights, and be over 30 years of age. The Senate is responsible for hearing cases brought by the representatives and can deprive a guilty person of a post by a two-thirds' majority.

THE EXECUTIVE

Executive power is exercised by the President and the Council of Ministers. There is a Vice-President, who is also President of the Congress and of the Senate. The President and Vice-President are directly elected by absolute majority, and remain in office for five years. They must be over 35 years of age and be natural citizens.

The Council of Ministers comprises the office holders in the ministries or their deputies, and is responsible for all acts of government and administration. It is presided over by the President of the Republic, who has a vote.

THE JUDICIARY

Judicial power is exercised by the five-member Supreme Court of Justice and by Tribunals and local courts; members of the Supreme Court must be over 40 years of age and be natural citizens, or legal citizens with 10 years' exercise and 25 years' residence, and must be lawyers of 10 years' standing, eight of them in public or fiscal ministry or judicature. Members serve for 10 years and can be re-elected after a break of five years. The Court nominates all other judges and judicial officials.

The Government

HEAD OF STATE

President: Dr TABARÉ RAMÓN VÁZQUEZ ROSAS (took office 1 March 2005).
Vice-President: RODOLFO NIN NOVOA (AP).

COUNCIL OF MINISTERS
(April 2008)

Minister of the Interior: DAISY TOURNÉ (PS).
Minister of Foreign Affairs: Dr GONZALO FERNÁNDEZ (PS).
Minister of National Defence: Dr JOSÉ BAYARDI (VA).
Minister of Social Development: MARINA ARISMENDI (PCU).
Minister of Economy and Finance: DANILO ASTORI (AU).
Minister of Industry, Energy and Mining: DANIEL MARTÍNEZ (PS).
Minister of Livestock, Agriculture and Fishing: ERNESTO AGAZZI (MPP).
Minister of Tourism and Sport: Dr HÉCTOR LESCANO (AP).
Minister of Transport and Public Works: VÍCTOR ROSSI (AP).
Minister of Labour and Social Security: EDUARDO BONOMI (MPP).
Minister of Education and Culture: MARÍA SIMÓN (Ind.).
Minister of Public Health: Dra MARÍA JULIA MUÑOZ (VA).
Minister of Housing, Territorial Regulation and the Environment: CARLOS COLACCE (Ind.).
Director of the Planning and Budget Office: ENRIQUE RUBIO (VA).

MINISTRIES

Office of the President: Casa de Gobierno, Edif. Libertad, Avda Luis Alberto de Herrera 3350, Montevideo; tel. (2) 4872110; fax (2) 4809397; internet www.presidencia.gub.uy.

Ministry of Economy and Finance: Colonia 1089, 3°, 11100 Montevideo; tel. (2) 7122910; fax (2) 7122919; e-mail seprimef@mef.gub.uy; internet www.mef.gub.uy.

Ministry of Education and Culture: Reconquista 535, 11000 Montevideo; tel. (2) 9161174; fax (2) 9161048; e-mail webmaster@mec.gub.uy; internet www.mec.gub.uy.

Ministry of Foreign Affairs: Avda 18 de Julio 1205, 11100 Montevideo; tel. (2) 9022132; fax (2) 9021349; e-mail webmaster@mrree.gub.uy; internet www.mrree.gub.uy.

Ministry of Housing, Territorial Regulation and the Environment: Zabala 1427, 11000 Montevideo; tel. (2) 9163989; fax (2) 9163914; e-mail secmtro@mvotma.gub.uy; internet www.mvotma.gub.uy.

Ministry of Industry, Energy and Mining: Paysandú esq. Libertador Brig. Gral Lavalleja 4°, Montevideo; tel. (2) 9009939; fax (2) 9021245; internet www.miem.gub.uy.

Ministry of the Interior: Mercedes 953, 11100 Montevideo; tel. (2) 9021665; fax (2) 9023142; e-mail webmaster@minterior.gub.uy; internet www.minterior.gub.uy.

Ministry of Labour and Social Security: Juncal 1511, 4°, 11000 Montevideo; tel. (2) 9162681; fax (2) 9162708; internet www.mtss.gub.uy.

Ministry of Livestock, Agriculture and Fishing: Avda Constituyente 1476, 11200 Montevideo; tel. (2) 4126326; fax (2) 4184051; e-mail webmaster@mgap.gub.uy; internet www.mgap.gub.uy.

Ministry of National Defence: Edif. General Artigas, Avda 8 de Octubre 2628, Montevideo; tel. (2) 4872828; fax (2) 4809397; e-mail rrpp.secretaria@mdn.gub.uy; internet www.mdn.gub.uy.

Ministry of Public Health: Avda 18 de Julio 1892, 11100 Montevideo; tel. (2) 4001086; fax (2) 4085360; e-mail msp@msp.gub.uy; internet www.msp.gub.uy.

Ministry of Social Development: Avda 18 de Julio 1453, 11200 Montevideo; tel. and fax (2) 4000302; e-mail dirgeneral@mides.gub.uy; internet www.mides.gub.uy.

Ministry of Tourism and Sport: Rambla 25 de Agosto 1825, esq. Yacaré, Montevideo; tel. (2) 1885100; fax (2) 9162487; e-mail difusion@mtop.gub.uy; internet www.turismo.gub.uy.

Ministry of Transport and Public Works: Rincón 561, 11000 Montevideo; tel. (2) 9160509; fax (2) 9165044; e-mail direcciongeneral@mtop.gub.uy; internet www.mtop.gub.uy.

Planning and Budget Office: Edif. Libertad, Luis A. de Herrera 3350, Montevideo; tel. (2) 4872110; fax (2) 2099730; e-mail direccion@opp.gub.uy; internet www.opp.gub.uy.

President and Legislature

PRESIDENT

Election, 31 October 2004

Candidate	% of vote
Tabaré Ramón Vázquez Rosas (Encuentro Progresista—Frente Amplio)	50.70
Jorge Larrañaga (Partido Nacional)	34.06
Guillermo Stirling (Partido Colorado)	10.32
Others	2.53
Invalid votes	2.39
Total	100.00

CONGRESO

Cámara de Senadores
(Senate)

Election, 31 October 2004

Party	Seats
Encuentro Progresista—Frente Amplio	16
Partido Nacional	11
Partido Colorado	3
Total*	30

* An additional seat is reserved for the Vice-President, who sits as President of the Senate.

URUGUAY

Cámara de Representantes
(Chamber of Representatives)

President: ENRIQUE PINTADO.

Election, 31 October 2004

Party	Seats
Encuentro Progresista—Frente Amplio	52
Partido Nacional	35
Partido Colorado	10
Other parties	2
Total	**99**

Election Commission

Corte Electoral: Ituzaingó 1474, Montevideo; tel. (2) 9159626; fax (2) 9155087; internet www.corteelectoral.gub.uy; f. 1967; Pres. CARLOS A. URRUTY NAVATTA.

Political Organizations

Alianza Libertadora Nacionalista: Montevideo; extreme right-wing; Leader OSVALDO MARTÍNEZ JAUME.

Encuentro Progresista—Frente Amplio (EP—FA): Col. 1367, 2°, 11100 Montevideo; tel. (2) 9022176; internet www.epfaprensa .org; f. 1971; left-wing grouping; Pres. JORGE BROVETTO; mems include:

Alianza Progresista 738 (AP): Col. y Edif. Acevedo, Montevideo; tel. and fax (2) 4016365; e-mail a738@adinet.com.uy; internet www.alianza738.org.uy; left-wing; Leader RODOLFO NIN NOVOA.

Asamblea Uruguay (AU): Carlos Quijano 1271, Montevideo; tel. (2) 9032121; fax (2) 9241147; e-mail jmahia@parlamento.gub.uy; internet www.asamblea.org.uy; f. 1994; centre-left; Leader DANILO ASTORI.

Frente Izquierda de Liberación (FIDEL): Montevideo; f. 1962; socialist; Leader ADOLFO AGUIRRE GONZÁLEZ.

Grupo Pregón: Montevideo; left-wing liberal party; Leaders SERGIO PREVITALI, ENRIQUE MORAS.

Movimiento de Acción Nacionalista (MAN): Montevideo; left-wing nationalist org.; Leader JOSÉ DURÁN MATOS.

Movimiento Blanco Popular y Progresista (MBPP): Montevideo; moderate left-wing; Leader A. FRANCISCO RODRÍGUEZ CAMUSSO.

Movimiento de Participación Popular (MPP): Germán Barbato 1491; tel. (2) 9086948; e-mail correos@mppuruguay.org; internet www.mppuruguay.org; f. 1989 by the MLN—Tupamaros (see below); grouping of left-wing parties; Leader JOSÉ (PEPE) MUJICA; mems include:

Movimiento de Liberación Nacional (MLN)—Tupamaros: Tristán Narvaja 1578, 11200 Montevideo; tel. (2) 4092298; fax (2) 4099957; e-mail mln@chasque.apc.org; internet www.chasque .net/mlnweb; f. 1962; radical socialist; during 1962–73 the MLN, operating under its popular name of the Tupamaros, conducted a campaign of urban guerrilla warfare until it was defeated by the Armed Forces in late 1973; following the return to civilian rule, in 1985, the MLN announced its decision to abandon its armed struggle; legally recognized in May 1989; Sec.-Gen. JOSÉ (PEPE) MUJICA.

Movimiento 26 de Marzo: Durazno 1118, 11200 Montevideo; tel. (2) 9011584; f. 1971; socialist; Pres. EDUARDO RUBIO; Sec.-Gen. FERNANDO VÁZQUEZ.

Partido Comunista de Uruguay (PCU): Río Negro 1525, 11100 Montevideo; tel. (2) 9017171; fax (2) 9011050; e-mail comitecentral@webpcu.org; internet www.webpcu.org; f. 1920; Sec.-Gen. MARINA ARISMENDI; c. 42,000 mems.

Partido de Democracia Avanzada: Montevideo; Communist.

Partido Socialista del Uruguay (PS): Casa del Pueblo, Soriano 1218, 11100 Montevideo; tel. (2) 9013344; fax (2) 9082548; e-mail info@ps.org.uy; internet www.ps.org.uy; f. 1910; Pres. REINALDO GARGANO; Sec.-Gen. EDUARDO (LALO) FERNÁNDEZ.

Partido por la Victoria del Pueblo (PVP): Mercedes 1551, esq. Tacuarembó, Montevideo; tel. (2) 4020370; e-mail cores567@ adinet.com.uy; internet www.pvp.org.uy; f. 1975 in Buenos Aires, Argentina; left-wing; Sec.-Gen. HUGO CORES.

Vertiente Artiguista (VA): San José 1191, 11200 Montevideo; tel. (2) 9000177; e-mail vertiente@vertiente.org.uy; internet www .vertiente.org.uy; f. 1989; left-wing; Leader MARCELO MANO.

Nuevo Espacio: Eduardo Acevedo 1615, 11200 Montevideo; tel. (2) 4026989; fax (2) 4026991; e-mail internacionales@nuevoespacio.org .uy; internet www.nuevoespacio.org.uy; f. 1994; social-democratic; allied to the EP—FA since Dec. 2002; moderate left-wing; Leader RAFAEL MICHELINI; Sec. EDGARDO CARVALHO.

Partido Azul (PA): Paul Harris 1722, Montevideo; tel. and fax (2) 6016327; e-mail hablacon@partidoazul.s5.com; internet www .partidoazul.s5.com; liberal; f. 1993; Leader Dr ROBERTO CANESSA; Gen. Sec. Ing. ARMANDO VAL.

Partido Colorado: Andrés Martínez Trueba 1271, 11100 Montevideo; tel. (2) 4090180; f. 1836; Sec.-Gen. JORGE LUIS BATLLE IBÁÑEZ; factions include:

Foro Batllista: Col. 1243, 11100 Montevideo; tel. (2) 9030154; e-mail info@forobatllista.com; internet www.forobatllista.com; Leader Dr JULIO MARÍA SANGUINETTI CAIROLO.

Lista 15: Leader JORGE LUIS BATLLE IBÁÑEZ.

Unión Colorada y Batllista (Pachequista): Buenos Aires 594, 11000 Montevideo; tel. (2) 9164648; right-wing.

Vanguardia Batllista: Casa de Vanguardia, Paysandú 1333, entre Ejido y Curiales, Montevideo; tel. (2) 9027779; e-mail albertoscavarelli@yahoo.com; internet www.scavarelli.com; f. 1999; Leader Dr ALBERTO SCAVARELLI.

Partido Demócrata Cristiano (PDC): Aquiles Lanza 1318 bis, Montevideo; tel. and fax (2) 9030704; e-mail pdc@chasque.apc.org; internet www.chasque.apc.org/pdc; f. 1962; fmrly Unión Cívica del Uruguay; allied to the Alianza Progresista since 1999; Pres. Dr HÉCTOR LESCANO; Sec.-Gen. FRANCISCO OTTONELLI.

Partido Justiciero: Montevideo; extreme right-wing; Leader BOLÍVAR ESPÍNDOLA.

Partido Nacional (Blanco): Juan Carlos Gómez 1384, Montevideo; tel. (2) 9163831; fax (2) 9163758; e-mail partidonacional@ partidonacional.com.uy; internet www.partidonacional.com.uy; f. 1836; Exec. Pres. LUIS ALBERTO LACALLE; Sec.-Gen. ALBERTO ZUMARÁN; tendencies within the party include:

Alianza Nacional: Leader JORGE LARRAÑAGA.

Consejo Nacional Herrerista: Leader LUIS ALBERTO LACALLE.

Desafío Nacional: Leader JUAN ANDRÉS RAMÍREZ.

Línea Nacional de Florida: Leader ARTURO HEBER.

Manos a la Obra: Plaza Cagancha 1145, 11100 Montevideo; tel. (2) 9028149; Leader ALBERTO VOLONTÉ.

Movimiento Nacional de Rocha—Corriente Popular Nacionalista: Avda Uruguay 1324, Montevideo; tel. (2) 9027502; Leader CARLOS JULIO PEREYRA.

Partido del Sol: Peatonal Yi 1385, 11000 Montevideo; tel. (2) 9001616; fax (2) 9006739; e-mail partidodelsol@adinet.com.uy; internet www.partidodelsoluruguay.org; ecologist, federal, pacifist; Leader HOMERO MIERES.

Partido de los Trabajadores: Convención 1196, 11100 Montevideo; tel. (2) 9082624; f. 1980; extreme left-wing; Leader JUAN VITAL ANDRADE.

Unión Cívica: Montevideo; tel. (2) 9005535; e-mail info@ unioncivica.org; internet www.dreamsmaker.com.uy/trabajos/ union-civica; f. 1912; recognized Christian Democrat faction, split from the Partido Demócrata Cristiano in 1980; Leader W. GERARDO AZAMBUYA.

Diplomatic Representation

EMBASSIES IN URUGUAY

Argentina: Cuareim 1470, 11800 Montevideo; tel. (2) 9028166; fax (2) 9028172; e-mail emargrou@adinet.com.uy; internet emb-uruguay.mrecic.gov.ar; Ambassador HERNÁN MARÍA PATIÑO MAYER.

Bolivia: Dr Prudencio de Peña 2469, 11300 Montevideo; tel. (2) 7083573; fax (2) 7080066; e-mail embouy@adinet.com; Ambassador MARCELO JANKO ALVAREZ.

Brazil: Blvr Artigas 1328, 11300 Montevideo; tel. (2) 7072119; fax (2) 7072086; e-mail montevideu@brasemb.org.uy; internet www.brasil .org.uy; Ambassador JOSÉ EDUARDO FELICIO.

Canada: Plaza Independencia 749, Of. 102, 11100 Montevideo; tel. (2) 9022030; fax (2) 9022029; e-mail mvdeo@international.gc.ca; internet www.dfait-maeci.gc.ca/uruguay; Ambassador ALAIN LATULIPPE.

Chile: 25 de Mayo 575, Montevideo; tel. (2) 9164090; fax (2) 9153804; e-mail echileuy@netgate.com.uy; Ambassador EDUARDO ARAYA ALEMPARTE.

China, People's Republic: Miraflores 1508, Carrasco, Casilla 18966, Montevideo; tel. (2) 6016126; fax (2) 6018508; e-mail

URUGUAY

embchina@adinet.com.uy; internet uy.china-embassy.org; Ambassador LI ZHONGLIANG.

Colombia: Edif. Tupí, Juncal 1305, 18°, 11000 Montevideo; tel. (2) 9161592; fax (2) 9161594; e-mail embajada@colombia.com.uy; internet www.colombia.com.uy; Ambassador CLAUDIA TURBAY QUINTERO.

Costa Rica: Casilla 12242, Montevideo; tel. (2) 7083645; fax (2) 7089727; e-mail embarica@adinet.com.uy; Ambassador MARCO VINICIO VARGAS PEREIRA.

Cuba: Echevarriarza 3471, Montevideo; tel. (2) 6232803; fax (2) 6232805; e-mail cancilleria@netgate.com.uy; Ambassador MARI-ELENA RUIZ CAPOTE.

Czech Republic: Luis B. Cavia 2996, Casilla 12262, 11300 Montevideo; tel. (2) 7087808; fax (2) 7096410; e-mail montevideo@embassy.mzv.cz; internet www.mzv.cz/montevideo; Ambassador PETR STIEGLER.

Dominican Republic: Tomás de Tezanos 1186, 11300 Montevideo; tel. (2) 6287766; fax (2) 6289655; e-mail embajadomuruguay@hotmail.com; Ambassador SILVIO ANTONIO HERASME PEÑA.

Ecuador: Pedro Berro 1217, entre Guayaquí y Pereira, Montevideo; tel. (2) 7076463; fax (2) 7076465; e-mail embajadaecuador@netgate.com.uy; Ambassador EDMUNDO VERA MANZO.

Egypt: Avda Brasil 2663, 11300 Montevideo; tel. (2) 7096412; fax (2) 7080977; e-mail boustanemontevideo@easymail.com.uy; Ambassador Dr OHIB ANWAR ES-SOUKKARY.

El Salvador: Melitón González 1157, Apto 501, Montevideo 11300; tel. (2) 6222005; fax (2) 6226842; e-mail embasauy@dedicado.net.uy; Ambassador JOSÉ MARIO AVILA ROMERO.

France: Avda Uruguay 853, Casilla 290, 11100 Montevideo; tel. (2) 9020077; fax (2) 9023711; e-mail ambafranceuruguay@gmail.com; internet www.ambafranceuruguay.org; Ambassador JEAN-CLAUDE MOYRET.

Germany: La Cumparsita 1417/1435, Casilla 20014, 11200 Montevideo; tel. (2) 9025222; fax (2) 9023422; e-mail info@montevideo.diplo.de; internet www.montevideo.diplo.de; Ambassador BERNHARD GRAF VON WALDERSEE.

Greece: Edif. Artigas, Rincón 487, 2°, 11100 Montevideo; tel. (2) 9165191; fax (2) 9150795; e-mail gremb.mvd@mfa.gr; Ambassador NICOLAOS DICTAKIS.

Guatemala: Costa Rica 1538, Carrasco, Montevideo; tel. and fax (2) 6012225; fax (2) 6014057; e-mail embajadaguatemala@netgate.com.uy; Ambassador RICARDO PUTZEYS.

Holy See: Blvr Artigas 1270, Casilla 1503, Montevideo (Apostolic Nunciature); tel. (2) 7072016; fax (2) 7072209; Apostolic Nuncio Most Rev. JANUSZ BOLONEK (Titular Archbishop of Madaurus).

Iran: Blvr Artigas 531, Montevideo; tel. (2) 7116657; fax (2) 7116659; e-mail embajada.iran@adinet.com.uy; Ambassador MORTEZA TAFRISHI.

Israel: Blvr Artigas 1585, 11200 Montevideo; tel. (2) 4004164; fax (2) 4095821; e-mail info@montevideo.mfa.gov.il; internet montevideo.mfa.gov.il; Ambassador YOEL BARNEA.

Italy: José Benito Lamas 2857, Casilla 268, 11300 Montevideo; tel. (2) 7084916; fax (2) 7084148; e-mail ambasciata.montevideo@esteri.it; internet www.ambmontevideo.esteri.it; Ambassador GUIDO SCALICI.

Japan: Blvr Artigas 953, 11300 Montevideo; tel. (2) 4187645; fax (2) 4187980; e-mail embjapon@adinet.com.uy; internet www.uy.emb-japan.go.jp; Ambassador MASAMI TAKEMOTO.

Korea, Republic: Edif. World Trade Center, Avda Luis Alberto de Herrera 1248, Torre 2, 10°, Montevideo; tel. (2) 6289374; fax (2) 6289376; e-mail ecorea@adinet.com.uy; Ambassador TAE-SHIN JAN.

Lebanon: Avda General Rivera 2278, Montevideo; tel. (2) 4086640; fax (2) 4086365; e-mail embliban@adinet.com.uy; Ambassador VICTOR GEORGES BITAR GHANEM.

Mexico: 25 de Mayo 512/514 esq. Treinta y Tres, 11100 Montevideo; tel. (2) 9166034; fax (2) 9166098; e-mail embajada-mexico@techtelnet.com.uy; internet www.sre.gob.mx/uruguay; Ambassador CASSIO MANUEL LUISELLI FERNÁNDEZ.

Netherlands: Leyenda Patria 2880, Of. 202, 2°, Casilla 1519, 11300 Montevideo; tel. (2) 7112956; fax (2) 7113301; e-mail mtv@minbuza.nl; internet www.holanda.org.uy; Ambassador ROBERT H. MEYS.

Panama: Juan Benito Blanco 3388, Montevideo; tel. (2) 6230301; fax (2) 6230300; e-mail empanuru@netgate.com.uy; Ambassador ELVIRA BARRIOS ICAZA.

Paraguay: Blvr Artigas 1256, Montevideo; tel. (2) 7072138; fax (2) 7083682; e-mail embapur@netgate.com.uy; internet www.geocities.com/embapur; Ambassador ANA MARÍA FIGUEREDO AMADO.

Peru: Obligado 1384, 11300 Montevideo; tel. (2) 7076862; fax (2) 7077793; e-mail emba8@embaperu.org.uy; internet www.angelfire.com/country/embaperu; Ambassador MAX DE LA FUENTE PREM.

Poland: Jorge Canning 2389, Casilla 1538, 11600 Montevideo; tel. (2) 4801313; fax (2) 4873389; e-mail ambmonte@netgate.com.uy; internet www.embajadapoloniauruguay.com; Ambassador LECH ZBIGNIEW KUBIAK.

Portugal: Avda Dr Francisco Soca 1128, Casilla 701, 11300 Montevideo; tel. (2) 7084061; fax (2) 7096456; e-mail embport@montevideu.dgaccp.pt; Ambassador LUISA BASTOS DE ALMEIDA.

Romania: Echevarriarza 3452, Casilla 12040, 11000 Montevideo; tel. (2) 6220876; fax (2) 6220135; e-mail bcemontevideo@adinet.com.uy; Chargé d'affaires a.i. GHEORGHE PETRE.

Russia: Blvr España 2741, 11300 Montevideo; tel. (2) 7081884; fax (2) 7086597; e-mail embaru@montevideo.com.uy; internet www.uruguay.mid.ru; Ambassador SERGUEY N. KOSHKIN.

South Africa: Echevarriarza 3335, Casilla 498, 11000 Montevideo; tel. (2) 6230161; fax (2) 6230066; e-mail safem@netgate.com.uy; Ambassador PETER GOOSEN (resident in Argentina).

Spain: Avda Libertad 2738, 11300 Montevideo; tel. (2) 7086010; fax (2) 7083291; e-mail embespuy@correo.mae.es; Ambassador FERNANDO VALDERRAMA Y DE PAREJA.

Switzerland: Ing. Federico Abadie 2936/40, 11°, Casilla 12261, 11300 Montevideo; tel. (2) 7115545; fax (2) 7115031; e-mail vertretung@mtv.rep.admin.ch; internet www.eda.admin.ch/montevideo; Ambassador MICHEL COQUOZ.

United Kingdom: Marco Bruto 1073, Casilla 16024, 11300 Montevideo; tel. (2) 6223630; fax (2) 6227815; e-mail bemonte@internet.com.uy; internet www.britishembassy.org.uy; Ambassador Dr HUGH SALVESSEN.

USA: Lauro Muller 1776, 11200 Montevideo; tel. (2) 4187777; fax (2) 4188611; e-mail webmastermvd@state.gov; internet uruguay.usembassy.gov; Ambassador FRANK E. BAXTER.

Venezuela: Iturriaga 3589, esq. Tomás de Tezanos, Puerto Buceo, Montevideo; tel. (2) 6221262; fax (2) 6282530; e-mail embaven@adinet.com.uy; internet www.repbolvenezuela.com.uy; Ambassador FRANKLIN GONZÁLEZ.

Judicial System

The Supreme Court of Justice comprises five members appointed at the suggestion of the executive, for a period of five years. It has original jurisdiction in constitutional, international and admiralty cases, and hears appeals from the appellate courts, of which there are seven, each with three judges.

Cases involving the functioning of the state administration are heard in the ordinary Administrative Courts and in the Supreme Administrative Court, which consists of five members appointed in the same way as members of the Supreme Court of Justice.

In Montevideo there are 19 civil courts, 10 criminal and correctional courts, 19 courts presided over by justices of the peace, three juvenile courts, three labour courts and courts for government and other cases. Each departmental capital, and some other cities, have a departmental court; each of the 224 judicial divisions has a justice of the peace.

The administration of justice became free of charge in 1980, with the placing of attorneys-at-law in all courts to assist those unable to pay for the services of a lawyer.

Supreme Court of Justice
H. Gutiérrez Ruiz 1310, Montevideo; tel. (2) 9001041; fax (2) 902350; e-mail secparga@poderjudicial.gub.uy; internet www.poderjudicial.gub.uy.

President of the Supreme Court of Justice: Dr DANIEL GUTIÉRREZ.

Supreme Administrative Court: Mercedes 961, 11100 Montevideo; tel. (2) 9008047; fax (2) 9080539.

Religion

Under the Constitution, the Church and the State were declared separate and toleration for all forms of worship was proclaimed. Roman Catholicism predominates.

CHRISTIANITY

Federación de Iglesias Evangélicas del Uruguay: Avda 8 de Octubre 3324, 11600 Montevideo; tel. and fax (2) 4875907; e-mail fieu@dcd.com.uy; internet www.chasque.net/obra/skontakt.htm; f. 1956; eight mem. churches; Pres. OSCAR BOLIOLI; Sec. OBED BODYAJIAN.

URUGUAY

The Roman Catholic Church

Uruguay comprises one archdiocese and nine dioceses. At 31 December 2005 there were an estimated 2,288,450 adherents in the country, representing about 71% of the total population.

Bishops' Conference

Conferencia Episcopal Uruguaya, Avda Uruguay 1319, 11100 Montevideo; tel. (2) 9002642; fax (2) 9011802; e-mail ceusecre@adinet.com.uy; internet www.iglesiauruguaya.com.

f. 1972; Pres. Rt Rev CARLOS MARÍA COLLAZZI IRAZÁBAL (Bishop of Mercedes).

Archbishop of Montevideo: Most Rev. NICOLÁS COTUGNO FANIZZI, Arzobispado, Treinta y Tres 1368, Casilla 356, 11000 Montevideo; tel. (2) 9158127; fax (2) 9158926; e-mail info@arquidiocesis.net; internet www.arquidiocesis.net.

The Anglican Communion

Uruguay constitutes a diocese in the Province of the Southern Cone of America. The presiding Bishop of the Iglesia Anglicana del Cono Sur de América is the Bishop of Northern Argentina.

Bishop of Uruguay: Rt Rev. MIGUEL TAMAYO ZALDÍVAR, Centro Diocesano, Reconquista 522, Casilla 6108, 11000 Montevideo; tel. (2) 9159627; fax (2) 9162519; e-mail mtamayo@netgate.com.uy; internet www.uruguay.anglican.org.

Other Churches

Baptist Evangelical Convention of Uruguay: Mercedes 1487, 11100 Montevideo; tel. and fax (2) 2167012; e-mail suspasos@adinet.com.uy; f. 1948; 4,500 mems; Pres. Dr JUAN CARLOS OTORMÍN.

Iglesia Adventista (Adventist Church): Castro 167, Montevideo; f. 1901; 4,000 mems; Principal Officers Dr GUILLERMO DURÁN, Dr ALEXIS PIRO.

Iglesia Evangélica Metodista en el Uruguay (Evangelical Methodist Church in Uruguay): San José 1457, 11200 Montevideo; tel. (2) 4136552; fax (2) 4136554; e-mail iemu@adinet.com.uy; internet www.gbgm-umc.org/iemu; f. 1878; 1,193 mems (1997); Pres. Rev. OSCAR BOLIOLI.

Iglesia Evangélica Valdense (Waldensian Evangelical Church): Avda 8 de Octubre 3039, 11600 Montevideo; tel. and fax (2) 4879406; e-mail ievm@internet.com.uy; f. 1952; 15,000 mems; Pastor ALVARO MICHELIN SALOMÓN.

Iglesia Pentecostal Unida Internacional en Uruguay (United Pentecostal Church International in Uruguay): Helvecia 4032, Piedras Blancas, 12200 Montevideo; tel. (2) 5133618; e-mail lrodrigu@montevideo.com.uy; internet members.tripod.com/~lrodrigu; Pastor LUIS RODRÍGUEZ.

Primera Iglesia Bautista (First Baptist Church): Avda Daniel Fernández Crespo 1741, Casilla 5051, 11200 Montevideo; tel. (2) 4098744; fax (2) 4094356; e-mail piebu@adinet.com.uy; f. 1911; 314 mems; Pastor LEMUEL J. LARROSA.

Other denominations active in Uruguay include the Iglesia Evangélica del Río de la Plata and the Iglesia Evangélica Menonita (Evangelical Mennonite Church).

BAHÁ'Í FAITH

National Spiritual Assembly of the Bahá'ís: Blvr Artigas 2440, 11600 Montevideo; tel. (2) 4875890; fax (2) 4802165; e-mail bahai@multi.com.uy; f. 1938; mems resident in 140 localities.

The Press

DAILIES

Montevideo

El Diario Español: Cerrito 551–555, Casilla 899, 11000 Montevideo; tel. (2) 9159481; fax (2) 9157389; f. 1905; morning (except Monday); newspaper of the Spanish community; Editor MARCELO REINANTE; circ. 20,000.

Diario Oficial: Avda 18 de Julio 1373, Montevideo; tel. (2) 9085042; fax (2) 9023098; e-mail impo@impo.com.uy; internet www.impo.com.uy; f. 1905; biweekly; publishes laws, official decrees, parliamentary debates, judicial decisions and legal transactions; Dir ALVARO PÉREZ MONZA.

La Mañana: Casilla 5005, Suc. 2, 11100 Montevideo; tel. (2) 9029055; fax (2) 9021326; f. 1917; supports the Partido Colorado; Editor Dr SALVADOR ALABÁN DEMARE; circ. 50,000.

El Observador: Cuareim 2052, 11800 Montevideo; tel. (2) 9247000; fax (2) 9248698; e-mail elobservador@observador.com.uy; internet www.observador.com.uy; f. 1991; morning; circ. 26,000.

El País: Zelmar Michelini 1287, 4°, 11100 Montevideo; tel. (2) 9020115; fax (2) 9020464; e-mail cartas@elpais.com.uy; internet www.elpais.com.uy; f. 1918; morning; supports the Partido Nacional; Editor MARTÍN AGUIRRE; circ. 106,000.

La República: Avda Gral Garibaldi 2579, 11600 Montevideo; tel. (2) 4873565; fax (2) 4873823; e-mail redaccion@diariolarepublica.com; internet www.larepublica.com.uy; f. 1988; morning; Editor FEDERICO FASANO MERTENS; circ. 20,000.

Ultimas Noticias: Paysandú 1179, 11100 Montevideo; tel. (2) 9020452; fax (2) 9024669; e-mail avisos@ultimasnoticias.com.uy; internet www.ultimasnoticias.com.uy; f. 1981; evening (except Saturday); owned by Impresora Polo; Publr Dr ALPHONSE EMANUILOFF-MAX; circ. 25,000.

Florida

El Heraldo: Independencia 824, 94000 Florida; tel. (35) 22229; fax (35) 24546; e-mail elheraldo@elheraldo.com.uy; internet www.elheraldo.com.uy; f. 1919; morning; independent; Dir ALVARO RIVA REY; circ. 20,000.

Maldonado

Correo de Punta del Este: Zelmar Michelini 815 bis, 20000 Maldonado; tel. and fax (42) 35633; e-mail gallardo@adinet.com.uy; internet www.diariocorreo.com; f. 1993; morning; Editor MARCELO GALLARDO; circ. 2,500.

Minas

La Unión: Florencio Sánchez 569, Minas; tel. (442) 2065; fax (442) 4011; e-mail union@chasque.apc.org; f. 1877; evening (except Sunday); Dir LAURA PUCHET MARTÍNEZ; Editor ALEJANDRO MAYA SOSA; circ. 2,600.

Paysandú

El Telégrafo: 18 de Julio 1027, 60000 Paysandú; tel. (722) 3141; fax (722) 7999; e-mail correo@eltelegrafo.com; internet www.eltelegrafo.com; f. 1910; morning; independent; Dir FERNANDO A. BACCARO; circ. 8,500.

Salto

El Pueblo: 18 de Julio 15, Salto; tel. (733) 4133; e-mail dipueblo@adinet.com.uy; internet www.diarioelpueblo.com.uy; morning; Dir ADRIANA MARTÍNEZ.

Tribuna Salteña: Joaquín Suárez 71, Salto; f. 1906; morning; Dir MODESTO LLANTADA FABINI; circ. 3,000.

PERIODICALS

Montevideo

Aquí: Zabala 1322, Of. 102, 11000 Montevideo; weekly; supports the Encuentro Progresista—Frente Amplio; Dir FRANCISCO JOSÉ O'HONELLI.

Brecha: Avda Uruguay 844, 11100 Montevideo; tel. (2) 9008777; fax (2) 9020388; e-mail brecha@brecha.com.uy; internet www.brecha.com.uy; f. 1985; weekly; politics, current affairs; Dir IVONNE TRÍAS; Editor-in-Chief DANIEL GATTI; circ. 8,500.

Búsqueda: Avda Uruguay 1146, 11100 Montevideo; tel. (2) 9021300; fax (2) 9022036; e-mail busqueda@adinet.com.uy; f. 1972; weekly; independent; politics and economics; Dir DANILO ARBILLA FRACHIA; circ. 25,000.

Charoná: Gutiérrez Ruiz 1276, Of. 201, Montevideo; tel. (2) 9086665; internet www.charona.com; f. 1968; fortnightly; children's; Dir SERGIO BOFFANO; circ. 25,000.

Colorín Colorado: Dalmiro Costa 4482, Montevideo; f. 1980; monthly; children's; Dir SARA MINSTER DE MURNINKAS; circ. 3,000.

Crónicas Económicas: Avda Libertador Brig.-Gen. Lavalleja 1532, Montevideo; tel. (2) 9004790; fax (2) 9020759; e-mail cronicas@netgate.com.uy; internet www.cronicas.com.uy; f. 1981; weekly; independent; business and economics; Dirs JULIO ARIEL FRANCO, WALTER HUGO PAGÉS, JORGE ESTELLANO.

La Gaceta Militar Naval: Montevideo; monthly.

Guambia: Rimac 1576, 11400 Montevideo; tel. (2) 6132703; fax (2) 6132703; e-mail info@guambia.com.uy; internet www.guambia.com.uy; f. 1983; monthly; satirical; Dir and Editor ANTONIO DABEZIES.

Indice Industrial-Anuario de la Industria Uruguaya: Sarandí 456, 11000 Montevideo; tel. (2) 9151963; f. 1957; annual; Dir W. M. TRIAS; circ. 6,000.

La Justicia Uruguaya: 25 de Mayo 555, 11000 Montevideo; tel. (2) 9157587; fax (2) 9159721; e-mail lajusticiauruguaya@lju.com.uy; internet www.lajusticiauruguaya.com.uy; f. 1940; bimonthly; jurisprudence; Dirs EDUARDO ALBANELL, ADOLFO ALBANELL; circ. 3,000.

La Juventud: 18 de Julio 1357, Of. 202, Montevideo; tel. (2) 9030305; e-mail weblajuve@yahoo.com.ar; internet www.chasque.apc.org/juventud; weekly; supports the Movimiento 26 de Marzo; Dir GUILLERMO FERNÁNDEZ; Editor JOSÉ L. BORGES.

Marketing Directo: Guaná 2237 bis, 11200 Montevideo; tel. (2) 4012174; fax (2) 4087221; e-mail consumo@adinet.com.uy; internet www.ciecc.org; f. 1988; monthly; Dir EDGARDO MARTÍNEZ ZIMARIOFF; circ. 9,500.

Mate Amargo: Tristán Narvaja 1578 bis, Montevideo; f. 1986; organ of the Movimiento de Liberación Nacional; circ. 22,500.

Opción: J. Barrios Amorín 1531, Casilla 102, 11100 Montevideo; f. 1981; weekly; Dir FRANCISCO JOSÉ OTTONELLI; circ. 15,000.

Patatín y Patatán: Montevideo; f. 1977; weekly; children's; Dir JUAN JOSÉ RAVAIOLI; circ. 3,000.

Patria: Montevideo; internet www.patria.com.uy; weekly; organ of the Partido Nacional; right-wing; Dir LUIS A. HEBER; Editor Dr JOSÉ LUIS BELLANI.

Revista Naval: Soriano 1117, 11100 Montevideo; tel. (2) 9087884; f. 1988; 3 a year; military; Editor GUSTAVO VANZINI; circ. 1,000.

PRESS ASSOCIATIONS

Asociación de Diarios del Uruguay: Río Negro 1308, 6°, 11100 Montevideo; f. 1922; Pres. BATLLE T. BARBATO.

Asociación de la Prensa Uruguaya: San José 1330, Montevideo; tel. and fax (2) 9013695; fax (2) 9013695; e-mail apu@adinet.com.uy; internet www.apu.org.uy; f. 1944; Pres. MANUEL MÉNDEZ.

Publishers

Autores Uruguayos: Paysandú 1561, 11200 Montevideo; e-mail mensajes@autoresuruguayos.com.uy; internet www.autoresuruguayos.com; publishes works by Uruguayan authors; Man. ADRIANA DOS SANTOS.

Editorial Arca: Ana Monterroso 2231, Montevideo; tel. (2) 4099796; fax (2) 4099788; f. 1963; general literature, social science and history; Man. Dir ENRIQUE PIQUÉ.

Ediciones de la Banda Oriental: Gaboto 1582, 11200 Montevideo; tel. (2) 4083206; fax (2) 4098138; e-mail ebo@chasque.net; general literature; Man. Dir HEBER RAVIOLO.

CENCI—Uruguay (Centro de Estadísticas Nacionales y Comercio Internacional): Misiones 1361, Casilla 1510, 11000 Montevideo; tel. (2) 9152930; fax (2) 9154578; e-mail cenci@cenci.com.uy; f. 1956; economics, statistics; Dir KENNETH BRUNNER.

Editorial y Librería Jurídica Amalio M. Fernández SRL: 25 de Mayo 589, 11000 Montevideo; tel. and fax (2) 9151782; e-mail amflibrosjurid@movinet.com.uy; f. 1951; law and sociology; Man. Dir CARLOS W. DEAMESTOY.

Editorial La Flor del Itapebí: Luis Piera 1917/401, Montevideo; tel. and fax (2) 7109267; internet www.itapebi.com.uy; f. 1991; cultural, technical, educational.

Fundación de Cultura Universitaria: 25 de Mayo 568, Casilla 1155, 11000 Montevideo; tel. (2) 9152532; fax (2) 9152549; e-mail ventas@fcu.com.uy; internet www.fcu.com.uy; f. 1968; law and social sciences; Pres. Dr PABLO DONNÁNGELO.

Hemisferio Sur: Buenos Aires 335, Casilla 1755, 11000 Montevideo; tel. (2) 9164515; fax (2) 9164520; e-mail editorial@hemisferiosur.com; internet www.hemisferiosur.com; f. 1951; agronomy and veterinary science.

Editorial Idea: Misiones 1424, 5°, 11000 Montevideo; tel. (2) 9165456; fax (2) 9150868; e-mail vescovi@fastlink.com.uy; law; Dir Dr GUILLERMO VESCOVI.

Librería Linardi y Risso: Juan C. Gómez 1435, 11000 Montevideo; tel. (2) 9157129; fax (2) 9157431; e-mail lyrbooks@linardiyrisso.com.uy; internet www.linardiyrisso.com.uy; f. 1944; general; Man. Dirs ALVARO RISSO, ANDRÉS LINARDI.

Editorial Medina SRL: Gaboto 1521, Montevideo; tel. (2) 4085800; f. 1933; general; Pres. MARCOS MEDINA VIDAL.

A. Monteverde & Cía, SA: Treinta y Tres 1475, Casilla 371, 11000 Montevideo; tel. (2) 9152939; fax (2) 9152012; f. 1879; educational; Man. Dir LILIANA MUSSINI.

Mosca Hermanos SA: Avda 18 de Julio 1578, 11300 Montevideo; tel. (2) 4093141; fax (2) 4088059; e-mail mosca@attmail.com.uy; f. 1888; general; Pres. Lic. ZSOLT AGARDY.

Librería Selecta Editorial: Guayabo 1865, 11200 Montevideo; tel. (2) 4086989; fax (2) 4086831; f. 1950; academic books; Dir FERNANDO MASA.

Ediciones Trilce: Durazno 1888, 11200 Montevideo; tel. (2) 4127662; fax (2) 4127722; e-mail trilce@trilce.com.uy; internet www.trilce.com.uy; f. 1985; science, politics, history.

Vintén Editor: Hocquart 1771, 11804 Montevideo; tel. (2) 2090223; internet vinten-uy.com; poetry, theatre, history, art, literature.

PUBLISHERS' ASSOCIATION

Cámara Uruguaya del Libro: Juan D. Jackson 1118, 11200 Montevideo; tel. (2) 4015732; fax (2) 4011860; e-mail camurlib@adinet.com.uy; f. 1944; Pres. ERNESTO SANJINÉS; Man. ANA CRISTINA RODRÍGUEZ.

Broadcasting and Communications

TELECOMMUNICATIONS

Administración Nacional de Telecomunicaciones (ANTEL): Complejo Torre de las Telecomunicaciones, Guatemala 1075, Montevideo; e-mail antel@antel.com.uy; internet www.antel.com.uy; f. 1974; state-owned; Pres. EDGARDO CARVALHO; Gen. Man. JOSÉ LUIS SALDÍAS.

    ANCEL: Pablo Galarza 3537, Montevideo; internet www.ancel.com.uy; f. 1974; state-owned mobile telephone co.

CTI Móvil: Montevideo; internet www.cti.com.uy; owned by América Móvil, SA de CV (Mexico); mobile cellular telephone services; launched wireless services in Dec. 2004.

Movistar Uruguay: Avda Constituyente, Edif. Torre el Gaucho, 1467 Montevideo; tel. (2) 4087502; internet www.movistar.com.uy; owned by Telefónica Móviles, SA (Spain); mobile telephone services.

Unidad Reguladora de Servicios de Comunicaciones (URSEC): Uruguay 988, Casilla 11100, Montevideo; tel. (2) 9028082; fax (2) 9005708; e-mail bergara@ursec.gub.uy; internet www.ursec.gub.uy; regulates telecommunications and postal sectors; Dir MARIO BERGERA.

BROADCASTING

Regulatory Authority

Asociación Nacional de Broadcasters Uruguayos (ANDEBU): Carlos Quijano 1264, 11100 Montevideo; tel. (2) 9021525; fax (2) 9021540; e-mail andebu@internet.com.uy; internet www.andebu.com.uy; f. 1933; 101 mems; Pres. CARLOS FALCO; Vice-Pres. Dr WALTER C. ROMAY.

Radio

El Espectador: Río Branco 1481, 11100 Montevideo; tel. (2) 9023531; fax (2) 9083192; e-mail ventas@espectador.com.uy; internet www.espectador.com; f. 1923; commercial; Gen. Man. ESTELA BARTOLIC.

Radio Carve: Mercedes 973, 11100 Montevideo; tel. (2) 9026162; fax (2) 9020126; e-mail carve@portalx.com.uy; internet www.carve.com.uy; f. 1928; commercial; Dir PABLO FONTAINA MINELLI.

Radio Montecarlo: Avda 18 de Julio 1224, 1°, 11100 Montevideo; tel. (2) 9030703; fax (2) 9017762; f. 1928; commercial; Dir DANIEL ROMAY.

Radio Sarandí: Enriqueta Compte y Riqué 1250, 11800 Montevideo; tel. (2) 2082612; fax (2) 2036906; e-mail direccion@sarandi690.com.uy; internet www.radiosarandi.com.uy; f. 1931; commercial; Pres. RAMIRO RODRÍGUEZ VALLAMIL RIVIERE.

Radio del Sol: tel. (2) 6283314; e-mail comoestamos@fmdelsol.com; internet www.comoestamos.com.uy.

Radio Universal: Avda 18 de Julio 1220, 3°, 11100 Montevideo; tel. (2) 9026022; fax (2) 9026050; e-mail info@22universal.com; internet www.22universal.com; f. 1929; commercial; Pres. OSCAR IMPERIO.

Radiodifusión Nacional SODRE: Sarandí 430, 11000 Montevideo; tel. (2) 957865; fax (2) 9161933; f. 1929; state-owned; Pres. JULIO CÉSAR OCAMPOS.

In 2002 there were some 16 AM and six FM radio stations in the Montevideo area. In addition, there were approximately 41 AM and 56 FM radio stations outside the capital.

Television

The Uruguayan Government holds a 10% stake in the regional television channel Telesur (q.v.), which began operations in May 2005 and is based in Caracas, Venezuela.

Canal 4 Monte Carlo: Paraguay 2253, 11800 Montevideo; tel. (2) 9244444; fax (2) 9247929; e-mail secretarias@montecarlotv.com.uy; internet www.canal4.com.uy; f. 1961; Dir HUGO ROMAY SALVO.

SAETA TV—Canal 10: Dr Lorenzo Carnelli 1234, 11200 Montevideo; tel. (2) 4102120; fax (2) 4009771; internet www.canal10.com.uy; f. 1956; Pres. JORGE DE FEO.

SODRE (Servicio Oficial de Difusión Radiotelevisión y Espectáculos): Blvr Artigas 2552, 11600 Montevideo; tel. (2) 4806448; fax (2)

URUGUAY

4808515; e-mail direccion@tveo.com.uy; internet www.sodre.gub.uy; f. 1963; Pres. Dra NELLY GOITIÑO.

Teledoce Televisora Color—Canal 12: Enriqueta Compte y Riqué 1276, 11800 Montevideo; tel. (2) 2083555; fax (2) 2037623; e-mail latele@teledoce.com; internet www.teledoce.com; f. 1962; Gen. Man. HORACIO SCHECK.

TV Ciudad: Javier Barrios Amorín 1460, Montevideo; tel. (2) 4021908; fax (2) 4001908; e-mail tvciudad@tvciudad.imm.gub.uy; internet www.montevideo.gub.uy/teveciudad; f. 1996; state-owned.

In 1999 there were 21 television stations outside the capital.

Finance

BANKING

(cap. = capital; res = reserves; dep. = deposits; m. = million; brs = branches; amounts in pesos uruguayos unless otherwise indicated)

State Banks

Banco Central del Uruguay: Avda Juan P. Fabini 777, Casilla 1467, 11100 Montevideo; tel. (2) 9085629; fax (2) 9021634; e-mail info@bcu.gub.uy; internet www.bcu.gub.uy; f. 1967; note-issuing bank, also controls private banking; cap. 1,547.7m., res −13,844.4m., dep. 103,138.6m. (Dec. 2005); Pres. WALTER CANCELA; Dir ALVARO CORREA.

Banco Hipotecario del Uruguay (BHU): Avda Daniel Fernández Crespo 1508, Montevideo; tel. (2) 4090000; fax (2) 4090782; e-mail info@bhu.net; internet www.bhu.net; f. 1892; state mortgage bank; in 1977 assumed responsibility for housing projects in Uruguay; Pres. MIGUEL PIPERNO.

Banco de la República Oriental del Uruguay (BROU): Cerrito y Zabala 351, 11000 Montevideo; tel. (2) 9150157; fax (2) 9162064; e-mail broupte@adinet.com.uy; internet www.brounet.com.uy; f. 1896; cap. 12,517.6m., res 2,825.1m., dep. 124,856.8m. (Dec. 2006); Pres. FERNANDO CALLOIA RAFFO; Gen. Man. FERNANDO JORAJURÍA; 117 brs.

Principal Commercial Banks

ABN AMRO Bank Uruguay NV: Julio Herrera y Obes 1365, Casilla 888, 11100 Montevideo; tel. (2) 9031073; fax (2) 9025011; internet www.abnamro.com.uy; f. 1952; owned by ABN AMRO Bank NV (Netherlands); Country Rep. FRANCISCO DI ROBERTO, Jr; 24 brs.

Banco Bilbao Vizcaya Argentaria Uruguay SA (BBVA): 25 de Mayo 401, esq. Zabala, 11000 Montevideo; tel. (2) 9161444; fax (2) 9162821; internet www.bbvabanco.com.uy; f. 1968; fmrly Unión de Bancos del Uruguay, and later Banesto Banco Uruguay, SA and Banco Francés Uruguay, SA; adopted current name in 2000 following merger with Banco Exterior de América, SA; cap. 883.0m., res 674.1m., dep. 10,336.3m. (Dec. 2004); Pres. TOMÁS DEANE; Vice-Pres. and Gen. Man. ANGEL SORIA; 14 brs.

Banco Galicia Uruguay, SA: Edif. World Trade Center, Luis A. Herrera 1248, 22°, Montevideo; tel. (2) 6281230; e-mail contactenos@bancogalicia.com.uy; internet www.bancogalicia.com.uy; f. 1999.

Banco Surinvest SA: Rincón 530, 11000 Montevideo; tel. (2) 9160177; fax (2) 9160241; e-mail bancosurinvest@surinvest.com.uy; internet www.surinvest.com.uy; f. 1981 as Surinvest Casa Bancaria; name changed as above 1991; cap. 249.3m., res 71.4m., dep. 2,351.2m. (Dec. 2004); Gen. Man. ALBERTO A. MELLO.

BNP Paribas (Uruguay) SA (France): Rincón 477, Of. 901/5, Montevideo; tel. (2) 9162768; fax (2) 9162609; e-mail uruguay@bnpparibas.com.ar; f. 1989 as BNP (Uruguay) SA; adopted present name in 2001.

Crédit Uruguay Banco SA: Rincón 500, 11000 Montevideo; tel. (2) 9150095; fax (2) 9164282; internet www.credituruguay.com.uy; f. 1998 as Banco Acac SA; adopted current name 2004; owned by Crédit Agricole (France); cap. 413.4m., res. 18.4m., dep. 11,616.1m. (Dec. 2005); Pres. GERMÁN VILLAR; Gen. Man. MARCELO OTEN.

Discount Bank (Latin America), SA: Rincón 390, 11000 Montevideo; tel. (2) 9164848; fax (2) 9160890; e-mail mensajes@discbank.com.uy; internet www.discbank.com.uy; f. 1978; owned by Israel Discount Bank of New York (USA); cap. US $12.8m., res $0.62m., dep. $179.3m. (Dec. 2002); Pres. and Chair. REUVEN SPIEGEL; Dir and Gen. Man. VALENTIN D. MALACHOWSKI; 4 brs.

HSBC Bank (Uruguay), SA: Ituzaingó 1389, 11000 Montevideo; tel. (2) 9153395; fax (2) 9160125; f. 1995; owned by HSBC Bank PLC (United Kingdom); CEO ALAN WILKINSON.

Nuevo Banco Comercial, SA (NBC): Misiones 1399, CP 11000 Montevideo; tel. (2) 1401300; fax (2) 1401185; e-mail servicioalcliente@nbc.com.uy; internet www.nbc.com.uy; f. 2003 by merger of Banco Comercial, Banco La Caja Obrera and Banco de Montevideo; fmrly state-owned, privatized in June 2006; dep.

US $923m., total assets $1,153m. (July 2006); Pres. ERNEST BACHRACH; Gen. Man. JOSÉ FUENTES; 46 brs.

Credit Co-operative

There are several credit co-operatives, which permit members to secure small business loans at preferential rates.

Federación Uruguaya de Cooperativas de Ahorro y Crédito (FUCAC): Blvr Artigas 1472, Montevideo; tel. and fax (2) 7088888; e-mail info@fucac.com.uy; internet www.fucac.com.uy; f. 1972; Pres. CARLOS ALBERTO ICASURIAGA SAMANO; Gen. Man. JAVIER HUMBERTO PI LEÓN.

Development Bank

Banco Bandes Uruguay: Sarandí 402, CP 111000, Montevideo; tel. (2) 9160100; internet www.cofac.com.uy; owned by the Banco de Desarrollo Económico y Social (BANDES) of Venezuela.

Bankers' Association

Asociación de Bancarios del Uruguay (Bankers' Association of Uruguay—AEBU): Camacuá 575, Montevideo; tel. (2) 9161060; e-mail secprensa@aebu.org.uy; internet www.aebu.org.uy; f. 1945; 7 mem. banks; Dir OSCAR JORGE VISSANI.

STOCK EXCHANGE

Bolsa de Valores de Montevideo: Edif. Bolsa de Comercio, Misiones 1400, 11000 Montevideo; tel. (2) 9165051; fax (2) 9161900; e-mail info@bolsademontevideo.com.uy; internet www.bolsademontevideo.com.uy; f. 1867; 75 mems; Pres. IGNACIO ROSPIDE.

INSURANCE

From mid-1994, following the introduction of legislation ending the state monopoly of most types of insurance, the Banco de Seguros del Estado lost its monopoly on all insurance except life, sea transport and fire risks, which have been traditionally open to private underwriters.

AIG Uruguay Compañía de Seguros, SA (USA): Colonia 993, 1°, Montevideo; tel. (2) 9000330; fax (2) 9084552; e-mail aig.uruguay@aig.com; internet www.aig.com; f. 1996; all classes; Gen. Man. JORGE FERRANTE.

Alico Compañía de Seguros de Vida, SA (USA): 18 de Julio 1738, Montevideo; tel. (2) 4033939; fax (2) 4033938; e-mail alico@alico.com.uy; internet www.alico.com; f. 1996; life; Gen. Man. JUAN ETCHEVERRY.

Banco de Seguros del Estado: Avda Libertador 1465, Montevideo; tel. (2) 9089303; fax (2) 9017030; e-mail directorio@bse.com.uy; internet www.bse.com.uy; f. 1912; state insurance org.; all risks; Pres. ENRIQUE ROIG CURBELO; Gen. Man. CARLOS VALDÉS.

Compañía de Seguros Aliança da Bahia Uruguay, SA (Brazil): Río Negro 1394, 7°, Montevideo; tel. (2) 9021086; fax (2) 9021087; e-mail avivo@netgate.com.uy; f. 1995; transport; Gen. Man. BERNARDO VIVO.

Mapfre Compañía de Seguros, SA (Spain): Blvr Artigas 459, Montevideo; tel. and fax (2) 7116595; e-mail info@mapfre.com.uy; internet www.mapfre.com.uy; f. 1994; general; Gen. Man. DIEGO SOBRINI.

Porto Seguro, Seguros del Uruguay SA (Brazil): Blvr Artigas 2025; tel. (2) 4028000; fax (2) 4030097; e-mail admin@portoseguro.com.uy; internet www.portoseguro.com.uy; f. 1995; property; Pres. LEANDRO SUÁREZ.

Real Uruguaya de Seguros SA (Netherlands): Avda 18 de Julio 988, Montevideo; tel. (2) 9025858; fax (2) 9024515; e-mail realseguros@abnamro.com; internet www.realseguros.com.uy; f. 1900; life and property; part of the ABN AMRO Group; Gen. Man. JOSÉ LUIZ TOMAZINI.

Royal & SunAlliance Seguros, SA (United Kingdom): Peatonal Sarandí 620, Montevideo; tel. (2) 9170505; fax (2) 9170490; internet www.royalsunalliance.com.uy; f. 1997; life and property; Dir Dr JUAN QUARTINO.

Surco, Compañía Cooperativa de Seguros: Blvr Artigas 1320, Montevideo; tel. (2) 7090089; fax (2) 7077313; e-mail surco@surco.com.uy; internet www.surco.com.uy; f. 1995; insurance co-operative; all classes; Gen. Man. ANDRÉS ELOLA.

L'UNION de Paris Compañía Uruguaya de Seguros, SA (France): Misiones 1549, Montevideo; tel. (2) 9160850; fax (2) 9160847; e-mail gabriel.penna@axa-seguros.com.uy; internet www.axa-seguros.com.uy; f. 1897 as L'Union IARD; present name adopted 2004; general; Gen. Man. GABRIEL PENNA.

INSURANCE ASSOCIATION

Asociación Uruguaya de Empresas Aseguradoras (AUDEA): Juncal 1305, Of. 1901, 11000 Montevideo; tel. (2) 9161465; fax (2) 9165991; e-mail audea@adinet.com.uy; Pres. Manuel Rodríguez; Gen. Man. Mauricio Castellanos.

Trade and Industry

GOVERNMENT AGENCIES

Administración Nacional de Combustibles, Alcohol y Portland (ANCAP): Paraguay 1598, 11100 Montevideo; tel. (2) 9020608; fax (2) 9021136; e-mail webmaster@ancap.com.uy; internet www.ancap.com.uy; f. 1931; deals with transport, refining and sale of petroleum products, and the manufacture of alcohol, spirit and cement; tanker services, also river transport; Pres. Raúl Sendic; Gen. Man. Sergio Lattanzio; Sec.-Gen. Jorge Urrutia.

Administración Nacional de Usinas y Transmisiones Eléctricas (UTE): Paraguay 2431, 10°, 11100 Montevideo; tel. (2) 2003424; fax (2) 2037082; e-mail ute@ute.com.uy; internet www.ute.com.uy; f. 1912; autonomous state body; sole purveyor of electricity until 1997; Pres. Ing. Beno Ruchansky; Gen. Man. Carlos Pombo.

Oficina de Planeamiento y Presupuesto de la Presidencia de la República: Edif. Libertad, Luis A. de Herrera 3350, Montevideo; tel. (2) 4872110; fax (2) 2099730; e-mail diropp@presidencia.gub.uy; internet www.opp.gub.uy; f. 1976; responsible for the implementation of devt plans; co-ordinates the policies of the various ministries; advises on the preparation of the budget of public enterprises; Dir Carlos Viera; Sub-Dir Daniel Mesa Peluffo.

Uruguay XXI (Instituto de Promoción de Inversiones y Exportaciones de Bienes y Servicios): Yaguarón 1407, Of. 1103, 11100 Montevideo; tel. (2) 9002912; fax (2) 9008298; e-mail info@uruguayxxi.gub.uy; internet www.uruguayxxi.gub.uy; f. 1996; govt agency to promote economic investment; Exec. Dir Victor Angenscheidt.

DEVELOPMENT ORGANIZATIONS

Corporación Nacional para el Desarrollo (CND): Rincón 528, 7°, Casilla 977, 11000 Montevideo; tel. (2) 9162680; fax (2) 9159662; e-mail cnd01@adinet.com.uy; internet www.cnd.org.uy; f. 1985; national devt corpn; mixed-capital org.; obtains 60% of funding from state; Pres. Alvaro García Rodríguez; Vice-Pres. Juan Arturo Echevarría; Gen. Man. Martín J. Dibarboure Rossini.

Asociación Nacional de Micro y Pequeños Empresarios (ANMYPE): Miguelete 1584, Montevideo; tel. (2) 9241010; e-mail anmype@anmype.net.uy; internet www.anmype.net.uy; promotes small businesses; f. 1988; Pres. Ricardo Posada.

Asociación Nacional de Organizaciones No Gubernamentales Orientadas al Desarrollo: Avda del Libertador 1985 esq. 202, Montevideo; tel. and fax (2) 9240812; e-mail anong@anong.com.uy; internet www.anong.org.uy; f. 1992; umbrella grouping of devt NGOs; Pres. María Elena Martínez.

Centro Interdisciplinario de Estudios sobre el Desarrollo, Uruguay (CIEDUR): 18 de Julio 1645-7, 11200 Montevideo; tel. and fax (2) 408 4520; e-mail ciedur@ciedur.org.uy; internet www.ciedur.org.uy; f. 1977; devt studies and training; Pres. Jaime Behar; Exec. Sec. Carlos Pérez Arrarte.

Fundación Uruguaya de Cooperación y Desarrollo Solidario (FUNDASOL) (Uruguayan Foundation for Supportive Co-operation and Development): Blvr Artigas 1119, esq. Maldonado, 11200 Montevideo; tel. (2) 4002020; fax (2) 4081485; e-mail consultas@fundasol.org.uy; internet www.fundasol.org.uy; f. 1979; Gen. Man. Jorge Naya.

Programa Alianzas para el Desarrollo Local en América Latina (ALOP): Montevideo; tel. and fax (2) 9007194; e-mail info@desarrollolocal.org; internet www.desarrollolocal.org; umbrella grouping of local devt orgs; Dir Enrique Gallicchio.

CHAMBERS OF COMMERCE

Cámara de Industrias del Uruguay (Chamber of Industries): Avda Italia 6101, 11500 Montevideo; tel. (2) 6040464; fax (2) 6040501; e-mail ciu@ciu.com.uy; internet www.ciu.com.uy; f. 1898; Pres. Diego Balestra.

Cámara Nacional de Comercio y Servicios del Uruguay (National Chamber of Commerce): Edif. Bolsa de Comercio, Rincón 454, 2°, Casilla 1000, 11000 Montevideo; tel. (2) 9161277; fax (2) 9161243; e-mail info@cncs.com.uy; internet www.cncs.com.uy; f. 1867; 1,500 mems; Pres. Julio Lacarte Muró; Man. Dr Claudio Piacenza.

Cámara Mercantil de Productos del País (Chamber of Commerce for Local Products): Avda General Rondeau 1908, 1°, 11800 Montevideo; tel. (2) 9240644; fax (2) 9240673; e-mail info@camaramercantil.com.uy; internet www.camaramercantil.com.uy; f. 1891; 180 mems; Pres. Ricardo Seizer; Gen. Man. Gonzalo González Piedras.

EMPLOYERS' ORGANIZATIONS

Asociación de Importadores y Mayoristas de Almacén (Importers' and Wholesalers' Asscn): Edif. Bolsa de Comercio, Of. 317/319, Rincón 454, 11000 Montevideo; tel. (2) 9156103; fax (2) 9160796; e-mail fmelissari@nidera.com.uy; f. 1926; 52 mems; Pres. Fernando Melissari.

Asociación Rural del Uruguay (ARU): Avda Uruguay 864, 11100 Montevideo; tel. (2) 9020484; fax (2) 9020489; e-mail consultas@aru.com.uy; internet www.aru.com.uy; f. 1871; 1,800 mems; Pres. Guzmán Tellechea Otero; Vice-Pres. Dr Juan García Requena.

Federación Rural: Avda 18 de Julio 965, 1°, Montevideo; tel. (2) 9005583; fax (2) 9004791; e-mail fedrural@gmail.com; internet www.federacionrural.org; f. 1915; 2,000 mems; Pres. Rodrigo Herrero.

Unión de Exportadores del Uruguay (Uruguayan Exporters' Asscn): Edif. Nacional de Aduanas, Yacaré s/n, 11000 Montevideo; tel. (2) 9170105; fax (2) 9165967; e-mail info@uruguayexporta.com; internet www.uruguayexporta.com; Pres. Rodolfo Merzario; Exec. Sec. Alejandro Bzurovski.

UTILITIES

Electricity

Administración Nacional de Usinas y Transmisiones Eléctricas (UTE): Paraguay 2431, 10°, 11100 Montevideo; tel. (2) 2003424; fax (2) 2037082; e-mail ute@ute.com.uy; internet www.ute.com.uy; f. 1912; autonomous state body; sole purveyor of electricity until 1997; Pres. Ing. Beno Ruchansky; Gen. Man. Carlos Pombo.

Gas

Conecta: Sanlúcar 1631, esq. Avda Rivera, Montevideo; tel. (2) 6008400; fax (2) 6006732; internet www.conecta.com.uy; gas distribution; Dir Francisco Llano.

MontevideoGas: 25 de Mayo 702, 11000 Montevideo; tel. (2) 9017454; e-mail mlcoitino@montevideogas.com.uy; internet www.montevideogas.com.uy; gas producers and service providers.

Water

Aguas de la Costa: Calle 1 y 20, La Barra, Maldonado; tel. (42) 771930; fax (42) 771932; e-mail adlcosta@adinet.com.uy; subsidiary of Aguas de Barcelona (Spain); operating in Uruguay since 1994, contract due to expire in 2019; management of water supply in Maldonado Dept.

Obras Sanitarias del Estado (OSE): Carlos Roxlo 1275, 11200 Montevideo; tel. (2) 4001151; fax (2) 4088069; e-mail oserou@adinet.com.uy; internet www.ose.com.uy; f. 1962; processing and distribution of drinking water, sinking wells, supplying industrial zones of the country; Pres. Ing. Jorge Carlos Colacce Molinari; Vice-Pres. Fernando Daniel Nopitsch D'Andrea.

TRADE UNION

Plenario Intersindical de Trabajadores—Convención Nacional de Trabajadores (PIT—CNT): Avda 18 de Julio 2190, Montevideo; tel. (2) 4096680; fax (2) 4004160; e-mail pitcnt@adinet.com.uy; f. 1966; org. comprising 83 trade unions, 17 labour federations; 320,000 mems; Pres. Jorge Castro; Exec. Sec. Juan Castillo.

Transport

Dirección Nacional de Transporte: Rincón 575, 5°, 11000 Montevideo; tel. (2) 9163122; fax (2) 9163122; e-mail pitcnt@adinet.com.uy; internet www.dnt.gub.uy; co-ordinates national and international transport services.

RAILWAYS

Administración de los Ferrocarriles del Estado (AFE): Avda del Libertador 1672, Montevideo; tel. (2) 9033030; e-mail rrpp-afe@adinet.com.uy; internet www.afe.com.uy; f. 1952; state org.; 3,002 km of track connecting all parts of the country; there are connections with the Argentine and Brazilian networks; passenger services ceased in 1988; passenger services linking Montevideo with Florida and Canelones were resumed in mid-1993; Pres. Antonio Gallicchio Queirolo.

ROADS

In 2006 Uruguay had an estimated 8,730 km of motorways (forming the most dense motorway network in South America), connecting

URUGUAY

Montevideo with the main towns of the interior and the Argentine and Brazilian frontiers. There was also a network of approximately 40,000 km of paved roads under departmental control.

Corporación Vial del Uruguay, SA: Rincón 528, 5°, 11000 Montevideo; tel. (2) 9261680; fax (2) 9170114; e-mail cvu@cnd.org.uy; internet www.cvu.com.uy; road construction agency; 100% owned by the Corporación Nacional para el Desarrollo; Pres. ALVARO GARCÍA; Gen. Man. ANDRÉS PEREYRA.

INLAND WATERWAYS

There are about 1,250 km of navigable waterways, which provide an important means of transport.

Nobleza Naviera, SA: Avda General Rondeau 2257, Montevideo; tel. (2) 9243222; fax (2) 9243218; e-mail nobleza@netgate.com.uy; operates cargo services on the River Plate, and the Uruguay and Paraná rivers; Chair. AMÉRICO DEAMBROSI; Man. Dir DORIS FERRARI.

SHIPPING

Administración Nacional de Puertos (ANP): Rambla 25 de Agosto de 1825 160, Montevideo; tel. (2) 9151441; fax (2) 9161704; e-mail presidencia@anp.com.uy; internet www.anp.com.uy; f. 1916; national ports admin; Pres. FERNANDO PUNTIGLIANO; Gen. Man. ALBERTO DÍAZ.

Prefectura Nacional Naval: Edif. Comando General de la Armada, 4°, Rambla 25 de Agosto de 1825 s/n, esq. Maciel, Montevideo; tel. (2) 9155500; fax (2) 9156786; internet www.armada.gub.uy/Prena; f. 1829; maritime supervisory body, responsible for rescue services, protection of sea against pollution, etc.; Prefect Rear-Adm. OSCAR DEBALI DE PALLEJA.

Navegación Atlántida, SA: Río Branco 1373, 11100 Montevideo; tel. (2) 9084449; f. 1967; ferry services for passengers and vehicles between Argentina and Uruguay; Pres. H. C. PIETRANERA.

Transportadora Marítima de Combustibles, SA (TRAMACO, SA): Rincón 540, Puerta Baja, 11000 Montevideo; tel. (2) 9165754; fax (2) 9165755; e-mail tramaco@tramaco.com.uy; owned by the Christopherson Group; Pres. JORGE FERNÁNDEZ BAUBETA.

CIVIL AVIATION

Civil aviation is controlled by the Dirección General de Aviación Civil and the Dirección General de Infraestructura Aeronáutica. The main airport is at Carrasco, 21 km from Montevideo, and there are also airports at Paysandú, Rivera, Salto, Melo, Artigas, Punta del Este and Durazno.

Primeras Líneas Uruguayas de Navegación Aérea (PLUNA): Colonia 1013, 11000 Montevideo; tel. (2) 9030273; fax (2) 9023916; e-mail info@pluna.com.uy; internet www.pluna.aero; f. 1936; nationalized 1951; partially privatized in 1994; 49% stake acquired by Aerolíneas Argentinas in 2004; operates international services to Argentina, Brazil, Chile, El Salvador, Paraguay, Spain and the USA; Pres. CARLOS BOUZAS.

Aeromás, SA: Avda de las Americas 5120, Montevideo; tel. (2) 6046359; e-mail aeromas@aeromas.com; internet www.aeromas.com; private hire, cargo, and air ambulance flights; internal mass transit services to Salto, Paysandú, Rivera, Tacuarembó and Artigas; f. 1983; Dir DANIEL DALMÁS.

Tourism

The sandy beaches and woodlands on the coast and the grasslands of the interior, with their variety of fauna and flora, provide the main tourist attractions. About 58% of tourists came from Argentina, and a further 10% from Brazil in 2005. Uruguay received 1.9m. visitors in that year, while tourism revenues totalled US $597m. in 2006.

Asociación Uruguaya de Agencias de Viajes (AUDAVI): Río Branco 1407, Of. 205, 11100 Montevideo; tel. (2) 9012326; fax (2) 9021972; e-mail audavi@netgate.com.uy; internet www.audavi.com.uy; f. 1951; 100 mems; Pres. GIORGIO VALENTI; Man. LEDO SILVA.

Cámara Uruguaya de Turismo: La Paz 3052, 11800 Montevideo; tel. and fax (2) 4016013; Pres. LUIS BORSARI.

Uruguay Natural: Rambla 25 de Agosto de 1825, esq. Yacaré s/n, Montevideo; tel. (2) 1885100; e-mail webmaster@mintur.gub.uy; internet www.uruguaynatural.com; f. 2003; state-run tourism promotion agency; Dir-Gen. Dr ANTONIO CARÁMBULA.

UZBEKISTAN

Introductory Survey

Location, Climate, Language, Religion, Flag, Capital

The Republic of Uzbekistan is located in Central Asia. It is bordered by Kazakhstan to the north, Turkmenistan to the south-west, Kyrgyzstan to the east, Tajikistan to the south-east and Afghanistan to the south. The climate is marked by extreme temperatures and low levels of precipitation. Summers are long and hot with average temperatures in July of 32°C (90°F); daytime temperatures often exceed 40°C (104°F). During the short winter there are frequent severe frosts, and temperatures can fall as low as −38°C (−36°F). The official language is Uzbek. Islam is the predominant religion. Most Uzbeks are Sunni Muslims, principally of the Hanafi school, although there are small communities of Salafis; Sufism is relatively well established in southern Uzbekistan. There are also Orthodox Christians among the Slavic communities. The national flag (proportions 1 by 2) consists of five unequal horizontal stripes of (from top to bottom) light blue, red, white, red and light green, with a white crescent and 12 white stars near the hoist on the top stripe. The capital is Tashkent (Toshkent).

Recent History

Soviet power was first established in parts of Uzbekistan in November 1917. In April 1918 the Turkestan Autonomous Soviet Socialist Republic (ASSR), a vast region in Central Asia including Uzbekistan, was proclaimed, but Soviet forces withdrew against opposition from the nationalist *basmachi* movement, the White Army and a British expeditionary force. Soviet power was re-established in September 1919, although armed opposition continued until the early 1920s. The khanates of Buxoro (Bukhara) and Xiva (Khiva) became nominally independent Soviet republics in 1920, but by 1924 had been incorporated into the Turkestan ASSR. On 27 October 1924 the Uzbek Soviet Socialist Republic (SSR) was established (including, until 1929, the Tajik ASSR). In May 1925 the Uzbek SSR became a constituent republic of the Union of Soviet Socialist Republics (USSR, which had been established in December 1922). In 1936 Qoraqalpog'iston (Karakalpakstan) was transferred from the Russian Federation to the Uzbek SSR, retaining its status as a nominally autonomous viloyat (oblast or region).

The National Delimitation of the Central Asian republics of 1924–25 established an Uzbek nation-state for the first time. Its formation was accompanied by the development of a new literary language. Literacy rose from 3.8% at the 1926 census to 52.5% in 1932, and there was an increase in the provision of educational facilities, which played a crucial role in the policy of secularization. Muslim schools, courts and mosques were closed, and Muslim clergy were persecuted.

There had been little industrial development in Central Asia under the tsarist regime, other than the extraction of raw materials. Under the first two Five-Year Plans (1928–33 and 1933–38), however, there was considerable economic growth, aided by the immigration of skilled workers from other republics of the USSR. Although economic expansion continued at a significant rate after the Second World War (during which Uzbekistan's industrial base was enlarged by the transfer of industries from the war-zone), most Uzbeks continued to lead a traditional rural life-style, affected only by the huge increase in the amount of cotton grown in the republic.

There was a greater measure of freedom of the press in the late 1980s, facilitated by the policies of the Soviet leader, Mikhail Gorbachev, which allowed discussion of previously unexamined aspects of Uzbek history and contemporary ecological and economic concerns. The over-irrigation of land to feed the vast cotton-fields had caused both salination of the soil and, most importantly, the desiccation of the Aral Sea, a vital element in the ecology of the entire region.

Environmental problems and the status of the Uzbek language were among the concerns on which Uzbekistan's first major non-communist political movement, Unity (Birlik), campaigned. Formed in 1988, it rapidly became the main challenger to the ruling Communist Party of Uzbekistan (CPU). However, the movement remained unregistered and was unsuccessful in the 1989 elections to the USSR's Congress of People's Deputies; nevertheless, its campaign led to the adoption of legislation declaring Uzbek to be the official language of the republic in October of that year.

On 18 February 1990 elections were held to the 500-seat Uzbekistani Supreme Soviet (Supreme Council—legislature), which came to be dominated by the CPU (members of Unity were not permitted to stand). The new Supreme Soviet convened in March and elected Islam Karimov, the First Secretary (leader) of the CPU, to the newly created post of executive President.

In April 1991 Uzbekistan agreed, together with eight other Soviet republics, to sign a new Union Treaty to redefine the state structure of the USSR. However, on 19 August, the day before the signing was to take place, there was an attempt to stage a coup by conservative communists in Moscow, the Russian and Soviet capital. President Karimov only expressed his opposition to the coup once it became clear that it had failed. On 31 August an extraordinary session of the Supreme Soviet voted to declare the republic independent, as the Republic of Uzbekistan. The CPU voted to dissociate itself from the Communist Party of the Soviet Union, and in November the party was restructured as the People's Democratic Party of Uzbekistan (PDPU), under Karimov's leadership.

On 21 December 1991 Karimov agreed, together with 10 other republican leaders, to dissolve the USSR and formally establish the Commonwealth of Independent States (CIS, see p. 215). On 29 December a direct presidential election was held for the first time in Uzbekistan, which was won by Karimov, with a reported 86% of the total votes cast. His sole rival (winning 12% of the votes) was the poet Muhammad Salih, the leader of the Freedom (Erk) party, which had been established as an offshoot of Unity in 1990. A referendum was held concurrently, in which 98.2% of participants endorsed Uzbekistan's independence.

Under Karimov's leadership, there was widespread repression of opposition and Islamist groups. Uzbekistan's new Constitution, adopted on 8 December 1992, firmly enshrined the concept of state secularism, although the formal provisions for a democratic multi-party system, freedom of expression and the observance of human rights were largely ignored, in practice. It also provided for a new, smaller legislature, the 250-member Oly Majlis (Supreme Assembly), to take effect from elections due to be held in late 1994. On the day of the adoption of the new Constitution three leading opposition members were seized by Uzbekistani security police in the Kyrgyzstani capital, Bishkek, on charges of sedition. On the following day Unity was banned. Restriction of the media also intensified: in mid-1993 the Government instructed all newspapers and periodicals to be re-registered with the State Committee for the Press; only organs of state and government were permitted official registration.

Only the PDPU and its ally, Progress of the Fatherland (PF), were permitted to register for the elections to the Oly Majlis in 1994. At the elections, held on 25 December (with a second round of voting in January 1995), the PDPU won 69 of the 250 seats, and the PF secured 14. The remaining 167 deputies elected had been nominated by local councils rather than by political parties; however, the majority of these deputies (some 120) were members of the PDPU, and thus the party's domination of the Majlis was retained. Some 94% of eligible voters were reported to have participated in the election.

In January 1995 Karimov announced that the Government would permit the formation of blocs in the Oly Majlis and in February a new political party, the Justice (Adolat) Social Democratic Party of Uzbekistan, was registered; it immediately declared its intention to establish such a parliamentary faction. A referendum held in March produced a 99.6% vote in favour of extending Karimov's presidential term, originally scheduled to end in 1997, until 2000, in which year parliamentary elections were due to be held. In May two new political formations emerged: the National Revival (Milliy Tiklanish) Democratic Party and the People's Unity (Xalq Birligi) Movement. Both were reported to be pro-Government, and were officially registered in June. In December 1995 O'tkir Sultonov, hitherto the Minister of Foreign Economic Relations, replaced Abdulkhashim Mutalov as Prime Minister. In June 1996 Karimov resigned from his position as Chairman of the PDPU.

During 1996 Karimov began to advocate the creation of a political opposition to the PDPU, and in December a new law on political parties was approved by the Oly Majlis. The legislation prohibited the organization of parties on a religious or ethnic basis and compelled prospective parties to provide evidence of some 5,000 members drawn from a majority of Uzbekistan's administrative regions.

In late 1997 there was an upsurge of violence in eastern Uzbekistan, particularly in the densely populated Farg'ona (Fergana) valley, which was attributed to groups of Islamist activists. In November the deputy head of the local administration of Namangan Viloyat (region) was assassinated, and in the following month four police officers were killed; government troops were dispatched to the area, whereupon they arrested hundreds of suspects. The Government's campaign against Islamist militancy intensified in early 1998. In February the Ministry of Foreign Affairs appealed to the Pakistani Government to extirpate military training camps in that country, where Uzbeks were allegedly being trained in dissident activities. (Pakistan denied the existence of any such camps.) In May the Oly Majlis adopted legislation that severely limited the activities of religious organizations in Uzbekistan and Karimov declared to the Majlis that he would be prepared personally to execute members of Islamist groups found guilty of terrorism. In May–July several suspected militant Islamists were sentenced to terms of imprisonment, and a member of an Islamist organization was sentenced to death following his conviction for the murder of five people and for his role in the training of militants in Afghanistan. In January 1999 five men allegedly linked with a former *imam* of a mosque in Tashkent, who had been in hiding since early 1998, were found guilty of attempting to overthrow the Government and establish an Islamist state. Meanwhile, in June 1998 new legislation was passed banning the purchase, sale or exchange of land.

In February 1999 a series of bombs exploded in the centre of Tashkent, killing an estimated 15 people. Government officials claimed that the explosions had been carried out in an attempt to assassinate President Karimov and destabilize the country. Following the trial, in June, of 22 people suspected of involvement in the bomb attacks, six of the accused were sentenced to death, and the other defendants received lengthy prison sentences. In August six members of the banned Freedom party were also given prison sentences of between eight and 15 years for their alleged involvement in the bombings. In November the Tashkent region was infiltrated by a group of about 15 armed militants, resulting in the shooting of three police officers and three civilians. (It was alleged that the group, who were subsequently killed by security forces, had been trained in the separatist Chechen Republic, Russia, and had entered Uzbekistan from Kyrgyzstan.) Following the violence, Karimov demanded increased security in the capital and appealed to the Organization of Security and Co-operation in Europe (OSCE, see p. 354) to assist Uzbekistan in combating international terrorism.

At elections to the Oly Majlis, held on 5 and 19 December 1999, the PDPU secured the largest representation of any single party in the legislature, winning 48 seats, but non-partisan local council nominees obtained a combined total of 110 seats. Of the 250 seats, only 184 were filled at the first round, on 5 December, which necessitated a second round of voting on 19 December, at which all but one deputy were elected. The rate of voter participation at the first round was reported to be some 93.5%. The OSCE had sent only a limited number of observers to the elections, since all of the parties participating were pro-Government, two opposition parties having been prevented from contesting.

President Karimov reportedly secured 91.9% of the votes cast at the presidential election held on 9 January 2000, compared with only 4.2% for his sole opponent, the leader of the PDPU, Abdulkhafiz Jalolov. He was duly inaugurated for another five-year term on 22 January. A reported 95% of the registered electorate participated in the poll. However, both the OSCE and the US Government criticized the election as undemocratic, as opposition parties had been barred from nominating candidates.

The trial of 12 defendants accused of involvement in the bomb attacks of February 1999 opened in October 2000. In November the spiritual leader of the banned militant group the Islamic Movement of Uzbekistan (IMU), Takhir Yoldoshev, and his field commander, Jumaboy Khojiyev (known as Juma Namangoniy), were sentenced to death, *in absentia*. The remaining 10 defendants (including, *in absentia*, Salih) were sentenced to between 12 and 20 years' imprisonment. In June 2001 10 further Islamist militants were reported to have received prison sentences for attempting to overthrow the Government. In December it was reported that Karimov had requested the extradition of Salih from the Czech capital, Prague. However, Salih was released by a Czech court later that month.

The Government's repression of minority groups continued in 2001. During March, in the towns of Samarqand and Buxoro, books in the Tajik language were removed from libraries and schools. In April allegations emerged that the Ministry of Education had commanded the destruction of books in the Tajik language elsewhere in the country.

The perceived threat of militant Islamist movements intensified in the latter half of 2001, following the suicide attacks in the USA on 11 September (see below), and Uzbekistan's decision to co-operate with the USA in its attempts to form an international coalition to combat the al-Qa'ida (Base) organization (elements of the leadership of which were harboured by the de facto ruling Taliban militia in Afghanistan). It was widely believed that Karimov expected to secure strategic benefits from such co-operation, notably the suppression of the IMU and the moderation of international criticism of his Government's position on economic reforms and human rights. In the mean time, further restrictions were placed on the media in an attempt to limit public reprisals against the country's co-operation with the USA. There were frequent allegations of the torture and arrest of suspected members of the IMU and Hizb-ut-Tahrir al-Islami (Hizb-ut-Tahrir—the Party of Islamic Liberation), a clandestine, transnational organization, which sought to re-establish a caliphate, apparently solely through peaceful means, and which was alleged to enjoy significant support in Uzbekistan and neighbouring countries, particularly in the Farg'ona valley region. In October an estimated 5,000–7,000 members of the IMU (which both the UN and the USA identified as a terrorist organization) were reported to be fighting alongside Taliban forces in Afghanistan.

On 27 January 2002 a referendum took place to seek approval for proposed constitutional amendments, which would extend the President's term of office for a further two years and change the legislative structure. Some 91.6% of the electorate participated, of whom 93.7% approved the establishment of a bicameral legislature and 91.8% endorsed the extension of the presidential term to seven years. In April the Oly Majlis approved a resolution delaying the next presidential election by two years, until 2007. (The amendments also prescribed that elections to all offices of state were henceforth to be held in the third week of December in the year in which the term of office expired, effectively awarding President Karimov constitutional legitimacy to extend his mandate for a further 11 months, until December 2007.)

In December 2002 the Oly Majlis passed legislation on the formation of the new, bicameral legislature; Karimov announced that the upper chamber, the Senat (Senate), would assume some of the duties formerly performed by the President. In April 2003 the Oly Majlis approved constitutional amendments permitting the redistribution of authority within the Government, with effect from the next legislative elections. Most notably, the amendments prohibited the same person from serving simultaneously as President and Prime Minister, with the latter leading the Cabinet of Ministers. In addition, a law granting former presidents lifelong immunity from prosecution and permanent membership of the Senat was endorsed, and the judiciary was restructured.

On 11 December 2003 the Oly Majlis confirmed the appointment by Karimov of a new Prime Minister, Shavkat Mirziyoyev, who had substantial experience in the agricultural sector; Sultonov became a Deputy Prime Minister, with responsibility for energy, petroleum and the chemicals sectors. In March 2004 the Deputy Prime Minister and Minister of the Economy, Rustam Azimov, revealed plans to improve the efficiency of the Government, which was reorganized to comprise 13 ministries and 11 state committees.

On 28–29 March 2004 three police officers were reportedly killed in two separate shooting incidents in Tashkent; on 29 March two apparent suicide bomb attacks in the city's Chorsu market resulted in further casualties. It was also reported that 10 people had been killed and 26 injured after bombs exploded in an apartment block in Buxoro, which police alleged was being used to manufacture explosives. On 30 March security forces carried out a raid in Tashkent, during which at least 16 suspected militants and three police officers were reported to have been killed. Karimov attributed the violence to militant Islamist organizations, and at the end of the month the Uzbekistani authorities began to make numerous arrests. A further bomb attack on 1 April killed one person and prompted the Government to temporarily close its land borders. By July some 85 people suspected of involvement in the attacks had been arrested. In August 15 of the accused were sentenced to between six and 18 years' imprisonment; in October a further 23 Islamist militants were sentenced to between three and 18 years' imprisonment; and in July 2005 another 20 men were given gaol sentences for their involvement in the attacks.

Meanwhile, in July 2004 seven people were killed as a result of suicide bomb attacks in Tashkent outside the Israeli and US embassies and outside the Office of the Prosecutor-General. President Karimov rejected allegations of IMU involvement in the attacks and accused Hizb-ut-Tahrir of bearing primary responsibility. In December the Office of the Prosecutor-General declared that all three of the suicide bombers had been Kazakhstani citizens.

Further civil unrest broke out in November 2004, with riots in Qoqand in the Farg'ona valley, where some 5,000–10,000 people protested against the introduction of new laws affecting market traders; the protests spread to markets in other towns in Uzbekistan, including Buxoro and Margilan. In December rights groups and opposition parties gathered outside the US embassy, urging the USA to encourage the Uzbekistani Government to promote democracy and respect for human rights in Uzbekistan, after three opposition parties (Unity, Freedom and the Free Peasants' Party) were refused permission to put forward candidates for the legislative elections scheduled for the end of the month.

Elections to the Qoqunchilik palatasi Kengashi (Legislative Chamber), as the lower chamber of the new 120-member bicameral legislature was designated, were held on 26 December 2004, with a second round of voting on 9 January 2005 in the 58 constituencies in which no candidate had obtained an absolute majority of votes cast. All five of the parties permitted to participate in the elections supported the Karimov regime. A party established in late 1993 led by Muhammadjon Ahmadjonov, the Movement of Entrepreneurs and Businessmen—Liberal Democratic Party of Uzbekistan, obtained 41 seats, securing the largest representation of any single party in the legislature. The PDPU obtained 28 seats, the Self-Sacrificers' National Democratic Party 18, the National Revival Democratic Party 11 and the Justice Social Democratic Party 10. The rate of voter participation at the first round was estimated to be 85.1%. A number of ministerial changes were effected in late 2004 and early 2005. On 14 January 2005 President Karimov announced the appointment of 16 members of the Senate; regional council members elected a further 84 senators on 17–20 January. The Senate's inaugural session took place on 27 January.

There were reports of heightened political tensions in early 2005, particularly in the Farg'ona valley, which were attributed to a number of factors, including dissatisfaction at widespread poverty, the influence of the political upheaval in neighbouring Kyrgyzstan in March (see the chapter on Kyrgyzstan), and discontent at restrictions on trade and on the freedom of association. From February daily peaceful protests, some of which were apparently attended by up to 1,000 people, were reported outside a court in Andijon, where 23 local business executives had been brought to trial on charges of belonging to a prohibited Islamist organization, referred to by the authorities as Akramiya, and which was alleged to have broken away from Hizb-ut-Tahrir. All 23 denied the charges brought against them. In the early hours of 13 May, several days before the trial of the alleged Islamists was due to conclude, a group of armed men stormed the gaol in Andijon, and released as many as 2,000 prisoners, including the 23 people charged with belonging to Akramiya. Armed rebels were reported to have taken control of the regional administration building in the city later that day, and several thousand people gathered in the main city square, apparently to protest against both the trial of the alleged militants and economic difficulties. Heavily armed state security forces, including troops in tanks, entered the city and opened fire on the demonstrators. The exact number of people killed was disputed, in part because of the strict restrictions placed on media coverage and on access to the region by foreign diplomatic representatives or members of non-governmental organizations. Protests continued in Andijon later in the month, and unrest was reported in Qorasuv, south-east of Andijon, on the border with Kyrgyzstan, where local Islamist rebels seized control of the local administration and re-opened a border crossing with Kyrgyzstan that had been closed since 2000. State forces subsequently recaptured the town. Meanwhile, Kyrgyzstan reported that it had registered more than 500 Uzbekistani refugees in the immediate aftermath of the violence in Andijon (see below).

President Karimov rejected requests by the international community for an independent investigation into the events in Andijon. In July 2005 the Prosecutor of Andijon Viloyat announced that 187 people had been killed as a result of the violence, including 94 terrorists, 57 civilians, 20 law-enforcement officials and 11 soldiers; in contrast, independent reports claimed that as many as 1,000 people, mainly civilians, had been killed. In September a report released by the Office of the Prosecutor-General stated that foreign-based Islamists had staged the violence. The report also claimed that in January–April instructors in Kyrgyzstan had trained some 70 Islamist fundamentalists in terrorist techniques. In August Karimov approved a decree abolishing capital punishment, with effect from 1 January 2008.

In September 2005 the First Deputy Prosecutor-General suggested that 'external forces' had instructed Western journalists to publish false information about the events in Andijon in the foreign media. Meanwhile, individuals and organizations providing accounts that undermined the credibility of the Government's version of events were subject to official harassment, and many were expelled from the country or imprisoned. In October the European Union (EU, see p. 244) imposed sanctions on Uzbekistan (including a ban on travel to EU states by officials suspected of involvement in the shooting of civilians in Andijon, and an embargo on the export of weapons and other related equipment), owing to the Government's refusal either to permit an international investigation into events at Andijon or to bring those who had perpetrated the killings to trial. (These sanctions were extended in November 2006 and again in May 2007.) By December more than 150 people had been sentenced to terms of imprisonment for their involvement in the protests in Andijon; in November the USA and the Office of the UN High Commissioner for Human Rights expressed concern that defendants were being convicted without being permitted a fair trial, and the international human rights organization Human Rights Watch condemned the use of closed trials. There were also allegations of the use of torture to extract confessions. In February 2006 the Government approved a resolution that made journalists deemed to be interfering in internal affairs or insulting Uzbekistani citizens liable to prosecution. In March the authorities requested that the UN High Commission for Refugees vacate its offices in Uzbekistan, asserting that it was no longer required in the country.

Meanwhile, frequent government and security personnel changes continued to be effected in 2005–06. In June 2005 the First Deputy Head of the Military Intelligence Directorate, Lt-Col Sanjar Ismoilov, was arrested on suspicion of spying for Russia and, following his conviction, was sentenced to 20 years' imprisonment in January 2006. Ismoilov appealed against his sentence but this was rejected by the Supreme Court in February. In November 2005 Karimov dismissed the Minister of Defence, Qodir G'ulomov, who was subsequently succeeded by Ruslan Mirzayev. (G'ulomov was given a five-year suspended prison sentence in July 2006 for offences committed during his term of office.) Later in November 2005 Rustam Azimov was appointed as Minister of Finance; Azimov, hitherto the Minister of Foreign Economic Relations, Investment and Trade, was replaced in that position by Alisher Shayxov. In December the Minister of Internal Affairs, Zokirjon Almatov (whom the EU held responsible for overseeing the violent repression of the protests in Andijon), resigned from his post, citing ill health. In January 2006 he was succeeded by Bahodir Matlyubov. In February Murat Shafirkhodjaev resigned as Speaker of the Senate, apparently for reasons of ill health; he was succeeded by Ilgizar Sobirov. In April Vyacheslav Golishev was dismissed from the position of Deputy Prime Minister, responsible for the Economic Sector and Foreign Economic Relations, and Minister of the Economy. Azimov, the Minister of Finance, replaced Golishev in the former post, and Botir Hojayev was appointed Minister of the Economy. In June Lt-Col Erkin Musayev, former head of the Ministry of Defence Directorate for International Military Co-operation, was sentenced to 15 years' imprisonment after being convicted of negligence, dereliction of duty and divulging secret information to the North Atlantic Treaty Organization (NATO). Elyor G'aniyev was replaced as Minister of

Foreign Affairs by Vladimir Norov in July, although he retained a post in the Cabinet as Minister of Foreign Economic Relations, Investment and Trade. In late 2006 several Hokims (regional governors) were replaced.

The arrest of human rights activists and political dissidents, and the closure of foreign-funded non-governmental organizations (NGOs), continued unabated in 2006–07. The operations in Uzbekistan of several NGOs were terminated at the behest of a Tashkent court, ostensibly owing to alleged financial offences, engagement in improper activities and dissemination of false information against the republic. In August the trial commenced in Tashkent of a popular musician and songwriter, Dodokhon Hasan, who was accused of defaming the President. In mid-September Jamshid Karimov, formerly a reporter for the United Kingdom-based NGO, the Institute for War and Peace Reporting (IWPR) and a nephew of President Karimov, was reported to have disappeared; it was subsequently announced that he had been detained at a psychiatric hospital in Samarqand. Another former reporter for IWPR, Ulughbek Haydarov, was convicted on charges of extortion in October and sentenced to six years' imprisonment. A human rights activist, Umida Niyazova, was convicted on charges of illegal cross-border smuggling and sentenced to seven years' imprisonment in May 2007, although this was subsequently commuted to a three-year suspended sentence. In June the six-year prison sentence of another human rights activist, Gulbahor Turayeva, convicted in April by an Andijon court for distributing press material that threatened public order, was also reduced on appeal to a three-year suspended sentence.

In September 2007 the Central Elections Commission announced that a presidential election was to take place on 23 December, following the expiry of Karimov's seven-year term in the previous January (in accordance with a constitutional stipulation that the election be held in December of the year in which the presidential term of office ended). Karimov subsequently confirmed that he would contest the election, despite a constitutional provision restricting the President to two consecutive terms in office; the authorities maintained that the extension of the presidential term to seven years from 2002 effectively meant that Karimov's previous terms in office would not be taken into account for the purposes of this restriction. In October EU foreign ministers, while extending the embargo on the export of armaments to Uzbekistan for a further year, adopted a decision to suspend for a period of six months the travel restrictions on senior Uzbekistani officials, including the Minister of Defence, with the stated aim of encouraging the authorities to improve the human rights situation in the country. Prior to the poll, a number of human rights activists were summarily arrested.

On 23 December 2007 Karimov was re-elected, receiving some 88.1% of votes cast at the presidential election (the other three candidates permitted to contest the election were all considered to be loyal to Karimov); voter turnout was officially recorded at 90.6%. An observer mission from the Office for Democratic Institutions and Human Rights of the OSCE stated that the poll had failed to meet democratic standards. At the end of December Karimov appointed Azimov (who retained the finance portfolio) as First Deputy Prime Minister, responsible for the Economic Sector and Foreign Economic Relations; new appointments were made to the posts of Minister of Justice and Minister of Higher and Secondary Specialized Education. The 2005 presidential decree abolishing the death penalty officially entered into effect on 1 January 2008. In January, following the removal of the Speaker of the lower legislative chamber, Erkin Halilov, for misuse of office, Dilorom Tashmuhamedov (who had contested the presidential election as a candidate of Adolat) was elected to the post.

Uzbekistan's closest relations are with the neighbouring Central Asian republics—Kazakhstan, Kyrgyzstan, Tajikistan and Turkmenistan. In September 1997 a Central Asian peacekeeping battalion participated, with troops from the USA and other countries, in military manoeuvres, which were held in Uzbekistan and elsewhere in the region under the auspices of NATO's 'Partnership for Peace' (see p. 342) programme of military co-operation. (Uzbekistan had joined the programme in 1994.) In January 2006 Uzbekistan acceded to membership of the Eurasian Economic Community (EURASEC, see p. 412); hitherto Uzbekistan had been the sole member of the Central Asian Co-operation Organization (CACO—which organization was thereby absorbed into EURASEC) which did not also belong to the former organization. Uzbekistan, alongside Kyrgyzstan and Tajikistan, was expected to accede to a EURASEC customs union, initially to comprise Belarus, Kazakhstan and Russia, by 2011. In April 1999 Uzbekistan joined the GUAM grouping, comprising Azerbaijan, Georgia, Moldova and Ukraine, which envisaged implementing joint economic and transportation initiatives and establishing a sub-regional free trade zone; the organization was therefore renamed GUUAM. However, Uzbekistan was not an active participant in the group, and in early May 2005 announced its intention to withdraw. In March 2006 President Karimov approved legislation passed by the Oly Majlis earlier in the year, which completed Uzbekistan's withdrawal from the organization (which was renamed the Organization for Democracy and Economic Development—GUAM, see p. 425—later in the year).

Uzbekistan was a member (alongside the People's Republic of China, Kazakhstan, Kyrgyzstan, Russia and Tajikistan) of the Shanghai Five, founded in 1996 to address border disputes, and acceded to that organization's successor, the Shanghai Co-operation Organization (SCO, see p. 425), signing the Shanghai Convention on Combating Terrorism, Separatism and Extremism. The organization subsequently established a regional anti-terrorism centre, located in Tashkent.

In August 2006 Karimov signed a protocol on Uzbekistan's membership of the Collective Security Treaty Organization (see p. 423), which had evolved from the CIS Collective Security Treaty into a more formal military-political organization focused on regional security, comprising seven of the CIS states.

In October 1998 Uzbekistan and Kazakhstan signed a Treaty of Eternal Friendship and agreed on a seven-year programme of bilateral economic co-operation. In November 2001 Uzbekistan and Kazakhstan signed a treaty demarcating most of their border. However, the demarcation of certain areas, including the villages of Bagys and Turkestanets, remained unresolved. The majority of citizens in Bagys were ethnic Kazakhs, and it had been hoped that the land, hitherto leased to Uzbekistan, would be returned to Kazakhstan following independence. In December residents declared an 'Independent Kazakh Republic of Bagys', and elected a president and legislature. The Uzbekistani security forces subsequently arrested a number of activists, and in April 2002 it was reported that troops had barricaded the villages. In September a new agreement delimiting the Kazakhstani–Uzbekistani border was signed by the countries' Presidents. However, at the end of 2002 Uzbekistan unexpectedly closed its border with Kazakhstan, following the introduction of new import taxes. The creation of a working group to finalize the demarcation of the border between the two countries was announced in August 2003. However, there was a reported increase in violent confrontations on the border between Uzbekistan and Kazakhstan following the arrests of Kazakhstani citizens in connection with a series of bombings in Uzbekistan in mid-2004 (see above), and in January 2005 representatives from the Uzbekistani Ministry of Defence reportedly announced that they considered Kazakhstan to be a potential military adversary and a base for militant groups opposed to the Uzbekistani regime. In the same month the Uzbekistani authorities announced proposals for the demolition of settlements along the border, apparently in response to cross-border smuggling. Demonstrations in February by residents demanding compensation for the destruction of their homes were met with a promise from the Khokim (Governor) of Tashkent Viloyat that an assessment of property values in the village would be conducted with the view of providing the residents with eventual compensation. In March President Karimov and the President of Kazakhstan, Nursultan Nazarbayev, agreed to establish a working group to create a future free trade zone.

Relations with Kyrgyzstan worsened in September 2000, when Uzbekistani government forces planted landmines along the Kyrgyzstani–Uzbekistani border, apparently without having informed Kyrgyzstani border guards, in order to prevent insurgents from entering Uzbekistan. Although it was announced in June 2001 that the mines were to be removed, there were claims in September that the laying of mines was continuing. As a result, the Kyrgyzstani legislature refused to ratify an agreement with Uzbekistan on arms supplies. Relations were again strained in mid-2005, when the Kyrgyzstani Government refused to return a large number of refugees, who had fled there from Uzbekistan following the violence in Andijon in May (see above). In July more than 400 refugees were deported from Kyrgyzstan to Romania, which Uzbekistan condemned as a violation of international law. There were subsequent reports that refugees repatriated to Uzbekistan had been tortured, and in August 2005 Uzbekistan annulled a bilateral agreement to supply natural gas to Kyrgyzstan. In the following month Uzbekistan issued a report accusing Kyrgyzstan of having permitted religious extremists to use bases in that country to foment unrest in Andijon. In August 2006 Kyrgyzstan deported to Uzbekistan refugees from the violence in Andijon, some of whom, it was reported, had been previously convicted of crimes in Uzbekistan. In early 2007 a bilateral agreement providing for visa-free travel between the two countries took effect.

In September 2000 Turkmenistan and Uzbekistan signed a treaty demarcating their 1,867-km border. Tighter control of the border, however, exacerbated tension (see the Turkmenistan chapter). In December 2002 Turkmenistani special forces entered the Uzbekistani embassy in the Turkmenistani capital, Aşgabat, purportedly in order to investigate reports that it was harbouring Boris Shikhmuradov, whom the Turkmenistani authorities blamed for an assassination attempt against that country's President, Saparmyrat Niyazov. Uzbekistan's ambassador to Turkmenistan was subsequently declared *persona non grata*, on the grounds that he had offered support to Shikhmuradov. The Uzbekistani authorities denied the allegations and reacted with hostility; open confrontation rapidly led to the deployment of troops from both countries along their mutual border, and an associated increase in border security. However, in November 2004 Presidents Karimov and Niyazov met for their first presidential summit in more than four years, in Buxoro, where they signed three bilateral agreements, pertaining to: friendship, mutual trust, and co-operation; simplifying regulations concerning cross-border travel for residents of border zones (where cross-border smuggling and related shooting incidents had become a problem in recent years); and a framework for sharing regional water resources. The Presidents declared that all bilateral issues had been resolved, and in January 2005 Uzbekistan appointed a new ambassador to Turkmenistan. President Karimov made an official visit to Turkmenistan in October 2007, meeting the President of Turkmenistan installed earlier in that year, Gurbanguly Berdymuhamedov.

Uzbekistan dispatched troops to Tajikistan in 1992, as part of a CIS peace-keeping contingent, and it tightened border controls with Tajikistan in an attempt to prevent the civil conflict in that country from extending into Uzbekistan (see the chapter on Tajikistan). In August 1997 Uzbekistan agreed to act as one of the guarantor states of a peace accord reached between the Tajikistani Government and opposition forces two months earlier. During a visit to Uzbekistan in January 1998, President Imamali Rakhmonov (later Rakhmon) of Tajikistan met Karimov, and the two leaders expressed their opposition to religious extremism. In the following month an intergovernmental agreement on restructuring Tajikistan's debt to Uzbekistan was agreed. In February 1999 Uzbekistan announced its intention to withdraw from the CIS Collective Security Treaty, owing to its opposition to Russia's attempts at closer integration within the CIS and, in particular, Russia's military presence in Tajikistan. In August the Uzbekistani Government accused Tajikistan of allowing militant groups to operate from its territory. From August 2000 armed Islamist militants made a series of incursions into the section of the Farg'ona valley in Uzbekistan from Tajikistan, leading to armed conflict with government forces. By September, however, the remaining militants were reported to have been killed by government troops. In the mean time, Uzbekistan, which had begun laying landmines along its border with Tajikistan from mid-2000, in an effort to prevent cross-border incursions by Islamist insurgents, officially informed Tajikistan of its actions only in May 2001. However, relations between the two countries subsequently improved. President Rakhmonov met President Karimov in Uzbekistan in December 2001; although no border agreement was reached, it was announced that the crossing between the Penjakent district in Tajikistan and Samarqand Viloyat, in Uzbekistan, was to reopen. The leaders also agreed to collaborate to combat terrorism, crime and the illegal drugs trade. At a meeting of the Tajikistani and Uzbekistani Prime Ministers in February 2002, an agreement on border-crossing procedures was reached. The continued influx of illegal drugs from Tajikistan also threatened relations. Later in the year, the Presidents of the two countries agreed on the demarcation of more than 85% of the two countries' shared borders.

Relations with Russia, the most influential member state of the CIS, have been intermittently strained by concerns regarding Uzbekistan's ethnic Russian population (which comprised an estimated 5.5% of the population in 1996, according to official figures). Uzbekistan has repeatedly refused to grant dual citizenship to its Russian minority, and since independence many thousands of these Russians have emigrated (Russians had comprised 8.3% of the population in 1989, according to census figures). In October 1998 Russia, Uzbekistan and Tajikistan signed a pact offering mutual military assistance, especially against 'the threat of religious extremism'; at the same time Russia and Uzbekistan signed a number of inter-governmental agreements. Russia supported the Uzbekistani Government's official report on the events in Andijon in May 2005. In June the Russian Minister of Foreign Affairs, Sergei Lavrov, alleged that Islamist militant groups had been involved in the violence. Uzbekistan forged closer relations with Russia in 2005 (as relations of both Uzbekistan and Russia with Western countries notably worsened), and in November Karimov and the Russian President, Vladimir Putin, signed a bilateral agreement, which provided for co-operation in: trade and security; the use of military facilities; and efforts to combat drugs-trafficking and terrorism. Notably, the two countries agreed to provide mutual support in the event that one of them came under attack.

Uzbekistan's concerns for the security of the Central Asian region, and the threat to stability caused by Islamist extremism, were augmented by the long-standing civil war in Afghanistan. In the early 1990s President Burhanuddin Rabbani of Afghanistan claimed that Uzbekistan was providing military and financial assistance to the Afghan militia leader, Gen. Abdul Rashid Dostam (an ethnic Uzbek), whose forces controlled parts of northern Afghanistan. In 1994 the Uzbekistani Government denied any military involvement in Afghanistan and declared that only humanitarian aid had been given. At a summit meeting attended by representatives of Russia and the Central Asian republics in October 1996, Karimov confirmed that no military assistance would be accorded to Gen. Dostam, but declared that Dostam's forces provided the only defence for the Central Asian republics against the Taliban militant Islamist grouping. Following the defeat of Dostam's forces in May 1997, increased numbers of troops were deployed on the Uzbekistani–Afghan border. In late 1997 the Uzbekistani Government denied having facilitated the return of Gen. Dostam to Afghanistan from exile in Turkey. In October 2000 Gen. Dostam rejected allegations that his troops fought alongside Uzbekistani government forces in August–September to repel incursions by Islamist militants. Relations with the de facto ruling Taliban regime in Afghanistan deteriorated after they granted political asylum to Khojiyev, the field commander of the IMU. Relations worsened further following reports in the Pakistani press in August 2001 that Khojiyev had been appointed the deputy Commander-in-Chief of the Taliban forces.

The Islamist militant threat intensified following the suicide attacks on the USA of 11 September 2001 (see the chapter on the USA). At the same time, Uzbekistan's relationship with the USA became closer. (Relations had already improved noticeably in the latter half of the 1990s, and during a visit to Tashkent in April 2000, the US Secretary of State had affirmed the USA's willingness to assist Uzbekistan in combating the spread of Islamist extremism.) Uzbekistan's decision to support the US-led 'coalition against global terrorism' was of great strategic importance to the USA, which hoped to benefit from access to the country's transportation facilities. On 23 September the Uzbekistani Government confirmed that US military aircraft had landed at an airfield near Tashkent. On 7 October Uzbekistan and the USA signed a co-operation agreement, whereby Uzbekistan agreed to make its airbases available for use in humanitarian and 'search-and-rescue' operations during the US-led aerial bombardment of Taliban and terrorist bases in Afghanistan. The USA also agreed to enter into urgent negotiations, should Uzbekistan's security be threatened. In October 2001 Uzbekistan commenced the deployment of its troops on the Uzbekistani–Afghan border. The Uzbekistani Government was reluctant to accept refugees from Afghanistan, even though 1.5m. of them were ethnic Uzbeks, citing security concerns. Initially, the Government also refused to open the border to allow humanitarian aid to reach Afghanistan. However, following the military successes of the anti-Taliban forces in November, the Government was persuaded to open the 'Friendship Bridge', the only transit point into Afghanistan, in the following month. Khojiyev was reported to have been killed during the US-led military action in Afghanistan. At an official summit of the heads of the Central Asian states in Tashkent in December 2001 (at which Turkmenistan was not represented), the leaders declared their support for the new Afghan Interim Administration, which was established following the defeat of the Taliban regime. In March 2002 the leaders of Uzbekistan and Afghanistan pledged jointly to combat terrorism and the drugs trade; the IMU, for example, continued to be a threat to both countries.

Meanwhile, in November 2001 Uzbekistan and the USA signed a number of agreements pledging to improve bilateral relations and to increase economic co-operation. The USA agreed to donate more than US $150m. in aid towards improving Uzbekistan's security and economic development. Further bilateral agreements on political, economic and military co-operation were signed in January and March 2002, and Karimov visited the USA in March. Disagreements over Uzbekistan's pace of democratization, however, persisted, and in July 2004 Uzbekistan's lack of progress in democratic reform and human rights practices led the USA to reduce its aid programme by $18m. In October the US Drug Enforcement Agency and Uzbekistan's Ministry of Internal Affairs, together with Azerbaijan, Georgia, Kazakhstan, Kyrgyzstan, Moldova, Russia, Tajikistan and Ukraine, initiated an operation to control the flow of illegal drugs.

Following the violence in Andijon in May 2005, the USA urged Uzbekistan to allow an international inquiry to be undertaken. In June a spokesman from the US Department of State stated that witnesses had reported the killing of hundreds of civilians by Uzbekistani government forces. Uzbekistan subsequently imposed restrictions on the USA's use of the Qarshi-Khanabad ('K-2') military base, which had been used by the USA since October 2001 to support military and other operations in Afghanistan (see above); Uzbekistan also proposed that the USA withdraw from the airbase. Uzbekistan denied allegations that its decision to impose restrictions on the USA's use of the base was prompted by that country's stance on the events in Andijon. However, in July 2005 the SCO issued a statement demanding that deadlines be imposed on the use of military bases in Central Asia by Western countries for operations in Afghanistan. Later in the month, following discussions with the USA, Uzbekistan renounced the agreement under which the USA was permitted to use the Qarshi-Khanabad airbase, and demanded that it vacate the base within six months. The last US military aircraft left the Qarshi-Khanabad base in November. In mid-2006 groups of Uzbekistani refugees from Andijon returned to Uzbekistan from the USA, having reportedly been guaranteed exemption from prosecution by the Uzbekistani Government. A new US ambassador to Uzbekistan appointed in late 2007, Richard Norland, announced his intention of helping to improve relations between the two countries.

Relations with the People's Republic of China improved in the 1990s, and in July 1996 Jiang Zemin became the first Chinese President to visit Uzbekistan; a joint declaration on bilateral relations and co-operation was signed. China and Uzbekistan signed further co-operation agreements in November 1999, including a joint communiqué on the development of bilateral relations. In October 2000 the two countries signed an agreement on combating terrorism. In May 2005 China praised Uzbekistan's management of the outbreak of violence in Andijon earlier that month.

Government

Under the terms of the Constitution of 8 December 1992, Uzbekistan is a secular, democratic presidential republic. The directly elected President is Head of State and also holds supreme executive power. In April 2002 the Oly Majlis adopted a resolution extending the presidential term from five to seven years, with immediate effect. The Government (Cabinet of Ministers) is subordinate to the President, who appoints the Prime Minister, Deputy Prime Ministers and Ministers (subject to the approval of the legislature). The highest legislative body is the bicameral Oly Majlis (Supreme Assembly). The Majlis may be dissolved by the President (with the approval of the Constitutional Court). The Oly Majlis comprises the 120-member lower chamber, the Qoqunchilik palatasi Kengashi (Legislative Chamber), whose members are directly elected for a five-year term. The upper chamber, the Senat (Senate), is composed of 84 members indirectly elected by regional Council members and 16 citizens appointed by the President. Uzbekistan is divided into 12 Viloyats (regions), the city of Toshkent (Tashkent), and one sovereign republic (Qoraqalpog'iston—Karakalpakstan).

Defence

The establishment of Uzbekistani national armed forces was initiated in 1992. As assessed at November 2007, active armed forces numbered some 67,000, comprising an army of 50,000 and an air force of some 17,000. There were also paramilitary forces numbering up to 20,000 (comprising a 1,000-strong National Guard attached to the Ministry of Defence and up to 19,000 troops attached to the Ministry of Internal Affairs). Compulsory military service lasts for 12 months. The budget for 2006 allocated an estimated 103,000m. sum to defence. In July 1994 Uzbekistan joined the North Atlantic Treaty Organization's (NATO) 'Partnership for Peace' (see p. 342) programme of military co-operation. In April 1999 Uzbekistan withdrew its membership of the Collective Security Treaty of the Commonwealth of Independent States (CIS, see p. 215).

Economic Affairs

In 2006, according to the World Bank, Uzbekistan's gross national income (GNI), measured at average 2004–06 prices, was US $16,179m., equivalent to $610 per head (or $2,250 per head on an international purchasing-power parity basis). During 1996–2006, it was estimated, the population increased by an annual average of 1.3%, while gross domestic product (GDP) per head increased, in real terms, at an average annual rate of 3.8%. Overall GDP increased, in real terms, by an average of 5.2% per year in 1996–2006. According to the Asian Development Bank (ADB, see p. 182), growth was 7.2% in 2006 and 9.5% in 2007.

In 2006, according to the World Bank, agriculture (including forestry) contributed 28.1% of GDP; the agricultural sector employed 29.1% of the working population in 2005. Some 60% of the country's land is covered by desert and steppe, while the remainder comprises fertile valleys watered by two major river systems. The massive irrigation of arid areas has greatly increased production of the major crop, cotton, but has caused devastating environmental problems (most urgently the desiccation of the Aral Sea). Uzbekistan is among the five largest producers of cotton in the world, and the crop accounted for 27.5% of the value of total exports in 2000. Other major crops include grain, rice, vegetables and fruit. Since independence the Government has striven to reduce the area under cultivation for cotton in order to produce more grain. Private farming was legalized in 1992, and by 1996 more than 98% of agricultural production originated in the non-state sector. According to World Bank figures, during 1996–2006 agricultural GDP increased, in real terms, by an annual average of 5.8%. Agricultural GDP increased by 6.2% in 2005 and by 6.0% in 2006.

According to the World Bank, industry (including mining, manufacturing, utilities and construction) contributed 29.4% of GDP in 2006. It provided 13.2% of total employment in 2005. According to World Bank figures, during 1996–2006 industrial GDP increased by an average of 3.3% annually, in real terms. GDP in the sector increased by 5.0% in 2005 and by 4.5% in 2006.

Uzbekistan is well endowed with mineral deposits, in particular gold, natural gas, petroleum and coal. It was estimated that Uzbekistan had sufficient reserves of crude petroleum to maintain output at mid-1990s levels for 30 years, and enough natural gas for 50 years. There are large reserves of silver, copper, lead, zinc and tungsten, and Uzbekistan is one of the world's largest producers of uranium and gold. In 2005 2,712 metric tons of uranium ore were produced; all uranium mined is exported. The Murantau mine, in the Kyzyl-kum desert, was reportedly the world's largest single open-cast gold mine, and produced a reported 74% of Uzbekistan's estimated output in 2003. In 2004 Oxus Gold (of the United Kingdom) and the Uzbekistani Government officially opened a further gold-mining complex in Amantaytau, 30 km from the Murantau mine. Each party had a 50% share in the mine, which had estimated reserves of some 1,400 metric tons, and was expected to produce some 14 tons of gold per year by 2007.

The manufacturing sector contributed 11.1% of GDP in 2006, according to the World Bank. Significant investment has been directed to the expansion of the raw-materials processing industry. According to the World Bank, the manufacturing sector grew at an average of 1.7% per year in 1996–2006. GDP for the sector decreased by 2.4% in 2005, but increased in 2006 by 4.0%.

Uzbekistan is self-sufficient in natural gas, crude petroleum and coal, and became a net exporter of crude petroleum in 1995. Energy products accounted for 4.2% of the value of imports in 2000. The opening of two petroleum refineries, which had a total refining capacity of 173,000 barrels per day (b/d), significantly increased Uzbekistan's hydrocarbons capacity. In 2004 74.0% of electricity was generated by natural gas, 12.8% was produced by hydroelectric power and 9.2% by petroleum.

According to the World Bank, the services sector contributed 42.5% of GDP in 2006. It employed 57.7% of the working population in 2005. According to World Bank figures, during

1996–2006 the GDP of the services sector increased, in real terms, by an average of 5.9% annually. Services GDP increased by 8.0% in 2005 and by 10.4% in 2006.

In 2006, according to the IMF, Uzbekistan recorded a visible trade surplus of an estimated US $2,054m., and there was a surplus of $3,136m. on the current account of the balance of payments. In 2006 the principal source of imports was Russia (accounting for 26.9% of the total value of imports). Other major suppliers were the Republic of Korea (accounting for 15.4%), the People's Republic of China 10.8%), Germany (7.4%) and Kazakhstan (7.2%). Russia was also the main market for exports in that year (accounting for 21.9% of the total value of exports); other important purchasers were China (11.0%), Turkey (7.9%), and Kazakhstan (5.9%). The principal exports in 2000 were cotton fibre, energy products, metals and food products. The main imports in that year were machinery and equipment, chemicals and plastics, food products and metals. By 2000 trade with republics of the former USSR represented only about 35% of Uzbekistan's total trade, compared with some 83% in 1990.

In 2006 Uzbekistan's overall budget surplus (including extra-budgetary operations) was some 2,000m. sum (equivalent to 0.01% of GDP). At the end of 2005 Uzbekistan's total external debt was US $4,226m., of which $3,639m. was long-term public debt. The average annual rate of inflation declined from 1,568% in 1994 to 26.6% in 2001. According to ADB figures, inflation amounted to 7.8% in 2005 and 6.8% in 2006. In 2006 some 26,000 people (0.2% of the economically active population) were registered as unemployed, although the actual level was believed to be considerably higher.

In 1992 Uzbekistan became a member of the IMF and the World Bank, also joining the European Bank for Reconstruction and Development (EBRD, see p. 239) as a 'Country of Operations'. In the same year Uzbekistan was admitted to the Economic Co-operation Organization (ECO, see p. 238). Uzbekistan became a member of the ADB in 1995, and in 2003 it joined the Islamic Development Bank (see p. 329). In January 2006 Uzbekistan became a member of the Eurasian Economic Community, a customs union founded in 2000 by the Presidents of Russia, Belarus, Kazakhstan, Kyrgyzstan, and Tajikistan. Uzbekistan is pursuing membership of the World Trade Organization (WTO, see p. 396).

Following the collapse of the USSR in 1991, GDP declined sharply and inflation increased rapidly. In April 2004 the EBRD announced that it was to limit its activities in Uzbekistan, owing to the Government's failure to implement reform; in July 2005, following the violence in the city of Andijon in May, the EBRD announced that it would not participate in any further public-sector projects in Uzbekistan. Meanwhile, in 2004 the Russian state-controlled natural gas company Gazprom and the Uzbekistani company Uzbekneftgazkurilish agreed a 15-year production-sharing agreement at the Shakhpakhty gas and condensate field in Uzbekistan, where annual production was expected to reach 500m. cu m by 2010. In December 2004 a consortium of three companies from Iran, Ukraine and the United Kingdom won a tender to increase liquefied gas production at Uzbekneftgazkurilish's Shurtan gas complex; this, together with other planned projects, was expected to increase annual output of liquefied gas to 615,000 metric tons by 2010, compared with 119,000 tons in 2002. In January 2006 Uzbekistan signed a production-sharing agreement with Gazprom for three further natural gas fields, and an agreement was also signed on joint exploration of the region for further resources. Uzbekistan has relied on, notably, Russia, China and Japan for the exploitation of its hydrocarbons sector. Output of natural gas increased 3.8% in 2006. According to the ADB, GDP increased by 9.5% in 2007. The strong growth was driven by the industry and services sectors, while increased exports (particularly of natural gas, cotton and gold) and remittances raised the current account surplus to 21.1% of GDP. The budget surplus, meanwhile, stood at 2.3% of GDP in 2007, slightly less than that recorded the previous year, while inflation increased markedly, according to the ADB, to 12.0%. GDP growth was forecast to slow to 7.8% in 2008. In early 2008 the Government introduced tax reforms, in particular the lowering of the unified tax rate for micro- and small-business and the lowering of the corporate income tax rate for banks. However, progress in the planned privatization of large enterprises continued to be limited. Further diversification of the economy, to reduce the reliance on the energy and commodity sectors, would also be required if robust growth were to be effectively sustained.

Education

Primary education, beginning at seven years of age, lasts for four years. Secondary education, beginning at 11 years of age, lasts for seven years, comprising a first cycle of five years and a second cycle of two years. The gross primary enrolment ratio in 1999, according to the Asian Development Bank, was equivalent to 85% of females and 86% of males in the relevant age-group, while the overall gross secondary enrolment ratio in 1994 was 94%. In 2004 6.2m. pupils were enrolled in general secondary schools. Higher education was provided in 63 institutes in that year. Legislation adopted in May 1993 banned private educational establishments in Uzbekistan; those already in existence were reportedly to be transferred to state control. In 1999 the Tashkent Islamic University was established by presidential decree. In 2004 government expenditure on education was an estimated 765,384.8m. sum (27.4% of total budgetary expenditure). The 2006 budget allocated some 1,285,078.5m. sum to education (29.8% of total budgetary expenditure).

Public Holidays

2008: 1 January (New Year's Day), 8 March (International Women's Day), 21 March (Navruz Bairam, Spring Holiday), 9 May (Victory Day), 1 September (Independence Day), 1 October* (Ruza Hayit, Id al-Fitr or end of Ramadan), 8 December (Constitution Day and Kurban Hayit, Id al-Adha or Feast of the Sacrifice*).

2009: 1 January (New Year's Day), 7–8 March (International Women's Day), 21 March (Navruz Bairam, Spring Holiday), 9 May (Victory Day), 1 September (Independence Day), 20 September* (Ruza Hayit, Id al-Fitr or end of Ramadan), 27 November* (Kurban Hayit, Id al-Adha or Feast of the Sacrifice), 8 December (Constitution Day).

* These holidays are dependent on the Islamic lunar calendar and may vary by one or two days from the dates given.

Weights and Measures

The metric system is in force.

UZBEKISTAN

Statistical Survey

Area and Population

AREA, POPULATION AND DENSITY

Area (sq km)	447,400*
Population (census results)†	
17 January 1979	15,389,307
12 January 1989	
Males	9,784,156
Females	10,025,921
Total	19,810,077
Population (UN estimates at mid-year)‡	
2005	26,593,000
2006	26,981,000
2007	27,372,000
Density (per sq km) at mid-2007	61.2

* 172,740 sq miles.
† Figures refer to *de jure* population. The *de facto* total at the 1989 census was 19,905,158.
‡ Source: UN, *World Population Prospects: The 2006 Revision*.

POPULATION BY ETHNIC GROUP
(1996, rounded estimates)

	%
Uzbek	80.0
Russian	5.5
Tajik	5.0
Kazakh	3.0
Kara-Kalpak	2.5
Tatar	1.5
Others	2.5
Total	**100.0**

Source: Ministry of Health, Tashkent.

ADMINISTRATIVE DIVISIONS
(1996, rounded figures, official estimates)

	Area (sq km)	Population	Density (per sq km)	Capital city (with population)
Sovereign Republic:				
Qoraqalpog'iston	165,600	1,400,000	8.5	Nukus (236,700)
Viloyats				
Andijon	4,200	1,899,000	452.1	Andijon (303,000)
Buxoro	39,400	1,384,700	35.2	Buxoro (263,400)
Farg'ona	6,800	2,597,000	381.9	Farg'ona (214,000)
Jizzax	20,500	910,500	44.4	Jizzax (127,200)
Namangan	7,900	1,862,000	235.7	Namangan (341,000)
Navoiy	110,800	767,500	6.9	Navoiy (128,000)
Qashqadaryo	28,400	2,029,000	71.4	Qarshi (177,000)
Samarqand	16,400	2,322,000	141.6	Samarqand (366,000)
Sirdaryo	5,100	648,100	127.1	Guliston (54,000)
Surxondaryo	20,800	1,676,000	80.6	Termiz (95,000)
Tashkent*	15,300	4,450,000	290.9	Tashkent (2,100,000)
Xorazm	6,300	1,200,000	190.5	Urgench (135,000)
Total	**447,400**	**23,145,800**	**51.7**	

* Including Tashkent City, which subsequently assumed a separate administrative status.

Source: Government of Uzbekistan.

PRINCIPAL TOWNS
(estimated population at 1 January 2001)

Toshkent (Tashkent, the capital)	2,137,218	Farg'ona	183,037
Namangan	391,297	Margilan	149,646
Samarqand	361,339	Chirchik	141,742
Andijon	338,366	Urgench	138,609
Buxoro	237,361	Navoiy	138,082
Nukus	212,012	Jizzax	131,512
Qarshi	204,690	Termiz	116,467
Qoqand	197,450	Olmaliq	113,114

Source: UN, *Demographic Yearbook*.

Mid-2007 ('000, incl. suburbs, UN estimate): Toshkent (Tashkent) 2,184 (Source: UN, *World Urbanization Prospects: The 2007 Revision*).

BIRTHS, MARRIAGES AND DEATHS

	Registered live births		Registered marriages		Registered deaths	
	Number	Rate (per 1,000)	Number	Rate (per 1,000)	Number	Rate (per 1,000)
1994	657,725	29.5	176,287	7.9	148,423	6.7
1995	677,999	29.9	170,828	7.5	145,439	6.4
1996	634,842	27.4	171,662	7.4	144,829	6.3
1997	602,694	25.6	181,126	7.7	137,331	5.8
1999*	553,745	23.1	170,525	7.1	140,526	5.9
2000	527,580	21.4	168,908	6.9	135,598	5.5
2001	512,950	20.5	170,101	6.8	132,542	5.3

* Figures for 1998 are not available.

Source: UN, *Demographic Yearbook*.

Registered live births: 553,700 in 1998; 532,500 in 2002; 508,400 in 2003; 540,400 in 2004 (Source: UNDP Country Office and Center for Economic Research, Tashkent, *Uzbekistan in Figures*).

2005: Birth rate 20.9 per 1,000; Death rate 5.0 per 1,000 (Source: Ministry of Health, Tashkent).

Expectation of life (years at birth, WHO estimates): 65.8 (males 632.9; females 68.9) in 2005 (Source: WHO, *World Health Statistics*)

UZBEKISTAN

EMPLOYMENT
(annual averages, '000 persons)

	1998	1999	2000
Agriculture*	3,467	3,213	3,083
Industry†	1,114	1,124	1,145
Construction	573	640	676
Transport and communications	362	370	382
Trade and catering‡	717	735	754
Other services	1,976	2,042	2,042
Housing, public utilities and personal services	235	240	246
Health care, social security, physical culture and sports	502	538	567
Education, culture and art	1,073	1,094	1,120
Banking and insurance	50	48	51
General administration	111	122	126
Information and computer services	5	—	—
Total (incl. others)	8,800	8,885	8,983

* Including forestry.
† Comprising manufacturing (except printing and publishing), mining and quarrying, electricity, gas, water, logging and fishing.
‡ Including material and technical supply.

Source: Centre for Economic Research, Tashkent, *Uzbek Economic Trends*.

2001 ('000 persons): Total employed 9,136 (Agriculture 3,062, Industry 1,160, Other 4,914). (Source: Asian Development Bank, *Key Indicators of Developing Asian and Pacific Countries*).

2002 ('000 persons): Total employed 9,333 (Agriculture 3,046, Industry 1,186, Other 5,101) (Source: Asian Development Bank, *Key Indicators of Developing Asian and Pacific Countries*).

2003 ('000 persons): Total employed 9,589 (Agriculture 3,063, Industry 1,223, Other 5,303) (Source: Asian Development Bank, *Key Indicators of Developing Asian and Pacific Countries*).

2004 ('000 persons): Total employed 9,911 (Agriculture 3,068, Industry 1,284, Other 5,559) (Source: Asian Development Bank, *Key Indicators of Developing Asian and Pacific Countries*).

2005 ('000 persons): Total employed 10,196 (Agriculture 2,970, Industry 1,348, Other 5,879) (Source: Asian Development Bank, *Key Indicators of Developing Asian and Pacific Countries*).

2006 ('000 persons): Total employed 10,467 (Source: Asian Development Bank, *Key Indicators of Developing Asian and Pacific Countries*).

Unemployed ('000 persons registered): 38 in 2001; 35 in 2002; 32 in 2003; 35 in 2004; 28 in 2005; 26 in 2006 (Source: Asian Development Bank, *Key Indicators of Developing Asian and Pacific Countries*).

Health and Welfare

KEY INDICATORS

Total fertility rate (children per woman, 2005)	2.6
Under-5 mortality rate (per 1,000 live births, 2005)	68
HIV/AIDS (% of persons aged 15–49, 2005)	0.2
Physicians (per 1,000 head, 2003)	2.74
Hospital beds (per 1,000 head, 2005)	5.2
Health expenditure (2004): US $ per head (PPP)	160.1
Health expenditure (2004): % of GDP	5.1
Health expenditure (2004): public (% of total)	46.6
Access to water (% of persons, 2004)	82
Access to sanitation (% of persons, 2004)	67
Human Development Index (2005): ranking	113
Human Development Index (2005): value	0.702

For sources and definitions, see explanatory note on p. vi.

Agriculture

PRINCIPAL CROPS
('000 metric tons)

	2004	2005	2006
Wheat	5,378	5,928	5,996
Rice (paddy)	181	166	220
Barley	108	109	73
Maize	156	164	194
Sorghum*	11	10	4
Potatoes	896	924	1,021
Dry broad beans*	5	4	4
Sunflower seed	11	10	9
Safflower seed	8	7	3
Sesame seed*	19	20	20
Cottonseed*	2,334	2,461	2,376
Cabbages and other brassicas	274	287	369
Tomatoes	1,245	1,317	1,584
Cucumbers and gherkins	184	200	259
Dry onions	539	546	591
Garlic	29	32	38
Carrots and turnips	500	506	745
Watermelons	572	615	744
Apples	390*	432*	514
Pears	32*	41*	54
Apricots	162*	180*	236
Sweet cherries	15*	17*	54
Peaches and nectarines	51*	56*	67
Plums and sloes	40*	44*	57
Grapes	589	642	804
Tobacco (leaves)	19†	20*	20
Jute*	20	20	20
Cotton (lint)	1,150	1,250	1,171

* FAO estimate(s).
† Unofficial figure.

Aggregate production ('000 metric tons, may include official, semi-official or estimated data): Total cereals 5,861 in 2004, 6,403 in 2005, 6,511 in 2006; Total roots and tubers 896 in 2004, 924 in 2005, 1,021 in 2006; Total vegetables (incl. melons) 3,908 in 2004, 4,133 in 2005, 5,001 in 2006; Total fruits (excl. melons) 1,478 in 2004, 1,629 in 2005, 2,062 in 2006.

Source: FAO.

LIVESTOCK
('000 head at 1 January)

	2004	2005	2006
Horses	152	158	162
Asses, mules or hinnies	269	289	293
Cattle	6,243	6,571	7,045
Camels	17	17	17
Pigs	87	87	93
Sheep	8,890	9,555	10,034
Goats	1,690	1,797	1,973
Chickens	18,833	20,540	24,188
Turkeys*	350	350	350
Rabbits and hares	76,800	92,000	101,400

* FAO estimates.

Source: FAO.

UZBEKISTAN

LIVESTOCK PRODUCTS
('000 metric tons)

	2004	2005	2006
Cattle meat	493.6	518.1	551.6
Sheep meat	69.6	73.6	83.6
Pig meat	13.8	16.0	18.1
Chicken meat	16.7	21.3	23.4
Cows' milk	4,211.9	4,447.2	4,821.4
Sheep's milk	31.7*	n.a.	n.a.
Goats' milk	68.4	107.5	34.2
Hen eggs	102.8	110.0†	116.5†
Other poultry eggs	1.6	3.2†	48.1†
Honey	1.9	2.1	2.0
Wool: greasy	18.6	20.1	21.4

* Unofficial figure.
† FAO estimate.

Source: FAO.

Fishing
(metric tons, live weight)

	2003	2004	2005*
Capture	1,349	1,230	1,625
Common carp	397	238	330
Crucian carp	216	191	240
Roach	122	234	320
Silver carp	348	106	160
Aquaculture	3,118	3,093	3,800
Common carp	560	574	700
Crucian carp	103	145	200
Grass carp (White amur)	67	249	300
Silver carp	1,318	1,189	1,400
Bighead carp	1,070	936	1,200
Total catch	**4,467**	**4,323**	**5,425**

* FAO estimates.

Source: FAO.

Mining
(metric tons, unless otherwise indicated)

	2003	2004	2005
Coal ('000 metric tons)*	1,913	2,699	3,033
Crude petroleum ('000 metric tons)†	7,169	6,617	5,449
Natural gas ('000 million cu metres)	58	59	60
Copper ore‡§	80,000	95,000	100,000
Molybdenum ore‡§	500	500	500
Silver ore (kilograms)‡§	80,000	80,000	83,000
Gold (kilograms)‡§	90,000	93,000	90,000
Kaolin ('000 metic tons)§	5,500	5,500	5,500
Feldspar§	4,300	4,300	4,300
Uranium ore (metric tons)‡	1,874	2,377	2,712

* Including lignite and brown coal.
† Including gas condensate.
‡ Figures refer to the metal content of ores.
§ Estimated production.

Sources: Asian Development Bank, *Key Indicators of Developing Asian and Pacific Economies*, and US Geological Survey.

2006 ('000 metric tons): Crude petroleum 5,384 (Source: Asian Development Bank, *Key Indicators of Developing Asian and Pacific Countries*).

Industry

SELECTED PRODUCTS
('000 metric tons, unless otherwise indicated)

	1998	1999	2000
Beer ('000 hectolitres)	569	422	609
Cigarettes (million)	7,582	10,668	7,766
Wool yarn (pure and mixed)	2	3	3
Cotton yarn (pure and mixed)	105	105	135
Woven cotton fabrics (million sq m)	314	333	360
Sulphuric acid	856	897	823
Nitrogenous fertilizers (a)*	755	707	717
Phosphate fertilizers (b)*	141	169	117
Motor spirit (petrol)	1,603	1,638	1,709
Gas-diesel (distillate fuel) oils	2,227	2,220	1,900
Residual fuel oils	1,977	1,750	1,700
Lubricating oils	229	223	238
Cement	3,331	3,284	3,722
Domestic refrigerators ('000)	16	2	1
Domestic washing machines ('000)	5	—	—
Television receivers ('000)	192	50	26
Electric energy (million kWh)†	54,790	55,581	56,401

* Production in terms of (a) nitrogen; (b) phosphoric acid.
† Source: Asian Development Bank, *Key Indicators of Developing Asian and Pacific Countries*.

Source (unless otherwise indicated): UN, *Industrial Commodity Statistics Yearbook*.

2001: Cement ('000 metric tons) 3,722; Electric energy (million kWh) 47,961 (Source: Asian Development Bank, *Key Indicators of Developing Asian and Pacific Countries*).

2002: Cement ('000 metric tons) 3,927; Electric energy (million kWh) 49,398 (Source: Asian Development Bank, *Key Indicators of Developing Asian and Pacific Countries*).

2003: Cement ('000 metric tons) 4,062 (Source: Asian Development Bank, *Key Indicators of Developing Asian and Pacific Countries*).

2004: Cement ('000 metric tons) 4,805 (Source: Asian Development Bank, *Key Indicators of Developing Asian and Pacific Countries*).

2005: Cement ('000 metric tons) 5,058; Electric energy (million kWh) 47,706 (Source: Asian Development Bank, *Key Indicators of Developing Asian and Pacific Countries*).

2006: Cement ('000 metric tons) 5,583; Electric energy (million kWh) 49,300 (Source: Asian Development Bank, *Key Indicators of Developing Asian and Pacific Countries*).

Finance

CURRENCY AND EXCHANGE RATES

Monetary Units
100 teen = 1 sum.

Sterling, Dollar and Euro Equivalents (30 November 2007)
£1 sterling = 2,642.9 sum;
US $1 = 1,279.0 sum;
€1 = 1,887.9 sum;
10,000 sum = £3.78 = $7.82 = €5.30.

Average Exchange Rate (sum per US $)
2000   236.61
2001   423.31
2002   769.50

Note: Prior to the introduction of the sum (see below), Uzbekistan used a transitional currency, the sum-coupon. This had been introduced in November 1993 to circulate alongside (and initially at par with) the Russian (formerly Soviet) rouble. Following the dissolution of the USSR in December 1991, Russia and several other former Soviet republics retained the rouble as their monetary unit. The Russian rouble ceased to be legal tender in Uzbekistan from 15 April 1994.

On 1 July 1994 a permanent currency, the sum, was introduced to replace the sum-coupon at 1 sum per 1,000 coupons. The initial exchange rate was set at US $1 = 7.00 sum. Sum-coupons continued to circulate, but from 15 October 1994 the sum became the sole legal tender. On 15 October 2003 the sum became fully convertible.

UZBEKISTAN

CONSOLIDATED BUDGET
('000 million sum)

Revenue	2004	2005	2006*
Tax revenue	2,770	3,312	4,118
Taxes on incomes and profits	776	987	1,294
Taxes on property	172	211	289
Taxes on goods and services	1,728	2,005	2,366
VAT	655	815	1,107
Excises	878	638	653
Customs duties	94	109	170
Other budget revenue	122	166	316
Social security contributions	771	991	1,364
Road fund and other extra-budgetary revenue	186	207	275
Education development tax	—	163	270
Grants	96	62	62
Total	**3,945**	**4,900**	**6,406**

Expenditure†	2004	2005	2006*
Socio-cultural expenditure	1,119	1,581	2,179
Social safety net	969	1,291	1,711
Low income support	219	280	332
Pension and employment fund	749	1,012	1,379
Pension fund	725	983	1,353
Employment fund	24	29	26
Economy	415	507	571
Public authorities and administration	74	97	118
Public investment	459	474	511
Interest expenditure	55	66	79
Other expenditure in the budget	531	627	886
Road fund	139	168	215
Extra-budgetary expenditure financed by grants	114	50	62
Total	**3,875**	**4,862**	**6,331**

* Estimates.
† Excluding net lending ('000 million): 64 in 2004; 84 in 2005; 73 in 2006 (estimate).

Source: IMF, *Republic of Uzbekistan: 2006 Article IV Consultation—Staff Report; Public Information Notice on the Executive Board Discussion; and Statement by the Executive Director for the Republic of Uzbekistan* (March 2007).

INTERNATIONAL RESERVES
(US $ million at 31 December)

	2002	2003	2004
Gold (national valuation)	505.8	558.0	418.5
IMF special drawing rights	1.1	0.1	0.0
Foreign exchange	709.8	1,101.2	1,728.0
Total	**1,215.0**	**1,659.3**	**2,146.5**

Total reserves (US $ million at 31 December): 2,895.0 in 2005; 4,604.0 in 2006.

Source: Asian Development Bank, *Key Indicators of Developing Asian and Pacific Countries*.

MONEY SUPPLY
(million sum at 31 December)

	2002	2003	2004
Currency outside banks	273,347	404,928	590,199
Demand deposits at deposit money banks	194,839	170,036	214,596
Total money	**468,186**	**574,964**	**804,795**

Source: Asian Development Bank, *Key Indicators of Developing Asian and Pacific Countries*.

COST OF LIVING
(Consumer Price Index; base: previous year = 100)

	2004	2005	2006
Food	98.8	106.7	103.9
Other goods	105.3	106.9	108.0
All items	**103.7**	**107.8**	**106.8**

Source: Asian Development Bank, *Key Indicators of Developing Asian and Pacific Countries*.

NATIONAL ACCOUNTS
('000 million sum at current prices)

Expenditure on the Gross Domestic Product

	2003	2004	2005
Final consumption expenditure	7,192.2	8,387.3	10,231.7
Households	}		
Non-profit institutions serving households	5,474.8	6,305.8	7,736.3
General government	1,717.4	2,081.5	2,495.4
Gross capital formation	2,042.8	2,913.1	3,499.5
Gross fixed capital formation	2,069.1	2,694.5	3,518.4
Acquisitions, less disposals, of valuables	}		
Changes in inventories	−26.3	218.6	−18.9
Total domestic expenditure	**9,235.0**	**11,300.4**	**13,731.2**
Exports of goods and services (net)	602.9	889.0	1,479.3
GDP in market prices	**9,837.8**	**12,189.5**	**15,210.4**

Gross Domestic Product by Economic Activity

	2003	2004	2005
Agriculture and forestry	2,812.6	3,260.9	3,801.6
Mining and quarrying	}		
Manufacturing	1,553.3	2,085.5	3,141.5
Electricity, gas and water			
Construction	442.4	551.0	741.9
Trade	921.1	1,101.8	1,403.9
Transport and communications	923.7	1,191.8	1,712.6
Finance	286.5	}	
Public administration	277.2	2,290.6	2,729.0
Other services	1,275.9		
GDP at factor cost	**8,492.8**	**10,481.7**	**13,530.5**
Indirect taxes	} 1,345.1	1,707.8	1,679.9
Less Subsidies			
GDP in purchasers' values	**9,837.8**	**12,189.5**	**15,210.4**

Source: Asian Development Bank, *Key Indicators of Developing Asian and Pacific Countries*.

UZBEKISTAN

BALANCE OF PAYMENTS
(US $ million)

	2004	2005	2006*
Exports of goods f.o.b.	4,263	4,757	5,842
Imports of goods f.o.b.	−3,061	−3,310	−3,787
Trade balance	1,202	1,446	2,054
Export of services	574	659	769
Import of services	−867	−790	−813
Balance on goods and services	909	1,315	2,010
Income (net)	−49	−24	−14
Current transfers (net)	354	658	1,139
Current balance	1,215	1,949	3,136
Capital account (net)	−132	31	−116
Foreign direct and portfolio investment (net)	187	88	164
Existing public and publicly-guaranteed debt (net)	−91	−241	−162
Commercial non-guaranteed (net)	18	34	42
Other capital and statistical discrepancy	−684	−1,093	−1,355
Overall balance	512	768	1,709

*Estimates.

Source: IMF, *Republic of Uzbekistan: 2006 Article IV Consultation—Staff Report; Public Information Notice on the Executive Board Discussion; and Statement by the Executive Director for the Republic of Uzbekistan* (March 2007).

External Trade

PRINCIPAL COMMODITIES
(US $ million)

Imports f.o.b.	1998	1999	2000
Chemicals and plastics	407.2	363.0	399.5
Metals	303.6	245.4	253.5
Machinery and equipment	1,553.7	1,393.5	1,044.1
Food products	512.2	408.1	361.1
Energy products	16.3	66.6	112.7
Total (incl. others)	3,288.7	3,110.7	2,696.4

Exports f.o.b.	1998	1999	2000
Cotton fibre	1,361.0	883.7	897.1
Chemicals and plastics	51.7	101.8	93.4
Metals	180.7	138.9	216.7
Machinery and equipment	146.6	103.2	111.8
Food products	111.9	206.7	176.4
Energy products	277.8	371.5	335.2
Total (incl. others)	3,528.2	3,235.8	3,264.7

Source: Center for Economic Research, Tashkent, *Uzbek Economic Trends*.

PRINCIPAL TRADING PARTNERS
(US $ million)

Imports	2004	2005	2006
China, People's Republic	182.9	253.2	446.7
France	43.2	n.a.	n.a.
Germany	242.9	313.4	306.5
Italy	76.3	68.2	44.9
Kazakhstan	221.9	253.5	297.4
Korea, Republic	395.0	542.4	636.4
Russia	843.6	946.6	1,112.3
Tajikistan	72.5	73.2	85.8
Turkey	159.7	166.2	193.5
Ukraine	141.4	165.7	194.4
USA	252.9	80.9	59.3
Total (incl. others)	3,163.8	3,559.1	4,142.2

Exports	2004	2005	2006
Bangladesh	101.4	163.1	206.6
China, People's Republic	371.3	410.0	514.4
Italy	48.7	65.4	n.a.
Japan	78.4	113.0	154.6
Kazakhstan	206.9	236.4	277.4
Korea, Republic	69.9	83.5	n.a.
Russia	556.2	820.0	1,025.8
Tajikistan	153.5	139.0	163.1
Turkey	162.4	235.9	368.6
Ukraine	63.3	186.7	219.0
USA	81.8	88.6	139.3
Total (incl. others)	2,696.6	3,442.7	4,681.8

Source: Asian Development Bank, *Key Indicators of Developing Asian and Pacific Countries*.

Transport

RAILWAYS
(traffic)

	2002	2003	2004
Passenger-km (million)	2	2	2
Freight ton-km (million)	18	19	18

Source: UN, *Statistical Yearbook*.

CIVIL AVIATION
(estimated traffic on scheduled services)

	2001	2002	2003
Kilometres flown (million)	57	39	40
Passengers carried ('000)	2,256	1,451	1,466
Passenger-km (million)	5,268	3,835	3,889
Total ton-km (million)	580	417	424

Source: UN, *Statistical Yearbook*.

Tourism

FOREIGN VISITOR ARRIVALS
('000, incl. excursionists)

Region of origin	2002	2003	2004
Africa	1.0	1.0	1.0
Americas	4.1	2.0	12.0
East Asia and the Pacific	195.1	145.0	140.0
Europe	99.8	51.0	68.6
Middle East	23.5	24.0	30.0
South Asia	8.0	8.0	10.0
Total	331.5	231.0	261.6

Tourism receipts (US $ million, excl. passenger transport): 68 in 2002; 48 in 2003; 57 in 2004.

Source: World Tourism Organization.

Communications Media

	2003	2004	2005
Telephones ('000 main lines in use)	1,717.1	1,750.4	1,793.5
Mobile cellular telephones ('000 subscribers)	320.8	544.1	720.0
Internet users ('000)	492.0	675.0	880.0
Broadband subscribers ('000)	2.8	5.5	8.3

Source: International Telecommunication Union.

2006: Internet users ('000) 1,700.0 (Source: International Telecommunication Union).

Book production: 1,003 titles and 30,914,000 copies in 1996 (Source: UNESCO, *Statistical Yearbook*).

Daily newspapers: 3 titles and 75,000 copies (average circulation) in 1996; 5 titles in 2004 (Sources: UNESCO, *Statistical Yearbook*; UNESCO Institute for Statistics).

Non-daily newspapers: 350 titles and 1,404,000 copies (average circulation) in 1996 (Source: UNESCO, *Statistical Yearbook*).

Other periodicals: 81 titles and 684,000 copies (average circulation) in 1996 (Source: UNESCO, *Statistical Yearbook*).

Radio receivers ('000 in use): 10,800 in 1997 (Source: UNESCO, *Statistical Yearbook*).

Television receivers ('000 in use): 7,000 in 2001 (Source: International Telecommunication Union).

Facsimile machines (number in use): 3,325 in 2001 (Source: International Telecommunication Union).

Education

(2006, unless otherwise indicated)

	Schools	Teachers	Students
Pre-primary	6,413	96,100*	562,200
Primary			1,905,693*
Secondary:	9,816†	463,100	
general			5,715,100
teacher training	n.a.	2,464‡	35,411‡
vocational	1,052	7,900*	214,500*
Higher	63§	18,400*	263,600§
Universities	20*	n.a.	131,100*

* 1994/95.
† Including 20 evening schools.
‡ 1993.
§ 2004.

Sources: UNESCO, *Statistical Yearbook* and Center for Economic Research, Tashkent.

Adult literacy rate (UNESCO estimates): 99.3% (males 99.6%; females 98.9%) in 2002 (Source: UN Development Programme, *Human Development Report*).

Directory

The Constitution

A new Constitution was adopted by the Supreme Council on 8 December 1992. It declares Uzbekistan to be a secular, democratic and presidential republic. Basic human rights are guaranteed. The principal features of the Constitution, as subsequently revised, are as follows:

THE OLY MAJLIS

The highest legislative body is the Oly Majlis (Supreme Assembly). The Oly Majlis comprises two chambers: the Qoqunchilik palatasi Kengashi (Legislative Chamber); and the Senat (Senate). The 120 deputies of the Qoqunchilik palatasi Kengashi are elected for a term of five years. Of the 100 members of the Senat, 84 members are indirectly elected by regional Council members, and 16 are appointed by the President of the Republic. The Oly Majlis may be dissolved by the President, with the agreement of the Constitutional Court. The Oly Majlis enacts legislation and constitutional legislation, elects its own officials, the judges of the higher courts and the Chairman of the State Committee for Environmental Protection. It confirms the President's appointments to ministerial office, the procuracy-general and the governorship of the Central Bank. It must ratify international treaties, changes to borders and presidential decrees on emergency situations. Legislation may be initiated by the deputies, by the President, by the higher courts, by the Procurator-General and by the Autonomous Republic of Qoraqalpogʻiston.

PRESIDENT OF THE REPUBLIC

The President of the Republic, who is directly elected by the people for a seven-year term, is Head of State and holds supreme executive power. (The term of office was extended, with immediate effect, from five to seven years in April 2002.) An individual may be elected President for a maximum of two consecutive terms*. The President is required to form and supervise the Cabinet of Ministers, appointing the Prime Minister and Ministers, subject to confirmation by the Oly Majlis. The President also nominates the candidates for appointment to the higher courts and certain offices of state, subject to confirmation by the Oly Majlis. The President appoints the judges of the lower courts and the hokims (governors) of the regions. Legislation may be initiated, reviewed and returned to the Oly Majlis by the President, who must promulgate all laws. The President may dissolve the Oly Majlis. The President is also Commander-in-Chief of the Armed Forces and may declare a state of emergency or a state of war, subject to confirmation by the Oly Majlis within three days.

* Despite this constitutional restriction, ISLAM KARIMOV was elected to a third consecutive term of office in December 2007, his second term having formally ended in January of that year.

THE CABINET OF MINISTERS

The Cabinet of Ministers is the Government of the republic; it is subordinate to the President, who appoints its Prime Minister, Deputy Prime Ministers and Ministers, subject to the approval of the legislature. Local government is carried out by elected councils and appointed hokims, the latter having significant personal authority and responsibility.

JUDICATURE

The exercise of judicial power is independent of government. The higher courts, of which the judges are nominated by the President and confirmed by the Oly Majlis, consist of the Constitutional Court, the Supreme Court and the High Economic Court. There is also a Supreme Court of the Sovereign Republic of Qoraqalpogʻiston. Lower courts, including economic courts, are based in the regions, districts and towns. The Procurator-General's office is responsible for supervising the observance of the law.

The Government

HEAD OF STATE

President of the Republic: ISLAM A. KARIMOV (elected by Supreme Soviet 24 March 1990; term of office extended by popular referendum 27 March 1995; re-elected 9 January 2000 and 23 December 2007; inaugurated 16 January 2008).

CABINET OF MINISTERS
(May 2008)

Prime Minister: SHAVKAT M. MIRZIYOYEV.

First Deputy Prime Minister, responsible for the Economic Sector and Foreign Economic Relations, and Minister of Finance: RUSTAM S. AZIMOV.

Deputy Prime Minister, responsible for the Construction Sector, Industry, Housing and Municipal Services and Transport: NODIRXON M. XANOV.

**Deputy Prime Minister, responsible for Machine-construction, Metallurgy, Petroleum and Natural Gas, Geology, Electrical Energy, Chemical Production, Standardization and Metrology and State Reserves: ERGASH R. SHOISMATOV.

Deputy Prime Minister, responsible for Information Systems and Telecommunications, Director-General of the Communications and Information Agency of Uzbekistan: ABDULLA N. ARIPOV.

Deputy Prime Minister: RUSTAM S. QOSIMOV.

Deputy Prime Minister, Chairman of the Committee of Women of Uzbekistan: SVETLANA T. INAMOVA.

Minister of the Economy: BATIR A. XODJAYEV.

Minister of Foreign Economic Relations, Investment and Trade: ELYOR M. G'ANIYEV.

Minister of Labour and Social Protection: AKTAM A. XAITOV (acting).

Minister of Culture and Sports: RUSTAM J. QURBONOV.

Minister of Internal Affairs: BAHODIR A. MATLYUBOV.

Minister of Foreign Affairs: VLADIMIR I. NOROV.

Minister of Defence: RUSLAN E. MIRZAEV.

Minister of National Education: G'AYRAT B. SHOUMAROV.

Minister of Higher and Secondary Specialized Education: AZIMJON P. PARPIEV.

Minister of Agriculture and Water Resources: SAYFIDDIN U. ISMOILOV.

Minister of Justice: RAVSHAN A. MUXYITDINOV.

Minister of Health: FERUZ G. NAZIROV.

Minister of Emergency Situations: QOBIL R. BERDIYEV.

Note: The Constitution provides for the Chairman of the Council of Ministers of the Republic of Qoraqalpog'iston to serve as an ex officio member of the Council of Ministers of the Republic of Uzbekistan. Since March 2006 this position has been held by BAXODIR YANGI-BOYEV. The following are also members of the Cabinet of Ministers: the Chairman of the Central Bank and chairmen of state committees and agencies.

MINISTRIES

Office of the President: 100163 Tashkent, O'zbekiston shoh ko'ch. 43; tel. (71) 139-54-04; fax (71) 139-53-25; e-mail presidents_office@press-service.uz; internet www.press-service.uz.

Office of the Cabinet of Ministers: 100078 Tashkent, Mustaqillik maydoni 5; tel. (71) 139-82-95; fax (71) 139-84-63; internet www.gov.uz.

Ministry of Agriculture and Water Resources: 100004 Tashkent, A. Navoiy ko'ch. 4; tel. (71) 244-21-30; fax (71) 232-21-59; e-mail qshv@intal.uz; internet www.agro.uz.

Ministry of Culture and Sport: 100159 Tashkent, Mustaqillik maydoni 5; tel. (71) 239-46-11; fax (71) 239-45-52; e-mail madaniyat@sport.uz; internet www.madaniyat.sport.uz.

Ministry of Defence: 100000 Tashkent, Ak. Abdullaev ko'ch. 100; tel. (71) 269-82-43; fax (71) 269-82-28.

Ministry of the Economy: 100003 Tashkent, O'zbekiston shoh ko'ch. 45A; tel. (71) 132-63-20; fax (71) 132-63-72; e-mail mineconomy@mmes.gov.uz; internet www.mineconomy.uz.

Ministry for Emergency Situations: 100084 Tashkent, Yunusobodn tumani, Kichik xalka yo'li–4; tel. (71) 239-16-85; fax (71) 233-09-55; e-mail mes@st.uz; internet www.mchs.uz.

Ministry of Finance: 100008 Tashkent, Mustaqillik maydoni 5; tel. (71) 233-70-73; fax (71) 244-56-43; e-mail info@mf.uz; internet www.mf.uz.

Ministry of Foreign Affairs: 100029 Tashkent, O'zbekiston shoh ko'ch. 9; tel. (71) 233-64-75; fax (71) 239-15-17; e-mail rnews@mfa.uz; internet www.mfa.uz.

Ministry of Foreign Economic Relations, Investment and Trade: 100029 Tashkent, Shevchenko ko'ch. 1; tel. (71) 238-50-00; fax (71) 238-51-00; e-mail secretary@mfer.uz; internet www.mfer.uz.

Ministry of Health: 100011 Tashkent, A. Navoiy ko'ch. 12; tel. (71) 241-16-91; fax (71) 241-10-33; e-mail minzdrav@med.uz; internet www.minzdr.uz.

Ministry of Higher and Specialized Secondary Education: 100100 Tashkent, Bobur ko'ch. 53; tel. (71) 252-77-45; fax 252-77-83; e-mail oliy@uzsci.net; internet www.edu.uz.

Ministry of Internal Affairs: 100029 Tashkent, Yu. Rajaby ko'ch. 1; tel. (71) 239-73-36; internet www.mvd.uz.

Ministry of Justice: 100047 Tashkent, Sayilgoh ko'ch. 5; tel. (71) 233-13-05; fax (71) 233-51-76; e-mail info@minjust.gov.uz; internet www.minjust.uz.

Ministry of Labour and Social Security: 100100 Tashkent, A. Avloniy ko'ch. 20A; tel. (71) 239-41-21; fax (71) 239-41-12; e-mail mehnat@uzpak.uz; internet www.mintrud.uz.

Ministry of National Education: 100078 Tashkent, Mustaqillik maydoni 5; tel. (71) 239-13-10; fax (71) 239-19-34; e-mail info@uzedu.uz; internet www.uzedu.uz.

President

Presidential Election, 23 December 2007

Candidate	Votes	%
Islam Karimov (Liberal Democratic Party of Uzbekistan)	13,008,357	88.10
Asliddin A. Rustamov (People's Democratic Party of Uzbekistan)	468,064	3.17
Akmal Saidov (Independent)	420,815	2.85
Dilorom Tashmuhamedov (Justice Social Democratic Party of Uzbekistan)	434,111	2.94
Total*	14,765,444	100.00

*Including 434,097 invalid votes (2.94% of the total).

Legislature

The Oly Majlis (Supreme Assembly) is a bicameral legislative body, comprising the 100-member upper chamber, the Senat (Senate), and the 120-member lower chamber, the Qoqunchilik palatasi Kengashi (Legislative Chamber).

Qoqunchilik palatasi Kengashi (Legislative Chamber)

100008 Tashkent, Xalqlar Do'stligi shoh ko'ch. 1; tel. (71) 139-87-07; fax (71) 139-41-51; internet www.parliament.gov.uz.

Speaker: DILOROM H. TASHMUHAMEDOV.

General Election, 26 December 2004 and 9 January 2005

Parties, etc.	Seats
Movement of Entrepreneurs and Businessmen—Liberal Democratic Party of Uzbekistan	41
People's Democratic Party of Uzbekistan	28
Self-Sacrificers' National Democratic Party (Fidokorlar)	18
National Revival Democratic Party of Uzbekistan (Milliy Tiklanish)	11
Justice Social Democratic Party of Uzbekistan (Adolat)	10
Citizens' groups	12
Total	**120**

Senat (Senate)

100029 Tashkent, Mustaqillik maydoni 6; tel. (71) 138-26-66; fax (71) 138-29-01; e-mail info@senat.uz; internet www.senat.gov.uz.

Of the 100 members of the chamber, 84 members are indirectly elected by regional Council members and 16 are appointed by the President of the Republic. The first presidential appointees to the Senate were announced on 14 January 2005, while the first indirect elections of senators were held on 17–20 January 2005. The inaugural session of the chamber convened on 27 January.

Speaker: ILGIZAR M. SOBIROV.

Election Commission

Central Election Commission (O'zbekiston Respublikasi Markaziy Saylov Kommissiyasi): 100000 Tashkent; tel. (71) 139-15-72; fax (71) 139-43-91; internet www.elections.uz; mems approved by the Oly Majlis; Chair. MIRZO-ULUG'BEK E. ABDUSALOMOV.

Political Organizations

Following Uzbekistan's independence (achieved in August 1991), the ruling People's Democratic Party of Uzbekistan (PDPU—the successor to the Communist Party of the Uzbek SSR) took increasingly repressive measures against opposition and Islamist parties. A new law on political parties was approved in 1996; among other provisions, the law prohibited the establishment of parties on a religious or ethnic basis and stipulated a minimum membership, per party, of 5,000 people (with stipulation that membership be distributed across the country's regions). From February 2004 the minimum membership requirement was increased to 20,000 people. Since independence a number of opposition elements have been based abroad, particularly in Russia.

Free Peasants' Party (Ozod Dehqonlar partiyasi—Ozod Dehqonlar): 100000 Tashkent; f. 2003; denied registration; Exec. Sec. of Political Council NIGORA HIDOYATOVA; Ideological Leader BABUR MALIKOV (in USA).

Freedom Democratic Party of Uzbekistan (O'zbekiston Erk Demokratik Partiyasi—Erk): 100055 Tashkent, Ipakchi ko'ch. 38; tel. (71) 120-65-30; e-mail erkparty@yahoo.com; f. 1990; banned in 1993; Chair. MUHAMMAD SALIH (based in Norway).

Islamic Renaissance Party: 100000 Tashkent; banned in 1991; advocates introduction of a political system based on the tenets of Islam; leader ABDULLAH UTAYEV 'disappeared' in 1992.

Justice Social Democratic Party of Uzbekistan ('Adolat' Sotsial Demokratik Partiyasi—Adolat): 100047 Tashkent, Musahanov ko'ch. 103; tel. (71) 133-26-75; f. 1995; advocates respect of human rights, improvement of social justice and consolidation of democratic reform; supports President Karimov; First Sec. TURG'UNPO'LAT O. DAMINOV; 50,000 mems (2003).

Liberal Democratic Party of Uzbekistan (O'zbekiston Liberal Demokratik Partiyasi—O'zlidep): 100015 Tashkent, Mirobod tumani, Nukus ko'ch. 73A; tel. (71) 133-28-46; e-mail uzlidep@intal.uz; f. 2003; supports President Karimov; Chair. MUHAMMADJON A. AHMADJONOV; 142,000 members (Dec. 2004).

National Revival Democratic Party of Uzbekistan (O'zbekiston Milliy Tiklanish Demokratik Partiyasi—Milliy Tiklanish): 100000 Tashkent, Navoiy ko'ch. 30; tel. (71) 144-81-28; f. 1995; supports President Karimov; Leader AZIZ KAYUMOV; Chair. of Central Council XURSHID N. DO'STMUHAMMEDOV; 50,000 mems (2003).

People's Democratic Party of Uzbekistan (O'zbekiston Xalq demokratik partiyasi): 100029 Tashkent, Mustaqillik maydoni 5/1; tel. (71) 139-83-11; fax (71) 133-59-34; f. 1991; successor of Communist Party of Uzbekistan; Leader ASLIDDIN A. RUSTAMOV; c. 580,000 mems (2003).

Self-Sacrificers' National Democratic Party (Fidokorlar Milliy Demokratik Partiyasi—Fidokorlar): 100000 Tashkent, Xalqlar Do'stligi ko'ch. 1; tel. (71) 139-45-53; f. 2000; incorporates fmr Watan Taraqqioti (Progress of the Fatherland) party; supports President Karimov; First Sec. AXTAM S. TURSUNOV; 61,000 mems (2003).

Unity People's Movement Party ('Birlik' Xalq Harakati Partiyasi—Birlik): c/o Union of Writers of Uzbekistan, 100000 Tashkent, Neru ko'ch. 1; tel. (71) 233-63-74; e-mail webmaster@birlik.net; internet www.birlik.net; f. 1988; leading opposition group, banned in 1992; registered as a social movement; refused registration as a political party 2004; Chair. Prof. ABDURAKHIM PULAT; Sec.-Gen. VASILA INOYATOVA.

The militant Islamist group **Islamic Movement of Uzbekistan (IMU)** was founded in 1999. It was banned by the Uzbek Government in 1999 and its leaders sentenced to death *in absentia* in 2000. The IMU's activities were believed to have been seriously curtailed after the death of one its leaders during the US-led military campaign in Afghanistan that commenced in late 2001. The transnational militant Islamist **Hizb-ut-Tahrir al-Islami (Party of Islamic Liberation)** was believed to operate in Uzbekistan. In 2004 President Karimov accused the organization of instigating a series of suicide bomb attacks. As in neighbouring states, the organization was proscribed in Uzbekistan. A related organization, **Akramiya**, also banned, was founded in 1996 by AKRAM YULDOSHEV, who was given a 17-year gaol sentence in 1999 for alleged involvement in terrorist activity. Akramiya apparently regards violence as an appropriate means of pursuing its goals.

Diplomatic Representation

EMBASSIES IN UZBEKISTAN

Afghanistan: 100047 Tashkent, Gulomov ko'ch. 73; tel. (71) 234-84-58; fax (71) 234-84-65; e-mail afgemuz@mail.tps.uz; Ambassador FAROOQ BARAKI.

Algeria: 100000 Tashkent, Murtozaev ko'ch. 6; tel. (71) 134-17-74; fax (711) 120-62-75; Ambassador HASEN LASKRI.

Azerbaijan: 100000 Tashkent, Sharq Tongi ko'ch. 25; tel. (71) 173-61-67; fax (71) 173-26-58; e-mail sefir@tsk.sarkor.uz; Ambassador NAMIQ ABBASOV.

Bangladesh: 100015 Tashkent, 1-chi Kunaev ko'ch. 17; tel. (71) 152-26-92; fax (71) 120-67-11; e-mail bdoot.tas@online.ru; Ambassador A. B. M. ABDUS SALAM.

Belarus: 100047 Tashkent, Ya. G'ulomov ko'ch. 75; tel. (71) 120-72-54; fax (71) 120-72-53; e-mail uzbekistan@belembassy.org; internet www.uzbekistan.belembassy.org; Ambassador Dr NIKOLAI N. DEMCHUK.

Bulgaria: 100000 Tashkent, Rakatboshi ko'ch. 52; tel. (71) 158-48-88; fax (71) 152-39-52; e-mail misiyabg@bcc.com.uz; internet www.mfa.bg/tashkent; Chargé d'affaires STOYANKA G. RUSINOVA.

China, People's Republic: 100047 Tashkent, Ya. G'ulomov ko'ch. 79; tel. (71) 133-80-88; fax (71) 133-47-35; e-mail chinaemb@bcc.com.uz; internet uz.china-embassy.org; Ambassador YU HONGJUN.

Czech Republic: 100041 Tashkent, Mirzo-Ulugbek Tumani, Navnihol ko'ch. 6; tel. (71) 120-60-71; fax (71) 120-60-75; e-mail tashkent@embassy.mzv.cz; internet www.mzv.cz/tashkent; Ambassador ALEŠ FOJTÍK.

Egypt: 100115 Tashkent, Chilonzor ko'ch. 53A; tel. (71) 120-50-08; fax (71) 120-64-52; Ambassador NADIA IBRAHIM KFAFI.

France: 100041 Tashkent, Oxunboboev ko'ch. 25; tel. (71) 133-53-82; fax (71) 133-51-97; e-mail presse@ambafrance-uz.org; internet www.ambafrance-uz.org; Ambassador HUGUES PERNET.

Georgia: 100170 Tashkent, A. Muhitdinov ko'ch. 6; tel. (711) 62-62-43; fax (711) 62-91-39; e-mail gruzemb@geo-embassy.co.uz; Chargé d'affaires GIORGI CHKHEIDZE.

Germany: 100017 Tashkent, Sh. Rashidov ko'ch. 15, POB 4337; tel. (71) 120-84-40; fax (71) 120-66-93; e-mail info@taschkent.diplo.de; internet www.taschkent.diplo.de; Ambassador MATTHIAS MEYER.

India: 100000 Tashkent, Qarabulak ko'ch. 15–16; tel. (71) 140-09-83; fax (71) 140-09-99; e-mail indhoc@buzton.com; internet www.indembassy.uz; Ambassador SKAND RANJAN TAYAL.

Indonesia: 100000 Tashkent, Ya. G'ulomov ko'ch. 73; tel. (71) 132-02-36; fax (71) 120-65-40; e-mail tashkent@indonesia.embassy.uz; internet www.indonesia.embassy.uz; Ambassador SJAHRIL SABARUDIN.

Iran: 100007 Tashkent, Parkent ko'ch. 20; tel. (71) 268-69-68; fax (71) 120-67-61; e-mail iriemuz@hotmail.com; Ambassador MOHAMMAD FATHALI.

Israel: 100000 Tashkent, A. Kahhor ko'ch. 3; tel. (71) 140-75-00; fax (71) 140-75-55; e-mail tashkent.mfa.gov.il; internet tashkent.mfa.gov.il; Ambassador AMI MEL.

Italy: 100031 Tashkent, Yusuf Xos Hojib ko'ch. 40; tel. (71) 152-11-19; fax (71) 120-66-06; e-mail segreteria.tashkent@esteri.it; internet www.ambtashkent.esteri.it; Ambassador GIOVANNI RICCIULLI.

Japan: 100047 Tashkent, S. Azimov ko'ch., 1-tor 28; tel. (71) 120-80-60; fax (71) 120-80-77; internet www.uz.emb-japan.go.jp; Ambassador TSYTOMU HIRAOKA.

Jordan: 100000 Tashkent, Farhod ko'ch. 9; tel. (71) 274-24-79; fax (71) 120-66-44; e-mail jordanembuzb@mail.ru; Ambassador MUHAMMAD NOUR OTHMAN YOUSEF BALKAR.

Kazakhstan: 100015 Tashkent, Chekhov ko'ch. 23; tel. (71) 152-16-54; fax (71) 152-16-50; e-mail kazembassy@kaz.uz; Ambassador ASKAR I. MYRZAHMETOV.

Korea, Democratic People's Republic: 100000 Tashkent, Usmon Nosir ko'ch. 95A; tel. (71) 152-63-16; fax (71) 152-63-15; Ambassador RI TONG PHAL.

Korea, Republic: 100000 Tashkent, Afrosiab ko'ch. 7; tel. (71) 152-31-51; fax (71) 120-62-48; e-mail admin1@korea.anet.uz; internet uzb.mofat.go.kr; Ambassador KYUN JE-MIN.

Kuwait: 100000 Tashkent, Batumi ko'ch. 2; tel. (71) 120-58-88; fax (71) 120-84-96; Ambassador VALID AHMAD AL-KANDARI.

Kyrgyzstan: 100000 Tashkent, X. Samatov ko'ch. 30; tel. (71) 137-47-94; fax (71) 120-72-94; e-mail erkindik@sarkor.uz; Ambassador AZIZBEK M. MADMAROV.

Latvia: 100000 Tashkent, A. Lashkarbegi ko'ch. 16A; tel. (71) 137-22-15; fax (71) 120-70-36; e-mail amblatv@bcc.com.uz; Ambassador IGORS APOKINS.

Malaysia: 100031 Tashkent, M. Yaqubov ko'ch. 28–30; tel. (71) 133-32-27; fax (71) 133-32-71; e-mail mwtskent@rol.uz; Ambassador (vacant).

Pakistan: 100115 Tashkent, Kichik Halqa Yoli ko'ch. 15; tel. (71) 148-05-25; fax (71) 144-92-33; e-mail parepuzb@online.ru; Ambassador SAJJAD KAMRAN.

Poland: 100084 Tashkent, Firdavsiy ko'ch. 66; tel. (71) 120-86-50; fax (71) 120-86-51; e-mail ambasada@bcc.com.uz; internet www.taszkent.polemb.net; Chargé d'affaires a.i. JERZY STANKIEWICZ.

Romania: 100000 Tashkent, Rejametov ko'ch. 44A; tel. (71) 152-63-55; fax (71) 120-75-67; e-mail romanian_embassy@sarkor.uz; Ambassador CONSTANTIN ALEXA.

Russia: 100015 Tashkent, Nukus ko'ch. 83; tel. (71) 120-35-04; fax (71) 120-35-09; e-mail rusemb@albatros.uz; internet www.uzbekistan.mid.ru; Ambassador FARIT M. MUKHAMETSHIN.

Saudi Arabia: 100000 Tashkent.

Slovakia: 100070 Tashkent, K. Beshyogoch ko'ch. 38; tel. (71) 120-68-52; fax (71) 120-68-51; e-mail slovakia@buzton.com; internet www.tashkent.mfa.sk; Ambassador JOSEF MAČISÁK.

Switzerland: 100070 Tashkent, U. Nosyr koʻch., tupik 1/4; tel. (71) 120-67-38; fax (71) 120-62-59; e-mail tas.vertretung@eda.admin.ch; internet www.eda.admin.ch/tashkent; Ambassador Dr PETER BURKHARD.

Tajikistan: 100000 Tashkent, A. Kahhor koʻch., 6-chi tor, 61; tel. (71) 254-99-66; fax (71) 254-89-69; e-mail tajembuz@yandex.ru; Ambassador BOBOKHON MAKHMADOV.

Turkey: 100000 Tashkent, Ya. Gʻulomov koʻch. 87; tel. (71) 133-03-00; fax (71) 113-03-33; e-mail turemb@bcc.com.uz; Ambassador RESHIT UMAN.

Turkmenistan: 100000 Tashkent, 1-chi Katta Mirobod koʻch. 10; tel. (71) 120-52-78; fax (71) 120-52-81; Ambassador SOLTAN PIRMUHAMEDOV.

Ukraine: 100000 Tashkent, Ya. Gʻulomov koʻch. 68; tel. (71) 236-08-12; fax (71) 233-10-89; e-mail emb_uz@mfa.gov.ua; internet www.ukraine.uz; Ambassador VYACHESLAV V. POKHVALSKY.

United Kingdom: 100000 Tashkent, ul. Ya. Gʻulomov koʻch. 67; tel. (71) 120-78-52; fax (71) 120-65-49; e-mail brit@emb.uz; internet www.britishembassy.gov.uk/uzbekistan; Ambassador IAIN KELLY.

USA: 100093 Tashkent, Moyqorghon koʻch. 3, Yunusobod District; tel. (71) 120-54-50; fax (71) 120-54-48; e-mail consulartashkent@state.gov; internet www.usembassy.uz; Ambassador RICHARD B. NORLAND.

Viet Nam: 100000 Tashkent, Sh. Rashidov koʻch. 100; tel. (71) 134-03-93; fax (71) 120-62-65; e-mail dsqvntas@online.ru; Ambassador DO VAN DONG.

Judicial System

Supreme Court of the Republic of Uzbekistan
(Oʻzbekistan Respublikasi Oliy sud)
100000 Tashkent, A. Qodiriy koʻch. 1; tel. and fax (71) 144-62-93; internet www.supcourt.gov.uz.
Chairman: FARUHA F. MUHITDINOVA.

Office of the Prosecutor-General: 100000 Tashkent, Ya. Gʻulomov koʻch. 66; tel. (71) 133-20-66; Prosecutor-Gen. RASHIDJON H. QODIROV.

Constitutional Court (Konstitutsiyaviy sud): 100000 Tashkent, Mustaqillik maydoni 6; tel. (71) 139-80-20; fax (71) 139-86-36; e-mail interconcourt@sarkor.uz; Chair. (vacant); Dep. Chair. BAKHTIYAR MIRBABAEV.

Supreme Economic Court (Oliy Xoʻjalik Sudi): 100097 Tashkent, Choʻp onota koʻch. 6; tel. (71) 367-36-18; fax (71) 173-84-78; e-mail economical-court@sarkor.uz; Chair. AMINDJAN D. ISHMETOV.

Religion

The Constitution of 8 December 1992 stipulates that, while there is freedom of worship and expression, there may be no state religion or ideology. A new law on religion was adopted in May 1998, which severely restricted the activities of religious organizations.

The most widespread religion in Uzbekistan is Islam; the majority of ethnic Uzbeks are Sunni Muslims (Hanafi school), but the number of Salafi (often referred to, inaccurately, as Wahhabi) communities is increasing. At 1 October 2002 there were 1,965 Islamic organizations registered in Uzbekistan, including 11 educational institutions. Most ethnic Slavs in Uzbekistan are adherents of Orthodox Christianity: there were 36 Russian Orthodox organizations registered in Uzbekistan at 1 October 2002. At the end of 1993 there were some 32,000 Jews in Uzbekistan; many Jews have since emigrated to Israel.

State Committee for Religious Affairs: 100069 Tashkent, 18-chi Zarqaynar koʻch., tupik 47A; tel. (71) 139-10-14; fax (71) 139-17-63; e-mail info@religions.uz; Chair. SHAAZIM SH. MINAVAROV.

ISLAM

Muslim Board of Central Asia: 100002 Tashkent, Zarkainar koʻch. 103, Madrese 'Barakhan'; tel. (71) 240-39-33; fax (71) 240-08-31; f. 1943 as state body with 'official' spiritual jurisdiction over Muslims in the Kyrgyz, Tajik, Turkmen and Uzbek SSRs; Chair. USMON OLIMOV (Chief Mufti of Mowarounnahr—Central Asia).

CHRISTIANITY

Roman Catholic Church

The Church is represented in Uzbekistan by an Apostolic Administration, established in January 2005. There were an estimated 4,000 adherents at 31 December 2005.

Apostolic Administrator: Most Rev. JERZY MACULEWICZ, 100047 Tashkent, Musahanov koʻch. 80/1; tel. (71) 133-70-25; fax (71) 133-70-35; e-mail adm.ap@agnuz.info.

Russian Orthodox Church (Moscow Patriarchate)

Eparchy of Tashkent and Central Asia (Moscow Patriarchate)—Orthodox Church of Central Asia: 100047 Tashkent, S. Azimov koʻch. 22; tel. (71) 133-33-21; fax (71) 136-79-39; e-mail church@albatros.uz; internet www.pravoslavie.uz; Metropolitan of Tashkent and Central Asia VLADIMIR (IKIM); has jurisdiction over Kyrgyzstan, Tajikistan, Turkmenistan and Uzbekistan.

JUDAISM

Chief Rabbi: Rabbi DAVID GUREVICH, 100100 Tashkent, Shohzhahon koʻch. 30; tel. (71) 152-59-78; fax (71) 120-64-31; e-mail jewish@jewish.uz; internet www.jewish.uz.

The Press

In 1997, according to official statistics, there were 495 newspapers published in Uzbekistan, including 385 published in Uzbek. The average daily circulation was 1,844,200 copies. There were 113 periodicals published, including 90 in Uzbek. Newspapers and periodicals were also published in Russian, Kazakh, Tajik, Korean, Arabic, English and Kara-Kalpak.

The publications listed below are in Uzbek, unless otherwise stated.

REGULATORY AUTHORITY

Uzbek Agency for Press and Information: 100129 Tashkent, Navoiy koʻch. 30; tel. (71) 133-65-03; fax (71) 133-66-45; e-mail info@aci.uz; internet aci.uz; f. 2002; Gen. Dir ABDULLA N. ARIPOV.

PRINCIPAL NEWSPAPERS

Adolat (Justice): 100000 Tashkent, Matbuotchilar koʻch. 32; tel. (71) 133-41-89; f. 1995; organ of the Justice Social Democratic Party of Uzbekistan (Adolat); Editor TOHTAMUROD TOSHEV; circ. 5,900.

Biznes-vestnik Vostoka (Business Bulletin of the East): 100000 Tashkent, Buxoro koʻch. 26; tel. (71) 132-27-30; fax (71) 132-27-29; e-mail info@uzreport.com; f. 1991; 3 a week; in Russian and English; economic and financial news; Editor-in-Chief RALIF NIGMATULLIN (acting); circ. 10,000 (Russian), 1,000 (English).

Fidokor (Self-Sacrificer): 100000 Tashkent, Xalqlar Doʻstligi koʻch. 1; tel. (71) 139-45-53; weekly; organ of the Fidokorlar (Self-Sacrificers') National Democratic Party; Editor JALOLIDDIN SAFAYEV; circ. 32,000.

Hurriyat (Freedom): 100000 Tashkent; tel. (71) 144-25-06; fax (71) 144-36-16; e-mail amir@uzpac.uz; f. 1996; independent; circ. 5,000.

Inson va Qonun (Person and Law): Ministry of Justice, 100047 Tashkent, Sayilgoh koʻch. 5; internet www.minjust.uz/uz/group.scm?groupId=4146; weekly; organ of the Ministry of Justice; Editor-in-Chief SHODIQUL HAMROEV.

Maʻrifat (Enlightenment): 100000 Tashkent, Matbuotchilar koʻch. 32; tel. (71) 133-50-55; e-mail mariat@ars-inform.uz; f. 1931; 2 a week; Editor KHALIM SAIDOV; circ. 33,000 (2006).

Menejer (Manager): 100000 Tashkent, Buyuk Turon koʻch. 41; tel. (71) 136-58-85; f. 1997; weekly; in Russian and Uzbek; commercial information and advertising; Editor KHOTAM ABDURAIMOV; circ. 15,000.

Mulkdor (Property Owner): 100083 Tashkent, Buyuk Turon koʻch. 41; tel. (71) 139-21-96; f. 1994; weekly; Editor-in-Chief MIRODIL ABDURAKHMANOV; circ. 10,000.

Novyi Vek (New Age): 100060 Tashkent, Movarounnaxr koʻch. 19; tel. (71) 133-48-55; fax (71) 133-76-84; f. 1992; fmrly *Kommercheskii Vestnik* (Commerical Herald); in Russian; Editor VALERII NIYAZMATOV; circ. 22,000.

Oʻzbekiston Adabiyoti va Sanʻati (Literature and Art of Uzbekistan): 100000 Tashkent, Matbuotchilar koʻch. 32; tel. (71) 133-52-91; f. 1956; weekly; organ of the Union of Writers of Uzbekistan; Editor AKHMAJON MELIBOYEV; circ. 10,300.

Oʻzbekiston ovozi/Golos Uzbekistana (Voice of Uzbekistan): 100000 Tashkent, Matbuotchilar koʻch. 32; tel. (71) 136-55-15; fax (71) 133-65-45; e-mail info@uzbekistonovozi.uz; internet www.uzbekistonovozi.uz; f. 1918; Uzbek and Russian edns; organ of the People's Democratic Party of Uzbekistan; Editor-in-Chief SAFAR OSTONOV.

Postda/Na postu: 100029 Tashkent, Yu. Rajaby koʻch. 1; f. 1930; Uzbek and Russian; military; Editor Z. ATAYEV.

Pravda Vostoka (Truth of the East): 100000 Tashkent, Matbuotchilar koʻch. 32; tel. (71) 133-56-33; fax (71) 133-70-98; e-mail pvbox@

mail.ru; internet www.pv.uz; f. 1917; 5 a week; in Russian; organ of the Cabinet of Ministers; Editor Abbaskhan Usmanov; circ. 12,000.

Savdogar (Trader): 100000 Tashkent, Buyuk Turon ko'ch. 41; tel. (71) 133-34-55; f. 1992; Editor Muhammad Orazmetov; circ. 17,000.

Soliq va Bojxona Xabarlari: 100011 Tashkent, Abaya ko'ch. 4; tel. (71) 144-02-01; e-mail normapress@mail.ru; f. 1994; weekly; Editor Mikhail Perper; circ. 25,000.

Sport: 100000 Tashkent, O'zbekiston shoh ko'ch. 98 A; tel. (71) 144-07-52; f. 1932; Editor Haydar Akbarov; circ. 8,490.

Toshkent Xakikati/Tashkentskaya Pravda (Tashkent Truth): 100000 Tashkent, Matbuotchilar ko'ch. 32; tel. (71) 133-64-95; fax (71) 133-58-85; internet www.th.uz; f. 1954; 2 a week; Uzbek and Russian edns; Editor Fatkhiddin Mukhitdinov; circ. 19,000 (Uzbek edn), 6,400 (Russian edn).

Turkiston (Turkestan): 100000 Tashkent, Matbuotchilar ko'ch. 32; tel. (71) 136-56-58; f. 1925 as *Yash Leninchy* (Young Leninist), renamed as above 1992; 2 a week; organ of the Kamolot Asscn of Youth of Uzbekistan; Editor Gafar Khatomov; circ. 12,580.

Xalk Suzi/Narodnoye Slovo (People's Word): 100000 Tashkent, Matbuotchilar ko'ch. 32; tel. (712) 133-15-22; e-mail info@narodnoeslovo.uz; internet www.narodnoeslovo.uz; f. 1991; Uzbek and Russian edns; 5 a week (Uzbek), weekly (Russian); organ of the Oly Majlis and the Cabinet of Ministers; Editor Abbaskhon Usmanov; circ. 41,580 (Uzbek edn), 12,750 (Russian edn).

Xamkor (Business Partner): 100077 Tashkent, Buyuk Ipak Yuli 75; tel. (71) 68-72-04; fax (71) 34-64-82; f. 1991; in Uzbek, Russian and English; Editor Ismat Hushev; circ. 20,000.

PRINCIPAL PERIODICALS

Monthly, unless otherwise indicated.

Erk (Freedom): 100055 Tashkent, Ipakchi ko'ch. 38; tel. (71) 120-65-30; e-mail erkgazetasi@yahoo.com; internet www.erkgazetasi.org; organ of Freedom Democratic Party of Uzbekistan (Erk); f. 1991; four a year; Uzbek and Russian edns; circ. 5,300 (2007).

Fan va turmush (Science and Life): 100000 Tashkent, Ya. G'ulomov ko'ch. 70; tel. (71) 133-07-05; f. 1933; every 2 months; publ. by the Fan (Science) Publishing House; popular scientific; Editor Murad Sharifkhojayev; circ. 28,000.

Gulxan (Bonfire): 100000 Tashkent, Buyuk Turon ko'ch. 41; tel. (71) 136-78-85; f. 1929; illustrated juvenile fiction; Editor Safar Barnoyev; circ. 26,000.

Guliston: 100000 Tashkent, Buyuk Turon ko'ch. 41; tel. (71) 136-78-90; f. 1925; present name adopted 1967; every 2 months; sociopolitical, literary; Editor-in-Chief Azim Suyun; circ. 4,000.

Guncha (Small Bud): 100000 Tashkent, Buyuk Turon ko'ch. 41; tel. (71) 136-78-80; f. 1958; illustrated; for pre-school-age children; Editor Erkin Malikov; circ. 35,000.

Jahon Adabiyoti (World Literature): 100129 Tashkent, A. Navoiy ko'ch. 30; tel. (71) 144-41-60; fax (71) 144-41-61; f. 1997; Editor Ozod Sharafiddinov; circ. 2,000.

Mushtum (Fist): 100000 Tashkent, Buyuk Turon ko'ch. 41; tel. (71) 133-99-72; internet www.mushtum.uz; f. 1923; fortnightly; satirical; Editor Ashurali Jurayev; circ. 10,650.

Obshchestvennye Nauki v Uzbekistane (Social Sciences in Uzbekistan): 100047 Tashkent, Ya. G'ulomov ko'ch. 70; tel. (71) 136-73-29; f. 1957; publ. by the Fan (Science) Publishing House of the Academy of Sciences of Uzbekistan; history, oriental studies, archaeology, economics, ethnology, etc.; in Russian and Uzbek; Editor A. Mukhamejanov; circ. 500.

O'zbek Tili va Adabiyoti (Uzbek Language and Literature): 100000 Tashkent, Muminov ko'ch. 9; tel. (71) 262-42-47; f. 1958; every 2 months; publ. by the Fan (Science) Publishing House; journal of the Academy of Sciences of Uzbekistan; history and modern development of the Uzbek language, folklore, etc.; Editor Azim Khajiyev; circ. 3,700.

Saodat (Happiness): 100083 Tashkent, Buyuk Turon ko'ch. 41; tel. (71) 133-68-10; f. 1925; 8 a year; women's popular; Editor Oidin Khajiyeva; circ. 70,000.

Sharq Yulduzi/Zvezda Vostoka (Star of the East): 100000 Tashkent, Buyuk Turon ko'ch. 41; tel. (71) 133-09-18; f. 1932; journal of the Union of Writers of Uzbekistan; fiction; Uzbek and Russian edns; Editor (Uzbek edn) Utkur Khashimov; Editor (Russian edn) Nikolai Krasilnikov; circ. 10,000 (Uzbek edn), 3,000 (Russian edn).

Sikhat Salomatlik (Health): 100000 Tashkent, Parkent ko'ch. 51; tel. (71) 268-17-54; f. 1990; every 2 months; Editor Damin A. Asadov; circ. 36,000.

Tafakkur (Contemplation): 100000 Tashkent, Movaraunnakhr ko'ch.; f. 1994; 4 a year; literary; organ of the (state-controlled) Republican Committee for Spirituality and Enlightenment; Editor-in-Chief Erkin A'zam.

Tong Yulduzi (Morning Star): 100129 Tashkent, A. Navoiy ko'ch. 30; tel. (71) 144-62-34; e-mail ijod@uzpak.uz; internet www.tongyulduzi.uz; f. 1929; weekly; children's; Editor Umida Abduazimova; circ. 60,000.

Yoshlik (Youth): 100000 Tashkent, Buyuk Turon ko'ch. 41; tel. (71) 133-09-18; f. 1932; literature and arts for young people; Editor Sabir Unarov; circ. 10,000.

NEWS AGENCIES

Jahon (World) Information Agency: 100029 Tashkent, O'zbekiston shoh ko'ch. 9; tel. (71) 133-65-91; fax (71) 120-64-43; e-mail aajahon@mfa.uz; internet jahon.mfa.uz; information agency of Ministry of Foreign Affairs; Dir Abror Gulyamov.

Turkiston Press: 100047 Tashkent, Xorazm ko'ch. 51; tel. (71) 133-78-54; fax (71) 133-95-38; e-mail tpress@sarkor.uz; Dir-Gen. Sagdula Hakimov.

Uzbekistan National News Agency (UzA): 100047 Tashkent, Musahanov ko'ch. 38; tel. (71) 133-16-22; fax (71) 133-24-45; internet www.uza.uz; Dir Mamatskul Khazratskulov.

Publishers

Uzbek Agency for Press and Information: 100129 Tashkent, A. Navoiy ko'ch. 30; tel. (71) 144-32-87; fax (71) 144-14-84; e-mail ozmaa@uzpak.uz; internet www.uzapi.gov.uz; f. 2002; mass media, press and information exchange; printing, publishing and distribution of periodicals; Gen. Dir Babur Alimov.

Chulpon (Morning Star) Publishers: 100129 Tashkent, A. Navoiy ko'ch. 30; tel. (71) 139-13-75; fax (71) 144-20-52; e-mail chulpan@sarkor.uz; internet www.chulpon.uz; Dir R. Zaparov.

Fan (Science) Publishers: 100047 Tashkent, Ya. G'ulomov ko'ch. 70/102; tel. (71) 133-69-61; scientific books and journals; Dir N. T. Khatamov.

Gafur Gulom Publishing House: 100129 Tashkent, A. Navoiy ko'ch. 30; tel. (71) 144-22-53; fax (71) 41-35-47; f. 1957; fiction, the arts; books in Uzbek, Russian and English; Dir Mizrob M. Buronov; Editor-in-Chief Nazira J. Jurayevna.

Mekhnat (Labour) Publishers: 100129 Tashkent, A. Navoiy ko'ch. 30; tel. (71) 144-22-27; f. 1985; Dir Rustam A. Mirzayev.

O'qituvchi (Teacher) Publishing-Printing and Creative House: 100129 Tashkent, A. Navoiy ko'ch. 30; tel. and fax (71) 144-26-89; f. 1936; literary textbooks, education manuals, popular science, juvenile; Dir R.O. Mirzayev.

O'zbekiston Milliy Entsiklopediyasi (Uzbekistan National Encyclopedias): 100129 Tashkent, A. Navoiy ko'ch. 30; tel. (71) 144-34-38; fax (71) 144-24-91; e-mail ume2@yandex.ru; internet www.ensiklopediya.uz; f. 1997; encyclopedias, dictionaries and reference books; Dir N. Tukhliyev.

O'zbekiston (Uzbekistan) Publishing and Printing Creative House: 100129 Tashkent, A. Navoiy ko'ch. 30; tel. (71) 144-34-01; fax (71) 144-38-10; e-mail aptpk@ars-inform.uz; f. 2004; politics, economics, law, history and art, illustrated, manuals and textbooks for schools and higher educational institutes; Dir Zair T. Isadjanov; Editor-in-Chief Shomuxitdin Sh. Mansurov.

Yozuvchi (Writer) Publishers: 100129 Tashkent, A. Navoiy ko'ch. 30; tel. (71) 144-29-97; f. 1990; Dir M. U. Toichiyev.

Broadcasting and Communications

TELECOMMUNICATIONS

Communications and Information Agency of Uzbekistan (O'zbekistol Aloqa Va Axborotlashtirish Agentligi): 100011 Tashkent, A. Navoiy ko'ch. 28A; tel. (71) 133-65-03; fax (71) 139-87-82; e-mail info@aci.uz; internet www.aci.uz; Dir-Gen. Abdulla N. Aripov.

Service Providers

Coscom: 100031 Tashkent, V. Vaxidov ko'ch. 118; tel. (71) 152-15-51; fax (71) 120-72-65; e-mail inform@coscom.uz; internet www.coscom.uz; f. 1996; Uzbekistani-US jt venture; mobile cellular telecommunications.

Unitel (Beeline): 100000 Tashkent, Buxoro ko'ch. 1; tel. (71) 133-33-30; fax (71) 132-12-22; internet www.beeline.uz; f. 1996; fmrly Daewoo Unitel; subsidiary of VympelKom-Bilain (Russia); mobile cellular telecommunications; more than 1m. subscribers (2007).

Uzbektelecom: 100000 Tashkent, Amir Temur ko'ch. 24; tel. (71) 133-42-59; fax (71) 136-01-88; e-mail uztelecom@intal.uz; internet www.uztelecom.uz; f. 2000; provides local, regional and interna-

UZBEKISTAN

tional telecommunications services; partial privatization pending; Gen. Dir KH. A. MUKHITDINOV.

Uzdunrobita: 100000 Tashkent, Amir Temur ko'ch. 24; tel. (97) 130-01-01; fax (97) 130-01-05; e-mail office@uzdunrobita.com.uz; internet www.uzdunrobita.uz; f. 1991; mobile cellular telecommunications; 74% owned by Mobile Telesystems (Russia); Gen. Dir BEKHZOD AKHMEDOV.

BROADCASTING

State Television and Radio Broadcasting Company of Uzbekistan (UZTELERADIO): 100011 Tashkent, A. Navoiy ko'ch. 69; tel. (71) 133-81-06; fax (71) 144-16-60; e-mail uztele@tkt.uz; local broadcasts, as well as relays from Egypt, France, India, Japan, Russia and Turkey; Chair. ALISHER KHUJAYEV.

Television

Uzbekistan Television and Radio Company (Uzteleradio): 100011 Tashkent, A. Navoiy ko'ch. 69; tel. (71) 133-81-06; fax (71) 144-16-60; e-mail uztcint@hotmail.com; four local programmes as well as relays from Russia, Kazakhstan, Egypt, India and Turkey; Chair. ALISHER KHADJAYEV.

Kamalak Television: 100084 Tashkent, Amir Temur ko'ch. 109; tel. (71) 137-51-77; fax (71) 120-62-28; e-mail kam.tv@kamalak.co.uz; f. 1992; jt venture between State Television and Radio Broadcasting Company and a US company; satellite broadcasts; relays from France, Germany, India, Russia, the United Kingdom and the USA; Gen. Dir PULAT UMAROV.

Finance

(cap. = capital; res = reserves; dep. = deposits; m. = million; amounts in Uzbek sum, unless otherwise stated; brs = branches)

BANKING

A reform of the banking sector was begun in 1994. A two-tier system was introduced, consisting of the Central Bank and about 30 commercial banks. An association of commercial banks was established in 1995 to co-ordinate the role of commercial banks in the national economy. At the end of 2002 there were reported to be 35 banks in Uzbekistan, of which 13 were under private ownership.

Central Bank

Central Bank of the Republic of Uzbekistan: 100001 Tashkent, O'zbekiston shoh ko'ch. 6; tel. (71) 112-61-94; fax (71) 133-00-44; e-mail webmaster@cbu.st.uz; internet www.cbu.uz; f. 1991; Chair. of Bd FAIZULLA M. MULLAJONOV.

State Commercial Bank

National Bank for Foreign Economic Activity of the Republic of Uzbekistan (NBU) (O'zbekiston Respublikasi Tashqi Iqtisodiy Faoliyat Milliy Banki): 100047 Tashkent, Oxunbabaev ko'ch. 23; tel. (71) 133-62-87; fax (71) 132-01-72; e-mail webmaster@central.nbu.com; internet www.nbu.com; f. 1991; cap. 22,385.7m., res 397,874.6m., dep. 2,276,197.1m. (Dec. 2005); Chair. SAIDAKHMAT B. RAKHIMOV; 95 brs.

State Joint-Stock Commercial Banks

Asaka—Specialized State Joint-Stock Commercial Bank: 100015 Tashkent, Nukus ko'ch. 67; tel. (71) 120-81-11; fax (71) 120-86-91; e-mail contact@asakabank.com; internet www.asakabank.com; f. 1995; cap. US $33.6m., res $15.2m., dep. $205.2m. (Dec. 2005); Chair. SHOKIR J. JURAYEV; 26 brs.

Ipoteka Bank: 100000 Tashkent, Pushkin ko'ch. 17; tel. (71) 133-11-22; fax (71) 132-13-23; e-mail info@ipotekabank.uz; internet www.ipotekabank.uz; f. 2005 by merger of UzJilSberBank and Zaminbank; cap. 15,814.6m., res 16,873.6m., dep. 378,338.7m. (Dec. 2006); Chair. RAVSHAN K. SHARAKHBAROV; 38 brs.

Other Banks

Alokabank: 100015 Tashkent, Oybek ko'ch. 30; tel. (71) 152-78-74; fax (71) 152-78-04; e-mail info@alokabank.uz; internet www.alokabank.uz; f. 1995; cap. 3,481m., res 1,031m., dep. 1,824m. (2004); Chair. FAKHRIDDIN T. YULDASHEV; 11 brs.

HamkorBank: 170111 Andijon, Babura ko'ch. 85; tel. and fax (74) 24-70-39; e-mail hamkorbank@mail.ru; internet www.hamkorbank.uz; f. 1991; Chair. IKRAM IBRAHIMOV; 15 brs.

Ipak Yuli Bank (Silk Road Bank): 100135 Tashkent, Farkod ko'ch. 12A; tel. (71) 120-00-09; fax (71) 120-38-86; e-mail info@ipakyulibank.com; internet www.ipakyulibank.com; f. 2000; Chair. of Bd ALISHER H. MUMINOV; Gen. Man. RUSTAMBEK R. RAHIMBEKOV.

O'zsanoatkurilishbank (Uzpromstroibank) (Uzbek Industrial Construction Bank): 100000 Tashkent, Shaxrisab ko'ch. 3; tel. (71) 133-24-88; fax (71) 132-06-14; e-mail cor_bank@uzpsb.com; internet www.uzpsb.com; f. 1922; cap. 23,843.7m., res 10,871.4m., dep. 485,679.6m. (Dec. 2005); Chair. KIYOMIDDIN K. RUSTAMOV; 47 brs, 79 sub-brs.

Paxta Bank (Pakhta Bank): 100096 Tashkent, Mukimi ko'ch. 43; tel. (71) 278-12-96; fax (71) 120-88-18; e-mail headoffice@pakhtabank.com; internet www.pakhtabank.com; f. 1995; cap. 39,351.7m., res 1,849.3m., dep. 319,035.2m. (Dec. 2006); Chair. ABDURAXMAT BOYMURATOV; 187 brs.

Savdogarbank: 100060 Tashkent, S. Barak ko'ch. 76; tel. (72) 254-19-91; fax (71) 256-56-71; internet www.savdogarbank.uz; Chair. MURSURMON N. NURMAMATOV.

Tadbirkor Bank: 100047 Tashkent, S. Azimov ko'ch. 52; tel. (71) 133-18-75; fax (71) 136-88-32; f. 2006; micro-credit bank; Chair. MUZAFFARBEK SABIROV.

Trustbank: 100038 Tashkent, A. Navoiy ko'ch. 7; tel. (71) 144-76-21; fax (71) 144-76-61; e-mail info@trustbank.uz; internet www.trustbank.uz; f. 1994; cap. 4,395.3m., res −103.2m., dep. 75,646.4m. (Dec. 2006); Chair. ILHOM F. SOLIYEV; 2 brs.

Turonbank: 100011 Tashkent, Abay 4A; tel. (71) 700-55-55; fax (71) 144-25-81; e-mail info@turonbank.uz; internet www.turonbank.uz; f. 1990; cap. US $4m., res $0.5m., dep. $8.2m. (2007); Chair. of Bd DANIYOR B. ARIFJANOV; 18 brs.

Uzbekistan-Turkish UT Bank: 100043 Tashkent, Xalqlar Do'stligi ko'ch. 15B; tel. (71) 173-83-25; fax (71) 120-63-62; e-mail utbank@utbk.com; internet www.utbk.com; f. 1993; 50% owned by Paxta Bank, 50% owned by Türkiye Cumhuriyeti Ziraat Bankası (Agricultural Bank of the Turkish Republic); cap. 2,909.2m., res 278.7m., dep. 10,214.7m. (Dec. 2005); Chair. AZIM TANGIRBERDIYEV.

INSURANCE

Ark Sug'urta: 100000 Tashkent, Pushkin ko'ch. 88; tel. (71) 140-03-69; fax (71) 267-70-28; e-mail info@arksugurta.uz; internet www.arksugurta.uz; f. 1991; life and non-life; Dir-Gen. ZAFAR O. TURSUNOV.

Ishonch: 100027 Tashkent, Xojaev ko'ch. 1A; tel. and fax (71) 138-69-55; internet www.ishonch-iic.uz; f. 1996; life and non-life; Dir-Gen. MIRSHAMSIDDIN M. XIKMATILLAEV.

Kalofat: 100000 Tashkent, Mustaqillik maydoni 5, 9th floor; tel. (71) 133-26-98; fax (71) 133-38-49; internet www.kalofatdask.uz; f. 1997; life and non-life; Dir-Gen. SHERALI B. IMAMOV.

O'zbekinvest (Uzbekinvest) National Export–Import Insurance Co: 100017 Tashkent, Suleimanov ko'ch. 49; tel. (71) 133-05-56; fax (71) 133-07-04; e-mail root@unic.gov.uz; internet www.unic.gov.uz; f. 1994, restructured 1997; jt venture with American International Group (AIG—USA); cap. US $60m.; Dir-Gen. SUNNAT A. UMAROV; Chief Exec. NODIR KALANDAROV.

Standard Insurance Group: 100015 Tashkent, Kunaev ko'ch 25; tel. (71) 150-99-99; fax (71) 120-31-13; e-mail office@sig-insurance.uz; internet www.sig-insurance.uz; f. 2005; non-life; Dir-Gen. UMUD U. KAMILOV.

Temir Yo'llari Sug'urta: 100060 Tashkent, Shevchenko ko'ch 7; tel. (71) 138-86-27; fax (71) 138-85-97; e-mail tys_KDilshod@mail.ru; internet www.tysugurta.sk.uz; f. 2002; non-life; Chair of Bd YOKUBZHON YU. MUHAMMEDOV; Dir-Gen. DILSHOD A. KADYROV.

COMMODITY EXCHANGE

Tashkent Republican Commodity and Raw Materials Exchange: 100003 Tashkent, O'zbekiston shoh ko'ch. 53; tel. (71) 139-83-77; fax (71) 139-83-92; Chair. of Bd NABIHON S. SAMATOV.

STOCK EXCHANGE

Tashkent Republican Stock Exchange (UZSE) (Respublika Fond Birjasi 'Toshkent'): 100047 Tashkent, Buxoro ko'ch. 10; tel. (71) 136-76-13; fax (71) 133-32-31; e-mail gairat@uzse.uz; internet www.uzse.uz; f. 1994; stocks and securities; Chair. BAKHTIYOR I. KHUDOYAROV.

Trade and Industry

GOVERNMENT AGENCIES

Foreign Investment Agency: 100077 Tashkent, Buyuk Ipak Yulli ko'ch. 75; tel. (71) 68-77-05; fax (71) 67-07-52; e-mail afi@mail.uznet.net; Gen. Dir SHAZIYATOV S. SHOAZIZ.

State Committee for De-monopolization and the Development of Competition (O'zbekiston Respublikasi Monopoliadan Chiqarish va Raqobatni Rivojlantirish Davlat Qo'mitasi): 100011 Tashkent, A. Navoiy ko'ch. 18A; tel. (71) 139-15-42; e-mail devonhona@antimon.uz; internet www.antimon.uz; Chair. BAIMUROD S. ULASHOV (acting).

State Committee for the Management of State Property and Support of Entrepreneurship (State Property Committee): 100003 Tashkent, O'zbekiston shoh ko'ch. 55; tel. (71) 139-44-46; fax (71) 139-14-84; e-mail ves@spc.gov.uz; internet www.spc.gov.uz; Chair. MAKHMUDJON A. ASKAROV.

CHAMBER OF COMMERCE

Chamber of Commerce and Industry of Uzbekistan (O'zbekiston Respublikasi Savdo-Sanoat Palatasi): 100047 Tashkent, Buxoro ko'ch. 6; tel. (71) 133-06-99; fax (71) 132-09-03; e-mail info@chamber.uz; internet www.chamber.uz; f. 1996 as Chamber of Commodity Producers and Entrepeneurs of Uzbekistan; re-established and renamed as above by presidential decree 2004; provides assistance, consultancy and support for businesses; Chair. ALISHER SHAIHOV.

STATE HYDROCARBONS COMPANY

Uzbekneftegaz (Uzbekistani Petroleum and Natural Gas Co): 100047 Tashkent, Akhunbabayev ko'ch. 21; tel. (71) 133-57-57; fax (71) 136-77-71; e-mail nhk@uzneftegaz.uz; internet www.uzneftegaz.uz; f. 1999; national petroleum and gas corpn; Chair. of Bd NURMUHAMMAD A. AHMETOV.

TRADE UNIONS

Federation of Trade Unions of Uzbekistan: 100000 Tashkent; Chair. of Council KHULKAR JAMALOV.

Transport

RAILWAYS

Uzbekistan's railway network is connected to those of the neighbouring republics of Kazakhstan, Kyrgyzstan, Tajikistan and Turkmenistan, and to that of Russia. There were 3,645 km of track in 2007.

O'zbekiston Temir Yo'llari (Uzbekistan State Railway Co): 100060 Tashkent, T. Shevchenko ko'ch. 7; tel. (71) 138-80-00; fax (71) 133-45-49; e-mail uzrailway@uzpak.uz; internet www.uzrailway.uz; f. 1994; state-owned joint-stock co.; Chair. of Bd ACHILBAY ZH. RAMATOV.

Toshkent metropoliteni (Tashkent Metro): 100027 Tashkent, O'zbekiston shoh ko'ch. 93A; tel. (71) 232-38-52; fax (71) 133-66-81; e-mail metro@sarkor.uz; f. 1977; three lines with total length of 36 km, and fourth line due to open by 2010; Chair. M. A. ODILOV.

ROADS

In 1999 the total length of the road network was estimated at 81,600 km, of which 87.3% was paved.

INLAND WATERWAYS

The extensive use of the waters of the Amu Dar'ya and Syr Dar'ya for irrigation lessened the flow of these rivers and caused the desiccation of the Aral Sea. This reduced a valuable transport asset. However, the Amu Dar'ya Steamship Co still operates important river traffic.

CIVIL AVIATION

There is an international airport at Tashkent. From 1996 the airports at Samarqand, Urgench and Buxoro were upgraded to stimulate tourism.

Uzbekistan Airways (Uzbekiston Havo Yollari): 100061 Tashkent, ul. Proletarskaya 41; tel. (71) 291-14-90; fax (71) 232-73-71; e-mail info@uzbekistan-airways.com; internet www.airways.uz; f. 1992; operates flights between Uzbekistan and destinations in Central Asia, South-East Asia, the USA, the Middle East and Europe; Dir-Gen. RAFIKOV GANIY; Gen. Dir VALERIY TYAN.

Tourism

Since independence Uzbekistan has sought to promote tourism as an important source of revenue. The republic has more than 4,000 historical monuments, many of which are associated with the ancient 'Silk Route', particularly the cities of Samarqand (Tamerlane's capital), Xiva (Khiva) and Buxoro (Bukhara), as well as other historic sites. Infrastructural limitations, however, have constrained development. In 2004 Uzbekistan received an estimated 261,600 foreign visitors (including excursionists). In that year tourism receipts totalled some US $57m.

Uzbektourism: 100047 Tashkent, Xorazm ko'ch. 47; tel. (71) 233-54-14; fax (71) 233-80-68; f. 1992; Chair. ZAHID L. XAKIMOV.

VANUATU

Introductory Survey

Location, Climate, Language, Religion, Flag, Capital

The Republic of Vanuatu comprises an irregular archipelago of 83 islands in the south-west Pacific Ocean, lying about 1,000 km (600 miles) west of Fiji and 400 km (250 miles) north-east of New Caledonia. The group extends over a distance of about 1,300 km (808 miles) from north to south. The islands have an oceanic tropical climate, with a season of south-east trade winds between May and October. Winds are variable, with occasional cyclones for the rest of the year, and annual rainfall varies between 2,300 mm (90 ins) in the south and 3,900 mm (154 ins) in the north. In Port Vila, in the centre of the group, mean temperatures vary between 22°C (72°F) and 27°C (81°F). The national language is Bislama, ni-Vanuatu pidgin. There are many Melanesian languages and dialects. English, French and Bislama are the official languages. Most of the inhabitants (about 80%) profess Christianity, of which a number of denominations are represented. The national flag (proportions 3 by 5) consists of two equal horizontal stripes, red above green, on which are superimposed a black-edged yellow horizontal 'Y' (with its base in the fly) and, at the hoist, a black triangle containing two crossed yellow mele leaves encircled by a curled yellow boar's tusk. The capital is Port Vila, on the island of Efate.

Recent History

During the 19th century the New Hebrides (now Vanuatu) were settled by British and French missionaries, planters and traders. The United Kingdom and France established a Joint Naval Commission for the islands in 1887. The two countries later agreed on a joint civil administration, and in 1906 the territory became the Anglo-French Condominium of the New Hebrides (Nouvelles-Hébrides). Under this arrangement, there were three elements in the structure of administration: the British National Service, the French National Service and the Condominium (Joint) Departments. Each power was responsible for its own citizens and other non-New Hebrideans who chose to be '*ressortissants*' of either power. Indigenous New Hebrideans were not permitted to claim either British or French citizenship. This resulted in two official languages, two police forces, three public services, three courts of law, three currencies, three national budgets, two resident commissioners in Port Vila (the capital) and two district commissioners in each of the four Districts.

Local political initiatives began after the Second World War, originating in New Hebridean concern over the alienation of native land. More than 36% of the New Hebrides was owned by foreigners. Na-Griamel, one of the first political groups to emerge, had its source in cult-like activities. In 1971 the leaders of Na-Griamel petitioned the UN to prevent further sales of land at a time when areas were being sold to US interests for development as tropical tourist resorts. In 1972 the New Hebrides National Party was formed, with support from Protestant missions and covert support from British interests. In response, French interests formed the Union des Communautés Néo-Hébridaises in 1974. Discussions in the United Kingdom in 1974 resulted in the replacement of the Advisory Council, established in 1957, by a Representative Assembly of 42 members, of whom 29 were directly elected in November 1975. The Assembly did not hold its first full working session until November 1976, and it was dissolved in early 1977, following a boycott by the National Party, which had changed its name to the Vanuaaku Pati (VP) in 1976. However, the VP reached an agreement with the Condominium powers on new elections for the Representative Assembly, based on universal suffrage for all seats.

In 1977, at a conference in France involving British, French and New Hebridean representatives, it was announced that the islands would become independent in 1980, following a referendum and elections. The VP boycotted this conference, as it demanded immediate independence. The VP also boycotted the elections in November 1977, and declared a 'People's Provisional Government'. Nevertheless, a reduced Assembly of 39 members was elected, and a measure of self-government was introduced in early 1978. A Council of Ministers and the office of Chief Minister (occupied by Georges Kalsakau) were created, and the French, British and Condominium Services began to be replaced by a single New Hebrides Public Service. In December a Government of National Unity was formed, with Fr Gérard Leymang as Chief Minister and Fr Walter Lini (the VP President) as Deputy Chief Minister.

At elections in November 1979 the VP won 26 of the 39 seats in the Assembly. The outcome of the election led to rioting by supporters of Na-Griamel on the island of Espiritu Santo, who threatened non-Santo 'foreigners'. However, the new Assembly elected Lini as Chief Minister.

In June 1980 Jimmy Stevens, the leader of Na-Griamel, declared Espiritu Santo independent of the rest of the New Hebrides, styling it the 'Independent State of Vemarana'. Members of his movement, allegedly assisted by French *colons* and supported by private US business interests, moved to the coast and imprisoned government officers and police, who were later released together with other European and indigenous public servants. British Royal Marines were deployed as a peace-keeping force, prompting strong criticism by the French authorities, which would not permit Britain's unilateral use of force on Espiritu Santo.

However, in mid-July 1980 agreement was reached between the two Condominium powers and Lini, and the New Hebrides became independent within the Commonwealth, under the name of Vanuatu, as planned, on 30 July. The first President was the former Deputy Chief Minister, George Kalkoa, who adopted the surname Sokomanu ('leader of thousands'), although the post was largely ceremonial. Lini became Prime Minister. The Republic of Vanuatu signed a defence pact with Papua New Guinea, and in August units of the Papua New Guinea Defence Force replaced the British and French troops on Espiritu Santo and arrested the Na-Griamel rebels.

At a general election in November 1983 the VP retained a majority in Parliament, taking 24 of the 39 seats. Sokomanu remained as President. In February 1984 Sokomanu resigned as President, after pleading guilty in court to the late payment of road taxes, but he was re-elected in the following month. In October 1987 the Government expelled the French ambassador (see below). The envoy was alleged to have provided 'substantial financial assistance' to the opposition Union of Moderate Parties (UMP). Parliament was expanded to 46 seats for the general election held in December. Of these, the VP won 26 seats, the UMP 19 and the Fren Melanesia one. Following the election, the Secretary-General of the VP, Barak Sope, unsuccessfully challenged Lini for the party presidency, but later accepted a portfolio in the Council of Ministers

In May 1988 a government decision to abolish a local land corporation, which had been a principal source of patronage for Sope, prompted a demonstration in Port Vila by Sope's supporters. Serious rioting ensued, in which one person was killed and several others injured. Lini accused Sope of being instrumental in provoking the riots, and subsequently dismissed him from the Council of Ministers. In July Sope and four colleagues resigned from the VP, and were subsequently dismissed from Parliament at Lini's behest. In addition, 18 members of the UMP were dismissed after they had boycotted successive parliamentary sittings in protest at the expulsions. In September Sope and his colleagues announced the formation of a new political party, the Melanesian Progressive Pati (MPP), and in October the VP expelled 128 of its own members for allegedly supporting the new party. In October the Court of Appeal ruled as unconstitutional the dismissal from Parliament of Sope and his colleagues, and reinstated them, but upheld the expulsion of the 18 members of the UMP. In November Sope resigned from Parliament, citing loss of confidence in its Speaker. In December President Sokomanu dissolved Parliament and announced that Sope would act as interim Prime Minister, pending a general election scheduled for February 1989. Lini immediately denounced Sokomanu's actions, and the Governments of Australia, New Zealand and Papua New Guinea refused to recognize the interim Government. The islands' police force remained loyal to Lini, and later in December Sokomanu, Sope and other members of the interim Government were arrested and charged with treason. In 1989

Sokomanu was sentenced to six years' imprisonment, and Sope and the then leader of the parliamentary opposition, Maxime Carlot Korman, were jailed for five-year terms, for seditious conspiracy and incitement to mutiny. However, representatives of the International Commission of Jurists, who had been present at the trials, criticized the rulings, and in April the Court of Appeal overturned the original judgment, citing insufficient evidence for the convictions. Fred Timakata, the former Minister of Health, replaced Sokomanu as President in January 1989.

Diminishing support for Lini's leadership led to the approval in August 1991 of a motion of no confidence in Lini as party leader at the VP's congress. Donald Kalpokas, the Secretary-General of the VP, was unanimously elected to replace Lini as President of the party. In September a motion of no confidence in the premiership of Lini was narrowly approved in Parliament, and Kalpokas was elected Prime Minister. Subsequently, Lini, with the support of a substantial number of defectors from the VP, formed the National United Party (NUP). At a general election in December the UMP secured 19 seats, while the VP and NUP each won 10 seats, the MPP four and Tan Union, Fren Melanesia and Na-Griamel one each. The leader of the UMP, Maxime Carlot Korman, was appointed Prime Minister, and a coalition Government was formed between the UMP and the NUP.

At a presidential election in February 1994 neither the UMP's candidate, Fr Luc Dini, nor Fr John Bani, who was supported by the opposition, attained the requisite two-thirds of total votes cast. The election was rescheduled for March. The VP subsequently agreed to vote with the ruling UMP, in return for a guaranteed role in a future coalition government. As a result of this agreement, the UMP's candidate, Jean-Marie Leye, was elected to the presidency with 41 votes. The VP subsequently withdrew its support for the UMP when Carlot refused to offer the party more than one ministerial post; the VP had requested three.

In May 1994 the 'breakaway' members of the NUP who had remained in their ministerial posts, Sethy Regenvanu, Edward Tabisari and Cecil Sinker, were expelled from the party. They subsequently formed a new grouping, the People's Democratic Party (PDP), and later that month signed an agreement with the UMP to form a new coalition Government, the third since the election of December 1991. The UMP-PDP coalition held a total of 26 legislative seats.

In October 1994 the Supreme Court granted the Government a restraining order against further actions by the President, pending the hearing of an application to the Supreme Court to overrule several of the President's recent decisions. Members of the Government and judiciary had become increasingly alarmed by Leye's exercise of his presidential powers, which had included orders to free 26 criminals (many of whom had been convicted on extremely serious offences) and to appoint a convicted criminal to the position of Police Commissioner (on the recommendation of the Prime Minister).

In April 1995 Carlot attracted severe criticism from the Vanuatu-based regional news agency, Pacnews, when he dismissed two senior government officials for making comments critical of the Government; moreover, the journalists who reported the comments were threatened with dismissal. The Prime Minister's increasing reputation for intolerance of criticism was compounded by allegations that, as part of his Government's policy of reducing the number of employees in the public service, civil servants believed to be opposition sympathizers were among the first to lose their jobs.

At a general election held in November 1995, the Unity Front coalition won 20 of the 50 seats in the newly enlarged Parliament and the UMP secured 17 seats. A period of intense political manoeuvring followed the election, as the two main parties sought to form coalitions with other members in an attempt to secure a parliamentary majority. The situation was compounded by the emergence of two factions within the UMP, one comprising the supporters of Carlot and another led by Serge Vohor (the party's President). The Carlot faction of the UMP and the Unity Front both sought the political allegiance of the NUP. The latter's decision to accept the offer of a coalition with the UMP effectively excluded the Unity Front (the grouping with the largest number of seats) from Government, and, in protest, its members boycotted the opening of Parliament in December, thus preventing a vote on the formation of a new government taking place. At a subsequent parliamentary session Vohor was elected as Prime Minister, despite continuing allegations of irregularities in the election of senior members of Government.

In early February 1996 seven dissident UMP members of Parliament proposed a motion of no confidence in Vohor, supported by 22 other opposition members. However, Vohor announced his resignation as Prime Minister, thus preventing the vote from taking place. A parliamentary session to elect a new premier was abandoned as a result of a boycott by supporters of Vohor, who was reported to have retracted his resignation. However, at a further sitting, Carlot was elected Prime Minister.

In July 1996 a report published by the national ombudsman revealed a serious financial scandal, involving the issuing of 10 bank guarantees with a total value of US $100m. The Minister of Finance, Barak Sope, who had issued the guarantees in April, had been persuaded by an Australian financial adviser, Peter Swanson, that the scheme could earn the country significant revenue. Swanson, who left Vanuatu after securing the guarantees, was subsequently traced and charged with criminal offences relating to his dealings with Sope. (In February 1998 the Supreme Court found Swanson guilty on seven charges arising from the scandal, sentencing him to 18 months' imprisonment.) Carlot, meanwhile, rejected demands for his resignation for his compliance with the scheme and resisted considerable pressure to dismiss Sope and the Governor of the Reserve Bank of Vanuatu. In the following month, however, Sope was dismissed following his defection to the opposition.

In an attempt to restore a measure of political stability, Carlot appealed for reconciliation among the various political groups in the country in August 1996 and invited members of the opposition to join the Government. The opposition responded by reiterating its demand for Carlot's resignation, and in September a motion of no confidence in the Government was approved and Vohor was elected Prime Minister. Vohor's coalition Government comprised the pro-Vohor faction of the UMP, the NUP, the MPP, Tan Union and Fren Melanesia. A new Council of Ministers, in which Sope was appointed Deputy Prime Minister, was announced in mid-October.

A dispute over unpaid allowances, dating from 1993, led members of the 300-strong Vanuatu Mobile Force (VMF—the country's paramilitary force) briefly to abduct the President and Deputy Prime Minister to demand a settlement. Both Leye and Sope expressed sympathy for the VMF members. Sope was replaced as Deputy Prime Minister by Donald Kalpokas, and Fr Walter Lini was appointed Minister of Justice. Following a further incident in November in connection with the pay dispute, in which an official from the Department of Finance was abducted and allegedly assaulted, Lini ordered the arrest of more than half of the members of the VMF. About 30 members were detained and charged with criminal offences. In June 1999 18 VMF members were charged with the alleged kidnapping of a number of government officers in 1996. One was found guilty and was to be referred to a court martial for sentencing.

In March 1997 a memorandum of agreement was signed between the VP, the NUP and the UMP, the three parties of the newly formed governing coalition. However, the defection in May of five NUP members of Parliament, including two cabinet ministers, to the VP led to the party's expulsion from the Government. As a result, a new coalition, comprising the UMP, the MPP, Tan Union and Fren Melanesia, was formed. The subsequent designation of a new Cabinet was controversial for the appointment of Sope to the position of Deputy Prime Minister and Minister of Commerce, Trade and Industry. Sope had been described in January by the national ombudsman, Marie-Noëlle Ferrieux-Patterson (in a further report on the financial scandal of the previous year), as unfit for public office. Ferrieux-Patterson also criticized the recent appointment of Willie Jimmy as Minister of Finance.

In July 1997 legal action was initiated to recover the estimated US $300,000 of public funds paid in 1993 by Jimmy, together with Carlot, as compensation to the 23 members dismissed from Parliament following their boycott of the legislature in 1988. In the same month it was reported that the Government was preparing to amend legislation governing the powers of the ombudsman, in an attempt to contain her increasingly vociferous criticism of certain public figures.

In September 1997 Vohor dismissed Jimmy from his position as Minister of Finance, apparently owing to a dispute between Jimmy and the Prime Minister over the latter's decision to remove several areas of responsibility from the Finance portfolio. Meanwhile, further allegations of financial impropriety were published by the ombudsman, this time concerning the illegal sale of ni-Vanuatu passports to foreign nationals. In September the Prime Minister ordered an investigation into the matter. With both Vohor and Jimmy alleging the involvement of the other, the dispute intensified the disunity within the UMP, which had now come to comprise three factions, led respectively by Vohor, Carlot and Jimmy.

In November 1997 Parliament approved legislation to repeal the Ombudsman Act and the Government announced that it was to establish a commission of inquiry to determine if the ombudsman had exceeded her constitutional powers. However, President Leye refused to promulgate the new law on the grounds that it was unconstitutional, and he referred it to the Supreme Court. Later in the month Carlot filed a motion of no confidence in Vohor's Government. When Vohor attempted to withdraw all proposed legislation in order to prevent debate on the motion, Leye announced the dissolution of Parliament. However, the Supreme Court revived the parliamentary session in December. The matter was referred to the Court of Appeal, and Vohor and Carlot agreed to co-operate temporarily pending its judgment, which was eventually delivered in January 1998 and which once again ordered the immediate dissolution of Parliament. Following Leye's announcement of a forthcoming general election, Carlot announced the formation of the Vanuatu Republikan Pati (VRP). Meanwhile, Ferrieux-Patterson released a report in December 1997 in which she recommended that Vohor be investigated for offences relating to the illegal sale of ni-Vanuatu passports. The release of outspoken reports by the ombudsman continued into early 1998 and was widely believed to have contributed significantly to the domination of the election campaign by allegations of government corruption.

At a general election held on 6 March 1998, the VP won 18 of the 52 seats in the newly enlarged Parliament, the UMP secured 12, the NUP won 11, the MPP obtained six, the John Frum Movement secured two, the VRP obtained one, and independent candidates won two seats. In mid-March the VP and the NUP agreed to form a coalition Government, with the support of Carlot (the VRP's sole representative) and one independent member. At the end of the month Donald Kalpokas was elected Prime Minister with 35 parliamentary votes, defeating Vohor (who secured 17). Kalpokas also assumed three ministerial portfolios, including that for Foreign Affairs, while Lini, who was appointed to the revived post of Deputy Prime Minister, also became Minister of Justice and Internal Affairs.

In June 1998, despite strong opposition, notably from the UMP, Parliament approved a new 'leadership code'. Regarded as a crucial element in ensuring greater accountability and transparency in public life, the code defined clear guide-lines for the conduct of state officials (including a requirement that all public figures submit an annual declaration of assets to Parliament), and laid down strict penalties for those convicted of corruption. Shortly before, the Supreme Court upheld the repeal of the Ombudsman Act, as approved by Parliament in November 1997. The Kalpokas Government emphasized its commitment to strengthening the role of the ombudsman, stating that new legislation governing the office would be prepared. Although the ombudsman was to continue to function in the mean time, in early August 1998 Ferrieux-Patterson issued a statement in which she expressed concern that her powers of jurisdiction had been diminished.

In October 1998 Kalpokas expelled the NUP from the governing coalition, following reports that Lini (who died in February 1999), the party's leader, had organized a series of meetings with prominent members of the opposition, with the aim of forming a new coalition government which would exclude the VP. NUP ministers were largely replaced by members of the UMP faction led by Jimmy, which included the Deputy President of the party, Vincent Boulekone, and its Secretary-General, Henri Taga; one ministerial post was allocated to the John Frum Movement. In March 1999 Fr John Bani was chosen by the electoral college to succeed Jean-Marie Leye as President of Vanuatu.

The issue of press freedom returned to the fore in May 1999 when the Pacific Islands News Association expressed concern at the alleged assault on a local newspaper publisher by an associate of the Deputy Prime Minister, Willie Jimmy. Jimmy was reportedly displeased with the newspaper's coverage of an election campaign. The news association urged the Government to act against the increasing number of cases of media intimidation on the island.

The governing coalition was threatened in August 1999 by a decision by the National Council of the UMP to oppose participation in the Government. The Council issued a directive to the 17 members of Jimmy's faction to resign from the Kalpokas administration. Following their refusal to comply with the directive, the National Council acted to suspend the members in October. However, later that month the suspensions were overruled by the Supreme Court. The two factions of the UMP had previously attempted reunification but negotiations had stalled over the demands of Vohor's faction for two of the four ministerial positions held by Jimmy's faction. (The UMP achieved reunification in November 2000.)

At the end of August 1999 four by-elections took place, three of which were won by opposition parties, thus eliminating the Government's majority in Parliament. In November the Government staged a boycott of Parliament to avoid a proposed vote of no confidence by opposition parties against the Kalpokas administration. However, the subsequent defection to the opposition of an independent representative, followed by that of the Minister of Health, forced the resignation of Kalpokas prior to a no confidence motion on 25 November. The Speaker, Edward Natapei, announced his resignation shortly afterwards and Paul Ren Tari of the NUP was elected as his replacement. The leader of the MPP, Barak Sope, was elected to lead a new Government the same day; he secured 28 votes compared with the 24 votes gained by Natapei as the newly appointed President of the VP. Sope formed a five-party coalition Government, comprising the MPP, the NUP, the Vohor faction of the UMP, the VRP and the John Frum Movement. The composition of the new Council of Ministers was swiftly announced; it included Vohor as Minister of Foreign Affairs and Carlot as Minister of Lands and Mineral Resources, both of whom, with Sope, had been the subject of critical reports by the ombudsman. The new Government pledged to reduce the country's dependence on foreign advisers, review the recently introduced value-added tax and ensure that adequate services were delivered to rural communities.

In May 2000 Parliament approved controversial legislation (the Public Services Amendment Bill and the Government Amendment Bill) giving the Government direct power to appoint and dismiss public servants. The opposition criticized the changes, claiming that they contravened the principles of the Comprehensive Reform Programme (a range of economic measures supported by the Asian Development Bank—ADB). President John Bani subsequently referred both pieces of legislation to the Supreme Court, which, in August, ordered that he approve them. The ADB reacted angrily to the development, arguing that it allowed for political bias in the public sector, and threatened to withhold further funds from Vanuatu. The bank's stance served to perpetuate an ongoing dispute between the organization and the Vanuatu Government, which had often expressed the view that the bank imposed harsh conditions in return for its finance.

An incident in August 2000 in which the Deputy Prime Minister, Reginald Stanley, was allegedly involved in the serious assault of two people and in causing criminal damage to property while under the influence of alcohol led to Stanley's dismissal from the post. He was replaced by the Minister of Trade Development, James Bule.

In September 2000 the opposition leader, Edward Natapei, invited the Vohor faction of the UMP to join the opposition and form a new government. Vohor declined the offer, saying that his priority was the stability of the current Government. The resignation of a VP member in October prevented the success of a motion of no confidence in the Prime Minister. Also in October the Government was forced to defend a controversial plan, which allowed a Thai company, Apex, to pay off a portion of government debt, allegedly in return for 'tax-haven' privileges. The President of Apex, Amarendra Nath Ghosh, was also Vanuatu's recently appointed honorary consul to Thailand. In January 2001 the Government deported Mark Neil-Jones, the publisher of the independent newspaper, *Trading Post*, on the grounds of instigating instability in the country. (The *Trading Post* had recently published several critical articles about the Government, including reports on the Government's financial dealings with Nath Ghosh.) However, the Supreme Court reversed the decision, declaring that the deportation order was illegal, and Neil-Jones was allowed to return to the country. An investigation was subsequently launched into the circumstances of the deportation.

In late January 2001 three members of the UMP resigned from the party, further reducing the Government's majority. The Government's problems intensified in March after the withdrawal of the UMP from the ruling coalition. Opposition attempts to vote on a motion of no confidence were delayed as

Sope initiated legal action against the motion, and the Speaker, Paul Ren Tari, refused to allow the vote while legal action was pending. The Chief Justice, however, ordered the vote to proceed, and after further postponements by the Speaker, the Sope Government was voted out of office in mid-April. A new Government, led by Edward Natapei of the VP, was elected. The incoming administration, a coalition of the VP and UMP, was duly sworn in, and pledged to continue the reform programme and to restore investor confidence. One of the Government's first acts was to remove Nath Ghosh from his diplomatic position. Vohor was appointed Deputy Prime Minister. In early May Parliament held an extraordinary session to debate a motion to remove Ren Tari as Speaker because of his conduct during the political crisis. Ren Tari responded by suspending Natapei, along with five other Members of Parliament who held cabinet posts, for breaching parliamentary procedure. Despite an order by the Chief Justice that they be allowed to return to Parliament to continue the extraordinary session, Ren Tari refused to open the legislature while he appealed to the Supreme Court against the order. In response, Ren Tari and his two deputies were arrested and charged with sedition. A new Speaker, Donald Kalpokas, President of the UMP, was elected, thus reducing Natapei's majority in Parliament to one. In September 2001 opposition leader Sope tabled a motion of no confidence against the ruling coalition but was defeated.

In November 2001 Sope was ordered to appear in court to answer charges that he had forged two government-supported Letters of Guarantee, worth US $23m., while he was Prime Minister. It was reported that police were also investigating the activities of the former Minister of Finance, Morkin Steven, whose signature appeared on the documents. Meanwhile, Sope was under investigation for possible involvement in the illegal issuing of diplomatic passports and in connection with allegations of bribery. The preliminary hearing of the forgery charges was postponed until February 2002, enabling Sope to contest the general election due to take place later in that year.

In March 2002 Parliament was dissolved after the Supreme Court ruled that its four-year term had expired. Prime Minister Natapei remained in charge of an interim Government until the general election, scheduled for early May. Also in March it was announced that the newly established People's Progressive Party (PPP) and Fren Melanesia were to form a coalition with the ruling NUP to contest the forthcoming election. It was reported that the general election was to be monitored by an independent group of observers. The future of the Comprehensive Reform Programme was widely perceived to be the main issue in the electoral campaign.

The general election was held on 2 May 2002. A total of 327 candidates contested the 52 seats available in Parliament. A record 138 candidates stood as independents, prompting Natapei to comment prior to the election that for Vanuatu to attain political stability the electoral constituency should vote only for party candidates. After some initial uncertainty, it was announced that the UMP had won 15 seats in the new Parliament and that the VP had secured 14. However, in accordance with the terms of the coalition agreement, the VP was permitted to nominate the next Prime Minister. The new Government was formed in early June, with Natapei duly re-elected Prime Minister.

In July 2002 former Prime Minister Barak Sope was convicted of fraud by the Supreme Court and sentenced to three years' imprisonment. It was alleged soon afterwards that New Zealand had interfered in Vanuatu's internal affairs by funding the investigation that had led to Sope's conviction. In early August, following the controversial appointment of Mael Apisai as Vanuatu's new Police Commissioner, disaffected police officers staged a raid during which they arrested Apisai, Attorney-General Hamilton Bulu and 14 other senior civil servants on charges of seditious conspiracy. Following an investigation, the charges were abandoned owing to a lack of evidence. Prime Minister Natapei subsequently assumed the police and VMF portfolios from the Minister of Internal Affairs, Joe Natuman, in what was thought to be an attempt to distance Natuman from some members of the police force, with whom he had reportedly become too closely involved. Later in the month members of the VMF surrounded the police headquarters in Port Vila to serve arrest warrants on 27 of those who had been involved in the raid, including the acting police commissioner, Holis Simon, and the commander of the VMF, Api Jack Marikembo. Shortly afterwards, in an attempt to bring an end to hostilities, the Government signed an agreement with representatives from the police department and the VMF during a traditional Melanesian reconciliation ceremony. The police officers involved, who had been suspended from their posts, were reinstated, the police and the VMF pledged to make no further arrests and it was agreed that Apisai's appointment would be reviewed by a newly appointed police services commission. At the same time it was decided that the allegations of conspiracy that had been brought against the 15 officials initially arrested would be considered by the judicial authorities. A new acting police commissioner, Lt-Gen. Arthur Coulton, was then appointed. In early October 2002 it was announced that the charges against 18 of those arrested in connection with the August raid would be abandoned, leaving eight senior officers to face trial on charges of mutiny and incitement to mutiny. In early December four of these police officers were found guilty by the Supreme Court on charges of mutiny, incitement to mutiny, kidnapping and false imprisonment and were given suspended two-year prison sentences. In the same month police intervened to prevent former Prime Minister Barak Sope from reclaiming his seat in Parliament, claiming that this was nullified by his conviction for fraud in July, despite receiving a pardon in November from President Bani. The pardon, which Bani stated he had made on the grounds of Sope's poor health, provoked widespread public opposition and led the Government to announce the appointment of a commission of inquiry to investigate the President's decision. However, in November 2003, at a by-election to the seat vacated by his conviction for fraud, Barak Sope was re-elected.

In April 2003 the election of Ham Lini (brother of Walter Lini, the late founder of the NUP) as President of the NUP led to the signing of a memorandum of understanding inviting that party to join the coalition Government. The NUP was expected to assume three ministerial portfolios (including finance) in a development which observers believed might lead to the reunification of the NUP with the VP (which had been a single political organization until the split of 1991). However, in late April the NUP rejected the VP's offer and announced its intention to remove the Government in a motion of no confidence. A further attempt to propose a motion of no confidence in the Government led Natapei to remove the UMP from the ruling coalition in a reorganization of cabinet portfolios in November. The party was replaced in the coalition by members of the NUP, the PPP, the Green Party and independents. Continued instability within the governing coalition prompted three further cabinet reorganizations during the first three months of 2004.

In April 2004 former Speaker Alfred Maseng Nalo was sworn in as Vanuatu's new President following a lengthy and closely contested election. Maseng defeated 31 other candidates during a total of four rounds of voting. However, the validity of the election was questioned when it was revealed that Maseng was serving a suspended prison sentence, having been convicted of misappropriation and receiving property dishonestly. In May, only four weeks after his appointment to the presidency, the Supreme Court ruled that Maseng should be removed from office; in August Kalkot Mataskelekele was elected as President. The likelihood that the Government, which held a minority of seats in Parliament, would be removed in an imminent vote of no confidence led to a decision by the Council of Ministers to dissolve Parliament in June.

A general election was held on 6 July 2004, at which no single party won an overall majority and 25 new members were elected, including many independent candidates. However, the validity of the election was jeopardized by an incident on Tanna in which ballot boxes *en route* to Port Vila for processing were ambushed and burnt. More than 40 people were arrested in connection with the incident, including the acting Minister of Finance, Jimmy Nickelim of the VP. In late July Serge Vohor was elected Prime Minister, defeating Ham Lini by 28 votes to 24. A Council of Ministers composed of five political groups and several independents was appointed shortly afterwards. However, the stability of the new administration was threatened by rumours of shifting allegiances and reports that several members were being persuaded to cross the floor of Parliament. Despite these suggestions, an opposition motion of no confidence in the new Government, proposed in September, was defeated, with Vohor's administration securing the support of 31 of the 52 members. Further doubts over Vohor's ability to continue as Prime Minister were cast when the country's police commissioner attempted to arrest him on charges of contempt, following comments made in Parliament accusing the Chief Justice, Vincent Lunabeck, of being unduly influenced by a desire to please foreign interests in the country. The Supreme Court, however, dismissed the charges against Vohor during an appeal in late September.

The Prime Minister became the focus of further serious controversy in November 2004 when he announced the establishment of diplomatic relations with Taiwan. The announcement, which Vohor defended by claiming that Taiwan's assistance was necessary to cover the budgetary deficit, was made only weeks after the Prime Minister had made an official visit to the People's Republic of China during which he had reiterated Vanuatu's allegiance to that country. The Council of Ministers, which had not given the necessary approval of the agreement with Taiwan, responded by demanding that Vohor renounce recognition of Taiwan or dismiss the entire cabinet. Controversy increased following reports that Vohor had assaulted the Chinese ambassador when questioned over the legitimacy of the Taiwanese flag flying in Port Vila. A parliamentary vote of no confidence in Vohor took place in early December, despite the Prime Minister's attempts to prevent the motion by means of a legal challenge, and was approved by 35 votes to 14. Ham Lini was elected Prime Minister and subsequently appointed a cabinet that included five former ministers who had crossed the floor of the legislature to vote against Vohor.

Lini's Government reversed the policy of the previous administration regarding Taiwan, and in July 2005 the Minister for Home Affairs made an official visit to China to sign a co-operation agreement providing for technical, logistical and financial support for the Vanuatu Police Force. Lini effected a cabinet reorganization in the same month. Further changes to the Council of Ministers reflected the decision of five opposition members to join the Green Party led by the Minister of Finance, Moana Carcasses Kalosil. Their defection resulted in the Green Party becoming Lini's most significant partner in the governing coalition. In November 2005, in a cabinet reorganization, Moana Carcasses was replaced as Minister of Finance by Willie Jimmy, hitherto Minister of Lands, Geology and Mines. In a further reallocation of portfolios announced in March 2006, Dunstan Hilton replaced Barak Sope as Minister of Agriculture, following reports that the former Prime Minister had been conducting negotiations aimed at attempting to oust the incumbent, Ham Lini, from office. In the same month the Prime Minister defeated by 30 parliamentary votes to 20 a motion of no confidence, which had been presented by the opposition partly as a result of criticism of the Government's handling of the ban on the import of Fijian biscuits, which had been imposed in retaliation for Fiji's ban on kava from Vanuatu.

As part of a programme of judicial reform, in early 2006 a new building accommodating a magistrate's court was opened in Port Vila. New court buildings were also to be constructed on three other islands, thus improving the population's access to the justice system. In June 2007 the Supreme Court building in Port Vila was destroyed in a fire; two men were charged with arson in early July. In late 2006 activists of the Vete association, which comprised inhabitants of Tongoa, vandalized unoccupied government buildings in Port Vila to publicize their campaign for land ownership rights. Vete claimed that prior to the declaration of areas of the capital as public land, no custom owner had been named. In December it was reported that members of Vete were occupying several empty government buildings, prompting police to warn of prosecution. In March 2007 allegations of witchcraft, following the death of a woman, led to civil unrest in outlying areas of Port Vila, with migrants from two islands engaging in violence that resulted in three fatalities and some 150 arrests. A two-week state of emergency, forbidding public gatherings and providing security forces with special powers, was declared. Nine people were later charged in relation to the violence, which was estimated to have displaced approximately 150 people. The unrest provoked renewed public debate about internal migration in Vanuatu.

In May 2007 the Minister of Agriculture, Forestry and Fisheries, Marcellino Pipite, was dismissed, having been accused of disloyalty to the Government; he was replaced by Donna Brounie in the same month. Following further cabinet changes in June, the VP was removed from the governing coalition and replaced by the UMP, whose President, Serge Vohor, was appointed Minister of Infrastructure and Public Utilities. The VP had reportedly allied itself with the UMP in the latter's attempt to oust the Government in a motion of no confidence, but the UMP subsequently retracted the motion. Vohor himself was dismissed in July, allegedly having been involved in an altercation with a government official. At the same time, the Deputy Prime Minister and Minister for Foreign Affairs, Sato Kilman, and the Minister of Youth and Sports, Dunstan Hilton, both of the PPP, were removed from office owing to allegations of fraud (in August Hilton was reported to have been charged in a fraud case involving funds misappropriated from the National Bank of Vanuatu). The VP rejoined the Government in order to ensure its retention of a majority and its members were allocated important portfolios including that of home affairs. Former Prime Minister and VP President Edward Natapei assumed the role of Deputy Prime Minister and returned to the infrastructure and public utilities portfolio. However, in April 2008 speculation arose about the strength of the coalition after it was reported that plans for another motion of no confidence had been discussed. The next general election was scheduled for September.

Meanwhile, Vanuatu has had an uneasy relationship with France. In 1981 the French ambassador to Vanuatu was expelled following the deportation from New Caledonia of the VP Secretary-General, who had been due to attend an assembly of the New Caledonian Independence Front. France immediately withdrew aid to Vanuatu, but this was subsequently restored and a new ambassador was appointed. However, the French ambassador was expelled again in 1987, for allegedly providing 'substantial financial assistance' to Vanuatu's opposition parties. In response to the expulsion, the French Government again announced that it would withdraw aid to Vanuatu. Maxime Carlot, Vanuatu's first francophone Prime Minister, made an official visit to France in May 1992, and the two countries fully restored diplomatic relations in October. In July, however, the Carlot Government reaffirmed its support for the Kanak independence movement on the French Territory of New Caledonia, following threats by Walter Lini to withdraw from the Government unless Carlot's pro-French policies were modified. Improved relations with France were confirmed in 1993 with the signing of a bilateral co-operation agreement. In mid-1995 the Carlot Government was virtually alone in the region in failing to condemn France's resumption of nuclear tests in French Polynesia. The opposition criticized the Government's stance as not reflecting the views of the vast majority of ni-Vanuatu. France provided food and other items for the relief effort in Port Vila following the communal violence of March 2007.

In March 1988 Vanuatu signed an agreement with Papua New Guinea and Solomon Islands to form the 'Spearhead Group', which aimed to preserve Melanesian cultural traditions and to lobby for independence for New Caledonia. In 1994 the Melanesian Spearhead Group concluded an agreement providing for the gradual establishment of a free trade area encompassing the three countries. Fiji joined the group in 1996. In March 2006 the Melanesian Spearhead Group met in Port Vila to discuss several issues concerning regional trade and security. Vanuatu had been accused of breaching the group's agreement by restricting its markets through the imposition of export licences for the sale of kava and other commodities. Negotiations were also taking place regarding the construction in Vanuatu of a permanent headquarters for the Melanesian Spearhead Group Secretariat. In August it was reported that a Chinese team was creating the designs for the new Port Vila headquarters. In March 2007 the members of the Melanesian Spearhead Group signed a constitution at a meeting in Vanuatu.

In August 2005 it was announced that discussions had taken place between the Prime Ministers of Vanuatu and Solomon Islands on the possibility of establishing an agreement governing border control and a patrol system. The issues were discussed amid concerns regarding drug- and people-trafficking, money-laundering and other border-related crime. It was hoped that a system of mutual co-operation similar to that operating between Solomon Islands and Papua New Guinea might be established. In December 2006 approximately 10 ni-Vanuatu police officers joined international peace-keeping forces in Timor-Leste.

Government

Vanuatu is a republic. Legislative power is vested in the unicameral Parliament, with 52 members who are elected by universal adult suffrage for four years. The Head of State is the President, elected for a five-year term by an electoral college consisting of Parliament and the Presidents of the Regional Councils. Executive power is vested in the Council of Ministers, appointed by the Prime Minister and responsible to Parliament. The Prime Minister is elected by and from members of Parliament. Legislation enacted in 1994 resulted in the replacement of the 11 local government councils by six provincial bodies, with greater executive powers. The six provincial authorities are Malampa, Penama, Sanma, Shefa, Tafea and Torba.

Economic Affairs

In 2006, according to estimates by the World Bank, Vanuatu's gross national income (GNI), measured at average 2004–06 prices, was US $370m., equivalent to $1,710 per head (or $3,280 per head on an international purchasing-power parity basis). During 1996–2006, it was estimated, the population increased at an average annual rate of 2.0%, while gross domestic product (GDP) per head decreased, in real terms, by an average of 0.5% per year. Overall GDP increased, in real terms, at an average annual rate of 1.5% in 1996–2006. According to the Asian Development Bank (ADB), GDP increased by 7.2% in 2006 and by 6.6% in 2007.

According to the ADB, the agricultural sector (including forestry and fishing) contributed 13.0% of GDP in 2006, compared with some 40% in the early 1980s. The GDP of the agricultural sector was estimated to have increased by an average annual rate of 2.1% in 1995–2005. The sector's GDP declined by 4.4% in 2005, before increasing by 2.4% in 2006 and by 4.9% in 2007. About 34% of the employed labour force were engaged in agricultural activities in 2005, according to FAO estimates. Coconuts, cocoa and coffee are grown largely for export (copra and cocoa being the most important of these), while yams, taro, cassava, breadfruit and vegetables are cultivated for subsistence purposes. Cattle, pigs, goats and poultry are the country's principal livestock, and beef is a significant export commodity. The forestry industry is also important, with timber having become a major export item. The Government derives substantial revenue from the sale of fishing rights to foreign fleets. In October 2005 the Government and the People's Republic of China signed an agreement that provided for the financing of the establishment of a new fish-processing plant near Port Vila. The facility would also be available for processing other products for export, such as beef.

The industrial sector (including manufacturing, utilities and construction) contributed about 8.6% of GDP in 2006, although only 3.5% of the employed labour force were engaged in the sector in 1989. According to figures from the ADB, in 1995–2005 the GDP of the industrial sector was estimated to have increased at an average annual rate of 0.5%. Compared with the previous year, industrial GDP increased by 7.0% in 2006 and by 7.3% in 2006. Construction activity alone contributed 3.2% of GDP in 2005.

Manufacturing, which contributed about 3.5% of GDP in 2005, is mainly concerned with the processing of agricultural products. In 1995–2005, however, the GDP of the manufacturing sector decreased by an average annual rate of 1.2%. The country's first kava extraction plant (for the manufacture of alcoholic beverages) was opened in 1998. However, in 2001 a ban was imposed on kava imports by several countries in Europe, owing to health concerns.

Various mineral deposits have been identified. These include manganese on the island of Efate, and there are reserves of gold, copper and petroleum around the islands of Malekula and Espiritu Santo. In March 2006 an agreement was signed by the Vanuatu Government to allow a Swiss-US company to extract manganese and to export the commodity.

Electricity generation is largely thermal. Long-term plans focus on the potential of renewable resources. Imports of mineral fuels comprised 11.9% of the value of total imports in 2006.

The economy depends heavily on the services sector, which accounted for 78.4% of GDP in 2006. According to figures from the ADB, in 1995–2005 the GDP of the services sector was estimated to have increased at an average annual rate of 2.1%. The GDP of the services sector increased by 8.4% in 2006 and by 6.9% in 2007. Tourism, offshore banking facilities and a shipping registry, providing a 'flag of convenience' to foreign-owned vessels, make a significant contribution to the country's income. In 2007, following an increase in the number of flights available, a total of 81,345 foreign tourists visited Vanuatu by air, compared with 68,179 in the previous year. However, the number of tourist arrivals by cruise-ship decreased slightly, from 85,922 in 2006 to 85,737 in 2007. Revenue from tourism was estimated to have increased from US $82m. in 2004 to $93m. in 2005.

In 2006 Vanuatu recorded a visible trade deficit of US $109.86m., and there was a deficit of $50.35m. on the current account of the balance of payments. In 2006 the principal sources of imports were Australia (41.3%), New Zealand (15.6%) and Fiji (8.9%), while Australia was also the principal market for exports (accounting for 25.4% of the total). The principal imports in 2006 were machinery and transport equipment (25.9% of total imports), food and live animals (18.3%) and basic manufactures (16.2%). Copra (which provided 8.9% of total export earnings), beef (9.1%), and timber (8.4%) were the main export commodities in 2006.

Budget estimates for 2006 projected a deficit of 424m. vatu; grants from abroad in that year totalled 851.3m. vatu. An overall deficit equivalent to 0.1% of GDP was anticipated in 2007. Australia, New Zealand, France, the United Kingdom and Japan are significant sources of development assistance. In 2007/08 Australia budgeted for aid of some $A44.5m., and in the same year development assistance from New Zealand was projected at $NZ15.0m. Vanuatu's total external debt reached US $86m. at the end of 2006. In that year the cost of debt-servicing was estimated to be equivalent to 1.7% of the value of exports of goods and services. The annual rate of inflation averaged 2.4% in 1996–2006. Consumer prices increased by 2.5% in 2007, according to the ADB.

Vanuatu is a member of the Pacific Community (see p. 377), the Pacific Islands Forum (see p. 380), the Asian Development Bank (ADB, see p. 182) and the UN Economic and Social Commission for Asia and the Pacific (ESCAP, see p. 35). The country is a signatory of the South Pacific Regional Trade and Economic Agreement (SPARTECA, see p. 381) and of the Lomé Conventions and the successor Cotonou Agreement (see p. 301) with the EU. Vanuatu is also a member of the Melanesian Spearhead Group, along with Fiji, Papua New Guinea and Solomon Islands; a free trade agreement concluded by members grants most-favoured nation status for all trading transactions.

Vanuatu's economic development has been impeded by its dependence on the agricultural sector, which is vulnerable to adverse weather conditions (notably cyclones) and by the relatively high rate of population growth. Furthermore, in contrast to the situation in other Pacific islands, opportunities for emigration and for engagement in overseas employment are limited. Successive administrations, therefore, have attempted to encourage the diversification of the country's economy, mainly through the development of the tourism sector, but such initiatives remain inhibited by a shortage of skilled indigenous labour and a weak infrastructure. The political instability of 2004 (see Recent History) impeded the timely implementation of the Prioritized Action Agenda, whereby the Comprehensive Reform Programme (CRP, which had been implemented in 1998) was to be linked to the Government's medium-term investment programme and annual budgetary plans. One of the principal challenges facing the incoming Government of Ham Lini following its assumption of office in December 2004 was the problem of rural hardship and the need to reverse the decline in income; the country's GDP per head was estimated to be below the level of the mid-1980s. The Government hoped to develop an effective regulatory framework for the utilities sector, in an effort to improve efficiency and to reduce costs in the fields of electricity, telecommunications and water supply. In rural areas access to such services had remained extremely limited. In March 2006 Vanuatu and the US Millennium Challenge Corporation signed an agreement providing the country with a grant of US $65.9m., to be disbursed between 2007 and 2011, for the purpose of financing various infrastructural projects. Although in 2007 strong GDP growth was recorded for the fifth consecutive year, the very high rate of population growth continued to impede any comparable rise in the country's per caput income. Expansion in tourism, aided by the introduction of additional flights from New Zealand, continued to support growth in 2007, with total arrivals rising by 8.5% in comparison with the previous year. GDP growth was forecast by the ADB to decelerate somewhat in 2008, to 5.7%.

Education

The abolition of nominal fees for primary education following independence resulted in a significant increase in enrolment at that level. Thus, at the beginning of the 1990s it was estimated that about 85% of children between the ages of six and 11 were enrolled at state-controlled primary institutions. Secondary education begins at 12 years of age, and comprises a preliminary cycle of four years and a second cycle of three years. In 2000/01 enrolment at pre-primary schools included 41% of pupils from the relevant age-group. In 2004/05 enrolment at primary schools included 93.9% of pupils in the relevant age-group, while in 2003/04 enrolment in secondary schools included 39.3% of pupils. Vocational education and teacher-training are also available. The relatively low level of secondary enrolment has been a cause of some concern to the Government, and a major programme for

VANUATU

Statistical Survey

the expansion of the education system was inaugurated in 1989. Low literacy rates have been another cause of concern.

An extension centre of the University of the South Pacific was opened in Port Vila in 1989. Students from Vanuatu can also receive higher education at the principal faculties of that university (in Suva, Fiji), in Papua New Guinea or in France.

The 2002 budget allocated an estimated 2,062m. vatu to education (20.1% of total recurrent expenditure by the central Government).

Public Holidays

2008: 1 January (New Year's Day), 21 February (Father Walter Lini Day), 5 March (Custom Chief's Day), 21–24 March (Easter), 1 May (Ascension Day, Labour Day), 24 July (Children's Day), 30 July (Independence Day), 15 August (Assumption), 5 October (Constitution Day), 29 November (Unity Day), 25 December (Christmas Day), 26 December (Family Day).

2009: 1 January (New Year's Day), 21 February (Father Walter Lini Day), 5 March (Custom Chief's Day), 10–13 April (Easter), 1 May (Labour Day), 21 May (Ascension Day), 24 July (Children's Day), 30 July (Independence Day), 15 August (Assumption), 5 October (Constitution Day), 30 November (Unity Day), 25 December (Christmas Day), 26 December (Family Day).

Weights and Measures

The metric system is in force.

Statistical Survey

Source (unless otherwise indicated): National Statistics Office, Ministry of Finance and Economic Management, PMB 9019, Port Vila; tel. (678) 22110; fax (678) 24583; e-mail stats@vanuatu.com.vu; internet www.spc.int/prism/country/vu/stats.

AREA AND POPULATION

Area: 12,190 sq km (4,707 sq miles); *By Island* (sq km): Espiritu Santo 4,010; Malekula 2,024; Efate 887; Erromango 887; Ambrym 666; Tanna 561; Pentecost 499; Epi 444; Ambae 399; Vanua Lava 343; Gaua 315; Maewo 300.

Population: 142,419 at census of 16 May 1989; 186,678 (males 95,682, females 90,996) at census of 16 November 1999. *Mid-2006* (official estimate): 221,417 (males 113,034, females 108,383). *By Island* (mid-1999, official estimates): Espiritu Santo 31,811; Malekula 19,766; Efate 43,295; Erromango 1,554; Ambrym 7,613; Tanna 26,306; Pentecost 14,837; Epi 4,706; Ambae 10,692; Vanua Lava 2,074; Gaua 1,924; Maewo 3,385.

Density (mid-2006): 18.2 per sq km.

Principal Towns (population at 1999 census): Port Vila (capital) 29,356; Luganville (Santo) 10,738. *Mid-2005* (incl. suburbs, UN estimate) Port Vila (capital) 36,000 (Source: UN, *World Urbanization Prospects: The 2005 Revision*).

Births and Deaths (annual averages, 2000–05, UN estimates): Birth rate 31.0 per 1,000; Death rate 5.7 per 1,000. Source: UN, *World Population Prospects: The 2006 Revision*.

Expectation of Life (years at birth, WHO estimates): 68.2 (males 66.9; females 69.7) in 2005. Source: WHO, *World Health Statistics*.

Economically Active Population (census of May 1989): Agriculture, forestry, hunting and fishing 40,889; Mining and quarrying 1; Manufacturing 891; Electricity, gas and water 109; Construction 1,302; Trade, restaurants and hotels 2,712; Transport, storage and communications 1,030; Financing, insurance, real estate and business services 646; Community, social and personal services 7,891; Activities not adequately defined 11,126; *Total labour force* 66,597 (males 35,692, females 30,905). *1999 Census* (persons aged 15 to 64 years): Subsistence farmers 51,309; Total employed (incl. others) 75,110; Unemployed (seeking work) 1,260; Total labour force 76,370 (males 42,072, females 34,298). *Mid-2005* (estimates): Agriculture, etc. 32,000; Total labour force 95,000 (Source: FAO).

HEALTH AND WELFARE
Key Indicators

Total Fertility Rate (children per woman, 2005): 3.9.

Under-5 Mortality Rate (per 1,000 live births, 2005): 38.

Physicians (per 1,000 head, 1997): 0.11.

Hospital Beds (per 1,000 head, 2003): 2.0.

Health Expenditure (2004): US $ per head (PPP): 123.2.

Health Expenditure (2004): % of GDP: 4.1.

Health Expenditure (2004): public (% of total): 76.8.

Access to Water (% of persons, 2004): 60.

Access to Sanitation (% of persons, 2004): 50.

Human Development Index (2005): ranking: 120.

Human Development Index (2005): value: 0.674.

For sources and definitions, see explanatory note on p. vi.

AGRICULTURE, ETC.

Principal Crops ('000 metric tons, 2006, FAO estimates): Coconuts 315; Copra 34.5; Roots and tubers 42.5; Vegetables and melons 10.8; Bananas 14.0; Other fruits 7.7; Groundnuts (in shell) 2.3; Maize 0.7; Cocoa beans 1.0.

Livestock ('000 head, year ending September 2006, FAO estimates): Cattle 152; Pigs 62; Goats 12; Horses 3; Chickens 340.

Livestock Products (metric tons, 2006, FAO estimates): Cattle meat 2,983; Pig meat 2,961; Chicken meat 517; Cows' milk 3,000; Hen eggs 320.

Forestry ('000 cu m, 2001): *Roundwood Removals* (excl. bark): Sawlogs and veneer logs 28; Fuel wood 91; Total 119. *Sawnwood Production* (all broadleaved, incl. railway sleepers): Total 28. *2002–06* (FAO estimates): Annual output as in 2001.

Fishing ('000 metric tons, live weight, 2005): Marine fishes 102.3 (Skipjack tuna 66.6; Yellowfin tuna 15.0; Bigeye tuna 4.8; Albacore 13.4); Marine crustaceans 48.6 (Antarctic krill 48.4); Total catch (incl. others) 151.1.

Source: FAO.

FINANCE

Currency and Exchange Rates: Currency is the vatu. *Sterling, Dollar and Euro Equivalents* (31 December 2007): £1 sterling = 211.71 vatu; US $1 = 104.81 vatu; €1 = 143.64 vatu; 1,000 vatu = £4.724 = $9.541 = €6.962. *Average Exchange Rate* (vatu per US $): 109.25 in 2005; 110.64 in 2006; 102.44 in 2007.

Budget (million vatu, 2006): *Revenue:* Tax revenue 8,125.7; Other current revenue 1,031.6; Total 9,157.3, excluding grants from abroad (851.3). *Expenditure:* Current expenditure 8,555.5; Transfers to government bodies 335.8; Capital expenditure 690.1; Total 9,581.4. Source: Reserve Bank of Vanuatu, *Quarterly Economic Review* (September 2007).

International Reserves (US $ million at 31 December 2007): IMF special drawing rights 1.89; Reserve position in IMF 3.94; Foreign exchange 113.79; Total 119.62. Source: IMF, *International Financial Statistics*.

Money Supply (million vatu at 31 December 2007): Currency outside banks 3,570; Demand deposits at banks 7,211; Total money 10,781. Source: IMF, *International Financial Statistics*.

Cost of Living (Consumer Price Index for Port Vila and Luganville, average of quarterly figures; base: 2000 = 100): All items 110.4 in 2004; 111.7 in 2005; 113.9 in 2006. Source: IMF, *International Financial Statistics*.

Gross Domestic Product (million vatu at constant 1983 prices): 15,936 in 2003; 16,812 in 2004; 17,953 in 2005. Source: Asian Development Bank, *Key Indicators of Developing Asian and Pacific Countries*.

Expenditure on the Gross Domestic Product (million vatu at current prices, 2005): Government final consumption expenditure 7,557; Private final consumption expenditure 24,729; Gross fixed capital formation 8,234; Statistical discrepancy 7,960; *Total domestic expenditure* 48,480; Exports of goods and services 16,002; *Less* Imports of goods and services 24,304; *GDP in purchasers' values* 40,178. Source: Asian Development Bank, *Key Indicators of Developing Asian and Pacific Countries*.

VANUATU

Directory

Gross Domestic Product by Economic Activity (million vatu at current prices, 2005): Agriculture, forestry and fishing 5,535; Manufacturing 1,487; Electricity, gas and water 810; Construction 1,337; Wholesale and retail trade 12,685; Hotels and restaurants 2,674; Transport, storage and communications 5,097; Finance and insurance 3,877; Real estate and business services 2,820; Government services 5,165; Personal and domestic services 928; *Sub-total* 42,416; *Less* Imputed bank service charge 2,238; *GDP in purchasers' values* 40,178.

Balance of Payments (US $ million, 2006): Exports of goods f.o.b. 37.69; Imports of goods f.o.b. −147.55; *Trade balance* −109.86; Exports of services 145.82; Imports of services −71.24; *Balance on goods and services* −35.29; Other income received 31.82; Other income paid −51.93; *Balance on goods, services and income* −55.40; Current transfers received 10.06; Current transfers paid −5.00; *Current balance* −50.35; Capital account (net) 25.20; Direct investment abroad −0.73; Direct investment from abroad 43.45; Portfolio investment assets −0.26; Other investment assets −27.47; Other investment liabilities 18.45; Net errors and omissions 4.59; *Overall balance* 12.88. Source: IMF, *International Financial Statistics*.

EXTERNAL TRADE

Principal Commodities (million vatu, 2006): *Imports c.i.f.:* Food and live animals 3,233; Beverages and tobacco 499; Mineral fuels, lubricants, etc. 2,098; Chemicals 1,693; Basic manufactures 2,856; Machinery and transport equipment 4,565; Miscellaneous manufactured articles 2,118; Total (incl. others) 17,645, excl. imports for re-export (99). *Exports f.o.b.:* Cocoa 277; Copra 324; Beef 332; Timber 306; Coconut oil 193; Shells 92; Kava 698; Total (incl. others) 3,651, excl. re-exports (428).

Principal Trading Partners (million vatu, 2006): *Imports c.i.f.* (excl. imports for re-export): Australia 7,289; Fiji 1,576; France 734; Japan 386; New Zealand 2,746; Singapore 957; Total (incl. others) 17,645. *Exports f.o.b.* (excl. re-exports): Australia 926; European Union countries 465; Japan 132; New Caledonia 320; New Zealand 158; Total (incl. others) 3,651.

TRANSPORT

Road Traffic ('000 motor vehicles in use, 2001, estimates): Passenger cars 2.6; Commercial vehicles 4.4. Source: UN, *Statistical Yearbook*.

Shipping: *Merchant Fleet* (registered at 31 December 2006): Vessels 419; Total displacement ('000 grt) 1,968.7 (Source: Lloyd's Register-Fairplay, *World Fleet Statistics*). *International Sea-borne Freight Traffic* ('000 metric tons, 1990, estimates): Goods loaded 80; Goods unloaded 55 (Source: UN, *Monthly Bulletin of Statistics*).

Civil Aviation (traffic on scheduled services, 2003): Kilometres flown (million) 3; Passengers carried ('000) 83; Passenger-km (million) 176; Total ton-km (million) 18. Source: UN, *Statistical Yearbook*.

TOURISM

Foreign Tourist Arrivals: 62,082 in 2005; 68,179 in 2006; 81,345 in 2007. Note: Figures refer to arrivals by air only; arrivals from cruise-ships were: 63,554 in 2005; 85,922 in 2006; 85,737 in 2007.

Tourist Arrivals by Country of Residence (2006): Australia 40,385; New Zealand 9,821; New Caledonia 7,480; Other Pacific 2,681; Europe 4,021; North America 1,896; Total (incl. others) 68,179.

Tourism Receipts (US $ million, incl. passenger transport): 71 in 2003; 82 in 2004; 93 in 2005.

Source: World Tourism Organization.

COMMUNICATIONS MEDIA

Radio Receivers (1997): 62,000 in use*.

Television Receivers (1999): 2,000 in use†.

Telephones (2006): 7,000 main lines in use‡.

Facsimile Machines (1996): 600 in use†.

Mobile Cellular Telephones (2006): 12,700 subscribers‡.

Internet Users (2006): 7,500‡.

Broadband Subscribers (2006): 100‡.

Personal Computers (2004): 3,000 in use‡.

Non-daily Newspapers (1996): 2 (estimated circulation 4,000)*.

* Source: UNESCO, *Statistical Yearbook*.
† Source: UN, *Statistical Yearbook*.
‡ Source: International Telecommunication Union.

EDUCATION

Pre-primary (1992, unless otherwise indicated): 252 schools; 49 teachers (1980); 5,178 pupils.

Primary (2002, unless otherwise indicated): 374 schools (1995); 1,614 teachers; 37,470 pupils.

Secondary (2002, unless otherwise indicated): 27 schools (1995); 591 teachers; 9,610 students.

Tertiary (2002): 2,124 students.

Secondary (Teacher Training): 1 college (1989); 13 teachers (1983); 124 students (1991).

Directory

The Constitution

A new Constitution came into effect at independence on 30 July 1980. The main provisions are as follows:

The Republic of Vanuatu is a sovereign democratic state, of which the Constitution is the supreme law. Bislama is the national language and the official languages are Bislama, English and French. The Constitution guarantees protection of all fundamental rights and freedoms and provides for the determination of citizenship.

The President, as head of the Republic, symbolizes the unity of the Republic and is elected for a five-year term of office by secret ballot by an electoral college consisting of Parliament and the Presidents of the Regional Councils.

Legislative power resides in the single-chamber Parliament, consisting of 39 members (amended to 46 members in 1987, to 50 in 1995 and further to 52 in 1998) elected for four years on the basis of universal franchise through an electoral system that includes an element of proportional representation to ensure fair representation of different political groups and opinions. Parliament is presided over by the Speaker elected by the members. Executive power is vested in the Council of Ministers which consists of the Prime Minister (elected by Parliament from among its members) and other ministers (appointed by the Prime Minister from among the members of Parliament). The number of ministers, including the Prime Minister, may not exceed a quarter of the number of members of Parliament.

Special attention is paid to custom law and to decentralization. The Constitution states that all land in the Republic belongs to the indigenous custom owners and their descendants. There is a National Council of Chiefs, composed of custom chiefs elected by their peers sitting in District Councils of Chiefs. It may discuss all matters relating to custom and tradition and may make recommendations to Parliament for the preservation and promotion of the culture and languages of Vanuatu. The Council may be consulted on any question in connection with any bill before Parliament. Each region may elect a regional council and the Constitution lays particular emphasis on the representation of custom chiefs within each one. (A reorganization of local government was initiated in May 1994, and resulted in September of that year in the replacement of 11 local councils with six provincial governments.)

The Constitution also makes provision for public finance, the Public Service, the Ombudsman, a leadership code and the judiciary (see Judicial System).

The Government

HEAD OF STATE

President: KALKOT MATASKELEKELE (appointed 16 August 2004).

COUNCIL OF MINISTERS
(April 2008)

Prime Minister: HAM LINI.

Deputy Prime Minister and Minister for Infrastructure and Public Utilities: EDWARD NATAPEI.

Minister for Foreign Affairs: GEORGE WELLS.

Minister for Home Affairs: JOE NATUMAN.

VANUATU

Minister of Agriculture, Forestry and Fisheries: DONNA BROUNIE.
Minister of Commerce and Industry: JAMES BULE.
Minister for Health: MORKIN STEVEN.
Minister of Education: THOMPSON SEINAVAO TASSO.
Minister for Finance and Economic Management: WILLIE JIMMY.
Minister of Justice and Social Welfare: ISABELLE DONALD.
Minister of Land: MAXIME CARLOT KORMAN.
Minister of Ni-Vanuatu Business Development: ISSACH JUDAH.
Minister of Youth Development and Training: (vacant).

MINISTRIES AND DEPARTMENTS

Prime Minister's Office: PMB 053, Port Vila; tel. 22413; fax 22863; internet www.vanuatugovernment.gov.vu.
Deputy Prime Minister's Office: PMB 057, Port Vila; tel. 22750; fax 27714.
Ministry of Agriculture, Livestock, Forestry and Fisheries: PMB 39, Port Vila; tel. 23406; fax 26498.
Ministry of Civil Aviation, Public Works and Transport: PMB 057, Port Vila; tel. 22790; fax 27214.
Ministry of the Comprehensive Reform Programme: POB 110, Port Vila.
Ministry of Culture, Home Affairs and Justice: PMB 036, Port Vila; tel. 22252; fax 27064.
Ministry of Education, Youth and Sports: PMB 028, Port Vila; tel. 22309; fax 24569.
Ministry of Energy, Lands, Mines and Rural Water Supply: PMB 007, Port Vila; tel. 27833; fax 25165.
Ministry of Finance: PMB 058, Port Vila; tel. 23032; fax 27937.
Ministry of Foreign Affairs: PMB 051, Port Vila; tel. 27750; fax 27832.
Ministry of Health: PMB 042, Port Vila; tel. 22545; fax 26113.
Ministry of Meteorology, Postal Services and Telecommunications: PMB 011, Port Vila; tel. 22790; fax 27714.
Ministry of Trade, Industry, Co-operatives and Commerce: PMB 056, Port Vila; tel. 25674; fax 25677.
Ministry of Women's Affairs: PMB 091, Port Vila; tel. 25099; fax 26353; e-mail emorris@vanuatu.gov.vu.

Legislature

PARLIAMENT

Speaker: SAM DAN AVOCK.
General Election, 6 July 2004

	Seats
National United Party	10
Union of Moderate Parties	8
Vanuaaku Pati	8
People's Progressive Party	4
Vanuatu Republikan Pati	4
Green Party	3
Melanesian Progressive Pati	3
National Community Association	2
Namangi Aute	1
People's Action Party	1
Independents	8
Total	**52**

Election Commission

Vanuatu Electoral Commission: PMB 033, Port Vila; tel. 23914; fax 26681; Principal Electoral Officer MARTIN TETE.

Political Organizations

Efate Laketu Party: Port Vila; f. 1982; regional party, based on the island of Efate.
Green Party: Port Vila; f. 2001; est. by breakaway group of the UMP; Leader MOANA CARCASSES KALOSIL.
Melanesian Progressive Pati (MPP): POB 39, Port Vila; tel. 23485; fax 23315; f. 1988; est. by breakaway group from the VP; Chair. BARAK SOPE; Sec.-Gen. GEORGES CALO.
National Democratic Party (NDP): Port Vila; f. 1986; advocates strengthening of links with France and the UK; Leader JOHN NAUPA.
National United Party (NUP): Port Vila; f. 1991; est. by supporters of Walter Lini, following his removal as leader of the VP; Pres. HAM LINI; Sec.-Gen. WILLIE TITONGOA.
People's Democratic Party (PDP): Port Vila; f. 1994; est. by breakaway faction of the NUP.
People's Progressive Party (PPP): Port Vila; f. 2001; formed coalition with National United Party (NUP) and Fren Melanesia to contest 2002 elections; Pres. SATO KILMAN.
Tu Vanuatu Kominiti: Port Vila; f. 1996; espouses traditional Melanesian and Christian values; Leader HILDA LINI.
Union of Moderate Parties (UMP): POB 698, Port Vila; f. 1980; Pres. SERGE VOHOR; the UMP is divided into two factions, one led by SERGE VOHOR and the other by WILLIE JIMMY.
Vanuaaku Pati (VP) (Our Land Party): POB 472, Port Vila; tel. 22584; f. 1971; est. as the New Hebrides National Party; advocates 'Melanesian socialism'; Pres. EDWARD NATAPEI; First Vice-Pres. IOLU ABBIL; Sec.-Gen. SELA MOLISA.
Vanuatu Independent Alliance Party (VIAP): Port Vila; f. 1982; supports free enterprise; Leaders THOMAS SERU, GEORGE WOREK, KALMER VOCOR.
Vanuatu Independent Movement: Port Vila; f. 2002; Pres. WILLIE TASSO.
Vanuatu Labour Party: Port Vila; f. 1986; trade-union based; Leader KENNETH SATUNGIA.
Vanuatu Republikan Pati (VRP): Port Vila; f. 1998; est. by breakaway faction of the UMP; Leader MAXIME CARLOT KORMAN.

The Na-Griamel (Leader FRANKLEY STEVENS), Namaki Aute, Tan Union (Leader VINCENT BULEKONE) and Fren Melanesia (Leader ALBERT RAVUTIA) represent rural interests on the islands of Espiritu Santo and Malekula. The John Frum Movement represents interests on the island of Tanna.

Diplomatic Representation

EMBASSIES AND HIGH COMMISSIONS IN VANUATU

Australia: Winston Churchill Ave, Port Vila; tel. 22777; fax 23948; e-mail australia_vanuatu@dfat.gov.au; internet www.vanuatu.embassy.gov.au; High Commissioner JOHN PILBEAM.
China, People's Republic: PMB 071, Rue d'Auvergne, Nambatu, Port Vila; tel. 23598; fax 24877; Ambassador CHENG SHUPING.
France: Kumul Highway, POB 60, Port Vila; tel. 22353; fax 22695; e-mail ambafra@vanuatu.com.vu; internet www.ambafrance-vu.org; Ambassador PIERRE MAYAUDON.
New Zealand: La Casa d'Andrea e Luciano, Rue Pierre Lamy St, Port Vila; tel. 22933; fax 22518; e-mail kiwi@vanuatu.com.vu; High Commissioner JEFF LANGLEY.

Judicial System

The Supreme Court has unlimited jurisdiction to hear and determine any civil or criminal proceedings. It consists of the Chief Justice, appointed by the President of the Republic after consultation with the Prime Minister and the leader of the opposition, and three other judges, who are appointed by the President of the Republic on the advice of the Judicial Service Commission.

The Court of Appeal is constituted by two or more judges of the Supreme Court sitting together. The Supreme Court is the court of first instance in constitutional matters and is composed of a single judge.

Magistrates' Courts have limited jurisdiction to hear and determine any civil or criminal proceedings. Island Courts have been established in several local government regions, and are constituted when three justices are sitting together to exercise civil or criminal jurisdiction, as defined in the warrant establishing the court. A magistrate nominated by the Chief Justice acts as Chairman. The Island Courts are competent to rule on land disputes.

In late 2001 legislation was introduced to establish a new Land Tribunal which was intended to expedite the hearing of land disputes. The tribunal was to have three levels, and no cases were to go beyond the tribunal and enter either the Supreme Court or the Island Courts. The tribunal was to be funded by the disputing parties.

VANUATU

In 1986 Papua New Guinea and Vanuatu signed a memorandum of understanding, under which Papua New Guinea Supreme Court judges were to conduct court hearings in Vanuatu, chiefly in the Court of Appeal.

Supreme Court of Vanuatu
PMB 041, rue de Querios, Port Vila; tel. 22420; fax 22692.
Attorney-General: Ishmael Kalsakau.
Chief Justice: Vincent Lunabeck.
Chief Prosecutor: Heather Lini Leo.

Religion

Most of Vanuatu's inhabitants profess Christianity. Presbyterians form the largest Christian group (with about one-half of the population being adherents), followed by Anglicans and Roman Catholics.

CHRISTIANITY

Vanuatu Christian Council: POB 13, Luganville, Santo; tel. 03232; f. 1967; est. as New Hebrides Christian Council; five mem. churches, two observers; Chair. (vacant); Sec. Rev. John Liu.

The Roman Catholic Church

Vanuatu forms the single diocese of Port Vila, suffragan to the archdiocese of Nouméa (New Caledonia). At 31 December 2005 there were an estimated 32,500 adherents in the country. The Bishop participates in the Catholic Bishops' Conference of the Pacific, based in Fiji.

Bishop of Port Vila: (vacant), Evêché, POB 59, Port Vila; tel. 22640; fax 25342; e-mail catholik@vanuatu.com.vu.

The Anglican Communion

Anglicans in Vanuatu are adherents of the Church of the Province of Melanesia, comprising eight dioceses: Vanuatu (which also includes New Caledonia), Banks and Torres and six dioceses in Solomon Islands. The Archbishop of the Province is the Bishop of Central Melanesia, resident in Honiara, Solomon Islands. In 1985 the Church had an estimated 16,000 adherents in Vanuatu.

Bishop of Vanuatu: Fr James Ligo, Bishop's House, POB 238, Luganville, Santo; tel. 37065; fax 36026.
Bishop of Banks and Torres: Rt Rev. Nathan Tome, Bishop's House, POB 19, Toutamwat, Torba Province.

Protestant Churches

Presbyterian Church of Vanuatu (Presbitirin Jyos long Vanuatu): POB 150, Port Vila; tel. 27184; fax 23650; f. 1948; 56,000 mems (1995); Moderator Pastor Bani Kalsinger; Assembly Clerk Pastor Fama Rakau.

Other denominations active in the country include the Apostolic Church, the Assemblies of God, the Churches of Christ in Vanuatu and the Seventh-day Adventist Church.

BAHÁ'Í FAITH

National Spiritual Assembly of the Bahá'ís of Vanuatu: POB 1017, Port Vila; tel. 22419; e-mail nsavanuatu@vanuatu.com.vu; f. 1953; Sec. Charles Pierce; mems resident in 216 localities.

The Press

Hapi Tumas Long Vanuatu: POB 1292, Port Vila; tel. 23642; fax 23343; quarterly tourist information; in English; Publr Marc Neil-Jones; circ. 12,000.

Pacific Island Profile: Port Vila; f. 1990; monthly; general interest; English and French; Editor Hilda Lini.

Port Vila Presse: 1st Floor, Raffea House, POB 637, Port Vila; tel. 22200; fax 27999; e-mail marke@presse.com.vu; internet www.presse.com.vu; f. 2000; daily; English and French; Publr Marke Lowen; Editor Ricky Binihi.

Vanuatu Daily Post: POB 1292, Port Vila; tel. 23111; fax 24111; e-mail tpost@vanuatu.com.vu; internet www.vanuatudaily.com.vu; daily; English; Publr Marc Neil-Jones; Editor Len Garae; circ. 2,000.

Vanuatu Weekly: PMB 049, Port Vila; tel. 22999; fax 22026; f. 1980; weekly; govt-owned; Bislama, English and French; circ. 1,700.

Viewpoints: Port Vila; weekly; newsletter of Vanuaaku Pati; Editor Peter Taurakoto.

Wantok Niuspepa: POB 1292, Port Vila; tel. 23642; fax 23343.

Broadcasting and Communications

TELECOMMUNICATIONS

Freedom Telecommunications Co (USA): Santo; f. 2000; provides services on Santo and islands in the north of Vanuatu.

Telecom Vanuatu Ltd (TVL): POB 146, Port Vila; tel. 22185; fax 22628; e-mail sales@tvl.net.vu; internet www.tvl.vu; f. 1989; est. as a jt venture between the Government of Vanuatu, Cable & Wireless Ltd and France Câbles et Radio; operates all national and international telecommunications services in Vanuatu; Man. Dir Michel Dupuis.

BROADCASTING

Radio

Vanuatu Broadcasting and Television Corpn (VBTC): PMB 049, Port Vila; tel. 22999; fax 22026; internet www.vbtc.com.vu; fmrly Government Media Services, name changed in 1992; Gen. Man. Joe Bomal Carlo; Chair. Godwin Ligo; Dir of Programmes A. Thompson.

Radio Vanuatu: PMB 049, Port Vila; tel. 22999; fax 22026; f. 1966; govt-owned; broadcasts in English, French and Bislama; Dir Joe Bomal Carlo.

Television

Vanuatu Broadcasting and Television Corpn (VBTC): see Radio

Television Blong Vanuatu: PMB 049, Port Vila; f. 1993; govt-owned; French-funded; broadcasts for four hours daily in French and English; Gen. Man. Claude Castelly; Programme Man. Gael Le Dantec.

Finance

(cap. = capital; res = reserves; dep. = deposits; amounts in vatu unless otherwise indicated)

Vanuatu has no personal income tax nor tax on company profits and is therefore attractive as a financial centre and 'tax haven'.

BANKING

Central Bank

Reserve Bank of Vanuatu: POB 62, Port Vila; tel. 23333; fax 24231; e-mail enquiries@rvb.gov.vu; internet www.rbv.gov.vu; f. 1981; est. as Central Bank of Vanuatu; name changed as above in 1989; govt-owned; cap. 100.0m., res 573.3m., dep. 5,186.6m. (Dec. 2004); Gov. Odo Tevi.

Development Bank

Development Bank of Vanuatu: rue de Paris, POB 241, Port Vila; tel. 22181; fax 24591; f. 1979; govt-owned; Man. Dir Augustine Garae.

National Bank

National Bank of Vanuatu: POB 249, Air Vanuatu House, rue de Paris, Port Vila; tel. 22201; fax 22761; e-mail nationalbank@vanuatu.com.vu; f. 1991; est. upon assumption of control of Vanuatu Co-operative Savings Bank; govt-owned; cap. 600m., dep. 4,662m. (Dec. 2005); Chair. John Ahuruhi; Man. Dir Bob Hughes; 19 brs.

Foreign Banks

ANZ Bank (Vanuatu) Ltd: PMB 9003, Port Vila; tel. 26355; fax 22814; e-mail anzvanuatu@anz.com; internet www.anz.com/vanuatu; f. 1971; cap. 3.7m., res 317.7m., dep. 24,734.2m. (Sept. 2003); Man. Dir Michael Flower; brs in Port Vila and Santo.

European Bank Ltd (USA): International Bldg, Fr Walter Lini Highway, POB 65, Port Vila; tel. 27700; fax 22884; e-mail info@europeanbank.net; internet www.europeanbank.net; 'offshore' and private banking; cap. US $0.8m., res US $1.3m., dep. US $35.0m. (Dec. 2005); Chair. Thomas Montgomery Bayer; Pres. Robert Murray Bohn.

Westpac Banking Corporation (Australia): Kumul Highway, POB 32, Port Vila; tel. 22084; fax 24773; Man. R. B. Wright; 2 brs.

Financial Institutions

The Financial Centre Association: POB 1128, Port Vila; tel. 24619; fax 26008; f. 1980; group of banking, legal, accounting and trust companies administering 'offshore' banking and investment; Chair. Jim Batty; Sec. Charles Kleiman.

Vanuatu Financial Services Commission (VFSC): Bougainville St, PMB 023, Port Vila; tel. 22247; fax 22242; e-mail info@vfsc.vu; internet www.vfsc.vu; f. 1993; regulation and supervision of non-banking financial services.

INSURANCE

Pacific Insurance Brokers: POB 229, Port Vila; tel. 23863; fax 23089.

QBE Insurance (Vanuatu) Ltd: La Casa D'Andrea Bldg, POB 186, Port Vila; tel. 22299; fax 23298; e-mail info.van@qbe.com; Gen. Man. GEOFFREY R. CUTTING.

Trade and Industry

GOVERNMENT AGENCY

Vanuatu Investment Promotion Authority: PMB 9011, Port Vila; tel. 24096; fax 25216; internet www.investinvanuatu.com; fmrly the Vanuatu Investment Board, name changed as above in 2000; CEO JOE LIGO.

CHAMBER OF COMMERCE

Chamber of Commerce and Industry of Vanuatu: POB 189, Port Vila; tel. 27543; fax 27542; e-mail vancci@vanuatu.com.vu; internet www.vanuatuchamber.com; Pres. JOSEPH JACOBE.

MARKETING BOARD

Vanuatu Commodities Marketing Board: POB 268, Luganville, Santo; f. 1982; sole exporter of major commodities, including copra, kava and cocoa; Gen. Man. GEORGE CALO.

UTILITIES
Electricity

Union Electrique du Vanuatu (Unelco Vanuatu Ltd): POB 26, rue Winston Churchill, Port Vila; tel. 22211; fax 25011; e-mail unelco@unelco.com.vu; private organization contracted for the generation and supply of electricity in Port Vila, Luganville, Tanna and Malekula, and for the supply of water in Port Vila; Dir-Gen. JEAN FRANÇOIS BARBEAU.

Village generators provide electricity in rural areas. The Government provides recirculated water supplies to about 85% of urban and 30% of rural households.

CO-OPERATIVES

During the early 1980s there were some 180 co-operative primary societies in Vanuatu and at least 85% of goods in the islands were distributed by co-operative organizations. Almost all rural ni-Vanuatu were members of a co-operative society, as were many urban dwellers. By the end of that decade, however, membership of co-operatives had declined, and the organizations' supervisory body, the Vanuatu Co-operative Federation, had been dissolved, after having accumulated debts totalling some $A1m.

TRADE UNIONS

Vanuatu Council of Trade Unions (VCTU): PMB 89, Port Vila; tel. 24517; fax 23679; Pres. OBED MASINGIOW; Sec.-Gen. EPHRAIM KALSAKAU.

National Union of Labour: Port Vila.

The principal trade unions include:

Oil and Gas Workers' Union: Port Vila; f. 1984.

Vanuatu Airline Workers' Union: Port Vila; f. 1984.

Vanuatu Public Service Association: Port Vila.

Vanuatu Teachers' Union: Port Vila; Gen. Sec. CHARLES KALO; Pres. OBED MASSING.

Vanuatu Waterside, Maritime and Allied Workers' Union: Port Vila.

Transport

ROADS

There are about 1,130 km of roads, of which 54 km, mostly on Efate Island, are sealed. In early 1998 Japan granted more than 400m. vatu to finance the sealing of the main road around Efate. In January 2002 an earthquake caused significant damage to the transport infrastructure around Efate. Several foreign donors, including New Zealand, contributed to funding urgent repairs to roads and bridges in the area. Two bridges on Efate were rebuilt with Japanese finance in 2004.

SHIPPING

The principal ports are Port Vila and Luganville. At the end of 2006 the merchant fleet comprised 419 vessels, with a total displacement of 1,968,700 grt. A shipping registry, based in Singapore, provides a 'flag of convenience' to foreign-owned vessels.

Vanuatu Maritime Authority: POB 320, Marine Quay, Port Vila; tel. 23128; fax 22949; e-mail iantchichine@vma.com.vu; domestic and international ship registry, maritime safety regulator; Commissioner of Maritime Affairs JOHN T. ROOSEN; Chair. LENNOX VUTI.

Ports and Harbour Department: PMB 9046, Port Vila; tel. 22339; fax 22475; e-mail nhamish@vanet.com; Harbour Master Capt. LUKE BEANDI; Dir NORRIS HAMISH.

Burns Philp (Vanuatu) Ltd: POB 27, Port Vila.

Ifira Shipping Agencies Ltd: POB 68, Port Vila; tel. 22929; fax 22052; f. 1986; Man. Dir CLAUDE BOUDIER.

Sami Ltd: Kumul Highway, POB 301, Port Vila; tel. 24106; fax 23405.

South Sea Shipping: POB 84, Port Vila; tel. 22205; fax 23304.

Vanua Navigation Ltd: POB 44, Port Vila; tel. 22027; f. 1977; by the Co-operative Federation and Sofrana Unilines; Chief Exec. GEOFFREY J. CLARKE.

The following services call regularly at Vanuatu: Compagnie Générale Maritime, Kyowa Shipping Co, Pacific Forum Line, Papua New Guinea Shipping Corpn, Sofrana-Unilines, Bank Line, Columbus Line and Bali Hai Shipping. Royal Viking Line, Sitmar and P & O cruises also call at Vanuatu.

CIVIL AVIATION

The principal airports are Bauerfield (Efate, for Port Vila) and Pekoa (Espiritu Santo, for Luganville). There are airstrips on all Vanuatu's principal islands, and an international airport at White Grass on Tanna was completed in 1998. In early 2000 it was announced that a further three airports were to be built on the islands of Pentecost, Malekula and Tanna. Major improvements providing for the accommodation of larger aircraft at both Bauerfield and Pekoa airports began in 2000. Moreover, in September 2000 plans for a new international airport at Teouma (Efate) were announced, with finance from a private Thai investor. In late 2003 plans for the construction of an international air terminal at Pekoa (Espiritu Santo) costing US $1.6m. were announced.

Civil Aviation Authority: POB 131, Port Vila; tel. 25111; fax 25532.

Air Vanuatu: 3rd Floor, Air Vanuatu House, rue de Paris, Port Vila; tel. 23838; fax 23250; e-mail reservations@airvanuatu.com.vu; internet www.airvanuatu.com; f. 1981; govt-owned national carrier since 1987; regular services between Port Vila and Sydney, Brisbane and Melbourne (Australia), Nadi (Fiji), Nouméa (New Caledonia), Auckland (New Zealand) and Honiara (Solomon Islands); the frequency of flights from Auckland, Sydney, Brisbane and Honiara to Port Vila was increased in mid-2004; CEO TERRY KERR.

Dovair: Port Vila; privately owned; operates domestic services.

Vanair: rue Pasteur, PMB 9069, Port Vila; tel. 22643; fax 23910; operates scheduled services to 29 destinations within the archipelago; management of the airline assumed by Air Vanuatu in Jan. 2005.

Tourism

Tourism is an important source of revenue for the Government of Vanuatu. Visitors are attracted by the islands' unspoilt landscape and rich local customs. There were some 120 hotels and guest houses in 2003, providing more than 1,300 rooms. In 2007 foreign visitor arrivals in Vanuatu totalled an estimated 81,345, compared with 50,400 in 2003. In 2006 some 60% of visitors were from Australia and 14% were from New Zealand. Receipts from tourism totalled some US $93m. in 2005. The development of the tourist industry has hitherto been concentrated on the islands of Efate, Espiritu Santo and Tanna; however, other islands are also being promoted as tourist centres.

Vanuatu Hotel and Resorts Association: POB 215, Port Vila; tel. 22040; fax 27579; Pres. JOHN GROCOCK.

Vanuatu Tourism Office: Lini Highway, POB 209, Port Vila; tel. 22685; fax 23889; e-mail tourism@vanuatu.com.vu; internet www.vanuatutourism.com; Gen. Man. ANNIE NIATU; Chair. BEN TARI.

THE VATICAN CITY
(THE HOLY SEE)

Introductory Survey

Location, Climate, Language, Religion, Flag

The State of the Vatican City is situated entirely within the Italian capital, Rome, on the right bank of the Tiber river. It covers an area of 0.44 sq km (0.17 sq mile). The climate is Mediterranean, with warm summers and mild winters (see Italy). Italian and Latin are the official languages. Roman Catholicism is the official religion. The state flag, which is square, consists of two vertical stripes of yellow and white, with the papal coat of arms superimposed on the white stripe.

History

For a period of nearly 1,000 years, dating roughly from the time of Charlemagne to the year 1870, the Popes ruled much of the central Italian peninsula, including the city of Rome. During the process of unification, the Kingdom of Italy gradually absorbed these States of the Church, the process being completed by the entry into Rome of King Victor Emmanuel's troops in September 1870. From 1860 to 1870 many attempts had been made to induce the Pope, Pius IX, to surrender his temporal possessions. Since, however, he regarded them as a sacred trust from a higher Power, to be guarded on behalf of the Church, he refused to do so. After the entry of the Royal Army into Rome, he retired to the Vatican from where no Pope emerged again until the ratification of the Lateran Treaty of 11 February 1929. By the Law of Guarantees of May 1871, Italy attempted to stabilize the position of the Papacy by recognizing the Pope's claim to use of the Palaces of the Lateran and the Vatican, the Papal villa of Castelgandolfo, and their gardens and annexes, and to certain privileges customary to sovereignty. This unilateral arrangement was not accepted by Pius IX, and his protest against it was repeated constantly by his successors.

In 1929 two agreements were made with the Italian Government—the Lateran Treaty and the Concordat. By the terms of the Lateran Treaty, the Holy See was given exclusive power and sovereign jurisdiction over the State of the Vatican City, which was declared neutral and inviolable territory. Financial compensation was also given for the earlier losses. Under the Concordat, Roman Catholicism became the state religion of Italy, with special privileges defined by law. The new Italian Constitution of 1947 reaffirmed adherence to the Lateran Treaty, but in 1967 negotiations began for a revision of the Concordat. In December 1978 the two sides agreed on a draft plan for a new Concordat, under which Catholicism would cease to be the official Italian state religion and most of the Catholic Church's special privileges in Italy would be removed. The revised version was signed in February 1984.

In 1917 the first legal code, the Code of Canon Law (Codex Iuris Canonici), was devised for the Catholic Church. In 1963 a pontifical commission was inaugurated to investigate possible reforms to the law, and in 1981 the Pope received more than 70 cardinals and bishops who had prepared the new code's 1,752 rules. Revisions included a reduction in the number of cases meriting excommunication and a general relaxing of penalties, with increased emphasis on the importance of the laity within the church. The code was ratified in January 1983, and came into force in November.

In October 1978 Cardinal Karol Wojtyła (then Archbishop of Kraków, Poland) became the first non-Italian Pope since the 16th century, taking the name John Paul II. Security surrounding the Pontiff was tightened considerably after an attempt on his life in May 1981 and another in May 1982. An Italian parliamentary inquiry, which published its findings in March 2006, concluded that the 1981 attempt was orchestrated by the former USSR.

In April 1984 Pope John Paul II announced a major reshuffle of offices in the Roman Curia, which included the delegation of most of his responsibility for the routine administration of the Vatican to the Secretariat of State. In July 1988 a number of reforms to the Curia were introduced. These consolidated the power of the Secretariat of State, as well as reorganizing some of the Congregations and Pontifical Commissions.

In February 1987 Italian judges issued a warrant for the arrest of Archbishop Paul Marcinkus, the Chairman of the Istituto per le Opere di Religione ('Vatican Bank'), and two other bank officials for alleged involvement in the fraudulent bankruptcy of the Banco Ambrosiano in Milan, which collapsed in 1982. In July 1987, however, the Italian Supreme Court cancelled the warrants for the arrest of the three bank officials, stating that the Vatican stood outside Italian jurisdiction and that, according to the Lateran Treaty, Italy did not have the right to interfere in the affairs of the central organs of the Roman Catholic Church. In May 1988, following an appeal, the Archbishop's immunity was endorsed by the Constitutional Court. In March 1989 the Vatican announced a wide-ranging reorganization of the Istituto per le Opere di Religione, by abolishing the post of Chairman, held by Marcinkus, and appointing a commission of five cardinals, nominated by the Pope, to preside over the bank, assisted by a committee of financial experts. Archbishop Marcinkus retired from papal service in October 1990 and died in February 2006.

In March 1998 the Vatican released its long-awaited 'definitive statement' condemning anti-Semitism and anti-Judaism, and repenting for Roman Catholic passivity during the Nazi Holocaust. However, a number of high-ranking Jewish officials expressed disappointment in the document and demanded an explicit apology for the attitude of Pope Pius XII and the Roman Catholic Church's failure to speak out, at the time, against Nazi atrocities. In March 2000, during a service in St Peter's Basilica in Rome, despite misgivings expressed by some theologians that such a statement would undermine the Church's authority, the Pope made a comprehensive and unprecedented plea for forgiveness for the 'past sins of the Church', including racial and ethnic discrimination and Christian mistreatment of minorities, women and native peoples. However, in July 2001 a panel of Catholic and Jewish historians was forced to halt its study of the Church's role in the Holocaust when the Vatican refused it access to files on Pope Pius XII, prompting allegations that the Vatican was seeking to conceal potentially damaging evidence. Following further pressure, however, archives covering the years 1922–39 were released in February 2003.

In February 2001 it was announced that the Constitution, dating back to the Lateran Treaty of 1929, was to be replaced by a new Basic Law incorporating a number of constitutional amendments made over the years. The Basic Law clarified the distinction between the legislative, executive and judicial branches.

In November 2001 Pope John Paul II issued an apology to victims of sexual abuse perpetrated by members of the Catholic clergy. Furthermore, in January 2002 new regulations were published by the Vatican, outlining the appropriate method of dealing with cases of alleged sexual abuse, notably against children, by members of the clergy. However, in mid-2002, in the most significant scandal to affect the Roman Catholic Church in many years, it was revealed that Cardinal Bernard Law, the Archbishop of Boston, Massachusetts, USA, had protected a number of priests who faced accusations of sexual misconduct against children. Hundreds of priests in the USA resigned or were subsequently suspended or sued in the wake of more than 200 allegations of sexual abuse involving members of the clergy in the Boston area. In April the Pope summoned 13 US cardinals to the Vatican to discuss the crisis. A 'zero tolerance' policy adopted by the US Conference of Catholic Bishops in June was subsequently rejected by the Vatican; a somewhat altered charter, which provided for the eventual dismissal of any priests found guilty of sexual abuse in a church tribunal, was accepted by the Vatican in December. Victims' groups were disappointed with the revisions, however, which reintroduced a 10-year statute of limitation on accusations. Following the filing of 450 lawsuits against Cardinal Law's archdiocese and the petition of 58 Boston priests, Law resigned in December 2002.

The publication in March 2003 of a *Lexicon On Ambiguous and Colloquial Terms About Family Life and Ethical Questions* caused controversy by its reaffirmation of the Catholic Church's uncompromising stance regarding birth control and homosexuality. In July a document was circulated to all bishops confirming the Vatican's opposition to the legalization of same-sex unions. Further controversy arose in October following claims by certain Vatican officials that the AIDS virus could be transferred through condoms, provoking much criticism from the World Health Organization. Of the 30 new cardinals elected at the ninth consistory of John Paul II's papacy, which took place in October, only six were Italian, while the representation from Africa and Latin America was increased. An additional cardinal was elevated *in pectore* (i.e. his name was not publicly divulged).

In August 2004, in an open letter to the bishops entitled 'On the collaboration of men and women in the Church and the World', the Pope criticized radical feminism for having created a culture of enmity between the sexes. In October the *Compendium of the Social Doctrine of the Church*, published by the Pontifical Council for Justice and Peace, called on Catholics to include their faith in the life and legislation of the State and reiterated the Church's oppositional stance on homosexuality and birth control.

Following a long period of ill health, Pope John Paul II died on 2 April 2005 at the age of 84. Only St Peter and Pius IX, in the mid-19th century, had enjoyed longer papacies. More than 3m. people visited the Vatican City in the period between the death of John Paul II and his funeral, which took place on 8 April and was attended by around 200 world leaders. By the time of his death, John Paul II had canonized 482 saints (more than all his predecessors combined since the 16th century), performed 1,338 beatifications and created 232 cardinals.

The conclave to elect a new Pope began on 18 April 2005 and was attended by 115 of the 117 cardinals of voting age (under 80 years old). On 19 April Cardinal Joseph Ratzinger was elected as the Supreme Pontiff, and took the name Benedict XVI. Ratzinger, who was aged 78, was hitherto the Dean of the College of Cardinals, the Prefect of the Congregation for the Doctrine of the Faith and President of the International Theological Commission and of the Pontifical Biblical Commission. He was widely viewed as a conservative theologian whose views were similar to those of his predecessor. The new Pope's inauguration as the 265th Roman pontiff took place on 24 April. Benedict XVI subsequently reappointed the officials of the Roman Curia, who had, according to custom, ceased to hold their offices on the death of John Paul II. In May Benedict announced the commencement of the process of beatification of John Paul II, waiving the five-year delay normally required after a person's death before beatification could begin. In his first addresses as Pope, Benedict pledged to continue his predecessor's attempts to improve ties with other religions and branches of Christianity. In October the first synod of Benedict XVI's papacy took place, at which the celibacy of the priesthood was reaffirmed.

In early 2006 it was reported that the Pope had decided to stop using one of his nine official titles, that of Patriarch of the West; this was regarded as a gesture of reconciliation towards the Orthodox churches. Pope Benedict's first encyclical, *Deus Caritas Est*, on the nature of love, was published in January. On 24 March Benedict appointed 15 new cardinals. Notable among the appointees was Joseph Zen Ze-kiun, Bishop of Hong Kong and an outspoken critic of the Chinese Government.

In September 2006 Cardinal Angelo Sodano retired as Secretary of State and was replaced by Cardinal Tarcisio Bertone, hitherto Archbishop of Genoa, Italy, while Cardinal Edmund Szoka was replaced as President of the Pontifical Commission for the Vatican City State and of the Governorate of the Vatican City State by Most Rev. Giovanni Lajolo, who had been Secretary of State for Relations with States—in effect the foreign minister. Most Rev. Dominique Mamberti was appointed Secretary of State for Relations with States.

In November 2007 Pope Benedict appointed 23 new cardinals, of whom 18 were of voting age, thus bringing the number of cardinals eligible to vote in the conclave to elect a new pontiff to 121.

The Vatican's prominence in international affairs increased from the late 1980s. In July 1989 diplomatic relations with Poland, severed in 1945, were restored. The Vatican had hitherto maintained no diplomatic relations with eastern European governments under communist rule, except for Yugoslavia. During the early 1990s diplomatic relations were restored or established with many former communist states, including with the USSR in 1990. In 1992 full diplomatic relations were restored, after more than 120 years of discord, between the Vatican and Mexico. In December 1993 the Vatican and Israel signed a mutual-recognition agreement, which led to the establishment of full diplomatic ties and the exchange of ambassadors in September 1994. Meanwhile, in February 1994 the Vatican established diplomatic relations with Jordan, in an apparent move to strengthen links with the Arab world to counterbalance its recent recognition of Israel. Similarly, in October of that year the Vatican instituted 'official relations' with the Palestine Liberation Organization.

Diplomatic relations between the Vatican and the People's Republic of China had been severed in 1951 following the communists' accession to power in Beijing. In August 1999 China vetoed plans for Pope John Paul II to visit Hong Kong later that year, owing to the Vatican's diplomatic ties with Taiwan. Any hope of a reconciliation between China and the Vatican looked increasingly unlikely in January 2000, when the state-controlled Patriotic Church in Beijing ordained five bishops in a ceremony timed to upstage official papal ordinations in the Vatican City. Relations further deteriorated following the Pope's announcement in September 2000 that he was to canonize 120 western and Chinese Catholics killed in China between 1648 and 1930. The controversy was exacerbated by the decision to hold the ceremony on China's National Day, the anniversary of the accession to power of communist rule (although the Vatican insisted that the date was merely coincidental). The canonizations were also denounced by Catholic organizations in China. However, in October 2001 Pope John Paul II issued an apology to China for the sins committed by Christians against the country; an appeal was also made for diplomatic relations between the two states to be restored. Informal talks recommenced in early 2003, but were adversely affected by the outspoken anti-Government stance of Hong Kong's Bishop (later Cardinal), Joseph Zen Ze-kiun. Relations were again strained in mid-2004, following allegations that some 23 Roman Catholics had been arrested in China. Following the accession of Benedict XVI, there appeared to be a growing emphasis on the need to improve Sino-Vatican relations. However, the ordination of a series of bishops by the Patriotic Church in April and May 2006 provoked criticism from the Pope. Despite ongoing disagreement over the ordination of bishops, attempts to improve relations between China and the Vatican continued in 2007. In July an open letter addressed to Chinese Catholics on behalf of the Pope called for 'respectful and constructive' relations. In September the Vatican approved the ordination of a bishop by the Patriotic Church, allaying fears that efforts toward reconciliation would be undermined by the death earlier that month of a Vatican-appointed bishop, John Han Dingxiang, while in detention by the Chinese authorities.

In February 2000 the Vatican and the Palestinian (National) Authority signed an historic agreement on joint interests, which appealed for a peaceful solution, through dialogue, to the Israeli-Palestinian conflict, and called for an internationally guaranteed special statute for the city of Jerusalem that safeguarded freedom of religion and conscience. The Israeli Government criticized the accord as representing unwelcome 'interference' by the Vatican in the ongoing Middle East peace talks. In early 2000 the Pope undertook a millennial pilgrimage to some of the principal biblical sites of the Middle East, including Mount Sinai in Egypt in February (the first visit by a pontiff to that country) and Israel, Jordan and the West Bank in March. Pope John Paul II's six-day visit to the politically volatile Holy Land constituted the first papal visit to that region for 36 years. In April 2002 an agreement was signed by the Vatican and the Turkish Government, promoting religious dialogue between Muslims and Christians.

In mid-2001 Pope John Paul II undertook visits to Greece and Syria, the first by a Roman pontiff since the division of Christianity into eastern and western churches. During his visit to Greece, the Pope attempted to heal the historic rift between the Roman Catholic and Orthodox churches by presenting an apology to the Orthodox community for wrongs committed over the centuries by the Roman Catholic Church. The Pope, despite not being granted the consent of the Russian Orthodox Patriarch, also visited Ukraine, where he called for an end to the 1,000-year schism between Roman Catholicism and the Orthodox Church in Ukraine and, by extension, the Russian Orthodox Church. The leaders of the Orthodox Church in Ukraine refused to meet the Pope, although his visit attracted much popular support. In September Pope John Paul II visited Armenia, becoming the first pontiff to visit the country.

Tensions between the Roman Catholic Church and the Russian Orthodox Church increased in February 2002 when the Vatican announced that the four apostolic administrations in Russia (officially considered to be temporary) had become dioceses. This move was interpreted by representatives of the Russian Orthodox Church as the establishment of an alternative church within the country, and a few days later a visit to Russia by the Head of the Pontifical Council for the Promotion of Christian Unity, Cardinal Walter Kasper, was cancelled by the Russian Orthodox Church.

In November 2002 John Paul II became the first pontiff to address the Italian Parliament, symbolically closing the Vatican's territorial dispute with Italy. His speech advocated institutional recognition by the European Union (EU, see p. 244) of Europe's Christian heritage. This followed an ultimately unsuccessful call in October for Christianity to be enshrined in the proposed EU constitution. In June 2004 John Paul II publicly criticized the lack of reference to Christianity in the approved text of the EU constitutional treaty, and in early 2005 the Vatican again criticized the increasing secularization of the EU states, with particular reference to plans by Spain's ruling socialist party to introduce same-sex marriage. In 2007 Pope Benedict XVI also criticized the Italian Government for its plans to give homosexual and unmarried couples equal legal status with married couples.

During late 2002 and early 2003 Pope John Paul II was prominent in opposing the prospect of US-led military intervention to remove the regime of Saddam Hussain in Iraq; he denounced the planned conflict as a 'defeat for humanity', and urged a diplomatic resolution to the crisis. During February and March the Pope granted a series of private audiences to important international figures, including the Deputy Prime Minister of Iraq, Tareq Aziz, the Secretary-General of the UN, Kofi Annan, the British Prime Minister, Tony Blair, and the Italian Prime Minister, Silvio Berlusconi. Papal envoys were also sent to Baghdad and Washington, DC. This was followed in March by an historic five-day meeting with a delegation from Israel's Chief Rabbinate. Later in the year the Pope continued to receive government representatives from various countries, including the Iranian and Israeli ministers responsible for foreign affairs and the Palestinian Prime Minister, Ahmad Quray.

While the number of foreign visits undertaken by John Paul II was reduced in 2003 owing to his increasing frailty, he continued to receive foreign leaders in the Vatican, including President Vladimir Putin of Russia in November. The Pope maintained his engagement with former Soviet bloc countries, visiting Slovakia in September and receiving the Prime Ministers of the former Yugoslav republic of Macedonia and Croatia. In September talks on an accord between Croatia and the Vatican stalled owing to differences of opinion over the Catholic Church's presence in the largely Orthodox country. The Dalai Lama, the head of the Tibetan Buddhist hierarchy, had a private audience with the Pope in November. In total, John Paul II made 104 journeys outside Italy during his papacy, making him by far the most widely travelled pontiff.

Pope John Paul II visited Switzerland in June 2004, and it was announced that diplomatic relations, which had been severed in 1873, were to be restored. In mid-2004 the Pope continued his policy of engagement with the Orthodox churches, with a visit by the Russian Minister of Foreign Affairs, Sergei Lavrov, and the return of a copy of the icon 'Our Lady of Kazan' to Moscow. On 1 July the Pope issued a joint statement with Patriarch Bartholomew I of Constantinople, the Orthodox Patriarch in Istanbul, Turkey, confirming their commitment to dialogue between the Roman Catholic and Orthodox churches.

Pope Benedict XVI's first major foreign visit as pontiff was to his native Germany in August 2005, during which he made a symbolic visit to a synagogue. In May 2006 the Pope made a trip to Poland, where he visited the Nazi concentration camp at Auschwitz.

Tensions between the Vatican and the Muslim world increased in September 2006 after Benedict XVI delivered a lecture at the University of Regensburg, Germany, in the course of which he quoted a medieval Byzantine emperor as saying that the Prophet Muhammad had contributed only 'evil and inhuman' things to the world. The Pope's remarks provoked widespread protest in Muslim countries. Benedict later apologized for causing offence, stating that the quotation did not reflect his personal belief. In November Benedict visited Turkey, where he was praised by Muslims for facing Mecca while praying in the Blue Mosque in Istanbul—only the second time that a Pope had entered a mosque (the first being during John Paul II's visit to Syria in 2001). He also held a joint service with Patriarch Bartholomew I, a gesture that was regarded as an attempt to heal the divisions between the Roman Catholic and Greek Orthodox churches.

Relations between Israel and the Vatican were strained in April 2007, when the Apostolic Nuncio to Israel, Archbishop Antonio Franco, announced his intention to boycott the Holocaust Memorial Day commemoration at the Yad Vashem Holocaust museum in protest at a caption the museum had attached to a photograph of Pope Pius XII, which condemned the late Pope's attitude to the extermination of the Jews. Franco later reversed his decision not to attend. Later that month it was announced that negotiations between the Vatican and Israel over tax and judicial matters would resume after five years of stalemate.

Following the controversy over a speech given by Pope Benedict XVI in September 2006 (see above), efforts to establish good relations between the Roman Catholic Church and the Muslim world intensified. In May 2007 it was announced that the Pontifical Council for Inter-Religious Dialogue was to be restored, thereby reversing a decision in March 2006 to place it under the direction of the Pontifical Council for Culture. (The decision to downgrade the Council, which had previously been led by an expert on Islamic affairs, had been criticized by Muslim leaders.) King Abdullah of Saudi Arabia visited the Vatican in November 2007 for talks with the Pope, representing the first meeting between a Saudi monarch and a pontiff. It was subsequently revealed that the discussions had focused on inter-faith relations and the 'necessity of finding a just solution' to the Israeli–Palestinian conflict. In December it was reported that Benedict had formally invited a delegation of Muslim religious leaders to participate in talks at the Vatican, following the publication in October of an open letter to the Pope, in which 138 Muslim leaders had urged increased co-operation between Roman Catholic and Muslim religious leaders. The talks duly took place at the Vatican in March 2008.

Pope Benedict XVI made a six-day trip to the USA in April 2008. During the visit, the Pope gave an address to the UN General Assembly in New York, in which he urged greater efforts on the part of UN members to protect human rights.

The population of the Vatican City was around 900 in 2004. Its inhabitants are of many nationalities, representing the presence of the Roman Catholic Church throughout the world. The papal guards, who number some 110, are of Swiss nationality.

Finance

The Vatican has three main sources of income: the Istituto per le Opere di Religione (see Directory), voluntary contributions to the Church, known as 'Peter's Pence' (Obolo di San Pietro), and interest on financial investments, managed by the Administration of the Patrimony of the Holy See. The euro is used as currency. The Vatican first revealed budget figures for the Holy See in 1979, when it disclosed a deficit of US $20.1m. This was incurred through the normal operating expenses of the Vatican bureaucracy, including the newspaper and radio services and overseas diplomatic missions. The alleged mismanagement of investments, banking scandals and the decline in the value of the US dollar contributed to a deficit of $56.7m. in 1986, when annual income reached $57m. The deficit was met by the receipt of $32m. from the 'Peter's Pence' levy, and by the withdrawal of $24.7m. from the 'Peter's Pence' reserve fund. In March 1988 the Vatican published an independently audited annual balance sheet, thereby, for the first time in its history, revealing the church's financial affairs to public scrutiny. During 1988–1990 the budget deficit continued to grow, and in April 1991 more than 100 representatives of bishops' conferences from around the world attended an unprecedented meeting held in the Vatican City, at which they discussed ways of making local dioceses systematically share the burden of the Vatican's annual budgetary deficit. In that year, however, the budgetary deficit reached a peak of $87.5m. The establishment of new diplomatic missions in the late 1980s and early 1990s (see History) entailed considerable capital expenditure for the papacy. However, in 1992 the deficit fell substantially and in 1993, after 23 years of budgetary deficits, a modest surplus, of $1.5m., was recorded. A small annual budgetary surplus was maintained throughout the 1990s, cumulating in a surplus of $8.5m. in 2000, a 70% rise compared with 1999, which reflected the greater receipts generated by activities associated with the jubilee year. The budget for 2001, in contrast, showed the first deficit since 1993, of $3.1m., as a result of a general slowdown in the global economy following the terrorist attacks in the USA on 11 September 2001; 'Peter's Pence' contributions for that year, not included in the consolidated budget, amounted to almost $52m. In 2002 another budget deficit, of $21m., was recorded. The considerable increase in the deficit was largely attributed to losses in investments of

$18.5m., compared with profits of $37m. from investments in 2001. 'Peter's Pence' contributions, however, rose by almost 86%, compared with the previous year, to $96.6m. in 2002. Another budget deficit, of $22.5m., was recorded in 2003. In 2004 a budget surplus of $3.7m. (€3.0m.) was recorded, the first since 2000, due in part to the sale of properties outside the Vatican. In 2005 the budget surplus increased to $12.3m., largely as a result of a seven-fold increase in returns on investments, assisted by favourable exchange rates. The surplus was achieved despite the costs incurred in conducting the funeral of John Paul II and the election of Benedict XVI. In 2006 a budget surplus of $3.2m. was recorded, despite a decline in the value of the Vatican's financial investments precipitated by a fall in the value of the US dollar against that of the euro. A large increase in 'Peter's Pence' contributions was recorded in that year, with donations totalling $102m.

Directory

Government

The State of the Vatican City came into existence with the Lateran Treaty of 1929. The Holy See (a term designating the papacy, i.e. the office of the Pope, and thus the central governing body of the Roman Catholic Church) is a distinct, pre-existing entity. Both entities are subjects of international law. Ambassadors and Ministers are accredited to the Holy See, which sends diplomatic representatives (nuncios and pro-nuncios) to more than 120 states, as well as having delegates or observers at the UN and other international organizations. The Vatican City is also a member of certain international organizations, including specialized agencies of the UN.

Both entities are indissolubly united in the person of the Pope, the Bishop of Rome, who is simultaneously ruler of the State and visible head of the Roman Catholic Church.

On 1 February 2001 a new Basic Law replaced the former Constitution dating back to the 1929 Lateran Treaty.

THE GOVERNMENT OF THE VATICAN CITY STATE

The Vatican City State is under the temporal jurisdiction of the Pope, the Supreme Pontiff elected for life by a conclave comprising members of the Sacred College of Cardinals. The Pope holds all legislative, executive and judicial power. Legislative power is vested in the Pontifical Commission for the Vatican State, which comprises a Cardinal President and six other cardinals, nominated by the Pope for a five-year period. Executive power is vested in the President of the Pontifical Commission (who is also the President of the Governorate of the Vatican City State), who is assisted by a Secretary-General. The State Councillors, including one General Councillor and eight other Councillors, are nominated by the Pope for a five-year period, and assist in the drawing-up of laws and report to the Pontifical Commission. Judiciary power is vested in a number of Tribunals and the Apostolic Penitentiary, who exercise their judicial authority in the name of the Pope. The Pontiff exclusively retains the right to grant pardons and amnesties.

Head of State

His Holiness Pope BENEDICT XVI (elected 19 April 2005).

Pontifical Commission for the Vatican City State

Most Rev. GIOVANNI LAJOLO (President).
Cardinal ANGELO SODANO.
Cardinal GIOVANNI BATTISTA RE.
Cardinal JOSÉ SARAIVA MARTINS.
Cardinal JEAN-LOUIS PIERRE TAURAN.
Cardinal RENATO RAFFAELE MARTINO.
Cardinal ATTILIO NICORA.

State Councillors

Prof. CESARE MIRABELLI (General Councillor).
There are nine additional councillors.

Governorate of the Vatican City State

President: Most Rev. GIOVANNI LAJOLO.
Secretary-General: Rt Rev. RENATO BOCCARDO (Titular Bishop of Aquipendium).
Vice Secretary-General: Rev. GIORGIO CORBELLINI.

THE SUPREME PONTIFF

His Holiness Pope Benedict XVI (Joseph Ratzinger), Bishop of Rome, Vicar of Christ, Successor of the Prince of the Apostles, Supreme Pontiff of the Universal Church, Primate of Italy, Archbishop and Metropolitan of the Province of Rome, Sovereign of the Vatican City State, Servant of the Servants of God, acceded on 19 April 2005 as the 265th Roman pontiff.

THE SACRED COLLEGE OF CARDINALS AND THE ROMAN CURIA

Members of the Sacred College of Cardinals are created by the Pope. The cardinals are divided into three orders: Bishops, Priests and Deacons. Under the decree of November 1970, *Ingravescentem Aetatem*, only cardinals under 80 years of age have the right to enter the conclave for the election of the Pope. Cardinals who reside in Rome, Italy, as the Pope's immediate advisers are styled Cardinals 'in Curia'. The Roman Curia acts as the Papal court and the principal administrative body of the Church. The College of Cardinals derives from the Church's earliest days. In March 1973 Pope Paul VI announced that the number of cardinals permitted to participate in the conclave would be limited to 120. This was increased to 135 by Pope John Paul II in February 2001. At 18 April 2005, as the conclave to elect John Paul II's successor began, there were 183 cardinals, of whom 117 were under the age of 80; 115 cardinals participated in the conclave. Following Benedict XVI's second consistory on 24 November 2007 there were 201 cardinals, of whom 121 were of voting age. There are usually six Cardinal Bishops, who are in titular charge of suburban sees of Rome. The order of Cardinal Bishops also includes the Cardinals of Patriarchal Sees of Oriental Rites. Cardinal Priests occupy titular churches in Rome, Italy, founded soon after Christianity originated. The administration of the Church's affairs is undertaken through the Secretariat of State and the Council for the Public Affairs of the Church, under the Cardinal Secretary of State, and through a number of Congregations, each under the direction of a cardinal or senior member of the Church, as well as through Tribunals, Offices, Commissions and Secretariats for special purposes.

The 'Apostolic Constitution' (*Regimini Ecclesiae Universae*), published in August 1967 and effective from 1 March 1968, reformed the Roman Curia. Among the changes were the creation of new organs and the restructuring of the Secretariat of State. In 1969 the Congregation of Rites was divided into two Congregations—one for Divine Worship and the other for the Causes of Saints. The Congregation for the Discipline of the Sacraments and the Congregation for Divine Worship were amalgamated in 1975, but separated again in 1984.

In July 1988 further reforms of the Curia were introduced. The Secretariat of State was divided into two sections: the first section dealing with 'General Affairs' and the second 'Relations with States'. The Congregation for Divine Worship was again amalgamated with the Congregation for the Discipline of the Sacraments.

Members in order of precedence:

Cardinal Bishops

ANGELO SODANO (Italy—Titular Bishop of Albano and of Ostia and Dean of the College of Cardinals).
ROGER ETCHEGARAY (France—Titular Bishop of Porto-Santa Rufina and Vice-Dean of the College of Cardinals).
GIOVANNI BATTISTA RE (Italy—Titular Bishop of Sabina-Poggio Mirteto, Prefect of the Congregation for the Bishops and President of the Pontifical Commission for Latin America).
FRANCIS A. ARINZE (Nigeria—Titular Bishop of Velletri-Segni, Prefect of the Congregation for Divine Worship and the Discipline of the Sacraments).
TARCISIO BERTONE (Italy—Titular Bishop of Frascati, Secretary of the Secretariat of State and Chamberlain of the Apostolic Chamber).

Cardinals of Patriarchal Sees of Oriental Rites

NASRALLAH PIERRE SFEIR (Lebanon—Maronite Patriarch of Antioch).
STÉPHANOS II GHATTAS (Egypt—Coptic Patriarch Emeritus of Alexandria).

THE VATICAN CITY

Ignace Moussa I Daoud (Syria—Prefect emeritus of the Congregation for the Eastern Churches).
Emmanuel III Delly (Iraq—Chaldean Patriarch of Babylon).

Cardinal Priests

Stephen Kim Sou-hwan (Republic of Korea).
Eugênio de Araújo Sales (Brazil).
Luis Aponte Martínez (Puerto Rico).
Paulo Evaristo Arns (Brazil).
William Wakefield Baum (USA).
Marco Cé (Italy).
Franciszek Macharski (Poland).
Michael Michai Kitbunchu (Thailand—Archbishop of Bangkok).
Alexandre do Nascimento (Angola).
Godfried Danneels (Belgium—Archbishop of Mechelen-Brussels).
Thomas Stafford Williams (New Zealand).
Carlo Maria Martini (Italy).
Józef Glemp (Poland).
Joachim Meisner (Germany—Archbishop of Cologne).
Duraisamy Simon Lourdusamy (India).
Antonio Innocenti (Italy).
Miguel Obando Bravo (Nicaragua).
Paul Augustin Mayer (Germany).
Ricardo Jamin Vidal (Philippines—Archbishop of Cebu).
Henryk Roman Gulbinowicz (Poland).
Jozef Tomko (Slovakia—President of the Pontifical Committee for International Eucharistic Congresses).
Andrzej Maria Deskur (Poland).
Paul Joseph Jean Poupard (France—President of the Pontifical Council for Culture).
Friedrich Wetter (Germany).
Silvano Piovanelli (Italy).
Adrianus Johannes Simonis (Netherlands).
Bernard Francis Law (USA—Archpriest of the Patriarchal Liberian Basilica of Santa Maria Maggiore).
Giacomo Biffi (Italy).
Eduardo Martínez Somalo (Spain).
Achille Silvestrini (Italy).
José Freire Falcão (Brazil).
Michele Giordano (Italy).
Alexandre José Maria dos Santos (Mozambique).
Giovanni Canestri (Italy).
Simon Ignatius Pimenta (India).
Edward Bede Clancy (Australia).
Edmund Casimir Szoka (USA).
László Paskai (Hungary).
Christian Wiyghan Tumi (Cameroon—Archbishop of Douala).
Jean Margéot (Mauritius).
Pio Laghi (Italy).
Edward Idris Cassidy (Australia).
Nicolás de Jesús López Rodríguez (Dominican Republic—Archbishop of Santo Domingo).
José Tomás Sánchez (Philippines).
Virgilio Noè (Italy).
Fiorenzo Angelini (Italy).
Roger Michael Mahony (USA—Archbishop of Los Angeles).
Anthony Joseph Bevilacqua (USA).
Giovanni Saldarini (Italy).
Cahal Brendan Daly (Ireland).
Camillo Ruini (Italy—Vicar-General of His Holiness for the Diocese of Rome, Archpriest of the Lateran Patriarchal Archbasilica, and Grand Chancellor of the Lateran Pontifical University).
Ján Chryzostom Korec (Slovakia).
Henri Schwéry (Switzerland).
Georg Maximilian Sterzinsky (Germany—Archbishop of Berlin).
Miloslav Vlk (Czech Republic—Archbishop of Prague).
Luigi Poggi (Italy).
Peter Seiichi Shirayanagi (Japan).
Carlo Furno (Italy).
Julius Riyadi Darmaatmadja (Indonesia—Archbishop of Jakarta).
Jaime Lucas Ortega y Alamino (Cuba—Archbishop of San Cristóbal de la Habana).
Gilberto Agustoni (Italy).
Emmanuel Wamala (Uganda).
William Henry Keeler (USA).
Jean-Claude Turcotte (Canada—Archbishop of Montreal).
Ricardo María Carles Gordó (Spain).
Adam Joseph Maida (USA—Archbishop of Detroit, and Superior of the Cayman Islands).
Vinko Puljić (Bosnia and Herzegovina—Archbishop of Vrhbosna).
Armand Gaétan Razafindratandra (Madagascar).
Paul Joseph Pham Đình Tung (Viet Nam).
Juan Sandoval Iñiguez (Mexico—Archbishop of Guadalajara).
Kazimierz Świątek (Belarus).
Ersilio Tonini (Italy).
Salvatore De Giorgi (Italy).
Serafim Fernandes de Araújo (Brazil).
Antonio María Rouco Varela (Spain—Archbishop of Madrid).
Aloysius Matthew Ambrozic (Canada).
Dionigi Tettamanzi (Italy—Archbishop of Milan).
Polycarp Pengo (Tanzania—Archbishop of Dar-es-Salaam).
Christoph Schönborn (Austria—Archbishop of Vienna).
Norberto Rivera Carrera (Mexico—Archbishop of Mexico City).
Francis Eugene George (USA—Archbishop of Chicago).
Paul Shan Kuo-hsi (Taiwan).
Marian Jaworski (Ukraine—Archbishop of Lviv—Latin Rite).
Jānis Pujats (Latvia—Archbishop of Rīga).
Antonio José González Zumárraga (Ecuador).
Ivan Dias (India—Prefect of the Congregation for the Evangelization of Peoples).
Geraldo Majella Agnelo (Brazil—Archbishop of São Salvador de Bahia).
Pedro Rubiano Sáenz (Colombia—Archbishop of Santafé de Bogotá).
Theodore Edgar McCarrick (USA).
Desmond Connell (Ireland).
Audrys Juozas Bačkis (Lithuania—Archbishop of Vilnius).
Francisco Javier Errázuriz Ossa (Chile—Archbishop of Santiago de Chile).
Julio Terrazas Sandoval (Bolivia—Archbishop of Santa Cruz de la Sierra).
Wilfrid Fox Napier (South Africa—Archbishop of Durban).
Óscar Andrés Rodríguez Maradiaga (Honduras—Archbishop of Tegucigalpa).
Bernard Agré (Côte d'Ivoire).
Juan Luis Cipriani Thorne (Peru—Archbishop of Lima).
Francisco Alvarez Martínez (Spain).
Cláudio Hummes (Brazil—Prefect of the Congregation for the Clergy).
Varkey Vithayathil (India—Major Archbishop of Ernakulam-Angamaly).
Jorge Mario Bergoglio (Argentina—Archbishop of Buenos Aires).
José da Cruz Policarpo (Portugal—Patriarch of Lisbon).
Severino Poletto (Italy—Archbishop of Turin).
Cormac Murphy-O'Connor (United Kingdom—Archbishop of Westminster).
Edward Michael Egan (USA—Archbishop of New York).
Lubomyr Husar (Ukraine—Archbishop-Major of Kyiv-Halyč, Byzantine Ukrainian Rite).
Karl Lehmann (Germany—Bishop of Mainz).
Jean Marcel Honoré (France).
Crescenzio Sepe (Italy—Archbishop of Naples).
Angelo Scola (Italy—Patriarch of Venice).
Anthony Olubunmi Okogie (Nigeria—Archbishop of Lagos).
Bernard Louis Auguste Panafieu (France).
Gabriel Zubeir Wako (Sudan—Archbishop of Khartoum).
Carlos Amigo Vallejo (Spain—Archbishop of Seville).
Justin Francis Rigali (USA—Archbishop of Philadelphia).
Keith Michael Patrick O'Brien (United Kingdom—Archbishop of St Andrews and Edinburgh).
Eusébio Oscar Scheid (Brazil—Archbishop of São Sebastião do Rio de Janeiro).
Ennio Antonelli (Italy—Archbishop of Florence).

THE VATICAN CITY

Peter Kodwo Appiah Turkson (Ghana—Archbishop of Cape Coast).
Telesphore Placidus Toppo (India—Archbishop of Ranchi).
George Pell (Australia—Archbishop of Sydney).
Josip Bozanić (Croatia—Archbishop of Zagreb).
Jean-Baptiste Pham Minh Mân (Viet Nam—Archbishop of Ho Chi Minh City).
Rodolfo Quezada Toruño (Guatemala—Archbishop of Guatemala City).
Philippe Xavier Ignace Barbarin (France—Archbishop of Lyon).
Péter Erdő (Hungary—Archbishop of Esztergom-Budapest).
Marc Ouellet (Canada—Archbishop of Québec).
Jorge Liberato Urosa Savino (Venezuela—Archbishop of Caracas—Santiago de Venezuela).
Gaudencio Borbon Rosales (Philippines—Archbishop of Manila).
Jean-Pierre Bernard Ricard (France—Archbishop of Bordeaux).
Antonio Cañizares Llovera (Spain—Archbishop of Toledo).
Nicholas Cheong Jin-Suk (Republic of Korea—Archbishop of Seoul).
Sean Patrick O'Malley (USA—Archbishop of Boston).
Stanisław Dziwisz (Poland—Archbishop of Kraków).
Carlo Caffarra (Italy—Archbishop of Bologna).
Joseph Zen Ze-kiun (Hong Kong—Bishop of Hong Kong).
Agustín García-Gasco y Vicente (Spain—Archbishop of Valencia).
Seán Baptist Brady (Ireland—Archbishop of Armagh).
Lluís Martínez Sistach (Spain—Archbishop of Barcelona).
André Armand Vingt-Trois (France—Archbishop of Paris).
Angelo Bagnasco (Italy—Archbishop of Genoa).
Théodore-Adrien Sarr (Senegal—Archbishop of Dakar).
Oswald Gracias (India—Archbishop of Mumbai).
Francisco Robles Ortega (Mexico—Archbishop of Monterrey).
Daniel Nicholas DiNardo (USA—Archbishop of Galveston-Houston).
Odilo Pedro Scherer (Brazil—Archbishop of São Paulo).
John Njue (Kenya—Archbishop of Nairobi).
Estanislao Esteban Karlic (Argentina).

Cardinal Deacons

Darío Castrillón Hoyos (Colombia—President of the Pontifical Commission 'Ecclesia Dei' and Protodeacon of the College of Cardinals).
Jorge Arturo Augustin Medina Estévez (Chile).
Lorenzo Antonetti (Italy—Pontifical Delegate for the Patriarchal Basilica of St Francis in Assisi).
James Francis Stafford (USA—Pro Grand Penitentiary of the Apostolic Penitentiary).
Giovanni Cheli (Italy).
Agostino Cacciavillan (Italy).
Sergio Sebastiani (Italy).
Zenon Grocholewski (Poland—Prefect of the Congregation for Catholic Education and Grand Chancellor of the Università Gregoriana).
José Saraiva Martins (Portugal—Prefect of the Congregation for the Causes of Saints).
Jorge María Mejía (Argentina).
Walter Kasper (Germany—President of the Pontifical Council for the Promotion of Christian Unity).
Roberto Tucci (Italy).
Avery Robert Dulles (USA).
Jean-Louis Pierre Tauran (France—Titular Archbishop of Thelepte and President of the Pontifical Council for Inter-Religious Dialogue).
Renato Raffaele Martino (Italy—Titular Bishop of Segerme, President of the Pontifical Council for Justice and Peace; President of the Pontifical Council for the Pastoral Care of Migrants and Itinerant People).
Francesco Marchisano (Italy—Titular Archbishop of Populonia, Archpriest of St Peter's Basilica, Vicar-General to His Holiness for the Vatican City).
Julián Herranz Casado (Spain—Titular Archbishop of Vertara, President of the Disciplinary Commission of the Roman Curia).
Javier Lozano Barragán (Mexico—President of the Pontifical Council for Health Pastoral Care).
Attilio Nicora (Italy—President of the Administration of the Patrimony of the Holy See).
Georges Marie Martin Cottier (Switzerland).
Thomáš Špidlík (Czech Republic).
Stanisław Kazimierz Nagy (Poland).
William Joseph Levada (USA—Prefect of the Congregation for the Doctrine of the Faith, Prefect of the Pontifical Biblical Commission, Prefect of the International Theological Commission).
Franc Rodé (Slovenia—Prefect of the Congregation for Institutes of Consecrated Life and for Societies of Apostolic Life).
Agostino Vallini (Italy—Prefect of the Supreme Tribunal of the Apostolic Signature).
Andrea Cordero Lanza di Montezemolo (Italy).
Albert Vanhoye (France).
Leonardo Sandri (Argentina—Prefect of the Congregation for the Oriental Churches).
John Patrick Foley (USA—Pro Grand Master of the Equestrian Order of the Holy Sepulchure of Jerusalem).
Giovanni Lajolo (Italy—President of the Governorate of the Vatican City State).
Paul Josef Cordes (Germany—President of the Pontifical Council 'Cor Unum').
Angelo Comastri (Italy—President of the Fabric of St Peter).
Stanisław Ryłko (Poland—President of the Pontifical Council for the Laity).
Raffaele Farina (Italy—Archivist of the Vatican Secret Archives).
Giovanni Coppa (Italy).
Urbano Navarrete Cortés (Spain).
Umberto Betti (Italy).

THE ROMAN CURIA

Secretariat of State: Palazzo Apostolico Vaticano, 00120 Città del Vaticano; tel. (06) 69883913; fax (06) 69885255; e-mail vati026@relstat-segstat.va; Sec. of State Cardinal Tarcisio Bertone.

First Section—General Affairs: Segreteria di Stato, 00120 Città del Vaticano; tel. (06) 69883438; fax (06) 69885088; e-mail vati023@genaff-segstat.va; Asst Sec. of State Most Rev. Fernando Filoni (Titular Archbishop of Volturnum).

Second Section—Relations with States: Palazzo Apostolico Vaticano, 00120 Città del Vaticano; tel. (06) 69883014; fax (06) 69885364; e-mail vati032@relstat-segstat.va; Sec. Most Rev. Dominique Mamberti (Titular Archbishop of Sagona).

Congregations

Congregation for the Doctrine of the Faith: Piazza del S. Uffizio 11, 00120 Città del Vaticano; tel. (06) 69883357; fax (06) 69883409; e-mail cdf@cfaith.va; concerned with questions of doctrine and morals; examines doctrines and gives a judgement on them; Prefect Cardinal William Joseph Levada; Sec. Most Rev. Angelo Amato (Titular Archbishop of Sila).

Congregation for the Oriental Churches: Palazzo del Bramante, Via della Conciliazione 34, 00193 Rome, Italy; tel. (06) 69884293; fax (06) 69884300; e-mail cco@orientchurch.va; f. 1862; exercises jurisdiction over all persons and things pertaining to the Oriental Rites; Prefect Cardinal Leonardo Sandri; Sec. Most Rev. Antonio Maria Vegliò (Titular Archbishop of Eclano).

Congregation for Divine Worship and the Discipline of the Sacraments: Palazzo delle Congregazioni, Piazza Pio XII 10, 00193 Rome, Italy; tel. (06) 69884316; fax (06) 69883499; considers all questions relating to divine worship, liturgy and the sacraments; Prefect Cardinal Francis Arinze; Sec. Most Rev. Albert Malcolm Ranjith Patabendige Don (Titular Archbishop of Umbriatico).

Congregation for the Causes of Saints: Palazzo delle Congregazioni, Piazza Pio XII 10, 00193 Rome, Italy; tel. (06) 69884247; fax (06) 69881935; e-mail vati335@csaints.va; concerned with the proceedings relating to beatification and canonization; Prefect Cardinal José Saraiva Martins; Sec. Most Rev. Michele Di Ruberto (Titular Archbishop of Biccari).

Congregation for the Bishops: Palazzo delle Congregazioni, Piazza Pio XII 10, 00193 Rome, Italy; tel. (06) 69884217; fax (06) 69885303; e-mail vati076@cbishops.va; designed for the preparation of matters for the erection and division of dioceses and the election of Bishops and for dealing with Apostolic Visitations; Prefect Cardinal Giovanni Battista Re; Sec. Most Rev. Francesco Monterisi (Titular Archbishop of Alba Maritima).

Congregation for the Evangelization of Peoples: Palazzo di Propaganda Fide, Piazza di Spagna 48, 00187 Rome, Italy; tel. (06) 69879299; fax (06) 69880118; e-mail cepsegreteria@evangel.va; exercises ecclesiastical jurisdiction over missionary countries; Prefect Cardinal Ivan Dias; Sec. Most Rev. Robert Sarah.

Congregation for the Clergy: Palazzo delle Congregazioni, Piazza Pio XII 3, 00193 Rome, Italy; tel. (06) 69884151; fax (06) 69884845; e-mail clero@cclergy.va; internet www.clerus.org; has jurisdiction

THE VATICAN CITY

over the life and discipline of the clergy and its permanent formation; parishes, chapters, pastoral and presbyteral councils; promotes catechesis and the preaching of the Word of God; deals with economic questions related to the compensation of the clergy and the patrimony of the Church; Prefect Cardinal CLÁUDIO HUMMES; Sec. Most Rev. MAURO PIACENZA (Titular Archbishop of Victoriana).

Congregation for Institutes of Consecrated Life and for Societies of Apostolic Life: Palazzo delle Congregazioni, Piazza Pio XII 3, 00193 Rome, Italy; tel. (06) 69884128; fax (06) 69884526; e-mail civcsva@ccscrlife.va; promotes and supervises practice of evangelical counsels, according to approved forms of consecrated life, and activities of societies of apostolic life; Prefect Cardinal FRANC RODÉ; Sec. Most Rev. GIANFRANCO AGOSTINO GARDIN (Titular Archbishop of Torcello).

Congregation for Catholic Education: Palazzo delle Congregazioni, Piazza Pio XII 3, 00193 Rome, Italy; tel. (06) 69884167; fax (06) 69884172; e-mail cec@cec.va; f. 1588; concerned with the direction, temporal administration and studies of Catholic universities, seminaries, schools and colleges; Prefect Cardinal ZENON GROCHOLEWSKI; Sec. Most Rev. JEAN-LOUIS BRUGUÈS.

Tribunals

Apostolic Penitentiary: Palazzo della Cancelleria, Piazza della Cancelleria 1, 00186 Rome, Italy; tel. (06) 69887526; fax (06) 69887557; e-mail rregente@apostpnt.va; internet www.penitenzieria.va; Pro Grand Penitentiary Cardinal JAMES FRANCIS STAFFORD; Regent Rt Rev. GIANFRANCO GIROTTI (Titular Bishop of Meta).

Supreme Tribunal of the Apostolic Signature: Palazzo della Cancelleria, Piazza della Cancelleria 1, 00186 Rome, Italy; tel. (06) 69887520; fax (06) 69887553; Prefect Cardinal AGOSTINO VALLINI; Sec. Rt Rev. FRANS DANEELS (Titular Bishop of Bita).

Tribunal of the Roman Rota: Palazzo della Cancelleria, Piazza della Cancelleria 1, 00186 Rome, Italy; tel. (06) 69887502; fax (06) 69887554; Dean Rt Rev. ANTONI STANKIEWICZ (Titular Bishop of Nova Petra).

Pontifical Councils

Pontifical Council for the Laity: Piazza S. Calisto 16, 00153 Rome, Italy; tel. (06) 69887396; fax (06) 69887214; e-mail pcpl@laity.va; advises and conducts research, on lay apostolic initiatives; Pres. Cardinal STANISŁAW RYŁKO (Titular Archbishop of Novica); Sec. Rt Rev. JOSEF CLEMENS (Titular Bishop of Segerme).

Pontifical Council for Promoting Christian Unity: Via della Conciliazione 5, 00193 Rome, Italy; tel. (06) 69884083; fax (06) 69885365; e-mail office1@chrstuni.va; f. 1964; Pres. Cardinal WALTER KASPER; Sec. Rt Rev. BRIAN FARRELL (Titular Bishop of Abitinae).

Pontifical Council for the Family: Piazza S. Calisto 16, 00153 Rome, Italy; tel. (06) 69887243; fax (06) 69887272; e-mail pcf@family.va; Pres. (vacant); Sec. (vacant).

Pontifical Council for Justice and Peace: Piazza S. Calisto 16, 00153 Rome, Italy; tel. (06) 69879911; fax (06) 69887205; e-mail pcjustpax@justpeace.va; to promote social justice, human rights, peace and development in needy areas; Pres. Cardinal RENATO RAFFAELE MARTINO; Sec. Rt Rev. GIAMPAOLO CREPALDI (Titular Bishop of Bisarcio).

Pontifical Council 'Cor Unum': Cor Unum, Via della Conciliazione 5, 00193 Rome, Italy; tel. (06) 69889411; fax (06) 69887301; e-mail corunum@corunum.va; f. 1971; cares for the needy, promotes human fellowship; Pres. Cardinal PAUL JOSEF CORDES (Titular Archbishop of Naissus); Sec. Rt Rev. Mgr KAREL KASTEEL.

Pontifical Council for the Pastoral Care of Migrants and Itinerant People: Piazza S. Calisto 16, 00153 Rome, Italy; tel. (06) 69887131; fax (06) 69887111; e-mail office@migrants.va; f. 1970; Pres. Cardinal RENATO RAFFAELE MARTINO; Sec. Most Rev. AGOSTINO MARCHETTO (Titular Archbishop of Astigi).

Pontifical Council for Health Pastoral Care: Via della Conciliazione 3, 00193 Rome, Italy; tel. (06) 69883138; fax (06) 69883139; e-mail opersanit@hlthwork.va; internet www.healthpastoral.org; Pres. Cardinal JAVIER LOZANO BARRAGÁN; Sec. Rt Rev. JOSÉ LUIS REDRADO MARCHITE (Titular Bishop of Ofena).

Pontifical Council for Legislative Texts: Palazzo delle Congregazioni, Piazza Pio XII 10, 00193 Rome, Italy; tel. (06) 69884008; fax (06) 69884710; e-mail vati100@legtxt.va; f. 1984; publishes *Communicationes* journal twice yearly; Pres. Most Rev. FRANCESCO COCCOPALMERIO (Titular Archbishop of Celiana); Vice-Pres. Most Rev. BRUNO BERTAGNA (Titular Archbishop of Drivasto); Sec. Rt Rev. JUAN IGNACIO ARRIETA OCHOA DE CHINCHETRU (Titular Bishop of Civitate).

Pontifical Council for Inter-Religious Dialogue: Via della Conciliazione 5, 00193 Rome, Italy; tel. (06) 69884321; fax (06) 69884494; e-mail dialogo@interrel.va; f. 1964; Pres. Cardinal JEAN-LOUIS TAURAN; Sec. Most Rev. PIER LUIGI CELATA (Titular Archbishop of Doclea).

Pontifical Council for Culture: Via della Conciliazione 5, 00193 Rome, Italy; tel. (06) 69893811; fax (06) 69887368; e-mail cultura@cultura.va; merged with Pontifical Council for Dialogue with Non-Believers in 1993; promotes understanding and dialogue between the Church, people from the field of learning, artists and non-believers; Pres. Most Rev. GIANFRANCO RAVASI.

Pontifical Council for Social Communications: Palazzo S. Carlo, 00120 Città del Vaticano; tel. (06) 69883197; fax (06) 69885373; e-mail pccs@pccs.va; f. 1948; to examine the relationship between the media and religious affairs; manages radio, TV, film and photographic work in the Vatican; Pres. Most Rev. CLAUDIO MARIA CELLI (Titular Archbishop of Cluentum).

Pontifical Commissions and Committees

Pontifical Commission for the Cultural Heritage of the Church: Palazzo della Cancelleria, Piazza della Cancelleria 1, 00186 Rome, Italy; tel. (06) 69887556; fax (06) 69887567; e-mail pcbcc@pcchc.va; f. 1988; Pres. Most Rev. GIANFRANCO RAVASI (Titular Archbishop of Villamagna in Proconsulari).

Pontifical Biblical Commission: Palazzo della Congregazione per la Dottrina della Fede, Piazza del S. Uffizio 11, 00193 Rome, Italy; tel. (06) 69884682; e-mail pcombiblica@cfaith.va; Prefect Cardinal WILLIAM JOSEPH LEVADA.

Pontifical Commission of Sacred Archaeology: Palazzo del Pontificio Istituto di Archeologia Cristiana, Via Napoleone III 1, 00185 Rome, Italy; tel. (06) 4465610; fax (06) 4467625; e-mail pcomm.arch@arcsacra.va; Pres. Rt Rev. GIANFRANCO RAVASI.

Pontifical Commission 'Ecclesia Dei': Palazzo della Congregazione per la Dottrina della Fede, Piazza del S. Uffizio 11, 00120 Città del Vaticano; tel. (06) 69885213; fax (06) 69883412; e-mail eccdei@ecclsdei.va; Pres. Cardinal DARÍO CASTRILLÓN HOYOS; Sec. Mgr CAMILLE PERL.

Pontifical Commission for Latin America: Palazzo di San Paolo, Via della Conciliazione 1, 00193 Rome, Italy; tel. (06) 69883131; fax (06) 69884260; e-mail pcal@latinamer.va; Pres. Cardinal GIOVANNI BATTISTA RE; Vice-Pres. Most Rev. JOSÉ OCTAVIO RUIZ ARENAS (Archbishop of Villavicencio).

International Theological Commission: Palazzo della Congregazione per la Dottrina della Fede, Piazza del S. Uffizio 11, 00193 Rome, Italy; tel. (06) 69884727; Prefect Cardinal WILLIAM JOSEPH LEVADA; Sec.-Gen. Fr LUIS LADARIA.

Pontifical Committee for International Eucharistic Congresses: Piazza S. Calisto 16, 00153 Rome, Italy; tel. and fax (06) 69887366; fax (06) 6987154; e-mail eucharistcongress@org.va; Pres. Most Rev. PIERO MARINI (Titular Archbishop of Martirano); Sec. Rev. Fr FERDINAND PRATZNER.

Pontifical Committee of Historical Sciences: Palazzo delle Congregazioni, Piazza Pio XII 3, 00193 Rome, Italy; tel. (06) 69884618; fax (06) 69873014; e-mail semeraro@unisal.it; Pres. Mgr WALTER BRANDEMÜLLER; Sec. Rev. Prof. COSIMO SEMERARO.

Archives of the Second Vatican Council: c/o Archivio Segreto Vaticano, 00120 Città del Vaticano; tel. (06) 69883314; fax (06) 69885574; e-mail asv@asv.va; Dir Rt Rev. SERGIO PAGANO (Titular Bishop of Celene).

Commission for Lawyers: Palazzo della Cancelleria, Piazza della Cancelleria 1, 00186 Rome, Italy; tel. (06) 69887523; fax (06) 698887557; f. 1988; Pres. Cardinal MARIO FRANCESCO POMPEDDA.

Disciplinary Commission of the Roman Curia: Palazzo delle Congregazioni, Piazza Pio XII 10, 00120 Città del Vaticano; tel. (06) 69884008; fax (06) 69884710; e-mail vati494@legtxt.va.

Offices

Apostolic Chamber: Palazzo Apostolico, 00120 Città del Vaticano; tel. (06) 69883554; Chamberlain of the Holy Roman Church Cardinal TARCISIO BERTONE; Vice-Chamberlain Most Rev. PAOLO SARDI (Titular Archbishop of Sutri).

Administration of the Patrimony of the Holy See: Palazzo Apostolico, 00120 Città del Vaticano; tel. (06) 69893403; fax (06) 69883141; e-mail apsa-ss@apsa.va; f. 1967; Pres. Cardinal ATTILIO NICORA; Sec. Most Rev. DOMENICO CALCAGNO.

Labour Office of the Apostolic See: Via della Conciliazione 1, 00193 Rome, Italy; tel. (06) 69884449; fax (06) 69883800; e-mail ulsa1@ulsa.va; Pres. Cardinal FRANCESCO MARCHISANO.

Prefecture for the Economic Affairs of the Holy See: Palazzo delle Congregazioni, Largo del Colonnato 3, 00193 Rome, Italy; tel. (06) 69884263; fax (06) 69885011; f. 1967; Pres. Most Rev. VELASIO DE PAOLIS; Sec. Rt Rev. VINCENZO DI MAURO (Titular Bishop of Arpi).

Prefecture of the Papal Household: 00120 Città del Vaticano; tel. (06) 69883114; fax (06) 69885863; f. 1967; responsible for domestic

THE VATICAN CITY

administration and organization; Prefect Most Rev. JAMES MICHAEL HARVEY (Titular Archbishop of Memphis).

Office of the Liturgical Celebrations of the Supreme Pontiff: Palazzo Apostolico, 00120 Città del Vaticano; tel. (06) 69883253; fax (06) 69885412.

Holy See Press Office: Palazzo dei Propilei, Via dei Corridori 32, 00193 Rome, Italy; tel. (06) 69892425; fax (06) 69883053; internet www.vatican.va; Dir Rev. Fr FEDERICO LOMBARDO; Vice-Dir Fr CIRO BENEDETTINI.

Central Statistical Office of the Church: Palazzo Apostolico, 00120 Città del Vaticano; tel. (06) 69883493; fax (06) 69883816; e-mail vformenti@statistica.va; Dir Mgr VITTORIO FORMENTI.

Pontifical Administration of the Patriarchal Basilica of San Paolo Fuori-le-Mura: 00120 Città del Vaticano; tel. (06) 5409374; fax (06) 54074049; e-mail spbasilica@org.va; Archpriest Cardinal ANDREA DI MONTEZEMOLO.

Diplomatic Representation

DIPLOMATIC MISSIONS IN ROME ACCREDITED TO THE HOLY SEE

Albania: Via Silla 7/1, 00192 Rome, Italy; tel. (06) 39754085; fax (06) 39733150; e-mail embassy.vatican@mfa.gov.al; Ambassador RROK LOGU.

Angola: Palazzo Odeschalchi, Piazza SS. Apostoli 81, 00166 Rome, Italy; tel. (06) 69190650; fax (06) 69788483; Ambassador ARMINDO FERNANDES DO ESPÍRITO SANTO VIEIRA.

Argentina: Via del Banco di Santo Spirito 42, 00186 Rome, Italy; tel. (06) 68801701; fax (06) 6879021; e-mail emba.argentina@flashnet.it; Ambassador CARLOS LUIS CUSTER.

Australia: Via Paola 24/10, 00186 Rome, Italy; tel. (06) 6877688; fax (06) 6896255; e-mail holysee.embassy@dfat.gov.au; internet www.holysee.embassy.gov.au; Ambassador ANNE PLUNKETT (resident in Dublin, Ireland).

Austria: Via Reno 9, 00198 Rome, Italy; tel. (06) 853725; fax (06) 8543058; e-mail vatikan-ob@bmeia.gv.at; Ambassador Dr MARTIN BOLLDORF.

Belgium: Via Giuseppe de Notaris 6A, 00197 Rome, Italy; tel. (06) 3224740; fax (06) 3226042; e-mail vatican@diplobel.be; internet www.diplomatie.be/vaticanfr; Ambassador FRANK DE CONINCK.

Bolivia: Via di Porta Angelica 15/2, 00193 Rome, Italy; tel. (06) 6874191; fax (06) 6874193; e-mail embolivat@rdn.it; Ambassador CARLOS FEDERICO DE LA RIVA GUERRA.

Bosnia and Herzegovina: Piazzale le Clodio 12, 00195 Rome, Italy; tel. (06) 39742411; fax (06) 39742484; e-mail embvavat@tin.it; Ambassador (vacant).

Brazil: Via della Conciliazione 22, 00193 Rome, Italy; tel. (06) 6875252; fax (06) 6872540; e-mail embaixada@vatemb.it; internet www.vatemb.it; Ambassador VERA BARROUIN MACHADO.

Bulgaria: Via di Porta Angelica 63, 00193 Roma, Italia; tel. (06) 6875717; fax (06) 6865223; e-mail ambulvat@yahoo.it; internet www.mfa.bg/vatican; Ambassador VALENTIN VASSILEV BOZHILOV.

Canada: Palazzo Pio, Via della Conciliazione 4D, 00193 Rome, Italy; tel. (06) 68307316; fax (06) 68806283; e-mail vatcn@international.gc.ca; internet geo.international.gc.ca/canada-europa/holysee; Ambassador DONALD W. SMITH.

Chile: Piazza Risorgimento 55, 00192 Rome, Italy; tel. (06) 6861232; fax (06) 6874992; e-mail echileva@uni.net; Ambassador PEDRO PABLO CABRERA GAETE.

China (Taiwan): Via della Conciliazione 4D, 00193 Rome, Italy; tel. (06) 68136206; fax (06) 68136199; e-mail taiwan@embroc.it; internet www.taiwanembassy.org/va; Ambassador CHU-SENG TOU.

Colombia: Via Cola di Rienzo 285/4B, 00192 Rome, Italy; tel. (06) 3211681; fax (06) 3211703; e-mail estasede@minrelext.gov.co; Ambassador JUAN PABLO MARÍA GÓMEZ MARTÍNEZ.

Congo, Democratic Republic: Via del Castro Pretorio 28/2, 00185 Rome, Italy; tel. (06) 45447860; Chargé d'affaires a.i. EDOUARD KAMBEMBO NGUNZA.

Congo, Republic: Rome, Italy; Ambassador PIERRE-CLAVER AKOUALA.

Costa Rica: Via G.B. Benedetti 3, 00197 Rome, Italy; tel. and fax (06) 80660390; e-mail embcr.vaticano@iol.it; Ambassador LUIS PARÍS CHAVERRI.

Côte d'Ivoire: Via Sforza Pallavicini 11, 00193 Rome, Italy; tel. (06) 6877503; fax (06) 6867925; e-mail ambco.va@flashnet.it; Ambassador KOUAMÉ BENJAMIN KONAN.

Croatia: Via della Conciliazione 44, 00193 Rome, Italy; tel. (06) 6877000; fax (06) 6877003; e-mail velrhvat@tin.it; internet va.mfa.hr; Ambassador Prof. EMILIO MARIN.

Cuba: Via Aurelia 137/5A, 00165 Rome, Italy; tel. (06) 39366680; fax (06) 636685; e-mail embajada@cubassede.com; Ambassador RAÚL ROA KOURÍ.

Czech Republic: Via Crescenzio 91/1B, 00193 Rome, Italy; tel. (06) 6874696; fax (06) 6879731; e-mail vatican@embassy.mzv.cz; internet www.mzv.cz/vatican; Ambassador PAVEL JAJTNER.

Dominican Republic: Lungotevere Marzio 3, 00186 Rome, Italy; tel. and fax (06) 6864084; e-mail embajadardss@tiscali.it; Ambassador RAFAEL MARION-LANDAIS.

Ecuador: Via di Porta Angelica 64, 00193 Rome, Italy; tel. (06) 6897179; fax (06) 68892786; e-mail mecuadorsantasede@ecuaemss.it; Ambassador FAUSTO CÓRDOVEZ CHIRIBOGA.

Egypt: Piazza della Città Leonina 9, 00193 Rome, Italy; tel. (06) 6865878; fax (06) 6832335; e-mail ambegyptvatican@tiscali.it; Ambassador NEVINE SIMAIKA HALIM ABDALLA.

El Salvador: Via Panama 22/2, 00198 Rome, Italy; tel. (06) 8540538; fax (06) 85301131; e-mail embasalssede@iol.it; Ambassador FRANCISCO SOLER.

France: Villa Bonaparte, Via Piave 23, 00186 Rome, Italy; tel. (06) 42030900; fax (06) 42030968; e-mail ambfrssg@tin.it; internet www.france-vatican.org; Chargé d'affaires a.i. PIERRE COCHARD.

Gabon: Piazzale Clodio 12, 00195 Rome, Italy; tel. (06) 39721584; fax (06) 39724847; Ambassador DÉSIRÉ KOUMBA.

Georgia: Via Emilia 25, 00187 Rome, Italy; tel. and fax (06) 42010664; e-mail georgiasantasede@gmail.com; Ambassador KETEVAN BAGRATION-MUKHRANBATONI.

Germany: Via di Villa Sacchetti 4–6, 00197 Rome, Italy; tel. (06) 809511; fax (06) 80951227; internet www.vatikan.diplo.de; Ambassador HANS-HENNING HORSTMANN.

Greece: Via Giuseppe Mercalli 6, 00197 Rome, Italy; tel. (06) 8070786; fax (06) 8079862; e-mail grembassyvat@grembassyvat.191.it; Ambassador MILTIADIS HISKAKIS.

Guatemala: Piazzale Gregorio VII 65A, 00165 Rome, Italy; tel. (06) 6381632; fax (06) 39376981; e-mail embsantasede@minex.gob.gt; Ambassador ACISCLO VALLADARES MOLINA.

Haiti: Via de Villa Patrizi 5B, 00161 Roma, Italy; tel. (06) 44242749; fax (06) 44236637; Chargé d'affaires a.i. PATRICK SAINT-HILAIRE.

Honduras: Via Boezio 45, 00192 Rome, Italy; tel. and fax (06) 6876051; e-mail honvati@fastwebnet.it; Ambassador ALEJANDRO EMILIO VALLADARES LANZA.

Hungary: Piazza Girolamo Fabrizio 2, 00161 Rome, Italy; tel. (06) 4402167; fax (06) 4402312; e-mail mission.vat@kum.hu; Ambassador GÁBOR ERDŐDY.

Indonesia: Piazzale Roberto Ardigò 42, 00142 Rome, Italy; tel. (06) 5940441; fax (06) 5417934; e-mail indonesia.vat@agora.stm.it; Ambassador SUPRAPTO MARTOSEMOTO.

Iran: Via Bruxelles 57, 00198 Rome, Italy; tel. (06) 8450443; e-mail chalac@libero.it; Ambassador MAHDI FARDI ZADEH.

Iraq: Via della Camilluccia 355, 00135 Rome, Italy; tel. (06) 3014508; fax (06) 35506416; e-mail ftkemb@iraqmofamail.net; Ambassador ALBERT EDWARD ISMAIL YELDA.

Ireland: Villa Spada, Via Giacomo Medici 1, 00153 Rome, Italy; tel. (06) 5810777; fax (06) 5895709; Ambassador NOEL FAHEY.

Israel: Via Michele Mercati 12, 00197 Rome, Italy; tel. (06) 36198690; fax (06) 36198626; e-mail info-vat@holysee.mfa.gov.il; internet vatican.mfa.gov.il; Ambassador MORDECHAI LEWY.

Italy: Palazzo Borromeo, Viale delle Belle Arti 2, 00196 Rome, Italy; tel. (06) 3264881; fax (06) 3201801; e-mail amb.scv@esteri.it; Ambassador ANTONIO ZANARDI LANDI.

Japan: Via Virgilio 30, 00193 Rome, Italy; tel. (06) 6875828; fax (06) 68807543; Ambassador KAGEFUMI UENO.

Lebanon: Via di Porta Angelica 15, 00193 Rome, Italy; tel. (06) 6833512; fax (06) 6833507; Ambassador ASSI NAJI ABI.

Libya: Via Orazio 31B, 00193 Rome, Italy; tel. (06) 97605051; fax (06) 45433476; Sec. of the People's Bureau ABD AL-HAFID GADDUR.

Lithuania: Corso Vittorio Emanuele II 308, 00186 Rome, Italy; tel. (06) 68192858; fax (06) 68809596; e-mail amb.va@urm.lt; internet va.mfa.lt; Ambassador ALGIRDAS SAUDARGAS.

Luxembourg: Via Casale di S. Pio V 20, 00165 Rome, Italy; tel. (06) 660560; fax (06) 66056309; Ambassador GEORGES SANTER (resident in Paris, France).

Macedonia, former Yugoslav Republic: Via di Porta Cavalleggeri 143, 00165 Rome, Italy; tel. (06) 635878; fax (06) 634826; e-mail vatican@mfa.gov.mk; Ambassador BARTOLOMEJ KAJTAZI.

Mexico: Via Ezio 49, 00192 Rome, Italy; tel. (06) 3230360; fax (06) 3230361; e-mail embamex-s.sede@mclink.it; internet portal.sre.gob.mx/vaticano; Ambassador LUIS FELIPE BRAVO MENA.

Monaco: Largo Nicola Spinelli 5, 00198 Rome, Italy; tel. (06) 8414357; fax (06) 8414507; e-mail ambmonacovat@alice.it; Ambassador JEAN-CLAUDE MICHEL.

THE VATICAN CITY

Montenegro: Via Crescenzio 97/II, 00193 Rome, Italy; tel. (06) 68134897; fax (06) 68130569; e-mail ambmont.vat@hotmail.it; Ambassador ANTUN SBUTEGA.

Morocco: Via delle Fornaci 203, 00165 Rome, Italy; tel. (06) 39388398; fax (06) 6374459; e-mail sifamavat@marocco.191.it; Ambassador ALI ACHOUR.

Netherlands: Piazza della Città Leonina 9, 00193 Rome, Italy; tel. (06) 6868044; fax (06) 6879593; e-mail vat@minbuza.nl; Ambassador MONIQUE P. A. FRANK.

Nicaragua: Via Luigi Luciani 42/1, 00197 Rome, Italy; tel. (06) 32600265; fax (06) 3207249; e-mail embanicsantasede@tin.it; Ambassador JOSÉ CUADRA CHAMORRO.

Panama: Largo di Torre Argentina 11/28, 00186 Rome, Italy; tel. (06) 68809764; fax (06) 68809812; e-mail embapass@tiscalinet.it; Chargé d'affaires a.i. JAVIER FRANCISCO TORRES GONZÁLEZ.

Paraguay: Via Alpinismo 24, 4° int. 1, Rome, Italy; tel. (06) 39751368; fax (06) 39745063; e-mail pyssede@mclink.it; Ambassador GERÓNIMO NARVÁEZ TORRES.

Peru: Via di Porta Angelica 63, 00193 Rome, Italy; tel. (06) 68308535; fax (06) 6896059; e-mail embaperuva@tin.it; Ambassador ALFONSO DÁMASO ANTONIO RIVERO MONSALVE.

Philippines: Via Paolo VI 29, 00193 Rome, Italy; tel. (06) 68308020; fax (06) 6834076; e-mail vaticanpe@philamsee.mysam.it; Ambassador LEONIDA L. VERA.

Poland: Via dei Delfini 16/3, 00186 Rome, Italy; tel. (06) 6990958; fax (06) 6990978; e-mail polamb.wat@agora.it; Ambassador HANNA SUCHOCKA.

Portugal: Villa Lusa, Via S. Valentino 9, 00197 Rome, Italy; tel. (06) 8091581; fax (06) 8077585; e-mail embportugalvatican@tiscalinet.it; Ambassador JOÃO ALBERTO BACELAR DA ROCHA PÁRIS.

Romania: Via Panama 92, 00198 Rome, Italy; tel. (06) 8541802; fax (06) 8554067; e-mail ambasciata@vatican.mae.ro; internet vatican.mae.ro; Ambassador MARIUS GABRIEL LAZURCA.

Russia: Via della Conciliazione 10, 00193 Rome, Italy; tel. (06) 6877078; fax (06) 6877168; Ambassador NIKOLAY SADCHIKOV.

San Marino: Piazza G. Winckelmann 14, 00162 Rome, Italy; tel. (06) 86321798; fax (06) 8610814; e-mail amb-sanmarino@libero.it; Ambassador GIOVANNI GALASSI.

Senegal: Via dei Monti Parioli 51, 00197 Rome, Italy; tel. (06) 3218892; fax (06) 3203624; e-mail senvat.iol.it; Ambassador FÉLIX OUDIANE.

Serbia: Via dei Monti Parioli 20, 00197 Rome, Italy; tel. (06) 3200099; fax (06) 3204530; e-mail amb.serbia.vatican@ambroma.com; Ambassador VLADETA JANKOVIĆ.

Slovakia: Via dei Prati della Farnesina 57, 00194 Rome, Italy; tel. (06) 33221132; fax (06) 33219582; e-mail slovakemvat@libero.it; Ambassador JOZEF DRAVECKÝ.

Slovenia: Via della Conciliazione 10, 00193 Rome, Italy; tel. (06) 6833009; fax (06) 68307942; e-mail vva@gov.si; Ambassador IVAN REBERNIK.

Spain: Palazzo di Spagna, Piazza di Spagna 57, 00187 Rome, Italy; tel. (06) 6784351; fax (06) 6784355; e-mail emb.santasede@mae.es; Ambassador FRANCISCO VÁZQUEZ Y VÁZQUEZ.

Turkey: Via Lovanio 24/1, 00198 Rome, Italy; tel. (06) 85508601; fax (06) 85508660; e-mail vatibe@libero.it; Ambassador MUAMMER DOGAN AKDUR.

Ukraine: Via A. G. Barrili 68A, Int. 5, 00152 Rome, Italy; tel. (06) 39378800; fax (06) 45439216; e-mail emb_va@mfa.gov.ua; Ambassador TETIANA IZHEVSKA.

United Kingdom: Via XX Settembre 80A, 00187 Rome, Italy; tel. (06) 42204000; fax (06) 42204205; e-mail holysee@fco.gov.uk; internet www.britishembassy.gov.uk/vatican; Ambassador FRANCIS MARTIN-XAVIER CAMPBELL.

USA: Villa Domiziana, Via delle Terme Deciane 26, 00153 Rome, Italy; tel. (06) 46743428; fax (06) 5758346; e-mail vaticaninfo@mail.usembassy.it; internet www.vatican.usembassy.gov; Ambassador MARY ANN GLENDON.

Uruguay: Via Antonio Gramsci 9/14, 00197 Rome, Italy; tel. (06) 3218904; fax (06) 3613249; e-mail uruvati@tin.it; Ambassador MARIO JUAN BOSCO CAYOTA ZAPPETTINI.

Venezuela: Via Antonio Gramsci 14, 00197 Rome, Italy; tel. (06) 3225868; fax (06) 36001505; e-mail evidano@iol.it; Ambassador IVÁN GUILLERMO RINCÓN URDANETA.

Ecclesiastical Organization

The organization of the Church consists of:
 (1) Patriarchs, Archbishops and Bishops in countries under the common law of the Church.
 (2) Abbots and Prelates 'nullius dioceseos'.
 (3) Vicars Apostolic and Prefects Apostolic in countries classified as Missionary and under Propaganda, the former having Episcopal dignity.

The population of the world adhering to the Roman Catholic faith, according to official estimates, was 1,131m. at 31 December 2006. Around 50% of adherents live in the Americas, 26% in Europe and 14% in Africa.

Among the Pope's official titles until early 2006, when Pope Benedict XVI decided no longer to use it, was that of Patriarch of the West. There are five other Patriarchates of the Latin Rite—Jerusalem, the West Indies, the East Indies, Lisbon and Venice. The Eastern Catholic Churches each have Patriarchs: Alexandria for the Coptic Rite, Babylon for the Chaldean Rite, Cilicia for the Armenian Rite, and Antioch for the Syrian, Maronite and Melkite Rites.

At 31 December 2007 there were 2,789 residential sees—13 patriarchates, four senior archbishoprics, 536 metropolitan archbishoprics, 75 archbishoprics and 2,161 bishoprics. Of the 2,062 titular sees (92 metropolitan archbishoprics, 91 archbishoprics and 1,879 bishoprics), 1,067 are filled by bishops who have been given these titles, but exercise no territorial jurisdiction. Other territorial divisions of the Church include 49 prelacies, 11 territorial abbacies, 25 exarchates of the Eastern Church, 35 military orders, 79 apostolic vicariates, 45 apostolic prefectures, nine apostolic administrations and nine missions 'sui iuris'.

The Press

Acta Apostolicae Sedis: Periodical Dept, Libreria Editrice Vaticana, 00120 Città del Vaticano; tel. (06) 69883529; fax (06) 39884716; e-mail mariasic2@publish.va; internet www.libreriaeditricevaticana.com; f. 1909; official bulletin issued by the Holy See; monthly, with special editions on special occasions; the record of Encyclicals and other Papal pronouncements, Acts of the Congregations and Offices, nominations, etc.; circ. 6,000.

Annuario Pontificio: Libreria Editrice Vaticana, Via del Tipografia, 00120 Città del Vaticano; tel. (06) 69883493; fax (06) 69885088; e-mail segreteria.lev@lev.va; official year book edited by Central Statistical Office; Dir Mgr VITTORIO FORMENTI.

L'Osservatore Romano: Tipografica Vaticana, Via del Pellegrino, 00120 Città del Vaticano; tel. (06) 69883461; fax (06) 69883675; e-mail ornet@ossrom.va; internet www.vatican.va/news_services/or/home_ita.html; f. 1861; an authoritative daily newspaper in Italian; its special columns devoted to the affairs of the Holy See may be described as semi-official; the news service covers religious matters and, in a limited measure, general affairs; weekly editions in English, French, German, Italian, Polish, Portuguese and Spanish; Editor-in-Chief GIOVANNI MARIA VIAN; Man. Editor CARLO DE LUCIA; circ. (Italian daily) 20,000.

Pro Dialogo: Via dell' Erba 1, 00193 Rome, Italy; tel. (06) 69884321; fax (06) 69884494; e-mail dialogo@interrel.va; three per year; publ. by the Pontifical Council for Inter-Religious Dialogue; Editor Most Rev. FELIX A. MACHADO.

Statistical Yearbook of the Church: c/o Secretariat of State, 00120 Città del Vaticano; tel. (06) 69883655; fax (06) 69885088; Dir Mgr VITTORIO FORMENTI.

NEWS AGENCY

Agenzia Internazionale FIDES: Palazzo de 'Propaganda Fide', Via di Propaganda 1C, 00187 Rome, Italy; tel. (06) 69880115; fax (06) 69880107; e-mail fides@fides.va; internet www.fides.org; f. 1926; handles news of missions throughout the world and publishes a weekly bulletin in six languages (circ. 3,000), provides a daily news service by e-mail; Dir LUCA DE MATA.

Publishers

Biblioteca Apostolica Vaticana: Cortile del Belvedere, 00120 Città del Vaticano; tel. (06) 69879402; fax (06) 69884795; e-mail bav@vatlib.it; internet www.vatican.va/library_archives/vat_library/index_it.htm; f. 1451; philology, classics, history, catalogues; Librarian of the Holy Roman Church Cardinal RAFFAELE FARINA.

Libreria Editrice Vaticana: Via della Tipografia, 00120 Città del Vaticano; tel. (06) 69883532; fax 69884716; e-mail lev@publish.va; internet www.libreriaeditricevaticana.com; f. 1926; religion, philosophy, literature, art, Latin philology, history; Pres. Mgr GUISEPPE SCOTTI; Dir Rev. GIUSEPPE COSTA.

Tipografia Vaticana (Vatican Press): Via della Tipografia, 00120 Città del Vaticano; tel. (06) 69883506; fax (06) 69884570; e-mail tipvat@tipografia.va; f. 1587; religion, theology, education, juveniles, natural and social sciences; prints *Acta Apostolicae Sedis* and *L'Osservatore Romano*; Dir-Gen. Rev. ELIO TORRIGIANI.

Broadcasting and Communications

RADIO

Radio Vaticana was founded in 1931 and is situated within the Vatican City. A transmitting centre, inaugurated by Pius XII in 1957, is located at Santa Maria di Galeria, about 20 km north-west of the Vatican. Under a special treaty between the Holy See and Italy, the site of this centre, which covers 420 ha, enjoys the same extra-territorial privileges as are recognized by international law for the diplomatic headquarters of foreign states.

The station operates an all-day service, normally in 40 languages, but with facilities for broadcasting liturgical and other religious services in additional languages, including Latin.

The purpose of the Vatican Radio is to broadcast papal teaching, to provide information on important events in the Roman Catholic Church, to express the Catholic point of view on problems affecting religion and morality, and, above all, to form a continuous link between the Holy See and Roman Catholics throughout the world.

Radio Vaticana: Palazzo Pio, Piazza Pia 3, 00193 Rome, Italy; tel. (06) 69883551; fax (06) 69883237; e-mail webteam@vaticanradio.org; internet www.vaticanradio.org; f. 1931; Dir-Gen. Rev. Fr FEDERICO LOMBARDI (SJ); Tech. Dir SANDRO PIERVENANZI (SJ); Administrative Dir ALBERTO GASBARRI (SJ); Dir of Programmes Rev. Fr ANDREJ KOPROWSKI (SJ).

TELEVISION

Centro Televisivo Vaticano (CTV) (Vatican Television Centre): Via del Pellegrino, 00120 Città del Vaticano; tel. (06) 69885467; fax (06) 69885192; e-mail ctv@ctv.va; f. 1983; produces and distributes religious programmes; Pres. Dott. EMILIO ROSSI; Dir-Gen. Rev. Fr FEDERICO LOMBARDI.

Finance

Istituto per le Opere di Religione (IOR): 00120 Città del Vaticano; tel. (06) 69883354; fax (06) 69883809; f. 1887; renamed in 1942; oversees the distribution of capital designated for religious works; its assets are believed to lie between US $3,000m. and $4,000m.; it takes deposits from religious bodies and Vatican residents; governed by a Board of Superintendence comprising five financial experts, overseen by a commission of five cardinals; Pres. Prof. ANGELO CALOIA; Dir-Gen. PAOLO CIPRIANI; Commission mems Cardinals TARCISIO BERTONE, ATTILIO NICORA, JEAN-LOUIS TAURAN, TELESPHORE PLACIDUS TOPPO, ODILO PEDRO SCHERER.

Lay Employees' Association

In 1989 Pope John Paul II agreed to establish a Labour Council to settle any disputes between the Holy See and its lay employees.

Associazione Dipendenti Laici Vaticani (Association of Vatican Lay Workers): Via della Posta, 00120 Città del Vaticano; tel. (06) 69885343; fax (06) 69884400; f. 1979; aims to safeguard the professional, legal, economic and moral interests of its members; Sec.-Gen. ALESSANDRO CANDI; 320 mems.

Transport

There is a small railway (863 m) which runs from the Vatican into Italy. It began to operate in 1934 and now carries supplies and goods. There is also a heliport used by visiting heads of state and Vatican officials.

VENEZUELA

Introductory Survey

Location, Climate, Language, Religion, Flag, Capital

The Bolivarian Republic of Venezuela lies on the north coast of South America, bordered by Colombia to the west, Guyana to the east and Brazil to the south. The climate varies with altitude from tropical to temperate; the average temperature in Caracas is 21°C (69°F). The language is Spanish. There is no state religion, but some 85% of the population is Roman Catholic. The national flag (proportions 2 by 3) has three horizontal stripes of yellow, blue and red, with eight five-pointed white stars, arranged in an arc, in the centre of the blue stripe. The state flag has, in addition, the national coat of arms (a shield bearing a gold wheat sheaf in the first division, a panoply of swords, an indigenous bow and arrow quiver, a machete, flags and a lance in the second, and a white running horse in the base, flanked by branches of laurel and palm and with two cornucopias at the crest) in the top left-hand corner. The capital is Caracas.

Recent History

Venezuela was a Spanish colony from 1499 until 1821 and, under the leadership of Simón Bolívar, achieved independence in 1830. The country was governed principally by dictators until 1945, when a military-civilian coup replaced Isaías Medina Angarita with Rómulo Betancourt as head of a revolutionary junta. Col (later Gen.) Marcos Pérez Jiménez seized power in December 1952 and took office as President in 1953. He remained in office until 1958, when he was overthrown by a military junta under Adm. Wolfgang Larrazábal. Betancourt was elected President in the same year.

A new Constitution was promulgated in 1961. Three years later President Betancourt became the first Venezuelan President to complete his term of office. Dr Raúl Leoni was elected President in December 1963. Supporters of former President Pérez staged an abortive military uprising in 1966. Dr Rafael Caldera Rodríguez became Venezuela's first Christian Democratic President in March 1969. He achieved some success in stabilizing the country politically and economically, although political assassinations and abductions committed by underground organizations continued into 1974. At elections in December 1973 Carlos Andrés Pérez Rodríguez, candidate of Acción Democrática (AD), the main opposition party, was chosen to succeed President Caldera. The new Government invested heavily in agriculture and industrial development, creating a more balanced economy, and also undertook to nationalize important sectors. The presidential election of December 1978 was won by the leader of the Partido Social-Cristiano (Comité de Organización Política Electoral Independiente—COPEI), Dr Luis Herrera Campíns, who took office in March 1979.

In 1981 a deteriorating economic situation provoked social unrest and a succession of guerrilla attacks. At a presidential election conducted in December 1983, Dr Jaime Lusinchi, the candidate of the AD, was elected with 57% of the votes cast. The AD also won the majority of seats in the Congreso Nacional; Lusinchi assumed power in February 1984.

At presidential and legislative elections conducted in December 1988, AD candidate Carlos Andrés Pérez Rodríguez became the first former President to be re-elected (he previously held office in 1974–79). However, the AD lost its overall majority in the Congreso Nacional. Following his inauguration in February 1989 President Pérez implemented a series of adjustments designed to halt Venezuela's economic decline. These measures, which included increases in the prices of petrol and public transport, provoked rioting throughout the country in late February. The Government introduced a curfew and suspended various constitutional rights in order to quell the disturbances, but it was estimated that some 246 people had died during the protests. In early March the curfew was revoked, and all constitutional rights were restored, after wages had been increased and the prices of some basic goods were frozen.

In May 1989 popular opposition to the Government's austerity programme became co-ordinated by the country's largest trade union, the Confederación de Trabajadores de Venezuela (CTV), which organized a 24-hour general strike (the first for 31 years) in favour of the introduction of pro-labour reforms. However, in July, despite its growing dissatisfaction with the stabilization plan then in progress, the CTV signed an agreement with the Government and the business sector to promote national harmony and to support the continuation of economic adjustment policies that had been agreed with the IMF in June.

In May 1991 a controversial new labour law came into effect, providing for a severance benefit scheme and a social security system. In the second half of that year a series of widespread demonstrations and strikes were staged to protest against monthly increases in the price of petrol, or to demand, *inter alia*, wage increases, the reintroduction of price controls on basic goods, and the suspension of planned public sector redundancies. The protesters often clashed with security forces and there were several fatalities.

On 4 February 1992 an attempt to overthrow the President by rebel army units was defeated by armed forces loyal to the Government. The rebels, identified as members of the 'Movimiento Bolivariano Revolucionario 200' (MBR-200), attempted to occupy the President's office, the Miraflores palace, and his official residence but were forced to capitulate. Simultaneous rebel action in the cities of Maracay, Valencia and Maracaibo ended when one of the leaders of the coup, Lt-Col Hugo Rafael Chávez Frías, broadcast an appeal for their surrender. More than 1,000 soldiers were arrested, and 33 officers were subsequently charged. A number of constitutional guarantees were immediately suspended, and press and television censorship was imposed to exclude coverage of Chávez, who had received considerable passive popular support. The rebels' stated primary reasons for staging the insurrection were the increasing social divisions and uneven distribution of wealth resulting from government economic policy, and widespread corruption in public life. In what was widely perceived as an attempt to appease disaffected sectors of society, immediately following the attempted coup Pérez authorized a 50% increase in the minimum wage and a 30% increase in the pay of middle-ranking officers of the armed forces. He also announced plans to bring forward a US $4,000m. social project, aimed at improving health care, social welfare and education.

In March 1992 Pérez announced a series of proposed political and economic reforms, including the introduction of legislation for immediate reform of the Constitution. In addition, the President announced the suspension of increases in the price of petrol and electricity, and the reintroduction of price controls on a number of basic foodstuffs and on medicine. In that month, in an effort to broaden the base of support for his Government, Pérez appointed two members of COPEI to the Council of Ministers. Full constitutional rights were finally restored in April. Nevertheless, widespread protests against government austerity measures and alleged official corruption continued in September and October. A series of bomb attacks, attributed to the rebel movements Los Justicieros de Venezuela and the Fuerzas Bolivarianos de Liberación (an organization claiming to have links with MBR-200), were directed at the residences of allegedly corrupt senior politicians.

On 27 November 1992 a further attempt by rebel members of the armed forces to overthrow the President was suppressed by forces loyal to the Government. The attempted coup, led by senior air force and navy officers, was reported to have been instigated by members of MRB-200. A videotaped statement by the imprisoned Lt-Col Chávez, transmitted from a captured government-owned television station, urged Venezuelans to stage public demonstrations in support of the rebels. Principal air force bases were seized, and rebel aircraft attacked the presidential palace and other strategically important installations. The Government introduced a state of emergency and suspended the Constitution. Sporadic fighting continued into the following day, but by 29 November order had been restored and some 1,300 rebel members of the armed forces had been arrested. President Pérez rejected demands from the press and opposition parties for his resignation. The curfew imposed during the coup was ended at the beginning of December, and further constitutional rights were restored later in the month.

Popular discontent with the Government was reflected further in regional and municipal elections held on 6 December 1992, which resulted in significant gains for COPEI as well as revealing increasing support for the left-wing Movimiento al Socialismo (MAS) and La Causa Radical (La Causa R), whose candidate, Aristóbulo Istúriz, was elected mayor of Caracas. In March 1993 the Supreme Court annulled the rulings of an extraordinary summary court martial, which had been established by presidential decree to try those implicated in the attempted coup of November 1992, on the grounds that the court was unconstitutional. Those sentenced by the court were to be retried by an ordinary court martial.

In May 1993 an extraordinary joint session of the Congreso Nacional voted to endorse a Supreme Court ruling that sufficient evidence existed for Pérez to be prosecuted on corruption charges. The charges concerned allegations that Pérez, and two former government ministers, had, in 1989, embezzled US $17m. from a secret government fund. Pérez was subsequently suspended from office and, in accordance with the terms of the Constitution, replaced by the President of the Senado, Octavio Lepage, pending the election by the Congreso Nacional of an interim President who would assume control until the expiry of the presidential term in February 1994, should Pérez be found guilty. On 5 June the Congreso Nacional elected Ramón José Velásquez, an independent senator, as interim President. Velásquez immediately undertook a broad-ranging reorganization of the Council of Ministers. In August the Congreso Nacional approved legislation enabling Velásquez to introduce urgent economic and financial measures by decree in order to address the growing economic crisis. In late August a special session of the Congreso Nacional voted in favour of the permanent suspension from office of Pérez, regardless of the outcome of the legal proceedings being conducted against him. (In May 1994 Pérez was arrested and imprisoned, pending trial by the Supreme Court on charges of corruption.)

The presidential and legislative elections of December 1993 proceeded peacefully. Dr Rafael Caldera Rodríguez, the candidate of a newly formed party, the Convergencia Nacional (CN), was elected President (having previously held office in 1969–74). However, the CN and its electoral ally, the MAS, secured only minority representation in the Congreso Nacional. Caldera took office in February 1994. In that month the AD and COPEI established a legislative pact using their combined majority representation in the Congreso Nacional in order to gain control of the major legislative committees. In response, Caldera warned that he would dissolve the legislature and organize elections to a Constituent Assembly should the government programme encounter obstructions in the Congreso Nacional. Also in February, in an attempt to consolidate relations with the armed forces, Caldera initiated proceedings providing for the release and pardon of all those charged with involvement in the coup attempts of February and November 1992.

In June 1994 the Government announced that it was to assume extraordinary powers, in view of the deepening economic crisis and the virtual collapse of the banking sector. Six articles of the Constitution were suspended concerning guarantees including freedom of movement and freedom from arbitrary arrest and the right to own property and to engage in legal economic activity. The Government also announced the introduction of price controls and a single fixed exchange rate, in order to address the problems of a rapidly depreciating currency and depleted foreign exchange reserves. Later that month Caldera issued a decree placing the financial system under government control. Of those banks affected by the crisis, 10 were closed permanently; the majority of those still operational were to be returned to private control. In July the Congreso Nacional voted to restore five of the six suspended constitutional guarantees. Despite protest, the Government promptly reintroduced the suspensions. Later that month, however, the legislative opposition, with the exception of La Causa R, which withdrew from the legislature in protest, endorsed emergency financial measures, including an extension of price controls and the strengthening of finance sector regulation, which were presented by the Government as a precursor to the restoration of full constitutional guarantees.

In March 1995 the arrest of some 500 alleged subversives (including activists of the MBR-200) by the security forces prompted demonstrations in the capital in support of demands for the release of those detained and in opposition to the deployment of the National Guard to patrol Venezuela's cities. In July the constitutional guarantees were restored, except in border areas with Brazil, in light of continued criminal activity there. In September 1997 the Congreso Nacional conferred extraordinary powers to enact legislation by an 'enabling law' ('ley habilitante') on President Caldera, in order to facilitate the implementation of emergency economic measures designed to reduce the huge fiscal deficit and to accelerate social security reforms.

In May 1996 former President Pérez was found guilty by the Supreme Court of misuse of public funds, although he was acquitted of charges of embezzlement. He was sentenced to two years and four months under house arrest, of which he had already served two years. In July the Senado voted to deny Pérez the seat-for-life in that chamber to which former Presidents of the country were normally entitled. In April 1998 Pérez was charged with misappropriation of public funds during his time in office, and was placed under house arrest pending full investigation of the charges. At legislative elections conducted in November (see below), however, he was successfully elected to the Senado, and was therefore entitled to parliamentary immunity from prosecution.

The legislative elections of 8 November 1998 were won by the Polo Patriótico, an alliance of small, mainly left-wing parties led by the Movimiento V República (MVR). The MVR had been founded in the previous year by the leader of the attempted coup of February 1992, Lt-Col (retd) Chávez; its electoral success was widely considered to reflect the popular rejection of apparent corruption in the country's major political parties. Proyecto Venezuela (PRVZL), the party created to support the presidential candidacy of the independent Henrique Salas Römer, also performed well. Success at the concurrent gubernatorial elections was shared equally between the Polo Patriótico and the AD, who each secured approximately one-third of the governorships.

In the light of the MVR's success in the legislative poll, prior to the presidential election the AD and COPEI withdrew their support for their respective candidates and united in support of Salas Römer, hoping to forestall the loss of their long-standing political predominance. However, Chávez, who had styled himself as a radical left-wing populist, promising social revolution and constitutional reform, was elected President on 6 December 1998, with 56% of the votes cast, ahead of Salas Römer, who received the support of some 40% of voters.

Chávez immediately announced plans for elections to a Constituent Assembly to draft a new constitution, and requested congressional permission to employ the enabling law to implement an extensive restructuring of public administration and a comprehensive economic recovery programme. Chávez was inaugurated as President on 2 February 1999 and a new Council of Ministers was installed. At the end of February Chávez announced details of an ambitious emergency social improvement plan (the Plan Bolívar 2000) to rehabilitate public property and land through voluntary civil and military action. Such pledges (together with a promise that the armed forces would not be used against the civilian population) prompted a series of rural and urban public land occupations, none of which was forcibly ended.

In April 1999, following prolonged negotiation and compromise, Chávez received congressional endorsement of his proposed use of the enabling law. On 25 April a national referendum, organized to ascertain levels of popular support for the convening of a Constituent Assembly and the regulations governing the election of such a body, demonstrated 82% support for the Assembly and 80% support for Chávez's proposals for electoral procedures. (The successful endorsement of the proposals was, however, qualified by the 60% rate of voter abstention.) Elections to the National Constituent Assembly (ANC) in late July resulted in an outright victory for Polo Patriótico, which won 120 out of the 131 seats. The leadership of COPEI and of the AD subsequently resigned. The ANC was formally inaugurated on 3 August and by late August had assumed most functions of the opposition-controlled Congreso Nacional; the Congreso itself was put into recess indefinitely. In response, the opposition accused the Government of establishing a de facto dictatorship. Chávez justified the control of the legislature, executive and judiciary as necessary in order to eradicate corruption and implement social reforms. A Judicial Emergency Commission was appointed in August with the task of investigating the notoriously corrupt judicial system. (By November 1999 200 judges had been dismissed or suspended.) In response, the Supreme Court President resigned. On 9 September the ANC and the Congreso Nacional signed an agreement of political coexistence that guaranteed the full functioning of the legislative branch from 2 October until a new constitution entered into force. However, relations between the Government and the Congreso Nacional were further strained when Chávez ignored congressional objections to the 2000 budget proposal and asked the ANC to approve it instead.

The draft of the new Constitution was signed by the ANC on 19 November 1999 and was approved by 71% of the popular vote in a referendum held on 15 December. The low rate of voter participation (only 46%) was largely blamed on torrential rain in much of the country (which resulted in the deaths of 30,000 and left a further 200,000 homeless in the central state of Vargas). The 350-article Constitution, which renamed the country the Bolivarian Republic of Venezuela, was promulgated on 30 December. It extended the President's term from five to six years, eliminated the Senate, permitted more state intervention in the economy, reduced civilian supervisory powers over the military, guaranteed the Government's oil monopoly and strengthened minority rights. The Government's political opponents challenged the Constitution because of its centralization of power in the executive branch. The Constitution also promoted public participation by giving the electorate the right to remove elected officials from office by referendum and to annul all but a handful of key laws with an absolute majority. The monitoring of such election processes was to be carried out by an independent National Electoral Council (Consejo Nacional Electoral—CNE). The Constitution also granted social security and labour benefits, including the reduction of the working week to 44 hours, which was strongly opposed by business leaders. The Congreso Nacional was officially dissolved on 4 January 2000. A new post of executive Vice-President was created, and on 24 January Chávez appointed Isaías Rodríguez (ANC Vice-President) to the position. In the same month the ANC appointed many of Chávez's nominees to head state institutions, ranging from the Tribunal Supremo de Justicia to the Central Bank, and including the Ombudsman, the Attorney-General and the Comptroller-General (national auditor). There was criticism that they were appointed without wider consultation and that they were all close associates of the President.

New elections for the President, governors, legislators and mayors, as stipulated under the new Constitution, were scheduled for 28 May 2000. The ANC was dissolved in January after it formally delegated its powers to a newly created 21-member Legislative Commission, which was designated as an interim body until the formation of a new Asamblea Nacional. For the first time in the country's history, the military were authorized to vote. Francisco Arias Cárdenas, Governor of the state of Zulia, and one of the four commanders who had led the abortive coup against President Pérez, was the main presidential challenger to Chávez. On 25 May, three days before voting was scheduled to take place, the Tribunal Supremo de Justicia suspended the elections, citing technical faults with the electronic voting system. Elections for the President, national legislators and governors were eventually held on 30 July, separate from the local elections, which were postponed until December. Despite the weak economic situation, popular support for the President, especially from the poorest sections of society, remained strong: Chávez won 59.7% of the valid votes cast in the presidential poll, compared with the 37.5% of the ballot polled by Arias and the 2.7% secured by Claudio Fermín (formerly Mayor of Caracas and member of the ANC). At the concurrent election to the new, 165-seat Asamblea Nacional, the ruling MVR secured a majority of 93 seats. The AD came second with 32 seats, Salas Römer's PRVZL gained eight seats, MAS won six seats, while the once powerful COPEI secured only five seats. However, the MVR's 93 seats fell short of the three-fifths' majority required to appoint members of the judiciary and the Attorney-General and Comptroller-General. In gubernatorial elections the MVR-led Polo Patriótico alliance dominated, narrowly gaining control of 14 regional executives. Chávez was sworn in as President on 16 August. His new administration was largely unchanged from the previous one. The Asamblea Nacional was convened for the first time in the same month.

In November 2000 Chávez's powers were further enhanced when the Asamblea Nacional approved an enabling law, allowing the President to decree, without legislative debate, a wide range of laws (in areas including public finance and land reform) for one year. In the same month the legislature passed controversial legislation that assigned the power to appoint important government posts, such as Attorney-General, public ombudsman and senior judges, to a 15-member congressional committee that was dominated by members of the ruling party. It also approved a government proposal to hold a referendum on whether the opposition-controlled CTV trade union should be suspended until new leadership elections could be held. Chávez accused the CTV leadership of corruption and undemocratic behaviour while his critics accused him of trying to eradicate a powerful opposition faction. In the previous month members of Fedepetrol, the petroleum workers' union, had gone on strike to demand a higher daily rate of pay. Their action proved successful and strikes by other unions swiftly followed. The trade unions declared the proposed referendum to be unconstitutional, but the Tribunal Supremo de Justicia rejected their arguments and the referendum proceeded on 3 December. In the event, the proposal to suspend trade union leaders for 180 days was approved by 65% of the vote, but the result was undermined by a very low rate of voter participation (23%). The MVR also performed well in municipal elections, held on the same day, although these were also affected by a high abstention rate.

In early February 2001 José Vicente Rangel became the first civilian to be appointed Minister of National Defence, to the consternation of many within the armed forces. However, tensions were eased the following day, when the President appointed Gen. Luis Amaya Chacón to the newly created post of Commander of the Armed Forces, effectively removing Rangel from the chain of military command.

In March 2001 a preliminary report by the Comptroller-General alleged widespread corruption within the Chávez administration's social programme, the Plan Bolívar 2000. In May thousands of petroleum and steel workers went on strike to demand recognition of trade union rights. By late November the Chávez administration had antagonized both the labour and business sectors sufficiently for them to find common cause. Earlier that month it was confirmed, amid government allegations of fraud and electoral malpractice, that Carlos Ortega had won the CTV leadership election, thus frustrating Chávez's efforts to establish a pro-Government trade union umbrella organization. The CTV allied itself with the country's largest business association, Fedecámaras (Federación Venezolana de Cámaras y Asociaciones de Comercio y Producción), to demand a nation-wide general strike. Fedecámaras was protesting against a recently decreed series of 49 laws (passed using the enabling law, thereby bypassing legislative scrutiny); these measures included land reform legislation allowing the Government to expropriate land it deemed unproductive, and a hydrocarbons law, which increased royalties on the petroleum industry. The CTV leaders objected to the hydrocarbons law, claiming that it threatened foreign investment and jobs. In the same month thousands of AD supporters marched on the Asamblea Nacional to demand the resignation of the President. A one-day general strike paralysed the country on 11 December and garnered support from a broad range of sectors.

In January 2002 Chávez replaced his Vice-President, Adina Bastidas, with his conspirator in the 1992 military coup attempt, Diosdado Cabello. Another participant in the 1992 coup attempt, Rámon Rodríguez Chacín, was appointed Minister of the Interior and Justice, while later in the month another former army colleague, Francisco Usón, was named Minister of Finance. The cabinet reorganization was interpreted by many as a move to the left that would increase political instability in the country. Also in February, four military officials, in separate statements, publicly demanded that Chávez resign, leading to further anti-Government protests and counter-demonstrations in support of the Government. In the same month, in the face of increasing economic uncertainty, the Government abandoned the fixed currency exchange regime and allowed the bolívar to float freely, in an attempt to halt mass capital flight. The bolívar subsequently lost nearly 19% of its value against the US dollar.

In early March 2002 business leaders, trade union leaders and representatives of the Catholic Church signed a pact calling for the installation of a government of national unity, and more transparency in government, as well as action against poverty and corruption. At the same time, industrial unrest continued to escalate. Following the appointment of a new management board of the state petroleum company Petróleos de Venezuela, SA (PDVSA), several thousand PDVSA managers marched through Caracas in protest; the managers claimed that the appointments were politically motivated. The demonstrators were supported by Fedepetrol, the petroleum workers' trade union, as well as by Fedecámaras. On 9 April a 48-hour general strike was organized by the CTV and Fedecámaras. It was subsequently announced that the strike would continue indefinitely, and on 11 April more than 150,000 people marched on the presidential palace to demand Chávez's resignation. In the subsequent clashes outside the Miraflores palace between protesters, government supporters and the security forces, 20 people were killed and more than 100 injured.

On 12 April 2002 a group of senior military officers announced that President Chávez had resigned amid allegations that pro-Government loyalists had fired on opposition protesters. It later emerged that Chávez had, in fact, refused to resign and that, in effect, a military coup had taken place. The military conspirators appointed Pedro Carmona, the President of Fedecámaras, interim President, while Chávez was held incommunicado. On assuming power, Carmona immediately dissolved the Asamblea Nacional and the Tribunal Supremo de Justicia and pronounced Chávez's Bolivarian Constitution to be null and void. The removal from office by the military of an elected head of state was immediately condemned by many Governments in the region; however, in contrast, the US Administration of George W. Bush blamed the crisis on Chávez and refused to call his ousting from power a coup (see below). Thousands of pro-Chávez and pro-democracy supporters immediately took to the streets to demand Chávez's reinstatement, while many senior military officers also expressed their continued loyalty to the deposed President. In the face of threats by officers loyal to Chávez to attack the presidential palace, Carmona immediately resigned; Vice-President Cabello was sworn in as interim President on 13 April. Chávez returned to the Miraflores palace within hours and, in a televised ceremony, resumed his presidential powers, less than two days after his ouster.

On reassuming the presidency, as a gesture of reconciliation, Chávez announced the resignation of the disputed PDVSA board of directors. He also declared that there would be no persecution of those who had supported his removal from office. Nevertheless, Carmona and 100 military personnel were arrested. (Carmona escaped from house arrest and was subsequently granted asylum in Colombia.) In late April 2002 the Asamblea Nacional approved the establishment of a Truth Commission to investigate the events surrounding the coup attempt. (In mid-October 2004 eight people, including workers, business leaders and students, were convicted and sentenced to prison sentences of between three and six years for their roles in the uprising.)

The country's political and economic situation continued to deteriorate in mid-2002. In August the Supreme Court ruled that there was insufficient evidence to prosecute four senior members of the military who had participated in the failed coup attempt in April. (However, this ruling was overturned in mid-March 2005.) In late October the opposition and its allies in the CTV labour union and Fedecámaras called a one-day strike, intended to force President Chávez to accept early presidential and legislative elections. The strike brought much of Venezuela to a halt, although the country's important oil industry was not seriously affected. On 23 October a group of 14 senior military officers declared themselves in rebellion against the Chávez Government. The men, many of whom had been involved in April's failed coup, occupied a square in eastern Caracas, where they were joined by hundreds of opposition activists. More than 100 junior officers later also expressed their rejection of Chávez's policies and joined the protest. All of the officers involved were subsequently dismissed from the armed forces. In an attempt to find a constitutional solution to the ongoing political crisis, 12 representatives of the opposition and the Government began round-table discussions in early November. The negotiations were chaired by the Secretary-General of the Organization of American States (OAS, see p. 360), César Gaviria Trujillo, and were also attended by representatives of the US-based Carter Center. The talks failed to make any immediate progress, however, and in late November the opposition, the CTV and Fedecámaras announced that a general strike would be held from 2 December to force President Chávez to call fresh elections or submit to a referendum. The general strike lasted a further nine weeks. The majority of large businesses and international companies observed the stoppage, although small shopkeepers and public transport continued to operate throughout. The strike had a particularly severe impact on the oil industry. The majority of managers and administrative staff at PDVSA observed the strike, and the company was obliged to declare *force majeure* on its exports of crude petroleum and petroleum products. The President of PDVSA, Alí Rodríguez Araque, sought to restart the industry by replacing the strikers with new staff, contract workers and retired employees. He eventually dismissed 18,000 of PDVSA's previous 33,000 full-time work-force for observing the strike, and production reportedly recovered to pre-strike levels by late March 2003. The strike caused enormous difficulties for the Government, which saw oil revenues collapse, while ordinary Venezuelans suffered from severe shortages of food and other basic products.

In mid-January 2003 President Chávez suspended trading in the national currency, the bolívar, in response to the economic crisis. Early the following month it was announced that the bolívar was to be 'pegged' to the US dollar, and that price controls were to be introduced on basic food items. None the less, the Government refused to negotiate on the issue of early elections, although discussions between the two sides, suspended at the start of the strike, began once more in late January. The general strike focused international attention on the ongoing crisis in Venezuela, and in late January six countries formed the 'Group of Friends of Venezuela', to support a peaceful solution to the crisis. The Group was composed of the USA, Brazil, Chile, Mexico, Portugal and Spain, despite President Chávez's call for the inclusion of countries more sympathetic to his revolutionary project, such as Cuba.

In early February 2003 the opposition parties, the CTV and Fedecámaras announced an end to the two-month general strike after failing to secure any concessions from the Government. The opposition, which had combined under the Coordinadora Democrática (CD) grouping, presented an estimated 4m. signatures in support of early elections. The Government did not respond to the petition, and several days later it announced new exchange rate rules, which critics alleged were designed to punish companies that had participated in the recent strike. In mid-February the Government and opposition representatives at the OAS-sponsored negotiations signed an agreement to seek to reduce political tension in Venezuela. The pact was immediately thrown into question, however, when the following day police arrested the President of Fedecámaras, Carlos Fernández Pérez, on charges including treason, relating to his role in organizing the recent general strike. A warrant was also issued for his fellow strike leader, the President of the CTV, Carlos Ortega, who went into hiding and later obtained political asylum in Costa Rica. (Ortega was expelled from that country in March 2004, and in December 2005 was found guilty of insurrection, incitement and use of false documents and sentenced to 15 years' imprisonment.) The opposition immediately accused President Chávez of authoritarianism and observers expressed fears that a further deterioration in the political situation was likely. In March an appeals court ordered the release without charge of Fernández Pérez, ruling that there was no evidence against him. At the same time, charges against six senior PDVSA managers who had supported the strike were also struck down.

In April 2003, following further OAS-sponsored negotiations, the Government and opposition agreed in principle that a referendum on the Chávez Government could be held if the opposition succeeded in collecting 2.4m. signatures in support of a vote. The agreement was finalized in the following month. The signatures collected by the opposition were to be verified by the CNE. However, since the Asamblea Nacional was unable to agree on appointments to the electoral body, responsibility passed, as stipulated by the Constitution, to the Tribunal Supremo de Justicia, which appointed, on 27 August, a new head of the electoral authority, as well as four other board members. One week earlier opposition parties had submitted a 2.4m.-signature petition to the CNE demanding a recall referendum. However, in early September the new board of the electoral authority ruled that the petition was not valid, as some of the signatures had been collected more than six months before the date on which a referendum could be held. Furthermore, in late September the CNE issued a new and more stringent set of referendum guidelines, which stipulated that, in the case of a binding presidential recall referendum, a President would then only be removed from office if a greater proportion of the electorate voted against him than had supported him in the most recent election (in the case of Chávez in the 2000 ballot, this would be greater than 59.7% of the votes). Also, if there were insufficient valid signatures collected (20% of the electorate, equivalent to some 2.4m. voters), no further recall petitions would be permitted during that President's term of office.

In October 2003 the CD presented a new recall referendum request to the CNE. In response, the MVR announced that it intended to compile more than 40 recall petitions on opposition deputies and state governors. The CNE ruled that any recall referendums would be restricted to members of the Asamblea Nacional and federal Government. It subsequently announced that signature-gathering for the recall of 37 opposition politicians would take place on 21–24 November, while that for the presidential (plus 33 MVR deputies) recall would be held one week later.

The CNE was scheduled to announce the validity of both sets of petitions by the end of December 2003. However, a series of technical problems and doubts over the validity of some petitions led to delays, provoking civil unrest in which eight protesters were killed in February 2004. Later that month the CNE announced that there would be a further delay, to allow about 1.1m. signatures to be revalidated. To this effect, in mid-March signatories of the petitions were to present themselves at electoral centres nation-wide to verify their signatures. Finally, following a rechecking of signatures that had technical irregularities at the end of May, in June the CNE ruled that the number of valid signatures collected was sufficient to force a presidential recall referendum. The Government accepted this ruling and the poll was duly held on 15 August. The motion to recall the President was defeated, with 3,989,008 votes (40.74% of those voting) in favour of Chávez's removal from office and 5,800,629 (59.25%) against. There was a voter turn-out of 70.0%. Despite assertions by the Carter Center, the OAS and other international observers that the ballot had been conducted fairly, the CD disputed the result, claiming that large-scale electoral fraud had been perpetrated by the Government. In late September the CNE rejected the CD's appeal against the referendum result, citing a lack of evidence. The CD alliance suffered further setbacks following the withdrawal of three parties (Causa R, Alianza Bravo Pueblo and Primero Justicia).

Immediately following the referendum in August 2004 President Chávez effected several changes to his Council of Ministers. Notably, Lt (retd) Jesse Chacón Escamillo replaced Lucas Rincón as Minister of the Interior and Justice. In the following month Chávez created two new portfolios—for food and for the mass economy. In late November Chávez unexpectedly dismissed Jesús Arnoldo Pérez as foreign minister, appointing Alí Rodríguez Araque, hitherto President of PDVSA, to the post. In early December Nelson Merentes Díaz was moved from the Ministry of Economic and Social Development to Finance, succeeding Tobías Nóbrega.

Meanwhile, in July 2004 the Tribunal Supremo de Justicia ratified a law that prohibited journalists from working if they did not hold a recognized qualification or belong to a recognized professional association. In mid-December Chávez promulgated a law imposing new broadcasting restrictions, ostensibly to protect children from unsuitable material and to prevent incitements to breaches of public order. Also in that month, the Asamblea Nacional approved amendments to the criminal code, which introduced prison sentences for those judged to have publicly insulted the President or other representatives of the state. The reforms, which took effect in mid-March 2005, were strongly criticized by a broad range of opposition groups, foreign governments and non-governmental organizations as a threat to civil liberties. In mid-April a journalist of the newspaper *El Nuevo País*, Patricia Poleo, was convicted of defaming interior minister Chacón Escamillo and sentenced to six months' imprisonment.

In November 2004 state prosecutor Danilo Anderson, who had been investigating the failed coup of April 2002, with a view to bringing charges against those involved, was assassinated in Caracas. In late November a former police commissioner of Caracas, Iván Simonovis, was arrested on suspicion of involvement with the murder; two other suspects were killed by police while allegedly resisting arrest. In October 2005 Attorney-General Isaías Rodríguez Díaz accused the US and Colombian intelligence services and Colombian paramilitaries of colluding in Anderson's assassination; both countries denied the accusation and cited a lack of supporting evidence. In November Patricia Poleo and three others were named in connection with the case. In mid-December 2004 the Asamblea Nacional approved the appointment of 12 more judges to the Tribunal Supremo de Justicia, in addition to the appointment of five replacements, increasing the total number of sitting judges from 20 to 32.

In January 2005 President Chávez signed a decree initiating a 90-day review process into both the level of productivity on privately owned land and into the validity of its ownership. Local authorities were granted powers to expropriate estates deemed unproductive by the review for redistribution to 'landless' farmers. The number of 'unproductive' estates was estimated at over 500, according to a preliminary government survey published earlier that month. In September President Chávez vowed to accelerate the process of land expropriations. In January 2006 the Government took control of 32 oilfields under private operation, in accordance with its policy of revising all private sector contracts for hydrocarbon exploitation in order to give the government-owned PDVSA a majority stake.

At elections to the Asamblea Nacional on 4 December 2005 the ruling MVR secured 114 of a total 167 seats, with the remaining seats won by parties allied to the Government. The overwhelming government victory was primarily owing to the boycott of the ballot by the main opposition parties (including the AD, Primero Justicia and Proyecto Venezuela), which claimed that the electronic voting system could not guarantee voters' anonymity. As a result, voter participation was estimated at just 25%. However, observers from the EU and the OAS declared the elections to be free and transparent; a report published by the EU observer group in March 2006 stated that the principal discernible problem in the elections had been a lack of confidence among some voters in the electoral process.

The Government announced further measures under its Bolivarian social reform programme in early 2006. In March it was stated that 150,000 new homes were to be built during the year to begin to address the housing crisis among impoverished sectors of society. In April a programme costing US $24m. to extend basic services to some 77,000 people living in rural areas was announced. Moreover, in November new measures aimed at extending access to higher education and at providing dental care for the poor were introduced. The Government's ongoing revision of its hydrocarbons operations also continued during 2006. In April the state assumed control of seven oilfields operated by foreign petroleum companies, five of which were relinquished under legislation introduced in 2001 and two of which were retaken without the agreement of the companies currently operating the sites. Further amendments to the hydrocarbon laws, approved in May 2006, provided for an increase in royalties required from foreign companies operating Venezuelan oilfields from one-sixth to one-third.

At the presidential election held on 3 December 2006 Chávez was decisively re-elected with 62.9% of the vote. The opposition's unity candidate Manuel Antonio Rosales Guerrero, secured 36.9% of votes cast. Observers from the EU declared themselves to be generally satisfied with the conduct of the election and praised the high rate of electoral participation in the poll (some 75% of registered voters took part). The victory was seen as a strong endorsement of the Government's so-called Bolivarian programme of social reform, and of Chávez himself, as a charismatic and popular national leader. Shortly after the election it was announced that the MVR was to be dissolved and replaced by a new political organization, the Partido Socialista Unido de Venezuela (PSUV), which was intended to unite the various leftwing parties allied to the Government. Chávez was inaugurated as President on 10 January 2007 and a new Council of Ministers was installed, comprising 12 members of the previous administration and 16 new appointees. In late January the Asamblea Nacional approved a wide-ranging enabling law granting the President powers to legislate by decree for a period of 18 months in 11 areas, including the reform of state institutions and public services. He announced that his administration's priorities would include major constitutional reform, the return to state ownership of privatized industries (particularly in the telecommunications, electricity and hydrocarbons sectors) and reforms to the education system. To this end, in February the Government agreed the terms of the purchase of shares in Electricidad de Caracas, and in early May it bought a majority share in the telecommunications concern Compañía Anónima Nacional Telefónos de Venezuela. In late June PDVSA gained control of petroleum operations in the Orinoco Belt, a large reserve of heavy crude petroleum, by acquiring majority stakes in four joint ventures with foreign companies. Two further companies refused to renegotiate their contracts with PDVSA and the projects in which they were involved came under full state ownership.

The Government was widely criticized for its attitude towards civil liberties following an announcement in December 2006 that it would not renew the broadcasting licence of Radio Caracas Televisión (RCTV), Venezuela's oldest television station, upon its expiry in May 2007. Chávez cited the station's support for the brief coup of 2002 and the anti-Government bias of its news reporting as reasons for the decision, which was condemned by RCTV (who disputed the dates of the lease) and by numerous international media organizations. The station duly ceased broadcasting in May and was replaced by a state-owned channel, Televisora Venezolana Social; however, RCTV recommended broadcasting via cable in July by means of its US-based subsidiary, RCTV International.

In mid-May 2007 the Minister of Health, Erick Rodríguez, resigned, ostensibly for personal reasons, and was replaced by Jesús Mantilla Oliveros. In July the Minister of National Defence, Gen. Raúl Isaías Baduel, announced his retirement, and was substituted by Gen. Gustavo Rangel Briceño.

In August 2007 Chávez presented to the Asamblea Nacional a proposal to amend 33 articles of the 1999 Constitution. The most significant of the amendments would have removed the restriction limiting the President to two consecutive terms in office—allowing him to be re-elected indefinitely—and increased the presidential term from six to seven years. The revised Constitution would have abolished the autonomy of the Banco Central de Venezuela and placed the country's international reserves under government control, defined a political role for the armed forces, and reduced the maximum working day from eight to six hours. In early November the Asamblea Nacional approved Chávez's proposed amendments, along with a further 36 proposed by the legislature. A referendum was held on 2 December on the two sets of amendments, both of which were rejected by a narrow margin. Baduel, the former Minister of National Defence, had been prominent in his opposition to the reform, claiming that it would have amounted to a coup.

Chávez carried out an extensive cabinet reorganization in early January 2008. Notably, Vice-President Jorge Rodríguez Gómez was dismissed and replaced by Ramón Alonso Carrizalez Rengifo, hitherto Minister of Housing, who was in turn replaced by Col (retd) Jorge Isaac Pérez Prado; Ramón Rodríguez Chacín substituted Pedro Carreño as Minister of the Interior and Justice; and Rafael Isea replaced Rodrigo Cabezas as Minister of Finance. (In March, however, Pérez Prado was himself dismissed and replaced by Edith Gómez.) Chávez announced that the departure of Vice-President Rodríguez would enable him to dedicate himself fully to the launch of the PSUV; the nascent party's inability thus far to unite the various left-wing forces, and the opposition of several of these parties to the constitutional reform, was regarded as a contributory factor in the referendum defeat. The appointment of more moderate figures to the Council of Ministers was also seen as a response to the referendum result. There were further cabinet changes during early 2008. Meanwhile, in April Chávez announced that the Government would take control of the cement industry in Venezuela, in order to guarantee supplies for state housing construction programmes.

In 1982 Venezuela refused to renew the 1970 Port of Spain Protocol, declaring a 12-year moratorium on the issue of Venezuela's claim to a large area of Guyana to the west of the Essequibo river, which expired in that year. Venezuela's border garrisons were strengthened and border violations were reported. In 1985 Venezuela and Guyana requested UN mediation in an attempt to resolve their dispute over the Essequibo region. A UN mediator was appointed in late 1989; however, negotiations remained deadlocked. The dispute resurfaced in 1999 when Guyana granted offshore oil concessions in the disputed waters to foreign oil firms, and in October of that year President Chávez renewed Venezuela's claim to the Essequibo region. The tension escalated in March 2000 when Guyana gave preliminary approval to the installation of a US satellite-launching facility in the disputed area. In March 2004 Chávez met his Guyanese counterpart, Bharrat Jagdeo; although no progress was made on resolving the dispute, the Venezuelan Government indicated its willingness to 'authorize' Guyanese mineral exploration in the Essequibo region. In mid-2005 Guyana signed the PetroCaribe energy accord with Venezuela, granting Guyana preferential terms for purchasing Venezuelan petroleum.

Venezuela also has a claim to some islands in the Netherlands Antilles, and a territorial dispute with Colombia concerning maritime boundaries in the Gulf of Venezuela. In March 1989 an agreement was reached with Colombia on the establishment of a border commission to negotiate a settlement for the territorial dispute. In March 1990 President Virgilio Barco of Colombia and President Pérez signed the 'San Pedro Alejandrino' document, by which they pledged to implement the commission's proposals. At a meeting of the Presidents of Colombia and Venezuela in Caracas in January 1992, Pérez publicly recognized that Colombia had legitimate territorial rights in the Gulf of Venezuela.

Periodic incursions into Venezuelan territory by Colombian combatants and criminal elements continually strained relations with Colombia. Despite agreements signed by both countries in 1997 and 2000 to increase co-operation in policing the border area, clashes between the Venezuelan military and Colombian guerrillas were frequent. Tensions were exacerbated in 2000, owing to Chávez's public opposition to the military component of 'Plan Colombia' (Colombia's US-supported anti-drugs strategy) and accusations by Colombia that Venezuela was covertly aiding the guerrilla forces. In November 2000 Colombia briefly recalled its ambassador to Venezuela after a representative of the Fuerzas Armadas Revolucionarias de Colombia—Ejército del Pueblo (FARC—EP, commonly known as the FARC) was allowed to speak in the Venezuelan Asamblea Nacional. In March 2001 Venezuela refused to extradite to Colombia a member of a guerrilla group accused of hijacking an aircraft in 1999. Although the right-wing Government of Alvaro Uribe Vélez repeatedly criticized President Chávez for failing to classify the FARC as a terrorist organization, in November there were indications of rapprochement following a meeting between the two Presidents to promote bilateral trade and security co-operation. However, the Venezuelan Government continued to demand improvements to border security arrangements, following confrontations with armed Colombian groups in December 2003 and September 2004 that resulted in the deaths of several Venezuelan soldiers. In a public demonstration of amity, Presidents Uribe and Chávez met in Cartagena, Colombia, in early November 2004 to discuss border security and economic co-operation. However, relations were severely strained in mid-December following the arrest by the Colombian authorities of Rodrigo Granda Escobar, the supposed international spokesperson of the FARC. It was subsequently alleged by the Venezuelan Government that Granda, although ultimately arrested in Cúcuta, Colombia, was first kidnapped in Caracas by Venezuelan and Colombian agents in the pay of the Colombian Government and with the collusion of US intelligence services; the Uribe and US Governments denied any involvement. In consequence, the Venezuelan ambassador to Colombia was recalled in January 2005 and restrictions on trade and passage between the two countries were imposed by the Chávez Government. Following an expression of regret by the Colombian Government in late January and a visit to Caracas by President Uribe in mid-February, relations between the two countries were normalized. Relations were strengthened in September following the Colombian authorities' refusal of political asylum to seven Venezuelan military officials and one diplomat accused of participating in the failed coup attempt of April 2002. However, in 2005 and early 2006 the Colombian and US Governments repeatedly expressed concern over Venezuela's rapid military expansion, which, it was argued, would upset the military balance of the region. In August 2007 Uribe engaged Chávez in negotiating with FARC leaders in respect of the release of hostages held by the guerrilla group. Relations between the two countries deteriorated significantly in November after Uribe abruptly cancelled Chávez's mediation attempt, accusing him of making contact with senior Colombian military officers against his orders; nevertheless, the Venezuelan President's subsequent role in securing the release of two of the hostages in January 2008 led to a slight improvement in relations. Chávez strongly condemned Uribe following Colombia's incursion into Ecuadorian territory in early March, during which time a senior FARC commander was killed; in response to the incident Chávez ordered the closure of the Venezuelan embassy in the Colombian capital, Bogotá, and sent troops to the Colombian border. Uribe subsequently alleged that evidence gathered during the raid indicated that Chávez had aided the FARC, and threatened to prosecute him in the International Criminal Court. However, diplomatic relations were swiftly restored a few days later after Chávez mediated a rapprochement between Uribe and the Ecuadorean President, Rafael Correa Delgado, at a Rio Group summit in the Dominican Republic.

Following his election in December 1998, President Chávez announced that his administration would seek greater integration in large regional organizations such as CARICOM (see p. 196) and Mercosur (see p. 391). In May 2005 Chávez launched PetroSur, an initiative to promote energy integration and offer preferential prices for petroleum in the Southern Cone region. In September Chávez unveiled similar initiatives for the Andean and Caribbean regions, called PetroAndina and PetroCaribe, respectively. Venezuela was admitted to Mercosur in July 2006, but its entry was subject to ratification by the group's existing members; in April 2008 Venezuela's accession had yet to be ratified by the legislatures of Brazil and Paraguay.

President Chávez made closer relations with Cuba a priority, and in October 2000 Chávez and the Cuban head of state Fidel Castro Ruz signed a co-operation agreement allowing the export of oil to Cuba on the same preferential terms enjoyed by a number of Central American and Caribbean countries. In 2003–04 improved relations between the two countries led to increased Cuban assistance for the Government's social-welfare programmes, and Venezuela continued to support Cuba's integration into regional trade associations.

Venezuela's relations with Mexico deteriorated in November 2005 at the Summit of the Americas in Mar del Plata, Argentina, owing to President Chávez's strident denunciation of an initiative promoted by Mexican President Vicente Fox Quesada for a free trade area of the Americas. The Venezuelan ambassador to Mexico was recalled later that month, as was the Mexican ambassador to Venezuela. Meanwhile, from early 2005 the Mexican authorities accused Venezuela with increasing frequency of failing to police adequately its sea and air ports in order to prevent the transshipment of illegal narcotics, primarily from Colombia, to Mexico. In April 2006 Mexican officials reportedly discovered 5.5 metric tons of cocaine on an aircraft that had arrived from Venezuela; the ultimate destination of the drugs was believed to be the USA. Relations with Mexico improved after Felipe Calderón Hinojosa took office as President of that country in late 2006, and in August 2007 an exchange of ambassadors marked the restoration of full diplomatic relations.

Relations between Venezuela and the USA (the main purchaser of Venezuelan crude petroleum) deteriorated markedly following the election of Chávez. In 2000 Chávez refused to authorize US drugs-surveillance flights over Venezuela. Furthermore, the President's close relationship with Fidel Castro led to further estrangement from the USA. The Venezuelan Government also signed a number of bilateral trade and cultural agreements with the People's Republic of China, India, Iran and Russia in 2001. (Further agreements on energy sector co-operation were signed with China and India in December 2004 and January 2005, respectively, and a bilateral investment agreement worth US $200m. was signed with Iran in February 2006.) Bilateral relations further deteriorated after the US Administration of George W. Bush refused to condemn the short-lived military ouster of Chávez in April 2002. It was subsequently revealed that US officials had met with opposition figures shortly before the failed coup; however, the US Government denied it had encouraged or supported the coup. Venezuela was highly critical of the US-led military campaign against the regime of Saddam Hussain in Iraq from March 2003. Relations with the USA remained hostile during the mid-2000s, owing in large part to Chávez's sustained personal criticism of President Bush and his outspoken rhetoric against US 'imperialism'. In April 2005 Venezuela suspended its military exchange programmes with the USA. In August of that year Chávez suspended co-operation with the US Drug Enforcement Agency (DEA), following its repeated criticism of Venezuela's counter-narcotics policies. Chávez accused DEA agents of spying on Venezuela and the US Government responded by 'decertifying' Venezuela for non-compliance in fulfilling its obligations to combat the trade in illegal drugs. None the less, in January 2006 Venezuela agreed to renew some co-operation with the DEA, although US agents from the organization were not to be allowed on Venezuelan territory. In the same month the US Department of State intervened to prevent the sale to Venezuela of Spanish military aircraft worth some $2,000m., ostensibly on the grounds that the aircraft contained US-built components requiring an export licence. However, in early February it was announced that the sale would proceed despite US opposition. Later that month Venezuela expelled a US naval attaché in Venezuela, Capt. John Correa, accusing him of espionage. The following day the USA expelled a Venezuelan diplomat in response. In early April President Chávez threatened to expel the US ambassador, William Brownfield, accusing him of abusing the principles of diplomatic protection after Brownfield had visited a poor neighbourhood of Caracas and distributed free baseball equipment, an act against which anti-US activists protested violently. Meanwhile, throughout 2005 and 2006 members of the Government, including President Chávez, repeatedly alleged that the USA was planning to invade Venezuela in order to secure its supply of petroleum and that the country's armed forces were being strengthened in preparation for this; the USA dismissed the allegation as unsubstantiated and accused Chávez of seeking to destabilize the region by expanding its military capability so significantly. During 2006 the Venezuelan Government continued to strengthen its armed forces, purchasing military aircraft from Russia as well as 100,000 assault rifles. In March the US authorities announced an embargo on all commercial arms sales to Venezuela. The US Government continued to express concern regarding Venezuela's close relations with countries including Cuba, Libya and Iran, with whose Government Chávez publicly stated his commitment to co-operate in the field of nuclear energy.

Venezuela has observer status in the Non-aligned Movement (see p. 424).

Government

Venezuela is a federal republic comprising 23 states, a Federal District (containing the capital) and 72 Federal Dependencies. Under the 1999 Constitution, legislative power is held by the unicameral Asamblea Nacional (National Assembly). Executive authority rests with the President. The President is elected for six years by universal adult suffrage. The President has extensive powers, and is assisted by a Council of Ministers. Each state has a directly elected executive governor and an elected legislature.

Defence

Military service is selective for two years and six months between 18 and 45 years of age. As assessed at November 2007, the armed forces numbered 115,000 men: an army of 63,000, a navy of 17,500 (including an estimated 7,000 marines), an air force of 11,500 and a National Guard of 23,000. There was an army reserve numbering 8,000. The defence budget for 2007 was 5,510,000m. bolívares.

Economic Affairs

In 2006, according to estimates by the World Bank, Venezuela's gross national income (GNI), measured at average 2004–06 prices, was US $163,996m., equivalent to $6,070 per head (or $7,440 per head on an international purchasing-power parity basis). During 1996–2006, it was estimated, the population increased by an annual average of 1.8%, while gross domestic product (GDP) per head decreased, in real terms, at an average of 0.8% per year. Overall GDP increased, in real terms, by an average annual rate of 2.7% in 1996–2006; according to World Bank estimates, GDP grew by 10.3% in 2006.

According to the World Bank, agriculture (including hunting, forestry and fishing) contributed an estimated 4.5% of GDP in 2003 and engaged an estimated 9.8% of the employed labour force in 2002. The principal crops are sugar cane, bananas, maize, rice, plantains, oranges, sorghum and cassava. Cattle are the principal livestock, but the practice of smuggling cattle across Venezuela's border into Colombia has had a severe effect on the livestock sector. According to the World Bank, agricultural GDP increased by an estimated annual average of 3.8% during 1996–2005. The sector's GDP decreased, in real terms, by 7.2% in 2005.

Industry (including mining, manufacturing, petroleum-related activities, construction and power) contributed a preliminary 42.9% of GDP in 2006 and engaged an estimated 20.9% of the employed labour force in 2002. According to the World Bank, industrial GDP decreased by an annual average of 0.4% during 1996–2005. Sectoral GDP decreased, in real terms, by a preliminary 8.1% in 2006.

Mining and quarrying (including petroleum and petroleum-related activities) contributed a preliminary 16.0% of GDP in 2006. However, in 2002 mining and quarrying engaged only 0.5% of the employed labour force. Petroleum and petroleum-related products provided 84.0% of export revenues in 2004. At the end of 2006 proven reserves totalled 80,000m. barrels, although if heavy and extra-heavy crude petroleum reserves were included, Venezuela's total reserves were estimated to be considerably higher. Production averaged 2.8m. barrels per day in 2006. As well as large reserves of petroleum, Venezuela has substantial deposits of natural gas, coal, diamonds, gold, zinc, copper, lead, silver, phosphates, manganese and titanium. The GDP of the mining sector increased by an average of 2.5% per year in 1995–2001; the sector increased, in real terms, by a preliminary 3.9% in 2006.

Manufacturing contributed a preliminary 17.5% of GDP in 2006 and engaged approximately 11.9% of the employed labour force in 2002. The most important sectors were food products, transport equipment, industrial chemicals and iron and steel. Manufacturing GDP increased by an annual average of 4.3% during 1996–2005. The sector's GDP increased, in real terms, by a preliminary 10.4% in 2006.

Energy is derived principally from domestic supplies of petroleum and coal, and from hydroelectric power. Hydroelectric power provided 74.9% of electricity production in 2005, according to the US Energy Information Administration, with thermal generation supplying the remainder. Imports of mineral fuels comprised 0.8% of the total value of merchandise imports in 2005.

The services sector (excluding hotels and restaurants) contributed a preliminary 50.9% of GDP in 2006 and engaged some 69.1% of the employed labour force in 2002. The sector increased by an annual average of 2.2% in 1996–2005. Sectoral GDP increased, in real terms, by a preliminary 13.9% in 2006.

In 2006 Venezuela recorded a visible trade surplus of US $32,712m., and there was a surplus of $27,149m. on the current account of the balance of payments. In 2004 the principal source of imports (31.2%) was the USA; other major suppliers were Colombia, Brazil, Mexico and Germany. The USA was also the principal market for exports (44.4%) in 2003; other major purchasers were the Netherlands Antilles, the Netherlands, Colombia and Cuba. The principal exports in 2004 were petroleum and related products (84.0%), steel, aluminium and chemical products. The principal imports in 2004 were machinery and transport equipment (41.9%), basic manufactures, and chemicals.

There was a budgetary deficit of 5,857,100m. bolívares in 2006. Venezuela's total external debt was US $44,201m. at the end of 2005, of which $29,317m. was long-term public debt. In that year the cost of servicing the debt was equivalent to 9.1% of the value of exports of goods and services. The average annual rate of inflation was 23.8% in 1996–2006. Consumer prices increased by an annual average of 13.6% in 2006. An estimated 10.3% of the labour force were unemployed in March 2007.

Venezuela is a member of the Inter-American Development Bank (IDB, see p. 308), the Latin American Integration Association (Asociación Latinoamericana de Integración—ALADI, see p. 331), the Organization of the Petroleum Exporting Countries (OPEC, see p. 373), the Latin American Economic System (Sistema Económico Latinoamericano—SELA, see p. 413) and the Group of Three (G3, see p. 412). In July 2004 Venezuela became an associate member of Mercosur (see p. 391), and in July 2006 the country gained full membership. In November 2005, at the Summit of the Americas in Mar del Plata, Argentina, President Chávez discounted the possibility of Venezuela joining the proposed Free Trade Area of the Americas (FTAA), advanced by the USA. In mid-April 2006 President Chávez withdrew Venezuela from the Andean Community of Nations (see p. 170). In the same month Chávez, and the Cuban and Bolivian heads of state, Fidel Castro Ruz and Evo Morales Aima, respectively, signed a trade agreement, the Bolivarian Alternative for Latin America (Alternativa Bolivariana para América Latina y el Caribe—ALBA), intended to be an alternative to the stalled FTAA. In December 2004 Venezuela was one of 12 countries that were signatories to the agreement, signed in Cusco, Peru, creating the South American Community of Nations (Comunidad Sudamericana de Naciones), intended to promote greater regional economic integration, due to become operational by 2007. In May 2007 Chávez announced that Venezuela was to withdraw from the IMF and the World Bank but reversed the decision later that year.

Venezuela's economy is largely dependent on the petroleum sector (providing some 43.8% of government revenue in 2006 and 84.0% of export revenue in 2004) and is therefore particularly vulnerable to fluctuations in global oil prices. The Chávez administration, inaugurated in 1999, introduced new pension benefits and health programmes, to be financed by surplus petroleum profits, known as the oil stabilization fund. While there was a large increase in public sector pay and in pensions in 2000, the non-petroleum private sector stagnated, partly because of an overvalued currency. In an attempt to reduce the growing fiscal deficit, a wide-ranging series of economic measures was approved by decree in late 2001. However, the controversial measures contained in the package (most notably, a hydrocarbons law that increased royalty taxes on the petroleum sector from 17% to 30%) led to widespread industrial unrest and political instability, which severely affected petroleum production rates in early 2002. The situation was compounded in February after a controlled devaluation plan was abandoned in favour of a floating exchange rate, in a bid to halt the flight of capital caused by the continuing political unrest. Investor confidence in Venezuela deteriorated following the attempted coup against President Chávez in April 2002 and the protracted industrial and social unrest in early 2003 (see Recent History). The failure of the coup, and of the opposition's attempt to unseat Chávez in a recall referendum in mid-2004, allowed the Government to consolidate its policy of increased state intervention. The Chávez Government increased petroleum taxes and royalties and in January 2006 appropriated 32 privately operated oilfields. Following his re-election in the previous December, in early 2007 Chávez signalled his intent further to advance his Bolivarian socialism project, with the nationalization of parts of the telecommunications and electricity sectors. In April 2008 Chávez announced that the cement industry was to be nationalized in an attempt to deal with severe housing shortages. The Chávez administration was also able to continue with its regional integration project, offering, *inter alia*, discounted petroleum to Caribbean and Latin American nations. Nevertheless, this economic largesse only remained possible while the price of oil remained high. Furthermore, the Government's policy of heightened state intervention continued to deter investment, as did the increasingly hostile relationship between Venezuela and the USA. Inflationary pressure increased from 17.0% in 2006 to an estimated 22.5% in 2007. GDP growth was projected to decline to 4.2% in 2008, compared with 8.4% in 2007. However, strong consumer demand concomitant with negative real interest rates was likely to undermine attempts to bring prices under control in 2008. Inflation was forecast to rise further to some 27.0% over 2008, although with year-on-year food prices increasing by 42.6% in March 2008, there were expectations that the annual average could be higher.

Education

Education is officially compulsory for 10 years, to be undertaken between six and 15 years of age. Primary education, which is available free of charge, begins at six years of age and lasts for nine years. Secondary education, beginning at the age of 15, lasts for a further two years. In 2005 enrolment at primary schools included 91.3% of children in the relevant age-group (males 90.9%; females 91.7%), while the secondary enrolment ratio was 63.0% (males 58.7%; females 67.5%). In 2003/04 there were 48 universities. Expenditure by the central Government on education and sport was an estimated 29,601.6m. bolívares in 2004.

Public Holidays

2008: 1 January (New Year's Day), 1–6 February (Carnival), 10 March (La Guaira only), 21–24 March (Easter), 19 April (Declaration of Independence), 1 May (Labour Day), 24 June (Battle of Carabobo), 5 July (Independence Day), 24 July (Birth of Simón Bolívar and Battle of Lago de Maracaibo), 4 September (Civil Servants' Day), 12 October (Discovery of America), 24 October (Maracaibo only), 24–25 December (Christmas), 31 December (New Year's Eve).

2009: 1 January (New Year's Day), 20–25 February (Carnival), 10 March (La Guaira only), 10–13 April (Easter), 19 April (Declaration of Independence), 1 May (Labour Day), 24 June (Battle of Carabobo), 5 July (Independence Day), 24 July (Birth of Simón Bolívar and Battle of Lago de Maracaibo), 4 September (Civil Servants' Day), 12 October (Discovery of America), 24 October (Maracaibo only), 24–25 December (Christmas), 31 December (New Year's Eve).

Banks and insurance companies also close on: 6 January (Epiphany), 19 March (St Joseph), Ascension Day (17 May 2007, 1 May 2008), 29 June (SS Peter and Paul), 15 August (Assumption), 1 November (All Saints' Day), and 8 December (Immaculate Conception).

Weights and Measures

The metric system is in force.

VENEZUELA

Statistical Survey

Statistical Survey

Sources (unless otherwise stated): Instituto Nacional de Estadística (formerly Oficina Central de Estadística e Informática), Edif. Fundación La Salle, Avda Boyacá, Caracas 1050; tel. (212) 782-1133; fax (212) 782-2243; e-mail ocei@platino.gov.ve; internet www.ine.gov.ve; Banco Central de Venezuela, Avda Urdaneta, esq. de las Carmelitas, Caracas 1010; tel. (212) 801-5111; fax (212) 861-0048; e-mail mbatista@bcv.org.ve; internet www.bcv.org.ve.

Area and Population

AREA, POPULATION AND DENSITY

Area (sq km)	916,445*
Population (census results)	
20 October 1990†	18,105,265
30 October 2001‡	
Males	11,402,869
Females	11,651,341
Total	23,054,210
Population (official postcensal estimates at mid-year)§	
2005	26,577,423
2006	27,030,656
2007	27,483,208
Density (per sq km) at mid-2007	30.0

* 353,841 sq miles.
† Excluding Indian jungle population and adjustment for underenumeration, estimated at 6.7%.
‡ Excluding Indian jungle population, enumerated at 183,143 in a separate census of indigenous communities in 2001. Also excluding adjustment for underenumeration, estimated at 6.7%.
§ Based on results of 2001 census, including Indian jungle population and adjustment for underenumeration.

ADMINISTRATIVE DIVISIONS
(official postcensal estimates at mid-2007)

	Area (sq km)	Population	Density (per sq km)	Capital
Federal District	433	2,085,488	4,816.4	Caracas
Amazonas	177,617	142,220	0.8	Puerto Ayacucho
Anzoátegui	43,300	1,477,926	34.1	Barcelona
Apure	76,500	473,941	6.2	San Fernando
Aragua	7,014	1,665,247	237.4	Maracay
Barinas	35,200	756,581	21.5	Barinas
Bolívar	240,528	1,534,825	6.4	Ciudad Bolívar
Carabobo	4,650	2,226,982	478.9	Valencia
Cojedes	14,800	300,288	20.2	San Carlos
Delta Amacuro	40,200	152,679	3.8	Tucupita
Falcón	24,800	901,518	36.4	Coro
Guárico	64,986	745,124	11.5	San Juan de los Morros
Lara	19,800	1,795,069	90.7	Barquisimeto
Mérida	11,300	843,830	74.7	Mérida
Miranda	7,950	2,857,943	359.5	Los Teques
Monagas	28,900	855,322	29.6	Maturín
Nueva Esparta	1,150	436,944	380.0	La Asunción
Portuguesa	15,200	873,375	57.5	Guanare
Sucre	11,800	916,646	77.7	Cumaná
Táchira	11,100	1,177,255	106.1	San Cristóbal
Trujillo	7,400	711,392	96.1	Trujillo
Vargas	1,497	332,938	222.4	La Guaira
Yaracuy	7,100	597,721	84.2	San Felipe
Zulia	63,100	3,620,189	57.4	Maracaibo
Federal Dependencies	120	1,765	14.7	—
Total	916,445	27,483,208	30.0	—

PRINCIPAL TOWNS
(city proper, estimated population at 1 July 2000)

Caracas (capital)	1,975,787	Mérida	230,101
Maracaibo	1,764,038	Barinas	228,598
Valencia	1,338,833	Turmero	226,084
Barquisimeto	875,790	Cabimas	214,000
Ciudad Guayana	704,168	Baruta	213,373
Petare	520,982	Puerto la Cruz	205,635
Maracay	459,007	Los Teques	183,142
Ciudad Bolívar	312,691	Guarenas	170,204
Barcelona	311,475	Puerto Cabello	169,959
San Cristóbal	307,184	Acarigua	166,720
Maturín	283,318	Coro	158,763
Cumaná	269,428		

Mid-2007 ('000, incl. suburbs, UN estimates): Caracas 2,985; Maracaibo 2,072; Valencia 1,770; Barquisimeto 1,116; Maracay 1,007 (Source: UN, *World Urbanization Prospects: The 2007 Revision*).

BIRTHS, MARRIAGES AND DEATHS*

	Registered live births Number	Rate (per 1,000)	Registered marriages Number	Rate (per 1,000)	Registered deaths Number	Rate (per 1,000)
2000	544,416	23.5	91,088	3.8	103,255	4.9
2001	529,552	23.2	81,516	3.3	107,867	5.0
2002	492,678	22.9	73,163	2.9	105,388	5.0
2003	555,614	22.6	74,562	2.9	118,562	5.0
2004	637,799	22.3	74,103	2.8	110,946	5.0
2005	665,997	22.0	86,093	3.2	110,301	5.0
2006	646,225	21.8	89,772	3.2	115,348	5.1

* Figures for numbers of births and deaths exclude adjustment for underenumeration. Rates are calculated using adjusted data.

Expectation of life (years at birth, WHO estimates): 75.5 (males 71.6; females 77.6) in 2005 (Source: WHO, *World Health Statistics*).

ECONOMICALLY ACTIVE POPULATION
(household surveys, '000 persons aged 10 years and over, 2006)*

	Males	Females	Total
Agriculture, hunting, forestry and fishing	939.4	76.7	1,016.0
Mining and quarrying	66.9	11.0	77.9
Manufacturing	936.6	414.3	1,350.9
Electricity, gas and water	39.5	10.9	50.4
Construction	1,009.0	48.7	1,057.6
Wholesale and retail trade, restaurants and hotels	1,289.8	1,330.2	2,620.0
Transport, storage and communications	819.5	94.1	913.6
Financing, insurance, real estate business services	355.6	195.4	551.0
Community, social and personal services	1,421.5	2,031.1	3,452.6
Activities not adequately defined	94.8	40.0	134.8
Total employed	6,972.5	4,252.7	11,224.8
Unemployed	626.0	529.0	1,154.9
Total labour force	7,598.5	4,781.7	12,379.7

* Figures exclude members of the armed forces.
Source: ILO.

2007 (persons aged 15 and over, January–March, estimates): Total employed 10,877,664; Unemployed 1,255,800; Total labour force 12,133,464 (males 7,467,783, females 4,665,681).

VENEZUELA

Health and Welfare

KEY INDICATORS

Total fertility rate (children per woman, 2005)	2.6
Under-5 mortality rate (per 1,000 live births, 2005)	21
HIV/AIDS (% of persons aged 15–49, 2005)	0.7
Physicians (per 1,000 head, 2001)	1.94
Hospital beds (per 1,000 head, 2003)	0.9
Health expenditure (2004): US $ per head (PPP)	284.8
Health expenditure (2004): % of GDP	4.7
Health expenditure (2004): public (% of total)	42.0
Access to water (% of persons, 2004)	83
Access to sanitation (% of persons, 2004)	68
Human Development Index (2005): ranking	74
Human Development Index (2005): value	0.792

For sources and definitions, see explanatory note on p. vi.

Agriculture

PRINCIPAL CROPS
('000 metric tons)

	2004	2005	2006
Rice (paddy)	974.1	1,006.7	1,114.6
Maize	2,126.3	2,278.1	2,374.7
Sorghum	563.3	391.2	588.7
Potatoes	350.1	433.1	454.1
Cassava (Manioc)	511.4	531.3	489.0
Yautia (Cocoyam)	47.3	59.2	75.1
Yams	69.9	76.9	87.0
Sugar cane	8,814.2	9,194.2	8,894.8
Coconuts	163.6	146.9	173.4
Oil palm fruit	283.4	304.5	291.5
Cabbages	78.4	92.6	101.4
Tomatoes	196.9	211.7	195.9
Green chillies and peppers	91.4	110.3	122.0
Dry onions	236.3	265.0	255.0
Carrots and turnips	184.8	185.0	209.4
Watermelons	257.9	285.7	150.7
Cantaloupes and other melons	232.1	293.6	131.6
Bananas	463.0	536.5	523.6
Plantains	426.3	492.0	335.3
Oranges	374.4	374.4	377.9
Tangerines, mandarins, etc.	91.5	95.7	93.0
Lemons and limes	54.7	65.5	49.6
Guavas, mangoes and mangosteens	68.6	74.9	74.4
Avocados	52.4	63.1	58.7
Pineapples	322.8	349.2	356.9
Papayas	131.8	118.1	151.4
Coffee (green)	71.5	64.5	74.3

Aggregate production ('000 metric tons, may include official, semi-official or estimated data): Total cereals 3,664 in 2004, 3,676 in 2005, 4,078 in 2006; Total roots and tubers 1,046 in 2004, 1,165 in 2005, 1,164 in 2006; Total vegetables (incl. melons) 1,503 in 2004, 1,668 in 2005, 1,420 in 2006; Total fruits (excl. melons) 2,138 in 2004, 2,352 in 2005, 2,183 in 2006.

Source: FAO.

LIVESTOCK
('000 head, year ending September)

	2003	2004	2005
Horses*	500	500	500
Asses, mules or hinnies*	512	512	512
Cattle	15,989	16,232	16,615
Pigs	2,922	3,047	3,264
Sheep	520	528	525
Goats	1,280	1,311	1,342
Chickens*	110,000	110,000	110,000

* FAO estimates.

2006: Figures assumed to be unchanged from 2005 (FAO estimates).

Source: FAO.

LIVESTOCK PRODUCTS
('000 metric tons)

	2003	2004	2005
Cattle meat	435.2	376.0	424.7
Pig meat	120.2	101.4	126.2
Chicken meat	675.5	685.6	739.4
Cows' milk	1,238.5	1,237.1	1,347.7
Hen eggs	147.0	146.5	147.5

2006: Production assumed to be unchanged from 2005 (FAO estimates).

Source: FAO.

Forestry

ROUNDWOOD REMOVALS
('000 cubic metres, excl. bark)

	2004	2005	2006
Sawlogs, veneer logs and logs for sleepers	805	1,027	1,051
Pulpwood	721*	416	622
Fuel wood*	3,793	3,843	3,884
Total	5,319	5,286	5,557

* FAO estimate(s).

Source: FAO.

SAWNWOOD PRODUCTION
('000 cubic metres, incl. railway sleepers)

	2004	2005	2006
Coniferous (softwood)	289	371	538
Broadleaved (hardwood)	190	191	300
Total	479	562	838

Source: FAO.

Fishing

('000 metric tons, live weight)

	2003	2004	2005
Capture	520.8	487.0*	470.0*
Round sardinella	141.9	141.9*	141.9*
Yellowfin tuna	98.1	62.1	48.5
Ark clams	45.9	45.9*	45.9*
Aquaculture	19.8	22.2	22.2*
Total catch	540.6	509.2*	492.2*

* FAO estimate.

Note: Figures exclude crocodiles, recorded by number rather than by weight. The number of spectacled caimans caught was: 33,942 in 2003; 63,902 in 2004; 65,915 in 2005.

Source: FAO.

VENEZUELA

Mining

('000 metric tons, unless otherwise indicated)

	2003	2004	2005*
Hard coal	7,034	8,107	8,200
Crude petroleum ('000 barrels)	1,025,508	1,100,000*	1,110,000
Natural gas (million cu metres)†	61,027	67,000*	67,000
Iron ore: gross weight	17,954	19,196	20,000
Iron ore: metal content	11,936	12,669	13,200
Nickel ore (metric tons)‡	20,700	20,468	20,000
Bauxite	5,446	5,842	5,900
Gold (kilograms)‡	8,190	9,690	10,000
Phosphate rock	260	300	392
Salt (evaporated)*	500	500	500
Diamonds (carats): Gem	11,080	40,000*	46,000
Diamonds (carats): Industrial	23,710	60,000*	69,000

* Estimated production.
† Figures refer to the gross volume of output. Marketed production (in million cu metres) was: 30,875 in 2003; 34,000 in 2004 (estimate); 34,000 in 2005 (estimate).
‡ Figures refer to the metal content of ores and concentrates.

Source: US Geological Survey.

Industry

PETROLEUM PRODUCTS
('000 barrels)

	2002	2003	2004*
Motor spirit (petrol)	64,386	52,374	75,000
Kerosene	77	117	120
Jet fuel	29,784	25,955	30,000
Distillate fuel oils	96,725	96,108	100,000
Residual fuel oils	84,479	85,052	80,000

* Estimated production.

2005: Production assumed to be unchanged from 2004 (US Geological Survey estimates).

Source: US Geological Survey.

SELECTED OTHER PRODUCTS
('000 metric tons, unless otherwise indicated)

	2001	2002	2003
Raw sugar*	612	637	736†
Fertilizers‡§	525	576	n.a.
Cement||	8,700†	7,000	7,000
Crude steel||	3,814	4,164	3,930
Aluminium||	571	605	601
Electric energy (million kWh)‡	85,211	87,406	n.a.

* FAO figures.
† Estimate.
‡ Data from UN Economic Commission for Latin America and the Caribbean.
§ Including phosphatic, nitrogenous and potassic fertilizers, year beginning 1 July.
\|\| Data from US Geological Survey.

Cement ('000 metric tons, estimates): 9,000 in 2004; 10,000 in 2005.

Crude steel ('000 metric tons, estimates): 4,575 in 2004; 4,907 in 2005.

Aluminium ('000 metric tons, estimates): 623.5 in 2004; 615.1 in 2005.

Finance

CURRENCY AND EXCHANGE RATES

Monetary Units
100 céntimos = 1 bolívar.

Sterling, Dollar and Euro Equivalents (30 November 2007)

£1 sterling = 4,436.56 bolívares;
US $1 = 2,147.00 bolívares;
€1 = 3,169.19 bolívares;
10,000 bolívares = £2.25 = $4.66 = €3.16.

Average Exchange Rate (bolívares per US dollar)
2004   1,891.33
2005   2,089.75
2006   2,147.00

Note: Venezuela adopted a new currency, the bolívar fuerte, equivalent to 1,000 of the former currency, on 1 January 2008; this was to become the sole legal tender from the end of June of the same year. Most of the relevant historical data in this survey continue to be presented in terms of Venezuelan bolívares.

BUDGET
('000 million bolívares, preliminary figures)

Revenue	2004	2005	2006
Current revenue	73,128.6	114,385.3	147,865.9
Tax revenue	24,243.3	36,756.2	49,056.5
Taxes on income	4,241.4	7,086.1	12,155.5
Social security contributions	1,333.5	1,889.9	2,743.4
Other	18,668.4	27,780.2	34,157.5
Non-tax revenue	48,876.4	77,599.7	98,801.6
State petroleum company surplus	35,524.2	53,181.0	64,725.6
Transfers	8.9	29.3	7.8
Capital revenue	2.6	27.5	0.5
Total revenue	73,131.2	114,412.8	147,866.5

Expenditure*	2004	2005	2006
Current expenditure	46,537.3	64,842.6	94,617.7
Operating expenditure	12,829.4	16,779.6	27,759.0
Wages and salaries	8,988.5	11,594.3	16,270.5
Interest and commission on public debt	7,989.1	9,046.1	8,223.0
Transfers	24,843.7	38,463.3	57,420.5
Other current expenditure	875.0	553.7	1,215.2
Capital expenditure	19,925.4	34,867.9	55,935.9
Acquisition of fixed capital	8,090.4	11,967.9	17,666.9
Capital transfers	11,835.0	22,900.0	38,269.0
Extrabudgetary expenditure	1,299.4	1,415.7	1,894.4
Total expenditure	67,762.1	101,126.1	152,448.0

* Excluding net lending (preliminary figures): 114.8 in 2004; 835.0 in 2005; 1,275.6 in 2006.

CENTRAL BANK RESERVES
(US $ million at 31 December)

	2005	2006	2007
Gold (national valuation)	5,718	7,255	9,281
IMF special drawing rights	5	—	1
Reserve position in IMF	460	484	509
Foreign exchange	23,454	28,933	23,686
Total	29,637	36,672	33,477

Source: IMF, *International Financial Statistics*.

VENEZUELA

MONEY SUPPLY
('000 million bolívares at 31 December)

	2003	2004	2005
Currency outside banks	4,778	6,506	8,926
Demand deposits at commercial banks	13,651	20,037	32,394
Total (incl. others)	19,056	27,927	42,922

Source: IMF, *International Financial Statistics*.

COST OF LIVING
(Consumer Price Index for Caracas; Base: 2000 = 100)

	2004	2005	2006
Food	274.6	332.5	399.3
Clothing and footwear	168.6	187.2	203.3
Rent	168.1	180.3	192.5
All items (incl. others)	219.9	255.0	289.8

Source: ILO.

NATIONAL ACCOUNTS
National Income and Product
(million bolívares at current prices)

	2001	2002	2003*
Compensation of employees	31,261.0	35,636.6	41,187.3
Net operating surplus	33,024.0	41,474.9	57,035.0
Net mixed income	12,196.8	14,368.3	17,064.9
Domestic primary incomes	76,481.8	91,479.8	115,287.2
Consumption of fixed capital	5,367.0	7,113.0	8,284.6
Gross domestic product (GDP) at factor cost	81,848.8	98,592.8	123,571.9
Taxes on production and imports	7,386.0	9,669.2	12,484.7
Less Subsidies	289.3	421.8	1,839.3
GDP in market prices	88,945.6	107,840.2	134,217.3
Primary incomes received from abroad	1,882.0	1,781.3	2,771.8
Less Primary incomes paid abroad	3,351.0	4,973.0	6,659.2
Gross national income (GNI)	87,476.6	104,648.5	130,329.9
Less Consumption of fixed capital	5,367.0	7,113.0	8,284.6
Net national income	82,109.6	97,535.4	122,045.2
Current transfers from abroad	257.9	335.0	416.9
Less Current transfers paid abroad	365.8	525.6	388.7
Net national disposable income	82,001.7	97,344.9	122,073.4

*Preliminary figures.

Expenditure on the Gross Domestic Product
('000 million bolívares at constant 1997 prices, preliminary)

	2004	2005	2006
Final consumption expenditure	31,318.7	36,322.1	42,319.0
Households / Non-profit institutions serving households	24,642.5	29,016.2	34,469.4
General government	6,676.2	7,305.9	7,849.6
Gross capital formation	10,689.0	13,620.9	17,687.9
Gross fixed capital formation / Acquisitions, less disposals, of valuables	8,559.4	11,806.6	15,757.0
Changes in inventories*	2,129.6	1,814.3	1,930.9
Total domestic expenditure	42,007.7	49,943.0	60,006.9
Exports of goods and services	11,295.9	11,756.6	11,260.1
Less Imports of goods and services	11,131.2	15,169.6	19,929.1
GDP in market prices	42,172.4	46,350.1	51,337.9

*Including statistical discrepancy.

Gross Domestic Product by Economic Activity
('000 million bolívares at constant 1997 prices, preliminary)

	2004	2005	2006
Petroleum-related activities	7,360.8	7,549.5	7,408.3
Non-petroleum activities	32,237.1	36,234.2	41,097.0
Mining and quarrying	322.2	316.7	329.0
Manufacturing	7,033.5	7,704.0	8,505.0
Electricity and water	1,021.5	1,109.2	1,178.4
Construction	2,069.0	2,547.0	3,365.8
Wholesale and retail trade; repair of motor vehicles, motorcycles and personal and household goods	3,629.8	4,414.5	5,294.8
Transport and storage	1,424.9	1,618.5	1,818.3
Communications	1,311.7	1,573.5	1,938.5
Financial intermediation and insurance	1,149.0	1,546.7	2,153.3
Real estate, renting and business activities	4,314.0	4,648.4	5,029.1
Community, social and personal services	2,085.3	2,294.2	2,668.1
Government services	5,211.6	5,584.8	5,794.6
Others*	2,664.5	2,876.7	3,022.1
Sub-total	39,597.9	43,783.7	48,505.3
Less Financial intermediation services indirectly measured	1,303.0	1,858.2	2,688.6
Gross value added in basic prices	38,294.9	41,925.5	45,816.7
Taxes on products / *Less* Subsidies on products	3,877.5	4,604.6	5,521.2
GDP in market prices	42,172.4	46,530.1	51,337.9

*Including agriculture and hotels and restaurants.

BALANCE OF PAYMENTS
(US $ million)

	2004	2005	2006
Exports of goods f.o.b.	39,668	55,647	65,210
Imports of goods f.o.b.	−17,021	−24,195	−32,498
Trade balance	22,647	31,452	32,712
Exports of services	1,114	1,341	1,572
Imports of services	−4,497	−5,349	−6,005
Balance on goods and services	19,264	27,444	28,279
Other income received	2,050	4,146	7,934
Other income paid	−5,723	−6,411	−9,026
Balance on goods, services and income	15,591	25,179	27,187
Current transfers received	227	249	296
Current transfers paid	−299	−318	−334
Current balance	15,519	25,110	27,149
Direct investment abroad	−619	−1,167	−2,076
Direct investment from abroad	1,483	2,602	−590
Portfolio investment assets	−813	−2,297	−5,382
Portfolio investment liabilities	−1,271	3,225	−3,982
Other investment assets	−8,233	−18,425	−7,020
Other investment liabilities	−1,408	−418	−194
Net errors and omissions	−2,503	−3,205	−2,828
Overall balance	2,155	5,425	5,077

Source: IMF, *International Financial Statistics*.

VENEZUELA

External Trade

PRINCIPAL COMMODITIES
(US $ million)

Imports f.o.b.	2002	2003	2004
Food and live animals	1,105.7	1,067.7	1,551.6
Cereals and cereal preparations	342.5	412.5	436.5
Mineral fuels	305.6	158.0	236.7
Petroleum and products	291.0	147.2	216.6
Animal and vegetable oils, fats and waxes	177.9	253.9	295.3
Chemicals and related products	1,872.8	1,736.3	2,437.5
Organic chemicals	295.0	258.5	428.7
Medicinal and pharmaceutical products	506.5	483.2	620.2
Medicaments (incl. veterinary)	418.9	391.8	496.3
Basic manufactures	1,572.7	1,046.6	2,073.1
Iron and steel	305.3	168.4	448.4
Machinery and transport equipment	5,036.5	2,979.4	6,158.2
Power generating equipment and machinery	287.1	317.6	333.7
Machinery specialized for particular industries	396.1	224.2	499.1
General industrial machinery equipment and parts	1,182.3	650.6	1,238.6
Heating and cooling equipment and parts	442.1	134.4	207.8
Telecommunications and sound recording and reproducing equipment	470.5	314.5	793.2
Telecommunications equipment parts and accessories	385.3	253.4	624.4
Other electrical machinery, apparatus, etc.	600.1	434.6	693.7
Road vehicles	1,225.9	590.9	1,548.7
Passenger motor vehicles (except buses)	801.7	261.2	928.6
Other transport equipment	604.6	252.4	552.0
Ships, boats and floating structures	361.9	103.2	477.6
Miscellaneous manufactured articles	1,194.3	773.55	1,264.4
Total (incl. others)	11,673.3	8,357.7	14,697.1

Exports f.o.b.	2002	2003	2004
Mineral fuels, lubricants and related materials	18,960.3	20,539.5	32,082.5
Petroleum, petroleum products and related materials	18,927.0	20,319.4	31,923.8
Crude petroleum	18,322.8	20,235.8	31,890.0
Petroleum products, refined	554.2	67.5	17.0
Chemicals and related products	978.2	778.9	939.2
Basic manufactures	2,344.9	2,240.5	3,457.0
Iron and steel	1,060.5	1,039.1	1,978.2
Aluminium	719.0	718.4	917.9
Total (incl. others)	23,987.2	24,974.3	38,001.1

Source: UN, *International Trade Statistics Yearbook*.

PRINCIPAL TRADING PARTNERS
(US $ million)

Imports f.o.b.	2002	2003	2004
Argentina	151.4	141.8	299.4
Bolivia	163.5	160.8	200.1
Brazil	755.4	555.4	1,238.3
Canada	320.1	219.6	433.4
Chile	189.9	135.2	237.5
China, People's Republic	224.8	176.0	424.9
Colombia	963.7	713.0	1,563.3
France (incl. Monaco)	221.7	222.1	202.0
Germany	52.9	347.8	468.1
Italy	504.9	272.0	418.3
Japan	435.9	194.5	534.8
Korea, Republic	226.3	82.6	192.4
Mexico	536.9	416.3	686.3
Netherlands	125.3	83.7	123.3
Netherlands Antilles	259.2	22.4	92.4
Panama	192.1	123.1	276.9
Spain	319.1	331.1	540.1
Switzerland-Liechtenstein	119.9	91.9	126.4
United Kingdom	279.3	234.9	482.8
USA	3,845.0	2,754.0	4,579.2
Total (incl. others)	11,673.4	8,357.7	14,697.1

Exports f.o.b.	2001	2002	2003
Brazil	674.9	562.3	259.6
Canada	474.8	289.8	294.7
Colombia	730.7	751.9	650.8
Costa Rica	258.5	294.6	210.4
Cuba	16.2	11.6	642.0
Dominican Republic	715.4	675.2	187.7
Ecuador	211.6	324.0	198.5
India	461.7	355.8	4.4
Mexico	360.9	338.5	376.4
Netherlands	291.7	330.8	2,058.9
Netherlands Antilles	1,543.9	1,520.8	4,140.9
Peru	295.7	197.4	237.7
Spain	426.3	521.5	211.6
Trinidad and Tobago	420.2	317.3	384.3
United Kingdom	191.9	213.5	396.6
USA	14,280.3	13,115.8	11,074.9
Total (incl. others)	25,304.3	23,293.3	24,974.3

Source: UN, *International Trade Statistics Yearbook*.

Transport

RAILWAYS
(traffic)

	1994	1995	1996
Passenger-kilometres (million)	31.4	12.5	0.1
Net ton-kilometres (million)	46.8	53.3	45.5

Net ton-kilometres (million): 54 in 1997; 79 in 1998; 54 in 1999; 59 in 2000; 81 in 2001; 32 in 2002; 12 in 2003; 22 in 2004.

Source: UN, *Statistical Yearbook*.

ROAD TRAFFIC
('000 motor vehicles in use)

	2002	2003	2004
Passenger cars	2,092	2,173	2,466
Commercial vehicles	615	630	677

Source: UN, *Statistical Yearbook*.

VENEZUELA

SHIPPING

Merchant Fleet
(registered at 31 December)

	2004	2005	2006
Number of vessels	286	305	321
Total displacement ('000 grt)	1,010.9	1,078.9	1,034.0

Source: Lloyd's Register-Fairplay, *World Fleet Statistics*.

CIVIL AVIATION
(traffic on scheduled services)

	2001	2002	2003
Kilometres flown (million)	79.7	77.5	50.4
Passengers carried ('000)	4,051.7	5,446.8	3,823.7
Passenger-km (million)	3,680.5	3,301.5	2,042.8
Freight ton-km (million)	30.5	6.6	2.0

Source: UN Economic Commission for Latin America and the Caribbean.

Tourism

ARRIVALS BY NATIONALITY

	2003	2004	2005
Argentina	14,108	18,708	25,862
Belgium	7,660	12,130	17,652
Brazil	9,929	13,404	18,667
Canada	20,588	31,794	46,533
Chile	6,345	8,402	11,607
Colombia	10,576	32,030	36,294
Denmark	6,325	9,573	13,916
France	14,362	21,041	30,629
Germany	42,320	65,733	96,414
Italy	20,166	27,867	39,176
Mexico	7,447	10,344	14,568
Netherlands	36,039	56,521	83,034
Spain	11,389	16,429	23,475
United Kingdom	19,624	24,399	43,279
USA	66,711	76,202	116,599
Total (incl. others)	336,974	486,401	706,103

Tourism receipts (US $ million, incl. passenger transport): 378 in 2003; 531 in 2004; 713 in 2005.

Source: World Tourism Organization.

Communications Media

	2004	2005	2006
Telephones ('000 main lines in use)	3,346.5	3,605.5	4,216.8
Mobile cellular telephones ('000 subscribers)	8,421.0	12,495.7	18,789.5
Personal computers ('000 in use)	2,145	n.a.	n.a.
Internet users ('000)	2,207.1	3,354.9	4,139.8
Broadband subscribers ('000)	210.3	356.3	537.5

Facsimile machines ('000 in use, 1997): 70.
Radio receivers ('000 in use, 1997, estimate): 10,750.
Television receivers ('000 in use, 2001): 10,750.
Book production (titles, 1997): 3,851*.
Daily newspapers (1996): 86 (estimated average circulation 4,600,000).
* First editions only.

Sources: UNESCO Institute for Statistics; UN, *Statistical Yearbook*; International Telecommunication Union.

Education

(2003/04)

	Institutions	Teachers	Students*
Pre-school	14,857†	59,178	984,224
Basic education:			
grades 1–6	17,521†	172,322	3,449,579
grades 7–9	4,667†	109,437	1,383,891
Further education:			
general	} 3,362† {	56,458	501,243
professional		8,844	68,372
Adult education	2,402	43,660	506,301
Special needs	1,999	8,723	317,687
Universities	48	51,459	626,837
Other higher	120‡	30,664	447,513‡

* Excluding students in out-of-school education: 720,726 in 2003/04.
† Data may be duplicated for institutions where education is offered at more than one level. The total number of pre-school, basic and further educational establishments in 2003/04 was 24,634.
‡ Estimate.

Sources: Ministry of Education, Caracas; National Council of Universities, Caracas.

Adult literacy rate (UNESCO estimates): 93.0% (males 93.3%; females 92.7%) in 2001 (Source: UNESCO Institute for Statistics).

Directory

The Constitution

The Bolivarian Constitution of Venezuela was promulgated on 30 December 1999.

The Bolivarian Republic of Venezuela is divided into 22 States, one Federal District and 72 Federal Dependencies. The States are autonomous but must comply with the laws and Constitution of the Republic.

LEGISLATURE

Legislative power is exercised by the unicameral National Assembly (Asamblea Nacional). This replaced the bicameral Congreso Nacional (National Congress) following the introduction of the 1999 Constitution.

Deputies are elected by direct universal and secret suffrage, the number representing each State being determined by population size on a proportional basis. A deputy must be of Venezuelan nationality and be over 21 years of age. Indigenous minorities have the right to select three representatives. Ordinary sessions of the Asamblea Nacional begin on the fifth day of January of each year and continue until the fifteenth day of the following August; thereafter, sessions are renewed from the fifteenth day of September to the fifteenth day of December, both dates inclusive. The Asamblea is empowered to initiate legislation. The Asamblea also elects a Comptroller-General to preside over the Audit Office (Contraloría General de la República), which investigates Treasury income and expenditure, and the finances of the autonomous institutes.

GOVERNMENT

Executive power is vested in a President of the Republic elected by universal suffrage every six years, who may serve one additional term. The President is empowered to discharge the Constitution and the laws, to nominate or remove Ministers, to take supreme command of the Armed Forces, to direct foreign relations of the State, to declare a state of emergency and withdraw the civil guarantees laid down in the Constitution, to convene extraordinary sessions of the Asamblea Nacional and to administer national finance.

JUDICIARY

Judicial power is exercised by the Supreme Tribunal of Justice (Tribunal Supremo de Justicia) and by the other tribunals. The Supreme Tribunal forms the highest court of the Republic and the Magistrates of the Supreme Tribunal are appointed by the Asamblea Nacional following recommendations from the Committee for Judicial Postulations, which consults with civil society groups. Magistrates serve a maximum of 12 years.

VENEZUELA   *Directory*

The 1999 Constitution created two new elements of power. The Moral Republican Council (Consejo Moral Republicano) is comprised of the Comptroller-General, the Attorney-General and the Peoples' Defender (or ombudsman). Its principal duty is to uphold the Constitution. The National Electoral Council (Consejo Nacional Electoral) administers and supervises elections.

The Government

HEAD OF STATE

President of the Republic: Lt-Col (retd) HUGO RAFAEL CHÁVEZ FRÍAS (took office 2 February 1999; re-elected 30 July 2000 and 3 December 2006).

COUNCIL OF MINISTERS
(April 2008)

Vice-President: RAMÓN ALONSO CARRIZALEZ RENGIFO.
Minister of Finance: RAFAEL ISEA.
Minister of the Interior and Justice: RAMÓN RODRÍGUEZ CHACÍN.
Minister of National Defence: Gen. GUSTAVO RANGEL BRICEÑO.
Minister of Basic Industry and Mining: RODOLFO SANZ.
Minister of Light Industry and Trade: WILLIAM CONTRERAS.
Minister of Energy and Petroleum: RAFAEL DARÍO RAMÍREZ CARREÑO.
Minister of Foreign Affairs: NICOLÁS MADURO MOROS.
Minister of Labour and Social Security: ROBERTO MANUEL HERNÁNDEZ WOHNSIEDLER.
Minister of the Mass Economy: PEDRO FRITZ MOREJÓN CARRILLO.
Minister of Food: FÉLIX OSORIO GUZMÁN.
Minister of Education: HÉCTOR NAVARRO.
Minister of Tourism: OLGA AZUAJE.
Minister of Health: Lt-Col JESÚS MANTILLA OLIVEROS.
Minister of Higher Education: LUIS AUGUSTO ACUÑA CEDEÑO.
Minister of Infrastructure: ISIDRO RONDÓN.
Minister of the Environment: YUVIRÍ DEL CARMEN ORTEGA LOVERA.
Minister of Agriculture and Lands: ELÍAS JAUA MILANO.
Minister of Planning and Development: HAIMAN EL TROUDI.
Minister of Science and Technology: NURIS ORIHUELA.
Minister of Participation and Social Protection: ERIKA FARÍAS.
Minister of Communications and Information: Lt (retd) ANDRÉS IZARRA.
Minister of Housing: EDITH GÓMEZ.
Minister of Sport: VICTORIA MATA.
Minister of Culture: FRANCISCO SESTO.
Minister of Telecommunications and Information Technology: SOCORRO HERNÁNDEZ.
Minister for Indigenous Peoples: NICIA MARINA MALDONADO.
Minister of Women's Affairs: MARÍA LEÓN.
Minister of the Presidency: Lt (retd) JESSE CHACÓN ESCAMILLO.

MINISTRIES

Ministry of Agriculture and Lands: Avda Urdaneta, entre esq. Platanal a Candilito, a media cuadra de la Plaza la Candelaria, Caracas; tel. (212) 509-0405; e-mail pda2007@mat.gob.ve; internet www.mat.gov.ve.

Ministry of Basic Industry and Mining: Torre Las Mercedes, 9°, Avda La Estancia, Chuao, Caracas; e-mail webmaster@mibam.gob.ve; tel. (212) 950-0311; internet www.mibam.gob.ve.

Ministry of Communications and Information: Torre MCT, 10°, Avda Universidad, esq. el Chorro, Caracas 1010; tel. (212) 505-3207; e-mail contactenos@mci.gob.ve; internet www.minci.gov.ve.

Ministry of Culture: Edif. Archivo General de la Nación, Avda Panteón, Foro Libertador, Caracas; tel. (212) 564-2207; e-mail mcu@ministeriodelacultura.gob.ve; internet www.ministeriodelacultura.gob.ve.

Ministry of Education: Edif. Ministerio de Educación, Mezzanina, esq. de Salas, Parroquia Altagracia, Caracas 1010; tel. (212) 506-8211; e-mail atencion_al_publico@me.gob.ve; internet www.me.gov.ve.

Ministry of Energy and Petroleum: Edif. Petróleos de Venezuela, Torre Oeste, Avda Libertador con Avda Empalme, La Campiña, Porroquia El Recreo, Caracas; tel. (212) 708-1299; fax (212) 708-7014; internet www.mem.gov.ve.

Ministry of the Environment: Torre Sur, 25°, Centro Simón Bolívar, Caracas 1010; tel. (212) 408-1111; fax (212) 408-1009; e-mail jfaria@marn.gov.ve; internet www.marn.gov.ve.

Ministry of Finance: Edif. Ministerio de Finanzas, esq. Carmelitas, Avda Urdaneta, Caracas 1010; tel. (212) 802-1404; fax (212) 802-1413; e-mail consultapublica@mf.gov.ve; internet www.mf.gov.ve.

Ministry of Food: Antiguo Edif. Seguros Orinoco, 11°, Avda Fuerzas Armadas, esq. Socarras, Caracas 1010; tel. (212) 564-2415; e-mail oirp@minal.gob.ve; internet www.minal.gob.ve.

Ministry of Foreign Affairs: Torre MRE, esq. Carmelitas, Avda Urdaneta, Caracas 1010; tel. (212) 862-1085; fax (212) 864-3633; e-mail criptogr@mre.gov.ve; internet www.mre.gov.ve.

Ministry of Health: Torre Sur, 9°, Centro Simón Bolívar, El Silencio, Caracas 1010; tel. (212) 408-0000; e-mail msds.gov.ve@msds.gov.ve; internet www.msds.gov.ve.

Ministry of Higher Education: Torre MCT, 6°, Avda Universidad, esq. el Chorro, Caracas 1010; tel. (212) 596-5293; e-mail enlacesmes@mes.gov.ve; internet www.mes.gov.ve.

Ministry of Housing: Caracas; tel. (212) 952-0515; fax (212) 952-7410; e-mail puestodemando@mhv.gov.ve; internet www.mhv.gob.ve.

Ministry for Indigenous Peoples: Caracas.

Ministry of Infrastructure: Torre Este, 50°, Parque Central, Caracas 1010; tel. (212) 509-1076; fax (212) 509-3682; internet www.infraestructura.gov.ve.

Ministry of the Interior and Justice: Edif. Ministerio del Interior y Justicia, esq. de Platanal, Avda Urdaneta, Caracas 1010; tel. (212) 506-1101; fax (212) 506-1559; e-mail webmaster@mij.gov.ve; internet www.mij.gov.ve.

Ministry of Labour and Social Security: Torre Sur, 5°, Centro Simón Bolívar, Caracas 1010; tel. (212) 481-1368; fax (212) 483-8914; internet www.mintra.gov.ve.

Ministry of Light Industry and Trade: Torre Este, 18°, Avda Lecuna, Parque Central, Caracas 1010; tel. (212) 509-0445; fax (212) 574-2432; e-mail ministro@milco.gob.ve; internet www.milco.gov.ve.

Ministry of the Mass Economy: Edif. INCE, Avda Nueva Granada, Caracas; tel. (212) 603-1965; fax (212) 633-4932; e-mail visitantes@minep.gov.ve; internet www.minep.gov.ve.

Ministry of National Defence: Edif. 17 de Diciembre, planta baja, Base Aérea Francisco de Miranda, La Carlota, Caracas; tel. (212) 908-1264; fax (212) 237-4974; e-mail prensamd@mindefensa.gov.ve; internet www.mindefensa.gov.ve.

Ministry of Participation and Social Protection: Avda Francisco de Miranda, Centro Empresarial Parque del Este, Los Dos Caminos, Caracas; tel. (212) 237-9113; internet www.mps.gob.ve.

Ministry of Planning and Development: Torre Oeste, 22°, Avda Lecuna, Parque Central, Caracas 1010; tel. (212) 507-0811; fax (212) 573-3076; e-mail webmaster@mpd.gov.ve; internet www.mpd.gov.ve.

Ministry of the Presidency: Palacio de Miraflores, final Avda Urdaneta, esq. de Bolero, Caracas; tel. (212) 806-3111; fax (212) 806-3229; e-mail mdpcomunicaciones@venezuela.gov.ve; internet www.venezuela.gov.ve.

Ministry of Science and Technology: Torre MCT, Avda Universidad, esq. El Chorro, Caracas; tel. (212) 210-3401; fax (212) 210-3536; e-mail mct@mct.gov.ve; internet www.mct.gov.ve.

Ministry of Sport: Sede del IND, Velódromo Teo Capriles, Avda Teherán (antigua prolongación La Vega), Caracas; tel. (212) 472-2376; internet www.ind.gob.ve.

Ministry of Telecommunications and Information Technology: Caracas.

Ministry of Tourism: Edif. Mintur, Avda Francisco de Miranda con Avda Principal de la Floresta, Municipio Chacao, Caracas; tel. (212) 208-4511; e-mail auditoria@mintur.gob.ve; internet www.mintur.gob.ve.

Ministry of Women's Affairs: Caracas.

State Agencies

Consejo de Defensa de la Nación (Codena): Edif. 2, 2°, Fuerte Tiuna, Caracas; tel. (212) 806-3104; fax (212) 806-3151; e-mail secodena@codena.gob.ve; internet www.codena.gob.ve; national defence council.

Contraloría General de la República (CGR): Edif. Contraloría, Avda Andrés Bello, Guaicaipuro, Caracas 1050; tel. (212) 508-3111; e-mail atencionciudadano@cgr.gov.ve; internet www.cgr.gov.ve; national audit office for Treasury income and expenditure, and for the finances of the autonomous institutes; Comptroller-Gen. CLODOSBALDO RUSSIÁN UZCÁTEGUI.

Defensoría del Pueblo: Edif. Defensoría del Pueblo, Plaza Morelos, Los Caobos, Caracas; tel. and fax (212) 578-3862; e-mail prensadefensoria@hotmail.com; internet www.defensoria.gov.ve; acts as an ombudsman and investigates complaints between citizens and the authorities; Defender of the People GERMÁN MUNDARAÍN.

Procuraduría General de la República: Paseo Los Ilustres con Avda Lazo Martí, Santa Mónica, Caracas; tel. (212) 693-0911; fax (212) 693-4657; e-mail webmaster@pgr.gov.ve; internet www.pgr.gob.ve; Procurator-Gen. GLADYS MARÍA GUTIÉRREZ ALVARADO.

President

Presidential Election, 3 December 2006

Candidates	Votes	% of total
Lt-Col (retd) Hugo Rafael Chávez Frías (MVR)	7,309,080	62.84
Manuel Antonio Rosales Guerrero (UNT)	4,292,466	36.91
Others	28,606	0.25
Total	11,630,152	100.00

In addition, there were 160,245 blank or spoiled ballots

Legislature

ASAMBLEA NACIONAL
(National Assembly)

President: CILIA A. FLORES.
First Vice-President: SAÚL ORTEGA.
Second Vice-President: JOSÉ ALBORNOZ.
Election, 4 December 2005*

Party	Seats
Movimiento V República (MVR)†	114
Por la Democracia Social (PODEMOS)	15
Patria para Todos (PPT)	11
Movimiento Electoral del Pueblo (MEP)	11
Partido Comunista de Venezuela (PCV)	8
Unión Popular Venezolana	8
Total	167

* The election was boycotted by opposition parties.
† Dissolved in December 2006 and replaced by the Partido Socialista Unido de Venezuela.

Election Commission

Consejo Nacional Electoral (CNE): Avda Washington, Quinta Adriana, El Paraíso, Caracas; tel. (212) 352-1032; fax (212) 352-6316; internet www.cne.gov.ve; f. 2002; 5 mems; Pres. TIBISAY LUCENA.

Political Organizations

Acción Democrática (AD): Casa Nacional Acción Democrática, Calle Los Cedros, La Florida, Caracas 1050; internet www.acciondemocratica.org.ve; f. 1936 as Partido Democrático Nacional; adopted present name and obtained legal recognition in 1941; social democratic; Sec-Gen. HENRY RAMOS ALLUP; Pres. JESÚS MÉNDEZ QUIJADA.

Alianza Bravo Pueblo: Caracas; oppositionist; Pres. ANTONIO LEDEZMA.

Asamblea del Pueblo (Asamblea Popular): Caracas; e-mail coordinadorweb@aporrea.org; internet www.aporrea.org; f. 2005; opposition group formed by dissident left-wing mems of AD, Bandera Roja and CD; Leader CLAUDIO FERMÍN.

Bandera Roja: Caracas; f. 1968; militant Marxist-Leninist grouping; Leader GABRIEL RAFAEL PUERTA APONTE.

Bloque Democrático: Caracas; e-mail contacto@bloquedemocratico.org; internet www.bloquedemocratico.org; hard-line opposition grouping; split from CD in 2004; Dir ROBERT ALONSO.

La Causa Radical (La Causa R): Santa Teresa a Cipreses, Residencias Santa Teresa, 2°, Ofs 21 y 22, Caracas; tel. (212) 545-7002; internet www.lacausar.org.ve; f. 1971; radical democratic; Leader ANDRÉS VELÁSQUEZ.

Convergencia Nacional (CN): Edif. Tajamar, 2°, Of. 215, Parque Central, Avda Lecuna, El Conde, Caracas 1010; tel. (212) 578-1177; fax (212) 578-0363; e-mail jjcaldera@convergencia.org.ve; internet www.convergencia.org.ve; f. 1993; Leader Dr RAFAEL CALDERA RODRÍGUEZ; Gen. Co-ordinator JUAN JOSÉ CALDERA.

Coordinadora Democrática (CD): Caracas; internet www.coordinadora-democratica.org; f. 2002; umbrella org. for 27 anti-Govt political parties and opposition groups; Leader ENRIQUE MENDOZA.

Fuerza Liberal: Caracas; e-mail alejandro@fuerzaliberalvenezuela.com.ve; e-mail fliberal@fuerzaliberalvenezuela.com.ve; internet www.fuerzaliberalvenezuela.com.ve; f. 2005; hard-line opposition party; right-wing; Pres. HAYDÉE DEUTSCH; Sec.-Gen. JOSÉ RIGOBERTO GONZÁLEZ.

Movimiento Electoral del Pueblo (MEP): Caracas; f. 1967 by left-wing AD dissidents; 100,000 mems; Pres. Dr LUIS BELTRÁN PRIETO FIGUEROA; Sec.-Gen. Dr JESÚS ÁNGEL PAZ GALARRAGA.

Movimiento Demócrata Liberal: 1°, Avda de Santa Eduvigis, entre 5° y 6° transversal, Quinta El Encuentro, Caracas; e-mail mpolesel@cantv.net; internet www.democrataliberales.org; liberal opposition party; Political Dir MARCO POLESEL.

Movimiento de Integración Nacional (MIN): Edif. José María Vargas, 1°, esq. Pajarito, Caracas; tel. (212) 563-7504; fax (212) 563-7553; f. 1977; Sec.-Gen. GONZALO PÉREZ HERNÁNDEZ.

Movimiento de Izquierda Revolucionaria (MIR): c/o Fracción Parlamentaria MIR, Edif. Tribunales, esq. Pajaritos, Caracas; f. 1960 by splinter group from AD; left-wing; Sec.-Gen. MOISÉS MOLEIRO.

Movimiento Republicano (MR): 4a transversal con Avda Andrés Bello, Residencia Guipelia, Apdo 4-A, Los Palos Grandes, Caracas 1060; tel. (212) 286-3137; e-mail movimientorepublicano@gmail.com; internet movimientorepublicano.blogspot.com; f. 1997; Pres. CARLOS PANDILLA; Sec.-Gen. MANUAL RIVAS.

Movimiento al Socialismo (MAS): Quinta Alemar, Avda Valencia, Las Palmas, Caracas 1050; tel. (212) 793-7800; fax (212) 761-9297; e-mail asamblea07@cantv.net; internet www.mas.org.ve; f. 1971 by PCV dissidents; opposition democratic-socialist party; split in 1997 over issue of support for presidential campaign of Lt-Col (retd) Hugo Rafael Chávez Frías; Pres. FELIPE MUJICA; Sec.-Gen. LEOPOLDO PUCHI.

Partido Comunista de Venezuela (PCV): Edif. Cantaclaro, esq. San Pedro, Apdo 20428, San Juan, Caracas; tel. (212) 484-0061; fax (212) 481-9737; internet www.pcv-venezuela.org; f. 1931; Pres. JERÓNIMO CARRERA.

Partido Social-Cristiano (Comité de Organización Política Electoral Independiente) (COPEI): esq. San Miguel, Avda Panteón cruce con Fuerzas Armadas, San José, Caracas 1010; internet www.partidocopei.org.ve; f. 1946; Christian democratic; more than 1,500,000 mems; Leader ENRIQUE MENDOZA; Sec.-Gen. CÉSAR PÉREZ.

Partido Socialista Unido de Venezuela (PSUV): Calle Lima, cruce con Avda Libertador, Los Caobos, Caracas; tel. (212) 782-3808; fax (212) 782-9720; internet www.militantepsuv.org.ve; f. 2007; successor party to the Movimiento V República (dissolved Dec. 2006); promotes Bolivarian revolution; Pres. Lt-Col (retd) HUGO RAFAEL CHÁVEZ FRÍAS.

Partido Unión: Caracas; f. 2001; Leader Lt-Col (retd) FRANCISCO ARIAS CÁRDENAS; Sec.-Gen. LUIS MANUEL ESCULPÍ.

Patria Para Todos (PPT): Caracas; tel. (212) 577-4545; e-mail ppt@cantv.net; internet www.ppt.org.ve; f. 1997; breakaway faction of La Causa Radical; revolutionary humanist party; Leaders JOSÉ ALBORNOZ, PABLO MEDINA.

Polo Patriótico (PP): f. 1998; grouping of small, mainly left-wing and nationalist political parties, incl. the MVR, in support of presidential election campaign of Lt-Col (retd) Hugo Rafael Chávez Frías.

Por la Democracia Social (PODEMOS): Caracas; e-mail contacto@podemos.org.ve; internet www.podemos.org.ve; f. 2001 by dissident mems of MAS (q.v.); Leader ISMAEL GARCÍA.

Primero Justicia: Centro Comercial Chacaíto, Nivel sótano, local 26, Caracas; tel. (212) 952-9733; e-mail pjelhaltillo@cantv.net; internet www.primerojusticia.org.ve; f. 2000; no fixed ideological stance; Nat. Co-ordinator JULIO BORGES; Sec.-Gen. GERARDO BLYDE.

Proyecto Venezuela (PRVZL): e-mail administrador@vpvonline.com; internet www.proyectovenezuela.org.ve; f. 1998; humanist party; ended alliance with Govt in Jan. 2002; Leader JORGE SUCRE.

Solidaridad: Caracas; f. 2001; Leader LUIS MIQUILENA.

Un Nuevo Tiempo (UNT): Caracas; internet www.unnuevotiempo.org.ve; f. 2005; opposition party; Pres. MANUEL ANTONIO ROSALES GUERRERO.

Unión Popular Venezolana (UPV): Caracas; f. 2004; Pres. LINA NINETTE RON PEREIRA.

VENEZUELA

OTHER ORGANIZATIONS

Asociación Civil Queremos Elegir: Edif. Industrial, 4°, Avda Sucre, Los Dos Caminos, Municipio Sucre, Caracas; tel. (212) 286-9785; e-mail info@queremoselegir.org; internet www.queremoselegir.org; f. 1991; opposition grouping promoting citizens' rights; mem. of Alianza Cívica de la Sociedad Venezolana; Principal Co-ordinator ELÍAS SANTANA.

COFAVIC: Edif. El Candil, 1°, Of. 1-A, Avda Urdaneta, esq. El Candilito, Apdo 16150, La Candelaria, Caracas 1011-A; tel. (212) 572-9631; fax (212) 572-9908; e-mail lortega@cofavic.org.ve; internet www.cofavic.org.ve; promotes human rights; Exec. Dir L. ORTEGA.

Movimiento 1011: tel. (414) 304-0432; e-mail contacto@movimiento1011.com; internet www.movimiento1011.com; civil asscn promoting educational reform; mem. of Alianza Cívica de la Sociedad Venezolana.

Rumbo Propio para Zulia: Edif. Boyscouts de Venezuela, planta baja, Avda 3E con Calle 73, Maracaibo; tel. (414) 638-1657; e-mail rumbopropio@hotmail.com; internet rumbopropio.org.ve; f. 2005; right-wing autonomist grouping; Pres. NÉSTOR SUÁREZ.

Súmate: Caracas; e-mail info@sumate.org; internet www.sumate.org; f. 2002; opposition grouping promoting citizens' rights; Leader MARÍA CORINA MACHADO.

Diplomatic Representation

EMBASSIES IN VENEZUELA

Algeria: 8a Transversal con 3a Avda, Quinta Azahar, Urb. Altamira, Caracas 1060; tel. (212) 263-2092; fax (212) 261-4254; e-mail ambalgcar@cantv.net; Ambassador MOHAMMED KHELLADI.

Argentina: Edif. Fedecámaras, 3°, Avda El Empalme, El Bosque, Apdo 569, Caracas; tel. (212) 731-3311; fax (212) 731-2659; e-mail argentina@impsat.net.ve; internet www.venezuela.embajada-argentina.gov.ar; Ambassador ALICIA AMALIA CASTRO.

Austria: Edif. Torre Las Mercedes, 4°, Of. 408, Avda La Estancia, Chuao, Apdo 61381, Caracas 1060-A; tel. (212) 991-3863; fax (212) 993-2753; e-mail caracas-ob@bmaa.gv.at; Ambassador MARIANNE FELDMANN.

Barbados: Edif. Los Frailes, 5°, Of. 501, Avda Principal con Calle La Guairita, Chuao, Caracas 1060; tel. (212) 992-0545; fax (212) 991-0333; e-mail caracas@foreign.gov.bb; Ambassador KEITH FRANKLIN.

Belgium: Quinta la Azulita, Avda 11, entre 6a y 7a Transversales, Apdo del Este 61550, Altamira, Caracas 1060; tel. (212) 263-3334; fax (212) 261-0309; e-mail caracas@diplobel.org; internet www.diplomatie.be/caracas; Ambassador CHRISTINE STEVENS.

Bolivia: Avda Luis Roche con 6a Transversal, Altamira, Caracas; tel. (212) 263-3015; fax (212) 261-3386; e-mail embaboliviaven@cantv.net; Ambassador JORGE ALVARO RIVAS.

Brazil: Avda Mohedano con Calle Los Chaguaramos, Centro Gerencial Mohedano, 6°, La Castellana, Caracas; tel. (212) 261-5505; fax (212) 261-9601; e-mail brasembcaracas@cantv.net; internet www.embajadabrasil.org.ve; Ambassador ANTONIO FERREIRA SIMÕES.

Bulgaria: Quinta Sofía, Calle Las Lomas, Urb. Las Mercedes, Apdo 68389, Caracas; tel. (212) 993-2714; fax (212) 993-4839; e-mail embulven@cantv.net; internet www.mfa.bg/caracas; Ambassador KIRIL GEORGIEV KOTSALIEV.

Canada: Edif. Embajada de Canadá, Avda Francisco de Miranda con Avda Sur, Altamira, Apdo 62302, Caracas 1060-A; tel. (212) 600-3101; fax (212) 261-8741; e-mail crcas@international.gc.ca; internet www.caracas.gc.ca; Ambassador PERRY CALDERWOOD.

Chile: Edif. Torre La Noria, 10°, Calle Paseo Enrique Eraso, Las Mercedes, Caracas; tel. (212) 992-3378; fax (212) 992-0614; e-mail echileve@cantv.net; internet www.embachileve.org; Ambassador ROLANDO DRAGO RODRÍGUEZ.

China, People's Republic: Avda El Paseo, Quinta El Oriente, Prados del Este, Caracas; tel. (212) 977-4949; fax (212) 978-0876; e-mail embcnven@cantv.net; internet ve.chineseembassy.org; Ambassador ZHANG TUO.

Colombia: Torre Credival, 11°, 2A Calle de Campo Alegre con Avda Francisco de Miranda, Apdo 60887, Caracas; tel. (212) 261-6596; fax (212) 261-1358; e-mail ecaracas@minrelext.gov.co; Ambassador FERNANDO MARÍN VALENCIA.

Costa Rica: Edif. For You P.H., Avda San Juan Bosco, entre 1a y 2a Transversal, Altamira, Apdo 62239, Caracas; tel. (212) 267-1104; fax (212) 265-4660; e-mail embaricavene@yahoo.com.mx; Ambassador WALTER RUBÉN HERNÁNDEZ JUÁREZ.

Cuba: Calle Roraima e Rio de Janeiro y Choroni, Chuao, Caracas 1060; tel. (212) 991-6611; fax (212) 993-5695; e-mail embacubavzla@cantv.net; Ambassador GERMÁN SÁNCHEZ OTERO.

Directory

Czech Republic: Calle Los Cedros, Quinta Isabel, Urb. Country Club, Altamira, Caracas 1060; tel. (212) 261-8528; fax (212) 266-3987; e-mail caracas@embassy.mzv.cz; internet www.mfa.cz/caracas; Ambassador Dr JIŘÍ JIRÁNEK.

Dominican Republic: Edif. Argentum, Ofs 1 y 2, 2a Transversal, entre 1a Avda y Avda Andrés Bello, Los Palos Grandes, Caracas 1060; tel. (212) 283-3709; fax (212) 283-3965; e-mail embdomvenezuela@serex.gov.do; Ambassador JAIME DURÁN HERNÁNDEZ.

Ecuador: Centro Andrés Bello, Torre Oeste, 13°, Avda Andrés Bello, Maripérez, Apdo 62124, Caracas 1060; tel. (212) 265-0801; fax (212) 264-6917; e-mail embajadaecuador@cantv.net; Ambassador Gen. (retd) RENÉ VARGAS PAZOS.

Egypt: Calle Caucagua con Calle Guaicaipuro, Quinta Maribel, Urb. San Román, Apdo 490007, Caracas; tel. (212) 992-6259; fax (212) 993-1555; e-mail egyptianembassy@cantv.net; Ambassador ESSAM SALEH AWAD MOUSTAFA.

El Salvador: Centro Comercial Ciudad Tamanaco (CCCT), Torre C, 4°, Of. 406, Chuao, Caracas; tel. (212) 959-0817; fax (212) 959-3920; e-mail embsalv@viptel.com; Chargé d'affaires a.i. RAFAEL HERNÁNDEZ.

Finland: Apdo 61118, Chacao, Caracas 1060; tel. (212) 952-4111; fax (212) 952-7536; e-mail sanomat.car@formin.fi; internet www.finland.org.ve/es; Ambassador MIKKO PYHÄLÄ.

France: Calle Madrid con Avda Trinidad, Las Mercedes, Apdo 60385, Caracas 1060; tel. (212) 909-6500; fax (212) 909-6630; e-mail infos@francia.org.ve; internet www.francia.org.ve; Ambassador HADELIN DE LA TOUR-DU-PIN.

Germany: Torre La Castellana, 10°, Avda Eugenio Mendoza, cruce con Avda José Angel Lamas, La Castellana, Caracas 1010-A; tel. (212) 261-0181; fax (212) 261-0641; e-mail info@caracas.diplo.de; internet www.caracas.diplo.de; Ambassador GEORG-CLEMENS DICK.

Greece: Quinta Maryland, Avda Principal del Avila, Alta Florida, Caracas 1050; tel. (212) 730-3833; fax (212) 731-0429; e-mail embgrccs@cantv.net; Ambassador EFSTATHIOS DARAS.

Grenada: Avda Norte 2, Quinta 330, Los Naranjos del Cafetal, Caracas; tel. (212) 985-5461; fax (212) 985-6391; e-mail mcphail@spiceisle.com; internet www.grenadaembassycaracas.org; Ambassador RICHARD PAUL MCPHAIL.

Guatemala: Avda de Francisco de Miranda, Torre Dozsa, 1°, Urb. El Rosal, Caracas; tel. (212) 952-1166; fax (212) 954-0051; e-mail embaguat@cantv.net; Ambassador IVAN ESPINOZA FARFÁN.

Guyana: Quinta 'Roraima', Avda El Paseo, Prados del Este, Apdo 51054, Caracas 1050; tel. (212) 977-1158; fax (212) 976-3765; e-mail embaguy@caracas.org.ve; Ambassador ODEEN ISHMAEL.

Haiti: Quinta Flor 59, Avda Las Rosas, La Florida, Caracas; tel. (212) 730-7220; fax (212) 730-4605; Chargé d'affaires a.i. GANDY THOMAS.

Holy See: Avda La Salle, Los Caobos, Apdo 29, Caracas 1010-A (Apostolic Nunciature); tel. (212) 781-8939; fax (212) 793-2403; e-mail nunapos@cantv.net; Apostolic Nuncio Most Rev. GIACINTO BERLOCO (Titular Archbishop of Fidene).

Honduras: Edif. Banco de Lara, 8°, Of. B2, Avda Principal de la Castellana con 1a Transversal de Altamira, La Castellana, Apdo 68259, Caracas; tel. (212) 264-0606; fax (212) 263-4379; e-mail honduven@cantv.net; Chargé d'affaires a.i. FERNANDO SUÁREZ LOCO.

India: Quinta Tagore, No. 12, Avda San Carlos, La Floresta, Caracas; tel. (212) 285-7887; fax (212) 286-5131; e-mail info@embindia.org; internet www.embindia.org; Ambassador YASHVARDHAN KUMAR SINHA.

Indonesia: Quinta La Trinidad, Avda El Paseo, Prados del Este, Apdo 80807, Caracas 1080; tel. (212) 976-2725; fax (212) 976-0550; e-mail kbri@telcel.net.ve; Ambassador ALFRED T. PALEMBANGAN.

Iran: Quinta Ommat, Calle Kemal Ataturk, Valle Arriba, Apdo 68460, Caracas; tel. (212) 992-3575; fax (212) 992-9989; e-mail embairanve@cantv.net; Ambassador ABDOLLAH ZIFAN.

Iraq: Quinta Babilonia, Avda Nicolás Cópernico con Calle Los Malabares, Valle Arriba, Caracas; tel. (212) 991-1627; fax (212) 992-0268.

Israel: Centro Empresarial Miranda, 4°, Avda Principal de los Ruices cruce con Francisco de Miranda, Apdo 70081, Los Ruices, Caracas; tel. (212) 239-4511; fax (212) 239-4320; e-mail caracas.mfa.gov.il; internet caracas.mfa.gov.il; Ambassador SHLOMO COHEN.

Italy: Edif. Atrium, Calle Sorocaima, entre Avdas Tamanaco y Venezuela, El Rosal, Apdo 3995, Caracas; tel. (212) 952-7311; fax (212) 952-4960; e-mail ambcaracas@esteri.it; internet www.ambcaracas.esteri.it; Ambassador LUIGI MACCOTTA.

Jamaica: Edif. Los Frailes, 5°, Calle La Guairita, Urb. Chuao, Caracas 1062; tel. (212) 991-6741; fax (212) 991-5708; e-mail embjaven@cantv.net; Ambassador AUDLEY RODRÍQUEZ.

Japan: Edif. Bancaracas, 10°, Avda San Felipe con 2a Transversal, La Castellana, Caracas; tel. (212) 261-8333; fax (212) 261-6780;

VENEZUELA

Directory

e-mail ajapon@genesisbci.net; internet www.ve.emb-japan.go.jp; Ambassador SHUJI SHIMOKOJI.

Korea, Republic: Avda Francisco de Miranda, Centro Lido, Torre B, 9°, Ofs 91-B y 92-B, El Rosal, Caracas; tel. (212) 954-1270; fax (212) 954-0619; e-mail venadmi@2net-uno.net; Ambassador SHIN SOONG CHULL.

Kuwait: Quinta El-Kuwait, Avda Las Magnolias con Calle Los Olivos, Los Chorros, Caracas; tel. (212) 239-4234; fax (212) 238-3878; Ambassador (vacant).

Lebanon: Edif. Embajada del Líbano, Prolongación Avda Parima, Colinas de Bello Monte, Calle Motatán, Caracas 1050; tel. (212) 751-5943; fax (212) 753-0726; e-mail emblibano@telcel.net.ve; Ambassador NICOLAS BECHARA KHAWAJA.

Malaysia: Centro Profesional Eurobuilding, 6°, Ofs 6D–G, Calle La Guairita, Apdo 65107, Chuao, Caracas 1060; tel. (212) 992-1011; fax (212) 992-1277; e-mail malcaracas@kln.gov.my; internet www.embajadamalasia.com; Ambassador RAMLAN KIMIN.

Mexico: Edif. Forum, Calle Guaicaipuro con Principal de las Mercedes, 5°, El Rosal, Apdo 61371, Caracas; tel. (212) 952-5777; fax (212) 952-3003; e-mail mexico@embamex.com.ve; internet www.embamex.com.ve; Ambassador JESÚS MARIO CHACÓN CARRILLO.

Morocco: Torre Multinvest, Plaza Isabel La Católica, Avda Eugenio Mendoza, 2°, La Castellana, Caracas; tel. (212) 265-9573; fax (212) 266-4681; e-mail embamaroccaracas@cantv.net; Ambassador Dr IBRAHIM HOUSSEIN MOUSSA.

Netherlands: Edif. San Juan Bosco, 9°, San Juan Bosco con 2a Transversal de Altamira, Caracas; tel. (212) 263-3622; fax (212) 263-0462; e-mail car@minbuza.nl; internet www.mfa.nl/car-es; Ambassador H. NIJENHUIS.

Nicaragua: Avda El Paseo, Quinta Doña Dilia, Prados del Este, Caracas; tel. (212) 977-3289; fax (212) 977-3973; e-mail embanic@cantv.net; internet www.ibw.com.net; Ambassador RAMÓN ENRIQUE LEETS CASTILLO.

Nigeria: Calle Chivacoa cruce con Calle Taría, Quinta Leticia, Urb. San Román, Apdo 62062, Chacao, Caracas 1060-A; tel. (212) 993-1520; fax (212) 993-7648; e-mail embnig@cantv.net; Ambassador A. OYESOLA.

Norway: Centro Lido, Torre A-92A, Avda Francisco de Miranda, El Rosal, Apdo 60532, Caracas 1060-A; tel. (212) 953-0269; fax (212) 953-6877; e-mail emb.caracas@mfa.no; internet www.noruega.org.ve; Ambassador MARTIN TORE BJØRNDAL.

Panama: Edif. Los Frailes, 6°, Calle La Guairita, Chuao, Apdo 1989, Caracas; tel. (212) 992-9093; fax (212) 992-8107; Ambassador CARMEN GABRIELA MENÉNDEZ GONZÁLEZ.

Paraguay: Quinta Paraguay, Avda Principal Macaracuay 1960, entre Avda Cuicas y Carretera del Este, Caracas; tel. (212) 257-2747; fax (212) 257-7256; e-mail embaparven@cantv.net; Ambassador FEDERICO GONZÁLEZ FRANCO.

Peru: Andres Bello, 7°, Ofs 71-72 (Torre Oeste) y 73-74 (Torre Este), Maripérez, Caracas; tel. (212) 264-1483; fax (212) 265-7592; e-mail leprucaracas@cantv.net; Ambassador Dr LUIS SANTA MARÍA CALDERÓN.

Philippines: 5a Transversal de Altamira, Quinta Filipinas, Altamira, Caracas 1060; tel. (212) 266-4725; fax (212) 266-6443; e-mail caracas@embassyph.com; Ambassador RONALD B. ALLAREY.

Poland: Quinta Ambar, Final Avda Nicolás Copérnico, Sector Los Naranjos, Las Mercedes, Apdo 62293, Caracas; tel. (212) 991-1461; fax (212) 992-2164; e-mail ambcarac@ambasada.org.ve; internet www.caracas.polemb.net; Ambassador KRZYSZTOF JACEK HINZ.

Portugal: Torre La Castellana, 3°, Avda Eugénio Mendoza, cruce con José Angel Lamas, La Castellana, Caracas 1062; tel. (212) 263-2529; fax (212) 266-4908; e-mail embajadaportugal@cantv.net; Ambassador JOÃO JOSÉ GOMES CAETANO DA SILVA.

Qatar: Avda Principal Lomas El Mirador, Alto Claro, Municipio Baruta, Caracas; tel. (212) 909-7800; fax (212) 993-2917; e-mail qatarven@cantv.net; Ambassador NASER RASHID MUHAMMAD A. AN-NUAMI.

Romania: 4a Avda entre 8a y 9a Transversales, Quinta Guardatinajas 94-14, Altamira, Caracas; tel. (212) 261-9480; fax (212) 263-7161; e-mail ambasadaccs@cantv.net; Ambassador MARINEL IOANA.

Russia: Quinta Soyuz, Calle Las Lomas, Las Mercedes, Caracas; tel. (212) 993-4395; fax (212) 993-6526; e-mail rusemb95@infoline.wtfe.com; Ambassador ALEKSEI ERMAKOV.

Saudi Arabia: Calle Andrés Pietri, Quinta Makkah, Los Chorros, Caracas 1071; tel. (212) 239-0290; fax (212) 239-6494; e-mail saudiembassycaracas@cantv.net; Ambassador JUDIYA AL-HATHAL.

South Africa: Edif. Atrium PH-A, Sorocaima con Avda Venezuela, El Rosal, Chacoa, Apdo 2613, Caracas 1064; tel. (212) 952-0026; fax (212) 951-3613; e-mail embajador.caracas@foreign.gov.za; Ambassador THAMI X. N. NGWEVELA.

Spain: Avda Mohedano entre 1a y 2a Transversal, La Castellana, Caracas; tel. (212) 263-2855; fax (212) 261-0892; internet www.maec.es/embajadas/caracas; Ambassador DÁMASO DE LARIO RAMÍREZ.

Suriname: 4a Avda entre 7a y 8a Transversal, Quinta 41, Altamira, Caracas; Apdo 61140, Chacao, Caracas; tel. (212) 261-2724; fax (212) 263-9006; e-mail emsurl@cantv.net; Ambassador SAMUEL PAWIRONADI.

Switzerland: Centro Letonia, Torre Ing-Bank, 15°, La Castellana, Apdo 62555, Chacao, Caracas 1060-A; tel. (212) 267-9585; fax (212) 267-7745; e-mail vertretung@car.rep.admin.ch; internet www.eda.admin.ch/caracas; Ambassador ARMIN RITZ.

Syria: Avda Casiquiare, Quinta Damasco, Colinas de Bello Monte, Caracas; tel. (212) 753-5375; fax (212) 751-6146; Ambassador MOHAMMAD SALEH KHAFIF.

Trinidad and Tobago: Quinta Serrana, 4a Avda entre 7 y 8 Transversales, Altamira, Caracas; tel. (212) 261-5796; fax (212) 261-9801; e-mail embassytt@cantv.net; Ambassador RAZIA ALI.

Turkey: Calle Kemal Atatürk, Quinta Turquesa 6, Valle Arriba, Apdo 62078, Caracas 1060-A; tel. (212) 991-0075; fax (212) 992-0442; e-mail turquia@cantv.net; Ambassador NIHAT AKYOL.

United Kingdom: Torre La Castellana, 11°, Avda Principal La Castellana, Caracas 1061; tel. (212) 263-8411; fax (212) 267-1275; e-mail britishembassy@internet.ve; internet www.britain.org.ve; Ambassador CATHERINE ROYLE.

USA: Calle Suapure con Calle F, Colinas de Valle Arriba, Caracas; tel. (212) 975-6411; fax (212) 975-6710; e-mail embajada@state.gov; internet caracas.usembassy.gov; Ambassador PATRICK DENNIS DUDDY.

Uruguay: Torre Delta, 8°, Ofs A y B, Avda Francisco de Miranda, Altamira Sur, Apdo 60366, Caracas 1060-A; tel. (212) 261-7603; fax (212) 266-9233; e-mail uruvene@infoline.wtfe.com; Ambassador JUAN JOSÉ ARTEAGA SAENZ DE ZUMARÁN.

Judicial System

The judicature is headed by the Supreme Tribunal of Justice, which replaced the Supreme Court of Justice after the promulgation of the December 1999 Constitution. The judges are divided into penal and civil and mercantile judges; there are military, juvenile, labour, administrative litigation, finance and agrarian tribunals. In each state there is a superior court and several secondary courts which act on civil and criminal cases. A number of reforms to the judicial system were introduced under the Organic Criminal Trial Code of March 1998. The Code replaced the inquisitorial system, based on the Napoleonic code, with an adversarial system in July 1999. In addition, citizen participation as lay judges and trial by jury was introduced, with training financed by the World Bank.

SUPREME TRIBUNAL OF JUSTICE

The Supreme Tribunal comprises 32 judges appointed by the Asamblea Nacional for 12 years. It is divided into six courts, each with three judges: political-administrative, civil, constitutional, electoral, social and criminal. When these act together the court is in full session. It has the power to abrogate any laws, regulations or other acts of the executive or legislative branches conflicting with the Constitution. It hears accusations against members of the Government and high public officials, cases involving diplomatic representatives and certain civil actions arising between the State and individuals.

Tribunal Supremo de Justicia

Final Avda Baralt, esq. Dos Pilitas, Foro Libertador, Caracas 1010; tel. (212) 801-9178; fax (212) 564-8596; e-mail cperez@tsj.gov.ve; internet www.tsj.gov.ve.

President: LUISA ESTELLA MORALES LAMUÑO.

President of the Constitutional Court: LUISA ESTELLA MORALES LAMUÑO.

President of the Political-Administrative Court: EVELYN MARGARITA MARRERO ORTÍZ.

President of the Court of Civil Cassation: ARMENIA PEÑA DE ANDUEZA.

President of the Court of Penal Cassation: DEYANIRA NIEVES BASTIDAS.

President of the Court of Social Cassation: OMAR ALFREDO MORA DÍAZ.

President of the Electoral Court: LUIS ALFREDO SUCRE CUBA.

Attorney-General: Dr JULIÁN ISAÍAS RODRÍGUEZ DÍAZ.

VENEZUELA
Directory

Religion

Roman Catholicism is the religion of the majority of the population, but there is complete freedom of worship.

CHRISTIANITY
The Roman Catholic Church

For ecclesiastical purposes, Venezuela comprises nine archdioceses, 23 dioceses and four Apostolic Vicariates. There are also apostolic exarchates for the Melkite and Syrian Rites. At 31 December 2005 there were an estimated 25.2m. adherents, accounting for 88% of the total population.

Latin Rite

Bishops' Conference
Conferencia Episcopal de Venezuela, Prolongación Avda Páez, Montalbán, Apdo 4897, Caracas 1010; tel. (212) 471-6284; fax (212) 472-7029; e-mail prensa@cev.org.ve; internet www.cev.org.ve. f. 1985; statutes approved in 2000; Pres. Most Rev. BALTAZAR ENRIQUE PORRAS CARDOZO (Archbishop of Mérida).

Archbishop of Barquisimeto: Most Rev. ANTONIO JOSÉ LÓPEZ CASTILLO, Arzobispado, Venezuela con Calle 29 y 30 Santa Iglesia Catedral, Nivel Sótano, Barquisimeto 3001; tel. (251) 231-3446; fax (251) 231-3724; e-mail arquidiocesisdebarquisimeto@hotmail.com.

Archbishop of Calabozo: (vacant), Arzobispado, Calle 4, No 11–82, Apdo 954, Calabozo 2312; tel. (246) 871-0483; fax (246) 871-2097; e-mail el.real@telcel.net.ve.

Archbishop of Caracas (Santiago de Venezuela): Most Rev. JORGE LIBERATO UROSA SAVINO, Arzobispado, Plaza Bolívar, Apdo 954, Caracas 1010-A; tel. (212) 542-1611; fax (212) 542-0297; e-mail arzobispado@cantv.net.

Archbishop of Ciudad Bolívar: Most Rev. MEDARDO LUIS LUZARDO ROMERO, Arzobispado, Avda Andrés Eloy Blanco con Calle Naiguatá, Apdo 43, Ciudad Bolívar 8001; tel. (285) 654-4960; fax (285) 654-0821; e-mail arzcb@cantv.net.ve.

Archbishop of Coro: Most Rev. ROBERTO LÜCKERT LEÓN, Arzobispado, Calle Federación esq. Palmasola, Apdo 7342, Coro; tel. (268) 251-7024; fax (268) 251-1636; e-mail dioceco@reaccium.ve.

Archbishop of Cumaná: Most Rev. DIEGO RAFAEL PADRÓN SÁNCHEZ, Arzobispado, Calle Bolívar 34 con Catedral, Apdo 134, Cumaná 6101-A; tel. (293) 431-4131; fax (293) 433-3413; e-mail dipa@cantv.net.

Archbishop of Maracaibo: Most Rev. UBALDO RAMÓN SANTANA SEQUERA, Arzobispado, Calle 95, entre Avdas 2 y 3, Apdo 439, Maracaibo; tel. (261) 722-5351; fax (261) 721-0805; e-mail ubrasan@hotmail.com.

Archbishop of Mérida: Most Rev. BALTAZAR ENRIQUE PORRAS CARDOZO, Arzobispado, Avda 4, Plaza Bolívar, Apdo 26, Mérida 5101-A; tel. (274) 252-5786; fax (274) 252-1238; e-mail arquimer@latinmail.com.

Archbishop of Valencia: Most Rev. REINALDO DEL PRETTE LISSOT, Arzobispado, Avda Urdaneta 100-54, Apdo 32, Valencia 2001-A; tel. (241) 858-5865; fax (241) 857-8061; e-mail arqui_valencia@cantv.net.

Melkite Rite

Apostolic Exarch: Rt Rev. GEORGES KAHHALÉ ZOUHAÏRATY, Iglesia San Jorge, Final 3a Urb. Montalbán II, Apdo 20120, Caracas; tel. (212) 472-5367; fax (212) 443-0131; e-mail georgeskhhale@cantv.net.

Syrian Rite

Apostolic Exarch: IWANNIS LOUIS AWAD, Parroquia Nuestra Señora de la Asunción, 1A Calle San Jacinto, Apdo 11, Maracay; tel. (243) 235-0821; fax (243) 235-7213.

The Anglican Communion

Anglicans in Venezuela are adherents of the Episcopal Church in the USA, in which the country forms a single, extra-provincial diocese attached to Province IX.

Bishop of Venezuela: Rt Rev. ORLANDO DE JESÚS GUERRERO, Avda Caroní 100, Apdo 49-143, Colinas de Bello Monte, Caracas 1042-A; tel. (212) 753-0723; fax (212) 751-3180; e-mail iglanglicanavzla@cantv.net.

Protestant Churches

Iglesia Evangélica Luterana en Venezuela: Apdo 68738, Caracas 1062-A; tel. and fax (212) 264-1868; e-mail iglesia_ielv@cantv.net; internet ielv.tripod.com; Pres. AKOS V. PUKY; 4,000 mems.

National Baptist Convention of Venezuela: Avda Santiago de Chile 12–14, Urb. Los Caobos, Caracas 1050; Apdo 61152, Chacao, Caracas 1060-A; tel. (212) 782-2308; fax (212) 781-9043; e-mail cnbv@telcel.net.ve; internet www.cnbv.org.ve; f. 1951; Pres. Rev. IVÁN MARTÍNEZ; Dir-Gen. Rev. ALEXANDER MONTERO.

ISLAM

Mezquita Sheikh Ibrahim bin-Abdulaziz bin-Ibrahim: Calle Real de Quebrada Honda, Los Caobos, Caracas; tel. (212) 577-7382; f. 1994; Leader OMAR KADWA.

BAHÁ'Í FAITH

National Spiritual Assembly of the Bahá'ís: Colinas de Bello Monte, Apdo 49133, Caracas; tel. and fax (212) 751-7669; e-mail aenbaven@telcel.net.ve; internet www.bci.org/venezuela; f. 1961; mems resident in 954 localities.

The Press

PRINCIPAL DAILIES
Caracas

Abril: Edif. Bloque DeArmas, final Avda San Martín cruce con Avda La Paz, Caracas; tel. (212) 406-4376; fax (212) 443-1575; e-mail ldelosreyes@dearmas.com; internet www.abril.com.ve; f. 1997; independent; morning; Mon. to Sat.; Pres. ANDRÉS DE ARMAS S.; Vice-Pres. MARTÍN DE ARMAS S.

Así es la Noticia: Maderero a Puente Nuevo, Caracas; tel. (212) 408-3444; fax (212) 408-3911; e-mail ipacheco@el-nacional.com; f. 1996; morning; Editor ERNESTINA HERRERA.

The Daily Journal: Avda Principal de Boleíta Norte, Apdo 76478, Caracas 1070-A; tel. (212) 237-9644; fax (212) 232-6831; e-mail redaccion@dj.com.ve; internet www.dj.com.ve; f. 1945; morning; English; Chief Editor RUSSELL M. DALLEN, Jr.

Diario 2001: Edif. Bloque DeArmas, final Avda San Martín cruce con Avda La Paz, Caracas; tel. (212) 406-4111; fax 443-4961; e-mail contacto@dearmas.com; internet www.2001.com.ve; f. 1973; Pres. ANDRÉS DE ARMAS S.; Dir ISRAEL MÁRQUEZ.

El Diario de Caracas: Calle Los Laboratorios, Torre B, 1°, Of. 101, Los Ruices, Caracas 1070; tel. (212) 238-0386; e-mail editor@eldiariodecaracas.net; internet www.eldiariodecaracas.net; f. 2003; Editor JULIO AUGUSTO LÓPEZ.

El Globo: Avda Principal de Maripérez, Transversal Colón con Avda Libertador, Apdo 16415, Caracas 1010-A; tel. (2) 576-4111; fax (212) 576-1730; f. 1990; Dir ANÍBAL J. LATUFF.

Meridiano: Edif. Bloque DeArmas, final Avda San Martín cruce con Avda La Paz, Caracas 1010; tel. (212) 406-4040; fax (212) 442-5836; e-mail meridian@dearmas.com; internet www.meridiano.com.ve; f. 1969; morning; sport; Dir ANDRÉS DE ARMAS S.; Vice-Pres. MARTÍN DE ARMAS S.

El Mundo: Torre de la Prensa, 4°, Plaza del Panteón, Apdo 1192, Caracas; tel. (212) 596-1911; fax (212) 596-1478; e-mail dgomez@la-cadena.com; internet www.elmundo.com.ve; f. 1958; evening; independent; Pres. MIGUEL ANGEL CAPRILES LÓPEZ; Dir ENRIQUE RONDÓN.

El Nacional: Edif. El Nacional, Puente Nuevo a Puerto Escondido, El Silencio, Apdo 209, Caracas; tel. (212) 408-3111; fax (212) 408-3169; e-mail contactenos@el-nacional.com; internet www.el-nacional.com; f. 1943; morning; right-wing; independent; Pres. and Editor MIGUEL HENRIQUE OTERO; Asst Editor YELITZA LINARES; circ. 12,000.

El Nuevo País: Pinto a Santa Rosalía 44, Caracas; tel. (212) 541-5211; fax (212) 545-9675; e-mail enpais1@telcel.net.ve; f. 1988; Exec. Pres. ZORAIDA GARCÍA VARA; Dir and Editor FRANCISCO ORTA.

Puerto: Avda Soublette, Maiquetia, Caracas; tel. (212) 331-2275; fax (212) 331-0886; e-mail diariopuerto@telcel.net.ve; f. 1975; Pres. CARLOS PARMIGIANI.

La Religión: Edif. Juan XXIII, Torre a Madrices, Caracas; tel. (212) 563-0600; fax (212) 563-5583; e-mail religion@cantv.ve; internet www.iglesia.org.ve; f. 1890; morning; independent; Dir ENNIO TORRES.

Reporte (Diario de la Economía): Torre Británica, 12°, Of. B, Avda Luis Roche, Altamira Sur, Caracas; tel. (212) 264-0591; fax (212) 264-6023; e-mail info@reporte.com.ve; internet www.diarioreportedelaeconomia.com; f. 1988; Pres. TANNOUS GERGES; Editor JOSÉ PALMAR.

TalCual: Edif. Menegrande, 5°, Of. 51, Avda Francisco de Miranda, Caracas; tel. (212) 286-7446; fax (212) 232-7446; e-mail tpekoff@talcualdigital.com; internet www.talcualdigital.com; f. 2000; morning; right-wing; Pres. TEODORO PETKOFF; Editor-in-Chief EDMUNDO BRACHO.

VENEZUELA

Ultimas Noticias: Torre de la Prensa, 3°, Plaza del Panteón, Apdo 1192, Caracas; tel. (212) 596-1911; fax (212) 596-1433; e-mail edrangel@cadena-capriles.com; internet www.ultimasnoticias.com.ve; f. 1941; morning; independent; Pres. MIGUEL ANGEL CAPRILES LÓPEZ; Dir ELEAZAR DÍAZ RANGEL.

El Universal: Edif. El Universal, Avda Urdaneta, esq. de Animas, Apdo 1909, Caracas; tel. (212) 505-2314; fax (212) 505-3710; e-mail consejoeditorial@eluniversal.com; internet www.eluniversal.com; f. 1909; morning; Dir ANDRÉS MATA OSORIO; Chief Editor ELIDES ROJAS.

Vea: Edif. San Martín, Sótano Uno, Parque Central, Caracas 1010; tel. (212) 516-1004; fax (212) 578-3031; e-mail webmaster@diariovea.com.ve; internet www.diariovea.com.ve; f. 2003; morning; left-wing; Editor and Dir GUILLERMO GARCÍA PONCE; Asst Editor MANUEL PÉREZ RODRÍGUEZ.

La Voz: C. C. Nueva Guarenas, Mezzanina, Urb. Trapichito, Sector 2, Caracas; tel. (212) 362-9702; fax (212) 362-0851; e-mail diariolavoz@cantv.net; internet www.diariolavoz.net; morning; right-wing; Exec. Dir FREDDY BLANCO; Editor ALEXIS CASTRO BLANDÍN.

Barcelona

El Norte: Avda Intercomunal Andrés Bello, Sector Colinas del Neverí, Barcelona; tel. (281) 682-5694; fax (281) 286-2884; e-mail administrac@elnorte.com.ve; internet www.elnorte.com.ve; f. 1989; morning; Exec. Dir MARIELA DÁVILA; circ. 133,000.

Barquisimeto

El Impulso: Avda Los Comuneros, entre Avda República y Calle 1a, Urb. El Parque, Apdo 602, Barquisimeto; tel. (251) 250-2222; fax (251) 250-2129; e-mail reaccion@elimpulso.com; internet www.elimpulso.com; f. 1904; morning; independent; Dir and Editor JUAN MANUEL CARMONA PERERA.

El Informador: Edif. El Informador, Carrera 21, esq. Calle 23, Barquisimeto; tel. (251) 231-1811; fax (251) 231-0624; e-mail mauriciogomez@elinformador.com.ve; internet www.elinformador.com.ve; f. 1968; morning; Dir-Gen. MAURICIO GÓMEZ.

Ciudad Bolívar

El Bolivarense: Calle Igualdad 26, Apdo 91, Ciudad Bolívar; tel. (414) 893-4443; fax (285) 632-5667; e-mail publicidad@elbolivarense.com; internet www.elbolivarense.com; f. 1957; morning; independent; Dir ALVARO NATERA.

El Expreso: Paseo Gáspari con Calle Democracia, Ciudad Bolívar; tel. and fax (285) 632-0334; e-mail webmaster@diarioelexpreso.com.ve; internet www.diarioelexpreso.com.ve; f. 1969; morning; independent; Dir LUIS ALBERTO GUZMÁN.

Maracaibo

Panorama: Avda 15, No 95–60, Apdo 425, Maracaibo; tel. (261) 725-6888; fax (261) 725-6911; e-mail editor@panodi.com; internet www.panodi.com; f. 1914; morning; independent; Pres. ESTEBAN PINEDA BELLOSO; Editorial Dir LUIS CAÑÓN; circ. 16,000.

Maracay

El Aragüeño: Calle 3a Oeste con Avda 1 Oeste, Urb. Ind. San Jacinto, Maracay; tel. (243) 235-9018; fax (243) 235-7866; e-mail el-aragueno@cantv.net; internet www.el-aragueno.com.ve; f. 1972; morning; Editor EVERT GARCÍA.

El Siglo: Edif. 'El Siglo', Avda Bolívar Oeste 244, La Romana, Maracay; tel. (243) 554-9521; fax (243) 554-5154; e-mail direccion@elsiglo.com.ve; internet www.elsiglo.com.ve; f. 1973; morning; independent; Editor TULIO CAPRILES.

El Periodiquito: Calle Páez Este 178, Maracay; tel. (243) 321-422; fax (243) 336-987; e-mail farandula@elperiodiquito.com; internet www.elperiodiquito.com; f. 1986; Editorial Co-ordinator PACO FRANK; circ. 45,000.

Puerto la Cruz

El Tiempo: Edif. Diario El Tiempo, Avda Municipal 153, Puerto La Cruz; tel. (281) 260-0600; fax (281) 260-0660; e-mail buzon@eltiempo.com.ve; internet www.eltiempo.com.ve; f. 1958; independent; Dir JESÚS MÁRQUEZ; Editorial Dir GIOCONDA DE MÁRQUEZ.

San Cristóbal

Diario Católico: Carrera 4a, No 3–41, San Cristóbal; tel. (276) 343-2819; fax (276) 343-4683; e-mail catolico@truevision.net; internet www.diariocatolico.com.ve; f. 1924; morning; Catholic; Man. Dir Mgr NELSON ARELLANO.

Diario La Nación: Edif. La Nación, Calle 4 con Carrera 6 bis, La Concordia, Apdo 651, San Cristóbal; tel. (276) 346-4263; fax (276) 346-5051; e-mail lanacion@lanacion.com.ve; internet www.lanacion.com.ve; f. 1968; morning; independent; Editor JOSÉ RAFAEL CORTEZ.

El Tigre

Antorcha: Edif. Antorcha, Avda Francisco de Miranda, El Tigre; tel. (283) 235-2383; fax (283) 235-3923; e-mail yurbina@diarioantorcha.com; internet www.diarioantorcha.com; f. 1954; morning; independent; Pres. and Editor ANTONIO BRICEÑO AMPARÁN.

Valencia

El Carabobeño: Edif. El Carabobeño, Avda Universidad, Urb. La Granja, Naguanagua, Valencia; tel. (241) 867-2918; fax (241) 867-3450; e-mail website@el-carabobeno.com; internet www.el-carabobeno.com; f. 1933; morning; Dir EDUARDO ALEMÁN PÉREZ.

Notitarde: Avda Boyacá entre Navas Spínola y Flores, Valencia; tel. (241) 850-1666; fax (241) 850-1534; e-mail lauodr@notitarde.com; internet www.notitarde.com; evening; Dir LAURENTZI ODRIOZOLA ECHEGARAY.

SELECTED PERIODICALS

Ambiente: Edif. Sur, Nivel Plaza Caracas, Local 9, Centro Simón Bolívar, Caracas; tel. (212) 408-1549; fax (212) 408-1546; e-mail fundamb@cantv.net; environmental issues; Gen. Man. AVRA MARINA SÁNCHEZ.

Artesanía y Folklore de Venezuela: C. C. Vista Mar, Local 20, Urbaneja, Lecherías, Estado Anzoátegui; tel. and fax (212) 286-2857; e-mail ismandacorrea@cantv.net; handicrafts and folklore; Dir ISMANDA CORREA.

Automóvil de Venezuela: Avda Caurimare, Quinta Expo, Colinas de Bello Monte, Caracas 1041; tel. (212) 751-1355; fax (212) 751-1122; e-mail ortizauto@cantv.net; internet www.automovildevenezuela.com; f. 1961; monthly; automotive trade; circ. 6,000; Editor MARÍA A. ORTIZ.

Barriles: Centro Parque Carabobo, Torre B, 20°, Of. 2003, Avda Universidad, La Candelaria, Caracas; e-mail informaciones@camarapetrolera.org; publ. of the Cámara Petrolera de Venezuela; Editor HAYDÉE REYES.

Bohemia: Edif. Bloque DeArmas, final Avda San Martín cruce con Avda La Paz, Apdo 575, Caracas; tel. (212) 406-4040; fax (212) 451-0762; e-mail bohemia@dearmas.com; f. 1966; weekly; general interest; Dir PEDRO RAMÓN ROMERA.

Business Venezuela: Torre Credival, Avda de Campo Alegre, Apdo 5181, Caracas 1010-A; tel. (212) 263-0833; fax (212) 263-2060; e-mail publicaciones@venamcham.org; internet www.bvonline.com.ve; every 2 months; business and economics journal in English; published by the Venezuelan-American Chamber of Commerce and Industry; Gen. Man. ANTONIO HERRERA.

Computer World: Edif. Marystella, Avda Carabobo, El Rosal, Caracas; tel. (212) 952-7427; fax (212) 953-3950; e-mail cernic@cwv.com.ve; Editor CLELIA SANTAMBROGIO.

Contrapunto: Edif. Unión, 1°, Of. 2, Avda El Parque, Las Acacias Sur, Caracas; tel. (212) 690-0431; Dir VÍCTOR VERA MORALES.

Convenciones: Torre Nonza, 4°, Plaza Venezuela, Caracas; tel. (212) 793-1962; e-mail redacta@tutopia.com; Dir MARIO ERNESTO ARBELÁEZ.

El Corresponsal: Conj. Residencial El Naranjal, Torre D, 8°, No 82-D, Urb. Los Samanes, Caracas; tel. and fax (212) 941-0409; Editor DOMINGO GARCÍA PÉREZ.

Dinero: Edif. Aco, Entrada A, 7°, Avda Principal Las Mercedes, Caracas; tel. (212) 993-5011; fax (212) 991-3132; e-mail lomonaco@gep.com.ve; internet www.dinero.com.ve; business and finance; Dir SALVATORE LOMONACO.

Exceso: Edif. Karam, Avda Urdaneta, 5°, Caracas; tel. (212) 564-1702; fax (212) 564-6760; e-mail baf-exceso@cantv.net; internet www.exceso.net; lifestyle; Dir BEN AMÍ FIHMAN; Editor ARMANDO COLL.

Gerente Venezuela: Avda Orinoco 3819, entre Muchuchies y Monterrey, Las Mercedes, Caracas 1060; tel. (212) 267-3733; fax (212) 267-6583; business and management; Editor LUIS RODÁN; circ. 15,000.

El Mirador: Edif. Pascal, Torre A, 1°, Of. 12-A, Avda Rómulo Gallegos, Santa Eduvigis, Caracas; tel. (212) 286-1661; fax (212) 283-5823; e-mail diarioelmirador@cantv.net; Dir JESÚS COUTO.

Mujer-Mujer: Centro Banaven, Nivel Sótano, No 13-A, Avda La Estancia, Chuao, Caracas; tel. (212) 959-5393; fax (212) 959-7864; e-mail ceciliapicon@hotmail.com.ve; women's interest; Dir and Editor CECILIA PICÓN DE TORRES.

Nueva Sociedad: Edif. IASA, 6°, Of. 606, Plaza La Castellana, Apdo 61712, Caracas; tel. (212) 265-9975; fax (212) 267-3397; e-mail nusoven@nuevasoc.org.ve; internet www.nuevasoc.org.ve; f. 1972; Latin American affairs; Editor DIETMAR DIRMOSER.

VENEZUELA

Primicia: Edif. El Nacional, 4°, Puente Nuevo a Puerto Escondido, Caracas; tel. (212) 408-3434; fax (212) 408-3485; e-mail primicia@el-nacional.com; current affairs and business; Editor FRANCHESCA CORDIDO.

La Razón: Edif. Valores, Sótano 'A', Avda Urdaneta, esq. de Urapal, Apdo 16362, La Candelaria, Caracas; tel. (212) 578-3143; fax (212) 578-2397; e-mail larazon@internet.ve; internet www.razon.com; weekly, on Sun.; independent; Dir PABLO LÓPEZ ULACIO.

La Red: Urb. Vista Alegre, Calle 7, Quinta Luisa Amelia, Caracas; tel. (212) 472-0703; fax (212) 471-7749; e-mail ldavila@lared.com.ve; internet www.lared.com.ve; f. 1996; information technology; Editor LUIS MANUEL DÁVILA.

Reporte Petrolero: Torre Británica, 12°, Of. B, Altamira Sur, Caracas; tel. (212) 264-6023; fax (212) 266-9991; e-mail reporte2002@hotmail.com; journal of the petroleum industry; Dir ENRIQUE ROMAI; Editor MIGUEL LÓPEZ TROCELT.

Sic: Edif. Centro de Valores, esq. de Luneta, Centro Gumilla, Caracas; tel. (212) 564-9803; fax (212) 564-7557; e-mail sic@gumilla.org.ve; internet www.gumilla.org.ve/sic.htm; f. 1938; monthly; liberal Jesuit publ.; Dir JESÚS MARÍA AGUIRRE.

Variedades: Edif. Bloque DeArmas, final Avda San Martín cruce con Avda La Paz, Caracas 1020; tel. (212) 406-4390; fax (212) 451-0762; e-mail mgonzalez@dearmas.com; women's weekly; Dir GLORIA FUENTES DE VALLADARES.

VenEconomía: Edif. Gran Sabana, 1°, Avda Abraham Lincoln 174, Blvr de Sabana Grande, Caracas; tel. (212) 761-8121; fax (212) 762-8160; e-mail editor@veneconomia.com; internet www.veneconomia.com; f. 1982; monthly; Spanish and English; business and economic issues; Editor TOBY BOTTOME.

Venezuela Gráfica: Torre de la Prensa, Plaza del Panteón, Apdo 2976, Caracas 101; tel. (212) 781-4931; f. 1951; weekly; illustrated news magazine, especially entertainment; Dir DIEGO FORTUNATO; Editor MIGUEL ANGEL CAPRILES.

Zeta: Pinto a Santa Rosalía 44, Apdo 14067, Santa Rosalía, Caracas; tel. (212) 541-5211; fax (212) 545-9675; e-mail enpaiscolumna@hotmail.com; f. 1974; weekly; politics and current affairs; Dir JURATE ROSALES; Editor RAFAEL POLEO.

Zulia Deportivo: Torre Luali, 5°, Of. 3, Piñango a Muñoz, Avda Baralt, Maracaibo; tel. (261) 787-2809; sports; Dir MANUEL COLINA HIDALGO.

PRESS ASSOCIATIONS

Asociación de Prensa Extranjera en Venezuela (APEX): Hotel Caracas Hilton, Torre Sur, 3°, Of. 301, Avda México, Caracas; tel. (212) 503-5301; fax (212) 576-9284; e-mail caracashilton@hotmail.com; Pres. PHILIP GUNSON.

Bloque de Prensa Venezolano (BEV): Edif. El Universal, 5°, Of. C, Avda Urdaneta, Caracas; tel. (212) 561-7704; fax (212) 561-9409; e-mail luichi@telcel.net.ve; asscn of newspaper owners; Pres. MIGUEL ANGEL MARTÍNEZ.

Colegio Nacional de Periodistas (CNP): Casa Nacional del Periodista, 2°, Avda Andrés Bello, Caracas; tel. and fax (212) 781-7601; e-mail cnpjdn@cantv.net; journalists' asscn; Pres. LEVY BENSHIMOL; Sec.-Gen. NOEL MOLINA.

STATE PRESS AGENCY

Venpres: Torre Oeste, 16°, Parque Central, Caracas; tel. (212) 572-7175; fax (212) 571-0563; internet www.venpres.gov.ve; Dir ORLANDO UTRERA REYES.

Publishers

Alfadil Ediciones: Calle Las Flores con Calle Paraíso, Sábana Grande, Apdo 50304, Caracas 1020-A; tel. (212) 762-3036; fax (212) 762-0210; f. 1980; general; Pres. LEONARDO MILLA A.

Armitano Editores, CA: Centro Industrial Boleita Sur, 4a Transversal de Boleita, Apdo 50853, Caracas 1070; tel. (212) 234-2565; fax (212) 234-1647; e-mail armiedit@telcel.net.ve; internet www.alfagrupo.com; art, architecture, ecology, botany, anthropology, history, geography; Pres. ERNESTO ARMITANO.

Ediciones La Casa Bello: Mercedes a Luneta, Apdo 134, Caracas 1010; tel. (212) 562-7100; f. 1973; literature, history; Pres. OSCAR SAMBRANO URDANETA.

Editorial El Ateneo, CA: Complejo Cultural, Plaza Morelos, Los Caobos, Apdo 662, Caracas; tel. (212) 573-4622; f. 1931; school-books and reference; Pres. MARÍA TERESA CASTILLO; Dir ANTONIO POLO.

Editorial Cincel Kapelusz Venezolana, SA: Avda Cajigal, Quinta K No 29, entre Avdas Panteón y Roraima, San Bernardino, Apdo 14234, Caracas 1011-A; f. 1963; school-books; Pres. DANTE TONI; Man. MAYELA MORGADO.

Directory

Colegial Bolivariana, CA: Edif. COBO, 1°, Avda Diego Cisneros (Principal), Los Ruices, Apdo 70324, Caracas 1071-A; tel. (212) 239-1433; internet www.co-bo.com; f. 1961; Dir ANTONIO JUZGADO ARIAS.

Ediciones Ekaré: Edif. Banco del Libro, final Avda Luis Roche, Altamira Sur, Apdo 68284, Caracas 1062; tel. (212) 264-7615; fax (212) 263-3291; e-mail editorial@ekare.com.ve; internet www.ekare.com; f. 1978; children's; Pres. CARMEN DIANA DEARDEN; Exec. Dir MARÍA FRANCISCA MAYOBRE.

Editora Ferga, CA: Torre Bazar Bolívar, 5°, Of. 501, Avda Francisco de Miranda, El Marqués, Apdo 16044, Caracas 1011-A; tel. (212) 239-1564; fax (212) 234-1008; e-mail ddex1@ibm.net; internet www.ddex.com; f. 1971; Venezuelan Exporters' Directory; Dir NELSON SÁNCHEZ MARTÍNEZ.

Fundación Biblioteca Ayacucho: Centro Financiero Latino, 12°, Ofs 1, 2 y 3, Avda Urdaneta, Animas a Plaza España, Apdo 14413, Caracas 1010; tel. (212) 561-6691; fax (212) 564-5643; e-mail biblioayacucho@cantv.net; internet www.bibliotecayacucho.gob.ve/fba; f. 1974; literature; Pres. STEFANIA MOSCA.

Fundación Bigott: Casa 10-11, Calle El Vigia, Plaza Sucre, Centro Histórico de Petare, Caracas 1010-A; tel. (212) 272-2020; fax (212) 272-5942; e-mail contacto@fundacionbigott.com; internet www.fundacionbigott.com; f. 1936; Venezuelan traditions, environment, agriculture; Admin. Co-ordinator NELSON REYES.

Fundación Editorial Salesiana: Paradero a Salesianos 6, Apdo 369, Caracas; tel. (212) 571-6109; fax (212) 574-9451; e-mail administracion@salesiana.com.ve; internet www.salesiana.com.ve; f. 1960; education; Gen. Man. JAIME GARCÍA.

Fundarte: Edif. Tajamar P. H., Avda Lecuna, Parque Central, Apdo 17559, Caracas 1015-A; tel. (212) 573-1719; fax (212) 574-2794; internet www.fundarte.gob.ve; f. 1975; literature, history; Pres. ALFREDO GOSEN; Dir ROBERTO LOVERA DE SOLA.

Editorial González Porto: Sociedad a Traposos 8, Avda Universidad, Caracas; Pres. Dr PABLO PERALES.

Ediciones IESA: Edif. IESA, 3°, Final Avda IESA, San Bernardino, Apdo 1640, Caracas 1010-A; tel. (212) 555-4298; e-mail ediesa@iesa.edu.ve; internet www.iesa.edu.ve/publicaciones/ediciones; f. 1984; economics, business; Pres. RAMÓN PIÑANGO.

Ediciones María Di Mase: Caracas; f. 1979; children's books; Pres. MARÍA DI MASE; Gen. Man. ANA RODRÍGUEZ.

Monte Avila Editores Latinoamericana, CA: Avda Principal La Castellana, Quinta Cristina, Apdo 70712, Caracas 1070; tel. (212) 265-6020; fax (212) 263-8783; e-mail maelca@telcel.net.ve; internet www.monteavila.gob.ve; f. 1968; general; Pres. MARIELA SÁNCHEZ URDANETA.

Nueva Sociedad: Edif. IASA, 6°, Of. 606, Plaza La Castellana, Apdo 61712, Chacao, Caracas 1060-A; tel. (212) 265-0593; fax (212) 267-3397; e-mail nuso@nuevasoc.org.ve; internet www.nuevasoc.org.ve; f. 1972; social sciences; Dir DIETMAR DIRMOSER.

Ediciones Panamericanas EP, SRL: Edif. Freites, 2°, Avda Libertador cruce con Santiago de Chile, Apdo 14054, Caracas; tel. (212) 782-9891; Man. JAIME SALGADO PALACIO.

Oscar Todtmann Editores: Avda Libertador, Centro Comercial El Bosque, Local 4, Caracas 1050; tel. (212) 763-0881; fax (212) 762-5244; science, literature, photography; Dir CARSTEN TODTMANN.

Vadell Hermanos Editores, CA: Edif. Golden, Avda Sur 15, esq. Peligro a Pele el Ojo, Caracas; tel. (212) 572-3108; fax (212) 572-5243; e-mail edvadell1@cantv.net.ve; internet www.vadellhermanos.com; f. 1973; science, social science; Gen. Man. MANUEL VADELL GRATEROL.

Ediciones Vega S.R.L.: Edif. Odeon, Plaza Las Tres Gracias, Los Chaguaramos, Caracas 1050-A; tel. (212) 662-2092; fax (212) 662-1397; f. 1965; educational; Man. Dir FERNANDO VEGA ALONSO.

PUBLISHERS' ASSOCIATION

Cámara Venezolana del Libro: Centro Andrés Bello, Torre Oeste, 11°, Of. 112-0, Avda Andrés Bello, Caracas 1050-A; tel. (212) 793-1347; fax (212) 793-1368; f. 1969; Pres. HANS SCHNELL; Sec. ISIDORO DUARTE.

Broadcasting and Communications

TELECOMMUNICATIONS

Regulatory Authority

Comisión Nacional de Telecomunicaciones (CONATEL): Torre Este, 35°, Parque Central, Caracas; tel. (212) 993-5389; e-mail conatel@conatel.gov.ve; internet www.conatel.gov.ve; regulatory body for telecommunications; Dir-Gen. Lt (retd) JESSE CHACÓN ESCAMILLO (Minister of Telecommunications).

VENEZUELA

Major Service Providers

AT&T Venezuela: Edif. Centro Banaven, Avda La Estancia A, Chuao, Caracas 1060; internet www.att.com.

Compañía Anónima Nacional Teléfonos de Venezuela (CANTV): Edif. NEA, 20, Avda Libertador, Caracas 1010-A; tel. (212) 500-3016; fax (212) 500-3512; e-mail amora@cantv.com.ve; internet www.cantv.net; privatized in 1991; renationalized in 2007; Pres. SOCORRO HERNÁNDEZ.

Movilnet: Edif. NEA, 20, Avda Libertador, Caracas 1010-A; tel. (202) 705-7901; e-mail info@movilnet.com.ve; internet www.movilnet.com.ve; f. 1992; mobile cellular telephone operator; owned by CANTV; 6.3m. subscribers (June 2006); Pres. JACQUELINE FARÍA.

Digicel, CA: Caracas; internet www.digicel.com.ve; owned by Banco Santander Central Hispano of Spain; fixed-line telecommunications; 110,200 subscribers (June 2006).

Digitel TIM: Caracas; e-mail 0412empres@digitel.com.ve; internet www.digitel.com.ve; f. 2000; mobile cellular telephone operator; owned by Telecom Italia Mobile (TIM) of Italy; 2.4m. subscribers (June 2006).

Intercable: Avda La Pedregosa Sur, cruce con Avda Los Próceres, Tapias; e-mail jguerrero@multimedios.net; internet www.intercable.net/default.asp; cable, internet and telecommunications services; Dir JUAN GERARDO GUERRERO.

Movistar: Edif. Parque Cristal, Torre Oeste, Avda Francisco Miranda, 14°, Los Palos Grandes, Caracas 1062; tel. (582) 201-8200; internet www.movistar.com.ve; f. 2005; subsidiary of Telefónica Móviles (Spain); 6.5m. subscribers (June 2006); Pres. LUIS MALVIDO.

NetUno: Edif. Insenica II, planta baja, Calle 7, La Urbina, Caracas; tel. (212) 710-0404; e-mail atccaracas@netuno.net; internet www.netuno.net; f. 1995; voice, data and video transmission services; Pres. GILBERT MINIONIS.

Telecom Venezuela: Puerto Ordaz; tel. (212) 393-1912; e-mail eauverana@cvgtelecom.com.ve; internet www.cvgtelecom.com.ve; f. 2004 as CVG Telecomunicaciones, CA; present name adopted Aug. 2007; state-owned telecommunications co; Pres. JULIO DURÁN MALAVER; Man. EVELYN AUVERANA.

Telecomunicaciones Gran Caribe: Caracas; f. 2007; owned by Telecom Venezuela (60%) and Transbit of Cuba (40%); construction and operation of 1,550 km fibre-optic cable connecting La Guaira (Venezuela) and Siboney (Cuba).

BROADCASTING

In 2007 there were 99 television stations, of which seven were state-owned, and 796 radio stations, of which 36 were run by the State.

Regulatory Authorities

Cámara Venezolana de la Industria de Radiodifusión: Avda Antonio José Istúriz entre Mohedano y Country Club, La Castellana, Caracas; tel. (212) 263-2228; fax (212) 261-4783; e-mail camradio@camradio.org.ve; internet www.camradio.org; Pres. CIRO GARCÍA.

Cámara Venezolana de Televisión por Suscripción: Edif. Venevisión, 4°, Colinas de Los Caobos, Caracas; tel. (212) 708-9223; fax (212) 708-9146; e-mail cavetesu@cavetesu.org.ve; internet www.cavetesu.org.ve; regulatory body for private stations; Man. EVELYN GONZÁLEZ.

Radio

Radio Nacional de Venezuela (RNV): Final Calle Las Marías, entre Chapellín y Country Club, La Florida, Caracas 1050; tel. (212) 730-6022; fax (212) 731-1457; e-mail rnv@rnv.gov.ve; internet www.rnv.gov.ve; f. 1936; state broadcasting org.; 15 stations; Gen. Man. HELENA SALCEDO.

There are also 20 cultural and some 500 commercial stations.

Television

Government Stations

Telesur (Televisora del Sur): Edif. Anexo VTV, 4°, Avda Principal Los Ruices, Caracas; tel. (212) 237-6365; e-mail contactenos@telesurtv.net; internet www.telesurtv.net; f. 2005; jtly owned by Govts of Venezuela (51%), Argentina (20%), Cuba (19%) and Uruguay (10%); regional current affairs and general interest; Pres. (vacant); Vice-Pres. ARAM AHARONIAN.

Televisora Venezolana Social—Canal 2 (TVes): Quinta Thaizza, Avda Principal Augusto César Sandino con 10a Transversal, Maripérez, Municipio Libertador, Caracas; tel. (212) 781-8069; e-mail info@tves.com.ve; internet tves.org.ve; f. May 2007 to replace private channel RCTV (q.v.); govt-owned; Pres. LIL RODRÍGUEZ.

Venezolana de Televisión (VTV)—Canal 8: Edif. VTV, Avda Principal Los Ruices, Caracas; tel. (212) 239-4870; fax (212) 239-8102; internet www.vtv.gob.ve; f. 1964; 26 relay stations; Pres. JESÚS ROMERO ANSELMI.

ViVe TV (Visión Venezuela): Edif. Biblioteca Nacional, AP-4, Final Avda Panteón, Foro Libertador, Altagracia, Caracas; tel. (212) 505-1611; e-mail dmercadeo@vive.gov.ve; internet www.vive.gob.ve; f. 2003; govt-run cultural channel; Pres. BLANCA EEKHOUT.

Private Stations

Corporación Venezolana de Televisión (Venevisión)—Canal 4: Edif. Venevisión, final Avda La Salle, Colinas de los Caobos, Apdo 6674, Caracas; tel. (212) 708-9224; fax (212) 708-9535; e-mail mponce@venevision.com.ve; internet www.venevision.net; f. 1961; privately owned; Pres. GUSTAVO CISNEROS.

Globovisión—Canal 33: Quinta Globovisión, Avda Los Pinos, Urb. Alta Florida, Caracas; tel. (212) 730-2290; fax (212) 731-4380; e-mail info@globovision.com; internet www.globovision.com; f. 1994; 24-hour news and current affairs channel; Pres. GUILLERMO ZULOAGA; Dir-Gen. ALBERTO RAVELL.

Meridiano Televisión: Caracas; e-mail opina@dearmas.com; f. 1982; sports programming; Pres. MARTÍN DE ARMAS; Dir-Gen. JUAN ANDRÉS DAZA.

Radio Caracas Televisión (RCTV): Edif. RCTV, Dolores a Puente Soublette, Quinta Crespo, Caracas; tel. (212) 401-2222; fax (212) 401-2647; e-mail marriaga@rctv.net; internet www.rctv.net; f. 1953; frmly broadcast on terrestrial channel as Radio Caracas Televisión—Canal 2; ceased broadcasting in May 2007; subsidiary RCTV International (based in Miami, FL, USA) recommenced broadcasting in Venezuela via cable in July 2007; Pres. MARCEL GRANIER.

Televén—Canal 10 (Televisión de Venezuela): Edif. Televén, 4a Transversal con Avda Rómulo Gallegos, Urb. Horizonte, Apdo 1070, Caracas; tel. (212) 280-0011; fax (212) 280-0204; e-mail aferro@televen.com; internet www.televen.com; f. 1988; privately owned; Pres. OMAR CAMERO ZAMORA.

Televisora Andina de Mérida (TAM)—Canal 6: Edif. Imperador, Entrada Independiente, Avda 6 y 7, Calle 23, Mérida 5101; tel. and fax (274) 251-0660; f. 1982; regional channel; Pres. Most Rev. BALTAZAR ENRIQUE PORRAS CARDOZO.

VALE TV (Valores Educativos Televisión)—Canal 5: Quinta VALE TV, final Avda La Salle, Colinas de los Caobos, Caracas 1050; tel. (212) 793-9215; fax (212) 708-9743; e-mail webmaster@valetv.com; internet www.valetv.com; f. 1998; Pres. JORGE CARDENAL L. UROSA SAVINO; Man. MARÍA ISABEL ROJAS.

Zuliana de Televisión—Canal 30: Edif. 95.5 América, Avda 11 (Veritas), Maracaibo; tel. (265) 641-0355; fax (265) 641-0565; e-mail elregionalredac@iamnet.com; Pres. GILBERTO URDANETA FIDOL.

Zuvisión: Maracaibo; f. 2007; regional channel for the state of Zulia; Pres. RAFAEL URDANETA.

Finance

(cap. = capital; res = reserves; dep. = deposits; m. = million; brs = branches; amounts in bolívares unless otherwise indicated)

BANKING

Regulatory Authority

Superintendencia de Bancos (SUDEBAN): Edif. Centro Empresarial Parque del Este, Avda Francisco de Miranda, Urb. La Carlota, Municipio Sucre del Estado Miranda, Apdo 6761, Caracas; tel. (212) 505-0933; e-mail sudeban@sudeban.gov.ve; internet www.sudeban.gov.ve; regulates banking sector; Supt TRINO A. DÍAZ.

Central Bank

Banco Central de Venezuela: Avda Urdaneta, esq. de Carmelitas, Caracas 1010; tel. (212) 801-5111; fax (212) 861-0048; e-mail info@bcv.org.ve; internet www.bcv.org.ve; f. 1940; bank of issue and clearing house for commercial banks; granted autonomy 1992; controls international reserves, interest rates and exchange rates; cap. 10m., res 8,171,432m., dep. 71,972,619m. (Dec. 2006); Pres. and Chair. DIEGO LUIS CASTELLANOS ESCALONA; 2 brs.

Commercial Banks

Banco del Caribe, CA: Edif. Banco del Caribe, 1°, Dr Paúl a esq. Salvador de León, Apdo 6704, Carmelitas, Caracas 1010; tel. (212) 505-5103; fax (212) 562-0460; e-mail producto@bancaribe.com.ve; internet www.bancaribe.com.ve; f. 1954; cap. 80,106.7m., res 66,919.6m., dep. 2,273,950.5m. (Dec. 2005); Pres. JUAN CARLOS DAO; Chair. MIGUEL IGNACIO PURROY; 70 brs and agencies.

Banco Caroní: Edif. Multicentro Banco Caroní, Vía Venezuela, Puerto Ordaz, Estado Bolívar; tel. (286) 23-2230; fax (286) 22-0995; e-mail carupsis@telcel.net.ve; internet www.bancocaroni.com.ve; Pres. ARÍSTIDES MAZA TIRADO.

VENEZUELA

Directory

Banco de Comercio Exterior (Bancoex): Central Gerencial Mohedano, 1°, Calle Los Chaguaramos, La Castellana, Caracas 1060; tel. (212) 265-1433; fax (212) 265-6722; e-mail exports@bancoex.com; internet www.bancoex.com; f. 1997 principally to promote non-traditional exports; state-owned; cap. US $200m.; Pres. Víctor Alvarez.

Banco Confederado: Edif. Centro Financiero Confederado, Blvr Gómez cruce con Calle Marcano, Porlamar, Estado Nuevo Esparta; tel. (95) 65-4230; fax (95) 63-7033; e-mail dbanel002@bancoconfederado.com; internet www.bancoconfederado.com; Pres. Hassan Saleh Saleh.

Banco Exterior, CA—Banco Universal: Edif. Banco Exterior, 1°, Avda Urdaneta, esq. Urapal a Río, Candelaria, Apdo 14278, Caracas 1011-A; tel. (212) 501-0211; fax (212) 501-0745; e-mail lperez@bancoexterior.com; internet www.bancoexterior.com; f. 1958; cap. 56,700m., res and surplus 56,117m., dep. 2,004,440m. (Dec. 2005); Chair. Francisco López Herrera; Pres. Sergio Sannia; 72 brs.

Banco Federal, CA: Avda Manaure, cruce con Avda Ruiz Pineda, Coro, Falcón; tel. (268) 51-4011; e-mail masterbf@bancofederal.com; internet www.bancofederal.com; f. 1982; Pres. Nelson Mezerhane; Exec. Pres. Rogelio Trujillo.

Banco de Fomento Regional Los Andes, CA: Avda 8, La Concordia con Calle 4, San Cristóbal, Táchira; tel. (276) 43-1269; f. 1951; Pres. Edgar A. Hernández; Exec. Vice-Pres. Pedro Roa Sánchez.

Banco de Fomento Regional Coro, CA: Avda Manaure, entre Calles Falcón y Zamora, Coro, Falcón; tel. (268) 51-4421; f. 1950; transferred to private ownership in 1994; Pres. Abraham Naín Senior Urbina.

Banco Guayana, CA: Edif. Los Bancos, Avda Guayana con Calle Caura, Puerto Ordaz, Bolívar; internet www.bancoguayana.net; f. 1955; state-owned; Pres. Oscar Eusebio Jiménez Ayesa.

Banco Industrial de Venezuela, CA: Torre Financiera BIV, Avda Las Delicias de Sabana Grande, cruce con Avda Francisco Solano López, Caracas 1010; tel. (212) 952-4051; fax (212) 952-6282; e-mail webmaster@biv.com.ve; internet www.biv.com.ve; f. 1937; 98% state-owned; cap. 100,000m. (Dec. 2001); Pres. Leonardo González Dellán; 60 brs.

Banco Mercantil, CA: Edif. Mercantil, 35°, Avda Andrés Bello 1, San Bernardino, Apdo 789, Caracas 1010-A; tel. (212) 503-1111; fax (212) 503-1075; e-mail mercan24@bancomercantil.com; internet www.bancomercantil.com; f. 1925; cap. 134,112m., res 179,298m., dep. 9,015,471m. (Dec. 2005); Chair. and CEO Dr Gustavo A. Marturet; 301 brs.

Banco Occidental de Descuento Banco Universal, CA: Calle 77, esq. Avda 17, Maracaibo 4001, Apdo 695, Zulia; tel. (261) 759-3011; fax (261) 594-9811; e-mail atclient@bodinternet.com; internet www.bodinternet.com; f. 1957; transferred to private ownership in 1991; cap. 169,675m., res 228,827m., dep. 6,948,220m. (Dec. 2006); Pres. Víctor Vargas Irausquin; Dir-Gen. Cándido Rodríguez Losada; 17 brs.

Banco Standard Chartered: Edif. Banaven, Torre D, 5°, Avda la Estancia A, Chuao, Caracas 1060; tel. (212) 993-3293; fax (212) 993-3130; internet www.standardchartered.com; f. 1980 as Banco Exterior de los Andes y de España; current name adopted in 1998 following acquisition by Standard Chartered Bank (United Kingdom); representative office only; CEO David Loretta; 3 brs.

Banco de los Trabajadores de Venezuela (BTV) CA: Edif. BTV, Avda Universidad, esq. Colón a esq. Dr Díaz, Caracas; tel. (212) 541-7322; f. 1968 to channel workers' savings for the financing of artisans and small industrial firms; came under state control in 1982; Pres. José Sánchez Piña; Man. Silverio Antonio Narváez; 11 agencies.

Banco de Venezuela, SA (Grupo Santander): Torre Banco de Venezuela, 16°, Avda Universidad, esq. Sociedad a Traposos, Apdo 6268, Caracas 1010-A; tel. (212) 501-2556; fax (212) 501-2546; internet www.bancodevenezuela.com; f. 1890; fmrly Banco de Venezuela CA; 93.38% share purchased by Banco Santander (Spain) in Dec. 1996; changed name to above in 1998; acquired Banco Caracas, CA in Dec. 2000; cap. 40,523.7m., res 459,119.7m., dep. 9,232,439.3m. (Dec. 2005); Exec. Pres. and Dir Michel J. Goguikian; 243 brs.

Banesco Banco Universal, CA: Edif. Banesco, 12°, Avda Guaicaipura con Avda Principal de Las Mercedes, Caracas; tel. (212) 952-4972; fax (212) 952-7124; e-mail atclient@banesco.com; internet www.banesco.com; cap. 554,373.0m., res 321,830.8m., dep. 16,405,178.4m. (Dec. 2006); Chair. Juan Carlos Escotet Rodríguez; Exec. Pres. Luis Xavier Luján Puigbó.

BBVA Banco Provincial, SA: Centro Financiero Provincial, 27°, Avda Vollmer con Avda Este O, San Bernadino, Apdo 1269, Caracas 1011; tel. (212) 504-5098; fax (212) 574-9408; e-mail calidad@provincial.com; internet www.provincial.com; f. 1952; 55.14% owned by Banco Bilbao Vizcaya Argentaria, 26.27% owned by Grupo Polar; cap. 165,301.5m., res 1,176,358.1m., dep. 13,678,404.1m. (Dec. 2006); Pres. Hernán Anzola Giménez; Exec. Pres. José Carlos Pla Royo.

Corp Banca, CA Banco Universal: Torre Corp Banca, Plaza la Castellana, Chacao, Caracas 1060; tel. (212) 206-3333; fax (212) 206-4950; e-mail calidad@corpbanca.com.ve; internet www.corpbanca.com.ve; f. 1969; fmrly Banco Consolidado, current name adopted in 1997; cap. 40,000m., res 47,423m., dep. 1,898,701m. (Dec. 2005); Chair. Jorge Selume Zaror; CEO Mario Chamorro; 116 brs.

Unibanca Banco Universal, CA: Torre Grupo Unión, Avda Universidad, esq. El Chorro, Apdo 2044, Caracas; tel. (212) 501-7031; fax (212) 563-0986; internet www.unibanca.com.ve; f. 2001 by merger of Banco Unión (f. 1943) and Caja Familia; Pres. Dr Ignacio Salvatierra; Vice-Pres. José Q. Salvatierra; 174 brs.

Venezolano de Crédito SA—Banco Universal: Edif. Banco Venezolano de Crédito, Avda Alameda, San Bernadino, Caracas 1011; tel. (212) 806-6111; fax (212) 541-2757; e-mail jurbano@venezolano.com; internet www.venezolano.com; f. 1925 as Banco Venezolano de Crédito, SACA; name changed as above in 2001; cap. 50,400.0m., res and surplus 80,944.2m., dep. 1,457,578.5m. (Dec. 2005); Pres. Dr Oscar García Mendoza; 95 brs in Venezuela and abroad.

Mortgage and Credit Institutions

Banco Hipotecario Unido, SA: Edif. Banco Hipotecario Unido, Avda Este 2, No 201, Los Caobos, Apdo 1896, Caracas 1010; tel. (212) 575-1111; fax (212) 571-1075; f. 1961; cap. 230m., res 143m., dep. 8,075m. (May 1990); Pres. Arturo J. Brillembourg; Gen. Man. Alfonso Espinosa M.

Banco Hipotecario de la Vivienda Popular, SA: Intersección Avda Roosevelt y Avda Los Ilustres, frente a la Plaza Los Símbolos, Caracas; tel. (212) 62-9971; f. 1961; cap. 100m., res 68.2m., dep. 259.3m. (Dec. 1987); Pres. Hely Malaret M.; First Vice-Pres. Alfredo Esquivar.

Banco Hipotecario del Zulia, CA: Avda 2, El Milagro con Calle 84, Maracaibo, Zulia; tel. (261) 91-6055; f. 1963; cap. 120m., res 133.5m., dep. 671.5m. (Nov. 1986); Pres. Alberto López Bracho.

Development Banks

Banco de Desarrollo Económico y Social de Venezuela (BANDES): Torre Bandes, Avda Universidad, Traposos a Colón, Caracas 1010; tel. (212) 505-8010; fax (212) 505-8030; e-mail apublicos@bandes.gov.ve; internet www.bandes.gov.ve; state-owned; Pres. Edgar Hernández Behrens.

Banco de Desarrollo de la Mujer (BANMUJER): Edif. Sudameris, planta baja, Avda Urdaneta, entre Plaza España y esq. de Animas, Caracas 1010; tel. (212) 564-3015; fax (212) 564-4087; e-mail banmujer@cantv.net; internet www.banmujer.gov.ve; f. 2001; state-owned bank offering loans to women; Pres. Nora Castañeda.

Banco del Pueblo Soberano CA: Edif. El Gallo de Oro, Gradillas a San Jacinto Parroquia Catedral, Caracas; tel. (212) 505-2800; fax (212) 505-2995; e-mail abarrera@bancodelpueblo.com.ve; internet www.bancodelpueblo.com.ve; f. 1999; microfinance; Pres. Humberto Ortega Díaz; Dir Jorge González.

Banco del Sur: Caracas; f. 2007 by Govts of Argentina, Bolivia, Brazil, Ecuador, Paraguay, Uruguay and Venezuela; regional devt bank; brs in Buenos Aires (Argentina) and La Paz (Bolivia).

Fondo de Desarrollo Microfinanciero (FONDEMI): Edif. Sudameras, 2°, Avda Urdaneta, esq. Fuerzas Armadas, Caracas 1010; tel. (212) 564-4327; fax (212) 564-0170; e-mail promocion@fondemi.gov.ve; internet www.fondemi.gov.ve; f. 2001; microfinancing devt fund; Pres. Isa Mercedes Sierra Flores.

Banking Association

Asociación Bancaria de Venezuela: Torre Asociación Bancaria de Venezuela, 1°, Avda Venezuela, El Rosal, Caracas; tel. (212) 951-4711; fax (212) 951-3696; e-mail abvinfo@asobanca.com.ve; internet www.asobanca.com.ve; f. 1959; 49 mems; Pres. Arístides Maza Tirado.

STOCK EXCHANGE

Bolsa de Valores de Caracas, CA: Edif. Atrium, Nivel C-1, Calle Sorocaima entre Avdas Tamanaco y Venezuela, Urb. El Rosal, Apdo 62724-A, Caracas 1060-A; tel. (212) 905-5511; fax (212) 952-2640; e-mail bvc@bolsadecaracas.com; internet www.bolsadecaracas.com; f. 1947; 65 mems; Pres. Nelson Ortiz Cusnier.

INSURANCE

Supervisory Board

Superintendencia de Seguros: Edif. Torre del Desarrollo P.H., Avda Venezuela, El Rosal, Chacao, Caracas 1060; tel. (212) 905-1611;

VENEZUELA

fax (212) 953-8615; e-mail sudeseg@sudeseg.gov.ve; internet www.sudeseg.gov.ve; Supt LUDMILA SOTO.

Principal Insurance Companies

Adriática, CA de Seguros: Edif. Adriática de Seguros, Avda Andrés Bello, esq. de Salesianos, Caracas; tel. (212) 571-5702; fax (212) 571-0812; e-mail adriatica@adriatica.com.ve; internet www.adriatica.com.ve; f. 1952; Pres. FRANÇOIS THOMAZEAU; Exec. Vice-Pres. GHISLAIN FABRE.

Avila, CA de Seguros: Edif. Centro Seguros La Paz, 7°, Avda Francisco de Miranda, Caracas; tel. (212) 239-7911; fax (212) 238-2470; f. 1936; Pres. RAMÓN RODRÍGUEZ; Vice-Pres. JUAN LUIS CASAÑAS.

Carabobo, CA de Seguros: Edif. Centro Empresarial Sábana Grande, 12°, Ofs 1 y 2, Calle Negrín, entre Avda Francisco Solano y Blvd de Sábana Grande, El Recreo, Caracas; tel. (212) 761-8514; fax (212) 761-5727; f. 1955; Pres. PAUL FRAYND; Gen. Man. ENRIQUE ABREU.

La Occidental, CA de Seguros: Edif. Seguros Occidental, Avda 4 (Bella Vista) esq. con Calle 71, No 10126, Maracaibo, Zulia; tel. (261) 798-4780; fax (261) 797-5422; e-mail relaciones@laoccidental.com; internet www.laoccidental.com; f. 1956; Pres. TOBÍAS CARRERO NÁCAR; Dir CARLOS MONÍZ ROCHA.

La Oriental, CA de Seguros: Avda Venezuela, cruce con Avda Sojo, Urb. El Rosal, Chacao, Caracas 1060; tel. (212) 905-9924; fax (212) 905-9652; internet www.laoriental.com; f. 1975; Pres. GONZALO LAURÍA ALCALÁ.

Seguros Los Andes, CA: Edif. Seguros Los Andes, Avda Las Pilas, Santa Inés, San Cristóbal, Táchira; tel. (276) 340-2611; fax (276) 340-2596; Pres. RAMÓN RODRÍGUEZ.

Seguros Caracas de Liberty Mutual, CAV: Torre Seguros Caracas C-4, Centro Comercial El Parque, Avda Francisco de Miranda, Los Palos Grandes, Caracas; tel. (212) 209-9111; fax (212) 209-9556; f. 1943; Pres. ROBERTO SALAS.

Seguros Catatumbo, CA: Edif. Seguros Catatumbo, Avda 4 (Bella Vista), No 77–55, Apdo 1083, Maracaibo; tel. (261) 700-5555; fax (261) 216-0037; e-mail mercado@seguroscatatumbo.com; internet www.seguroscatatumbo.com; f. 1957; cap. 9,300m. (2003); Pres. ATENÁGORAS VERGEL RIVERA.

Seguros Mapfre La Seguridad, CA: Calle 3A, Frente a La Torre Express, La Urbina Sur, Apdo 473, Caracas 1010; tel. (212) 204-8000; fax (212) 204-8751; f. 1943; owned by Seguros Mapfre (Spain); Pres. ARISTÓBULO BAUSELA.

Seguros Mercantil, CA: Edif. Seguros Mercantil, Avda Libertador con calle Andrés Galarraga, Chacao, Caracas; tel. (212) 276-2000; fax (212) 276-2596; e-mail rcubillanb@segurosmercantil.com; internet www.segurosmercantil.com; f. 1988; acquired Seguros Orinoco in 2002; Pres. ALBERTO BENSHIMOL; Gen. Man. RAFAEL CUBILLÁN.

Seguros Nuevo Mundo, SA: Edif. Seguros Nuevo Mundo, Avda Luis Roche con 3a Transversal, Altamira, Apdo 2062, Caracas; tel. (212) 201-1111; fax (212) 263-1435; internet www.nmbc.com.ve; f. 1856; cap. 100m. (2003); Pres. RAFAEL PEÑA ALVAREZ; Exec. Vice-Pres. RAFAEL VALENTINO.

Seguros La Previsora, CNA: Torre La Previsora, Avda Abraham Lincoln, Sábana Grande, Caracas; tel. (212) 709-1555; fax (212) 709-1976; internet www.previsora.com; f. 1914; Pres. ALBERTO QUINTANA; Exec. Vice-Pres. JUAN CARLOS MALDONADO.

Seguros Venezuela, CA: Edif. Seguros Venezuela, 8° y 9°, Avda Francisco de Miranda, Urb. Campo Alegre, Caracas; tel. (212) 901-7111; fax (212) 901-7218; e-mail carmen.guillen@segurosvenezuela.com; internet www.segurosvenezuela.com; part of American International group; Exec. Pres. ENRIQUE BANCHIERI ORTIZ.

Universitas de Seguros, CA: Edif. Impres Médico, 2°, Avda Tamanaco, El Rosal, Caracas; tel. (212) 951-6711; fax (212) 901-7506; e-mail tbarrera@universitasdeseguros.com; internet www.universitasdeseguros.com; cap. 6,500m.; Pres. ANA TERESA FERRINI.

Insurance Association

Cámara de Aseguradores de Venezuela: Torre Taeca, 2°, Avda Guaicaipuro, El Rosal, Apdo 3460, Caracas 1010-A; tel. (212) 952-4411; fax (212) 951-3268; e-mail rrpp@camaraseg.org; internet www.camaraseg.org; f. 1951; 42 mems; Pres. CARLOS LUENGO; Exec. Pres. JUAN B. BLANCO-URIBE.

Trade and Industry

GOVERNMENT AGENCIES

Comisión de Administración de Divisas (CADIVI): Antiguo Edif. PDVSA Servicios, 6°, Avda Leonardo Da Vinci, Los Chaguaramos, Caracas; tel. (212) 606-3904; fax (212) 606-3026; e-mail info@cadivi.gov.ve; internet www.cadivi.gov.ve; f. 2003; regulates access to foreign currency; Pres. MANUEL ANTONIO BARROSO.

Corporación Venezolana de Guayana (CVG): Edif. General, 2°, Avda La Estancia, Apdo 7000, Chuao, Caracas; tel. (212) 992-9764; fax (212) 993-0554; e-mail presidenciaccs@cvg.com; internet www.cvg.com; f. 1960 to organize devt of Guayana area, particularly its metal ore and hydroelectric resources; Pres. RODOLFO SANZ (Minister of Basic Industry and Mining).

Fondo Intergubermental para la Decentralización (FIDES): Avda Las Acacias, cruce con Avda Casanova, Torre Banhorient, Sábana Grande, Caracas; tel. (212) 708-0000; fax (212) 708-3642; e-mail info@fides.gov.ve; internet www.fides.gov.ve; f. 1993; part of the Ministry of Planning and Development; co-ordinates investment; Pres. JOSÉ JULIÁN VILLALBA.

Instituto Nacional de Nutrición (INN): Edif. INN, Avda Baralt, esq. El Carmen, Quinta Crespo, Caracas; tel. (212) 483-5142; Dir RHAITZA MENDOZA.

Instituto Nacional de Tierras (INTI): Avda Lecuna, Torre Oeste, 37°, Parque Central, Caracas; tel. (212) 574-8554; fax (212) 576-2201; internet www.inti.gov.ve; f. 1945 as Instituto Agrario Nacional (IAN); present name adopted in 2001; established under Agrarian Law to assure ownership of the land to those who worked on it; now authorized to expropriate and redistribute idle or unproductive lands; Pres. RICHARD VIVAS.

Instituto Nacional de la Vivienda: Torre Inavi, Avda Francisco de Miranda entre Guaicaipuro y San Ignacio de Loyola, Chacao, Caracas; tel. (212) 206-9279; e-mail sugerencias@inavi.gov.ve; internet www.inavi.gov.ve; f. 1975; administers govt housing projects; Pres. JESÚS HERNÁNDEZ GONZÁLEZ.

Mercal, CA: Edif. Torres Seguros Orinoco, Avda Fuerzas Armadas, esq. Socarras, Caracas; tel. (212) 564-3856; e-mail gestioncomunicacional@mercal.gov.ve; internet www.mercal.gov.ve; responsible for marketing agricultural products; fmrly Corporación de Mercadeo Agrícola; Pres. FÉLIX OSORIO GUZMÁN.

Superintendencia de Inversiones Extranjeras (SIEX): Edif. La Perla, Bolsa a Mercaderes, 3°, Apdo 213, Caracas 1010; tel. (212) 483-6666; fax (212) 484-4368; e-mail siexdespacho@cantv.net; internet www.siex.gov.ve; f. 1974; supervises foreign investment in Venezuela; Supt MIRIAM BEATRIZ AGUILERA DE BLANCO.

DEVELOPMENT ORGANIZATIONS

Corporación de Desarrollo de la Pequeña y Mediana Industria (Corpoindustria): Aragua; tel. (243) 23459; internet www.sain.org.ve/corpoind/cedinco.htm; promotes the devt of small and medium-sized industries; Pres. Dr CARLOS GONZÁLEZ-LÓPEZ.

Fondo de Desarrollo Agropecuario, Pesquero, Forestal y Afines (FONDAFA): Edif. FONDAFA, esq. Salvador de León a Socarras, La Hoyada, Caracas; tel. (212) 542-3570; fax (212) 542-5887; e-mail fondafa@fondafa.gov.ve; internet www.fondafa.gov.ve; f. 1974; devt of agriculture, fishing and forestry; Pres. ALIRIO RONDÓN.

Fondo de Desarrollo Microfinanciero (FONDEMI): see Finance—Development Banks.

CHAMBERS OF COMMERCE AND INDUSTRY

Federación Venezolana de Cámaras y Asociaciones de Comercio y Producción (Fedecámaras): Edif. Fedecámaras, Avda El Empalme, Urb. El Bosque, Apdo 2568, Caracas; tel. (212) 731-1711; fax (212) 730-2097; e-mail direje@fedecameras.org.ve; internet www.fedecamaras.org.ve; f. 1944; 307 mems; Pres. JOSÉ LUIS BETANCOURT RAMÍREZ; Gen. Man. GILBERTO DELGADO G.

Cámara de Comercio, Industria y Servicios de Caracas: Edif. Cámara de Comercio de Caracas, 8°, Avda Andrés Eloy Blanco 215, Los Caobos, Caracas; tel. (212) 571-3222; fax (212) 571-0050; e-mail camaradecaracas@cantv.net; f. 1893; 650 mems; Pres. Dr ALEJO PLANCHART; Exec. Dir VLADIMIR CHELMINSKI.

Cámara de Industriales de Caracas: Edif. Cámara de Industriales, 3°, Avda Las Industrias, esq. Pte Anauco, La Candelaria, Apdo 14255, Caracas 1011; tel. (212) 571-4224; fax (212) 571-2009; e-mail ciccs@telcel.net.ve; internet www.cic.org.ve; f. 1939; 550 mems; Pres. ROBERTO J. BALL.

Cámara Venezolano-Americana de Industria y Comercio (Venamcham): Torre Credival, 10°, Of. A, 2a Avda Campo Alegre, Apdo 5181, Caracas 1011; tel. (212) 263-0833; fax (212) 263-2060; e-mail venam@venamcham.org; internet www.venamcham.org; f. 1950; Pres. EDMUND SAADE; Gen. Man. CARLOS TEJERA.

There are chambers of commerce and industry in all major provincial centres.

VENEZUELA

EMPLOYERS' ORGANIZATIONS

Caracas

Asociación Nacional de Industriales Metalúrgicos y de Minería de Venezuela: Edif. Cámara de Industriales, 9°, Puente Anauco a Puente República, Apdo 14139, Caracas; metallurgy and mining; Pres. José Luis Gómez; Exec. Dir Luis Córdova Brito.

Asociación Textil Venezolana: Edif. Textilera Gran Colombia, Calle el Club 8, Los Cortijos de Lourdes, Caracas; tel. (212) 238-1744; fax (212) 239-4089; f. 1957; textiles; Pres. David Fihman; 68 mems.

Asociación Venezolana de Exportadores (AVEX): Centro Comercial Coneresa, Redoma de Prados del Este 435, 2°, Prados del Este, Caracas; tel. (212) 979-5042; fax (212) 979-4542; e-mail directorejecutivo@avex.com.ve; internet www.avex.com.ve; Pres. Francisco Mendoza.

Cámara Petrolera: Torre Domus, 3°, Of. 3-A, Avda Abraham Lincoln con Calle Olimpo, Sábana Grande, Caracas; tel. (212) 794-1222; fax (212) 793-8529; e-mail informacion@camarapetrolera.org; internet www.camarapetrolera.org; f. 1978; asscn of petroleum-sector cos; Pres. Antonio Vincentelli.

Confederación Venezolana de Industriales (CONINDUSTRIA): Edif. CIEMI, Avda Principal de Chuao, Caracas 1061; tel. (212) 991-2116; fax (212) 991-7737; e-mail comunicaciones@conindustria.org; internet www.conindustria.org; asscn of industrialists; Pres. Eduardo Gómez Sigala; Exec. Pres. Juan Francisco Mejía B.

Confederación Nacional de Asociaciones de Productores Agropecuarios (FEDEAGRO): Edif. Casa de Italia, planta baja, Avda La Industria, San Bernardino, Caracas 1010; tel. (212) 571-4035; fax (212) 573-4423; e-mail fedeagro@fedeagro.org; internet www.fedeagro.org; f. 1960; agricultural producers; 133 affiliated asscns; Pres. Gustavo Moreno Lleras.

Federación Nacional de Ganaderos de Venezuela (FEDENAGA): Avda Urdaneta, Centro Financiero Latino, 18°, Ofs 18-2 y 18-4, La Candelaria, Caracas; tel. (212) 563-2153; fax (212) 564-7273; e-mail fedenagat@cantv.net; cattle owners; Pres. José Luis Betancourt.

Unión Patronal Venezolana del Comercio: Edif. General Urdaneta, 2°, Marrón a Pelota, Apdo 6578, Caracas; tel. (582) 561-7025; fax (582) 561-4321; trade; Sec. H. Espinoza Banders.

Other Towns

Asociación de Comerciantes e Industriales del Zulia (ACIZ): Edif. Los Cerros, 3°, Calle 77 con Avda 3C, Apdo 91, Maracaibo, Zulia; tel. (261) 91-7174; fax (261) 91-2570; f. 1941; traders and industrialists; Pres. Jorge Avila.

Asociación Nacional de Cultivadores de Algodón (ANCA) (National Cotton Growers' Association): Edif. Portuguesa, Avda Los Pioneros, Sector Aspiga-Acarigua; tel. (255) 621-5111; fax (255) 621-4368; Sec. Concepción Quijada G.

Asociación Nacional de Empresarios y Trabajadores de la Pesca: Cumaná; fishermen's org.

Unión Nacional de Cultivadores de Tabaco: Urb. Industrial La Hamaca, Avda Hustaf Dalen, Maracay; tobacco growers.

STATE HYDROCARBONS COMPANIES

Corporación Petroquímica de Venezuela (CPV): Torre Pequiven, Avda Francisco de Miranda, Chacao, Apdo 2066, Caracas 1010-A; tel. (212) 201-4011; fax (212) 201-3189; e-mail webmaster@pdvsa.com; internet www.pequiven.com; f. 1956 as Instituto Venezolano de Petroquímica; became Pequiven in 1977; name changed as above in 2005 following independence from PDVSA; involved in many joint ventures with foreign and private Venezuelan interests for expanding petrochemical industry; active in regional economic integration; an affiliate of PDVSA from 1978 until 2005; Pres. Saúl Ameliach.

Petróleos de Venezuela, SA (PDVSA): Edif. Petróleos de Venezuela, Torre Este, Avda Libertador, La Campiña, Apdo 169, Caracas 1010-A; tel. (212) 708-4743; fax (212) 708-4661; e-mail saladeprensa@pdvsa.com; internet www.pdvsa.com; f. 1975; holding co for national petroleum industry; responsible for petrochemical sector since 1978 and for devt of coal resources in western Venezuela since 1985; Pres. Rafael Darío Ramírez Carreño (Minister of Energy and Petroleum); Vice-Pres. of Exploration and Production Luis Vierma; Vice-Pres. of Refining Alejandro Granado; the following are subsidiaries of PDVSA:

  Bariven, SA: Edif. PDVSA Los Chaguaramos, 6°, Avda Leonardo Da Vinci, Urb. Los Chaguaramos, Apdo 1889, Caracas 1010-A; tel. (212) 606-4060; fax (212) 606-2741; handles the petroleum, petrochemical and hydrocarbons industries' overseas purchases of equipment and materials.

  Bitúmenes Orinoco, SA (PDVSA-BITOR): Edif. PDVSA Exploración, Producción y Mejoramiento, 9°, Avda Ernesto Blohm, La Estancia, Chuao, Apdo 3470, Caracas 1010-A; tel. (212) 908-2811; fax (212) 908-3982; e-mail abreuew@pdvsa.com; plans, develops and markets the bitumen resources of the Orinoco belt; produces Venezuela's trademark boiler fuel, Orimulsion.

  Corporación Venezolana del Petróleo (CVP): Edif. Pawa, Calle Cali con Avda Veracruz, Las Mercedes, Caracas; internet www.pdvsa.com/index2.html; f. 1960, reformed 2003; responsible for PDVSA's negotiations with other petroleum cos.

  Deltaven, SA: Edif. PDVSA Deltaven, Avda Principal de La Floresta, La Floresta, Caracas 1060; tel. (212) 208-1111; internet www.pdvsa.com/index2.html; f. 1997; markets PDVSA products and services within Venezuela.

  INTERVEN Venezuela, SA: Edif. Chacofi II, planta baja, entrepiso y 2°, Avda del Libertador 602, Buenos Aires, Argentina; tel. (11) 4813-9652; f. 1986; manages PDVSA's interests in South America.

  Intevep, SA: Centro de Investigación y Apoyo Tecnológico, Edif. Sede Central, Urb. Santa Rosa, Sector El Tambor, Los Teques, Apdo 76343, Caracas 1070-A; tel. (212) 330-6011; fax (212) 330-6448; internet www.intevep.pdvsa.com/index2.html; f. 1973 as Fundación para la Investigación de Hidrocarburos y Petroquímica; present name adopted in 1979; research and devt br. of PDVSA; undertakes applied research and devt in new products and processes and provides specialized technical services for the petroleum and petrochemical industries.

  Palmaven: Edif. PDVSA La Floresta, Torre Palmaven, 7°, Avda Principal, Urb. La Floresta, Caracas; tel. (212) 204-4511; internet www.pdvsa.com/index2.html; sustainable devt agency of PDVSA; Man. Dir Eddie Ramírez.

  PDV Marina: Edif. Petróleos de Venezuela Refinación, Suministro y Comercio, Torre Oeste, 9°, Avda Libertador, La Campiña, Apdo 2103, Caracas 1010-A; tel. (212) 708-1111; fax (212) 708-2200; internet www.pdvsa.com/index2.html; f. 1990; responsible for the distribution, by ship, of PDVSA products; Pres. Fernando Camejo Arenas.

  PDVSA Gas: Edif. Sucre, Avda Francisco de Miranda, La Floresta, Caracas; tel. (212) 208-6212; fax (212) 208-6288; e-mail messina@pdvsa.com; internet www.pdvsa.com/index2.html; f. 1998; gas exploration and extraction; Pres. Nelson Martínez; Dir-Gen. Juan José García.

UTILITIES

Electricity

CADAFE (Compañía de Administración y Fomento Eléctrico): Edif. Cadafe, 14°, Avda Sanz, El Marqués, Caracas; tel. (212) 280-8583; fax (212) 280-8667; e-mail dirgestion@cadafe.com.ve; internet www.cadafe.com.ve; f. 1958; electricity transmission; Pres. María Gabriela González; six subsidiaries:

  CADELA (Compañía Anónima Electricidad de los Andes): San Cristobál; tel. (276) 341-6128; fax (276) 300-3066; e-mail webmaster@cadela.gov.ve; internet www.cadela.gov.ve; f. 1991; electricity transmission in Táchira, Mérida, Barinas and Trujillo; Pres. Jhonny Castro; Dir-Gen. Carlos Esteban Sánchez.

  DESURCA (Desarrollo Uribante Caparo Compañía Anónima): Centro Comercial El Pinar, nivel sótano, Urb. Las Acacias, San Cristóbal; tel. (276) 347-1404; fax (276) 347-4428; internet www.cadafe.gov.ve/ns/desurca; f. 1990; oversees construction of the Uribante-Caparo hydroelectric complex.

  ELECENTRO (Compañía Anónima Electricidad del Centro): Avda Rómulo Gallegos, frente a Domesa, Puerto Ayacucho; tel. (248) 521-1584; internet www.elecentro.gov.ve; f. 1991; electricity transmission in Aragua, Miranda, Guárico, Apure and Amazonas.

  ELEOCCIDENTE (Compañía Anónima Electricidad de Occidente): Edif. Centro Profesional MASCOLO, Calle 28, entre Avdas 30 y 31, Acarigua; tel. (255) 600-2026; fax (255) 600-2071; internet eleoccidente.gob.ve; f. 1991; electricity transmission in Falcón, Lara, Yaracuy, Carabobo, Cojedes and Portuguesa; Dir Khaled Ortíz Villegas.

  ELEORIENTE (Compañía Anónima Electricidad de Oriente): Edif. Eleoriente, Avda Universidad, Cumana; tel. (293) 400-1177; fax (293) 400-1188; internet www.eleoriente.com.ve; f. 1991; electricity transmission in Anzoátegui, Bolívar and Sucre.

  Semda (Sistema Eléctrico de Monagas y Delta Amacuro): Edif. Nicamale, Calle Mariño con Piar, Maturín; tel. (291) 641-3654; fax (291) 641-3613; f. 1998; generation and transmission of electricity in Monagas and Delta Amacuro.

La Electricidad de Caracas (EDC): Edif. La Electricidad de Caracas, Avda Vollmer, San Bernadino, Caracas; tel. (212) 502-2111; e-mail info@edc-ven.com; supplies electricity to capital; owned by AES Corpn; scheduled for renationalization in 2007; Pres. Andrés Gluski.

VENEZUELA

Electrificación del Caroní, CA (Edelca): Edif. General, planta baja, Avda La Estancia, Chuao, Caracas; tel. (212) 950-2111; fax (212) 950-2808; e-mail wriera@edelca.com.ve; internet www.edelca.com.ve; affiliate of Corporación Venezolana de Guayana; supplies some 70% of the country's electricity; Pres. HIPÓLITO IZQUIERDO.

Enelco (Energía Eléctrica de la Costa Oriental): tel. (264) 370-5555; e-mail atencionalcliente@enelco.com.ve; internet www.enelco.com.ve; electricity services to the eastern coast of the Lago de Maracaibo region.

Sistema Eléctrico de Nueva Esparta (Seneca): Caracas; tel. (295) 260-1412; fax (295) 260-1419; e-mail seneca@seneca.com.ve; internet www.seneca.com.ve; electricity co; privatized in Oct. 1998.

Gas

ENAGAS (Ente Nacional del Gas): Edif. PDVSA, Torre Sur, 9° y 10°, Avda Libertador, Caracas; tel. (212) 706-6654; fax (212) 706-6471; e-mail webmaster@enagas.gov.ve; internet www.enagas.gov.ve; f. 1999; autonomous agency attached to the Ministry of Energy and Petroleum; regulatory body.

Water

Hidroven: Edif. Hidroven, Avda Augusto César Sandino con 9a Transversal, Maripérez, Caracas; tel. (212) 781-4778; fax (212) 781-6424; e-mail hvenpres@cantv.net; internet www.hidroven.gov.ve; national water co; owns Hidroandes, Hidrocapital, Hidrocaribe, Hidrofalcon, Hidrolago, Hidrollanos, Hidropaez, Hidrosuroeste, Aguas de Monagas, Aguas de Ejido, Hidrolara, Aguas de Anaco, Aguas de Cojedes, Aguas de Mérida, Aguas de Apure, Aguas de Yaracuy, Aguas de Portuguesa; Pres. CRISTÓBAL FRANCISCO ORTIZ; Vice-Pres. FRANCISCO DURÁN.

Compañía Anónima Hidrológica de la Región Capital (Hidrocapital): Edif. Hidroven, Avda Augusto César Sandino con 9a Transversal, Maripérez, Caracas; tel. (212) 793-1638; fax (212) 793-6794; e-mail 73070.2174@compuserve.com; internet www.hidrocapital.com.ve; f. 1992; owned by Hidroven; operates water supply in Federal District and states of Miranda and Vargas; Pres. ALEJANDRO HITCHER.

TRADE UNIONS

About one-quarter of the labour force in Venezuela belongs to a trade union. Most unions in Venezuela are legally recognized. The country's union movement is strongest in the public sector.

Confederación de Trabajadores de Venezuela (CTV) (Confederation of Venezuelan Workers): Edif. José Vargas, 17°, Avda Este 2, Los Caobos, Caracas; tel. (212) 575-0005; e-mail mcova@ctv.org.ve; internet www.ctv.org.ve; f. 1936; largest trade union confederation; principally active in public sector; Chávez Govt disputes legitimacy of election of CTV leadership; Pres. CARLOS ALFONSO ORTEGA CARVAJAL; Sec.-Gen. MANUEL JOSÉ COVA FERMÍN; 1,000,000 mems from 24 regional and 16 industrial feds.

Fedepetrol: union of petroleum workers; Pres. RAFAEL ROSALES.

Federación Campesina (FC): peasant union; CTV affiliate; Leader RUBÉN LANZ.

Fetrametal: union of metal workers; Leader JOSÉ MOLLEGAS.

Fuerza Bolivariana de Trabajadores (FBT): f. 2000; pro-Govt union.

Movimiento Nacional de Trabajadores para la Liberación (MONTRAL): Edif. Don Miguel, 6°, esq. Cipreses, Caracas; f. 1974; affiliated to CLAT and WFTU; Pres. LAUREANO ORTIZ BRAEAMONTE; Sec.-Gen. DAGOBERTO GONZÁLEZ; co-ordinating body for the following trade unions:

Central Nacional Campesina (CNC): Pres. REINALDO VÁSQUEZ.

Cooperativa Nacional de Trabajadores de Servicios Múltiples (CNTSM).

Federación Nacional de Sindicatos Autónomos de Trabajadores de la Educación de Venezuela (FENASATREV): Pres. LUIS EFRAÍN ORTA.

Federación de los Trabajadores de Hidrocarburos de Venezuela (FETRAHIDROCARBUROS).

Frente de Trabajadores Copeyanos (FTC): Sec.-Gen. DAGOBERTO GONZÁLEZ.

Movimiento Agrario Social-Cristiano (MASC): Sec.-Gen. GUSTAVO MENDOZA.

Movimiento Magisterial Social-Cristiano (MMSC): Sec.-Gen. FELIPE MONTILLA.

Movimiento Nacional de Trabajadores de Comunicaciones (MONTRAC).

Movimiento Nacional de Trabajadores Estatales de Venezuela (MONTREV).

Unión Nacional de Trabajadores (UNT): f. 2003; pro-Govt federation; Nat. Co-ordinators STALIN PÉREZ BORGES, ORLANDO CHIRINO.

Transport

RAILWAYS

In 1999 work began on lines linking Acarigua and Turén (45 km) and Morón and Riecito (100 km). Construction of the first section (Caracas–Cúa) of a line linking the capital to the existing network at Puerto Cabello (219 km in total) was also begun. Services on the underground system began in 1983 on a two-line system: east to west from Palos Verdes to Propatria; north to south from Capitolio/El Silencio to Zoológico. A southern extension from Plaza Venezuela to El Valle opened in 1995. Further extensions to the lines were under way in 2007.

CVG Ferrominera Orinoco, CA: Vía Caracas, Puerto Ordaz, Apdo 399, Bolívar; tel. (286) 30-3451; fax (286) 30-3333; e-mail 104721.2354@compuserve.com; f. 1976; state-owned; operates two lines San Isidro mine–Puerto Ordaz (316 km) and El Pao–Palua (55 km) for transporting iron ore; Pres. Ing. LEOPOLDO SUCRE FIGARELLA; Man. M. ARO G.

Ferrocarril de CVG Bauxilum—Operadora de Bauxita: Caracas; tel. (212) 40-1716; fax (212) 40-1707; f. 1989; state-owned; operates line linking Los Pijiguaos with river Orinoco port of Gumilla (52 km) for transporting bauxite; Pres. P. MORALES.

Instituto Autónomo de Ferrocarriles del Estado (IAFE): Edif. Torre Británica de Seguros, 7° y 8°, Avda José Féliz Sosa, Urb. Altamira, Chacao, Caracas 1062-A; tel. (212) 201-8911; e-mail relacp@cantv.net; state co; operates 336 km of track; Pres. RAFAEL ALVAREZ; Vice-Pres. INOVA CASTRO PÉREZ.

CA Metro de Caracas: Multicentro Empresarial del Este, Edif. Miranda, Torre B, 7°, Avda Francisco de Miranda, Apdo 61036, Caracas; tel. (212) 206-7111; fax (212) 266-3346; internet www.metrodecaracas.com.ve; f. 1976 to supervise the construction and use of the underground railway system; state-owned; Pres. DANIEL DAVIS.

ROADS

In 2004 there were an estimated 96,200 km of roads, of which 32,300 km were paved.

Of the three great highways, the first (960 km) runs from Caracas to Ciudad Bolívar. The second, the Pan-American Highway (1,290 km), runs from Caracas to the Colombian frontier and is continued as far as Cúcuta. A branch runs from Valencia to Puerto Cabello. The third highway runs southwards from Coro to La Ceiba, on Lake Maracaibo.

A new 'marginal highway' was under construction along the western fringe of the Amazon Basin in Venezuela, Colombia, Ecuador, Peru, Bolivia and Paraguay. The Venezuelan section now runs for over 440 km and is fully paved.

INLAND WATERWAYS

Instituto Nacional de Canalizaciones: Edif. INC, Calle Caracas, al lado de la Torre Diamen, Chuao, Caracas; tel. (212) 908-5106; fax (212) 959-6906; internet www.incanal.gov.ve; f. 1952; semi-autonomous institution connected with the Ministry of Infrastructure; Pres. Cmmdr WOLFGANG LÓPEZ CARRASQUEL; Vice-Pres. LUZKARIM CORNETT PABÓN.

Compañía Anónima La Translacustre: Maracaibo; freight and passenger service serving Lake Maracaibo, principally from Maracaibo to the road terminal from Caracas at Palmarejo.

SHIPPING

There are 13 major ports, 34 petroleum and mineral ports and five fishing ports. Formerly the main port for imports, La Guaira, the port for Caracas, was affected by mudslides caused by heavy rains in November 1999. Venezuela's main port is now Puerto Cabello, which handles raw materials for the industrial region around Valencia. Maracaibo is the chief port for the petroleum industry. Puerto Ordaz, on the Orinoco River, was also developed to deal with the shipments of iron from Cerro Bolívar.

Instituto Nacional de Puertos: Caracas; tel. (212) 92-2811; f. 1976 as the sole port authority; Pres. Vice-Adm. FREDDY J. MOTA CARPIO.

Consolidada de Ferrys, CA (CONFERRY): Torre Banhorient, 3°, Avda Las Acacias y Avda Casanova, Apdo 87, Sabana Grande, Caracas 1010-A; tel. (212) 781-9711; fax (212) 781-8739; f. 1970; Dir RAFAEL MATA.

Consorcio Naviero Venezolano (Conavén): Torre Uno, 4°, Avda Orinoco, Las Mercedes, Caracas; tel. (212) 993-2922; fax (212) 993-1636; e-mail conavent@conaven.com.

VENEZUELA

Corpoven, SA: Edif. Petróleos de Venezuela, Avda Libertador, La Campiña, Apdo 61373, Caracas 1060-A; tel. (212) 708-1111; fax (212) 708-1833; Pres. Dr ROBERTO MANDINI; Vice-Pres. JUAN CARLOS GÓMEZ; 2 oil tankers.

Lagoven, SA: Edif. Lagovén, Avda Leonardo da Vinci, Los Chaguaramos, Apdo 889, Caracas; tel. (212) 606-3311; fax (212) 606-3637; f. 1978 as a result of the nationalization of the petroleum industry; fmrly Creole Petroleum Group; transports crude petroleum and by-products between Maracaibo, Aniba and other ports in the area; Pres. B. R. NATERA; Marine Man. P. D. CAREZIS; 10 tankers.

Tacarigua Marina, CA: Torre Lincoln 7A-B, Avda Lincoln, Apdo 51107, Sábana Grande, Caracas 1050-A; tel. (212) 781-1315; Pres. R. BELLIZZI.

Transpapel, CA: Edif. Centro, 11°, Of. 111, Centro Parque Boyaca, Avda Sucre, Los Dos Caminos, Apdo 61316, Caracas 1071; tel. (212) 283-8366; fax (212) 285-7749; e-mail nmaldonado@cantv.net; f. 1985; Chair. GUILLERMO ESPINOSA F.; Man. Dir Capt. NELSON MALDONADO.

Transporte Industrial, SA: Edif. Anzoátegui, Planta Vencemos, Pertigalete, Carretera Guanta, Km 5, Apdo 4356, Puerto la Cruz; tel. (281) 68-5607; fax (281) 68-5683; f. 1955; bulk handling and cement bulk carrier; Chair. VÍCTOR ROMO; Man. Dir RAFAEL ANEE.

CIVIL AVIATION

There are two adjacent airports 13 km from Caracas: Maiquetía for domestic and Simón Bolívar for international services. There are 61 commercial airports, 11 of which are international airports.

National Airlines

Aeropostal (Alas de Venezuela): Torre Polar Oeste, 22°, Plaza Venezuela, Los Caobos, Caracas 1051; tel. (212) 708-6211; fax (212) 782-6323; internet www.aeropostal.com; f. 1933; transferred to private ownership in Sept. 1996, acquired by Venezuelan/US consortium Corporación Alas de Venezuela; domestic services and flights to destinations in the Caribbean, South America and the USA; Pres. and CEO NELSON RAMIZ.

Aerovías Venezolanas, SA (AVENSA): Torre Humboldt, 1°, Avda Rio Caura, Prados del Este, Caracas; tel. (212) 976-5240; fax (212) 563-0225; e-mail info@avensa.com.ve; internet www.avensa.com.ve; f. 1943; provides domestic services from Caracas and services to Europe and the USA; govt-owned; Pres. WILMAR CASTRO SOTELDO.

Aserca Airlines: Torre Exterior, 8°, Avda Bolívar Norte, Valencia, Carabobo 2002; tel. (241) 237-111; fax (241) 220-210; e-mail rsv@asercaairlines.com; internet www.asercaairlines.com; f. 1968; domestic services and flights to Caribbean destinations; Pres. SIMEÓN GARCÍA.

LASER (Línea Aérea de Servicio Ejecutivo Regional): Torre Bazar Bolívar, 8°, Avda Francisco de Miranda, El Marqués, Caracas; tel. (212) 202-0100; fax (212) 235-8359; internet www.laser.com.ve; f. 1994; scheduled and charter passenger and cargo services to domestic and international destinations; Pres. INOCENCIO ALVAREZ; Gen. Man. JORGE ANDRADE HIDALGO.

Línea Turística Aereotuy, CA: Edif. Gran Sábana, 5°, Blvd de Sábana Grande, Apdo 2923, Carmelitas, Caracas 1050; tel. (212) 761-6231; fax (212) 762-5254; e-mail tuysales@etheron.net; internet www.tuy.com; f. 1982; operates on domestic and international routes; Pres. PETER BOTTOME; Gen. Man. JUAN C. MÁRQUEZ.

Santa Barbara Airlines: Avda 3H, No 78-51, Res. República, Local 01, Maracaibo; tel. (261) 922-090; fax (261) 927-977; internet www.sbairlines.com; f. 1996; domestic and international services; Pres. FRANCISCO GONZÁLEZ YANES.

Tourism

In 2005 Venezuela received 706,103 tourists. Receipts from tourism in 2004 amounted to US $531m. Venezuela's high crime levels, political instability and high prices relative to regional competitors have deterred tour operators. An estimated 90% of tourists visit the island of Margarita, while only 20% of tourists visit the mainland.

Asociación Venezolana de Agencias de Viajes y Turismo (AVAVIT): Caracas; e-mail turvspecialtours@cantv.net; internet www.avavit.com; Pres. ELIAS M. RAJBE S.

Corporación Nacional de Hoteles y Turismo (CONAHOTU): Caracas; f. 1969; govt agency; Pres. ERASTO FERNÁNDEZ.

INATUR: Hotel Caracas Hilton, Torre Sur, 4°, Of. 424, Caracas; tel. (212) 503-5423; fax (212) 503-5424; e-mail inatur@inatur.gov.ve; internet www.inatur.gov.ve; govt tourism devt agency; Exec. Dir AIXA RONDÓN.

VIET NAM

Introductory Survey

Location, Climate, Language, Religion, Flag, Capital

The Socialist Republic of Viet Nam is situated in South-East Asia, bordered to the north by the People's Republic of China, to the west by Laos and Cambodia, and to the east by the South China Sea. The climate is humid during both the hot summer and the relatively cold winter, and there are monsoon rains in both seasons. Temperatures in Hanoi are generally between 13°C (55°F) and 33°C (91°F). The language is Vietnamese. The principal religion is Buddhism. There are also Daoist, Confucian, Hoa Hao, Caodaist and Christian (mainly Roman Catholic) minorities. The national flag (proportions 2 by 3) is red, with a large five-pointed yellow star in the centre. The capital is Hanoi.

Recent History

Cochin-China (the southernmost part of Viet Nam) became a French colony in 1867. Annam and Tonkin (central and northern Viet Nam) were proclaimed French protectorates in 1883. Later all three were merged with Cambodia and Laos to form French Indo-China. Throughout the French colonial period, but especially after 1920, nationalist and revolutionary groups operated in Viet Nam. The best-organized was the Vietnamese Revolutionary Youth League, founded by Ho Chi Minh. The League was succeeded in 1930 by the Communist Party of Indo-China, also led by Ho Chi Minh.

In September 1940 Japanese forces began to occupy Viet Nam, although (Vichy) France retained administrative authority, and in June 1941 the nationalists formed the Viet Nam Doc Lap Dong Minh Hoi (Revolutionary League for the Independence of Viet Nam), or Viet Minh. In March 1945 French control was ended by a Japanese coup. Following Japan's surrender in August, Viet Minh forces entered Hanoi, and on 2 September the new regime proclaimed independence as the Democratic Republic of Viet Nam (DRV), with Ho Chi Minh as President. The Communist Party, formally dissolved in 1945, continued to be the dominant group within the Viet Minh Government. In March 1946, after French forces re-entered Viet Nam, an agreement between France and the DRV recognized Viet Nam as a 'free' state within the French Union. However, the DRV Government continued to seek complete independence. Negotiations with France broke down, and full-scale hostilities began in December 1946.

In March 1949 the French established the State of Viet Nam in the South. Meanwhile, in the North the Viet Minh was dissolved in 1951, and the Communists formed the Dang Lao Dong Viet Nam (Viet Nam Workers' Party), with Ho Chi Minh as Chairman of the Central Committee. After the defeat of French forces at Dien Bien Phu in May 1954, terms for a cease-fire were settled in Geneva, Switzerland. Agreements signed in July provided for the provisional partition of Viet Nam into two military zones, with French forces south of latitude 17°N and DRV forces in the north. Later in 1954 the French withdrew from South Viet Nam. Ngo Dinh Diem became Prime Minister of the State of Viet Nam, and in 1955, following a referendum, proclaimed himself President of the Republic of Viet Nam. He thereby deposed Bao Dai, Emperor of Viet Nam from 1932 until his forced abdication in 1945, who had become Head of the State of Viet Nam in 1949. (The former Emperor died in exile in France in 1997.) Diem refused to participate in elections envisaged by the Geneva agreement. In the DRV Ho Chi Minh was succeeded as Prime Minister by Pham Van Dong in 1955, but remained Head of State and party Chairman.

The anti-communist Diem regime in the South was opposed by former members of the Viet Minh, who became known as the Viet Cong. Diem was overthrown by a coup in November 1963, and a series of short-lived military regimes held power until June 1965, when some stability was restored by the National Leadership Committee, with Lt-Gen. Nguyen Van Thieu as Chairman and Air Vice-Marshal Nguyen Cao Ky as Prime Minister. In 1967 Gen. Thieu was elected President, with Marshal Ky as Vice-President, and in 1971, after splitting with Ky, President Thieu was re-elected unopposed.

From 1959 the DRV actively assisted the insurgent movement in South Viet Nam, supporting the establishment there of the communist-dominated National Liberation Front (NLF) in December 1960. In 1961 the USA joined the war on the side of the anti-communist regime in the South, later bombing the North extensively from 1965 to 1968. In November 1968 peace talks between the four participants in the Viet Nam war began in Paris, France, but remained deadlocked as the fighting continued. In June 1969 the NLF formed the Provisional Revolutionary Government (PRG) in the South. Ho Chi Minh died in September 1969: he was succeeded as Head of State by Ton Duc Thang, while political leadership passed to Le Duan, First Secretary of the Viet Nam Workers' Party since 1960.

In 1972 PRG and North Vietnamese forces launched a major offensive in South Viet Nam, and US bombing of the North was renewed with greater intensity. In January 1973 a peace agreement was finally signed in Paris, providing for a cease-fire in the South, the withdrawal of US forces, the eventual peaceful reunification of the whole country, and US aid to the Government in the North to assist in reconstruction. US troops withdrew, and in December 1974 combined PRG and North Vietnamese forces began a final offensive, taking the southern capital, Saigon, in April 1975. By May the new regime was in complete control of the South.

While South Viet Nam, under the PRG, remained technically separate from the DRV, effective control of the whole country passed to Hanoi. In July 1976 the country's reunification was proclaimed under the name of the Socialist Republic of Viet Nam, and Saigon was renamed Ho Chi Minh City. A new Government was appointed, dominated by members of the former Government of the DRV but including some members of the PRG. In December Le Duan was appointed General Secretary of the Communist Party of Viet Nam (formerly the Viet Nam Workers' Party). President Ton Duc Thang died in March 1980. A new Constitution was adopted in December of that year. Truong Chinh was appointed President of the Council of State (Head of State) in July 1981, but real power remained with Le Duan.

Le Duan died in July 1986, and was succeeded as General Secretary of the Communist Party by Truong Chinh. At the Sixth Party Congress, held in December, the country's three most senior leaders, Truong Chinh, Pham Van Dong and Le Duc Tho, announced their retirement from the party Political Bureau (Politburo). However, they continued to attend politburo meetings in an advisory capacity. Truong Chinh and Pham Van Dong retained their respective posts as President of the Council of State and Chairman of the Council of Ministers (Prime Minister) until 1987, and Le Duc Tho continued to wield considerable political influence until his death in October 1990. The Congress appointed Nguyen Van Linh, a long-standing party official, as General Secretary of the Party.

In February 1987 an extensive government reorganization involved the dismissal of 12 ministers, as well as the merger or restructuring of several ministries, apparently with a view to the implementation of economic reforms. An election to the National Assembly took place in April. There were 829 candidates for the 496 seats (compared with 613 candidates at the previous election). In June the new Assembly elected Vo Chi Cong and Pham Hung, both former Vice-Chairmen of the Council of Ministers, to the posts of President of the Council of State and Chairman of the Council of Ministers respectively. Although a veteran of the struggle with the South, and reputedly a strict conservative, Pham Hung gave his support to the programme of economic reform, referred to as *doi moi* (renovation), initiated by Nguyen Van Linh. The new liberalism of the regime was demonstrated by the release in September of 480 political prisoners from 're-education' camps, as part of an amnesty for more than 6,600 prisoners on the anniversary of independence from France in 1945. In February 1988 more than 1,000 political prisoners were released. In March Pham Hung died. The Council of State appointed Vo Van Kiet, a Vice-Chairman of the Council of Ministers and the Chairman of the State Commission for Planning, as acting Chairman of the Council of Ministers.

At the meeting of the National Assembly in June, members from the south took the unprecedented step of nominating the reformist Vo Van Kiet to oppose the Central Committee's more conservative candidate, Do Muoi (ranked third in the Politburo), in the election for the chairmanship of the Council of Ministers. Do Muoi was elected to the position, but Vo Van Kiet received unexpectedly strong support. Despite his reputation, Do Muoi declared his commitment to the advancement of reform. Widespread dissatisfaction with the condition of the economy led to the removal of hundreds of cadres from government posts in a 'purification' of the party. In an attempt to improve international relations, and thus secure much-needed Western aid, Viet Nam amended its Constitution in December, removing derogatory references to the USA, the People's Republic of China, France and Japan. In March 1989 a reorganization of senior economic ministers adjusted the balance further towards reform and strengthened the position of Nguyen Van Linh.

In August 1989 68 members of a US-based exiles' movement, the National Front for the Liberation of Viet Nam, were arrested while crossing from Thailand into Laos. Viet Nam formally protested to Thailand for supporting the group, which had allegedly attempted to incite a rebellion in southern Viet Nam, although the Thai Government denied involvement. In January 1990 38 suspected rebels were extradited to Viet Nam; in October they were sentenced to long terms of imprisonment.

Municipal elections to provincial and district councils took place in November 1989. Under new legislation, candidates who were not members of the Communist Party were allowed to participate for the first time. In December the National Assembly approved legislation imposing new restrictions on the press: the appointment of editors became subject to government approval, and journalists were required to reveal sources of information on request. Open dissension towards Communist Party policy also became a criminal offence. In late 1989 progress towards political reform under *doi moi* was adversely affected by government concern regarding the demise of socialism in Eastern Europe. At a meeting of the Central Committee in March 1990, disagreement on the issue of political pluralism resulted in the dismissal of a member of the Politburo, Tran Xuan Bach, who had openly advocated reform.

In the second half of 1990 the Government dismissed or brought charges against more than 18,000 officials, in an attempt to eradicate corruption. In December the Central Committee produced draft political and economic reports, reaffirming the party's commitment to socialism and to the process of economic liberalization, which were to be submitted to the next Party Congress. In the same month Bui Tin, the Deputy Editor of the official organ of the Communist Party, *Nhan Dan*, criticized government policy. He was subsequently expelled from the Politburo and dismissed as Deputy Editor. Following a request by the Central Committee for public comment on the reports, in early 1991 the party journal, *Tap Chi Cong San* (Communist Review), published articles by prominent intellectuals that severely criticized the reports and questioned the effectiveness of the socialist system. The Communist Party subsequently increased surveillance of dissidents and instructed the press to publish retaliatory articles condemning party critics. In June the Communist Party Congress approved the reports. It elected Do Muoi to replace Nguyen Van Linh as General Secretary of the Party; seven members of the Politburo were removed from their posts, including Nguyen Van Linh, although he, together with Pham Van Dong and the President of the Council of State, Vo Chi Cong, remained in the Central Committee in an advisory capacity. At a session of the National Assembly held in late July and early August, the reformist Vo Van Kiet was elected to replace Do Muoi as Chairman of the Council of Ministers. In addition, the National Assembly studied proposals, made by a constitutional commission, for amendments to the Constitution.

A new draft Constitution was published in December 1991 and, after being reviewed in public discussions, was adopted by the National Assembly in April 1992. Like the previous (1980) Constitution, it emphasized the central role of the Communist Party; however, the new document stipulated that the party must be subject to the law. While affirming adherence to a state-regulated socialist economy, the new Constitution guaranteed protection for foreign investment in Viet Nam, and permitted foreign travel and overseas investment for Vietnamese. Land was to remain the property of the State, although the right was granted to procure long-term leases, which could be inherited or sold. The National Assembly was to be reduced in number, but was to have greater power. The Council of State was to be replaced by a single President as Head of State, to be responsible for appointing (subject to the approval of the National Assembly) a Prime Minister and senior members of the judiciary. The new Constitution was to enter into effect after the July 1992 general election.

In July 1992 a total of 601 candidates contested 395 seats in the National Assembly. Almost 90% were members of the Communist Party: although independent candidates (i.e. not endorsed by the Viet Nam Fatherland Front—the grouping of mass organizations, such as trade unions, affiliated to the Communist Party) were for the first time permitted to seek election, in the event only two were deemed to qualify, and neither was elected.

At the first session of the new National Assembly, in September 1992, the conservative Gen. Le Duc Anh (a member of the Politburo and a former Minister of Defence) was elected to the new post of executive President. Vo Van Kiet was appointed Prime Minister (the equivalent of his former post) by the Assembly in October. Only four ministers, all of whom had been implicated in corruption scandals, were not reappointed. During 1993 the Government emphasized its determination to continue progress towards a market-led economy and to encourage foreign investment. However, there was no tolerance of political dissent. In August 14 people were sentenced to terms of imprisonment, after having been convicted of conspiring to overthrow the Government, and in November several Buddhist monks were imprisoned for allegedly inciting anti-Government demonstrations. In January 1994 four new members were appointed to the Politburo, including the Minister of Foreign Affairs, Nguyen Manh Cam, and 20 new members (all under the age of 55) were elected to the Communist Party's Central Committee. In June the National Assembly approved a labour law that guaranteed the right to strike (providing that the 'social life of the community' was not adversely affected). Strikes followed in some southern provinces, and in August the first incident of industrial action in Hanoi was reported. At the fourth Congress of the Fatherland Front, in August, a new, 200-member Central Committee was elected. Elections to provincial and district councils took place during December 1994.

In February 1995 a prominent human rights organization, Amnesty International, protested to the Vietnamese Government about the recent detention of members of the anti-Government Unified Buddhist Church of Viet Nam. In August the People's Court of Ho Chi Minh City sentenced nine political activists, who had attempted to organize pro-democracy conferences, to terms of imprisonment. (Two of those sentenced, who held joint US-Vietnamese nationality, were released in November following a request from the US Government.) In October the National Assembly adopted an extensive civil code (drafted over a period of 10 years), guaranteeing the rights of the individual and enshrining existing rights concerning land usage and inheritance of property. In November two former prominent members of the Communist Party, Do Trung Hieu and Hoang Minh Chinh, were sentenced to custodial terms on charges of damaging national security: Hieu had been involved with an organization demanding political pluralism, while Chinh had published articles urging the restoration of senior party officials removed in the 1960s.

In April 1996 the Central Committee of the Communist Party released draft reports on political and economic policy, which were to be submitted to the Eighth Communist Party Congress at the end of June, indicating that the party intended to maintain state control of the economy (while remaining committed to economic growth) and to continue to reject political pluralism. Also in April the Vice-Chairman of the National Assembly was dismissed from the Politburo and from the Communist Party; it was reported that he had been accused of treason in connection with the Viet Nam war. In June the Congress elected a new, 170-member Central Committee and an expanded (19-member) Politburo. A five-member Standing Board, which included Do Muoi, Le Duc Anh and Vo Van Kiet, was created. In November 12 ministers were dismissed in an extensive cabinet reorganization. Later in the month Le Duc Anh withdrew temporarily from politics, owing to ill health: this prompted considerable speculation regarding the eventual leadership succession. In subsequent months Lt-Gen. Le Kha Phieu, a member of the new Standing Board, came to the fore as a likely successor to Do Muoi as General Secretary of the Communist Party. Widely seen as a conservative, Le Kha Phieu was expected to seek an increased political role for the military. Le Duc Anh returned to active politics in April 1997.

In December 1996 the Politburo issued a directive requiring the establishment of Communist Party cells in all foreign-invested enterprises. In January 1997 an unprecedentedly high-profile corruption case was brought to trial: the case involved former senior officials of Tamexco (an import-export company owned by the Communist Party), along with officials from Vietcombank (the state foreign trade bank) and the financial sector. The 20 defendants were accused of a range of financial crimes, principally embezzlement of socialist property. In late January four death sentences were pronounced, together with one sentence of life imprisonment, two suspended sentences and a combined total of 103 years' imprisonment for the remaining defendants. In February 1997 a judge of the Supreme People's Court was sentenced to two years' imprisonment, having been found to have abused a position of influence for personal gain, and was thus the first member of Viet Nam's judiciary to be convicted of corruption.

In May 1997 substantial amendments to the criminal code were approved by the National Assembly in respect of corruption, bribery, child abuse and drugs-trafficking. The acceptance of bribes in excess of 50m. dông, and possession of 5 kg of opium or 100 grams of heroin, became crimes punishable by death or life imprisonment; increased penalties were introduced for first-time offenders in cases of corruption. In the same month a group of 22 people, including police, customs and border officials, stood trial for drugs-trafficking: all were convicted, with eight sentenced to death and eight to life imprisonment. In July two people were sentenced to death, and three others to life imprisonment, following what was reported as Viet Nam's first terrorism trial, having been convicted of involvement in a bomb attack in Ho Chi Minh City in October 1994. Official reports stated that the defendants were members of the National Resistance Front for the Restoration of Viet Nam, which was alleged to have issued death threats to foreign nationals who had established businesses in Viet Nam.

Elections to the 10th National Assembly took place on 20 July 1997. A record 663 candidates contested 450 seats (expanded from 395 seats). Under a modified selection process, 112 non-Communist Party members registered as potential candidates. However, following rigorous screening procedures, only 11 independent ('self-nominated') candidates qualified to contest the elections, of whom three secured seats in the Assembly. Do Muoi was among senior figures who did not seek re-election, and, in total, fewer than one-third of the members of the outgoing Assembly returned to office. At the first session of the new National Assembly in late September, Tran Duc Luong, hitherto a Deputy Prime Minister, was elected as President in succession to Le Duc Anh, who, owing to continued ill health, did not seek re-election. The Assembly subsequently endorsed the appointment of Nguyen Thi Binh as Vice-President, Nong Duc Manh as Chairman of the National Assembly Standing Committee, and Phan Van Khai as Prime Minister. (Vo Van Kiet had also stepped down.) A reorganization of the Cabinet was approved at the end of September: the new Cabinet included an increased number of Deputy Prime Ministers, each of whom held a wide portfolio of responsibilities. In October Do Que Luong was appointed acting Governor of the State Bank of Viet Nam (a cabinet post), following the refusal of the National Assembly to re-elect the incumbent Cao Si Kiem, deemed responsible for recent corruption scandals in the banking sector.

Reports emerged during September 1997 of violent unrest in the northern province of Thai Binh. The unrest, which had begun in May and intensified in June as hundreds of farmers protested against taxes and local corruption, had remained largely unreported earlier in the year as the province had been closed to foreign journalists. There was violence in November in the predominantly Roman Catholic province of Dong Nai, in southern Viet Nam, as thousands of protesters demonstrated against corruption in local government and attempts to confiscate church land. At the end of November the Government pledged to provide financial aid to Thai Binh province, and in February 1998 President Luong made an official tour of the province. In July 1998 more than 30 people were sentenced to terms of imprisonment for their involvement in the previous year's violent unrest in Thai Binh.

In December 1997 Le Kha Phieu was elected to succeed Do Muoi as General Secretary of the Central Committee of the Communist Party. At the same time Do Muoi, Le Duch Anh and Vo Van Kiet resigned from the Politburo; all three were subsequently appointed as advisers to the Central Committee. Four new members were elected to the Politburo, and in January 1998 the election by the Politburo of a new Standing Board, comprising Le Kha Phieu, Tran Duc Luong, Phan Van Khai, Nong Duc Manh and Pham The Duyet, was announced. The new appointments were widely perceived to reflect the consolidation of the conservative tendency within the leadership, to the detriment of reformists, among them the Prime Minister. In March, in an illustration of the Government's commitment to countering corruption, the Communist Party announced that in 1997 it had disciplined and expelled some 18,000 members, and sentenced 469 to terms of imprisonment. Further members of the party were reported to have been disciplined over corruption-related offences in July.

In a general amnesty announced by the Government to mark Viet Nam's National Day on 2 September 1998, more than 5,000 prisoners, including four of the country's most prominent dissidents—Doan Viet Hoat, Nguyen Dan Que, Thich Quang Do and Thich Tue Sy—were released from detention; however, the release of at least two of the dissidents was reported to be dependent upon their immediate exile from Viet Nam. In October amnesty was granted to a further 2,630 prisoners. Also in October, the former Editor-in-Chief of *Doanh Nghiep*, Nguyen Hoang Linh, was convicted of 'abusing freedom and democratic rights to violate the interests of the State', following the publication in his newspaper of articles detailing alleged government corruption; Nguyen Hoang Linh was sentenced to more than 12 months' imprisonment, but was released almost immediately as his sentence represented the exact time he had served in detention while awaiting trial. In October the Special Rapporteur on religious intolerance of the UN Commission on Human Rights, Abdelfattah Amor, visited Viet Nam to investigate assertions made by the Vietnamese authorities that greater freedom of religious expression was being afforded in the country. However, at the end of his visit, Amor stated that his investigation had been obstructed by government officials and that he had been prevented from meeting key religious dissidents.

In January 1999 the leadership of the Communist Party announced that it had expelled Gen. (retd) Tran Do from the party in response to his explicit criticism of the establishment. His expulsion caused renewed speculation about party divisions, and also set the precedent for the continued suppression of political dissent. In March the prominent writer and geophysicist, Nguyen Thanh Giang, whose critiques of the Communist Party were reported to have been widely disseminated both within Viet Nam and abroad, was arrested on the grounds of 'propagandizing against the socialist regime'; he was released in May, but reportedly remained under house arrest. In September the trial opened of 24 members of the dissident People's Action Party, charged with 'exiting the country illegally for the purpose of undermining the people's administration'; all 24 defendants were subsequently convicted and sentenced to terms of imprisonment ranging from two to 20 years. Prior to the trial Le Kha Phieu, speaking at the Seventh Plenum of the Eighth Party Central Committee in August, had emphasized the Communist Party's opposition to political pluralism.

In 1999 the issue of corruption remained a major source of concern for the Communist Party. The trial of 74 people accused of smuggling (more than one-half of whom were reported to be former government officials) opened in March, with two of the defendants being subsequently sentenced to death, and the remainder to terms of imprisonment. In May 77 businessmen, bankers and government officials appeared in court charged with the fraudulent procurement of state loans; in August six of the defendants were sentenced to death (although two of these subsequently had their sentences commuted to life imprisonment), and the remainder to various terms of imprisonment. In December, in a further demonstration of the efforts of the Communist Party to address corruption, Deputy Prime Minister Ngo Xuan Loc was dismissed from the Cabinet following his implication in a corrupt land deal related to a private sector project. However, in April 2000 he was reinstated to a government post and resumed responsibility for the sectors connected to the initial accusations against him, thus attracting speculation as to the extent of the Government's attempts to eliminate corruption. In September 2001 eight officials were tried on charges of fraud in Hanoi in connection with the land deal. One businessman received a 20-year prison sentence; the remaining defendants were either released or sentenced to prison terms of nine months or less.

In October 2000 the Politburo issued orders to develop the country's information technology (IT) capabilities and raise them to a level comparable to other countries in the region by 2010. The order emphasized the application of IT for the development of economics, culture and society, along with defence and security. Also in October the Ministry of Public Security announced a nation-wide campaign against the use of illicit drugs. In November Communist Party documents divulged to the US-based human rights group Freedom House emphasized the leadership's level of concern regarding the increasing number of ethnic minorities converting to Christianity, and the fear that religion would be used by the USA and other countries to undermine communism in Viet Nam. In December the Minister of National Defence, Lt-Gen. Pham Van Tra, instructed the army not to become depoliticized, and to remain vigilant and safeguard the Communist Party and the socialist system.

Ethnic violence broke out in the Central Highland provinces of Gia Lai and Dak Lak in February 2001, as local hill minorities (known as Montagnards) protested against perceived injustices caused by the migration of ethnic Vietnamese from the densely populated coastal regions and by the deforestation resulting from the establishment of coffee plantations. Some 5,000 protesters in the provincial capitals of Pleiku and Buon Ma Thuot respectively attacked state offices and blocked roads. The Vietnamese authorities deployed troops, riot police, water cannon and helicopters to quell the unrest, and injuries were reported on both sides. Some 20 people were arrested in connection with instigating the violence, which was attributed to 'extremists' seeking to use religion to foment unrest. The protesters had demanded autonomy, freedom to practise their Protestant religion, the return of ancestral lands confiscated for use as coffee plantations and the right to preserve their traditional way of life. The Ministry of Public Security accused the US-based Montagnard Foundation of organizing the violence, stating that several of those arrested were former members of the United Front for the Liberation of Oppressed Races (FULRO), a guerrilla unit that had close ties to the US military and Central Intelligence Agency (CIA) during the Viet Nam war. The Vietnamese authorities also stated that during 2000 there had been several incursions into the country by agents of Free Viet Nam, a movement based in Thailand. The unrest coincided with a climate of increasing repression of religion, and it was feared that 'hardliners' in the Communist Party might use the incident to strengthen their position and to delay economic and political reforms. In March the authorities denounced a Catholic priest, Nguyen Van Ly, for writing to the US Congress and urging it not to ratify a bilateral trade agreement, owing to human rights abuses in Viet Nam. In October Nguyen Van Ly was sentenced to 15 years in prison after a court convicted him of undermining national unity and contravening a detention order. (His sentence was reduced by five years in July 2003 and by a further five years in June 2004, and in February 2005 he was released from prison, having been granted amnesty. However, he was imprisoned again in March 2007—see below.) Exiled Vietnamese Buddhist leaders also claimed that their followers in Viet Nam were routinely harassed. In September 2001 Ho Tan Anh, leader of the Buddhist Youth Movement, burnt himself to death in protest at the restrictions that had been imposed upon his organization.

The Ninth Party Congress was held in April 2001, and resulted in the election of a new 150-member Central Committee, 15-member Politburo and nine-member Secretariat. Nong Duc Manh was appointed General Secretary, replacing Le Kha Phieu, who was accused of using military intelligence against party members and of slowing the pace of reforms. Phieu had agreed to step down under pressure from the Central Committee. Nong Duc Manh, who was rumoured to be the illegitimate son of Ho Chi Minh, was the first ethnic Tay to attain such a senior position. Some 84 members of the previous Central Committee were re-elected. President Tran Duc Luong and Prime Minister Phan Van Khai retained their party posts, but former President Le Duc Anh, former Prime Minister Vo Van Kiet and former General Secretary Do Muoi lost their positions as senior advisers to the Central Committee upon the abolition of the posts. Manh was believed to favour economic reforms and greater democracy, the latter a major theme at the Congress. However, the Congress reiterated its commitment to socialism as a means to national industrialization and modernization. In June 2001 Nguyen Van An, a member of the Politburo, was elected to the chairmanship of the National Assembly, succeeding Nong Duc Manh.

In September 2001 14 Montagnards received sentences of between six and 12 years' imprisonment for participating in the protests of February of that year. In October a further six men were convicted of distributing propaganda and inciting ethnic unrest in the city of Buon Ma Thuot during the disturbances. A critical report issued by the international organization Human Rights Watch in April 2002 warned of further violence in the Central Highlands if the Government continued to implement its repressive policies towards ethnic minorities. In November 2002 it was alleged that the Government had executed three Montagnards in the previous month, reportedly owing to their involvement in the violence of February 2001. In December a further eight people were convicted of charges of undermining national unity, having allegedly aided people attempting to leave the region following the violence. In January 2003, according to Human Rights Watch, 70 Montagnards were known to be imprisoned in Viet Nam owing to their political or religious beliefs. In April a report issued by Human Rights Watch claimed that government persecution of the Montagnards had escalated since January. In May 15 Montagnards were convicted of causing social disorder during the protests of February 2001 and sentenced to lengthy prison terms. In April 2004 Human Rights Watch again accused the Vietnamese Government of repression, following reports that a rally held by Montagnards in that month in Dak Lak province, in protest against land confiscation and religious persecution, had been violently suppressed by government officials. Human Rights Watch claimed that at least 10 Montagnards had been killed, although the Vietnamese Government insisted that only two people had died. In May Human Rights Watch reported that the Vietnamese authorities had arrested a number of Montagnard church leaders, as well as Montagnards with relatives in the USA. In August nine Montagnards, who were alleged to be former members of the FULRO, were convicted of fomenting disorder and undermining national unity during the demonstrations of February 2001 and thereafter. They were sentenced to prison terms of between five and 12 years.

In December 2001 the National Assembly gave its approval to several constitutional amendments, including one allowing politicians to instigate mid-term votes of no confidence if they considered any minister to be performing unsatisfactorily. The amendments were intended to encourage the development of Viet Nam's market economy and improve democracy, thus facilitating the country's further integration into the international community.

It was reported in January 2002 that the Communist Party had passed a decree authorizing the police to engage in the destruction of publications that had not been approved by the party. Books written by several leading dissidents, including Gen. Tran Do, had subsequently been destroyed. In March the Politburo was reported to have established a special investigation into allegations that more than 50 government officials had colluded in organized crime. Several of those accused were reported to have accepted bribes to protect a gang whose alleged leader, Truong Van Cam, also known as Nam Cam, was undergoing investigation on murder charges. As the investigation continued, more than 100 government officials and an estimated 50 police officers were implicated; two members of the Central Committee (the Director-General of the state radio station Voice of Viet Nam, Tran Mai Hanh, and Pham Sy Chien) were expelled from the Communist Party in July owing to their involvement. In November the Deputy Minister of Public Security, Maj.-Gen. Haong Ngoc Nhat, was dismissed from his position and demoted in rank, owing to his alleged complicity. In January 2003 the director of the Economic Commission of the Politburo, Truong Tan San, became the most senior member of the Communist Party to be punished in relation to the investigation; he was formally reprimanded for 'dereliction of duty' during his tenure as secretary of the party in Ho Chi Minh City in 1996–2000.

Meanwhile, in March 2002 the Communist Party decided that it would formally permit its members to engage in private business, indicating the Government's desire to encourage the expansion of the role of the private sector within the economy. In April 59 people went on trial in Ho Chi Minh City charged with embezzling state assets and violating commercial law in connection with the Chinese-owned Viet Hoa bank. In the following month all those tried were found guilty of the charges against them; 43 were sentenced to prison terms of varying lengths, while those remaining were given suspended sentences. The trial was widely perceived to constitute a further attempt on the part of the Government to take firm action against corruption.

Elections to the 11th National Assembly took place on 19 May 2002. The 498 seats available were contested by 759 candidates, only 13 of whom were independent. Non-Communist Party candidates won 51 seats and independents two, the remainder being secured by party members. In July and August the newly elected National Assembly held its first session, during which significant reorganizations of both the Standing Committee and the Cabinet were approved. Three new ministries were created during the extensive reorganization, in which Vu Khoan, the former Minister of Trade, was promoted to the position of Deputy Prime Minister. President Tran Duc Luong, Prime Minister Phan Van Khai and the Chairman of the National Assembly, Nguyen Van An, were all formally re-elected to their posts, while Truong My Hoa succeeded Nguyen Thi Binh as Vice-President.

In November 2002 Le Chi Quang, a lawyer, was convicted of committing 'acts of propaganda' against the State, after allegedly publishing material critical of the Government on the internet. He was sentenced to a four-year prison term (but was released early, in June 2004, to serve a three-year term of house arrest). In December 2002 another dissident, Nguyen Khac Toan, was sentenced to 12 years in prison, having been convicted of using the internet for espionage purposes; he was subsequently granted amnesty and released in January 2006. In March 2003 the dissident Nguyen Dan Que, who had spent over 18 years in prison for campaigning for improved democracy and human rights in Viet Nam and had been freed five years previously, was arrested again after publishing an essay on the internet concerning Viet Nam's control of the media. In July 2004 he was sentenced to a 30-month prison term, but was granted amnesty and released in February 2005, one of an estimated 12 political or religious prisoners to be granted early release during the course of that year. Meanwhile, at the Seventh Plenum of the Central Committee of the Communist Party held in January 2003, a resolution was passed intended to increase the Party's control over religious affairs. At the Plenum Nguyen Van Chi was appointed to the Party Secretariat.

In February 2003 the trial of Nam Cam and 154 other defendants on a number of charges, including murder, organized gambling, bribery, drugs-trafficking and extortion, began in Ho Chi Minh City. Among the defendants were 21 former state and government officials. The hearings constituted Viet Nam's largest corruption trial to date. In June Nam Cam was convicted of all the charges against him and sentenced to death. In the same month many more defendants in the trial were convicted of the charges against them, including Tran Mai Hanh, who received a 10-year prison term, and Pham Sy Chien, who was to serve a six-year sentence. Five other defendants were given death sentences. In June 2004 Nam Cam and four of his co-defendants were executed by firing squad, the death sentence of the fifth having been commuted to life imprisonment.

In April 2003 Prime Minister Phan Van Khai held talks with Thich Huyen Quang, leader of the anti-Government Unified Buddhist Church of Viet Nam, who had been held under house arrest since the group was proscribed almost 20 years previously. While the meeting was welcomed by international diplomats, there was speculation that the Communist Party might use it to respond to continued criticism of its human rights record, while avoiding making any more substantial reforms. In May Thich Huyen Quang was permitted to meet with his deputy, Thich Quang Do, for only the third time in 21 years. In June Thich Quang Do was released from house arrest, two months before the end of his two-year sentence. In the same month, however, Pham Hong Son, a doctor, was sentenced to a 13-year prison term, to be followed by three years of house arrest, having been found guilty of charges of espionage and disseminating false information about the State on the internet. The Government later reduced the length of his prison sentence to five years. In October a one-day 'stand-off' was reported to have taken place in Binh Dinh province between government security forces and supporters of the Unified Buddhist Church of Viet Nam, following an attempt by Thich Huyen Quang and Thich Quang Do to depart for Ho Chi Minh City. In November both the US House of Representatives and the European Parliament approved resolutions condemning the continuing official repression of non-recognized religious organizations in Viet Nam and calling for the release of Thich Huyen Quang.

In November 2003 the trial opened in Hanoi of two former junior agriculture ministers, Nguyen Thien Luan and Nguyen Quang Ha, together with La Thi Kim Oanh, the former director of a company controlled by the Ministry of Agriculture and Rural Development, and five other officials, on embezzlement charges. The opening of the trial was televised as part of the Government's ongoing campaign to combat corruption. In December all those tried were found guilty of the charges against them. La Thi Kim Oanh was sentenced to death, while the remaining defendants received prison sentences of various lengths. Meanwhile, in the same month former journalist Nguyen Vu Binh was sentenced to a seven-year prison term, having been convicted of espionage charges. (Nguyen Vu Binh was granted a presidential amnesty in June 2007, shortly before a visit by the Vietnamese President to the USA, which had pressed for the dissident's release.) In June 2004 the National Assembly approved the dismissal of the Minister of Agriculture and Development, Le Huy Ngo, on the grounds that he had failed adequately to monitor his subordinates and organizations under his administration in connection with the embezzlement case; he was replaced by Cao Duc Phat.

In March 2004 police arrested four members of the Mennonite Church, which was not officially recognized by the Government, after scuffles broke out when a number of Mennonites attempted to photograph police officers who were posted outside the headquarters of the Church. In June Nguyen Hong Quang, the Secretary-General of the Mennonite Church in Viet Nam, was also arrested for his involvement in the incident, and a sixth church member was detained the following month. In November Quang was sentenced to three years' imprisonment for preventing officials from carrying out their duties, while the five other defendants received custodial sentences of between nine months and two years.

Two veteran dissidents, Tran Van Khue, a retired academic, and Pham Que Duong, a military historian, were sentenced to 19 months' imprisonment in July 2004, having been convicted of abusing democratic freedoms to undermine the interests of the State. Both men had posted articles critical of the Government on the internet. However, they were released at the end of the month, as they had been in detention since December 2002. In late July 2004 the Minister of Posts and Telecommunications, Do Trung Ta, issued new regulations aimed at controlling access to the internet by allowing internet service providers to suspend contracts with cafés that allowed customers to view pornographic websites or those deemed to threaten national security. In the following month a special police unit was established to combat internet crime and prevent the spread of banned materials.

Also in July 2004 the President promulgated an Ordinance on Beliefs and Religions, which came into effect in November. A coalition of non-recognized Protestant churches condemned the new law, which, while upholding the right of citizens to freedom of religious belief, decreed that only state-authorized clergy be entitled to preach and only within defined territorial jurisdictions. The ordinance also provided for the suspension of religious activities that were deemed to jeopardize national security, public order or national unity. In February 2005 it was reported that the Government had issued a decree allowing outlawed Protestant churches to operate if they renounced connections to the FULRO.

Details emerged in September 2004 of a major corruption scandal in which local textile companies had been allegedly obliged to pay large bribes to trade officials in order to secure export quotas to the USA. Some 19 people were subsequently arrested in connection with the case; the most prominent of these was Deputy Minister of Trade Mai Van Dau, who was charged with abuse of power and dismissed from the Government in November. Mai Van Dau's trial was conducted in March 2007: the former Deputy Minister of Trade was convicted of receiving bribes and sentenced to 14 years' imprisonment, while 12 other defendants received sentences ranging from one year to 17 years; Mai Van Dau's sentence was reduced to 12 years in June. Meanwhile, in October 2004 Prime Minister Phan Van Khai announced plans to establish an anti-corruption agency. In November the National Assembly approved new legislation on national security, which stipulated the principles of security policy and the powers and responsibilities of the agencies in charge of national security.

In December 2004 two retired state physicists, Tran Van Luong and Nguyen Thi Minh Hoan, were sentenced, respectively, to 21 months' and eight months' imprisonment for sending to state agencies documents and petitions that were critical of the Government and the Communist Party. In January 2005 the Government announced that 8,323 prisoners, including six political dissidents and 33 foreigners, were to be released in an amnesty to mark Tet (the lunar New Year). In March the Government issued a decree aimed at tightening control over demonstrations and banning unauthorized gatherings. It was reported that the decree required the approval in advance of all gatherings not organized by the Communist Party or state organs.

It was reported in June 2005 that, according to the Ministry of Public Security, 176,534 economic crimes had been exposed in the 12 previous years; 9,960 of those were said to be related to corruption. In November the National Assembly ratified a long-awaited Anti-Corruption Law, the terms of which required all officials, and their close relatives, to disclose fully their assets. There was considerable scepticism as to how effectively this would be enforced, especially in view of the protection given to the authorities by state control of the media. In the previous month the deputy head of the State Inspectorate's department of economic inspection, Luong Cao Khai, was arrested amid claims that he had accepted bribes and had abused his position to provide relatives with employment; in November 2007 he was convicted of the charges against him and sentenced to 21 years' imprisonment, while two other former senior officials from the State Inspectorate received shorter custodial terms for accepting bribes.

In April 2006 the Minister of Transport and Communications, Dao Dinh Binh, tendered his resignation from the Cabinet, following allegations concerning an apparent misappropriation of state funds by staff members within his ministry. It was claimed that officials had stolen money allocated to construction projects and had accepted numerous bribes. Binh announced that he would accept full responsibility for the actions of those employed in his ministry. The Deputy Minister of Transport and Communications, Nguyen Viet Tien, was arrested in connection with the embezzlement of state funds. In August 2007 eight people were sentenced to between seven and 13 years' imprisonment for their involvement in the scandal, while a ninth defendant received a suspended two-year term. Criminal charges against Nguyen Viet Tien were withdrawn in March 2008.

The 10th Communist Party Congress was held in late April 2006, during which elections were held for a new 160-member Central Committee, 14-member Politburo and eight-member Secretariat. Nong Duc Manh was retained as General Secretary of the Party; five other members of the previous Politburo also secured re-election. President Tran Duc Luong, Prime Minister Phan Van Khai and Chairman of the National Assembly Standing Committee, Nguyen Van An, all announced that they were to resign, thus preparing the way for a younger generation of officials to assume prominent positions within the party leadership. The Congress reaffirmed its commitment to socialism, announced its aim of Viet Nam achieving the status of a developed country by 2020 and adopted the Report and Five-Year Plan of Action on Socio-economic Development Goals for 2006–10; the issue of corruption within the party was also given considerable focus, with General Secretary Manh vowing in his opening speech to 'intensify' the fight against it. In June 2006, at its annual session, the National Assembly formally approved the resignations of Tran Duc Luong, Phan Van Khai and Nguyen Van An. Phan Van Kai's nominee, Nguyen Tan Dung, was confirmed as Prime Minister, while Nguyen Minh Triet succeeded Tran Duc Luong as President. Nguyen Phu Trong was elected Chairman of the National Assembly Standing Committee. Soon after, a cabinet reorganization was approved: Minister of Finance Nguyen Sinh Hung, who had been promoted to the position of Deputy Prime Minister, was replaced by Vu Van Ninh, while another Deputy Prime Minister, Pham Gia Khiem, took additional charge of the foreign affairs portfolio. Among the new appointees were Truong Vinh Trong as Deputy Prime Minister and Lt-Gen. Phung Quang Thanh as Minister of National Defence (to replace Lt-Gen. Pham Van Tra following his retirement); however, several other ministers retained their portfolios. Vu Khoan, who had retired from the post of Deputy Prime Minister, was later appointed as the Prime Minister's special envoy for foreign affairs.

At the end of June 2006 the new Prime Minister's decision to waive possible disciplinary action against the retiring former Minister of Transport and Communications, Dao Dinh Binh, encountered significant, although unsuccessful, opposition within the National Assembly. In October it appeared that the campaign against corruption was progressing, with the establishment of the Central Steering Committee for Corruption Prevention and Control, chaired by Nguyen Tan Dung. The committee, which was created to oversee and co-ordinate national anti-corruption operations, would have the power to suspend government officials for unlawful practices. In the following month the Government was reported to have established a department to address the issue of corruption, as part of the General Directorate of Police, with links to the Ministry of Public Security. In late January 2007 a Communist Party Central Committee plan for partial privatization was announced, with the military and the party projected to relinquish ownership of several businesses; however, the details of the programme were yet to be revealed. Earlier in the month a list of state companies due to sell shares to the public (with the Government remaining majority shareholder) by 2010, including Viet Nam Airlines, had been authorized by the Prime Minister.

Meanwhile, in August 2006 Pham Hong Son (see above) was one of thousands of prisoners freed under an amnesty to commemorate National Day in the following month. In November seven people, three of them US nationals, were convicted on terrorism charges and sentenced to 15 months' imprisonment. In the same month the USA's decision to remove Viet Nam from its list of 'countries of particular concern' in relation to religious freedom provoked criticism from Thich Quang Do. Although the decision recognized the country's progress towards greater religious freedom, reports of cases against dissidents continued: in March 2007 a Catholic priest, Father Nguyen Van Ly, was convicted of disseminating information against the State and sentenced to eight years' imprisonment. None the less, relations between the Vietnamese Government and the Roman Catholic Church were improving. In January 2007 Nguyen Tan Dung became the first Vietnamese Prime Minister to visit the Vatican, where he held talks with Pope Benedict XVI, and in March a delegation from the Vatican visited Viet Nam to discuss the possibility of establishing full diplomatic relations. Moreover, during 2007 the Government's Committee for Religious Affairs granted operating licences to several additional religions, including the Mennonite Church, the Baptist Church and the Bahá'í faith.

Elections to the 12th National Assembly held on 20 May 2007 were contested by 875 candidates, including 30 independents. Of the 493 deputies elected, only one was an independent, while a further 42 were non-Communist Party members. A high turn-out, of 99.6%, was recorded. Earlier that month several political dissidents were convicted of spreading propaganda intended to undermine the State. Le Nguyen Sang, Nguyen Bac Truyen, Huynh Nguyen Dao and Tran Quoc Hien received prison terms ranging from three to five years in Ho Chi Minh City, while the Hanoi People's Court sentenced two human rights lawyers, Nguyen Van Dai and Le Thi Cong Nhan, to terms of five years and four years, respectively.

The first session of the newly elected National Assembly commenced in July 2007. Nguyen Minh Triet, Nguyen Tan Dung and Nguyen Phu Trong were all re-elected to their respective positions as President, Prime Minister and Chairman of the National Assembly Standing Committee, while Nguyen Thi Doan succeeded Truong My Hoa as Vice-President. In early August the National Assembly endorsed a cabinet reorganization, which included a reduction in the number of ministries from 26 to 22 and the appointment of Hoang Trung Hai and Nguyen Thien Nhan, both relatively young and with economic backgrounds, as additional Deputy Prime Ministers (joining Nguyen Sinh Hung, Pham Gia Khiem and Truong Vinh Trong), with Nhan also remaining Minister of Education and Training. The incumbent Ministers of National Defence, Public Security, Finance and Foreign Affairs all remained in the Cabinet, while new appointees were allocated responsibility for some of the less strategic portfolios. A reduction in the term of the 12th National Assembly from five years to four years was also approved. Meanwhile, hundreds of peasant farmers from the Mekong River Delta protested in Ho Chi Minh City in July against the seizure of their land and alleged abuse of legislation on land usage by local government officials; a smaller demonstration also took place in Hanoi. Deputy Prime Minister Truong Vinh Trong urged local leaders to conduct a swift investigation into the farmers' complaints.

Six political activists, including one French, one Thai and two US nationals, were arrested in Ho Chi Minh City in November 2007, reportedly after participating in pro-democracy discussions. The US and French citizens were members of the US-based Viet Tan (Vietnam Reform Party), which stated that its aim was to promote democratic reform in Viet Nam through peaceful means, although it was described as a terrorist organization by the Vietnamese state media. Six days later two other US nationals were detained for allegedly attempting to enter Viet Nam with a firearm; Viet Tan denied any link to them. They were freed in mid-December, as were the French citizen and one of the two US members of Viet Tan, following international demands for their release, although the others remained in detention. Meanwhile, rising inflation provoked labour unrest in late 2007 and early 2008, with large increases in food prices of particular concern.

By the end of 1976, meanwhile, Viet Nam had established diplomatic relations with many countries, including all of its South-East Asian neighbours. However, tension arose over the growing number of Vietnamese refugees (particularly ethnic Chinese) arriving in Thailand and other nearby countries. In 1979 more than 200,000 fled Viet Nam, and in July an international conference was convened in Geneva to discuss the situation. The Orderly Departure Programme, sponsored by the office of the UN High Commissioner for Refugees (UNHCR, see p. 66), whereby Viet Nam agreed to legal departures, was negotiated, and by the end of 1988 about 140,000 people had left the country in this way. However, illegal departures continued, and the increasing reluctance of Western countries to provide resettlement opportunities led to a meeting in Malaysia in March 1989, at which representatives of 30 nations were present and a comprehensive programme of action was drafted. Members of the Association of South East Asian Nations (ASEAN, see p. 185) subsequently ceased to accept refugees for automatic resettlement and planned to institute a screening procedure to distinguish genuine refugees from economic migrants. A similar procedure had been in effect since June 1988 in Hong Kong, and an agreement had been signed in November, whereby Viet Nam agreed to accept voluntary repatriation of refugees from Hong Kong, funded by UNHCR and the United Kingdom, with UN supervision to protect the returning refugees from punitive measures by the Vietnamese Government.

In June 1989 a UN-sponsored conference adopted the so-called Comprehensive Action Plan that had been drafted in March, introducing the desired screening procedures to distinguish political refugees from economic migrants (who might be forcibly repatriated if efforts to secure their voluntary return proved unsuccessful). In December the United Kingdom forcibly repatriated a group of 51 Vietnamese from Hong Kong, provoking international criticism; this policy was abandoned as a result both of opposition by the USA and of Viet Nam's refusal to accept further deportations. In July 1990, however, the USA accepted in principle the 'involuntary' repatriation of refugees classed as economic migrants who did not actively oppose deportation. In September the United Kingdom, Viet Nam and UNHCR reached an agreement whereby the Vietnamese Government would no longer refuse refugees who had been repatriated 'involuntarily'. In May 1992 the United Kingdom and Viet Nam signed an agreement providing for the compulsory repatriation of all economic migrants from Hong Kong. In 1991–95 some 66,132 Vietnamese were voluntarily repatriated, while an additional 1,562 were forcibly returned. In January 1996 ASEAN member states, including Viet Nam (see below), agreed that all Vietnamese residing in South-East Asian refugee camps (apart from those in Hong Kong) would be repatriated by the end of June of that year. (China had already indicated that all Vietnamese refugees in Hong Kong should be returned prior to the transfer of the territory to Chinese sovereignty in June 1997.) In March 1996 UNHCR announced that it would suspend funding of Vietnamese refugee camps from the end of June. In April a new initiative, proposed by the US Government in an effort to accelerate the repatriation programme, whereby refugees who returned to Viet Nam would be eligible to apply for settlement in the USA under a new screening process, was received with caution by the Vietnamese authorities. By February 1997 Malaysia, Singapore, Indonesia and Thailand had closed their camps, following the repatriation of all Vietnamese refugees from those countries, leaving Hong Kong as the only South-East Asian country with a significant number (12,000 in November 1996). In December 1996 repatriates were prohibited from engaging in any type of political activity, and from January 1997 anti-communist activists and critics of the Government were banned from returning to Viet Nam. In mid-June the main Vietnamese detention centre in Hong Kong was closed. However, the scheduled repatriation of all remaining Vietnamese (estimated at some 1,600 people qualifying as refugees and 700 non-refugees) before the end of the month was not achieved. In July 1999 Hong Kong announced that the Vietnamese who remained in the territory—estimated to number around 1,400, some classed as refugees, others as 'stateless' persons—would be given permanent residency in Hong Kong; the last remaining camp for Vietnamese refugees in Hong Kong was closed in May 2000.

Following the unrest in the Central Highlands in February 2001 (see above), many Montagnards fled over the border into Cambodia, where they were accommodated in two camps situated in the provinces of Mondol Kiri and Rotanak Kiri. By December the camps housed 805 refugees, who sought a supervised return to the Highlands, accompanied by a guarantee that they would be given permission to reoccupy their ancestral lands. In January 2002 Viet Nam and Cambodia signed a joint repatriation agreement with UNHCR, and in February 15 refugees left the camps to return to their home in Kon Tum province. Later in the same month the Vietnamese Government criticized UNHCR for the delay in the repatriation of the refugees (of whom there were now more than 1,000). It had imposed a deadline of 30 April 2002 for the completion of the repatriation process. The programme was later suspended, as UNHCR claimed that by imposing the deadline the Government was undermining the voluntary nature of returns. In March 2002 UNHCR announced its withdrawal from the agreement, owing to the frequent intimidation of both refugees and UN staff at the camps. Its decision was precipitated by an incident in which more than 400 Vietnamese had crossed the border with Cambodia and threatened inmates and staff at the Mondol Kiri camp. Following the termination of the agreement, the US Government stated that it was prepared to offer asylum to the refugees who remained in Cambodia. The Cambodian Government announced in April that, while it would authorize the resettlement of the Montagnard refugees in the USA, it planned to close down the camps housing the refugees and cease its provision of asylum within one month. In April 2003 the Cambodian Government also announced its intention to shut the refugee transit centre operated by UNHCR in Phnom-Penh as soon as the remaining refugees housed there had been resettled. Following the repression of a protest rally in the Central Highland province of Dak Lak in April 2004 (see above), there was a further influx of Montagnards into Cambodia. In January 2005 UNHCR and the Governments of Cambodia and Viet Nam signed an agreement on the resettlement to third countries or the repatriation to Viet Nam of some 750 Montagnards in Cambodia. The Vietnamese Government guaranteed that returnees would not be punished, discriminated against or prosecuted for their departure. In March the first group of 43 Montagnards who had opted for repatriation returned to Viet Nam; by that time a further 297 had decided to accept resettlement in third countries, including the USA, Finland and Canada. The Cambodian Government insisted that it would not allow the Montagnards to remain in Cambodia.

Relations with Kampuchea (known as Cambodia until 1976 and again from 1989) deteriorated during 1977, and in December Viet Nam launched a major offensive into eastern Kampuchea. Sporadic fighting continued, and in December 1978 Viet Nam invaded Kampuchea in support of elements opposed to the regime of the Khmers Rouges (see the chapter on Cambodia). By January 1979 the Government of Pol Pot had been overthrown and a pro-Vietnamese regime was installed. The invasion prompted much international criticism, and in February 1979 Chinese forces launched a punitive attack across the border into Viet Nam. Peace talks began in April but made little progress, and in March 1980 they were suspended by China. In March 1983 Viet Nam rejected a five-point peace plan, proposed by China, aimed at resolving the dispute over Kampuchea. In 1984 Chinese and Vietnamese troops engaged in heavy fighting, accusing each other of persistent border violations. China refused to normalize relations with Viet Nam until the withdrawal of Vietnamese troops from Kampuchea. Throughout 1986 and 1987 further armed clashes between Vietnamese and Chinese soldiers occurred on the Sino-Vietnamese border. Both sides denied responsibility for initiating the attacks. In early 1988 the tension between the two countries was exacerbated by the re-emergence of conflict over the Spratly Islands in the South China Sea, when the Vietnamese Government alleged that China had dispatched warships to the islands. (For many years the sovereignty of the islands had been contested, not only by Viet Nam and China, which engaged in military conflict over the issue in 1974, but also by the neighbouring states of Brunei, Malaysia, the Philippines and Taiwan.)

In March 1984 Viet Nam agreed in principle that it would eventually withdraw its troops from Kampuchea, and in August 1985 it was announced that all Vietnamese troops would be withdrawn by 1990. An eight-point peace plan, proposed by Kampuchean resistance leaders in March 1986 (involving the installation of a quadripartite government in Kampuchea, to be followed by UN-supervised elections), was rejected by Viet Nam. Viet Nam's urgent need of Western aid, together with increasing pressure from the USSR, prompted an announcement in May 1988 that Viet Nam would withdraw 50,000 (of an estimated total of 100,000) troops from Kampuchea by the end of the year.

The Vietnamese military high command left Kampuchea in June, placing the remainder of the Vietnamese forces under Kampuchean control.

In April 1989 the Vietnamese Government and the Heng Samrin regime in Kampuchea declared that Vietnamese troops would withdraw by September even if a political settlement had not been reached, on condition that military assistance to the three other Kampuchean factions also ceased by that date. China responded that it would halt military aid to the Khmers Rouges only after a complete withdrawal of Vietnamese troops had been verified. The Vietnamese Government claimed that the withdrawal of troops had been completed by the end of September. However, the absence of a UN commission to verify the troops' departure led to claims by the Government-in-exile of Democratic Kampuchea that a number of troops remained in the country, while China, the ASEAN countries and the USA initially refused to recognize the alleged withdrawal. In July 1990 the USA finally acknowledged that all troops had been withdrawn.

In September 1990 secret negotiations took place between Viet Nam and China, during which the Vietnamese endorsed a new UN Security Council agreement to resolve the conflict in Cambodia (q.v.). It was widely believed that the Chinese had promised an improvement in Sino-Vietnamese relations in exchange for Vietnamese support for the UN plan. In October 1991 Viet Nam was a signatory to a peace agreement whereby an interim Supreme National Council was established in Cambodia, representing all four factions there, as a prelude to the holding of UN-supervised elections. The agreement allowed immediate progress towards ending Viet Nam's diplomatic and economic isolation (see below). During 1992–93 there were several massacres of civilians of Vietnamese origin living in Cambodia. In January 1995 the First Prime Minister of Cambodia, Prince Norodom Ranariddh, visited Viet Nam for discussions. In November of that year Viet Nam accused the Cambodian Government of supporting a dissident Vietnamese movement, based in Phnom-Penh. In January 1996 it was reported that Cambodian troops had opened fire in a southern border area; Cambodia subsequently claimed that Vietnamese forces had made incursions into Cambodian territory. Discussions between Vietnamese and Cambodian government officials on the border issue took place in April and May. In March 1997 Viet Nam and Cambodia signed an agreement on bilateral co-operation in combating crime and, during 2000, security officials from the two countries signed a number of agreements aimed at combating drugs-trafficking and strengthening border controls. In November 2005 Viet Nam and Cambodia signed a supplementary border treaty to an existing one concluded in 1985; under the new agreement, the demarcation of the border between the two countries was to be finalized by the end of 2008.

From the mid-1970s Viet Nam developed closer relations with the USSR, and became increasingly dependent on its support. In 1990–91 the USSR substantially reduced financial assistance to Viet Nam. After the dissolution of the USSR, the Vietnamese Government pursued close relations with its successor states. In June 1994 Vo Van Kiet visited Ukraine, Kazakhstan and Russia to discuss economic and defence co-operation issues. During a visit by the Russian Minister of Foreign Affairs in July 1995, it was agreed that Russian vessels would continue to use the former Soviet naval base at Cam Ranh Bay, in central Viet Nam. In February 1997 Russia announced plans further to develop its defence ties with Viet Nam, and in November of that year the Russian Prime Minister, Viktor Chernomyrdin, paid an official visit to Viet Nam; Tran Duc Luong made a reciprocal visit to Russia in August 1998. The Russian Deputy Prime Minister, Viktor Khristenko, visited Viet Nam in July 2000 to discuss Russian involvement in oil and gas development, and Viet Nam's outstanding 11,000m. rouble Soviet-era debt. Agreement on the latter was reached in September, when it was arranged that Viet Nam would repay Russia US $1,700m. over 23 years, mostly in the form of business concessions. A major concern for Russia was its continued use of the naval base at Cam Ranh Bay. Under a 1978 agreement, Russia was to have access to the facilities until 2004. In February–March 2001 the Russian President, Vladimir Putin, became the first Russian (or Soviet) Head of State to visit Viet Nam. The two countries agreed to strengthen co-operation in economic, energy, and military and defence matters, and proclaimed a new 'strategic partnership'. In May 2002 control of the naval base at Cam Ranh Bay was formally transferred to the Vietnamese Government, two years ahead of the agreed date. President Tran Duc Luong visited Ukraine in April 2000 and pledged to increase bilateral economic and political co-operation. Viet Nam also signed a military co-operation agreement with Ukraine in May. In May 2004 President Tran Duc Luong visited Russia and held talks with President Putin on bilateral relations, focusing particularly on expanding economic co-operation. Both leaders confirmed their commitment to the 'strategic partnership'. In April 2007 Russia and Viet Nam reached agreement in principle on reducing barriers to bilateral trade, and in June the two countries initialled a memorandum of understanding on Russia's bid for accession to the World Trade Organization (WTO, see p. 396), which Viet Nam had joined in January. Trade and investment were also the main areas of discussion during visits by Prime Minister Nguyen Tan Dung to Russia, the Czech Republic and Poland in September.

The collapse of communism in Eastern Europe prompted renewed efforts by Viet Nam to restore political and economic links with China. Relations between Viet Nam and China improved significantly in the second half of 1990, owing to the co-operation of the Vietnamese Government concerning Cambodia. After the conclusion of the Cambodian peace agreement in October 1991, Vo Van Kiet and Do Muoi paid an official visit to China in November, during which normal diplomatic relations were restored and agreements were concluded on trade and on border affairs, while in March 1992 further agreements were signed on the resumption of transport and communications links (severed in 1979), and on the reopening of border posts. In May 1992 Viet Nam protested to China when the latter unilaterally granted exploration rights to a US petroleum company in an area of the South China Sea regarded by Viet Nam as part of its continental shelf. Several more protests were lodged later in the year over the presence of Chinese vessels in disputed areas. In November the Chinese Premier, Li Peng, made an official visit to Viet Nam (the first visit by a Chinese head of government since 1971): new agreements on economic, scientific and cultural co-operation were signed, and the two Governments agreed to accelerate negotiations on disputed territory that had begun in the previous month. In October 1993 Viet Nam and China concluded an agreement to avoid the use of force when resolving territorial disputes. In November 1994 the two countries agreed to co-operate in seeking an early resolution to all border disputes. During an official visit by Do Muoi to China in November 1995, it was agreed that rail links between the two countries would be restored (they were subsequently reopened in February 1996). In April 1996 the state-owned petroleum company, Petrovietnam, signed a joint exploration contract with a US enterprise that covered part of the South China Sea where the Chinese Government had granted exploration rights in May 1992. In May 1996 China agreed to abide by the UN Convention on the Law of the Sea, which provided for international arbitration, but at the same time announced a new delineation of its sea border, attracting criticism from Viet Nam and other nations in the region.

In March 1997 Chinese vessels entered Vietnamese waters around the disputed Spratly Islands and were believed to be carrying out exploratory activities. China defended its actions, declaring a legitimate claim to the territory. In April China agreed to hold talks with Viet Nam over the issue; however, China withdrew the vessels before the discussions took place, stating that its operation in the area had been completed. In May China ratified the opening to traffic of a sea route between north-eastern Viet Nam and China. In July Do Muoi visited China and met with President Jiang Zemin to discuss the development of bilateral relations. In October 1998 Phan Van Khai made an official visit to China, during which it was agreed that Viet Nam and China would increase efforts to reach a settlement on their various border disputes; in November, however, Viet Nam reiterated its territorial claim to the disputed Spratly Islands. In February 1999 Le Kha Phieu paid an official visit to China, and in December the Chinese Premier, Zhu Rongji, visited Viet Nam. Also in December a formal border treaty was signed by Viet Nam and China. Vietnamese leaders travelled to China in June 2000 to attend an ideological symposium on methods of introducing market reforms without incurring any loss of political control. The visit was regarded as a major improvement in bilateral relations, and was followed by a second symposium in Hanoi in November. The two countries also made further progress in delineating their mutual land border, which took effect from July 2000, and finalized their border in the Gulf of Tonkin in late December, the latter agreement demarcating their economic and fishing zones. Chinese military delegations visited Viet Nam in July 2000 and February 2001 to enhance military co-operation, and President Tran Duc Luong visited China in December 2000 and 2001. In February 2002 Chinese President Jiang Zemin paid an official visit to Viet Nam, his second since the restoration of normal bilateral relations in 1991. His visit coincided with campaigns mounted by several dissidents expressing concern over the agreements that had been signed to demarcate the Sino-Vietnamese border. An ongoing dispute over fishing rights in the Gulf of Tonkin prevented the ratification of any agreement to delineate the shared maritime boundary. During the Chinese President's visit modest agreements on technical and economic co-operation were signed, and the framework was agreed for a Chinese loan of US $12m. to Viet Nam. In April 2002 it was reported that the two countries had begun demarcating their land border. In November of that year, following an ASEAN summit meeting attended by China, a declaration was issued outlining a code of conduct to be observed by those countries contesting the Spratly Islands. It was hoped that the agreement would end Viet Nam's dispute with China over the issue. However, China strongly opposed Viet Nam's decision, in March 2004, to allow tourists to visit the Spratly Islands, claiming that the tours infringed its territorial sovereignty. Viet Nam and China accelerated efforts to delineate their border in early 2005, and an 11th round of talks was held on the issue in Hanoi in February and March. In October Viet Nam and China agreed to conduct joint military patrols of the Gulf of Tonkin. Later that month Chinese President Hu Jintao made a three-day state visit to Viet Nam, during which he met with President Tran Duc Luong and General Secretary of the Central Committee of the Communist Party Nong Duc Manh. Bilateral relations were discussed, as were issues of regional and international concern, and both countries pledged to work together to promote mutual trust and encourage further bilateral co-operation. President Nguyen Minh Triet visited China in May 2007, holding talks with Hu Jintao and Premier Wen Jiabao. Several agreements on co-operation were signed during the visit, including nine economic accords. Notably, a joint working group was established to formulate a five-year plan for the further development of economic and trade co-operation between Viet Nam and China. Border issues were also addressed, with Presidents Triet and Hu pledging to complete the demarcation of the land border in 2008 and to accelerate negotiations on the delineation of boundaries in the Gulf of Tonkin. However, the territorial dispute in the South China Sea continued to provoke tensions, and in July 2007 a Chinese naval vessel fired on Vietnamese fishing boats near the Spratly Islands, sinking one boat; one fisherman died in the incident and several others were injured. In late November, moreover, Viet Nam protested after China conducted naval exercises near the Paracel Islands, and in the following month Vietnamese students demonstrated outside China's embassy in Hanoi and its consulate in Ho Chi Minh City, following reports that China was to create a new municipality incorporating the Spratly and Paracel Islands.

In the late 1990s Viet Nam developed closer links with India, ostensibly because of mutual concerns about China. The Indian Minister of Defence visited Viet Nam in March 2000 and signed a wide-ranging defence agreement that would allow Viet Nam to train the Indian army in jungle warfare and counter-insurgency methods, and India to assist in the modernization of the Vietnamese military. The two countries also agreed to take action to combat piracy in the South China Sea. The Indian Minister of External Affairs, Jaswant Singh, and Prime Minister Atal Bihari Vajpayee made separate visits to Viet Nam in November 2000 and January 2001 respectively and agreed to co-ordinate their positions in the Non-Aligned Movement (NAM), South-South Co-operation and regional forums. India's Oil and Natural Gas Company became an investor in Viet Nam's Nam Con Son gas field in 2000, and India pledged some US $238m. of investment in the Vietnamese petroleum and gas industries. In September 2001 the Minister of Foreign Affairs, Nguyen Dy Nien, visited India, and in March 2002 Vice-President Nguyen Thi Binh also visited the country to discuss the possibility of closer bilateral co-operation. Relations were further strengthened in July 2007 by a state visit to India by Prime Minister Nguyen Tan Dung, during which a joint declaration was signed on the establishment of a 'strategic partnership' between India and Viet Nam, covering bilateral co-operation in the areas of politics, the economy, security, defence, culture, science and technology. In March 2008 the Vietnamese Minister of Public Security, Le Hong Anh, and the Indian Minister of Home Affairs, Shivraj Patil, signed a memorandum of understanding on bilateral co-operation in combating international terrorism and drugs-trafficking.

From 1984 Viet Nam indicated that it would welcome a return to normal diplomatic relations with the USA, but the latter rejected any re-establishment of relations until agreements were made concerning the return to the USA of the remains of US soldiers 'missing in action' (MIA) from Viet Nam, and the proposed resettlement in the USA of some 10,000 Vietnamese 'political prisoners'. A number of senior US officials visited Hanoi during 1985 and 1986 for discussions about missing soldiers (estimated to total 1,797), and Viet Nam arranged for the return of some of the remains. In September 1987 the Vietnamese Government agreed to investigate the fate of some 70 soldiers who were believed to have been captured alive, while the US Government, in turn, agreed to facilitate humanitarian aid for Viet Nam from US charities and private groups, which had hitherto been illegal. In July 1988 Viet Nam agreed in principle to the resettlement of former political detainees in the USA or elsewhere. In early 1991 a US representative was stationed in Hanoi to supervise inquiries into MIA, the first official US presence in Viet Nam since 1975. In April 1991 the USA proposed a four-stage programme for the resumption of normal diplomatic relations with Viet Nam, conditional on Vietnamese co-operation in reaching a diplomatic settlement in Cambodia and in accounting for the remaining MIA. Following the conclusion of the peace agreement on Cambodia in October, Viet Nam made a plea for the removal of the US economic embargo, and in November discussions on the establishment of normal trade relations began. In early 1992 the US Government agreed to provide humanitarian aid for Viet Nam, but refused to end the economic embargo, reiterating that relations would not fully return to normal until after the UN-supervised elections in Cambodia, due to take place in early 1993. The embargo was renewed for another year in September 1992, although in December the US Government announced that US companies would now be allowed to open offices and sign contracts in Viet Nam, in anticipation of a future removal of the embargo. In July 1993 the new administration of President Bill Clinton revoked the US veto on assistance from the IMF and the World Bank for Viet Nam. In September the USA permitted US companies to take part in projects in Viet Nam that were financed by international aid agencies. The trade embargo was finally removed in February 1994.

In January 1995 Viet Nam and the USA signed an agreement that permitted the two countries to establish liaison offices in each other's capitals (these were opened immediately), and which resolved a long-standing dispute concerning former US diplomatic properties seized by the Vietnamese authorities in 1975. The establishment of full diplomatic relations was announced in July 1995. In May 1996 Clinton formally ended Viet Nam's official classification as a combat zone. In March 1997 military relations were established between the two countries. In April Douglas Peterson was appointed as the first US ambassador to Viet Nam, and in May Le Van Bang was formally appointed the first Vietnamese ambassador to the USA. In June Madeleine Albright became the first US Secretary of State to visit the country since the end of the Viet Nam war. During a visit to Washington, DC, by the Vietnamese Minister of Planning and Investment, an agreement was signed to promote greater economic co-operation. This was facilitated in March 1998, when Clinton signed a waiver to the 'Jackson-Vanik amendment' to 1974 US trade legislation, which restricted trade with communist countries. (In August 1999 the US House of Representatives voted in favour of an extension of the waiver of the amendment for Viet Nam.) In September 1998 the Vietnamese Deputy Prime Minister and Minister of Foreign Affairs, Nguyen Manh Cam, made an official visit to the USA. In July 1999 Viet Nam and the USA reached agreement in principle on the establishment of normal trade relations. Madeleine Albright made another official visit to Viet Nam in September. In March 2000 the US Secretary of Defense, William Cohen, made the first visit to Viet Nam by a US Secretary of Defense since the end of the Viet Nam war.

Although in early 2000 the US Government continued to refuse to acknowledge the responsibility of the chemical defoliant Agent Orange, sprayed in large quantities over areas of Viet Nam by the USA during the Viet Nam war, for widespread health problems (including birth defects) among the Vietnamese, Cohen, during his visit in March, reportedly indicated that the US Government would be willing to conduct joint research with the Vietnamese Government into the effects of the chemical. In

May the US House of Representatives passed a resolution calling for the release of all political and religious prisoners in Viet Nam, a motion that was criticized as 'impudent interference' by Viet Nam. A landmark bilateral trade agreement between the USA and Viet Nam was signed in Washington, DC, in July 2000, paving the way for an increase in exports to, and investment from, the USA. The agreement was subject to an annual review by the US Congress. US President Bill Clinton made a highly significant visit to Viet Nam in November, the first since a brief stop-over by Richard Nixon in 1969. Although warmly received by the Vietnamese people, Clinton's calls for greater freedoms were rebuffed by General Secretary Le Kha Phieu, who defended the socialist system. In March 2001 Viet Nam accused US-based groups of fomenting the recent unrest in the Central Highlands (see above). In April a helicopter carrying nine Vietnamese and seven US citizens, searching for the remains of MIA, crashed in the highlands, killing all on board. Some 1,498 US servicemen and 300,000 Vietnamese remained unaccounted for in Viet Nam.

Following the September 2001 attacks on the USA (see the chapter on the USA) the Vietnamese Government expressed its support for the US-led war on terrorism. In October the severe penalty imposed on the dissident Roman Catholic priest Father Nguyen Van Ly (see above) accelerated the passage of the Viet Nam Human Rights Act through the US House of Representatives. The act was intended to make US non-humanitarian aid to Viet Nam conditional upon the improvement of its human rights record, thus angering the Vietnamese Government, but was subsequently blocked and never voted on in the Senate. (The act was reintroduced and approved again by the US House of Representatives in July 2004, but subsequently stalled in the Senate. The House of Representatives adopted another version of the act in September 2007.) In November 2001 the National Assembly finally ratified the bilateral trade agreement, marking the complete restoration of normal relations between the two countries. In March 2002 Vietnamese and US scientists attended an unprecedented joint conference in Hanoi, at which the effects of Agent Orange were discussed. As a result, the two countries formally agreed to conduct joint research into the effects of the defoliant. However, relations with the USA threatened to deteriorate once more when the US Government expressed its concern for the safety of refugees returning to the Central Highlands from Cambodia. In March 2002, following the collapse of Viet Nam's agreement with UNHCR, the USA offered asylum to those refugees who remained in Cambodia. In the same month relations were further strained when the US Government issued a critical report on Viet Nam's human rights record.

In early 2003 the Vietnamese Government condemned the US-led campaign to oust the regime of Saddam Hussain in Iraq. However, in November relations improved when Minister of National Defence Lt-Gen. Pham Can Tra visited Washington, DC, and held talks with US Secretary of Defense Donald Rumsfeld. In the same month a US frigate spent four days in the port of Ho Chi Minh City, the first visit to Viet Nam by a US warship since the end of the Viet Nam war in 1975. In December 2003 an aviation agreement was signed with the USA, enabling direct flights between the two countries for the first time; the first US flight arrived in Ho Chi Minh City in December 2004. In February 2004, during a visit to the country, Adm. Thomas Fargo, head of the US Pacific Command, reportedly became the first foreign official to visit the naval base at Da Nang. Meanwhile, an independent organization, the Vietnam Association for Victims of Agent Orange, submitted a lawsuit to the US Federal Court, on behalf of three Vietnamese people who had been affected by the defoliant, against the US companies that were responsible for its manufacture. The lawsuit was the first of its kind to have been filed. In March 2005, however, the US Federal Court dismissed the lawsuit, ruling that there was no legal basis for the claims of the plaintiffs. In February 2008 an appeal against the judgment was rejected. The Vietnam Association for Victims of Agent Orange condemned the decision and announced its intention to file an appeal with the US Supreme Court. In September 2004 the US Secretary of State designated Viet Nam as a 'country of particular concern' under the International Religious Freedom Act for particularly severe violations of religious freedom. (Viet Nam was removed from the list in November 2006.) The Department of State again urged the Vietnamese Government to release prisoners detained for their religious beliefs and to reopen churches closed in the Central Highlands. The designation was denounced by the Vietnamese Government, which lodged an official protest with the US Government. In June 2005 Prime Minister Phan Van Khai, accompanied by a delegation of government officials, made an official state visit to the USA. He thus became the most senior Vietnamese official to visit the USA since the end of the Viet Nam war three decades previously. During his visit, he met with US President George W. Bush. Among the issues discussed were Viet Nam's application to join the WTO, human rights, religious freedom and corporate development. In May 2006 the two countries signed a bilateral trade agreement, marking the final stage of Viet Nam's accession to the WTO. US Secretary of Defense Rumsfeld's visit to Viet Nam in June was followed by a visit from President Bush in November. In December the US Congress approved legislation permitting 'permanent normal trade relations' with Viet Nam. It appeared that progress was being made with regard to the ongoing Agent Orange issue when the Bush Administration approved funding of US $400,000 towards a $1m. study into the decontamination of its former base in Da Nang in February 2007. In June Nguyen Minh Triet became the first Vietnamese Head of State to visit the USA since the end of the Viet Nam war. Triet held talks with President Bush during the visit, and several bilateral economic agreements were signed, including a Trade and Investment Framework Agreement (TIFA). However, while the two Presidents were meeting, hundreds of protesters, including many Vietnamese exiles, demanded the release of Vietnamese political prisoners. The first ministerial-level meeting on the TIFA took place in Washington, DC, in December, focusing on Viet Nam's implementation of its WTO commitments, following its accession to that organization in January, as well as measures to expand bilateral trade and investment ties.

In October 1990 the European Community (now the European Union—EU, see p. 244) announced the restoration of diplomatic relations with Viet Nam. In October 1991 a group of industrialized countries, led by France, agreed to assist Viet Nam in paying its arrears to the IMF, thereby enabling it to qualify for future IMF loans (which nevertheless remained dependent on the approval of the USA, as the IMF's principal vote-holder). In February 1993 President Mitterrand of France made an official visit to Viet Nam (the first Western Head of State to do so since the country's reunification). France's Geopetrol oil company formed part of a consortium to develop Vietnamese offshore oil and gas deposits. In October 2002 President Tran Duc Luong paid the first visit to France by a Vietnamese leader since the establishment of diplomatic relations with France in 1973. President Jacques Chirac of France made an official visit to Viet Nam in early October 2004, attending the fifth biennial Asia-Europe Meeting, which took place in Hanoi. Several agreements on bilateral co-operation were signed during the visit, and President Chirac pledged his country's support for Viet Nam's bid to join the WTO. Prime Minister Nguyen Tan Dung visited Germany, Ireland and the United Kingdom in March 2008, agreeing with his counterparts in the three countries to strengthen bilateral co-operation in a range of areas. In January 1992 a Japanese government mission visited Viet Nam to negotiate the repayment of Vietnamese debts, and in November Japan (which—although a principal trading partner—had hitherto imposed a ban on official economic co-operation) began to provide financial assistance to Viet Nam. In March 1999 Prime Minister Phan Van Khai made an official visit to Japan. During 2000 Viet Nam and Japan also strengthened their defence links, with the aim of promoting regional security. In June 2001 Phan Van Khai paid a further visit to Japan.

The Cambodian peace agreement of 1991 allowed Viet Nam to initiate closer relations with ASEAN member states: Vo Van Kiet visited Indonesia, Thailand and Singapore in October and November 1991 and Malaysia, Brunei and the Philippines in early 1992; agreements on economic co-operation were concluded with these countries, including guarantees of protection for future investment by them in Viet Nam. In July 1992 Viet Nam signed the ASEAN agreement (of 1976) on regional amity and co-operation, and in July 1995 became a full member of the organization. In September 1992 an agreement was signed with Singapore on the mutual provision of 'most-favoured nation' trading status. In April 1995 Viet Nam, Thailand, Laos and Cambodia signed an agreement providing for the establishment of the Mekong River Commission (see p. 413), which was to co-ordinate the sustainable development of the resources of the Lower Mekong River basin. In October 1997 Viet Nam and Thailand reached an agreement to demarcate their maritime boundary, following a series of incidents between Vietnamese and Thai fishing vessels. In December 1998 Viet Nam hosted the sixth summit meeting of the heads of state and government of the

ASEAN grouping of countries. During 2000 Viet Nam reaffirmed sovereignty over the Spratly and Paracel Islands, but reassured ASEAN that it was committed to a peaceful solution to the territorial dispute through multilateral negotiations. It was hoped that the declaration of November 2002, which established a code of conduct to be adhered to by the claimants of the islands, would provide such a solution. Vietnamese and Laotian officials held several meetings during the course of 2000, and Viet Nam provided assistance to Laos in its fight against ethnic Hmong rebels. In November 2001 President Tran Duc Long held talks with President Gloria Macapagal Arroyo while on an official visit to the Philippines. The two countries agreed to the enhancement of economic relations and to co-operation in trade, investment and tourism. In February 2002 the Prime Minister met with the Prime Ministers of Cambodia and of Laos in Ho Chi Minh City. The three countries agreed to promote co-operation in the development of tourism and infrastructure within the 'development triangle'. In February 2004 the first joint meeting of the Cabinets of Viet Nam and Thailand took place. During the meeting, several co-operation agreements were signed concerning various social and economic issues. Prime Minister Phan Van Khai paid a four-day visit to Singapore (the largest foreign investor in Viet Nam) in March, during which a comprehensive co-operation framework document was signed. Following the announcement also in March that Viet Nam intended to allow tourists to begin visiting the Spratly Islands, the first tour took place in April, despite opposition from other claimants to the disputed islands. In May Viet Nam announced that it was renovating a disused runway on one of the islands to further its tourism plans. As part of efforts to strengthen relations with other ASEAN member states, particularly in the area of economic co-operation, Vietnamese Prime Minister Nguyen Tan Dung visited Brunei, Indonesia, Myanmar, the Philippines and Singapore in August 2007. In February 2008 Viet Nam, Cambodia and Laos concluded a draft agreement on defining the intersection point of their borders. In the following month Viet Nam ratified the new ASEAN Charter, which codified the principles and purposes of the Association and had been signed in November 2007 at the 13th summit meeting in Singapore.

In mid-November 1997 Viet Nam hosted the seventh summit meeting of francophone states (La Francophonie), which was attended by representatives of 49 countries. In April 2000 President Tran Duc Luong attended the Group of 77 (G-77) South Summit meeting of developing countries, held in Havana, Cuba.

Viet Nam has sought to expand its participation in international organizations in recent years. Two significant achievements were made in this regard in 2007: accession to the WTO in January and election as a non-permanent member of the UN Security Council for 2008–09 in October.

Government

The 1992 Constitution declares the supremacy of the Communist Party. Legislative power is vested in the National Assembly, which is elected for a four-year term by universal adult suffrage and, from 2007, had 493 members. The President, elected by the National Assembly from among its members, is the Head of State and Commander-in-Chief of the armed forces. The President appoints a Prime Minister (from among the members of the National Assembly, and subject to their approval), who forms a government (again, subject to ratification by the National Assembly). The country is divided into provinces and municipalities, which are subordinate to the central government. Local government is entrusted to locally elected People's Councils.

Defence

As assessed at November 2007, the active ('Main Force') armed forces of Viet Nam had an estimated total strength of 455,000: an estimated 412,000 in the army, an estimated 13,000 in the navy, and 30,000 in the air and air defence forces. Military service is compulsory and usually lasts for two years. Paramilitary forces number in excess of 40,000 and include the urban People's Self-Defence Force and the rural People's Militia. The defence budget for 2007 was estimated at US $3,730m.

Economic Affairs

In 2006, according to estimates by the World Bank, Viet Nam's gross national income (GNI), measured at average 2004–06 prices, was US $58,143m., equivalent to $690 per head (or $3,300 per head on an international purchasing-power parity basis). During 1996–2006, it was estimated, the population increased at an average annual rate of 1.2%, while gross domestic product (GDP) per head increased, in real terms, by an average of 5.8% per year. Overall GDP increased, in real terms, at an average annual rate of 7.1% in 1996–2006. According to the Asian Development Bank (ADB), GDP grew by 8.2% in 2006 and by 8.5% in 2007.

Agriculture (including forestry and fishing) contributed an estimated 20.4% of GDP in 2006, according to the ADB, and engaged 55.7% of the employed labour force in the same year. The staple crop is rice, which also provided 3.3% of total export earnings in 2006. In addition, Viet Nam is a major producer of coffee; this commodity accounted for 2.8% of export revenue in 2006. Other important cash crops include sugar cane, groundnuts, cashew nuts, rubber, tea and cotton. According to the ADB, exports of wood and wood products increased from US $1,562m. in 2005 to $1,904m. in 2006, when they accounted for 4.8% of total export earnings. Livestock-rearing and fishing are also important. In 2006 marine products accounted for some 8.4% of export revenues, according to preliminary data. According to figures from the ADB, agricultural GDP increased by an estimated annual average of 4.1% in 1995–2006. Despite adverse weather conditions and outbreaks of livestock diseases, the sector's GDP expanded by 3.4% in 2007.

In 2006 industry (comprising manufacturing, mining and quarrying, construction and utilities) contributed an estimated 41.6% of GDP, according to the ADB. In the same year, the industrial sector engaged 19.1% of the labour force. According to figures from the ADB, industrial GDP increased by an annual average of 10.4% per year in 1995–2006. The sector's GDP expanded by 10.6% in 2007.

In 2006 mining and quarrying contributed an estimated 10.3% of GDP. In 2004 the mining sector engaged 0.7% of the labour force. Viet Nam's principal mineral exports are petroleum and coal. Tin, zinc, iron, antimony, chromium, natural phosphates, bauxite and gold are also mined. Significant reserves of offshore natural gas were discovered in 1993. In 2004 exports of crude petroleum accounted for 22.0% of total merchandise exports. According to figures from the ADB, mining GDP increased by an annual average of 7.5% in 1995–2006. Mining GDP increased by 1.7% in 2006.

Manufacturing contributed an estimated 21.3% of GDP in 2006, and accounted for 11.7% of employment in 2004. The main manufacturing sectors in 2000, measured by gross value of output, included food-processing, cigarettes and tobacco, textiles, chemicals and electrical goods. According to the ADB, the value of textile exports reached US $5,802m. in 2006, when they accounted for 14.6% of total export revenue. Manufacturing GDP increased by an annual average of 11.5% in 1995–2006. The sector's GDP expanded by 12.2% in 2006.

Energy is derived principally from natural gas, which in 2004 accounted for 42.7% of the total electricity produced, hydroelectric power (38.4%), coal (15.3%) and petroleum (3.7%). In 2005 fuel imports accounted for 14.6% of the value of total merchandise imports. Imports of mineral fuels accounted for 10.9% of total imports in 2003. Construction of Viet Nam's first petroleum refinery at Dung Quat commenced in late 2005 and was expected to be completed in early 2009. Viet Nam operates a 500-kW nuclear research reactor at Da Lat, in the Central Highlands, with Russian assistance. In February 2006 the Government announced its intention to construct a 2,000-MW nuclear power plant by 2020.

The services sector contributed an estimated 38.1% of GDP in 2006, according to the ADB, and employed 25.2% of the labour force. Tourism is an important source of foreign exchange; receipts from tourism totalled US $1,880m. in 2005. In 2006 around 3.6m. foreign tourists visited Viet Nam. According to figures from the ADB, the GDP of the services sector increased by an average of 6.5% per year in 1995–2006. The sector's GDP rose by 8.7% in 2007.

In 2006 Viet Nam recorded a visible trade deficit of US $2,776m. The surplus on the current account of the balance of payments in that year was an estimated $164m. In 2005, according to preliminary figures, the People's Republic of China was Viet Nam's principal source of imports, supplying 15.6% of total imports; other major sources were Singapore (12.4%), Japan (11.1%) and the Republic of Korea (9.7%). The principal market for exports in that year was the USA (18.3%); other important purchasers were Japan (13.6%) and China (9.1%). The principal exports in 2005 were light industrial and handicraft goods (40.3%), agricultural products and mineral fuels. In 2005 the principal imports were fuels and raw materials (68.1%), machinery, instruments and accessories, and pharmaceutical and medicinal products.

In 2006 the budgetary deficit was recorded at 3,400,000m. dông. In 2007 the budgetary deficit was forecast at some 38,800,000m. dông. The fiscal deficit was projected to be equivalent to 7.9% of GDP in that year. Viet Nam's total external debt was estimated by the ADB at US $21,300m. in 2007. In that year the cost of servicing the debt was equivalent to 5.5% of the value of exports of goods and services. The annual rate of inflation averaged 4.5% in 1995–2006. According to the ADB, the rate of inflation reached 8.3% in 2007. In that year an estimated 4.6% of the labour force were unemployed.

Viet Nam is a member of the Asian Development Bank (ADB, see p. 182), the Association of South East Asian Nations (ASEAN, see p. 185), the Asia-Pacific Economic Co-operation (APEC, see p. 176), the UN Economic and Social Commission for Asia and the Pacific (ESCAP, see p. 35) and the Mekong River Commission (see p. 413). Viet Nam also joined the ASEAN Free Trade Area (AFTA) in 1996 and was granted until 2003 to comply with the requisite tariff reductions (to between 0% and 5%). The area was formally established on 1 January 2002. Viet Nam joined the World Trade Organization (WTO, see p. 396) in January 2007.

From 1990 the process of *doi moi* (renovation) aimed to transform Viet Nam's centralized economy to a market-orientated system. Agricultural production was stimulated by the removal of price controls, by a new system of land tenure and by the relaxation of the state monopoly on rice exports, with the result that by the mid-1990s Viet Nam had become one of the world's principal rice exporters. The establishment of the country's first stock exchange in July 2000 was an important development, and by 2007 34 Vietnamese companies were listed on the exchange. During 2001–05 about 3,590 of a total of 5,655 state enterprises were restructured, 2,347 of which were subject to 'equitization' (privatization). The 2006–11 socio-economic development plan, which envisaged average annual GDP growth of 7.5%–8.0%, included measures to stimulate the private sector. Limits on foreign ownership in firms were to be relaxed. Viet Nam's accession to the WTO, which took effect in January 2007, was expected to improve the country's investment potential. According to the ADB, foreign direct investment totalled US $2,400m. in 2007, compared with $2,315m. in the previous year. The level of private domestic investment also continued to rise, and by 2007 was estimated to account for 40% of total investment in Viet Nam. Growth remained strong in 2007; however, this led to an increase in imports as domestic resources became depleted, concomitant with a scarcity of skilled labour, while inadequacies in the country's infrastructure remained evident. Furthermore, as the unrestrained economic growth continued, by early 2008 inflationary pressures were mounting. Although interest rates were raised in early 2008, a very substantial rise in consumer prices, notably for essential foodstuffs, was forecast for the year. Nevertheless, the ADB predicted GDP growth of about 7.0%.

Education

Primary education, which is compulsory, begins at six years of age and lasts for five years. Secondary education, beginning at the age of 11, lasts for seven years, comprising a first cycle of four years and a second cycle of three years. In 2004/05 total preprimary enrolment included 61% of children in the relevant agegroup. In the same year enrolment within primary education included 93% of children in the relevant age-group (males 96%; females 90%), while secondary enrolment included 75% of the relevant age-group (males 76%, females 94%). In 2004/05 there were 10,376 pre-primary institutions, 14,518 primary schools and 12,299 secondary schools, as well as 230 higher education institutions at which over 1.3m. students were enrolled. In 1989 Viet Nam's first private college since 1954 was opened in Hanoi; Thang Long College was to cater for university students. Of total planned budgetary expenditure by the central Government in 2005, 20,500,000m. dông (9.1%) was allocated to education.

Public Holidays

2008: 1 January (New Year's Day), 3 February (Founding of the Communist Party), 7–9 February* (Tet, lunar new year), 30 April (Liberation of Saigon), 1 May (May Day), 2 September (National Day).

2009: 1 January (New Year's Day), 26–27 January* (Tet, lunar new year), 3 February (Founding of the Communist Party), 30 April (Liberation of Saigon), 1 May (May Day), 2 September (National Day).

* Varies according to the lunar calendar.

Weights and Measures

The metric system is in force.

Statistical Survey

Sources (unless otherwise stated): General Statistics Office of Viet Nam, 2 Hoang Van Thu, Ba Dinh District, Hanoi; tel. (4) 7332997; e-mail banbientap@gso.gov.vn; internet www.gso.gov.vn; Communist Party of Viet Nam, 1 Hoang Van Thu, Hanoi; e-mail cpv@hn.vnn.vn; internet www.cpv.org.vn.

Area and Population

AREA, POPULATION AND DENSITY

Area (sq km)	331,212*
Population (census results)	
1 April 1989	64,411,713
1 April 1999	
Males	37,469,117
Females	38,854,056
Total	76,323,173
Population (official estimates of annual averages)	
2004	82,031,700
2005	83,106,300
2006	84,155,800†
Density (per sq km) at 2006	254.1

* 127,881 sq miles.
† Preliminary.

ADMINISTRATIVE DIVISIONS

(2006, annual averages, preliminary figures)

	Area (sq km)	Population ('000)	Density (per sq km)
Red River Delta	14,862.5	18,207.7	1,255
Hanoi	921.8	3,216.7	3,490
Vinh Phuc	1,373.2	1,180.4	860
Bac Ninh	823.1	1,009.8	1,227
Ha Tay	2,198.0	2,543.5	1,157
Hai Duong	1,652.8	1,722.5	1,042
Haiphong	1,520.7	1,803.4	1,186
Hung Yen	923.5	1,142.7	1,237
Thai Binh	1,546.5	1,865.4	1,206
Ha Nam	859.7	826.6	961
Nam Dinh	1,650.8	1,974.3	1,196
Ninh Binh	1,392.4	922.6	663
North East	64,025.2	9,458.5	148
Ha Giang	7,945.8	683.5	86
Cao Bang	6,724.6	518.9	77
Bac Kan	4,868.4	301.5	62
Tuyen Quang	5,870.4	732.3	125
Lao Cai	6,383.9	585.8	92
Yen Bai	6,899.5	740.7	107
Thai Nguyen	3,546.6	1,127.2	318
Lang Son	8,331.2	746.4	90
Quang Ninh	6,099.0	1,091.3	179
Bac Giang	3,827.4	1,594.3	417
Phu Tho	3,528.4	1,336.6	379

VIET NAM

Statistical Survey

—continued

	Area (sq km)	Population ('000)	Density (per sq km)
North West	37,533.8	2,606.9	69
Dien Bien	9,562.9	459.1	48
Lai Chau	9,112.3	319.9	35
Son La	14,174.4	1,007.5	71
Hoa Binh	4,684.2	820.4	175
North Central Coast	51,552.0	10,668.3	207
Thanh Hoa	11,136.3	3,680.4	330
Nghe An	16,498.5	3,064.3	186
Ha Tinh	6,026.5	1,306.4	217
Quand Binh	8,065.3	847.9	105
Quang Tri	4,760.1	625.8	131
Thua Thien-Hué	5,065.3	1,143.5	226
South Central Coast	33,166.1	7,131.3	215
Da Nang	1,257.3	788.5	627
Quang Nam	10,438.3	1,472.7	141
Quang Ngai	5,152.7	1,295.6	251
Binh Dinh	6,039.6	1,556.3	259
Phu Yen	5,060.6	873.3	173
Khanh Hoa	5,217.6	1,135.0	218
Central Highlands	54,659.6	4,868.9	89
Kon Tum	9,690.5	383.1	40
Gia Lai	15,536.9	1,161.7	75
Dak Lak	13,139.2	1,737.6	132
Dak Nong	6,516.9	407.3	62
Lam Dong	9,776.1	1,179.2	121
South East	34,807.7	13,798.6	396
Ninh Thuan	3,363.1	567.9	169
Binh Thuan	7,836.9	1,163.0	148
Binh Phuoc	6,883.4	809.5	118
Tay Ninh	4,035.9	1,047.1	259
Binh Duong	2,696.2	964.0	358
Dong Nai	5,903.9	2,214.8	375
Ba Ria-Vung Tau	1,989.6	926.3	466
Ho Chi Minh City	2,098.7	6,106.0	2,909
Mekong River Delta	40,604.7	17,415.6	429
Long An	4,493.8	1,423.1	317
Tien Giang	2,484.2	1,717.4	691
Ben Tre	2,360.2	1,353.3	573
Tra Vinh	2,295.1	1,036.8	452
Vinh Long	1,479.1	1,057.0	715
Dong Thap	3,376.4	1,667.8	494
An Giang	3,536.8	2,210.4	625
Kien Giang	6,348.3	1,684.6	265
Can Tho	1,401.6	1,139.9	813
Hau Giang	1,601.1	796.9	498
Soc Trang	3,312.3	1,276.2	385
Bac Lieu	2,584.1	820.1	317
Ca Mau	5,331.7	1,232.0	231
Total	331,211.6	84,155.8	254

PRINCIPAL TOWNS
(excl. suburbs, estimated population at mid-1992)

Ho Chi Minh City (formerly Saigon)	3,015,743*	Nam Dinh		171,699
Hanoi (capital)	1,073,760	Qui Nhon		163,385
Haiphong	783,133	Vung Tau		145,145
Da Nang	382,674	Rach Gia		141,132
Buon Ma Thuot	282,095	Long Xuyen		132,681
Nha Trang	221,331	Thai Nguyen		127,643
Hué	219,149	Hong Gai		127,484
Can Tho	215,587	Vinh		112,455
Cam Pha	209,086			

* Including Cholon.

Source: UN, *Demographic Yearbook*.

Mid-2007 ('000, incl. suburbs, UN estimates): Ho Chi Minh City 5,723; Hanoi 4,378; Haiphong 2,129 (Source: UN, *World Urbanization Prospects: The 2007 Revision*).

BIRTHS AND DEATHS
(annual averages, UN estimates)

	1990–95	1995–2000	2000–05
Birth rate (per 1,000)	28.2	21.4	20.2
Death rate (per 1,000)	6.9	5.7	5.2

Source: UN, *World Population Prospects: The 2006 Revision*.

Expectation of life (years at birth, WHO estimates): 71.6 (males 69.1; females 74.3) in 2005 (Source: WHO, *World Health Statistics*).

EMPLOYMENT
('000 persons aged 15 years and over, averages at mid-year)

	2004	2005	2006*
Agriculture, hunting and forestry	23,026.1	22,860.0	22,567.0
Fishing	1,404.6	1,482.4	1,555.8
Construction	1,922.9	2,181.3	2,438.8
Other industry	5,293.6	5,601.1	5,841.1
Trade	4,767.0	4,991.7	5,251.1
Hotels and restaurants	755.3	767.5	783.4
Transport, storage and communications	1,202.2	1,204.5	1,212.3
Culture, health and education	1,657.4	1,726.1	1,806.0
Other services	1,557.2	1,712.3	1,891.7
Total employed	41,586.3	42,526.9	43,347.2

* Preliminary figures.

Health and Welfare

KEY INDICATORS

Total fertility rate (children per woman, 2005)	2.2
Under-5 mortality rate (per 1,000 live births, 2005)	19
HIV/AIDS (% of persons aged 15–49, 2005)	0.5
Physicians (per 1,000 head, 2001)	0.53
Hospital beds (per 1,000 head, 2002)	1.40
Health expenditure (2004): US $ per head (PPP)	184.1
Health expenditure (2004): % of GDP	5.5
Health expenditure (2004): public (% of total)	27.1
Access to water (% of persons, 2004)	85
Access to sanitation (% of persons, 2004)	61
Human Development Index (2005): ranking	105
Human Development Index (2005): value	0.733

For sources and definitions, see explanatory note on p. vi.

Agriculture

PRINCIPAL CROPS
('000 metric tons)

	2004	2005	2006
Rice (paddy)	36,149	35,791	35,827
Maize	3,431	3,756	3,819
Potatoes*	365	370	370
Sweet potatoes	1,512	1,461	1,455
Cassava (Manioc)	5,821	6,646	7,714
Sugar cane	15,649	14,949	15,679
Dry beans	157	158*	158*
Cashew nuts	819	961	942
Soybeans (Soya beans)	246	293	258
Groundnuts (in shell)	469	489	465
Coconuts	960	977	982
Cabbages and other brassicas*	650	700	700
Dry onions*	225	225	225
Watermelons*	410	420	420
Bananas	1,329	1,344	1,344
Oranges	541	601	601
Guavas, mangoes and mangosteens	338	368	368
Pineapples	415	470	470
Coffee (green)	836	752	854
Tea (made)	120	133	142
Tobacco (leaves)	23	26	43
Natural rubber	419	482	546

* FAO estimate(s).

Aggregate production ('000 metric tons, may include official, semi-official or estimated data): Total cereals 39,581 in 2004, 39,549 in 2005, 39,648 in 2006; Total roots and tubers 7,698 in 2004, 8,477 in 2005, 9,539 in 2006; Total vegetables (incl. melons) 7,780 in 2004, 7,991 in 2005, 7,991 in 2006; Total fruits (excl. melons) 5,481 in 2004, 5,691 in 2005, 5,691 in 2006.

Source: FAO.

VIET NAM

LIVESTOCK
('000 head, year ending September)

	2004	2005	2006
Horses	113.4	110.4	110.4*
Cattle	4,907.7	5,540.7†	6,510.8
Buffaloes	2,869.8	2,922.2	2,921.0
Pigs	26,143.7	27,434.9	26,855.3
Goats	1,020.2	1,314.1	1,492.0
Chickens	152,706	153,937	150,220
Ducks	65,446	65,973	64,380

* FAO estimate.
† Unofficial figure.
Source: FAO.

LIVESTOCK PRODUCTS
('000 metric tons)

	2004	2005	2006*
Cattle meat	119.8	153.2	181.0
Buffalo meat*	101.1	103.2	103.2
Pig meat	2,012.0	2,288.3	2,446.0
Chicken meat	316.4	321.9	322.0
Duck meat*	88.2	88.2	86.0
Cows' milk	151.3	197.7	215.0
Buffaloes' milk*	31.0	31.0	31.0
Hen eggs*	197.0	225.0	225.0
Silk-worm cocoons*	3.0	3.0	3.0

* FAO estimates.
Source: FAO.

Forestry

ROUNDWOOD REMOVALS
('000 cubic metres, excl. bark)

	2004	2005	2006
Sawlogs, veneer logs and logs for sleepers*†	2,737	2,737	2,737
Pulpwood	1,850	1,067	1,291
Other industrial wood	650	650	650
Fuel wood*	21,250	26,350	26,151
Total	26,487	30,804	30,829

* FAO estimates.
† Annual output assumed to be unchanged from 2000.
Source: FAO.

SAWNWOOD PRODUCTION
('000 cubic metres, incl. railway sleepers)

	2004	2005	2006
Total (all broadleaved)	2,900	3,232	3,414

Source: FAO.

Fishing

('000 metric tons, live weight)

	2002	2003	2004
Capture*	1,802.6	1,856.1	1,879.5
Freshwater fishes	163.6	149.0	134.1
Marine fishes	1,168.7	1,210.0	1,315.8
Prawns and shrimps*	95.0	102.8	107.1
Cephalopods	189.7	199.0*	185.0*
Aquaculture*	703.0	937.5	1,198.6
Freshwater fishes	441.8	599.8	761.6
Giant tiger prawns*	126.4	150.0	185.6
Marine molluscs	75.0*	100.0*	155.2
Total catch*	2,505.6	2,793.6	3,078.1

* FAO estimate(s).
Note: Figures exclude aquatic plants ('000 metric tons, all aquaculture, FAO estimates): 25 in 2002; 30 in 2003; 30 in 2004.
Source: FAO.

Mining

('000 metric tons)

	2004	2005	2006*
Crude petroleum ('000 barrels)	141,930	131,003	119,300
Natural gas (million cubic metres)†	6,266	6,342	6,766
Coal (anthracite)	27,349	34,100	38,900
Chromium ore—gross weight	82	89	90
Ilmenite—gross weight	145	150	150
Gold (kilograms)	2,065	2,138	2,500
Kaolin*	650	650	650
Barite (metric tons)	120,000	130,000*	130,000
Phosphate rock:			
gross weight	902	1,066	1,220
P_2O_5 content	271*	320*	366
Salt (unrefined)	906	925	950

* Estimate(s).
† Gross production.
Source: US Geological Survey.

Industry

SELECTED PRODUCTS
('000 metric tons, unless otherwise indicated)

	2003	2004	2005*
Raw sugar	1,360	1,434	1,175
Beer (million litres)	1,119	1,343	1,427
Cigarettes (million packets)	3,871	4,192	4,429
Fabrics (million metres)	496	502	503
Chemical fertilizers	1,294	1,714	2,306
Insecticides	41	55	56
Bricks (million)	12,810	14,661	16,728
Cement	24,127	26,153	28,050
Crude steel	2,954	3,280	3,888
Diesel motors (pieces)	184,418	182,443	145,450
Television receivers ('000)	2,188	2,660	2,515
Electric engines (pieces)	95,779	132,320	134,445
Bicycle tyres ('000)	26,686	26,008	29,545
Bicycle tubes ('000)	36,083	32,386	35,490
Rice milling equipment (pieces)	10,112	5,749	6,480
Transformers (pieces)	33,364	50,146	45,541
Electric energy (million kWh)	40,546	46,202	53,320

* Preliminary figures.

Electric energy (million kWh): 40,500 in 2003; 46,205 in 2004; 53,320 in 2005 (Source: Asian Development Bank, *Key Indicators of Developing Asian and Pacific Countries*).

VIET NAM

Statistical Survey

Finance

CURRENCY AND EXCHANGE RATES

Monetary Units
  100 xu = 1 new dông.

Sterling, Dollar and Euro Equivalents (29 May 2007)
  £1 sterling = 31,808.8 dông;
  US $1 = 16,087.0 dông;
  €1 = 21,641.8 dông;
  100,000 new dông = £3.14 = $6.22 = €4.62.

Average Exchange Rate (new dông per US $)
  2004   n.a.
  2005   15,858.9
  2006   15,994.3

Note: The new dông, equivalent to 10 former dông, was introduced in September 1985.

BUDGET
('000,000 million dông)

Revenue (incl. grants)	2005	2006	2007*
Tax revenue	166.2	210.3	231.4
Corporate income tax	71.7	100.8	99.0
Individual income tax	4.2	5.2	6.1
Tax on the transfer of properties	2.8	3.4	3.8
Value-added tax (VAT)	45.7	54.8	78.9
Excises	15.7	17.1	17.1
Taxes on international trade	23.6	26.3	23.8
Other taxes	2.3	2.8	2.7
Non-tax and capital revenue	48.5	50.3	47.5
Fees and charges	21.0	23.1	23.1
Income from natural resources	21.9	20.2	19.9
Capital revenues	0.9	1.5	0.8
Grants	2.3	3.6	3.0
Total	217.1	264.2	281.9

Expenditure (cash basis)†	2005	2006	2007*
Current expenditure	155.0	181.5	221.3
General administrative services	16.8	19.0	24.8
Economic services	12.8	15.0	16.3
Social services	77.3	91.4	97.3
Education	29.1	33.8	38.1
Health	10.7	12.7	14.7
Social subsidies	23.6	28.7	26.8
Other services (incl. defence)	13.8	16.3	17.8
Interest on public debt	7.0	8.9	11.7
Capital expenditure	72.0	86.1	99.5
Total	226.9	267.6	320.7

* Forecasts.
† Excluding off-budget investment expenditure ('000,000 million dông): 39.4 in 2005; 33.7 in 2006; 39.4 in 2007 (forecast).

Source: IMF, *Vietnam: Statistical Appendix* (December 2007).

INTERNATIONAL RESERVES
(US $ million at 31 December)

	2004	2005	2006
Gold (market valuation)	144.6	165.9	206.9
IMF special drawing rights	0.5	0.9	1.6
Foreign exchange	7,041.0	9,049.7	13,382.5
Total	7,186.1	9,216.5	13,591.0

Source: IMF, *International Financial Statistics*.

MONEY SUPPLY
('000 million dông at 31 December)

	2004	2005	2006
Currency outside banks	109,097	131,179	158,809
Demand deposits at banks	88,891	110,823	133,405
Total money	197,989	242,002	292,215

Source: IMF, *International Financial Statistics*.

COST OF LIVING
(Consumer Price Index; annual averages, base: 2001 = 100)

	2004	2005	2006
Staple foods	125.6	136.8	168.3
Other foods	125.7	140.9	163.2
Beverages and tobacco	110.0	114.3	126.5
Clothing (incl. footwear)	107.9	112.4	125.4
Household goods	105.2	109.7	121.9
Housing and construction	118.0	126.5	149.8
Transport and communications	97.1	105.2	115.9
All items (incl. others)	115.6	125.1	143.3

Source: IMF, *Vietnam: Statistical Appendix* (December 2007).

NATIONAL ACCOUNTS
('000 million dông at current prices)

Expenditure on the Gross Domestic Product

	2004	2005	2006
Government final consumption expenditure	45,715	51,652	57,334
Private final consumption expenditure	465,506	533,141	611,206
Increase in stocks	15,818	22,702	28,880
Gross fixed capital formation	237,868	275,841	319,020
Total domestic expenditure	764,907	883,336	1,016,440
Exports of goods and services	470,216	582,069	715,369
Less Imports of goods and services	524,216	617,157	747,840
Sub-total	710,907	848,248	983,969
Statistical discrepancy	4,400	−9,037	−10,178
GDP in purchasers' values	715,307	839,211	973,790
GDP at constant 1994 prices	362,435	392,989	425,135

Gross Domestic Product by Economic Activity

	2004	2005	2006
Agriculture, forestry and fishing	155,992	175,984	198,266
Mining and quarrying	72,492	88,897	99,919
Manufacturing	145,475	173,122	206,945
Electricity, gas and water	25,090	28,929	33,386
Construction	44,558	53,276	64,503
Trade	96,995	113,768	132,794
Transport, storage and communications	30,402	36,629	43,825
Finance	12,737	15,072	17,607
Public administration	61,255	66,556	76,165
Other community, social and personal services	70,310	86,978	100,380
Total	715,307	839,211	973,790

Source: Asian Development Bank, *Key Indicators of Developing Asian and Pacific Countries*.

BALANCE OF PAYMENTS
(US $ million)

	2004	2005	2006
Exports of goods f.o.b.	26,485	32,447	39,826
Imports of goods f.o.b.	−28,772	−34,886	−42,602
Trade balance	−2,287	−2,439	−2,776
Exports of services	3,867	4,176	5,100
Imports of services	−4,739	−4,395	−5,108
Balance on goods and services	−3,159	−2,658	−2,784
Other income received	188	364	668
Other income paid	−1,079	−1,583	−2,098
Balance on goods, services and income	−4,050	−3,877	−4,214
Current transfers received	2,485	3,380	4,049
Current balance	−1,565	−497	−164
Direct investment abroad	−536	−524	−643
Direct investment from abroad	1,878	1,954	2,400
Medium and long-term loans (net)	1,396	1,360	1,139
Portfolio investment assets	—	865	1,313
Short-term capital (net)	−291	−1,027	277
Overall balance	883	2,131	4,322

Source: IMF, *Vietnam: Statistical Appendix* (December 2007).

VIET NAM

External Trade

SELECTED COMMODITIES
(distribution by SITC, US $ million)

Imports c.i.f.	2001	2002	2003
Food and live animals	834	939	1,262
Beverages and tobacco	108	149	153
Crude materials (inedible) except fuels	690	816	1,001
Mineral fuels, etc.	1,970	2,166	2,714
Animal and vegetable fats, and oils	83	131	152
Chemicals and related products	2,490	2,933	3,623
Basic manufactures	3,730	5,415	6,672
Machinery and transport equipment	4,865	5,758	7,922
Miscellaneous manufactured goods	1,447	1,427	1,575
Total (incl. others)	16,218	19,746	25,256

Exports f.o.b.	2001	2002	2003
Food and live animals	4,052	4,118	4,432
Beverages and tobacco	46	75	160
Crude materials (inedible) except fuels	413	517	631
Mineral fuels, etc.	3,469	3,568	4,151
Chemicals and related products	222	262	340
Basic manufactures	990	1,125	1,355
Machinery and transport equipment	1,399	1,337	1,793
Miscellaneous manufactured goods	4,408	5,691	7,260
Total (incl. others)	15,029	16,706	20,149

Source: Asian Development Bank, *Key Indicators of Developing Asian and Pacific Countries*.

2004 (US $ million): *Imports*: Machinery, instruments and accessories 9,207.5; Fuels and raw materials 20,625.9; Food products 776.4; Pharmaceutical and medicinal products 439.6; Total (incl. others) 31,968.8. *Exports*: Heavy industrial products and minerals 9,641.9; Light industrial and handicraft goods 10,870.7; Agricultural products 3,383.6; Forest products 180.6; Aquatic products 2,408.3; Total 26,485.0.

2005 (US $ million, preliminary figures): *Imports*: Machinery, instruments and accessories 9,688.3; Fuels and raw materials 25,182.0; Pharmaceutical and medicinal products 495.0; Total (incl. others) 36,978.0. *Exports*: Heavy industrial products and minerals 10,965.4; Light industrial and handicraft goods 13,074.0; Agricultural and forest products 5,663.8; Aquatic products 2,738.7; Total 32,441.9.

2006 (US $ million, preliminary figures): Total imports 44,891.1; Total exports 39,826.2.

PRINCIPAL TRADING PARTNERS
(US $ million)

Imports c.i.f.	2003	2004	2005*
China, People's Republic	3,138.6	4,595.1	5,778.9
Germany	614.6	694.3	662.5
Hong Kong	990.9	1,074.3	1,235.8
Japan	2,982.1	3,552.6	4,093.0
Korea, Republic	2,625.4	3,359.4	3,600.5
Malaysia	925.0	1,215.3	1,258.6
Russia	491.8	671.5	768.0
Singapore	2,875.8	3,618.4	4,597.6
Thailand	1,282.2	1,858.6	2,393.2
USA	1,143.3	1,133.9	864.4
Total (incl. others)	25,255.8	31,968.8	36,978.0

Exports f.o.b.	2003	2004	2005*
Australia	1,420.9	1,884.7	2,570.2
China, People's Republic	1,883.1	2,899.1	2,961.0
France	496.1	555.1	652.7
Germany	854.7	1,064.7	1,086.7
Japan	2,908.6	3,542.1	4,411.2
Korea, Republic	492.1	608.1	630.9
Netherlands	493.0	606.7	603.9
Singapore	1,024.7	1,485.3	1,808.5
United Kingdom	754.8	1,010.3	1,015.8
USA	3,938.6	5,024.8	5,930.6
Total (incl. others)	20,149.3	26,485.0	32,441.9

* Preliminary figures.

Transport

RAILWAYS
(traffic)

	2003	2004	2005*
Passengers carried (million)	11.6	12.9	12.8
Passenger-km (million)	4,069.0	4,376.3	4,580.0
Freight carried ('000 metric tons)	8,385.0	8,873.6	8,838.1
Freight ton-km (million)	2,725.4	2,745.3	2,948.4

* Preliminary figures.

2006 (preliminary): 11.6m. passengers carried.

ROAD TRAFFIC

	2003	2004	2005*
Passengers carried (million)	926.2	1,011.5	1,094.4
Passenger-km (million)	29,180.8	31,471.9	34,354.3
Freight carried (million metric tons)	172.8	196.0	212.3
Freight ton-km (million)	9,285.0	10,593.1	11,567.7

* Preliminary figures.

Commercial vehicles ('000 in use): 49.4 in 1998; 57.8 in 1999; 69.9 in 2000 (Source: UN, *Statistical Yearbook*).

INLAND WATERWAYS

	2003	2004	2005*
Passengers carried (million)	161.7	166.2	171.4
Passenger-km (million)	3,282.4	3,398.6	3,584.5
Freight carried (million metric tons)	55.3	59.2	63.0
Freight ton-km (million)	5,140.5	5,271.4	5,524.4

* Preliminary figures.

SHIPPING

Merchant Fleet
(registered at 31 December)

	2004	2005	2006
Number of vessels	797	883	1,191
Total displacement ('000 grt)	1,427.5	1,677.9	2,053.8

Source: Lloyd's Register-Fairplay, *World Fleet Statistics*.

International Sea-Borne Shipping
(freight traffic)

	2002	2003	2004*
Freight carried (million metric tons)	18.5	21.8	24.4
Freight ton-km ('000 million)	40.3	43.5	48.3

* Preliminary figures.

VIET NAM

CIVIL AVIATION
(traffic on scheduled services)

	2003	2004	2005*
Domestic:			
Passengers carried ('000)	2,688.0	3,120.0	3,932.0
Passenger-km (million)	2,688.0	2,565.0	3,730.8
Freight carried ('000 metric tons)	48.2	51.8	58.7
Freight ton-km (million)	53.8	59.6	62.7
International:			
Passengers carried ('000)	1,831.0	2,411.0	2,907.0
Passenger-km (million)	5,028.2	6,811.0	8,228.9
Freight carried ('000 metric tons)	41.5	46.4	46.4
Freight ton-km (million)	156.9	176.2	180.4

*Preliminary figures.

Tourism

TOURIST ARRIVALS BY COUNTRY OF RESIDENCE

Country	2004	2005	2006
Australia	128,661	145,359	172,519
Cambodia	90,838	186,543	154,956
China, People's Republic	778,431	752,576	516,286
France	104,025	126,402	132,304
Japan	267,210	320,605	383,896
Korea, Republic	232,995	317,213	421,741
Laos	34,215	44,462	33,980
Malaysia	55,717	76,755	105,558
Singapore	50,942	77,676	104,947
Taiwan	256,906	286,324	274,663
Thailand	53,682	84,100	123,804
United Kingdom	71,016	80,884	84,264
USA	272,473	333,566	385,654
Total (incl. others)	2,927,876	3,467,757	3,583,486

Source: Viet Nam National Administration of Tourism.

Tourism receipts (US $ million): 1,400 in 2003; 1,700 in 2004; 1,880 in 2005. Source: World Tourism Organization.

Communications Media

	2004	2005	2006
Telephones ('000 main lines in use)	10,124.9	15,845.0	n.a.
Mobile cellular telephones ('000 subscribers)	4,960.0	9,593.2	15,505.4
Personal computers ('000 in use)	1,044	n.a.	n.a.
Internet users ('000)	6,345	10,711	14,684
Broadband subscribers ('000)	52.7	210.0	516.6

Facsimile machines ('000 in use): 31 in 1999.

Radio receivers ('000 in use): 8,200 in 1997.

Television receivers ('000 in use): 14,750 in 2000.

Book production: 11,455 titles (166,500,000 copies) in 2001.

Daily newspapers: 5 (with estimated circulation of 450,000 copies) in 1999.

Sources: partly International Telecommunication Union; UN, *Statistical Yearbook*; UNESCO, *Statistical Yearbook*.

Education

(2005/06)

	Teachers ('000)	Students ('000)
Pre-primary	117.2	2,426.9
Primary	354.8	7,304.0
Lower secondary	310.2	6,371.3
Upper secondary	115.5	2,973.9
Higher	48.5	1,404.7

Institutions (2004/05): Pre-primary 10,376; Primary 14,518; Lower secondary 9,041; Upper secondary 1,828; Primary and lower secondary 1,034; Lower and upper secondary 396; Higher 230.

Adult literacy rate (UNESCO estimates): 90.3% (males 93.9%; females 86.9%) in 1999 (Source: UNESCO Institute for Statistics).

Directory

The Constitution

On 15 April 1992 the National Assembly adopted a new Constitution, a revised version of that adopted in December 1980 (which in turn replaced the 1959 Constitution of the Democratic Republic of Viet Nam). The National Assembly approved amendments to 24 articles of the Constitution on 12 December 2001. The main provisions of the Constitution (which originally entered into force after elections in July 1992) are summarized as follows:

POLITICAL SYSTEM

All state power belongs to the people. The Communist Party of Viet Nam is a leading force of the state and society. All party organizations operate within the framework of the Constitution and the law. The people exercise power through the National Assembly and the People's Councils.

ECONOMIC SYSTEM

The State develops a multi-sectoral economy, in accordance with a market mechanism based on state management and socialist orientations. All lands are under state management. The State allots land to organizations and individuals for use on a stabilized and long-term basis: they may transfer the right to the use of land allotted to them. Individuals may establish businesses with no restrictions on size or means of production, and the State shall encourage foreign investment. Legal property of individuals and organizations, and business enterprises with foreign invested capital, shall not be subjected to nationalization.

THE NATIONAL ASSEMBLY

The National Assembly is the people's highest representative agency, and the highest organ of state power, exercising its supreme right of supervision over all operations of the State. It elects the President and Vice-President, the Prime Minister and senior judicial officers, and ratifies the Prime Minister's proposals for appointing members of the Government. It decides the country's socio-economic development plans, national financial and monetary policies, and foreign policy. The term of each legislature is five years. The National Assembly Standing Committee supervises the enforcement of laws and the activities of the Government. Amendments to the Constitution may only be made by a majority vote of at least two-thirds of the Assembly's members.

THE PRESIDENT OF THE STATE

The President, as Head of State, represents Viet Nam in domestic and foreign affairs. The President is elected by the National Assembly from among its deputies, and is responsible to the National Assembly. The President's term of office is the same as that of the National Assembly. He or she is Commander-in-Chief of the people's armed forces, and chairs the National Defence and Security Council. The President asks the National Assembly to appoint or dismiss the Vice-President, the Prime Minister, the Chief Justice of the Supreme People's Court and the Chief Procurator of the Supreme People's Organ of Control. According to resolutions of the National Assembly or of its Standing Committee, the President appoints or dismisses members of the Government, and declares war or a state of emergency.

VIET NAM

THE GOVERNMENT

The Government comprises the Prime Minister, the Vice-Prime Ministers, ministers and other members. Apart from the Prime Minister, ministers do not have to be members of the National Assembly. The Prime Minister is responsible to the National Assembly, and the term of office of any Government is the same as that of the National Assembly, which ratifies the appointment or dismissal of members of the Government.

LOCAL GOVERNMENT

The country is divided into provinces and municipalities, which are subordinate to the central Government; municipalities are divided into districts, precincts and cities, and districts are divided into villages and townships. People's Councils are elected by the local people.

JUDICIAL SYSTEM

The judicial system comprises the Supreme People's Court, local People's Courts, military tribunals and other courts. The term of office of the presiding judge of the Supreme People's Court corresponds to the term of the National Assembly, and he or she is responsible to the National Assembly. The Supreme People's Organ of Control ensures the observance of the law and exercises the right of public prosecution. Its Chief Procurator is responsible to the National Assembly. There are local People's Organs of Control and Military Organs of Control.

The Government

HEAD OF STATE

President: NGUYEN MINH TRIET (appointment approved by the 11th National Assembly on 27 June 2006; re-elected 25 July 2007).
Vice-President: NGUYEN THI DOAN.

CABINET
(April 2008)

Prime Minister: NGUYEN TAN DUNG.
Standing Deputy Prime Minister: NGUYEN SINH HUNG.
Deputy Prime Minister and Minister of Foreign Affairs: PHAM GIA KHIEM.
Deputy Prime Minister and Minister of Education and Training: NGUYEN THIEN NHAN.
Deputy Prime Ministers: TRUONG VINH TRONG, HOANG TRUNG HAI.
Minister of National Defence: Gen. PHUNG QUANG THANH.
Minister of Public Security: LE HONG ANH.
Minister of Justice: HA HUNG CUONG.
Minister of Finance: VU VAN NINH.
Minister of Labour, War Invalids and Social Affairs: NGUYEN THI KIM NGAN.
Minister of Health: NGUYEN QUOC TRIEU.
Minister of Culture, Sport and Tourism: HOANG TUAN ANH.
Minister of Construction: NGUYEN HONG QUAN.
Minister of Transportation: HO NGHIA DUNG.
Minister of Internal Services: TRAN VAN TUAN.
Minister of Agriculture and Rural Development: CAO DUC PHAT.
Minister of Industry and Trade: VU HUY HOANG.
Minister of Planning and Investment: VO HONG PHUC.
Minister of Sciences and Technology: HOANG VAN PHONG.
Minister of Natural Resources and the Environment: PHAM KHOI NGUYEN.
Minister of Information and Communication: LE DOAN HOP.
Chief Government Inspector: TRAN VAN TRUYEN.
Minister, Chairman of Ethnic Minorities Committee: GIANG SEO PHU.
Minister, Chairman of the Government Office: NGUYEN XUAN PHUC.
Minister, Chairman of Sports and Physical Training Affairs: NGUYEN DANH THAI.
Minister, Chairwoman of Population, Family and Children Committee: LE THI THU.

MINISTRIES AND COMMISSIONS

Ministry of Agriculture and Rural Development: 2 Ngoc Ha, Ba Dinh District, Hanoi; tel. (4) 8468160; fax (4) 8454319; e-mail icard@agroviet.gov.vn; internet www.agroviet.gov.vn.
Ministry of Construction: 37 Le Dai Hanh, Hai Ba Trung District, Hanoi; tel. (4) 9760271; fax (4) 9762153; e-mail bxd-vp@hn.vnn.vn; internet www.moc.gov.vn.
Ministry of Culture and Information: 51–53 Ngo Quyen, Hoan Kiem District, Hanoi; tel. (4) 9438231; fax (4) 9439009; internet www.cinet.gov.vn.
Ministry of Education and Training: 49 Dai Co Viet, Hai Ba Trung District, Hanoi; tel. (4) 8694904; fax (4) 8694085; e-mail intlaff@iupui.edu; internet www.edu.net.vn.
Ministry of Finance: 28 Tran Hung Dao, Hoan Kiem District, Hanoi; tel. (4) 2202828; fax (4) 2208129; e-mail support@mof.gov.vn; internet www.mof.gov.vn.
Ministry of Fisheries: 10 Nguyen Cong Hoan, Hanoi; tel. (4) 7716396; fax (4) 7716702; e-mail mofi@mofi.gov.vn; internet www.mofi.gov.vn.
Ministry of Foreign Affairs: 1 Ton That Dam, Ba Dinh District, Hanoi; tel. (4) 8452980; fax (4) 82318725; e-mail banbientap@mofa.gov.vn; internet www.mofa.gov.vn.
Ministry of Industry: 54 Hai Ba Trung, Hoan Kiem District, Hanoi; tel. (4) 8258311; fax (4) 8265303; e-mail webmaster@moi.gov.vn; internet www.moi.gov.vn.
Ministry of Internal Services: 137A Nguyen Binh Khiem, Hai Ba Trung District, Hanoi; tel. (4) 9760370; fax (4) 9781005; e-mail ngoc-hien@hn.vnn.vn.
Ministry of Justice: 60 Tran Phu, Ba Dinh District, Hanoi; tel. (4) 8438847; fax (4) 8431431; e-mail vpb@moj.gov.vn; internet www.moj.gov.vn.
Ministry of Labour, Invalids and Social Affairs: 12 Ngo Quyen, Hoan Kiem District, Hanoi; tel. (4) 8269557; fax (4) 8248036; e-mail tapchildxh@molisa.gov.vn; internet www.molisa.gov.vn.
Ministry of National Defence: 1A Hoang Dieu, Ba Dinh District, Hanoi; tel. (4) 069 882041; fax (4) 069 532090.
Ministry of Natural Resources and the Environment: 83 Nguyen Chi Thanh, Dong Da District, Hanoi; tel. (4) 8343911; fax (4) 8359221; e-mail webmaster@monroe.gov.vn; internet www.monre.gov.vn.
Ministry of Planning and Investment: 2 Hoang Van Thu, Ba Dinh District, Hanoi; tel. (4) 8453027; fax (4) 8234453; internet www.mpi.gov.vn.
Ministry of Posts and Telecommunications: 18 Nguyen Du, Hanoi; tel. (4) 8226410; fax (4) 8263477; e-mail tt_tt@mpt.gov.vn; internet www.mpt.gov.vn.
Ministry of Public Health: 138A Giang Vo, Ba Dinh District, Hanoi; tel. (4) 8464416; fax (4) 8464051; internet www.moh.gov.vn.
Ministry of Public Security: 44 Yet Kieu, Hoan Kiem District, Hanoi; tel. (4) 8226602; fax (4) 9420223.
Ministry of Science and Technology: 39 Tran Hung Dao, Hoan Kiem District, Hanoi; tel. (4) 9439057; fax (4) 8252733; e-mail ttth@most.gov.vn; internet www.most.gov.vn.
Ministry of Trade: 21 Ngo Quyen, Hanoi; tel. (4) 8262522; fax (4) 8264696; e-mail bitec@mot.gov.vn; internet www.mot.gov.vn.
Ministry of Transport: 80 Tran Hung Dao, Hoan Kiem District, Hanoi; tel. (4) 9424015; fax (4) 8267291; internet www.mt.gov.vn.
National Commission for Population, Family and Children: 33 Tran Phu, Ba Dinh District, Hanoi; tel. (4) 7473851; fax (4) 8237983; e-mail banbientap@vcfpc.gov.vn; internet www.vcpfc.gov.vn.
Government Inspection Committee: 220 Doi Can, Ba Dinh District, Hanoi; tel. (4) 8325558; fax (4) 8325786; e-mail ttcp@thanhtra.gov.vn; internet www.thanhtra.gov.vn.

NATIONAL DEFENCE AND SECURITY COUNCIL

President: NGUYEN MINH TRIET.
Vice-President: NGUYEN TAN DUNG.
Members: NGUYEN PHU TRONG, PHAM GIA KHIEM, PHUNG QUANG THANH, LE HONG ANH.

Legislature

QUOC HOI
(National Assembly)

Elections to the 12th National Assembly were held on 20 May 2007. The new Assembly comprised 493 members (compared with 498 in the previous legislature), elected from among 875 candidates; 42 non-party candidates and one independent were elected.

Standing Committee

Chairman: NGUYEN PHU TRONG.
Vice-Chairmen: NGUYEN DUC KHIEN, UONG CHU LUU, TONG THI PHONG, HUYNH NGOC SON.

VIET NAM

Political Organizations

COMMUNIST PARTY

Dang Cong San Viet Nam (Communist Party of Viet Nam): 1 Hoang Van Thu, Hanoi; internet www.cpv.org.vn; f. 1976; ruling party; fmrly the Viet Nam Workers' Party, f. 1951 as the successor to the Communist Party of Indo-China, f. 1930; c. 3.1m. mems (2006); Gen. Sec. of Cen. Cttee NONG DUC MANH.

Political Bureau (Politburo)

Members: NONG DUC MANH, LE HONG ANH, NGUYEN MINH TRIET, NGUYEN TAN DUNG, TRUONG TAN SANG, NGUYEN PHU TRONG, PHAM GIA KHIEM, PHAM QUANG NGHI, NGUYEN SINH HUNG, NGUYEN VAN CHI, HO DUC VIET, Sr Lt-Gen. PHUNG QUANG THANH, TRUONG VINH TRONG, LE THANH HAI.

Secretariat

Members: NONG DUC MANH, TRUONG TAN SANG, TRUONG VINH TRONG, NGUYEN VAN CHI, PHAM QUANG NGHI, Sr Lt-Gen. LE VAN DUNG, TONG THI PHONG, TO HUY RUA.

OTHER POLITICAL ORGANIZATIONS

Ho Chi Minh Communist Youth Union: 60 Ba Trieu, Hanoi; tel. (4) 9435709; fax (4) 9348439; e-mail cydeco@hn.vnn.vn; f. 1931; 4m. mems; First Sec. VO VAN THUONG.

People's Action Party (PAP): POB 4752, San Jose, CA 95150-4752, USA; e-mail dang@ndhd.net; internet www.dndhd.org; Chair. NGUYEN SI BINH.

Viet Nam Fatherland Front: 46 Trang Thi, Hanoi; e-mail pttmattran@hn.vnn.vn; internet www.mattran.org.vn; f. 1930; replaced the Lien Viet (Viet Nam National League), the successor to Viet Nam Doc Lap Dong Minh Hoi (Revolutionary League for the Independence of Viet Nam) or Viet Minh; in 1977 the original org. merged with the National Front for the Liberation of South Viet Nam and the Alliance of National, Democratic and Peace Forces in South Viet Nam to form a single front; 200-member Cen. Cttee; Pres. Presidium of Cen. Cttee HUYNH DAM; Gen. Sec. VU TRONG KIM.

Vietnam Women's Union (VWU): 39 Hang Chuoi, Hanoi; tel. (4) 9713436; fax (4) 9713143; internet hoilhpn.org.vn; f. 1930; 11m. mems; Pres. HA THI KHIET.

Diplomatic Representation

EMBASSIES IN VIET NAM

Algeria: 13 Phan Chu Trinh, Hanoi; tel. (4) 8253865; fax (4) 8260830; e-mail ambalghanoi@ambalgvn.org.vn; internet www.ambalgvn.org.vn; Ambassador NACEUR BOUCHERIT.

Argentina: 8th Floor, Office Tower, Daeha Business Centre, 360 Kim Ma, Ba Dinh District, Hanoi; tel. (4) 8315262; fax (4) 8315577; e-mail embarg@hn.vnn.vn; internet www.embargentina.org.vn; Ambassador TOMÁS FERRARI.

Australia: 8 Dao Tan, Ba Dinh District, Hanoi; tel. (4) 8317755; fax (4) 8317711; e-mail austemb@fpt.vn; internet www.vietnam.embassy.gov.au; Ambassador BILL TWEDDELL.

Austria: Prime Centre, 8th Floor, 53 Quang Trung, Hai Ba Trung District, Hanoi; tel. (4) 9433050; fax (4) 9433055; e-mail hanoi-ob@bmeia.gv.at; internet www.aussenministerium.at/hanoi; Ambassador Dr JOHANNES PETERLIK.

Bangladesh: 7th Floor, Daeha Business Centre, 360 Kim Ma, Ba Dinh District, Hanoi; tel. (4) 7716625; fax (4) 7716628; Ambassador MOHD ENAMUL KABIR.

Belarus: 11th Floor, 44b Ly Thuong Kiet, Hanoi; tel. (4) 9344416; fax (4) 9344417; e-mail check@hn.vnn.vn; Ambassador ALYAKSANDR KUTSALAY.

Belgium: 9th Floor, Hanoi Towers, 49 Hai Ba Trung, Hanoi; tel. (4) 9346179; fax (4) 9346183; e-mail hanoi@diplobel.be; internet www.diplomatie.be/hanoi; Ambassador HUBERT COOREMAN.

Brazil: 14 Thuy Khue, T72 Hanoi; tel. (4) 8430817; fax (4) 8432542; e-mail vetbrem@netnam.org.vn; internet www.brazil.org.vn; Ambassador JOÃO DE MENDONÇA LIMA NETO.

Brunei: Villa No. 8 & 9, Van Phuc Diplomatic Quarter, 44/8 Van Bao, Ba Dinh District, Hanoi; tel. (4) 7262001; fax (4) 7262010; e-mail bruemviet@hn.vnn.vn; Ambassador Dato Paduka Haji MAHADI BIN WASLI (designate).

Bulgaria: Van Phuc Quarter, 5 Nui Truc, Hanoi; tel. (4) 8452095; fax (4) 8460856; e-mail bgremb@fpt.vn; internet www.mfa.bg/hanoi; Ambassador GEORGI VASSILIEV.

Cambodia: 71 Tran Hung Dao, Hanoi; tel. (4) 8253788; fax (4) 9423225; e-mail arch@fpt.vn; Ambassador (vacant).

Canada: 31 Hung Vuong, Hanoi; tel. (4) 7345000; fax (4) 7345049; e-mail hanoi@international.gc.ca; internet www.dfait-maeci.gc.ca/vietnam; Ambassador GABRIEL M. LESSARD.

Chile: Suite 1201–1203, 12th Floor, 2 Ngo Quyen, Tung Shing Sq. Bldg, Hoan Kiem District, Hanoi; tel. (4) 9351147; fax (4) 9351150; e-mail embajada1@chile.org.vn; Ambassador JORGE CANELAS UGALDE.

China, People's Republic: 46 Hoang Dieu, Hanoi; tel. (4) 8453736; fax (4) 8232826; e-mail eossc@hn.vnn.vn; internet vn.chineseembassy.org; Ambassador HU QIANWEN.

Cuba: 65A Ly Thuong Kiet, Hanoi; tel. (4) 9424775; fax (4) 9422426; e-mail embacuba@netnam.org.vn; internet embacuba.cubaminrex.cu/vietnaming; Ambassador JESÚS AISE SOTOLONGO.

Czech Republic: 13 Chu Van An, Hanoi; tel. (4) 8454131; fax (4) 8233996; internet www.mfa.cz/hanoi; Ambassador IVO ŽDÁREK.

Denmark: 19 Dien Bien Phu, Hanoi; tel. (4) 8231888; fax (4) 8231999; e-mail hanamb@um.dk; internet www.ambhanoi.um.dk; Ambassador PETER LYSHOLT HANSEN.

Egypt: 63 To Ngoc Van, Quang An, Tay Ho District, Hanoi; tel. (4) 8294999; fax (4) 8294997; e-mail arabegypt@ftp.vn; Ambassador MUHAMMAD ALAA EL-DEIN SAAD EL-LEISI.

Finland: Suite 63, 6th Floor, Central Bldg, 31 Hai Ba Trung, Hanoi; tel. (4) 8266788; fax (4) 8266766; e-mail sanomat.han@formin.fi; internet www.finland.org.vn; Ambassador PEKKA HYVÖNEN.

France: 57 Tran Hung Dao, Hanoi; tel. (4) 9437719; fax (4) 9437236; internet www.ambafrance-vn.org; Ambassador HERVÉ BOLOT.

Germany: 29 Tran Phu, Hanoi; tel. (4) 8453836; fax (4) 8453838; e-mail germanemb.hanoi@fpt.vn; internet www.hanoi.diplo.de; Ambassador ROLF SCHULZE.

Hungary: Daeha Business Centre, 12th Floor, 360 Kim Ma, Ba Dinh District, Hanoi; tel. (4) 7715714; fax (4) 7715716; e-mail hungemb@hn.vnn.vn; internet www.mfa.gov.hu/emb/hanoi; Ambassador LASZLO VIZI.

India: 58–60 Tran Hung Dao, Hanoi; tel. (4) 8244990; fax (4) 8244998; e-mail india@netnam.org.vn; internet www.indembassy.com.vn; Ambassador LAL THLA MUANA.

Indonesia: 50 Ngo Quyen, Hanoi; tel. (4) 8253353; fax (4) 8259274; e-mail komhan@hn.vnn.vn; internet www.indonesia-hanoi.org.vn; Ambassador ARTAULI RATNA MENARA PANGGABEAN TOBING.

Iran: 54 Tran Phu, Ba Dinh District, Hanoi; tel. (4) 8232068; fax (4) 8232120; e-mail iriemb@fpt.vn; Ambassador JAVAD GHAVAM SHAHIDI.

Iraq: 66 Tran Hung Dao, Hanoi; tel. (4) 9424141; fax (4) 9424055; e-mail hanemb@iraqmofamail.net; Ambassador AMAL ABOOD FAIROOZ.

Ireland: Vincom City Towers, 8th Floor, 191 Ba Trieu, Hai Ba Trung District, Hanoi; tel. (4) 9743291; fax (4) 9743295; e-mail irishembassyhanoi@dfanet.ie; Ambassador MAEVE COLLINS.

Israel: 68 Nguyen Thai Hoc, Dong Da, Hanoi; tel. (4) 8433141; fax (4) 8435760; e-mail info@hanoi.mfa.gov.il; internet hanoi.mfa.gov.il; Ambassador EPHRAIM BEN-MATITYAU.

Italy: 9 Le Phung Hieu, Hoan Kiem District, Hanoi; tel. (4) 8256256; fax (4) 8267602; e-mail ambasciata.hanoi@esteri.it; internet www.ambhanoi.esteri.it; Ambassador ALFREDO MATACOTTA CORDELLA.

Japan: 27 Lieu Giai, Ba Dinh District, Hanoi; tel. (4) 8463000; fax (4) 8463043; e-mail soumuhan@vnn.vn; internet www.vn.emb-japan.go.jp; Ambassador MITSUO SAKABA.

Korea, Democratic People's Republic: 25 Cao Ba Quat, Hanoi; tel. (4) 8453008; fax (4) 8231221; e-mail emb.dprk@hn.vnn.vn; Ambassador MA CHOL SU.

Korea, Republic: 4th Floor, Daeha Business Centre, 360 Kim Ma, Ba Dinh District, Hanoi; tel. (4) 8315111; fax (4) 8315117; e-mail korembviet@mofat.go.kr; internet vnm-hanoi.mofat.go.kr; Ambassador IM HONG-JAE.

Laos: 22 Tran Binh Trong, Hanoi; tel. (4) 9424576; fax (4) 8228414; Ambassador SOUNTHONE SAYACHAK.

Libya: A3 Van Phuc Residential Quarter, Hanoi; tel. (4) 8453379; fax (4) 8454977; e-mail libpbha@yahoo.com; Secretary SALEM ALI SALEM DANNAH.

Malaysia: 43-45 Dien Bien Phu, Ba Dinh District, Hanoi; tel. (4) 7343836; fax (4) 7343832; e-mail mwhanoi@hn.vnn.vn; internet www.kln.gov.my/perwakilan/hanoi; Ambassador LIM KIM ENG.

Mexico: 14 Thuy Khue, T-11, Hanoi; tel. (4) 8470948; fax (4) 8470949; e-mail embvietnam@sre.gob.mx; Ambassador RICARDO CÁMARA SÁNCHEZ.

Mongolia: Villa 5, Van Phuc Diplomatic Quarter, Hanoi; tel. (4) 8453009; fax (4) 8454954; e-mail mongembhanoi@hn.vnn.vn; Ambassador GANBOLD BAASANJAV.

Morocco: Sofitel Plaza, 1 Thanh Nien, Hanoi; tel. (4) 7345586; fax (4) 7345589; e-mail embamaroc-hanoi@vnn.vn; Ambassador EL HOUCINE FARDANI.

Myanmar: A-3 (101–104), Van Phuc Diplomatic Quarter, Kim Ma, Hanoi; tel. (4) 8453369; fax (4) 8452404; e-mail myan.emb@fpt.vn; Ambassador U KHIN AUNG.

Netherlands: Daeha Office Tower, 6th Floor, 360 Kim Ma, Ba Dinh District, Hanoi; tel. (4) 8315650; fax (4) 8315655; e-mail han@minbuza.nl; internet www.netherlands-embassy.org.vn; Ambassador ANDRÉ HASPELS.

New Zealand: Level 5, 63 Ly Thai To, Hanoi; tel. (4) 8241481; fax (4) 8241480; e-mail nzembhan@fpt.vn; Ambassador JAMES KEMBER.

Norway: 10th Floor, Block B, Vincom City Towers, 191 Ba Trieu, Hanoi; tel. (4) 9742930; fax (4) 9743301; e-mail emb.hanoi@mfa.no; internet www.norway.org.vn; Ambassador KJELL STORLØKKEN.

Pakistan: 44/2 Van Bao, Van Phuc Diplomatic Quarter, Hanoi; tel. (4) 7262251; fax (4) 7262253; e-mail parep-hanoi@hn.vnn.vn; Ambassador GHULAM RASOOL BALUCH.

Panama: 18th Floor, 44th St, Ly Thuong Kiet, Hanoi; tel. (4) 9365213; Ambassador LIZIA LU.

Philippines: 27B Tran Hung Dao, Hanoi; tel. (4) 9437873; fax (4) 9435760; e-mail hanoipe@dfa.gov.ph; Ambassador ESTRELLA BERENGUEL.

Poland: 3 Chua Mot Cot, Hanoi; tel. (4) 8452027; fax (4) 8236914; e-mail polamb@hn.vnn.vn; Ambassador MIROSŁAW GAJEWSKI.

Romania: 5 Le Hong Phong, Hanoi; tel. (4) 8452014; fax (4) 8430922; e-mail rombcehan@fpt.vn; Ambassador DUMITRU OLARU.

Russia: 191 La Thanh, Hanoi; tel. (4) 8336991; fax (4) 8336995; e-mail moscow.vietnam@hn.vnn.vn; Ambassador VADIM VIKTOROVICH SERAFIMOV.

Singapore: Pacific Place, Unit V804–808, 8th Floor, 83B, Ly Thuong Kiet, Hanoi; tel. (4) 9460808; fax (4) 9460821; e-mail singemb_hanoi@sgmfa.gov.sg; internet www.mfa.gov.sg/hanoi; Ambassador LIM THUAN KUAN.

South Africa: 3rd Floor, Central Bldg, 31 Hai Ba Trung, Hanoi; tel. (4) 9362000; fax (4) 9361991; e-mail hanoi@foreign.gov.za; Ambassador RATUBATSI SUPER MOLOI.

Spain: 15th Floor, Daeha Business Centre, 360 Kim Ma, Ba Dinh District, Hanoi; tel. (4) 7715207; fax (4) 7715206; e-mail embespvn@fpt.vn; Ambassador MARÍA SOLEDAD FUENTES GÓMEZ.

Sri Lanka: 55B Tran Phu, Ba Dinh District, Hanoi; tel. (4) 7341894; fax (4) 7341897; e-mail slembvn@fpt.vn; internet www.slembvn.org; Ambassador A. L. RATNAPALA.

Sweden: 2 Nui Truc, Ba Dinh District, Hanoi; tel. (4) 7260400; fax (4) 8232195; e-mail ambassaden.hanoi@foreign.ministry.se; internet www.swedenabroad.com/hanoi; Ambassador ROLF BERGMAN.

Switzerland: 44B Ly Thuong Kiet, 15th Floor, Hanoi; tel. (4) 9346589; fax (4) 9346591; e-mail vertretung@han.rep.admin.ch; internet www.eda.admin.ch/hanoi; Ambassador JEAN HUBERT LEBET.

Thailand: 63–65 Hoang Dieu, Hanoi; tel. (4) 8235092; fax (4) 8235088; e-mail thaiemhn@netnam.org.vn; internet www.thaiembassy.org.vn; Ambassador KITTIPHONG NA RANONG.

Turkey: 4th Floor, North Star Bldg, 4 Da Truong, Hanoi; tel. (4) 8222460; fax (4) 8222458; e-mail turkeyhn@fpt.vn; Ambassador (vacant).

Ukraine: 6B Le Hong Phong, Hanoi; tel. (4) 7344484; fax (4) 7344497; e-mail emb_vn@mfa.gov.ua; internet www.mfa.gov.ua/vietnam; Ambassador PAVLO SULTANSKY.

United Kingdom: Central Bldg, 4th Floor, 31 Hai Ba Trung, Hanoi; tel. (4) 9360500; fax (4) 9360561; e-mail behanoi@hn.vnn.vn; internet www.uk-vietnam.org; Ambassador MARK ANDREW GEOFFREY KENT.

USA: 7 Lang Ha, Ba Dinh District, Hanoi; tel. (4) 7721500; fax (4) 7721510; e-mail irchanoi@state.gov; internet vietnam.usembassy.gov; Ambassador MICHAEL W. MICHALAK.

Venezuela: 368 Lac Long Quan, Tay Ho District, Hanoi; tel. (4) 7588891; fax (4) 7588893; e-mail embavenezhanoi@yahoo.com; Ambassador JORGE JOSÉ RONDÓN UZCÁTEGUI.

Judicial System

Supreme People's Court
48 Ly Thuong Kiet, Hanoi.

The Supreme People's Court in Hanoi is the highest court and exercises civil and criminal jurisdiction over all lower courts. The Supreme Court may also conduct trials of the first instance in certain cases. There are People's Courts in each province and city which exercise jurisdiction in the first and second instance. Military courts hear cases involving members of the People's Army and cases involving national security. In 1993 legislation was adopted on the establishment of economic courts to consider business disputes. The observance of the law by ministries, government offices and all citizens is the concern of the People's Organs of Control, under a Supreme People's Organ of Control. The Chief Justice of the Supreme People's Court and the Chief Procurator of the Supreme People's Organ of Control are elected by the National Assembly, on the recommendation of the President.

Chief Justice of the Supreme People's Court: TRUONG HOA BINH.

Chief Procurator of the Supreme People's Organ of Control: TRAN QUOC VUONG.

Religion

Traditional Vietnamese religion included elements of Indian and all three Chinese religions: Mahayana Buddhism, Daoism and Confucianism. Its most widespread feature was the cult of ancestors, practised in individual households and clan temples. Various Buddhist sects belong to the 'new' religions of Caodaism and Hoa Hao. The Protestant and Roman Catholic Churches are also represented. In 2007 operating licences were granted to several additional religions, including the Mennonite Church, the Baptist Church and the Bahá'í faith.

BUDDHISM

In the North a Buddhist organization, grouping Buddhists loyal to the Democratic Republic of Viet Nam, was formed in 1954. In the South the United Buddhist Church was formed in 1964, incorporating several disparate groups, including the 'militant' An-Quang group (mainly natives of central Viet Nam), the group of Thich Tam Chau (mainly northern emigrés in Saigon) and the southern Buddhists of the Xa Loi temple. In 1982 most of the Buddhist sects were amalgamated into the state-approved Viet Nam Buddhist Church (which comes under the authority of the Viet Nam Fatherland Front). The number of adherents was estimated at 10m. in 2005, approximately 12% of the total population. The Unified Buddhist Church of Viet Nam is an anti-Government organization.

Viet Nam Buddhist Church: Pres. Exec. Council Most Ven. THICH TRI TINH; Gen. Sec. THICH MING CHAU.

Unified Buddhist Church of Viet Nam: Patriarch THICH HUYEN QUANG.

CAODAISM

Formally inaugurated in 1926, this is a syncretic religion based on spiritualist seances with a predominantly ethical content, but sometimes with political overtones. There are 13 different sects, of which the most politically involved (1940–75) was that of Tay Ninh. Another sect, the Tien Thien, was represented in the National Liberation Front from its inception. There were an estimated 2.4m. adherents in 2005, resident mainly in the South.

Leader: Cardinal THAI HUU THANH.

CHRISTIANITY

In 2005 the number of Christian adherents represented an estimated 7.2% of the total population.

The Roman Catholic Church

The Roman Catholic Church has been active in Viet Nam since the 17th century, and since 1933 has been led mainly by Vietnamese priests. Many Roman Catholics moved from North to South Viet Nam in 1954–55, but some remained in the North. The total number of adherents was estimated at 5,844,452 in December 2005, representing 5.5% of the population. For ecclesiastical purposes, Viet Nam comprises three archdioceses and 23 dioceses.

Bishops' Conference

Conférence Episcopale du Viêt Nam, 22 Tran Phu, Khank Hoa, Nha Trang; tel. (58) 822842; fax (58) 815494; e-mail vangia@dng.vnn.vn. f. 1980; Pres. Most Rev. PAUL NGUYEN VAN HÒA (Bishop of Nha Trang).

Archbishop of Hanoi: Most Rev. JOSEPH NGO QUANG KIET, Archevêché, 40 Pho Nha Chung, Hanoi; tel. (4) 8254424; fax (4) 9285073; e-mail ttgmhn@hn.vnn.vn.

Archbishop of Ho Chi Minh City: Cardinal JEAN-BAPTISTE PHAM MINH MÂN, Archevêché, 180 Nguyen Dinh Chieu, Ho Chi Minh City 3; tel. (8) 9303828; fax (8) 9300598.

Archbishop of Hué: Most Rev. ETIENNE NGUYEN NHU THE, Archevêché, 6 Nguyen Truong To, Hué; tel. (54) 824937; fax (54) 833656; e-mail tgmhue@dng.vnn.vn.

Committee for Solidarity of Patriotic Vietnamese Catholics: 59 Trang Thi, Hanoi; Pres. Rev. VUONG DINH AI.

The Protestant Church

Introduced in 1920 with 500 adherents; the total number was estimated at 500,000 in 2005.

VIET NAM *Directory*

HOA HAO
A new manifestation of an older religion called Buu Son Ky Huong, the Hoa Hao sect was founded by Nguyen Phu So in 1939. There were an estimated 1.6m. adherents in 2005.

ISLAM
The number of Muslims was estimated at 65,000 in 2005.

The Press

The Ministry of Culture and Information supervises the activities of newspapers, news agencies and periodicals.

DAILIES

Hanoi

Le Courrier du Viet Nam: 33 Le Thanh Tong, Hanoi; tel. (4) 9334587; fax (4) 8258368; e-mail courrier@vnagency.com.vn; internet lecourrier.vnagency.com.vn; French; publ. by the Viet Nam News Agency; Editor-in-Chief TRAN SON MACH.

Dan Tri (Intellectual People's Standard): 2/48 Giang Vo, Dong Da District, Hanoi; tel. (4) 7366491; fax (4) 7366490; e-mail dantri@gmail.com; internet www.dantri.com.vn; f. 1982, fmrly known as *Tin Tuc* (News); publ. by the Viet Nam News Agency; afternoon; Vietnamese; Editor-in-Chief HUY HOAN PHAM.

Hanoi Moi (New Hanoi): 44 Le Thai To, Hoan Kiem District, Hanoi; tel. (4) 8253067; fax (4) 8287327; e-mail quangcao@hanoimoi.com.vn; internet www.hanoimoi.com.vn; f. 1976; organ of Hanoi Cttee of the Communist Party of Viet Nam; Editor HO XUAN SON; circ. 35,000.

Lao Dong (Labour): 15/167 Tay Son, Dong Da District, Hanoi; tel. (4) 5330305; fax (4) 5370141; e-mail webmaster@laodong.com.vn; internet www.laodong.com.vn; f. 1929; organ of the Viet Nam General Confederation of Labour; Editor-in-Chief VUONG VAN VIET; circ. 80,000.

Nhan Dan (The People): 71 Hang Trong, Hoan Kiem District, Hanoi; tel. (4) 8254231; fax (4) 8255593; e-mail toasoan@nhandan.org.vn; internet www.nhandan.org.vn; f. 1946; official organ of the Communist Party of Viet Nam; Editor-in-Chief DINH THE HUYNH; circ. 180,000.

Quan Doi Nhan Dan (People's Army): 7 Phan Dinh Phung, Hanoi; tel. (4) 8254118; f. 1950; organ of the armed forces; Editor NGUYEN QANG HAI; circ. 60,000.

Thanh Nien: 248 Cong Quynh St, District 1, Hanoi; tel. (8) 8394046; fax (8) 8322025; internet www.thanhniennews.com; f. 1986; flagship publication of the Viet Nam National Youth Federation; Chief Editor NGUYEN CONG KHE.

Viet Nam Economic Times: 96 Hoang Quoc Viet, Cau Giay District, Hanoi; tel. (4) 7552060; fax (4) 7552046; e-mail vet@hn.vnn.vn; internet www.vneconomy.com.vn; f. 1994; in Vietnamese (with monthly edn in English); Editor-in-Chief Prof. DAO NGUYEN CAT; Dep. Editor-in-Chief NGUYEN THI VAN ANH; circ 38,900.

Viet Nam News: 11 Tran Hung Dao, Hanoi; tel. (4) 9332314; fax 9332311; e-mail vnnews@vnagency.com.vn; internet vietnamnews.vnanet.vn; f. 1991; English; publ. by the Viet Nam News Agency; Editor-in-Chief TRAN MAI HUONG; circ. 60,000.

Ho Chi Minh City

Sai Gon Giai Phong (Liberated Saigon): 432–438 Nguyen Thi Minh Khai, District 3, Ho Chi Minh City; tel. (8) 8395942; fax (8) 8324958; internet www.sggp.org.vn; f. 1975; organ of Ho Chi Minh City Cttee of the Communist Party of Viet Nam; Editor-in-Chief TRAN THE TUYEN; circ. 100,000.

Saigon Times: 35 Nam Ky Khoi Nghia, District 1, Ho Chi Minh City; tel. (8) 8295936; fax (8) 8294294; e-mail sgt@thesaigontimes.vn; internet www.saigontimes.com.vn; f. 1991; Vietnamese and English; business issues; Editor-in-Chief TRAN THI NGOC HUE.

PERIODICALS

Dai Doan Ket (Great Unity): 66 Ba Trieu, Hanoi; tel. (4) 8262420; internet www.mattran.org.vn/Daidoanket; f. 1977; weekly; organ of the Viet Nam Fatherland Front; Editor NGUYEN QUANG CANH.

Dau Tu: 175 Nguyen Thai Hoc, Hanoi; tel. (4) 8450537; fax (4) 8457937; e-mail vir@hn.vnn.vn; internet www.vir.com.vn/Client/dautu/default.asp; 3 a week; business newspaper publ. in Vietnamese; Editor-in-Chief Dr NGUYEN ANH TUAN; circ. 40,000.

Dau Tu Chung Khoan: 175 Nguyen Thai Hoc, Hanoi; tel. (4) 8450537; fax (4) 8457937; e-mail vir@hn.vnn.vn; internet www.vir.com.vn/CLIENT/DautuChungkhoan/default.asp; weekly; stock market news publ. in Vietnamese; Editor-in-Chief Dr NGUYEN ANH TUAN; circ. 50,000.

Giao Duc Thoi Dai (People's Teacher): 29B Ngo Quyen, Hoan Kiem District, Hanoi; tel. (4) 8241781; fax (4) 9345611; e-mail gdtd@fpt.vn; internet www.gdtd.com.vn; f. 1959; weekly; organ of the Ministry of Education and Training; Editor TRAN DANG THAO.

Giao Thong-Van Tai (Communications and Transport): 1 Nha Tho, Hanoi; tel. (4) 8255387; f. 1962; weekly; organ of the Ministry of Transport; Editor NGUYEN VAN LUU; circ. 30,000.

Hoa Hoc Tro (Pupils' Flowers): 5 Hoa Ma, Hanoi; tel. (4) 8211065; internet www.hoahoctro.com; weekly; Editor NGUYEN PHONG DOANH; circ. 150,000.

Khoa Hoc Ky Thuat Kinh Te The Gioi (World Science, Technology and Economy): 5 Ly Thuong Kiet, Hanoi; tel. (4) 8252931; f. 1982; weekly.

Khoa Hoc va Doi Song (Science and Life): 70 Tran Hung Dao, Hanoi; tel. (4) 8253427; f. 1959; weekly; Editor-in-Chief TRAN CU; circ. 30,000.

Nghe Thuat Dien Anh (Cinematography): 65 Tran Hung Dao, Hanoi; tel. (4) 8262473; f. 1984; fortnightly; Editor DANG NHAT MINH.

Nguoi Cong Giao Viet Nam (Vietnamese Catholic): 59 Trang Thi, Hanoi; tel. (4) 8256242; f. 1984; weekly; organ of the Cttee for Solidarity of Patriotic Vietnamese Catholics; Editor-in-Chief SO CHI.

Nguoi Dai Bieu Nhan Dan (People's Deputy): 35 Ngo Quyen, Hanoi; tel. (4) 08046231; fax (4) 08046659; e-mail ndbnd@hn.vnn.vn; f. 1988; bi-weekly; disseminates resolutions of the National Assembly and People's Council; Editor-in-Chief HO ANH TAI (acting); circ. 2m.

Nguoi Hanoi (The Hanoian): 19 Hang Buom, Hanoi; tel. (4) 8255662; f. 1984; Editor VU QUAN PHUONG.

Nha Bao Va Cong Luan (The Journalist and Public Opinion): 59 Ly Thai To, Hanoi; tel. (4) 8253609; fax (4) 8250797; f. 1985; monthly review; organ of the Viet Nam Journalists' Asscn; Editor-in-Chief PHAN DUOC TOAN; circ. 40,000.

Nong Nghiep Viet Nam (Viet Nam Agriculture): 14 Ngo Quyen, Hanoi; tel. (4) 8256492; fax (4) 8252923; f. 1987; weekly; Editor LE NAM SON.

Outlook: 11 Tran Hung Dao, Hanoi; tel. (4) 8222884; fax (4) 9424908; e-mail vnnews@vnagency.com.vn; internet vietnamnews.vnanet.com.vn; f. 2002; monthly news magazine; Editor-in-Chief TRAN MAI HUONG; circ. 6,000.

Phu Nu (Woman): Vietnam Women's Union, International Relations Dept, 39 Hang Chuoi, Hanoi; e-mail VWUnion@netnam.org.vn; f. 1997; fortnightly; women's magazine; circ. 100,000.

Phu Nu Thu Do (Capital Women): 72 Quan Su, Hanoi; tel. (4) 8247228; fax (4) 8223989; f. 1987; weekly; magazine of the Hanoi Women's Union; Editor-in-Chief MAI THUC.

Phu Nu Viet Nam (Vietnamese Women): 39 Hang Chuoi, Hanoi; tel. (4) 8253500; weekly; magazine of the Vietnam Women's Union; Editor-in-Chief PHUONG MINH.

Suc Khoe Va Doi Song (Health and Life): 138A Giang Vo, Hanoi; tel. (4) 8443144; weekly; published by the Ministry of Public Health; Editor LE THAU; circ. 20,000.

Tap Chi Cong San (Communist Review): 52 Nguyen Chi Thanh, Hanoi; tel. (4) 7753605; fax (4) 7753633; e-mail bbttccs@hn.vnn.vn; internet www.tapchicongsan.org.vn; f. 1955 as *Hoc Tap*; fortnightly; political and theoretical organ of the Communist Party of Viet Nam; Editor-in-Chief TA NGOC TAN; circ. 50,000.

Tap Chi Nghien Cuu Van Hoc (Literature Research Magazine): 20 Ly Thai To, Hanoi; tel. (4) 8252895; e-mail tcvapmail@vnn.vn; monthly; published by the Institute of Literature; Editor-in-Chief PHAN TRONG THUONG.

Tap Chi San Khau (Theatre Magazine): 51 Tran Hung Dao, Hanoi; tel. (4) 9434423; fax (4) 9434293; e-mail trongkhoi@hn.vnn.vn; f. 1973; monthly; Editor NGO THAO.

Tap Chi Tac Pham Van Hoc: 65 Nguyen Du, Hanoi; tel. (4) 8252442; f. 1987; monthly; organ of the Viet Nam Writers' Asscn; Editor-in-Chief NGUYEN DINH THI; circ. 15,000.

Tap Chi Tu Tuong Van Hoa (Ideology and Culture Review): Hanoi; f. 1990; organ of the Central Committee Department of Ideology and Culture; Editor PHAM HUY VAN.

The Thao Van Hoa (Sports and Culture): 5 Ly Thuong Kiet, Hanoi; tel. (4) 8267043; fax (4) 8264901; f. 1982; weekly; Editor-in-Chief NGUYEN HUU VINH; circ. 100,000.

The Thao Viet Nam (Viet Nam Sports): 18 Ly Van Phuc, Hanoi; tel. (4) 7340217; fax (4) 7341494; e-mail baottvn@yahoo.com; internet www.thethaovietnam.com.vn; f. 1968; weekly; Editor HOANG DUR.

Thieu Nhi Dan Toc (The Ethnic Young): 5 Hoa Ma, Hanoi; tel. (4) 9317133; bi-monthly; Editor PHAM THANH LONG; circ. 60,000.

Thieu Nien Tien Phong (Young Pioneers): 5 Hoa Ma, Hanoi; tel. (4) 9713133; fax (4) 8215710; e-mail toasoan@tntp.org.vn; internet www.tntp.org.vn; three a week; Editor PHAM THANH LONG; circ. 210,000.

Thoi Bao Kinh Te Viet Nam: 175 Nguyen Thai Hoc, Hanoi; tel. (4) 8452411; fax (4) 8432755; f. 1993; 2 a week; Editor-in-Chief Pavef Daonguyencat; circ. 37,000.

Thoi Trang Tre (New Fashion): 12 Ho Xuan Huong, Hanoi; tel. (4) 8254032; fax (4) 8226002; f. 1993; monthly; Editor Vu Quang Vinh; circ. 80,000.

Thuong Mai (Commerce): 100 Lo Duc, Hanoi; tel. (4) 8263150; f. 1990; weekly; organ of the Ministry of Trade; Editor Tran Nam Vinh.

Tien Phong (Vanguard): 15 Ho Xuan Huong, Hanoi; tel. (4) 8264301; fax (4) 8225032; f. 1953; four a week; organ of the Ho Chi Minh Communist Youth Union and of the Forum of Vietnamese Youth; Editor Duong Xuan Nam; circ. 165,000.

Van Hoa (Culture and Arts): 26 Dien Bien Phu, Hanoi; tel. (4) 8257781; f. 1957; fortnightly; Editor Phi Van Tuong.

Van Nghe (Arts and Letters): 17 Tran Quoc Toan, Hanoi; tel. (4) 8264430; f. 1949; weekly; organ of the Vietnamese Writers' Union; Editor Huu Thinh; circ. 40,000.

Van Nghe Quan Doi (Army Literature and Arts): 4 Ly Nam De, Hanoi; tel. (4) 8254370; f. 1957; monthly; Editor Nguyen Tri Huan; circ. 50,000.

Viet Nam Business Forum: 9 Dao Duy Anh, 4th Floor, Dong Da District, Hanoi; tel. (4) 5743985; fax (4) 5743063; e-mail vbfhn@hn.vnn.vn; internet vibforum.vcci.com.vn; f. 1995; weekly magazine in English; publ. by the Viet Nam Chamber of Commerce and Industry; Editor-in-Chief Doan Duy Khuong.

Viet Nam Courier: 5 Ly Thuong Kiet, Hanoi; tel. (4) 8261847; fax (4) 8242317; weekly; English; publ. by the Viet Nam News Agency; Editor-in-Chief Nguyen Duc Giap.

Viet Nam Cultural Window: 46 Tran Hung Dao, Hanoi; tel. (4) 8253841; fax (4) 8269578; e-mail vncw@hn.vnn.vn; f. 1998; every two months; English; Dir Tran Doan Lam.

Viet Nam Investment Review (VIR): 175 Nguyen Thai Hoc, Hanoi; tel. (4) 8450537; fax (4) 8235281; e-mail vir@hn.vnn.vn; internet www.vir.com.vn/Client/VIR/Default.asp; f. 1990; weekly; business newspaper publ. in English; Editor-in-Chief Dr Nguyen Phu Ky; circ 40,000.

Vietnam Pictorial: 11 Tran Hung Dao, Hanoi; tel. (4) 9332303; fax (4) 9332291; e-mail baodientuba@fpt.vn; internet vietnampictorial@vnanet.vn; f. 1954; monthly online, in Vietnamese, English, French, Chinese, Japanese, Spanish and Russian; fmrly Viet Nam Review; Editor-in-Chief Nguyen Vinh Quang; circ. 138,000.

Viet Nam Renovation: Hanoi; f. 1994; quarterly magazine on reform of the agricultural sector; in Vietnamese, Chinese and English.

Viet Nam Social Sciences: 27 Tran Xuan Soan, Hanoi; tel. (4) 9784578; fax (4) 9783869; e-mail 21.6.tapchikhxh@fpt.vn; f. 1984; every 2 months; publ. in English and Vietnamese; organ of Viet Nam Social Academy; Editor-in-Chief Dr Le Dinh Cuc.

Vietnamese Studies: 46 Tran Hung Dao, Hanoi; tel. (4) 8253841; fax (4) 8269578; e-mail thegioi@hn.vnn.vn; internet www.thegioipublishers.com.vn; f. 1964; quarterly; English and French edns; Dir and Chief Editor Dr Tran Doan Lâm.

NEWS AGENCY

Viet Nam News Agency (VNA): 5 Ly Thuong Kiet, Hoan Kiem District, Hanoi; tel. (4) 8252931; fax (4) 8252984; e-mail btk@vnanet.vn; internet www.vnanet.vn; f. 1945; mem. of Organization of Asian and Pacific News Agencies; Gen. Dir Nguyen Quoc Uy.

PRESS ASSOCIATION

Viet Nam Journalists' Association (VJA): 59 Ly Thai To, Hanoi; tel. (4) 8269747; fax (4) 8250797; e-mail sumocon@gmail.com; internet www.vja.org.vn; f. 1950; asscn of editors, reporters and photographers working in the press, radio, television and news agencies; 16,000 mems (2006); Pres. Dinh The Huynh; Vice-Pres. Le Quoc Trung.

Publishers

Am Nhac Dia Hat (Music) Publishing House: 61 Ly Thai To, Hoan Kiem District, Hanoi; tel. (4) 8256208; f. 1986; produces cassettes, videocassettes, books and printed music; Dir Pham Duc Loc.

Cong An Nhan Dan (People's Public Security) Publishing House: 167 Mai Hac De, Hai Ba Trung District, Hanoi; tel. (4) 8260910; f. 1981; cultural and artistic information, public order and security; Dir Pham Van Tham.

Giao Thong Van Tai (Communications and Transport) Publishing House: 80B Tran Hung Dao, Hanoi; tel. (4) 8255620; fax (4) 8224784; f. 1983; managed by the Ministry of Transport and Communications; 350 titles annually; Dir Le Tu Giang.

Khoa Hoc Va Ky Thuat (Science and Technology) Publishing House: 70 Tran Hung Dao, Hanoi; tel. (4) 9424786; fax (4) 8220658; e-mail nxbkhkt@hn.vnn.vn; internet www.nxbkhkt.com.vn; f. 1960; scientific and technical works, guide books, dictionaries, popular and management books; Dir Prof. Dr To Dang Hai.

Khoa Hoc Xa Hoi (Social Sciences) Publishing House: 61 Phan Chu Trinh, Hanoi; tel. (4) 8255428; f. 1967; managed by the Institute of Social Science; Dir Dr Nguyen Duc Zieu.

Kim Dong Publishing House: 55 Quang Trung, Hanoi; tel. (4) 9434730; fax (4) 8229085; e-mail kimdong@hn.vnn.vn; internet www.nxbkimdong.com.vn; f. 1957; children's; managed by the Ho Chi Minh Communist Youth Union; Dir Pham Quang Vinh; Editor-in-Chief Le Thi Dat.

Lao Dong (Labour) Publishing House: 54 Giang Vo, Hanoi; tel. (4) 8515380; f. 1945; translations and political works; managed by the Viet Nam General Confederation of Labour; Dir Le Thanh Tong.

My Thuat (Fine Arts) Publishing House: 44B Hamlong, Hanoi; tel. (4) 8253036; f. 1987; managed by the Plastic Arts Workers' Association; Dir Truong Hanh.

Nha Xuat Ban Giao Duc (Education) Publishing House: 81 Tran Hung Dao, Hanoi; tel. (4) 8220073; fax (4) 9422010; f. 1957; managed by the Ministry of Education and Training; Dir Ngo Tran Ai; Editor-in-Chief Nguyen Quy Thao.

Nha Xuat Ban Hoi Nha Van (Writers' Association) Publishing House: 65 Nguyen Du, Hoan Kiem District, Hanoi; tel. and fax (4) 8222135; f. 1957; managed by the Vietnamese Writers' Association; Editor-in-Chief and Dir (acting) Ngo Van Phu.

Nong Nghiep (Agriculture) Publishing House: DH 14, Phoung Mai Ward, Dong Da District, Hanoi; tel. (4) 8523887; f. 1976; managed by the Ministry of Agriculture and Rural Development; Dir Duong Quang Dieu.

Phu Nu (Women) Publishing House: 16 Alexandre De Rhodes, Hanoi; tel. (4) 8294459; f. 1957; managed by the Vietnamese Women's Union; Dir Tran Thu Huong.

Quan Doi Nhan Dan (People's Army) Publishing House: 25 Ly Nam De, Hanoi; tel. (4) 8255766; managed by the Ministry of National Defence; Dir Doan Chuong.

San Khau (Theatre) Publishing House: 51 Tran Hung Dao, Hanoi; tel. (4) 8264423; f. 1986; managed by the Stage Artists' Association.

Su That (Truth) Publishing House: 24 Quang Trung, Hanoi; tel. (4) 8252008; fax (4) 8251881; f. 1945; managed by the Communist Party of Viet Nam; Marxist-Leninist classics, politics and philosophy; Dir Tran Nham.

Thanh Nien (Youth) Publishing House: 270 Nguyen Dinh Chieu, District 3, Hanoi; tel. and fax (4) 8222612; f. 1954; managed by the Ho Chi Minh Communist Youth Union; Dir Bui Van Ngoi.

The Duc The Thao (Physical Education and Sports) Publishing House: 7 Trinh Hoai Duc, Hanoi; tel. (4) 8256155; f. 1974; managed by the Ministry of Culture and Information; Dir Nguyen Hieu.

The Gioi Publishers: 46 Tran Hung Dao, Hanoi; tel. (4) 8253841; fax (4) 8269578; e-mail thegioi@hn.vnn.vn; internet www.thegioipublishers.com.vn; f. 1957; foreign language publications; managed by the Ministry of Culture and Information; Dir and Chief Editor Dr Tran Doan Lâm.

Thong Ke (Statistics) Publishing House: 96 Thuy Khe, Hanoi; tel. (4) 8257814; f. 1980; managed by the Gen. Statistics Office; Dir Nguyen Dao.

Van Hoa (Culture) Publishing House: 43 Lo Duc, Hanoi; tel. (4) 8253517; f. 1971; managed by the Ministry of Culture and Information; Dir Quang Huy.

Van Hoc (Literature) Publishing House: 19 Nguyen Truong To, Ba Dinh,, Hanoi; tel. (4) 8294783; fax (4) 8294781; f. 1948; managed by the Ministry of Culture and Information; Dir Nguyen Van Cu.

Xay Dung (Building) Publishing House: 37 Le Dai Hanh, Hanoi; tel. (4) 8268271; fax (4) 8215369; f. 1976; managed by the Ministry of Construction; Dir Nguyen Luong Bich.

Y Hoc (Medicine) Publishing House: 4 Le Thanh Ton, Phan Chu Trinh, Hoan Kiem District, Hanoi; tel. (4) 8255281; e-mail xuatbanhoc@netnam.vn; managed by the Ministry of Public Health; Dir Hoang Trong Quang.

VIET NAM   *Directory*

Broadcasting and Communications

TELECOMMUNICATIONS

Directorate General for Posts and Telecommunications (DGPT): Department of Science-Technology and International Cooperation, 18 Nguyen Du, Hanoi; tel. (4) 8226580; fax (4) 8226590; industry regulator; Sec.-Gen. Dr MAI LIEM TRUC.

Board of the Technical and Economic Programme on Information Technology: 39 Tran Hung Dao, Hanoi; e-mail nyenet@itnet.gov.vn; Gen. Dir Dr DO VAN LOC.

Electricity of Viet Nam Telecommunications Co (EVN Telecom): 18 Tran Nguyen Han, Hanoi; tel. (4) 8249508; fax (4) 8249461; internet www.evntelecom.com; provides fixed and cellular telephone services, as well as broadband internet services.

Hanoi Telecommunications Co (Hanoi Telecom): 149C Truong Dinh, District 3, Ho Chi Minh City; tel. (8) 9351744; fax (8) 9351745; e-mail info@hanoitelecom.com; internet www.hanoitelecom.com; f. 2005; cellular telephone service provider.

Saigon Post and Telecommunications Service Corpn: 45 Le Duan, District 1, Ho Chi Minh City; tel. (8) 4040608; fax (8) 4040609; e-mail saigonpostel@saigonpostel.com.vn; internet www.saigonpostel.com.vn; f. 1995; partially owned by the State; nationwide post and telecommunications services; Chair. TRAN THI NGOC BINH; Pres. PHAM NGOC TUAN.

Viet Nam Military Electronics and Telecommunications Corpn (Viettel): 16 Phao Dai Lang, Dong Da District, Hanoi; tel. (4) 8461453; fax (4) 7733585; internet www.viettel.com.vn; f. 1998; offers range of post and telecommunication services, including cellular telephone and broadband internet services; Dir HOANG ANG XUAN.

Viet Nam Posts and Telecommunications Corpn (VNPT): 18 Nguyen Du, Hai Ba Trung District, Hanoi; tel. (4) 5113859; fax (4) 5182808; e-mail vnpt_website@vnpt.com.vn; internet www.vnpt.com.vn; f. 1995; state-owned communications co; Chair. PHAM LONG TRAN (acting); Pres. and CEO VU TUAN HUNG.

Viet Nam Mobile Telecommunication Services Co (MobiFone): Hanoi; internet www.mobifone.com.vn; f. 1993; mobile cellular telephone service provider.

Viet Nam Telecommunication Services Co (VinaPhone): 57A Huynh Thuc Khang, Dong Da District, Hanoi; tel. (4) 8358816; fax (4) 7731745; internet www.vinaphone.com.vn; f. 1996; provides mobile cellular telephone services; Dir HOANG TRUNG HAI.

Vietnam Power Telecommunications Co (VP Telecom): Hanoi; f. 2004; cellular telephone service provider.

RADIO

In 1998 there were 390 FM stations, 567 district radio stations and 6,505 commune radio stations in Viet Nam. The Ministry of Culture and Information is responsible for the management of radio services.

Voice of Viet Nam (VOV): 58 Quan Su, Hanoi; tel. (4) 9344231; fax (4) 9344230; e-mail english@vovnews.vn; internet www.vov.org.vn; f. 1945; four domestic channels in Vietnamese; two foreign service channels in English, Japanese, French, Khmer, Laotian, Spanish, Thai, Cantonese, Mandarin, Indonesian, Vietnamese and Russian; Dir-Gen. Dr VU VAN HIEN.

TELEVISION

At the end of 1994 there were 53 provincial television stations and 232 relay stations in Viet Nam. The Ministry of Culture and Information is responsible for the management of television services.

Viet Nam Television (VTV): 43 Nguyen Chi Thanh, Hanoi; tel. (4) 8354992; fax (4) 8350882; e-mail webmaster@vtv.org.vn; internet www.vtv.org.vn; television was introduced in South Viet Nam in 1966 and in North Viet Nam in 1970; broadcasts from Hanoi (via satellite) to the whole country, the Asia region, Western Europe and North America; Vietnamese, French, English; Dir-Gen. Dr VU VAN HIEN.

Finance

(cap. = capital; p.u. = paid up; res = reserves; dep. = deposits; m. = million; brs = branches; amounts in new dông unless otherwise indicated)

BANKING

In 2002 the Vietnamese banking system comprised five state-owned commercial banks, one policy bank, five joint-venture banks, 26 foreign bank branches, 36 joint-stock commercial banks and approximately 900 People's Credit Funds. From March 2006 foreign banks were for the first time allowed to offer a full range of banking services.

Central Bank

State Bank of Viet Nam: 47–49 Ly Thai To, Hanoi; tel. (4) 8242479; fax (4) 8268765; e-mail nhnn@sbv.gov.vn; internet www.sbv.gov.vn; f. 1951; central bank of issue; provides a national network of banking services and supervises the operation of the state banking system; Gov. NGUYEN VAN GIAU; 61 brs and sub-brs.

State Banks

Bank for Agriculture and Rural Development: 2 Lang Ha, Ba Dinh District, Hanoi; tel. (4) 8313694; fax (4) 8313717; e-mail webmaster@vbard.com; internet www.vbard.com; f. 1988; cap. 6,113,660m., res −5,630,041m., dep. 145,499,224m. (Dec. 2004); Chair. NGOC DO TAT; Gen. Dir VAN SO LE; 1,291 brs.

Bank for Foreign Trade of Viet Nam (Vietcombank): 198 Tran Quang Khai, Hanoi; tel. (4) 8251322; fax (4) 8269067; e-mail webmaster@vietcombank.com.vn; internet www.vietcombank.com.vn; f. 1963; authorized to deal in foreign currencies and all other international banking business; undergoing equitization in mid-2005; cap. (p.u.) 5,455,546m., res 2,812,846m., dep. 123,039,203m. (Dec. 2005); Chair. NGUYEN HOA BINH; Dir-Gen. VU VIET NGOAN; 23 brs.

Bank for Investment and Development of Vietnam (Vietinde Bank): Vincom City Tower, Block A, 191 Ba Trieu, Hai Ba Trung District, Hanoi; tel. (4) 2200422; fax (4) 2200399; e-mail fi@bidv.com.vn; internet www.bidv.com.vn; cap. 4,077,401m., res 3,437,687m., dep. 149,352,743m. (Dec. 2006); Chair. VU QUOC SAU; Gen. Dir TRAN BAC HA.

Saigon Bank for Industry and Trade: 2C Pho Duc Chinh, District 1, Ho Chi Minh City; tel. (8) 9143183; fax (8) 9143193; internet www.saigonbank.com.vn; cap. 400,000m., res 98,294m., dep. 3,475,260m. (Dec. 2005); specializes in trade and industry activities; Chair. NGUYEN PHUC MINH; Dir-Gen. TRAN THI VIET ANH; 11 brs and 7 sub-brs.

Vietnam Bank for Industry and Trade (VietinBank): 108 Tran Hung Dao, Hanoi; tel. (4) 9421030; fax (4) 9421032; e-mail webteam@icbv.com; internet www.icb.com.vn; f. 1987; fmrly Industrial and Commercial Bank of Viet Nam (Incombank); state-owned; authorized to receive personal savings, extend loans, issue stocks and invest in export-orientated cos and jt ventures with foreign interests; cap. 3,405,705m., res 1,262,749m., dep. 100,571,938m. (Dec. 2005); Chair. PHAM HUY HUNG; Gen. Dir PHAM XUAN LAP; 131 brs.

Vietnam Export-Import Commercial Joint-Stock Bank (Vietnam Eximbank): 7 Le Thi Hong Gam, District 1, Ho Chi Minh City; tel. (8) 8210055; fax (8) 8296063; internet www.eximbank.com.vn; f. 1989 as Vietnam Export Import Bank, name changed as above 1992; authorized to undertake banking transactions for the production and processing of export products and export-import operations; cap. 715,396m., res 105,790m., dep. 10,309,077m. (Dec. 2005); Chair. NGUYEN THANH LONG; Dir-Gen. NGUYEN GIA DINH; 5 brs.

Viet Nam Technological and Commercial Joint-Stock Bank (Techcombank): 15 Dao Duy Tu, Hoan Kiem District, Hanoi; tel. (4) 8243941; fax (4) 8250545; internet www.techcombank.vn; cap. 1,500,000m., res 90,566m., dep. 14,955,526m. (Dec. 2006); Chair. NGUYEN THI NGA; Pres. and CEO NGUYEN DUC VINH.

Joint-Stock and Other Banks

CBD (Codo Rural Share Commercial Bank): Co Do, Thoi Dong, O Mon, Can Tho Province; tel. (71) 61642; Dir TRAN NGOC HA.

DS Bank (Dongthap Commercial Joint-Stock Bank): 48 Rad 30/4, Cao Lanh Town, Dong Thap Province; tel. (67) 51441; fax (67) 51878; Dir HOANG VAN TU.

Ficombank (Denhat Joint-Stock Commercial Bank): 67A Le Quang Sung, District 6, Ho Chi Minh City; tel. (8) 8556066; fax (8) 8557093; Dir VAN DUONG.

Indovina Bank Ltd: 39 Ham Nghi, District 1, Ho Chi Minh City; tel. (8) 8224995; fax (8) 8230131; internet www.indovinabank.com.vn; f. 1990; jt venture of the Cathay United Bank (Taiwan) and the Industrial and Commercial Bank of Viet Nam; also has brs in Hanoi, Haiphong, Binh Duong, Can Tho and Dong Nai; cap. US $25m., res $3.4m., dep. $151m. (Dec. 2004); Chair. ROGER MING HSIEN LEE; Gen. Dir JAN YEI FONG; 5 brs.

Maritime Bank: 5A Nguyen Tri Phuong, Haiphong; tel. (3) 1823076; fax (3) 1823063; internet www.msb.com.vn; f. 1991; cap. 109,310m. dông (2003); Pres. TRAN BA VINH; 9 brs.

Phuong Nam Commercial Joint-Stock Bank (Southern Bank): 279 Ly Thuong Kiet, District 11, Ho Chi Minh City; tel. (8) 8663890; fax (8) 8663904; internet www.southernbank.com.vn; f. 1993; Chair. TRUONG TY.

Quedo Joint-Stock Bank: 1-3-5 Can Giuoc, District 8, Ho Chi Minh City; tel. (8) 8562418; fax (8) 8553596; Dir BAO LAN.

Sacombank (Saigon Thuong Tin Commercial Joint-Stock Bank): 278 Nam Ky Khoi Nghia St, District 3, Ho Chi Minh City; tel. (8) 9320420; fax (8) 9320424; e-mail sacombank@vnn.vn; internet www.sacombank.com.vn; f. 1991; became the first bank to list on the Securities Trading Centre in July 2006; Chair. Dang Van Thanh; Gen. Dir Tran Xuan Huy.

Shinhanvina Bank: 3-5 Ho Tung Mau, District 1, Ho Chi Minh City; tel. (8) 8291581; fax (8) 8291583; e-mail hcmc.fvb@hcm.vnn.vn; f. 1993; jt venture between the Bank for Foreign Trade of Viet Nam and Korea First Bank; fmrly known as Chohung Vina Bank; cap. US $20.0m., res $1.3m., dep. $116.3m. (Dec. 2004); Chair. Phu Thai Vu; Dir-Gen. Sung Ho Noh.

VID Public Bank: Ground Floor, Hanoi Tungshing Square, 2 Ngo Quyen, Hanoi; tel. (4) 8268307; fax (4) 8268228; e-mail vpb.han@hn.vnn.vn; internet www.vidpublicbank.com.vn; f. 1992; jt venture between the Bank for Investment and Development (Viet Nam) and the Public Bank Berhad (Malaysia); commercial bank; cap. US $20m. (2001); Chair. Tran Anh Tuan (acting); Gen. Dir Tay Hong Heng; 5 brs.

VinaSiam Bank: 2 Pho Duc Chinh, District 1, Ho Chi Minh City; tel. (8) 8210557; fax (8) 8210585; internet www.vinasiambank.com; f. 1995; jt venture between Bank for Agriculture and Rural Development, Siam Commercial Bank (Thailand) and Charoen Pokphand Group (Thailand); cap. US $20.0m., res. $1.1m., dep. $37.2m. (Dec. 2005); Chair. Le Van So; Gen. Man. Viroj Thanapitak.

VP Bank (Viet Nam Commercial Joint-Stock Bank for Private Enterprises): 18B Le Thanh Tong, Hanoi; tel. (4) 8245246; fax (4) 8260182; internet www.vpb.com.vn; Chair. Lam Hoang Loc.

STOCK EXCHANGE

Ho Chi Minh Stock Exchange: 45–47 Ben Chuong Duong, Nguyen Thai Binh District, Ho Chi Minh City; tel. (8) 8217713; fax (8) 8217452; internet www.vse.org.vn; f. 2000 by the State Securities Commission (see Development Organization); fmrly Securities Trading Centre; name changed as above in 2007.

INSURANCE

In January 1994 it was announced that foreign insurance companies were to be permitted to operate in Viet Nam and in 1995 it was announced that Baoviet's monopoly of the insurance industry was to be ended. A number of new insurance companies were subsequently established. By September 2006 there were 22 insurance companies operating in the country.

Aon Vietnam Ltd: Suites 1403/6/7, 14th Floor, Vietcombank Tower, 198 Tran Quang Khai, Hoan Kiem District, Hanoi; tel. (4) 8260832; fax (4) 8243983; e-mail vu_my_lan@aon-asia.com; f. 1993; fmrly Inchibrok Insurance; Man. Dir Vu My Lan.

Bao Long (Nha Rong Joint-Stock Insurance Co): 185 Dien Bien Phu, District 1, Ho Chi Minh City; tel. (8) 8239219; fax (8) 8239223; internet www.nharong.com; Dir Tran Van Binh.

Bao Minh Insurance Co (Ho Chi Minh City Insurance Co): 26 Ton That Dam, District 1, Ho Chi Minh City; tel. (8) 8294180; fax (8) 8294185; e-mail baominh@baominh.com.vn; internet www.baominh.com.vn; f. 1995; life and non-life; Chair. and CEO Vinh Duc Tran.

Baoviet (Viet Nam Insurance Co): 35 Hai Ba Trung, Hoan Kiem District, Hanoi; tel. (4) 8245935; fax (4) 8257188; internet www.baoviet.com.vn; f. 1965; property and casualty, personal accident, liability and life insurance; total assets 8,817,000m. dông (2004); CEO Nguyen Thi Phuc Lam; Chair. Le Quang Binh.

Dai-ichi Life Insurance Co of Vietnam Ltd: 3rd Floor, Saigon Riverside Office Center, 2A–4A, Ton Duc Thang, District 1, Ho Chi Minh City; tel. (8) 8291919; fax (8) 8293131; e-mail info@dai-ichi-life.com.vn; internet www.dai-ichi-life.com.vn; f. 2007.

Manulife (Vietnam) Ltd: Manulife Plaza, 75 Hoang Van Thai, Tan Phu Ward, District 7, Ho Chi Minh City; tel. (8) 4166888; fax (8) 4161818; e-mail manulifevn_info@manulife.com; internet www.manulife.com.vn; f. 1999; fmrly Chinfon-Manulife Life Insurance Co Ltd; first wholly foreign-owned life insurance co to operate in Viet Nam; Gen. Dir David Wong.

Petrolimex Joint-Stock Insurance Co (PJICO Insurance): 532 Lang Ha, Dong Da District, Hanoi; tel. (4) 7760865; fax (4) 7760868; e-mail pjico@petrolimex.com.vn; internet www.pjico.com.vn; f. 1995; non-life insurance; Chair. Bui Ngoc Bao; CEO Nguyen Anh Dung.

PetroVietnam Insurance Joint Stock Corpn (PVI): 154 Nguyen Thai Hoc, Ba Dinh District, Hanoi; tel. (4) 7335588; fax (4) 7336284; e-mail contact@pvi.com.vn; internet www.pvi.com.vn; f. 1996; non-life insurance; Man. Dir Le Van Hung.

Viet Nam International Assurance Co (VIA): 3rd Floor, Petro-Vietnam Tower, 1–5 Le Duan, District 1, Ho Chi Minh City; tel. (8) 8221340; fax (8) 8221338; e-mail hcm@via.com.vn; internet www.via.com.vn; f. 1996; jt-venture co, 51% owned by Baoviet, 49% owned by Tokyo Marine and Fire Insurance Co (Japan); non-life insurance and reinsurance for foreign cos; Marketing Man. Peter Huy.

INSURANCE ASSOCIATION

Association of Vietnamese Insurers: 8th Floor, 141 Le Duan, Hanoi; tel. (4) 9428106; fax (4) 9422601; internet www.avi.org.vn; Chair. Trinh Quang Tuyen.

Trade and Industry

GOVERNMENT AGENCIES

State Financial and Monetary Council (SFMC): f. 1998; established to supervise, review and resolve matters relating to national financial and monetary policy.

Vietrade (Viet Nam Trade Promotion Agency): 20 Ly Thuong Kiet, Hanoi; tel. (4) 9347628; fax (4) 9344260; e-mail xttm@vietrade.gov.vn; internet www.vietrade.gov.vn; part of the Ministry of Trade; responsible for state management, co-ordination and implementation of trade and trade-related investment promotion and development activities; Dir-Gen. Do Thang Hai.

Vinacontrol (The Viet Nam Superintendence and Inspection Joint Stock Co): 54 Tran Nhan Tong, Hanoi; tel. (4) 9436011; fax (4) 9433844; e-mail vinacontrolvn@hn.vnn.vn; internet www.vinacontrol.com.vn; f. 1957; brs in all main Vietnamese ports and trade centres; controls quality and volume of exports and imports and transit of goods, and conducts inspections of deliveries and production processes; price, assets and enterprise valuation, marine survey, damage survey, claim settling and adjustment; Chair. Bui Duy Chinh; Gen. Dir Mai Tien Dung; 600 employees.

DEVELOPMENT ORGANIZATION

State Securities Commission: 164 Tran Quang Khai, Hanoi; tel. (4) 9340750; fax (4) 9340740; internet www.ssc.gov.vn; f. 1997; responsible for developing the capital markets, incl. the establishment of a stock exchange; 14 mems; Chair. Bang Vu.

CHAMBER OF COMMERCE

VCCI (Viet Nam Chamber of Commerce and Industry): 9 Dao Duy Anh, 4th Floor, Hanoi; tel. (4) 5743985; fax (4) 5743063; e-mail vcci@fmail.vnn.vn; internet www.vcci.com.vn; f. 1963; offices in Ho Chi Minh City, Da Nang, Haiphong, Can Tho, Vung Tau, Nha Trang, Nghe An, Thanh Hoa and Vinh; promotes business and investment between foreign and Vietnamese cos; protects interests of businesses; organizes training activities, exhbns and fairs in Viet Nam and abroad; provides information about and consultancy in Viet Nam's trade and industry; represents foreign applicants for patents and trade mark registration; issues certificates of origin and other documentation; helps domestic and foreign businesses to settle disputes by negotiation or arbitration; in 1993 foreign businesses operating in Viet Nam and Vietnamese businesses operating abroad were permitted to become assoc. mems; Pres. and Chair. Dr Vu Tien Loc; Sec.-Gen. Pham Gia Tuc; associated organizations: Viet Nam International Arbitration Centre, Viet Nam General Average Adjustment Committee, Advisory Board.

> **Viet Nam International Arbitration Centre (VIAC):** 9 Dao Duy Anh, 6th Floor, Dong Da District, Hanoi; tel. (4) 5742021; fax (4) 5743001; e-mail viac-vcci@hn.vnn.vn; internet www.viac.org.vn; f. 1993; adjudicates in disputes concerning both domestic and international economic relations.

INDUSTRIAL AND TRADE ORGANIZATIONS

Agrex Saigon (Agricultural Products and Foodstuffs Export Co): 58 Vo Van Tan, District 3, Ho Chi Minh City; tel. (8) 9306606; fax (8) 9303451; e-mail agrexsaigon@hcm.vnn.vn; internet www.agrexsaigon.com.vn; f. 1976; exports agricultural produce, coffee, frozen foods and aquatic products; imports agricultural and industrial materials, machinery and equipment, and consumer goods; Gen. Dir Duong Ky Hung; 1,200 employees.

Agrimex (Viet Nam National Agricultural Products Corpn): 173 Hai Ba Trung, District 3, Ho Chi Minh City; tel. (8) 8241049; fax (8) 8291349; e-mail agrimex@hcm.fpt.vn; f. 1956; imports and exports agricultural products; Gen. Dir Nguyen Bach Tuyet.

Airimex (General Civil Aviation Import-Export and Forwarding Co): 100 Nguyen Van Cu, Gia Lam, Long Bien District, Hanoi; tel. (4) 8271939; fax (4) 8271925; e-mail airimex@fpt.vn; f. 1989; imports and exports aircraft, spare parts and accessories for aircraft and air communications; Gen. Dir Pham Doa Hong.

An Giang Afiex Co (An Giang Agriculture and Foods Import and Export Co): 34–36 Hai Ba Trung, Long Xuyen Town, An Giang Province; tel. (76) 841021; fax (76) 843199; e-mail xnknstpagg@hcm

VIET NAM

.vnn.net; f. 1992; mfr and sale of agricultural products, also beverages; Dir Pham Van Bay.

Artexport–Hanoi (Viet Nam Handicrafts and Art Articles Export-Import Corpn): 31–33 Ngo Quyen, Hanoi; tel. (4) 8252760; fax (4) 8259275; e-mail artexport.hn@fpt.vn; internet www.artexport.com.vn; f. 1964; deals in craft products and art articles; Gen. Dir Do Van Khoi.

Barotex (Viet Nam National Bamboo and Rattan Export-Import Co): 100 Thai Thinh, Dong Da District, Hanoi; tel. (4) 8573428; fax (4) 8573036; e-mail info@barotex.com.vn; internet www.barotex.com.vn; f. 1971; specializes in art and handicrafts made from natural materials, sports shoes, ceramic and lacquer wares, gifts and other housewares, fibres, agricultural and forest products; Gen. Dir Ta Quoc Toan.

Bimson Cement Co: Badinh, Bimson Town, Thanh Hoa Province; tel. (37) 824242; fax (37) 824046; e-mail ktkh_bs@yahoo.com; internet www.ximangbimson.com.vn; mfr of cement; Dir Le Van Chung.

Binh Tay Import-Export Joint Stock Co (BITEX): 110–112 Hau Giang, District 6, Ho Chi Minh City; tel. (8) 9604325; fax (8) 9602478; e-mail bitexvn@bitexvn.com; internet www.bitexvn.com; trade in miscellaneous goods; Dir Nguyen Van Thien.

B12 Petroleum Co: Cai Lan, Bay Chay Sub-District, Ha Long City, Quang Ninh Province; tel. (33) 846360; fax (33) 846349; internet www.b12petroleum.com.vn; distribution of petroleum products; Dir Vu Ngoc Hai.

Centrimex (Viet Nam National General Import-Export Corpn): 247 Giang Vo, Dong Da District, Hanoi; tel. (58) 8512986; fax (58) 8512974; e-mail centrimexhn@fpt.vn; internet www.centrimexhn.com.vn; f. 1986; exports and imports goods for five provinces in the south-central region of Viet Nam; Gen. Dir Hoang Dinh Dung.

Coalimex (Vinacoal Import-Export Joint Stock Co): 33 Trang Thi, Hanoi; tel. (4) 9723845; fax (4) 9723846; e-mail coalimexhn@vnn.vn; internet www.coalimex.com.vn; f. 1982; exports coal, imports mining machinery and equipment; Gen. Dir Ninh Xuan Son.

Cocenex (Central Production Import-Export Corpn): 80 Hang Gai, Hanoi; tel. (4) 8254535; fax (4) 8294306; f. 1988; Gen. Dir Bui Thi Thu Huong.

Coffee Supply, Processing and Materials Co: 38B Nguyen Bieu, Nha Trang City, Khanh Hoa Province; tel. (58) 21176; coffee producer.

Cokyvina (Post and Telecommunication Equipment Import-Export Service Corpn): 178 Trieu Viet Vuong, Hanoi; tel. (4) 9782362; fax (4) 9782368; e-mail cokyvina@hn.vnn.vn; f. 1987; imports and exports telecom equipment, provides technical advice on related subjects, undertakes authorized imports, jt ventures, jt co-ordination and co-operation on investment with foreign and domestic economic organizations; Dir Nguyen Kim Ky.

Constrexim (Viet Nam Construction Investment and Export-Import Holdings Corpn): 39 Nguyen Dinh Chieu, Hanoi; tel. (4) 9744836; fax (4) 9742701; e-mail constrexim@fpt.vn; internet www.constrexim.com.vn; f. 1982; exports and imports building materials, equipment and machinery; undertakes construction projects in Viet Nam and abroad, and production of building materials with foreign partners; also involved in investment promotion and projects management, real estate development, and human resources development and training; Gen. Dir Ly Ngoc Tuan.

Culturimex (State Enterprise for the Export and Import of Works of Art and other Cultural Commodities): 22B Hai Ba Trung, Hanoi; tel. (4) 8252226; fax (4) 8259224; e-mail namson@fpt.vn; f. 1988; exports cultural items and imports materials for the cultural industry; Gen. Dir Nguyen Lai.

Dau Tieng Rubber Corpn: Dau Tieng Townlet, Dau Tieng District, Binh Duong Province; tel. (650) 561847; fax (650) 561488; f. 1981; planting, processing and export of natural rubber; Man. Dir Le Van Khoa.

Epco Ltd (Export Import and Tourism Co Ltd): 1 Nyuyen Thuong Hien, District 3, Ho Chi Minh City; tel. (8) 8324392; fax (8) 8324744; f. 1986; processes seafood; tourism and hotel business; Gen. Dir Nguyen Loc Ri.

Foocosa (Food Co Ho Chi Min City): 57 Nguyen Thi Minh Khai, District 1, Ho Chi Minh City; tel. (8) 9309070; fax (8) 9304552; e-mail foocosa@hcm.vnn.vn; internet www.foocosa.com; mfr and distributor of food products (rice, instant noodles, porridge, sauces, biscuits); Dir Ngo Van Tan; 3,500 employees.

Forexco Quang Nam (Quang Nam Forest Products Export Joint Stock Co): Dien Ngoc Village, Dien Ban District, Quangnam Province; tel. (510) 843595; fax (510) 843619; e-mail forexcoqnam@dng.vnn.vn; internet www.forexco.com.vn; f. 1986; mfr and exporter of furniture and other wood products; Gen. Dir Dang Ngoc Ba.

Garmex Saigon (Saigon Garment Manufacturing Import-Export Co): 213 An Duong Vuong, District 5, Ho Chi Minh City; tel. (8) 8557166; fax (8) 8557299; e-mail gmsg@hcm.fpt.vn; f. 1993; garment production and export; Gen. Dir Le Quang Hung.

Genecofov (General Co of Foods and Services): 64 Ba Huyen Thanh Quan, District 3, Ho Chi Minh City; tel. (8) 9325366; fax (8) 9325428; e-mail gecofov@hcm.fpt.vn; f. 1956; import and export of food products, handicrafts and ceramics, garage services, vehicle trading; under the Ministry of Trade; Dir To Van Phat.

Generalexim (Viet Nam National General Export-Import Corpn): 46 Ngo Quyen, Hoan Kiem, Hanoi; tel. (4) 8264009; fax (4) 8259894; e-mail gexim@generalexim.com.vn; f. 1981; export and import on behalf of production and trading organizations, also garment processing for export and manufacture of toys; Gen. Dir Hoang Tuan Khai.

Generalimex (General II Import-Export Joint Stock Co): 216/4 Dien Bien Phu, Ward 7, District 3, Ho Chi Minh City; tel. (8) 2907517; fax (8) 2907518; e-mail generalimex@hcm.fpt.vn; internet www.generalimex.com.vn; exports of agricultural products and spices, imports of machinery, vehicles, chemicals and fertilizers; Gen. Dir Nguyen Van Hoang.

Geruco (Viet Nam General Rubber Corpn): 236 Nam Ky Khoi Nghia, District 3, Ho Chi Minh City; tel. (8) 9327857; fax (8) 9327341; e-mail grc@vngeruco.com; internet www.vngeruco.com; merged with Rubexim (rubber export-import corpn) in 1991; manages and controls the Vietnamese rubber industry, including the planting, processing and trading of natural rubber and rubber wood products; also imports chemicals, machinery and spare parts for the industry; Chair. Tran Ngoc Thanh; Dir-Gen. Le Quang Thung.

Haprosimex (Hanoi General Production and Import-Export Company): Km 11, National Highway 1A, Van Dien, Hanoi; tel. (4) 8618341; fax (4) 8615390; e-mail business@hapro.com.vn; internet www.hapro.com.vn; specializes in handicrafts, textiles, clothing and agricultural and forestry products; Gen. Dir Nguyen Minh Tuan.

Hatien 1 Cement Joint Stock Co: Km 8 Highway Hanoi, Thu Duc, Ho Chi Minh City; tel. (8) 8966608; fax (8) 8967635; e-mail hatien1@hatien1.com.vn; internet www.hatien1.com.vn; mfr of cement; Dir Nguyen Ngoc Anh.

Hatien Cement Co No 2: Kien Luong Town, Ha Tien, Kien Giang Province; tel. (77) 53004; fax (77) 53005; e-mail xmht2@vnn.vn; internet www.xmht2.com; mfr of cement; Dir Nguyen Manh.

Haugiang Petrolimex (Haugiang Petrol and Oil Co): 21 Cach Mang Thang 8, Can Tho City, Can Tho Province; tel. (71) 21657; fax (71) 12746; distributor of fuel; Dir Trinh Mang Thang.

Hoang Thach Cement Co: Minh Tan Hamlet, Kim Mon, Hai Hung Province; tel. (32) 821092; fax (32) 821098; sale of construction materials; Dir Nguyen Duc Hoan.

Intimex Import-Export Corpn: 96 Tran Hung Dao, Hanoi; tel. (4) 9423240; fax (4) 9424250; internet www.intimexco.com; f. 1979; exports mainly agricultural products and processed items; imports mainly consumer goods, motorcycles and raw materials, machinery and equipment for the construction industry; Gen. Dir Vu Anh.

Lefaso (Viet Nam Leather and Footwear Asscn): Rm 120–2, Block 9, 7 Dao Duy Anh, Hanoi; tel. (4) 5770983; fax (4) 5770984; e-mail hhdg@hn.vnn.vn; internet www.lefaso.org.vn; f. 1990 to promote external trade relations, to provide technical support and technological training and to disseminate market information; Chair. Nguyen Gia Thao; Gen. Sec. Nguyen Thi Tong.

Machinoimport (Viet Nam Machinery and Spare Parts Co): 8 Trang Thi, Hoan Kiem, Hanoi; tel. (4) 8253703; fax (4) 8254050; e-mail machinokhdt@hn.vnn.vn; internet www.machinoimport.com.vn; f. 1956 as Vietnam National Machinery Export-Import Corpn; reorganised in 2003; now controlled by Ministry of Trade; imports and exports machinery, spare parts and tools; consultancy, investment, jt-venture, and manufacturing services; comprises 12 cos; Chair. Nguyen Tran Dat; Gen. Dir Tran Duc Truong.

Marine Supply (Marine Technical Materials Import-Export and Supplies): 276A Da Nang, Ngo Quyen, Haiphong; tel. (31) 847308; fax (31) 845159; f. 1985; imports and exports technical materials for marine transportation industry; Dir Phan Trang Chan.

Mecanimex (Viet Nam National Mechanical Products Export-Import Co): 37 Trang Thi, Hoan Kiem District, Hanoi; tel. (4) 8257459; fax (4) 9349904; e-mail mecahn@fpt.vn; internet mecanimex.com.vn; exports and imports mechanical products and hand tools; Gen. Dir Tran Bao Gioc.

Minexport (Viet Nam National Minerals Export-Import Corpn): 28 Ba Trieu, Hanoi; tel. (4) 8253674; fax (4) 5532669; e-mail minexport@fpt.vn; f. 1956; 30% state-owned; exports minerals and metals, quarry products, chemical products and footwear; imports metals, chemical products, industrial materials, fertilizers and consumer goods; Gen. Dir Anh Tran Thi Lan.

Nafobird (Viet Nam Forest and Native Birds, Animals and Ornamental Plants Export-Import Enterprises): 64 Truong Dinh, District 3, Ho Chi Minh City; tel. (8) 8290211; fax (8) 8293735; f. 1987; exports

VIET NAM

native birds, animals and plants, and imports materials for forestry; Dir Vo Ha An.

Naforimex (Hanoi Forest Products Export-Import and Production Corpn): 19 Ba Trieu, Hoan Kiem District, Hanoi; tel. (4) 8261255; fax (4) 8259264; e-mail naforimexhanoi@fpt.vn; f. 1960; imports chemicals, machinery and spare parts for the forestry industry and water supply network; exports oils, forest products, gum benzoin and resin; CEO Nguyen Ba Hung.

Nitagrex (Ninh Thuan Agricultural Products Import-Export Co): 158 Bac Ai, Do Vinh Ward, Phan Rang Thap Cham, Ninh Thuan Province; tel. (68) 888779; fax (68) 888842; e-mail nitagrex@hcm.vnn.vn; internet www.nitagrex.com.vn; f. 1999; production and export of agricultural products; import of consumer goods, transport vehicles and agricultural materials and equipment; Gen. Dir Dao Van Chan.

Packexport (Viet Nam National Packaging Technology and Import-Export Co): 31 Hang Thung, Hanoi; tel. (4) 8262792; fax (4) 8269227; e-mail packexport-vn@vnn.vn; f. 1976; manufactures packaging for domestic and export demand, and imports materials for the packaging industry; Gen. Dir Trinh Le Kieu.

Petec Trading and Investment Corpn: 194 Nam Ky Khoi Nghia, District 3, Ho Chi Minh City; tel. (8) 9303633; fax (8) 9305686; e-mail petectonghop@hcm.vnn.vn; internet www.petec.com.vn; f. 1981; imports equipment and technology for oil drilling, exploration and oil production; exports crude petroleum, rice, coffee and agricultural products; invests in silk, coffee, financial and transport sectors; Gen. Dir Tran Huu Lac.

Petrol and Oil Co (Zone 1): Duc Gliang Town, Gia Lam, Hanoi; tel. (4) 8271400; fax (4) 8272432; sales of oil and gas; Dir Phan Van Du.

Petrolimex (Viet Nam National Petroleum Corpn): 1 Kham Thien, Dong Da District, Hanoi; tel. (4) 8512603; fax (4) 8519203; e-mail xttm@petrolimex.com.vn; internet www.petrolimex.com.vn; f. 1956; import, export and distribution of petroleum products and liquefied petroleum gas; Chair. Nguyen Manh Tien; Dir-Gen. Tran Van Khoi.

Petrolimex Saigon Petroleum Co (Zone 2): 15 Le Duan, District 1, Ho Chi Minh City; tel. (8) 8292081; fax (8) 8222082; sales of petroleum products; Dir Tran Van Thang.

Petrovietnam (The Viet Nam Oil and Gas Corpn): 22 Ngo Quyen, Hoan Kiem District, Hanoi; tel. (4) 8252526; fax (4) 8265942; e-mail webmaster@hn.pv.com.vn; internet www.petrovietnam.com.vn; f. 1975; exploration and production of petroleum and gas; Chair. Dr Pham Quang Du; Pres. and CEO Dr Tran Ngoc Canh.

Saigon Beer Alcohol Beverage Corpn (Sabeco): 6 Hai Ba Trung, Ben Nghe District, Ho Chi Minh City; tel. (8) 8294081; fax (8) 8296856; e-mail biasaigon@sabeco.com.vn; internet www.sabeco.com.vn; producer of beer; Pres. Nguyen Anh Dzung.

Seaco (Sundries Electric Appliances Co): 64 Pho Duc Chinh, District 1, Ho Chi Minh City; tel. (8) 8210961; fax (8) 8210974; deals in miscellaneous electrical goods; Dir Mai Minh Cuong.

Seaprodex Hanoi (Hanoi Sea Products Export-Import Co): 20 Lang Ha, Hanoi; tel. (4) 8344437; fax (4) 8354125; e-mail seahn@seaprodexhanoi.com.vn; internet www.seaprodexhanoi.com.vn; Dir Dang Dinh Bao.

Seaprodex Saigon (Ho Chi Minh City Sea Products Import-Export Corpn): 87 Ham Nghi, District 1, Ho Chi Minh City; tel. (8) 8293669; fax (8) 9142236; internet www.seaprodexsg.com; f. 1978; exports frozen and processed sea products; imports machinery and materials for fishing and processing; Gen. Dir Phung Quoc Man.

SJC (Saigon Jewellery Co): 115 Nguyen Cong Tru, District 1, Ho Chi Minh City; tel. (8) 9144056; fax (8) 9144057; e-mail sjc@hcm.vnn.vn; f. 1998; manufacturing, processing and trading of gold, gemstones, silver and jewellery; Man. Dir Nguyen Thanh Long.

Technimex JSC (Technology Import-Export Joint Stock Company): 70 Tran Hung Dao, Hanoi; tel. (4) 9423751; fax (4) 8220377; e-mail technimex@hn.vnn.vn; internet www.technimexvn.com; f. 1982 under the name Viet Nam Technology Import-Export Corpn; name changed as above in 2001; exports and imports machines, equipment, instruments, etc.; Dir Nguyen Huy Binh.

Technoimport (Viet Nam National Complete Equipment and Technics Import-Export Corpn): 16–18 Trang Thi, Hanoi; tel. (4) 8254974; fax (4) 8254059; e-mail technohn@netnam.vn; internet www.technoimport.com.vn; f. 1959; imports and exports equipment, machinery, transport equipment, spare parts, materials and various consumer commodities; exports products by co-investment and jt-venture enterprises; provides consulting services for trade and investment, transport and forwarding services; acts as import-export brokering and trading agents; Gen. Dir Vu Chu Hien.

Terraprodex (Corpn for Processing and Export-Import of Rare Earth and Other Specialities): 35 Dien Bien Phu, Hanoi; tel. (4) 8232010; fax (4) 8256446; f. 1989; processing and export of rare earth products and other minerals; Dir Tran Duc Hiep.

Tocontap Saigon (Saigon Sundries Export-Import Joint Stock Co): 35 Le Quy Don, District 3, Ho Chi Minh City; tel. (8) 9325687; fax (8) 9325963; e-mail tocontapsaigon@hcm.vnn.vn; internet www.tocontapsaigon.com; f. 1956; imports and exports apparel, agricultural products, art and handicrafts and sundries; Gen. Dir Le Thi Thanh Huong.

Tracimexco (Transport Investment Co-operation and Import-Export Corpn): 22 Nguyen Van Troi, Phu Nhuan District, Ho Chi Minh City; tel. (8) 8442993; fax (8) 8445240; e-mail tralico@hn.vnn.vn; internet www.tracimexco.vnn.vn; fmrly Vietranscimex; exports and imports specialized equipment and materials for transportation and communication; Gen. Dir Pham Quang Vinh.

Vama (Viet Nam Automobile Manufacturers' Association): 13 Quang Trung, Go Vap District, Ho Chi Minh City; tel. (8) 8959100; fax (8) 8958714; e-mail vama.office@gmail.com; internet www.vama.org.vn; f. 2000; 18 mems; Chair. and Pres. Udo F. Loersch.

Vasep (Viet Nam Asscn of Seafood Exporters and Producers): 10–12 Nguyen Cong Hoan, Ba Dinh District, Hanoi; tel. (4) 7715055; fax (4) 7715084; e-mail vasep@hn.vnn.vn; internet www.vasep.com.vn; f. 1998; exports seafood products; provides essential market information to Viet Nam's seafood industry; organizes and implements activities designed to develop and promote the industry; Chair. Dr Ho Quoc Luc.

Vegetexco (Viet Nam National Vegetables and Fruit Export-Import Corpn): 2 Pham Ngoc Thach, Dong Da District, Hanoi; tel. (4) 5740779; fax (4) 8523926; e-mail vegetexcovn@fpt.vn; internet vegetexcovn.tripod.com; f. 1971; exports fresh and processed vegetables and fruit, spices and flowers, and other agricultural products; imports vegetable seeds and processing materials; Gen. Dir Le Van Anh.

Vietrans (Viet Nam National Foreign Trade Forwarding and Warehousing Corpn): 13 Ly Nam De, Hoan Kiem District, Hanoi; tel. (4) 8457417; fax (4) 8455829; e-mail vietrans@hn.vnn.vn; internet www.vietrans.com.vn; f. 1970; agent for forwarding and transport of exports and imports, diplomatic cargoes and other goods, warehousing, shipping and insurance; Gen. Dir Thai Duy Long.

Viettronimex (Viet Nam Electronics Import-Export Corpn): 74–76 Nguyen Hue, District 1, Ho Chi Minh City; tel. (8) 8298201; fax (8) 8294873; e-mail vtr@hcm.vnn.vn; f. 1981; imports and exports electronic goods; Dir Nguyen Huu Thinh.

Vigecam (Viet Nam General Corpn of Agricultural Materials): 16 Ngo Tat To, Dong Da District, Hanoi; tel. (4) 8231972; fax (4) 7474647; exports and imports agricultural products; Gen. Dir Tran Van Kanh.

Viglacera (Viet Nam Glass and Ceramics Corpn): 628 Hoang Hoa Tham, Ba Dinh District, Hanoi; tel. (4) 8326982; fax (4) 7613292; e-mail vgc@hn.vnn.vn; internet www.viglacera.com.vn; f. 1974; mfr of building materials; Gen. Dir Nguyen Tran Nam Huy.

Vimedimex II (Vimedimex Medi-Pharma Joint Stock Co): 246 Cong Quynh, District 1, Ho Chi Minh City; tel. (8) 8398441; fax (8) 8325953; e-mail vietpharma@hcm.vnn.vn; internet www.vietpharm.com.vn; f. 1984; exports and imports medicinal and pharmaceutical materials and products, medical instruments; Gen. Dir Nguyen Tien Hung.

Vimico (Viet Nam National Minerals Corpn): 562 Nguyen Van Cu, Gia Lam District, Hanoi; tel. (4) 8770010; fax (8) 8770006; e-mail vimico@hn.vnn.vn; internet www.vimicovn.com; Chair. Vu Xuan Khoat; Gen. Dir Ngo Van Troi.

Vinacafe (Viet Nam National Coffee Import-Export Corpn): 240 Nguyen Dinh Chinh, 11 Ward, Phu Nuan District, Ho Chi Minh City; tel. (8) 4495514; fax (8) 4495513; e-mail vinacafe@hn.vnn.vn; internet www.vinacafe.com.vn; f. 1995; state-owned; exports coffee, and imports equipment and chemicals for coffee production; Pres. and CEO Do Van Nam.

Vinachem (Viet Nam National Chemical Corpn): 1A Trang Tien, Hoan Kiem District, Hanoi; tel. (4) 8240551; fax (4) 8252995; e-mail vinachem@hn.vnn.vn; internet www.vinachem.com.vn; production, import and export of chemicals and fertilizers; Chair. Nguyen Quoc Tuan; Pres. and CEO Do Duy Phi.

Vinachimex (Viet Nam National Chemicals Import-Export Corpn): 4 Pham Ngu Lao, Hanoi; tel. (4) 8256377; fax (4) 8257727; f. 1969; exports and imports chemical products, minerals, rubber, fertilizers, machinery and spare parts; Dir Nguyen Van Son.

Vinafilm (Viet Nam Film Import, Export and Film Service Corpn): 73 Nguyen Trai, Dong Da District, Hanoi; tel. (4) 8244566; f. 1987; export and import of films and video tapes; film distribution; organization of film shows and participation of Vietnamese films in international film festivals; Gen. Man. Ngo Manh Lan.

Vinafimex (Viet Nam National Agricultural Produce and Foodstuffs Import and Export Corpn): 58 Ly Thai To, Hanoi; tel. (4) 8255768; fax (4) 8255476; e-mail fime@hn.vnn.vn; internet www.vinafimex.com.vn; f. 1984; exports cashews, peanuts, coffee, rubber and other agricultural products, and garments; imports malt, fertilizer,

VIET NAM   Directory

insecticide, seeds, machinery and equipment, etc.; Pres. NGUYEN TOAN THANG; Gen. Dir NGUYEN VAN THANG.

Vinafood Hanoi (Hanoi Food Import-Export Co): 6 Ngo Quyen, Hoan Kiem District, Hanoi; tel. (4) 8256771; fax (4) 8258528; f. 1988; exports rice, maize, tapioca; imports fertilizers, insecticides, wheat and wheat flour; Dir NGUYEN DUC HY.

Vinalivesco (Vietnam National Livestock Corpn): 519 Minh Khai, Hanoi; tel. (4) 8626763; fax (4) 8623645; f. 1996; imports and exports animal and poultry products, animal feeds and other agro-products, and foodstuffs; Gen. Dir NGUYEN VAN KHAC.

Vinamilk (Viet Nam Milk Co): 184–188 Nguyen Dinh Chieu, Ward 6, District 3, Ho Chi Minh City; tel. (8) 9305197; fax (8) 9304880; e-mail vinamilk@vinamilk.com.vn; internet www.vinamilk.com.vn; f. 1976; producer of dairy products; Dir MAI TRIUE LIEN.

Vinapimex (Viet Nam Paper Corpn): 25A Ly Thuong Kiet, Hanoi; tel. (4) 8260143; fax (4) 8260381; f. 1995; production and marketing of paper; Pres. and CEO VO SY DONG.

Vinaplast (Viet Nam Plastics Corpn): 92–94 Ly Tu Trong, District 1, Ho Chi Minh City; tel. (8) 8238011; fax (8) 8237956; internet www.vinaplast.com.vn; f. 1976; import and export of products for plastic processing industry; production and trade of plastic products; Gen. Dir NGUYEN KHAC LONG.

Vinasteel (Viet Nam National Steel Corpn): D2 Ton That Tung, Dong Da District, Hanoi; tel. (4) 8525537; fax (4) 8262657; distributor of metal products; Dir NGO HUY PHAN.

Vinataba (Viet Nam National Tobacco Corpn): 25A Ly Thuong Kiet, Hoan Kiem District, Hanoi; tel. (4) 8265778; fax (4) 8265777; internet www.vinataba.com.vn; mfr of tobacco products; Chair. NGUYEN THAI SINH; Gen. Dir NGUYEN NAM HAI.

Vinatea (Viet Nam National Tea Development Investment and Export-Import Co): 92 Vo Thi Sau, Hanoi; tel. (4) 6226990; fax (4) 6226991; e-mail info@vinatea.com.vn; internet www.vinatea.com.vn; exports tea, imports tea-processing materials; Gen. Dir NGUYEN THIEN TOAN.

Vinatex (Viet Nam National Textile and Garment Corpn): 25 Ba Trieu, Hoan Kiem District, Hanoi; tel. (4) 8257700; fax (4) 8262269; e-mail vinatexhn@vinatex.com.vn; internet www.vinatex.com; f. 1995; imports raw material, textile and sewing machinery, spare parts, accessories, dyestuffs; exports textiles, ready-made garments, carpets, jute, silk; Gen. Dir VU DUC THINH.

Vitas (Viet Nam Tea Association): 92 Vo Thu Sau, Hai Ba Trung District, Hanoi; tel. (4) 6250908; e-mail vitas@fpt.vn; internet www.vitas.org.vn; f. 1988; promotes the trading and marketing of tea products; offers advice and information, both to the Govt and to farmers, regarding development schemes and policies; Chair. and Pres. NGUYEN KIM PHONG.

VNCC (Viet Nam Cement Industry Corpn—Vinacement): 228 Le Duan, Dong Da District, Hanoi; tel. (4) 8510593; fax (4) 8512778; e-mail banbt@vinacement.com.vn; internet www.vinacement.com.vn; f. 1980; manufactures and exports cement and clinker; Chair. LE VAN CHUNG; Gen. Dir NGUYEN NGOC ANH.

Vocarimex (National Co for Vegetable Oils, Aromas, and Cosmetics of Viet Nam): 58 Nguyen Binh Khiem, District 1, Ho Chi Minh City; tel. (8) 8294513; fax (8) 8290586; e-mail vocar@hcm.vnn.vn; internet www.vocarimex.com; f. 1976; producing and trading vegetable oils, oil-based products and special industry machinery; packaging; operating port facilities; Gen. Dir DO NGOC KAI.

Xunhasaba (Viet Nam State Corpn for Export and Import of Books, Periodicals and other Cultural Commodities): 32 Hai Ba Trung, Hanoi; tel. (4) 8262989; fax (4) 8252860; e-mail xunhasaba@hn.vnn.vn; internet www.xunhasaba.com.vn; f. 1957; exports and imports books, periodicals, postage stamps, greetings cards, calendars and paintings; Dir HA TRIEU KIEN.

UTILITIES

Electricity

Electricity of Viet Nam (EVN): 18 Tran Nguyen Han, Hanoi; tel. (4) 8249508; fax (4) 8249461; e-mail vp@evn.com.vn; internet www.evn.com.vn; produces, transmits and distributes electrical power; Chair. DAO VAN HUNG; Pres. and CEO PHAM LE TANH.

Power Co No 1 (PC1): 20 Tran Nguyen Han, Hoan Kiem, Hanoi; tel. (4) 8255074; fax (4) 8244033; e-mail anhdn@pc1.com.vn; manages the generation, transmission and distribution of electrical power in northern Viet Nam; Dir DO VAN LOC.

Power Co No 2 (PC2): 72 Hai Ba Trung, District 1, Ho Chi Minh City; tel. (8) 8231303; fax (8) 8299680; manages the distribution of electrical power in southern Viet Nam; Dir NGUYEN THANH DUY.

Power Co No 3 (PC3): 315 Trung Nu Vuong, Hai Chau District, Da Nang; tel. (511) 621028; fax (511) 625071; f. 1975; manages the generation, transmission and distribution of electrical power in central Viet Nam; Gen. Dir TA CANH.

Water

Hanoi Water Business Co: 44 Yen Phu, Hanoi; tel. (4) 8292478; fax (4) 8294069; f. 1954; responsible for the supply of water to Hanoi and its five urban and two suburban districts; Dir-Gen. BUI VAN MAT.

Saigon Water Corpn (SAWACO): 1 Cong Truong Quoc Te, District 3, Ho Chi Minh City; tel. (8) 8291974; fax (8) 8241644; e-mail hcmcwater@hcm.vnn.vn; f. 1966; manages the water services and water construction works of Ho Chi Minh City; Gen. Dir DINH PHU TRAN.

CO-OPERATIVES

Viet Nam Co-operative Alliance (VCA): 77 Nguyen Thai Hoc, Ba Dinh District, Hanoi; tel. (4) 8431689; fax (4) 8431883; e-mail vca@vietnamcoop.org; internet www.vca.org.vn; f. 1993; fmrly Viet Nam Co-operatives Council; Pres. Dr NGUYEN TIEN QUAN.

TRADE UNIONS

Tong Lien doan Lao dong Viet Nam (Viet Nam General Confederation of Labour): 82 Tran Hung Dao, POB 627, Hanoi; tel. (4) 9421794; fax (4) 9423781; e-mail doingoaitld@hn.vnn.vn; internet www.congdoanvn.org.vn; f. 1929; merged in 1976 with the South Viet Nam Trade Union Fed. for Liberation; 4,000,000 mems; 18 affiliated unions; Pres. DANG NGOC TUNG; Vice-Pres. NGUYEN HOA BINH.

Cong Doan Nong Nghiep Cong Nghiep Thu Pham Viet Nam (Viet Nam Agriculture and Food Industry Trade Union): Hanoi; f. 1987; 550,000 mems.

National Union of Building Workers: 12 Cua Dong, Hoan Kiem, Hanoi; tel. (4) 8253781; fax (4) 8281407; f. 1957; Pres. NGUYEN VIET HAI.

Vietnam National Union of Industrial Workers: 54 Hai Ba Trung, Hanoi; tel. (4) 9344426; fax (4) 8245306; f. 1997; Pres. VU TIEN SAU.

Vietnam National Union of Post and Telecoms Workers: 30 Hang Chuoi, Hai Ba Trung, Hanoi; tel. (4) 9713514; fax (4) 9720236; f. 1947; Chair. HOANG DUY CAN.

Transport

RAILWAYS

In 2007 the Government approved plans to construct a new rail link between Hanoi and Ho Chi Minh City, which would reduce the journey time from 29 hours to 10 hours. Construction was expected to take six years. In 2008 construction commenced of a metro system in Ho Chi Minh City. The 19.7 km route was due for completion in 2014.

Duong Sat Viet Nam (DSVN) (Viet Nam Railways): 118 Le Duan, Hanoi; tel. (4) 8220537; fax (4) 9422866; e-mail vr.hn.irstd@fpt.vn; internet www.vr.com.vn; 2,600 km of main lines (1996); lines in operation are: Hanoi–Ho Chi Minh City (1,726 km), Hanoi–Haiphong (102 km), Hanoi–Dong Dang (167 km), Hanoi–Lao Cai (296 km), Hanoi–Thai Nguyen (75 km), Thai Nguyen–Kep–Bai Chay (106 km); Chair. PHAN VAN GIAN; Gen. Dir Dr NGUYEN HUU BANG.

ROADS

In 2004 there were an estimated 137,359 km of roads, of which 53,610 km were asphalted and 6,681 km were stone-paved. In 1995 the Government announced plans to upgrade 430 km of the national highway, which runs from Hanoi in the north to Ho Chi Minh City in the south. In 1997 the Government announced plans to build a new 1,880-km north–south highway in the east of the country. In 2001 the Government also announced plans to upgrade the section of the national highway that runs between the northern provinces of Hoa Binh and Son La. In 2006 an upgrade of National Highway No. 2, linking An Giang province in Viet Nam to Takeo province in Cambodia, was completed; 95% of the funding of US $13m. was provided by Japan. In the following year the Government announced plans to upgrade the section of National Highway No. 1 in the central province of Thua Thien-Hue; construction was scheduled for completion in 2010.

SHIPPING

The principal port facilities are at Haiphong, Da Nang and Ho Chi Minh City. In 2006 the Vietnamese merchant fleet (1,191 vessels) had a combined displacement totalling 2,053,800 grt.

Cong Ty Co Phan Dai Ly Hang Hai Viet Nam (VOSA Corpn): Unit 1003, 10th Floor, Harbour View Tower, 35 Nguyen Hue, District 1, Ho Chi Minh City; tel. (8) 8211290; fax (8) 8214919; e-mail vosagroup@hcm.vnn.vn; internet www.vosagroup.com; f. 1957; fmrly the Viet Nam Ocean Shipping Agency; controlled by the Viet Nam National Shipping Lines (VINALINES); in charge of merchant shipping; arranges ship repairs, salvage, passenger services, air and sea freight forwarding services; main br. offices in Haiphong, Quang

Ninh, Ha Noi, Ben Thuy, Da nang, Qui Nhon, Nha Trang, Ho Chi Minh City, Vung Tau and Can Tho; brs in Mong Cai, Cua Ong, Cam Pha, Vung Ang, Dung Quat, Chan May, Van Phong, Ca Mau and Kien Giang; Dir-Gen. TRAN DUNG KHANG (acting).

Cong Ty Van Tai Duong Bien Viet Nam (VOSCO) (Viet Nam Ocean Shipping Joint Stock Co): 215 Tran Quoc Toan, Ngo Quyen District, Haiphong; tel. (31) 846951; fax (31) 845107; e-mail vosco.1@hn.vnn.vn; internet www.vosco.com.vn; controlled by the Viet Nam Gen. Dept of Marine Transport; Gen. Dir VU HUU CHINH.

Transport and Chartering Corpn (Vietfracht): 74 Nguyen Du, Hai Ba Trung, Hanoi; tel. (4) 9422355; fax (4) 9423679; e-mail vfhan@hn.vnn.vn; internet www.vietfracht.com.vn; f. 1963; ship broking, chartering, ship management, shipping agency, international freight forwarding; logistic and consultancy services, import-export services; Chair. NGUYEN QUANG THOAI; CEO TRAN VAN QUY.

Viet Nam Sea Transport and Chartering Co (Vitranschart): 428–432 Nguyen Tat Thanh, District 4, Ho Chi Minh City; tel. (8) 9404027; fax (8) 9404711; e-mail vtc-hcm@vitranschart.com.vn; internet www.vitranschart.com.vn; Dir VO PHUNG LONG.

CIVIL AVIATION

Viet Nam's principal airports are Tan Son Nhat International Airport (Ho Chi Minh City) and Noi Bai International Airport (Hanoi), which cater for both overseas and domestic traffic. There is a third international airport at Da Nang. In 1997 it was announced that numerous abandoned wartime airstrips were to be repaired and returned to service under a programme scheduled for completion in 2010, by which time the Government also aimed to expand the annual capacity of Tan Son Nhat to 30m. passengers and 1m. metric tons of freight. In January 2004 plans were announced for the construction of a new international airport at Long Thang, in Dong Nai province; work on the project was expected to commence in 2010. The airport, with a projected passenger capacity of 20m. a year, was to have four runways and four terminals, the first of which were scheduled to become operational in 2015. Five new airports to handle domestic traffic were opened in 2004, at Ca Mau, Can Tho, Con Son, Chu Lai and Nha Trang. As of late 2006 there were 20 domestic airports in Viet Nam.

Viet Nam Airlines: Gialem Airport, Hanoi; tel. (4) 8731484; fax (4) 8272291; internet www.vietnamairlines.com; fmrly the Gen. Civil Aviation Admin. of Viet Nam, then Hang Khong Viet Nam; remained wholly state-owned in 2006, with plans for transfer to private sector; operates domestic passenger services from Hanoi and from Ho Chi Minh City to the principal Vietnamese cities, and international services to 18 countries; Pres. and CEO PHAM NGOC MINH; Chair. NGUYEN SY HUNG.

Pacific Airlines: 112 Hong Ha, Tan Binh District, Ho Chi Minh City; tel. (8) 8487145; fax (8) 8450085; e-mail quang.dongoc@pacificairlines.com.vn; internet www.pacificairlines.com.vn; f. 1991; operates charter cargo flights, also scheduled passenger and cargo services to Taiwan and Hong Kong; purchased by Qantas (Australia) in 2008; to be renamed Jetstar Pacific; Chair. PHAM VU HIEN; CEO LUONG HOAI NAM.

Tourism

In the 1990s the Vietnamese Government encouraged tourism as a source of much-needed foreign exchange, with the objective of attracting some 4m. tourists annually by the year 2005. The total number of tourist arrivals in that year fell just short of this target, at about 3.5m.; a modest increase, to approximately 3.6m., was recorded in 2006. According to the Viet Nam National Administration of Tourism, approximately 4.1m. tourists visited the country in 2007. In 2005 revenue from tourism totalled US $1,880m.

Viet Nam National Administration of Tourism (VNAT): 80 Quan Su, Hanoi; tel. (4) 9423998; fax (4) 9424115; e-mail titc@vietnamtourism-info.com; internet www.vietnamtourism.com; f. 1960; Gen. Dir NGO HUY PHUONG.

Hanoi Tourism Service Co (HANOI TOSERCO): 273 Kim Ma, Hanoi; tel. (4) 7262626; fax (4) 7262571; e-mail hanoitoserco@hn.vnn.vn; internet www.tosercohanoi.com; f. 1988; manages the development of tourism, hotels and restaurants in the capital and other services including staff training; Dir TRAN TIEN HUNG.

Tong Cong ty Du lich Saigon (Saigon Tourist Holding Co): 23 Le Loi, District 1, Ho Chi Minh City; tel. (8) 8225887; fax (8) 8291026; e-mail saigontourist@sgtourist.com.vn; internet www.saigon-tourist.com; f. 1975; holding co controlling 11 tour operators, 56 hotels, 10 resorts and 24 restaurants; Gen. Dir NGUYEN HUU THO.

YEMEN

Introductory Survey

Location, Climate, Language, Religion, Flag, Capital

The Republic of Yemen is situated in the south of the Arabian peninsula, bounded to the north by Saudi Arabia, to the east by Oman, to the south by the Gulf of Aden, and to the west by the Red Sea. The islands of Perim and Kamaran at the southern end of the Red Sea, the island of Socotra, at the entrance to the Gulf of Aden, and the Kuria Muria islands, near the coast of Oman, are also part of the Republic. The climate in the semi-desert coastal strip is hot, with high humidity and temperatures rising to more than 38°C (100°F); inland, the climate is somewhat milder, with cool winters and relatively heavy rainfall in the highlands. The eastern plateau slopes into desert. The language is Arabic. The population is almost entirely Muslim, and mainly of the Sunni Shafi'a sect. The national flag (proportions 2 by 3) has three equal horizontal stripes, of red, white and black. The capital is San'a.

Recent History

The Republic of Yemen was formed in May 1990 by the amalgamation of the Yemen Arab Republic (YAR) and the People's Democratic Republic of Yemen (PDRY). The YAR (from 1967 also known as North Yemen) had formerly been a kingdom. When Turkey's Ottoman Empire was dissolved in 1918, the Imam Yahya, leader of the Zaidi community, was left in control. In 1948 Yahya was assassinated in a palace coup, when power was seized by forces opposed to his feudal rule. However, Yahya's son, Ahmad, defeated the rebel forces to become Imam. In 1958 Yemen and the United Arab Republic (Egypt and Syria) formed a federation called the United Arab States, though this was dissolved in 1961. The Imam Ahmad died in September 1962 and was succeeded by his son, Muhammad. Less than a week later army officers, led by Col (later Marshal) Abdullah as-Sallal, removed the Imam and proclaimed the YAR. Civil war ensued between royalist forces, supported by Saudi Arabia, and republicans, aided by Egyptian troops. The republicans prevailed and Egyptian forces withdrew in 1967. In November President Sallal was deposed by a Republican Council.

The People's Republic of Southern Yemen, comprising Aden and the former Protectorate of South Arabia, was formed on 30 November 1967. Aden had been under British rule since 1839 and the Protectorate was developed by a series of treaties between the United Kingdom and local leaders. Prior to the British withdrawal, two rival factions, the National Liberation Front (NLF) and the Front for the Liberation of Occupied South Yemen, fought for control. The Marxist NLF eventually prevailed and assumed power as the National Front (NF). The country's first President, Qahtan ash-Sha'abi, was forced out of office in June 1969, when a Presidential Council, led by Salem Rubayi Ali, took power. Muhammad Ali Haitham became Prime Minister. In November 1970, on the third anniversary of independence, the country was renamed the PDRY. In May 1971 a provisional Supreme People's Council (SPC) was established as the national legislature. In August Haitham was replaced as Prime Minister by Ali Nasser Muhammad. Following the introduction of repressive measures against dissidents by the Government after independence, more than 300,000 Southern Yemenis fled to the YAR. Backed by Saudi Arabia and Libya, many of the refugees joined mercenary organizations, aimed at the overthrow of the Marxist regime in Southern Yemen, and conducted cross-border raids.

Intermittent fighting, beginning in early 1971, flared into open warfare between the two Yemens in October 1972, with the YAR receiving aid from Saudi Arabia and the PDRY being supplied with Soviet arms. A cease-fire was arranged in the same month, under the auspices of the League of Arab States (Arab League, see p. 332), and soon afterwards both sides agreed to the union of the two Yemens within 18 months. The union was not, however, implemented.

On 13 June 1974 a 10-member Military Command Council (MCC) seized power in the YAR, under the leadership of the pro-Saudi Lt-Col Ibrahim al-Hamadi. Mohsin al-Aini was appointed Prime Minister, but was replaced by Abd al-Aziz Abd al-Ghani in January 1975. An unsuccessful pro-royalist coup was reported in August. Al-Hamadi subsequently attempted to reduce the influence of the USSR, and endeavoured to re-equip the army with US weapons, making use of financial assistance from Saudi Arabia. In October 1977, however, al-Hamadi was killed by unknown assassins in San'a. Another member of the MCC, Lt-Col Ahmad bin Hussain al-Ghashmi, took over as Chairman, and martial law was imposed. In February 1978 the MCC appointed a Constituent People's Assembly, and in April the Assembly elected al-Ghashmi President of the Republic. The MCC was then dissolved.

In June 1978 the proposed union of the two Yemens was seriously hampered when President al-Ghashmi of the YAR was assassinated by a bomb carried in the suitcase of a PDRY envoy. In the following month the Constituent People's Assembly elected a senior military officer, Lt-Col (later Gen., and subsequently Field Marshal) Ali Abdullah Saleh, as President of the YAR. During recriminations that followed the assassination, President Rubayi Ali of the PDRY was deposed and executed by opponents within the ruling party, which had been known as the United Political Organization—National Front (UPO—NF) since its merger with two smaller parties in October 1975. The Prime Minister, Ali Nasser Muhammad, became interim Head of State. Two days after the overthrow of Rubayi Ali, it was announced that the UPO—NF had agreed to form a Marxist-Leninist 'vanguard' party. At the constituent congress of this Yemen Socialist Party (YSP), held in October 1978, Abd al-Fattah Ismail, who favoured uncompromising Marxist policies, became Secretary-General. A new SPC was elected in December and appointed Ismail to be Head of State. In April 1980 Ali Nasser Muhammad replaced Ismail as Head of State, Chairman of the Presidium of the SPC and Secretary-General of the YSP, while retaining the post of Prime Minister; his posts were confirmed at an extraordinary congress of the YSP in October.

Renewed fighting broke out between the YAR and the PDRY in February and March 1979, when the National Democratic Front (NDF), an alliance of disaffected YAR politicians, won the support of the PDRY and began a revolt. Later in the same month, however, at a meeting between the North and South Yemeni Heads of State in Kuwait, arranged by the Arab League, an agreement was signed pledging unification of the two states. Following a series of meetings, in December 1981 the two sides signed a draft Constitution for a unified state and established a joint YAR/PDRY Yemen Council to monitor progress towards unification. NDF forces rebelled again in 1982, but they were defeated and forced over the border into the PDRY.

Abd al-Aziz Abd al-Ghani was replaced as Prime Minister of the YAR in October 1980, but was reappointed in November 1983. Meanwhile, in May 1983 President Saleh submitted his resignation at an extraordinary meeting of the Constituent People's Assembly, declaring his intention to nominate himself for a presidential election. His five-year term of office was due to end in July. However, he was nominated and unanimously re-elected by the Assembly for a further five-year term. Elections to the Assembly itself, scheduled for early 1983, were postponed.

In the PDRY, President Muhammad relinquished the post of Prime Minister in February 1985, nominating the Minister of Construction, Haidar Abu Bakr al-Attas, as his successor (while retaining his other senior posts). The former President, Abd al-Fattah Ismail, returned from exile in the USSR in the same month, and was reappointed to the Secretariat of the YSP's Central Committee. At the party's third General Congress, in October, President Muhammad was re-elected to the posts of Secretary-General of the YSP and of its Political Bureau for a further five years. However, his control over the party was weakened by the enlargement of the Political Bureau from 13 members to 16 (including his rival, Ismail), and by an increase in membership of the Central Committee from 47 to 77, to incorporate a number of his critics.

On 13 January 1986 President Muhammad attempted to eliminate his opponents in the Political Bureau: his personal guard opened fire on six members who had assembled for a meeting with the President. Three were killed, and three escaped, including Ismail (who was, however, officially declared to have been killed in subsequent fighting). Muhammad was reported to have left Aden for his tribal stronghold in Abyan province, to the east of the city. In Aden itself, rival elements of the armed forces fought for control, causing widespread destruction, and the conflict quickly spread to the rest of the country, despite diplomatic efforts by the USSR. Apparently prompted by reports of massacres by President Muhammad's supporters, the army intervened decisively, turning back pro-Muhammad tribesmen from Abyan who were advancing on Aden. On 24 January al-Attas, the Prime Minister, who had been abroad when the troubles began, was named by the YSP Central Committee as head of an interim administration in Aden, and Muhammad was stripped of all his party and state posts; he reportedly fled to Ethiopia. An estimated 5,000 people died in the conflict. A new Government of the PDRY was formed in February. Al-Attas was confirmed as President, Chairman of the Presidium of the SPC and Secretary-General of the YSP Political Bureau. The former Deputy Prime Minister and Minister of Fisheries, Dr Yasin Said Numan, was named as Prime Minister. The new Council of Ministers contained only three members of the previous Government. In March a general amnesty was proclaimed, inviting supporters of Muhammad to return from the YAR, where some 10,000 of them had sought refuge. In October a general election took place for a 111-member SPC. Al-Attas was unanimously elected Chairman of the YSP. In December the Supreme Court sentenced Muhammad to death, *in absentia*, for treason; 34 other men received the same sentence, although it was only carried out in five cases.

In July 1988 the first general election took place in the YAR for 128 seats in the new 159-member Consultative Council, which replaced the non-elected Constituent People's Assembly. The remaining 31 seats were filled by presidential decree. More than 1m. people registered to vote and more than 1,200 candidates contested the poll. Approximately 25% of the elective seats were won by candidates sympathetic to the Muslim Brotherhood, a militant Islamist organization. Later in the month President Saleh was re-elected by the Consultative Council for a third five-year term, winning 96% of the votes, while the Vice-President, Abd al-Karim al-Arashi, was elected as Speaker of the Consultative Council. Al-Ghani was reappointed Prime Minister.

The first session of the joint YAR/PDRY Yemen Council (which had been established in 1981) was held in San'a in August 1983 and discussed the state of progress towards unification. These sessions were scheduled to take place every six months and to alternate between San'a and Aden. A joint committee on foreign policy met for the first time in March 1984 in Aden. In July 1986 Presidents Saleh of the YAR and al-Attas of the PDRY met for the first time in Libya to discuss unification. In early 1987 Kuwait acted as a mediator between the two Yemens in an effort to solve the problem of the thousands of refugees from the PDRY who had recently sought refuge in the north. In July it was reported that more than 50% of these refugees had returned to the PDRY.

In May 1988 the Governments of the YAR and the PDRY agreed to withdraw troops from their mutual border and to create a demilitarized zone, covering an area of 2,200 sq km, between Marib and Shabwah, where they intended to carry out joint projects involving exploration for petroleum. The movement of citizens between the two states was also to be facilitated. In July a programme of wide-ranging political and economic reforms was introduced in the PDRY, indicating the country's intention to create a free-market economy. In November President Saleh and the Secretary-General of the Central Committee of the YSP, Ali Salim al-Baid, signed an agreement to unify the two states. On 1 December a draft Constitution for the unified state was published: it was to be ratified by both countries within six months, and was subsequently to be approved by a referendum. At the end of December the Governments of the YAR and the PDRY agreed to release all political prisoners in their respective countries.

The first joint meeting of the two Councils of Ministers was held in San'a in January 1990 and resulted in restrictions on travel between the two countries being rescinded. In February President Saleh held talks with King Fahd of Saudi Arabia, who pledged his official support for the unification of the YAR and the PDRY. However, opposition to unification developed in the YAR in early 1990. The Muslim Brotherhood, which believed that *Shari'a* (Islamic) law should be enshrined in the Constitution of the unified state (as in the YAR Constitution), condemned the draft Constitution, which was based principally, but not solely, on *Shari'a* law, and advocated a boycott of the referendum on the Constitution. In the PDRY, meanwhile, there were demonstrations by women, who feared that the increasing influence of Islamist militancy might jeopardize their freedom, and demanded that their existing rights in the secular Republic be guaranteed in the new Constitution.

In May 1990 the armed forces of the YAR and the PDRY were declared to be technically dissolved, prior to their unification, and it was announced that they were to be withdrawn from their respective capitals to designated military zones. In the same month a draft law embodying the freedom of the press was signed. The unification of the YAR and the PDRY was proclaimed on 22 May, six months ahead of the agreed deadline, apparently in order to counter the threat to the unification process posed by disruption in the north of the YAR. The unification agreement had been ratified on the previous day by both countries' legislatures. The new country was to be known as the Republic of Yemen, with San'a as its political capital and Aden its economic and commercial centre. President Saleh of the YAR became President of the new state, while al-Baid was elected Vice-President. The President of the PDRY, al-Attas, became Prime Minister, leading a transitional coalition Council of Ministers with 39 members, of whom 20 were from the YAR (members of the General People's Congress—GPC—a broad grouping of supporters of President Saleh) and 19 from the PDRY (all members of the YSP, under the continued leadership of al-Baid). A five-member Presidential Council (chaired by Saleh) was formed, together with a 45-member advisory council. The two legislatures were amalgamated to form the House of Representatives, pending elections to be held after a 30-month transitional period; an additional 31 members, including opponents of the YAR and PDRY governments, were nominated by President Saleh. In September it was reported that more than 30 new political parties had been formed since unification. The Yemeni Congregation for Reform (al-Islah), an Islamic grouping with considerable support in the House of Representatives, was regarded as the most influential of the new parties.

In May 1991 the people of Yemen voted in a referendum on the Constitution for the unified state. Religious fundamentalists and sympathizers, including al-Islah members, had urged a boycott of the referendum, owing to the proposed role of Islam. Those who participated in the referendum approved the new Constitution by a large majority, although less than 50% of the electorate registered to vote. Members of al-Islah and other opposition groups claimed that irregularities in the voting procedure had invalidated the result.

During late 1991 and early 1992 the deteriorating economic situation prompted domestic unrest. A shooting incident in San'a in October 1991 led to two days of rioting, in which nine people were believed to have died. In March 1992 workers in some parts of the country held a one-day strike, in support of demands for salary increases and the establishment of a job-creation programme for the estimated 850,000 returnees from Saudi Arabia (see below). In December at least 15 people were killed in riots in several towns, apparently caused by a sharp rise in consumer prices.

At legislative elections held on 27 April 1993, an estimated 4,730 candidates contested the 301 elective seats in the House of Representatives, of whom approximately 30% were affiliated to political parties. International observers were largely satisfied with the conduct of the elections. The GPC secured 123 of the 300 seats for which results were announced. Al-Islah won 62 seats, and the YSP 56, with independents securing 47 of the remaining seats. In May the two former ruling parties, the GPC and YSP, agreed to merge, thereby creating a single political group with an overall majority in the new House of Representatives. The subsequent election of al-Islah's leader, Sheikh Abdullah bin Hussain al-Ahmar, as Speaker of the House was regarded as a concession to his party, whose influence had been weakened by the merger. At the end of the month, however, a 31-member coalition Government was announced, including representatives of all three leading parties. Al-Attas was reappointed Prime Minister.

In August 1993 the YSP leader, al-Baid, ceased to participate in the political process and withdrew from San'a to Aden. This followed a visit to the USA, apparently without the approval of President Saleh, for talks with the US Vice-President, Al Gore. Al-Baid claimed that Saleh had made no attempt to halt the numerous armed attacks by northern officials on southerners, and claimed that as many as 150 YSP members had been assassinated since unification. He also protested at what he perceived to be the increasing marginalization of the south, particularly with regard to the distribution of petroleum revenues. In October the House of Representatives elected a new five-member Presidential Council, and later in the month the Council, in the absence of al-Baid, re-elected Saleh as its Chairman, and, accordingly, as President of the Republic of Yemen, for a further four-year term. Al-Baid was unanimously re-elected as Vice-President, but was not sworn in.

The political deadlock persisted into November 1993. Reports emerged that the armed forces of the former YAR and the PDRY (which had failed to integrate since unification) were being deployed along the former frontier. In September al-Baid, who remained in Aden, had submitted an 18-point programme of conditions for his return to San'a. Although President Saleh accepted the programme in December, there was no indication of any improvement in the political situation. In January 1994, following Jordanian mediation, representatives of the main political parties signed a 'Document of Pledge and Agreement' designed to resolve the crisis. In February Saleh and al-Baid signed the document, which contained certain security guarantees, as well as providing for a degree of decentralization, and for a review of the Constitution and of the country's economic policies. Nevertheless, both leaders remained active in mustering support for their positions throughout the region. At the same time there were reports of clashes between rival army units.

In March 1994 Saleh and al-Baid held talks in Oman, but at the end of the month al-Baid, together with Salim Salih Muhammad, refused to attend a meeting of the Presidential Council, which he had boycotted since August 1993. At the end of April 1994 the First Deputy Prime Minister, Hassan Muhammad Makki, was wounded during an assassination attempt in San'a. A series of pitched battles followed between battalions stationed in the territory of their former neighbour. On 5 May President Saleh declared a 30-day state of emergency, and dismissed al-Baid from his position as Vice-President, together with four other southern members of the Government, including Salim Muhammad. On the same day missile attacks were launched against economic and military targets, including San'a, Aden and other main airports. On 9 May Saleh announced that al-Attas had been replaced as Prime Minister by the Minister of Industry, Muhammad Said al-Attar, and that the Minister of Petroleum and Minerals had also been replaced. By this time fighting had become concentrated around Aden, and along the former north–south frontier. Several thousand southern reservists were mobilized, as the forces of the former YAR attempted to isolate and capture Aden. Meanwhile, President Saleh rejected appeals for a negotiated settlement to the civil war, and demanded that al-Baid surrender.

On 21 May 1994, the fourth anniversary of the unification of Yemen, al-Baid, in a televised address, declared the independence of a new Democratic Republic of Yemen (DRY), with Aden as its capital. He also announced the formation of a Presidential Council, with himself as President and Abd ar-Rahman al-Jifri, the leader of the League of the Sons of Yemen (LSY), as Vice-President. The composition of the Council reflected al-Baid's need to achieve a consensus of the different political and tribal groups of the former PDRY. Saleh denounced the secession as illegitimate, and offered an amnesty to all in the PDRY who rejected it, with the exception of 16 YSP leaders (including al-Baid).

At the beginning of June 1994, with the northern army attacking Aden on three fronts to the north and east of the city, the UN Security Council adopted Resolution 924, demanding a cease-fire and the resumption of dialogue in Yemen, and ordering the dispatch of a UN commission of inquiry to the region. Although welcomed by the authorities in Aden, the resolution was initially rejected by the Government in San'a, which urged the Arab League to support the unity of Yemen. Subsequently, however, the San'a Government declared itself positively disposed towards the resolution.

On 1 June 1994 the House of Representatives voted to extend the state of emergency for a further 30 days. On the following day al-Baid announced the composition of a DRY Government, in which al-Attas was to be Prime Minister and Minister of Finance. Although most of the ministers were from the YSP, the Government contained a range of religious, political and tribal representatives. As northern forces made further territorial gains around Aden, it was reported that al-Baid had transferred his centre of operations to Mukalla, east of Aden. On 7 July Aden came under the control of Saleh's troops. Many of the southern secessionist leaders fled to neighbouring Arab states, and it was officially announced that the civil war had ended. Al-Baid was believed to have requested political asylum in Oman. In March 1998 al-Baid, al-Attas and three other rebel leaders were sentenced to death *in absentia*.

According to official sources, 931 civilians and soldiers were killed, and 5,000 wounded, in the civil war, although this was generally regarded as a conservative estimate. President Saleh immediately undertook measures to consolidate his position and bring stability to the country, ending the state of emergency and reiterating the general amnesty; by August 1994, when the amnesty expired, more than 5,000 Yemenis had returned to the country. In the same month, in an attempt to undermine the strength of southern military units loyal to the YSP, President Saleh announced that party membership would no longer be permitted within the armed forces. In September, moreover, Saleh introduced amendments to the Constitution intended to strengthen his position further: the Presidential Council was abolished, and in future the President would be elected by universal suffrage. *Shari'a* would also serve as the basis of all legislation. On 1 October Saleh was re-elected President; he appointed Abd ar-Rabbur Mansur Hadi as his deputy, and Abd al-Aziz Abd al-Ghani (hitherto a member of the Presidential Council) as Prime Minister. In the new Council of Ministers members of the GPC retained the key portfolios, the YSP was denied representation and al-Islah was rewarded for its allegiance during the civil war by the allocation of nine ministerial posts. In a reorganization of the Council of Ministers in June 1995, the GPC increased its share of portfolios at the expense of independents, leading to a Government composed entirely of GPC and al-Islah members. Also in June President Saleh was re-elected Chairman of the GPC at the party's first general assembly since 1988.

In July 1994 UN-sponsored negotiations between the Yemeni leadership and the secessionists proved inconclusive. President Saleh announced that any further discussions would have to be conducted in Yemen, effectively terminating dialogue, as the YSP leaders remained in exile. In August a faction of the YSP in Yemen declared itself the new party leadership. In October, nevertheless, exiled leaders of the YSP announced the formation of a coalition, the National Opposition Front, which included former Prime Minister al-Attas and Abd ar-Rahman al-Jifri, leader of the LSY. The role of the YSP in Yemeni politics subsequently diminished considerably. In February 1995 another opposition grouping, the Democratic Coalition of Opposition, was formed, embracing 13 political parties and organizations, including a faction of the YSP and the LSY.

The economic repercussions of the civil war on the population were significant, particularly in the south. During March and April 1994, following the devaluation of the riyal (YR) and the doubling of the price of fuel, demonstrators clashed with police in Aden, San'a and Dhamar, resulting in three deaths and more than 50 arrests. The activities of militant Islamists, meanwhile, posed an additional threat to internal stability. In September some 20 people were reportedly killed in clashes with the security forces in Abyan province, following the destruction of three Muslim saints' shrines by Islamists who deemed them idolatrous. In September 1995 security forces arrested six alleged members of the Islamic Jihad group for their apparent involvement in acts of terrorism in Aden.

Tensions between al-Islah and the GPC became increasingly evident during 1995. Al-Islah expressed its opposition to economic reforms recommended by the World Bank, and criticized the GPC for attending an economic summit meeting in Jordan, in October, at which Israeli officials were present. Moreover, in December the al-Islah Minister of Trade and Supply, Muhammad Ahmad Afandi, resigned from his post, citing political and economic differences with the GPC.

In June 1996 it was reported that the Government was considering a redefinition of the boundaries of several governorates in the former border region, prior to forthcoming parliamentary elections, in order to discourage further factionalism in the area. In December al-Islah deputies withdrew from parliamentary sessions dedicated to the approval of the 1997 budget, citing insufficient opportunity to discuss its provisions. There was speculation that the deputies had adopted this confrontational stance as a result of government proposals to merge future budget allocations for religious schools (previously administered by al-Islah members) with those for general expenditure on education. In April four cabinet ministers resigned in order to seek election at the forthcoming poll.

The results of elections, conducted on 27 April 1997, demonstrated a decisive victory for the GPC, which increased its parliamentary representation from 123 to 187 seats. Al-Islah secured 53 seats (compared with 62 in 1993), and independent candidates won 54 seats. The remaining seats were shared between Nasserite and Baathist parties. The GPC's position was further consolidated by the stated intention of 39 newly elected independent deputies to demonstrate parliamentary allegiance to the GPC.

Prime Minister al-Ghani presented his own resignation, and that of the Council of Ministers, to President Saleh in May 1997. Two days later Faraj Said bin Ghanim, a political independent, was appointed Prime Minister. All but four members of the new Council of Ministers were drawn from the GPC. In April 1998 bin Ghanim resigned; the Deputy Prime Minister and Minister of Foreign Affairs, Abd al-Karim al-Iryani, was appointed Prime Minister, and he announced his new Government in May. A substantial increase in the price of petrol and basic foodstuffs in June led to public demonstrations in which more than 50 people died. Further unrest was reported during 1998 and, in September, a series of explosions in Yemen was attributed by the Government to 'foreign elements'.

The suppression of lawlessness, which had been exacerbated by the widespread ownership of weapons dating from the period of internal unrest, was a persistent domestic problem in the late 1990s. A number of armed kidnappings, frequently of tourist visitors, attracted international attention during 1997 and 1998, and in December 1998 16 foreign tourists were taken hostage; four were later killed during an attempt to release them. Yemen was criticized for failing to warn foreign embassies of an increased terrorist threat to tourists and for its precipitate use of force to free the hostages. The trial of the kidnappers, who belonged to the Islamic Aden-Abyan Army, a small extremist Islamist movement, began in January 1999. At their trial all denied the charges, claiming that their earlier confessions had been obtained under duress and that they had been tortured. Despite having no extradition treaty with the United Kingdom, the Yemeni authorities also requested the extradition from that country of a prominent Muslim cleric, a relative of two of the defendants, who they claimed had funded and masterminded a series of terrorist incidents in Yemen, including the kidnapping of the tourists in December 1998. Relations with the United Kingdom had deteriorated as a result both of Yemeni actions to end the hostage situation (three of the tourists who died were British) and of Yemeni accusations of British support for international terrorism, which were vehemently denied. The lawyer representing the defendants was himself arrested in February 1999, shortly before he was due to publicize allegations of torture against them; he was subsequently expelled from the country. In May three of the kidnappers were sentenced to death, a fourth defendant received a 20-year prison sentence and the remainder were acquitted. Two of the death sentences were eventually commuted to life imprisonment and in October the leader of the Islamic Aden-Abyan Army, Ziene al-Abidine al-Mihdar, was executed. His was the first execution under legislation, enacted in August 1998, providing for the use of capital punishment in kidnapping cases. By the end of January 1999 eight British citizens and two Algerians had been arrested on suspicion of plotting terrorist attacks on British targets in Aden; they were also reported to have links to the Islamic Aden-Abyan Army. In August all 10 were found guilty; three of the Britons were sentenced to the time they had already served and the remaining seven defendants were sentenced to between three and seven years' imprisonment. (In October 2002 the Islamic Aden-Abyan Army attacked a French supertanker, the *Limburg*, off the coast of Yemen. A spokesman for the group declared the attack, which killed a crew member, to be revenge for the execution of al-Mihdar.)

On 23 September 1999 the first direct presidential elections were held in Yemen. Saleh was re-elected, winning 96.3% of the votes; his only opponent was Najib Qahtan ash-Sha'bi, a member of the GPC who stood as an independent. The elections, which were boycotted by the YSP, were criticized for their lack of a credible candidate to oppose President Saleh.

Some internal instability was reported in 1999, with a number of bomb explosions in San'a. In February 2000 clashes occurred between members of Islamic Jihad and the security forces, while three soldiers were killed in clashes with tribesmen in ad-Dali governorate, north of Aden. In March a demonstration was held in ad-Dali in protest at the detention of two YSP officials; in April 15 YSP officials were arrested in Abyan governorate and the Secretary-General was arrested at San'a airport on his return to the country. Kidnappings continued throughout 1999 and early 2000, involving hostages from a number of Western nations; all were released unharmed. However, in June a Norwegian diplomat was killed during a police operation to release him and his son from kidnappers in San'a. In October Hatim Muhsin bin Farid, the alleged new leader of the Islamic Aden-Abyan Army, was sentenced to a seven-year term of imprisonment, having been convicted of kidnapping charges. Owing to a lack of evidence, he was cleared of charges relating to his leadership of the movement and to the possession of heavy weapons.

In mid-October 2000 a suicide bomb attack on a US destroyer, the USS *Cole*, in Aden harbour, as a result of which 17 US naval personnel were killed, was linked by many commentators to the escalating crisis in the Middle East. The Yemeni authorities responded by arresting several Islamist militants, including leading members of Islamic Jihad from Yemen, Egypt, Algeria and other Arab states. The USA blamed agents of Osama bin Laden, the Saudi-born fundamentalist Islamist believed at that time to be based in Afghanistan, for the attack, and claimed to have evidence that the two suicide bombers were Saudi nationals. Only days after the USS *Cole* bombing, the British embassy in San'a was the target of an attack, although it was unclear as to whether the two incidents were linked. (In July 2001 four Yemenis were found guilty of plotting and orchestrating the embassy bombing, and sentenced to between four and 15 years' imprisonment.)

In November 2000 Yemen and the USA signed an anti-terrorism agreement whereby the Yemeni authorities agreed to allow the US Federal Bureau of Investigation to assist in investigations into the USS *Cole* explosion, and to extradite any persons accused of involvement in terrorism against foreign targets. It was announced in the following month that investigations into the bombing had been completed and that six Yemeni nationals would stand trial in early 2001. In January, however, the Yemeni Government agreed to a postponement of the trial, following a request by US officials for more time to gather additional evidence. A further two Yemenis entering the country from Afghanistan were detained in February; another three suspects were reportedly arrested in April. In November a Yemeni newspaper published claims that the individual suspected of planning the attack had subsequently sought refuge in Afghanistan. The man was named as Muhammad Omar al-Harazi, and was also believed to have been one of the principal organizers of the 1998 attacks on the US embassies in Kenya and Tanzania. In February 2002 it was reported that the trial of eight of the suspects in the bombing of the USS *Cole* had been postponed at the request of the US authorities because of the possibility that new information about the case would be obtained during interrogation of al-Qa'ida (see below) and Taliban prisoners captured by US military forces in Afghanistan in late 2001. Two senior al-Qa'ida operatives believed to have been responsible for planning the attack on USS *Cole* were arrested by US forces and Pakistani police in November 2002 and April 2003, respectively. In April 2003 10 of the Yemenis accused of involvement in the USS *Cole* attack escaped from a high security prison; two of the fugitives were captured in May, and charged with the murder of US military personnel. The remaining eight, in addition to one further suspect, were reportedly captured in March 2004. In September two men (a Yemeni and a Saudi) were sentenced to death for their role in the attack. Four other Yemeni nationals received prison sentences of between five and 10 years. In February 2005 an appeal court ruling upheld one of the death sentences, but commuted the other to 15 years in prison and reduced the sentence of one of the other men from eight to five years.

In January 2001 the formation of a new opposition grouping, the Opposition Co-ordination Council, was announced in Yemen. The bloc, which included the YSP, was created in anticipation of the forthcoming municipal elections, Yemen's first since unification, which were held on 20 February. A national referendum was held concurrently on proposed amendments to the Constitution that would extend the President's term of office from five to seven years and the duration of the House of Representatives from four to six years, abolish the right of the President to issue decree laws when parliament is not in session and provide for the creation of a 111-member Consultative Council. According to official sources, 77.5% of voters endorsed the constitutional changes. There were claims of electoral irregularities and harassment of opposition candidates, and violent clashes were reported (principally between supporters of the GPC and those of al-Islah) in which, according to certain sources, up to 45 people were killed. The elections were boycotted by some opposition parties and were criticized by human rights groups, which claimed that the President and the GPC were seeking to consolidate their dominant position at the expense of further democratization.

In March 2001 President Saleh dismissed Prime Minister Abd al-Karim al-Iryani and declared the formation of a new Government, to be led by the former Deputy Prime Minister and Minister of Foreign Affairs, Abd al-Qadir Bajammal. The new Council of Ministers was composed exclusively of GPC members; several new ministers were appointed (including Yemen's first female minister), with only 12 remaining from the previous administration. Commentators believed that al-Iryani's dismissal was an attempt to hasten the country's reform programme. In April the President elected a new Consultative Council, which for the first time included three female politicians.

In early 2003 22 political parties were registered for a parliamentary election, which was held on 27 April. The GPC recorded another decisive victory, winning 228 of the 301 seats, while al-Islah secured 47 seats, independents 14 and the YSP seven. (Final results were published following three by-elections held in July.) Voter turn-out was reported to total 76% of the electorate. The European Union (EU, see p. 244) expressed its satisfaction with the elections, although the US-based National Democratic Institute for International Affairs claimed that the electoral process was flawed, and cited instances of under-age voting, ballot-buying and inappropriate behaviour by security forces. Moreover, opposition parties threatened to boycott the new Parliament after widespread claims of ballot-rigging, fraud and intimidation. None the less, on 10 May the President re-appointed Bajammal as Prime Minister. Bajammal's new Council of Ministers, which was sworn in on 19 May, included 17 new appointees, among them a Minister of Human Rights, Amat al-Alim as-Susua. However, the key portfolios of defence, the interior, petroleum and mineral resources, and foreign affairs remained unchanged.

Meanwhile, also in May 2003 President Saleh declared an amnesty for five exiled southern secessionist leaders who had been sentenced to death *in absentia* in 1998. In June 2003 the House of Representatives endorsed a government proposal that Yemen's counter-terrorism organization should become a separate department overseen by the Ministry of the Interior; the resources allocated to the unit were also increased. In July security forces killed six suspected Islamist militants during an operation in Abyan province, where alleged members of the Islamic Aden-Abyan Army had taken refuge after attacking a military detachment. The Government had previously maintained that the Islamic Aden-Abyan Army had ceased to exist following the execution of its leader in 1999.

In August 2003 it was reported that the Government was determined to remove imams suspected of affiliation to al-Islah. A senior official accused al-Islah of seeking to dominate the mosques and called on all political forces to fight against religious fanaticism. Later, the Minister of Religious Endowments and Guidance announced that the Government had formulated a programme to train imams to promote moderation and tolerance and was determined to prevent the preaching of *jihad* against the West or Israel. In June 2004 the Director of the Ministry of Religious Endowments and Guidance stated that the authorities would not allow Islamist parties to share control over state-controlled mosques and use them as platforms to preach extremism. Firm measures would be taken against imams who preached opposition to the Government and incited worshippers to violence. In late June the Council of Ministers gave orders to close down all unlicensed religious schools in an effort to combat extremism, and stated that an extensive review of religious education in public schools was urgently needed to ensure that teaching about Islam advocated moderation. Some commentators argued that the Government was merely responding to pressure from the US Administration.

As part of efforts to combat violence and extremism, the Government stated in 2003 that it had spent over US $32m. since 2002 buying up weapons on sale on the open market and seeking to persuade ordinary citizens to sell their weapons to the authorities. (According to the Government, 60m.–80m. guns were owned by the country's population, which numbered some 19m.) Officials indicated, however, that they were unable to continue the scheme due to a lack of resources and had approached the USA for financial assistance. An initiative endorsed by President Saleh to prevent the public from carrying firearms resulted in riots in February 2005, in which five people died in northern Yemen. Saudi Arabia had recently complained to Yemen over reports of the smuggling of arms into the kingdom, and in 2004 began the construction of a 'separation wall' along the Saudi–Yemen border (see below).

In June 2004 violent clashes took place in the mountainous north-western province of Saada between the security forces and supporters of a militant Zaidi cleric, Hussain al-Houthi, leader of Ash-Shabab al-Mo'men (Believing Youth). The authorities alleged that al-Houthi's movement had formed its own militia near the border with Saudi Arabia and had launched attacks against government buildings and mosques in Saada. Although the group appeared to be motivated by opposition to the USA and Israel and to have a militant Islamist agenda, it was not thought to have links to al-Qa'ida. Reports estimated that al-Houthi had some 3,000 armed supporters, of whom some 200–300 had been killed since the conflict began, with hundreds of rebels wounded or arrested. In September al-Houthi was killed by members of the security forces; the Government declared this development to have effectively ended the uprising. However, renewed fighting broke out with followers of the cleric in April 2005; five Yemeni soldiers and eight members of Ash-Shabab al-Mo'men were understood to have been killed. On 12 April it was reported that the conflict had decreased in intensity and that government forces were seeking al-Houthi's relatives: in particular his brother, Abd al-Malik al-Houthi, and his father, Badr ad-Din al-Houthi, who were believed to have acceded to the leadership of the movement. After several months of relative peace, fighting broke out again in November when two days of conflict reportedly left 16 rebels and eight government soldiers dead. Further violent clashes occurred in February 2006.

In 2005 and early 2006 the President faced political pressure from the USA over the Chairman of al-Islah's Shura Council, Sheikh Abd al-Majid az-Zindani. Az-Zindani was described as a 'financier of terrorism' by the UN Security Council and as a 'global terrorist' by the USA; it was understood that the latter might increase the pressure on the Yemeni Government to arrest or extradite az-Zindani. Despite having announced in July 2005 that he would not seek re-election to the presidency in September 2006, President Saleh was re-elected as Chairman of the GPC in December 2005, prompting speculation that he would in fact continue in office.

In late 2005 and 2006 a series of kidnappings further undermined Yemen's image abroad. Meanwhile, in July 2005 at least 39 people were killed in severe riots in San'a, Aden and several other towns in protest at the Government's decision to remove subsidies on fuel and the consequent doubling in the price of petroleum products. The GPC accused opposition parties of instigating the riots after they publicly criticized the price increases. The opposition denied the allegations and condemned the killing of civilians by security forces. At the end of July the Government announced a partial reduction in fuel prices.

President Saleh effected a comprehensive reshuffle of the Council of Ministers, which was also increased in size, to 34 members (including two new female ministers), in February 2006. The ministers in charge of the key portfolios of defence, oil, finance and planning were all removed from their posts and a further 18 positions were altered; however, the Minister of the Interior, Gen. Rashid al-Alimi, who had been under pressure following the escape of 23 suspected al-Qa'ida sympathizers (including Jamal al-Badawi, who had been convicted for the bombing of USS *Cole* in 2000—see above) from a San'a prison earlier in the month, was promoted to Deputy Prime Minister. The President claimed that the changes would add new impetus to the process of economic and political reform, although the opposition suggested that the reorganization was targeted at strengthening the regime before the presidential and municipal elections, which were scheduled for September.

Also in February 2006 the authorities charged three journalists (from separate publications) with denigrating Islam after they reprinted cartoons regarded as extremely offensive to Muslims that had been originally published in Denmark in late 2005. The arrests came amid complaints that the freedom of the press was being reduced ahead of the 2006 presidential election. (In November 2006 the editor of *Ar-Ra'i al-'Am*, Kamal Alufi, was convicted and sentenced to one year's imprisonment. Muhammad al-Asaadi, editor-in-chief of the *Yemen Observer*, was convicted in December and fined YR 500,000. In the same month *Al-Huriya* was ordered to cease publication for one month, and its editor, Abd al-Halim Akram Sabra, and a senior reporter were both sentenced to four months' imprisonment.)

The presidential election was held on 20 September 2006, with turn-out estimated at approximately 65% of the 9.2m. registered voters. As widely predicted, Saleh, who had rescinded his statement that he would not seek re-election, was chosen to serve another seven-year term, attracting 77.17% of the total ballot, according to official results published by the Supreme Commission for Elections and Referendums (SCER). Saleh's primary opponent, Faisal bin Shamlan of the Joint Meeting Parties (an opposition bloc that included the YSP and the Al-Haq party), garnered 21.82% of the ballot, although Shamlan's supporters rejected the results, claiming that he had received at least 40% of all votes; three other candidates each won less than 0.5% of the total number of votes cast. The SCER acknowledged that tens of thousands of votes had had to be discounted due to 'voter error'; however, the Minister of Foreign Affairs, Abu Bakr al-Kurbi, denied claims of electoral fraud, and accused those making such allegations of being opposed to democracy and the will of the Yemeni people. (One week prior to the polls at least 51 people died, and more than 230 were injured, during a stampede at an election campaign rally for the incumbent Saleh.)

In September 2006 the Ministry of the Interior announced that security forces had foiled two co-ordinated suicide attacks intended to destroy oil facilities in Marib and Hadramout. Security guards identified vehicles laden with explosives at both locations, and destroyed the vehicles before they reached their intended targets, killing all four assailants and one security guard. In October it was reported that Yemeni security forces had killed two of the 23 suspected al-Qa'ida sympathizers who had escaped from prison in February during a gun battle on the outskirts of San'a. In November a militant Islamist group calling itself 'al-Qa'ida in Yemen' issued a statement on the internet in which it claimed responsibility for the attempted bombing of oil facilities and pledged further attacks in the country. The Government responded by promising to 'strike with an iron fist' against any groups or individuals who posed a threat to national security.

In its Worldwide Press Freedom Index 2006, published in October of that year, the international non-governmental organization Reporters sans frontières ranked Yemen among the 20 worst violators of press freedom. Harassment, intimidation and imprisonment of journalists were reported to be widespread in Yemen, and the Ministry of Information was highlighted as one of the main sponsors of the violations. In January 2007 the Minister of Social Affairs and Labour, Amat ar-Razzak Ali Hamad, declared that child-trafficking was a 'burning problem' that the Government could not afford to ignore, and announced plans to establish a new centre in San'a intended to address the issues confronting the country's children.

Renewed violence broke out in the province of Saada in late January 2007, when at least six soldiers were killed in attacks on military bases by armed rebels led by Abd al-Malik al-Houthi. Earlier that month al-Houthi supporters had allegedly threatened to kill members of a small Jewish community in Saada if they did not leave the country. At the beginning of February an ambush on an army roadblock, which was also thought to have been carried out by al-Houthi insurgents, resulted in the deaths of a further 10 soldiers. A few days later 42 army and police personnel were reported to have been killed in further clashes with rebels in Saada. The latter disturbance came just a few days after President Saleh had issued an ultimatum warning of a full military campaign against the rebels if they did not surrender their weapons. Thousands of additional troops were subsequently deployed to the region, but the violence escalated in late February. In early March it was reported that more than 500 people, including more than 400 troops, had died in the fighting since the beginning of the year.

A presidential decree was issued at the end of March 2007 appointing Ali Muhammad Mujawar, hitherto Minister of Electricity, as Prime Minister, to replace Bajammal, whose dismissal was reported to be the result of weak anti-corruption policies. A new Council of Ministers was formed in early April. Key portfolios remained unchanged, with the Ministers of Foreign Affairs, Defence, the Interior, Information, and Oil and Minerals all being retained. The Ministry of Expatriate Affairs was reintroduced, to be headed by Saleh Hassan Sumi'e, and there were 11 other new appointments, including those of Noman Taher as-Souhaibi as Minister of Finance and Abd al-Qader Ali Hilal as Minister of Local Government. Addressing the new cabinet for the first time, President Saleh urged ministers to: adopt a tougher stance against corruption; abandon nepotism; tackle rising inflation; and improve living standards.

President Saleh dismissed Yahya ash-Shami, the Governor of Saada province, in mid-April 2007, as confrontations between the al-Houthi rebels and the security forces continued, causing further fatalities on both sides, and appointed Mutahar Rashad al-Masri, hitherto Deputy Minister of the Interior, in his place. In mid-May it was reported that government forces had succeeded in regaining control of the as-Saifi district of Saada, hitherto a significant al-Houthi stronghold, following fierce fighting in the area. Also in May a small bomb exploded outside the Ministry of Defence in San'a, injuring at least two people. Meanwhile, two of the 23 suspected al-Qa'ida affiliates who had escaped from prison in February 2006 surrendered to the authorities; the Yemen authorities reportedly rejected a US request for the extradition of one of the men, Jabir al-Bana. Following mediation by Qatar, in mid-June 2007 the Government and the leaders of the al-Houthi rebellion reached a cease-fire agreement, which required the rebels to relinquish their weapons and the Government to release imprisoned rebels, fund reconstruction efforts in areas affected by the fighting and facilitate the return to their homes of displaced people (estimated at more than 50,000 by the International Committee of the Red Cross); in addition, Abd al-Malik al-Houthi, two of his brothers and another rebel leader were to move to the Qatari capital, Doha, for an unspecified period of exile. A committee was established to monitor the implementation of the agreement. However, later that month it was reported that the rebel leaders remained in Saada and that insurgents were continuing to attack government troops in the province, amid some dissent within the al-Houthi movement regarding the accord with the Government. The rebels had apparently issued a new set of demands, most notably the return of the body of Hussain al-Houthi (who had been killed by the security forces in 2004—see above). Also in June Reporters sans frontières criticized the Yemeni Government for banning services that distributed news to mobile telephones and blocking access to opposition websites. The Government was also accused of attempting to prevent journalists from covering the conflict in Saada. At the end of the month a new anti-corruption body was established, its 11 members being elected by the legislature.

The threat to national security posed by purported Islamist militants also increased in 2007. A suicide bomber drove an explosives-laden car into a convoy of tourist vehicles in Marib in early July, killing eight Spanish tourists and two local drivers. Several arrests were made in connection with the attack, for which the Government held al-Qa'ida responsible, and later that month the authorities announced the discovery of explosive devices in two cars in Aden. Meanwhile, there were rumours of divisions within al-Qa'ida in Yemen over methods of operation, with some members reportedly opposed to the perpetration of suicide bombings on Yemeni territory. By this time a total of nine of the 23 suspected al-Qa'ida sympathizers who had escaped from prison in February 2006 had apparently surrendered to the authorities; five had been killed in various clashes with the Yemeni security forces; one had been killed by US forces in Somalia; one was under arrest in Kenya; and seven—including Nasir al-Wuhayshi (reported to be the new leader of the al-Qa'ida affiliate), Kassem ar-Raimi (who, together with al-Wuhayshi, was believed to have been involved in the July 2007 attack) and Jamal al-Badawi—remained at large. In August three al-Qa'ida militants were killed by Yemeni security forces. Al-Badawi surrendered to the Yemeni authorities in October; initial reports that he had been placed under house arrest, after declaring his allegiance to President Saleh, prompted criticism from the USA, although in November it was claimed that he remained in custody. In early November 32 people were found guilty of planning the attacks on oil facilities in Marib and Hadramout in September 2006 and sentenced to prison terms of between two and 15 years; six of those convicted, including ar-Raimi and al-Wuhayshi, had been tried *in absentia*, while four other defendants were acquitted owing to a lack of evidence.

Thousands of military and security officers who had been forced to retire after the civil war in 1994 demonstrated in Aden in July 2007, demanding to be allowed to return to work and to be paid wages for the intervening years. A few days earlier President Saleh had ordered the return to service of more than 600 officers, but this was regarded as inadequate by the protesters, some of whom advocated the redivision of Yemen. Unrest persisted in the south of the country in the following months, provoked not only by the issue of the military retirees, but also by economic concerns. In mid-August sit-ins were staged outside local government buildings in several towns in protest against water shortages, increases in consumer prices, unemployment, poverty and corruption; it was reported that more than 10,000 people participated in Taiz. Further demonstrations took place in Aden and Mukalla, the capital of Hadramout, in early

September, during which 40 protesters were reportedly arrested on suspicion of treason for chanting secessionist slogans. Six people were believed to have been killed in clashes between the security forces and protesters in Aden and Lahij in mid-October. Meanwhile, in a renewed effort to improve security and reassure foreign investors and tourists, in late August the Ministry of the Interior decided to enforce a ban on carrying firearms in San'a and provincial capitals, noting that some 5,000 people had been killed and 18,500 others injured in gun-related incidents during the previous three years. (By late April 2008 more than 100,000 weapons had been confiscated under the initiative.)

In September 2007, at a meeting with the leaders of a number of political organizations (although not those of the Joint Meeting Parties), President Saleh announced proposals for constitutional reform, including reductions in the presidential mandate from seven years to five and in the terms of office of the House of Representatives and the Consultative Council from six years to four; the reservation of 15% of seats in both bodies for women; and various changes related to local government.

The cease-fire between government forces and al-Houthi insurgents in Saada was breached in mid-October 2007, when at least three armed rebels and one soldier were killed in clashes resulting from the rebels' refusal to surrender their weapons. Four soldiers died in further fighting later that month after al-Houthi supporters reportedly attacked a police station. Insecurity was not confined to Saada in late 2007. Six civilians and 10 soldiers were killed in the south-eastern province of Shabwa in November when violence erupted between tribesman and troops protecting employees of a Ukrainian oil company. In December, furthermore, it was reported that two bomb explosions at military posts in Hadramout had resulted in the deaths of two security officials, while three soldiers were killed in attacks in Taiz.

Sheikh Abdullah bin Hussain al-Ahmar, Speaker of the House of Representatives since 1993 and Chairman of al-Islah, died in late December 2007. In February 2008 Yahya Ali ar-Ra'ei, of the GPC, was elected to succeed al-Ahmar as Speaker, while Sheikh Muhammad Ali al-Yadoumi became acting Chairman of al-Islah.

Clashes between government forces and al-Houthi rebels continued in Saada in early 2008, resulting in further deaths on both sides, while further demonstrations against the perceived marginalization of the south took place in Aden and other southern towns. At the same time a series of attacks and bomb explosions, mainly targeting Western interests, exacerbated tensions. In mid-January 2008 two Belgian tourists and their Yemeni driver were killed in Hadramout by gunmen who ambushed their convoy. Another al-Qa'ida-affiliated group, calling itself Jund al-Yaman (Soldiers of Yemen), later claimed responsibility for the attack, as well as that perpetrated against Spanish tourists in July 2007. In February 2008 it was announced that the security forces had foiled an attempt to blow up an oil pipeline in Marib. A grenade attack believed to have been aimed at the US embassy in San'a wounded 13 pupils at a neighbouring school, as well as several soldiers, in mid-March. In early April three explosions took place at a residential compound housing Western workers in the capital, but no injuries were reported. Two days later the US embassy announced that it was evacuating non-essential personnel from Yemen. In mid-April three police officers were killed in a bomb attack in Marib, and later that month there were two explosions in San'a near the Italian embassy.

Public unrest in the south of the country intensified in late March 2008, as large demonstrations degenerated into rioting in the provinces of Aden, Lahij and ad-Dali. The protesters had various demands, ranging from an improvement in living standards to the secession of south Yemen, while youths claimed that the authorities had reneged on promises to offer them employment in the army. In response, the Government heightened security in the region and arrested those believed to be organizing the rallies. The Prime Minister stated that 283 people had been detained in connection with the disturbances between 30 March and 9 April, but that 161 had been released. Several members of the YSP were reported to be among those arrested.

Meanwhile, with the security situation in Saada deteriorating further, the Qatari Government renewed its efforts to mediate between the Yemeni Government and the al-Houthi insurgents, and at the beginning of February 2008 a document was signed outlining measures for the implementation of the initial agreement reached in June 2007; the full details of the new accord were not disclosed. Some progress in restoring stability in Saada was achieved in the following weeks. In mid-February 2008 it was reported that hostilities had ceased and that the rebels had freed two military commanders who had been captured in January. Furthermore, by early March the Government had released 376 detainees arrested in connection with the rebellion. However, the Government subsequently accused the rebels of violating the cease-fire agreement and of killing a detainee whom they had recently abducted, and sporadic violence resumed. Two soldiers were reportedly killed and six al-Houthi rebels wounded in clashes in the district of Hidan in mid-March. Fighting broke out between al-Houthi followers and al-Bakhtan tribesmen in Saada in early April, after the pro-Government tribe accused the rebels of killing one of its members two months previously; more than 20 people died in the confrontations. In mid-April a GPC member of the House of Representatives, Saleh al-Hindi Daghsan, was killed, together with his son and a bodyguard, in an ambush carried out by unknown gunmen in Saada. Later that month Abd al-Malik al-Houthi asserted that efforts to implement the peace agreement had failed, owing to the Government's refusal to withdraw its forces from the areas in which they were deployed during the conflict with the rebels. A few days later further clashes resulted in the deaths of eight al-Houthi followers and three soldiers. In early May at least 15 people were killed and up to 60 injured in a bombing at a mosque frequented by military personnel in Saada. Abd al-Malik al-Houthi denied claims of his followers' involvement in the incident. Heavy fighting reportedly took place between rebels and troops in mid-May, resulting in a number of fatalities. Meanwhile, four al-Houthi insurgents were sentenced to death (three *in absentia*) after being convicted of killing two soldiers and injuring two others in 2006.

Gubernatorial elections were held for the first time on 17 May 2008, governors having hitherto been appointed by the President.

An agreement on the long-disputed former PDRY–Omani border was signed in San'a in October 1992 and ratified in December. Demarcation was completed in June 1995. Oman withdrew an estimated 15,000 troops from the last of the disputed territories on the Yemeni border in July 1996, in accordance with the 1992 agreement. In May 1997 officials from both countries signed the demarcation maps at a ceremony in Muscat, Oman. In January 2004 the two countries signed an agreement on their sea border during wider discussions over the establishment of a joint free trade zone.

The Iraqi invasion of Kuwait in August 1990 proved problematic for the Yemeni Government, as the economy was heavily dependent on trade with, and aid from, Iraq, and also on aid from Saudi Arabia, which was host to a considerable number of Yemeni expatriate workers. In December Yemen assumed the chair of the UN Security Council (which rotates on a monthly basis), and the Government increased its efforts to mediate in the Gulf crisis. It was, however, unable to prevent the outbreak of war, despite a peace plan, presented in January 1991, and further diplomatic initiatives. Yemen condemned the US-led military offensive against Iraq, and large demonstrations were held in support of Iraq. Later in January it was confirmed that US aid to Yemen was to be suspended indefinitely, apparently as a result of Yemen's policy towards Iraq, although reduced US economic aid was resumed in August. Yemen continued to support Iraq and in December 1998 it requested an Arab League summit on Iraq and called for an end to the sanctions. The Yemeni Government expressed its concerns regarding the US-led military operations against Iraqi air defence targets in 1999–2002.

Following the suicide attacks apparently perpetrated by Osama bin Laden's al-Qa'ida (Base) network against New York and Washington, DC, USA on 11 September 2001, the Yemeni Government arrested a number of suspected Islamist militants and froze the assets of individuals and organizations deemed to have links with al-Qa'ida. In December up to 30 people (including about 19 soldiers) were reportedly killed during clashes in the central Marib governorate, when local residents apparently fought to prevent the Yemeni security forces from arresting a group of alleged militants. (President Saleh had, during a visit to Washington in November, been presented with a list of suspected al-Qa'ida members residing in Yemen.) Meanwhile, at least 100 foreign students enrolled at the country's Islamic institutes were said to have been arrested on charges of violating residency requirements. In January 2002 the US embassy in San'a was closed amid fears of an imminent terrorist attack; two grenades were thrown at the building in March, although no injuries were reported. There were reports in March that the US Administration was considering the deployment of several hundred US troops to Yemen to assist the authorities in their struggle against militant Islamist organizations. In April an explosion was reported close to the home of a leading security official involved in the search for al-Qa'ida militants; a previously unknown group styled the al-Qa'ida Sympathizers was suspected of having carried out the bombing. Despite increasing popular resentment towards US activities in the Middle East among Yemenis, President Saleh continued to co-operate with the USA over anti-terrorism initiatives, and in November an unmanned US aircraft killed six men in northern Yemen believed to have links with al-Qa'ida. In December three US missionaries were murdered by a Yemeni who confessed to having links with bin Laden's network.

In February 2002 President Saleh was reported to have warned the US Government that a US-led attack on the regime of Saddam Hussain in Iraq, as part of its 'war on terror', would jeopardize the continued support of its traditional allies in the Arab region. However, Saleh was careful to emphasize his own ongoing efforts to persuade the Iraqi authorities to accept the return of UN weapons inspectors. When the US-led military campaign commenced in Iraq in March 2003, some 30,000 protesters, some of them armed, marched on the US embassy in San'a. Public resentment also continued to increase towards President Saleh's regime, as a result of its perceived co-operation with the USA. In June, however, the Director of the US Federal Bureau of Investigation, Robert Mueller, met Saleh in Aden to discuss further co-operation on security and intelligence. In September the human rights organization Amnesty International released a report claiming that the authorities were holding some 200 people without trial in an effort to assuage US concerns that Yemen was not co-operating fully with the 'war on terror'. In November Muhammad Hamdi al-Ahdal, who, according to the USA, had been among the 20 most significant al-Qa'ida members still at large, was captured by security forces; al-Ahdal was suspected of having organized the bombings of the USS *Cole* in 2000 and the French petroleum tanker, the *Limburg*, in 2002 (see above). Another reported senior al-Qa'ida operative, who had apparently survived a US attempt to assassinate him in 2002, was arrested by security forces in March 2004.

In early 2004 the Government signed a memorandum of understanding with the USA, which was regarded as the first step towards a free trade pact between the countries. The agreement also provided Yemen with an extra US $7.6m. in aid. In March Yemen welcomed the signing of an interim constitution in Iraq, describing it as a step towards Iraq recovering its sovereignty, but continued to press for the USA and its allies to withdraw their forces from the country. In August the Minister of Foreign Affairs confirmed that Yemen was preparing a peace-keeping force for Iraq under mandates from the Arab League and the UN, but would only send the troops should the US-led coalition forces withdraw from Iraq. In December 2006 the US embassy in San'a was again closed after a man bearing a semi-automatic rifle had opened fire at the compound. Security guards on site returned fire, incapacitating the gunman and allowing him to be arrested; no embassy staff were injured in the incident and the embassy was reopened on the following day. Discussions held between Saleh and US President George W. Bush in May 2007, during a visit by the Yemeni President to Washington, focused on efforts to combat terrorism and developments in the Middle East, as well as bilateral relations. In November Saleh al-Ammari was convicted of shooting at the embassy in December 2006 and sentenced to five years' imprisonment; an appeals court reduced his sentence to three years in May 2008.

Relations with Saudi Arabia deteriorated as a result of Yemen's initially strong opposition to the presence of foreign armed forces in the Gulf and to the ambiguous stance it had subsequently adopted in this respect. In September 1990, apparently in retaliation, Saudi Arabia announced that it had withdrawn the privileges that Yemeni workers had previously enjoyed. This resulted in an exodus from Saudi Arabia of some 850,000 Yemeni workers during October and November, which caused widespread economic and social disruption. The expulsion and consequent return to Yemen of the workers not only caused a reduction in the country's income from remittances, but also led to a serious increase in unemployment. During 1995, at negotiations proceeding from the February 1995 memorandum of understanding—see below—it was reported that the Saudi authorities had agreed to allow Yemenis sponsored by Saudi nationals to seek employment in the kingdom. In 1998 Saudi Arabia began issuing visas to Yemeni workers.

The Governments of Yemen and Saudi Arabia held negotiations concerning the demarcation of their common border during 1992–94; however, in December 1994 Yemen accused Saudi Arabia of trespassing on Yemeni territory and alleged that three of its soldiers had been killed during clashes earlier in that month. Further clashes were reported in January 1995 following the failure of the two countries to renew the 1934 Ta'if agreement (renewable every 20 years), which delineated their existing frontier. Intense mediation by Syria culminated in a joint statement in mid-January 1995, in which Yemen and Saudi Arabia pledged to cease all military activity in the border area. It was subsequently announced that the demarcation of the disputed border would be undertaken by a joint committee. In February the Yemeni and Saudi Governments signed a memorandum of understanding that reaffirmed their commitment to the Ta'if agreement and provided for the establishment of six joint committees to delineate the land and sea borders and develop economic and commercial ties. In June President Saleh led a high-ranking delegation to Saudi Arabia, constituting the first official visit to that country since February 1990. The two Governments expressed their satisfaction with the memorandum of understanding and, in addition, pledged their commitment to strengthening economic, commercial and cultural co-operation.

In July 1996 Yemen and Saudi Arabia signed a bilateral security agreement which included provisions intended to counter the cross-border trafficking of illicit drugs. Friction over border claims, however, was revived in 1997, and in May 1998 it was reported that Saudi Arabia had occupied an uninhabited island in the Red Sea regarded by Yemen as within its national boundaries. In the same month Saudi Arabia sent a memorandum to the UN stating that it did not recognize the 1992 border agreement between Yemen and Oman and claiming that parts of the area involved were Saudi Arabian territory. The Saudi objection to the accord was widely believed to be related to its attempts to gain land access to the Arabian Sea, via a corridor between Yemen and Oman, which it had thus far been denied in its negotiations with Yemen. In July 1998 Yemen submitted a memorandum to the Arab League refuting the Saudi claim to the land, and stating that the Saudi protests contravened the Ta'if agreement signed by that country. In the same month three Yemeni troops were killed during fighting with a Saudi border patrol on the disputed island of Duwaima in the Red Sea; Saudi Arabia claimed its actions on the island were in self-defence and that, under the Ta'if agreement, three-quarters of the island belonged to Saudi Arabia. Meanwhile, bilateral discussions continued and the Saudi Minister of Foreign Affairs visited Yemen at the end of July. The Yemeni Prime Minister cancelled a planned visit to Saudi Arabia in October 1999, reportedly owing to the failure of the two Governments to agree on the issues to be discussed.

Despite reported clashes in the border area during 1999, however, relations continued to improve. In June 2000, at a ceremony in Riyadh, Saudi Arabia, the Saudi Arabian and Yemeni ministers responsible for foreign affairs signed a final border treaty demarcating their joint land and sea border. The treaty incorporated both the 1934 Ta'if agreement and the 1995 memorandum of understanding, although it failed to define the eastern section of the Saudi–Yemeni land frontier. The two countries also agreed to further economic, commercial and cultural ties, and each pledged not to permit its territory to be used as a base for political or military aggression against the other. In the months following the signing of the treaty, however, clashes were reported between rival tribal groups near the border. In December 2000 a meeting was held of the Saudi-Yemeni Co-operation Council (the first since before the Gulf conflict), at which Saudi officials pledged financial assistance to Yemen for development projects. However, talks concerning the proposed construction of a petroleum pipeline between the two countries had reportedly been unsuccessful. In April 2001 Yemen and Saudi Arabia were said to have agreed on the location of four crossing-points on their joint border. At the same time reports suggested that the withdrawal of Yemeni and Saudi troops from their respective sides of the border was almost complete. Renewed tensions surfaced in early 2004 after the Saudi Government began construction of a 'separation wall' along the border that some considered to be in violation of the treaty of June 2000 on border demarcation. The construction of the wall reflected unease on the part of the Saudis regarding the capacity of the Yemeni authorities to maintain their own border security. In June 2006 the Saudi and Yemeni ministers responsible for internal affairs signed an agreement on the final demarcation of their shared border.

In November 1995 there were reports that Eritrean troops had attempted to land on the Red Sea island of Greater Hanish, one of three islands (the others being Lesser Hanish and Zuqar) claimed by both Yemen and Eritrea. The attempted invasion had apparently been prompted by Yemen's announced intention to develop Greater Hanish as a tourist resort, and its subsequent refusal to comply with an Eritrean demand that the island be evacuated. Negotiations in Yemen and Eritrea failed to defuse the crisis, and on 15 December fighting broke out between the two sides, resulting in the deaths of six Eritrean and three Yemeni soldiers. On 17 December Yemen and Eritrea agreed to a cease-fire. None the less, fighting was renewed the following day and Eritrean forces succeeded in occupying Greater Hanish. The cease-fire was adhered to thenceforth, and some 180 Yemeni soldiers (captured during the fighting) were released at the end of the month.

In May 1996, following French mediation, it was announced that Yemen and Eritrea would sign an arbitration agreement, whereby both countries would renounce the use of force and submit their dispute to an international tribunal. France subsequently undertook to observe and supervise military movements in the area around the disputed islands. Eritrean troops occupied Lesser Hanish in mid-August, but were withdrawn later in the month after representations by France and a UN Security Council edict to evacuate the island forthwith. At a meeting held in Paris, France, in October, representatives of Eritrea and Yemen confirmed that they would submit the dispute to an international tribunal. In October 1998 the tribunal ruled that Yemen had sovereignty over Greater and Lesser Hanish, and all islands to their north-west, while Eritrea had sovereignty over the Mohabaka islands. The court recommended that the fishing traditions around the islands be maintained, thereby granting access to the Hanish islands to Eritrean and Yemeni fishermen. Both countries accepted the ruling, and shortly afterwards they agreed to establish a joint committee to strengthen bilateral co-operation. In May 1999 the Presidents of Eritrea and Yemen held talks to discuss bilateral relations. A final ruling on the Hanish islands, issued by the tribunal in December, delineated the joint maritime border as the median line between their mainland coastlines. This was welcomed by both countries and in January 2000 the Yemeni Vice-President made an official visit to Eritrea for talks with President Afewerki. In March Eritrea denied reports that it had appealed against the tribunal's decision on the islands. In June 2003 a number of Yemeni fishing boats and 133 crew members were arrested by Eritrean naval patrols in the area around the Hanish islands. Although the men were released in July, this latest development was an indication of increased tension between the countries since the decision of the tribunal.

Since the mid-1990s President Saleh has increasingly sought to widen the range of Yemen's international contacts, particularly in relation to aid and co-operation agreements. In November 1997 an accord was reached with the 'Paris Club' of official creditors for the amelioration of Yemen's burden of external debt. In the same month, on an official visit to the United Kingdom (during which a co-operation agreement was signed with the EU), President Saleh made a formal application for Yemen to join the Commonwealth (see p. 206). Saleh made a state visit to the People's Republic of China in February 1998, during which extensive agreements were negotiated for Yemen to receive technical and economic assistance. In early 2000 Saleh made official visits to Canada, the USA, Italy and Iran; at the same time Yemen repeatedly denied reports that it had had secret contacts with Israel and that it was seeking to normalize relations with that country. According to reports, in early 2004 the Government sought to borrow some US $700m. from Italy and Poland to finance sea patrols in order to improve coastal security. Meanwhile, in December 2003 Yemen concreted its improved relations with two of its neighbours to the west, Sudan and Ethiopia, with the establishment of the Tripartite San'a Co-operation Forum. Eritrea, however, accused the group of collaborating against it. In December 2005 Yemen offered to mediate between Ethiopia and Eritrea over the two countries' border demarcation dispute. At a meeting held in London, United Kingdom, in November 2006, international donors pledged some US $5,000m. in development assistance for Yemen. In August 2007 Yemen signed a 10-year development partnership agreement with the United Kingdom.

In September 2005 Yemen signed a security agreement with Bahrain; the two states agreed to co-operate on training, combating crime and terrorism, and exchanging intelligence. In mid-May 2007 the staging of a demonstration intended to protest against perceived Iranian and Libyan interference in Yemeni domestic affairs was prevented by the Ministry of the Interior, provoking outrage among, in particular, many in Saada, who were angered by alleged Iranian and Libyan support for those rebels loyal to al-Houthi who were thought to be responsible for much of the violence in that region. A few days previously Yemen had recalled its ambassadors from both countries. The Iranian and Libyan Governments both denied any involvement in the rebellion in Saada and sought to ease tensions with Yemen. Later in May the Libyan leader dispatched an envoy to San'a to deliver a letter to President Saleh expressing support for the Yemeni Government's efforts to quash the insurgency, and in July Muhammad Reza Baqeri, the Iranian Deputy Foreign Minister for Arab and African Affairs, visited Yemen in an effort to improve bilateral relations.

President Saleh sought to mediate in the dispute that arose between rival Palestinian political factions the Islamic Resistance Movement (Hamas) and Fatah after Hamas had seized control of the Gaza Strip in June 2007. In late March 2008 the Yemeni President brokered a reconciliation agreement, the San'a Declaration, which was signed by the two organizations (for further details, see the chapter on the Palestinian Autonomous Areas).

Government

Legislative power is vested in the House of Representatives, with 301 members directly elected by universal adult suffrage. Under the revised Constitution, the President of the Republic (Head of State) is to be elected directly by voters for a period of seven years, renewable once. The President appoints a Council of Ministers, headed by a Prime Minister.

Defence

As assessed at November 2007, the armed forces of the Republic of Yemen totalled 66,700: army 60,000; navy 1,700; air force 3,000; air defence 2,000. There was a paramilitary force with a strength in excess of 71,200, comprising the 50,000-strong Ministry of the Interior Forces and tribal levies numbering at least 20,000. Military conscription was ended in May 2001, and in 2004 a voluntary programme of military service was introduced. The defence budget for 2007 was forecast at YR 179,000m.

Economic Affairs

In 2006, according to estimates by the World Bank, Yemen's gross national income (GNI), measured at average 2004–06 prices, was US $16,444m., equivalent to $760 per head (or $920 per head on an international purchasing-power parity basis). During 1996–2006, it was estimated, the population increased at an average annual rate of 3.2%, while gross domestic product (GDP) per head increased, in real terms, by an average of 2.2% per year. Overall GDP increased, in real terms, at an average annual rate of 4.5% in 1996–2006; GDP growth in 2006 was 3.2%.

Agriculture (including forestry and fishing) contributed an estimated 10.0% of GDP in 2006, and the sector engaged 31.0% of the working population at the 2004 census. According to FAO estimates, however, the sector engaged 45.3% of the total labour force in mid-2005. The principal cash crops are coffee, cotton and fruits. Subsistence crops include sorghum, wheat, barley and potatoes. Livestock-rearing (particularly in the east and north) and fishing are also important activities. Livestock, hides and skins and fish are all exported on a small scale. Estimates indicated growth in the agricultural sector averaging 2.7% annually in 2002–06. Real agricultural GDP increased by 7.2% in 2006, according to provisional estimates.

Industry (including mining, manufacturing, construction and power) contributed an estimated 48.5% of GDP in 2006, and 16.3% of the working population were employed in the sector at the 2004 census. According to estimates, industrial GDP increased at an average annual rate of 3.2% in 2002–06. Real growth in industrial GDP was provisionally estimated at 2.6% in 2006.

Mining and quarrying contributed an estimated 34.7% of GDP in 2006 and employed 0.5% of the working population at the 2004 census. Yemen's proven petroleum reserves totalled 2,900m. barrels at the end of 2006, sufficient to maintain production at that year's levels for 20 years. Petroleum production averaged 390,000 barrels per day (b/d) during 2006, considerably lower than the Government's planned output. The value of exports of petroleum and petroleum products accounted for 91.5% of the value of total exports in 2004. There are also significant reserves of natural gas: proven reserves at the end of 2006 were 490,000m. cu m. Salt and gypsum are also exploited on a large scale. In addition, there are deposits of copper, lead, zinc, gold, sulphur and molybdenum. GDP of the mining sector decreased at an estimated average annual rate of 3.7% in 2002–06; real mining GDP contracted by 7.7% in 2006, according to provisional estimates.

The manufacturing sector contributed an estimated 7.6% of GDP in 2006; at the 2004 census 5.9% of the working population were employed in the sector. The most important branches of manufacturing are food-processing, petroleum refining, construction materials (particularly cement and iron and steel), paper and paper products and traditional light industries (including textiles, leather goods and jewellery). The Aden oil refinery recommenced operations in 1994 and was being considered for partial privatization in the mid-2000s; some imported crude oil is also refined. Plans for the construction of a new refinery at Hadramout were completed in 2004; the facility was scheduled to commence supply of petroleum products to eastern Yemen in 2007. Real growth in manufacturing GDP was estimated at an average of 5.9% annually in 2002–06; according to provisional estimates, the sector's real GDP increased by 6.2% in 2006.

Some domestic energy requirements are served by locally produced petroleum, but the country is somewhat reliant on fuel imports (particularly petroleum from other producers in the region). Imports of fuel and energy comprised 21.4% of the value of total imports in 2005. The northern and southern electricity grids were linked in 1997.

The services sector contributed an estimated 41.5% of GDP in 2006, and employed 52.7% of the working population at the 2004 census. A free trade zone at Aden was inaugurated in May 1991. A series of kidnappings in 2005–06 further damaged Yemen's image in the West, and consequently its attractiveness as a destination for tourists and investment. The real GDP of the services sector increased at an estimated average annual rate of 7.5% in 2002–06. Real services GDP expanded by 7.4% in 2006, according to provisional estimates.

In 2006 Yemen recorded a visible trade surplus of US $1,390.3m., and there was a surplus of $205.7m. on the current account of the balance of payments. In 2006 the principal source of imports (22.0%) was the United Arab Emirates (UAE); other major suppliers were Saudi Arabia, Switzerland and the People's Republic of China. In that year India was the main export destination (24.0%). Other important export markets were China, Thailand, the USA and the UAE. The principal exports in 2004 were petroleum and petroleum products (91.5%). The main imports in that year were food and live animals (especially cereals and cereal preparations), machinery and transport equipment, and basic manufactures.

A preliminary budget deficit of YR 69,700m. was recorded in 2005. Total external debt at the end of 2005 was estimated to be US $5,363m., of which $4,717m. was long-term public debt. In that year the cost of debt-servicing was equivalent to 2.6% of the value of exports of goods and services. According to ILO, the annual rate of inflation averaged 10.0% in 1996–2006; consumer prices increased by 21.3% in 2006. The rate of unemployment is estimated to be as high as 25% of the labour force.

Yemen is a member of the Arab Fund for Economic and Social Development (AFESD, see p. 174) and the Council of Arab Economic Unity (see p. 222).

Between the establishment of the Republic of Yemen in 1990 and the civil war of 1994 the economy declined substantially, resulting, by 1994, in an annual inflation rate averaging 55%, a budget deficit of 16.7% of GDP and high levels of external debt. Following a series of economic reforms implemented by the Government, the budget deficit was narrowed and several years of stable inflation were achieved; however, in 2006 Yemen recorded inflation of over 20% as a result of high government spending and rapid monetary growth. In mid-2007 the IMF held bilateral discussions with Yemen, and highlighted the country's three principal macroeconomic challenges: lowering inflation to below 10%; achieving fiscal security in the face of diminishing oil reserves; and promoting growth in sectors other than hydrocarbons in order to combat poverty and create employment opportunities. The Fund's concerns largely corresponded with those issues prioritized by the Government in its third five-year development plan (for 2006–10), which aimed, *inter alia*, to increase growth in the non-petroleum sectors and to lower both unemployment and poverty rates. Yemen's economy remains closely tied to international petroleum prices: the IMF forecast low GDP growth, of 2.6%, in 2007, and a decline of 10.1% in hydrocarbons GDP, as petroleum reserves and subsequently oil exports were expected to decline. The situation was thought likely to be exacerbated by falling productivity in the exploitation of existing resources and lower-than-anticipated output from some newer oilfields. Yemen remains one of the least developed countries in the world, ranking 153 out of 177 countries in the UN Development Programme's Human Development Index for 2007/08. With one of the highest population growth rates in the world, the country faces serious problems with rising levels of unemployment and stagnant per capita income, which in 2005 stood at only US $600. Moreover, increased security concerns in 2007–08 have further damaged Yemen's image as far as potential investors are concerned. In late 2006 the Government asked foreign donors to pledge $10,000m. in aid over a five-year period to assist Yemen in its preparations for membership of the Co-operation Council for the Arab States of the Gulf—Gulf Co-operation Council (GCC, see p. 219).

Education

Primary education, between the ages of six and 15, is compulsory. Secondary education, beginning at 15, lasts for a further three years. In 2005/06 enrolment at primary schools included 75% of children in the relevant age-group (85% of boys; 65% of girls), according to UNESCO estimates; in 2004/05 the total number of students in primary education was estimated at 4,072,294. Enrolment at secondary schools in 2005/06, according to UNESCO estimates, included 37% of students (48% of boys; 26% of girls) in the appropriate age-group; in 2004/05 the total number of students in secondary education was estimated at 595,114. In 2004/05 some 188,124 students were enrolled at institutions of higher education. In 2000 public expenditure on education was forecast at YR 90,054m., equivalent to 21.3% of total government spending; in 2004 this had increased to an equivalent of 32.8% of total government expenditure. A Basic Education Development project aimed to improve the quality of education and to increase enrolment at primary schools to 85% over 40 years; the World Bank approved the project in September 2004 and provided a loan of US $65m. to assist with its implementation.

Public Holidays

2008: 1 January (New Year's Day), 10 January*† (Muharram, Islamic New Year), 19 January* (Ashoura), 8 March (International Women's Day), 20 March* (Mouloud, Birth of the Prophet), 1 May (Labour Day), 13 June (Corrective Movement Anniversary), 30 July* (Leilat al-Meiraj, Ascension of the Prophet), 2 September* (Ramadan begins), 1 October* (Id al-Fitr, end of Ramadan), 14 October (National Day), 9 December* (Id al-Adha, Feast of the Sacrifice), 29 December*† (Muharram, Islamic New Year).

2009: 1 January (New Year's Day), 7 January*‡ (Ashoura), 8 March (International Women's Day), 9 March* (Mouloud, Birth of the Prophet), 1 May (Labour Day), 13 June (Corrective Movement Anniversary), 19 July* (Leilat al-Meiraj, Ascension of the Prophet), 22 August* (Ramadan begins), 20 September* (Id al-Fitr, end of Ramadan), 14 October (National Day), 27 November* (Id al-Adha, Feast of the Sacrifice), 18 December* (Muharram, Islamic New Year), 27 December*‡ (Ashoura).

* These holidays are dependent on the Islamic lunar calendar and may vary by one or two days from the dates given.

† This festival occurs twice (marking the start of the Islamic years AH 1429 and 1430) within the same Gregorian year.

‡ This festival occurs twice (in the Islamic years AH 1430 and 1431) within the same Gregorian year.

Weights and Measures

Local weights and measures are used, and vary according to location.

Statistical Survey

Sources (unless otherwise indicated): Republic of Yemen Central Statistical Organization, POB 13434, San'a; tel. (1) 250619; fax (1) 250664; e-mail csoi@y.net.ye; internet www.cso-yemen.org; Central Bank of Yemen, POB 59, Ali Abd al-Mughni St, San'a; tel. (1) 274314; fax (1) 274360; e-mail info@centralbank.gov.ye; internet www.centralbank.gov.ye.

Area and Population

AREA, POPULATION AND DENSITY

Area (sq km)	536,869*
Population (census results)	
16 December 1994†	14,587,807
16 December 2004‡	
Males	10,036,953
Females	9,648,208
Total	19,685,161
Population (UN estimates at mid-year)§	
2005	21,096,000
2006	21,732,000
2007	22,389,000
Density (per sq km) at mid-2007	41.7

* 207,286 sq miles.
† Excluding adjustment for underenumeration.
‡ Population is *de jure*.
§ Source: UN, *World Population Prospects: The 2006 Revision*.

PRINCIPAL TOWNS
(population at 1994 census)

San'a (capital)	954,448	Hodeida	298,452
Aden	398,294	Mukalla	122,359
Taiz	317,571	Ibb	103,312

Source: UN, *Demographic Yearbook*.

Mid-2007 ('000, incl. suburbs, UN estimate): San'a 2,008 (Source: UN, *World Urbanization Prospects: The 2007 Revision*).

BIRTHS, MARRIAGES AND DEATHS
(annual averages, UN estimates)

	1990–95	1995–2000	2000–05
Birth rate (per 1,000)	48.6	42.9	39.3
Death rate (per 1,000)	11.9	10.1	8.6

Source: UN, *World Population Prospects: The 2006 Revision*.

Registered births: 153,945 in 2004; 152,792 in 2005.

Registered deaths: 22,255 in 2004; 19,653 in 2005.

Marriages (2002, estimate): 10,934 (Source: UN, *Demographic Yearbook*).

Expectation of life (years at birth, WHO estimates): 60.5 (males 58.9; females 62.2) in 2005 (Source: WHO, *World Health Statistics*).

EMPLOYMENT
('000 persons aged 15 years and over, 2004 census results)

	Males	Females	Total
Agriculture, forestry and fishing	973	130	1,103
Mining and quarrying	17	1	18
Manufacturing	185	25	210
Electricity, gas and water	16	1	17
Construction	331	2	333
Trade, restaurants and hotels	736	20	756
Transport, storage and communications	188	4	192
Finance, insurance and real estate	39	5	44
Education	217	70	287
Health and social welfare	33	17	50
Personal and social services	49	4	53
Public administration and defence	444	25	469
Private households with employed persons	13	6	19
Extra-territorial organizations	3	1	4
Total	**3,244**	**311**	**3,555**

Mid-2005 (estimates in '000): Agriculture, etc. 3,091; Total labour force 6,820 (Source: FAO).

Health and Welfare

KEY INDICATORS

Total fertility rate (children per woman, 2005)	5.9
Under-5 mortality rate (per 1,000 live births, 2005)	102
HIV/AIDS (% of persons aged 15–49, 2003)	0.1
Physicians (per 1,000 head, 2004)	0.33
Hospital beds (per 1,000 head, 2005)	0.60
Health expenditure (2004): US $ per head (PPP)	81.6
Health expenditure (2004): % of GDP	5.0
Health expenditure (2004): public (% of total)	38.3
Access to water (% of persons, 2004)	67
Access to sanitation (% of persons, 2004)	43
Human Development Index (2005): ranking	153
Human Development Index (2005): value	0.508

For sources and definitions, see explanatory note on p. vi.

Agriculture

PRINCIPAL CROPS
('000 metric tons)

	2004	2005	2006
Wheat	103	113	149
Barley	25	21	28
Maize	32	31	66
Millet	66	67	82
Sorghum	263	264	402
Potatoes	198	218	226
Chick-peas	38	37	54
Sesame seed	19	19	22
Cottonseed	13	14	15
Tomatoes	200	204	212
Cucumbers and gherkins	8	10	13
Chillies and green peppers	19	17	17
Dry onions	154	173	174
Garlic*	3	3	3
Green beans	1	3	3
Carrots and turnips	14	12	13
Okra	17	18	19
Watermelons	141	144	148
Cantaloupes and other melons	29	28	27
Bananas	86	90	112
Oranges	71	84	101
Tangerines, mandarins, etc.	12	13	20
Grapes	104	108	118
Mangoes, mangosteens and guavas	351	345	349
Dates	29	30	50
Papayas	21	21	22
Coffee (green)	10	11	17
Tobacco (leaves)	17	18	20

* FAO estimates.

Aggregate production ('000 metric tons, may include official, semi-official or estimated data): Total cereals 490 in 2004, 496 in 2005, 727 in 2006; Total roots and tubers 198 in 2004, 218 in 2005, 227 in 2006; Total vegetables (incl. melons) 673 in 2004, 695 in 2005, 712 in 2006; Total fruits (excl. melons) 746 in 2004, 768 in 2005, 866 in 2006.

Source: FAO.

YEMEN

LIVESTOCK
('000 head, year ending September)

	2004	2005	2006
Horses*	3	3	3
Asses, mules or hinnies*	500	500	500
Cattle	1,433	1,447	1,464
Camels	353	357	347
Sheep	7,899	7,980	8,197
Goats	7,785	7,864	8,042
Chickens (million)	n.a.	n.a.	48*

* FAO estimate(s).

Source: FAO.

LIVESTOCK PRODUCTS
('000 metric tons)

	2003	2004	2005
Cattle meat	69.5	70.9	72.6
Sheep meat*	33.6	34.3	35.0
Goat meat*	26.0	26.0	26.0
Chicken meat	108.0	111.0	113.2
Camels' milk*	13.6	13.6	13.6
Cows' milk	208.3	212.5	216.6
Sheep's milk*	22.4	22.4	22.4
Goats' milk*	34.8	34.7	34.7
Hen eggs	46.3†	47.2*	48.4*
Wool (greasy)*	6.2	6.4	6.5

* FAO estimate(s).
† Unofficial figure.

2006: Cattle meat 72.7; Sheep meat 31.9 (FAO estimate); Goat meat 25.6 (FAO estimate); Chicken meat 117.7; Camels' milk 17.7 (FAO estimate); Cows' milk 224.2; Sheep's milk 27.2 (FAO estimate); Goats' milk 37.5 (FAO estimate); Hen eggs 48.4 (FAO estimate); Wool (greasy) 6.5 (FAO estimate).

Source: FAO.

Forestry

ROUNDWOOD REMOVALS
('000 cubic metres, excl. bark, estimates)

	2004	2005	2006
Total (all fuel wood)	353	367	381

Source: FAO.

Fishing

('000 metric tons, live weight of capture)

	2003	2004	2005*
Demersal percomorphs	10.9	12.4*	12.7
Indian oil sardine*	9.4	10.7	11.0
Yellowfin tuna	29.2	31.3	32.0
Pelagic percomorphs*	105.0	119.5	122.7
Sharks, rays and skates, etc.*	11.0	12.5	12.8
Cuttlefish and bobtail squids	11.3	12.8*	13.2
Total catch (incl. others)*	228.1	256.3	263.0

* FAO estimate(s).

Source: FAO.

Mining
('000 metric tons, unless otherwise indicated)

	2003	2004*	2005*
Crude petroleum ('000 barrels)	157,000	147,000	149,000
Natural gas (million cu m)†	30,000	28,500	29,500
Salt	116	88	90
Gypsum (crude)	42	37	38

* Estimates.
† Gross production.

Source: US Geological Survey.

Industry

SELECTED PRODUCTS
('000 barrels, unless otherwise indicated)

	2003	2004	2005
Mineral water (million litres)	146	153	n.a.
Soft drinks (million litres)	105*	127	154
Cigarettes (million packets)	298*	90	109
Liquefied petroleum gas	1,100	800	900
Benzene	7,400	8,100	8,100
Kerosene	3,510	3,100	3,300
Distillate fuel oils	16,000	16,900	17,000
Residual fuel oils	10,000	9,000	9,000
Cement ('000 metric tons)	1,541	1,546	1,550
Paints ('000 litres)	15,564	15,664	n.a.
Plastic bags ('000 metric tons)	10,891	10,993	n.a.
Electric energy (million kWh)	4,094*	4,366	4,767

* Provisional figure.

Source: partly US Geological Survey.

Finance

CURRENCY AND EXCHANGE RATES

Monetary Units
100 fils = 1 Yemeni riyal (YR).

Sterling, Dollar and Euro Equivalents (30 November 2007)
£1 sterling = YR 411.50;
US $1 = YR 199.14;
€1 = YR 293.95;
YR 1,000 = £2.43 = $5.02 = €3.40.

Average Exchange Rate (YR per US $)
2004   184.776
2005   191.509
2006   197.049

Note: The exchange rate of US $1 = YR 9.76, established in the YAR in 1988, remained in force until February 1990, when a new rate of $1 = YR 12.01 was introduced. Following the merger of the two Yemens in May 1990, the YAR's currency was adopted as the currency of the unified country. In March 1995 the official exchange rate was amended from YR 12.01 to YR 50.04 per US dollar. The rate has since been adjusted. From mid-1996 data refer to a market-determined exchange rate, applicable to most private transactions.

YEMEN

CENTRAL GOVERNMENT BUDGET
(YR '000 million)

Revenue*	2003	2004	2005†
Oil and gas	480.2	579.1	842.2
Exports	316.4	360.7	502.6
Domestic revenues	163.8	218.4	339.6
Non-oil revenues	184.3	203.4	265.8
Tax revenues	145.3	177.3	215.7
Non-tax revenues	39.0	26.1	50.1
Total	664.5	782.5	1,108.0

Expenditure	2003	2004	2005†
Current expenditure	581.2	618.5	907.9
Civil wages and salaries	143.2	159.5	197.6
Materials and services	51.7	14.2	27.3
Defence	148.1	135.9	193.3
Interest	38.0	54.0	70.7
Domestic	29.2	44.9	60.1
Foreign	8.8	9.1	10.6
Transfers and subsidies	177.2	230.6	384.9
Current transfers	70.3	78.2	98.9
Subsidies	106.9	152.4	286.0
Other current expenditure	23.0	24.3	34.1
Capital development expenditure	197.1	198.9	212.0
Net lending	0.0	40.5	57.7
Total	778.3	858.0	1,177.7

* Excluding grants received (YR '000 million): 8.3 in 2003; 18.7 in 2004; 0.0 in 2005 (preliminary).
† Preliminary.

INTERNATIONAL RESERVES
(US $ million at 31 December)

	2005	2006	2007
Gold (national valuation)	27.2	32.9	44.2
IMF special drawing rights	18.8	7.1	—
Foreign exchange	6,096.6	7,504.4	7,715.4
Total	6,142.6	7,544.7	7,759.6

Source: IMF, *International Financial Statistics*.

MONEY SUPPLY
(YR million at 31 December)

	2005	2006	2007
Currency outside banks	330,620	412,520	425,840
Demand deposits at commercial banks	69,368	99,625	130,417
Total money (incl. others)	442,464	558,461	613,748

Source: IMF, *International Financial Statistics*.

COST OF LIVING
(Consumer Price Index; base: 2000 = 100)

	2004	2005	2006
Food	168.3	199.9	269.5
Rent	132.3	139.7	146.8
Clothing	118.8	121.9	120.0
All items (incl. others)	156.6	174.5	211.6

Source: ILO.

NATIONAL ACCOUNTS
(YR million at current prices)

National Income and Product

	2004	2005*	2006†
Domestic factor incomes	2,425,066	3,158,788	3,662,281
Consumption of fixed capital	195,752	210,683	272,055
Gross domestic product (GDP) at factor cost	2,620,818	3,369,471	3,934,336
Indirect taxes, *less* subsidies	−57,328	−160,970	−174,298
GDP in purchasers' values	2,563,490	3,208,501	3,760,038
Factor income from abroad (net)	−235,531	−295,678	−229,847
Gross national product (GNP)	2,327,959	2,912,823	3,530,191
Less Consumption of fixed capital	195,752	210,683	272,055
National income in purchasers' values	2,132,207	2,702,140	3,258,136
Other transfers from abroad (net)	253,400	255,689	253,862
National disposable income	2,385,607	2,957,829	3,511,998

Expenditure on the Gross Domestic Product

	2004	2005*	2006†
Government final consumption expenditure	321,897	392,941	517,272
Private final consumption expenditure	1,698,053	2,058,537	2,289,922
Changes in stocks	−18,560	−15,675	−29,955
Gross fixed capital formation	538,428	610,198	645,991
Total domestic expenditure	2,539,818	3,046,001	3,423,230
Exports of goods and services	932,382	1,311,034	1,546,773
Less Imports of goods and services	908,710	1,148,534	1,209,965
GDP in purchasers' values	2,563,490	3,208,501	3,760,038
GDP at constant 1990 prices	298,761	315,466	325,469

Gross Domestic Product by Economic Activity

	2004	2005*	2006†
Agriculture, hunting, forestry and fishing‡	300,706	338,422	381,528
Mining and quarrying	796,401	1,145,553	1,322,025
Manufacturing	188,863	228,804	291,711
Electricity, gas and water	21,219	22,968	27,480
Construction	151,293	174,501	210,504
Trade, restaurants and hotels	357,910	411,077	491,409
Transport, storage and communications	291,301	351,858	407,512
Finance, insurance, real estate and business services	183,114	214,533	234,526
Government services	246,875	307,032	391,444
Other community, social and personal services	34,489	42,382	54,575
Private non-profit services and services to households	1,964	2,136	2,458
Sub-total	2,574,135	3,239,266	3,815,172
Import duties	51,897	51,945	36,129
Less Imputed bank service charge	62,542	82,710	91,263
GDP in purchasers' values	2,563,490	3,208,501	3,760,038

* Provisional.
† Preliminary estimates.
‡ Including production of qat.

YEMEN

Statistical Survey

BALANCE OF PAYMENTS
(US $ million)

	2004	2005	2006
Exports of goods f.o.b.	4,675.7	6,413.2	7,316.4
Imports of goods f.o.b.	−3,858.6	−4,712.9	−5,926.1
Trade balance	817.1	1,700.3	1,390.3
Exports of services	369.7	372.1	548.8
Imports of services	−1,059.4	−1,241.4	−1,855.0
Balance on goods and services	127.3	830.9	84.0
Other income received	103.6	178.2	316.2
Other income paid	−1,450.1	−1,790.7	−1,550.5
Balance on goods, services and income	−1,219.1	−781.5	−1,150.3
Current transfers received	1,493.1	1,458.4	1,401.7
Current transfers paid	−49.4	−52.8	−45.7
Current balance	224.6	624.1	205.7
Capital account (net)	163.3	202.3	94.4
Direct investment from abroad	143.6	−302.1	1,121.0
Portfolio investment assets	−6.4	−14.2	−34.0
Other investment assets	−25.4	−81.6	−387.1
Other investment liabilities	−180.4	−208.0	−68.2
Net errors and omissions	53.3	213.3	179.8
Overall balance	372.5	433.8	1,111.7

Source: IMF, *International Financial Statistics*.

External Trade

PRINCIPAL COMMODITIES
(distribution by SITC, US $ million)

Imports c.i.f.	2002	2003	2004
Food and live animals	722.2	866.4	915.3
Dairy products and birds' eggs	94.6	113.7	104.6
Cereals and cereal preparations	318.8	335.1	417.4
Sugar, sugar preparations and honey	112.0	165.2	98.5
Beverages and tobacco	42.1	59.8	56.0
Mineral fuels, lubricants, etc.	427.7	546.0	481.6
Petroleum, petroleum products, etc.	427.7	545.8	481.3
Animal and vegetable oils and fats	52.4	69.6	73.3
Vegetable oils and fats	49.5	60.5	69.6
Chemicals and related products	204.8	236.7	303.6
Medical and pharmaceutical	104.1	120.1	106.4
Basic manufactures	420.9	570.8	556.9
Iron and steel	110.2	152.2	192.7
Machinery and transport equipment	707.5	920.1	1,015.9
Machinery specialized in particular industries	157.0	189.1	192.5
Road vehicles	167.2	174.9	209.2
Miscellaneous manufactured articles	161.7	213.0	272.7
Total (incl. others)	2,920.7	3,674.7	3,734.0

Exports f.o.b.	2002	2003	2004
Food and live animals	156.1	161.9	163.2
Fish, crustacea and molluscs, and preparations thereof	91.0	88.9	89.4
Mineral fuels, lubricants, etc.	2,870.4	3,372.0	3,726.0
Petroleum, petroleum products, etc.	2,867.4	3,335.9	3,705.1
Total (incl. others)	3,077.8	3,733.4	4,050.8

Source: UN, *International Trade Statistics Yearbook*.

PRINCIPAL TRADING PARTNERS
(YR million)

Imports c.i.f.	2004	2005	2006
Argentina	8,221.4	15,978.0	10,929.1
Australia	12,067.6	6,415.0	4,332.2
Bahrain	302.2	1,298.7	462.3
Brazil	23,280.8	28,729.7	27,603.8
China, People's Republic	47,179.0	56,516.8	76,455.7
Djibouti	2,757.3	1,966.4	3,153.3
Egypt	16,399.9	21,257.8	18,377.5
France (incl. Monaco)	23,991.5	20,248.5	21,446.8
Germany	26,574.9	26,313.9	26,866.7
India	29,781.5	26,101.3	33,234.7
Indonesia	6,853.8	6,212.9	7,376.3
Italy	13,943.6	13,064.5	11,038.5
Japan	28,531.6	18,413.9	43,381.1
Korea, Republic	7,234.0	11,429.1	12,073.6
Kuwait	45,585.6	6,115.4	69,863.0
Malaysia	14,514.7	18,592.8	20,380.0
Netherlands	12,440.5	9,224.1	7,228.3
Oman	11,188.7	12,485.9	14,219.2
Saudi Arabia	64,630.7	81,841.2	101,192.4
Singapore	9,809.1	8,844.3	9,540.5
Switzerland	28,513.9	78,618.8	94,972.9
Thailand	11,379.7	7,216.4	8,886.8
Turkey	18,162.1	28,486.7	25,484.2
United Arab Emirates	122,814.4	173,561.3	229,768.4
United Kingdom	33,823.1	25,642.8	26,066.8
USA	34,373.8	41,398.8	25,470.7
Total (incl. others)	736,533.1	931,599.2	1,043,119.4

Exports f.o.b.	2004	2005	2006
China, People's Republic	215,926.3	378,022.7	296,618.5
India	99,750.3	173,885.6	315,245.9
Italy	1,105.9	1,071.0	1,732.6
Korea, Republic	24,115.6	67,525.2	33,867.8
Kuwait	10,904.2	22,390.8	31,557.5
Malaysia	55,381.7	42,596.8	2,406.5
Saudi Arabia	16,110.4	18,766.3	25,775.5
Singapore	35,594.8	76,532.2	8,459.6
South Africa	20,957.0	31.2	8,399.3
Switzerland	43,436.9	56,461.7	46,910.9
Thailand	218,179.3	127,592.8	190,130.0
United Arab Emirates	5,963.2	2,967.2	69,512.3
USA	8,389.9	34,154.1	74,856.4
Total (incl. others)	731,781.1	1,040,657.9	1,316,197.7

Transport

ROAD TRAFFIC
(vehicles in use at 31 December)

	1994	1995	1996
Passenger cars	227,854	229,084	240,567
Buses and coaches	2,712	2,835	3,437
Goods vehicles	279,154	279,780	291,149

2004: Private cars 285,335; Taxi cars 36,371; Buses 22,214; Lorries 127,213; Motorcycles 64,845.

Source: IRF, *World Road Statistics*.

SHIPPING

Merchant Fleet
(registered at 31 December)

	2004	2005	2006
Number of vessels	49	48	47
Total displacement ('000 grt)	33.0	33.6	29.2

Source: Lloyd's Register-Fairplay, *World Fleet Statistics*.

YEMEN

International Sea-borne Freight Traffic
('000 metric tons unless otherwise indicated, excluding dhows)

	2004	2005	2006
Vessels called (number)	2,828	3,089	3,177
Dry cargo:*			
goods loaded	308	309	400
goods unloaded	6,800	7,917	7,473
Oil products:			
goods loaded	4,560	4,615	4,610
goods unloaded	8,537	9,158	9,516

* Excluding livestock and vehicles.

CIVIL AVIATION
(traffic on scheduled services)

	2001	2002	2003
Kilometres flown (million)	18	16	18
Passengers carried ('000)	841	869	844
Passenger-km (million)	1,580	1,598	1,956
Total ton-km (million)	174	180	225

Source: UN, *Statistical Yearbook*.

Tourism

TOURISM ARRIVALS

	2004	2005	2006
Africa	7,798	10,449	10,204
Sudan	3,055	2,179	2,821
Americas	17,099	18,253	18,771
Europe	28,608	26,456	32,788
France	3,101	3,078	5,465
Germany	2,757	2,975	2,705
Italy	2,332	3,054	2,436
United Kingdom	7,061	4,348	9,230
Middle East	178,734	240,703	281,206
Egypt	8,464	6,947	10,915
Iraq	3,945	1,687	3,464
Jordan	5,129	3,483	6,060
Saudi Arabia	123,799	162,160	178,670
Syria	7,307	7,622	11,044
Total (incl. others)	273,732	335,870	382,332

Tourism receipts (US $ million, incl. passenger transport): 139 in 2003; 139 in 2004; 181 in 2005.

Source: partly World Tourism Organization.

Communications Media

	2003	2004	2005
Telephones ('000 main lines in use)	684.9	798.1	968.4
Mobile cellular telephones ('000 subscribers)	700.0	1,072.0	2,000.0
Personal computers ('000 in use)	200	300	300
Internet users ('000)	120.0	180.0	220.5

2006: Internet users ('000) 270.0.

Source: International Telecommunication Union.

Radio receivers ('000 in use): 1,050 in 1997.

Television receivers ('000 in use): 5,200 in 2000.

Facsimile machines ('000 in use, estimate): 2,784 in 1995.

Daily newspapers: 6 titles (total circulation 83,300 copies) in 2004.

Sources: UN, *Statistical Yearbook*; UNESCO, *Statistical Yearbook*; UNESCO Institute for Statistics.

Education

(2004/05)

	Schools	Teachers	Males	Females	Total
Pre-primary	63	615	4,911	4,272	9,183
Primary	11,045	99,839	2,450,272	1,622,022	4,072,294
Secondary	307	6,217	409,896	185,218	595,114
Higher	16	6,164	138,039	50,085	188,124

Adult literacy rate (UNESCO estimates): 54.1% (males 73.1%; females 34.7%) in 2004 (Source: UNESCO Institute for Statistics).

Directory

The Constitution

A draft Constitution for the united Republic of Yemen, based on that endorsed by the Yemen Arab Republic (YAR) and the People's Democratic Republic of Yemen (PDRY) in December 1981, was published in December 1989; it was approved by a popular referendum on 15–16 May 1991.

On 29 September 1994 52 articles were amended, 29 added and one cancelled, leaving a total of 159 articles in the Constitution. Further amendments to the Constitution were adopted by the House of Representatives in late November 2000 and approved in a national referendum on 20 February 2001.

The Constitution defines the Yemeni Republic as an independent and sovereign Arab and Islamic country. The document states that the Republic 'is an indivisible whole, and it is impermissible to concede any part of it. The Yemeni people are part of the Arab and Islamic nation'. The Islamic *Shari'a* is identified as the basis of all laws.

The revised Constitution provides for the election, by direct universal suffrage, of the President of the Republic; the President is elected for a seven-year term (increased from five years by the amendments approved in 2001). The President is empowered to appoint a Vice-President. The President of the Republic is, ex officio, Supreme Commander of the Armed Forces. The Constitution as amended in 2001 requires presidential candidates to obtain the endorsement of 5% of a combined vote of the appointed Consultative Council and the elected House of Representatives (in place of 10% of the latter chamber alone).

Legislative authority is vested in the 301-member House of Representatives, which is elected, by universal suffrage, for a six-year term (increased from four years by amendment in 2001). The role of the House of Representatives is defined as to 'monitor' the executive. The President is empowered to dissolve the legislature and call new elections within a period of 60 days.

The upper house of the legislature, the Consultative Council, has 111 members (increased from 59 by amendment in 2001), nominated by the President.

The President of the Republic appoints the Prime Minister and other members of the Government on the advice of the Prime Minister.

The Constitution delineates the separation of the powers of the organs of State, and guarantees the independence of the judiciary. The existence of a multi-party political system is confirmed. Serving members of the police and armed forces are banned from political activity.

The Government

HEAD OF STATE

President: Field Marshal Ali Abdullah Saleh (took office 24 May 1990; re-elected 1 October 1994, 23 September 1999 and 20 September 2006).

Vice-President: Maj.-Gen. Abd ar-Rabbuh Mansur al-Hadi.

COUNCIL OF MINISTERS
(May 2008)

Prime Minister: Ali Muhammad Mujawar.
Deputy Prime Minister for Defence and Security Affairs: Dr Rashid Muhammad al-Alimi.
Deputy Prime Minister for Economic Affairs and Minister of Planning and International Co-operation: Abd al-Karim Ismail al-Arhabi.
Deputy Prime Minister for Local Authority Affairs: Sadiq Ahmin Abu Ras.
Minister of the Interior: Maj.-Gen. Mutahar Rashid al-Masri.
Minister of Finance: Noman Taher as-Souhaibi.
Minister of Oil and Minerals: Amir Salim al-Aidarous.
Minister of Social Affairs and Labour: Amat ar-Razzak Ali Hamad.
Minister of Local Government: Abd al-Qader Ali Hilal.
Minister of Human Rights: Huda Abd al-Latif al-Ban.
Minister of Transport: Khalid Ibrahim al-Wazir.
Minister of Information: Hassan Ahmad al-Lawzi.
Minister of Foreign Affairs: Abu Bakr al-Kurbi.
Minister of Expatriate Affairs: Ahmad Musaead Hussein.
Minister of Electricity: Awadh Sa'ad as-Suqatri.
Minister of Legal Affairs: Rashad Ahmad ar-Rassas.
Minister of Religious Endowments and Guidance: Hamoud Abd al-Hamid al-Hitar.
Minister of Culture: Muhammad Abu Bakr al-Maflahi.
Minister of Agriculture and Irrigation: Mansour Ahmad al-Houshabi.
Minister of Industry and Commerce: Yahya al-Mutawakel.
Minister of Public Health and Population: Abd al-Karim Ras'e.
Minister of Education: Abd as-Salam al-Jawfi.
Minister of Fisheries: Muhammad Saleh Shamlan.
Minister of Justice: Ghazi Shayef al-Aghbari.
Minister of Higher Education and Scientific Research: Saleh Ali Basorra.
Minister of Technical Education and Vocational Training: Ibrahim Omar Hajri.
Minister of Tourism: Nabil Hassan al-Faqih.
Minister of the Civil Service and Social Security: Dr Yahya ash-Shuaibi.
Minister of Communications and Information Technology: Kamal Hussein al-Jabri.
Minister of Defence: Muhammad Nasser Ahmad Ali.
Minister of Public Works and Urban Development: Omar Abdullah al-Kurshumi.
Minister of Water and the Environment: Abd ar-Rahman al-Iryani.
Minister of Youth and Sports: Hamoud Muhammad Ubad.
Minister of State for Parliament and Shoura Council Affairs: Khalid ash-Sharif.
Minister of State and Mayor of San'a: Yahya Muhammad ash-Shaibi.
Minister of State: Abd ar-Rahman Tarmoum.

MINISTRIES

Ministry of Agriculture and Irrigation: POB 2805, San'a; tel. (1) 282966; fax (1) 289509.
Ministry of Communications and Information Technology: POB 17045, San'a; tel. (1) 331469; fax (1) 331473; e-mail mtit@mtit.gov.ye; internet www.mtit.gov.ye.
Ministry of Culture and Tourism: POB 129, San'a; tel. (1) 235114; fax (1) 235113.
Ministry of Defence: POB 4131, San'a; tel. (1) 252640; fax (1) 252375.
Ministry of Education: San'a; tel. (1) 274548; fax (1) 274555; e-mail moed@yemen.net.ye.
Ministry of Electricity: POB 11422, San'a; tel. (1) 326191; fax (1) 326214; e-mail yempec@y.net.ye.
Ministry of Expatriate Affairs: San'a; tel. (1) 402643; fax (1) 400710.
Ministry of Finance: POB 190, San'a; tel. (1) 260370; fax (1) 263040.
Ministry of Fisheries: San'a; tel. (1) 268583; fax (1) 263182.
Ministry of Foreign Affairs: POB 1994, San'a; tel. (1) 276612; fax (1) 286618; e-mail mofa1@mofa.gov.ye; internet www.mofa.gov.ye.
Ministry of Industry and Commerce: POB 22210, San'a; tel. (1) 252345; fax (1) 251557; e-mail most@y.net.ye.
Ministry of Information: POB 3040, San'a; tel. (1) 274011; fax (1) 282004; e-mail yemen-info@y.net.ye; internet www.infoyemen.net.
Ministry of the Interior: San'a; tel. (1) 274147; fax (1) 332511; internet www.moi.gov.ye.
Ministry of Legal Affairs: POB 2192, San'a; tel. (1) 402743; fax (1) 402695.
Ministry of Local Government: POB 2198, San'a; tel. (1) 252532; fax (1) 251513.
Ministry of Oil and Minerals: POB 81, San'a; tel. (1) 202306; fax (1) 202314; e-mail mom@y.net.ye; internet www.mom.gov.ye.
Ministry of Planning and International Co-operation: POB 175, San'a; tel. (1) 250101; fax (1) 251665; internet www.mpic-yemen.org.
Ministry of Public Health and Population: POB 274160, San'a; tel. (1) 252193; fax (1) 252247; internet www.mophp-ye.org.
Ministry of Public Works and Urban Development: San'a; tel. (1) 262602; fax (1) 262609; e-mail info@mpwud.gov.ye; internet www.mpwud.gov.ye.
Ministry of Social Affairs and Labour: San'a; tel. (1) 274921; fax (1) 262806.
Ministry of Transportation: POB 2781, San'a; tel. (1) 260903; fax (1) 260901.
Ministry of Water and the Environment: San'a; tel. (1) 418290; fax (1) 418282.

President and Legislature

PRESIDENT

Presidential Election, 20 September 2006

Candidates	Valid votes cast	% of valid votes
Field Marshal Ali Abdullah Saleh	4,149,673	77.17
Faisal bin Shamlan	1,173,025	21.81
Fathi al-Azab	24,524	0.46
Yassin Abdo Said	21,642	0.40
Ahmad al-Majidi	8,324	0.15
Total	**5,377,188***	**100.00**

* Excluding 648,580 invalid votes.

HOUSE OF REPRESENTATIVES

Speaker: Yahya Ali ar-Ra'ei.

General Election, 27 April 2003

Party	Seats*
General People's Congress (GPC)	228
Yemeni Congregation for Reform (al-Islah)	47
Independents	14
Yemeni Socialist Party (YSP)	7
Nasserite Unionist Popular Organization	3
Arab Socialist Baath Party	2
Total	**301**

* Includes the results of three by-elections held in July 2003.

Election Commission

Supreme Commission for Elections and Referendums (SCER): San'a; tel. (1) 202325; e-mail scer@y.net.ye; internet www.scer.org.ye; f. 2001; Chair. Khaled A. ash-Sharif.

Political Organizations

In the former PDRY the Yemen Socialist Party (YSP) was the only legal political party until December 1989, when the formation of opposition parties was legalized. There were no political parties in the former YAR. The two leading parties that emerged in the unified Yemen were the General People's Congress and the YSP. During 1990 an estimated 30–40 further political parties were reported to have been formed, and in 1991 a law was passed regulating the formation of political parties. Following the civil war from May to July 1994, President Saleh excluded the YSP from the new Government formed in October. There were 22 registered political parties in April 2003.

Democratic Coalition of Opposition: San'a; f. 1995 as a coalition of 13 political parties and organizations, incl. a splinter faction of the YSP and the LSY.

General People's Congress (GPC): San'a; e-mail gpc@y.net.ye; internet www.gpc.org.ye; a broad grouping of supporters of President Saleh; Chair. Field Marshal ALI ABDULLAH SALEH; Vice-Chair. Maj.-Gen. ABD AR-RABBUH MANSUR HADI; Sec.-Gen. Dr ABD AL-QADIR BAJAMMAL.

Al-Haq: San'a; conservative Islamic party; Sec.-Gen. Sheikh AHMAD ASH-SHAMI.

League of the Sons of Yemen (LSY): Aden; f. 1951; represents interests of southern tribes; Leader ABD AR-RAHMAN AL-JIFRI; Sec.-Gen. MOHSEN FARID.

Nasserite Unionist Popular Organization: Aden; f. 1989 as a legal party; Sec.-Gen. SULTAN AL-ATWANI.

National Opposition Co-ordination Council: San'a; f. 2001 as a coalition of opposition parties, incl. the YSP.

Yemen Socialist Party (YSP): San'a; f. 1978 to succeed the United Political Organization—National Front (UPO—NF); fmrly Marxist-Leninist 'vanguard' party based on 'scientific socialism'; has Political Bureau and Cen. Cttee; Leader Dr YASIN SAID NUMAN.

Yemeni Congregation for Reform (al-Islah): POB 23090, San'a; tel. (1) 213281; fax (1) 213311; f. 1990 by mems of the legislature, other political figures and tribal leaders; seeks constitutional reform based on Islamic law; Chair. Sheikh MUHAMMAD ALI AL-YADOUMI (acting).

Yemeni Unionist Rally Party: Aden; f. 1990 by intellectuals and politicians from the fmr YAR and PDRY to safeguard human rights; Leader OMAR AL-JAWI.

Other parties in Yemen include the **Arab Socialist Baath Party**; the **Federation of Popular Forces**; the **Liberation Front Party**; the **Nasserite Democratic Party**; the **National Democratic Front**; the **National Social Party**; the **Popular Nasserite Reformation Party**; the **Social Green Party**; the **Yemen League** and the **Yemeni Unionist Congregation Party**.

Diplomatic Representation

EMBASSIES IN YEMEN

Algeria: POB 509, 67 Amman St, San'a; tel. (1) 209689; fax (1) 209688; Ambassador BEN SAAD BIN AL-ABED.

Bulgaria: POB 1518, Asr, St 4, Residence 5, San'a; tel. (1) 208469; fax (1) 207924; e-mail bgemb_yem@y.net.ye; Chargé d'affaires a.i. ALEXI ALAXIEV.

China, People's Republic: POB 482, az-Zubairy St, San'a; tel. (1) 275337; fax (1) 275341; e-mail chinaem@y.net.ye; internet ye.chineseembassy.org; Ambassador LUO XIAOGUANG.

Cuba: POB 15256, St 6B, Block 9, House 3, Safia Zone, nr Amman St, San'a; tel. (1) 442321; fax (1) 442322; e-mail embacubayemen@y.net.ye; Ambassador BIENVENIDO GARCÍA NEGRÍN.

Czech Republic: POB 2501, Safiya Janoobia, St 16, House 6, San'a; tel. (1) 440946; fax (1) 440762; e-mail sanaa@embassy.mzv.cz; internet www.mzv.cz/sanaa; Ambassador JOZEF VRABEC.

Djibouti: POB 3322, 6 Amman St, San'a; tel. (1) 445236; fax (1) 445237; e-mail youssouf@y.net.ye; Ambassador YOUSSOUF OMAR DOUALEH.

Egypt: POB 1134, Gamal Abd an-Nasser St, San'a; tel. (1) 275948; fax (1) 274196; Ambassador MUHAMMAD MORSY MUHAMMAD AWAD.

Eritrea: POB 11040, Western Safia Bldg, San'a; tel. (1) 209422; fax (1) 214088; Ambassador MOUSA YASSIN SHEIKH.

Ethiopia: POB 234, Al-Hamadani St, San'a; tel. (1) 208833; fax (1) 213780; e-mail ethoembs@y.net.ye; Ambassador TOFIKI ABDULAHI.

France: POB 1286, cnr Sts 2 and 21, San'a; tel. (1) 268888; fax (1) 269160; e-mail ambaf@y.net.ye; internet www.ambafrance-ye.org; Ambassador GILLES GAUTHIER.

Germany: POB 2562, Hadda, San'a; tel. (1) 413174; fax (1) 413179; e-mail info@sanaa.diplo.de; internet www.sanaa.diplo.de; Ambassador MICHAEL KLOR-BERCHTOLD.

India: POB 1154, Bldg 12, Djibouti St, San'a; tel. (1) 441251; fax (1) 441257; e-mail indiaemb@y.net.ye; internet www.eoisanaa.com.ye; Ambassador R. M. AGGARWAL.

Indonesia: POB 19873, Bldg 16, Beirut St, Haddah, San'a; tel. (1) 414633; fax (1) 412956; e-mail indosan@y.net.ye; Ambassador KEMAS FACHRUDDIN.

Iran: POB 1437, Haddah St, San'a; tel. (1) 413552; fax (1) 414139; e-mail iriranemb@y.net.ye; internet www.iranyemen.com.ye; Ambassador HOSSEIN KAMALIAN.

Iraq: POB 498, South Airport Rd, San'a; tel. (1) 440184; fax (1) 440187; e-mail snaemb@iraqmofamail.net; Ambassador TALAL JAMEEL SALEH AL-OBAYDI.

Italy: POB 1152, No. 5 Bldg, St No. 29, San'a; tel. (1) 269164; fax (1) 266137; e-mail ambasciata.sanaa@esteri.it; internet www.ambsanaa.esteri.it; Ambassador MARIO BOFFO.

Japan: POB 817, Haddah Area, San'a; tel. (1) 423700; fax (1) 417850; internet www.ye.emb-japan.go.jp; Ambassador MASAKAZU TOSHIKAGE.

Jordan: POB 2152, Hadat Damascus St, San'a; tel. (1) 413276; fax (1) 414516; e-mail sanaa@fm.gov.jo; Ambassador AHMAD ALI JARADAT.

Korea, Democratic People's Republic: POB 1209, al-Hasaba, Mazda Rd, San'a; tel. (1) 232340; Ambassador CHANG MYONG SON.

Kuwait: POB 3746, South Ring Rd, San'a; tel. (1) 268876; fax (1) 268875; Ambassador ABD AR-RAHMAN SAYED AL-OTAEBI.

Lebanon: POB 38, St 3, San'a; tel. (1) 203959; fax (1) 201120; e-mail lebem@y.net.ye; Ambassador HASSAN MUSILMANI.

Libya: POB 1506, Ring Rd, St No. 8, House No. 145, San'a; Secretary of Libyan Brotherhood Office MUSTAFA HWAIDI.

Malaysia: POB 16157, San'a; tel. (1) 415605; fax (1) 416181; e-mail mwsanaa@y.net.ye; Ambassador Dato' ABD-ASSAMD BIN OTHMAN.

Mauritania: POB 19383, No. 6, Algeria St, San'a; tel. (1) 264188; fax (1) 215926; Ambassador AHMED OULD SIDY.

Morocco: Faj Attan, Hay Assormi, ave Beyrouth, San'a; tel. (1) 426628; fax (1) 426627; e-mail sifama_yemen@hotmail.com; Ambassador MUHAMMAD TOUHAMI.

Netherlands: POB 463, off 14th October St, San'a; tel. (1) 421800; fax 421035; e-mail holland@y.net.ye; internet www.holland.com.ye; Ambassador R. H. BUIKEMA.

Oman: POB 6163, 14th October St, al-Gala Quarter, Bldg 2, Khormaskar, San'a; tel. (1) 208874; fax (1) 204586; e-mail omanembassy@y.net.ye; Ambassador ABDULLAH BIN HAMAD AL-BADI.

Pakistan: POB 2848, Ring Rd, off Haddah St, San'a; tel. (1) 248814; fax (1) 248866; e-mail pakembassy@yemen.net.ye; Ambassador NAWAB AMIR ABDUL REHMAN NOUSHERWANI.

Poland: POB 16168, Haddah St, San'a; tel. (1) 413523; fax (1) 413647; e-mail polemb@y.net.ye; internet www.sana.polemb.net; Chargé d'affaires a.i. HENRYK PIASZCZYK.

Qatar: POB 19717, San'a; tel. (1) 304640; fax (1) 304645; e-mail sanaa@mofa.gov.qa; Ambassador JASIM ABU AL-INAYN.

Russia: POB 1087, 26 September St, San'a; tel. (1) 278719; fax (1) 283142; e-mail remb@y.net.ye; Ambassador ALEXANDER ZASYPKIN.

Saudi Arabia: POB 1184, Zuhara House, Hadda Rd, San'a; tel. (1) 240429; Ambassador ALI BIN MUHAMMAD AL-HAMDAN.

Somalia: San'a; tel. (1) 208864; Ambassador HASSAN MOHAMED SIAD BARRE.

Sudan: POB 2561, 82 Abou al-Hassan al-Hamadani St, San'a; tel. (1) 265231; fax (1) 265234; Ambassador OMAR AS-SAID TAHA.

Syria: POB 494, Hadda Rd, Damascus St 1, San'a; tel. (1) 414891; Ambassador ABD AL-GHAFOUR SABOUNI.

Tunisia: POB 2561, Diplomatic area, St No. 22, San'a; tel. (1) 240458; Ambassador (vacant).

Turkey: POB 18371, as-Safiya, San'a; tel. and fax (1) 241395; Ambassador TÜREL ÖZKARO.

United Arab Emirates: POB 2250, Ring Rd, San'a; tel. (1) 248777; Ambassador ALI SAIF SULTAN AL-AWANI.

United Kingdom: POB 1287, 938 Thaher Himiyar St, East Ring Rd, San'a; tel. (1) 302450; fax (1) 302454; e-mail britishembassysanaa@fco.gov.uk; internet www.britishembassy.gov.uk/yemen; Ambassador TIM TORLOT.

USA: POB 22347, Sa'awan St, Sheraton Hotel District, San'a; tel. (1) 7552000; fax (1) 303182; e-mail consularsanaa@state.gov; internet yemen.usembassy.gov; Ambassador STEPHEN A. SECHE.

Judicial System

Yemen's Constitution guarantees the independence of the judiciary and identifies Islamic law (*Shari'a*) as the basis of all laws.

Yemen is divided into 20 governorates in addition to the Capital Secretariat of San'a (a municipality), each of which is further divided into districts. Each district has a Court of First Instance in which all cases are heard by a single magistrate. Appeals against decisions of the Courts of First Instance are referred to a Court of Appeal. Each governorate has a Court of Appeal with four divisions: Civil, Criminal, Matrimonial and Commercial, each of which consists of three judges.

The Supreme Court of the Republic, which sits in San'a, rules on matters concerning the Constitution, appeals against decisions of the Courts of Appeal and cases brought against members of the Legislature. The Supreme Court has eight divisions, each of which consists of five judges.

The Supreme Judicial Council supervises the proper function of the courts and its Chairman is the President of the Republic.

Religion

ISLAM

The majority of the population are Muslims. Most are Sunni Muslims of the Shafi'a sect, except in the north-west of the country, where Zaidism (a moderate sect of the Shi'a order) is the dominant persuasion.

CHRISTIANITY

The Roman Catholic Church

Apostolic Vicariate of Arabia: POB 54, Abu Dhabi, United Arab Emirates; tel. (2) 4461895; fax (2) 4465177; e-mail vicapar@emirates.net.ae; f. 1889; responsible for a territory comprising most of the Arabian peninsula (including Saudi Arabia, the UAE, Oman, Qatar, Bahrain and Yemen), containing an estimated 1,500,100 Roman Catholics (31 December 2005); Vicar Apostolic PAUL FRIDOLIN HINDER (Titular Bishop of Macon, Georgia, resident in the UAE); Vicar Delegate for Yemen Rev. GEORGE PUDUSSERY.

The Anglican Communion

Within the Episcopal Church in Jerusalem and the Middle East, Yemen forms part of the diocese of Cyprus and the Gulf. The Anglican congregations in San'a and Aden are entirely expatriate; the Bishop in Cyprus and the Gulf is resident in Cyprus, while the Archdeacon in the Gulf is resident in Bahrain.

HINDUISM

There is a small Hindu community.

The Press

Legislation embodying the freedom of the press in the unified Republic of Yemen was enacted in May 1990. The lists below include publications which appeared in the YAR and the PDRY prior to their unification in May 1990.

DAILIES

Al-Jumhuriya: Taiz Information Office, Taiz; tel. (4) 216748; Arabic; circ. 100,000.

Ar-Rabi' 'Ashar Min Uktubar (14 October): POB 4227, Crater, Aden; f. 1968; not publ. on Sat; Arabic; Editorial Dir FAROUQ MUSTAFA RIFAT; Chief Editor MUHAMMAD HUSSAIN MUHAMMAD; circ. 20,000.

Ash-Sharara (The Spark): 14 October Corpn for Printing, Publishing, Distribution and Advertising, POB 4227, Crater, Aden; Arabic; circ. 6,000.

Ath-Thawra (The Revolution): POB 2195, San'a; tel. (1) 262626; fax (1) 274139; e-mail contact@althawranews.net; internet www.althawranews.net; Arabic; govt-owned; Editor MUHAMMAD AZ-ZORKAH; circ. 110,000.

WEEKLIES AND OTHERS

Attijarah (Trade): POB 3370, Hodeida; tel. (3) 213784; fax (3) 211528; e-mail hodcci@y.net.ye; monthly; Arabic; commercial.

Al-Ayyam: POB 648, al-Khalij al-Imami, Crater, Aden; tel. (2) 255170; fax (2) 255692; e-mail editor@al-ayyam-yemen.com; internet www.al-ayyam.info; Editor HISHAM BASHRAHEEL.

Al-Bilad (The Country): POB 1438, San'a; weekly; Arabic; centre-right; Editor-in-Chief ABD AL-MALIK AL-FAISHANI.

Dar as-Salam (Peace): POB 1790, San'a; tel. (1) 272946; f. 1948; weekly; Arabic; political, economic and general essays; Editor ABDULLAH MUKBOOL AS-SICGUL.

Al-Fanoon: Ministry of Culture and Tourism, POB 1187, Tawahi 102, Aden; tel. (2) 23831; f. 1980; Arabic; monthly arts review; Editor FAISAL SOFY; circ. 15,500.

Al-Gundi (The Soldier): Ministry of Defence, Madinat ash-Sha'ab; fortnightly; Arabic; circ. 8,500.

Al-Hares: Aden; fortnightly; Arabic; circ. 8,000.

Al-Hikma (Wisdom): POB 4227, Crater, Aden; monthly; Arabic; publ. by the Writers' Union; circ. 5,000.

Al-Ma'in (Spring): Ministry of Information, San'a; monthly; general interest.

Majallat al-Jaish (Army Magazine): POB 2182, San'a; tel. (1) 231181; monthly; publ. by Ministry of Defence.

Al-Maseerah (Journey): Ministry of Information, POB 2182, San'a; tel. (1) 231181; monthly; general interest.

Al-Mithaq (The Charter): San'a; weekly; organ of the General People's Congress.

Ar-Ra'i al-'Am (Public Opinion): POB 293, San'a; tel. (1) 253785; e-mail alraialaam2002@yahoo.com; internet www.alraialaam.com.ye; weekly; independent; Editor KAMAL ALUFI.

Ar-Risalah: POB 55777, 26 September St, Taiz; tel. (4) 214215; fax (4) 221164; e-mail alaws@y.net.ye; f. 1968; weekly; Arabic.

As-Sahwa (Awakening): POB 11126, Hadda Road, San'a; tel. (1) 247892; fax (1) 269218; internet www.alsahwa-yemen.net; weekly; Islamist fundamentalist; Editor MUHAMMAD AL-YADDOUMI.

As-Salam (Peace): POB 181, San'a; tel. (1) 272946; weekly.

San'a: POB 193, San'a; fortnightly; Arabic; left-wing.

Sawt al-'Ummal (The Workers' Voice): POB 4227, Crater, Aden; weekly; Arabic.

Sawt al-Yemen (Voice of Yemen): POB 302, San'a; weekly; Arabic.

Ash-Shura: POB 15114, San'a; tel. (1) 213584; fax (1) 213468; e-mail shoura@y.net.ye; internet www.y.net.ye/shoura; Editor ABD AL-KARIM AL-KHAIWANI; circ. 15,000.

At-Ta'awun (Co-operation): at-Ta'awun Bldg, az-Zubairy St, San'a; weekly; Arabic; supports co-operative societies.

Ath-Thawri (The Revolutionary): POB 4227, Crater, Aden; weekly, on Sat.; Arabic; organ of Cen. Cttee of YSP; Editor Dr KHALED IBRAHIM SALMAN.

26 September: 26 September Publishing, POB 17, San'a; tel. (1) 262626; fax (1) 234129; e-mail webmaster@26september.com; internet www.26sept.info; armed forces weekly; circ. 25,000.

Al-Wahda al-Watani (National Unity): Al-Baath Printing House, POB 193, San'a; tel. (1) 77511; f. 1982; fmrly Al-Omal; monthly; Editor MUHAMMAD SALEM ALI; circ. 40,000.

Al-Yemen: Yemen Printing and Publishing Co, POB 1081, San'a; tel. (1) 72376; f. 1971; weekly; Arabic; centre-right; Editor MUHAMMAD AHMAD AS-SABAGH.

Yemen Observer: POB 19183, 38 Algeria St, San'a; tel. (1) 203393; fax (1) 207239; e-mail info@yobserver.com; internet www.yobserver.com; f. 1996; twice-weekly; English; independent; Editor-in-Chief ZAID AL-ALYA'A.

The Yemen Times: POB 2579, Hadda St, San'a; tel. (1) 268661; fax (1) 268276; e-mail editor@yementimes.com; internet www.yementimes.com; f. 1991; privately owned; Mon. and Thur.; English; Editor-in-Chief NADIA AS-SAQQAF; circ. 30,000.

Yemeni Women: POB 4227, Crater, Aden; monthly; circ. 5,000.

NEWS AGENCY

Yemen News Agency (SABA): Five Story Office Bldg and Printing Plant, al-Jama'ah al-Arabia St, al-Hasaba, San'a; tel. (1) 252944; fax (1) 251586; e-mail info@sabanews.net; internet www.sabanews.net; f. 1990 by merger of Saba News Agency and Aden News Agency following reunification of Yemen; mem. of the Federation of Arab News Agencies and of the Non-Aligned News Agencies; Editor-in-Chief NASR TAHA MUSTAFA.

Publishers

Armed Forces Printing Press: POB 17, San'a; tel. (1) 274240.

14 October Corpn for Printing, Publishing, Distribution and Advertising: POB 4227, Crater, Aden; under control of the Ministry of Information; Chair. and Gen. Man. SALIH AHMAD SALAH.

26 September Publishing: POB 17, San'a; tel. (1) 274240.

Ath-Thawrah Corpn: POB 2195, San'a; fax (1) 251505; Chair. M.R. AZ-ZURKAH.

Yemen Printing and Publishing Co: POB 1081, San'a; Chair. Ahmad Muhammad Hadi.

Broadcasting and Communications

TELECOMMUNICATIONS

Public Telecommunications Corpn: POB 17045, Airport Rd, al-Jiraf, San'a; tel. (1) 250040; Dir-Gen. Muhammad al-Kassous.

BROADCASTING

Yemen Radio and Television Corpn: POB 2182, San'a; tel. (1) 230654; fax (1) 230761; e-mail info@yemenradio.net; internet www.yemenradio.net; state-controlled; Chair. Abdullah az-Zalab; Gen. Man. Ahmad T. Shayany.

Finance

(cap. = capital; res = reserves; dep. = deposits; m. = million; brs = branches; amounts in Yemeni riyals, unless otherwise indicated)

BANKING

Central Bank

Central Bank of Yemen: POB 59, Ali Abd al-Mughni St, San'a; tel. (1) 274314; fax (1) 274360; e-mail cbyh@y.net.ye; internet www.centralbank.gov.ye; f. 1971; merged with Bank of Yemen in 1990; cap. 2,000.0m., res 181,571.48m., dep. 611,209.8m. (Dec. 2005); Gov. Ahmad Abd ar-Rahman as-Samawi; Dep. Gov. Muhammad Awad bin Humam; 22 brs.

Principal Banks

Co-operative and Agricultural Credit Bank: POB 2015, Banks Complex, az-Zubairy St, San'a; tel. (1) 220090; fax (1) 220088; e-mail cacbank@y.net.ye; f. 1976; cap. 293m., total assets 4,930m. (Dec. 2000); Chair. Dr Muhammad H. al-Wadan; Dir-Gen. Yahia as-Sabri; 27 brs.

International Bank of Yemen YSC: POB 4444, 106 az-Zubairy St, San'a; tel. (1) 407000; fax (1) 407020; e-mail info@ibyemen.com; internet www.ibyemen.com; f. 1980; commercial bank; 75% private Yemeni interests; 25% foreign shareholders; cap. 3,400.0m., res 347.7m., dep. 94,209.9m. (Dec. 2006); Chair. Hayel A. Haq Besher; Gen. Man. Ahmad T. N. al-Absi; 11 brs.

Islamic Bank of Yemen for Finance and Investment: POB 18452, Mareb Yemen Insurance Co Bldg, az-Zubairy St, San'a; tel. (1) 206117; fax (1) 206116; internet www.islbank.com; f. 1996; savings, commercial, investment and retail banking; cap. 2,011.2m., res 142.6m., dep. 13,220.1m. (Dec. 2006); Chair. Abd al-Karem al-Aswadi; Gen. Man. Abd al-Malik Thabet.

National Bank of Yemen: POB 5, Arwa Rd, Crater, Aden; tel. (2) 253753; fax (2) 252325; e-mail nby.ho@y.net.ye; internet www.nbyemen.com; f. 1970 as National Bank of South Yemen; reorg. 1971; 100% state-owned; cap. 5,500.0m., res 1,996.0m., dep. 71,765.8m. (Dec. 2006); Chair. and Gen. Man. Abd ar-Rahman Muhammad al-Kuhali; 27 brs.

Shamil Bank of Yemen and Bahrain: POB 19382, Hadah St, San'a; tel. (1) 264702; fax (1) 264703; e-mail shamilbank@y.net.ye; internet www.sbyb.net; f. 2002; cap. and res 2,000.0m., dep. 9,163.8m. (Dec. 2004); Chair. Ahmad Abubaker Omer Bazara; Gen. Man. Muhammad Najib Ahmad Saad.

Tadhamon International Islamic Bank: POB 2411, as-Saeed Commercial Bldg, az-Zubairy St, San'a; e-mail tib@y.net.ye; internet www.tib.com.ye; f. 1995 as Yemen Bank for Investment and Development; became Tadhamon Islamic Bank in 1996; name changed as above in 2002; cap. 9,101.3m., res 6,233.0m., dep. 46,261.5m. (Dec. 2006); Chair. Abd al-Gabbar Hayel Said; Gen. Man. Amer M. Tawqan; 18 brs.

Watani Bank for Trade and Investment: POB 3058, az-Zubairy St, San'a; tel. (1) 206613; fax (1) 205706; e-mail watanibank@y.net.ye; f. 1998; cap. 1,301.0m., res 55.9m., dep. 20,282.9m. (Dec. 2003); Chair. Dr Ahmad Ali al-Hamdani; Gen. Man. and CEO Shabih S. Mehdi Naqvi.

Yemen Bank for Reconstruction and Development (YBRD): POB 541, 26 September St, San'a; tel. (1) 271626; fax (1) 271684; e-mail ybrdho@y.net.ye; internet www.ybrd.com.ye; f. 1962; 51% state; 49% public shareholders; cap. 2,800.0m., res 2,685.0m., dep. 55,206.4m. (Dec. 2005); Chair. Abdullah Salim al-Gifri; Gen. Man. Hussain Fadhle Muhammad; 41 brs.

Yemen Commercial Bank: POB 19845, ar-Rowaishan Bldg, az-Zubairy St, San'a; tel. (1) 277224; fax (1) 277291; e-mail info@ycb.com.ye; internet www.ycb.com.ye; f. 1993; cap. 3,650.2m., res 250.4m.,dep. 34,946.6m. (Dec. 2006); Chair. Sheikh Muhammad bin Yahya ar-Rowaishan; Chief Exec. and Gen. Man. Ayed al-Mashni; 13 brs.

INSURANCE

Aman Insurance Co (YSC): POB 1133, az-Zubairy St, San'a; tel. (1) 202106; fax (1) 209452; e-mail aman-ins@y.net.ye; internet www.y.net.ye/amaninsurance; all classes of insurance; Chair. Muhammad Abdullah as-Sunidar; Man. Dir Akil as-Sakkaf.

Mareb Yemen Insurance Co: POB 2284, az-Zubairy St, San'a; tel. (1) 206111; fax (1) 206118; e-mail maryinsco74@y.net.ye; internet www.marebinsurance.com.ye; f. 1974; all classes of insurance; cap. 150m.; Chair. and CEO Ali Muhammad Hashim; Gen. Man. Ali Abd ar-Rashid.

National Insurance and Re-insurance Co: POB 456, Aden; tel. (2) 51464; e-mail yireico@y.net.ye; f. 1970; Lloyd's Agents; cap. 5m. Yemeni dinars; Gen. Man. Abubakr S. al-Qoti.

Saba Yemen Insurance Co: POB 19214, Ishaq Bldg, az-Zubairy St, San'a; tel. (1) 240908; fax (1) 240943; e-mail info@saba-insurance.com; internet www.saba-insurance.com; f. 1990; all classes of insurance; cap. 400m. (Jan. 2006); Chair. Sheikh Muhammad bin Yahiah ar-Rowaishan; Man. Dir Muhammad Hussein Zawiyah.

Trust Yemen Insurance and Reinsurance Co: POB 18392, San'a; tel. (1) 425007; fax (1) 412570; e-mail trust-yemen@y.net.ye; internet www.trustgroup.net/Main; all classes of insurance; Chair. Ali Dhib; Gen. Man. Hussain Ayyoub.

United Insurance Co: POB 1883, as-Saeed Commercial Bldg, 2nd Floor, az-Zubairy St, San'a; tel. (1) 555555; fax (1) 214012; e-mail uuicyemen@uicyemen.com; internet www.uicyemen.com; f. 1981; general and life insurance; cap. 400m. (2005); Chair. Ahmad Said; Gen. Man. Tarek A. Hayel Said.

Al-Watania Insurance Co (YSC): POB 15497, al-Kasr St, San'a; tel. (1) 272874; fax (1) 272924; e-mail alwatania-ins@y.net.ye; f. 1993; all classes of insurance; cap. 100m. (2005); Exec. Chair. Yousuf Abd al-Wadud.

Yemen General Insurance Co (SYC): POB 2709, YGI Bldg, 25 Algiers St, San'a; tel. (1) 442489; fax (1) 442492; e-mail ygi-san@y.net.ye; internet www.yginsurance.com; f. 1977; all classes of insurance; cap. 500m. (2005); Chair. Abd al-Gabbar Thabet; Gen. Man. Bakir al-Munshi.

Yemen Insurance Co: POB 8437, San'a; tel. (1) 272806; fax (1) 274177; e-mail sanaa@yemenins.com; internet yemenins.com; f. 1990; all classes of insurance; cap. 100m.; Chair. Muhammad Mubarak Adhban; Gen. Man. Khalid Bashir Tahir.

Trade and Industry

GOVERNMENT AGENCIES

General Corpn for Foreign Trade and Grains: POB 710, San'a; tel. (1) 202361; fax (1) 209511; f. 1976; Dir-Gen. Abd ar-Rahman al-Madwahi.

General Corpn for Manufacturing and Marketing of Cement: POB 1920, San'a; tel. (1) 215691; fax (1) 263168; Chair. Amin Abd al-Wahid Ahmad.

General Investment Authority (GIAY): POB 19022, al-Quds St, San'a; tel. (1) 262962; fax (1) 262964; e-mail gias@y.net.ye; internet www.giay.org; f. 1992; Pres. Saleh Muhammad Said al-Attar.

National Co for Foreign Trade: POB 90, Crater, Aden; tel. (2) 42793; fax (2) 42631; f. 1969; incorporates main foreign trading businesses (nationalized in 1970) and arranges their supply to the National Co for Home Trade; Gen. Man. Ahmad Muhammad Saleh (acting).

National Co for Home Trade: POB 90, Crater, Aden; tel. (2) 41483; fax (2) 41226; f. 1969; marketing of general consumer goods, building materials, electrical goods, motor cars and spare parts, agricultural machinery, etc.; Man. Dir Abd ar-Rahman as-Sailani.

National Dockyards Co: POB 1244, Hedjuff, Aden; tel. (2) 244503; fax (2) 241681; f. 1969; Man. Dir Abdullah Ali Muhammad.

National Drug Co (YEDCO): POB 192, Crater, Aden; tel. (2) 04912; fax (2) 21242; f. 1972; import of pharmaceutical products, chemicals, medical supplies, baby foods and scientific instruments; Chair. and Gen. Man. Dr Awadh Salam Issa Bamatraf.

Public Corpn for Building and Housing: POB 7022, al-Mansoura, Aden; tel. (2) 342296; fax (2) 345726; f. 1973; govt contractors and contractors of private housing projects; Dir-Gen. Hussain Muhammad al-Wali.

Public Corpn for Maritime Affairs (PCMA): POB 19396, San'a; tel. (1) 414412; fax (1) 414645; f. 1990; protection of the marine environment; registration of ships; implementation of international maritime conventions; Chair. Said Yafai.

Yemen Co for Industry and Commerce Ltd (YCIC): POB 5423, Taiz; tel. (4) 218058; fax (4) 218054; e-mail ycic@y.net.ye; internet www.ycic.com; f. 1970; Chair. ALI MUHAMMAD SAID.

Yemen Co for Investment and Finance Ltd (YCIF): POB 2789, San'a; tel. (1) 276372; fax (1) 274178; f. 1981; cap. YR 100m.; Chair. and Gen. Man. ABDULLAH MUHAMMAD ISHAQ.

Yemen Drug Co for Industry and Commerce: POB 40, San'a; tel. (1) 370210; fax (1) 370209; Chair. MUHAMMAD AL-KOHLANI; Gen. Man. MUHAMMAD ALI AL-KADIR.

Yemen Economical Corpn: POB 1207, San'a; tel. (1) 262501; fax (1) 262508; e-mail info@yeco.biz; internet www.yeco.biz; f. 1973; Gen. Man. ALI MUHAMMAD AL-KUHLANI.

Yemen Land Transport Corpn: POB 279, Taiz St, San'a; tel. (1) 268307; f. 1961; Chair. YAHYA AHMED AL-KOHLANI; Gen. Man. SALEH ABDULLAH ABD AL-WALI.

Yemen Trading and Construction Co: POB 1092, San'a; tel. (1) 264005; fax (1) 240624; e-mail ytcc@y.net.ye; f. 1979; initial cap. YR 100m.

DEVELOPMENT ORGANIZATIONS

Agricultural Research and Extension Authority: POB 87148, Dhamar; tel. (6) 509413; fax (6) 509414; e-mail muharram@y.net.ye; internet www.area.gov.ye; Chair. Dr ISMAIL A. MUHARRAM.

General Board for Development of Eastern Region: San'a.

General Board for Development of Tihama: POB 49, Lufthansa Bldg, az-Zubairy St, San'a; tel. (1) 219436; fax (1) 219203; e-mail titra@y.net.ye; internet www.tihama-group.com; Chair. AMIN DIRHEM; Dir MUHAMMAD A. DIRHEM.

Social Fund for Development (SFD): POB 15485, Fij Attan, San'a; tel. (1) 449669; fax (1) 449670; e-mail sfd@sfd-yemen.org; internet www.sfd-yemen.org; f. 1997; autonomous devt agency, governed by a bd of dirs representing the Govt, non-governmental orgs and the private sector, chaired by the Prime Minister.

Yemen Free Zone Public Authority: Aden; tel. (2) 241210; fax (2) 221237; supervises creation of a free zone for industrial investment; Chair. ABD AL-QADIR BAJAMMAL.

CHAMBERS OF COMMERCE

Chamber of Commerce and Industry—Aden: POB 473, Crater 101, Aden; tel. (2) 251104; fax (2) 255446; e-mail info@adenchamber.org; internet www.adenchamber.org; f. 1886; 7,708 mems (July 2006); Chair. MUHAMMAD OMER BAMASHMUS; Dir-Gen. G. AHMAD HADI SALEM.

Federation of Chambers of Commerce: POB 16992, San'a; tel. (1) 232445; fax (1) 221765; e-mail fucci@y.net.ye; internet www.fycci.org.ye; Chair. MUHAMMAD ABDO SAID AN'AM; Dir-Gen. MUHAMMAD AL-MAITAMI.

Hodeida Chamber of Commerce: POB 3370, 20 az-Zubairy St, Hodeida; tel. (3) 217401; fax (3) 211528; e-mail hodcci@y.net.ye; f. 1960; 6,500 mems; cap. YR 10m.; Dir NABIL AL-WAGEEH.

Ibb Chamber of Commerce and Industry: POB 70004, Ibb; tel. (4) 404868; fax (4) 403893.

Saadah Chamber of Commerce and Industry: POB 2566, Saadah; tel. (51) 230244.

San'a Chamber of Commerce and Industry: Airport Rd, al-Hasabah St, POB 195, San'a; tel. (1) 232361; fax (1) 232412; e-mail sanaacomyemen@y.net.ye; internet www.scci.com.ye; f. 1963; over 15,000 mems; Pres. Al-Haj HUSSAIN AL-WATARI; Gen. Man. ABDULLAH H. AR-RUBAIDI.

Taiz Chamber of Commerce and Industry: POB 5029, Chamber St, Taiz; tel. (4) 210580; fax (4) 212335; e-mail info@taizchamber.com; internet www.taizchamber.com; f. 1962; 5,600 mems; Chair. AHMED HAYEL SAID; Dir MOFID A. SAIF.

Thamar Chamber of Commerce and Industry: POB 87010, Thamar; tel. (5) 502200; fax (6) 501191.

Yemen Chamber of Commerce and Industry: POB 16690, San'a; tel. (1) 223539; fax (1) 251555.

STATE HYDROCARBONS COMPANIES

General Corpn for Oil and Mineral Resources: San'a; f. 1990; state petroleum co; Pres. AHMAD BARAKAT.

Ministry of Oil and Minerals: POB 81, San'a; tel. (1) 202306; fax (1) 202314; e-mail mom@y.net.ye; internet www.mom.gov.ye; responsible for the refining and marketing of petroleum products, and for prospecting and exploitation of indigenous hydrocarbons and other minerals; subsidiaries include:

   Aden Refinery Co: POB 3003, Aden 110; tel. (2) 376214; fax (2) 376600; e-mail info@arc-ye.com; internet www.arc-ye.com; f. 1952; operates petroleum refinery; capacity 8.6m. metric tons per year; output 4.2m. tons (1990); operates one oil tanker; Exec. Dir FATHI SALEM ALI; Refinery Man. MUHAMMAD YESLAM.

Petroleum Exploration and Production Authority (PEPA): POB 7196, Hadda St, San'a; tel. (1) 442630; fax (1) 442632; e-mail pepa-expo.com@y.net.ye; internet www.pepa.com.ye; f. 1990; manages petroleum concessions; Chair. AHMED ALI ABDULLAH.

Yemen National Oil Co: POB 5050, Maalla, Aden; importer and distributor of petroleum products; Gen. Man. MUHAMMAD ABD HUSSEIN.

UTILITIES

Electricity

Public Electricity Corpn: POB 178, Airport Rd, San'a; tel. (1) 328141; fax (1) 328150; e-mail ypecnt@y.net.ye; Man. Dir AHMAD AL-AINI.

Water

General Authority for Rural Water Supply Projects (GARWSP): San'a; govt agency responsible for water supply in rural areas.

National Water Resources Authority (NWRA): POB 8944, Amran St, Al-Hassaba, San'a; tel. (1) 231733; e-mail info@nwra-yemen.org; internet www.nwra-yemen.org; govt agency responsible for management of water resources; Chair. SALEM HASSAN BASHUEB.

National Water and Sewerage Authority (NWSA): POB 104, San'a; tel. (1) 250158; fax (1) 251536; e-mail NWSA@y.net.ye; govt agency responsible for water supply in urban areas.

TRADE UNIONS

Agricultural Co-operatives Union: POB 649, San'a; tel. (1) 270685; fax (1) 274125.

General Confederation of Workers: POB 1162, Maalla, Aden; f. 1956; affiliated to WFTU; 35,000 mems; Pres. RAJEH SALEH NAJI; Gen. Sec. ABD AR-RAZAK SHAIF.

Trade Union Federation: San'a; Pres. ALI SAIF MUQBIL.

Transport

RAILWAYS

There are no railways in Yemen.

ROADS

In 1996 Yemen had a total road network of 64,725 km, including 5,234 km of main roads and 2,474 km of secondary roads. In 2006 there were an estimated 73,200 km of roads, of which 13.7% was paved.

General Corpn for Roads and Bridges: POB 1185, az-Zubairy St, Asir Rd, San'a; tel. (1) 202278; fax (1) 209571; e-mail gcrb@y.net.ye; responsible for maintenance and construction.

Yemen Land Transport Co: Aden; f. 1980; incorporates fmr Yemen Bus Co and all other public transport of the fmr PDRY; Chair. ABD AL-JALIL TAHIR BADR; Gen. Man. SALEH AWAD AL-AMUDI.

SHIPPING

Aden is the main port. Aden Main Harbour has 28 first-class berths. In addition there is ample room to accommodate vessels of light draught at anchor in the 18-ft dredged area. There is also 800 ft of cargo wharf accommodating vessels of 300 ft length and 18 ft draught. Aden Oil Harbour accommodates four tankers of 57,000 metric tons and up to 40 ft draught. In 1999 work was completed on a US $580m. programme to expand container handling facilities at Aden, with the aim of establishing the port as a major transhipment centre. A 35-year concession to operate Aden Container Terminal was signed by Dubai Ports World, of the United Arab Emirates, in late 2005, incorporating an estimated $490m. upgrade programme and an initial capacity expansion investment of $370m.; this was expected to increase the annual capacity to 1.5m. containers by 2007. Hodeida port, on the Red Sea, was expanded with aid from the USSR and now handles a considerable amount of traffic; there are also ports at Maalla, Mocha, Nishtun and Salif.

At 31 December 2006 Yemen's merchant fleet comprised 47 vessels, with a combined displacement of 29,169 grt.

Yemen Ports Authority: POB 1316, Steamer Point, Tawahi, Aden; tel. (2) 202666; fax (2) 203521; e-mail info@portofaden.com; internet www.portofaden.com; f. 1888; Chair. MUHAMMAD A. MUBARAK BIN AEFAN; Port Officer Capt. BARAKAT ALI DERWISH.

Principal Shipping Companies

Aden Refinery Co: POB 3003, Aden 110; tel. (2) 430743; fax (2) 376600; f. 1952; two general tankers and one chemical tanker; Exec. Dir FATHI SALEM ALI.

Arabian Gulf Navigation Co (Yemen) Ltd: POB 3740, Hodeida; tel. (3) 2442; one general cargo vessel.

Elkirshi Shipping and Stevedoring Co: POB 3813, al-Hamdi St, Hodeida; tel. (3) 204448; fax (3) 241199; operates at ports of Hodeida, Mocha and Salif; Contact FATHI ALI MUHAMMAD.

Hodeida Shipping and Transport Co Ltd: POB 3337, Hodeida; tel. (3) 228543; fax (3) 228533; e-mail hodship_1969@y.net.ye; internet www.hodship.aden.com.ye; shipping agents, stevedoring, Lloyd's agents; clearance, haulage, land transportation, cargo and vessel surveys; Chair. MUHAMMAD ABDO THABET.

Al-Katiri Shipping Corpn: POB 716, Aden; tel. (2) 255538; fax (2) 251152; one general cargo vessel.

Middle East Shipping Co Ltd (Mideast): POB 3700, Hayel Saeed Bldg, at-Tahreer St, Hodeida; tel. (3) 203977; fax (3) 203910; e-mail mideast@mideastshipping.com; internet www.mideastshipping.com; f. 1962; Chair. ABD AL-WASA HAYEL SAID; Gen. Man. AHMAD GAZEM SAID; brs in Mocha, Aden, Taiz, Mukalla, San'a, Salif, Ras Isa, ash-Shihr.

National Shipping Co: POB 1228, Steamer Point, Aden; tel. (2) 204861; fax (2) 202644; e-mail natship@y.net.ye; shipping, bunkering, clearing and forwarding, and travel agents; Dir-Gen. MOHSEN SALEM BIN BREIK.

Yemen Navigation Line: POB 4190, Aden; tel. (2) 24861; fleet of three general cargo vessels.

Yemen Shipping Development Co Ltd: POB 3686, Hodeida; tel. (3) 224103; fax (3) 211584; one general cargo vessel; Shipping Man. FAHDLE A. KARIM.

Yeslam Salem Alshagga: POB 778, Aden; one general cargo vessel.

CIVIL AVIATION

There are six international airports—San'a International (13 km from the city), Aden Civil Airport (at Khormaksar, 11 km from the port of Aden), al-Ganad (at Taiz), Mukalla (Riyan), Seyoun and Hodeida Airport. A US $500m. expansion of San'a international airport was ongoing in 2008, with completion scheduled for 2009.

Yemen Airways (Yemenia): POB 1183, Airport Rd, San'a; tel. (1) 232400; fax (1) 252991; e-mail admin@yemenia.com; internet www.yemenia.com; f. 1961 as Yemen Airlines; nationalized as Yemen Airways Corpn 1972; present name adopted 1978; merged with airlines of fmr PDRY in 1996; owned 51% by Yemeni Govt and 49% by Govt of Saudi Arabia; scheduled for privatization; supervised by a ministerial cttee under the Ministry of Transportation; internal services and external services to 29 destinations in the Middle East, Asia, Africa, Europe and the USA; Chair. and CEO ABD AL-KALEK S. AL-KADI.

Tourism

The former YAR formed a joint tourism company with the PDRY in 1980. Yemen boasts areas of beautiful scenery, a favourable climate and towns of historic and architectural importance. UNESCO has named San'a and Shibam as World Heritage sites. However, the growth of tourism has, in recent years, been hampered by political instability. In 2006 some 382,332 tourists visited Yemen; tourism receipts totalled US $181m. in 2005. The Government designated 2006 its Year of Tourism in an effort to encourage more robust growth in the industry.

Association of Yemen Tourism and Travel Agencies: San'a; e-mail ysaleh@y.net.ye; internet www.aytta.org.ye; f. 1996; Chair. YAHYA M. A. SALEH.

General Authority of Tourism: POB 129, San'a; tel. (1) 252319; fax (1) 252317; e-mail gtda@gtda.gov.ye; internet www.gtda.gov.ye; Chair. MUTAHAR TAQI.

Yemen Tourism Promotion Board: POB 5607, 48 Amman St, San'a; tel. (1) 251033; fax (1) 251034; e-mail ytpb@yementourism.com; internet www.yementourism.com; Man. ABDU LUTF; Public Relations and Information Man. KHALED M. AD-DUAIS.

ZAMBIA

Introductory Survey

Location, Climate, Language, Religion, Flag, Capital

The Republic of Zambia is a land-locked state in southern central Africa, bordered to the north by Tanzania and the Democratic Republic of the Congo, to the east by Malawi and Mozambique, to the south by Zimbabwe, Botswana and Namibia, and to the west by Angola. The climate is tropical, modified by altitude, with average temperatures from 18°C to 24°C (65°F–75°F). The official language is English. The principal African languages are Nyanja, Bemba, Tonga, Lozi, Lunda and Luvale. Christians comprise an estimated 50% of the population and are roughly divided between Protestants and Roman Catholics. A sizeable proportion of the population follow traditional animist beliefs. Most Asians are Muslims, although some are Hindus. The national flag (proportions 2 by 3) is green, with equal red, black and orange vertical stripes in the lower fly corner, and an orange eagle in flight in the upper fly corner. The capital is Lusaka.

Recent History

In 1924 control of Northern Rhodesia was transferred from the British South Africa Company to the Government of the United Kingdom. In 1953 the protectorate united with Southern Rhodesia (now Zimbabwe) and Nyasaland (now Malawi) to form the Federation of Rhodesia and Nyasaland. In 1962, following a campaign of civil disobedience organized by the United National Independence Party (UNIP), in support of demands that Northern Rhodesia be granted independence, the British Government introduced a new Constitution, which provided for a limited African franchise. In December 1963 the Federation was formally dissolved. Northern Rhodesia, which was henceforth known as Zambia, became an independent republic within the Commonwealth on 24 October 1964, with the leader of UNIP, Dr Kenneth Kaunda, as the country's first President.

Following its accession to power, the Kaunda administration supported African liberation groups operating in Southern Rhodesia (then known as Rhodesia) and Mozambique; repeated clashes along the border with both countries were reported, while incidents of internal political violence, particularly in the Copperbelt region, also occurred. In December 1972 Zambia was declared a one-party state. In January 1973 the Rhodesian administration closed the border with Zambia. Kaunda, the sole candidate, was re-elected to the presidency in 1978, 1983 and 1988.

In May 1990 Kaunda announced that a popular referendum on the subject of multi-party politics would take place in October of that year, and that supporters of such a system (which Kaunda and UNIP opposed) would be permitted to campaign and hold public meetings. Accordingly, in July the Movement for Multiparty Democracy (MMD), an unofficial alliance of political opponents of the Government, was formed. The MMD, which was led by a former government minister, Arthur Wina, and the Chairman of the Zambian Congress of Trade Unions (ZCTU), Frederick Chiluba, swiftly gained widespread public support. Later in July Kaunda announced that the referendum was to be postponed until August 1991, to facilitate the registration of a large section of the electorate. In September 1990, however, following the recommendation by Kaunda that a multi-party political system be reintroduced, that multi-party elections be organized by October 1991, that the national referendum be abandoned, and that a commission be appointed to revise the Constitution, the National Council of UNIP endorsed proposals for multi-party legislative and presidential elections, and accepted the recommendations of a parliamentary committee regarding the restructuring of the party.

In December 1990 constitutional amendments were adopted that permitted the formation of other political associations to contest the forthcoming elections. The MMD was subsequently granted official recognition. In early 1991 several prominent members of UNIP resigned from the party and declared their support for the MMD, while the ZCTU officially transferred allegiance to the MMD. Several other opposition movements were also established.

In June 1991 the constitutional commission presented a series of recommendations, including the creation of the post of Vice-President, the expansion of the National Assembly to 150 members and the establishment of a constitutional court. Kaunda accepted the majority of the proposed constitutional amendments, which were subsequently submitted for approval by the National Assembly. The MMD, however, rejected the draft, and announced that it would boycott the forthcoming elections if the National Assembly accepted the proposals. In July, following discussions between Kaunda, Chiluba and delegates from seven other political associations, Kaunda agreed to suspend the review of the draft Constitution in the National Assembly pending further negotiations. Subsequent discussions between the MMD and UNIP resulted in the establishment of a joint commission to revise the draft Constitution. In late July Kaunda conceded to opposition demands that ministers be appointed only from the National Assembly and that proposals for a constitutional court be abandoned. A provision granting the President the power to impose martial law was also rescinded.

On 2 August 1991 the National Assembly formally adopted the new Constitution. At the UNIP congress in the same month Kaunda was unanimously re-elected as President of the party. Kaunda also announced the dissociation of the armed forces from UNIP; senior officers in the armed forces were subsequently obliged to retire from the party's Central Committee. In September Kaunda officially dissociated UNIP from the State; workers in the public sector were henceforth prohibited from engaging in political activity.

On 31 October 1991 Chiluba, with 75.8% of votes cast, defeated Kaunda in the presidential election. In the concurrent legislative elections, contested by 330 candidates representing six political parties, the MMD secured 125 seats in the National Assembly, while UNIP won the remaining 25 seats; only four members of the previous Government were returned to the National Assembly. Kaunda's failure to secure re-election was attributed to widespread perceptions of economic mismanagement by his administration. On 2 November Chiluba was inaugurated as President. He appointed Levy Mwanawasa, a constitutional lawyer, as Vice-President and Leader of the National Assembly, and formed a new Cabinet. Chiluba subsequently initiated a major restructuring of the civil service and of parastatal organizations, as part of efforts to reverse the country's significant economic decline and eradicate widespread corruption among officials.

In mid-1992 widespread opposition to government policies was reported. In May a dissident faction of academics within the MMD, the Caucus for National Unity (CNU), emerged and demanded that Chiluba review procedures for the appointment of cabinet ministers and heads of parastatal organizations, to ensure that all ethnic groups were represented. The CNU, together with other pressure groups, also advocated the establishment of a constitutional commission to curtail the executive power vested in the President and the Cabinet. In July two cabinet ministers (who reportedly supported the CNU) resigned in protest at what they alleged was the Government's failure to suppress corruption and to institute democratic measures, following the refusal of the National Assembly to accept a report that implicated several government members in alleged financial malpractice. Later that month the CNU registered as an independent political party. In September Kaunda formally resigned from active participation in UNIP; Kebby Musokotwane (Prime Minister in 1985–89) was subsequently elected as the party's President.

In March 1993 Chiluba declared a state of emergency, following the discovery of UNIP documents that allegedly revealed details of a conspiracy to destabilize the Government. Several prominent members of UNIP, including Kaunda's three sons, were subsequently arrested. Musokotwane admitted the existence of the documents; however, Kaunda claimed that the conspiracy had been fabricated by Zambian security forces, with the assistance of US intelligence services, in an attempt to undermine the opposition.

Divisions within the MMD became apparent in August 1993, when 15 prominent members (11 of whom held seats in the National Assembly) resigned from the party: they accused the

Government of protecting corrupt cabinet ministers and of failing to respond to numerous reports linking senior party officials with the illegal drugs trade. Their opposition to the Government was consolidated later in the month by the formation of a new political group, the National Party (NP). In November Chiluba appointed a 22-member commission to revise the Constitution; it was announced that the draft document was to be submitted for approval by a Constituent Assembly, and subsequently by a national referendum. At partial elections for 10 of the 11 vacated seats in the National Assembly, which took place in November 1993 and April 1994, the MMD regained five seats, while the NP secured four and UNIP took one. The remaining seat was secured by UNIP at a by-election in December.

Meanwhile, in July 1994 Mwanawasa resigned as Vice-President, citing long-standing differences with Chiluba, and was subsequently replaced by Brig.-Gen. Godfrey Miyanda. Also in July Kaunda stated that he intended to contest the presidential election due in 1996; however, UNIP officials indicated that he would only be allowed to resume the leadership of the party if he were officially elected by members.

In June 1995 some members of the Constitutional Review Commission rejected a final draft of the Constitution, objecting, in particular, to restrictions on the independent press, and on public gatherings and demonstrations; they claimed that the four members of the Commission who had prepared the draft had taken payments from the Government, and accused the Chairman of complicity with the authorities. Later that month, however, the draft Constitution was submitted for approval. At the end of June Kaunda was elected President of UNIP, defeating Musokotwane; he reiterated his intention of seeking re-election to the state presidency, despite provisions in the draft Constitution that effectively debarred his candidature, on the grounds that he had already served two terms of office and that he was not of direct Zambian descent (his parents originated from Malawi). At by-elections in 13 constituencies in September–October 1995, the MMD secured seven seats, and UNIP six. In October the Minister for Legal Affairs announced that Kaunda had not officially relinquished Malawian citizenship until 1970 (and had therefore governed illegally for six years), and that he had not obtained Zambian citizenship through the correct procedures. However, following widespread reports that the authorities intended to deport Kaunda, the Government ordered security forces to suspend investigations into the former President's citizenship (apparently owing to fears of civil unrest).

In January 1996 seven opposition parties, including UNIP and the NP, established an informal alliance to campaign in favour of democratic elections and the establishment of a Constituent Assembly to approve the draft Constitution by a process of national consensus. Opposition parties subsequently demanded that the Government abandon the draft Constitution and negotiate with them regarding electoral reform. Later that month UNIP deputies withdrew from a parliamentary debate on the draft, which was subsequently approved by a large majority in the National Assembly. On 28 May the Constitution was officially adopted by Chiluba. In early June Western donor Governments suspended aid to Zambia, in protest at the constitutional provisions that effectively precluded Kaunda from contesting the presidency, while Kaunda announced that he intended to defy the ban.

In August 1996 Chiluba and Kaunda met for discussions, as part of a programme of dialogue between the Government and opposition parties. Following Kaunda's decision to boycott a scheduled second round of discussions in September, the Government made minor concessions regarding the conduct of forthcoming elections, including assurances that votes would be counted at polling stations and that the Electoral Commission (appointed by Chiluba) would be independent; UNIP's request that the elections be conducted according to the 1991 Constitution was rejected. In mid-October 1996 Chiluba dissolved the National Assembly and announced that presidential and legislative elections would take place on 18 November. UNIP, still dissatisfied with the electoral system, announced its intention to boycott the elections and organize a campaign of civil disobedience; by early November a further six political parties had also decided to boycott the elections. There was widespread criticism of the voter registration process, in which fewer than one-half of the estimated 4.6m. eligible voters had been listed.

Despite appeals for a postponement, the elections were held as planned, and Chiluba and the MMD were returned to power by a large majority. In the presidential election Chiluba defeated the four other candidates with 72.5% of the valid votes cast. His nearest rival (with only 12.5%) was Dean Mung'omba of the Zambia Democratic Congress (ZADECO), an erstwhile opponent of Chiluba within the MMD. The MMD secured 131 of the 150 seats in the National Assembly. Of the eight other parties that contested the elections, only the NP (five seats), ZADECO (two seats) and Agenda for Zambia (AZ—two seats) won parliamentary representation, with independent candidates taking the remaining 10 seats.

Chiluba was inaugurated for a second presidential term on 21 November 1996. Amid demands for his resignation and for fresh elections to be held, Chiluba dissolved the Cabinet and placed the military on alert at the end of the month. In early December a new Government was appointed, although the main portfolios remained largely unchanged.

Political tension increased in the second half of 1997. In response to reports in June claiming that Kaunda and Roger Chongwe, the leader of the Liberal Progressive Front, were appealing for international assistance to overcome a political crisis in Zambia, the MMD denied that any such crisis existed. Later that month the MMD's chairman in Lusaka called for the declaration of a state of emergency, on the grounds that the opposition, by refusing to enter into talks with the MMD, were advocating a civil war. Chongwe insisted that the opposition would welcome dialogue, but only if the 1996 elections were annulled and the Constitution repealed. Meanwhile, the opposition's campaign of civil disobedience continued. In August 1997 Kaunda and Chongwe were shot and wounded (Chongwe seriously) when the security forces opened fire on an opposition gathering in Kabwe, north of Lusaka. Kaunda's subsequent allegation that the shooting was an assassination attempt organized by the Government was strongly denied by Chiluba.

On 28 October 1997 rebel army officers briefly captured the national television and radio station from where they proclaimed the formation of a military regime. The attempted coup was swiftly suppressed by regular military units; 15 people were arrested during the operation. Allegations by Kaunda that the Government had orchestrated the coup in order to be in a position to detain prominent members of the opposition were repeated by other opposition figures after Chiluba declared a state of emergency on 29 October, providing for the detention for 28 days without trial of people suspected of involvement in the attempted coup.

Chiluba carried out an extensive cabinet reshuffle in early December 1997. Observers interpreted the transfer to lesser cabinet posts of Miyanda and of Benjamin Mwila, hitherto the Minister of Defence, as an attempt to forestall the emergence of potential rivals to Chiluba within the MMD. Lt-Gen. Christon Tembo, hitherto the Minister of Mines and Mineral Development, replaced Miyanda as Vice-President.

On 25 December 1997 Kaunda was arrested under emergency powers and imprisoned, shortly after his return to Zambia from more than two months abroad. Numerous regional and international Governments expressed serious concern at the detention of Kaunda. On the following day Kaunda was placed under house arrest at his home in Lusaka. He was arraigned in court in January 1998, and in mid-February he was formally notified that he was to stand trial for 'misprision of treason', on the grounds that he had failed to report in advance to the authorities details allegedly known to him of the attempted coup of October 1997. Meanwhile, in late January 1998 the National Assembly voted to extend the state of emergency for a further three months; Chiluba eventually revoked the state of emergency on 17 March, following pressure from external donors. Also in March, Chiluba effected a minor cabinet reshuffle, most notably dismissing the Minister of Finance and Economic Development, Ronald Penza. In April 80 people who were being detained in connection with the attempted coup, including Kaunda and Mung'omba, were committed to summary trial in the High Court. Kaunda was released from detention in June, after charges against him were withdrawn, apparently owing to lack of evidence.

In November 1998 Penza was murdered at his home by a gang of masked men. Shortly afterwards five of the six suspects were shot dead by police-officers, who claimed the motive for Penza's murder was robbery, although it was reported that nothing had been stolen. The police action, and Chiluba's subsequent approval of legislation providing for Zambia's intelligence service to be armed, were of considerable concern to human rights organizations. In December Mung'omba was granted bail, as no witnesses had provided evidence against him since his detention on charges of treason following the failed coup attempt of October 1997.

In mid-February 1999 opposition parties demanded the dismissal of Tembo and Benjamin Mwila, the Minister of Energy and Water Development (previously responsible for defence), who had been implicated, along with the former Minister of Commerce, Trade and Industry, Enoch Kavindele, in Angolan claims that Zambia was supporting the Angolan rebel movement, União Nacional para a Independência Total de Angola (UNITA)—allegations that the Zambian authorities strongly denied. In late February a number of bombs exploded in Lusaka, one of which seriously damaged the Angolan embassy, killing a security guard, while several further explosive devices were discovered and defused. In mid-March it was reported that two Zambians had been arrested, and two foreigners deported, in connection with the bombings.

At the end of March 1999 the High Court delivered its judgment in a case concerning Kaunda's citizenship, declaring him to be a stateless person. The following day Kaunda appealed to the Supreme Court against the ruling, and later that day he escaped a reported assassination attempt, when a group of armed men opened fire on his car. In April five opposition parties, including the AZ and ZADECO, formed a new alliance, the Zambia Alliance for Progress (ZAP). However, the authorities refused to register the ZAP on the grounds that its constituent parties had not been dissolved. The ZAP initially disputed the ruling and announced its intention to appeal to the High Court, but in August ZADECO formally announced its dissolution, thus effectively losing its parliamentary seat. Meanwhile, in June Chiluba effected a minor cabinet reshuffle, notably appointing Katele Kalumba as Minister of Finance and Economic Development.

In September 1999 59 soldiers were sentenced to death for their part in the failed coup against the Chiluba administration in October 1997. A further soldier was sentenced to 21 years' imprisonment for concealing information regarding the coup attempt from the authorities, while another eight soldiers were acquitted of charges of treason, owing to lack of evidence. In October 1999 55 of the soldiers sentenced to death launched an appeal against the convictions.

In March 2000 Kaunda announced his resignation as President of UNIP and his retirement from active politics. At an extraordinary congress, which was convened in Ndola in May, Francis Nkhoma, a former governor of the Bank of Zambia, was elected to replace Kaunda as President of UNIP, while Kaunda's son, Tilyenji, became the party's new Secretary-General.

In May 2000 the Minister of the Environment and Natural Resources and MMD National Treasurer, Benjamin Mwila, announced that he intended to stand in the presidential election scheduled for 2001; Chiluba had previously prohibited members of his Cabinet from publicly discussing their potential candidacy for the presidency upon the expiry of the two terms permitted to him by the Constitution. Mwila was subsequently dismissed from the Government and expelled from the MMD. In July Mwila and a number of other MMD members formed a new political movement, the Republican Party (RP); Mwila reiterated his intention to seek election to the presidency. The RP merged with the ZAP in February 2001, Mwila becoming leader of the new movement, known as the Zambia Republican Party (ZRP).

In early 2001 a number of prominent figures in the MMD publicly advocated Chiluba's election to a third presidential term, despite such an event being prohibited by the Constitution. Chiluba, while declining to reveal his intentions, was reported to have expressed a willingness to listen to the outcome of any public debate on the issue. Opposition parties and some leading MMD members (including Tembo) demanded that Chiluba announce that he would not seek re-election. In April, amid increasing controversy, a convention of the MMD approved a motion removing the stipulation that the party's President should serve a maximum of two five-year terms. Tembo, Miyanda and seven other ministers expressed their opposition to the convention's decision and were expelled from the party; their supporters subsequently alleged that intimidation by supporters of Chiluba had caused some who opposed the motion not to attend the conference. Several Western donor governments also expressed their opposition to Chiluba's re-election. In April Tilyenji Kaunda was adopted as the President of UNIP.

In May 2001 a motion to impeach Chiluba for misconduct, proposed by two MMD deputies, was signed by more than one-third of the members of the National Assembly. The following day Chiluba announced that he would not seek re-election and dissolved the Cabinet. A new Cabinet was appointed some days later, with the ministers who had opposed Chiluba all being replaced—Tembo was succeeded as Vice-President by Kavindele, the Vice-President of the MMD and hitherto Minister of Health. In July the FDD won a by-election in Lusaka, occasioned by the resignation of Tembo after his expulsion from the MMD; violent confrontations between rival supporters from the MMD and FDD were reported. Tembo was elected President of the FDD in October. Meanwhile, Miyanda had established a further opposition party, the Heritage Party (HP).

The MMD adopted former Vice-President Mwanawasa as its presidential candidate in August 2001. Later that month seven opposition parties, including UNIP and the FDD, agreed to form a government of national unity following the forthcoming legislative elections, in order to provide effective opposition in the event of the MMD securing the presidency. In September Michael Sata resigned as Minister without Portfolio and as National Secretary of the MMD, in protest at the nomination of Mwanawasa as presidential candidate. He subsequently formed a new political party, the Patriotic Front (PF). In October Tembo was elected as the FDD's presidential candidate.

The presidential and legislative elections took place on 27 December 2001. On 1 January 2002 (the scheduled date for the announcement of the election results) violent confrontations took place between anti-Government demonstrators and the security forces in Lusaka and Kitwe, amid allegations that the MMD had engaged in electoral fraud and voter intimidation. Mwanawasa was officially declared President on the following day, with 29.2% of the valid votes cast, narrowly defeating Anderson Mazoka, the leader of the United Party for National Development (UPND, established in 1998), who secured 27.2%, while Tembo won 13.2% and Tilyenji Kaunda 10.1%. The High Court had rejected a petition for the further postponement of the declaration of the results by opposition parties, which were demanding an investigation into their allegations. The MMD secured 69 of the 150 elective seats in the National Assembly (and subsequently all eight of the seats nominated by the President); the UPND became the second largest party in the National Assembly, with 49 seats. Other parties to gain legislative representation were UNIP (with 13 seats), the FDD (12 seats), the HP (four seats), and the PF and the ZRP (one seat each); one independent candidate was also elected.

Although the MMD held only 77 of the 158 seats in the National Assembly, Mwanawasa refused to form a coalition with any of the opposition parties to ensure a working majority, and appointed a new Cabinet in early January, retaining many ministers from the previous administration. Kavindele remained Vice-President, and Kalumba was appointed as Minister of Foreign Affairs, while Mwanawasa assumed the defence portfolio himself. A report published in February by an observer mission of the European Union criticized the Electoral Commission of Zambia for misadministration of the recent elections, and later in that month the Supreme Court began hearing a legal challenge to the election results from UNIP, the FDD and the HP, which alleged that the MMD had won the polls fraudulently. Later that month senior members of the FDD expressed their support for the new President, praising his stated commitment to curbing corruption and alleviating poverty. In February 2005 the Supreme Court ruled that although there had been irregularities in the electoral process, the overall result of the elections had not been affected.

In July 2002 the Minister of Foreign Affairs and the Chief Justice resigned, apparently in response to pressure from Mwanawasa, exerted in what was regarded as an attempt to rid the administration of corrupt officials. Later that month the National Assembly voted to remove Chiluba's immunity from prosecution, pending a review by the High Court, in order to allow his trial on charges of corruption against him to proceed. Mwanawasa offered Chiluba a full pardon, on condition that he return the assets he was alleged to have embezzled. The decision to remove his immunity was upheld by the High Court in August. In February 2003 the Supreme Court ruled that Chiluba's immunity could not be restored, and a few days later he was arrested and charged with stealing more than US $2m. of public funds while President.

In August 2003 Chiluba, who had been released on bail following his arrest in February, was rearrested and charged with the theft of US $29.7m. while in office. In October, amid an intensification of demands for political reform, President Mwanawasa convened a four-day national conference. The principal opposition parties and reformist civil organizations refused to participate in the conference, however. In December two concurrent trials of Chiluba commenced. The former President was reportedly arraigned on 264 charges of stealing a total of some $40m., in collaboration, in some instances, with other former government officials. In March 2004 Vice-President Mumba announced that about 150 former government officials and businessmen linked to Chiluba's administration were under investigation in connection with the theft of public funds. By January 2005 the charges against Chiluba had been reduced to six counts of theft of some $488,000. In mid-2005 Chiluba's lawyers halted the trial for four months, demanding access to confidential prosecution documents; however, the High Court rejected their claims and in November ordered that proceedings be resumed. In November 2006 a magistrate's court ruled that Chiluba was not fit to stand trial because of a chronic heart condition. The court ordered the release of his passport so that he could undergo medical treatment in South Africa.

In early August 2004 the National Assembly approved legislation postponing local elections—scheduled to take place in November—until 2006, when they were to be held concurrent with legislative and presidential elections. The legislation also extended the terms of office for mayors and councillors from three to five years. In late September the Constitutional Review Commission (CRC) made recommendations that included, the appointment of a non-executive President and the adoption of an electoral process based on proportional representation. In October President Mwanawasa announced that the Constitution could only be amended with the support of at least two-thirds of the National Assembly. In late June 2006 the CRC published its report and a draft constitution, which included, *inter alia*, an updated bill of rights, the requirement for a presidential candidate to win more than 50% of the vote and certain limitations on the President's statutory powers. After considering the draft, in mid-January 2006 it was reported that Mwanawasa was prepared to accept the recommendations and implement constitutional reform prior to that year's elections. However, in early February he announced that the elections would be held under the terms of the existing Constitution and that a referendum and a national census were necessary before a new constitution could be enacted. Meanwhile, minor government reorganizations were effected in August and October 2005, and in March 2006. Concerns over Mwanawasa's health surfaced in April after he suffered a stroke. He resumed light duties after some weeks and subsequently declared himself fit to stand for re-election to the presidency.

During the presidential election campaign Mwanawasa focused on his Government's economic reforms and anti-corruption drive that had elicited international praise. His main challenger for the presidency was Michael Sata, the candidate for the PF, who made poverty his main campaign theme, and threatened to deport Chinese, Indian and Lebanese businessmen who he accused of exploiting Zambian workers. While this enhanced his populist credentials among the electorate, it damaged his reputation internationally, and led the Chinese Government to warn that it would consider the suspension of diplomatic ties with Zambia if Sata was elected. Sata, who commanded the support of Chiluba, increased his populist rhetoric by praising Zimbabwean President Robert Mugabe's policy of seizing white-owned land.

In the event, Mwanawasa secured a second presidential term on 28 September 2006, with 42.98% of the votes cast. Sata took 29.37%, while Hakainde Hichilema of the opposition United Democratic Alliance (UDA) coalition, won 25.32%. Voter turnout was estimated at 70.8%. Sata alleged electoral fraud, claiming that as many as 400,000 votes appeared not to have been counted in areas where he had expected to win support. Clashes between PF supporters and the security forces broke out in Lusaka when the Electoral Commission announced that Sata had fallen from first place to third in interim vote counts. Protesters threw stones at police who responded with tear gas and by firing live ammunition into the air. The subsequent violence, which lasted two days, and allegations of irregularities contrasted with the voting on election day, which international observers proclaimed took place in a generally efficient and transparent manner. In concurrently held parliamentary elections, the MMD took 72 seats, the PF won 43 and the UDA secured 26. Voting in two constituencies was postponed until 26 October, owing to the deaths of candidates.

Mwanawasa was in sworn in as President on 3 October 2006 and a new Cabinet was announced a few days later: Rupiah Banda was named as Vice-President, while Mundia Sikatana and George Mpombo were appointed to the foreign affairs and defence portfolios, respectively. In December Sata was arrested for allegedly making a false declaration of his assets before the presidential elections; however, the charges were dropped later that month.

Meanwhile, in October 2006 Zambia announced its first discoveries of oil and gas reserves in the Chavuma and Zambezi districts, close to the border with Angola. Mwanawasa announced that the Government would appoint a special cabinet committee to select foreign petroleum firms to conduct comprehensive exploration. In February 2007 Chinese President Hu Jintao announced new investment worth US $800m. in Zambia after talks in Lusaka with Mwanawasa. The two leaders stated that a special economic zone would be created in Zambia's copper-mining area in Chambishi, north of Lusaka, where Chinese firms could operate without paying import or value-added taxes. Part of Zambia's bilateral debt to the People's Republic of China was also written off. Later in February a High Court judge ruled that Zambia must pay a substantial sum to a so-called 'vulture fund' (companies which buy up the debt of poor nations cheaply when it is about to be written off, then sue for the full value of the debt plus interest). British Virgin Islands-based Donegal International paid less than $4m. for a debt Zambia owed, but sued Zambia for a $42m. repayment. There were concerns that such funds were eradicating the benefits that international debt relief was envisaged to bring to poor countries.

In March 2007 police demolished some 250 houses in Lusaka which the authorities maintained were built without official approval. The Government announced that it was the beginning of a campaign to eradicate corruption in the way land plots were distributed. Earlier that month the Minister of Lands, Gladys Nyirongo, was dismissed for allocating plots of land to family members; in April Minister of Information and Broadcasting Services Vernon Mwaanga was removed from office. In May a further governmental reorganization was effected in which Minister of Health Angela Chifire was replaced by Brig.-Gen. Brian Chituwo, hitherto Minister of Science, Technology and Vocational Training. In August Minister of Foreign Affairs Mundia Sikatana was replaced by Kabinga Pande in another cabinet reshuffle. Pande was succeeded at the Ministry of Tourism, the Environment and Natural Resources by Michael Kaingu.

In 1986 South African troops launched attacks on alleged bases of the African National Congress of South Africa (ANC) in Zambia; a number of foreigners and Zambian citizens were subsequently arrested in Zambia on suspicion of spying for South Africa. In August of that year Zambia undertook to impose economic sanctions against South Africa, and the South African Government retaliated by temporarily enforcing trade restrictions on Zambia. Further attacks on ANC targets took place during 1987–89. During the 1980s President Kaunda's support for the Governments of Angola and Mozambique resulted in attacks on Zambian civilians by Angolan rebels (with assistance from the Governments of South Africa and the USA) and by Mozambican rebels (also allegedly supported by South Africa). In September 1992 the Governments of Zambia and Angola signed a security agreement providing for common border controls. In early 1996 Zambia contributed some 1,000 troops to the UN Angola Verification Mission. Zambia consistently denied allegations, made by the Angolan Government in 1997–98, that it was providing military and logistical support to UNITA rebels.

In early 1999, however, tension between the two countries intensified, as the accusations resurfaced and a bomb severely damaged the Angolan embassy in Lusaka (see above). In March the Angolan Government delivered a letter to the UN explaining its accusations against Zambia. The Zambian Government again refuted all allegations against it. In April, however, relations appeared to have improved, when both countries were reported to have signed an agreement aimed at resolving their differences, under the mediation of Swaziland's King Mswati III. In June the Zambian and Angolan Governments signed a further agreement, which provided for the reactivation of the joint permanent commission on defence and security and the organization of a summit between Chiluba and the Angolan President, José Eduardo dos Santos. In December it was reported that Angolan jets had bombed Zambian territory in pursuit of UNITA rebels, and in January 2000 it was announced that some 21,000 Angolan refugees had entered Zambia since October 1999. During January–February 2000 UNITA rebels carried out a series of raids on Zambian villages, which prompted Chiluba to announce that he would not permit UNITA troops to operate from Zambia. In February, following the convention of the joint permanent commission on defence and security to discuss the security situation along the common border, both sides resolved to strengthen measures against UNITA forces operating in the common border area. In September the Zambian Government declined a request from the Angolan Government for its forces to be allowed to use Zambian territory to attack UNITA positions near the frontier.

In February 2001 the Governments of Zambia, Angola and Namibia agreed to establish a tripartite mechanism for political and security co-operation in an attempt to improve security on their joint borders. However, armed Angolans raided three Zambian villages close to the border in November, reportedly abducting some 100 Zambians and subsequently killing seven of them; Zambian forces claimed to have killed 10 Angolans in retaliation. Reports in the Zambian press attributed the attacks on the villages to the Angolan armed forces, which admitted occupying UNITA bases in the area, but claimed to have observed UNITA rebels crossing the border shortly before the attacks. At the end of 2002 there were 188,436 Angolan refugees in Zambia, compared with 218,154 at the beginning of the year, and by the end of 2006, according to the office of the UN High Commissioner for Refugees (UNHCR) that figure had been reduced to 42,675.

In early March 1997 the Zambian Government appealed for international assistance in coping with the influx of refugees fleeing the civil conflict in Zaire (now the Democratic Republic of the Congo—DRC); by March some 6,000 Zairean refugees had arrived in Zambia. In January 1998 Zambia and the DRC agreed to establish a joint permanent commission on defence and security. During late 1998 and early 1999 the Zambian Government was involved in regional efforts to find a political solution to the conflict in the DRC, after a rebellion was mounted against the Government in August 1998; President Chiluba was appointed to co-ordinate peace initiatives on the crisis by the Southern African Development Community and the Organization of African Unity (OAU, now the African Union, see p. 164). Meanwhile, thousands of Congolese entered Zambia, fleeing the renewed fighting, prompting the Government to appeal to the international community for immediate assistance to cope with the refugees, which, by then, reportedly numbered more than 30,000. In addition, several hundred DRC soldiers crossed into Zambia seeking refuge, but were subsequently repatriated. At a summit held in Lusaka during June–July 1999 a cease-fire document was formulated, providing for the withdrawal of foreign forces from the DRC and for political reform in the country. The accord was signed by the President of the DRC and the leaders of the five other countries involved in the conflict in July, and by rebel leaders in August. Nevertheless, progress with its implementation was slow. Zambia's involvement in mediation efforts aimed at achieving a definitive end to the conflict in the DRC diminished in the early 2000s, although a number of regional summit meetings were held in Lusaka. In March 2004 it was reported that more than 1,000 DRC nationals had entered Zambia, fleeing renewed fighting between government and rebel forces in south-eastern DRC. At the end of 2006 there were more than 64,000 refugees living in UNHCR refugee camps in Zambia, of whom 43,788 were from the DRC. In addition, UNHCR estimated that a further 75,000 refugees (including 49,000 Angolans) had settled among the Zambian population. In July 2007 some 100 Angolan refugees refused to be repatriated until the Zambian Government paid wages due for construction work carried out in 2003. The refugees had been employed on a casual basis by a government agency that had since been dissolved. Other refugees had returned to Angola in late 2006 without receiving their wages, despite being assured that they would receive payment.

Government

Under the provisions of the Constitution, which was formally adopted in May 1996, Zambia is a multi-party state. Executive power is vested in the President, who is the constitutional Head of State. Legislative power is vested in a National Assembly, which comprises 158 members, of whom 150 are elected by universal adult suffrage, and eight nominated by the President. The President and the National Assembly are elected simultaneously by universal adult suffrage for a five-year term. The maximum duration of the President's tenure of office is limited to two five-year terms. The President governs with the assistance of a Vice-President and a Cabinet, whom he appoints from members of the National Assembly. The Constitution also provides for a 27-member House of Chiefs, which represents traditional tribal authorities. Each of Zambia's nine provinces has a minister, who is appointed by the President.

Defence

The total strength of armed forces, as assessed at November 2007, was 15,100, with 13,500 in the army and 1,600 in the air force. Paramilitary forces numbered 1,400. Military service is voluntary. There is also a National Defence Force responsible to the Government. The defence budget for 2007 was estimated at K933,000m.

Economic Affairs

In 2006, according to estimates by the World Bank, Zambia's gross national income (GNI), measured at average 2004–06 prices, was US $7,476m., equivalent to $630 per head (or $1,000 per head on an international purchasing-power parity basis). During 1996–2006, it was estimated, the population increased at an average annual rate of 1.9%, while gross domestic product (GDP) per head increased, in real terms, by an average of 1.7% per year. Overall GDP increased, in real terms, at an average annual rate of 3.7% in 1996–2006; growth in 2006 was 6.0%.

Agriculture (including forestry and fishing) contributed 19.9% of GDP in 2006. According to the 2000 census, 71.6% of those employed were engaged in the sector. However, in 2006 only 11.7% of those in paid employment were engaged in agriculture. The principal crops are sugar cane, cassava, maize, wheat, cotton, sweet potatoes and groundnuts. Millet, rice, sorghum, tobacco, sunflower seeds and horticultural produce are also cultivated. Cattle-rearing remains important. During 1996–2006, according to the World Bank, agricultural GDP increased by an average of 1.1% per year. However, agricultural GDP declined by 0.6% per year in 2005 and 2006.

Industry (including mining, manufacturing, construction and power) contributed 31.3% of GDP in 2006, and engaged 22.7% of all those in paid employment in that year. According to the World Bank, industrial GDP grew at an average annual rate of 4.5% in 1996–2006. Industrial GDP increased by 6.7% in 2006.

In 2006 mining and quarrying contributed 4.1% of GDP, according to official figures, and engaged 5.5% of those in paid employment. According to balance of payments data, exports of copper contributed 76.9% of the value of total exports in 2006. Output of copper ore increased from 426,900 metric tons in 2004 to 514,000 tons in 2006. Cobalt is also an important export, while coal, gold, emeralds, amethyst, limestone and selenium are also mined. The issuing of licences for the mining of uranium was expected to commence in mid-2008. In addition, Zambia has reserves of phosphates, fluorspar and iron ore. During 2002–06, according to the IMF, mining GDP increased by an estimated average of 8.1% per year. Mining GDP increased by 7.3% in 2006.

Manufacturing contributed 10.2% of GDP in 2006, and engaged 11.6% of those in paid employment. The principal manufacturing activities are food-processing, the smelting and refining of copper and other metals, vehicle assembly, petroleum-refining, and the production of fertilizers, explosives, textiles, bottles, batteries, bricks and copper wire. During 1996–2006, according to the World Bank, manufacturing GDP increased at an average annual rate of 4.3%. Manufacturing GDP increased by 5.0% in 2006.

Energy is derived principally from hydroelectric power (99.4% in 2004), in which Zambia is self-sufficient. Imports of mineral fuels accounted for 15.0% of the value of merchandise imports in 2006. In an effort to address the problem of power shortages and expand availability of electricity, construction was planned of three new hydroelectric plants during 2009–15, for which a financing requirement of some US $1,200m. was anticipated.

In 2006 the services sector contributed 48.9% of GDP, and engaged 65.6% of those in paid employment. According to the World Bank, the GDP of the services sector increased by an average of 4.8% per year in 1996–2006. Services GDP increased by 8.5% in 2006.

In 2006 Zambia recorded a trade surplus of US $1,183m., while there was a surplus of $120m. on the current account of the balance of payments. In 2006 the principal source of imports (47.3%) was South Africa; other major suppliers were the United Arab Emirates and Zimbabwe. The principal market for exports in 2006 was Switzerland (accounting for 38.3% of the total); other significant purchasers were South Africa, Thailand and the People's Republic of China. The principal exports in 2006 were basic manufactures and crude materials. The principal imports in that year were machinery and transport equipment, mineral fuels, chemicals and related products, basic manufactures and food and live animals.

In 2006 there was an overall budgetary surplus of K7,291,000m., equivalent to 18.6% of GDP. Zambia's total external debt was US $5,668m. at the end of 2005, of which $4,085m. was long-term public debt. In 1996–2006 the average annual rate of inflation was 21.1%. Consumer prices increased by 9.0% in 2006.

Zambia is a member of the Southern African Development Community (see p. 386) and the Common Market for Eastern and Southern Africa (see p. 205).

By 2006–07 Zambia was experiencing a period of robust economic growth, attributable principally to the impact of high international prices for its principal export, copper, in conjunction with extensive debt-relief and the consolidation of economic restructuring under the supervision of the IMF and World Bank. Inflation had been brought beneath 10% by the end of 2006, and was held at this level in 2007, despite the strong upward pressure of world petroleum prices. Expansion in the mining sector, with increased output as a result of new infrastructural projects expected to offset an eventual slowing of copper prices, was accompanied by strong performance in the construction and telecommnications sectors, while diversification was being pursued in non-traditional sectors such as tourism and agri-business. As a result of relief under the terms of the heavily indebted poor countries and multilateral debt relief initiatives, Zambia's debt-to-GDP ratio fell from some 85% at the end of 2005 to 9% at the end of 2006. In the assessment of the IMF, under consultations expected to result in agreement of a new Poverty Reduction and Growth Facility (PRGF) in support of Zambia's Fifth National Development Plan (2006–10)—the previous PRGF having expired in September 2007—real annual GDP growth of 6.5% was expected in 2008–09, while year-end inflation was expected to slow to 7%, with a further contraction to 5% achievable by 2010. Under the Plan, the Government aimed to increase expenditure on poverty-reduction programmes and infrastructural investment, while promoting diversification notably through creating an economic environment attractive to the private sector. Infrastructural developments in the mining sector were to be accompanied by progress towards participation in the international Extractive Industries Transparency Initiative. Policy in the agricultural sector was to focus on increased productivity and food security. The 2008 budget envisaged an overall increase of 14% in exenditure, with particular priority in areas of general public services, education and health. A 17% increase in tax revenue was to be derived principally from proposed changes to the tax regime for the mining sector, notably including a new 'windfall' tax for each base metal and a 15% levy on exports of copper concentrates. It was also aimed to capitalize on the strong export market for copper by maintaining international reserves at not less than three months' import cover. Meanwhile, a principal obstacle to further economic diversification, and thus a reduction in dependence on the copper sector, remained infrastructural inadequacies, particularly in the energy sector. To accompany efforts to rehabilitate and expand capacity for electricity generation, the IMF emphasized the necessity of improving the governance and efficiency of the state power monopoly, ZESCO Ltd, notably to include the negotiation of a new pricing structure for mining companies hitherto guaranteed priority supply at below-cost prices.

Education

Between 1964 and 1979 enrolment in schools increased by more than 260%. Primary education, which is compulsory, begins at seven years of age and lasts for seven years. Secondary education, beginning at the age of 14, lasts for a further five years, comprising a first cycle of two years and a second of three years. According to UNESCO estimates, in 2003/04 80% of children (80% of boys; 80% of girls) in the relevant age-group attended primary schools, while enrolment at secondary schools included 24% of children (27% of boys; 21% of girls) in the relevant age-group. There are two universities: the University of Zambia at Lusaka, and the Copperbelt University at Kitwe (which is to be transferred to Ndola). There are 14 teacher training colleges. In 2005 expenditure on education was K1,062.0m. The 2006 budgetary allocation for education was K1,647.0m., some 26.9% of the overall budget. The Government recruited an additional 8,000 teachers in 2005 and planned to recruit a further 4,500 in 2006.

Public Holidays

2008: 1 January (New Year's Day), 8 March ((International Women's Day), 11 March (Youth Day), 21–24 March (Easter), 1 May (Labour Day), 25 May (African Freedom Day, anniversary of OAU's foundation), 7 July (Heroes' Day), 8 July (Unity Day), 4 August (Farmers' Day), 24 October (Independence Day), 25 December (Christmas Day).

2009: 1 January (New Year's Day), 8 March ((International Women's Day), 11 March (Youth Day), 10–13 April (Easter), 1 May (Labour Day), 25 May (African Freedom Day, anniversary of OAU's foundation), 6 July (Heroes' Day), 7 July (Unity Day), 3 August (Farmers' Day), 24 October (Independence Day), 25 December (Christmas Day).

Weights and Measures

The metric system is in use.

Statistical Survey

Source (unless otherwise indicated): Central Statistical Office, POB 31908, Lusaka; tel. (1) 211231; internet www.zamstats.gov.zm.

Area and Population

AREA, POPULATION AND DENSITY

Area (sq km)	752,612*
Population (census results)	
20 August 1990	7,383,097
25 October 2000	
Males	4,946,298
Females	4,939,293
Total	9,885,591
Population (UN estimates at mid-year)†	
2005	11,478,000
2006	11,696,000
2007	11,922,000
Density (per sq km) at mid-2007	15.8

* 290,585 sq miles.
† Source: UN, *World Population Prospects: The 2006 Revision*.

PROVINCES
(2000 census)

	Area	Population	Density
Central	94,394	1,012,257	10.7
Copperbelt	31,328	1,581,221	50.5
Eastern	69,106	1,306,173	18.9
Luapula	50,567	775,353	15.3
Lusaka	21,896	1,391,329	63.5
Northern	147,826	1,258,696	8.5
North-Western	125,826	583,350	4.6
Southern	85,283	1,212,124	14.2
Western	126,386	765,088	6.1
Total	752,612	9,885,591	13.1

ZAMBIA

PRINCIPAL TOWNS
(population at 2000 census)

Lusaka (capital)	1,084,703	Lundazi	236,833
Kitwe	376,124	Petauke	235,879
Ndola	374,757	Choma	204,898
Chipata	367,539	Solwezi	203,797
Chibombo	241,612	Mazabuka	203,219

Mid-2007 ('000, incl. suburbs, UN estimate): Lusaka 1,328 (Source: UN, *World Urbanization Prospects: The 2007 Revision*).

BIRTHS AND DEATHS
(annual averages, UN estimates)

	1990–95	1995–2000	2000–05
Birth rate (per 1,000)	43.9	43.8	41.9
Death rate (per 1,000)	17.5	21.3	21.7

Source: UN, *World Population Prospects: The 2006 Revision*.

Expectation of life (years at birth, WHO estimates): 40.4 (males 40.2; females 40.5) in 2005 (Source: WHO, *World Health Statistics*).

EMPLOYMENT
(Usually active population aged 12 years and over at 2000 census)

Agriculture, hunting, forestry and fishing	2,014,028
Mining and quarrying	36,463
Manufacturing	77,515
Electricity, gas and water	11,016
Construction	36,790
Wholesale and retail trade; restaurants and hotels	190,354
Transport, storage and communication	53,736
Financial, insurance, real estate and business services	29,151
Community, social and personal services	363,375
Total	**2,812,428**

Source: ILO.

2006 (persons in paid employment, labour force survey, January): Agriculture, forestry and fishing 56,139; Mining and quarrying 26,253; Manufacturing 55,709; Electricity and water 12,399; Construction 14,343; Wholesale and retail trade 65,012; Transport and communication 19,378; Finance and insurance 54,032; Public administration 176,062; *Total* 479,327 (Source: IMF, *Zambia: Statistical Appendix* (January 2008)).

Health and Welfare

KEY INDICATORS

Total fertility rate (children per woman, 2005)	5.4
Under-5 mortality rate (per 1,000 live births, 2005)	182
HIV/AIDS (% of persons aged 15–49, 2005)	17.0
Physicians (per 1,000 head, 2004)	0.12
Hospital beds (per 1,000 head, 2004)	0.20
Health expenditure (2004): US $ per head (PPP)	62.8
Health expenditure (2004): % of GDP	6.3
Health expenditure (2004): public (% of total)	54.7
Access to water (% of persons, 2004)	58
Access to sanitation (% of persons, 2004)	55
Human Development Index (2005): ranking	165
Human Development Index (2005): value	0.434

For sources and definitions, see explanatory note on p. vi.

Agriculture

PRINCIPAL CROPS
('000 metric tons)

	2004	2005	2006
Wheat	85*	137	137†
Rice (paddy)	12	13	13†
Maize	1,214.0	866.2	865.0†
Millet	39.8	29.6	36.0†
Sorghum	24.5	18.7	19.0†
Potatoes	11†	14	14†
Sweet potatoes	53†	67	67†
Cassava (Manioc)	957	900	950†
Sugar cane	n.a.	n.a.	2,700†
Soybeans (Soya beans)*	14	12	12
Groundnuts (in shell)*	40	40	40
Sunflower seed*	9	8	8
Cottonseed†	12	11	11
Dry onions†	27	27	27
Tomatoes†	24	23	23
Cotton (lint)	n.a.	n.a.	43†
Tobacco (leaves)†	4.8	4.8	4.8

* Unofficial figure(s).
† FAO estimate(s).

Aggregate production ('000 metric tons, may include official, semi-official or estimated data): Total cereals 1,377 in 2004, 1,067 in 2005, 1,072 in 2006; Total pulses 17 in 2004, 17 in 2005, 17 in 2006; Total roots and tubers 1,021 in 2004, 981 in 2005, 1,031 in 2006; Total vegetables (incl. melons) 266 in 2004, 266 in 2005, 266 in 2006; Total fruits (excl. melons) 101 in 2004, 101 in 2005, 101 in 2006.

Source: FAO.

LIVESTOCK
('000 head, year ending September)

	1999	2000	2001*
Cattle	2,905	2,621	2,600
Sheep	120†	140†	150
Goats	1,069†	1,249†	1,270
Pigs	324†	309	340
Chickens*	28,000	29,000	30,000

* FAO estimates.
† Unofficial figure.

2002–06: Figures assumed to be unchanged from 2001 (FAO estimates).
Source: FAO.

LIVESTOCK PRODUCTS
('000 metric tons, FAO estimates)

	1999	2000	2001
Cattle meat	46.5	40.8	40.8
Pig meat	10.6	10.1	11.0
Chicken meat	33.5	35.0	36.5
Other meat	37.4	38.6	38.8
Cows' milk	61.5	64.2	64.2
Hen eggs	44.8	46.4	48.0
Cattle hides	6.3	5.4	5.4

2002–06: Hen eggs 46.4 in 2003, all other figures assumed to be unchanged from 2001 (FAO estimates).

Source: FAO.

Forestry

ROUNDWOOD REMOVALS
('000 cubic metres, FAO estimates)

	2004	2005	2006
Sawlogs, veneer logs and logs for sleepers	319	319	319
Other industrial wood	515	515	515
Fuel wood	7,219	7,219	8,573
Total	8,053	8,053	9,407

Source: FAO.

SAWNWOOD PRODUCTION
('000 cubic metres, incl. railway sleepers, FAO estimates)

	1995	1996	1997
Coniferous (softwood)	300	230	145
Broadleaved (hardwood)	20	15	12
Total	320	245	157

1998–2006: Figures assumed to be unchanged from 1997 (FAO estimates).
Source: FAO.

Fishing

('000 metric tons, live weight)

	2003	2004	2005*
Capture	65.0*	65.0*	65.0
Dagaas	8.5*	8.5*	8.5
Other freshwater fishes	56.5*	56.5*	56.5
Aquaculture	4.5	5.1	5.1
Three-spotted tilapia	2.3	2.0	2.0
Total catch*	69.5	70.1	70.1

* FAO estimate(s).

Note: Figures exclude aquatic animals, recorded by number rather than weight. The number of Nile crocodiles caught was: 28,019 in 2003; 26,353 in 2004; 23,133 in 2005.
Source: FAO.

Mining

(estimates)

	2004	2005	2006
Coal ('000 metric tons)	240.0	240.0	100.0
Copper ore ('000 metric tons)*	426.9	447.0	514.0
Cobalt ore (metric tons)*	10,000	9,300	8,000
Amethysts ('000 kilograms)	1,100	1,100	1,200

* Figures refer to the metal content of ore.
Source: US Geological Survey.

Industry

SELECTED PRODUCTS
('000 metric tons, unless otherwise indicated, estimates)

	2004	2005	2006
Cement	390	435	650
Copper (unwrought): smelter	280	270	290
Copper (unwrought): refined	410	399	460
Cobalt (refined, metric tons)	5,791	5,422	4,665

* Estimates.

Raw sugar ('000 metric tons): 189 in 2000; 279 in 2001; 232 in 2002.
Electric energy (million kWh): 8,448 in 2004; 8,255 in 2005; 8,906 in 2006.

Sources: FAO; US Geological Survey; UN, *Industrial Commodity Statistics Yearbook*; IMF, *Zambia: Statistical Appendix* (January 2008).

Finance

CURRENCY AND EXCHANGE RATES

Monetary Units
100 ngwee = 1 Zambian kwacha (K).

Sterling, Dollar and Euro Equivalents (30 November 2007)
£1 sterling = 7,763.2 kwacha;
US $1 = 3,756.9 kwacha;
€1 = 5,545.5 kwacha;
10,000 Zambian kwacha = £1.29 = $2.66 = €1.80.

Average Exchange Rate (Zambian kwacha per US $)
2004 4,778.88
2005 4,463.50
2006 3,603.07

CENTRAL GOVERNMENT BUDGET
(K '000 million)*

Revenue	2004	2005	2006
Tax revenue	4,546	5,512	6,317
Income tax	2,028	2,416	2,902
Excise taxes	607	768	821
Value-added tax (VAT)	1,362	1,633	1,792
Customs duty	544	656	744
Extractive industries royalty	4	39	59
Non-tax revenue	194	130	301
Total†	4,740	5,642	6,618

Expenditure	2004	2005	2006
Current expenditure	4,569	5,828	7,203
Wages and salaries	2,012	2,455	2,833
Goods and services	784	1,249	1,779
Interest payments	898	865	749
Domestic	746	731	689
External	152	133	60
Other current expenditure	876	1,259	1,842
Capital expenditure	2,265	2,267	1,601
Domestic arrears payments	84	254	247
Total	6,919	8,350	9,051

* The budgetary out-turn includes a statistical discrepancy; a negative value indicates overfinancing (K '000 million): n.a. in 2004; 24 in 2005; −483 in 2006.
† Excluding grants received (K '000 million): 1,433 in 2004; 1,825 in 2005; 10,207 in 2006.

Sources: IMF, *Zambia: Statistical Appendix* (January 2008) and *Zambia: 2007 Article IV Consultation—Staff Report; Staff Statement; Public Information Notice on the Executive Board Discussion; and Statement by the Executive Director for Zambia*.

ZAMBIA

INTERNATIONAL RESERVES
(US $ million at 31 December)

	2005	2006	2007
IMF special drawing rights	15.7	13.3	9.7
Foreign exchange	544.0	706.4	1,080.2
Total	559.8	719.7	1,089.9

Source: IMF, *International Financial Statistics*.

MONEY SUPPLY
(K '000 million at 31 December)

	2005	2006	2007
Currency outside banks	818.9	1,066.4	1,299.8
Demand deposits at commercial banks	1,338.3	2,264.8	2,511.8
Total money (incl. others)	2,168.2	3,340.1	3,828.9

Source: IMF, *International Financial Statistics*.

COST OF LIVING
(Consumer Price Index; low-income group; base: 2000 = 100)

	2001	2002	2003
Food (incl. alcohol and tobacco)	118.9	151.1	184.5
Clothing and footwear	120.5	139.4	168.8
Fuel and rent	121.4	145.1	176.5
All items (incl. others)	121.4	148.4	180.1

Food (incl. alcohol and tobacco): 214.7 in 2004; 254.5 in 2005; 267.1 in 2006.

All items: 212.5 in 2004; 251.4 in 2005; 274.1 in 2006.

Source: ILO.

NATIONAL ACCOUNTS
Expenditure on the Gross Domestic Product
(US $ million at current prices)

	2004	2005	2006
Final consumption expenditure	4,695.00	5,805.43	8,193.24
Households	3,676.67	4,809.90	6,753.33
General government	1,018.33	995.53	1,439.91
Gross fixed capital formation	1,617.30	1,669.82	2,576.73
Total domestic expenditure	6,312.40	7,475.25	10,769.97
Exports of goods and services	1,525.61	2,465.15	3,304.85
Less Imports of goods and services	2,397.84	2,670.38	3,130.27
GDP in purchasers' values	5,440.07	7,270.02	10,944.55

Source: African Development Bank.

Gross Domestic Product by Economic Activity
(K '000 million at current prices)

	2004	2005	2006
Agriculture, forestry and fishing	5,568	6,724	7,800
Mining and quarrying	810	1,031	1,613
Manufacturing	2,828	3,430	4,016
Electricity, gas and water	695	923	1,166
Construction	2,402	3,728	5,463
Wholesale and retail trade, restaurants and hotels	4,844	5,869	6,525
Transport and communications	1,252	1,396	1,629
Finance and insurance	2,283	2,772	3,247
Real estate and business services	1,692	1,979	2,296
Restaurants and hotels	671	894	1,120
Community, social and personal services*	2,047	2,710	3,366
Other services	907	1,001	983
Sub-total	25,997	32,456	39,223
Import duties	2,219	2,594	2,849
Less imputed bank service charge	1,312	1,593	1,866
GDP in purchasers' values	26,904	33,457	40,207

*Includes public administration, defence, sanitary services, education, health, recreation, and personal services.

Source: IMF, *Zambia: Statistical Appendix* (January 2008).

BALANCE OF PAYMENTS
(US $ million, preliminary)

	2004	2005	2006
Exports of goods f.o.b.	1,847	2,210	3,819
Imports of goods f.o.b.	−1,872	−2,161	−2,636
Trade balance	−25	50	1,183
Services (net)	−215	−199	−284
Balance on goods and services	−240	−150	899
Income (net)	−397	−619	−960
Interest payments	−121	−110	−17
Balance on goods, services and income	−637	−769	−61
Current transfers (net)	19	107	180
Current account	−618	−662	120
Capital and financial accounts (net)	258	704	1,013
Net errors and omissions	139	−172	−311
Overall balance	−220	−129	822

Source: IMF, *Zambia: Statistical Appendix* (January 2008).

External Trade

PRINCIPAL COMMODITIES
(US $ million)

Imports c.i.f.	2004	2005	2006
Food and live animals	98.2	113.1	175.1
Beverages and tobacco	2.3	3.2	10.3
Crude materials except fuels	68.9	89.6	83.1
Mineral fuels, lubricants and related materials	244.1	279.1	453.2
Animal and vegetable oils, fats and waxes	41.2	41.7	48.9
Chemicals	345.3	457.5	446.1
Basic manufactures	314.2	405.8	429.1
Machinery and transport equipment	670.6	814.2	1,207.2
Miscellaneous manufactured articles	364.8	372.4	169.3
Total (incl. others)	2,149.6	2,576.6	3,022.4

Exports f.o.b.	2004	2005	2006
Food and live animals	152.1	172.9	139.4
Beverages and tobacco	61.1	74.1	74.9
Crude materials except fuels	237.6	258.4	536.8
Mineral fuels, lubricants and related materials	27.8	13.9	22.6
Chemicals	41.6	15.7	23.2
Basic manufactures	1,016.0	1,558.0	2,772.1
Machinery and transport equipment	17.5	23.4	101.5
Miscellaneous manufactured articles	22.2	59.3	10.0
Other	270.4	34.2	138.0
Total (incl. others)	1,846.9	2,210.4	3,819.2

Source: IMF, *Zambia: Statistical Appendix* (January 2008).

ZAMBIA

PRINCIPAL TRADING PARTNERS
(US $ million)

Imports c.i.f.	2004	2005	2006
China, People's Repub.	46.1	83.8	81.4
Congo, Democratic Repub.	14.1	23.3	30.5
Finland	22.7	12.1	12.9
France	72.2	93.6	22.1
Germany	22.1	35.8	44.1
India	50.6	80.6	85.2
Japan	28.8	41.9	47.6
Kenya	34.1	38.0	55.3
Netherlands	11.2	30.6	45.5
South Africa	993.5	1,228.5	1,430.6
Tanzania	30.1	68.5	54.1
United Arab Emirates	145.1	96.1	313.0
United Kingdom	317.8	312.7	111.4
USA	34.9	41.9	57.2
Zimbabwe	124.6	110.2	171.5
Total (incl. others)	2,149.6	2,576.6	3,022.4

Exports f.o.b.	2004	2005	2006
Belgium	36.6	31.4	9.0
Botswana	2.9	40.4	6.0
China, People's Repub.	33.9	192.1	257.7
Congo, Democratic Repub.	106.0	102.0	128.4
Egypt	0.7	79.5	151.1
India	16.8	32.8	133.3
Japan	7.0	29.8	3.7
Korea, Repub.	0.0	65.1	44.4
Malawi	48.1	70.8	57.6
Malaysia	0.0	52.7	77.2
Netherlands	47.8	46.0	44.3
Pakistan	0.0	24.6	49.2
Saudi Arabia	0.0	60.2	84.3
South Africa	386.4	195.9	401.4
Switzerland	255.5	754.1	1,462.6
Taiwan	44.7	2.9	71.4
Tanzania	120.9	11.5	13.8
Thailand	1.1	98.9	284.7
United Kingdom	275.1	74.5	99.4
Zimbabwe	89.4	76.4	51.7
Total (incl. others)	1,846.9	2,210.4	3,819.2

Source: IMF, *Zambia: Statistical Appendix* (January 2008).

Transport

ROAD TRAFFIC
(estimates, '000 motor vehicles in use at 31 December)

	1994	1995	1996
Passenger cars	123	142	157
Lorries and vans	68	74	81

Source: IRF, *World Road Statistics*.

CIVIL AVIATION
(traffic on scheduled services)

	2001	2002	2003
Kilometres flown (million)	2	2	2
Passengers carried ('000)	49	47	45
Passenger-km (million)	16	16	14
Total ton-km (million)	1	1	1

Source: UN, *Statistical Yearbook*.

Tourism

VISITOR ARRIVALS BY NATIONALITY
(provisional figures)

	2003	2004	2005
Australia	5,597	7,490	16,336
South Africa	62,604	110,710	110,272
Tanzania	30,776	33,502	65,881
United Kingdom	31,072	37,520	44,369
USA	15,879	20,547	23,895
Zimbabwe	138,288	123,573	148,436
Total (incl. others)	412,675	515,000	668,862

Tourism receipts (US $ million, incl. passenger transport): 149 in 2003; 161 in 2004; 164 in 2005.

Source: World Tourism Organization.

Communications Media

	2004	2005	2006
Telephones ('000 main lines in use)	91.7	94.7	93.4
Mobile cellular telephones ('000 subscribers)	464.4	949.6	1,663.3
Personal computers ('000 in use)	113	113	n.a.
Internet users ('000)	231.0	334.8	500.0
Broadband subscribers ('000)	0.2	0.2	2.3

Radio receivers ('000 in use): 1,436 in 1999.

Television receivers ('000 in use): 540 in 2001.

Facsimile machines (number in use): 1,005 (estimate) in year ending 31 March 1999.

Daily newspapers: 3 (average circulation 114,000 copies) in 1996; 3 in 2004.

Sources: UNESCO, *Statistical Yearbook*; UNESCO Institute for Statistics; UN, *Statistical Yearbook*; International Telecommunication Union.

Education

(2004/05 unless otherwise indicated)

	Institutions	Teachers	Students
Primary	4,221*	50,224	2,565,419
Secondary	n.a.	33,964†	408,971
Tertiary	n.a.	n.a.	24,553‡

* 1998 figure.
† 2002/03 estimate.
‡ 1999/2000 estimate.

Source: UNESCO Institute for Statistics.

Adult literacy rate (UNESCO estimates): 68.0% (males 76.3%; females 59.8%) in 1999 (Source: UNESCO Institute for Statistics).

Directory

The Constitution

The Constitution for the Republic of Zambia, which was formally adopted on 28 May 1996 (amending the Constitution of 1991), provides for a multi-party form of government. The Head of State is the President of the Republic, who is elected by popular vote at the same time as elections to the National Assembly. The President's tenure of office is limited to two five-year terms. Foreign nationals and those with foreign parentage are prohibited from contesting the presidency. The legislature comprises a National Assembly of 158 members: 150 are elected by universal adult suffrage, while the remaining eight are nominated by the President. The President appoints a Vice-President and a Cabinet from members of the National Assembly.

The Constitution also provides for a House of Chiefs numbering 27: four from each of the Northern, Western, Southern and Eastern Provinces, three each from the North-Western, Luapula and Central Provinces and two from the Copperbelt Province. It may submit resolutions to be debated by the Assembly and consider those matters referred to it by the President.

The Supreme Court of Zambia is the final Court of Appeal. The Chief Justice and other judges are appointed by the President. Subsidiary to the Supreme Court is the High Court, which has unlimited jurisdiction to hear and determine any civil or criminal proceedings under any Zambian law.

The Government

HEAD OF STATE

President: LEVY PATRICK MWANAWASA (took office 2 January 2002; re-elected 28 September 2006).

THE CABINET
(April 2008)

President: LEVY PATRICK MWANAWASA.
Vice-President: RUPIAH BANDA.
Minister of Home Affairs: RONNIE SHIKAPWASHA.
Minister of Foreign Affairs: KABINGA PANDE.
Minister of Defence: GEORGE MPOMBO.
Minister of Finance and National Planning: NG'ANDU PETER MAGANDE.
Minister of Commerce, Trade and Industry: FELIX MUTATI.
Minister of Justice: GEORGE KUNDA.
Minister of Agriculture, Food and Fisheries: BEN KAPITA.
Minister of Communications and Transport: SARAH SAYIFWANDA.
Minister of Energy and Water Development: KENNETH KONGA.
Minister of Tourism, the Environment and Natural Resources: MICHAEL KAINGU.
Minister of Education: GEOFFREY LUNGWANGWA.
Minister of Science, Technology and Vocational Training: PETER DAKA.
Minister of Health: Brig.-Gen. Dr BRIAN CHITUWO.
Minister of Local Government and Housing: SYLVIA MASEBO.
Minister of Works and Supply: KAPEMBWA SIMBAO.
Minister of Community Development and Social Services: CATHERINE NAMUGALA.
Minister of Sport, Youth and Child Development: GABRIEL NAMULAMBE.
Minister of Lands: BRADFORD MACHILA.
Minister of Labour and Social Security: RONALD MUYKUMA.
Minister of Mines and Mineral Development: KALOMBO MWANSA.
Minister of Information and Broadcasting Services: MIKE MULONGOTI.
Minister of Gender and Development: PATRICIA MULASIKAWANDA.

There are, in addition, 23 Deputy Ministers.

MINISTRIES

Office of the President: POB 30135, Lusaka; tel. (1) 266147; fax (1) 266092; internet www.statehouse.gov.zm.
Ministry of Agriculture, Food and Fisheries: Mulungushi House, Independence Ave, Nationalist Rd, POB RW50291, Lusaka; tel. (1) 213551.
Ministry of Commerce, Trade and Industry: Kwacha Annex, Cairo Rd, POB 31968, Lusaka; tel. (1) 213767.
Ministry of Communications and Transport: Fairley Rd, POB 50065, Lusaka; tel. (1) 251444; fax (1) 253260.
Ministry of Community Development and Social Welfare: Fidelity House, POB 31958, Lusaka; tel. (1) 228321; fax (1) 225327.
Ministry of Defence: POB 31931, Lusaka; tel. (1) 252366.
Ministry of Education: 15102 Ridgeway, POB RW50093, Lusaka; tel. (1) 227636; fax (1) 222396.
Ministry of Energy and Water Development: Mulungushi House, Independence Ave, Nationalist Rd, POB 36079, Lusaka; tel. and fax (1) 252589.
Ministry of Finance and National Planning: Finance Bldg, POB 50062, Lusaka; tel. (1) 253512; fax (1) 251078.
Ministry of Foreign Affairs: POB RW50069, Lusaka; tel. (1) 213822; fax (1) 222440.
Ministry of Gender and Development: Lusaka.
Ministry of Health: Woodgate House, 1st–2nd Floors, Cairo Rd, POB 30205, Lusaka; tel. (1) 227745; fax (1) 228385.
Ministry of Home Affairs: POB 32862, Lusaka; tel. (1) 213505.
Ministry of Information and Broadcasting Services: Independence Ave, POB 32245, Lusaka; tel. (1) 228202; fax (1) 253457.
Ministry of Justice: Fairley Rd, POB 50106, 15101, Ridgeway, Lusaka; tel. (1) 228522.
Ministry of Labour and Social Security: Lechwe House, Freedom Way, POB 32186, Lusaka; tel. (1) 212020.
Ministry of Lands: POB 50694, Lusaka; tel. (1) 252288; fax (1) 250120.
Ministry of Local Government and Housing: Church Rd, POB 34204, Lusaka; tel. (1) 253077; fax (1) 252680.
Ministry of Mines and Mineral Development: Chilufya Mulenga Rd, POB 31969, 10101 Lusaka; tel. (1) 251402; fax (1) 252095.
Ministry of Science, Technology and Vocational Training: POB 50464, Lusaka; tel. (1) 229673; fax (1) 252951.
Ministry of Sport, Youth and Child Development: Memaco House, POB 50195, Lusaka; tel. (1) 227158; fax (1) 223996.
Ministry of Tourism, the Environment and Natural Resources: Electra House, Cairo Rd, POB 30575, Lusaka; tel. (1) 227645; fax (1) 222189.
Ministry of Works and Supply: POB 50003, Lusaka; tel. (1) 253088; fax (1) 253404.

President and Legislature

PRESIDENT

Presidential Election, 28 September 2006

Candidate	Votes	% of votes
Levy Patrick Mwanawasa (MMD)	1,177,846	42.98
Michael C. Sata (PF)	804,748	29.37
Hakainde Hichilema (UDA)	693,772	25.32
Brig.-Gen. Godfrey K. Miyanda (HP)	42,891	1.57
Winright K. Ngondo (APC)	20,921	0.76
Total	**2,740,178**	**100.00**

NATIONAL ASSEMBLY

Speaker: AMUSAA KATUNDA MWANAMWAMBWA.

General Election, 28 September 2006*

Party	Seats
Movement for Multi-party Democracy (MMD)	75
Patriotic Front (PF)	43
United Democratic Alliance (UDA)†	26
Independents	3
United Liberal Party (ULP)	2
National Democratic Focus (NDF)	1
Total	**150**

* Includes the results of voting in two constituencies where the elections were postponed until 26 October 2006, owing to the deaths of candidates.

† Coalition of the Forum for Democracy and Development (FDD), the United National Independence Party (UNIP) and the United Party for National Development (UPND).

ZAMBIA   *Directory*

House of Chiefs

The House of Chiefs is an advisory body which may submit resolutions for debate by the National Assembly. There are 27 Chiefs, four each from the Northern, Western, Southern and Eastern Provinces, three each from the North-Western, Luapula and Central Provinces, and two from the Copperbelt Province.

Election Commission

Electoral Commission of Zambia (ECZ): Ndeke Annex, Haile Selassie Ave, POB 50274, Longacres, Lusaka; tel. (1) 253155; fax (1) 253884; e-mail elections@electcom.org.zm; internet www.elections.org.zm; f. 1996; independent; Chair. IRENE MAMBILIMA; Dir DAN KALALE.

Political Organizations

Democratic Party (DP): Plot C4, President Ave (North), POB 71628, Ndola; f. 1991; Pres. EMMANUEL MWAMBA.

Heritage Party (HP): POB 51055, Lusaka; f. 2001 by expelled mems of the MMD; Pres. Brig.-Gen. GODFREY K. MIYANDA.

Liberal Progressive Front (LPF): POB 31190, Lusaka; f. 1993; Pres. Dr RODGER CHONGWE.

Movement for Multi-party Democracy (MMD): POB 30708, Lusaka; f. 1990; governing party since Nov. 1991; Nat. Chair. BONIFACE KAWIMBE; Nat. Sec. VERNON MWAANGA.

National Democratic Front: Lusaka; f. 2006 to contest the presidential election; Acting Chair. NEVERS MUMBA (RP).

Comprising:

All Peoples' Congress Party (APC): Lusaka; f. 2005 by fmr mems of the FDD; Pres. WINRIGHT K. NGONDO.

Party for Unity, Democracy and Development (PUDD): Lusaka; f. 2004 by fmr mems of the MMD; Pres. CHITALU SAMPA.

Reform Party: Lusaka; f. 2005 by fmr mems of the MMD; Pres. NEVERS MUMBA; Nat. Chair. EVA SANDERSON; Sec.-Gen. CLEMENT MICHELO.

Zambia Democratic Conference (ZADECO): Lusaka; f. 1998 as the Zambia Democratic Congress Popular Front by fmr mems of the Zambia Democratic Congress; disbanded in 1999; reformed after 2001 election by fmr mems of the ZAP; Pres. Rev. Dr DAN PULE.

Zambia Republican Party (ZRP): Lusaka; f. 2001 by merger of the Republican Party (f. 2000) and the Zambia Alliance for Progress (f. 1999); Gen. Sec. SILVIA MASEBO; Nat. Chair. BEN KAPITA.

National Leadership for Development (NLD): POB 34161, Lusaka; f. 2000; Pres. Dr YOBERT K. SHAMAPANDE.

National Party (NP): POB 37840, Lusaka 10101; tel. (1) 8491431; e-mail nationalparty1993@yahoo.com; f. 1993; by fmr mems of MMD; promotes human rights; Pres. Rev. RICHARD KAMBULU; Sec.-Gen. NDANISO BANDA.

Patriotic Front (PF): f. 2001 by expelled mems of the MMD; Pres. MICHAEL C. SATA; Sec.-Gen. GUY SCOTT.

United Democratic Alliance (UDA): Kenneth Kaunda House, Cairo Rd, Lusaka; f. 2006 to contest that year's elections; Nat. Chair. TILYENJI KAUNDA (FDD).

Comprising:

Forum for Democracy and Development (FDD): POB 35868, Lusaka; f. 2001 by expelled mems of the MMD; Pres. EDITH NAWAKWI; Chair. SIMON ZUKAS.

United National Independence Party (UNIP): POB 30302, Lusaka; tel. (1) 221197; fax (1) 221327; f. 1959; sole legal party 1972–90; Pres. TILYENJI KAUNDA; Nat. Chair. KEN KAIRA.

United Party for National Development (UPND): POB 33199, Lusaka; internet www.upnd.org; f. 1998; incl. fmr mems of the Progressive People's Party and Zambia Dem. Party; Pres. HAKAINDE HICHILEMA.

Unity Party for Democrats (UPD): POB RW28, Ridgeway, Lusaka; f. 1997; Pres. MATHEW PIKITI.

Zambia Alliance for Progress (ZAP): Lusaka; f. 1999; re-registered as ZAP in 2001 after splitting from Zambia Republican Party; Pres. (vacant).

Diplomatic Representation

EMBASSIES AND HIGH COMMISSIONS IN ZAMBIA

Angola: Plot 108, Great East Rd, Northmead, POB 31595, 10101 Lusaka; tel. (1) 34764; fax (1) 221210; Ambassador PEDRO DE MORAIS NETO.

Botswana: 5201 Pandit Nehru Rd, Diplomatic Triangle, POB 31910, 10101 Lusaka; tel. (1) 250555; fax (1) 250804; High Commissioner LAPOLOGANG CAESAR LEKOA.

Brazil: 74 Anglo American Bldg, Independence Ave, POB 33300; tel. (1) 250400; fax (1) 251652; e-mail brasemblusaca@iconnect.zm; Chargé d'affaires a.i. PAULO M. G. DE SOUSA.

Canada: Plot 5199, United Nations Ave, POB 31313, 10101 Lusaka; tel. (1) 250833; fax (1) 254176; e-mail lsaka@international.gc.ca; High Commissioner JOHN DEYELL.

China, People's Republic: Plot 7430, United Nations Ave, Longacres, POB 31975, 10101 Lusaka; tel. (1) 251169; fax (1) 251157; Ambassador LI QIANGMIN.

Congo, Democratic Republic: Plot 1124, Parirenyatwa Rd, POB 31287, 10101 Lusaka; tel. and fax (1) 235679; Ambassador JOHNSON WA BINANA.

Cuba: 5574 Mogoye Rd, Kalundu, POB 33132, 10101 Lusaka; tel. (1) 291308; fax (1) 291586; e-mail ambassador@iconnect.zm; Ambassador NARCISO MARTÍN MORA DÍAZ.

Denmark: 4 Manenekela Rd, POB 50299, Lusaka; tel. (1) 254277; fax (1) 254618; e-mail lunamb@um.dk; internet www.amblusaka.um.dk/en; Ambassador ORLA BAKDAL.

Egypt: Plot 5206, United Nations Ave, Longacres, POB 32428, Lusaka 10101; tel. (1) 250229; fax (1) 254149; Ambassador MOHAMED TAMER SAAD ELDIN MANSOUR.

Finland: Haile Selassie Ave, opp. Ndeke House, Longacres, POB 50819, 15101 Lusaka; tel. (1) 251988; fax (1) 253783; e-mail sanomat.lus@formin.fi; internet www.finland.org.zm; Ambassador SINIKKA ANTILA.

France: Anglo American Bldg, 4th Floor, 74 Independence Ave, POB 30062, 10101 Lusaka; tel. (1) 251322; fax (1) 254475; e-mail france@ambafrance-zm.org; internet www.ambafrance-zm.org; Ambassador FRANCIS SAUDUBRAY.

Germany: Plot 5209, United Nations Ave, POB 50120, 15101 Ridgeway, Lusaka; tel. (1) 250644; fax (1) 254014; e-mail info@lusaka.diplo.de; internet www.lusaka.diplo.de; Ambassador Dr IRENE HINRICHSEN.

Holy See: 283 Los Angeles Blvd, POB 31445, 10101 Lusaka; tel. (1) 251033; fax (1) 250601; e-mail nuntius@coppernet.zm; Apostolic Nuncio Most Rev. NICOLA GIRASOLI (Titular Archbishop of Egnazia Appula).

India: 1 Pandit Nehru Rd, POB 32111, 10101 Lusaka; tel. (1) 253159; fax (1) 254118; High Commissioner YOGESH K. GUPTA.

Ireland: 6663 Katima Mulilo Rd, Olympia Park, POB 34923, 10101 Lusaka; tel. (1) 290650; fax (1) 290482; Ambassador BILL NOLAN.

Italy: Plot 5211, Embassy Park, Diplomatic Triangle, POB 50497, Lusaka; tel. (1) 250781; fax (1) 254929; e-mail ambasciata.lusaka@esteri.it; internet www.amblusaka.esteri.it; Ambassador Dr GIOVANNI CERUTI.

Japan: Plot 5218, Haile Selassie Ave, POB 34190, 10101 Lusaka; tel. (1) 251555; fax (1) 254425; internet www.zm.emb-japan.go.jp; Ambassador MASAAKI MIYASHITA.

Kenya: 5207 United Nations Ave, POB 50298, 10101 Lusaka; tel. (1) 250722; fax (1) 253829; e-mail kenhigh@zamnet.zm; High Commissioner LAZARUS O. AMAYO.

Libya: 251 Ngwee Rd, off United Nations Ave, Longacres, POB 35319, 10101 Lusaka; tel. (1) 253055; fax (1) 251239; Ambassador KHALIFA OMER SWIEXI.

Malawi: 31 Bishops Rd, Kabulonga, POB 50425, Lusaka; tel. (1) 213750; fax (1) 265764; e-mail mhcomm@zamtel.zm; High Commissioner Dr CHRISSIE MUGHOGHO.

Mozambique: Kacha Rd, Plot 9592, POB 34877, 10101 Lusaka; tel. (1) 220333; fax (1) 220345; High Commissioner SHAHARUDDIN MOHAMMED SOM.

Namibia: 30B Mutende Rd, Woodlands, POB 30577, 10101 Lusaka; tel. (1) 260407; fax (1) 263858; High Commissioner FRIEDA NANGULA ITHETE.

Netherlands: 5208 United Nations Ave, POB 31905, 10101 Lusaka; tel. (1) 253819; fax (1) 253733; e-mail lus@minbuza.nl; internet www.netherlandsembassy.org.zm; Ambassador EDUARD J. M. MIDDELDORP.

Nigeria: 17 Broads Rd, Fairview, POB 32598, Lusaka; tel. (1) 229860; fax (1) 223791; High Commissioner Chief IBIRONKE O. VAUGHAN-ADEFOPE.

ZAMBIA   *Directory*

Norway: cnr Birdcage Walk and Haile Selassie Ave, Longacres, POB 34570, 10101 Lusaka; tel. (1) 252188; fax (1) 253915; e-mail emb.lusaka@mfa.no; internet www.norway.org.zm; Ambassador TERJE VIGTEL.
Russia: Plot 6407, Diplomatic Triangle, POB 32355, 10101 Lusaka; tel. (1) 252120; fax (1) 253582; internet www.russianembassy.biz/zambia-lusaka.htm; Ambassador ANVAR AZIMOV.
Saudi Arabia: 27BC Leopards Hill Rd, Kabulonga, POB 34411, 10101 Lusaka; tel. (1) 266861; fax (1) 266863; e-mail saudiemb@uudial.zm; Ambassador TALAT SALEM RADWAN.
Serbia: Independence Ave 5216, POB 33379, 10101 Lusaka; tel. (1) 250235; fax (1) 253889; e-mail serbianemba@zamnet.zm; Chargé d'affaires a.i. MIRKO MANOJLOVIC.
Somalia: G3/377A Kabulonga Rd, POB 34051, Lusaka; tel. (1) 262119; Ambassador Dr OMAN UMAL.
South Africa: D26, Cheetah Rd, Kabulonga, Private Bag W369, Lusaka; tel. (1) 260999; fax (1) 263001; e-mail sahcadmin@samnet.zm; High Commissioner MOSES MABOKELA CHIKANE.
Sudan: 31 Ng'umbo Rd, Longacres, POB RW179X, 15200 Lusaka; tel. (1) 215570; fax (1) 40653; Ambassador ABDALLAH KHIDIR BASHIR.
Sweden: Haile Selassie Ave, POB 50264, 10101 Lusaka; tel. (1) 251711; fax (1) 254049; e-mail ambassaden.lusaka@foreign.ministry.se; internet www.swedenabroad.com/lusaka; Ambassador LARS RONNÅS.
Tanzania: Ujamaa House, Plot 5200, United Nations Ave, POB 31219, 10101 Lusaka; tel. (1) 253222; fax (1) 254861; e-mail tzreplsk@zamnet.zm; High Commissioner GEORGE MWANJABALA.
United Kingdom: Plot 5201, Independence Ave, POB 50050, 15101 Ridgeway, Lusaka; tel. (1) 251133; fax (1) 253798; High Commissioner ALISTAIR HARRISON.
USA: cnr Independence and United Nations Aves, POB 31617, Lusaka; tel. (1) 250955; fax (1) 252225; internet zambia.usembassy.gov; Ambassador CARMEN M. MARTINEZ.
Zimbabwe: 11058, Haile Selassie Ave, Longacres, POB 33491, 10101 Lusaka; tel. (1) 254012; fax (1) 227474; Ambassador KOSHO DUBE.

Judicial System

The judicial system of Zambia comprises a Supreme Court, composed of a Chief Justice, a Deputy Chief Justice and five Justices; a High Court comprising the Chief Justice and 30 Judges; Senior Resident and Resident Magistrates' Courts, which sit at various centres; and Local Courts, which deal principally with customary law, but which also have limited criminal jurisdiction.

Supreme Court of Zambia
Independence Ave, POB 50067, Ridgeway, Lusaka; tel. (1) 251330; fax (1) 251743.
Chief Justice: ERNEST L. SAKALA.
Deputy Chief Justice: DAVID M. LEWANIKA.
Supreme Court Judges: LOMBE CHIBESAKUNDA, DENNIS CHIRWA, PETER CHITENGI, IREEN MAMBILIMA, SANDSON SILOMBA.

Religion

CHRISTIANITY
Council of Churches in Zambia: Church House, Cairo Rd, POB 30315, Lusaka; tel. (1) 229551; fax (1) 224308; e-mail info@ccz.org.zm; f. 1945; Chair. Rt Rev. THUMA HAMUKANG'ANDU (Brethren in Christ Church); Gen. Sec. JAPHET NDHLOVU; 22 mem. churches and 18 affiliate mem. orgs.

The Anglican Communion
Anglicans are adherents of the Church of the Province of Central Africa, covering Botswana, Malawi, Zambia and Zimbabwe. The Church comprises 15 dioceses, including five in Zambia. The Archbishop of the Province is the Bishop of Upper Shire in Malawi. There are an estimated 80,000 adherents in Zambia.
Bishop of Central Zambia: Rt Rev. DEREK G. KAMUKWAMBA, POB 70172, Ndola; tel. (2) 612431; fax (2) 615954; e-mail adcznla@zamnet.zm.
Bishop of Eastern Zambia: Rt Rev. WILLIAM MUCHOMBO, POB 510154, Chipata; tel. and fax (6) 221294; e-mail dioeastzm@zamnet.zm.
Bishop of Luapula: Rt Rev. ROBERT MUMBI, POB 710210, Mansa, Luapula.
Bishop of Lusaka: Rt Rev. DAVID NJOVU, Bishop's Lodge, POB 30183, Lusaka; tel. (1) 264515; fax (1) 262379; e-mail angdiolu@zamnet.zm.
Bishop of Northern Zambia: Rt Rev. ALBERT CHAMA, POB 20798, Kitwe; tel. (2) 223264; fax (2) 224778; e-mail dionorth@zamnet.zm.

Protestant Churches
At mid-2000 there were an estimated 2.7m. Protestants.
African Methodist Episcopal Church: Carousel Bldg, Lumumba Rd, POB 36628, Lusaka; tel. (1) 95708031; fax (1) 225067; Presiding Elder Rev. PAUL KAWIMBE; 440 congregations, 880,000 mems.
Baptist Church: Lubu Rd, POB 30636, Lusaka; tel. (1) 253620.
Baptist Mission of Zambia: Baptist Bldg, 3062 Great East Rd, POB 50599, 15101 Ridgeway, Lusaka; tel. (1) 222492; fax (1) 227520; internet bmoz.org.
Brethren in Christ Church: POB 630115, Choma; tel. (3) 20228; fax (3) 20127; e-mail biccz@zamtel.zm; internet www.bic.org; f. 1906; Bishop Rev. E. SHAMAPANI; 165 congregations, 17,623 mems.
Reformed Church in Zambia: POB 38255, Lusaka; tel. (1) 295369; e-mail info@rczsynod.co.zm; internet www.rczsynod.co.zm; f. 1899; African successor to the Dutch Reformed Church mission; Gen. Sec. Rev. WILLIAM ZULU (acting); 147 congregations, 400,000 mems.
Seventh-day Adventist Church: Plot 9221, cnr Burma Rd and Independence Ave, POB 36010, Lusaka; tel. and fax (1) 254036; e-mail lcsdac@zamnet.zm; internet www.lcsdac.net.zm; f. 1905; Pres. Dr CORNELIUS MULENGA MATANDIKO; Sec. HARRINGTON SIMUI AKOMBWA; 534,126 mems.
United Church of Zambia: Synod Headquarters, Nationalist Rd at Burma Rd, POB 50122, Lusaka; tel. (1) 250641; fax (1) 252198; e-mail uczsynod@zamnet.zm; f. 1965; Synod Bishop Rev. MUTALE MULUMBWA (Interim Synod Bishop); Gen. Sec. Rev. Prof. TEDDY KALONGO; c. 3m. mems.

Other denominations active in Zambia include the Assemblies of God, the Church of Christ, the Church of the Nazarene, the Evangelical Fellowship of Zambia, the Kimbanguist Church, the Presbyterian Church of Southern Africa, the Religious Society of Friends (Quakers) and the United Pentecostal Church. At mid-2000 there were an estimated 2m. adherents professing other forms of Christianity.

The Roman Catholic Church
Zambia comprises two archdioceses and eight dioceses. At 31 December 2005 there were an estimated 3,768,719 adherents in the country, equivalent to 29.9% of the total population.

Bishops' Conference
Catholic Secretariat, Unity House, cnr Freedom Way and Katunjila Rd, POB 31965, 20201 Lusaka; tel. (1) 212070; fax (1) 220996.
f. 1984; Pres. Rt Rev. TELESPHORE GEORGE MPUNDU (Bishop of Mpika).
Archbishop of Kasama: Most Rev. JAMES SPAITA, Archbishop's House, POB 410143, Kasama; tel. (4) 221248; fax (4) 222202; e-mail archkasa@zamtel.zm.
Archbishop of Lusaka: Most Rev. TELESPHORE GEORGE MPUNDU, 41 Wamulwa Rd, POB 32754, 10101 Lusaka; tel. (1) 255973; fax (1) 255975; e-mail adl@zamnet.zm.

ISLAM
There are about 10,000 members of the Muslim Association in Zambia.

BAHÁ'Í FAITH
National Spiritual Assembly: Sekou Touré Rd, Plot 4371, Private Bag RW227X, Ridgeway 15102, Lusaka; tel. and fax (1) 254505; f. 1952; Sec.-Gen. MARGARET K. LENGWE; mems resident in 1,456 localities.

The Press

DAILIES
The Post: 36 Bwinjimfumu Rd, Rhodespark, Private Bag E352, Lusaka; tel. (97) 788200; fax (1) 229271; internet www.postzambia.com; f. 1991; privately owned; Editor-in-Chief FRED M'MEMBE; circ. 29,000.
The Times of Zambia: Kabelenga Ave, POB 70069, Ndola; tel. and fax (2) 614469; e-mail times@zamtel.zm; internet www.times.co.zm; f. 1943; govt-owned; English; Deputy Editor-in-Chief DAVEY SAKALA; circ. 25,000.
Zambia Daily Mail: Zambia Publishing Company, POB 31421, Lusaka; tel. (1) 225131; fax (1) 225881; internet www.daily-mail.co

ZAMBIA

Directory

.zm; f. 1968; govt-owned; English; Man. Editor Emmanuel Nyirenda; circ. 40,000.

PERIODICALS

African Social Research: Institute of Economic and Social Research, University of Zambia, POB 32379, Lusaka; tel. (1) 294131; fax (1) 253952; f. 1944; two a year; Editor Mubanga E. Kashoki; circ. 1,000.

The Challenge: Mission Press, Chifubu Rd, POB 71581, Ndola; tel. (2) 680456; fax (2) 680484; e-mail info@missionpress.org; internet www.missionpress.org; f. 1999; quarterly; English; social, educational and religious; Roman Catholic; edited by Franciscan friars; Ed. Fr Miha Drevensek; circ. 9,000.

Chipembele Magazine: POB 30255, Lusaka; tel. (1) 254226; six a year; publ. by Wildlife Conservation Soc. of Zambia; circ. 20,000.

Chronicle: Lusaka; bi-weekly; independent.

Farming in Zambia: POB 50197, Lusaka; tel. (1) 213551; f. 1965; quarterly; publ. by Ministry of Agriculture, Food and Fisheries; Editor L. P. Chirwa; circ. 3,000.

Imbila: POB RW20, Lusaka; tel. (1) 217254; f. 1953; monthly; publ. by Zambia Information Services; Bemba; Editor D. Mukaka; circ. 20,000.

Intanda: POB RW20, Lusaka; tel. (1) 219675; f. 1958; monthly; publ. by Zambia Information Services; Tonga; Editor J. Sikaulu; circ. 6,000.

Journal of Adult Education: University of Zambia, POB 50516, Lusaka; tel. (1) 216767; f. 1982; Exec. Editor Francis Kasoma.

Journal of Science and Technology: School of Natural Sciences, Dept of Biological Sciences, University of Zambia, POB 32379, Lusaka 10101; tel. (1) 293008; fax (1) 253952; f. 1996; science and technology journal of the Univ. of Zambia; two a year; Editor-in-Chief Prof. J. N. Zulu (acting).

Konkola: Zambia Consolidated Copper Mines Ltd, PR Dept, POB 71505, Ndola; tel. (2) 640142; f. 1973 as *Mining Mirror*; monthly; English; Editor G. Mukuwa; circ. 30,000.

Leisure Magazine: Farmers House, Cairo Rd, POB 8138, Woodlands, Lusaka; monthly; general interest.

Liseli: POB RW20, Lusaka; tel. (1) 219675; monthly; publ. by Zambia Information Services; Lozi; Editor F. Amnsaa; circ. 8,000.

The Lowdown: Lusaka; internet www.lowdown.co.zm; f. 1995; monthly; English; Editor Heather Chalcraft.

Lukanga News: POB 919, Kabwe; tel. (5) 217254; publ. by Zambia Information Services; Lenje; Editor J. H. N. Nkomanga; circ. 5,500.

National Mirror: Multimedia Zambia, 15701 Woodlands, POB 320199, Lusaka; tel. (1) 263864; fax (1) 263050; f. 1972; fortnightly; news, current affairs and foreign affairs; publ. by Multimedia Zambia; Editor Simon Mwanza; circ. 40,000.

Ngoma: POB RW20, Lusaka; tel. (1) 219675; monthly; Lunda, Kaonde and Luvale; publ. by Zambia Information Services; Editor B. A. Luhila; circ. 3,000.

Outlook: TBM Publicity Enterprises Ltd, POB 40, Kitwe; f. 1971; monthly; general interest.

Speak Out!: POB 70244, Ndola; tel. (2) 612241; fax (2) 620630; e-mail speakout@zamnet.zm; f. 1984; six a year; Christian; aimed at youth readership up to 35 years; Man. Editor Constantia Treppe; circ. 25,000.

The Sportsman: POB 31762, Lusaka; tel. (1) 214250; f. 1980; monthly; Man. Editor Sam Sikazwe; circ. 18,000.

Sunday Express: Lusaka; f. 1991; weekly; Man. Editor John Mukela.

Sunday Times of Zambia: Kabelenga Ave, POB 70069, Ndola; tel. (2) 614469; fax (2) 617096; e-mail times@zamtel.zm; internet www.times.co.zm/sunday; f. 1965; owned by UNIP; English; Man. Editor Arthur Simuchoba; circ. 78,000.

Tsopano: POB RW20, Lusaka; tel. (1) 217254; f. 1958; monthly; publ. by Zambia Information Services; Nyanja; Editor S. S. Banda; circ. 9,000.

Voters' Voice: Lusaka; monthly; independent.

Workers' Voice: POB 20652, Kitwe; tel. (2) 211999; f. 1972; fortnightly; publ. by Zambia Congress of Trade Unions.

Youth: POB 30302, Lusaka; tel. (1) 211411; f. 1974; quarterly; publ. by UNIP Youth League; Editor-in-Chief N. Anamela; circ. 20,000.

Zambia Government Gazette: POB 30136, Lusaka; tel. (1) 228724; fax (1) 224486; f. 1911; weekly; English; official notices.

NEWS AGENCY

Zambia News Agency (ZANA): Mass Media Complex, 2nd Floor, Alick Nkhata Rd, POB 30007, Lusaka; tel. (1) 219673; fax (1) 251631; internet www.zana.gov.zm; f. 1969; Dir Lewis Mwanangombe;
Editor-in-Chief Villie Lombanya; headquarters in Lusaka and nine regional offices.

PRESS ASSOCIATION

Press Association of Zambia (PAZA): Bishops Rd, Multi-Media Centre, POB 37065, Lusaka; tel. (1) 263595; fax (1) 263110; f. 1983; Pres. Andrew Sakala; Vice-Pres. Amos Chanda.

Publishers

Africa: Literature Centre, POB 21319, Kitwe; tel. (2) 210765; fax (2) 210716; general, educational, religious; Dir Jackson Mbewe.

African Social Research: Institute of Economic and Social Research, University of Zambia, POB 32379, Lusaka; tel. (1) 294131; fax (1) 253952; social research in Africa; Editor Mubanga E. Kashoki.

Bookworld Ltd: Plot 10442 off Lumumba Rd, POB 31838, Lusaka; tel. (1) 230606; fax (1) 230614; e-mail bookworld@realtime.zm.

Daystar Publications Ltd: POB 32211, Lusaka; f. 1966; religious; Man. Dir S. E. M. Pheko.

Directory Publishers of Zambia Ltd: Mabalenga Rd, POB 30963, Lusaka; tel. (1) 257133; fax (1) 257137; e-mail dpz@coppernet.zm; f. 1958; trade directories; Gen. Man. W. D. Wratten.

Multimedia Zambia: Woodlands, POB 320199, Lusaka; tel. and fax (1) 261193; f. 1971; religious and educational books, audio-visual materials; Exec. Dir Eddy Mupeso.

University of Zambia Press (UNZA Press): POB 32379, 10101 Lusaka; tel. (1) 290740; fax (1) 290409; f. 1938; academic books, papers and journals.

Zambia Educational Publishing House: Chishango Rd, POB 32708, 10101 Lusaka; tel. (1) 222324; fax (1) 225073; f. 1967; educational and general; Man. Dir Beniko E. Mulota.

Zambia Printing Co Ltd: POB 34798, 10101 Lusaka; tel. (1) 227673; fax (1) 225026; Gen. Man. Bernard Lubumbashi.

GOVERNMENT PUBLISHING HOUSES

Government Printer: POB 30136, Lusaka; tel. (1) 228724; fax (1) 224486; official documents and statistical bulletins.

Zambia Information Services: POB 50020, Lusaka; tel. (1) 219673; state-controlled; Dir Benson Sianga.

PUBLISHERS' ASSOCIATION

Booksellers' and Publishers' Association of Zambia: POB 31838, Lusaka; tel. (1) 222647; fax (1) 225195; Chair. Ray Munamwimbu; Sec. Basil Mbewe.

Broadcasting and Communications

TELECOMMUNICATIONS

Celtel Zambia: POB 320001, Nyerere Rd, Woodlands, Lusaka; tel. (1) 250707; e-mail customerservice@zm.celtel.com; internet www.zm.celtel.com; f. 1997 as ZamCell Ltd; acquired by Celtel Int. BV, Netherlands, in 1998; mobile cellular telephone operator; Chair. George Sokota; Man. Dir David Venn; c. 500,000 subscribers.

MTN (Zambia) Ltd: POB 35464, Lusaka; tel. (1) 750072; fax (1) 750750; internet www.mtnzambia.co.zm; f. 1997 as Telecel (Zambia) Ltd; acquired by MTN Group, South Africa, in 2005; mobile cellular telecommunications provider; CEO Mike Blackburn; 152,000 subscribers (2006).

Zambia Telecommunications Co Ltd (ZAMTEL): Provident House, POB 71660, Ndola; tel. (2) 611111; fax (2) 611399; internet www.zamtel.zm; transfer to private sector abandoned in 2005; commercialization pending; operates Cell-Z cellular network (f. 1995); Chair. Basil Sichali; Man. Dir Simon Tembo.

BROADCASTING

Zambia National Broadcasting Corpn: Mass Media Complex, Alick Nkhata Rd, POB 50015, Lusaka; tel. (1) 252005; fax (1) 254013; internet www.znbc.co.zm; f. 1961; state-owned; two national radio stations (Radio 1 and Radio 2) and one line-of-rail station (Radio 4); television broadcasts along the line of rail, from Livingstone to Chililabombwe; services in English and seven Zambian languages; Dir-Gen. Eddy Mupeso.

Radio

Breeze FM: POB 511178, Chipata; tel. (216) 221175; fax (216) 221823; e-mail breezefm@zamtel.zm; internet www.breezefm.com;

f. 2003; Nyanja and English; community based commercial radio; broadcasts to the Eastern Province; signal is also received in parts of north-west Malawi and border areas of Tete Province in Mozambique; Man. Dir MIKE DAKA.

Educational Broadcasting Services: Headquarters: POB 50231, Lusaka; tel. (1) 251724; radio broadcasts from Lusaka; audio-visual aids service from POB 50295, Lusaka; Controller MICHAEL MULOMBE.

Radio Maria Zambia: POB 510307, Chipata; tel. and fax (6) 221154; e-mail info.zam@radiomaria.org; internet www.radiomaria.org; f. 1999; part of The World Family of Radio Maria, Italy; Roman Catholic religious programming; broadcasts to Eastern Province; Dir MWANZA GABRIEL KWAKU.

Radio Phoenix: Private Bag E702, Lusaka; tel. (1) 223581; fax (1) 226839; e-mail rphoenix@zamnet.zm; commercial radio station; Chair. ERROL T. HICKEY.

Yatsani Radio: Leopards Hill Rd, Bauleni Catholic Church, POB 320147, Lusaka; tel. (1) 261082; fax (1) 265842; internet yatsani.com; f. 1999; owned by the Archdiocese of Lusaka; Roman Catholic religious community; broadcasts to Lusaka; Dir Most Rev. MEDARDO JOSEPH MAZOMBWE (Archbishop of Lusaka).

Television

Educational Broadcasting Services: POB 21106, Kitwe; television for schools; Controller MICHAEL MULOMBE.

Finance

(cap. = capital; auth. = authorized; res = reserves; dep. = deposits; m. = million; br(s). = branch(es); amounts in kwacha)

BANKING

From 30 June 1996 all banks operating in Zambia were required to have capital of not less than K2,000m. in order to receive a banking licence or to continue to function.

Central Bank

Bank of Zambia: Bank Sq., Cairo Rd, POB 30080, 10101 Lusaka; tel. (1) 228888; fax (1) 221722; internet www.boz.zm; f. 1964; bank of issue; cap. 10m., res 31,675m., dep. 2,459,106m. (Dec. 2002); Gov. and Chair. Dr CALEB FUNDANGA; br. in Ndola.

Commercial Banks

Finance Bank Zambia Ltd: 2101 Chanik House, Cairo Rd, POB 37102, 10101 Lusaka; tel. (1) 229733; fax (1) 227290; e-mail fbz@financebank.co.zm; internet www.financebank.co.zm; f. 1987; cap. and res 92,636m., dep. 390,086m. (Dec. 2002); Chair. Dr R. L. MAHTANI; Man. Dir DICK KING; 32 brs and 9 agencies.

National Savings and Credit Bank of Zambia: Plot 248B, Cairo Rd, POB 30067, Lusaka; tel. (1) 228985; fax (1) 223296; internet www.natsave.co.zm; f. 1972; total assets 6,598m. (Dec. 1998); Man. Dir LEONARD Z. MWANZA.

New Capital Bank PLC: Anchor House, Mezzanine Floor, Sapele Rd, POB 36452, Lusaka; tel. (1) 229508; fax (1) 224055; f. 1992; cap. and res 4,510m., total assets 18,538m. (Dec. 2001); Chair. WILA D. MUNG'OMBA; CEO and Gen. Man. GODFREY P. MSISKA.

Zambia National Commercial Bank PLC (ZNCB): POB 33611, Lusaka; tel. (1) 228979; fax (1) 223106; e-mail support@zanaco.co.zm; internet www.zanaco.co.zm; f. 1969; partial privatization agreed in 2005: 25% to remain govt-owned; 25.8% to be sold to Zambian citizens through the Zambian Privatisation Trust Fund; cap. and res 63,370m., total assets 584,667m. (Dec. 2000); Chair. MBIKUSITA W. LEWANIKA; Man. Dir LIKOLO NDALAMEI; 43 brs.

Foreign Banks

Bank of China (Zambia) Ltd (China): Amandra House, Ben Bella Rd, POB 34550, Lusaka; tel. (1) 235349; fax (1) 235350; e-mail service_zm@bank-of-china.com; f. 1997; cap. and res 5,731m., total assets 73,237m. (Dec. 2001); Chair. PING YUE; Gen. Man. HONG XINSHENG.

Barclays Bank of Zambia PLC (United Kingdom): Kafue House, Cairo Rd, POB 31936, Lusaka; tel. (1) 228858; fax (1) 222519; e-mail barclays.zambia@barclays.com; internet www.africa.barclays.com; f. 1971; cap. and res 114,618m., total assets 809,515m. (Dec. 2001); Chair. A. BRUCE MUNYAMA; Man. Dir MARGARET MWANAKATWE; 5 brs.

Citibank Zambia Ltd (USA): Citibank House, Cha Cha Cha Rd, POB 30037, Southend, Lusaka; tel. (1) 229025; fax (1) 226264; internet www.citibank.com/eastafrica/zambia; f. 1979; cap. 521.2m., dep. 237,176m. (Dec. 2001); 2 brs.

Indo-Zambia Bank (IZB): Plot 6907, Cairo Rd, POB 35411, Lusaka; tel. (1) 224653; fax (1) 225090; e-mail izb@zamnet.zm; internet www.izb.co.zm; f. 1984; cap. and res 34,312m., dep. 200,770m. (March 2002); Chair. ORLENE Y. MOYO; Man. Dir CYRIL PATRO; 7 brs.

Stanbic Bank Zambia Ltd: Woodgate House, 6th Floor, Nairobi Place, Cairo Rd, POB 31955, Lusaka; tel. (1) 229071; fax (1) 221152; internet www.stanbic.co.zm; f. 1971; wholly owned by Standard Bank Investment Corpn; cap. and res 55,064m., total assets 425,746m. (Dec. 2001); Chair. D. A. R. PHIRI; Man. Dir A. H. S. MACLEOD; 7 brs.

Standard Chartered Bank Zambia Ltd (United Kingdom): Standard House, Cairo Rd, POB 32238, Lusaka; tel. (1) 229242; fax (1) 222092; f. 1971; cap. 2,048m., res 75,575m., dep. 450,784m. (Dec. 2001); Chair. A. K. MAZOKA; Man. Dir J. A. H. JANES; 14 brs.

Development Banks

Development Bank of Zambia: Development House, Katondo St, POB 33955, Lusaka; tel. (1) 228576; fax (1) 222821; e-mail projects@dbz.co.zm; internet www.dbz.co.zm; f. 1973; 99% state-owned; provides medium- and long-term loans and administers special funds placed at its disposal; cap. and res 7,580.0m., total assets 145,976.6m. (March 1998); Chair. NAMUKULO MUKUTU; Man. Dir RICHARD PHIRI; 2 brs.

Lima Bank: Kulima House, Cha Cha Cha Rd, POB 32607, Lusaka; tel. (1) 213111; fax (1) 228077; cap. 57m. (March 1986); Chair. N. MUKUTU; Man. Dir K. V. KASAPATU.

Zambia Agricultural Development Bank: Society House, Cairo Rd, POB 30847, Lusaka; tel. (1) 219251; f. 1982; loan finance for devt of agriculture and fishing; auth. cap. 75m.; Chair. K. MAKASA; Man. Dir AMON CHIBIYA.

Zambia Export and Import Bank Ltd: Society House, Cairo Rd, POB 33046, Lusaka; tel. (1) 229486; fax (1) 222313; f. 1987; cap. 50m. (March 1992), dep. 50.9m. (March 1990); Man. Dir LIKANDO NAWA.

STOCK EXCHANGE

Lusaka Stock Exchange (LuSE): Farmers House, 3rd Floor, Cairo Rd, POB 34523, Lusaka; tel. (1) 228537; fax (1) 225969; e-mail info@luse.co.zm; internet www.luse.co.zm; f. 1994; Chair. JOHN JANES; Gen. Man. JOSEPH CHIKOLWA.

INSURANCE

African Life Assurance Zambia: Mukuba Pension House, 4th Floor, Dedan Kimathi Rd, POB 31991; tel. (1) 225452; fax (1) 225435; e-mail customercare@african-life.com.zm; f. 2002; life insurance; CEO STEVE WILLIAMS.

Cavmont Capital Insurance Corpn Ltd: Farmers House, 3rd Floor, POB 38474, Lusaka; tel. (1) 228929; e-mail info@cavmont.com.zm; f. 2003; subsidiary of Cavmont Capital Holdings Ltd; Man. Dir MOSES MALUNGA.

Goldman Insurance Ltd: Zambia National Savings and Credit Bank Bldg, 2nd Floor, Cairo Rd, Private Bag W395, Lusaka; tel. (1) 235234; fax (1) 227262; f. 1992; Chair. BWALYA CHITI.

Madison Insurance Co Ltd: Plot 255, Kaleya Rd, Roma, POB 37013, Lusaka; tel. (1) 295311; fax (1) 295320; internet www.madisonzambia.com; f. 1992; general and micro-insurance; Chair. DAVID A. R. PHIRI; Man. Dir LAWRENCE S. SIKUTWA.

NICO Insurance Zambia Ltd (NIZA): 1131 Parirenyatwa Rd, Fairview, POB 32825, Lusaka; tel. (1) 222862; fax (1) 222863; e-mail nicozam@zamnet.zm; internet www.nicomw.com/zambia; f. 1997; subsidiary of NICO Group, Malawi; general insurance; Chair. JOHN MWANAKATWE; Gen. Man. TITUS KALENGA.

Professional Insurance Corpn Zambia Ltd (PICZ): Professional Insurance House, Heroes Pl., POB 34264, Lusaka; tel. (1) 227509; fax (1) 222151; e-mail ho@picz.co.zm; internet www.picz.co.zm; f. 1992; Exec. Dir GEORGE SILUTONGWE; Man. Dir ASHOK CHAWLA.

Zambia State Insurance Corpn Ltd: Premium House, Independence Ave, POB 30894, Lusaka; tel. (1) 229343; fax (1) 222263; e-mail zsic@zsic.co.zm; internet www.zsic.co.zm; f. 1968; sole authorized insurance provider in Zambia 1971–92; transfer to private sector pending; Chair. ALBERT WOOD; Man. Dir IRENE MUYENGA.

ZIGI Insurance Co Ltd: Mukuba Pension House, 5th Floor, POB37782, Lusaka; tel. (1) 226835; fax (1) 231564; e-mail zigi@zamnet.zm; f. 1998; Chair. and CEO SAVIOUR H. KONIE.

Trade and Industry

GOVERNMENT AGENCIES

Export Board of Zambia (EBZ): Woodgate House, 5th Floor, Cairo Rd, Heroes Pl., POB 30064, Lusaka; tel. (1) 228106; fax (1) 222509; e-mail ebz@ebz.co.zm; internet www.ebz.co.zm; f. 1985; develops and promotes non-traditional exports.

ZAMBIA

Export Processing Zones Authority (EPZA): Plot No. 18939, cnr Great East and Katima Mulilo Rds, POB 337110, Lusaka; tel. (1) 212403; fax (1) 212406; e-mail zepza@uudial.zm; f. 2002; Chair. LOVEMORE CHIHOTA.

Small Enterprises Development Board (SEDB): SEDB House, Cairo Rd (South End), POB 35373, Lusaka; tel. and fax (1) 222176; f. 1981 as the Small Industries Devt Org.; to promote devt of small and village industries.

Zambia Investment Centre: Los Angeles Blvd, POB 34580, 10101 Lusaka; tel. (1) 255240; fax (1) 252150; f. 1991; Dir-Gen. JACOB LUSHINGA.

Zambia Privatisation Agency: Privatisation House, Nasser Rd, POB 30819, Lusaka; tel. (1) 223859; fax (1) 225270; e-mail zpa@zpa.org.zm; internet www.zpa.org.zm; f. 1992; responsible for the divestment of various state-owned enterprises; 262 cos privatized by mid-2006, 22 privatizations pending; Chair. LUKE MBEWE; CEO ANDREW CHIPWENDE.

DEVELOPMENT ORGANIZATIONS

Industrial Development Corpn of Zambia Ltd (INDECO): Indeco House, Buteko Place, POB 31935, Lusaka; tel. (1) 228026; fax (1) 228868; f. 1960; auth. cap. K300m.; taken over by the Nat. Housing Authority in May 2005; Chair. R. L. BWALYA; Man. Dir S. K. TAMELE.

Mpongwe Development Company: Block 4450, Mpongwe, POB 90599, Luanshya; tel. (2) 510584; fax (2) 511713; promotes the production of crops for domestic and regional markets; CEO HENK MARMELSTEIN.

CHAMBERS OF COMMERCE

Zambia Association of Chambers of Commerce and Industry: Great East Rd, Showgrounds, POB 30844, Lusaka; tel. (1) 252483; fax (1) 253020; e-mail secretariat@zacci.co.zm; internet www.zacci.org.zm; f. 1938; Chair. WAMULUME KALABO; 10 district chambers.

Member chambers and associations include:

Chamber of Mines of Zambia: POB 22100, Kitwe; tel. (2) 214122; f. 1941 as Northern Rhodesia Chamber of Mines; replaced by the Copper Industry Service Bureau 1965–2000; represents mining employers; 19 mems; Pres. NATHAN CHISHIMBA; Gen. Man. FREDERICK BANTUBONSE.

Zambia Association of Manufacturers: POB 30036, Lusaka; tel. (1) 242780; fax (1) 222912; e-mail babbar@zamnet.zm; f. 1985; Chair. D. BABBAR; 180 mems.

Chamber of Small and Medium Business Associations.

INDUSTRIAL AND TRADE ASSOCIATIONS

Tobacco Board of Zambia (TBZ): POB 31963, Lusaka; tel. (1) 288995; fax (1) 287118; e-mail tbz@zamnet.zm; promotes, monitors and controls tobacco production; Sec. JONATHAN M. CHIZUNI.

Zambia Farm Employers' Association (ZFEA): Farmers' Village, Lusaka Agricultural and Commercial Showgrounds, POB 30395, Lusaka; tel. (1) 252649; fax (1) 252648; e-mail znfu@zamnet.zm; Chair. R. DENLY; 350 mems.

Other associations include: the Bankers Asscn of Zambia; the Cotton Asscn of Zambia; the Environmental Conservation Asscn of Zambia; the Insurance Brokers Asscn of Zambia; the Kapenta Fishermen Asscn; the National Aquaculture Asscn of Zambia; the National Council for Construction; the Poultry Asscn of Zambia; Tobacco Asscn of Zambia; the Wildlife Producers Asscn of Zambia; the Young Farmers Clubs of Zambia; the Zambia Asscn of Clearing and Forwarding; the Zambia Asscn of Manufacturers; the Zambia Coffee Growers Asscn; the Zambia Export Growers Asscn; and the Zambian Women in Agriculture.

UTILITIES

Electricity

ZESCO (Zambia Electricity Supply Corpn) Ltd: Stand 6949, Great East Rd, POB 33304, Lusaka; tel. (1) 226084; fax (1) 222753; e-mail mchisela@zesco.co.zm; internet www.zesco.co.zm; f. 1970; state-owned; Man. Dir RHODNIE P. SISALA.

Copperbelt Energy Corpn PLC (CEC): Private Bag E835, Postnet No. 145, Chindo Rd, Kabulonga, Lusaka; tel. (1) 261647; fax (1) 261640; e-mail info@cec.com.zm; internet www.copperbeltenergy.com; f. 1997 upon privatization of the power div. of Zambia Consolidated Copper Mines; privately owned co supplying power generated by ZESCO to mining cos in the Copperbelt; Exec. Chair HANSON SINDOWE.

CO-OPERATIVES

Zambia Co-operative Federation Ltd: Co-operative House, Cha Cha Cha Rd, POB 33579, Lusaka; tel. (1) 220157; fax (1) 222516; f. 1973; agricultural marketing; supply of agricultural chemicals and implements; cargo haulage; insurance; agricultural credit; auditing and accounting; property and co-operative devt; Chair. B. TETAMASHIMBA; Man. Dir G. Z. SIBALE.

TRADE UNIONS

Zambia Congress of Trade Unions (ZCTU): Solidarity House, Oxford Rd, POB 20652, Kitwe; tel. (2) 211999; fax (2) 228284; e-mail zctu@microlink.zm; f. 1965; Pres. LEONARD HIKAUMBA; Sec.-Gen. SYLVESTER TEMBO; c. 400,000 mems.

Affiliated Unions

Airways and Allied Workers' Union of Zambia: Lusaka International Airport, 2nd Floor, Terminal Bldg, POB 30175, 10101 Lusaka; affiliated to the Int. Transport Workers' Fed.; Pres. F. MULENGA; Gen. Sec. B. CHINYANTA.

Civil Servants' Union of Zambia (CSAWUZ): Plot 5045A, Mumbwa Rd, POB 50160, Lusaka; tel. and fax (1) 287106; e-mail csuz@zamnet.zm; f. 1975; Chair. L. C. HIKAUMBA; Gen. Sec. DARISON CHAALA; 35,000 mems.

Guards Union of Zambia (GUZ): POB 21882, Kitwe; tel. (2) 216189; e-mail uni-africa@union-network.org; f. 1972; affiliated to the Union Network Int.; Chair. D. N. S. SILUNGWE; Gen. Sec. MICHAEL S. SIMFUKWE; 13,500 mems.

Hotel Catering Workers' Union of Zambia: POB 35693, Lusaka; affiliated to the Int. Union of Food, Agricultural, Hotel, Restaurant, Catering, Tobacco and Allied Workers' Asscns; Chair. IAN MKANDAWIRE; Gen. Sec. STOIC KAPUTU; 9,000 mems.

Mineworkers' Union of Zambia (MUZ): POB 20448, Kitwe; tel. (2) 214022; affiliated to the Int. Fed. of Chemical, Energy, Mine and Gen. Workers' Unions; Pres. ANDREW MWANZA; Sec.-Gen. OSWELL MUNYENYEMBE; 50,000 mems.

National Union of Building, Engineering and General Workers (NUBEGW): City Sq., Millers Bldg, Plot No. 1094, POB 21515, Kitwe; tel. (2) 224468; fax (2) 661119; e-mail nubegw@zamtel.zm; affiliated to the Building and Wood Workers Int. and the Int. Metalworkers' Fed.; Chair. LUCIANO MUTALE (acting); Gen. Sec. P. N. NZIMA; 18,000 mems.

National Union of Commercial and Industrial Workers (NUCIW): 17 Obote Ave, POB 21735, Kitwe; tel. (2) 228607; fax (2) 225211; e-mail nuciw@zamtel.zm; f. 1982; affiliated to the Int. Fed. of Chemical, Energy, Mine and Gen. Workers' Unions, the Int. Textile, Garment and Leather Workers' Fed., the Int. Union of Food, Agricultural, Hotel, Restaurant, Catering, Tobacco and Allied Workers' Asscns and the Union Network Int.; Chair. I. M. KASUMBU; Gen. Sec. JOHN M. BWALYA; 16,000 mems.

National Union of Communication Workers: POB 70751, Ndola; tel. (2) 611345; fax (2) 614679; e-mail nucw@zamtel.zm; affiliated to the Union Network Int.; Pres. PATRICK KAONGA; Gen. Sec. CHELLA WELLINGTON; 5,000 mems.

National Union of Plantation and Agricultural Workers: POB 80529, Kabwe; tel. (5) 224548; affiliated to the Int. Union of Food, Agricultural, Hotel, Restaurant, Catering, Tobacco and Allied Workers' Asscns; Pres. MUDENDA RISHER; Gen. Sec. MAILONI KABULAYI; 15,155 mems.

National Union of Public Services' Workers (NUPSW): POB 32523, Lusaka; tel. (1) 227451; fax (1) 287105; e-mail znslib@zamtel.zm; affiliated to the Public Services Int.; Gen. Sec. DAVIS J. CHINGONI.

National Union of Transport and Allied Workers (NUTAW): Cha Cha Cha House, Rm 4, 1st Floor, POB 30068, Cario Rd, Lusaka; tel. (1) 214756; e-mail sapphiri2005@yahoo.com; Pres. PATRICK C. CHANDA; Gen. Sec. SAM A. P. PHIRI.

Railway Workers' Union of Zambia: POB 80302, Kabwe; tel. (5) 224006; affiliated to the Int. Transport Workers' Fed.; Chair. H. K. NDAMANA; Gen. Sec. BENSON L. NGULA; 10,228 mems.

University of Zambia and Allied Workers' Union: POB 32379, Lusaka; tel. (1) 213221; f. 1968; Chair. BERIATE SUNKUTU; Gen. Sec. SAINI PHIRI.

Zambia Electricity Workers' Union: POB 70859, Ndola; f. 1972; Chair. COSMAS MPAMPI; Gen. Sec. ADAM KALUBA; 3,000 mems.

Zambia National Farmers' Union: ZNFU Head Office, Tiyende Pamodzi Rd, opp. Polo Grounds, Farmers' Village, Zambia Agricultural and Commercial Showgrounds, POB 30395, Lusaka; tel. (1) 252649; fax (1) 252648; e-mail znfu@zamnet.zm; internet www.znfu.org.zm; Exec. Dir SONGOWAYO ZYAMBO.

Zambia National Union of Teachers: POB 31914, Lusaka; tel. (1) 214623; fax (1) 214624; e-mail znut@microlink.zm; affiliated to Education Int; Chair. RICHARD M. LIYWALII; Gen. Sec. ROY MWABA; 2,120 mems.

Zambia Graphical and Allied Workers' Union (ZATAWU): c/o UNI-Africa, POB 71760, Ndola; tel. (2) 612889; fax (2) 613054; e-mail zatawu@yahoo.com; affiliated to the Union Network Int.; Gen. Sec. David S. Mwaba.

Zambia Union of Journalists: POB 30394, Lusaka; tel. (1) 227348; fax (1) 221695; e-mail zuj.zambia@yahoo.com; Vice-Pres. Morgan Chonya; Gen. Sec. Nigel Mulenga.

Zambia Union of Local Government Officers: f. 1997; Pres. Isaac Mwanza.

Zambia Union of Skilled Mineworkers: f. 1998; Chair. Alex Moloi.

Zambia United Local Authorities Workers' Union (ZULAWU): Mugala House, POB 70575, Ndola; tel. (2) 615022; affiliated to the Public Services Int.; Chair. Abraham M. Mutakila; Gen. Sec. Amon Daka (acting).

Principal Non-Affiliated Union

Zambian African Mining Union: Kitwe; f. 1967; 40,000 mems.

Transport

RAILWAYS

Total length of railways in Zambia was 2,162 km (including 891 km of the Tanzania–Zambia railway) in 2000. There are two major railway networks: the Zambia Railways network, which traverses the country from the Copperbelt in northern Zambia and links with the National Railways of Zimbabwe to provide access to South African ports, and the Tanzania–Zambia Railway (Tazara) network, linking New Kapiri-Mposhi in Zambia with Dar es Salaam in Tanzania. The Tazara railway line increased its capacity from 1976, in order to reduce the dependence of southern African countries on trade routes through South Africa. A 10-year rehabilitation programme, assisted by the USA and EC (now EU) countries, began in 1985. In April 1987 the Governments of Zambia, Angola and Zaire (now the Democratic Republic of the Congo) declared their intention to reopen the Benguela railway, linking Zambian copper mines with the Angolan port of Lobito, following its closure to international traffic in 1975 as a result of the guerrilla insurgency in Angola. In 1997 a programme of repairs was begun, and plans were announced in June 2002 to rebuild the Benguela railway. It was announced in 2003 that a line would be built linking the Zambian port of Mpulungu to the Tazara network. In April 2005 Northwest Railways undertook to develop a new line between Chingola, in the Copperbelt Province, and Lumwana, in the North-Western Province. It was anticipated that the line could eventually be linked to the Benguela railway.

Tanzania–Zambia Railway Authority (Tazara): POB T01, Mpika; Head Office: POB 2834, Dar es Salaam, Tanzania; tel. (4) 370684; fax (4) 370228; f. 1975; operates passenger and freight services linking New Kapiri-Mposhi, north of Lusaka, with Dar es Salaam in Tanzania, a distance of 1,860 km, of which 891 km is in Zambia; jtly owned and administered by the Govts of Tanzania and Zambia; Chair. Salim H. Msoma; Man. Dir Clement Mwiya.

Zambia Railways Ltd: cnr Buntungwa St and Ghana Ave, POB 80935, Kabwe; tel. (5) 222201; fax (5) 224411; f. 1967; management assumed in 1998 by consortium of Hifab Int. AB, Sweden, and DE Consult, Germany; concession of assets and operations to consortium of New Limpopo Bridge Project Investments Ltd and Spoornet, South Africa, agreed in early 2003; Chair. B. Nonde; Man. Dir Göran Malmberg.

ROADS

In 2001 there was a total road network of 91,440 km, including 4,222 km of main roads and 8,948 km of secondary roads. The main arterial roads run from Beitbridge (Zimbabwe) to Tunduma (the Great North Road), through the copper-mining area to Chingola and Chililabombwe (hitherto the Zaire Border Road), from Livingstone to the junction of the Kafue river and the Great North Road, and from Lusaka to the Malawi border (the Great East Road). In 1984 the 300-km BotZam highway linking Kazungula with Nata, in Botswana, was formally opened. A 1,930-km main road (the TanZam highway) links Zambia and Tanzania. In 1998 the Government initiated a 10-year Road Sector Investment Programme with funding from the World Bank, and in its second phase the European Union.

Road Development Agency: POB 50003, Lusaka; tel. (1) 253801; fax (1) 253404; e-mail rda_hq@roads.gov.zm; internet www.rda.org.zm; f. 2002; fmrly Dept of Roads; CEO Watson Ng'ambi.

CIVIL AVIATION

In 1984 there were 127 airports, aerodromes and air strips. An international airport, 22.5 km from Lusaka, was opened in 1967.

National Airports Corpn Ltd (NACL): Airport Rd, 10101 Lusaka; tel. (1) 271313; fax (1) 271048; e-mail nacl@zamnet.zm; internet www.lun.aero; f. 1973; air cargo services; Man. Dir Robinson Misitala (acting).

Zambia Skyways (Eastern Air): Plot 6, Addis Ababa Rd, POB 32661, Lusaka; tel. (1) 250987; fax (1) 250767; e-mail yzumla@zambiaskyways.aero; internet www.zambiaskyways.aero; f. 1995; operates scheduled passenger services to domestic destinations and South Africa; Chair. Yoosuf Zumla.

Zambian Airways: Lusaka International Airport, POB 34777, Lusaka; tel. (1) 271230; fax (1) 271054; e-mail reservations@zambianairways.com; internet www.zambianairways.co.zm; f. 1988 as Roan Air; present name adopted in 1999; operates domestic and regional routes; CEO Donald MacDonald.

Tourism

Zambia's main tourist attractions, in addition to the Victoria Falls, are its wildlife, unspoilt scenery and diverse cultural heritage; there are 19 national parks and 36 game management areas. In 2005 668,862 tourists visited Zambia, up from 515,000 in the previous year; tourism receipts increased from US $149m. in 2003 to $164m. in 2005.

Tourism Council of Zambia: Holiday Inn Cottage, Church Rd, Lusaka; tel. (1) 252859; fax (1) 255337; e-mail tcz@zamnet.zm; internet www.zambiatourism.com/travel/localnews/tcz.htm; Chair. Bruce Chapman.

Zambia National Tourist Board: Century House, Lusaka Sq., POB 30017, Lusaka; tel. (1) 229087; fax (1) 225174; e-mail zntb@zambiatourism.org.zm; internet www.zambiatourism.com; Chair. Errol Hickey; Man. Dir Chanda Charity Lumpa.

ZIMBABWE

Introductory Survey

Location, Climate, Language, Religion, Flag, Capital

The Republic of Zimbabwe is a land-locked state in southern Africa, with Mozambique to the east, Zambia to the north-west, Botswana to the south-west and South Africa to the south. The climate is tropical, modified considerably by altitude. Average monthly temperatures range from 13°C (55°F) to 22°C (72°F) on the Highveld, and from 20°C (68°F) to 30°C (86°F) in the low-lying valley of the Zambezi river. The rainy season is from November to March. The official languages are English, ChiShona and SiNdebele. About 55% of the population are Christians. A large number of the African population follow traditional beliefs, while the Asian minority comprises both Muslims and Hindus. The national flag (proportions 1 by 2) has seven equal horizontal stripes, of green, gold, red, black, red, gold and green, with a white triangle, bearing a red five-pointed star on which a gold 'Great Zimbabwe bird' is superimposed, at the hoist. The capital is Harare.

Recent History

In 1923 responsibility for Southern Rhodesia (now Zimbabwe) was transferred from the British South Africa Company to the Government of the United Kingdom, and the territory became a British colony. It had full self-government (except for African interests and some other matters) under an administration controlled by European settlers. African voting rights were restricted.

In 1953 the colony united with two British protectorates, Northern Rhodesia (now Zambia) and Nyasaland (now Malawi), to form the Federation of Rhodesia and Nyasaland. A new Constitution, which ended most of the United Kingdom's legal controls and provided for a limited African franchise, came into effect in November 1962. At elections in December the Prime Minister, Sir Edgar Whitehead, lost power to the Rhodesian Front (RF), a coalition of white opposition groups committed to maintaining racial segregation. The leader of the RF, Winston Field, became Prime Minister.

As a result of pressure from African nationalist movements in Northern Rhodesia and Nyasaland, the Federation was dissolved in December 1963. African nationalists were also active in Southern Rhodesia. The African National Congress, founded in 1934, was revived in 1957, with Joshua Nkomo as President. Following the banning of the Congress in February 1959, some of its members formed the National Democratic Party (NDP) in January 1960. Nkomo, although in exile, was elected President of the NDP in October. When the NDP was banned in December 1961, Nkomo formed the Zimbabwe African People's Union (ZAPU), which was declared an unlawful organization in September 1962. ZAPU split in July 1963, and a breakaway group, led by the Rev. Ndabaningi Sithole, formed the Zimbabwe African National Union (ZANU) in August. Robert Mugabe became Secretary-General of ZANU.

In April 1964 Field was succeeded as Prime Minister of Southern Rhodesia by his deputy, Ian Smith. The new regime rejected British conditions for independence, including acceptance by the whole Rhodesian population and unimpeded progress to majority rule. In August ZANU was banned. After Northern Rhodesia became independent as Zambia in October, Southern Rhodesia became generally (although not officially) known as Rhodesia. On 5 November 1965 a state of emergency (to be renewed annually) was declared, and on 11 November Smith made a unilateral declaration of independence (UDI) and proclaimed a new Constitution, naming the country Rhodesia. The British Government regarded Rhodesia's independence as unconstitutional and illegal, and no other country formally recognized it. The United Kingdom terminated all relations with Rhodesia, while the UN applied economic sanctions. Both ZAPU and ZANU took up arms against the RF regime.

Following a referendum in June 1969, Rhodesia was declared a republic in March 1970. The 1969 Constitution provided for a bicameral Legislative Assembly, comprising a 23-member Senate and a 66-member House of Assembly (50 Europeans and 16 Africans). The President had only formal powers, and Smith remained Prime Minister. The RF won all 50 European seats in the House of Assembly in 1970, 1974 and 1977.

In November 1971 the British and Rhodesian Governments agreed on draft proposals for a constitutional settlement, subject to their acceptability to the Rhodesian people 'as a whole'. In December the African National Council (ANC), led by Bishop Abel Muzorewa, was formed to co-ordinate opposition to the plan. In December 1974, however, the Rhodesian Government and leaders of four nationalist organizations (including ZAPU, ZANU and the ANC) agreed the terms of a cease-fire, conditional on the release of African political detainees and on the convening of a constitutional conference in 1975. The African organizations agreed to unite within the ANC, with Muzorewa as President. Mugabe opposed the incorporation of ZANU into the ANC, and in mid-1975 left Rhodesia for neighbouring Mozambique, where he took control of ZANU's external wing, and challenged Sithole's leadership of the party. In September the ANC split into rival factions, led by Muzorewa and Nkomo. Constitutional talks between the Government and the Nkomo faction began in December 1975, but were abandoned in March 1976. In September, under pressure from South Africa, Smith announced his Government's acceptance of proposals leading to majority rule within two years. In late 1976 representatives of the RF, the African nationalists and the British Government met to discuss the transition to majority rule. The nationalists were led by Muzorewa, Sithole, Nkomo and Mugabe (by then the recognized leader of ZANU). Nkomo and Mugabe adopted a joint position as the Patriotic Front (PF).

In January 1977 Angola, Botswana, Mozambique, Tanzania and Zambia (the 'front-line' states) declared their support for the PF. Smith rejected British proposals for an interim administration, and received a mandate from the RF to repeal racially discriminatory laws and to seek agreement with such African factions as he chose. In November Smith accepted the principle of universal adult suffrage, and talks on an internal settlement were initiated with Muzorewa's United African National Council (UANC), Sithole's faction of the ANC and the Zimbabwe United People's Organization, led by Chief Jeremiah Chirau. These talks led to the signing of an internal settlement on 3 March 1978, providing for an interim power-sharing administration to prepare for independence on 31 December. The proposals were rejected by the PF and by the UN Security Council. In May 1978 the newly created Executive Council, consisting of Smith, Sithole, Muzorewa and Chirau, ordered the release of all political detainees in an attempt to bring about a cease-fire.

In January 1979 a 'majority rule' Constitution, with entrenched safeguards for the white minority, was approved by the House of Assembly and endorsed by a referendum of European voters. In April elections to the new House of Assembly (the first by universal adult suffrage) were held in two stages: for 20 directly elected European members (chosen by non-African voters only) and then for 72 African members (chosen by the whole electorate). The elections were boycotted by the PF. The UANC emerged as the majority party, with 51 seats, while the RF won all 20 seats for whites. In May the new Parliament elected Josiah Gumede as President. Muzorewa became Prime Minister of the country (renamed Zimbabwe Rhodesia) in June. In accordance with the Constitution, Muzorewa formed a government of national unity, including European members (Smith became Minister without Portfolio). However, international recognition was not forthcoming, and UN sanctions remained in force.

New impetus for a lasting and internationally recognized settlement followed the Commonwealth Conference in Zambia in August 1979. In September a Rhodesian Constitutional Conference in London, United Kingdom, was attended by delegations under Muzorewa and the joint leaders of the PF. The PF reluctantly agreed to special representation for the whites under the proposed new Constitution, which was eventually accepted by both parties; complete agreement was reached on transitional arrangements in November, and a cease-fire between the guerrillas of the PF and the Rhodesian security forces was finalized the following month. On 11 December the Zimbabwe Rhodesia

Parliament voted to renounce independence and to revert to the status of a British colony, as Southern Rhodesia. Illegal rule ended on the following day, when Parliament was dissolved, the President, Prime Minister and Cabinet resigned, and the British-appointed Governor, Lord Soames, was vested with full executive and legislative authority for the duration of the transition to legal independence. The United Kingdom immediately revoked economic sanctions.

Lord Soames ended the ban on the two wings of the PF (ZAPU and ZANU) and ordered the release of most of the detainees who were held under the 'emergency powers' laws. Elections to a new House of Assembly proceeded in February 1980 (again in two stages) under the supervision of a British Electoral Commissioner. Mugabe's ZANU—PF emerged as the largest single party, winning 57 of the 80 African seats; Nkomo's PF—ZAPU took 20 seats and the UANC only three. In a separate poll of white voters, the RF secured all 20 reserved seats. The new state of Zimbabwe became legally independent, within the Commonwealth, on 18 April, with Rev. Canaan Banana as President (with largely ceremonial duties) and Mugabe as Prime Minister, at the head of a coalition Government.

Relations within the Government were strained, particularly between Mugabe and Nkomo. The latter was removed from the Cabinet, with two PF colleagues, in February 1982, under suspicion of plotting against Mugabe. By May 1984 the RF, now restyled the Republican Front, retained only seven of the 20 seats reserved for whites, the remaining 13 being held by independents. In July the RF was renamed the Conservative Alliance of Zimbabwe (CAZ), and opened its membership to all races.

There were several outbreaks of violence prior to a general election in June–July 1985. ZANU—PF was returned to power with an increased majority, winning 63 of the 79 'common roll' seats in the House of Assembly (and an additional seat at a by-election in August). ZAPU won 15 seats, retaining its traditional hold over Matabeleland, and ZANU—Sithole took a single seat. The UANC failed to gain representation. Of the 20 seats reserved for whites, 15 were secured by the CAZ. However, the CAZ was not represented in the new Cabinet.

During mid-1985 a large number of ZAPU officials were detained for questioning about dissident activity in Matabeleland. Later in the year, however, ZANU and ZAPU reached broad agreement on the terms of a merger of the two parties, in the interests of national unity; negotiations continued during 1986, but were suspended in April 1987. The failure, in August, of further talks aimed at uniting ZANU and ZAPU led to renewed rebel activity, whereupon the Government took steps to prevent ZAPU from functioning effectively. Furthermore, ZANU declined to endorse seven ZAPU-nominated candidates for the parliamentary seats made vacant in September by the abolition of seats reserved for whites (see below). In December Mugabe and Nkomo finally signed an agreement of unity, which was ratified by both parties in April 1988 and implemented in December 1989 (see below). In January 1988 Nkomo was appointed as one of the Senior Ministers in the President's Office, and two other ZAPU officials were given government posts. Following the unity agreement there was a significant improvement in the security situation in Matabeleland. However, the state of emergency remained in force, owing to incursions into eastern Zimbabwe by the Mozambican rebel movement, the Resistência Nacional Moçambicana (Renamo, see below).

Two major constitutional reforms were enacted during 1987. In September the reservation for whites of 20 seats in the House of Assembly and 10 seats in the Senate was abolished, as permitted by the Constitution, subject to a majority vote in the House. In October the 80 remaining members of the House of Assembly elected 20 candidates, who were nominated by ZANU, including 11 whites, to fill the vacant seats in the House of Assembly until the next general election. In the same month Parliament approved the replacement of the ceremonial presidency by an executive presidency. The post of Prime Minister was to be incorporated into the presidency. President Banana (who, as the only candidate, had been sworn in for a second term of office as President in April 1986) retired in December 1987, and at the end of that month Mugabe (the sole candidate) was inaugurated as Zimbabwe's first executive President.

In April 1989 Edgar Tekere, a former Secretary-General of ZANU, founded the Zimbabwe Unity Movement (ZUM), intending to challenge ZANU at the next general election. In December ZANU and ZAPU merged to form a single party, named the Zimbabwe African National Union—Patriotic Front (ZANU—PF). The united party aimed to establish a one-party state with a Marxist-Leninist doctrine. Mugabe was appointed President of ZANU—PF, while Nkomo became one of its two Vice-Presidents.

Presidential and parliamentary elections were held concurrently in March 1990; at these elections legislation approved in late 1989 came into effect, abolishing the Senate and increasing the number of seats in the House of Assembly from 100 to 150 (of which 120 were to be directly elected; 12 were to be allocated to presidential nominees, 10 to traditional Chiefs and eight to provincial governors). Mugabe won nearly 80% of all votes cast at the presidential election and at the parliamentary elections ZANU—PF secured 117 of the 120 elective seats in the House of Assembly; the ZUM (which had entered into an informal electoral alliance with the CAZ) won only two seats, and the UANC took one seat. Although ZANU—PF won an outright victory, only 54% of the electorate voted, and representatives of the ruling party were accused of intimidating voters. Following the elections Nkomo was appointed as one of two Vice-Presidents (the other being Simon Muzenda, also a Vice-President of ZANU—PF), and remained one of the Senior Ministers in the President's Office. In August 1990 the state of emergency was finally revoked.

In March 1992 the House of Assembly approved legislation (the Land Acquisition Act) that permitted the compulsory acquisition of land by the Government; this was intended to facilitate the redistribution of land ownership from Europeans (who owned about one-third of farming land in early 1992) to Africans. In May 1993 the Government published a list of properties allotted for transfer to the State under the Act, provoking a strong protest from the white-dominated Commercial Farmers' Union (CFU). The High Court subsequently ruled against three white farmers who had attempted to prove that the confiscation of their land was unconstitutional. A lack of available funds impeded the progress of the Government's land resettlement programme.

ZANU—PF won an overwhelming victory at legislative elections in April 1995, receiving more than 82% of the votes cast and securing 118 of the 120 elective seats in the House of Assembly (55 of which were uncontested). The remaining two elective seats were taken by ZANU—Ndonga (formerly ZANU—Sithole). Following the allocation of nominated and reserved seats, ZANU—PF controlled 148 of the total 150 seats. However, only 54% of the electorate voted, and the elections were boycotted by eight opposition groups, including the ZUM. In mid-April Mugabe appointed a reorganized and enlarged Cabinet; Nkomo and Muzenda remained as Vice-Presidents.

Mugabe retained the presidency at an election in March 1996, winning 92.7% of the votes cast. Turn-out was, however, low. In late March Mugabe was sworn in for a third term as President. Between August and November there were a number of national strikes by public-sector workers demanding pay increases. In October it was announced that ZANU—PF was abandoning Marxism-Leninism as its guiding principle. In August the Government announced that the independence war veterans (an increasingly powerful lobby) were to be awarded a number of substantial, unbudgeted benefits.

In October 1997 Mugabe announced that the pace of the land resettlement programme would be accelerated, declaring that the constitutional right of white commercial farmers to receive full and fair compensation for confiscated land would not be honoured and (unsuccessfully) challenging the United Kingdom, in its role as former colonial power, to take responsibility for assisting them. A list of 1,503 properties to be reallocated forthwith was published in November. In January 1998, however, the IMF stipulated on an assurance from the Mugabe administration that it would respect the Constitution during the land resettlement procedure as a condition for the release of financial assistance; such an assurance was eventually given in March, when it was announced that 120 farms would be acquired in the near future in exchange for full and fair compensation. In August Mugabe introduced the second phase of the programme, to resettle 150,000 families on 1m. ha of land each year for the next seven years. Under pressure from Western donors, the Government agreed to reduce its plans, and was restricted to using 118 farms that it had already been offered. In November, however, 841 white-owned farms were ordered to be confiscated by the state: compensation was to be deferred. Pressure exerted by the IMF in light of a forthcoming release of aid brought an assurance from Mugabe that his administration would not break agreements for a gradual land reform programme; however, at the end of March 1999 the President contravened the agreement when he announced a new plan to acquire a further 529 white-owned farms. Mugabe accused the USA and the United Kingdom of 'destabilizing' Zimbabwe through their alleged control over the IMF, which was delaying financial assistance to the country. In May the Government agreed a plan that aimed to resettle 77,700 black families on 1m. ha by 2001. Some of this land was to come from the 118 farms that had already been offered. The remainder would be the result of uncontested acquisitions under the Government's reduced list of 800 farms for compulsory purchase. The plan was to be partially funded by the World Bank, and was broadly accepted by the white landowners' association.

Meanwhile, labour unrest escalated in December 1997, when a general strike was organized by the Zimbabwe Congress of Trade Unions (ZCTU), in protest at the imposition by the Government of three unpopular new taxes in order to finance the provision of benefits to war veterans (see above); the authorities capitulated, withdrawing two of the taxes immediately. Shortly after the demonstrations had subsided, Morgan Tsvangirai, the Secretary-General of ZCTU, was attacked in his office by unknown assailants. The weak Zimbabwe currency and soaring food prices aggravated the nation-wide mood of discontent. In January 1998 riots erupted in most of the country's urban areas in protest at rises in the price of maize meal, the staple food. In response Mugabe agreed to withdraw the most recent price increase. However, the army was deployed to suppress the disturbances and was authorized to open fire on protesters; nine people were reportedly killed and some 800 rioters were arrested. The ZCTU organized a further two-day strike in March, to protest against the continuing rise in living costs.

In September 1998 threats for a five-day stoppage in support of demands for tax cuts resulted in government concessions. Meanwhile, further consumer price increases were followed by renewed rioting. A series of one-day strikes over pay were called by unions, and action took place until banned by Mugabe. In February 1999, however, the ban was ruled to be illegal. In that month growing unrest followed an address to the nation by Mugabe in which he attacked the judiciary, the independent media and 'British agents'. He also accused whites of 'fomenting unrest' and disturbances continued throughout 1999.

Meanwhile, in October 1998 the Government discussed potential amendments to Zimbabwe's Constitution with an opposition grouping, known as the National Constitutional Assembly (NCA). In March 1999 Mugabe appointed a commission of inquiry to make recommendations for a new constitution. The NCA refused to participate, owing to the alleged high risk of presidential manipulation.

An international constitutional conference was held in November 1999, but several experts suspected that the draft constitution had already been written, and that they had been invited primarily to give the process global credibility. In late November a document bearing no relation to that prepared by the 400-member constitutional commission, a drafting committee overseen by ZANU—PF having deleted crucial clauses (particularly relating to the reduction of the President's powers and the introduction of a parliamentary system), was declared to have been 'adopted by acclamation', despite vigorous protests. In January 2000 Mugabe announced that a referendum on the new constitution would take place on 12–13 February. Confusion before the polls over such issues as eligibility to vote and the location of polling stations was believed by the opposition to have been orchestrated by ZANU—PF to maximize Mugabe's chances of victory. Despite fears that a lack of supervision of the ballot had led to widespread irregularities on ZANU—PF's part, 54.6% of the 26% of the electorate who participated in the polls voted to reject the draft constitution. The level of participation was highest in urban areas where support for the recently formed opposition party, the Movement for Democratic Change (MDC), led by Tsvangirai, was strong.

The Government embarked on a campaign to restore its popularity prior to the legislative elections, which, it was announced in March 2000, were to be held in May rather than April. Illegal occupations of white-owned farms by black 'war veterans' (many of whom, too young to have taken part in the war of independence, were suspected of having been paid to participate), which began in late February, were rumoured to have been organized by the Government in an attempt to regain support through the land issue. The security forces refused to act against the occupiers, declaring that the 'political issue' lay outside their jurisdiction. Occupations increased, and the police also failed to take steps to evict the protesters, following a ruling by the High Court in mid-March in favour of the white farmers (which was ignored by the veterans). Mugabe repeatedly denied that his administration was behind the occupations, but made no secret of his support for them. The invasions became increasingly violent, and two farmers were killed in April. The international community condemned the Government's increasingly militant stance, which also extended to the treatment of the opposition, in particular the MDC, which was subjected to a campaign of intimidation and aggression. A constitutional amendment approved in April stated that white farmers dispossessed of their land would have to apply to the 'former colonial power', the United Kingdom, for compensation (see below). Many farmers were aggrieved, as their land had been purchased under Zimbabwean law. In May Mugabe met with war veterans and white farmers and announced the creation of a land commission to redistribute farmland. Shortly afterwards, however, he signed a law allowing the seizure of 841 white-owned farms without compensation. Violence continued unabated throughout the month. In June a list was published of 804 farms that were to be confiscated. Farmers were to be granted approximately one month to contest the list.

International aid to Zimbabwe was suspended in October 1999 owing to the Government's failure to meet reform targets. The budget deficit continued to increase and huge arrears to overseas suppliers of fuel, partly owing to a desperate shortage of foreign currency reserves, led to the suspension of oil supplies in December. Mugabe, however, refused to acquiesce to demands from farmers and financial institutions to devalue the currency.

Prior to legislative elections, which took place on 24–25 June 2000, there were reports of violence towards observers, and a UN team, sent to co-ordinate the polls, was recalled following obstruction by the Government. The authorities also refused to permit the accreditation of some 200 foreign monitors. ZANU—PF secured 48.6% of the votes cast and 62 of the 120 elective seats in the House of Assembly, the MDC won 47.0% of the ballot and 57 seats, while ZANU—Ndonga received one seat. Morgan Tsvangirai failed to win his constituency, as did the Ministers of Justice and Home Affairs. There were reports of widespread irregularities in the polls, which international observers declared not to have been free and fair. The MDC announced that it was to submit 10 dossiers listing alleged incidents of electoral fraud to the High Court. In total, the MDC challenged the results in 37 constituencies. In April 2001 the Court announced that results in two constituencies, including that contested by Tsvangirai, were to be nullified and new elections held; the MDC had previously abandoned proceedings relating to two other constituencies, and had been defeated in its challenge to the result in another. In June one further result was nullified, and one upheld.

Shortly after the legislative elections, Mugabe announced that some 500 additional white-owned farms would be appropriated for resettlement. In December 2000 a court ruling upheld previous opinions that declared the appropriation of white-owned farms without compensation payments to be unlawful, and urged the Government to produce a feasible land-reform programme by June 2001; Mugabe announced that sufficient white-owned land had been appropriated for resettlement, but repeated his assertion that he would not accept court-imposed impediments to any further land-reform measures. Negotiations between the Government and farmers' representatives resumed in January 2001.

In March 2001 the Commonwealth announced that it would send a delegation comprising the foreign ministers of Australia, Barbados and Nigeria to Zimbabwe for discussions with the Government. Mugabe refused to meet the delegation, however, claiming that the decision had been inspired by the United Kingdom. Similar criticisms were made of an attempt by the European Union (EU, see p. 244) to establish a dialogue with Zimbabwe regarding its record on human rights. In April Mugabe dismissed speculation that he would resign and arrange a presidential election for July, by stating that he intended to contest the election at its scheduled time in 2002. In the same month various foreign diplomatic missions in Harare reported receiving threats from war veterans; the Government refused to guarantee the safety of diplomatic personnel if they 'became involved in local politics'. In early June Mugabe urged war veterans to intensify the occupation of white-owned farms, and in the following days attacks against such farms throughout the country were reported to have increased, causing the death of at least one farm worker. The Zimbabwean Government criticized US and British media coverage of the events, and in mid-

June it imposed severe restrictions on journalists visiting the country. Later that month the Government listed a further 2,030 farms for compulsory acquisition, and in early August Joseph Made, the Minister of Lands, Agriculture and Rural Development announced the Government's intention to appropriate 8.3m. ha of commercial farmland. Further unrest occurred later that month in the north of the country, where approximately 100 white-owned farms were reported to have been evacuated following attacks by war veterans.

In early September 2001 a meeting of Commonwealth ministers was convened in Abuja, Nigeria, to discuss Mugabe's land resettlement programme; it was agreed that illegal farm seizures would cease and that international donors would compensate white farmers for the distribution of their land to landless black families. The agreement was broadly supported by both ZANU—PF and the MDC. By the end of September, however, more than 20 new farm invasions were reported to have taken place, resulting in several deaths, and talks between the Government and the CFU collapsed. Mugabe's intention to disregard the terms of the Abuja agreement became apparent in early October, when he ordered the Supreme Court to recognize the land reform programme as legal, reversing the ruling of December 2000; widespread criticism was directed at the Government for its manipulation of the judiciary. Commonwealth ministers and officials visited Zimbabwe later in October 2001 to monitor the Government's adherence to the Abuja agreement, but failed to persuade the Government to comply with its terms. Government repression intensified in November, when it amended the Land Act by decree. According to the revised legislation, any farm issued with a 'notice of acquisition' would become the property of the state with immediate effect; previously, a farm owner had been served 90 days' notice.

In November 2001 the Government ordered *The Daily News* to close its offices, alleging financial irregularities; it was widely believed, however, that the measure was taken to suppress criticism of the Government. The editor of that newspaper was charged with false reporting and undermining the Government in October 2002, under the Public Order and Security Act (see below), and resigned in December. In December 2001 Mugabe was nominated as the presidential candidate of ZANU—PF and announced that the election would take place in March 2002.

International concern about the situation in Zimbabwe intensified at the end of 2001. South African President Thabo Mbeki expressed doubts about whether conditions were suitable for a free and fair election, and the Commonwealth Ministerial Action Group on the Harare Declaration, meeting in London, United Kingdom, in late December, warned the Zimbabwean Government that it risked suspension from the organization unless it ended violent land seizures and political intimidation of the media and opposition groups. Despite Zimbabwe's growing isolation in the international community, in January 2002 further controversial legislation, aimed at suppressing opposition to Mugabe, was introduced: the Public Order and Security Bill prohibited the publication of documents that incited public disorder or undermined the security services, and banned public gatherings that incited rioting; the General Laws Amendment Bill prohibited foreign and independent missions from monitoring the elections, and forbade voter education (the Bill was repealed by the Supreme Court in February, following a challenge from the MDC); and the Access to Information Bill made it an offence for foreign news services to report from Zimbabwe unless authorized by the Zimbabwean Government. The EU finally imposed so-called 'smart' sanctions on Zimbabwe in mid-February, after the leader of its electoral observer mission was expelled from the country. (Mugabe had previously attempted to ban certain EU member states, including the United Kingdom, from participating in the mission.) The sanctions included an embargo on the sale of arms to Zimbabwe, the suspension of €128m. of aid scheduled to be disbursed during 2002–07, and the freezing of the assets of 19 Zimbabwean officials, including Mugabe, who were also prohibited from visiting any EU state; the USA imposed similar measures several days later. In July the EU applied the sanctions to a further 53 people, including all cabinet members. The EU extended sanctions for a further 12 months in February 2003, although Mugabe attended the Franco-African summit in Paris, France, later that month. (However, he was not invited to the Franco-African summit in Cannes, France in February 2007.) The USA also extended its sanctions to more than 70 senior officials in March 2003.

Meanwhile, in late February 2002 Tsvangirai and two other senior members of the MDC were arrested and charged with treason for allegedly plotting to assassinate Mugabe, after an Australian television network broadcast footage that purportedly showed Tsvangirai suggesting the possibility of 'eliminating' Mugabe. The three men appeared in court in mid-March and were released on bail.

The presidential election took place on 9–10 March 2002, but voting was extended to 11 March by the High Court, in response to a request from the MDC, which had claimed that the number of polling stations in areas with strong MDC support was inadequate, and that certain stations had closed on 10 March before many people had been able to vote. Mugabe was declared the winner on 13 March, with 56.2% of the valid votes cast; Tsvangirai secured 42.0%. Independent observers were divided in their judgement of whether the election was free and fair; most observers from African countries declared the election result legitimate, while the Norwegian delegation (the only European representatives) and independent Zimbabwean observers condemned the result and reported widespread electoral fraud and intimidation of the electorate and of observers by members of ZANU—PF. The MDC claimed that a number of its agents had been abducted from certain polling stations and detained by the police. Tsvangirai mounted a legal challenge to have the results declared null and void; however, after a protracted case, the High Court eventually ruled against him in 2005 and the Supreme Court dismissed his application in February 2006.

Prior to the presidential election the Commonwealth had nominated the Nigerian President, Olusegun Obasanjo, President Mbeki and the Australian Prime Minister, John Howard, to consider the conduct of the election and to formulate the organization's response. Mbeki and Obasanjo visited Zimbabwe following the election and urged Mugabe and the MDC to form a government of national unity; however, the MDC refused to co-operate unless the election was held again. The Commonwealth suspended Zimbabwe from meetings of the organization for one year in mid-March, stating that the election result had been undermined by politically motivated violence and that conditions did not permit the free will of the electorate to be expressed. (The suspension was extended for a further nine months in March 2003.) Immediately after the election the Government enacted the Access to Information and Protection of Privacy Act (AIPPA), which required all journalists reporting in Zimbabwe to be approved by the state; seven journalists had been detained under the Act by early May. In April the NCA organized demonstrations in support of demands for a new constitution and a rerun of the presidential election, at which more than 80 demonstrators were arrested. Violence directed at supporters of the MDC intensified following the election, allegedly committed by ZANU—PF supporters, and more than 50 people were reported to have been killed between the election and the end of April.

Land seizures also escalated, and in late March 2002 the Government listed almost 400 white-owned farms for compulsory acquisition, bringing the area scheduled for redistribution to the black population to around 85% of total commercial farmland. In June Mugabe issued an order listing some 2,900 white-owned farms for seizure; farmers were obliged to cease working their land on 25 June, or face up to two years' imprisonment, and to leave their properties by early August. Some 860 farmers had vacated their properties by the deadline, while 1,700 refused to leave. (Some 300 had left their farms temporarily to avoid confrontation.) In a speech in August Mugabe stated that white farmers who were 'loyal' to the Government had the option of staying, although later that month it was reported that almost 200 farmers had been arrested for refusing to leave their properties, while others had gone into hiding. In September the Land Acquisition Act was amended to allow the eviction of white farmers within seven days, as opposed to the 90 days previously required.

In April 2002 ZANU—PF and the MDC engaged in talks in an effort to end the political crisis, but negotiations collapsed in the following month, when ZANU—PF withdrew, citing the MDC's petition to the High Court, seeking to overturn the election results, which ZANU—PF regarded as unlawful. In August Mugabe dissolved his Cabinet and appointed a new Government a few days later, retaining several ministers from the previous administration. In February 2003 the trial of Tsvangirai and two other senior MDC officials for allegedly plotting to assassinate Mugabe (see above) began in Harare, but was adjourned until May. In March the MDC led a 'mass action' against the Government, aimed at forcing it to repeal what the party called repressive legislation and to release political prisoners; the

Government claimed that the MDC had detonated bombs in Kadoma, south-west of Harare, and it was reported that up to 500 members of the opposition had been arrested and many more driven from their homes and beaten. In early June Tsvangirai was arrested at the conclusion of further demonstrations against the Government organized by the MDC, reportedly in connection with statements he had made in May; he was released on bail in late June.

In September 2003 the closure of The Daily News, owing to the failure of its publisher to register with the Government's Media and Information Commission (MIC), provoked international condemnation. A court ruling that the newspaper should be allowed to resume publication pending the result of an application that it had made to register with the MIC was initially disregarded by the police. Publication of The Daily News did subsequently resume, despite the refusal of the MIC to grant it a licence, but was suspended again in February 2004 when the Supreme Court confirmed that its unlicensed appearance was illegal. (By early 2005 four newspapers had been closed under the Act: The Daily News, the Daily News on Sunday, The Tribune and The Weekly Times.)

The death, in September 2003, of Simon Muzenda, one of Zimbabwe's two Vice-Presidents, reignited speculation regarding an eventual successor to President Mugabe. It was reported in December that leading ZANU—PF officials had persuaded Mugabe to retire before the expiry of his term of office in 2008, but the annual conference of the party, held in December, elicited no indication of the President's intentions in this respect. Nor was there any confirmation of speculation that ZANU—PF was willing to engage in dialogue with the MDC in order to resolve Zimbabwe's political crisis.

From October 2003 increased concern was expressed at divisions within the Commonwealth over the political crisis in Zimbabwe. The decision, taken at a meeting of Commonwealth Heads of Government held in Abuja, Nigeria, in December, to extend Zimbabwe's suspension from the organization indefinitely, until the country had restored democracy and the rule of law, confirmed the existence of a rift between African Commonwealth members and their Western counterparts. The 12 members from southern Africa criticized the decision, and Mbeki claimed that other Commonwealth members had failed to understand the question of land ownership in Zimbabwe and that they were mistaken in their belief that the presidential election held in Zimbabwe in 2002 had been unfair. Zimbabwe, for its part, announced its decision to withdraw from the Commonwealth shortly before the conclusion of the Heads of Government meeting.

In January 2004, giving evidence for the first time in his trial for treason, Tsvangirai denied that he had ever plotted to assassinate President Mugabe or to overthrow the Government. Tsvangirai was acquitted of the assassination charges in mid-October 2004; the outstanding treason charge was finally dropped in August 2005. In February 2004 a cabinet reorganization was effected in which, among other changes, Herbert Murerwa was replaced as Minister of Finance and Economic Development by Chris Kuruneri. In late April, however, Kuruneri was arrested on charges of illegally trading foreign currency; his arrest was stated by the authorities to be part of an anti-corruption campaign inaugurated earlier in the year; Murerwa, who was now serving as the Minister of Higher Education and Technology, was subsequently appointed to replace Kuruneri on an acting basis. (Kuruneri's trial began in May 2005. The Governor of the Reserve Bank of Zimbabwe, Gideon Gono, gave evidence that the currency in question had been legitimately obtained by Kuruneri. Kuruneri was granted bail in late July but placed under house arrest.) Meanwhile, in February 2004 the EU renewed sanctions imposed upon the Mugabe regime, extending the travel ban and assets freeze to cover a total of 95 Zimbabwean officials, and in March the USA imposed a further series of sanctions on Zimbabwe, notably targeting government-owned enterprises.

In late 2004 a power struggle developed within ZANU—PF. There was speculation that Mugabe was actively assigning key posts in the administration to members of his own Zezuru clan, replacing members of the majority Karanga clan. At the annual ZANU—PF conference in December Joyce Mujuru, the incumbent Minister of Water Resources, Infrastructural Development and Small and Medium Enterprises, was appointed to the post of Vice-President, which had been vacant since the death of Muzenda in September 2003. In December 2004 the country's voting constituencies were redrawn, reportedly increasing the number of seats available in traditional ZANU—PF strongholds, while reducing those available in areas where the MDC commanded popular support.

In January 2005 Mugabe approved an amendment to the AIPPA that made it an offence for any journalist to work without accreditation from the MIC. In mid-February Mugabe dismissed the Minister of State for Information and Publicity, Jonathan Moyo, from the Cabinet after Moyo had announced his intention to stand as an independent candidate at the legislative elections in March. Moyo was also expelled from ZANU—PF and barred from taking his seat in the House of Assembly.

According to provisional results of the legislative elections held on 31 March 2005, Mugabe's ruling ZANU—PF party won 78 out of the 120 seats available, taking 56.4% of the vote. The opposition MDC took 41 seats with 42.1% of the votes cast; Moyo, was elected as an independent candidate. Under the Constitution the President could allocate 12 seats in the House of Assembly to candidates of his choosing and appoint the eight provincial governors; a further 10 seats were reserved for tribal chiefs, also loyal to Mugabe. The overall result therefore gave ZANU—PF a two-thirds majority in the Assembly which would allow Mugabe to amend the Constitution. International observers from the African Union (AU, see p. 164) and the Southern African Development Community (SADC, see p. 386) endorsed the results; observers from the Commonwealth, the EU and the USA were not invited owing to their perceived hostility towards the Mugabe Government. The Governments of Malawi, Mozambique, South Africa and Zambia were among those who accepted the elections as free and fair; however, the results were dismissed by Australia, the EU and the USA. (The observers from the AU later reversed their opinion and called for investigations into allegations of electoral fraud.) The MDC contested the results citing electoral irregularities in 76 out of the 120 constituencies, and claimed that it should, in fact, have won 94 seats. In mid-April the MDC released a report alleging that some 134,000 people had been turned away from polling stations and that ballot boxes had been filled with votes for ZANU—PF after the polls had closed. The MDC filed petitions at the Electoral Court challenging the results in 13 constituencies. Meanwhile, the outgoing Minister responsible for Land Reform and Resettlement, John Nkomo, announced that white farmers who had lost their farms during the resettlement programme would be compensated for the value of assets and improvements but not for the land itself, which the Government maintained was the responsibility of the United Kingdom. It was estimated that the white population in Zimbabwe had fallen from 200,000 in 2000 to around 25,000 at March 2005; of these some 500 were farmers.

The EU renewed its sanctions against Zimbabwe in February 2005, but in early April Italy was obliged to allow Mugabe to travel through the country to the Vatican City in order to attend the funeral of the Supreme Pontiff of the Roman Catholic Church, Pope John Paul II. The Zimbabwe Government exploited international treaties which obliged countries to allow foreign government officials to travel to international organizations hosted within those countries. In July 2005 Gono and Murerwa both attended a meeting of the IMF in New York, USA, despite sanctions which otherwise would have prevented them travelling to that country, while in October Mugabe attended a conference of the Food and Agriculture Organization in Rome, Italy.

In April 2005 Mugabe announced his new Government, which he described as a 'development Cabinet': the former Zimbabwean ambassador to the United Kingdom, Simbarashe Mumbengegwi, was appointed Minister of Foreign Affairs replacing Stanislaus Mudenge, who moved to head the Ministry of Higher and Tertiary Education; Tichaona Jokonya, formerly Zimbabwe's Permanent Representative to the United Nations, assumed the hitherto vacant post of Minister of State for Information and Publicity; Murerwa was confirmed as Minister of Finance. Sixteen ministers retained their portfolios, including Patrick Chinamasa as Minister of Justice, Legal and Parliamentary Affairs. Didymus Mutasa was appointed Minister of State for National Security and head of the Central Intelligence Organization, and in mid-May also assumed overall responsibility for the land redistribution programme.

In late May 2005 the Government launched Operation Murambatsvina ('Sweep Away the Rubbish'), which targeted black market trading—principally in foreign currency and fuel—and 'general lawlessness'. The MDC claimed that it was a punitive action against the urban poor who had voted against ZANU—PF in the elections in March. Shanty towns were razed to the ground in Harare and other major cities, including Bulawayo and Gweru. The operation attracted widespread international condemnation and, according to a report by UN-Habitat published in late July, some 700,000 people were made homeless; however, the Government refused offers of humanitarian aid. In late June President Mugabe announced that some Z.$3,000,000m. was to be spent on new housing and commercial premises under a three-year redevelopment programme entitled Operation Garikai/Hlalani Kuhle. (In September 2006 the human rights organization Amnesty International reported that the Government had not met its housing obligations as just 3,325 new homes had been built, while 92,460 had been demolished.) In late 2005 July Vice-President Mujuru announced the official end of Operation Murambatsvina and appealed for humanitarian aid; nevertheless the Government reaffirmed that it would not make an official appeal to the UN for food aid. In early October, as part of Operation Siyapambili/Hatidzokereshure ('Going Forward/No Turning Back'), police arrested more than 14,000 people in Harare on charges of illegal street trading and foreign currency dealing.

In late August 2005 the House of Assembly approved a bill which provided for a number of changes to the Constitution. The bill also included legislation designed to conclude the land redistribution programme: courts would no longer be able to hear appeals on land acquisition and ones listed for appropriation land would immediately become state property. (However, in early 2006 banks were still refusing to extend loans to resettled farmers because they were not in possession of the title deeds to the land.) Under the bill it became a criminal offence for Zimbabweans to endorse sanctions or military action against their country, and the Zimbabwe Electoral Commission (ZEC) was established in place of the Electoral Supervisory Commission. In addition, the bill provided for the reintroduction of a 66-member Senate (abolished in 1990) as the second chamber of the legislature; senatorial elections were held in late November 2005. The MDC was deeply divided over the issue of participating in the elections. Tsvangirai opposed electoral participation, advocating mass protests and 'democratic resistance'; however, a faction led by the party's Secretary-General, Welshman Ncube, fielded 26 candidates. ZANU—PF won 43 of the 50 elected seats, receiving 73.7% of the vote; MDC candidates took the remaining seven seats with 20.3% of the vote. The MDC effectively split in two, a 'pro-Senate' faction electing Arthur Mutumbara as its leader in February 2006. The rump of the party re-elected Tsvangirai as its President in late March at a conference reportedly attended by some 15,000 supporters.

In July 2006 five senior members of the MDC were injured in an attack as they left the Harare suburb of Mabvuku. A statement from the pro-Senate faction blamed the attack on Tsvangirai. However, Tsvangirai's spokesman suggested that the attack was the work of government agents attempting to sow division within the party. In late December Lovemore Madhuku, the Chairman of the NCA, was the victim of an arson attack on his home; the NCA alleged that it was the third attempt on Madhuku's life in four years and the attack occurred as the organization was mobilizing supporters to resist a proposed extension of Mugabe's term in office until 2010. An alliance of 23 opposition parties, church and civic groups had agreed to unite under the 'Save Zimbabwe' banner to campaign against any such extension.

Meanwhile, in March 2006 the IMF postponed a decision to expel Zimbabwe after it repaid US $120m. of its debt to the fund and pledged to clear its remaining obligations by November. In December the IMF recommended sharp reductions in public spending to lower inflation (the annual rate was recorded as 1,594% in January 2007) as well as the reform of exchange rates, the liberalization of price controls, the removal of restrictions on current account payments and the strengthening of private property rights. In August 2006 the Reserve Bank of Zimbabwe unexpectedly devalued the Zimbabwe dollar by 59.3%, and removed three zeros from the currency, in an attempt to stem both corruption and hyperinflation. New banknotes were introduced later that month, which led to the seizure of more than US $50m. worth of old banknotes at roadblocks and border posts in a crackdown on money launderers. In June the People's Republic of China had signed an agreement worth $1,300m. with Zimbabwe to help relieve an acute shortage of energy. In exchange for chrome from Zimbabwe, Chinese companies agreed to build new coal mines and three thermal power stations in the Zambezi valley on the Zambian border. In December Zimbabwe opened talks with China regarding a US $2,000m. loan in an attempt to secure much needed funding to boost its rapidly deteriorating economy.

In February 2007 President Mugabe dismissed Murerwa, and made a number of other changes to the Cabinet. Murerwa had been involved in a prolonged public disagreement with Gono over economic policies, in particular over the latter's refusal further to devalue the national currency, and had also been subjected to sustained criticism with regard to the subsidizing of the prices of grain, fuel and electricity; Mugabe had also denounced a number of Murerwa's decisions as 'disastrous'. In the same month more than 60 junior doctors were dismissed from Harare Central Hospital after commencing industrial action. Some 350 doctors across the country had been demanding increased pay and better working conditions, while urban workers struggled to cope with the soaring costs of consumer goods, public transport fares and medical fees.

Between November 2006 and February 2007 more than 31,000 people were arrested in a major police crackdown, known as Operation Chikorokoza Chapera ('The End of Illegal Gold Dealings'). With the rate of unemployment reportedly standing at more than 80%, many Zimbabweans turned to gold- or diamond-prospecting following the collapse of commercial agriculture. Earlier in February the Government had announced that the last white farmers, numbering some 400, could remain on their land long enough to harvest their crops, even though the deadline to leave had passed. In the previous month the US-based Famine Early Warning System warned that Zimbabwe was likely to record a shortfall in maize of some 850,000 metric tons in 2007.

In mid-February 2007 police used tear gas and water cannons to prevent an MDC rally from proceeding in Harare, despite the organization obtaining a High Court order allowing the rally to take place. In late February, in a rare act of violent defiance against the authorities, anti-Government protesters took control of Budiriro township in Harare for several hours, setting up roadblocks of boulders and burning tyres. Political tensions intensified further when Tsvangirai was arrested in mid-March along with five other members of the MDC after riot police violently dispersed a 'Save Zimbabwe' prayer meeting in Harare's Highfield township. One activist was killed by the police and Tsvangirai suffered severe injuries while in police custody. The Government stated that the rally breached a recently introduced three-month ban on political gatherings. The incident provoked widespread international condemnation and demands for the release of those detained. Following an SADC summit in Dar es Salaam, Tanzania, in late March, it was announced that Mbeki had agreed to mediate between the MDC and the Zimbabwean Government; however, there were further reports of the mistreatment of MDC activists in police custody, provoking renewed opposition protests and repeated calls for Mugabe to relinquish the presidency. Nevertheless, in early April ZANU—PF declared that Mugabe would stand as the party's candidate in the 2008 presidential election.

The first round of private talks between the MDC and the Government were held in May 2007, hosted by South African officials. Further discussions were held in early June to establish the agenda for formal negotiations, scheduled for later that month. Meanwhile, in mid-May Zimbabwe was elected to lead the UN Commission on Sustainable Development, prompting widespread objections from EU and US officials, who had opposed Zimbabwe's candidacy and questioned the nation's ability to assume such a role.

In early June 2007 constitutional amendments were proposed that would allow the legislative elections to be brought forward to coincide with the presidential election in 2008, harmonizing the presidential and parliamentary terms of office. The proposals also contained provisions for amendments to the structure of the House of Assembly and the Senate. The MDC opposed the proposals, which would, inter alia, allow the House of Assembly to nominate a new President should the incumbent stand down; under the existing structure, new elections would be required if the presidency were vacated. The MDC continued to be weakened by divisions between party members and in July it was announced that the two factions planned to field separate candidates in the presidential and legislative elections. Meanwhile, South African-led mediation between the MDC and ZANU—PF faltered amid worsening political and economic conditions; however, Mbeki denied that negotiations would collapse.

On 30 October 2007 a number of changes to the Constitution were officially adopted. With effect from the 2008 elections, the

House of Assembly was to be enlarged to comprise 210 directly elected members, while the total number of members of the Senate was to be increased to 93. Of these, 60 were to be directly elected, five were to be nominated by the President and 10 seats were reserved for provincial governors; the remaining 18 were to include the President and the Deputy President of the Council of Chiefs and 16 traditional Chiefs. The presidential term was reduced to five years. However, talks between ZANU—PF and the opposition failed to produce any agreement on electoral procedures and negotiations continued. ZANU—PF representatives insisted that further negotiations, expected to continue throughout November, would not delay the March 2008 elections.

In January 2008 Mugabe confirmed that presidential and legislative elections would be held concurrently on 29 March, resulting in complaints from the opposition which continued to demand further electoral and constitutional reforms. The MDC announced that it was to organize a mass protest against the Government's decision not to delay elections, claiming that Mugabe had reneged on agreements reached during the earlier talks mediated by Mbeki. In February Simba Makoni, a senior member of ZANU—PF who had served as Minister of Finance and Economic Development in 2000–02, announced his intention to challenge Mugabe for the presidency; Makoni was later expelled from the ruling party.

Presidential and legislative elections took place as scheduled on 29 March 2008. According to results released by the ZEC, the faction of the MDC led by Tsvangirai secured 99 of the 210 seats in the House of Assembly, while ZANU—PF took 97 seats; the MDC faction led by Mutambara secured 10 seats. However, no immediate announcement was made regarding the outcome of the presidential poll. Widespread irregularities were reported and observers expressed concern that the delay in releasing official results was allowing the ruling party to manipulate ballot papers. A recount of the legislative votes in 23 constituencies—the majority of which had been awarded to the MDC after the first count—commenced in mid-April. Following completion of the recount, the ZEC confirmed that the original results remained unchanged. It was subsequently announced that the two MDC factions intended to reunite, consolidating that party's legislative majority. In mid-May it was reported that ZANU—PF party had filed legal petitions challenging the results in 53 constituencies, while the MDC had challenged the election of 52 deputies. Provisional results of the senatorial elections indicated that ZANU—PF had secured 30 of the 60 directly elected seats in the upper chamber; Tsvangirai's faction of the MDC took 24 seats, while the Mutambara-led faction won six.

Following a period of sustained regional and international pressure, on 2 May 2008 the ZEC released results of the disputed presidential election. According to the Commission, Tsvangirai secured 47.9% of the votes cast, while Mugabe took 43.2%. Makoni was placed third with 8.3%. As no candidate secured the requisite 50% of the votes, a second round of voting was to be conducted, although no date was immediately established for the second round and, following an alleged campaign of violent intimidation of MDC supporters by ZANU—PF loyalists, Tsvangirai refused to confirm his participation in the run-off. On 10 May, however, Tsvangirai, who had temporarily relocated to South Africa, announced that he would take part in the second round. Nevertheless, the Chairman of the ZEC expressed doubt that the run-off would take place within three weeks of the announcement of the election results, as stipulated by the Electoral Law.

Meanwhile, in mid-March 2008 Mugabe signed a controversial nationalization law requiring 51% of all companies operating in Zimbabwe to be owned by black Zimbabweans. The legislation also banned mergers and restructuring of businesses unless the majority share was owned by black interests.

Zimbabwe severed diplomatic relations with South Africa in September 1980 and subsequently played an important role in international attempts to stabilize southern Africa and to end apartheid in South Africa. In July 1987 the Cabinet rejected a proposal by Mugabe to impose sanctions against South Africa, and the Government opted instead for less stringent economic measures. South Africa is believed to have been responsible for intermittent attacks during the 1980s against the then banned African National Congress of South Africa (ANC) in Zimbabwe. A meeting between President Mugabe and a South African government official in April 1991 (following the implementation of a programme of political reforms by President F. W. de Klerk of South Africa in February 1990) constituted the first direct contact between the Zimbabwean and South African Governments since 1980. The two countries re-established diplomatic relations following the holding of the first democratic elections in South Africa in April 1994, and in March 1997 a mutual defence co-operation agreement was concluded. Relations deteriorated in 1998 owing to South Africa's opposition to Zimbabwe's military intervention in the civil war in the DRC (see below). Relations were also strained from 1999, owing to Zimbabwe's increasingly negative economic and political circumstances (see above). In February 2000 South Africa denied reports that it had offered a substantial loan to Zimbabwe to help the country to resolve its financial crisis. However, President Mbeki offered to negotiate on Zimbabwe's behalf with the IMF and the World Bank for emergency aid to prevent the collapse of the economy. By May the increasingly turbulent land reform situation in Zimbabwe had adversely affected South Africa's economy, prompting Mbeki to appeal to foreign donors to fund the transfer of white-owned land to black farmers.

During the 1980s and early 1990s Zimbabwe provided support to the Mozambican Government against Renamo rebels; in late 1992–early 1993, under the terms of the peace agreement in Mozambique (q.v.), Zimbabwean troops, who had been stationed in Mozambique since 1982, were withdrawn. During the mid-1990s a group of armed Zimbabwean dissidents, known as the Chimwenjes, were reportedly active in western Mozambique (see above). In January 1996 the Mozambican Government announced its intention to expel the rebels, and in January 1997 an accord was signed by representatives of Mozambique and Zimbabwe on the co-ordination of activities against the rebels. Plans for the repatriation of some 145,000 Mozambican refugees were announced in March 1993; this scheme, co-ordinated by the office of the UN High Commissioner for Refugees, was completed by May 1995.

Following an SADC summit in Harare in August 1998, the Zimbabwean Government dispatched troops and arms to the DRC to support the regime of President Laurent-Désiré Kabila against advancing rebel forces. Despite repeated summits attempting to find a peaceful solution to the conflict, by May 1999 it was reported that Zimbabwe had spent at least $500m. on the continuing unpopular military action. A cease-fire agreement was signed at Lusaka, Zambia, on 10 July and troop withdrawals were to follow within the next few months. However, a few days later, both the rebels and the allies of the DRC were accused of violating the accord. The Zimbabwe and DRC Governments unveiled a plan in September to establish a joint diamond and gold marketing venture to finance the war. Nevertheless, in early 2000 the Zimbabwean Government was reportedly unable to pay allowances to its troops fighting in the region owing to the critical shortage of foreign currency (see above). Public opinion was further turned against the continuation of the conflict in February when heavy rains and a cyclone struck Mozambique and neighbouring provinces of eastern Zimbabwe. There was a desperate shortage of helicopters, which were needed to bring aid to those affected, owing to their deployment in the DRC. The war also caused tensions between Zimbabwe and the IMF, the latter suspending assistance partly because of Zimbabwe's false accounting of expenses relating to the conflict. In March Congolese rebels breached the cease-fire, capturing a town in the eastern DRC, and continued to advance westwards.

In August 2000 a further conference was held in Lusaka, at which all the governments involved reiterated their support for the accord agreed at the previous meeting; President Kabila subsequently stated that he had no confidence in the process, however. Kabila was assassinated in January 2001 and was succeeded by his son, Joseph. Efforts to agree a solution to the conflict increased, and all countries involved in the conflict agreed to withdraw their forces by May, pending the deployment of a UN force. Nevertheless, in April 2002 the Zimbabwean army announced that some 6,000–7,000 of its troops remained in the DRC, from an initial deployment of around 11,000. However, following a number of positive developments in the peace process, the last Zimbabwean troops withdrew from the DRC in October.

Relations with the United Kingdom centred on land reform in 1999–2001. In November 1999, while on a private visit to London, Mugabe was assaulted by protesters in support of homosexual rights. The President subsequently alleged at a Commonwealth summit that the British Government had organized the incident to register its disapproval of plans to redistribute land (see above), and declared Prime Minister Tony Blair unfit to govern. Mugabe's anger had been aroused by a speech by

ZIMBABWE

Introductory Survey

Blair criticizing certain African countries' inactivity concerning AIDS. Mugabe repeated his allegations in an outburst in March 2000, also accusing the United Kingdom of orchestrating an international hate campaign against Zimbabwe.

Relations between the United Kingdom and Zimbabwe remained strained throughout 2000 and 2001. In September 2002, at the UN World Summit on Sustainable Development in South Africa, tensions increased when Mugabe criticized Blair for his part in imposing EU sanctions on Zimbabwe and for interfering in the country's domestic politics; later that month the Government informed British diplomats that they could not leave Harare without permission from the Ministry of Foreign Affairs. In November Mugabe imposed a ban on senior British officials, including Blair, from travelling to Zimbabwe; the measure was taken in response to the United Kingdom's introduction of a requirement for Zimbabwean nationals to apply for a visa in order to visit that country. In 2006 Annan offered to intercede in order to foster better relations between the United Kingdom and Zimbabwe but cancelled his trip to Harare in July 2006 after the former Tanzanian President, Benjamin Mkapa, assumed the role of mediator, apparently with the approval of Mugabe. The British Prime Minister, Gordon Brown, boycotted a summit of EU and African states held in Lisbon, Portugal, in December 2007 in opposition to Mugabe's attendance.

In March 2004, at the international airport in Harare, the Zimbabwean authorities detained 70 men alleged to be involved in a plot to overthrow the Government of Equatorial Guinea, after impounding the aircraft in which 67 of them had travelled from South Africa. South African government officials suggested that the suspected mercenaries had landed in Harare en route to Equatorial Guinea in order to collect weapons, although the company that had chartered the aircraft insisted that the men had stopped to obtain mining-related supplies before flying to Burundi and the DRC to work as security guards. Later that month the 70 defendants appeared in a prison court near Harare, charged with a number of offences including conspiring against the Government of Equatorial Guinea and violating immigration laws. In June Zimbabwe and Equatorial Guinea agreed to open embassies in their respective capitals and it was reported that President Mugabe had agreed to extradite the 70 men accused of involvement in the coup plot in exchange for petroleum to the value of US $1,200m. Simon Mann, a South African-based British security consultant and the alleged leader of the coup plot, was convicted in September of attempting illegally to procure weapons and was sentenced to seven years' imprisonment (subsequently reduced to four) in Zimbabwe. At the completion of that sentence in 2007, the Equato-Guinean authorities sought to extradite Mann in order to undergo further legal proceedings. That request was granted by a Zimbabwean judge in May and in early February 2008 Mann was transported to custody in Equatorial Guinea.

Government

Under the terms of the 1980 Constitution (as subsequently amended), legislative power is vested in the President and a bicameral Parliament, consisting of a House of Assembly and a Senate. The House of Assembly comprises 210 members, who are directly elected by universal adult suffrage. Members of the House of Assembly serve for five years. The Senate comprises 93 members, 60 of whom are directly elected by universal adult suffrage (six in each of the 10 Provinces), five are appointed by the President, 10 are provincial governors, two are the President and the Deputy President of the Council of Chiefs and 16 are traditional Chiefs. Members of the Senate serve for five years. Executive authority is vested in the President, elected by universal adult suffrage for five years. The President appoints, and acts on the advice of, a Cabinet, which comprises no more than two Vice-Presidents and other Ministers and Deputy Ministers. The Cabinet must have the confidence of Parliament, to which it is responsible.

Defence

As assessed at November 2007, total armed forces numbered about 29,000: 25,000 in the army and 4,000 in the air force. Paramilitary forces comprise a police force of 19,500 and a police support unit of 2,300. Defence expenditure was budgeted at Z.$25,200m. for 2006.

Economic Affairs

In 2005, according to the World Bank, Zimbabwe's gross national income (GNI), measured at average 2003–2005 prices, was US $4,467m., equivalent to $340 per head (or $1,950 per head on an international purchasing-power parity basis). During 1996–2006, it was estimated, the population increased at an average annual rate of 0.9%, while gross domestic product (GDP) per head decreased, in real terms, by an average of 3.5% per year during 1996–2006. Overall GDP decreased, in real terms, at an average annual rate of 3.8% in 1996–2006; GDP declined by 4.8% in 2006.

Agriculture (including forestry and fishing) contributed 21.9% of GDP in 2006, according to the World Bank, and engaged 15.5% of the employed labour force in 2004. According to FAO estimates, however, the sector employed 59.7% of the total labour force in 2005. The principal cash crops are tobacco (which accounted for an estimated 13.5% of export earnings in 2004), maize, cotton, coffee and sugar. In addition, wheat, soybeans and groundnuts are cultivated. Beef production was traditionally an important activity; however, at December 2004 the Cattle Producers' Association reported that the commercial beef herd numbered fewer than 125,000 head of cattle, down from 1.4m. in 2000. Production of tobacco and maize was severely affected by the farm invasions that took place from the late 1990s (see Recent History). Zimbabwe's cereals deficit in 2007 was estimated at some 1m. metric tons. Of a maize requirement of 1.8m. tons, the country's own harvest was in the region of 300,000 tons, and the Government undertook to distribute a further 400,000 tons. Some 1.7m. people were estimated to require food aid in that year. During 1996–2006 agricultural GDP declined by an average of 3.4% per year. Agricultural GDP decreased by 5.8% in 2006.

Industry (including mining, manufacturing, construction and power) contributed 27.4% of GDP in 2006, according to the World Bank, and engaged 22.2% of the employed labour force in 2004. During 1996–2006 industrial GDP decreased at an average annual rate of 7.0%. Industrial GDP declined by 5.8% in 2006.

Mining contributed 1.8% of GDP and engaged 5.0% of the employed labour force in 2004. Gold, nickel and asbestos are the major mineral exports. Chromium ore, copper, silver, emeralds, lithium, tin, iron ore, cobalt, magnesite, niobium, tantalum, limestone, phosphate rock, coal and diamonds are also mined. In October 1999 the discovery of significant diamond deposits in Zimbabwe was announced; in 2003 Rio Tinto opened Zimbabwe's second diamond mine, at Murowa, near Zvishavane. In 2003 Anglo Platinum announced its intention to mine reserves of platinum ore located at Unki, on the Great Dyke. Zimbabwe also has large reserves of kyanite and smaller reserves of zinc and lead. In 2004 the export of minerals comprised an estimated 36.0% of the value of total exports. Mining GDP declined by an estimated 11.0% in 2000. According to government figures, mining GDP increased by 11.6% in 2004.

Manufacturing contributed 15.5% of GDP in 2006, according to the World Bank, and engaged 13.6% of the employed labour force in 2004. The most important sectors, measured by gross value of output, are food-processing, metals (mainly ferrochrome and steel), chemicals and textiles. According to the Confederation of Zimbabwe Industries, 840 manufacturing companies closed between 2000 and 2003. During 1996–2006 manufacturing GDP decreased by an average of 8.6% per year. Manufacturing GDP declined by 5.8% in 2006.

In 2004 56.8% of Zimbabwe's electricity production was derived from hydroelectric power, and 43.0% from coal. In 1998 a new project was introduced to supply electricity to villages by solar energy systems, funded by Italy. The Italian Government cancelled the project in September 1999, however, owing to Zimbabwe's political and economic difficulties. Imports of fuel and electricity comprised an estimated 23.2% of the value of total imports in 2004. In 2002 Zimbabwe purchased 24.2% of its electrical energy from neighbouring countries.

The services sector contributed 50.7% of GDP in 2006, according to the World Bank, and engaged 62.4% of the employed labour force in 2004. During 1996–2006 the GDP of the services sector decreased at an average annual rate of 4.7%. Services GDP declined by 28.8 in 2005, but increased by 10.8% in 2006.

In 2004, according to the African Development Bank, Zimbabwe had a visible trade surplus of US $5m., while there was a deficit of $139m. on the current account of the balance of payments. In 2004 South Africa was the principal source of imports (50.5%) and the principal market for exports (30.2%). Other major trading partners were Botswana, Switzerland, the People's Republic of China, Zambia, the United Kingdom, Germany, Japan and Malawi. The principal exports in 2004 were gold, tobacco, ferrous alloys, platinum, and cotton lint. The main imports in that year were fuel and electricity, machinery and transport equipment, chemicals and food.

In 2006 there was a budgetary deficit of Z.$46,037,300m. At the end of 2005 Zimbabwe's external debt totalled US $4,257m., of which $3,222m. was long-term public debt. In 2004 external debt was estimated to be equivalent to 77% of GDP and the cost of debt-servicing to 8.3% of GDP. The annual rate of inflation averaged 163.3% in 1996–2006. Consumer prices increased by an annual average of 1,096.7% in 2006. The official rate of inflation reached 3,719% in the year to April 2007, from 2,200% in the year to March. By February 2008 it was reported to have reached 164,900%. According to official figures, 6.0% of the total labour force were unemployed in 1999, although the actual rate was believed to be significantly greater: according to the Zimbabwe Congress of Trade Unions, some 80% of the labour force were unemployed in early 2007.

Zimbabwe is a member of the Southern African Development Community (see p. 386), which aims to promote closer economic integration among its members, and also belongs to the Common Market for Eastern and Southern Africa (see p. 205).

During the 1980s and 1990s Zimbabwe benefited from a well-developed infrastructure, mineral wealth and a highly diversified manufacturing sector, all of which contributed to relative resilience to the effects of fluctuations in international prices for the country's export commodities, and to the negative impact on agricultural output in years of poor rains. However, from 1999 the economy entered a prolonged period of crisis, and by the mid-2000s Zimbabwe was suffering hyperinflation, extremely high levels of unemployment, and a chronic shortage of foreign exchange to finance imports of essential foodstuffs, fuel, agricultural inputs and capital goods for the mining and manufacturing sectors. International humanitarian groups considered that the Government's land redistribution and urban clearance programmes (see Recent History) had contributed to a widening of disparities in incomes and were impeding the access of vulnerable groups to adequate food supplies, education, water, sanitation and health care. The Zimbabwean authorities attributed the country's severe economic decline to the actions of the international community, citing the impact of economic sanctions and lack of credit lines, balance of payments support and foreign direct investment. Despite the discharge of arrears to the IMF's General Resources Account in February 2006, and the consequent annulment of proceedings for the compulsory withdrawal of Zimbabwe from the Fund, Zimbabwe has been in continuous arrears to the IMF since 2001, and is the only case of prolonged arrears (totalling some SDR 86m. in early 2007) to the Fund's Poverty Reduction and Growth Facility-Exogenous Shocks Facility (PRGF-ESF) Trust. In view of the deterioration in economic performance, and Zimbabwe's continuing arrears to the Fund, the IMF in early 2007 maintained its earlier measures of sanction: a declaration of non-co-operation; the suspension of technical assistance; and the removal of Zimbabwe from eligibility under the PRGF-ESF. At mid-2006 Zimbabwe's external debt was put by the Ministry of Finance at almost US $4,000m., including arrears of US $2,100m. Targeted GDP growth under the supplementary budget of 0.3%–0.6% was not achieved that year and Zimbabwe had thus recorded negative growth each year since 1999. A new currency was issued by the Reserve Bank of Zimbabwe (RBZ) in August 2006, when Z.$1 replaced Z.$1,000 of the former currency. An accompanying devaluation was made of 59.3% in the official interbank exchange rate, to Z.$250 = US 1. In April 2007 the Governor of the RBZ announced a new foreign currency bond, intended to raise funds to address severe food shortages: the proceeds of the issue were to be directed to a new Drought Mitigation and Stabilization Fund. While the Government and the RBZ continued to resist demands for a further devaluation of the currency, a new rate of an effective Z.$15,000 = US $1 was set for foreign currency to be acquired for the new fund. Despite the announcement of new price support for producers of gold and tobacco, these sectors considered that the 'skewed' exchange rate would have a severe negative impact on their trading. The prevailing parallel exchange rate at this time was in the region of Z.$20,000—Z.$25,000 = US $1. In May President Mugabe signed legislation to establish a new Incomes and Pricing Commission, which was to have sole authority to set rates for price-controlled items including basic foodstuffs, school fees and public transport. Critics of the policy considered that such controls would force suppliers out of business and further divert goods to the parallel market. In September the Government finally effected a devaluation of the Zimbabwe dollar and abolished the two-tier exchange rate. Henceforth, an exchange rate of Z.$30,000 = US $1 was applicable to all purchases and sales of foreign exchange. The 2008 budget, which was announced in November 2007, provided for a reduction in the rate of personal tax and the removal of value-added tax on pork products. These measures were, however, expected to have little positive impact on the economy, particularly as inflation continued to increase at an extraordinary rate each month. Although recognizing a fall in maize production of 36%, the Minister of Finance, Samuel Mumbengegwi, claimed that agricultural production had actually increased by 4% during 2007, leading many analysts to question the legitimacy of the Government's figures. Meanwhile, the Government's credibility was further brought into question after the People's Republic of China, one of Zimbabwe's few remaining international allies, reportedly announced the cessation of all financial assistance to Zimbabwe with the exception of humanitarian aid. The political instability precipitated by the disputed legislative and presidential elections of March 2008 (see Recent History) was expected to exacerbate economic disruption. It was estimated that GDP per head in Zimbabwe had fallen from around US $200 in 1996 to just US $9 in 2007. According to IMF estimates, GDP contracted by 6.1% in 2007.

Education

Primary education, which begins at six years of age and lasts for seven years, has been compulsory since 1987. Secondary education begins at the age of 13 and lasts for six years. According to UNESCO estimates, in 2002/03 enrolment at primary schools included 82% of children in the relevant age-group (males 81%; females 82%), while the comparable ratio for secondary enrolment was 34% of children (males 35%; females 33%). In 1998 some 11,451 students were attending universities, while 36,830 students were enrolled at institutions of higher education. There are two state-run universities, the University of Zimbabwe, which is located in Harare, and the University of Science and Technology, at Bulawayo. There are also two private universities, Africa University in Mutare and Solusi University in Figtree. Education was allocated Z.$6,800,000m. by the central Government in the budget for 2005, equivalent to 24.7% of total expenditure for that year.

Public Holidays

2008: 1 January (New Year's Day), 21–24 March (Easter), 18 April (Independence Day), 1 May (Workers' Day), 25 May (Africa Day, anniversary of OAU's foundation), 11 August (Heroes' Day), 12 August (Defence Forces National Day), 22 December (National Unity Day), 25–26 December (Christmas).

2009: 1 January (New Year's Day), 10–13 April (Easter), 18 April (Independence Day), 1 May (Workers' Day), 25 May (Africa Day, anniversary of OAU's foundation), 11 August (Heroes' Day), 12 August (Defence Forces National Day), 22 December (National Unity Day), 25–26 December (Christmas).

Weights and Measures

The metric system is in use.

Statistical Survey

Source (unless otherwise stated): Central Statistical Office, Ministry of Finance and Economic Development, Blocks B, E and G, Composite Bldg, cnr Samora Machel Ave and Fourth St, Private Bag 7705, Causeway, Harare; tel. (4) 706681; fax (4) 728529; internet www.mofed.gov.zw.

Area and Population

AREA, POPULATION AND DENSITY

Area (sq km)	390,757*
Population (census results)	
18 August 1997	11,789,274
17 August 2002†	
Males	5,634,180
Females	5,997,477
Total	11,631,657
Population (UN estimates at mid-year)‡	
2005	13,120,000
2006	13,228,000
2007	13,349,000
Density (per sq km) at mid-2007	34.2

* 150,872 sq miles.
† Source: UN, *Population and Vital Statistics Report*.
‡ Source: UN, *World Population Prospects: The 2006 Revision*.

PRINCIPAL TOWNS
(population at census of August 1992)

Harare (capital)	1,189,103	Masvingo	51,743
Bulawayo	621,742	Chinhoyi (Sinoia)	43,054
Chitungwiza	274,912	Hwange (Wankie)	42,581
Mutare (Umtali)	131,367	Marondera (Marandellas)	39,384
Gweru (Gwelo)	128,037	Zvishavane (Shabani)	32,984
Kwekwe (Que Que)	75,425	Redcliff	29,959
Kadoma (Gatooma)	67,750		

Mid-2007 ('000, incl. suburbs, UN estimate): Harare 1,572 (Source: UN, *World Urbanization Prospects: The 2007 Revision*).

BIRTHS AND DEATHS
(annual averages, UN estimates)

	1990–95	1995–2000	2000–05
Birth rate (per 1,000)	35.5	31.9	28.9
Death rate (per 1,000)	8.7	15.3	20.5

Source: UN, *World Population Prospects: The 2006 Revision*.

Expectation of life (years at birth, WHO estimates): 42.4 (males 43.3; females 41.5) in 2005 (Source: WHO, *World Health Statistics*).

ECONOMICALLY ACTIVE POPULATION
(sample survey, persons aged 15 years and over, 1999)

	Males	Females	Total
Agriculture, hunting, forestry and fishing	1,215,661	1,584,839	2,800,500
Mining and quarrying	46,946	3,367	50,313
Manufacturing	283,090	94,667	377,757
Electricity, gas and water	10,158	n.a.	10,158
Construction	98,908	6,659	105,567
Trade, restaurants and hotels	154,198	178,341	332,539
Transport, storage and communications	93,289	8,288	101,577
Financing, insurance, real estate and business services	100,425	20,749	121,174
Community, social and personal services	320,020	258,505	578,525
Activities not adequately defined	63,052	124,286	187,338
Total employed	2,385,747	2,279,701	4,665,448
Unemployed	187,142	110,669	297,811
Total labour force	2,572,889	2,390,370	4,963,259

2004 ('000 employees, annual average): Agriculture, hunting, forestry and fishing 154; Mining and quarrying 50; Manufacturing 136; Electricity, gas and water 11; Construction 25; Trade, restaurants and hotels 114; Transport, storage and communications 38; Financing, insurance, real estate and business services 38; Public administration 68; Education 151; Health 26; Domestic 102; Other services 88; *Total employed* 999 (Source: IMF, *Zimbabwe: Selected Issues and Statistical Appendix*—October 2005).

Mid-2005 (estimates in '000): Agriculture, etc. 3,688; Total labour force 6,180 (Source: FAO).

Health and Welfare

KEY INDICATORS

Total fertility rate (children per woman, 2005)	3.4
Under-5 mortality rate (per 1,000 live births, 2005)	86
HIV/AIDS (% of persons aged 15–49, 2005)	20.1
Physicians (per 1,000 head, 2004)	0.16
Hospital beds (per 1,000 head, 1990)	0.51
Health expenditure (2004): US $ per head (PPP)	138.6
Health expenditure (2004): % of GDP	7.5
Health expenditure (2004): public (% of total)	46.1
Access to water (% of persons, 2004)	81
Access to sanitation (% of persons, 2004)	53
Human Development Index (2005): ranking	151
Human Development Index (2005): value	0.513

For sources and definitions, see explanatory note on p. vi.

ZIMBABWE

Agriculture

PRINCIPAL CROPS
('000 metric tons)

	2004	2005	2006
Wheat	140*	140*	140†
Barley	25*	29†	29†
Maize	550.0*	900.0*	900.0†
Millet	40.0*	40.0*	35.0†
Sorghum	80.0*	80.0*	75.0†
Potatoes†	34	34	34
Cassava (Manioc)†	198	207	207
Dry beans†	52	52	52
Sugar cane	4,121*	3,290*	3,600†
Soybeans (Soya beans)	84*	100*	90†
Groundnuts (in shell)†	152	160	160
Sunflower seed*	10	13	10
Oranges†	96	99	99
Bananas†	86	87	87
Coffee (green)*	6	4	5
Tea (made)†	22	22	22
Tobacco (leaves)	62.3*	65.0†	65.0†
Cotton (lint)*	100	75	72

* Unofficial figure(s).
† FAO estimate(s).

Aggregate production ('000 metric tons, may include official, semi-official or estimated data): Total cereals 837 in 2004, 1,192 in 2005, 1,182 in 2006; Total roots and tubers 235 in 2004, 244 in 2005, 244 in 2006; Total vegetables (incl. melons) 163 in 2004, 163 in 2005, 163 in 2006; Total fruits (excl. melons) 231 in 2004, 235 in 2005, 235 in 2006.

Source: FAO.

LIVESTOCK
('000 head, year ending September, FAO estimates)

	2004	2005	2006
Horses	27.5	28.0	28.0
Asses, mules or hinnies	113	113	113
Cattle	5,400	5,400	5,400
Sheep	610	610	610
Pigs	620	610	610
Goats	2,970	2,970	3,000
Chickens	22,000	23,000	23,000

Source: FAO.

LIVESTOCK PRODUCTS
('000 metric tons, FAO estimates)

	2004	2005	2006
Cattle meat	96.8	96.8	97.0
Goat meat	12.8	12.8	13.0
Pig meat	27.1	27.5	27.5
Chicken meat	44.7	46.1	40.0
Cows' milk	248	248	248
Hen eggs	22	22	22

Source: FAO.

Forestry

ROUNDWOOD REMOVALS
('000 cubic metres, excl. bark)

	2004	2005	2006
Sawlogs, veneer logs and logs for sleepers	786*	632	578
Pulpwood*	94	83	81
Other industrial wood*	112	112	112
Fuel wood*	8,115	8,115	8,380
Total*	9,108	8,942	9,151

* FAO estimate(s).
Source: FAO.

SAWNWOOD PRODUCTION
('000 cubic metres, incl. railway sleepers)

	2004*	2005	2006
Coniferous (softwood)	354	594	533
Broadleaved (hardwood)	43	22	32
Total	397	617	565

* FAO estimates.
Source: FAO.

Fishing

('000 metric tons, live weight, FAO estimates)

	2003	2004	2005
Capture	13.0	13.0	13.0
Tilapias	0.8	0.8	0.8
Other freshwater fishes	1.8	1.8	1.8
Dagaas	10.4	10.4	10.4
Aquaculture	2.6	3.0	2.5
Total catch	15.6	16.0	15.5

Note: Figures exclude aquatic animals, recorded by number rather than weight. The number of Nile crocodiles caught was: 73,707 in 2003; 60,185 in 2004; 76,970 in 2005 (all FAO estimates).

Source: FAO.

Mining

('000 metric tons, unless otherwise indicated)

	2004	2005	2006*
Asbestos	104	122	97
Chromium ore	668.4	614.7	700.0
Coal	2,476	2,891	2,107
Cobalt ore (metric tons)†	59	281	26
Copper ore‡	2.4	2.6	2.6
Gold (kilograms)	21,330	14,024	11,354
Iron ore	283	377	104
Limestone	41	84	50§
Magnesite (metric tons)	749	893	939
Nickel ore (metric tons)	9,776	8,556	8,825
Phosphate rock	83.4	45.7	65.8
Silver (kilograms)	3,216	187	500§

* Preliminary figures.
† Figures include metal content of compounds and salts and may include cobalt recovered from nickel-copper matte.
‡ Figures refer to the metal content of ores and concentrates.
§ Estimate.

Source: US Geological Survey.

Industry

SELECTED PRODUCTS
('000 metric tons, unless otherwise indicated)

	2004	2005	2006*
Coke (metallurgical)	180	200	160
Cement	500	600	700
Pig-iron	125	129	70†
Ferro-chromium	193.1	218.1	200.7
Crude steel	135	107	60†
Refined copper—unwrought (metric tons)†	2,000	2,000	2,000
Refined nickel—unwrought (metric tons)	15,700†	13,200†	14,500

* Preliminary figures.
† Estimate(s).
Source: US Geological Survey.

Raw sugar ('000 metric tons): 585 in 2000; 639 in 2001 (Source: UN, *Industrial Commodity Statistics Yearbook*).

Electric energy (million kWh): 8,587 in 2002; 8,789 in 2003; 9,908 in 2004 (Source: UN, *Industrial Commodity Statistics Yearbook*).

Finance

CURRENCY AND EXCHANGE RATES

Monetary Units
100 cents = 1 Zimbabwe dollar (Z.$).

Sterling, US Dollar and Euro Equivalents (31 August 2007)
£1 sterling = Z.$515.3169;
US $1 = Z.$255.1200;
€1 = Z.$349.6418;
Z.$1,000 = £1.94 = US $3.92 = €2.86.

Average Exchange Rate (Z.$ per US dollar)
2004   5,068.66
2005   22,363.60
2006   164,361.00

BUDGET
(Z.$ '000 million)

Revenue*	2004	2005	2006
Tax revenue	7,868.0	32,530.9	404,322.3
Income and profits	4,096.0	16,325.3	232,161.0
Customs duties	930.0	3,854.6	42,647.7
Excise duties	278.8	1,062.1	14,136.7
Value-added tax	2,377.0	10,546.0	109,705.9
Other taxes	186.2	742.9	5,670.9
Non-tax revenue	308.7	674.9	12,973.6
Total	8,176.7	33,205.8	417,295.8

Expenditure†	2004	2005	2006
Current expenditure	7,991.3	32,487.6	349,773.2
Goods and services	5,519.6	21,153.7	215,771.3
Salaries and wages	3,657.6	13,800.0	138,678.6
Other	1,862.0	7,353.7	77,092.7
Interest on debt	737.3	5,153.8	62,255.7
Foreign	3.3	52.8	5,623.3
Domestic	734.0	5,101.0	56,632.3
Transfers	1,734.4	6,180.1	71,746.2
Capital	1,220.2	3,406.2	112,450.6
Statistical discrepancy	358.3	—	—
Total	9,569.5	35,893.8	462,223.8

* Excluding grants and foreign interest arrears (Z.$ '000 million): 23.3 in 2004; 10.7 in 2005; 10.2 in 2006.
† Excluding net lending (Z.$ '000 million): 139.8 in 2004; 288.6 in 2005; 1,119.5 in 2006.

INTERNATIONAL RESERVES
(US $ million at 31 December)

	2000	2001	2002
Gold*	45.4	27.5	22.7
IMF special drawing rights	0.2	—	—
Reserve position in IMF	0.4	0.4	0.4
Foreign exchange	192.5	64.3	82.9
Total	238.5	92.2	106.0

*Valued at a market-related price which is determined each month.
2003–07 (US $ million at 31 December): Reserve position in IMF 0.5.
Source: IMF, *International Financial Statistics*.

MONEY SUPPLY
(Z.$ '000 million at 31 December)

	2004	2005	2006
Currency outside banks	1,656	9,876	228,064
Demand deposits at deposit money banks	5,148	34,048	404,965
Total money (incl. others)	6,857	44,746	636,799

Source: IMF, *International Financial Statistics*.

COST OF LIVING
(Consumer Price Index; base: 2000 = 100)

	2004	2005	2006
Food	8,792.0	42,868.1	n.a.
All items (incl. others)	8,625.7	34,688.3	415,106.7

Source: ILO.

NATIONAL ACCOUNTS

Expenditure on the Gross National Product
(US $ million at current prices, estimates)

	2004	2005	2006
Government final consumption expenditure	153.99	142.52	248.64
Private final consumption expenditure	4,730.58	3,442.12	6,545.78
Gross capital formation	240.73	150.47	243.57
Total domestic expenditure	5,125.30	3,735.11	7,037.99
Exports of goods and services	2,006.24	1,443.83	1,838.76
Less Imports of goods and services	2,419.48	1,806.43	1,843.03
GDP in purchasers' values	4,712.06	3,372.50	7,033.72

Source: African Development Bank.

Gross Domestic Product by Economic Activity
(Z.$ million, at factor cost)

	1997	1998	1999
Agriculture, hunting, forestry and fishing	17,042	27,135	35,812
Mining and quarrying	1,400	2,400	3,380
Manufacturing	16,208	20,708	30,538
Electricity and water	2,849	3,139	5,171
Construction	2,544	3,640	5,132
Trade, restaurants and hotels	17,163	22,652	36,261
Transport, storage and communications	5,192	6,712	11,373
Finance, insurance and real estate	9,797	15,679	26,917
Government services	13,640	16,916	22,913
Other services	5,320	6,806	8,273
Sub-total	91,155	125,762	185,770
Less Imputed bank service charges	1,149	1,242	1,357
Total	90,006	124,540	184,413

ZIMBABWE

BALANCE OF PAYMENTS
(US $ million)

	2002	2003	2004*
Exports of goods f.o.b.	1,802	1,670	1,680
Imports of goods f.o.b.	−1,821	−1,778	−1,989
Trade balance	−18	−108	−310
Exports of services	217	185	317
Imports of services	−398	−401	−424
Balance on goods and services	−199	−324	−417
Investment income (net)	−242	−191	−208
Balance on goods, services and income	−441	−515	−625
Private transfers (net)	228	169	204
Current balance	−213	−346	−421
Official transfers (net)	38	38	24
Direct investment (net)	23	4	9
Portfolio investment (net)	−2	4	2
Long-term capital (net)	−281	−228	−221
Short-term capital (net)	−94	−27	17
Net errors and omissions	74	79	344
Overall balance	−456	−476	−247

* Estimates.

Source: IMF, *Zimbabwe: Selected Issues and Statistical Appendix* (October 2005).

External Trade

PRINCIPAL COMMODITIES
(US $ million)

Imports f.o.b.	2002	2003	2004*
Food	337	206	161
Tobacco and beverages	39	36	44
Crude materials	87	79	96
Fuel and electricity	352	456	462
Petroleum products	149	110	342
Oils and fats	27	25	30
Chemicals	361	328	401
Machinery and transport equipment	375	341	417
Other manufactured goods	241	220	269
Total (incl. others)	1,821	1,778	1,989

Exports†	2002	2003	2004*
Agricultural exports	646.6	516.0	384.2
Tobacco	434.7	321.3	226.7
Sugar	64.2	54.8	53.9
Cold Storage Co beef	2.3	0.2	—
Coffee	5.4	5.9	4.1
Horticulture	126.6	118.7	84.1
Mineral exports	297.8	390.8	604.2
Gold‡	159.5	152.3	262.8
Asbestos	39.3	42.4	19.4
Nickel	31.8	68.5	95.7
Platinum	14.5	77.4	174.4
Copper	8.9	4.6	2.6
Manufacturing exports	287.3	691.2	620.9
Ferrous alloys	106.8	119.8	185.1
Cotton lint	53.2	67.2	122.1
Iron and steel	22.3	39.9	22.9
Textiles and clothing	17.7	28.2	13.8
Machinery and equipment	5.2	12.8	1.9
Chemicals	3.5	5.1	9.6
Total (incl. others)§	1,397.9	1,670.3	1,679.7

* Estimates.
† Value of exports based on official exchange rates.
‡ Based on unit value of US dollar per ounce.
§ Excluding unidentified exports and internal freight.

Source: IMF, *Zimbabwe: Selected Issues and Statistical Appendix* (October 2005).

PRINCIPAL TRADING PARTNERS
(US $ million)

Imports f.o.b.	2001	2002	2004
Botswana	33.6	47.2	88.9
Congo, Democratic Repub.	96.1	2.9	7.1
France (incl. Monaco)	27.7	31.9	20.4
Germany	47.7	134.3	37.5
Japan	29.5	72.4	24.0
Kuwait	6.9	54.1	44.3
Mozambique	89.9	46.7	49.7
South Africa	802.6	1,297.8	1,159.8
United Kingdom	54.3	120.7	83.2
USA	48.4	87.0	41.4
Total (incl. others)	1,714.9	2,466.7	2,203.8

Exports f.o.b.	2001	2002	2004
Botswana	12.8	68.0	48.3
China, People's Repub.	104.8	13.3	110.5
Germany	155.8	109.6	77.2
Japan	117.1	122.3	55.5
Malawi	10.6	120.1	47.6
Mozambique	3.7	69.0	19.5
Netherlands	25.8	89.8	27.0
South Africa	122.3	431.4	565.2
Spain	32.5	70.5	29.2
Switzerland (incl. Liechtenstein)	12.5	303.7	133.7
United Arab Emirates	3.4	8.9	12.0
United Kingdom	130.3	140.4	131.3
USA	61.5	104.7	41.0
Zambia	11.6	215.5	71.6
Total (incl. others)	1,206.8	2,327.4	1,926.1

* Figures for 2003 unavailable.

Source: UN, *International Trade Statistics Yearbook*.

Transport

RAIL TRAFFIC
(National Railways of Zimbabwe, including operations in Botswana)

	1998	1999	2000
Total number of passengers ('000)	1,787	1,896	1,614
Revenue-earning metric tons hauled ('000)	12,421	12,028	9,422
Gross metric ton-km (million)	9,248	8,962	6,953
Net metric ton-km (million)	4,549	4,375	3,326

ROAD TRAFFIC
('000 motor vehicles in use, estimates)

	1998	1999	2000
Passenger cars	540	555	573
Commercial vehicles	37	38	39

2002: Passenger cars 570,866; Lorries and vans 84,456; Motorcycles 45.

CIVIL AVIATION
(traffic on scheduled services)

	2001	2002	2003
Kilometres flown (million)	15	8	6
Passengers carried ('000)	308	251	201
Passenger-km (million)	723	674	437
Total ton-km (million)	224	87	58

Source: UN, *Statistical Yearbook*.

ZIMBABWE

Tourism

VISITOR ARRIVALS BY NATIONALITY

	2003	2004	2005
Australia and New Zealand	40,141	28,540	13,369
Botswana	242,750	135,860	189,751
Canada and USA	54,572	60,093	39,779
Mozambique	313,954	299,122	183,792
South Africa	882,726	653,352	626,677
United Kingdom	58,354	42,260	42,525
Zambia	295,103	220,060	194,311
Total (incl. others)	2,256,205	1,854,488	1,558,501

Tourism receipts (US $ million, incl. passenger transport): 61 in 2003; 194 in 2004; 99 in 2005.

Source: World Tourism Organization.

Communications Media

	2004	2005	2006
Telephones ('000 main lines in use)	317.0	328.0	331.7
Mobile cellular telephones ('000 subscribers)	423.6	668.0	832.5
Personal computers ('000 in use)	1,000	1,200	n.a.
Internet users ('000)	820	1,000	1,222
Broadband subscribers ('000)	9.0	10.2	10.2

Radio receivers ('000 in use): 4,488 in 1999.

Television receivers ('000 in use): 410 in 2000.

Facsimile machines: 4,100 in use in year ending 30 June 1995.

Daily newspapers: 2 (average circulation 209,000 copies) in 1996; 3 in 2004.

Sources: UNESCO, *Statistical Yearbook*; UNESCO Institute for Statistics; UN, *Statistical Yearbook*; Inter-national Telecommunication Union.

Education

(2002/03, unless otherwise indicated)

	Institutions*	Teachers	Students
Pre-primary	n.a.	19,588	448,124
Primary	4,699	61,521	2,361,588
Secondary	1,539	33,964	758,229
Tertiary	n.a.	n.a.	21,631†

* 1998 figures.
† Estimate.

Source: mainly UNESCO Institute for Statistics.

Adult literacy rate (UNESCO estimates): 89.4% (males 92.7%; females 86.2%) in 2004 (Source: UNESCO Institute for Statistics).

Directory

The Constitution

The Constitution of the Republic of Zimbabwe took effect at independence on 18 April 1980. Amendments to the Constitution must have the approval of two-thirds of the members of the House of Assembly (see below). The provisions of the 1980 Constitution (with subsequent amendments) are summarized below:

THE REPUBLIC

Zimbabwe is a sovereign republic and the Constitution is the supreme law.

DECLARATION OF RIGHTS

The declaration of rights guarantees the fundamental rights and freedoms of the individual, regardless of race, tribe, place of origin, political opinions, colour, creed or sex.

THE PRESIDENT

Executive power is vested in the President, and may be exercised by him/her directly or through the Cabinet, a Vice-President, a Minister or a Deputy Minister. The President is Head of State, Head of Government and Commander-in-Chief of the Defence Forces. The President appoints no more than two Vice-Presidents and other Ministers and Deputy Ministers, to be members of the Cabinet. The President holds office for five years and is eligible for re-election.

PARLIAMENT

Legislative power is vested in the Legislature, which consists of the President and a bicameral Parliament, comprising the Senate and the House of Assembly. The Senate comprises 93 members, of whom 60 are directly elected by universal adult suffrage (six are elected in each of the 10 provinces by voters registered in the 60 senatorial constituencies), five are nominated by the President, 10 are provincial governors, two are the President and the Deputy President of the Council of Chiefs and 16 are traditional Chiefs. The life of the Senate is ordinarily to be five years. The House of Assembly comprises 210 members, all of whom are directly elected by universal adult suffrage. The life of the House of Assembly is ordinarily to be five years.

OTHER PROVISIONS

A Public Protector shall be appointed by the President, acting on the advice of the Judicial Service Commission, to investigate complaints against actions taken by employees of the Government or of a local authority.

Chiefs shall be appointed by the President, and shall form a Council of Chiefs from their number in accordance with customary principles of succession.

Other provisions relate to the Judicature, Defence and Police Forces, public service and finance.

The Government

HEAD OF STATE

President: ROBERT GABRIEL MUGABE (took office 31 December 1987; re-elected March 1990, 16–17 March 1996 and 9–11 March 2002).

THE CABINET
(March 2008)

Vice-President: JOSEPH MSIKA.
Vice-President: JOYCE MUJURU.

ZIMBABWE

Minister of Special Affairs in the President's Office, responsible for Lands, Land Reform and Resettlement: FLORA BHUKA.
Minister of Defence: SYDNEY SEKERAMAYI.
Minister of Home Affairs: KEMBO MOHADI.
Minister of Justice, Legal and Parliamentary Affairs: PATRICK ANTHONY CHINAMASA.
Minister of Public Service, Labour and Social Welfare: NICHOLAS GOCHE.
Minister of Local Government, Public Works and National Housing: Dr IGNATIUS MORGAN CHIMINYA CHOMBO.
Minister of Agriculture and Rural Resettlement: RUGARE GUMBO.
Minister of Rural Housing and Social Amenities: EMMERSON MNANGAGWA.
Minister of Industry and International Trade: OBERT MPOFU.
Minister of Energy and Power Development: MICHAEL NYAMBUYA.
Minister of Mines and Mining Development: AMOS MIDZI.
Minister of the Environment and Tourism: FRANCIS NHEMA.
Minister of Foreign Affairs: SIMBARASHE MUMBENGEGWI.
Minister of Finance: SAMUEL MUMBENGEGWI.
Minister of Economic Development: SYLVESTER NGUNI.
Minister of Higher and Tertiary Education: I. STANISLAUS GORERAZVO MUDENGE.
Minister of Education, Sports and Culture: AENEAS CHIGWEDERE.
Minister of Health and Child Welfare: DAVID PARIRENYATWA.
Minister for Information and Publicity: Dr SKHANYISO NDLOVU.
Minister of Science and Technology: OLIVIA MUCHENA.
Minister of Transport and Communications: CHRIS MUSHOHWE.
Minister of Women Affairs, Gender and Community Development: OPPAH MUCHINGURI.
Minister of Small and Medium Enterprises Development: SITHEMBISO NYONI.
Minister of Youth Development, Gender and Employment Creation: Brig. (retd) AMBROSE MUTINHIRI.
Minister of Water Resources and Infrastructural Development: MUNACHO MUTEZO.
Minister of State for National Security: DIDYMUS MUTASA.
Minister of State for Policy Implementation: WEBSTER SHAMU.
Minister of State for Indigenization and Empowerment: MUNYARADZI PAUL MANGWANA.
Minister of State for State Enterprises, Anti-Monopolies and Anti-Corruption: SAMUEL UNDENGE.
Minister without Portfolio: ELLIOT MANYIKA.

The Constitution provides for the Attorney-General to serve as an ex officio member of the Cabinet.

MINISTRIES

Office of the President: Munhumutapa Bldg, Samora Machel Ave, Private Bag 7700, Causeway, Harare; tel. (4) 707091.
Office of the Vice-Presidents: Munhumutapa Bldg, Samora Machel Ave, Private Bag 7700, Causeway, Harare; tel. (4) 707091.
Ministry of Agriculture and Rural Resettlement: Ngungunyana Bldg, Private Bag 7701, Causeway, Harare; tel. (4) 700596; fax (4) 734646; internet www.moa.gov.zw.
Ministry of Defence: Defence House, cnr Kwame Nkuruma and 3rd Sts, Harare; tel. (4) 700155; fax (4) 727501; internet www.mod.gov.zw.
Ministry of Economic Development: New Complex Bldg, Government Composite Offices, cnr 3rd St and Samora Machel Ave, Harare; e-mail moed@gta.gov.zw; internet www.mofed.gov.zw.
Ministry of Education, Sports and Culture: Ambassador House, Union Ave, POB CY121, Causeway, Harare; tel. (4) 734051; fax (4) 707599; internet www.moesc.gov.zw.
Ministry of Energy and Power Development: Chaminuka Bldg, Private Bag 7758, Causeway, Harare; tel. (4) 791760; fax (4) 797956; e-mail energy@gta.gov.zw; internet www.energy.gov.zw.
Ministry of the Environment and Tourism: Kaguvi Bldg, 12th Floor, cnr 4th St and Central Ave, Private Bag 7753, Causeway, Harare; tel. (4) 701681; fax (4) 252673; e-mail metlib@zarnet.ac.zw; internet www.met.gov.zw.
Ministry of Finance: Blocks B, E and G, Composite Bldg, cnr Samora Machel Ave and Fourth St, Private Bag 7705, Causeway, Harare; tel. (4) 738603; fax (4) 792750; internet www.mofed.gov.zw.
Ministry of Foreign Affairs: Munhumutapa Bldg, Samora Machel Ave, POB 4240, Causeway, Harare; tel. (4) 727005; fax (4) 705161; internet www.zimfa.gov.zw.
Ministry of Health and Child Welfare: Kaguvi Bldg, Fourth St, POB CY198, Causeway, Harare; tel. (4) 730011; fax (4) 729154; internet www.mohcw.gov.zw.
Ministry of Higher Education and Technology: Government Composite Bldg, cnr Fourth St and Samora Machel Ave, Union Ave, POB UA275, Harare; tel. (4) 796440; fax (4) 790923; e-mail thesecretary@mhet.ac.zw; internet www.mhet.ac.zw.
Ministry of Home Affairs: Mukwati Bldg, Private Bag 7703, Causeway, Harare; tel. (4) 703641; fax (4) 707231; e-mail moha@gvt.co.zw; internet www.moha.gov.zw.
Ministry of Indigenization and Empowerment: Harare.
Ministry of Industry and International Trade: Mukwati Bldg, Fourth St, Private Bag 7708, Causeway, Harare; tel. (4) 702731; fax (4) 729311; internet www.miit.gov.zw.
Ministry of Information and Publicity: Linquenda House, Baker Ave, POB CY825, Causeway, Harare; tel. (4) 703894; fax (4) 707213.
Ministry of Justice, Legal and Parliamentary Affairs: Corner House, cnr Samora Machel Ave and Leopold Takawira St, Private Bag 7751, Causeway, Harare; tel. (4) 774620; fax (4) 772999; internet www.justice.gov.zw.
Ministry of Local Government, Public Works and National Housing: Mukwati Bldg, Fourth St, Private Bag 7755, Causeway, Harare; tel. (4) 7282019; fax (4) 708493; internet www.mlgpwud.gov.zw.
Ministry of Mines and Mining Development: ZIMRE Centre, 6th Floor, cnr Leopold Takawira St and Kwame Nkrumah Ave, Private Bag 7709, Causeway, Harare; tel. (4) 777022; fax (4) 777044; e-mail minsec@technopark.co.zw; internet www.mines.gov.zw.
Ministry of National Security: Chaminuka Bldg, POB 2278, Harare; tel. (4) 700501; fax (4) 732660.
Ministry of Policy Implementation: Harare.
Ministry of Public Service, Labour and Social Welfare: Compensation House, cnr Central Ave and Fourth St, Private Bag 7707, Causeway, Harare; tel. (4) 790871; fax (4) 794568; e-mail mpslsw@gta.gov.zw; internet www.pslsw.gov.zw.
Ministry of Transport and Communications: Kaguvi Bldg, POB CY595, Causeway, Harare; tel. (4) 700991; fax (4) 708225; internet www.transcom.gov.zw.
Ministry of Water Resources, Infrastructural Development, and Small and Medium Enterprises: Kurima House, cnr Nelson Madela Ave and Fourth St, Private Bag CY 7767, Harare; tel. (4) 700596; fax (4) 738165; internet www.water.gov.zw.
Ministry of Youth Development, Gender and Employment Creation: ZANU—PF Bldg, Private Bag 7762, Causeway, Harare; tel. (4) 734691; fax (4) 732709; e-mail mydgec@zarnet.ac.zw; internet www.mydgec.gov.zw.

PROVINCIAL GOVERNORS
(March 2008)

Bulawayo: CAIN MATHEMA.
Harare: DAVID KARIMANZIRA.
Manicaland: TINAYE CHIGUDU.
Mashonaland Central: EPHRAIM MASAWI.
Mashonaland East: RAY KAUKONDE.
Mashonaland West: NELSON SAMKANGE.
Masvingo: WILLARD CHIWEWE.
Matabeleland North: THOKOZILE MATHUTHU.
Matabeleland South: ANGELINA MASUKU.
Midlands: CEPHAS MSIPA.

President and Legislature

PRESIDENT

Election, 9–11 March 2002

Candidate	Votes	% of votes
Robert Gabriel Mugabe	1,685,212	56.2
Morgan Tsvangirai	1,258,401	42.0
Wilson Kumbala	31,368	1.0
Shakespeare Maya	11,906	0.4
Paul Siwela	11,871	0.4
Total	**2,998,758**	**100.0**

ZIMBABWE

HOUSE OF ASSEMBLY

Speaker: JOHN NKOMO.

General Election, 29 March 2008, provisional results

Party	Votes	% of votes	Seats
MDC—Tsvangirai	1,041,176	42.99	99
ZANU—PF	1,110,649	45.86	97
MDC—Mutambara	202,259	8.35	10
Independents	54,254	2.24	1
Others	13,635	0.56	—
Total	**2,421,973**	**100.00**	**207***

* Voting was postponed in three constituencies, owing to the deaths of candidates.

SENATE

Speaker: EDNA MADZONGWE.

General Election, 29 March 2008, provisional results

Party	Seats
ZANU—PF	30
MDC—Tsvangirai	24
MDC—Mutambara	6
Total	**60***

* In addition to the 60 directly elective seats, five are held by nominees of the President, 10 by provincial governors, two by the President and the Deputy President of the Council of Chiefs and 16 by traditional Chiefs.

Election Commission

Zimbabwe Electoral Commission (ZEC): Century House East, Private Bag 7782, Causeway, Harare; tel. (4) 759130; fax (4) 781903; e-mail zecpr@gta.gov.zw; internet www.zimbabweelectoralcommission.org; f. 2005; the President appoints six commrs, three of whom must be women, and also the Chair. in consultation with the Judicial Service Commission; superseded and replaced the Electoral Supervisory Commission (abolished Aug. 2005); responsible for establishing constituency boundaries, voter registration and conducting elections; Chair. GEORGE CHIWESHE.

Political Organizations

Committee for a Democratic Society (CODESO): f. 1993; Karanga-supported grouping, based in Matabeleland; Leader SOUL NDLOVU.

Christian Democratic Party: Leader WILLIAM GWATA.

Federal Democratic Union: f. 2008; Leader PAUL SIWELA.

Forum Party of Zimbabwe (FPZ): POB 74, Bulawayo; f. 1993; conservative; Pres. WASHINGTON SANSOLE.

General Conference of Patriots: Harare; f. 1998; opposes the Govt; aims to organize and direct dissent; Leader OBEY MUDZINGWA.

Movement for Democratic Change (MDC): Harvest House, 6th Floor, cnr Angwa St and Nelson Mandela Ave, Harare; internet www.mdczimbabwe.org; f. 1999; allied to Zimbabwe Congress of Trade Unions; opposes the Mugabe Govt; a 'pro-Senate' splinter faction emerged in Dec. 2005 led by Prof. ARTHUR MUTAMBARA and WELSHMAN NCUBE; Pres. MORGAN TSVANGIRAI; Sec.-Gen. TENDAI BITI.

National Progressive Alliance: f. 1991; Chair. CANCIWELL NZIRAMASANGA.

United National Federal Party (UNFP): Harare; f. 1978; conservative; seeks a federation of Mashonaland and Matabeleland; Leader Chief KAYISA NDIWENI.

United People's Party (UPP): f. 2006; Leader DANIEL SHUMBA.

Zimbabwe Active People's Unity Party: Bulawayo; f. 1989; Leader NEWMAN MATUTU NDELA.

Zimbabwe African National Union—Ndonga (ZANU—Ndonga): POB UA525, Union Ave, Harare; tel. and fax (4) 481180; f. 1977; breakaway faction from ZANU, also includes fmr mems of United African Nat. Council; supports free market economy; Pres. (vacant); Sec.-Gen. EDWIN C. NGUWA.

Zimbabwe African National Union—Patriotic Front (ZANU—PF): cnr Rotten Row and Samora Machel Ave, POB 4530, Harare; tel. (4) 753329; fax (4) 774146; internet www.zanupfpub.co.zw; f. 1989 by merger of PF—ZAPU and ZANU—PF; Pres. ROBERT GABRIEL MUGABE; Vice-Pres SIMON VENGAYI MUZENDA, JOSEPH W. MSIKA; Nat. Chair. JOHN LANDAU NKOMO.

Zimbabwe Congress Party: Harare; f. 1994; Pres. KENNETH MANO.

Zimbabwe Development Party: Harare; Leader KISINOTI MUKWAZHE.

Zimbabwe Federal Party (ZFPO): Stand 214, Nketa 6, P.O. Nkulumane, Bulawayo; f. 1994; aims to create national federation of five provinces; Leader RICHARD NCUBE.

Zimbabwe Integrated Programme: f. 1999; seeks economic reforms; Pres. Prof. HENEDI DZINOCHIKIWEYI.

Zimbabwe Peoples' Democratic Party: POB 4001, Harare; e-mail mail@zpdp.org; internet www.zpdp.org; f. 1991; Chair. ISABEL SHANANGURAI MADANGURE; Sec.-Gen. DUDLEY GURA.

Zimbabwe Progressive People's Democratic Party: Harare; Leader TAFIRENYIKA MUDAVANHU.

Zimbabwe Unity Movement (ZUM): f. 1989 by a breakaway faction from ZANU—PF; merged with United African National Council in 1994; Leader EDGAR TEKERE.

Zimbabwe Youth in Alliance: Leader MOSES MUTYASIRA.

Diplomatic Representation

EMBASSIES IN ZIMBABWE

Angola: 26 Speke Ave, POB 3590, Harare; tel. (4) 770075; fax (4) 770077; Ambassador FILIPE MONIMAMBU.

Australia: 1 Green Close, Borrowdale, Harare, POB 4541, Harare; tel. (4) 852471; fax (4) 870566; e-mail zimbabwe.embassy@dfat.gov.au; internet www.dfat.gov.au/missions/countries/zw.html; Ambassador JON COURTNEY.

Austria: 13 Duthie Rd, Alexandra Park, POB 4120, Harare; tel. (4) 702921; fax (4) 705877; e-mail harare-ob@bmeia.gv.at; Ambassador Dr GERHARD ZIEGLER.

Bangladesh: 9 Birchenough Rd, POB 3040, Harare; tel. (4) 727004; Ambassador NASIMA HAIDER.

Botswana: 22 Phillips Ave, Belgravia, POB 563, Harare; tel. (4) 729551; fax (4) 721360; Ambassador PELOKGALE SELOMA.

Brazil: Old Mutual Centre, 9th Floor, Jason Moyo Ave, POB 2530, Harare; tel. (4) 790740; fax (4) 790754; e-mail brasemb@ecoweb.co.zw; Chargé d'affaires a.i. FRANCISCO CARLOS SOARES LUZ.

Bulgaria: 15 Maasdorp Ave, Alexandra Park, POB 1809, Harare; tel. (4) 730509; fax (4) 732504; e-mail bgembhre@ecoweb.co.zw; Ambassador CHRISTO TEPAVITCHAROV.

Canada: 45 Baines Ave, POB 1430, Harare; tel. (4) 252181; fax (4) 252186; e-mail hrare@dfait-maeci.gc.ca; internet www.harare.gc.ca; Ambassador ROXANNE DUBÉ.

China, People's Republic: 30 Baines Ave, POB 4749, Harare; tel. and fax (4) 794155; e-mail chinaemb_zw@mfa.gov.cn; internet www.chinaembassy.org.zw; Ambassador NANSHENG YUAN.

Congo, Democratic Republic: 5 Pevensey Rd, Highlands, POB 2446, Harare; tel. (4) 481172; fax (4) 796421; Ambassador Dr KIKAYA BIN KARUB (acting).

Cuba: 5 Phillips Ave, Belgravia, POB 4139, Harare; tel. (4) 720256; Ambassador BUENAVENTURA REYES ACOSTA.

Czech Republic: 4 Sandringham Dr., Alexandra Park, GPO 4474, Harare; tel. (4) 700636; fax (4) 720930; e-mail harare@embassy.mzv.cz; internet www.mzv.cz/harare; Ambassador VÁCLAV JÍLEK.

Egypt: 7 Aberdeen Rd, Avondale, POB A433, Harare; tel. (4) 303445; fax (4) 303115; Ambassador MUHAMMAD FARED MONEIB.

Ethiopia: 14 Lanark Rd, Belgravia, POB 2745, Harare; tel. (4) 701514; fax (4) 701516; e-mail embassy@ecoweb.co.zw; Ambassador DINA MUFTI.

France: Bank Chambers, 11th Floor, 74–76 Samora Machel Ave, POB 1378, Harare; tel. (4) 703216; fax (4) 730078; internet www.ambafrance-zw.org; Ambassador GABRIEL JUGNET.

Germany: 30 Ceres Rd, Avondale, Harare; tel. (4) 308655; fax (4) 303455; e-mail botschaft_harare@gmx.de; Ambassador KARIN BLUMBERGER-SAUERTEIG.

Ghana: 11 Downie Ave, Belgravia, POB 4445, Harare; tel. (4) 700982; fax (4) 701014; e-mail ghcom25@africaonline.co.zw; Ambassador JOHN K. GBENAH.

Greece: 8 Deary Ave, Belgravia, POB 4809, Harare; tel. (4) 793208; fax (4) 703662; e-mail grembha@zol.co.zw; Ambassador DIMITRI M. ALEXANDRAKIS.

Holy See: 5 St Kilda Rd, Mount Pleasant, POB MP191, Harare (Apostolic Nunciature); tel. (4) 744547; fax (4) 744412; e-mail nunzim@zol.co.zw; Apostolic Nuncio Most Rev. EDWARD JOSEPH ADAMS (Titular Archbishop of Scala).

ZIMBABWE

Hungary: 20 Lanark Rd, Belgravia, POB 3594, Harare; tel. (4) 733528; fax (4) 730512; Ambassador TAMÁS GÁSPÁR GÁL.

India: 12 Natal Rd, Belgravia, POB 4620, Harare; tel. (4) 795955; fax (4) 722324; e-mail hci@samara.co.zw; Ambassador AJIT KUMAR.

Indonesia: 3 Duthie Ave, Belgravia, POB CY 69 Causeway, Harare; tel. (4) 251799; fax (4) 796587; e-mail indohar@ecoweb.co.zw; internet www.indonesia-harare.org; Ambassador HUPUDIO SUPARDI.

Iran: 8 Allan Wilson Ave, Avondale, POB A293, Harare; tel. (4) 726942; Ambassador RASOUL MOMENI.

Italy: 7 Bartholomew Close, Greendale North, POB 1062, Harare; tel. (4) 498190; fax (4) 498199; e-mail segreteria.ambzimbabwe@esteri.it; internet www.ambitalia.co.zw; Ambassador MARIO BOLOGNA.

Japan: Social Security Centre, 4th Floor, cnr Julius Nyerere Way and Sam Nujoma St, POB 2710, Harare; tel. (4) 250025; fax (4) 250111; internet www.zw.emb-japan.go.jp; Ambassador TAKEO YOSHIKAWA.

Kenya: 95 Park Lane, POB 4069, Harare; tel. (4) 704820; fax (4) 723042; Ambassador Prof. JOHN ABDUBA.

Korea, Democratic People's Republic: 102 Josiah Chinamano Ave, Greenwood, POB 4754, Harare; tel. (4) 724052; Ambassador RI MYONG CHOL.

Kuwait: 1 Bath Rd, Avondale, POB A485, Harare; Ambassador SAUD FAISAL AL-DAWESS.

Libya: 124 Harare St, POB 4310, Harare; tel. (4) 728381; Ambassador MAHMOUD YOUSEF AZZABI.

Malawi: 9–11 Duthie Rd, Alexandra Park, POB 321, Harare; tel. (4) 798584; fax (4) 799006; e-mail malahigh@africaonline.co.zw; Ambassador Dr BENSON M. TEMBO.

Malaysia: 40 Downie Ave, Avondale, POB 5570, Harare; tel. (4) 334413; fax (4) 334415; e-mail malharare@kln.gov.my; Ambassador CHEAH CHOONG KIT.

Mozambique: 152 cnr Herbert Chitepo Ave, and Leopold Takawira St, POB 4608, Harare; tel. (4) 790837; fax (4) 732898; Ambassador VINCENTE MEBUNIA VEKOSO.

Netherlands: 2 Arden Rd, Highlands, POB HG601, Harare; tel. (4) 776701; fax (4) 776700; e-mail nlgovhar@mweb.co.zw; Ambassador JOSEPH WETERINGS.

Nigeria: 36 Samora Machel Ave, POB 4742, Harare; tel. (4) 253900; Ambassador ANTHONY U. OSULA.

Norway: 5 Lanark Rd, Belgravia, POB A510, Avondale, Harare; tel. (4) 252426; fax (4) 252430; e-mail emb.harare@mfa.no; internet www.norway.org.zw; Ambassador PER GULLIK STAVNUM.

Pakistan: 314 Pipendale Rd, Barrowadalf, Harare; tel. (4) 720293; fax (4) 722446; e-mail pakhar@icon.zw; Ambassador RIFFAT IQBAL.

Poland: 16 Cork Rd, Belgravia, POB 3932, Harare; tel. (4) 253442; fax (4) 253710; Ambassador JAN WIELINSKI.

Portugal: 12 Harvey Brown Ave, Milton Park, Harare; tel. (4) 253023; fax (4) 253637; e-mail embport@harare.dgaccp.pt; Ambassador JOÃO CARLOS VERSTEEG.

Romania: 105 Fourth St, POB 4797, Harare; tel. (4) 700853; fax (4) 725493; Chargé d'affaires a.i. LUMINITA FLORESCU.

Russia: 70 Fife Ave, POB 4250, Harare; tel. (4) 701957; fax (4) 700534; e-mail russemb@africaonline.co.zw; internet www.zimbabwe.mid.ru; Ambassador SERGEI KRYUKOV.

South Africa: 7 Elcombe Rd, Belgravia, POB A1654, Harare; tel. (4) 753147; fax (4) 749657; e-mail admin@saembassy.co.zw; Ambassador MLUNGISI MAKALIMA.

Spain: 16 Phillips Ave, Belgravia, POB 3300, Harare; tel. (4) 250740; fax (4) 795261; e-mail emb.harare@mae.es; Ambassador SANTIAGO MARTÍNEZ-CARO DE LA CONCHA-CASTAÑEDA.

Sudan: 4 Pascoe Ave, Harare; tel. (4) 700111; fax (4) 703450; e-mail sudan@africaonline.co.zw; internet www.sudaniharare.org.zw; Ambassador HASSAN AHMED FAGEERI.

Sweden: 32 Aberdeen Rd, Avondale, POB 4110, Harare; tel. (4) 302636; fax (4) 302236; e-mail ambassaden.harare@foreign.ministry.se; internet www.swedenabroad.com; Ambassador STEN RYLANDER.

Switzerland: 9 Lanark Rd, POB 3440, Harare; tel. (4) 703997; fax (4) 794925; e-mail har.vertretung@eda.admin.ch; Ambassador MARCEL STUTZ.

Tanzania: Ujamaa House, 23 Baines Ave, POB 4841, Harare; tel. (4) 792714; fax (4) 792747; e-mail tanrep@icon.co.zw; Ambassador ADADI RAJABU.

Tunisia: Harare; tel. (4) 791570; fax (4) 727224; Ambassador HAMID ZAOUCHE.

United Kingdom: Corner House, cnr Samora Machel Ave and Leopold Takawira St, POB 4490, Harare; tel. (4) 772990; fax (4) 774617; e-mail consular.harare@fco.gov.uk; internet www.britishembassy.gov.uk/zimbabwe; Ambassador Dr ANDREW POCOCK.

USA: 172 Herbert Chitepo Ave, POB 3340, Harare; tel. (4) 758803; fax (4) 796488; e-mail hararepas@state.gov; internet harare.usembassy.gov; Ambassador JAMES D. MCGEE.

Zambia: Zambia House, cnr Union and Julius Nyerere Aves, POB 4698, Harare; tel. (4) 773777; fax (4) 773782; Ambassador Prof. E. C. MUMBA.

Judicial System

The legal system is Roman-Dutch, based on the system which was in force in the Cape of Good Hope on 10 June 1891, as modified by subsequent legislation.

The Supreme Court has original jurisdiction in matters in which an infringement of Chapter III of the Constitution defining fundamental rights is alleged. In all other matters it has appellate jurisdiction only. It consists of the Chief Justice, a Deputy Chief Justice and such other judges of the Supreme Court, being not less than two, as the President may deem necessary.

The High Court consists of the Chief Justice, the Judge President, and such other judges of the High Court as may from time to time be appointed. Below the High Court are Regional Courts and Magistrates' Courts with both civil and criminal jurisdiction presided over by full-time professional magistrates.

The Customary Law and Local Courts Act, adopted in 1990, abolished the village and community courts and replaced them with customary law and local courts, presided over by chiefs and headmen; in the case of chiefs, jurisdiction to try customary law cases is limited to those where the monetary values concerned do not exceed Z.$1,000 and in the case of a headman's court Z.$500. Appeals from the Chiefs' Courts are heard in Magistrates' Courts and, ultimately, the Supreme Court. All magistrates now have jurisdiction to try cases determinable by customary law.

Chief Justice: GODFREY CHIDYAUSIKU.

Judges of Appeal: W. SANDURA, ANELE MATIKA, TADIUS KARWI, SUSAN MAVANGIRA, LAVENDER MAKONI.

Judge President: PADDINGTON GARWE.

Attorney-General: SOBUZA GULA-NDEBELE.

Religion

AFRICAN RELIGIONS

Many Zimbabweans follow traditional beliefs.

CHRISTIANITY

About 55% of the population are Christians.

Zimbabwe Council of Churches: 128 Mbuya Nehanda St, POB 3566, Harare; tel. (4) 772043; fax (4) 773650; e-mail zcc@africaonline.co.zw; f. 1964; Pres. Rt Rev. Dr WILSON SITSHEBO; Gen. Sec. DENSEN MAFIYANI; 24 mem. churches, nine assoc. mems.

The Anglican Communion

Anglicans are adherents of the Church of the Province of Central Africa, covering Botswana, Malawi, Zambia and Zimbabwe. The Church comprises 15 dioceses, including five in Zimbabwe. The current Archbishop of the Province is the Bishop of Upper Shire, Malawi. The Church had an estimated 320,000 members at mid-2000.

Bishop of Central Zimbabwe: Rt Rev. ISHMAEL MUKUWANDA, POB 25, Gweru; tel. (54) 21030; fax (54) 21097.

Bishop of Harare: Rt Rev. Dr NOLBERT KUNONGA, Bishopsmount Close, POB UA7, Harare; tel. (4) 702253; fax (4) 700419; e-mail angbishophre@mango.zw.

Bishop of Manicaland: (vacant), 115 Herbert Chitepo St, Mutare; tel. (20) 64194; fax (20) 63076; e-mail diomani@syscom.co.zw; internet www.anglicandioceseofmanicaland.co.zw.

Bishop of Masvingo: Rt Rev. GODFREY TOANEZVI, POB 1421, Masvingo; tel. (39) 362536; e-mail anglicandiomsv@comone.co.zw.

Bishop of Matabeleland: Rt Rev. WILSON SITSHEBO, POB 2422, Bulawayo; tel. (9) 61370; fax (9) 68353; e-mail angdiomat@telconet.co.zw.

The Roman Catholic Church

For ecclesiastical purposes, Zimbabwe comprises two archdioceses and six dioceses. At 31 December 2005 there were some 1.3m. adherents, equivalent to an estimated 8.9% of the total population.

Zimbabwe Catholic Bishops' Conference (ZCBC)

Catholic Secretariat, Causeway, 29 Selous Ave, POB 8135, Harare; tel. (4) 705368; fax (4) 705369; internet www.zcbc.co.zw.

f. 1969; Pres. Most Rev. ROBERT C. NDLOVU (Archbishop of Harare).

ZIMBABWE   Directory

Archbishop of Bulawayo: Most Rev. Martin Scarp, cnr Lobengula St and 9th Ave, POB 837, Bulawayo; tel. (9) 63590; fax (9) 60359; e-mail archdbyo@mweb.co.zw.

Archbishop of Harare: Most Rev. Robert C. Ndlovu, Archbishop's House, 66 Fifth St, POB CY330, Causeway, Harare; tel. (4) 727386; fax (4) 721598; e-mail hrearch@zol.co.zw.

Other Christian Churches

At mid-2000 there were an estimated 4.8m. adherents professing other forms of Christianity.

Dutch Reformed Church in Zimbabwe (Nederduitse Gereformeerde Kerk): 35 Samora Machel Ave, POB 503, Harare; tel. (4) 774738; fax (4) 774739; e-mail pvanvuuren@mango.zw; f. 1895; 10 congregations in Zimbabwe and two in Zambia; Chair. Rev. Piet F. J. van Vuuren; Sec. Rev. J. Haasbroek; 1,400 mems.

Evangelical Lutheran Church: 7 Lawley Rd, POB 2175, Bulawayo; tel. (9) 254991; fax (9) 254993; e-mail elczhead@mweb.co.zw; f. 1903; Sec. Rt Rev. L. M. Dube; 57,000 mems.

Greek Orthodox Church: POB 2832, Harare; tel. and fax (4) 744991; e-mail zimbabwe@greekorthodox-alexandria.org; internet www.greekorthodox-zimbabwe.org; Archbishop George.

Methodist Church in Zimbabwe: POB CY71, Causeway, Harare; tel. (4) 250523; fax (4) 723709; e-mail methodistconn@zol.co.zw; f. 1891; Presiding Bishop Rev. Simbarashe Sithole; Sec. of Conference Rev. Amos Ndhlumbi.

United Congregational Church of Southern Africa: 40 Jason Moyo St, POB 2451, Bulawayo; tel. (9) 63686; internet www.uccsa.org.za/zimbabwe-synod; Chair. Rev. B. Mathema (acting); Sec. Rev. Majaha Nthliziyo.

United Methodist Church: POB 3408, Harare; tel. (4) 704127; f. 1890; Bishop of Zimbabwe Abel Tendekayi Muzorewa; 45,000 mems.

Among other denominations active in Zimbabwe are the African Methodist Church, the African Methodist Episcopal Church, the African Reformed Church, the Christian Marching Church, the Church of Christ in Zimbabwe, the Independent African Church, the Presbyterian Church (and the City Presbyterian Church), the United Church of Christ, the Zimbabwe Assemblies of God and the Ziwezano Church.

JUDAISM

The Jewish community numbered 897 members at 31 December 1997; by 2006 that number had fallen to around 300.

Zimbabwe Jewish Board of Deputies: POB 1954, Harare; tel. (4) 702507; fax (4) 702506; Pres. P. Sternberg; Sec. E. Alhadeff.

BAHÁ'Í FAITH

National Spiritual Assembly: POB GD380, Greendale, Harare; tel. (4) 495945; fax (4) 744611; internet www.bahai.co.zw; Nat. Sec. Derek Sithole; f. 1970; mems resident in 57 clusters.

The Press

DAILIES

The Chronicle: 9th Ave and George Silundika St, POB 585, Bulawayo; tel. (9) 888871; fax (9) 888884; e-mail editor@chronicle.co.zw; internet www.chronicle.co.zw; f. 1894; publ. by the Govt-controlled co Zimpapers; circulates throughout south-west Zimbabwe; English; English; Editor Makuwerere Bwititi; circ. 25,000 (2004).

Daily Mirror (Zim Mirror): Charter House, 70 Samora Machel Ave, Harare; tel. (4) 725251; fax (4) 729607; internet www.zimmirror.co.zw; f. 2002; publ. by Zimbabwe Mirror Newspapers Group; also publ. *Sunday Mirror* (f. 1997 as *The Zimbabwe Mirror Weekly*, circ. c. 15,000); English; CEO and Editor-in-Chief Ibbo Mandaza.

The Daily News: 18 Sam Nujoma St and cnr Speke Ave, Harare; tel. (4) 753027; fax (4) 753024; publ. by Associated Newspapers of Zimbabwe; English; publ. suspended Sept. 2003; Editor Nqobile Nyathi; CEO Sam Sipepa Nkomo; Chair. Strive Masiyiwa; circ. c. 80,000 (2004).

The Herald: POB 396, Harare; tel. (4) 795771; fax (4) 700305; internet www.herald.co.zw; f. 1891; publ. by the Govt-controlled co Zimpapers; English; Editor Pikirayi Deketeke; circ. 60,000 (2006).

WEEKLIES

Financial Gazette: Coal House, 5th Floor, cnr Nelson Mandela Ave and Leopold Takawira St, Harare; tel. (4) 781571; fax (4) 781578; e-mail schamunorwa@fingaz.co.zw; internet www.fingaz.co.zw; f. 1969; publ. by ZimInd Publrs (Pvt) Ltd; affiliated to the ZANU—PF party; Editor-in-Chief Sunsleey Chamunorwa; Gen. Man. Jacob Chisese; circ. c. 40,000 (2004).

Indonsakusa/Ilanga: c/o CNG, POB 6520, Harare; tel. (4) 796855; fax (4) 703873; publ. by Community Newspaper Group (Mass Media Trust); distributed in north and south Matabeleland; circ c. 10,000.

Kwayedza: POB 396, Harare; tel. (4) 795771; fax (4) 791311; internet www.kwayedza.co.zw; publ. by the Govt-controlled co Zimpapers; f. 1985; ChiShona; Editor Gervase M. Chitewe; circ. c. 15,000 (2003).

Manica Post: POB 960, Mutare; tel. (20) 61212; fax (20) 61149; f. 1893; publ. by the Govt-controlled co Zimpapers; English; Editor Paul Mambo; circ. 15,000 (2004).

Mashonaland Guardian/Telegraph: c/o CNG, POB 6520, Harare; tel. (4) 796855; fax (4) 703873; publ. by Community Newspaper Group (Mass Media Trust); distributed in Mashonaland; circ. c. 10,000.

Masvingo Mirror: POB 1214, Masvingo; tel. (39) 64372; fax (39) 64484; independent; Editor Norna Edwards.

Masvingo Star: 2–3 New Market Centre, R. Tangwena Ave, POB 138, Masvingo; tel. and fax (39) 63978; publ. by Community Newspaper Group (Mass Media Trust); English; distributed in Masvingo province; Editor Tapera Chikuwira; circ. c. 10,000.

Midlands Observer: POB 533, Kwekwe; tel. (55) 22248; fax (55) 23985; e-mail nelson_mashiri@yahoo.com; f. 1953; weekly; English; Editor R. Jarijari; circ. 20,000.

North Midlands Gazette: POB 222, Kadoma; tel. and fax (68) 3731; f. 1912; Editor C. B. Kidia.

The Standard: 1st Block, 3rd Floor, Ernst and Young Bldg, 1 Kwame Nkrumah Ave, POB 661730, Kopje, Harare; tel. 1750401; fax 1773854; internet www.thestandard.co.zw; f. 1997; publ. by ZimInd Publrs (Pvt) Ltd; Sun.; Exec. Chair and CEO Trevor Ncube; circ. 42,000 (2004).

Sunday Mail: POB 396, Harare; tel. (4) 795771; fax (4) 700305; internet www.sundaymail.co.zw; f. 1935; publ. by the Govt-controlled co Zimpapers; English; Chair. Thomas Sithole; Editor William Chikoto; circ. 110,000 (2004).

Sunday News: POB 585, Bulawayo; tel. (9) 540071; fax (9) 540084; f. 1930; publ. by the Govt-controlled co Zimpapers; English; Editor Brezhnev Malaba; circ. 30,000 (2004).

The Times: c/o CNG, POB 6520, Harare; tel. (4) 796855; fax (4) 703873; f. 1897; fmrly *The Gweru Times*; publ. by Community Newspaper Group (Mass Media Trust); distributed in Mashonaland; English; circ. c. 5,000.

uMthunywa (The Messenger): 9th Ave and George Silundika, POB 585 Bulawayo; tel. (09) 880888; fax (09) 888884; e-mail advertising@chronicle.co.zw; internet www.umthunywa.co.zw; f. 2004; SiNdebele; publ. by the Govt-controlled co Zimpapers; Editor Bhekithemba J. Ncube.

The Vanguard: Zimbabwe National Students' Union, 21 Wembley Cres., Eastlea, Harare; tel. (4) 788135; e-mail zinasu@gmail.com; internet www.zinasu.org/vanguards/latest.html; publ. by the Zimbabwe Nat. Students' Union.

The Zimbabwean: POB 248, Hythe, SO45 4WX, United Kingdom; e-mail feedback@thezimbabwean.co.uk; internet www.thezimbabwean.co.uk; f. 2005; independent; publ. in the United Kingdom and South Africa; focus on news in Zimbabwe and life in exile; Publr and Editor Wilf Mbanga.

Zimbabwe Independent: Zimind Publishers (Pvt) Ltd, Suites 23/24, 1 Union Ave, POB BE1165, Belvedere, Harare; e-mail trevorn@mg.co.za; internet www.theindependent.co.zw; f. 1996; publ. by ZimInd Publrs (Pvt) Ltd; English; Publr Trevor Ncube; Editor Dumisani Muleya; circ. 30,500 (2005).

Zimbabwean Government Gazette: POB 8062, Causeway, Harare; official notices; Editor L. Takawira.

PERIODICALS

The Agenda: Information Department, 348 Herbert Chitepo Ave, Harare; tel. (4) 736338; fax (4)721146; e-mail info@nca.org.zw; internet www.nca.org.zw; f. 1997; publ. by the Nat. Constitutional Assembly; quarterly; civil rights issues.

Central African Journal of Medicine (CAJM): University of Zimbabwe Publications, POB A195, Avondale, Harare; tel. (4) 791630; fax (4) 791995; e-mail cajm@medsch.uz.ac.zw; internet www.ajol.info; f. 1955; monthly; Editor-in-Chief Prof. G. I. Muguti.

Chamber of Mines Journal: Stewart House, North Wing, 4 Central Ave, POB 712, Harare; tel. (4) 702841; fax (4) 707983; e-mail chamines@utande.co.zw; publ. by Thomson Publs; monthly.

Chaminuka News: POB 650, Marondera; f. 1988; publ. by Community Newspaper Group (Mass Media Trust); fortnightly; English and ChiShona; distributed in Manicaland and Mashonaland North provinces; Editor M. Mugabe; circ. c. 10,000.

Indonsakusa: Hwange; f. 1988; monthly; English and SiNdebele; Editor D. NTABENI; circ. 10,000.

The Insider: Insider Publications, POB FM 415, Famona, Bulawayo; tel. (11) 789-739; e-mail charlesrukuni@insiderzim.com; e-mail charlesrukuni@yahoo.com; internet www.insiderzim.com; f. 1990; monthly; digital newsletter; news and current affairs; Editor and Publr CHARLES RUKUNI.

JASSA: Journal of Applied Science in Southern Africa: University of Zimbabwe Publications, POB MP203, Mount Pleasant, Harare; tel. (4) 303211; fax (4) 333407; e-mail uzpub@admin.uz.ac.zw; internet www.uz.ac.zw/publications; applied science journal of the Univ. of Zimbabwe; 2 a year; Editor-in-Chief Prof. C. F. B. NHACHI.

Journal of Social Development in Africa: School of Social Work, University of Zimbabwe, Private Bag 66022, Kopje, Harare; tel. and fax (4) 751903; e-mail sswprinc@mweb.co.zw; 2 a year; Editor Prof. RODRECK MUPEDZISWA.

Mahogany: POB UA589, Harare; tel. (4) 752063; fax (4) 752062; f. 1980; 6 a year; English; women's interest; Editor TENDAI DONDO; circ. 240,000.

Masiye Pambili (Let Us Go Forward): POB 591, Bulawayo; tel. (9) 75011; fax (9) 69701; f. 1964; 2 a year; English; Editor M. N. NDLOVU; circ. 25,000.

Moto (Fire): POB 890, Gweru; tel. (54) 24886; fax (54) 28194; e-mail moto@telco.co.zw; f. 1959; monthly; publ. by the Govt-controlled co Zimpapers; banned in 1974; relaunched in 1980 as a weekly newspaper, then in magazine format in 1982; Roman Catholic; Editor SYDNEY SHOKO; circ. 22,000.

Mukai-Vukani Jesuit Journal for Zimbabwe: Jesuit Communications, 1 Churchill Ave, Alexandra Park, POB ST194, Southerton, Harare; tel. (4) 744571; fax (4) 744284; e-mail owermter@zol.co.zw; internet www.jescom.co.zw; 4–6 a year; Catholic; Editor Fr OSKAR WERMTER; circ. 2,000.

Nehanda Guardian: Bindura; f. 1988; weekly; English and ChiShona; Editor K. MWANAKA; circ. 10,000.

New Farmer: Herald House, cnr George Sikundika and Sam Nujoma Sts, POB 55, Harare; tel. (4) 708296; fax (4) 702400; e-mail advertising@chronicle.co.zw; internet www.newfarmer.co.zw; f. 2002; publ. by the Govt-controlled co Zimpapers; weekly; English; Editor GEORGE CHISOKO.

The Outpost: POB HG106, Highlands; tel. (4) 724571; fax (4) 703631; e-mail theoutpostmag@yahoo.com; f. 1911; publ. of the Zimbabwe Republic Police; monthly; English; Editor NKOSANA DLAMINI; circ. c. 25,000 (2005).

Railroader: National Railways of Zimbabwe, cnr Fife St and 10th Ave, POB 596, Bulawayo; tel. (9) 363716; fax (9) 363502; f. 1952; publ. by Nat. Railways of Zimbabwe; monthly; Editor M. GUMEDE; circ. 10,000.

Southern African Political and Economic Monthly (SAPEM): Southern Africa Political Economy Series Trust, 2–6 Deary Ave, Belgravia, POB MP111, Mt Pleasant, Harare; tel. (4) 252962; fax (4) 252964; f. 1987; monthly; publ. by the SAPES Trust; incorporating *Southern African Economist*; Editor-in-Chief KHABELE MATLOSA; circ. 16,000.

Trends: 9th Ave and George Silundika St, POB 585 Bulawayo; tel. (09) 880888; fax (09) 888884; e-mail advertising@chronicle.co.zw; internet www.zimtrends.co.zw; f. 2003; publ. by the Govt-controlled co Zimpapers; monthly; English; leisure and entertainment; Editor EDWIN DUBE.

The Worker: ZCTU, Chester House, 9th Floor, Speke Ave and Third St, POB 3549, Harare; tel. (4) 794742; fax (4) 728484; e-mail info@zctu.co.zw; publ. by the Zimbabwe Congress of Trade Unions; News Editor BRIGHT CHIBVURI.

Zambezia: University of Zimbabwe Publications, POB MP203, Mount Pleasant, Harare; tel. (4) 303211; fax (4) 333407; e-mail uzpub@admin.uz.ac.zw; internet www.uz.ac.zw/publications; publ. by the Univ. of Zimbabwe; 2 a year; humanities and general interest; Editor Dr ZIFIKILE MGUNI-GAMBAHAYA.

Zimbabwe Agricultural Journal: Dept of Research and Specialist Services, 5th St, Extension, POB CY594, Causeway, Harare; tel. (4) 704531; fax (4) 728317; f. 1903; 6 a year; Editor R. J. FENNER; circ. 2,000.

Zimbabwean Travel: Herald House, cnr George Sikundika and Sam Nujoma Sts, POB 55, Harare; tel. (4) 708296; fax (4) 702400; e-mail advertising@chronicle.co.zw; internet www.zimtravel.com; f. 2003; publ. by the Govt-controlled co Zimpapers; monthly; English; Editor NOMSA NKALA.

Zimbabwe National Army Magazine: Ministry of Defence, Defence House, cnr Kwame Nkuruma Ave and 3rd St, Harare; tel. (4) 700316; f. 1982; 4 a year; Dir of Communications Col LIVINGSTONE CHINEKA; circ. 5,000.

The Zimbabwe Farmer: POB 1683, Harare; tel. (4) 736836; fax (4) 749803; monthly; fmrly *Tobacco News*; present name adopted in 2003; publ. by Thomson Publs; Editor D. MILLER; circ. 2,000.

Zimbabwe Journal of Educational Research: HRRC, Faculty of Education, University of Zimbabwe, POB MP167, Mount Pleasant, Harare; e-mail hrrc@education.uz.ac.zw; internet www.uz.ac.zw/education/zjer; 3 a year; Editor-in-Chief Prof. F. ZINDI.

Zimbabwe Veterinary Journal: Zimbabwe Veterinary Asscn, POB A415, Avondale, Harare; e-mail rjestewart@yahoo.com; f. 1970; journal of the Zimbabwe Veterinary Asscn; 2 a year; Editor-in-Chief S. MUKARATIRWA; Editing Man. Dr RACHEL STEWART.

NEWS AGENCY

NewZiana (Pvt) Ltd: Mass Media House, 19 Selous Ave, POB CY511, Causeway, Harare; tel. (4) 251754; fax (4) 794336; e-mail mukrati@ziana.co.zw; internet www.newziana.co.zw; f. 1981 as Zimbabwe Inter-Africa News Agency; present name adopted in 2003; owned by the Govt-controlled co Multimedia Investment Trust (fmrly Zimbabwe Mass Media Trust); operates 10 community newspapers; CEO MUNYARADZI MATANYAIRE.

Publishers

Academic Books (Pvt) Ltd: POB 567, Harare; tel. (4) 755408; fax (4) 781913; educational; Editorial Dir IRENE STAUNTON.

Amalgamated Publications (Pvt) Ltd: POB 1683, Harare; tel. (4) 736835; fax (4) 749803; f. 1949; trade journals.

Anvil Press: POB 4209, Harare; tel. (4) 751202; fax (4) 739681; f. 1988; general; Man. Dir PAUL BRICKHILL.

The Argosy Press: POB 2677, Harare; tel. (4) 755084; magazine publrs; Gen. Man. A. W. HARVEY.

Baobab Books (Pvt) Ltd: POB 567, Harare; tel. (4) 665187; fax (4) 665155; general, literature, children's.

The Bulletin: POB 1595, Bulawayo; tel. (9) 78831; fax (9) 78835; fmrly Directory Publrs Ltd; educational; CEO BRUCE BEALE.

College Press Publishers (Pvt) Ltd: 15 Douglas Rd, POB 3041, Workington, Harare; tel. (4) 754145; fax (4) 754256; f. 1968; educational and general; Man. Dir B. B. MUGABE.

Harare Publishing House: Chiremba Rd, Hatfield, Harare; tel. (4) 570342; f. 1982; Dir Dr T. M. SAMKANGE.

HarperCollins Publishers Zimbabwe (Pvt) Ltd: Union Ave, POB UA201, Harare; tel. (4) 721413; fax (4) 732436; Man. S. D. MCMILLAN.

Longman Zimbabwe (Pvt) Ltd: POB ST125, Southerton, Harare; tel. (4) 62711; fax (4) 62716; f. 1964; general and educational; Man. Dir N. L. DLODLO.

Mambo Press: Senga Rd, POB 779, Gweru; tel. (54) 24017; fax (54) 21991; f. 1958; religious, educational and fiction in English and African languages.

Modus Publications (Pvt) Ltd: Modus House, 27–29 Charter Rd, POB 66070, Kopje, Harare; tel. (4) 738722; Man. Dir ELIAS RUSIKE.

Munn Publishing (Pvt) Ltd: POB UA460, Union Ave, Harare; tel. (4) 481048; fax (4) 7481081; Man. Dir I. D. MUNN.

Standard Publications (Pvt) Ltd: POB 3745, Harare; Dir G. F. BOOT.

Southern African Printing and Publishing House (SAPPHO): 109 Coventry Rd, Workington, POB MP1005, Mount Pleasant, Harare; tel. (4) 621681; fax (4) 666061; internet www.zimmirror.co.zw; Editor-in-Chief Dr IBBO MANDAZA.

University of Zimbabwe Publications: University of Zimbabwe, POB MP203, Mount Pleasant, Harare; tel. (4) 303211; fax (4) 333407; e-mail uzpub@admin.uz.ac.zw; internet www.uz.ac.zw/publications; f. 1969; Dir MUNANI SAM MTETWA.

Zimbabwe Newspapers (1980) Ltd (Zimpapers): POB 55, Harare; tel. (4) 704088; fax (4) 702400; e-mail theherald@zimpapers.co.zw; internet www.herald.co.zw; f. 1981; 51% state-owned; publ. the newspapers *The Herald*, *The Sunday Mail*, *The Manica Post*, *The Chronicle*, *The Sunday News*, *Kwayedza*, *Umthunywa* and *The Southern Times* (based in Namibia); and magazines incl. *The Zimbabwean Travel*, *Trends Magazine* and *New Farmer Magazine*; Chair. HERBERT NKALA; Group CEO JUSTIN MUTASA.

ZPH Publishers (Pvt) Ltd: 183 Arcturus Rd, Kamfinsa, GD510, Greendale, Harare; tel. (4) 497548; fax (4) 497554; e-mail tafi@zph.co.zw; f. 1982 as Zimbabwe Publishing House Ltd; Chair. BLAZIO G. TAFIREYI.

ZIMBABWE   *Directory*

Broadcasting and Communications

TELECOMMUNICATIONS

Econet Wireless Zimbabwe: Econet Park, No.2 Old Mutare Rd, Msasa, POB BE1298, Belvedere, Harare; tel. (91) 793500; fax (4) 486120; e-mail info@econet.co.zw; internet www.econet.co.zw; f. 1998; mobile cellular telecommunications operator; Chair. Tawanda Nyambirai; CEO Douglas Mboweni.

Net.One Ltd: POB CY579, Causeway, Harare; tel. (4) 707138; e-mail marketing@netone.co.zw; internet www.netone.co.zw; f. 1998; state-owned; mobile cellular telecommunications operator; Chair. Callistus Ndlovu; CEO Reward Kangai.

Posts and Telecommunications Corpn (PTC): POB CY331, Causeway, Harare; tel. (4) 728811; fax (4) 731980; Chair. Dr M. Mhloyi; CEO Brian Mutandiro.

Telecel Zimbabwe: 148 Seke Rd, Graniteside, POB CY232, Causeway, Harare; tel. (4) 748321; fax (4) 748328; e-mail info@telecelzim.co.zw; internet www.telecel.co.zw; f. 1998; 60% owned by Telecel Int. and 40% owned by Empowerment Corpn; mobile cellular telecommunications operator; Chair. James Makamba; Man. Dir John Swaim.

TelOne: Runhare House, 107 Union Ave, POBCY331, Causeway, Harare; tel. (4) 798111; e-mail webmaster@telone.co.zw; internet www.telone.co.zw; state-owned; sole fixed-line telecommunications operator.

BROADCASTING

There are four govt-controlled radio stations (National FM, Power FM, Radio Zimbabwe and Spot FM) and one television station. Radio Voice of the People was established as an alternative to state broadcasting. An independent radio station, SW Radio Africa, broadcasts to Zimbabwe from London, United Kingdom. Since 2003 Voice of America has broadcast a weekday news and entertainment programme (Studio 7) from the USA in ChiShona, English and SiNdebele.

Radio

Voice of the People (VOP): POB 5750, Harare; tel. (4) 707123; e-mail voxpopzim@yahoo.co.uk; internet www.vopradio.co.zw; f. 2000 by fmr ZBC staff; broadcasts one hour per day; relayed by Radio Netherlands transmitters in Madagascar; news and information in ChiShona, SiNdebele and English; Chair. David Masunda; Exec. Dir John Masuku.

Zimbabwe Broadcasting Corpn: Broadcasting Center, Pockets Hill, POB HG444, Highlands, Harare; tel. (4) 498610; fax (4) 498613; e-mail zbc@zbc.co.zw; internet www.zbc.co.zw; f. 1957; programmes in English, ChiShona, SiNdebele and 14 minority languages, incl. Chichewa, Venda and Xhosa; broadcasts a general service (mainly in English), vernacular languages service, light entertainment, and educational programmes; Editor-in-Chief Christina Taruvinga.

Television

Zimbabwe Broadcasting Corpn: (see Radio).
The main broadcasting centre is in Harare, with a second studio in Bulawayo; broadcasts ZBC-TV 24 hours per day.

Finance

(cap. = capital; res = reserves; dep. = deposits; m. = million; br(s). = branch(es); amounts in Zimbabwe dollars)

BANKING

Central Bank

Reserve Bank of Zimbabwe: 80 Samora Machel Ave, POB 1283, Harare; tel. (4) 703000; fax (4) 706450; e-mail lchitapi@rbz.co.zw; internet www.rbz.co.zw; f. 1964; bank of issue; cap. 2m., res 6m., dep. 11,734,195m. (Dec. 2004); Gov. Dr Gideon Gono.

Commercial Banks

Barclays Bank of Zimbabwe Ltd: Barclays House, cnr First St and Jason Moyo Ave, POB 1279, Harare; tel. (4) 758281; fax (4) 752913; e-mail barclays.zimbabwe@barclays.com; internet www.barclays.co.zw; f. 1912; commercial and merchant banking; cap. 1,000m., res 19,000m., dep. 1,779,000m. (Dec. 2004); Chair. Dr Robbie Matongo Mupawose; CEO Charity Jinya; 44 brs.

Jewel Bank: Union House, 60 Union Ave, POB 3313, Harare; tel. (4) 758081; fax (4) 758085; e-mail cbzinfo@africaonline.co.zw; state-owned; cap. and res 2,551m., total assets 36,057m. (Dec. 2001); f. 1980; fmrly Commercial Bank of Zimbabwe; present name adopted 2004; Chair. Richard V. Wilde; 9 brs.

Kingdom Bank Ltd: 6th Floor, Karigamombe Centre, 53 Samora Machel Ave, Harare; tel. (4) 749400; fax (4) 755201; e-mail kmb@kingdom.co.zw; internet www.kingdom.co.zw; f. 2000; cap. 102m., res 14,655m., dep. 522,437m.; Man. Dir Mark Wood.

Stanbic Bank Zimbabwe Ltd: Stanbic Centre, 1st Floor, 59 Samora Machel Ave, POB 300, Harare; tel. (4) 759480; fax (4) 751324; e-mail zimbabweinfo@stanbic.com; internet www.stanbic.co.zw; f. 1990; cap. 1,000m., res 1,761,842m., dep. 7,386,055m. (Dec. 2005); Chair. S. Moyo; Man. Dir Pindie Nyandoro; 16 brs.

Standard Chartered Bank Zimbabwe Ltd: John Boyne House, cnr Inez Terrace and Speke Ave, POB 373, Harare; tel. (4) 252623; fax (4) 758076; internet www.standardchartered.com/zw; f. 1983; cap. and res 3,422.7m., total assets 558,124m. (2003); Chair. H. P. Mkushi; CEO Washington Matsaira; 28 brs.

Trade and Investment Bank Ltd: Cabs Centre, 10th Floor, 74 Jason Moyo Ave, POB CY1064, Causeway, Harare; tel. (4) 703791; fax (4) 705491; f. 1997; cap. and res 32m., total assets 421m. (Dec. 1997); Chair. Dr Bernard Thomas Chidzero; CEO Dr Kombo James Moyana.

Zimbabwe Banking Corpn Ltd (Zimbank): Zimbank House, Speke Ave and First St, POB 3198, Harare; tel. (4) 757471; fax (4) 757497; e-mail finhold@finhold.co.zw; internet www.finhold.co.zw; f. 1951; state-owned; cap. 102m., res 178,293m., dep. 821,214m. (Sept. 2004); Chair. Richard Chemist Hove; Group CEO Elisha N. Mushayakarara; 35 brs.

Development Banks

African Export-Import Bank (Afreximbank): Eastgate Bldg, 3rd Floor, Gold Bridge (North Wing), Second St, POB 1600 Causeway, Harare; tel. (4) 729751; fax (4) 729756; internet www.afreximbank.com.

Infrastructure Development Bank of Zimbabwe (IDBZ): 99 Rotten Row, Harare; tel. (4) 774226; fax (4) 774225; e-mail enquiries@zdb.co.zw; internet www.zdb.co.zw; f. 2005.

Zimbabwe Development Bank (ZDB): ZDB House, 99 Rotten Row, POB 1720, Harare; tel. (4) 774226; fax (4) 774225; internet www.zdb.co.zw; f. 1985; 33.3% state-owned; cap. and res 355m., total assets 2,317m. (Dec. 2001); Chair. Dr T. Masaya; Man. Dir Cornelius Maradza; 3 brs.

Merchant Banks

African Banking Corpn of Zimbabwe Ltd (ABC): ABC House, 1 Endeavour Cres., Mount Pleasant Business Park, Mount Pleasant, POB 2786, Harare; tel. (4) 369260; fax (4) 369939; e-mail abcmail@africanbankingcorp.com; internet www.africanbankingcorp.com; f. 1956 as Rhodesian Acceptances Ltd; name changed to First Merchant Bank of Zimbabwe Ltd in 1990; merged with Heritage Investment Bank in 1997; present name adopted in 2002; subsidiary of ABC Holdings Ltd, Botswana; cap. and res 36.8m., total assets 475.6m. (Dec. 2001); Chair. O. M. Chidawu; Man. Dir F. M. Dzanya; 1 br.

MBCA Bank Ltd: Old Mutual Centre, 14th Floor, cnr Third St and Jason Moyo Ave, POB 3200, Harare; tel. (4) 701636; fax (4) 708005; e-mail mbca@mbca.co.zw; internet www.mbca.co.zw; f. 1956; cap. 500.1m., res 10,946.7m., dep. 3,366,941.3m. (Dec. 2004); Chair. E. D. Chiura; Man. Dir D. Denya.

NMB Bank Ltd: Unity Court, 4th Floor, cnr Union Ave and First St, POB 2564, Harare; tel. (4) 759651; fax (4) 759648; e-mail enquiries@nmbz.co.zw; internet www.nmbz.com; f. 1993; fmrly Nat. Merchant Bank of Zimbabwe; cap. 32m., res 391,485m., dep. 2,610,982m. (Dec. 2005); Chair. Dr Gibson Manyowa Mandishona; CEO Dr David T. Hatendi; 10 brs.

Standard Chartered Merchant Bank Zimbabwe Ltd: Standard Chartered Bank Bldg, cnr Second St and Nelson Mandela Ave, POB 60, Harare; tel. (4) 708585; fax (4) 725667; f. 1971; cap. and res 78m., dep. 83m. (Dec. 1998); Chair. Barry Hamilton; Man. Dir Ebby Essoka.

Discount Houses

African Banking Corpn Securities Ltd: 69 Samora Machel Ave, POB 3321, Harare; tel. (4) 752756; fax (4) 790641; cap. and res 68m. (Dec. 1999); fmrly Bard Discount House Ltd; Chair. N. Kudenga; Man. Dir D. Dube.

The Discount Co of Zimbabwe (DCZ): 70 Park Lane, POB 3424, Harare; tel. (4) 705414; fax (4) 731670; cap. and res 8.9m., total assets 377.4m. (Feb. 1995); Chair. S. J. Chihambakwe.

Intermarket Discount House: Unity Court, 5th Floor, Union Ave, POB 3290, Harare.

National Discount House Ltd: MIPF House, 5th Floor, Central Ave, Harare; tel. (4) 700771; fax (4) 792927; internet www.ndh.co.zw; cap. and res 168.4m., total assets 2,365.2m. (Dec. 2000); Chair. Edwin Manikai; Man. Dir Lawrence Tamayi.

ZIMBABWE

Banking Organizations

Bankers' Association of Zimbabwe (BAZ): Kuwana House, 4th Floor, Union Ave and First St, POB UA550, Harare; tel. (4) 728646; Pres. ELISHA MUSHAYAKARA; Dir FRANK READ.

Institute of Bankers of Zimbabwe: Union Ave, POB UA521, Harare; tel. (4) 752474; fax (4) 750281; e-mail info@iobz.co.zw; internet www.iobz.co.zw; f. 1973; Chair. S. BIYAM; Pres. M. L. WOOD; Dir I. E. H. HELBY; 7,000 mems.

STOCK EXCHANGE

Zimbabwe Stock Exchange: Chiyedza House, 5th Floor, cnr First St and Kwame Nkrumah Ave, POB UA234, Harare; tel. (4) 736861; fax (4) 791045; e-mail zse@econet.co.zw; internet www.zse.co.zw; f. 1946; Chair. G. MHLANGA; CEO EMMANUEL MUNYUKWI.

INSURANCE

Export Credit Guarantee Corpn of Zimbabwe (Pvt): 6 Earles Rd, Alexandra Park, POB CY2995, Causeway, Harare; tel. and fax (4) 744644; e-mail ecgc@telco.co.zw; internet www.ecgc.co.zw; f. 1999 as national export credit insurance agency; also provides export finance guarantee facilities; 100% owned by Reserve Bank of Zimbabwe; Chair. J. A. L. CARTER; Man. Dir RAPHAEL G. NYADZAYO.

Credit Insurance Zimbabwe (Credsure): Credsure House, 69 Sam Nujoma St, POB CY1584, Causeway, Harare; tel. (4) 706101; fax (4) 706105; e-mail headoffice@credsure.co.zw; export credit insurance; Man. Dir BRIAN HILLEN-MOORE.

Fidelity Life Assurance of Zimbabwe (Pvt) Ltd: 66 Julius Nyerere Way, POB 435, Harare; tel. (4) 750927; fax (4) 751723; f. 1977; 52% owned by Zimre Holdings Ltd; pensions and life assurance; Chair. J. P. MKUSHI; Man. Dir SIMON B. CHAPAREKA.

Intermarket Life Assurance Ltd: Intermarket Life Towers, 77 Jason Moyo Ave, POB 969, Harare; tel. (4) 708801; fax (4) 703186; e-mail info@interlife.co.zw; internet www.intermarket.co.zw; f. 1964; life insurance; Man. Dir AMBROSE G. CHINEMBIRI.

NICOZ Diamond: Shell House, Samora Machel and Leopold Takawira Ave, POB 1256, Harare; tel. (4) 704911; fax (4) 704134; internet www.nicozdiamond.co.zw; f. 2003 by merger of National Insurance Co of Zimbabwe and Diamond Insurance of Zimbabwe; Chair. PHINEAS S. CHINGONO; Man. Dir GRACE MURADZIKWA.

Old Mutual PLC: Old Mutual Central Africa CABS Bldg, Northend Close, Northridge Park, Highlands, Harare; POB 1346, Harare; tel. (4) 851484; fax (4) 485480; e-mail info@oldmutual.co.zw; internet www.oldmutual.co.zw; f. 1845; life and general insurance, asset management, and banking services; Chair. M. J. LEVETT; CEO J. H. SUTCLIFFE.

Zimnat Lion Insurance Co Ltd: Zimnat House, cnr Nelson Mandela Ave and Third St, POB CY1155, Causeway, Harare; tel. (4) 701177; fax (4) 735060; f. 1998 by merger of Zimnat Insurance Co Ltd and Lion of Zimbabwe Insurance; merged with AIG Zimbabwe in 2005; short-term insurance; Chair. S. MUTASA; Man. Dir CARLSON CHISWO.

Trade and Industry

GOVERNMENT AGENCIES

Export Processing Zones Authority (EPZA): POB 661484, Kopje, Harare; tel. (4) 780147; fax (4) 773843; e-mail info@epz.co.zw; internet www.epz.co.zw; f. 1996; administers and regulates export processing zones established since 1994; Chair. LOVEMORE CHIHOTA; Chief Exec. WALTER CHIDHAKWA.

Industrial Development Corpn of Zimbabwe (IDC): 93 Park Lane, POB CY1431, Causeway, Harare; tel. (4) 706971; fax (4) 250385; e-mail administrator@idc.co.zw; internet www.idc.co.zw; f. 1963; state investment agency; Gen. Man. MIKE NDUDZO.

Privatisation Agency of Zimbabwe (PAZ): Club Chambers, 9th Floor, cnr Nelson Mandela Ave and Third St, Private Bag 7728, Causeway, Harare; tel. (4) 251620; fax (4) 253723; internet www.paz.co.zw; f. 1999; CEO ANDREW N. BVUMBE.

Zimbabwe Investment Centre (ZIC): Investment House, 109 Rotten Row, POB 5950, Harare; tel. (4) 757931; fax (4) 757937; e-mail info@zic.co.zw; internet www.zic.co.zw; f. 1993; promotes domestic and foreign investment; CEO RICHARD MBAIWA (acting).

ZimTrade: 904 Premium Close, Mount Pleasant Business Park, POB 2738, Harare; tel. (4) 369330; fax (4) 369244; internet www.zimtrade.co.zw; f. 1991; national export promotion org.; Chair. FLORENCE SIGUDU MATAMBO; CEO ELIZABETH NERWANDE.

DEVELOPMENT ORGANIZATIONS

Alternative Business Association (ABA): Stand No. 15295, cnr First St and Eighth Cres., Sunningdale, Harare; tel. (4) 589625; fax (4) 799600; f. 1999 to address urban and rural poverty; programme areas include, agriculture, micro-mining, cross-border trade, micro-enterprise devt and micro-finance; Dir ISRAEL MABHOU.

Indigenous Business Development Centre (IBDC): Pocket Bldg, 1st Floor, Jason Moyo Ave, POB 3331, Causeway, Harare; tel. (4) 748345; f. 1990; Pres. BEN MUCHECHE; Sec.-Gen. Enoch KAMUSHINDA.

Indigenous Business Women's Organisation (IBWO): 73B Central Ave, POB 3710, Harare; tel. (4) 702076; fax (4) 614012; Pres. JANE MUTASA.

Zidco Holdings: 88 Robert Mugabe Rd, POB 1275, Harare; tel. (4) 253682; fax (4) 704391; f. 1981; fmrly Zimbabwe Devt Corpn; privatized in 2001; CEO (vacant).

Zimbabwe Human Rights NGO Forum: Blue Bridge, 8th Floor, Eastgate, POB 9077, Harare; tel. (4) 250511; fax (4) 250494; e-mail admin@hrforum.co.zw; internet www.hrforumzim.com; f. 1998; provides legal and 'psycho-social' assistance to the victims of organized violence; comprises 16 mem. orgs.

Zimbabwe Women's Bureau: 43 Hillside Rd, POB CR 120, Cranborne, Harare; tel. (4) 747809; fax (4) 707905; e-mail zwbtc@africaonline.co.zw; f. 1978; promotes entrepreneurial and rural community devt; Dir BERTHA MSORA.

CHAMBERS OF COMMERCE

Manicaland Chamber of Industries: 91 Third St, POB 92, Mutare; tel. (20) 61718; f. 1945; Pres. KUMBIRAI KATSANDE; 60 mems.

Mashonaland Chamber of Industries: POB 3794, Harare; tel. (4) 772763; fax (4) 750953; f. 1922; Pres. CHESTER MHENDE; 729 mems.

Matabeleland Chamber of Industries: 104 Parirenyatwa St, POB 2317, Bulawayo; tel. (9) 60642; fax (9) 60814; f. 1931; Pres. FELIX TSHUMA; 75 mems (2003).

Midlands Chamber of Industries: POB 213, Gweru; tel. (54) 2812; Pres. Dr BILL MOORE; 50 mems.

Zimbabwe National Chamber of Commerce (ZNCC): ZNCC Business House, 42 Harare St, POB 1934, Harare; tel. (4) 749335; fax (4) 750375; internet www.zncc.co.zw; f. 1983; represents small and medium businesses; Pres. LUXON ZEMBE; CEO CAIN MPOFU (acting); 2,500 mems; 8 brs.

INDUSTRIAL AND TRADE ASSOCIATIONS

Chamber of Mines of Zimbabwe: Stewart House, North Wing, 4 Central Ave, POB 712, Harare; tel. (4) 702841; fax (4) 707983; internet www.chamines.co.zw; f. 1939 by merger of the Rhodesian Chamber of Mines (Bulawayo) and Salisbury Chamber of Mines; Pres. Dr JACK MUREHWA; Chief Exec. and Sec. DAVID E. H. MURANGARI.

Confederation of Zimbabwe Industries (CZI): 31 Josiah Chinamano Ave, POB 3794, Harare; tel. (4) 251490; fax (4) 252424; e-mail cmsileya@czi.co.zw; internet www.czi.org.zw; f. 1957; Pres. CALLISTO M. JOKONYA; CEO CLIFFORD M. SILEYA.

Specialized affiliate trade associations include:

CropLife Zimbabwe: POB AY78, Amby, Harare; tel. (4) 620191; fax (4) 660590; e-mail maxm@ecomed.co.zw; fmrly Agricultural Chemical Industry Asscn; Chair. MAX MAKUVISE.

Furniture Manufacturers' Association: c/o CZI, 31 Josiah Chinamano Ave, POB 3794, Harare; Pres. MATT SNYMAN.

Zimbabwe Association of Packaging: 17 Conventry Rd, Workington, Harare; tel. (4) 753800; fax (4) 882020.

Construction Industry Federation of Zimbabwe: Conquenar House, 256 Samora Machel Ave East, POB 1502, Harare; tel. (4) 746661; fax (4) 746937; Pres. GILBERT MATIKA; CEO MARTIN CHINGAIRA; c. 460 mems.

Grain Marketing Board (GMB): Dura Bldg, 179–187 Samora Machel Ave, POB CY77, Harare; tel. (4) 701870; fax (4) 251294; e-mail seedco@seedcogroup.com; f. 1931; responsible for maintaining national grain reserves and ensuring food security; CEO SAMUEL MUVUTI (acting).

Indigenous Petroleum Group of Zimbabwe (IPGZ): Harare; f. 2004 following split from Petroleum Marketers' Asscn of Zimbabwe; Chair. HUBERT NYAMBUYA; represents 68 importers.

Minerals Marketing Corpn of Zimbabwe (MMCZ): 90 Mutare Rd, Msasa, POB 2628, Harare; tel. (4) 487200; fax (4) 487161; internet www.mmcz.co.zw; f. 1982; sole authority for marketing of mineral production (except gold); Chair. MERCY MKUSHI (acting); Gen. Man. and CEO ONESIMO MAZAI MOYO.

Petroleum Marketers' Association of Zimbabwe (PMAZ): 142 Samora Machel Ave, Harare; tel. (4) 797556; represents private importers of petroleum-based products; Chair. GORDON MUSARIRA.

Timber Council of Zimbabwe: Conquenar House, 256 Samora Machel Ave, POB 3645, Harare; tel. (4) 746645; fax (4) 746013; Exec. Dir MARTIN DAVIDSON.

ZIMBABWE

Tobacco Growers' Trust (TGT): POB AY331, Harare; tel. (4) 781167; fax (4) 781722; f. 2001; manages 20% of tobacco industry foreign exchange earnings on behalf of Reserve Bank of Zimbabwe; affiliated orgs include Zimbabwe Tobacco Assen and Zimbabwe Farmers' Union; Chair. WILFANOS MASHINGAIDZE; Gen. Man. ALBERT JAURE.

Tobacco Industry and Marketing Board: POB 10214, Harare; tel. (4) 613310; fax (4) 613264; e-mail timb@timb.co.zw; internet www.timb.co.zw; f. 1936; Chair. NJODZI MACHIRORI; CEO STANLEY MUTEPFA.

Tobacco Trade Association: c/o 4–12 Paisley Rd, POB ST180, Southerton, Harare; tel. (4) 773858; fax (4) 773859; e-mail tta@zol.co.zw; f. 1948; represents manufacturers and merchants.

Zimbabwe National Traditional Healers' Association (ZINATHA): Red Cross House, 2nd Floor, Rm 202, 98 Cameron St, POB 1116, Harare; tel. and fax (11) 606771; f. 1980; certifies and oversees traditional healers and practitioners of herbal medicine through the Traditional Medical Practitioners Council; promotes indigenous methods of prevention and treatment of HIV/AIDS; Pres. Prof. GORDON CHAVUNDUKA; 55,000 mems (2004).

Zimbabwe Tobacco Association (ZTA): 108 Prince Edward St, POB 1781, Harare; tel. (4) 796931; fax (4) 791855; e-mail fctobacco@zta.co.zw; internet www.zta.co.zw; f. 1928; represents growers; Pres. ANDREW FERREIRA; CEO RODNEY AMBROSE; c. 5,500 mems.

EMPLOYERS' ASSOCIATIONS

Commercial Farmers' Union (CFU): Agriculture House, cnr Adylinn Rd and Marlborough Dr., Marlborough; POB WGT390, Westgate, Harare; tel. (4) 309800; fax (4) 309849; e-mail aisd3@cfu.co.zw; internet www.cfu.co.zw; f. 1942; Pres. DOUGLAS TAYLOR-FREEME; Dir HENDRIK W. OLIVIER; 1,200 mems.

Cattle Producers' Association (CPA): Agriculture House, cnr Adylinn Rd and Marlborough Dr., Marlborough; POB WGT390, Westgate, Harare; tel. and fax (4) 309837; e-mail cpa@cfu.co.zw; Chair. MARYNA ERASMUS.

Coffee Growers' Association: Agriculture House, cnr Adylinn Rd and Marlborough Dr., Marlborough; POB WGT390, Westgate, Harare; tel. and fax (4) 750238; e-mail pres@cfu.co.zw; f. 1961; Chair. T. GIFFORD; Dir H. OLIVIER.

Commercial Cotton Growers' Association: Agriculture House, cnr Adylinn Rd and Marlborough Dr., Marlborough; POB WGT390, Westgate, Harare; tel. (4) 309800; fax (4) 309849; f. 1951; Chair. NEVILLE BROWN.

Crops Association: Agriculture House, cnr Adylinn Rd and Marlborough Dr., Marlborough; POB WGT390, Westgate, Harare; tel. (4) 309843; fax (4) 309850; e-mail copa@cfu.co.zw; comprises the Commercial Oilseeds Producers' Assen (COPA), the Zimbabwe Cereal Producers' Assen (ZCPA) and the Zimbabwe Grain Producers' Assen (ZGPA); Chair. DENNIS LAPHAM; Man. (Crops) GEORGE HUTCHISON; represents c. 800 producers.

National Association of Dairy Farmers: Agriculture House, cnr Adylinn Rd and Marlborough Dr., Marlborough; POB WGT390, Westgate, Harare; tel. (4) 309800; fax (4) 309837; e-mail nadf@cfu.co.zw; f. 1953; CEO ROB J. VAN VUUREN; 174 mems.

Ostrich Producers' Association of Zimbabwe (TOPAZ): Agriculture House, cnr Adylinn Rd and Marlborough Dr., Marlborough; POB WGT390, Westgate, Harare; tel. (4) 309800; fax (4) 309862; Chair. CEDRIC WILDE; Exec. Dir CLARE DAVIES.

Zimbabwe Association of Tobacco Growers (ZATG): Agriculture House, cnr Adylinn Rd and Marlborough Dr., Marlborough; POB WGT390, Westgate, Harare; f. 2001; Pres. JULIUS NGORIMA; CEO CANAAN RUSHIZHA; 1,500 mems.

Zimbabwe Poultry Association (Commercial Poultry Producers' Association): Agriculture House, cnr Adylinn Rd and Marlborough Dr., Marlborough; POB WGT390, Westgate, Harare; tel. (4) 309800; fax (4) 309849; Chair. PETER DRUMMOND; represents c. 200 producers.

Employers' Confederation of Zimbabwe (EMCOZ): Stewart House, 4 Central Ave, 2nd Floor, POB 158, Harare; tel. (4) 739647; fax (4) 739630; e-mail emcoz@emcoz.co.zw; Pres. MIKE C. BIMHA; Exec. Dir JOHN W. MUFUKARE.

Horticultural Promotion Council (HPC): 12 Maasdorp Ave, Alexandra Park; POB WGT290, Westgate, Harare; tel. (4) 745492; fax (4) 745480; Chief Exec. BASILIO SANDAMU; represents c. 1,000 producers.

Export Flower Growers' Association of Zimbabwe (EFGAZ): 12 Maasdorp Ave, Alexandra Park; POB WGT290, Westgate, Harare; tel. (4) 725130; fax (4) 795303; Dir MARY DUNPHY; c. 300 mems.

National Employment Council for the Construction Industry of Zimbabwe: St Barbara House, Nelson Mandela Ave and Leopold Takawira St, POB 2995, Harare; tel. (4) 773966; fax (4) 773967; CEO STANLEY R. MAKONI; represents over 19,000 mem. cos (2002).

National Employment Council for the Engineering and Iron and Steel Industry: Adven House, 5th Floor, cnr Inez Terrace and Speke Ave, POB 1922, Harare; tel. (4) 775144; fax (4) 775918; f. 1943; Gen. Sec. E. E. SHARPE.

Zimbabwe Association of Consulting Engineers (ZACE): 16 Murandy Sq. East, POB HG836, Highlands, Harare; tel. (4) 746010; fax (4) 746010; e-mail zace@mango.zw.

Zimbabwe Building Contractors' Association: Caspi House, Block C, 4 Harare St, Harare; tel. (4) 780411; represents small-scale building contractors; CEO CONCORDIA MUKODZI.

Zimbabwe Commercial Farmers' Union (ZCFU): 53 Third St, Mutare; tel. (20) 67163; fmrly Indigenous Commercial Farmers' Union; Pres. DAVISON MUGABE; Dir. JOHN MAUTSA; represents c. 11,000 black farmers (2003).

Zimbabwe Farmers' Union (ZFU): POB 3755, Harare; tel. (4) 704763; fax (4) 700829; Pres. SILAS HUNGWE; Exec. Dir KWENDA DZAVIRA; represents c. 200,000 small-scale black farmers (2002).

UTILITIES

Electricity

Rural Electrification Agency (REA): Megawatt House, 6th Floor, 44 Samora Machel Ave Harare, POB 311, Harare; tel. (4) 770666; fax (4) 101661; e-mail emidzi@zesa.co.zw; f. 2002; manages the Rural Electrification Fund to expand and accelerate the electrification of rural areas; Chair. Dr SYDNEY GATA; CEO EMMANUEL MIDZI.

Zimbabwe Electricity Regulatory Commission (ZERC): Harare; f. 2004 to oversee the unbundling from ZESA of the Zimbabwe Power Co, the Zimbabwe Electricity Transmission Co and the Zimbabwe Electricity Distribution Co; Dir-Gen. MAVIS CHIDZONGA.

Zimbabwe Electricity Supply Authority (ZESA): 25 Samora Machel Ave, POB 377, Harare; tel. (4) 774508; fax (4) 774542; operates one hydroelectric and four thermal power stations; Chair. and CEO Dr SIDNEY GATA; dependable generation capacity of 1,700 MW.

Oil

National Oil Company of Zimbabwe (Pvt) Ltd (NOCZIM): NOCZIM House, 100 Leopold Takawira St, POB CY223, Causeway, Harare; tel. (4) 748543; fax (4) 748525; responsible for importing liquid fuels; Chair. CHARLES CHIPATO; Man. Dir ZVINECHIMWE CHURA.

Water

Zimbabwe National Water Authority (ZINWA): POB CY1215, Causeway, Harare; tel. and fax (4) 793139; e-mail mtetwa@utande.co.zw; f. 2001; fmrly Dept of Water, privatized in 2001; construction of dams, water supply, resources planning and protection; Chief Exec. ALBERT MUYAMBO.

TRADE UNIONS

Zimbabwe Congress of Trade Unions (ZCTU): Chester House, 9th Floor, Speke Ave and Third St, POB 3549, Harare; tel. (4) 794742; fax (4) 728484; e-mail info@zctu.co.zw; internet www.zctu.co.zw; f. 1981 by merger of the African Trade Union Congress, the Nat. African Trade Union Congress, the Trade Union Congress of Zimbabwe, the United Trade Unions of Zimbabwe, the Zimbabwe Fed. of Labour and the Zimbabwe Trade Union Congress; affiliated to the Int. Trade Union Confed., the Org. of African Trade Union Unity and the Southern African Trade Union Co-ordination Council; co-ordinating org. for trade unions; Pres. LOVEMORE MATOMBO; Sec.-Gen. WELLINGTON CHIBEBE; c. 163,000 mems (2002).

In 2005 there were 35 affiliated unions. Affiliates with over 3,000 mems include:

Associated Mineworkers' of Zimbabwe (AMWZ): St. Andrew's House, 4th Floor, Leopold Takawira St and Samora Machel Ave, POB 384, Harare; tel. (4) 700287; fax (4) 706543; e-mail amwz@mweb.co.zw; affiliated to the Int. Fed. of Chemical, Energy, Mine and Gen. Workers' Unions; Nat. Pres. TINAGO EDMUND RUZIVE; 10,000 mems (2002).

Commercial Workers' Union of Zimbabwe (CWUZ): CWUZ House, 15 Sixth Ave, Parktown; POB 3922 Harare; tel. (4) 664701; e-mail cwuz@africaonline.co.zw; Pres. TAITUS MAGAYA; Gen. Sec. LOVEMORE MUSHONGA (acting); 22,000 mems (2003).

Communication and Allied Services Workers Union of Zimbabwe (CASWUZ): Morgan House, 4th Floor, G. Silundika Ave, POB 739, Harare; tel. (4) 794763; e-mail caswuz@africaonline.co.zw; fmrly the Zimbabwe Post and Telecommunication Workers' Union; present name adopted 2002; Gen. Sec. REWARD S. MUSIWOKUWAYA; 5,700 mems (2002).

ZIMBABWE

Federation of Food and Allied Workers' Union of Zimbabwe (FFAWUZ): c/o ZCTU, Chester House, 9th Floor, Speke Ave and Third St, POB 3549, Harare; tel. (4) 74150; f. 1962; affiliated to the Int. Union of Food, Agricultural, Hotel, Restaurant, Catering, Tobacco and Allied Workers' Asscns; Gen. Sec. LEONARD KUZONDISHAYA; 3,000 mems (2002).

General Agricultural and Plantation Workers' Union (GAPWUZ): POB 1952, Harare; tel. (4) 734141; fax (4) 797918; e-mail alb@cfu.co.zw; affiliated to the Building and Wood Workers Int. and the Int. Union of Food, Agricultural, Hotel, Restaurant, Catering, Tobacco and Allied Workers' Asscns; Gen. Sec. GERTRUDE HAMBIRA; 5,000 mems (2002).

National Engineering Workers' Union (NEWU): St Barbara House, cnr Nelson Mandela Ave and Leopold Takawira St, Harare; tel. (4) 759597; fax (4) 759598; e-mail information@newu.org.zw; affiliated to the Int. Metalworkers' Fed.; Pres. ISAAC MATONGO; Gen. Sec. JAPHET MOYO; 9,000 mems (2002).

National Union of Clothing Industry Workers' Union (NUCI): Union House, 139A Lobengula St with 13th Ave, POB RY28, Raylton, Bulawayo; tel. (9) 64432; fax (9) 71089; affiliated to the Int. Textile, Garment and Leather Workers' Fed.; Gen. Sec. FRED MPOFU; 4,500 mems (2002).

Progressive Teachers' Union of Zimbabwe (PTUZ): 14 McLaren Rd, Milton Park, Harare; POB CR620, Cranborne, Harare; tel. (4) 757746; fax (4) 741937; e-mail ptuz@mweb.co.zw; f. 1997; Pres. TAKAVAFIREI ZHOU; Sec.-Gen. RAYMOND MAJONGWE; 12,000 mems (2002).

Public Service Association: PSA House, 9 Livingstone Ave, POB 179, Harare; tel. (4) 726506; fax (4) 704971; e-mail psahq@mweb.co.zw; f. 1919; affiliated to the Public Services Int.; Pres. CECILIA ALEXANDER; Gen. Sec. MAXWELL KAITANO; 20,689 mems (2003).

Mem. orgs incl. the Administrative and Exec. Officers Asscn, the Govt Officers Asscn, the Govt Workers Asscn, Professional and Technical Officers Asscn and:

Civil Service Employees' Association (CSEA): PSA House, 3rd floor, 9 Livingstone Ave, POB CY 202, Causeway, Harare; tel. (4) 701123; fax (4) 707208; e-mail civilsea@africaonline.co.zw; f. 1966; represents public-sector employees; Pres. MASIMBA KADZIMU; Gen. Sec. GEORGE NASHO WILSON; 5,000 mems (2006).

Zimbabwe Amalgamated Railwaymen's Union (ZARU): Unity House, 13th Ave, Herbert Chitepo St, POB 556, Bulawayo 10; tel. (9) 60948; affiliated to the Int. Transport Workers' Fed.; Gen. Sec. GIDEON P. SHOKO; 7,000 mems (2002).

Zimbabwe Banks and Allied Workers' Union (ZIBAWU): 1 Meredith Dr., Eastlea, POB 966, Harare; tel. (4) 703744; e-mail bankunion@zol.co.zw; Pres. GEORGE KAWENDA; Gen. Sec. COLLEN GWIYO; 4,560 mems (2002).

Zimbabwe Catering and Hotel Workers' Union (ZCHWU): Nialis Bldg, 1st Floor, Manyika, POB 3913, Harare; tel. (4) 753338; affiliated to the Int. Union of Food, Agricultural, Hotel, Restaurant, Catering, Tobacco and Allied Workers' Asscns; 8,500 mems (2002).

Zimbabwe Chemical, Plastics and Allied Workers' Union (ZCPAWU): St Andrew's House, 2nd Floor, Leopold Takawira St and Samora Machel Ave, POB 4810, Harare; tel. (4) 796533; Gen. Sec. F. P. GOMBEDZA; 3,723 mems (2002).

Zimbabwe Construction and Allied Trades Workers' Union (ZCAWU): St Barbara House, Office 306, cnr Nelson Mandela Ave and Leopold Takawira St, POB 1291, Harare; tel. (4) 750159; fax (4) 773967; affiliated to the Building and Wood Workers Int.; Gen. Sec. CHARLES GUMBO; 3,000 mems (2002).

Zimbabwe Electricity and Energy Workers' Union (ZEEWU): Crossroads House, 43 Julius Nyere Way, POB 5537, Harare; tel. and fax (4) 724430; e-mail zeewu@comone.co.zw; affiliated to the Int. Fed. of Chemical, Energy, Mine and Gen. Workers' Unions and the Building and Wood Workers Int.; Gen. Sec. IAN MUNJOMA; 3,075 mems (2002).

Zimbabwe Furniture, Timber and Allied Trades Union (ZFTATU): St Andrew's House, 4th Floor, Samora Machel Ave, POB 4793, Harare; tel. (4) 728056; fax (4) 737686; e-mail invioftbb@yahoo.com; affiliated to the affiliated to the Building and Wood Workers Int.; Gen. Sec. L. CHISHAKWE; 3,500 mems (2002).

Zimbabwe Graphical Workers' Union (ZGWU): 6 Harare St, POB 494, Harare; tel. (4) 775627; fax (4) 775727; represents employees in the printing and packaging industries; Gen. Sec. MADZIVO CHIMHUKA; 5,000 mems (2005).

Zimbabwe Leather Shoe and Allied Workers' Union (ZLSAWU): POB 4450, Harare; tel. (4) 727925; fax (4) 727926; e-mail zlsawu@telco.co.zw; affiliated to the Int. Textile, Garment and Leather Workers' Fed.; Gen. Sec. ISIDORE MANHANDO ZINDOGA; 6,745 mems (2002).

Zimbabwe Textile Workers' Union (ZTWU): 50 Jason Moyo Ave, Pockets Bldg, 2nd Floor, South Wing, Hillside, POB 10245, Harare; tel. (4) 770226; fax (4) 758233; e-mail ztwu@mweb.co.zw; affiliated to the Int. Textile, Garment and Leather Workers' Fed.; Gen. Sec. SILAS KUVEYA; 11,636 mems (2004).

Zimbabwe Tobacco Industry Workers' Union (ZTIWU): St Andrew's House, 2nd Floor, Samora Machel Ave, POB 2757, Harare; tel. (4) 702339; Gen. Sec. ESTEVAO CUMBULANE; 3,000 mems (2002).

Zimbabwe Urban Councils Workers' Union (ZUCWU): POB CY 1859, Causeway, Harare; tel. (4) 729412; f. 1990; represents workers in engineering, housing and community services, health and emergency services, and clerical and treasury services; affiliated to the Public Services Int.; Pres. SIMON TAYALI; Gen. Sec. MOSES TSHIMKENI-MAHLANGU; 10,200 mems (2003).

Other ZCTU affiliates include the Automotive and Allied Workers' Union, the Cement and Lime Workers' Union, the Employment Council Workers' Union, the National Airways Workers' Union, the Railway Artisans' Union, the Railway Association of Enginemen, Transport and General Workers' Union, the Zimbabwe Domestic and Allied Workers' Union, the Zimbabwe Education, Scientific and Social Welfare Workers' Union, the Zimbabwe Ferro-alloys Workers' Union, the Zimbabwe Pulp and Paper Workers' Union, the Zimbabwe Sugar Milling Workers' Union, the Zimbabwe Soft Drinks Manufacturing Workers' Union, and the Zimbabwe Radio, Television, Electronics Manufacturing Union.

Zimbabwe Federation of Trade Unions: Makombe Complex, Causeway, Harare; f. 1996 as alternative to ZCTU; 23 affiliated unions (2006); Gen. Sec. ADAMS VERENGA.

Affiliated unions include:

Zimbabwe Teachers' Union (ZITU): POB GV1, Glen View, Harare; tel. (4) 692454; fax (4) 708929; f. 2002; Gen. Sec. SIMPLISIO K. MATUMBA.

Other reported ZFTU affiliates include the Clothing Industry Workers' Union, the Zimbabwe Mining, Quarrying, Iron and Steel Workers' Union and the Zimbabwe National Drivers' Union.

Non-affiliated Unions

Zimbabwe National Students' Union (ZINASU): 21 Wembley Cres., Eastlea, Harare; tel. (4) 788135; e-mail zinasu@gmail.com; internet www.zinasu.org; represents students in more than 43 tertiary institutions; Sec.-Gen. BELOVED CHIWESHE; Nat. Co-ordinator WASHINGTON KATEMA; c. 260,000 mems (2006).

Zimbabwe Nurses' Association (ZINA): 47 Livingstone Ave, POB 2610, Harare; tel. and fax (4) 700479; e-mail zimnurse@mweb.co.zw; f. 1980; affiliated to the Public Services Int.; Gen. Sec. VANZAI MAJADA; 4,500 mems (2003).

Zimbabwe Teachers' Association (ZIMTA): POB 1440, Harare, Zimbabwe; tel. (4) 728438; fax (4) 791042; e-mail zimta@telco.co.zw; affiliated to Education Int.; Pres. TENDAI CHIKOWORE; Sec.-Gen. RICHARD GUNDANI (acting); 55,000 mems (2004).

Transport

RAILWAYS

In 1998 the rail network totalled 2,592 km, of which 313 km was electrified. Trunk lines run from Bulawayo south to the border with Botswana, connecting with the Botswana railways system, which, in turn, connects with the South African railways system; north-west to the Victoria Falls, where there is a connection with Zambia Railways; and north-east to Harare and Mutare connecting with the Mozambique Railways' line from Beira. From a point near Gweru, a line runs to the south-east, making a connection with the Mozambique Railways' Limpopo line and with the Mozambican port of Maputo. A connection runs from Rutenga to the South African Railways system at Beitbridge. A 320-km line from Beitbridge to Bulawayo was opened in 1999.

National Railways of Zimbabwe (NRZ): cnr Fife St and 10th Ave, POB 596, Bulawayo; tel. (9) 363716; fax (9) 363502; f. 1899; reorg. 1967; privatization under way; Chair. Brig. DOUGLAS NYIKAYARAMBA; Gen. Man. Air Commodore MIKE TICHAFA KARAKADZAI.

ROADS

In 2002 the road system in Zimbabwe totalled an estimated 97,267 km; some 18,481 km of the total network was paved. In December 2005 tollgates were introduced at the borders to raise funds to maintain the road network.

CIVIL AVIATION

AirZim operates an effective monopoly over air travel and transport within Zimbabwe. International and domestic air services connect most of the larger towns.

Civil Aviation Authority of Zimbabwe (CAAZ): Harare Int. Airport Terminal, Level 3, Private Bag CY7716, Causeway, Harare; tel. (4) 585009; fax (4) 585112; e-mail ais@caaz.co.zw; internet www.caaz.co.zw; f. 1999; operates eight airports incl. Harare Int. Airport and Joshua Mqabuko Nkomo Int. Airport (fmrly Bulawayo Airport); CEO DAVID CHAWOTA.

Air Zimbabwe (Pvt) Ltd (AirZim): POB AP1, Harare Airport, Harare; tel. (4) 575111; fax (4) 575068; internet www.airzimbabwe.com; f. 1967; scheduled domestic and international passenger and cargo services to Africa, Australia and Europe; plans were announced in Apr. 2006 to separate operations, creating the new cos Air Zimbabwe Technical, Air Zimbabwe Cargo, Nat. Handling Services and Galileo Zimbabwe, in addition to Air Zimbabwe; Chair. MIKE BIMHA; CEO Dr PETER CHIKUMBA.

Tourism

The principal tourist attractions are the Victoria Falls, the Kariba Dam and the Hwange Game Reserve and National Park. Zimbabwe Ruins, near Fort Victoria, and World's View, in the Matapos Hills, are also of interest. There is climbing and trout-fishing in the Eastern Districts, around Umtali. In 2005 1,558,501 tourists visited Zimbabwe, down from 1,854,488 in 2004 and 2,256,205 in 2003; however, revenue from tourism rose sharply in 2004, to US $194m., from US $61m. in the previous year, before declining to US $99m. in 2005.

Zimbabwe Tourism Authority (ZTA): POB CY286, Causeway, Harare; tel. (4) 758748; fax (4) 758826; e-mail info@ztazim.co.zw; internet www.zimbabwetourism.co.zw; f. 1984; promotes tourism domestically and from abroad; Chair. EMMANUEL FUNDIRA.

Associations licensed by the ZTA include:

Zimbabwe Association of Tour and Safari Operators (ZATSO): 18 Walter Hill Ave, Eastlea, Harare; tel. (4) 702402; fax (4) 707306; e-mail enquiries@soaz.net; CEO PAUL MATAMISA (acting).

INDEX OF TERRITORIES IN VOLUMES I AND II

	Page
Abu Dhabi	4577
Afghanistan	475
Ajman	4577
Åland Islands	1768
Albania	502
Alderney	4671
Algeria	522
American Samoa	4839
Andorra	549
Angola	556
Anguilla	4680
Antarctic Territory, Australian	678
Antarctic Territory, British	4694
Antarctica	575
Antigua and Barbuda	577
Argentina	587
Armenia	616
Aruba	3301
Ascension	4737
Ashmore Islands	678
Australia	634
Australian Antarctic Territory	678
Austria	680
Azad Kashmir	3516
Azerbaijan	708
Bahamas	727
Bahrain	738
Baker Island	4857
Bangladesh	755
Barbados	780
Barbuda	577
Belarus	790
Belau (see Palau)	
Belgium	810
Belize	840
Benin	851
Bermuda	4687
Bhutan	869
Bolivia	885
Bosnia and Herzegovina	906
Botswana	931
Bouvetøya	3452
Brazil	946
Brecqhou	4671
British Antarctic Territory	4694
British Indian Ocean Territory	4695
British Virgin Islands	4696
Brunei	980
Bulgaria	992
Burkina Faso	1012
Burma (see Myanmar)	
Burundi	1029
Caicos Islands	4739
Cambodia	1048
Cameroon	1070
Canada	1088
Cape Verde	1128
Cartier Island	678
Cayman Islands	4703
Central African Republic	1137
Ceuta	4145
Chad	1153
Channel Islands	4668
Chile	1171
China, People's Republic	1197
China (Taiwan)	1284
Christmas Island	670

	Page
Cocos Islands	672
Colombia	1317
Comoros	1342
Congo, Democratic Republic	1354
Congo, Republic	1375
Cook Islands	3349
Coral Sea Islands Territory	678
Costa Rica	1391
Côte d'Ivoire	1407
Croatia	1431
Cuba	1451
Cyprus	1475
Czech Republic	1501
Democratic People's Republic of Korea	2613
Democratic Republic of the Congo	1354
Denmark	1521
Djibouti	1558
Dominica	1567
Dominican Republic	1576
Dronning Maud Land	3452
Dubai	4577
East Timor (see Timor-Leste)	
Ecuador	1594
Egypt	1618
El Salvador	1649
Equatorial Guinea	1666
Eritrea	1676
Estonia	1689
Ethiopia	1708
Falkland Islands	4711
Faroe Islands	1546
Federated States of Micronesia	3084
Fiji	1729
Finland	1745
Former Yugoslav republic of Macedonia	2880
France	1772
French Guiana	1825
French Polynesia	1854
French Southern and Antarctic Territories	1882
Fujairah	4577
Futuna Islands	1875
Gabon	1896
Gambia	1912
Georgia	1926
Germany	1949
Ghana	1999
Gibraltar	4717
Great Britain	4595
Greece	2019
Greenland	1552
Grenada	2040
Grenadines	3838
Guadeloupe	1832
Guam	4844
Guatemala	2050
Guernsey	4668
Guinea	2070
Guinea-Bissau	2086
Guyana	2100
Haiti	2113
Heard Island	678
Herm	4671

5034
www.europaworld.com

INDEX OF TERRITORIES IN VOLUMES I AND II

	Page		Page
Herzegovina	906	Montenegro	3140
Holy See	4907	Montserrat	4724
Honduras	2134	Morocco	3149
Hong Kong	1248	Mozambique	3174
Howland Island	4857	Myanmar	3193
Hungary	2149		
		Namibia	3221
Iceland	2170	Nauru	3239
India	2183	Navassa Island	4858
Indian Ocean Territory, British	4695	Nepal	3247
Indonesia	2242	Netherlands	3274
Iran	2282	Netherlands Antilles	3308
Iraq	2315	Nevis	3817
Ireland	2348	New Caledonia	1883
Isle of Man	4675	New Zealand	3320
Israel	2374	Nicaragua	3362
Italy	2415	Niger	3382
Ivory Coast (see Côte d'Ivoire)		Nigeria	3400
		Niue	3356
		Norfolk Island	674
Jamaica	2455	North Korea	2613
Jan Mayen	3452	Northern Areas (Pakistan)	3516
Japan	2471	Northern Ireland	4595
Jarvis Island	4857	Northern Mariana Islands	4821
Jersey	4672	Norway	3426
Jethou	4671		
Johnston Atoll	4857		
Jordan	2521	Oman	3453
Kazakhstan	2563	Pakistan	3467
Keeling Islands	672	Palau	3517
Kenya	2583	Palestinian Autonomous Areas	3524
Kingman Reef	4857	Palmyra	4858
Kiribati	2605	Panama	3550
Korea, Democratic People's Republic	2613	Papua New Guinea	3568
Korea, Republic	2643	Paraguay	3591
Kosovo	2681	People's Republic of China	1197
Kuwait	2687	Peru	3608
Kyrgyzstan	2707	Peter I Øy	3452
		Philippines	3632
		Pitcairn Islands	4731
Laos	2725	Poland	3670
Latvia	2741	Portugal	3696
Lebanon	2759	Príncipe	3864
Lesotho	2789	Puerto Rico	4827
Liberia	2802		
Libya	2819	Qatar	3721
Liechtenstein	2839		
Lihou	4671		
Lithuania	2847	Ras al-Khaimah	4577
Luxembourg	2868	Republic of China (Taiwan)	1284
		Republic of the Congo	1375
		Republic of Korea	2643
Macao	1270	Réunion	1846
Macedonia, former Yugoslav republic	2880	Romania	3734
Madagascar	2899	Ross Dependency	3344
Malawi	2917	Russian Federation	3759
Malaysia	2934	Rwanda	3800
Maldives	2973		
Mali	2986		
Malta	3003	Saint-Barthélemy	1871
Man, Isle of	4675	Saint Christopher and Nevis	3817
Marshall Islands	3014	Saint Helena	4734
Martinique	1840	Saint Lucia	3827
Mauritania	3022	Saint-Martin	1871
Mauritius	3038	Saint Pierre and Miquelon	1872
Mayotte	1866	Saint Vincent and the Grenadines	3838
McDonald Islands	678	Samoa	3848
Melilla	4150	San Marino	3857
Mexico	3054	São Tomé and Príncipe	3864
Micronesia, Federated States	3084	Sark	4671
Midway Atoll	4858	Saudi Arabia	3874
Miquelon	1872	Senegal	3897
Moldova	3091	Serbia	3921
Monaco	3109	Seychelles	3946
Mongolia	3116	Sharjah	4577

INDEX OF TERRITORIES IN VOLUMES I AND II

	Page		Page
Sierra Leone	3954	Turkey	4467
Singapore	3971	'Turkish Republic of Northern Cyprus'	1475
Slovakia	3997	Turkmenistan	4503
Slovenia	4017	Turks and Caicos Islands	4739
Solomon Islands	4034	Tuvalu	4521
Somalia	4048		
South Africa	4066		
South Georgia	4738	Uganda	4528
South Korea	2643	Ukraine	4547
South Sandwich Islands	4738	Umm al-Qaiwain	4577
Spain	4101	United Arab Emirates	4577
Spanish North Africa	4145	United Kingdom	4595
Sri Lanka	4155	United States of America	4746
St Kitts (Saint Christopher)	3817	United States Virgin Islands	4851
Sudan	4185	Uruguay	4859
Suriname	4211	Uzbekistan	4877
Svalbard	3450		
Swaziland	4224		
Sweden	4238	Vanuatu	4896
Switzerland	4264	Vatican City	4907
Syria	4289	Venezuela	4917
		Viet Nam	4944
		Virgin Islands, British	4696
Taiwan	1284	Virgin Islands, US	4851
Tajikistan	4313		
Tanzania	4332		
Thailand	4353	Wake Island	4858
Timor-Leste	4384	Wallis and Futuna Islands	1875
Tobago	4430	Western Samoa (see Samoa)	
Togo	4402		
Tokelau	3344		
Tonga	4420	Yemen	4972
Trinidad and Tobago	4430		
Tristan da Cunha	4738	Zambia	4993
Tunisia	4448	Zimbabwe	5010

THE EUROPA REGIONAL SURVEYS OF THE WORLD

'Europa's Regional Surveys of the World are justly renowned for their exceptionally high levels of production, content and accuracy.'
– Reference Reviews

A nine-volume library of historical, political, geographical and economic data, providing an accurate and impartial overview of the major regions of the world.

These exhaustive surveys bring together a unique collection of information, from description and analysis of the principal issues affecting each region, to statistical data and directory information. They provide a combination of contemporary material and important historical perspectives to offer a definitive guide to all regions of the world.

Meticulously researched and updated every year, the *Europa Regional Surveys of the World* are an indispensable information source on which you can rely.

The nine titles that make up the series are as follows:

Africa South of the Sahara; Central and South-Eastern Europe; Eastern Europe, Russia and Central Asia; The Far East and Australasia; The Middle East and North Africa; South America, Central America and the Caribbean; South Asia; The USA and Canada; Western Europe.

To order call: UK & Rest of World Customers: **+44 (0)1235 400524**
North & South American Customers: **1-800-634-7064**

www.routledge.com/reference   Email: reference@routledge.com

EUROPA WORLD *PLUS*

Europa World and the Europa Regional Surveys of the World Online

www.europaworld.com

ALSO AVAILABLE

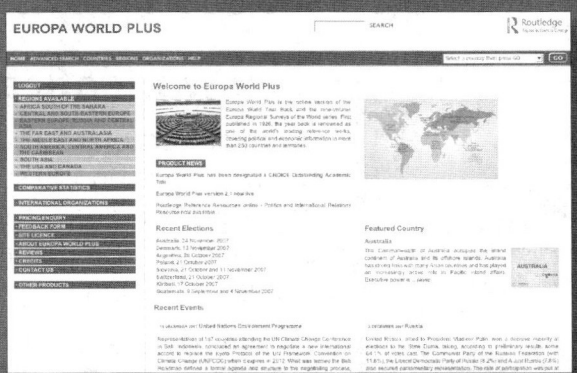

Europa World Plus provides immediate online access to the latest versions of the *Europa World Year Book* and the *Europa Regional Surveys of the World* and merges them into an easy, intuitive interface, with updates throughout the year and powerful search capabilities.

Designated a CHOICE Outstanding Academic Title

For more information, free trials or rate quotes please contact your sales representative

UK & Rest of World Customers:
Carlos Gimeno, Tel: +44 (0) 20 7017 6062 or Email: online.sales@tandf.co.uk

North & South American Customers:
Tel: (888)318-2367 or Email: e-reference@taylorandfrancis.com

Routledge
Taylor & Francis Group

	DATE DUE